Tax Acts

2005

Tottel
publishing

Tax Acts

2005

Editor **Philip Brennan** AITI

Tottel
publishing

Tottel Publishing, Maxwelton House, 41–43 Boltro Road, Haywards Heath, West Sussex, RH16 1BJ

A CIP Catalogue record for this book is available from the British Library.

ISBN 1845921410

ISBN 1-84592-141-0

9 781845 921415

Typeset in Dublin by Marie Armah-Kwantreng
Printed and bound in Great Britain by CPI Bath

CONTENTS

A destination table, which may be used to trace the present location of older legislation as re-enacted in the Taxes Consolidation Act 1997, may be ordered in electronic format from amy.hayes@tottelpublishing.com.

The statutory references of the older legislation are also given in the notes following each section of the Taxes Consolidation Act 1997.

Legislation

Statutory Instruments

HOW TO USE THIS WORK

Tracing legislation

This book sets out the text of the Irish tax law relating to income tax, corporation tax, and capital gains tax. Each section is annotated in respect of amendments, cross-references, definitions, construction, statutory instruments, statements of practice and former enactments.

The legislation is set out in the following manner:

(*a*) the full text of an amending provision is normally omitted, but effect is given to the amendment in the amended provision,

(*b*) the full text of a repealing provision is normally omitted, but effect is given to the repeal in the repealed provision.

Section and Schedule headings of repealed or amended legislation are retained for the purposes of clarity.

For ease of reference, section and Schedule numbers are conspicuously marked at the top of the page. If the section or Schedule is known, it can be found immediately because the legislation is printed in chronological order. Where only the subject matter is known, it may be traced through the index. The present location of the text of former enactments may be traced through the destination table.

The publishers welcome suggestions for the improvement of this work.

Standard abbreviations

The following are the standard abbreviations used in LexisNexis Tax publications:

General

s, ss	section (or sections) of an Act
subs, subss	subsection (or subsections) of a section
Sch	Schedule to an Act
para, paras	paragraph (or paragraphs) of a Schedule
subpara, subparas	subparagraph (or subparagraphs) of a Schedule
Pt	Part (of an Act)
Ch	Chapter (of a Part of an Act)
r, reg	regulation (of a statutory instrument)

Statutes

CA	Companies Act
CABA 1996	Criminal Assets Bureau Act 1996
CATCA 2003	Capital Acquisitions Tax Consolidation Act 2003
CGTA 1975	Capital Gains Tax Act 1975
CGT(A)A 1978	Capital Gains Tax (Amendment) Act 1978
CTA 1976	Corporation Tax Act 1976
DCITPA 1996	Disclosure of Certain Information for Taxation and Other Purposes Act 1996
FA	Finance Act
F(No 2)A	Finance (No 2) Act
F(MP)A	Finance (Miscellaneous Provisions) Act
IA 1937	Interpretation Act 1937
IRRA 1890	Inland Revenue Regulation Act 1890
ITA 1967	Income Tax Act 1967
PCTA 1927	Provisional Collection of Taxes Act 1927
SDCA 1999	Stamp Duties Consolidation Act 1999
TCA 1997	Taxes Consolidation Act 1997

TD(SC)A 1942	Taxes and Duties (Special Circumstances) Act 1942
VATA 1972	Value Added Tax 1972
Statutory Instruments	
ITECR	Income Tax (Employments) (Consolidated) Regulations
SI 28/1960	Statutory Instrument Number 28 of 1960
IT(RC)R	Income Tax (Relevant Contracts) Regulations
Practice	
SP	Statement of Practice
Case law	
ITR	Irish Tax Reports
IR	Irish Reports
STC	Simon's Tax Cases
TC	Tax Cases
TL	Tax leaflet
ITC	Irish Tax Cases
ECJ	European Court of Justice

PROVISIONAL COLLECTION OF TAXES ACT 1927

(1927 Number 7)

ARRANGEMENT OF SECTIONS

An Act to give statutory effect for a limited period to resolutions of the committee on finance of Dáil Éireann imposing, renewing, varying, or abolishing taxation, and to make provision with respect to payments, deductions, assessments, charges, and other things made or done on account of any temporary tax in anticipation of the renewal of the tax by the Oireachtas. [19th March, 1927]

1 Definitions

In this Act—

the expression **"Committee on Finance"** means the Committee on Finance of Dáil Éireann when and so long as such Committee is a committee of the whole House;

[the expression **"new tax"** when used in relation to a resolution under this Act means a tax which was not in force immediately before the date on which the resolution is expressed to take effect or, where no such date is expressed, the passing of the resolution by Dáil Éireann;][1]

the expression **"permanent tax"** means a tax which was last imposed without any limit of time being fixed for its duration;

the expression **"temporary tax"** means a tax which was last imposed or renewed for a limited period only;

the expression **"normal expiration"** when used in relation to a temporary tax means the end of the limited period for which the tax was last imposed or renewed;

the word **"tax"** includes duties of customs, duties of excise, income tax, ...[2] ...[3] [and value-added tax][4] [and capital gains tax][5] ...[6] [and corporation tax][7] [and gift tax and inheritance tax][8] [and residential property tax][9] [and stamp duties][10] [and gift tax and inheritance tax][11] but no other tax or duty.

Amendments

1 Definition of "new tax" substituted by FA 2002 s 139(*a*) with effect from 25 March 2002.

2 Words "and super-tax" repealed by FA 1974 s 86 and Sch 2 Pt I for 1974–75 and later tax years.

3 Words "and also turnover tax" repealed by VATA 1972 s 41.
4 Inserted by VATA 1972 s 38.
5 Inserted by CGTA 1975 s 50.
6 Words "and wealth tax" deleted by FA 1978 s 38.
7 Inserted by CTA 1976 s 6.
8 Inserted by CATA 1976 s 69.
9 Inserted by FA 1983 s 114(1).
10 Inserted by FA 1986 s 100.
11 Inserted by CATCA 2003 s 115(1).

2 Certain resolutions to have statutory effect

Whenever a resolution (in this Act referred to as a resolution under this Act) is passed by [Dáil Éireann][1] resolving—

(*a*) that a new tax specified in the resolution be imposed, or

(*b*) that a specified permanent tax in force [immediately before the date on which the resolution is expressed to take effect or, where no such date is expressed, the passing of the resolution by Dáil Éireann][2] be increased, reduced, or otherwise varied, or be abolished, or

(*c*) that a specified temporary tax in force [immediately before the date on which the resolution is expressed to take effect or, where no such date is expressed, the passing of the resolution by Dáil Éireann][2] be renewed (whether at the same or a different rate and whether with or without modification) as from the date of its normal expiration or from an earlier date or be discontinued on a date prior to the date of its normal expiration,

and the resolution contains a declaration that it is expedient in the public interest that the resolution should have statutory effect under the provisions of this Act, the resolution shall, subject to the provisions of this Act, have statutory effect as if contained in an Act of the Oireachtas.

Amendments

1 Substituted by FA 1974 s 85(1)(*a*) with effect from 23 October 1974 (SI 312/1974); previously "the Committee on Finance".

2 Substituted by FA 2002 s 139(*b*) with effect from 25 March 2002; previously "immediately before the end of the previous financial year".

3 Application of general taxing enactments

(1) Whenever a new tax is imposed by a resolution under this Act and such resolution describes the tax as a duty of customs or as a duty of excise or as an income tax ...[1], the enactments which [immediately before the date on which the resolution is expressed to take effect or, where no such date is expressed, the passing of the resolution by Dáil Éireann][2] were in force in relation to customs duties generally, or excise duties generally, or income tax generally, ...[3] (as the case may require) shall, subject to the provisions of this Act, apply to and have full force and effect in respect of such new tax so long as the resolution continues to have statutory effect.

(2) Whenever a permanent tax is increased, reduced, or otherwise varied by a resolution under this Act, all enactments which were in force with respect to that tax [immediately before the date on which the resolution is expressed to take effect or, where no such date

is expressed, the passing of the resolution by Dáil Éireann][2] shall, so long as the resolution continues to have statutory effect and subject to the provisions of this Act, have full force and effect with respect to the tax as so increased, reduced, or otherwise varied.

(3) Whenever a temporary tax is renewed (whether at the same or a different rate and whether with or without modification) by a resolution under this Act, all enactments which were in force with respect to that tax [immediately before the date on which the resolution is expressed to take effect or, where no such date is expressed, the passing of the resolution by Dáil Éireann][2] shall, so long as the resolution continues to have statutory effect and subject to the provisions of this Act, have full force and effect with respect to the tax as renewed by the resolution.

Amendments

1 Words "or as a super-tax" repealed by FA 1974 s 86 and Sch 2 Pt 1 for 1974–75 and later tax years.

2 Substituted by FA 2002 s 139(*b*) with effect from 25 March 2002; previously "immediately before the end of the previous financial year".

3 Words "or super-tax generally" repealed by FA 1974 s 86 and Sch 2 Pt 1 for 1974–75 and later tax years.

4 Duration of statutory effect of resolution

[A resolution under this Act shall cease to have statutory effect upon the happening of whichever of the following events first occurs, that is to say:

[(*a*) subject to section 4A of this Act, if a Bill containing provisions to the same effect (with or without modifications) as the resolution is not read a second time by Dáil Éireann—

(i) where Dáil Éireann is in recess on any day between the eighty-second and the eighty-fourth day after the resolution is passed by Dáil Éireann, within the next five sitting days of the resumption of Dáil Éireann after that recess,

(ii) in any other case, within the next eighty-four days after the resolution is passed by Dáil Éireann,][1]

(*b*) if those provisions of the said bill are rejected by Dáil Éireann during the passage of the Bill through the Oireachtas;

(*c*) the coming into operation of an Act of the Oireachtas containing provisions to the same effect (with or without modification) as the resolution;

(*d*) [subject to section 4A of this Act][2] the expiration of a period of four months from that date on which the resolution is expressed to take effect or, where no such date is expressed, from the passing of the resolution by Dáil Éireann.][3]

Amendments

1 Para (*a*) substituted by Appropriation Act 1991 s 2(*a*)(i).

2 Inserted by Appropriation Act 1991 s 2(*a*)(ii).

3 Section 4 substituted by FA 1974 s 85(1)(*b*) with effect from 23 October 1974 (SI 312/1974).

4A Effect of dissolution of Dáil Éireann

[Where Dáil Éireann, having passed a resolution under this Act, has been dissolved on the date the resolution was so passed or within four months of that date, then the period of dissolution shall be disregarded for the purposes of calculating any period to which paragraph (*a*) or (*d*) of section 4 of this Act relates.][1]

Amendments

1 Section originally inserted by Appropriation Act 1991; substituted by FA 1992 s 250.

Definitions

"Dáil Éireann": IA 1937 Sch.

5 Repayment of certain payments and deductions

(1) Whenever a resolution under this Act ceases to have statutory effect by reason of the happening of any event other than the coming into operation of an Act of the Oireachtas containing provisions to the same effect (with or without modification) as the resolution, all moneys paid in pursuance of the resolution shall be repaid or made good and every deduction made in pursuance of the resolution shall be deemed to be an unauthorised deduction.

(2) ...[1].

(3) Whenever an Act of the Oireachtas comes into operation containing provisions to the same effect with modifications as a resolution under this Act and such resolution ceases by virtue of such coming into operation to have statutory effect, all moneys paid in pursuance of such resolution which would not be payable under such Act shall be repaid or made good and every deduction made in pursuance of such resolution which would not be authorised by such Act shall be deemed to be an unauthorised deduction.

Amendments

1 Subs (2) repealed by FA 1974 s 85(1)(*c*) with effect from 23 October 1974 (SI 312/1974).

6 Certain payments and deductions deemed to be legal

(1) Any payment or deduction on account of a temporary tax to which this section applies made within two months after the expiration of such tax in respect of a period or event occurring after such expiration shall, if such payment or deduction would have been a legal payment or deduction if the tax had not expired, be deemed to be a legal payment or deduction subject to the conditions that—

(*a*) if a resolution under this Act renewing the tax (with or without modification) is not passed by [Dáil Éireann][1] within two months after the expiration of the tax, the amount of such payment or deduction shall be repaid or made good on the expiration of such two months, and

(*b*) if (such resolution having been so passed) an Act of the Oireachtas renewing the tax (with or without modification) does not come into operation when or before such resolution ceases to have statutory effect, the amount of such payment or deduction shall be repaid or made good on such cesser, and

(*c*) if (such Act having been so passed) the tax is renewed by such Act with such modifications that the whole or some portion of such payment or deduction is not a legal payment or deduction under such Act, the whole or such portion (as the case may be) of such payment or deduction shall be repaid or made good on the coming into operation of such Act.

(2) This section applies only to a temporary tax which was last imposed or renewed for a limited period not exceeding eighteen months and was in force immediately before the end of the financial year next preceding the financial year in which the payment or deduction under this section is made.

Amendments

1 Substituted by FA 1974 s 85(1)(*d*) with effect from 23 October 1974 (SI 312/1974); previously "the Committee on Finance".

7 Repeal

The Provisional Collection of Taxes Act, 1913, is hereby repealed.

8 Short title

This Act may be cited as the Provisional Collection of Taxes Act, 1927.

INTERPRETATION ACT 1937

(Number 38 of 1937)

ARRANGEMENT OF SECTIONS

PART I

PRELIMINARY AND GENERAL

Section

PART II

FORM, CITATION, AND OPERATION OF ACTS OF THE OIREACHTAS

PART III

MEANING AND CONSTRUCTION OF PARTICULAR WORDS AND EXPRESSIONS

PART IV

STATUTORY POWERS AND DUTIES

PART V

EFFECT OF REPEALS AND REVOCATIONS

SCHEDULE

INTERPRETATION OF PARTICULAR EXPRESSIONS AND WORDS

An Act to make, for the purpose of the Constitution of Ireland lately enacted by the people, divers provisions in relation to the form, operation, and interpretation of Acts of the Oireachtas and of Instruments made under such Acts. [8th December, 1937]

PART I

PRELIMINARY AND GENERAL

1 Short title

This Act may be cited as the Interpretation Act, 1937.

2 Commencement

This Act shall come into operation immediately after the coming into operation of the Constitution of Ireland lately enacted by the People.

3 Definitions

In this Act —

the word **"statute"** includes (in addition to Acts of the Oireachtas) Acts of the Oireachtas of Saorstát Éireann, Acts of the Parliament of the former United Kingdom of Great Britain and Ireland, and Acts of a Parliament sitting in Ireland at any time before the coming into force of the Union with Ireland Act, 1800;

the word **"instrument"** means an order, regulation, rule, bye-law, warrant, licence, certificate, or other like document;

the expression **"statutory instrument"** means an instrument made, issued, or granted under a power or authority conferred by statute;

references to instruments made wholly or partly under an Act of the Oireachtas shall be construed as referring to instruments made, issued, or granted under a power or authority conferred by an Act of the Oireachtas or conferred by the joint operation of an Act of the Oireachtas and some other statute.

4 Application to certain Acts of the Oireachtas of Saorstát Éireann

Save as is otherwise expressly provided by this Act, every provision of this Act which relates to Acts of the Oireachtas shall apply and have effect in relation to this Act and every other Act of the Oireachtas of Saorstát Éireann (whether passed before or after this Act) which is expressed to come into operation immediately after the coming into operation of the Constitution, and accordingly this Act and every such other Act shall, for the purpose of such application but no further or otherwise, be deemed to be an Act of the Oireachtas and (save as is otherwise expressly provided by this Act) the expression **"Act of the Oireachtas"** shall in this Act be construed and have effect as including this Act and every such other Act of the Oireachtas of Saorstát Éireann.

5 Non-application of the Interpretation Act, 1923

(1) The Interpretation Act, 1923 (No 46 of 1923), shall not apply to any Act of the Oireachtas or to any instrument made wholly or partly under any such Act.

(2) The foregoing subsection of this section shall not preclude or prejudice the application to this Act and to other Acts of the Oireachtas of Saorstát Éireann which are expressed to come into operation immediately after the coming into operation of the Constitution of so much of the Interpretation Act, 1923 (No 46 of 1923), as concerns events happening or things to be done in relation to an Act before it comes into operation.

Definitions
"instrument": s 3; "Act of the Oireachtas": s 4.

PART II

FORM, CITATION, AND OPERATION OF ACTS OF THE OIREACHTAS

6 Form of Acts of the Oireachtas

(1) Every Act of the Oireachtas shall be a public document and shall be judicially noticed.

(2) Every Act of the Oireachtas shall be divided into sections numbered consecutively and any such section may be sub-divided in such manner and to such extent as is convenient.

(3) The sections of an Act of the Oireachtas may, where convenient, be grouped in Parts, Chapters, or other divisions numbered consecutively.

Definitions
Act of the Oireachtas: s 4.

7 Citation of Acts of the Oireachtas

(1) Every Act of the Oireachtas may be cited in any other Act of the Oireachtas or in any instrument or other document either by the short title of the Act so cited or by the calendar year in which the Act so cited was passed and the consecutive number of such Act in such year.

(2) Any enactment contained in an Act of the Oireachtas may be cited in any other Act of the Oireachtas or in any instrument or other document by reference to the Part, section, subsection, or other sub-division of the first-mentioned Act which contains the enactment so cited.

Definitions
"Act of the Oireachtas": s 4.

8 Date of passing of Acts of the Oireachtas

(1) The date of the passing of every Act of the Oireachtas shall be the date of the day on which the Bill for such Act is signed by the President.

(2) Immediately after the passing of every Act of the Oireachtas the Clerk of Dáil Éireann shall endorse on such Act, immediately after the title thereof, the date of the passing of such Act, and such date shall be taken to be part of such Act.

(3) Every enactment contained in an Act of the Oireachtas shall, unless the contrary intention is expressed in such Act, be deemed to be in operation as from the end of the day before the date of the passing of such Act.

(4) This section shall not apply to this Act or to any other Act of the Oireachtas of Saorstát Éireann which is expressed to come into operation immediately after the coming into operation of the Constitution, and accordingly the expression **"Act of the Oireachtas"** shall not in this section include any such Act of the Oireachtas of Saorstát Éireann.

Definitions
"Act of the Oireachtas": s 4.

9 Commencement of Acts and instruments

(1) Where an Act of the Oireachtas, or a portion of any such Act, or an instrument made wholly or partly under any such Act, or a portion of any such instrument is expressed to come into operation on a particular day (whether such day is before or after the date of the passing of such Act or the making of such instrument and whether such day is named in such Act or instrument or is to be fixed or ascertained in any particular manner), such Act, portion of an Act, instrument, or portion of an instrument shall come into operation at the end of the day before such particular day.

(2) Every instrument made wholly or partly under an Act of the Oireachtas shall, unless the contrary intention is expressed in such instrument, be deemed to be in operation as from the end of the day before the day on which the instrument is made.

Definitions
"instrument": s 3; "Act of the Oireachtas": s 4.

10 Exercise of statutory powers before commencement of the Act

(1) Where an Act of the Oireachtas or any particular enactment contained in any such Act is expressed to come into operation on a day subsequent to the date of the passing of such Act, the following provisions shall have effect, that is to say:—

(*a*) if the day on which such Act or such enactment (as the case may be) comes into operation is to be fixed or ascertained in any particular manner, the instrument, act, or thing whereby such day is fixed or ascertained may, subject to any restrictions imposed by such Act, be made or done at any time after the passing of such Act;

(*b*) if such Act confers a power to make or do, for the purposes of such Act or such enactment (as the case may be), any instrument, act, or thing the making or doing of which is necessary or expedient to enable such Act or enactment to have full force and effect immediately upon its coming into operation, such power may, subject to any restrictions imposed by such Act, be exercised at any time after the passing of such Act.

(2) In the application of this section to an Act of the Oireachtas of Saorstát Éireann which is expressed to come into operation immediately after the coming into operation of the Constitution, nothing in this section shall operate to enable any instrument, act, or thing to be made or done under or in relation to any such Act before the coming into operation of the Constitution.

Definitions
"instrument": s 3; "Act of the Oireachtas": s 4.

PART III

MEANING AND CONSTRUCTION OF PARTICULAR WORDS AND EXPRESSIONS

11 Certain general rules of construction

The following provisions shall apply and have effect in relation to the construction of every Act of the Oireachtas and of every instrument made wholly or partly under any such Act, that is to say:—

(*a*) *Singular and plural.* Every word importing the singular shall, unless the contrary intention appears, be construed as if it also imported the plural, and every word importing the plural shall, unless the contrary intention appears, be construed as if it also imported the singular;

(*b*) *Masculine and feminine.* Every word importing the masculine gender shall, unless the contrary intention appears, be construed as if it also imported the feminine gender;

(*c*) *Person.* The word **"person"** shall, unless the contrary intention appears, be construed as importing a body corporate (whether a corporation aggregate or a corporation sole) and an unincorporated body of persons as well as an individual;

(*d*) *Time.* Every word or expression relating to time and every reference to a point of time shall, unless the contrary intention appears, be construed as relating or referring to Greenwich mean time, but subject to the provisions of any enactment whereunder the time in Ireland differs from Greenwich mean time during a specified period;

(*e*) *Distance*. Every word or expression relating to the distance between two points and every reference to the distance from or to a point shall, unless the contrary intention appears, be construed as relating or referring to such distance measured in a straight line on a horizontal plane;

(*f*) *Citations*. Every description of or citation from any statute, instrument, or other document shall, unless the contrary intention appears, be construed as including the word, subsection, section, or other portion mentioned or referred to as forming the beginning or as forming the end of the portion comprised in the description or citation or as being the point from which or to which such portion extends;

(*g*) *Marginal notes*. No marginal note placed at the side of any section or provision to indicate the subject, contents, or effect of such section or provision and no heading or cross-line placed at the head or beginning of a Part, section or provision or a group of sections or provisions to indicate the subject, contents, or effect of such Part, section, provision, or group shall be taken to be part of the Act or instrument or be considered or judicially noticed in relation to the construction or interpretation of the Act or instrument or any portion thereof;

(*h*) *Periods of time*. Where a period of time is expressed to begin on or be reckoned from a particular day, that day shall, unless the contrary intention appears, be deemed to be included in such period, and, where a period of time is expressed to end on or be reckoned to a particular day, that day shall, unless the contrary intention appears, be deemed to be included in such period;

(*i*) *Offences by corporations*. References to a person in relation to an offence (whether punishable on indictment or on summary conviction) shall, unless the contrary intention appears, be construed as including references to a body corporate.

Cross-references

Para (*b*): as regards legislation passed after 22 December 1993, every word importing the feminine gender, unless the contrary intention appears, also imports the masculine gender: Interpretation (Amendment) Act 1993.

Case law

Words in a charging provision, in the absence of a definition, to be interpreted according to normal usage: *De Brún v Kiernan* [1982] ITR Vol III p 19.

Interpretation, misclassification of goods under customs tariff, negligence of Revenue Commissioners, legitimate expectation: *Carbery Milk Products Ltd v Minister for Agriculture,* (High Court, 23 April 1993) ITR Vol IV p 492.

Definitions

"person": s 11(*c*); "instrument": s 3; "Act of the Oireachtas": s 4.

12 Interpretation of the expressions and words in the Schedule

In every Act of the Oireachtas and every instrument made wholly or partly under any such Act, every word and every expression to which a particular meaning, construction, or effect is assigned in the Schedule to this Act shall, unless the contrary intention appears, have the meaning, construction, or effect so assigned to it.

Case law

Words in a charging provision, in the absence of a definition, to be interpreted according to normal usage: *De Brún v Kiernan* [1982] ITR Vol III p 19.

Definitions

"instrument": s 3; "Act of the Oireachtas": s 4.

13 Construction of certain statutory instruments

Every expression and every word used in an instrument made wholly or partly under an Act of the Oireachtas shall, unless the contrary intention appears, have in such instrument the same meaning as it has in the Act or Acts under which such instrument is made.

Definitions

"instrument": s 3; "Act of the Oireachtas": s 4.

14 Offences under two or more laws

Where any act, whether of commission or omission, constitutes an offence under two or more statutes or under a statute and at common law, the offender shall, unless the contrary intention appears, be liable to be prosecuted and punished under either or any of those statutes or at common law, but shall not be liable to be punished twice for the same offence.

Definitions

"statute": s 3.

PART IV

STATUTORY POWERS AND DUTIES

15 Construction and exercise of statutory powers

(1) Every power conferred by an Act of the Oireachtas or by an instrument made wholly or partly under any such Act may, unless the contrary intention appears in such Act or instrument, be exercised from time to time as occasion requires.

(2) Every power conferred by an Act of the Oireachtas or by an instrument made wholly or partly under any such Act on the holder of an office as such shall, unless the contrary intention appears in such Act or instrument, be deemed to be conferred on and may accordingly be exercised by the holder for the time being of such office.

(3) Every power conferred by an Act of the Oireachtas to make any regulations, rules, or bye-laws shall, unless the contrary intention appears in such Act, be construed as including a power, exercisable in the like manner and subject to the like consent and conditions (if any), to revoke or amend any regulations, rules, or bye-laws made under such power and (where requisite) to make other regulations, rules, or bye-laws in lieu of those so revoked.

Definitions
"instrument": s 3; "Act of the Oireachtas": s 4.

16 Construction and performance of statutory duties

(1) Every duty imposed by an Act of the Oireachtas or by an instrument made wholly or partly under any such Act shall, unless the contrary intention appears in such Act or instrument, be performed from time to time as occasion requires.

(2) Every duty imposed by an Act of the Oireachtas or by an instrument made wholly or partly under any such Act on the holder of an office as such shall, unless the contrary intention appears in such Act or instrument, be deemed to be imposed on and shall accordingly be performed by the holder for the time being of such office.

Definitions
"instrument": s 3; "Act of the Oireachtas": s 4.

17 Rules of Court

Whenever an Act of the Oireachtas confers any new jurisdiction on a court of justice or extends or varies an existing jurisdiction of a court of justice, the authority having for the time being power to make rules or orders regulating the practice and procedure of such court shall have, and may at any time exercise, power to make rules or orders for regulating the practice and procedure of such court in the exercise of the jurisdiction so conferred, extended, or varied.

Definitions
"Act of the Oireachtas": s 4.

18 Service by post

Where an Act of the Oireachtas or an instrument made wholly or partly under any such Act authorises or requires a document to be served by post, whether the word "serve" or any of the words "give", "deliver", or "send", or any other word is used, then, unless the contrary intention appears, the service of such document may be effected by properly addressing, prepaying (where requisite), and posting a letter containing such document, and in such case the service of such document shall, unless the contrary is proved, be deemed to have been effected at the time at which such letter would be delivered in the ordinary course of post.

Definitions
"instrument": s 3; "Act of the Oireachtas": s 4.

PART V

EFFECT OF REPEALS AND REVOCATIONS

19 Date of operation of repeals and revocations

(1) Where an Act of the Oireachtas repeals the whole or a portion of a previous statute and substitutes other provisions for the statute or portion of a statute so repealed, the

statute or portion of a statute so repealed shall, unless the contrary is expressly provided in the repealing Act, continue in force until the said substituted provisions come into operation.

(2) Where an instrument made wholly or partly under an Act of the Oireachtas revokes the whole or a portion of a previous statutory instrument (whether made wholly or partly under such Act or under another statute) and substitutes other provisions for the instrument or portion of an instrument so revoked, the instrument or portion of an instrument so revoked shall, unless the contrary is expressly provided in the revoking instrument, continue in force until the said substituted provisions come into operation.

Definitions
"statute", "instrument", "statutory instrument": s 3; "Act of the Oireachtas": s 4.

20 Construction of references to repealed statutes and revoked instruments

(1) Whenever any statute or portion of a statute is repealed and re-enacted, with or without modification, by an Act of the Oireachtas, references in any other statute or in any statutory instrument to the statute or portion of a statute so repealed and re-enacted shall, unless the contrary intention appears, be construed as references to the portion of such Act of the Oireachtas containing such re-enactment.

(2) Whenever a statutory instrument or a portion of a statutory instrument is revoked and re-enacted, with or without modification, by an instrument made wholly or partly under an Act of the Oireachtas, references in any other statutory instrument to the statutory instrument or portion of a statutory instrument so revoked and re-enacted shall, unless the contrary intention appears, be construed as references to the said instrument containing such re-enactment.

Definitions
"statute", "instrument", "statutory instrument": s 3; "Act of the Oireachtas": s 4.

21 Operation of repeals, cessers, and terminations of statutes

(1) Where an Act of the Oireachtas repeals the whole or a portion of a previous statute, then, unless the contrary intention appears, such repeal shall not —

(*a*) revive anything not in force or not existing immediately before such repeal takes effect, or

(*b*) affect the previous operation of the statute or portion of a statue so repealed or anything duly done or suffered thereunder, or

(*c*) affect any right, privilege, obligation, or liability acquired, accrued, or incurred under the statute or portion of a statue so repealed, or

(*d*) affect any penalty, forfeiture, or punishment incurred in respect of any offence against or contravention of the statute or portion of a statute so repealed which was committed before such repeal, or

(*e*) prejudice or affect any legal proceedings, civil or criminal, pending at the time of such repeal of any such right, privilege, obligation, liability, offence, or contravention as aforesaid.

(2) Where an Act of the Oireachtas repeals the whole or a portion of a previous statute, then, unless the contrary intention appears, any legal proceedings, civil or criminal, in respect of any right, privilege, obligation, or liability acquired, accrued, or incurred under or any offence against or contravention of the statute or portion of a statute so repealed may be instituted, continued or enforced, and any penalty, forfeiture, or punishment in respect of any such offence or contravention may be imposed and carried out as if such statute or portion of a statute had not been repealed.

(3) Where an Act of the Oireachtas or a portion of any such Act ceases by any means or for any reason (other than repeal by a subsequent Act of the Oireachtas) to be in force, the preceding subsections of this section shall apply and have effect in relation to such Act or portion of an Act as if such cesser were caused by a repeal effected by an Act of the Oireachtas, and accordingly, for the purposes of such application, every reference in either of the said preceding subsections to a repeal shall be construed as a reference to a cesser by any means or for any reason (other than such repeal) to be in force.

Definitions

"statute": s 3; "Act of the Oireachtas": s 4.

22 Operation of revocations, cessers and terminations of statutory instruments

(1) Where an instrument made wholly or partly under an Act of the Oireachtas revokes the whole or a portion of a previous statutory instrument, then, unless the contrary intention appears, such revocation shall not —

(*a*) revive anything not in force or not existing immediately before such revocation takes effect, or

(*b*) affect the previous operation of the statutory instrument or portion of a statutory instrument so revoked or anything duly done or suffered thereunder, or

(*c*) affect any right, privilege, obligation, or liability acquired, accrued, or incurred under the statutory instrument or portion of a statutory instrument so revoked, or

(*d*) affect any penalty, forfeiture, or punishment incurred in respect of any offence against or contravention of the statutory instrument or portion of a statutory instrument so revoked which was committed before such revocation, or

(*e*) prejudice or affect any legal proceedings, civil or criminal, pending at the time of such revocation in respect of any such right, privilege, obligation, liability, offence, or contravention as aforesaid.

(2) Where an instrument made wholly or partly under an Act of the Oireachtas revokes the whole or a portion of a previous statutory instrument, then, unless the contrary intention appears, any legal proceedings, civil or criminal, in respect of any right, privilege, obligation, or liability acquired, accrued, or incurred under or any offence against or contravention of the statutory instrument or portion of the statutory instrument so revoked may be instituted, continued, or enforced and any penalty, forfeiture, or punishment in respect of any such offence or contravention may be

imposed and carried out as if such statutory instrument or portion of a statutory instrument had not been revoked.

(3) Where an instrument made wholly or partly under an Act of the Oireachtas or a portion of an instrument so made ceases by any means or for any reason (other than revocation by a subsequent such instrument) to be in force, the preceding subsections of this section shall apply and have effect in relation to such instrument or portion of an instrument as if such cesser were caused by a revocation effected by a subsequent such instrument, and accordingly, for the purposes of such application, every reference in either of the said preceding subsections to a revocation shall be construed as a reference to a cesser by any means or for any reason (other than such revocation) to be in force.

Definitions
"instrument", "statutory instrument": s 3; "Act of the Oireachtas": s 4.

SCHEDULE

INTERPRETATION OF PARTICULAR EXPRESSIONS AND WORDS

1. The word **"affidavit"**, in the case of persons for the time being allowed by law to declare instead of swearing, includes declaration.

2. The expression **"the Bank of Ireland"** means either, as the context requires, the Governor and Company of the Bank of Ireland or the bank of the said Governor and Company.

3. The expression **"British statute"** means an Act of the Parliament of the late United Kingdom of Great Britain and Ireland.

4. The expression **"the Circuit Court"**, means the Circuit Court of Justice as established and for the time being maintained by law.

5. The word **"commencement"**, when used in relation to a statute or a statutory instrument or a portion of a statute or statutory instrument, means the time at which such statute, statutory instrument, or portion of a statute or statutory instrument comes into operation.

6. The expression **"consular officer"** means a person in the Civil Service of Ireland who is a consul-general, a consul, or a vice-consul.

7. The expression **"the Constitution"** means the Constitution of Ireland enacted by the people on the 1st day of July, 1937.

8. The expression **"Dáil Éireann"** means the House of the Oireachtas to which that name is given by section 1 of Article 15 of the Constitution.

9. The expression **"the District Court"** means the District Court of Justice as established and for the time being maintained by law.

10. ...[1].

11. The expression **"the Government"** means the Government mentioned in Article 28 of the Constitution.

12. The expression **"Great Britain"** does not include the Channel Islands or the Isle of Man.

13. The expression **"the High Court"** means the High Court of Justice established and for the time being maintained by law in pursuance of Article 34 of the Constitution.

14. The word **"land"** includes messuages, tenements, and hereditaments, houses and buildings, of any tenure.

15. The expression **"the Lands Clauses Acts"** means the Lands Clauses Consolidation Act, 1845, the Lands Clauses Consolidation Acts Amendment Act, 1860, the Railways Act (Ireland), 1851, the Railways Act (Ireland), 1860, the Railways Act (Ireland), 1864, the Railways Traverse Act, the Acquisition of Land (Assessment of Compensation) Act, 1919, and every statute for the time being in force amending those Acts or any of them.

16. ...[1].

17. The word **"midnight"** means, in relation to any particular day, the point of time at which such day ends.

18. The expression [**"Minister of the Government"**][2] means a member of the Government having charge of a Department of State.

19. The word **"month"** means a calendar month.

20. The word **"oath"**, in the case of persons for the time being allowed by law to affirm instead of swearing, includes affirmation.

21. The expression **"the Oireachtas"** means the National Parliament provided for by Article 15 of the Constitution.

22. The expression **"ordnance map"** means a map made under the powers conferred by the Survey (Ireland) Acts, 1825 to 1870, and the statutes for the time being in force amending those Acts or any of them.

23. The expression **"the President"** means the President of Ireland and includes any commission or other body or authority for the time being lawfully exercising the powers and performing the duties of the President.

24. The expression **"pre-union Irish statute"** means an Act passed by a Parliament sitting in Ireland at any time before the coming into force of the Union with Ireland Act, 1800.

25. The expression **"rateable valuation"** means the valuation under the Valuation Acts of the property in relation to which the expression is used.

26. The expression **"rules of court"** means rules made by the authority for the time being having power to make rules regulating the practice and procedure of the court in relation to which the expression is used.

27. The expression **"Saorstát Éireann statute"** means an Act of the Oireachtas of Saorstát Éireann.

28. The expression **"Seanad Éireann"** means the House of the Oireachtas to which that name is given by section 1 of Article 15 of the Constitution.

29. The expression **"statutory declaration"** means a declaration made by virtue of the Statutory Declarations Act, 1835.

30. The expression **"the Supreme Court"** means the Supreme Court of Justice as established and for the time being maintained by law in pursuance of Article 34 of the Constitution.

31. The word **"swear"**, in the case of persons for the time being allowed by law to affirm or declare instead of swearing, includes affirm and declare.

32. The word **"town"** means the area comprised in a town (not being an urban district) in which the Towns Improvement (Ireland) Act, 1854, is in operation.

33. The expression **"Valuation Acts"** means the Acts for the time being in force relating to the valuation of rateable property.

34. The word **"week"**, when used without qualification, means the period between midnight on any Saturday and midnight on the next following Saturday.

35. The word **"week-day"** means a day which is not a Sunday.

36. The word **"writing"** includes printing, type-writing, lithography, photography, and other modes of representing or reproducing words in visible form, and cognate words shall be construed accordingly.

37. The word **"year"**, when used without qualification, means a period of twelve months beginning on the 1st day of the month of January in any year.

Amendments

1 Repealed by Exchequer and Local Financial Years Act 1974 s 2 except in relation to before 1 January 1975.

2 Substituted by the Ministers and Secretaries (Amendment) (No 2) Act 1977.

Definitions

"person": s 11(*c*).

---

29. The expression "statutory declaration" means a declaration made by virtue of the Statutory Declarations Act, 1835.

30. The expression "the Supreme Court" means the Supreme Court of Justice as established and for the time being maintained by law in pursuance of Article 34 of the Constitution.

31. The word "swear" in the case of persons for the time being allowed by law to affirm or declare instead of swearing, includes affirm and declare.

32. The word "town" means the area comprised in a town (not being an urban district) in which the Towns Improvement (Ireland) Act, 1854 is in operation.

33. The expression "Valuation Acts" means the Acts for the time being in force relating to the valuation of rateable property.

34. The word "week", when used without qualification, means the period between midnight on any Saturday and midnight on the next following Saturday.

35. The word "week-day" means a day which is not a Sunday.

36. The word "writing" includes printing, type-writing, lithography, photography, and other modes of representing or reproducing words in visible form, and cognate words shall be construed accordingly.

37. The word "year", when used without qualification, means a period of twelve months beginning on the 1st day of the month of January in any year.

Amendments:

1 Repealed by Exchequer and Local Financial Years Act 1974 s.5 except in relation to Clause 1 January 1975.

2 Substituted by the Ministers and Secretaries (Amendment) (No. 2) Act 1977.

Definitions:

"person": s11(c).

WAIVER OF CERTAIN TAX, INTEREST AND PENALTIES ACT 1993

(Number 24 of 1993)

ARRANGEMENT OF SECTIONS

Section

An Act to waive certain tax and interest and penalties on certain tax, to amend the provisions of the Income Tax Act, 1967, by amending section 512 and Schedule 15 to that Act and by substituting a new provision for section 516 of that Act, to provide for the furnishing of certain information by financial institutions to inspectors of the Revenue Commissioners and to provide for connected matters [14th July, 1993]

Cross-references

Concealing facts disclosed by documents: s 1078A(1)(*a*), (2)(i).
Presumptions in proceedings: s 1078B(1), (2).
Provision of information to juries: s 1078C(1).

1 Interpretation

(*a*) In this Act, except where the context otherwise requires–

"arrears of tax", subject to section 2(5)(*a*), has the meaning assigned to it by section 3(2);

"Chief Special Collector" has the meaning assigned to it by section 7(3);

"the declared amounts" has the meaning assigned to it by section 2(3)(*a*)(iii);

"estimate" means an estimate of, or an assessment to, tax made in accordance with the provisions of–

(i) section 7 or 8 of the Finance Act, 1968,

(ii) section 17 of the Finance Act, 1970, and the regulations made thereunder, or

(iii) section 22 or 23 of the Value-Added Tax Act, 1972,

as the case may be;

"functions" includes powers and duties;

"inspector" means an inspector of taxes appointed under section 161 of the Income Tax Act, 1967;

"the Minister" means the Minister for Finance;

"relevant interest" means interest payable in accordance with the specified provisions;

"the relevant period" means any period ending on or before the 5th day of April, 1991;

"relevant tax" has the meaning assigned to it by section 2(2);

"settlement amount" has the meaning assigned to it by section 2(3)(*b*);

"the specified period" means the period beginning with the passing of this Act and ending on the [21st day of December] [1];

"the specified provisions" means any provision of the Acts (within the meaning of section 2 or 3, as the case may be) pursuant to which a person may be liable–

(i) to interest in respect of tax (within the aforesaid meaning) which is unpaid, including interest on an undercharge of such tax which is attributable to fraud or neglect, or

(ii) to a fine or other penalty in respect of an offence or default.

(*b*) References in this Act to tax (within the meaning of section 2 or 3, as the case may be) being due and payable by a person include references to such tax which would have been due and payable by him if any return, statement or declaration (being a return, statement or declaration, as the case may be, which should have, but had not, been made by him in accordance with any provision of the Acts (within the aforesaid meaning)) had been so made and if that tax had been contained in an assessment made on the person or in an estimate issued to the person.

Amendments

1 Substituted by FA 1994 s 163(1) with effect from 14 July 1993; previously "30th day of November".

Definitions

"inspector": ITA 1967 ss 1(1), 161; "person": IA 1937 s 11(*c*).

2 Waiver of certain tax and related interest and penalties

(1) In this section–

"the Acts" means–

(*a*) the Income Tax Acts (other than Chapter IV of Part V of the Income Tax Act, 1967, and section 17 of the Finance Act, 1970),

(*b*) the Capital Gains Tax Acts,

(*c*) section 16 of the Finance Act, 1983,

(*d*) the Health Contributions Act, 1979, and

(*e*) the Youth Employment Agency Act, 1981,

and any instruments made thereunder;

"income" means total income from all sources as estimated in accordance with the provisions of the Income Tax Acts after deducting from the income so much of any deduction allowed by virtue of the provisions referred to in section 33 of the Finance Act, 1975, as is to be deducted from or set off against that income in charging it to income tax;

"tax" means any tax, levy or contributions payable in accordance with any provision of the Acts.

(2) This section applies to an individual who, for the relevant period, was in receipt of income or had chargeable gains in respect of which any tax (referred to in this Act as **"relevant tax"**) due and payable by him in accordance with any provision of the Acts has not been paid:

Provided that–

(*a*) this section shall not apply to an individual if, before the 25th day of May, 1993 (hereafter in this proviso referred to as **"the designated date"**), he had been notified in writing by an inspector–

(i) that the inspector intended to make any enquiries or take any actions as are specified in section 15 of the Finance Act, 1988, in relation to the liability to tax of the individual for the relevant period, or

(ii) that any matter which occasions or may occasion a liability or further liability to tax of the individual for the relevant period is under investigation or enquiry by the inspector,

and such enquiries or actions, or investigation or enquiry, as the case may be, had not been concluded on or before the designated date, and for the purposes of this paragraph the aforesaid enquiries or actions, or investigation or enquiry, shall be deemed not to have been concluded unless an agreement has been reached between the individual and the inspector as to the liability to tax of the individual for the relevant period,

(*b*) relevant tax shall not include any sum–

(i) which, before the designated date, was certified in a certificate issued, and not withdrawn, under section 485 of the Income Tax Act, 1967,

(ii) which, before the designated date, was the subject of proceedings initiated, and not withdrawn, as a debt due to the Minister, in any court of competent jurisdiction,

(iii) which was tax contained in an assessment which was on the designated date the subject of an appeal to which the provisions of Part XXVI of the Income Tax Act, 1967, apply,

(iv) which, before the designated date, was entered as a specified amount in a notice of attachment issued, and not revoked, under section 73 of the Finance Act, 1988,

(v) which was not paid on or before the designated date by virtue of an arrangement or scheme the main purpose, or one of the main purposes, of which was the avoidance of liability to tax,

(vi) which, following enquiries made, or action taken, by an inspector pursuant to section 15 of the Finance Act, 1988, or any other investigation by an inspector, had been agreed before the designated date by an individual and an inspector as being the individual's tax liability,

(vii) being tax in respect of income or chargeable gains which arose from, or by reason of, an illegal source or activity (other than the evasion of tax or the non-compliance with the provisions relating to exchange control), or

(viii) paid or remitted in accordance with the provisions of section 3 in respect of arrears of tax.

(3) An individual to whom this section applies shall–

(*a*) within the specified period give a declaration in writing to the Chief Special Collector which–

(i) is made and signed by the individual,

(ii) is in a form prescribed by the Revenue Commissioners and approved of by the Minister,

(iii) contains, in relation to the individual, a full and true statement of the respective amounts (referred to in this Act as **"the declared amounts"**) of–

(I) the income, and

(II) the chargeable gains,

referred to in subsection (2), and

(iv) declares that neither the declared amounts nor any part of those amounts arose from, or by reason of, an unlawful source or activity (other than the evasion of tax or the non-compliance with the provisions relating to exchange control), and

(*b*) not earlier than the giving of the declaration referred to in paragraph (*a*) but on or before the 14th day of January, 1994, remit to the Chief Special Collector an amount (referred to in this Act as **"the settlement amount"**) equal to 15 per cent of the declared amounts.

(4) On receipt by him of the declaration referred to in subsection (3) and the settlement amount, the Chief Special Collector shall give to the individual concerned–

(*a*) a certificate, in a form prescribed by the Revenue Commissioners and approved of by the Minister, stating, in relation to that individual–

(i) his name and address,

(ii) the settlement amount paid by him, and

(iii) the respective amounts of the declared amounts, and

(*b*) evidence, in a form prescribed by the Revenue Commissioners and approved of by the Minister, that such a certificate has been given.

(5) Notwithstanding any other provision of the Acts but subject to section 4, where an individual to whom this section applies complies with the provisions of subsection (3)--

(*a*) his liability to relevant tax in respect of the declared amounts—

(i) shall be deemed to be satisfied by the settlement amount, and

(ii) shall not be arrears of tax,

(*b*) any amount of relevant interest which the individual may have become liable for in relation to relevant tax in respect of the declared amounts shall be waived, and

(*c*) proceedings shall not be initiated or continued for the recovery of any fine or penalty to which the individual may be liable under any of the specified provisions in relation to relevant tax in respect of the declared amounts, nor shall the Revenue Commissioners seek or demand from the individual payment of any sum in lieu of such fine or penalty.

Cross-references

Penalties (subs (2) and (3)(*a*)): mitigation of: ITA 1967 s 512(1)(proviso); ITA 1967 s 516(4).
Inspector's enquiries (subs (40): s 5.

Case law

Subs (4): Held taxpayer could not rely on an certificate under subs (4)(*a*) where proceedings had been issued before 25 May 1993: *Irwin v Grimes* (High Court, 27 July 1995).

Definitions

"chargeable gain": CGTA 1975 ss 2(1), 11(2); CTA 1976 ss 1(5)(*c*), 155(5); "Income Tax Acts": ITA 1967 s 3; "inspector": ITA 1967 ss 1(1), 161; "total income": ITA 1967 s 1(1); "writing": IA 1937 Sch.

---

3 Waiver of certain interest and penalties in respect of certain tax

(1) (*a*) In this section–

"the Acts" means–

(i) the Acts within the meaning of section 2,

(ii) Chapter IV of Part V of the Income Tax Act 1967,

(iii) section 17 of the Finance Act, 1970,

(iv) the Corporation Tax Acts,

(v) Part V of the Finance Act, 1920, and the enactments amending or extending that Part,

(vi) the Value-Added Tax Act, 1972, and the enactments amending or extending that Act,

(vii) the Capital Acquisitions Tax Act, 1976, and the enactments amending or extending that Act,

(viii) the Stamp Act, 1891, and the enactments amending or extending that Act, and

(ix) Part VI of the Finance Act, 1983, and the enactments amending or extending that Part,

and any instruments made thereunder;

"the due date" means, in relation to an amount of tax, the date on which a person becomes liable to interest under any of the specified provisions in respect of the late payment of that tax;

"tax" means any tax, duty, levy or contributions payable in accordance with any provision of the Acts.

(*b*) The reference in subsection (2) to an amount of tax due and payable shall, in a case where tax is assessed or estimated in an assessment or estimate against which an appeal has been made, be construed as a reference to the amount of tax which becomes due and payable on the determination of the appeal (within the meaning of section 550(2A)(*c*) of the Income Tax Act, 1967) or, pending such determination, the tax as assessed or estimated.

(2) This section applies to a person who had not paid or remitted before the due date an amount of tax (in this-Act referred to as "arrears of tax") due and payable by him, or chargeable, in accordance with any provision of the Acts in respect of or during the relevant period.

(3) Where a person to whom this section applies has unpaid arrears of tax on the passing of this Act, he shall on or before the 14th day of January, 1994, and subject to the provisions of subsection (6), pay or remit those arrears of tax.

(4) Notwithstanding any other provision of the Acts but subject to the provisions of subsection (5) and section 4, where a person has paid or remitted, on or before the 14th day of January, 1994, his arrears of tax–

(*a*) any amount of relevant interest to which the person may be liable in relation to arrears of tax and which is unpaid at the date of the payment or remittance referred to in subsection (3) shall be waived,

(*b*) any amount of relevant interest in relation to arrears of tax which is paid by the person on or after the 26th day of May, 1993, shall be refunded to him, and (*c*) proceedings shall not be initiated or continued for the recovery of any fine or penalty to which the person may be liable under any of the specified provisions in relation to arrears of tax, nor shall the Revenue Commissioners seek or demand from the person payment of any sum in lieu of such fine or penalty.

(5) This section shall not apply to any interest, fine or other penalty that–

(*a*) in the case of a fine or other penalty, is imposed by a court under any of the Acts,

(*b*) in the case of interest, is ordered by a court in any proceedings for the recovery of tax or interest to be paid by a person, or

(*c*) in any case, is included in a specified sum such as is referred to in subsection (2)(*c*) of section 23 of the Finance Act, 1983, where the full amount of the specified sum was not paid on or before the 25th day of May, 1993.

(6) (*a*) Where a payment or remittance in accordance with the provisions of subsection (3) *is* made by an individual who also remits a settlement amount, then, without prejudice to the amount of that payment or remittance, so much of that payment or remittance as is referable to value-added tax may be remitted to the Chief Special Collector.

(*b*) Where, in accordance with paragraph (*a*), an individual makes a remittance to the Chief Special Collector, the individual by whom the remittance is made shall on the earlier of–

(i) the date of payment, or

(ii) a date within the specified period,

give a declaration in writing to the Chief Special Collector which–

(I) is made and signed by the individual,

(II) is in a form prescribed by the Revenue Commissioners and approved of by the Minister, and

(III) contains, in relation to that individual, a full and true statement of the amount of value-added tax comprised in the arrears of tax.

(*c*) On receipt by him of the declaration referred to in paragraph (*b*) and the remittance referred to in paragraph (*a*), the Chief Special Collector shall give to the individual by whom the remittance is made–

(i) a certificate, in a form prescribed by the Revenue Commissioners and approved of by the Minister, stating, in relation to that individual–

(I) his name and address, and

(II) the amount of the said remittance, and

(ii) evidence, in a form prescribed by the Revenue Commissioners and approved of by the Minister, that such a certificate has been given.

(7) ....

Note

Subs (7) substituted FA 1983 s 23(4)(*aa*).

Cross-references

Inspector's enquiries: s 5.

Penalties (subs (2) and (6)(*b*)): mitigation of: ITA 1967 s 512(1)(proviso); ITA 1967 s 516(4).

Defaulters availing of these provisions, non-publication of names: FA 1983 s 23(4).

Definitions

"the Corporation Tax Acts": CTA 1976 s 155(1); "person": IA 1937 s 11(*c*); "writing": IA 1937 Sch.

4 Non-application of sections 2(5) and 3(4)

(1) The provisions of sections 2(5) and 3(4) shall not apply, and those provisions shall be deemed never to have applied, to a person where–

(*a*) such person fails–

(i) if he is an individual, for the year of assessment 1992–93, or

(ii) in any other case, for any accounting period ending in the year beginning on the 1st day of January, 1993, and ending on the 31st day of December, 1993,

to duly deliver a return of income on or before the specified date in relation to that return, or

(*b*) (i) a declaration given by such person to the Chief Special Collector under subsection (3)(*a*) of section 2—

(I) did not contain a full and true statement of the kind referred to in subparagraph (iii) of the said subsection, or

(II) is proven to be false in so far as the requirements of subparagraph (iv) of the said subsection are concerned,

or

(ii) a declaration given by him to the Chief Special Collector under subsection (6)(*b*) of section 3 did not contain a full and true statement of the kind referred to in subparagraph (III) of the said subsection, or

(*c*) the amount paid or remitted by him in respect of arrears of tax was less than the arrears of tax due and payable by him,

and any certificate issued to that person pursuant to section 2(4) or section 3(6)(*c*) shall be null and void.

(2) Where, by virtue of this section, section 2(5) does not apply and is deemed never to have applied to an individual, the amount paid by him as the settlement amount shall be treated as a payment on account of relevant tax.

(3) (*a*) In subsection (1) **"return of income"** and **"specified date"** have the meanings assigned to them by section 48 of the Finance Act, 1986.

(*b*) The provisions of subsection (1)(*b*) of section 48 of the Finance Act, 1986, shall apply for the purposes of subsection (1)(*a*) of this section as they apply for the purposes of that section.

5 Enquiries or action by inspector or other officer

(1) Where, in relation to any liability to tax (within the meaning of section 2 or 3, as the case may be) of an individual for the relevant period, being tax which has been remitted to the Chief Special Collector, an inspector or other officer of the Revenue Commissioners commences to make such enquiries, or take such action, as are within his powers, or gives a notice in writing to an individual of his intention to make such enquiries or take such action in relation to such liability to tax and the individual produces to the inspector or other officer, not later than 30 days from the commencement of the said enquiries or the taking of the said action, or the giving of the notice as aforesaid, a certificate referred to in section 2(4) or 3(6)(*c*), as the case may be, in respect of such liability to tax given to him by the Chief Special Collector, the inspector or other officer shall, on production to him of the said certificate and on validation of that certificate in accordance with the provisions of paragraph (*a*) of the proviso to section 7(4), be precluded from continuing with or commencing the said enquiries or continuing with or commencing the said action unless, on application by him to the Appeal Commissioners, he shows to the satisfaction of those Commissioners that–

(*a*) enquiries made or action taken in relation to the liability to tax (within the aforesaid meaning) of the individual for any period commencing on or after the 6th day of April, 1991, indicate, or

(*b*) there are other reasonable grounds which indicate,

that a declaration made by the individual to the Chief Special Collector under section 2(3)(*a*) or 3(6)(*b*) did not contain a full and true statement of the declared amounts or the amount of value-added tax comprised in the [arrears of tax, as the case may be, or that the declaration made by the individual under section 2(3)(*a*)(iv) is false].[1]

(2) (*a*) An application by the inspector or other officer under subsection (1) shall be made by him by notice in writing to the Appeal Commissioners within 30 days of the receipt by him from the individual concerned of the certificate referred to in section 2(4) or 3(6)(*c*), as the case may be, given to that individual by the Chief Special Collector, and a copy of the application shall be furnished as soon as practicable by the inspector or other officer to the individual concerned.

(*b*) An application under subsection (1) shall, with any necessary modifications, be heard by the Appeal Commissioners as if it were an appeal against an assessment to income tax.

(*c*) Any action required to be taken by the individual and any further action proposed to be taken by the inspector or other officer pursuant to the inspector's or other officer's enquiry or action shall be suspended pending decision by the Appeal Commissioners on the application.

(*d*) Where, on the hearing of the application by an inspector or other officer under subsection (1), the Appeal Commissioners–

(i) decide that there are no reasonable grounds to suggest that the declaration made by the individual to the Chief Special Collector under section 2(3)(*a*) or 3(6)(*b*) did not contain a full and true statement of the declared amounts or the amount of value-added tax comprised in the arrears of tax, as the case may be, then the individual shall not be required to take any action pursuant to the inspector's or other officer's enquiry or action and the inspector or other officer shall be prohibited from pursuing his enquiry or action, or

(ii) decide that there are such reasonable grounds, then the inspector or other officer may continue with his enquiry or action.

Amendments

1 Substituted by Criminal Assets Bureau Act 1996 s 25; previously "arrears of tax, as the case may be".

Definitions

"Appeal Commissioners": ITA 1967 s 1(1), 156; "inspector": ITA 1967 ss 1(1), 161; "person": IA 1937 s 11(*c*); "year of assessment": CGTA 1975 s 2(1), ITA 1967 s 1(1).

6 Demands or other requests for payment

Where, in relation to an individual–

(*a*) the Revenue Commissioners, the Collector-General or any of their or his officers authorised in that behalf, have demanded or otherwise requested the payment of any tax–

(i) in respect of which a settlement amount has been remitted to the Chief Special Collector, or

(ii) which is value-added tax in respect of which a remittance has been made to the Chief Special Collector in accordance with section 3(6)(*a*), and

(*b*) the individual has been given a certificate as is referred to in section 2(4) or 3(6)(*c*) in respect of such tax,

the individual shall produce to the Revenue Commissioners, the Collector-General or the authorised officer, as the case may be, within 30 days of–

(i) the date of the making of the demand or request, or

(ii) if later, the date he received the certificate,

the evidence referred to in section 2(4)(*b*) or section 3(6)(*c*), as the case may be, and the demand or request shall be withdrawn and the amount of tax specified in the demand or request shall be discharged:

Provided that, where subsection (5) of section 2 and subsection (4) of section 3 do not apply by virtue of the provisions of section 4—

(i) the amount of tax discharged shall be reinstated, and

(ii) any additional assessments or estimates necessary to give effect to this proviso shall be made.

7 Confidentiality

(1) In this section–

"declaration of confidentiality" means the declaration of confidentiality contained in the Schedule to this Act;

"special collection function" means any function or duty related to–

(*a*) the receipt and retention of declarations referred to in section 2(3)(*a*) or 3(6)(*b*),

(*b*) the receipt, recording and lodgement of–

(i) settlement amounts, or

(ii) so much of any payment or remittance referred to in section 3(6)(*a*) as is referable to value-added tax, or

(*c*) the issue and recording of certificates referred to in section 2(4) or 3(6)(*c*),

which could result in the person or persons discharging that function or performing that duty acquiring, or having access to, any information in respect of such declarations, amounts or certificates, and a reference to the discharge of a special collection function shall be construed as a reference to the discharge of such a function or performance of such a duty;

"special collector" means any officer or employee of the Revenue Commissioners who–

(*a*) has been nominated by the Revenue Commissioners to discharge a special collection function, and has not had his nomination revoked, and

(*b*) has made and subscribed the declaration of confidentiality.

(2) (*a*) Special collection functions may only be discharged by special collectors.

(*b*) Every person nominated by the Revenue Commissioners to be a special collector shall, upon making and subscribing to the declaration of confidentiality, become a special collector.

(*c*) Declarations of confidentiality shall be made before a peace commissioner or other person duly authorised to take and receive statutory declarations.

(3) (*a*) Special collection functions shall be under the control and direction of a special collector, to be known as and is referred to in this Act as **"the Chief Special Collector"**, who is designated to be such by the Revenue Commissioners.

(*b*) Whenever there is no Chief Special Collector, the Revenue Commissioners shall designate as soon as is practicable thereafter a special collector to be the Chief Special Collector and all other special collectors shall observe and follow the orders, instructions and directions of the Chief Special Collector in relation to any special collection function:

Provided that nothing in paragraph (*b*) shall be construed so as to affect the proviso to subsection (6).

(*c*) For the purposes of the receipt of any declaration, amount or remittance, or the issue of any certificate or evidence, in accordance with section 2 or 3, references to the Chief Special Collector shall be construed as including a reference to any other special collector acting on behalf of the Chief Special Collector in that matter.

(*d*) If and so long as the Chief Special Collector is unable through illness, absence or other cause to fulfil his duties, another special collector designated in that behalf by the Revenue Commissioners shall act as Chief Special Collector, and any reference in this Act to the Chief Special Collector shall be construed as including, where appropriate, a reference to a special collector designated under this paragraph.

(4) A special collector shall be deemed to have contravened his declaration of confidentiality if he discloses, or causes to be disclosed, to a person who is not a special collector, any information which he could have acquired, or had access to, only by virtue of being a special collector:

Provided that a special collector shall not be deemed to have contravened his declaration of confidentiality where–

(*a*) having been requested to validate a certificate or evidence referred to in section 2(4) or 3(6)(*c*) by an officer of the Revenue Commissioners to whom that certificate or evidence has been produced for the purposes of section 5 or 6, as the case may be, he informs that officer whether or not that certificate or evidence, as the case may be, was given by a special collector,

(*b*) he provides to the Minister or the Revenue Commissioners such information, in the form of aggregates and in that form only, as the Minister or the Commissioners, as the case may be, may request in relation to–

(i) the total amount of–

(I) the declared amounts,

(II) settlement amounts, or

(III) such amounts of any payments or remittances referred to in section 3(6)(*a*) as are referable to value-added tax remitted to the Chief Special Collector,

and

(ii) the total respective numbers of individuals who remitted amounts to the Chief Special Collector in respect of income, chargeable gains or value-added tax,

or

(*c*) he provides to the Comptroller and Auditor General or the Accounting Officer of the Revenue Commissioners such information as the Comptroller and Auditor General or that Accounting Officer, as the case may be, may request and reasonably require to ensure that any special collection function has been discharged in accordance with this Act

(5) Any information acquired by the Comptroller and Auditor General or the Accounting Officer of the Revenue Commissioners by virtue of paragraph (*c*) of the proviso to subsection (4) shall be used by the Comptroller and Auditor General or that Accounting Officer, as the case may be, only for the purpose of ensuring that any special collection function has been discharged in accordance with this Act:

Provided that the foregoing provisions of this subsection shall not prevent the Comptroller and Auditor General from carrying out his functions, including exercising his reporting duty to Dáil Éireann.

(6) The Revenue Commissioners may make such nominations as are required for the purposes of this section and may at any time also revoke any such nomination:

Provided that the Revenue Commissioners may only revoke at any time the nomination of the special collector who is the Chief Special Collector where they also designate, with effect from that time, a special collector to be his successor as Chief Special Collector.

Definitions

"chargeable gain": CGTA 1975 ss 2(1), 11(2); CTA 1976 ss 1(5)(*c*), 155(5); "statutory declaration": IA 1937 Sch.

8 Remittances

Any remittance made to the Chief Special Collector under section 2(3)(*b*) or 3(6)(*a*) shall–

(*a*) where it is made otherwise than in cash, be made payable to the Revenue Commissioners, and

(*b*) be lodged to the General Account of the Revenue Commissioners in the Central Bank of Ireland as soon as prompt recording, and secure transmission to that account, of that remittance permits.

9 Penalty for failure to comply with section 2(3)(*a*) or 3(6)(*b*)

(1) Where an individual, being an individual to whom section 2 applies, or a person to whom section 3 applies–

(*a*) (i) has knowingly or wilfully failed to comply with any provision of the Acts requiring–

(I) the furnishing of a return of income, profits or gains, or of sources of income, profits or gains, for the purposes of any tax,

(II) the furnishing of any other return, certificate, notification, particulars, or any statement or evidence, for the purposes of any tax, or

(ii) has knowingly or wilfully delivered any incorrect return, statement or accounts or knowingly or wilfully furnished any incorrect information in connection with any tax,

in respect of the relevant period, and

(*b*) (i) fails to give a declaration required by section 2(3)(*a*), or

(ii) gives such a declaration as aforesaid or a declaration under section 3(6)(*b*) which is false or fails to comply with the requirements of subparagraph (iii) or (iv) of the said section 2(3)(*a*) or subparagraph (III) of the said section 3(6)(*b*) to the extent that any of the said subparagraphs apply to him,

he shall, without prejudice to any other penalty to which he may be liable, be guilty of an offence and shall be liable–

(I) on summary conviction where the amount of the specified difference is–

(A) less than £1,200, to a fine not exceeding 25 per cent of the amount of the specified difference or, at the discretion of the court, to a term of imprisonment not exceeding 12 months or to both,

(B) equal to or greater than £1,200, to a fine not exceeding £1,200 or, at the discretion of the court, to a term of imprisonment not exceeding 12 months or to both,

(II) on conviction on indictment where the amount of the specified difference is–

(A) less than £5,000, to a fine not exceeding 25 per cent of the amount of the specified difference or, at the discretion of the court, to a term of imprisonment not exceeding 2 years or to both,

(B) equal to or greater than £5,000 but less than £10,000, to a fine not exceeding 50 per cent of the amount of the specified difference or, at the discretion of the court, to a term of imprisonment not exceeding 3 years or to both,

(C) equal to or greater than £10,000 but less than £25,000, to a fine not exceeding the amount of the specified difference or, at the discretion of the court, to a term of imprisonment not exceeding 4 years or to both,

(D) equal to or greater than £25,000 but less than £100,000, to a fine not exceeding twice the amount of the specified difference or, at the discretion of the court, to a term of imprisonment not exceeding 8 years or to both,

(E) equal to or greater than £100,000, to a fine not exceeding twice the amount of the specified difference and to a term of imprisonment not exceeding 8 years.

(2) Subsections (4), (6), (7) and (8) of section 94 of the Finance Act, 1983, shall, with any necessary modifications, apply and have effect for the purposes of this section as they apply and have effect for the purposes of that section.

(3) In this section–

"the Acts" and **"tax"** have the meanings assigned to them, respectively, by section 2 or 3, as appropriate;

"the specified difference" means the difference between–

(*a*) the amount of tax payable for the relevant period by the individual, and

(*b*) the amount which would have been so payable if–

(i) any return, certificate, notification or particulars or any statement of evidence, referred to in subsection (1)(*a*)(i), not furnished by him, had, in fact, been so furnished and the details therein had been correct, or

(ii) any incorrect return, statement or accounts, or any incorrect information, referred to in subsection (1)(*a*)(ii), in connection with any tax had, in fact, been correct.

Definitions

"month": IA 1937 Sch; "profits": CTA 1976 s 1(5)(*c*); "year": IA 1937 Sch.

10 Amendment of section 512 (mitigation and application of fines and penalties) of Income Tax Act, 1967

Amendments

Repealed by Taxes Consolidation Act 1997 s 1098 and Sch 30.

11 Penalty for false statement to obtain allowance

Amendments

Repealed by Taxes Consolidation Act 1997 s 1098 and Sch 30.

12 Amendment of Schedule 15 to Income Tax Act, 1967

Amendments

Repealed by Taxes Consolidation Act 1997 s 1098 and Sch 30.

13 Furnishing of certain information by financial institutions

Amendments

Repealed by Taxes Consolidation Act 1997 s 1098 and Sch 30.

14 Care and management

Subject to section 7(3)(*a*), all matters relating to this Act are hereby placed under the care and management of the Revenue Commissioners.

15 Short title, construction and collective citation

(1) This Act may be cited as the Waiver of Certain Tax, Interest and Penalties Act, 1993.

(2) This Act shall be construed–

(*a*) so far as relating to income tax and sur-tax, together with the Income Tax Acts,

(*b*) so far as relating to corporation profits tax, together with Part V of the Finance Act, 1920, and the enactments amending or extending that Part,

(*c*) so far as relating to corporation tax, together with the Corporation Tax Acts,

(*d*) so far as relating to capital gains tax, together with the Capital Gains Tax Acts, (*e*) so far as relating to value-added tax, together with the Value-Added Tax Acts, 1972 to 1993,

(*f*) so far as relating to stamp duty, together with the Stamp Act, 1891, and the enactments amending or extending that Act,

(*g*) so far as relating to capital acquisitions tax, together with the Capital Acquisitions Tax Act, 1976, and the enactments amending or extending that Act,

(*h*) so far as relating to residential property tax, together with Part VI of the Finance Act, 1983, and the enactments amending or extending that Part,

(*i*) so far as relating to income levy, together with section 16 of the Finance Act, 1983, and the enactments amending or extending that section,

(*j*) so far as relating to health contributions, together with the Health Contributions Act, 1979, and the enactments amending or extending that Act, and

(*k*) so far as relating to employment and training levy, together with the Youth Employment Agency Act, 1981, and the enactments amending or extending that Act.

(3) The collective citation "the Value-Added Tax Acts, 1972 to 1993" shall include this Act in so far as it relates to value-added tax.

(4) Any reference in this Act to any other enactment shall, except so far as the context otherwise requires, be construed as a reference to that enactment as amended by or under any other enactment including this Act.

(5) In this Act, a reference to a section is to a section of this Act, unless it is indicated that reference to some other enactment is intended.

(6) In this Act, a reference to a subsection, paragraph or subparagraph is to the subsection, paragraph or subparagraph of the provision in which the reference occurs, unless it is indicated that reference to some other provision is intended.

Definitions

"Corporation Tax Acts": CTA 1976 s 155(1); "Income Tax Acts": ITA 1967 s 3.

SCHEDULE

FORM OF DECLARATION OF CONFIDENTIALITY TO BE MADE BY SPECIAL COLLECTORS

"I, A.B., do solemnly declare that I have read and understand section 7 of the Waiver of Certain Tax, Interest and Penalties Act, 1993, and that I will not disclose, or cause to be disclosed, to a person who is not a special collector (within the meaning of that section) any information which I acquire, or have access to, in the course of discharging special collection functions (within the meaning of the said section) save where the disclosure of such information is deemed, by virtue of the proviso to subsection (4) of the said section 7, not to be a contravention of this declaration.".

TAXES CONSOLIDATION ACT 1997

(1997 Number 39)

ARRANGEMENT OF SECTIONS

INTERPRETATION AND BASIC CHARGING PROVISIONS

PART 1
INTERPRETATION

Section

PART 2
THE CHARGE TO TAX

CHAPTER 1
Income Tax

CHAPTER 2
Corporation Tax

CHAPTER 3
Capital Gains Tax

INCOME TAX AND CORPORATION TAX: THE MAIN PROVISIONS

PART 3
PROVISIONS RELATING TO THE SCHEDULE C CHARGE AND GOVERNMENT AND OTHER PUBLIC SECURITIES

CHAPTER 1
Principal Provisions Relating to the Schedule C Charge

CHAPTER 2
Government and Other Public Securities: Interest Payable Without Deduction of Tax

CHAPTER 3
Government and Other Public Securities: Exemptions from Tax

CHAPTER 4
Miscellaneous Provisions

PART 4
PRINCIPAL PROVISIONS RELATING TO THE SCHEDULE D CHARGE

CHAPTER 1
Supplementary Charging Provisions

CHAPTER 2
Foreign Dividends

CHAPTER 3
Income Tax: Basis of Assessment under Cases I and II

CHAPTER 4
Income Tax: Basis of Assessment under Cases III, IV and V

CHAPTER 5
Computational Provisions: Corporation Tax

CHAPTER 6
Computational Provisions: General

CHAPTER 7
Special Measures on Discontinuance of, and Change of Basis of Computation of Profits or Gains of, a Trade or Profession

CHAPTER 8
Taxation of Rents and Certain Other Payments

CHAPTER 9
Miscellaneous Provisions

PART 5
PRINCIPAL PROVISIONS RELATING TO THE SCHEDULE E CHARGE

CHAPTER 1
Basis of Assessment, Persons Chargeable and Extent of Charge

CHAPTER 2
Computational Provisions

CHAPTER 3
Expenses Allowances and Provisions Relating to the General Benefits in Kind Charge

CHAPTER 3
Distributions and Tax Credits — General

CHAPTER 4
Distributions Out of Certain Exempt Profits or Gains or Out of Certain Relieved Income

CHAPTER 5
Distributions Out of Certain Income of Manufacturing Companies

CHAPTER 6
Distributions — Supplemental

CHAPTER 7
Franked Investment Income

CHAPTER 8
Advance Corporation Tax

PART 7
INCOME TAX AND CORPORATION TAX EXEMPTIONS

CHAPTER 1
Income Tax

CHAPTER 2
Corporation Tax

CHAPTER 3
Income Tax and Corporation Tax

PART 8
ANNUAL PAYMENTS, CHARGES AND INTEREST

CHAPTER 1
Annual Payments

CHAPTER 2

Charges on Income for Corporation Tax Purposes

CHAPTER 3

Principal Provisions Relating to the Payment of Interest

CHAPTER 4

Interest Payments by Certain Deposit Takers

CHAPTER 5

Dividend Payments by Credit Unions

CHAPTER 6

Implementation of Council Directive 2003/49/EC of 3 June 2003 on a common system of taxation applicable to interest and royalty payments made between associated companies of different Member States.

CHAPTER 7

Certain interest from sources within the European Communities

PART 9

PRINCIPAL PROVISIONS RELATING TO RELIEF FOR CAPITAL EXPENDITURE

CHAPTER 1

Industrial Buildings or Structures: Industrial Building Allowances, Writing-Down Allowances, Balancing Allowances and Balancing Charges

CHAPTER 2

Machinery or Plant: Initial Allowances, Wear and Tear Allowances, Balancing Allowances and Balancing Charges

CHAPTER 3

Dredging: Initial Allowances and Annual Allowances

CHAPTER 4

Miscellaneous and General

PART 10

INCOME TAX AND CORPORATION TAX: RELIEFS FOR RENEWAL AND IMPROVEMENT OF CERTAIN URBAN AREAS, CERTAIN RESORT AREAS AND CERTAIN ISLANDS

CHAPTER 1

Custom House Docks Area

CHAPTER 2

Temple Bar Area

CHAPTER 3
Designated Areas, Designated Streets, Enterprise Areas and Multi-Storey Car Parks in Certain Urban Areas

CHAPTER 4
Qualifying Resort Areas

372F Rented residential accommodation: deduction for certain expenditure on construction
372G Rented residential accommodation: deduction for certain expenditure on conversion
372H Rented residential accommodation: deduction for certain expenditure on refurbishment
372I Residential accommodation: allowance to owner-occupiers in respect of certain expenditure on construction or refurbishment
372J Provisions supplementary to sections 372F to 372I
372K Non-application of relief in certain cases and provision against double relief

CHAPTER 8
Qualifying Rural Areas

372L Interpretation (Chapter 8)
372M Accelerated capital allowances in relation to construction or refurbishment of certain industrial buildings or structures
372N Capital allowances in relation to construction or refurbishment of certain commercial buildings or structures
372O Double rent allowance in respect of rent paid for certain business premises
372P Rented residential accommodation: deduction for certain expenditure on construction
372Q Rented residential accommodation: deduction for certain expenditure on conversion
372R Rented residential accommodation: deduction for certain expenditure on refurbishment
372RA Residential accommodation: allowance to owner-occupiers in respect of certain expenditure on construction or refurbishment
372S Provisions supplementary to sections 372P to 372R
372T Non-application of relief in certain cases and provision against double relief

CHAPTER 9
Park and Ride Facilities and Certain Related Developments

372U Interpretation
372V Capital allowances in relation to construction or refurbishment of certain park and ride facilities
372W Capital allowances in relation to construction or refurbishment of certain commercial premises
372X Rented residential accommodation: deduction for certain expenditure on construction
372Y Residential accommodation: allowance to owner-occupiers in respect of certain expenditure on construction
372Z Provisions supplementary to sections 372X and 372Y

CHAPTER 10
Designated areas of certain towns

372AA Interpretation and application (Chapter 10)

CHAPTER 11

Reliefs for lessors and owner-occupiers in respect of expenditure incurred on the provision of certain residential accommodation

PART 11

CAPITAL ALLOWANCES AND EXPENSES FOR CERTAIN ROAD VEHICLES

PART 11A

INCOME TAX AND CORPORATION TAX: DEDUCTION FOR EXPENDITURE ON CONSTRUCTION, CONVERSION AND REFURBISHMENT OF CERTAIN RESIDENTIAL ACCOMMODATION FOR CERTAIN STUDENTS

PART 11B

INCOME TAX AND CORPORATION TAX: DEDUCTION FOR EXPENDITURE ON REFURBISHMENT OF CERTAIN RESIDENTIAL ACCOMMODATION

PART 12

PRINCIPAL PROVISIONS RELATING TO LOSS RELIEF, TREATMENT OF CERTAIN LOSSES AND CAPITAL ALLOWANCES, AND GROUP RELIEF

CHAPTER 1

Income Tax: Loss Relief

CHAPTER 2

Income Tax: Loss Relief— Teatment of Capital Allowances

CHAPTER 3
Corporation Tax: Loss Relief

CHAPTER 4
Income Tax and Corporation Tax: Treatment of Certain Losses and Certain Capital Allowances

CHAPTER 5
Group Relief

PART 13

CLOSE COMPANIES

CHAPTER 1

Interpretation and General

CHAPTER 2

Additional Matters to be Treated as Distributions, Charges to Tax in Respect of Certain Loans and Surcharges on Certain Undistributed Income

PART 14

TAXATION OF COMPANIES ENGAGED IN MANUFACTURING TRADES, CERTAIN TRADING OPERATIONS CARRIED ON IN SHANNON AIRPORT AND CERTAIN TRADING OPERATIONS CARRIED ON IN THE CUSTOM HOUSE DOCKS AREA

CHAPTER 1

Interpretation and General

CHAPTER 2

Principal Provisions

PART 15

PERSONAL ALLOWANCES AND RELIEFS AND CERTAIN OTHER INCOME TAX AND CORPORATION TAX RELIEFS

CHAPTER 1

Personal Allowances and Reliefs

CHAPTER 2

Income Tax and Corporation Tax: Reliefs Applicable to Both

CHAPTER 3

Corporation Tax Reliefs

PART 16

INCOME TAX RELIEF FOR INVESTMENT IN CORPORATE TRADES— BUSINESS EXPANSION SCHEME AND SEED CAPITAL SCHEME

PART 17

PROFIT SHARING SCHEMES AND EMPLOYEE SHARE OWNERSHIP TRUSTS

CHAPTER 1

Profit Sharing Schemes

CHAPTER 2

Employee Share Ownership Trusts

CHAPTER 2

Computation of Chargeable Gains and Allowable Losses

CHAPTER 3

Assets Held in a Fiduciary or Representative Capacity, Inheritances and Settlements

CHAPTER 4
Shares and Securities

CHAPTER 5
Life Assurance and Deferred Annuities

CHAPTER 6
Transfers of Business Assets

CHAPTER 2
Provisions Where Companies Cease to be Resident in the State

PART 21
MERGERS, DIVISIONS, TRANSFERS OF ASSETS AND EXCHANGES OF SHARES CONCERNING COMPANIES OF DIFFERENT MEMBER STATES

TRANSACTIONS IN LAND

PART 22
PROVISIONS RELATING TO DEALING IN OR DEVELOPING LAND AND DISPOSALS OF DEVELOPMENT LAND

CHAPTER 1
Income Tax and Corporation Tax: Profits or Gains from Dealing in or Developing Land

CHAPTER 2
Capital Gains Tax: Disposals of Development Land

OTHER SPECIAL PROVISIONS

PART 23
FARMING AND MARKET GARDENING

CHAPTER 1
Interpretation and General

CHAPTER 2
Farming: Relief for Increase in Stock Values

CHAPTER 3
Milk Quotas

PART 24
TAXATION OF PROFITS OF CERTAIN MINES AND PETROLEUM TAXATION

CHAPTER 1
Taxation of Profits of Certain Mines

CHAPTER 2
Petroleum Taxation

PART 24A
SHIPPING: TONNAGE TAX

PART 25
INDUSTRIAL AND PROVIDENT SOCIETIES, BUILDING SOCIETIES, AND TRUSTEE SAVINGS BANKS

CHAPTER 1
Industrial and Provident Societies

CHAPTER 2
Building Societies

CHAPTER 3
Trustee Savings Banks

PART 26
LIFE ASSURANCE COMPANIES

CHAPTER 1
General Provisions

CHAPTER 2
Special Investment Policies

CHAPTER 3
Provisions Applying to Overseas Life Assurance Companies

CHAPTER 4
Taxation of Assurance Companies — New Basis

CHAPTER 5
Policyholders — New Basis

Chapter 6
Certain Foreign Life Policies — Taxation and Returns

PART 27
UNIT TRUSTS AND OFFSHORE FUNDS

CHAPTER 1
Unit Trusts

CHAPTER 1A
Investment Undertakings

CHAPTER 2
Offshore Funds

CHAPTER 3
Offshore Funds: Supplementary Provisions

CHAPTER 4
Certain Offshore Funds — Taxation and Returns

PART 28
PURCHASE AND SALE OF SECURITIES

CHAPTER 1
Purchase and Sale of Securities

CHAPTER 2
Purchases of Shares by Financial Concerns and Persons Exempted from Tax, and Restriction on Relief for Losses by Repayment of Tax in Case of Dividends Paid Out of Accumulated Profits

PART 29

PATENTS, SCIENTIFIC AND CERTAIN OTHER RESEARCH, KNOW-HOW AND CERTAIN TRAINING

CHAPTER 1
Patents

CHAPTER 2
Scientific and Certain Other Research

CHAPTER 3
Know-How and Certain Training

CHAPTER 4
Transmission Capacity Rights

PART 30

OCCUPATIONAL PENSION SCHEMES, RETIREMENT ANNUITIES, PURCHASED LIFE ANNUITIES AND CERTAIN PENSIONS

CHAPTER 1

Occupational Pension Schemes

CHAPTER 2

Retirement Annuities

CHAPTER 2A

Personal Retirement Savings Accounts

CHAPTER 2B
Overseas Pension Plans: Migrant Member Relief

CHAPTER 3
Purchased Life Annuities

CHAPTER 4
Miscellaneous

PART 31
TAXATION OF SETTLORS, ETC IN RESPECT OF SETTLED OR TRANSFERRED INCOME

CHAPTER 1
Revocable Dispositions for Short Periods and Certain Dispositions in Favour of Children

CHAPTER 2
Settlements on Children Generally

PART 32
ESTATES OF DECEASED PERSONS IN COURSE OF ADMINISTRATION AND SURCHARGE ON CERTAIN INCOME OF TRUSTEES

CHAPTER 1
Estates of Deceased Persons in Course of Administration

CHAPTER 2

Surcharge on Certain Income of Trustees

PART 33

ANTI-AVOIDANCE

CHAPTER 1

Transfer of Assets Abroad

CHAPTER 2

Miscellaneous

PART 34

PROVISIONS RELATING TO THE RESIDENCE OF INDIVIDUALS

PART 35
Double taxation relief

CHAPTER 1
Principal Reliefs

CHAPTER 2
Miscellaneous

PART 36
Miscellaneous special provisions

PART 36A

SPECIAL SAVINGS INCENTIVE ACCOUNTS

MANAGEMENT PROVISIONS

PART 37

ADMINISTRATION

PART 38

Returns of Income and Gains, Other Obligations and Returns, and Revenue Powers

CHAPTER 1

Income Tax: Returns of Income

CHAPTER 2

Corporation Tax: Returns of Profits

CHAPTER 3

Other Obligations and Returns

CHAPTER 5

Capital Gains Tax: Returns, Information, etc

CHAPTER 6

Electronic Transmission of Returns of Income, Profits, etc, and of Other Revenue Returns

PART 39
ASSESSMENTS

CHAPTER 1
Income Tax and Corporation Tax

CHAPTER 2
Provision Against Double Assessment and Relief for Error or Mistake

CHAPTER 3
Capital Gains Tax

PART 40
APPEALS

CHAPTER 1
Appeals Against Income Tax and Corporation Tax Assessments

CHAPTER 2
Appeals Against Capital Gains Tax Assessments

CHAPTER 3
Miscellaneous

PART 41
SELF ASSESSMENT

PART 42
COLLECTION AND RECOVERY

CHAPTER 1
Income Tax

CHAPTER 2
Corporation Tax

CHAPTER 3
Capital Gains Tax

CHAPTER 4
Collection and Recovery of Income Tax on Certain Emoluments (PAYE System)

CHAPTER 2
Capital Gains Tax

PART 47
PENALTIES, REVENUE OFFENCES, INTEREST ON OVERDUE TAX AND OTHER SANCTIONS

CHAPTER 1
Income Tax and Corporation Tax Penalties

CHAPTER 2
Other Corporation Tax Penalties

CHAPTER 3
Capital Gains Tax Penalties

CHAPTER 4
Revenue Offences

CHAPTER 5
Interest on Overdue Tax

CHAPTER 6
Other Sanctions

PART 48
MISCELLANEOUS AND SUPPLEMENTAL

PART 49
COMMENCEMENT, REPEALS, TRANSITIONAL PROVISIONS, ETC

SCHEDULE 1

SUPPLEMENTARY PROVISIONS CONCERNING THE EXTENSION OF CHARGE TO TAX TO PROFITS AND INCOME DERIVED FROM ACTIVITIES CARRIED ON AND EMPLOYMENTS EXERCISED ON THE CONTINENTAL SHELF

SCHEDULE 2

MACHINERY FOR ASSESSMENT, CHARGE AND PAYMENT OF TAX UNDER SCHEDULE C AND, IN CERTAIN CASES, SCHEDULE D

SCHEDULE 2A

DIVIDEND WITHHOLDING TAX

SCHEDULE 2B

INVESTMENT UNDERTAKINGS: DECLARATIONS

SCHEDULE 3

RELIEFS IN RESPECT OF INCOME TAX CHARGED ON PAYMENTS ON RETIREMENT, ETC

SCHEDULE 4

EXEMPTION OF SPECIFIED NON-COMMERCIAL STATE SPONSORED BODIES FROM CERTAIN TAX PROVISIONS

SCHEDULE 5

DESCRIPTION OF CUSTOM HOUSE DOCKS AREA

SCHEDULE 6

DESCRIPTION OF TEMPLE BAR AREA

SCHEDULE 7

DESCRIPTION OF CERTAIN ENTERPRISE AREAS

SCHEDULE 8

DESCRIPTION OF QUALIFYING RESORT AREAS

SCHEDULE 8A

DESCRIPTION OF QUALIFYING RURAL AREAS

SCHEDULE 9

CHANGE IN OWNERSHIP OF COMPANY: DISALLOWANCE OF TRADING LOSSES

SCHEDULE 10

RELIEF FOR INVESTMENT IN CORPORATE TRADES: SUBSIDIARIES

SCHEDULE 11

PROFIT SHARING SCHEMES

SCHEDULE 22
DIVIDENDS REGARDED AS PAID OUT OF PROFITS ACCUMULATED BEFORE GIVEN DATE

SCHEDULE 23
OCCUPATIONAL PENSION SCHEMES

SCHEDULE 23A
SPECIFIED OCCUPATIONS AND PROFESSIONS

SCHEDULE 24
RELIEF FROM INCOME TAX AND CORPORATION TAX BY MEANS OF CREDIT IN RESPECT OF FOREIGN TAX

SCHEDULE 25
CONVENTION BETWEEN THE GOVERNMENT OF IRELAND AND THE GOVERNMENT OF THE UNITED STATES OF AMERICA FOR THE AVOIDANCE OF DOUBLE TAXATION AND THE PREVENTION OF FISCAL EVASION WITH RESPECT TO TAXES ON INCOME

SCHEDULE 25A
EXEMPTION FROM TAX IN THE CASE OF GAINS ON CERTAIN DISPOSALS OF SHARES

SCHEDULE 26
REPLACEMENT OF HARBOUR AUTHORITIES BY PORT COMPANIES

SCHEDULE 26A
DONATIONS TO APPROVED BODIES, ETC

SCHEDULE 27
FORMS OF DECLARATIONS TO BE MADE BY CERTAIN PERSONS

SCHEDULE 28
STATEMENTS, LISTS AND DECLARATIONS

SCHEDULE 29
PROVISIONS REFERRED TO IN SECTIONS 1052, 1053 AND 1054

SCHEDULE 30
REPEALS

SCHEDULE 31
CONSEQUENTIAL AMENDMENTS

SCHEDULE 32
TRANSITIONAL PROVISIONS

AN ACT TO CONSOLIDATE ENACTMENTS RELATING TO INCOME TAX, CORPORATION TAX AND CAPITAL GAINS TAX, INCLUDING CERTAIN ENACTMENTS RELATING ALSO TO CERTAIN OTHER TAXES AND DUTIES. [*30TH NOVEMBER, 1997*]

Cross-references

Civil Liability and Courts Act 2004, s 28(1)(*b*)(i) (income undeclared for tax purposes).

Civil Registration Act 2004, s 66(1h) (power of Ard-Chláraitheoir to give information to others).

Health Contributions Act 1979, s 7B, (inserted by Social Welfare (Miscellaneous Provisions) Act 2004, s 20), certain arrangements entered into with Revenue Commissioners.

National Traning Fund Act 2000, s 4(14)(inserted by Social Welfare (Miscellaneous Provisions) Act 2004, s 21), rate of levy and supplemental provisions.

Social Welfare (Consolidation) Act 1993, s 10(11) (inserted by Social Welfare (Miscellaneous Provisions) Act 2004, s 14), employment contribution; s 18(3) (inserted by Social Welfare (Miscellaneous Provisions) Act 2004, s 15), rates of self employment contribution and related matters.

INTERPRETATION AND BASIC CHARGING PROVISIONS

PART 1
INTERPRETATION

1 Interpretation of this Act

(1) In this Act, except where the context otherwise requires, **"repealed enactments"** has the meaning assigned to it by section 1098.

(2) In this Act and in any Act passed after this Act, except where the context otherwise requires—

"the Capital Gains Tax Acts" means the enactments relating to capital gains tax in this Act and in any other enactment;

"the Corporation Tax Acts" means the enactments relating to corporation tax in this Act and in any other enactment, together with the Income Tax Acts in so far as those Acts apply for the purposes of corporation tax;

"the Income Tax Acts" means the enactments relating to income tax in this Act and in any other enactment;

"the Tax Acts" means the Income Tax Acts and the Corporation Tax Acts.

(3) References in this Act to any enactment shall, except where the context otherwise requires, be construed as references to that enactment as amended or extended by any subsequent enactment.

(4) In this Act a reference to a Part, section or Schedule is to a Part or section of, or Schedule to, this Act, unless it is indicated that reference to some other enactment is intended.

(5) In this Act a reference to a subsection, paragraph, subparagraph, clause or subclause is to the subsection, paragraph, subparagraph, clause or subclause of the provision (including a Schedule) in which the reference occurs, unless it is indicated that reference to some other provision is intended.

Cross-references

Companies Act 1990, s 205E (inserted by Companies (Auditing and Accounting Act 2003), directors' compliance statement and related statement, references to "Tax Acts" and "Capital Gains Tax Act" in definition in that section of "tax law".

Residential Institutions Redress Act 2002, s 22(2), income and award, meaning of "Income Tax Acts" applied.

Former enactments

ITA 1967 s 3; FA 1974 s 86 and Sch 2 Pt I; CGTA 1975 s 1(1); CTA 1976 s 155(1)–(2); CGT(A)A 1978 s 1(1); FA 1980 s 9.

2 Interpretation of Tax Acts

(1) In the Tax Acts, except where otherwise provided or the context otherwise requires—

"Appeal Commissioners" has the meaning assigned to it by section 850;

"body of persons" means any body politic, corporate or collegiate, and any company, fraternity, fellowship and society of persons, whether corporate or not corporate;

"capital allowance" means any allowance (other than an allowance or deduction to be made in computing profits or gains) under—

(*a*) Part 9,
(*b*) [Part 23,][1]
(*c*) Chapter 1 of Part 24, or
(*d*) Part 29,

and **"capital allowances"** shall be construed accordingly;

"Clerk to the Appeal Commissioners" means the person for the time being authorised by the Appeal Commissioners to act as such;

"Collector-General" means the Collector-General appointed under section 851;

"inspector" means an inspector of taxes appointed under section 852;

"local authority" means—

(*a*) the corporation of a county or other borough,
(*b*) the council of a county, or
(*c*) the council of an urban district;

"ordinary share capital", in relation to a company, means all the issued share capital (by whatever name called) of the company, other than capital the holders of which have a right to a dividend at a fixed rate, but have no other right to share in the profits of the company;

"profession" includes vocation;

"resident" and **"ordinarily resident"**, in relation to an individual, shall be construed in accordance with Part 34;

"statute" has the same meaning as in section 3 of the Interpretation Act, 1937;

...[2]

[**"year of assessment"** means—

(*a*) in relation to a period prior to 6 April 2001, a year beginning on 6 April in one year and ending on 5 April in the next year,
(*b*) the period beginning on 6 April 2001 and ending on 31 December 2001, which period is referred to as the "year of assessment 2001", and

(*c*) thereafter, a calendar year and, accordingly, the "year of assessment 2002" means the year beginning on 1 January 2002 and any corresponding expression in which a subsequent year of assessment is similarly mentioned means the year beginning on 1 January in that year;][3]

"the year 1997–98" means the year of assessment beginning on the 6th day of April, 1997, and any corresponding expression in which 2 years are similarly mentioned means the year of assessment beginning on the 6th day of April in the first-mentioned of those 2 years;

a source of income is within the charge to corporation tax or income tax if that tax is chargeable on the income arising from it, or would be so chargeable if there were any such income, and references to a person, or to income, being within the charge to tax, shall be similarly construed.

(2) Except where the context otherwise requires, in the Tax Acts, and in any enactment passed after this Act which by an express provision is to be construed as one with those Acts, **"tax"**, where neither income tax nor corporation tax is specified, means either of those taxes.

(3) Subsection (2) is without prejudice to section 76 (which applies income tax law for certain purposes of corporation tax), and accordingly the use of **"income tax"** rather than **"tax"** in any provision of the Income Tax Acts is not a conclusive indication that that provision is not applied to corporation tax by section 76.

[(3A) In the Tax Acts, a reference to a tax credit, in relation to a distribution, shall be construed as a reference to a tax credit as computed in accordance with those Acts as they applied at the time of the making of the distribution.][4]

...[5]

Note

In regard to the definition of "local authority", it should be noted that, by virtue of Local Government Act 2001 s 3(2) and Sch 2, reference in any other enactment to "county borough corporation", "borough corporation" (not being a country borough corporation), "council of a county" and "council of an urban district", and to similar or analagous expressions, are now to be construed as references to "City council", "Borough council of a borough mentioned in Chapter 1 of Part 1 of Schedule 6 to the Local Government Act 2001", "City council" and "Town council of a town mentioned in Chapter 2 of Part 1 of Schedule 6 to the Local Government Act 2001", respectively.

Amendments

1 Para (*b*) of definition of "capital allowance" substituted by FA 2000 s 61(*a*) with effect from 6 April 2000.

2 Definition of "tax credit" repealed by FA 2000 s 69(2) and Sch 2 Part 2 with effect from 6 April 1999 in the case of income tax and from accounting periods commencing on or after that date in the case of corporation tax.

3 Definition of "year of assessment" substituted by FA 2001 s 77(1)(*a*) with effect from 6 April 2001.

4 Subs (3A) inserted by FA 2000 s 69(1) and Sch 2 Part 1 para (*a*) with effect from 6 April 1999 in the case of income tax and from accounting periods commencing on or after that date in the case of corporation tax.

5 Subs (4) repealed by FA 2000 s 69(2) and Sch 2 Part 2 with effect from 6 April 1999 in the case of income tax and from accounting periods commencing on or after that date in the case of corporation tax.

Cross-references

Capital acquisitions tax, general interpretation, meaning of "year of assessment" applied: CATCA 2003 s 2(1).
Capital gains tax share reinvestment relief, meaning of "ordinary share capital" applied: s 591(1).
Employee share ownership trusts, interpretation, meaning of "ordinary share capital" applied: Sch 12 para 1.

Personal Retirement Savings Accounts (PRSAs), relevant earnings and net relevant earnings, meaning of "capital allowance" applied: s 787B(3).
Reduced rate of capital gains tax on disposal by individuals of shares in unquoted companies, meaning of "ordinary share capital" applied: s 592(1).

Case law

Advantage was taken of this definition of "ordinary share capital" to effect a tax free sale in: *Burman v Hedges and Butler Ltd* [1979] STC 136.

Revenue precedents

Issue: Whether covenants are deductible in arriving at total income.
Decision: Payments made under tax effective covenants (ie covenants which are effective under Irish tax law) are deductible in arriving at total income.

Definitions

chargeable gain: ss 5(1), 545; charges on income: ss 4(1), 243(1); company: ss 4(1), 5(1); Income Tax Acts: s 1(2); the Oireachtas: IA 1937 Sch; profits: s 4(1); Tax Acts: s 1(2); person: IA 1937 s 11(*c*); total income: s 3(1); year of assessment: ss 2(1), 5(1).

Former enactments

ITA 1967 s 1(1); CTA 1976 s 155(3), (4)–(5); CTA 1976 s 171; F(MP)A 1968 s 3(2) and Sch Pt I; FA 1974 s 1; FA 1975 s 33(1); FA 1977 s 41(1); FA 1997 s 146(1) and Sch 9 Pt I para 1(1).

3 Interpretation of Income Tax Acts

(1) In the Income Tax Acts, except where otherwise provided or the context otherwise requires—

[**"chargeable tax"**, in relation to an individual for a year of assessment, means the amount of income tax to which the individual is chargeable for that year of assessment under section 15 in respect of his or her total income for that year including, in the case of an individual assessed to tax in accordance with the provisions of section 1017, the total income, if any, of the individual's spouse;][1]

[**"general tax credit"**, in relation to an individual for a year of assessment, means any relief (other than a credit under section 59) applicable for that year of assessment, not by way of deduction from income, but by way of reduction of or deduction from the chargeable tax or by way of repayment thereof when paid, other than a personal tax credit, and such credit shall be determined by reference to the amount of the reduction, deduction or repayment as the case may be;][1]

"higher rate", in relation to tax, means the rate of tax known by that description and provided for in section 15;

"incapacitated person" means any minor or person of unsound mind;

[**"income tax payable"**, in relation to an individual for a year of assessment, means the chargeable tax less the aggregate of the personal tax credits and general tax credits;][2]

[**"personal tax credit"**, in relation to an individual for a year of assessment, means a tax credit specified in sections 461, 461A, 462, 463, 464, 465, 466, 466A, 468 and 472;][2]

"relative" includes any person of whom the person claiming [relief][3] had the custody and whom he or she maintained at his or her own expense while that person was under the age of 16 years;

"standard rate", in relation to tax, means the rate of tax known by that description and provided for in section 15;

"tax" means income tax;

"taxable income" has the meaning assigned to it by section 458;

"total income" means total income from all sources as estimated in accordance with the Income Tax Acts;

"trade" includes every trade, manufacture, adventure or concern in the nature of trade.

(2) (*a*) Subject to subsection (3), in the Income Tax Acts, **"earned income"**, in relation to an individual, means—

(i) any income arising in respect of any remuneration from any office or employment of profit held by the individual, or in respect of any pension, superannuation or other allowance, deferred pay, or compensation for loss of office, given in respect of the past services of the individual or of the husband or parent of the individual in any office or employment of profit, or given to the individual in respect of the past services of any deceased person, whether or not the individual or husband or parent of the individual shall have contributed to such pension, superannuation allowance or deferred pay,

(ii) any income from any property which is attached to or forms part of the emoluments of any office or employment of profit held by the individual, and

(iii) any income charged under Schedule D and immediately derived by the individual from the carrying on or exercise by the individual of his or her trade or profession, either as an individual or, in the case of a partnership, as a partner personally acting in the partnership.

(*b*) In cases where the profits of a wife are deemed to be profits of the husband, any reference in this subsection to an individual includes either the husband or the wife.

(3) Without prejudice to the generality of subsection (2), in the Income Tax Acts, except where otherwise expressly provided, **"earned income"** includes—

(*a*) any annuity made payable to an individual under the terms of an annuity contract or trust scheme for the time being approved by the Revenue Commissioners for the purposes of Chapter 2 of Part 30 to the extent to which such annuity is payable in return for any amount on which relief is given under section 787, and

(*b*) any payment or other sum which is or is deemed to be income chargeable to tax under Schedule E for any purpose of the Income Tax Acts.

(4) References to profits or gains in the Income Tax Acts shall not include references to chargeable gains within the meaning of the Capital Gains Tax Acts.

Amendments

1 Definitions of "chargeable tax" and "general tax credit" inserted by FA 2001 s 2(3) and Sch 1 para 1(*a*)(i) for short tax "year" 2001 and later tax years.

2 Definitions of "income tax payable" and "personal tax credit" inserted by FA 2001 s 2(3) and Sch 1 para 1(*a*)(ii) for short tax "year" 2001 and later tax years.

3 Substituted by FA 2000 s 14 and Sch 1 para 1 with effect from 6 April 2000; previously "a deduction".

Cross-references

Age exemption and associated marginal relief, meaning of "income tax payable" applied, but without regard to any reduction of tax under s 244; meaning of "total income" applied, but so as to include income arising outside the State which is not chargeable to tax: s 188(1).
Income Tax (Employments) (Consolidated) Regulations 2001, SI No 559 of 2001, meanings of "general tax credit" and "personal tax credit" applied: Reg 2(1).
"investment income" does not include earned income: s 434(1).
Investment undertakings (interpretation and application), meaning of "standard rate" applied: s 739B(1).
Life assurance, payment in respect of a foreign life policy, meaning of "standard rate" applied: s 730J(*a*).
Undertaking for collective investment, meaning of "standard rate" applied, subs (1): s 738(1)(*a*).

Definitions

person: IA 1937 s 11(*c*); year of assessment: s 2(1).

Former enactments

ITA 1967 ss 1(1), 2; FA 1969 s 65 and Sch 5; FA 1974 s 1; CGTA 1975 s 2(5); FA 1991 s 2(3) and Sch 1 Pt I para 1; FA 1993 s 2(2) and Sch 1 Pt I; FA 1994 s 2(2); FA 1996 s 132(1) and Sch 5 Pt I para 1(1).

4 Interpretation of Corporation Tax Acts

(1) In the Corporation Tax Acts, except where the context otherwise requires—

"accounting date" means the date to which a company makes up its accounts, and **"period of account"** means the period for which a company does so;

"allowable loss" does not include, for the purposes of corporation tax in respect of chargeable gains, a loss accruing to a company in such circumstances that if a gain accrued the company would be exempt from corporation tax in respect of the gain;

"branch or agency" means any factorship, agency, receivership, branch or management;

"chargeable gain" has the same meaning as in the Capital Gains Tax Acts, but does not include a gain accruing on a disposal made before the 6th day of April, 1976;

"charges on income" has the meaning assigned to it by section 243(1);

"close company" has the meaning assigned to it by sections 430 and 431;

"company" means any body corporate and includes a trustee savings bank within the meaning of the Trustee Savings Banks Act, 1989, but does not include—

(*a*) [the Health Service Executive][1],
(*b*) a grouping within the meaning of section 1014,
(*c*) a vocational educational committee established under the Vocational Education Act, 1930,
(*d*) a committee of agriculture established under the Agriculture Act, 1931, or
(*e*) a local authority, and for this purpose **"local authority"** has the meaning assigned to it by section 2(2) of the Local Government Act, 1941, and includes a body established under the Local Government Services (Corporate Bodies) Act, 1971;

"distribution" has the meaning assigned to it by Chapter 2 of Part 6 and [sections 436 and 437, and subsection (2)(*b*) of section 816];[2]

"the financial year" followed by a reference to the year 1996 or any other year means the year beginning on the 1st day of January of such year;

"franked investment income" and **"franked payment"** shall be construed in accordance with section 156;

[**"generally accepted accounting practice"** means—

(*a*) in relation to the affairs of a company or other entity that prepares accounts (in this section referred to as **"IAS accounts"**) in accordance with international accounting standards, generally accepted accounting practice with respect to such accounts;

(*b*) in any other case, Irish generally accepted accounting practice;][3]

"group relief" has the meaning assigned to it by section 411;

"interest" means both annual or yearly interest and interest other than annual or yearly interest;

[**"international accounting standards"** means the international accounting standards, within the meaning of Regulation (EC) No 1606/2002 of the European Parliament and the Council of 19 July 2002 on the application of international accounting standards (in this section referred to as **"the Regulation"**);][4]

[**"Irish generally accepted accounting practice"** means generally accepted accounting practice with respect to accounts (other than IAS accounts) of companies incorporated or formed under the laws of the State, being accounts that are intended to give a true and fair view;][5]

"preference dividend" means a dividend payable on a preferred share or preferred stock at a fixed rate per cent or, where a dividend is payable on a preferred share or preferred stock partly at a fixed rate per cent and partly at a variable rate, such part of that dividend as is payable at a fixed rate per cent;

"profits" means income and chargeable gains;

[**"standard credit rate"** for a year of assessment means—

(*a*) for the year of assessment 1997–98—

(i) 21 per cent where it has application in relation to a distribution made or treated as having been made by a company before the 3rd day of December, 1997, and

(ii) 11 per cent where it has application in relation to a distribution made or treated as having been made by a company on or after the 3rd day of December, 1997,

and

(*b*) for the year of assessment 1998–99, 11 per cent,

and, accordingly, **"standard credit rate per cent"** for the year of assessment 1997–98 means 21 or 11, as the case may be, and for the year of assessment 1998–99 means 11;][6]

"standard rate per cent" for a year of assessment means 26 where the standard rate for that year is 26 per cent and similarly as regards any reference to the standard rate per cent for a year of assessment for which the standard rate is other than 26 per cent;

"trade" includes vocation and includes also an office or employment.

(2) Except where otherwise provided by the Corporation Tax Acts and except where the context otherwise requires, words and expressions used in the Income Tax Acts have the same meaning in the Corporation Tax Acts as in those Acts; but no provision of the Corporation Tax Acts as to the interpretation of any word or expression, other than a provision expressed to extend to the use of that word or expression in the Income Tax Acts, shall be taken to affect its meaning in those Acts as they apply for the purposes of corporation tax.

(3) References in the Corporation Tax Acts to distributions or payments received by a company apply to any distributions or payments received by another person on behalf of or in trust for the company but not to any distributions or payments received by the company on behalf of or in trust for another person.

(4) References in the Corporation Tax Acts to—

(*a*) profits brought into charge to corporation tax are references to the amount of those profits chargeable to corporation tax before any deduction from those profits for charges on income, expenses of management or other amounts which can be deducted from or set against or treated as reducing profits of more than one description,

(*b*) total income brought into charge to corporation tax are references to the amount, calculated before any deduction mentioned in paragraph (*a*), of the total income from all sources included in any profits brought into charge to corporation tax, and

(*c*) an amount of profits on which corporation tax falls finally to be borne are references to the amount of those profits after making all deductions and giving all reliefs that for the purposes of corporation tax are made or given from or against those profits, including deductions and reliefs which under any provision are treated as reducing them for those purposes.

(5) For the purposes of the Corporation Tax Acts, except where otherwise provided, dividends shall be treated as paid on the date when they become due and payable.

(6) Except where otherwise provided by the Corporation Tax Acts, any apportionment to different periods to be made under the Corporation Tax Acts shall be made on a time basis according to the respective lengths of those periods.

[(7) For the purposes of this section, where the European Commission in accordance with the Regulation adopts an international accounting standard with modifications, then as regards matters covered by that standard—

(*a*) generally accepted accounting practice with respect to IAS accounts shall be regarded as permitting the use of the standard either with or without the modifications, and

(*b*) accounts prepared on either basis shall be regarded as prepared in accordance with international accounting standards.][7]

Amendments

1 Substituted by FA 2005 s 147 and Sch 6 para 1(*a*) with effect from 25 March 2005; previously "a health board".

2 Substituted by FA 1998 s 43(1)(*b*) as respects shares issued by a company on or after 3 December 1997; previously "sections 436 and 437".

3 Definition of "generally accepted accounting practice" inserted by FA 2005 s 48(1)(*a*)(i)(I) as respects any period of account beginning on or after 1 January 2005.

4 Definition of "international accounting standards" inserted by FA 2005 s 48(1)(*a*)(i)(II) as respects any period of account beginning on or after 1 January 2005.

5 Definition of "Irish generally accepted accounting practice" inserted by FA 2005 s 48(1)(*a*)(i)(II) as respects any period of account beginning on or after 1 January 2005.

6 Definition of "standard credit rate" substituted by FA 1998 s 51(1) with effect from 3 December 1997.

7 Subs (7) inserted by FA 2005 s 48(1)(*a*)(ii) as respects any period of account beginning on or after 1 January 2005.

Cross-references

Connected persons, meaning of "company" applied: s 10(1).
Deposit interest retention tax, interpretation, meaning of "standard rate per cent" applied: s 256(1) (para (*c*) of definition of "appropriate tax").
Employee share options schemes, meaning of "branch or agency" and "company" applied: s 128(1)(*a*).
Farming stock relief, meaning of "company" applied: s 665.
Foreign life policies, taxation and returns of certain policies, interpretation and application, meaning of "standard rate per cent" applied: s 730H(1).
Investment undertakings, gain arising on a chargeable event, meaning of "standard rate per cent" applied: s 739D(5A).
Life assurance companies, deduction of tax on the happening of a chargeable event, meaning of "standard rate per cent" applied: s 730F(1) (paras (*a*) and (*b*) of definition of "appropriate tax").
Manufacturing (10%) relief and higher rate of corporation tax, interaction: s 448(5A)(*b*).
Offshore funds, taxation and returns of certain funds, interpretation and application, meaning of "standard rate per cent" applied: s 747B(1).
Restriction of relief to individuals in respect of loans applied in acquiring interest in companies, meaning of "distribution" applied: s 250A(1).
Returns by nominee holders of securities, meaning of "company" applied: s 892(1).
Ring-fence on use of certain capital allowances on certain industrial buildings and other premises, meaning of "company" applied: s 409E(1).
Securitisation: s 110(6)(*a*).
Stamp duties, levy on certain financial institutions, meaning of "company" applied: SDCA 1999 s 126A(1)(*a*).
Undertaking for collective investment, meaning of "distribution" and "standard rate per cent" applied, subs (1): s 738(1)(*a*); subs (6): s 738(1)(*c*).

Former enactments

CTA 1976 s 1(5)(*a*)–(*d*), s 155(5), (9)–(13); FA 1986 s 57(1); FA 1990 s 29(4); FA 1993 s 42; FA 1997 s 37(1).

5 Interpretation of Capital Gains Tax Acts

(1) In the Capital Gains Tax Acts, except where the context otherwise requires—

"Appeal Commissioners" has the meaning assigned to it by section 850;

"body of persons" has the same meaning as in section 2;

"branch or agency" means any factorship, agency, receivership, branch or management, but does not include the brokerage or agency of a broker or agent referred to in section 1039;

"local authority" has the meaning assigned to it by section 2(2) of the Local Government Act, 1941, and includes a body established under the Local Government Services (Corporate Bodies) Act, 1971;

"allowable loss" has the meaning assigned to it by section 546;

"capital allowance" means any allowance under the provisions of the Tax Acts which relate to allowances in respect of capital expenditure, and includes an allowance under section 284;

"chargeable gain" has the same meaning as in section 545;

"charity" has the same meaning as in section 208;

"class", in relation to shares or securities, means a class of shares or securities of any one company;

"close company" has the meaning assigned to it by section 430;

"company" means any body corporate, but does not include a grouping within the meaning of section 1014;

"control" shall be construed in accordance with section 432;

"inspector" means an inspector of taxes appointed under section 852;

"land" includes any interest in land;

"lease"—

(*a*) in relation to land, includes an underlease, sub-lease or any tenancy or licence, and any agreement for a lease, underlease, sub-lease or tenancy or licence and, in the case of land outside the State, any interest corresponding to a lease as so defined, and

(*b*) in relation to any description of property other than land, means any kind of agreement or arrangement under which payments are made for the use of, or otherwise in respect of, property,

and **"lessor"**, **"lessee"** and **"rent"** shall be construed accordingly;

"legatee" includes any person taking under a testamentary disposition or an intestacy or partial intestacy or by virtue of the Succession Act, 1965, or by survivorship, whether such person takes beneficially or as trustee, and a person taking under a donatio mortis causa shall be treated as a legatee and such person's acquisition as made at the time of the donor's death and, for the purposes of this definition and of any reference to a person acquiring an asset as legatee, property taken under a testamentary disposition or on an intestacy or partial intestacy or by virtue of the Succession Act, 1965, includes any asset appropriated by the personal representatives in or towards the satisfaction of a pecuniary legacy or any other interest or share in the property devolving under the disposition or intestacy or by virtue of the Succession Act, 1965;

"market value" shall be construed in accordance with section 548;

"minerals" has the same meaning as in section 3 of the Minerals Development Act, 1940;

"mining" means mining operations in the State for the purpose of obtaining, whether by underground or surface working, any minerals;

"part disposal" has the meaning assigned to it by section 534;

"personal representative" has the same meaning as in section 799;

"prescribed" means prescribed by the Revenue Commissioners;

"profession" includes vocation;

"resident" and **"ordinarily resident"**, in relation to an individual, shall be construed in accordance with Part 34;

"settled property" means any property held in trust other than property to which section 567 applies, but does not include any property held by a trustee or assignee in bankruptcy or under a deed of arrangement;

"settlement" and **"settlor"** have the same meanings respectively as in section 10, and **"settled property"** shall be construed accordingly;

"shares" includes stock, and shares or debentures comprised in any letter of allotment or similar instrument shall be treated as issued unless the right to the shares or debentures conferred by such letter or instrument remains provisional until accepted and there has been no acceptance;

"trade" has the same meaning as in the Income Tax Acts;

"trading stock" has the same meaning as in section 89;

"unit trust" means any arrangements made for the purpose, or having the effect, of providing facilities for the participation by the holders of units, as beneficiaries under a trust, in profits or income arising from the acquisition, holding, management or disposal of securities or any other property whatever;

"units", in relation to a unit trust, means any units (whether described as units or otherwise) into which are divided the beneficial interests in the assets subject to the trusts of a unit trust;

"unit holder", in relation to a unit trust, means a holder of units of the unit trust;

"wasting asset" has the meaning assigned to it by section 560 and paragraph 2 of Schedule 14;

[**"year of assessment"** means—

(*a*) in relation to a period prior to 6 April 2001, a year beginning on 6 April in one year and ending on 5 April in the next year,

(*b*) the period beginning on 6 April 2001 and ending on 31 December 2001, which period is referred to as the "year of assessment 2001", and

(*c*) thereafter, a calendar year and, accordingly, the "year of assessment 2002" means the year beginning on 1 January 2002 and any corresponding expression in which a subsequent year of assessment is similarly mentioned means the year beginning on 1 January in that year;][1]

"the year 1997–98" means the year of assessment beginning on the 6th day of April, 1997, and any corresponding expression in which 2 years are similarly mentioned means the year of assessment beginning on the 6th day of April in the first-mentioned of those 2 years.

(2) (*a*) References in the Capital Gains Tax Acts to a married woman living with her husband shall be construed in accordance with section 1015(2).

(*b*) For the purposes of paragraph (*a*), the reference in section 1015(2) to a wife shall be construed as a reference to a married woman.

(3) Any provision in the Capital Gains Tax Acts introducing the assumption that assets are sold and immediately reacquired shall not imply that any expenditure is incurred as incidental to the sale or reacquisition.

Note

In regard to the definition of "local authority", it should be noted that, by virtue of Local Authority Act 2001 s 3(2) and Sch 2, references in any other enactment to "local authority for the purposes of the Local Government Act, 1941", and to similar or analogous expressions, are now to be construed as references to "a county council, city council and town council, and where the context so required includes a joint body", within the meaning respectively assigned to each of those terms in the Local Government Act 2001.

Amendments

[1] Definition of "year of assessment" substituted by FA 2001 s 77(1)(*b*) with effect from 6 April 2001.

Cross-references

Industrial and provident societies, transfer of shares to members, meaning of "company" applied: s 701(1).

Case law

Meaning of "settlement": *Young v Pearce* [1996] STC 743.

Definitions

Income Tax Acts: s 1(2); land: IA 1937 Sch; person: IA 1937 s 11(*c*).

Former enactments

CGTA 1975 s 2(1), (3)–(4); CTA 1976 s 140(2) and Sch 2 Pt II para 1; FA 1980 s 61(*a*); FA 1990 s 29(3); FA 1997 s 146(1) and Sch 9 Pt I para 9(1).

6 Construction of references to child in Tax Acts and Capital Gains Tax Acts

For the purposes of the Tax Acts and the Capital Gains Tax Acts, except where the contrary intention appears—

(*a*) references in any of those Acts to a child (including references to a son or a daughter) include references to—

(i) a stepchild, and

(ii) a child who is—

(I) adopted under the Adoption Acts, 1952 to 1991, or

(II) the subject of a foreign adoption (within the meaning of section 1 of the Adoption Act, 1991) which is deemed to have been effected by a valid adoption order made under the Adoption Acts, 1952 to 1991,

and

(*b*) the relationship between a child referred to in paragraph (*a*)(ii) and any other person, or between other persons, that would exist if such child had been born to the child's adoptor or adoptors in lawful wedlock, shall be deemed to exist between such child and that other person, or between those other persons, and the relationship of any such child and any person that existed prior to the child being so adopted shall be deemed to have ceased,

and **"adopted child"** shall be construed in accordance with this section.

Definitions

person: IA 1937 s 11(*c*); Tax Acts: s 1(2).

Former enactments

FA 1977 s 36; FA 1992 s 16.

7 Application to certain taxing statutes of Age of Majority Act, 1985

(1) Notwithstanding subsection (4) of section 2 of the Age of Majority Act, 1985 (in this section referred to as **"the Act of 1985"**), subsections (2) and (3) of that section shall, subject to subsection (2), apply for the purposes of the Income Tax Acts and any other statutory provision (within the meaning of the Act of 1985) dealing with the imposition, repeal, remission, alteration or regulation of any tax or other duty under the care and management of the Revenue Commissioners, and accordingly section 2(4)(*b*)(vii) of the Act of 1985 shall cease to apply.

(2) Nothing in subsection (1) shall affect a claimant's entitlement to [relief][1] under section 462 or 465.

Amendments

1 Substituted by FA 2000 s 14 and Sch 1 para 2 with effect from 6 April 2000; previously "a deduction".

Cross-references

This section to be construed together with the Customs Acts, in so far as relating to customs, and with the statutes which relate to excise duty, in so far as relating to that duty: s 1104(2).

This section to be construed together with the Value Added Tax Acts 1972–1997, in so far as relating to value added tax: s 1104(3).

This section to be construed together with the Stamp Act 1891 and the enactments amending or extending that Act, in so far as relating to stamp duties: s 1104(4).

This section to be construed together with the Capital Acquisitions Tax Act 1976, and the enactments amending or extending that Act, in so far as relating to capital acquisitions tax: s 1104(5).

This section to be construed together with FA 1983 Pt VI and the enactments amending or extending that Part, in so far as relating to residential property tax: s 1104(6).

Definitions

Income Tax Acts: s 1(2).

Former enactments

FA 1986 s 112(1)–(2).

8 Construction of certain taxing statutes in accordance with Status of Children Act, 1987

(1) In this section, **"the Acts"** means—

- (*a*) the Tax Acts,
- (*b*) the Capital Gains Tax Acts,
- (*c*) the [Capital Acquisitions Tax Consolidation Act 2003][1], and the enactments amending or extending that Act, and
- (*d*) the statutes relating to stamp duty,

and any instruments made thereunder.

(2) Notwithstanding any provision of the Acts or the dates on which they were passed, in deducing any relationship between persons for the purposes of the Acts, the Acts shall be construed in accordance with section 3 of the Status of Children Act, 1987.

Amendments

1 Substituted by CATCA 2003 s 119 and Sch 3 with effect from 21 February 2003; previously "Capital Acquisitions Tax Act 1976".

Definitions

person: IA 1937 s 11(*c*); Tax Acts: s 1(2); Capital Gains Tax Acts: s 1(2).

Former enactments

FA 1988 s 74(1)–(2).

9 Subsidiaries

(1) For the purposes of the Tax Acts, except where otherwise provided, a company shall be deemed to be—

(*a*) a **"51 per cent subsidiary"** of another company if and so long as more than 50 per cent of its ordinary share capital is owned directly or indirectly by that other company,

(*b*) a **"75 per cent subsidiary"** of another company if and so long as not less than 75 per cent of its ordinary share capital is owned directly or indirectly by that other company,

(*c*) a **"90 per cent subsidiary"** of another company if and so long as not less than 90 per cent of its ordinary share capital is directly owned by that other [company,][1]

[(*d*) a **"wholly-owned subsidiary"** of another company if and so long as 100 per cent of its ordinary share capital is directly owned by that other company.][2]

(2) In paragraphs (*a*) and (*b*) of subsection (1), **"owned directly or indirectly"** by a company means owned whether directly or through another company or other companies or partly directly and partly through another company or other companies.

(3) In this section, references to ownership shall be construed as references to beneficial ownership.

(4) For the purposes of this section, the amount of ordinary share capital of one company owned by a second company through another company or other companies, or partly directly and partly through another company or other companies, shall be determined in accordance with subsections (5) to (10).

(5) Where, in the case of a number of companies, the first directly owns ordinary share capital of the second and the second directly owns ordinary share capital of the third, then, for the purposes of this section, the first shall be deemed to own ordinary share capital of the third through the second and, if the third directly owns ordinary share capital of a fourth, the first shall be deemed to own ordinary share capital of the fourth through the second and third, and the second shall be deemed to own ordinary share capital of the fourth through the third, and so on.

(6) In this section—

(*a*) any number of companies of which the first directly owns ordinary share capital of the next and the next directly owns ordinary share capital of the next but one and so on, and, if there are more than 3, any 3 or more of them, are referred to as a **"series"**;

(*b*) in any series—

(i) that company which owns ordinary share capital of another through the remainder is referred to as "the first owner";

(ii) that other company the ordinary share capital of which is so owned is referred to as "the last owned company";

(iii) the remainder, if one only, is referred to as an "intermediary" and, if more than one, are referred to as "a chain of intermediaries";

(*c*) a company in a series which directly owns ordinary share capital of another company in the series is referred to as an **"owner"**;

(*d*) any 2 companies in a series of which one owns ordinary share capital of the other directly, and not through one or more of the other companies in the series, are referred to as being directly related to one another.

(7) Where every owner in a series owns the whole of the ordinary share capital of the company to which it is directly related, the first owner shall be deemed to own through the intermediary or chain of intermediaries the whole of the ordinary share capital of the last owned company.

(8) Where one of the owners in a series owns a fraction of the ordinary share capital of the company to which it is directly related, and every other owner in the series owns the whole of the ordinary share capital of the company to which it is directly related, the first owner shall be deemed to own that fraction of the ordinary share capital of the last owned company through the intermediary or chain of intermediaries.

(9) Where—

(*a*) each of 2 or more of the owners in a series owns a fraction, and every other owner in the series owns the whole, of the ordinary share capital of the company to which it is directly related, or

(*b*) every owner in a series owns a fraction of the ordinary share capital of the company to which it is directly related,

the first owner shall be deemed to own through the intermediary or chain of intermediaries such fraction of the ordinary share capital of the last owned company as results from the multiplication of those fractions.

(10) Where the first owner in any series owns a fraction of the ordinary share capital of the last owned company in that series through the intermediary or chain of intermediaries in that series, and also owns another fraction or other fractions of the ordinary share capital of the last owned company, either—

(*a*) directly,

(*b*) through an intermediary which is not a member, or intermediaries which are not members, of that series,

(*c*) through a chain or chains of intermediaries of which one or some or all are not members of that series, or

(*d*) in a case where the series consists of more than 3 companies, through an intermediary which is a member, or intermediaries which are members, of the series, or through a chain or chains of intermediaries consisting of some but not all of the companies of which the chain of intermediaries in the series consists,

then, for the purpose of ascertaining the amount of the ordinary share capital of the last owned company owned by the first owner, all those fractions shall be aggregated and the first owner shall be deemed to own the sum of those fractions.

Amendments

1 Substituted by FA 2001 s 79(*a*)(i) with effect from 6 April 2001; previously "company.".

2 Subs (1)(*d*) inserted by FA 2001 s 79(*a*)(ii) with effect from 6 April 2001.

Cross-references

Capital gains tax share reinvestment relief, 51% subsidiary: s 591(1).

Change of ownership of a company, disallowance of trading losses, subss (5)–(10) applied by: Sch 9 para 6(*c*).

Companies' chargeable gains, groups of companies, meaning of "75% subsidiary" applied: s 616(1)(*b*)(*d*).

Company reconstructions without change of ownership, subss (5)–(10) applied by: s 400(3)(*c*).

Company residence: s 23A(1)(*b*)(i)(II).

Disposal of business or farm on "retirement", 75% subsidiary: s 598(1)(*a*).

Distributions to certain non-residents, subss (2)–(10) applied: s 153(3A)(*a*).

Dividend withholding tax, exemption for certain non-residents, subss (2)–(10) applied: s 172D(6)(*a*).

Employee loan to acquire an interest in employing company, 90% subsidiary: s 250(1).

Exemption from tax in the case of gains on certain disposals of shares, subss (2) to (10) applied: s 626B(1)(i)(A).

Exploration expenditure incurred by bodies corporate, subss (5)–(10) applied: s 675(4).

Stamp duties, levy on certain financial institutions, meaning of "51 per cent subsidiary" applied: SDCA 1999 s 126A(1)(*b*).

Case law

A company in liquidation cannot qualify as a parent company as it is no longer the beneficial owner of its assets: *Ayerst v C & K Construction Ltd* [1975] STC 1; *IRC v Olive Mill Spinners Ltd* (1963) 41 TC 77.

Held a 75% parent company which granted an option to another shareholder to purchase 5% of its 75% sharing remained a 75% parent: *Sainsbury plc v O'Connor* [1991] 5 TC 318.

Definitions

company: ss 4(1), 5(1); Corporation Tax Acts: s 1(2); land: IA 1937 Sch; ordinary share capital: s 2(1); person: IA 1937 s 11(*c*).

Former enactments

CTA 1976 s 156.

10 Connected persons

(1) In this section—

"close company" has the meaning assigned to it by sections 430 and 431;

"company" has the same meaning as in section 4(1);

"control" shall be construed in accordance with section 432;

"relative" means brother, sister, ancestor or lineal descendant and, for the purposes of the Capital Gains Tax Acts, also means uncle, aunt, niece or nephew;

"settlement" includes any disposition, trust, covenant, agreement or arrangement, and any transfer of money or other property or of any right to money or other property;

"settlor", in relation to a settlement, means any person by whom the settlement was made, and a person shall be deemed for the purposes of this section to have made a settlement if the person has made or entered into the settlement directly or indirectly and, in particular (but without prejudice to the generality of the preceding words), if the person has provided or undertaken to provide funds directly or indirectly for the purpose of the settlement, or has made with any other person a reciprocal arrangement for that other person to make or enter into the settlement.

(2) For the purposes of the Tax Acts and the Capital Gains Tax Acts, except where the context otherwise requires, any question whether a person is connected with another person shall be determined in accordance with subsections (3) to (8) (any provision that one person is connected with another person being taken to mean that they are connected with one another).

(3) A person shall be connected with an individual if that person is the individual's husband or wife, or is a relative, or the husband or wife of a relative, of the individual or of the individual's husband or wife.

(4) A person in the capacity as trustee of a settlement shall be connected with—

(*a*) any individual who in relation to the settlement is a settlor,

(*b*) any person connected with such an individual, and

(*c*) a body corporate which is deemed to be connected with that settlement, and a body corporate shall be deemed to be connected with a settlement in any accounting period or, as the case may be, year of assessment if, at any time in that period or year, as the case may be, it is a close company (or only not a close company because it is not resident in the State) and the participators then include the trustees of or a beneficiary under the settlement.

(5) Except in relation to acquisitions or disposals of partnership assets pursuant to bona fide commercial arrangements, a person shall be connected with any person with whom such person is in partnership, and with the spouse or a relative of any individual with whom such person is in partnership.

(6) A company shall be connected with another company—

(*a*) if the same person has control of both companies, or a person (in this paragraph referred to as **"the first-mentioned person"**) has control of one company and persons connected with the first-mentioned person, or the first-mentioned person and persons connected with the first-mentioned person, have control of the other company, or

(*b*) if a group of 2 or more persons has control of each company, and the groups either consist of the same persons or could be regarded as consisting of the same persons by treating (in one or more cases) a member of either group as replaced by a person with whom such member is connected.

(7) A company shall be connected with another person if that person has control of the company or if that person and persons connected with that person together have control of the company.

(8) Any 2 or more persons acting together to secure or exercise control of, or to acquire a holding in, a company shall be treated in relation to that company as connected with one another and with any person acting on the direction of any of them to secure or exercise control of, or to acquire a holding in, the company.

Cross-references

Approved savings-related share option schemes, interpretation, this section applied: Sch 12A para 1(2).

Approved share option schemes, interpretation, this section applied: Sch 12C para 1(2).

Benefit in kind charge, "connected person" rules applied: s 118(8).

Company acquiring its own shares, different "connected persons" rules applied: s 186.

Company loan to acquiring interest in another company, interest relief: s 247(1)(*b*).

Credit in respect of tax deducted from emoluments of certain directors, "connected persons" rules applied: s 997A(1)(*b*)(ii).

Employee loan to acquire an interest in employing company, "connected person" rules applied: s 250(5)(*a*).

Enterprise areas, capital allowances, "connected persons" rules applied: s 343(11)(*b*).

General rule as to deductions under Cases I and II of Schedule D, "connected persons" rules applied: s 81(2)(*n*).

Information to be furnished by financial institutions, "connected persons" rules applied: s 906A(1).

Life assurance, personal portfolio life policies, "connected person" rules applied: s 730BA(2)(*b*).

Notional loans relating to shares, etc, meaning of "connected person" applied: s 122A(1).

Park and ride facilities, capital allowances in relation to construction or refurbishment of, and capital allowances in relation to construction or refurbishment of certain commercial premises in, "connected persons" rules applied: s 372V(2A)(*b*); s 372W(3A)(*b*).

Particulars to be supplied by new companies, meaning of "settlor" and "settlement" applied: s 882(1)(*a*).

Qualifying areas, non-application of relief in certain cases and provision against double relief, "connected persons" rules applied: s 372K(1)(*a*)(ii).

Qualifying rural areas, non-application of relief in certain cases and provision against double relief, "connected persons" rules applied: s 372T(1)(*a*)(ii).

Restriction on use of income tax losses on approved buildings, "connected person" rules applied: s 409C(2)(*c*)(i).

Retirement annuities, interpretation, meaning of "connected person" applied: s 783(1)(*a*).

Scholarship income exemption, meaning of "settlement" applied: s 193(1)(*b*).

Special savings incentive accounts, acquisition of qualifying assets, meaning of "connected person" applied: s 848G(1)(*b*), (*c*).

Special trusts for permanently incapacitated individuals, "connected person" rules applied: s 189A(1), para (*c*) of definition of "qualifying trust".

Stamp duty, intellectual property, "connected persons" rules applied, "Stamp Duties Consolidation Act 1999, s 101(7).

Tax credit for research and development expenditure: s 766(1)(*a*) ("expenditure on research and development)".

Taxation of reverse premiums, "connected person" rules applied: s 98A(1)(*b*).

Tax clearance certificates for licences, meaning of "connected person" applied: s 1094(3).

Tax clearance certificates, general scheme, meaning of "connected person" applied: s 1095(5).

Transfer of assets abroad, power to obtain information, meaning of "settlement" and "settlor" applied: s 808(1).

Valuation of trading stock on discontinuance of a trade, "connected persons" rules applied: s 89(1)(*b*)(ii)(*a*).

Case law

Ongoing implementation of a shareholders' agreement held to constitute the necessary continued activity to ensure control was retained: *Steele v European Vinyl Corp (Holdings) Ltd* [1995] STC 31; [1996] STI 853.

Revenue precedents

Issue: Is a daughter-in-law or son-in-law connected with her/his father-in-law?

Decision: Yes.

Definitions

close company: ss 4(1), 430, 431; company: ss 4(1), 5(1); Corporation Tax Acts: s 1(2); disposition: s 791; land: IA 1937 Sch; person: IA 1937 s 11(*c*); relative: s 3(1); settlement: ss 5(1); year of assessment: ss 2(1), 5(1).

Corresponding UK tax provision

Income and Corporation Taxes Act 1988 s 839.

Former enactments

FA 1996 s 131(1)–(8).

11 Meaning of "control" in certain contexts

For the purposes of, and subject to, the provisions of the Corporation Tax Acts which apply this section, **"control"**, in relation to a company, means the power of a person to secure—

(*a*) by means of the holding of shares or the possession of voting power in or in relation to that or any other company, or

(*b*) by virtue of any powers conferred by the articles of association or other document regulating that or any other company,

that the affairs of the first-mentioned company are conducted in accordance with the wishes of that person and, in relation to a partnership, means the right to a share of more than 50 per cent of the assets, or of more than 50 per cent of the income, of the partnership.

Cross-references

BES investments, subsidiaries: s 507(2)(*b*).
BES relief: s 493(7).
Company acquiring its own shares: s 173(1).
Matters to be treated as distributions: s 130(5)(*b*).
Group, transfer of company to another: s 424(1).
Profit sharing schemes: s 511(6)(*c*).
Tonnage tax, transactions between associated persons and between tonnage tax trade and other activities of same company: s 697LA(1).
Valuation of trading stock on discontinuance of a trade: s 89(1)(*b*)(ii).

Definitions

company: ss 4(1), 5(1); Corporation Tax Acts: s 1(2); person: IA 1937 s 11(*c*).

Former enactments

CTA 1976 s 158.

Corresponding UK tax provision

Income and Corporation Taxes Act 1988 s 840.

PART 2
THE CHARGE TO TAX

CHAPTER 1
Income Tax

12 The charge to income tax

Income tax shall, subject to the Income Tax Acts, be charged in respect of all property, profits or gains respectively described or comprised in the Schedules contained in the sections enumerated below—
Schedule C — Section 17;
Schedule D — Section 18;
Schedule E — Section 19;
Schedule F — Section 20;
and in accordance with the provisions of the Income Tax Acts applicable to those Schedules.

Former enactments

ITA 1967 s 4; FA 1980 s 55.

Corresponding UK tax provision

Income and Corporation Taxes Act 1988 s 1.

13 Extension of charge to income tax to profits and income derived from activities carried on and employments exercised on the Continental Shelf

(1) In this section and in Schedule 1—

"designated area" means an area designated by order under section 2 of the Continental Shelf Act, 1968;

"exploration or exploitation activities" means activities carried on in connection with the exploration or exploitation of so much of the sea bed and subsoil and their natural resources as is situated in the State or in a designated area;

"exploration or exploitation rights" means rights to assets to be produced by exploration or exploitation activities or to interests in or to the benefit of such assets.

(2) Any profits or gains from exploration or exploitation activities carried on in a designated area or from exploration or exploitation rights shall be treated for income tax purposes as profits or gains from activities or property in the State.

(3) Any profits or gains arising to any person not resident in the State from exploration or exploitation activities carried on in the State or in a designated area or from exploration or exploitation rights shall be treated for income tax purposes as profits or gains of a trade carried on by that person in the State through a branch or agency.

[(4) Where exploration or exploitation activities are carried on by a person on behalf of the holder of a licence or lease granted under the Petroleum and Other Minerals Development Act, 1960, such holder shall, for the purpose of an assessment to income tax, be deemed to be the agent of that person.][1]

(5) Any emoluments from an office or employment in respect of duties performed in a designated area in connection with exploration or exploitation activities shall be treated for income tax purposes as emoluments in respect of duties performed in the State.

(6) Schedule 1 shall apply for the purpose of supplementing this section.

Amendments

1 Subs (4) substituted by FA 2001 s 44(*a*) with effect from 6 April 2001.

Cross-references

Capital gains tax, deduction from consideration on disposal of certain assets, meaning of "exploration or exploitation rights": s 980(1).

Supplementary provisions: Sch 1 paras 1(*a*), 2(1); subs (5): Sch 1 para 3.

Definitions

person: IA 1937 s 11(*c*); trade: s 3(1).

Former enactments

FA 1973 s 33(1)(*a*)–(*c*), (2), (5) and (7); FA 1974 s 86 and Sch 2 Pt I; CTA 1976 s 164 and Sch 3 Pt II.

14 Fractions of a pound and yearly assessments

(1) The due proportion of income tax shall be charged for every fractional part of [one euro][1], but no income tax shall be charged on a lower denomination than [one cent][2].

[(2) Every assessment and charge to income tax shall be made for a year of assessment.][3]

Amendments

1 Substituted by FA 2001 s 240(1), (2)(*a*) and Sch 5 Pt 1 for 2002 and later tax years; previously "one pound".

2 Substituted by FA 2001 s 240(1), (2)(*a*) and Sch 5 Pt 1 for 2002 and later tax years; previously "one cent".

3 Subs (2) substituted by FA 2001 s 77(1)(*c*) with effect from 6 April 2001.

Former enactments

ITA 1967 s 5 and 6; FA 1970 s 3.

Corresponding UK tax provision

Income and Corporation Taxes Act 1988 s 2.

15 Rate of charge

(1) Subject to subsection (2), income tax shall be charged for each year of assessment at the rate of tax specified in the Table to this section as the standard rate.

[(2) Where a person who is charged to income tax for any year of assessment is an individual (other than an individual acting in a fiduciary or representative capacity), such individual shall, notwithstanding anything in the Income Tax Acts but subject to section 16(2), be charged to tax on such individual's taxable income—

(*a*) in a case in which such individual is assessed to tax otherwise than in accordance with section 1017 and is not an individual referred to in paragraph (*b*), at the rates specified in Part 1 of the Table to this section, or

(*b*) in a case in which the individual is assessed to tax otherwise than in accordance with section 1017 and is entitled to a reduction of tax provided for in section 462, at the rates specified in Part 2 of the Table to this section, or

(*c*) subject to subsections (3) and (5), in a case in which such individual is assessed to tax in accordance with section 1017, at the rates specified in Part 3 of the Table to this section,

and the rates in each Part of that Table shall be known respectively by the description specified in column (3) in each such Part opposite the mention of the rate or rates, as the case may be, in column (2) of that Part.][1]

(3) Subject to subsections (4) and (5)—

(*a*) where an individual is charged to tax for a year of assessment in accordance with section 1017, and

(*b*) both the individual and his or her spouse are each in receipt of income in respect of which the individual is chargeable to tax in accordance with that section,

the part of his or her taxable income chargeable to tax at the standard rate specified in column (1) of Part 3 of the Table to this section shall be increased by an amount which is the lesser of—

(i) [€20,400][2], and

(ii) the specified income of the individual or the specified income of the individual's spouse, whichever is the lesser.

[(4) For the purposes of subsection (3), **"specified income"** means total income after deducting from such income any deduction attributable to a specific source of income and any relevant interest within the meaning of Chapter 4 of Part 8.][3]

(5) Where all or any part of an increase under subsection (3) in the amount of an individual's taxable income chargeable to income tax at the standard rate is attributable to emoluments from which tax is deductible in accordance with the provisions of Chapter 4 of Part 42 and any regulations made thereunder, then, the full amount of the increase, or that part of the increase, as may be appropriate in the circumstances, shall only be used in accordance with the provisions of that Chapter and those regulations in calculating the amount of tax to be deducted from those emoluments.

[TABLE

Part 1

Part of taxable income	Rate of tax	Description of rate
(1)	(2)	(3)
The first €29,400	20 per cent	the standard rate
The remainder	42 per cent	the higher rate

Part 2

Part of taxable income	Rate of tax	Description of rate
(1)	(2)	(3)
The first €33,400	20 per cent	the standard rate
The remainder	42 per cent	the higher rate

Part 3

Part of taxable income	Rate of tax	Description of rate
(1)	(2)	(3)
The first €38,400	20 per cent	the standard rate
The remainder	42 per cent	the higher rate][4]

Amendments

1 Subs (2) substituted by FA 2000 s 3(*a*) for 2000–2001 and later tax years.

2 Substituted by FA 2005 s 2(*a*) for 2005 and subsequent years of assessment; previously "€19,000".

3 Subs (4) substituted by FA 2001 s 3(*a*) for 2001 and later tax years.

4 Substituted by FA 2005 s 2(*b*) for 2005 and subsequent years of assessment.

Cross-references

Distributions to certain non-residents, subs (2): s 153(6)(*a*).
Foreign life policies, payments in respect of certain policies: s 730J(*a*)(i), (ii).
Home carer tax credit, subs (3): s 466A(8).
Income Tax (Employments) (Consolidated) Regulations 2001, SI No 559 of 2001, meanings of "higher rate of tax" and "standard rate of tax" applied: reg 2(1).
Interpretation of Income Tax Acts: s 3(1) ("chargeable tax").
Life assurance, payment in respect of a foreign life policy: s 730J(*a*)(ii)(I), (II).
Method of apportioning reliefs and charging tax in cases of separate assessment: s 1024(2)(*c*), (4).
Offshore funds, taxation and returns of certain funds, disposal of an interest in offshore fund: s 747E(1); payments in respect of offshore funds: s 747D.

Definitions

Income Tax Acts: s 1(2); person: IA 1937 s 11(*c*); taxable income: ss 3(1), 458; year of assessment: s 2(1).

Former enactments

FA 1991 s 2 and FA 1997 s 2(1)–(2).

16 Income tax charged by deduction

(1) In estimating under the Income Tax Acts the total income of any person, any income chargeable with tax by means of deduction at the standard rate in force for any year shall be deemed to be income of that year, and any deductions allowable on account of sums

payable under deduction of tax at the standard rate in force for any year out of the property or profits of that person shall be allowed as deductions in respect of that year, notwithstanding that the income or sums, as the case may be, accrued or will accrue in whole or in part before or after that year.

(2) Where a person is required to be assessed and charged with tax in respect of any property, profits or gains out of which such person makes any payment in respect of any annual interest, annuity or other annual sum, or any royalty or other sum in respect of the user of a patent, such person shall, in respect of so much of the property, profits or gains as is equal to that payment and may be deducted in computing such person's total income, be charged at the standard rate only.

Cross-references

Alarm systems for the elderly: s 478(2).
Home loan interest (subs (2)): s 244(2)(*b*).
Provisions relating to reductions in tax: s 458(1A).
Rate of charge is subject to subs (2): s 15(2).
Reduction in income tax for certain income earned outside the State: s 825A(1).
Relief for fees paid for third level education: s 473A(2).
Relief for insurance against expenses of illness: s 470(2).
Relief for trade union subscriptions: s 472C(2).
Rent paid: s 473(2).
Service charges: s 477(2).
Training courses: s 476(2).

Definitions

Income Tax Acts: s 1(2); person: IA 1937 s 11(*c*); standard rate: ss 3(1), 15; total income: s 3(1).

Former enactments

FA 1974 s 5(2)–(3).

17 Schedule C

(1) The Schedule referred to as Schedule C is as follows:

SCHEDULE C

1. Tax under this Schedule shall be charged in respect of all profits arising from public revenue dividends payable in the State in any year of assessment.
2. Where a banker or any other person in the State, by means of coupons received from another person or otherwise on that other person's behalf, obtains payment of any foreign public revenue dividends, tax under this Schedule shall be charged in respect of the dividends.
3. Where a banker in the State sells or otherwise realises coupons for any foreign public revenue dividends and pays over the proceeds of such realisation to or carries such proceeds to the account of any person, tax under this Schedule shall be charged in respect of the proceeds of the realisation.
4. Where a dealer in coupons in the State purchases coupons for any foreign public revenue dividends otherwise than from a banker or another dealer in coupons, tax under this Schedule shall be charged in respect of the price paid on the purchase.
5. Nothing in paragraph 1 shall apply to any annuities which are not of a public nature.

6. The tax under this Schedule shall be charged for every [one euro][1] of the annual amount of the profits, dividends, proceeds of realisation or price paid on purchase charged.

(2) Section 32 shall apply for the interpretation of Schedule C.

[(3) Subsection (1) shall not apply to a banker by virtue only of the clearing of a cheque, or the arranging for the clearing of a cheque, by the banker.][2]

Amendments

1 Substituted by FA 2001 s 240(1) and (2)(*a*) and Sch 5 Pt 1 for 2002 and later tax years; previously "one pound".

2 Subs (3) inserted by FA 2005 s 46(1)(*a*) as respects any payment on or after 25 March 2005.

Cross-references

General charge: s 12.
Machinery for assessment, charge and payment of tax under Schedule C, and in certain cases, Schedule D: Sch 2 para 23.
Provisions relating to residence of individuals: s 821(1).

Definitions

dividends, foreign public revenue dividends, banker, coupons, coupons for any foreign public revenue dividends: s 32; person: IA 1937 s 11(*c*); tax: s 3(1); year of assessment: s 3(1).

Former enactments

ITA 1967 s 47 and s 51.

18 Schedule D

(1) The Schedule referred to as Schedule D is as follows:

SCHEDULE D

1. Tax under this Schedule shall be charged in respect of—

(*a*) the annual profits or gains arising or accruing to—

(i) any person residing in the State from any kind of property whatever, whether situate in the State or elsewhere,

(ii) any person residing in the State from any trade, profession or employment, whether carried on in the State or elsewhere,

(iii) any person, whether a citizen of Ireland or not, although not resident in the State, from any property whatever in the State, or from any trade, profession or employment exercised in the State, and

(iv) any person, whether a citizen of Ireland or not, although not resident in the State, from the sale of any goods, wares or merchandise manufactured or partly manufactured by such person in the State,

and

(*b*) all interest of money, annuities and other annual profits or gains not charged under Schedule C or Schedule E, and not specially exempted from tax,

in each case for every [one euro][1] of the annual amount of the profits or gains.

2. Profits or gains arising or accruing to any person from an office, employment or pension shall not by virtue of paragraph 1 be chargeable to tax under this Schedule unless they are chargeable to tax under Case III of this Schedule.

(2) Tax under Schedule D shall be charged under the following Cases:

Case I— Tax in respect of—

(*a*) any trade;

(*b*) profits or gains arising out of lands, tenements and hereditaments in the case of any of the following concerns—

(i) quarries of stone, slate, limestone or chalk, or quarries or pits of sand, gravel or clay,

(ii) mines of coal, tin, lead, copper, pyrites, iron and other mines, and

(iii) ironworks, gasworks, salt springs or works, alum mines or works, waterworks, streams of water, canals, inland navigations, docks, drains or levels, fishings, rights of markets and fairs, tolls, railways and other ways, bridges, ferries and other concerns of the like nature having profits from or arising out of any lands, tenements or hereditaments;

Case II— Tax in respect of any profession not contained in any other Schedule;

Case III— Tax in respect of—

(*a*) any interest of money, whether yearly or otherwise, or any annuity, or other annual payment, whether such payment is payable in or outside the State, either as a charge on any property of the person paying the same by virtue of any deed or will or otherwise, or as a reservation out of it, or as a personal debt or obligation by virtue of any contract, or whether the same is received and payable half-yearly or at any shorter or more distant periods, but not including any payment chargeable under Case V of Schedule D;

(*b*) all discounts;

(*c*) profits on securities bearing interest payable out of the public revenue other than those charged under Schedule C;

(*d*) interest on any securities issued, or deemed within the meaning of section 36 to be issued, under the authority of the Minister for Finance, in cases where such interest is paid without deduction of tax;

(*e*) income arising from securities outside the State except such income as is charged under Schedule C;

(*f*) income arising from possessions outside the State;

Case IV— Tax in respect of any annual profits or gains not within any other Case of Schedule D and not charged by virtue of any other Schedule;

Case V— Tax in respect of any rent in respect of any premises or any receipts in respect of any easement;

and subject to and in accordance with the provisions of the Income Tax Acts applicable to those Cases respectively.

(3) This section is without prejudice to any other provision of the Income Tax Acts directing tax to be charged under Schedule D or under one or other of the Cases mentioned in subsection (2), and tax so directed to be charged shall be charged accordingly.

Amendments

1 Substituted by FA 2001 s 240(1) and (2)(*a*) and Sch 5 Pt 1 for 2002 and later tax years; previously "one pound".

Cross-references

Approved retirement fund: s 784A(3)(*a*).

Benefit in kind from employment taxed under Sch D Case III: s 57(1).

Certain rents and other payments, (subs (2), s 104(1)(*a*)(i).

Charge to income tax of pensions under Schedule E: s 779(1).

Corporation tax, miscellaneous special rules for computation of income (subs (2)): Sch D Case III paras (*e*)-(*f*)): s 77(7).

Deduction of five-twelfths of rateable valuation (subs (2)): s 85(3).

General charge: s 12.

Relieving provision to TCA 1997 s 1035 (profits from agencies): s 1035A(3).

Residence of individuals, subs (1): s 821(1).

Retirement annuities, relief for premiums: s 784(2B)(*a*), (7).

Taxation of payments from a Personal Retirement Savings Account (PRSA): s 787G(1)(*a*).

Case I

Case I(*b*): Lands owned and occupied; trades conducted by charities: s 208(2)(*a*).

Case III

Para (*d*): government securities beneficially owned by non-residents, Minister for Finance may exempt capital and interest from tax: s 43; securities of semi-state and public bodies owned by non-ordinarily resident non-domiciled persons, Minister for Finance may exempt capital and interest from tax: s 49.

Para (*f*): foreign pensions exempt: s 200(3).

Case law

In determining whether a trade is exercised within the UK, the place where the contracts for sale are concluded is an important factor: *Erichsen v Last* (1881) 4 TC 422; *Maclaine & Co v Eccott* (1924) 10 TC 481; as is the place where the operations occur from which the profits arise: *FL Smidth & Co v Greenwood* (1921) 8 TC 193.

Held trust income arose to trustees jointly not severally and where one of the trustees resided outside the UK the other trustee could not be assessed to income tax under 1(*a*)(i): *Dawson v IRC* [1988] STC 684.

Applying the decision in *The San Paulo (Brazilian) Railway Company Ltd v Carter* 3 TC 407, a trade cannot be said to be wholly carried on abroad if it is under the control and management of persons resident in Ireland even if those persons are acting through agents and managers resident abroad.

Case I: capital receipts

Irish

Compensation payments made to a company on the ending of an arrangement whereby a department was to supply goods to a subsidiary: *O'Dwyer v Irish Exporters and Importers Ltd (in liquidation)* ITR Vol I p 629.

Ex-gratia payments made by British Government for business losses incurred by a trader: *Robinson (T/A J Pim and Son) v Dolan* ITR Vol I p 427.

Profits arising on the compulsory acquisition by the State of raw materials: *Guinness v Commissioners of Inland Revenue*, 1 ITR Vol I p 1.

UK

Compensation received for loss of entire profit-making apparatus: *Van den Bergh Ltd v Clark* (1935) 19 TC 390; *Barr Crombie Ltd v IRC* (1945) 26 TC 406; *British-Borneo Petroleum Syndicate v Cropper* (1968) 45 TC 201; *Creed v H & M Levinston Ltd* [1981] STC 585.

Currency gains on deposits made by agents abroad: *Davies v The Shell Company of China Ltd* (1951) 32 TC 133. See also *Beauchamp v Woolworth* [1989] STC 510, *Overseas Containers Finance Ltd v Storer* [1989] STC 364.

Government grants: *Burman v Thorn Domestic Appliances (Electrical) Ltd* [1982] STC 179; *Poulter v Grayjohn Processes Ltd* [1985] STC 174.

Receipt for disposal of goodwill in a foreign country: *Wolf Electric Tools Ltd v Wilson* (1969) 45 TC 326.

Receipt for not mining certain fireday deposits: *Glenboig Union Fireday Co Ltd v IRC* (1922) 12 TC 427.

Receipt from petrol company for redecoration of petrol station: *McLaren v Needham* (1960) 39 TC 37.

Payment by lessor to induce lessee to enter into an onerous lease: *CIR v Wattie* [1998] STC 1160.

Case I: whether "trading"

Irish

A body of persons performing statutory functions not regarded as chargeable to tax on surplus income derived from registration and annual fees: *Veterinary Council v Corr* ITR Vol II p 204.

A company engaged in loan business regarded as taxable on profits from the realisation of investments: *Agricultural Credit Corporation Ltd v Vale* ITR Vol I p 474.

A company producing grass meal (from the use of land that was part of a military establishment) regarded as chargeable under Case I: *O'Connell v Shackleton and Sons* [1982] ILRM 451.

A company receiving investment income after the disposal of its shipping assets held to be carrying on business even after the appointment of a liquidator: *City of Dublin Steampacket Co v Revenue Commissioners* ITR Vol I p 318.

A railway company with substantial investment income which leased its property and rights on a rental basis held to be carrying on a trade: *Commissioners of Inland Revenue v Dublin and Kingston Railway Co* 1 ITC 131; [1930] IR 317.

A statutory body set up to effect a compulsory insurance scheme treated as carrying on a taxable trade: *Exported Live Stock (Insurance) Board v Carroll* ITR Vol II p 211.

Profits arising on resale to the distillery of whiskey, which had increased in value while in bond, regarded as a taxable trading venture: *Personal Representatives of PJ McCall (deceased) v Commissioners of Inland Revenue* ITR Vol I p 28.

The fact that property is purchased with a view to resale does not of itself establish that the transaction is an adventure in the nature of trade – *Spa Estates v O' hArgain* [1975] (High Court).

The disposal of an investment cannot constitute a trading transaction – *Mara v Hummingbird* ITR Vol II 667.

If a transaction as a whole appears not to be a trading transaction but an artificial device remote from a trade to secure a tax advantage, then the presence of trading elements in it will not secure its classification as a trading transaction – approved by O' Hanlon J in *MacCarthaigh v Daly* 3 ITR 253.

Damages representing loss of profits in respect of a breach of contract were treated as taxable in *Hickey & Co v Roches* [1980] ILRM.

UK

Held to be trading:

Agricultural machinery merchant using elaborate sales campaign to sell airforce linen: *Martin v Lowry* (1926) 11 TC 297.

Buying and selling of land: *California Copper Syndicate Ltd v Harris* (1904) 5 TC 159, *Turner v Last* (1965) 42 TC 517, *Clark v Follett* (1973) 48 TC 677 (but see *Leeming v Jones, Kirkham v Williams* below).

Buying and selling of shares: *Lewis Emmanuel & Son Ltd v White* (1965) 42 TC 369 (but see *Salt v Chamberlain* below).

Sale of large quantity of toilet paper: *Rutledge v IRC* (1929) 14 TC 490.

Syndicate selling assets of mill-owning companies: *Pickford v Quirke* (1927) 13 TC 251.

Trustees cultivating crops and fattening cattle after deceased's death: *Patullo's Trustees v IRC* (1955) 36 TC 87.

Woodcutter selling whiskey: *IRC v Fraser* (1942) 24 TC 498.

Prostitute: *CIR v Aken* [1990] STC 1374.

Limited partnership set up to finance film production: *Ensign Tankers (Leasing) v Stokes* [1992] STC 226.

Held not trading:

Buying and selling land: *Kirkham v Williams* [1991] STC 342.

Buying and selling of a rubber estate: *Leeming v Jones* (1930) 15 TC 333.

Buying and selling shares: *Salt v Chamberlain* [1975] STC 750.

Executors completing a contract initiated by the deceased: *Cohan's Executors v IRC* (1924) 12 TC 602.

Selling of houses due to rent control and rising expenses: *West v Phillips* (1958) 38 TC 203.

Trustees selling deceased's cattle: *IRC v Donaldson* (1963) 41 TC 161.

Company advancing finance to joint venture: *Stone & Temple v Waters* [1995] STC 1.

Commodity broker trading from home: *Wannell v Rothwell* [1996] STC 450.

Case I: revenue receipts

Irish

Compensation for compulsory official detention of ships: *Alliance and Dublin Gas Consumers Co v McWilliams* ITR Vol I p 426.

Industrial Development Authority training grant: *O'Cléirigh v Jacobs International Ltd* ITR Vol III p 165.

Profits arising on disposal of government stock required to be held solely for statutory liquidity purposes: *Browne v Bank of Ireland Finance Ltd* ITR Vol III p 644.

Sale proceeds from a loss of profits policy: *Corr v Larkin* ITR Vol II p 164.

Statutory levies received by a public body not chargeable to tax as a trading receipt: *The Racing Board v O'Culacháin* ITR Vol IV p 73.

UK

Compensation for loss of trading stock or profits: *Green v Gliksten & Co Ltd* (1929) 14 TC 364; *R v British Columbia Fir and Cedar Lumber Co Ltd* (1932) 15 ATC 624.

Compensation for loss of use of an asset: *London and Thames Haven Oil v Attwooll* (1966) 43 TC 491.

Compensation for partial loss of profit making apparatus: *Wiseburgh v Domville* (1956) 36 TC 527.

Compensation payment to tenant: *Donald Fisher (Ealing) Ltd v Spencer* [1989] STC 256.

EC payment for temporary loss of income on conversion from dairy to beef production: *White v G & M Davies* [1979] STC 415; *IRC v Biggar* [1982] STC 677.

Ex gratia payment on termination of contract: *Rolfe v Nagel* [1981] STC 585.

Gain on sale of foreign currency: *Imperial Tobacco Co of Great Britain and Ireland v Kelly* (1943) 25 TC 292; *Landes Bros v Simpson* (1935) 19 TC 62.

Held no taxable profit when foreign currency transactions matched: *Pattison v Marine Midland Ltd* [1984] STC 10.

Medical research grant: *Duff v Williamson* (1973) 49 TC 1.

Proceeds for know how sold to countries to which the company could not export: *Jeffrey v Rolls Royce Ltd* (1962) 40 TC 443.

Reimbursement of promotion expenses: *Evans v Wheatley* (1958) 38 TC 216.

Cash injection into subsidiary prior to its sale to protect goodwill of the business: *Lawson v Johnson Matthey plc* [1992] STC 466.

Damages for negligence recovered by Lloyds names from managing agents: *Deeny v Gooda Walker* [1996] STC 299.

Case I: accounting rules

Irish

Goods bought on "forward contracts" but not received are to be excluded as part of the closing stock of an accounting period: *Green and Co (Cork) Ltd v Revenue Commissioners* ITR Vol I p 130; *Revenue Commissioners v Latchford and Sons Ltd*, 1 ITC 238.

Historical cost accounting (not current cost accounting) to be used for determination of profits: *P J Carroll and Co Ltd v O'Culacháin* ITR Vol IV p 135.

UK

In calculating taxable profits, sound commercial accounting principles should be followed unless they conflict with taxation principles: *Heather v P-E Consulting Group Limited* (1975) 48 TC 293; *Willingale v International Commercial Bank Ltd* [1978] STC 75; *Threlfall v Jones* [1993] STC 534; *Johnston v Brittania Airways Ltd* [1994] STC 763.

Stock in trade in profit and loss account should be valued at the lower of cost and market value: *Whimster v CIR* (1928) 12 TC 823.

Where sound accounting principles are employed, accounts cannot be revised in the light of circumstances as they subsequently transpire: *Symons v Weeks* [1986] IR 355.

Profits should be calculated on the basis of generally accepted principles of commercial accounting – *Herbert Smith v Honour* [1999] STC 173.

Case II

Irish

A barrister who on appointment as judge transferred his interest in uncollected fees to a company was held to be personally chargeable on such receipts: *O'Coindealbháin v Gannon* ITR Vol III p 484.

A local manager for the Department of Social Welfare required to provide premises and staff held to be self-employed: *O'Coindealbháin v Mooney* ITR Vol IV p 45.

Bookmaker's profits arising from dealing in drawn sweepstake tickets not regarded as separate to his general business activities: *HH v Forbes* ITR Vol III p 178.

Insurance agent not subject to any restrictions or direct control of his activities by the company for which he acted regarded as within the charge to Case II: *MacDermott v Loy*, (High Court ,29 July 1982).

Jockey held to be chargeable under Case II: *Wing v O'Connell* ITR Vol I p 155.

Members of a fishing crew entitled to share of the proceeds of the catch regarded as self-employed: *McLoughlin v Director of Public Prosecutions* ITR Vol III p 387.

Advertising agency does carry on a profession – *MacGiolla Mhaith v Cronin & Associates Ltd* 3 ITR 211.

UK

Held sale by author of his working papers and manuscripts for a sum payable in several yearly instalments assessable as a profit of his profession: *Wain v Cameron* [1995] STI 732.

Held to be exercising a profession:

Actress: *Davies v Braithwaite* (1931) 18 TC 198.

Barrister: *Seldon v Croom-Johnston* (1932) 16 TC 740.

Independent local inquiry inspector held assessable under Schedule E and not Schedule D: *Edwards v Clinch* [1981] STC 617.

Journalist: *CIR v Maxse* (1919) 12 TC 41.

Optician: *CIR v North and Ingram* (1918) 2 KB 705.

Held not to be exercising a profession:

Dance band leader: *Loss v CIR* (1945) 2 All ER 683.

Insurance broker: *Durant v CIR* (1921) 12 TC 245.

Professional gambler: *Graham v Green* (1925) 2 TC 309.

Case III(a)

Irish

An assignment of the benefits of a pension previously chargeable under Case III by a taxpayer involved the cesser of that source despite the continuing direct receipt of the pension by the taxpayer: *Cronin v C* ITR Vol II p 592.

Deposit interest arising to a liquidator chargeable under Case III: *Irish Provident Assurance Co Ltd (in liquidation) v Kavanagh* ITR Vol I p 45.

Payments made to an Irish resident former managing director of an English company were not a succession of gifts but chargeable Case III income: *McHugh v A* ITR Vol II p 393.

Retirement pensions payable by British Government chargeable under Case III: *Forbes v Dundon* 3 ITC 365 [1964] IR 447.

Sums received by a life tenant of property for its upkeep and maintenance not regarded as chargeable income of the recipient: *Marchioness Conyngham v Revenue Commissioners* 1 ITC 259 [1928] ILRM 57.

UK

An 'annual payment' is a payment which is pure income profit in the hands of the recipient: *Re Hanbury (dec'd)* (1939) 38 TC 588; and does not include payment of insurance premiums: *Earl Howe v IRC* (1919) 7 TC 289; payment for the use of assets: *Hanbury (dec'd)* (above); or payment of training fees: *Essex County Council v Ellam* [1989] STC 317.

Court awarded interest held assessable under Case III: *Schulze v Bensted (No 1)* (1915) 7 TC 30; *Riches v Westminster Bank Ltd* (1947) 28 TC 159; *The Norseman* (1957) 36 ATC 173.

Element of repayments in excess of capital borrowed held to represent interest chargeable under Case III: *Bennett v Ogston* (1930) 15 TC 374.

Payment for delay in discharging contractual obligations is not a payment of interest: *Re Euro Hotel (Belgravia) Ltd* [1975] STC 682.

Portion of sale proceeds representing interest held assessable under Case III: *Hudson Bay Co v Thew* (1919) 7 TC 206; *Ruskin Investments Ltd v Copeman* (1943) 25 TC 187.

Interest accruing and being compounded was interest when paid: *Girvan v Orange Communication Services* [1998] STC 567.

Case III(b)

UK

Held discount and premium on notes were capital payments not assessable under Case III: *Lomax v Peter Dixon & Son Ltd* (1943) 25 TC 353.

Held the difference between cost of Treasury bill and amount realised was a profit on a discount: *National Provident Institution v Brown* (1921) 8 TC 57; see also *Ditchfield v Sharp* [1982] STC 124.

Case III(e)

Irish

Foreign currency income received on investments compulsorily acquired by the State taxable on the Irish monetary equivalent value: *O'Sullivan v J O'Gorman (as Administrator of estate of E O'Brien, deceased)*, 2 ITC 352 [1947] IR 416.

Underwriting profits arising abroad held not to be a separate Case III source: *O'Connell v R* ITR Vol II p 304.

Case III(f)

Irish

Australian farming business in respect of which powers of management had been delegated by power of attorney to Australian residents by UK and Irish resident taxpayer trustees held not to be taxable in Ireland or UK but in Australia – *Executors and Trustees of AC Ferguson (deceased) v Donovan* 1 ITR 183.

UK

A dividend from a company incorporated in the US but resident in the UK is not income from a foreign possession: *Bradbury v English Sewing Cotton Co Ltd* (1923) 8 TC 481.

A trade controlled from abroad is taxable as a foreign possession: *Colquhoun v Brooks* (1889) 2 TC 490; *San Paolo (Brazilian) Railway Company Ltd v Carter* (1896) 3 TC 407; *Newstead v Frost* [1980] STC 123.

A trade controlled from the UK is assessable under Case I: *Ogilvie v Kitton* (1908) 5 TC 338; *Egyptian Hotels Ltd v Mitchel* (1915) 6 TC 542.

A UK resident in receipt of foreign alimony or a foreign annuity is in receipt of income from a foreign possession: *IRC v Anderstrom* (1928) 13 TC 482; *Chamney v Lewis* (1932) 17 TC 318.

Where a distribution from a company represents a return of capital, it is not income from foreign possession: *Rae v Lazard Investment Co Ltd* (1963) 41 TC 1; *Courtaulds Investments Ltd v Fleming* (1969) 46 TC 111.

Where remuneration is paid in the UK, it is not income from a foreign office or employment even though all the duties are performed abroad: *Pickles v Foulsham* (1925) 9 TC 261; *Bennett v Marshall* (1938) 22 TC 73.

Case IV

Irish

Receipts of money by a statutory board may be subject to considerations different from those pertaining to the receipts of an ordinary profit-making concern depending on how the legislation governing the board directs how profits should be dealt with – *Moville District Board of Conservatory v Ua Clothasaigh* [1950] IR 301.

UK

Annual profits or gains held to include:

casual commissions: *Ryall v Hoare* (1925) 8 TC 521; *Grey v Tiley* (1932) 16 TC 414;

income from letting racehorses: *Norman v Evans* (1964) 42 TC 188;

income under a consultancy agreement where the services rendered were negligible: *Hale v Shea* (1964) 42 TC 260;

payment by newspaper for exclusive publication rights: *Alloway v Phillips* [1980] STC 490.

profits from dealings in futures: *Cooper v Stubbs* (1925) 10 TC 29; *Townsend v Grundy* (1933) 18 TC 140;

profits of a company from exploiting the services of a actress: *Black Nominees Ltd v Nicol* [1975] STC 372.

Revenue precedents

Issue: Whether video tapes in use in video rental shops should be classed as fixed assets or stock in trade.

Decision: The ordinary rules of commercial accounting apply. It is necessary to examine the facts of each case to determine whether video tapes are fixed assets or stock in trade.

Issue: Whether the special seller's prize paid by the national lottery to lotto-agents who sell winning lotto tickets is taxable.

Decision: Such prizes are taxable under Schedule D Case I.

Issue: Is income earned abroad by Irish resident entertainers taxable in Ireland under Schedule D Case II?

Decision: Yes.

Issue: Is court interest chargeable to income tax in the hands of the recipient?

Decision: Yes, under Schedule D Case III.

Issue: Are disability benefits receivable by Irish residents under US insurance policies taxable here?

Decision: Yes, under Schedule D Case III.

Issue: What rate is applied for the purpose of converting dividend income to Irish pounds?

Decision: The rate of exchange which applied to the dividend on encashment.

Issue: Taxation of resettlement expenses and certain allowances paid by the Agency for Personnel Services Overseas (APSO) to its volunteers.

Decision: It was agreed to concessionally exempt from tax certain allowances paid to APSO volunteers.

Issue: Whether gifts to amateur sportsmen are taxable receipts in the hands of those sportsmen.

Decision: In general, where the recipient is a sportsperson who engages in the sport purely for recreational purposes (ie is not carrying on a trade or profession as a sportsperson or is not an employee of the club etc which provides the gift, it would be regarded as a gift which would not give rise to an Income Tax liability. However, the circumstances of each case would need to be considered, before giving a definitive answer.

Issue: Whether payment over and above fee charged was income within s 18.

Decision: Revenue accept CCJ decision that payment was not a receipt of the profession but a personal gift.

Issue: How is credit for US tax shown in a Lloyds account given?

Decision: Credit is given against the tax for the year of assessment for which the accounts form the basis of assessment. If there are losses, the effective rate of Irish tax is nil. In these circumstances the amount of the US tax is allowed as a deduction.

Issue: Whether a bookmakers stand/patch at a racecourse constitutes a permanent establishment.

Decision: A bookmakers stand/patch at a racecourse constitutes a permanent establishment.

Issue: Whether Boarding Out Allowances paid under Statutory Instrument 225 of 1993 by Health Boards to people who board out elderly persons are taxable.
Decision: The allowances are taxable. There is no exempting provision.
Issue: Where a company acts as a trustee and the settlors are not resident, ordinarily resident or domiciled in Ireland and funds upon the trust are settled in currencies other than Irish pounds and/or property situated outside Ireland, is the trust treated as non-resident.
Decision: Yes.
Issue: Profit sharing income.
Decision: Two individuals both in Brussels since 1989 both in receipt of profit sharing income employed by a 3M group company – paid from Belgium while in Belgium. In addition, received a small portion of salary together with profit sharing income which was paid in Ireland. Neither resident nor ordinarily resident in Ireland for the relevant years and all the duties of employment were exercised outside the State. Exclusion order requested. Referred to C.I'.s for decision. Decision from C.I.'s - the profit sharing income in this case is remuneration arising from the employment and it is difficult to divorce such income from normal earnings. Consequently, in this case, the "profit sharing income" is exempt from Irish tax by virtue of TCA 1997 s 18. This is not a general ruling. All cases of this nature should be examined on an individual basis looking at the facts and particulars of that case.

Statement of practice

Currency and/or interest swap agreements, regular receipts directly relating to allowable interest of a trade are part of trading income and corresponding payments are deductible revenue expenses; similarly, regular receipts directly relating to interest allowable under Sch D Case V are part of Sch D Case V income and corresponding payments are deductible in the Sch D Case V computation: SP CT/1/91.

Tax Briefing

TB31 Apr 1998 p 13 Interest received under the Prompt Payment of Accounts Act, 1997 is taxable in the hands of the recipient. Although strictly chargeable under Sch. D Case III, it may be included as a trade receipt and assessed under Sch. D Case I.

TB33 Sept 1998 p 15 — Employed or Self-Employed — Guidelines.

TB43 Apr 2001 pp 3–7 — Employed or Self-Employed — Report of the Employment Status Group and Code of Practice.

TB57 Oct 2004 pp 10–12 — Classification of Activities as Trading — CT.

Revenue Information Notice

Deposit Interest — Whether a Trading Receipt? — March 2003.

Guidance on Revenue opinions on classification of activities as trading — May 2003.

Trading Opinions

Cases submitted to Revenue for an opinion on the classification of activities which were finalised in the period 1 January 2003 to 30 April 2004.

Date received: Dec 02.
No of employees in Ireland: None.
Description of activity: Provision of aircraft warehousing facility until airline is in a position to take full ownership and delivery of aircraft. Under the arrangement an Irish SPC will take an assignment of a purchase contract between an aircraft manufacturer and an airline and will enter into an agreement with the manufacturer to store the aircraft until required by the airline. The SPC will charge the airline a fee for the warehousing arrangement.
Opinion given: Not Case 1.
Reason: SPC is a conduit company, there is no real activity, it did not negotiate the original purchase contracts and merely takes assignment of the contract. There is no real profit motive in the transaction.
Date received: Dec 02.
No of employees in Ireland: 1 senior manager. Work outsourced to other group companies who would have in excess of 35 employees engaged in the activity.
Description of activity: Construction and operation of an electricity generation project.
Opinion given: Case 1 confirmed.
Reason: Case 1 confirmed on basis that the company will be generating and selling electricity. The senior manager has overall responsibility for the operations including the outsourced operations.
Date received: Jan 03.
No of employees in Ireland: 5.

Description of activity: The company will be involved in web hosting, online marketing of pharmaceuticals, marketing and distribution of medical devices and health and beauty products, and administrative and support services for online and retail sales and marketing organisations within the worldwide group.
Opinion given: Case 1 confirmed.
Reason: Case 1 confirmed on the basis of the level of activities involved and staff with the appropriate level of skills and expertise are employed by the company.
Date received: Jan 03.
No of employees in Ireland: Not stated.
Description of activity: Franchise operation.
Opinion given: No opinion given.
Reason: Not enough information given in relation to operation of company. Further information requested in May 2003 but the case was not pursued by agents.
Date received: Feb 03.
No of employees in Ireland: Not stated.
Description of activity: Joint venture company established to finance the purchase of aircraft. The company will set up an SPC for each transaction. The SPC will borrow from its parent or a 3rd party and on-lend or finance lease to the airline.
Opinion given: Not Case 1.
Reason: Not Case 1 as the SPC is essentially passive. The characteristics of a trade are absent. The activities undertaken are not sufficient to be regarded as trading activities. The real decision making and planning takes place elsewhere.
Date received: Mar 03.
No of employees in Ireland: None.
Description of activity: Company will be responsible for the group's global brand management activity for which it will receive royalty income from group companies and third parties.
Opinion given: Not Case 1.
Reason: Under the new structure, the work involved in targetting, evaluating and negotiating contracts with suitable partners would be undertaken by other group companies. The company is carrying on investment activities from which royalties are derived. Case IV is the more appropriate classification.
Date received: Mar 03.
No of employees in Ireland: Outsourced initially.
Description of activity: Company will be involved in (1) group financing and treasury operations and (2) charter of vessel on a long-term basis to other group company.
Opinion given: (1) Case 1 confirmed (2) Not Case 1.
Reason: (1) Case 1 confirmed for finance and treasury activities. The Irish company will be actively managing the business and will make the strategic decisions in relation to the financing and treasury operations. The outsourcing arrangement will be managed and controlled by Irish resident directors who have the appropriate level of expertise in this area (2) In relation to vessel charter, the companies will not be carrying on sufficient activities to be regarded as trading. The companies are not involved in the strategic and high level decision making process and it seems that the real authority, responsibility and decision making lie elsewhere in the group. The income in this case arises from ownership of an income bearing asset rather than from trading.
Date received: Mar 03.
No of employees in Ireland: No additional employees.
Description of activity: Company wants to treat (as an extension of its Case 1 trade) the income arising from licensing to a US subsidiary of the right to use an existing customer relationship.
Opinion given: Not Case 1.
Reason: Unable to confirm Case 1 treatment. There is not sufficient ongoing work involved in maintaining the customer relationship for the exploitation of the customer base to be regarded as a trading activity.
Date received: Mar 03.
No of employees in Ireland: 4.
Description of activity: Company will provide agency treasury services to other group companies involving investment and cash management services.
Opinion given: Case 1 confirmed.
Reason: Case 1 confirmed on the basis that the company will be carrying out real trading activities, and that the company's employees possess the requisite skill and expertise to undertake the transactions and that the company exercises decision-making and control and directors will hold meetings in Ireland.
Date received: Mar 03.
No of employees in Ireland: 2 initially.

Description of activity: Partnership formed to purchase vessels. Partnership will then lease the vessels to each of the partners who will in turn sub-lease to group operating companies. Irish partner will be managing partner and be responsible for fleet management as well as negotiating and arranging for own leasing activities.
Opinion given: Case 1 confirmed.
Reason: Case 1 confirmed because the Irish company will be the managing partner and, in addition to having full authority to negotiate and manage its own leases, has also been given authority under the Partnership agreement to manage the entire fleet as well as responsibility for allocating the vessels between the partners.
Date received: Apr 03.
No of employees in Ireland: Outsourced to employees of two other companies.
Description of activity: Two companies involved. Both will acquire and lease aircraft.
Opinion given: Case 1 confirmed.
Reason: The companies will be actively seeking new customers and negotiating leases for the aircraft. Activities will be carried out by people with the appropriate knowledge and expertise, the companies will have responsibility for strategic decisions and each will act independently in carrying out its trading activities. The directors of the companies will take an active part in the management of the outsourcing contract and will be responsible for setting the strategic policy of the companies.
Date received: May 03.
No of employees in Ireland: 3 increasing to 7 after one year.
Description of activity: The Irish company will be responsible for the management, control and development of money transfer services. This will involve treasury management and administrative activities.
Opinion given: Case 1 confirmed.
Reason: Case 1 confirmed on the basis that the Irish company is a genuine stand-alone operation, staffed by people with appropriate skills and experience and that real strategic business decisions will be made by the company.
Date received: Jun 03.
No of employees in Ireland: 2–3.
Description of activity: The company will provide cash management and pooling services, foreign exchange hedging and processing and financial settlement of payment for other group companies.
Opinion given: Case 1 confirmed.
Reason: Case 1 confirmed on basis that the activities will be carried on by people with appropriate skills and experience and that the real strategic business decisions will be made by company.
Date received: Jul 03.
No of employees in Ireland: Outsourced to other group company which has 44 skilled employees.
Description of activity: The company will be responsible for funding UK operations of the group and in particular its inventory funding requirements. This will involve a series of short term loans which close out on a fortnightly basis.
Opinion given: Case 1 confirmed.
Reason: Case 1 confirmed on the basis of the level of activity to be carried on. The directors of the company will be responsible for strategic business planning and agreeing parameters and loan agreements.
Date received: Aug 03.
No of employees in Ireland: 17/20 within 2 years.
Description of activity: Company will (1) licence other group companies to use a proprietary system which will enable information to be delivered to clients over the internet. The Irish company owns the software, hardware and infracture and (2) also provide helpdesk and on-line sales in the provision of international media information.
Opinion given: (1) Not Case 1 (2) Case 1 confirmed.
Reason: (1) Unable to confirm Case 1 for this as the income flows from ownership of an asset rather than being generated from activities undertaken by the company. The Irish company did not have full control and responsibility for the licensing and development of the system. All of the key decisions makers in this area are located abroad and report to other group companies. (2) Case 1 confirmed for income from on-line sales and help desk functions as there will be sufficient activities in these areas to constitute a trade.
Date received: Sep 03.
No of employees in Ireland: 1.
Description of activity: Irish company will conduct financing activities with other group companies in various jurisdictions around the world. Initially this will consist of one long term loan. Further loans may be made but this is dependant on other factors within the group.
Opinion given: Not Case 1.

Reason: Unable to confirm Case 1 treatment. The company was not actively involved in sourcing and negotiating the loan arrangement. The decision to make the loan was made elsewhere in the group. The profits were not generated by the company's activities.
Date received: Oct 03.
No of employees in Ireland: 12.
Description of activity: The company subcontracts the manufacturing activities to a group company abroad and is also responsible for European sales of the products.
Opinion given: Case 1 confirmed.
Reason: The subcontracted activities are part of an existing Irish trade. The company will be managed by six senior executives who have responsibility for the day to day management of the trade including the outsourced operations. Revenue was satisfied that the executives had the capacity, in a restructured scenario, to manage the outsourced activities. The Irish company is also responsible for quality control of the goods and a team of six will audit the subcontractor to ensure that technical standards are met.
Date received: Oct 03.
No of employees in Ireland: None.
Description of activity: The company is being established to develop, manufacture, market and sell a technological system.
Opinion given: No opinion given.
Reason: It would not be appropriate to give an opinion on trading status. The strategic decisions and day to day management of the company will be carried out by a board of directors that will not be based in Ireland. The company does not have any senior personnel based in Ireland with the authority and skills to carry out the functions involved in the management of the R&D, and manufacture and sale of the company's products. The R& D phase of the operation would not be regarded as trading.
Date received: Nov 03.
No of employees in Ireland: None.
Description of activity: The company will acquire a share in a fleet of aircraft which will be leased to US airline
Opinion given: Not Case 1.
Reason: Unable to confirm Case 1 as there is insufficient activity in the company to constitute a trade. The company will not be actively seeking business.
Date received: Nov 03.
No of employees in Ireland: None — work outsourced.
Description of activity: The parent company will loan money to a new company to acquire title to two planes which newco will then lease to an airline for a seven year period.
Opinion given: Not Case 1.
Reason: Newco has not been involved in the negotiations leading to the purchase and on-lease of the planes.It is not actively involved in a trade of leasing. It will not be actively seeking new business. Correctly assessable Case IV.
Date received: Nov 03.
No of employees in Ireland: 4.
Description of activity: Company will act as inter group financing and treasury company.
Opinion given: Case 1 confirmed.
Reason: Confirmation given on the basis that company will be actively involved in negotiating and arranging loans for other group companies and also cash pooling and currency management requirements of group.
Date received: Nov 03.
No of employees in Ireland: 3+.
Description of activity: The Irish branch will be responsible for the investment management functions of the reinsurance operations of a large multi-national insurance group. It will be responsible for actively trading the existing corporate bond portfolio of the group. This will involve new purchases, sales of existing bonds,swaps etc.
Opinion given: Case 1 confirmed.
Reason: Case 1 confirmed on the basis that the branch operation will be actively trading the portfolio and is responsible for and has the capacity to make the key strategic decisions on purchases, sales etc
Date received: Jan 04.
No of employees in Ireland: None.
Description of activity: Special purpose company set up to purchase and on lease aircraft. The company is being set up solely to purchase and on-lease to a specific customer.
Opinion given: Not Case 1.
Reason: The company was not involved in the negotiation or decision making process Nor will it be looking for new business. As such it is not carrying on a Case 1 trade. Income is more appropriately taxed under Case IV.

Date received: Feb 04.
No of employees in Ireland: Outsourced to company who will have already have 5 employees engaged on this type of work and may have to engage one other depending on future volume of business.
Description of activity: Irish company will lend to other group companies, place surplus cash on deposit and undertake hedging activities for the group.
Opinion given: Case 1 confirmed
Reason: The company will deal with a large number of customers and transactions annually. The work is outsourced but Irish directors evaluate and have responsibility for ongoing decisions on loans, approval of credit limits, interest rates etc.
Date received: Feb 04.
No of employees in Ireland: 2–3.
Description of activity: Irish company will licence third parties to exploit trademarks in Europe and Asia. In the long term the company also Intends to expand its activities to include distribution and the provision of certain shared services for other group companies.
Opinion given: Case 1 confirmed.
Reason: The company will be actively trading with the licences. Company employees are responsible for continuous monitoring and review of existing licences and licensees, seeking out potential new licensees, ensuring maintenance of brand image by driving and advising on marketing strategies.
Date received: Feb 04.
No of employees in Ireland: Outsourced initially.
Description of activity: Established to protect and exploit the IP of a non-resident.
Opinion given: Not Case 1.
Unable to confirm that activites of company constitutes a Case I trade because the company is not involved in the key activities giving rise to the income. None of the main players in the case are located in Ireland and the company's involvement is essentially passive. Case IV would apply if company resident in Ireland.
Date received: Mar 04.
No of employees in Ireland: 12.
Description of activity: The company will serve as the primary group entity that enters into third party foreign exchange and other derivative transactions for the group.
Opinion given: Case 1 confirmed.
Reason: Case 1 confirmed on the basis of the level of activities involved and that the employees and company management involved possess the appropriate level of skills, expertise and authority necessary.
Date received: Mar 04.
No of employees in Ireland: None — outsourced.
Description of activity: Established to carry on an aircraft leasing and financing trade in Ireland.
Opinion given: Not Case 1.
Reason: Not satisfied that activities of company constitute a Case I trade. Would expect that a leasing company would have been actively involved in acquisition and leasing of asset. Company was not involved in negotiations leading to purchase and on-lease of asset nor will it be seeking other business. In these circumstances the income is more correctly assessable under Case IV.

Definitions

person: IA 1937 s 11(*c*); land: IA 1937 Sch; profession: s 2(1); trade: s 3(1).

Former enactments

ITA 1967 s 52 and s 53; FA 1969 s 33(1) and Sch 4 Pt I, s 65 and Sch 5 Pt I.

Corresponding UK tax provision

Income and Corporation Taxes Act 1988 s 18.

19 Schedule E

(1) The Schedule referred to as Schedule E is as follows:

SCHEDULE E

1. In this Schedule, **"annuity"** and **"pension"** include respectively an annuity which is paid voluntarily or is capable of being discontinued and a pension which is so paid or is so capable.

2. Tax under this Schedule shall be charged in respect of every public office or employment of profit, and in respect of every annuity, pension or stipend payable out of the public revenue of the State, other than annuities charged under Schedule C, for every [one euro][1] of the annual amount thereof.
3. Tax under this Schedule shall also be charged in respect of any office, employment or pension the profits or gains arising or accruing from which would be chargeable to tax under Schedule D but for paragraph 2 of that Schedule.
4. Paragraphs 1 to 3 are without prejudice to any other provision of the Income Tax Acts directing tax to be charged under this Schedule, and tax so directed to be charged shall be charged accordingly.
5. Subsection (2) and sections 114, 115 and 925 shall apply in relation to the tax to be charged under this Schedule.

(2) Tax under Schedule E shall be paid in respect of all public offices and employments of profit in the State or by the officers respectively described below—

(*a*) offices belonging to either House of the Oireachtas;
(*b*) offices belonging to any court in the State;
(*c*) public offices under the State;
(*d*) officers of the Defence Forces;
(*e*) offices or employments of profit under any ecclesiastical body;
(*f*) offices or employments of profit under any company or society, whether corporate or not corporate;
(*g*) offices or employments of profit under any public institution, or on any public foundation of whatever nature, or for whatever purpose established;
(*h*) offices or employments of profit under any public corporation or local authority, or under any trustees or guardians of any public funds, tolls or duties;
(*i*) all other public offices or employments of profit of a public nature.

Amendments

[1] Substituted by FA 2001 s 240(1) and (2)(*a*) and Sch 5 Pt 1 for 2002 and later tax years; previously "one pound".

Cross-references

Approved retirement fund: s 784A(3)(*a*).
Charge to income tax of pensions under Schedule E: s 779(1).
General charge: s 12.
Reporting of offences: section 59(1) ("relevant person") of the Criminal Justice (Theft and Fraud Offences) Act 2001.
Retirement annuities, relief for premiums: s 784(2B)(*a*), (7).
Taxation of payments from a Personal Retirement Savings Account (PRSA): s 787G(1)(*a*).

Case law

4: Held provision envisaged items chargeable under Schedule E in addition to emoluments: *Nicols v Gibson* [1994] STC 102

Revenue precedents

Issue: Taxation of employees of embassies who are not exempt from tax under the Diplomatic Relations and Immunities Act, 1967 and who are not relieved from double taxation because no Double Taxation Convention exists with the country.
Decision: In the case of certain employees in the Turkish Embassy it was agreed to allow that they would be assessed to Irish tax on the net amount of earnings received after deduction of tax imposed by the Turkish authorities.
Issue: Bilateral Aid Programme — General.

Decision: Public Office. Individuals who go abroad on the Irish Bilateral Aid Programme should not be regarded as acquiring "public office" by the mere fact of being engaged in the Programme. An individual who holds "public office" and is seconded to the programme would, however, retain his "public office" status. A person who gets leave of absence from his "public office" and joins the programme would not retain his "public office" status.

Issue: EU Human Capital and Mobility Programme. Tax status of holders of grants or research fellowship under the EU Human Capital and Mobility Programme. Holders of grants or research fellowships under the EU Human Capital and Mobility Programme are employees of the Irish Institute to which they are attached.

Decision: The income (including the mobility allowance) payable to such individuals is chargeable to Irish tax under Schedule E and subject to the operation of P.A.Y.E., unless relieved by the provisions of a Double Taxation Treaty.

Statement of Practice

Treatment of Remuneration of Members of State and State Sponsored Committees and Boards: SP IT1/04.

Tax Briefing

TB33 Sept 1998 p 15 — Employed or Self-Employed — Guidelines.

TB43 Apr 2001 pp 3–7 Employed or Self-Employed — Report of the Employment Status Group and Code of Practice.

Former enactments

ITA 1967 s 109 and Sch 2 rule 2.

Corresponding UK tax provision

Income and Corporation Taxes Act 1988 s 19.

20 Schedule F

(1) The Schedule referred to as Schedule F is as follows:

SCHEDULE F

1. In this Schedule, **"distribution"** has the meaning assigned to it by Chapter 2 of Part 6 and [sections 436 and 437, and subsection (2)(b) of section 816].[1]
2. Income tax under this Schedule shall be chargeable for any year of assessment in respect of all dividends and other distributions in that year of a company resident in the State which are not specially excluded from income tax, and for the purposes of income tax all such distributions shall be regarded as income however they are to be dealt with in the hands of the recipient.

...[2]

(2) No distribution chargeable under Schedule F shall be chargeable under any other provision of the Income Tax Acts.

Amendments

1 Substituted by FA 1998 s 43(1)(*c*) as respects shares issued by a company on or after 3 December 1997; previously "sections 436 and 437".

2 Para 3 repealed by FA 2000 s 69(2) and Sch 2 Part 2 with effect from 6 April 1999 in the case of income tax and for accounting periods commencing on or after that date in the case of corporation tax.

Cross-references

Dividend withholding tax (interpretation), meaning of distribution applied: s 172(1)(*a*)("relevant distribution").

General charge: s 12.

Definitions

company: ss 4(1), 5(1); distribution: ss 4(1), 436, 437; Income Tax Acts: s 1(2); interest: s 4(1); person: IA 1937 s 11(*c*); resident: s 5(1); Tax Acts: s 1(2); tax: s 3(1); writing: IA 1937 Sch; year of assessment: ss 2(1), 5(1).

Former enactments

CTA 1976 s 83(2)–(3).

Corresponding UK tax provision

Income and Corporation Taxes Act 1988 s 20.

CHAPTER 2
Corporation Tax

21 The charge to corporation tax and exclusion of income tax and capital gains tax

[(1) Corporation tax shall be charged on the profits of companies at the rate of—

(*a*) 32 per cent for the financial year 1998,

(*b*) 28 per cent for the financial year 1999,

(*c*) 24 per cent for the financial year 2000,

(*d*) 20 per cent for the financial year 2001,

(*e*) 16 per cent for the financial year 2002,

(*f*) 12½ per cent for the financial year 2003 and each subsequent financial year.][1]

[(1A)(*a*) In this subsection—

"qualifying shipping activities" and **"qualifying shipping trade"** have the same meanings respectively as in section 407;

(*b*) Notwithstanding subsection (1), for the financial year 2001 and 2002, in relation to a company carrying on a qualifying shipping trade, profits from qualifying shipping activities carried on in the course of the qualifying shipping trade shall be charged to corporation tax at the rate of 12½ per cent.

[(*c*) Notwithstanding subsection (1), for the financial year 2002, in relation to a tonnage tax company (within the meaning of Part 24A), tonnage tax profits shall be charged to corporation tax at the rate of 12½ per cent.][2]][3]

(2) The provisions of the Income Tax Acts relating to the charge of income tax shall not apply to income of a company (not arising to it in a fiduciary or representative capacity) if—

(*a*) the company is resident in the State, or

(*b*) the income is, in the case of a company not so resident, within the chargeable profits of the company as defined for the purposes of corporation tax.

(3) Subject to section 649, a company shall not be chargeable to capital gains tax in respect of gains accruing to it so that it is chargeable in respect of them to corporation tax.

Amendments

1 Subs (1) substituted by FA 1999 s 71 with effect from 6 April 1999.

2 Subs (1A)(*c*) inserted by FA 2002 s 53(3) and (5) (as amended by FA 2003 s 62) with effect from 28 March 2003.

3 Subs (1A) inserted by FA 2001 s 82(1)(*a*) with effect from 1 January 2001.

Cross-references

Bank levy credit: 487(1)(*a*).

Computation of companies' chargeable gains (subs (1)): s 78(3).

Double tax relief: s 450(5).

Group relief, relief for certain losses on a value basis: s 420B(3)(*b*), (4)(*b*)(ii).

Higher rate of corporation tax: s 21A(3)(*a*).

Life assurance companies, chargeable gains of life business: s 711(1)(*c*)(ii), (*d*).

Life assurance companies, investment income reserved for policy holders, subs (1): s 713(3).

Life assurance companies, management expenses deduction, subs (1): s 707(4).
Making of claims etc, subs (2): s 864(2)(*a*).
Partnerships involving companies, subs (2): s 1009(4)(*b*), (*c*).
Persons chargeable in a representative capacity: s 1044(1).
Petroleum taxation, reduced rate: s 686(2).
Reduction of corporation tax liability in respect of certain trading income: s 22A(2)(*a*)(i).
Relief for certain charges on a value basis: s 243B(4)(b)(ii).
Relief for certain trading losses on a value basis: s 396B(3)(*b*), (5)(*b*)(ii).
Undertakings for collective investment, subs (1): s 738(2)(*c*); taxation of unit holders, subs (3): s 739(4)(*a*)(i).

Definitions

chargeable gain: ss 4(1), 5(1); company: s 4(1); the financial year: s 4(1); Income Tax Acts: s 1(2); profits: s 4(1).

Notes

Previous rates:	*Rate:*	*Authority:*
1 April 1997 to 31 December 1997	36%	FA 1998 s 55(1)
1 April 1995 to 31 March 1997:	38%	FA 1995 s 54(1)
1 April 1991 to 31 March 1995:	40%	FA 1990 s 37(1)
1 April 1989 to 31 March 1991:	43%	FA 1988 s 33(1)
1 April 1988 to 31 March 1989:	47%	FA 1988 s 33(1)
1 January 1982 to 31 March 1988:	50%	FA 1982 s 26(1)
1 January 1977 to 31 December 1981:	45%	FA 1977 s 15
6 April 1976 to 31 December 1976:	50%	CTA 1976 s 1 as enacted

Revenue Information Notice

Guidance on Revenue opinions on classification of activities as trading — May 2003.

Tax Briefing

TB 57 Oct 2004 pp 10–12 — Classification of Activities as Trading — CT.

Former enactments

CTA 1976 s 1(1)–(3); FA 1997 s 59(1).

21A Higher rate of corporation tax

[(1) In this section—

"construction operations" means operations of any of the descriptions referred to in the definition of "construction operations" in section 530(1), other than operations referred to in paragraph (*f*) of that definition;

"dealing in or developing land" shall be construed in accordance with Chapter 1 of Part 22;

"excepted operations" means any one or more of the following operations or activities—

[(*a*) dealing in or developing land, other than such part of that operation or activity as consists of—

(i) construction operations, or

(ii) dealing by a company in land which, in relation to the company, is qualifying land,][1]

(*b*) working minerals, and

(*c*) petroleum activities;

"excepted trade" means a trade consisting only of trading operations or activities which are excepted operations or, in the case of a trade consisting partly of excepted operations and partly of other operations or activities, the part of the trade consisting only of excepted operations which is treated as a separate trade by virtue of subsection (2);

[**"exempt development"** means a development within Class 1 of Part 1 of the Second Schedule to the Local Government Planning and Development Regulations, 1994 (SI No 86 of 1994), which complies with the conditions and limitations specified in column 2 of that Part which relate to that Class;][2]

"land" includes foreshore and land covered with water, and **"dry land"** means land not permanently covered by water;

"minerals" means all substances (other than the agricultural surface of the ground and other than turf or peat) in, on or under land, whether obtainable by underground or by surface working, and includes all mines, whether or not they are already opened or in work, and also includes the cubic space occupied or formerly occupied by minerals;

"petroleum" has the same meaning as in section 2(1) of the Petroleum and Other Minerals Development Act, 1960;

"petroleum activities" means any one or more of the following activities—

(*a*) petroleum exploration activities,
(*b*) petroleum extraction activities, and
(*c*) the acquisition, enjoyment or exploitation of petroleum rights;

"petroleum exploration activities" means activities carried on in searching for deposits of petroleum, in testing or appraising such deposits or in winning access to such deposits for the purposes of such searching, testing or appraising;

"petroleum extraction activities" means activities carried on in—

(*a*) winning petroleum from any land, including searching in that land and winning access to such petroleum,
(*b*) transporting as far as dry land petroleum so won from a place not on dry land, or
(*c*) effecting the initial treatment and storage of petroleum so won from any land;

"petroleum rights" means rights to petroleum to be extracted or to interests in, or to the benefit of, petroleum;

[**"qualifying land"**, in relation to a company, means land which is disposed of at any time by the company, being land—

(*a*) on which a building or structure had been constructed by or for the company before that time, and
(*b*) which had been developed by or for the company to such an extent that it could reasonably be expected at that time that no further development (within the meaning of section 639) of the land would be carried out in the period of 20 years beginning at that time (other than a development which is not material and which is intended to facilitate the occupation of, and the use or enjoyment

of, the building or structure for the purposes for which it was constructed) and for those purposes a development of land on which a building or buildings had been constructed shall not be material if it consists of one or both of the following—

(i) an exempt development, and

(ii) a development, not being an exempt development, if the total floor area of the building or buildings on the land after such development is not greater than 120 per cent of the total floor area of the building or buildings on the land calculated without regard to that development;][3]

"working", in relation to minerals, includes digging, searching for, mining, getting, raising, taking, carrying away and treating minerals and the sale or other disposal of minerals.

(2) For the purposes of this section, where a trade consists partly of excepted operations and partly of other operations or activities, the part of the trade consisting of excepted operations and the part of the trade consisting of other operations or activities shall each be treated as a separate trade, and there shall be apportioned to each such part such proportion of the total amount receivable from sales made and services rendered in the course of the trade, and of expenses incurred in the course of the trade, as is just and reasonable.

[(3) (*a*) Notwithstanding section 21, but subject to subsection (4), corporation tax shall be charged on the profits of companies, in so far as those profits consist of income chargeable to corporation tax under Case III, IV or V of Schedule D or of income of an excepted trade, at the rate of 25 per cent for the financial year 2000 and subsequent financial years.

(*b*) For the purposes of paragraph (*a*), the profits of a company for an accounting period shall be treated as consisting of income of an excepted trade to the extent of the income of the trade for the accounting period after deducting from the amount of that income the amount of charges on income paid in the accounting period wholly and exclusively for the purposes of that trade.

(4) This section shall not apply to the profits of a company for any accounting period—

(*a*) to the extent that those profits consist of income from the sale of goods within the meaning of section 454, and

(*b*) to the extent that those profits consist of income which arises in the course of any of the following trades—

(i) non-life insurance,

(ii) reinsurance, and

(iii) life business, in so far as the income is attributable to shareholders of the company.

(5) (*a*) Notwithstanding subsection (1), as respects an accounting period ending before 1 January 2001, operations carried out in relation to residential development land (within the meaning of section 644A) shall be treated for the purposes of this section as not being construction operations if they consist of—

(i) the demolition or dismantling of any building or structure on the land,

(ii) the construction or demolition of any works forming part of the land, being roadworks, water mains, wells, sewers or installations for the purposes of land drainage, or

(iii) any other operations which are preparatory to residential development on the land other than the laying of foundations for such development.

(*b*) For the purposes of this subsection, where an accounting period of a company begins before 1 January 2001 and ends on or after that day, it shall be divided into two parts, one beginning on the day on which the accounting period begins and ending on 31 December 2000 and the other beginning on 1 January 2001 and ending on the day on which the accounting period ends, and both parts shall be treated for the purpose of this section as if they were separate accounting periods of the company.][4]][5]

Amendments

1 Definition of "excepted operations" para (*a*) substituted by FA 2000 s 75(1)(*a*)(i) with effect for 2000 and later financial years.

2 Definition of "exempt development" inserted by FA 2000 s 75(1)(*a*)(ii) with effect for 2000 and later financial years.

3 Definition of "qualifying land" inserted by FA 2000 s 75(1)(*a*)(iii) with effect for 2000 and later financial years.

4 Subss (3)–(5) substituted for subss (3)–(4) by FA 2000 s 75(1)(*b*) with effect for 2000 and later financial years.

5 Section 21A inserted by FA 1999 s 73 with effect from 6 April 1999.

Cross-references

Close company surcharges, distributions to be taken into account and meaning of distributable estate and investment income, meaning of "excepted trade" applied: s 434(1)("relevant charges"), (5)(*b*)(iii).

Disposal of an interest in offshore funds, subs (3): s 747E(1)(*a*).

Group relief, relevant losses and charges: s 420A(1) ("relevevant trading loss"); subs (4)(*b*): s 420A(3)(*a*)(i).

Life assurance companies, investment income reserved for policy holders: s 713(3).

Manufacturing (10%) relief and higher rate of corporation tax, interaction: s 448(5A).

Reduction of corporation tax liability in respect of certain trading income, meaning of "excepted trade" applied: s 22A(1) ("relevant charges on income", "relevant trading income", "relevant trading loss"); subs (2) applied: s 22A(11).

Relief for relevant trading losses, meaning of "excepted trade" applied: s 396A(1)("relevant trading loss"); subs (4)(*b*): s 396A(3).

Relief from corporation tax in respect of income from dealing in residential development land, meaning of "excepted trade" applied: s 644B(1); meaning of "construction operations" applied: s 644B(2)(*b*)(i)(I), (II); s 644B(2)(*b*)(ii), (4)(*a*).

Relief from income tax and corporation tax by means of credit in respect of foreign tax: Sch 24 paras 4(4)(*a*), 9E(2).

Restriction of relevant charges on income, meaning of "excepted trade" applied: s 243A(1)("relevant trading charges on income", "relevant trading income"); subs (4)(*b*): s 243A(3)(*a*).

Restriction of reliefs where individual is not actively participating in certain trades, meaning of "petroleum activities" applied: s 409D(1) ("specified trade").

Revenue Information Notice

Deposit Interest – whether a trading receipt? – March 2003.

Guidance on Revenue opinions on classification of activities as trading – May 2003.

Definitions

company: s 4(1); land: IA 1937 Sch; profits: s 4(1); trade: ss 3(1), 4(1).

---

22 Reduced rate of corporation tax for certain income

Amendments

Section 22 repealed by FA 1999 s 72(2) with effect from 1 January 2000.

22A Reduction of corporation tax liability in respect of certain trading income

[(1) In this section—

"income from the sale of goods", in relation to an accounting period of a company, means such income as is income from the sale of those goods in the course of a trade carried on by the company for the purposes of a claim under section 448(3);

"net relevant trading income", in relation to an accounting period of a company, means the excess of the amount of relevant trading income of the company for the accounting period over the aggregate of the amounts of—

(*a*) relevant charges on income paid by the company in the accounting period, and

(*b*) any relevant trading loss incurred by the company in the accounting period;

"relevant charges on income", in relation to an accounting period of a company, means the charges on income paid by the company in the accounting period wholly and exclusively for the purposes of a trade carried on by the company other than so much of those charges as are—

(*a*) charges on income paid for the purposes of the sale of goods within the meaning of section 454, or

(*b*) charges on income paid for the purposes of an excepted trade within the meaning of section 21A;

"relevant trading income", in relation to an accounting period of a company, means the trading income of the company for the accounting period (not being income chargeable to tax under Case III of Schedule D) other than so much of that income as is—

(*a*) income from the sale of goods, or

(*b*) income of an excepted trade within the meaning of section 21A;

"relevant trading loss", in relation to an accounting period of a company, means a loss incurred in the accounting period in a trade carried on by the company other than so much of the loss as is—

(i) a loss from the sale of goods within the meaning of section 455, or

(ii) a loss incurred in an excepted trade within the meaning of section 21A;

"trading income", in relation to an accounting period of a company, means the income which is to be included in respect of a trade or trades in the total profits of the company for the accounting period as reduced by the amount of any loss set off against that income under section 396(1).

(2) Subject to subsections (7) and (8), where in any accounting period ending on or after 1 January 2000 the net relevant trading income of a company does not exceed the upper relevant maximum amount, then the corporation tax charged on the company for that accounting period shall be reduced—

(*a*) where the net relevant trading income of the company does not exceed the lower relevant maximum amount, by such amount as will secure that the corporation tax charged on the company for the accounting period does not exceed the corporation tax which, apart from this section, would have been charged on the company for the accounting period if—

(i) in section 21 for paragraphs (*c*) to (*f*) of subsection (1) there were substituted the following paragraph:

"(*c*) 12.5 per cent for the financial year 2000 and each subsequent financial year.",

and

(ii) in section 448 for paragraphs (*c*) to (*f*) of subsection (2) there were substituted the following paragraph:

"(*c*) by one-fifth, in so far as it is corporation tax charged on profits which under section 26(3) are apportioned to the financial year 2000 or any subsequent financial year.",

and

(*b*) where the net relevant trading income of the company exceeds the lower relevant maximum amount, by a sum equal to—

[(i) as respects an accounting period falling within the financial year 2001, 30 per cent, and

(ii) as respects an accounting period falling within the financial year, 2002, 14 per cent,][1]

of the excess of the upper relevant maximum amount over the net relevant trading income for the accounting period.

(3) The lower and upper relevant maximum amounts mentioned in subsection (2) shall be determined as follows:

(*a*) where the company has no associated company in the accounting period, those amounts are [€254,000][2] and [€317,500][2], respectively,

(*b*) where the company has one or more associated companies in the accounting period, the lower relevant maximum amount is [€254,000][2] divided by one plus the number of those associated companies and the upper relevant maximum amount is [€317,500][2] divided by one plus the number of those associated companies.

(4) (*a*) In this subsection **"control"** shall be construed in accordance with section 432.

(*b*) In applying this section to any accounting period of a company, an associated company which has no net relevant trading income for that accounting period (or, if an associated company during part only of that accounting period, for that part of that accounting period) shall be disregarded and, for the purposes of this section, a company shall be treated as an "associated company" of another company at a given time if at that time one of the two has control of the other or both are under the control of the same person or persons.

(5) In determining how many associated companies a company has in an accounting period or whether a company has an associated company in an accounting period, an

associated company shall be counted even if it was an associated company for part only of the accounting period, and two or more associated companies shall be counted even if they were associated companies for different parts of the accounting period.

(6) For an accounting period of less than 12 months the relevant maximum amounts determined in accordance with subsection (3) shall be proportionately reduced.

(7) (*a*) Where, in the case of a company which has one or more associated companies in an accounting period—

(i) the accounting period of the company ends on a date on which accounting periods of all of the associated companies end, and

(ii) the company and all of the associated companies jointly elect in writing that this subsection shall apply,

then—

(I) the relief under subsection (2) shall be computed as if, in relation to the accounting period, the company and all of the associated companies were a single company (with no associated companies) with an accounting period ending on that date and beginning at the earliest date on which the accounting period of the company, or of any of the associated companies, begins, and

(II) the relief as so computed shall be allocated to the accounting period of the company and to the accounting periods of its associated companies in such manner as is specified in the election, and the amount so allocated to a company shall be deemed to be the relief under this section in relation to the accounting period of the company.

(*b*) Notwithstanding paragraph (*a*)—

(i) the aggregate of amounts allocated under subparagraph (II) of that paragraph for an accounting period shall not exceed the relief computed under subparagraph (I) of that paragraph, and

(ii) the amount allocated to an accounting period of a company shall not exceed the amount which would have been the relief in relation to the accounting period if the company had no associated companies in the accounting period.

(8) (*a*) Subject to paragraph (*b*), where, in the case of a company which has one or more associated companies in an accounting period, the end of the accounting period of the company and the end of an accounting period of each of its associated companies do not coincide—

(i) subsection (7) shall apply as respects any period (in this subsection referred to as a "relevant period") which falls into the accounting period of the company and an accounting period of each of the associated companies as if the relevant period were an accounting period of the company and of the associated companies,

(ii) the relief allocated to any company in respect of a relevant period shall be deemed to be the relief in relation to that period, and

(iii) where an amount of relief has been allocated to a company in respect of a relevant period falling into an accounting period of the company, the relief for the accounting period of the company shall be the aggregate of—

(I) any relief in relation to relevant periods falling into the accounting period, and

(II) the amounts which would be the relief in relation to any periods (which are not relevant periods) within the accounting period if each of those periods was treated as an accounting period.

(*b*) The relief under paragraph (*a*) in relation to an accounting period of a company shall not exceed the amount which would be the relief in relation to the accounting period if the company had no associated companies in the accounting period.

(9) For the purposes of this section, where an accounting period of a company begins before 1 January of a financial year and ends on or after that date, it shall be divided into 2 parts, one beginning on the date on which the accounting period begins and ending on 31 December of the preceding financial year and the other beginning on 1 January of the financial year and ending on the date on which the accounting period ends, and both parts shall be treated as if they were separate accounting periods of the company.

(10)(*a*) A company shall include in the return required to be delivered under section 951—

(i) a statement specifying—

(I) the amount of relief to be given to it under this section, and

(II) the number of companies which are its associated companies in relation to the accounting period,

and

(ii) a copy of any election made under subsection (7).

(*b*) A company which has specified an amount under paragraph (*a*) shall not he entitled to alter the amount so specified.

(11) Subsection (2) of section 21A shall apply for the purposes of this section.][4]

Amendments

1 Subs (2)(*b*)(i)–(iii) substituted by FA 2001 s 83(1)(*a*) for the financial year 2001 and later financial years.

2 Substituted by FA 2001 s 83(1)(*b*)(ii) for the financial year 2002 and later financial years; previously "£50,000" and "£75,000" (short tax "year" 2001: £200,00, £250,000: FA 2001 s 83(1)(*b*)(i)).

3 Section 22A inserted by FA 2000 s 76 with effect from 6 April 2000.

Cross-reference

Close company surcharges, distributions to be taken into account and meaning of distributable estate and investment income, subs (2): s 434(5A)(*a*)("distributable trading income").
Relief from corporation tax: s 448(1)(*d*).

Definitions

company: ss 4(1), 5(1); profits: s 2(1); trade: s 4(1); writing: IA 1937 Sch.

23 Application of section 13 for purposes of corporation tax

Section 13 shall apply for the purposes of corporation tax as it applies for the purposes of income tax.

Cross-references

Supplementary provisions: Sch 1 para 2(1).

Former enactments

CTA 1976 s 140(1) and Sch 2 Pt I para 34.

23A Company residence

[(1) (*a*) In this section—

"arrangements" means arrangements having the force of law by virtue of section [826(1)(*a*)][1] ;

"relevant company" means a company—

(i) which is under the control, whether directly or indirectly, of a person or persons who is or are—

(I) by virtue of the law of any relevant territory, resident for the purposes of tax in a relevant territory or relevant territories, and

(II) not under the control, whether directly or indirectly, of a person who is, or persons who are, not so resident,

or

(ii) which is, or is related to, a company the principal class of the shares of which is substantially and regularly traded on one or more than one recognised stock exchange in a relevant territory or territories;

"relevant territory" means—

(i) a Member State of the European Communities, or

(ii) not being such a Member State, a territory with the government of which arrangements have been made;

"tax", in relation to a relevant territory other than the State, means any tax imposed in that territory which corresponds to income tax or corporation tax.

(*b*) For the purposes of—

(i) this section—

(I) a company shall be treated as related to another company if one company is a 50 per cent subsidiary of the other company or both companies are 50 per cent subsidiaries of a third company,

[(II) section 9 shall apply as it would apply for the purposes of the Tax Acts if in paragraph (*b*) of subsection (1) of that section "50 per cent" were substituted for "75 per cent" in both places where it occurs, and][2]

(III) sections 412 to 418 shall apply as those sections would apply for the purposes of Chapter 5 of Part 12 if—

(A) "50 per cent" were substituted for "75 per cent" in each place where it occurs in those sections, and

(B) ...[3] section 411(1)(*c*) were deleted,

and

(ii) the definition of "relevant company", control shall be construed in accordance with subsections (2) to (6) of section 432 as if in subsection (6) of that section for "5 or fewer participators" there were substituted—

(I) in so far as paragraph (i)(I) of that definition is concerned, "persons who, by virtue of the law of any relevant territory (within the meaning of section 23A), are resident for the purposes of tax in a relevant territory or relevant territories", and

(II) in so far as paragraph (i)(II) of that definition is concerned, "persons not resident for the purposes of tax in a relevant territory (within the meaning of section 23A).

(2) Subject to subsections (3) and (4), a company which is incorporated in the State shall be regarded for the purposes of the Tax Acts and the Capital Gains Tax Acts as resident in the State.

(3) Subsection (2) shall not apply to a company incorporated in the State if the company is a relevant company and—

(*a*) carries on a trade in the State, or

(*b*) is related to a company which carries on a trade in the State.

(4) Notwithstanding subsection (2), a company which is regarded for the purposes of any arrangements as resident in a territory other than the State and not resident in the State shall be treated for the purposes of the Tax Acts and the Capital Gains Tax Acts as not resident in the State.][4]

Amendments

1 Substituted by FA 2004 s 89 and Sch 3 para 1(*a*) with effect from 25 March 2004; previously "section 826".

2 Subs (1)(*b*)(i)(II) substituted by FA 2000 s 77(1)(*a*) with effect from 10 February 2000.

3 Deleted by FA 2000 s 77(1)(*b*) with effect from 10 February 2000; previously "subparagraph (iii) of".

4 Section 23A inserted by FA 1999 s 82 with effect from 11 February 1999 for companies incorporated on or after 11 February 1999, and from 1 October 1999 for companies which were incorporated before 11 February 1999.

Cross-references

Particulars to be supplied by new companies, meaning of "relevant territory" applied: s 882(2)(ii)(III)(A); subss (2), (3): s 882(2)(ii)(II); subs (4): s 882(2)(ii)(III).

Tax Briefing

TB 37 Oct 1999 pp 5–6 — Irish registered non-resident companies update.

Definitions

Capital Gains Tax Acts: s 1(2); company: ss 4(1), 5(1); person: IA 1937 s 11(*c*); Tax Acts: s 1(2); trade: ss 3(1), 4(1).

24 Companies resident in the State: income tax on payments made or received

(1) No payment made by a company resident in the State shall by virtue of this section or otherwise be treated for any purpose of the Income Tax Acts as paid out of profits or gains brought into charge to income tax, nor shall any right or obligation under the Income Tax Acts to deduct income tax from any payment be affected by the fact that the recipient is a company not chargeable to income tax in respect of the payment.

(2) Subject to the Corporation Tax Acts, where a company resident in the State receives any payment on which it bears income tax by deduction, the income tax on that payment shall be set off against any corporation tax assessable on the company by an assessment made for the accounting period in which that payment is to be taken into account for corporation tax (or would be taken into account but for any exemption from corporation tax), and accordingly in respect of that payment the company, unless wholly exempt from corporation tax, shall not be entitled to a repayment of income tax before the assessment for that accounting period is finally determined and it appears that a repayment is due.

(3) References in this section to payments received by a company apply to any payments received by another person on behalf of or in trust for the company, but not to any payments received by the company on behalf of or in trust for another person.

Cross-references

Making of claims etc, subs (2): s 864(2)(*a*).

Shipping tonnage tax, exclusion of reliefs, deductions and set-offs, subs (2): s 697M(3)(*c*).

Definitions

company: ss 4(1), 5(1); Income Tax Acts: s 1(2); person: IA 1937 s 11(*c*); profits: s 4(1).

Former enactments

CTA 1976 s 3.

---

25 Companies not resident in the State

(1) A company not resident in the State shall not be within the charge to corporation tax unless it carries on a trade in the State through a branch or agency, but if it does so it shall, subject to any exceptions provided for by the Corporation Tax Acts, be chargeable to corporation tax on all its chargeable profits wherever arising.

(2) For the purposes of corporation tax, the chargeable profits of a company not resident in the State but carrying on a trade in the State through a branch or agency shall be—

(*a*) any trading income arising directly or indirectly through or from the branch or agency, and any income from property or rights used by, or held by or for, the branch or agency, but this paragraph shall not include distributions received from companies resident in the State, and

(*b*) such chargeable gains as but for the Corporation Tax Acts would be chargeable to capital gains tax in the case of a company not resident in the State;

but such chargeable profits shall not include chargeable gains accruing to the company on the disposal of assets which, at or before the time when the chargeable gains accrued, were not used in or for the purposes of the trade and were not used or held or acquired for the purposes of the branch or agency.

(3) Subject to section 729, where a company not resident in the State receives any payment on which it bears income tax by deduction, and that payment forms part of, or is to be taken into account in computing, the company's income chargeable to corporation tax, the income tax on that payment shall be set off against any corporation tax assessable on that income by an assessment made for the accounting period in which the payment is to be taken into account for corporation tax, and accordingly in respect of that payment the company shall not be entitled to a repayment of income tax before the

assessment for that accounting period is finally determined and it appears that a repayment is due.

Cross-references

Attribution to shareholders of chargeable gains accruing to non-resident company, subs (2)(*b*): s 590(7)(*c*).

Charge to income tax of offshore income gain, subs (2)(*b*): s 745(2).

Making of claims etc, subs (3): s 864(2).

Overseas life assurance companies, income tax, foreign tax and tax credit, subs (3): s 729(2).

Relief to companies on loans applied in acquiring interest in other companies, subs (2)(*a*): s 247(5).

Shipping tonnage tax, exclusion of reliefs, deductions and set-offs, subs (3): s 697M(3)(*c*).

Case law

Irish

Non-resident company transporting persons from an Irish base held not to be chargeable where the arrangements and payments involved were made abroad: *Cunard Steamship Co Ltd v Revenue Commissioners* ITR Vol I p 330.

Whether interest earned on monies deposited in the Swiss bank account were subject to corporation tax under TCA 1997 s 25 (2)(a) as being income from property "used by" the Dublin branch or "held by" or "held for" that branch. Held that these monies were not "used by" the Irish branch but were used by the company which controlled the bank account and whose decision it was to transfer some of the monies to the Dublin branch – *Murphy v Dataproducts (Dublin) Ltd* (High Court, 29 January 1988).

UK

A company resides where its central management and control is located: *Calcutta Jute Mills Co Ltd v Nicholson* (1876) 1 TC 83; *De Beers Consolidated Mines Ltd v Howe* (1906) 5 TC 198; and not necessarily where it is incorporated: *Todd v Egyptian Delta Land and Investment Co Ltd* (1928) 14 TC 119; or registered: *Bullock v The Unit Construction Co Ltd* (1959) 38 TC 712.

A company may be resident in more than one country: *Swedish Central Railway Co Ltd v Thompson* (1924) 9 TC 342; *Union Corporation v CIR* (1952) 34 TC 207.

Tax Briefing

TB 26 Criteria & Guidelines on Permanent Establishment.

Definitions

branch or agency: s 5(1); chargeable gain: ss 5(1), 545; company: ss 4(1), 5(1); distribution: ss 4(1), 436, 437; person: IA 1937 s 11(*c*); profits: s 4(1); trade: ss 3(1), 4(1), 5(1); within the charge to (tax): s 2(1).

Former enactments

CTA 1976 s 8(1)–(3).

26 General scheme of corporation tax

(1) Subject to any exceptions provided for by the Corporation Tax Acts, a company shall be chargeable to corporation tax on all its profits wherever arising.

(2) A company shall be chargeable to corporation tax on profits accruing for its benefit under any trust, or arising under any partnership, in any case in which it would be so chargeable if the profits accrued to it directly, and a company shall be chargeable to corporation tax on profits arising in the winding up of the company, but shall not otherwise be chargeable to corporation tax on profits accruing to it in a fiduciary or representative capacity except as respects its own beneficial interest (if any) in those profits.

(3) Corporation tax for any financial year shall be charged on profits arising in that year; but assessments to corporation tax shall be made on a company by reference to accounting periods, and the amount chargeable (after making all proper deductions) of the profits arising in an accounting period shall where necessary be apportioned between the financial years in which the accounting period falls.

(4) Subsection (3) shall apply as respects accounting periods ending on or after the 1st day of April, 1997, as if—

(*a*) the period beginning on the 1st day of January, 1996, and ending on the 31st day of March, 1997, and

(*b*) the period beginning on the 1st day of April, 1997, and ending on the [31st day of December, 1997],[1]

were each a financial year.

Amendments

[1] Substituted by FA 1998 s 55(2) and Sch 6 para 1 with effect from 6 April 1998; previously "31st day of December, 1998".

Cross-references

Manufacturing (10%) rate, computation: s 448(2).
Reduction of corporation tax liability in respect of certain trading income: s 22A(2)(*c*)(ii).
Relief from corporation tax by means of credit in respect of foreign tax, unilateral relief, subs (3): Sch 24 para 9D(1)(*b*)(i)(I) and (II), (2)(*a*) and (*b*).

Definitions

company: ss 4(1), 5(1); the financial year: s 4(1); month: IA 1937 Sch; profits: s 4(1).

Former enactments

CTA 1976 s 6(1)–(3); FA 1997 s 59(2) and Sch 6 Pt I para 1.

27 Basis of, and periods for, assessment

(1) Except where otherwise provided by the Corporation Tax Acts, corporation tax shall be assessed and charged for any accounting period of a company on the full amount of the profits arising in that period (whether or not received in or remitted to the State) without any deduction other than one authorised by the Corporation Tax Acts.

(2) An accounting period of a company shall begin for the purposes of corporation tax whenever—

(*a*) the company, not then being within the charge to corporation tax, comes within it whether by the coming into force of any provision of the Corporation Tax Acts, or by the company becoming resident in the State or acquiring a source of income, or otherwise, or

(*b*) an accounting period of the company ends without the company then ceasing to be within the charge to corporation tax.

(3) An accounting period of a company shall end for the purposes of corporation tax on the first occurrence of any of the following—

(*a*) the expiration of 12 months from the beginning of the accounting period,

(*b*) an accounting date of the company or, if there is a period for which the company does not make up accounts, the end of that period,

(*c*) the company beginning or ceasing to trade or to be, in respect of the trade or (if more than one) of all the trades carried on by it, within the charge to corporation tax,

(*d*) the company beginning or ceasing to be resident in the State, and

(*e*) the company ceasing to be within the charge to corporation tax.

(4) For the purposes of this section, a company resident in the State, if not otherwise within the charge to corporation tax, shall be treated as coming within the charge to corporation tax at the time when it commences to carry on business.

(5) Where a company carrying on more than one trade makes up accounts of any of those trades to different dates and does not make up general accounts for the whole of the company's activities, subsection (3)(*b*) shall apply with reference to the accounting date of such one of the trades as the Revenue Commissioners may determine.

(6) Where a chargeable gain or allowable loss accrues to a company at a time not otherwise within an accounting period of the company, an accounting period of the company shall then begin for the purposes of corporation tax and the gain or loss shall accrue in that accounting period.

(7) (*a*) Notwithstanding anything in subsections (1) to (6), where a company is wound up, an accounting period shall end and a new one shall begin with the commencement of the winding up, and thereafter an accounting period shall not end otherwise than by the expiration of 12 months from its beginning or by the completion of the winding up.

(*b*) For the purposes of paragraph (*a*), a winding up shall be taken to commence on the passing by the company of a resolution for the winding up of the company, or on the presentation of a winding up petition if no such resolution has previously been passed and a winding up order is made on the petition, or on the doing of any other act for a like purpose in the case of a winding up otherwise than under the Companies Act, 1963.

(8) Where it appears to the inspector that the beginning or end of any accounting period of a company is uncertain, he or she may make an assessment on the company for such a period, not exceeding 12 months, as appears to him or her appropriate, and that period shall be treated for all purposes as an accounting period of the company unless—

(*a*) the inspector on further facts coming to his or her knowledge sees fit to revise it, or

(*b*) on an appeal against the assessment in respect of some other matter, the company shows the true accounting periods,

and, if on an appeal against an assessment made by virtue of this subsection the company shows the true accounting periods, the assessment appealed against shall, as regards the period to which it relates, have effect as an assessment or assessments for the true accounting periods, and such other assessments may be made for any such periods or any of them as might have been made at the time when the assessment appealed against was made.

Cross-references

Farming stock relief, meaning of "accounting period" applied: s 665.

Restrictive covenants, meaning of "accounting period" applied: s 127(1).

Seed capital investments, meaning of "accounting period" applied: s 494(6).

Stamp duties, cash cards, meaning of "accounting period" applied: SDCA 1999 s 123(1); debit cards, meaning of "accounting period" applied: SDCA 1999 s 123A(1).

Case law

Irish

Two related companies were given advance rulings as to the scope of future taxation charges on patent income. Claims for judicial review, certiorari and mandamus to enforce Revenue rulings refused by the court: *Osprey Ltd and Pandion Haliaetus Ltd v Revenue Commissioners* ITR Vol III p 670.

UK

(8): Held the test of uncertainty was a subjective not an objective one: *Kelsall v Stipplechoice* [1995] STC 681.

Definitions

accounting date: s 4(1); allowable loss: ss 4(1), 5(1), 546; chargeable gain: ss 5(1), 545; company: ss 4(1), 5(1); inspector: ss 2(1), 5(1), 852; month: IA 1937 Sch; profits: s 4(1); trade: ss 3(1), 4(1), 5(1); within the charge to (tax): s 2(1).

Former enactments

CTA 1976 s 9.

Corresponding UK tax provision

Income and Corporation Taxes Act 1988 s 12.

CHAPTER 3
Capital Gains Tax

Revenue information

Information leaflet CGT1 — Guide to Capital Gains Tax.

28 Taxation of capital gains and rate of charge

(1) Capital gains tax shall be charged in accordance with the Capital Gains Tax Acts in respect of capital gains, that is, in respect of chargeable gains computed in accordance with those Acts and accruing to a person on the disposal of assets.

(2) Capital gains tax shall be assessed and charged for years of assessment in respect of chargeable gains accruing in those years.

(3) Except where otherwise provided by the Capital Gains Tax Acts, the rate of capital gains tax in respect of a chargeable gain accruing to a person on the disposal of an asset shall be [20 per cent],[1] and any reference in those Acts to the rate specified in this section shall be construed accordingly.

Amendments

1 Substituted by FA 1998 s 65(1)(*a*) in relation to disposals made on or after 3 December 1997; previously "40 per cent".

Cross-references

Charging and assessment of persons not resident or ordinarily resident, modification of general rules, subs (2): s 1042(1).

Development land (relevant disposals): rate of charge, subs (3): s 649A.

Foreign life assurance and deferred annuities: taxation and returns, subs (3): s 594(2)(*f*).

Gifts, recovery of capital gains tax from donee, subs (3): s 978(2).

Life assurance companies, chargeable gains, subs (3): s 711(1)(*c*).

Offshore funds, capital gains tax: rate of change, subs (3): s 747A(4).

Reduced rate of capital gains tax on disposal by individuals of shares in unquoted companies, subs (3): s 592(1).

Special investment schemes, subs (3): s 737(6)(*b*)(ii).

Taxation of unit holders in investment undertakings: s 739G(1).

Undertakings for collective investment, subs (3): s 738(2)(*c*).

Unit trusts, special arrangements for qualifying unit trusts, subs (3): s 732(3).

Case law

Sum received for abandonment of an option held to be a disposal of an asset: *Dilleen v Kearns* ITR Vol IV p 547. See also *Golding v Kaufmann* [1985] STC 152; *Welbeck Securities Ltd v Powlson* [1987] STC 468.

Definitions

chargeable gain: ss 5(1), 545; person: IA 1937 s 11(*c*).

Former enactments

CGTA 1975 s 3(1)–(3); FA 1992 s 60(1)(*a*).

Corresponding UK tax provision

Taxation of Chargeable Gains Act 1992 s 1.

29 Persons chargeable

(1) In this section—

"designated area" means an area designated by order under section 2 of the Continental Shelf Act, 1968;

"exploration or exploitation rights" has the same meaning as in section 13;

"shares" includes stock and any security;

"security" includes securities not creating or evidencing a charge on assets, and interest paid by a company on money advanced without the issue of a security for the advance, or other consideration given by a company for the use of money so advanced, shall be treated as if paid or given in respect of a security issued for the advance by the company;

references to the disposal of assets mentioned in paragraphs (*a*) and (*b*) of subsection (3) and in subsection (6) include references to the disposal of shares deriving their value or the greater part of their value directly or indirectly from those assets, other than shares quoted on a stock exchange.

(2) Subject to any exceptions in the Capital Gains Tax Acts, a person shall be chargeable to capital gains tax in respect of chargeable gains accruing to such person in a year of assessment for which such person is resident or ordinarily resident in the State.

(3) Subject to any exceptions in the Capital Gains Tax Acts, a person who is neither resident nor ordinarily resident in the State shall be chargeable to capital gains tax for a year of assessment in respect of chargeable gains accruing to such person in that year on the disposal of—

(*a*) land in the State,

(*b*) minerals in the State or any rights, interests or other assets in relation to mining or minerals or the searching for minerals,

(*c*) assets situated in the State which at or before the time when the chargeable gains accrued were used in or for the purposes of a trade carried on by such person in the State through a branch or agency, or which at or before that time were used or held or acquired for use by or for the purposes of the branch or [agency,][1]

[(*d*) assets situated outside the State of an overseas life assurance company (within the meaning of section 706(1)), being assets which were held in connection with the life business (within the meaning of section 706(1)) carried on by the company, which at or before the time the chargeable gains accrued were used or held by or for the purposes of that company's branch or agency in the State.][2]

(4) Subsection (2) shall not apply in respect of chargeable gains accruing from the disposal of assets situated outside the State and the United Kingdom to an individual who satisfies the Revenue Commissioners that he or she is not domiciled in the State; but—

(*a*) the tax shall be charged on the amounts received in the State in respect of those chargeable gains,

(*b*) any such amounts shall be treated for the purposes of the Capital Gains Tax Acts as gains accruing when they are received in the State, and

(*c*) any losses accruing to the individual on the disposal of assets situated outside the State and the United Kingdom shall not be allowable losses for the purposes of the Capital Gains Tax Acts.

(5) For the purposes of subsection (4), all amounts paid, used or enjoyed in or in any manner or form transmitted or brought to the State shall be treated as received in the State in respect of any gain, and section 72 shall apply as it would apply if the gain were income arising from possessions outside of the State.

(6) Any gains accruing on the disposal of exploration or exploitation rights in a designated area shall be treated for the purposes of the Capital Gains Tax Acts as gains accruing on the disposal of assets situated in the State.

(7) Any gains accruing to a person who is neither resident nor ordinarily resident in the State on the disposal of assets mentioned in subsections (3)(*b*) and (6) shall be treated for the purposes of capital gains tax as gains accruing on the disposal of assets used for the purposes of a trade carried on by that person in the State through a branch or agency.

(8) Any person aggrieved by a decision of the Revenue Commissioners on any question as to domicile or ordinary residence arising under the Capital Gains Tax Acts may, by notice in writing to that effect given to the Revenue Commissioners within 2 months from the date on which notice of the decision is given to such person, make an application to have such person's claim for relief heard and determined by the Appeal Commissioners.

(9) Where an application is made under subsection (8), the Appeal Commissioners shall hear and determine the claim in the like manner as an appeal made to them against an assessment, and the provisions of the Income Tax Acts relating to such an appeal (including the provisions relating to the rehearing of an appeal and to the statement of a case for the opinion of the High Court on a point of law) shall apply accordingly with any necessary modifications.

Amendments

[1] Substituted by FA 2005 s 41(1)(*a*) as respects accounting periods ending on or after 1 March 2005; previously "agency.".

[2] Subs (3)(*d*) inserted by FA 2005 s 41(1)(*b*) as respects accounting periods ending on or after 1 March 2005.

Cross-references

Allowable losses: s 546(4).

Attribution to shareholders of chargeable gains accruing to non-resident company: s 590(7)(*c*).

Charge to income tax of offshore income gain, subs (3)(*c*), delete "situated in the State": s 745(2), (3); subss (4)–(5): s 745(4).
Exemption from tax in the case of gains on certain disposals of shares, subs (3)(*a*), (*b*): s 626B(3)(*d*).
Location of assets: s 533.
Overseas life assurance companies, investment income, subss (3), (6): s 726(6)(*a*).
Transactions between connected persons: s 549(8)(*a*).

Revenue precedents

Issue: Calculation of liability in respect of assets disposed of after leaving Ireland.
Decision: A Diplomatic Agent is exempt in respect of gains on assets other than investments made in commercial undertakings in the State. In practice, this exemption will be treated as covering a period of up to one year after the end of their posting. If the disposal is at a later date, the gains will be apportioned.
Issue: Is the OTC Bulletin Board a stock exchange?
Decision: The OTC Bulletin Board is not a Stock Exchange for the purpose of TCA 1997 s 29. However, where a company has applied for a full listing on NASDAQ, its ADRs will be treated as "shares quoted on a Stock Exchange" for the purpose of the said s 29.

Definitions

allowable loss: ss 4(1), 5(1), 546; branch or agency: ss 4(1), 5(1); chargeable gain: ss 5(1), 545; company: s 5(1); minerals: s 5(1); mining: s 5(1); person: IA 1937 s 11(*c*); profession: ss 2(1), 5(1); resident: s 5(1); shares: s 5(1); trade: ss 3(1), 4(1), 5(1); year of assessment: ss 2(1), 5(1).

Former enactments

CGTA 1975 ss 4(1)–(4) and (6)–(8), 51(1) and Sch 4 para 2; FA 1977 s 54(1)(*a*) and Sch 2 Pt I.

Corresponding UK tax provision

Taxation of Chargeable Gains Act 1992 s 2.

29A Temporary non-residents

[(1) (*a*) In this section—

"intervening year", in relation to an individual, means any year of assessment falling within the period commencing with the first day of the year of assessment immediately following the year of his or her departure and ending with the last day of the year of assessment immediately preceding the year of his or her return;

"relevant assets", in relation to an individual, means shares in a company, or rights to acquire shares in a company, being shares or rights which he or she beneficially owned on the last day of the year of his or her departure and the market value of which on that day—

(i) is equal to, or exceeds, 5 per cent of the value of the issued share capital of the company, or

(ii) exceeds €500,000;

"year of departure", in relation to an individual, means the last year of assessment before the year of return, for which the individual is resident in the State, and references to year of his or her departure shall be construed accordingly;

"year of return", in relation to an individual, has the meaning assigned to it by subsection (2), and references to year of his or her return shall be construed accordingly.

(*b*) References in this section to an individual being resident in the State for a year of assessment shall be construed as references to an individual—

(i) who is resident in the State for the year of assessment, and

(ii) who could be taxed in the State for that year in respect of gains on a disposal, on each day of that year, of his or her relevant assets, if such a disposal were made by the individual on that day and gains accrued on the disposal.

(*c*) References in this section to an individual being not resident in the State for a year of assessment shall be construed as references to an individual who could not be taxed in the State for that year in respect of gains on a disposal in that year, or part of that year, of his or her relevant assets, or part of those assets, if the individual had made such a disposal in that year, or, as the case may be, that part of that year, and gains accrued on the disposal.

(2) This section applies to an individual where—

(*a*) the individual has relevant assets,

(*b*) the individual is resident in the State for a year of assessment (in this section referred to as the **"year of return"**),

(*c*) the individual was not resident in the State for one or more years of assessment immediately preceding the year of his or her return; but there is a year of assessment before the year of return for which the individual was resident in the State and, at any time during that year, the individual was domiciled in the State, and

(*d*) there are not more than 5 years of assessment falling between the year of his or her departure and the year of his or her return.

(3) Where an individual to whom this section applies, disposes of his or her relevant assets or any part of them (as the case may be) in one or more intervening years, the individual shall, for the purposes of the Capital Gains Tax Acts, be deemed to have disposed of and immediately reacquired, the relevant assets or that part of them (as the case may be), on the last day of the year of his or her departure, for a consideration equal to their market value on that day.

(4) Where by virtue of subsection (3), an individual is chargeable to capital gains tax in respect of a deemed disposal of his or her relevant assets or any part of them (as the case may be), credit shall be allowed against such tax in respect of tax (in this section referred to as **"foreign tax"**) payable on the subsequent disposal by the individual of those relevant assets or that part of them (as the case may be) under the law of any territory outside the State, the government of which has entered into arrangements having the force of law by virtue of [section 826(1)(*a*)][1], and the amount of such credit—

(*a*) shall be calculated having regard to the provisions of Schedule 24, and

(*b*) notwithstanding those provisions, shall not exceed the amount by which capital gains tax payable by the individual would be reduced if the individual had not been deemed to have disposed of relevant assets or that part of them (as the case may be).

(5) Where by virtue of subsection (3) a chargeable gain accrues to an individual, the provisions of Part 41 shall apply in relation to the chargeable gain, as if the year of his or her departure were the year of his or her return.][2]

Amendments

1 Substituted by FA 2004 s 89 and Sch 3 para 1(*b*) with effect from 25 March 2004; previously "section 826".

2 Section 29A inserted by FA 2003 s 69(1) as respects an individual who ceases to be resident in the State for the year of assessment 2003, or a subsequent year of assessment, but does not apply as respects an individual who before 24 February 2003 ceases to be resident in the State for the year of assessment 2003, but who would not have so ceased, but for the fact that for these purposes and individual is treated as resident in the State for a year of assessment so long as he or she could be taxed in the State for that year in respect of gains on a disposal, on each day of that year, of his or her relevant assets, if such a disposal were made by the individual on that day and gains accrued on the disposal. (For these purposes an individual is resident in the State for a year of assessment so long as he or she is resident in the State for the year of assessment, and could be taxed in the State for that year in respect of gains on a disposal, on each day of that year, of his or her relevant assets, if such a disposal were made by the individual on that day and gains accrued on the disposal).

Tax Briefing

TB52 May 2003 p 14 — FA 2003 s 69 measure.

Definitions

Capital Gains Tax Acts: s 1(2); chargeable gain: s 5(1); company: s 5(1); market value: s 5(1); shares: s 5(1); year of assessment: s 5(1).

30 Partnerships

Where 2 or more persons carry on a trade, business or profession in partnership—

(*a*) capital gains tax in respect of chargeable gains accruing to those persons on the disposal of any partnership assets shall be assessed and charged on them separately, and

(*b*) any partnership dealings in assets shall be treated as dealings by the partners and not by the firm as such.

Cross-references

Charge to income tax of offshore income gain: s 745(2), (3).
Transactions between connected persons: s 549(8)(*a*).
Tax treatment of profits, losses and capital gains of a European Economic Interest Grouping: s 1014(3).

Former enactments

CGTA 1975 s 4(5).

Corresponding UK tax provision

Taxation of Chargeable Gains Act 1992 s 59.

31 Amount chargeable

Capital gains tax shall be charged on the total amount of chargeable gains accruing to the person chargeable in the year of assessment, after deducting—

(*a*) any allowable losses accruing to that person in that year of assessment, and

(*b*) in so far as they have not been allowed as a deduction from chargeable gains accruing in any previous year of assessment, any allowable losses accruing to that person in any previous year of assessment (not earlier than the year 1974–75).

Cross-references

Allowable losses: s 546(6).
Annual exempt amount: s 601(1), (2).
Attribution of gains to beneficiaries: s 579A(3).

Capital gains tax share reinvestment, withdrawal of relief: s 591(11)(*b*)(i).
Chargeable gains of life business: s 711(3)(*a*).
Charging and assessment of persons not resident or ordinarily resident, modification of general rules: s 1042(1), (2).
Computation of companies' chargeable gains: s 78(2).
Development land disposals: s 653(2).
Disposals where assets lost or destroyed or become of negligible value: s 538(2A)(*a*).
Exchange of Irish Government bonds: s 751B(6)(*a*).
Foreign life assurance and deferred annuities: s 594(2)(*d*).
Married persons: s 1028(3), (4).
Non-resident trust: s 579(2)(*a*).
Shipping tonnage tax, chargeable gains: s 697N(4).
Special investment schemes: s 737(8)(*b*)(i).
Special portfolio investment accounts: s 838(4)(*bb*).
Undertakings for collective investment: s 738(6)(*a*).

Definitions

allowable loss: ss 4(1), 5(1), 546; chargeable gain: ss 5(1), 545; person: IA 1937 s 11(*c*); resident: s 5(1); year of assessment: ss 2(1), 5(1).

Former enactments

CGTA 1975 s 5(1).

INCOME TAX AND CORPORATION TAX: THE MAIN PROVISIONS

PART 3
PROVISIONS RELATING TO THE SCHEDULE C CHARGE AND GOVERNMENT AND OTHER PUBLIC SECURITIES

CHAPTER 1
Principal Provisions Relating to the Schedule C Charge

Cross-references

Machinery for assessment, charge and payment of tax under Schedule C, and in certain cases, Schedule D: Sch 2 paras 1, 23.
Residence of individuals: s 821(1).

32 Interpretation (Chapter 1)

In this Chapter—

"banker" includes a person acting as a banker;

"coupons" and **"coupons for any foreign public revenue dividends"** include warrants for or bills of exchange purporting to be drawn or made in payment of any foreign public revenue dividends;

"dividends", except in the phrase **"stock, dividends or interest"**, means any interest, annuities, dividends or shares of annuities;

"foreign public revenue dividends" means dividends payable elsewhere than in the State (whether they are or are not also payable in the State) out of any public revenue other than the public revenue of the State;

"public revenue", except where the context otherwise requires, includes the public revenue of any Government whatever and the revenue of any public authority or institution in any country outside the State;

"public revenue dividends" means dividends payable out of any public revenue.

Cross-references

Charge to tax: s 17(2).

Interest on quoted Eurobonds: s 64(1)(meaning of "relevant foreign securities").

Machinery for assessment: Sch 2 para 1.

Former enactments

ITA 1967 s 51.

Corresponding UK tax provision

Income and Corporation Taxes Act 1988 s 45 (now repealed).

33 Method of charge and payment

(1) Tax under Schedule C shall be charged by the Commissioners designated for that purpose by the Income Tax Acts, and shall be paid on behalf of the persons entitled to the profits, dividends, proceeds of realisation or price paid on purchase which are the subject of the tax—

(*a*) in the case of tax charged under paragraph 1 of that Schedule, by the persons and bodies of persons respectively entrusted with payment;

(*b*) in the case of tax charged under paragraph 2, 3 or 4 of that Schedule, by the banker or other person, or by the banker or by the dealer in coupons, as the case may be.

(2) Schedule 2 shall apply in relation to the assessment, charge and payment of tax under Schedule C.

Definitions

dividends, banker: s 32; person: IA 1937 s 11(*c*); tax: s 3(1).

Former enactments

ITA 1967 s 48.

Corresponding UK tax provision

Income and Corporation Taxes Act 1988 s 44.

34 Stock, dividends or interest belonging to the State

(1) No tax shall be chargeable in respect of the stock, dividends or interest transferred to accounts in the books of the Bank of Ireland in the name of the Minister for Finance in pursuance of any statute, but the Bank of Ireland shall transmit to the Revenue Commissioners an account of the total amount of such stock, dividends or interest.

(2) No tax shall be chargeable in respect of the stock, dividends or interest belonging to the State in whatever name they may stand in the books of the Bank of Ireland.

Definitions

Bank of Ireland: IA 1937 Sch; dividends: s 32; statute: IA 1937 s 3; tax: s 3(1).

Former enactments

ITA 1967 s 49(1)–(2); F(MP)A 1968 s 3(3) and Sch Pt II.

Corresponding UK tax provision

Income and Corporation Taxes Act 1988 s 49.

35 Securities of foreign territories

(1) (*a*) No tax shall be chargeable in respect of the dividends on any securities of any territory outside the State which are payable in the State, where it is proved to the satisfaction of the Revenue Commissioners that the person owning the securities and entitled to the dividends is not resident in the State; but, except where provided by the Income Tax Acts, no allowance shall be given or repayment made in respect of the tax on the dividends on the securities of any such territory which are payable in the State.

(*b*) Where the securities of any territory outside the State are held under any trust, and the person who is the beneficiary in possession under the trust is the sole beneficiary in possession and can, by means either of the revocation of the trust or of the exercise of any powers under the trust, call on the trustees at any time to transfer the securities to such person absolutely free from any trust, that person shall for the purposes of this section be deemed to be the person owning the securities.

(2) Relief under this section may be given by the Revenue Commissioners either by means of allowance or repayment on a claim being made to them for that purpose.

(3) Any person aggrieved by a decision of the Revenue Commissioners on any question as to residence arising under this section may, by notice in writing to that effect given to the Revenue Commissioners within 2 months from the date on which notice of the decision is given to such person, make an application to have such person's claim for relief heard and determined by the Appeal Commissioners.

(4) Where an application is made under subsection (3), the Appeal Commissioners shall hear and determine the claim in the like manner as an appeal made to them against an assessment, and the provisions of the Income Tax Acts relating to such an appeal (including the provisions relating to the rehearing of an appeal and to the statement of a case for the opinion of the High Court on a point of law) shall apply accordingly with any necessary modifications.

Cross-references

Transfer of assets abroad, income not exempted: s 809.

Corporation tax: treatment of tax free income of non resident banks, insurance businesses etc: s 845(3), (5).

Definitions

Appeal Commissioners: s 2(1); dividends: s 32; High Court: IA 1937 Sch; month: IA 1937 Sch; person: IA 1937 s 11(*c*); tax: s 3(1); writing: IA 1937 Sch.

Former enactments

ITA 1967 s 50; F(MP)A 1968 s 3(2) and Sch Pt I.

Corresponding UK tax provision

Income and Corporation Taxes Act 1988 s 48.

CHAPTER 2
Government and Other Public Securities: Interest Payable Without Deduction of Tax

36 Government securities

(1) The Minister for Finance may direct that any securities already issued or to be issued under that Minister's authority shall be deemed to have been, or shall be, issued subject

to the condition that the interest on those securities shall be paid without deduction of tax.

(2) The interest on all securities issued, or deemed to have been issued, subject to the condition referred to in subsection (1) shall be paid without deduction of tax, but all such interest shall be chargeable under Case III of Schedule D and, where any funds under the control of any court or public department are invested in any such securities, the person in whose name the securities are invested shall be the person so chargeable in respect of the interest on those securities.

(3) Where interest on any security is paid under this section without deduction of tax, every person by whom such interest is paid, every person who receives such interest on behalf of a registered or inscribed holder of the security, and every person who has acted as an intermediary in the purchase of the security, shall, on being so required by the Revenue Commissioners, furnish to them—

(*a*) the name and address of the person to whom such interest has been paid, or on whose behalf such interest has been received, and the amount of the interest so paid or received, or, as the case may require,

(*b*) the name and address of the person on whose behalf such security was purchased and the amount of such security.

Cross-references

Charge to tax under Schedule D Case III: s 18(2).
Exchange of Irish Government bonds: s 751B(1)(securities).
Interest paid by companies and to non-residents: s 246(2)(*e*).
Securities issued by body designated under section 4(1) of the Securitisation (Proceeds of Certain Mortgages) Act 1995 deemed to be securities issued under this section: s 41.
Securities issued by International Bank for Reconstruction and Development deemed to be securities issued under this section: s 40(2).
Securities issued by State-owned companies deemed to be securities issued under this section: s 37(3).
Securities of European Bodies deemed to be securities issued under this section: s 39(2).
State-guaranteed securities deemed to be securities issued under this section: s 38(2).
Transitional: Sch 32 para 1(1).

Definitions

person: IA 1937 s 11(*c*).

Former enactments

ITA 1967 s 466; FA 1997 s 146(1) and Sch 9 Pt I para 1(31).

Corresponding UK tax provision

Income and Corporation Taxes Act 1988 s 50.

37 Securities of certain State-owned companies

(1) In this section, **"securities"** means any bonds, certificates of charge, debentures, debenture stock, notes, stock or other forms of security.

(2) The securities specified in the Table to this section shall be deemed to be securities issued under the authority of the Minister for Finance under section 36, and that section shall apply accordingly.

(3) Notwithstanding anything in the Tax Acts, in computing for the purposes of assessment under Schedule D the amount of the profits or gains of a company (being a company referred to in the Table to this section) for any accounting period, the amount

of the interest on any securities which, by direction of the Minister for Finance given under section 36, as applied by subsection (2), is paid by the company without deduction of tax for such period shall be allowed as a deduction.

TABLE

...[1]

Securities issued on or after the 13th day of July, 1954, by the Electricity Supply Board.

Securities issued on or after the 13th day of July, 1954, by Córas Iompair Éireann.

Securities issued on or after the 18th day of July, 1957, by Bord na Móna.

Securities issued on or after the 2nd day of July, 1964, by Aer Lingus, Teoranta.

Securities issued on or after the 2nd day of July, 1964, by Aer Rianta, Teoranta.

Securities issued on or after the 2nd day of July, 1964, by Aerlínte Éireann, Teoranta.

...[2]

...[2]

Securities issued on or after the 24th day of May, 1989, by Radio Telefís Éireann.

...[3]

Securities issued on or after the 28th day of May, 1992, by Bord Gáis Éireann.

Amendments

1 Repealed by ACC Bank Act 2001 s 12(1) and Sch with effect from such date as the Minister for Finance may appoint by order. By virtue of the ACC Bank Act 2001 (Sections 6, 8, 10, 11(2) and 12) (Commencement) Order 2002, SI No 69 of 2002, this amendment came into operation with effect from 28 February 2002.

2 Deleted by FA 2001 s 241(*a*) as respects any securities issued by Bord Telecom Éireann or Irish Telecommunications Investments plc on or after 15 February 2001; previously "Securities issued on or after the 25th day of May, 1988, by Bord Telecom Éireann" and "Securities issued on or after the 25th day of May, 1988, by Irish Telecommunications Investments plc.".

3 Repealed by ICC Bank Act 2000 s 7, and ICC Bank Act 2000 (Sections 5 and 7) (Commencement) Order 2001 (SI No 396 of 2001), as respects securities issued on or after 12 February 2001; previously "Securities issued on or after the 24th day of May, 1989, by ICC Bank plc.".

Cross-references

Capital and income, exemption from tax: s 49(1).
Exemption on premiums on certain securities, excludes securities listed in the Table: s 48(1)(*b*).
State guaranteed securities: s 38(1).

Former enactments

FA 1997 s 144.

38 Certain State-guaranteed securities

[(1) This section applies to any securities which are issued by a body corporate and in respect of which the payment of interest and the repayment of principal are guaranteed by a Minister of the Government under statutory authority; but does not apply to securities—

(*a*) specified in the Table to section 37, or

(*b*) issued by a company formed by the National Development Finance Agency in accordance with section 5 of the National Development Finance Agency Act 2002.][1]

(2) Any securities to which this section applies shall be deemed to be securities issued under the authority of the Minister for Finance under section 36, and that section shall apply accordingly.

(3) Notwithstanding anything in the Tax Acts, in computing for the purposes of assessment under Case I of Schedule D the amount of the profits or gains of a body corporate by which the securities to which this section applies are issued, for any period for which accounts are made up, the amount of the interest on such securities which, by direction of the Minister for Finance under section 36, as applied by this section, is paid by the body corporate without deduction of tax for such period shall be allowed as a deduction.

Amendments

1 Subs (1) substituted by FA 2003 s 43(1)(*a*) with effect from 6 February 2003.

Cross-references

Capital and income, exemption from tax: s 49(1).

Definitions

Tax Acts: s 1(2).

Former enactments

FA 1970 s 59(1)–(3); FA 1997 s 146(1) and Sch 9 Pt I para 4(3).

39 Securities of certain European bodies

(1) This section shall apply to any stock or other form of security issued in the State by the European Community, the European Coal and Steel Community, the European Atomic Energy Community or the European Investment Bank.

(2) Any stock or other form of security to which this section applies shall be deemed to be a security issued under the authority of the Minister for Finance under section 36, and that section shall apply accordingly.

Cross-references

Capital and income, exemption from tax: s 49(1).

Former enactments

FA 1973 s 92(1)–(2)(*a*); FA 1989 s 98(1).

40 Securities of International Bank for Reconstruction and Development

(1) This section shall apply to any stock or other form of security issued by the International Bank for Reconstruction and Development.

(2) Any stock or other form of security to which this section applies shall be deemed to be a security issued under the authority of the Minister for Finance under section 36, and that section shall apply accordingly.

Cross-references

Capital and income, exemption from tax: s 49(1).

Former enactments

FA 1994 s 161(1)–(2)(*a*).

41 Securities of designated bodies under the Securitisation (Proceeds of Certain Mortgages) Act, 1995

Any stock or other form of security issued by a body designated under section 4(1) of the Securitisation (Proceeds of Certain Mortgages) Act, 1995, shall be deemed to be a security issued under the authority of the Minister for Finance under section 36, and that section shall apply accordingly.

Cross-references

Capital and income, exemption from tax: s 49(1).

Former enactments

FA 1996 s 39(1) and (3).

CHAPTER 3

Government and Other Public Securities: Exemptions from Tax

42 Exemption of interest on savings certificates

The accumulated interest payable in respect of any savings certificate issued by the Minister for Finance, under which the purchaser, by virtue of an immediate payment of a specified sum, becomes entitled after a specified period to receive a larger sum consisting of the specified sum originally paid and accumulated interest on that specified sum, shall not be liable to tax so long as the amount of such certificates held by the person who is for the time being the holder of the certificate does not exceed the amount which that person is for the time being authorised to hold under regulations made by the Minister for Finance.

Cross-references

Implementation of Council Directive 2003/48/EC of 3 June 2003 on Taxation of Savings Income in the Form of Interest Payments, interest payment: s 898E(1)(*a*).

Definitions

person: IA 1937 s 11(*c*).

Former enactments

ITA 1967 s 463.

43 Certain securities issued by Minister for Finance

(1) Any security which the Minister for Finance has power to issue for the purpose of raising any money or loan may be issued with a condition that neither the capital of nor the interest on such security shall be liable to tax so long as it is shown in the manner to be prescribed by the Minister for Finance that such security is in the beneficial ownership of a person who is not, or persons who are not, ordinarily resident in the State, and accordingly every security issued with such condition shall be exempt from tax.

(2) (*a*) Notwithstanding subsection (1), where a security has been issued with the condition referred to in that subsection and the security is held by or for a branch or agency through which a company carries on a trade or business in the State, which is such a trade or business, as the case may be, that, if the security had been issued without that condition, interest on, or other profits or gains from, the security accruing to the company would be chargeable to corporation tax under Case I or, as respects interest and other profits or gains accruing on or after the 21st day of April, 1997, from the security, Case IV of Schedule D, or in accordance with section 726, then, such interest and profits or gains shall be charged to tax as if the security had been issued without such condition.

(*b*) Paragraph (*a*) shall apply as respects securities acquired by a company after the 29th day of January, 1992, whether they were issued before or after that date.

Cross-references

Corporation tax: treatment of tax free income of non resident banks, insurance businesses etc: s 845(2).
Foreign life assurance funds: s 718(3)(*a*).
Offshore funds, Irish equivalent profits: Sch 19 para 5(5).
Transfer of assets abroad, income not exempted: s 809.

Definitions

person: IA 1937 s 11(*c*).

Former enactments

ITA 1967 s 464; FA 1992 s 42(1)(*a*); FA 1997 s 45.

44 Exemption from corporation tax of certain securities issued by Minister for Finance

(1) In this section—

"control" shall be construed in accordance with subsections (2) to (6) of section 432, with the substitution in subsection (6) of that section for **"5 or fewer participators"** of **"persons resident in a relevant territory"**;

"foreign company" means a company which is—

(*a*) not resident in the State, and
(*b*) under the control of a person or persons resident in a relevant territory;

"qualifying company" means a company—

(*a*) (i) which is resident in the State and not resident elsewhere,

(ii) whose business consists wholly or mainly of—

(I) the carrying on of a relevant trade or relevant trades, or
(II) the holding of stocks, shares or securities of a company which exists wholly or mainly for the purpose of the carrying on of a relevant trade or relevant trades,

and

(iii) of which not less than 90 per cent of its issued share capital is held by a foreign company or foreign companies, or by a person or persons directly or indirectly controlled by a foreign company or foreign companies,

or

(*b*) which is a foreign company carrying on a relevant trade through a branch or agency in the State;

"relevant territory" means ...[1] a territory with the government of which arrangements having the force of law by virtue of [section 826(1)(*a*)][2] have been made;

"relevant trade" means a trade carried on wholly or mainly in the State, but does not include a trade consisting wholly or partly of—

(*a*) banking within the meaning of the Central Bank Act, 1971,

(*b*) assurance business within the meaning of section 3 of the Insurance Act, 1936,

(*c*) selling goods by retail, or

(*d*) dealing in securities,

but goods shall be deemed for the purposes of this definition not to be sold by retail if they are sold to—

(i) a person who carries on a trade of selling goods of the class to which the goods so sold to such person belong,

(ii) a person who uses goods of that class for the purposes of a trade carried on by such person, or

(iii) a person, other than an individual, who uses goods of that class for the purposes of an undertaking carried on by such person.

(2) Any security which the Minister for Finance has power to issue for the purpose of raising any money or loan may be issued with a condition that any interest arising on such security shall not be liable to corporation tax so long as the security is held continuously from the date of issue in the beneficial ownership of a qualifying company to which the security was issued.

Amendments

1 Deleted by FA 1998 s 48 and Sch 3 para 1 from 1 January 1998; previously "the United States of America or".

2 Substituted by FA 2004 s 89 and Sch 3 para 1(*c*) with effect from 25 March 2004; previously "section 826".

Revenue precedents

Issue: Whether profit or loss arising on the disposal of foreign currency under a hedging contract linked to s 44 securities is exempt from CGT by virtue of s 607.

Decision: No, the s 44 securities and the foreign currency are separate assets.

Definitions

branch or agency: ss 4(1), 5(1); company: ss 4(1), 5(1); person: IA 1937 s 11(*c*); shares: s 5(1); trade: s 3(1).

Former enactments

FA 1985 s 69.

45 Exemption of non-interest-bearing securities

(1) The excess of the amount received on the redemption of a unit of non-interest-bearing securities issued by the Minister for Finance under section 4 of the Central Fund Act, 1965, over the amount paid for the unit on its issue shall, except where the excess is to be taken into account in computing for the purposes of taxation the profits of a trade, be exempt from tax.

(2) Subsection (1) shall not apply to issues of securities to which subsection (3) applies made after the 25th day of January, 1984, unless a tender for any such securities was submitted on or before that date.

(3) The securities to which this subsection applies are—

(*a*) non-interest-bearing securities issued by the Minister for Finance at a discount, including Exchequer Bills and Exchequer Notes, and

(*b*) Agricultural Commodities Intervention Bills issued by the Minister for Agriculture and Food.

(4) (*a*) In this subsection, **"owner"**, in relation to securities, means at any time the person who would be entitled, if the securities were redeemed at that time by the issuer, to the proceeds of the redemption.

(*b*) Notwithstanding subsection (2), where the owner of a security to which subsection (3) applies—

(i) sells or otherwise disposes of the security, or

(ii) receives on redemption of the security an amount greater than the amount paid by such owner for that security either on its issue or otherwise,

then, any profit, gain or excess arising to the owner from such sale, disposal or receipt shall be exempt from tax where the owner is not ordinarily resident in the State; but this subsection shall not apply in respect of corporation tax chargeable on the income of an Irish branch or agency of a company not resident in the State.

Cross-references

Exemption of premiums on certain securities, excludes securities to which subs (1) applies: s 48(1)(*a*).

Definitions

branch or agency: ss 4(1), 5(1); company: ss 4(1), 5(1); resident: s 5(1); trade: s 3(1).

Former enactments

ITA 1967 s 465; FA 1974 s 86 and Sch 2 Pt I; FA 1984 s 28 and FA 1990 s 138.

46 Exemption of premiums on Investment Bonds

The excess of the amount received on the redemption of a unit of securities created and issued by the Minister for Finance under the Central Fund (Permanent Provisions) Act, 1965, and known as Investment Bonds, over the amount which was paid for the unit on its issue shall, except where the excess is to be taken into account in computing for the purposes of taxation the profits of a trade, be exempt from tax.

Cross-references

Exemption of premiums on certain securities: s 48(1)(*a*).

Definitions

trade: s 3(1).

Former enactments

F(No 2) A 1968 s 8; FA 1974 s 86 and Sch 2 Pt I.

47 Certain securities of ACC Bank plc

Debentures, debenture stock and certificates of charge issued by ACC Bank plc, shall not be liable to tax so long as it is shown in the manner to be prescribed by the Minister for Finance that they are in the beneficial ownership of persons neither domiciled nor ordinarily resident in the State.

Notes

This section was repealed by the ACC Bank Act 2001 s 12(1) and Sch, other than as respects debentures, debenture stock and certificates of charge issued before the commencement of this repeal. By virtue of the ACC Bank Act 2001 (Sections 6, 8, 10, 11(2) and 12) (Commencement) Order 2002, SI No 69 of 2002, the commencement date is 28 February 2002.

Cross-references

Transfer of assets abroad, income not exempted: s 809.

Former enactments

ITA 1967 s 468(3).

48 Exemption of premiums on certain securities

(1) The securities to which this subsection applies are—

(*a*) securities created and issued by the Minister for Finance under the Central Fund (Permanent Provisions) Act, 1965, or under any other statutory powers conferred on that Minister, and any stock, debenture, debenture stock, certificate of charge or other security issued with the approval of the Minister for Finance given under any Act of the Oireachtas and in respect of which the payment of interest and repayment of capital is guaranteed by the Minister for Finance under that Act, but excluding securities to which section 4 of the Central Fund Act, 1965, or section 45(1) or 46 applies,

(*b*) securities (other than securities specified in the Table to section 37) issued by a body corporate and in respect of which the payment of interest and the repayment of principal is guaranteed by a Minister of the Government under statutory authority,

(*c*) any stock or other form of security issued in the State by the European Community, the European Coal and Steel Community, the European Atomic Energy Community or the European Investment Bank, and

(*d*) any stock or other form of security issued by the International Bank for Reconstruction and Development.

(2) The excess of the amount received on the redemption of a unit of securities to which subsection (1) applies over the amount paid for the unit on its issue shall, except where the excess is to be taken into account in computing for the purposes of taxation the profits of a trade, be exempt from tax.

(3) Subsection (2) shall not apply to issues of securities to which subsection (4) applies made after the 25th day of January, 1984, unless a tender for any such securities was submitted on or before that date.

(4) The securities to which this subsection applies are—

(*a*) non-interest-bearing securities issued by the Minister for Finance at a discount, including Exchequer Bills and Exchequer Notes,

(*b*) Agricultural Commodities Intervention Bills issued by the Minister for Agriculture and Food, and

(*c*) strips within the meaning of section 54(10) of the Finance Act, 1970 (inserted by section 161 of the Finance Act, 1997).

(5) (*a*) In this subsection, **"owner"**, in relation to securities, means at any time the person who would be entitled, if the securities were redeemed at that time by the issuer, to the proceeds of the redemption.

(*b*) Notwithstanding subsection (3), where the owner of a security to which subsection (4) applies—

(i) sells or otherwise disposes of the security, or

(ii) receives on redemption of the security an amount greater than the amount paid by the owner for that security either on its issue or otherwise,

any profit, gain or excess arising to the owner from such sale, disposal or receipt shall be exempt from tax where the owner is not ordinarily resident in the State; but this subsection shall not apply in respect of corporation tax chargeable on the income of an Irish branch or agency of a company not resident in the State.

Definitions

the Oireachtas: IA 1937 Sch; trade: s 3(1).

Former enactments

FA 1969 s 63; FA 1970 s 59(1) and (6); FA 1973 s 92(1), (2)(*b*); FA 1974 s 86 and Sch 2 Pt I; FA 1984 s 28; FA 1989 s 98(1); FA 1990 s 138; FA 1994 s 161(1), (2)(*b*); FA 1997 s 34.

49 Exemption of certain securities

(1) This section shall apply to any stock or other security on which interest is payable without deduction of tax by virtue of a direction given by the Minister for Finance in pursuance of section 37, 38, 39, 40 or 41.

(2) Any stock or other security to which this section applies may be issued with either or both of the following conditions—

(*a*) that neither the capital of nor the interest on the stock or other security shall be liable to tax so long as it is shown in the manner directed by the Minister for Finance that the stock or other security is in the beneficial ownership of persons who are neither domiciled nor ordinarily resident in the State, and

(*b*) that the interest on the stock or other security shall not be liable to tax so long as it is shown in the manner directed by the Minister for Finance that the stock or other security is in the beneficial ownership of persons who, though domiciled in the State, are not ordinarily resident in the State,

and accordingly, as respects every such stock or other security so issued, exemption from tax shall be granted.

(3) (*a*) Notwithstanding subsection (2), where a security to which this section applies has been issued with either or both of the conditions referred to in that subsection and the security is held by or for a branch or agency through which a company carries on a trade or business in the State, which is such a trade or business, as the case may be, that, if the security had been issued without either of those conditions, interest on, or other profits or gains from, the security accruing to the company would be chargeable to corporation tax under Case I or, as respects interest and other profits or gains accruing on or after the 21st day of April, 1997, from the security, Case IV of Schedule D, or in accordance

with section 726, then, such interest and profits or gains shall be charged to tax as if the security had been issued without either of those conditions.

(*b*) Paragraph (*a*) shall apply as respects securities acquired by a company after the 15th day of May, 1992, whether they were issued before or after that date.

Cross-references

Corporation tax: treatment of tax free income of non resident banks, insurance businesses etc: s 845(2).

Foreign life assurance funds: s 718(3)(*b*).

Offshore funds, Irish equivalent profits: Sch 19 para 5(5).

Transfer of assets abroad, income not exempted: s 809.

Transitional, subs (1) applies as if "or paragraph 1 of Schedule 32" were inserted after "or 41": Sch 32 para 1(2).

Definitions

person: IA 1937 s 11(*c*).

Former enactments

ITA 1967 s 474; FA 1992 s 42(1)(*c*); FA 1997 ss 47, 146(1) and Sch 9 Pt I para 1(32).

50 Securities of Irish local authorities issued abroad

(1) In this section, **"local authority"** includes any public body recognised as a local authority for the purpose of this section by the Minister for the Environment and Local Government.

(2) Securities issued outside the State by a local authority in the State for the purpose of raising any money which the local authority is authorised to borrow, if issued under the authority of the Minister for Finance, shall not be liable to tax, except—

(*a*) where they are held by persons domiciled in the State or ordinarily resident in the State, or

(*b*) as respects securities acquired by a company after the 15th day of May, 1992, whether they were issued before or after that date, where they are held by or for a branch or agency through which a company carries on a trade or business in the State which is such a trade or business, as the case may be, that, if this section had not been enacted, interest on, or other profits or gains from, the securities accruing to the company would be chargeable to corporation tax under Case I or, as respects interest and other profits or gains accruing on or after the 21st day of April, 1997, from the securities, Case IV of Schedule D, or in accordance with section 726.

Cross-references

Corporation tax: treatment of tax free income of non resident banks, insurance businesses etc: s 845(2).

Offshore funds, Irish equivalent profits: Sch 19 para 5(5).

Transfer of assets abroad, income not exempted: s 809.

Definitions

branch or agency: ss 4(1), 5(1); company: ss 4(1), 5(1); local authority: s 2(1); person: IA 1937 s 11(*c*); trade: s 3(1).

Former enactments

ITA 1967 s 470; FA 1992 s 42(1)(*b*); FA 1997 s 46.

CHAPTER 4
Miscellaneous Provisions

51 Funding bonds issued in respect of interest on certain debts

(1) In this section, **"funding bonds"** includes all bonds, stocks, shares, securities and certificates of indebtedness.

(2) This section shall apply to all debts owing by any government, public authority or public institution whatever or wherever and to all debts owing by any body corporate whatever or wherever.

(3) Where any funding bonds are issued to a creditor in respect of any liability to pay interest on a debt to which this section applies, the issue of those bonds shall be treated for the purposes of the Tax Acts as if it were the payment of an amount of the interest equal to the value of the bonds at the time of the issue of the bonds, and the redemption of the bonds shall not be treated for any of the purposes of the Tax Acts as payment of the interest or any part of the interest.

Former enactments

ITA 1967 s 475; CTA 1976 Sch 2 Pt I para 26.

Corresponding UK tax provision

Income and Corporation Taxes Act 1988 s 582.

PART 4
PRINCIPAL PROVISIONS RELATING TO THE SCHEDULE D CHARGE

CHAPTER 1
Supplementary Charging Provisions

52 Persons chargeable

Income tax under Schedule D shall be charged on and paid by the persons or bodies of persons receiving or entitled to the income in respect of which tax under that Schedule is directed in the Income Tax Acts to be charged.

Revenue precedents

Issue: What regime of tax should apply to payments by individuals to a trust for funeral expenses?
Decision: Arrangements have been agreed for the taxation and administration of trusts established by funeral directors to hold payments made in advance by individuals to meet their future funeral costs. The conditions for the operation of these trusts are as follows: a) 18% tax to be applied to all gross income of the trust with credit for DIRT allowed. No refund of DIRT is available; b) the individual has no further tax liability; c) no individual may invest more than £4,000 (this limit is subject to review); d) no individual may have more than one investment; e) details need not be included in the individuals tax return; f) the scheme is subject to review to ensure that it is operating satisfactorily.

Definitions

body of persons: s 2(1).

Former enactments

ITA 1967 s 105.

Corresponding UK tax provision

Income and Corporation Taxes Act 1988 s 59.

53 Cattle and milk dealers

(1) In this section—

"farm land" means land in the State wholly or mainly occupied for the purposes of husbandry, other than market garden land within the meaning of section 654;

"occupation", in relation to any land, means having the use of that land.

(2) The occupation by a dealer in cattle, or a dealer in or a seller of milk, of farm land which is insufficient for the keep of the cattle brought on to the land shall be treated as the carrying on of a trade, and the profits or gains thereof shall be charged under Case I of Schedule D.

Definitions

trade: s 3(1).

Former enactments

FA 1969 s 19; FA 1996 s 132(1) and Sch 5 Pt I para 4.

54 Interest, etc paid without deduction of tax under Schedule C

(1) This section shall apply to all interest, dividends, annuities and shares of annuities payable out of any public revenue of the State or out of any public revenue of Great Britain or of Northern Ireland or of Great Britain and Northern Ireland.

(2) Where any interest, dividends, annuities or shares of annuities to which this section applies or the profits attached to any such interest, dividends or annuities are to be charged under the provisions applicable to Schedule C but are in fact not assessed for any year under that Schedule, tax on such interest, dividends, annuities, shares of annuities or profits may be charged and assessed on and shall be payable by the person entitled to receive such interest, dividends or other annual payments for that year under the appropriate Case of Schedule D.

Definitions

Great Britain: IA 1937 Sch; person: IA 1937 s 11(*c*).

Former enactments

ITA 1967 s 55.

55 Taxation of strips of securities

(1) In this section—

"chargeable period" has the same meaning as in section 321(2);

"market value" shall be construed in accordance with section 548;

"nominal value", in relation to a unit of a security, means—

(*a*) where the interest on the unit of the security is expressed to be payable by reference to a given value, that value, and

(*b*) in any other case, the amount paid for the unit of the security on its issue;

"opening value", in relation to a unit of a security from which at any time strips of the unit have been created by a person, means—

(*a*) in the case of a person who is carrying on a trade which consists wholly or partly of dealing in securities of which the unit of the security is an asset in respect of which any profits or gains are chargeable to tax under Case I of Schedule D, an amount equal to the market value of the unit of the security at the time the strips were created, and

(*b*) in the case of any other person, an amount equal to the lesser of—

(i) the market value of the unit of the security at the time the strips were created, and

(ii) the nominal value of the unit of the security;

"relevant day", in relation to a person who holds a strip, means—

(*a*) where the person is not a company within the charge to corporation tax, [31 December][1] in a year of assessment, and

(*b*) where the person is a company within the charge to corporation tax, the day on which an accounting period of the company ends;

"securities" has the same meaning as in section 815(1), and a unit of a security shall be construed accordingly;

"strip", in relation to a unit of a security, means an obligation of the person who issued the security to make a payment, whether of interest or of principal, which has been separated from other obligations of that person to make payments in respect of the unit of the security.

(2) Where at any time a person who owns a unit of a security creates strips of that unit—

(*a*) the unit of the security shall be deemed to have been sold at that time by that person for an amount equal to its market value at that time,

(*b*) that person shall be deemed to have acquired at that time each strip for the amount which bears the same proportion to the opening value of the unit of the security as the market value of the strip at that time bears to the aggregate of the market value at that time of each of the strips of the unit of the security, and

(*c*) each strip shall be deemed to be a non-interest-bearing security any profits or gains arising on a disposal or redemption of which shall, subject to subsection (5), be chargeable to tax under Case III of Schedule D unless charged to tax under Case I of that Schedule.

(3) Where a person, other than a person carrying on a trade which consists wholly or partly of dealing in securities in respect of which any profits or gains are chargeable to tax under Case I of Schedule D, acquires a strip in respect of a unit of a security referred to in section 607, otherwise than in accordance with subsection (2), the person shall be deemed to have acquired the strip for an amount equal to the lesser of—

(*a*) the amount which bears the same proportion to the nominal value of the unit of the security as the market value of the strip at the time of issue of the security would have borne to the aggregate of the market value at that time of each of the strips of the unit of the security if the strip had been created at the time of issue of the security, and

(*b*) the amount paid by the person for the acquisition of the strip.

(4) Where at any time strips of a unit of a security are reconstituted into a unit of the security by any person—

(*a*) each of the strips shall be deemed to have been sold at that time by that person for an amount equal to its market value at that time, and

(*b*) that person shall be deemed to have acquired at that time the unit of the security for an amount equal to the aggregate of the market value at that time of each of the strips.

(5) Where a person holds a strip on a relevant day, that person shall on that day be deemed to have disposed of and immediately reacquired the strip at the market value of the strip on that day.

(6) Where under subsection (5) a person is deemed to have disposed of a strip on a relevant day, the amount to be included in the profits or gains chargeable to tax under Case III of Schedule D for the chargeable period in which the relevant day falls shall be the aggregate of the amounts of any profits or gains arising on such deemed disposals in the chargeable period after deducting the aggregate of the amounts of any losses arising on such deemed disposals in that chargeable period and, in so far as they have not been allowed as a deduction from profits or gains in any previous chargeable period, any losses arising on such deemed disposals in any previous chargeable period.

Amendments

1 Substituted by FA 2001 s 77(2) and Sch 2 para 1 with effect from 6 April 2001; previously "the 5th day of April".

Cross-references

Implementation of Council Directive 2003/48/EC of 3 June 2003 on Taxation of Savings Income in the Form of Interest Payments, interpretation, meaning of "strip of a security" applied: s 898B(1).

Former enactments

FA 1997 s 33.

Corresponding UK tax provision

Income and Corporation Taxes Act 1988 s 722A.

---

56 Tax on quarries, mines and other concerns chargeable under Case I(*b*) of Schedule D

(1) Subject to this section, Chapter 3 of this Part and section 108 shall apply in relation to the concerns which by virtue of section 18 are chargeable under Case I(*b*) of Schedule D.

(2) Tax under Case I of Schedule D shall be assessed and charged on the person or body of persons carrying on such concern or on the agents or other officers who have the direction or management of the concern or receive the profits of the concern.

(3) (*a*) The computation in respect of any mine carried on by a company of adventurers shall be made and stated jointly in one sum, but any adventurer may be assessed and charged separately if that adventurer makes a declaration of that adventurer's proportion or share in the concern for that purpose.

(*b*) Any adventurer so separately assessed and charged may set off against that adventurer's profits from one or more of such concerns the amount of that adventurer's loss sustained in any other such concern as certified by the inspector.

(*c*) In any such case one assessment and charge only shall be made on the balance of profit and loss, and shall be made in the assessment district where the adventurer is chargeable to the greatest amount.

Definitions

body of persons: s 2(1); inspector: ss 2(1), 5(1), 852; person: IA 1937 s 11(*c*).

Former enactments

ITA 1967 s 56(1)–(3).

Corresponding UK tax provision

Income and Corporation Taxes Act 1988 s 55.

57 Extension of charge to tax under Case III of Schedule D in certain circumstances

(1) This section shall apply to any sum received or benefit derived by an employee in respect of which there would be a charge to tax by virtue of Chapter 3 of Part 5 if the office or employment held by the employee were one the profits or gains from which were chargeable to tax under Schedule E.

(2) Where a person holds an office or employment and—

(*a*) the profits or gains arising to the person from that office or employment are chargeable to tax under Case III of Schedule D by virtue of section 18, and

(*b*) the person receives a sum in respect of expenses or derives a benefit, being a sum or benefit to which this section applies,

the profits or gains from that office or employment assessable to tax shall include the specified amount and shall be charged to tax accordingly.

(3) The specified amount referred to in subsection (2) shall be the amount which by virtue of Chapter 3 of Part 5 would be chargeable to tax in respect of the sum or benefit to which this section applies if the profits or gains from the office or employment referred to in that subsection were chargeable to tax under Schedule E.

Former enactments

FA 1976 s 22.

58 Charge to tax of profits or gains from unknown or unlawful source

(1) Profits or gains shall be chargeable to tax notwithstanding that at the time an assessment to tax in respect of those profits or gains was made—

(*a*) the source from which those profits or gains arose was not known to the inspector,

(*b*) the profits or gains were not known to the inspector to have arisen wholly or partly from a lawful source or activity, or

(*c*) the profits or gains arose and were known to the inspector to have arisen from an unlawful source or activity, and any question whether those profits or gains arose wholly or partly from an unknown or unlawful source or activity shall be disregarded in determining the chargeability to tax of those profits or gains.

(2) Notwithstanding anything in the Tax Acts, any profits or gains which are charged to tax by virtue of subsection (1) or charged to tax by virtue of or following any investigation by any body (in this subsection referred to as **"the body"**) established by or under statute or by the Government, the purpose or one of the principal purposes of which is—

(*a*) the identification of the assets of persons which derive or are suspected to derive, directly or indirectly, from criminal activity,

(*b*) the taking of appropriate action under the law to deprive or to deny those persons of the assets or the benefit of such assets, in whole or in part, as may be appropriate, and

(*c*) the pursuit of any investigation or the doing of any other preparatory work in relation to any proceedings arising from the purposes mentioned in paragraphs (*a*) and (*b*),

shall be charged under Case IV of Schedule D and shall be described in the assessment to tax concerned as **"miscellaneous income"**, and in respect of such profits and gains so assessed—

(i) the assessment—

(I) may be made solely in the name of the body, and

(II) shall not be discharged by the Appeal Commissioners or by a court by reason only of the fact that the income should apart from this section have been described in some other manner or by reason only of the fact that the profits or gains arose wholly or partly from an unknown or unlawful source or activity,

and

(ii) (I) the tax charged in the assessment may be demanded solely in the name of the body, and

(II) on payment to it of the tax so demanded, the body shall issue a receipt in its name and shall forthwith—

(A) lodge the tax paid to the General Account of the Revenue Commissioners in the Central Bank of Ireland, and

(B) transmit to the Collector-General particulars of the tax assessed and payment received in respect of that tax.

Cross-references

Anonymity, meaning of "the body" applied: s 859(1).

Case law

Prior to the introduction of this section the superior courts had held that profits from illegal activities were not taxable. See *Hayes v Duggan* ITR Vol I p 195; *Collins and others v Mulvey* ITR Vol II p 291.

CAB has express statutory power under this section to raise assessments, demand the relevant tax charged and issue a receipt in its own name. These express statutory powers carry an implicit power to sue and execute judgment in its own name: *Criminal Assets Bureau v H(S) and H(R)*.

Definitions

Appeal Commissioners: s 2(1); inspector: ss 2(1), 5(1), 852; profits: s 4(1); Tax Acts: s 1(2).

Former enactments

FA 1983 s 19(1)–(2); DCITPA 1996 s 11.

59 Charge to tax of income from which tax has been deducted

Where income (in this section referred to as **"the relevant income"**)—

(*a*) from which tax is deductible by virtue of Schedule C or D, or

(*b*) from which tax is deductible by virtue of section 237 or 238,

is to be taken into account in computing the total income of an individual for any year of assessment, then, for the purpose of charging that total income to tax at the rate or rates of tax charged for that year of assessment, the following provisions shall apply:

(i) the relevant income shall be regarded as income chargeable to tax under Case IV of Schedule D and shall be charged accordingly, and

(ii) in determining the amount of tax payable on that total income, credit shall be given for the tax deducted from the relevant income and the amount of the credit shall be the amount of tax deducted from the relevant income.

Cross-references

Deposit interest retention tax included under para (*a*): s 261(*c*)(ii)(I).

Interpretation of Income Tax Acts: s 3(1)("general tax credit").

Loans to participators, effect of release of debt, para (ii): s 439(1)(*d*).

Payments in respect of personal injuries, exemption: s 189(2)(*a*)("relevant income").

Special trusts for permanently incapacitated individuals, exemption: s 189A(2), (4)("relevant income").

Thalidomide children, investment income exempt: s 192(2).

Revenue precedents

Issue: Whether credit for DIRT under s 59 available for set off against PRSI liability.

Decision: No - the credit is available only in computing tax payable on total income.

Definitions

total income: s 3(1); year of assessment: ss 2(1), 5(1).

Former enactments

FA 1974 s 4; CTA 1976 s 140(1) and Sch 2 Pt I para 41 and s 164 and Sch 3 Pt I; FA 1996 s 132(2) and Sch 5 Pt II.

CHAPTER 2
Foreign Dividends

Cross-references

Implementation of Council Directive 90/435/EEC concerning the common system of taxation applicable in the case of parent companies and subsidiaries of different member States, meaning of "arrangements" applied: s 831(2)(*b*).

Making of assessments under Schedules C, D, E and F: s 918(1)(*a*).

Machinery for assessment, charge and payment of tax under Schedule C, and in certain cases, Schedule D: Sch 2 paras 1, 14(1)(*b*)–(*e*), 23.

Taxation of income deemed to arise from transfers of right to receive interest on securities: s 812(2)(*a*)(iv), (*c*), (4)(*b*).

60 Interpretation (Chapter 2)

In this Chapter—

"dividends to which this Chapter applies" means any interest, dividends or other annual payments payable out of or in respect of the stocks, funds, shares or securities of any body of persons not resident in the State, but does not include any payment to which section 237 or 238 applies, and references to dividends shall be construed accordingly;

"banker" includes a person acting as a banker;

references to coupons in relation to any dividends include warrants for or bills of exchange purporting to be drawn or made in payment of those dividends.

Cross-references

Machinery for assessment, charge and payment of tax under Schedule C, and in certain cases, Schedule D: Sch 2 para 1.

Revenue precedents

Issue: Liabilities taken over — do they represent consideration?

Decision: Liabilities of the business included in the transfer rank as consideration for the transfer because the discharge of liabilities of the transferor by the transferee is equivalent to the payment of cash by the transferee to the transferor. In practice, however, where an individual transfers a business to a company, in exchange for shares only and assets exceed liabilities, bona fide trade creditors taken over will not be treated as consideration.

Definitions

body of persons: s 2(1); person: IA 1937 s 11(*c*).

Former enactments

ITA 1967 s 459.

Corresponding UK tax provision

Income and Corporation Taxes Act 1988 s 123 [repealed].

61 Dividends entrusted for payment in the State

Where dividends to which this Chapter applies are entrusted to any person in the State for payment to any persons in the State—

(*a*) the dividends shall be assessed and charged to tax under Schedule D by the Revenue Commissioners, and

(*b*) Parts 1, 4 and 5 of Schedule 2 shall extend to the tax to be assessed and charged under this section.

Definitions

person: IA 1937 s 11(*c*).

Former enactments

ITA 1967 s 460; F(MP)A 1968 s 3(3) and Sch Pt II.

62 Dividends paid outside the State and proceeds of sale of dividend coupons

[(1)][1] Where—

(*a*) a banker or any other person in the State, by means of coupons received from another person or otherwise on that other person's behalf, obtains payment of any dividends to which this Chapter applies elsewhere than in the State, (*b*) a banker in the State sells or otherwise realises coupons for any dividends to which this Chapter applies and pays over the proceeds of such realisation to or carries such proceeds to the account of any person, or

(*c*) a dealer in coupons in the State purchases coupons for any dividends to which this Chapter applies otherwise than from a banker or another dealer in coupons,

then, the tax under Schedule D shall extend—

(i) in the case mentioned in paragraph (*a*), to the dividends,

(ii) in the case mentioned in paragraph (*b*), to the proceeds of the realisation, and

(iii) in the case mentioned in paragraph (*c*), to the price paid on such purchase,

and Parts 1, 4 and 5 of Schedule 2 shall apply in relation to the assessment, charge and payment of the tax.

[(2) This section does not apply to a banker by virtue only of the clearing of a cheque, or the arranging for the clearing of a cheque, by the banker.][2]

Amendments

[1] Renumbered as subs (1) by FA 2005 s 46(1)(*b*)(i) as respects any payment on or after 25 March 2005.

[2] Subs (2) inserted by FA 2005 s 46(1)(*b*)(ii) as respects any payment on or after 25 March 2005.

Cross-references

Quoted Eurobonds: s 64(1)(meaning of "relevant person"), this section applies but in para (*a*) for "applies elsewhere than in the State" substitute:

"applies and-

(i) the payment of those dividends was not made by or entrusted to any person in the State, or

(ii) the stocks, funds and securities in respect of which those dividends are paid are held in a recognised clearing system".

and treat Sch 2 Pt 4 para 14(1)(*a*)–(*b*) as deleted: s 64(5)(*a*) and (*c*).

Definitions

person: IA 1937 s 11(*c*).

Former enactments

ITA 1967 s 461.

63 Exemption of dividends of non-residents

(1) (*a*) No tax shall be chargeable in respect of dividends to which this Chapter applies which are payable in the State where it is proved to the satisfaction of the Revenue Commissioners that the person owning the stocks, funds, shares or securities and entitled to the income arising from those stocks, funds, shares or securities is not resident in the State but, except where provided by the Income Tax Acts, no allowance shall be given or repayment made in respect of the tax on dividends to which this Chapter applies which are payable in the State.

(*b*) Where the dividends referred to in paragraph (*a*) are from stocks, funds, shares or securities which are held under any trust, and the person who is the beneficiary in possession under the trust is the sole beneficiary in possession and can, by means either of the revocation of the trust or of the exercise of any powers under the trust, call on the trustees at any time to transfer the stocks, funds, shares or securities to such person absolutely free from any trust, such person shall for the purposes of this section be deemed to be the person owning the stocks, funds, shares or securities.

(2) Relief under this section may be given by the Revenue Commissioners either by means of allowance or repayment on a claim being made to them for that purpose.

(3) Any person aggrieved by a decision of the Revenue Commissioners on any question as to residence arising under this section may, by notice in writing to that effect given to the Revenue Commissioners within 2 months from the date on which notice of the decision is given to such person, make an application to have such person's claim for relief heard and determined by the Appeal Commissioners.

(4) Where an application is made under subsection (3), the Appeal Commissioners shall hear and determine the claim in the like manner as an appeal made to them against an assessment, and the provisions of the Income Tax Acts relating to such an appeal (including the provisions relating to the rehearing of an appeal and to the statement of a case for the opinion of the High Court on a point of law) shall apply accordingly with any necessary modifications.

Cross-references

Corporation tax: treatment of tax free income of non resident banks, insurance businesses etc: s 845(3), (5).
Offshore funds, Irish equivalent profits: Sch 19 para 5(5).
Quoted Eurobonds, this section applies but for subs (1)(*a*) substitute:

"(1)(*a*) No tax shall be chargeable in respect of dividends to which this Chapter applies which are payable in the State where the person who is the beneficial owner of the stocks, funds, shares or securities and who is beneficially entitled to the dividends is not resident in the State and has made a declaration of the kind mentioned in section 64(7)."

and treat Sch 2 Pt 4 para 14(1)(*a*)–(*b*) as deleted: s 64(5)(*b*) and (*c*).
Transfer of assets abroad, income not exempted: s 809(*b*).

Definitions

Appeal Commissioners: s 2(1); High Court: IA 1937 Sch; month: IA 1937 Sch; person: IA 1937 s 11(*c*); writing: IA 1937 Sch.

Former enactments

ITA 1967 s 462; F(MP)A 1968 s 3(2) and Sch Pt I.

64 Interest on quoted Eurobonds

(1) In this section—

"appropriate inspector" means the inspector authorised by the Revenue Commissioners for the purposes of this section;

"quoted Eurobond" means a security which—

(*a*) is issued by a company,
(*b*) is quoted on a recognised stock exchange,
(*c*) is in bearer form, and
(*d*) carries a right to interest;

...[1]

"relevant foreign securities" means—

(*a*) any such stocks, funds, shares or securities as give rise to dividends to which this Chapter applies, or
(*b*) any such securities as give rise to foreign public revenue dividends within the meaning of section 32;

"relevant person" means—

(*a*) the person by or through whom interest is paid, or

(*b*) a banker or any other person, or a dealer in coupons, referred to in section 62,

as the case may be.

[(1A) The definition of **"recognised clearing system"** in section 246A(2) applies for the purposes of this section as it applies for the purposes of section 246A.][2]

(2) Section 246(2) shall not apply to interest paid on any quoted Eurobond where—

(*a*) the person by or through whom the payment is made is not in the State, or

(*b*) the payment is made by or through a person in the State, and—

(i) the quoted Eurobond is held in a recognised clearing system, or

(ii) the person who is the beneficial owner of the quoted Eurobond and who is beneficially entitled to the interest is not resident in the State and has made a declaration of the kind mentioned in subsection (7).

(3) In a case within subsection (2)(*b*), the person by or through whom the payment is made shall deliver to the appropriate inspector—

(*a*) on demand by the appropriate inspector, an account of the amount of any such payment, and

(*b*) not later than 12 months after making any such payment and unless within that time that person delivers an account with respect to the payment under paragraph (*a*), a written statement specifying that person's name and address and describing the payment.

(4) Where by virtue of any provision of the Tax Acts interest paid on any quoted Eurobond is deemed to be income of a person other than the person who is the beneficial owner of the quoted Eurobond, subsection (2)(*b*)(ii) shall apply as if it referred to that other person.

(5) Sections 62 and 63 and, in so far as it relates to section 62, Schedule 2 shall apply in relation to interest on quoted Eurobonds as they would apply in relation to dividends to which this Chapter applies—

(*a*) if in paragraph (*a*) of section 62 the following were substituted for **"applies elsewhere than in the State"**:

"applies and—

(i) the payment of those dividends was not made by or entrusted to any person in the State, or

(ii) the stocks, funds and securities in respect of which those dividends are paid are held in a recognised clearing system",

(*b*) if in section 63 the following were substituted for subsection (1)(*a*):

"(1) (*a*) No tax shall be chargeable in respect of dividends to which this Chapter applies which are payable in the State where the person who is the beneficial owner of the stocks, funds, shares or securities and who is beneficially entitled to the dividends is not resident in the State and has made a declaration of the kind mentioned in section 64(7).",

and

(*c*) if in paragraph 14(1) of Part 4 of Schedule 2 clauses (*a*) and (*b*) were deleted.

...[3]

(7) The declaration referred to in subsection (2)(*b*)(ii) or in subsection (1)(*a*) of section 63 (as construed by reference to subsection (5)(*b*)) shall be a declaration in writing to a relevant person which—

(*a*) is made by a person (in this section referred to as **"the declarer"**) to whom any interest in respect of which the declaration is made is payable by the relevant person, and is signed by the declarer,

(*b*) is made in such form as may be prescribed or authorised by the Revenue Commissioners,

(*c*) declares that at the time the declaration is made the person who is beneficially entitled to the interest is not resident in the State,

(*d*) contains as respects the person mentioned in paragraph (*c*)—

(i) the name of the person,

(ii) the address of that person's principal place of residence, and

(iii) the name of the country in which that person is resident at the time the declaration is made,

(*e*) contains an undertaking by the declarer that, if the person referred to in paragraph (*c*) becomes resident in the State, the declarer will notify the relevant person accordingly, and

(*f*) contains such other information as the Revenue Commissioners may reasonably require for the purposes of this section.

(8) (*a*) A relevant person shall—

(i) keep and retain for the longer of the following periods—

(I) a period of 6 years, and

(II) a period which ends not earlier than 3 years after the latest date on which interest in respect of which the declaration was made is paid,

and

(ii) on being so required by notice given in writing by an inspector, make available to the inspector within the time specified in the notice,

all declarations of the kind mentioned in this section which have been made in respect of interest paid by the relevant person.

(*b*) The inspector may examine or take extracts from or copies of any declarations made available under paragraph (*a*).

Amendments

1 Definition of "recognised clearing system" deleted by FA 2003 s 49(3)(*a*)(i) as respects a "quoted eurobond" (within the meaning of TCA 1997 s 64) issued on or after 28 March 2003.

2 Subs (1A) inserted by FA 2003 s 49(3)(*a*)(ii) as respects a "quoted eurobond" (within the meaning of TCA 1997 s 64) issued on or after 28 March 2003.

3 Subs (6) deleted by FA 2003 s 49(3)(*a*)(iii) as respects a "quoted eurobond" (within the meaning of TCA 1997 s 64) issued on or after 28 March 2003.

Cross-references

Certain interest not to be chargeable: s 198(1)(*e*).
Corporation tax, charges on income: s 243(5)(*a*)(III).
Interest in respect of wholesale debt instruments, Revenue may designate by order one or more systems for clearing securities to be a "recognised clearing system for TCA 1997 ss 246A and 739B and this section: s 246A(1)(*b*).

Definitions

company: ss 4(1), 5(1); inspector: ss 2(1), 5(1), 852; interest: s 4(1); tax: s 3(1); person: IA 1937 s 11(*c*); writing: IA 1937 Sch;

Former enactments

ITA 1967 s 462A; FA 1994 s 15.

Corresponding UK tax provision

Income and Corporation Taxes Act 1988 s 124 [repealed].

CHAPTER 3
Income Tax: Basis of Assessment Under Cases I and II

Cross-references

Farming and market gardening, Schedule D Case I: s 655(2).
Farming, averaging of farming profits: s 657(7), (8)(*a*).
Farming buildings expenditure: s 658(4).
Returns of income: s 879(3).
This Chapter applies to concerns chargeable under Case I(*b*): s 56(1).

65 Cases I and II: basis of assessment

(1) Subject to this Chapter, income tax shall be charged under Case I or II of Schedule D on the full amount of the profits or gains of the year of assessment.

(2) Where in the case of any trade or profession it has been customary to make up accounts—

(*a*) if only one account was made up to a date within the year of assessment and that account was for a period of one year, the profits or gains of the year ending on that date shall be taken to be the profits or gains of the year of assessment;

(*b*) if an account, other than an account to which paragraph (*a*) applies, was made up to a date in the year of assessment, or if more accounts than one were made up to dates in the year of assessment, the profits or gains of the year ending on that date or on the last of those dates, as the case may be, shall be taken to be the profits or gains of the year of assessment;

(*c*) in any other case, the profits or gains of the year of assessment shall be determined in accordance with subsection (1).

(3) Where the profits or gains of a year of assessment have been computed on the basis of a period in accordance with paragraph (*b*) or (*c*) of subsection (2) and the profits of the corresponding period relating to the preceding year of assessment exceed the profits or gains charged to income tax for that year, then, [notwithstanding anything to the contrary in section 66(2),][1] the profits of that corresponding period shall be taken to be the profits or gains of that preceding year of assessment and the assessment shall be amended accordingly.

[(3A) As respects the year of assessment 2001, subsection (2) shall apply as if in both paragraph (*a*) and paragraph (*b*) of that subsection "74 per cent of the profits or gains of the year ending on that date" were substituted for "the profits or gains of the year ending on that date".

(3B) For the purposes of subsection (2)(*a*), an account made up for a period of one year to a date falling in the period from 1 January 2002 to 5 April 2002 shall, in addition to being an account made up to a date in the year of assessment 2002, be deemed to be an account for a period of one year made up to a date within the year of assessment 2001, and the corresponding period in relation to the year of assessment 2000–2001 for the purposes of subsection (3) shall be determined accordingly.

(3C) Notwithstanding subsection (3), where the profits or gains of the year of assessment 2001 have been taken to be the full amount of the profits or gains of that year of assessment in accordance with subsection (2)(*c*), and the full amount of the profits or gains of the year of assessment 2000–2001 exceed the profits or gains charged to income tax for that year of assessment, then, the profits or gains of the year of assessment 2000–2001 shall be taken to be the full amount of the profits or gains of that year of assessment and the assessment shall be amended accordingly.

(3D) Notwithstanding subsection (3), where the profits or gains of a period of one year ending in the year of assessment 2002 have been taken to be the profits or gains of that year of assessment in accordance with subsection (2)(*b*), and the profits or gains charged to income tax for the year of assessment 2001 are less than 74 per cent of the profits or gains of the corresponding period relating to the year of assessment 2001, then, the profits or gains of the year of assessment 2001 shall be taken to be 74 per cent of the profits or gains of that corresponding period and the assessment shall be amended accordingly.

(3E) For the purposes of subsection (3D), where, apart from this subsection, a period (in this subsection referred to as the **"relevant period"**) would not be treated as the corresponding period relating to the year of assessment 2001 by virtue of the fact that the relevant period ends on a date falling in the period from 1 January 2001 to 5 April 2001, the relevant period shall, notwithstanding any other provision of the Income Tax Acts, be treated as the corresponding period relating to that year of assessment.

(3F) Notwithstanding subsection (3), where the profits or gains of the year of assessment 2002 have been taken to be the full amount of the profits or gains of that year of assessment in accordance with subsection (2)(*c*), and the full amount of the profits or gains of the year of assessment 2001 exceed the profits or gains charged to income tax for that year of assessment, then, the profits or gains of the year of assessment 2001 shall be taken to be the full amount of the profits or gains of that year of assessment and the assessment shall be amended accordingly.][2]

(4) In the case of the death of a person who, if he or she had not died, would under this section have become chargeable to income tax for any year of assessment, the tax which would have been so chargeable shall be assessed and charged on such person's executors or administrators, and shall be a debt due from and payable out of such person's estate.

Amendments

[1] Inserted by FA 2003 s 11 with effect from 1 January 2003.

[2] Subs (3A)–(3F) substituted by FA 2001 s 77(2) and Sch 2 para 2 with effect from 6 April 2001.

Cross-references

Farming, averaging of farming profits, subs (1): s 657(4)(*b*), (9).
Farming, compulsory disposals of livestock: s 668(6)(*a*).
Professional Services Withholding Tax, interpretation, subs (2)(*a*) and (3B): s 520(3).
Profits or gains do not include chargeable gains within the meaning of the Capital Gains Tax Acts: s 3(4).
Self assessment, date for payment of tax, subs (3): s 958(8)(*a*), (*c*).
Self assessment, obligation to make a return, subs (3): s 951(1).
Separate assessment of partners: s 1008(2)(*b*).

Case law

Irish

Change of activity from fruit to coal merchants considered to be a separate trading activity: *O'Loan v Noone and Co* ITR Vol II p 146.
Evidence of a separate trade would include separate bank accounts – *HH v Forbes* 2 ITR 614.

UK

Company held to be still trading when it sold all its stocks during a 'retirement from business' sale: *O'Kane & Co v IRC* (1922) 12 TC 303; *Gloucester Railway Carriage & Wagon Co Ltd* (1925) 12 TC 720.
Company held to have commenced trading on de facto transfer to it of business of a partnership: *Angel v Hollingworth* (1956) 37 TC 714.
Company held to have commenced trading when raw materials it purchased were processed: *Birmingham and District Cattle By-Products Ltd v IRC* (1928) 12 TC 92.
Held taxpayers who bought second shop continued an existing trade and did not commence a new one: *Maidment v Kirby and another* [1993] STC 494.
Held profits should be calculated on the basis of generally accepted principle of commercial accounting: *Herbert Smith v Honour* [1999] STC 173.
Activities of milling and baking constitute a single trade – *Bolands Ltd v Davis* [1925] 1 ITC 91.

Revenue precedents

Issue: Are there any special arrangements for the taxation of athletes?
Decision: No. Athletes are taxable in the normal way ie the income earned from all sources, less expenses which have been incurred wholly and exclusively, is assessable.
Issue: Are payments received from the Department of Agriculture in respect of the grubbing-up of orchards chargeable?
Decision: No. These appear to be capital in nature and would be chargeable under the Capital Gains Tax rules.
Issue: Can self-employed medical practitioners who must be registered with the Medical Council in order to practice and who pay a retention fee to the council in order to remain on the register claim a deduction for the payment in computing their profits?
Decision: Yes.
Issue: Are payments made under the Emergency Aid Grant, paid by an Bord Iascaigh Mhara to compensate fishermen for poor earnings during adverse weather conditions, taxable receipts liable to Income Tax?
Decision: Yes.
Issue: Is the sale of copyright subject to Income Tax or Capital Gains Tax?
Decision: The UK case of *Nethersole v Withers* (28 TC 501) which was concerned with the sale of copyright in a play is relevant. It contains a useful summary of the case law on the point. To apply the decision to a case it would first be necessary to decide if the activities of the taxpayer are in the nature of a trade. If so, the payments are liable to Income Tax and there is no consideration for Capital Gains Tax Purposes. If not, they are capital and liable to Capital Gains Tax.
Issue: A farmer avails of the EC set-a-side scheme and instead of leaving the land fallow grows trees. Are the set-a-side payments in respect of that woodland, which is managed on a commercial basis and with a view to the realisation of profits, exempt from income tax?
Decision: Payments under the EC schemes for set-aside of land are assessable under the rules of Case 1 of Schedule D. The payments are to reimburse the farmer for the loss of income which would have accrued had he continued to till the land. Where a farmer receives payments under the set-aside scheme, and afforests the set-aside land, the payments will not be derived from the occupation of woodlands. They will still represent loss of income which would have accrued had tillage continued, and are not therefore exempt under TCA 1997 s 232.

Issue: How are the activities of a racehorse trainer taxed? What deductions are allowable?
Decision: Where a racehorse trainer, who holds a licence, trains horses which he or she owns or part owns, the activity is regarded as part of the trade of training. Accordingly, the expenses of training those horses may be allowed as a Case I deduction, and any income from prize money or the sale of horses is part of the income of that trade.
Issue: Do Revenue accept that income arising from holiday cottages registered with Bord Fáilte are Case I trading receipts?
Decision: No. The question of whether the income arising from a particular scheme of holiday cottages is chargeable under the rules of Case 1 or Case V of Schedule D is one which can only be determined by reference to the facts of each case.

Tax Briefing

TB45 Oct 2001 pp 15–18 — Case I and Case II Basis of Assessment and the Calendar Tax Year.
TB50 Oct 2002 pp 7–8 — Director's remuneration and the short tax "year" 2001.

Definitions

person: IA 1937 s 11(*c*); profession: s 2(1); trade: s 3(1); year of assessment: s 3(1).

Former enactments

ITA 1967 s 58(1) and s 60; FA 1990 ss 14(1)(*a*), 15; FA 1997 s 146(1) and Sch 9 Pt I para 1(2).

Corresponding UK tax provision

Income and Corporation Taxes Act 1988 s 60.

66 Special basis at commencement of trade or profession

(1) Where a trade or profession has been set up and commenced within the year of assessment, the computation of the profits or gains chargeable under Case I or II of Schedule D shall be made either on the full amount of the profits or gains arising in the year of assessment or according to the average of such period, not being greater than one year, as the case may require and as may be directed by the inspector.

[(2) Any person chargeable with income tax in respect of the profits or gains of any trade or profession which has been set up and commenced within one year preceding the year of assessment shall be charged—

(*a*) if only one account was made up to a date within the year of assessment and that account was for a period of one year, on the full amount of the profits or gains of the year ending on that date,

(*b*) if—

(i) an account, other than an account to which paragraph (*a*) applies, was made up to a date in the year of assessment or more accounts than one were made up to dates in the year of assessment, and

(ii) the trade or profession was set up and commenced not less than 12 months before the first-mentioned date in subparagraph (i) or, as the case may be, the last of the second-mentioned dates in that subparagraph,

on the full amount of the profits or gains of the year ending on that first-mentioned date or, as the case may be, the last of those second-mentioned dates, or

(*c*) in any other case, on the full amount of the profits or gains of the year of assessment.][1]

(3) Any person chargeable with income tax in respect of the profits or gains of any trade or profession which has been set up and commenced within the year next before the year preceding the year of assessment shall be entitled, [on including a claim in that behalf

with the return required under section 951 for the year of assessment],[2] to have the assessment reduced by the amount (if any) by which the amount of the assessment for the year preceding the year of assessment exceeds the full amount of the profits or gains of that preceding year; but, where the excess is greater than the amount of the assessment, the difference between the excess and the amount of the assessment shall be treated for the purposes of section 382 as if it were a loss sustained in a trade in that year of assessment.

[(3A) As respects the year of assessment 2001, subsection (2) shall apply as if in both paragraph (*a*) and paragraph (*b*) of that subsection "74 per cent of the full amount of the profits or gains" were substituted for "the full amount of the profits or gains".

(3B) As respects the year of assessment 2002—

(*a*) subsection (2) shall apply as if "within the period from 6 April 2001 to 31 December 2001" were substituted for "within one year preceding the year of assessment", and

(*b*) subsection (3) shall apply as if "within the period from 6 April 2000 to 5 April 2001" were substituted for within the year next before the year preceding the year of assessment".

(3C) As respects the year of assessment 2003, subsection (3) shall apply as if "within the period from 6 April 2001 to 31 December 2001" were substituted for "within the year next before the year preceding the year of assessment".][3]

Amendments

1 Subs (2) substituted by FA 1998 s 8 for 1998–99 and later tax years.

2 Substituted by FA 2001 s 78(2)(*a*) for the short tax "year" 2001 and later tax years; previously "on giving notice in writing to the inspector with the return required under section 951 for the year of assessment".

3 Subs (3A)–(3C) substituted by FA 2001 s 77(2) and Sch 2 para 3 with effect from 6 April 2001.

Cross-references

Cases I and II, basis of assessment, subs (2): s 65(3).

Profits or gains do not include chargeable gains within the meaning of the Capital Gains Tax Acts: s 3(4).

Surcharge for late returns, subs (1): s 1084(4)(*a*).

Caselaw

UK

Gascoine v Wharton (1996) STC 1481.

Revenue precedents

Issue: Where a trade is set up and commenced on the 6th April do the profits of the first year to 5th April represent the amount on which the person is charged for the first year of assessment and the second year of assessment?

Decision: Yes.

Revenue information

Information leaflet IT48 — Starting in Business — A Revenue Guide.

Tax Briefing

TB 35 Mar 1999 pp 8–9 — Income Tax Commencement Rules.

TB 45 Oct 2001 pp 17–18 — Income Tax Commencement Rules: Calendar Tax Year changes.

Definitions

person: IA 1937 s 11(*c*); profession: s 2(1); inspector: ss 2(1), 5(1), 852; trade: s 3(1); writing: IA 1937 Sch; year of assessment: s 3(1).

Former enactments

ITA 1967 s 58(2)–(4); FA 1990 s 14(1)(*b*).

Corresponding UK tax provision

Income and Corporation Taxes Act 1988 s 61.

67 Special basis on discontinuance of trade or profession

(1) (*a*) Where in any year of assessment a trade or profession is permanently discontinued, then, notwithstanding anything in the Income Tax Acts—

(i) the person charged or chargeable with income tax in respect of the trade or profession shall be charged for that year on the amount of the profits or gains of the period beginning on [the first day of the year of assessment][1] and ending on the date of the discontinuance, subject to any deduction or set- off to which such person may be entitled under section 382 and, if such person has been charged otherwise than in accordance with this paragraph, any tax overpaid shall be repaid, or an additional assessment may be made on such person, as the case may require;

[(ii) if the full amount of the profits or gains of the year of assessment preceding the year of assessment in which the discontinuance occurs exceeds the amount on which that person has been charged for that preceding year of assessment, or would have been charged if no such deduction or set-off to which such person may be entitled under section 382 had been allowed, an additional assessment may be made on such person, so that such person shall be charged for that preceding year of assessment on the full amount of the profits or gains of that preceding year of assessment, subject to any such deduction or set-off to which such person may be entitled.][2]

(*b*) In the case of the death of a person who, if he or she had not died, would under this subsection have become chargeable to income tax for any year, the tax which would have been so chargeable shall be assessed and charged on such person's executors or administrators, and shall be a debt due from and payable out of such person's estate.

(2) The reference in subsection (1) to the discontinuance of a trade or profession shall be construed as referring to a discontinuance occurring by reason of the death while carrying on such trade or profession of the person carrying on the same, as well as to a discontinuance occurring in the lifetime of such person, and for the purposes of subsection (1) such death shall be deemed to cause a discontinuance and such discontinuance shall be deemed to take place on the day of such death.

Amendments

1 Substituted by FA 2001 s 77(2) and Sch 2 para 4(*a*) with effect from 6 April 2001; previously "the 6th day of April in that year".

2 Subs (1)(*a*)(ii) substituted by FA 2001 s 77(2) and Sch 2 para 4(*b*) with effect from 6 April 2001.

Cross-references

Farming, averaging of farming profits: s 657(10).

Profits or gains do not include chargeable gains within the meaning of the Capital Gains Tax Acts: s 3(4).

Short-lived businesses, subs (2) applied: s 68(3).

Caselaw relating to the corresponding UK provision

Gilmore v Inspector of Taxes (1999) STC 269.

Watts v Hart (1984) STC 548.

Tax Briefing

TB36 June 1999 pp 17–18 — Cessation of a trade or profession: basis of assessment.

TB43 April 2001 p 27 — Cessation of a trade: tax treatment.

TB45 Oct 2001 p 18 — Cessation of a trade: changes to assessment rules consequent on changeover to a calendar tax year.

Former enactments

ITA 1967 s 58(5)–(6); FA 1971 s 3; FA 1990 s 14(2); FA 1996 s 132(2) and Sch 5 Pt II.

Corresponding UK tax provision

Income and Corporation Taxes Act 1988 s 63.

68 Short-lived businesses

(1) This section shall apply to a trade or profession—

(*a*) which has been set up and commenced in a year of assessment,

(*b*) which is permanently discontinued within the second year of assessment following that year of assessment, and

(*c*) in respect of which the aggregate of the profits or gains on which any person has been charged, or would be charged to income tax, by virtue of any other provision of the Income Tax Acts, exceeds the aggregate of the profits or gains arising in the period beginning on the date of set up and commencement and ending on the date of permanent discontinuance of the trade or profession.

(2) Any person chargeable to income tax on the profits or gains of a trade or profession to which this section applies shall be entitled, on giving notice in writing to the inspector on or before the specified return date (within the meaning of section 950) for the year of assessment in which the trade or profession is permanently discontinued, to have the assessment for the year of assessment immediately preceding that year reduced by the amount by which the amount of the assessment for that immediately preceding year exceeds the full amount of the profits or gains arising in that same year.

(3) Subsection (2) of section 67 shall apply to this section as if references in that subsection to subsection (1) of that section included references to this section.

Cross-references

Profits or gains do not include chargeable gains within the meaning of the Capital Gains Tax Acts: s 3(4).

Definitions

inspector: ss 2(1), 5(1), 852; profession: s 2(1); tax: s 3(1); trade: s 3(1); writing: IA 1937 Sch; year of assessment: s 3(1).

Former enactments

ITA 1967 s 58A; FA 1995 s 19.

69 Changes of proprietorship

(1) Where at any time a trade or profession which immediately before that time was carried on by an individual (in this subsection referred to as **"the predecessor"**) becomes carried on by another individual or by a partnership of persons (including a partnership in which the predecessor is a partner), the income tax payable for all years of assessment by the predecessor shall be computed as if the trade or profession had been permanently discontinued at that time.

(2) Where at any time an individual (in this subsection referred to as **"the successor"**) succeeds to a trade or profession which immediately before that time was carried on by another individual or by a partnership of persons (including a partnership in which the successor was a partner), the income tax payable for all years of assessment by the successor shall be computed as if the successor had set up or commenced the trade or profession at that time.

(3) In the case of the death of a person who, if he or she had not died, would under this section have become chargeable to income tax for any year, the tax which would have been so chargeable shall be assessed and charged on such person's executors or administrators, and shall be a debt due from and payable out of such person's estate.

Cross-references

It is established Revenue practice that where a widow succeeds to the trade of her deceased husband, the trade is not treated as ceasing and recommencing.

Property that is in use for the purposes of a trade (which continues to be used by a successor to that trade) is treated as having been sold by the person ceasing to the successor: s 313(1); this also applies where a person or partnership succeeds to a partnership trade: s 1010(4).

Case law

UK

Watts v Hart (1984) STC 548.

Definitions

person: IA 1937 s 11(*c*); profession: s 2(1); trade: s 3(1).

Former enactments

ITA 1967 s 59.

Corresponding UK tax provision

Income and Corporation Taxes Act 1988 s 113.

CHAPTER 4

Income Tax: Basis of Assessment under Cases III, IV and V

70 Case III: basis of assessment

(1) Income or profits chargeable under Case III of Schedule D shall, for the purposes of ascertaining liability to income tax, be deemed to issue from a single source, and this section shall apply accordingly.

(2) Income tax under Case III of Schedule D shall be computed on the full amount of the profits or income arising within the year of assessment.

(3) Income tax shall, subject to section 71, be paid on the actual amount computed in accordance with subsection (2) without any deduction.

(4) Subsection (2) shall, in cases where income tax is to be computed by reference to the amount of income received in the State, apply as if the reference in that subsection to income arising were a reference to income so received.

Cross-references

Foreign securities and possessions: s 71(1), (3).

Income from possessions in Great Britain or Northern Ireland: to apply as if s 71(2) were deleted: s 73(2)(*a*).

Overseas life assurance companies, investment income, subs (1): s 726(7).

Patent royalty income exemption, not a cessation of source: s 234(5).

UK double taxation agreement: s 832(2).

Caselaw relating to the corresponding UK provision

Girvan v Orange Personal Communication Services Ltd (1998) STC 567.

Revenue precedents

Issue: Basis of assessment of interest received by partnership

Decision: Interest should be returned on the strict basis ie on the basis of the year to 5 April (31 December, for the short tax "year" 2001 and later tax years).

Definitions

person: IA 1937 s 11(*c*); trade: s 3(1); year of assessment: s 3(1).

Former enactments

ITA 1967 s 75 and s 77(1), (2) and (5); FA 1990 s 17(1)(*a*)(i) and (iii) and (2); FA 1997 s 146(1) and Sch 9 Pt I para 1(5).

Corresponding UK tax provision

Income and Corporation Taxes Act 1988 s 64.

71 Foreign securities and possessions

(1) Subject to this section and section 70, income tax chargeable under Case III of Schedule D in respect of income arising from securities and possessions in any place outside the State shall be computed on the full amount of such income arising in the year of assessment whether the income has been or will be received in the State or not, subject to, in the case of income not received in the State—

(*a*) the same deductions and allowances as if it had been so received,

(*b*) the deduction, where such deduction cannot be made under, and is not forbidden by, any other provision of the Income Tax Acts, of any sum paid in respect of income tax in the place where the income has arisen, and

(*c*) a deduction on account of any annuity or other annual payment (apart from annual interest) payable out of the income to a person not resident in the State,

and the provisions of the Income Tax Acts (including those relating to the delivery of statements) shall apply accordingly.

(2) Subsection (1) shall not apply to any person who satisfies the Revenue Commissioners that he or she is not domiciled in the State, or that, being a citizen of Ireland, he or she is not ordinarily resident in the State.

(3) In the cases mentioned in subsection (2), the tax shall, subject to section 70, be computed on the full amount of the actual sums received in the State from remittances payable in the State, or from property imported, or from money or value arising from property not imported, or from money or value so received on credit or on account in respect of such remittances, property, money or value brought into the State in the year of assessment without any deduction or abatement.

(4) Income arising outside the State which if it had arisen in the State would be chargeable under Case V of Schedule D shall be deemed to be income to which sections 75 and 97 apply, in so far as those sections relate to deductions to be made by reference to section 97(2)(*e*).

[(4A) For the purposes of subsection (4), section 97 shall apply as if references to the 23rd day of April, 1998, in subsections (2A), (2B), (2C) and (2E) of that section, were references to the 7th day of May, 1998.][1]

(5) Any person aggrieved by a decision of the Revenue Commissioners on any question as to domicile or ordinary residence arising under subsection (2) may, by notice in writing to that effect given to the Revenue Commissioners within 2 months from the date on which notice of the decision is given to him or her, make an application to have his or her claim for relief heard and determined by the Appeal Commissioners.

(6) Where an application is made under this section, the Appeal Commissioners shall hear and determine the claim in the like manner as an appeal made to them against an assessment, and the provisions of the Income Tax Acts relating to such an appeal (including the provisions relating to the rehearing of an appeal and to the statement of a case for the opinion of the High Court on a point of law) shall apply accordingly with any necessary modifications.

Amendments

1 Subs (4A) inserted by F(No 2)A 1998 s 1(2) with effect from 20 May 1998.

Cross-references

Corporation tax, computation of income, application of income tax principles: s 76(7), 77(1).
Employee share options schemes, subs (3): s 128(1)(*b*)(ii)(II).
Income from possessions in Great Britain and Northern Ireland: subs (2) treated as deleted: s 73(2)(*a*).
Offshore funds, Irish equivalent profits, subs (1): Sch 19 para 5(4)(*c*).
Reduction in income tax for certain income earned outside the State, subs (3): s 825A(2)(*a*).
Remittance basis (subs (3)), sums applied outside the State in repaying certain loans: s 72(2).
Residence of individuals, deduction for income earned outside the State: s 823(2)(*b*)(i).
Retirement payments, "foreign service" means under an employment not taxed under subs (1): s 201(1)(*a*).
Seafarer allowance, subs (3): s 472B(3)(*b*)(i).
Split year residence subs (3): s 822(3)(*a*).
Transfer of assets abroad, liability of non-transferors, subs (3): s 807A(5).
UK double taxation agreement: s 832(2).

Case law

Irish

Subs (1): Underwriting profits arising abroad held not to be a separate source of Case III: *O'Connell v R* 3 ITC 167; [1956] IR 97.

Subs (2): Taxpayers born in Ireland who claimed English domicile but had indefinite or limited intentions as regards future Irish residence held not to have discharged the onus placed on them to have established a domicile of choice: *Captain Prior-Wandesforde v Revenue Commissioners* 1 ITC 248; *Earl of Iveagh v Revenue Commissioners* 1 ITC 316; [1930] IR 386.

It is a question of fact whether the person has formed the necessary settled purpose of acquiring a domicile of choice: *In re Sillar* [1956] IR 350.

The fact that an individual had come from the UK with his family in order to take up employment in Ireland and had lived here for two years was too meagre a basis on which to infer the acquisition of an Irish domicile of choice – "freedom of movement and mobility of employment are the order of the day under the [EU] treaty" – *MT v NT* [1982] ILRM 217.

It does not follow from the fact that a husband decided to accept the tax and other advantages that Ireland offered, that the setting up of a family residence here for an indefinite period established per se an intention on his part to make his permanent home in Ireland and to abandon his domicile of origin – *M v M* [1988] ILRM 456.

The reference to an "indefinite" period in *M v M* should be construed as reference to a period of residence contingent on the happening of a certain event – *PL v An t'Ard Chlaraitheoir* [1995] 2 ILRM 241.

In order to abandon a domicile of choice and resurrect his domicile of origin, a person must return to reside in his country of origin: *In re Rowan (deceased)* [1988] ILRM 65.

UK

Actual residence in the country in question is essential before a domicile of choice can be acquired: *IRC v Duchess of Portland* [1982] STC 149; *Plummer v IRC* [1987] STC 698.

Taxpayer held not to have abandoned his domicile of origin despite lengthy residence in the UK as he had not formed the necessary intention to acquire a new domicile: *Buswell v IRC* [1971] STC 266; *IRC v Bullock* [1976] STC 409.

Subs (3): Held only remittances of income are subject to income tax: *Kneen v Martin* (1935) 19 TC 33.

Taxpayer held to have remitted US income when UK bank lodged in his UK account the sterling value of a cheque in dollars drawn by him: *Thomson v Moyse* (1960) 39 TC 328.

Where a sum received in UK could be directly traced to the taxpayer's South African salary, he was held to have remitted his income: *Harmel v Wright* (1974) 49 TC 149.

Possession connoted a legal identifiable entity which included an incorporeal right to money: *Albon v IRC* [1998] STC 1181.

Definitions

Appeal Commissioners: s 2(1); High Court: IA 1937 Sch; month: IA 1937 Sch; person: IA 1937 s 11(*c*); writing: IA 1937 Sch; year of assessment: s 3(1).

Former enactments

ITA 1967 s 76(1), (2)(*a*), (3), (5)–(6); F(MP)A 1968 s 3(2) and Sch Pt I; FA 1974 s 46; FA 1990 s 17(1)(*a*)(ii); FA 1997 s 146(1) and Sch 9 Pt I para 1(4).

Corresponding UK tax provision

Income and Corporation Taxes Act 1988 s 65.

72 Charge to tax on sums applied outside the State in repaying certain loans

(1) For the purposes of this section—

(*a*) a debt for money loaned shall, to the extent to which that money is applied in or towards satisfying another debt, be deemed to be a debt incurred for satisfying that other debt, and a debt incurred for satisfying in whole or in part a debt within subsection (2)(*c*) shall itself be treated as within that subsection, and

(*b*) **"lender"**, in relation to any money loaned, includes any person for the time being entitled to repayment.

(2) For the purposes of section 71(3), any income arising from securities and possessions in any place outside the State which is applied outside the State by a person ordinarily resident in the State in or towards satisfaction of—

(*a*) any debt for money loaned to such person in the State or for interest on money so loaned,

(*b*) any debt for money loaned to such person outside the State and received in or brought to the State, or

(*c*) any debt incurred for satisfying in whole or in part a debt within paragraph (*a*) or (*b*),

shall be treated as received by such person in the State and as so received from remittances payable in the State.

(3) Where a person ordinarily resident in the State receives in or brings to the State money loaned to such person outside the State, but the debt for that money is wholly or partly satisfied before such person does so, subsection (2) shall apply as if the money had been received in or brought to the State before the debt was so satisfied, except that any sums treated by virtue of that subsection as received in the State shall be treated as so received at the time when the money so loaned is actually received in or brought to the State.

(4) Where a person is indebted for money loaned to him or her, income applied by the person in such a way that the money or property representing the income is held by the lender on behalf of or to the account of the person in such circumstances as to be available to the lender for the purpose of satisfying or reducing the debt by set-off or otherwise shall be treated as applied by the person in or towards its satisfaction if, under any arrangement between the person and the lender, the amount for the time being of the person's indebtedness to the lender, or the time at which it is to be repaid in whole or in part, depends in any respect directly or indirectly on the amount or value so held by the lender.

(5) In relation to income applied in or towards satisfaction of a debt for money loaned on or after the 20th day of February, 1997, or a debt incurred for satisfying in whole or in part any such debt, this section shall apply as if the references to ordinarily resident in the State in subsections (2) and (3) were references to resident or ordinarily resident in the State.

Cross-references

Capital gains tax, this section applied by: s 29(5).
Transfer of assets abroad, liability of non-transferors: s 807A(5).

Definitions

person: IA 1937 s 11(*c*).

Former enactments

FA 1971 s 4(1)–(4) and (6); FA 1997 s 15.

Corresponding UK tax provision

Income and Corporation Taxes Act 1988 s 65(6).

73 Income from certain possessions in Great Britain or Northern Ireland

(1) In this section, **"rents"** includes any payment in the nature of a royalty and any annual or periodical payment in the nature of a rent derived from any lands, tenements or hereditaments, including lands, tenements and hereditaments to which section 56 would apply or would have applied if such lands, tenements and hereditaments were situate in the State.

(2) In respect of property situate and profits or gains arising in Great Britain or Northern Ireland—

(*a*) sections 70 and 71 shall apply as if section 71(2) were deleted, and

(*b*) subsection (3) shall apply for the purposes of Case III of Schedule D, notwithstanding anything to the contrary in section 70 or 71.

(3) (*a*) Income tax in respect of income arising from possessions in Great Britain or Northern Ireland, other than stocks, shares, rents or the occupation of land, shall be computed either—

(i) on the full amount of such income arising in the year of assessment, or

(ii) on the full amount of such income on an average of such period as the case may require and as may be directed by the Appeal Commissioners,

so that according to the nature of the income the tax may be computed on the same basis as that on which it would have been computed if the income had arisen in the State, and subject in either case to a deduction on account of any annuity or other annual payment (apart from annual interest) payable out of the income to a person not resident in the State, and the provisions of the Income Tax Acts (including those relating to the delivery of statements) shall apply accordingly.

(*b*) The person chargeable and assessable in accordance with paragraph (*a*) shall be entitled to the same allowances, deductions and reliefs as if the income had arisen in the State.

Cross-references

Residence of individuals, deduction for income earned outside the State: s 823(2)(*b*)(ii).
UK double taxation agreement: s 832(2), (3).

Definitions

Appeal Commissioners: s 2(1); Great Britain: IA 1937 Sch; land: IA 1937 Sch; person: IA 1937 s 11(*c*); year of assessment: s 3(1).

Former enactments

ITA 1967 Sch 6 Pt III para 1; F(MP)A 1968 s 3(2) and Sch Pt I; FA 1969 s 21; FA 1990 s 17(1)(*b*); FA 1997 s 146(1) and Sch 9 Pt I para 1(36).

Corresponding UK tax provision

Income and Corporation Taxes Act 1988 s 68.

74 Case IV: basis of assessment

(1) Income tax under Case IV of Schedule D shall be computed either on the full amount of the profits or gains arising in the year of assessment or according to the average of such a period, not being greater than one year, as the case may require and as may be directed by the inspector.

(2) The nature of the profits or gains chargeable to income tax under Case IV of Schedule D, and the basis on which the amount of such profits or gains has been computed, including the average, if any, taken on such profits or gains, shall be stated to the inspector.

(3) Every such statement and computation shall be made to the best of the knowledge and belief of the person in receipt of or entitled to the profits or gains.

Revenue precedents

Issue: The taxpayer won the grand prize in a U.S. state lottery and under the U.S. tax code the winnings were treated as income. The winnings were to be paid to the taxpayer in 20 annual payments. How would these payments be treated if the taxpayer became resident here?

Decision: On the basis of the information provided it appears that the taxpayer is receiving a series of income payments which would be liable to Income Tax here.

Statement of practice

Currency and/or interest swap agreements, irregular receipts chargeable under this section: SP CT/1/91.

Definitions

person: IA 1937 s 11(*c*); year of assessment: s 3(1).

Former enactments

ITA 1967 s 79; FA 1996 s 132(1) and Sch 5 Pt I para 1(2).

Corresponding UK tax provision

Income and Corporation Taxes Act 1988 s 65.

75 Case V: basis of assessment

(1) Without prejudice to any other provision of the Income Tax Acts, the profits or gains arising from—

(*a*) any rent in respect of any premises, and

(*b*) any receipts in respect of any easement,

shall, subject to and in accordance with the provisions of the Income Tax Acts, be deemed for the purposes of those Acts to be annual profits or gains within Schedule D, and the person entitled to such profits or gains shall be chargeable in respect of such profits or gains under Case V of that Schedule; but such rent or such receipts shall not include any payments to which section 104 applies.

(2) Profits or gains chargeable under Case V of Schedule D shall, for the purposes of ascertaining liability to income tax, be deemed to issue from a single source, and subsection (3) shall apply accordingly.

(3) Tax under Case V of Schedule D shall be computed on the full amount of the profits or gains arising within the year of assessment.

(4) Neither this section nor section 97 or 384 shall apply to a case in which the rent reserved under a lease (including, in the case of a lease granted on or after the 6th day of April, 1963, the duration of which does not exceed 50 years, an appropriate sum in respect of any premium payable under the lease) is insufficient, taking one year with another, to defray the cost to the lessor of fulfilling such lessor's obligations under the lease and of meeting any expense of maintenance, repairs, insurance and management of the premises subject to the lease which falls to be borne by such lessor.

(5) Section 96 shall apply for the interpretation of this section as it applies for the interpretation of Chapter 8 of this Part.

Cross-references

Capital gains tax, exclusion of premiums taxed under Sch D Case V: Sch 14 para 6(5).
Premiums treated as rent: s 98(1).
Pre-letting expenditure, no deduction: s 105(1).
Transactions in land, Schedule D Case I, subs (1)(*b*): s 641(2)(*e*).
Woodlands: s 232(2).

Revenue information

Information Leaflet IT70 — A Revenue Guide to Rental Income.

Revenue precedents

Issue: How is the leasing of milk quota taxed?
Decision: The milk quota is treated as attaching to the land. Income from leasing of the quota would be assessable under the rules of Case V of Schedule D, ie on the profits arising in the year of assessment, and not on the profits received. If the agreement provides that the full amount of the payment in respect of the lease will arise (ie become payable) in the first year, then it will be taxed in that year. If the agreement provides that the amount will become payable over each of the five years, then it will be taxed accordingly.
Issue: Whether rent paid as an up-front lump sum is taxable in year of receipt.
Decision: On the basis that the upfront payment represents a single payment of rent, it is taxable in the year in which it is received. A trader making such a payment would be required to spread it in accordance with the matching principle in preparing accounts.

Statement of practice

Accountancy fees are an allowable deduction: ***Tax Briefing 25***, February 1997.

Former enactments

ITA 1967 s 81(1)–(3)(*a*) and s 86; FA 1969 s 22, s 33(1) and Sch 4 Pt I and s 65(1) and Sch 5 Pt I; FA 1990 s 18(1)(*a*).

Corresponding UK tax provision

Income and Corporation Taxes Act 1988 s 65.

CHAPTER 5

Computational Provisions: Corporation Tax

76 Computation of income: application of income tax principles

(1) Except where otherwise provided by the Tax Acts, the amount of any income shall for the purposes of corporation tax be computed in accordance with income tax principles, all questions as to the amounts which are or are not to be taken into account

as income, or in computing income, or charged to tax as a person's income, or as to the time when any such amount is to be treated as arising, being determined in accordance with income tax law and practice as if accounting periods were years of assessment.

(2) For the purposes of this section, **"income tax law"**, in relation to any accounting period, means the law applying to the charge on individuals of income tax for the year of assessment in which that accounting period ends, but does not include such of the enactments of the Income Tax Acts so applying as make special provision for individuals in relation to matters referred to in subsection (1).

(3) Accordingly, for the purposes of corporation tax, income shall be computed and the assessment shall be made under the like Schedules and Cases as apply for the purposes of income tax, and in accordance with the provisions applicable to those Schedules and Cases, but (subject to the Corporation Tax Acts) the amounts so computed for several sources of income, if more than one, together with any amounts to be included in respect of chargeable gains, shall be aggregated to arrive at the total profits.

(4) Nothing in this section shall be taken to mean that income arising in any period is to be computed by reference to any other period (except in so far as this results from apportioning to different parts of a period income of the whole period).

(5) Subject to section 77 and to any enactment applied by this section which expressly authorises such a deduction, no deduction shall be made for the purposes of the Corporation Tax Acts in computing income from any source—

(*a*) in respect of dividends or other distributions, or

(*b*) in respect of any yearly interest, annuity or other annual payment or any other payments mentioned in section 104 or 237(2), but not including sums which are, or but for any exemption would be, chargeable under Case V of Schedule D.

(6) Without prejudice to the generality of subsection (1), any provision of the Income Tax Acts, or of any other statute, which confers an exemption from income tax, provides for the disregarding of a loss, or provides for a person to be charged to income tax on any amount (whether expressed to be income or not, and whether an actual amount or not), shall, except where otherwise provided, have the like effect for the purposes of corporation tax.

(7) This section shall not have effect so as to apply for the purposes of corporation tax anything in section 71.

(8) Where by virtue of this section or otherwise any enactment applies both to income tax and to corporation tax—

(*a*) that enactment shall not be affected in its operation by the fact that income tax and corporation tax are distinct taxes but, in so far as is consistent with the Corporation Tax Acts, shall apply in relation to income tax and corporation tax as if they were one tax, so that, in particular, a matter which in a case involving 2 individuals is relevant for both of them in relation to income tax shall in a like case involving an individual and a company be relevant for such individual in relation to income tax and for such company in relation to corporation tax, and (*b*) for that purpose, references in any such enactment to a relief from or charge to income tax or to a specified provision of the Income Tax Acts shall, in the absence of or subject to any express adaptation, be construed as being or including a reference to any corresponding relief from or charge to corporation tax or to any corresponding provision of the Corporation Tax Acts.

Cross-references

Corporation tax, treatment of tax free income of non resident banks, insurance businesses etc: s 845(3).

Deposit interest retention tax, repayment of tax (subs (6)): s 267(2)(*b*).

Investment undertakings, gain arising on a chargeable event, subs (6): s 739D(6)(*f*)(i)(II).

Life assurance companies, general annuity business: s 716(4)(*b*)(ii).

Life assurance companies, pension business, subs (5): s 717(6).

Life assurance companies, policyholders — new basis, gains arising on a chargeable event, subs (6): s 730D(2)(*b*)(iii)(II); declarations, subs (6): s 730E(3)(*e*)(iii)(II).

Patent income distributions (subs (6)) exempt from income tax: s 141(1).

Use of term "income tax": s 2(3).

Definitions

chargeable gain: ss 5(1), 545; company: ss 4(1), 5(1); Corporation Tax Acts: s 1(2); distribution: ss 4(1), 436, 437; Income Tax Acts: s 1(2); interest: s 4(1); person: IA 1937 s 11(*c*); profits: s 4(1); statute: s 2(1), IA 1937 s 3; year of assessment: ss 2(1), 5(1).

Former enactments

CTA 1976 s 11(1), (2)(*b*), (3)–(8); FA 1996 s 132(2) and Sch 5 Pt II.

Corresponding UK tax provision

Income and Corporation Taxes Act 1988 s 70.

76A Computation of profits or gains of a company — accounting standards

(1) For the purposes of Case I or II of Schedule D the profits or gains of a trade or profession carried on by a company shall be computed in accordance with generally accepted accounting practice subject to any adjustment required or authorised by law in computing such profits or gains for those purposes.

(2) Schedule 17A shall apply to a company where—

(*a*) for an accounting period profits or gains of a trade or profession carried on by the company are computed in accordance with relevant accounting standards (within the meaning of that Schedule), and

(*b*) for preceding accounting periods profits or gains of a trade or profession carried on by the company are computed in accordance with standards other than relevant accounting standards (within the meaning of that Schedule).

Amendments

[1] Section 76A inserted by FA 2005 s 48(1)(*b*) as respects any period of account beginning on or after 1 January 2005.

Cross-references

Treatment of unrealised gains and losses in certain cases: s 76B(1).

Definitions

accounting period: s 27; company: ss 4(1), 5(1); generally accepted accounting practice: s 4(1); profession: s 2(1); profits: s 4(1); trade: ss 3(1), 4(1).

76B Treatment of unrealised gains and losses in certain circumstances

(1) (*a*) In this section and paragraph 4 of Schedule 17A, **"fair value"**, **"financial asset"** and **"financial liability"** have the meanings assigned to them by international accounting standards.

(*b*) For the purposes of this section, section 76A and paragraph 4 of Schedule 17A—

(i) references to profits or gains include references to losses, and

(ii) the amount of a loss incurred in a trade or profession in an accounting period shall be computed in like manner as profits or gains from the trade or profession in the accounting period would have been computed.

(2) A profit or gain from a financial asset or a financial liability of a company that, in accordance with relevant accounting standards (within the meaning of Schedule 17A), is—

(*a*) calculated on the basis of fair values of the asset or the liability in an accounting period, and

(*b*) included in the profit or loss of the company for the accounting period,

shall be taken into account on that basis in computing profits or gains of the company for that accounting period for the purposes of Case I or II of Schedule D.

Amendments

1 Section 76B inserted by FA 2005 s 48(1)(*b*) as respects any period of account beginning on or after 1 January 2005.

Definitions

accounting period: s 27; company: ss 4(1), 5(1); international accounting standards: s 4(1); profession: s 2(1); profits: s 4(1); trade: ss 3(1); 4(1).

76C Use of different accounting policies within a group of companies

(1) (*a*) In this section **"tax advantage"** means—

(i) a reduction, avoidance or deferral of any charge or assessment to tax, including any potential or prospective charge or assessment, or

(ii) a refund of or a payment of an amount of tax, or an increase in an amount of tax refundable or otherwise payable to a person, including any potential or prospective amount so refundable or payable.

(*b*) For the purposes of this section, a series of transactions is not prevented from being a series of transactions in relation to companies by reason only of the fact that one or more of the following is the case—

(i) there is no transaction in the series to which both those companies are parties;

(ii) that parties to any arrangement in pursuance of which the transactions in the series are entered into do not include one or both of those companies;

(iii) there are one or more transactions in the series to which neither of those companies is a party.

(2) Where—

(*a*) a company within the charge to tax under Case I or II of Schedule D prepares accounts in accordance with international accounting standards, (*b*) another company within the charge to tax under Case I or II of Schedule D, being a company which is an associated company (within the meaning of section 432) of the company referred to in paragraph (*a*), prepares accounts in accordance with Irish generally accepted accounting practice,

(*c*) there is a transaction between, or a series of transactions involving, those companies, and

(*d*) a tax advantage would, apart from this section, accrue to the company which prepares its accounts in accordance with international accounting standards compared with its position if it had prepared its accounts in accordance with Irish generally accepted accounting practice in relation to the transaction or series of transactions,

then the Corporation Tax Acts shall apply for the purposes of computing profits or gains of that company from that transaction or series of transactions as if that company prepared its accounts in accordance with Irish generally accepted accounting practice.][1]

Amendments

1 Section 76C inserted by FA 2005 s 48(1)(*b*) as respects any period of account beginning on or after 1 January 2005.

Definitions

company: ss 4(1), 5(1); Corporation Tax Acts: s 1(2); international accounting standards: s 4(1); Irish generally accepted accounting practice: s 4(1); person: IA 1937 s 11(*c*); profits: s 4(1).

---

77 Miscellaneous special rules for computation of income

(1) For the purposes of corporation tax, income tax law as applied by section 76 shall apply subject to subsections (2) to (7).

(2) (*a*) Where a company begins or ceases to carry on a trade, or to be within the charge to corporation tax in respect of a trade, the company's income shall be computed as if that were the commencement or, as the case may be, discontinuance of the trade, whether or not the trade is in fact commenced or discontinued.

(*b*) Notwithstanding paragraph (*a*), where any provision of the Income Tax Acts is applied for corporation tax by the Corporation Tax Acts, this subsection shall not apply for any purpose of that provision if under any enactment a trade is not to be treated as permanently discontinued for the corresponding income tax purpose.

(3) In computing income from a trade, section 76(5)(*b*) shall not prevent the deduction of yearly interest.

(4) In computing a company's income for any accounting period from the letting of rights to work minerals in the State, there may be deducted any sums disbursed by the company wholly, exclusively and necessarily as expenses of management or supervision of those minerals in that period; but any enactments restricting the relief from income tax that might be given under section 111 shall apply to restrict in the like manner the deductions that may be made under this subsection.

(5) Where a company is chargeable to corporation tax in respect of a trade under Case III of Schedule D, the income from the trade shall be computed in accordance with the provisions applicable to Case I of Schedule D.

(6) The amount of any income arising from securities and possessions in any place outside the State shall be treated as reduced (where such a deduction cannot be made under, and is not forbidden by, any provision of the Income Tax Acts applied by the Corporation Tax Acts) by any sum paid in respect of income tax in the place where the income has arisen.

(7) Paragraphs (*e*) and (*f*) of Case III of Schedule D in section 18(2) shall for the purposes of corporation tax extend to companies not resident in the State, in so far as those companies are chargeable to tax on income of descriptions which, in the case of companies resident in the State, are within those paragraphs (but without prejudice to any provision of the Income Tax Acts specially exempting non-residents from income tax on any particular description of income).

Cross-references

Corporation tax, computation of income, application of income tax principles: s 76(5).
Overseas life assurance companies, income tax, foreign tax and tax credit, subs (6): s 729(1).
Offshore funds, Irish equivalent profits, subs (6): Sch 19 para 5(4)(*c*).

Definitions

company: ss 4(1), 5(1); Income Tax Acts: s 1(2); interest: s 4(1); minerals: s 5(1); trade: ss 3(1), 4(1), 5(1); within the charge to (tax): s 2(1).

Former enactments

CTA 1976 s 12(1)–(7).

78 Computation of companies' chargeable gains

(1) Subject to this section, the amount to be included in respect of chargeable gains in a company's total profits for any accounting period shall be determined in accordance with subsection (3) after taking into account subsection (2).

(2) Where for an accounting period chargeable gains accrue to a company, an amount of capital gains tax shall be calculated as if, notwithstanding any provision to the contrary in the Corporation Tax Acts, capital gains tax were to be charged on the company in respect of those gains in accordance with the Capital Gains Tax Acts, and as if accounting periods were years of assessment; but, in calculating the amount of capital gains tax, section 31 shall apply as if the reference in that section to deducting allowable losses were a reference to deducting relevant allowable losses.

(3) (*a*) The amount referred to in subsection (1) shall be an amount which, if (before making any deduction from the amount) it were charged to corporation tax as profits of the company arising in the accounting period at the rate specified in section 21(1), would produce an amount of corporation tax equal to the amount of capital gains tax calculated for that accounting period in accordance with subsection (2).

(*b*) For the purposes of paragraph (*a*), where part of the accounting period falls in one financial year (in this paragraph referred to as the **"first-mentioned financial year"**) and the other part falls in the financial year succeeding the first-mentioned financial year and different rates are in force under section

21(1) for each of those years, **"the rate specified in section 21(1)"** shall be deemed to be a rate per cent determined by the formula—

$$\frac{(A \times C)}{E} + \frac{(B \times D)}{E}$$

where—

A is the rate per cent in force for the first-mentioned financial year,

B is the rate per cent in force for the financial year succeeding the first-mentioned financial year,

C is the length of that part of the accounting period falling in the first-mentioned financial year,

D is the length of that part of the accounting period falling in the financial year succeeding the first-mentioned financial year, and

E is the length of the accounting period.

(*c*) Paragraph (*b*) shall apply as respects accounting periods ending on or after the 1st day of April, 1997, as if—

(i) the period beginning on the 1st day of January, 1996, and ending on the 31st day of March, 1997, and

(ii) the period beginning on the 1st day of April, 1997, and ending on the [31st day of December, 1997],[1]

were each a financial year.

(4) In subsection (2)—

"chargeable gains" does not include chargeable gains accruing on relevant disposals within the meaning of section 648;

"relevant allowable losses" means any allowable losses accruing to the company in the accounting period and any allowable losses previously accruing to the company while it has been within the charge to corporation tax in so far as they have not been allowed as a deduction from chargeable gains accruing in any previous accounting period.

(5) Except where otherwise provided by the Corporation Tax Acts, chargeable gains and allowable losses shall for the purposes of corporation tax be computed in accordance with the principles applying for capital gains tax, all questions as to the amounts which are or are not to be taken into account as chargeable gains or as allowable losses, or in computing gains or losses, or charged to tax as a person's gain, or as to the time when any such amount is to be treated as accruing, being determined in accordance with the provisions relating to capital gains tax as if accounting periods were years of assessment.

(6) Subject to subsection (8), where the enactments relating to capital gains tax contain any reference to income tax or to the Income Tax Acts, the reference shall, in relation to a company, be construed as a reference to corporation tax or to the Corporation Tax Acts; but—

(*a*) this subsection shall not affect the references to income tax in section 554(2), and (*b*) in so far as those enactments operate by reference to matters of any specified description, for corporation tax account shall be taken of matters of that description which are confined to companies, but not of any such matters which are confined to individuals.

(7) The Capital Gains Tax Acts as extended by this section shall not be affected in their operation by the fact that capital gains tax and corporation tax are distinct taxes but, in so far as is consistent with the Corporation Tax Acts, shall apply in relation to capital gains tax and corporation tax on chargeable gains as if they were one tax, so that, in particular, a matter which in a case involving 2 individuals is relevant for both of them in relation to capital gains tax shall in a like case involving an individual and a company be relevant for such individual in relation to capital gains tax and for such company in relation to corporation tax.

(8) Where assets of a company are vested in a liquidator, this section and the enactments applied by this section shall apply as if the assets were vested in, and the acts of the liquidator in relation to the assets were the acts of, the company (acquisitions from or disposals to the liquidator by the company being disregarded accordingly).

Amendments

1 Substituted by FA 1998 s 55(2) and Sch 6 para 2 with effect from 6 April 1998; previously "31st day of December, 1998".

Cross-references

Bank levy credit subs (3)(*b*): 487(1)(*a*).
Development land disposals, subss (2), (4): s 653(2).
Disposals by liquidators and other persons: s 571(3)(*b*), (6).
EU Council Directive 90/434/EEC, transfer of development land, subs (4): s 633.
Life assurance companies, benefits from life policies issued before 6 April 1974: s 722(2).
Life assurance companies, chargeable gains, subs (2): s 711(1)(*c*).
Overseas life assurance companies, investment income, subs (1): s 726(6)(*b*).
Restriction on set-off of pre-entry losses: Sch 18A para 3(1), (2).
Shipping tonnage tax, chargeable gains: s 697N(4); subs (2): s 697N(4).
Undertakings for collective investment, subs (2): s 738(2)(*c*); taxation of unit holders: s 739(4)(*a*)(ii).
Unit trusts, special arrangements for qualifying unit trusts, subs (1): s 732(5).

Definitions

allowable loss: s 4(1), 5(1), 546; chargeable gain s 4(1), 5(1), 545; company: s 4(1), Corporation Tax Acts: s 1(2); the financial year: s 4(1); Income Tax Acts: s 1(2); person: IA 1937 s 11(*c*); profits: s 4(1); within the charge to (tax): s 2(1).

Former enactments

CTA 1976 s 13(1)–(2) (3)(*a*)–(*c*), (4)–(5); CGT(A)A 1978 s 17 and Sch 2; FA 1982 s 31(1); FA 1988 Sch 3 Pt I para 1(*b*); FA 1997 s 59(2) and Sch 6 Pt I para 1.

79 Foreign currency: computation of income and chargeable gains

(1) (*a*) In this section—

"profit and loss account" means—

(i) in the case of a company (in this definition referred to as the **"resident company"**) resident in the State, the account of that company, and

(ii) in the case of a company (in this definition referred to as the **"non-resident company"**) not resident in the State but carrying on a trade in the

State through a branch or agency, the account of the business of the company carried on through or from such branch or agency,

which, in the opinion of the auditor appointed under section 160 of the Companies Act, 1963, or under the law of the State in which the resident company or non-resident company, as the case may be, is incorporated and which corresponds to that section, presents a true and fair view of the profit or loss of the resident company or the business of the non-resident company, as the case may be;

"rate of exchange" means a rate at which 2 currencies might reasonably be expected to be exchanged for each other by persons dealing at arm's length or, where the context so requires, an average of such rates;

"relevant contract", in relation to a company, means any contract entered into by the company for the purpose of eliminating or reducing the risk of loss being incurred by the company due to a change in the value of a relevant monetary item, being a change resulting directly from a change in a rate of exchange;

"relevant monetary item", in relation to a company, means money held or payable by the company for the purposes of a trade carried on by it;

"relevant tax contract", in relation to an accounting period of a company, means any contract entered into by the company for the purpose of eliminating or reducing the risk of loss being incurred by the company due to a change in the value of money payable in discharge of a liability of the company to corporation tax for the accounting period, being a change resulting directly from a change in a rate of exchange of the functional currency (within the meaning of section 402) of the company for the currency of the State.

(*b*) The treatment of a contract entered into by a company as a relevant contract for the purposes of this section shall be disregarded for any other purpose of the Tax Acts.

[(*c*) For the purposes of this section a gain or loss arising to a company which results directly from a change in a rate of exchange shall include a gain or loss which results directly from an event which substitutes for the currency of a State another currency of that State where the other currency, as a result of the event, becomes the functional currency (within the meaning of section 402) of the company.][1]

(2) Notwithstanding section 76, for the purposes of corporation tax, the amount of any gain or loss, whether realised or unrealised, which—

(*a*) is attributable to any relevant monetary item or relevant contract of a company,

(*b*) results directly from a change in a rate of exchange, and

(*c*) is properly credited or debited, as the case may be, to the profit and loss account of the company,

shall be taken into account in computing the trading income of the company.

(3) (*a*) Notwithstanding section 78, for the purposes of corporation tax, where any gain or loss arises to a company in respect of—

(i) a relevant contract of the company, or

(ii) money held by the company for the purposes of a trade carried on by it,

so much of that gain or loss as results directly from a change in a rate of exchange shall not be a chargeable gain or an allowable loss, as the case may be, of the company.

(*b*) This subsection shall not apply as respects any gain or loss arising to a company carrying on life business within the meaning of section 706(1), being a company which is not charged to corporation tax in respect of that business under Case I of Schedule D.

(4) Notwithstanding section 78, so much of the amount of any gain or loss arising to a company which carries on a trade in the State in an accounting period as—

(*a*) is attributable to any relevant tax contract in relation to the accounting period,

(*b*) results directly from a change in a rate of exchange, and

(*c*) (i) where it is a gain, does not exceed the amount of the loss which, if the company had not entered into the relevant tax contract, would have been incurred by the company, and

(ii) where it is a loss, does not exceed the amount of the gain which, if the company had not entered into the relevant tax contract, would have arisen to the company,

due to a change in the value of money payable in discharge of a liability of the company to corporation tax for the accounting period,

shall not be a chargeable gain or an allowable loss, as the case may be, of the company.

Amendments

1 Subs (1)(*c*) inserted by FA 1998 s 47 and Sch 2 para 1 with effect from such date as the Minister for Finance may appoint by order. Subs (1)(*c*) comes into operation from 31 December 1998 — Finance Act 1998 (Section 47) (Commencement) Order 1998, SI No 502 of 1998 refers.

Cross-references

Foreign currency, capital allowances and trading losses, "profit and loss account", "rate of exchange", meaning applied: s 402(1)(*a*).

Matching of relevant foreign currency assets with foreign currency liabilities, meaning of "rate of exchange" and "relevant monetary item" applied: s 79A(1).

Shipping tonnage tax, calculation of profits of tonnage tax company: s 697C(2); relevant shipping income, foreign currency gains: s 697J(1); treatment of finance costs: s 697LB(1) ("finance costs").

Tax Briefing

TB 31 Apr 1998 p 5 — The Euro and Tax: Exchange gains and losses in trading companies.

Definitions

branch or agency: ss 4(1), 5(1); company: ss 4(1), 5(1); person: IA 1937 s 11(*c*). profits: s 4(1); resident: s 5(1); tax: s 3(1); trade: ss 3(1), 4(1).

Former enactments

CTA 1976 s 12A; FA 1994 s 56(*a*); FA 1996 s 45(1).

79A Matching of relevant foreign currency assets with foreign currency liabilities

[(1) (*a*) In this section—

"foreign currency asset", in relation to a company, means an asset, not being a relevant monetary item (within the meaning of section 79), of the company the consideration for the acquisition of which consisted solely of an amount denominated in a currency other than the currency of the State;

"foreign currency liability", in relation to a company, means—

(i) a liability, not being a relevant monetary item (within the meaning of section 79), or

(ii) a sum subscribed for paid up share capital or contributed to the capital,

of the company which is denominated in a currency other than the currency of the State;

"rate of exchange" has the meaning assigned to it by section 79.

(*b*) For the purposes of this section—

(i) a foreign currency asset is a relevant foreign currency asset in relation to a company if it consists of shares in another company acquired by the company and immediately after the acquisition by the company of the shares in the other company—

(I) the company owns not less than 25 per cent of the share capital of the other company, and

(II) the other company is a trading company or a holding company of a trading company,

(ii) where at any time a company disposes of a relevant foreign currency asset which has been matched with a corresponding foreign currency liability and the company does not discharge the liability at that time, the company shall be deemed to discharge the liability, and to incur a new liability equal to the amount of the liability, at that time,

(iii) where in accordance with subsection (2) a company specifies that a relevant foreign currency asset acquired by it at any time is to be matched with a corresponding foreign currency liability incurred by it before that time, the company shall be deemed to discharge the foreign currency liability, and to incur a new liability equal to the amount of the liability, at that time, and

(iv) the amount of a gain or loss on the discharge of a foreign currency liability shall be the amount which would be the gain accruing to, or as the case may be the loss incurred by, the company on the disposal of an asset acquired by it at the time the liability was incurred and disposed of at the time at which the liability was discharged if—

(I) the amount given by the company to discharge the liability was the amount given by the company as consideration for the acquisition of the asset, and

(II) the amount of the liability incurred by the company was the consideration received by the company on the disposal of the asset.

(2) (*a*) A company may, by giving notice in writing to the inspector, specify that a relevant foreign currency asset denominated in a currency other than the currency of the State shall be matched with such corresponding foreign currency liability denominated in that currency as is specified by the company.

(*b*) A notice under paragraph (*a*) shall be given within 3 weeks after the acquisition by the company concerned of the relevant foreign currency asset.

(3) Where in an accounting period a company disposes of a relevant foreign currency asset which has been matched by the company under subsection (2) with a foreign currency liability of the company, any chargeable gain or allowable loss on the relevant foreign currency asset shall be computed for the purposes of capital gains tax as if the consideration received for the disposal of the asset—

(*a*) where the company incurs a loss on discharge of the liability which loss results directly from a change in a rate of exchange, was reduced by an amount equal to the amount of that loss, but the amount of any such reduction shall not exceed the amount of so much of any gain on the disposal of the asset as results directly from a change in a rate of exchange, and

(*b*) where the company realises a gain on discharge of the liability which gain results directly from a change in a rate of exchange, was increased by an amount equal to the amount of that gain, but the amount of any such increase shall not exceed the amount of so much of any loss incurred on the disposal of the asset which loss results directly from a change in a rate of exchange.][1]

Amendments

1 Section 79A inserted by FA 2003 s 37(1) as respects accounting periods ending on or after 6 February 2003.

Definitions

chargeable gain: s 5(1); company: ss 4(1), 5(1); inspector: ss 2(1), 5(1); shares: s 5(1); writing: IA 1937 Sch.

80 Taxation of certain foreign currencies

(1) In this section—

"relevant liability", in relation to an accounting period, means relevant principal—

(*a*) denominated in a currency other than the currency of the State, and

(*b*) the interest in respect of which—

(i) is to be treated as a distribution for the purposes of the Corporation Tax Acts, and

(ii) is computed on the basis of a rate which, at any time in that accounting period, exceeds 80 per cent of the specified rate at that time;

"relevant principal" means an amount of money advanced to a borrower by a company, the ordinary trading activities of which include the lending of money, where—

(*a*) the consideration given by the borrower for that amount is a security within subparagraph (ii), (iii)(I) or (v) of section 130(2)(*d*), and

(*b*) interest or any other distribution is paid out of the assets of the borrower in respect of that security;

"specified rate" means—

[(*a*) the rate known as the 3 month European Interbank Offered Rate, or][1]

(*b*) where such a record was not maintained, the rate known as the Interbank market 3 month fixed rate as published in the statistical appendices of the bulletins and annual reports of the Central Bank of Ireland.

(2) Notwithstanding any other provision of the Tax Acts or the Capital Gains Tax Acts, a profit or loss from any foreign exchange transaction, being a profit or loss which arises in an accounting period—

(*a*) in connection with relevant principal which, in relation to the accounting period, is a relevant liability, and

(*b*) to a company which, in relation to that relevant liability, is the borrower,

shall for the purposes of those Acts be deemed to be a profit or gain or a loss, as the case may be, of the trade carried on by the borrower in the course of which trade the relevant liability is used.

Amendments

1 Definition of "specified rate" para (*a*) substituted by FA 1998 s 47 and Sch 2 para 2 with effect from such date as the Minister for Finance may appoint by order; previously:

"(*a*) the rate known as the 3 month Dublin Interbank Offered Rate, a record of which is maintained by the Central Bank of Ireland, or".

The substitution comes into operation from 1 January 1999 — Finance Act 1998 (Section 47) (Commencement) Order 1998, SI No 502 of 1998, refers.

Cross-references

Manufacturing (10%) rate: s 443(18).

Definitions

company: ss 4(1), 5(1); distribution: ss 4(1), 436, 437; Tax Acts: s 1(2); trade: ss 3(1), 4(1).

Former enactments

FA 1993 s 47(1)–(2).

80A Taxation of certain short-term leases of plant and machinery

[(1) In this section—

"asset" means machinery or plant;

"fair value", in relation to a leased asset, means an amount equal to such consideration as might be expected to be paid for the asset at the inception of the lease on a sale negotiated on an arm's length basis, less any grants receivable by the lessor towards the purchase of the asset;

"inception of the lease" means the date on which the leased asset is brought into use by the lessee or the date from which lease payments under the lease first accrue, whichever is the earlier;

"lease payments" means the lease payments over the term of the lease to be paid to the lessor in relation to the leased asset, and includes any residual amount to be paid to the lessor at or after the end of the term of the lease and guaranteed by the lessee or by a person connected with the lessee or under the terms of any scheme or arrangement between the lessee and any other person;

"lessee" and **"lessor"** have the same meanings, respectively, as in section 403;

"normal accounting practice" means normal accounting practice in relation to the accounts of companies incorporated in the State.

"predictable useful life", in relation to an asset, means the useful life of the asset estimated at the inception of the lease, having regard to the purpose for which the asset was acquired and on the assumption that—

(*a*) its life will end when it ceases to be useful for the purpose for which it was acquired, and

(*b*) it will be used in the normal manner and to the normal extent throughout its life;

"relevant period" means the period—

(*a*) beginning at the inception of the lease, and

(*b*) ending at the earliest time at which the aggregate of amounts of the discounted present value at the inception of the lease of lease payments under the terms of the lease which are payable at or before that time amounts to 90 per cent or more of the fair value of the leased asset, and, for the purposes of this definition, relevant lease payments shall be discounted at a rate which, when applied at the inception of the lease to the amount of the relevant lease payments, produces discounted present values the aggregate of which equals the amount of the fair value of the leased asset at the inception of the lease;

"relevant short-term asset" in relation to a company means an asset—

(*a*) the predictable useful life of which does not exceed 8 years, and

(*b*) the expenditure on which is incurred by the company on or after the date referred to in subsection (3);

"relevant short-term lease" means a lease—

(*a*) of a relevant short-term asset, and

(*b*) the relevant period in relation to which does not exceed 8 years;

(2) Where a company makes a claim under this section—

(*a*) the amount to be included in the trading income of the company in respect of all relevant short-term leases is the amount of income from such leases computed in accordance with normal accounting practice,

(*b*) the company will not be entitled to any allowance in respect of expenditure incurred on assets which are the subject of relevant short-term leases under Part 9, section 670, Part 29 or any other provision of the Tax Acts relating to the making of allowances in accordance with Part 9, and

(*c*) the income from relevant short-term leases will be treated for the purposes of section 403 as if it were not income from a trade of leasing.

(3) A claim by a company under this section shall be made by the time by which a return under section 951 falls to be made for an accounting period of the company and shall apply as respects expenditure incurred on or after the date on which the accounting period begins.][1]

Amendments

1 Section 80A inserted by FA 2004 s 35(1) as respects accounting periods ending on or after 4 February 2004.

Tax Briefing

TB55 April 2004 pp 7–8 — Short term leases of plant and machinery.

Definitions

company: s 4(1); connected: s 10; person: IA 1937 s 11(*c*); year: IA 1937 Sch.

CHAPTER 6
Computational Provisions: General

81 General rule as to deductions

(1) The tax under Cases I and II of Schedule D shall be charged without any deduction other than is allowed by the Tax Acts.

(2) Subject to the Tax Acts, in computing the amount of the profits or gains to be charged to tax under Case I or II of Schedule D, no sum shall be deducted in respect of—

(*a*) any disbursement or expenses, not being money wholly and exclusively laid out or expended for the purposes of the trade or profession;

(*b*) any disbursements or expenses of maintenance of the parties, their families or establishments, or any sums expended for any other domestic or private purposes distinct from the purposes of such trade or profession;

(*c*) the rent of any dwelling house or domestic offices or any part of any dwelling house or domestic offices, except such part thereof as is used for the purposes of the trade or profession, and, where any such part is so used, the sum so deducted shall be such as may be determined by the inspector and shall not, unless in any particular case the inspector is of the opinion that having regard to all the circumstances some greater sum ought to be deducted, exceed two-thirds of the rent bona fide paid for that dwelling house or those domestic offices;

(*d*) any sum expended for repairs of premises occupied, or for the supply, repairs or alterations of any implements, utensils or articles employed, for the purposes of the trade or profession, over and above the sum actually expended for those purposes;

(*e*) any loss not connected with or arising out of the trade or profession;

(*f*) any capital withdrawn from, or any sum employed or intended to be employed as capital in, the trade or profession;

(*g*) any capital employed in improvements of premises occupied for the purposes of the trade or profession;

(*h*) any interest which might have been made if any such sums as aforesaid had been laid out at interest;

(*i*) any debts, except bad debts proved to be such to the satisfaction of the inspector and doubtful debts to the extent that they are respectively estimated to be bad and, in the case of the bankruptcy or insolvency of a debtor, the amount which may reasonably be expected to be received on any such debts shall be deemed to be the value of any such debts;

(*j*) any average loss over and above the actual amount of loss after adjustment;

(*k*) any sum recoverable under an insurance or contract of indemnity;

(*l*) any annuity or other annual payment (other than interest) payable out of the profits or gains;

(*m*) any royalty or other sum paid in respect of the user of a [patent;][1]

[(*n*) without prejudice to the preceding paragraphs any consideration given for goods or services, or to an employee or director of a company, which consists, directly or indirectly, of shares in the company, or a connected company (within the meaning of section 10), or a right to receive such shares, except to the extent—

(i) of expenditure incurred by the company on the acquisition of the shares at a price which does not exceed the price which would have been payable, if the shares were acquired by way of a bargain made at arm's length, or

(ii) where the shares are shares in a connected company, of any payment by the company to the connected company for the issue or transfer by that company of the shares, being a payment which does not exceed the amount which would have been payable in a transaction between independent persons acting at arm's length.][2]

[(3) (*a*) In respect of a company—

(i) interest payable by the company, and

(ii) expenditure on research and development incurred by the company,

shall not be prevented from being regarded for tax purposes as deductible in computing profits or gains of the company for the purposes of Case I or II of Schedule D by virtue only of the fact that for accounting purposes they are brought into account in determining the value of an asset.

(*b*) Any amount shall not be regarded by virtue of paragraph (*a*) as deductible in computing profits or gains of a company for the purposes of Case I or II of Schedule D for an accounting period to the extent that—

(i) a deduction has been made in respect of that amount in computing such profits or gains for a previous accounting period, or

(ii) the company has benefited from a tax relief under any provision in respect of that amount for a previous accounting period.][3]

Amendments

1 Substituted by FA 2005 s 48(1)(*c*)(i) as respects any period of account beginning on or after 1 January 2005; previously "patent.".

2 Subs (2)(*n*) inserted by FA 2005 s 48(1)(*c*)(i) as respects any period of account beginning on or after 1 January 2005.

3 Subs (3) inserted by FA 2005 s 48(1)(*c*)(ii) as respects any period of account beginning on or after 1 January 2005.

Cross-references

Patents, relief for expenses: s 758(1).

Certain rents and other payments, subs (2)(*m*): s 104(2)(*a*)(ii).

Implementation of Council Directive 2003/49/EC of 3 June 2003 on a common system of taxation applicable to interest and royalty payments made between associated companies of different Member States, application: s 267H(1)(*a*)(ii).

Restrictive covenants, business expense deduction subs (2): s 127(4).

Tonnage tax, treatment of finance costs: s 697LB(1) ("finance costs").

Trade marks, registration costs: s 86.

Case law

Case I: capital expenditure

Irish

A company which rebuilt premises had its claim that part of the expenditure should be considered as repair of the old premises and treated as a revenue disbursement rejected: *Curtin v M Ltd* ITR Vol II p 360.

Cost of fitting out temporary premises pending re-building of original premises destroyed by fire treated as capital: *Fitzgerald v Commissioners of Inland Revenue* ITR Vol I p 91.

Installation costs of sanitary facilities at the direction of a public health authority held to be capital expenditure: *Vale v Martin Mahony and Co Ltd* ITR Vol II p 32.

Legal costs incurred by a builder in defending an action under a construction contract not allowable as revenue expenditure: *Casey v AB Ltd* ITR Vol II p 500.

Loss arising on investments forming part of a statutory dividend equalisation fund of a company treated as referable to capital: *Alliance and Dublin Consumer Gas Co v Davis* ITR Vol I p 104.

A payment of a premium on a lease, even if paid in instalments, will constitute capital expenditure – *O'Sullivan v P Ltd* 2 ITR 464.

UK

Compensation payment made for loss of a construction contract held to be capital expenditure: *Countess Warwick Steamship Co Ltd v Ogg* [1924] 8 TC 652; *Watneys London Ltd v Pike* [1982] STC 733.

Cost of replacing a chimney which was a separate structure held to be capital expenditure: *O'Grady v Bullcroft Main Collieries Ltd* (1932) 17 TC 93; but where the chimney is part of the factory, the expenditure is revenue expenditure: *Samuel Jones & Co (Devondale) Ltd v IRC* (1956) 37 TC 69.

Expenditure on extensive repairs which was a condition of the lease, treated as a capital expenditure: *Jackson v Laskers Home Furnishers Ltd* (1956) 37 TC 69.

Expenditure on repairs to a ship held to be capital expenditure: *Law Shipping Co Ltd v IRC* (1923) 12 TC 621.

Expenditure on repairs to a spectator stand held to be capital expenditure: *Brown v Burnley Football & Athletic Club Co Ltd* [1980] STC 424.

Payment for release from an onerous contract held to be capital expenditure: *Whitehead v Tubbs (Elastics) Ltd* [1984] STC 1.

Payment of cash to business partner to enable him to carry on the business: *Stone & Temple v Waters* [1995] STC 1.

Expenditure incurred on the insertion of polyethylene pipes into existing old leaking cast iron pipes held to constitute an improvement over the old system and capital in nature – *Auckland Gas Company v CIR* [2000] STC 527.

Case I: deductible expenditure

Irish

Payment by company to get rid of a director to preserve the good name of the company held wholly and exclusively incurred for company's trade: *Noble v Mitchell* (1927) 11 TC 372.

Compensation and legal costs paid to tenants adjoining a new factory for loss of rights held to be allowable revenue expenditure: *Davis v X Ltd* ITR Vol II p 45.

Expenses of promoting a parliamentary bill allowed as revenue expenditure to a statutory undertaking: *McGarry v Limerick Gas Committee* ITR Vol I p 375.

Expenses of removing the top soil of a quarry regarded as revenue expenditure: *Milverton Quarries Ltd v Revenue Commissioners* ITR Vol II p 382.

Instalment payments for the supply of technical information treated as capital: *S Ltd v O'Sullivan* ITR Vol II p 602.

Lump sum payments and improvement grants made to petrol retailers by a main distributor in return for exclusive dealing in the company's product held by Supreme Court to be revenue expenditure: *Dolan v AB Company Ltd* ITR Vol II p 515.

Replacement of plant and fixtures with different specifications but which did not contain any element of improvement allowed in full as revenue expenditure: *Hodgkins v Plunder and Pollack (Ireland) Ltd* ITR Vol III p 267.

Interest paid on loan taken out to redeem preference shares was held to be paid out wholly and exclusively for the purpsoe of the company's trade (Canadian case of *Trans Prairie Pipe Lines Limited v Minister of National Revenue* 70 DTC 6351, cited): Supreme Court *Mac Aonghusa v Ringmahon Company.*

Loss on foreign currency transactions: *Brosnan v Mutual Enterprise Ltd* [1995] 2 ILRM 304.

Interest on a loan taken out to redeem the preference share capital of the taxpayer company was deductible in calculating the taxpayers profits – *MacAonghusa (IOT) v Ringmahon* 2001 ITR 117.

UK

Bad debt created through choosing to offset receipt against loan account instead of trading account: *Sycamore plc and Maple Ltd v Fir* [1996] STI 51.

Estimated anticipated liabilities under warranties unexpired at the end of the accounting period in which vehicles sold held deductible: *CIR v Mitsubishi Motors New Zealand Ltd* [1995] STC 989.

Advance payment on a five-year agreement held to be revenue expenditure: *Bolam v Regent Oil Co Ltd* (1956) 37 TC 56; *Lawson v Johnson Matthey plc* [1992] STC 466.

Campaign expenses incurred to prevent nationalisation of taxpayer's trade held fully deductible: *Morgan v Tate & Lyle Ltd* (1954) 35 TC 367.

Expenditure on repairs to a factory chimney held to be revenue expenditure: *Samuel Jones & Co (Devondale) Ltd v IRC* (1951) 32 TC 513.

Expenses incurred by a brick-layer in travelling from home to building sites held fully deductible: *Horton v Young* (1971) 47 TC 60.

Legal expenses incurred in defending company's title to land held to be revenue expenditure: *Southern v Borax Consolidated Ltd* (1940) 23 TC 597.

Payment to terminate an onerous agency agreement held to be revenue expenditure: *Anglo-Persian Oil Ltd v Dale* (1931) 16 TC 253.

Repairs to a cinema held to be revenue expenditure: *Odeon Associated Theatres Ltd v Jones* (1971) 48 TC 257.

Payment made to preserve the goodwill of a business: *Lawson v Johnson Matthey plc* [1992] STC 466.

Payment to be released from onerous fee agreement: *Vodafone Cellular Ltd v Shaw* [1997] STC 734.

Stockbrokers' fines for breaching stock exchange regulations: *McKnight v Sheppard* [1997] STC 846.

Sum expended to buy back shares of dissident shareholders and to alter the charter of the company held to be revenue expenditure: *Commissioners of Inland Revenue v Carron* 45 TC 18.

A gas supplier's expenditure on polyethylene inserted into pipes otherwise at risk of fracture was revenue in nature. The process did not enhance the capacity or longevity of the pipeline system – *Transco Plc v Dyall (IOT)* [2002] STC (SCD) 199 (Sp Comm).

Case I: non-deductible expenditure

Irish

A reorganisation of company shares resulting in a reduced holding for all shareholders not regarded by the Supreme Court as a loss on realisation of investments giving rise to a deduction against profits of a bank: *Davis v Hibernian Bank* 2 ITC 111.

Currency devaluation loss arising on amounts credited to but not transferred to a foreign resident company not to be allowed as revenue expenditure against the profits of the Irish permanent establishment: *Revenue Commissioners v L and Co* 3 ITC 205.

Expenses relating to the formation of a "holding company" not allowable as a deduction against trading profits: *Kealy v O'Mara Ltd* ITR Vol I p 642.

UK

Bad debt arising when company lent money to another held not incurred for the purpose of the trade: *English Crown Spelter Co Ltd v Baker* (1908) 5 TC 327.

Compensation paid to a guest injured at the taxpayer's licensed premised held not deductible: *Strong and Co of Romsey Ltd v Woodifield* (1906) 5 TC 215.

Cost of barrister's clothing for court appearances held not deductible: *Mallalieu v Drummond* [1981] STC 391.

Cost of living accommodation above public house: *McLaren v Mumford* [1996] STC 1134.

Hospital expenses not allowed although taxpayer conducted his business from his hospital bed: *Murgatroyd v Evans Jackson* (1966) 43 TC 581.

Legal expenses incurred in a dispute between partners held not deductible: *C Connelly & Co v Wilbey* [1992] STC 783.

Legal fees incurred in appealing tax assessment disallowed: *Allen v Farquharson Brothers & Co* (1932) 17 TC 59; *Smith's Potato Estates Ltd v Bolland* (1948) 30 TC 267.

Lunch expenses of a self-employed carpenter not allowed: *Caillebotte v Quinn* [1975] STC 265.

Food and accommodation expenses: *Prior v Saunders* [1993] STC 562.

Notional costs held not deductible: *Rolfe v Wimpey Waste Management Ltd* [1988] STC 329.

Partner's removal expenses paid by the firm not allowed: *MacKinlay v Arthur Young McClelland Moore & Co* [1989] STC 898.

Portion of directors' salaries considered excessive held not deductible: *Boarland v Kramat Pulai Ltd* (1953) 35 TC 1.

Revenue precedents

Issue: Whether interest which qualifies as a deduction for a trading company under this section may be allowed even where it is capitalised in the accounts.

Decision: Yes.

Issue: Whether a deduction due in respect of a provision for a loss on a court case.

Decision: In principle there is no statutory rule against charging a provision for a liability which has not materialised at the accounts date, provided such a provision will result in the accounts providing a true and fair view of the profits of the period and the amount of the provision can be estimated with reasonable accuracy. Where the claim includes a claim for a return of fees already earned, this aspect should be dealt with in the same manner as the rest of the claim.

Issue: Are registration fees/licence renewal fees which are required by law to be paid by a trader or professional deductible?
Decision: Yes. Provided they are laid out wholly and exclusively for the purposes of the trade.
Issue: Is a trader, who offers a "free gift" to a customer who purchases certain items, entitled to a deduction for the cost of the "free gift" or is the cost disallowed under s 840? eg a trader starts a sales promotion whereby the purchaser of a washing machine will receive a radio to the value of €20.
Decision: It appears that in these circumstances the contract between the customer and the trader involves both the washing machine and the radio. In effect the radio is not a "free gift" and as such would not come within the provisions of s 840. It is the Revenue view that the cost of each radio is allowable in computing the profits of the trade.
Issue: Are legal fees incurred in connection with the ownership of a business property deductible in arriving at trading profits?
Decision: The allowability of legal expenditure will depend on whether it is attributable to Revenue or Capital. This matter has been considered in a number of tax cases and the main findings appear to be that legal expenses incurred in acquiring a capital asset are treated as capital expenditure, yet expenditure incurred in protecting the title to a capital asset, when it has been acquired, may be deductible revenue expenditure. The case of *Southern v Borax Consolidated Ltd* 23 TC 597 is relevant.
Issue: Whether professional penalty fees incurred in connection with a tax appeal are deductible.
Decision: Such fees are not deductible. Normal recurring professional fees incurred in preparing accounts or agreeing liabilities are allowable.
Issue: Whether interest on a loan to finance the payment of income tax is allowable.
Decision: Such interest is not allowable. It is not wholly and exclusively laid out for the purposes of the trade.
Issue. Whether, in a trade or profession, interest paid on borrowings used to fund drawings is allowable.
Decision: Where a capital account is in a debit position and the debit balance arises from an excess of drawings over profits available to fund those drawings, the interest portion of the bank borrowings used to fund the deficit is not allowable.
Issue: Refunds of a percentage of fees paid by self employed practitioners to the Medical Protection Society are made by Health Boards. Tax relief on the gross fees is estimated by the boards when they are calculating the refunds. Do these refunds have to be taken into account when preparing accounts and on what amounts is tax relief due to the practitioners?
Decision: Refunds of fees received must be taken into account. As a result tax relief will be due on the net amount paid in each case ie the gross payment made less the actual refund received.
Issue: Can a partnership claim a deduction for rent paid in respect of a premises which is owned by the individual partners in the firm?
Decision: No. It appears that the lease involved between the partnership and the partners has no legal standing. The case of *Rye v Rye* 1962 A.C. 496 is relevant.
Issue: Is the superlevy penalty collected by Co-ops from farmers for exceeding their milk quota allowed as a charge against farming profits?
Decision: It is accepted that payments by farmers under the European Communities (Milk Levy) Regulations, 1985 are an expense of the trade.
Issue: Amateur sportsmen in receipt of payments from media.
Decision: Payments are chargeable to tax and should be included in returns.
Issue: Whether insurance premiums and insurance claims paid by a compensation fund which is a trade protection association are allowable as deductions against income of the fund.
Decision: Both insurance premiums and insurance claims are allowable deductions.
Issue: Whether unbilled disbursements on behalf of clients can be deducted in the period in which paid.
Decision: Where there are unbilled disbursements, there is no known liability in the majority of cases. The presumption is that the disbursement will be billed to the client on whose behalf it was incurred. In so far as it cannot be so billed or the client refuses to pay it the amount can be written off at that stage.
Issue: Treatment of tapes owned by a video library.
Decision: In the circumstances of a particular case, it was agreed that tapes could be treated as trading stock.

Revenue information

Information leaflet IT52 — Taxation Treatment of Finance Leases.

Statement of practice

Currency and/or interest swap agreements, regular receipts directly relating to allowable interest of a trade are part of trading income and corresponding payments are deductible revenue expenses: SP CT/1/91.

Tax Briefing

TB11 July 1993 para 1.4 — Allowability of Keyman Insurance Premia.

TB29 Dec 1997 p 7 — Tax treatment of subscriptions to Trade and Professional Associations.

TB31 Apr 1998 p 7 — Euro/Year 2000 Changeover Costs.

TB31 Apr 1998 p 13 Interest paid under Prompt Payment of Accounts Act, 1997 regarded as a trade expense which is tax deductible in computing the profits of the person making the payment.

TB31 Apr 1998 p 16 — Allowable food and subsistence expenses of self-employed individuals.

Definitions

accounting period: s 27; company: s 3(1); inspector: ss 2(1), 5(1), 852; person: IA 1937 s 11(*c*); profession: s 2(1); profits: s 4(1); profits or gains: s 3(4); Tax Acts: s 1(2); trade: s 3(1).

Former enactments

ITA 1967 s 57 and s 61; FA 1969 s 65(1) and Sch 5 Pt I; FA 1974 s 42(1); FA 1997 s 146(1) and Sch 9 Pt I para 1(3).

Corresponding UK tax provision

Income and Corporation Taxes Act 1988 s 74.

81A Restriction of deductions for employee benefit contributions

[(1) (*a*) In this section—

"accident benefit scheme" means an employee benefit scheme under which benefits may be provided only by reason of a person's disablement, or death, caused by an accident occurring during the person's service as an employee of the employer;

"chargeable period" has the same meaning as in section 321;

"employee benefit scheme" means a trust, scheme or other arrangement for the benefit of persons who are employees of an employer;

"qualifying expenses", in relation to a third party and an employee benefit scheme, does not include expenses that, if incurred by the employer, would not be allowed as a deduction in calculating the profits or gains of the employer to be charged to tax under Case I or II of Schedule D but, subject to the foregoing, includes any expenses of the third party (apart from the provision of benefits to employees of the employer) incurred in the operation of the employee benefit scheme.

(*b*) For the purposes of this section—

(i) an employer makes an employee benefit contribution if—

(I) the employer pays money or transfers an asset to another person (referred to in this section as the **"third party"**), and

(II) the third party is entitled or required, under the provisions of an employee benefit scheme, to retain or use the money or asset for or in connection with the provision of benefits to employees of the employer,

(ii) qualifying benefits are provided where there is a payment of money or a transfer of assets, otherwise than by way of a loan, and the recipient or a person other than the recipient is or would, if resident, ordinarily resident and domiciled in the State, be chargeable to income tax in respect of the provision of such benefits, and

(iii) a reference to a person's employee includes a reference to the holder of an office under that person.

(2) (*a*) This section applies where—

(i) a calculation is made of the amount of a person's profits or gains to be charged to tax under Case I or II of Schedule D for a chargeable period beginning on or after 3 February 2005, and

(ii) a deduction would, but for this section, be allowed by the Tax Acts for that period in respect of employee benefit contributions made, or to be made, by that person (referred to in this section as the "employer").

(*b*) Notwithstanding paragraph (*a*), this section does not apply in respect of a deduction referred to in subsection (7).

(3) (*a*) A deduction in respect of employee benefit contributions referred to in subsection (2)(*a*) shall be allowed only to the extent that, during the chargeable period in question or within 9 months from the end of it—

(i) qualifying benefits are provided out of the contributions, or

(ii) qualifying expenses are paid out of the contributions.

(*b*) (i) For the purposes of paragraph (*a*), any qualifying benefits provided or qualifying expenses paid by the third party after the receipt by the third party of employee benefit contributions shall be regarded as being provided or paid out of those contributions, up to the total amount of the contributions as reduced by the amount of any benefits or expenses previously provided or paid as referred to in paragraph (*a*).

(ii) In the application of this paragraph, no account shall be taken of any other amount received or paid by the third party.

(4) (*a*) An amount which is disallowed under subsection (3) shall be allowed as a deduction for a subsequent chargeable period to the extent that qualifying benefits are provided out of the employee benefit contributions in question before the end of that subsequent chargeable period.

(*b*) (i) For the purposes of paragraph (*a*), any qualifying benefits provided by the third party after the receipt by the third party of employee benefit contributions shall be regarded as being provided out of those contributions, up to the total amount of the contributions as reduced by the amount of any benefits or expenses previously provided or paid as referred to in subsection (3)(*a*) or paragraph (*a*) of this subsection.

(ii) In the application of this paragraph, no account shall be taken of any other amount received or paid by the third party.

(5) (*a*) This subsection applies where the provision of a qualifying benefit takes the form of the transfer of an asset.

(*b*) The amount provided shall be taken for the purposes of this section to be the total of—

(i) (I) the amount, if any, expended on the asset by the third party, or

(II) where the asset consists of new shares in the third party, or rights in respect of such shares, issued by the third party, the market value of those shares or rights, as the case may be, at the time of the transfer, and

(ii) in a case in which the asset was transferred to the third party by the employer, the amount of the deduction that would be allowed as referred to in subsection (2) in respect of the transfer.

(*c*) Where the amount calculated in accordance with paragraph (*b*) is greater than the amount (referred to in this paragraph as the "second-mentioned amount") in respect of which an employee is chargeable to income tax in respect of the transfer, the deduction to be allowed in accordance with subsection (3) or (4) shall not exceed the second-mentioned amount.

(6) In any case where the calculation referred to in subsection (2)(*a*) is made before the end of the 9 month period mentioned in subsection (3)—

(*a*) for the purposes of making the calculation, subsection (3) shall be construed as if the reference to that 9 month period were a reference to the period ending at the time when the calculation is made, and

(*b*) after the end of the 9 month period the calculation shall if necessary be adjusted to take account of any benefits provided, expenses paid or contributions made within that period but after the time of the calculation.

(7) This section does not apply in relation to any deduction that is allowable—

(*a*) in respect of anything given as consideration for goods or services provided in the course of a trade or profession,

(*b*) in respect of contributions under an accident benefit scheme,

(*c*) under Part 17, or

(*d*) under Part 30.][1].

Amendments

1 Section 81A inserted by FA 2005 s 17 with effect from 3 February 2005.

Definitions

month: IA 1937 Sch; person: IA 1937: s 11(*c*); profession: s 2(1); profits or gains: s 3(4); Tax Acts: s 1(2); trade: ss 3(1), 4(1).

82 Pre-trading expenditure

(1) This section shall apply to expenditure incurred for the purposes of a trade or profession set up and commenced on or after the 22nd day of January, 1997.

(2) Subject to subsection (3), where a person incurs expenditure for the purposes of a trade or profession before the time that the trade or profession has been set up and commenced by that person, and such expenditure—

(*a*) is incurred not more than 3 years before that time, and

(*b*) is apart from this section not allowable as a deduction for the purpose of computing the profits or gains of the trade or profession for the purposes of Case I or II of Schedule D, but would have been so allowable if it had been incurred after that time,

then, the expenditure shall be treated for that purpose as having been incurred at that time.

(3) The amount of any expenditure to be treated under [subsection (2)][1] as incurred at the time that a trade or profession has been set up and commenced shall not be so treated for the purposes of section 381, 396(2), 420, 455(3) or 456.

(4) An allowance or deduction shall not be made under any provision of the Tax Acts other than this section in respect of any expenditure or payment treated under this section as incurred on the day on which a trade or profession is set up and commenced.

Amendments

1 Substituted by FA 1998 s 136 and Sch 9 para 1 with effect from 6 April 1997; previously "subsection (1)".

Tax Briefing

TB27 Aug 1997 p 1 — Relief for pre-trading expenses.

Former enactments

FA 1997 s 29(1) and (4)–(6).

Corresponding UK tax provision

Income and Corporation Taxes Act 1988 s 401.

83 Expenses of management of investment companies

(1) For the purposes of this section and of the other provisions of the Corporation Tax Acts relating to expenses of management, **"investment company"** means any company whose business consists wholly or mainly of the making of investments, and the principal part of whose income is derived from the making of investments, but includes any savings bank or other bank for savings.

(2) In computing for the purposes of corporation tax the total profits for any accounting period of an investment company resident in the State—

(*a*) there shall be deducted any sums disbursed as expenses of management (including commissions) for that period, except any such expenses as are deductible in computing income for the purposes of Case V of Schedule D; but

(*b*) there shall be deducted from the amount treated as expenses of management the amount of any income derived from sources not charged to tax, other than franked investment income.

(3) Where in any accounting period of an investment company the expenses of management deductible under subsection (2), together with any charges on income paid in the accounting period wholly and exclusively for the purposes of the company's business, exceed the amount of the profits from which they are deductible, the excess shall be carried forward to the succeeding accounting period, and the amount so carried forward shall be treated for the purposes of this section ...,[1] including any further application of this subsection, as if it had been disbursed as expenses of management for that accounting period.

(4) For the purposes of subsections (2) and (3), there shall be added to a company's expenses of management in any accounting period the amount of any allowances to be made to the company for that period by virtue of section 109 or 774.

...[2]

Amendments

1 Deleted by FA 2003 s 41(1)(*a*)(i) as respects accounting periods ending on or after 6 February 2003; previously "(other than subsection (5))".

2 Subss (5) and (6) deleted by FA 2003 s 41(1)(*a*)(ii) as respects accounting periods ending on or after 6 February 2003.

Cross-references

Approved pension schemes, exemptions and reliefs: s 774(6)(*b*).
Approved share option schemes: s 519D(6)(*b*), (*c*).
Business entertainment expenses: s 840(2)(*b*).
Cars, limit on renewals allowance: s 375(*c*); restriction of deduction in respect of running expenses: s 376(1).

Close company surcharges, estate and investment income, meaning, subs (2): s 434(5)(*a*)(II).
Corporation tax, relief for trading losses other than terminal losses: s 396(5)(*b*).
Cost of establishing profit sharing schemes: s 518(2)(*b*).
Cost of establishing savings-related share option schemes: s 519B(2)(*b*), (2A)(*b*).
Employee share ownership trusts: s 519(2).
Franked investment income, set off of losses (subs (5)): s 157(5)(*a*).
Group relief, losses that may be surrendered: s 420(3), (5), (7).
Life assurance companies, acquisition expenses, subs (3): s 708(4)(*a*).
Life assurance companies, chargeable gains: s 711(1)(*d*).
Life assurance companies, management expenses deduction: s 707(1)(*b*); subs (2): s 707(2)(*b*); subs (3): s 707(2)(*c*).
Life assurance companies, profits of life business, subs (3): s 710(5)(*b*)(i).
Offshore funds, commodity income: Sch 19 para 4(3)(*b*).
Personal Retirement Savings Accounts (PRSAs), allowance to employer: s 787J(2).
Profit sharing schemes, payments to trustees: s 517(1)(*b*), (3)(*b*)(ii).
Redundancy payments, deduction: s 109(3).
Restrictive covenants, management expense deduction: s 127(5).
Tonnage tax, transactions between associated persons and between tonnage tax trade and other activities of same company, subs (3): s 697LA(1) ("losses").

Case law

Irish

An estate company not an "investment company": *Howth Estate Co v Davis* ITR Vol I p 447; *Casey v Monteagle Estate Co* ITR Vol II 429.
Expenses incurred in research and evaluating potential investments held not management expenses: *Hibernian Insurance Company Ltd v MacUimis* ITR Vol V p 495.

UK

Provision of housing at a reduced profit held to be "making an investment": *Cook v Medway* [1997] STC 90.
Management expenses held not to include expenses related to properties held as investments: *London & Northern Estates Co Ltd v Harris* (1937) 21 TC 197; *Southern v Aldwych Property Trust Ltd* (1940) 23 TC 707.
Brokerage and stamp duty expenses of an insurance company held not management expenses: *Sun Life Assurance Society v Davidson* (1957) 37 TC 330; *Hoechst Finance Ltd v Gumbrell* [1983] STC 150.
Directors fees related to management duties held deductible: *Berry (LG) Investments Ltd v Attwooll* (1961) 41 TC 547.
Excessive service charges held not deductible: *Fragmap Developments Ltd v Cooper* (1967) 44 TC 366.
Johnson v The Prudential Assurance Co Ltd (1988) STC 439.

Definitions

Appeal Commissioners: s 2(1); charges on income: ss 4(1), 243(1); company: ss 4(1), 5(1); franked investment income: ss 4(1), 156; High Court: IA 1937 Sch; Income Tax Acts: s 1(2); inspector: ss 2(1), 5(1), 852; interest: s 4(1); profits: s 4(1); tax credit: ss 2(1), 136; writing: IA 1937 Sch.

Former enactments

CTA 1976 s 15.

Corresponding UK tax provision

Income and Corporation Taxes Act 1988 s 75.

---

84 Expenses in relation to establishment or alteration of superannuation schemes

Where a superannuation scheme is established in connection with a trade or undertaking or a superannuation scheme so established is altered, and the person by whom the trade or undertaking is carried on makes a payment in respect of expenses (including a payment in respect of professional fees, but not including a payment by means of contribution towards the cost of providing the benefits payable under the scheme) in connection with such establishment or alteration, then, if the scheme or, as the case may be, the altered scheme is approved by the Revenue Commissioners under section 772, the amount of the payment shall be allowed to be deducted in the computation, for the purposes of assessment to tax, of the profits or gains of the trade or undertaking as an expense incurred when the payment is made.

Definitions

person: IA 1937 s 11(*c*); trade: s 3(1).

Former enactments

ITA 1967 s 63; FA 1972 s 13(4) and Sch 1 Pt III para 1, s 46(2) and Sch 4 Pt II.

85 Deduction for certain industrial premises

(1) In this section, **"premises"** means an industrial building or structure within the meaning of section 268 which is not a building or structure to which section 272 applies.

(2) In estimating the amount of annual profits or gains arising or accruing from any trade the profits of which are chargeable to tax under Case I of Schedule D, there shall be allowed to be deducted, as expenses incurred in any year on account of any premises owned by the person carrying on that trade and occupied by such person for the purposes of that trade, a deduction equal to five-twelfths of the rateable valuation of those premises.

(3) In estimating the profits for any year of any of the concerns which by virtue of section 18(2) are charged under Case I(*b*) of Schedule D, there shall be allowed to be deducted, as expenses incurred in any year on account of any premises owned by the person carrying on the concern and occupied by such person for the purposes of that concern, a deduction equal to five-twelfths of the rateable valuation of those premises.

(4) (*a*) Where, in the case of property valued under the Valuation Acts as a unit, a part is and a part is not premises, the rateable valuation of each part shall be arrived at by apportionment of the rateable valuation of the property.

(*b*) Any apportionment required by this subsection shall be made by the inspector according to the best of his or her knowledge and judgment.

(*c*) An apportionment made under paragraph (*b*) may be amended by the Appeal Commissioners or by the Circuit Court on the hearing or the rehearing of an appeal against an assessment made on the basis of the apportionment; but, on the hearing or the rehearing of any such appeal, a certificate of the Commissioner of Valuation tendered by either party to the appeal and stating, as regards property valued under the Valuation Acts as a unit, the amount of the rateable valuation of the property attributable to any part of the property shall be evidence of the amount so attributable.

Cross-references

Capital expenditure on scientific research: s 765(4).

Mine development allowance: s 670(8).

Definitions

Appeal Commissioners: s 2(1); Circuit Court: IA 1937 Sch; inspector: ss 2(1), 5(1), 852; rateable valuation: IA 1937 Sch: IA 1937 Sch; person: IA 1937 s 11(*c*); trade: s 3(1); Valuation Acts: IA 1937 Sch.

Former enactments

ITA 1967 s 67(1)–(3A); FA 1969 s 31.

86 Cost of registration of trade marks

Notwithstanding anything in section 81, in computing the amount of the profits or gains of any trade, there shall be allowed to be deducted as expenses any fees paid or expenses incurred in obtaining for the purposes of the trade the registration of a trade mark or the renewal of registration of a trade mark.

Definitions

trade: s 3(1).

Former enactments

FA 1971 s 5.

87 Debts set off against profits and subsequently released

(1) Where, in computing for tax purposes the profits or gains of a trade or profession, a deduction has been allowed for any debt incurred for the purposes of the trade or profession, then, if the whole or any part of that debt is thereafter released, the amount released shall be treated as a receipt of the trade or profession arising in the period in which the release is effected.

(2) If in any case referred to in subsection (1) the trade or profession has been permanently discontinued at or after the end of the period for which the deduction was allowed and before the release was effected, or is treated for tax purposes as if it had been so discontinued, section 91 shall apply as if the amount released were a sum received after the discontinuance.

Definitions

profession: s 2(1); trade: s 3(1).

Former enactments

FA 1970 s 24(1)–(2)(*a*).

Corresponding UK tax provision

Income and Corporation Taxes Act 1988 s 94.

87A Deductions for gifts to Foundation for Investing in Communities

Amendments

[1] Section 87A (which was inserted by FA 2001 s 84(1)–(2) with effect from 1 August 2000) deleted by FA 2001 s 84(3) with effect from 6 April 2001.

88 Deduction for gifts to Enterprise Trust Ltd

Amendments

Section 88 repealed by TCA 1997 s 848A(13) (inserted by FA 2001 s 45) with effect from 6 April 2001.

88A Double deduction in respect of certain emoluments

[(1) In this section—

"chargeable period" has the same meaning as in section 321(2);

"emoluments", **"employment"**, **"employment scheme"**, **"qualifying employment"**, and **"qualifying individual"** have the same meanings, respectively, as in section 472A;

"qualifying period", in relation to a qualifying employment, means the period of 36 months beginning on the date when that employment commences.

(2) (*a*) Where in the computation of the amount of the profits or gains of a trade or profession for a chargeable period, a person is, apart from this section, entitled to a deduction (in this subsection referred to as **"the first-mentioned deduction"**) on account of—

(i) emoluments payable to a qualifying individual in respect of a qualifying employment, and

(ii) the employer's contribution to the Social Insurance Fund payable, in respect of those emoluments, under the Social Welfare Acts,

that person shall be entitled in that computation to a further deduction (in this subsection referred to as **"the second-mentioned deduction"**) equal to the amount of the first-mentioned deduction as respects that qualifying employment.

(*b*) Relief under this section, in respect of a qualifying employment, shall not be granted—

(i) in respect of a second-mentioned deduction which relates to a chargeable period or part of a chargeable period outside the qualifying period in relation to such qualifying employment, or

(ii) if the claimant or the qualifying individual is benefiting, or has benefited, under an employment scheme, whether statutory or otherwise.

(*c*) For the purposes of this section, an activity, programme or course mentioned in section 472A(1)(*b*)(i) shall be deemed not to be an employment scheme.][1]

Amendments

1 Section 88A inserted by FA 1998 s 16(*a*) with effect from 6 April 1998.

Revenue information

Information leaflet IT59 — Revenue Job Assist Information for Employers.

Definitions

person: IA 1937 s 11(*c*); profession: s 2(1); trade: ss 3(1), 4(1), 5(1).

CHAPTER 7

Special Measures on Discontinuance Of, and Change of Basis of Computation of Profits or Gains Of, a Trade or Profession

89 Valuation of trading stock at discontinuance of trade

(1) (*a*) In this section, **"trading stock"** means, subject to paragraph (*b*), property of any description, whether real or personal, which is either—

(i) property such as is sold in the ordinary course of the trade in relation to which the expression is used or would be so sold if it were mature or if its manufacture, preparation or construction were complete, or

(ii) materials such as are used in the manufacture, preparation or construction of property such as is sold in the ordinary course of that trade.

[(*b*) For the purposes of this section—

(i) **"trading stock"**, in relation to a trade, includes any services, article or material which, if the trade were a profession, would be treated as work in progress of the profession for the purposes of section 90, and references to the sale or transfer of trading stock shall be construed accordingly;

(ii) two persons are connected with each other if—

(*a*) they are connected with each other within the meaning of section 10;

(*b*) one of them is a partnership and the other has a right to a share in the partnership;

(*c*) one of them is a body corporate and the other has control over that body;

(*d*) both of them are partnerships and some other person has a right to a share in each of them; or

(*e*) both of them are bodies corporate or one of them is a partnership and the other is a body corporate and, in either case, some other person has control over both of them;

and in this subparagraph the references to a right to a share in a partnership are references to a share of the assets or income of the partnership and control has the meaning given by section 11.][1]

(*c*) References in this section to a trade having been discontinued or to the discontinuance of a trade shall be construed as not referring to or including any case where such trade was carried on by a single individual and is discontinued by reason of such individual's death (whether such trade is or is not continued by another person after such death), but shall be construed as referring to and including every other case where a trade has been discontinued or is, by virtue of any of the provisions of the Tax Acts, treated as having been discontinued for the purpose of computing tax.

(2) In computing the profits or gains of a trade which has been discontinued, any trading stock belonging to the trade at the discontinuance of the trade shall be valued in accordance with the following provisions:

(*a*) in the case of any such trading stock—

(i) which is sold, or is transferred for valuable consideration, to a person who carries on or intends to carry on a trade in the State, and

(ii) the cost of which to such person on such sale or transfer may be deducted by such person as an expense in computing for any purpose of the Tax Acts the profits or gains of the trade carried on or intended to be carried on by such person,

the value of such trading stock shall be taken to be [the amount determined in accordance with subsections (3) and (4)][2];

(*b*) in the case of any other such trading stock, the value of such other trading stock shall be taken to be the amount which it would have realised if it had been sold in the open market at the discontinuance of the trade.

[(3) Subject to subsection (4), paragraph 2(2) of Schedule 16 and paragraph 4(2) of Schedule 17, the value of any trading stock falling to be valued under subsection (2)(*a*) shall be taken—

(*a*) except where the person to whom it is sold or transferred is connected with the person who makes the sale or transfer, to be the amount (in this subsection and subsection (4) referred to as **"the price actually received for it"**) realised on the sale or, as the case may be, which is in fact the value of the consideration given for the transfer, and

(*b*) if those persons are connected with each other, to be what would have been the price actually received for it had the sale or transfer been a transaction between independent persons dealing at arm's length.

(4) If—

(*a*) trading stock is sold or transferred to a person in circumstances where subsection (3)(*b*) would, apart from this subsection, apply for determining the value of stock so sold or transferred,

(*b*) the amount which would be taken in accordance with subsection (3)(*b*) to be the value of the stock sold or transferred to that person is more than the acquisition value of that stock and also more than the price actually received for it, and

(*c*) the person by whom the stock is sold or transferred includes in a return required to be delivered under section 951 for the chargeable period in which the trade is discontinued an election signed by both parties to the sale or transfer that this subsection shall apply,

then the stock so sold or transferred shall be taken to have a value equal to whichever is the greater (taking all the stock so sold or transferred together) of its acquisition value and the price actually received for it or, in a case where they are the same, to either of them.

(5) In subsection (4) **"acquisition value"**, in relation to any trading stock, means the amount which, in computing for any tax purposes the profits or gains of the discontinued trade, would have been deductible as representing the purchase price of that stock if—

(*a*) the stock had, immediately before the discontinuance, been sold in the course of the trade for a price equal to whatever would be its value in accordance with subsection (3)(*b*), and

(*b*) the period for which those profits or gains were to be computed began immediately before the sale.

(6) Where any trading stock falls to be valued under subsection (2)(*a*), the amount determined in accordance with subsections (3) and (4) to be the amount to be brought into account as the value of that stock in computing profits or gains of the discontinued trade shall also be taken, for the purpose of making any deduction in computing the profits or gains of any trade carried on by the purchaser, to be the cost of that stock to the purchaser.][3]

Amendments

1 Subs (1)(*b*) substituted by FA 2001 s 42(1)(*a*) with effect from 6 December 2000.

2 Substituted by FA 2001 s 42(1)(*b*) with effect from 6 December 2000; previously "the price paid for such trading stock on such sale or the value of the consideration given for such trading stock on such transfer, as the case may be".

3 Subs (3)–(6) inserted by FA 2001 s 42(1)(*c*) with effect from 6 December 2000.

Cross-references

Building societies, change in status, financial assets: Sch 16 para 2(2).
Companies' chargeable gains, reconstruction or amalgamation, meaning of "trading stock" applied: s 615(1).
Farming stock relief, meaning of "trading stock" applied: s 665.
Farming, trading stock of discontinued trade, subs (2)(*b*): s 656(2)(*a*).
Reorganisation into companies of Trustee Savings Banks, financial assets: Sch 17 para 4(1), (2).
Transactions in land, meaning of "trading stock" applied: s 639(1).

Case law

Where trading stock was withdrawn from the trade (and appropriated to personal use), the figure to be credited in the accounts was the market value of the trading stock at the time of withdrawal – *Sharkey v Wernher* 36 TC 275.
Reed v Nova Securities Ltd (1985) STC 124.

Revenue precedents

Issue: Does a transfer of stock at a grossly inflated price come within the provisions of s 89(2)(*a*)?
Decision: No. In order for a transaction to come within this provision the purchaser must be entitled to deduct the cost in computing his/her trading profits. Where the value at which stock is transferred does not come within the realms of being a bona fide transaction the purchaser would not be entitled to a deduction for such cost.
Issue: Does natural love and affection constitute "valuable consideration" for the purposes of this section?
Decision: No.

Definitions

person: IA 1937 s 11(*c*); profits or gains: s 3(1); trade: ss 3(1), 4(1).

Former enactments

ITA 1967 s 62(1)(apart from proviso) and (2); FA 1970 s 23(4).

Corresponding UK tax provision

Income and Corporation Taxes Act 1988 s 100.

90 Valuation of work in progress at discontinuance of profession

(1) Where, in computing for any of the purposes of the Tax Acts the profits or gains of a profession which has been discontinued, a valuation is taken of the work of the profession in progress at the discontinuance, that work shall be valued as follows:

(*a*) if the work is transferred for money or any other valuable consideration to a person who carries on or intends to carry on a profession in the State, and the cost of the work may be deducted by that person as an expense in computing for any such purpose the profits or gains of that profession, the value of the work shall be taken to be the amount paid or other consideration given for the transfer;

(*b*) if the work is not to be valued under paragraph (*a*), its value shall be taken to be the amount which would have been paid for a transfer of the work on the date of the discontinuance as between parties at arm's length.

(2) Where a profession is discontinued and the person by whom it was carried on immediately before the discontinuance so elects, by notice in writing sent to the inspector at any time within 24 months after the discontinuance, the amount, if any, by which the value of the work in progress at the discontinuance (as ascertained under

subsection (1)) exceeds the actual cost of the work shall not be taken into account in computing the profits or gains of the period immediately before the discontinuance, but the amount by which any sums received for the transfer of the work exceed the actual cost of the work shall be included in the sums chargeable to tax under section 91 as if it were a sum to which that section applies received after the discontinuance.

(3) Subsections (1) and (2) shall apply where a profession is treated for any of the purposes of the Tax Acts as permanently discontinued as they apply in the case of an actual discontinuance, but shall not apply in a case where a profession carried on by a single individual is discontinued by reason of such individual's death.

(4) References in this section to work in progress at the discontinuance of a profession shall be construed as references to—

(*a*) any services performed in the ordinary course of the profession, the performance of which was wholly or partly completed at the time of the discontinuance and for which it would be reasonable to expect that a charge would have been made on their completion if the profession had not been discontinued, and

(*b*) any article produced, and any such material as is used, in the performance of any such services,

and references in this section to the transfer of work in progress shall include references to the transfer of any benefits and rights which accrue, or might reasonably be expected to accrue, from the carrying out of the work.

Cross-references

"Trading stock" at discontinuance of trade includes work in progress: s 89(1)(*b*).

Definitions

Income Tax Acts: s 1(2); inspector: ss 2(1), 5(1), 852; month: IA 1937 Sch; person: IA 1937 s 11(*c*); profession: s 2(1); trade: s 3(1); writing: IA 1937 Sch.

Former enactments

FA 1970 s 23(1)–(3) and (5); FA 1981 s 9(*d*).

Corresponding UK tax provision

Income and Corporation Taxes Act 1988 s 101.

91 Receipts accruing after discontinuance of trade or profession

(1) Subject to subsection (2), this section shall apply to all sums arising from the carrying on of a trade or profession during any period before the discontinuance of the trade or profession (not being sums otherwise chargeable to tax), in so far as the amount or value of the sums was not taken into account in computing the profits or gains for any period before the discontinuance, and whether or not the profits or gains for the period were computed on an earnings basis or on a conventional basis.

(2) This section shall not apply to any of the following sums—

(*a*) sums received by a person beneficially entitled to such sums who is not resident in the State, or by a person acting on such person's behalf, which represent income arising directly or indirectly from a country or territory outside the State, (*b*) a lump sum paid to the personal representatives of the author of a literary, dramatic, musical or artistic work as a consideration for the assignment by them, wholly or partially, of the copyright in the work,

(*c*) sums realised by the transfer of trading stock belonging to a trade at the discontinuance of the trade or, in a case in which the profits or gains of a profession were computed on an earnings basis at the discontinuance of the profession, sums realised by the transfer of the work of the profession in progress at the discontinuance, and

(*d*) sums arising to an individual from a work which is such that any profits or gains that might have arisen to the individual from its publication, production or sale, as the case might be, would in accordance with section 195(3) have been disregarded for the purposes of the Income Tax Acts if they had arisen before the discontinuance of that individual's profession.

(3) Where any trade or profession, the profits or gains of which are chargeable to tax under Case I or II of Schedule D, has been permanently discontinued, tax shall be charged under Case IV of that Schedule in respect of any sums to which this section applies received after the discontinuance subject to any such deduction as is authorised by subsection (4).

(4) In computing the charge to tax in respect of sums received by any person which are chargeable to tax by virtue of this section (including amounts treated as sums received by such person by virtue of section 87), there shall be deducted from the amount which apart from this subsection would be chargeable to tax—

(*a*) any loss, expense or debit (not being a loss, expense or debit arising directly or indirectly from the discontinuance itself) which, if the trade or profession had not been discontinued, would have been deducted in computing for tax purposes the profits or gains of the person by whom the trade or profession was carried on before the discontinuance, or would have been deducted from or set off against those profits or gains as so computed, and

(*b*) any capital allowance to which the person who carried on the trade or profession was entitled immediately before the discontinuance and to which effect has not been given by means of relief before the discontinuance.

(5) For the purposes of this Chapter—

(*a*) the profits or gains of a trade or profession in any period shall be treated as computed by reference to earnings where all credits and liabilities accruing during that period as a consequence of the carrying on of the trade or profession are taken into account in computing those profits or gains for tax purposes, and not otherwise, and **"earnings basis"** shall be construed accordingly,

(*b*) the profits or gains of a trade or profession in any period shall be treated as computed on a conventional basis where they are computed otherwise than by reference to earnings, and

(*c*) the value of any sum received in payment of a debt shall be treated as not taken into account in the computation to the extent that a deduction has been allowed in respect of that sum under section 81(2)(i).

Definitions

Income Tax Acts: s 1(2); person: IA 1937 s 11(*c*); profession: s 2(1); trade: s 3(1).

Former enactments

FA 1970 s 20(1)–(4)–(5)(*b*)–(*d*); FA 1975 s 33(2) and Sch 1 Pt II.

Corresponding UK tax provision

Income and Corporation Taxes Act 1988 s 103.

92 Receipts and losses accruing after change treated as discontinuance

(1) This section shall apply in any case where, as a result of a change in the persons engaged in carrying on a trade or profession, the trade or profession is treated for any of the purposes of the Tax Acts as if it had been permanently discontinued and a new trade or profession set up and commenced.

(2) (*a*) Sections 91 and 95 shall apply in the case of any such change as if the trade or profession had been permanently discontinued.

(*b*) Notwithstanding paragraph (*a*), where the right to receive any sums to which section 91 applies is or was transferred at the time of the change to the persons carrying on the trade or profession after the change, tax shall not be charged by virtue of that section, but any sums received by those persons by virtue of the transfer shall be treated for all purposes as receipts to be taken into the computation of profits or gains of the trade or profession in the period in which they are received.

(3) In computing for tax purposes the profits or gains of the trade or profession in any period after the change, there may be deducted a sum equal to any amount proved during that period to be irrecoverable in respect of any debts credited in computing for tax purposes the profits or gains for any period before the change (being debts the benefit of which was assigned to the persons carrying on the trade or profession after the change), in so far as the total amount proved to be irrecoverable in respect of those debts exceeds any deduction allowed in respect of them under section 81(2)(i) in a computation for any period before the change.

Definitions

Income Tax Acts: s 1(2); person: IA 1937 s 11(*c*); profession: s 2(1); trade: s 3(1).

Former enactments

FA 1970 s 22.

Corresponding UK tax provision

Income and Corporation Taxes Act 1988 s 104.

93 Cash basis, etc: relief for certain individuals

(1) In this section—

"the net amount" with which a person is chargeable to tax under section 91 means the amount with which such person is so chargeable after making any deduction authorised by section 91(4) but before giving any relief under this section;

"relevant date" means—

(*a*) in relation to tax under section 91, the date of the permanent discontinuance, and

(*b*) in relation to tax under section 94, the date of the change of basis.

(2) Where an individual born before the 6th day of April, 1919, or the personal representative of such an individual, is chargeable to tax under section 91 or 94 and—

(*a*) the individual was engaged in carrying on the trade or profession on the 4th day of August, 1970, and

(*b*) the profits or gains of the trade or profession were not computed by reference to earnings in the period in which the date specified in paragraph (*a*) fell, or in any subsequent period ending before or on the relevant date,

the net amount with which such individual is so chargeable to tax shall be reduced by multiplying that net amount by the fraction specified in subsection (4).

(3) Where section 94 applies in relation to a change of basis taking place on a date before the 4th day of August, 1970, then, in relation to tax chargeable by reference to that change of basis, subsection (2) shall apply as if—

(*a*) that earlier date were substituted for the date specified in paragraph (*a*) of that subsection, and

(*b*) paragraph (*b*) of that subsection were deleted.

(4) The fraction referred to in subsection (2) is—

(*a*) where on the 6th day of April, 1970, the individual had not attained the age of 52 years, nineteen-twentieths,

(*b*) where on that date the individual had attained the age of 52 years, but had not attained the age of 53 years, eighteen-twentieths, and so on, reducing the fraction by one-twentieth for each year the individual had attained, up to the age of 64 years,

(*c*) where on that date the individual had attained the age of 65 years or any greater age, five-twentieths.

Definitions

person: IA 1937 s 11(*c*); profession: s 2(1); trade: s 3(1).

Former enactments

FA 1970 s 25.

94 Conventional basis: general charge on receipts after change of basis

(1) Where in the case of any trade or profession the profits or gains of which are chargeable to tax under Case I or II of Schedule D there has been—

(*a*) a change from a conventional basis to the earnings basis, or

(*b*) a change of conventional basis which may result in receipts dropping out of computation,

tax shall be charged under Case IV of Schedule D in respect of sums to which this subsection applies which are received after the change and before the trade or profession is permanently discontinued.

(2) Subsection (1) shall apply to all sums arising from the carrying on of the trade or profession during any period before the change (not being sums otherwise chargeable to

tax) in so far as their amount or value was not taken into account in computing the profits or gains for any period.

(3) Where in the case of any profession the profits or gains of which are chargeable to tax under Case II of Schedule D—

(*a*) there has been a change from a conventional basis to the earnings basis, or a change of conventional basis, and

(*b*) the value of work in progress at the time of the change was debited in the accounts and allowed as a deduction in computing profits for tax purposes for a period after the change,

then, in so far as no counterbalancing credit was taken into account in computing profits for tax purposes for any period ending before or on the date of the change, tax shall be charged under subsection (1) in respect of that amount for the year of assessment in which the change occurred as if that amount were a sum to which subsection (2) applies and the change of basis were a change of the kind described in subsection (1).

(4) In this section, references to work in progress at the time of a change of basis shall be construed in accordance with section 90(4) but as if references in that section to the change of basis were references to the discontinuance.

(5) There shall be a change from a conventional basis to the earnings basis at the end of a period, the profits or gains of which were computed on a conventional basis, if the profits or gains of the next succeeding period are computed by reference to earnings and, if the profits or gains of 2 successive periods are computed on different conventional bases, a change of conventional basis shall occur at the end of the earlier period.

Case law

Meaning of "conventional basis": *Walker v O'Connor* UK Special Commissioners [1996] STI 16.

Revenue precedents

Issue: Can a farmer who has been on the profile basis change to the accounts basis in his final year of trading?
Decision: Yes. However a charge under s 94(1) is likely to arise in respect of sums arising from the carrying on of the trade prior to the changeover which are not brought into the accounts in computing the profits of the trade.

Definitions

profession: s 2(1); trade: s 3(1); year of assessment: ss 2(1), 5(1).

Former enactments

FA 1970 s 26(1)–(4).

Corresponding UK tax provision

Income and Corporation Taxes Act 1988 s 104.

---

95 Supplementary provisions as to tax under section 91 or 94

(1) In the case of a transfer for value of the right to receive any sums described in section 91(1) or 94, any tax chargeable by virtue of either of those sections shall be charged in respect of the amount or value of the consideration (or, in the case of a transfer otherwise than at arm's length, in respect of the value of the right transferred as between

parties at arm's length), and references in those sections to sums received shall be construed accordingly.

(2) Where an individual is chargeable to tax by virtue of section 91 in respect of any sums received after the discontinuance of a trade or profession, and the profits or gains of the trade or profession to which such individual was entitled before the discontinuance fell to be treated as earned income for the purposes of the Income Tax Acts, those sums shall also be treated as earned income for those purposes but after any reduction in those sums under section 93.

(3) Where any sum chargeable to tax by virtue of section 91 or 94 is received in any year of assessment beginning not later than 10 years after the discontinuance or, as the case may be, change of basis by the person by whom the trade or profession was carried on before the discontinuance or change or by such person's personal representatives, such person or (in either case) such person's personal representatives may, by notice in writing sent to the inspector within 2 years after the end of that year of assessment, elect that the tax so chargeable shall be charged as if the sum in question were received on the date on which the discontinuance took place or, as the case may be, on the last day of the period at the end of which the change took place, and, in any such case, an additional assessment shall (notwithstanding anything in section 924(2)) be made accordingly and, in connection with that assessment, no further deduction or relief shall be made or given in respect of any loss or allowance deducted in pursuance of section 91(4).

(4) Where work in progress at the discontinuance of a profession, or the responsibility for its completion, is transferred, the sums to which section 91 applies include any sums received by means of consideration for the transfer and any sums received by means of realisation by the transferee on behalf of the transferor of the work in progress transferred.

(5) No amount shall be deducted under section 91(4) if that amount has been allowed under any other provision of the Tax Acts.

(6) No amount shall be deducted more than once under section 91(4) and, as between sums chargeable for one year of assessment and sums chargeable for a subsequent year of assessment, any deduction in respect of a loss or capital allowance shall be made against sums chargeable for the earlier year of assessment but, in the case of a loss which by virtue of this subsection or section 91(4) is to be allowed after the discontinuance, a deduction shall not be made from any sum chargeable for a year of assessment preceding that in which the loss is incurred.

Definitions

Income Tax Acts: s 1(2); inspector: ss 2(1), 5(1), 852; person: IA 1937 s 11(*c*); profession: s 2(1); trade: s 3(1); writing: IA 1937 Sch; year of assessment: ss 2(1), 5(1).

Former enactments

FA 1970 s 21; CTA 1976 s 164 and Sch 3 Pt II.

Corresponding UK tax provision

Income and Corporation Taxes Act 1988 s 102.

CHAPTER 8
Taxation of Rents and Certain Other Payments

Cross-references

Capital gains tax, exclusion of premiums taxed under Sch D Case V: Sch 14 para 6(5).

Leased farm land exemption, definitions of "lease", "lessee", "lessor" and "rent" applied: s 664(1)(*a*).

Loss relief, meaning of "the person chargeable" applied: s 384(1).

Plant and machinery wear and tear allowance: s 284(6).

Returns etc by lessors, lessees and agents, definitions of "lease", "lessee", "lessor", "premises" and "rent" applied: s 888(1), (2).

Ring-fence on use of certain capital allowances on certain industrial buildings and other premises, meaning of "rent" applied: s 409E(1).

Transactions in land: s 639(3).

Renewal incentives

Custom House Dock area

Double rent allowance, definitions of "lease", "lessee", "lessor" and "rent" applied: s 324(1);

Temple Bar area

Double rent allowance, definitions of "lease", "lessee", "lessor" and "rent" applied: s 333(1);

Designated areas and streets, and enterprise areas

Interpretation, definitions of "lease", "lessee", "lessor", "premium" and "rent" applied: s 339(1);

Resort areas

Interpretation, definitions of "lease", "lessee", "lessor", and "rent" applied: s 351;

Qualifying areas and qualifying streets

Interpretation, definitions of "lease", "lessee", "lessor", "premium" and "rent" applied: s 372A(1).

Qualifying rural areas

Interpretation, definitions of "lease", "lessee", "lessor", "premium" and "rent" applied: s 372L.

Designated areas in certain towns

Interpretation, definitions of "lease", "lessee", "lessor", "premium" and "rent" applied: s 372AA(1).

Reliefs for lessors and owner-occupiers in respect of expenditure incurred on the provision of certain rented residential accommodation

Interpretation, definition of "lease", "lessee", "lessor", "premium" and "rent" applied: s 372AK(1).

Qualifying lease: s 372AO(2)(*a*).

Revenue information

Information leaflet IT70 — A Revenue Guide to Rental Income.

96 Interpretation (Chapter 8)

(1) In this Chapter, except where the context otherwise requires—

"easement" includes any right, privilege or benefit in, over or derived from premises;

"lease" includes an agreement for a lease and any tenancy, but does not include a mortgage, and **"lessee"** and **"lessor"** shall be construed accordingly, and **"lessee"** and **"lessor"** include respectively the successors in title of a lessee or a lessor;

"the person chargeable" means the person entitled to the profits or gains arising from—

(*a*) any rent in respect of any premises, and

(*b*) any receipts in respect of any easement;

"premises" means any lands, tenements or hereditaments in the State;

"premium" includes any like sum, whether payable to the immediate or a superior lessor or to a person connected with the immediate or superior lessor;

"rent" includes—

(*a*) any rentcharge, fee farm rent and any payment in the nature of rent, notwithstanding that the payment may relate partly to premises and partly to goods or services, and

(*b*) any payment made by the lessee to defray the cost of work of maintenance of or repairs to the premises, not being work required by the lease to be carried out by the lessee.

[**"rented residential premises"** means a residential premises in respect of which any person is entitled to a rent or receipts from any easements;

"residential premises" means any building or part of a building used or suitable for use as a dwelling and any outoffice, yard, garden or other land appurtenant to or usually enjoyed with that building or part of a building.][1]

(2) (*a*) In ascertaining for the purposes of this Chapter the duration of a lease, the following provisions shall apply:

(i) where any of the terms of the lease (whether relating to forfeiture or to any other matter) or any other circumstances render it unlikely that the lease will continue beyond a date falling before the expiration of the term of the lease and the premium was not substantially greater than it would have been (on the assumptions required by paragraph (*b*)) if the term had been one expiring on that date, the lease shall not be treated as having been granted for a term longer than one ending on that date;

(ii) where the terms of the lease include provision for the extension of the lease beyond a particular date by notice given by the lessee, account may be taken of any circumstances making it likely that the lease will be so extended;

(iii) where the lessee or a person connected with the lessee is or may become entitled to a further lease or the grant of a further lease (whenever commencing) of the same premises or of premises including the whole or part of the same premises, the term of the lease may be treated as not expiring before the term of the further lease.

(*b*) Paragraph (*a*) shall be applied by reference to the facts which were known or ascertainable at the time of the grant of the lease or, in relation to tax under section 98(4), at the time when the contract providing for a variation or waiver of a kind referred to in section 98(4) is entered into, and in applying paragraph (*a*)—

(i) it shall be assumed that all parties concerned, whatever their relationship, act as they would act if they were at arm's length, and

(ii) if by the lease or in connection with the granting of it—

(I) benefits were conferred other than vacant possession and beneficial occupation of the premises or the right to receive rent at a reasonable commercial rate in respect of the premises, or

(II) payments were made which would not be expected to be made by parties so acting if no other benefits had been so conferred, it shall be further assumed, unless it is shown that the benefits were not conferred or the payments were not made for the purpose of securing a tax advantage in the application of this Chapter, that the benefits would not have been conferred nor the payments made had the lease been for a term ending on the date mentioned in paragraph (*a*).

(3) Where the estate or interest of any lessor of any premises is the subject of a mortgage and either the mortgagee is in possession or the rents and profits are being received by a receiver appointed by or on the application of the mortgagee, that estate or interest shall be deemed for the purposes of this Chapter to be vested in the mortgagee, and references to a lessor shall be construed accordingly; but the amount of the liability to tax of any such mortgagee shall be computed as if the mortgagor was still in possession or, as the case may be, no receiver had been appointed and as if it were the amount of the liability of the mortgagor that was being computed.

(4) Where an inspector has reason to believe that a person has information relevant to the ascertainment of the duration of a lease in accordance with subsection (2), the inspector may by notice in writing require such person to give, within 21 days after the date of the notice or such longer period as the inspector may allow, such information relevant to the ascertainment of the duration of the lease on the matters specified in the notice as is in such person's possession.

Amendments

[1] Definitions of "rented residential premises" and "residential premises" inserted by F(No 2)A 1998 s 1(1)(*a*) with effect from 23 April 1998.

Cross-references

Farming and market gardening, meaning of "easement" applied: s 654.

Premiums treated as rent, subs (2)(*a*): s 98(7).

Restriction of relief in respect of loans applied in acquiring interest in companies and partnerships, definitions of "premises" and "rented residential premises" applied: s 248A(1).

Sch D Case V basis of assessment, this section applied: s 75(5).

Statement of practice

Currency and/or interest swap agreements, regular receipts directly relating to interest allowable under Sch D Case V are part of Sch D Case V income and corresponding payments are deductible in the Sch D Case V computation: SP CT/1/91.

Tax Briefing

TB21 Mar 1996 p 10 — Income from conacre letting is "a payment in the nature of rent" and is chargeable under Case V of Schedule D.

TB42 Dec 2000 p 28 — Income from the letting of plant in a leased building.

Definitions

land: IA 1937 Sch; person: IA 1937 s 11(*c*); writing: IA 1937 Sch.

Former enactments

ITA 1967 s 80(1)–(2), (4)–(5) and s 81(1)(the person chargeable); FA 1969 s 27; FA 1975 s 19 and Sch 2 Pt I paras 1–2.

Corresponding UK tax provision

Income and Corporation Taxes Act 1988 s 24.

97 Computational rules and allowable deductions

(1) Subject to this Chapter, the amount of the profits or gains arising in any year shall for the purposes of Case V of Schedule D be computed as follows:

(*a*) the amount of any rent shall be taken to be the gross amount of that rent before any deduction for income tax;

(*b*) the amount of the profits or gains arising in any year shall be the aggregate of the surpluses computed in accordance with paragraph (*c*), reduced by the aggregate of the deficiencies as so computed;

(*c*) the amount of the surplus or deficiency in respect of each rent or in respect of the total receipts from easements shall be computed by making the deductions authorised by subsection (2) from the rent or total receipts from easements, as the case may be, to which the person chargeable becomes entitled in any year.

(2) The deductions authorised by this subsection shall be deductions by reference to any or all of the following matters—

(*a*) the amount of any rent payable by the person chargeable in respect of the premises or in respect of a part of the premises;

(*b*) any sums borne by the person chargeable—

(i) in the case of a rent under a lease, in accordance with the conditions of the lease, and

(ii) in any other case, relating to and constituting an expense of the transaction or transactions under which the rents or receipts were received,

in respect of any rate levied by a local authority, whether such sums are by law chargeable on such person or on some other person;

(*c*) the cost to the person chargeable of any services rendered or goods provided by such person, otherwise than as maintenance or repairs, being services or goods which—

(i) in the case of a rent under a lease, such person is legally bound under the lease to render or provide but in respect of which such person receives no separate consideration, and

(ii) in any other case, relate to and constitute an expense of the transaction or transactions under which the rents or receipts were received, not being an expense of a capital nature;

(*d*) the cost of maintenance, repairs, insurance and management of the premises borne by the person chargeable and relating to and constituting an expense of the transaction or transactions under which the rents or receipts were received, not being an expense of a capital nature;

(*e*) interest on borrowed money employed in the purchase, improvement or repair of the premises.

[(2A) Notwithstanding subsection (2) but subject to the other provisions of this section, a deduction shall not be authorised by paragraph (*e*) of that subsection by reference to interest on borrowed money employed on or after the 23rd day of April, 1998, in the purchase, improvement or repair of a premises which, at any time during the year, is a residential premises.

(2B) Subject to subsection (2C), subsection (2A) shall not apply in relation to interest on borrowed money employed—

(*a*) on or before the [31st day of March, 1999],[1] in the purchase of a residential premises in pursuance of a contract which was evidenced in writing prior to the 23rd day of April, 1998, for the purchase of that premises, (*b*) in the improvement or repair of a premises which on the 23rd day of April, 1998, or at any time during the 12 month period ending on that day, is or was a rented residential premises—

(i) in which the person chargeable had an estate or interest on that day, or

(ii) in respect of which the person chargeable is, or would be, entitled, by virtue of paragraph (*a*), to a deduction authorised by subsection (2)(*e*) by reference to interest on borrowed money employed in its purchase,

(*c*) in the purchase, improvement or repair of premises which is—

(i) a building or structure to which section 352 applies by virtue of the building or structure being a holiday cottage of the type referred to in section 268(3), or

(ii) a building or structure which is a qualifying premises within the meaning of section 353 by virtue of the building or structure being—

(I) a holiday apartment registered under Part III of the Tourist Traffic Act, 1939, or

(II) other self-catering accommodation specified in a list published under section 9 of the Tourist Traffic Act, 1957,

or

(iii) a qualifying premises within the meaning of section 356, 357 or 358,

(*d*) in the purchase, improvement or repair of any premises, other than premises to which paragraph (*c*) applies, the site of which is wholly within a qualifying rural area within the meaning of Chapter 8 of Part 10 of the Taxes Consolidation Act, [1997,][2]

(*e*) in the purchase, improvement or repair of premises, other than premises to which paragraphs (*c*) and (*d*) apply, where—

(i) the premises is a holiday cottage, holiday apartment or other self-catering accommodation either registered under Part III of the Tourist Traffic Act, 1939, or specified in a list published under section 9 of the Tourist Traffic Act, 1957,

(ii) an application for planning permission for the development of the premises was received by a planning authority before the 23rd day of April, 1998, and

(iii) the terms under which planning permission in respect of the development of the premises was granted by the planning authority contain the condition that the premises may not be used by any person for residential use in excess of 2 consecutive calendar months at any one time and such condition is in force [during the year, or][3]

[(*f*) in the purchase, improvement or repair of a premises which complies with the conditions of subsection (2F).][4]

(2C)(*a*) For the purposes of subsections (2A) and (2B), borrowed money employed on or after the 23rd day of April, 1998, on the construction of a building or part of a building for use or suitable for use as a dwelling on land in which the person chargeable has an estate or interest shall, together with any borrowed money which that person employed in the acquisition of such land, be deemed to be borrowed money employed in the purchase of a residential premises.

(b) In any case where paragraph (a) applies, subsection (2B)(a) shall apply only where the money is employed on or before the [31st day of March, 1999],[4] and the person chargeable—

(i) has before the 23rd day of April, 1998, either—

(I) an estate or interest in land, or

(II) entered into a contract evidenced in writing to acquire an estate or interest in land,

and

(ii) in respect of any building or part of any building for use or suitable for use as a dwelling to be constructed on that land, either—

(I) has entered into a contract evidenced in writing before the 23rd day of April, 1998, for the construction of that building or that part of that building, or

(II) if no such contract exists, satisfies the Revenue Commissioners that the foundation for that building or that part of that building was laid in its entirety before the 23rd day of April, 1998.

(2D) Where—

(a) any premises in respect of which the person chargeable is entitled to a rent or to receipts from any easement consists in part of residential premises and in part of premises which are not residential premises, and

(b) subsection (2A) applies,

then, the amount of the deduction which is authorised under subsection (2)(e) by reference to interest on borrowed money employed in the purchase, improvement or repair of those premises shall be the amount of interest on that part of the borrowed money which can, on a just and reasonable basis, be attributed to that part of the premises which are not residential premises.

(2E) Notwithstanding anything contained in this section, where a premises in respect of which the person chargeable is entitled to a rent or to receipts from any easement is at any time on or after the 23rd day of April, 1998, the sole or main residence of that person, a deduction shall not be authorised by subsection (2)(e) by reference to any interest payable for any year or part of a year commencing after the date on which the premises ceases to be the sole or main residence of that person.][5]

[(2F)(a) The conditions of this subsection are—

(i) the premises was converted into multiple residential units prior to 1 October 1964,

(ii) the premises was acquired by the chargeable person under a contract which was evidenced in writing on or after 5 January 2001,

(iii) subsequent to the acquisition by the chargeable person of the premises, the number of residential units is not, subject to subparagraph (iv), reduced to less than 50 per cent of the total number of residential units contained in the premises at date of acquisition,

(iv) the premises consists throughout the year of a minimum of 3 residential units,

(v) at all times during the year (except for reasonable periods of temporary disuse between the ending of one lease and the commencement of another lease) not less than 50 per cent of the residential units in the premises are let under a lease where the lessee in the case of each such letting is either—

(I) a local authority, or a person nominated by a local authority under an agreement in writing between the lessor and that local authority, or

(II) a person who, at the commencement of the tenancy, is entitled to a payment under section 179 of the Social Welfare (Consolidation) Act, 1993, in respect of rent,

and

(vi) all the requirements of the following Regulations—

(I) the Housing (Standards for Rented Houses) Regulations, 1993 (SI No 147 of 1993),

(II) the Housing (Rent Books) Regulations, 1993 (SI No 146 of 1993), and

(III) the Housing (Registration of Rented Houses) Regulations, 1996 (SI No 30 of 1996), as amended by the Housing (Registration of Rented Houses) (Amendment) Regulations, 2000 (SI No 12 of 2000),

are complied with in relation to the premises throughout the year,

and

(*b*) in this subsection—

"local authority", in relation to a premises, means the council of a county or the corporation of a county or other borough or, where appropriate, the council of an urban district in whose functional area the premises is located;

"residential unit" means a separately contained part of a residential premises used or suitable for use as a dwelling.][6]

[(2G) Subsections (2A) to (2F) shall not apply or have effect in relation to interest on borrowed money employed [in the purchase, other than from the spouse of the person chargeable],[7] improvement or repair of residential premises where that interest accrues on or after 1 January 2002 and, for the purposes of this subsection, interest on such borrowed money shall be treated as accruing from day to day.][8]

[(2H) The reference to "spouse" in subsection (2G) does not include a spouse to a marriage—

(*a*) in which the spouses are separated under an order of a court of competent jurisdiction or by deed of separation, or

(*b*) that has been dissolved under either—

(i) section 5 of the Family Law (Divorce) Act 1996, or

(ii) the law of a country or jurisdiction other than the State, being a divorce that is entitled to be recognised as valid in the State.][9]

(3) (*a*) The amount of the deductions authorised by subsection (2) shall be the amount which would be deducted in computing profits or gains under the provisions applicable to Case I of Schedule D if the receipt of rent were deemed to be a trade carried on by the person chargeable—

(i) in the case of a rent under a lease, during the currency of the lease, and

(ii) in the case of a rent not under a lease, during the period during which the person chargeable was entitled to the rent,

and the premises comprised in the lease or to which the rent relates were deemed to be occupied for the purpose of that trade.

(*b*) For the purpose of this subsection, the currency of a lease shall be deemed to include a period immediately following its termination, during which the lessor immediately before the termination was not in occupation of the premises or any part of the premises, but was entitled to possession of the premises, if at the end of that period the premises have become subject to another lease granted by the lessor.

(4) (*a*) Where the person chargeable is entitled in respect of any premises (in this subsection referred to as **"the relevant premises"**) to a rent or to receipts from any easement and a sum by reference to which a deduction is authorised to be made by subsection (2) is payable by such person in respect of premises which comprise the whole or a part of the relevant premises and other premises, the inspector shall make, according to the best of his or her knowledge and judgment, any appropriate apportionment of the sum in determining the amount of any deduction under that subsection.

(*b*) Where the person chargeable retains possession of a part of any premises and that part is used in common by persons respectively occupying other parts of the premises, paragraph (*a*) shall apply as if a payment made in respect of the part used in common had been made in respect of those other parts.

(5) Any amount or part of an amount shall not be deducted under subsection (2) if it has otherwise been allowed as a deduction in computing the income of any person for the purposes of tax.

Amendments

1 Substituted by FA 1999 s 31(1) with effect from 20 May 1998; previously "31st day of December, 1998".

2 Substituted by FA 2001 s 34(*a*)(i) with effect from 6 April 2001; previously "1997, or".

3 Substituted by FA 2001 s 34(*a*)(ii) with effect from 6 April 2001; previously "during the year.".

4 Subs (2B)(*f*) inserted by FA 2001 s 34(*a*)(iii) with effect from 6 April 2001.

5 Subs (2A)–(2E) inserted by F(No 2)A 1998 s 1(1)(*b*) with effect from 23 April 1998.

6 Subs (2F) inserted by FA 2001 s 34(*b*) with effect from 6 April 2001.

7 Substituted by FA 2003 s 16(1)(*a*)(i) in relation to interest referred to in subs (2G) and s 248A(2) which accrues on or after 6 February 2003 and, for such purposes, such interest shall be treated as accruing from day to day; previously "in the purchase".

8 Subs (2G) inserted by FA 2002 s 17(*a*) with effect from 1 January 2002.

9 Subs (2H) inserted by FA 2003 s 16(1)(*a*)(ii) in relation to interest referred to in subs (2G) and s 248A(2) which accrues on or after 6 February 2003 and, for such purposes, such interest shall be treated as accruing from day to day.

Cross-references

Corporation tax, relief for Schedule D Case IV or V losses, subs (1): s 399(2).

Foreign securities and possessions, subss (2A)–(2C), (2E): s 71(4A).

Implementation of Council Directive 2003/49/EC of 3 June 2003 on a common system of taxation applicable to interest and royalty payments made between associated companies of different Member States, application: s 267H(1)(*a*)(ii).

Industrial and provident societies, computation, subs (2)(*e*): s 700(3).

Leased farm land exemption, meaning of "surplus" applied, subs (1): s 664(1)(*a*)(specified amount), (2)(*b*).

Loss relief, subs (1): s 384(2).

Pre-letting expenditure, no deduction, subs (2): s 105(2).
Premiums treated as rent, subs (2): s 98(2)(*b*).
Redundancy payments, deduction: s 109(4).
Reliefs for lessors and owner-occupiers in respect of exenditure incurred on the provision of certain residential accommodation: s 372AP(4)(*b*); subs (1): s 372AP(2)(*a*); subs (2): s 372AP(2)(*b*), s 372AM(9A)(*c*).
Ring-fence on use of certain capital allowances on certain industrial buildings and other premises, subs (1): s 409E(1) ("specified amount of rent").
Sch D Case V basis of assessment: s 75(4).

Case law

Subs (2): Letting and legal fees incurred in respect of the initial letting of property allowable deductions: *Stephen Court Ltd v Browne* (High Court, 7 June 1983) TL 120.

Revenue precedents

Issue: Whether a deduction is allowable under s 97(2)(*e*) where a loan which falls into the subsection is replaced by other borrowings for genuine commercial reasons only.
Decision: Yes.
Issue: Is a balancing charge made in charging a person's income under Case V of Schedule D a Case V surplus for the purposes of s 97(1)?
Decision: Yes.
Issue: Whether interest is allowable in respect of a replacement loan on a rented property.
Decision: Interest on borrowed money employed in the purchase, repair or improvement of a rented premises is allowable. In certain situations, Revenue allows interest where the original loan is replaced by another loan. In determining whether such interest is to be allowed, the inspector will take into account all the circumstances of the case, including whether the transaction was a genuine commercial transaction.
Issue: Whether interest paid on a loan used to repay a loan for which relief allowable under s 97 would be allowed under s 97.
Decision: Yes; provided the redemption of the earlier loan was for bona fide commercial reasons and not for the avoidance of tax, the interest could be allowed in computing profit rent.
Issue: Whether pre-letting expenditure is allowable under TCA 1997 s 97(3) given that pre-trading expenditure is allowable under TCA 1997 s 82.
Decision: Pre-letting expenditure is not allowable under s 97(3). The only Case V deductions allowable are those set out in s 97(2). Under s 97(3), the amount of the deductions authorised under s 97(2) is the amount which would be deducted under Case I if the receipt of rent were deemed to be a trade carried on during the currency of the lease or the period during which the recipient of the rent was entitled to that rent. In a pre-letting situation there is no receipt of rent. Accordingly, s 97(3) does not invoke s 82 for the purposes of authorising a deduction for pre-letting expenditure.

Tax Briefing

TB21 – Income from conacre lettings of farmland is "in the nature of rent" and thus falls to be charged to be taxed under Schedule D Case V.
TB25 Feb 1997 p 11 & TB31 Apr 1998 p 20 — Allowability of accountancy fees and other administrative costs.
TB31 Apr 1998 p 20 — No deduction is allowable for pre-letting expenses.
TB32 June 1998 p 20 & TB33 Sept 1998 p 13 — Clarification of impact of subsection (2A) to (2E) on deductibility of loan interest.
TB32 June 1998 pp 21–25 Subsections (2A) — (2E): deductibility of loan interest.
TB44 – Receipts from letting a self-contained unit within a residential premises may qualify for "Rent-a-Room" Relief.
TB50 Oct 2002 pp 13–15 — Finance Act 2002 — Rental Income — Deductibility of Loan Interest and Related Isses.
TB53 Aug 2003 p 16 — Mortgage Protection Policy Premiums — clarification as to deductibility.

Definitions

Income Tax Acts: s 1(2); land: IA 1937 Sch; month: IA 1937 Sch; person: IA 1937 s 11(*c*); trade: s 3(1); writing: IA 1937 Sch; year of assessment: s 3(1).

Former enactments

ITA 1967 s 81(4)–(8); FA 1969 s 22; FA 1997 s 146(1) and Sch 9 Pt I para 1(6).

Corresponding UK tax provision

Income and Corporation Taxes Act 1988 s 25 [repealed].

98 Treatment of premiums, etc as rent

(1) Where the payment of any premium is required under a lease or otherwise under the terms subject to which a lease is granted and the duration of the lease does not exceed 50 years, the lessor shall be treated for the purposes of section 75 as becoming entitled when the lease is granted to an amount as rent (in addition to any actual rent) equal to the amount of the premium reduced by 2 per cent of that amount for each complete period of 12 months, other than the first, comprised in the term of the lease.

(2) (*a*) Where the terms subject to which a lease of any premises is granted impose on the lessee an obligation to carry out any work on the premises, the lease shall be deemed for the purposes of this section to have required the payment of a premium to the lessor (in addition to any other premium) of an amount equal to the amount by which the value of the lessor's estate or interest immediately after the commencement of the lease falls short of what its then value would have been if the work had been carried out, but otherwise than at the expense of the lessee, and the rent were increased accordingly.

(*b*) Notwithstanding paragraph (*a*), this subsection shall not apply in so far as the obligation requires the carrying out of work payment for which, if the lessor and not the lessee were obliged to carry it out, would be deductible from the rent under section 97(2).

(3) Where under the terms subject to which a lease is granted a sum becomes payable by the lessee in place of the whole or a part of the rent for any period, or as consideration for the surrender of the lease, the lease shall be deemed for the purposes of this section to have required the payment of a premium to the lessor (in addition to any other premium) of the amount of that sum; but—

(*a*) in computing tax chargeable by virtue of this subsection in respect of a sum payable in place of rent, the term of the lease shall be treated as not including any period other than that in relation to which the sum is payable, and

(*b*) notwithstanding subsection (1), rent treated as arising by virtue of this subsection shall be deemed to become due when the sum in question becomes payable by the lessee.

(4) Where as consideration for the variation or waiver of any of the terms of a lease a sum becomes payable by the lessee otherwise than as rent, the lease shall be deemed for the purposes of this section to have required the payment of a premium to the lessor (in addition to any other premium) of the amount of that sum; but—

(*a*) in computing tax chargeable by virtue of this subsection, the term of the lease shall be treated as not including any period which precedes the time at which the variation or waiver takes effect or falls after the time at which the variation or waiver ceases to have effect, and

(*b*) notwithstanding subsection (1), rent treated as arising by virtue of this subsection shall be deemed to become due when the contract providing for the variation or waiver is entered into.

(5) Where a payment mentioned in subsection (1), (3) or (4) is due to a person other than the lessor, subsection (1), (3) or (4), as the case may be, shall not apply in relation to that payment, but any amount which would have been treated as rent if the payment had been

due to the lessor shall be treated as an annual profit or gain of that other person and chargeable to tax under Case IV of Schedule D; but, where the amount relates to a payment within subsection (4), it shall not be so treated unless the payment is due to a person connected with the lessor.

(6) For the purposes of this section, any sum other than rent paid on or in connection with the granting of a lease shall be presumed to have been paid by means of a premium except in so far as other sufficient consideration for the payment is shown to have been given.

(7) Where subparagraph (iii) of section 96(2)(*a*) applies, the premium, or an appropriate part of the premium, payable for or in connection with any lease mentioned in that subparagraph may be treated as having been required under any other lease.

(8) Where an amount by reference to which a person is chargeable to income tax or corporation tax by virtue of this section is payable by instalments, the tax chargeable may, if the person chargeable satisfies the Revenue Commissioners that such person would otherwise suffer undue hardship, be paid at such person's option by such instalments as the Revenue Commissioners may allow over a period not exceeding 8 years and ending not later than the time at which the last of the first-mentioned instalments is payable.

(9) Reference in this section to a sum shall be construed as including the value of any consideration, and references to a sum paid or payable or to the payment of a sum shall be construed accordingly.

Cross-references

Appeals against determination made under this section: s 947(1).

Capital gains tax, exclusion of premiums taxed under Sch D Case V: Sch 14 para 6(1), (2): subs (3)–(4): Sch 14 para 6(4).

Capital gains tax, expenditure by lessee under terms of lease, subs (2): Sch 14 para 8.

Charge on assignment of lease granted at undervalue, subs (1): s 99(1).

Deduction by reference to premiums etc in computation of rental income: s 103(1)(*a*).

Deduction by reference to premiums etc in computation of trading or professional profits: s 102(1)(*a*), (2)(*a*), (3).

Making of assessments under Schedules C, D, E and F: s 918(4).

Restriction of balancing allowance on sale of industrial building, meaning of "premium" applied: s 275(1).

Transactions in land, Schedule D Case I: s 641(2)(*a*).

Case law

Subs (8): Where a lessor had opted for liability on the basis of instalments in respect of the payment of a premium under a sale and leaseback arrangement within s 102 between a parent and its wholly owned subsidiary, this did not debar a deduction to the lessee for the full amount of the premium: *Hammond Lane Metal Co Ltd v O'Culacháin* ITR Vol IV p 187.

Definitions

month: IA 1937 Sch; person: IA 1937 s 11(*c*).

Former enactments

ITA 1967 s 83; FA 1969 s 33(1) and Sch 4 Pt I; FA 1975 s 20 and Sch 2 Pt I paras 1 and 2; CTA 1976 Sch 2 Pt I para 3.

Corresponding UK tax provision

Income and Corporation Taxes Act 1988 s 98.

98A Taxation of reverse premiums

[(1) (*a*) In this section—

"chargeable period" means an accounting period of a company or a year of assessment;

"first relevant chargeable period" means—

(*a*) the chargeable period in which a relevant transaction is entered into, or

(*b*) if a relevant transaction is entered into—

(i) by a person receiving a reverse premium, and

(ii) for the purposes of a trade or profession which that person is about to carry on,

the chargeable period in which the person commences to carry on the trade or profession;

"relevant arrangements" means a relevant transaction and any arrangements entered into in connection with it, whether before, at the same time or after it;

"relevant transaction" means a transaction under which a person is granted an estate or interest in, or a right in or over, land;

"reverse premium" means a payment or other benefit received by a person by way of inducement in connection with a relevant transaction being entered into by that person or by a person connected with that person;

"sale and lease-back arrangement" means an arrangement under which a person disposes of the full estate or interest held by that person in land to another person and the terms subject to which the disposal is made provide for the grant of a lease of an interest in or a right in or over the land concerned to the person by that other person.

(*b*) For the purposes of this section persons are connected with each other if they are connected within the meaning of section 10 at any time during the chargeable period or periods when the relevant arrangements are entered into.

(2) A reverse premium shall, for the purposes of the Tax Acts, be regarded as a receipt of a revenue nature.

(3) Subject to subsections (4) and (6), the amount or value of a reverse premium shall be treated as if it were an amount of rent.

(4) Where a relevant transaction is entered into—

(*a*) by a person receiving a reverse premium, and

(*b*) for the purposes of a trade or profession carried on or to be carried on by that person,

the amount or value of the reverse premium shall be taken into account in computing the profits or gains of that trade or profession under Case I or II of Schedule D, as the case may be, as if it were a receipt of that trade or profession.

(5) Where—

(*a*) two or more of the persons who enter into relevant arrangements are connected with each other, and

(*b*) the terms of those arrangements are not such as would reasonably have been expected if those persons had been dealing at arm's length,

the whole of the amount or value of the reverse premium shall, for the purposes of subsections (3) and (4) be treated as accruing in the first relevant chargeable period.

(6) Where a reverse premium is received by an assurance company (within the meaning of section 706) carrying on life business (within the meaning of section 706) in respect of which it is chargeable to tax otherwise than in accordance with the rules applicable to Case I of Schedule D, the amount or value of the reverse premium shall be deducted from the amount treated as the company's expenses of management for the chargeable period in which the reverse premium is received.

(7) This section does not apply to a payment or benefit—

(*a*) received by an individual in connection with a relevant transaction and the transaction relates to the grant of an estate or interest in, or a right in or over premises occupied or to be occupied by that individual as his or her only or main residence,

(*b*) to the extent that it is consideration for the transfer of an estate or interest in land which constitutes the sale in a sale and lease-back arrangement where the terms of that arrangement at the time the arrangement is entered into are on bona fide commercial terms, or

(*c*) to the extent that, apart from this section, it is taken into account in computing the profits or gains of a trade or profession under Case I or II of Schedule D, as the case may be, as a receipt of that trade or profession.][1]

Amendments

1 Section 98A inserted by FA 2002 s 18 and applies as on and from 7 June 2001 in respect of a reverse premium received on or after that date.

Definitions

land: IA1937 Sch; person: IA 1937 s 11(c); profession: s 2(1); profits or gains: s 3(4); Tax Acts: s 1(2); trade: ss 3(1), 4(1); year of assessment: s 2(1).

99 Charge on assignment of lease granted at undervalue

(1) Where the terms subject to which a lease of a duration not exceeding 50 years was granted are such that the lessor, having regard to values prevailing at the time the lease was granted, and on the assumption that the negotiations for the lease were at arm's length, could have required the payment of an additional sum (in this section referred to as **"the amount forgone"**) by means of a premium or an additional premium for the grant of the lease, then, on any assignment of the lease for a consideration—

(*a*) where the lease has not previously been assigned, exceeding the premium (if any) for which it was granted, or

(*b*) where the lease has been previously assigned, exceeding the consideration for which it was last assigned, the amount of the excess, in so far as it is not greater than the amount forgone reduced by the amount of any such excess arising on a previous assignment of the lease, shall, in the same proportion as the amount forgone would under section 98(1) have been treated as rent if it had been a premium under a lease, be treated as profits or gains of the assignor chargeable to the tax under Case IV of Schedule D.

(2) In computing the profits or gains of a trade of dealing in land, any trading receipts within this section shall be treated as reduced by the amount on which tax is chargeable by virtue of this section.

Cross-references

Appeals against determination made under this section: s 947(1).
Deduction by reference to premiums etc in computation of rental income: s 103(1)(*b*), (3).
Deduction by reference to premiums etc in computation of trading or professional profits: s 102(1)(*b*), (2)(*a*).
Disallowance of premiums treated as rent under superior lease: Sch 14 para 7(2).
Making of assessments under Schedules C, D, E and F: s 918(4).
Transactions in land, Schedule D Case IV, subs (2): s 643(9)(*b*).

Definitions

land: IA 1937 Sch; person: IA 1937 s 11(*c*); trade: s 3(1).

Former enactments

ITA 1967 s 84; FA 1969 s 33(1) and Sch 4.

Corresponding UK tax provision

Income and Corporation Taxes Act 1988 s 35.

100 Charge on sale of land with right to reconveyance

(1) Where the terms subject to which an estate or interest in land is sold provide that it shall be, or may be required to be, reconveyed at a future date to the vendor or a person connected with the vendor, the vendor shall be chargeable to tax under Case IV of Schedule D on any amount by which the price at which the estate or interest is sold exceeds the price at which it is to be reconveyed or, if the earliest date at which in accordance with those terms it would fall to be reconveyed is a date 2 years or more after the sale, on that excess reduced by 2 per cent of that excess for each complete year (other than the first) in the period between the sale and that date.

(2) Where under the terms of the sale the date of the reconveyance is not fixed, then—

- (*a*) if the price on reconveyance varies with the date, the price shall be taken for the purposes of this section to be the lowest possible under the terms of the sale;
- (*b*) the vendor may, before the expiration of 6 years after the date on which the reconveyance takes place, claim repayment of any amount by which tax assessed on such vendor by virtue of this section exceeded the amount which would have been so assessed if that date had been treated for the purposes of this section as the date fixed by the terms of the sale.

(3) Where the terms of the sale provide for the grant of a lease directly or indirectly out of the estate or interest to the vendor or a person connected with the vendor, this section shall apply as if the grant of the lease were a reconveyance of the estate or interest at a price equal to the sum of the amount of the premium (if any) for the lease and the value at the date of the sale of the right to receive a conveyance of the reversion immediately after the lease begins to run; but this subsection shall not apply if the lease is granted, and begins to run, within one month after the sale.

(4) In computing the profits or gains of a trade of dealing in land, any trading receipts within this section shall be treated as reduced by the amount on which tax is chargeable by virtue of this section; but where, on a claim being made under subsection (2)(*b*), the amount on which tax is chargeable by virtue of this section is treated as reduced, this subsection shall be deemed to have applied to the amount as reduced, and such adjustment of liability to tax shall be made (for all relevant years of assessment), whether by means of an additional assessment or otherwise, as may be necessary.

Cross-references

Appeals against determination made under this section: s 947(1).

Capital gains tax, exclusion of premiums taxed under Sch D Case V: Sch 14 para 6(3)(*a*).

Deduction by reference to premiums etc in computation of rental income: s 103(1)(*c*), (3), (7).

Deduction by reference to premiums etc in computation of trading or professional profits: s 102(1)(*c*), (2)(*a*),(4).

Disallowance of premiums treated as rent under superior lease, subs (2)(*b*): Sch 14 para 7(3).

Making of assessments under Schedules C, D, E and F: s 918(4).

Transactions in land, Schedule D Case IV, subs (4): s 643(9)(*b*).

Definitions

land: IA 1937 Sch; month: IA 1937 Sch; person: IA 1937 s 11(*c*); trade: s 3(1).

Former enactments

ITA 1967 s 85.

Corresponding UK tax provision

Income and Corporation Taxes Act 1988 s 36.

101 Relief for amount not received

Where on a claim in that behalf the person chargeable proves—

(*a*) that such person has not received an amount to which such person is entitled and which is to be taken into account in computing the profits or gains on which such person is chargeable by virtue of this Chapter under Case IV or V of Schedule D, and

(*b*) (i) if the non-receipt of the amount was attributable to the default of the person by whom it was payable, that the amount is irrecoverable, or

(ii) if the person chargeable has waived payment of the amount, that the waiver was made without consideration and was reasonably made in order to avoid hardship,

then, the person chargeable shall be treated for tax purposes for all relevant years of assessment as if such person had not been entitled to receive the amount, and such adjustment shall be made by repayment or otherwise, as the case may require; but, if all or any part of the amount is subsequently received, such person's liability to tax for all relevant years of assessment shall be appropriately readjusted by additional assessment or otherwise.

Definitions

person: IA 1937 s 11(*c*).

Former enactments

ITA 1967 s 90; FA 1969 s 28.

Corresponding UK tax provision

Income and Corporation Taxes Act 1988 s 41 [repealed].

102 Deduction by reference to premium, etc paid in computation of profits for purposes of Schedule D, Cases I and II

(1) In this section, **"the relevant period"** means—

(*a*) where the amount chargeable arose under section 98, the period treated in computing that amount as being the duration of the lease;

(*b*) where the amount chargeable arose under section 99, the period treated in computing that amount as being the duration of the lease remaining at the date of the assignment;

(*c*) where the amount chargeable arose under section 100, the period beginning with the sale and ending on the date fixed under the terms of the sale as the date of the reconveyance or grant, or, if that date is not so fixed, ending with the earliest date at which the reconveyance or grant could take place in accordance with the terms of the sale.

(2) Where in relation to any premises an amount (in this section referred to as **"the amount chargeable**")—

(*a*) has become chargeable to tax under subsection (1), (2), (3), (4) or (5) of section 98 or under section 99 or 100, or

(*b*) would have become so chargeable but for section 103(3) or any exemption from tax,

and during any part of the relevant period the premises are wholly or partly occupied by the person for the time being entitled to the lease, estate or interest as respects which the amount chargeable arose for the purposes of a trade or profession carried on by such person, such person shall be treated, for the purpose of computing the profits or gains of the trade or profession for assessment under Case I or II of Schedule D, as paying in respect of the premises rent for any part of the relevant period during which the premises are occupied by such person (in addition to any rent actually paid) of an amount which bears to the amount chargeable the same proportion as that part of the relevant period bears to the whole, and such rent shall be taken as accruing from day to day.

(3) Where the amount chargeable arose under section 98(2) by reason of an obligation which included the incurring of expenditure in respect of which any allowance has been or will be made under Part 9, this section shall apply as if the obligation had not included the incurring of that expenditure and the amount chargeable had been calculated accordingly.

(4) Where the amount chargeable arose under section 100 and the reconveyance or grant in question takes place at a price different from that taken in calculating that amount or on a date different from that taken in determining the relevant period, subsections (1) to (3) shall be deemed to have applied (for all relevant years of assessment) as they would have applied if the actual price or date had been so taken and such adjustments of liability to tax shall be made, by means of additional assessment or otherwise, as may be necessary.

Definitions

person: IA 1937 s 11(*c*); profession: s 2(1); trade: s 3(1).

Former enactments

ITA 1967 s 91; FA 1975 s 22(3) and Sch 2 Pt III.

Corresponding UK tax provision

Income and Corporation Taxes Act 1988 s 37.

103 Deduction by reference to premiums, etc paid in computation of profits for purposes of this Chapter

(1) In this section, **"the relevant period"** means, in relation to any amount—

(*a*) where the amount arose under section 98, the period treated in computing that amount as being the duration of the lease;

(*b*) where the amount arose under section 99, the period treated in computing that amount as being the duration of the lease remaining at the date of the assignment;

(*c*) where the amount arose under section 100, the period beginning with the sale and ending on the date fixed under the terms of the sale as the date of the reconveyance or grant, or, if that date is not so fixed, ending with the earliest date at which the reconveyance or grant could take place in accordance with the terms of the sale.

(2) Where in relation to any premises an amount has become or would have become chargeable to tax as mentioned in section 102(2) by reference to a lease, estate or interest, the person for the time being entitled to that lease, estate or interest shall, subject to this section, be treated for the purposes of section 97(2) as paying rent accruing from day to day in respect of the premises (in addition to any rent actually paid) during any part of the relevant period in relation to the amount for which such person is entitled to the lease, estate or interest and in all bearing to that amount the same proportion as that part of the relevant period bears to the whole.

(3) Where in relation to any premises an amount has become or would have become chargeable to tax as mentioned in section 102(2), and by reference to a lease granted out of, or a disposition of, the lease, estate or interest by reference to which the amount (in this section referred to as **"the prior chargeable amount"**) so became or would have so become chargeable, a person would apart from this subsection be chargeable under section 98, 99 or 100 on any amount (in this section referred to as **"the later chargeable amount"**), the amount on which the person is so chargeable shall be the excess, if any, of the later chargeable amount over the appropriate fraction of the prior chargeable amount or, where the lease or disposition by reference to which the person would be so chargeable extends to a part only of that premises, the excess, if any, of the later chargeable amount over so much of the appropriate fraction of the prior chargeable amount as on a just apportionment is attributable to that part of the premises.

(4) (*a*) In a case in which subsection (3) operates to reduce the amount on which apart from that subsection a person would be chargeable by reference to a lease or disposition, subsection (2) shall apply for the relevant period in relation to the later chargeable amount only if the appropriate fraction of the prior chargeable amount exceeds the later chargeable amount and shall then apply as if the prior chargeable amount were reduced in the proportion which the excess bears to that appropriate fraction.

(*b*) Notwithstanding paragraph (*a*), where the lease or disposition extends to a part only of the premises mentioned in subsection (3), subsection (2) and this subsection shall be applied separately in relation to that part and to the remainder of the premises, but as if for any reference to the prior chargeable amount there were substituted a reference to that amount proportionately adjusted.

(5) For the purposes of subsections (3) and (4), the appropriate fraction of the prior chargeable amount shall be the sum which bears to that amount the same proportion as the length of the relevant period in relation to the later chargeable amount bears to the length of the relevant period in relation to the prior chargeable amount.

(6) Where the prior chargeable amount arose under section 98(2) by reason of an obligation which included the incurring of expenditure in respect of which any allowance has been or will be made under Part 9, this section shall apply as if the obligation had not included the incurring of that expenditure and the prior chargeable amount had been calculated accordingly.

(7) Where the prior chargeable amount arose under section 100 and the reconveyance or grant in question takes place at a price different from that taken in calculating that amount or on a date different from that taken in determining the relevant period in relation to that amount, subsections (1) to (6) shall be deemed to have applied (for all relevant years of assessment) as they would have applied if the actual price or date had been so taken and such adjustments of liability to tax shall be made, by means of additional assessment or otherwise, as may be necessary.

Cross-references

Deduction by reference to premiums etc in computation of profits, subs (3): s 102(2)(*b*).

Disallowance of premiums treated as rent under superior lease, subs (2): Sch 14 para 7(1).

Definitions

person: IA 1937 s 11(*c*).

Former enactments

ITA 1967 s 92; FA 1969 s 33(1) and Sch 4 Pt I; FA 1975 s 22 and Sch 2 Pt III.

Corresponding UK tax provision

Income and Corporation Taxes Act 1988 s 37.

104 Taxation of certain rents and other payments

(1) (*a*) This section shall apply to the following payments—

(i) any rent payable in respect of any premises or easements where the premises or easements are used, occupied or enjoyed in connection with any of the concerns the profits or gains arising out of which are chargeable to tax under Case I(*b*) of Schedule D by virtue of section 18(2), and

(ii) any yearly interest, annuity or other annual payment reserved in respect of, or charged on or issuing out of any premises, not being a rent or a payment in respect of an easement.

(*b*) In paragraph (*a*)(i), the reference to rent shall be deemed to include a reference to a toll, duty, royalty or annual or periodical payment in the nature of rent, whether payable in money, money's worth or otherwise.

(2) (*a*) Any payment to which this section applies shall—

(i) in so far as it is not within any other Case of Schedule D, be charged with tax under Case IV of that Schedule, and

(ii) be treated for the purposes of sections 81(2)(*m*), 237 and 238 as if it were a royalty paid in respect of the user of a patent.

(*b*) Notwithstanding paragraph (*a*), where a rent mentioned in subsection (1)(*a*) is rendered in produce of the concern, this subsection shall apply as if paragraph (*a*)(ii) were deleted, and the value of the produce so rendered shall be taken to be the amount of profits or gains arising from that produce.

Cross-references

Charge and deduction of income tax not charged or deducted before passing of annual Act: s 1087(2).

Corporation tax, allowance of charges on income, this section applies: s 243(4).

Corporation tax, computation of income, application of income tax principles: s 76(5)(*b*).

Sch D Case V basis of assessment: s 75(1).

Former enactments

ITA 1967 s 93(1)–(2); FA 1969 s 29.

105 Taxation of rents: restriction in respect of certain rent and interest

(1) This section shall apply to—

(*a*) rent in respect of premises, or

(*b*) interest on borrowed money employed in the purchase, improvement or repair of premises,

payable by a person chargeable to tax in accordance with section 75 on the profits or gains arising from rent in respect of those premises for a period before the date on which the premises are first occupied by a lessee for the purpose of a trade or undertaking or for use as a residence.

(2) No deduction shall be allowed for any year of assessment under section 97(2) in respect of rent or interest to which this section applies.

Definitions

person: IA 1937 s 11(*c*); trade: s 3(1); year of assessment: ss 2(1).

Former enactments

FA 1974 s 62(1)–(2).

106 Tax treatment of receipts and outgoings on sale of premises

(1) Where by virtue of a contract for the sale of an estate or interest in premises there is to be apportioned between the parties a receipt or outgoing in respect of the estate or interest which becomes due after the making of the contract but before the time at which the apportionment is to be made, and a part of the receipt is therefore receivable by the vendor in trust for the purchaser or, as the case may be, a part of the outgoing is paid by the vendor as trustee for the purchaser, the purchaser shall be treated for the purposes of tax under Case V of Schedule D as if that part had become receivable or payable on the purchaser's behalf immediately after the time at which the apportionment is to be made.

(2) Where by virtue of such a contract there is to be apportioned between the parties a receipt or outgoing in respect of the estate or interest which became due before the making of the contract, the parties shall be treated for the purposes of tax under Case V of Schedule D as if the contract had been entered into before the receipt or outgoing became due, and subsection (1) shall apply accordingly.

(3) Where on the sale of an estate or interest in premises there is apportioned to the vendor a part of a receipt or outgoing in respect of the estate or interest which becomes receivable or is paid by the purchaser after the making of the apportionment, then, for the purposes of tax under Case V of Schedule D—

(*a*) when the receipt becomes due or, as the case may be, the outgoing is paid, the amount of the receipt or outgoing, as the case may be, shall be treated as reduced by so much of that amount as was apportioned to the vendor, and

(*b*) the part apportioned to the vendor shall be treated as if it were of the same nature as the receipt or outgoing and had become receivable, or had been paid, directly by the vendor and, where it is a part of an outgoing, had become due, immediately before the time at which the apportionment is made.

(4) Any reference in subsection (1) or (2) to a party to a contract shall include a person to whom the rights and obligations of that party under the contract have passed by assignment or otherwise.

Definitions

person: IA 1937 s 11(*c*).

Former enactments

FA 1969 s 26(1)–(4).

Corresponding UK tax provision

Income and Corporation Taxes Act 1988 s 40.

106A Transfer of rent

[(1) (*a*) In this section—

"relevant transaction" means any scheme, arrangement or understanding under which a person becomes entitled to receive a capital sum and the consideration given for the entitlement to receive the sum consists wholly or mainly of the direct or indirect transfer to another person of a right to receive rent which, in the absence of the scheme, arrangement or understanding, could reasonably have been expected to accrue to the first-mentioned person or to a person connected with that person;

"rent" includes any sum which—

(i) is chargeable to tax under Case V of Schedule D, or

(ii) would be so chargeable if the source of the sum were in the State.

(*b*) For the purposes of this section, a scheme, arrangement or understanding under which a person grants a lease in connection with which—

(i) the person is entitled to a capital sum,

(ii) rent is payable to another person, and

(iii) the consideration given for the entitlement to receive the capital sum consists wholly or mainly of the grant to the other person or a person connected with the other person of a right to rent under the lease,

shall be treated as a relevant transaction and this section applies as if the capital sum were a capital sum under the relevant transaction.

(2) (*a*) Subject to paragraph (*b*), where a person other than a company becomes entitled to receive a capital sum under a relevant transaction, the capital sum shall be treated for the purposes of the Tax Acts as being an amount of income of the person chargeable to tax under Case IV of Schedule D for the year of assessment—

(i) in which the person becomes entitled to the capital sum, or

(ii) if it is earlier, in which the sum was received.

(*b*) Paragraph (*a*) does not apply to a person, other than an individual, if the consideration for the capital sum—

(i) was given by the person, and

(ii) is a qualifying asset (within the meaning of section 110) acquired by a qualifying company (within the meaning of that section) in the course of its business.

(3) Any profits or gains arising by virtue of a relevant transaction to the person to whom the right to receive rent was transferred shall be computed in accordance with section 97, and shall, notwithstanding any other provision of the Tax Acts, be chargeable to tax under Case V of Schedule D: but this subsection does not apply in relation to a person if—

(*a*) the consideration received by the person for the capital sum is a qualifying asset (within the meaning of section 110) acquired by a qualifying company (within the meaning of that section) in the course of its business, and

(*b*) the asset was acquired from a person other than an individual.][1]

Amendments

1 This section inserted by FA 2003 s 36(1) and applies in the case of subs (2) as respects of any capital sum received on or after 6 February 2003 and in the case of subs (3) as respects amounts received on or after that date.

Definitions

company s 4(1); connected: s 10; person: IA 1937 s 11(*c*); Tax Acts: s 1(2); year of assessment: s 2(1).

CHAPTER 9
Miscellaneous Provisions

107 Apportionment of profits

(1) Where in the case of any profits or gains chargeable under Case I, II or IV of Schedule D it is necessary, in order to determine the profits or gains or losses of any year of assessment or other period, to divide and apportion to specific periods the profits or gains or losses for any period for which the accounts have been made up, or to aggregate any such profits or gains or losses or any apportioned parts of such profits or

gains or losses, it shall be lawful to make such division and apportionment or aggregation.

(2) Any apportionment under this section shall be made in proportion to the number of months or fractions of months in the respective periods.

Cross-references

Separate assessment of partners: s 1008(2)(*b*).

Definitions

month: IA 1937 Sch; year of assessment: s 3(1).

Former enactments

ITA 1967 s 107; FA 1969 s 65(1) and Sch 5 Pt I.

108 Statement of profits

Every statement of profits to be charged under Schedule D which is made by any person—

(*a*) on that person's own account, or

(*b*) on account of another person for whom that person is chargeable, or who is chargeable in that person's name,

shall include every source of income so chargeable.

Cross-references

This section applies to concerns chargeable under Case I(*b*): s 56(1).

Definitions

body of persons: s 2(1); person: IA 1937 s 11(*c*).

Former enactments

ITA 1967 s 68(1); FA 1997 s 146(2) and Sch 9 Pt II.

109 Payments in respect of redundancy

(1) In this section, **"lump sum"** and **"rebate"** have the same meanings respectively as in the Redundancy Payments Act, 1967.

(2) Where a lump sum is paid by an employer in respect of employment wholly in a trade or profession carried on by the employer and within the charge to income tax or corporation tax, the amount of the lump sum shall (if not otherwise so allowable) be allowable as a deduction in computing for the purposes of Schedule D the profits or gains or losses of the trade or profession, but if it is so allowed by virtue of this section the amount of the rebate recoverable shall (if it is not otherwise to be so treated) be treated as a receipt to be taken into account in computing those profits or gains and, if the lump sum was paid after the discontinuance of the trade or profession, the net amount so deductible shall be treated as if it were a payment made on the last day on which the trade or profession was carried on.

(3) Where a lump sum is paid by an employer in respect of employment wholly in a business carried on by the employer and expenses of management of the business are eligible for relief under [section 83 or 707],[1] the amount by which the lump sum exceeds the amount of the rebate recoverable shall (if not otherwise so allowable) be allowable as expenses of management eligible for relief under that section and, if the lump sum was

paid after the discontinuance of the business, the net amount so allowable shall be treated as if it were expenses of management incurred on the last day on which the business was carried on.

(4) Where a lump sum is paid by an employer in respect of employment wholly in maintaining or managing premises and the expenses of maintaining or managing the premises were deductible under section 97, the amount by which the lump sum exceeds the amount of the rebate recoverable shall (if not otherwise allowable under that section) be treated for the purposes of section 97 as a payment made by the employer in respect of the maintenance or management of the premises and, if the payment was made after the latest time when it could be taken into account under section 97 as a payment in respect of the maintenance or management of the property, it shall be treated as having been made at that time.

(5) Relief shall not be given under subsections (2) to (4), or otherwise, more than once in respect of any lump sum and, if the employee was being employed by the employer in such a way that different parts of the employee's remuneration fell to be treated for income tax purposes in different ways, the amount (in this subsection referred to as **"the excess amount"**) by which the lump sum exceeds the amount of the rebate recoverable shall be apportioned to the different capacities in which the employee was employed, and subsections (2) to (4) shall apply separately to the employment in those capacities, and by reference to the apportioned part of the excess amount, instead of by reference to the full amount of the lump sum and the full amount of the rebate.

(6) Where under section 32 of the Redundancy Payments Act, 1967, a payment of the whole or part of a lump sum is made by the Minister for Enterprise, Trade and Employment, the payment shall, in so far as the employer has reimbursed that Minister, be deemed for the purposes of this section to have been made by the employer.

Amendments

1 Substituted by FA 1998 s 136 and Sch 9 para 2 with effect from 6 April 1997; previously "section 83 or 709".

Cross-references

Management expenses of investment companies: s 83(4).

Definitions

person: IA 1937 s 11(*c*); profession: s 2(1); trade: s 3(1); week: IA 1937 Sch.

Former enactments

FA 1968 s 37(1) and (3)–(7); FA 1974 s 86 and Sch 2 Pt I; CTA 1976 s 140(1) and Sch 2 Pt I para 30; FA 1977 s 42 and Sch 1 Pt IV para 2.

110 Securitisation

[(1) In this section—

"authorised officer" means an officer of the Revenue Commissioners authorised by them in writing for the purposes of this section;

"qualifying asset", in relation to a qualifying company, means an asset which consists of, or of an interest in, a financial asset;

"financial asset" includes—

(*a*) shares, bonds and other securities,

(*b*) futures, options, swaps, derivatives and similar instruments,

(*c*) invoices and all types of receivables,

(*d*) obligations evidencing debt (including loans and deposits),

(*e*) leases and loan and lease portfolios,

(*f*) hire purchase contracts,

(*g*) acceptance credits and all other documents of title relating to the movement of goods, and

(*h*) bills of exchange, commercial paper, promissory notes and all other kinds of negotiable or transferable instruments;

"qualifying company" means a company—

(*a*) which is resident in the State,

(*b*) which—

(i) acquires qualifying assets from a person,

(ii) as a result of an arrangement with another person holds or manages qualifying assets, or

(iii) has entered into a legally enforceable arrangement with another person which arrangement itself constitutes a qualifying asset,

(*c*) which carries on in the State a business of holding, managing, or both the holding and management of, qualifying assets,

(*d*) which, apart from activities ancillary to that business, carries on no other activities,

(*e*) in relation to which company—

(i) the market value of all qualifying assets held or managed, or

(ii) the market value of all qualifying assets in respect of which the company has entered into legally enforceable arrangements,

is not less than €10,000,000 on the day on which the qualifying assets are first acquired, first held, or an arrangement referred to in subparagraph (iii) of paragraph (*b*) is first entered into, by the company, and

(*f*) which has notified in writing the authorised officer in a form prescribed by the Revenue Commissioners that it is or intends to be a company to which paragraphs (*a*) to (*e*) apply and has supplied such other particulars relating to the company as may be specified on the prescribed form,

but a company shall not be a qualifying company if any transaction or arrangement is entered into by it otherwise than by way of a bargain made at arm's length, apart from a transaction or arrangement where subsection (4) applies to any interest or other distribution payable under the transaction or arrangement unless the transaction or arrangement concerned is excluded from that provision by virtue of subsection (5).

(2) For the purposes of the Tax Acts, profits arising to a qualifying company, in relation to activities carried out by it in the course of its business, shall, notwithstanding any other provisions of the Tax Acts, be treated as annual profits or gains within Schedule D

and shall be chargeable to corporation tax under Case III of that Schedule, and for that purpose—

(*a*) the profits or gains shall be computed in accordance with the provisions applicable to Case I of that Schedule,

(*b*) there shall be deducted, in computing the amount of the profits or gains to be charged to tax, the amount, in so far as it is not—

(i) otherwise deductible, or

(ii) recoverable from any other person or under any insurance, contract of indemnity or otherwise,

of any debt which is proved to be bad and of a doubtful debt to the extent that it is estimated to be bad, and

(*c*) where at any time an amount or part of an amount which had been deducted under paragraph (*b*) is recovered or is no longer estimated to be bad, the amount which had been deducted shall, in so far as it is recovered or no longer estimated to be bad, be treated as income of the qualifying company at that time.

(3) (*a*) Notwithstanding Chapter 5 of Part 12, a qualifying company shall not be eligible to surrender in accordance with that Chapter any amount eligible for relief from corporation tax.

(*b*) (i) Where in an accounting period a qualifying company incurs a loss, the company may make a claim requiring that the amount of the loss be set off against the amount of any profits of the company for any subsequent accounting period for so long as the company continues to be a qualifying company, and the company's profits for any accounting period shall be treated as reduced by the amount of the loss.

(ii) The claim referred to in subparagraph (i) shall be included with the return which the company is required to make under section 951 for the subsequent accounting period concerned.

(iii) The amount of a loss incurred by a qualifying company in an accounting period shall be computed for the purposes of this paragraph in the same way as any profits of the company in that period would have been computed under subsection (2).

(4) Any interest or other distribution which is paid out of the assets of a qualifying company to another person and is so paid in respect of a security referred to in section 130(2)(*d*)(iii) shall not be a distribution by virtue only of section 130(2)(*d*)(iii) unless the application of this subsection is excluded by subsection (5).

(5) (*a*) Subject to paragraph (*b*), subsection (4) shall not apply in respect of any interest or other distribution paid or payable out of the assets of a qualifying company if such interest or other distribution has been paid as part of a scheme or arrangement the main purpose or one of the main purposes of which is to obtain a tax relief or the reduction of a tax liability, in either case arising from the operation of subsection (4), by a person within the charge to corporation tax (in this subsection referred to as the **"beneficiary"**) and the beneficiary is the person—

(i) from whom the assets were acquired by the qualifying company, or

(ii) with whom the qualifying company has entered into an arrangement referred to in subparagraph (ii) or (iii) of paragraph (*b*) of the definition of "qualifying company".

(*b*) Paragraph (*a*) shall only apply where the qualifying company concerned is, at the time of the acquisition of the asset or the entering into of the arrangement, in possession, or aware, of information which can reasonably be used by it to identify the beneficiary.][1]

[(6) (*a*) Subject to paragraph (*b*), section 76A shall have effect in relation to a qualifying company as it would if, in section 4, the following were substituted for the definition of generally accepted accounting practice:

"**'generally accepted accounting practice'** means Irish generally accepted accounting practice as it applied for a period of account ending on 31 December 2004.".

(*b*) A qualifying company may, as respect any accounting period, by notice in writing given to the inspector by the specified return date (within the meaning of section 950) for the accounting period, elect that this subsection shall not apply as respects that or any subsequent accounting period; and any election under this paragraph shall be irrevocable.

(*c*) Schedule 17A shall apply with any necessary modifications to a company which makes an election under paragraph (*b*).][2]

Amendments

1 Section 110 substituted by FA 2003 s 48(1) as respects any asset acquired or, as a result of an arrangement with another person, held or managed, by a qualifying company (within the meaning of TCA 1997 s 110), or in relation to which a qualifying company (within that meaning) has entered into a legally enforceable arrangement with another person, on or after 6 February 2003.

2 Subs (6) inserted by FA 2005 s 48(1)(*d*) as respects any period of account beginning on or after 1 January 2005.

Cross-references

Certain trading operations carried on in Custom House Docks Area, meaning of "qualifying company" applied: s 446(2D), (7)(*c*)(ii)(V).

Companies (Auditing and Accounting) Act 2003, s 48(1)(*j*)(i), Minister's power to make regulations, meaning of "qualifying companies" in this section applied.

Interest, certain interest not to be chargeable, meaning of "qualifying company" applied: s 198(1)(*c*)(iv).

Interest payments by companies and to non-residents, meaning of "qualifying company" applied: s 246(3)(*cc*), (*ccc*).

Transfer of rent, meanings of "qualifying asset" and "qualifying company" applied: s 106A(2)(*b*)(ii), (3)(*a*).

Definitions

company: ss 4(1), 5(1); distribution: s 4(1); inspector: ss 2(1), 5(1); Irish generally accepted accounting practice: s 4(1); person: IA 1937 s 11(*c*); Tax Acts: s 1(2); writing: IA 1937 Sch.

Former enactments

FA 1991 s 31; FA 1996 s 55(1).

111 Allowance to owner of let mineral rights for expenses of management of minerals

(1) (*a*) Where for any year of assessment rights to work minerals in the State are let, the lessor shall be entitled on making a claim in that behalf to be repaid so much of the income tax paid by such lessor by deduction or otherwise in respect of the rent or royalties for that year as is equal to the amount of the tax on any sums proved to have been wholly, exclusively and necessarily disbursed

by such lessor as expenses of management or supervision of those minerals in that year.

(*b*) Notwithstanding paragraph (*a*), no repayment of tax under that paragraph shall be made—

(i) except on proof of payment of tax on the aggregate amount of the rent or royalties, or

(ii) if, or to such extent as, the expenses of management or supervision have been otherwise allowed as a deduction in computing income for the purposes of income tax.

(2) Notice of any claim under this section together with the particulars of the claim shall be given in writing within 24 months after the expiration of the year of assessment in respect of which the claim is made, and where the inspector objects to such claim the Appeal Commissioners shall hear and determine the claim in the like manner as in the case of an appeal to them against an assessment under Schedule D, and the provisions of the Income Tax Acts relating to the statement of a case for the opinion of the High Court on a point of law shall apply.

Cross-references

Corporation tax, computation of income, application of income tax principles: s 77(4).

Definitions

Appeal Commissioners: s 2(1); High Court: IA 1937 Sch; inspector: ss 2(1), 5(1), 852; month: IA 1937 Sch; minerals: s 5(1); IA 1937 Sch; writing: IA 1937 Sch; year of assessment: s 3(1).

Former enactments

ITA 1967 s 553; F(MP)A 1968 s 3(2) and Sch Pt I and s3(5) and Sch Pt IV; FA 1981 s 9(*c*).

Corresponding UK tax provision

Income and Corporation Taxes Act 1988 s 131.

PART 5
PRINCIPAL PROVISIONS RELATING TO THE SCHEDULE E CHARGE

Statement of Practice

Tax Treatment of Remuneration of Members of State and State Sponsored Committees and Boards: SP IT 1/04.

Tax Briefing

TB40 June 2000 pp 23–26 — Taxation of Fringe Benefits.

Revenue precedents

Issue: Re-instatement of employee following a decision of the tribunal.
Decision: As the decision of the tribunal related to the reinstatement of the employee, the award is in respect of the earnings that he was entitled to and are chargeable as ordinary emoluments under TCA 1997 s 112.
Issue: Employer had a bonus scheme and the employees were obliged to expend their benefits under the bonus scheme in a particular way.
Decision: The benefits form part of the gross emoluments of the employees.

CHAPTER 1
Basis of Assessment, Persons Chargeable and Extent of Charge

112 Basis of assessment, persons chargeable and extent of charge

(1) Income tax under Schedule E [shall be charged for each year of assessment][1] on every person having or exercising an office or employment of profit mentioned in that

Schedule, or to whom any annuity, pension or stipend chargeable under that Schedule is payable, in respect of all salaries, fees, wages, perquisites or profits whatever therefrom, and shall be computed on the amount of all such salaries, fees, wages, perquisites or profits whatever therefrom for the year of assessment.

(2) (*a*) In this subsection, **"emoluments"** means anything assessable to income tax under Schedule E.

(*b*) Where apart from this subsection emoluments from an office or employment would be for a year of assessment in which a person does not hold the office or employment, the following provisions shall apply for the purposes of subsection (1):

(i) if in the year concerned the office or employment has never been held, the emoluments shall be treated as emoluments for the first year of assessment in which the office or employment is held, and

(ii) if in the year concerned the office or employment is no longer held, the emoluments shall be treated as emoluments for the last year of assessment in which the office or employment was held.

Amendments

1 Substituted by FA 2001 s 77(2) and Sch 2 para 5 with effect from 6 April 2001; previously "shall be charged annually".

Cross-references

Additional assessments, subs (2): s 924(2)(*d*)(ii).
Application of section 985 (PAYE method of collection) to certain perquisites, etc: s 985A(1)(*a*).
Benefit in kind charge: s 118(1).
Deduction for income earned outside the State: s 823(1)("the specified amount").
Employer preferential loan: s 122(2).
Expenses allowances taxed as perquisite: s 117(1).
Income Tax (Employments) (Consolidated) Regulations 2001, deduction of tax in respect of certain notional payments: ITECR 2001 reg 17A(1)(*c*).
Oireachtas severance payments, subs (1): s 124(2)(*a*).
Permanent health benefit scheme benefits, subs (1): s 125(3)(*b*).
Restrictive covenants: s 127(2).
Social welfare benefits, tax treatment, subs (1): s 126(3)(*b*)(i).
Taxation of certain perquisites: s 112A(2).

Case law

Exercising an office or employment

Irish

A local manager for the Dept of Social Welfare required to provide premises and staff held to be self-employed and accordingly not liable under Schedule E: *O'Coindealbháin v Mooney* ITR Vol IV p 45.
An insurance agent not subject to any restrictions or direct control of his activities by the company for which he worked regarded as not in receipt of emoluments: *MacDermott v Loy* TL 118, (High Court, 29 July 1982).
Contributory children's pensions payable in conjunction with other entitlements of a Garda widow not to be regarded as the income of the mother: *O'Coindealbháin v O'Carroll* ITR Vol IV p 221. See also *Inspector of Taxes v Neenan* (High Court, July 1996).
Members of a fishing crew entitled to a share of the proceeds of sale of the catch held not to be employees: *McLoughlin v Director of Public Prosecutions* ITR Vol III p 467.
Members of Drogheda Deepsea Dockers' Association (who shared pooled earnings) held to be employees (contract of service) of the stevedores: *Louth and others v Minister for Social Welfare* [1995] 1 IR 238.
Temporary typist's contract was with the employment bureau, not the company using the bureau's service, therefore she was not an employee: *Minister for Labour v PMPA Insurance Company Ltd* ITR Vol III p 505.
An agreement to deliver newspapers between individuals and a distributor of newspapers held to be a contract for services: *McAuliffe v Minister for Social Welfare* [1995] 1IR 238.

A demonstrator of food products at supermarkets held to have a contract of service: *Denny & Sons (Ireland) Ltd v the Minister for Social Welfare* ITR Vol V p 238.
The tax treatment of an employment is not conclusive for other purposes – *Re Sunday Tribune Ltd* [1984] IR 505.
In *FAS v Minister of Social Welfare, Abbott and Ryan* Egan J in the High Court held that no employee PRSI contributions were due in respect of an illegal contract of service. In the Supreme Court, it was held that the contract in question was ultra vires the employer rather than illegal consequently the court was able to exercise its discretion and refused to invalidate the contract.
UK
A professional dancer prohibited by contract from performing elsewhere without the consent of the theatre management held assessable under Schedule E: *Fall v Hitchen* (1973) 49 TC 433.
A TV vision mixer working for 20 TV production companies held to be self-employed and not assessable under Schedule E: *Hall v Lorimer* [1992] STI 554.
Actress who executed a separate contract for each play and radio appearance held assessable under Schedule D and not E: *Davies v Braithwaite* (1931) 18 TC 198.
An independent local inquiry inspector held not the holder of an office and assessable under Schedule D: *Edwards v Clinch* [1981] STC 617.
If the provider of services performs them as a person in business on his own account, the contract is one for services assessable under Schedule D, otherwise it is a contract of services assessable under Schedule E: *Market Investigations Ltd v Minister for Social Security* [1968] 3 All ER 732.
Part-time hospital consultant held assessable under Schedule E as the holder of an office: *Mitchell v Ross* (1961) 40 TC 11.
Barrister's clerk working for each member of chambers for a percentage of gross earnings held assessable under Schedule D: *McMenamin v Diggles* [1991] STC 419.
Potato workers held employees of individual under whose general control and management they worked: *Andrews v King* [1991] STC 481.
Video and television technician held to be self-employed: *Barnett v Brabyn* [1996] STC 716.

Emoluments

Irish
A teaching nun required by the constitution of her order to pay over all her earnings to the order held to be directly chargeable under Schedule E on her emoluments: *Dolan v K* ITR Vol I p 656.
Tax on emoluments to be computed on earnings and not receipts basis: *McKeown v Roe* 1 ITC 206; [1928] IR 195; see also *Bedford v Hannon* TL 105(High Court, 30 May 1968).
A teacher who took night classes under a separate contract with the same local authority that employed her was held to fall within Schedule E in respect thereof – *Fuge v McLelland* 36 ITC 571.
UK
A perquisite is money or that which can be turned to pecuniary account: *Tennant v Smith* (1892) 3 TC 158.
The payment must be a reward for past, present or future services and must be made by reference to the service rendered by the employee: *Hochstrasser v Mayes* (1958) 38 TC 673.
The taxpayer is assessed on the market value of the perquisite and not on the cost to the employer: *Wilkins v Rogerson* (1960) 39 TC 344.
Bonus payment held assessable for year in which it was earned and not for year in which it was paid: *Griffin v Standish* [1995] STC 825.

Benefits taxed under Schedule E include:

Irish
Bonus paid to a jockey by his employer: *Wing v O'Connell* ITR Vol II p 452.
Value of rental payment made by employer for house occupied voluntarily by employee: *Connolly v McNamara*, 3 ITC 341.
Inducement payment (*Shilton v Wilmshurst* [1991] STC 88 approved): Supreme Court, *O'Connell v Keleghan*.
UK
Compensation for surrendering rights under employment protection legislation: *Hamblett v Godfrey* [1987] STC 60.
Compensation paid for the surrender of contractual rights: *Bolam v Muller* (1947) 28 TC 471.
Compensation paid for the withdrawal of a company car: *Bird v Maitland, Bird v Allen* [1982] STC 603.
Compensation paid under a contract of service: *Dale v de Soissons* (1950) 32 TC 118.
Compensation paid under the terms of the articles of association on resignation of a director: *Henry v Foster* (1932) 16 TC 605.
Easter offerings paid by a church to its vicar: *Cooper v Blakiston* (1907) 5 TC 347.

Payment by football club to induce player to take up a position with another club: *Shilton v Wilmshurst* [1991] STC 88.

Payment made for storing company property: *Beecham Group Ltd v Fair* [1984] STC 15.

Payment made to induce the taxpayer to become an employee of the paying company: *Glantre Engineering Ltd v Goodhand* [1983] STC 1.

Payment of employee's income tax by employer: *Hartland v Diggines* (1926) 10 TC 247.

Payment to clergyman of a grant from the diocesan fund: *Herbert v McQuade* (1902) 4 TC 489.

Payment to professional cricketer of sum collected from crowd provided for in his contract: *Moorhouse v Dooland* (1955) 36 TC 1.

Taxi driver's tips: *Calvert v Wainwright* (1947) 27 TC 475.

Payment by employer of school fees of child of employee: *Glynn v Hong Kong Commissioners of Inland Revenue* [1990] STC 227.

Income from loan by employer to non-resident trust for benefit of employee: *O'Leary v McKinley* [1991] STC 42.

Allowance for purchase of newspapers and periodicals by journalists: *Smith v Abbott* [1994] STC 237; *Fitzpatrick v CIR* [1994] STC 237.

Payment originally intended as supplementary to statutory redundancy but subsequently made to all employees whether made redundant or not: *Allan v IRC, Cullen v IRC* [1994] STC 943.

Termination payment to employee treated by firm in many respects as a partner: *Horner v Hasted* [1995] STC 766.

Receipts not liable under Schedule E:

Irish

A share of estate rents payable to an individual (including also a reduced share of any property sold) receivable in return for managing the properties held by the Supreme Court to be conditional gifts and not Schedule E income: *O'Reilly v Casey* ITR Vol I p 601.

A full-time employee of a company provided assistance and advice to another company on the liquidation of which he was made an "ex gratia" payment which was held not to be taxable: *McGarry v EF* ITR Vol II p 261.

In *Cerberus Software v Rowley* [2001] IRLR 160, the Court upheld the right of the employer not to exercise its discretion not to make a payment in lieu of notice but to breach the contract instead. It seems clear that such a payment as was made in *Cerberus* would not be taxable on general principles under TCA 1997 s 112.

UK

Bonus paid to team captain on winning the world cup: *Moore v Griffiths* (1972) 48 TC 388.

Compensation for giving up pension rights: *Wales v Tiley* (1942) 25 TC 136.

Compensation paid to indemnify employee against loss on the sale of his house due to job transfer: *Hochstrasser v Mayes* (1959) 38 TC 673.

Compensation payment for cancellation of employment contract: *DuCros v Ryall* (1935) 19 TC 444; *Henley v Murray* (1950) 31 TC 351.

Ex gratia payment from Department of Economic Development: *Mairs v Haughey* [1993] STC 569.

Expenses connected with membership of European Parliament: *Lord Bruce of Donnington v Aspden* [1981] STC 761.

Payment for surrendering right to compensation under articles of association: *Hunter v Dewhurst* (1932) 16 TC 605.

Signing on fee paid by rugby league on change by taxpayer from amateur to professional status: *Jarrold v Boustead* (1964) 41 TC 701.

Transfer of shares made to induce taxpayer to give up his position of employment: *Pritchard v Arundale* (1971) 47 TC 680.

Sponsorship payments: *Walters v Tickner* [1993] STC 624.

Payments for loss of rights under share option scheme: *Wilcock v Eve* [1995] STC 18.

See also: *Singh v Williams* (2000) STC (SCO) 404.

Revenue precedents

Issue: Employer lodges an allowance to the credit card account of an employee. Is it a perquisite or benefit?

Decision: It is a perquisite. The payment ranks no differently from an employer lodging wages to his employees bank accounts. The PAYE system applies to such allowances.

Issue: Whether a payment to a member of staff, who introduces a potential employee, is taxable.

Decision: As the payment arises from the employment, it is taxable under TCA 1997 s 112.

Issue: Informal sickness benefit scheme operates which is funded jointly by employer and employees.

Decision: Tax relief is not allowed for the employees contributions. Benefits received by employees are chargeable to tax to the extent that they represent the employers contribution to the fund (under PAYE). Tax is not chargeable on the employees at the time the employers contributions are made to the fund.

Revenue information

Information leaflet IT11 — Employee's Guide to PAYE.

Statement of Practice

Tax Treatment of Remuneration of Members of State and State Sponsored Committees and Boards: IT 1/04.

Tax Briefing

TB28 Oct 1997 — Part-time lecturers/teachers/trainers are, in general, employees.

TB31 Apr 1998 — Agency workers are, in general, treated as employees, and person contractually obliged to pay the employed agency worker is the employer for PAYE purposes.

TB32 June 1998 — Inducement payments to take up employment are taxable under this section and PAYE must be deducted at time of payment, generally when employment offer is made and accepted.

TB42 Dec 2000 p 48 — Taxation treatment of provision of home leave travel for expatriate employees — where employer bears or reimburses the cost of one trip per year to the home location for the expatriate and his/her family, no assessment will be made on the employee in respect of the benefit received.

TB51 Jan 2003 p 20 — What is the tax treatment of legal costs recovered by an employee from an employer as part of a court action to recover compensation for loss of office or employment, etc? Revenue are prepared to accept that no income tax charge will be imposed on the employee in respect of the payment of legal costs where the payment is made by the former employer directly to the former employee's solicitor, is in full or partial discharge of the solicitor's bill of costs incurred by the employee only in connection with the termination of his/her employment and is under a specific term in the settlement agreement. This treatment applies only to legal costs and applies to payments made either under a court order or where a settlement is reached outside of court.

TB58 Dec 2004 p 13 — Third Party Benefits.

Definitions

person: IA 1937 s 11(*c*); year of assessment: s 3(1).

Former enactments

ITA 1967 s 110; FA 1990 s 19(*a*); FA 1991 s 6.

Corresponding UK tax provision

Income and Corporation Taxes Act 1988 s 131.

112A Taxation of certain perquisites

[(1) In this section—

"appropriate percentage", **"authorised insurer"**, **"relevant contract"** and **"relievable amount"** have the same meanings, respectively, as in section 470, and

"qualifying insurer" and **"qualifying long-term care policy"** have the same meanings, respectively, as in section 470A.

(2) Section 112 shall apply in relation to a perquisite comprising the payment to—

(*a*) an authorised insurer under a relevant contract, or

(*b*) a qualifying insurer under a qualifying long-term care policy

as if any deduction authorised by—

(i) in a case in which paragraph (*a*) applies, section 470(3)(*a*), or

(ii) in a case in which paragraph (*b*) applies, section 470A(8)(*a*),

had not been made.

(3) Where, for any year of assessment, an employer (within the meaning of section 983)—

(*a*) makes a payment of emoluments consisting of a perquisite of the kind mentioned in subsection (2), and

(*b*) deducts therefrom and retains in accordance with—

(i) section 470(3)(*a*), an amount equal to the appropriate percentage for the year of assessment of the relievable amount in relation to the payment, or

(ii) section 470A(8)(*a*), an amount equal to the appropriate percentage for the year of assessment of the payment,

the employer shall be assessed and charged to income tax in an amount equal to the amount so deducted and retained and that amount shall be allowable as a deduction in charging to tax the profits or gains of such employer.

(4) Subsections (3) to (6) of section 238 shall apply, with necessary modifications, in relation to a payment referred to in subsection (3) as they apply in relation to a payment to which that section applies.]

Amendments

[1] Section 112A inserted by FA 2001 s 21 for short tax "year" 2001 and later tax years.

Cross-references

application of section 985 (PAYE method of collection) to certain perquisites, etc: s 985A(1)(*a*)(iii).

Tax Briefing

TB43 April 2001 p 24 — Employer Paid Medical Insurance Premiums.
TB49 Aug 2002 p 18 — Employer Paid Medical Insurance Premiums.

Definitions

profits or gains: s 3(4); year of assessment: s 2(1).

CHAPTER 2
Computational Provisions

113 Making of deductions

(1) In this section, **"emoluments"** means all salaries, fees, wages, perquisites or profits or gains whatever arising from an office or employment, or the amount of any annuity, pension or stipend, as the case may be.

(2) Any deduction from emoluments allowed under the Income Tax Acts for the purpose of computing an assessment to income tax under Schedule E shall be made by reference to the amount paid or borne for the year or portion of the year on the emoluments of which the computation is made.

Cross-references

Benefit of use of a car, meaning of emoluments applied: s 121(1)(*a*).
Notional loans relating to shares, etc, meaning of "emoluments" applied: s 122A(1).

Former enactments

ITA 1967 s 111(4) and s 112; FA 1990 s 19(*b*)(proviso).

Corresponding UK tax provision

Income and Corporation Taxes Act 1988 s 131.

114 General rule as to deductions

Where the holder of an office or employment of profit is necessarily obliged to incur and defray out of the emoluments of the office or employment of profit expenses of travelling in the performance of the duties of that office or employment, or otherwise to expend money wholly, exclusively and necessarily in the performance of those duties, there may be deducted from the emoluments to be assessed the expenses so necessarily incurred and defrayed.

Cross-references

Allowance for expenses of members of the Oireachtas: s 836(2).

Benefit in kind charge: s 118(1).

Business entertainment expenses: s 840(2)(*c*).

Expense allowances taxed as perquisite: s 117(1).

Expenses subject to benefit in kind: s 116(3)(*a*).

Judiciary, tax treatment of expenses of, this rule does not apply to allowances payable in accordance with Courts of Justice Act 1953 s 5: s 196(3).

Schedule E: s 19(1).

Case law

Irish

Cost of travelling to a place of employment not allowable as expenses against emoluments: *Phillips v Keane* ITR Vol I p 64.

Expenses payments by local government engineers which were not incurred during the course of the employments not allowable as Schedule E deductions: *O'Broin v MacGiolla Meidhre and Pigott* ITR Vol II p 366.

Payments made by an army officer arising from but not incurred in the course of his public employment, including payments to a batman, regarded as inadmissible: *Kelly v H* ITR Vol II p 460.

While the main expenses of a director of a number of companies involving international travel were reimbursed other incidental expenses for which no records were kept were not. Relief for income tax purposes refused: *MacDaibhéid v Carroll* TL 115; [1982] ILRM 430.

UK

Expense of travelling to place of employment not allowable: *Ricketts v Colquhoun* (1926) 10 TC 118; unless employment begins at home: *Pook v Owen* (1969) 45 TC 571; or taxpayer travelling between bases: *Taylor v Provan* [1973] STC 170. A taxpayer who was director of his own company whose registered office was in his home could not claim travelling expenses to another company to which his services had been contracted: *Miners v Atkinson* [1997] STC 58.

Unrelieved expenses cannot be deducted from Schedule D Case III income: *Shaw v Tonkin* [1988] STC 186.

Expenses not allowable include:

Annual club subscription: *Brown v Bulloch* (1961) 40 TC 1.

Lecture fees: *Humbles v Brooks* (1962) 40 TC 500.

Examination fees: *Lupton v Potts* (1969) 45 TC 643.

Cost to journalists of purchasing newspapers: *Fitzpatrick v IRC* [1992] STC 406; unless used in the performance of their duties: *Smith v Abbot* [1993] STC 316.

Sch E tax arising on benefit in kind of salesman's car not a "travelling expense": *Clark v Bye* [1997] STC 311.

Ansell (Inspector of Taxes) v Brown (2001) STC 1166.

Snowdon v Charnock (Inspector of Taxes) (2001) STC 152.

Kirkwood (Inspector of Taxes) v Evans (2001) STC (SCO) 231.

Revenue information

Information leaflet IT51 — Employees' Motoring Expenses.

Information leaflet IT54 — Employees' Subsistence Expenses.

Tax Briefing

TB52 p 17 — What is the tax treatment of expenses paid to or incurred by soccer players and other sportspersons employed by clubs?

TB Supplement May 2004 pp 28–30 — Schedule E Expenses 2003 and 2004.

TB57 Oct 2004 p 13 — Domestic (Civil Service) Subsistence Rates effective from 1 September 2004.

Former enactments

ITA 1967 Sch 2 rule 3; FA 1996 s 132 and Sch 5 Pt II.

Corresponding UK tax provision

Income and Corporation Taxes Act 1988 s 198.

115 Fixed deduction for certain classes of persons

Where the Minister for Finance is satisfied, with respect to any class of persons in receipt of any salary, fees or emoluments payable out of the public revenue, that such persons are obliged to lay out and expend money wholly, exclusively and necessarily in the performance of the duties in respect of which such salary, fees or emoluments are payable, the Minister for Finance may fix such sum as in that Minister's opinion represents a fair equivalent of [the average amount for a year of assessment][1] so laid out and expended by persons of that class, and in charging the tax on such salary, fees or emoluments, there shall be deducted from the amount of such salary, fees or emoluments the sums so fixed by the Minister for Finance; but, if any person would but for this section be entitled to deduct a larger amount than the sum so fixed, that sum may be deducted instead of the sum so fixed.

Amendments

1 Substituted by FA 2001 s 77(2) and Sch 2 para 6 with effect from 6 April 2001; previously "the average annual amount".

Cross-references

Allowance for expenses of members of the Oireachtas: s 836(2).

Judiciary, tax treatment of expenses of, this rule does not apply to allowances payable in accordance with Courts of Justice Act 1953 s 5: s 196(3).

Schedule E: s 19(1).

Definitions

person: IA 1937 s 11(*c*).

Former enactments

ITA 1967 Sch 2 rule 4.

CHAPTER 3

Expenses Allowances and Provisions Relating to the General Benefits in Kind Charge

Cross-references

Additional assessments: s 924(2)(*d*)(ii).

Benefit of use of car, this Chapter does not apply in relation to expense incurred in connection with provision of car: s 121(2)(*b*)(i).

Benefit of use of van, this Chapter does not apply in relation to expense incurred in connection with provision of van: s 121A(1)(*b*)(i).

Employee share purchase schemes, meaning of "director" applied: s 479(1)(*a*).

Loans of art objects: s 236(3)(*a*).

Relief for contributions to permanent health benefit schemes: s 471(3).

Revenue information

An Employer's Guide to operating PAYE and PRSI on certain benefits is available on Revenue's website (www.revenue.ie) under PAYE/Benefits in Kind.

116 Interpretation (Chapter 3)

(1) In this Chapter—

"business premises", in relation to a body corporate, includes all premises occupied by that body for the purpose of any trade carried on by it and, except when the reference is expressly to premises which include living accommodation, includes so much of any such premises so occupied as is used wholly or mainly as living accommodation for any of the directors of the body corporate or for any persons employed by the body corporate in any employment to which this Chapter applies;

[**"business use"**, in relation to the use of an asset by a person, means the use of that asset by the person in the performance of the duties of the person's office or employment;][1]

"control", in relation to a body corporate, means the power of a person to secure—

(*a*) by means of the holding of shares or the possession of voting power in or in relation to that or any other body corporate, or

(*b*) by virtue of any powers conferred by the articles of association or other document regulating that or any other body corporate,

that the affairs of the first-mentioned body corporate are conducted in accordance with the wishes of that person;

"director" means—

(*a*) in relation to a body corporate the affairs of which are managed by a board of directors or similar body, a member of that board or body,

(*b*) in relation to a body corporate the affairs of which are managed by a single director or similar person, that director or person,

(*c*) in relation to a body corporate the affairs of which are managed by the members themselves, a member of the body corporate,

and includes any person in accordance with whose directions or instructions the directors of a body corporate, defined in accordance with the preceding provisions of this definition, are accustomed to act, but a person shall not, within the meaning of this definition, be deemed to be a person in accordance with whose directions or instructions the directors of a body corporate are accustomed to act by reason only that those directors act on advice given by the person in a professional capacity;

"employment" means an employment such that any emoluments of the employment would be assessed under Schedule E, and references to persons employed by, or employees of, a body corporate include any person who takes part in the management of the affairs of the body corporate and is not a director of the body corporate.

[**"premises"** includes lands;][2]

[**"private use"**, in relation to an asset, means use of the asset other than business use.][3]

(2) Any reference in this Chapter to anything provided for a director or employee shall, unless the reference is expressly to something provided for the director or employee personally, be construed as including a reference to anything provided for the spouse, family, servants, dependants or guests of that director or employee, and the reference in

the definition of **"business premises"** to living accommodation for directors or employees shall be construed accordingly.

(3) (*a*) Subject to subsection (4) and paragraphs (*b*) and (*c*), the employments to which this Chapter applies shall be employments the emoluments of which, estimated for the year of assessment in question according to the Income Tax Acts and on the basis that they are employments to which this Chapter applies, and without any deduction being made under section 114 in respect of money expended in performing the duties of those employments, are [€1,905][4] or more.

(*b*) Where a person is employed in 2 or more employments by the same body corporate and the total of the emoluments of those employments for the year of assessment in question estimated in accordance with paragraph (*a*) is [€1,905][5] or more, all those employments shall be treated as employments to which this Chapter applies.

(*c*) Where a person is a director of a body corporate, all employments in which the person is employed by the body corporate shall be treated as employments to which this Chapter applies.

(4) All the directors of, and persons employed by, a body corporate over which another body corporate has control shall be treated for the purposes of paragraphs (*b*) and (*c*) of subsection (3) (but not for any other purpose) as if they were directors of that other body corporate or, as the case may be, as if the employment were an employment by that other body corporate.

Amendments

1 Definition of "business use" inserted by FA 2004 s 8(1)(*a*)(i) with effect from 1 January 2004.

2 Definition of "premises" inserted by FA 2005 s 7 with effect from 1 January 2005.

3 Definition of "private use" inserted by FA 2004 s 8(1)(*a*)(ii) with effect from 1 January 2004.

4 Substituted by FA 2001 s 240(1), (2)(*a*) and Sch 5 Pt 1 for 2002 and later tax years; previously "£1,500" (£1,110: short tax "year" 2001).

5 Substituted by FA 2002 s 138 and Sch 6 paras 3(*a*) and 6(*c*)(i) with effect from 1 January 2002; previously "£1,500" (£1,110: short tax "year" 2001).

Cross-references

Capital gains tax share reinvestment relief, meaning of "director" applied: s 591(1).

Returns of employees' emoluments, meaning of "director" applied: s 897(3).

Self assessment, meaning of "chargeable person": s 950(1).

Surcharge for late returns, meaning of "director" applied: s 1084(3).

Tax on non-resident company recoverable from another group member or controlling director, meaning of "director" applied: s 629(1).

Unincorporated bodies, partnerships and individuals, definition of "control" (subs (1)) applied: s 120(1), (2)(*b*).

Definitions

trade: s 3(1); year of assessment: s 3(1).

Former enactments

ITA 1967 ss 119 and 122.

Corresponding UK tax provision

Income and Corporation Taxes Act 1988 s 153.

117 Expenses allowances

(1) Subject to this Chapter, any sum paid in respect of expenses by a body corporate to any of its directors or to any person employed by it in an employment to which this Chapter applies shall, if not otherwise chargeable to income tax as income of that

director or employee, be treated for the purposes of section 112 as a perquisite of the office or employment of that director or employee and included in the emoluments of that office or employment assessable to income tax accordingly; but nothing in this subsection shall prevent a claim for a deduction being made under section 114 in respect of any money expended wholly, exclusively and necessarily in performing the duties of the office or employment.

(2) The reference in subsection (1) to any sum paid in respect of expenses includes a reference to any sum put by a body corporate at the disposal of a director or employee and paid away by him or her.

Revenue information

Information leaflet IT20 — Benefits from Employment
Information leaflet IT51 — Employees' Motoring Expenses
Information leaflet IT54 — Employees' Subsistence Expenses
Information leaflet IT69 — eWorking and Tax

Revenue information

An Employer's Guide to operating PAYE and PRSI on certain benefits is available on Revenue's website (www.revenue.ie) under PAYE/Benefits in Kind.

Statement of practice

Genuine cases of employee removal/relocation expenses: SP IT/1/91.

Tax Briefing

TB27 Aug 1997 p 5 — Employees' Subsistence Expenses.

TB31 Apr 1998 p 9 — Re Statement of Practice SP/IT/91 — from April 1998 specific prior approval by Revenue no longer required to make removal/relocation expenses covered by the Statement of Practice free of tax.

TB36 June 1999 p 9 — where Revenue approval to pay expenses without deduction of tax was given prior to introduction of information leaflet IT54, only those arrangements within the scope of that leaflet can continue to be paid without deduction of tax.

TB52 p 17 — What is the tax treatment of expenses paid to or incurred by soccer players and other sportspersons employed by clubs?

TB Supplement May 2004 pp 13–14 — Employees' Motoring and Subsistence Expenses — Civil Service Rates.

TB 57 Oct 2004 p 13 — Domestic (Civil Service) Subsistence Rates effective from 1 September 2004.

Definitions

director, employment: s 116.

Former enactments

ITA 1967 s 116; FA 1974 s 86 and Sch 2 Pt I.

Corresponding UK tax provision

Income and Corporation Tax Act 1988 s 153.

---

118 Benefits in kind: general charging provision

(1) Subject to this Chapter, where—

(*a*) a body corporate incurs expense in or in connection with the provision, for any of its directors or for any person employed by it in an employment to which this Chapter applies, of—

(i) living or other accommodation,

(ii) entertainment,

(iii) domestic or other services, or

(iv) other benefits or facilities of whatever nature, and

(*b*) apart from this section the expense would not be chargeable to income tax as income of the director or employee,

then, sections 112, 114 and 897 shall apply in relation to so much of the expense as is not made good to the body corporate by the director or employee as if the expense had been incurred by the director or employee and the amount of the expense had been refunded to the director or employee by the body corporate by means of a payment in respect of expenses, and income tax shall be chargeable accordingly.

(2) Subsection (1) shall not apply to expense incurred by the body corporate in or in connection with the provision for a director or employee in any of its business premises of any accommodation, supplies or services provided for the director or employee personally and used by the director or employee solely in performing the duties of his or her office or employment.

(3) Subsection (1) shall not apply to expense incurred by the body corporate in or in connection with the provision of living accommodation for an employee in part of any of its business premises which include living accommodation if the employee is, for the purpose of enabling the employee properly to perform his or her duties, required by the terms of his or her employment to reside in the accommodation and either—

(*a*) the accommodation is provided in accordance with a practice which since before the 30th day of July, 1948, has commonly prevailed in trades of the class in question as respects employees of the class in question, or

(*b*) it is necessary in the case of trades of the class in question that employees of the class in question should reside on premises of the class in question;

but this subsection shall not apply where the employee is a director of the body corporate in question or of any other body corporate over which that body corporate has control or which has control over that body corporate or which is under the control of a person who also has control over that body corporate.

(4) Subsection (1) shall not apply to expense incurred by the body corporate in or in connection with the provision of meals in any canteen in which meals are provided for the staff generally.

[(5) Subsection (1) shall not apply to expense incurred by the body corporate in or in connection with the provision for a director or employee, or for the director's or employee's spouse, children or dependants, of any pension, annuity, lump sum, gratuity or other like benefit to be given on the death or retirement of the director or employee, other than an expense incurred by way of contribution by the body corporate to a PRSA (within the meaning of Chapter 2A of Part 30).][1]

[(5A)(*a*) Subsection (1) shall not apply to expense incurred by the body corporate in or in connection with the provision for a director or employee of a monthly or annual bus, railway or ferry travel pass issued by or on behalf of one or more approved transport providers.

(*b*) In this subsection—

"approved transport provider" means—

(*a*) Córas Iompair Éireann or any of its subsidiaries,

(*b*) a holder of a passenger licence granted under section 7 of the Road Transport Act 1932, (*c*) a person who provides a passenger transport service under an arrangement entered into with Córas Iompair Éireann in accordance with section 13(1) of the Transport Act 1950,

(*d*) the Railway Procurement Agency or any of its subsidiaries,

(*e*) a person who has entered into an arrangement with the Railway Procurement Agency, in accordance with section 43(6) of the Transport (Railway Infrastructure) Act 2001 to operate a railway, or

(*f*) a person who provides a ferry service within the State, operating a vessel which holds a current valid—

(i) passenger ship safety certificate,

(ii) passenger boat licence, or

(iii) high-speed craft safety certificate,

issued by the Minister for Communications, Marine and Natural Resources;

"railway pass" includes a pass issued by a railway designated as a light railway or as a metro in a railway order made under section 43 of the Transport (Railway Infrastructure) Act 2001.][2]

[(5B)(*a*) Subsection (1) shall not apply to expense incurred by the body corporate in or in connection with the provision, without any transfer of the property in it, for a director or employee of a mobile telephone for business use where private use of the mobile telephone is incidental.

(*b*) The mobile telephones to which the exemption provided by this subsection applies include any mobile telephone provided in connection with a car or van notwithstanding that the vehicle is made available as referred to in section 121 or 121A, as the case may be.

(*c*) In this subsection **"mobile telephone"** means telephone apparatus which—

(i) is not physically connected to a landline, and

(ii) is not a cordless telephone.

(*d*) For the purposes of paragraph (*c*)—

"cordless telephone" means telephone apparatus designed or adapted to provide a wireless extension to a telephone, and used only as such an extension to a telephone that is physically connected to a land-line;

"telephone apparatus" means wireless telegraphy apparatus designed or adapted for the purposes of transmitting and receiving either or both spoken messages and information (being information for the same purposes as the Electronic Commerce Act 2000) and connected to a public telecommunications network (as defined in the European Communities (Telecommunications Services) Regulations 1992 (SI No 45 of 1992)).

(5C)(*a*) Subsection (1) shall not apply to expense incurred by the body corporate in or in connection with the provision for a director or employee of a high-speed internet connection to the director's or employee's home for business use where private use of the connection is incidental.

(*b*) In this subsection **"high-speed internet connection"** means a connection capable of transmitting information (being information for the same purposes as the Electronic Commerce Act 2000) at a rate equal to or greater than 250 kilobits per second.

(5D)(*a*) Subsection (1) shall not apply to expense incurred by the body corporate in or in connection with the provision, without any transfer of the property in it, for a director or employee of computer equipment for business use where private use of the computer equipment is incidental.

(*b*) In this section **"computer equipment"**, in addition to a computer, includes—

(i) a facsimile machine, and

(ii) printers, scanners, modems, discs, disc drives, and other peripheral devices designed to be used by being connected to or inserted in a computer and computer software to be used in such equipment.

(5E)(*a*) Subsection (1) shall not apply to expense incurred by the body corporate, or incurred by a director or employee and reimbursed by the body corporate, in or in connection with the payment on behalf of a director or employee of the annual membership fees of a professional body where membership of that body by the director or employee is relevant to the business of the body corporate.

(*b*) Membership of a professional body by a director or employee of a body corporate may be regarded as relevant to the business of that body corporate where—

(i) it is necessary for the performance of the duties of the office or employment of the director or employee, or

(ii) it facilitates the acquisition of knowledge which—

(I) is necessary for or directly related to the performance of the duties of the office or employment of the director or employee, or

(II) would be necessary for or directly related to the performance of prospective duties of the office or employment of the director or employee with that body corporate.

(5F) Subsection (1) shall not apply to expense incurred by the body corporate in or in connection with the provision, without any transfer of the property in it, for a director or employee of a mechanically propelled road vehicle which is—

(*a*) designed or constructed solely or mainly for the carriage of goods or other burden, and

(b) of a type not commonly used as a private vehicle and unsuitable to be so used.][3]

(6) Any reference in this section to expense incurred in or in connection with any matter includes a reference to a proper proportion of any expense incurred partly in or in connection with that matter.

(7) Where expense is incurred by a person connected with a body corporate, being expense which if incurred by the body corporate would be expense of the kind mentioned in subsection (1)(*a*), the body corporate shall be deemed for the purposes of this section to have incurred the expense, and subsection (1) shall apply accordingly in relation to any person, being a director or employee of the body corporate, in respect of whom the expense was incurred.

(8) A person shall be regarded as connected with a body corporate for the purposes of subsection (7) if the person is—

(*a*) a trustee of a settlement (within the meaning of section 794) made by the body corporate, or

(*b*) a body corporate,

and would be regarded as connected with the body corporate for the purposes of section 10.

Amendments

1 Subs (5) substituted by Pensions (Amendment) Act 2002 s 4(1)(*a*) with effect from such date or dates as the Minister for Social, Community and Family Affairs may appoint by order. By virtue of Pensions (Amendment) Act, 2002 (Commencement) Order, 2002, SI No 502 of 2002, this amendment comes into operation on 7 November 2002.

2 Subs (5A) substituted by FA 2005 s 8 with effect from 1 January 2005.

3 Subs (5B)–(5F) inserted by FA 2004 s 8(1)(*b*) with effect from 1 January 2004.

Cross-references

Application of section 985 (PAYE method of collection) to certain perquisites, etc: s 985A(1)(*a*)(i).
Deduction for income earned outside the State: s 823(1)("the specified amount").
Costs and expenses in respect of personal security assets and services, subs (1) of this section does not apply: s 118A(4).
Exemption from benefit-in-kind of certain childcare facilities, subs (1) of this section does not apply: s 120A(2).
Expenses for participators and associates: 436(4).
Loans of art objects, exemption: s 236(3).
Personal Retirement Savings Accounts (PRSAs), extent of relief, subs (5): s 787E(2).
Valuation of benefit in kind: s 119(1), (2), (3) and (4).

Case law

Irish

Subs (1): The assessment of benefits in kind received by a sales representative from the use of a car supplied by an employer not unconstitutional: *Browne and others v Attorney General and others* ITR Vol IV p 323.
Subs (3): Value of rental payment made by employer for a house occupied voluntarily by an employee taxable: *Connolly v McNamara* ITR Vol II p 452.

UK

Expense of loft conversion of an employee who worked from home taxed as a benefit in kind: *Templeton v Jacobs* [1996] STC 991.
Subs (3): Payment by a company of coal, electricity and garden maintenance expenses held not covered by exemption: *Butter v Bennett* (1962) 40 TC 402.
Held it was neither necessary for performance of his duties nor the custom of the trade to provide living accommodation for a nursery foreman: *Vertigan v Brady* [1988] STC 91.
Held taxpayer assessable on benefit in kind of rent free accommodation despite claim that management services rendered in return for accommodation: *Stones v Hall* [1989] STC 138.
Subs (6): Where employee obliged to reside in house owned by company in order to entertain customers, expenses borne by the company should be apportioned in accordance with use for the benefit of the company and use for the benefit of the employee: *Wescott v Bryan* (1969) 45 TC 476.
R v Dimpsey; *R v Allen* (1999) STC 846.
Sports Club plc and Other v Inspector of Taxes (2000) STC (SCO) 443.

Revenue information

Information leaflet IT20 — Benefits from Employment.
An Employer's Guide to operating PAYE and PRSI on certain benefits is available on Revenue's website (www.revenue.ie) under PAYE/Benefits in Kind.
Information Leaflet IT69 — eWorking and Tax.

Tax Briefing

TB41 Sept 2000 p 22 — Benefit-in-kind — Bus and Train Passes Exemption/"Salary Sacrifice" Arrangements.
TB52 May 2003 p 8 — Benefits-in-kind: application of PAYE and PRSI (Finance Act 2003 changes).

Definitions

"business premises", "control", "director", "employment": s 116; person: IA 1937 s 11(*c*); trade: s 3(1).

Former enactments

ITA 1967 s 117; FA 1973 s 41; FA 1974 s 86 and Sch 2 Pt I; FA 1996 s 131(9)(*a*).

Corresponding UK tax provision

Income and Corporation Taxes Act 1988 s 154.

118A Costs and expenses in respect of personal security assets and services

[(1) In this section—

"asset" includes equipment or a structure, but not any mode of transport or a dwelling or grounds appurtenant to a dwelling;

"service" does not include a dwelling or grounds appurtenant to a dwelling.

(2) This section applies where there is a credible and serious threat to a director's or an employee's personal physical security, which arises wholly or mainly because of the director's or employee's office or employment.

(3) This section applies to expense incurred by the body corporate, or incurred by a director or employee and reimbursed to the director or employee by the body corporate—

(*a*) in—

(i) the provision or use of, or

(ii) expenses connected with,

an asset or service for the improvement of personal security which is provided for or used by the director or employee to meet the threat to his or her personal physical security, and

(*b*) with the sole object of meeting that threat.

(4) Subject to subsections (6) and (7), where this section applies, section 118(1) shall not apply to an expense to which this section applies.

(5) Where the body corporate intends the asset to be used solely to improve personal physical security, any use of the asset incidental to that purpose shall be ignored.

(6) Where the body corporate intends the asset to be used only partly to improve personal physical security, subsection (4) shall apply only to that part of the expense incurred in relation to the asset which is attributable to the intended use for that purpose.

(7) Subsection (4) shall only apply to an expense incurred in relation to a service referred to in subsection (3) where the benefit resulting to the director or employee consists wholly or mainly of an improvement of his or her personal physical security.

(8) In determining whether or not this section applies in relation to an asset or service, the fact that—

(*a*) the asset becomes fixed to land (whether the land constitutes a dwelling or otherwise), or

(*b*) the director or employee is, or becomes, entitled

(i) to the property in the asset, or

(ii) if the asset is a fixture, to any estate or interest in the land concerned, or (*c*) the asset or the service improves the personal physical security of a member of the director's or employee's family or household, as well as that of the director or employee,

does not exclude the expense incurred by the body corporate from coming within subsection (4).][1]

Amendments

1 Section 118A inserted by FA 2005 s 10 with effect from 1 January 2005.

Definitions

director: s 116; employment: s 116; land: IA 1937 Sch.

119 Valuation of benefits in kind

(1) Any expense incurred by a body corporate in the acquisition or production of an asset which remains its own property shall be disregarded for the purposes of section 118.

(2) Where the making of any provision mentioned in section 118(1) takes the form of a transfer of the property in any asset of the body corporate and, since the acquisition or production of that asset by the body corporate, that asset has been used or has depreciated, the body corporate shall be deemed to have incurred in the making of that provision expense equal to the value of that asset at the time of the transfer.

(3) Where an asset which continues to belong to the body corporate is used wholly or partly in the making of any provision mentioned in section 118(1), the body corporate shall be deemed for the purposes of that section to incur (in addition to any other expense incurred by it in connection with the asset, not being expense to which subsection (1) applies) annual expense in connection with the asset of an amount equal to the annual value of the use of the asset, but where any sum by means of rent or hire is payable by the body corporate in respect of the asset—

(*a*) if the annual amount of the rent or hire is equal to or greater than the annual value of the use of the asset, this subsection shall not apply, and

(*b*) if the annual amount of the rent or hire is less than the annual value of the use of the asset, the rent or hire shall be disregarded for the purposes of section 118(1).

[(4) For the purposes of subsection (3), the annual value of the use of an asset shall be taken to be—

(*a*) in the case of an asset being premises, the rent which might reasonably be expected to be obtained on a letting from year to year if the tenant undertook to pay all usual tenant's rates, and if the landlord undertook to bear the costs of repairs and insurance, and the other expenses, if any, necessary for maintaining the premises in a state to command that rent, and

(*b*) in the case of any other asset, 5 per cent of the market value (within the meaning of section 548) of the asset at the time when it was first applied by the body corporate in making any provision mentioned in section 118(1).][1]

Amendments

[1] Subs (4) substituted by FA 2003 s 6(1)(*a*) with effect from 1 January 2004; previously "(4) In the case of an asset being premises, the annual value of the use of the asset shall be taken for the purposes of subsection (3) to be the rent which might reasonably be expected to be obtained on a letting from year to year if the tenant undertook to pay all usual tenant's rates, and if the landlord undertook to bear the costs of the repairs and insurance, and the other expenses, if any, necessary for maintaining the premises in a state to command that rent.".

Cross-references

Income Tax (Employments) (Consolidated) Regulations 2001, deduction of tax in respect of certain notional payments, subs (3): ITECR 2001 reg 17A(2)(*d*).

Case Law

Benefit-in-kind assessment on taxpayer in respect of discounted fees for his children at his employer's school held to be the additional costs incurred by the school in providing places for his children (net of fees paid by him) – *Pepper v Hart* [1992] STC 898.

Former enactments

ITA 1967 s 118(1)–(2) and (4); FA 1969 s 32(*b*)–(*c*).

Corresponding UK tax provision

Income and Corporation Taxes Act 1988 s 156.

120 Unincorporated bodies, partnerships and individuals

(1) This Chapter shall apply in relation to unincorporated societies and other bodies as it applies in relation to bodies corporate and, in connection with this Chapter, the definition of **"control"** in section 116(1) shall, with the necessary modifications, also so apply.

(2) This Chapter shall apply in relation to any partnership carrying on any trade or profession as it would apply in relation to a body corporate carrying on a trade if so much of this Chapter as relates to directors of the body corporate or persons taking part in the management of the affairs of the body corporate were deleted; but—

(*a*) **"control"**, in relation to a partnership, means the right to a share of more than 50 per cent of the assets, or of more than 50 per cent of the income, of the partnership, and

(*b*) where a partnership carrying on any trade or profession has control over a body corporate to which this Chapter applies (**"control"** being construed for this purpose in accordance with the definition of that term in section 116(1))—

(i) any employment of any director of that body corporate by the partnership shall be an employment to which this Chapter applies, and

(ii) all the employments of any person who is employed both by the partnership and by the body corporate (being employments by the partnership or the body corporate) shall, for the purpose of ascertaining whether those employments or any of them are employments to which this Chapter applies, be treated as if they were employments by the body corporate.

(3) Subsection (2) shall apply in relation to individuals as it applies in relation to partnerships, but nothing in this subsection shall be construed as requiring an individual to be treated in any circumstances as under the control of another person.

Definitions

trade: s 3(1).

Former enactments

ITA 1967 s 123.

120A Exemption from benefit-in-kind of certain childcare facilities

[(1) In this section—

"childcare service" means any form of child minding service or supervised activity to care for children, whether or not provided on a regular basis;

"qualifying premises" means premises which—

(*a*) are made available solely by the employer,

(*b*) are made available by the employer jointly with other persons and the employer is wholly or partly responsible for financing and managing the provision of the childcare [service],[1]

(*c*) are made available by any other person or persons and the employer is wholly or partly responsible for financing and managing the provision of the childcare service, [or][2]

[(*d*) are made available by the employer jointly with other persons or are made available by any other person or persons and the employer is wholly or partly responsible for capital expenditure on the construction or refurbishment of the premises,][3]

and in respect of which it can be shown that the requirements of Article 9, 10 or 11, as appropriate, of the Child Care (Pre-School Services) Regulations, 1996 (SI No 398 of 1996), have been complied with.

(2) Subsection (1) of section 118 shall not apply to any expense incurred by a body corporate in or in connection with the provision of a childcare service in qualifying premises for a child of a director or employee.

[(3) In the case of a qualifying premises within the meaning of paragraph (*d*) of the definition of **"qualifying premises"**, the exemption provided for in subsection (2) shall be limited to the amount expended by the employer on capital expenditure on the construction or refurbishment of the premises.][4]][5]

Amendments

1 Substituted by FA 2001 s 25(*a*) with effect from 6 April 2001; previously "service, or".

2 Inserted by FA 2001 s 25(*a*) with effect from 6 April 2001.

3 Para (*d*) inserted by FA 2001 s 25(*b*) with effect from 6 April 2001.

4 Subs (3) inserted by FA 2001 s 25(*c*) with effect from 6 April 2001.

5 Section 120A inserted by FA 1999 s 34 with effect from 6 April 1999.

Tax Briefing

TB37 Oct 1999 p 10 — Childcare facilities provided by employers for employees.

Definitions

director: s 116(1); person: IA 1937 s 11(*c*).

CHAPTER 4

Other Benefit in Kind Charges

121 Benefit of use of car

(1) (*a*) In this section—

"business mileage for a year of assessment", in relation to a person, means the total number of whole miles travelled in the year in the course of business use by that person of a car or cars in respect of which this section applies in relation to that person;

"business use", in relation to a car in respect of which this section applies in relation to a person, means travelling in the car which that person is necessarily obliged to do in the performance of the duties of his or her employment;

[**"car"** means any mechanically propelled road vehicle designed, constructed or adapted for the carriage of the driver or the driver and one or more other persons other than—

(*a*) a motor-cycle,

(*b*) a van (within the meaning of section 121A), or

(*c*) a vehicle of a type not commonly used as a private vehicle and unsuitable to be so used;][1]

"employment" means an office or employment of profit such that any emoluments (within the meaning of section 113) of the office or employment would be charged to tax, and cognate expressions shall be construed accordingly;

[**"motor-cycle"** means a mechanically propelled vehicle with less than four wheels and the weight of which unladen does not exceed 410 kilograms;][2]

"private use", in relation to a car, means use of the car other than business use;

"relevant log book", in relation to a person and a year of assessment, means a record maintained on a daily basis of the person's business use for the year of assessment of a car or cars in respect of which this section applies in relation to that person for that year of assessment which —

(i) contains relevant details of distances travelled, nature and location of business transacted and amount of time spent away from the employer's place of business, and

(ii) is certified by the employer as being to the best of the employer's knowledge and belief true and accurate.

(*b*) For the purposes of this section—

(i) (I) a car made available in any year to an employee by reason of his or her employment shall be deemed to be available in that year for his or her private use unless the terms on which the car is so made available prohibit such use and no such use is made of the car in that year;

(II) a car made available to an employee by his or her employer or by a person connected with the employer shall be deemed to be made available to him or her by reason of his or her employment (unless the employer is an individual and it can be shown that the car was made so available in the normal course of his or her domestic, family or personal relationships);

(III) a car shall be treated as available to a person and for his or her private use if it is available to a member or members of his or her family or household;

(IV) references to a person's family or household are references to the person's spouse, sons and daughters and their spouses, parents and servants, dependants and guests;

(ii) in relation to a car in respect of which this section applies, expenditure in respect of any costs borne by a person connected with the employer shall be treated as borne by the employer;

(iii) the original market value of a car shall be the price (including any duty of customs, duty of excise or value-added tax chargeable on the car) which the car might reasonably have been expected to fetch if sold in the State singly in a retail sale in the open market immediately before the date of its first registration in the State under section 6 of the Roads Act, 1920, or under corresponding earlier legislation, or elsewhere under the corresponding legislation of any country or territory.

(2) (*a*) In relation to a person chargeable to tax in respect of an employment, this section shall apply for a year of assessment in relation to a car which, by reason of the employment, is made available (without a transfer of the property in it) to the person and is available for his or her private use in that year.

(*b*) In relation to a car in respect of which this section applies for a year of assessment—

(i) Chapter 3 of this Part shall not apply for that year in relation to the expense incurred in connection with the provision of the car, and

[(ii) there shall be treated for that year as emoluments of the employment by reason of which the car is made available, and accordingly chargeable to income tax, the amount, if any, by which the cash equivalent of the benefit of the car for the year exceeds the aggregate for the year of the amount which the employee is required to make good and actually makes good to the employer in respect of any part of the costs of providing or running the car.][3]

(3) [(*a*) The cash equivalent of the benefit of a car for a year of assessment shall be 30 per cent of the original market value of the car.][4]

(*b*) Where a car in respect of which this section applies in relation to a person for a year of assessment is made available to the person for part only of that year, the cash equivalent of the benefit of that car as respects that person for that year shall be an amount which bears to the full amount of the cash equivalent of the car for that year (ascertained under paragraph (*a*)) the same proportion as that part of the year bears to that year.

[(*c*) Notwithstanding paragraphs (*a*) and (*b*), the cash equivalent of the benefit of a car for the year of assessment 2001 shall be 74 per cent of the amount of the cash equivalent of the car for that year as ascertained under those paragraphs.][5]

(4) [(*a*) Where in relation to a person the business mileage for a year of assessment exceeds 15,000 miles the cash equivalent of the benefit of the car for that year, instead of being the amount ascertained under subsection (3) shall be the percentage of the original market value of the car applicable to the business mileage under the Table to this subsection.][6]

(*b*) In the Table to this subsection, any percentage shown in column (3) shall be that applicable to any business mileage for a year of assessment which—

(i) exceeds the lower limit shown in column (1), and

(ii) does not exceed the upper limit (if any) shown in column (2),

opposite the mention of that percentage in column (3).

[(*c*) Where a car in respect of which this section applies in relation to a person for a year of assessment is made available to the person for part only of that year, the cash equivalent of the benefit of that car as respects that person for that year shall be an amount determined by applying paragraph (*a*) as if—

(i) the figure 15,000 referred to in that paragraph were replaced by a figure (in this paragraph referred to as the "new figure") determined by the formula—

$$15{,}000 \times \frac{A}{365}$$

where—

A is the number of days in the part of the year, and

(ii) each figure in columns (1), (2) and (3) of the Table to this section were reduced in the same proportion as the new figure bears to 15,000.][7]

"[TABLE

Business Mileage		Percentage of original market value
lower limit	upper limit	
(1)	(2)	(3)
miles	miles	per cent
15,000	20,000	24
20,000	25,000	18
25,000	30,000	12
30,000	—	6][8]

[(4A) As respects the year of assessment 2001, subsection (4) shall apply—

(*a*) as if in paragraph (*a*) of that subsection "11,100 miles" were substituted for "15,000 miles",

and

(*b*) as if the following were substituted for the Table to that subsection:

"TABLE

Business mileage		*Percentage*
lower limit	*upper limit*	
(1)	(2)	(3)
Miles	Miles	
11,100	11,840	97.5 per cent
11,840	12,580	95 per cent
12,580	13,320	90 per cent
13,320	14,060	85 per cent
14,060	14,800	80 per cent
14,800	15,540	75 per cent
15,540	16,280	70 per cent
16,280	17,020	65 per cent
17,020	17,760	60 per cent
17,760	18,500	55 per cent
18,500	19,240	50 per cent
19,240	19,980	45 per cent
19,980	20,720	40 per cent
20,720	21,460	35 per cent
21,460	22,200	30 per cent
22,200	—	25 per cent][9]

(5) (*a*) Where for a year of assessment—

(i) a person, in the performance of the duties of his or her employment, spends 70 per cent or more of his or her time engaged on such duties away from the place of business of his or her employer, and

(ii) in relation to that person, the business mileage exceeds 5,000 miles,

then, if the person so elects in writing to the inspector, the cash equivalent of the benefit of the car for that year of assessment in relation to the person shall, instead of being the amount ascertained under subsection (3) or (4), as may otherwise be appropriate, be 80 per cent of the amount ascertained under subsection (3).

[(*aa*) As respects the year of assessment 2001, paragraph (*a*) shall apply as if in subparagraph (ii) of that paragraph "3,700 miles" were substituted for "5,000 miles".][10]

(*b*) When requested in writing by the inspector, a person who makes an election under paragraph (*a*) for a year of assessment shall within 30 days of the date of such request furnish to the inspector a relevant log book in relation to that year of assessment.

(*c*) This subsection shall not apply as respects a year of assessment where—

(i) when requested to do so, a person fails to deliver to the inspector within the time specified in paragraph (*b*) a relevant log book in relation to that year of assessment, or

(ii) the time spent by a person in the performance of the duties of his or her employment in that year of assessment is on average less than 20 hours per week.

(*d*) Subsection (7)(*e*) shall apply for the purposes of this subsection as it applies for the purposes of subsection (7).

(*e*) Where a person makes an election under paragraph (*a*) for a year of assessment, such person shall retain the relevant log book in relation to that year of assessment for a period of 6 years after that end of that year or for such shorter period as the inspector may authorise in writing.

(6) (*a*) Where any amount is to be treated as emoluments of an employment under subsection (2)(*b*)(ii) for a year of assessment, it shall be the duty of the person chargeable to tax in respect of that amount to deliver in writing to the inspector, not later than 30 days after the end of that year of assessment, particulars of the car, of its original market value and of the business mileage and private mileage for that year of assessment.

(*b*) Where in relation to a year of assessment—

(i) a person makes default in the delivery of particulars in relation to —

(I) the original market value of a car in respect of which this section applies in relation to him or her,

(II) his or her business mileage for the year, or

(III) his or her private mileage for the year,

or

(ii) the inspector is not satisfied with the particulars which have been delivered by the person,

then, the original market value or business mileage or private mileage which is to be taken into account for the purpose of computing the amount of the tax to which that person is to be charged shall be such value or mileage, as the case may be, as according to the best of the inspector's judgment ought to be so taken into account and, in the absence of sufficient evidence to the contrary, the business mileage for a year of assessment in relation to a person shall be determined by deducting 5,000 from the total number of miles travelled in that year by that person in a car or cars in respect of which this section applies in relation to that person.

[(*bb*) As respects the year of assessment 2001, paragraph (*b*) shall apply as if "3,700 miles" were substituted for "5,000 miles".][11]

...[12]

(*d*) A value or mileage taken into account under paragraph (*b*) may be amended by the Appeal Commissioners or the Circuit Court on the hearing or the rehearing of an appeal against an assessment in respect of the employment in the performance of the duties of which the business mileage is done.

(7) (*a*) This subsection shall apply to any car in the case of which the inspector is satisfied (whether on a claim under this subsection or otherwise) that it has for any year been included in a car pool for the use of the employees of one or more employers.

(*b*) A car shall be treated as having been so included for a year if—

(i) in that year the car was made available to and actually used by more than one of those employees and in the case of each of them was made available to him or her by reason of his or her employment but was not in that year ordinarily used by any one of them to the exclusion of the others,

(ii) in the case of each of them, any private use of the car made by him or her in that year was merely incidental to his or her other use of the car in the year, and

(iii) the car was in that year not normally kept overnight on or in the vicinity of any residential premises where any of the employees was residing, except while being kept overnight on premises occupied by the person making the car available to them.

(*c*) Where this subsection applies to a car, the car shall be treated under this section as not having been available for the private use of any of the employees for the year in question.

(*d*) A claim under this subsection in respect of a car for any year may be made by any one of the employees mentioned in paragraph (*b*)(i) (they being referred to in paragraph (*e*) as **"the employees concerned"**) or by the employer on behalf of all of them.

(*e*) (i) Any person aggrieved by a decision of the inspector on any question arising under this subsection may, by notice in writing to that effect given to the inspector within 2 months from the date on which notice of the decision is given to that person, make an application to have his or her claim for relief heard and determined by the Appeal Commissioners.

(ii) Where an application is made under subparagraph (i), the Appeal Commissioners shall hear and determine the claim in the like manner as an appeal made to them against an assessment, and the provisions of the Income Tax Acts relating to such an appeal (including the provisions relating to the rehearing of an appeal and to the statement of a case for the opinion of the High Court on a point of law) shall apply accordingly with any necessary modifications.

(iii) On an appeal against the decision of the inspector on a claim under this section all the employees concerned may take part in the proceedings, and the determination of the Appeal Commissioners or the Circuit Court, as the case may be, shall be binding on all those employees, whether or not they have taken part in the proceedings.

(iv) Where an appeal against the decision of the inspector on a claim under this subsection has been determined, no appeal against the inspector's decision on any other such claim in respect of the same car while in the same car pool and the same year shall be entertained.

Amendments

1 Definition of "car" substituted by FA 2003 s 6(1)(*b*)(i)(I) with effect from 1 January 2004; previously "'car' means any mechanically propelled road vehicle constructed or adapted for the carriage of passengers, other than a vehicle of a type not commonly used as a private vehicle and unsuitable to be so used;".

2 Definition of "motor-cycle" inserted by FA 2003 s 6(1)(*b*)(i)(II) with effect from 1 January 2004;

3 Subs (2)(*b*)(ii) substituted by FA 2003 s 6(1)(*b*)(ii) with effect from 1 January 2004; previously "(ii) there shall be treated for that year as emoluments of the employment by reason of which the car is made available, and accordingly chargeable to income tax, the amount, if any, by which the cash equivalent of the benefit of the car for the year exceeds the aggregate for the year of the amounts which the employee is required to make good and actually makes good to the employer in respect of any part of the costs of providing or running the car; but any part of such aggregate in respect of which the cash equivalent is reduced under subsection (3)(*a*) shall be disregarded for the purposes of this subparagraph.".

4 Subs (3)(*a*) substituted by FA 2003 s 6(1)(*b*)(iii) with effect from 1 January 2004; previously

"(*a*) The cash equivalent of the benefit of a car for a year of assessment shall be 30 per cent of the original market value of the car, but shall be reduced—

(i) where no part of the cost for that year of the fuel used in the course of the private use of the car by the employee is borne directly or indirectly by the employer, by 4.5 per cent of the original market value of the car,

(ii) where no part of the cost for that year of the insurance of the car is borne directly or indirectly by the employer, by 3 per cent of the original market value of the car,

(iii) where no part of the cost for that year of repair and servicing of the car is borne directly or indirectly by the employer, by 3 per cent of the original market value of the car, and

(iv) where no part of the excise duty for that year on the licence under section 1 of the Finance (Excise Duties) (Vehicles) Act, 1952, relating to the car is borne directly or indirectly by the employer, by 1 per cent of the original market value of the car.".

5 Subs (3)(*c*) inserted by FA 2001 s 77(2) and Sch 2 para 8(*a*) with effect from 6 April 2001.

6 Subs (4)(*a*) substituted by FA 2003 s 6(1)(*b*)(iv)(I) with effect from 1 January 2004; previously "(*a*) Where in relation to a person the business mileage for a year of assessment exceeds 15,000 miles, the cash equivalent of the benefit of the car for that year, instead of being the amount ascertained under subsection (3), shall be the percentage of that amount applicable to that business mileage under the Table to this subsection.".

7 Subs (4)(*c*) inserted by FA 2003 s 6(1)(*b*)(iv)(II) with effect from 1 January 2004.

8 Subs (4)(Table) inserted by FA 2003 s 6(1)(*b*)(iv)(III) with effect from 1 January 2004; previously "TABLE

Business mileage		Percentage
lower limit	upper limit	
(1)	(2)	(3)
Miles	Miles	
15,000	16,000	97.5 per cent
16,000	17,000	95 per cent
17,000	18,000	90 per cent
18,000	19,000	85 per cent
19,000	20,000	80 per cent
20,000	21,000	75 per cent
21,000	22,000	70 per cent
22,000	23,000	65 per cent
23,000	24,000	60 per cent
24,000	25,000	55 per cent
25,000	26,000	50 per cent
26,000	27,000	45 per cent
27,000	28,000	40 per cent
28,000	29,000	35 per cent
29,000	30,000	30 per cent
30,000	—	25 per cent

9 Subs (4A) inserted by FA 2001 s 77(2) and Sch 2 para 8(*b*) with effect from 6 April 2001.

10 Subs (5)(*aa*) inserted by FA 2001 s 77(2) and Sch 2 para 8(*c*) with effect from 6 April 2001.

11 Subs (6)(*bb*) inserted by FA 2001 s 77(2) and Sch 2 para 8(*d*) with effect from 6 April 2001.

12 Subs (6)(*c*) deleted by FA 2003 s 6(1)(*b*)(v) with effect from 1 January 2004; previously "(*c*) The inspector, in making a computation for the purposes of an assessment or of the [Income Tax (Employments) (Consolidated) Regulations 2001 (SI No 559 of 2001)][5], before the end of the year of assessment to which the computation relates, in relation to a person in relation to whom this section applies for that year of assessment, shall make an estimate of that person's business mileage for the purpose of the computation, and section 926 shall, with any necessary modifications, apply in relation to the estimate so made as it applies in relation to an estimate made under that section.

5 Substituted by FA 2002 s 138 and Sch 6 paras 3(*b*) and 6(*c*)(i) with effect from 1 January 2002; previously 'Income Tax (Employments) Regulations, 1960 (SI No 28 of 1960)'.".

Cross-references

Application of section 985 (PAYE method of collection) to certain perquisites, etc: s 985A(1)(*b*).
Benefit in kind, general charging provision: s 118(5B)(*b*).
Benefit of use of van, subss (1) (other than definition of "car" in para (*a*)), (3)(*b*), (6) and (7) applied: s 121A(4).
Deduction for income earned outside the State, subs (2)(*b*)(ii): s 823(1)("the specified amount").
Income tax (Employments) (Consolidated) Regulations 2001, deduction of tax in respect of certain notional payments: ITEC 2001 reg 17A(1)(*a*).
Notional loans relating to shares, etc, meaning of "employment" applied: s 122A(1).
Returns of employees' emoluments: s 897(2)(*b*).
Penalty: Sch 29 column 1.

Case law

Irish

Arguments that this section is unconstitutional were unsuccessful: *Paul Brown and others v Attorney General and others* ITR Vol IV p 323.

UK

Subs (1): Held employee did not have private use of a company car where he believed private use of the car was prohibited by the company: *Gilbert v Hemsley* [1981] STC 703.
IRC v Quigley (1995) STC 931.

Revenue information

Information leaflet IT20 — Benefits from Employment.
An Employer's Guide to operating PAYE and PRSI on certain benefits is available on Revenue's website (www.revenue.ie) under PAYE/Benefits in Kind.

Tax Briefing

TB21 Mar 1996 p 8 — Overseas Duties and Car Benefit-in-Kind.
TB28 Oct 1997 p 10 — Benefit-in-Kind on Company Cars.
TB52 May 2003 p 8 — Benefits-in-Kind: application of PAYE and PRSI (Finance Act 2003 changes).
TB58 Dec 2004 p 13 — Third Party Benefits.

Definitions

Appeal Commissioners: s 2(1); Circuit Court: IA 1937 Sch; group relief: ss 4(1), 411; Income Tax Acts: s 1(2); inspector: ss 2(1), 5(1), 852; month: IA 1937 Sch; person: IA 1937 s 11(*c*); writing: IA 1937 Sch; year of assessment: ss 2(1), 5(1).

Former enactments

FA 1982 s 4(2)–(6) and (9)(*a*), (*b*)(i), (ii) and (iv); FA 1992 s 8(*a*), (*b*)(i) and (ii)(V) and Sch 1 PtV; FA 1996 s 6.

Corresponding UK tax provision

Income and Corporation Taxes Act 1988 s 157.

121A Benefit of use of van

[(1) In this section—

[**"gross vehicle weight"**, in relation to a vehicle, means the weight which the vehicle is designed or adapted not to exceed when in normal use and travelling on the road laden.][1]

"van" means a mechanically propelled road vehicle which—

(*a*) is designed or constructed solely or mainly for the carriage of goods or other burden,

(*b*) has a roofed area or areas to the rear of the driver's seat, ...[2]

(*c*) has no side windows or seating fitted in that roofed area or [areas, and][3]

[(*d*) has a gross vehicle weight not exceeding 3,500 kilograms.][4]

(2) (*a*) In relation to a person chargeable to tax in respect of an employment, this section shall apply for a year of assessment in relation to a van which, by reason of the employment, is made available (without a transfer of the property in it) to the person and is available for his or her private use in that year.

(*b*) In relation to a van in respect of which this section applies for a year of assessment—

(i) Chapter 3 of this Part shall not apply for that year in relation to the expense incurred in connection with the provision of the van, and

(ii) there shall be treated for that year as emoluments of the employment by reason of which the van is made available, and accordingly chargeable to income tax, the amount, if any, by which the cash equivalent of the benefit of the van for the year exceeds the aggregate for the year of the amounts which the employee is required to make good and actually makes good to the employer in respect of any part of the costs of providing or running the van.

[(2A) Subsection (2) shall not apply for a year of assessment in respect of the private use of a van made available to a person (in this subsection referred to as the **"employee"**) as set out in that subsection where the following conditions are met—

(*a*) the van made available to the employee is necessary for the performance of the duties of the employee's employment,

(*b*) the employee is required by the person who made the van available to keep it, when not in use in the performance of the duties of the employee's employment, at or in the vicinity of the employee's private residence,

(*c*) apart from travel between the employee's private residence and workplace, other private use of the van is prohibited by the person making the van available and there is no such other private use, and

(*d*) in the performance of the duties of his or her employment, the employee spends at least 80 per cent of his or her time engaged on such duties away from the premises of the employer to which the employee is attached.][5]

(3) The cash equivalent of the benefit of a van for a year of assessment shall be 5 per cent of the original market value of the van.

(4) The provisions of subsections (1) (other than the definition of car in paragraph (*a*)), paragraph (*b*) of subsection (3), (6) and (7) of section 121 shall apply, with any necessary modifications in relation to a van, for the purposes of this section as they apply in relation to a car for the purposes of that section.][6]

Amendments

1 Definition of "gross vehicle weight" inserted by FA 2004 s 8(1)(*c*)(i)(I) with effect from 1 January 2004.

2 Deleted by FA 2004 s 8(1)(*c*)(i)(II)(A) with effect from 1 January 2004; previously "and".

3 Substituted by FA 2004 s 8(1)(*c*)(i)(II)(B) with effect from 1 January 2004; previously "areas.".

4 Definition of "van" para (*d*) inserted by FA 2004 s 8(1)(*c*)(i)(II)(C) with effect from 1 January 2004.

5 Subs (2A) inserted by FA 2004 s 8(1)(*c*)(ii) with effect from 1 January 2004.

6 Section 121A inserted by FA 2003 s 6(1)(*c*) with effect from 1 January 2004.

Cross-references

Application of section 985 (PAYE method of collection) to certain perquisites, etc: s 985A(1)(*c*).
Benefit of use of car, meaning of "van" applied: s 121(1)(*a*)("car").
Benefits in kind, general charging provision: s 118(5B)(*b*).
Income Tax (Employments)(Consolidated) Regulations 2001, deduction of tax in respect of certain notional payments: ITECR 2001 reg 17A(1)(*b*).

Tax Briefing

TB52 May 2003 p 8 — Benefits-in-kind: application of PAYE and PRSI (Finance Act 2003 changes).
TB58 Dec 2004 p 13 — Third Party Benefits.

Definitions

person: IA 1937 s 11(*c*); year of assessment: ss 2(1), 5(1).

122 Preferential loan arrangements

(1) (*a*) In this section—

[**"employee"**, in relation to an employer, means an individual employed by the employer in an employment—

(*a*) to which Chapter 3 of this Part applies, or

(*b*) the profits or gains of which are chargeable to tax under Case III of Schedule D,

including, in a case where the employer is a body corporate, a director (within the meaning of that Chapter) of the body corporate;][1]

"employer", in relation to an individual, means—

[(i) a person of whom the individual or the spouse of the individual is or was an employee,][2]

(ii) a person of whom the individual becomes an employee subsequent to the making of a loan by the person to the individual, and while any part of the loan, or of another loan replacing it, is outstanding, or

(iii) a person connected with a person referred to in paragraph (i) or (ii);

"loan" includes any form of credit, and references to a loan include references to any other loan applied directly or indirectly towards the replacement of another loan;

"preferential loan" [means, in relation to an individual, a loan, in respect of which no interest is payable or interest is payable at a preferential rate, made directly or indirectly to the individual][3] or to the spouse of the individual by a person who in relation to the individual or the spouse is an employer, but does not include any such loan in respect of which interest is payable at a rate that is not less than the rate of interest at which the employer in the course of the employer's trade makes equivalent loans for similar purposes at arm's length to persons other than employees or their spouses;

"preferential rate" means a rate less than the specified rate;

"the specified rate", in relation to a preferential loan, means—

(i) in a case where—

(I) the interest paid on the preferential loan qualifies for relief under section 244, or

(II) if no interest is paid on the preferential loan, the interest which would have been paid on that loan (if interest had been payable) would have so qualified,

the rate of [3.5 per cent][4] per annum or such other rate (if any) prescribed by the Minister for Finance by regulations,

(ii) in a case where—

(I) the preferential loan is made to an employee by an employer,

(II) the making of loans for the purposes of purchasing a dwelling house for occupation by the borrower as a residence, for a stated term of years at a rate of interest which does not vary for the duration of the loan, forms part of the trade of the employer, and

(III) the rate of interest at which, in the course of the employer's trade at the time the preferential loan is or was made, the employer makes or made loans at arm's length to persons, other than employees, for the purposes of purchasing a dwelling house for occupation by the borrower as a residence is less than [3.5 per cent][4] per annum or such other rate (if any) prescribed by the Minister for Finance by regulations,

the first-mentioned rate in subparagraph (III), or

(iii) in any other case, the rate of [11 per cent][5] per annum or such other rate (if any) prescribed by the Minister for Finance by regulations.

(*b*) For the purposes of this section, a person shall be regarded as connected with another person if such person would be so regarded for the purposes of section 250.

(*c*) In this section, a reference to a loan being made by a person includes a reference to a person assuming the rights and liabilities of the person who originally made the loan and to a person arranging, guaranteeing or in any way facilitating a loan or the continuation of a loan already in existence.

[(2)Where, for the whole or part of a year of assessment, there is outstanding, in relation to an individual, a preferential loan, the individual shall, subject to subsection (4), be treated for the purposes of section 112 or a charge to tax under Case III of Schedule D, as having received in that year of assessment, as a perquisite of the office or employment with the employer who made the loan, a sum equal to—

(*a*) if no interest is payable on the preferential loan or loans, the amount of interest which would have been payable in that year, if interest had been payable on the loan or loans at the specified rate, or

(*b*) if interest is paid or payable at a preferential rate or rates, the difference between the aggregate amount of interest paid or payable in that year and the amount of interest which would have been payable in that year, if interest had been payable on the loan or loans at the specified rate, and the individual or, in the case of an individual who is a wife whose husband is chargeable to tax for the year of assessment in accordance with the provisions of section 1017, the spouse of the individual, shall be charged to tax accordingly.][6]

(3) Where an individual has a loan made to him or her directly or indirectly in any year of assessment by a person who at the time the loan is made is, or who at a time subsequent to the making of the loan becomes, an employer in relation to the individual and the loan or any interest payable on the loan is released or written off in whole or in part—

(*a*) the individual shall be deemed for the purposes of section 112 or, in a case where profits or gains from an employment with that person would be chargeable to tax under Case III of Schedule D, for the purposes of a charge to tax under that Case to have received in the year of assessment in which the release or writing off took place as a perquisite of an office or employment with that person a sum equal to the amount which is released or written off, and

(*b*) the individual or, in the case of an individual whose spouse is chargeable to tax for the year of assessment in accordance with section 1017, the spouse of the individual shall be charged to tax accordingly.

(4) Where for any year of assessment a sum is chargeable to tax under subsection (2) in respect of a preferential loan or loans or under subsection (3) in respect of an amount of interest written off or released, the individual to whom the loan or loans was or were made shall be deemed for the purposes of section 244 to have paid in the year of assessment an amount or additional amount of interest, as the case may be, on the loan or loans equal to such sum or the individual by whom the interest written off or released was payable shall be deemed for those purposes to have paid in the year of assessment the interest released or written off.

(5) This section shall not apply to a loan made by an employer, being an individual, and shown to have been made in the normal course of his or her domestic, family or personal relationships.

(6) Any amount chargeable to tax by virtue of this section shall not be emoluments for the purpose of section 472.

(7) Every regulation made under this section shall be laid before Dáil Éireann as soon as may be after it is made and, if a resolution annulling the regulation is passed by Dáil Éireann within the next 21 days on which Dáil Éireann has sat after the regulation is laid before it, the regulation shall be annulled accordingly, but without prejudice to the validity of anything previously done thereunder.

Amendments

1 Definition of "employee" substituted by FA 2005 s 9(*a*)(i) with effect from 1 January 2005.

2 Definition of "employer" para (i) substituted by FA 2004 s 10(1)(*a*) as respects loans made on or after 4 February 2004.

3 Substituted by FA 2005 s 9(*a*)(ii) with effect from 1 January 2005; previously "means a loan, in respect of which no interest is payable or interest is payable at a preferential rate, made directly or indirectly to an individual".

4 Substituted by FA 2004 s 10(1)(*b*) with effect from 1 January 2004; previously "4.5 per cent".

5 Substituted by FA 2003 s 4(*b*) for 2003 and later tax years; previously "12 per cent".

6 Subs (2) substituted by FA 2005 s 9(*b*) with effect from 1 January 2005.

Cross-references

Application of section 985 (PAYE method of collection) to certain perquisites, etc: s 985A(1)(*a*)(ii).

Deduction for income earned outside the State: s 823(1)("the specified amount").

Income Tax (Employments) (Consolidated) Regulations 2001, deduction of tax in respect of certain notional payments: ITECR 2001 reg 17A(1)(*c*).

Notional loans relating to shares, etc, meaning of "employee", "employer" and "preferential loan" applied: s 122A(1); subs (3): s 122A(6).

Returns of employees' emoluments: s 897(2)(*c*).

Revenue precedents

Issue: Employer wished to provide loans to employees to enable them purchase computers. The loans would be repaid by salary deduction over a 12 month period. The employer sought to have the provisions in TCA 1997 s 122 dispensed with, by concession.

Decision: Concession not acceded to.

Revenue information

Information leaflet IT20 — Benefits from Employment.

An Employer's Guide to operating PAYE and PRSI on certain benefits is available on Revenue's website (www.revenue.ie) under PAYE/Benefits in Kind.

Case law

UK

"Any form of credit" included provision of services, payment for which was made at year end: *Grant v Watton* [1999] STC 330.

Definitions

Dáil Éireann: IA 1937 Sch; person: IA 1937 s 11(*c*); trade: s 3(1); year of assessment: ss 2(1), 5(1).

Former enactments

ITA 1967 s 195B(3) and (6); FA 1982 s 8(1)–(5), (7) and (9); FA 1989 s 6; FA 1993 s 10(1); FA 1995 s 9; FA 1997 s 146(1) and Sch 9 Pt I para 12(1).

Corresponding UK tax provision

Income and Corporation Taxes Act 1988 s 160.

122A Notional loans relating to shares, etc

[(1) In this section—

"acquisition", in relation to shares, includes receipt by way of allotment or assignment;

"connected person" has the same meaning as in section 10;

"emoluments" has the same meaning as in section 113;

"employee" and **"employer"** have the same meanings, respectively, assigned to them by section 122;

"employment" has the same meaning as in section 121;

"market value" shall be construed in accordance with section 548;

"preferential loan" has the same meaning as in section 122;

"shares" includes securities within the meaning of section 135 and stock.

(2) Where an employee, or a person connected with him or her, acquires shares in a company (whether the employing company or not) and those shares are acquired at an under-value in pursuance of a right or opportunity available by reason of his or her employment, he or she shall be deemed to have the benefit of a loan on which no interest is payable (in this section referred to as the "notional loan") made directly or indirectly

to him or her by a person who at the time the loan is made is, or who at a time subsequent to the making of the loan becomes, an employer in relation to the individual and such notional loan shall be deemed to be a preferential loan to which section 122 applies.

(3) This section shall apply, subject to Chapter 1 of Part 17, for a year of assessment in which an individual has, in accordance with subsection (2), a notional loan and in this section—

(*a*) references to shares being acquired at an under-value are references to shares being acquired either without payment for them at the time or being acquired for an amount then paid which is less than the market value of fully paid-up shares of that class (in either case with or without obligation to make payment or further payment at some later time), and

(*b*) any reference, in relation to any shares, to the undervalue on acquisition is a reference to the market value of fully paid-up shares of that class less any payment then made for the shares.

(4) The amount initially outstanding of the notional loan shall be so much of the under-value on acquisition as is not chargeable to tax as an emolument of the employee, and—

(*a*) the loan shall remain outstanding until terminated under subsection (5), and

(*b*) payments or further payments made for the shares after the initial acquisition shall go to reduce the amount outstanding of the notional loan.

(5) The notional loan shall terminate on the occurrence of any of the following events—

(*a*) the whole amount of it outstanding is made good by means of payments or further payments made for the shares;

(*b*) the case being one in which the shares were not at the time of acquisition fully paid up, any outstanding or contingent obligation to pay for them is released, transferred or adjusted so as no longer to bind the employee or any person connected with him or her;

(*c*) the shares are so disposed of by surrender or otherwise that neither he nor she nor any such person any longer has a beneficial interest in the shares;

(*d*) the employee dies.

(6) If the notional loan terminates in a manner referred to in subsection (5)(*b*) or (*c*), the provisions of section 122(3) shall apply as if an amount equal to the then outstanding amount of the notional loan had been released or written off from a loan within that section.

(7) Where shares are acquired, whether or not at an undervalue but otherwise as mentioned in subsection (2), and—

(*a*) the shares are subsequently disposed of by surrender or otherwise so that neither the employee nor any person connected with him or her any longer has a beneficial interest in them, and

(*b*) the disposal is for a consideration which exceeds the then market value of the shares, then, for the year in which the disposal is effected, the outstanding amount of the excess shall be treated as emoluments of the employee's employment and accordingly chargeable to income tax under Schedule D or Schedule E.

(8) If at the time of the event giving rise to a charge by virtue of subsection (6) the employment in question has terminated, that subsection shall apply as if it had not.

(9) No charge arises under subsection (6) by reference to any disposal effected after the death of the employee, whether by his or her personal representatives or otherwise.

(10) This section applies in relation to acquisition and disposal of an interest in shares less than full beneficial ownership (including an interest in the proceeds of sale of part of the shares but not including a share option) as it applies in relation to the acquisition and disposal of shares, subject to the following:

(*a*) reference to the shares acquired shall be construed as reference to the interest in shares acquired,

(*b*) reference to the market value of the shares acquired shall be construed as reference to the proportion corresponding to the size of the interest of the market value of the shares in which the interest subsists,

(*c*) reference to shares of the same class as those acquired shall be construed as reference to shares of the same class as those in which the interest subsists,

(*d*) reference to the market value of fully paid-up shares of that class shall be construed as reference to the proportion of that value corresponding to the size of the interest.

(11) In this section, any reference to payment for shares includes giving any consideration in money or money's worth or making any subscription, whether in pursuance of a legal liability or not.][1]

Amendments

[1] Section 122A inserted by FA 1998 s 15(1) and applies, as regards subs (2), with effect from 4 March 1998 as respects shares whenever acquired (where shares were acquired before 4 March 1998, the notional loan is deemed to have been made on that date in an amount equal to the amount of the loan outstanding at that date); as regards subs (6), in respect of the termination of a loan on or after 4 March 1998; as regards subs (7), in respect of disposals made on or after 4 March 1998.

Tax Briefing

TB32 June 1998 p 6 — Revenue accept that subs (2) and (6) do **not** apply to shares obtained by directors/employees under rights acquired between 6/4/1986 and 28/1/1992 under an approved share option scheme (FA 1986 s10 refers) or to shares obtained by directors/employees under Revenue approved profit sharing schemes (Chapter 1 of Part 17 refers).

Definitions

person: IA 1937 s 11(*c*).

Corresponding UK tax provision

Income and Corporation Taxes Act 1988 s 162.

CHAPTER 5

Miscellaneous Charging Provisions

123 General tax treatment of payments on retirement or removal from office or employment

(1) This section shall apply to any payment (not otherwise chargeable to income tax) which is made, whether in pursuance of any legal obligation or not, either directly or

indirectly in consideration or in consequence of, or otherwise in connection with, the termination of the holding of an office or employment or any change in its functions or emoluments, including any payment in commutation of annual or periodical payments (whether chargeable to tax or not) which would otherwise have been so made.

(2) Subject to section 201, income tax shall be charged under Schedule E in respect of any payment to which this section applies made to the holder or past holder of any office or employment, or to his or her executors or administrators, whether made by the person under whom he or she holds or held the office or employment or by any other person.

(3) For the purposes of this section and section 201, any payment made to the spouse or any relative or dependant of a person who holds or has held an office or employment, or made on behalf of or to the order of that person, shall be treated as made to that person, and any valuable consideration other than money shall be treated as a payment of money equal to the value of that consideration at the date when it is given.

(4) Any payment chargeable to tax by virtue of this section shall be treated as income received on the following date—

(*a*) in the case of a payment in commutation of annual or other periodical payments, the date on which the commutation is effected, and

(*b*) in the case of any other payment, the date of the termination or change in respect of which the payment is made,

and shall be treated as emoluments of the holder or past holder of the office or employment assessable to income tax under Schedule E.

(5) In the case of the death of any person who if he or she had not died would have been chargeable to tax in respect of any such payment, the tax which would have been so chargeable shall be assessed and charged on his or her executors or administrators, and shall be a debt due from and payable out of his or her estate.

(6) Where any payment chargeable to tax under this section is made to any person in any year of assessment, it shall be the duty of the person by whom that payment is made to deliver particulars of the payment in writing to the inspector not later than 14 days after the end of that year.

Cross-references

Additional assessments, subs (4): s 924(2)(*d*)(ii).

Agreed pay restructuring relief to be reduced: s 202(7).

Associated employers, payments made by: s 201(1)(*c*).

Basic exemption: s 201(5).

Deduction for income earned outside the State: s 823(1)("the specified amount").

Disturbance and compensation payments: s 480(2)(*b*)(i).

Exemption in respect of certain payments under employment law, subs (1): s 192A(5)(*b*).

Exemptions: s 201(2), (2A).

Foreign service: s 201(4).

Penalty, subs (6): Sch 29 column 3.

Reliefs in respect of income tax charged on payments on retirement etc: Sch 3 paras 2, 4, 6–12.

Time limit: s 201(6).

"Top slicing" relief: s 201(7).

Revenue precedents

Issue: Payment of compensation arising from an unfair dismissals case.

Decision: Treated as a payment chargeable under s 123, with appropriate reliefs. Note: The award was not in respect of actual salary, which would be chargeable under s 112.

Issue: Whether the item included in the severance agreement and described as "Damages" is liable to tax.

Decision: A payment made in consideration or in consequence of, or otherwise in connection with the termination of an employment however described - is chargeable to tax under TCA 1997 s 123, unless it is otherwise chargeable to tax.

Issue: Whether a charge arises on a termination lump sum payment made to a non-resident individual.

Decision: It is taxable in this country by reference to the length of Irish service. The amount qualifies for relief under the foreign service provisions, SCSB and top slicing relief provisions.

Tax Briefing

TB22 June 1996 p 14 — Redundancy payments and re-engagement of employees.

TB28 Oct 1997 p 7 — Taxation treatment of redundancy/termination payments.

TB51 Jan 2003 p 20 — What is the tax treatment of legal costs recovered by an employee from an employer as part of a court action to recover compensation for loss of office or employment, etc? Revenue are prepared to accept that no income tax charge will be imposed on the employee in respect of the payment of legal costs where the payment is made by the former employer directly to the former employee's solicitor, is in full or partial discharge of the solicitor's bill of costs incurred by the employee only in connection with the termination of his/her employments, and is under a specific term in the settlement agreement. This treatment applies only to legal costs and applies to payments made either under a court order or where a court order or where a settlement is reached outside of the court.

TB54 Dec 2003 p 10 — Redundancy payments.

Case law

Irish

Subs (1): A monetary grant additional to maximum pension and gratuity entitlements given by University College Dublin to a retiring President for unrewarded services treated as a non-taxable gift: *Mulvey v Coffey* ITR Vol I p 618.

UK

Subs (1): Held payment on termination of employment repayable if the firm had to make payment under a policy of insurance was not a loan and was assessable under Schedule E: *Horner v Hasted* [1995] STC 766.

Richardson (Inspector of Taxes) v Delaney (2001) STC 1328.

Definitions

inspector: ss 2(1), 5(1), 852; relative: s 3(1); writing: IA 1937 Sch; year of assessment: s 3(1).

Former enactments

ITA 1967 s 114(1)–(5) and (7).

Corresponding UK tax provision

Income and Corporation Taxes Act 1988 s 148.

124 Tax treatment of certain severance payments

(1) This section shall apply to the following payments—

(*a*) a termination allowance (other than that part of the allowance which comprises a lump sum) payable in accordance with section 5 of the Oireachtas (Allowances to Members) and Ministerial and Parliamentary Offices (Amendment) Act, 1992, and any regulations made under that section, and

(*b*) a severance allowance or a special allowance payable in accordance with Part V (inserted by the Oireachtas (Allowances to Members) and Ministerial and Parliamentary Offices (Amendment) Act, 1992) of the Ministerial and Parliamentary Offices Act, 1938.

(2) Notwithstanding any other provision of the Income Tax Acts, payments to which this section applies shall be deemed to be—

(*a*) profits or gains accruing from an office or employment (and accordingly tax under Schedule E shall be charged on those payments, and tax so chargeable shall be computed under section 112(1)), and

(*b*) emoluments to which Chapter 4 of Part 42 is applied by section 984.

Definitions

Income Tax Acts: s 1(2).

Former enactments

FA 1993 s 7(2).

125 Tax treatment of benefits received under permanent health benefit schemes

(1) In this section—

"benefit" means a payment made to a person under a permanent health benefit scheme in the event of loss or diminution of income in consequence of ill health;

"permanent health benefit scheme" means any scheme, contract, policy or other arrangement, approved by the Revenue Commissioners for the purposes of this section, which provides for periodic payments to an individual in the event of loss or diminution of income in consequence of ill health.

(2) (*a*) A policy of permanent health insurance, sickness insurance or other similar insurance issued in respect of an insurance made on or after the 6th day of April, 1986, shall be a permanent health benefit scheme within the meaning of this section if it conforms with a form which, at the time the policy is issued, is either—

(i) a standard form approved by the Revenue Commissioners as a standard form of permanent health benefit scheme, or

(ii) a form varying from a standard form so approved in no other respect than by making such alterations to that standard form as are, at the time the policy is issued, approved by the Revenue Commissioners as being compatible with a permanent health benefit scheme when made to that standard form and satisfying any conditions subject to which the alterations are so approved.

(*b*) In approving a policy as a standard form of permanent health benefit scheme in pursuance of paragraph (*a*), the Revenue Commissioners may disregard any provision of the policy which appears to them insignificant.

(3) (*a*) Any benefit received by a person under a permanent health benefit scheme, whether as of right or not, shall be deemed to be—

(i) profits or gains arising or accruing from an employment, and

(ii) emoluments within the meaning of Chapter 4 of Part 42.

(*b*) Tax under Schedule E shall be charged on every person to whom any benefit referred to in paragraph (*a*) is paid in respect of all such benefits paid to such person, and tax so chargeable shall be computed under section 112(1).

(4) The Revenue Commissioners may nominate any of their officers, including an inspector, to perform any acts and discharge any functions authorised by this section to be performed or discharged by them.

Cross-references

Relief for contributions to permanent health benefit schemes, meanings of "benefit" and "permanent health benefit" applied: s 471(1).

Definitions

Income Tax Acts: s 1(2); person: IA 1937 s 11(*c*); tax: s 3(1); Tax Acts: s 1(2); total income: s 3(1); week: IA 1937 Sch; year of assessment: ss 2(1), 5(1).

Former enactments

FA 1979 s 8(1), (4), (4A) and (6); FA 1986 s 7; FA 1992 s 7.

126 Tax treatment of certain benefits payable under Social Welfare Acts

(1) In this section, **"the Acts"** means the Social Welfare (Consolidation) Act, 1993, and any subsequent enactment together with which that Act may be cited.

(2) (*a*) This subsection shall apply to the following benefits payable under the Acts—

(i) widow's (contributory) pension,

(ii) orphan's (contributory) allowance,

(iii) retirement pension, and

(iv) old age (contributory) pension.

(*b*) Payments of benefits to which this subsection applies shall be deemed to be emoluments to which Chapter 4 of Part 42 applies.

(3) (*a*) This subsection shall apply to the following benefits payable under the Acts—

(i) disability benefit,

(ii) unemployment benefit,

(iii) injury benefit which is comprised in occupational injuries benefit, and

(iv) pay-related benefit.

(*b*) Amounts to be paid on foot of the benefits to which this subsection applies (other than amounts so payable in respect of a qualified child within the meaning of section 2(3)(*a*) of the Social Welfare (Consolidation) Act, 1993) shall be deemed—

(i) to be profits or gains arising or accruing from an employment (and accordingly tax under Schedule E shall be charged on every person to whom any such benefit is payable in respect of amounts to be paid on foot of such benefits, and tax so chargeable shall be computed under section 112(1)), and

(ii) to be emoluments to which Chapter 4 of Part 42 is applied by section 984.

(4) (*a*) In this subsection, **"income tax week"** means one of the successive periods of 7 days in a year of assessment beginning on the 1st day of that year, or on any 7th day after that day, and the last day of a year of assessment (or the last 2 days of a year of assessment ending in a leap year) shall be taken as included in the last income tax week of that year of assessment.

(*b*) Notwithstanding subsection (3), the first [€13][1] of the aggregate of the amounts of unemployment benefit payable to a person in respect of one or more days of unemployment comprised in any income tax week (other than an amount so payable in respect of a qualified child within the meaning of section 2(3)(*a*) of the Social Welfare (Consolidation) Act, 1993) shall be disregarded for the purposes of the Income Tax Acts.

(5) Notwithstanding subsection (3), the aggregate of the amounts of disability benefit, injury benefit or both disability benefit and injury benefit payable to a person in respect of—

(*a*) for the year of assessment 1997–98, the first 18 days, and

(*b*) for the year of assessment 1998–99 and subsequent years of assessment, the first 36 days,

incapacity for work for which the person is entitled to payment of either disability benefit or injury benefit shall be disregarded for the purposes of the Income Tax Acts.

(6) (*a*) Subsection (3) shall come into operation on such day or days as may be fixed for that purpose by order or orders of the Minister for Finance, either generally or with reference to any particular benefit to which that subsection applies, or with reference to any category of person in receipt of any particular benefit to which that subsection applies, and different days may be so fixed for different benefits or categories of persons in receipt of benefits.

(*b*) Where an order is proposed to be made under this subsection, a draft of the order shall be laid before Dáil Éireann, and the order shall not be made until a resolution approving of the draft has been passed by Dáil Éireann.

(7) [(*a*) The Revenue Commissioners may, in order to provide for the efficient collection and recovery of any tax due in respect of benefits to which subsection (3) applies, make regulations modifying the [Income Tax (Employments) (Consolidated) Regulations 2001 (SI No 559 of 2001)][2], in their application to those benefits, the employees in receipt of those benefits, the reliefs from income tax appropriate to such employees, and employers of such employees or certificates of tax credits and standard rate cut-off point or tax deduction cards held by employers of such employees in respect of those employees.

(*b*) Without prejudice to the generality of paragraph (*a*), regulations under that paragraph may include provision for the reallocation by the Revenue Commissioners (without the issue of amended notices of determination of tax credits and standard rate cut-off point, amended certificates of tax credits and standard rate cut-off point and amended tax deduction cards) of the reliefs from income tax appropriate to employees between the benefits to which subsection (3) applies and other emoluments receivable by them.][3]

(*c*) Every regulation made under this subsection shall be laid before Dáil Éireann as soon as may be after it is made and, if a resolution annulling the regulation is passed by Dáil Éireann within the next 21 days on which Dáil Éireann has sat after the regulation is laid before it, the regulation shall be annulled accordingly, but without prejudice to the validity of anything previously done thereunder.

(8) (*a*) In this subsection, **"short-time employment"** has the same meaning as it has for the purposes of the Social Welfare Acts, but also includes an employment referred to in section 79(2)(*b*) of the Social Welfare (Consolidation) Act, 1993.

[(*b*) Notwithstanding subsection (3) and the Finance Act 1992 (Commencement of Section 15) (Unemployment Benefit and Pay-Related Benefit) Order 1994 (SI No 19 of 1994), subsection (3)(*b*) shall not apply in relation to unemployment benefit paid or payable, in the period commencing on 6 April 1997 and ending on 31 December 2006, to a person employed in short-time employment.][4]

Note

By virtue of the Finance Act 1992 (Commencement of Section 15) (Disability Benefit and Injury Benefit) Order 1993, SI No 66/1993, subs (3) came into operation on 6 April 1993 as respects disability benefit and injury benefit. By virtue of the Finance Act 1992 (Commencement of Section 15) (Unemployment Benefit and Pay-Related Benefit) Order 1994, SI No 19/1994, subs (3) came into operation on 6 April 1994 as respects unemployment benefit and pay-related benefit.

Amendments

1 Substituted by FA 2001 s 240(1) and (2)(*a*) and Sch 5 Pt 1 for 2002 and later tax years; previously "£10".

2 Substituted by FA 2002 s 138 and Sch 6 paras 3(*c*) and 6(*c*)(i) with effect from 1 January 2002; previously "Income Tax (Employments) Regulations, 1960 (SI No 28 of 1960)".

3 Subs (7)(*a*)–(*b*) substituted by FA 2001 s 2(3) and Sch 1 para 1(*b*) for short tax "year" 2001 and later tax years.

4 Sub(8)(*b*) substituted by FA 2004 s 5.

Cross-references

Income Tax (Employments) (Consolidated) Regulations 2001, SI No 559 of 2001: Regulation 43 (interpretation — Pt 8).

Revenue information

Information leaflet IT22 — Taxation of Disability Benefit.

An information note on the Taxation of Social Welfare Short-Term Benefits is available on Revenue's website — www.revenue.ie — under Whats New/Archive/July 2004.

Tax Briefing

TB10 Apr 1993 par 2.18 & TB26 Apr 1997 p 13 — Taxation of Disability Benefit and Occupational Injury Benefit.

Former enactments

ITA 1967 s 224(1), (2) and (4); FA 1971 s 12; FA 1992 s 15; FA 1995 s 10(1); FA 1997 s 4.

Corresponding UK tax provision

Income and Corporation Taxes Act 1988 s 151.

127 Tax treatment of restrictive covenants

(1) In this section—

"accounting period" means an accounting period determined in accordance with section 27;

"basis period" means the period on the profits or gains of which income tax is to be finally computed under Schedule D or, where by virtue of the Income Tax Acts the profits or gains of any other period are to be taken to be the profits or gains of that period, that other period;

"office or employment" means any office or employment whatever such that the emoluments of that office or employment, if any, are or would be chargeable to income tax under Schedule E or under Case III of Schedule D for any year of assessment;

references to the giving of valuable consideration shall not include references to the mere assumption of an obligation to make over or provide valuable property, rights or advantages, but shall include references to the doing of anything in or towards the discharge of such an obligation.

(2) Where—

(*a*) an individual who holds, has held or is about to hold an office or employment gives, in connection with the holding of the office or employment, an undertaking (whether absolute or qualified and whether legally valid or not), the tenor or effect of which is to restrict the individual as to his or her conduct or activities,

(*b*) in respect of the giving of that undertaking by the individual, or of the total or partial fulfilment of that undertaking by the individual, any sum is paid either to the individual or to any other person, and

(*c*) apart from this section, the sum paid would not be treated as profits or gains from the office or employment,

the sum paid shall be deemed—

(i) to be profits or gains arising or accruing from the office or employment, and accordingly—

(I) in a case where the profits or gains from the office or employment are or would be chargeable to tax under [Schedule E][1], tax under that Schedule shall be charged on that sum, and tax so chargeable shall be computed under section 112(1), or

(II) in a case where the profits or gains from the office or employment are or would be chargeable to tax under Case III of Schedule D, tax under that Case shall be charged on that sum,

and

(ii) in a case within paragraph (i)(I), to be emoluments to which Chapter 4 of Part 42 is applied by section 984,

for the year of assessment in which the sum is paid; but where the individual has died before the payment of the sum this subsection shall apply as if the sum had been paid immediately before the individual's death.

(3) Where valuable consideration otherwise than in the form of money is given in respect of the giving of, or of the total or partial fulfilment of, any undertaking, subsection (2) shall apply as if a sum had instead been paid equal to the value of that consideration.

(4) Notwithstanding section 81(2), where any sum paid or valuable consideration given by a person carrying on a trade or profession is chargeable to tax in accordance with subsection (2), the sum paid or the value of the consideration given, as the case may be, may be deducted as an expense in computing for the purposes of Schedule D the profits or gains of that person's trade or profession, as the case may be—

(*a*) in the case of a person chargeable to income tax, for the basis period, or

(*b*) in the case of a person chargeable to corporation tax, for the accounting period, in which the sum is paid or valuable consideration is given.

(5) Where any sum paid or valuable consideration given by an investment company (within the meaning of section 83), or a company to which section 83 applies by virtue of section 707, is chargeable to tax in accordance with subsection (2), the sum paid or the value of consideration given, as the case may be, shall for the purposes of section 83 be treated as an expense of management for the accounting period in which the sum is paid or valuable consideration is given.

(6) This section shall apply in relation to any sum paid or consideration given in respect of the giving of, or the total or partial fulfilment of, any undertaking whenever given.

Amendments

1 Substituted by FA 2005 s 147 and Sch 6 para 1(*b*) with effect from 25 March 2005; previously "the Schedule E".

Cross-references

Deduction for income earned outside the State, subs (2): s 823(1)("the specified amount").

Exempt payments: s 201(2)(*b*).

Relief from income tax in respect of income from dealing in residential development land, meaning of "basis period" applied: s 644A(1).

Revenue information

Information leaflet IT22 — Taxation of Disability and Short-term Occupational Injury Benefits.

Information leaflet IT24 — Taxation of Unemployment Benefit.

Definitions

person: IA 1937 s 11(*c*); trade: s 3(1).

Former enactments

ITA 1967 s 525; FA 1992 s 18(1) and (3); FA 1997 s 146(1) and Sch 9 Pt I para 1(35).

128 Tax treatment of directors of companies and employees granted rights to acquire shares or other assets

(1) (*a*) In this section, except where the context otherwise requires—

"company" has the same meaning as in section 4;

[**"branch or agency"** has the same meaning as in section 4;][1]

"director" and **"employee"** have the meanings respectively assigned to them by section 770(1);

"right" means a right to acquire any asset or assets including shares in any company;

"market value" shall be construed in accordance with section 548;

"shares" includes securities within the meaning of section 135 and stock.

(*b*) In this section—

(i) references to the release of a right include references to agreeing to the restriction of the exercise of the right;

(ii) a person shall be regarded as acquiring a right as a director of a company or as an employee—

(I) if by reason of the person's office or employment it is granted to the person, or to another person who assigns the right to the person, and

(II) if section 71(3) does not apply in charging to tax the profits or gains of that office or employment,

and clauses (I) and (II) shall apply to a right granted by reason of a person's office or employment before the person has commenced to hold it or after the person has ceased to hold it as they would apply if the person had commenced to hold the office or employment or had not ceased to hold the office or employment, as the case may be.

(2) Where a person realises a gain by the exercise of, or by the assignment or release of, a right obtained by the person on or after the 6th day of April, 1986, as a director of a company or employee, the person shall be chargeable to tax under Schedule E for the year of assessment in which the gain is so realised on an amount equal to the amount of his or her gain as computed in accordance with this section [and shall be so chargeable notwithstanding that he or she was not resident in the State on the date on which the right was obtained][2].

[(2A) Notwithstanding any other provision of the Tax Acts, where a person is, by virtue of this section, chargeable to tax under Schedule E for a year of assessment in respect of an amount equal to the gain realised from the exercise, assignment or release of a right, he or she shall be a chargeable person for that year for the purposes of Part 41, unless—

...[3]

(*b*) the person has been exempted by an inspector from the requirements of section 951 by reason of a notice given under subsection (6) of that section.][4]

(3) Subject to subsection (5), where tax may by virtue of this section become chargeable in respect of any gain which may be realised by the exercise of a right, tax shall not be chargeable under any other provision of the Tax Acts in respect of the receipt of the right.

(4) The gain realised by—

(*a*) the exercise of any right at any time shall be taken to be the difference between the market value of the asset or assets, as the case may be, at the time of acquisition and the aggregate amount or value of the consideration, if any, given for the asset or assets and for the grant of the right, and

(*b*) the assignment or release of any right shall be taken to be the difference between the amount or value of the consideration for the assignment or release and the amount or value of the consideration, if any, given for the grant of the right,

and for this purpose the inspector may make a just apportionment of any entire consideration given for the grant of the right or for the grant of the right and for something besides; but neither the consideration given for the grant of the right nor any such entire consideration shall be taken to include the performance of any duties in or in connection with an office or employment, and no part of the amount or value of the consideration given for the grant shall be deducted more than once under this subsection.

(5) (*a*) Where a right mentioned in subsection (2) is obtained as mentioned in that subsection and the right is capable of being exercised later than 7 years after it

is obtained, subsection (3) shall not prevent the charging of tax under any other provision of the Tax Acts in respect of the receipt of the right; but where tax is charged under such provision it shall be deducted from any tax which under subsection (2) is chargeable by reference to the gain realised by the exercise, assignment or release of the right.

(*b*) For the purpose of any charge to tax enabled to be made by this subsection, the value of a right shall be taken to be not less than the market value at the time the right is obtained of the asset or assets which may be acquired by the exercise of the right or of any asset or assets for which the asset or assets so acquired may be exchanged, reduced by the amount or value (or, if variable, the least amount or value) of the consideration for which the asset or assets may be so acquired.

(6) Subject to subsection (7), a person shall, in the case of a right granted by reason of the person's office or employment, be chargeable to tax under this section in respect of a gain realised by another person—

(*a*) if the right was granted to that other person, or

(*b*) if the other person acquired the right otherwise than by or under an assignment made by means of a bargain at arm's length, or if the 2 persons are connected persons at the time when the gain is realised;

but in a case within paragraph (*b*) the gain realised shall be treated as reduced by the amount of any gain realised by a previous holder on an assignment of the right.

(7) A person shall not be chargeable to tax by virtue of subsection (6)(*b*) in respect of any gain realised by another person if the first-mentioned person was divested of the right by operation of law on the first-mentioned person's bankruptcy or otherwise, but the other person shall be chargeable to tax in respect of the gain under Case IV of Schedule D.

(8) Where a right is assigned or released in whole or in part for a consideration which consists of or comprises another right, that other right shall not be treated as consideration for the assignment or release; but this section shall apply in relation to that other right as it applies in relation to the right assigned or released and as if the consideration for its acquisition did not include the value of [the right assigned or released but did include the amount or value of][5] the consideration given for the grant of the right assigned or released in so far as that has not been offset by any valuable consideration for the assignment or release other than the consideration consisting of the other right.

(9) (*a*) Where as a result of 2 or more transactions a person ceases to hold a right and the person or a connected person comes to hold another right (whether or not acquired from the person to whom the other right was assigned) and any of those transactions was effected under arrangements to which 2 or more persons holding rights in respect of which tax may be chargeable under this section were parties, those transactions shall be treated for the purposes of subsection (8) as a single transaction whereby the one right is assigned for a consideration which consists of or comprises the other right.

(*b*) This subsection shall apply in relation to 2 or more transactions, whether they involve an assignment preceding, coinciding with, or subsequent to, an acquisition.

(10) Where a gain chargeable to tax under subsection (2) or (6) is realised by the exercise of a right, section 552 shall apply as if a sum equal to the amount of the gain so chargeable to tax formed part of the consideration given by the person acquiring the shares for their acquisition by that person.

(11) Where in any year of assessment a person grants a right in respect of which tax may be chargeable under this section, or allots any shares or transfers any asset in pursuance of such a right, or gives any consideration for the assignment or release in whole or in part of such a right, or receives written notice of the assignment of such a right, the person shall deliver particulars thereof in writing to the inspector not later than [[31 March][6] in the year of assessment following][7] that year.

...[8]

[(12) Where in relation to any right—

(*a*) the person referred to in subsection (11) is not resident in the State, and

(*b*) the person who obtains the right is a director or employee of a company which is either—

(i) resident in the State, or

(ii) not resident in the State but carries on a trade, profession or vocation in the State through a branch or agency in which the director or employee is employed,

subsection (11) shall, as regards a company referred to in paragraph (*b*)(i) apply to the company, and, as regards a company referred to in paragraph (*b*)(ii) apply to its agent, manager, factor or other representative.][9]

Amendments

1 Definition of "branch or agency" inserted by FA 2002 s 11(1)(*a*) with effect from 25 March 2002.

2 Inserted by FA 2005 s 16(1) as respects a right (within the meaning of TCA 1997 s 128) obtained on or after such day as the Minister for Finance may appoint by order.

3 Subs (2A)(*a*) deleted by FA 2003 s 8(1)(*b*) in respect of the exercise, assignment or release of a right (within the meaning of TCA 1997 s 128) on or after 30 June 2003.

4 Subs (2A) inserted by FA 2000 s 27(*a*)(i) with effect from 6 April 2000.

5 Inserted by FA 1998 s 136 and Sch 9 para 3 with effect from 6 April 1997.

6 Substituted by FA 2002 s 11(1)(*b*) for 2002 and later tax years; previously "30 June".

7 Substituted by FA 2000 s 27(*a*)(ii) with effect from 6 April 2000; previously "30 days after the end of".

8 Subs (11A), which was inserted by FA 2000 s 27(*a*)(iii) with effect from 6 April 2000, substituted by subs (12) (inserted by FA 2002 s 11(1)(*c*)) with effect from 25 March 2002.

9 Subs (12) inserted by FA 2002 s 11(1)(*c*) with effect from 25 March 2002.

Cross-references

Approved share option schemes, transitional: Sch 32 para 7(2)(*a*).

Deduction for income earned outside the State: s 823(1)("the specified amount").

Deferral of payment of tax under section 128: s 128A(1)(*a*), (*b*), (4A)(*a*), (*b*), (*c*), (*d*), (*f*), (*g*), (*h*), (*j*), (4B), (6).

Payment of tax under section 128: s 128B(1); subs (4): s 128B(2).

Penalty, subss (11), (11A): Sch 29 column 3.

Revenue precedents

Issue: Whether income chargeable to tax under TCA 1997 s 128 should be included in the calculation of FED, TCA 1997 s 823.

Decision: Yes, the income chargeable to tax under TCA 1997 s 128 should be included in calculating the Foreign Earnings Deduction.

Issue: Whether income chargeable to tax under TCA 1997 s 128 should be included as an emolument for the purposes of calculating SCSB.

Decision: Yes, the income chargeable to tax under TCA 1997 s 128 should be included in the calculation.

Revenue information

Information leaflet CG16 — Relevant tax on a share option.

Tax Briefing

TB31 Apr 1998 p 11 and TB35 Mar 1999 p 18 — Tax treatment of shares acquired under share schemes which are subject to a restriction or clog prohibiting disposal of the shares for a number of years.

TB31 Apr 1998 p 12 — Share option schemes and residence.

TB36 June 1999 p 16 — Unapproved share option schemes: returns and assessments.

TB40 June 2000 pp 27–28 — Share options and other rights: tax treatment.

TB50 Oct 2002 p 4 — Any cash payment chargeable under Schedule E, by virtue of the release of a share option, should be paid through the company payroll and is subject to PAYE and PRSI in the normal manner.

Definitions

company: ss 4(1), 5(1); inspector: ss 2(1), 5(1), 852; person: IA 1937 s 11(*c*); profession: s 2(1); resident: s 2(1); shares: s 5(1); Tax Acts: s 1(2); trade: s 2(1); writing: IA 1937 Sch; year of assessment: ss 2(1), 5(1).

Former enactments

FA 1986 s 9(1)(*a*), (*b*)(i), (iii) and (2)–(11)(*a*).

128A Deferral of payment of tax under section 128

[(1) Subject to subsection (2), in any case where—

(*a*) for any year of assessment a person is chargeable to tax under Schedule E, by virtue of section 128, on an amount equal to a gain realised by the exercise of a right to acquire shares in a company ("the relevant shares"), which right was exercised [in the period from 6 April 2000 to the date of the passing of the Finance Act 2003][1], and

(*b*) following an assessment for the year in which that right was exercised ("the relevant year") an amount of tax, chargeable by virtue of section 128 in respect of the amount referred to in paragraph (*a*), is payable to the Collector- General, and

(*c*) the person concerned makes an election in accordance with subsection (3),

he or she shall be entitled to defer payment of the tax in accordance with subsection (4).

(2) Subsection (1) shall not apply where the relevant shares are disposed of by the person concerned in the relevant year.

[(3) An election under this section shall be made by notice in writing to the inspector on or before—

(*a*) where the relevant year is the year of assessment 2000–2001, 31 January 2002, and

(*b*) where the relevant year is the year of assessment 2001 or any subsequent year of assessment, 31 October in the year of assessment following the relevant year.][2]

(4) Where an election has been made under this section the tax referred to in subsection (1)(*b*) shall, notwithstanding any other provision of the Income Tax Acts, but subject to the provisions of this section, be paid on or before the earlier of—

(*a*) [31 October][3] in the year of assessment following the year of assessment in which the relevant shares are disposed of, or

(*b*) [31 October][3] in the year of assessment following the year of assessment beginning 7 years after the relevant year.

[(4A)(*a*) Notwithstanding subsection (4), where an election has been made in accordance with subsection (3) and—

(i) relevant shares are disposed of (in this subparagraph referred to as the **"first-mentioned disposal"**), and

(I) but for this subparagraph, tax would be payable, by reference to the first-mentioned disposal, in accordance with subsection (4)(*a*), and

(II) the market value of those shares at the date of the first-mentioned disposal is less than the tax chargeable under section 128, by reference to the exercise of an option to acquire those shares,

then an amount, being an amount equal to that market value, shall be due and payable to the Collector-General within 30 days after the date of the first-mentioned disposal or, if later, on or before 30 June 2003, and the balance of the tax chargeable remaining unpaid after that payment shall be payable in the event of, and by reference to, disposals of any shares in a company in a year of assessment, in accordance with paragraph (*d*), being disposals after the date of the first-mentioned disposal, or

(ii) relevant shares are held at 31 December in the year of assessment beginning 7 years after the relevant year (in this subparagraph referred to as the **"first-mentioned date"**), and

(I) but for this subparagraph, tax would be payable in accordance with subsection (4)(*b*), and

(II) the market value of the relevant shares is, at the first-mentioned date, less than the tax chargeable under section 128, by reference to the exercise of an option to acquire those shares,

then an amount, being an amount equal to that market value, shall be due and payable to the Collector-General within 30 days after the date of the first-mentioned date and the balance of the tax chargeable remaining unpaid after that payment shall be payable in the event of, and by reference to, disposals of any shares in a company in a year of assessment, in accordance with paragraph (*d*), being disposals after the first-mentioned date.

(*b*) Where a person who is entitled to make an election in accordance with subsection (3), after 6 February 2003 and on or before 31 October in the year of assessment following the relevant year in respect of relevant shares, does not do so, or tax chargeable under section 128, in respect of any gain realised by the exercise before 6 February 2003 of a right to acquire shares, is due after 6

February 2003 but on or before 31 October in the year of assessment following the relevant year, and the market value of the shares on—

(i) that 31 October, or

(ii) where the shares are disposed of before that date, the date of the disposal (referred to in this paragraph as the **"first-mentioned disposal"**) of the shares,

is less than the tax chargeable under section 128, then an amount, being an amount equal to that market value, shall be due and payable to the Collector-General within 30 days after the said 31 October, and the balance of the tax chargeable remaining unpaid after that payment shall be payable in the event of, and by reference to, disposals of any shares in a company in a year of assessment, in accordance with paragraph (*d*), being disposals after the said 31 October or the date of the first-mentioned disposal of the shares, as the case may be.

(*c*) In all cases other than those referred to in paragraph (*a*) or (*b*), where tax is chargeable under section 128 on an amount equal to a gain realised by the exercise, at any time before 6 February 2003, of a right to acquire shares in a company, and the market value of the shares on—

(i) that date, or

(ii) where the shares are disposed of before that date, the date of the disposal of the shares,

is less than the tax chargeable under section 128, then an amount, being an amount equal to that market value, shall be due and payable to the Collector-General on or before 30 June 2003, and the balance of the tax chargeable remaining unpaid after that payment shall be payable in the event of, and by reference to, disposals of any shares in a company in a year of assessment, in accordance with paragraph (*d*), being disposals after 6 February 2003.

(*d*) (i) A payment that is to be made in the event of, and by reference to, disposals of any shares in a year of assessment shall be a payment which is the lesser of—

(I) the aggregate of the balances of unpaid tax referred to in paragraphs (*a*), (*b*) and (*c*), as reduced by tax payable in accordance with this paragraph by reference to disposals of shares in a previous year of assessment, and

(II) the aggregate of the net gains (if any) arising in respect of disposals of shares in the year of assessment.

(ii) For the purposes of subparagraph (i)(II), the net gain arising in relation to a disposal of shares shall be the market value at the date of disposal of those shares reduced by so much of the aggregate of—

(I) the amount of the consideration, if any, given for the shares (including, where relevant, the grant of a right to acquire the shares),

(II) (A) where this subsection does not apply to the payment of income tax chargeable under section 128 by reference to the acquisition of the shares, the amount of the income tax so chargeable, or

(B) where this subsection does apply to the payment of income tax chargeable under section 128 by reference to the acquisition of the shares, the total amount paid, before the date of the disposal, in respect of that income tax,

and

(III) capital gains tax chargeable by reference to the disposal of the shares, as does not exceed that market value.

(iii) For the purposes of subparagraph (ii), the income tax or capital gains tax, as the case may be, so chargeable shall be the amount by which the income tax or capital gains tax, as the case may be, chargeable on the taxpayer for the year of assessment would have been reduced if the acquisition or disposal of the shares, as the case may be, had not taken place.

(iv) Payments referred to in paragraph (*d*)(i) which are to be made by reference to disposals of shares shall be due and payable to the Collector-General on or before 31 October in the year following the year of assessment in which the disposal of those shares takes place.

(*e*) (i) A taxpayer who wishes to be entitled to avail of the provisions of this subsection shall so elect, by giving notice in writing to the inspector, on or before 1 June 2003 in a form prescribed or authorised by the Revenue Commissioners, and the notice shall contain details of—

(I) the date of exercise of the option,

(II) the number of shares acquired by exercise of the option,

(III) the market value of the shares at date of exercise of that option, and

(IV) such further particulars for the purposes of this subsection as may be required or indicated by the Revenue Commissioners.

(ii) The inspector or such other officer as the Revenue Commissioners shall appoint in that behalf may admit a late election under subparagraph (i) in circumstances where he or she is satisfied that the delay in making the election was due to absence, illness or other reasonable cause.

(*f*) In any case where, at any time, the requirements of this subsection have not been fully complied with, any amount of tax chargeable under section 128 which is unpaid shall be due and payable as if this subsection had not been enacted.

(*g*) Any tax chargeable under section 128 which is due and payable in accordance with subsection (4) or this subsection, which remains unpaid at the date of death of the chargeable person, shall be discharged by the Revenue Commissioners.

(*h*) Any amount paid before 6 February 2003 in respect of tax chargeable under section 128 shall not be repaid by reference to any provision of this subsection.

(*i*) The reference in paragraph (*d*) to the disposal of shares includes a reference to the disposal of shares by the spouse of the person chargeable—

(I) in a case where section 1017 applies, or

(II) in a case where that section does not apply, but the disposal by the spouse is subsequent to a transfer, on or after 25 February 2003, of the shares from the other spouse, except where the spouses are separated in the circumstances referred to in paragraph (*a*) or (*b*) of section 1015(2), or their marriage has been dissolved under either section 5 of the Family Law (Divorce) Act 1996, or the law of a country or jurisdiction other than the State, being a dissolution that is entitled to be recognised as valid in the State.

(*j*) A person shall not, at any time, be entitled to avail of the provisions of this subsection where, at that time, he or she has not paid, or agreed an arrangement acceptable to the Collector-General for the payment of, tax due and payable which is chargeable under section 128 in respect of the exercise of a right to acquire shares to which this subsection does not apply.

(*k*) In this subsection—

"market value" shall be construed in accordance with section 548;

"shares" includes securities within the meaning of section 135 and stock.

(4B) In any case where the provisions of subsection (4A) apply, the amount by which the market value of the shares at the time of acquisition exceeds the market value at the date of disposal of those shares, or any part of that amount, shall not be an allowable loss for the purposes of the Capital Gains Tax Acts until such time as the tax liability of the person under section 128 has been paid in full to the Collector-General.][4]

(5) The reference in [subsections (4)(*a*) and (4A)][5] to the relevant shares being disposed of includes a part disposal of such shares, and in the case of a part disposal, the tax to be paid shall be determined in a manner that is just and reasonable.

(6) Subject to any other provision of the Income Tax Acts requiring income of any description to be treated as the highest part of a person's income, in determining for the purposes of paragraph (*b*) of subsection (1) what tax is chargeable on a person by virtue of section 128 in respect of an amount referred to in paragraph (*a*) of that subsection, that amount shall be treated as the highest part of his or her income for the relevant year.

(7) Notwithstanding any other provision of the Income Tax Acts, the due date in relation to tax, the payment of which has been deferred by virtue of an election under this section, shall, for the purposes of section 1080, be the date when the amount becomes due and payable under [subsections (4) and (4A) but notwithstanding any provisions of subsection (4A) that subsection shall have no effect as respects the payment of any tax in relation to a gain realised by the exercise on or after 6 February 2003 of a right to acquire shares.][6].][7]

Amendments

1 Substituted by FA 2003 s 7(*a*) with effect from 1 January 2003; previously "on or after 6 April 2000";

2 Subs (3) substituted by FA 2003 s 34(1)(*a*) with effect from 6 April 2001.

3 Substituted by FA 2001 s 77(2) and Sch 2 para 9(*b*) with effect from 6 April 2001; previously "1 November".

4 Subss (4A) and (4B) inserted by FA 2003 s 7(*b*) with effect from 1 January 2003.

5 Substituted by FA 2003 s 7(*c*) with effect from 1 January 2003; previously "subsection (4)(*a*)".

6 Substituted by FA 2003 s 7(*d*) with effect from 1 January 2003; previously "subsection (4)".

7 Section 128A inserted by FA 2000 s 27(*b*) with effect from 6 April 2000.

Revenue information

Information leaflet CG16 — Relevant tax on a share option.

Tax Briefing

TB40 June 2000 pp 27–28 — Share options and other rights: tax treatment.
TB41 Sept 2000 p 28 — Share options — deferral of payment of income tax.
TB46 Dec 2001 p 25 — Share options — deferral of payment of income tax and inplications for preliminary tax.
TB48 June 2002 p 18 — Deferral of payment of income tax under section 128 TCA 1997.
TB50 Oct 2002 p 4 — Deferral of income tax on the exercise of a share option — what information must be included on a return of income?
TB52 May 2003 pp 26–31 — Share options — Payment of Tax (Finance Act 2003 changes).

Definitions

Capital Gains Tax Acts: s 1(2); Collector-General: s 2(1); company: s 4(1); Income Tax Acts: s 1(2); inspector: s 2(1); part disposal: s 5(1); person: IA 1937 s 11(*c*); writing: IA 1937 Sch; year of assessment: ss 2(1), 5(1).

128B Payment of tax under section 128

[(1) This section applies where, by virtue of section 128, a person (in this section referred to as a **"taxable person"**) is chargeable to tax under Schedule E for a year of assessment on an amount equal to the gain realised by the exercise, on or after 30 June 2003, of a right to acquire shares (in this section referred to as **"relevant shares"**) in a company.

(2) Where this section applies for a year of assessment, the taxable person shall pay an amount of tax (in this section referred to as **"relevant tax"**) in respect of the gain realised by the exercise of the right to acquire relevant shares, and that amount of tax shall be determined by the formula—

$$A \times B$$

where—

A is the amount of that gain computed in accordance with section 128(4), and

B is the percentage which is equal to the higher rate in force for the year of assessment in which the taxable person exercises the right to acquire the relevant shares.

(3) Relevant tax shall be due and payable to the Collector-General within 30 days after the exercise of the right to acquire the relevant shares, and shall be so due and payable without the making of an assessment, but relevant tax which has become so due and payable may be assessed on the taxable person (whether or not it has been paid when the assessment is made) if the tax or any part of it is not paid on or before the due date.

(4) Each payment of relevant tax shall be accompanied by a return containing, in relation to the taxable person by whom the payment is made, details of the amount of the gain referred to in subsection (1) and of the relevant tax due in respect of that gain and such other particulars as may be required by the return.

(5) Every return under this section shall be in a form prescribed or authorised by the Revenue Commissioners, and shall include a declaration to the effect that the return is correct and complete.

(6) The Collector-General shall give the taxable person a receipt for the amount of relevant tax paid by the taxable person.

(7) Where it appears to an officer of the Revenue Commissioners that there is any amount of relevant tax which ought to have been but has not been included in a return

under subsection (4), or where such officer is dissatisfied with any such return, such officer may make an assessment on the taxable person concerned to the best of such officer's judgement, and any amount of relevant tax due under an assessment made by virtue of this subsection shall be treated for the purposes of interest on unpaid tax as having been payable at the time specified in subsection (3).

(8) Where any item has been incorrectly included in a return under subsection (4) as a gain in respect of which relevant tax is required to be paid, an officer of the Revenue Commissioners may make such assessments, adjustments or set-offs as may in his or her judgement be required for securing that the resulting liability to relevant tax, including interest on unpaid tax, of the taxable person is, in so far as possible, the same as it would have been if the item had not been so included.

(9) (*a*) The provisions of the Income Tax Acts relating to—

(i) assessments to income tax,

(ii) appeals against such assessments (including the rehearing of appeals and the statement of a case for the opinion of the High Court), and

(iii) the collection and recovery of income tax,

shall, in so far as they are applicable, apply to the assessment, collection and recovery of relevant tax.

(*b*) Any amount of relevant tax payable in accordance with this section without the making of an assessment shall carry interest at the rate of 0.0322 per cent for each day or part of a day from the date when the amount becomes due and payable until payment.

(*c*) [Subsections (3) to (5) of section 1080][1] shall apply in relation to interest payable under paragraph (*b*) as they apply in relation to interest payable under that section.

(*d*) In its application to any relevant tax charged by any assessment made in accordance with this section, section 1080 shall apply as if [subsection (2)(*b*)][2] of that section were deleted.

(10) Where a taxable person has paid relevant tax in respect of a gain realised by the exercise, in any year of assessment, of a right to acquire relevant shares, the taxable person may claim to have that relevant tax set against the income tax chargeable on the taxable person for that year of assessment and, where that relevant tax exceeds such income tax, to have the excess refunded to the taxable person.

(11) Relevant tax payable by a taxable person in respect of a gain realised by the exercise, in any year of assessment, of a right to acquire relevant shares shall not be regarded as a payment of, or on account of, preliminary tax for the purposes of sections 952 and 958.

(12) Relevant tax payable by a taxable person in respect of a gain realised by the exercise, in any year of assessment, of a right to acquire relevant shares—

(*a*) shall not, for the purposes of section 952(2), form part of the income tax which in the opinion of the taxable person is likely to become payable by that person for that year of assessment, (*b*) shall not, for the purposes of section 958(3A), be regarded as either part of the income tax paid or part of the income tax payable by that person for that year of assessment, and

(*c*) shall not, for the purposes of section 958(4), be regarded as income tax payable by the taxable person for that year of assessment.

(13) Notwithstanding any other provision of this section, any gain realised by the exercise, in any year of assessment, of a right to acquire relevant shares and in respect of which relevant tax is payable by a taxable person shall be included in the return required to be delivered by that person under section 951.

(14) Where, on an application in writing having been made to them in that behalf, the Revenue Commissioners are satisfied that an individual is likely to be chargeable to income tax for a year of assessment at the standard rate only, the reference in the meaning of B in subsection (2) to the higher rate shall be construed for the purposes of the payment or payments required to be made by the individual for that year in accordance with subsection (2), as a reference to the standard rate.][3]

Amendments

1 Substituted by FA 2005 s 145(7)(*a*) and Sch 5 Pt 1 in relation to any unpaid income tax, corporation tax or capital gains tax, as the case may be, that has not been paid before 1 April 2005 regardless of when that tax became due and payable and notwithstanding anything to the contrary in any other enactment other than TCA 1997 s 1082; previously "Subsections (3) and (4) of section 1080".

2 Substituted by FA 2005 s 145(7)(*a*) and Sch 5 Pt 1 in relation to any unpaid income tax, corporation tax or capital gains tax, as the case may be, that has not been paid before 1 April 2005 regardless of when that tax became due and payable and notwithstanding anything to the contrary in any other enactment other than TCA 1997 s 1082; previously "subsection (1)(*b*)".

3 Section 128B inserted by FA 2003 s 8(1)(*a*) with effect from 30 June 2003.

Revenue information

Information Leaflet CG16 — Relevant tax on a share option.

Tax Briefing

TB52 May 2003 p 8 — Share options — payment of tax under TCA 1997 s 128B.

TB53 Aug 2003 p 9 — Payment of tax on share options.

TB55 April 2004 p 14 — Relevant tax on share options and interaction with preliminary tax obligations.

Definitions

Collector-General: s 2(1); company: s 4(1); High Court: IA 1937 Sch; higher rate: s 3(1); Income Tax Acts: s 1(2); right: s 128(1); shares: s 128(1); standard rate: s 3(1); tax: s 3(1); writing: IA 1937 Sch; year of assessment: s 2(1).

PART 6
COMPANY DISTRIBUTIONS, TAX CREDITS, FRANKED INVESTMENT INCOME AND ADVANCE CORPORATION TAX

CHAPTER 1
Taxation of Company Distributions

129 Irish resident company distributions not generally chargeable to corporation tax

Except where otherwise provided by the Corporation Tax Acts, corporation tax shall not be chargeable on dividends and other distributions of a company resident in the State, nor shall any such dividends or distributions be taken into account in computing income for corporation tax.

Cross-references

Company acquiring its own shares, shares bought by issuing company or its subsidiary, taxation of dealer's receipts: s 174(2).

Dividend withholding tax on relevant distributions: s 172B(5).

Investment income, meaning: s 434(1).

Tax credit for recipients of distributions: s 136(3)(*b*).

Life assurance companies, distributions received from Irish resident companies: s 712(1).

Life assurance companies, computation of profits: s 714(1).

Life assurance companies, pension business: s 717(4).

Undertaking for collective investment; distributions received: s 738(3)(*a*)(i).

Definitions

company: ss 4(1), 5(1); distribution: ss 4(1), 436, 437; profits: s 4(1).

Former enactments

CTA 1976 s 2.

Corresponding UK tax provision

Income and Corporation Taxes Act 1988 s 208.

CHAPTER 2
Meaning of Distribution

Cross-references

Charge and deduction of income tax not charged or deducted before passing of annual Act: s 1087(3).

Schedule F, meaning of "distribution" applied: s 20(1).

130 Matters to be treated as distributions

(1) The following provisions of this Chapter, together with [sections 436 and 437, and subsection (2)(*b*) of section 816],[1] shall, subject to any express exceptions, apply with respect to the meaning in the Corporation Tax Acts of **"distribution"** and for determining the persons to whom certain distributions are to be treated as made; but references in the Corporation Tax Acts to distributions of a company shall not apply to distributions made in respect of share capital in a winding up.

(2) In relation to any company, **"distribution"** means—

(*a*) any dividend paid by the company, including a capital dividend;

(*b*) any other distribution out of assets of the company (whether in cash or otherwise) in respect of shares in the company, except, subject to section 132, so much of the distribution, if any, as represents a repayment of capital on the shares or is, when it is made, equal in amount or value to any new consideration received by the company for the distribution;

(*c*) any amount met out of assets of the company (whether in cash or otherwise) in respect of the redemption of any security issued by the company in respect of shares in, or securities of, the company otherwise than wholly for new consideration, or in the redemption of such part of any such security so issued as is not properly referable to new consideration;

(*d*) any interest or other distribution out of assets of the company in respect of securities of the company (except so much, if any, of any such distribution as represents the principal thereby secured, and, without prejudice to section 135(9), for this purpose no amount shall be regarded as representing the principal secured by a security in so far as it exceeds any new consideration received by the company for the issue of the security), where the securities are—

(i) securities issued as mentioned in paragraph (*c*), but excluding securities issued before the 27th day of November, 1975,

(ii) securities convertible directly or indirectly into shares in the company or securities carrying any right to receive shares in or securities of the company, not being (in either case) securities quoted on a recognised stock exchange nor issued on terms which are reasonably comparable with the terms of issue of securities so quoted,

(iii) securities under which—

(I) the consideration given by the company for the use of the principal secured is to any extent dependent on the results of the company's business or any part of the company's business, or

(II) the consideration so given represents more than a reasonable commercial return for the use of that principal; but this shall not operate so as to treat as a distribution so much of the interest or other distribution as represents a reasonable commercial return for the use of that principal,

(iv) securities issued by the company and held by a company not resident in the State, where—

(I) the company which issued the securities is a 75 per cent subsidiary of the other company,

(II) both companies are 75 per cent subsidiaries of a third company which is not resident in the State, or

(III) except where 90 per cent or more of the share capital of the company which issued the securities is directly owned by a company resident in the State, both the company which issued the securities and the company not resident in the State are 75 per cent subsidiaries of a third company which is resident in the State,

or

(v) securities connected with shares in the company, where "connected with" means that, in consequence of the nature of the rights attaching to the securities or shares, and in particular of any terms or conditions attaching to the right to transfer the shares or securities, it is necessary or advantageous for a person who has, or disposes of or acquires, any of the securities also to have, or to dispose of or acquire, a proportionate holding of the shares;

(*e*) any amount required to be treated as a distribution by subsection (3) or by [section 131;][2]

[(*f*) any qualifying amount (within the meaning of subsection (2C)) paid to an individual who at the time that amount is paid—

(i) is a beneficiary under the terms of a trust deed of an employee share ownership trust approved of by the Revenue Commissioners under Schedule 12 and for which approval has not been withdrawn and which trust deed contains provision for the transfer of securities to the trustees of a scheme approved of by the Revenue Commissioners under Schedule 11 and for which approval has not been withdrawn, and

(ii) would be eligible to have securities appropriated to him or her, had such securities been available for appropriation, under the scheme referred to in subparagraph (i).][3]

[(2A) For the purposes of subsection (2)(*d*)(iii)(I), the consideration given by the company for the use of the principal received shall not be treated as being to any extent dependent on the results of the company's business or any part of the company's business by reason only of the fact that the terms (however expressed) of the security provide—

(*a*) for the consideration to be reduced in the event of the results improving, or

(*b*) for the consideration to be increased in the event of the results deteriorating.][4]

[(2B) Subsection (2)(*d*)(iv) shall not apply as respects interest, other than interest to which section 452 or 845A applies, paid to a company which is a resident of a Member State of the European Communities other than the State and, for the purposes of this subsection, a company is a resident of a Member State of the European Communities if the company is by virtue of the law of that Member State resident for the purposes of tax (being any tax imposed in the Member State which corresponds to corporation tax in the State) in such Member State.][5]

[(2C) Notwithstanding section 519(6) and paragraph 13(4) of Schedule 12, **"qualifying amount"** means an amount paid solely out of income consisting of dividends received in a chargeable period (within the meaning of section 321) in respect of securities (within the meaning of Schedule 12) held by the trustees of the employee share ownership trust referred to in subsection (2)(*f*)(i), but only to the extent that such income exceeds the aggregate of—

(*a*) any sum or sums spent to meet expenses of the trust,

(*b*) any interest paid on sums borrowed by the trust,

(*c*) any sum or sums paid to the personal representatives of a deceased person who was a beneficiary under the terms of the trust deed,

(*d*) any amount spent on the repayment of sums borrowed including any amount capable of being so spent, having regard to the conditions referred to in paragraph 11(2B)(*d*) or 11A(5)(*d*) of Schedule 12, and

(*e*) any amount spent on the acquisition of securities (within the meaning of Schedule 12) including any amount capable, at any particular time, of being so spent on such securities at their market value (within the meaning of section 548) at that time,

in the chargeable period.][6]

(3) (*a*) Where on a transfer of assets or liabilities by a company to its members or to a company by its members the amount or value of the benefit received by a member (taken according to its market value) exceeds the amount or value (so

taken) of any new consideration given by the member, the company shall be treated as making a distribution to the member of an amount equal to the difference (in paragraph (*b*) referred to as **"the relevant amount"**).

(*b*) Notwithstanding paragraph (*a*), where the company and the member receiving the benefit are both resident in the State and either the former is a subsidiary of the latter or both are subsidiaries of a third company [, being a company which, by virtue of the law of a [relevant Member State][7], is resident for the purposes of tax in such a Member State],[8] the relevant amount shall not be treated as a distribution.

[(*c*) For the purposes of this subsection and subsection (4), **"tax"**, in relation to a [relevant Member State][9] other than the State, means any tax imposed in the Member State which corresponds to corporation tax in the State.][10]

[(*d*) For the purposes of this subsection and subsection (4)—

"EEA Agreement" means the Agreement on the European Economic Area signed at Oporto on 2 May 1992, as adjusted by the Protocol signed at Brussels on 17 March 1993;

"EEA State" means a state which is a contracting party to the EEA Agreement;

"relevant Member State" means—

(i) a Member State of the European Communities, or

(ii) not being such a Member State, an EEA State which is a territory with the government of which arrangements having the force of law by virtue of [section 826(1)(*a*)][11] have been made.][12]

(4) The question whether one company is a subsidiary of another company for the purpose of subsection (3) shall be determined as a question whether it is a 51 per cent subsidiary of that other company, except that that other company shall be treated as not being the owner of—

(*a*) any share capital which it owns directly in a company, if a profit on a sale of the shares would be treated as a trading receipt of its trade,

(*b*) any share capital which it owns indirectly and which is owned directly by a company for which a profit on the sale of the shares would be a trading receipt, or

(*c*) any share capital which it owns directly or indirectly in a company [, not being a company which, by virtue of the law of a [relevant Member State][13], is resident for the purposes of tax in such a Member State].[14]

(5) (*a*) No transfer of assets (other than cash) or of liabilities between one company and another company shall constitute, or be treated as giving rise to, a distribution by virtue of subsection (2)(*b*) or (3) if they are companies—

(i) both of which are resident in the State and neither of which is a 51 per cent subsidiary of a company not so resident, and

(ii) which neither at the time of the transfer nor as a result of it are under common control.

(*b*) For the purposes of this subsection, 2 companies shall be under common control if they are under the control of the same person or persons, and for this purpose **"control"** shall be construed in accordance with section 11.

(*c*) Any amount which would be a distribution by virtue of subsection (3)(*a*) shall not constitute a distribution by virtue of subsection (2)(*b*).

Amendments

1 Substituted by FA 1998 s 43(1)(*d*) as respects shares issued by a company on or after 3 December 1997; previously "sections 436 and 437".

2 Substituted by FA 2005 s 18(1)(*a*) with effect from 3 February 2005; previously "section 131.".

3 Subs (2)(*f*) inserted by FA 2005 s 18(1)(*b*) with effect from 3 February 2005.

4 Subs (2A) inserted by FA 2001 s 85(1) for payments made on or after 15 February 2001.

5 Subs (2B) inserted by FA 2003 s 61(1) as respects any interest paid or other distribution made on or after 6 February 2003.

6 Subs (2C) inserted by FA 2005 s 18(1)(*c*) with effect from 3 February 2005.

7 Substituted by FA 2002 s 39(*a*)(i) with effect from 1 January 2002; previously "Member State of the European Communities".

8 Substituted by FA 1999 s 79(1)(*a*)(i) for accounting periods ending on or after 1 July 1998; previously "also so resident"

9 Substituted by FA 2002 s 39(*a*)(ii) with effect from 1 January 2002; previously "Member State of the European Communities".

10 Subs (3)(*c*) inserted by FA 1999 s 79(1)(*a*)(ii) for accounting periods ending on or after 1 July 1998.

11 Substituted by FA 2004 s 89 and Sch 3 para 1(*d*) with effect from 25 March 2004; previously "section 826".

12 Subs (3)(*d*) inserted by FA 2002 s 39(*a*)(iii) with effect from 1 January 2002.

13 Substituted by FA 2002 s 39(*b*) with effect from 1 January 2002; previously "Member State of the European Communities".

14 Substituted by FA 1999 s 79(1)(*b*) for accounting periods ending on or after 1 July 1998; previously "not resident in the State". The substitution came into operation from 1 January 1999 — Finance Act 1998, (Section 47) (Commencement) Order, 1998, SI No 502 of 1998, refers.

Cross-references

Application of this section to certain interest, certain interest not to be treated as a distribution, subs (2)(*d*)(iv): s 452(2) and (3).

Attribution of dividends to accounting periods (subs (2)(*d*)(ii), (iii)(I), (v)): 154(3)(*b*).

Bonus issues, disallowance of reliefs, subs (2)(*c*)–(*d*): s 137(1)(*a*).

Distribution (subs (2)(*b*)), meaning in relation to a company that is a member of a 90% group: s 135(4)(*b*).

Expenses for participators and associates: s 436(1).

Foreign currencies, taxation of (subs (2)(*d*)(ii), (iii)(I), (v)): s 80(1).

Interest not treated as a distribution (subs (2)(*d*)(ii), (iii)(I), (v)), advance corporation tax: s 170(1).

Interest paid to directors, directors' associates, subs (1): s 437(3).

Interest treated as a distribution (subs (2)(*d*)(ii), (iii)(I), (v)): s 133(2), (4); s 134(3)(*b*), (4).

Non-application of this section in case of certain interest paid by banks, subs (2)(*d*)(iv): s 845A(2), (3).

Petroleum trade, subs (2)(*d*)(iv) not to apply: s 690(2).

Profit sharing schemes (subs (2)(*c*))), company reconstructions etc: s 514(3)(*b*).

Repayment of share capital following bonus issue: s 132(2)(*a*).

Securitisation of assets, subs (2)(*d*)(iii): s 110(4).

Revenue precedents

Issue: Would interest payable by a qualified company within the meaning of TCA 1997 s 446 on borrowings from group companies in non-treaty countries be treated as a distribution under TCA 1997 s 130(2)(*d*)(iv)?

Decision: Interest would not be treated as a distribution under TCA 1997 s 130(2)(*d*)(iv) subject to the following conditions: a) the interest is charged at a commercial rate; b) the interest would otherwise be recognised (apart from the aforementioned section) as an expense to be set against income of the trade; c) the funds borrowed are used solely for qualifying activities certified by the Minister for Finance under TCA 1997 s 446; d) an application for this treatment must be made in letter form to the Revenue Commissioners, Direct Taxes: Incentives Branch, Dublin Castle, Dublin 2.

Issue: Redemption of shares in stock exchange where stock broker retires.

Decision: The redemption would not be treated as a distribution under TCA 1997 s 130 but would be treated as a disposal for CGT purposes.

Tax Briefing

TB45 Oct 2001 p 9 — Review of operation of TCA 1997 s 130(2)(*d*)(iv) in relation to payments of interest to residents of countries with which Ireland has a double taxation treaty and to residents of EU Member States.

Definitions

company: ss 4(1), 5(1); distribution: ss 4(1), 436, 437; interest: s 4(1); person: IA 1937 s 11(*c*); trade: ss 3(1), 4(1), 5(1).

Former enactments

CTA 1976 s 84.

Corresponding UK tax provision

Income and Corporation Taxes Act 1988 s 209.

---

131 Bonus issues following repayment of share capital

(1) In this section—

"ordinary shares" means shares other than preference shares;

"preference shares" means shares—

(*a*) which do not carry any right to dividends other than dividends at a rate per cent of the nominal value of the shares which is fixed, and

(*b*) which carry rights in respect of dividends and capital which are comparable with those general for fixed-dividend shares quoted on a stock exchange in the State;

"new consideration not derived from ordinary shares" means new consideration other than consideration consisting of the surrender, transfer or cancellation of ordinary shares of the company or any other company or consisting of the variation of rights in ordinary shares of the company or any other company, and other than consideration derived from a repayment of share capital paid in respect of ordinary shares of the company or of any other company.

(2) Where a company—

(*a*) repays any share capital or has done so at any time on or after the 27th day of November, 1975, and

(*b*) at or after the time of that repayment, issues as paid up, otherwise than by the receipt of new consideration, any share capital,

the amount so paid up shall be treated as a distribution made in respect of the shares on which it is paid up, except in so far as that amount exceeds the amount or aggregate amount of share capital so repaid less any amounts previously so paid up and treated by virtue of this subsection as distributions.

(3) Subsection (2) shall not apply where the repaid share capital consists of fully paid up preference shares—

(*a*) if those shares existed as issued and fully paid preference shares on the 27th day of November, 1975, and throughout the period from that date until the repayment those shares continued to be fully paid preference shares, or

(*b*) if those shares were issued after the 27th day of November, 1975, as fully paid preference shares wholly for new consideration not derived from ordinary shares and throughout the period from their issue until the repayment those shares continued to be fully paid preference shares.

(4) Except in relation to a close company within the meaning of section 430, this section shall not apply if the issue of share capital mentioned in subsection (2)(*b*)—

(*a*) is of share capital other than redeemable share capital, and

(*b*) takes place more than 10 years after the repayment of share capital mentioned in subsection (2)(*a*).

Cross-references

Bonus issues, disallowance of reliefs: s 137(1)(*b*).

Distribution, meaning: s 130(2)(*e*).

Profit sharing schemes (subs (2)(*c*)), company reconstructions etc: s 514(3)(*a*).

Repayment of share capital following bonus issue: s 132(2)(*a*).

Tax Briefing

TB45 Oct 2001 p 9 — Review of operation of TCA 1997 s 130(2)(*d*)(iv) in relation to payments of interest to residents of countries with which Ireland has a double taxation treaty and to residents of EU Member States.

Definitions

close company: ss 4(1), 430, 431; company: ss 4(1), 5(1); distribution: ss 4(1), 436, 437.

Former enactments

CTA 1976 s 85.

Corresponding UK tax provision

Income and Corporation Taxes Act 1988 s 210.

---

132 Matters to be treated or not treated as repayments of share capital

(1) In this section, **"relevant distribution"** means so much of any distribution made in respect of shares representing the relevant share capital as apart from subsection (2)(*a*) would be treated as a repayment of share capital, but by virtue of that subsection cannot be so treated.

(2) (*a*) Where—

(i) a company issues any share capital as paid up otherwise than by the receipt of new consideration, or has done so on or after the 27th day of November, 1975, and

(ii) any amount so paid up is not to be treated as a distribution,

then, for the purposes of sections 130 and 131, distributions made afterwards by the company in respect of shares representing that share capital shall not be treated as repayments of share capital, except to the extent to which those distributions, together with any relevant distributions previously so made, exceed the amounts so paid up (then or previously) on such shares after that date and not treated as distributions.

(*b*) For the purposes of paragraph (*a*), all shares of the same class shall be treated as representing the same share capital, and where shares are issued in respect of other shares, or are directly or indirectly converted into or exchanged for other shares, all such shares shall be treated as representing the same share capital.

(3) Where share capital is issued at a premium representing new consideration, the amount of the premium shall be treated as forming part of that share capital for the

purpose of determining under this Chapter whether any distribution made in respect of shares representing the share capital is to be treated as a repayment of share capital; but this subsection shall not apply in relation to any part of the premium after that part has been applied in paying up share capital.

(4) Subject to subsection (3), premiums paid on redemption of share capital shall not be treated as repayments of capital.

(5) Except in relation to a close company within the meaning of section 430, subsection (2)(*a*) shall not prevent a distribution being treated as a repayment of share capital if it is made—

(*a*) more than 10 years after the issue of share capital mentioned in subsection (2)(*a*)(i), and

(*b*) in respect of share capital other than redeemable share capital.

Cross-references

Bonus issues, disallowance of reliefs (subs (2)(*a*)): s 137(1)(*c*).

Distribution, meaning: s 130(2)(*b*); new consideration, subs (3): s 135(1)(*b*).

Profit sharing schemes (subs (2)), company reconstructions etc: s 514(3)(*b*).

Definitions

class (of shares): s 5(1); close company: ss 4(1), 430, 431; company: ss 4(1), 5(1); distribution: ss 4(1), 428, 429.

Former enactments

CTA 1976 s 86.

Corresponding UK tax provision

Income and Corporation Taxes Act 1988 s 211.

133 Limitation on meaning of "distribution"— general

(1) (*a*) In this section—

"agricultural society" and **"fishery society"** have the meanings respectively assigned to them by section 443(16);

"relevant principal" means an amount of money advanced to a borrower by a company which is within the charge to corporation tax and the ordinary trading activities of which include the lending of money, where—

(i) the consideration given by the borrower for that amount is a relevant security, and

(ii) interest or any other distribution is paid out of the assets of the borrower in respect of that security;

"selling by wholesale" means selling goods of any class to a person who carries on a business of selling goods of that class or uses goods of that class for the purposes of a trade or undertaking carried on by the person;

"specified trade" means, subject to paragraphs (*b*), (*d*) and (*e*), a trade which consists wholly or mainly of the manufacture of goods, including activities which, if the borrower were to make a claim for relief in respect of the trade under Part 14, would be regarded for the purposes of that Part as the manufacture of goods, but not including trading activities in respect of which a certificate has been given by the Minister for Finance under section 445.

(*b*) Where the borrower mentioned in subsection (5) is a 75 per cent subsidiary of—

(i) an agricultural society, or

(ii) a fishery society,

"specified trade", in that subsection, means a trade of the borrower which consists wholly or mainly of either or both of—

(I) the manufacture of goods within the meaning of the definition of "specified trade" in paragraph (*a*), and

(II) the selling by wholesale of—

(A) where subparagraph (i) applies, agricultural products, or

(B) where subparagraph (ii) applies, fish.

(*c*) For the purposes of the definition of **"specified trade"** in paragraph (*a*) and of paragraph (*b*), a trade shall be regarded, as respects an accounting period, as consisting wholly or mainly of particular activities only if the total amount receivable by the borrower from sales made in the course of those activities in the accounting period is not less than 75 per cent of the total amount receivable by the borrower from all sales made in the course of the trade in that period.

(*d*) A qualifying shipping trade (within the meaning of section 407) shall not be regarded as a specified trade for the purposes of this section.

(*e*) This section shall apply as respects any interest paid to a company in respect of relevant principal advanced before the 20th day of April, 1990, by the company to another company which carries on in the State a trade which but for section 443(6) would be a specified trade as if that trade were a specified trade.

(2) Any interest or other distribution which—

(*a*) is paid out of assets of a company (in this section referred to as **"the borrower"**) to another company within the charge to corporation tax, and

(*b*) is so paid in respect of a security (in this section referred to as a **"relevant security"**) within subparagraph (ii), (iii)(I) or (v) of section 130(2)(*d*),

shall not be a distribution for the purposes of the Corporation Tax Acts unless the application of this subsection is excluded by subsection (3), (4) or (5).

(3) Subsection (2) shall not apply where the principal secured has been advanced by a company out of money subscribed for the share capital of the company and that share capital is beneficially owned directly or indirectly by a person or persons resident outside the State.

(4) Subsection (2) shall not apply in a case where the consideration given by the borrower for the use of the principal secured represents more than a reasonable commercial return for the use of that principal; but, where this subsection applies, nothing in subparagraph (ii), (iii)(I) or (v) of section 130(2)(*d*) shall operate so as to treat as a distribution for the purposes of the Corporation Tax Acts so much of the interest or other distribution as represents a reasonable commercial return for the use of that principal.

(5) Subject to subsections (6) and (7), subsection (2) shall not apply to any interest paid by the borrower, in an accounting period of the borrower, to another company in respect of relevant principal advanced by that other company, where—

(*a*) in that accounting period the borrower carries on in the State a specified trade,

(*b*) the relevant principal in respect of which the interest is paid is used in the course of the specified trade—

(i) for the activities of the trade which consist of the manufacture of goods within the meaning of the definition of "specified trade" in paragraph (*a*) of subsection (1), or

(ii) where paragraph (*b*) of subsection (1) applies, for the activities of the trade which consist of such selling by wholesale as is referred to in paragraph (II) of the definition of "specified trade" in that paragraph,

and

(*c*) the interest, if it were not a distribution, would be treated as a trading expense of that trade for that accounting period.

(6) Subsection (5) shall not apply to interest paid in respect of relevant principal to a company which on the 12th day of April, 1989, had no outstanding amounts of relevant principal advanced.

(7) Notwithstanding subsection (5), where at any time after the 12th day of April, 1989, the total of the amounts of relevant principal (in this subsection referred to as **"the current amounts of relevant principal"**) advanced by a company in respect of relevant securities held directly or indirectly by the company at that time is in excess of a limit, being a limit equal to 110 per cent of the total of the amounts of relevant principal advanced by the company in respect of relevant securities held directly or indirectly by the company on the 12th day of April, 1989, then, such part of any interest paid at that time to the company in respect of relevant principal as bears, in relation to the total amount of interest so paid to the company, the same proportion as the excess bears in relation to the current amounts of relevant principal shall not be treated as a distribution for the purposes of the Corporation Tax Acts in the hands of the company.

(8) (*a*) In this subsection and in subsection (10), **"specified period"**, in relation to relevant principal, means the period commencing on the date on which the relevant principal was advanced and ending on the date on which the relevant principal is to be repaid under the terms of the agreement to advance the relevant principal or, if earlier—

(i) in the case of relevant principal advanced before the 11th day of April, 1994, the 11th day of April, 2001, and

(ii) in any other case, a date which is 7 years after the date on which the relevant principal was advanced.

(*b*) Notwithstanding subsection (5), where at any time on or after the 31st day of January, 1990, the total of the amounts of relevant principal (in this subsection and in subsections (9) and (10) referred to as **"the current amounts of relevant principal"**) advanced by a company in respect of relevant securities held directly or indirectly by the company at that time is in excess of a limit, being a limit equal to 75 per cent of the total of the amounts of relevant principal advanced by the company in respect of relevant securities held directly or indirectly by the company on the 12th day of April, 1989, then, any interest paid to the company in respect of relevant principal advanced by the company on or after the 31st day of January, 1990, being relevant principal which is included in the current amounts of relevant principal, shall not be treated as a distribution for the purposes of the Corporation Tax Acts in the hands of the company.

(*c*) Where apart from this paragraph any part of any interest paid to a company in respect of relevant principal advanced by the company on or after the 31st day of January, 1990, would not be treated as a distribution for the purposes of the Corporation Tax Acts in the hands of the company by virtue only of paragraph (*b*), then, that paragraph shall not apply in relation to so much of that interest as is paid for a specified period in respect of relevant principal advanced and which was, at the time the relevant principal was advanced, specified in the list referred to in subparagraph (iv) if—

(i) the relevant principal is advanced by the company to a borrower who was in negotiation before the 31st day of January, 1990, with any company for an amount of relevant principal,

(ii) the borrower had received before the 31st day of January, 1990, a written offer of grant aid from the Industrial Development Authority, the Shannon Free Airport Development Company Limited or Údarás na Gaeltachta in respect of a specified trade or a proposed specified trade for the purposes of which trade the relevant principal is borrowed,

(iii) the specified trade is a trade which the borrower commenced to carry on after the 31st day of January, 1990, or is a specified trade of the borrower in respect of which the borrower is committed, under a business plan approved by the Industrial Development Authority, the Shannon Free Airport Development Company Limited or Údarás na Gaeltachta, to the creation of additional employment,

(iv) before the 25th day of March, 1992, the specified trade of the borrower was included in a list prepared by the Industrial Development Authority and approved before that day by the Minister for Industry and Commerce and the Minister for Finance, being a list specifying a particular amount of relevant principal in respect of each trade which amount is considered to be essential for the success of that trade, and

(v) the borrower or a company connected with the borrower is not a company which commenced to carry on relevant trading operations (within the meaning of section 446) after the 20th day of April, 1990, or intends to commence to carry on such trading operations;

but this paragraph shall not apply to any interest in respect of any relevant principal advanced after the time when the total of the amounts of relevant principal to which this paragraph applies, advanced by all lenders who have made such advances, exceeds [€215,855,473.33][1].

(*d*) For the purposes of this subsection and subsections (9) and (10)—

(i) relevant principal advanced by a company at any time on or after a day includes any relevant principal advanced on or after that day to a borrower under an agreement entered into before that day,

(ii) where on or after the 6th day of May, 1993, a period of repayment of relevant principal advanced by a company is extended (whether or not the right to such an extension arose out of the terms of the agreement to advance the relevant principal), the company shall be treated as having—

(I) received repayment of the relevant principal, and

(II) advanced a corresponding amount of relevant principal,

on the date on which apart from the extension the relevant principal fell to be repaid, and

(iii) where at any time after an amount of relevant principal is specified in a list in accordance with paragraph (*c*)(iv) or subsection (9)(*c*)(ii) or (10)(*b*)(ii) a company advances, or is treated as advancing, to a borrower relevant principal the interest in respect of which is treated as a distribution by virtue only of paragraph (*c*) or subsection (9)(*c*) or (10)(*b*), the amount of relevant principal specified in the list shall be treated as reduced by the amount of relevant principal so advanced, or treated as advanced, and the amount so reduced shall be treated as the amount specified in that list.

(*e*) For the purposes of this subsection and subsections (9) and (10), where a company which has on or after the 31st day of January, 1990, advanced relevant principal to a borrower under the terms of an agreement and, under the terms of that or any other agreement, the company assigns to another company part or all of its rights and obligations under the first-mentioned agreement in relation to the relevant principal, such assignment shall be deemed not to have taken place.

(9) (*a*) Notwithstanding subsections (5), (7) and (8), where at any time on or after the 31st day of December, 1991, the current amounts of relevant principal advanced by a company in respect of relevant securities held directly or indirectly by the company at that time is in excess of a limit, being a limit equal to 40 per cent of the total of the amounts of relevant principal advanced by the company in respect of the relevant securities held directly or indirectly by the company on the 12th day of April, 1989, then, any interest paid to the company in respect of relevant principal advanced by the company on or after the 31st day of December, 1991, being relevant principal which is included in the current amounts of relevant principal, shall not be treated as a distribution for the purposes of the Corporation Tax Acts in the hands of the company.

(*b*) (i) Where the total of the amounts of relevant principal advanced by a company in respect of relevant securities held directly or indirectly by the company at any time on or after the 31st day of December, 1991, is less than the limit referred to in paragraph (*a*), that paragraph shall apply as if that limit were the total of the amounts of relevant principal so advanced as at that time unless the company proves that it has as far as possible, at all times on or after the 31st day of December, 1991, advanced to borrowers relevant principal in respect of the interest on which paragraph (*a*) does not, or would not, apply by virtue of paragraph (*c*).

(ii) Where at any time during the period commencing on the 18th day of April, 1991, and ending immediately before the 31st day of December, 1991, an amount of relevant principal which was advanced to a borrower, being a company which carries on one or more trading operations (within the meaning of section 445(1)), is repaid, this section shall apply as if—

(I) references in subparagraph (i) and in paragraph (*a*) to the 31st day of December, 1991, were references to the day on which the amount is repaid, and

(II) during that period—

(A) the reference in subparagraph (i) to relevant principal in respect of the interest on which paragraph (*a*) does not, or would not, apply by virtue of paragraph (*c*) were a reference to such principal in respect of the interest on which paragraph (*b*) of subsection (8) does not, or would not, apply by virtue of paragraph (*c*) of that subsection, and

(B) the reference in paragraph (*c*) of subsection (8) to paragraph (*b*) of that subsection were a reference to paragraph (*a*).

(*c*) Where apart from this paragraph any part of any interest paid to a company in respect of relevant principal advanced by the company on or after the 31st day of December, 1991, would not be treated as a distribution for the purposes of the Corporation Tax Acts in the hands of the company by virtue only of paragraph (*a*), then, subject to subsection (11), that paragraph shall not apply in relation to so much of that interest as is paid if—

(i) the specified trade is a trade which the borrower commenced to carry on after the 31st day of January, 1990, or is a specified trade of the borrower in respect of which the borrower is committed, under a business plan approved by the Industrial Development Authority, the Shannon Free Airport Development Company Limited or Údarás na Gaeltachta, to the creation of additional employment,

(ii) the specified trade of the borrower was selected by the Industrial Development Authority for inclusion in a list, approved by the Minister for Industry and Commerce and the Minister for Finance, being a list specifying a particular amount of relevant principal in respect of each trade which amount is considered to be essential for the success of that trade, and

(iii) the borrower or a company connected with the borrower is not a company which commenced to carry on relevant trading operations (within the meaning of section 446) after the 20th day of April, 1990, or intends to commence to carry on such trading operations.

(10)(*a*) Notwithstanding subsections (5) and (7) to (9), any interest paid to a company in respect of relevant principal advanced by the company on or after the 20th day of December, 1991, shall not be treated as a distribution for the purposes of the Corporation Tax Acts in the hands of the company.

(*b*) Where apart from this paragraph any interest paid to a company in respect of relevant principal advanced by the company on or after the 20th day of December, 1991, would not be treated as a distribution for the purposes of the Corporation Tax Acts in the hands of the company by virtue only of paragraph (*a*), then, subject to subsection (11), that paragraph shall not apply in relation to so much of that interest as is paid for a specified period in respect of relevant principal advanced and which was, at the time the relevant principal was advanced, specified in the list referred to in subparagraph (ii) if—

(i) the specified trade is a trade which the borrower commenced to carry on after the 31st day of January, 1990, or is a specified trade of the borrower in respect of which the borrower is committed, under a business plan approved by the Industrial Development Authority, the Shannon Free Airport Development Company Limited or Údarás na Gaeltachta, to the creation of additional employment,

(ii) before the 25th day of March, 1992, the specified trade of the borrower was included in a list prepared by the Industrial Development Authority and approved before that day by the Minister for Industry and Commerce and the Minister for Finance, being a list specifying a particular amount of relevant principal in respect of each trade which amount is considered to be essential for the success of that trade, and

(iii) the borrower is not a company which carries on relevant trading operations (within the meaning of section 446) or intends to carry on such trading operations.

(11) Subsections (9)(*c*) and (10)(*b*) shall not apply to any interest in respect of any relevant principal advanced after the time when the total of the amounts of relevant principal to which those subsections apply, advanced by all lenders who have made such advances, exceeds the aggregate of—

(*a*) [€317,434,519.61][2], and

(*b*) the excess, if any, of [€215,855,473.33][3] over the total of the amounts of relevant principal to which subsection (8)(*c*) applies advanced by all lenders who have made such advances.

(12)(*a*) In this subsection, **"scheduled repayment date"**, in relation to any relevant principal, means the date on which that relevant principal is to be repaid under the terms of the agreement to advance that relevant principal.

(*b*) Where at any time before the 7th day of December, 1993—

(i) relevant principal (in this subsection referred to as "the first-mentioned relevant principal"), the interest in respect of which was treated as a distribution by virtue only of subsection (8)(*c*), (9)(*c*) or (10)(*b*), advanced by a company to a borrower was repaid by the borrower before the scheduled repayment date, and

(ii) a further amount or further amounts of relevant principal, the interest in respect of which is to be treated as a distribution by virtue only of subsection (8)(*c*), (9)(*c*) or (10)(*b*), was or were advanced to that borrower,

then, subsection (8)(*d*)(iii) shall not apply in relation to so much of—

(I) the further amount of relevant principal advanced as does not exceed the amount of relevant principal repaid, or

(II) where there are more further amounts advanced than one, the aggregate of the further amounts of relevant principal advanced as does not exceed the relevant principal repaid.

(*c*) Where by virtue of paragraph (*b*) subsection (8)(*d*)(iii) does not apply in relation to any amount of relevant principal advanced by a company, the company shall be treated as having—

(i) received a repayment of that amount of relevant principal, and

(ii) advanced a corresponding amount of relevant principal,

on the scheduled repayment date of the first-mentioned relevant principal.

(*d*) For the purposes of this subsection, where there are more further advances of relevant principal than one, the amount to which subsection (8)(*d*)(iii) does not apply shall be referable as far as possible to an earlier rather than a later such further advance.

(*e*) Notwithstanding paragraphs (*b*) to (*d*), interest which but for this paragraph would not be treated as a distribution by virtue only of subsection (8)(*d*)(iii) may be treated as a distribution if it is paid in respect of relevant principal advanced before the 7th day of December, 1993.

(13)(*a*) In this subsection, **"relevant period"** means a period which commences at a time at which, in accordance with the terms of the agreement under which relevant principal secured by a relevant security is advanced, an amount representing the interest for the use of the relevant principal is to be paid, and ends at a time immediately before the next time at which such an amount is to be paid.

(*b*) Interest paid to a company in respect of—

(i) relevant principal denominated in a currency other than Irish currency, and

(ii) a relevant period which begins on or after the 30th day of January, 1991,

shall not be a distribution for the purposes of the Corporation Tax Acts in the hands of the company if, at any time during that period, the rate on the basis of which interest is computed exceeds 80 per cent of [the rate known as the 3 month European Interbank Offered Rate].[4]

(*c*) Paragraph (*b*) shall not apply to any interest paid to a company in respect of relevant principal advanced by the company—

(i) before the 30th day of January, 1991, under an agreement entered into before that day if on that day the rate on the basis of which interest in respect of the relevant security is to be computed exceeds 80 per cent of [the rate known as the 3 month European Interbank Offered Rate];[2] but this subparagraph shall not apply as respects any relevant period commencing on or after the 20th day of December, 1991, if in that relevant period that rate exceeds the rate on the basis of which interest would have been computed if the relevant principal had continued to be denominated in the currency in which it was denominated on the 30th day of January, 1991,

(ii) on or after the 30th day of January, 1991—

(I) which is included in a list referred to in subsection (8)(*c*)(iv), (9)(*c*)(ii) or (10)(*b*)(ii), and

(II) for the purposes of a specified trade of a borrower who is certified by the Minister for Enterprise, Trade and Employment as having received an undertaking that the interest would be treated as a distribution;

but this subparagraph shall not apply as respects any relevant period commencing on or after the 20th day of December, 1991, if in that relevant period the rate on the basis of which interest in respect of the relevant security is to be computed exceeds—

(A) a rate approved by the Minister for Finance in consultation with the Minister for Enterprise, Trade and Employment, or

(B) where it is lower than the rate so approved and the relevant principal was advanced on or after the 30th day of January, 1991, and before the 20th day of December, 1991, the rate which would have applied if the relevant principal had continued to be denominated in the currency in which it was denominated when it was advanced,

(iii) on or after the 18th day of April, 1991, where the rate on the basis of which that interest is computed exceeds 80 per cent of [the rate known as the 3 month European Interbank Offered Rate][5] by reason only that the relevant principal advanced is denominated in sterling, or

(iv) to a borrower which is a company carrying on one or more trading operations within the meaning of section 445(1).

Amendments

1 Substituted by FA 2001 s 240(1) and (2)(*c*) and Sch 5 Pt 1 for accounting periods ending on or after 1 January 2002; previously "£170,000,000".

2 Substituted by FA 2001 s 240(1) and (2)(*c*) and Sch 5 Pt 1 for accounting periods ending on or after 1 January 2002; previously "£250,000,000".

3 Substituted by FA 2001 s 240(1) and (2)(*c*) and Sch 5 Pt 1 for accounting periods ending on or after 1 January 2002; previously "£170,000,000".

4 Substituted by FA 1998 s 47 and Sch 2 para 4(*a*) with effect from such date as the Minister for Finance may appoint by order; previously "the rate known as the 3 month Dublin Interbank Offered Rate on Irish pounds (in this subsection referred to as 'the 3 month Dublin Interbank Offered Rate') a record of which is maintained by the Central Bank of Ireland".

5 Substituted by FA 1998 s 47 and Sch 2 para 4(*b*)(i)–(ii) with effect from such date as the Minister for Finance may appoint by order; previously "the 3 month Dublin Interbank Offered Rate".

The substitutions come into operation from 1 January 1999 — Finance Act 1998 (Section 47) (Commencement) Order, 1998, SI No 502 of 1998, refers.

Cross-references

Industrial building allowance for IDA list projects (subs (8)(*c*)(iv)): s 271(3)(*c*).

Industrial building accelerated annual allowance, for IDA list projects (subs (8)(*c*)(iv)): s 273(7)(*a*).

Leased machinery or plant, restriction of on use of allowances (subs (8)(*c*)(iv)): s 404(1)(*b*)(ii).

Plant and machinery initial allowance for IDA list projects (subs (8)(*c*)(iv)): s 283(5).

Plant and machinery accelerated wear and tear allowance for IDA list projects (subs (8)(*c*)(iv)): s 285(7)(*a*).

Case law

Subs (2)(*d*)(iv): These provisions were held to take priority over the application of Article 12 (Interest) of the Ireland/Japan Double Taxation Convention (SI 259/1974): *Murphy v Asahi Synthetic Fibres (Ireland) Ltd* ITR Vol III p 246.

Revenue precedents

Issue: Treatment of interest in accordance with s 133 of the TCA, 1997 (was CTA 1976 s 84(2)(*d*)(iv)) and the Ireland/Netherlands Double Taxation Convention.

Decision: Interest paid to a Dutch parent company by its Irish subsidiary will be regarded as interest and will be allowed as trading expense to the paying company.

Issue: Conflict in the treatment of interest which is treated as a distribution within the meaning of TCA 1997 s 133 (CTA 1976 s 84(2)(*d*)(iv)) and interest which is treated as such for the purposes of a Double Taxation Convention.
Decision: Where a conflict arises the Double Taxation Convention provisions will apply unless a claim to the contrary is made by the company.

Definitions

company: ss 4(1), 5(1); distribution: ss 4(1), 436, 437; interest: s 4(1); person: IA 1937 s 11(*c*); trade: ss 3(1), 4(1), 5(1); within the charge to (tax): s 2(1).

Former enactments

CTA 1976 s 84A, FA 1987 s 28(5)(*b*); FA 1989 s 21(1)(*a*) and (2); FA 1990 s 41(4) and s 46; FA 1991 s 28; FA 1992 s 40; FA 1993 s 45; FA 1994 s 50; FA 1997 s 146(1) and Sch 9 Pt I para 10(2)(*b*).

134 Limitation on meaning of "distribution" in relation to certain payments made in respect of "foreign source" finance

(1) (*a*) In this section—

"agricultural society" and **"fishery society"** have the meanings respectively assigned to them by section 443(16);

"selling by wholesale" means selling goods of any class to a person who carries on a business of selling goods of that class or uses goods of that class for the purposes of a trade or undertaking carried on by the person;

"specified trade" means, subject to paragraphs (*b*) and (*d*) and to subsection (6), a trade which consists wholly or mainly of—

(i) the manufacture of goods, including activities which, if the borrower were to make a claim for relief in respect of the trade under Part 14, would be regarded for the purposes of that Part as the manufacture of goods, or

(ii) the rendering of services in the course of a service undertaking in respect of which an employment grant was made by the Industrial Development Authority under section 2 of the Industrial Development (No. 2) Act, 1981.

(*b*) Where the borrower mentioned in subsection (5) is a 75 per cent subsidiary of—

(i) an agricultural society, or

(ii) a fishery society,

"specified trade", in that subsection, means a trade of the borrower which consists wholly or mainly of either or both of—

(I) the manufacture of goods within the meaning of the definition of "specified trade" in paragraph (*a*), and

(II) the selling by wholesale of—

(A) where subparagraph (i) applies, agricultural products, or

(B) where subparagraph (ii) applies, fish.

(*c*) For the purposes of the definition of **"specified trade"** and of paragraph (*b*), a trade shall be regarded, as respects an accounting period, as consisting wholly or mainly of particular activities only if the total amount receivable by the borrower from sales made or, as the case may be, in payment for services rendered in the course of those activities in the accounting period is not less than 75 per cent of the total amount receivable by the borrower from all sales made in the course of the trade in that period.

(*d*) A qualifying shipping trade (within the meaning of section 407) shall not be regarded as a specified trade for the purposes of this section.

(2) This section shall apply only where the principal secured has been advanced by a company out of money subscribed for the share capital of the company and that share capital is beneficially owned directly or indirectly by a person or persons resident outside the State.

(3) Any interest or other distribution which—

(*a*) is paid out of assets of a company (in this section referred to as **"the borrower"**) to another company within the charge to corporation tax, and

(*b*) is so paid in respect of a security (in this section referred to as a **"relevant security"**) within subparagraph (ii), (iii)(I) or (v) of section 130(2)(*d*),

shall not be a distribution for the purposes of the Corporation Tax Acts unless the application of this subsection is excluded by subsection (4) or (5).

(4) Subsection (3) shall not apply in a case where the consideration given by the borrower for the use of the principal secured represents more than a reasonable commercial return for the use of that principal; but, where this subsection applies, nothing in subparagraph (ii), (iii)(I) or (v) of section 130(2)(*d*) shall operate so as to treat as a distribution for the purposes of the Corporation Tax Acts so much of the interest or other distribution as represents a reasonable commercial return for the use of that principal.

(5) Subsection (3) shall not apply to any interest paid by the borrower, in an accounting period of the borrower, to another company the ordinary trading activities of which include the lending of money, where—

(*a*) in that accounting period the borrower carries on in the State a specified trade, and

(*b*) the interest, if it were not a distribution, would be treated as a trading expense of that trade for that accounting period.

(6) (*a*) This subsection shall apply to any interest or other distribution which apart from this subsection would be a distribution for the purposes of the Corporation Tax Acts, other than any interest or other distribution which is paid by the borrower under an obligation entered into—

(i) before the 13th day of May, 1986, or

(ii) before the 1st day of September, 1986, in accordance with negotiations which were in progress between the borrower and a lender before the 13th day of May, 1986.

(*b*) Subsection (5) shall apply as respects any interest or other distribution to which this subsection applies as if paragraph (ii) of the definition of **"specified trade"** in subsection (1)(*a*) were deleted.

(*c*) For the purposes of paragraph (*a*)—

(i) an obligation shall be treated as having been entered into before a particular date only if before that date there was in existence a binding contract in writing under which that obligation arose, and

(ii) negotiations in accordance with which an obligation was entered into shall not be regarded as having been in progress before the 13th day of May, 1986, unless on or before that date preliminary commitments or agreements in relation to that obligation had been entered into between the lender referred to in that paragraph and the borrower.

Definitions

Company: ss 4(1), 5(1); distribution: ss 4(1), 436, 437; interest: 54(1); person: IA 1937 s 11(*c*); trade: ss 3(1), 4(1); within the charge to (tax): s 2(1).

Former enactments

CTA 1976 s 84A(1)–(6) and (9)–(10); FA 1984 s 41; FA 1986 s 54; FA 1987 s 28(5)(*b*); FA 1989 s 21(2)(*a*); FA 1997 s 146(1) and Sch 9 Pt I para 10(2)(*a*).

135 Distributions: supplemental

(1) (*a*) In this Chapter, **"new consideration"** means consideration not provided directly or indirectly out of the assets of the company, but does not include amounts retained by the company by means of capitalising a distribution.

(*b*) Notwithstanding paragraph (*a*), where share capital has been issued at a premium representing new consideration, any part of that premium applied afterwards in paying up share capital shall also be treated as new consideration for that share capital, except in so far as the premium has been taken into account under section 132(3) so as to enable a distribution to be treated as a repayment of share capital.

(2) (*a*) No consideration derived from the value of any share capital or security of a company, or from voting or other rights in a company, shall be regarded for the purposes of this Chapter as new consideration received by the company unless the consideration consists of—

(i) money or value received from the company as a distribution,

(ii) money received from the company as a payment which for those purposes constitutes a repayment of that share capital or of the principal secured by that security, or

(iii) the giving up of the right to that share capital or security on its cancellation, extinguishment or acquisition by the company.

(*b*) No amount shall be regarded as new consideration by virtue of subparagraph (ii) or (iii) of paragraph (*a*) in so far as it exceeds any new consideration received by the company for the issue of the share capital or security in question or, in the case of share capital which constituted a distribution on issue, the nominal value of that share capital.

(3) Where 2 or more companies enter into arrangements to make distributions to each other's members, all parties concerned may for the purposes of this Chapter be treated as if anything done by any of those companies had been done by any other, and this subsection shall apply however many companies participate in the arrangements.

(4) (*a*) In this Chapter and in section 137, **"in respect of shares in the company"** and **"in respect of securities of the company"**, in relation to a company which is a member of a 90 per cent group, mean respectively in respect of shares in that company or any other company in the group and in respect of securities of that company or any other company in the group.

(*b*) Without prejudice to section 130(2)(*b*) as extended by paragraph (*a*), in relation to a company which is a member of a 90 per cent group, **"distribution"** includes anything distributed out of assets of the company (whether in cash or otherwise) in respect of shares in or securities of another company in the group.

(*c*) Nothing in this subsection shall require a company to be treated as making a distribution to any other company which is in the same group and is resident in the State.

(*d*) For the purposes of this subsection, a principal company and all its 90 per cent subsidiaries form a 90 per cent group, and **"principal company"** means a company of which another company is a subsidiary.

(*e*) Nothing in this subsection shall require any company which is a subsidiary (within the meaning of section 155 of the Companies Act, 1963) of another company to be treated as making a distribution where it acquires shares in the other company in accordance with section 9(1) of the Insurance Act, 1990.

(5) A distribution shall be treated under this Chapter as made, or consideration as provided, out of assets of a company if the cost falls on the company.

(6) In this Chapter and in section 137, **"share"** includes stock and any other interest of a member in a company.

(7) References in this Chapter to issuing share capital as paid up apply also to the paying up of any issued share capital.

(8) For the purposes of this Chapter and of section 137, **"security"** includes securities not creating or evidencing a charge on assets, and interest paid by a company on money advanced without the issue of a security for the advance, or other consideration given by a company for the use of money so advanced, shall be treated as if paid or given in respect of a security issued for the advance by the company.

(9) Where securities are issued at a price less than the amount repayable on them and are not quoted on a recognised stock exchange, the principal secured shall not be taken for the purposes of this Chapter to exceed the issue price unless the securities are issued on terms reasonably comparable with the terms of issue of securities so quoted.

(10) For the purposes of this Chapter and of section 137, a thing shall be regarded as done in respect of a share if it is done to a person as being the holder of the share, or as having at a particular time been the holder of the share, or is done in pursuance of a right granted or offer made in respect of a share, and anything done in respect of shares by reference to share holdings at a particular time shall be regarded as done to the then holder of the shares or the personal representatives of any shareholder then dead.

(11) Subsection (10) shall apply in relation to securities as it applies in relation to shares.

Cross-references

Company buying its own shares, meaning of "new consideration" applied: s 174(1).

Deferral of payment of tax under section 128 (tax treatment of share options), meaning of "securities" applied: s 128A(4A)(*k*).

Distribution (subs (9)), meaning: s 130(2)(*d*).

Employee share options schemes, "shares" includes securities within this section: s 128(1)(*a*).

Notional loans relating to shares, etc, "shares" includes "securities" within this section: s 122A(1).

Notional winding up, meaning of "new consideration" applied: s 415(4).

Profits or assets available for distribution, meaning of "new consideration" applied: s 413(2).

Surcharge on undistributed investment and estate income: s 440(2)(*b*).

Schemes to avoid liability to tax under Sch F, meaning of "new consideration" applied: s 817(1)(*a*).

Definitions

company: ss 4(1), 5(1); distribution: ss 4(1), 436, 437; interest: s 4(1); person: IA 1937 s 11(*c*); personal representatives: s 5(1), 784.

Former enactments

CTA 1976 s 87; FA 1991 s 29.

CHAPTER 3
Distributions and Tax Credits — General

136 Tax credit for certain recipients of distributions

Amendments

Section 136 repealed by FA 2000 s 69(2) and Sch 2 Part 2 with effect from 6 April 1999 in the case of income tax and for accounting periods commencing on or after that date in the case of corporation tax.

137 Disallowance of reliefs in respect of bonus issues

(1) This section shall apply where any person (in this section referred to as **"the recipient"**) receives an amount treated as a distribution by virtue of—

(*a*) paragraph (*c*) or (*d*) of section 130(2),
(*b*) section 131, or
(*c*) section 132(2)(*a*),

and, in this section, a distribution within paragraph (*a*), (*b*) or (*c*) is referred to as a **"bonus issue"**....[1]

(2) Subject to subsection (5), where the recipient is entitled by reason of—

(*a*) any exemption from tax,
(*b*) the setting-off of losses against profits or income, or
(*c*) the payment of interest,

to recover tax in respect of any distribution which the recipient has received, no account shall be taken, for the purposes of any such exemption, set-off or payment of interest, of any bonus issue ...[2] which the recipient has received.

(3) Subject to subsection (5), a bonus issue ...[3] shall be treated as not being franked investment income within the meaning of section 156.

...[4]

(5) Nothing in [subsections (2) and (3)][5] shall affect the proportion (if any) of any bonus issue made in respect of any shares or securities which, if that bonus issue were declared as a dividend, would represent a normal return to the recipient on the consideration provided by the recipient for the relevant shares or securities, that is, those in respect of which the bonus issue was made and, if those securities are derived from shares or securities previously acquired by the recipient, the shares or securities which were previously acquired....[6]

(6) For the purposes of subsection (5)—

(*a*) if the consideration provided by the recipient for any of the relevant shares or securities was in excess of their market value at the time the recipient acquired them, or if no consideration was provided by the recipient for any of the relevant shares or securities, the recipient shall be taken to have provided for those shares or securities consideration equal to their market value at the time the recipient acquired them, and

(*b*) in determining whether an amount received by means of dividend exceeds a normal return, regard shall be had to the length of time before the receipt of that amount that the recipient first acquired any of the relevant shares or securities and to any dividends and other distributions made in respect of the relevant shares or securities during that time.

Amendments

1 Repealed by FA 2000 s 69(2) and Sch 2 Part 2 with effect from 6 April 1999 in the case of income tax and for accounting periods commencing on or after that date in the case of corporation tax; previously ", and 'relevant tax credit'" to "in respect of the bonus issue".

2 Repealed by FA 2000 s 69(2) and Sch 2 Part 2 with effect from 6 April 1999 in the case of income tax and for accounting periods commencing on or after that date in the case of corporation tax; previously " or relevant tax credit".

3 Deleted by FA 2003 s 41(1)(*b*) as respects accounting periods ending on or after 6 February 2003; previously "and the relevant tax credit".

4 Subs (4) repealed by FA 2000 s 69(2) and Sch 2 Part 2 with effect from 6 April 1999 in the case of income tax and for accounting periods commencing on or after that date in the case of corporation tax.

5 Substituted by FA 2000 s 69(1) and Sch 2 Part 1 para (*b*) with effect from 6 April 1999 in the case of income tax and for accounting periods commencing on or after that date in the case of corporation tax; previously "subsections (2) to (4)".

6 Repealed by FA 2000 s 69(2) and Sch 2 Part 2 with effect from 6 April 2000; previously "; and nothing in those subsections shall affect the like proportion of the relevant tax credit relating to that bonus issue".

Cross-references

Meaning of "in respect of shares in the company", "in respect of securities of the company" in relation to a company that is a member of a 90% group: s 135(4)(*a*).

Security, meaning: s 135(8).

Share, meaning: s 135(6); meaning of a thing regarded as done in respect of a share: s 135(10).

Definitions

distribution: ss 4(1), 436, 437; franked investment income: ss 4(1), 156; franked payment: ss 4(1), 156; interest: s 4(1); person: IA 1937 s 11(*c*); profits: s 4(1).

Former enactments

CTA 1976 s 89.

Corresponding UK tax provision

Income and Corporation Taxes Act 1988 s 237 [repealed in relation to distributions made after 5 April 1999].

138 Treatment of dividends on certain preference shares

(1) In this section—

"preference shares" does not include preference shares—

(*a*) which are quoted on a stock exchange in the State,

(*b*) which are not so quoted but which carry rights in respect of dividends and capital comparable with those general for fixed-dividend shares quoted on a stock exchange in the State, or

(*c*) which are non-transferable shares issued on or after the 6th day of April, 1989, by a company in the course of carrying on relevant trading operations within the meaning of section 445 or 446, to a company—

(i) none of the shares of which is beneficially owned, whether directly or indirectly, by a person resident in the State, and

(ii) which, if this paragraph had not been enacted, would not be chargeable to corporation tax in respect of any profits other than dividends which would be so chargeable by virtue of this section;

"shares" includes stock.

(2) This section shall apply to any dividend which—

(*a*) is paid by a company (in this section referred to as **"the issuer"**) to another company (in this section referred to as **"the subscriber"**) within the charge to corporation tax, and

(*b*) is so paid in respect of preference shares of the issuer.

(3) Notwithstanding any provision of the Tax Acts—

...[1]

(*b*) the dividend shall be chargeable to corporation tax under Case IV of Schedule D.

Amendments

1 Subs (3)(*a*) repealed by FA 2000 s 69(2) and Sch 2 Part 2 with effect from 6 April 1999 in the case of income tax and for accounting periods commencing on or after that date in the case of corporation tax.

Cross-references

Attribution of distributions to accounting periods (subs (1)): s 154(3)(*c*).

Definitions

company: ss 4(1), 5(1); person: IA 1937 s 11(*c*); profits: s 4(1); shares: s 5(1); Tax Acts: s 1(2); within the charge to (tax): s 2(1); writing: IA 1937 Sch.

Former enactments

FA 1984 s 42(1)–(3); FA 1989 s 26.

139 Dividends and other distributions at gross rate or of gross amount

Amendments

Section 139 repealed by FA 2000 s 69(2) and Sch 2 Part 2 with effect from 6 April 1999 in the case of income tax and for accounting periods commencing on or after that date in the case of corporation tax.

CHAPTER 4

Distributions Out of Certain Exempt Profits or Gains or Out of Certain Relieved Income

140 Distributions out of profits or gains from stallion fees, stud greyhound services fees and occupation of certain woodlands

(1) In this section—

"exempt profits" means profits or gains which by virtue of section 231, 232 or 233 were not charged to tax;

"other profits" includes a dividend or other distribution of a company resident in the State, but does not include a distribution to which subsection (3)(*a*)(i) applies.

(2) Where a distribution for an accounting period is made by a company in part out of exempt profits and in part out of other profits, the distribution shall be treated as if it consisted of 2 distributions respectively made out of exempt profits and out of other profits.

(3) (*a*) So much of any distribution as has been made out of exempt profits—

(i) shall, where the recipient of that distribution is a company, be deemed for the purposes of the Corporation Tax Acts to be exempt profits of the company, and

(ii) shall not be regarded as income for any purpose of the Income Tax Acts.

...[1]

...[2]

(5) In relation to any distribution ...,[3] including part of a distribution treated under subsection (2) as a distribution, made by a company out of exempt profits, section 152 shall apply to the company so that the statements provided for by that section shall show as respects each such distribution, in addition to the particulars required to be given apart from this section, that the distribution is made out of exempt profits.

...[4]

(7) Where a company makes a distribution for an accounting period, the distribution shall be regarded for the purposes of this section as having been made out of the distributable income (within the meaning of section 144(8)) of that period to the extent of that income and, in relation to the excess of the distribution over that income, out of the most recently accumulated income.

[(8) Where a period of account for or in respect of which a company makes a distribution is not an accounting period and part of the period of account is within an accounting period, the proportion of the distribution to be treated for the purposes of this section as being for or in respect of the accounting period shall be the same proportion as that part of the period of account bears to the whole of that period.

(9) Where a company makes a distribution which is not expressed to be for or in respect of a specified period, the distribution shall be treated for the purposes of this section as having been made for the accounting period in which it is made.][5]

Amendments

1 Subs (3)(*b*) repealed by FA 2000 s 69(2) and Sch 2 Part 2 with effect from 6 April 1999 in the case of income tax and for accounting periods commencing on or after that date in the case of corporation tax.

2 Subs (4) repealed by FA 2000 s 69(2) and Sch 2 Part 2 with effect from 6 April 1999 in the case of income tax and for accounting periods commencing on or after that date in the case of corporation tax.

3 Repealed by FA 2000 s 69(2) and Sch 2 Part 2 with effect from 6 April 1999 in the case of income tax and for accounting periods commencing on or after that date in the case of corporation tax; previously "(not being a supplementary distribution under this section)".

4 Subs (6) repealed by FA 2000 s 69(2) and Sch 2 Part 2 with effect from 6 April 1999 in the case of income tax and for accounting periods commencing on or after that date in the case of corporation tax.

5 Subs (8)–(9) substituted for subs (8) by FA 2000 s 69(1) and Sch 2 Part 1 para (*c*) with effect from 6 April 1999 in the case of income tax and for accounting periods commencing on or after that date in the case of corporation tax.

Cross-references

Attribution of dividends to accounting periods: 154(1).

Close company surcharges, distributions to be taken into account, meaning of "exempt profits" applied: s 434(1)("franked investment income").

Distributions out of income from patent royalties, subs (8) and (9): s 141(10).

Distributions out of profits of certain mines, subs (8) and (9): s 142(6).

Distributions out of profits from coal, gypsum and anhydrite mining, subss (8) and (9): s 143(10).

Dividend withholding tax on relevant distributions does not apply to distributions made out of "exempt profits" (within the meaning of this section): s 172B(7)(*a*).

Distributions out of profits from trading in Shannon Airport, subs (3)(*a*): s 144(8)("T"); subs (8) and (9): s 144(9).

Restriction of reliefs (subs (3)(*a*)): s 155(3).

Definitions

company: ss 4(1), 5(1); distribution: ss 4(1), 436, 437; profits: s 4(1).

Former enactments

CTA 1976 s 93; FA 1996 s 25(3); FA 1997 s 146(1) and Sch 9 Pt I para 10(3).

141 Distributions out of income from patent royalties

(1) In this section—

"disregarded income" means—

(*a*) as respects distributions made out of specified income accruing to a company on or after the 28th day of March, 1996—

(i) income from a qualifying patent which by virtue of section 234(2) has been disregarded for the purposes of income tax, and

(ii) income from a qualifying patent which by virtue of section 234(2) and section 76(6) has been disregarded for the purposes of corporation tax,

but does not include income (in this section referred to as **"specified income"**) from a qualifying patent (within the meaning of section 234) which would not be income from a qualifying patent if paragraph (*a*) of the definition of **"income from a qualifying patent"** in section 234(1) had not been enacted, and

(*b*) as respects any other distributions—

(i) income which by virtue of section 234(2) has been disregarded for the purposes of income tax, and

(ii) income which by virtue of section 234(2) and section 76(6) has been disregarded for the purposes of corporation tax;

"eligible shares", in relation to a company, means shares forming part of the ordinary share capital of the company which—

(*a*) are fully paid up,

(*b*) carry no present or future preferential right to dividends or to the company's assets on its winding up and no present or future preferential right to be redeemed, and

(*c*) are not subject to any different treatment from the treatment which applies to all shares of the same class, in particular different treatment in respect of—

(i) the dividend payable,

(ii) repayment,

(iii) restrictions attaching to the shares, or

(iv) any offer of substituted or additional shares, securities or rights of any description in respect of the shares;

"other profits" includes a dividend or other distribution of a company resident in the State, but does not include a distribution to which subsection (3)(*a*)(ii) applies.

(2) Where a distribution for an accounting period is made by a company in part out of disregarded income and in part out of other profits, the distribution shall be treated as if it consisted of 2 distributions respectively made out of disregarded income and out of other profits.

(3) (*a*) So much of any distribution as has been made out of disregarded income—

(i) shall, subject to subsection (4)(*a*), not be regarded as income for any purpose of the Income Tax Acts, and

(ii) shall, where the recipient of that distribution is a company and the distribution is in respect of eligible shares, be deemed for the purposes of this section to be disregarded income.

...[1]

(4) (*a*) Subsection (3)(*a*)(i) shall not apply to any distribution received by a person unless it is a distribution—

(i) in respect of eligible shares, or

(ii) made out of disregarded income, being income (in this subsection referred to in relation to a person as "relevant income") which is referable to a qualifying patent in relation to which the person carried out, either solely or jointly with another person, the research, planning, processing, experimenting, testing, devising, designing, development or other similar activity leading to the invention which is the subject of the qualifying patent.

(*b*) For the purposes of paragraph (*a*), where a distribution for an accounting period is made by a company to a person in part out of relevant income, in relation to the person, and in part out of other disregarded income, the distribution shall be treated as if it consisted of 2 distributions respectively made out of relevant income and out of other disregarded income.

(5) (*a*) In this subsection—

"the amount of aggregate expenditure on research and development incurred by a company in relation to an accounting period" means the amount of expenditure on research and development activities incurred in the State by the company in the accounting period and the previous 2 accounting periods; but, where in an accounting period a company incurs expenditure on research and development activities and not less than 75 per cent of that expenditure was incurred in the State, all of that expenditure shall be deemed to have been incurred in the State;

"the amount of the expenditure on research and development activities", in relation to expenditure incurred by a company in an accounting period, means non-capital expenditure incurred by the company, being the aggregate of the amounts of—

(i) such part of the emoluments paid by the company to employees of the company engaged in carrying out research and development activities related to the company's trade as is laid out for the purposes of those activities,

(ii) expenditure incurred by the company on materials or goods used solely by the company in the carrying out of research and development activities related to the company's trade, and

(iii) a sum paid to another person, not being a person connected with the company, in order that such person may carry out research and development activities related to the company's trade,

but, where the company (in this definition referred to as **"the first company"**) is a member of a group, then, for the purposes of this section, the amount of expenditure on research and development activities incurred in an accounting period by another company which in the accounting period is a member of the group shall, on a joint election in writing being made on that behalf by the first company and the other company, be treated as being expenditure incurred on research and development activities in the accounting period by the first company and not by the other company;

"reseach and development activities" has the meaning that it would have in section 766 if section 33 of the Finance Act 2004 had not been enacted.][2]

(*b*) For the purpose of this subsection —

(i) 2 companies shall be deemed to be members of a group if both companies are wholly or mainly under the control of the same individual or individuals or if one company is a 75 per cent subsidiary of another company or both companies are 75 per cent subsidiaries of a third company and, in determining whether one company is a 75 per cent subsidiary of another company, the other company shall be treated as not being the owner of —

(I) any share capital which it owns directly in a company if a profit on sale of the shares would be treated as a trading receipt of its trade, or

(II) any share capital which it owns indirectly and which is owned directly by a company for which a profit on the sale of the shares would be a trading receipt;

(ii) a company shall be wholly or mainly under the control of an individual or individuals if not less that 75 per cent of the ordinary share capital of the company is owned directly or indirectly by the individual or, as the case may be, by individuals each of whom owns directly or indirectly part of that share capital;

(iii) sections 412 to 418 shall apply for the purposes of this paragraph as they apply for the purposes of Chapter 5 of Part 12 and, where 2 companies are deemed to be members of a group by reason that both companies are wholly or mainly under the control of the same individual or individuals, those sections shall apply as they would apply for the purposes of that Chapter if the references in those sections to a parent company included a reference to an individual or individuals who hold shares in a company.

(*c*) Where for an accounting period a company makes one or more distributions out of specified income which accrued to the company on or after the 28th day of March, 1996, so much of the amount of that distribution, or the aggregate of such distributions, as does not exceed the amount of aggregate expenditure on research and development incurred by the company in relation to the accounting period shall be treated as a distribution made out of disregarded income.

(*d*) (i) Notwithstanding paragraph (*c*) but subject to subparagraph (ii), if in an accounting period the beneficial recipient (in this paragraph referred to as "the recipient") of the specified income shows in writing to the satisfaction of the Revenue Commissioners that the specified income is income from a qualifying patent in respect of an invention which—

(I) involved radical innovation, and

(II) was patented for bona fide commercial reasons and not primarily for the purpose of avoiding liability to taxation,

the Revenue Commissioners shall, after consideration of any evidence in relation to the matter which the recipient submits to them and after such consultations (if any) as may seem to them to be necessary with such persons as in their opinion may be of assistance to them, determine whether all distributions made out of specified income accruing to the recipient for that accounting period and all subsequent accounting periods shall be treated as distributions made out of disregarded income and the recipient shall be notified in writing of the determination.

(ii) A recipient aggrieved by a determination of the Revenue Commissioners under subparagraph (i) may, by notice in writing given to the Revenue Commissioners within 30 days of the date of notification advising of the determination, appeal to the Appeal Commissioners and the Appeal Commissioners shall hear and determine the appeal made to them as if it were an appeal against an assessment to income tax, and the provisions of the Income Tax Acts relating to the rehearing of an appeal and to the statement of a case for the opinion of the High Court on a point of law shall apply accordingly with any necessary modifications.

(*e*) The Revenue Commissioners may nominate any of their officers to perform any acts and discharge any functions authorised by this subsection to be performed or discharged by the Revenue Commissioners, and references in this subsection to the Revenue Commissioners shall, with any necessary modifications, be construed as including references to an officer so nominated.

...[3]

(7) In relation to any distribution ...,[4] including part of a distribution treated under subsection (2) as a distribution, made by a company out of disregarded income, section 152 shall apply to the company so that the statements provided for by that section shall show as respects each such distribution, in addition to the particulars required to be given apart from this section, that the distribution is made out of disregarded income.

...[5]

(9) Where a company makes a distribution for an accounting period, the distribution shall be regarded for the purposes of this section as having been made out of the distributable income (within the meaning of section 144(8)) of that period to the extent of that income and, in relation to the excess of the distributions over that income, out of the most recently accumulated income.

(10) [Subsections (8) and (9) of section 140][6] shall apply for the purposes of this section as they apply for the purposes of that section.

Amendments

1 Subs (3)(*b*) repealed by FA 2000 s 69(2) and Sch 2 Part 2 with effect from 6 April 1999 in the case of income tax and for accounting periods commencing on or after that date in the case of corporation tax.

2 Definition of "research and development activities" substituted by FA 2004 s 33(1)(*b*) with effect from such day as the Minister for Finance may appoint by order and has effect as respects expenditure incurred on or after that day; previously "**'research and development activities'** has the same meaning as in section 766.". By virtue of the Finance Act 2004 (Section 33) (Commencement) Order 2004, SI No 425 of 2004, this amendment comes into operation with effect from 1 January 2004.

3 Subs (6) repealed by FA 2000 s 69(2) and Sch 2 Part 2 with effect from 6 April 1999 in the case of income tax and for accounting periods commencing on or after that date in the case of corporation tax.

4 Repealed by FA 2000 s 69(2) and Sch 2 Part 2 with effect from 6 April 1999 in the case of income tax and for accounting periods commencing on or after that date in the case of corporation tax; previously "(not being a supplementary distribution under this section)".

5 Subs (8) repealed by FA 2000 s 69(2) and Sch 2 Part 2 with effect from 6 April 1999 in the case of income tax and for accounting periods commencing on or after that date in the case of corporation tax.

6 Substituted by FA 2000 s 69(1) and Sch 2 Part 1 para (*d*) with effect from 6 April 1999 in the case of income tax and for accounting periods commencing on or after that date in the case of corporation tax; previously "Subsections (6) and (7) of section 145".

Cross-references

Attribution of dividends to accounting periods: 154(1).

Close company surcharge, distributions to be taken into account, meaning of "disregarded income" applied: s 434(1)("franked investment income").

Distributions out of profits from trading in Shannon Airport, subs (3)(*a*): s 144(8)("T").

Dividends withholding tax on relevant distributions does not apply to distributions made out of "disregarded income" (within the meaning of this section) to which subsection (3)(*a*) of this section applies: s 172B(7)(*b*).

Restriction of reliefs (subs (3)(*a*)): s 155(3).

Tax Briefing

TB38 Dec 1999 pp 18–19 — Patent Royalties Income and Distributions.

Revenue information

A list of companies who received a favourable radical innovation determination under subsection (5)(*d*) of this section since 2003 is available on Revenue's website — www.revenue.ie — under Publications/Lists.

Definitions

company: ss 4(1), 5(1); distribution: ss 4(1), 436, 437; Income Tax Acts: s 1(2); person: IA 1937 s 11(*c*); 75 per cent subsidiary: s 9.

Former enactments

CTA 1976 s 170; FA 1992 s 19(2); FA 1996 s 32(2)–(3)(*b*); FA 1997 s 146(1) and Sch 9 Pt I para 10(9).

142 Distributions out of profits of certain mines

(1) In this section—

"exempted income" means income in respect of which a company has obtained relief under—

(*a*) the Finance (Profits of Certain Mines) (Temporary Relief from Taxation) Act, 1956, or

(*b*) Chapter II (Profits of Certain Mines) of Part XXV of the Income Tax Act, 1967;

"other income" means income of a company which is not exempted income.

(2) Where a distribution for an accounting period is made by a company wholly out of exempted income, the distribution shall not be regarded as income for any purpose of the Income Tax Acts ....[1]

(3) Where a distribution for an accounting period is made by a company in part out of exempted income and in part out of other income, the distribution shall be treated as if it consisted of 2 distributions respectively made out of exempted income and other income, and subsection (2) shall apply to such part of the distribution as is made out of exempted income as it applies to a distribution made wholly out of exempted income.

(4) Any distribution, including part of a distribution treated under subsection (3) as a distribution, made out of exempted income shall, where the recipient is a company resident in the State, be deemed for the purposes of this section to be exempted income of the company.

...[2]

(6) Subsections (7) and (8) of section 144 and [subsections (8) and (9) of section 140][3] shall apply for the purposes of this section as they apply for the purposes of those sections.

(7) In relation to any distribution ...,[4] including part of a distribution treated under subsection (3) as a distribution, made out of exempted income, section 152 shall apply so that the statements provided for by that section shall show, in addition to the particulars required to be given apart from this section, that the distribution is made out of exempted income.

Amendments

1 Repealed by FA 2000 s 69(2) and Sch 2 Part 2 with effect from 6 April 1999 in the case of income tax and for accounting periods commencing on or after that date in the case of corporation tax; previously "and, notwithstanding section 136, the recipient of the distribution shall not be entitled to a tax credit in respect of it".

2 Subs (5) repealed by FA 2000 s 69(2) and Sch 2 Part 2 with effect from 6 April 1999 in the case of income tax and for accounting periods commencing on or after that date in the case of corporation tax.

3 Substituted by FA 2000 s 69(1) and Sch 2 Part 1 para (*e*) with effect from 6 April 1999 in the case of income tax and for accounting periods commencing on or after that date in the case of corporation tax; previously "subsections (6) and (7) of section 145".

4 Repealed by FA 2000 s 69(2) and Sch 2 Part 2 with effect from 6 April 1999 in the case of income tax and for accounting periods commencing on or after that date in the case of corporation tax; previously "(not being a supplementary distribution under this section)".

Cross-references

Close company surcharges, meaning of "exempted income" applied: s 434(1)("franked investment income").
Distributions out of profits from trading in Shannon Airport, subs (4): s 144(8)("T").
Dividend withholding tax on relevant distributions does not apply to distributions made out of "exempted income" (within the meaning of this section) : s 172B(7)(*c*).

Definitions

company: ss 4(1), 5(1); distribution: ss 4(1), 436, 437; Income Tax Acts: s 1(2); mining: s 5(1); profits: s 4(1).

Former enactments

CTA 1976 s 81.

143 Distributions out of profits from coal, gypsum and anhydrite mining operations

(1) In this section, **"relieved income"** means the income of a company—

(*a*) on which income tax was paid at a reduced rate by virtue of—

(i) section 395(1) of the Income Tax Act, 1967,

(ii) section 7 or 8 of the Finance (Miscellaneous Provisions) Act, 1956, or

(iii) section 32 of the Finance Act, 1960,

(*b*) on which income tax was borne by deduction at a reduced rate under—

(i) section 396(1) of the Income Tax Act, 1967, or

(ii) section 9 of the Finance (Miscellaneous Provisions) Act, 1956,

or

(*c*) which is franked investment income, [which consists of a distribution made out of relieved income].[1]

...[2]

(3) Where a distribution is made in part out of relieved income and in part out of other income, the distribution shall be treated as if it consisted of 2 distributions respectively made out of relieved income and out of other income ....[3]

(4) Any distribution, including part of a distribution treated under subsection (3) as a distribution, made out of relieved income shall, where the recipient is a company resident in the State, be deemed for the purposes of this section to be relieved income of the company.

...[4]

(6) Where for a year of assessment the taxable income of an individual which is chargeable at the standard rate includes income represented by distributions made out of relieved income, the individual's liability to income tax in respect of the income represented by such distributions shall be an amount equal to the tax on that income calculated at 50 per cent of the standard rate for the year of assessment in which the distributions were made.

(7) Where for a year of assessment the taxable income of an individual which is chargeable at the higher rate includes income represented by distributions made out of relieved income, the individual's liability to income tax at the higher rate in respect of the income represented by such distributions shall be an amount equal to the tax, calculated at the higher rate for the year of assessment in which the distributions were made, on the income reduced by 50 per cent ....[5]

...[6]

...[7]

(10) Subsections (7) and (8) of section 144 and [subsections (8) and (9) of section 140][8] shall apply for the purposes of this section as they apply for the purposes of those sections.

(11) In relation to any distribution ...,[9] including part of a distribution treated under subsection (3) as a distribution, made by a company out of relieved income, section 152 shall apply so that the statements provided for by that section shall show, in addition to the particulars required to be given apart from this section, that the distribution is made out of relieved income ....[10]

Amendments

1 Substituted by FA 2000 s 69(1) and Sch 2 Part 1 para (*f*)(i) with effect from 6 April 1999 in the case of income tax and for accounting periods commencing on or after that date in the case of corporation tax; previously "the tax credit comprised in which has been reduced under this section".

2 Subs (2) repealed by FA 2000 s 69(2) and Sch 2 Part 2 with effect from 6 April 1999 in the case of income tax and for accounting periods commencing on or after that date in the case of corporation tax.

3 Repealed by FA 2000 s 69(2) and Sch 2 Part 2 with effect from 6 April 1999 in the case of income tax and for accounting periods commencing on or after that date in the case of corporation tax; previously ", and the tax credit in respect of each such distribution shall be calculated in accordance with subsection (2) and section 136 respectively".

4 Subs (5) repealed by FA 2000 s 69(2) and Sch 2 Part 2 with effect from 6 April 1999 in the case of income tax and for accounting periods commencing on or after that date in the case of corporation tax.

5 Repealed by FA 2000 s 69(2) and Sch 2 Part 2 with effect from 6 April 1999 in the case of income tax and for accounting periods commencing on or after that date in the case of corporation tax; previously ", and, where" to "so reduced".

6 Subs (8) repealed by FA 2000 s 69(2) and Sch 2 Part 2 with effect from 6 April 1999 in the case of income tax and for accounting periods commencing on or after that date in the case of corporation tax.

7 Subs (9) repealed by FA 2000 s 69(2) and Sch 2 Part 2 with effect from 6 April 1999 in the case of income tax and for accounting periods commencing on or after that date in the case of corporation tax.

8 Substituted by FA 2000 s 69(1) and Sch 2 Part 1 para (*f*)(ii) with effect from 6 April 1999 in the case of income tax and for accounting periods commencing on or after that date in the case of corporation tax; previously "subsections (6) and (7) of section 145".

9 Repealed by FA 2000 s 69(2) and Sch 2 Part 2 with effect from 6 April 1999 in the case of income tax and for accounting periods commencing on or after that date in the case of corporation tax; previously "(not being a supplementary distribution under this section".

10 Repealed by FA 2000 s 69(2) and Sch 2 Part 2 with effect from 6 April 1999 in the case of income tax and for accounting periods commencing on or after that date in the case of corporation tax; previously "and the amount of the tax credit which would apply in respect of the distribution if it were not made out of relieved income".

Definitions

company: ss 4(1), 5(1); distribution: ss 4(1), 436, 437; franked investment income: ss 4(1), 156; higher rate: ss 3(1), 15; mining: s 5(1); person: IA 1937 s 11(*c*); profits: s 4(1); taxable income: ss 3(1), 458; year of assessment: ss 2(1), 5(1).

Former enactments

CTA 1976 s 82; FA 1977 s 5(2) and Sch 1 Pt II; FA 1997 s 37 and Sch 2 para 1.

144 Distributions out of profits from trading within Shannon Airport

(1) In this section—

"exempted trading operations" means trading operations which were exempted trading operations for the purposes for Part V of the Corporation Tax Act, 1976;

"other profits" includes a dividend or other distribution of a body corporate resident in the State, but does not include a distribution to which subsection (3)(*a*) applies.

(2) Where a distribution for an accounting period is made by a body corporate in part out of income from exempted trading operations and in part out of other profits, the distribution shall be treated as if it consists of 2 distributions respectively made out of income from exempted trading operations and out of other profits.

(3) (*a*) So much of any distribution as has been made out of income from exempted trading operations shall, where the recipient of that distribution is a body corporate, be deemed for the purposes of this section to be income from exempted trading operations.

...[1]

...[2]

(5) In relation to any distribution ...,[3] including part of a distribution treated under subsection (2) as a distribution, made by a body corporate out of income from exempted trading operations, section 152 shall apply to the body corporate so that the statements provided for by that section shall show, as respects each such distribution, in addition to the particulars required to be given apart from this section, that the distribution is made out of income from exempted trading operations.

...[4]

(7) Where a body corporate makes a distribution for an accounting period, the distribution shall be regarded for the purposes of this section as having been made out of the distributable income of that period to the extent of that income and in relation to the excess of the distribution over that income out of the most recently accumulated income.

(8) For the purposes of subsection (7), the distributable income of a company for an accounting period shall be an amount determined by the formula—

$$(R - S) + T$$

[where

R is the amount of income of the company charged to corporation tax for the accounting period with the addition of any amount of income of the company which would be charged to corporation tax for the accounting period but for section 231, 232, 233 or 234, or section 71 of the Corporation Tax Act, 1976; and, for the purposes of this definition—

(*a*) the income of a company for an accounting period shall be taken to be the amount of its profits for that period on which corporation tax falls finally to be borne exclusive of the part of the profits attributable to chargeable gains, and

(*b*) the part referred to in paragraph (*a*) shall be taken to be the amount brought into the company's profits for that period for the purposes of corporation tax in respect of chargeable gains before any deduction for charges on income, expenses of management or other amounts which can be deducted from or set against or treated as reducing profits of more than one description,

S is the amount of the corporation tax which, before any set-off of or credit for tax, including foreign tax, and after any relief under section 448 or paragraph 16 or 18 of Schedule 32, or section 58 of the Corporation Tax Act, 1976, is chargeable for the accounting period, exclusive of the corporation tax, before any credit for foreign tax, chargeable on the part of the company's profits attributable to chargeable gains for that period; and that part shall be taken to be the amount brought into the company's profits for that period for the purposes of corporation tax in respect of chargeable gains before any deduction for charges on income, expenses of management or other amounts which can be deducted from or set against or treated as reducing profits of more than one description, and

[T is the amount of the distributions received by the company in the accounting period which is included in its franked investment income of the accounting period with the addition of any amount received by the company in the accounting period to which section 140(3)(*a*), 141(3)(*a*), 142(4) or 144(3)(*a*) applies.][5]][6]

(9) [Subsections (8) and (9) of section 140][7] shall apply for the purposes of this section as they apply for purposes of that section.

Amendments

1 Subs (3)(*b*) repealed by FA 2000 s 69(2) and Sch 2 Part 2 with effect from 6 April 1999 in the case of income tax and for accounting periods commencing on or after that date in the case of corporation tax.

2 Subs (4) repealed by FA 2000 s 69(2) and Sch 2 Part 2 with effect from 6 April 1999 in the case of income tax and for accounting periods commencing on or after that date in the case of corporation tax.

3 Repealed by FA 2000 s 69(2) and Sch 2 Part 2 with effect from 6 April 1999 in the case of income tax and for accounting periods commencing on or after that date in the case of corporation tax; previously "(not being a supplementary distribution under this section)".

4 Subs (6) repealed by FA 2000 s 69(2) and Sch 2 Part 2 with effect from 6 April 1999 in the case of income tax and for accounting periods commencing on or after that date in the case of corporation tax.

5 Substituted by FA 2003 s 41(1)(*c*) as respects accounting periods ending on or after 6 February 2003.

6 Substituted by FA 2000 s 69(1) and Sch 2 Part 1 para (*g*)(i) with effect from 6 April 1999 in the case of income tax and for accounting periods commencing on or after that date in the case of corporation tax; previously "where R, S and T have the same meanings respectively as in sections 147(1)(*a*)".

7 Substituted by FA 2000 s 69(1) and Sch 2 Part 1 para (*g*)(ii) with effect from 6 April 1999 in the case of income tax and for accounting periods commencing on or after that date in the case of corporation tax; previously "Subsections (6) and (7) of section 145".

Cross-references

Attribution of dividends to accounting periods: 154(1).

Distributions from exempt profits (subs (8)): s 140(7).

Mining distributions, subss (7)–(8) applied: s 142(6); coal, gypsum and anhydrite, subss (7)–(8) applied: s 143(10).

Patent income distributions (subs (8)): s 141(9).

Restriction of reliefs (subs (3)(*a*)): s 155(3).

Definitions

charges on income: ss 4(1), 243(1); company: ss 4(1), 5(1); distribution: ss 4(1), 436, 437; Income Tax Acts: s 1(2); profits: s 4(1); tax credit: ss 2(1), 136; trade: ss 3(1), 4(1), 5(1).

Former enactments

CTA 1976 s 76(1), (2)(*a*)(ii) and (*b*) and (3)–(8); FA 1992 s 35(*b*); FA 1997 s 146(2) and Sch 9 Pt II; FA 1997 s 146(1) and Sch 9 Pt I para 10(1).

145 Distributions out of profits from export of certain goods

Amendments

Section 145 repealed by FA 2000 s 69(2) and Sch 2 Part 2 with effect from 6 April 1999 in the case of income tax and for accounting periods commencing on or after that date in the case of corporation tax.

146 Provisions supplementary to section 145

Amendments

Section 146 repealed by FA 2000 s 69(2) and Sch 2 Part 2 with effect from 6 April 1999 in the case of income tax and for accounting periods commencing on or after that date in the case of corporation tax.

CHAPTER 5

Distributions Out of Certain Income of Manufacturing Companies

147 Distributions

Amendments

Repealed by FA 2000 s 69(2) and Sch 2 Part 2 with effect from 6 April 1999 in the case of income tax and for accounting periods commencing on or after that date in the case of corporation tax.

148 Treatment of certain deductions in relation to relevant distributions

Amendments

Repealed by FA 2000 s 69(2) and Sch 2 Part 2 with effect from 6 April 1999 in the case of income tax and for accounting periods commencing on or after that date in the case of corporation tax.

149 Dividends and other distributions at gross rate or of gross amount

Amendments

Repealed by FA 2000 s 69(2) and Sch 2 Part 2 with effect from 6 April 1999 in the case of income tax and for accounting periods commencing on or after that date in the case of corporation tax.

150 Tax credits for recipients of certain distributions

Amendments

Repealed by FA 2000 s 69(2) and Sch 2 Part 2 with effect from 6 April 1999 in the case of income tax and for accounting periods commencing on or after that date in the case of corporation tax.

151 Appeals

Amendments

Repealed by FA 2000 s 69(2) and Sch 2 Part 2 with effect from 6 April 1999 in the case of income tax and for accounting periods commencing on or after that date in the case of corporation tax.

CHAPTER 6
Distributions — Supplemental

152 Explanation of tax credit to be annexed to interest and dividend warrants

(1) Every warrant, cheque or other order drawn or made, or purporting to be drawn or made, in payment by any company of any dividend, or of any interest which is a distribution, shall have annexed to it or be accompanied by a statement in writing showing

(*a*) the amount of the dividend (distinguishing a dividend or any part of it which is paid out of capital profits of the company) or interest paid, [and][1]

...[2]

(*c*) the period for which that dividend or interest is paid.

(2) Where a company fails to comply with any of the provisions of subsection (1), the company shall incur a penalty of [€10][3] in respect of each offence, but the aggregate amount of the penalties imposed under this section on any company in respect of offences connected with any one distribution of dividends or interest shall not exceed [€125][4].

(3) (*a*) A company which makes a distribution (not being a distribution to which subsection (1) refers) shall, if the recipient so requests in writing, furnish to the recipient a statement in writing showing the amount or value of the distribution ...[5].

(*b*) The duty imposed by this subsection shall be enforceable at the suit or instance of the person requesting the statement.

Amendments

1 Inserted by FA 2000 s 69(1) and Sch 2 Part 1 para (*h*) with effect from 6 April 1999 in the case of income tax and for accounting periods commencing on or after that date in the case of corporation tax.

2 Subs (1)(*b*) repealed by FA 2000 s 69(2) and Sch 2 Part 2 with effect from 6 April 1999 in the case of income tax and for accounting periods commencing on or after that date in the case of corporation tax.

3 Substituted by FA 2001 s 240(1) and (2)(*k*) and Sch 5 Pt 1 as respects any act or omission which takes place or begins on or after 1 January 2002; previously "£10".

4 Substituted by FA 2001 s 240(1) and (2)(*k*) and Sch 5 Pt 1 as respects any act or omission which takes place or begins on or after 1 January 2002; previously "£100".

5 Repealed by FA 2000 s 69(2) and Sch 2 Part 2 with effect from 6 April 1999 in the case of income tax and for accounting periods commencing on or after that date in the case of corporation tax; previously "and (whether" to "entitled in respect of the distribution".

Cross-references

Company acquiring its own shares, shares bought by issuing company or its subsidiary, taxation of dealer's receipts: s 174(2).
Distributions from exempt profits: s 140(5), (6).
Dividend withholding tax, statement to be given to recipients of relevant distributions, subs (1): s 172I(2), (3); subs (2): s 172I(3).
Mining distributions: s 142(7); coal, gypsum and anhydrite mining distributions: s 143(11).
Patent royalty distributions: s 141(7).
Shannon company distributions: s 144(5).
Shares issued in place of cash dividends: s 816(3).

Definitions

company: ss 4(1), 5(1); distribution: ss 4(1), 436, 437; Income Tax Acts: s 1(2); interest: s 4(1); person: IA 1937 s 11(*c*); profits: s 4(1); resident: s 5(1); Tax Acts: s 1(2); tax: s 3(1); writing: IA 1937 Sch; year of assessment: ss 2(1), 5(1).

Former enactments

CTA 1976 s 5 and s 83(5).

Corresponding UK tax provision

Income and Corporation Taxes Act 1988 ss 234 and 234A.

153 Distributions to certain non-residents

[(1) In this section—

[**"qualifying non-resident person"**, in relation to a distribution, means the person beneficially entitled to the distribution, being—

(*a*) a person, other than a company, who—

(i) is neither resident nor ordinarily resident in the State, and

(ii) is, by virtue of the law of a relevant territory, resident for the purposes of tax in the relevant territory,

or

(*b*) a company which is not resident in the State and—

(i) is, by virtue of the law of a relevant territory, resident for the purposes of tax in the relevant territory, but is not under the control, whether directly or indirectly, of a person or persons who is or are resident in the State,

(ii) is under the control, whether directly or indirectly, of a person or persons who, by virtue of the law of a relevant territory, is or are resident for the purposes of tax in the relevant territory and who is or are, as the case may be, not under the control, whether directly or indirectly, of a person who is, or persons who are, not so resident, or

(iii) the principal class of the shares of which, or—

(I) where the company is a 75 per cent subsidiary of another company, of that other company, or

(II) where the company is wholly-owned by 2 or more companies, of each of those companies,

is substantially and regularly traded on one or more than one recognised stock exchange in a relevant territory or territories or on such other stock exchange as may be approved of by the Minister for Finance for the purposes of this section;][1]

"relevant territory" means—

(*a*) a Member State of the European Communities other than the State, or

(*b*) not being such a Member State, a territory with the government of which arrangements having the force of law by virtue of [section 826(1)(*a*)][2] have been made;

"tax", in relation to a relevant territory, means any tax imposed in that territory which corresponds to income tax or corporation tax in the State.

[(1A) For the purposes of paragraph (*b*)(i) of the definition of "qualifying non-resident person", "control" shall be construed in accordance with subsections (2) to (6) of section 432 as if in subsection (6) of that section for "5 or fewer participators" there were substituted "persons resident in the State".][3]

(2) For the purposes of [paragraph (*b*)(ii) of the definition of "qualifying non-resident person"][4] in subsection (1), "control" shall be construed in accordance with subsections (2) to (6) of section 432 as if in subsection (6) of that section for "5 or fewer participators" there were substituted—

(*a*) in so far as the first mention of "control" in that paragraph is concerned, "persons who, by virtue of the law of a relevant territory (within the meaning assigned by section 153), are resident for the purposes of tax in such a relevant territory (within that meaning)", and

(*b*) in so far as the second mention of "control" in that paragraph is concerned, "persons who are not resident for the purposes of tax in a relevant territory (within that meaning)".

(3) For the purposes of [paragraph (*b*)(iii)(I) of the definition of "qualifying non-resident person"][5] in subsection (1), sections 412 to 418 shall apply as those sections would apply for the purposes of Chapter 5 of Part 12 if ...[6] section 411(1)(*c*) were deleted.

[(3A) For the purposes of paragraph (*b*)(iii)(II) of the definition of "qualifying non-resident person", a company (in this subsection referred to as an "aggregated 100 per cent subsidiary") shall be treated as being wholly-owned by 2 or more companies (in this subsection referred to as the "joint parent companies") if and so long as 100 per cent of its ordinary share capital is owned directly or indirectly by the joint parent companies, and for the purposes of this subsection—

(*a*) subsections (2) to (10) of section 9 shall apply as those subsections apply for the purposes of that section, and

(*b*) sections 412 to 418 shall apply with any necessary modifications as those sections would apply for the purposes of Chapter 5 of Part 12 if—

(i) section 411(1)(*c*) were deleted, and

(ii) the following subsection were substituted for subsection (1) of section 412:

"(1) Notwithstanding that at any time a company is an aggregated 100 per cent subsidiary (within the meaning assigned by section 153(3A)) of the joint parent companies (within the meaning so assigned), it shall not be treated at that time as such a subsidiary unless additionally at that time—

(*a*) the joint parent companies are between them beneficially entitled to not less than 100 per cent of any profits available for distribution to equity holders of the company, and

(*b*) the joint parent companies would be beneficially entitled between them to not less than 100 per cent of any assets of the company available for distribution to its equity holders on a winding up.][7]

(4) Where for any year of assessment the income of a person who for that year of assessment is a [qualifying non-resident person][8] includes an amount in respect of a distribution made by a company resident in the State—

(*a*) income tax shall not be chargeable in respect of that distribution, and

(*b*) the amount or value of the distribution shall be treated for the purposes of sections 237 and 238 as not brought into charge to income tax.

(5) Where, by virtue of section 831(5), Chapter 8A of Part 6 (other than section 172K) does not apply to a distribution made to a parent company (within the meaning of section 831) which is not resident in the State by its subsidiary (within the meaning of that section) which is a company resident in the State—

(*a*) income tax shall not be chargeable in respect of that distribution, and

(*b*) the amount or value of the distribution shall be treated for the purposes of section 237 and 238 as not brought into charge to income tax.

[(6) Where for any year of assessment the income of a person, being an individual who for that year of assessment is neither resident nor ordinarily resident in the State but is not a qualifying non-resident person, includes an amount in respect of a distribution made by a company resident in the State, then—

(*a*) notwithstanding section 15(2), income tax shall not be chargeable in respect of that distribution at a rate in excess of the standard rate, and

(*b*) the amount or value of the distribution shall be treated for the purposes of sections 237 and 238 as not brought into charge to income tax.][9]][10]

Amendments

1 Definition of "qualifying non-resident person" substituted by FA 2000 s 31(*a*) with effect from 6 April 2000.

2 Substituted by FA 2004 s 89 and Sch 3 para 1(*e*) with effect from 25 March 2004; previously "section 826".

3 Subs (1A) inserted by FA 2000 s 31(*b*) with effect from 6 April 2000.

4 Substituted by FA 2000 s 31(*c*) with effect from 6 April 2000; previously "paragraph (*b*)(i) of the definition of 'non-resident person'".

5 Substituted by FA 2000 s 31(*d*)(i) with effect from 6 April 2000; previously "paragraph (*b*)(ii)(II) of the definition of 'non-resident person'".

6 Deleted by FA 2000 s 31(*d*)(ii) with effect from 6 April 2000; previously "subparagraph (iii) of".

7 Subs (3A) inserted by FA 2000 s 31(*e*) with effect from 6 April 2000.

8 Substituted by FA 2000 s 31(*f*) with effect from 6 April 2000; previously "non-resident person".

9 Subs (6) inserted by FA 2000 s 31(*g*) with effect from 6 April 2000.

10 Section 153 substituted by FA 1999 s 28(1) in respect of distributions made on or after 6 April 1999.

Cross-references

Life assurance companies, distributions received from Irish resident companies, subss (4), (5): s 712(1).

Definitions

company: ss 4(1), 5(1); distribution: ss 4(1), 436, 437; person: IA 1937 s 11(*c*); year of assessment: ss 2(1), 5(1); 75 per cent subsidiary: s 9.

Former enactments

CTA 1976 s 83(4); FA 1992 s 38(2); FA 1994 s 27(*a*); FA 1995 s 39.

Corresponding UK tax provision

Income and Corporation Taxes Act 1988 s 232.

154 Attribution of distributions to accounting periods

(1) (*a*) Notwithstanding sections 140, 141 [and 144][1] but subject to subsections (2) and (3), where a company which makes a distribution specifies, by notice in writing given to the inspector within 6 months of the end of the accounting period in which the distribution is made, the extent to which the distribution is to be treated for the purposes of sections 140, 141 [and 144][1] as made for any accounting period or periods, the distribution shall be so treated for those purposes irrespective of the period of account for which it was made.

(*b*) A part of a distribution treated under paragraph (*a*) as made for an accounting period shall be treated for the purposes of sections 140, 141 [and 144][1] ...[2] as a separate distribution.

(2) A company may specify in accordance with subsection (1) that only so much of a distribution, or more than one distribution, made on any day is made—

(*a*) for any accounting period, as does not exceed the undistributed income of the company for that accounting period on that day, and

(*b*) for an accounting period or accounting periods ending more than 9 years before that day, as does not exceed the amount by which the amount of the distribution or the aggregate amount of the distributions, as the case may be, exceeds the aggregate of the undistributed income of the company on that day for accounting periods ending before, but not more than 9 years before, that day.

(3) Except where a distribution made by a company is—

(*a*) an interim dividend paid before [1 January 2003][3] by the directors of the company, pursuant to powers conferred on them by the articles of association of the company, in respect of the profits of the accounting period in which it is paid,

(*b*) a distribution by virtue only of subparagraph (ii), (iii)(I) or (v) of section 130(2)(*d*),

(*c*) a distribution made in respect of shares of a type referred to in paragraph (*c*) of the definition of **"preference shares"** in section 138(1), or

(*d*) made in an accounting period in which the company ceases or commences to be within the charge to corporation tax,

the company shall not be entitled to specify in accordance with subsection (1) that the distribution is to be treated as made for the accounting period in which it is made.

...[4]

...[5]

[(6) For the purposes of this section, the amount of the undistributed income of a company for an accounting period shall be the amount determined by the formula—

$$(R - S) + T - W$$

reduced by the amount of each distribution, or part of each distribution, made before [the day in question][6] and on or after 6 April 1989, which is to be treated under this section, or which was treated under section 147, as made for that accounting period,

where—

R, S and T have the same meanings respectively as in section 144(8), and W is the amount of the distributions made by the company before 6 April 1989, which—

(*a*) were made for the accounting period,

(*b*) are, by virtue of subsection (7), deemed to have been made for the accounting period, or

(*c*) would be deemed to have been made for the accounting period by virtue of subsection (9) of section 140 if that subsection were treated as applying for the purposes of this section as it applies for the purpose of that section.

(7) For the purposes of this section—

(*a*) where the total amount of the distributions made by a company for an accounting period exceeds the amount determined by the formula—

$$(R - S) + T$$

for that accounting period (where R, S and T have the same meanings respectively as in section 144(8)), the excess shall be deemed for the purposes of this section to be a distribution for the immediately preceding accounting period, and

(*b*) where the total amount of the distributions made or deemed under paragraph (*a*) to have been made by a company for the immediately preceding accounting period referred to in paragraph (*a*) exceeds the amount determined for that accounting period in accordance with the formula mentioned in paragraph (*a*), the excess shall be deemed to be a distribution for the immediately preceding accounting period and so on.][7]

Amendments

1 Substituted by FA 2003 s 41(1)(*d*)(i) as respects accounting periods ending on or after 6 February 2003; previously ", 144 and 145".

2 Substituted by FA 2000 s 69(1) and Sch 2 Pt 1 para (*i*)(i)(II) with effect from 6 April 2000; previously "144, 145 and 147".

3 Substituted by FA 2001 s 77(2) and Sch 2 para 10 with effect from 6 April 2001; previously "the 6th day of April, 2002,".

4 Subs (4) repealed by FA 2000 s 69(2) and Sch 2 Part 2 with effect from 6 April 2000.

5 Subs (5) repealed by FA 2000 s 69(2) and Sch 2 Part 2 with effect from 6 April 2000.

6 Substituted by FA 2003 s 41(1)(*d*)(ii) as respects accounting periods ending on or after 6 February 2003; previously "that day".

7 Subs (6)–(7) substituted for subs (6) by FA 2000 s 69(1) and Sch 2 Pt 1 para (*i*)(ii) with effect from 6 April 2000.

Definitions

company: ss 4(1), 5(1); distribution: ss 4(1), 436, 437; inspector: ss 2(1), 5(1), 852; month: IA 1937 Sch; profits: s 4(1); resident: s 5(1); tax credit: ss 2(1), 136; shares: s 5(1); within the charge to (tax): s 2(1); writing: IA 1937 Sch.

Former enactments

FA 1989 s 25; FA 1992 s 37; FA 1997 s 38.

155 Restriction of certain reliefs in respect of distributions out of certain exempt or relieved profits

(1) In this section, **"distribution"** has the same meaning as in the Corporation Tax Acts.

(2) (*a*) This section shall apply to shares in a company where any agreement, arrangement or understanding exists which could reasonably be considered to eliminate the risk that the person beneficially owning those shares—

(i) might, at or after a time specified in or implied by that agreement, arrangement or understanding, be unable to realise directly or indirectly in money or money's worth an amount so specified or implied, other than a distribution, in respect of those shares, or

(ii) might not receive an amount so specified or implied of distributions in respect of those shares.

(*b*) The reference in this subsection to the person beneficially owning shares shall be deemed to be a reference to both that person and any person connected with that person.

(*c*) For the purposes of this subsection, an amount specified or implied shall include an amount specified or implied in a foreign currency.

(3) Where any person receives a distribution in respect of shares to which this section applies and, apart from the application of this subsection to the distribution, section 140(3)(*a*), 141(3)(*a*) [or 144(3)(*a*)][1] would apply to the distribution, then, notwithstanding any provision of the Tax Acts other than subsection (4) and for the purposes of those Acts—

(*a*) none of those sections shall apply to the distribution, [and][2]

...[3]

(*c*) the distribution shall be treated as income chargeable to income tax or corporation tax, as the case may be, under Case IV of Schedule D.

(4) Subsection (3) shall not apply to a distribution received—

(*a*) by a company—

(i) none of the shares of which is beneficially owned by a person resident in the State, and

(ii) which, if this subsection had not been enacted, would not be chargeable to corporation tax in respect of any profits other than distributions which would be so chargeable by virtue of this section, or

(*b*) by a person not resident in the State.

(5) Notwithstanding subsection (4), the liability to income tax or corporation tax of any person resident in the State, other than a company to which paragraph (*a*) of that subsection relates, shall be determined as if that subsection had not been enacted.

Amendments

1 Substituted by FA 2003 s 41(1)(*e*) as respects accounting periods ending on or after 6 February 2003; previously ", 144(3)(*a*) or 145".

2 Inserted by FA 2000 s 69(1) and Sch 2 Part 1 para (*k*) with effect from 6 April 1999 in the case of income tax and for accounting periods commencing on or after that date in the case of corporation tax.

3 Subs (3)(*b*) repealed by FA 2000 s 69(2) and Sch 2 Part 2 with effect from 6 April 1999 in the case of income tax and for accounting periods commencing on or after that date in the case of corporation tax.

Definitions

distribution: ss 4(1), 436, 437; person: IA 1937 s 11(*c*); profits: s 4(1); shares: s 5(1).

Former enactments

FA 1990 s 34(1)(*a*) and (*b*)(ii), (2)–(3), (5)–(6).

CHAPTER 7
Franked Investment Income

156 Franked investment income and franked payments

[(1) Income of a company resident in the State which consists of a distribution made by another company resident in the State shall be referred to in the Corporation Tax Acts as "franked investment income" of the company, and the amount of the franked investment income of such a company shall be the amount or value of the distribution.

(2) A reference in the Corporation Tax Acts to a "franked payment" in relation to a company resident in the State which makes a distribution shall be construed as a reference to the amount or value of the distribution and references to any accounting or other period in which a franked payment is made are references to the period in which the distribution is made.][1]

Amendments

1 Section 156 substituted by FA 2003 s 41(1)(*f*)(i) as respects accounting periods ending on or after 6 February 2003.

Cross-references

Bonus issue and relevant tax credit not franked investment income: s 137(3).
Life assurance companies, distributions received from Irish resident companies: s 712(2)(*b*).

Definitions

company: ss 4(1), 5(1); corporation Tax Acts: s 1(2); distribution: ss 4(1), 436, 437.

Former enactments

CTA 1976 s 24.

157 Set-off of losses, etc against franked investment income

Amendments

Section 157 deleted by FA 2003 s 41(1)(*f*)(ii) as respects accounting periods ending on or after 6 February 2003.

158 Set-off of loss brought forward or terminal loss against franked investment income in the case of financial concerns

Amendments

Section 158 deleted by FA 2003 s 41(1)(*f*)(ii) as respects accounting periods ending on or after 6 February 2003.

CHAPTER 8
Advance Corporation Tax

Cross-references

Bank levy credit: 487(1)(*a*).
Payment of tax by donation of heritage items: s 1003(1)(*a*).

159 Liability for advance corporation tax

Amendments

Section 159 deleted by FA 2003 s 41(1)(*g*) as respects accounting periods ending on or after 6 February 2003.

Cross-references

Set-off of surplus advance corporation tax: s 845B(1).

160 Set-off of advance corporation tax

Amendments

Section 160 deleted by FA 2003 s 41(1)(*g*) as respects accounting periods ending on or after 6 February 2003.

161 Rectification of excessive set-off of advance corporation tax

Amendments

Section 161 deleted by FA 2003 s 41(1)(*g*) as respects accounting periods ending on or after 6 February 2003.

162 Calculation of advance corporation tax where company receives distributions

Amendments

Section 162 deleted by FA 2003 s 41(1)(*g*) as respects accounting periods ending on or after 6 February 2003.

163 Tax credit recovered from company

Amendments

Section 163 deleted by FA 2003 s 41(1)(*g*) as respects accounting periods ending on or after 6 February 2003.

164 Restrictions as to payment of tax credit

Amendments

Section 164 deleted by FA 2003 s 41(1)(*g*) as respects accounting periods ending on or after 6 February 2003.

165 Group dividends

Amendments

Section 165 repealed by FA 2000 s 69(2) and Sch 2 Part 2 with effect from 6 April 1999 in the case of income tax and for accounting periods commencing on or after that date in the case of corporation tax.

166 Surrender of advance corporation tax

Amendments

Section 166 deleted by FA 2003 s 41(1)(*g*) as respects accounting periods ending on or after 6 February 2003.

167 Change of ownership of company: calculation and treatment of advance corporation tax

Amendments

Section 167 deleted by FA 2003 s 41(1)(*g*) as respects accounting periods ending on or after 6 February 2003.

168 Distributions to certain non-resident companies

Amendments

Section 168 repealed by FA 2000 s 69(2) and Sch 2 Part 2 with effect from 6 April 1999 in the case of income tax and for accounting periods commencing on or after that date in the case of corporation tax.

169 Non-distributing investment companies

Amendments

Section 169 repealed by FA 2000 s 69(2) and Sch 2 Part 2 with effect from 6 April 1999 in the case of income tax and for accounting periods commencing on or after that date in the case of corporation tax.

170 Interest in respect of certain securities

Amendments

Section 170 repealed by FA 2000 s 69(2) and Sch 2 Part 2 with effect from 6 April 1999 in the case of income tax and for accounting periods commencing on or after that date in the case of corporation tax.

171 Returns, payment and collection of advance corporation tax

Amendments

Section 171 repealed by FA 2000 s 69(2) and Sch 2 Part 2 with effect from 6 April 1999 in the case of income tax and for accounting periods commencing on or after that date in the case of corporation tax.

172 Application of Corporation Tax Acts

Amendments

Section 172 repealed by FA 2000 s 69(2) and Sch 2 Part 2 with effect from 6 April 1999 in the case of income tax and for accounting periods commencing on or after that date in the case of corporation tax.

[CHAPTER 8A
Dividend withholding tax][1]

Amendments

[1] Inserted by FA 1999 s 27(*a*) with effect from 6 April 1999.

Cross-references

Declarations to be made by non-liable persons in relation to dividend withholding tax: Sch 2A, paras 3(*g*), 4(*h*), 5(*h*), 6(*g*), 7(*h*), 8(*i*), 9(*i*).

Distributions to certain non-residents: s 153(5).

Implementation of Parents/Subsidiaries Directive: s 831(5), (6).

Power of inspection, returns and collection of dividend withholding tax: s 904I(1)("records"), (2), (3)(*a*).

Restriction of relief in respect of loans applied in acquiring interest in companies: s 250A(3)(*a*), (*b*).

Revenue offences, meaning of dividend withholding tax applied: s 1078(2)(*dd*)(i), (iv), (v).

Treatment of distributions to certain parent companies, non-application of this Chapter other than s 172K: s 831A(2).

Tax Briefing

TB35 Mar 1999 pp 10–18 — Dividend Withholding Tax.

TB41 Sept 2000 pp 24–27 — Dividend Withholding Tax — Summary of Scheme/Refunds.

TB56 p 18 — DWT Stapled Stock Arrangements.

Revenue Information

A list of Authorised Qualifying Intermediaries and Authorised Withholding Agents, together with Associated Nominee Companies, is available on Revenue's website — www.revenue.ie under Publications/Lists.
Dividend Withholding Tax Information Leaflet (DWT INFO 1V2).
Refunds of Dividend Withholding Tax.
Dividend Withholding Tax — A guide to the submission of returns in electronic form.
Qualifying Intermediary Annual Return of Dividend Withholding Tax Information — a guide to the submission of QI Returns in electronic form.

172A Interpretation

[(1) (*a*) In this Chapter and in Schedule 2A—

"American depositary receipt" has the same meaning as in section 207 of the Finance Act, 1992;

[**"approved body of persons"** has the same meaning as in section 235;][1]

[**"approved minimum retirement fund"** has the same meaning as in section 784C;][2]

[**"approved retirement fund"** has the same meaning as in section 784A;][2]

"auditor", in relation to a company, means the person or persons appointed as auditor of the company for the purposes of the Companies Acts, 1963 to 1990, or under the law of the territory in which the company is incorporated and which corresponds to those Acts;

"authorised withholding agent", in relation to a relevant distribution, has the meaning assigned to it by section 172G;

[**"collective investment undertaking"** means—

(i) a collective investment undertaking within the meaning of section 734,

(ii) an undertaking for collective investment within the meaning of section 738, ...[3]

(iii) an investment undertaking within the meaning of section 739B (inserted by the Finance Act, 2000), [or][4]

[(iv) a common contractual fund within the meaning of section 739I (inserted by the Finance Act 2005),][5]

not being an offshore fund within the meaning of section 743;][6]

[**"designated broker"** has the same meaning as in section 838;][7]

"dividend withholding tax", in relation to a relevant distribution, means a sum representing income tax on the amount of the relevant distribution at the standard rate in force at the time the relevant distribution is made;

"excluded person", in relation to a relevant distribution, has the meaning assigned to it by section 172C(2);

"intermediary" means a person who carries on a trade which consists of or includes—

(i) the receipt of relevant distributions from a company or companies resident in the State, or

(ii) the receipt of amounts or other assets representing such distributions from another intermediary or intermediaries,

on behalf of other persons;

"non-liable person", in relation to a relevant distribution, means the person beneficially entitled to the relevant distribution, being an excluded person or a qualifying non-resident person;

"pension scheme" means an exempt approved scheme within the meaning of section 774 or a retirement annuity contract or a trust scheme to which section 784 or 785 applies;

[**"PRSA administrator"** has the same meaning as in section 787A;

"PRSA assets" has the same meaning as in section 787A;][8]

"qualifying employee share ownership trust" means an employee share ownership trust which the Revenue Commissioners have approved of as a qualifying employee share ownership trust in accordance with Schedule 12 and which approval has not been withdrawn;

[**"qualifying fund manager"** has the same meaning as in section 784A;][9]

"qualifying intermediary", in relation to a relevant distribution, has the meaning assigned to it by section 172E;

"qualifying non-resident person", in relation to a relevant distribution, has the meaning assigned to it by section 172D(3);

[**"qualifying savings manager"** has the same meaning as in section 848B (inserted by the Finance Act, 2001);][10]

"relevant distribution" means—

[(i) a distribution within the meaning of paragraph 1 of Schedule F in section 20(1), other than such a distribution made to—

(I) a Minister of the Government in his or her capacity as such Minister, or

(II) the National Pensions Reserve Fund Commission,

and][11]

(ii) any amount assessable and chargeable to tax under Case IV of Schedule D by virtue of section 816;

"relevant person", in relation to a relevant distribution, means—

(i) where the relevant distribution is made by a company directly to the person beneficially entitled to the distribution, the company making the relevant distribution, and

(ii) where the relevant distribution is not made by the company directly to the person beneficially entitled to the relevant distribution but is made to that person through one or more than one qualifying intermediary, the qualifying intermediary from whom the relevant distribution, or an amount or other asset representing the relevant distribution, is receivable by the person beneficially entitled to the distribution;

"relevant territory" means—

(i) a Member State of the European Communities other than the State, or

(ii) not being such a Member State, a territory with the government of which arrangements having the force of law by virtue of [section 826(1)(*a*)][12] have been made;

[**"special portfolio investment account"** has the same meaning as in section 838;][13]

[**"special savings incentive account"** has the same meaning as in section 848M (inserted by the Finance Act, 2001);][14]

"specified person", in relation to a relevant distribution, means the person to whom the relevant distribution is made, whether or not that person is beneficially entitled to the relevant distribution;

"tax", in relation to a relevant territory, means any tax imposed in that territory which corresponds to income tax or corporation tax in the State;

"tax reference number" has the same meaning as in section 885.

(*b*) In this Chapter and in Schedule 2A, references to the making of a relevant distribution by a company, or to a relevant distribution to be made by a company, or to the receipt of a relevant distribution from a company do not include, respectively, references to the making of a relevant distribution by a collective investment undertaking, or to a relevant distribution to be made by a collective investment undertaking, or to the receipt of a relevant distribution from a collective investment undertaking.

(2) For the purposes of this Chapter, the amount of a relevant distribution shall be an amount equal to—

(*a*) where the relevant distribution consists of a payment in cash, the amount of the payment,

(*b*) where the relevant distribution consists of an amount which is treated under section 816 as a distribution made by a company, the amount so treated,

(*c*) where the relevant distribution consists of an amount which is assessable and chargeable to tax under Case IV of Schedule D by virtue of section 816, the amount so assessable and chargeable, and

(*d*) where the relevant distribution consists of a non-cash distribution, not being a relevant distribution to which paragraph (*b*) or (*c*) applies, an amount which is equal to the value of the distribution,

and a reference in this Chapter to the amount of a relevant distribution shall be construed as a reference to the amount which would be the amount of the relevant distribution if no dividend withholding tax were to be deducted from the relevant distribution.

(3) Schedule 2A shall have effect for the purposes of supplementing this Chapter.][15]

Amendments

1 Definition of "approved body of persons" inserted by FA 2000 s 30(1)(*a*)(i) with effect from 6 April 2000.

2 Definition of "approved minimum retirement fund" and "approved retirement fund" inserted by FA 2001 s 43(1)(*a*)(i) with effect from 6 April 2001.

3 Deleted by FA 2005 s 44(*a*)(i) with effect from 1 January 2005; previously "or".

4 Inserted by FA 2005 s 44(*a*)(ii) with effect from 1 January 2005.

5 Definition of "collective investment undertaking" subpara (iv) inserted by FA 2005 s 44(*a*)(iii) with effect from 1 January 2005.

6 Definition of "collective investment undertaking" substituted by FA 2000 s 59 with effect from 6 April 2000.

7 Definition of "designated broker" inserted by FA 2000 s 30(1)(*a*)(ii) with effect from 6 April 2000.

8 Definitions of "PRSA administrator" and "PRSA assets" inserted by FA 2005 s 47(1)(*a*) with effect from 3 February 2005.

9 Definition of "qualifying fund manager" inserted by FA 2001 s 43(1)(*a*)(ii) with effect from 6 April 2001.

10 Definition of "qualifying savings manager" inserted by FA 2001 s 43(1)(*a*)(iii) with effect from 6 April 2001.

11 Definition of "relevant distribution" para (i) substituted by National Pensions Reserve Fund Act 2000 s 30(*a*) with effect from 10 December 2000.

12 Substituted by FA 2004 s 89 and Sch 3 para 1(*f*) with effect from 25 March 2004; previously "section 826".

13 Definition of "special portfolio investment account" inserted by FA 2000 s 30(1)(*a*)(iii) with effect from 6 April 2000.

14 Definition of "special savings incentive account" inserted by FA 2001 s 43(1)(*a*)(iv) with effect from 6 April 2001.

15 Section 172A inserted by FA 1999 s 27(*a*) with effect from 6 April 1999.

Cross-references

Approved retirement fund, definition of "qualifying fund manager", meaning of "collective investment undertaking" applied: s 784A(1)(*a*).

Cross-border pension schemes, exemption of — for the purposes of section 172A(1), the reference to "an exempt approved scheme within the meaning of section 774" in the definition of "pension scheme" in s 172A(1) is deemed to include a reference to a scheme referred to in s 790B(2): s 790B(4).

Dividend withholding tax on relevant distributions; paras (*b*), (*c*) of subs (2): s 172B(2).

Exemption from dividend withholding tax for certain non-resident persons: s 172D(4).

Implementation of Parents/Subsidiaries Directive: s 831(6).

Power of inspection, returns and collection of dividend withholding tax, meaning of "authorised withholding agent", "dividend withholding tax" and "relevant distribution" applied: s 904I(1).

Definitions

company: s 4(1); Minister of the Government: IA 1937 Sch; person: IA 1937s 11(*c*); standard rate: ss 3(1), 15; trade: ss 3(1), 4(1), 5(1).

172B Dividend withholding tax on relevant distributions

[(1) Except where otherwise provided by this Chapter, where, on or after the 6th day of April, 1999, a company resident in the State makes a relevant distribution to a specified person—

(*a*) the company shall deduct out of the amount of the relevant distribution dividend withholding tax in relation to the relevant distribution,

(*b*) the specified person shall allow such deduction on the receipt of the residue of the relevant distribution, and

(*c*) the company shall be acquitted and discharged of so much money as is represented by the deduction as if that amount of money had actually been paid to the specified person.

(2) Except where otherwise provided by this Chapter, where, at any time on or after the 6th day of April, 1999, a company resident in the State makes a relevant distribution to a specified person and the relevant distribution consists of an amount referred to in paragraph (*b*) or (*c*) of section 172A(2) (being an amount equal to the amount which the specified person would have received if that person had received the relevant

distribution in cash instead of in the form of additional share capital of the company), subsection (1) shall not apply, but—

(*a*) the company shall reduce the amount of the additional share capital to be issued to the specified person by such amount as will secure that the value at that time of the additional share capital issued to the specified person does not exceed an amount equal to the amount which the person would have received, after deduction of dividend withholding tax, if the person had received the relevant distribution in cash instead of in the form of additional share capital of the company,

(*b*) the specified person shall allow such reduction on the receipt of the residue of the additional share capital,

(*c*) the company shall be acquitted and discharged of so much money as is represented by the reduction in the value of the additional share capital as if that amount of money had actually been paid to the specified person,

(*d*) the company shall be liable to pay to the Collector-General an amount (which shall be treated for the purposes of this Chapter as if it were a deduction of dividend withholding tax in relation to the relevant distribution) equal to the dividend withholding tax which, but for this subsection, would have been required to be deducted from the relevant distribution, and

(*e*) the company shall be liable to pay that amount in the same manner in all respects as if it were the dividend withholding tax which, but for this subsection, would have been required to be deducted from the relevant distribution.

(3) Except where otherwise provided by this Chapter, where, on or after the 6th day of April, 1999, a company resident in the State makes a relevant distribution to a specified person and the relevant distribution consists of a non-cash distribution, not being a relevant distribution to which subsection (2) applies, subsection (1) shall not apply, but the company—

(*a*) shall be liable to pay to the Collector-General an amount (which shall be treated for the purposes of this Chapter as if it were a deduction of dividend withholding tax in relation to the relevant distribution) equal to the dividend withholding tax which, but for this subsection, would have been required to be deducted from the amount of the relevant distribution,

(*b*) shall be liable to pay that amount in the same manner in all respects as if it were the dividend withholding tax which, but for this subsection, would have been required to be deducted from the relevant distribution, and

(*c*) shall be entitled to recover a sum equal to that amount from the specified person as a simple contract debt in any court of competent jurisdiction.

(4) A company resident in the State shall treat every relevant distribution to be made by it on or after the 6th day of April, 1999, to a specified person as a distribution to which this section applies, but, where the company has satisfied itself that a relevant distribution to be made by it to a specified person is not, by virtue of the following provisions of this Chapter, a distribution to which this section applies, the company shall, subject to those provisions, be entitled to so treat relevant distributions to be made by it to the specified person until such time as it is in possession of information which

can reasonably be taken to indicate that a relevant distribution to be made to the specified person is or may be a relevant distribution to which this section applies.

[(4A)(*a*) A company resident in the State shall keep and retain for the longer of the following periods—

(i) a period of 6 years, or

(ii) a period which, in relation to the relevant distributions in respect of which the declaration or notification is made or, as the case may be, given, ends not earlier than 3 years after the date on which the company has ceased to make relevant distributions to the person who made the declaration or, as the case may be, gave the notification to the company,

all declarations (and accompanying certificates) and notifications (not being a notice given to the company by the Revenue Commissioners) which are made or, as the case may be, given to the company in accordance with this Chapter and Schedule 2A.

(*b*) A company resident in the State shall, on being so required by notice in writing given to the company by the Revenue Commissioners, make available to the Commissioners, within the time specified in the notice—

(i) all declarations, certificates or notifications referred to in paragraph (*a*) which have been made or, as the case may be, given to the company, or

(ii) such class or classes of such declarations, certificates or notifications as may be specified in the notice.

(*c*) The Revenue Commissioners may examine or take extracts from or copies of any declarations, certificates or notifications made available to the Commissioners under paragraph (*b*).][1]

(5) The provisions of the Tax Acts relating to the computation of profits or gains shall not be affected by the deduction of dividend withholding tax in relation to relevant distributions in accordance with this section and, accordingly, the amount of such relevant distributions shall, subject to section 129, be taken into account in computing for tax purposes the profits or gains of persons beneficially entitled to such distributions.

[(6) This section shall not apply to a relevant distribution where section 831(5) applies in relation to that distribution.][2]

[(7) This section shall not apply where a relevant distribution is made by a company resident in the State and that distribution is—

(*a*) a distribution made out of exempt profits within the meaning of section 140,

(*b*) a distribution made out of disregarded income within the meaning of section 141 and to which subsection (3)(*a*) of that section applies, or

(*c*) a distribution made out of exempted income within the meaning of section 142.][3]

[(8) This section shall not apply where a relevant distribution is made by a company resident in the State to another company so resident and the company making the relevant distribution is a 51 per cent subsidiary of that other company.][4]][5]

Amendments

1 Subs (4A) inserted by FA 2000 s 30(1)(*b*)(i) with effect from 6 April 2000.
2 Subs (6) substituted by FA 2000 s 30(1)(*b*)(ii) with effect from 6 April 2000.
3 Subs (7) inserted by FA 2000 s 30(1)(*b*)(iii) with effect from 6 April 2000.
4 Subs (8) inserted by FA 2001 s 43(1)(*b*) with effect from 6 April 2001.
5 Section 172B inserted by FA 1999 s 27(*a*) with effect from 6 April 1999.

Cross-references

Authorised withholding agent: s 172G(1).
Exemption from dividend withholding tax for certain non-resident persons: s 172D(1), (2).
Exemption from dividend withholding tax for certain persons: s 172C(1); subs (8): s 172C(2)(*a*).
Obligations of authorised withholding agent in relation to relevant distributions: s 172H(2), (3).
Obligations of qualifying intermediary in relation to relevant distributions: s 172F(6).
Qualifying intermediary: s 172E(1).
Returns, payment and collection of dividend withholding tax, subs (7): s 172K(1)(*h*).
Revenue offences: subs (1): s 1078(2)(*dd*)(i); subs (2): s 1078(2)(*dd*)(iii); subs (2)(*d*): s 1078(2)(*dd*)(iv); subs (3)(*a*): s 1078(2)(*dd*)(v).

Definitions

Collector-General: ss 2(1), 851; company: s 4(1); dividend withholding tax: s 172A(1)(*a*); person: IA 1937 s 11(*c*); relevant distribution, specified person: s 172A(1)(*a*); Tax Acts: s 1(2); writing: IA 1937 Sch; 51 per cent subsidiary: s 9.

172C Exemption from dividend withholding tax for certain persons

[(1) Section 172B shall not apply where a company resident in the State makes a relevant distribution to an excluded person.

(2) For the purposes of this Chapter, a person shall be an excluded person in relation to a relevant distribution if the person is beneficially entitled to the relevant distribution and is—

(*a*) a company resident in the State which has made a declaration to the relevant person in relation to the relevant distribution in accordance with paragraph 3 of Schedule 2A [, but this paragraph is without prejudice to the operation of section 172B(8)][1],

(*b*) a pension scheme which has made a declaration to the relevant person in relation to the relevant distribution in accordance with paragraph 4 of Schedule 2A,

[(*ba*) a qualifying fund manager or a qualifying savings manager who—

(i) is receiving the relevant distribution as income arising in respect of assets held—

(I) in the case of a qualifying fund manager, in an approved retirement fund or an approved minimum retirement fund, and

(II) in the case of a qualifying savings manager, in a special savings incentive account,

and

(ii) has made a declaration to the relevant person in relation to the relevant distribution in accordance with paragraph 4A of Schedule 2A,][2]

[(*bb*) a PRSA administrator who is receiving the relevant distribution as income arising in respect of PRSA assets, and has made a declaration to the relevant person in relation to the relevant distribution in accordance with paragraph 10 of Schedule 2A,][3]

(*c*) a qualifying employee share ownership trust which has made a declaration to the relevant person in relation to the relevant distribution in accordance with paragraph 5 of Schedule 2A,

(*d*) a collective investment undertaking which has made a declaration to the relevant person in relation to the relevant distribution in accordance with paragraph 6 of Schedule 2A, ...[4]

[(*da*) a person who—

(i) is entitled to exemption from income tax under Schedule F in respect of the relevant distribution by virtue of section 189(2), subsection (2) or (3)(*b*) of section 189A or section 192(2), and

(ii) has made a declaration to the relevant person in relation to the relevant distribution in accordance with paragraph 6A of Schedule 2A,][5]

[(*db*) a unit trust to which section 731(5)(*a*) applies and which has made a declaration to the relevant person in relation to the relevant distribution in accordance with paragraph 11 of Schedule 2A,][6]

(*e*) a person who—

(i) is entitled to exemption from income tax under Schedule F in respect of the relevant distribution by virtue of section 207(1)(*b*), and

(ii) has made a declaration to the relevant person in relation to the relevant distribution in accordance with paragraph 7 of [Schedule 2A,][7]

[(*f*) an approved body of persons which—

(i) is entitled to exemption from income tax under Schedule F in respect of the relevant distribution by virtue of section 235(2), and

(ii) has made a declaration to the relevant person in relation to the relevant distribution in accordance with paragraph 7A of Schedule 2A,

or

(*g*) a designated broker who—

(i) is receiving the relevant distribution as all or part of the relevant income or gains (within the meaning of section 838) of a special portfolio investment account, and

(ii) has made a declaration to the relevant person in relation to the relevant distribution in accordance with paragraph 7B of Schedule 2A.][8]

[(3) For the purposes of subsection (2) and Schedule 2A—

(*a*) a collective investment undertaking which receives a relevant distribution, ...[9]

(*b*) a designated broker who receives a relevant distribution as all or part of the relevant income or gains (within the meaning of section 838) of a special portfolio investment account,

[(*c*) a qualifying fund manager or a qualifying savings manager who receives a relevant distribution as income arising in respect of assets held—

(i) in the case of a qualifying fund manager, in an approved retirement fund or an approved minimum retirement fund, and

(ii) in the case of a qualifying savings manager, in a special savings incentive account,

[(*ca*) a PRSA administrator who receives a relevant distribution as income arising in respect of PRSA assets,

(*cb*) a unit trust to which section 731(5)(*a*) applies which receives a relevant distribution in relation to units in that unit trust,][10]

and

(*d*) the trustees of a qualifying trust (within the meaning of section 189A) who receive a relevant distribution as income arising in respect of the trust funds (within the meaning of that section),][11]

shall be treated as being beneficially entitled to the relevant distribution.][12]][13]

Amendments

1 Inserted by FA 2001 s 43(1)(*c*)(i)(I) with effect from 6 April 2001.
2 Subs (2)(*ba*) inserted by FA 2001 s 43(1)(*c*)(i)(II) with effect from 6 April 2001.
3 Subs (2)(*bb*) inserted by FA 2005 s 47(1)(*b*)(i)(I) with effect from 3 February 2005.
4 Deleted by FA 2000 s 30(1)(*c*)(i)(I) with effect from 6 April 2000; previously "or".
5 Subs (2)(*da*) inserted by FA 2001 s 43(1)(*c*)(i)(III) with effect from 6 April 2001.
6 Subs (2)(*db*) inserted by FA 2005 s 47(1)(*b*)(i)(II) with effect from 3 February 2005.
7 Substituted by FA 2000 s 30(1)(*c*)(i)(I) with effect from 6 April 2000; previously "Schedule 2A.".
8 Subss (2)(*f*)–(*g*) inserted by FA 2000 s 30(1)(*c*)(i)(II) with effect from 6 April 2000.
9 Deleted by FA 2001 s 43(1)(*c*)(ii)(I) with effect from 6 April 2001; previously "and".
10 Subs (3)(*ca*)–(*cb*) inserted by FA 2005 s 47(1)(*b*)(ii) with effect from 3 February 2005.
11 Subs (3)(*c*)–(*d*) inserted by FA 2001 s 43(1)(*c*)(ii)(II) with effect from 6 April 2001.
12 Subs (3) inserted by FA 2000 s 30(1)(*c*)(ii) with effect from 6 April 2000.
13 Section 172C inserted by FA 1999 s 27(*a*) with effect from 6 April 1999.

Cross-references

Declarations of exemption from dividend withholding tax, subs (2)(*a*): Sch 2A para 3; subs (2)(*b*): Sch 2A para 4; subs (2)(*ba*): Sch 2A para 4A; subs (2)(*bb*): Sch 2A para 10; subs (2)(*c*): Sch 2A para 5; subs (2)(*d*): Sch 2A para 6; subs (2)(*da*): Sch 2A para 6A; subs (2)(*db*): Sch 2A para 11; subs (2)(*e*)(i): Sch 2A para 7(*d*); subs (2)(*e*)(ii): Sch 2A para 7; subs (2)(*f*)(i): Sch 2A para 7A(*d*); subs (2)(*f*)(ii): Sch 2A para 7A; Subs (2)(*g*)(i): Sch 2A para 7B(*d*); subs (2)(*g*)(ii): Sch 2A para 7B.

Dividend withholding tax (interpretation), meaning of excluded person applied for purposes of Pt 6 Ch 8A and of Sch 2A: s 172A(1)(*a*).

Obligations of qualifying intermediary in relation to relevant distributions: s 172F(3)(*a*)(i), (7)(*a*)(iv).

Definitions

approved body of persons, approved minimum retirement fund, approved retirement fund, collective investment undertaking, designated broker: s 172A(1)(*a*); company: s 4(1); pension scheme: s 172A(1)(*a*); person: IA 1937 s:11(*c*); qualifying employee share ownership trust, qualifying fund manager, qualifying savings manager, relevant distribution, relevant person: s 172A(1)(*a*).

172D Exemption from dividend withholding tax for certain non-resident persons

[...[1]

(2) Section 172B shall not apply where, on or after the 6th day of April, 2000, a company resident in the State makes a relevant distribution to a qualifying non-resident person.

(3) For the purposes of this Chapter, a person shall be a qualifying non-resident person in relation to a relevant distribution if the person is beneficially entitled to the relevant distribution and is—

(*a*) a person, not being a company, who—

(i) is neither resident nor ordinarily resident in the State,

(ii) is, by virtue of the law of a relevant territory, resident for the purposes of tax in the relevant territory, and

(iii) has made a declaration to the relevant person in relation to the relevant distribution in accordance with paragraph 8 of Schedule 2A and in relation to which declaration the certificate referred to in subparagraph (*f*) of that paragraph is a current certificate (within the meaning of paragraph 2 of that Schedule) at the time of the making of the relevant distribution,

or

[(*b*) a company which is not resident in the State and—

(i) is, by virtue of the law of a relevant territory, resident for the purposes of tax in the relevant territory, but is not under the control, whether directly or indirectly, of a person or persons who is or are resident in the State,

(ii) is under the control, whether directly or indirectly, of a person or persons who, by virtue of the law of a relevant territory, is or are resident for the purposes of tax in the relevant territory and who is or are, as the case may be, not under the control, whether directly or indirectly, of a person who is, or persons who are, not so resident, or

(iii) the principal class of the shares of which, or—

(I) where the company is a 75 per cent subsidiary of another company, of that other company, or

(II) where the company is wholly-owned by 2 or more companies, of each of those companies,

is substantially and regularly traded on one or more than one recognised stock exchange in a relevant territory or territories or on such other stock exchange as may be approved of by the Minister for Finance for the purposes of this Chapter,

and which has made a declaration to the relevant person in relation to the relevant distribution in accordance with paragraph 9 of Schedule 2A and in relation to which declaration each of the certificates referred to in clause (i), the certificate referred to in clause (ii) or, as the case may be, the certificate referred to in clause (iii), of subparagraph (*f*) of that paragraph is a current certificate (within the meaning of paragraph 2 of that Schedule) at the time of the making of the relevant distribution.][2]

[(3A) For the purposes of subsection (3)(*b*)(i), "control" shall be construed in accordance with subsections (2) to (6) of section 432 as if in subsection (6) of that section for "5 or fewer participators" there were substituted "persons resident in the State".][3]

(4) For the purposes of [subsection (3)(*b*)(ii)],[4] "control" shall be construed in accordance with subsections (2) to (6) of section 432 as if in subsection (6) of that section for "5 or fewer participators" there were substituted—

(*a*) in so far as the first mention of "control" in [subsection (3)(*b*)(ii)][4] is concerned, "persons who, by virtue of the law of a relevant territory (within the meaning assigned by section 172A), are resident for the purposes of tax in such a relevant territory (within that meaning)", and

(*b*) in so far as the second mention of "control" in [subsection (3)(*b*)(ii)][4] is concerned, "persons who are not resident for the purposes of tax in a relevant territory (within that meaning)".

(5) For the purposes of [subsection (3)(*b*)(iii)(I)],[5] sections 412 to 418 shall apply as those sections would apply for the purposes of Chapter 5 of Part 12 if ...[6] section 411(1)(*c*) were deleted.

[(6) For the purposes of subsection (3)(*b*)(iii)(II), a company (in this subsection referred to as an "aggregated 100 per cent subsidiary") shall be treated as being wholly-owned by 2 or more companies (in this subsection referred to as the "joint parent companies") if and so long as 100 per cent of its ordinary share capital is owned directly or indirectly by the joint parent companies, and for the purposes of this subsection—

(*a*) subsections (2) to (10) of section 9 shall apply as those subsections apply for the purposes of that section, and

(*b*) sections 412 to 418 shall apply with any necessary modifications as those sections would apply for the purposes of Chapter 5 of Part 12—

(i) if section 411(1)(*c*) were deleted, and

(ii) if the following subsection were substituted for subsection (1) of section 412:

"(1) Notwithstanding that at any time a company is an aggregated 100 per cent subsidiary (within the meaning assigned by section 172D(6)) of the joint parent companies (within the meaning assigned by that section), it shall not be treated at that time as such a subsidiary unless additionally at that time—

(*a*) the joint parent companies are between them beneficially entitled to not less than 100 per cent of any profits available for distribution to equity holders of the company, and

(*b*) the joint parent companies would be beneficially entitled between them to not less than 100 per cent of any assets of the company available for distribution to its equity holders on a winding-up."]7][8]

Amendments

1 Subs (1) deleted by FA 2001 s 43(1)(*d*) with effect from 6 April 2001.

2 Subs (3)(*b*) substituted by FA 2000 s 30(1)(*d*)(i) with effect from 6 April 2000.

3 Subs (3A) inserted by FA 2000 s 30(1)(*d*)(ii) with effect from 6 April 2000.

4 Substituted by FA 2000 s 30(1)(*d*)(iii) with effect from 6 April 2000; previously "subsection (3)(*b*)(i)".

5 Substituted by FA 2000 s 30(1)(*d*)(iv)(I) with effect from 6 April 2000; previously "subsection (3)(*b*)(ii)(II)".

6 Deleted by FA 2000 s 30(1)(*d*)(iv)(II) with effect from 6 April 2000; previously "subparagraph (iii) of".

7 Subs (6) inserted by FA 2000 s 30(1)(*d*)(v) with effect from 6 April 2000.

8 Section 172D inserted by FA 1999 s 27(*a*) with effect from 6 April 1999.

Cross-references

Declaration of exemption from dividend withholding tax, subs (3)(*a*)(iii): Sch 2A para 8; subs (3)(*b*): Sch 2A para 9; subs (3A): Sch 2A para 9(*f*)(i); subs (4)(*a*), (*b*): Sch 2A para 9(*f*)(ii); subs (5), (6): Sch 2A para 9(*f*)(ii).

Dividend withholding tax (interpretation), meaning of qualifying non-resident person applied for purposes of Pt 6 Ch 8A and of Sch 2A: s 172A(1)(*a*).

Obligations of qualifying intermediary in relation to relevant distributions: s 172F(3)(*a*)(ii), (7)(*a*)(iv).

Definitions

company: s 4(1); intermediary: s 172A(1)(*a*); person: IA 1937 s 11(*c*); relevant distribution, relevant person, relevant territory, specified person, tax (in relation to a relevant territory, 75 per cent subsidiary: s 9.

172E Qualifying intermediaries

[(1) Subject to section 172F(6), section 172B shall not apply where a company resident in the State makes a relevant distribution through one or more than one qualifying intermediary for the benefit of a person beneficially entitled to the relevant distribution who is a non-liable person in relation to the relevant distribution.

(2) For the purposes of this Chapter, a person shall be a qualifying intermediary in relation to relevant distributions to be made to the person by a company resident in the State, and in relation to amounts or other assets representing such distributions to be paid or given to the person by another qualifying intermediary, if the person is an intermediary who—

(*a*) is resident in the State or who, by virtue of the law of a relevant territory, is resident for the purposes of tax in the relevant territory,

(*b*) has entered into a qualifying intermediary agreement with the Revenue Commissioners, and

(*c*) has been authorised by the Revenue Commissioners, by way of notice in writing, to be a qualifying intermediary in relation to relevant distributions to be made to the person by companies resident in the State, and in relation to amounts or other assets representing such distributions to be paid or given to the person by another qualifying intermediary, for the benefit of other persons who are beneficially entitled to the relevant distributions, which authorisation has not been revoked under subsection (6).

(3) A qualifying intermediary agreement shall be an agreement entered into between the Revenue Commissioners and an intermediary under the terms of which the intermediary undertakes—

[(*a*) to accept, and to retain for the longer of the following periods—

(i) a period of 6 years, or

(ii) a period which, in relation to the relevant distributions in respect of which the declaration or notification is made or, as the case may be, given, ends not earlier than 3 years after the date on which the intermediary has ceased to receive relevant distributions on behalf of the person who made the declaration or, as the case may be, gave the notification to the intermediary,

all declarations (and accompanying certificates) and notifications (not being a notice given to the intermediary by the Revenue Commissioners) which are made or, as the case may be, given to the intermediary in accordance with this Chapter and Schedule 2A,

(*b*) on being so required by notice in writing given to the intermediary by the Revenue Commissioners, to make available to the Commissioners, within the time specified in the notice—

(i) all declarations, certificates or notifications referred to in paragraph (*a*) which have been made or, as the case may be, given to the intermediary, or

(ii) such class or classes of such declarations, certificates or notifications as may be specified in the notice,][1]

(*c*) to inform the Revenue Commissioners if the intermediary has reasonable grounds to believe that any such declaration or notification made or given by any person was not, or may not have been, a true and correct declaration or notification at the time of the making of the declaration or the giving of the notification, as the case may be,

(*d*) to inform the Revenue Commissioners if the intermediary has at any time reasonable grounds to believe that any such declaration made by any person would not, or might not, be a true and correct declaration if made at that time,

(*e*) to operate the provisions of section 172F in a correct and efficient manner and provide to the Revenue Commissioners the return referred to in subsection (7) of that section within the time specified in that behalf in subsection (8) of that section,

[(*f*) to provide to the Revenue Commissioners, not later than 3 months after the end of the first year of the operation of the agreement by the intermediary, a report on the intermediary's compliance with the agreement in that year, which report shall be signed by—

(i) if the intermediary is a company, the auditor of the company, or

(ii) if the intermediary is not a company, a person who, if the intermediary were a company, would be qualified to be appointed auditor of the company,

and thereafter, on being required by notice in writing given to the intermediary by the Revenue Commissioners, to provide to the Commissioners, within the time specified in the notice, a similar report in relation to such other period of the operation of the agreement by the intermediary as may be specified in the notice,][2]

(*g*) if required by the Revenue Commissioners, to give a bond or guarantee to the Revenue Commissioners which is sufficient to indemnify the Commissioners against any loss arising by virtue of the fraud or negligence of the intermediary in relation to the operation by the intermediary of the agreement and the provisions of this Chapter,

(*h*) in the case where the intermediary is a depositary bank holding shares in trust for, or on behalf of, the holders of American depositary receipts—

(i) if authorised to do so by the Revenue Commissioners, to operate the provisions of subsection (3)(*d*) of section 172F, and

(ii) to comply with any conditions in relation to such operation as may be specified in the agreement,

and

(*i*) to allow for the verification by the Revenue Commissioners of the intermediary's compliance with the agreement and the provisions of this Chapter in any other manner considered necessary by the Commissioners.

[(3A) The Revenue Commissioners may examine or take extracts from or copies of any declarations, certificates or notifications made available to the Commissioners under subsection (3)(*b*).][3]

(4) The Revenue Commissioners shall not authorise an intermediary to be a qualifying intermediary unless the intermediary—

(*a*) is a company which holds a licence granted under section 9 of the Central Bank Act, 1971, or a person who holds a licence or other similar authorisation under the law of any relevant territory which corresponds to that section,

(*b*) is a person who is wholly owned by a company or person referred to in paragraph (*a*),

(*c*) is a member firm of the Irish Stock Exchange Limited or of a recognised stock exchange in a relevant territory, or

(*d*) is in the opinion of the Revenue Commissioners a person suitable to be a qualifying intermediary for the purposes of this Chapter.

(5) The Revenue Commissioners shall maintain a list of intermediaries who have been authorised by the Commissioners to be qualifying intermediaries for the purposes of this Chapter and whose authorisations have not been revoked under subsection (6), and, notwithstanding any obligations as to secrecy or other restriction upon disclosure of information imposed by or under any statute or otherwise, the Revenue Commissioners may make available to any person the name and address of any such qualifying intermediary.

(6) Where, at any time after the Revenue Commissioners have authorised an intermediary to be a qualifying intermediary for the purposes of this Chapter, the Commissioners are satisfied that the intermediary—

(*a*) has failed to comply with the agreement referred to in subsection (3) or the provisions of this Chapter, or

(*b*) is otherwise unsuitable to be a qualifying intermediary,

they may, by notice in writing served by registered post on the intermediary, revoke the authorisation with effect from such date as may be specified in the notice.

(7) Notice of a revocation under subsection (6) shall be published as soon as may be in Iris Oifigiúil.

[(8) Without prejudice to the operation of subsection (6), the authorisation by the Revenue Commissioners of an intermediary as a qualifying intermediary for the purposes of this Chapter shall cease to have effect on the day before the seventh anniversary of the date from which such authorisation applied; but this shall not prevent—

(*a*) the intermediary and the Revenue Commissioners from agreeing to renew the qualifying intermediary agreement entered into between them in accordance with subsection (3) or to enter into a further such agreement, and

(*b*) a further authorisation by the Revenue Commissioners of the intermediary as a qualifying intermediary for the purposes of this Chapter.][4][5]

Amendments

1 Subs (3)(*a*)–(*b*) substituted by FA 2000 s 30(1)(*e*)(i)(I) with effect from 6 April 2000.

2 Subs (3)(*f*) substituted by FA 2000 s 30(1)(*e*)(i)(II) with effect from 6 April 2000.

3 Subs (3A) inserted by FA 2000 s 30(1)(*e*)(ii) with effect from 6 April 2000.

4 Subs (8) inserted FA 2000 s 30(1)(*e*)(iii) with effect from 6 April 2000.

5 Section 172E inserted by FA 1999 s 27(*a*) with effect from 6 April 1999.

Cross-references

Dividend withholding tax (interpretation), meaning of qualifying intermediary applied for purposes of Pt 6 Ch 8A and of Sch 2A: s 172(1)(*a*).

Obligations of qualifying intermediary in relation to relevant distributions, subs (1): s 172F(5); subs (4)(*a*), (*b*), (*c*), (*d*): s 172F(2)(*e*).

Definitions

American depositary receipt, auditor: s 172A(1)(*a*); company: s 4(1); intermediary: s 172A(1); month: IA 1937 Sch; non-liable person: s 172A(1)(*a*); person: IA 1937 s 11(*c*); relevant distribution, relevant territory, tax (in relation to a relevant territory: s 172A(1)(*a*); writing, year: IA 1937 Sch.

172F Obligations of qualifying intermediaries in relation to relevant distributions

[(1) A qualifying intermediary which is to receive on behalf of other persons—

(*a*) any relevant distributions to be made by any company resident in the State, or

(*b*) from another qualifying intermediary amounts or other assets (in this section referred to as "payments") representing such distributions,

shall create and maintain, in relation to such distributions and payments, 2 separate and distinct categories to be known, respectively, as the "Exempt Fund" and the "Liable Fund", and the qualifying intermediary shall notify that company or that other qualifying intermediary, as the case may be, by way of notice in writing, whether the relevant distributions to be made to it by that company, or, as the case may be, the payments representing such distributions to be made to it by that other qualifying intermediary, are to be received by it for the benefit of a person included in the Exempt Fund or a person included in the Liable Fund.

(2) Subject to subsections (3) and (5), a qualifying intermediary shall include in its Exempt Fund in relation to such distributions and payments only those persons on whose behalf it is to receive such distributions or payments, being—

(*a*) persons beneficially entitled to such distributions or payments who are non-liable persons in relation to such distributions, and

(*b*) any further qualifying intermediary to whom such distributions or payments (or amounts or other assets representing such distributions or payments) are to be given by the qualifying intermediary and are to be received by that further qualifying intermediary for the benefit of persons included in that further qualifying intermediary's Exempt Fund.

(3) (*a*) A qualifying intermediary shall not include a person referred to in subsection (2)(*a*) in its Exempt Fund unless it has received from that person—

(i) a declaration made by that person in accordance with section 172C(2), or

(ii) a declaration made by that person in accordance with section 172D(3) in relation to which—

(I) the certificate referred to in paragraph 8(*f*) of Schedule 2A is a current certificate (within the meaning of paragraph 2 of that Schedule), or

(II) the certificates referred to in [paragraph 9(*f*)][1] of that Schedule are current certificates (within the meaning of paragraph 2 of that Schedule),

as the case may be, at the time of the making of the relevant distributions.

(*b*) A qualifying intermediary shall not include a further qualifying intermediary referred to in subsection (2)(*b*) in its Exempt Fund unless the qualifying intermediary has received from that further qualifying intermediary a notification in writing given to the qualifying intermediary by that further qualifying intermediary in accordance with subsection (1) to the effect that the relevant distributions made by the company resident in the State, or, as the case may be, the payments representing such distributions, which are to be given by the qualifying intermediary to that further qualifying intermediary are to be received by that further qualifying intermediary for the benefit of a person included in that further qualifying intermediary's Exempt Fund.

(*c*) Notwithstanding paragraphs (*a*) and (*b*), a qualifying intermediary, being a depositary bank holding shares in trust for, or on behalf of, the holders of American depositary receipts, shall, if provided for in the qualifying intermediary agreement and subject to any conditions specified in that agreement, operate the provisions of paragraph (*d*).

(*d*) Where this paragraph applies in relation to a qualifying intermediary, the qualifying intermediary shall include in its Exempt Fund—

(i) any person on whose behalf it is to receive any relevant distributions to be made by a company resident in the State, or on whose behalf it is to receive from another qualifying intermediary payments representing such distributions, being a person who is beneficially entitled to such distributions or payments, who is the holder of an American depositary receipt and whose address on the qualifying intermediary's register of depositary receipts is located in the United States of America, and

(ii) any specified intermediary to which such distributions or payments (or amounts or other assets representing such distributions or payments) are to be given by the qualifying intermediary and are to be received by that specified intermediary for the benefit of—

(I) persons who are beneficially entitled to such distributions or payments, who are the holders of American depositary receipts, whose address on that specified intermediary's register of depositary receipts is located in the United States of America, and who in accordance with paragraph (*e*)(iii)(I) are to be included in that specified intermediary's Exempt Fund, or

(II) any further specified intermediary to which such distributions or payments (or amounts or other assets representing such distributions or payments) are to be given by the first-mentioned specified intermediary and are to be received by that further specified intermediary for the benefit of persons who in accordance with clauses (I) and (II) of paragraph (*e*)(iii) are to be included in that further specified intermediary's Exempt Fund.

(*e*) [For the purposes of this section, but subject to paragraphs (*g*) and (*h*)],[2] an intermediary shall be treated as a specified intermediary if the intermediary—

(i) is not a qualifying intermediary but is a person referred to in paragraph (*a*), (*b*), (*c*) or (*d*) of section 172E(4) who is operating as an intermediary in an establishment situated in the United States of America,

(ii) creates and maintains, in relation to such distributions or payments (or amounts or other assets representing such distributions or payments) to be received by it on behalf of other persons from a qualifying intermediary or another specified intermediary, an Exempt Fund and a Liable Fund in accordance with subsections (1) and (5), but subject to subparagraphs (iii) and (iv), as if it were a qualifying intermediary,

(iii) includes in its Exempt Fund in relation to such distributions or payments (or amounts or other assets representing such distributions or payments), only—

(I) those persons who are beneficially entitled to such distributions or payments, being persons who are the holders of American depositary receipts and whose address on its register of depositary receipts is located in the United States of America, and

(II) any further specified intermediary to which such distributions or payments (or amounts or other assets representing such distributions or payments) are to be given by the intermediary and are to be received by that further specified intermediary for the benefit of persons who in accordance with this subparagraph are to be included in that further specified intermediary's Exempt Fund,

(iv) includes in its Liable Fund in relation to such distributions or payments (or amounts or other assets representing such distributions or payments), all other persons (being persons who are the holders of American depositary receipts) on whose behalf such distributions or payments (or amounts or other assets representing such distributions or payments) are to be received by it from a qualifying intermediary or a further specified intermediary, other than those persons included in its Exempt Fund,

(v) notifies, [by way of notice in writing or in electronic format],[3] the qualifying intermediary or, as the case may be, the further specified intermediary from whom it is to receive, on behalf of other persons, such distributions or payments (or amounts or other assets representing such distributions or payments), whether such distributions or payments (or amounts or other assets representing such distributions or payments) are to be so received by it for the benefit of persons included in its Exempt Fund or persons included in its [Liable Fund, and][4]

[(vi) enters into an agreement with the qualifying intermediary or further specified intermediary, as the case may be, under the terms of which it agrees that if and when required to comply with subsection (7A) it will do so.][5]

(*f*) Where, by virtue of the preceding provisions of this subsection, any person, being a person who, apart from this paragraph, would not be a non-liable person in relation to the distributions or payments (or amounts or other assets representing such distributions or payments) to be received on that person's behalf by a qualifying intermediary or a specified intermediary, is included in the Exempt Fund of the qualifying intermediary or, as the case may be, of the specified intermediary, that person shall, notwithstanding any other provision of this Chapter, be treated as a non-liable person in relation to such distributions.

[(*g*) Notwithstanding paragraph (*e*), where the Revenue Commissioners are satisfied that an intermediary, being a specified intermediary or other specified intermediary referred to in subsection (7A), has failed to comply with that subsection—

(i) the Commissioners may, by notice in writing given to the intermediary, notify it that it shall cease to be treated as a specified intermediary for the purposes of this section from such date as may be specified in the notice, and

(ii) notwithstanding any obligations as to secrecy or other restriction upon disclosure of information imposed by or under statute or otherwise, the Commissioners may make available to any qualifying intermediary (being a depositary bank holding shares in trust for, or on behalf of, the holders of American depositary receipts) or specified intermediary a copy of such notice.

(*h*) Where subsequently the Revenue Commissioners are satisfied that the intermediary has furnished the information required under subsection (7A) and will in future comply with that subsection if and when requested to do so, the Commissioners may, by further notice in writing given to the intermediary, revoke the notice given to the intermediary under paragraph (*g*) from such date as may be specified in the further notice, and a copy of that further notice shall be given to any person to whom a copy of the notice under paragraph (*g*) was given.][6]

(4) Subject to subsection (5), a qualifying intermediary shall include in its Liable Fund in relation to relevant distributions to be made to it by a company resident in the State and payments representing such distributions to be made to it by another qualifying intermediary all persons on whose behalf the qualifying intermediary is to receive such distributions or payments, other than those persons included in its Exempt Fund in relation to such distributions and payments.

(5) A qualifying intermediary shall update its Exempt Fund and Liable Fund, in relation to relevant distributions to be made to it by a company resident in the State and payments representing such distributions to be made to it by another qualifying intermediary, as often as may be necessary to ensure that the provisions of section 172E(1) and subsections (2) to (4) of this section are complied with, and shall notify the company or, as the case may be, that other qualifying intermediary, by way of notice in writing, of all such updates.

(6) Where at any time a company resident in the State makes a relevant distribution to a qualifying intermediary and, apart from this subsection, the relevant distribution would be treated as being made to the qualifying intermediary for the benefit of a person beneficially entitled to the relevant distribution who is a non-liable person in relation to that distribution, the distribution shall be treated as if it were not made to the qualifying intermediary for the benefit of such a person unless, at or before that time, the qualifying intermediary has notified the company in accordance with subsection (1) or (5), as the case may be, that the relevant distribution is to be received by the qualifying

intermediary for the benefit of a person included in the qualifying intermediary's Exempt Fund in relation to relevant distributions to be made to the qualifying intermediary by the company, and accordingly, in the absence of such a notification, section 172B shall apply in relation to the relevant distribution.

[(7) (*a*) A qualifying intermediary shall, on being so required by notice in writing given to the qualifying intermediary by the Revenue Commissioners, make a return to the Commissioners, within the time specified in the notice (which shall not be less than 30 days) and as respects such year of assessment as may be specified in the notice (being the year of assessment 1999–2000 or any subsequent year of assessment), showing—

(i) the name and address of—

(I) each company resident in the State from which the qualifying intermediary received, on behalf of another person, a relevant distribution made by that company in the year of assessment to which the return refers, and

(II) each other person from whom the qualifying intermediary received, on behalf of another person, an amount or other asset representing a relevant distribution made by a company resident in the State in the year of assessment to which the return refers,

(ii) the amount of each such relevant distribution,

(iii) the name and address of each person to whom such a relevant distribution, or an amount or other asset representing such a relevant distribution, has been given by the qualifying intermediary, and

(iv) the name and address of each person referred to in subparagraph (iii) in respect of whom a declaration under section 172C(2) or 172D(3) has been received by the qualifying intermediary.

(*b*) A return required to be made by a qualifying intermediary under paragraph (*a*) may be confined to such class or classes of relevant distributions as may be specified in the notice given to the qualifying intermediary by the Revenue Commissioners under that paragraph.

(7A)(*a*) This subsection shall apply where a qualifying intermediary has been required to make a return to the Revenue Commissioners under subsection (7)(*a*) and a relevant distribution (or an amount or other asset representing a relevant distribution), the details of which are required to be included in that return, has been given by the qualifying intermediary to a specified intermediary.

(*b*) The qualifying intermediary shall, immediately on receipt of the notice referred to in subsection (7)(*a*), request the specified intermediary, by way of notice in writing or in electronic format, to notify the qualifying intermediary or the Revenue Commissioners of the name and address of each person to whom the specified intermediary gave such a distribution (or an amount or other asset representing such a distribution) and of the amount of each such distribution.

(*c*) The specified intermediary shall, within 21 days of the receipt of a notice under paragraph (*b*), furnish to the qualifying intermediary or, at the discretion of the specified intermediary, to the Revenue Commissioners, by way of notice in writing or in electronic format, the information required under that paragraph.

(*d*) Where the specified intermediary furnishes the information required under paragraph (*b*)—

(i) to the qualifying intermediary, the qualifying intermediary shall include that information in the return required to be made by it under subsection (7)(*a*), or

(ii) to the Revenue Commissioners, the specified intermediary shall, by way of notice in writing or in electronic format, immediately advise the qualifying intermediary of that fact and the qualifying intermediary shall include in the return required to be made by it under subsection (7)(*a*) a statement to the effect that it has been so advised by the specified intermediary.

(*e*) If any person to whom a specified intermediary gave such a distribution (or an amount or other asset representing such a distribution) is another specified intermediary, the specified intermediary shall, immediately on the receipt of a notice under paragraph (*b*), request the other specified intermediary, by way of notice in writing or in electronic format, to notify the specified intermediary or the Revenue Commissioners of the name and address of each person to whom it gave such a distribution (or an amount or other asset representing such a distribution) and of the amount of each such distribution.

(*f*) The other specified intermediary shall, within 21 days of the receipt of a notice under paragraph (*e*), furnish to the specified intermediary or, at the discretion of the other specified intermediary, to the Revenue Commissioners, by way of notice in writing or in electronic format, the information required under that paragraph.

(*g*) Where the other specified intermediary furnishes the information required under paragraph (*e*)—

(i) to the specified intermediary, the specified intermediary shall, by way of notice in writing or in electronic format, immediately transmit that information to the person referred to in paragraph (*d*) (being the qualifying intermediary or the Revenue Commissioners, as the case may be) to whom it furnishes the information required under paragraph (*b*), and—

(I) if that person is the qualifying intermediary, the qualifying intermediary shall include that information in the return required to be made by it under subsection (7)(*a*), or

(II) if that person is the Revenue Commissioners, the specified intermediary shall, by way of notice in writing or in electronic format, immediately advise the qualifying intermediary of the fact that the information required to be furnished by the other specified intermediary under paragraph (*e*) has been furnished to the specified intermediary and transmitted by the specified intermediary to the Revenue Commissioners in accordance with this paragraph and the qualifying intermediary shall include in the return to be made by it under subsection (7)(*a*) a statement to the effect that it has been so advised by the specified intermediary,

or

(ii) to the Revenue Commissioners, the other specified intermediary shall, by way of notice in writing or in electronic format, immediately advise the specified intermediary of that fact, the specified intermediary shall in turn, by way of similar notice, immediately advise the qualifying intermediary of that fact and the qualifying intermediary shall include in the return required to be made by it under subsection (7)(*a*) a statement to the effect that it has been so advised by the specified intermediary.

(*h*) Where, in accordance with this subsection, the specified intermediary or the other specified intermediary furnishes information to the Revenue Commissioners in electronic format, such format shall be agreed in advance with the Revenue Commissioners.][7]

(8) Subject to subsection (9), every return by a qualifying intermediary under subsection (7) shall be made ...[8] in an electronic format approved by the Revenue Commissioners and shall be accompanied by a declaration made by the qualifying intermediary, on a form prescribed or authorised for that purpose by the Revenue Commissioners, to the effect that the return is correct and complete.

(9) Where the Revenue Commissioners are satisfied that a qualifying intermediary does not have the facilities to make a return under subsection (7) in the format referred to in subsection (8), the return shall be made in writing in a form prescribed or authorised by the Revenue Commissioners and shall be accompanied by a declaration made by the qualifying intermediary, on a form prescribed or authorised for that purpose by the Revenue Commissioners, to the effect that the return is correct and complete.][9]

Amendments

1 Substituted by FA 2001 s 43(1)(*e*) with effect from 6 April 2001; previously "subparagraphs (*f*) and (*g*) of paragraph 9".

2 Substituted by FA 2000 s 30(1)(*f*)(i)(I) with effect from 6 April 2000; previously "For the purposes of paragraph (*d*)".

3 Substituted by FA 2000 s 30(1)(*f*)(i)(II) with effect from 6 April 2000; previously "by way of notice in writing given in accordance with subsection (1)".

4 Substituted by FA 2000 s 30(1)(*f*)(i)(II) with effect from 6 April 2000; previously "Liable Fund,".

5 Subs (3)(*e*)(vi) and (vii) substituted by FA 2000 s 30(1)(*f*)(i)(III) with effect from 6 April 2000.

6 Subs (3)(*g*)–(*h*) inserted by FA 2000 s 30(1)(*f*)(i)(IV) with effect from 6 April 2000.

7 Subs (7) substituted by FA 2000 s 30(1)(*f*)(ii) with effect from 6 April 2000.

8 Deleted by FA 2000 s 30(1)(*f*)(iii) with effect from 6 April 2000; previously ", not later than the 21st day of May following the year of assessment to which the return refers,".

9 Section 172F inserted by FA 1999 s 27(*a*) with effect from 6 April 1999.

Cross-references

Qualifying intermediaries, subs (6): s 172E(1).

Definitions

American depositary receipt: s 172A(1)(*a*); company: s 4(1); non-liable person: s 172A(1)(*a*); person: IA 1937 s 11(*c*); qualifying intermediary, relevant distribution: s 172A(1)(*a*); writing: IA 1937 Sch; year of assessment: s 2(1).

172G Authorised withholding agent

[(1) Subject to section 172H, section 172B shall not apply where a company resident in the State makes a relevant distribution to an authorised withholding agent for the benefit of a person beneficially entitled to the relevant distribution, not being the authorised withholding agent.

(2) For the purposes of this Chapter, a person shall be an authorised withholding agent in relation to relevant distributions to be made to the person by a company resident in the State if the person is an intermediary who—

(*a*) (i) is resident in the State, or

(ii) if not resident in the State, is, by virtue of the law of a relevant territory, resident for the purposes of tax in the relevant territory, and carries on through a branch or agency in the State a trade which consists of or includes the receipt of relevant distributions from a company or companies resident in the State on behalf of other persons,

(*b*) has entered into an authorised withholding agent agreement with the Revenue Commissioners, and

(*c*) has been authorised by the Revenue Commissioners, by way of notice in writing, to be an authorised withholding agent in relation to relevant distributions to be made to the person by companies resident in the State for the benefit of other persons who are beneficially entitled to the relevant distributions, which authorisation has not been revoked under subsection (6).

(3) An authorised withholding agent agreement shall be an agreement entered into between the Revenue Commissioners and an intermediary under the terms of which the intermediary undertakes—

[(*a*) to accept, and to retain for the longer of the following periods—

(i) a period of 6 years, or

(ii) a period which, in relation to the relevant distributions in respect of which the declaration or notification is made or, as the case may be, given, ends not earlier than 3 years after the date on which the intermediary has ceased to receive relevant distributions on behalf of the person who made the declaration or, as the case may be, gave the notification to the intermediary,

all declarations (and accompanying certificates) and notifications (not being a notice given to the intermediary by the Revenue Commissioners) which are made or, as the case may be, given to the intermediary in accordance with this Chapter and Schedule 2A,

(*b*) on being so required by notice in writing given to the intermediary by the Revenue Commissioners, to make available to the Commissioners, within the time specified in the notice—

(i) all declarations, certificates or notifications referred to in paragraph (*a*) which have been made or, as the case may be, given to the intermediary, or

(ii) such class or classes of such declarations, certificates or notifications as may be specified in the notice,][1]

(*c*) to inform the Revenue Commissioners if the intermediary has reasonable grounds to believe that any such declaration or notification made or given by any person was not, or may not have been, a true and correct declaration or notification at the time of the making of the declaration or the giving of the notification, as the case may be,

(*d*) to inform the Revenue Commissioners if the intermediary has at any time reasonable grounds to believe that any such declaration made by any person would not, or might not, be a true and correct declaration if made at that time,

(*e*) to operate the provisions of section 172H in a correct and efficient manner,

(*f*) to provide to the Collector-General the return referred to in section 172K(1), and to pay to the Collector-General any dividend withholding tax required to be included in such a return, within the time specified in that behalf in that section,

[(*g*) to provide to the Revenue Commissioners, not later than 3 months after the end of the first year of the operation of the agreement by the intermediary, a report on the intermediary's compliance with the agreement in that year, which report shall be signed by—

(i) if the intermediary is a company, the auditor of the company, or

(ii) if the intermediary is not a company, a person who, if the intermediary were a company, would be qualified to be appointed auditor of the company,

and thereafter, on being required by notice in writing given to the intermediary by the Revenue Commissioners, to provide to the Commissioners, within the time specified in the notice, a similar report in relation to such other period of the operation of the agreement by the intermediary as may be specified in the notice,

and][2]

(*h*) to allow for the verification by the Revenue Commissioners of the intermediary's compliance with the agreement and the provisions of this Chapter in any other manner considered necessary by the Commissioners.

[(3A) The Revenue Commissioners may examine or take extracts from or copies of any declarations, certificates or notifications made available to the Commissioners under subsection (3)(*b*).][3]

(4) The Revenue Commissioners shall not authorise an intermediary to be an authorised withholding agent unless the intermediary—

(*a*) is a company which holds a licence granted under section 9 of the Central Bank Act, 1971, or a person who holds a licence or other similar authorisation under the law of any relevant territory which corresponds to that section,

(*b*) is a person who is wholly owned by a company or person referred to in paragraph (*a*),

(*c*) is a member of the Irish Stock Exchange Limited or of a recognised stock exchange in a relevant territory, or

(*d*) is in the opinion of the Revenue Commissioners a person suitable to be an authorised withholding agent for the purposes of this Chapter.

(5) The Revenue Commissioners shall maintain a list of intermediaries who have been authorised by the Commissioners to be authorised withholding agents for the purposes of this Chapter and whose authorisations have not been revoked under subsection (6),

and, notwithstanding any obligation as to secrecy or other restriction upon disclosure of information imposed by or under any statute or otherwise, the Revenue Commissioners may make available to any person the name and address of any such authorised withholding agent.

(6) Where, at any time after the Revenue Commissioners have authorised an intermediary to be an authorised withholding agent for the purposes of this Chapter, the Commissioners are satisfied that the intermediary—

(*a*) has failed to comply with the agreement referred to in subsection (3) or the provisions of this Chapter, or

(*b*) is otherwise unsuitable to be an authorised withholding agent,

they may, by notice in writing served by registered post on the intermediary, revoke the authorisation with effect from such date as may be specified in the notice.

(7) Notice of a revocation under subsection (6) shall be published as soon as may be in Iris Oifigiúil.

[(8) Without prejudice to the operation of subsection (6), the authorisation by the Revenue Commissioners of an intermediary as an authorised withholding agent for the purposes of this Chapter shall cease to have effect on the day before the seventh anniversary of the date from which such authorisation applied; but this shall not prevent—

(*a*) the intermediary and the Revenue Commissioners from agreeing to renew the authorised withholding agent agreement entered into between them in accordance with subsection (3) or to enter into a further such agreement, and

(*b*) a further authorisation by the Revenue Commissioners of the intermediary as an authorised withholding agent for the purposes of this Chapter.][4]][5]

Amendments

1 Subs (3)(*a*)–(*b*) substituted by FA 2000 s 30(1)(*g*)(i)(I) with effect from 6 April 2000.

2 Subs (3)(*g*) substituted by FA 2000 s 30(1)(*g*)(i)(II) with effect from 6 April 2000.

3 Subs (3A) inserted by FA 2000 s 30(1)(*g*)(ii) with effect from 6 April 2000.

4 Subs (8) inserted by FA 2000 s 30(1)(*g*)(iii) with effect from 6 April 2000.

5 Section 172G inserted by FA 1999 s 27(*a*) with effect from 6 April 1999.

Cross-references

Dividend withholding tax (interpretation), meaning of authorised withholding agent applied for purposes of Pt 6 Ch 8A and of Sch 2A: s 172A(1)(a).

Definitions

auditor: s 172A(1)(*a*); Collector-General: ss 2(1), 851; company: s 4(1); dividend withholding tax, intermediary: s 172A(1)(*a*); month: IA 1937 Sch; person: IA 1937 s 11(*c*); relevant distribution, relevant territory, tax (in relation to a relevant territory): s 172A(1)(*a*); writing: IA 1937 Sch.

172H Obligations of authorised withholding agent in relation to relevant distributions

[(1) An authorised withholding agent which is to receive, on behalf of other persons, any relevant distributions to be made to it by any company resident in the State shall notify that company, by way of notice in writing, that it is an authorised withholding agent in relation to those distributions.

(2) Where an authorised withholding agent receives, on behalf of another person, a relevant distribution from a company resident in the State, and gives that distribution, or an amount or other asset representing that distribution, to that other person, this Chapter shall apply, with any necessary modifications, as if—

(*a*) the authorised withholding agent were the company which made the distribution, and

(*b*) the giving by the authorised withholding agent of the relevant distribution, or an amount or other asset representing that distribution, to that other person were the making of the relevant distribution by the authorised withholding agent to that other person at the time of the making of the relevant distribution to the authorised withholding agent by the company,

and accordingly, except where otherwise provided by this Chapter, section 172B shall apply in relation to that relevant distribution and the authorised withholding agent shall be obliged to pay and account for the dividend withholding tax (if any) due in relation to the relevant distribution.

(3) Where at any time a company resident in the State makes a relevant distribution to a person and, apart from this subsection, the relevant distribution would be treated as being made to an authorised withholding agent for the benefit of another person, the distribution shall be treated as if it were not made to the authorised withholding agent for the benefit of that other person unless, at or before that time, the authorised withholding agent has notified the company in accordance with subsection (1) that it is an authorised withholding agent in relation to the relevant distribution, and accordingly, in the absence of such a notification, section 172B shall apply in relation to the relevant distribution.][1]

Amendments

1 Section 172H inserted by FA 1999 s 27(*a*) with effect from 6 April 1999.

Cross-references

Authorised withholding agent: s 172G(1), (3)(*e*).

Power of inspection, returns and collection of dividend withholding tax: s 904I(1)(*b*).

Returns, payment and collection of dividend withholding tax: s 172K(1), (1)(*g*).

Definitions

authorised withholding agent: s 172A(1)(*a*); company: s 4(1); dividend withholding tax: s 172A(1)(*a*); person: IA 1937 s 11(*c*); relevant distribution: s 172A(1)(*a*); writing: IA 1937 Sch.

172I Statement to be given to recipients of relevant distributions

[(1) Every person (in this section referred to as "the payer") who makes, or who (being an authorised withholding agent) is treated as making, a relevant distribution shall, at the time of the making of the relevant distribution or, in the case of an authorised withholding agent, at the time of the giving by the authorised withholding agent of the relevant distribution, or an amount or other asset representing that distribution, to another person, give the recipient of the relevant distribution or, as the case may be, that other person a statement in writing showing—

(*a*) the name and address of the payer and, if the payer is not the company making the relevant distribution, the name and address of that company,

(*b*) the name and address of the person to whom the relevant distribution is made,

(*c*) the date the relevant distribution is made,
(*d*) the amount of the relevant distribution, and
(*e*) the amount of the dividend withholding tax (if any) deducted in relation to the relevant distribution.

(2) The requirements of subsection (1) shall be satisfied by the inclusion of the information referred to in that subsection in a statement in writing made in relation to the distribution in accordance with section 152(1).

(3) Where a person fails to comply with any of the provisions of subsection (1), subsection (2) of section 152 shall apply as it applies where a company fails to comply with any of the provisions of subsection (1) of that section.][1]

Amendments

[1] Section 172I inserted by FA 1999 s 27(*a*) with effect from 6 April 1999.

Cross-references

Credit for, or repayment of, dividend withholding tax: s 172J(4).

Definitions

authorised withholding agent, dividend withholding tax: s 172A(1)(*a*); person: IA 1937 s 11(*c*); relevant distribution: s 172A(1)(*a*); writing: IA 1937 Sch.

172J Credit for, or repayment of, dividend withholding tax borne

[(1) Where, in relation to any year of assessment, a person is within the charge to income tax and has borne dividend withholding tax in relation to a relevant distribution to which the person is beneficially entitled which tax is referable to that year of assessment, the person may claim to have that dividend withholding tax set against income tax chargeable for that year of assessment and, where that dividend withholding tax exceeds such income tax, to have the excess refunded to the person.

(2) Where, in relation to any year of assessment, a person is not within the charge to income tax and has borne dividend withholding tax in relation to a relevant distribution to which the person is beneficially entitled which tax is referable to that year of assessment, the person may claim to have the amount of that dividend withholding tax refunded to the person.

(3) Where a person has borne dividend withholding tax in relation to a relevant distribution to which the person is beneficially entitled, and the person—

(*a*) is a non-liable person in relation to the relevant distribution, or
(*b*) would have been a non-liable person in relation to the relevant distribution if the requirement for the person to make the appropriate declaration referred to in Schedule 2A had not been necessary,

the person may claim to have the amount of that dividend withholding tax refunded to the person.

(4) A person making a claim under this section shall furnish, in respect of each amount of dividend withholding tax to which the claim relates, the statement in writing given to the person in accordance with section 172I(1) by the person who made, or who (being an authorised withholding agent) was treated as making, the relevant distribution in relation to which the dividend withholding tax was deducted.

(5) The Revenue Commissioners shall not authorise the setting-off of dividend withholding tax against income tax chargeable on a person for a year of assessment, or pay a refund of dividend withholding tax to a person, unless the Commissioners receive such evidence as they consider necessary that the person is entitled to that setting-off or refund.][1]

Amendments

1 Section 172J inserted by FA 1999 s 27(*a*) with effect from 6 April 1999.

Definitions

dividend withholding tax: s 172A(1)(*a*); person: IA 1937 s 11(*c*); relevant distribution: s 172A(1)(*a*); year of assessment: s 2(1); writing: IA 1937 Sch.

172K Returns, payment and collection of dividend withholding tax

[(1) Any person (in this section referred to as "the accountable person"), being a company resident in the State which makes, or an authorised withholding agent who is treated under section 172H as making, any relevant distributions to specified persons in any month shall, within 14 days of the end of that month, make a return to the Collector-General which shall contain details of—

(*a*) the name and tax reference number of the company which actually made the relevant distributions,

(*b*) if different from the company which actually made the relevant distributions, the name of the accountable person, being an authorised withholding agent, in relation to those distributions,

(*c*) the name and address of each person to whom a relevant distribution was made or, as the case may be, was treated as being made by the accountable person in the month to which the return refers,

(*d*) the date on which the relevant distribution was made to that person,

(*e*) the amount of the relevant distribution made to that person,

(*f*) the amount of the dividend withholding tax (if any) in relation to the relevant distribution deducted by the accountable person or, as the case may be, the amount (if any) to be paid to the Collector-General by the accountable person in relation to that distribution as if it were a deduction of dividend withholding tax, ...[1]

(*g*) the aggregate of the amounts referred to in paragraph (*f*) in relation to all relevant distributions made or treated under section 172H as being made by the accountable person to specified persons in the month to which the return [refers, and][2]

[(*h*) in a case where section 172B has not applied to a relevant distribution by virtue of the operation of subsection (7) of that section, whether the relevant distribution is a distribution within paragraph (*a*), (*b*) or (*c*) of that subsection.][3]

(2) Dividend withholding tax which is required to be included in a return under subsection (1) shall be due at the time by which the return is to be made and shall be paid by the accountable person to the Collector-General, and the dividend withholding tax so due shall be payable by the accountable person without the making of an assessment, but dividend withholding tax which has become so due may be assessed on

the accountable person (whether or not it has been paid when the assessment is made) if that tax or any part of it is not paid on or before the due date.

(3) Where it appears to the inspector that there is any amount of dividend withholding tax in relation to a relevant distribution which ought to have been but has not been included in a return under subsection (2), or where the inspector is dissatisfied with any such return, the inspector may make an assessment on the accountable person in relation to the relevant distribution to the best of the inspector's judgment, and any amount of dividend withholding tax in relation to a relevant distribution due under an assessment made by virtue of this subsection shall be treated for the purposes of interest on unpaid tax as having been payable at the time when it would have been payable if a correct return under subsection (1) had been made.

(4) Where any item has been incorrectly included in a return under subsection (1) as a relevant distribution in relation to which dividend withholding tax is required to be deducted, the inspector may make such assessments, adjustments or set-offs as may in his or her judgment be required for securing that the resulting liabilities to tax, including interest on unpaid tax, whether of the accountable person in relation to the relevant distribution or any other person, are in so far as possible the same as they would have been if the item had not been so included.

(5) Any dividend withholding tax assessed on an accountable person under this Chapter shall be due within one month after the issue of the notice of assessment (unless that tax is due earlier under subsection (2)) subject to any appeal against the assessment, but no such appeal shall affect the date when any amount is due under subsection (2).

(6) (*a*) The provisions of the Income Tax Acts relating to—

(i) assessments to income tax,

(ii) appeals against such assessments (including the rehearing of appeals and the statement of a case for the opinion of the High Court), and

(iii) the collection and recovery of income tax,

shall, in so far as they are applicable, apply to the assessment, collection and recovery of dividend withholding tax.

(*b*) Any amount of dividend withholding tax payable in accordance with this Chapter without the making of an assessment shall carry interest at the rate of [0.0322 per cent for each day or part of a day][4] from the date when the amount becomes due and payable until payment.

(*c*) [Subsections (3) to (5) of section 1080][5] shall apply in relation to interest payable under paragraph (*b*) as they apply in relation to interest payable under section 1080.

(*d*) In its application to any dividend withholding tax charged by any assessment made in accordance with this Chapter, section 1080 shall apply as if [subsection (2)(*b*)][6] of that section were deleted.

(7) Subject to subsection (8), every return by an accountable person under subsection (1) shall be made in an electronic format approved by the Revenue Commissioners and shall be accompanied by a declaration made by the accountable person, on a form prescribed or authorised for that purpose by the Revenue Commissioners, to the effect that the return is correct and complete.

(8) Where the Revenue Commissioners are satisfied that an accountable person does not have the facilities to make a return under subsection (1) in the format referred to in subsection (7), the return shall be made in writing in a form prescribed or authorised by the Revenue Commissioners and shall be accompanied by a declaration made by the accountable person, on a form prescribed or authorised for that purpose by the Revenue Commissioners, to the effect that the return is correct and complete.][7]

Amendments

1 Deleted by FA 2000 s 30(1)(*h*)(i) with effect from 6 April 2000; previously "and".
2 Substituted by FA 2000 s 30(1)(*h*)(i) with effect from 6 April 2000; previously "refers.".
3 Inserted by FA 2000 s 30(1)(*h*)(ii) with effect from 6 April 2000.
4 Substituted by FA 2002 s 129(1)(*a*) with effect from 1 September 2002 as regards interest chargeable in respect of an amount due to be paid or remitted, whether before, on, or after that date; previously "1 per cent for each month or part of a month".
5 Substituted by FA 2005 s 145(7)(*a*) and Sch 5 Pt 1 in relation to any unpaid income tax, corporation tax or capital gains tax, as the case may be, that has not been paid before 1 April 2005 regardless of when that tax became due and payable and notwithstanding anything to the contrary in any other enactment other than TCA 1997 s 1082; previously "Subsections (2) to (4) of section 1080".
6 Substituted by FA 2005 s 145(7)(*a*) and Sch 5 Pt 1 in relation to any unpaid income tax, corporation tax or capital gains tax, as the case may be, that has not been paid before 1 April 2005 regardless of when that tax became due and payable and notwithstanding anything to the contrary in any other enactment other than TCA 1997 s 1082; previously "subsection (1)(*b*)".
7 Section 172K inserted by FA 1999 s 27(*a*) with effect from 6 April 1999.

Cross-references

Authorised withholding agent, subs (1): s 172G(3)(*f*).
Distributions to certain non-residents: s 153(5).
Implementation of Parents/Subsidiaries Directive: s 831(5).
Power of inspection, returns and collection of dividend withholding tax: s 904I(2).
Revenue offences, subs (2): s 1078(2)(*dd*)(ii), (iv), (v).
Treatment of distributions to certain parent companies, application of this section: s 831A(2).

Definitions

authorised withholding agent: s 172A(1)(*a*); Collector-General: ss 2(1), 851; company: s 4(1); dividend withholding tax: s 172A(1)(*a*); Income Tax Acts: s 1(2); inspector: ss 2(1), 852; month: IA 1937 Sch; person: IA 1937 s 11(*c*); relevant distribution, tax reference number: s 172A(1)(*a*).

172L Reporting of distributions made under stapled stock arrangements

[(1) For the purposes of this section, a distribution made to a person by a company which is not resident in the State (in this section referred to as "the non-resident company") shall be treated as made under a stapled stock arrangement where—

(*a*) the person has, under any agreement, arrangement or understanding, whether made or entered into on, before or after the 6th day of April, 1999, exercised a right, whether directly or through a nominee or other person acting on behalf of the person, to receive distributions from the non-resident company instead of receiving relevant distributions from a company resident in the State (in this section referred to as "the resident company"), and

(*b*) that right has not been revoked.

(2) Where on or after the 6th day of April, 1999, the non-resident company makes distributions to persons under a stapled stock arrangement, the resident company shall, within 14 days of the end of each month in which those distributions were made, make a return to the Revenue Commissioners which shall contain details of—

(*a*) the name and tax reference number of the resident company,

(*b*) the name and address of the non-resident company which made those distributions,

(*c*) the name and address of each person to whom such a distribution was made in the month to which the return refers,

(*d*) the date on which such distribution was made to that person, and

(*e*) the amount of such distribution made to that person.

(3) Subject to subsection (4), every return by a company under subsection (2) shall be made in an electronic format approved by the Revenue Commissioners and shall be accompanied by a declaration made by the company, on a form prescribed or authorised for that purpose by the Revenue Commissioners, to the effect that the return is correct and complete.

(4) Where the Revenue Commissioners are satisfied that a company does not have the facilities to make a return under subsection (2) in the format referred to in subsection (3), the return shall be made in writing in a form prescribed or authorised by the Revenue Commissioners and shall be accompanied by a declaration made by the company, on a form prescribed or authorised for that purpose by the Revenue Commissioners, to the effect that the return is correct and complete.][1]

Amendments

1 Section 172L inserted by FA 1999 s 27(*a*) with effect from 6 April 1999.

Tax Briefing

TB 56 July 2004 p 18 — DWT Stapled Stock Arrangements.

Definitions

company: s 4(1); month: IA 1937 Sch; relevant distribution, tax reference number: s 172A(1)(*a*); writing: IA 1937 Sch.

172LA Deduction of dividend withholding tax on settlement of market claims

[(1) In this section, **"stockbroker"** means a member firm of the Irish Stock Exchange or of a recognised stock exchange in another territory.

(2) For the purposes of this section, a market claim shall be deemed to have arisen in relation to a relevant distribution where—

(*a*) a company resident in the State has made a relevant distribution to a person (in this section referred to as the "recorded owner") on the basis of the information on the share register of the company at a particular date,

(*b*) it subsequently transpires, as a result of an event (in this section referred to as the "specified event"), being—

(i) the sale or purchase of, or

(ii) the happening, or failure to happen, of another event in relation to,

the shares or other securities in respect of which the relevant distribution was made, that another person (in this section referred to as the "proper owner") had actually been entitled to receive the relevant distribution, and

(*c*) a person (in this section referred to as an "accountable person"), being—

(i) the relevant stockbroker who has acted for the recorded owner in the specified event, or

(ii) if the recorded owner is a qualifying intermediary or an authorised withholding agent, that intermediary or agent,

is obliged to pay the relevant distribution to the proper owner or, as may be appropriate, to the relevant stockbroker who has acted for the proper owner in the specified event, which action is in this section referred to as the "settlement of the market claim".

(3) Notwithstanding any other provision of this Chapter, where a market claim arises, then, if dividend withholding tax had not already been deducted out of the amount of the relevant distribution made by the company resident in the State to the recorded owner—

(*a*) the accountable person shall, on the settlement of the market claim, deduct out of the amount of the relevant distribution dividend withholding tax in relation to the relevant distribution,

(*b*) the proper owner or, as may be appropriate, the relevant stockbroker who has acted for the proper owner in the specified event shall allow such deduction on the receipt of the residue of the relevant distribution, and

(*c*) the accountable person shall be acquitted and discharged of so much money as is represented by the deduction as if that amount of money had actually been paid to the proper owner or, as may be appropriate, to the relevant stockbroker who has acted for the proper owner in the specified event.

(4) Where subsection (3) applies, the accountable person shall, on the settlement of the market claim, give the proper owner or, as may be appropriate, the relevant stockbroker who has acted for the proper owner in the specified event a statement in writing showing—

(*a*) the name and address of the accountable person,

(*b*) the name and address of the company which made the relevant distribution,

(*c*) the amount of the relevant distribution, and

(*d*) the amount of the dividend withholding tax deducted in relation to the relevant distribution.

(5) Dividend withholding tax which is required to be deducted by the accountable person under subsection (3) shall be paid by the accountable person to the Collector-General within 14 days of the end of the month in which that tax was required to be so deducted, and the dividend withholding tax so due shall be payable without the making of an assessment, but dividend withholding tax which has become so due may be assessed on the accountable person if that tax or any part of it is not paid on or before the due date.

(6) Dividend withholding tax which is required to be paid in accordance with subsection (5) shall be accompanied by a statement in writing from the accountable person making the payment showing—

(*a*) the name and address of that accountable person,

(*b*) the name and address of the company or companies which made the relevant distribution or distributions to which the payment relates, and

(*c*) the amount of the dividend withholding tax included in the payment.

(7) An accountable person shall, as respects each year of assessment (being the year of assessment 1999–2000 or any subsequent year of assessment) in which subsection (3) applied in relation to the accountable person and not later than [15 February][1] following that year of assessment, make a return to the Revenue Commissioners showing—

(*a*) the name and address of the accountable person, and

(*b*) the following details in relation to each market claim to which subsection (3) applied in that year:

(i) the name and address of the company resident in the State which made the relevant distribution to which the market claim relates,

(ii) the amount of the relevant distribution concerned, and

(iii) the amount of the dividend withholding tax in relation to the relevant distribution deducted by the accountable person.

(8) Subject to subsection (9), every return by an accountable person under subsection (7) shall be made in an electronic format approved by the Revenue Commissioners and shall be accompanied by a declaration made by the accountable person, on a form prescribed or authorised for that purpose by the Revenue Commissioners, to the effect that the return is correct and complete.

(9) Where the Revenue Commissioners are satisfied that an accountable person does not have the facilities to make a return under subsection (7) in the format referred to in subsection (8), the return shall be made in writing in a form prescribed or authorised by the Revenue Commissioners and shall be accompanied by a declaration made by the accountable person, on a form prescribed or authorised for that purpose by the Revenue Commissioners, to the effect that the return is correct and complete.

(10)(*a*) An accountable person shall keep and retain for a period of 6 years the accountable person's documents and records relating to market claims arising from relevant distributions made by companies resident in the State.

(*b*) An accountable person shall allow the Revenue Commissioners to inspect such documents and records and to verify the accountable person's compliance with this section in any other manner considered necessary by the Commissioners.][2]

Amendments

1 Substituted by FA 2001 s 77(2) and Sch 2 paras 11 and 61(*c*) for short tax "year" 2001 and later tax years; previously "the 21st day of May".

2 Section 172LA inserted by FA 2000 s 30(1)(*i*) with effect from 10 February 2000.

Definitions

authorised withholding agent: s 172A(1); Collector-General: ss 2(1), 851; company: s 4(1); dividend withholding tax: s 172A(1); person: IA 1937 s 11(*c*); qualifying intermediary, relevant distribution: s 172A(1); writing: IA 1937 Sch; year of assessment: s 2(1).

172M Delegation of powers and functions of Revenue Commissioners

[The Revenue Commissioners may nominate any of their officers to perform any acts and discharge any functions authorised by this Chapter or Schedule 2A to be performed or discharged by the Revenue Commissioners.][1]

Amendments

1 Section 172M inserted by FA 1999 s 27(*a*) with effect from 6 April 1999.

CHAPTER 9
Taxation of Acquisition by a Company of its Own Shares

173 Interpretation (Chapter 9)

(1) In this Chapter—

"chargeable period" means an accounting period of a company or a year of assessment;

"control" shall be construed in accordance with section 11;

"group" means a company which has one or more 51 per cent subsidiaries together with those subsidiaries;

"holding company" means a company whose business, disregarding any trade carried on by it, consists wholly or mainly of the holding of the shares or securities of one or more companies which are its 51 per cent subsidiaries;

"inspector", in relation to any matter, means an inspector of taxes appointed under section 852, and includes such other officer as the Revenue Commissioners shall appoint in that behalf;

"personal representative" has the same meaning as in section 799;

"quoted company" means a company whose shares, or any class of whose shares, are listed in the official list of a stock exchange or dealt in on an unlisted securities market;

"shares" includes stock;

"trade" does not include dealing in shares, securities, land, futures or traded options, and **"trading activities"** shall be construed accordingly;

"trading company" means a company whose business consists wholly or mainly of the carrying on of a trade or trades;

"trading group" means a group the business of whose members taken together consists wholly or mainly of the carrying on of a trade or trades.

(2) References in this Chapter to the owner of shares shall be treated as references to the beneficial owner except where the shares are held on trusts other than bare trusts, or are comprised in the estate of a deceased person, and in such a case shall be treated as references to the trustees or, as the case may be, to the deceased's personal representatives.

(3) References in this Chapter to a payment made by a company include references to anything else that is, or but for section 175 or 176 would be, a distribution.

(4) References in this Chapter to a company being unquoted shall be treated as references to a company which is neither a quoted company nor a 51 per cent subsidiary of a quoted company.

Definitions

company: ss 4(1), 5(1); distribution: ss 4(1), 436, 437; inspector: ss 2(1), 5(1), 852; person: IA 1937 s 11(*c*); personal representative: s 5(1), 799; shares: s 5(1); trade: s 3(1); year of assessment: ss 2(1), 5(1).

Former enactments

FA 1991 s 59; FA 1997 s 39(1)(*a*).

---

174 Taxation of dealer's receipts on purchase of shares by issuing company or by its subsidiary

(1) In this section—

"fixed-rate preference shares" means shares which—

(*a*) were issued wholly for new consideration,

(*b*) do not carry any right either to conversion into shares or securities of any other description or to the acquisition of any additional shares or securities,

(*c*) do not carry any right to dividends other than dividends which are of a fixed amount or at a fixed rate per cent of the nominal value of the shares, and

(*d*) carry rights in respect of dividends and capital which are comparable with those general for fixed-dividend shares quoted on a stock exchange in the State;

"new consideration" has the meaning assigned to it by section 135.

(2) Where—

(*a*) a company purchases its own shares from a dealer, or

(*b*) a company, which is a subsidiary (within the meaning of section 155 of the Companies Act, 1963) of another company, purchases the other company's shares from a dealer,

the purchase price shall be taken into account in computing the profits of the dealer chargeable to tax under Case I or II of Schedule D, and accordingly—

(i) tax shall not be chargeable under Schedule F in respect of any distribution represented by any part of the price, [and][1]

...[2]

(iii) sections 129 and 152 shall not apply to the distribution.

(3) For the purposes of subsection (2), a person shall be a dealer in relation to shares of a company if the price received on their sale by the person other than to the company, or to a company which is a subsidiary (within the meaning of section 155 of the Companies Act, 1963) of the company, would be taken into account in computing the person's profits chargeable to tax under Case I or II of Schedule D.

(4) Subject to subsection (5), in subsection (2)—

(*a*) the reference to the purchase of shares includes a reference to the redemption or repayment of shares and the purchase of rights to acquire shares, and

(*b*) the reference to the purchase price includes a reference to any sum payable on redemption or repayment.

(5) Subsection (2) shall not apply in relation to—

(*a*) the redemption of fixed-rate preference shares, or

(*b*) the redemption, on binding terms settled before the 18th day of April, 1991, of other preference shares issued before that date,

if in either case the shares were issued to and continuously held by the person from whom they are redeemed.

Amendments

[1] Inserted by FA 2000 s 69(1) and Sch 2 Part 1 Part 1 para (*m*) with effect from 6 April 1999 in the case of income tax and for accounting periods commencing on or after that date in the case of corporation tax.

[2] Subs (2)(ii) repealed by FA 2000 s 69(2) and Sch 2 Part 2 with effect from 6 April 1999 in the case of income tax and for accounting periods commencing on or after that date in the case of corporation tax.

Definitions

company: ss 4(1), 5(1); distribution: ss 4(1), 436, 437; person: IA 1937 s 11(*c*); shares: s 173(1).

Former enactments

FA 1991 s 60.

Corresponding UK tax provision

Finance (No 2) Act 1997 s 24.

175 Purchase of own shares by quoted company

(1) Notwithstanding Chapter 2 of this Part, references in the Tax Acts to distributions of a company shall be construed so as not to include references to a payment made on or after the 26th day of March, 1997, by a quoted company on the redemption, repayment or purchase of its own shares.

(2) References in subsection (1) to a quoted company shall include references to a company which is a member of a group of which a quoted company is a member.

Cross-references

Interpretation: s 173(3).

Tax Briefing

TB53 Aug 2003 p 3 — First Active plc — repayment of capital to its shareholders, CGT treatment.

TB53 Aug 2003 pp 21–23 — Jefferson Smurfit shares, CGT implications for shareholders on takeover of company.

Former enactments

FA 1991 s 60A; FA 1997 s 39(1)(*b*), (2).

176 Purchase of unquoted shares by issuing company or its subsidiary

(1) Notwithstanding Chapter 2 of this Part, references in the Tax Acts to distributions of a company, other than any such references in sections 440 and 441, shall be construed so as not to include references to a payment made by a company on the redemption, repayment or purchase of its own shares if the company is an unquoted trading company or the unquoted holding company of a trading group and either—

(*a*) (i) the redemption, repayment or purchase—

(I) is made wholly or mainly for the purpose of benefiting a trade carried on by the company or by any of its 51 per cent subsidiaries, and

(II) does not form part of a scheme or arrangement the main purpose or one of the main purposes of which is to enable the owner of the shares to participate in the profits of the company or of any of its 51 per cent subsidiaries without receiving a dividend,

and

(ii) the conditions specified in sections 177 to 181, in so far as applicable, are satisfied in relation to the owner of the shares, or (*b*) the person to whom the payment is made—

(i) applies the whole or substantially the whole of the payment (apart from any sum applied in discharging that person's liability to capital gains tax, if any, in respect of the redemption, repayment or purchase) to discharging—

(I) within 4 months of the valuation date (within the meaning of [section 30 of the Capital Acquisitions Tax Consolidation Act 2003][1]) of a taxable inheritance of the company's shares taken by that person, a liability to inheritance tax in respect of that inheritance, or

(II) within one week of the day on which the payment is made, a debt incurred by that person for the purpose of discharging that liability to inheritance tax,

and

(ii) could not without undue hardship have otherwise discharged that liability to inheritance tax and, where appropriate, the debt so incurred.

(2) Where subsection (1) would apply to a payment made by a company which is a subsidiary (within the meaning of section 155 of the Companies Act, 1963) of another company on the acquisition of shares of the other company if for the purposes of the Tax Acts other than this subsection—

(*a*) the payment were to be treated as a payment by the other company on the purchase of its own shares, and

(*b*) the acquisition by the subsidiary of the shares were to be treated as a purchase by the other company of its own shares,

then, notwithstanding Chapter 2 of this Part, references in the Tax Acts to distributions of a company, other than references in sections 440 and 441, shall be construed so as not to include references to the payment made by the subsidiary.

Amendments

1 Substituted by CATCA 2003 s 119 and Sch 3 with effect from 21 February 2003; previously "section 21 of the Capital Acquisitions Tax 1976".

Cross-references

Associated persons: s 185.

Connected persons: s 186.

Information, subss (1)(*a*), (2): s 183.

Interpretation: s 173(3).

Relaxation of conditions, subs (1)(*a*): s 181.

Residence conditions and ownership period, subs (1)(*a*): s 177(1).

Returns, subss (1)–(2): s 182(2).

Tax Briefing

TB25 Feb 1997 p 9 — Company Buy-Back of Shares — "Trade Benefit Test".

Definitions

company: ss 4(1), 5(1); distribution: ss 4(1), 436, 437; holding company: s 173(1); month: IA 1937 Sch; person: IA 1937 s 11(*c*); shares: s 173(1); Tax Acts: s 1(2); trade: s 173(1); trading group: s 173(1); week: IA 1937 Sch.

Former enactments

FA 1991 s 61.

Corresponding UK tax provision

Income and Corporation Taxes Act 1988 s 219.

---

177 Conditions as to residence and period of ownership

(1) In this section and in sections 178 to 181—

"the purchase" means the redemption, repayment or purchase referred to in section 176(1)(*a*);

"the vendor" means the owner of the shares immediately before the purchase is made.

(2) The vendor shall be resident and ordinarily resident in the State for the chargeable period in which the purchase is made and, if the shares are held through a nominee, the nominee shall also be so resident and ordinarily resident.

(3) The residence and ordinary residence of trustees shall be determined for the purposes of this section as they are determined under section 574 for the purposes of the Capital Gains Tax Acts.

(4) The residence and ordinary residence of personal representatives shall be taken for the purposes of this section to be the same as the residence and ordinary residence of the deceased immediately before his or her death.

(5) The references in this section to a person's ordinary residence shall be disregarded in the case of a company.

[(6) The shares shall have been owned by the vendor throughout the period of—

(*a*) where the shares were appropriated to the vendor under an approved scheme (within the meaning of Chapter 1 of Part 17), and to which the provisions of subsections (4) to (7) of section 515 do not apply, 3 years, and

(*b*) in any other case, 5 years,

ending on the date of redemption, repayment or purchase, as the case may be.][1]

(7) Where at any time during that period the shares were transferred to the vendor by a person who was then the vendor's spouse living with the vendor, then, unless that person is alive at the date of the purchase but is no longer the vendor's spouse living with the vendor, any period during which the shares were owned by that person shall be treated for the purposes of subsection (6) as a period of ownership by the vendor.

(8) Where the vendor became entitled to the shares under the will or on the intestacy of a previous owner or is the personal representative of a previous owner—

(*a*) any period during which the shares were owned by the previous owner or the previous owner's personal representatives shall be treated for the purposes of subsection (6) as a period of ownership by the vendor, and

(*b*) that subsection shall apply as if it referred to 3 years instead of 5 years.

(9) In determining whether the condition in subsection (6) is satisfied in a case where the vendor acquired shares of the same class at different times—

(*a*) shares acquired earlier shall be taken into account before shares acquired later, and

(*b*) any previous disposal by the vendor of shares of that class shall be assumed to be a disposal of shares acquired later rather than of shares acquired earlier.

(10) Where for the purposes of capital gains tax the time when a person acquired shares would be determined under section 584, 585, 586, 587 or 600, then, unless the person is to be treated under section 584(4) as giving or becoming liable to give any consideration, other than the old holding, for the acquisition of those shares, it shall be determined in the same way for the purposes of this section.

Amendments

1 Subs (6) substituted by FA 2001 s 35 as respects a redemption, repayment or purchase of its own shares by a company to which s 176 applies on or after 15 February 2001.

Cross-references

Associated persons: s 185.

Connected persons: s 186.

Unquoted company buying its own shares: s 176(1).

Definitions

company: ss 4(1), 5(1); chargeable period: s 173(1); person: IA 1937 s 11(*c*); personal representative: s 173(1); shares: s 173(1); resident: s 5(1).

Former enactments

FA 1991 s 62.

Corresponding UK tax provision

Income and Corporation Taxes Act 1988 s 220.

178 Conditions as to reduction of vendor's interest as shareholder

(1) Where immediately after the purchase the vendor owns shares in the company, the vendor's interest as a shareholder shall, subject to section 181, be substantially reduced.

(2) Where immediately after the purchase any associate of the vendor owns shares in the company, the combined interest as shareholders of the vendor and the vendor's associates shall, subject to section 181, be substantially reduced.

(3) The question whether the combined interests as shareholders of the vendor and the vendor's associates are substantially reduced shall be determined in the same way as is (under subsections (4) to (7)) the question whether a vendor's interest as a shareholder is substantially reduced, except that the vendor shall be assumed to have the interests of the vendor's associates as well as the vendor's own interests.

(4) Subject to subsection (5), the vendor's interest as a shareholder shall be taken to be substantially reduced only if the total nominal value of the shares owned by the vendor immediately after the purchase, expressed as a percentage of the issued share capital of the company at that time, does not exceed 75 per cent of the corresponding percentage immediately before the purchase.

(5) The vendor's interest as a shareholder shall not be taken to be substantially reduced where—

(*a*) the vendor would, if the company distributed all its profits available for the distribution immediately after the purchase, be entitled to a share of those profits, and

(*b*) that share, expressed as a percentage of the total of those profits, exceeds 75 per cent of the corresponding percentage immediately before the purchase.

(6) In determining for the purposes of subsection (5) the division of profits among the persons entitled to them, a person entitled to periodic distributions calculated by reference to fixed rates or amounts shall be regarded as entitled to a distribution of the amount or maximum amount to which the person would be entitled for a year.

(7) In subsection (5), **"profits available for distribution"** has the same meaning as it has for the purposes of Part IV of the Companies (Amendment) Act, 1983, except that for the purposes of that subsection the amount of the profits available for distribution (whether immediately before or immediately after the purchase) shall be treated as increased—

(*a*) in the case of every company, by [€100][1], and

(*b*) in the case of a company from which any person is entitled to periodic distributions of the kind mentioned in subsection (6), by a further amount equal to that required to make the distribution to which that person is entitled in accordance with that subsection,

and, where the aggregate of the sums payable by the company on the purchase and on any contemporaneous redemption, repayment or purchase of other shares of the company exceeds the amount of the profits available for distribution immediately before the purchase, that amount shall be treated as further increased by an amount equal to the excess.

(8) References in this section to entitlement are, except in the case of trustees and personal representatives, references to beneficial entitlement.

Amendments

1 Substituted by FA 2001 s 240(1) and (2)(*c*) and Sch 5 Pt 1 for accounting periods ending on or after 1 January 2002; previously "£100".

Cross-references

Associated persons: s 185.

Conditions applying where buyer company is member of a group, subss (6)–(7) applied: s 179(12).

Connected persons: s 186.

Relaxation of conditions: s 181.

Residence conditions and ownership period: s 177(1).

Unquoted company buying its own shares: s 176(1).

Vendor not connected with buying company: s 180(3).

Definitions

company: ss 4(1), 5(1); distribution: ss 4(1), 436, 437; person: IA 1937 s 11(*c*); personal representative: s 173(1); shares: s 173(1).

Former enactments

FA 1991 s 63.

Corresponding UK tax provision

Income and Corporation Taxes Act 1988 s 221.

179 Conditions applicable where purchasing company is member of a group

(1) Subject to subsections (2) to (4), in this section, **"group"** means a company which has one or more 51 per cent subsidiaries but is not itself a 51 per cent subsidiary of any other company, together with those subsidiaries.

(2) Where the whole or a significant part of the business carried on by an unquoted company (in this section referred to as **"the successor company"**) was previously carried on by—

(*a*) the company making the purchase, or

(*b*) a company which apart from this subsection is a member of a group to which the company making the purchase belongs,

the successor company and any company of which it is a 51 per cent subsidiary shall be treated as being a member of the same group as the company making the purchase, whether or not apart from this subsection the company making the purchase is a member of a group.

(3) Subsection (2) shall not apply if the successor company first carried on the business referred to in that subsection more than 3 years before the time of the purchase.

(4) For the purposes of this section, a company which has ceased to be a 51 per cent subsidiary of another company before the time of the purchase shall be treated as continuing to be such a subsidiary if at that time there exist arrangements under which it could again become such a subsidiary.

(5) Subject to section 181, where the company making the purchase is immediately before the purchase a member of a group and immediately after the purchase—

(*a*) the vendor owns shares in one or more other members of the group, whether or not the vendor then owns shares in the company making the purchase, or

(*b*) the vendor owns shares in the company making the purchase and immediately before the purchase the vendor owned shares in one or more members of the group,

the vendor's interest as a shareholder in the group shall be substantially reduced.

(6) Subject to section 181, where the company making the purchase is immediately before the purchase a member of a group, and at that time an associate of the vendor owns shares in any member of the group, the combined interests as shareholders in the group of the vendor and the vendor's associates shall be substantially reduced.

(7) Subject to subsection (8), in subsections (9) to (11), **"relevant company"** means the company making the purchase and any other company—

(*a*) in which the vendor owns shares, and

(*b*) which is a member of the same group as the company making the purchase,

immediately before or immediately after the purchase.

(8) The question whether the combined interests as shareholders in the group of the vendor and the vendor's associates are substantially reduced shall be determined in the same way as is (under this section) the question whether a vendor's interest as a shareholder in a group is substantially reduced, except that the vendor shall be assumed to have the interests of the vendor's associates as well as the vendor's own interests, and references in subsections (9) to (11) to a relevant company shall be construed accordingly.

(9) The vendor's interest as a shareholder in the group shall be ascertained by—

(*a*) expressing the total nominal value of the shares owned by the vendor in each relevant company as a percentage of the issued share capital of the company,

(*b*) adding together the percentages so obtained, and

(*c*) dividing the result by the number of relevant companies (including any in which the vendor owns no shares).

(10) Subject to subsection (11), the vendor's interest as a shareholder in the group shall be taken to be substantially reduced only if it does not exceed 75 per cent of the corresponding interest immediately before the purchase.

(11) The vendor's interest as a shareholder in the group shall not be taken to be substantially reduced where—

(*a*) the vendor would, if every member of the group distributed all its profits available for distribution immediately after the purchase (including any profits received by it on a distribution by another member), be entitled to a share of the profits of one or more or them, and

(*b*) that share, or the aggregate of those shares, expressed as a percentage of the aggregate of the profits available for distribution of every member of the group which is—

(i) a relevant company, or

(ii) a 51 per cent subsidiary of a relevant company,

exceeds 75 per cent of the corresponding percentage immediately before the purchase.

(12) Subsections (6) and (7) of section 178 shall apply for the purposes of subsection (11) as they apply for the purposes of subsection (5) of that section.

Cross-references

Additional conditions, meaning of "group" applied: s 180(1).
Associated persons: s 185.
Connected persons: s 186.
Relaxation of conditions: s 181.
Residence conditions and ownership period: s 177(1).
Unquoted company buying its own shares: s 176(1).
Vendor not connected with buying company: s 180, (3).

Definitions

company: ss 4(1), 5(1); distribution: ss 4(1), 436, 437; shares: s 173(1).

Former enactments

FA 1991 s 64.

Corresponding UK tax provision

Income and Corporation Taxes Act 1988 s 222.

180 Additional conditions

(1) In this section, **"group"** has the same meaning as in section 179.

(2) Subject to section 181, the vendor shall not immediately after the purchase be connected with the company making the purchase or with any company which is a member of the same group as that company.

(3) Subject to section 181, the purchase shall not be part of a scheme or arrangement which is designed or likely to result in the vendor or any associate of the vendor having interests in any company such that, if the vendor or any associate of the vendor had those interests immediately after the purchase, any of the conditions in sections 178 and 179 and subsection (2) could not be satisfied.

(4) A transaction occurring within one year after the purchase shall be deemed for the purposes of subsection (3) to be part of a scheme or arrangement of which the purchase is also part.

Cross-references

Associated persons: s 185.
Connected persons: s 186.
Information (subs (3): s 183(1)–(2).
Residence conditions and ownership period: s 177(1).
Relaxation of conditions: s 181.
Unquoted company buying its own shares: s 176(1).

Definitions

company: ss 4(1), 5(1).

Former enactments

FA 1991 s 65.

Corresponding UK tax provision

Income and Corporation Taxes Act 1988 s 223.

181 Relaxation of conditions in certain cases

Where—

(*a*) any of the conditions in sections 178 to 180 which are applicable are not satisfied in relation to the vendor, but

(*b*) the vendor proposed or agreed to the purchase in order to produce the result that the condition in section 178(2) or 179(6), which could not otherwise be satisfied in respect of the redemption, repayment or purchase of shares owned by a person of whom the vendor is an associate, could be satisfied in that respect,

then, if that result is produced by virtue of the purchase, section 176(1)(*a*) shall apply, as respects so much of the purchase as was necessary to produce that result, as if the conditions in sections 178 to 180 were satisfied in relation to the vendor.

Cross-references

Associated persons: s 185.
Conditions applying where buyer company is member of a group: s 179(5), (6).
Connected persons: s 186.
Reduction of vendor's interest: s 178(1).
Residence conditions and ownership period: s 177(1).
Unquoted company buying its own shares: s 176(1).
Vendor not connected with buying company: s 180(2), (3).

Definitions

person: IA 1937 s 11(*c*); shares: s 173(1).

Former enactments

FA 1991 s 66.

Corresponding UK tax provision

Income and Corporation Taxes Act 1988 s 224.

182 Returns

(1) In this section, **"appropriate inspector"** and **"prescribed form"** have the same meanings respectively as in Part 41.

(2) Where a company makes a payment which it treats as one to which subsection (1) or (2) of section 176 applies, the company shall make a return in a prescribed form to the appropriate inspector of—

- (*a*) the payment,
- (*b*) the circumstances by reason of which that subsection is regarded as applying to it, and
- (*c*) such further particulars as may be required by the prescribed form.

(3) A company shall make a return under this section—

- (*a*) within 9 months from the end of the accounting period in which it makes the payment, or
- (*b*) if, at any time after the payment is made, the inspector by notice in writing requests such a form, within the time (which shall not be less than 30 days) limited by such notice.

(4) Section 1071 shall, with any necessary modifications, apply in relation to a return under this section as it applies in relation to a return under section 884.

Cross-references

Associated persons: s 185.

Connected persons: s 186.

Definitions

company: ss 4(1), 5(1); inspector: s 173(1); month: IA 1937 Sch; writing: IA 1937 Sch.

Former enactments

FA 1991 s 67.

Corresponding UK tax provision

Income and Corporation Taxes Act 1988 s 225.

183 Information

(1) Where a company treats a payment made by it as one to which subsection (1)(*a*) or (2) of section 176 applies, any person connected with the company who knows of any such scheme or arrangement affecting the payment as is mentioned in section 180(3) shall, within 60 days after that person first knows of both the payment and the scheme or arrangement, give a notice to the inspector containing particulars of the scheme or arrangement.

(2) Where the inspector has reason to believe that a payment treated by the company making it as one to which subsection (1)(*a*) or (2) of section 176 applies may form part of a scheme or arrangement of the kind referred to in that section or in section 180(3), the inspector may by notice require the company or any person connected with the company to furnish to the inspector within such time, not being less than 60 days, as may be specified in the notice—

(*a*) a declaration in writing stating whether or not, according to information which the company or that person has or can reasonably obtain, any such scheme or arrangement exists or has existed, and

(*b*) such other information as the inspector may reasonably require for the purposes of the provision in question and the company or that person has or can reasonably obtain.

(3) (*a*) The recipient of a payment treated by the company making it as a payment to which subsection (1)(*a*) or (2) of section 176 applies shall, if so required by the inspector, state whether the payment in question is received on behalf of any person other than such recipient and, if so, the name and address of that person.

(*b*) Any person on whose behalf a payment referred to in paragraph (*a*) is received shall, if so required by the inspector, state whether the payment in question is received on behalf of any person other than that person and, if so, the name and address of that other person.

Cross-references

Associated persons: s 185.

Connected persons: s 186.

Penalty: Sch 29 column 2.

Definitions

company: ss 4(1), 5(1); inspector: s 173(1); person: IA 1937 s 11(*c*); writing: IA 1937 Sch.

Former enactments

FA 1991 s 68(1)–(3).

Corresponding UK tax provision

Income and Corporation Taxes Act 1988 s 226.

184 Treasury shares

(1) For the purposes of the Tax Acts and the Capital Gains Tax Acts—

(*a*) any shares which are—

(i) held by the company as treasury shares, and

(ii) not cancelled by the company,

shall be deemed to be cancelled immediately on their acquisition by the company,

(*b*) a deemed or actual cancellation of shares shall be treated as giving rise to neither a chargeable gain nor an allowable loss, and

(*c*) a reissue by the company of treasury shares shall be treated as an issue of new shares by it.

(2) For the purposes of this section, a reference to treasury shares shall be a reference to treasury shares within the meaning of section 209 of the Companies Act, 1990.

Definitions

allowable loss: ss 4(1), 5(1), 546; chargeable gain: ss 4(1), 5(1), 534; company: ss 4(1), 5(1); shares: s 173(1); Tax Acts: s 1(2).

Former enactments

FA 1991 s 70.

185 Associated persons

(1) Any question whether a person is an associate of another person in relation to a company shall be determined for the purposes of sections 176 to 183 and section 186 in accordance with the following provisions:

(*a*) a husband and wife living together shall be associates of one another, a person under the age of 18 shall be an associate of his or her parents, and his or her parents shall be the person's associates;

(*b*) a person who has control of a company shall be an associate of the company and the company shall be the person's associate;

(*c*) where a person who has control of one company has control of another company, the second company shall be an associate of the first company;

(*d*) where shares in a company are held by trustees other than bare trustees, then, in relation to that company but subject to subsection (2), the trustees shall be associates of—

(i) any person who directly or indirectly provided property to the trustees or has made a reciprocal arrangement for another person to do so,

(ii) any person who is by virtue of paragraph (*a*) an associate of a person within subparagraph (i), and

(iii) any person who is or may become beneficially entitled to a material interest in the shares,

and any such person shall be an associate of the trustees;

(*e*) where shares in a company are comprised in the estate of a deceased person, then, in relation to that company, the deceased's personal representatives shall be associates of any person who is or may become beneficially entitled to a material interest in the shares, and any such person shall be an associate of the personal representatives;

(*f*) where one person is accustomed to act on the directions of another person in relation to the affairs of a company, then, in relation to that company, the 2 persons shall be associates of one another.

(2) Subsection (1)(*d*) shall not apply to shares held on trusts which—

(*a*) relate exclusively to an exempt approved scheme within the meaning of Chapter 1 of Part 30, or

(*b*) are exclusively for the benefit of the employees, or the employees and directors, of the company referred to in subsection (1)(*d*) or of companies in a group to which that company belongs, or their dependants, and are not wholly or mainly for the benefit of directors or their relatives,

and for the purposes of this subsection **"group"** means a company which has one or more 51 per cent subsidiaries, together with those subsidiaries.

(3) For the purposes of paragraphs (*d*) and (*e*) of subsection (1), a person's interest shall be a material interest if its value exceeds 5 per cent of the value of all the property held on the trusts or, as the case may be, comprised in the estate concerned, excluding any property in which the person is not and cannot become beneficially entitled to an interest.

Definitions

company: ss 4(1), 5(1); control: s 173(1); person: IA 1937 s 11(*c*); personal representative: s 173(1); relative: s 3(1); "shares": s 173(1).

Former enactments

FA 1991 s 71.

Corresponding UK tax provision

Income and Corporation Taxes Act 1988 s227.

186 Connected persons

(1) Any question whether a person is connected with a company shall, notwithstanding section 10, be determined for the purposes of sections 176 to 183 in accordance with the following provisions:

(*a*) a person shall, subject to subsection (2), be connected with a company if the person directly or indirectly possesses or is entitled to acquire more than 30 per cent of—

(i) the issued ordinary share capital of the company,

(ii) the loan capital and issued share capital of the company, or

(iii) the voting power in the company;

(*b*) a person shall be connected with a company if the person directly or indirectly possesses or is entitled to acquire such rights as would, in the event of the winding up of the company or in any other circumstances, entitle the person to receive more than 30 per cent of the assets of the company which would then be available for distribution to equity holders of the company, and for the purposes of this paragraph—

(i) the persons who are equity holders of the company, and

(ii) the percentage of the assets of the company to which a person would be entitled,

shall be determined in accordance with sections 413 and 415, but construing references in section 415 to the first company as references to an equity holder and references to a winding up as including references to other circumstances in which assets of the company are available for distribution to its equity holders;

(*c*) a person shall be connected with a company if the person has control of the company.

(2) Where a person—

(*a*) acquired or became entitled to acquire loan capital of a company in the ordinary course of a business carried on by the person, being a business which includes the lending of money, and

(*b*) takes no part in the management or conduct of the company,

the person's interest in that loan capital shall be disregarded for the purposes of subsection (1)(*a*).

(3) References in this section to the loan capital of a company are references to any debt incurred by the company—

(*a*) for any money borrowed or capital assets acquired by the company, (*b*) for any right to receive income created in favour of the company, or

(*c*) for consideration the value of which to the company was at the time when the debt was incurred substantially less than the amount of the debt, including any premium on the debt.

(4) For the purposes of this section—

(*a*) a person shall be treated as entitled to acquire anything which the person is entitled to acquire at a future date or will at a future date be entitled to acquire, and

(*b*) a person shall be assumed to have the rights or powers of the person's associates as well as the person's own rights or powers.

Cross-references

Associated persons: s 185.

Definitions

company: ss 4(1), 5(1); control: s 173(1); distribution: ss 4(1), 436, 437; ordinary share capital: s 2(1); person: IA 1937 s 11(*c*).

Former enactments

FA 1991 s 72; FA 1996 s 131(9)(*a*).

Corresponding UK tax provision

Income and Corporation Taxes Act 1988 s 228.

PART 7
INCOME TAX AND CORPORATION TAX EXEMPTIONS

CHAPTER 1
Income Tax

187 Exemption from income tax and associated marginal relief

[(1) In this section, "the specified amount" means, subject to subsection (2)—

(*a*) in a case where the individual would apart from this section be entitled to a tax credit specified in section 461(*a*) (inserted by the Finance Act, 2001), [€10,420],[1] and

(*b*) in any other case, [€5,210].[2]][3]

(2) (*a*) For the purposes of this section and section 188, where a claimant proves that he or she has living at any time during the year of assessment any qualifying child, then, subject to subsection (3), the specified amount (within the meaning of this section or section 188, as the case may be) shall be increased for that year of assessment by—

(i) [€575][4] in respect of the first such child,

(ii) [€575][4] in respect of the second such child, and

(iii) [€830][5] in respect of each such child in excess of 2.

(*b*) Any question as to whether a child is a qualifying child for the purposes of this section or section 188 shall be determined on the same basis as it would be for the purposes of section 462, but without regard to [subsections (1)(*b*), (2) and (3) of that section.][6]

(3) Where for any year of assessment 2 or more individuals are, or but for this subsection would be, entitled under subsection (2) to an increase in the specified amount (within the meaning of this section or section 188, as the case may be) in respect of the same child, the following provisions shall apply:

(*a*) only one such increase under subsection (2) shall be allowed in respect of each child;

(*b*) where such child is maintained by one individual only, that individual only shall be entitled to claim the increase;

(*c*) where such child is maintained by more than one individual, each individual shall be entitled to claim such part of the increase as is proportionate to the amount expended on the child by that individual in relation to the total amount paid by all individuals towards the maintenance of the child;

(*d*) in ascertaining for the purposes of this subsection whether an individual maintains a child and, if so, to what extent, any payment made by the individual for or towards the maintenance of the child which that individual is entitled to deduct in computing his or her total income for the purposes of the Income Tax Acts shall be deemed not to be a payment for or towards the maintenance of the child.

(4) Where for any year of assessment—

(*a*) an individual makes a claim for the purpose, makes a return in the prescribed form of his or her total income for that year and proves that such total income does not exceed the specified amount, the individual shall be entitled to exemption from income tax, or

(*b*) an individual makes a claim for the purpose, makes a return in the prescribed form of his or her total income for that year and proves that such total income does not exceed a sum equal to twice the specified amount, the individual shall be entitled to have the amount of income tax payable in respect of his or her total income for that year, if that amount would but for this subsection exceed a sum equal to 40 per cent of the amount by which his or her total income exceeds the specified amount, reduced to that sum.

Amendments

1 Substituted by FA 2001 s 2(3) and Sch 1 para 2(*a*)(i) for 2002 and later tax years; previously "£6,068".

2 Substituted by FA 2001 s 2(3) and Sch 1 para 2(*a*)(i) for 2002 and later tax years; previously "£3,034".

3 Subs (1) substituted by FA 2001 s 2(3) and Sch 1 para 1(*d*)(i) for the short tax "year" 2001 and later tax years.

4 Substituted by FA 2001 s 2(3) and Sch 1 para 2(*a*)(ii) for 2002 and later tax years; previously "£450" (short tax "year" 2001: £333).

5 Substituted by FA 2001 s 2(3) and Sch 1 para 2(*a*)(ii) for 2002 and later tax years; previously "£650" (short tax "year" 2001: £481).

6 Substituted by FA 2002 s 138 and Sch 6 paras 3(*d*) and 6(*c*)(ii) with effect from 6 April 2001; previously "subsections (1)(*b*), (2), (3) and (5) of that section".

Cross-references

Age exemption: s 188(1); subs (2): s 188(2).
Home loan interest: s 244(2)(*c*).
Method of apportioning reliefs and charging tax in cases of separate assessment, subs (4)(*b*): s 1024(2)(*b*).
Relief from income tax in respect of income from dealing in residential development land: s 644A(3)(*b*).
Taxation of relevant interest (deposit interest retention tax): s 261(*c*).

Revenue precedents

Issue: Are the exemption limits available to a person who is not resident in Ireland (ss 187 and 188)?
Decision: Yes. "Total Income" for these purposes includes income arising outside the State which is not chargeable to tax in the State.

Revenue information

Information leaflet IT8 — Tax Exemption and Marginal Relief.

Tax Briefing

TB18 No.2 of 1995 par2.2 — Deposit interest retention tax and computation of marginal relief.

Definitions

Income Tax Acts: s 1(2); year of assessment: ss 2(1), 5(1).

Former enactments

FA 1980 s 1; FA 1981 s 1(*a*)(i); FA 1989 s 1(*a*); FA 1991 s 1(*a*)(iii); FA 1994 s 1(*a*); FA 1995 s 1(*a*); FA 1997 s 1(*a*).

188 Age exemption and associated marginal relief

[(1) In this section and in section 187—

"income tax payable" has the same meaning (inserted by the Finance Act, 2001) as in section 3, but without regard to any reduction of tax under section 244;

"total income" has the same meaning as in section 3, but includes income arising outside the State which is not chargeable to tax.

(2) In this section, **"the specified amount"** means, subject to section 187(2)—

(*a*) in a case where the individual would apart from this section be entitled to a tax credit specified in section 461(*a*) (inserted by the Finance Act, 2001), [€33,000],[1] and

(*b*) in any other case, [€16,500].[2]][3]

(3) This section shall apply for any year of assessment to an individual who makes a claim for the purpose, makes a return in the prescribed form of his or her total income for that year and proves that, at some time during the year of assessment, either the individual or, in a case where the individual would apart from this section be entitled to [a tax credit specified in section 461(*a*)],[4] the spouse of the individual was of the age of 65 years or over.

(4) Where an individual to whom this section applies proves that his or her total income for a year of assessment for which this section applies does not exceed the specified amount, the individual shall be entitled to exemption from income tax for that year.

(5) Where an individual to whom this section applies proves that his or her total income for a year of assessment for which this section applies does not exceed a sum equal to twice the specified amount, the individual shall be entitled to have the amount of income tax payable in respect of his or her total income for that year, if that amount would but for this subsection exceed a sum equal to 40 per cent of the amount by which his or her total income exceeds the specified amount, reduced to that sum.

(6) (*a*) Subsections (1) and (2) of section 459 and section 460 shall apply in relation to exemption from tax or any reduction of tax under this section or under section 187 as they apply to any allowance, deduction, relief or reduction under the provisions specified in the Table to section 458.

(*b*) Subsections (3) and (4) of section 459 and paragraph 8 of Schedule 28 shall, with any necessary modifications, apply in relation to exemption from tax or any reduction of tax under this section or under section 187.

Amendments

1 Substituted by FA 2005 s 4 for 2005 and subsequent years of assessment; previously "€31,000".

2 Substituted by FA 2005 s 4 for 2005 and subsequent years of assessment; previously ""€15,500".

3 Subss (1)–(2) substituted by FA 2001 s 4(*a*)(i) for short tax "year" 2001 and later tax years.

4 Substituted by FA 2001 s 4(*a*)(ii) for short tax "year" 2001 and later tax tears; previously "relief under section 461(2) as an individual referred to in paragraph (*a*)(i) of the definition of 'specified amount' in subsection (1) of that section".

Cross-references

Children: s 187(2).
Home loan interest: s 244(2)(*c*).
Low income exemption: s 187(3).
Method of apportioning reliefs and charging tax in cases of separate assessment, subs (5): s 1024(2)(*b*).
Relief from income tax in respect of income from dealing in residential development land: s 644A(3)(*b*).
Taxation of relevant interest (deposit interest retention tax): s 261(*c*).

Revenue information

Information leaflet IT8 — Tax Exemption and Marginal Relief

Tax Briefing

TB18 No.2 of 1995 para 2.2 — Deposit interest retention tax and computation of marginal relief

Definitions

Income Tax Acts: s 1(2); year of assessment: ss 2(1), 5(1).

Former enactments

FA 1980 s 2(1)–(4) and (6)–(7); FA 1981 s 1(*b*)(i); FA 1989 s 1(*b*); FA 1994 s 1(*b*); FA 1996 s 132 and Sch 5 Pt I para 12; FA 1997 s 1(*b*).

189 Payments in respect of personal injuries

(1) This section shall apply to any payment made—

(*a*) to or in respect of an individual who is permanently and totally incapacitated by reason of mental or physical infirmity from maintaining himself or herself, and

[(*b*) (i) pursuant to the issue of an order to pay under section 38 of the Personal Injuries Assessment Board Act 2003, or

(ii) following the institution by or on behalf of the individual of a civil action for damages,

in respect of personal injury giving rise to that mental or physical infirmity.][1]

[(2) (*a*) In this subsection—

"relevant gains" means chargeable gains (including allowable losses) within the meaning of the Capital Gains Tax Acts, which accrue to an individual, to or in respect of whom payments to which this section applies are made, from the disposal of—

(*a*) assets acquired with such payments,

(*b*) assets acquired with relevant income, or

(*c*) assets acquired directly or indirectly with the proceeds from the disposal of assets referred to in paragraphs (*a*) and (*b*);

"relevant income" means income which arises to an individual, to or in respect of whom payments to which this section applies are made, from the investment—

(*a*) in whole or in part of such payments, or

(*b*) of income derived directly or indirectly from such payments,

being income consisting of dividends or other income which, but for this section, would be chargeable to tax under Schedule C or under Case III, IV (by virtue of section 59 or section 745) or V of Schedule D or under Schedule F.

(*b*) Where for any year of assessment the aggregate of the relevant income arising to and the relevant gains accruing to an individual exceeds 50 per cent of the aggregate of the total income arising to and the total chargeable gains (including allowable losses) accruing to the individual for that year of assessment—

(i) the relevant income shall be exempt from income tax and shall not be reckoned in computing total income for the purposes of the Income Tax Acts, but the provisions of those Acts relating to the making of returns shall apply as if this section had not been enacted, and

(ii) the relevant gains shall be exempt from capital gains tax, but the provisions of the Capital Gains Tax Acts relating to the making of returns shall apply as if this section had not been enacted.

(*c*) For the purposes of computing whether a chargeable gain is, in whole or in part, a relevant gain, or whether income is, in whole or in part, relevant income, all such apportionments shall be made as are, in the circumstances, just and reasonable.][2]

Amendments

1 Subs (1)(*b*) substituted by FA 2004 s 6 with effect from 1 January 2004.

2 Subs (2) substituted by FA 2004 s 17(1)(*a*) with effect for 2004 and subsequent years of assessment.

Note

By virtue of Residential Institutions Redress Act 2002 s 22(1)—

(*a*) income consisting of an award under that Act is to be disregarded for the purposes of income tax assessment, and

(*b*) any payment in respect of an award under that Act is to be treated for the purposes of the Income Tax Acts as if it were a payment made following the institution, by or on behalf of the applicant to whom the payment is made, of a civil action for damages in respect of personal injury.

Cross-references

Deposit interest retention tax, repayment of tax: s 267(3).
Dividend withholding tax, exemption for certain persons, subs (2): s 172C(2)(*da*)(i).
Life assurance companies, taxation of policyholders — new basis, repayment of appropriate tax: s 730GA.
Taxation of unit holders in investment undertakings: s 739G(2)(*j*).

Revenue information

Information leaflet IT13 — Personal Injury Compensation Payments.

Tax Briefing

TB9 Jan 1993 para 1.6 — Personal Injuries — Exemption of Income.
TB44 June 2001 p 29 — Personal Injuries — Exemption of Income.

Definitions

allowable loss: s 5(1); Capital Gains Tax Acts: s 1(2); chargeable gain: s 5(1); Income Tax Acts: s 1(2); total income: s 3(1); year of assessment: ss 2(1), 5(1).

Former enactments

FA 1990 s 5(1)–(2).

Corresponding UK tax provision

Income and Corporation Taxes Act 1988 s 329.

189A Special trusts for permanently incapacitated individuals

[(1) In this section—

"incapacitated individual" means an individual who is permanently and totally incapacitated, by reason of mental or physical infirmity, from being able to maintain himself or herself;

"public subscriptions" means subscriptions, in the form of money or other property, raised, following an appeal made in that behalf to members of the public, for the benefit of one or more incapacitated individual or individuals, whose identity or identities is or are known to the persons making the subscriptions, being subscriptions that meet either of the following conditions, namely—

(*a*) the total amount of the subscriptions does not exceed [€381,000][1], or

(*b*) no amount of the subscriptions, at any time on or after the specified return date for the chargeable period for which exemption is first claimed under either subsection (2) or (3), constitutes a subscription made by any one person that is greater than 30 per cent of the total amount of the subscriptions;

"qualifying trust" means a trust established by deed in respect of which it is shown to the satisfaction of the inspector or, on appeal, to the Appeal Commissioners, that—

(*a*) the trust has been established exclusively for the benefit of one or more specified incapacitated individual or individuals, for whose benefit public subscriptions, within the meaning of this section, have been raised,

(*b*) the trust requires that—

(i) the trust funds be applied for the benefit of that individual or those individuals, as the case may be, at the discretion of the trustees of the trust, and

(ii) in the event of the death of that individual or those individuals, as the case may be, the undistributed part of the trust funds be applied for charitable purposes or be appointed in favour of the trustees of charitable bodies,

and

(*c*) none of the trustees of the trust is connected (within the meaning of section 10) with that individual or any of those individuals, as the case may be;

"specified return date for the chargeable period" has the same meaning as in section 950;

"trust funds" means, in relation to a qualifying trust—

(*a*) public subscriptions, raised for the benefit of the incapacitated individual or individuals, the subject or subjects of the trust, and

(*b*) all moneys and other property derived directly or indirectly from such public subscriptions.

(2) Income arising to the trustees of a qualifying trust in respect of the trust funds, being income consisting of dividends or other income which but for this section would be chargeable to tax under Schedule C or under Case Ill, IV (by virtue of section 59 or section 745) or V of Schedule D or under Schedule F, shall be exempt from income tax and shall not be reckoned in computing total income for the purposes of the Income Tax Acts.

[(3) Gains accruing to trustees of a qualifying trust in respect of the trust funds shall not be chargeable gains for the purposes of the Capital Gains Tax Acts.

(4) (*a*) In this subsection—

"relevant gains" means chargeable gains (including allowable losses) within the meaning of the Capital Gains Tax Acts, which accrue to an incapacitated individual from the disposal of—

(*a*) assets acquired with payments made by the trustees of a qualifying trust,

(*b*) assets acquired with relevant income, or

(*c*) assets acquired directly or indirectly with the proceeds from the disposal of assets referred to in paragraphs (*a*) and (*b*);

"relevant income" means income which—

(*a*) consists of payments made by the trustees of a qualifying trust to or in respect of an incapacitated individual, being a subject of the trust, or

(*b*) arises to such an incapacitated individual from the investment—

(i) in whole or in part of payments, made by the trustees of a qualifying trust, or

(ii) of income derived directly or indirectly from such payments,

being income consisting of dividends or other income which, but for this section, would be chargeable to tax under Schedule C or under Case III, IV (by virtue of section 59 or section 745) or V of Schedule D or under Schedule F.

(*b*) Where for any year of assessment the aggregate of relevant income arising to and the relevant gains accruing to an individual exceeds 50 per cent of the aggregate of the total income arising to and the total chargeable gains (including allowable losses) accruing to the individual in that year of assessment—

(i) the relevant income shall be exempt from income tax and shall not be reckoned in computing total income for the purposes of the Income Tax Acts, but the provisions of those Acts relating to the making of returns shall apply as if this section had not been enacted, and

(ii) the relevant gains shall be exempt from capital gains tax, but the provisions of the Capital Gains Tax Acts relating to the making of returns shall apply as if this section had not been enacted.

(*c*) For the purposes of computing whether a chargeable gain is, in whole or in part, a relevant gain, or whether income is, in whole or in part, relevant income, all such apportionments shall be made as are, in the circumstances, just and reasonable.][2]

(5) This section shall have effect as respects the year 1997–98 and subsequent years of assessment.][3]

Amendments

[1] Substituted by FA 2001 s 240(1) and (2)(*a*) and Sch 5 Pt 1 for 2002 and later tax years; previously "£300,000".

[1] Subs (3) and (4) substituted by FA 2004 s 17(1)(*b*) with effect for 2004 and subsequent years of assessment.

[2] Section 198A inserted by FA 1999 s 12(*a*) with effect from 6 April 1999.

Cross-references

Capital acquisitions tax, exemption of certain receipts, meanings of "incapacitated individual", "trust funds" and "qualifying trust" applied: CATCA 2003 s 82(3)(*a*).

Deposit interest retention tax, repayment of tax: s 267(2)(*a*), (3).

Dividend withholding tax, exemption for certain persons, subs (2), (3)(*b*): s 172C(2)(*da*); meaning of "qualifying trust" and "trust funds" applied: s 172C(3)(*d*).

Life assurance companies, taxation of policyholders — new basis, repayment of appropriate tax: s 730GA.

Taxation of unit holders in investment undertakings: s 739G(2)(*j*).

Tax Briefing

TB38 Dec 1999 pp 7–8 Special Trusts — Permanently Incapacitated Individuals.

TB44 June 2001 p 29 — Personal Injuries — Exemption of Income.

Definitions

allowable loss: s 5(1); Appeal Commissioners: s 2(1); Capital Gains Tax Acts: s 1(2); chargeable gain: s 5(1); Income Tax Acts: s 1(2); inspector: ss 2(1), 5(1); person: IA 1937 s 11(*c*); total income: s 3(1); year of assessment: ss 2(1), 5(1).

190 Certain payments made by the Haemophilia HIV Trust

(1) In this section, **"the Trust"** means the trust established by deed dated the 22nd day of November, 1989, between the Minister for Health and certain other persons, and referred to in that deed as **"the Haemophilia H.I.V. Trust"** or **"the HHT"**.

(2) This section shall apply to income consisting of payments made by the trustees of the Trust to or in respect of a beneficiary under the Trust.

(3) Notwithstanding any provision of the Income Tax Acts, income to which this section applies shall be disregarded for the purposes of those Acts.

Definitions

Income Tax Acts: s 1(2); person: IA 1937 s 11(*c*).

Former enactments

FA 1990 s 7.

191 Taxation treatment of Hepatitis C [and HIV] compensation payments

[(1) In this section—

"the Act" means the Hepatitis C Compensation Tribunal Act, 1997;

"the Tribunal" means the Tribunal known as the Hepatitis C Compensation Tribunal established under section 3 of the Act. [**See Note below**]

(2) This section shall apply to any payment in respect of compensation—

(*a*) by the Tribunal in accordance with the Act, or

(*b*) following the institution by or on behalf of a person of a civil action for damages in respect of personal injury, to a person referred to—

(i) in subsection (1) of section 4 of the Act, in respect of matters referred to in that section, or

(ii) in any regulations made under section 9 of the Act, in respect of matters referred to in those regulations.][1]

(3) For the purposes of [the Income Tax Acts and the Capital Gains Tax Acts][2] and notwithstanding any provision of those Acts to the contrary—

(*a*) income consisting of payments to which this section applies shall be disregarded, and

(*b*) any payment by the Tribunal to which this section applies shall be treated in all respects as if it were a payment made following the institution, by or on behalf of the person to or in respect of whom the payment is made, of a civil action for damages in respect of personal injury.

Note

By virtue of the Hepatitis C Compensation Tribunal (Amendment) Act 2002 ss 2 and 11, and the Hepatitis C Compensation Tribunal (Amendment) Act 2002 (Commencement) Order 2002, the Tribunal established by the Hepatatis C Compensation Tribunal Act 1997 is, with effect from 9 October 2002, to be known as the Hepatitis C and HIV Compensation Tribunal, and references in the latter Act and any other Act of the Oireachtas and any instrument made under any Act of the Oireachtas to the Hepatitis C Compensation Tribunal are to be construed as references to the Hepatitis C and HIV Compensation Tribunal.

Amendments

1 Subss (1)–(2) substituted by FA 1998 s 9 as on and from 1 November 1997.

2 Substituted by FA 2004 s 17(1)(*c*) with effect for 2004 and subsequent years of assessment; previously "the Income Tax Acts".

Tax Briefing

TB35 Mar 1999 p 6 — Hepatitis C Compensation Payments.

TB44 June 2001 p 28 — Hepatitis C Compensation Payments and the issue of exemption under TCA 1997 s 189 for income arising from the investment of compensation payments. Where it is medically certified that an individual is suffering from a degenerative condition which will ultimately cause a permanent and total incapacity by reason of mental or physical infirmity and the condition gave rise to the compensation payment, Revenue accepts that the requirements of TCA 1997 s 189(1)(*a*) are met.

Definitions

Capital Gains Tax Acts: s 1(2); Income Tax Acts: s 1(2).

Former enactments

FA 1996 s 9.

192 Payments in respect of thalidomide children

(1) This section shall apply to any payment made by the Minister for Health and Children or by the foundation known as Hilfswerk fur behinderte Kinder to or in respect of any individual handicapped by reason of infirmity which can be linked with the taking by the individual's mother during her pregnancy of preparations containing thalidomide.

(2) Income which—

(*a*) consists of a payment to which this section applies, or

(*b*) arises to a person to or in respect of whom payments to which this section applies are made, from the investment in whole or in part of such payments or of the income derived from such payments, being income consisting of dividends or other income which but for this section would be chargeable to tax under Schedule C or under Case III, IV [(by virtue of section 59 or section 745)][1] or V of Schedule D or under Schedule F,

shall be exempt from income tax and shall not be reckoned in computing total income for the purposes of the Income Tax Acts; but the provisions of those Acts relating to the making of returns of total income shall apply as if this section had not been enacted.

[(3) Gains which accrue to a person, to or in respect of whom payments to which this section applies are made, from the disposal of—

(*a*) assets acquired with such payments,

(*b*) assets acquired with income exempted from income tax under subsection (2), or

(*c*) assets acquired directly or indirectly with the proceeds from the disposal of assets referred to in paragraphs (*a*) and (*b*),

shall not be chargeable gains for the purposes of the Capital Gains Tax Acts.

(4) For the purposes of computing whether by virtue of this section a gain is, in whole or in part, a chargeable gain, or whether income is, in whole or in part, exempt from income tax, all such apportionments shall be made as are, in the circumstances, just and reasonable.][2]

Amendments

1 Substituted by FA 1999 s 13(*b*) with effect from 6 April 1999; previously "(by virtue of section 59)".

1 Subs (3) and (4) inserted by FA 2004 s 17(1)(*d*) with effect for 2004 and subsequent years of assessment.

Cross-references

Deposit interest retention tax, repayment of tax: s 267(3).

Dividend withholding tax, exemption of certain persons, subs (2): s 172C(2)(*da*)(i).

Life assurance companies, taxation of policyholders — new basis, repayment of appropriate tax: s 730GA.

Taxation of unit holders in investment undertakings: s 739G(2)(*j*).

Tax Briefing

TB44 June 2001 p 29 — Personal Injuries — Exemption of Income.

Definitions

Capital Gains Tax Acts: s 1(2); chargeable gain: s 5(1); Income Tax Acts: s 1(2); total income: s 3(1).

Former enactments

FA 1973 s 19(1)–(2); FA 1978 s 7.

192A Exemption in respect of certain payments under employment law

[(1) In this section—

"relevant Act" means an enactment which contains provisions for the protection of employees' rights and entitlements or for the obligations of employers towards their employees;

"relevant authority" means any of the following—

(*a*) a rights commissioner,

(*b*) the Director of Equality Investigations,

(*c*) the Employment Appeals Tribunal,

(*d*) the Labour Court,

(*e*) the Circuit Court, or

(*f*) the High Court.

(2) Subject to subsections (3) and (5), this section applies to a payment under a relevant Act, to an employee or former employee by his or her employer or former employer, as the case may be, which is made, on or after 4 February 2004, in accordance with a recommendation, decision or a determination by a relevant authority in accordance with the provisions of that Act.

(3) A payment made in accordance with a settlement arrived at under a mediation process provided for in a relevant Act shall be treated as if it had been made in accordance with a recommendation, decision or determination under that Act of a relevant authority.

(4) (*a*) Subject to subsection (5) and without prejudice to any of the terms or conditions of an agreement referred to in this subsection, this section shall apply to a payment—

(i) made, on or after 4 February 2004, under an agreement evidenced in writing, being an agreement between persons who are not connected with each other (within the meaning of section 10), in settlement of a claim which—

(I) had it been made to a relevant authority, would have been a *bona fide* claim made under the provisions of a relevant Act,

(II) is evidenced in writing, and

(III) had the claim not been settled by the agreement, is likely to have been the subject of a recommendation, decision or determination under that Act by a relevant authority that a payment be made to the person making the claim,

(ii) the amount of which does not exceed the maximum payment which, in accordance with a decision or determination by a relevant authority (other than the Circuit Court or the High Court) under the relevant Act, could have been made under that Act in relation to the claim, had the claim not been settled by agreement, and

(iii) where—

(I) copies of the agreement and the statement of claim are kept and retained by the employer, by or on behalf of whom the payment was made, for a period of six years from the day on which the payment was made, and

(II) the employer has made copies of the agreement and the statement of claim available to an officer of the Revenue Commissioners where the officer has requested the employer to make those copies available to him or her.

(*b*) (i) On being so requested by an officer of the Revenue Commissioners, an employer shall make available to the officer all copies of—

(I) such agreements as are referred to in paragraph (*a*) entered into by or on behalf of the employer, and

(II) the statements of claim related to those agreements,

kept and retained by the employer in accordance with subparagraph (iii) of that paragraph.

(ii) The officer may examine and take extracts from or copies of any documents made available to him or her under this subsection.

(5) This section shall not apply to so much of a payment under a relevant Act or an agreement referred to in subsection (4) as is—

(*a*) a payment, however described, in respect of remuneration including arrears of remuneration, or

(*b*) a payment referred to in section 123(1) or 480(2)(*a*).

(6) Payments to which this section applies shall be exempt from income tax and shall not be reckoned in computing total income for the purposes of the Income Tax Acts.][1]

Amendments

1 Section 192A inserted by FA 2004 s 7 with effect from 1 January 2004.

Definitions

Circuit Court: IA 1937 Sch; High Court: IA 1937 Sch; Income Tax Acts: s 1(2); person: IA 1937 s 11(*c*); total income: s 3(1); writing: IA 1937 Sch.

192B Foster care payments etc

[(1) In this section—

"carer" means an individual who is or was a foster parent or relative or who takes care of an individual on behalf of the Health Service Executive;

"foster parent" has the meaning assigned to it in the Child Care (Placement of Children in Foster Care) Regulations 1995 (SI No 260 of 1995);

"relative" has the meaning assigned to it in the Child Care (Placement of Children with Relatives) Regulations 1995 (SI No 261 of 1995).

(2) This section applies to payments made—

(*a*) to a carer by the Health Service Executive in accordance with—

(i) article 14 of the Child Care (Placement of Children in Foster Care) Regulations 1995, or

(ii) article 14 of the Child Care (Placement of Children with Relatives) Regulations 1995,

(*b*) at the discretion of the Health Service Executive to a carer in respect of an individual—

(i) who had been in the care of a carer until attaining the age of 18 years,

(ii) in respect of whom a payment referred to in paragraph (*a*) had been paid until the individual attained the age of 18 years,

(iii) who since attaining the age of 18 years continues to reside with a carer, and

(iv) who has not attained the age of 21 years or where the person has attained such age, suffers from a disability or is in receipt of full-time instruction at any university, college, school or other educational establishment and such disability or instruction commenced before the person attained the age of 21 years,

or

(*c*) in accordance with the law of any other Member State of the European Communities which corresponds to the payments referred to in paragraph (*a*) or (*b*).

(3) Payments to which this section applies are exempt from income tax and shall not be taken into account in computing total income for the purposes of the Income Tax Acts.][1]

Amendments

1 Section 192B inserted by FA 2005 s 11 with effect from 1 January 2005.

Definitions

Income Tax Acts: s 1(2); total income: s 3(1).

193 Income from scholarships

(1) (*a*) In this section—

"relevant body" means a body corporate, unincorporated body, partnership, individual or other body;

"relevant scholarship" means a scholarship provision for which is made, either directly or indirectly, by a relevant body or a person connected with the relevant body and where payments are made, either directly or indirectly, in respect of such a scholarship to—

(i) an employee or, where the relevant body is a body corporate, a director of the relevant body, or

(ii) the spouse, family, dependants or servants of such employee or director;

"scholarship" includes an exhibition, bursary or other similar educational endowment.

(*b*) A person shall be regarded as connected with a relevant body for the purposes of this subsection if that person is—

(i) a trustee of a settlement, within the meaning of section 10, made by the relevant body, or

(ii) a relevant body,

and that person would be regarded as connected with the relevant body for the purposes of that section.

(2) Income arising from a scholarship held by a person receiving full-time instruction at a university, college, school or other educational establishment shall be exempt from income tax, and no account shall be taken of any such income in computing the amount of income for the purposes of the Income Tax Acts.

(3) Nothing in subsection (2) shall be construed as conferring on any person other than the person holding the scholarship in question any exemption from a charge to income tax.

(4) Notwithstanding subsection (3), a payment of income arising from a relevant scholarship which is—

(*a*) provided from a trust fund or under a scheme, and

(*b*) held by a person receiving full-time instruction at a university, college, school or other educational establishment,

shall be exempt from income tax if, in the year of assessment in which the payment is made, not more than 25 per cent of the total amount of the payments made from that fund, or under that scheme, in respect of scholarships held as mentioned in paragraph (*b*) is attributable to relevant scholarships.

(5) If any question arises whether any income is income arising from a scholarship held by a person receiving full-time instruction at a university, college, school or other educational establishment, the Revenue Commissioners may consult the Minister for Education and Science.

(6) Where a payment is made before the 6th day of April, 1998, in respect of a scholarship awarded before the 26th day of March, 1997, this section shall apply subject to paragraph 2 of Schedule 32.

Cross-references

Returns of employees' emoluments: s 897(2)(*d*).

For income payments made before 6 April 1998, in respect of a scholarship awarded before 26 March 1997, in subs (1) treat definitions of "relevant body", "relevant scholarship" and para (*b*) as deleted and treat subss (3)-(4) as deleted: Sch 32 para 2.

Case law

Scholarships awarded to children of employees out of fund set up by employer held within the exemption: *Wicks v Firth* (1984) 56 TC 318.

Payments by Home Office of post graduate course fees held exempt: *Walters v Tickner* [1993] STC 1059.

Definitions

person: IA 1937 s 11(*c*).

Former enactments

ITA 1967 s 353; FA 1997 s 11(1)–(2).

Corresponding UK tax provision

Income and Corporation Taxes Act 1988 s 331.

194 Child benefit

Child benefit payable under Part IV of the Social Welfare (Consolidation) Act, 1993, or any subsequent Act together with which that Act may be cited, shall be exempt from income tax and shall not be reckoned in computing income for the purposes of the Income Tax Acts.

Definitions

Income Tax Acts: s 1(2).

Former enactments

ITA 1967 s 354; FA 1997 s 146(1) and Sch 9 Pt I para 1(26).

Corresponding UK tax provision

Income and Corporation Taxes Act 1988 s 617.

195 Exemption of certain earnings of writers, composers and artists

(1) In this section, **"work"** means an original and creative work which is within one of the following categories—

(*a*) a book or other writing;

(*b*) a play;
(*c*) a musical composition;
(*d*) a painting or other like picture;
(*e*) a sculpture.

(2) (*a*) This section shall apply to an individual—

(i) who is—

(I) resident in the State and not resident elsewhere, or

(II) ordinarily resident and domiciled in the State and not resident elsewhere, and

(ii) (I) who is determined by the Revenue Commissioners, after consideration of any evidence in relation to the matter which the individual submits to them and after such consultation (if any) as may seem to them to be necessary with such person or body of persons as in their opinion may be of assistance to them, to have written, composed or executed, as the case may be, either solely or jointly with another individual, a work or works generally recognised as having cultural or artistic merit, or

(II) who has written, composed or executed, as the case may be, either solely or jointly with another individual, a particular work which the Revenue Commissioners, after consideration of the work and of any evidence in relation to the matter which the individual submits to them and after such consultation (if any) as may seem to them to be necessary with such person or body of persons as in their opinion may be of assistance to them, determine to be a work having cultural or artistic merit.

(*b*) The Revenue Commissioners shall not make a determination under this subsection unless—

(i) the individual concerned duly makes a claim to the Revenue Commissioners for the determination, being (where the determination is sought under paragraph (*a*)(ii)(II)) a claim made after the publication, production or sale, as the case may be, of the work in relation to which the determination is sought, and

(ii) the individual complies with any request to him or her under subsection (4).

(3) (*a*) An individual to whom this section applies and who duly makes a claim to the Revenue Commissioners in that behalf shall, subject to paragraph (*b*), be entitled to have the profits or gains arising to him or her from the publication, production or sale, as the case may be, of a work or works in relation to which the Revenue Commissioners have made a determination under clause (I) or (II) of subsection (2)(*a*)(ii), or of a work of the individual in the same category as that work, and which apart from this section would be included in an assessment made on him or her under Case II of Schedule D, disregarded for the purposes of the Income Tax Acts.

(*b*) The exemption authorised by this section shall not apply for any year of assessment before the year of assessment in which the individual concerned makes a claim under clause (I) or (II) of subsection (2)(*a*)(ii) in respect of which the Revenue Commissioners make a determination referred to in clause (I) or (II) of subsection (2)(*a*)(ii), as the case may be.

(*c*) The relief provided by this section may be given by repayment or otherwise.

(4) (*a*) Where an individual makes a claim to which subsection (2)(*a*)(ii)(I) relates, the Revenue Commissioners may serve on the individual a notice or notices in writing requesting the individual to furnish to them within such period as may be specified in the notice or notices such information, books, documents or other evidence as may appear to them to be necessary for the purposes of a determination under subsection (2)(*a*)(ii)(I).

(*b*) Where an individual makes a claim to which subsection (2)(*a*)(ii)(II) relates, the individual shall—

(i) in the case of a book or other writing or a play or musical composition, if the Revenue Commissioners so request, furnish to them 3 copies, and

(ii) in the case of a painting or other like picture or a sculpture, if the Revenue Commissioners so request, provide, or arrange for the provision of, such facilities as the Revenue Commissioners may consider necessary for the purposes of a determination under subsection (2)(*a*)(ii)(II) (including any requisite permissions or consents of the person who owns or possesses the painting, picture or sculpture).

(5) The Revenue Commissioners may serve on an individual who makes a claim under subsection (3) a notice or notices in writing requiring the individual to make available within such time as may be specified in the notice all such books, accounts and documents in the individual's possession or power as may be requested, being books, accounts and documents relating to the publication, production or sale, as the case may be, of the work in respect of the profits or gains of which exemption is claimed.

(6) (*a*) In this subsection, **"relevant period"** means, as respects a claim in relation to a work or works or a particular work, the period of 6 months commencing on the date on which a claim is first made in respect of that work or those works or the particular work, as the case may be.

(*b*) Where—

(i) an individual—

(I) has made due claim (in this subsection referred to as a **"claim"**) to the Revenue Commissioners for a determination under clause (I) or (II) of subsection (2)(*a*)(ii) in relation to a work or works or a particular work, as the case may be, that the individual has written, composed or executed, as the case may be, solely or jointly with another individual, and

(II) as respects the claim, has complied with any request made to the individual under subsection (4) or (5) in the relevant period,

and

(ii) the Revenue Commissioners fail to make a determination under clause (I) or (II) of subsection (2)(*a*)(ii) in relation to the claim in the relevant period, the individual may, by notice in writing given to the Revenue Commissioners within 30 days after the end of the relevant period, appeal to the Appeal Commissioners on the grounds that—

(A) the work or works is or are generally recognised as having cultural or artistic merit, or

(B) the particular work has cultural or artistic merit,

as the case may be.

(7) The Appeal Commissioners shall hear and determine an appeal made to them under subsection (6) as if it were an appeal against an assessment to income tax and, subject to subsection (8), the provisions of the Income Tax Acts relating to such appeals and to the rehearing of an appeal and to the statement of a case for the opinion of the High Court on a point of law shall apply accordingly with any necessary modifications.

(8) (*a*) On the hearing of an appeal made under subsection (6), the Appeal Commissioners may—

(i) after consideration of—

(I) any evidence in relation to the matter submitted to them by or on behalf of the individual concerned and by or on behalf of the Revenue Commissioners, and

(II) in relation to a work or works or a particular work, the work or works or the particular work,

and

(ii) after such consultation (if any) as may seem to them to be necessary with such person or body of persons as in their opinion may be of assistance to them,

determine that the individual concerned has written, composed or executed, as the case may be, either solely or jointly with another individual—

(A) a work or works generally recognised as having cultural or artistic merit, or

(B) a particular work which has cultural or artistic merit,

and, where the Appeal Commissioners so determine, the individual shall be entitled to relief under subsection (3)(*a*) as if the determination had been made by the Revenue Commissioners under clause (I) or (II) of subsection (2)(*a*)(ii), as the case may be.

(*b*) This subsection shall, subject to any necessary modifications, apply to the rehearing of an appeal by a judge of the Circuit Court and, to the extent necessary, to the determination by the High Court of any question or questions of law arising on the statement of a case for the opinion of the High Court.

(9) For the purposes of the hearing or rehearing of an appeal made under subsection (6), the Revenue Commissioners may nominate any of their officers to act on their behalf.

(10) For the purposes of determining the amount of the profits or gains to be disregarded under this section for the purposes of the Income Tax Acts, the Revenue Commissioners may make such apportionment of receipts and expenses as may be necessary.

(11) Notwithstanding any exemption provided by this section, the provisions of the Income Tax Acts regarding the making by the individual of a return of his or her total income shall apply as if the exemption had not been authorised.

(12)(*a*) An Comhairle Ealaíon and the Minister for Arts, Heritage, Gaeltacht and the Islands shall, with the consent of the Minister for Finance, draw up guidelines for determining for the purposes of this section whether a work within a category specified in subsection (1) is an original and creative work and whether it has, or is generally recognised as having, cultural or artistic merit.

(*b*) Without prejudice to the generality of paragraph (*a*), a guideline under that paragraph may—

(i) consist of a specification of types or kinds of works that are not original and creative or that have not, or are not generally recognised as having, cultural or artistic merit, including a specification of works that are published, produced or sold for a specified purpose, and

(ii) specify criteria by reference to which the questions whether works are original or creative and whether they have, or are generally recognised as having, cultural or artistic merit are to be determined.

(13)(*a*) Where a claim for a determination under subsection (2) is made to the Revenue Commissioners, the Revenue Commissioners shall not determine that the work concerned is original and creative or has, or is generally recognised as having, cultural or artistic merit unless it complies with the guidelines under subsection (12) for the time being in force.

(*b*) Paragraph (*a*) shall, with any necessary modifications, apply to—

(i) a determination by the Appeal Commissioners under subsection (8) on an appeal to them under subsection (6) in relation to a claim mentioned in paragraph (*a*), and

(ii) a rehearing by a judge of the Circuit Court of an appeal mentioned in subparagraph (i) and, to the extent necessary, to the determination by the High Court of any question of law arising on such an appeal or rehearing and specified in the statement of a case for the opinion of the High Court, by the Appeal Commissioners or, as the case may be, a judge of the Circuit Court.

(14) Where a determination has been or is made under clause (I) or (II) of subsection (2)(*a*)(ii) in relation to a work or works of a person, subsection (3)(*a*) shall not apply to any other work of that person that is in the same category as such work or works and is or was first published, produced or sold on or after the 3rd day of May, 1994, unless that other work is one that complies with the guidelines under subsection (12) for the time being in force and would qualify to be determined by the Revenue Commissioners as an original or creative work and as having, or being generally recognised as having, cultural or artistic merit.

(15) On application to the Revenue Commissioners in that behalf by any person, the Revenue Commissioners shall supply the person free of charge with a copy of any guidelines under subsection (12) for the time being in force.

Cross-references

Receipts accruing after discontinuance of profession, subs (3): s 91(2)(*d*).

Case law

Subs (2)(*a*): Exemption refused to a journalist for general work despite a successful claim in respect of a book based on earlier activities: *Healy v Breathnach* ITR Vol III p 496 [1986] IR 105; but granted to author of a series of history books: *Revenue Commissioners v O'Loinsigh* [1995] 1 IR 509.

Tax Briefing

TB18 No.2 of 1995 par 2.1 — Guidelines for determining whether works are original and creative and whether they are recognised as having artistic or cultural merit.

TB42 Dec 2000 pp 17–19 — Artists Exemption — Question and Answers.

TB56 July 2004 p 12 — Meaning of "not resident elsewhere" for the purposes of sections 195 and 234 Taxes Consolidation Act 1997.

TB57 Oct 2004 p 15 — "not resident elsewhere": Correction of error in TB56.

Definitions

Appeal Commissioners: s 2(1); body of persons: s 2(1); Circuit Court: IA 1937 Sch; High Court: IA 1937 Sch; Income Tax Acts: s 1(2); month: IA 1937 Sch; person: IA 1937 s 11(*c*); total income: s 3(1); writing: IA 1937 Sch; year of assessment: ss 2(1), 5(1).

Former enactments

FA 1969 s 2; FA 1989 s 5; FA 1994 s 14; FA 1995 s 173(2); FA 1996 s 14; FA 1997 s 146(1) and Sch 9 Pt I para 18(1).

Corresponding UK tax provision

Income and Corporation Taxes Act 1988 s 538.

196 Expenses of members of judiciary

(1) In this section, **"a member of the Judiciary"** means—

(*a*) a judge of the Supreme Court,

(*b*) a judge of the High Court,

(*c*) a judge of the Circuit Court, or

(*d*) a judge of the District Court.

(2) An allowance payable by means of an annual sum to a member of the Judiciary in accordance with section 5 of the Courts of Justice Act, 1953, and which has been determined, in accordance with subsection (2)(*c*) of that section, by the Minister for Justice, Equality and Law Reform in consultation with the Minister for Finance to be in full settlement of the expenses which such a person is obliged to incur in the performance of his or her duties as a member of the Judiciary, and which are not otherwise reimbursed either directly or indirectly out of moneys provided by the Oireachtas, shall be exempt from income tax and shall not be reckoned in computing income for the purposes of the Income Tax Acts.

(3) Sections 114 and 115 shall not apply in relation to expenses in full settlement of which an allowance referred to in subsection (2) is payable, and no claim shall lie under those sections in respect of those expenses.

Definitions

person: IA 1937 s 11(*c*); Circuit Court: IA 1937 Sch; High Court: IA 1937 Sch; the Supreme Court: IA 1937 Sch.

Former enactments

FA 1994 s 164.

196A State employees: foreign service allowances

[(1) Where any allowance to, or emoluments of, an officer of the State are certified by the Minister for Finance, having consulted with the Minister for Foreign Affairs, or with such Minister of the Government as the Minister for Finance considers appropriate in the circumstances, to represent compensation for the extra cost of having to live outside the State in order to perform his or her duties, that allowance, or those emoluments, shall be disregarded as income for the purposes of the Income Tax Acts.

(2) In this section—

"emoluments" means emoluments to which section 985A applies;

"officer of the State" means—

(*a*) a civil servant within the meaning of section 1(1) of the Civil Service Regulation Act 1956,

(*b*) a member of the Garda Síochána, or

(*c*) a member of the Permanent Defence Force.

(3) This section is deemed to have applied as on and from 1 January 2005.][1].

Amendments

1 Section 196A inserted by FA 2005 s 12 with effect from 1 January 2005.

Definitions

Income Tax Acts: s 1(2).

197 Bonus or interest paid under instalment savings schemes

Any bonus or interest payable to an individual under an instalment savings scheme (within the meaning of section 53 of the Finance Act, 1970) shall be disregarded for the purposes of the Income Tax Acts if, or in so far as, the bonus or interest is payable in respect of an amount not exceeding the amount permitted under the scheme to be paid by the individual.

Definitions

Income Tax Acts: s 1(2).

Notes

FA 1970 s 53 authorises the setting up of instalment savings schemes which are either (*a*) established and administered by the Minister for Finance or (*b*) established and administered by a bank, trustee savings bank or building society, and approved by the Minister for Finance.

Former enactments

FA 1970 s 18.

198 Certain interest not to be chargeable

[(1) (*a*) In this subsection—

"arrangements" means arrangements having the force of law by virtue of [section 826(1)(*a*)][1];

"relevant territory" means—

(i) a Member State of the European Communities other than the State, or

(ii) not being such a Member State, a territory with the government of which arrangements have been made;

"tax", in relation to a relevant territory, means any tax imposed in that territory which corresponds to [income tax or corporation tax, as is appropriate,][2] in the State.

(*b*) For the purposes of this subsection, a [person][3] shall be regarded as being a resident of a relevant territory if—

(i) in a case where the relevant territory is a territory with the government of which arrangements have been made, the [person][3] is regarded as being a resident of that territory under those arrangements, and

(ii) in any other case, the [person][3] is by virtue of the law of the relevant territory resident for the purposes of tax in that territory.

(*c*) Notwithstanding any other provision of the Income Tax Acts but without prejudice to any charge under the Corporation Tax Acts on the profits of such a person—

(i) a company not resident in the State or a person not ordinarily resident in the State shall not be chargeable to income tax in respect of interest paid by—

(I) a company in the course of carrying on relevant trading operations (within the meaning of section 445 or 446), or

(II) a specified collective investment undertaking (within the meaning of section 734),

...[4]

(ii) a company shall not be chargeable to income tax in respect of interest paid by a relevant person (within the meaning of section 246) in the ordinary course of a trade or business carried on by that person if the company—

(I) is not resident in the State, and

(II) is regarded for the purposes of this subsection as being a resident of a [relevant territory,][5] ...[6]][7]

[(iii) a person shall not be chargeable to income tax in respect of interest [paid][8] by a company if the person is not a resident of the State and is regarded as being a resident of a relevant territory for the purposes of this subsection, and the interest is interest to which section 64(2) applies or interest paid in respect of an asset covered security within the meaning of [section 3 of the Asset Covered Securities Act 2001, and][9]][10]

[(iv) a person shall not be chargeable to income tax in respect of interest paid by a qualifying company (within the meaning of section 110) if the person is not a resident of the State and is regarded as being a resident of a relevant territory for the purposes of this subsection, and the interest is paid out of the assets of the qualifying company.][11]

[(2) In relation to interest paid in respect of a relevant security (within the meaning of section 246), subsection (1) shall apply—

[(*a*) as if in section 445 the following subsection were substituted for subsection (2) of that section:

"(2) Subject to subsections (7) and (8), the Minister may give a certificate certifying that such trading operations of a qualified company as are specified in the certificate are, with effect from a date specified in the certificate, relevant trading operations for the purpose of this section.",

and

(*b*) as if in section 446 the following subsection were substituted for subsection (2) of that section:

"(2) Subject to subsections (7) and (9), the Minister may give a certificate certifying that such trading operations of a company as are specified in the certificate are, with effect from a date specified in the certificate, relevant trading operations for the purpose of this section.".][12]][13]

Amendments

1 Substituted by FA 2004 s 89 and Sch 3 para 1(*g*) with effect from 25 March 2004; previously "section 826".

2 Substituted by FA 2001 s 36(1)(*a*) in respect of interest paid on or after 30 March 2001; previously "corporation tax"

3 Substituted by FA 2001 s 36(1)(*b*) in respect of interest paid on or after 30 March 2001; previously "company".

4 Deleted by FA 2001 s 36(1)(*c*) in respect of interest paid on or after 30 March 2001; previously "and".

5 Substituted by FA 2001 s 36(1)(*d*) in respect of interest paid on or after 30 March 2001; previously "relevant territory".

6 Deleted by FA 2003 s 48(3)(*a*) as respects interest paid on or after 6 February 2003; previously "and".

7 Subs (1) substituted by FA 2000 s 34(1) as respects interest paid in 2000–2001 and later tax years.

8 Substituted by FA 2003 s 48(3)(*b*)(i) as respects interest paid on or after 6 February 2003; previously "payable".

9 Substituted by FA 2003 s 48(3)(*b*)(ii) as respects interest paid on or after 6 February 2003; previously "section 2 of the Asset Covered Securities Act 2001.".

10 Subs (1)(*c*)(iii) substituted by Asset Covered Securities Act 2001 s 106 and Sch 2, Pt 2. By virtue of the Asset Covered Securities Act 2001 (Commencement) Order 2002 (SI No 94 of 2002) this amendment came into operation on 22 March 2002.

11 Subs (1)(*c*)(iv) inserted by FA 2003 s 48(3)(*c*) as respects interest paid on or after 6 February 2003.

12 Subs (2)(*a*)–(*b*) substituted by FA 1999 s 85(*a*) with effect from 6 April 1999.

13 Subs (2) inserted by FA 1998 s 54(*b*) with effect from 6 April 1998.

Cross-references

Restriction on deductibility of certain interest: s 817C(3).

Definitions

company: s 4(1); Corporation Tax Acts: s 1(2); Income Tax Acts: s 1(2); person: IA 1937 s 11(*c*).

Former enactments

FA 1995 s 40.

199 Interest on certain securities

Income tax shall not be chargeable in respect of the interest on securities issued by the Minister for Finance for the purpose of being used in payment of income tax, and such interest shall not be reckoned in computing income for the purposes of the Income Tax Acts.

Definitions

Income Tax Acts: s 1(2).

Former enactments

ITA 1967 s 345; FA 1974 s 86 and Sch 2 Pt I.

200 Certain foreign pensions

(1) In this section, **"tax"**, in relation to any country, means a tax which is chargeable and payable under the law of that country and which corresponds to income tax in the State.

(2) This section shall apply to any pension, benefit or allowance which—

(*a*) is given in respect of past services in an office or employment or is payable under the provisions of the law of the country in which it arises which correspond to the provisions of Chapter 12, 16 or 17 of Part II of, or Chapter 4 or 6 of Part III of, the Social Welfare (Consolidation) Act, 1993, or any subsequent Act together with which that Act may be cited, and

(*b*) if it were received by a person who, for the purposes of tax of the country in which it arises, is resident in that country and is not resident elsewhere, would not be regarded as income for those purposes.

[(2A) Notwithstanding subsection (2), this section shall not apply to a pension to which subparagraph (*b*) of paragraph 1 of Article 18 (Pensions, Social Security, Annuities, Alimony and Child Support) of the Convention between the Government of Ireland and the Government of the United States of America for the Avoidance of Double Taxation and the Prevention of Fiscal Evasion with respect to Taxes on Income and Capital Gains signed at Dublin on the 28th day of July, 1997 applies.][1]

(3) In section 18(2), the reference in paragraph (*f*) of Case III to income arising from possessions outside the State shall be deemed not to include a reference to any pension, benefit or allowance to which this section applies.

Amendments

1 Subs (2A) inserted by FA 1998 s 18 with effect from 6 April 1998.

Cross-references

Approved minimum retirement fund: s 784(4)(*b*).

Tax Briefing

TB33 Sept 1998 — US Social Security Pensions payable to Irish residents taxable in Ireland only.

Definitions

person: IA 1937 s 11(*c*); year of assessment: ss 2(1), 5(1).

Former enactments

F(MP)A 1968 s 9; FA 1997 s 146(1) and Sch 9 Pt I para 3.

Corresponding UK tax provision

Income and Corporation Taxes Act 1988 s 58.

---

201 Exemptions and reliefs in respect of tax under section 123

(1) (*a*) In this section and in Schedule 3—

"the basic exemption" means [€10,160][1] together with [€765][2] for each complete year of the service, up to the relevant date, of the holder in the office or employment in respect of which the payment is made;

"foreign service", in relation to an office or employment, means service such that—

(i) tax was not chargeable in respect of the emoluments of the office or employment,

(ii) the office or employment being an office or employment within Schedule E, tax under that Schedule was not chargeable in respect of the whole of the emoluments of that office or employment, or

(iii) the office or employment being regarded as a possession in a place outside the State within the meaning of Case III of Schedule D, tax in respect of the income arising from that office or employment did not fall to be computed in accordance with section 71(1);

"the relevant date", in relation to a payment not being a payment in commutation of annual or other periodical payments, means the date of the termination or change in respect of which it is made and, in relation to a payment in commutation of annual or other periodical payments, means the date of the termination or change in respect of which those payments would have been made.

(*b*) In this section—

"control", in relation to a body corporate, means the power of a person to secure—

(i) by means of the holding of shares or the possession of voting power in or in relation to that or any other body corporate, or

(ii) by virtue of any power conferred by the articles of association or other document regulating that or any other body corporate,

that the affairs of the first-mentioned body corporate are conducted in accordance with the wishes of that person and, in relation to a partnership, means the right to a share of more than 50 per cent of the assets, or of more than 50 per cent of the income, of the partnership;

references to an employer or to a person controlling or controlled by an employer include references to such employer's or such person's successors.

(*c*) For the purposes of this section and of Schedule 3, offices or employments in respect of which payments to which section 123 applies are made shall be treated as held under associated employers if, on the date which is the relevant date in relation to any of those payments, one of those employers is under the control of the other or of a third person who controls or is under the control of the other on that or any other such date.

(2) Income tax shall not be charged by virtue of section 123 in respect of the following payments—

(*a*) any payment made in connection with the termination of the holding of an office or employment by the death of the holder, or made on account of injury to or disability of the holder of an office or employment;

(*b*) any sum chargeable to tax under section 127;

(*c*) a benefit provided in pursuance of any retirement benefits scheme where under section 777 the employee (within the meaning of that section) was chargeable to tax in respect of sums paid, or treated as paid, with a view to the provision of the benefit;

(*d*) a benefit paid in pursuance of any scheme or fund described in section 778(1).

[(2A) Where a payment is not chargeable to tax under section 123 by virtue of subsection (2)(*a*), the person by whom the payment was made shall deliver to the inspector, not later than 46 days after the end of the year of assessment in which the payment was made, the following particulars—

(*a*) the name and address of the person to whom the payment was made,

(*b*) the personal public service number (within the meaning of section 223 of the Social Welfare (Consolidation) Act 1993) of the person who received the payment,

(*c*) the amount of the payment, and

(*d*) the basis on which the payment is not chargeable to tax under section 123, indicating, in the case of a payment made on account of injury or disability, the extent of the injury or disability, as the case may be.][3]

(3) Subsection (2)(*d*) shall not apply to the following payments—

(*a*) a termination allowance payable in accordance with section 5 of the Oireachtas (Allowances to Members) and Ministerial and Parliamentary Offices (Amendment) Act, 1992, and any regulations made under that section,

(*b*) a severance allowance or a special allowance payable in accordance with Part V (inserted by the Oireachtas (Allowances to Members) and Ministerial and Parliamentary Offices (Amendment) Act, 1992) of the Ministerial and Parliamentary Offices Act, 1938,

(*c*) a special severance gratuity payable under section 7 of the Superannuation and Pensions Act, 1963, or any analogous payment payable under or by virtue of any other enactment, or

(*d*) a benefit paid in pursuance of any statutory scheme (within the meaning of Chapter 1 of Part 30) established or amended after the 10th day of May, 1997, other than a payment representing normal retirement benefits, which is made in consideration or in consequence of, or otherwise in connection with, the termination of the holding of an office or employment in circumstances—

(I) of redundancy or abolition of office, or

(II) for the purposes of facilitating improvements in the organisation of the employing company, organisation, Department or other body by which greater efficiency or economy can be effected,

and, for the purposes of this paragraph, **"normal retirement benefits"** means recognised superannuation benefits customarily payable to an individual on retirement at normal retirement date under the relevant statutory scheme, notwithstanding that, in relation to the termination of an office or employment in the circumstances described in this paragraph, such benefits may be paid earlier than the designated retirement date or may be calculated by reference to a period greater than the individual's actual period of service in the office or employment, and includes benefits described as short service gratuities which are calculated on a basis approved by the Minister for Finance.

(4) Income tax shall not be charged by virtue of section 123 in respect of a payment in respect of an office or employment in which the holder's service included foreign service where the foreign service comprised—

(*a*) in any case, three-quarters of the whole period of service down to the relevant date,

(*b*) where the period of service down to the relevant date exceeded 10 years, the whole of the last 10 years, or

(*c*) where the period of service down to the relevant date exceeded 20 years, one-half of that period, including any 10 of the last 20 years.

(5) (*a*) Income tax shall not be charged by virtue of section 123 in respect of a payment of an amount not exceeding the basic exemption and, in the case of a payment which exceeds that amount, shall be charged only in respect of the excess.

(*b*) Notwithstanding paragraph (*a*), where 2 or more payments in respect of which tax is chargeable by virtue of section 123, or would be so chargeable apart from paragraph (*a*), are made to or in respect of the same person in respect of the same office or employment, or in respect of different offices or employments held under the same employer or under associated employers, that paragraph shall apply as if those payments were a single payment of an amount equal to that aggregate amount, and the amount of any one payment chargeable to tax shall be ascertained as follows:

(i) where the payments are treated as income of different years of assessment, the amount of the basic exemption shall be deducted from a payment treated as income of an earlier year before any payment treated as income of a later year, and

(ii) subject to subparagraph (i), the amount of the basic exemption shall be deducted rateably from the payments according to their respective amounts.

(6) The person chargeable to income tax by virtue of section 123 in respect of any payment may, before the expiration of [4 years][4] after the end of the year of assessment of which that payment is treated as income, by notice in writing to the inspector claim any such relief in respect of the payment as is applicable to the payment under Schedule 3 and, where such a claim is duly made and allowed, all such repayments and assessments of income tax shall be made as are necessary to give effect to such a claim.

(7) For the purposes of any provision of the Income Tax Acts requiring income of any description to be treated as the highest part of a person's income, that income shall be calculated without regard to any payment chargeable to tax by virtue of section 123.

Amendments

1 Substituted by FA 2001 s 240(1) and (2)(*l*)(ii) and Sch 5 Pt 1 as respects payments made on or after 1 January 2002; previously "£8,000" ; previously "£6,000" (FA 1999 s 14: 1 December 1998).

2 Substituted by FA 2001 s 240(1) and (2)(*l*)(ii) and Sch 5 Pt 1 as respects payments made on or after 1 January 2002; previously "£600"; previously "£500" (FA 1999 s 14: 1 December 1998).

3 Subs (2A) inserted by FA 2005 s 19(1)(*a*)(i) as respects payments made on or after 25 March 2005.

4 Substituted by FA 2005 s 19(1)(*a*)(ii) as respects payments made on or after 25 March 2005; previously "6 years".

Cross-references

Agreed pay restructuring relief to be reduced, subs (5): s 202(7); no double deduction: s 202(8).

Payments on retirement or removal from employment: s 123(2), (3).

Reliefs in respect of income tax charged on payments on retirement etc, subs (5): Sch 3 paras 2, 4, 8.

Case law

Subs (2)(*a*): In the civil proceedings *Glover v BLN Ltd* [1973] IR 432, it was held that a decree for a lump sum payment under an employment contract was not, apart from any charge under s 123, chargeable to tax.

Termination payments made to disabled employees were redundancy payments and were not "on account of" disabilities: *Harding, Coughlan and others v O'Cahill* ITR Vol IV p 233.

Ex gratia payment to employee who resigned due to ill-health was a payment on account of injury or disability: *O'Shea v Mulqueen* [1995] 1 IR 504.

Revenue precedents

Issue: Does the exemption in TCA 1997 s 201(2)(*a*) apply to a payment made in connection with the termination of an office or employment where the individual suffers from an injury or disability?

Decision: To qualify for relief, the payment must be made on account of injury or disability of the holder of the office or employment. Termination of the office or employment is not relevant. Where the payment is made in connection with the termination of the office or employment, it does not qualify for exemption under TCA 1997 s 201(2)(*a*).

Issue: Whether an individual employed in the State by a non-resident employer (PAYE not operating) is entitled to the exemptions and reliefs in TCA 1997 s 201.

Decision: The individual is entitled to the exemptions and reliefs as the charge under TCA 1997 s 123 depends on holding an office or employment. The basis of assessment of the emoluments is not the issue.

Revenue information

Information leaflet IT21 — Lump Sum Payments on Redundancy/Retirement.

Tax Briefing

TB11 July 1993 par1.3 — Termination Payments.

TB22 June 1996 p 14 — Redundancy payments and re-engagement of employees.

TB28 Oct 1997 p 7 — Taxation Treatment of Redundancy/Termination Payments.

TB36 June 1999 p 13 — Career Breaks: service pre and post career break may be added together for the purposes of determining "each complete year of service", periods where individual was on career break is not reckonable service; for SCSB purposes (see Schedule 3), where employee has less than 3 years paid service in the immediate period prior to date of termination, emoluments of the last 36 months of paid service are taken into account in determining the average for one year of the holder's emoluments for the last 3 years of service.

TB36 June 1999 p 13 — Job-Sharers: length of service should be taken as the number of complete years of service with no apportionment to take account of the part-time nature of the employment.

TB38 Dec 1999 p 17 — The value of any rights arising to an employee under an approved profit sharing scheme may be regarded as emoluments for the purposes of Schedule 3 for the purposes of calculating standard capital superannuation benefit.

TB54 Dec 2003 p 10 — Redundancy Payments and Re-engagement of Employees.

Definitions

higher rate: ss 3(1), 15; inspector: ss 2(1), 5(1), 852; person: IA 1937 s 11(*c*); writing: IA 1937 Sch; year of assessment: s 3(1).

Former enactments

ITA 1967 s 115 and Sch 3 paras 12–13; FA 1972 Sch 1 Pt III para 2; FA 1980 s 10(1)(*a*), (*c*); FA 1992 s 18(2); FA 1993 s 7(1) and s 8(*a*); FA 1997 s 12.

Corresponding UK tax provision

Income and Corporation Taxes Act 1988 s 188 [repealed].

202 Relief for agreed pay restructuring

(1) (*a*) In this section—

"basic pay", in relation to a participating employee of a qualifying company, means the employee's emoluments (other than non-pecuniary emoluments) from the company in respect of an employment held with the company;

"collective agreement" means an agreement entered into by a company with, or on behalf of, one or more than one body representative of employees of the company where each such body is either the holder of a negotiation licence under the Trade Union Act, 1941 or is an excepted body within the meaning of section 6 of that Act as amended by the Trade Union Act, 1942;

"control", in relation to a qualifying company, means the power of a person to secure—

(i) by means of the holding of shares or the possession of voting power in or in relation to the qualifying company or any other qualifying company, or

(ii) by virtue of any power conferred by the articles of association or any other document regulating the qualifying company or any other qualifying company,

that the affairs of the first-mentioned qualifying company are conducted in accordance with the wishes of such person and, in relation to a partnership, means the right to a share of more than 50 per cent of the assets, or of more than 50 per cent of the income, of the partnership;

"emoluments" has the same meaning as in section 472;

"employment" means an office or employment of profit such that any emoluments of the office or employment of profit are to be charged to tax under Schedule E;

"the Minister" means the Minister for Enterprise, Trade and Employment;

"participating employee", in relation to a qualifying company, means a qualifying employee who is a participant in a relevant agreement with the company;

"qualifying company" means a company to which the Minister has issued a certificate under subsection (2) which has not been withdrawn under that subsection;

"qualifying employee", in relation to a qualifying company, means an employee of the company in receipt of emoluments from the company;

"reduced basic pay", in relation to a participating employee, means the basic pay of the employee as reduced by the substantial reduction provided for in the relevant agreement concerned;

[**"relevant agreement"**, in relation to a qualifying company, means a collective agreement—

(*a*) that applies to—

(i) more than **50 per cent** of the total number of qualifying employees of the company, or

(ii) more than **75 per cent** of a bona fide class or classes of qualifying employees of the company if the number of participating employees in the class or classes, as the case may be, comprises at least **25 per cent** of the total number of qualifying employees of the company,

(*b*) that provides amongst other things for—

(i) a substantial reduction in the basic pay of the participating employees to which it relates,

(ii) the payment of the reduced basic pay to the participating employees to which it relates for the duration of the relevant period, and

(iii) the payment to them of a lump sum to compensate for that reduction, and

(*c*) that is registered with the Labour Relations Commission;][1]

"relevant date", in relation to a relevant agreement, means the date the relevant agreement was registered with the Labour Relations Commission;

"relevant period", in relation to a relevant agreement, means the period of 5 years commencing on the relevant date in relation to that agreement;

[**"specified amount"**, in relation to a participating employee, means—

(*a*) in a case where the basic pay of the employee is subject to a reduction of at least 10 per cent but not exceeding 15 per cent, [€7,620][2] together with [€255][3] for each complete year of service (subject to a maximum of 20 years), up to the relevant date, of the employee in the service of the qualifying company,

(*b*) in a case where the basic pay of the employee is subject to a reduction exceeding 15 per cent but not exceeding 20 per cent, [€7,620][2] together with [€635][4] for each complete year of service (subject to a maximum of 20 years), up to the relevant date, of the employee in the service of the qualifying company, and

(*c*) in a case where the basic pay of the employee is subject to a reduction exceeding 20 per cent, [€10,160][5] together with [€765][6] for each complete year of service (subject to a maximum of 20 years), up to the relevant date, of the employee in the service of the qualifying company.][7]

(*b*) For the purposes of this section—

(i) a reduction in the basic pay of a participating employee shall not be regarded as substantial unless it amounts to at least 10 per cent of the average for one year of the employee's basic pay ascertained by reference to such pay for the 2 year period ending on the relevant date, and

(ii) employments in respect of which payments to which this section applies are made shall be treated as held with associated qualifying companies if, on the date of any of those payments, one of those companies is under the control of the other company or of a third person who controls or is under the control of the other company on that or any other such date.

[(*c*) In determining for the purposes of the definition of "relevant agreement" whether qualifying employees of a qualifying company are comprised in a bona fide class or classes, as the case may be, regard shall be had to matters such as common work practices, skills, established collective bargaining arrangements and the organisational structure and arrangements within the company.][8]

(2) (*a*) The Minister, on the making of an application in that behalf by a company, may, in accordance with guidelines laid down for the purpose by the Minister with the agreement of the Minister for Finance, give a certificate to a company

stating that for the purposes of this section it may be treated as a qualifying company.

(*b*) The Minister may not grant a certificate to a company under this subsection unless the Minister is satisfied, on advice from the Labour Relations Commission, that—

[(i) the company is confronted with a substantial adverse change to its competitive environment which will determine its current or continued viability,

(ii) to accommodate that change and maintain its viability, it is necessary for it to enter into a relevant agreement with its qualifying employees, and][9]

(iii) the relevant agreement into which it is proposed to enter is designed for the sole purpose of addressing, and can be reasonably expected to address, that change.

(*c*) An application under paragraph (*a*) shall be in such form as the Minister may direct and shall contain such information in relation to the company, its trade or business and the terms of the relevant agreement into which it proposes to enter with its qualifying employees as may be specified in the guidelines referred to in that paragraph.

(*d*) A certificate issued by the Minister under paragraph (*a*) shall contain such conditions as the Minister considers appropriate and specifies in the certificate.

(*e*) Any cost incurred by the Labour Relations Commission in providing advice to the Minister in accordance with paragraph (*b*) shall be reimbursed by the company concerned to the Commission.

(*f*) Where during the relevant period a qualifying company fails to comply with any of the conditions to which a certificate given to it under paragraph (*a*) is subject, the Minister may, by notice in writing to the company, revoke the certificate.

(*g*) The Minister may not give a certificate under paragraph (*a*) at any time on or after [1 January 2004].[10]

(3) (*a*) An agreement shall not be a relevant agreement for the purposes of this section unless and until it has been registered with the Labour Relations Commission.

(*b*) A qualifying company shall, within the period of one month from the date of each of the first 5 anniversaries of the relevant date or such longer period as the Labour Relations Commission may in writing allow, confirm to the Commission, in such form as the Commission shall direct, that all the terms of the relevant agreement, to the extent that they are still relevant, continue to be in force.

(4) Nothing in this section shall be construed as preventing a participating employee from receiving during the relevant period an increase in basic pay—

(*a*) which is—

(i) provided for under the terms of the agreement known as Partnership 2000 for Inclusion, Employment and Competitiveness entered into by the Government and the Social Partners in December, 1996, or any similar increase under an agreement, whether negotiated on a national basis or otherwise, which succeeds that agreement or which succeeds an agreement which succeeds the first-mentioned agreement, or

(ii) part of an incremental scale under the terms of the employee's contract of employment and which was in place 12 months before the relevant date,

and

(*b*) which is determined by reference to the employee's reduced basic pay or that pay as subsequently increased as provided for in paragraph (*a*).

(5) (*a*) This section shall apply to a payment made to a participating employee by a qualifying company under a relevant agreement.

(*b*) A payment to which this section applies shall, to the extent that the payment does not exceed the specified amount, be exempt from any charge to income tax.

(*c*) Where 2 or more payments to which this section applies are made to or in respect of the same person in respect of the same employment or in respect of different employments held with the same qualifying company or an associated qualifying company, this subsection shall apply as if those payments were a single payment of an amount equal to the aggregate of those payments, and the amount of any payment chargeable to income tax shall be ascertained as follows:

(i) where the payments are treated as income of different years of assessment, the specified amount shall be deducted from a payment treated as income of an earlier year before any payment treated as income of a later year, and

(ii) subject to subparagraph (i), the specified amount shall be deducted from a payment made earlier in a year of assessment before any payment made later in that year.

(6) Where during the relevant period—

(*a*) the Minister revokes, in accordance with paragraph (*f*) of subsection (2), a certificate given to a company under paragraph (*a*) of that subsection,

(*b*) a qualifying company fails to meet the requirements of subsection (3)(*b*), or

(*c*) a participating employee receives an increase in reduced basic pay other than as provided for in subsection (4),

then, any relief granted under this section, where paragraph (*a*) or (*b*) applies, to all the participating employees of the company or, where paragraph (*c*) applies, to the participating employee concerned, shall be withdrawn by the making of an assessment to income tax under Case IV of Schedule D for the year of assessment for which the relief was granted.

(7) Where during the relevant period a participating employee receives a payment from a qualifying company, other than a payment to which this section applies, which is chargeable to tax by virtue of section 123, any relief from tax in respect of that payment under section 201(5) or Schedule 3 shall be reduced by the amount of any relief given under this section in respect of a payment to which this section applies made in the relevant period.

(8) Section 201 and Schedule 3 and section 480 shall not apply in relation to a payment to which this section applies.

Amendments

1 Definition of "relevant agreement" substituted by FA 1998 s 10(*a*)(i) with effect from 6 April 1998.

2 Substituted by FA 2001 s 240(1) and (2)(*l*)(ii) and Sch 5 Pt 1 as respects payments made on or after 1 January 2002; previously "£6,000".

3 Substituted by FA 2001 s 240(1) and (2)(*l*)(ii) and Sch 5 Pt 1 as respects payments made on or after 1 January 2002; previously "£200".

4 Substituted by FA 2001 s 240(1) and (2)(*l*)(ii) and Sch 5 Pt 1 as respects payments made on or after 1 January 2002; previously "£500".

5 Substituted by FA 2001 s 240(1) and (2)(*l*)(ii) and Sch 5 Pt 1 as respects payments made on or after 1 January 2002; previously "£8,000".

6 Substituted by FA 2001 s 240(1) and (2)(*l*)(ii) and Sch 5 Pt 1 as respects payments made on or after 1 January 2002; previously "£600".

7 Definition of "specified amount" substituted by FA 2000 s 18(1)(*a*) as respects payments made under a relevant agreement (within the meaning of section 202 of the Principal Act) the relevant date (within that meaning) of which is after 20 July 1999.

8 Subs (1)(*c*) inserted by FA 1998 s 10(*a*)(ii) with effect from 6 April 1998.

9 Subs (2)(*b*)(i)–(ii) substituted by FA 1998 s 10(*b*) with effect from 6 April 1998.

10 Substituted by FA 2001 s 77(2) and Sch 2 para 12 with effect from 6 April 2001; previously "6 April 2003".

Definitions

company: s 4(1); year: IA 1937 Sch.

Former enactments

FA 1997 s 14.

203 Payments in respect of redundancy

(1) In this section, **"lump sum"** and **"weekly payment"** have the same meanings respectively as in the Redundancy Payments Act, 1967.

(2) Any lump sum or weekly payment and any payment to or on behalf of an employed or unemployed person in accordance with regulations under section 46 of the Redundancy Payments Act, 1967, shall be exempt from income tax under Schedule E.

Revenue information

Information leaflet IT21 — Lump Sum Payments on Redundancy/Retirement.

Former enactments

FA 1968 s 37(1)–(2).

Corresponding UK tax provision

Income and Corporation Taxes Act 1988 s 579.

204 Military and other pensions, gratuities and allowances

(1) This section shall apply to—

(*a*) all wound and disability pensions, and all increases in such pensions, granted under the Army Pensions Acts, 1923 to 1980, or those Acts and any subsequent Act together with which those Acts may be cited; but, where the amount of any pension to which this paragraph applies is not solely attributable to disability, the relief conferred by this section shall extend only to such part as is certified by the Minister for Defence to be attributable to disability;

(*b*) all gratuities in respect of wounds or disabilities similarly granted under any enactment referred to in paragraph (*a*);

(*c*) military gratuities and demobilisation pay granted to officers of the National Forces or the Defence Forces of Ireland on demobilisation;

(*d*) deferred pay within the meaning of any regulations under the Defence Act, 1954, which is credited to the pay account of a member of the Defence Forces;

(*e*) gratuities granted in respect of service with the Defence Forces.

(2) Income to which this section applies shall be exempt from income tax and shall not be reckoned in computing income for the purposes of the Income Tax Acts.

Definitions

Income Tax Acts: s 1(2).

Former enactments

ITA 1967 s 340(1), (2)(*a*), (*b*) and (*c*).

Corresponding UK tax provision

Income and Corporation Taxes Act 1988 s 315.

205 Veterans of War of Independence

(1) In this section—

"military service" means the performance of duty as a member of an organisation to which Part II of the Army Pensions Act, 1932, applies, but includes military service within the meaning of that Part of that Act, military service within the meaning of the Military Service Pensions Act, 1924, and service in the Forces within the meaning of the Military Service Pensions Act, 1934;

"relevant legislation" means the Army Pensions Acts, 1923 to 1980, the Military Service Pensions Acts, 1924 to 1964, the Connaught Rangers (Pensions) Acts, 1936 to 1964, any Act amending any of those Acts and any regulation (in so far as it affects a pension, allowance, benefit or gratuity under any of those Acts or any other Act amending any of those Acts) made under the Pensions (Increase) Act, 1964, or under any of those Acts or any other Act amending any of those Acts;

"relevant military service" means military service during any part of a period referred to in section 5(2) of the Army Pensions Act, 1932, or, in the case of a qualified person within the meaning of the Connaught Rangers (Pensions) Act, 1936, the circumstances referred to in paragraphs (*a*), (*b*) and (*c*) of section 2 of that Act;

"veteran of the War of Independence" means a person who was—

(*a*) a member of an organisation to which Part II of the Army Pensions Act, 1932, applies, or a qualified person within the meaning of the Connaught Rangers (Pensions) Act, 1936, and

(*b*) engaged in relevant military service.

(2) A pension, allowance, benefit or gratuity, in so far as it is related to the relevant military service of a veteran of the War of Independence, or to an event which happened during or in consequence of such relevant military service, which is paid under the relevant legislation to—

(*a*) such veteran, or

(*b*) the wife, widow, child or other dependant or partial dependant of such veteran,

shall be exempt from income tax and shall not be reckoned in computing income for the purposes of the Income Tax Acts.

Definitions

Income Tax Acts: s 1(2); person: IA 1937 s 11(*c*).

Former enactments

FA 1982 s 9(1)–(2).

Corresponding UK tax provision

Income and Corporation Taxes Act 1988 ss 315 and 317.

206 Income from investments under Social Welfare (Consolidation) Act, 1993

The Minister for Finance shall be entitled to exemption from tax in respect of the income derived from investments made under section 7 of the Social Welfare (Consolidation) Act, 1993.

Former enactments

ITA 1967 s 338.

207 Rents of properties belonging to hospitals and other charities

(1) Exemption shall be granted—

(*a*) from income tax chargeable under Schedule D in respect of the rents and profits of any property belonging to any hospital, public school or almshouse, or vested in trustees for charitable purposes, in so far as those rents and profits are applied to charitable purposes only;

(*b*) from income tax chargeable—

(i) under Schedule C in respect of any interest, annuities, dividends or shares of annuities,

(ii) under Schedule D in respect of any yearly interest or other annual payment, and

(iii) under Schedule F in respect of any distribution,

forming part of the income of any body of persons or trust established for charitable purposes only, or which, according to the rules or regulations established by statute, charter, decree, deed of trust or will, are applicable to charitable purposes only, and in so far as the same are applied to charitable purposes only;

(*c*) from income tax chargeable under Schedule C in respect of any interest, annuities, dividends or shares of annuities in the names of trustees applicable solely towards the repairs of any cathedral, college, church or chapel, or any building used solely for the purposes of divine worship, and in so far as the same are applied to those purposes.

(2) (*a*) This subsection shall apply to every gift (within the meaning of the Charities Act, 1961) made before the 1st day of July, 1961, which, if it had been made on or after that day, would by virtue of section 50 of that Act (which relates to gifts for graves and memorials) have been, to the extent provided in that section, a gift for charitable purposes.

(*b*) Subsection (1) shall apply in relation to a gift to which this subsection applies as if the gift had been made on or after the 1st day of July, 1961.

(3) Every claim under this section shall be verified by affidavit, and proof of the claim may be given by the treasurer, trustee or any duly authorised agent.

(4) A person who makes a false or fraudulent claim for exemption under this section in respect of any interest, annuities, dividends or shares of annuities charged or chargeable under Schedule C shall forfeit the sum of [€125][1].

Amendments

1 Substituted by FA 2001 s 240(1) and (2)(*k*) and Sch 5 Pt 1 as respects acts or omissions which take place or begin on or after 1 January 2002; previously "£100".

Cross-references

Bodies having consultative status with United Nations and/or Council of Europe, relief: s 209.
Corporation donations to eligible charities: s 486A(3)(*c*).
Deposit interest retention tax, deposits of charities: s 266; interpretation: s 256(1)("relevant deposit", para (*h*)(ii)); repayment of tax, subs (1)(*b*): s 267(2).
Donations to approved bodies: Sch 26A Pt 3 para 3.
Exemption from dividend withholding tax for certain persons, subs (1)(*b*): s 172C(2)(*e*).
Investment undertakings (gain arising on a chargeable event): s 739D(6)(*f*)(i)(I).
Life assurance companies, taxation of policyholders — new basis, gains arising on a chargeable event, subs (1)(*b*): s 730D(2)(*b*)(iii); declaration: s 730E(3)(*e*)(iii).
Professional services withholding tax, interpretation: s 520(1) "relevant payment").

Case law

Irish

Subs (1)(*b*): A statutory body established for the regulation of the pharmacy profession in Ireland was refused exemption as a body established for charitable purposes only: *Pharmaceutical Society of Ireland v Revenue Commissioners* ITR Vol I p 542.
Foreign charity with activities based in Ireland held entitled to the exemption: *Revenue Commissioners v Sisters of Charity of the Incarnate Word* [1998] ITR 65.
A hospital established for the relief of the sick poor also admitted paying patients for treatment in an annexe. Although the whole undertaking was accepted as a charitable institution it was held that the acceptance of private patients was the carrying on of a trade and since the rest of the undertaking was non-trading, it was not permissible to set off the expenses of the non-trading activities against the trading profits – *Davis v Superioress, Mater Misericordiae Hospital Dublin* 1 ITR 387.
Professional services withholding tax, interpretation: s 520(1) ("relevant payment").

UK

A power of appointment for non-charitable purposes prevented a successful claim for exemption: *R v Special Commissioners (ex parte Rank's Trustees)* (1922) 8 TC 286.
A payment by one charity to another held to be a payment for charitable purposes: *IRC v Helen Slater Charitable Trust Ltd* [1981] STC 471.
No exemption allowed where a charity was entitled to the residual share in the winding-up of an employer's share scheme: *Guild and others v IRC* [1993] STC 444.

Revenue precedents

Issue: Accumulation of Funds.
Decision: It is acceptable that a charity can accumulate funds for more than two years provided that it is for a specific charitable purpose approved by the charities section and accounts to be submitted and checked annually.
Issue: Health Boards.
Decision: Health Boards are charitable. There is no need for a Governing Instrument as they are set up under the Health Act, 1970.
Issue: Fund raising as a charitable object.
Decision: Bodies whose main object is the raising of funds for charitable organisations may be regarded as established for charitable purposes.
Issue: Fisheries Development Societies.
Decision: Fisheries Societies are charitable in law and exemption is in order.
Issue: Insurance.
Decision: The provision of insurance is not a charitable object.
Issue: Co-Operative Societies.

Decision: Per Revenue Solicitors opinion it is in order for a Co-operative to be considered charitable as long as the possibility of any benefit to members is removed.
Issue: Christian Fellowships.
Decision: Christian Fellowships are charitable under the advancement of religion.
Issue: Amending a Deed of Trust.
Decision: In the absence of a Deed of Variation a Charitable Trust cannot be amended or altered but as an alternative undertakings may be accepted from the Charity.
Issue: The provision of advice.
Decision: The provision of advice whether financial or legal for the benefit of the community is charitable.
Issue: Is a Festival a charitable activity?
Decision: The promotion of a Festival in itself is not a charitable objective, unless it is for the advancement of the Arts eg music, theatre etc.
Issue: Tidy Towns.
Decision: Tidy Towns are considered to be charitable under the fourth Pemsel category.
Issue: When is a private Trust charitable?
Decision: A gift to a narrow class of persons for the relief of poverty is a valid charitable gift. But the gift must be one which is expressly for the relief of poverty and if an intention to relieve poverty is not expressed, the Courts will not infer same.
Issue: When a Case cannot proceed to Appeal.
Decision: A case cannot proceed to Appeal if: (1) the applicant is not constituted ie no completed Governing Instrument (2) there is no income in respect of which exemption is being sought. It also has to prove that tax was suffered.
Issue: Two Governing Instruments for an organisation.
Decision: The Co-operative Society or any other organisation should not have two Governing Instruments. However, under this Society's Rules it is possible to amend the Governing Instrument under Clause 15 of the Rules.
Issue: Lions Clubs.
Decision: A Lions Club is not considered charitable.
Issue: Tax suffered during the administration of an Estate.
Decision: Charities are not entitled to claim a repayment of income tax/DIRT suffered on the income during the administration of an Estate.
Issue: Social Services Councils.
Decision: Social Services Councils may or may not be charitable depending on their main objects (the co-ordination of charitable bodies in itself is not regarded as a charitable object).
Issue: Retirement Home for Priests of a particular Order.
Decision: Charitable exemption can be granted under the category of advancement of religion, where the main objects of an organisation are the relief of the infirm, sick and aged Priests of a particular Order (precended case - *Forster, Gellatly v Palmer*).
Issue: Protection of Lives or Property of the Community.
Decision: A gift for the protection of lives or property of the Community was held to be charitable eg lifeboat or a public fire brigade.
Issue: Promotion of Tourism.
Decision: Generally, the promotion of Tourism is not a charitable objective, however, each application with the promotion of tourism as a main object must be examined on its own merits.
Issue: Mutual Investment Fund.
Decision: Mutual Investment Funds are not charitable in law.
Issue: Local Authorities.
Decision: Local Authorities are not charitable, however, there is relief from income tax available to them, in accordance with s 13 of the Finance Act, 1990.
Issue: Trust for benefit of members of an industry.
Decision: The Asst. Revenue Solicitor agreed with the view that a trust for the benefit of individuals engaged in a particular industry is a Trust which is for a sufficiently large section of the community to render it charitable in law.
Issue: Would a distribution to a charity by a unit trust which invested only in rental property be regarded as rental income in the hands of the charity.
Decision: Yes.

Revenue information

Information leaflet CHY1 — Applying for Relief from Tax on the Income and Property of Charities.
A list of bodies with Charitable Tax Exemption under the Tax Acts is available on Revenue's website — www.revenue.ie — under Publications/Lists.

Definitions

affidavit: IA 1937 Sch; body of persons: s 2(1); person: IA 1937 s 11(*c*); statute: IA 1937 s 3; s 1(1).

Former enactments

ITA 1967 s 333 and s339(2) and (4); F(MP)A 1968 s 3(4) and Sch Pt III; FA 1969 s 65(1) and Sch 5 Pt I; CTA 1976 s 140 and Sch 2 Pt I para 13.

Corresponding UK tax provision

Income and Corporation Taxes Act 1988 s 505.

208 Lands owned and occupied, and trades carried on by, charities

(1) In this section, **"charity"** means any body of persons or trust established for charitable purposes only.

(2) Exemption shall be granted—

(*a*) from income tax chargeable under Case I (*b*) of Schedule D by virtue of section 18(2) where the profits or gains so chargeable arise out of lands, tenements or hereditaments which are owned and occupied by a charity;

(*b*) from income tax chargeable under Schedule D in respect of the profits of a trade carried on by any charity, if the profits are applied solely to the purposes of the charity and either—

(i) the trade is exercised in the course of the actual carrying out of a primary purpose of the charity, or

(ii) the work in connection with the trade is mainly carried on by beneficiaries of the charity.

(3) Subsection (2)(*b*) shall apply in respect of the profits of a trade of farming carried on by a charity as if the words after **"solely to the purposes of the charity"** were deleted.

Cross-references

Charge to income tax of offshore income gain, meaning of "charity" applied: s 745(5)(*a*).
Industrial building or structure, meaning of: s 268(2A)("qualifying hospital").

Case law

Irish

A business bequeathed to a society established for charitable purposes, which employed a man who would otherwise have been an object of the society, was refused exemption: *Beirne v St Vincent de Paul Society Wexford* ITR Vol I p 393.
A hospital entitled to charitable exemption was held to be taxable in respect of profits derived from an annexe used as a private nursing home: *Davis v Mater Misericordiae Hospital* ITR Vol I p 387.
Foreign charity with activities based in Ireland held entitled to the exemption: *Revenue Commissioners v Sisters of Charity of Incarnate Word* [1998] ITR 65.

UK

Charitable purposes consist of the relief of poverty the advancement of education, the advancement of religion or other purposes of a charitable nature beneficial to the community not falling within these three categories: *Special Commissioners v Pemsel* (1891) 3 TC 53.
Charitable purposes have been held to include:
the relief of the poor of a particular church: *Re Wall, Pomeroy v Willway* (1889) 43 Ch D 774;
the encouragement of choral singing: *Royal Choral Society v IRC* (1943) 25 TC 263;
the promotion of an annual chess tournament for boys: *Re Dupree's Deed Trusts* [1944] 2 All ER 443;

the establishment of a rest home for hospital nurses: *Re White's Will Trusts, Tindall v United Sheffield Hospital Board of Governors* [1951] 1 All ER 528;
the relief of poor widows and orphans of deceased bank officers: *Re Coulthurst* [1951] All ER 774;
the publication of law reports: *Incorporated Council of law Reporting v AG* (1971) 47 TC 341.
The following have been held to be non-charitable:
the formation of a council to secure legislative and other temperance reform: *IRC v Temperance Council of the Christian Churches of England and Wales* (1926) 10 TC 748;
the advancement of education in political matters in the interests of one political party: *Bonar Law Memorial Trust v IRC* (1933) 17 TC 508;
private body set up to develop industry and enterprise and provide vocational education to the public: *IRC v Oldham Training and Enterprise Council* [1996] STC 1218.
the suppression of vivisection: *IRC v National Anti-Vivisection Society* (1948) 28 TC 311.

Revenue information

Information leaflet CHY1 — Applying for Relief from Tax on the Income and Property of Charities.
Information leaflet CHY7 — Trading by Charities — Exemption from Tax.
A list of bodies with Charitable Tax Exemption under the Tax Acts is available on Revenue's website — www.revenue.ie — under Publications/Lists.

Definitions

body of persons: s 2(1); land: IA 1937 Sch; person: IA 1937 s 11(*c*); trade: s 3(1).

Former enactments

ITA 1967 s 334(1)(*a*), (*c*); FA 1969 s 33(1) and Sch 4 Pt I and s 65(1) and Sch 5 Pt I; FA 1981 s 11.

Corresponding UK tax provision

Income and Corporation Taxes Act 1988 s 505.

209 Bodies for the promotion of Universal Declaration of Human Rights and the implementation of European Convention for the Protection of Human Rights and Fundamental Freedoms

Where any body of persons having consultative status with the United Nations Organisation or the Council of Europe—

(*a*) has as its sole or main object the promotion of observance of the Universal Declaration of Human Rights or the implementation of the European Convention for the Protection of Human Rights and Fundamental Freedoms or both the promotion of observance of that Declaration and the implementation of that Convention, and

(*b*) is precluded by its rules or constitution from the direct or indirect payment or transfer, otherwise than for valuable and sufficient consideration, to any of its members of any of its income or property by means of dividend, gift, division, bonus or otherwise however by means of profit,

there shall, on a claim in that behalf being made to the Revenue Commissioners, be allowed, in the case of the body, such exemption from income tax as is to be allowed under section 207 in the case of a body of persons established for charitable purposes only the whole income of which is applied to charitable purposes only.

Cross-references

Donations to approved bodies: Sch 26A Pt 1 para 17.

Definitions

body of persons: s 2(1); person: IA 1937 s 11(*c*).

Former enactments

FA 1973 s 20.

210 The Great Book of Ireland Trust

(1) In this section, **"the Trust"** means **"The Great Book of Ireland Trust"** established by trust deed dated the 12th day of December, 1990, for the purposes of—

(*a*) making and carrying to completion and selling a unique manuscript volume (in this section referred to as **"The Great Book of Ireland"**), and

(*b*) using the proceeds of the sale of The Great Book of Ireland for the benefit of—

(i) a company incorporated on the 5th day of August, 1986, as Clashganna Mills Trust Limited, and

(ii) a company incorporated on the 1st day of March, 1991, as Poetry Ireland Limited.

(2) Notwithstanding any provision of the Income Tax Acts—

(*a*) income arising to the trustees of the Trust in respect of the sale by it of The Great Book of Ireland, and

(*b*) payments made to the companies referred to in subsection (1)(*b*) under the Trust by the trustees of the Trust,

shall be disregarded for the purposes of those Acts.

Definitions

company: ss 4(1), 5(1); Income Tax Acts: s 1(2).

Former enactments

FA 1991 s 13.

211 Friendly societies

(1) An unregistered friendly society whose income does not exceed [€205][1] shall be entitled to exemption from income tax, and a registered friendly society which is precluded by statute or by its rules from assuring to any person a sum exceeding [€1,270][2] by means of gross sum, or [€70][3] a year by means of annuity, shall be entitled to exemption from income tax under Schedules C, D and F.

(2) A registered friendly society shall not be entitled to exemption from tax under this section in relation to any year of assessment if the Revenue Commissioners determine, for the purposes of entitlement to exemption for that year, that the society does not satisfy the following conditions—

(*a*) that it was established solely for any or all of the purposes set out in section 8(1) of the Friendly Societies Act, 1896, and not for the purpose of securing a tax advantage, and

(*b*) that since its establishment it has engaged solely in activities directed to achieving the purposes for which it was so established and has not engaged in trading activities, other than by means of insurance in respect of members, with a view to the realisation of profits.

(3) In making a determination under this section in relation to a registered friendly society, the Revenue Commissioners shall consider any evidence in relation to the matter submitted to them by the society.

(4) In any case where a friendly society is aggrieved by a determination of the Revenue Commissioners under this section in relation to the society, the society shall be entitled to appeal to the Appeal Commissioners against the determination of the Revenue Commissioners and the Appeal Commissioners shall hear and determine the appeal as if it were an appeal against an assessment to income tax, and the provisions of the Income Tax Acts relating to the rehearing of an appeal and to the statement of a case for the opinion of the High Court on a point of law shall apply accordingly with any necessary modifications.

(5) Every claim under this section shall be verified by affidavit, and proof of the claim may be given by the treasurer, trustee or any duly authorised agent.

(6) A person who makes a false or fraudulent claim for exemption under this section in respect of any interest, annuities, dividends or shares of annuities charged or chargeable under Schedule C shall forfeit the sum of [€125][4].

Amendments

1 Substituted by FA 2001 s 240(1) and (2)(*a*) and Sch 5 Pt 1 for 2002 and later tax years; previously "£160".
2 Substituted by FA 2001 s 240(1) and (2)(*a*) and Sch 5 Pt 1 for 2002 and later tax years; previously "£1,000".
3 Substituted by FA 2001 s 240(1) and (2)(*a*) and Sch 5 Pt 1 for 2002 and later tax years; previously "£52".
4 Substituted by FA 2001 s 240(1) and (2)(*k*) and Sch 5 Pt 1 as respects acts or omissions which take place or begin on or after 1 January 2002; previously "£100".

Revenue precedents

Issue: Charge to tax in respect of trade unions.
Decision: Income to which s 211 exemption does not apply is chargeable to income tax at the standard rate.

Definitions

Appeal Commissioners: s 2(1); High Court: IA 1937 Sch; person: IA 1937 s 11(*c*); statute: IA 1937 s 3; s 1(1); year of assessment: s 3(1).

Former enactments

ITA 1967 s 335 and s 339(2) and (4); FA 1967 s 7; F(MP)A 1968 s 3(4) and Sch Pt III; FA 1973 s 44; CTA 1976 s 140 and Sch 2 Pt I para 14.

Corresponding UK tax provision

Income and Corporation Taxes Act 1988 ss 459–466.

212 Credit unions

Amendments

Section 212 repealed by FA 1998 s 58(2) with effect from 6 April 1998 (but see section 219A).

213 Trade unions

(1) In this section, **"provident benefits"** includes any payment expressly authorised by the registered rules of the trade union and made to a member during sickness or incapacity from personal injury or while out of work, or to an aged member by means of superannuation, or to a member who has met with an accident, or has lost his or her tools by fire or theft, and includes a payment in discharge or aid of funeral expenses on the death of a member, or the wife of a member, or as provision for the children of a deceased member.

[(2) A registered trade union which is precluded by statute or by its rules from assuring to any persons a sum exceeding [€10,160][1] by means of gross sum or [€2,540][2] a year by means of annuity shall be entitled to exemption from income tax under Schedules C, D and F in respect of its interest and dividends which are applicable and applied solely for one or more of the following purposes—

(*a*) provident benefits, and

(*b*) the education, training or retraining of its members and dependent children of members.

(3) Every claim under this section shall be verified in such manner (including by affidavit) as may be specified by the Revenue Commissioners and proof of the claim may be given by the treasurer, trustee or any duly authorised agent of the trade union concerned.][3]

(4) A person who makes a false or fraudulent claim for exemption under this section in respect of any interest, annuities, dividends or shares of annuities charged or chargeable under Schedule C shall forfeit the sum of [€125][4].

Amendments

1 Substituted by FA 2001 s 240(1) and (2)(*a*) and Sch 5 Pt 1 for 2002 and later tax years; previously "£8,000".

2 Substituted by FA 2001 s 240(1) and (2)(*a*) and Sch 5 Pt 1 for 2002 and later tax years; previously "£2,000".

3 Subss (2)–(3) substituted by FA 2000 s 74 with effect from 6 April 2000.

4 Substituted by FA 2001 s 240(1) and (2)(*k*) and Sch 5 Pt 1 as respects acts or omissions which take place or begin on or after 1 January 2002; previously "£100".

Revenue precedents

Issue: Does the term "provident benefits" in s 213 include dental, optical and legal benefits?
Decision: Yes.

Definitions

affidavit: IA 1937 Sch; person: IA 1937 s 11(*c*); statute: IA 1937 s 3.

Former enactments

ITA 1967 s 336 and s339(2) and (4); F(MP)A 1968 s 3(4) and Sch Pt III; CTA 1976 s 140 and Sch 2 Pt I para 15; FA 1980 s 11.

Corresponding UK tax provision

Income and Corporation Taxes Act 1988 s 467.

214 Local authorities, etc

(1) In this section, **"local authority"** has the meaning assigned to it by section 2(2) of the Local Government Act, 1941, and includes a body established under the Local Government Services (Corporate Bodies) Act, 1971.

(2) This section shall apply to each of the following bodies—

(*a*) a local authority;

(*b*) [the Health Service Executive][1];

(*c*) a vocational education committee established under the Vocational Education Acts, 1930 to 1993;

(*d*) a committee of agriculture established under the Agriculture Acts, 1931 to 1980.

(3) Notwithstanding any provision of the Income Tax Acts, other than Chapter 4 of Part 8, income arising to a body to which this section applies shall be exempt from income tax.

Amendments

1 Substituted by FA 2005 s 147 and Sch 6 para 1(*c*) with effect from 25 March 2005; previously "a health board".

Note

In regard to the definition of "local authority", it should be noted that, by virtue of Local Government Act 2001 s 3(2) and Sch 2, references in any other enactment to "local authority for the purposes of the Local Government Act, 1941", and to similar or analogous expressions, are now to be construed as references to "a county council, city council and town council, and where the context so requires includes a joint body", within the meaning respectively assigned to each of those terms in the Local Government Act 2001.

Definitions

Income Tax Acts: s 1(2); local authority: ss 2(1), 5(1); year of assessment: ss 2(1), 5(1).

Former enactments

FA 1990 s 13.

Corresponding UK tax provision

Income and Corporation Taxes Act 1988 s 517.

215 Certain profits of agricultural societies

(1) In this section, **"agricultural society"** means any society or institution established for the purpose of promoting the interests of agriculture, horticulture, livestock breeding or forestry.

(2) Any profits or gains arising to an agricultural society from an exhibition or show held for the purposes of the society shall, if they are applied solely to the purposes of the society, be exempt from income tax.

Case law

A body of trustees established for the promotion of horse racing not regarded as an "agricultural society": *Trustees of Ward Union Hunt Races v Hughes* ITR Vol I p 538.

Revenue precedents

Issue: Trade Protection Association.

Decision: The above case did not qualify as an Agricultural Society but it may be considered as a trade protection association. An application for such recognition can be obtained from the Office of the Chief Inspector of Taxes.

Former enactments

ITA 1967 s 348.

Corresponding UK tax provision

Income and Corporation Taxes Act 1988 s 510.

216 Profits from lotteries

Exemption from income tax shall be granted in respect of profits from a lottery to which a licence under Part IV of the Gaming and Lotteries Act, 1956, applies.

Former enactments

ITA 1967 s 350.

Corresponding UK tax provision

Income and Corporation Taxes Act 1988 s 505.

216A Rent-a-room relief

[(1) In this section—

"qualifying residence", in relation to an individual for a year of assessment, means a residential premises situated in the State which is occupied by the individual as his or her sole or main residence during the year of assessment;

"relevant sums" means all sums arising in respect of the use for the purposes of residential accommodation, of a room or rooms in a qualifying residence and includes sums arising in respect of meals, cleaning, laundry and other similar goods and services which are incidentally supplied in connection with that use;

"residential premises" means a building or part of a building used as a dwelling.

(2) (*a*) This subsection applies if—

(i) relevant sums, chargeable to income tax under Case IV or Case V of Schedule D, arise to an individual (regardless of whether the relevant sums are chargeable to income tax under Case IV or Case V or under both Case IV and Case V), and

(ii) the amount of the relevant sums does not exceed the individual's limit for the year of assessment.

(*b*) In ascertaining the amount of relevant sums for the purposes of this subsection no deduction shall be made in respect of expenses or any other matter.

(*c*) Where this subsection applies the following shall be treated as nil for the purposes of the Income Tax Acts—

(i) the profits or gains of the year of assessment, and

(ii) the losses of any such year of assessment,

in respect of relevant sums arising to an individual.

(*d*) Where an individual has relevant sums chargeable to income tax under Case V of Schedule D and an election under subsection (3)(*a*) has not been made, an allowance under section 284, which would on due claim being made be granted, shall be deemed to have been granted.

(3) (*a*) Subsection (2) shall not apply for a year of assessment if an individual so elects by notice in writing to the inspector on or before the specified return date for the chargeable period (within the meaning of section 950).

(*b*) An election under this subsection shall have effect only for the year of assessment for which it is made.

(4) The provisions of the Income Tax Acts relating to the making of returns shall apply as if this section had not been enacted.

(5) Subject to subsections (6) and (7), the limit of an individual referred to in subsection (2) is [€7,620][1].

...[2]

(7) Where relevant sums arise to more than one individual in respect of a qualifying residence the limits referred to in subsections (5) and (6) shall be divided by the number of such individuals.

(8) Where subsection (2) applies, the receipt of relevant sums shall not operate so as to restrict or reduce any entitlement to relief under section 244 or 604.][3]

Amendments

[1] Substituted by FA 2001 s 32(2)(*a*) for 2002 and later tax years; previously "£6,000".

[2] Subs (6) deleted by FA 2001 s 32(2)(*b*) for 2002 and later tax years.

[3] Section 216A inserted by FA 2001 s 32(1) with effect from 6 April 2001.

Tax Briefing

TB43 April 2001 p 17 — Rent-a-room relief.

TB44 June 2001 p 41 — Rent-a-room relief — topical questions.

Definitions

Income Tax Acts: s 1(2); profits or gains: s 3(4); year of assessment: s 2(1).

216B Payments under Scéim na bhFoghlaimeoirí Gaeilge

[(1) This section shall apply, in the case of a qualified applicant under a scheme administered by the Minister for Community, Rural and Gaeltacht Affairs and known as Scéim na bhFoghlaimeoirí Gaeilge, to any income received under that scheme in respect of a person who is temporarily resident with the qualified applicant, together with any other income received in the ordinary course in respect of such temporary resident.

(2) Notwithstanding any provision of the Income Tax Acts, income to which this section applies shall be disregarded for the purposes of those Acts.][1]

Amendments

[1] Section 216B inserted by FA 2004 s 12 with effect from 1 January 2004.

Definitions

Income Tax Acts: s 1(2).

CHAPTER 2
Corporation Tax

217 Certain income of Nítrigin Éireann Teoranta

Notwithstanding any provision of the Corporation Tax Acts, income—

(*a*) arising to Nítrigin Éireann Teoranta in any accounting period ending in the period commencing on the 1st day of January, 1987, and ending on the 31st day of December, 1999, from the business of supplying gas purchased from Bord Gáis Éireann to Irish Fertilizer Industries Limited under a contract between Nítrigin Éireann Teoranta and Irish Fertilizer Industries Limited, and

(*b*) which but for this section would have been chargeable to corporation tax under Case I of Schedule D,

shall be exempt from corporation tax.

Definitions

Corporation Tax Acts: s 1(2).

Former enactments

FA 1988 s 39; FA 1992 s 57.

218 Certain income of Housing Finance Agency plc

Notwithstanding any provision of the Corporation Tax Acts, income arising to the Housing Finance Agency plc—

(*a*) from the business of making loans and advances under section 5 of the Housing Finance Agency Act, 1981, which income would but for this section have been chargeable to corporation tax under Case I of Schedule D, and

(*b*) which income would but for this section have been chargeable to corporation tax under Case III of Schedule D,

shall be exempt from corporation tax.

Definitions

Corporation Tax Acts: s 1(2).

Former enactments

FA 1985 s 24; FA 1990 s 56.

219 Income of body designated under Irish Takeover Panel Act, 1997

Notwithstanding any provision of the Corporation Tax Acts, income arising in any accounting period ending after the 30th day of April, 1997, to the body designated by the Minister for Enterprise, Trade and Employment under section 3 of the Irish Takeover Panel Act, 1997, shall be exempt from corporation tax.

Definitions

Corporation Tax Acts: s 1(2).

Former enactments

FA 1997 s 63.

219A Income of credit unions

[(1) In this section **"the Act"** means the Credit Union Act, 1997.

(2) Income arising to a credit union which is—

(*a*) registered as such under the Act, or

(*b*) deemed to be so registered by virtue of section 5(3) of the Act,

shall, with effect from the date of the registration or the deemed registration, as the case may be, of the credit union under the Act, be exempt from corporation tax.][1]

Amendments

1 Section 419A inserted by FA 1998 s 58(1) with effect from 6 April 1998.

Corresponding UK tax provision

Income and Corporation Taxes Act 1988 s 487.

219B Income of Investor Compensation Company Ltd

[(1) In this section, **"the company"** means the company incorporated on the 10th day of September, 1998, as The Investor Compensation Company Limited.

(2) Notwithstanding any provision of the Corporation Tax Acts, profits arising in any accounting period ending on or after the 10th day of September, 1998, to the company shall be exempt from corporation tax.][1]

Amendments

1 Section 219B inserted by FA 1999 s 76(1)(*a*) with effect from 6 April 1999.

Definitions

company: s 4(1); Corporation Tax Acts: s 1(2); profits: s 4(1).

220 Profits of certain bodies corporate

Notwithstanding any provision of the Corporation Tax Acts, profits arising to any of the bodies corporate specified in the Table to this section shall be exempt from corporation tax.

TABLE

...[1]

2. A company authorised by virtue of a licence granted by the Minister of Finance under the National Lottery Act, 1986.

3. The Dublin Docklands Development [Authority and any of its wholly-owned subsidiaries.][2]

4. An Bord Pinsean— The Pensions Board.

5. [Horse Racing Ireland.][3]

6. The company incorporated on the 1st day of December, 1994, as Irish Thoroughbred Marketing Limited.

7. The company incorporated on the 1st day of December, 1994, as Tote Ireland Limited.

[8. The Commission for Electricity Regulation.][4]

Amendments

1 Para 1 deleted by FA 1999 s 77 (Table para 1) for accounting periods beginning on or after 25 March 1999; previously "1. Bord Gáis Éireann.".

2 Substituted by FA 2001 s 79(*b*) for accounting periods ending on or after 6 April 2001; previously "Authority.".

3 Substituted by Horse and Greyhound Racing Act 2001 s 11 with effect from "the establishment day"; previously "The Irish Horseracing Authority". By virtue of the Horse and Greyhound Racing Act 2001 (Establishment Day) Order 2001, SI No 630 of 2001, 18 December 2001 is "the establishment day".

4 Para 8 inserted by FA 2000 s 84(1) with effect from 14 July 1999.

Definitions

company: ss 4(1), 5(1); Corporation Tax Acts: s 1(2); inspector: ss 2(1), 5(1), 852; profits: s 4(1); wholly-owned subsidiary: s 9.

Former enactments

FA 1983 s 32; FA 1987 s 34; FA 1988 s 42; FA 1991 s 41; FA 1995 s 44(1)–(2); FA 1997 s 49(1)–(2).

221 Certain payments to National Co-operative Farm Relief Services Ltd and certain payments made to its members

(1) In this section—

"the first agreement" means the agreement in writing dated the 4th day of July, 1991, between the Minister for Agriculture, Food and Forestry and the National Co-operative for the provision of financial support for farm relief services, together with every amendment of the agreement in accordance with Article 9.1 of that agreement;

"the second agreement" means the agreement in writing dated the 16th day of May, 1995, between the Minister for Agriculture, Food and Forestry and the National Co-operative for the provision of financial support for the development of agricultural services, together with every amendment of the agreement in accordance with Article 9.1 of that agreement;

"a member co-operative" means a society engaged in the provision of farm relief services which has been admitted to membership of the National Co-operative;

"the Minister" means the Minister for Agriculture and Food;

"the National Co-operative" means the society registered on the 13th day of August, 1980, as National Co-operative Farm Relief Services Limited;

"society" means a society registered under the Industrial and Provident Societies Acts, 1893 to 1978.

(2) Notwithstanding any provision of the Corporation Tax Acts—

(*a*) a grant made under Article 3.1 of the first agreement by the Minister to the National Co-operative,

(*b*) a transfer of moneys under Article 3.6 of the first agreement by the National Co-operative to a member co-operative,

(*c*) a payment made under Article 3.1(*a*) of the second agreement by the Minister to the National Co-operative, and

(*d*) a transmission of moneys under Article 3.4 in respect of payments under Article 3.1(*a*) of the second agreement by the National Co-operative to a member co-operative,

shall be disregarded for the purposes of those Acts.

Definitions

Corporation Tax Acts: s 1(2); writing: IA 1937 Sch.

Former enactments

FA 1994 s 52; FA 1995 s 57.

222 Certain dividends from a non-resident subsidiary

(1) (*a*) In this section—

"approved investment plan" means an investment plan in respect of which the Minister has given a certificate in accordance with subsection (2) to the company concerned;

"investment plan" means a plan of a company resident in the State which is directed towards the creation or maintenance of employment in the State in trading operations carried on, or to be carried on, in the State and which has been submitted—

(i) before the commencement of its implementation, or

(ii) where the Minister is satisfied that there was reasonable cause for it to be submitted after the commencement of its implementation, within one year from that commencement,

to the Minister by the company for the purpose of enabling it to claim relief under this section;

"the Minister" means the Minister for Finance;

"relevant dividends" means dividends, received by a company resident in the State (being the company claiming relief under this section) from a foreign subsidiary of the company, which are—

(i) [specified in a certificate given before 15 February 2001 by the Minister][1] under subsection (2), and

(ii) applied within a period—

(I) which begins one year before the first day on which the dividends so specified are received in the State, or at such earlier time as the Revenue Commissioners may by notice in writing allow, and

(II) which ends 2 years after the first day on which the dividends so specified are received in the State, or at such later time as the Revenue Commissioners may by notice in writing allow,

for the purposes of an approved investment plan;

"relief under this section", in relation to a company for an accounting period, means the amount by which any corporation tax payable by the company is reduced by virtue of subsection (3).

(*b*) (i) The reference in the definition of "relevant dividends" to "a foreign subsidiary" means a 51 per cent subsidiary of a company where the company is resident in the State and the subsidiary is a resident ...[2] of a territory with the government of which arrangements having the force of law by virtue of [section 826(1)(*a*)][3] have been made.

(ii) For the purposes of subparagraph (i)—

...[4]

a company shall be regarded as being a resident of a territory ...[5] if it is so regarded under arrangements made with the government of that territory and having the force of law by virtue of [section 826(1)(*a*)][3].

(2) Where an investment plan has been duly submitted by a company, and the Minister—

(*a*) is satisfied that the plan is directed towards the creation or maintenance of employment in the State in trading operations carried on, or to be carried on, in the State, and

(*b*) has been informed in writing by the company of the amount of dividends concerned, the Minister may give a certificate to the company certifying that an amount of dividends specified in the certificate shall be an amount of relevant dividends.

(3) Subject to subsection (4), where a company claims and proves that it has received in an accounting period any amount of relevant dividends, the amount of the company's income for the period represented by those dividends shall not be taken into account in computing the income of the company for that accounting period for the purposes of corporation tax.

(4) Where in relation to a certificate given to a company under subsection (2) the Minister considers that, as regards the approved investment plan concerned, all or part of the relevant dividends have not been applied within the period provided for in the definition of **"relevant dividends"**, the Minister may, by notice in writing to the company, reduce the amount of the relevant dividends specified in the certificate by so much as has not been so applied, and accordingly where the amount of the relevant dividends specified in a certificate is so reduced—

(*a*) in a case where relief under this section has been granted in respect of the amount of the relevant dividends specified in the certificate before such a reduction of that amount, the inspector shall make such assessments or additional assessments as are necessary to recover the relief given in respect of the amount of the reduction, and

(*b*) in a case where a claim for relief has not yet been made, relief shall not be due under this section in respect of the amount of the reduction.

(5) A claim for relief under this section shall be made in writing to the inspector and shall be submitted together with the company's return of profits for the period in which the relevant dividends are received in the State.

Amendments

1 Substituted by FA 2001 s 86 with effect from 6 April 2001; previously "specified in a certificate given by the Minister".

2 Deleted by FA 1998 s 48 and Sch 3 para 3(*a*) from 1 January 1998; previously "of the United States of America or".

3 Substituted by FA 2004 s 89 and Sch 3 para 1(*h*) with effect from 25 March 2004; previously "section 826".

4 Definition of "resident of the United States of America" deleted by FA 1998 s 48 and Sch 3 para 3(*b*)(i) from 1 January 1998.

5 Deleted by FA 1998 s 48 and Sch 3 para 3(*b*)(ii) from 1 January 1998; previously "other than the United States of America".

Definitions

company: ss 4(1), 5(1); profits: s 4(1); writing: IA 1937 Sch.

Former enactments

FA 1988 s 41; FA 1991 s 40.

CHAPTER 3
Income Tax and Corporation Tax

223 Small enterprise grants

(1) This section shall apply to a grant made under section 10(5)(*a*) of the Údarás na Gaeltachta Act, 1979, or section 21(5)(*a*) (as amended by the Industrial Development

(Amendment) Act, 1991) of the Industrial Development Act, 1986, being an employment grant—

(*a*) in the case of section 10(5)(*a*) of the Údarás na Gaeltachta Act, 1979, under the scheme known as **"Deontais Fhostaíochta Údarás na Gaeltachta do Thionscnaimh Sheirbhíse Idir-Náisiúnta"** or the scheme known as **"Deontais Fhostaíochta ó Údarás na Gaeltachta do Thionscail Bheaga Dhéantúsaíochta"**, or

(*b*) in the case of section 21(5)(*a*) of the Industrial Development Act, 1986 (as so amended), under the scheme known as **"Scheme Governing the Making of Employment Grants to Small Industrial Undertakings"**.

(2) A grant to which this section applies shall be disregarded for the purposes of the Tax Acts.

Definitions

Tax Acts: s 1(2).

Former enactments

FA 1993 s 37.

224 Grants to medium and large industrial undertakings

(1) This section shall apply to a grant made under section 10(5)(*a*) of the Údarás na Gaeltachta Act, 1979, or section 21(5)(*a*) (as amended by the Industrial Development (Amendment) Act, 1991) of the Industrial Development Act, 1986, being an employment grant—

(*a*) in the case of section 10(5)(*a*) of the Údarás na Gaeltachta Act, 1979, under the scheme known as **"Deontais Fhostaíochta ó Údarás na Gaeltachta do Ghnóthais Mhóra/Mhénmhéide Thionsclaíocha"**, or

(*b*) in the case of section 21(5)(*a*) of the Industrial Development Act, 1986 (as so amended), under the scheme known as **"Scheme Governing the Making of Employment Grants to Medium/Large Industrial Undertakings"**.

(2) A grant to which this section applies shall be disregarded for the purposes of the Tax Acts.

Definitions

Tax Acts: s 1(2).

Former enactments

FA 1995 s 43.

225 Employment grants

(1) This section shall apply to an employment grant made under—

[(*a*) section 3 or 4 (as amended by the Shannon Free Airport Development Company Limited (Amendment) Act, 1983) of the Shannon Free Airport Development Company Limited (Amendment) Act, 1970,

(*b*) section 25 of the Industrial Development Act, 1986, or

(*c*) section 12 of the Industrial Development Act, 1993.][1]

(2) A grant to which this section applies shall be disregarded for the purposes of the Tax Acts.

Amendments

1 Subs (1)(*a*)–(*b*) substituted by FA 1999 s 38 as respects a grant made on or after 6 April 1996.

Definitions

Tax Acts: s 1(2).

Former enactments

FA 1982 s 18; FA 1997 s 146(1) and Sch 9 Pt I para 12(2).

226 Certain employment grants and recruitment subsidies

(1) This section shall apply to an employment grant or recruitment subsidy made to an employer in respect of a person employed by such employer under—

(*a*) the Back to Work Allowance Scheme, being a scheme established on the 1st day of October, 1993, and administered by the Minister for Social, Community and Family Affairs,

(*b*) any scheme which may be established by the Minister for Enterprise, Trade and Employment with the approval of the Minister for Finance for the purposes of promoting the employment of individuals who have been unemployed for 3 years or more and which is to be administered by An Foras Áiseanna Saothair,

(*c*) paragraph 13 of Annex B to an operating agreement between the Minister for Enterprise, Trade and Employment and a County Enterprise Board, being a board specified in the Schedule to the Industrial Development Act, 1995,

(*d*) as respects grants or subsidies paid on or after the 6th day of April, 1997, the Employment Support Scheme, being a scheme established on the 1st day of January, 1993, and administered by the National Rehabilitation Board,

(*e*) as respects grants or subsidies paid on or after the 6th day of April, 1997, the Pilot Programme for the Employment of People with Disabilities, being a programme administered by a company incorporated on the 7th day of March, 1995, as The Rehab Group,

(*f*) the European Union Leader II Community Initiative 1994 to 1999, and which is administered in accordance with operating rules determined by the Minister for Agriculture and Food,

(*g*) the European Union Operational Programme for Local Urban and Rural Development which is to be administered by the company incorporated under the Companies Acts, 1963 to 1990, on the 14th day of October, 1992, as Area Development Management Limited,

(*h*) the Special European Union Programme for Peace and Reconciliation in Northern Ireland and the Border Counties of Ireland which was approved by the European Commission on the 28th day of July, 1995,

(*i*) the Joint Northern Ireland/Ireland INTERREG Programme 1994 to 1999, which was approved by the European Commission on the 27th day of February, 1995, or

(*j*) any initiative of the International Fund for Ireland, which was designated by the International Fund for Ireland (Designation and Immunities) Order, 1986 (SI No 394 of 1986), as an organisation to which Part VIII of the Diplomatic Relations and Immunities Act, 1967, applies.

(2) An employment grant or recruitment subsidy to which this section applies shall be disregarded for the purposes of the Tax Acts.

Definitions

company: ss 4(1), 5(1); person: IA 1937 s 11(*c*); Tax Acts: s 1(2).

Former enactments

FA 1996 s 40(1)–(2); FA 1997 s 40.

227 Certain income arising to specified non-commercial state-sponsored bodies

(1) In this section, **"non-commercial state-sponsored body"** means a body specified in Schedule 4.

(2) For the purposes of this section, the Minister for Finance may by order amend Schedule 4 by the addition to that Schedule of any body or the deletion from that Schedule of any body standing specified.

(3) Where an order is proposed to be made under subsection (2), a draft of the order shall be laid before Dáil Éireann and the order shall not be made until a resolution approving of the draft has been passed by Dáil Éireann.

(4) Notwithstanding any provision of the Tax Acts other than the provisions (apart from section 261(*c*)) of Chapter 4 of Part 8, income arising to a non-commercial state-sponsored body—

(*a*) which but for this section would have been chargeable to tax under Case III, IV or V of Schedule D, and

(*b*) from the date that such body was incorporated under the Companies Acts, 1963 to 1990, or was established by or under any other enactment,

shall be disregarded for the purposes of the Tax Acts; but a non-commercial state-sponsored body—

(i) which has paid income tax or corporation tax shall not be entitled to repayment of that tax, and

(ii) shall not be treated as—

(I) a company within the charge to corporation tax in respect of interest for the purposes of paragraph (*f*) of the definition of "relevant deposit" in section 256, or

(II) a person to whom section 267 applies.

Definitions

company: ss 4(1), 5(1); interest: s 4(1); tax: s 3(1); Tax Acts: s 1(2).

Former enactments

FA 1994 s 32(1)–(4).

228 Income arising to designated bodies under the Securitisation (Proceeds of Certain Mortgages) Act, 1995

Notwithstanding any provision of the Tax Acts, income arising to a body designated under section 4(1) of the Securitisation (Proceeds of Certain Mortgages) Act, 1995, shall be exempt from income tax and corporation tax.

Definitions

Tax Acts: s 1(2).

Former enactments

FA 1996 s 39(1)–(2).

229 Harbour authorities and port companies

(1) (*a*) In this section—

"relevant body" means—

(i) a harbour authority within the meaning of the Harbours Act, 1946,

(ii) a company established pursuant to section 7 of the Harbours Act, 1996, and

(iii) any other company which controls a harbour and carries on a trade which consists wholly or partly of the provision in that harbour of such facilities and accommodation for vessels, goods and passengers as are ordinarily provided by harbour authorities specified in paragraph (i), and companies specified in paragraph (ii) which control harbours, situate within the State, in those harbours;

"relevant profits or gains" means so much of the profits or gains of a relevant body controlling a harbour situate within the State as arise from the provision in that harbour of such facilities and accommodation for vessels, goods and passengers as are ordinarily provided by—

(i) harbour authorities specified in paragraph (i), and

(ii) companies specified in paragraph (ii),

of the definition of **"relevant body"**, which control harbours, situate within the State, in those harbours.

(*b*) For the purposes of this section, where an accounting period falls partly in a period, the part of the accounting period falling in the period shall be regarded as a separate accounting period.

(2) Exemption shall be granted from tax under Schedule D in respect of relevant profits or gains in the period beginning on the 1st day of January, 1997, and ending on the 31st day of December, 1998.

(3) Subsection (2) shall apply to a relevant body which is a harbour authority referred to in paragraph (i) of the definition of **"relevant body"** as if **"in the period beginning on the 1st day of January, 1997, and ending on the 31st day of December, 1998"** were deleted.

(4) Where a relevant body is chargeable to tax under Schedule D in respect of relevant profits or gains, the relevant profits or gains shall be reduced by an amount equal to—

(*a*) as respects accounting periods falling wholly or partly in the year 1999, two-thirds of those relevant profits or gains, and

(*b*) as respects accounting periods falling wholly or partly in the year 2000, one-third of those relevant profits or gains.

Former enactments

FA 1997 s 60(1) and (3)–(5).

230 National Treasury Management Agency

(1) Notwithstanding any provision of the Corporation Tax Acts, profits arising to the National Treasury Management Agency in any accounting period shall be exempt from corporation tax.

(2) Notwithstanding any provision of the Tax Acts, any interest, annuity or other annual payment paid by the National Treasury Management Agency shall be paid without deduction of income tax.

Definitions

Corporation Tax Acts: s 1(2); profits: s 4(1).

Former enactments

FA 1991 s 20(1) and (3).

230A National Pensions Reserve Fund Commission

[Notwithstanding any provision of the Corporation Tax Acts, profits arising to the National Pensions Reserve Fund Commission shall be exempt from corporation tax.][1]

Amendments

1 Section 230A inserted by National Pensions Reserve Fund Act 2000 s 30(*b*) with effect from 10 December 2000.

Definitions

Corporation Tax Acts: s 1(2); profits: s 4(1).

230AB National Development Finance Agency

[(1) Notwithstanding any provision of the Corporation Tax Acts, profits arising to the National Development Finance Agency in any accounting period shall be exempt from corporation tax.

(2) Notwithstanding any provision of the Tax Acts, any interest, annuity or other annual payment paid by the National Development Finance Agency shall be paid without deduction of income tax.][1]

Amendments

1 Section 230AB inserted by FA 2003 s 43(1)(*b*) with effect from 6 February 2003.

Definitions

Corporation Tax Acts: s 1(2); profits: s 4(1); Tax Acts: s 1(2).

231 Profits or gains from stallion fees

[(1)][1] The profits or gains arising —

(*a*) (i) to the owner of a stallion, which is ordinarily kept on land in the State, from the sale of services of mares within the State by the stallion, or

(ii) to the part-owner of such a stallion from the sale of such services or of rights to such services, or (*b*) to the part-owner of a stallion, which is ordinarily kept on land outside the State, from the sale of services of mares by the stallion or of rights to such services, where the part-owner carries on in the State a trade which consists of or includes bloodstock breeding and it is shown to the satisfaction of the inspector, or on appeal to the satisfaction of the Appeal Commissioners, that the part-ownership of the stallion was acquired and is held primarily for the purposes of the service by the stallion of mares owned or partly-owned by the part-owner of the stallion in the course of that trade,

[shall be exempt from income tax and corporation tax][2].

[(2) As respects the making of a return of income (being a return which a chargeable person, within the meaning of section 950, is required to deliver under section 951), the Tax Acts shall apply—

(*a*) as if subsection (1) had not been enacted,

(*b*) notwithstanding anything to the contrary in Part 41, as if a person to whom profits or gains referred to in subsection (1) arise for any chargeable period (within the meaning of section 321(2)) were, if such person would not otherwise be, a chargeable person (within the meaning of section 950) for that chargeable period,

(*c*) where a person to whom profits or gains referred to in subsection (1) arise for any chargeable period (within the meaning of section 321(2)) is a person to whom a notice under section 951(6) has been issued, as if such a notice had not been issued, and

(*d*) in so far as those Acts relate to the keeping of records (within the meaning of section 886) and the making available of such records for inspection, as if such profits or gains were chargeable to income tax or corporation tax, as the case may be.

(3) For the purposes of subsection (2)—

(*a*) profits or gains referred to in subsection (1) or a loss referred to in paragraph (*b*) shall be computed in accordance with the Tax Acts as if subsection (1) had not been enacted, and

(*b*) where a loss is incurred for any chargeable period (within the meaning of section 321(2)), the amount of that loss shall be included in the return of income referred to in subsection (2) for that chargeable period.][3]

Amendments

1 Renumbered by FA 2003 s 35(1)(*a*)(i) as respects any chargeable period (within the meaning of TCA 1997 s 321(2)) commencing on or after 1 January 2004.

2 Substituted by FA 2003 s 35(1)(*a*)(ii) as respects any chargeable period (within the meaning of TCA 1997 s 321(2)) commencing on or after 1 January 2004; previously "shall not be taken into account for any purpose of the Tax Acts".

3 Subss (2) and (3) inserted by FA 2003 s 35(1)(*a*)(iii) as respects any chargeable period (within the meaning of TCA 1997 s 321(2)) commencing on or after 1 January 2004.

Cross-references

Distributions from exempt profits: s 140(1).

Distributions out of profits from trading in Shannon Airport: s 144(8)("R").

Tax Briefing

TB33 Sept 1998 p 19 — "Dual hemisphere" or "shuttle" stallions treated as ordinarily kept on land in the State.
TB48 June 2002 p 18 — Dual hemisphere or shuttle stallions.

Definitions

Appeal Commissioners: s 2(1); land: IA 1937 Sch; person: IA 1937 s 11(*c*); Tax Acts: s 1(2); trade: ss 3(1), 4(1).

Former enactments

FA 1969 s 18(2)(*b*); CTA 1976 s 11(6); FA 1985 s 14(1).

232 Profits from occupation of certain woodlands

(1) In this section—

"occupation", in relation to any land, means having the use of that land;

"woodlands" means woodlands in the State.

(2) Except where otherwise provided by section 75, the profits or gains arising from the occupation of woodlands managed on a commercial basis and with a view to the realisation of profits [shall be exempt from income tax and corporation tax][1].

[(3) As respects the making of a return of income (being a return which a chargeable person, within the meaning of section 950, is required to deliver under section 951), the Tax Acts shall apply—

(*a*) as if subsection (2) had not been enacted,

(*b*) notwithstanding anything to the contrary in Part 41, as if a person to whom profits or gains referred to in subsection (2) arise for any chargeable period (within the meaning of section 321(2)) were, if such person would not otherwise be, a chargeable person (within the meaning of section 950) for that chargeable period,

(*c*) where a person to whom profits or gains referred to in subsection (2) arise for any chargeable period (within the meaning of section 321(2)) is a person to whom a notice under section 951(6) has been issued, as if such a notice had not been issued, and

(*d*) in so far as those Acts relate to the keeping of records (within the meaning of section 886) and the making available of such records for inspection, as if such profits or gains were chargeable to income tax or corporation tax, as the case may be.

(4) For the purposes of subsection (3)—

(*a*) profits or gains referred to in subsection (2) or a loss referred to in paragraph (*b*) shall be computed in accordance with the Tax Acts as if subsection (2) had not been enacted, and

(*b*) where a loss is incurred for any chargeable period (within the meaning of section 321(2)), the amount of that loss shall be included in the return of income referred to in subsection (3) for that chargeable period.][2]

Amendments

1 Substituted by FA 2003 s 35(1)(*b*)(i) as respects any chargeable period (within the meaning of TCA 1997 s 321(2)) commencing on or after 1 January 2004; previously "shall not be taken into account for any purpose of the Tax Acts".

[2] Subss (3) and (4) inserted by FA 2003 s 35(1)(*b*)(ii) as respects any chargeable period (within the meaning of TCA 1997 s 321(2)) commencing on or after 1 January 2004.

Cross-references

Distributions from exempt profits: s 140(1).

Distributions out of profits from trading in Shannon Airport: s 144(8)("R").

Case law

Irish

Words in a charging provision, in the absence of a definition, to be interpreted according to normal usage: *De Brún v Kiernan* [1982] ITR Vol III p 19.

In construing the phrase "have the use of", two principles apply (1) it's necessary to look at the effect of the actual use of the land in question by the taxpayer, and (2) where there are two concurrent users of the land in question, it's only the predominant use that should be taken into account – *O'Conaill v Z Ltd* 2 ITR 636.

UK

Owner of woodlands and sawmills held exempt from tax on profits from sale of timber out of the sawmills: *IRC v Williamson Bros* (1950) 31 TC 370; *Collins v Fraser* (1969) 46 TC 143.

Individuals who purchased, felled and removed the timber and not the landowner held to be the occupiers of the woodlands: *Russell v Hird* [1983] STC 541.

Revenue precedents

Issue: Are profits from the planting and harvesting of Christmas trees exempt under the section?

Decision: Yes.

Issue: A person intends to plant a small area of holly. Small amounts of foliage can be harvested after 3 years but the main harvest will arise after 6 to 10 years. Is the profit arising from the sale of the holly exempt under TCA 1997 s 232?

Decision: The profits from the sale of foliage from holly bushes are not regarded as profits arising from the occupation of woodlands and are therefore not exempt.

Statement of practice

New forest premium scheme, EC Council Regulation 797/85, premiums are not to be taken into account for any purpose of the Income Tax Acts by virtue of this section: SP IT/1/90, July 1990.

Definitions

land: IA 1937 Sch; person: IA 1937 s 11(*c*); Tax Acts: s 1(2); trade: s 3(1).

Former enactments

FA 1969 s 18(1)–(2)(*c*); CTA 1976 s 11(6); FA 1996 s 132(2) and Sch 5 Pt II.

Corresponding UK tax provision

Income and Corporation Taxes Act 1988 ss 53(4) and 54.

233 Stud greyhound service fees

(1) In this section—

"greyhound bitches" means female greyhounds registered in the Irish Greyhound Stud Book or in any other greyhound stud book recognised for the purposes of the Irish Greyhound Stud Book;

"stud greyhound" means a male greyhound registered as a sire for stud purposes in the Irish Greyhound Stud Book or in any other greyhound stud book recognised for the purposes of the Irish Greyhound Stud Book.

(2) The profits or gains arising—

(*a*) (i) to the owner of a stud greyhound, which is ordinarily kept in the State, from the sale of services of greyhound bitches within the State by the stud greyhound, or

(ii) to the part-owner of such a stud greyhound from the sale of such services or of rights to such services, or (*b*) to the part-owner of a stud greyhound, which is ordinarily kept outside the State, from the sale of services of greyhound bitches by the stud greyhound or of rights to such services, where the part-owner carries on in the State a trade which consists of or includes greyhound breeding and it is shown to the satisfaction of the inspector, or on appeal to the satisfaction of the Appeal Commissioners, that the part-ownership of the stud greyhound was acquired and is held primarily for the purposes of the service by the stud greyhound of greyhound bitches owned or partly-owned by the part-owner of the stud greyhound in the course of that trade,

[shall be exempt from income tax and corporation tax][1].

[(3) As respects the making of a return of income (being a return which a chargeable person, within the meaning of section 950, is required to deliver under section 951), the Tax Acts shall apply—

(*a*) as if subsection (2) had not been enacted,

(*b*) notwithstanding anything to the contrary in Part 41, as if a person to whom profits or gains referred to in subsection (2) arise for any chargeable period (within the meaning of section 321(2)) were, if such person would not otherwise be, a chargeable person (within the meaning of section 950) for that chargeable period,

(*c*) where a person to whom profits or gains referred to in subsection (2) arise for any chargeable period (within the meaning of section 321(2)) is a person to whom a notice under section 951(6) has been issued, as if such a notice had not been issued, and

(*d*) in so far as those Acts relate to the keeping of records (within the meaning of section 886) and the making available of such records for inspection, as if such profits or gains were chargeable to income tax or corporation tax, as the case may be.

(4) For the purposes of subsection (3)—

(*a*) profits or gains referred to in subsection (2) or a loss referred to in paragraph (*b*) shall be computed in accordance with the Tax Acts as if subsection (2) had not been enacted, and

(*b*) where a loss is incurred for any chargeable period (within the meaning of section 321(2)), the amount of that loss shall be included in the return of income referred to in subsection (3) for that chargeable period.][2]

Amendments

1 Substituted by FA 2003 s 35(1)(*c*)(i) as respects any chargeable period (within the meaning of TCA 1997 s 321(2)) commencing on or after 1 January 2004; previously "shall not be taken into account for any purpose of the Tax Acts".

2 Subss (3) and (4) inserted by FA 2003 s 35(1)(*c*)(ii) as respects any chargeable period (within the meaning of TCA 1997 s 321(2)) commencing on or after 1 January 2004.

Cross-references

Distributions from exempt profits: s 140(1).

Distributions out of profits from trading in Shannon Airport: s 144(8)("R").

Definitions

Appeal Commissioners: s 2(1); person: IA 1937 s 11(*c*); Tax Acts: s 1(2); trade: ss 3(1), 4(1).

Former enactments

FA 1996 s 25(1)–(2).

234 Certain income derived from patent royalties

(1) In this section—

"income from a qualifying patent" means any royalty or other sum paid in respect of the user of the invention to which the qualifying patent relates, including any sum paid for the grant of a licence to exercise rights under such patent, where that royalty or other sum is paid—

(*a*) for the purposes of activities which—

(i) would be regarded, otherwise than by virtue of paragraph (*b*) or (*c*) of section 445(7) or section 446, as the manufacture of goods for the purpose of relief under Part 14, or

(ii) would be so regarded if they were carried on in the State by a company,

but, as respects a royalty or other sum paid on or after the 23rd day of April, 1996, where the royalty or other sum exceeds the royalty or other sum which would have been paid if the payer of the royalty or other sum and the beneficial recipient of the royalty or other sum were independent persons acting at arm's length, the excess shall not be income from a qualifying patent,

or

(*b*) by a person who—

(i) is not connected (within the meaning of section 10 as it applies for the purposes of capital gains tax) with the person who is the beneficial recipient of the royalty or other sum, and

(ii) has not entered into any arrangement in connection with the royalty or other sum the main purpose or one of the main purposes of which was to satisfy subparagraph (i);

"qualifying patent" means a patent in relation to which the research, planning, processing, experimenting, testing, devising, designing, developing or similar activity leading to the invention which is the subject of the patent was carried out in the State;

"resident of the State" means any person resident in the State for the purposes of income tax and not resident elsewhere;

a company shall be regarded as a resident of the State if it is managed and controlled in the State.

(2) (*a*) A resident of the State who makes a claim in that behalf and makes a return in the prescribed form of his or her total income from all sources, as estimated in accordance with the Income Tax Acts, shall be entitled to have any income from a qualifying patent arising to him or her disregarded for the purposes of the Income Tax Acts.

(*b*) In paragraph (*a*), the reference to a return of total income from all sources as estimated in accordance with the Income Tax Acts shall apply for corporation tax as if it were or included a reference to a return under section 884.

(3) Notwithstanding subsection (2), an individual shall not be entitled to have any amount of income from a qualifying patent arising to him or her disregarded for any purpose of the Income Tax Acts unless the individual carried out, either solely or jointly

with another person, the research, planning, processing, experimenting, testing, devising, designing, developing or other similar activity leading to the invention which is the subject of the qualifying patent.

(4) Where, under section 77 of the Patents Act, 1992, or any corresponding provision of the law of any other country, an invention which is the subject of a qualifying patent is made, used, exercised or vended by or for the service of the State or the government of the country concerned, this section shall apply as if the making, user, exercise or vending of the invention had taken place in pursuance of a licence and any sums paid in respect of the licence were income from a qualifying patent.

(5) Where any income arising to a person is by virtue of this section to be disregarded, the person shall not be treated, by reason of such disregarding, as having ceased to possess the whole of a single source within the meaning of section 70(1).

(6) For the purpose of determining the amount of income to be disregarded under this section for the purposes of the Income Tax Acts, the Revenue Commissioners may make such apportionments of receipts and expenses as may be necessary.

(7) The relief provided by this section may be given by repayment or otherwise.

(8) Subsections (3) and (4) of section 459 and paragraph 8 of Schedule 28 shall, with any necessary modifications, apply in relation to exemptions from tax under this section.

Cross-references

Distributions out of profits from trading in Shannon Airport: s 144(8)("R").

Patent income distributions (subs (2)) exempt from income tax: s 141(1).

Tax credit for research and development expenditure, meaning of "qualifying patent" applied: s 766(1)(*a*)("expenditure on research and development").

Case law

Opinion given by an inspector was not an advance ruling and the inspector was not bound by that opinion: *Pandion Haliaetus Ltd, Ospreycare Ltd and Osprey Systems Design Ltd v Revenue Commissioners* ITR Vol III p 670.

Revenue precedents

Issue: Interaction of Ireland/UK Double Taxation convention and s 234.

Decision: Where a person is a resident of Ireland and not a resident of the UK in accordance with the Irl/UK Double Taxation convention, that person is a resident of Ireland for the purposes of s 234.

Issue: Does exempt income from patents have to be declared on a return of income Form 11?

Decision: Yes.

Tax Briefing

TB38 Dec 1999 pp 18–19 Patent Royalties Income and Distributions.

TB53 Aug 2003 p 16 — Patent Royalty Income exemption (in the context of phasing out of manufacturing relief).

TB56 July 2004 p 12 — Meaning of "not resident elsewhere" for the purposes of sections 195 and 234 Taxes Consolidation Act 1997.

TB57 Oct 2004 p 15 — "not resident elsewhere": Correction of error in TB56.

Definitions

Income Tax Acts: s 1(2); person: IA 1937 s 11(*c*); taxable income: ss 3(1), 458; total income: s 3(1).

Former enactments

FA 1973 s 34; CTA 1976 Sch 2 Pt I para 35; FA 1981 s 19; FA 1992 s 19(1); FA 1994 s 28; FA 1996 s 32(1) and (3)(*a*) and s132(1) and Sch 5 Pt I para 7; FA 1997 s 146(1) and Sch 9 Pt I para 6(2).

Corresponding UK tax provision

Income and Corporation Taxes Act 1988 s 529.

235 Bodies established for promotion of athletic or amateur games or sports

(1) In this section, **"approved body of persons"** means—

(*a*) any body of persons established for and existing for the sole purpose of promoting athletic or amateur games or sports, and

(*b*) (i) any body of persons that, as respects the year 1983–84 or any earlier year of assessment, was granted exemption from income tax under section 349 of the Income Tax Act, 1967, before that section was substituted by section 9 of the Finance Act, 1984, or

(ii) any company that, as respects any accounting period ending before the 6th day of April, 1984, was granted exemption from corporation tax under section 349 (before the substitution referred to in subparagraph (i)) of the Income Tax Act, 1967, as applied for corporation tax by section 11(6) of the Corporation Tax Act, 1976;

but does not include any such body of persons to which the Revenue Commissioners, after such consultation (if any) as may seem to them to be necessary with such person or body of persons as in their opinion may be of assistance to them, give a notice in writing stating that they are satisfied that the body—

(I) was not established for the sole purpose specified in paragraph (*a*) or was established wholly or partly for the purpose of securing a tax advantage, or

(II) being established for the sole purpose specified in paragraph (*a*), no longer exists for such purpose or commences to exist wholly or partly for the purpose of securing a tax advantage.

(2) Exemption from income tax or, as the case may be, corporation tax shall be granted in respect of so much of the income of any approved body of persons as is shown to the satisfaction of the Revenue Commissioners to be income which has been or will be applied to the sole purpose specified in subsection (1)(*a*).

(3) Where a notice is given under subsection (1), the exemption from income tax or, as the case may be, corporation tax accorded to the body of persons to which it relates shall cease to have effect—

(*a*) if the notice is a notice to which paragraph (I) of that subsection applies—

(i) as respects income tax, for the year of assessment in which the body of persons was established or the year 1984–85, whichever is the later, and for each subsequent year of assessment, or

(ii) as respects corporation tax, for the first accounting period of the body of persons which commences on or after the 6th day of April, 1984, and for each subsequent accounting period;

(*b*) if the notice is a notice to which paragraph (II) of that subsection applies—

(i) as respects income tax, for the year of assessment in which in the opinion of the Revenue Commissioners the body of persons ceased to exist for the sole purpose specified in subsection (1)(*a*) or the year in which it commenced to exist wholly or partly for the purpose of securing a tax advantage, whichever is the earlier, but not being a year earlier than the year 1984–85, and for each subsequent year of assessment, or

(ii) as respects corporation tax, for the accounting period in which in the opinion of the Revenue Commissioners the body of persons ceased to exist for the sole purpose specified in subsection (1)(*a*) or the accounting period in which it commenced to exist wholly or partly for the purpose of securing a tax advantage, whichever is the earlier, but not being an accounting period which ends before the 6th day of April, 1984, and for each subsequent accounting period.

(4) Section 949 shall apply to a notice under subsection (1) as if the notice were a determination by the Revenue Commissioners of a claim to an exemption under the Income Tax Acts.

(5) Anything required or permitted to be done by the Revenue Commissioners or any power or function conferred or imposed on them by this section may be done, exercised or performed, as appropriate, by an officer of the Revenue Commissioners authorised by them in that behalf.

Cross-references

Capital Gains Tax, exempt bodies, meaning of "approved body" applied: Sch 15 Pt 1 para 37.

Dividend withholding tax, interpretation, meaning of "approved body of persons" applied: s 172A(1).

Dividend withholding tax, exemption for certain persons: s 172C(2)(*f*)(i).

Donations to certain sports bodies: s 847A(1)("approved sports body"), subs (2): s 847A(19).

Case law

The underlying legislation was substituted following the case of *O'Reilly and others v Revenue Commissioners* [1984] ILRM 406. In the particular case the courts held that the exemption was not available to a private sports club. The present section allows withdrawal of relief by the Revenue Commissioners.

Revenue precedents

Issue: Whether a sporting body entitled to exemption under TCA 1997 s 235 would be entitled to receive interest without deduction of tax on the basis of a declaration under TCA 1997 s 265.

Decision: No; since the sporting body would not be within the charge to corporation tax in respect of the interest, Also, the body in question could not complete a declaration to the effect that the interest will be included in the profits of the company on which it will be charged to Corporation Tax, as required by s 265.

Revenue information

Information Leaflet GS 1 — Relief from Income Tax and Corporation Tax for Certain Sporting Bodies.

A list of Sports Bodies with a Tax Exemption under the Tax Acts is available on Revenue's website — www.revenue.ie — under Publications/Lists.

Tax Briefing

TB44 June 2001 p 20 — Games and Sports Bodies — Relief from Income Tax and Corporation Tax.

Definitions

body of persons: s 2(1); person: IA 1937 s 11(*c*); writing: IA 1937 Sch; year of assessment: s 3(1).

Former enactments

ITA 1967 s 349; FA 1984 s 9; FA 1997 s 146(1) and Sch 9 Pt I para 1(25).

236 Loan of certain art objects

(1) In this section—

"art object" has the meaning assigned to it by subsection (2)(*a*);

"authorised person" means—

(*a*) an inspector or other officer of the Revenue Commissioners authorised by them in writing for the purposes of this section, or

(*b*) a person authorised by the Minister in writing for the purposes of this section;

"the Minister" means the Minister for Arts, Heritage, Gaeltacht and the Islands;

"relevant building" means an approved building within the meaning of section 482;

"relevant garden" means an approved garden within the meaning of section 482.

(2) (*a*) In this section, **"art object"** means any work of art (including a picture, sculpture, print, book, manuscript, piece of jewellery, furniture or other similar object) or scientific collection which, on application to them in that behalf by a person who owns or occupies a relevant building or a relevant garden, as the case may be, is determined—

(i) by the Minister, after consideration of any evidence in relation to the matter which the individual submits to the Minister and after such consultation (if any) as may seem to the Minister to be necessary with such person or body of persons as in the opinion of the Minister may be of assistance to the Minister, to be an object which is intrinsically of significant national, scientific, historical or aesthetic interest, and

(ii) by the Revenue Commissioners, to be an object reasonable access to which is afforded, and in respect of which reasonable facilities for viewing are provided, to the public.

(*b*) Without prejudice to the generality of the requirement that reasonable access be afforded, and that reasonable facilities for viewing be provided, to the public, access to and facilities for the viewing of an art object shall not be regarded as being reasonable access afforded, or the provision of reasonable facilities for viewing, to the public unless—

(i) subject to such temporary removal as is necessary for the purposes of the repair, maintenance or restoration of the object as is reasonable, access to it is afforded and facilities for viewing it are provided for not less than 60 days (including not less than 40 days during the period commencing on the 1st day of May and ending on the 30th day of September) in any year and, on each such day, such access is afforded and such facilities for viewing are provided in a reasonable manner and at reasonable times for a period, or periods in the aggregate, of not less than 4 hours,

(ii) such access is afforded and such facilities are provided to the public on the same days and at the same times as access is afforded to the public to the relevant building or the relevant garden, as the case may be, in which the object is kept, and

(iii) the price, if any, paid by the public in return for such access is in the opinion of the Revenue Commissioners reasonable in amount and does not operate to preclude the public from seeking access to the object.

(*c*) Where the Revenue Commissioners make a determination under paragraph (*a*) in relation to an art object, and reasonable access to the object ceases to be afforded, or reasonable facilities for the viewing of the object cease to be provided, to the public, the Revenue Commissioners may, by notice in writing given to the owner or occupier of the relevant building or relevant garden, as the case may be, in which the object is kept, revoke the determination with effect from the date on which they consider that such access or such facilities for viewing so ceased, and—

(i) this subsection shall cease to apply to the object from that date, and

(ii) for the year of assessment in which this subsection ceases to apply to the object, subsection (3) shall cease to apply to any expense referred to in paragraph (*a*) of that subsection incurred or deemed to have been incurred by the body corporate concerned.

(3) Subject to this section, where—

(*a*) a body corporate incurs an expense solely in, or solely in connection with, or is deemed to incur an expense in connection with, the provision to an individual (being an individual who is employed by the body corporate in an employment to which Chapter 3 of Part 5 applies, or who is a director, within the meaning of that Chapter, of the body corporate) of a benefit or facility which consists of the loan of an art object of which the body corporate is the beneficial owner, and

(*b*) the object is kept in a relevant building or a relevant garden, as the case may be, owned or occupied by the individual,

then, section 436(3) shall not apply to any such expense and section 118(1) shall not apply to any such expense for any year of assessment for which a claim in that behalf is made by the individual to the Revenue Commissioners.

(4) (*a*) Where an individual makes an application under subsection (2) or a claim under subsection (3), an authorised person may at any reasonable time enter the relevant building or relevant garden concerned for the purpose of inspecting the art object to which the application or claim relates.

(*b*) Whenever an authorised person exercises any power conferred on him or her by this subsection, the authorised person shall on request produce his or her authorisation to any person concerned.

(*c*) Any person who obstructs or interferes with an authorised person in the course of exercising a power conferred on the authorised person by this subsection shall be guilty of an offence and shall be liable on summary conviction to a fine not exceeding [€630][1].

(5) An application under subsection (2) or a claim under subsection (3)—

(*a*) shall be made in such form as the Revenue Commissioners may from time to time prescribe, and

(*b*) in the case of a claim under subsection (3), shall be accompanied by such statements in writing as may be required by the prescribed form in relation to the expense in respect of which the claim is made, including statements by the body corporate which incurred the expense.

(6) Section 606 shall not apply to an object which is an art object.

Amendments

[1] Substituted by FA 2001 s 240(1) and (2)(*k*) and Sch 5 Pt 1 as respects acts or omissions which begin or take place on or after 1 January 2002; previously "£500".

Definitions

body of persons: s 2(1); inspector: ss 2(1), 5(1), 852; interest: s 4(1); person: IA 1937 s 11(*c*); year of assessment: ss 2(1), 5(1).

Former enactments

FA 1994 s 19(1)–(6).

PART 8
ANNUAL PAYMENTS, CHARGES AND INTEREST

Cross-references

Implementation of Council Directive 2003/49/EC of 3 June 2003 on a common system of taxation applicable to interest and royalty payments made between associated companies of different Member States, application: s 267H(1)(*a*)(ii).

Restriction of relief for payments of interest: s 817A(1).

Tax credit for research and development expenditure: s 766(1)(*a*)("expenditure on research and development").

Tonnage tax, treatment of finance costs: s 697LB(1) ("finance costs").

CHAPTER 1
Annual Payments

237 Annual payments payable wholly out of taxed income

(1) Where any annuity or any other annual payment apart from yearly interest of money (whether payable in or outside the State, either as a charge on any property of the person paying the same by virtue of any deed or will or otherwise, or as a reservation thereout, or as a personal debt or obligation by virtue of any contract, or whether payable half-yearly or at any shorter or more distant periods), is payable wholly out of profits or gains brought into charge to income tax—

- (*a*) the whole of those profits or gains shall be assessed and charged with income tax on the person liable to the annuity or annual payment, without distinguishing the same,
- (*b*) the person liable to make such payment, whether out of the profits or gains charged with tax or out of any annual payment liable to deduction, or from which a deduction has been made, shall be entitled on making such payment to deduct and retain out of such payment a sum representing the amount of the income tax on such payment at the standard rate of income tax for the year in which the amount payable becomes due,
- (*c*) the person to whom such payment is made shall allow such deduction on the receipt of the residue of such payment, and
- (*d*) the person making such deduction shall be acquitted and discharged of so much money as is represented by the deduction as if that sum had been actually paid.

(2) Where any royalty or other sum is paid in respect of the user of a patent wholly out of profits or gains brought into charge to income tax, the person paying the royalty or other sum shall be entitled on making the payment to deduct and retain out of the payment a sum representing the amount of income tax on the payment at the standard rate of income tax for the year in which the royalty or other sum payable becomes due.

(3) This section shall not apply to any rents or other sums in respect of which the person entitled to them is chargeable to tax under Case V of Schedule D or would be so chargeable but for any exemption from tax.

Cross-references

Capital expenditure, references to: s 316(1).

Charge to tax of income from which tax has been deducted: s 59.

Corporation tax, allowance of charges on income, subs (2): s 243(4)(*a*).

Corporation tax, computation of income, application of income tax principles, subs (2): s 76(5)(*b*).
Dividends regarded as paid out of profits accumulated before given date: Sch 22 para 5(3)(*f*)(i).
Loans to participators, effect of release of debt: s 439(1)(*c*).
Non-residents, distributions to: s 153(4)(*b*), (5)(*b*), (6)(*b*).
Partnerships and European Economic Interest Groupings, meaning of "annual payment" applied: s 1007(1).
Patents, spreading revenue payments over several years: s 759(2).
Petroleum trade, interest and charges on income: s 690(4).
Purchased life annuities: s 789(4)(*b*).
Certain rents under long leases and other payments: s 104(2)(*a*)(i).
Self assessment, meaning of "chargeable person": s 950(1).

Case law

Distinction between purchased life annuities and other annuities highlighted by Murphy J in the Supreme Court in *McCabe v South City and County Investment Co. Ltd* [1997] 5 ITR 107.
Tax on payments made gross due to a mistake in law cannot be recouped from subsequent payments unless the payments are in arrears: *Shrewsbury v Shrewsbury* (1907) 23 TLR 224; *Taylor v Taylor* [1938] 1 KB 320.
Annual payments cannot be made "wholly out of profits or gains brought into charge to tax" where there is no taxable income because of losses: *Luipaard's Vlei Estate & Gold Mining Co Ltd v IRC* (1930) 15 TC 573; *Trinidad Petroleum Development Co Ltd v IRC* (1936) 21 TC 1.
An 'annual payment' is a payment which is pure income profit in the hands of the recipient: *In re Hanbury (dec'd)* (1939) 38 TC 588 and does not include payment of insurance premiums: *Earl Howe v IRC* (1919) 7 TC 289; payment for the use of assets: *In re Hanbury dec'd* (above); payment of training fees: *Essex County Council v Ellam* [1989] STC 317; nor payments to charity where taxpayers received sums in return and accordingly did not reduce their actual income: *Moodie v CIR & Sinnett* [1993] 2 All ER 49.

Revenue precedents

Issue: Whether copyright royalties are "annual payments" within the scope of s 237 and 238.
Decision: No.

Statement of practice

Currency and/or interest swap agreements, not annual payments, tax need not be deducted: SP CT/1/91.

Definitions

person: IA 1937 s 11(*c*).

Former enactments

ITA 1967 s 433; FA 1969 s 33 and Sch 4 Pt I; FA 1974 s 5(1); CTA 1976 s 164 and Sch 4 Pt I; FA 1989 s 89(1); FA 1996 s 132(1) and Sch 5 Pt I para 1(19).

Corresponding UK tax provision

Income and Corporation Taxes Act 1988 s 348.

238 Annual payments not payable out of taxed income

(1) In this section, **"the inspector"** means such inspector as the Revenue Commissioners may direct.

(2) On payment of any annuity or other annual payment (apart from yearly interest of money) charged with tax under Schedule D, or of any royalty or other sum paid in respect of the user of a patent, not payable or not wholly payable out of profits or gains brought into charge, the person by or through whom any such payment is made shall deduct out of such payment a sum representing the amount of the income tax on such payment at the standard rate of tax in force at the time of the payment.

(3) Where any such payment is made by or through any person, that person shall forthwith deliver to the Revenue Commissioners an account of the payment, or of so much of the payment as is not made out of profits or gains brought into charge, and of the income tax deducted out of the payment or out of that part of the payment, and the inspector shall assess and charge the payment of which an account is so delivered on that person.

(4) The inspector may, where any person has made default in delivering an account required by this section, or where he or she is not satisfied with the account so delivered, make an assessment according to the best of his or her judgment.

(5) The provisions of the Income Tax Acts relating to—

(*a*) persons who are to be chargeable with income tax,
(*b*) income tax assessments,
(*c*) appeals against such assessments,
(*d*) the collection and recovery of income tax,
(*e*) the rehearing of appeals, and
(*f*) cases to be stated for the opinion of the High Court,

shall, in so far as they are applicable, apply to the charge, assessment, collection and recovery of income tax under this section.

(6) Subsections (3) to (5) shall apply subject to sections 239 and 241 with respect to the time and manner in which certain companies resident in the State are to account for and pay income tax in respect of—

(*a*) payments from which tax is deductible, and
(*b*) any amount deemed to be an annual payment.

(7) Except where provided by section 1041(1), this section shall not apply to any rents or other sums in respect of which the person entitled to them is chargeable to tax under Case V of Schedule D or would be so chargeable but for any exemption from tax.

Cross-references

Allowance of charges on income: s 243(5)(*c*).
Amount of s 237 assessment to be allowed as a loss: s 390.
Capital expenditure, references to: s 316(1).
Charge to tax of income from which tax has been deducted: s 59.
Charges on capital sums received for sale of patent rights: s 757(2), (4)(*b*).
Corporation tax, charges on income: s 243(5)(*a*).
Dividends regarded as paid out of profits accumulated before given date: Sch 22 para 5(3)(*f*)(i).
Group payments: s 410(4).
Implementation of Council Directive 2003/49/EC of 3 June 2003 on a common system of taxation applicable to interest and royalty payments made between associated companies of different Member States, exemptions from tax and withholding tax: s 267I(1).
Income tax on payments by non-resident companies, subs (3): s 241(1)(*a*), subs (2): (2)(*a*).
Income tax on payments by resident companies (subss (3)–(5)), "relevant payment" includes annual payments under this section: s 239(1)(*a*).
Interest payments by companies and to non-residents, subss (1), (3)–(5): s 246(2).
Loans to participators, effect of release of debt: s 439(1)(*a*), (*c*).
Non-residents, distributions to: s 153(4)(*b*), (5)(*b*), (6)(*b*).
Patents, spreading revenue payments over several years: s 759(2), (4).
Penalty, subs (3): Sch 29 column 3.
Profit sharing schemes, assessment of trustees in respect of sums received: s 516(*b*).
Purchase and sale of securities, persons entitled to exemption: s 750(*a*).
Purchase and sale of securities, traders other than dealers in securities: s 751(2)(*a*).
Purchases of shares by financial concerns and persons exempted from tax: s 752(4).
Rents payable to non-residents: s 1041(1).
Certain rents under long leases and other payments: s 104(2)(*a*)(i).
Returns of profits, subss (3)–(5): s 884(2)(*d*).
Scheduled mineral assets, charge to tax on sums received from sale: s 683(3)(*b*), (*c*), (4).
Self assessment, meaning of "chargeable person": s 950(1).
Taxation of certain perquisites, subs (3)–(6): s 112A(4).

Transactions in land, Schedule D Case IV: s 644(2).

Case law

Irish

Liability on "annual payments" confined to amount chargeable to income tax: *In re estate of T Downing deceased* ITR Vol I p 487.

Interest paid on funds in court is not subject to the provisions of the section. Liability to be accounted even where no formal assessment, when final allocation of funds being made: *Colclough and others v Colclough and another* [1965] IR 668.

Payments by trustees out of capital because the trust income loss insufficient to pay beneficiary's annuity held to be annual payments not wholly payable out of profits brought into charge: *Michelham's Trustees v IRC* (1930) 15 TC 737; *Brodie's Will Trustees v IRC* (1933) 17 TC 432; *Lindus and Hortin v IRC* (1993) 17 TC 442.

UK

Tax not deducted from payments made cannot be recouped from subsequent payments: *Tenbry Investments Limited v Peugeot Talbot Motor Co Ltd* [1992] STC 791.

Appointment of 22 sums out of capital over a 2 year period to a single beneficiary to defray costs of medical treatment and residential care of elderly beneficiary held not to be income in nature – *Stevenson v Wishart* [1987] STC 266.

Revenue precedents

Issue: Whether copyright royalties are annual payments for the purposes of TCA 1997 s 238.

Decision: Copyright royalties are not annual payments for the purposes of TCA 1997 s 238.

Issue: Is interest paid on an award made by an arbitrator under s 34 of the Arbitrator's Act 1954 "interest of money" within the meaning of TCA 1997 s 238?

Decision: Yes.

Issue: Are film royalties annual payments?

Decision: Generally, yes, since they are normally pure income profit.

Statement of practice

Currency and/or interest swap agreements, not annual payments, tax need not be deducted: SP CT/1/91.

Definitions

High Court: IA 1937 Sch; inspector: ss 2(1), 5(1), 852; person: IA 1937 s 11(*c*).

Former enactments

ITA 1967 s 434(1)–(5A) and (8); FA 1969 s 33 and Sch 4; FA 1974 s 11 and Sch 1 Pt II; CTA 1976 s 151(14); FA 1990 s 51(3); FA 1996 s 132(1) and Sch 5 Pt I para 1(20).

Corresponding UK tax provision

Income and Corporation Taxes Act 1988 ss 349–350.

---

239 Income tax on payments by resident companies

(1) In this section, **"relevant payment"** means—

(*a*) any payment from which income tax is deductible and to which subsections (3) to (5) of section 238 apply, and

(*b*) any amount which under section 438 is deemed to be an annual payment.

(2) This section shall apply for the purpose of regulating the time and manner in which companies resident in the State—

(*a*) are to account for and pay income tax in respect of relevant payments, and

(*b*) are to be repaid income tax in respect of payments received by them.

(3) A company shall make for each of its accounting periods in accordance with this section a return to the inspector of the relevant payments made by it in that period and of the income tax for which the company is accountable in respect of those payments.

(4) A return for any period for which a return is required to be made under this section shall be made within 9 months from the end of that period.

(5) Income tax in respect of any payment required to be included in a return under this section shall be due at the time by which preliminary tax (if any) for the accounting period for which the return is required to be made under subsection (3) is due and payable, and income tax so due shall be payable by the company without the making of any assessment; but income tax which has become so due may be assessed on the company (whether or not it has been paid when the assessment is made).

(6) Where it appears to the inspector that there is a relevant payment which ought to have been but has not been included in a return, or where the inspector is dissatisfied with any return, the inspector may make an assessment on the company to the best of his or her judgment, and any income tax due under an assessment made by virtue of this subsection shall be treated for the purposes of interest on unpaid tax as having been payable at the time when it would have been payable if a correct return had been made.

(7) Where in any accounting period a company receives any payment on which it bears income tax by deduction, the company may claim to have the income tax on that payment set against any income tax which it is liable to pay under this section in respect of payments made by it in that period, and any such claim shall be included in the return made under subsection (3) for the accounting period in question, and (where necessary) income tax paid by the company under this section for that accounting period and before the claim is allowed shall be repaid accordingly.

(8) (*a*) Where a claim has been made under subsection (7), no proceedings for collecting tax which would be discharged if the claim were allowed shall be instituted pending the final determination of the claim, but this subsection shall not affect the date when the tax is due, and when the claim is finally determined any tax underpaid in consequence of this subsection shall be paid.

(*b*) Where proceedings are instituted for collecting tax assessed, or interest on tax assessed, under subsection (5) or (6), effect shall not be given to any claim under subsection (7) made after the institution of the proceedings so as to affect or delay the collection or recovery of the tax charged by the assessment or of interest on that tax.

(9) Income tax set against other tax under subsection (7) shall be treated as paid or repaid, as the case may be, and the same tax shall not be taken into account both under this subsection and under section 24(2).

(10)(*a*) Where a company makes a relevant payment on a date which does not fall within an accounting period, the company shall make a return of that payment within 6 months from that date, and the income tax for which the company is accountable in respect of that payment shall be due at the time by which the return is to be made.

(*b*) Any assessment in respect of tax payable under this subsection shall be treated as relating to the year of assessment in which the payment is made.

(*c*) Subsection (11) shall not apply to an assessment under this subsection.

(11)(*a*) Subject to subsection (10)(*b*), income tax payable (after income tax borne by the company by deduction has been set, by virtue of any claim under subsection (7), against income tax which it is liable to pay under subsection (5)) in respect of relevant payments in an accounting period shall, for the purposes of the charge, assessment, collection and recovery from the company making the payments of that tax and of any interest or penalties on that tax, be treated and described as corporation tax payable by that company for that accounting period, notwithstanding that for all other purposes of the Tax Acts it is income tax.

(*b*) Tax paid by a company which is treated as corporation tax by virtue of this subsection shall be repaid to the company if it would have been so repaid under subsection (7) had it been treated as income tax paid by the company.

(*c*) Any tax assessable under one or more of the provisions of this section may be included in one assessment if the tax so included is all due on the same date.

(12) Nothing in this section shall be taken to prejudice any powers conferred by the Tax Acts for the recovery of tax by means of an assessment or otherwise.

(13)(*a*) The Revenue Commissioners may, by regulations made for the purposes mentioned in subsection (2), modify, supplement or replace any of the provisions of this section, and references in the Corporation Tax Acts and in any other enactment to this section shall be construed as including references to any such regulations and, without prejudice to the generality of the foregoing, such regulations may, in relation to tax charged by this section, modify any provision of the Tax Acts relating to returns, assessments, claims or appeals, or may apply any such provision with or without modification.

(*b*) Regulations under this subsection may—

(i) make different provision for different descriptions of companies and for different circumstances, and may authorise the Revenue Commissioners, where in their opinion there are special circumstances justifying it, to make special arrangements as respects income tax for which a company is liable to account or the repayment of income tax borne by a company;

(ii) include such transitional and other supplemental provisions as appear to the Revenue Commissioners to be expedient or necessary.

(*c*) Every regulation made under this subsection shall be laid before Dáil Éireann as soon as may be after it is made and, if a resolution annulling the regulation is passed by Dáil Éireann within the next 21 days on which Dáil Éireann has sat after the regulation is laid before it, the regulation shall be annulled accordingly, but without prejudice to the validity of anything previously done thereunder.

Cross-references

Annual payments not payable out of taxed income: s 238(6).

Group relief, relief for certain losses on a value basis: s 420B(1)("relevant corporation tax").

Income tax collection and appeals procedures (subs (10)) applied by: s 240.

Loans to participators etc: s 438(1)(*b*).

Manufacturing (10%) rate, meaning of "relevant corporation tax": s 448(1)(*d*)(i).

Penalties for failure to furnish certain information and for incorrect information: s 1075(2).

Profits of life business: s 710(3)(*b*)(i).

Relief for certain charges on income on a value basis: s 243B(1)("relevant corporation tax").

Relief for certain trading losses on a value basis: s 396B(1)("relevant corporation tax").

Relief in respect of unrelieved losses and capital allowances carried forward from 1975–76: Sch 32 para 16(1).

Self assessment, meaning of "chargeable person": s 950(1).

Definitions

company: ss 4(1), 5(1); Dáil Éireann: IA 1937 Sch; inspector: ss 2(1), 5(1), 852; month: IA 1937 Sch; Tax Acts: s 1(2); year of assessment: ss 2(1), 5(1).

Former enactments

CTA 1976 s 151(1)–(13) (apart from subs (8)(*c*)); FA 1990 s 49.

Corresponding UK tax provision

Income and Corporation Taxes Act 1988 ss 349–350.

240 Provisions as to tax under section 239

(1) Subsections (2) to (4) shall apply only in respect of a company to which section 239(10) relates.

(2) The provisions of the Income Tax Acts relating to—

(*a*) persons who are to be chargeable to income tax,
(*b*) income tax assessments,
(*c*) appeals against such assessments (including the rehearing of appeals and the statement of a case for the opinion of the High Court), and
(*d*) the collection and recovery of income tax,

shall, in so far as they are applicable, apply to the charge, assessment, collection and recovery of income tax under section 239.

(3) (*a*) Any tax payable in accordance with section 239 without the making of an assessment shall carry interest at the rate of [0.0322 per cent for each day or part of a day][1] from the date when the tax becomes due and payable until payment.

(*b*) [Subsections (3) to (5) of section 1080][2] shall apply in relation to interest payable under this subsection as they apply in relation to interest payable under section 1080.

(4) In its application to any tax charged by an assessment to income tax in accordance with section 239, section 1080 shall apply as if [subsection (2)(*b*)][3] of that section were deleted.

(5) Section 1081(1) shall not apply where by virtue of section 438(4) there is any discharge or repayment of tax assessed under section 239.

Amendments

1 Substituted by FA 2002 s 129(1)(*a*) with effect from 1 September 2002 as regards interest chargeable in respect of an amount due to be paid or remitted, whether before, on, or after that date; previously "1 per cent for each month or part of a month".

2 Substituted by FA 2005 s 145(7)(*a*) and Sch 5 Pt 1 in relation to any unpaid income tax, corporation tax or capital gains tax, as the case may be, that has not been paid before 1 April 2005 regardless of when that tax became due and payable and notwithstanding anything to the contrary in any other enactment other than TCA 1997 s 1082; previously "Subsections (2) to (4) of section 1080".

3 Substituted by FA 2005 s 145(7)(*a*) and Sch 5 Pt 1 in relation to any unpaid income tax, corporation tax or capital gains tax, as the case may be, that has not been paid before 1 April 2005 regardless of when that tax became due and payable and notwithstanding anything to the contrary in any other enactment other than TCA 1997 s 1082; previously "subsection (1)(*b*)".

Definitions

company: ss 4(1), 5(1); High Court: IA 1937 Sch; Income Tax Acts: s 1(2); month: IA 1937 Sch.

Former enactments

CTA 1976 s 152; FA 1978 s 46(1)(*f*), (2)–(3); FA 1981 s 22; FA 1990 s 50; FA 1997 s 146(2) and Sch 9 Pt II.

Corresponding UK tax provision

Income and Corporation Taxes Act 1988 s 350.

241 Income tax on payments by non-resident companies

(1) This section shall apply in relation to an accounting period of a company not resident in the State if the company is—

(*a*) required by virtue of section 238(3) to deliver an account to the Revenue Commissioners, and

(*b*) within the charge to corporation tax in respect of the accounting period.

(2) Where this section applies in relation to an accounting period of a company, then—

(*a*) the company shall make a return to the inspector of—

(i) payments made by the company in the accounting period and in respect of which income tax is required to be deducted by virtue of section 238(2), and

(ii) the tax deducted out of those payments by virtue of section 238(2),

and

(*b*) income tax in respect of which a return is to be made under paragraph (*a*) shall, for the purposes of the charge, assessment, collection and recovery from the company making the payments of that tax and of any interest or penalties on that tax, be treated as if it were corporation tax chargeable for the accounting period for which the return is required under paragraph (*a*).

Cross-references

Annual payments not payable out of taxed income: s 238(6).
Corporation tax, charges on income: s 243(5)(*a*).
Group relief, relief for certain losses on a value basis: s 420B(1)("relevant corporation tax").
Manufacturing (10%) rate, meaning of "relevant corporation tax": s 448(1)(*d*)(i).
Relief for certain charges on income on a value basis: s 243B(1)("relevant corporation tax").
Relief for certain trading losses on a value basis: s 396B(1)("relevant corporation tax").
Relief in respect of unrelieved losses and capital allowances carried forward from 1975–76: Sch 32 para 16(1).

Definitions

company: ss 4(1), 5(1); inspector: s 2(1), 852; within the charge to (tax): s 2(1).

Former enactments

FA 1990 s 51(1)–(2).

242 Annual payments for non-taxable consideration

(1) This section shall apply to any payment which is—

(*a*) an annuity or other annual payment charged with tax under Case III of Schedule D, other than—

(i) interest,

(ii) an annuity granted in the ordinary course of a business of granting annuities, or

(iii) a payment made to an individual under a liability incurred in consideration of the individual surrendering, assigning or releasing an interest in settled property to or in favour of a person having a subsequent interest,

and

(*b*) made under a liability incurred for consideration in money or money's worth, where all or any part of such consideration is not required to be taken into account in computing for the purposes of income tax or corporation tax the income of the person making the payment.

(2) Any payment to which this section applies—

(*a*) shall be made without deduction of income tax,

(*b*) shall not be allowed as a deduction in computing the income or total income of the person by whom it is made, and

(*c*) shall not be a charge on income for the purposes of corporation tax.

Definitions

person: IA 1937 s 11(*c*); settled property: s 5(1); total income: s 3(1).

Former enactments

FA 1989 s 89(2).

Corresponding UK tax provision

Income and Corporation Taxes Act 1988 s 125.

CHAPTER 2
Charges on Income for Corporation Tax Purposes

243 Allowance of charges on income

(1) Subject to this section and to any other express exceptions, **"charges on income"** means, for the purposes of corporation tax, payments of any description mentioned in subsection (4), not being dividends or other distributions of the company; but no payment deductible in computing profits or any description of profits for the purposes of corporation tax shall be treated as a charge on income.

[(1A) For the purposes of this section, **"bank"** [has the meaning assigned to it by section 845A and][1] includes building society within the meaning of section 256(1).][2]

(2) In computing the corporation tax chargeable for any accounting period of a company, any charges on income paid by the company in the accounting period, in so far as paid out of the company's profits brought into charge to corporation tax, shall be allowed as deductions against the total profits for the period reduced by any other relief from corporation tax other than group relief [in accordance with section 420][3].

(3) (*a*) This subsection shall apply to expenditure incurred for the purposes of a trade or profession set up and commenced on or after the 22nd day of January, 1997.

(*b*) Where—

(i) a company pays any charges on income before the time it sets up and commences a trade, and

(ii) the payment is made wholly and exclusively for the purposes of that trade,

that payment, to the extent that it is not otherwise deducted from total profits of the company, shall be treated for the purposes of corporation tax as paid at that time.

(*c*) An allowance or deduction shall not be made under any provision of the Tax Acts, other than this subsection, in respect of any expenditure or payment treated under this section as incurred on the day on which a trade or profession is set up and commenced.

(4) Subject to subsections (5) to (8), the payments referred to in subsection (1) are—

(*a*) any yearly interest, annuity or other annual payment and any other payments mentioned in section 104 or 237(2), and

(*b*) any other [interest payable on an advance][4] from—

(i) a bank carrying on a bona fide banking business [in a Member State of the European Communities][5], or

(ii) a person who in the opinion of the Revenue Commissioners is bona fide carrying on business as a member of a stock exchange [in a Member State of the European Communities][5] or bona fide carrying on the business of a discount house in the State,

and for the purposes of this section any interest payable by a company as is mentioned in paragraph (*b*) shall be treated as paid on such interest being debited to the company's account in the books of the person to whom it is payable.

(5) No payment mentioned in subsection (4)(*a*) made by a company to a person not resident in the State shall be treated as a charge on income unless it is a payment—

(*a*) from which, in accordance with—

(i) section 238, or

(ii) that section as applied by section 246,

[except where—

(I) the company has been authorised by the Revenue Commissioners to do otherwise, ...[6]

[(II) the interest is interest referred to in paragraph (*a*), (*b*) or (*h*) of section 246(3), or

(III) the interest is interest to which section 64(2) applies,][7]

the company deducts income tax which it accounts for under sections 238 and 239, or under sections 238 and 241, [as the case may be,][8]][9]

(*b*) which is payable out of income brought into charge to tax under Case III of Schedule D and which arises from securities and possessions outside [the State, or][10]

[(*c*) to which section 238 or 246(2) do not apply by virtue of section 267I.][11]

(6) No such payment made by a company as is mentioned in subsection (4) shall be treated as a charge on income if—

(*a*) the payment is charged to capital or the payment is not ultimately borne by the company, or

(*b*) the payment is not made under a liability incurred for a valuable and sufficient consideration and, in the case of a company not resident in the State, incurred wholly and exclusively for the purposes of a trade carried on by the company in the State through a branch or agency, and for the purposes of this paragraph a payment within subparagraph (ii) or (iii) of section 792(1)(*b*) shall be treated as incurred for valuable and sufficient consideration.

(7) Subject to subsection (8), interest shall not be treated as a charge on income.

(8) Subject to subsection (9), subsection (7) shall not apply to any payment of interest on a loan to a company to defray money applied for a purpose mentioned in subsection (2) of section 247, if the conditions specified in subsections (3) and (4) of that section are fulfilled.

(9) Section 249 shall apply for corporation tax as for income tax, and accordingly references in that section to section 247, to the investing company and to the borrower, to interest eligible for relief, and to affording relief for interest shall apply as if they were or included respectively references to subsection (8), to such a company as is mentioned in that subsection, to interest to be treated as a charge on income, and to treating part only of a payment of interest as a charge on income.

Amendments

1 Inserted by FA 2005 s 49(1)(*a*) as respects accounting periods ending on or after 3 February 2005.

2 Subs (1A) inserted by FA 2001 s 37(1)(*a*)(i) in respect of interest paid on or after 30 March 2001.

3 Inserted by FA 2005 s 49(1)(*b*) as respects accounting periods ending on or after 3 February 2005.

4 Substituted by FA 2005 s 49(1)(*c*)(i) as respects accounting periods ending on or after 3 February 2005; previously "interest payable in the State on an advance".

5 Substituted by FA 2005 s 49(1)(*c*)(ii) as respects accounting periods ending on or after 3 February 2005; previously "in the State".

6 Deleted by FA 2001 s 37(1)(*a*)(ii)(I) in respect of interest paid on or after 30 March 2001; previously "or".

7 Subs (5)(*a*)(II)–(III) inserted by FA 2001 s 37(1)(*a*)(ii)(II) in respect of interest paid on or after 30 March 2001.

8 Substituted by FA 2005 s 49(1)(*d*)(i) as respects accounting periods ending on or after 3 February 2005; previously "as the case may be, or".

9 Substituted by FA 2000 s 65(1) with effect from 10 February 2000; previously "except where the company has been authorised by the Revenue Commissioners to do otherwise, the company deducts income tax which it accounts for under sections 238 and 239, or under sections 238 and 241, as the case may be, or".

10 Substituted by FA 2005 s 49(1)(*d*)(ii) as respects accounting periods ending on or after 3 February 2005; previously "the State.".

11 Subs (5)(*c*) inserted by FA 2005 s 49(1)(*d*)(iii) as respects accounting periods ending on or after 3 February 2005.

Cross-references

Close company surcharges, distributions to be taken into account and meaning of distributable estate and investment income: s 434(1)("relevant charges").
Corporation tax, relief for terminal losses: s 397(3).
Dividends regarded as paid out of profits accumulated before given date, subs (2): Sch 22 para 5(3)(*f*).
Franked investment income, set off of losses: s 157(2)(*a*), (7)(*a*).
Group payments, subs (7): s 410(5)(*a*).
Group relief, relation to other relief: s 421(2).
Industrial and provident societies, computation: s 700(3); delete "yearly" in subs (4)(*a*): s 700(2).
Limited partnerships, specified provisions: s 1013(1).
Loans to participators etc: s 438(1)(*c*).
Partnerships involving companies, transfer of relief: s 426(3)(*b*).
Petroleum trade, interest and charges on income: s 690(3), (6).
Restriction of certain charges on income: s 454(2).
Restriction of relevant charges on income: s 243A(2).
Seed capital investments, meaning of charges on income applied: s 494(5)(*c*).
Self assessment, meaning of "chargeable person": s 950(1).
Tax free securities, exclusion of interest on borrowed money: s 846(2)(*b*).

Case law

Subs (2): Held reference to relief did not include double tax relief: *Commercial Union Assurance Co Plc v Shaw* [1998] STC 48.

Subs (3): Held interest treated as paid on its being debited to the company's account applied equally to yearly interest: *Macarthur v Greycoat Estates Mayfair Ltd* [1996] STC 1.

If a payment of interest has been guaranteed, it would seem that a payment by the guarantor is a payment of interest – *Westminster Bank Executor and Trustee Co (Channel Islands) Ltd v National Bank of Greece* 46 TC 472.

Tax Briefing

TB44 June 2001 pp 39–40 — CT Losses, Charges and Group Relief Offset (following enactment of FA 2001, s 90).

Definitions

branch or agency: ss 4(1), 5(1); company: ss 4(1), 5(1); distribution: ss 4(1), 436, 437; group relief: ss 4(1), 411; interest: s 4(1); lease: s 5(1); month: IA 1937 Sch; person: IA 1937 s 11(*c*); profits: s 4(1); trade: ss 3(1), 4(1), 5(1).

Former enactments

CTA 1976 s 10; FA 1982 s 23(3); FA 1983 s 25(2); FA 1990 s 43; FA 1997 s 29(2), (5)–(6).

Corresponding UK tax provision

Income and Corporation Taxes Act 1988 s 338.

243A Restriction of relevant charges on income

[(1) In this section—

"relevant trading charges on income", in relation to an accounting period of a company, means the charges on income paid by the company in the accounting period wholly and exclusively for the purposes of a trade carried on by the company, other than so much of those charges as are charges on income paid for the purposes of an excepted trade within the meaning of section 21A;

"relevant trading income", in relation to an accounting period of a company, means the trading income of the company for the accounting period (not being income chargeable to tax under Case III of Schedule D) other than so much of that income as is income of an excepted trade within the meaning of section 21A;

(2) Notwithstanding section 243, relevant trading charges on income paid by a company in an accounting period shall not be allowed as deductions against the total profits of the company for the accounting period.

(3) Subject to section 454, where a company pays relevant trading charges on income in an accounting period and, apart from subsection (2), those charges would be allowed as deductions against the total profits of the company for the accounting period, those charges shall be allowed as deductions against—

(*a*) income specified in section 21A(4)(*b*), and

(*b*) relevant trading income,

of the company for the accounting period as reduced by any amount set off against that income under section 396A.][1]

Amendments

1 Section 243A inserted by FA 2001 s 90(1)(*a*) as respects an accounting period ending on or after 6 March 2001.

Note

For the purposes of computing the amount of relevant trading charges on income within the meaning of TCA 1997 s 243A, where an accounting period of a company begins before 6 March 2001 and ends on or after that date, it shall be divided into 2 parts, one beginning on the date on which the accounting period begins and ending on 5 March 2001 and the other beginning on 6 March 2001 and ending on the date on which the accounting period ends, and both parts shall be treated as if they were separate accounting periods of the company — see FA 2001 s 90(4) as substituted by FA 2002 s 55.

Cross-references

Close companies, distributions to be taken into account and meaning of distributable estate and investment income: s 434(3)(*g*).

Corporation tax, relief for terminal losses: s 397(3).

Group relief, relevant losses and charges, meaning of "relevant trading charges on income" and "relevant trading income" applied: s 420A(1); 420(3)(*a*); relief for certain losses on a value basis, meaning of "relevant trading charges on income" applied: s 420B(1); s 420B(2)(*a*).

Manufacturing (10%) relief: s 448(4).

Relief for certain charges on income on a value basis, meaning of "relevant trading charges on income" applied: s 243B(1); s 243B(2)(*a*).

Relief for relevant trading losses, meaning of "relevant trading income" applied: s 396A(1).

Restriction of certain charges on income, meaning of "relevant trading income" applied: s 454(2); s 454(2); subs (2): s 454(3).

Tax Briefing

TB44 June 2001 pp 39–40 — CT Losses, Charges and Group Relief Offset (following enactment of FA 2001 s 90).

Definitions

charges on income: ss 4(1), 243(1); company: s 4(1); profits: s 4(1); trade: s 4(1).

243B Relief for certain charges on income on a value basis

[(1) In this section—

"charges on income paid for the purposes of the sale of goods" has the same meaning as in section 454;

"relevant corporation tax", in relation to an accounting period of a company, means the corporation tax which, apart from this section and sections 239, 241, 396B, 420B, 440 and 441, would be chargeable on the company for the accounting period;

"relevant trading charges on income" has the same meaning as in section 243A.

(2) Where a company pays relevant trading charges on income in an accounting period and the amount so paid exceeds an amount equal to the aggregate of the amounts allowed as deductions against—

(*a*) the income of the company in accordance with section 243A, and

(*b*) the income from the sale of goods in accordance with section 454,

of the company for the accounting period, the company may claim relief under this section for the accounting period in respect of the excess.

(3) Where for any accounting period a company claims relief under this section in respect of the excess, the relevant corporation tax of the company for the accounting period shall be reduced—

(*a*) in so far as the excess consists of charges on income paid for the purpose of the sale of goods (within the meaning of section 454), by an amount equal to 10 per cent of those charges on income paid for the purpose of the sale of goods, and (*b*) in so far as the excess consists of charges on income (in this section referred to as "other relevant trading charges on income") which are not charges on income paid for the purposes of the sale of goods (within the meaning of section 454), by an amount determined by the formula—

$$C \times \frac{R}{100}$$

where—

C is the amount of the other relevant trading charges on income, and

R is the rate per cent of corporation tax which, by virtue of section 21, applies in relation to the accounting period.

(4) (*a*) Where a company makes a claim for relief under this section in respect of any relevant trading charges on income paid in an accounting period, an amount (which shall not exceed the amount of the excess in respect of which a claim under this section may be made), determined in accordance with paragraph (*b*), shall be treated for the purposes of the Tax Acts as relieved under this section.

(*b*) [The][1] amount determined in accordance with this paragraph in relation to an accounting period is an amount equal to the aggregate of the following amounts:

(i) where relief is given under paragraph (*a*) of subsection (3) for the accounting period, an amount equal to 10 times the amount by which the relevant corporation tax for the accounting period is reduced by virtue of that paragraph, and

(ii) where relief is given under paragraph (*b*) of subsection (3) for the accounting period, an amount determined by the formula—

$$T \times \frac{100}{R}$$

where—

T is the amount by which the relevant corporation tax for the accounting period is reduced by virtue of that paragraph, and

R is the rate per cent of corporation tax which, by virtue of section 21, applies in relation to the accounting period.][2]

Amendments

1 Substituted by FA 2003 s 59(1)(*a*) as respects accounting periods ending on or after 6 February 2003; previously "Subject to paragraph (*c*), the".

2 Section 243B inserted by FA 2002 s 54(1)(*a*) as respects an accounting period ending on or after 6 March 2001 (for the purposes of computing the amount of charges on income paid for the purposes of the sale of goods (within the meaning of TCA 1997 s 454), a loss from the sale of goods (within the meaning of TCA 1997 s 455), relevant trading charges on income (within the meaning of TCA 1997 s 243A), and relevant trading losses (within the meaning of TCA 1997 s 396A), in respect of which relief may be claimed by virtue of FA 2002 s 54, where an accounting period of a company begins before 6 March 2001 and ends on or after that date, it shall be divided into 2 parts, one beginning on the date on which the accounting period begins and ending on 5 March 2001 and the other beginning on 6 March 2001 and ending on the date on which the accounting period ends, and both parts shall be treated as if they were separate accounting periods of the company).

Cross-references

Relief for trading losses other than terminal losses: s 396(7).

Revenue information

Tax certificates issued by the Minister for Finance under sections 445(2) and 446(2) of the Taxes Consolidation Act 1997 to IFSC/Shannon companies contain a condition restricting the offset of losses to the trading activities referred to in the certificate. The Department of Finance has confirmed that section 54 of the Finance Act 2002 may be applied to these companies on the same basis as it applies to non-certified companies.

Tax Briefing

TB51 Jan 2003 pp 14–18 — Losses, Charges and Group Relief — relief for certain losses on a value basis [FA 2002 s 54].

Definitions

company: s 4(1); Tax Acts: s 1(2).

CHAPTER 3

Principal Provisions Relating to the Payment of Interest

244 Relief for interest paid on certain home loans

(1) (*a*) In this section—

["**dependent relative**" in relation to an individual, means any of the persons mentioned in paragraph *(a)* or *(b)* of subsection (2) of section 466 in respect of whom the individual is entitled to a tax credit under that section.][1]

"**loan**" means any loan or advance or any other arrangement whatever by virtue of which interest is paid or payable;

"**qualifying interest**", in relation to an individual and a year of assessment, means the amount of interest paid by the individual in the year of assessment in respect of a qualifying loan;

"**qualifying loan**", in relation to an individual, means a loan or loans which, without having been used for any other purpose, is or are used by the individual solely for the purpose of defraying money employed in the purchase, repair, development or improvement of a qualifying residence or in paying off another loan or loans used for such purpose;

"**qualifying residence**", in relation to an individual, means a residential premises situated in the State, Northern Ireland or Great Britain, which is used as the sole or main residence of—

(i) the individual,

(ii) a former or separated spouse of the individual, or

(iii) a person who in relation to the individual is a dependent relative, and which is, where the residential premises is provided by the individual, provided rent-free and without any other consideration;

["**relievable interest**", in relation to an individual and a year of assessment, means—

(i) in the case of—

(I) an individual assessed to tax for the year of assessment in accordance with section 1017, or

(II) a widowed individual,

the amount of qualifying interest paid by the individual in the year of assessment or, if less, [€5,080][2],

(ii) in the case of any other individual, the amount of qualifying interest paid by the individual in the year of assessment or, if less, [€2,540][3],

but, notwithstanding the preceding provisions of this definition and subject to paragraph (*c*), as respects the first [7 years][4] of assessment for which there is an entitlement to relief under this section in respect of a qualifying loan, "relievable interest", in relation to an individual and a year of assessment, shall mean—

(iii) in the case of—

(I) an individual assessed to tax for the year of assessment in accordance with section 1017, or

(II) a widowed individual,

the amount of qualifying interest paid by the individual in the year of assessment or, if less, [€8,000][5],

(iv) in the case of any other individual, the amount of qualifying interest paid by the individual in the year of assessment or, if less, [€4,000][6];][7]

"residential premises" means—

(i) a building or part of a building used, or suitable for use, as a dwelling, and

(ii) land which the occupier of a building or part of a building used as a dwelling has for the occupier's own occupation and enjoyment with that building or that part of a building as its garden or grounds of an ornamental nature;

"separated" means separated under an order of a court of competent jurisdiction or by deed of separation or in such circumstances that the separation is likely to be permanent.

(*b*) For the purposes of this section, in the case of an individual assessed to tax for a year of assessment in accordance with section 1017, any payment of qualifying interest made by the individual's spouse, in respect of which the individual's spouse would have been entitled to relief under this section if that spouse were assessed to tax for the year of assessment in accordance with section 1016 (apart from subsection (2) of that section) shall be deemed to have been made by the individual.

[(*c*) The number of years of assessment for which the amount of relievable interest is to be determined by reference to subparagraph (iii) or (iv) of the definition of "relievable interest" shall be reduced by one year of assessment for each year of assessment in which an individual was entitled to relief for a year of assessment before the year 1997–1998 under section 76(1) or 496 of, or paragraph 1(2) of Part III of Schedule 6 to, the Income Tax Act, 1967.][8]

(2) (*a*) In this subsection, **"appropriate percentage"**, in relation to a year of assessment, means a percentage equal to the standard rate of tax for that year.

(*b*) Where an individual for a year of assessment proves that in the year of assessment such individual paid an amount of qualifying interest, then, the income tax to be charged, other than in accordance with section 16(2), on such individual for that year of assessment shall be reduced by an amount which is the lesser of—

(i) the amount equal to the appropriate percentage of the relievable interest, and

(ii) the amount which reduces that income tax to nil.

(*c*) Except for the purposes of sections 187 and 188, no account shall be taken of relievable interest in calculating the total income of the individual by whom the relievable interest is paid.

(3) [(*a*) Where the amount of relievable interest is determined by reference to subparagraph (iii) or (iv) of the definition of "relievable interest", then, notwithstanding any other provision of the Tax Acts, in the case of an individual who has elected or could be deemed to have duly elected to be assessed to tax for the year of assessment in accordance with section 1017, where either—

(i) the individual, or

(ii) the individual's spouse,

was previously entitled to relief under this section or under section 76(1) or 496 of, or paragraph 1(2) of Part III of Schedule 6 to, the Income Tax Act, 1967, and the other person was not so entitled—

(I) the relief to be given under this section, other than that part of the relief (in this subsection referred to as "the additional relief") which is represented by the difference between the relievable interest and the amount which would have been the amount of the relievable interest if this had been determined by reference to subparagraph (i) or (ii) of that definition, shall be treated as given in equal proportions to the individual and that individual's spouse for that year of assessment, and

(II) the additional relief shall be reduced by 50 per cent and the additional relief, as so reduced, shall be given only to the person who was not previously entitled to relief under this section or under section 76(1) or 496 of, or paragraph 1(2) of Part III of Schedule 6 to, the Income Tax Act, 1967.][9]

(*b*) Paragraph (*a*) shall apply notwithstanding that—

(i) section 1023 may have applied for the year of assessment, and

(ii) the payments in respect of which relief is given may not have been made in equal proportions.

(4) (*a*) Notwithstanding anything in this section, a loan shall not be a qualifying loan, in relation to an individual, if it is used for the purpose of defraying money applied in—

(i) the purchase of a residential premises or any interest in such premises from an individual who is the spouse of the purchaser,

(ii) the purchase of a residential premises or any interest in such premises if, at any time after the 25th day of March, 1982, that premises or interest was disposed of by the purchaser or by his or her spouse or if any interest which is reversionary to the interest purchased was so disposed of after that date, or

(iii) the purchase, repair, development or improvement of a residential premises, and the person who, directly or indirectly, received the money is connected with the individual and it appears that the purchase price of the premises substantially exceeds the value of what is acquired or, as the case may be, the cost of the repair, development or improvement substantially exceeds the value of the work done.

(*b*) Subparagraphs (i) and (ii) of paragraph (*a*) shall not apply in the case of a husband and wife who are separated.

(5) Where an individual acquires a new sole or main residence but does not dispose of the previous sole or main residence owned by the individual and it is shown to the satisfaction of the inspector that it was the individual's intention, at the time of the acquisition of the new sole or main residence, to dispose of the previous sole or main residence and that the individual has taken and continues to take all reasonable steps necessary to dispose of it, the previous sole or main residence shall be treated as a qualifying residence, in relation to the individual, for the period of 12 months commencing on the date of the acquisition of the new sole or main residence.

(6) (*a*) In this subsection, **"personal representative"** has the same meaning as in section 799.

(*b*) Where any interest paid on a loan used for a purpose mentioned in the definition of **"qualifying loan"** by persons as the personal representatives of a deceased person or as trustees of a settlement made by the will of a deceased person would, on the assumptions stated in paragraph (*c*), be eligible for relief under this section and, in a case where the condition stated in that paragraph applies, that condition is satisfied, that interest shall be so eligible notwithstanding the preceding provisions of this section.

(*c*) For the purposes of paragraph (*b*), it shall be assumed that the deceased person would have survived and been the borrower and if, at the time of the person's death, the residential premises was used as that person's sole or main residence, it shall be further assumed that the person would have continued so to use it and the following condition shall then apply, namely, that the residential premises was, at the time the interest was paid, used as the sole or main residence of the deceased's widow or widower or of any dependent relative of the deceased.

Amendments

1 Definition of "dependant relative" substituted by FA 2002 s 138 and Sch 6 paras 3(*e*) and 6(*c*)(ii) with effect from 6 April 2001.

2 Substituted by FA 2001 s 240(1), (2)(*a*) and Sch 5 Pt 1 for 2002 and later tax years; previously "£4,000" (short tax "year" 2001: £2,960 (FA 2001 s 77(2) and Sch 2 paras 13 and 61(*a*))).

3 Substituted by FA 2001 s 240(1), (2)(*a*) and Sch 5 Pt 1 for 2002 and later tax years; previously "£2,000" (short tax "year" 2001: £1,480 (FA 2001 s 77(2) and Sch 2 paras 13 and 61(*a*))).

4 Substituted by FA 2003 s 9(1)(*a*) with effect from 1 January 2003 but shall not apply to an individual for whom the fifth year of assessment for which he or she had an entitlement to relief under TCA 1997 s 244 in respect of a qualifying loan (within the meaning of that section) was prior to the year of assessment 2002; previously "5 years".

5 Substituted by FA 2003 s 9(1)(*b*) with effect from 1 January 2003 but shall not apply to an individual for whom the fifth year of assessment for which he or she had an entitlement to relief under TCA 1997 s 244 in respect of a qualifying loan (within the meaning of that section) was prior to the year of assessment 2002; previously "€6,350".

6 Substituted by FA 2003 s 9(1)(*c*) with effect from 1 January 2003 but shall not apply to an individual for whom the fifth year of assessment for which he or she had an entitlement to relief under TCA 1997 s 244 in respect of a qualifying loan (within the meaning of that section) was prior to the year of assessment 2002; previously "€3,175".

7 Definition of "relievable interest" substituted by FA 2000 s 17(*a*)(ii) for 2000–2001 and later tax years.

8 Subs (1)(*c*) substituted by FA 2000 s 17(*a*)(iii) for 2000–2001 and later tax years.

9 Subs (3)(*a*) substituted by FA 2000 s 17(*b*) for 2000–2001 and later tax years.

Cross-references

Age exemption and associated marginal relief: s 188(1)("income tax payable").
Bridging loans: s 245(1).
Deductions allowed in ascertaining taxable income and provisions relating to reductions in tax: s 458(1), (2); s 459(1), (2).
Employer preferential loan: s 122(4).
Method of apportioning reliefs and charging tax in cases of separate assessment: s 1024(2)(*a*)(i).
Mortgage Interest (Relief at Source) Regulations 2001, SI No 558 of 2001, Regulation 2(1) (interpretation).
Rate of tax at which repayments are to be made: s 460.
Rent-a-room relief: s 216A(8).
Tax relief at source for certain interest, meanings of "appropriate percentage", "qualifying interest", "qualifying loan", "qualifying residence" and "relievable interest" applied: s 244A(1)(*a*); s 244A(1)(*b*), (2)(*a*).

Revenue precedents

Issue: What is regarded as "qualifying loan" where borrower of home improvement loan has option of insurance policy to cover himself against accident?
Decision: Interest charged on insurance premium would not qualify for relief but element of loan relating solely to home improvement regarded as "qualifying loan".

Tax Briefing

TB34 Dec 1998 p 9 — Relief for Home Loan Interest — Rules & Guidelines.

Former enactments

FA 1997 s 145.

Corresponding UK tax provision

Income and Corporation Taxes Act 1988 ss 356A–356D.

244A Application of section 244 (relief for interest paid on certain home loans) of Principal Act

[(1) (*a*) In this section—

(i) **"qualifying dwelling"**, in relation to an individual, means a qualifying residence situated in the State;

"qualifying lender" has the meaning assigned to it by subsection (3);

"qualifying mortgage interest", in relation to an individual and a year of assessment, means the qualifying interest paid by the individual in the year of assessment in respect of a qualifying mortgage loan;

"qualifying mortgage loan", in relation to an individual, means a qualifying loan or loans secured by the mortgage of freehold or leasehold estate or interest in a qualifying dwelling, and

(ii) **"appropriate percentage"**, **"qualifying interest"**, **"qualifying loan"**, **"qualifying residence"** and **"relievable interest"** have the same meanings, respectively, as they have in section 244.

(*b*) This section provides for a scheme whereby relief due under section 244 shall, in certain circumstances, be given by way of deduction at source (**"the tax relief at source scheme"**) under subsection (2)(*a*) and in no other manner.

(2) (*a*) Where an individual makes a payment of qualifying mortgage interest to a qualifying lender in respect of which relief is due under section 244, the individual shall be entitled in accordance with regulations to deduct and retain out of it an amount equal to the appropriate percentage, for the year of assessment in which the payment is due, of the relievable interest.

(*b*) A qualifying lender to which a payment referred to in paragraph (*a*) is made—

(i) shall accept in accordance with regulations the amount paid after deduction in discharge of the individual's liability to the same extent as if the deduction had not been made, and

(ii) may, on making a claim in accordance with regulations, recover from the Revenue Commissioners an amount equal to the amount deducted.

(3) The following bodies shall be qualifying lenders—

(*a*) a bank holding a licence under section 9 of the Central Bank Act, 1971;

(*b*) a building society incorporated or deemed to be incorporated under the Building Societies Act, 1989;

(*c*) a trustee savings bank within the meaning of the Trustee Savings Banks Act, 1989;

(*d*) ACC Bank plc;

(*e*) a local authority;

(*f*) a body which—

(i) (I) holds a licence or similar authorisation, corresponding to a licence referred to in paragraph (*a*), or

(II) has been incorporated in a manner corresponding to that referred to in paragraph (*b*),

under the law of any other Member State of the European Communities,

and

(ii) provides qualifying mortgage loans;

and

(*g*) a body which applies to the Revenue Commissioners for registration as a qualifying lender and in respect of which the Revenue Commissioners, having regard to the activities and objects of the body, are satisfied is entitled to be so registered.

(4) (*a*) The Revenue Commissioners shall maintain, and publish in such manner as they consider appropriate, a register for the purposes of subsection (3).

(*b*) If the Revenue Commissioners are satisfied that an applicant for registration is entitled to be registered, they shall register the applicant with effect from such date as may be specified by them.

(*c*) If it appears to the Revenue Commissioners at any time that a body which is registered under this subsection would not be entitled to be registered if it applied for registration at that time, the Revenue Commissioners may, by written notice given to the body, cancel its registration with effect from such date as may be specified by them in the notice.

(*d*) Any body which is aggrieved by the failure of the Revenue Commissioners to register it or by the cancellation of its registration, may, by notice given to the

Revenue Commissioners before the end of the period of 30 days beginning with the date on which the body is notified of the Revenue Commissioners' decision, require the matter to be determined by the Appeal Commissioners and the Appeal Commissioners shall hear and determine the matter in like manner as an appeal.

(5) (*a*) The Revenue Commissioners shall make regulations providing generally as to administration of this section and those regulations may, in particular and without prejudice to the generality of the foregoing, include provision—

(i) that a claim under subsection (2)(*b*)(ii) shall be—

(I) made in such form and manner,
(II) made at such time, and
(III) accompanied by such documents,

as provided for in the regulations,

(ii) that, in circumstances specified in regulations, a claim may be made under subsection (2)(*b*)(ii) where a payment is due but not made;

(iii) for the making by qualifying lenders, in such form and manner as may be prescribed, of monthly returns containing particulars in relation to—

(I) each individual making payments of qualifying mortgage interest,
(II) the amount of qualifying mortgage interest paid or due by the individual to date in the year of assessment,
(III) the amount deducted by the individual, or the amount he or she would have been entitled to deduct, under subsection (2)(*a*),
(IV) the estimated qualifying mortgage interest to be paid by the individual in the year of assessment,
(V) the total amount of qualifying mortgage loans of the qualifying lender outstanding at the date of the return,
(VI) the total amount claimed by the qualifying lender under subsection (2)(*b*)(ii) for the month to which the return relates,
(VII) qualifying mortgage loans repaid in full in that month, and
(VIII) such other matters as may be specified;

(iv) for the transmission by the Revenue Commissioners to qualifying lenders, on a monthly basis, of such details as may be specified in the regulations in relation to—

(I) qualifying mortgage loans, and
(II) individuals with qualifying mortgage loans,

which are necessary for the operation of this section;

(v) in relation to the obligations and entitlements of individuals with qualifying mortgage loans under the tax relief at source scheme;

(vi) in relation to the obligations and entitlements of qualifying lenders under the tax relief at source scheme;

(vii) for deeming of certain qualifying mortgage loans, in such circumstances as may be specified in the regulations, as being no longer entitled to relief under this section;

(viii) for the granting of appropriate relief in any case where inadequate or excessive relief has been granted under this section; and

(ix) for the implementation of this section where a qualifying lender disposes of all or part of its qualifying mortgage loans.

(*b*) Every regulation made under this section shall be laid before Dáil Éireann as soon as may be after it is made and, if a resolution annulling the regulation is passed by Dáil Éireann within the next 21 days on which Dáil Éireann has sat after the regulation is laid before it, the regulation shall be annulled accordingly, but without prejudice to the validity of anything previously done thereunder.

(6) (*a*) Where any amount is paid to a qualifying lender by the Revenue Commissioners as an amount recoverable by virtue of subsection (2)(*b*)(ii) but is an amount to which that qualifying lender is not entitled, that amount shall be repaid by the qualifying lender.

(*b*) There shall be made such assessments, adjustments or set-offs as may be required for securing repayment of the amount referred to in paragraph (*a*) and the provisions of this Act relating to the assessment, collection and recovery of income tax shall, in so far as they are applicable and with necessary modification, apply in relation to the recovery of such amount.][1]

Amendments

1 Section 244A inserted by FA 2001 s 23(1) for 2002 and later tax years.

Cross-references

Penalties: Sch 29, column 1.

Power of inspection, claims by qualifying lenders, meaning of "qualifying lender" and "qualifying mortgage loan" applied: s 904F(1); subs (2)(*b*)(ii): s 904F(2).

Provision of certain information, transitional, meaning of "qualifying lender" applied: FA 2001 s 24(1); FA 2001 s 24(3).

Regulations

Mortgage Interest (Relief at Source) Regulations 2001, SI No 558 of 2001.

Revenue information

Information Leaflet CG 13 — Mortgage Interest — Tax Relief at Source.

Definitions

Appeal Commissioners, ss 2(1), 850; Dáil Éireann: IA 1937 Sch; local authority: s 2(1); month: IA 1937 Sch; writing: IA 1937 Sch; year of assessment: s 2(1).

245 Relief for certain bridging loans

(1) Where a person—

(*a*) disposes of such person's only or main residence and acquires another residence for use as such person's only or main residence,

(*b*) obtains a loan, the proceeds of which are used to defray in whole or in part the cost of the acquisition or the disposal or both, and

(*c*) pays interest on the loan (and on any subsequent loan the proceeds of which are used to repay in whole or in part the first-mentioned loan or any such subsequent loan or to pay interest on any such loan) in respect of the period of 12 months from the date of the making of the first-mentioned loan, such person shall be entitled on proof of those facts to a reduction in tax under section 244 on the amount of that interest as if no other interest had been paid by such person in respect of the period of 12 months from the date of the making of the first-mentioned loan.

(2) Subsection (1) shall not apply to a loan the proceeds of which are applied for some other purpose before being applied for the purpose specified in that subsection.

Cross-references

Limited partnerships, specified provisions: s 1013(1).

Tax Briefing

TB34 Dec 1998 p 15 — Bridging Finance Guidelines.

Definitions

month: IA 1937 Sch; person: IA 1937 s 11(*c*).

Former enactments

FA 1974 s 32; FA 1997 s 146(1) and Sch 9 Pt I para 8(1).

246 Interest payments by companies and to non-residents

(1) In this section—

[**"bank"** includes building society within the meaning of section 256(1);][1]

"company" means any body corporate;

[**"investment undertaking"** means—

(*a*) a unit trust mentioned in section 731(5)(*a*),

(*b*) a special investment scheme within the meaning given to it in section 737, ...[2]

(*c*) an investment undertaking within the meaning given to it in [section 739B, or][3]][4]

[(*d*) a common contractual fund within the meaning given to it in section 739I (inserted by the Finance Act 2005);][5]

[**"relevant person"** means—

(*a*) a company, or

(*b*) an investment undertaking;"][4]

"relevant security" means a security issued by a company [in the course of carrying on relevant trading operations within the meaning of section 445 or 446],[6] on terms which oblige the company to redeem the security within a period of 15 years after the date on which the security was [issued;][7]

[**"relevant territory"** means—

(*a*) a Member State of the European Communities other than the State, or

(*b*) not being such a Member State, a territory with the government of which arrangements having the force of law by virtue of [section 826(1)(*a*)][8] have been [made;][9]][10]

[**"tax"**, in relation to a relevant territory, means any tax imposed in such territory which corresponds to income tax or corporation tax in the State.][11]

(2) Where any yearly interest charged with tax under Schedule D is paid—

(*a*) by a company, otherwise than when paid in a fiduciary or representative capacity, to a person whose usual place of abode is in the State, or

(*b*) by any person to another person whose usual place of abode is outside the State,

the person by or through whom the payment is made shall on making the payment deduct out of the payment a sum representing the amount of the tax on the payment at the standard rate in force at the time of the payment, and subsections (1) and (3) to (5) of section 238 shall apply to such payments as they apply to payments specified in subsection (2) of that section.

(3) Subsection (2) shall not apply to—

(*a*) interest paid in the State on an advance from a bank carrying on a bona fide banking business in the State,

(*b*) interest paid by such a bank in the ordinary course of such business,

[(*bb*) interest paid in the State by a company to another company, being a company to which paragraph (*a*) of subsection (5) applies, for so long as that other company is a company to which that paragraph applies,][12]

(*c*) interest paid to a person whose usual place of abode is outside the State by—

(i) a company in the course of carrying on relevant trading operations within the meaning of section 445 or 446, or

(ii) a specified collective investment undertaking within the meaning of section 734,

[(*cc*) interest paid in the State to a qualifying company (within the meaning of section 110),

(*ccc*) interest paid by a qualifying company (within the meaning of section 110) to a person who, by virtue of the law of a relevant territory, is resident for the purposes of tax in the relevant territory, except, in a case where the person is a company, where such interest is paid to the company in connection with a trade or business which is carried on in the State by the company through a branch or agency,][13]

(*d*) interest paid by a company authorised by the Revenue Commissioners to pay interest without deduction of income tax,

(*e*) interest on any securities in respect of which the Minister for Finance has given a direction under section 36,

(*f*) interest paid without deduction of tax by virtue of [section 700,][14]

(*g*) interest which under section 437 is a [distribution, or][15]

[(*h*) interest, other than interest referred to in paragraphs (*a*) to (*g*), paid by a relevant person in the ordinary course of a trade or business carried on by that person to a company [which, by virtue of the law of a relevant territory, is resident for the purposes of tax in the relevant territory,][16] except where such interest is paid to that company in connection with a trade or business which is carried on in the State by that company through a branch or agency.][17]

(4) In relation to interest paid in respect of a relevant security subsection (3)(*c*) shall apply—

[(*a*) as if in section 445 the following subsection were substituted for subsection (2) of that section:

"(2) Subject to subsections (7) and (8), the Minister may give a certificate certifying that such trading operations of a qualified company as are specified in the certificate are, with effect from a date specified in the certificate, relevant trading operations for the purposes of this section.",

and

(*b*) as if in section 446 the following subsection were substituted for subsection (2) of that section:

"(2) Subject to subsections (7) and (9), the Minister may give a certificate certifying that such trading operations of a company as are specified in the certificate are, with effect from a date specified in the certificate, relevant trading operations for the purposes of this section.".][18]

[(5) (*a*) This paragraph shall apply to a company—

(i) which advances money in the ordinary course of a trade which includes the lending of money,

(ii) in whose hands any interest payable in respect of money so advanced is taken into account in computing the trading income of the company, and

(iii) which—

(I) has notified in writing the appropriate inspector to whom the company makes the return referred to in section 951 that it meets the requirements of subparagraphs (i) and (ii), and

(II) (A) has notified the first company referred to in subsection (3)(*bb*) in writing that it is a company which meets those requirements and that it has made the notification referred to in subparagraph (iii)(I), and

(B) has provided the first company referred to in subsection (3)(*bb*) with its tax reference number (within the meaning of section 885).

(*b*) A company which is no longer a company to which paragraph *(a)* applies shall, upon that paragraph ceasing to apply to it, immediately notify in writing the inspector referred to in subparagraph (iii)(I) of paragraph *(a)* and the company referred to in subparagraph (iii)(II) accordingly.][19]

Amendments

1 Substituted by FA 2001 s 37(1)(*b*)(i) in respect of interest paid on or after 30 March 2001.

2 Deleted by FA 2005 s 44(*b*)(i) with effect from 1 January 2005; previously "or".

3 Substituted by FA 2005 s 44(*b*)(ii) with effect from 1 January 2005; previously "section 739B;".

4 Definition of "investment undertaking" inserted and definition of "relevant person" substituted by FA 2001 s 37(1)(*b*)(ii) in respect of interest paid on or after 30 March 2001.

5 Definition of "investment undertaking" para (*d*) inserted by FA 2005 s 44(*b*)(iii) with effect from 1 January 2005.

6 Substituted by FA 1999 s 39(*a*)(iii)(I) with effect from 6 April 1999; previously "on or before the 31st day of December, 2005".

7 Substituted by FA 1999 s 39(*a*)(iii)(II) with effect from 6 April 1999; previously "issued.".

8 Substituted by FA 2004 s 89 and Sch 3 para 1(*i*) with effect from 25 March 2004; previously "section 826".
9 Substituted by FA 2000 s 66(1)(*a*) with effect from 10 February 2000; previously "made.".
10 Definition of "relevant territory" inserted by FA 1999 s 39(*a*)(iv) with effect from 6 April 1999.
11 Definition of "tax" inserted by FA 2000 s 66(1)(*a*) with effect from 10 February 2000.
12 Subs (3)(*bb*) inserted by FA 2002 s 19(1)(*a*) as respects interest paid on or after 25 March 2002.
13 Subs (3)(*cc*) and (*ccc*) inserted by FA 2003 s 48(2) as respects interest paid on or after 6 February 2003.
14 Substituted by FA 1999 s 39(*b*)(i) with effect from 6 April 1999; previously "section 700, or".
15 Substituted by FA 1999 s 39(*b*)(ii) with effect from 6 April 1999; previously "distribution.".
16 Substituted by FA 2000 s 66(1)(*b*) with effect from 10 February 2000; previously "resident in a relevant territory".
17 Subs (3)(*h*) inserted by FA 1999 s 39(*b*)(iii) with effect from 6 April 1999.
18 Subs (4)(*a*)–(*b*) substituted by FA 1999 s 39(*c*) with effect from 6 April 1999.
19 Subs (5) inserted by FA 2002 s 19(1)(*b*) as respects interest paid on or after 25 March 2002.

Cross-references

Allowance of charges on income, subs (2): s 243(5)(*c*).
Amount of s 238 assessment to be allowed as a loss, subs (2): s 390(3).
Certain interest not to be chargeable, meaning of "relevant person" applied: s 198(1)(*c*)(ii), meaning of "relevant security" applied: s 198(2).
Corporation tax, charges on income: s 243(5)(*a*).
Group payments: s 410(4).
Implementation of Council Directive 2003/49/EC of 3 June 2003 on a common system of taxation applicable to interest and royalty payments made between associated companies of different Member States, exemptions from tax and withholding tax: s 267I(1).
Interest in respect of wholesale debt instruments, subs (2): s 246A(3)(*a*)(A), (b)(ii)(A).
Limited partnerships, specified provisions: s 1013(1).
Payments within deposit interest retention tax not within subs (1): s 257(3).
Quoted Eurobonds, subs (2) does not apply: s 64(2).
Returns of interest paid to non-residents, meaning of "relevant person" applied: s 891A(1); subs (2), (3)(*h*): s 891A(1)(relevant interest).

Case law

Yearly interest is interest payable in respect of a loan which is likely to be outstanding for longer than one year: *Goslings & Sharpe v Blake* (1889) 2 TC 450; *Cairns v MacDiarmuid* [1983] STC 178; *Minsham Properties Ltd v Price* [1990] STC 718.

Interest which is merely capitalised is not regarded as paid unless and until the amount due is actually discharged – *IRC v Oswald* 26 TC 435.

A debtor company which issued bonds in discharge of its liability to pay interest was held not to have paid the interest, this would only be achieved when the bonds were redeemed by the issuer – *Cross v London and Provincial Trust Ltd* 21 TC 705.

Revenue precedents

Issue: Whether interest payable on borrowings between companies carrying on relevant trading operations within the meaning of TCA 1997 s 445 or 446 may be paid without deduction of tax.

Decision: Yes, provided that the following conditions are satisfied: a) the loan is in a foreign currency; b) the making of the loan is covered by the terms of the certificate of the lending company ie it's licensed trading operations include lending to other IFSC/Shannon companies (in this connection, the lender should provide written confirmation that this is the case and that it will remain so throughout the period of the loan); c) the loan is applied by the borrower for the purpose of it's own licensed trading operations; d) authorisations are granted on a case by case basis. Applications for exemption should be made in letter form to the Revenue Commissioners, Direct Taxes: Incentives Branch, Dublin Castle, Dublin 2.

Issue: Whether obligation to deduct and account for tax applies where payment is made from taxed profits.

Decision: Yes; s 246 treats a payment of interest as one to which s 238 TCA applies ie the payment is treated as made out of profits or gains not brought into charge to tax.

Issue: Where a local authority is late in making a payment of an amount under a compulsory purchase order and is required to pay interest on such amount because it is late, is the interest "yearly interest" within the meaning of TCA 1997 s 246?

Decision: Yes.

Tax Briefing

TB31 Apr 1998 p 13 Interest paid under the Prompt Payment of Accounts Act, 1997 is yearly interest and this section may apply thereto (tax need not be deducted from penalty interest under £100).

TB52 May 2003 p 25 — Interest paid under the Late Payment in Commercial Transactions Regulations, SI No 388 of 2002 is not yearly interest and, accordingly, TCA 1997 s 246 does not apply where penalty interest is paid.
TB55 April 2004 p 14 — Interest Payments — Exemption from Withholding Tax.

Definitions

company: s 4(1); person: IA 1937 s 11(*c*); inspector: s 2(1); standard rate: ss 3(1), 15; trade: ss 3(1), (4)(1); writing: IA 1937 Sch.

Former enactments

FA 1974 s 31; CTA 1976 s 140(1) and Sch 2 Pt I para 42; FA 1988 s 38; FA 1996 s 33 and s 132(2) and Sch 5 Pt II; FA 1997 s 36.

Corresponding UK tax provision

Income and Corporation Taxes Act 1988 s 246.

246A Interest in respect of wholesale debt instruments

[(1) In this section—

"approved denomination", in relation to a wholesale debt instrument, means a denomination of not less than—

(*a*) in the case of an instrument denominated in euro, €500,000;

(*b*) in the case of an instrument denominated in United States Dollars, US$500,000; or

(*c*) in the case of an instrument denominated in a currency other than euro or United States Dollars, the equivalent in that other currency of €500,000;

and, for the purposes of this definition, the equivalent of an amount of euro in another currency shall be determined by reference to the rate of exchange—

(i) in the case of instruments issued under a programme, at the time the programme under which the instrument is to be issued is first publicised; or

(ii) in the case of all other instruments, on the date of issue of the instrument;

"Revenue officer" means an officer of the Revenue Commissioners;

"certificate of deposit" means an instrument, either in physical or electronic form, relating to money in any currency which has been deposited with the issuer or some other person, being an instrument—

(*a*) issued by a financial institution,

(*b*) which recognises an obligation to pay a stated amount to bearer or to order, with or without interest, and

(*c*) (i) in the case of instruments held in physical form, by the delivery of which, with or without endorsement, the right to receive the stated amount is transferable, or

(ii) in the case of instruments held in electronic form, in respect of which the right to receive the stated amount is transferable;

"commercial paper" means a debt instrument, either in physical or electronic form, relating to money in any currency, which—

(*a*) is issued by—

(i) a financial institution, or

(ii) a company that is not a financial institution,

(*b*) recognises an obligation to pay a stated amount,

(*c*) carries a right to interest or is issued at a discount or at a premium, and

(*d*) matures within 2 years;

"financial institution" has the same meaning as it has in section 906A;

"relevant person" means the person by or through whom a payment in respect of a wholesale debt instrument is made;

"tax reference number" has the meaning assigned to it by section 885;

"wholesale debt instrument" means a certificate of deposit or commercial paper, as appropriate.

(2) (*a*) In this section and in any other provision of the Tax Acts or the Capital Gains Tax Acts which applies this subsection, **"recognised clearing system"** means the following clearing systems—

(i) Bank One NA, Depository and Clearing Centre,

(ii) Central Moneymarkets Office,

(iii) Clearstream Banking SA,

(iv) Clearstream Banking AG,

(v) CREST,

(vi) Depository Trust Company of New York,

(vii) Euroclear,

(viii) Monte Titoli SPA,

(ix) Netherlands Centraal Instituut voor Giraal Effectenverkeer BV,

(x) National Securities Clearing System,

(xi) Sicovam SA,

(xii) SIS Sega Intersettle AG, and

(xiii) any other system for clearing securities which is for the time being designated, for the purposes of this section or any other provision of the Tax Acts or the Capital Gains Tax Acts which applies this subsection, by order of the Revenue Commissioners under paragraph (*b*) as a recognised clearing system.

(*b*) For the purposes of this section and sections 64 and 739B, the Revenue Commissioners may, designate by order one or more than one system for clearing securities as a "recognised clearing system".

(*c*) An order of the Revenue Commissioners under paragraph (*b*) may—

(i) contain such transitional and other supplemental provisions as appear to the Revenue Commissioners to be necessary or expedient, and

(ii) be varied or revoked by a subsequent order.

(3) As respects any payment made in respect of a wholesale debt instrument—

(*a*) if either—

(i) the person by whom the payment is made, or

(ii) the person through whom the payment is made,

is not resident in the State and the payment is not made by or through a branch or agency through which a company not resident in the State carries on a trade or business in the State, and

(I) the wholesale debt instrument is held in a recognised clearing system, and

(II) the wholesale debt instrument is of an approved denomination,

then—

(A) section 246(2) shall not apply to that payment, and

(B) the wholesale debt instrument shall not be treated as a relevant deposit (within the meaning of section 256) for the purposes of Chapter 4 of this Part,

or

(*b*) (i) if either—

(I) the person by whom the payment is made, or

(II) the person through whom the payment is made,

is resident in the State or the payment is made either by or through a branch or agency through which a company not resident in the State carries on a trade or business in the State,

and

(ii) (I) the wholesale debt instrument is held in a recognised clearing system and is of an approved denomination, or

(II) the person who is beneficially entitled to the interest is a resident of the State and has provided the person's tax reference number to the relevant person, or

(III) the person who is the beneficial owner of the wholesale debt instrument and who is beneficially entitled to the interest is not resident in the State and has made a declaration of the kind described in subsection (5),

then, subject to subsection (4) or (5)—

(A) section 246(2) shall not apply to that payment, and

(B) the wholesale debt instrument shall not be treated as a relevant deposit (within the meaning of section 256) for the purposes of Chapter 4 of this Part.

(4) A relevant person who makes a payment in respect of a wholesale debt instrument shall as respects a case which is within paragraph (*b*)(ii)(I) or (*b*)(ii)(II), as the case may be, of subsection (3) and which is not within paragraph (*a*) of that subsection—

(*a*) (i) be regarded as a person to whom section 891(1) applies as respects that case, if that provision would not otherwise apply to that person,

(ii) be regarded as a "relevant person" (within the meaning of section 894) for the purposes of that section as respects that case, if that person would not otherwise be a "relevant person" (within that meaning), and

(iii) in addition to the matters to be included in a return to be made under section 891 for a chargeable period (within the meaning of section 321(2)), include on that return, in respect of that case, the tax reference number of the person to whom the payment was made,

and

(*b*) on being so required by notice given in writing by a Revenue officer, in relation to any person named by the officer in the notice, deliver an account in writing of the amount of any payment made in respect of a wholesale debt instrument to that person together with details of the person's name and address and tax reference number if such details have not been included in a return made by that person under section 891.

(5) The declaration referred to in subsection (3)(*b*)(ii)(III) is a declaration in writing to a relevant person which—

(*a*) is made by a person (in this section referred to as **"the declarer"**) to whom any payment in respect of which the declaration is made is payable by the relevant person, and is signed by the declarer,

(*b*) is made in such form as may be prescribed or authorised by the Revenue Commissioners,

(*c*) declares that at the time the declaration is made the person who is beneficially entitled to the interest is not resident in the State,

(*d*) contains as respect the person mentioned in paragraph (*c*)—

(i) the name of the person,

(ii) the address of that person's principal place of residence, and

(iii) the name of the country in which that person is resident at the time that the declaration is made,

(*e*) contains an undertaking by the declarer that, if the person referred to in paragraph (*c*) becomes resident in the State, the declarer shall notify the relevant person accordingly, and

(*f*) contains such other information as the Revenue Commissioners may reasonably require for the purposes of this section.

(6) Where a relevant person is satisfied that any payment made by that person in respect of a wholesale debt instrument has been made to a person to whom paragraph (*b*)(ii)(II) or (*b*)(ii)(III), as the case may be, of subsection (3) applies, the relevant person shall be entitled to continue to treat that person as a person to whom that paragraph applies until such time as the relevant person is in possession, or aware, of information which can reasonably be taken to indicate that that paragraph no longer applies to that person.

(7)(*a*) A relevant person shall—

(i) keep and retain for the longer of the following—

(I) a period of 6 years after the declaration is made, and

(II) a period which ends not earlier than 3 years after the latest date on which any payment in respect of which the declaration was made is paid,

and

(ii) on being required by notice given in writing by a Revenue officer, make available to that officer within the time specified in the notice,

all declarations of the kind mentioned in this section that have been made in respect of any payment made by the relevant person.

(*b*) A Revenue officer may examine or take extracts from or copies of any declarations made available under paragraph (*a*).][1]

Amendments

1 Section 246A inserted by FA 2003 s 49(1) as respects a wholesale debt instrument (within the meaning of TCA 1997 s 246A) issued on or after such day as the Minister for Finance may appoint by order. By virtue of Finance Act 2003 (Section 49(1)) (Date of Application) Order 2003, SI No 245 of 2003, the 13th of June 2003 is appointed as the day on which FA 2003 s 49(1) is to apply in relation to wholesale debt instruments issued on or after that day.

Cross-references

Interest on quoted eurobonds, subs (2) definition of "recognised clearing system" applied: s 64(1A).

Investment undertaking, interpretation and application, subs (2) definition of "recognised clearing system" applied: s 739B(1A).

Power of inspection, returns and collection of appropriate tax (DIRT), subs (3)(*b*)(ii): s 904A(3)(*b*)(ii)

Definitions

Capital Gains Tax Acts: s 1(2); company: s 4(1); resident: s 2(1); Tax Acts: s 1(2); trade: ss 3(1), 4(1); writing: IA 1937 Sch.

247 Relief to companies on loans applied in acquiring interest in other companies

(1) (*a*) In this section and in sections 248 and 249—

"control" shall be construed in accordance with section 432;

"material interest", in relation to a company, means the beneficial ownership of, or the ability to control, directly or through the medium of a connected company or connected companies or by any other indirect means, more than 5 per cent of the ordinary share capital of the company.

(*b*) For the purposes of this section and sections 248 and 249, a company shall be regarded as connected with another company if it would be so regarded for the purposes of the Tax Acts by virtue of section 10 and if it is a company referred to in subsection (2)(*a*).

(2) This section shall apply to a loan to a company (in this section and in section 249(1) referred to as **"the investing company"**) to defray money applied—

(*a*) in acquiring any part of the ordinary share capital of—

(i) a company which exists wholly or mainly for the purpose of carrying on a trade or trades or a company whose income consists wholly or mainly of profits or gains chargeable under Case V of Schedule D, or

(ii) a company whose business consists wholly or mainly of the holding of stocks, shares or securities of a company referred to in subparagraph (i),

(*b*) in lending to a company referred to in paragraph (*a*) money which is used wholly and exclusively for the purposes of the trade or business of the company or of a connected company, or

(*c*) in paying off another loan where relief could have been obtained under this section for interest on that other loan if it had not been paid off (on the assumption, if the loan was free of interest, that it carried interest).

(3) Relief shall be given in respect of any payment of the interest by the investing company on the loan if—

(*a*) when the interest is paid the investing company has a material interest in the company or in a connected company,

(*b*) during the period taken as a whole from the application of the proceeds of the loan until the interest was paid at least one director of the investing company was also a director of the company or of a connected company, and

(*c*) the investing company shows that in the period referred to in paragraph (*b*) it has not recovered any capital from the company or from a connected company apart from any amount taken into account under section 249.

(4) Subsection (2) shall not apply to a loan unless it is made in connection with the application of the money and either on the occasion of its application or within what is in the circumstances a reasonable time from the application of the money, and that subsection shall not apply to a loan the proceeds of which are applied for some other purpose before being applied as described in that subsection.

[(5) Interest eligible for relief under this section shall be deducted from or set off against the income (not being income referred to in subsection (2)(*a*) of section 25) of the borrower for the year of assessment in which the interest is paid and tax shall be discharged or repaid accordingly.

(6) Where relief is given under this section in respect of interest on a loan, no relief or deduction under any other provision of the Tax Acts shall be given or allowed in respect of interest on the loan.][1]

Amendments

1 Subs (5) substituted by FA 2000 s 67 with effect from 6 April 1997.

Cross-references

Corporation tax, charges on income, subs (2): s 243(8).

Limited partnerships, specified provisions: s 1013(1).

Recovery of capital: s 249(1)(*a*)(i) ("relevant period"), (ii), (iii), (2)(*aa*); subs (2): s 249(1)(*a*)(ii)(II), (2)(*aa*)(i), (3); subs (3): s 249(3).

Restriction of relief: s 248A(2).

Case Law

See *Macniven v Westmoreland Investments Ltd* [2001] STC 237 for application of anti-avoidance legislation disallowing relief for interest paid where a scheme has been effected or arrangements have been made such that the sole or main benefit expected to accrue to the borrower from the transaction under which the interest is paid is a reduction in liability to tax (Irish equivalent legislation in s 817A).

Revenue precedents

Issue: Whether the cessation of a trading activity by the company in which shares have been acquired triggers withdrawal of the relief.

Decision: No.

Issue: Whether a "company" for s 247(2)(*a*)(i) must be resident in the State or within the charge to Irish.

Decision: No.

Definitions

Tax Acts: s 1(2); trade: s 3(1); year of assessment: s 2(1).

Former enactments

FA 1974 s 33 and s 35(4)–(5); CTA 1976 s 140(1) and Sch 2 Pt I para 43; FA 1996 s 131(9)(*a*).

248 Relief to individuals on loans applied in acquiring interest in companies

(1) This section shall apply to a loan to an individual to defray money applied—

(*a*) in acquiring any part of the ordinary share capital of—

(i) a company which exists wholly or mainly for the purpose of carrying on a trade or trades or a company whose income consists wholly or mainly of profits or gains chargeable under Case V of Schedule D, or

(ii) a company whose business consists wholly or mainly of the holding of stocks, shares or securities of a company referred to in subparagraph (i),

(*b*) in lending to such a company referred to in paragraph (*a*) money which is used wholly and exclusively for the purpose of the trade or business of the company or of a connected company, or

(*c*) in paying off another loan where relief could have been obtained under this section for interest on that other loan if it had not been paid off (on the assumption, if the loan was free of interest, that it carried interest).

(2) Relief shall be given in respect of any payment of interest by the individual on the loan if—

(*a*) when the interest is paid the individual has a material interest in the company or in a connected company,

(*b*) during the period taken as a whole from the application of the proceeds of the loan until the interest was paid, the individual has worked for the greater part of his or her time in the actual management or conduct of the business of the company or of a connected company, and

(*c*) the individual shows that in the period referred to in paragraph (*b*) he or she has not recovered any capital from the company or from a connected company, apart from any amount taken into account under section 249.

(3) Relief shall not be given in respect of any payment of interest by an individual on a loan applied on or after the 24th day of April, 1992, for any of the purposes specified in subsection (1) unless the loan is applied for bona fide commercial purposes and not as part of a scheme or arrangement the main purpose or one of the main purposes of which is the avoidance of tax.

(4) Subsection (1) shall not apply to a loan unless it is made in connection with the application of the money and either on the occasion of its application or within what is in the circumstances a reasonable time from the application of the money, and that subsection shall not apply to a loan the proceeds of which are applied for some other purpose before being applied as described in that subsection.

(5) Interest eligible for relief under this section shall be deducted from or set off against the income of the borrower for the year of assessment in which the interest is paid and tax shall be discharged or repaid accordingly, and such interest shall not be eligible for relief under any provision of the Income Tax Acts apart from this section.

Cross-references

"Control", "material interest", "connected", meaning: s 247(1)(*a*).

BES relief or film relief, no interest relief: s 251(*a*).

Companies which become quoted companies, restriction of relief: s 252(1).

Employee loan to acquire an interest in employing company: s 250(2); public companies, subs (1)(*a*)(i): s 250(5)(*e*).
Limited partnerships, specified provisions: s 1013(1).
Recovery of capital: s 249(1)(*a*)(iv), (*b*); subs (1)(*c*) and (2): s 249(3).
Restriction of relief: s 248A(2), (4).
Restriction of relief to individuals in respect of loans applied in acquiring interest in companies: s 250A(1)("eligible loan", "specified provisions"), (2); subs (1)(*a*), (*b*): s 250A(3)(*a*), (*b*).

Revenue precedents

Issue: Whether cessation of the trade by the company would result in the relief being withdrawn.
Decision: Not in itself, however unless trading was resumed within a reasonable period the individual would be unable to satisfy the requirements of subs (2) (*b*) and relief would be withdrawn.
Issue: Individuals borrowed money which was applied in acquiring an interest in a company. The company subsequently ceased to trade. Can the individuals still claim relief under TCA 1997 s 248.
Decision: Relief is not due. The company no longer existed for the purposes set out in the section. Separately, at the time the interest was paid, the individuals did not have a material interest in the company or a connected company.
Issue: Whether interest on money advance to company allowable, where the company had been struck off the companies register.
Decision: No; if the company was restored to the register, interest would be allowed for the periods during which it was struck off.
Issue: Borrowings on a loan were used for 1) financing a qualifying home loan and 2) for a qualifying loan to a company.
Decision: Subject to satisfying the necessary conditions, relief may be allowed on the interest paid under the relevant sections of the act, based on the appropriate percentage of the loan.

Definitions

trade: s 3(1).

Former enactments

FA 1974 s 34 and s 35(4)–(5); FA 1992 s 14(4).

Corresponding UK tax provision

Income and Corporation Taxes Act 1988 ss 360 and 361.

248A Restriction of relief in respect of loans applied in acquiring interest in companies and partnerships

[(1) In this section—

"chargeable period" has the same meaning as in section 321(2);

"premises" and **"rented residential premises"** have the same meanings, respectively, as in section 96.

(2) Where—

(*a*) a loan, being a loan to which section 247, 248 or 253 applies, is applied on or after the 7th day of May, 1998, to defray money for any of the purposes specified in those sections, and

(*b*) the money so defrayed is used, in whole or in part, directly or indirectly—

(i) in the purchase, improvement or repair of a premises, or

(ii) in paying off a loan used in the purchase, improvement or repair of a premises,

then the relief to be given for a chargeable period under those sections in respect of that loan shall, for any chargeable period in which the premises is at any time a rented residential premises, be reduced by the interest attributable to so much of the money used for the purposes specified in subparagraphs (i) and (ii) of paragraph (*b*).][1]

[(3) This section shall not apply or have effect in relation to interest referred to in subsection (2) which accrues on or after 1 January 2002 and, for the purposes of this subsection, such interest shall be treated as accruing from day to day.][2]

[(4) Notwithstanding subsection (3), subsection (2) shall apply in relation to interest referred to in subsection (2) where the purpose of the loan is the purchase of a residential premises from the spouse of the individual to whom relief is given under section 248 or 253.

(5) The reference to "spouse" in subsection (4) does not include a spouse to a marriage—

(*a*) in which the spouses are separated under an order of a court of competent jurisdiction or by deed of separation, or

(*b*) that has been dissolved under either—

(i) section 5 of the Family Law (Divorce) Act 1996, or

(ii) the law of a country or jurisdiction other than the State, being a divorce that is entitled to be recognised as valid in the State.][3]

Amendments

1 Section 248A inserted by F(No 2)A 1998 s 2 with effect from 20 May 1998.

2 Subs (3) inserted by FA 2002 s 17(*b*) with effect from 1 January 2002.

3 Subss (4) and (5) inserted by FA 2003 s 16(1)(*b*) in relation to interest referred to in ss 97(1)(2G) and s 248A(2) which accrues on or after 6 February 2003 and, for such purposes, such interest shall be treated as accruing from day to day.

249 Rules relating to recovery of capital and replacement loans

(1)[(*a*) (i) In this section—

"specified loan", in relation to a company, means—

(I) any loan or advance made to the company before 6 February 2003 (other than a loan referred to in paragraph (II)), or

(II) any loan or advance in respect of which any interest paid is, or if charged would be, deductible if the company were within the charge to Irish tax—

(A) in computing the company's profits or gains for the purposes of Case I of Schedule D, or

(B) in computing the company's profits or gains for the purposes of Case V of Schedule D;

"relevant period", in relation to a loan to which section 247 applies, means the period beginning 2 years before the date of application of the proceeds of the loan and ending on the date of application of the proceeds of the loan.

(ii) Where at any time in the relevant period in relation to a loan to which section 247 applies the investing company recovered any amount of capital from the company concerned, other than a repayment in respect of a specified loan, the investing company shall immediately after the application of the loan to which section 247 applies be treated for the purposes of this section as if the investing company had repaid out of the loan an amount equal to the amount of capital recovered and so that out of the interest otherwise eligible for relief and payable for any period after that time there shall be deducted an amount equal to interest on the amount of capital so recovered, but this subparagraph shall not apply to so much of the capital so recovered as was applied by the investing company—

(I) before the application of the loan to which section 247 applies, in repayment of any other loan to which section 247 applies, or

(II) in accordance with paragraph (*a*) or (*b*) of section 247(2);

and, for the purposes of this section, the investing company shall not be treated as having repaid so much of an amount out of a loan as does not exceed the amount, if any, of capital so recovered which has been previously treated under this section as being in repayment of a loan.

(iii) Where at any time after the application of the proceeds of the loan to which section 247 applies the investing company—

(I) has recovered any amount of capital from the company concerned or from a connected company, or

(II) is deemed, under subsection (2)(*aa*), to have recovered any amount of capital from the company concerned,

without using the amount recovered or an amount equal to the amount deemed to have been recovered in repayment of the loan, the investing company shall be treated for the purposes of this section as if the investing company had at that time repaid out of the loan an amount equal to the amount of capital recovered or deemed to have been recovered and so that out of the interest otherwise eligible for relief and payable for any period after that time there shall be deducted an amount equal to interest on the amount of capital so recovered or so deemed to have been recovered.

(iii) Where, after the application of the proceeds of a loan to which section 248 applies, the individual has recovered any amount of capital from the company concerned or from a connected company without using that amount in repayment of the loan, the individual shall be treated for the purposes of this section as if the individual had repaid that amount out of the loan and so that out of the interest otherwise eligible for relief and payable for any period after that time there shall be deducted an amount equal to interest on the amount of capital so recovered.][1]

(*b*) Where part only of a loan referred to in paragraph (*a*) fulfils the conditions in section 247 or 248 so as to afford relief for interest on that part, the deduction to be made under this subsection shall be made wholly out of interest on that part.

(2) [(*a*) The investing company or the individual, as the case may be (in this paragraph referred to as the **"borrower"**) shall be treated as having recovered an amount of capital from the company concerned or from a connected company if—

(i) the borrower receives consideration of that amount or value for the sale of any part of the ordinary share capital of the company concerned or of a connected company or any consideration of that amount or value by means of repayment of any part of that ordinary share capital,

(ii) the company concerned or a connected company repays that amount of a loan or advance from the borrower,

(iii) the borrower receives consideration of that amount or value for assigning any debt due to the borrower from the company concerned or from a connected company.

(*aa*) (i) Where the company concerned is a company to which section 247(2)(*a*)(ii) applies, the investing company shall be deemed to have recovered from the company concerned an amount equal to so much of any capital recovered by the company concerned from another company, being a company more than 50 per cent of the ordinary share capital of which was directly owned by the company concerned, as is not applied by the company concerned—

(I) in repayment of any loan or part of a loan made to it by the investing company,

(II) in redemption, repayment or purchase of any of its ordinary share capital acquired by the investing company,

(III) in accordance with paragraph (*a*) or (*b*) of section 247(2), or

(IV) in repayment of a loan to which section 247 applies.

(ii) The company concerned shall be treated as having recovered an amount of capital from another company if—

(I) the company concerned receives consideration of that amount or value for the sale of any part of the ordinary share capital of the other company or any consideration of that amount or value by means of repayment of any part of that ordinary share capital,

(II) the other company repays that amount of a loan or advance from the company concerned, other than a repayment in respect of a specified loan,

(III) the company concerned receives consideration of that amount or value for assigning any debt due to the company concerned from the other company.

(iii) Where subparagraph (i) applies and more than one investing company has either—

(I) made a loan to the company concerned, or

(II) acquired any part of its share capital,

the amount deemed to have been recovered under that subparagraph shall be apportioned between the investing companies in proportion to the aggregate amount of any loan made and any money applied in acquiring that share capital by each company, but if the companies concerned agree between them to such other apportionment of the amount as they may consider appropriate and jointly specify in writing to the inspector, then the amount deemed to have been so recovered shall be apportioned accordingly.][2]

(*b*) In the case of a sale or assignment otherwise than by means of a bargain made at arm's length, the sale or assignment shall be deemed to be for consideration of an amount equal to the market value of what is disposed of.

(3) Sections 247(3) and 248(2) and subsections (1) and (2) shall apply to a loan referred to in section 247(2)(*c*) or 248(1)(*c*) as if such loan and any loan it replaces were one loan, and as if—

(*a*) references in sections 247(3) and 248(2) and in subsection (1) to the application of the proceeds of the loan were references to the application of the proceeds of the original loan, and

(*b*) any restriction under subsection (1) which applied to any loan which has been replaced applied also to the loan which replaces that loan.

Amendments

1 Subs (1)(*a*) substituted by FA 2003 s 46(1)(*a*) as respects any recovery of capital or deemed recovery of capital (within the meaning of TCA 1997 s 249) effected from 6 February 2003.

2 Subs (2)(*a*) substituted by FA 2003 s 46(1)(*b*) as respects any recovery of capital or deemed recovery of capital (within the meaning of TCA 1997 s 249) effected from 6 February 2003.

Cross-references

"Control", "material interest", "connected", meaning: s 247(1)(*a*).
Company loan to acquire interest in another company: s 247(3)(*c*).
Individual loan to acquire interest in a company: s 248(2)(*c*).
Corporation tax, charges on income: s 243(9).
Limited partnerships, specified provisions: s 1013(1).

Definitions

company: s 4(1); connected: s 247(1)(*b*); inspector: s 2(1); ordinary share capital: s 2(1); writing: IA 1937 Sch.

Former enactments

FA 1974 s 35(1)–(3).

Corresponding UK tax provision

Income and Corporation Taxes Act 1988 s 363.

250 Extension of relief under section 248 to certain individuals in relation to loans applied in acquiring interest in certain companies

(1) In this section—

"90 per cent subsidiary" has the meaning assigned to it by section 9;

"full-time employee" and **"full-time director"**, in relation to a company, mean an employee or director, as the case may be, who is required to devote substantially the whole of his or her time to the service of the company;

"holding company" has the same meaning as in section 411;

"part-time employee" and **"part-time director"**, in relation to a company, mean an employee or director, as the case may be, who is not required to devote substantially the whole of his or her time to the service of the company;

"private company" has the meaning assigned to it by section 33 of the Companies Act, 1963.

(2) Notwithstanding that an individual does not satisfy one or both of the conditions set out in paragraphs (*a*) and (*b*) of section 248(2), the individual shall be entitled to relief

under section 248 for any interest paid on any loan to him or her applied for a purpose specified in section 248(1) if—

(*a*) the company part of whose ordinary share capital is acquired or, as the case may be, to which the money is loaned is—

(i) both a company referred to in paragraph (*a*)(i) of section 248(1) and a company in relation to which the individual was a full-time employee, part-time employee, full-time director or part-time director during the period taken as a whole from the application of the proceeds of the loan until the interest was paid, or

(ii) both a company referred to in paragraph (*a*)(ii) of section 248(1) and a private company in relation to which, or in relation to any company which would be regarded as connected with it for the purposes of section 248, the individual was during that period a full-time director or a full-time employee,

and

(*b*) the company or any person connected with the company has not, during the period specified in paragraph (*a*)(i), made any loans or advanced any money to the individual or a person connected with the individual other than a loan made or money advanced in the ordinary course of a business which included the lending of money, being business carried on by the company or, as the case may be, by the person connected with the company.

(3) In relation to any payment or payments of interest on any loan or loans applied—

(*a*) in acquiring any part of the ordinary share capital of a company other than a private company,

(*b*) in lending money to such a company, or

(*c*) in paying off any other loan or loans applied for a purpose specified in paragraphs (*a*) and (*b*),

no relief shall be given for any year of assessment by virtue of this section other than to a full-time employee or full-time director of the company and no such relief shall be given to such employee or director on the excess of that payment, or the aggregate amount of those payments, for that year of assessment over [€3,050][1].

(4) Where relief is given by virtue of this section to an individual and any loan made or money advanced to the individual or to a person connected with the individual is, in accordance with paragraph (*c*) of subsection (5) and by virtue of subparagraph (ii), (iii), (iv) or (v) of that paragraph, subsequently regarded as not having been made or advanced in the ordinary course of a business, any relief so given, which would not have been given if, at the time the relief was given, the loan or money advanced had been so regarded, shall be withdrawn and there shall be made all such assessments or additional assessments as are necessary to give effect to this subsection.

(5) For the purposes of this section—

(*a*) any question whether a person is connected with another person shall be determined in accordance with section 10 (as it applies for the purposes of the Tax Acts) and paragraph (*b*), (*b*) a person shall be connected with any other person to whom such person has, otherwise than in the ordinary course of a business carried on by such person which includes the lending of money, made any loans or advanced any money, and with any person to whom that other person has so made any loan or advanced any money and so on,

(*c*) a loan shall not be regarded as having been made, or money shall not be regarded as having been advanced, in the ordinary course of a business if—

(i) the loan is made or the money is advanced on terms which are not reasonably comparable with the terms which would have been applied in respect of that loan or the advance of that money on the basis that the negotiations for the loan or the advance of the money had been at arm's length,

(ii) at the time the loan was made or the money was advanced the terms were such that subparagraph (i) did not apply, those terms are subsequently altered and the terms as so altered are such that if they had applied at the time the loan was made or the money was advanced subparagraph (i) would have applied,

(iii) any interest payable on the loan or on the money advanced is waived,

(iv) any interest payable on the loan or on the money advanced is not paid within 12 months from the date on which it became payable, or

(v) the loan or the money advanced or any part of the loan or money advanced is not repaid within 12 months of the date on which it becomes repayable,

(*d*) the cases in which any person is to be regarded as making a loan to any other person include a case where—

(i) that other person incurs a debt to that person, or

(ii) a debt due from that other person to a third party is assigned to that person;

but subparagraph (i) shall not apply to a debt incurred for the supply by that person of goods or services in the ordinary course of that person's trade or business unless the period for which credit is given exceeds 6 months or is longer than normally given by that person,

(*e*) a company other than a private company shall be deemed to be a company referred to in section 248(1)(*a*)(i) if it is a holding company and is resident in the State, and

(*f*) an individual shall be deemed to be a full-time employee or full-time director of a company referred to in paragraph (*e*) if the individual is a full-time employee or full-time director of any company which is a 90 per cent subsidiary of that company.

Amendments

[1] Substituted by FA 2001 s 240(1), (2)(*a*) and Sch 5 Pt 1 for 2002 and later tax years; previously "£2,400" (short tax "year" 2001: £1,776: FA 2001 s 77(2) and Sch 2 paras 14 and 61(*a*)).

Cross-references

Approved savings-related share option schemes, interpretation, meaning of "full-time director" applied: Sch 12A para 1(1).

BES relief or film relief, no interest relief: s 251(*a*).

Business, meanings of "full-time employee" and "full-time director" applied: s 488(1).

Capital gains tax share reinvestment relief, meanings of "full-time employee", "full-time director", "part-time employee" and "part-time director" applied: s 591(1).

Companies which become quoted companies, restriction of relief: s 252(1).
Employer preferential loans, connected person rules applied: s 122(1)(*b*).
Limited partnerships, specified provisions: s 1013(1).
Restriction of relief to individuals in respect of loans applied in acquiring interest in companies: s 250A(1)("specified provisions").

Revenue precedents

Issue: Can employees of a subsidiary company claim relief on loans acquired to buy shares in the holding company?
Decision: Employees of a company, which is a 100% subsidiary of a second company, which in turn is a subsidiary of a third company, can claim relief.
Issue: Whether relief is allowed where a holding company is also a trading company (subss 5(*e*) & (*f*).
Decision: Relief is allowed.
Issue: Would a registered Industrial & Provident Society be regarded as a private company for relief under s 250?
Decision: Such a society would not be regarded as a private company for the purposes of granting interest relief under s 250.

Definitions

company: ss 4(1), 5(1); month: IA 1937 Sch; ordinary share capital: s 2(1); person: IA 1937 s 11(*c*); trade: s 3(1); year of assessment: ss 2(1), 5(1).

Former enactments

FA 1978 s 8; FA 1979 s 9; FA 1996 s 131(9)(*a*).

250A Restriction of relief to individuals in respect of loans applied in acquiring interest in companies

[(1) In this section—

"distribution" has the same meaning as it has for the purposes of the Corporation Tax Acts by virtue of section 4;

"eligible loan" in relation to an individual and a company, means a loan, being a loan to which section 248 applies, to the individual to defray money applied for any of the purposes specified in that section;

"relevant interest" has the same meaning as in section 269;

"residue of expenditure" shall be construed in accordance with section 277;

"specified amount" in relation to an eligible loan, means the amount of the eligible loan or so much of the eligible loan where the money or, as the case may be, part of the money which was defrayed by that loan and which was applied by the individual—

(*a*) is used after 1 January 2003 by the company directly or indirectly—

(i) in the acquisition (whether by the company or by any other person) of the relevant interest in relation to any capital expenditure incurred or deemed to be incurred on the construction or refurbishment of a specified building,

(ii) in replacing money used in such acquisition of such an interest, or

(iii) in paying off a loan used in such acquisition of such an interest,

(*b*) pays off another eligible loan or so much of another eligible loan where the money or, as the case may be, part of the money which was defrayed by that other loan (or any previous loan or loans which it replaced) and which was applied by the individual was used after 1 January 2003 by the company directly or indirectly for any of the purposes referred to in paragraph (*a*), or (*c*) was applied in acquiring, on or after 20 February 2004, any part of the ordinary share capital of a company at least 75 per cent of whose income consists of profits or gains chargeable under Case V of Schedule D in respect of one or more specified buildings;

"specified building" means a building or structure, or a part of a building or structure—

(*a*) (i) which is or is to be an industrial building or structure by reason of its use or deemed use for a purpose specified in section 268(1) and in relation to which an allowance has been, or is to be, made to a company under Chapter 1 of Part 9, or

(ii) in relation to which an allowance has been, or is to be, so made to a company by virtue of Part 10 or section 843 or 843A,

in respect of—

(I) the capital expenditure incurred or deemed to be incurred on the construction or refurbishment of the building or structure or, as the case may be, the part of the building or structure, or

(II) the residue of that expenditure,

(*b*) in relation to which at any time beginning on or after 1 January 2003 the company referred to in paragraph (*a*) is entitled to the relevant interest in relation to the capital expenditure referred to in that paragraph, and

(*c*) in relation to which any other company (not being the company referred to in paragraph (*a*)) is entitled, at any time subsequent to the time referred to in paragraph (*b*), to an allowance under Chapter 1 of Part 9, in respect of the capital expenditure referred to in paragraph (*a*) or the residue of that expenditure, following the acquisition of the relevant interest or any part of the relevant interest in relation to that capital expenditure, whether or not, subsequent to the time referred to in paragraph (*b*), any other person or persons had previously become entitled to that relevant interest or that part of that relevant interest;

"specified provisions" means section 248 and that section as extended by section 250.

(2) Notwithstanding anything in the specified provisions, relief under section 248 for any year of assessment in relation to any payment or payments of interest on the specified amount of an eligible loan by the individual concerned shall not exceed that individual's return from the company concerned in that year in relation to that specified amount.

(3) Subject to subsection (4), an individual's return from a company in relation to a specified amount of an eligible loan in any year of assessment is—

(*a*) where the specified amount defrays an amount of money applied by the individual for the purpose specified in section 248(1)(*a*) or (*b*), the amount, if any, of the distributions (before deduction of any dividend withholding tax under Chapter 8A of Part 6), or, as the case may be, the amount, if any, of the interest, received by the individual from the company in that year as a result of the application by the individual of that amount of money, or

(*b*) where the specified amount defrays an amount of money applied by the individual, directly or indirectly, in paying off the specified amount of another eligible loan where the earlier specified amount defrayed an amount of money (subsequently referred to in this paragraph as "that earlier amount of money") which was applied by the individual for the purpose specified in section 248(1)(*a*) or (*b*), the amount, if any, of the distributions (before deduction of any dividend withholding tax under Chapter 8A of Part 6), or, as the case may be, the amount, if any, of the interest, received by the individual from the company in that year as a result of the application by the individual of that earlier amount of money.

(4) In determining for the purposes of this section—

(*a*) the amount of any payment or payments of interest by an individual on the specified amount of an eligible loan, or

(*b*) the amount of interest received by an individual as a result of the application by the individual of an amount of money which was defrayed by the specified amount of an eligible loan,

such apportionment, where necessary, of the total payments of interest by the individual on the eligible loan, or, as the case may be, the total amount of interest received by the individual as a result of the application of all the money defrayed by the eligible loan, shall be made in the same proportion which the specified amount of the eligible loan bears to the amount of the eligible loan.][1]

Amendments

[1] Section 250A inserted by FA 2004 s 22(1) and applies in relation to any payment or payments of interest by an individual (*a*) on or after 19 March 2003, or (*b*) where FA 2004 s 22 applies by virtue of para (*c*) of the definition of "specified amount" (within the meaning of section 250A), on or after 20 February 2004.

Tax Briefing

TB55 April 2004 pp 5–6 — Loans applied in acquiring interest in companies.

Definitions

company: s 4(1); ordinary share capital: s 2(1); person: IA 1937 s 11(*c*); year of assessment: s 2(1).

251 Restriction of relief to individuals on loans applied in acquiring shares in companies where a claim for "BES relief" or "film relief" is made in respect of amount subscribed for shares

Notwithstanding sections 248 and 250, relief shall not be given under either section in respect of any payment of interest on any loan applied in acquiring shares (being shares forming part of the ordinary share capital of a company) issued—

(*a*) on or after the 20th day of April, 1990, if a claim for relief under Part 16 is made in respect of the amount subscribed for those shares, or

(*b*) on or after the 6th day of May, 1993, if a claim for relief under section 481 is made in respect of the amount subscribed for those shares.

Cross-references

Limited partnerships, specified provisions: s 1013(1).

Definitions

company: ss 4(1), 5(1); ordinary share capital: s 2(1); shares: s 5(1).

Former enactments

FA 1990 s 11; FA 1993 s 6.

252 Restriction of relief to individuals on loans applied in acquiring interest in companies which become quoted companies

(1) In this section—

"loan" means a loan applied for any of the purposes specified in the principal section;

"the principal section" means section 248 as extended by section 250;

"quoted company" means a company whose shares or any class of whose shares—

(*a*) are listed in the official list of the Irish Stock Exchange or any other stock exchange, or

(*b*) are quoted on an unlisted securities market of any stock exchange;

"the specified date", in relation to a loan, means—

(*a*) (i) in a case where the loan was applied on or before the 5th day of April, 1989, the 6th day of April, 1992,

(ii) in a case where the loan was applied on or after the 6th day of April, 1989, but on or before the 5th day of April, 1990, the 6th day of April, 1993, and

(iii) in a case where the loan was applied on or after the 6th day of April, 1990, the 6th day of April, 1994,

or

(*b*) if later, [1 January][1] in the second year of assessment next after the year of assessment in which the company, part of whose ordinary share capital was acquired or, as the case may be, to which the money was loaned, becomes a quoted company.

(2) Subject to subsection (3), if the company, part of whose ordinary share capital was acquired or, as the case may be, to which the money was loaned, is, at the specified date in relation to the loan, a quoted company, entitlement to relief under the principal section in respect of interest paid on a loan shall be determined subject to the following provisions:

(*a*) as respects the year of assessment commencing with the specified date, relief shall not be given in respect of the excess of the amount, or of the aggregate amount, of the interest over 70 per cent of the amount, or of the aggregate amount, of the interest in respect of which apart from this paragraph relief would otherwise have been given under the principal section;

(*b*) as respects the next year of assessment, relief shall not be given in respect of the excess of the amount, or of the aggregate amount, of the interest over 40 per cent of the amount, or of the aggregate amount, of the interest in respect of which apart from this paragraph relief would otherwise have been given under the principal section;

(*c*) as respects any subsequent year of assessment, no relief shall be given under the principal section.

(3) Notwithstanding anything in subsection (2) or the principal section, the principal section shall not apply in relation to any payment of interest on a loan applied on or after the 29th day of January, 1992, if, at the time the loan is applied, the company, part of

whose ordinary share capital was or is acquired or, as the case may be, to which the money was or is loaned, is a quoted company.

Amendments

1 Substituted by FA 2001 s 77(2) and Sch 2 paras 15 and 61(*d*) with effect from 1 January 2002; previously "the 6th day of April".

Cross-references

Limited partnerships, specified provisions: s 1013(1).

Definitions

class (of shares): s 5(1); company: ss 4(1), 5(1); ordinary share capital: s 2(1); year of assessment: ss 2(1), 5(1).

Former enactments

FA 1992 s 14(1)–(3); FA 1997 s 10.

253 Relief to individuals on loans applied in acquiring interest in partnerships

(1) This section shall apply to a loan to an individual to defray money applied—

(*a*) in purchasing a share in a partnership,

(*b*) in contributing money to a partnership by means of capital or a premium, or in advancing money to the partnership, where the money contributed or advanced is used wholly and exclusively for the purposes of the trade or profession carried on by the partnership, or

(*c*) in paying off another loan where relief could have been obtained under this section for interest on that other loan if it had not been paid off (on the assumption, if the loan was free of interest, that it carried interest).

(2) Relief shall be given in respect of any payment of interest by the individual on the loan if—

(*a*) throughout the period from the application of the proceeds of the loan until the interest was paid the individual has personally acted in the conduct of the trade or profession carried on by the partnership as a partner therein, and

(*b*) the individual shows that in that period he or she has not recovered any capital from the partnership, apart from any amount taken into account under subsection (3).

(3) (*a*) Where at any time after the application of the proceeds of the loan the individual has recovered any amount of capital from the partnership without using that amount in repayment of the loan, the individual shall be treated for the purposes of this section as if he or she had at that time repaid that amount out of the loan, and accordingly there shall be deducted out of the interest otherwise eligible for relief and payable for any period after that time an amount equal to interest on the amount of capital so recovered.

(*b*) Where part only of a loan fulfils the conditions in this section so as to afford relief for interest on that part, the deduction to be made under this subsection shall be made wholly out of interest on that part.

(4) (*a*) The individual shall be treated as having recovered an amount of capital from the partnership if—

(i) the individual receives a consideration of that amount or value for the sale of any part of his or her interest in the partnership,

(ii) the partnership returns any amount of capital to the individual or repays any amount advanced by the individual, or

(iii) the individual receives a consideration of that amount or value for assigning any debt due to the individual from the partnership.

(*b*) In the case of a sale or assignment otherwise than by means of a bargain made at arm's length, the sale or assignment shall be deemed to be for consideration of an amount equal to the market value of what is disposed of.

(5) Subsections (2) to (4) shall apply to a loan referred to in subsection (1)(*c*) as if such loan and any loan it replaces were one loan, and as if—

(*a*) references in subsections (2) to (4) to the application of the proceeds of the loan were references to the application of the proceeds of the original loan, and

(*b*) any restriction under subsection (3) which applied to any loan which has been replaced applied also as respects the loan which replaces that loan.

(6) Subsection (1) shall not apply to a loan unless it is made in connection with the application of the money and either on the occasion of its application or within what is in the circumstances a reasonable time from the application of the money, and that subsection shall not apply to a loan the proceeds of which are applied for some other purpose before being applied as described in that subsection.

(7) Interest eligible for relief under this section shall be deducted from or set off against the income of the individual for the year of assessment in which the interest is paid and tax shall be discharged or repaid accordingly, and such interest shall not be eligible for relief under any provision of the Income Tax Acts apart from this section.

Cross-references

Limited partnerships, specified provisions: s 1013(1).

Restriction of relief: s 248A(2), (4).

Definitions

Income Tax Acts: s 1(2); profession: s 2(1); trade: s 3(1); year of assessment: ss 2(1), 5(1).

Former enactments

FA 1974 s 36.

Corresponding UK tax provision

Income and Corporation Taxes Act 1988 s 362.

---

254 Interest on borrowings to replace capital withdrawn in certain circumstances from a business

Where a person borrows money to replace in whole or in part capital in any form formerly employed in any trade, profession or other business carried on by the person in respect of the profits or gains of which tax is charged under Schedule D, being capital which within the 5 years preceding the date of replacement was withdrawn from such use for use otherwise than in connection with a trade, profession or other business carried on by the person, interest on such borrowed money shall not be regarded as interest wholly and exclusively laid out or expended for the purposes of a trade, profession or other business.

Cross-references

Limited partnerships, specified provisions: s 1013(1).

Definitions

person: IA 1937 s 11(*c*); profession: s 2(1); trade: s 3(1).

Former enactments

FA 1974 s 37.

255 Arrangements for payment of interest less tax or of fixed net amount

(1) Any agreement made, whether orally or in writing, for the payment of interest **"less tax"**, or using words to that effect, shall be construed, in relation to interest payable without deduction of tax, as if the words **"less tax"** or the equivalent words were not included.

(2) In relation to interest on which the recipient is chargeable to tax under Schedule D and which is payable without deduction of tax, any agreement, whether orally or in writing and however worded, for the payment of interest at such a rate (in this subsection referred to as **"the gross rate"**) as shall, after deduction of tax at the standard rate of tax for the time being in force, be equal to a stated rate, shall be construed as if it were an agreement requiring the payment of interest at the gross rate.

Cross-references

Limited partnerships, specified provisions: s 1013(1).

Definitions

standard rate: ss 3(1), 15; writing: IA 1937 Sch.

Former enactments

FA 1974 s 39.

Corresponding UK tax provision

Income and Corporation Taxes Act 1988 s 818.

CHAPTER 4

Interest Payments by Certain Deposit Takers

Notes

Dormant accounts, claims for repayment, accrued interest is defined for the purposes of this Chapter to be a payment of an amount of "relevant interest" paid by the institution on the date of the payment to the claimant: Dormant Account Act 2001 s 19(6).

Dormant accounts, investment of funds by NTMA, interest received by NTMA in respect of moneys invested by way of deposit with credit institution is deemed for purposes of this Chapter to be beneficially owned by NTMA: Dormant Accounts Act 2001 s 18(5).

Cross-references

Approved retirement fund, a deposit consisting of money held by a qualifying fund manager in that capacity is not a relevant deposit for purposes of this Chapter: s 784A(6).

Chargeable gains accruing to certain unit trusts: s 731(5)(*c*).

Common contractual funds, this Chapter applies to a deposit (within the meaning of this Chapter) to which a common contractual fund is entitled as if such deposit is not a relevant deposit within the meaning of this Chapter.

Designated charities, repayment of tax in respect of donations, meaning of "appropriate tax" applied: s 848(1)(*a*).

Dividend payments by credit unions, election to open a special share account or a special term share account: s 267B(2)(*b*), (3)(*b*); interpretation: s 267A(1)("special share account"); supplementary provisions: s 267F(2).

Donations to approved bodies, meaning of "appropriate tax" applied: s 848A(1)(*a*)("appropriate certificate").

Donations to certain sports bodies, meaning of "appropriate tax" applied: s 847A(1)("appropriate certificate").

Interest in respect of wholesale debt instruments: s 246A(3)(*a*)(B), (3)(*b*)(ii)(B).

Investment undertakings (charge to tax), a deposit to which an investment undertaking is entitled is not a relevant deposit for purposes of this Chapter: s 739C(2).
Local authority exemption applies to income other than under this Chapter: s 214(3).
Non-commercial State-sponsored bodies, exemption applies to income other than under this Chapter: s 227(4).
Power of inspection: returns and collection of appropriate tax: s 904A(2).
Rate of charge, meaning of "relevant interest" applied: s 15(4).
Revenue offences: s 1078(2)(*e*)(iii).
Special investment schemes: s 737(7)(*c*).
Special portfolio investment accounts, Part 8 Chapter 4 (other than s 259) applies as it applies to special savings accounts: s 838(3); Part 8 Chapter 4 to be construed as if:
a reference to a "deposit" is a reference to a "specified deposit" within s 838(1)(*a*);
a reference to "interest" is a reference to "income or gains" within s 838(1)(*a*);
a reference to a "relevant deposit" is a reference to a "relevant investment" within s 838(1)(*a*);
a reference to a "relevant deposit taker" is a reference to a "designated broker" within s 838(1)(*a*);
a reference to "relevant interest" is a reference to "relevant income or gains" within s 838(1)(*a*);
a reference to a "special savings account" is a reference to a "special portfolio investment account" within s 838(1)(*a*); and as if s 258(4)–(5) and s 259 had not been enacted: s 838(1)(*b*).
Special savings incentive accounts, payment of tax credit: s 848E(3).
Undertaking for collective investment: s 738(3)(*c*).

Statement of practice

SP-Gen 1/01 — "Underlying Tax" on Funds Deposited in Bogus Non-Resident Accounts.

Revenue information

Deposit Interest Retention Tax — Guidance Notes for Deposit-Takers are available on Revenue's website (www.revenue.ie) under Publications/Technical Guidelines.
Information leaflet IT5 — Refund of Deposit Interest Retention Tax.
Information leaflet IT17 — Special Savings Accounts and other Special Investment Products.

Tax Briefing

TB43 April 2001 p 18 — Taxation of Credit Union dividends and interest.
TB49 Aug 2002 pp 1–5 — Bogus Non-Resident Accounts.
TB51 Jan 2003 p 7 — Bogus Non-Resident Accounts — Consequences of Non-Co-operation.

256 Interpretation (Chapter 4)

(1) In this Chapter—

"amount on account of appropriate tax" shall be construed in accordance with section 258(4);

[**"appropriate tax"**, in relation to a payment of relevant interest, means a sum representing income tax on the amount of the payment—

[(*a*) in the case of interest paid in respect of a relevant deposit or relevant deposits held in—

(i) a special savings account, or

(ii) a special term account,

at the rate of 20 per cent,][1]

(*b*) subject to paragraph (*c*), in the case of interest paid in respect of any other relevant deposit, at the standard rate in force at the time of payment, and

(*c*) in the case of interest paid in respect of a relevant deposit, being a deposit made on or after 23 March 2000, other than interest which is—

(i) referred to in paragraph (*a*), or

(ii) payable annually or at more frequent intervals, or

(iii) specified interest within the meaning of section 260,

at a rate determined by the formula—

(S + 3) per cent

where S is the standard rate per cent (within the meaning of section 4(1)) in force at the time of payment;][2]

"building society" means a building society within the meaning of the Building Societies Act, 1989, or a society established in accordance with the law of any other Member State of the European Communities which corresponds to that Act;

[**"credit union"** means a society registered under the Credit Union Act, 1997, including a society deemed to be so registered under section 5(3) of that Act;][3]

[**"deposit"** means a sum of money paid to a relevant deposit taker on terms under which it, or any part of it, may be repaid with or without interest and either on demand or at a time or in circumstances agreed by or on behalf of the person making the payment and the person to whom it is made, notwithstanding that the amount to be repaid may be to any extent linked to or determined by changes in a stock exchange index or any other financial index;][4]

"foreign currency" means a currency other than the currency of the State;

[**"interest"** means any interest of money whether yearly or otherwise, including any amount, whether or not described as interest, paid in consideration of the making of a deposit, and, as respects—

(*a*) a deposit, where the amount to be repaid may be to any extent linked to or determined by changes in a stock exchange index or any other financial index, includes any amount which is or is to be repaid over and above the amount of the deposit,

(*b*) a building society, includes any dividend or other distribution in respect of shares in the society,

...[5],][6]

[**"long term account"** means an account opened by an individual with a relevant deposit taker on terms under which the individual has agreed that each relevant deposit held in the account is to be held in the account for a period of not less than 5 years;][7]

[**"medium term account"** means an account opened by an individual with a relevant deposit taker on terms under which the individual has agreed that each relevant deposit held in the account is to be held in the account for a period of not less than 3 years;][7]

"pension scheme" means an exempt approved scheme within the meaning of section 774 or a retirement annuity contract or a trust scheme to which section 784 or 785 applies;

"relevant deposit" means a deposit held by a relevant deposit taker, other than a deposit—

(*a*) which is made by, and the interest on which is beneficially owned by—

(i) a relevant deposit taker,

(ii) the National Treasury Management Agency,

(iii) the State acting through the National Treasury Management Agency,

[(iii*a*) the National Pensions Reserve Fund Commission,

(iii*b*) the State acting through the National Pensions Reserve Fund Commission,][8]

[(iii*c*) the National Development Finance Agency,][9]

[(iv) the Central Bank of Ireland,

(v) The Investor Compensation Company Limited, or

(vi) Icarom plc,][10]

(*b*) which is a debt on a security issued by the relevant deposit taker and listed on a stock exchange,

(*c*) which, in the case of a relevant deposit taker resident in the State for the purposes of corporation tax, is held at a branch of the relevant deposit taker situated outside the State,

(*d*) which, in the case of a relevant deposit taker not resident in the State for the purposes of corporation tax, is held otherwise than at a branch of the relevant deposit taker situated in the State,

(*e*) which is a deposit denominated in a foreign currency made—

(i) by a person other than an individual before the 1st day of January, 1993, or

(ii) by an individual before the 1st day of June, 1991,

but, where on or after the 1st day of June, 1991, and before the 1st day of January, 1993, a deposit denominated in a foreign currency is made by an individual to a relevant deposit taker with whom the individual had a deposit denominated in the same foreign currency immediately before the 1st day of June, 1991, such a deposit shall not be regarded as a relevant deposit,

(*f*) (i) which is made on or after the 1st day of January, 1993, by, and the interest on which is beneficially owned by—

(I) a company which is or will be within the charge to corporation tax in respect of the interest, or

(II) a pension scheme,

and

[(ii) in respect of which the company or pension scheme which is the beneficial owner of the interest has provided the relevant deposit taker with that person's tax reference number (within the meaning of section 885) or where, in the case of a pension scheme, there is no such number, with the number assigned by the Revenue Commissioners to the employer to whom that pension scheme relates,][11]

(*g*) in respect of which—

(i) no person resident in the State is beneficially entitled to any interest, and

(ii) a declaration of the kind mentioned in section 263 has been made to the relevant deposit taker, or

(*h*) (i) the interest on which is exempt—

(I) from income tax under Schedule D by virtue of section 207(1)(*b*), or

(II) from corporation tax by virtue of section 207(1)(*b*) as it applies for the purposes of corporation tax under section 76(6),

and

[(ii) in respect of which the beneficial owner of the interest has provided the relevant deposit taker with the reference number assigned to that person by the Revenue Commissioners in recognition of that person's entitlement to exemption from tax under section 207 and known as the charity (CHY) number;][12]

"relevant deposit taker" means any of the following persons—

(*a*) a person who is a holder of a licence granted under section 9 of the Central Bank Act, 1971, or a person who holds a licence or other similar authorisation under the law of any other Member State of the European Communities which corresponds to a licence granted under that section,

(*b*) a building society,

(*c*) a trustee savings bank within the meaning of the Trustee Savings Banks Acts, 1863 to 1989,

[(*ca*) a credit union,][13]

...[14]

...[15]

...[15]

(*g*) the Post Office Savings Bank;

[**"relevant interest"** means, subject to section 261A, interest paid in respect of a relevant deposit;][16]

"return" means a return under section 258(2);

"special savings account" means an account opened [on or after 1 January 1993 and before 6 April 2001],[17] in which a relevant deposit or relevant deposits made by an individual is or are held and in respect of which—

(*a*) the conditions in section 264(1) are satisfied, and

(*b*) a declaration of the kind mentioned in section 264(2) has been made to the relevant [deposit taker;][18]

[**"special term account"** means—

(*a*) a medium term account, or

(*b*) a long term account,

being an account in which a relevant deposit or relevant deposits made by an individual is or are held and in respect of which—

(i) the conditions specified in section 264A(1) are satisfied, and

(ii) a declaration of the kind mentioned in section 264A(2) has been made to the relevant deposit [taker;][19]][20]

[**"special term share account"** has the same meaning as in section 267A.][21]

(2) For the purposes of this Chapter—

(*a*) any amount credited as interest in respect of a relevant deposit shall be treated as a payment of interest, and references in this Chapter to relevant interest being paid shall be construed accordingly, (*b*) any reference in this Chapter to the amount of a payment of relevant interest shall be construed as a reference to the amount which would be the amount of that payment if no appropriate tax were to be deducted from that payment, and

(*c*) a deposit shall be treated as held at a branch of a relevant deposit taker if it is recorded in its books as a liability of that branch.

Amendments

1 Definition of "appropriate tax" para (*a*) substituted by FA 2001 s 57(1)(*a*)(i)(I) with effect from such date as the Minister for Finance may by order or orders appoint; previously:

"(*a*) in the case of interest paid in respect of a relevant deposit or relevant deposits held in a special savings account, at the rate of 20 per cent,".

This amendment came into operation with effect from 1 January 2002 — Finance Act, 2001 (Section 57) (Commencement) Order 2001, SI No 596 of 2001, refers.

2 Definition of "appropriate tax" substituted by FA 2001 s 55(*a*)(i)(II) with effect from 6 April 2001; previously from 6 April 2000 (FA 2001 s 55(*a*)(i)(I)):

"'appropriate tax', in relation to a payment of relevant interest, means a sum representing income tax on the amount of the payment—

(*a*) in the case of a relevant deposit or relevant deposits held in a special savings account, at the rate of 20 per cent,

(*b*) subject to paragraph (*c*), in the case of any other relevant deposit, at the standard rate in force at the time of payment, and

(*c*) in the case of a relevant deposit, being a deposit made on or after 23 March 2000, other than a relevant deposit—

(i) referred to in paragraph (*a*), or

(ii) the interest in respect of which is payable annually or at more frequent intervals, or

(iii) which is a specified deposit within the meaning of section 260,

at a rate determined by the formula—

(S + 3) per cent

where S is the standard rate per cent (within the meaning of section 4(1)) in force at the time of payment;"

3 Definition of "credit union" inserted by FA 2001 s 57(1)(*a*)(i)(II) with effect from such date as the Minister for Finance may by order or orders appoint. This amendment came into operation with effect from 1 January 2002 — Finance Act, 2001 (Section 57) (Commencement) Order 2001, SI No 596 of 2001, refers.

4 Definition of "deposit" substituted by FA 2001 s 55(*a*)(ii) as respects a deposit made on or after 6 April 2001.

5 Repealed by ACC Bank Act 2001 s 12(1) and Sch with effect from such day as the Minister for Finance may appoint by order; previously "but any amount consisting of an excess of the amount received on the redemption of any holding of ACC Bonus Bonds — First Series, issued by ACC Bank plc, over the amount paid for the holding shall not be treated as interest for the purposes of this Chapter". By virtue of the ACC Bank Act 2001 (Sections 6, 8, 10, 11(2) and 12) (Commencement) Order 2002, SI No 69 of 2002, this amendment came into operation with effect from 28 February 2002.

6 Definition of "interest" substituted by FA 2001 s 55(*a*)(iii) as respects a deposit made on or after 6 April 2001.

7 Definitions of "long term account" and "medium term account" inserted by FA 2001 s 57(1)(*a*)(i)(III) with effect from such date as the Minister for Finance may by order or orders appoint. This amendment came into operation with effect from 1 January 2002 — Finance Act 2001 (Section 57) (Commencement) Order 2001, SI No 596 of 2001, refers.

8 Definition of "relevant deposit" paras (*a*)(iii*a*) and (*a*)(iii*b*) inserted by National Pensions Reserve Fund Act 2000 s 30(*c*) with effect from 10 December 2000.

9 Definition of "relevant deposit" para (*a*)(iii*c*) inserted by FA 2003 s 43(1)(*c*) with effect from 6 February 2003.

10 Definition of "relevant deposit" para (*b*)(iv)–(v) substituted by FA 1999 s 76(1)(*b*) with effect from 10 September 1998.

11 Definition of "relevant deposit" para (*f*)(ii) substituted by FA 2002 s 20(1)(*a*)(i) as respects deposits made on or after 25 March 2002.

12 Definition of "relevant deposit" para (*h*)(ii) substituted by FA 2002 s 20(1)(*a*)(ii) as respects deposits made on or after 25 March 2002.

13 Definition of "relevant deposit taker" para (*ca*) inserted by FA 2001 s 57(1)(*a*)(i)(IV) with effect from such date as the Minister for Finance may by order or orders appoint. This amendment came into operation with effect from 1 January 2002 — Finance Act 2001 (Section 57) (Commencement) Order 2001, SI No 596 of 2001, refers.

14 Definition of "relevant deposit taker" para (*d*) repealed by ACC Bank Act 2001 s 12(1) and Sch with effect from such date as the Minister for Finance may appoint by order. By virtue of the ACC Bank Act 2001 (Sections 6, 8, 10, 11(2), 12) (Commencement) Order 2002, SI No 69 of 2002, this amendment came into operation with effect from 28 February 2002.

15 Definition of "relevant deposit taker" paras (*e*) and (*f*) repealed by ICC Bank Act 2000 s 7 and the ICC Bank Act 2000 (Sections 5 and 7) (Commencement) Order 2001 (SI No 396 of 2001) with effect from 12 February 2001; previously "(*e*) ICC Bank plc." and "(*f*) ICC Investment Bank Limited.".

16 Definition of "relevant interest" inserted by FA 2001 s 57(1)(*a*)(i)(V) with effect from such date as the Minister for Finance may by order or orders appoint. This amendment came into operation with effect from 1 January 2002 — Finance Act 2001 (Section 57) (Commencement) Order 2001, SI No 596 of 2001, refers.

17 Substituted by FA 2001 s 55(*a*)(iv); previously "on or after the 1st day of January, 1993".

18 Substituted by FA 2001 s 57(1)(*a*)(i)(VI) with effect from such date as the Minister for Finance may by order or orders appoint; previously "deposit taker.". This amendment came into operation with effect from 1 January 2002 — Finance Act 2001 (Section 57) (Commencement) Order 2001, SI No 596 of 2001, refers.

19 Substituted by FA 2002 s 21(*a*)(i) with effect from 1 January 2002; previously "taker.".

20 Definition of "special term account" inserted by FA 2001 s 57(1)(*a*)(i)(VII) with effect from such date as the Minister for Finance may by order or orders appoint. This amendment came into operation with effect from 1 January 2002 — Finance Act 2001 (Section 57) (Commencement) Order 2001, SI No 596 of 2001, refers.

21 Definition of "special term share account" inserted by FA 2002 s 21(*a*)(ii) with effect from 1 January 2002.

Cross-references

Allowance of charges on income, meaning of "building society" applied: s 243(1A).

Approved retirement fund, definition of "qualifying fund manager", meaning of "building society" applied: s 784A(1)(*a*).

Chargeable gains accruing to certain unit trusts, meanings of "deposit" and "relevant deposit" applied: s 731(5)(*c*).

Conditions and declarations relating to special savings accounts, para (*a*) of definition of "special savings account": s 264(1).

Conditions and declarations relating to special term accounts, subparas (i) and (ii) of defintion of "special term account": s 264A(1), (2).

Cross-border pension schemes, exemption of — for purposes of s 256(1), the reference to "an exempt approved scheme within the meaning of section 774" in the definition of "pension scheme" in s 256(1) is deemed to include a reference to a scheme referred to in s 790B(2): s 790B(4).

Declarations relating to deposits of non-residents, para (*g*)(ii) of definition of "relevant deposit": s 263(1).

Deposits of companies and pension schemes, para (*f*) of definition of "relevant deposit": s 265.

Deposits of charities, para (*h*) of definition of "relevant deposit": s 266.

Dividend payments by credit unions, interpretation, meaning of "appropriate tax", "relevant deposit", "relevant deposit taker" "relevant interest" and "special term account" applied: s 267A(1).

Employee share ownership trusts, definition of "relevant deposit taker" applied: Sch 12 para 13(*c*).

Implementation of Council Directive 2003/48/EC of 3 June 2003 on Taxation of Savings Income in the Form of Interest Payments, interpretation, meaning of "building society" and "credit union" applied: s 898B(1).

Information to be furnished by financial institutions, meaning of "deposit" and "interest" applied: s 906A(1).

Interest, etc under certified contractual savings schemes, meaning of "building society" applied: s 519C(1); meaning of "relevant deposit taker" applied: s 519C(3); meaning of "relevant deposit" applied: s 519(4)(*a*).

Interest in respect of wholesale debt instruments, meaning of "relevant deposit" applied: s 246A(3)(*a*)(B), (3)(*b*)(ii)(B).

Interest payments by companies and to non-residents, meaning of "building society" applied: s 246(1)("bank").

Life assurance, personal portfolio life policy, meaning of "building society" applied: s 730BA(1).

Limits to special investments, subs (1): s 839(1)(*a*), (5)(*a*).

Non-commercial State-sponsored bodies, not to be treated as a company within the charge to corporation tax (definition of "relevant deposit" para (*f*)): s 227(4).

Power of inspection: returns and collection of appropriate tax, meaning of "amount on account of appropriate tax", "appropriate tax", "deposit interest", "relevant deposit taker", "relevant interest" and "return" applied: s 904A(1); s 904A(3)(*b*)(ii)(II).
Report to Committee of Public Accounts, publication, etc, meaning of "appropriate tax" and "relevant deposit taker" applied: s 904B(1).
Tax rate applicable to certain deposit interest (arising in a Member State of the European Communities other than the State) received by individuals, meaning of "relevant deposit" applied with modifications: s 267M(1) ("specified interest"); definition of "relevant deposit taker" adapted: s 267M(1)("specified interest").
Taxation of relevant interest, paras (*b*) and (*c*) of the definition of "appropriate tax": s 261(*c*)(i)(II), (III).
Special portfolio investment accounts, subs (1): s 838(3).
Special savings accounts conditions, subs (1): s 264(1)–(2).
Special savings incentive accounts, interpretation, meaning of "deposit" applied: s 848B(1)("deposit account"); meaning of "building society" applied: s 848B(1)("qualifying savings manager"); payment of tax credit, meaning of "deposit" applied: s 848E(3).
Stamp duty, levy on certain financial institutions, meaning of "appropriate tax" applied: SDCA 1999 s 126A(1)(*a*).

Revenue precedents

Issue: Whether a sporting body entitled to exemption under TCA 1997 s 235 would be entitled to receive interest without deduction of tax on the basis of a declaration under TCA 1997 s 265.
Decision: No; since the sporting body would not be within the charge to corporation tax in respect of the interest. Also, the body in question could not complete a declaration to the effect that the interest will be included in the profits of the company on which it will be charged to Corporation Tax, as required by s 265.
Issue: Repayments of DIRT and double taxation conventions.
Decision: Double taxation conventions over-ride the DIRT provisions which preclude repayment of DIRT except in certain circumstances. Where deposit held in trust for non-resident such that the non resident had an absolute interest in the deposit, the interest retains its character as relevant interest when paid to her by the trustee.
Issue: Whether notification of change of residence necessary to make a deposit in relation to which a non-resident declaration was completed a relevant deposit.
Decision: No; where the person who is beneficially entitled to the interest becomes ordinarily resident (now resident) in the State, the deposit automatically becomes a relevant deposit, although we might not seek to penalise a relevant deposit taker who continued to treat such a deposit as not a relevant deposit in good faith.
Issue: Whether deposit held in the name of the EU Commission is a relevant deposit within the meaning of TCA 1997 s 256.
Decision: Deposit is not a relevant deposit, in view of the EC accession treaty and the protocol on privileges and immunities of the European Community.

Definitions

distribution: ss 4(1), 436, 437; person: IA 1937 s 11(*c*); shares: s 5(1); standard rate: ss 3(1), 15; year: IA 1937 Sch.

Former enactments

FA 1986 s 31; FA 1991 s 11; FA 1992 s 22(1)(*a*); F(No 2)A 1992 s 3(*a*); FA 1993 s 15(1)(*a*); FA 1995 s 11(1) and s 167.

Corresponding UK tax provision

Income and Corporation Taxes Act 1988 s 481.

---

257 Deduction of tax from relevant interest

(1) Where a relevant deposit taker makes a payment of relevant interest—

(*a*) the relevant deposit taker shall deduct out of the amount of the payment the appropriate tax in relation to the payment,

(*b*) the person to whom such payment is made shall allow such deduction on the receipt of the residue of the payment, and

(*c*) the relevant deposit taker shall be acquitted and discharged of so much money as is represented by the deduction as if that amount of money had actually been paid to the person.

(2) A relevant deposit taker shall treat every deposit made with it as a relevant deposit unless satisfied that such a deposit is not a relevant deposit; but, where a relevant deposit taker has satisfied itself that a deposit is not a relevant deposit, it shall be entitled to continue to so treat the deposit until such time as it is in possession of information which can reasonably be taken to indicate that the deposit is or may be a relevant deposit.

(3) Any payment of relevant interest which is within subsection (1) shall be treated as not being within section 246.

Cross-references

Dividend payments by credit unions, taxation of dividends on special term share accounts, subs (1): s 267C(5)(*b*)(i); subs (1)(*b*), (*c*): s 267C(5)(*b*)(ii)(II).

Implementation of Council Directive 2003/49/EC of 3 June 2003 on a common system of taxation applicable to interest and royalty payments made between associated companies of different Member States, exemptions from tax and withholding tax: s 267I(1).

Interest accrued but not paid, bringing forward of payment date for deposit interest retention tax: s 260(3)(*a*).

Interest, etc under certified contractual savings schemes: s 519C(3).

Penalty, subs (1): Sch 29 column 3.

Power of inspection: returns and collection of appropriate tax, subs (2): s 904A(3)(*a*).

Returns and collection of appropriate tax: s 258(4B)(*a*)(i).

Revenue offences, subs (1): s 1078(2)(*e*)(i).

Special portfolio investment accounts: s 838(6)(*a*).

Taxation of interest on special term accounts, subs (1): s 261A(7)(i); subs (1)(*b*), (*c*): s 261A(7)(ii)(II).

Revenue precedents

Issue: Is a nil deposit a relevant deposit for the purposes of s 257?

Decision: No.

Issue: Where a parent gives money to a child to open a deposit account and enters into a verbal agreement that the child is to pay over to the parent the deposit interest arising on the deposit, who is beneficially entitled to the deposit interest?

Decision: The parent is beneficially entitled to the deposit interest.

Definitions

appropriate tax, deposit: s 256(1); person: IA 1937 s 11(*c*); relevant deposit, relevant deposit taker, relevant interest: s 256(1).

Former enactments

FA 1986 s 32.

Corresponding UK tax provision

Income and Corporation Taxes Act 1988 ss 480A–480C.

258 Returns and collection of appropriate tax

(1) Notwithstanding any other provision of the Tax Acts, this section shall apply for the purpose of regulating the time and manner in which appropriate tax in relation to a payment of relevant interest shall be accounted for and paid.

(2) Subject to subsection (5), a relevant deposit taker shall make for each year of assessment, within 15 days from the end of the year of assessment, a return to the Collector-General of the relevant interest paid by it in that year and of the appropriate tax in relation to the payment of that interest.

(3) The appropriate tax in relation to a payment of relevant interest which is required to be included in a return shall be due at the time by which the return is to be made and shall be paid by the relevant deposit taker to the Collector-General, and the appropriate tax so due shall be payable by the relevant deposit taker without the making of an

assessment; but appropriate tax which has become so due may be assessed on the relevant deposit taker (whether or not it has been paid when the assessment is made) if that tax or any part of it is not paid on or before the due date.

(4) (*a*) Notwithstanding subsection (3), a relevant deposit taker shall for each year of assessment pay to the Collector-General, within 15 days of the 5th day of October in that year of assessment, an amount on account of appropriate tax.

(*b*) An amount on account of appropriate tax payable under this subsection shall be not less than the amount of appropriate tax which would be due and payable by the relevant deposit taker for the year of assessment concerned under subsection (3) if the total amount of the relevant interest which had accrued in the period commencing on [1 January][1] and ending on the 5th day of October in that year of assessment on all relevant deposits held by the relevant deposit taker in that period (and no more) had been paid by it in that year of assessment.

(*c*) Any amount on account of appropriate tax so paid by the relevant deposit taker for any year of assessment shall be treated as far as may be as a payment on account of any appropriate tax due and payable by it for that year of assessment under subsection (3).

(*d*) For the purposes of paragraph (*b*), interest shall be treated as accruing from day to day if not otherwise so treated.

(*e*) Where the amount on account of appropriate tax paid by a relevant deposit taker for any year of assessment under this subsection exceeds the amount of appropriate tax due and payable by it for that year of assessment under subsection (3), the excess shall be carried forward and shall be set off against any amount due and payable under this subsection or subsection (3) by the relevant deposit taker for any subsequent year of assessment (any such set-off being effected as far as may be against an amount so due and payable at an earlier date rather than at a later date).

[(4A) For the purposes of this section and subject to subsection (4B), interest payable by a relevant deposit taker in respect of a relevant deposit, other than interest which cannot be determined until the date of payment of such interest, notwithstanding that the terms under which the deposit was made are complied with fully, shall be deemed—

(*a*) to accrue from day to day, and

(*b*) to be relevant interest paid by the relevant deposit taker on 31 December in each year of assessment to the extent that—

(i) it is deemed to accrue in that year of assessment, and

(ii) it is not paid in that year of assessment,

and the relevant deposit taker shall account for appropriate tax accordingly.

(4B)(*a*) Where, apart from subsection (4A), a relevant deposit taker makes a payment of relevant interest which is or includes interest (in paragraph (*b*) referred to as **"accrued interest"**) which, by virtue of that subsection, is deemed to have been paid by the relevant deposit taker on 31 December in a year of assessment, the relevant deposit taker shall—

(i) deduct out of the whole of the amount of that payment the appropriate tax in relation to that payment in accordance with section 257, and

(ii) account for that appropriate tax under this section,

and that appropriate tax shall be due and payable by the relevant deposit taker in accordance with this section.

(*b*) So much of the appropriate tax paid by the relevant deposit taker by virtue of subsection (4A) as is referable to accrued interest included in a payment of relevant interest referred to in paragraph (*a*) shall be set off against any amount of appropriate tax due and payable by the relevant deposit taker for the year of assessment in which that payment of interest is made or against any amount, or amount on account of, appropriate tax due and payable by it for a year of assessment subsequent to that year (any such set-off being effected as far as may be against an amount so due and payable at an earlier date rather than a later date).][2]

(5) (*a*) Any amount on account of appropriate tax payable by a relevant deposit taker under subsection (4) shall be so payable without the making of an assessment.

(*b*) The provisions of this Chapter relating to the collection and recovery of appropriate tax shall, with any necessary modifications, apply to the collection and recovery of any amount on account of appropriate tax.

(*c*) A return required to be made by a relevant deposit taker for any year of assessment shall contain a statement of the amount of interest in respect of which an amount on account of appropriate tax is due and payable by the relevant deposit taker for that year of assessment and of the amount on account of appropriate tax so due and payable, and a return shall be so required to be made by a relevant deposit taker for a year of assessment notwithstanding that no relevant interest was paid by it in the year of assessment.

(6) Where it appears to the inspector that there is any amount of appropriate tax in relation to a payment of relevant interest which ought to have been but has not been included in a return, or where the inspector is dissatisfied with any return, the inspector may make an assessment on the relevant deposit taker to the best of his or her judgment, and any amount of appropriate tax in relation to a payment of relevant interest due under an assessment made by virtue of this subsection shall be treated for the purposes of interest on unpaid tax as having been payable at the time when it would have been payable if a correct return had been made.

(7) Where any item has been incorrectly included in a return as a payment of relevant interest, the inspector may make such assessments, adjustments or set-offs as may in his or her judgment be required for securing that the resulting liabilities to tax, including interest on unpaid tax, whether of the relevant deposit taker or any other person, are in so far as possible the same as they would have been if the item had not been so included.

(8) (*a*) Any appropriate tax assessed on a relevant deposit taker under this Chapter shall be due within one month after the issue of the notice of assessment (unless that tax or any amount treated as an amount on account of that tax is due earlier under subsection (3) or (4)) subject to any appeal against the assessment, but no such appeal shall affect the date when any amount is due under subsection (3) or (4).

(*b*) On the determination of an appeal against an assessment under this Chapter, any appropriate tax overpaid shall be repaid.

(9) (*a*) The provisions of the Income Tax Acts relating to—

(i) assessments to income tax,

(ii) appeals against such assessments (including the rehearing of appeals and the statement of a case for the opinion of the High Court), and

(iii) the collection and recovery of income tax,

shall, in so far as they are applicable, apply to the assessment, collection and recovery of appropriate tax.

(*b*) Any amount of appropriate tax or amount on account of appropriate tax payable in accordance with this Chapter without the making of an assessment shall carry interest at the rate of 1.25 per cent for each month or part of a month from the date when the amount becomes due and payable until payment.

(*c*) [Subsections (3) to (5) of section 1080][3] shall apply in relation to interest payable under paragraph (*b*) as they apply in relation to interest payable under section 1080.

(*d*) In its application to any appropriate tax charged by any assessment made in accordance with this Chapter, section 1080 shall apply as if [subsection (2)(*b*)][4] of that section were deleted.

(10) Every return shall be in a form prescribed by the Revenue Commissioners and shall include a declaration to the effect that the return is correct and complete.

Amendments

1 Substituted by FA 2001 s 77(2) and Sch 2 paras 16(*a*) and 61(*e*) for 2002 and later tax years; previously "the 6th day of April".

2 Subs (4A)–(4B) inserted by FA 2001 s 77(2) and Sch 2 paras 16(*b*) and 61(*c*) for short tax "year" 2001 and later tax years.

3 Substituted by FA 2005 s 145(7)(*a*) and Sch 5 Pt 1 in relation to any unpaid income tax, corporation tax or capital gains tax, as the case may be, that has not been paid before 1 April 2005 regardless of when that tax became due and payable and notwithstanding anything to the contrary in any other enactment other than TCA 1997 s 1082; previously "Subsections (2) to (4) of section 1080".

4 Substituted by FA 2005 s 145(7)(*a*) and Sch 5 Pt 1 in relation to any unpaid income tax, corporation tax or capital gains tax, as the case may be, that has not been paid before 1 April 2005 regardless of when that tax became due and payable and notwithstanding anything to the contrary in any other enactment other than TCA 1997 s 1082; previously "subsection (1)(*b*)".

Cross-references

Appropriate tax, amount to be paid on account, alternative calculation: s 259(2)–(4).

Dividend payments by credit unions, supplementary provisions, in applying Pt 8 Ch 4 s 258(4) does not apply: s 267F(2).

Interest accrued but not paid, bringing forward of payment date for deposit interest retention tax: s 260(2)–(4).

Penalty, subs (2): Sch 29 column 2.

Return, subs (2), definition applied: s 256(1).

Revenue offences, subs (3): s 1078(2)(*e*)(ii); subs (4): s 1078(2)(*e*)(iii).

Special portfolio investment accounts: s 838(6)(*a*); subs (2) to apply as if "on or before 31 October following that year of assessment" were substituted for "within 15 days from the end of the year of assessment": s 838(6)(*c*).

Stamp duty, levy on certain financial institutions: SDCA 1999 s 126A(1)(*a*)("relevant person", "relevant retention tax"), (3)(*a*).

Definitions

appropriate tax: s 256(1); Collector General: ss 2(1), 851; High Court: IA 1937 Sch; Income Tax Acts: s 1(2); inspector: ss 2(1), 5(1), 852; month: IA 1937 Sch; person: IA 1937 s 11(*c*); relevant deposit taker, relevant interest: s 256(1); Tax Acts: s 1(2); year of assessment: ss 2(1), 5(1).

Former enactments

FA 1986 s 33(1)–(9)(*d*) and (10); FA 1997 s 146(2) and Sch 9 Pt II.

Corresponding UK tax provision

Income and Corporation Taxes Act 1988 s 482.

259 Alternative amount on account of appropriate tax

(1) For the purposes of this section—

(*a*) interest shall be treated, if not otherwise so treated, as accruing from day to day, and

(*b*) references to **"general crediting date"**, as respects a relevant deposit taker, shall be construed as references to a date on which the relevant deposit taker credits to all, or to the majority, of relevant deposits held by it on that date interest accrued due on those deposits (whether or not the interest is added to the balances on the relevant deposits on that date for the purpose of calculating interest due at some future date).

(2) Where for any year of assessment the amount of appropriate tax due and payable by a relevant deposit taker for that year under section 258 is less than the amount of appropriate tax which would have been so due and payable by the relevant deposit taker for that year if the total amount of the interest which had accrued, in the period of 12 months ending on—

(*a*) the general crediting date as respects that relevant deposit taker falling in that year of assessment,

(*b*) if there is more than one general crediting date as respects that relevant deposit taker falling in that year of assessment, the last such date, or

(*c*) if there is no general crediting date as respects that relevant deposit taker falling in that year of assessment, [31 December][1] in that year,

on all relevant deposits held by the relevant deposit taker in that period (and no more) had been paid by it in that period, this section shall apply to that relevant deposit taker for the year of assessment succeeding that year of assessment and for each subsequent year of assessment.

(3) Notwithstanding anything in section 258, where this section applies to a relevant deposit taker for any year of assessment, section 258(4) shall not apply to the relevant deposit taker for that year of assessment but subsection (4) shall apply to that relevant deposit taker for that year and, as respects that relevant deposit taker for that year, any reference in the Tax Acts (apart from this section) to section 258(4) shall be construed as a reference to subsection (4).

(4) (*a*) Notwithstanding section 258(3), a relevant deposit taker shall for each year of assessment pay to the Collector-General, within 15 days of the 5th day of October in that year of assessment, an amount on account of appropriate tax which shall be not less than the amount determined by the formula set out in the Table to this paragraph, and any amount on account of appropriate tax so paid by the relevant deposit taker for a year of assessment shall be treated as far as may be as a payment on account of any appropriate tax due and payable by it for that year of assessment under section 258(3).

TABLE

A - (B - C)

where—

A is the amount of appropriate tax which would be due and payable by the relevant deposit taker for the year of assessment (in this Table referred to as **"the relevant year"**) in accordance with section 258(3) if the total amount of the relevant interest which had accrued in the period of 12 months ending on the 5th day of October in the relevant year on all relevant deposits held by the relevant deposit taker in that period (and no more) had been paid by it in the relevant year,

B is the amount of appropriate tax which was due and payable by the relevant deposit taker for the year of assessment preceding the relevant year in accordance with section 258(3), and

C is an amount equal to the lesser of the amount at B and the amount treated, in accordance with this subsection or section 258(4), as paid by the relevant deposit taker on account of the appropriate tax due and payable by it for the year of assessment preceding the relevant year.

(*b*) Where the amount on account of appropriate tax paid by a relevant deposit taker for any year of assessment under this subsection exceeds the amount of appropriate tax due and payable by it for that year of assessment under section 258(3), the excess shall be carried forward and shall be set off against any amount due and payable under this subsection or section 258(3) by the relevant deposit taker for any subsequent year of assessment (any such set-off being effected as far as may be against an amount so due and payable at an earlier date rather than at a later date).

Amendments

[1] Substituted by FA 2001 s 77(2) and Sch 2 paras 17(*b*) and 61(*c*) for short tax "year" 2001 and later tax years; previously "the 5th day of April".

Cross-references

Interest accrued but not paid bringing forward of payment date for deposit interest retention tax: s 260(4).

Special portfolio investment accounts: s 838(3).

Stamp duty, levy on certain financial institutions: SDCA 1999 s 126A(1)(*a*) ("relevant person", "relevant retention tax"), (3)(*a*).

Definitions

appropriate tax: s 256(1); Collector-General: ss 2(1), 851; deposit, interest: s 256(1); month: IA 1937 Sch; relevant deposit, relevant deposit taker, relevant interest: s 256(1)(*a*); Tax Acts: s 1(2); year of assessment: ss 2(1), 5(1).

Former enactments

FA 1987 s 7(1)(*a*)–(*b*) and (2)–(4).

260 Provisions supplemental to sections 258 and 259

(1) In this section—

"specified deposit" means a relevant deposit made on or after the 28th day of March, 1996, in respect of which specified interest is payable other than such a deposit—

(*a*) which is held in a special savings account, or

(*b*) in respect of which—

(i) the interest payable is to any extent linked to or determined by changes in a stock exchange index or any other financial index,

(ii) arrangements were, or were being put, in place by the relevant deposit taker before the 28th day of March, 1996, to accept such a deposit, and

(iii) the deposit is made on or before the 7th day of June, 1996;

"specified interest" means interest in respect of a specified deposit, other than so much of the amount of that interest as—

(*a*) is payable annually or at more frequent intervals, or

(*b*) cannot be determined until the date of payment of such interest, notwithstanding that the terms under which the deposit was made are complied with fully.

(2) (*a*) Subject to this section, specified interest shall for the purposes of section 258 be deemed—

(i) to accrue from day to day, and

(ii) to be relevant interest paid by the relevant deposit taker in each year of assessment to the extent that—

(I) it is deemed to accrue in that year of assessment, and

(II) it is not paid in that year of assessment,

and the relevant deposit taker shall account for appropriate tax accordingly.

(*b*) The amount of specified interest deemed to be relevant interest paid by a relevant deposit taker in any year of assessment by virtue of this subsection shall not be less than such amount as would be deductible in respect of interest or any other amount payable on the specified deposit in computing the income of the relevant deposit taker for the year of assessment if the year of assessment were an accounting period of the relevant deposit taker.

(3) (*a*) Where apart from subsection (2) a relevant deposit taker makes a payment of relevant interest which is or includes specified interest, the relevant deposit taker shall—

(i) deduct out of the whole of the amount of that payment the appropriate tax in relation to that payment in accordance with section 257, and

(ii) account for that appropriate tax under section 258,

and that appropriate tax shall be due and payable by the relevant deposit taker in accordance with section 258.

(*b*) So much of the amount of appropriate tax paid by the relevant deposit taker by virtue of subsection (2) as is referable to specified interest included in a payment of relevant interest referred to in paragraph (*a*) shall be set off against any amount of appropriate tax due and payable by the relevant deposit taker for the year of assessment in which that payment of interest is made or against any amount, or amount on account of, appropriate tax due and payable by it for a year of assessment subsequent to that year (any such set-off being effected as far as may be against an amount so due and payable at an earlier date rather than at a later date).

(4) Subsection (2) shall not apply for any year of assessment where, for that year of assessment and all preceding years of assessment—

(*a*) in accordance with section 258(4) or 259(4), as may be appropriate, a relevant deposit taker makes a payment on account of appropriate tax in respect of specified interest as if, in relation to each specified deposit held by it, the references—

(i) in section 258(4), to the period beginning on [1 January][1] and ending on the 5th day of October in the year of assessment, and

(ii) in section 259(4), where it occurs in the meaning assigned to **"A"**, to the period of 12 months ending on the 5th day of October in the relevant year,

were a reference to the period beginning on the date on which the specified deposit was made and ending on the 5th day of October in the year of assessment, and

(*b*) the full amount payable on account of appropriate tax by the relevant deposit taker in that year of assessment in accordance with section 258(4) or 259(4), including any amount payable in accordance with those sections as modified by paragraph (*a*), before the set-off of any amount on account of appropriate tax paid in an earlier year of assessment, does not exceed the appropriate tax payable by the relevant deposit taker for that year of assessment.

Amendments

1 Substituted by FA 2001 s 77(2) and Sch 2 paras 18 and 61(*e*) for 2002 and later tax years; previously "the 6th day of April".

Cross-references

Interpretation, meaning of "specified interest" applied: s 256(1)(para (*c*)(iii) of definition of "appropriate tax").

Definitions

appropriate tax, interest, relevant deposit, relevant deposit taker, relevant interest: s 256(1); year of assessment: s 2(1).

Former enactments

FA 1986 s 33A; FA 1996 s 42; FA 1997 s 146(1) and Sch 9 Pt I para 14.

261 Taxation of relevant interest, etc

Notwithstanding anything in the Tax Acts—

(*a*) no part of any interest paid by a building society in respect of any shares in the society shall be treated for the purposes of the Corporation Tax Acts as a distribution of the society or as franked investment income of any company resident in the State;

(*b*) except where otherwise provided for in section 267, no repayment of appropriate tax in respect of any relevant interest shall be made to any person receiving or entitled to the payment of the relevant interest who is not a company within the charge to corporation tax in respect of the payment;

(*c*) [(i) the amount of any payment of relevant interest shall be regarded as income chargeable to tax under Case IV of Schedule D, and under no other Case or Schedule, and shall be taken into account in computing the total income of the person entitled to that amount, but, in relation to such a person (being an individual)—

(I) except for the purposes of a claim to repayment under section 267(3), the specified amount within the meaning of section 187 or 188 shall, as respects the year of assessment for which he or she is to be charged to income tax in respect of the relevant interest, be increased by the amount of that payment,

(II) the part of taxable income on which he or she is charged to income tax at the standard rate for that year shall be increased by the part of such relevant interest which comes within [paragraph (*b*) of the definition][1] of "appropriate tax" in section 256(1), and

(III) as respects any part of relevant interest which comes within paragraph (*c*) of the definition of "appropriate tax" in section 256(1), the person shall be chargeable to tax at the rate at which tax was deducted from that relevant interest,

and][2]

(ii) where the specified amount is so increased, references in sections 187 and 188 to—

(I) income tax payable shall be construed as references to the income tax payable after credit is given by virtue of section 59 for appropriate tax deducted from the payment of relevant interest, and

(II) a sum equal to twice the specified amount shall be construed as references to a sum equal to the aggregate of—

(A) twice the specified amount (before it is so increased), and

(B) the amount of the payment of relevant interest;

(*d*) section 59 shall apply as if a reference to appropriate tax deductible by virtue of this Chapter were contained in paragraph (*a*) of that section.

Amendments

1 Substituted by FA 2001 s 55(*c*) with effect from 6 April 2001; previously "paragraph (*b*) or the definition".

2 Para (*c*)(i) substituted by FA 2000 s 28(2) with effect from 6 April 2000.

Cross-references

Dividend payments by credit unions, supplementary provisions, s 261 to apply, in relation to any dividends paid on shares held in a special share account or a special term share account which under s 267B is treated in whole or in part as relevant interest paid in respect of a relevant deposit, as if the following were substituted for para (*c*):

"(*c*) the amount of any payment of relevant interest paid in respect of a relevant deposit shall not, except for the purposes of a claim to repayment under section 267(3) in respect of appropriate tax deducted from such relevant interest, be reckoned in computing total income for the purposes of the Income Tax Acts;": s 267F(3)."

Exploration expenditure, para (*b*): s 679(5)(*b*).

Repayment of tax in certain cases (para (*b*)): s 267(2), (3).

Special savings accounts, for para (*c*) read:

"(*c*) the amount of any payment of relevant interest (being relevant interest paid in respect of any relevant deposit held in a special savings account) shall not, except for the purposes of a claim to repayment under section 267(3) in respect of the appropriate tax deducted from such relevant interest, be reckoned in computing total income for the purposes of the Income Tax Acts,": s 264(4).

Taxation of interest on special term accounts, for para (*c*) read:

"(*c*) the amount of any payment of relevant interest paid in respect of any relevant deposit held in a special term account shall not, except for the purposes of a claim to repayment under section 267(3) in respect of the appropriate tax deducted from such relevant interest, be reckoned in computing total income for the purposes of the Income Tax Acts,": s 261A(6).

Non-commercial State sponsored bodies, income exemption applies to income other than under than this Part apart from para (*c*): s 227(4).

Statement of practice

SP-Gen 1/01 — "Underlying Tax" on Funds Deposited in Bogus Non-Resident Accounts.

Tax Briefing

TB18 No 2 of 1995 par 2.2 — Deposit interest retention tax and computation of marginal relief under section 187 or 188.

TB49 August 2002 pp 1–5 — Bogus Non-Resident Accounts.

Definitions

appropriate tax: s 256(1); company: ss 4(1), 5(1); Corporation Tax Acts: s 1(2); distribution: ss 4(1), 436, 437; franked investment income: ss 4(1), 156; interest: s 256(1); higher rate: ss 3(1), 15; person: IA 1937 s 11(*c*); relevant interest: s 256(1); shares: s 5(1); tax: s 3(1); taxable income: ss 3(1), 458: Tax Acts: s 1(2); total income: s 3(1); within the charge to (tax): s 2(1); year of assessment: ss 2(1), 5(1).

Former enactments

FA 1986 s 35(1)(*a*)–(*cc*); FA 1993 s 15(1)(*b*); FA 1994 s 12(1)(*a*).

261A Taxation of interest on special term accounts

[(1) Where interest is paid by a relevant deposit taker in respect of a relevant deposit held in a special term account, such interest shall be relevant interest for the purposes of this Chapter only to the extent provided for in this section.

[(2) Interest paid in a year of assessment in respect of a relevant deposit held in a medium term account shall—

(*a*) be relevant interest only to the extent that such interest exceeds €480, and

(*b*) as respects the first €480 of such interest, be exempt from income tax and shall not be reckoned in computing total income for the purposes of the Income Tax Acts.

(3) Interest paid in a year of assessment in respect of a relevant deposit held in a long term account shall—

(*a*) be relevant interest only to the extent that such interest exceeds €635, and

(*b*) as respects the first €635 of such interest, be exempt from income tax and shall not be reckoned in computing total income for the purposes of the Income Tax Acts.][1]

(4) Where an individual opens a medium term account, the individual may subsequently make an election in writing to the relevant deposit taker to have the account converted to a long term account.

[(5) Where an election is made in accordance with subsection (4), interest paid in a year of assessment which commences on or after the date the election is made shall—

(*a*) be relevant interest only to the extent that such interest exceeds €635, and

(*b*) as respects the first €635 of such interest, be exempt from income tax and shall not be reckoned in computing total income for the purposes of the Income Tax Acts.][2]

(6) Subject to subsection (8), section 261 shall apply in relation to any relevant interest paid in respect of a relevant deposit held in a special term account, as if the following paragraph were substituted for paragraph (*c*) of that section:

"(*c*) the amount of any payment of relevant interest paid in respect of any relevant deposit held in a special term account shall not, except for the purposes of a claim to repayment under section 267(3) in respect of the appropriate tax deducted from such relevant interest, be reckoned in computing total income for the purposes of the Income Tax Acts;".

(7) An account shall cease to be a special term account if any of the conditions specified in section 264A(1) cease to be satisfied, and where that occurs—

(*a*) all interest paid on or after the occurrence in respect of relevant deposits held in the account shall be relevant interest,

(*b*) all interest (in this paragraph referred to as **"past interest"**) paid prior to the occurrence, in respect of relevant deposits held in the account, shall be treated by the relevant deposit taker as relevant interest to the extent that such interest has not already been treated as relevant interest, and—

(i) the provisions of section 257(1) shall apply as if the payment of past interest was being made on the date of the occurrence, and

(ii) where on that date the past interest has already been withdrawn from the account—

(I) the relevant deposit taker shall deduct from the relevant deposits held in the account on that date, an amount equal to the amount of the appropriate tax which would have been deducted from the past interest under subparagraph (i), but for the withdrawal, and such amount shall be treated as appropriate tax, and

(II) the provisions of paragraphs (*b*) and (*c*) of section 257(1) shall apply to such deduction as they apply to a deduction from relevant interest.

(8) Subsection (6) shall not apply to any interest in respect of any relevant deposit held in the account which is paid, or by virtue of subsection (7) treated as paid, on or after the date on which the account ceases to be a special term account.][3]

Amendments

1 Subss (2)–(3) substituted by FA 2002 s 21(*b*)(i) with effect from 1 January 2002.

2 Subs (5) substituted by FA 2002 s 21(*b*)(ii) with effect from 1 January 2002.

3 Section 261A inserted by FA 2001 s 57(1)(*a*)(ii) with effect from such date as the Minister for Finance may by order or orders appoint. This amendment came into operation with effect from 1 January 2002 — Finance Act 2001 (Section 57) (Commencement) Order 2001, SI No 596 of 2001, refers.

Cross-references

Interpretation: s 256(1)("relevant interest").

Definitions

appropriate tax, interest, long term account, medium term account, relevant deposit, relevant deposit taker, relevant interest, special term account: s 256(1); Income Tax Acts: s 1(2); total income: s 3(1); writing: IA 1937 Sch; year of assessment: s 2(1).

262 Statement furnished by relevant deposit taker

A relevant deposit taker shall, when requested to do so by any person entitled to any relevant interest on a relevant deposit held by the relevant deposit taker, furnish to that person, as respects any payment of such relevant interest, a statement showing—

(*a*) the amount of that payment,

(*b*) the amount of appropriate tax deducted from that payment,

(*c*) the net amount of that payment, and

(*d*) the date of that payment.

Definitions

appropriate tax, relevant deposit, relevant deposit taker, relevant interest: s 256(1); person: IA 1937 s 11(*c*).

Former enactments

FA 1986 s 36.

263 Declarations relating to deposits of non-residents

(1) The declaration referred to in paragraph (*g*)(ii) of the definition of **"relevant deposit"** in section 256(1) shall be a declaration in writing to a relevant deposit taker which—

(*a*) is made by a person (in this section referred to as **"the declarer"**) to whom any interest on the deposit in respect of which the declaration is made is payable by the relevant deposit taker and is signed by the declarer,

(*b*) is made in such form as may be prescribed or authorised by the Revenue Commissioners,

(*c*) declares that at the time when the declaration is made the person beneficially entitled to the interest in relation to the deposit is not, or, as the case may be, all of the persons so entitled are not, resident in the State,

(*d*) contains as respects the person or, as the case may be, each of the persons mentioned in paragraph (*c*)—

(i) the name of the person,

(ii) the address of the person's principal place of residence, and

(iii) the name of the country in which the person is resident at the time the declaration is made,

(*e*) contains an undertaking by the declarer that if the person or, as the case may be, any of the persons mentioned in paragraph (*c*) becomes resident in the State, the declarer will notify the relevant deposit taker accordingly, and

(*f*) contains such other information as the Revenue Commissioners may reasonably require for the purposes of this Chapter;

and a declaration made before the 27th day of May, 1986, in a form authorised by the Revenue Commissioners under paragraph (22) of Financial Resolution No. 12 passed by Dáil Éireann on the 30th day of January, 1986, shall be deemed for the purposes of this Chapter to be a declaration of the kind mentioned in this subsection.

(2) (*a*) A relevant deposit taker shall—

(i) keep and retain for the longer of the following periods—

(I) a period of 6 years, and

(II) a period which, in relation to the deposit in respect of which the declaration is made, ends not earlier than 3 years after the date on which the deposit is repaid or, as the case may be, becomes a relevant deposit, and

(ii) on being so required by notice given to it in writing by an inspector, make available to the inspector, within the time specified in the notice,

all declarations of the kind mentioned in subsection (1) which have been made in respect of deposits held by the relevant deposit taker.

(*b*) The inspector may examine or take extracts from or copies of any declarations made available to him or her under paragraph (*a*).

Cross-references

Application to Appeal Commissioners: information from financial institutions, subs (1): s 907(1)(*b*).

Application to High Court seeking order requiring information from financial institutions, subs (1): s 908(1)(a taxpayer).

Conditions relating to an approved minimum retirement fund, subs (2): s 784D(4).

Conditions relating to an approved retirement fund, subs (2): s 784B(4).

Dividend payments by credit unions, conditions and declarations relating to special term share accounts, subs (2) applied by: s 267D(3).

Power of inspection, returns and collection of appropriate tax: s 904A(3)(*b*)(ii)(I).

"Relevant deposit": para (*g*)(ii): s 256(1).

Special savings accounts, subs (2) applied by: s 264(3).

Special term accounts, subs (2) applied by: s 264A(3).

Revenue precedents

Issue: Would micro-film copies of non-resident declarations be sufficient for Revenue Purposes?

Decision: No; the original declarations should be maintained.

Definitions

Dáil Éireann: IA 1937 Sch; deposit: s 256(1); inspector: s 2(1), 852; interest: s 256(1); person: IA 1937 s 11(*c*); relevant deposit taker: s 256(1); writing: IA 1937 Sch; year: IA 1937 Sch.

Former enactments

FA 1986 s 37(1) (apart from para (i) of the proviso) and (2); FA 1995 s 167.

Corresponding UK tax provision

Income and Corporation Taxes Act 1988 s 482A [repealed].

---

264 Conditions and declarations relating to special savings accounts

(1) The following are the conditions referred to in paragraph (*a*) of the definition of **"special savings account"** in section 256(1):

(*a*) the account shall be designated by the relevant deposit taker as a special savings account;

(*b*) the account shall not be denominated in a foreign currency;

(*c*) the account shall not be connected with any other account held by the account holder or any other person; and for this purpose an account shall be connected with another account if—

(i) (I) either account was opened with reference to the other account, or with a view to enabling the other account to be opened on particular terms, or with a view to facilitating the opening of the other account on particular terms, and

(II) the terms on which either account was opened would have been significantly less favourable to the account holder if the other account had not been opened,

or

(ii) the terms on which either account is operated are altered or affected in any way whatever because of the existence of the other account;

(*d*) no withdrawal of money shall be made from the account within the period of 3 months commencing on the date on which it is opened;

(*e*) the terms under which the account is opened shall require the individual to give a minimum notice of 30 days to the relevant deposit taker in relation to the withdrawal of any money from the account;

(*f*) all moneys held in the account shall be subject to the same terms;

(*g*) there shall not be any agreement, arrangement or understanding in existence, whether express or implied, which influences or determines, or could influence or determine, the rate (other than an unspecified and variable rate) of interest which is paid or payable, in respect of the relevant deposit or relevant deposits held in the account, in or in respect of any period which is more than 24 months;

(*h*) interest paid or payable in respect of the relevant deposit or relevant deposits held in the account shall not directly or indirectly be linked to or determined by any change in the price or value of any shares, stocks, debentures or securities listed on a stock exchange or dealt in on an unlisted securities market;

(*i*) the relevant deposit or the aggregate of the relevant deposits held in the account, including any relevant interest added to that deposit or those deposits, shall not at any time exceed [€63,500][1];

(*j*) the account shall not be opened by or held in the name of an individual who is not of full age;

(*k*) the account shall be opened by and held in the name of the individual beneficially entitled to the relevant interest payable in respect of the relevant deposit or relevant deposits held in the account;

(*l*) except in the case of an account opened and held jointly only by a couple married to each other, the account shall not be a joint account;

(*m*) except in the case of an account opened and held jointly only by a couple married to each other, either the same or any other relevant deposit taker shall not simultaneously hold another special savings account opened and held by an individual;

(*n*) in the case of an account opened and held jointly only by a couple married to each other, they shall not simultaneously hold (either with the same or any other relevant deposit taker) any other special savings account either individually or jointly other than one other such account opened and held jointly by them.

(2) The declaration referred to in paragraph (*b*) of the definition of "**special savings account**" in section 256(1) shall be a declaration in writing to a relevant deposit taker which—

(*a*) is made by the individual (in this section referred to as "**the declarer**") to whom any interest payable in respect of the relevant deposit or relevant deposits held in the account in respect of which the declaration is made is payable by the relevant deposit taker, and is signed by the declarer,

(*b*) is made in such form as may be prescribed or authorised by the Revenue Commissioners,

(*c*) declares that at the time when the declaration is made the conditions referred to in paragraphs (*j*) to (*n*) of subsection (1) are satisfied in relation to the account in respect of which the declaration is made,

(*d*) contains the full name and address of the individual beneficially entitled to the interest payable in respect of the relevant deposit or relevant deposits held in the account in respect of which the declaration is made,

(*e*) contains an undertaking by the declarer that, if the conditions referred to in paragraphs (*j*) to (*n*) of subsection (1) cease to be satisfied in respect of the account in respect of which the declaration is made, the declarer will notify the relevant deposit taker accordingly, and

(*f*) contains such other information as the Revenue Commissioners may reasonably require for the purposes of this Chapter.

(3) Subsection (2) of section 263 shall apply as respects declarations of the kind mentioned in this section as it applies as respects declarations of the kind mentioned in that section.

(4) Section 261 shall apply in relation to any relevant interest paid in respect of any relevant deposit held in a special savings account as if the following paragraph were substituted for paragraph (*c*) of that section:

"(*c*) the amount of any payment of relevant interest (being relevant interest paid in respect of any relevant deposit held in a special savings account) shall not, except for the purposes of a claim to repayment under section 267(3) in respect of the appropriate tax deducted from such relevant interest, be reckoned in computing total income for the purposes of the Income Tax Acts,".

(5) An account shall cease to be a special savings account if any of the conditions mentioned in subsection (1) cease to be satisfied, and subsection (4) shall not apply to any relevant interest in respect of any relevant deposit held in the account which is paid on or after the date on which the account ceases to be a special savings account.

Amendments

1 Substituted by FA 2001 s 240(1), (2)(*a*) and Sch 5 Pt 1 for 2002 and later tax years; previously "£50,000".

Cross-references

Limits to special investments, subs (1)(i): s 839(2)(*a*)(i), (*b*)(ii)(I), (3).

"Special savings account", subss (1)–(2): s 256(1).

Special portfolio investment accounts, Part 8 Chapter 4 applies as if subs (1)(*d*)–(i) had not been enacted, and the conditions in s 838(2) had been included in s 264(1): s 838(1)(*c*).

Revenue precedents

Issue: In calculating tax payable under the 1993 Amnesty, whether account is to be taken of DIRT which has been or should have been deducted.

Decision: No account is to be taken of DIRT which has been or should have been deducted. Tax due under amnesty is calculated on income - no credit for DIRT is given against such tax due.

Issue: Whether re-negotiation of interest rates on special savings accounts at two yearly intervals breaches the condition for SSA's that interest cannot be fixed for periods longer than 2 years.

Decision: Whether the condition is breached will depend on the terms of an SSA product. If the interest rate is fixed for two years and genuinely reset after this time, the condition will not be regarded as breached.

Issue: Where a certificate of interest which incorporates DIRT deductions at different rates (ie where the DIRT rate changed from one tax year to the next and the certificate is in respect of a calendar year) how is credit given for the purposes of a repayment of DIRT?

Decision: The amount of DIRT for which credit is to be given is the actual amount of DIRT deducted. In circumstances, it may be necessary to gross up the DIRT at one of the two rates of tax in order to give effect to allowing the correct credit.

Issue: May an SSA be transferred between branches of the same financial institution without triggering closure of the SSA?

Decision: Yes, provided no payment is made to the depositor.

Issue: Where joint SSA held by married couple and one spouse dies can surviving spouse convert the joint account into a single account?

Decision: Yes. Provided that a single SSA declaration is made within a reasonable period and the single SSA limit is observed.

Issue: In the event of an SSA exceeding the £50,000 limit, is time given in which to reduce account balance below the limit (ceases to be SSA over £50,000)?

Decision: Yes. Three working days.

Issue: Are disabled persons required to make and sign an SSA declaration themselves?

Decision: Yes. But if mentally or physically incapable of doing so, another person may do it for them. Revenue requires a medical certificate and details of relationship.

Definitions

appropriate tax, interest, relevant deposit, relevant deposit taker, relevant interest: s 256(1).

Former enactments

FA 1986 s 37A; FA 1992 s 22(1)(*c*); F(No 2)A 1992 s 3(*b*); FA 1993 s 15(1)(*c*); FA 1994 s 12(1)(*b*).

Corresponding UK tax provision

Income and Corporation Taxes Act 1988 s 326A.

264A Conditions and declarations relating to special term accounts

[(1) The following are the conditions referred to in subparagraph (i) of the definition of "special term account" in section 256(1):

(*a*) the account shall be opened and designated by the relevant deposit taker as a medium term account or, as the case may be, a long term account;

(*b*) the account shall not be denominated in a foreign currency;

(*c*) the account shall not be connected with any other account held by the account holder or any other person; and for this purpose an account shall be connected with another account if—

(i) (I) either account was opened with reference to the other account, or with a view to enabling the other account to be opened on particular terms, or with a view to facilitating the opening of the other account on particular terms, and

(II) the terms on which either account was opened would have been significantly less favourable to the account holder if the other account had not been opened,

or

(ii) the terms on which either account is operated are altered or affected in any way whatever because of the existence of the other account;

(*d*) all relevant deposits held in the account shall be subject to the same terms;

(*e*) there shall not be any agreement, arrangement or understanding in existence, whether express or implied, which influences or determines, or could influence or determine, the rate (other than an unspecified and variable rate) of interest which is paid or payable, in respect of the relevant deposit or relevant deposits held in the account, in or in respect of any period which is more than 12 months;

(*f*) interest paid or payable in respect of the relevant deposit or relevant deposits held in the account shall not directly or indirectly be linked to or determined by any change in the price or value of any shares, stocks, debentures or securities listed on a stock exchange or dealt in on an unlisted securities market;

(*g*) the account shall not be opened by or held in the name of an individual who is under 16 years of age;

(*h*) the account shall be opened by and held in the name of the individual beneficially entitled to the relevant interest payable in respect of the relevant deposit or relevant deposits held in the account;

(*i*) the account may be held jointly by not more than 2 individuals;

[(*j*) an individual shall not simultaneously hold whether solely or jointly—

(I) a special term share account, or

(II) subject to paragraph (*k*), another special term account;][1]

(*k*) where the account is held jointly by individuals who are married to each other they may simultaneously hold one other such account jointly;

(*l*) subject to paragraphs (*m*) and (*n*), the amount of a deposit or the aggregate amount of deposits which may be made to an account in any one month shall not exceed [€635];[2]

(*m*) at the time an individual opens an account with a relevant deposit taker, a deposit consisting of all or part of the relevant deposits of the individual which are at that time held by the same relevant deposit taker, may be transferred to the account;

(*n*) otherwise than by way of a transfer under paragraph (*m*) a deposit of not more than [€7,620][3] may be made by an individual once and only once to an account during the period in which the account is a special term account;

(*o*) any interest credited to the account by the relevant deposit taker shall not be treated as a deposit for the purposes of paragraph (l) or (p), but such interest may not be withdrawn from the account, otherwise than in accordance with paragraph (q), unless the withdrawal is made within the period of 12 months from the date it was so credited;

(*p*) subject to paragraph (q), a deposit may not be withdrawn from an account held by an individual within—

(i) 3 years from the date the deposit was made, in the case of a medium term account, and

(ii) 5 years from the date the deposit was made, in the case of a long term account,

otherwise than on the death of the individual or, where the account is an account held jointly by 2 individuals, on the death of one of them;

(*q*) one and only one withdrawal may be made from an account by an individual who is 60 years of age or over on the date of the withdrawal, provided that the account was opened when the individual was under that age.

(2) The declaration referred to in subparagraph (ii) of the definition of "special term account" in section 256(1) shall be a declaration in writing to a relevant deposit taker which—

(*a*) is made by the individual (in this subsection referred to as **"the declarer"**) who holds the account in respect of which the declaration is made ...,[4]

(*b*) is signed by the declarer,

(*c*) is made in such form as may be prescribed or authorised by the Revenue Commissioners,

(*d*) declares that at the time when the declaration is made the conditions referred to in paragraphs (*g*), (*h*), (*j*) and (*k*) of subsection (1) are satisfied in relation to the account in respect of which the declaration is made,

(*e*) contains the full name and address of the declarer,

(*f*) contains an undertaking by the declarer that, if the conditions referred to in paragraphs (*g*), (*h*), (*j*) and (*k*) of subsection (1) cease to be satisfied in respect of the account in respect of which the declaration is made, the declarer will notify the relevant deposit taker accordingly, and

(*g*) contains such other information as the Revenue Commissioners may reasonably require for the purposes of this Chapter.

(3) Section 263(2) shall apply as respects declarations of the kind mentioned in this section as it applies as respects declarations of the kind mentioned in that section.][5]

Amendments

1 Subs (1)(*j*) substituted by FA 2002 s 21(*c*)(i) with effect from 1 January 2002.

2 Substituted by FA 2001 s 57(1)(*a*)(v)(I) for 2002 and later tax years; previously "£500".

3 Substituted by FA 2001 s 57(1)(*a*)(v)(II) for 2002 and later tax years; previously "£6,000".

4 Deleted by FA 2002 s 21(*c*)(ii) with effect from 1 January 2002; previously "is payable".

5 Section 264A inserted by FA 2001 s 57(1)(*a*)(iv) with effect from such date as the Minister for Finance may by order or orders appoint. This amendment came into operation with effect from 1 January 2002 — Finance Act 2001 (Section 57) (Commencement) Order 2001, SI No 596 of 2001, refers.

Cross-references

Interpretation, subs (1) and (2): s 256(1)("special term account").
Taxation of interest on special term accounts, subs (1): s 261A(7).

Definitions

deposit, interest, long term account, medium term account, relevant deposit, relevant deposit taker, special term account: s 256(1); month: IA 1937 Sch; person: IA 1937 s 11(*c*); writing, year: IA 1937 Sch.

264B Returns of special term accounts by relevant deposit takers

[(1) In this section **"appropriate inspector"** means—

(*a*) the inspector who has last given notice in writing to the relevant deposit taker that he or she is the inspector to whom the relevant deposit taker is required to deliver the return referred to in subsection (2), or

(*b*) where there is no such inspector as is referred to in paragraph (*a*), the inspector of returns specified in section 950.

(2) On or before 31 March in each year of assessment, every relevant deposit taker shall prepare and deliver to the appropriate inspector a return, in such form as may be prescribed or authorised by the Revenue Commissioners specifying—

(*a*) the name and address of the holder or holders, as the case may be, of each special term account which was opened during the previous year of assessment,

(*b*) whether such account is a medium term account or a long term account, and

(*c*) the date of opening of such account.

(3) Sections 1052 and 1054 shall apply to a failure by a relevant deposit taker to deliver a return required by subsection (2) and to each and every such failure, as they apply to a failure to deliver a return referred to in section 1052.][1]

Amendments

1 Section 264B inserted by FA 2001 s 57(1)(*a*)(iv) with effect from such date as the Minister for Finance may by order or orders appoint. This amendment came into operation with effect from 1 January 2002 — Finance Act 2001 (Section 57) (Commencement) Order 2001, SI No 596 of 2001, refers.

Cross-references

Penalties: Sch 29, column 2.

Definitions

long term account, medium term account, relevant deposit taker, special term account: s 256(1); inspector: ss 2(1), 852; writing: IA 1937 Sch; year of assessment: s 2(1).

265 Deposits of companies and pension schemes

[Where a return is required to be made by a relevant deposit taker under section 891 in respect of interest on a deposit which is a deposit of a kind referred to in paragraph (*f*) of the definition of "relevant deposit" in section 256, that return shall, in addition to the matters which shall be included on the return by virtue of section 891, include the tax reference number (within the meaning of section 885) of the person beneficially entitled to the interest and where, in the case of a pension scheme, there is no such number, with the number assigned by the Revenue Commissioners to the employer to whom the pension scheme relates.][1]

Amendments

1 Section 265 substituted by FA 2002 s 20(1)(*b*) and applies as respects deposits made on or after 25 March 2002 but, by virtue of FA 2002 s 20(2) (as substituted by FA 2003 s 49(5)) applies, in so far as it relates to a pension scheme, to interest paid or credited on or after 1 January 2003 in respect of a deposit made on or after 25 March 2002.

Cross-references

"Relevant deposit" para (*f*)(ii): s 256(1).

Definitions

deposit, interest, relevant deposit, relevant deposit taker: s 256(1); person, IA 1937 s 11(*c*).

Former enactments

FA 1986 s 37B; FA 1992 s 22(1)(*c*); F(No 2)A 1992 s 3(*c*).

266 Deposits of charities

[Where a return is required to be made by a relevant deposit taker under section 891 in respect of interest on a deposit which is a deposit of a kind referred to in paragraph (*h*) of the definition of "relevant deposit" in section 256, that return shall, in addition to the matters which shall be included on that return by virtue of section 891, include the reference number assigned to that person by the Revenue Commissioners in recognition of that person's entitlement to exemption from tax under section 207 and known as the charity (CHY) number.][1]

Amendments

1 Section 266 substituted by FA 2002 s 20(1)(*c*) and applies (by virtue of FA 2002 s 20(2) (as substituted by FA 2003 s 49(5)) to interest paid or credited on or after 1 January 2003 in respect of a deposit made on or after 25 March 2002.

Revenue information

Information leaflet CHY1 — Applying for Relief from Tax on the Income and Property of Charities.

Definitions

deposit, interest, relevant deposit, relevant deposit taker: s 256(1); `person: IA 1937 s 11(*c*).

Former enactments

FA 1986 s 38.

267 Repayment of appropriate tax in certain cases

(1) In this section, **"relevant person"** means an individual who proves to the satisfaction of the inspector or, on appeal, to the Appeal Commissioners that—

(*a*) at some time during the relevant year the individual or his or her spouse was of the age of 65 years or over, or

(*b*) throughout the relevant year the individual or his or her spouse was, or as on and from some time during the relevant year the individual or his or her spouse became, permanently incapacitated by reason of mental or physical infirmity from maintaining himself or herself.

(2) Notwithstanding section 261(*b*), repayment of appropriate tax in respect of any relevant interest shall be made to a person entitled to exemption in respect of that interest—

(*a*) from income tax under Schedule D by virtue of [section 189A(2) or][1] section 207(1)(*b*), or

(*b*) from corporation tax by virtue of section 207(1)(*b*) as it applies for the purposes of corporation tax by virtue of section 76(6).

(3) Where in any year of assessment (in this subsection referred to as **"the relevant year"**) the total income of a relevant person includes any relevant interest [or would, but for the provisions of section 189(2), section 189A(3) or section 192(2), have included relevant interest,][2] and apart from section 261(*b*) the relevant person would be entitled to repayment of the whole or any part of the appropriate tax deducted from that relevant interest, then, notwithstanding section 261(*b*), the repayment to which the relevant person would be so entitled may be made to the relevant person on the making by the relevant person to the inspector, not earlier than the end of the relevant year, of a claim in that behalf.

Amendments

1 Inserted by FA 1999 s 12(*b*)(i) in respect of relevant interest paid on or after 6 April 1997.

2 Inserted by FA 1999 s 12(*b*)(ii) in respect of relevant interest paid on or after 6 April 1997.

Cross-references

Conditions and declarations relating to special savings accounts, sub (3): s 264(4).

Dividend payments by credit unions, supplementary provisions, subs (3): s 267F(3).

Non-commercial State-sponsored bodies, not to be treated as a person to whom this section applies: s 227(4).

Taxation of interest on special term accounts, subs (3): s 261(6).
Taxation of relevant interest: s 261(*b*), (*c*)(i)(I).

Revenue precedents

Issue: Whether DIRT can be repaid to a mining company where DIRT was deducted from deposit interest because the company failed to complete a declaration under TCA 1997 s 265.
Decision: DIRT cannot be repaid.
Issue: Whether a person suffering from depression and/or ME is considered to be permanently incapacitated for the purposes of entitlement to a repayment of DIRT.
Decision: A person suffering from depression and/or ME will be considered to be permanently incapacitated for the purposes of a DIRT repayment where there is medical evidence to show the condition is permanent.

Revenue information

Information leaflet IT5 — Refund of Deposit Interest Retention Tax.

Definitions

Appeal Commissioners: s 2(1); appropriate tax: s 256(1); inspector: ss 2(1), 5(1), 852; person: IA 1937 s 11(*c*); relevant interest: 256(1); total income: s 3(1); year of assessment: ss 2(1), 5(1).

Former enactments

FA 1986 s 39.

[CHAPTER 5
Dividend Payments by Credit Unions][1]

Amendments

1 Part 8 Ch 5 inserted by FA 2001 s 57(1)(*a*)(vi) with effect from such date as the Minister for Finance may by order or orders appoint. This amendment came into operation with effect from 1 January 2002 — Finance Act 2001 (Section 57) (Commencement) Order 2001, SI No 596 of 2001, refers.

Tax Briefing

TB43 2001 p 18 — Taxation of Credit Union Dividends and Interest.

267A Interpretation (Chapter 5)

[(1) In this Chapter—

"appropriate tax" has the same meaning as in section 256(1);

"dividend" means a dividend on shares declared by a credit union at an annual general meeting of that credit union;

"long term share account" means an account opened by a member (being an individual) with a credit union on terms under which the member has agreed that each share subscribed for by the member to be held in the account is to be held in the account for a period of not less than 5 years;

"medium term share account" means an account opened by a member (being an individual) with a credit union on terms under which the member has agreed that each share subscribed for by the member to be held in the account is to be held in the account for a period of not less than 3 years;

"relevant deposit" has the same meaning as in section 256(1);

"relevant deposit taker" has the same meaning as in section 256(1);

"relevant interest" has the same meaning as in section 256(1);

"savings" includes shares and deposits;

"share" has the same meaning as in section 2(1) of the Credit Union Act, 1997;

"special share account" means an account in which shares subscribed for by a member are held by a credit union on terms under which the member has agreed with the credit union that for the purposes of Chapter 4 of this Part—

(*a*) the value of the shares held in the account at any time is to be treated as an amount of a relevant deposit held by the credit union at that time, and

(*b*) the value of any dividend paid on those shares at any time is to be treated as an amount of relevant interest paid in respect of such relevant deposit by the credit union at that time;

[**"special term account"** has the same meaning as in section 256(1);][1]

"special term share account" means—

(*a*) a medium term share account, or

(*b*) a long term share account,

being an account in which shares subscribed for by a member are held by a credit union and in respect of which—

(i) the conditions specified in section 267D(1) are satisfied, and

(ii) a declaration of the kind mentioned in section 267D(2) has been made to the credit union][2]

[(2) For the purposes of this Chapter the amount of any dividend credited to a member's account shall be treated as if it were a dividend paid, and references in this Chapter to any dividend paid shall be construed accordingly.][3]

Amendments

1 Definition of "special term account" inserted by FA 2002 s 21(*d*)(i) with effect from 1 January 2002.

2 Section 267A inserted by FA 2001 s 57(1)(*a*)(vi) with effect from such date as the Minister for Finance may by order or orders appoint. This amendment came into operation with effect from 1 January 2002 — Finance Act 2001 (Section 57) (Commencement) Order 2001, SI No 596 of 2001, refers.

3 Subs (2) inserted by FA 2002 s 21(*d*)(ii) with effect from 1 January 2002.

Cross-references

Conditions and declarations relating to special term share accounts, subparas (i) and (ii) of definition of "special term share account": s 267D(1), (2).

Deposit interest retention tax, interpretation, meaning of "special term share account" applied: s 256(1).

Special savings incentive accounts, payment of tax credit, meaning of "special share account" applied: s 848C(3A).

Definitions

credit union: s 256(1); year: IA 1937 Sch.

267B Election to open a special share account or a special term share account

[(1) A person, who is a member or is about to become a member of a credit union, may either or both—

(*a*) make an election in writing to the credit union to open an account which is a special share account, and

(*b*) where the person is an individual, make an election in writing to the credit union to open either a medium term share account or a long term share account.

(2) Where an election is made in accordance with subsection (1)(*a*), the credit union shall designate the account as a special share account and shall treat—

(*a*) the value of the shares held in the account at any time, as an amount of a relevant deposit held by it at that time, and

(*b*) the value of any dividend paid on those shares at any time, as an amount of relevant interest paid at that time in respect of such relevant deposit and the provisions of Chapter 4 of this Part shall apply to such relevant interest treated as paid by a credit union as they apply to relevant interest paid by a relevant deposit taker, and the appropriate tax in respect of such relevant interest shall be at a rate of 20 per cent.

(3) Where an election is made in accordance with subsection (1)(*b*), the credit union shall treat—

(*a*) the value of the shares held in the account at any time, as an amount of a relevant deposit held by it at that time, and

(*c*) subject to section 267C, the value of any dividend paid on those shares at any time, as an amount of relevant interest paid at that time in respect of such relevant deposit and the provisions of Chapter 4 of this Part shall apply to such relevant interest treated as paid by the credit union as they apply to relevant interest paid by a relevant deposit taker, and the appropriate tax in respect of such relevant interest shall be at a rate of 20 per cent.][1]

Amendments

[1] Section 267B inserted by FA 2001 s 57(1)(*a*)(vi) with effect from such date as the Minister for Finance may by order or orders appoint. This amendment came into operation with effect from 1 January 2002 — Finance Act 2001 (Section 57) (Commencement) Order 2001, SI No 596 of 2001, refers.

Cross-references

Penalties: Sch 29 column 3.
Special savings incentive accounts, payment of tax credit, subs (2): s 848C(3A).
Supplementary provisions: s 267F(3).

Definitions

appropriate tax: s 267A(1); credit union: s 256(1); dividend, long term share account, medium term share account: s 267A(1); person: IA 1937 s 11(*c*); relevant deposit, relevant deposit taker, relevant interest, share, special share account: s 267A(1); writing: IA 1937 Sch.

267C Taxation of dividends on special term share accounts

[(1) The value of the dividend paid in a year of assessment on shares held in a medium term share account shall—

(*a*) be treated as an amount of relevant interest paid in that year of assessment only to the extent that such value exceeds €480, and

(*b*) as respects the first €480 of such value, be exempt from income tax and shall not be reckoned in computing total income for the purposes of the Income Tax Acts.

(2) The value of the dividend paid in a year of assessment on shares held in a long term share account shall—

(*a*) be treated as an amount of relevant interest paid in that year of assessment only to the extent that such value exceeds €635, and (*b*) as respects the first €635 of such value, be exempt from income tax and shall not be reckoned in computing total income for the purposes of the Income Tax Acts.][1]

(3) Where an account is opened by a member as a medium term share account, the member may subsequently make an election in writing to the credit union to have the account converted to a long term share account.

[(4) Where an election is made in accordance with subsection (3), the value of the dividend paid on shares in a year of assessment which commences on or after the date the election is made shall—

(*a*) be treated as an amount of relevant interest paid in that year of assessment only to the extent that such value exceeds €635, and

(*b*) as respects the first €635 of such value, be exempt from income tax and shall not be reckoned in computing total income for the purposes of the Income Tax Acts.][2]

(5) An account shall cease to be a special term share account if any of the conditions specified in subsection (1) of section 267D cease to be satisfied, and where that occurs—

(*a*) the account shall be treated as a special share account from the time of the occurrence, and

(*b*) the value of all dividends (in this paragraph referred to as **"past dividends"**) paid prior to the occurrence, on shares held in the account, shall be treated by the credit union as an amount of relevant interest to the extent that the value of such dividends has not already been treated as an amount of relevant interest, and—

(i) the provisions of section 257(1) shall apply as if the payment of past dividends was being made on the date of the occurrence, and

(ii) where on that date the past dividends have already been withdrawn from the account—

(I) the credit union shall deduct from the value of the shares in the account on that date, an amount equal to the amount of the appropriate tax which would have been deducted from the past dividends under subparagraph (i), but for the withdrawal, and such amount shall be treated as appropriate tax, and

(II) the provisions of paragraphs (*b*) and (*c*) of section 257(1) shall apply to such deduction as they apply to a deduction from relevant interest.][3]

Amendments

1 Subss (1)–(2) substituted by FA 2002 s 21(*e*)(i) with effect from 1 January 2002.

2 Subs (4) substituted by FA 2002 s 21(*e*)(ii) with effect from 1 January 2002.

3 Section 267C inserted by FA 2001 s 57(1)(*a*)(vi) with effect from such date as the Minister for Finance may by order or orders appoint. This amendment came into operation with effect from 1 January 2002 — Finance Act 2001 (Section 57) (Commencement) Order 2001, SI No 596 of 2001, refers.

Cross-references

Election to open a special share account or a special term share account: s 267B(3)(*b*).

Definitions

appropriate tax: s 267A(1); credit union: s 256(1); dividend, long term share account, medium term share account, relevant interest, shares, special share account, special term share account: s 267A(1); Income Tax Acts: s 1(2); total income: s 3(1); writing: IA 1937 Sch; year of assessment: s 2(1).

267D Conditions and declarations relating to special term share accounts

[(1) The following are the conditions referred to in subparagraph (i) of the definition of **"special term share account"** in section 267A(1):

(*a*) the account shall be opened and designated by the credit union as a medium term share account or, as the case may be, a long term share account;

(*b*) the account shall not be denominated in a foreign currency;

(*c*) the account shall not be connected with any other share account or deposit account held by the member or any other person; and for this purpose an account shall be connected with another account if—

(i) (I) either account was opened with reference to the other account, or with a view to enabling the other account to be opened on particular terms, or with a view to facilitating the opening of the other account on particular terms, and

(II) the terms on which either account was opened would have been significantly less favourable to the member if the other account had not been opened,

or

(ii) the terms on which either account is operated are altered or affected in any way whatever because of the existence of the other account;

(*d*) all shares held in the account shall be subject to the same terms;

(*e*) there shall not be any agreement, arrangement or understanding in existence, whether express or implied, which influences or determines, or could influence or determine, the rate (other than an unspecified and variable rate) of dividend which is paid or payable, in respect of the share or shares held in the account, in or in respect of any period which is more than 12 months;

(*f*) dividends paid or payable in respect of the share or shares held in the account shall not directly or indirectly be linked to or determined by any change in the price or value of any shares, stocks, debentures or securities listed on a stock exchange or dealt in on an unlisted securities market;

(*g*) the account shall not be opened by or held in the name of a member who is under 16 years of age;

(*h*) the account shall be opened by and held in the name of the member beneficially entitled to the dividend payable in respect of the share or shares held in the account;

(*i*) an account may be held jointly by not more than 2 individual members;

[(*j*) a member shall not simultaneously hold whether solely or jointly—

(I) a special term account, or

(II) subject to paragraph (*k*), another special term share account;][1]

(*k*) where the account is held jointly by individuals who are married to each other they may simultaneously hold one other such account jointly;

(*l*) subject to paragraphs (*m*) and (*n*) the amount of a subscription or aggregate amount of subscriptions for shares which may be added to an account in any one month shall not exceed [€635];[2]

(*m*) at the time a member opens an account with a credit union, a single subscription for shares consisting of all or part of the savings of the member which are already held by the same credit union, may be transferred to the account;

(*n*) otherwise than by way of a transfer under paragraph (*m*), shares at a cost of not more than [€7,620][3] may be added by a member once and only once to an account during the period in which the account is a special term share account;

(*o*) any disbursement of the surplus funds of a credit union, in the form of dividends or rebate of loan interest, which is added to the account shall not be treated as a subscription for shares for the purposes of paragraph (*l*) or (*p*), but such dividend or rebate of loan interest may not be withdrawn from the account, otherwise than in accordance with paragraph (*q*), unless the withdrawal is made within the period of 12 months from the date it was so added;

(*p*) subject to paragraph (*q*), a share may not be withdrawn from an account held by a member within—

- (i) 3 years from the date the share was subscribed for, in the case of a medium term share account, and
- (ii) 5 years from the date the share was subscribed for, in the case of a long term share account,

otherwise than on the death of the member or, where the account is an account held jointly by 2 members, on the death of one of them;

(*q*) one and only one withdrawal may be made from an account by a member who is 60 years of age or over on the date of the withdrawal, provided that the account was opened when the member was under that age;

(*r*) a transfer of shares from an account by a credit union to reduce a balance outstanding on a loan from the credit union to a member shall not be treated as a withdrawal from the account for the purposes of paragraph (*p*) where—

- (i) such shares were pledged as security for the loan at the time the loan was granted,
- (ii) a default (whether of interest or otherwise) in the terms of the repayment of the loan of not less than 6 months has occurred, and
- (iii) the credit union has followed its standard procedures in seeking to recover the loan.

(2) The declaration referred to in subparagraph (ii) of the definition of **"special term share account"** in section 267A(1) shall be a declaration in writing to the credit union which—

(*a*) is made by the member (in this subsection referred to as **"the declarer"**) who holds the account in respect of which the declaration is made …[4],

(*b*) is signed by the declarer,

(*c*) is made in such form as may be prescribed or authorised by the Revenue Commissioners, (*d*) declares that at the time when the declaration is made the conditions referred to in paragraphs (*g*), (*h*), (*j*) and (*k*) of subsection (1) are satisfied in relation to the account in respect of which the declaration is made,

(*e*) contains the full name and address of the declarer,

(*f*) contains an undertaking by the declarer that, if the conditions referred to in paragraphs (*g*), (*h*), (*j*) and (*k*) of subsection (1) cease to be satisfied in respect of the account in respect of which the declaration is made, the declarer will notify the credit union accordingly, and

(*g*) contains such other information as the Revenue Commissioners may reasonably require for the purposes of this Chapter.

(3) Section 263(2) shall apply as respects declarations of the kind mentioned in this section as it applies as respects declarations of the kind mentioned in that section.][5]

Amendments

1 Subs (1)(*j*) substituted by FA 2002 s 21(*f*)(i) with effect from 1 January 2002.

2 Substituted by FA 2001 s 57(1)(*a*)(viii)(I) for 2002 and later tax years; previously "£500".

3 Substituted by FA 2001 s 57(1)(*a*)(viii)(II) for 2002 and later tax years; previously "£6,000".

4 Deleted by FA 2002 s 21(*f*)(ii) with effect from 1 January 2002; previously "is payable".

5 Section 267D inserted by FA 2001 s 57(1)(*a*)(vi) with effect from such date as the Minister for Finance may by order or orders appoint. This amendment came into operation with effect from 1 January 2002 — Finance Act 2001 (Section 57) (Commencement) Order 2001, SI No 596 of 2001, refers.

Cross-references

Interpretation, subs (1): s 267A(1)("special term share account").

Taxation of dividends on special term share accounts, subs (1): s 267C(5).

Definitions

credit union: s 256(1); dividend, long term share account, medium term share account: s 267A(1); month: IA 1937 Sch; person: IA 1937 s 11(*c*); share, special term share account: s 267A(1); year, writing: IA 1937 Sch.

267E Returns of special term share accounts by credit unions

[(1) In this section **"appropriate inspector"** means—

(*a*) the inspector who has last given notice in writing to the credit union that he or she is the inspector to whom the credit union is required to deliver the return required under subsection (2), or

(*b*) where there is no such inspector as is referred to in paragraph (*a*), the inspector of returns specified in section 950;

(2) On or before 31 March in each year of assessment, every credit union shall prepare and deliver to the appropriate inspector a return, in such form as may be prescribed or authorised by the Revenue Commissioners specifying—

(*a*) the name and address of the holder or holders, as the case may be, of each special term share account which was opened during the previous year of assessment,

(*b*) whether the account is a medium term share account or a long term share account, and

(*c*) the date of opening of such account.

(3) Sections 1052 and 1054 shall apply to a failure by a credit union to deliver a return required by subsection (2) and to each and every such failure, as they apply to a failure to deliver a return referred to in section 1052.][1]

Amendments

[1] Section 267E inserted by FA 2001 s 57(1)(*a*)(vi) with effect from such date as the Minister for Finance may by order or orders appoint. This amendment came into operation with effect from 1 January 2002 — Finance Act 2001 (Section 57) (Commencement) Order 2001, SI No 596 of 2001, refers.

Cross-references

Penalties: Sch 29, column 2.

Definitions

credit union: s 256(1); inspector: ss 2(1), 852; long term share account, medium term share account, special term share account: s 267A(1); writing: IA 1937 Sch; year of assessment: s 2(1).

267F Supplementary provisions (Chapter 5)

[(1) The provisions of section 904A shall apply to a credit union, treated under this Chapter as paying relevant interest, as they apply to a relevant deposit taker paying relevant interest.

(2) In applying Chapter 4 of this Part for the purposes of this Chapter, section 258(4) shall not apply.

(3) Section 261 shall apply in relation to any dividend paid on shares held in a special share account or a special term share account which under section 267B is treated in whole or in part as relevant interest paid in respect of a relevant deposit, as if the following paragraph were substituted for paragraph (*c*) of that section:

"(*c*) the amount of any payment of relevant interest paid in respect of a relevant deposit shall not, except for the purposes of a claim to repayment under section 267(3) in respect of the appropriate tax deducted from such relevant interest, be reckoned in computing total income for the purposes of the Income Tax Acts;".][1]

Amendments

[1] Section 267F inserted by FA 2001 s 57(1)(*a*)(vi) with effect from such date as the Minister for Finance may by order or orders appoint. This amendment came into operation with effect from 1 January 2002 — Finance Act 2001 (Section 57) (Commencement) Order 2001, SI No 596 of 2001, refers.

Definitions

appropriate tax: s 267A(1); credit union: s 256(1); dividend: s 267A(1); Income Tax Acts: s 1(2); relevant deposit, relevant deposit taker, relevant interest, special share account, special term share account: s 267A(1).

[CHAPTER 6

Implementation of Council Directive 2003/49/EC of 3 June 2003 on a common system of taxation applicable to interest and royalty payments made between associated companies of different Member States

Amendments

[1] Chapter 6 (ss 267G–267K) substituted by FA 2004 s 41(1) and Sch 1 (originally inserted by the European Communities (Abolition of Withholding Tax on Certain Interest and Royalties) Regulations 2003 which were revoked by FA 2004 s 41(2)).

267G Interpretation (Chapter 6)

[(1) In this Chapter—

"arrangements" means arrangements having the force of law by virtue of section 826(1)(*a*);

"bilateral agreement" means any arrangements, protocol or other agreement between the Government and the government of another state;

"permanent establishment" means a fixed place of business through which the business of a company of a Member State is wholly or partly carried on which place of business is situated in a territory other than that Member State;

"company" means a company of a Member State;

"company of a Member State" has the meaning assigned to it by Article 3(*a*) of the Directive;

[**"the Directive"** means Council Directive 2003/49/EC of 3 June 2003 [OJ No L 157, 26.6.2003, p 49] as amended by Council Directive 2004/66/EC of 26 April 2004 [OJ No L 168, 1.5.2004, p 35] and Council Directive 2004/76/EC of 29 April 2004 [OJ No L 195, 2.6.2004,p.33];][1]

"interest" means income from debt-claims of every kind, whether or not secured by mortgage and whether or not carrying a right to participate in the debtor's profits, and in particular, income from securities and income from bonds or debentures, including premiums and prizes attaching to such securities, bonds or debentures but does not include penalty charges for late payment;

"Member State" means a Member State of the European Communities;

"royalties" means payments of any kind as consideration for

(*a*) the use of, or the right to use—

(i) any copyright of literary, artistic or scientific work, including cinematograph films and software,

(ii) any patent, trade mark, design or model, plan, secret formula or process,

(*b*) information concerning industrial, commercial or scientific experience;

(*c*) the use of, or the right to use, industrial, commercial or scientific equipment;

"tax", in relation to a Member State other than the State, means any tax imposed in that Member State which is specified in Article 3(*a*)(iii) of the Directive.

(2) For the purposes of this Chapter—

(*a*) a company shall be treated as an **"associated company"** of another company during an uninterrupted period of at least 2 years throughout which—

(i) one of them directly controls not less than 25 per cent of the voting power of the other company, or

(ii) in respect of those companies, a third company directly controls not less than 25 per cent of the voting power of each of them, (*b*) a permanent establishment of a company in a Member State shall be treated as being the beneficial owner of interest or royalties if—

(i) the debt-claim, right or asset in respect of which the interest arises, or as the case may be the royalties arise, consists of property or rights used by, or held by or for, the permanent establishment, and

(ii) the interest or royalties are taken into account in computing income of the permanent establishment which is subject to one of the taxes specified in Article 1.5(*b*) or Article 3(*a*)(iii) of the Directive,

(*c*) a word or expression used in this Chapter and in the Directive has, unless the contrary intention appears, the same meaning in this Chapter as in the Directive.][2]

Amendments

2 Definition of "the Directive" substituted by European Communities (Exemption from Tax for Certain Interest and Royalties Payments) Regulations 2004 (2004 No 644) reg 4 with effect for payments made on or after 1 May 2004.

2 Section 267G substituted by FA 2004 s 41(1) and Sch 1.

Cross-references

Application of this Chapter to certain payments made to companies in Switzerland: s 267L(2), (3).

Miscellaneous: s 267K(1).

Definitions

company: ss 4(1), 5(1); profits: s 4(1); year: IA 1937 Sch.

267H Application (Chapter 6)

[(1) Subject to subsection (2), this Chapter shall apply to a payment, being interest or royalties, made—

(*a*) by either—

(i) a company resident in the State, or

(ii) a company not so resident which carries on a trade in the State through a permanent establishment if, in relation to the trade the interest gives, or as the case may be the royalties give, rise to a deduction under section 81 or 97 or relief under Part 8,

(*b*) to or for the benefit of—

(i) where subparagraph (ii) does not apply, a company which—

(I) is the beneficial owner of the interest, or as the case may be the royalties, and

(II) is, by virtue of the law of a Member State other than the State, resident for the purposes of tax in such a Member State,

or

(ii) a permanent establishment—

(I) which is situated in a Member State (in this subparagraph referred to as the **"first Member State"**) other than the State,

(II) which is treated as the beneficial owner of the interest, or as the case may be the royalties, and

(III) through which a company, which is (by virtue of the law of a Member State other than the State) resident for the purposes of tax in such a Member State, carries on a business in the first Member State,

if the company referred to in paragraph (*a*) is an associated company of the company referred to in paragraph (*b*).

(2) This Chapter shall not apply to—

(*a*) interest or royalties paid—

(i) to a company where the debt-claim, right or asset in respect of which the payment is made consists of property or rights used by, or held by or for, a permanent establishment of the company through which the company carries on a trade—

(I) in the State, or

(II) in a territory which is not a Member State,

or

(ii) by a company for the purposes of a business carried on by it through a permanent establishment in a territory which is not a Member State,

(*b*) interest on a debt-claim in respect of which there is no provision for repayment of the principal amount or where the repayment is due more than 50 years after the creation of the debt, or

(*c*) so much of any royalties paid as exceeds the amount which would have been agreed by the payer, and the beneficial owner, of the royalties if they were independent persons acting at arms' length.

Amendments

1 Section 267H substituted by FA 2004 s 41(1) and Sch 1.

Cross-references

Application of this Chapter to certain payments made to companies in Switzerland: s 267L(2), (3).
Miscellaneous: s 267K(1).

Definitions

company: ss 4(1), 5(1); interest: s 267G(1); Member State: s 267G(1); permanent establishment: s 267G(1); person: IA 1937 s 11(*c*); royalties: s 267G(1); tax: s 267G(1); trade: ss 3(1), 4(1), 5(1); year: IA 1937 Sch.

267I Exemptions from tax and withholding tax

(1) Where, apart from this section, section 238, 246(2) or 257 would apply to a payment of interest or royalties to which this Chapter applies, those sections shall not apply to that payment.

(2) A company which, by virtue of the law of a Member State other than the State, is resident for the purposes of tax in that Member State, shall not be chargeable to corporation tax or income tax in respect of interest or royalties to which this Chapter applies except where the interest is, or as the case may be the royalties are, paid to the company in connection with a trade which is carried on in the State by that company through a permanent establishment.

Amendments

1 Section 267I substituted by FA 2004 s 41(1) and Sch 1.

Cross-references

Allowance of charges on income: s 243(5)(*c*).

Application of this Chapter to certain payments made to companies in Switzerland: s 267L(2), (3).

Miscellaneous: s 267K(1).

Definitions

company: ss 4(1), 5(1); interest: s 267G(1); Member State: s 267G(1); permanent establishment: s 267G(1); royalties: s 267G(1); tax: s 267G(1); trade: ss 3(1), 4(1), 5(1).

267J Credit for foreign tax

[[(1) Where interest or royalties are received by a company resident in the State from an associated company, credit shall be allowed for any withholding tax charged on the interest or royalties by a Member State pursuant to the derogations duly given from Article 6 of the Directive against corporation tax in respect of such interest and royalties to the extent that credit for such withholding tax would not otherwise be so allowed.][1]

[(2) Where by virtue of subsection (1) a company is to be allowed credit for tax payable under the laws of a Member State other than the State, Schedule 24 shall apply for the purposes of that subsection as if that subsection were arrangements providing that the tax so payable shall be allowed as a credit against tax payable in the State.][2]

(3) This section applies without prejudice to a provision of a bilateral agreement.][3]

Amendments

1 Subs (1) substituted by European Communities (Exemption from Tax for Certain Interest and Royalties Payments) Regulations 2004 (2004 No 644) reg 4 with effect for payments made on or after 1 May 2004.

2 Subs (2) substituted by FA 2005 s 147 and Sch 6 para 1(*d*) with effect from 1 January 2004.

3 Section 267J substituted by FA 2004 s 41(1) and Sch 1.

Cross-references

Miscellaneous: s 267K(1).

Definitions

bilateral agreement: s 267G(1); company: ss 4(1), 5(1); the Directive: s 267G(1); interest: s 267G(1); Member State: s 267G(1); royalties: s 267G(1); tax: s 267G(1).

267K Miscellaneous

(1) Sections 267G, 267H, 267I and 267J shall not apply to interest or royalties unless it can be shown that the payment of the interest or royalties was made for bona fide commercial reasons and does not form part of any arrangement or scheme of which the main purpose or one of the main purposes is avoidance of liability to income tax, corporation tax or capital gains tax.

(2) Where a company which—

(*a*) is entitled to receive a payment of interest or royalties from any person, and

(*b*) had received from that person a payment of interest or royalties which was exempt from tax in accordance with the Directive,

ceases to fulfil the requirements specified in the Directive for exemption to apply, the company shall without delay inform that person that it has so ceased.][1]

Amendments

[1] Section 267K substitued by FA 2004 s 41(1) and Sch 1.

Cross-references

Application of this Chapter to certain payments made to companies in Switzerland, this section applies in relation to s 267L as it applies in relation to ss 267G to 267I: s 267L(3).
Miscellaneous: s 267K(1).

Definitions

company: ss 4(1), 5(1); the Directive: s 267G(1); interest: s 267G(1); person: IA 1937 s 11(c); royalties: s 267G(1); tax: s 267G(1).

267L Application of this Chapter to certain payments made to companies in Switzerland

[(1) This section applies to a payment, being interest or royalties, made to or for the benefit of—

(*a*) where paragraph (*b*) does not apply, a company which—

(i) is the beneficial owner of the interest, or as the case may be the royalties,

(ii) is, by virtue of the law of Switzerland, resident for the purposes of tax in Switzerland, and

(iii) is not treated, by virtue of any arrangements made by the government of Switzerland with the government of any territory for the purposes of tax, as resident in any territory which is not—

(I) a Member State of the European Communities, or

(II) Switzerland,

or

(*b*) a permanent establishment situated in Switzerland through which a company carries on business in Switzerland, being a permanent establishment which would, in accordance with the Directive, be treated as the beneficial owner of the interest, or as the case may be the royalties.

(2) Sections 267G to 267I shall have effect in relation to a payment to which this section applies as if—

(*a*) a reference in those sections to a Member State of the European Communities included a reference to Switzerland,

(*b*) a reference in those sections to a company of a Member State included a company (being a company which takes one of the forms specified in Article 15 of the Agreement attached to the Council Decision (2004/911/EC) of 2 June 2004 on the signing and conclusion of the Agreement between the European Community and the Swiss Confederation providing for measures equivalent to those laid down in Council Directive 2003/48/EC of 3 June 2003 on taxation of savings income in the form of interest payments and the accompanying Memorandum of Understanding (OJ No L385, 29.12.2004, p 28)) resident for the purposes of tax in Switzerland, and

(*c*) a reference in those sections to tax included any tax imposed in Switzerland which corresponds to income tax or corporation tax in the State.

(3) Section 267K applies in relation to this section as it applies in relation to sections 267G to 267I.][1]

Amendments

[1] Section 267L inserted by FA 2005 s 50(1) as respects any payment made on or after 1 July 2005.

Definitions

company: ss 4(1), 5(1); company of a Member State: s 267G(1); the Directive: s 267G(1); interest: s 267G(1); permanent establishment: s 267G(1); royalties: s 267G(1); tax: s 267G(1).

[CHAPTER 7
Certain interest from sources within the European Communities][1]

Amendments

[1] Chapter 7 (s 267M) inserted by FA 2005 s 20(1) for 2005 and subsequent years of assessment.

267M Tax rate applicable to certain deposit interest received by individuals

[(1) In this section—

"specified interest" means interest arising in a Member State of the European Communities other than the State which would be interest payable in respect of a relevant deposit within the meaning of section 256(1) if—

(*a*) in the definition of **"relevant deposit"** in section 256(1)—

(i) the following were substituted for paragraphs (*c*) and (*d*):

"(*c*) which, in the case of a relevant deposit taker which, by virtue of the law of a Member State of the European Communities other than the State, is resident for the purposes of tax in such a Member State, is held at a branch of the relevant deposit taker situated in a territory which is not a Member State,

(*d*) which, in the case of a relevant deposit taker not so resident in a Member State of the European Communities for the purposes of tax, is held otherwise than at a branch of the relevant deposit taker situated in a Member State,"

and

(ii) paragraph (*g*) were deleted,

and

(*b*) there were included in the definition of **"relevant deposit taker"** in section 256(1) bodies established in accordance with the law of any Member State of the European Communities other than the State which corresponds to—

(i) the Credit Union Act 1997,

(ii) the Trustee Savings Banks Acts 1989 and 2001, or

(iii) the Post Office Savings Bank Acts 1861 to 1958;

"tax" in relation to a Member State other than the State means tax which corresponds to income tax or corporation tax in the State.

(2) (*a*) Notwithstanding any provision of the Income Tax Acts and subject to paragraph (*b*), the amount of taxable income on which a person who is an individual is charged to income tax at the standard rate for any year shall be increased by an amount equal to the amount of specified interest of that person on which income tax for that year falls to be computed.

(*b*) Paragraph (*a*) shall not apply where any liability of the individual for a year of assessment in respect of the specified interest has not been discharged on or before the specified return date for the chargeable period (within the meaning of section 950) for that year.][1]

Amendments

1 Section 267M inserted by FA 2005 s 20(1) for 2005 and subsequent years of assessment.

Definitions

Income Tax Acts: s 1(2); standard rate: s 3(1); taxable income: s 3(1); year of assessment: s 2(1).

PART 9
PRINCIPAL PROVISIONS RELATING TO RELIEF FOR CAPITAL EXPENDITURE

Cross-references

Business entertainment expenses: s 840(3)(*a*).

Capital allowances for buildings used for certain childcare purposes: s 843A(2)(*a*).

Capital allowances for buildings used for third level educational purposes: s 843(2)(*a*).

Capital expenditure on scientific research: 765(5).

Capital gains tax, exclusion of sums chargeable to income tax: s 551(3).

Change in ownership of a company, disallowance of trading losses: s 401(5).

Farming buildings expenditure: s 658(6).

Group relief, exclusion of double allowances etc: s 428(6).

Industrial and provident societies, expenses: s 699(2)(*a*).

Leased plant and machinery, restriction on use of allowances: s 404(4)(*a*).

Loss relief, meaning of "balancing charges" applied: s 391(1).

Mine development allowance: s 670(6).

Mine rehabilitation expenditure: s 681(9).

Mining machinery or plant: s 678(7).

Multi-storey car parks, transitional: Sch 32 para 9(2).

Non-resident company within the charge to corporation tax in respect of one source and income tax in respect of another: s 309.

Partnerships and European Economic Interest Groupings, meaning of "balancing charge" applied: s 1007(1).

Petroleum trade, abandonment expenditure and loss relief: s 695(8).

Petroleum trade, exploration expenditure: s 693(12), (13).

Reorganisation of companies into Trustee Savings Banks, capital allowances: Sch 17 para 2(1)(*a*).

Restriction of loss relief: s 455(6).

Shipping tonnage tax, capital allowances, general: s 697O(1), (2), (3); deferment of balancing charge on re-investment: Sch 18B, para 18(1)(*a*); exit, plant and machinery: Sch 18B, para 19(1), (2), (3)(*b*); exit, plant and machinery: Sch 18B, para 19(1), (2), (3)(*b*); plant and machinery used wholly for tonnage tax trade: Sch 18B, para 10(1)(*b*)(ii), (2)(*b*)(ii)(III)(C), (*c*)(iii); plant and machinery used partly for tonnage tax trade: Sch 18B, para 11(2)(*b*); plant and machinery, new expenditure partly for tonnage tax trade: Sch 18B, para 12(2); plant and machinery, change of use of tonnage tax asset: Sch 18B, para 13(2)(*a*), (*b*)(ii); plant and machinery, provisions relating to balancing charges: Sch 18B, para 15(1), (4); reduction in balancing charge by reference to time in tonnage tax: Sch 18B, para 16; set-off of accrued losses against balancing charges: Sch 18B, para 17.

Taxation of certain short-term leases of plant and machinery: s 80A(2)(*b*).

Tax credit for research and development expenditure: s 766(1)(*a*)("expenditure on research and development").

Tax credit on expenditure on buildings or structures used for research and and development: s 766A(1)(*a*)("relevant expenditure on a building or structure").

Training of local staff before commencement of trading: s 769(3).

CHAPTER 1

Industrial Buildings or Structures: Industrial Building Allowances, Writing-Down Allowances, Balancing Allowances and Balancing Charges

Cross-references

Farming buildings expenditure: s 658(12).
Farming pollution control capital expenditure: s 659(11).
Petroleum trade, development expenditure: s 692(4).
Restriction of relief to individuals in respect of loans applied in acquiring interest in companies: s 250A(1)("specified building").
Restriction on use of capital allowances on certain hotels: s 409B(2)–(4).
Restriction on use of capital allowances on certain industrial buildings and other premises: s 409A(1) (specified building), (2), (3), (5).
Ring-fence on use of certain capital allowances on certain industrial buildings and other premises: s 409E(1)("specified building"), (2)(*c*), (3)(*a*).
Shipping tonnage tax, industrial buildings: Sch 18B, para 20(1), (4).

Renewal incentives

Custom House Dock area, commercial premises: s 323(2)(*a*); double rent allowance: s 324(1)(*a*) (qualifying premises).
Designated area or street, commercial premises: s 342(2)(*a*); double rent allowance: s 345(1)(*a*) (qualifying premises).
Designated areas in certain towns, capital allowances for commercial premises: s 372AD(2)(*a*)(i).
Dublin Docklands Area, commercial premises: s 369(2)(*a*); double rent allowance: s 370(1)(*a*) (qualifying premises), (5).
Enterprise area building: s 343(7)(*a*).
Multi-storey car parks: s 344(2)(*a*), (8).
Park and ride facilities, capital allowances for qualifying park and ride facilities: s 372V(1)(*a*); capital allowances for certain commercial premises: s 372W(2)(*a*)(i).
Qualifying areas, commercial premises: s 372D(2)(*a*); double rent allowance: s 372E(1) (qualifying premises), (5), (6).
Qualifying rural areas, commercial buildings or structures: s 372N(2)(*a*); double rent allowance: s 372O(1) (qualifying premises).
Resort areas, commercial premises: s 353(2)(*a*), (8); double rent allowance: s 354(1) (qualifying premises); holiday cottages, disclaimer of capital allowances: s 355(2)(*a*), (*b*), (3)(*a*).
Room ownership schemes, denial of allowances: s 409(4).
Temple Bar area, buildings: s 332(2)(*a*); double rent allowance: s 333(1)(*a*) (qualifying premises).

Tax Briefing

TB37 Oct 1999 p 9 — Capital allowances — property held in joint names (married couples).
TB42 Dec 2000 p 28–29 — Plant in leased buildings.

268 Meaning of "industrial building or structure"

(1) In this Part, **"industrial building or structure"** means a building or structure in use—

(*a*) for the purposes of a trade carried on in—

(i) a mill, factory or other similar premises, or

(ii) a laboratory the sole or main function of which is the analysis of minerals (including oil and natural gas) in connection with the exploration for, or the extraction of, such minerals,

(*b*) for the purposes of a dock undertaking,

(*c*) for the purposes of growing fruit, vegetables or other produce in the course of a trade of market gardening within the meaning of section 654,

(*d*) for the purposes of the trade of hotel-keeping,

(*e*) for the purposes of the intensive production of cattle, sheep, pigs, poultry or eggs in the course of a trade other than the trade of farming within the meaning of [section 654,][1]

(*f*) for the purposes of a trade which consists of the operation or management of an airport and which is an airport runway or an airport apron used solely or mainly by aircraft carrying passengers or cargo for hire or reward,

[(*g*) for the purposes of a trade which consists of the operation or management of a nursing home [(in this section referred to as a "registered nursing home")][2] within the meaning of section 2 of the Health (Nursing Homes) Act, 1990, being a nursing home which is registered under [section 4 of that Act,][3]][4]

[(*h*) for the purposes of a trade which consists of the operation or management of an airport, other than a building or structure to which [paragraph (*f*) relates, ...[5]][6]][7]

[(*i*) for the purposes of a trade which consists of the operation or management of a convalescent home for the provision of medical and nursing care for persons recovering from treatment in a hospital, being a hospital that provides treatment for acutely ill patients, and in respect of which convalescent home [the Health Service Executive][8] is satisfied that the convalescent home satisfies the requirements of sections 4 and 6 of the Health (Nursing Homes) Act, 1990, and any regulations made under section 6 of that Act as if it were a nursing home within the meaning of section 2 of [that Act, ...[9]][10]][11]

[(*j*) for the purposes of a trade which consists of the operation or management of a [qualifying hospital, or][12]][13]

[(*k*) for the purposes of a trade which consists of the operation or management of a qualifying sports injuries clinic,][14]

and in particular, in relation to capital expenditure incurred on or after the 6th day of April, 1969, includes any building or structure provided by the person carrying on such a trade or undertaking for the recreation or welfare of workers employed in that trade or undertaking and in use for that purpose.

[(1A) Where the relevant interest in relation to capital expenditure incurred on the construction of a building or structure in use for the purposes specified in subsection (1)(*j*) is held by—

(*a*) a company,

(*b*) the trustees of a trust,

(*c*) an individual who is involved in the operation or management of the qualifying hospital concerned either as an employee or director or in any other capacity, or

(*d*) a property developer (within the meaning of section 372A), in the case where either such property developer or a person connected with such property developer incurred the capital expenditure on the construction of that building or structure,

then, notwithstanding that subsection, that building or structure [shall not, as regards a claim for any allowance under this Part by any such person, be regarded as an industrial building or structure][15] for the purposes of this Part, irrespective of whether that relevant interest is held by the person referred to in paragraph (*a*), (*b*), (*c*) or (*d*), as the case may be, in a sole capacity or jointly or in partnership with another person or persons.][16]

[(1B) Where the relevant interest in relation to capital expenditure incurred on the construction of a building or structure in use for the purposes specified in subsection (1)(*k*) is held by—

(*a*) a company,

(*b*) the trustees of a trust,

(*c*) an individual who is involved in the operation or management of the qualifying sports injuries clinic concerned either as an employee or director or in any other capacity, or

(*d*) a property developer (within the meaning of section 372A), in the case where either such property developer or a person connected with such property developer incurred the capital expenditure on the construction of that building or structure,

then, notwithstanding that subsection, that building or structure [shall not, as regards a claim for any allowance under this Part by any such person, be regarded as an industrial building or structure][17] for the purposes of this Part, irrespective of whether that relevant interest is held by the person referred to in paragraph (*a*), (*b*), (*c*) or (*d*), as the case may be, in a sole capacity or jointly or in partnership with another person or persons.][18]

(2) In this section, **"dock"** includes any harbour, wharf, pier or jetty or other works in or at which vessels can ship or unship merchandise or passengers, not being a pier or jetty primarily used for recreation, and **"dock undertaking"** shall be construed accordingly.

[(2A) In this section—

...[19]

"qualifying hospital" means a hospital (within the meaning of the Tobacco (Health Promotion and Protection) Regulations, 1995 (SI No 359 of 1995)) which—

(*a*) is a private hospital (within the meaning of the Health Insurance Act, 1994 (Minimum Benefits) Regulations, 1996 (SI No 83 of 1996)),

...[20]

(*c*) has the capacity to provide and normally provides medical and surgical services to persons every day of the year,

[(*d*) has the capacity to provide—

(i) out-patient services and accommodation on an overnight basis of not less than 70 in-patient beds, or

(ii) day-case and out-patient medical and surgical services and accommodation for such services of not less than 40 beds,][21]

(*e*) contains an operating theatre or theatres and related on-site diagnostic and therapeutic facilities,

(*f*) contains facilities to provide not less than 5 of the following services:

(i) accident and emergency,

(ii) cardiology and vascular,

(iii) eye, ear, nose and throat,

(iv) gastroenterology,

(v) geriatrics,

(vi) haematology,

(vii) maternity,
(viii) medical,
(ix) neurology,
(x) oncology,
(xi) orthopaedic,
(xii) respiratory,
(xiii) rheumatology, and
(xiv) paediatric,

(*g*) undertakes to [the Health Service Executive][22]—

(i) to make available annually, for the treatment of persons who have been awaiting in-patient or out-patient hospital services as public patients, not less than 20 per cent of its capacity, subject to service requirements to be specified by [the Health Service Executive][23] in advance and to the proviso that nothing in this subparagraph shall require the [the Health Service Executive][23] to take up all or any part of the capacity made available to [the Health Service Executive][23] by the hospital, and

(ii) in relation to the fees to be charged in respect of the treatment afforded to any such person, that such fees shall not be more than 90 per cent of the fees which would be charged in respect of similar treatment afforded to a person who has private medical insurance,

and

(*h*) in respect of which [the Health Service Executive][24], in consultation with the Minister for Health and Children and with the consent of the Minister for Finance, [gives, during the period of 7 years referred to in section 272(4)(*h*), an annual certificate in writing][25] stating that it is satisfied that the hospital complies with the conditions mentioned in paragraphs (*a*), (*c*), (*d*), (*e*), (*f*) and (*g*),

[and—

(I) includes any part of the hospital which consists of rooms used exclusively for the assessment or treatment of patients, but

(II) does not include any part of the hospital which consists of consultants' rooms or offices.][26][27]

[(2B) In this section "qualifying sports injuries clinic" means a medical clinic—

(*a*) which does not (other than by virtue of paragraph (*e*)) provide health care services to a person pursuant to his or her entitlements under Chapter II of Part IV of the Health Act 1970,

(*b*) in which the sole or main business carried on is the provision, by or under the control of medical or surgical specialists, of health care consisting of the diagnosis, alleviation and treatment of physical injuries sustained by persons in participating, or in training for participation, in athletic games or sports,

(*c*) which has the capacity to provide day-patient, in-patient and out-patient medical and surgical services and in-patient accommodation of not less than 20 beds,

(*d*) which contains an operating theatre or theatres and related on-site diagnostic and therapeutic facilities, (*e*) which undertakes to [the Health Service Executive][28]—

(i) to make available annually, for the treatment of persons who have been awaiting day-patient, in-patient or out-patient hospital services as public patients, not less than 20 per cent of its capacity, subject to service requirements to be specified by [the Health Service Executive][29] in advance and to the condition that nothing in this subparagraph shall require [the Health Service Executive][29] to take up all or any part of the capacity made available to [the Health Service Executive][29] by the medical clinic, and

(ii) in relation to the fees to be charged in respect of the treatment afforded to any such person, that such fees shall not be more than 90 per cent of the fees which would be charged in respect of similar treatment afforded to a person who has private medical insurance,

and

(*f*) in respect of which [the Health Service Executive][30], in consultation with the Minister for Health and Children and with the consent of the Minister for Finance, gives, during the period of 7 years referred to in section 272(4)(*h*), an annual certificate in writing stating that it is satisfied that the medical clinic complies with the conditions mentioned in paragraphs (*a*) to (*e*),

and—

(I) includes any part of the clinic which consists of rooms used exclusively for the assessment or treatment of patients, but

(II) does not include any part of the clinic which consists of consultants' rooms or offices.][31]

[(2C) For the purposes of this Part, a building or structure (other than a building or structure which is in use for the purposes of the trade of hotel-keeping) which is in use as—

(*a*) a guest house and is registered in the register of guest houses kept under the Tourist Traffic Acts 1939 to 2003, or

(*b*) a holiday hostel and is registered in the register of holiday hostels kept under the Tourist Traffic Acts 1939 to 2003,

shall, as respects capital expenditure incurred on or after 3 February 2005 on its construction (within the meaning of section 270), be deemed to be a building or structure in use for the purposes of the trade of hotel-keeping.][32]

(3) For the purpose of this Part, a building or structure in use as [a holiday camp registered in the register of holiday camps kept under the Tourist Traffic Acts 1939 to 2003][33] or, in relation to capital expenditure incurred on or after the 1st day of July, 1968, a building or structure in use as a holiday cottage and comprised in premises registered in any register of holiday cottages established by Bord Fáilte Éireann under any Act of the Oireachtas passed on or after the 29th day of July, 1969, [shall, subject to subsection (13), be deemed][34] to be a building or structure in use for the purposes of the trade of hotel-keeping.

[(3A) In this section **"qualifying residential unit"** means a house which—

(*a*) is constructed on the site of, or on a site which is immediately adjacent to the site of, a registered nursing home,

(*b*) is—

(i) a single storey house, or

(ii) a house that is [comprised in a building of one or more storeys in relation to which building a fire safety certificate under Part III of the Building Control Regulations 1997 (SI No 496 of 1997) (as amended from time to time) is required, and prior to the commencement of the construction works on the building, is granted by the building control authority (within the meaning of section 2 of the Building Control Act 1990, as amended by the Local Government (Dublin) Act 1993 and the Local Government Act 2001) in whose functional area the building is situated],[35]

where—

(I) the house is, or (as the case may be) the house and the building in which it is comprised are, designed and constructed to meet the needs of persons with disabilities, including in particular the needs of persons who are confined to wheelchairs, and

(II) the house consists of 1 or 2 bedrooms, a kitchen, a living room, bath or shower facilities, toilet facilities and a nurse call system linked to the registered nursing home,

(*c*) is comprised in a development of [not less than 10 qualifying residential units][36] where—

(i) that development also includes a day-care centre,

(ii) those units are operated or managed by the registered nursing home and an on-site caretaker is provided,

(iii) back-up medical care, including nursing care, is provided by the registered nursing home to the occupants of those units when required by those occupants,

(iv) not less than 20 per cent of those units are made available for renting to persons who are eligible for a rent subsidy from [the Health Service Executive][37], subject to service requirements to be specified by [the Health Service Executive][38] in advance and to the condition that nothing in this subparagraph shall require [the Health Service Executive][38] board to take up all or any of the units so made available, and

(v) the rent to be charged in respect of any such unit made available in accordance with subparagraph (iv) is not more than 90 per cent of the rent which would be charged if that unit were rented to a person who is not in receipt of a subsidy referred to in that subparagraph,

and

(*d*) is leased to a person or persons who has or have been certified, by a person who is registered in the register established under section 26 of the Medical Practitioners Act, 1978, as requiring such accommodation by reason of old age or infirmity.

(3B) For the purposes of this Part but subject to subsection (3C), as respects capital expenditure incurred in the period of 5 years commencing on the date of the passing of the Finance Act, 2002, a building or structure in use as a qualifying residential unit shall be deemed to be a building or structure in use for the purposes of a trade referred to in subsection (1)(*g*).

(3C) Subsection (3B) shall not apply in respect of expenditure incurred on the construction of a qualifying residential unit where any part of that expenditure has been or is to be met, directly or indirectly, by grant assistance or any other assistance which is granted by or through the State, any board established by statute, any public or local authority or any other agency of the State.][39]

(4) Where capital expenditure is incurred on preparing, cutting, tunnelling or levelling land for the purposes of preparing the land as a site for the installation of machinery or plant, the machinery or plant shall, as regards that expenditure, be treated for the purposes of this Chapter as a building or structure.

(5) For the purposes of this Part, expenditure incurred by a person on or after the 23rd day of April, 1996, either on the construction of, or on the acquisition of the relevant interest in, a building or structure not situated in the State shall not be treated as expenditure on a building or structure within the meaning of this section unless, being a building or structure not situated in the State—

(*a*) it is a building or structure which is to be constructed or which is in the course of construction and in respect of which it can be shown that—

(i) the person has either entered into a binding contract in writing for the acquisition of the site for the building or structure or has entered into an agreement in writing in relation to an option to acquire that site on or before the 23rd day of April, 1996,

(ii) the person has entered into a binding contract in writing for the construction of the building or structure on or before the 1st day of July, 1996, and

(iii) the construction of the building or structure had commenced on or before the 1st day of July, 1996, and had been completed before the [30th day of September, 1998][40],

and

(*b*) it is a building or structure to be constructed or which is being constructed which will be used for the purposes of a trade the profits or gains from which are taxable in the State.

(6) Subsection (1) shall apply in relation to a part of a trade as it applies in relation to a trade but, where part only of a trade complies with the conditions set out in that subsection, a building or structure shall not by virtue of this subsection be an industrial building or structure unless it is in use for the purposes of that part of that trade.

(7) (*a*) In this subsection, **"retail shop"** includes any premises of a similar character where retail trade or business (including repair work) is carried on.

(*b*) Notwithstanding anything in subsections (1) to (6) but subject to subsection (8), in this Part, **"industrial building or structure"** does not include any building or structure in use as, or as part of, a dwelling house (other than a holiday cottage referred to in subsection (3) [or a qualifying residential unit][41]), retail shop, showroom or office or for any purpose ancillary to the purposes of a dwelling house (other than a holiday cottage referred to in subsection (3) [or a qualifying residential unit][41]), retail shop, showroom or office.

(8) Where part of the whole of a building or structure is, and part of the whole of the building or structure is not, an industrial building or structure, and the capital expenditure incurred on the construction of the second-mentioned part is not more than 10 per cent of the total capital expenditure incurred on the construction of the whole building or structure, the whole building or structure and every part of the whole of the building or structure shall be treated as an industrial building or structure.

(9) Subsection (1) shall apply—

(*a*) by reference to paragraph (*a*)(ii), as respects capital expenditure incurred on or after the 25th day of January, 1984,

(*b*) by reference to paragraph (*e*), as respects capital expenditure incurred on or after the 6th day of April, 1971, ...[42]

(*c*) by reference to paragraph (*f*), as respects capital expenditure incurred on or after the 24th day of April, [1992,][43]

[(*d*) by reference to paragraph (*g*), as respects capital expenditure incurred on or after the 3rd day of December, 1997, ...[44]][45]

[(*e*) by reference to paragraph (*h*), as respects capital expenditure incurred—

(i) by Aer Rianta cuideachta phoiblí theoranta on or after the vesting day, and

[(ii) by any other person on or after the date of the passing of the Finance Act, 1998, ...[46]][47]][48]

[(*f*) by reference to paragraph (*i*), as respects capital expenditure incurred on or after the 2nd day of December, [1998, ...[49]][50]][51]

[(*g*) by reference to paragraph (*j*), as respects capital expenditure incurred on or after the date of the coming into operation of section 64 of the Finance Act, [2001, and][52]][53]

[(*h*) by reference to paragraph (*k*), as respects capital expenditure incurred on or after the date of the coming into operation of section 32 of the Finance Act 2002.][54]

[(10) For the purposes of this Part, **"the vesting day"** has the same meaning as it has in the Bill presented to Dáil Éireann by the Minister for Public Enterprise on the 2nd day of October, 1997, providing, amongst other things, for the vesting of Dublin Airport, Shannon Airport and Cork Airport in Aer Rianta cuideachta phoibli theoranta.][55]

[(11) Notwithstanding any other provision of this section, as respects capital expenditure incurred on or after 20 March 2001, a building or structure in use for the purposes of the trade of hotel-keeping shall not be treated as an industrial building or structure where any part of that expenditure has been or is to be met, directly or indirectly, by [grant assistance or any other assistance which is granted by or through the State, any board established by statute, any public or local authority or any other agency of the State][56].

(12) Notwithstanding any other provision of this section, as respects capital expenditure incurred on the construction or refurbishment of a building or structure in respect of which construction or refurbishment first commences on or after [6 April 2001 (being capital expenditure in respect of which but for this subsection a writing-down allowance

in excess of 4 per cent would be available under section 272 for a chargeable period),][57] a building or structure in use for the purposes of the trade of hotel-keeping shall not be treated as an industrial building or structure unless, on the making of an application by the person who incurs the capital expenditure on the construction or refurbishment of the building or structure, Bord Fáilte Éireann gives a certificate in writing to that person, in relation to that expenditure, stating—

[(*a*) that it has received a declaration from that person as to whether or not that person is—

(i) a small or medium-sized enterprise within the meaning of Annex I to Commission Regulation (EC) No 70/2001 of 12 January 2001 on the application of Articles 87 and 88 of the European Communities Treaty to State aid to small and medium-sized enterprises (OJ No L10 of 13 January 2001, p 33), or

(ii) a micro, small or medium-sized enterprise within the meaning of the Annex to Commission Recommendation of 6 May 2003 concerning the definition of micro, small and medium-sized enterprises (OJ No L124 of 20 May 2003, p 36),][58]

[(*b*) that the expenditure concerned falls within the meaning of "initial investment" contained in point 4.4 of the "Guidelines on National Regional Aid" (OJ No C 74, 10.3.1998, p 9) prepared by the Commission of the European Communities,

[(*c*) that, in the case of expenditure incurred on or after 1 January 2003 on the construction or refurbishment of a building or structure provided for the purposes of a project which is subject to the notification requirements of—

(i) the "Multisectoral framework on regional aid for large investment projects" (OJ No C 107, 7.4.1998, p.7) prepared by the Commission of the European Communities and dated 7 April 1998, or

(ii) the "Multisectoral framework on regional aid for large investment projects" (OJ No C 70, 19.3.2002, p.8) prepared by the Commission of the European Communities and dated 19 March 2002,

as the case may be, approval of the potential capital allowances involved has been received from that Commission by the Minister for Finance, or by such other Minister of the Government, agency or body as may be nominated for that purpose by the Minister for Finance, and][59]

(*d*) that such person has undertaken to furnish to the Minister for Finance, or to such other Minister of the Government, agency or body as may be nominated for that purpose by the Minister for Finance, upon request in writing by the Minister concerned or that agency or body, such further information as may be necessary to enable compliance with the reporting requirements of—

(i) [the Regulation or Recommendation][60] referred to in paragraph *(a)* or the Multisectoral framework referred to in paragraph (*c*),

(ii) "Community guidelines on State aid for rescuing and restructuring firms in difficulty" (OJ No C 288, 9.10.1999, p 2) prepared by the Commission of the European Communities [or, as the case may be, "Community guidelines on State aid for rescuing and restructuring firms in difficulty" (OJ No C244 of 1 October 2004, p 2) prepared by that Commission][61], or

(iii) any other European Communities Regulation or Directive under the European Communities Treaty governing the granting of State aid in specific sectors.][62][63]

[(13)(*a*) Notwithstanding subsection (3) but subject to paragraph (*b*), a holiday cottage referred to in that subsection shall not, as respects capital expenditure incurred on or after 4 December 2002 on its construction (within the meaning of section 270), be deemed to be a building or structure in use for the purposes of the trade of hotel-keeping.

(*b*) This subsection shall not apply as respects expenditure incurred on or before [31 July 2006][64] on the construction or refurbishment of a holiday cottage if—

(i) (I) a planning application (not being an application for outline permission within the meaning of section 36 of the Planning and Development Act 2000)[, in so far as planning permission is required,][65] in respect of the holiday cottage is made in accordance with the Planning and Development Regulations 2001 to 2002,

(II) an acknowledgement of the application, which confirms that the application was received on or before [31 December 2004][66], is issued by the planning authority in accordance with article 26(2) of the Planning and Development Regulations 2001 (SI No 600 of 2001), and

(III) the application is not an invalid application in respect of which a notice is issued by the planning authority in accordance with article 26(5) of those regulations,

...[67]

(ii) (I) [a planning application, in so far as planning permission was required,][68] in respect of the holiday cottage was made in accordance with the Local Government (Planning and Development) Regulations 1994 (SI No 86 of 1994), not being an application for outline permission within the meaning of article 3 of those regulations,

(II) an acknowledgement of the application, which confirms that the application was received on or before 10 March 2002, was issued by the planning authority in accordance with article 29(2)(*a*) of the regulations referred to in clause (I), and

(III) the application was not an invalid application in respect of which a notice was issued by the planning authority in accordance with article 29(2)(*b*)(i) of those [regulations,][69]

[or

(iii) where the construction or refurbishment work on the holiday cottage represented by that expenditure is exempted development for the purposes of the Planning and Development Act 2000 by virtue of section 4 of that Act or by virtue of Part 2 of the Planning and Development Regulations 2001 (SI No 600 of 2001) and—

(I) a detailed plan in relation to the development work is prepared,

(II) a binding contract in writing, under which the expenditure on the development is incurred, is in existence, and

(III) work to the value of 5 per cent of the development costs is carried out, not later than 31 December 2004.][70]][71]

[(14) Subject to subsection (15), a building or structure in use for the purposes of the trade of hotel-keeping (but not including a building or structure deemed to be such a building or structure) shall not, as respects capital expenditure incurred on or after 3 February 2005 on its construction (within the meaning of section 270), be treated as an industrial building or structure unless the building or structure is registered in the register of hotels kept under the Tourist Traffic Acts 1939 to 2003.

(15) Subsection (14) shall not apply as respects capital expenditure incurred on or before 31 July 2006 on the construction or refurbishment of a building or structure in use for the purposes of the trade of hotel-keeping if—

(*a*) (i) a planning application (not being an application for outline permission within the meaning of section 36 of the Planning and Development Act 2000), in so far as planning permission was required, in respect of the construction or refurbishment work on the building or structure represented by that expenditure, was made in accordance with the Planning and Development Regulations 2001 to 2004,

(ii) an acknowledgement of the application, which confirms that the application was received on or before 31 December 2004, was issued by the planning authority in accordance with article 26(2) of the Planning and Development Regulations 2001 (SI No 600 of 2001), and

(iii) the application was not an invalid application in respect of which a notice was issued by the planning authority in accordance with article 26(5) of those regulations,

(*b*) (i) a planning application, in so far as planning permission was required, in respect of the construction or refurbishment work on the building or structure represented by that expenditure, was made in accordance with the Local Government (Planning and Development) Regulations 1994 (SI No 86 of 1994), not being an application for outline permission within the meaning of article 3 of those regulations,

(ii) an acknowledgement of the application, which confirms that the application was received on or before 10 March 2002, was issued by the planning authority in accordance with article 29(2)(*a*) of the regulations referred to in subparagraph (i), and

(iii) the application was not an invalid application in respect of which a notice was issued by the planning authority in accordance with article 29(2)(*b*)(i) of those regulations,

(*c*) where the construction or refurbishment work on the building or structure represented by that expenditure is exempted development for the purposes of the Planning and Development Act 2000 by virtue of section 4 of that Act or by virtue of Part 2 of the Planning and Development Regulations 2001 (SI No 600 of 2001), and—

(i) a detailed plan in relation to the development work was prepared,

(ii) a binding contract in writing, under which the expenditure on the development is incurred, was in existence, and

(iii) work to the value of 5 per cent of the development costs was carried out, not later than 31 December 2004, or

(*d*) (i) the construction or refurbishment of the building or structure is a development in respect of which an application for a certificate under section 25(7)(*a*)(ii) of the Dublin Docklands Development Authority Act 1997 was made to the Authority (within the meaning of that Act),

(ii) an acknowledgement of the application, which confirms that the application was received on or before 31 December 2004, was issued by that Authority, and

(iii) the application was not an invalid application.][72]

Notes

The Air Navigation and Transport (Amendment) Act, 1998 (Vesting Day) Order 1998, SI No 326 of 1998, appointed 1 January 1999 as vesting day for the purposes of the Air Navigation and Transport (Amendment) Act, 1998.

Amendments

1 Substituted by FA 1998 s 22(*a*)(i)(I) with effect from 6 April 1998; previously "section 654, or".

2 Inserted by FA 2002 s 33(*a*) with effect from 1 January 2002.

3 Substituted by FA 1999 s 48(*a*)(i)(I) with effect from 6 April 1999; previously "section 4 of that Act, or".

4 Subs (1)(*g*) inserted by FA 1998 s 22(*a*)(i)(II) with effect from 6 April 1998.

5 Substituted by FA 1999 s 48(*a*)(i)(II) with effect from 6 April 1999; previously "paragraph (*f*) relates,".

6 Deleted by FA 2001 s 64(1)(*a*)(i)(I) with effect from such day as the Minister for Finance may by order appoint; previously "or,". By virtue of the Finance Act, 2001 (Commencement of Section 64) Order 2002, FA 2001 s 64 comes into operation as on and from 15 May 2002.

7 Subs (1)(*h*) inserted by FA 1998 s 20(*a*)(i) with effect from 6 April 1998.

8 Substituted by FA 2005 s 147 and Sch 6 para 1(*e*)(i) with effect from 25 March 2005; previously "the health board in whose functional area the convalescent home is situated,".

9 Deleted by FA 2002 s 34(1)(*a*)(i)(I) with effect from such day as the Minister for Finance may by order appoint; previously "or". By virtue of the Finance Act, 2002 (Commencement of Section 34) Order 2002, FA 2002 s 34 comes into operation as on and from 15 May 2002.

10 Substituted by FA 2001 s 64(1)(*a*)(i)(II) with effect from such day as the Minister for Finance may by order appoint; previously "that Act.". By virtue of the Finance Act, 2001 (Commencement of Section 64) Order 2002, FA 2001 s 64 comes into operation as on and from 15 May 2002.

11 Subs (1)(*i*) substituted by FA 2000 s 36 with effect from 6 April 2000.

12 Substituted by FA 2002 s 34(1)(*a*)(i)(I) with effect from such day as the Minister for Finance may by order appoint; previously "qualifying hospital". By virtue of the Finance Act, 2002 (Commencement of Section 34) Order 2002, FA 2002 s 34 comes into operation as on and from 15 May 2002.

13 Subs (1)(*j*) inserted by FA 2001 s 64(1)(*a*)(i)(III) with effect from such day as the Minister for Finance may by order appoint. By virtue of the Finance Act, 2001 (Commencement of Section 64) Order 2002, FA 2001 s 64 comes into operation as on and from 15 May 2002.

14 Subs (1)(*k*) inserted by FA 2002 s 34(1)(*a*)(i)(II) with effect from such day as the Minister for Finance may by order appoint. By virtue of the Finance Act, 2002 (Commencement of Section 34) Order 2002, FA 2002 s 34 comes into operation as on and from 15 May 2002.

15 Substituted by FA 2004 s 24(1)(*a*) as respects capital expenditure incurred on the construction or refurbishment of a building or structure on or after 1 May 2004; previously "shall not be regarded as an industrial building or structure".

16 Subs (1A) inserted by FA 2002 s 32(*a*) with effect from 1 January 2002.

17 Substituted by FA 2004 s 24(1)(*b*) as respects capital expenditure incurred on the construction or refurbishment of a building or structure on or after 1 May 2004; previously "shall not be regarded as an industrial building or structure".

18 Subs (1B) inserted by FA 2002 s 34(1)(*a*)(ii) with effect from such day as the Minister for Finance may by order appoint. By virtue of the Finance Act, 2002 (Commencement of Section 34) Order 2002, FA 2002 s 34 comes into operation as on and from 15 May 2002.

19 Definition of "health board" deleted by FA 2005 s 147 and Sch 6 para 1(*e*)(ii)(I) with effect from 25 March 2005.

20 Definition of "qualifying hospital" para (*b*) deleted by FA 2002 s 32(*b*)(i) with effect from 1 January 2002.

21 Definition of "qualifying hospital" para (d) substituted by FA 2003 s 24(1) as respects capital expenditure incurred on or after 28 March 2003 on the construction (within the meaning of TCA 1997 s 270) of a building or structure.

22 Substituted by FA 2005 s 147 and Sch 6 para 1(*e*)(ii)(II)(A) with effect from 25 March 2005; previously "the health board in whose functional area it is situated".

23 Substituted by FA 2005 s 147 and Sch 6 para 1(*e*)(ii)(II)(B) with effect from 25 March 2005; previously "the health board".

24 Substituted by FA 2005 s 147 and Sch 6 para 1(*e*)(ii)(II)(C) with effect from 25 March 2005; previously "that health board".

25 Substituted by FA 2002 s 32(*b*)(iii) with effect from 1 January 2002; previously "gives a certificate in writing".

26 Substituted by FA 2002 s 32(*b*)(iv) with effect from 1 January 2002; previously "but does not include any part of the hospital which consists of consultants' rooms or offices.".

27 Subs (2A) inserted by FA 2001 s 64(1)(*a*)(ii) with effect from such day as the Minister for Finance may by order appoint. By virtue of the Finance Act, 2001 (Commencement of Section 64) Order 2002, FA 2001 s 64 comes into operation as on and from 15 May 2002.

28 Substituted by FA 2005 s 147 and Sch 6 para 1(*e*)(iii)(I)(A) with effect from 25 March 2005; previously "the health board in whose functional area it is situated".

29 Substituted by FA 2005 s 147 and Sch 6 para 1(*e*)(iii)(I)(B) with effect from 25 March 2005; previously "the health board".

30 Substituted by FA 2005 s 147 and Sch 6 para 1(*e*)(iii)(II) with effect from 25 March 2005; previously "that health board".

31 Subs (2B) inserted by FA 2002 s 34(1)(*a*)(iii) with effect from such day as the Minister for Finance may by order appoint. By virtue of the Finance Act, 2002 (Commencement of Section 34) Order 2002, FA 2002 s 34 comes into operation as on and from 15 May 2002.

32 Subs (2C) inserted by FA 2005 s 34(*a*)(i) with effect from 1 January 2005.

33 Substituted by FA 2005 s 34(*a*)(ii) with effect from 1 January 2005; previously "a holiday camp".

34 Substituted by FA 2003 s 25(1)(*a*)(i) with effect from 4 December 2002; previously "shall be deemed".

35 Substituted by FA 2004 s 23(1)(*a*) as respects capital expenditure incurred on or after 4 February 2004; previously "comprised in a two storey building".

36 Substituted by FA 2004 s 23(1)(*b*) as respects capital expenditure incurred on or after 4 February 2004; previously "not less than 20 qualifying residential units".

37 Substituted by FA 2005 s 147 and Sch 6 para 1(*e*)(iv)(I) with effect from 25 March 2005; previously "the health board in whose functional area it is situated".

38 Substituted by FA 2005 s 147 and Sch 6 para 1(*e*)(iv)(II) with effect from 25 March 2005; previously "that health board".

39 Subss (3A)–(3C) inserted by FA 2002 s 33(*b*) with effect from 1 January 2002.

40 Substituted by FA 1998 s 19 with effect from 6 April 1998; previously "31st day of December, 1997".

41 Inserted by FA 2002 s 33(*c*) with effect from 1 January 2002.

42 Deleted by FA 1998 s 22(*a*)(ii)(I) with effect from 6 April 1998; previously "and".

43 Substituted by FA 1998 s 22(*a*)(ii)(II) with effect from 6 April 1998; previously "1992.".

44 Deleted by FA 1999 s 48(*a*)(ii)(I) with effect from 6 April 1999; previously "and".

45 Subs (9)(*d*) inserted by FA 1998 s 22(*a*)(ii)(III) with effect from 6 April 1998.

46 Deleted by FA 2001 s 64(1)(*a*)(iii)(I) with effect from such day as the Minister for Finance may by order appoint; previously "and". By virtue of the Finance Act, 2001 (Commencement of Section 64) Order 2002, FA 2001 s 64 comes into operation as on and from 15 May 2002.

47 Subs (9)(*e*)(ii) substituted by FA 1999 s 48(*a*)(ii)(II) with effect from 6 April 1999.

48 Subs (9)(*e*) inserted by FA 1998 s 20(*a*)(ii) with effect from 6 April 1998.

49 Deleted by FA 2002 s 34(1)(*a*)(iv)(I) with effect from such day as the Minister for Finance may by order appoint; previously "and". By virtue of the Finance Act, 2002 (Commencement of Section 34) Order 2002, FA 2002 s 34 comes into operation as on and from 15 May 2002.

50 Substituted by FA 2001 s 64(1)(*a*)(iii)(II) with effect from such day as the Minister for Finance may by order appoint; previously "1998.". By virtue of the Finance Act, 2001 (Commencement of Section 64) Order 2002, FA 2001 s 64 comes into operation as on and from 15 May 2002.

51 Subs (9)(*f*) inserted by FA 1999 s 48(*a*)(ii)(III) with effect from 6 April 1999.

52 Substituted by FA 2002 s 34(1)(*a*)(iv)(I) with effect from such day as the Minister for Finance may by order appoint; previously "2001.". By virtue of the Finance Act, 2002 (Commencement of Section 34) Order 2002, FA 2002 s 34 comes into operation as on and from 15 May 2002.

53 Subs (9)(*g*) inserted by FA 2001 s 64(1)(*a*)(iii)(III) with effect from such day as the Minister for Finance may by order appoint. By virtue of the Finance Act, 2001 (Commencement of Section 64) Order 2002, FA 2001 s 64 comes into operation as on and from 15 May 2002.

54 Subs (9)(*h*) inserted by FA 2002 s 34(1)(*a*)(iv)(II) with effect from such day as the Minister for Finance may by order appoint. By virtue of the Finance Act, 2002 (Commencement of Section 34) Order 2002, FA 2002 s 34 comes into operation as on and from 15 May 2002.

55 Subs (10) inserted by FA 1998 s 20(*a*)(iii) with effect from 6 April 1998.

56 Substituted by FA 2002 s 22(1)(*a*) as respects expenditure incurred on or after 1 January 2002; previously "grant assistance from the State or from any other person".

57 Substituted by FA 2003 s 25(1)(*a*)(ii)(I) with effect from 4 December 2002; previously "6 April 2001,".

58 Subs (12)(*a*) substituted by FA 2005 s 34(*a*)(iii)(I) with effect from 1 January 2005.

59 Subs (12)(*c*) substituted by FA 2003 s 25(1)(*a*)(ii)(II) with effect from 1 January 2003.

60 Substituted by FA 2005 s 34(*a*)(iii)(II) with effect from 1 January 2005; previously "the Regulation".

61 Inserted by FA 2005 s 34(*a*)(iii)(III) with effect from 1 January 2005.

62 Subs (12)(*b*) substituted and subs (12)(*c*)–(*d*) inserted by FA 2002 s 22(1)(*b*)(ii) as respects expenditure incurred on or after 1 January 2002.

63 Subs (11)–(12) inserted by FA 2001 s 81 with effect from 6 April 2001.

64 Substituted by FA 2004 s 25(1)(*a*)(i) with effect from 1 January 2004; previously "31 December 2004".

65 Inserted by FA 2004 s 25(1)(*a*)(ii) with effect from 4 December 2002.

66 Substituted by FA 2004 s 25(1)(*a*)(iii) with effect from 1 January 2004; previously "31 May 2003".

67 Deleted by FA 2004 s 25(1)(*a*)(iv) with effect from 4 December 2002; previously "or".

68 Substituted by FA 2004 s 25(1)(*a*)(v) with effect from 1 January 2004; previously "a planning application".

69 Substituted by FA 2004 s 25(1)(*a*)(vi) with effect from 1 January 2004; previously "regulations.".

70 Subs (13)(*b*)(iii) inserted by FA 2004 s 25(1)(*a*)(vii) with effect from 1 January 2004.

71 Subs (13) inserted by FA 2003 s 25(1)(*a*)(iii) with effect from 4 December 2002.

72 Subss (14) and (15) inserted by FA 2005 s 34(*a*)(iv) with effect from 1 January 2005.

Cross-references

Balancing allowances and charges: s 274(1)(*b*), (6), (7).

Capital allowances for buildings used for certain childcare purposes: s 843A(1)(qualifying premises); subs (1)(*a*): s 843A(2)(*a*).

Capital allowances for buildings used for third level education: s 843(1)(qualifying premises); subs (1)(*a*): s 843(2)(*a*).

Capital expenditure on an industrial building cannot qualify for plant and machinery wear and tear allowance: s 284(5).

Case V, Schedule D, computational rules and allowable deductions: s 97(2B)(*c*)(i).

Deduction of five-twelfths of rateable valuation, meaning of "premises" applied: s 85(1).

Dredging, qualifying trade, subs (1): s 302(1).

Industrial building allowance (subs (1)(*a*)–(*b*)), 50% continued for certain approved projects: s 271(4)(*a*).

Industrial building allowance (subs (1)(*c*), (*e*)), 20% continued for certain approved projects: s 271(4)(*b*).

Interpretation of certain references to expenditure and time when expenditure is incurred, subs (3): s 316(2A).

Limited partnerships, specified provisions: s 1013(5)(*b*).

Multi-storey car parks, transitional, subs (1)(*a*): Sch 32 para 9(2).

Restriction of relief to individuals in respect of loans applied in acquiring interest in companies, subs (1): s 250A(1)("specified building").

Restriction on use of capital allowances on certain hotels, subs (1)(*d*) and (3): s 409B(1) (specified building).

Restriction on use of capital allowances on certain industrial buildings and other premises, subs (1) and (1)(*d*): s 409A(1) (specified building).

Ring-fence on use of certain capital allowances on certain industrial buildings and other premises, subs (1): s 409E(1)("specified building").

Writing down allowances: s 272(3); (3A), (3B), (4), (7).

Mill, factory, laboratory, dock undertaking

2% annual allowance where expenditure incurred before 16 January 1975: s 272(3)(*a*)(i); 50 year writing down life: s 272(4)(*a*)(i);

4% annual allowance where expenditure incurred on or after 16 January 1975: s 272(3)(*a*)(ii); 25 year writing down life: s h272(4)(*a*)(ii);

accelerated annual allowance, qualifying expenditure (subs (1)(*a*), (*b*), (*d*)): s 273(1); restriction: s 273(2)–(3); extension for certain projects: s 273(3)–(7);
balancing allowances and charges: s 274(1)(*b*)(i).

Market gardening structures and buildings for the intensive production of cattle, sheep, pigs, or poultry
10% annual allowance: s 272(3)(*b*);
10 year writing down life: s 272(4)(*b*);
balancing allowances and charges: s 274(1)(*b*)(ii);
conversion of hotel to nursing home: s 272(7).

Hotel
10% annual allowance where the expenditure is incurred before 27 January 1994: s 272(3)(*c*)(i); 10 year writing down life: s 272(4)(*c*)(i);
15% annual allowance for six years, 10% in the seventh year, where the expenditure is incurred on or after 27 January 1994: s 272(3)(*c*)(ii); 7 year writing down life: s 272(4)(*c*)(ii);
(subject to certain transitional arrangements which preserve 15% annual allowance (10% in year 7) and 7 year writing down life for certain expenditure incurred up to 31 July 2006) 4% annual allowance where the expenditure is incurred on or after 4 December 2002: s 272(3)(c)(iii); 25 year writing down life: s 272(4)(*c*)(iii).
accelerated annual allowance, qualifying expenditure (subs (1)(*d*)): s 273(1); restriction: s 273(2)–(3); extension for certain projects: s 273(3)–(7);
balancing allowances and charges: s 274(1)(*b*)(iii);
conversion of hotel to nursing home: s 272(7).

Holiday cottage
10 year writing down life: s 272(4)(*d*);
accelerated annual allowance, qualifying expenditure (subs (1)(*d*)): s 273(1); restriction: s 273(2)–(3); extension for certain projects: s 273(3)–(7);
annual allowance: s 272(3)(*d*);
anti-avoidance: s 274(6)–(7);
balancing allowances and charges: s 274(1)(*b*)(iv);
resort area, disclaimer of capital allowances: s 355(1)(*a*);
restriction on use of allowances: s 405(1);
(Subject to certain transitional arrangements which preserve 10% annual allowances and 10 year writing down life for certain expenditure incurred up to 31 July 2006) no allowances apply where the expenditure is incurred on or after 4 December 2002: s 268(13).

Guest houses and holiday hostels
4% annual allowance: s 272(3)(*da*);
25 year writing down life: s 272(4)(*da*);
balancing allowances and charges: s 274(1)(*b*)(iv*a*).

Airport runway or apron
4% annual allowance: s 272(3)(*e*);
25 year writing down life: s 272(4)(*e*);
balancing allowances and charges: s 274(1)(*b*)(v).

Nursing homes (and associated housing for the aged or infirm) and convalescent homes
15% annual allowance for six years, 10% in seventh year: s 272(3)(*f*);
7 year writing down life: s 272(4)(*f*);
balancing allowances and charges: s 274(1)(*b*)(ii).

Other airport buildings or structures
4% annual allowance: s 272(3)(*g*);
25 year writing down life: s 272(4)(*g*);
balancing allowances and charges: s 274(1)(*b*)(vi).

Qualifying private hospitals and qualifying sports injuries clinics
15% annual allowance for six years, 10% in seventh year: s 272(3)(*h*);
7 year writing down life: s 272(4)(*h*);
balancing allowances and charges: s 274(1)(*b*)(vii).

Renewal incentives

Custom House Dock Area
Commercial premises: s 323(1)(*a*), (2)(*a*); double rent allowance: s 324(1)(*a*) (qualifying premises).

Temple Bar Area
Industrial building (subs (1)(*a*), (*d*)): s 331(1)(*b*).
Commercial premises: s 332(1)(*b*), (2)(*a*); double rent allowance: s 333(1)(*a*) (qualifying premises).
Designated area or street
Industrial building (subs (1)(*a*)): s 341(1).
Commercial premises: s 342(1)(*a*), (2)(*a*).
Double rent allowance, qualifying premises: s 345(1), (6).
Enterprise areas
Industrial building: s 343(7)(*a*).
Multi-storey car parks
Industrial building: s 344(2)(*a*).
Resort areas
Industrial building, subs (1)(*d*): s 352(1).
Commercial premises: s 353(1).
Double rent allowance, qualifying premises, subs (1)(*d*): s 354(1).
Dublin Docklands Areas
Industrial building, subs (1)(*a*): s 368(1).
Commercial premises, subs (1)(*a*): s 369(2)(*a*)(i).
Double rent allowance, subs (1)(*d*): s 370(1) (qualifying premises), (5).
Qualifying areas
Industrial buildings, subs (1)(*a*): s 372C(1).
Commercial premises: s 372D(1), (2)(*a*).
Double rent allowance, subs (1)(*a*), (*d*): s 372E(1) (qualifying premises), subs (1)(*d*): s 372E(5)(*a*), (6).
Qualifying rural areas
Industrial buildings, subs (1)(*a*), (*b*): s 372M(1).
Commercial buildings: s 372N(1), (2)(*a*).
Double rent allowance, subs (1)(*a*): s 372O(1) (qualifying premises).
Park and ride facilities
Qualifying park and ride facility, subs (1)(*a*): s 372V(1)(*a*).
Commercial premises: subs (1): s 372W(1)(qualifying premises); subs (1)(*a*): s 372W(2)(*a*)(i).
Designated areas in certain towns
Commercial premises: s 372AD(1)(qualifying premises); subs (1)(*a*): s 372AD(2)(*a*)(i).

Case law

Irish

Subs (1)(*b*): Storage sheds used by shipping agents regarded as buildings in use for the purpose of a "dock undertaking": *Patrick Monahan (Drogheda) Ltd v O'Connell* ITR Vol III p 661.

Part of building housing computer and computer facilities regarded as an industrial building but showroom and general administration offices were not: *O'Connell v JJ Limited* ITR Vol III p 65.

UK

Subs (1): held cold stores qualified as an industrial building: *Ellerker v Union Cold Storage Co Ltd* (1938) 22 TC 195.

Held grain elevator qualified as an industrial building: *IRC v Leith Harbours & Docks Commissioners* (1941) 24 TC 118.

Drawing office of engineering company held qualified as an industrial building: *IRC v Lambhill Ironworks Ltd* (1950) 31 TC 393.

Building used for cleaning and repairing equipment held did not qualify as an industrial building: *Vibroplant Ltd v Holland* [1982] STC 164.

A building housing machines used to process large volumes of cheques and other documents not a mill or similar premises: *Girobank v Clarke* [1996] STI 451.

Subs (7): Warehouse used for storage and distribution was in use for purpose ancillary to a retail shop: *Sarsfield v Dixon Group plc* [1998] STC 938.

Subs (8): A separate building housing administrative activities, although attached to the factory by a covered passageway and heated by the same heating system did not qualify as it was not sufficiently part of the factory: *Abbott Laboratories v Carmody* (1968) 44 TC 569.

A building all of which was used concurrently for both qualifying and non-qualifying purposes was eligible for industrial building allowances – *Saxone Lilley* & Skinner *(Holdings) Ltd v IRC* 44 TC 122.

Revenue precedents

Issue: In order for a holiday camp to qualify for industrial buildings allowances is it necessary for it to be registered as a holiday camp with Bord Fáilte?

Decision: There is no requirement that a holiday camp be registered as a holiday camp with Bord Fáilte. Section 37 of the Tourist Traffic Act 1939 states that: "It shall not be lawful to describe or holdout or permit any person to describe or holdout any premises as a holiday camp unless such premises are registered in the Register of Holiday camps and such proprietor is registered as the registered proprietor of the holiday camp". Thus, while it is illegal to hold out a premises as a holiday camp unless it is registered with Bord Fáilte, the fact that it is not registered does not mean that it is not a holiday camp - just that it cannot be held out as such.

Issue: Does a hotel have to be registered as a hotel with Bord Fáilte in order for it to be regarded as a building or structure in use for the purposes of the trade of hotel keeping?

Decision: There is no requirement that a building be registered as a hotel with Bord Fáilte for it to be regarded as a building in use for the purposes of the trade of hotel keeping.

Issue: Are hostels and other budget accommodation facilities which feature common rooms, dormitories, self catering kitchens and other self use facilities regarded by Revenue as buildings in use for the purposes of the trade of hotel keeping.

Decision: No.

Issue: Capital Allowances.

Decision: Industrial Buildings Allowance was granted in respect of the facilities at a salmon hatchery.

Issue: Industrial building allowance for caravan parks.

Decision: Granted for caravan parks registered with Bord Fáilte.

Issue: Is a building in which grain is subjected to a process of drying an industrial building?

Decision: On the basis of the case of *CIR v Leith Harbour and Docks Commissioners* the building in this case appears to be similar to a mill.

Issue: Does expenditure incurred on golf courses qualify for capital allowances either as a building or structure in use for the purposes of the trade of hotel keeping, or as plant?

Decision: No. It is the Revenue view that such expenditure does not qualify under either of these headings.

Issue: An individual incurs expenditure on the construction of a holiday cottage and leases it to an operator. If the operator rather than the individual registers the cottage in the Register of Holiday Cottages maintained by Bord Fáilte will the building be regarded as an industrial building within the meaning of s 268.

Decision: The section is silent on who actually registers the property. Therefore an operator may register properties owned by other parties.

Issue: Whether a jetty on the Shannon used for charter cruisers is an industrial building or structure.

Decision: TCA 1997 s 268(2) provides that a dock includes a jetty at which vessels can ship or unship passengers, not being a jetty primarily used for receation. The occupants of bareboat charters may be regarded as passengers and boarding these vessels comes within the test to "ship or unship". The jetty itself is not used primarily for recreation; it is used to gain access to the boats. It therefore comes within the meaning of industrial building or structure.

Issue: Can capital allowances be claimed on the office comprised in the premises which is registered by Bord Fáilte under the Registration and Renewal of Holiday Cottages regulations?

Decision: TCA 1997 s 268(3) provides that a building in use as a holiday cottage and comprised in premises registered in any register of holiday cottages established by Bord Failte Éireann shall be deemed to be a building in use for the purposes of the trade of hotel-keeping. Therefore only the building used as a holiday cottage qualifies for allowances and not the office.

Tax Briefing

TB47 Apr 2002 pp 11–13 Finance Act 2002 changes — Private Hospitals, Registered Nursing Homes, Sports Injuries Clinics.

TB50 Oct 2002 pp 5–6 Registered Nursing Homes.

TB52 May 2003 p 11 Finance Act 2003 changes — Capital Allowances for Hotels and Holiday Cottages.

Definitions

the Oireachtas: IA 1937 Sch; land: IA 1937 Sch; person: IA 1937 s 11(*c*); trade: s 3(1); writing: IA 1937 Sch; year of assessment: ss 2(1), 5(1).

Former enactments

ITA 1967 s 255(1)–(5), s 257 and 263(4); FA 1969 s 64(1), (2) and (5), FA 1975 s 34(1) and (3); FA 1984 s 36; FA 1992 s 27; FA 1996 s 29.

Corresponding UK tax provision

Capital Allowances Act 2001 s 271.

269 Meaning of "the relevant interest"

(1) Subject to this section, in this Chapter, **"the relevant interest"**, in relation to any expenditure incurred on the construction of a building or structure, means the interest in that building or structure to which the person who incurred the expenditure was entitled when the person incurred the expenditure.

(2) Where, when a person incurs expenditure on the construction of a building or structure, the person is entitled to 2 or more interests in the building or structure and one of those interests is an interest which is reversionary on all the others, that interest shall be the relevant interest for the purposes of this Chapter.

(3) An interest shall not cease to be the relevant interest for the purposes of this Chapter by reason of the creation of any lease or other interest to which that interest is subject, and where the relevant interest is a leasehold interest and is extinguished by reason of the surrender of the leasehold interest, or on the person entitled to the leasehold interest acquiring the interest which is reversionary on the leasehold interest, the interest into which that leasehold interest merges shall thereupon become the relevant interest.

Cross-references

Capital allowances for buildings used for childcare purposes: s 843A(5).

Designated areas in certain towns, non-application of relief in certain cases and provision against double relief: s 372AJ(1)(*ab*), (*b*), (*c*).

Designated areas, double rent allowance: s 345(6)(*c*).

Enterprise areas, capital allowances: s 343(11)(*a*).

Holiday cottages, disclaimer of capital allowance: s 355(3)(*c*).

Park and ride facilities, capital allowances in relation to construction or refurbishment of, and capital allowances in relation to construction or refurbishment of certain commercial premises in, meaning of relevant interest applied: s 372V(2A)(*a*); s 372W(3A)(*a*).

Qualifying areas, double rent allowance: s 372E(6)(*c*); non-application of relief in certain cases and provision against double relief: s 372K(1)(*a*)(i), (*b*).

Qualifying rural areas, non-application of relief in certain cases and provision against double relief: s 372T(1)(*a*)(i), (*b*).

Restriction of relief to individuals in respect of loans applied in acquring interest in companies, meaning of relevant interest applied: s 250A(1).

Ring-fence on use of certain capital allowances on certain industrial buildings and other premises: s 409E(1).

Former enactments

ITA 1967 s 268.

Corresponding UK tax provision

Capital Allowances Act 2001 s 286.

270 Meaning of "expenditure on construction of building or structure"

(1) In this section, **"refurbishment"**, in relation to a building or structure, means any work of construction, reconstruction, repair or renewal, including the provision of water, sewerage or heating facilities carried out in the course of the repair or restoration, or maintenance in the nature of repair or restoration, of the building or structure.

(2) A reference in this Chapter to expenditure incurred on the construction of a building or structure includes expenditure on the refurbishment of the building or structure, but does not include—

(*a*) any expenditure incurred on the acquisition of, or of rights in or over, any land, (*b*) any expenditure on the provision of machinery or plant or on any asset treated for any chargeable period as machinery or plant, or

(*c*) any expenditure in respect of which an allowance is or may be made for the same or for any other chargeable period under section 670 or 765(1).

(3) Where a building or structure which is to be an industrial building or structure forms part of a building or is one of a number of buildings in a single development, or forms a part of a building which is itself one of a number of buildings in a single development, there shall be made such apportionment as is necessary of the expenditure incurred on the construction of the whole building or number of buildings, as the case may be, for the purpose of determining the expenditure incurred on the construction of the building or structure which is to be an industrial building or structure.

Cross-references

Industrial building or structure, meaning of: s 268(2C), (13)(*a*), (14).

Industrial buildings, balancing allowances and balancing charges: s 274(1)(*b*)(iii)(IIII).

Industrial buildings, writing-down allowances: s 272(3)(*c*)(iii), (*da*), (4)(*c*)(iii), (*da*).

Industrial buildings bought unused: s 279(1).

Interpretation of certain references to expenditure and time when expenditure is incurred: s 316(2A).

Definitions

land: IA 1937 Sch.

Former enactments

ITA 1967 s 256, s 263(4); CTA 1976 s 21(1) and Sch 1 para 18; FA 1994 s 22(1)(*b*); FA 1997 s 146(1) and Sch 9 Pt I para 1(18).

Corresponding UK tax provision

Capital Allowances Act 2001 s 272.

271 Industrial building allowances

(1) In this section—

"industrial development agency" means the Industrial Development Authority, the Shannon Free Airport Development Company Limited or Údarás na Gaeltachta;

"appropriate chargeable period", in relation to any person who has incurred expenditure on the construction of a building or structure, means the chargeable period related to the expenditure or, if it is later, the chargeable period related to the event (which shall be regarded as an event within the meaning of section 321(2)(*b*)), where such event is—

(*a*) the commencement of the tenancy in a case in which the first use to which the building or structure is put is a use by a person occupying it by virtue of a tenancy to which the relevant interest is reversionary, or

(*b*) in a case to which subsection (2)(*b*)(ii) refers, the commencement of the tenancy to which the relevant interest is reversionary;

"relevant lease" means a lease to which the relevant interest is reversionary.

(2) (*a*) Subject to the Tax Acts, where a person incurs capital expenditure on the construction of a building or structure—

(i) which is to be an industrial building or structure to which subsection (3) applies, and

(ii) which is to be occupied for the purposes of a trade carried on either by the person or by a lessee mentioned in paragraph (*b*),

there shall be made to the person who incurred the expenditure, for the appropriate chargeable period, an allowance (in this Chapter referred to as an **"industrial building allowance"**).

(*b*) The lessee referred to in paragraph (*a*) is a lessee occupying the building or structure on the construction of which the expenditure was incurred and who so occupies it—

(i) under a relevant lease, or

(ii) under a lease to which a relevant lease granted to an industrial development agency is reversionary.

(3) This subsection shall apply to—

(*a*) an industrial building or structure provided—

(i) before the 23rd day of April, 1996, for use for the purposes of trading operations, or

(ii) on or after the 23rd day of April, 1996, by a company for use for the purposes of trading operations carried on by the company,

which are relevant trading operations within the meaning of section 445 or 446 but, in relation to capital expenditure incurred on the provision of an industrial building or structure on or after the 6th day of May, 1993, excluding an industrial building or structure provided by a lessor to a lessee other than in the course of the carrying on by the lessor of those relevant trading operations,

(*b*) an industrial building or structure provided for the purposes of a project approved by an industrial development agency on or before the 31st day of December, 1988, and in respect of the provision of which expenditure was incurred before the 31st day of December, 1995; but, as respects an industrial building or structure provided for the purposes of a project approved by an industrial development agency in the period from the 1st day of January, 1986, to the 31st day of December, 1988, this paragraph shall apply as if the reference to the 31st day of December, 1995, were a reference to the 31st day of December, 1996,

and

(*c*) an industrial building or structure provided for the purposes of a project approved for grant assistance by an industrial development agency in the period from the 1st day of January, 1989, to the 31st day of December, 1990, and in respect of the provision of which expenditure is incurred before the 31st day of December, 1997 [, or before the 30th day of June, 1998, if such expenditure would have been incurred before the 31st day of December, 1997, but for the existence of circumstances which resulted in legal proceedings being initiated, being proceedings which were the subject of an order of the High Court made before the 1st day of January, 1998];[1] but, as respects an industrial building or structure provided for the purposes of any such project specified in the list referred to in section 133(8)(*c*)(iv), this paragraph shall apply as if the reference to the 31st day of December, 1997, [where it first occurs,][2] were a reference to the 31st day of December, 2002.

(4) An industrial building allowance shall be of an amount equal to—

(*a*) where the building or structure is to be used for a purpose specified in paragraph (*a*) or (*b*) of section 268(1), 50 per cent of the capital expenditure mentioned in subsection (2); but, in the case of a building or structure to which subsection (3)(*a*) applies, this paragraph shall apply only if that expenditure is incurred before the 25th day of January, 1999,

(*b*) where the building or structure is to be used for a purpose specified in paragraph (*c*) or (*e*) of section 268(1), 20 per cent of the capital expenditure mentioned in subsection (2), and

(*c*) in any other case, 10 per cent of the capital expenditure mentioned in subsection (2).

(5) Where an industrial building allowance in respect of capital expenditure incurred on the construction of a building or structure to which subsection (3)(*c*) applies is made under this section for any chargeable period—

(*a*) no allowance in relation to that capital expenditure shall be made under section 272 for that chargeable period, and

(*b*) an allowance in relation to that capital expenditure which is to be made under section 272 for any chargeable period subsequent to that chargeable period shall not be increased under section 273.

(6) Notwithstanding any other provision of this section, no industrial building allowance shall be made in respect of any expenditure on a building or structure if the building or structure, when it comes to be used, is not an industrial building or structure, and where an industrial building allowance has been granted in respect of any expenditure on any such building or structure, any necessary additional assessments may be made to give effect to this subsection.

Amendments

1 Inserted by FA 1998 s 21(*a*)(i) with effect from 6 April 1998.

2 Inserted by FA 1998 s 21(*a*)(ii) with effect from 6 April 1998.

Cross-references

Corporation tax: allowances and charges in taxing a trade: s 307(2)(*b*)(i).

Holiday cottages, restriction on use of allowances: s 405(1).

Income tax: allowances and charges in taxing a trade: s 304(3)(*a*).

Industrial buildings bought unused: s 279(2)(*a*).

Machinery or plant: initial allowances, subs (3)(*c*): s 283(5).

Machinery or plant: accelerated wear and tear allowances, subs (3)(*c*): s 285(7)(*a*)(i).

Pre-trading capital expenditure: s 316(3).

Property investment, restriction of tax incentives on: s 408(2).

Renewal incentives

Custom House Dock area

Commercial premises construction expenditure, in subs (1) delete the definition of "industrial development agency", in subs (2)(*a*)(i) delete "to which subsection (3) applies", delete subss (3) and (5) and for subs (4) read:

"(4) An industrial building allowance shall be of an amount equal to 50 per cent of the capital expenditure mentioned in subsection (2).": s 323(3)(*a*)(i).

Dublin Docklands Area

Industrial building construction or refurbishment expenditure, in subs (1) delete the definition of "industrial development agency", in subs (2)(*a*)(i) delete "to which subsection (3) applies", delete subs (3), for subs (4) read

"(4) An industrial building allowance shall be of an amount equal to 50 per cent of the capital expenditure mentioned in subsection (2).": s 368(2); qualifying period: s 368(5).

Commercial premises construction or refurbishment expenditure, in subs (1) delete the definition of "industrial development agency", in subs (2)(*a*)(i) delete "to which subsection (3) applies", delete subs (3), for subs (4) read:

"(4) An industrial building allowance shall be of an amount equal to 50 per cent of the capital expenditure mentioned in subsection (2).": s 369(4)(*a*); qualifying period: s 369(7).

Double rent allowance: s 370(1) (qualifying premises).

Temple Bar Area

Industrial premises construction expenditure, in subs (1) delete the definition of "industrial development agency", in subs (2)(*a*)(i) delete "to which subsection (3) applies", delete subss (3) and (5) and for subs (4) read:

"(4) An industrial building allowance shall be of an amount equal to 25 per cent of the capital expenditure mentioned in subsection (2).": s 331(2).

Industrial building refurbishment expenditure, in subs (1) delete the definition of "industrial development agency", in subs (2)(*a*)(i) delete "to which subsection (3) applies", delete subss (3) and (5) and for subs (4) read:

"(4) An industrial building allowance shall be of an amount equal to 50 per cent of the capital expenditure mentioned in subsection (2).": s 331(2); qualifying period: s 331(6).

Commercial premises construction or refurbishment expenditure, in subs (1) delete the definition of "industrial development agency", in subs (2)(*a*)(i) delete "to which subsection (3) applies", delete subss (3) and (5) and for subs (4) read:

"(4) An industrial building allowance shall be of an amount equal to 50 per cent of the capital expenditure mentioned in subsection (2).": s 332(3); qualifying period: s 332(8).

Designated areas or street

Industrial building, construction or refurbishment expenditure, in subs (1) delete the definition of "industrial development agency", in subs (2)(*a*)(i) delete "to which subsection (3) applies", delete subs (3), for subs (4) read:

"(4) An industrial building allowance shall be of an amount equal to 25 per cent of the capital expenditure mentioned in subsection (2)." and delete "to which subsection (3)(*c*) applies" from subs (5): s 341(2); qualifying period: s 341(6).

Commercial premises, construction or refurbishment expenditure: in subs (1) delete the definition of "industrial development agency", in subs (2)(*a*)(i) delete "to which subsection (3) applies", delete subs (3), for subs (4) read:

"(4) An industrial building allowance shall be of an amount equal to 50 per cent of the capital expenditure mentioned in subsection (2)." and delete "to which subsection (3)(*c*) applies" from subs (5): s 342(4)(*a*); qualifying period: s 342(7).

Double rent allowance: s 345(1) (qualifying premises).

Enterprise areas

Qualifying building construction or refurbishment expenditure, in subs (1) delete the definition of "industrial development agency", in subs (2)(*a*)(i) delete "to which subsection (3) applies", delete subs (3), for subs (4) read:

"(4) An industrial building allowance, in the case of a qualifying building (within the meaning of section 343(1)), shall be of an amount equal to—

(*a*) 25 per cent, or

(*b*) in the case of such a building the site of which is wholly within an area described in an order referred to in section 340(2)(i), 50 per cent,

of the capital expenditure mentioned in subsection (2)."

and delete "to which subsection (3)(*c*) applies" from subs (5): s 343(8)(*a*); qualifying period: s 343(10).

Qualifying areas

Industrial building, construction or refurbishment expenditure, in subs (1) delete the definition of "industrial development agency", in subs (2)(*a*)(i) delete "to which subsection (3) applies", delete subs (3), for subs (4) read:

"(4) An industrial building allowance shall be of an amount equal to 50 per cent of the capital expenditure mentioned in subsection (2).", and delete "to which subsection (3)(*c*) applies" from subs (5): s 372C(2); qualifying period: s 372C(6).

Commercial premises, construction or refurbishment expenditure, in subs (1) delete the definition of "industrial development agency", in subs (2)(*a*)(i) delete "to which subsection (3) applies", delete subs (3), for subs (4) read:

> "(4) An industrial building allowance shall be of an amount equal to 50 per cent of the capital expenditure mentioned in subsection (2).", and delete "to which subsection (3)(*c*) applies" from subs (5): s 372D(4)(*a*).

Double rent allowance: s 372E(1) (qualifying premises).

Qualifying rural areas

Industrial building, construction or refurbishment expenditure, in subs (1) delete the definition of "industrial development agency", in subs (2)(*a*)(i) delete "to which subsection (3) applies", delete subs (3), for subs (4) read:

> "(4) An industrial building allowance shall be of an amount equal to 50 per cent of the capital expenditure mentioned in subsection (2).", and delete "to which subsection (3)(*c*) applies" from subs (5): s 372M(2); qualifying period: s 372M(6).

Commercial buildings or structures, construction or refurbishment expenditure, in subs (1) delete the definition of "industrial development agency", in subs (2)(*a*)(i) delete "to which subsection (3) applies", delete subs (3), for subs (4) read:

> "(4) An industrial building allowance shall be of an amount equal to 50 per cent of the capital expenditure mentioned in subsection (2).", and delete "to which subsection (3)(*c*) applies" from subs (5): s 372N(4)(*a*).

Double rent allowance: s 372O(1) (qualifying premises).

Multi-storey car parks

Qualifying car park construction or refurbishment expenditure, in subs (1) delete the definition of "industrial development agency", in subs (2)(*a*)(i) delete "to which subsection (3) applies", delete subs (3), for subs (4) read:

> "(4) An industrial building allowance shall be of an amount equal to 50 per cent of the capital expenditure mentioned in subsection (2)." and delete "to which subsection (3)(*c*) applies" from subs (5): s 344(4)(*a*); qualifying period: s 344(7).

Resort areas

Industrial building, construction or refurbishment expenditure, in subs (1) delete the definition of "industrial development agency", in subs (2)(*a*)(i) delete "to which subsection (3) applies", delete subs (3), for subs (4) read:

> "(4) An industrial building allowance shall be of an amount equal to 50 per cent of the capital expenditure mentioned in subsection (2)." and delete "to which subsection (3)(*c*) applies" from subs (5): s 352(2); qualifying period: s 352(6).

Commercial premises construction or refurbishment expenditure, in subs (1) delete the definition of "industrial development agency", in subs (2)(*a*)(i) delete "to which subsection (3) applies", delete subs (3), for subs (4) read:

> "(4) An industrial building allowance shall be of an amount equal to 50 per cent of the capital expenditure mentioned in subsection (2)." and delete "to which subsection (3)(*c*) applies" from subs (5): s 353(4)(*a*); qualifying period: s 353(7).

Double rent allowance: s 354(1) (qualifying premises).

Holiday cottages, disclaimer of capital allowance: s 355(4).

Park and ride facilities

Qualifying park and ride facilities, construction or refurbishment expenditure, in subs (1) delete the definition of "industrial development agency", in subs (2)(*a*)(i) delete "to which subsection (3) applies", delete subs (3), for subs (4) read:

> "(4) An industrial building allowance shall be of an amount equal to 50 per cent of the capital expenditure mentioned in subsection (2)."
>
> and delete "to which subsection (3)(i) applies" from subs (5): s 372V(3)(*a*);

and in definition of "appropriate chargeable period" in subs (1) for "the chargeable period related to the expenditure" read "the chargeable period in which the building or structure becomes an industrial building or structure" and in subs (6) for "if the building or structure, when it comes to be used, is not an industrial building or structure" read "if, within 5 years of the building or structure coming to be used, it is not an industrial building or structure": s 372V(4A)(*a*).

Commercial premises, construction or refurbishment expenditure, in subs (1) delete the definition of "industrial development agency", in subs (2)(*a*)(i) delete "to which subsection (3) applies", delete subs (3), for subs (4) read:

> "(4) An industrial building allowance shall be of an amount equal to 50 per cent of the capital expenditure mentioned in subsection (2).", and delete "to which subsection (3)(*c*) applies" from subs (5): s 372W(4)(*a*);

and in definition of "appropriate chargeable period" in subs (1) for "the chargeable period related to the expenditure" read "the chargeable period in which the building or structure becomes an industrial building or structure" and in subs (6) for "if the building or structure, when it comes to be used, is not an industrial building or structure" read "if, within 5 years of the building or structure coming to be used, it is not an industrial building or structure": s 372W(5A)(*a*).

Designated areas in certain towns

Industrial building, construction or refurbishment expenditure, in subs (1) delete the definition of "industrial development agency", in subs (2)(*a*)(i) delete "to which subsection (3) applies", delete subs (3), for subs (4) read:

> "(4) An industrial building allowance shall be of an amount equal to 50 per cent of the capital expenditure mentioned in subsection (2).",
>
> and in subs (5) delete "to which subsection (3)(*c*) applies": s 372AC(2).

Commercial building, construction or refurbishment expenditure, in subs (1) delete the definition of "industrial development agency", in subs (2)(*a*)(i) delete "to which subsection (3) applies", delete subs (3), for subs (4) read:

> "(4) An industrial building allowance shall be of an amount equal to 50 per cent of the capital expenditure mentioned in subsection (2).",
>
> and in subs (5) delete "to which subsection (3)(*c*) applies": s 372AD(3).

Childcare facilities

Buildings used for childcare purposes, qualifying expenditure incurred on or after 1 December 1999, in subs (1) delete the definition of "industrial development agency", in subs (2)(*a*)(i) delete "to which subsection (3) applies", delete subs (3), for subs (4) read:

> "(4) An industrial building allowance shall be of an amount equal to 100 per cent of the capital expenditure mentioned in subsection (2)", and delete subs (5): s 843A(3A)(*a*).

Revenue precedents

Issue: Whether IBA due where property occupied by tenant of lessee who carries on qualifying trade - lessee does not carry on such a trade.

Decision: IBA not due unless the lessee is IDA, SFADCO or Udaras na Gaeilge. Otherwise, the trade to be considered is that carried on by the lessee who must occupy it for the purposes of that trade.

Definitions

High Court: IA 1937 s 11(*c*); person: IA 1937 s 11(*c*); statute: IA 1937 s 3; s 1(1); trade: s 3(1).

Former enactments

ITA 1967 s 254(1)(*a*), (*b*) and (*c*), (2A), (2B), (3) and (7); FA 1975 s 34(2)(*a*)(i); CTA 1976 s 21(1) and Sch 1 para 17 and para 72; FA 1981 s 27; FA 1988 s 51(1)(*a*) and (*cc*), (4)(*a*) and (6); FA 1989 s 14; FA 1990 ss 74, 80 and 81(1)(*a*) and (4); FA 1991 s 22(1); FA 1993 s 33(1); FA 1995 s 26 and s 27; FA 1996 s 27 and s 43.

272 Writing-down allowances

(1) A building or structure shall be one to which this section applies only if the capital expenditure incurred on the construction of it has been incurred on or after the 30th day of September, 1956.

(2) Subject to this Part, where—

(*a*) any person is, at the end of a chargeable period or its basis period, entitled to an interest in a building or structure to which this section applies,

(*b*) at the end of the chargeable period or its basis period, the building or structure is an industrial building or structure, and (*c*) that interest is the relevant interest in relation to the capital expenditure incurred on the construction of that building or structure,

an allowance (in this Chapter referred to as a **"writing-down allowance"**) shall be made to such person for that chargeable period.

(3) A writing-down allowance shall be of an amount equal to—

(*a*) in relation to a building or structure which is to be regarded as an industrial building or structure within the meaning of paragraph (*a*) or (*b*) of section 268(1)—

(i) 2 per cent of the expenditure referred to in subsection (2)(*c*), if that expenditure was incurred before the 16th day of January, 1975, or

(ii) 4 per cent of the expenditure referred to in subsection (2)(*c*), if that expenditure is incurred on or after the 16th day of January, 1975,

(*b*) in relation to a building or structure which is to be regarded as an industrial building or structure within the meaning of paragraph (*c*) or (*e*) of section 268(1), 10 per cent of the expenditure referred to in subsection (2)(*c*),

(*c*) in relation to a building or structure which is to be regarded as an industrial building or structure within the meaning of section 268(1)(*d*), other than a building or structure to which [paragraph (*d*) or (*da*)][1] relates—

(i) 10 per cent of the expenditure referred to in subsection (2)(*c*), if that expenditure was incurred before the 27th day of January, 1994, ...[2]

(ii) 15 per cent of the expenditure referred to in subsection (2)(*c*), if that expenditure is incurred on or after the 27th day of January, 1994, [or][3]

[(iii) subject to subsection (8), 4 per cent of the expenditure referred to in subsection (2)(*c*), if the capital expenditure on the construction (within the meaning of section 270) of the building or structure is incurred on or after 4 December 2002,][4]

(*d*) in relation to a building or structure which is to be regarded as an industrial building or structure within the meaning of section 268(1)(*d*) by reason of its use as a holiday cottage, 10 per cent of the expenditure referred to in subsection (2)(*c*), ...[5]

[(*da*) in relation to a building or structure which is to be regarded as an industrial building or structure within the meaning of section 268(1)(*d*) by reason of its use as a guest house or a holiday hostel to which section 268(2C) applies, 4 per cent of the capital expenditure on the construction (within the meaning of section 270) of the building or structure which is incurred on or after 3 February 2005,][6]

(*e*) in relation to a building or structure which is to be regarded as an industrial building or structure within the meaning of section 268(1)(*f*), 4 per cent of the expenditure referred to in [subsection (2)(*c*),][7]

[(*f*) in relation to a building or structure which is to be regarded as an industrial building or structure within the meaning of paragraph (*g*) or (*i*) of section 268(1), 15 per cent of the expenditure referred to in subsection (2)(*c*), ...[8]][9]

[(*g*) in relation to a building or structure which is to be regarded as an industrial building or structure within the meaning of section 268(1)(*h*), 4 per cent of the expenditure referred to in [subsection (2)(*c*), and][10]][11] [(*h*) in relation to a building or structure which is to be regarded as an industrial building or structure within the meaning of [paragraph (*j*) or (*k*) of section 268(1)][12], 15 per cent of the expenditure referred to in subsection (2)(*c*).][13]

[(3A)(*a*) This subsection shall apply to a building or structure in existence on—

(i) in the case of Aer Rianta cuideachta phoiblí theoranta, the vesting day, and

(ii) in the case of any other person, the date of the passing of the Finance Act, 1998,

and in use for the purposes of a trade which consists of the operation or management of an airport, not being either machinery or plant or a building or structure to which section 268(1)(*f*) applies.

(*b*) For the purposes of this Part, in relation to a building or structure to which this subsection applies, expenditure shall be deemed to have been incurred on—

(i) in the case of Aer Rianta cuideachta phoiblí theoranta, the vesting day, and

(ii) in the case of any other person, the date of the passing of the Finance Act, 1998,

on the construction of the building or structure of an amount determined by the formula—

$$A - B$$

where—

A is the amount of the capital expenditure originally incurred on the construction of the building or structure, and

B is the amount of the writing-down allowances which would have been made under this section in respect of the capital expenditure referred to in A if the building or structure had at all times been an industrial building or structure within the meaning of section 268(1)(*h*) and on the assumption that that section had applied as respects capital expenditure incurred before—

(I) in the case of Aer Rianta cuideachta phoiblí theoranta, the vesting day, and

(II) in the case of any other person, the date of the passing of the Finance Act, 1998.

(3B)(*a*) This subsection shall apply to a building or structure to which section 268(1)(*f*) applies, being a building or structure in existence on the vesting day and vested in Aer Rianta cuideachta phoiblí theoranta on that day.

(*b*) For the purposes of this Part, in the case of a building or structure to which this subsection applies, expenditure shall be deemed to have been incurred by Aer Rianta cuideachta phoiblí theoranta on the vesting day on the construction of the building or structure of an amount determined by the formula—

$$A - B$$

where—

A is the amount of the capital expenditure originally incurred on the construction of the building or structure, and

B is the amount of the writing-down allowances which would have been made under this section in respect of the capital expenditure referred to in A for the period to the day before the vesting day if a claim for those allowances had been duly made and allowed.][14]

(4) Where the interest in a building or structure which is the relevant interest in relation to any expenditure is sold while the building or structure is an industrial building or structure, then, subject to any further adjustment under this subsection on a later sale, the writing-down allowance for any chargeable period, if that chargeable period or its basis period ends after the time of the sale, shall be the residue (within the meaning of section 277) of that expenditure immediately after the sale, reduced in the proportion (if it is less than one) which the length of the chargeable period bears to the part unexpired at the date of the sale of the period of—

(*a*) in relation to a building or structure which is to be regarded as an industrial building or structure within the meaning of paragraph (*a*) or (*b*) of section 268(1)—

(i) 50 years beginning with the time when the building or structure was first used, in the case where the capital expenditure on the construction of the building or structure was incurred before the 16th day of January, 1975, or

(ii) 25 years beginning with the time when the building or structure was first used, in the case where the capital expenditure on the construction of the building or structure is incurred on or after the 16th day of January, 1975,

(*b*) in relation to a building or structure which is to be regarded as an industrial building or structure within the meaning of paragraph (*c*) or (*e*) of section 268(1), 10 years beginning with the time when the building or structure was first used,

(*c*) in relation to a building or structure which is to be regarded as an industrial building or structure within the meaning of section 268(1)(*d*), other than a building or structure referred to in [paragraph (*d*) or (*da*)][15]—

(i) 10 years beginning with the time when the building or structure was first used, in the case where the capital expenditure on the construction of the building or structure was incurred before the 27th day of January, 1994, ...[16]

(ii) 7 years beginning with the time when the building or structure was first used, in the case where the capital expenditure on the construction of the building or structure is incurred on or after the 27th day of January, 1994, [or][17]

[(iii) subject to subsection (8), 25 years beginning with the time when the building or structure was first used, in the case where the capital expenditure on the construction (within the meaning of section 270) of the building or structure is incurred on or after 4 December 2002,][18]

(*d*) in relation to a building or structure which is to be regarded as an industrial building or structure within the meaning of section 268(1)(*d*) by reason of its use as a holiday cottage, 10 years beginning with the time when the building or structure was first used, ...[19]

[(*da*) in relation to a building or structure which is to be regarded as an industrial building or structure within the meaning of section 268(1)(*d*) by reason of its use as a guest house or a holiday hostel to which section 268(2C) applies, 25 years beginning with the time when the building or structure was first used, in the case where the capital expenditure on the construction (within the meaning of section 270) of the building or structure is incurred on or after 3 February 2005,][20]

[(*e*) in relation to a building or structure which is to be regarded as an industrial building or structure within the meaning of section 268(1)(*f*), 25 years beginning with—

(i) the time when the building or structure was first used, or

(ii) in the case of a building or structure to which subsection (3B) applies, the vesting day,][21]

[(*f*) in relation to a building or structure which is to be regarded as an industrial building or structure within the meaning of paragraph (*g*) or (*i*) of section 268(1), 7 years beginning with the time when the building or structure was first used, ...[22]][23]

[(*g*) in relation to a building or structure which is to be regarded as an industrial building or structure within the meaning of section 268(1)(*h*), 25 years beginning with—

(i) the time when the building or structure was first used, or

(ii) as respects a building or structure to which subsection (3A) applies—

(I) in the case of Aer Rianta cuideachta phoiblí theoranta, the vesting day, and

(II) in the case of any other person, the date of the passing of the Finance Act, [1998,][24]][25]

[and

(*h*) in relation to a building or structure which is to be regarded as an industrial building or structure within the meaning of [paragraph (*j*) or (*k*) of section 268(1)][26], 7 years beginning with the time when the building or structure was first used.][27]

(5) In ascertaining a writing-down allowance to be made to a person under subsection (4), the residue of expenditure mentioned in that subsection shall, where it exceeds the amount of expenditure incurred by that person in respect of the sale, be taken to be the amount of the expenditure so incurred.

(6) Notwithstanding any other provision of this section, in no case shall the amount of a writing-down allowance made to a person for any chargeable period in respect of any expenditure exceed what, apart from the writing off to be made by reason of the making of that allowance, would be the residue of that expenditure at the end of that chargeable period or its basis period.

[(7) For the purposes of this section, where a writing-down allowance has been made to a person for any chargeable period in respect of capital expenditure incurred on the construction of a building or structure within the meaning of paragraph (*d*) of section 268(1) and at the end of a chargeable period or its basis period the building or structure is not in use for the purposes specified in that paragraph, then, in relation to that expenditure—

(*a*) the building or structure shall not be treated as ceasing to be an industrial building or structure if, on the cessation of its use for the purposes specified in paragraph (*d*) of section 268(1), it is converted to use for the purposes specified in paragraph (*g*) of that section and at the end of the chargeable period or its basis period it is in use for those latter purposes, and

(*b*) as respects that chargeable period or its basis period and any subsequent chargeable period or basis period of it, the building or structure shall, notwithstanding the cessation of its use for the purposes specified in paragraph (*d*) of section 268(1), be treated as if it were in use for those purposes if at the end of the chargeable period or its basis period the building or structure is in use for the purposes specified in paragraph (*g*) of that section.][28]

[(8) Subsections (3)(*c*)(iii) and (4)(*c*)(iii) (as inserted by the Finance Act 2003) shall not apply as respects capital expenditure incurred on or before [31 July 2006][29] on the construction or refurbishment of a building or structure if—

(*a*) (i) a planning application (not being an application for outline permission within the meaning of section 36 of the Planning and Development Act 2000)[, in so far as planning permission is required,][30] in respect of the building or structure is made in accordance with the Planning and Development Regulations 2001 to 2002,

(ii) an acknowledgement of the application, which confirms that the application was received on or before [31 December 2004][31], is issued by the planning authority in accordance with article 26(2) of the Planning and Development Regulations 2001 (SI No 600 of 2001), and

(iii) the application is not an invalid application in respect of which a notice is issued by the planning authority in accordance with article 26(5) of those regulations,

(*b*) (i) [a planning application, in so far as planning permission was required,][32] in respect of the building or structure was made in accordance with the Local Government (Planning and Development) Regulations 1994 (SI No 86 of 1994), not being an application for outline permission within the meaning of article 3 of those regulations,

(ii) an acknowledgement of the application, which confirms that the application was received on or before 10 March 2002, was issued by the planning authority in accordance with article 29(2)(*a*) of the regulations referred to in subparagraph (i), and

(iii) the application was not an invalid application in respect of which a notice was issued by the planning authority in accordance with article 29(2)(*b*)(i) of those regulations,

[(*ba*) where the construction or refurbishment work on the building or structure represented by that expenditure is exempted development for the purposes of the Planning and Development Act 2000 by virtue of section 4 of that Act or by virtue of Part 2 of the Planning and Development Regulations 2001 (SI No 600 of 2001) and—

(i) a detailed plan in relation to the development work is prepared,

(ii) a binding contract in writing, under which the expenditure on the development is incurred, is in existence, and

(iii) work to the value of 5 per cent of the development costs is carried out,

not later than 31 December 2004.][33]

or

(*c*) (i) the construction or refurbishment of the building or structure is a development in respect of which an application for a certificate under section 25(7)(*a*)(ii) of the Dublin Docklands Development Authority Act 1997 is made to the Authority (within the meaning of that Act),

(ii) an acknowledgement of the application, which confirms that the application was received on or before [31 December 2004][34], is issued by that Authority, and

(iii) the application is not an invalid application.][35]

Notes

Re subss (3A) and (3B): the Air Navigation and Transport (Amendment) Act, 1998 (Vesting Day) Order 1998, SI No 326 of 1998, appointed 1 January 1999 as vesting day for the purposes of the Air Navigation and Transport (Amendment) Act, 1998.

Amendments

1 Substituted by FA 2005 s 34(*b*)(i)(I) with effect from 1 January 2005; previously "paragraph (*d*)".

2 Deleted by FA 2003 s 25(1)(*b*)(i)(I) with effect from 4 December 2002; previously "or".

3 Inserted by FA 2003 s 25(1)(*b*)(i)(II) with effect from 4 December 2002.

4 Subs (3)(*c*)(iii) inserted by FA 2003 s 25(1)(*b*)(i)(III) with effect from 4 December 2002.

5 Deleted by FA 1998 s 22(*b*)(i)(I) with effect from 6 April 1998 ; previously "and".

6 Subs (3)(*da*) inserted FA 2005 s 34(*b*)(i)(II) with effect from 1 January 2005.

7 Substituted by FA 1998 s 22(*b*)(i)(II) with effect from 6 April 1998; previously "subsection (2)(*c*).".

8 Deleted inserted by FA 2001 s 64(1)(*b*)(i)(I) with effect from such date as the Minister for Finance may by order appoint; previously "and". By virtue of the Finance Act, 2001 (Commencement of Section 64) Order 2002, FA 2001 s 64 comes into operation as on and from 15 May 2002.

9 Subs (3)(*f*) substituted by FA 1999 s 49(*b*)(i) with effect from 6 April 1999.

10 Substituted by FA 2001 s 64(1)(*b*)(i)(II) with effect from such date as the Minister for Finance may by order appoint; previously "subsection (2)(*c*), and". By virtue of the Finance Act, 2001 (Commencement of Section 64) Order 2002, FA 2001 s 64 comes into operation as on and from 15 May 2002.

11 Subs (3)(*g*) inserted by FA 1998 s 20(*b*)(i) with effect from 6 April 1998.

12 Substituted by FA 2002 s 34(1)(*b*) with effect from such day as the Minister for Finance may by order appoint; previously "section 268(1)(*j*)". By virtue of the Finance Act, 2002 (Commencement of Section 34) Order 2002, FA 2002 s 34 comes into operation as on and from 15 May 2002.

13 Subs (3)(*h*) inserted by FA 2001 s 64(1)(*b*)(i)(III) with effect from such date as the Minister for Finance may by order appoint. By virtue of the Finance Act, 2001 (Commencement of Section 64) Order 2002, FA 2001 s 64 comes into operation as on and from 15 May 2002.

14 Subss (3A)–(3B) inserted by FA 1998 s 20(*b*)(ii) with effect from 6 April 1998.

15 Substituted by FA 2005 s 34(*b*)(ii)(I) with effect from 1 January 2005; previously "paragraph (*d*)".

16 Deleted by FA 2003 s 25(1)(*b*)(ii)(I) with effect from 4 December 2002; previously "or".

17 Inserted by FA 2003 s 25(1)(*b*)(ii)(II) with effect from 4 December 2002.

18 Subs (4)(*c*)(iii) inserted by FA 2003 s 25(1)(*b*)(ii)(III) with effect from 4 December 2002.

19 Deleted by FA 1998 s 20(*b*)(iii)(I) with effect from 6 April 1998; previously "and".

20 Subs (4)(*da*) inserted by FA 2005 s 34(*b*)(ii)(II) with effect from 1 January 2005.

21 Subs (4)(*e*) substituted by FA 1998 s 20(*b*)(iii)(II) with effect from 6 April 1998.

22 Deleted by FA 2001 s 64(1)(*b*)(ii)(I) with effect from such date as the Minister for Finance may by order appoint; previously "and". By virtue of the Finance Act, 2001 (Commencement of Section 64) Order 2002, FA 2001 s 64 comes into operation as on and from 15 May 2002.

23 Subs (4)(*f*) substituted by FA 1999 s 49(*b*)(ii) with effect from 6 April 1999.

24 Substituted by FA 2001 s 64(1)(*b*)(i)(II) with effect from such date as the Minister for Finance may by order appoint; previously "1998.". By virtue of the Finance Act, 2001 (Commencement of Section 64) Order 2002, FA 2001 s 64 comes into operation as on and from 15 May 2002.

25 Subs (4)(*g*) inserted by FA 1998 s 20(*b*)(iii)(III) with effect from 6 April 1998.

26 Substituted by FA 2002 s 34(1)(*b*) with effect from such day as the Minister for Finance may by order appoint; previously "section 268(1)(*j*)". By virtue of the Finance Act, 2002 (Commencement of Section 34) Order 2002, FA 2002 s 34 comes into operation as on and from 15 May 2002.

27 Subs (4)(*h*) inserted by FA 2001 s 64(1)(*b*)(ii)(III) with effect from such date as the Minister for Finance may by order appoint. By virtue of the Finance Act, 2001 (Commencement of Section 64) Order 2002, FA 2001 s 64 comes into operation as on and from 15 May 2002.

28 Subs (7) inserted by FA 1998 s 22(*b*)(iii) with effect from 6 April 1998.

29 Substituted by FA 2004 s 25(1)(*b*)(i) with effect from 1 January 2004; previously "31 December 2004".

30 Inserted by FA 2004 s 25(1)(*b*)(ii) with effect from 4 December 2002.

31 Substituted by FA 2004 s 25(1)(*b*)(iii) with effect from 4 December 2002; previously "31 May 2003".

32 Substituted by FA 2004 s 25(1)(*b*)(iv) with effect from 1 January 2004; previously "a planning application".

33 Subs (8)(*ba*) inserted by FA 2004 s 25(1)(*b*)(v) with effect from 1 January 2004.

34 Substituted by FA 2004 s 25(1)(*b*)(vi) with effect from 1 January 2004; previously "31 May 2003".

35 Subs (8) inserted by FA 2003 s 25(1)(*b*)(iii) with effect from 4 December 2002.

Cross-references

Capital allowances for buildings used for certain childcare purposes, in subs (3)(*a*)(ii) for "4 per cent" read "15 per cent", in subs (4)(*a*)(ii) for "25 years" read "7 years": s 843A(3).

Capital allowances for buildings used for third level education, in subs (3)(*a*)(ii) for "4 per cent" read "15 per cent", in subs (4)(*a*)(ii) for "25 years" read "7 years": s 843(3).

Contribution to local authority for treatment of trade effluents or provision of water supply: s 310(2).

Deduction of five-twelfths of rateable valuation: s 85(1).

Holiday cottages, balancing charges, anti-avoidance: s 274(6); restriction on use of allowances: s 405(1).

Industrial building allowance for IDA list projects, no increased or accelerated allowance: s 271(5).

Industrial buildings bought unused: s 279(2)(*a*).

Industrial building or structure, meaning of: s 268(12); subs (4)(*h*): s 268(2A)(*h*), (2B)(*f*).

Property investment, restriction of tax incentives on: s 408(2).

Relevant period, subs (6): s 274(5)(*c*).

Restriction of balancing allowance on sale of industrial building, refurbishment expenditure: in subs (4), for "the building or structure was first used" substitute "the capital expenditure on refurbishment of the building or structure was incurred": s 276(2).

Writing off expenditure (subs (4)), and meaning of "residue of expenditure": s 277(4)(*a*).

Renewal incentives

Resort areas

Commercial building construction or refurbishment expenditure, for subs (3), read "(3) A writing down allowance shall be of an amount equal to 5 per cent of the expenditure referred to in subsection (2)(*c*).": s 353(4)(*b*).

Double rent allowance: s 354(1)(qualifying premises).

Holiday cottages, disclaimer of capital allowance: s 355(4).

Industrial building construction or refurbishment expenditure, for subs (3), read "(3) A writing down allowance shall be of an amount equal to 5 per cent of the expenditure referred to in subsection (2)(*c*).": s 352(3).

Park and ride facilities

Qualifying park and ride facilities, construction or refurbishment expenditure, in subs (4)(*a*)(ii) for "beginning with the time when the building or structure was first used" read: "beginning with the time when the building or structure was first used as an industrial building or structure": s 372V(4A)(*b*).

Commercial premises, construction or refurbishment expenditure, in subs (4)(*a*)(ii) for "beginning with the time when the building or structure was first used" read: "beginning with the time when the building or structure was first used as an industrial building or structure": s 372W(5A)(*b*).

Revenue precedents

Issue: Abbatoirs, whether qualify as industrial buildings.

Decision: Yes, unless ancillary to a retail outlet.

Issue: Whether industrial buildings allowances apply to sawmill.

Decision: Yes, provided treatment or processing carried on in the mill and machinery is involved.

Issue: A company received Industrial Development Authority grants in respect of an industrial building. These grants were repayable in the event of the company ceasing to trade. The company ceased trading and sold the industrial building for a nominal sum conditional on the purchaser entering into an agreement with the IDA to assume liability for the vendors grants if the purchaser ceased to trade. Is this contingent liability regarded as expenditure incurred for the purposes of TCA 1997 s 272(5)?

Decision: Expenditure is incurred on the date on which it becomes payable. If the liability is contingent on some future uncertain event it cannot be regarded as payable until that event is no longer contingent but certain. It therefore follows that the current expenditure incurred is the nominal sum.

Issue: S 22 Finance Act 1994 changed the industrial building writing down allowance from 10% to 15%. Does the new rate apply to existing hotels on or after 27/01/94? In the event of a sale after 27 January 1994, is the residue after sale written off over 7 years?

Decision: Section 22 of the Finance Act 1994 provides that the 15% allowance and 7 year life only apply where the expenditure on construction is incurred on or after 27 January 1994. Where the construction expenditure is incurred before this date, there is a 10% allowance, and the building has a 10 year life. A person who purchases a hotel second hand does not incur expenditure on the construction of the hotel. If, on or after 27 January 1994, a person purchases second hand a hotel, the construction expenditure on which was incurred before that date, the building still has a 10 year life, and the industrial buildings annual allowances will be by reference to the residue of the expenditure over the remainder of that 10 year.

Issue: Where warehousing facilities provided to person carrying on a qualifying trade for IBA purposes is building in use for qualifying trade.

Decision: Where the building is let to a person carrying on a trade carried on in a mill, factory or other similar premises, it is in use for the lessee's trade. Where the person providing the warehousing facilities does so as part of a trade, the building is in use for the purposes of the trade of that person and is not in use for the purposes of a qualifying trade.

Issue: Does a distribution in specie constitute a sale for the purposes of the section?

Decision: No.

Issue: A building was used for the purpose of a trade carried on in a factory for a number of years. No industrial buildings writing down allowances were claimed. The building was subsequently sold while it was an industrial building by the IDA. What allowance is the purchaser entitled to?

Decision: The allowance available to the purchaser is the expenditure incurred on the construction written off over the unexpired part of the tax life of the building.

Tax Briefing

TB52 May 2003 p 11 — Capital Allowances for Hotels and Holiday Cottages (Finance Act 2003 changes).

Definitions

person: IA 1937 s 11(*c*); vesting day: s 268(10); writing: IA 1937 Sch.

Former enactments

ITA 1967 s 264; FA 1975 s 34(2)(*a*)(ii) and (iii) and (3); CTA 1976 s 21(1) and Sch 1 paras 23, 72; FA 1986 s 52(2); FA 1994 s 22(1)(*c*) and (2); FA 1996 s 28(1).

Corresponding UK tax provision

Capital Allowances Act 2001 ss 309–312.

273 Acceleration of writing-down allowances in respect of certain expenditure on certain industrial buildings or structures

(1) In this section—

"industrial development agency" means the Industrial Development Authority, Shannon Free Airport Development Company Limited or Údarás na Gaeltachta;

"qualifying expenditure" means capital expenditure incurred on or after the 2nd day of February, 1978, by the person to whom the allowance under section 272 is to be made on the construction of a building or structure which is to be an industrial building or structure occupied by that person for a purpose specified in paragraph (*a*), (*b*) or (*d*) of section 268(1), but excluding such expenditure incurred for the purposes of the trade of hotel-keeping unless it is incurred on the construction of premises which are registered in a register kept by Bord Fáilte Éireann under the Tourist Traffic Acts, 1939 to 1995.

(2) (*a*) Subject to this section, where for any chargeable period an allowance is to be made under section 272 in respect of qualifying expenditure, the allowance shall, subject to subsection (6) of that section, be increased by such amount as is specified by the person to whom the allowance is to be made and, in relation to a case in which this subsection has applied, any reference in the Tax Acts to an allowance made under section 272 shall be construed as a reference to that allowance as increased under this section.

(*b*) As respects any qualifying expenditure incurred on or after the 1st day of April, 1988, any allowance made under section 272 and increased under paragraph (*a*) in respect of that expenditure, whether claimed for one chargeable period or more than one such period, shall not in the aggregate exceed—

(i) if the qualifying expenditure was incurred before the 1st day of April, 1989, 75 per cent,

(ii) if the qualifying expenditure was incurred on or after the 1st day of April, 1989, and before the 1st day of April, 1991, 50 per cent, or

(iii) if the qualifying expenditure was incurred on or after the 1st day of April, 1991, and before the 1st day of April, 1992, 25 per cent,

of the amount of that qualifying expenditure.

(3) Notwithstanding subsection (2), but subject to subsections (4) and (6)—

(*a*) no allowance made under section 272 in respect of qualifying expenditure incurred on or after the 1st day of April, 1992, shall be increased under this section, and

(*b*) as respects chargeable periods ending on or after the 6th day of April, 1999, no allowance made under section 272 in respect of qualifying expenditure incurred before the 1st day of April, 1992, shall be increased under this section.

(4) This section shall apply in relation to capital expenditure incurred on the construction of an industrial building or structure to which subsection (5) applies as if subsections (2)(*b*) and (3) were deleted.

(5) This subsection shall apply to—

(*a*) an industrial building or structure provided—

(i) before the 23rd day of April, 1996, for use for the purposes of trading operations, or

(ii) on or after the 23rd day of April, 1996, by a company for use for the purposes of trading operations carried on by the company,

which are relevant trading operations within the meaning of section 445 or 446 but, in relation to capital expenditure incurred on the provision of an industrial building or structure on or after the 6th day of May, 1993, excluding an industrial building or structure provided by a lessor to a lessee other than in the course of the carrying on by the lessor of those relevant trading operations,

(*b*) an industrial building or structure the expenditure on the provision of which was incurred before the 31st day of December, 1995, under a binding contract entered into on or before the 27th day of January, 1988, and (*c*) an industrial building or structure provided for the purposes of a project approved by an industrial development agency on or before the 31st day of December, 1988, and in respect of the provision of which expenditure was incurred before the 31st day of December, 1995; but, as respects an industrial building or structure provided for the purposes of a project approved by an industrial development agency in the period from the 1st day of January, 1986, to the 31st day of December, 1988, this paragraph shall apply as if the reference to the 31st day of December, 1995, were a reference to the 31st day of December, 1996.

(6) This section shall apply in relation to capital expenditure incurred on the construction of a building or structure which is to be an industrial building or structure to which subsection (7)(*a*) applies—

(*a*) as if in subsection (2)(*b*)—

(i) the following subparagraph were substituted for subparagraph (ii):

"(ii) if the qualifying expenditure is incurred on or after the 1st day of April, 1989, 50 per cent,",

and

(ii) subparagraph (iii) were deleted,

and

(*b*) as if subsection (3) were deleted.

(7) (*a*) This subsection shall apply to—

(i) an industrial building or structure provided for the purposes of a project approved for grant assistance by an industrial development agency in the period from the 1st day of January, 1989, to the 31st day of December, 1990, and in respect of the provision of which expenditure is incurred before the 31st day of December, 1997 [, or before the 30th day of June, 1998, if such expenditure would have been incurred before the 31st day of December, 1997, but for the existence of circumstances which resulted in legal proceedings being initiated, being proceedings which were the subject of an order of the High Court made before the 1st day of January, 1998];[1] but, as respects an industrial building or structure provided for the purposes of any such project specified in the list referred to in section 133(8)(*c*)(iv), this paragraph shall apply as if the reference to the 31st day of December, 1997, [where it first occurs,][2] were a reference to the 31st day of December, 2002, and

(ii) a building or structure which is to be an industrial building or structure within the meaning of section 268(1)(*d*) and in respect of the provision of which expenditure was incurred before the 31st day of December, 1995, where a binding contract for the provision of the building or structure was entered into before the 31st day of December, 1990.

(*b*) Paragraph (*a*)(ii) shall not apply if the building or structure referred to in that paragraph is not registered within 6 months after the date of the completion of that building or structure in a register kept by Bord Fáilte Éireann under the Tourist Traffic Acts, 1939 to 1995, and where by virtue of this section any allowance or increased allowance has been granted, any necessary additional assessments may be made to give effect to this paragraph.

(8) Where for any chargeable period an allowance under section 272 in respect of qualifying expenditure is increased under this section, no allowance under section 271 shall be made in respect of that qualifying expenditure for that or any subsequent chargeable period.

Amendments

1 Inserted by FA 1998 s 21(*a*)(i) with effect from 6 April 1998.

2 Inserted by FA 1998 s 21(*a*)(ii) with effect from 6 April 1998.

Cross-references

Industrial building allowance for IDA list projects, no increased or accelerated allowance: s 271(5).
Machinery or plant: initial allowance, subs (7)(*a*)(i): s 283(5).
Machinery or plant: accelerated wear and tear allowances, subs (7)(*a*)(i): s 285(7)(*a*)(i).
Multi-storey car parks, transitional: Sch 32 para 9(2).

Renewal incentives

Custom House Dock area

Commercial premises construction expenditure, in subs (1) delete the definition of "industrial development agency", and delete subss (2)(*b*) and (3)–(7): s 323(3)(*a*)(ii).

Dublin Docklands Area

Industrial building construction or refurbishment expenditure, in subs (1) delete the definition of "industrial development agency", and delete subss (2)(*b*) and (3)–(7): s 368(3); qualifying period: s 368(5).
Commercial premises construction or refurbishment expenditure, in subs (1) delete the definition of "industrial development agency" and delete subss (2)(*b*) and (3)–(7): s 369(4)(*b*); qualifying period: s 369(7).
Double rent allowance: s 370(1)(qualifying premises).

Temple Bar Area

Industrial building construction expenditure, in subs (1) delete the definition of "industrial development agency", for subs (2)(*b*) read: "(*b*) As respects any qualifying expenditure, any allowance made under section 272, and increased under paragraph (*a*), in respect of that expenditure, whether claimed in one chargeable period or more than one such period, shall not in the aggregate exceed 50 per cent of the amount of that qualifying expenditure", and delete subss (3)–(7): s 331(3)(*a*); qualifying period: s 331(6).
Industrial building refurbishment expenditure, in subs (1) delete the definition of "industrial development agency", and delete subss (2)(*b*) and (3)–(7): s 331(3)(*b*); qualifying period: s 331(6).
Commercial premises construction or refurbishment expenditure, in subs (1) delete the definition of "industrial development agency", and delete subss (2)(*b*) and (3)–(7): s 332(4); qualifying period: s 332(8).

Designated areas or street

Industrial building, construction or refurbishment expenditure, in subs (1) delete the definition of "industrial development agency", for subs (2)(*b*) read:
"(*b*) As respects any qualifying expenditure, any allowance made under section 272 and increased under paragraph (*a*) in respect of that expenditure, whether claimed for one chargeable period or more than one such period, shall not in the aggregate exceed 50 per cent of the amount of that qualifying expenditure." and delete subss (3)–(5): s 341(3); qualifying period: s 341(6).
Commercial premises, construction or refurbishment expenditure: in subs (1) delete the definition of "industrial development agency", and delete subss (2)(*b*), and (3)–(7): s 342(4)(*b*); qualifying period: s 342(7).
Double rent allowance: s 345(1) (qualifying premises).

Enterprise areas

Qualifying building construction or refurbishment expenditure, in subs (1) delete the definition of "industrial development agency", for subs (2)(*b*) read:
"(*b*) As respects any qualifying expenditure, any allowance made under section 272 and increased under paragraph (*a*) in respect of that expenditure, whether claimed for one chargeable period or more than one such period, shall not in the aggregate exceed 50 per cent of the amount of that qualifying expenditure." and delete subss (3)–(7): s 343(8)(*b*); qualifying period: s 343(10).

Multi-storey car parks

Qualifying car park, construction or refurbishment expenditure: in subs (1) delete the definition of "industrial development agency", and delete subss (2)(*b*), and (3)–(7): s 344(4)(*b*); qualifying period: s 344(7).

Qualifying areas

Industrial buildings, construction or refurbishment expenditure, in subs (1) delete the definition of "industrial development agency", for subs (2)(*b*) read:

"(*b*) As respects any qualifying expenditure, any allowance made under section 272 and increased under paragraph (*a*) in respect of that expenditure, whether claimed for one chargeable period or more than one such period, shall not in the aggregate exceed 50 per cent of the amount of that qualifying expenditure." and delete subs (3) to (7): s 372C(3); qualifying period: s 372C(6).

Commercial premises, construction or refurbishment expenditure, in subs (1) delete the definition of "industrial development agency", for subs (2)(*b*) read:

"(*b*) As respects any qualifying expenditure, any allowance made under section 272 and increased under paragraph (*a*) in respect of that expenditure, whether claimed for one chargeable period or more than one such period, shall not in the aggregate exceed 50 per cent of the amount of that qualifying expenditure." and delete subs (3) to (7): s 372D(4)(*b*).

Double rent allowance: s 372E(1) (qualifying premises).

Qualifying rural areas

Industrial buildings, construction or refurbishment expenditure, in subs (1) delete the definition of "industrial development agency", for subs (2)(*b*) read:

"(*b*) As respects any qualifying expenditure, any allowance made under section 272 and increased under paragraph (*a*) in respect of that expenditure, whether claimed for one chargeable period or more than one such period, shall not in the aggregate exceed 50 per cent of the amount of that qualifying expenditure." and delete subs (3) to (7): s 372M(3); qualifying period: s 372M(6).

Commercial buildings or structures, construction or refurbishment expenditure, in subs (1) delete the definition of "industrial development agency", for subs (2)(*b*) read:

"(*b*) As respects any qualifying expenditure, any allowance made under section 272 and increased under paragraph (*a*) in respect of that expenditure, whether claimed for one chargeable period or more than one such period, shall not in the aggregate exceed 50 per cent of the amount of that qualifying expenditure." and delete subs (3) to (7).": s 372N(4)(*b*).

Double rent allowance: s 372O(1) (qualifying premises).

Resort areas

Industrial building, construction or refurbishment expenditure, in subs (1) delete the definition of "industrial development agency", for subs (2)(*b*) read:

"(*b*) As respects any qualifying expenditure, any allowance made under section 272 and increased under paragraph (*a*) in respect of that expenditure, whether claimed for one chargeable period or more than one such period, shall not in the aggregate exceed 75 per cent of the amount of that qualifying expenditure." and delete subss (3)–(7): s 352(4); qualifying period: s 352(6).

Commercial premises, construction or refurbishment expenditure, in subs (1) delete the definition of "industrial development agency", for subs (2)(*b*) read:

"(*b*) As respects any qualifying expenditure, any allowance made under section 272 and increased under paragraph (*a*) in respect of that expenditure, whether claimed for one chargeable period or more than one such period, shall not in the aggregate exceed 75 per cent of the amount of that qualifying expenditure." and delete subss (3)–(7): s 353(4); qualifying period: s 353(7).

Double rent allowance: s 354(1) (qualifying premises).

Park and ride facilities

Qualifying park and ride facilities, construction or refurbishment expenditure, in subs (1) delete definition of "industrial development agency" and delete subss (2)(*b*) and (3) to (7): s 372V(3)(*b*).

Commercial premises, construction or refurbishment expenditure, in subs (1) delete definition of "industrial development agency" and delete subss (2)(*b*) and (3) to (7): s 372W(4)(*b*).

Designated areas in certain towns

Industrial building, construction or refurbishment expenditure, in subs (1) delete the definition of "industrial development agency", for subs (2)(*b*) read:

"(*b*) As respects any qualifying expenditure, any allowance made under section 272 and increased under paragraph (*a*) in respect of that expenditure, whether claimed for one chargeable period or more than one such period, shall not in the aggregate exceed 50 per cent of the amount of that expenditure.", and delete subs (3) to (7): s 372AC(3).

Commercial premises, construction or refurbishment expenditure, in subs (1) delete the definition of "industrial development agency", for subs (2)(*b*) read:

"(*b*) As respects any qualifying expenditure, any allowance made under section 272 and increased under paragraph (*a*) in respect of that expenditure, whether claimed for one chargeable period or more than one such period, shall not in the aggregate exceed 50 per cent of the amount of that expenditure.", and delete subs (3) to (7): s 372AD(3)(*b*).

Childcare facilities

Buildings used for childcare purposes, qualifying expenditure incurred on or after 1 December 1999, in subs (1) delete definition of "industrial development agency" and delete subss (2)(*b*) and (3) to (7): s 843(3A)(*b*).

Revenue precedents

Issue: Are owners of holiday apartments, listed with Bord Fáilte, who let such premises to tourists entitled to free depreciation under the section?

Decision: No. The owners are lessors and not owner-occupiers.

Issue: Did capital expenditure on a new industrial building provided for the purposes of a project approved by the IDA on or before 31/12/90 qualify for accelerated capital allowances?

Decision: It was agreed that this new building will be used in connection with the same enterprise which was outlined in the IDA approval, although the manufacturing process and the final product were not the same as the original due to changes in production technology which resulted in a more sophisticated product.

Definitions

High Court: IA 1937 Sch; Income Tax Acts: s 1(2); person: IA 1937 s 11(*c*); trade: s 3(1).

Former enactments

FA 1978 s 25; FA 1979 s 25; FA 1988 s 48 and s 51(1)(*a*), (*c*) and (*cc*), (4)(*b*) and (6); FA 1989 s 16; FA 1990 s 76, s 80 and s 81(1)(*a*) and (*b*) and proviso to (1) and (5); FA 1993 s 33; FA 1995 s 26 and s 27; FA 1996 s 43 and s 132(1) and Sch 5 Pt I para 11.

274 Balancing allowances and balancing charges

(1) (*a*) Where any capital expenditure has been incurred on the construction of a building or structure in respect of which an allowance has been made under this Chapter, and any of the following events occurs—

(i) the relevant interest in the building or structure is sold,

(ii) that interest, being a leasehold interest, comes to an end otherwise than on the person entitled to the leasehold interest acquiring the interest which is reversionary on the leasehold interest,

(iii) the building or structure is demolished or destroyed or, without being demolished or destroyed, ceases altogether to be used, or

(iv) subject to subsection (2), where consideration (other than rent or an amount treated or, as respects consideration received on or after the 26th day of March, 1997, partly treated as rent under section 98) is received by the person entitled to the relevant interest in respect of an interest which is subject to that relevant interest,

an allowance or charge (in this Chapter referred to as a **"balancing allowance"** or a **"balancing charge"**) shall, in the circumstances mentioned in this section, be made to or on, as the case may be, the person entitled to the relevant interest immediately before that event occurs, for the chargeable period related to that event.

(*b*) Notwithstanding paragraph (*a*), no balancing allowance or balancing charge shall be made by reason of any event referred to in that paragraph occurring more than—

(i) in relation to a building or structure which is to be regarded as an industrial building or structure within the meaning of paragraph (*a*) or (*b*) of section 268(1)—

(I) 50 years after the building or structure was first used, in the case where the capital expenditure on the construction of the building or structure was incurred before the 16th day of January, 1975, or

(II) 25 years after the building or structure was first used, in the case where the capital expenditure on the construction of the building or structure is incurred on or after the 16th day of January, 1975,

[(ii) in relation to a building or structure which is to be regarded as an industrial building or structure within the meaning of paragraph (*c*), (*e*), (*g*) or (*i*) of section 268(1), 10 years after the building or structure was first used,][1]

(iii) in relation to a building or structure which is to be regarded as an industrial building or structure within the meaning of section 268(1)(*d*), other than a building or structure to which [subparagraph (iv) or (iv*a*)][2] relates—

(I) 10 years after the building or structure was first used, in the case where the capital expenditure on the construction of the building or structure was incurred before the 27th day of January, 1994, ...[3]

(II) 7 years after the building or structure was first used, in the case where the capital expenditure on the construction of the building or structure is incurred on or after the 27th day of January, 1994, [or][4]

[(III) subject to subsection (1A), 25 years after the building or structure was first used, in the case where the capital expenditure on the construction (within the meaning of section 270) of the building or structure is incurred on or after 4 December 2002,][5]

(iv) in relation to a building or structure which is to be regarded as an industrial building or structure within the meaning of section 268(1)(*d*) by reason of its use as a holiday cottage, 10 years after the building or structure was first used, ...[6]

[(iv*a*) in relation to a building or structure which is to be regarded as an industrial building or structure within the meaning of section 268(1)(*d*) by reason of its use as a guest house or a holiday hostel to which section 268(2C) applies, 25 years after the building or structure was first used, in the case where the capital expenditure on the construction (within the meaning of section 270) of the building or structure is incurred on or after 3 February 2005,][7]

[(v) in relation to a building or structure which is to be regarded as an industrial building or structure within the meaning of section 268(1)(*f*), 25 years after—

(I) the building or structure was first used, or

(II) in the case of a building or structure to which section 272(3B) applies, the vesting day, ...[8]][9]

[(vi) in relation to a building or structure which is to be regarded as an industrial building or structure within the meaning of section 268(1)(*h*), 25 years after—

(I) the building or structure was first used, or

(II) as respects a building or structure to which section 272(3A) applies—

(A) in the case of Aer Rianta cuideachta phoiblí theoranta, the vesting day, and

(B) in the case of any other person, the date of the passing of the Finance Act, [1998,][10]][11]

[and

(vii) in relation to a building or structure which is to be regarded as an industrial building or structure within the meaning of [paragraph (*j*) or (*k*) of section 268(1)][12], 10 years beginning with the time when the building or structure was first used.][13]

[(1A) Subsection (1)(*b*)(iii)(III) (as inserted by the Finance Act 2003) shall not apply as respects capital expenditure incurred on or before [31 July 2006][14] on the construction or refurbishment of a building or structure if—

(*a*) (i) a planning application (not being an application for outline permission within the meaning of section 36 of the Planning and Development Act 2000)[, in so far as planning permission is required,][15] in respect of the building or structure is made in accordance with the Planning and Development Regulations 2001 to 2002,

(ii) an acknowledgement of the application, which confirms that the application was received on or before [31 December 2004][16], is issued by the planning authority in accordance with article 26(2) of the Planning and Development Regulations 2001 (SI No 600 of 2001), and

(iii) the application is not an invalid application in respect of which a notice is issued by the planning authority in accordance with article 26(5) of those regulations,

(*b*) (i) [a planning application, in so far as planning permission was required,][17] in respect of the building or structure was made in accordance with the Local Government (Planning and Development) Regulations 1994 (SI No 86 of 1994), not being an application for outline permission within the meaning of article 3 of those regulations,

(ii) an acknowledgement of the application, which confirms that the application was received on or before 10 March 2002, was issued by the planning authority in accordance with article 29(2)(*a*) of the regulations referred to in subparagraph (i), and

(iii) the application was not an invalid application in respect of which a notice was issued by the planning authority in accordance with article 29(2)(*b*)(i) of those regulations,

[(*ba*) where the construction or refurbishment work on the building or structure represented by that expenditure is exempted development for the purposes of the Planning and Development Act 2000 by virtue of section 4 of that Act or by virtue of Part 2 of the Planning and Development Regulations 2001 (SI No 600 of 2001) and—

(i) a detailed plan in relation to the development work is prepared,

(ii) a binding contract in writing, under which the expenditure on the development is incurred, is in existence, and

(iii) work to the value of 5 per cent of the development costs is carried out, not later than 31 December 2004.][18]

or

(*c*) (i) the construction or refurbishment of the building or structure is a development in respect of which an application for a certificate under section 25(7)(*a*)(ii) of the Dublin Docklands Development Authority Act 1997 is made to the Authority (within the meaning of that Act),

(ii) an acknowledgement of the application, which confirms that the application was received on or before [31 December 2004][19], is issued by that Authority, and

(iii) the application is not an invalid application.][20]

(2) Subsection (1)(*a*)(iv) shall not apply as respects the relevant interest in a building or structure in use for the purposes of a trade or part of a trade of hotel-keeping where a binding contract for the provision of the building or structure was entered into after the 27th day of January, 1988, and before the 1st day of June, 1988.

(3) Where there are no sale, insurance, salvage or compensation moneys, or consideration of the type referred to in subsection (1)(*a*)(iv), or where the residue of the expenditure immediately before the event exceeds those moneys or that consideration, a balancing allowance shall be made, and the amount of that allowance shall be the amount of that residue or, as the case may be, of the excess of that residue over those moneys [or that consideration; but this subsection shall not apply in the case of consideration of the type referred to in subsection (1)(*a*)(iv) which is received on or after 5 March 2001.][21]

(4) Where the sale, insurance, salvage or compensation moneys, or consideration of the type referred to in subsection (1)(*a*)(iv), exceed the residue, if any, of the expenditure immediately before the event, a balancing charge shall be made, and the amount on which it is made shall be an amount equal to the excess or, where the residue is nil, to those moneys or that consideration.

(5) (*a*) In this subsection, **"the relevant period"** means the period beginning when the building or structure was first used for any purpose and ending—

(i) if the event giving rise to the balancing allowance or balancing charge occurs on the last day of a chargeable period or its basis period, on that day, or

(ii) in any other case, on the latest date before that event which is the last day of a chargeable period or its basis period;

but where before that event the building or structure has been sold while an industrial building or structure, the relevant period shall begin on the day following that sale or, if there has been more than one such sale, the last such sale.

(*b*) Where a balancing allowance or a balancing charge is to be made to or on a person, and any part of the relevant period is not comprised in a chargeable period for which a writing-down allowance has been made to such person or is not comprised in the basis period for such chargeable period, the amount of the balancing allowance or, as the case may be, the amount on which the balancing charge is to be made shall be reduced in the proportion which the part or parts so comprised bears to the whole of the relevant period.

(*c*) Notwithstanding paragraph (*b*), where but for section 272(6) or 321(5) a writing-down allowance would have been made to a person for any chargeable period, the part of the relevant period comprised in that chargeable period or its basis period shall be deemed for the purposes of this subsection to be comprised in a chargeable period for which a writing-down allowance was made to the person.

(6) Where a building or structure which is to be regarded as an industrial building or structure within the meaning of section 268(1)(*d*) by reason of its use as a holiday cottage ceases to be comprised in premises registered in a register referred to in section 268 in such circumstances that apart from this subsection this section would not apply in relation to the building or structure, the relevant interest in the building or structure shall for the purposes of this Chapter (other than section 272(4)) be deemed on such cesser to have been sold while the building or structure was an industrial building or structure and the net proceeds of the sale shall be deemed for those purposes to be an amount equal to the capital expenditure incurred on the construction of the building or structure.

(7) Where a balancing charge is made under this section by virtue of subsection (6) and the relevant interest in the building or structure is not subsequently sold by the person on whom the charge is made while the building or structure is not an industrial building or structure, such person shall, if the building or structure again becomes comprised in a premises registered in a register referred to in section 268, be treated for the purposes of this Chapter as if, at the time of the cesser referred to in subsection (6), such person were the buyer of the relevant interest deemed under that subsection to have been sold.

(8) Notwithstanding any other provision of this section, in no case shall the amount on which a balancing charge is made on a person in respect of any expenditure on the construction of a building or structure exceed the amount of the industrial building allowance, if any, made to such person in respect of that expenditure together with the amount of any writing-down allowances made to such person in respect of that expenditure for chargeable periods which end on or before the date of the event giving rise to the charge or, as the case may be, for chargeable periods for which the basis periods end on or before that date.

Notes

Re subs (1)(*b*)(v), (vi): the Air Navigation and Transport (Amendment) Act, 1998 (Vesting Day) Order 1998, SI No 326 of 1998, appointed 1 January 1999 as vesting day for the purposes of the Air Navigation and Transport (Amendment) Act, 1998.

Amendments

1 Subs(1)(*b*)(ii) substituted by FA 1999 s 48(*c*) with effect from 6 April 1999.

2 Substituted by FA 2005 s 34(*c*)(i) with effect from 1 January 2005; previously "subparagraph (iv)".

3 Deleted by FA 2003 s 25(1)(*c*)(i)(I) with effect from 4 December 2002; previously "or".

4 Inserted by FA 2003 s 25(1)(*c*)(i)(II) with effect from 4 December 2002.

5 Subs (1)(*b*)(iii)(III) inserted by FA 2003 s 25(1)(*c*)(i)(III) with effect from 4 December 2002.

6 Deleted by FA 1998 s 20(*c*)(i) with effect from 6 April 1998; previously "and".

7 Subs (1)(*b*)(iva) inserted by FA 2005 s 34(*c*)(ii) with effect from 1 January 2005.

8 Deleted by FA 2001 s 64(1)(*c*)(i) with effect from such date as the Minister for Finance may by order appoint; previously "and". By virtue of the Finance Act, 2001 (Commencement of Section 64) Order 2002, FA 2001 s 64 comes into operation as on and from 15 May 2002.

9 Subs (1)(*b*)(v) substituted by FA 1998 s 20(*c*)(ii) with effect from 6 April 1998.

10 Substituted by FA 2001 s 64(1)(*c*)(ii) with effect from such date as the Minister for Finance may by order appoint; previously "1998.". By virtue of the Finance Act, 2001 (Commencement of Section 64) Order 2002, FA 2001 s 64 comes into operation as on and from 15 May 2002.

11 Subs (1)(*b*)(vi) inserted by FA 1998 s 20(*c*)(iii) with effect from 6 April 1998.

12 Substituted by FA 2002 s 34(1)(*b*) with effect from such day as the Minister for Finance may by order appoint; previously "section 268(1)(*j*)". By virtue of the Finance Act, 2002 (Commencement of Section 34) Order 2002, FA 2002 s 34 comes into operation as on and from 15 May 2002.

13 Subs (1)(*b*)(vii) inserted by FA 2001 s 64(1)(*c*)(iii) with effect from such date as the Minister for Finance may by order appoint. By virtue of the Finance Act, 2001 (Commencement of Section 64) Order 2002, FA 2001 s 64 comes into operation as on and from 15 May 2002.

14 Substituted by FA 2004 s 25(1)(*c*)(i) with effect from 1 January 2004; previously "31 December 2004".

15 Inserted by FA 2004 s 25(1)(*c*)(ii) with effect from 4 December 2002.

16 Substituted by FA 2004 s 25(1)(*c*)(iii) with effect from 4 December 2002; previously "31 May 2003".

17 Substituted by FA 2004 s 25(1)(*c*)(iv) with effect from 1 January 2004; previously "a planning application".

18 Subs (1A)(*ba*) inserted by FA 2004 s 25(1)(*c*)(v) with effect from 1 January 2004.

19 Substituted by FA 2004 s 25(1)(*c*)(vi) with effect from 1 January 2004; previously "31 May 2003".

20 Subs (1A) inserted by FA 2003 s 25(1)(*c*)(ii) with effect from 4 December 2002.

21 Substituted by FA 2001 s 54 with effect from 6 April 2001; previously "or that consideration.".

Cross-references

Capital allowances for buildings used for certain childcare services: s 843A(4).
Capital allowances for buildings used for third level education, subs (1): s 843(5).
Industrial and provident societies, expenses, subs (8): s 699(2)(*a*).
Industrial buildings bought unused: s 279(2)(*a*).
Restriction of balancing allowance on sale of industrial building: s 275(2)(*b*), (3); refurbishment expenditure: in subs (1)(*b*), for "the building or structure was first used" substitute "the capital expenditure on refurbishment of the building or structure was incurred": s 276(2).
Writing off expenditure (subs (1)(*a*)(iv)), and meaning of "residue of expenditure": s 277(7).

Renewal incentives

Custom House Dock area
Commercial premises writing down life: s 323(4).
Dublin Docklands Area
Commercial premises writing down life: s 369(5), (6)(*d*).
Double rent allowance: s 370(6)(*b*).
Temple Bar Area
Commercial premises writing down life: s 332(6).
Industrial building writing down life: s 331(5).
Commercial premises in designated areas or street
Industrial building, writing down life: s 341(5).
Commercial premises writing down life: s 342(5).
Double rent allowance: s 345(6)(*b*).
Enterprise areas
Qualifying building writing down life: s 343(9).
Multi-storey car parks
Qualifying car park writing down life: s 344(5).
Qualifying areas
Industrial building writing down life: s 372C(5).
Commercial premises writing down life: s 372D(5).
Double rent allowance: s 372E(6)(*b*).
Qualifying rural areas
Industrial building writing down life: s 372M(5).
Commercial buildings writing down life: s 372N(5).
Resort areas
Commercial premises writing down life: s 353(6).
Holiday cottages, disclaimer of capital allowance: s 355(3)(*b*).
Tourist facilities that cease to be registered: s 353(5).

Park and ride facilities

Qualifying park and ride facilities, writing down life: s 372V(4); and in subs (1)(*b*)(i)(II) for "after the building or structure was first used" read "after the building or structure was first used as an industrial building or structure" and in subs (5)(*a*) for "when the building or structure was first used for any purpose" read "when the building or structure was first used as an industrial building or structure": s 372V(4A)(*c*).

Commercial premises writing down life: s 372W(5); and in subs (1)(*b*)(i)(II) for "after the building or structure was first used" read "after the building or structure was first used as an industrial building or structure" and in subs (5)(*a*) for "when the building or structure was first used for any purpose" read "when the building or structure was first used as an industrial building or structure": s 372W(5A)(*c*).

Designated areas in certain towns

Industrial buildings, writing down life: s 372AC(4).

Commercial buildings, writing down life: s 372AD(4).

Revenue precedents

Issue: Is the death of an individual a balancing event for the purposes of the section?

Decision: No.

Issue: If there is a termination of a "relevant period", as defined in TCA 1997 TCA 1997 s 1007, in relation to a non-trading partnership does a balancing charge arise?

Decision: The provisions of Part 43 apply to trades and professions carried on in partnership. They do not apply to non-trading or non-professional partnerships, such as a partnership which exists solely to own and let property. The provisions of TCA 1997 s 274 will determine if and when a balancing allowance/charge will arise in the case of such non-trading partnerships.

Definitions

person: IA 1937 s 11(*c*); trade: s 3(1); vesting day: s 268(10); writing: IA 1937 Sch.

Former enactments

ITA 1967 s 265; FA 1969 s 64(3)–(4); FA 1975 s 34(2)(*a*)(iii); CTA 1976 s 21(1) and Sch 1 paras 24 and 72; FA 1980 s 58; FA 1988 s 45 and s51(1)(*d*) and (5); FA 1990 s 78; FA 1994 s 22(1)(*d*) and (2); FA 1995 s 24; FA 1996 s 28(2); FA 1997 s 23(1)(*a*) and (2).

Corresponding UK tax provision

Capital Allowances Act 2001 ss 314–324.

275 Restriction of balancing allowances on sale of industrial building or structure

(1) In this section—

"inferior interest" means any interest in or right over the building or structure in question, whether granted by the relevant person or by someone else;

"premium" includes any capital consideration except so much of any sum as corresponds to any amount of rent or profits which is to be computed by reference to that sum under section 98;

"capital consideration" means consideration which consists of a capital sum or would be a capital sum if it had taken the form of a money payment;

"rent" includes any consideration which is not capital consideration;

"commercial rent" means such rent as might reasonably be expected to have been required in respect of the inferior interest in question, having regard to any premium payable for the grant of the interest, if the transaction had been at arm's length.

(2) This section shall apply where—

(*a*) the relevant interest in a building is sold subject to an inferior interest,

(*b*) by virtue of the sale a balancing allowance under section 274 would apart from this section be made to or for the benefit of the person (in this section referred to as **"the relevant person"**) who was entitled to the relevant interest immediately before the sale, and

(*c*) either—

(i) the relevant person, the person to whom the relevant interest is sold and the grantee of the inferior interest, or any 2 of them, are connected with each other, or

(ii) it appears with respect to the sale or the grant of the inferior interest, or with respect to transactions including the sale or grant, that the sole or main benefit which but for this section might have been expected to accrue to the parties or any of them was the obtaining of an allowance or deduction under this Chapter.

(3) For the purposes of section 274, the net proceeds to the relevant person of the sale—

(*a*) shall be taken to be increased by an amount equal to any premium receivable by the relevant person for the grant of the inferior interest, and

(*b*) where no rent or no commercial rent is payable in respect of the inferior interest, shall be taken to be the sum of—

(i) what those proceeds would have been if a commercial rent had been payable and the relevant interest had been sold in the open market, and

(ii) any amount to be added under paragraph (*a*);

but the net proceeds of the sale shall not by virtue of this subsection be taken to be greater than such amount as will secure that no balancing allowance is to be made.

(4) Where subsection (3) operates in relation to a sale to deny or reduce a balancing allowance in respect of any expenditure, the residue of that expenditure immediately after the sale shall be calculated for the purposes of this Chapter as if that balancing allowance had been made or, as the case may be, had not been reduced.

(5) Where the terms on which the inferior interest is granted are varied before the sale of the relevant interest, any capital consideration for the variation shall be treated for the purposes of this section as a premium for the grant of the interest, and the question whether any and, if so, what rent is payable in respect of the interest shall be determined by reference to the terms as in force immediately before the sale.

Definitions

person: IA 1937 s 11(*c*).

Former enactments

FA 1973 s 40(1)–(5).

Corresponding UK tax provision

Capital Allowances Act 2001 ss 325–326.

276 Application of sections 272 and 274 in relation to capital expenditure on refurbishment

(1) In this section, **"refurbishment"** means any work of construction, reconstruction, repair or renewal, including the provision or improvement of water, sewerage or heating facilities, carried out in the course of repair or restoration, or maintenance in the nature of repair or restoration, of a building or structure.

(2) Notwithstanding any other provision of the Tax Acts, where on or after the 6th day of April, 1991, any capital expenditure has been incurred on the refurbishment of a building or structure in respect of which an allowance is to be made for the purposes of income tax or corporation tax, as the case may be, under this Chapter, sections 272 and 274 shall apply as if **"the capital expenditure on refurbishment of the building or structure was incurred"** were substituted for **"the building or structure was first used"** in each place where it occurs in section 272(4) and 274(1)(*b*).

(3) For the purposes of giving effect to this section in so far as the computation of a balancing allowance or balancing charge is concerned, all such apportionments shall be made as are in the circumstances just and reasonable.

Cross-references

Renewal incentives

Custom House Dock area, commercial premises writing down life: s 323(4).
Designated area or street, industrial building writing down life: s 341(5); commercial premises writing down life: s 342(5).
Designated areas in certain towns, industrial buildings, writing down life: s 372AC(4); commercial buildings, writing down life: s 372AD(4).
Dublin Docklands Area, commercial premises writing down life: s 369(5).
Enterprise area buildings, qualifying premises writing down life: s 343(9).
Multi-storey carparks, qualifying car park writing down life: s 344(5).
Park and ride facilities, qualifying park and ride facilities writing down life: s 372V(4)(*b*); commercial premises writing down life: s 372W(5)(*b*).
Qualifying area, industrial building writing down life: s 372C(5); commercial premises writing down life: s 372D(5).
Qualifying rural area, industrial building writing down life: s 372M(5); commercial building writing down life: s 372N(5).
Temple Bar area, commercial premises writing down life: s 332(6).

Definitions

Tax Acts: s 1(2).

Former enactments

FA 1991 s 26.

277 Writing off of expenditure and meaning of "residue of expenditure"

(1) For the purposes of this Chapter, any expenditure incurred on the construction of any building or structure shall be treated as written off to the extent and at the times specified in this section, and references in this Chapter to the residue of any such expenditure shall be construed accordingly.

(2) Where an industrial building allowance is made in respect of the expenditure, the amount of that allowance shall be written off at the time when the building or structure is first used.

(3) Where, by reason of the building or structure being at any time an industrial building or structure, a writing-down allowance is made for any chargeable period in respect of the expenditure, the amount of that allowance shall be written off at that time; but, where at that time an event occurs which gives rise or may give rise to a balancing allowance or balancing charge, the amount directed to be written off by this subsection at that time shall be taken into account in computing the residue of that expenditure immediately before that event for the purpose of determining whether any, and if so what, balancing allowance or balancing charge is to be made.

(4) (*a*) Where, for any period or periods between the time when the building or structure was first used for any purpose and the time at which the residue of the expenditure is to be ascertained, the building or structure has not been in use as an industrial building or structure, there shall in ascertaining that residue be treated as having been previously written off in respect of that period or those periods amounts equal to writing-down allowances made for chargeable periods of a total length equal to the length of that period, or the aggregate length of those periods, as the case may be, at such rate or rates as would have been appropriate having regard to any sale on which section 272(4) operated.

(*b*) Where the building or structure was in use as an industrial building or structure at the end of the basis period for any year of assessment before the year 1960–61, an amount equal to 2 per cent of the expenditure shall be treated as written off at the end of the previous year of assessment.

(5) Where on the occasion of a sale a balancing allowance is made in respect of the expenditure, there shall be written off at the time of the sale the amount by which the residue of the expenditure before the sale exceeds the net proceeds of the sale.

(6) Where on the occasion of a sale a balancing charge is made in respect of the expenditure, the residue of the expenditure shall be deemed for the purposes of this Chapter to be increased at the time of the sale by the amount on which the charge is made.

(7) Where, on receipt of consideration of the type referred to in section 274(1)(*a*)(iv), a balancing allowance is made in respect of the expenditure, there shall be written off at the time of the event giving rise to the balancing allowance or, if later, on the 26th day of March, 1997, the amount by which the residue of the expenditure before that event exceeds that consideration.

Cross-references

Designated areas, double rent allowance: s 345(6)(*b*).

Dublin Docklands Area, double rent allowance: s 370(6)(*b*).

Holiday cottages, disclaimer of capital allowance: s 355(3)(*b*).

Industrial building annual allowance, meaning of "residue" applied: s 272(4).

Industrial buildings bought unused: s 279(2)(*a*).

Park and ride facilities, qualifying park and ride facilities, construction or refurbishment, in subs (2) for "when the building or structure is first used" read "when the building or structure is first used as an industrial building or structure" and in subs (4)(*a*) for "when the building or structure was first used for any purpose" read "when the building or structure was first used as an industrial building or structure": s 372V(4A)(*d*).

Park and ride facilities, commercial premises, construction or refurbishment, in subs (2) for "when the building or structure is first used" read "when the building or structure is first used as an industrial building or structure" and in subs (4)(*a*) for "when the building or structure was first used for any purpose" read "when the building or structure was first used as an industrial building or structure": s 372W(5A)(*d*).

Qualifying areas, double rent allowance: s 372E(6)(*b*).

Restriction of relief in respect of loans applied in acquiring interest in companies, "residue of expenditure" to be construed in accordance with this section: s 250A(1).

Ring-fence on use of certain capital allowances on certain industrial buildings and other premises: s 409E(1).

Shipping tonnage tax, industrial buildings: Sch 18B, para 20(3).

Definitions

year of assessment: s 3(1).

Former enactments

ITA 1967 s 266; CTA 1976 s 21(1) and Sch 1 para 25 and para 72; ITA 1967 s 266(7); FA 1997 s 23(1)(*b*).

Corresponding UK tax provision

Capital Allowances Act 2001 s 512.

278 Manner of making allowances and charges

(1) Except in the cases mentioned in this section, any allowance or charge made to or on a person under the preceding provisions of this Part shall be made to or on such person in taxing such person's trade or, as the case may require, in charging such person's income under Case V of Schedule D.

(2) An industrial building allowance shall be made to a person by discharge or repayment of tax if such person's interest in the building or structure is subject to any lease when the expenditure is incurred or becomes subject to any lease before the building or structure is first used for any purpose ...;[1] but this subsection shall not apply as respects income chargeable under Case V of Schedule D.

(3) A writing-down allowance shall be made to a person for a chargeable period by means of discharge or repayment of tax if such person's interest is subject to any lease at the end of that chargeable period or its basis period; but this subsection shall not apply as respects income chargeable under Case V of Schedule D.

(4) A balancing allowance shall be made to a person by means of discharge or repayment of tax if such person's interest is subject to any lease immediately before the event giving rise to the allowance; but this subsection shall not apply as respects income chargeable under Case V of Schedule D.

(5) A balancing charge shall be made on a person under Case IV of Schedule D if such person's interest is subject to any lease immediately before the event giving rise to the charge and the corresponding income is chargeable under that Case.

(6) Any allowance which under subsections (1) to (4) is to be made otherwise than in taxing a trade shall be available primarily against the following income—

- (*a*) where the income (whether arising by means of rent or receipts in respect of premises or easements or otherwise) from the industrial building or structure in respect of the capital expenditure on which the allowance is given is chargeable under Case V of Schedule D, against income chargeable under that Case,
- (*b*) where the income (whether arising by means of rent or receipts in respect of premises or easements or otherwise) from the industrial building or structure in respect of the capital expenditure on which the allowance is given is chargeable under Case IV of Schedule D, against income chargeable under that Case, or
- (*c*) income chargeable under Case IV or V of Schedule D respectively which is the subject of a balancing charge.

Amendments

[1] Deleted by FA 2000 s 40(*a*) with effect from 6 April 2000; previously "and, where it is so made, section 304(4) shall not apply".

Cross-references

Park and ride facilities, qualifying park and ride facilities, construction or refurbishment, in subs (2) for "before the building or structure is first used for any purpose" read "before the building or structure is first used as an industrial building or structure": s 372V(4A)(*e*).

Park and ride facilities, commercial premises, construction or refurbishment, in subs (2) for "before the building or structure is first used for any purpose" read "before the building or structure is first used as an industrial building or structure": s 372W(5A)(*e*).

Ring-fence on use of certain capital allowances on certain industrial buildings and other premises: s 409E(3)(*b*).

Revenue precedents

Issue: What is the manner of making industrial buildings allowances in respect of expenditure incurred on buildings situated outside the State?

Decision: Revenue is prepared to accept that industrial buildings allowances may be made in charging a person's income under Case III of Sch D. If the amount of the allowance is greater than the person's Case III income the excess may be offset against all other income.

Former enactments

ITA 1967 s 254(1)(*d*) and (*e*) and s 267; CTA 1976 s 21(1) and Sch 1 para 17 and para 26.

Corresponding UK tax provision

Capital Allowances Act 2001 s 529.

279 Purchases of certain buildings or structures

(1) For the purposes of this section—

...[1]

"the net price paid" means the amount represented by A in the equation—

$$A = B \times \frac{C}{C + D}$$

where—

B is the amount paid by a person on the purchase of the relevant interest in a building or structure,

C is the amount of the expenditure actually incurred on the construction of the building or structure, and

D is the amount of any expenditure actually incurred which is expenditure for the purposes of paragraph (*a*), (*b*) or (*c*) of section 270(2).

(2) Where expenditure is incurred on the construction of a building or structure and, before the building or structure is used or within a period of one year after it commences to be used, the relevant interest in the building or structure is sold, then, if an allowance has not been claimed by any other person in respect of that building or structure under this Chapter—

(*a*) the expenditure actually incurred on the construction of the building or structure shall be disregarded for the purposes of sections 271, 272, 274 and 277, but

(*b*) the person who buys that interest shall be deemed for those purposes to have incurred, on the date when the purchase price becomes payable, expenditure on the construction of the building or structure equal to that expenditure or to the net price paid by such person for that interest, whichever is the less;

but, where the relevant interest in the building or structure is sold more than once before the building or structure is used or within the period of one year after it commences to be used, paragraph (*b*) shall apply only in relation to the last of those sales.

(3) Where the expenditure incurred on the construction of a building or structure was incurred by a person carrying on a trade which consists, as to the whole or any part of the trade, of the construction of buildings or structures with a view to their sale and, before the building or structure is used or within a period of one year after it commences to be used, such person sells the relevant interest in the building or structure in the course of that trade or, as the case may be, of that part of that trade, subsection (2) shall apply subject to the following modifications—

(*a*) if that sale is the only sale of the relevant interest before the building or structure is used or within the period of one year after it commences to be used, subsection (2) shall apply as if in paragraph (*b*) of that subsection **"that expenditure or to"** and **", whichever is the less"** were deleted, and

(*b*) if there is more than one sale of the relevant interest before the building or structure is used or within the period of one year after it commences to be used, subsection (2) shall apply as if the reference to the expenditure actually incurred on the construction of the building or structure were a reference to the price paid on that sale.

Amendments

1 Deleted by FA 1998 s 136 and Sch 9 para 5 with effect from 6 April 1997; previously "'expenditure incurred on the construction of a building or structure' excludes any expenditure within the meaning of section 270(2);".

Cross-references

Custom House Docks area, double rent allowance: s 324(1)(*a*) (qualifying premises).

Designated areas, double rent allowance: s 345(1) (qualifying premises), (6)(*c*).

Dublin Docklands Area, double rent allowance: s 370(1) (qualifying premises).

Holiday cottages, disclaimer of capital allowance: s 355(3)(*c*).

Park and ride facilities, qualifying park and ride facilities, construction or refurbishment, in subs (2) and (3) for "before the building or structure is used or within the period of one year after it commences to be used" (in each place it occurs) read "before the building or structure is used as an industrial building or structure or within the period of one year after it commences to be so used": s 372V(4A)(*f*).

Park and ride facilities, commercial premises, construction or refurbishment, in subs (2) and (3) for "before the building or structure is used or within the period of one year after it commences to be used" (in each place it occurs) read "before the building or structure is used as an industrial building or structure or within the period of one year after it commences to be so used": s 372W(5A)(*f*).

Qualifying areas, double rent allowance: s 372E(1) (qualifying premises), (6)(*c*).

Qualifying rural areas: s 372O(1) (qualifying premises).

Restriction on use of capital allowances on certain industrial buildings and other premises: s 409A(1)(specified building), (5).

Resort areas, double rent allowance: s 354(1) (qualifying premises).

Temple Bar area, double rent allowance: s 333(1)(*a*) (qualifying premises).

Tax Briefing

TB29 Dec 1997 p 4 — Operation of TCA 1997 s 279.

TB42 Dec 2000 p 48 — when buildings are purchased new and unused from a developer rather than constructed by the taxpayer, Revenue's view is that the amount paid on the purchase of the relevant interest in the building does not include the cost of professional fees and stamp duty. Accordingly, such costs should not be included in "B" in the formula in subs (1).

Definitions

Income Tax Acts: s 1(2); person: IA 1937 s 11(*c*); trade: s 3(1).

Former enactments

FA 1970 s 19(1)–(2A); FA 1990 s 75; FA 1991 s 23; FA 1997 s 146(1) and Sch 9 Pt I para 4(2).

280 Temporary disuse of building or structure

(1) For the purposes of this Chapter, a building or structure shall not be deemed to cease altogether to be used by reason that it is temporarily out of use and where, immediately before any period of temporary disuse, a building or structure is an industrial building or structure, it shall be deemed to continue to be an industrial building or structure during the period of temporary disuse.

(2) (*a*) Notwithstanding any other provision of this Part as to the manner of making allowances and charges but subject to paragraph (*b*), where by virtue of

subsection (1) a building or structure is deemed to continue to be an industrial building or structure while temporarily out of use, then, if—

(i) on the last occasion on which the building or structure was in use as an industrial building or structure, it was in use for the purposes of a trade which has since been permanently discontinued, or

(ii) on the last occasion on which the building or structure was in use as an industrial building or structure, the relevant interest in the building or structure was subject to a lease which has since come to an end,

any writing-down allowance or balancing allowance to be made to any person in respect of the building or structure during any period for which the temporary disuse continues after the discontinuance of the trade or the coming to an end of the lease shall be made by means of discharge or repayment of tax, and any balancing charge to be made on any person in respect of the building or structure during that period shall be made under Case IV of Schedule D.

(*b*) Where for a chargeable period the person has income chargeable to tax under Case V of Schedule D and at the end of the chargeable period or its basis period the building or structure is one to which paragraph (*a*) applies, any writing-down allowance or balancing allowance or balancing charge to be made to or on the person in respect of the building or structure shall be made in charging that person's income under Case V of Schedule D.

(3) The reference in this section to the permanent discontinuance of a trade does not include a reference to the happening of any event which by virtue of the Income Tax Acts is to be treated as equivalent to the discontinuance of the trade.

Definitions

person: IA 1937 s 11(*c*); trade: s 3(1).

Former enactments

ITA 1967 s 270; CTA 1976 s 21(1) and Sch 1 para 27.

Corresponding UK tax provision

Capital Allowances Act 2001 ss 285 and 354.

---

281 Special provisions in regard to leases

(1) Where with the consent of the lessor a lessee of any building or structure remains in possession of that building or structure after the termination of the lease without a new lease being granted to the lessee, that lease shall be deemed for the purposes of this Chapter to continue so long as the lessee remains so in possession.

(2) Where on the termination of a lease a new lease is granted to the lessee consequent on the lessee being entitled by statute to a new lease or in pursuance of an option available to the lessee under the terms of the first lease, this Chapter shall apply as if the second lease were a continuation of the first lease.

(3) Where on the termination of a lease the lessor pays any sum to the lessee in respect of a building or structure comprised in the lease, this Chapter shall apply as if the lease had come to an end by reason of the surrender of the lease in consideration of the payment.

Definitions

statute: IA 1937 s 3; s 1(1).

Former enactments

ITA 1967 s 269.

Corresponding UK tax provision

Capital Allowances Act 2001 s 359.

282 Supplementary provisions (Chapter 1)

(1) A person who has incurred expenditure on the construction of a building or structure shall be deemed, for the purposes of any provision of this Chapter referring to such person's interest in the building or structure at the time when the expenditure was incurred, to have had the same interest in the building or structure as such person would have had if the construction of the building or structure had been completed at that time.

(2) Without prejudice to any other provision of this Part relating to the apportionment of sale, insurance, salvage or compensation moneys, the sum paid on the sale of the relevant interest in a building or structure, or any other sale, insurance, salvage or compensation moneys payable in respect of any building or structure, shall for the purposes of this Chapter be deemed to be reduced by an amount equal to so much of that sum or those moneys, as the case may be, as on a just apportionment is attributable to assets representing expenditure other than expenditure in respect of which an allowance may be made under this Chapter.

Former enactments

ITA 1967 s 263(2)–(3).

Corresponding UK tax provision

Capital Allowances Act 2001 s 287.

CHAPTER 2
Machinery or Plant: Initial Allowances, Wear and Tear Allowances, Balancing Allowances and Balancing Charges

Cross-references

Cars costing more than the specified amount: s 374(2).; hire purchase provisions: s 378(2).

Farming, deemed wear and tear allowance, meanings of "balancing allowance" and "balancing charge" applied: s 660(1).

Profits or assets available for distribution: s 413(5)(*b*).

Tax Briefing

TB42 Dec 2000 pp 28–29 — Plant in Leased Buildings — Wear and Tear Allowances.

283 Initial allowances

(1) In this section—

"industrial development agency" means the Industrial Development Authority, Shannon Free Airport Development Company Limited or Údarás na Gaeltachta;

"new" means unused and not secondhand, but a ship shall be deemed to be new even if it has been used or is secondhand.

(2) Subject to the Tax Acts, where—

(*a*) a person carrying on a trade, the profits or gains of which are chargeable under Case I of Schedule D, incurs capital expenditure on the provision for the purposes of the trade of new machinery or new plant, other than vehicles suitable for the conveyance by road of persons or goods or the haulage by road of other vehicles,

(*b*) that machinery or plant is machinery or plant to which subsection (4) or (5) applies, and

(*c*) that machinery or plant while used for the purposes of that trade is wholly and exclusively so used,

there shall be made to such person for the chargeable period related to the expenditure an allowance (in this Chapter referred to as an **"initial allowance"**).

(3) An initial allowance shall be of an amount equal to—

(*a*) in the case of machinery or plant to which subsection (4) applies, 100 per cent of the capital expenditure mentioned in subsection (2), or

(*b*) in the case of machinery or plant to which subsection (5) applies, 50 per cent of the capital expenditure mentioned in subsection (2).

(4) This subsection shall apply to—

(*a*) machinery or plant provided—

(i) before the 23rd day of April, 1996, for use for the purposes of trading operations, or

(ii) on or after the 23rd day of April, 1996, by a company for use for the purposes of trading operations carried on by the company,

which are relevant trading operations within the meaning of section 445 or 446 but, in relation to capital expenditure incurred on the provision of machinery or plant on or after the 6th day of May, 1993, excluding machinery or plant provided by a lessor to a lessee other than in the course of the carrying on by the lessor of those relevant trading operations, and

(*b*) machinery or plant provided for the purposes of a project approved by an industrial development agency in the period from the 1st day of January, 1986, to the 31st day of December, 1988, and in respect of the provision of which expenditure was incurred before the 31st day of December, 1996.

(5) This subsection shall apply to machinery or plant provided for the purposes of a project approved for grant assistance by an industrial development agency in the period from the 1st day of January, 1989, to the 31st day of December, 1990, and in respect of the provision of which expenditure is incurred before the 31st day of December, 1997 [, or before the 30th day of June, 1998, if its provision is solely for use in an industrial building or structure referred to in sections 271(3)(*c*) and 273(7)(*a*)(i) and expenditure in respect of such provision would have been incurred before the 31st day of December, 1997, but for the existence of circumstances which resulted in legal proceedings being initiated, being proceedings which were the subject of an order of the High Court made before the 1st day of January, 1998];[1] but, as respects machinery or plant provided for the purposes of any such project specified in the list referred to in section 133(8)(*c*)(iv),

this subsection shall apply as if the reference to the 31st day of December, 1997, [where it first occurs,][2] were a reference to the 31st day of December, 2002.

(6) Where an initial allowance in respect of capital expenditure incurred on or after the 1st day of April, 1989, on the provision of machinery or plant, other than machinery or plant to which subsection (4) applies, is made under this section for any chargeable period—

(*a*) no allowance for wear and tear of that machinery or plant shall be made under section 284 for that chargeable period, and

(*b*) an allowance for wear and tear of that machinery or plant which is to be made under section 284 for any chargeable period subsequent to that chargeable period shall not be increased under section 285.

(7) Any initial allowance under this section made to a person for any chargeable period in respect of machinery or plant shall not exceed such sum as will, when added to—

(*a*) the amount of any allowance in respect of the machinery or plant made to the person under section 284 for that chargeable period, and

(*b*) the aggregate amount of any allowances made to the person in respect of the machinery or plant under this section and section 284 for earlier chargeable periods,

equal the amount of the expenditure incurred by such person on the provision of the machinery or plant.

Amendments

1 Inserted by FA 1998 s 21(*b*)(i) with effect from 6 April 1998.

2 Inserted by FA 1998 s 21(*b*)(ii) with effect from 6 April 1998.

Cross-references

Added to plant and machinery wear and tear allowance: s 284(4)(*b*).
Corporation tax: allowances and charges in taxing a trade: s 307(2).
Grants, treatment of: s 317(2)–(4).
Leased plant and machinery, restriction on use of allowances: s 404(1)(*b*)(ii)(II).
Lessees, allowance to: s 299(1).
Lessors, allowance to: s 298(1)(*a*).
Petroleum trade, development expenditure: s 692(4)(*b*).
Pre-trading capital expenditure: s 316(3).
Professions and employments, application to: s 301.

Case law

Held the withdrawal by the Revenue of advance clearance by inspector in relation to a claim for initial allowances was not unfair and did not amount to an abuse of power: *Matrix-Securities Ltd v IRC* [1994] STC 272.

Revenue precedents

Issue: Whether new machines incorporating a limited number of recycled parts but sold as a "new build" machine would be regarded as "unused and not secondhand" ie "new" for the purposes of s 283.
Decision: Yes.
Issue: Are large ocean going dredgers considered as ships for the purposes of TCA 1997 s 283(1)?
Decision: Large vessels of burden that substantially go to sea may be regarded as ships. Accordingly, large ocean going dredgers may be considered ships for the purposes of TCA 1997 s 283(1).
Issue: If a project for the design and manufacture of communications products constituted the same project as that approved in 1988 for the design of expert systems and therefore qualified for accelerated capital allowances?
Decision: This was not regarded as the same project as the proposed activities were in a different line of business and at a different location to the project approved.

Issue: Whether expenditure to replace existing plant, which was provided under a grant assisted project, with state of the art plant qualifies for accelerated capital allowances?
Decision: It was agreed that this expenditure came within the provisions of TCA 1997 s 283(4)(*b*) as the new plant was provided to make the same products in a more environmentally friendly way using more advanced computer controlled technology.

Definitions

High Court: IA 1937 Sch; person: IA 1937 s 11(*c*).

Former enactments

ITA 1967 s 251(1), (4)(*bb*)(ii) and (*d*), (6)–(7); FA 1973 s 9(2) (apart from the proviso); CTA 1976 s 21(1) and Sch 1 para 15 and para 61; FA 1988 s 43(*b*), s 51(1)(*a*) and (*cc*) (proviso thereto), (2)(*a*), (*c*) and (*d*) and (6); FA 1989 s 13; FA 1990 s 73(*a*) and (*b*), s 80, s 81(1)(*a*), (2)(*a*)–(*b*); FA 1993 s 33; FA 1995 s 27; FA 1996 s 43.

Corresponding UK tax provision

Capital Allowances Act 2001 ss 39–51.

284 Wear and tear allowances

(1) Subject to the Tax Acts, where a person carrying on a trade in any chargeable period has incurred capital expenditure on the provision of machinery or plant for the purposes of the trade, an allowance (in this Chapter referred to as a **"wear and tear allowance"**) shall be made to such person for that chargeable period on account of the wear and tear of any of the machinery or plant which belongs to such person and is in use for the purposes of the trade at the end of that chargeable period or its basis period and which, while used for the purposes of the trade, is wholly and exclusively so used.

(2) (*a*) Subject to [paragraphs (*aa*), (*ab*) and (*ad*)][1] and][2] subsection (4), the amount of the wear and tear allowance to be made shall be an amount equal to—

(i) in the case of machinery or plant, other than machinery or plant of the type referred to in subparagraph (ii), 15 per cent of the actual cost of the machinery or plant, including in that actual cost any expenditure in the nature of capital expenditure on the machinery or plant by means of renewal, improvement or reinstatement, or

(ii) in the case of machinery or plant which consists of a vehicle suitable for the conveyance by road of persons or goods or the haulage by road of other vehicles, 20 per cent of the value of that machinery or plant at the commencement of the chargeable period.

[(*aa*) Notwithstanding paragraph (*a*), where capital expenditure is incurred on or after 1 January 2001 on the provision of—

(i) machinery or plant, other than machinery or plant to which paragraph (*a*)(ii) and subsection (3A) relates, or

(ii) machinery or plant to which paragraph (*a*)(ii) relates, other than a car within the meaning of section 286 used for qualifying purposes within the meaning of that section,

the amount of the wear and tear allowance to be made shall be an amount equal to 20 per cent of the actual cost of the machinery or plant, including in that actual cost any expenditure in the nature of capital expenditure on the machinery or plant by means of renewal, improvement or reinstatement.][3]

[(*ab*) Where for any chargeable period ending on or after 1 January 2002 a wear and tear allowance would be due to be made to a person in respect of machinery or plant in accordance with paragraph *(a)*, the person may elect that the amount of the wear and tear allowance to be made for that chargeable period and any subsequent chargeable period in respect of each and every item of the machinery or plant concerned shall, subject to subsection (4), instead of being the amount referred to in paragraph *(a)*, be an amount equal to—

(i) where, apart from this paragraph, the allowance would be made in accordance with paragraph *(a)*(i), 20 per cent of the amount of the capital expenditure incurred on the provision of that machinery or plant which is still unallowed as at the commencement of the first-mentioned chargeable period, and

(ii) where, apart from this paragraph, the allowance would be made in accordance with paragraph *(a)*(ii), 20 per cent of the value of that machinery or plant at the commencement of the first-mentioned chargeable period.

(ac) An election under paragraph *(ab)* shall be irrevocable, and shall be included—

(i) where such an election is made by a chargeable person within the meaning of Part 41, in the return required to be made by that person under section 951 for the first chargeable period, and

(ii) where such an election is made by any other person, in the annual statement of profits or gains required to be delivered by that person under the Income Tax Acts, for the first year of assessment,

for which a wear and tear allowance in respect of machinery or plant is to be made in accordance with that paragraph.][4]

[*(ad)* Notwithstanding any other provision of this subsection but subject to subsection (4), where capital expenditure is incurred on or after 4 December 2002 on the provision of machinery or plant, the amount of the wear and tear allowance to be made shall be an amount equal to 12.5 per cent of the actual cost of the machinery or plant, including in that actual cost any expenditure in the nature of capital expenditure on the machinery or plant by means of renewal, improvement or reinstatement; but this paragraph shall not apply in the case of—

(i) machinery or plant to which subsection (3A) relates,

(ii) machinery or plant which consists of a car within the meaning of section 286, used for qualifying purposes, within the meaning of that section, or

(iii) machinery or plant provided under the terms of a binding contract evidenced in writing before 4 December 2002 and in respect of the provision of which capital expenditure is incurred on or before 31 January 2003.][5]

(b) Where a chargeable period or its basis period consists of a period less than one year in length, the wear and tear allowance shall not exceed such portion of [the amount specified in any other provision of this subsection][6] as bears to that amount the same proportion as the length of the chargeable period or its basis period bears to a period of one year.

(3) [For the purposes of paragraphs *(a)*(ii) and *(ab)*(ii) of subsection (2), the value at the commencement of a chargeable period][7] of the machinery or plant shall be taken to be

the actual cost to the person of such machinery or plant reduced by the total of any wear and tear allowances made to that person in relation to the machinery or plant for previous chargeable periods.

[(3A)(*a*) This subsection applies to machinery or plant consisting of a sea fishing boat registered in the Register of Fishing Boats and in respect of which capital expenditure is incurred in the period of [6 years][8] commencing on the appointed day, being expenditure that is certified by Bord Iascaigh Mhara as capital expenditure incurred for the purposes of fleet renewal in the polyvalent and beam trawl segments of the fishing fleet.

(*b*) Notwithstanding subsection (2), but subject to [paragraph (*ba*) and subsection (4)][9], wear and tear allowances to be made to any person in respect of machinery or plant to which this subsection applies shall be made during a writing-down period of 8 years beginning with the first chargeable period or its basis period at the end of which the machinery or plant belongs to that person and is in use for the purposes of that person's trade, and shall be of an amount equal to—

(i) as respects the first year of the writing-down period, 50 per cent of the actual cost of the machinery or plant, including in that actual cost any expenditure in the nature of capital expenditure on that machinery or plant by means of renewal, improvement or reinstatement,

(ii) as respects each of the next 6 years of the writing-down period, 15 per cent of the balance of that actual cost after the deduction of any allowance made by virtue of subparagraph (i), and

(iii) as respects the last year of the writing-down period, 10 per cent of the balance of that actual cost after the deduction of any allowance made by virtue of subparagraph (i).

[(*ba*) Notwithstanding subsection (2), but subject to subsection (4), wear and tear allowances to be made to any person in respect of machinery or plant to which this subsection applies, and in respect of which capital expenditure is incurred on or after the date of the coming into operation of section 51 of the Finance Act, 2001, shall be made during a writing-down period of 6 years beginning with the first chargeable period or its basis period at the end of which the machinery or plant belongs to that person and is in use for the purposes of that person's trade, and shall be of an amount equal to—

(i) as respects the first year of the writing-down period, 50 per cent of the actual cost of the machinery or plant, including in that actual cost any expenditure in the nature of capital expenditure on that machinery or plant by means of renewal, improvement or reinstatement, and

(ii) as respects the next 5 years of the writing-down period, 20 per cent of the balance of that actual cost after the deduction of any allowance made by virtue of subparagraph (i).][10]

(*c*) Where a chargeable period or its basis period consists of a period less than one year in length, the wear and tear allowance shall not exceed such portion of the amount specified in subparagraph (i), (ii) or (iii), as may be appropriate, of paragraph (*b*), [or in subparagraph (i) or (ii), as may be appropriate, of paragraph (*ba*)][11] as bears to that amount the same proportion as the length of the chargeable period or its basis period bears to a period of one year.

(*d*) This subsection shall come into operation on such day (in this subsection referred to as the **"appointed day"**) as the Minister for Finance may, by order, appoint.][12]

[(3B) For the purposes of subsections (2)(*b*) and (3A)(*c*), and notwithstanding any other provision of the Income Tax Acts, the length of the basis period for the year of assessment 2001 shall be deemed to be—

(*a*) the length of that period as determined in accordance with section 306, or

(*b*) 270 days,

whichever is the lesser.][13]

(4) No wear and tear allowance or repayment on account of any such allowance shall be made for any chargeable period if such allowance, when added to—

(*a*) the allowances on that account, and

(*b*) any initial allowances in relation to the machinery or plant under section 283,

made for any previous chargeable periods to the person by whom the trade is carried on, will make the aggregate amount of the allowances exceed the actual cost to that person of the machinery or plant, including in that actual cost any expenditure in the nature of capital expenditure on the machinery or plant by means of renewal, improvement or reinstatement.

(5) No wear and tear allowance shall be made under this section in respect of capital expenditure incurred on the construction of a building or structure which is or is deemed to be an industrial building or structure within the meaning of section 268.

(6) Subject to subsection (7), this section shall, with any necessary modifications, apply in relation to the letting of any premises the profits or gains from which are chargeable under Chapter 8 of Part 4 as it applies in relation to trades.

(7) Where by virtue of subsection (6) this section applies to the letting of any premises, it shall apply as respects the year of assessment 1997–98 and subsequent years of assessment in respect of capital expenditure incurred on the provision of machinery or plant within the meaning of subsection (2)(*a*)(i) where—

(*a*) such expenditure is incurred wholly and exclusively in respect of a house used solely as a dwelling which is or is to be let as a furnished house, and

(*b*) that furnished house is provided for renting or letting on bona fide commercial terms in the open market.

[(8) For the purposes of this Part, Aer Rianta cuideachta phoiblí theoranta shall be deemed to have incurred, on the vesting day, capital expenditure on the provision of machinery or plant, being the machinery or plant vested in Aer Rianta cuideachta phoiblí theoranta on that day, and the actual cost of that machinery or plant shall be deemed to be an amount determined by the formula—

$$A - B$$

where—

A is the original actual cost of the machinery or plant, including in that cost any expenditure in the nature of capital expenditure on the machinery or plant by means of renewal, improvement or reinstatement, and

B is the amount of any wear and tear allowances which would have been made under this section in respect of the machinery or plant since the original provision of the machinery or plant if a claim for those allowances had been duly made and allowed.][14]

Notes

Re subs (8): the Air Navigation and Transport (Amendment) Act, 1998 (Vesting Day) Order 1998, SI No 326 of 1998, appointed 1 January 1999 as vesting day for the purposes of the Air Navigation and Transport (Amendment) Act, 1998.

Amendments

1 Substituted by FA 2003 s 23(1)(*a*)(i) with effect from 4 December 2002; previously "paragraphs (*aa*) and (*ab*)".

2 Inserted by FA 2001 s 53(*a*) as respects capital expenditure incurred on or after 1 January 2001.

3 Subs (2)(*aa*) inserted by FA 2001 s 53(*b*) as respects capital expenditure incurred on or after 1 January 2001.

4 Subs (2)(*ab*)–(*ac*) inserted by FA 2002 s 31(1)(*a*)(ii) with effect from 1 January 2002.

5 Subs (2)(*ad*) inserted by FA 2003 s 23(1)(*a*)(ii) with effect from 4 December 2002.

6 Substituted by FA 2003 s 23(1)(*a*)(iii) with effect from 4 December 2002; previously "the amount specified in subparagraph (i) or (ii) of paragraph (*a*), the amount specified in paragraph (*aa*) or, as the case may be, the amount specified in subparagraph (i) or (ii) of paragraph (*ab*)".

7 Substituted by FA 2002 s 31(1)(*b*) with effect from 1 January 2002; previously "For the purposes of subsection (2)(*a*)(ii), the value at the commencement of the chargeable period".

8 Substituted by FA 2001 s 52(1)(*a*) from such date as the Minister may by order appoint; previously "3 years". By virtue of Finance Act 2001 (Commencement of Section 52) Order 2004, SI No 124/2004, this amendment came into operation on 24 March 2004.

9 Substituted by FA 2001 s 52(1)(*b*) from such date as the Minister may by order appoint; previously "subsection (4)". By virtue of Finance Act 2001 (Commencement of Section 52) Order 2004, SI No 124/2004, this amendment came into operation on 24 March 2004.

10 Subs (3A)(*ba*) inserted by FA 2001 s 52(1)(*c*) from such date as the Minister may by order appoint. By virtue of Finance Act 2001 (Commencement of Section 52) Order 2004, SI No 124/2004, this amendment came into operation on 24 March 2004.

11 Inserted by FA 2001 s 52(1)(*d*) from such date as the Minister may by order appoint. By virtue of Finance Act 2001 (Commencement of Section 52) Order 2004, SI No 124/2004, this amendment came into operation on 24 March 2004.

12 Subs (3A) inserted by FA 1998 s 23(*a*) with effect from such day as the Minister for Finance may appoint by order. Subs (3A) comes into operation from 4 September 1998 — Taxes Consolidation Act, 1997 (Section 284(3A)) (Commencement) Order 1998, SI No 321 of 1998 refers.

13 Subs (3B) inserted FA 2001 s 77(2) and Sch 2 para 19 with effect from 6 April 2001.

14 Subs (8) inserted by FA 1998 s 20(*d*) with effect from 6 April 1998.

Cross-references

Capital expenditure on scientific research: s 765(3)(*b*), (4).

Capital expenditure, references to: s 316(2).

Cars costing more than the specified amount: s 374(1), (2)

Contribution to local authority for treatment of trade effluents or provision of water supply: s 310(2), (3); also for s 310(2) purposes the reference in s 284(2)(*aa*) to "20 per cent of the actual cost of the machinery or plant, including .... or reinstatement" is treated as a reference to "20 per cent of the capital sum contributed in the chargeable period or its basis period" and the reference in s 284(2)(ad) to "12.5 per cent of the actual cost of the machinery or plant, including .... or reinstatement" is treated as a reference to "12.5 per cent of the capital sum contributed in the chargeable period or its basis period": s 310(2A).

Deemed wear and tear allowance where none claimed: s 287(1), (2).

Farming, deemed wear and tear allowance: s 660(1).

Furnished lettings, restriction on use of allowances, subs (7): s 406.

Grants, treatment of: s 317(2)–(4).

Leased assets, restriction on use of allowances: s 403(8)(*b*).

Lessees, allowance to: s 299(1).

Lessors, allowance to: s 298(1)(*b*).
Manner of making allowances and charges, subs (6): s 300(1).
Mine development allowance: s 670(7).
Mining machinery or plant, subs (4): s 678(3).
Petroleum trade, development expenditure: s 692(5)(*a*); subs (1): s 692(3); in subs (2) for "15 per cent", "20 per cent" and "12.5 per cent" read "100 per cent": s 692(2).
Plant and machinery accelerated wear and tear allowance: s 285(2)(*a*), (3), (8).
Plant and machinery initial allowance, wear and tear may not be claimed in addition to: s 283(6), (7).
Professions, employments, offices, application to: s 301.
Rent a room relief: s 216A(2)(*d*).
Restriction on use by certain partnerships of certain losses, etc, transitional arrangements; subs (3A): s 1013(2C)(*d*).
Restriction on use of capital allowances for certain leased assets, meaning of "appointed day" applied, subs (3A): s 403(5A).
Shipping tonnage tax, exit, plant and machinery, subs (2): Sch 18B, para 19(3)(*d*).
Taxis and rental cars, increased allowance, in subs (2)(*a*)(ii) for "20 per cent" read "40 per cent": s 286(2).
Wear and tear allowances for licences for public hire (taxi) vehicles, subs (1): s 286A(2)(*b*); subs (2)(*aa*) to apply for purposes of s 286A as if machinery or plant to which subs (2) of that section refers were machinery or plant to which subs (2)(*aa*) applies and as if reference in subs (2)(*aa*) to "on or after 1 January 2001" were a reference to "on 21 November 1997": s 286A(4).

Case law

Burden of wear and tear: *MacSaga Investment Co Ltd v Lupton*, 44 TC 659.

Regarded as "plant"

Irish

Barrister's books: *Breathnach v McCann*, (High Court, 3 October 1983) TL 121.
A structure specially designed for egg production*: O'Srianáin v Lakeview Ltd* ITR Vol III, 219.
Petrol filling station canopy: *O'Culacháin v McMullan Brothers* ITR Vol IV p 284; [1995] IR 217.
Racecourse stand (excluding bar areas): *O'Grady v Roscommon Race Committee* ITR Vol IV p 425 (Supreme Court, 26 March 1996).
A business suit: *Gaffney v Inspector of Taxes* – [1989] ITR 481.

UK

A horse: *Yarmouth v France* (1887) QBD 647.
Loose tools, knives and lasts: *Hinton v Maden & Ireland Ltd* (1959) 38 TC 391.
Movable office partitions: *Jarrold v John Good & Sons Ltd* (1962) 40 TC 681.
A dry dock: *IRC v Barclay, Curle & Co Ltd* (1969) 45 TC 221.
A swimming pool: *Cooke v Beach Station Caravans Ltd* [1974] STC 402.
Grain silos: *Schofield v R & H Hall Ltd* [1975] STC 353.
Certain electrical installations: *Cole Brothers Ltd v Phillips* [1982] STC 307.
Light fittings and mural in a hotel: *IRC v Scottish & Newcastle Breweries Ltd* [1982] STC 296.
Decorative panels: *Leeds Permanent Building Society v Proctor* [1982] STC 821.
Mezzanine platforms in warehouses: *Hunt v Henry Quick Ltd; King v Bridisco Ltd* [1992] STC 633.

Not regarded as "plant"

Irish

A suspended ceiling in a supermarket: *Dunnes Stores (Oakville) Ltd v Cronin* ITR Vol IV p 68.

UK

Car wash site: *Attwood v Anduff Car Wash Ltd* [1996] STC 110.
Furniture for a flat: *Mason v Tyson* [1980] STC 284.
Football spectator stand: *Brown v Burnley Football & Athletic Club Ltd* [1980] STC 424.
Garage canopy: *Dixon v Fitch's Garage Ltd* [1975] STC 486 (not followed by Irish courts in *O'Culacháin v McMullan Brothers* ITR Vol IV p 284.
Glasshouses: *Gray v Seymour's Garden Centre (Horticulture)* [1995] STC 706.
Held lessor not entitled to capital allowance on plant and equipment installed as fixtures in buildings that did not belong to them: *Melluish v BMI* [1995] STC 964.
Inflatable tennis court cover: *Thomas v Reynolds* [1987] STC 135.
Kennels: *Carr v Sayer* [1992] STC 396.
Ship used as a floating restaurant: *Benson v Yard Arm Club Ltd* [1979] STC 266.
Suspended ceiling: *Hampton v Forte Autogrill Ltd* [1980] STC 80.
Underground bunker for electricity transformer: *Bradley v London Electric plc* [1996] STC 231 [1996] STC 1054.
Wallpaper pattern books: *Rose & Co (Wallpaper & Paints) Ltd v Campbell* (1967) 44 TC 500.

Other

Expenditure on plant funded by non-recourse borrowings allowable: *Airspace Investments Ltd v Moore* [1994] 2 ILRM 15. Contrast *Ensign Tankers (Leasing) Ltd v Stokes* [1992] STC 226.

Revenue precedents

Issue: Does expenditure incurred on golf courses qualify for capital allowances either as a building or structure in use for the purposes of the trade of hotel keeping, or as plant?

Decision: No. It is the Revenue view that such expenditure does not qualify under either of these headings.

Issue: Vehicles used for towing aircraft, stairways for aircraft and luggage at airport - whether vehicle suitable for conveyance by road of persons or goods.

Decision: Not a vehicle suitable for conveyance by road of persons or goods.

Issue: Can a taxpayer opt not to claim capital allowances on a particular asset in a particular basis period, while preserving the written down value forward for future claims?

Decision: Following the decision in the UK cases of *Elliss v BP Oil Northern Ireland Refinery Ltd*, and *Elliss v BP Tyne Tanker Co Ltd*, capital allowances are not automatically deductible in computing the profits of a company for corporation tax purposes, and a company, if it so desires, may disclaim capital allowances for a particular accounting period. It should be noted that in the case of plant and machinery, the provisions of TCA 1997 s 287 will apply.

Issue: Is a suspended ceiling which forms one side of an air conditioning plenum regarded as plant?

Decision: It is the view of Revenue that the ceiling is not apparatus used by the company for the carrying on of its business but functions primarily as part of the setting in which that business is carried on.

Issue: Is a roller shutter fire door regarded as plant?

Decision: The treatment of expenditure on fire safety equipment differs here from that in the UK, where capital allowances are available for equipment purchased to comply with a notice served under the Fire Precautions Act, 1971. There is no similar tax legislation in this country. That the doors are part of the premises cannot be disputed. It is the view of this Office that they do not function as part of the plant with which the business is carried on, and are therefore no more than the setting.

Issue: What is the amount of the wear and tear allowance to be made in the case of refuse trucks?

Decision: The Revenue Commissioners are prepared to regard refuse trucks as not suitable for the conveyance by road of goods. Therefore allowances claimed under s 284 are given at the rate of 15% (now 20%) per annum on a straight line basis.

Issue: Do Revenue consider that tennis courts constitute plant for capital allowances purposes?

Decision: No.

Issue: What safety equipment on a sea fishing boat registered in the Register of Fishing Boats qualifies for accelerated allowances?

Decision: The accelerated allowances are available in respect of the safety equipment listed on page 5 of the booklet "Programme for the Renewal of the Whitefish Fleet" issued June 1998 by BIM.

Issue: What marina furniture used in a commercial marina for berthing boats and other craft is considered plant?

Decision: The following items are considered plant: pontoons, anchors, gangways, equipment and conduit for utilities, and the movable access bridge but not the piles.

Issue: Is the amount of the wear allowances available for farm tractors 15% of actual cost or 20% on a reducing balance basis?

Decision: In strictness farm tractors would be regarded as vehicles suitable for the conveyance by road of persons or goods or the haulage by road of other vehicles and therefore the reducing balance method should apply. Revenue is prepared to accept a claim for allowance based on 15% of the actual cost.

Tax Briefing

TB14 May 1994 par3.5 — Capital allowances on video tapes.

TB24 Dec 1996 p 16–18, 20 — Finance Leasing.

TB25 Feb 1997 p 1–3 — Finance Leasing.

TB47 Apr 2002 p 11 — Finance Act 2002 Changes.

Definitions

Appeal Commissioners: s 2(1); Income Tax Acts: s 1(2); inspector: ss 2(1), 5(1), 852; month: IA 1937 Sch; person: IA 1937 s 11(*c*); profits or gains: s 3(4); trade: s 3(1); vesting day: s 268(10); writing: IA 1937 Sch; year of assessment: s 3(1).

Former enactments

ITA 1967 s 241(1)(*a*) and (*b*) and proviso to (1), (1A), (6)–(6A) and (10)–(11); CTA 1976 s 21(1) and Sch 1 para 6; FA 1992 s 26(4); FA 1996 s 132(1) and Sch 5 Pt I para 1(12)(*a*); FA 1997 s 22, s 146(1) and Sch 9 Pt I para 1(16).

285 Acceleration of wear and tear allowances

(1) In this section—

"designated area" means a designated area for the purposes of the Industrial Development Act, 1969;

"industrial development agency" means the Industrial Development Authority, Shannon Free Airport Development Company Limited or Údarás na Gaeltachta;

"qualifying building or structure" means a building or structure which is to be an industrial building or structure within the meaning of section 268(1)(*d*), and in respect of the provision of which expenditure was incurred before the 31st day of December, 1995, where a binding contract for the provision of the building or structure was entered into before the 31st day of December, 1990;

"qualifying machinery or plant" means machinery or plant, other than vehicles suitable for the conveyance by road of persons or goods or the haulage by road of other vehicles, provided—

(*a*) on or after the 1st day of April, 1967, for use in any designated area, or

(*b*) on or after the 1st day of April, 1971, for use in any area other than a designated area,

for the purposes of a trade and which at the time it is so provided is unused and not secondhand.

(2) (*a*) Subject to this section and section 299(2), where for any chargeable period a wear and tear allowance is to be made under section 284 in relation to any qualifying machinery or plant, the allowance shall, subject to section 284(4), be increased by such amount as is specified by the person to whom the allowance is to be made and, in relation to a case in which this subsection has applied, any reference in the Tax Acts to an allowance made under section 284 shall be construed as a reference to that allowance as increased under this subsection.

(*b*) Subject to subsections (4) and (6), as respects any machinery or plant provided for use on or after the 1st day of April, 1988, any wear and tear allowance made under section 284 and increased under paragraph (*a*) in respect of that machinery or plant, whether claimed for one chargeable period or more than one such period, shall not in the aggregate exceed—

(i) if the machinery or plant was provided for use before the 1st day of April, 1989, 75 per cent,

(ii) if the machinery or plant was provided for use on or after the 1st day of April, 1989, and before the 1st day of April, 1991, 50 per cent, or

(iii) if the machinery or plant was provided for use on or after the 1st day of April, 1991, and before the 1st day of April, 1992, 25 per cent,

of the capital expenditure incurred on the provision of that machinery or plant.

(3) Notwithstanding subsection (2) but subject to subsections (4) and (6)—

(*a*) no allowance made under section 284 for wear and tear of any qualifying machinery or plant provided for use on or after the 1st day of April, 1992, shall be increased under this section, and

(*b*) as respects chargeable periods ending on or after the 6th day of April, 1999, no allowance made under section 284 for wear and tear of any qualifying machinery or plant provided for use before the 1st day of April, 1992, shall be increased under this section.

(4) This section shall apply in relation to machinery or plant to which subsection (5) applies as if subsections (2)(*b*) and (3) were deleted.

(5) This subsection shall apply to—

(*a*) machinery or plant provided—

(i) before the 23rd day of April, 1996, for use for the purposes of trading operations, or

(ii) on or after the 23rd day of April, 1996, by a company for use for the purposes of trading operations carried on by the company,

which are relevant trading operations within the meaning of section 445 or 446 but, in relation to capital expenditure incurred on the provision of machinery or plant on or after the 6th day of May, 1993, excluding machinery or plant provided by a lessor to a lessee other than in the course of the carrying on by the lessor of those relevant trading operations,

(*b*) machinery or plant the expenditure on the provision of which was incurred before the 31st day of December, 1995, under a binding contract entered into on or before the 27th day of January, 1988,

(*c*) machinery or plant provided for the purposes of a project approved by an industrial development agency on or before the 31st day of December, 1988, and in respect of the provision of which expenditure was incurred before the 31st day of December, 1995; but, as respects machinery or plant provided for the purposes of a project approved by an industrial development agency in the period from the 1st day of January, 1986, to the 31st day of December, 1988, this paragraph shall apply as if the reference to the 31st day of December, 1995, were a reference to the 31st day of December, 1996,

and

(*d*) machinery or plant provided before the 1st day of April, 1991, for the purposes of a trade or part of a trade of hotel-keeping carried on in a building or structure or part of a building or structure, including machinery or plant provided by a lessor to a lessee for use in such a trade or part of a trade, where a binding contract for the provision of that building or structure was entered into after the 27th day of January, 1988, and before the 1st day of June, 1988.

(6) This section shall apply in relation to machinery or plant to which subsection (7)(*a*) applies—

(*a*) as if in subsection (2)(*b*)—

(i) the following subparagraph were substituted for subparagraph (ii):

"(ii) if the machinery or plant is provided for use on or after the 1st day of April, 1989, 50 per cent.",

and

(ii) subparagraph (iii) were deleted,

and

(*b*) as if subsection (3) were deleted.

(7) (*a*) This subsection shall apply to—

(i) machinery or plant provided for the purposes of a project approved for grant assistance by an industrial development agency in the period from the 1st day of January, 1989, to the 31st day of December, 1990, and in respect of the provision of which expenditure is incurred before the 31st day of December, 1997 [, or before the 30th day of June, 1998, if its provision is solely for use in an industrial building or structure referred to in sections 271(3)(*c*) and 273(7)(*a*)(i) and expenditure in respect of such provision would have been incurred before the 31st day of December, 1997, but for the existence of circumstances which resulted in legal proceedings being initiated, being proceedings which were the subject of an order of the High Court made before the 1st day of January, 1998];[1] but, as respects machinery or plant provided for the purposes of any such project specified in the list referred to in section 133(8)(*c*)(iv), this subparagraph shall apply as if the reference to the 31st day of December, 1997, [where it first occurs,][2] were a reference to the 31st day of December, 2002,

and

(ii) machinery or plant provided for the purposes of a trade or part of a trade of hotel-keeping carried on in a qualifying building or structure and in respect of the provision of which expenditure was incurred before the 31st day of December, 1995.

(*b*) Paragraph (*a*)(ii) shall not apply if the qualifying building or structure is not registered within 6 months after the date of the completion of that building or structure in a register kept by Bord Fáilte Éireann under the Tourist Traffic Acts, 1939 to 1995, and where by virtue of this section any allowance or increased allowance has been granted any necessary additional assessments may be made to give effect to this paragraph.

(8) Where for any chargeable period a wear and tear allowance under section 284 in relation to any machinery or plant is increased under this section, no allowance under section 283 shall be made in relation to the machinery or plant for that or any subsequent chargeable period.

Amendments

1 Inserted by FA 1998 s 21(*b*)(i) with effect from 6 April 1998.

2 Inserted by FA 1998 s 21(*b*)(ii) with effect from 6 April 1998.

Cross-references

Deemed wear and tear allowance where none claimed: s 287(1).
Initial allowance, no accelerated wear and tear allowance: s 283(6)(*b*).
Leased assets, restriction on use of allowances: s 403(8)(*b*).
Leased plant and machinery, restriction on use of allowances, subs (7)(*a*)(i): s 404(1)(*b*)(ii)(II), (8)(*b*).
Lessees, allowance to, subs (2): s 299(2).
Professions and employments: s 301.
Mining machinery or plant: s 678(1).

Definitions

High Court: IA 1937 Sch; Income Tax Acts: s 1(2); person: IA 1937 s 11(*c*); trade: s 3(1).

Former enactments

FA 1967 s 11(1)–(2A) and (4); FA 1971 s 26(1)–(2A) and (4); CTA 1976 s 21(1) and Sch 1 para 53 and para 60; FA 1978 s 22; FA 1988 s 46, s 47 and s 51(1)(*a*), (*c*), (*cc*) and the proviso thereto and (*d*), (3) and (6); FA 1990 s 71, s 72, s 80 and s81(1)(*a*) and (*c*), proviso to (1), and (3); FA 1995 s 26 and s 27; FA 1996 s 43 and 132(1) and Sch 5 Pt I paras 2 and 5.

286 Increased wear and tear allowances for taxis and cars for short-term hire

(1) (*a*) In this section—

"car" means any mechanically propelled road vehicle, being a vehicle which has been constructed or adapted to be primarily suited to the carriage of passengers and not to the conveyance of goods or burden of any description or to the haulage by road of other vehicles, and which is a vehicle of a type commonly used as a private vehicle and suitable to be so used, and includes a vehicle in use for the purpose referred to in paragraph (ii) of the definition of **"qualifying purposes"**;

"qualifying purposes" means, subject to paragraphs (*c*) and (*d*), the use in the ordinary course of trade of a car for the purposes of—

(i) short-term hire to members of the public, or

(ii) the carriage of members of the public while the car is a licensed public hire vehicle fitted with a taximeter in accordance with the Road Traffic (Public Service Vehicles) Regulations, 1963 (SI No 191 of 1963);

"short-term hire", in relation to a car and subject to paragraph (*b*), means the hire of the car to a person under a hire-drive agreement (within the meaning of section 3 of the Road Traffic Act, 1961) for a continuous period which does not exceed 8 weeks.

(*b*) Where a period of hire of a car to a person by another person is followed within 7 days of the end of that period by a further period of hire of a car (whether the same car or not) to that person by that other person, the 2 periods shall be deemed for the purposes of this section, including any subsequent application of this paragraph, to constitute together a single continuous period of hire so that, where that continuous period of hire exceeds 8 weeks, the period of hire of any car included in that continuous period of hire shall not be treated as a period of short-term hire, and for the purposes of this paragraph any reference to a person shall be treated as including a reference to any other person who is connected with that person.

(*c*) For the purposes of this section, a car shall be regarded as used by a person for qualifying purposes as respects a chargeable period only if not less than 75 per cent of its use (determined by reference to the periods of time in which the car is used, or available for use, for any purpose) by that person in the chargeable period or its basis period is for qualifying purposes.

(*d*) Notwithstanding paragraph (*c*), where as respects a chargeable period the use of a car for qualifying purposes does not satisfy the requirements of that paragraph but would have satisfied those requirements if the reference in that paragraph to 75 per cent were a reference to 50 per cent, the car shall be deemed to be used for qualifying purposes as respects that chargeable period if the use of the car by that person for qualifying purposes satisfied the requirements of that paragraph as respects the immediately preceding chargeable period, or the car shall be deemed to be so used if that use of the car has satisfied those requirements as respects the immediately succeeding chargeable period, and the inspector shall accordingly adjust the amount of capital allowances to be made in taxing the person's trade and any amount of tax overpaid shall be repaid.

(2) In determining what capital allowances are to be made to a person for any chargeable period in taxing a trade which consists of or includes the carrying on of qualifying purposes, section 284 shall apply to a car which as respects that period has been used by the person for qualifying purposes as if the reference in subsection (2)(*a*)(ii) of that section to 20 per cent were a reference to 40 per cent.

Cross-references

Professions and employments, non-application of this section: s 301(1).

Wear and tear allowances, general regime, meaning of "car" applied: s 284(2)(*aa*).

Definitions

capital allowance: ss 2(1), 5(1); inspector: ss 2(1), 5(1), 852; person: IA 1937 s 11(*c*); trade: s 3(1); week: IA 1937 Sch.

Former enactments

FA 1987 s 24; FA 1996 s 131, s 132(1) and Sch 5 Pt I para 16.

286A Wear and tear allowances for licences for public hire vehicles

[(1) In this section—

"licence" means a taxi licence or a wheelchair accessible taxi licence granted in respect of a small public service vehicle by a licensing authority in accordance with the Road Traffic (Public Service Vehicles) Regulations, 1963 to 2000, made under section 82 of the Road Traffic Act, 1961, as amended by section 57 of the Road Traffic Act, 1968;

"qualifying expenditure" means—

(*a*) capital expenditure incurred on the acquisition of a licence on or before 21 November 2000 and for the purposes of this section, where capital expenditure is so incurred it shall be deemed to have been incurred on 21 November 1997 or, if later, on the day on which the trade commenced, or

(*b*) where a licence formed part of an inheritance taken by an individual on or before 21 November 2000 and inheritance tax or probate tax was paid in relation to that licence, an amount equal to the open market value of the licence used for the purpose of inheritance tax or probate tax if that amount is greater than the amount of the capital expenditure incurred on the acquisition of the licence and, where this paragraph applies, the first-mentioned amount shall be deemed to have been capital expenditure incurred on the acquisition of a licence on 21 November 1997 or, if later, on the date on which the trade commenced;

"qualifying trade", means a trade carried on by an individual which consists of the carriage of members of the public for reward in a vehicle in respect of which a licence has been granted but excluding any trade or part of a trade which consists of the letting of such a vehicle.

(2) (*a*) Where an individual carrying on a qualifying trade proves to have incurred qualifying expenditure, then, for the purposes of this Chapter, other than sections 298 and 299, and for the purposes of Chapter 4 of this Part—

(i) the licence shall, subject to paragraph (*c*), be treated as machinery or plant,

(ii) such machinery or plant shall be treated as having been provided for the purposes of the trade, and

(iii) for so long as the individual is entitled to the licence, that machinery or plant shall be treated as belonging to that individual.

(*b*) Where an individual who has incurred qualifying expenditure carries on a qualifying trade and uses a vehicle, being the vehicle to which the machinery or plant referred to in paragraph (*a*) relates, partly for letting to another person and partly for the purposes of the qualifying trade, the machinery or plant shall be deemed for the purposes of section 284(1) to be used only for the purposes of the qualifying trade.

(*c*) Notwithstanding paragraph (*a*), where an individual who has incurred qualifying expenditure in relation to more than one licence carries on a qualifying trade and lets more than one of the vehicles, which are used for the purposes of the trade, being the vehicles to which the machinery or plant referred to in paragraph (*a*) relates, to another person or persons for use also by that other person or persons, paragraph (*a*) shall apply in respect of so much of that machinery or plant as relates to one licence only (in this section referred to as **"the relevant licence"**).

(3) Where an individual who is not, apart from this subsection, entitled to allowances under this Chapter by virtue of this section, becomes the beneficial owner of a licence on the death of his or her spouse, and that spouse—

(*a*) had incurred qualifying expenditure in respect of the licence, and

(*b*) had carried on a qualifying trade,

then, for the purposes of this section, if the individual lets the vehicle to which the licence relates, or lets the licence, for use for the purposes of a qualifying trade carried on by another person—

(i) the individual shall be deemed to have incurred the qualifying expenditure in respect of the licence,

(ii) that licence shall be treated as machinery or plant, and

(iii) the letting of that vehicle or of that licence by the individual shall be deemed to be a qualifying trade carried on by the individual which commenced on the date of the first letting of that vehicle, but this subsection shall apply in relation to an individual as respects one licence only.

(4) In determining what capital allowances are to be made in taxing the trade of an individual to which subsection (2) refers for any year of assessment, section 284(2)(*aa*) (inserted by the Finance Act, 2001) shall apply—

(*a*) as if the machinery or plant to which subsection (2) refers were machinery or plant to which section 284(2)(*aa*) applies, and

(*b*) as if the reference to "on or after 1 January 2001" in section 284(2)(*aa*) were a reference to "on 21 November 1997".

(5) (*a*) This subsection shall apply to an individual to whom paragraph (*b*) or (*c*) of subsection (2) relates who lets a vehicle to which subsection (2)(*b*) relates or a vehicle relating to a relevant licence.

(*b*) Notwithstanding section 381, where relief is claimed under that section in respect of a loss sustained in a qualifying trade, the amount of that loss, in so far as by virtue of section 392 it is referable to an allowance under this section, shall be treated for the purposes of subsections (1) and (3)(*b*) of section 381 as reducing income only from a letting to which paragraph (*a*) refers and shall not be treated as reducing any other income.

(6) Subsection (7) of section 953 shall apply to an excess, referred to in that subsection, arising by virtue of an allowance made under this section as if the reference in paragraph (*a*)(ii) of that subsection to "section 438(4)" were a reference to this section.

(7) This section shall be deemed to have come into operation as on and from 6 April 1997.][1]

Amendments

1 Section 286A inserted by FA 2001 s 51 and is deemed to been in operation from 6 April 1997.

Definitions

person: IA 1937 s 11(*c*); trade: s 3(1).

287 Wear and tear allowances deemed to have been made in certain cases

(1) In this section—

"wear and tear allowance" means an allowance made under section 284 otherwise than by virtue of section 285;

"normal wear and tear allowance" means such wear and tear allowance or greater wear and tear allowance, if any, as would have been made to a person in respect of any machinery or plant used by such person during any chargeable period if all the conditions specified in subsection (3) had been fulfilled in relation to that chargeable period.

(2) Where for any chargeable period during which any machinery or plant has been used by a person no wear and tear allowance or a wear and tear allowance less than the normal wear and tear allowance is made to such person in respect of the machinery or plant, the normal wear and tear allowance shall be deemed for the purposes of subsections (3) and (4) of section 284 to have been made to such person in respect of the machinery or plant for that chargeable period.

(3) The conditions referred to in subsection (1) are—

(*a*) that the trade had been carried on by the person in question since the date on which such person acquired the machinery or plant and had been so carried on by such person in such circumstances that the full amount of the profits or gains of the trade was liable to be charged to tax,

(*b*) that the trade had at no time consisted wholly or partly of exempted trading operations within the meaning of Chapter I of Part XXV of the Income Tax Act, 1967, or Part V of the Corporation Tax Act, 1976,

(*c*) that the machinery or plant had been used by such person solely for the purposes of the trade since that date,

(*d*) that a proper claim had been duly made by such person for wear and tear allowance in respect of the machinery or plant for every relevant chargeable period, and

(*e*) that no question arose in connection with any chargeable period as to there being payable to such person directly or indirectly any sums in respect of, or taking account of, the wear and tear of the machinery or plant.

(4) In the case of a company, subsection (3)(*a*) shall not alter the periods which are to be taken as chargeable periods but if, during any time after the year 1975–76 and after the company acquired the machinery or plant, the company has not been within the charge to corporation tax, any year of assessment or part of a year of assessment falling within that time shall be taken as a chargeable period as if it had been an accounting period of the company.

Cross-references

Professions, employments, offices, application to: s 301.

Shipping tonnage tax, plant and machinery used wholly for tonnage tax trade: Sch 18B, para 10(1)(*b*)(iii).

Definitions

person: IA 1937 s 11(*c*).

Former enactments

FA 1970 s 14(1), (2)–(3); CTA 1976 s 21(1) and Sch 1 para 56; FA 1997 s 146(1) and Sch 9 Pt I para 4(1).

288 Balancing allowances and balancing charges

(1) Subject to this section, where any of the following events occurs in the case of any machinery or plant in respect of which an initial allowance or a wear and tear allowance has been made for any chargeable period to a person carrying on a trade—

(*a*) any event occurring after the setting up and before the permanent discontinuance of the trade whereby the machinery or plant ceases to belong to the person carrying on the trade (whether on a sale of the machinery or plant or in any other circumstances of any description),

(*b*) any event occurring after the setting up and before the permanent discontinuance of the trade whereby the machinery or plant (while continuing to belong to the person carrying on the trade) permanently ceases to be used for the purposes of a trade carried on by the person,

(*c*) the permanent discontinuance of the trade, the machinery or plant not having previously ceased to belong to the person carrying on the trade,

(*d*) in the case of machinery or plant consisting of computer software or the right to use or otherwise deal with computer software, any event whereby the person grants to another person a right to use or otherwise deal with the whole or part of [that machinery or plant][1] in circumstances where the consideration in money for the grant constitutes (or, if there were consideration in money for the grant, would constitute) a capital sum,

an allowance or charge (in this Chapter referred to as a **"balancing allowance"** or a **"balancing charge"**) shall, in the circumstances mentioned in this section, be made to or, as the case may be, on that person for the chargeable period related to that event.

(2) Where there are no sale, insurance, salvage or compensation moneys or where the amount of the capital expenditure of the person in question on the provision of the machinery or plant still unallowed as at the time of the event exceeds those moneys, a balancing allowance shall be made, and the amount of the allowance shall be the amount of the expenditure still unallowed as at that time or, as the case may be, of the excess of that expenditure still unallowed as at that time over those moneys.

(3) Where the sale, insurance, salvage or compensation moneys exceed the amount, if any, of that expenditure still unallowed as at the time of the event, a balancing charge shall be made, and the amount on which it is made shall be an amount equal to—

(*a*) the excess, or

(*b*) where the amount still unallowed is nil, those moneys.

[(3A) Where, in relation to an event referred to in subsection (1)(*d*), a balancing allowance or balancing charge is to be made to or, as the case may be, on a person for the chargeable period related to that event and following that event, the person retains an interest in the machinery or plant, then, for the purposes of this Chapter—

(*a*) the amount of capital expenditure still unallowed at the time of the event, which is to be taken into account in calculating the balancing allowance or balancing charge, shall be such portion of the unallowed expenditure relating to the machinery or plant in question as the sale, insurance, salvage or compensation moneys bear to the aggregate of those moneys and the market value of the machinery or plant which remains undisposed of, and the balance of the unallowed expenditure shall be attributed to the machinery or plant which remains undisposed of, and

(*b*) the amount of capital expenditure incurred on the machinery or plant in question shall be treated as reduced by such portion of that expenditure as the sale, insurance, salvage or compensation moneys bear to the aggregate of those moneys and the market value of the machinery or plant which remains undisposed of.][2]

[(3B) Notwithstanding subsection (3), a balancing charge shall not be made where the amount of the sale, insurance, salvage or compensation moneys received by the person in question in respect of the machinery or plant is less than €2,000; but this subsection shall not apply in the case of the sale or other disposal of the machinery or plant to a connected person.][3]

(4) (*a*) In this subsection, **"scientific research allowance"** means—

(i) in relation to any expenditure incurred before the 6th day of April, 1965, the total amount of any allowances made in respect of that expenditure under section 244(3) of the Income Tax Act, 1967, increased by the amount of any allowance made under section 244(4)(*b*) of that Act or, as the case may be, reduced by any amount treated as a trading receipt in accordance with section 244(4)(*c*) of that Act, and

(ii) in relation to any expenditure incurred on or after the 6th day of April, 1965, the amount of any allowance made in respect of that expenditure under subsection (1) or (2) of section 765, reduced by any amount treated as a trading receipt in accordance with section 765(3)(*a*).

(*b*) Notwithstanding anything in subsection (3), in no case shall the amount on which a balancing charge is made on a person exceed the aggregate of the following amounts—

(i) the amount of the initial allowance, if any, made to the person in respect of the expenditure in question,

(ii) the amount of any wear and tear allowance made to the person in respect of the machinery or plant in question,

(iii) the amount of any scientific research allowance made to the person in respect of the expenditure, and

(iv) the amount of any balancing allowance previously made to the person in respect of the expenditure.

[(*c*) Where subsection (3A) applies, the amount of any allowances referred to in paragraph (*b*) made in respect of the machinery or plant in question shall, for the purposes of this Chapter, be apportioned so that:

(i) such portion of those allowances as the sale, insurance, salvage or compensation moneys bear to the aggregate of those moneys and the market value of the machinery or plant which remains undisposed of, shall be attributed to the grant of the right to use or otherwise deal with, referred to in subsection (1)(*d*), and

(ii) the balance of those allowances shall be attributed to the machinery or plant which remains undisposed of.][4]

(5) (*a*) Where the aggregate amount of initial allowances and wear and tear allowances made to any person in respect of any machinery or plant exceeds the actual amount of the expenditure incurred by that person on the provision of that machinery or plant, the amount of such excess (in this paragraph referred to as **"the excess amount"**) shall, on the occurrence of an event within paragraph (*a*), (*b*), (*c*) or (*d*) of subsection (1), be deemed to be a payment of an equal amount received by that person on account of sale, insurance, salvage or compensation moneys and shall be added to any other such moneys received in respect of that machinery or plant, and a balancing charge shall be made and the amount on which it is made shall be an amount equal to—

(i) where there are no sale, insurance, salvage or compensation moneys, the excess amount, or

(ii) where there are sale, insurance, salvage or compensation moneys, the aggregate of such moneys and the excess amount.

(*b*) Where as respects any machinery or plant an event within paragraph (*a*), (*b*), (*c*) or (*d*) of subsection (1) is followed by another event within any of those paragraphs, any balancing allowance or balancing charge made to or on the person by virtue of the happening of the later event shall take account of any balancing allowance or balancing charge previously made to or on that person in respect of the expenditure incurred by the person on the provision of that machinery or plant.

(6) (*a*) Where—

(i) the sale, insurance, salvage or compensation moneys consist of a payment or payments to a person under the scheme for compensation in respect of the decommissioning of fishing vessels implemented by the Minister for the Marine and Natural Resources in accordance with Council Regulation (EC) No 3699/93 of 21 December 1993, (OJ No L 346, 31.12.1993, p1) and

(ii) on account of the receipt by the person of such payment or payments, a balancing charge is to be made on the person for any chargeable period other than by virtue of paragraph (*b*),

then, the amount on which the balancing charge is to be made for that chargeable period shall be an amount equal to one-third of the amount (in this subsection referred to as **"the original amount"**) on which the balancing charge would but for this subsection have been made.

(*b*) Notwithstanding paragraph (*a*), there shall be made on the person for each of the 2 immediately succeeding chargeable periods a balancing charge, and the amount on which that charge is made for each of those periods shall be an amount equal to one-third of the original amount.

Amendments

1 Substituted by FA 2000 s 41(*a*)(i) with effect from 29 February 2000; previously "the computer software concerned".

2 Subs (3A) inserted by FA 2000 s 41(*a*)(ii) with effect from 29 February 2000.

3 Subs (3B) inserted by FA 2002 s 31(2) with effect from 1 January 2002.

4 Subs (4)(*c*) inserted by FA 2000 s 41(*a*)(iii) with effect from 29 February 2000.

Cross-references

Deemed wear and tear allowance, subs (4): s 296(5).

Farming, deemed wear and tear allowance: s 660(1).

Meaning of "amount still unallowed", subs (4)(*a*): s 292(*c*).

Option (subs (1)), in case of replacement: s 290.

Partnerships (subs (4)), application to: s 293(1)(*b*); sale or gift of plant or machinery: s 293(3).

Professions, employments, offices, application to: s 301.

Shipping tonnage tax, plant and machinery used wholly for tonnage tax trade: Sch 18B, para 10(1)(*b*)(i); (2)(*b*)(ii); subs (2): Sch 18B, para 10(2)(*b*)(i); plant and machinery, change of use of non-tonnage tax asset: Sch 18B, para 14(2)(*b*); deferment of balancing charge on re-investment: Sch 18B, para 18(2).

Subsidy towards wear and tear, subs (4): s 297(2).

Revenue precedents

Issue: (1) Whether it is acceptable to reclassify as stocks rather than fixed assets linen used by companies providing a hiring and cleaning service in respect of linen; (2) Whether s 288 applies to the re-Classification as if it were a sale at the open market price.

Decision: (1) Yes. (2) Yes.

Issue: Prior to 1973 a person could claim initial allowances and wear and tear allowances amounting to more than the cost of the plant and machinery. Section 11 Finance Act 1973 provided for the charging of the excess of the allowances over the actual cost. The question that arises is whether the actual cost is the cost as reduced by grants. At the time grants were not deducted in arriving at the qualifying expenditure for wear and tear purposes but were deducted for the purpose of a balancing charge.

Decision: A strict application of the section could have had the effect of imposing a balancing charge on the excess of the allowances made over the expenditure incurred as reduced by grants. The Revenue Commissioners are prepared to accept that the provisions of Section 11 Finance Act 1973 (now Section 288(5) Taxes Consolidation Act 1997) will not apply to this excess. The provision is only applied where the capital allowances granted exceed the gross cost.

Definitions

person: IA 1937 s 11(*c*); trade: s 3(1).

Former enactments

ITA 1967 s 272(1)–(4), (5)(*a*) and (*b*) and (6) and definition of "scientific research allowance" in ITA 1967 s 271; CTA 1976 s 21(1) and Sch 1 para 28 and para 29; FA 1994 s 24(*b*); FA 1995 s 25(1).

Corresponding UK tax provision

Capital Allowances Act 2001 ss 61 and 62.

289 Calculation of balancing allowances and balancing charges in certain cases

(1) In this section, **"open-market price"**, in relation to any machinery or plant, means the price which the machinery or plant would have fetched if sold in the open market at the time of the event in question.

(2) Where—

(*a*) an event occurs which gives rise or might give rise to a balancing allowance or balancing charge in respect of machinery or plant,

(*b*) the event is the permanent discontinuance of a trade, and

(*c*) at or about the time of the discontinuance there occurs in relation to the machinery or plant any event mentioned in paragraphs (*a*) to (*c*) of section 318, not being a sale at less than open-market price other than a sale to which section 312 applies,

then, for the purpose of determining—

(i) whether the discontinuance gives rise to a balancing allowance or balancing charge, and, if so,

(ii) the amount of the allowance or, as the case may be, the amount on which the charge is to be made,

the amount of the net proceeds, compensation, receipts or insurance moneys mentioned in paragraphs (*a*) to (*c*) of section 318 which arise on the last-mentioned event shall be deemed to be an amount of sale, insurance, salvage or compensation moneys arising on the permanent discontinuance of the trade.

(3) (*a*) Subject to subsections (4) and (6), paragraph (*b*) shall apply where an event occurs which gives rise or might give rise to a balancing allowance or balancing charge in respect of machinery or plant, and—

(i) the event is the permanent discontinuance of the trade and immediately after the time of the discontinuance the machinery or plant continues to belong to the person by whom the trade was carried on immediately before that time and the case is not one within subsection (2),

(ii) the event is the permanent discontinuance of the trade and at the time of the discontinuance the machinery or plant is either sold at less than the open-market price, the sale not being one to which section 312 applies, or the machinery or plant is given away,

(iii) the event is the sale of the machinery or plant at less than the open-market price, not being a sale to which section 312 applies, or is the gift of the machinery or plant, or

(iv) the event is that, after the setting up and before the permanent discontinuance of the trade, the machinery or plant permanently ceases to be used for the purposes of a trade carried on by the person by whom the first-mentioned trade is being carried on, and so ceases either by reason of that person's transferring the machinery or plant to other use or, on a transfer of the trade which is not treated as involving a discontinuance of the trade, by reason of the retention of the machinery or plant by the transferor.

(*b*) For the purpose of determining whether a balancing allowance or balancing charge is to be made and, if so, the amount of the allowance or, as the case may be, the amount on which the charge is to be made, the event shall be treated as if it had given rise to sale, insurance, salvage or compensation moneys of an amount equal to the open-market price of the machinery or plant.

(4) References in subsection (3) to the sale of machinery or plant at less than the open-market price do not include references to the sale of machinery or plant in such circumstances that there is a charge to income tax under Schedule E by virtue of Chapter 3 of Part 5, and subsection (3)(*b*) shall not apply by reason of the gift of machinery or plant if the machinery or plant is given away in any such circumstances.

(5) Subject to subsection (6), where subsection (3)(*b*) applies by reason of the gift or sale of machinery or plant to any person, and that person receives or purchases the machinery or plant with a view to using it for the purposes of a trade carried on by that person, then, in determining whether any, and if so what, wear and tear allowances, balancing allowances or balancing charges are to be made in connection with that trade, the like consequences shall ensue as if the recipient or purchaser had purchased the machinery or plant at the open-market price.

(6) [Subject to subsection (6A), where in a case within subsection (5)][1] the recipient or purchaser and the donor or seller, by notice in writing to the inspector, jointly so elect, the following provisions shall apply:

(*a*) subsections (3)(*b*) and (5) shall apply as if for the references in those subsections to the open-market price there were substituted references to that price or the amount of the expenditure on the provision of the machinery or plant still unallowed immediately before the gift or sale, whichever is the lower;

(*b*) notwithstanding anything in this Chapter, such balancing charge, if any, shall be made on the recipient or purchaser on any event occurring after the date of the gift or sale as would have been made on the donor or seller if the donor or seller had continued to own the machinery or plant and had done all such things and been allowed all such allowances in connection with the machinery or plant as were done by or allowed to the recipient or purchaser.

[(6A)(*a*) Subsection (6) shall only apply in a case where the donor or seller is connected with the recipient or purchaser.

(*b*) Notwithstanding paragraph (*a*), subsection (6) shall not apply in any case where the donor or seller is not a company and the recipient or purchaser is a company.][2]

Amendments

1 Substituted by FA 2003 s 47(1)(*a*) as respects a gift or sale of machinery or plant on or after 6 February 2003.

2 Subs (6A) inserted by FA 2003 s 47(1)(*b*) as respects a gift or sale of machinery or plant on or after 6 February 2003.

Cross-references

Capital gains tax, restriction of losses by reference to capital allowances, subs (6): s 555(2).
Cars costing more than the specified amount: s 374(1).
Professions, employments, offices, application to: s 301.
Shipping tonnage tax, plant and machinery used wholly for tonnage tax trade, subs (3): Sch 18B, para 10(2)(*b*)(ii); plant and machinery, change of use of non-tonnage tax asset, subs (3): Sch 18B, para 14(*b*)(iii).

Definitions

company: s 4(1); connected: s 10; inspector: ss 2(1), 5(1), 852; person: IA 1937 s 11(*c*); trade: s 3(1); writing: IA 1937 Sch.

Former enactments

ITA 1967 s 277.

Corresponding UK tax provision

Capital Allowances Act 2001 s 196.

290 Option in case of replacement

Where machinery or plant, in the case of which any of the events mentioned in section 288(1) has occurred, is replaced by the owner of the machinery or plant and a balancing charge is to be made on that owner by reason of that event, or but for this section a balancing charge would have been made on that owner by reason of that event, then, if by notice in writing to the inspector that owner so elects, the following provisions shall apply:

(*a*) if the amount on which the charge would have been made is greater than the capital expenditure on providing the new machinery or plant—

(i) the charge shall be made only on an amount equal to the difference,

(ii) no initial allowance, no balancing allowance and no wear and tear allowance shall be made in respect of the new machinery or plant or the expenditure on the provision of the new machinery or plant, and

(iii) in considering whether any, and if so what, balancing charge is to be made in respect of the expenditure on the new machinery or plant, there shall be deemed to have been made in respect of that expenditure an initial allowance equal to the full amount of that expenditure;

(*b*) if the capital expenditure on providing the new machinery or plant is equal to or greater than the amount on which the charge would have been made—

(i) the charge shall not be made,

(ii) the amount of any initial allowance in respect of that expenditure and the amount of any wear and tear allowance shall be calculated as if the expenditure had been reduced by the amount on which the charge would have been made, and

(iii) in considering whether any, and if so what, balancing allowance or balancing charge is to be made in respect of the new machinery or plant, there shall be deemed to have been granted in respect of the new machinery or plant an initial allowance equal to the amount on which the charge would have been made, in addition to any initial allowance actually granted in respect of the new machinery or plant.

Cross-references

Cars costing more than the specified amount: s 374(5).
Capital gains tax, restriction of losses by reference to capital allowances: s 555(3).
Professions, employments, offices, application to: s 301.
Shipping tonnage tax, deferment of balancing charge on re-investment: Sch 18B, para 18(4).

Revenue precedents

Issue: Where a balancing charge arises on the disposal of a motor vehicle what amount is deducted from the replacement cost? ie is it the amount of the charge before or after adjustment has been made for private use?
Decision: The amount to be deducted is the amount of the charge after adjustment has been made for private use.

Definitions

inspector: ss 2(1), 5(1), 852.

Former enactments

ITA 1967 s 273(1).

291 Computer software

(1) Where a person carrying on a trade incurs capital expenditure in acquiring for the purposes of the trade a right to use or otherwise deal with computer software, then, for the purposes of this Chapter and Chapter 4 of this Part—

(*a*) the right and the software to which the right relates shall be treated as machinery or plant,
(*b*) such machinery or plant shall be treated as having been provided for the purposes of the trade, and
(*c*) for so long as the person is entitled to the right, that machinery or plant shall be treated as belonging to that person.

(2) In any case where—

(*a*) a person carrying on a trade incurs capital expenditure on the provision of computer software for the purposes of the trade, and
(*b*) in consequence of the person incurring that expenditure, the computer software belongs to that person but does not constitute machinery or plant,

then, for the purposes of this Chapter and Chapter 4 of this Part, the computer software shall be treated as machinery or plant.

Cross-references

Professions, employments, offices, application to: s 301.

Definitions

person: IA 1937 s 11(*c*); trade: s 3(1).

Former enactments

ITA 1967 s 241A(1)–(2); FA 1994 s 24(*a*).

Corresponding UK tax provision

Capital Allowances Act 2001 s 71.

292 Meaning of "amount still unallowed"

References in this Chapter to the amount still unallowed as at any time of any expenditure on the provision of machinery or plant shall be construed as references to the amount of that expenditure less—

(*a*) any initial allowance made or deemed under this Chapter to have been made in respect of that expenditure to the person who incurred the expenditure,

(*b*) any wear and tear allowances made or deemed under this Chapter to have been made to that person in respect of the machinery or plant on the provision of which the expenditure was incurred, being allowances made for any chargeable period such that the chargeable period or its basis period ended before the time in question,

(*c*) any scientific research allowance (within the meaning of section 288(4)(*a*)) made to that person in respect of the expenditure, and

(*d*) any balancing allowance made to that person in respect of the expenditure.

Cross-references

Professions, employments, offices, application to: s 301.

Definitions

person: IA 1937 s 11(*c*).

Former enactments

ITA 1967 s 274; CTA 1976 s 21(1) and Sch 1 para 30.

293 Application to partnerships

(1) (*a*) Where, after the setting up and on or before the permanent discontinuance of a trade which at any time is carried on in partnership, any event occurs which gives rise or may give rise to a balancing allowance or balancing charge in respect of machinery or plant—

(i) any balancing allowance or balancing charge which, if the trade had at all times been carried on by one and the same person, would have been made to or on that person in respect of that machinery or plant by reason of that event shall, subject to section 1010, be made to or on the person or persons carrying on the trade in the chargeable period related to that event (in this paragraph referred to as **"the relevant person or persons"**), and

(ii) the amount of any such allowance or charge shall be computed as if the relevant person or persons had at all times been carrying on the trade and as if everything done to or by the predecessors of the relevant person or persons in the carrying on of the trade had been done to or by the relevant person or persons.

(*b*) Notwithstanding paragraph (*a*), in applying section 288(4) to any balancing charge to be made in accordance with that paragraph, the allowances made in respect of the machinery or plant for the year beginning on the 6th day of April, 1959, or for any earlier year of assessment shall not be taken to include allowances made to, or attributable to the shares of, persons who were not, either alone or in partnership with other persons, carrying on the trade at the beginning of the year beginning on the 6th day of April, 1959.

(2) (*a*) In this subsection, **"several trade"** has the meaning assigned to it by section 1008.

(*b*) In taxing the several trade of any partner in a partnership, the same allowances and charges shall be made in respect of machinery or plant used for the purposes of that trade, and belonging to one or more of the partners but not being partnership property, as would be made if the machinery or plant had at all material times belonged to all the partners and been partnership property and everything done by or to any of the partners in relation to the machinery or plant had been done by or to all the partners.

(3) Notwithstanding section 288, a sale or gift of machinery or plant used for the purposes of a trade carried on in partnership, being a sale or gift by one or more of the partners to one or more of the partners, shall not be treated as an event giving rise to a balancing allowance or balancing charge if the machinery or plant continues to be used after the sale or gift for the purposes of that trade.

(4) References in subsections (2) and (3) to use for the purposes of a trade do not include references to use in pursuance of a letting by the partner or partners in question to the partnership or to use in consideration of the making to the partner or partners in question of any payment which may be deducted in computing under section 1008(3) the profits or gains of the trade.

Cross-references

Professions, employments, offices, application to: s 301.

Definitions

person: IA 1937 s 11(*c*); trade: s 3(1); year of assessment: s 3(1).

Former enactments

ITA 1967 s 275; CTA 1976 s 21(1) and Sch 1 para 31.

294 Machinery or plant used partly for non-trading purposes

Where an event occurs which gives rise or might give rise to a balancing allowance or balancing charge to or on any person and the machinery or plant concerned is machinery or plant which—

(*a*) has been used by that person for the purposes of a trade carried on by that person and, in relation to machinery or plant provided for use for the purposes of a trade on or after the 1st day of April, 1990, while so used, was used wholly and exclusively for those purposes, and

(*b*) has also been used for other purposes,

then, in determining the amount of the allowance or, as the case may be, the amount on which the charge is to be made, regard shall be had to all the relevant circumstances and in particular to the extent of the use for those other purposes, and there shall be made to or on that person an allowance of such an amount or a charge on such an amount, as the case may be, as may be just and reasonable.

Cross-references

Professions, employments, offices, application to: s 301.

Definitions

person: IA 1937 s 11(*c*); trade: s 3(1).

Former enactments

ITA 1967 s 276; FA 1990 s 79.

Corresponding UK tax provision

Capital Allowances Act 2001 s 11.

295 Option in case of succession under will or intestacy

Where a person succeeds to a trade as a beneficiary under the will or on the intestacy of a deceased person who carried on that trade, the following provisions shall, if the beneficiary by notice in writing to the inspector so elects, apply in relation to any machinery or plant previously owned by the deceased person and used by the deceased person for the purposes of that trade:

(*a*) the reference in section 313 to the price which the machinery or plant would have fetched if sold in the open market shall, in relation to the succession and any previous succession occurring on or after the death of the deceased, be deemed to be a reference to that price or the amount of the expenditure on the provision of the machinery or plant still unallowed immediately before the succession in question, whichever is the lower, and

(*b*) notwithstanding anything in that section, such balancing charge, if any, shall be made on the beneficiary on any event occurring after the succession as would have been made on the deceased if he or she had not died and had continued to own the machinery or plant and had done all such things and been allowed all such allowances in connection with the machinery or plant as were done by or allowed to the beneficiary or the successor on any previous succession mentioned in paragraph (*a*).

Cross-references

Capital gains tax, restriction of losses by reference to capital allowances: s 555(2)(*a*).

Professions, employments, offices, application to: s 301.

Definitions

inspector: ss 2(1), 5(1), 852; person: IA 1937 s 11(*c*); trade: s 3(1); writing: IA 1937 Sch.

Former enactments

ITA 1967 s 278.

296 Balancing allowances and balancing charges: wear and tear allowances deemed to have been made in certain cases

(1) In determining whether any, and if so what, balancing allowance or balancing charge is to be made to or on any person for any chargeable period in taxing a trade, there shall be deemed to have been made to that person, for every previous chargeable period in which the machinery or plant belonged to that person and which is a chargeable period to be taken into account for the purpose of this section, such wear and tear allowance or greater wear and tear allowance, if any, in respect of the machinery or plant as would have been made to that person if all the conditions specified in subsection (3) had been fulfilled in relation to every such previous chargeable period.

(2) There shall be taken into account for the purposes of this section every previous chargeable period in which the machinery or plant belonged to the person and—

(*a*) during which the machinery or plant was not used by the person for the purposes of the trade,

(*b*) during which the trade was not carried on by the person,

(*c*) during which the trade was carried on by the person in such circumstances that, otherwise than by virtue of Chapter I of Part XXV of the Income Tax Act, 1967, or Part V of the Corporation Tax Act, 1976, the full amount of the profits or gains of the trade was not liable to be charged to tax,

(*d*) for which the whole or a part of the tax chargeable in respect of the profits of the trade was not payable by virtue of Chapter II of Part XXV of the Income Tax Act, 1967, or

(*e*) for which the tax payable in respect of the profits of the trade was reduced by virtue of Chapter III or IV of Part XXV of the Income Tax Act, 1967, or Part IV of the Corporation Tax Act, 1976.

(3) The conditions referred to in subsection (1) are—

(*a*) that the trade had been carried on by the person in question since the date on which that person acquired the machinery or plant and had been so carried on by that person in such circumstances that the full amount of the profits or gains of the trade was liable to be charged to tax,

(*b*) that the trade had at no time consisted wholly or partly of exempted trading operations within the meaning of Chapter I of Part XXV of the Income Tax Act, 1967, or Part V of the Corporation Tax Act, 1976,

(*c*) that the machinery or plant had been used by that person solely for the purposes of the trade since that date, and

(*d*) that a proper claim had been duly made by that person for wear and tear allowance in respect of the machinery or plant for every relevant chargeable period.

(4) In the case of a company (within the meaning of section 4(1)), subsection (3)(*a*) shall not alter the periods which are to be taken as chargeable periods but, if during any time after the 5th day of April, 1976, and after the company acquired the machinery or plant, the company has not been within the charge to corporation tax, any year of assessment or part of a year of assessment falling within that time shall be taken as a chargeable period as if it had been an accounting period of the company.

(5) Nothing in this section shall affect section 288(4).

Cross-references

Professions, employments, offices, application to: s 301.

Shipping tonnage tax, plant and machinery, change of use of non-tonnage tax asset: Sch 18B, para 14(2)(*b*)(i), (ii).

Definitions

person: IA 1937 s 11(*c*); trade: s 3(1).

Former enactments

ITA 1967 s 279; CTA 1976 s 21(1) and Sch 1 para 32.

---

297 Subsidies towards wear and tear

(1) Where—

(*a*) an event occurs which gives rise or might give rise to a balancing allowance or balancing charge to or on any person in respect of any machinery or plant provided or used by that person for the purposes of a trade, and

(*b*) any sums which—

(i) are in respect of, or take account of, the wear and tear to the machinery or plant occasioned by its use for the purposes of the trade, and

(ii) do not fall to be taken into account as that person's income or in computing the profits or gains of any trade carried on by that person,

have been paid, or are to be payable, to that person directly or indirectly,

then, in determining whether any and, if so, what balancing allowance or balancing charge is to be made to or on that person, there shall be deemed to have been made to that person for the chargeable period related to the event a wear and tear allowance in respect of the machinery or plant of an amount equal to the total amount of those sums.

(2) Nothing in this section shall affect section 288(4).

Cross-references

Professions, employments, offices, application to: s 301.

Former enactments

ITA 1967 s 280; CTA 1976 s 21(1) and Sch 1 para 33.

298 Allowances to lessors

(1) Where machinery or plant is let on such terms that the burden of the wear and tear of the machinery or plant falls directly on the lessor, the lessor shall be entitled, on making a claim to the inspector within 24 months after the end of the chargeable period, to—

(*a*) an initial allowance under section 283, and

(*b*) a wear and tear allowance under section 284,

in relation to the machinery or plant, equal to the amount which might have been allowed if during the period of the letting the machinery or plant were in use for the purposes of a trade carried on by the lessor.

(2) Where machinery or plant is let on such terms as are referred to in subsection (1), the preceding provisions of this Chapter, in so far as they relate to balancing allowances and balancing charges, shall apply in relation to the lessor as if the machinery or plant were, during the term of the letting, in use for the purposes of a trade carried on by the lessor.

Cross-references

Manner of making allowances and charges: s 300.

Professions, employments, offices, application to: s 301.

Wear and tear allowances for licences for public hire (taxi) vehicles: s 286A(2)(*a*).

Definitions

trade: s 3(1).

Former enactments

ITA 1967 s 241(5), s 252 and s 281; CTA 1976 s 21(1) and Sch 1 para 6 and para 16; FA 1980 s 17(3).

Corresponding UK tax provision

Capital Allowances Act 2001 ss 177–180.

299 Allowances to lessees

(1) Where machinery or plant is let to the person by whom the trade is carried on, on the terms of that person being bound to maintain the machinery or plant and deliver it over in good condition at the end of the lease, and if the burden of the wear and tear of the machinery or plant will in fact fall directly on that person, then, for the purposes of sections 283 and 284, the capital expenditure on the provision of the machinery or plant shall be deemed to have been incurred by that person and the machinery or plant shall be deemed to belong to that person.

(2) Subsection (2) of section 285 shall not apply to qualifying machinery or plant (within the meaning of that section) which is let to a person on the terms mentioned in subsection (1), unless the contract of letting provides that the person shall or may become the owner of the machinery or plant on the performance of the contract, and, where the contract so provides but without becoming the owner of the machinery or plant the person ceases to be entitled (otherwise than on his or her death) to the benefit of the contract in so far as it relates to the machinery or plant, subsection (2) of section 285 shall be deemed not to have applied in relation to the machinery or plant, and accordingly there shall be made all such additional assessments and adjustments of assessments as may be appropriate.

Cross-references

Plant and machinery accelerated wear and tear allowance, subs (2): s 285(2)(*a*).

Professions, employments, offices, application to: s 301.

Wear and tear allowances for licences for public hire (taxi) vehicles: s 286A(2)(*a*).

Former enactments

ITA 1967 s 241(2) and s 252; FA 1967 s 11(3); FA 1971 s 26(3); CTA 1976 s 21(1) and Sch 1 para 6, para 16, para 53 and para 60.

300 Manner of making allowances and charges

(1) Any allowance or charge made to or on any person under the preceding provisions of this Chapter shall, unless it is made under or by virtue of [section 284(6) or 298],[1] be made to or on that person in taxing such person's trade.

(2) Any initial allowance or wear and tear allowance made under or by virtue of section 298(1) or any balancing allowance made under or by virtue of section 298(2) shall be made by means of discharge or repayment of tax, and shall be available primarily against income from the letting of machinery or plant.

(3) Any balancing charge made under or by virtue of section 298(2) shall be made under Case IV of Schedule D.

[(4) Any wear and tear allowance made to any person under or by virtue of section 284(6) shall be made in charging that person's income under Case V of Schedule D.][2]

Amendments

1 Substituted by FA 2000 s 40(*b*)(i) with effect from 6 April 2000; previously "section 298".

2 Subs (4) inserted by FA 2000 s 40(*b*)(ii) with effect from 6 April 2000.

Cross-references

Professions, employments, offices, application to: s 301.

Definitions

person: IA 1937 s 11(*c*); trade: ss 3(1), 4(1).

Former enactments

ITA 1967 s 241(1)(*c*), s 251(1) and s 282; CTA 1976 s 21(1) and Sch 1 para 15, para 34; FA 1996 s 132(1) and Sch 5 Pt I para 1(12).

301 Application to professions, employments and offices

(1) The preceding provisions of this Chapter (other than sections 283, 285 and 286) shall, with any necessary modifications, apply in relation to professions, employments and offices as they apply in relation to trades.

(2) Sections 283 and 285 shall, with any necessary modifications, apply in relation to professions as they apply in relation to trades.

Definitions

person: IA 1937 s 11(*c*); profession: s 2(1); trade: s 3(1).

Former enactments

ITA 1967 s 241(10), s 241A(3), s 253 and s 283(1); FA 1970 s 14(4); CTA 1976 s 21(1) and Sch 1 para 6; FA 1997 s 22 and s 146(1) and Sch 9 Pt I para 1(17)

Corresponding UK tax provision

Capital Allowances Act 2001 s 251.

CHAPTER 3

Dredging: Initial Allowances and Annual Allowances

Cross-references

Petroleum trade, development expenditure: s 692(4).

302 Interpretation (Chapter 3)

(1) In this Chapter—

"dredging" does not include things done otherwise than in the interests of navigation, but (subject to that) includes the removal of anything forming part of or projecting from the bed of the sea or of any inland water, by whatever means it is removed and whether or not at the time of removal it is wholly or partly above water, and also includes the widening of an inland waterway in the interests of navigation;

"qualifying trade" means any trade or undertaking which, or a part of which, complies with either of the following conditions—

(*a*) that it consists of the maintenance or improvement of the navigation of a harbour, estuary or waterway, or

(*b*) that it is for a purpose set out in section 268(1),

but, where part only of a trade or undertaking complies with paragraph (*a*) or (*b*), section 303(5) shall apply as if the part which does and the part which does not so comply were separate trades.

(2) For the purposes of this Chapter, the first relevant chargeable period, in relation to expenditure incurred by any person, shall be the chargeable period related to the following event or occasion—

(*a*) the incurring of the expenditure, or

(*b*) in the case of expenditure for which allowances are to be made by virtue of section 303(6), the occasion when that person first both carries on the trade or part of the trade for the purposes of which the expenditure was incurred, and occupies for the purposes of that trade or part of the trade the dock or other premises in connection with which the expenditure was incurred.

Former enactments

ITA 1967 s 294(6), (8) and (10); CTA 1976 s 21(1) and Sch 1 para 43.

Corresponding UK tax provision

Capital Allowances Act 2001 s 484.

303 Allowances for expenditure on dredging

(1) (*a*) Subject to this section, where for the purposes of any qualifying trade carried on by a person the person incurs capital expenditure on dredging, and either the trade consists of the maintenance or improvement of the navigation of a harbour, estuary or waterway or the dredging is for the benefit of vessels coming to, leaving or using any dock or other premises occupied by the person for the purposes of the trade, then—

(i) an initial allowance equal to 10 per cent of the expenditure shall be made for the first relevant chargeable period to the person incurring the expenditure, and

(ii) writing-down allowances shall be made in respect of that expenditure to the person for the time being carrying on the trade during a writing-down period of 50 years beginning with the first relevant chargeable period; but, where a writing-down allowance is to be made for a year of assessment to such a person and such person is within the charge to income tax in respect of the trade for part only of that year, that part shall be treated as a separate chargeable period for the purposes of computing allowances under this section.

(*b*) This subsection shall not apply to any expenditure incurred before the 30th day of September, 1956.

(2) Where the trade is permanently discontinued in any chargeable period, then, for that chargeable period there shall be made to the person last carrying on the trade, in addition to any other allowance made to that person, an allowance equal to the amount of the expenditure less the allowances made in respect of the expenditure under subsection (1) for that and previous chargeable periods.

(3) For the purposes of this section, a trade shall not be treated by virtue of the Income Tax Acts as discontinued on a change in the persons engaged in carrying it on.

(4) Any allowance under this section shall be made in taxing the trade.

(5) Where expenditure is incurred partly for the purposes of a qualifying trade and partly for other purposes, subsection (1) shall apply to so much only of that expenditure as on a just apportionment ought fairly to be treated as incurred for the purposes of that trade.

(6) Where a person incurs capital expenditure for the purposes of a trade or part of a trade not yet carried on by the person but with a view to carrying it on, or incurs capital expenditure in connection with a dock or other premises not yet occupied by the person for the purposes of a qualifying trade but with a view to so occupying the dock or premises, subsections (1) to (5) shall apply as if the person had been carrying on the trade or part of the trade or occupying the dock or premises for the purposes of the qualifying trade, as the case may be, at the time when the expenditure was incurred.

(7) Where a person contributes a capital sum to expenditure on dredging incurred by another person, the person shall for the purposes of this section be treated as incurring capital expenditure on that dredging equal to the amount of the contribution, and the capital expenditure incurred by the other person on that dredging shall for those purposes be deemed to be reduced by the amount of the contribution.

(8) No allowance shall be made by virtue of this section in respect of any expenditure if for the same or any other chargeable period an allowance is or can be made in respect of that expenditure under Chapter 1 of this Part.

(9) Notwithstanding any other provision of this section, in determining the allowances to be made under this section in any particular case, there shall be deemed to have been made in that case all such allowances (other than initial allowances) as could have been made if this section had always applied.

Cross-references

Corporation tax: allowances and charges in taxing a trade, subs (1)(*a*): s 307(2)(*b*)(i).
First relevant chargeable period, subs (6): s 302(2)(*b*).
Qualifying trade, subs (5): s 302(1).

Definitions

trade: s 3(1); person: IA 1937 s 11(*c*); year of assessment: s 3(1).

Former enactments

ITA 1967 s 294(1)–(5), (7), (9), (11)–(12); CTA 1976 s 21(1) and Sch 1 para 43.

Corresponding UK tax provision

Capital Allowances Act 2001 s 485.

CHAPTER 4
Miscellaneous and General

Cross-references

Farming, capital allowances for milk quotas, application of this Chapter: s 669E(1), (2).
Patents, capital sums: effect of death, winding up and partnership changes: s 760(4)(*b*).
Transmission capacity rights, capital allowances for expenditure on, application of this Chapter: s 769E(1), (2).
Wear and tear allowances for licences for public hire (taxi) vehicles: s 286A(2)(*a*).

304 Income tax: allowances and charges in taxing a trade, etc

(1) This section and section 305 shall apply as respects allowances and charges which are to be made under this Part ...[1] for the purposes of income tax.

(2) Any claim by a person for an allowance under this Part in charging profits or gains of any description shall be included in the annual statement required to be delivered under

the Income Tax Acts of those profits or gains, and the allowance shall be made as a deduction in charging those profits or gains.

(3) (*a*) A claim for an industrial building allowance under section 271 shall be accompanied by a certificate signed by the claimant (which shall be deemed to form part of the claim) stating that the expenditure was incurred on the construction of an industrial building or structure and giving such particulars as show that the allowance is to be made.

(*b*) A claim for an initial allowance under section 283 shall be accompanied by a certificate signed by the claimant (which shall be deemed to form part of the claim) stating that the expenditure was incurred on new machinery or new plant and giving such particulars as show that the allowance is to be made.

(4) ...[2] where full effect cannot be given in any year to any allowance to be made under this Part in taxing a trade [, or in charging profits or gains of any description, as the case may be,][3] owing to there being no profits or gains chargeable for that year, or owing to the profits or gains chargeable being less than the allowance, then, the allowance or part of the allowance to which effect has not been given, as the case may be, shall, for the purpose of making the assessment to income tax for the following year, be added to the amount of the allowances to be made under this Part in taxing the trade [or in charging the profits or gains, as the case may be,][4] for that following year, and be deemed to be part of those allowances, or, if there is no such allowance for that following year, be deemed to be the allowance for that following year, and so on for succeeding years.

(5) Any charge to be made under this Part on a person for any chargeable period in taxing the person's trade or in charging the person's income under Case V of Schedule D shall be made by means of an assessment in addition to any other assessment to be made on the person for that period.

(6) (*a*) The preceding provisions of this section (other than subsection (3)) shall apply in relation to professions, employments and offices as they apply in relation to trades.

(*b*) Subsection (3)(*b*) shall, with any necessary modifications, apply in relation to professions as it applies in relation to trades.

[(*c*) Subsection (4) shall not apply as respects an allowance given by means of discharge or repayment of tax or in charging income under Case V of Schedule D.][5]

Amendments

1 Deleted by FA 2000 s 40(*c*)(i) with effect from 6 April 2000; previously "as it applies".
2 Deleted by FA 2000 s 40(*c*)(ii)(I) with effect from 6 April 2000; previously "Subject to section 278(2),".
3 Inserted by FA 2000 s 40(*c*)(ii)(II) with effect from 6 April 2000.
4 Inserted by FA 2000 s 40(*c*)(ii)(III) with effect from 6 April 2000.
5 Subs (6)(*c*) inserted by FA 2000 s 40(*c*)(iii) with effect from 6 April 2000.

Cross-references

Capital expenditure on scientific research, subs (4): 765(5).
Farming buildings expenditure, subs (4): s 658(6).
Farming pollution control capital expenditure, subs (4): s 659(5).
Farming stock relief, subs (4): s 666(3)(*b*).
Mine development allowance, subs (4): s 670(6).
Mine rehabilitation expenditure, subs (4) applied by: s 681(9).
Mining machinery or plant, subs (4): s 678(7).

Petroleum trade, exploration expenditure, subs (4): s 693(9).
Reorganisation of companies into Trustee Savings Banks, capital allowances, subs (4): Sch 17 para 2(3).
Training of local staff before commencement of trading, subs (4): s 769(3).

Definitions

person: IA 1937 s 11(*c*); profession: s 2(1); trade: s 3(1).

Former enactments

ITA 1967 s 241(3)–(4), s 251(5), s 252, s 254(5)–(6), s 295, CTA 1976 s 21(1) and Sch 1 para 6, para 15, para 16, para 17 and para 44.

305 Income tax: manner of granting, and effect of, allowances made by means of discharge or repayment of tax

(1) (*a*) Where under this Part an allowance is to be made to a person for any year of assessment which is to be given by means of discharge or repayment of tax [or in charging income under Case V of Schedule D],[1] and is to be available or available primarily against a specified class of income, the amount of the allowance shall be deducted from or set off against the person's income of that class for that year of assessment and, if the amount to be allowed is greater than the amount of the person's income of that class for that year of assessment, the balance shall be deducted from or set off against the person's income of that class for the next year of assessment, and so on for subsequent years of assessment, and tax shall be discharged or repaid accordingly.

[(*b*) (i) Notwithstanding paragraph (*a*), where an allowance referred to in that paragraph is available primarily against income of the specified class and the amount of the allowance is greater than the amount of the person's income of that class for the first-mentioned year of assessment (after deducting or setting off any allowances for earlier years), then the person may, by notice in writing given to the inspector not later than 2 years after the end of the year of assessment, elect that the excess shall be deducted from or set off—

(I) in the case of an individual—

(A) against the individual's other income for that year of assessment, or

(B) where the individual, or, being a husband or wife, the individual's spouse, is assessed to tax in accordance with section 1017, firstly, against the individual's other income for that year of assessment and, subsequently, against the income of the individual's husband or wife, as the case may be, for that year of assessment,

(II) in the case of a person other than an individual, against the person's other income for that year of assessment.

(ii) Where an election is made in accordance with subparagraph (i), the excess shall be deducted from or set off against the income referred to in subclause (A) or (B) of clause (I) or in clause (II), as the case may be, and tax shall be discharged or repaid accordingly and only the balance, if any, of the amount of the excess over all the income referred to in subclause (A) or (B) of clause (I) or in clause (II), as the case may be, for that year of assessment shall be deducted from or set off against the person's income of the specified class for succeeding years.][2]

[(*c*) Notwithstanding any other provision of this subsection, where under this Part an allowance, the amount of which has been determined in accordance with section 409E(3)(*a*)(i), is to be made to an individual for any year of assessment and the allowance is to be—

(*a*) made in charging the specified amount of rent (within the meaning of section 409E) under Case V of Schedule D for that year of assessment, and

(*b*) is to be available only in charging that specified amount of rent,

then—

(i) in charging income under Case V of Schedule D the amount of that allowance shall be deducted from or set off against that specified amount of rent, and

(ii) if the amount of the allowance which would have been made in charging income under Case V of Schedule D if section 409E had not been enacted is greater than that specified amount of rent, the excess shall—

(I) be added to the amount of the allowance to be made to the individual for the next year of assessment under Chapter 1 of this Part in respect of the capital expenditure incurred on the construction or refurbishment of the specified building (within the meaning of section 409E) or the residue of that expenditure (within the meaning of section 409E), and be deemed to be part of the allowance to be so made for that next year, or

(II) if there is no such allowance for that next year, be deemed to be the allowance for that next year,

and so on for subsequent years of assessment, and section 409E(3) shall apply in relation to the resulting allowance to be made for that next year or, as the case may be, for any subsequent year of assessment.][3]

(2) Any claim for an allowance mentioned in subsection (1) shall be made to and determined by the inspector, but any person aggrieved by any decision of the inspector on any such claim may, on giving notice in writing to the inspector within 21 days after the notification to that person of the decision, appeal to the Appeal Commissioners.

(3) The Appeal Commissioners shall hear and determine an appeal to them under subsection (2) as if it were an appeal against an assessment to income tax, and the provisions of the Income Tax Acts relating to the rehearing of an appeal and to the statement of a case for the opinion of the High Court on a point of law shall, with the necessary modifications, apply accordingly.

(4) Where any person, for the purpose of obtaining for that person or any other person any relief from or repayment of tax in respect of an allowance mentioned in subsection (1), knowingly makes any false statement or false representation, that person shall be liable to a penalty of [€630][4].

Amendments

1 Inserted by FA 2000 s 40(*d*)(i) with effect from 6 April 2000.

2 Subs (1)(*b*) substituted by FA 2000 s 40(d)(ii) with effect from 6 April 2000.

[3] Subs (1)(*c*) inserted by FA 2003 s 14(2) with effect from 1 January 2003.

[4] Substituted by FA 2001 s 240(1) and (2)(*k*) and Sch 5 Pt 1 as respects acts or omissions which take place or begin on or after 1 January 2002; previously "£500".

Cross-references

Holiday cottages, disclaimer of capital allowance, subs (1)(*b*): s 355(4)(*a*); restriction on use of allowances, subs (1)(*b*): s 405(1)(*b*).

Income tax: allowances and charges in taxing a trade: s 304(1).

Leased assets, restriction on use of allowances, subs (1)(*b*): s 403(5), (5A).

Leased plant and machinery, restriction on use of allowances, subs (1)(*b*): s 404(2)(*b*), (4)(*c*).

Limited partnerships, specified provisions: s 1013(1).

Petroleum trade, treatment of losses, subs (1)(*b*): s 687(3)(*a*).

Property investment, restriction of tax incentives on, subs (1)(*b*): s 408(1), (2).

Recovery of penalties: s 1061(1).

Restriction of reliefs where individual is not actively participating in certain trades: s 409D(1)("specified provisions").

Restriction on use of capital allowances on certain hotels, subs (1)(*b*): s 409B(2).

Restriction on use of capital allowances on certain industrial buildings and other premises, subs (1)(*b*): s 409A(2).

Restriction on use of capital allowances on fixtures and fittings for furnished residential accommodation, subs (1)(b): s 406.

Restriction on use of capital allowances on holiday cottages, subs (1)(*b*): s 405(1)(*a*).

Ring-fence on use of certain capital allowances on certain industrial buildings and other premises, subs (1)(*c*): s 409E(3)(*c*).

Revenue precedents

Issue: Where capital allowances in a year of assessment are due against Case V income arising in that year, are the capital allowances set against the Case V income before or after losses forward are taken into account?

Decision: The capital allowances should be set off against the Case V income of the year of assessment in which the allowances arise ie before losses forward are taken into account.

Issue: What is the order of setoff of capital allowances where there are annual allowances to be allowed against Case V income in a year of assessment and also excess Case V allowances carried forward from a previous year?

Decision: The capital allowances of the year of assessment are the allowances which are available primarily against the Case V income and should be allowed before the excess Case V allowances coming forward from the earlier year are deducted or set off.

Issue: Where a claim is made to have excess capital allowances for a year set against other income and an excess still arises which is carried forward to a subsequent year, can the excess carried forward be again set against other income?

Decision: No. The excess carried forward to the succeeding year can be set against income from the specified class only.

Definitions

Appeal Commissioners: s 2(1); High Court: IA 1937 Sch; inspector: ss 2(1), 5(1), 852; person: IA 1937 s 11(*c*); writing: IA 1937 Sch; year of assessment: s 3(1).

Former enactments

ITA 1967 s 254(1)(*e*), s 296(1), (3)–(5), F(MP)A 1968 s 3(2) and Sch 1; CTA 1976 s 21(1) and Sch 1 para 17; FA 1980 s 17(1).

---

306 Meaning of basis period

(1) In this Part, as it applies for income tax purposes, **"basis period"** has the meaning assigned to it by this section.

(2) (*a*) Subject to paragraph (*b*), in the case of a person to whom an allowance or on whom a charge is to be made under Case I of Schedule D in charging the profits or gains of the person's trade or under Case V of Schedule D in charging income arising from rents or receipts in respect of premises or easements, the person's basis period for any year of assessment shall be the

period on the profits or gains of which income tax for that year is to be finally computed under Case I of Schedule D in respect of the trade in question or, as the case may be, under Case V of Schedule D in respect of the income arising from rents or receipts in respect of premises or easements or, where by virtue of the Income Tax Acts the profits or gains or income of any other period are to be taken to be the profits or gains or income of that period, that other period.

(*b*) In the case of any trade—

(i) where 2 basis periods overlap, the period common to both shall be deemed for the purpose of this subsection to fall in the first basis period only,

(ii) where there is an interval between the end of the basis period for one year of assessment and the basis period for the next year of assessment, then, unless the second-mentioned year of assessment is the year of the permanent discontinuance of the trade, the interval shall be deemed to be part of the second basis period, and

(iii) where there is an interval between the end of the basis period for the year of assessment preceding that in which the trade is permanently discontinued and the basis period for the year in which the permanent discontinuance occurs, the interval shall be deemed to form part of the first basis period.

(3) (*a*) Any reference in subsection (2)(*b*) to the overlapping of 2 periods shall be construed as including a reference to the coincidence of 2 periods or to the inclusion of one period in another, and references to the period common to both of 2 periods shall be construed accordingly.

(*b*) Any reference in subsection (2)(*b*) to the permanent discontinuance of a trade shall be construed as including a reference to the occurring of any event which under the Income Tax Acts is to be treated as equivalent to the permanent discontinuance of a trade.

(4) Where an allowance or charge is to be made under Chapter 2 of this Part to or on a person carrying on or holding a profession, employment or office, subsections (1) to (3) shall apply as if the references to a trade included references to a profession, employment or office and as if the references to Case I of Schedule D included references to Case II of Schedule D and Schedule E.

(5) In the case of any other person to whom an allowance or on whom a charge is to be made under this Part, that other person's basis period for any year of assessment shall be the year of assessment itself.

Cross-references

Farming pollution control capital expenditure, meaning of "basis period" applied: s 659(4).
Mine rehabilitation expenditure, subss (2)–(3) applied by: s 681(1)(*c*).
Mining machinery or plant, subss (2)–(3) applied by: s 678(5)(*e*).
Petroleum trade, exploration expenditure, subss (2)–(3) applied by: s 693(11).

Definitions

person: IA 1937 s 11(*c*); profession: s 2(1); trade: s 3(1); year of assessment: s 3(1).

Former enactments

ITA 1967 s 297; CTA 1976 s 21(1) and Sch 1 para 45; FA 1990 s 22(1)(*b*); FA 1996 s 132(1) and Sch 5 Pt I para 1(13).

307 Corporation tax: allowances and charges in taxing a trade

(1) In computing for the purposes of corporation tax a company's profits for any accounting period, there shall be made in accordance with this section and section 308 all such deductions and additions as are required to give effect to the provisions of the Tax Acts which relate to allowances (including investment allowances) and charges in respect of capital expenditure, and subsection (2) and section 308 shall apply as respects allowances and charges to be made under those provisions as they apply for the purposes of corporation tax.

(2) (*a*) Allowances and charges to be made for any accounting period in taxing a trade shall be given effect by treating the amount of any allowance as a trading expense of the trade in that period and by treating the amount on which any such charge is to be made as a trading receipt of the trade in that period.

(*b*) (i) A company to which an industrial building allowance under section 271, an initial allowance under section 283 or an initial allowance under section 303(1)(*a*) is to be made in taxing a trade for any accounting period may disclaim the allowance by notice in writing given to the inspector not later than 2 years after the end of that period.

(ii) Any such notice shall be accompanied by a certificate signed by the person by whom the notice is given giving such particulars as show that the allowance would be made if no such notice were given and the amount which would be so made.

(iii) Where notice is given under subparagraph (i) for any accounting period, the inspector may make an assessment to corporation tax on the company for that accounting period on the amount or the further amount which in the inspector's opinion ought to be charged.

Cross-references

Building societies, change of status: Sch 16 para 1(1), (2).

Dividends regarded as paid out of profits accumulated before given date: Sch 22 para 5(3)(*e*).

EU Council Directive 90/434/EEC, mergers, divisions: s 631(2)(*a*), (*b*).

Farming or market gardening, restriction of losses: s 663(2)(*b*)(i).

Farming stock relief: s 666(2).

Leased assets, restriction on use of allowances: s 403(4).

Leased plant and machinery, restriction on use of allowances: s 404(4)(*c*)(i)(II).

Petroleum trade, exploration expenditure, subs (2)(*a*): s 693(9).

Profit sharing schemes, payments to trustees: s 517(3)(*a*).

Reorganisation of companies into Trustee Savings Banks, capital allowances: Sch 17 para 2(1)(*b*), (3).

Shipping tonnage age, set-off of accrued losses against balancing charge: Sch 18B para 17.

Tax credit for research and development expenditure: s 766(1)(*a*)("expenditure on research and development").

Definitions

company: ss 4(1), 5(1); Tax Acts: s 1(2); inspector: ss 2(1), 5(1), 852; person: IA 1937 s 11(*c*); trade: ss 3(1), 4(1), 5(1); within the charge to (tax): s 2(1); writing: IA 1937 Sch.

Former enactments

CTA 1976 s 14(1)–(2).

---

308 Corporation tax: manner of granting, and effect of, allowances made by means of discharge or repayment of tax

(1) Where an allowance is to be made to a company for any accounting period which is to be given by discharge or repayment of tax or in charging its income under Case V of Schedule D, and is to be available primarily against a specified class of income, it shall, as far as may be, be given effect by deducting the amount of the allowance from any income of the period, being income of the specified class.

(2) Balancing charges for any accounting period which are not to be made in taxing a trade shall, notwithstanding any provision for them to be made under Case IV or V of Schedule D, as the case may be, be given effect by treating the amount on which the charge is to be made as income of the same class as that against which the corresponding allowances are available or primarily available.

(3) Where an allowance which is to be made for any accounting period by means of discharge or repayment of tax, or in charging income under Case V of Schedule D, as the case may be, cannot be given full effect under subsection (1) in that period by reason of a want or deficiency of income of the relevant class, then, so long as the company remains within the charge to corporation tax, the amount unallowed shall be carried forward to the succeeding accounting period, except in so far as effect is given to it under subsection (4), and the amount so carried forward shall be treated for the purposes of this section, including any further application of this subsection, as the amount of a corresponding allowance for that period.

(4) Where an allowance (other than an allowance carried forward from an earlier accounting period) which is to be made for any accounting period by means of discharge or repayment of tax, or in charging income under Case V of Schedule D, as the case may be, and which is available primarily against income of a specified class cannot be given full effect under subsection (1) in that period by reason of a want or deficiency of income of that class, the company may claim that effect shall be given to the allowance against the profits (of whatever description) of that accounting period and, if the company was then within the charge to corporation tax, of preceding accounting periods ending within the time specified in subsection (5), and, subject to that subsection and to any relief for earlier allowances or for losses, the profits of any of those accounting periods shall then be treated as reduced by the amount unallowed under subsection (1), or by so much of that amount as cannot be given effect under this subsection against profits of a later accounting period.

(5) The time referred to in subsection (4) is a time immediately preceding the accounting period first mentioned in subsection (4) equal in length to the accounting period for which the allowance is to be made; but the amount or aggregate amount of the reduction which may be made under that subsection in the profits of an accounting period falling partly before that time shall not, with the amount of any reduction to be made in those profits under any corresponding provision of the Corporation Tax Acts relating to losses, exceed a part of those profits proportionate to the part of the period falling within that time.

(6) A claim under subsection (4) shall be made by notice in writing given to the inspector not later that 2 years from the end of the accounting period in which an allowance cannot be given full effect under subsection (1).

Cross-references

Building societies, change of status: Sch 16 para 1(1), (2).
Corporation tax — late returns, restriction of relief, subs (4): s 1085(2)(*a*).
Corporation tax: allowances and charges in taxing a trade: s 307(1).
EU Council Directive 90/434/EEC, mergers, divisions: s 631(2)(*a*), (*b*).
Farming or market gardening, restriction of losses: s 663(2)(*b*)(i).
Farming stock relief: s 666(2).
Franked investment income (subs (4)), set off of losses: s 157(2)(*b*), (4), (7)(*a*).
Group relief, relation to other relief: s 421(1)(*a*), (3).
Holiday cottages, disclaimer of capital allowance: s 355(4)(*a*); restriction on use of allowances: s 405(1).
Leased assets, restriction on use of allowances: s 403(4), (5), (5A).
Leased plant and machinery, restriction on use of allowances: s 404(2)(*b*), (4)(*c*)(i)(II).
Limited partnerships, specified provisions, subs (4): s 1013(1).
Petroleum trade, treatment of losses, subs (4): s 687(3).
Profit sharing schemes, payments to trustees: s 517(3)(*a*).
Property investment, restriction of tax incentives on, subs (4): s 408(1), (2).
Relief for certain trading losses on a value basis, subs (4): s 396B(5)(*c*)(i).
Reorganisation of companies into Trustee Savings Banks, capital allowances: Sch 17 para 2(1)(*b*), (3).
Restriction on use of capital allowances for fixtures and fittings for furnished residential accommodation, subs (4): s 406.
Restriction on use of capital allowances for holiday cottages, subs (4): s 405(1)(*a*).
Shipping tonnage tax, set-off of accrued losses against balancing charge: Sch 18B para 17.

Former enactments

CTA 1976 s 14(3)–(8).

309 Companies not resident in the State

Where a company not resident in the State is within the charge to corporation tax in respect of one source of income and to income tax in respect of another source, then, in applying—

(*a*) this Part,
(*b*) section 374,
(*c*) sections 658 and 660,
(*d*) sections 670 and 672 to 678,
(*e*) sections 764 and 765,
(*f*) section 769, and
(*g*) any other provision of the Tax Acts relating to the making of allowances or charges under or in accordance with the provisions referred to in paragraphs (*a*) to (*f*),

allowances relating to any source of income shall be given effect against income chargeable to the same tax as is chargeable on income from that source.

Definitions

company: s 4(1); within the charge to (tax): s 2(1).

Former enactments

CTA 1976 s 21(4).

310 Allowances in respect of certain contributions to capital expenditure of local authorities

(1) In this section—

"approved scheme" means a scheme undertaken by a local authority with the approval of the Minister for the Environment and Local Government which has as its object or among its objects the treatment of trade effluents;

[**"local authority"**, means the council of a county or the corporation of a county or other borough or the council of an urban district;][1]

"trade effluents" means liquid or other matter discharged into public sewers from premises occupied for the purposes of a trade.

[(2) Where a person, for the purposes of a trade carried on or to be carried on by the person, contributes a capital sum to capital expenditure incurred by a local authority on or after 15 February 2001 on the provision of an asset to be used for the purposes of—

(*a*) an approved scheme, in so far as the scheme relates to the treatment of trade effluents, or

(*b*) the supply of water under an agreement in writing between the person and the local authority,

then, such allowances, if any, shall be made to the person under section 272 or 284 as would have been made to the person if the capital sum contributed in the chargeable period or its basis period had been expenditure on the provision for the purposes of that trade of a similar asset and that asset had continued at all material times to be in use for the purposes of the trade.][2]

[(2A) Where, by virtue of subsection (2), a person is entitled to an allowance under section 284 then, for the purposes of determining the amount of wear and tear allowances to be made for any chargeable period or its basis period for the purposes of this section, section 284 shall apply—

(*a*) as if the reference in paragraph (*aa*) of subsection (2) of that section to "20 per cent of the actual cost of the machinery or plant, including in that actual cost any expenditure in the nature of capital expenditure on the machinery or plant by means of renewal, improvement or reinstatement" were a reference to "20 per cent of the capital sum contributed in the chargeable period or its basis period", and

(*b*) as if the reference in paragraph (*ad*) of subsection (2) of that section to "12.5 per cent of the actual cost of the machinery or plant, including in that actual cost any expenditure in the nature of capital expenditure on the machinery or plant by means of renewal, improvement or reinstatement" were a reference to "12.5 per cent of the capital sum contributed in the chargeable period or its basis period".][3]

(3) The following provisions shall apply in relation to a transfer of a trade or part of a trade for the purposes of which a contribution referred to in subsection (2) was made:

(*a*) where the transfer is of the whole trade, allowances which, if the transfer had not taken place, would have been made to the transferor under section 272 or

284 for chargeable periods ending after the date of the transfer shall be made to the transferee and shall not be made to the transferor;

(*b*) where the transfer is of part only of the trade, paragraph (*a*) shall apply in relation to so much of the allowance as is properly referable to the part of the trade transferred.

Note

In regard to the definition of "local Authority", it should be noted that, by virtue of Local Government Act 2001 s 3(2) and Sch 2, reference in any other enactment to "county borough corporation", "borough corporation" (not being a county borough corporation), "council of a county" and "council of an urban district", and to similar or analogous expressions, are now to be construed as references to "City council", "Borough council of a borough mentioned in Chapter 1 of Part 1 of Schedule 6 to the Local Government Act 2001, "County council" and "Town council of a town mentioned in Chapter 2 of Part 1 of Schedule 6 to the Local Government Act 2001", respectively.

Amendments

1 Definition of "local authority" inserted by FA 2001 s 50(1)(*a*) from such date as the Minister for Finance may by order appoint. By virtue of the Finance Act 2001 (Commencement of Section 50) Order 2001, SI No 471 of 2001, this amendment came into operation with effect from 22 October 2001.

2 Subs (2) substituted by FA 2001 s 50(1)(*b*) from such date as the Minister for Finance may by order appoint. By virtue of the Finance Act 2001 (Commencement of Section 50) Order 2001, SI No 471 of 2001, this amendment came into operation with effect from 22 October 2001.

3 Subs (2A) substituted by FA 2003 s 23(1)(*b*) with effect from 4 December 2002.

Definitions

chargeable period or its basis period: s 321(2); person: IA 1937 s 11(*c*); person: IA 1937 Sch.

Former enactments

FA 1978 s 26.

311 Apportionment of consideration and exchanges and surrenders of leasehold interests

(1) (*a*) Any reference in this Part to the sale of any property includes a reference to the sale of that property together with any other property and, where property is sold together with other property, so much of the net proceeds of the sale of the whole property as on a just apportionment is properly attributable to the first-mentioned property shall for the purposes of this Part be deemed to be the net proceeds of the sale of the first-mentioned property, and references to expenditure incurred on the provision or the purchase of property shall be construed accordingly.

(*b*) For the purposes of this subsection, all the property which is sold in pursuance of one bargain shall be deemed to be sold together, notwithstanding that separate prices are, or purport to be, agreed for separate items of that property or that there are, or purport to be, separate sales of separate items of that property.

(2) Subsection (1) shall, with the necessary modifications, apply in relation to other sale, insurance, salvage or compensation moneys as it applies in relation to the net proceeds of sales.

(3) This Part shall apply as if any reference in this Part to the sale of any property included a reference to the exchange of any property and, in the case of a leasehold interest, also included a reference to the surrender of that interest for valuable consideration, and any provisions of this Part referring to the sales shall apply

accordingly with the necessary modifications and in particular with the modifications that references to the net proceeds of sale and to the price shall be taken to include references to the consideration for the exchange or surrender, and references to capital sums included in the price shall be taken to include references to so much of the consideration as would have been a capital sum if the consideration had taken the form of a money payment.

(4) This section shall, with the necessary modifications, apply in relation to Chapter 1 of Part 24 and sections 764 and 765 as if that Chapter and those sections were contained in this Part.

Revenue precedents

Issue: Can the purchase price of a property be apportioned between the plant and machinery element and the building element where the contract does not distinguish same?

Decision: Yes - a professional valuation should be provided.

Former enactments

ITA 1967 s 298; FA 1996 s 132(1) and Sch 5 Pt I para 1(14).

312 Special provisions as to certain sales

(1) In this section, **"control"**, in relation to a body corporate, means the power of a person to secure—

(*a*) by means of the holding of shares or the possession of voting power in or in relation to that or any other body corporate, or

(*b*) by virtue of any powers conferred by the articles of association or other document regulating that or any other body corporate,

that the affairs of the first-mentioned body corporate are conducted in accordance with the wishes of that person and, in relation to a partnership, means the right to a share of more than 50 per cent of the assets, or of more than 50 per cent of the income, of the partnership.

(2) (*a*) This section shall apply in relation to sales of any property where either—

(i) the buyer is a body of persons over whom the seller has control, or the seller is a body of persons over whom the buyer has control, or both the seller and the buyer are bodies of persons and some other person has control over both of them, or

(ii) it appears with respect to the sale, or with respect to transactions of which the sale is one, that the sole or main benefit which apart from this section might have been expected to accrue to the parties or any of them was the obtaining of an allowance under this Part or under Chapter 1 of Part 24 or section 764 or 765.

(*b*) References in this subsection to a body of persons include references to a partnership.

(3) Where the property is sold at a price other than the price it would have fetched if sold in the open market, then, subject to subsections (4) and (5), the like consequences shall ensue for the purposes of the enactments mentioned in subsection (2), in their application to the tax of all persons concerned, as would have ensued if the property had been sold for the price it would have fetched if sold in the open market.

(4) (*a*) Subject to paragraph (*b*), where the sale is a sale of machinery or plant—

(i) no initial allowance shall be made to the buyer, and

(ii) subject to subsection (5), if the price which the property would have fetched if sold in the open market is greater than the amount which, for the purpose of determining whether any, and if so, what, balancing charge should be made on the seller in respect of the property under Chapter 2 of this Part, would be taken to be the amount of the capital expenditure incurred by the seller on the provision of the property, subsection (3) shall apply as if for each of the references to the price which the property would have fetched if sold in the open market there were substituted a reference to that amount.

(*b*) This subsection shall not apply in relation to a sale of machinery or plant which was never used if the business or part of the business of the seller was the manufacture or supply of machinery or plant of that class and the sale was effected in the ordinary course of the seller's business.

(5) (*a*) Subject to subsection (6), where the sale is one to which subsection (2)(*a*)(i) applies and subsection (2)(*a*)(ii) does not apply, and the parties to the sale by notice in writing to the inspector so elect, the following provisions shall apply:

(i) subsection (3) shall apply as if for each of the references to the price which the property would have fetched if sold in the open market there were substituted a reference to that price or to the sum mentioned in paragraph (*b*), whichever is the lower;

(ii) subsection (4)(*a*)(ii) shall not apply;

(iii) notwithstanding anything in the preceding provisions of this section, such balancing charge, if any, shall be made on the buyer on any event occurring after the date of the sale as would have been made on the seller if the seller had continued to own the property and had done all such things and been allowed all such allowances or deductions in connection with the property as were done by or allowed to the buyer.

(*b*) The sum referred to in paragraph (*a*)(i) is—

(i) in the case of an industrial building or structure, the residue of the expenditure on the construction of that building or structure immediately before the sale, computed in accordance with section 277, and

(ii) in the case of machinery or plant, the amount of the expenditure on the provision of the machinery or plant still unallowed immediately before the sale, computed in accordance with section 292.

(6) (*a*) An election under subsection (5)(*a*) may not be made if—

(i) any of the parties to the sale is not resident in the State at the time of the sale, and

(ii) the circumstances are not at that time such that an allowance or charge under this Part is to be or might be made to or on that party in consequence of the sale.

(*b*) Except where referred to in paragraph (*a*), this section shall apply in relation to a sale notwithstanding that it is not fully applicable by reason of the non-residence of a party to the sale or otherwise.

Cross-references

Calculation of balancing allowances and charges: s 289(2)(*c*), (3)(*a*)(ii)–(iii).

Capital gains tax, restriction of losses by reference to capital allowances, subs (5): s 555(2).

Cars costing more than the specified amount: s 374(4).

Know-how allowance, meaning of "control" applied: s 768(1).

Farming, capital allowances for milk quotas, subs 5(*a*)(i), the reference to the sum mentioned in para (*b*) in the case of a qualifying quota is to be construed as a reference to the amount of capital expenditure on the acquisition of the qualifying quota remaining unallowed, computed in accordance with s 669C: s 669E(2).

Patents, subs (5)(*a*)(i), the reference to the sum mentioned in para (*b*) in the case of patents rights is to be construed as a reference to the amount of capital expenditure on the acquisition of the patent rights remaining unallowed, computed in accordance with s 756: s 762(2)(*a*).

Petroleum trade, exploration expenditure: s 693(13)(*a*).

Transmission capacity rights, capital allowances for expenditure on, subs (5)(*a*)(i), the reference to the sum mentioned in paragraph (*b*) in the case of capacity rights is to be construed as a reference to the amount of capital expenditure on the acquisition of the capacity rights remaining unallowed, computed in accordance with section 769C: s 769E(2).

Definitions

body of persons: s 2(1); inspector: ss 2(1), 5(1), 852; person: IA 1937 s 11(*c*); writing: IA 1937 Sch.

Former enactments

ITA 1967 s 299 other than subs (4)(*b*)(iii); CTA 1976 s 21(1) Sch 1 para 46; FA 1996 s 132(1) and Sch 5 Pt I para 1(15).

Corresponding UK tax provision

Capital Allowances Act 2001 ss 567 and 568.

313 Effect, in certain cases, of succession to trade, etc

(1) Where a person succeeds to any trade or profession which until that time was carried on by another person and by virtue of section 69 the trade or profession is to be treated as discontinued, any property which, immediately before the succession takes place, was in use for the purposes of the discontinued trade or profession and without being sold is, immediately after the succession takes place, in use for the purposes of the new trade or profession shall for the purposes of this Part be treated as if it had been sold to the successor when the succession takes place and as if the net proceeds of that sale had been the price which that property would have fetched if sold in the open market.

(2) Where, after the setting up and before the permanent discontinuance of a trade or profession which at any time is carried on in partnership anything is done for the purposes of that trade or profession, any allowance or charge which, if the trade or profession had at all times been carried on by one and the same person, would have been made to or on that person under this Part shall, subject to section 1010, be made to or on the person or persons from time to time carrying on that trade or profession (in this subsection referred to as **"the relevant person or persons"**), and the amount of any such allowance or charge shall be computed as if the relevant person or persons had at all times been carrying on the trade or profession and as if everything done to or by the predecessors of the relevant person or persons in the carrying on of that trade or profession had been done to or by the relevant person or persons.

(3) In relation to machinery or plant, this section shall apply subject to Chapter 2 of this Part in so far as that Chapter relates to balancing allowances and balancing charges.

Cross-references

Balancing allowances and charges: s 295(*a*).

Capital allowances and balancing charges in partnership cases, subs (1): s 1010(4).

Cars costing more than the specified amount: s 374(4).

Definitions

person: IA 1937 s 11(*c*); profession: s 2(1); trade: s 3(1).

Former enactments

ITA 1967 s 300; FA 1996 s 132(2) and Sch 5 Pt II.

Corresponding UK tax provision

Capital Allowances Act 2001 s 559.

314 Procedure on apportionment

(1) Where under or by virtue of this Part any sum is to be apportioned and at the time of the apportionment it appears that it is material as respects the liability to tax (for whatever chargeable period) of 2 or more persons, any question which arises as to the manner in which the sum is to be apportioned shall be determined, for the purposes of the tax of all those persons, by the Appeal Commissioners in the like manner as if it were an appeal against an assessment to income tax under Schedule D, and the provisions of the Income Tax Acts relating to such an appeal shall apply accordingly with any necessary modifications, and all those persons shall be entitled to appear and be heard by the Appeal Commissioners or to make representations to them in writing.

(2) This section shall apply in relation to any determination for the purposes of this Part of the price which property would have fetched if sold in the open market as it applies in relation to apportionments.

Definitions

Appeal Commissioners: s 2(1); person: IA 1937 s 11(*c*); writing: IA 1937 Sch.

Former enactments

ITA 1967 s 301; CTA 1976 s 21(1) and Sch 1 para 47.

Corresponding UK tax provision

Capital Allowances Act 2001 s 563.

315 Property used for purposes of "exempted trading operations"

(1) Where an event occurs which gives rise, or would but for this section give rise, to a balancing allowance or balancing charge in respect of any property to or on a company in relation to which a certificate under section 374(2) of the Income Tax Act, 1967, or section 70(2) of the Corporation Tax Act, 1976, has been given, then, whether the certificate is still in force or not, this section shall apply.

(2) Where the property has been used by the company exclusively for the purposes of its exempted trading operations within the meaning of Chapter I of Part XXV of the Income Tax Act, 1967, or Part V of the Corporation Tax Act, 1976, no balancing allowance or balancing charge shall be made.

(3) Where the property has been used partly for the purposes of the company's exempted trading operations and partly for the purposes of its other trading operations, regard shall be had to all the relevant circumstances of the case and there shall be made to or on the company an allowance of such an amount, or, as the case may be, a charge on such an amount, as may be just and reasonable.

Former enactments

ITA 1967 s 302; CTA 1976 s 21(1) and Sch 1 para 48.

316 Interpretation of certain references to expenditure and time when expenditure is incurred

(1) References in this Part to capital expenditure and capital sums—

(*a*) in relation to the person incurring the expenditure or paying the sums, do not include any expenditure or sum allowed to be deducted in computing for the purposes of tax the profits or gains of a trade, profession, office or employment carried on or held by that person, and

(*b*) in relation to the person receiving the amounts expended or the sums in question, do not include references to any amounts or sums which are to be taken into account as receipts in computing the profits or gains of any trade, profession, office or employment carried on or held by that person,

and do not include, in relation to any person referred to in paragraphs (*a*) and (*b*), any expenditure or sum in the case of which a deduction of tax is to be or may be made under section 237 or 238.

(2) Any reference in this Part to the date on which expenditure is incurred shall be construed as a reference to the date when the sums in question become payable; but, for the purposes of section 284, this subsection shall apply only in respect of machinery and plant provided for use for the purposes of a trade on or after the 6th day of April 1996.

[(2A) For the purposes only of determining, in relation to a claim for an allowance under Chapter 1 of this Part, whether and to what extent capital expenditure incurred on the construction (within the meaning of section 270) of:

(*a*) a building or structure in use for the purposes of the trade of hotel keeping, or

(*b*) a building or structure deemed to be a building or structure in use for such purposes by virtue of section 268(3),

is incurred or not incurred on or before 31 July 2006, only such an amount of that capital expenditure as is properly attributable to work on the construction or refurbishment of the building or structure actually carried out on or before 31 July 2006 shall (notwithstanding subsection (2) and any other provision of the Tax Acts as to the time when any capital expenditure is or is to be treated as incurred) be treated as having been incurred on or before that date.][1]

(3) For the purposes of sections 271 and 283, any expenditure incurred for the purposes of a trade by a person about to carry on the trade shall be treated as if it had been incurred by that person on the first day on which that person carries on the trade.

Amendments

1 Subs (2A) inserted by FA 2004 s 25(1)(*d*) with effect from 1 January 2004.

Cross-references

Patents, subs (1), the reference to any expenditure or sum in the case of which a deduction to of tax is to be or may be, made under s 237 or s 238 shall not include a sum in the case of which such a deduction is to be or may be so made by virtue of section 757: s 762(2)(*b*).

Petroleum trade, abandonment expenditure and loss relief, subss (1)–(2): s 695(8).

Petroleum trade, exploration expenditure, subss (1)–(2): s 693(13)(*b*).

Provisions of general application in relation to the making of allowances and charges: s 321(2A).

Definitions

local authority: s 2(1); person: IA 1937 s 11(*c*); statute: IA 1937 s 3; s 1(1); profession: s 2(1); Tax Acts: s 1(2); trade: s 3(1).

Former enactments

ITA 1967 s 241(9A), s251(2), s 254(4)(*a*), 260, 261, 303(1), (2); CTA 1976 s 21(1) and Sch 1 para 15, para 17, para 21 and para 49; FA 1996 s 132(1) and Sch 5 Pt I para 1(12)(*b*).

317 Treatment of grants

(1) In this section—

"food processing trade" means a trade which consists of or includes the manufacture of processed food;

"processed food" means goods manufactured in the State in the course of a trade by a company, being goods which—

(*a*) are intended for human consumption as a food, and

(*b*) have been manufactured by a process involving the use of machinery or plant whereby the goods produced by the application of that process differ substantially in form and value from the materials to which the process has been applied and whereby, without prejudice to the generality of the foregoing, the process does not consist primarily of—

(i) the acceleration, retardation, alteration or application of a natural process, or

(ii) the application of methods of preservation, pasteurisation or any similar treatment;

"qualifying machinery or plant" means machinery or plant used solely in the course of a process of manufacture whereby processed food is produced.

(2) Subject to subsection (3), expenditure shall not be regarded for any of the purposes of this Part, other than sections 283 and 284, as having been incurred by a person in so far as the expenditure has been or is to be met directly or indirectly—

(*a*) in relation to expenditure incurred before the 6th day of May, 1993, by the State, by any board established by statute or by any public or local authority, and

(*b*) in relation to expenditure incurred on or after the 6th day of May, 1993, by the State or by any person other than the first-mentioned person.

(3) (*a*) Subject to paragraph (*b*) and subsection (4), where an allowance is to be made for the purposes of income tax or corporation tax, as the case may be, under section 283 or 284 and the capital expenditure incurred on the provision of the machinery or plant in respect of which the allowance is to be made was incurred on or after the 29th day of January, 1986, the following provisions shall apply:

(i) expenditure shall not be regarded as having been incurred by a person in so far as the expenditure has been or is to be met directly or indirectly—

(I) in relation to expenditure incurred before the 6th day of May, 1993, by the State, by any board established by statute or by any public or local authority, and

(II) in relation to expenditure incurred on or after the 6th day of May, 1993, by the State or by any person other than the first-mentioned person, and

(ii) the actual cost of any machinery or plant to any person shall for the purposes of section 284 be taken to be the amount of capital expenditure incurred on the provision of such machinery or plant less any expenditure referred to in subparagraph (i).

(*b*) Paragraph (*a*) shall not apply in relation to any capital expenditure which is met or is to be met in the manner mentioned in paragraph (*a*)(i)—

(i) under the terms of an agreement finally approved on or before the 29th day of January, 1986, by a Department of State, any board established by statute or any public or local authority, or

(ii) under the terms of an agreement which—

(I) was the subject of negotiations which were in progress on the 29th day of January, 1986, with a Department of State, any board established by statute or any public or local authority, and

(II) was finally approved by such Department, board or authority not later than the 31st day of December, 1986.

(4) (*a*) Subsection (3) shall not apply where an allowance is to be made under section 283 or 284 in taxing a food processing trade carried on by a company and the capital expenditure in respect of which the allowance is to be made was incurred by that company and was so incurred in respect of qualifying machinery or plant.

(*b*) The reference in paragraph (*a*) to expenditure incurred by a company shall not include any expenditure which it is deemed to have incurred in accordance with section 299.

Cross-references

Capital allowances for buildings used for third level educational purposes, subs (2): s 843(2).

Cars costing more than the specified amount, subs (2): s 374(6).

Petroleum trade, abandonment expenditure and loss relief, subs (2): s 695(8).

Petroleum trade, exploration expenditure, subs (2): s 693(13)(*c*).

Revenue precedents

Issue: Whether malt for use in the brewing industry is intended for human consumption as a food" such that s 317 relief applies.

Decision: No.

Issue: Capital allowances for Industrial Buildings and Plant and Machinery are computed on a net of grant basis. In the event of a grant being repaid, may the grant be treated as expenditure incurred and qualifying for capital allowances?

Decision: The grant repaid may be treated as expenditure incurred for the purposes of claiming capital allowances on industrial buildings, machinery and plant. The date on which the expenditure is incurred may be taken as the date when the grants are repaid.

Issue: Where a company is engaged in a food processing trade, as defined, and receives grants in respect of machinery and plant which it uses in that trade can the grants be excluded when calculating the capital allowances?

Decision: The grants may only be excluded in respect of machinery and plant which is used solely in the course of manufacturing processed food and which is not used in any other process.

Definitions

capital allowance: ss 2(1), 5(1); company: ss 4(1), 5(1); local authority: ss 2(1), 5(1); person: IA 1937 s 11(*c*); statute: s 2(1), IA 1937 s 3; trade: s 3(1).

Former enactments

ITA 1967 s 254(4)(*b*), s 303(3); FA 1986 s 52(1), FA 1987 s 25; CTA 1976 s 21(1) and Sch 1 para 1, para 17 and para 49; FA 1993 s 34(1)(*a*) and (*b*) and (3).

318 Meaning of "sale, insurance, salvage or compensation moneys"

In this Part, except where the context otherwise requires, **"sale, insurance, salvage or compensation moneys"**, in relation to an event which gives rise or might give rise to a balancing allowance or a balancing charge to or on any person, means—

(*a*) where the event is a sale of any property, including the sale of a right to use or otherwise deal in machinery or plant consisting of computer software, the net proceeds to that person of the sale,

[(*aa*) as respects machinery or plant consisting of computer software or the right to use or otherwise deal with computer software, where the event is the grant of a right to use or otherwise deal with the whole or part of that machinery or plant, the consideration in money or money's worth received by that person for the grant of the right,][1]

(*b*) where the event is the demolition or destruction of any property, the net amount received by that person for the remains of the property, together with any insurance moneys received by that person in respect of the demolition or destruction and any other compensation of any description received by that person in respect of the demolition or destruction, in so far as that compensation consists of capital sums,

(*c*) as respects machinery or plant, where the event is the permanent loss of the machinery or plant otherwise than in consequence of its demolition or destruction, any insurance moneys received by that person in respect of any loss and any other compensation of any description received by that person in respect of that loss, in so far as that compensation consists of capital sums, and

(*d*) where the event is that a building or structure ceases altogether to be used, any compensation of any description received by that person in respect of that event, in so far as that compensation consists of capital sums.

Amendments

1 Para (*aa*) inserted by FA 2000 s 41(*b*) with effect from 29 February 2000.

Cross-references

Calculation of balancing allowances and charges (paras (*a*)–(*c*)): s 289(2).

Petroleum trade, exploration expenditure: s 693(13)(*d*).

Definitions

person: IA 1937 s 11(*c*); trade: s 3(1).

Former enactments

ITA 1967 s 304(1); CTA 1976 s 21(1) and Sch 1 para 50; FA 1994 s 24(*c*).

319 Adjustment of allowances by reference to value-added tax

(1) In computing any deduction, allowance or relief for the purposes of—

(*a*) this Part,

(*b*) sections 658 and 659,

(*c*) Chapter 1 of Part 24, or
(*d*) sections 764, 765 and 769,

the cost to a person of any machinery or plant, or the amount of any expenditure incurred by a person, shall not take account of any amount included in such cost or expenditure for value-added tax in respect of which the person may claim—

(i) a deduction under section 12 of the Value-Added Tax Act, 1972, or
(ii) a refund of value-added tax under an order under section 20(3) of that Act.

(2) In calculating for the purposes of this Part the amount of sale, insurance, salvage or compensation moneys to be taken into account in computing a balancing allowance or balancing charge to be made to or on a person, no account shall be taken of the amount of value-added tax (if any) chargeable to the person in respect of those moneys.

Cross-references

Petroleum trade, exploration expenditure: s 693(15).

Definitions

person: IA 1937 s 11(*c*).

Former enactments

FA 1975 s 29; FA 1997 s 20(14).

320 Other interpretation (Part 9)

(1) In this Part, except where the context otherwise requires—

"income" includes any amount on which a charge to tax is authorised to be made under this Part;

"lease" includes an agreement for a lease where the term to be covered by the lease has begun, and any tenancy, but does not include a mortgage, and **"lessee"**, **"lessor"** and **"leasehold interest"** shall be construed accordingly.

(2) Any reference in this Part to any building, structure, machinery or plant shall be construed as including a reference to a part of any building, structure, machinery or plant except, in relation to a building or structure, where the reference is comprised in a reference to the whole of a building or structure.

(3) This Part shall apply in relation to a share in machinery or plant as it applies in relation to a part of machinery or plant and, for the purposes of this Part, a share in machinery or plant shall be deemed to be used for the purposes of a trade only so long as the machinery or plant is used for the purposes of the trade.

(4) Any reference in this Part to the time of any sale shall be construed as a reference to the time of completion or the time when possession is given, whichever is the earlier.

(5) Any reference in this Part to the setting up or permanent discontinuance of a trade includes, except where the contrary is expressly provided, a reference to the occurring of any event which under any provision of the Income Tax Acts is to be treated as equivalent to the setting up or permanent discontinuance of a trade.

(6) Any reference in this Part to an allowance made includes a reference to an allowance which would be made but for an insufficiency of profits or gains, or other income, against which to make the allowance.

Cross-references

Change in ownership of a company, disallowance of trading losses: s 401(5)(*a*).

Group relief, exclusion of double allowances etc, subs (6): s 428(6).

Petroleum trade, abandonment expenditure and loss relief, subs (5): s 695(8).

Petroleum trade, exploration expenditure, subss (4)–(5): s 693(13)(*e*).

Former enactments

ITA 1967 s 254(1)(*c*), s 255(6) and s 304(1)–(6); CTA 1976 s 21(1) and Sch 1 para 17 and para 50; FA 1997 s 146(1) and Sch 9 Pt I para 1(20).

321 Provisions of general application in relation to the making of allowances and charges

(1) Subsections (2) to (7) shall apply for the interpretation of—

(*a*) this Part,

(*b*) section 374,

(*c*) sections 658 to 660

(*d*) Chapter 1 of Part 24,

(*e*) sections 764 and 765

(*f*) section 769, and

(*g*) any other provision of the Tax Acts relating to the making of allowances or charges under or in accordance with the provisions referred to in paragraphs (*a*) to (*f*).

(2) **"Chargeable period"** means an accounting period of a company or a year of assessment, and—

(*a*) a reference to a chargeable period or its basis period is a reference to the chargeable period if it is an accounting period and to the basis period for it if it is a year of assessment;

(*b*) a reference to a chargeable period related to expenditure, or a sale or other event, is a reference to the chargeable period in which, or to that in the basis period for which, the expenditure is incurred or the sale or other event takes place, and means the latter only if the chargeable period is a year of assessment.

[(2A) Subject to section 316, references to expenditure in relation to an asset—

(*a*) include expenditure on labour costs including emoluments paid to employees of the company, and

(*b*) do not include interest payable,

which for accounting purposes is taken into account by the company in determining the value of the asset.][1]

(3) References to tax for a chargeable period shall be construed in relation to corporation tax as referring to the tax for any financial year which is chargeable in respect of that period.

(4) A reference to allowances or charges being made in taxing a trade is a reference to their being made in computing the trading income for corporation tax or in charging the profits or gains of the trade to income tax.

(5) (*a*) Where it is provided that writing-down allowances shall be made in respect of any expenditure during a writing-down period of a specified length, there shall for any chargeable period wholly or partly comprised in the writing-down period be made an allowance equal to the appropriate fraction of the expenditure and, subject to any provision to the contrary, the appropriate fraction shall be such fraction of the writing-down period as falls within the chargeable period.

(*b*) Notwithstanding paragraph (*a*), the aggregate amount of the writing-down allowances made, whether to the same or to different persons, together with the amount of any initial allowance (but not of any investment allowance), shall not exceed the amount of the expenditure.

(6) Where the reference is partly to years of assessment before the year 1976–77—

(*a*) a writing-down allowance includes an annual allowance, and

(*b*) an allowance on account of wear and tear of machinery or plant includes a deduction on account of wear and tear of machinery or plant,

in the sense which in the context those expressions had immediately before the commencement of the Corporation Tax Act, 1976.

(7) Where any enactment referred to in subsection (1) provides for an amount of a writing-down allowance or an allowance on account of wear and tear of machinery or plant to be determined by a fraction or percentage, specified numerically, of any expenditure or other sum, or by reference to a percentage determined or deemed to be determined for a chargeable period of one year, then for a chargeable period of less than a year the fraction or percentage shall be proportionately reduced.

(8) Except where the context otherwise requires, in any provision of the Income Tax Acts not referred to in subsection (1) any reference to an allowance or charge for a year of assessment under a provision referred to in that subsection shall include the like allowance or charge for an accounting period of a company, and any reference to the making of an allowance or charge in charging profits or gains of a trade shall be construed as a reference to making the allowance in taxing a trade.

(9) Any provision of the Income Tax Acts whereby, for the purposes of—

(*a*) this Part,

(*b*) section 670,

(*c*) section 764 or 765,

(*d*) section 769, or

(*e*) any provision of the Income Tax Acts relating to the making of allowances or charges under or in accordance with the provisions referred to in paragraphs (*a*) to (*d*),

a trade is or is not to be treated as permanently discontinued or a new trade as set up and commenced shall apply in the like manner in the case of a trade so treated by virtue of the Corporation Tax Acts.

Amendments

1 Subs (2A) inserted by FA 2005 s 48(1)(*e*) as respects any period of account beginning on or after 1 January 2005.

Cross-references

Allowance for certain capital expenditure on roads, bridges — transitional, meaning of "chargeable period" and "chargeable period or its basis period" applied, subs (2): Sch 32 para 10(1).

Charge to income tax of offshore income gain, meaning of "chargeable period" applied, subs (2): s 745(1)(*b*).

Distributions, matters to be treated as, meaning of "chargeable period" applied: s 130(2C).

Double deduction in respect of certain emoluments, meaning of "chargeable period" applied: s 88A(1).

Exchange of Irish Government bonds, meaning of "chargeable period" applied, subs (2): s 751B(1).

Farming stock relief, meaning of "chargeable period" applied, subs (2): s 665.

Foreign life policies, taxation and returns of certain policies, interpretation and application, meaning of "chargeable period" applied: s 730H(1).

Interest in respect of wholesale debt instruments, meaning of "chargeable period" applied: s 246A(4)(*a*)(iii).

Interest on overdue income tax, corporation tax and capital gains tax, meaning of "chargeable period" applied: s 1080(1).

Leased assets, restriction on use of allowances, meaning of "chargeable period or its basis period" applied: s 403(1).

Leased plant and machinery, restriction on use of allowances, meanings of "chargeable period", "chargeable period related to" and "chargeable period or its basis period" applied: s 404(1).

Offshore funds, taxation and returns of certain funds, interpretation and application, meaning of "chargeable period" applied: s 747B(1).

Personal Retirement Savings Accounts (PRSAs), allowance to employer, meaning of "chargeable period or its basis period" applied: s 787J(1).

Petroleum trade, exploration expenditure, subss (2)–(7) applied by: s 693(10).

Profits from occupation of certain woodlands, meaning of "chargeable period" applied: s 232(3)(*b*), (*c*), (4)(*b*).

Profits or gains from stallion fees, meaning of "chargeable period" applied: s 231(2)(*b*), (*c*), (3)(*b*).

Relevant period, subs (5): s 274(5)(*c*).

Repayment of tax, meaning of "chargeable period" applied, subs (2); s 865(1).

Relief to lessors in respect of expenditure incurred on the provision of certain residential accommodation, qualifying premises and special qualifying premises, meaning of "chargeable period" applied: s 372AM(9A)(*c*).

Restriction of deductions for employee benefit contributions, meaning of "chargeable period" applied: s 81A.

Restriction of relief in respect of loans applied in acquiring interest in companies and partnerships, meaning of "chargeable period" applied: s 248A(1).

Returns of interest paid to non-residents, meaning of "chargeable period" applied, subs (2): s 891A(1).

Returns in relation to certain offshore products, meaning of "chargeable period" applied, subs (2): s 896(1).

Returns in relation to foreign accounts, meaning of "chargeable period" applied, subs (2): s 895(1).

Returns of certain information by third parties, meaning of "chargeable period" applied, subs (2): s 894(1).

Self assessment, meaning of "chargeable period" applied, subs (2): s 950(1).

Significant buildings, meaning of "chargeable period" applied, subs (2): s 482(1)(*a*).

Strips of securities, meaning of "chargeable period" applied, subs (2): s 55(1).

Stud greyhound service fees, meaning of "chargeable period" applied: s 233(3)(*b*), (*c*), (4)(*b*).

Surcharge for late returns, meaning of "chargeable period" applied: s 1084(1)(*b*)(*ib*).

Taxation of collective investment undertakings: s 734(1)(*a*).

Definitions

accounting period: s 27; company: s 4(1); Corporation Tax Acts: s 1(2); Income Tax Acts: s 1(2); Tax Acts: s 1(2); trade: ss 3(1), 4(1); year of assessment: s 2(1).

Former enactments

CTA 1976 Sch 1 para 1, 2, 3; FA 1997 s 20(4).

PART 10
INCOME TAX AND CORPORATION TAX: RELIEFS FOR RENEWAL AND IMPROVEMENT OF CERTAIN URBAN AREAS, CERTAIN RESORT AREAS AND CERTAIN ISLANDS

Cross-references

Restriction of relief in respect of loans applied in acquiring interest in companies: s 250A(1)("specified building").

Restriction on use of capital allowances on certain industrial buildings or other premises: s 409A(1) (specified building), (5).
Ring-fence on use of certain capital allowances on certain industrial buildings and other premises: s 409E(1) (specified building).

Revenue information

Information leaflet IT26 — Urban Renewal Relief.
A spreadsheet summarising the tax reliefs available under the various property incentive schemes [Urban, Rural, etc] is available on Revenue's website (WWW.REVENUE.IE/SERVICES/SCHEMES.XLS).

CHAPTER 1
Custom House Docks Area

322 Interpretation (Chapter 1)

(1) In this Chapter, but subject to subsection (2)—

"the Custom House Docks Area" means the area described in paragraph 2 of Schedule 5;

[**"the specified period"** means the period commencing on the 25th day of January, 1988, and ending on—

(*a*) the 24th day of January, 1999, for the purposes of section 324,

(*b*) the 31st day of December, 1999, for the purposes of sections 325 to 328, and

(*c*) the 31st day of December, 1999, for the purposes of section 323; but where, in relation to the construction of a qualifying premises within the meaning of that section, at least 51 per cent of the total capital expenditure which is incurred on the construction of the premises is incurred before the 1st day of January, 2000, the reference in this paragraph to the 31st day of December, 1999, shall be construed as a reference to the 30th day of June, 2000.][1]

(2) For the purposes of this Chapter, the Minister for Finance, after consultation with the Minister for the Environment and Local Government, may by order direct that—

(*a*) the definition of **"the Custom House Docks Area"** shall include such area or areas described in the order which but for the order would not be included in that definition, and

[(*b*) as respect any such area so described, the definition of **"the specified period"** shall be construed as a reference to such period as shall be specified in the order in relation to that area; but no such period specified in the order shall commence before the 26th day of January, 1994, or end after—

(i) the 24th day of January, 1999, for the purposes of section 324,

(ii) the 31st day of December, 1999, for the purposes of section 325 to 328, and

(iii) the 31st day of December, 1999, for the purposes of section 323; but where, in relation to the construction of a qualifying premises within the meaning of that section, at least 51 per cent of the total capital expenditure which is incurred on the construction of the premises is incurred before the 1st day of January, 2000, the reference in this subparagraph to the 31st day of December, 1999, shall be construed as a reference to the 30th day of June, 2000,][2] and, where the Minister for Finance so orders, the definition of **"the Custom House Docks Area"** shall be deemed to include that area or those areas and the definition of **"the specified period"** shall be construed as a reference to the period specified in the order.

(3) The Minister for Finance may make orders for the purpose of this section and any order made under this section shall be laid before Dáil Éireann as soon as may be after it is made and, if a resolution annulling the order is passed by Dáil Éireann within the next 21 days on which Dáil Éireann has sat after the order is laid before it, the order shall be annulled accordingly, but without prejudice to the validity of anything previously done thereunder.

(4) Schedule 5 shall apply for the purposes of supplementing this Chapter.

Amendments

1 Substituted by Urban Renewal Act 1998 s 20(1)(*a*)(i) with effect from such date as the Minister for Finance may appoint by order* — Urban Renewal Act 1998 s 2(5), as substituted by FA 1999 s 42, refers (previously "the specified period" means the period commencing on the 25th day of January 1998, and ending on the 24th day of January 1999"). An earlier amendment effected by FA 1998 s 25(1)(*a*)(i), which extended "the specified period" to 31 December 1999 from such date as the Minister for Finance was to appoint by order, was repealed with effect from 28 May 1998 by Urban Renewal Act 1998 s 20(2).

2 Substituted Urban Renewal Act 1998 s 20(1)(*a*)(ii) with effect from such date as the Minister for Finance may appoint by order* — Urban Renewal Act 1998 s 2(5), as substituted by FA 1999 s 42, refers (previously a period specified in an order could not end after 24 January 1999). An earlier amendment effected by FA 1998 s 25(1)(*a*)(ii), which changed 24 January 1999 to 31 December 1999 from such date as the Minister for Finance was to appoint by order, was repealed with effect from 28 May 1998 by Urban Renewal Act 1998 s 20(2).

* The Urban Renewal Act, 1998 (Section 20) (Commencement) Order, 2000 provided that these amendments came into operation on 5 January 2000.

Cross-references

BES relief, qualifying trades, meaning of the Custom House Docks Area applied: s 496(2)(*a*)(iv), (xv).

Double rent allowance in respect of rent paid for certain business premises, subs (2): s 324(5)(*a*)(i).

Manufacturing (10%) rate, International Financial Services Centre: s 446(1), (12).

See also Urban Renewal Act 1998 s 2(5)(commencement), reference therein to "the specified period" within the meaning of this section.

Ministerial Orders

Finance Act, 1987 (Designation of Urban Renewal Areas) Order, 1986 (SI No 56 of 1996).

Taxes Consolidation Act, 1997 (Designation of Urban Renewal Areas and Tax Relief on Income from Certain Trading Operations) Order, 1997 (SI No 483 of 1997).

Taxes Consolidation Act, 1997 (Extension of the Specified Period — Custom House Docks Area) Order, 2000.

Definitions

Dáil Éireann: IA 1937 Sch; rent: s 5(1).

Former enactments

FA 1986 s 41; FA 1987 s 27(1)(*b*) and (2); FA 1994 s 36(*c*) and (*d*); FA 1995 s 32(1)(*a*) and s 33.

323 Capital allowances in relation to construction of certain commercial premises

(1) In this section, **"qualifying premises"** means a building or structure the site of which is wholly within the Custom House Docks Area and which—

(*a*) apart from this section is not an industrial building or structure within the meaning of section 268(1), and

(*b*) (i) is in use for the purposes of a trade or profession, or

(ii) whether or not it is so used, is let on bona fide commercial terms for such consideration as might be expected to be paid in a letting of the building or structure negotiated on an arm's length basis,

but does not include any building or structure in use as or as part of a dwelling house.

(2) (*a*) Subject to subsections (3) to (5), the provisions of the Tax Acts relating to the making of allowances or charges in respect of capital expenditure incurred on the construction of an industrial building or structure shall, notwithstanding anything to the contrary in those provisions, apply—

(i) as if a qualifying premises were, at all times at which it is a qualifying premises, a building or structure in respect of which an allowance is to be made for the purposes of income tax or corporation tax, as the case may be, under Chapter 1 of Part 9 by reason of its use for a purpose specified in section 268(1)(*a*), and

(ii) where any activity carried on in the qualifying premises is not a trade, as if it were a trade.

(*b*) An allowance shall be given by virtue of this subsection in respect of any capital expenditure incurred on the construction of a qualifying premises only in so far as that expenditure is incurred in the specified period.

(3) (*a*) For the purposes of the application, by subsection (2), of sections 271 and 273 in relation to capital expenditure incurred in the specified period on the construction of a qualifying premises—

(i) section 271 shall apply as if—

(I) in subsection (1) of that section the definition of "industrial development agency" were deleted,

(II) in subsection (2)(*a*)(i) of that section "to which subsection (3) applies" were deleted,

(III) subsections (3) and (5) of that section were deleted, and

(IV) the following subsection were substituted for subsection (4) of that section:

"(4) An industrial building allowance shall be of an amount equal to 50 per cent of the capital expenditure mentioned in subsection (2).",

and

(ii) section 273 shall apply as if—

(I) in subsection (1) of that section the definition of "industrial development agency" were deleted, and

(II) subsections (2)(*b*) and (3) to (7) of that section were deleted.

...[1]

(4) Notwithstanding section 274(1), no balancing charge shall be made in relation to a qualifying premises by reason of any of the events specified in that section which occurs—

(*a*) more than 13 years after the qualifying premises was first used, or

(*b*) in a case where section 276 applies, more than 13 years after the capital expenditure on refurbishment of the qualifying premises was incurred.

(5) For the purposes only of determining, in relation to a claim for an allowance by virtue of subsection (2), whether and to what extent capital expenditure incurred on the construction of a qualifying premises is incurred in the specified period, only such an amount of that capital expenditure as is determined by the inspector, according to the best of the inspector's knowledge and judgment, to be properly attributable to work on the construction of the premises actually carried out during the specified period shall (notwithstanding any other provision of the Tax Acts as to the time when any capital expenditure is or is to be treated as incurred) be treated as having been incurred in that period, and any amount which by virtue of this subsection is determined by the inspector may be amended by the Appeal Commissioners or by the Circuit Court on the hearing or the rehearing of an appeal against that determination.

Amendments

1 Subs (3)(*b*) deleted by Urban Renewal Act 1998 s 20(1)(*b*) with effect from such date as the Minister for Finance may appoint by order — Urban Renewal Act 1998 s 2(5), as substituted by FA 1999 s 42, refers. This deletion had previously been effected by FA 1998 s 25(1)(*b*) but Urban Renewal Act 1998 s 20(2) repealed that section with effect from 28 May 1998; and the deletion was re-enacted by Urban Renewal Act 1998 s 20(1)(*b*). Subs (3)(*b*) had read:

"(*b* Notwithstanding paragraph (*a*), as respects any capital expenditure incurred on or after the 25th day of January, 1998, on the construction of any qualifying premises—

(i) any allowance made under section 272 and increased under section 273(2)(*a*) in respect of that expenditure, whether claimed for one chargeable period or more than one such period, shall not in the aggregate exceed 54 per cent of the amount of that expenditure, and

(ii) where any allowance made under section 272 in respect of that expenditure is increased under section 273 for any chargeable period, no allowance shall be made in respect of that expenditure under section 271."

The Urban Renewal Act, 1998 (Section 20) (Commencement) Order, 2000 provided that this deletion came into operation on 5 January 2000.

Cross-references

Interpretation: s 322(1)(the specified period), (2)(*b*)(iii).
Restriction of loss relief, subs (2): s 455(7).
Restriction of group relief, subs (2): s 456(4).

Definitions

Appeal Commissioners: s 2(1); Circuit Court: IA 1937 Sch; inspector: ss 2(1), 852; local authority: s 2(1); person: IA 1937 s 11(*c*); profession: ss 2(1), 5(1); Tax Acts: s 1(2); trade: ss 3(1), 4(1), 5(1); writing: IA 1937 Sch.

Former enactments

FA 1986 s 42(1), (2), proviso to (4), and (7); FA 1992 s 29(*b*)(ii); FA 1993 s 30(1)(*a*)(ii); FA 1995 s 32(1)(*b*).

324 Double rent allowance in respect of rent paid for certain business premises

(1) (*a*) In this section—

"lease", **"lessee"**, **"lessor"** and **"rent"** have the same meanings respectively as in Chapter 8 of Part 4;

"market value", in relation to a building or structure, means the price which the unencumbered fee simple of the building or structure would fetch if sold in the open market in such manner and subject to such conditions as might reasonably be calculated to obtain for the vendor the best price for the building or structure, less the part of that price which would be attributable to the acquisition of, or of rights in or over, the land on which the building or structure is constructed;

"qualifying lease" means, subject to subsection (4), a lease in respect of a qualifying premises granted in the specified period, or within the period of 2 years from the day next after the end of the specified period, on bona fide commercial terms by a lessor to a lessee not connected with the lessor, or with any other person entitled to a rent in respect of the qualifying premises, whether under that lease or any other lease;

"qualifying premises" means a building or structure the site of which is wholly within the Custom House Docks Area and—

(i) (I) which is an industrial building or structure within the meaning of section 268(1), and in respect of which capital expenditure is incurred in the specified period for which an allowance is to be made for the purposes of income tax or corporation tax, as the case may be, under Chapter 1 of Part 9, or

(II) in respect of which an allowance is to be made, or, as respects rent payable under a qualifying lease entered into on or after the 18th day of April, 1991, will by virtue of section 279 be made, for the purposes of income tax or corporation tax, as the case may be, under Chapter 1 of Part 9 by virtue of section 323, and

(ii) which is let on bona fide commercial terms for such consideration as might be expected to be paid on a letting of the building or structure negotiated on an arm's length basis,

but, as respects rent payable under a qualifying lease entered into on or after the 6th day of May, 1993, where capital expenditure is incurred in the specified period on the refurbishment of a building or structure in respect of which an allowance is to be made for the purposes of income tax or corporation tax, as the case may be, under Chapter 1 of Part 9, the building or structure shall not be regarded as a qualifying premises unless the total amount of the expenditure so incurred is not less than an amount equal to 10 per cent of the market value of the building or structure immediately before that expenditure is incurred;

"refurbishment", in relation to a building or structure, means any work of construction, reconstruction, repair or renewal, including the provision or improvement of water, sewerage or heating facilities, carried out in the course of repair or restoration, or maintenance in the nature of repair or restoration, of the building or structure.

(*b*) For the purposes of this section but subject to paragraph (*c*), so much of a period, being a period when rent is payable by a person in relation to a qualifying premises under a qualifying lease, shall be a relevant rental period as does not exceed—

(i) 10 years, or

(ii) the period by which 10 years exceeds—

(I) any preceding period, or

(II) if there is more than one preceding period, the aggregate of those periods, for which rent was payable—

(A) by that person or any other person, or

(B) as respects rent payable in relation to any qualifying premises under a qualifying lease entered into before the 11th day of April, 1994, by that person or any person connected with that person,

in relation to that premises under a qualifying lease.

(*c*) As respects rent payable in relation to any qualifying premises under a qualifying lease entered into before the 18th day of April, 1991, **"relevant rental period"**, in relation to a qualifying premises, means the period of 10 years commencing on the day on which rent in respect of that premises is first payable under any qualifying lease.

(2) Subject to subsection (3), where in the computation of the amount of the profits or gains of a trade or profession a person is apart from this section entitled to any deduction (in this subsection referred to as **"the first-mentioned deduction")** on account of rent in respect of a qualifying premises occupied by such person for the purposes of that trade or profession which is payable by such person—

(*a*) for a relevant rental period, or

(*b*) as respects rent payable in relation to any qualifying premises under a qualifying lease entered into before the 18th day of April, 1991, in the relevant rental period,

in relation to that qualifying premises under a qualifying lease, such person shall be entitled in that computation to a further deduction (in this subsection referred to as **"the second-mentioned deduction"**) equal to the amount of the first-mentioned deduction but, as respects a qualifying lease granted on or after the 21st day of April, 1997, where the first-mentioned deduction is on account of rent payable by such person to a connected person, such person shall not be entitled in that computation to the second-mentioned deduction.

(3) Where a person holds an interest in a qualifying premises out of which interest a qualifying lease is created directly or indirectly in respect of the qualifying premises and in respect of rent payable under the qualifying lease a claim for a further deduction under this section is made, and such person or, as respects rent payable in relation to any qualifying premises under a qualifying lease entered into on or after the 6th day of May, 1993, either such person or another person connected with such person—

(*a*) takes under a qualifying lease a qualifying premises (in this subsection referred to as **"the second-mentioned premises"**) occupied by such person or such other person, as the case may be, for the purposes of a trade or profession, and

(*b*) is apart from this section entitled, in the computation of the amount of the profits or gains of that trade or profession, to a deduction on account of rent in respect of the second-mentioned premises,

then, unless such person or such other person, as the case may be, shows that the taking on lease of the second-mentioned premises was not undertaken for the sole or main benefit of obtaining a further deduction on account of rent under this section, such person or such other person, as the case may be, shall not be entitled in the computation of the amount of the profits or gains of that trade or profession to any further deduction on account of rent in respect of the second-mentioned premises.

(4) (*a*) In this subsection—

"current value", in relation to minimum lease payments, means the value of those payments discounted to their present value at a rate which, when applied at the inception of the lease to—

(i) those payments, including any initial payment but excluding any payment or part of any payment for which the lessor will be accountable to the lessee, and

(ii) any unguaranteed residual value of the qualifying premises, excluding any part of such value for which the lessor will be accountable to the lessee,

produces discounted present values the aggregate amount of which equals the amount of the fair value of the qualifying premises;

"fair value", in relation to a qualifying premises, means an amount equal to such consideration as might be expected to be paid for the premises on a sale negotiated on an arm's length basis less any grants receivable towards the purchase of the qualifying premises;

"inception of the lease" means the earlier of the time the qualifying premises is brought into use or the date from which rentals under the lease first accrue;

"minimum lease payments" means the minimum payments over the remaining part of the term of the lease to be paid to the lessor, and includes any residual amount to be paid to the lessor at the end of the term of the lease and guaranteed by the lessee or by a person connected with the lessee;

"unguaranteed residual value", in relation to a qualifying premises, means that part of the residual value of that premises at the end of a term of a lease, as estimated at the inception of the lease, the realisation of which by the lessor is not assured or is guaranteed solely by a person connected with the lessor.

(*b*) A finance lease, that is—

(i) a lease in respect of a qualifying premises where, at the inception of the lease, the aggregate of the current value of the minimum lease payments (including any initial payment but excluding any payment or part of any payment for which the lessor will be accountable to the lessee) payable by the lessee in relation to the lease amounts to 90 per cent or more of the fair value of the qualifying premises, or

(ii) a lease which in all the circumstances is considered to provide in substance for the lessee the risks and benefits associated with ownership of the qualifying premises other than legal title to that premises,

shall not be a qualifying lease for the purposes of this section.

[(5) Notwithstanding any other provision of this section, subsection (2) shall not apply—

(*a*) in respect of rent payable, under a qualifying lease, for any part of a relevant rental period between 3 December 1998 and 31 December 2003 unless—

(i) in the case of a qualifying premises within an area or areas included in the definition of "the Customs House Docks Area" by virtue of being described in an order of the Minister for Finance made under section 322(2), an agreement in writing or a contract in writing to secure the development of the building or structure, which comprises the qualifying premises or in which the qualifying premises is located, was entered into in the specified period, but by 2 December 1998, with the Dublin Docklands Development Authority (within the meaning of section 14 of the Dublin Docklands Development Authority Act, 1997), or

(ii) in the case of any other qualifying premises, an agreement in writing or a contract in writing to secure the development of the building or structure, which comprises the qualifying premises or in which the qualifying premises is located, was entered into in the specified period, but by 2 December 1998, and such development was wholly or mainly completed before 1 January 2000,

(*b*) in respect of rent payable, under a qualifying lease, for any part of a relevant rental period between 1 January 2004 and 31 December 2008, in the case of a qualifying premises to which subsection (2) applies by virtue of paragraph (*a*)(i),

(*c*) in respect of rent payable, under a qualifying lease, for any part of a relevant rental period between 1 January 2004 and 31 December 2008, in the case of a qualifying premises to which subsection (2) applies by virtue of paragraph (*a*)(ii), unless—

(i) the construction or refurbishment of the qualifying premises, which is the subject of the qualifying lease, was completed prior to 1 April 1998, or

(ii) (I) the construction or refurbishment of the qualifying premises, which is the subject of the qualifying lease, commenced prior to 1 April 1998, and

(II) such premises was occupied by a lessee, under a qualifying lease, prior to 9 February 1999,

or

(*d*) in respect of rent payable, under a qualifying lease, for any part of a relevant rental period after 31 December 2008.][1]

Amendments

[1] Subs (5) inserted by FA 2000 s 39(1) with effect from 3 December 1998.

Cross-references

Interpretation: s 322(1)(the specified period), (2)(*b*)(i).
Life assurance companies, acquisition expenses: s 708(1).
Restriction on use by certain partnerships of certain losses, etc, transitional arrangements, subs (2): s 1013(2C)(*a*)("specified deduction").

Revenue precedents

Issue: Whether payment of irrecoverable VAT under s 4 VAT Act 1972 qualifies for double rent deduction.
Decision: No, since the payment is not rent. The deduction is not given on account of rent. If given, it is on account of the VAT payable by the lessee.
Issue: Whether payments for certain service charges made in accordance with the terms of a qualifying lease qualify for double rent deduction.

Decision: The payments must be in the nature of rent as defined in TCA 1997 s 96. Not all payments made in accordance with the terms of a lease would be in the nature of rent. If the payments do not arise from the holding of the premises but from the use to which the premises are put they are less likely to be in the nature of rent. If the payments would arise irrespective of the nature of the occupier's interest in the premises, they are not in the nature of rent.

Definitions

lease: s 5(1); person: IA 1937 s 11(*c*); profession: ss 2(1), 5(1); profits: s 4(1); rent: s 5(1); trade: s 3(1).

Former enactments

FA 1986 s 45(1)(*a*) and (*c*) and (2) (apart from 1st proviso para (*a*) and 2nd proviso thereto); FA 1990 s 32 and s 33(1)–(2)(*a*); FA 1991 s 21; FA 1992 s 29(*d*)(ii); FA 1993 s 30(1)(*c*) and (2)(*b*); FA 1994 s 35(1)(*d*) and (2)(*c*); FA 1996 s 131; FA 1997 s 27.

325 Rented residential accommodation: deduction for certain expenditure on construction

Amendments

[1] Section 325 repealed by FA 2002 s 24(3)(*a*) with effect from 1 January 2002; but see now TCA 1997 Pt 10 Ch 11 (ss 372AK–372AV) which codified, with effect from 1 January 2002, reliefs for lessors and owner-occupiers in respect of expenditure incurred on the provision of certain residential accommodation, and in particular s 372AU which provides a saver for relief due, and for a clawback of relief given, under old schemes.

326 Rented residential accommodation: deduction for certain expenditure on conversion

Amendments

[1] Section 326 repealed by FA 2002 s 24(3)(*a*) with effect from 1 January 2002; but see now TCA 1997 Pt 10 Ch 11 (ss 372AK–372AV) which codified, with effect from 1 January 2002, reliefs for lessors and owner-occupiers in respect of expenditure incurred on the provision of certain residential accommodation, and in particular s 372AU which provides a saver for relief due, and for a clawback of relief given, under old schemes.

327 Rented residential accommodation: deduction for certain expenditure on refurbishment

Amendments

[1] Section 327 repealed by FA 2002 s 24(3)(*a*) with effect from 1 January 2002; but see now TCA 1997 Pt 10 Ch 11 (ss 372AK–372AV) which codified, with effect from 1 January 2002, reliefs for lessors and owner-occupiers in respect of expenditure incurred on the provision of certain residential accommodation, and in particular s 372AU which provides a saver for relief due, and for a clawback of relief given, under old schemes.

328 Residential accommodation: allowance to owner-occupiers in respect of certain expenditure on construction or refurbishment

Amendments

[1] Section 328 repealed by FA 2002 s 24(3)(*a*) with effect from 1 January 2002; but see now TCA 1997 Pt 10 Ch 11 (ss 372AK–372AV) which codified, with effect from 1 January 2002, reliefs for lessors and owner-occupiers in respect of expenditure incurred on the provision of certain residential accommodation, and in particular s 372AU which provides a saver for relief due, and for a clawback of relief given, under old schemes.

329 Provisions supplementary to sections 325 to 328

Amendments

1 Section 329 repealed by FA 2002 s 24(3)(*a*) with effect from 1 January 2002; but see now TCA 1997 Pt 10 Ch 11 (ss 372AK–372AV) which codified, with effect from 1 January 2002, reliefs for lessors and owner-occupiers in respect of expenditure incurred on the provision of certain residential accommodation, and in particular s 372AU which provides a saver for relief due, and for a clawback of relief given, under old schemes.

CHAPTER 2
Temple Bar Area

330 Interpretation (Chapter 2)

(1) In this Chapter—

[**"qualifying period"** means the period commencing—

(*a*) for the purposes of any provision of this Chapter other than section 334, 335 or 336, the 6th day of April, 1991, or

(*b*) for the purposes of sections 334 to 336, the 30th day of January, 1991,

and ending on—

(i) the 5th day of April, 1999, or

(ii) the 31st day of December, 1999, where, in relation to the construction of, conversion into, refurbishment of, or, as the case may be, construction or refurbishment of a house which is a qualifying premises within the meaning of section 334, 335, 336 or 337, the corporation of the county borough of Dublin gives a certificate in writing, on or before the 31st day of July, 1999, to the person constructing, converting or refurbishing, as the case may be, the house stating that it is satisfied that not less than 50 per cent of the total cost of the house and the site thereof had been incurred on or before the 5th day of April, 1999;][1]

"refurbishment" means any work of construction, reconstruction, repair or renewal, including the provision or improvement of water, sewerage or heating facilities, carried out in the course of repair or restoration, or maintenance in the nature of repair or restoration, of a building or structure, which is consistent with the original character or fabric of the building or structure;

"the Temple Bar Area" means the area described in paragraph 2 of Schedule 6.

(2) The provisions specified in this Chapter as applying in relation to capital or other expenditure incurred or rent payable in relation to any building or premises (however described in this Chapter) in the Temple Bar Area shall apply only if the relevant building or premises, in relation to which that capital or other expenditure was incurred or rent is so payable, is approved for the purposes of this Chapter by the company known as Temple Bar Renewal Limited.

(3) Notwithstanding any other provision of the Tax Acts, where part of a building or structure is used for commercial purposes and part is used for residential purposes, the

total amount of the expenditure incurred on the construction or refurbishment of the building or structure shall be apportioned as between the respective parts of the building or structure in such manner as is just and reasonable for the purpose of giving effect to this Chapter.

(4) Schedule 6 shall apply for the purposes of supplementing this Chapter.

Amendments

1 Definition of "qualifying period" substituted by FA 1999 s 43 with effect from 6 April 1999.

Revenue precedents

Issue: If in the course of "refurbishment" of a building in Temple Bar an extension is built on to part of the building will the expenditure on the addition qualify as "refurbishment"?
Decision: No. Such expenditure is not considered to be carried out on the repair or restoration of the building, rather it is considered to be new construction.

Former enactments

FA 1997 s 147.

331 Accelerated capital allowances in relation to construction or refurbishment of certain industrial buildings or structures

(1) This section shall apply to a building or structure—

(*a*) which is—

(i) constructed in the Temple Bar Area in the qualifying period, or

(ii) an existing building or structure in the Temple Bar Area as on the 1st day of January, 1991, and is the subject of refurbishment in the qualifying period,

and

(*b*) which is to be an industrial building or structure by reason of its use for a purpose specified in paragraph (*a*) or (*d*) of section 268(1).

(2) Section 271 shall apply in relation to capital expenditure incurred in the qualifying period on the construction or refurbishment of a building or structure to which this section applies as if—

(*a*) in subsection (1) of that section the definition of "industrial development agency" were deleted,

(*b*) in subsection (2)(*a*)(i) of that section "to which subsection (3) applies" were deleted,

(*c*) subsections (3) and (5) of that section were deleted, and

(*d*) (i) in the case where the capital expenditure is incurred on the construction of the building or structure, the following subsection were substituted for subsection (4) of that section:

"(4) An industrial building allowance shall be of an amount equal to 25 per cent of the capital expenditure mentioned in subsection (2).",

and

(ii) in the case where the capital expenditure is incurred on the refurbishment of the building or structure, the following subsection were substituted for subsection (4) of that section:

"(4) An industrial building allowance shall be of an amount equal to 50 per cent of the capital expenditure mentioned in subsection (2).".

(3) Section 273 shall apply in relation to capital expenditure incurred in the qualifying period on the construction or refurbishment of a building or structure to which this section applies—

(*a*) in the case where the capital expenditure is incurred on the construction of the building or structure as if—

(i) the definition of "industrial development agency" in subsection (1) of that section were deleted,

(ii) the following paragraph were substituted for paragraph (*b*) of subsection (2) of that section:

"(*b*) As respects any qualifying expenditure, any allowance made under section 272 and increased under paragraph (*a*) in respect of that expenditure, whether claimed for one chargeable period or more than one such period, shall not in the aggregate exceed 50 per cent of the amount of that qualifying expenditure.",

and

(iii) subsections (3) to (7) of that section were deleted,

and

(*b*) in the case where the capital expenditure is incurred on the refurbishment of the building or structure as if—

(i) in subsection (1) of that section the definition of "industrial development agency" were deleted, and

(ii) subsections (2)(*b*) and (3) to (7) of that section were deleted.

(4) For the purposes of this section, where capital expenditure is incurred in the qualifying period on the refurbishment of a building or structure to which this section applies, such expenditure shall be deemed to include the lesser of—

(*a*) any expenditure incurred on the purchase of the building or structure, other than expenditure incurred on the acquisition of, or of rights in or over, any land, and

(*b*) an amount which is equal to the value of the building or structure on the 1st day of January, 1991, other than any amount of such value as is attributable to, or to rights in or over, any land,

if the expenditure referred to in paragraph (*a*) or the amount referred to in paragraph (*b*), as the case may be, is not greater than the amount of the capital expenditure actually incurred in the qualifying period on the refurbishment of the building or structure.

(5) Notwithstanding section 274(1), in the case of a building or structure to which this section applies by reason of its use for a purpose specified in section 268(1)(*a*), no balancing charge shall be made by reason of any of the events specified in section 274(1) which occurs—

(*a*) more than 13 years after the building or structure was first used, or

(*b*) in a case where section 276 applies, more than 13 years after the capital expenditure on refurbishment of the building or structure was incurred.

(6) For the purposes only of determining, in relation to a claim for an allowance under section 271 or 273 as applied by this section, whether and to what extent capital expenditure incurred on the construction or refurbishment of an industrial building or structure is incurred or not incurred in the qualifying period, only such an amount of that capital expenditure as is properly attributable to work on the construction or, as the case may be, refurbishment of the building or structure actually carried out during the qualifying period shall (notwithstanding any other provision of the Tax Acts as to the time when any capital expenditure is or is to be treated as incurred) be treated as having been incurred in that period; but nothing in this subsection shall affect the operation of subsection (4).

(7) Where, in relation to capital expenditure incurred in the qualifying period on the construction or refurbishment of a building or structure to which this section applies, any allowance or charge has been made under the provisions of the Tax Acts relating to the making of allowances and charges in respect of capital expenditure incurred on the construction or refurbishment of an industrial building or structure by virtue of section 42 of the Finance Act, 1986, as applied by section 55 of the Finance Act, 1991, that allowance or charge shall be deemed to have been made under those provisions by virtue of this section.

Tax Briefing

TB29 Dec 1997 p 4 — Purchase of refurbished buildings: operation of TCA 1997 s 279 in context of Temple Bar "uplift" provided by subs (4).

Former enactments

FA 1997 s 148.

332 Capital allowances in relation to construction or refurbishment of certain commercial premises

(1) In this section—

"multi-storey car park" means a building or structure consisting of 3 or more storeys wholly or mainly in use for the purpose of providing, for members of the public generally without preference for any particular class of person, on payment of an appropriate charge, parking space for mechanically propelled vehicles;

"qualifying premises" means a building or structure which—

(*a*) (i) is constructed in the Temple Bar Area in the qualifying period, or

(ii) is an existing building or structure in the Temple Bar Area as on the 1st day of January, 1991, and is the subject of refurbishment in the qualifying period,

(*b*) apart from this section is not an industrial building or structure within the meaning of section 268, and (*c*) (i) is in use for the purposes of a trade or profession, or

(ii) whether or not it is so used, is let on bona fide commercial terms for such consideration as might be expected to be paid in a letting of the building or structure negotiated on an arm's length basis,

but does not include any part of a building or structure in use as or as part of a dwelling house.

(2) (*a*) Subject to subsections (3) to (8), the provisions of the Tax Acts relating to the making of allowances or charges in respect of capital expenditure incurred on the construction or refurbishment of an industrial building or structure shall, notwithstanding anything to the contrary in those provisions, apply—

(i) as if a qualifying premises were, at all times at which it is a qualifying premises, a building or structure in respect of which an allowance is to be made for the purposes of income tax or corporation tax, as the case may be, under Chapter 1 of Part 9 by reason of its use for a purpose specified in section 268(1)(*a*), and

(ii) where any activity carried on in the qualifying premises is not a trade, as if it were a trade.

(*b*) An allowance shall be given by virtue of this subsection in respect of any capital expenditure incurred on the construction or refurbishment of a qualifying premises only in so far as that expenditure is incurred in the qualifying period.

(3) Section 271 shall apply in relation to capital expenditure incurred in the qualifying period on the construction or refurbishment of a qualifying premises as if—

(*a*) in subsection (1) of that section the definition of "industrial development agency" were deleted,

(*b*) in subsection (2)(*a*)(i) of that section "to which subsection (3) applies" were deleted,

(*c*) subsections (3) and (5) of that section were deleted, and

(*d*) the following subsection were substituted for subsection (4) of that section:

"(4) An industrial building allowance shall be of an amount equal to 50 per cent of the capital expenditure mentioned in subsection (2).".

(4) Section 273 shall apply in relation to capital expenditure incurred in the qualifying period on the construction or refurbishment of a qualifying premises as if—

(*a*) in subsection (1) of that section the definition of "industrial development agency" were deleted, and

(*b*) subsections (2)(*b*) and (3) to (7) of that section were deleted.

(5) For the purposes of this section, where capital expenditure is incurred in the qualifying period on the refurbishment of a qualifying premises, such expenditure shall be deemed to include the lesser of—

(*a*) any expenditure incurred on the purchase of the building or structure, other than expenditure incurred on the acquisition of, or of rights in or over, any land, and (*b*) an amount which is equal to the value of the building or structure as on the 1st day of January, 1991, other than any amount of such value as is attributable to, or to rights in or over, any land,

if the expenditure referred to in paragraph (*a*) or the amount referred to in paragraph (*b*), as the case may be, is not greater than the amount of the capital expenditure actually incurred in the qualifying period on the refurbishment of the qualifying premises.

(6) Notwithstanding section 274(1), no balancing charge shall be made in relation to a qualifying premises by reason of any of the events specified in that section which occurs—

(*a*) more than 13 years after the qualifying premises was first used, or

(*b*) in a case where section 276 applies, more than 13 years after the capital expenditure on refurbishment of the qualifying premises was incurred.

(7) (*a*) Notwithstanding subsections (2) to (4), any allowance or charge which apart from this subsection would be made by virtue of subsection (2) in respect of capital expenditure incurred on the construction of a qualifying premises, other than a qualifying premises which is a multi-storey car park, shall be reduced to one-half of the amount which apart from this subsection would be the amount of that allowance or charge.

(*b*) For the purposes of paragraph (*a*), the amount of an allowance or charge to be reduced to one-half shall be computed as if—

(i) this subsection had not been enacted, and

(ii) effect had been given to all allowances taken into account in so computing that amount.

(*c*) Nothing in this subsection shall affect the operation of section 274(8).

(8) For the purposes only of determining, in relation to a claim for an allowance by virtue of subsection (2), whether and to what extent capital expenditure incurred on the construction or refurbishment of a qualifying premises is incurred or not incurred in the qualifying period, only such an amount of that capital expenditure as is properly attributable to work on the construction or, as the case may be, refurbishment of the premises actually carried out during the qualifying period shall (notwithstanding any other provision of the Tax Acts as to the time when any capital expenditure is or is to be treated as incurred) be treated as having been incurred in that period; but nothing in this subsection shall affect the operation of subsection (5).

(9) Where, in relation to capital expenditure incurred in the qualifying period on the construction or refurbishment of a qualifying premises, any allowance or charge has been made under the provisions of the Tax Acts relating to the making of allowances and charges in respect of capital expenditure incurred on the construction or refurbishment of an industrial building or structure by virtue of section 42 of the Finance Act, 1986, as applied by section 55 of the Finance Act, 1991, that allowance or charge shall be deemed to have been made under those provisions by virtue of this section.

Cross-references

Double rent allowance: s 333(1)(*a*) (qualifying premises).

Revenue precedents

Issue: Where retail units are contained in a development which incorporates a multi-storey car-park, are the retail units treated as part of the multi-storey car-park and do they accordingly qualify for capital allowances at the same rate as the carpark?

Decision: No. The retail units must be looked at in their own right and will qualify at the rate appropriate to them.

Tax Briefing

TB29 Dec 1997 p 4 — Purchase of refurbished buildings: operation of TCA 1997 s.279 in context of Temple Bar "uplift" provided by subs (5).

Former enactments

FA 1997 s 149.

333 Double rent allowance in respect of rent paid for certain business premises

(1) (*a*) In this section—

"lease", **"lessee"**, **"lessor"** and **"rent"** have the same meanings respectively as in Chapter 8 of Part 4;

"market value", in relation to a building or structure, means the price which the unencumbered fee simple of the building or structure would fetch if sold in the open market in such manner and subject to such conditions as might reasonably be calculated to obtain for the vendor the best price for the building or structure, less the part of that price which would be attributable to the acquisition of, or of rights in or over, the land on which the building or structure is constructed;

[**"qualifying lease"** means, subject to subsection (4), a lease in respect of a qualifying premises granted in the qualifying period, or granted in any subsequent period ending on or before 31 December 1999, on bona fide commercial terms by a lessor to a lessee not connected with the lessor, or with any other person entitled to a rent in respect of the qualifying premises, whether under that lease or any other lease;][1]

"qualifying premises" means a building or structure in the Temple Bar Area—

(i) (I) which is an industrial building or structure within the meaning of section 268(1), and in respect of which capital expenditure is incurred in the qualifying period for which an allowance is to be made for the purposes of income tax or corporation tax, as the case may be, under Chapter 1 of Part 9, or

(II) in respect of which an allowance is to be made, or, as respects rent payable under a qualifying lease entered into on or after the 18th day of April, 1991, will by virtue of section 279 be made, for the purposes of income tax or corporation tax, as the case may be, under Chapter 1 of Part 9 by virtue of section 332, and

(ii) which is let on bona fide commercial terms for such consideration as might be expected to be paid in a letting of the building or structure negotiated on an arm's length basis,

but, as respects rent payable under a qualifying lease entered into on or after the 6th day of May, 1993, where capital expenditure is incurred in the qualifying period on the refurbishment of a building or structure in respect of which an allowance is to be made for the purposes of income tax or corporation tax, as the case may be, under Chapter 1 of Part 9, the building or structure shall not be regarded as a qualifying premises unless the total amount of the expenditure so incurred is not less than an amount equal to 10 per cent of the market value of the building or structure immediately before that expenditure is incurred.

(*b*) For the purposes of this section but subject to paragraph (*c*), so much of a period, being a period when rent is payable by a person in relation to a qualifying premises under a qualifying lease, shall be a relevant rental period as does not exceed—

(i) 10 years, or

(ii) the period by which 10 years exceeds—

(I) any preceding period, or

(II) if there is more than one preceding period, the aggregate of those periods,

for which rent was payable—

(A) by that person or any other person, or

(B) as respects rent payable in relation to any qualifying premises under a qualifying lease entered into before the 11th day of April, 1994, by that person or any person connected with that person,

in relation to that premises under a qualifying lease.

(*c*) As respects rent payable in relation to any qualifying premises under a qualifying lease entered into before the 18th day of April, 1991, **"relevant rental period"**, in relation to a qualifying premises, means the period of 10 years commencing on the day on which rent in respect of that premises is first payable under any qualifying lease.

(2) Subject to subsection (3), where in the computation of the amount of the profits or gains of a trade or profession a person is apart from this section entitled to any deduction (in this subsection referred to as **"the first-mentioned deduction"**) on account of rent in respect of a qualifying premises occupied by such person for the purposes of that trade or profession which is payable by such person—

(*a*) for a relevant rental period, or

(*b*) as respects rent payable in relation to any qualifying premises under a qualifying lease entered into before the 18th day of April, 1991, in the relevant rental period,

in relation to that qualifying premises under a qualifying lease, such person shall be entitled in that computation to a further deduction (in this subsection referred to as **"the**

second-mentioned deduction") equal to the amount of the first-mentioned deduction but, as respects a qualifying lease granted on or after the 21st day of April, 1997, where the first-mentioned deduction is on account of rent payable by such person to a connected person, such person shall not be entitled in that computation to the second-mentioned deduction.

(3) Where a person holds an interest in a qualifying premises out of which interest a qualifying lease is created directly or indirectly in respect of that qualifying premises and in respect of rent payable under the qualifying lease a claim for a further deduction under this section is made, and such person or, as respects rent payable in relation to any qualifying premises under a qualifying lease entered into on or after the 6th day of May, 1993, either such person or another person connected with such person—

(*a*) takes under a qualifying lease a qualifying premises (in this subsection referred to as **"the second-mentioned premises"**) occupied by such person or such other person, as the case may be, for the purposes of a trade or profession, and

(*b*) is apart from this section entitled, in the computation of the amount of the profits or gains of that trade or profession, to a deduction on account of rent in respect of the second-mentioned premises,

then, unless such person or such other person, as the case may be, shows that the taking on lease of the second-mentioned premises was not undertaken for the sole or main benefit of obtaining a further deduction on account of rent under this section, such person or such other person, as the case may be, shall not be entitled in the computation of the amount of the profits or gains of that trade or profession to any further deduction on account of rent in respect of the second-mentioned premises.

(4) (*a*) In this subsection—

"current value", in relation to minimum lease payments, means the value of those payments discounted to their present value at a rate which, when applied at the inception of the lease to—

(i) those payments, including any initial payment but excluding any payment or part of any payment for which the lessor will be accountable to the lessee, and

(ii) any unguaranteed residual value of the qualifying premises, excluding any part of such value for which the lessor will be accountable to the lessee,

produces discounted present values the aggregate amount of which equals the amount of the fair value of the qualifying premises;

"fair value", in relation to a qualifying premises, means an amount equal to such consideration as might be expected to be paid for the premises on a sale negotiated on an arm's length basis less any grants receivable towards the purchase of the qualifying premises;

"inception of the lease" means the earlier of the time the qualifying premises is brought into use or the date from which rentals under the lease first accrue;

"minimum lease payments" means the minimum payments over the remaining part of the term of the lease to be paid to the lessor, and includes any residual amount to be paid to the lessor at the end of the term of the lease and guaranteed by the lessee or by a person connected with the lessee;

"unguaranteed residual value", in relation to a qualifying premises, means that part of the residual value of that premises at the end of a term of a lease, as estimated at the inception of the lease, the realisation of which by the lessor is not assured or is guaranteed solely by a person connected with the lessor.

(*b*) A finance lease, that is—

(i) a lease in respect of a qualifying premises where, at the inception of the lease, the aggregate of the current value of the minimum lease payments (including any initial payment but excluding any payment or part of any payment for which the lessor will be accountable to the lessee) payable by the lessee in relation to the lease amounts to 90 per cent or more of the fair value of the qualifying premises, or

(ii) a lease which in all the circumstances is considered to provide in substance for the lessee the risks and benefits associated with ownership of the qualifying premises other than legal title to that premises,

shall not be a qualifying lease for the purposes of this section.

(5) In determining whether a period is a relevant rental period for the purposes of this section, rent payable by any person in relation to a premises in respect of which a further deduction was given under section 45 of the Finance Act, 1986, as applied by section 55 of the Finance Act, 1991 (or would have been so given but for the operation of paragraph (*b*) of the proviso to subsection (2) of section 45 of the Finance Act, 1986), shall be treated as having been payable by that person in relation to the premises under a qualifying lease.

Amendments

1 Definition of "qualifying lease" substituted by FA 2000 s 37 with effect from 6 April 2000.

Cross-references

Life assurance companies, acquisition expenses: s 708(1).

Restriction on use by certain partnerships of certain losses, etc, transitional arrangements, subs (2): s 1017(2C)(*a*) ("specified deduction").

Revenue precedents

Issue: The total amount of expenditure incurred on refurbishment may not be less than an amount equal to 10% of the market value of the building immediately before that expenditure is incurred. The issue arises as to whether in computing that total amount, the expenditure incurred by the lessee as well as the lessor may be taken into account.

Decision: The total amount of the expenditure incurred on refurbishment includes the expenditure incurred by the vendor as well as the purchaser. In such a case, the market value to be used is the market value immediately before the expenditure incurred by the vendor.

Former enactments

FA 1997 s 150; FA 1990 s 33(1), (2)(*a*).

334 Rented residential accommodation: deduction for certain expenditure on construction

Amendments

1 Section 334 repealed by FA 2002 s 24(3)(*b*) with effect from 1 January 2002; but see now TCA 1997 Pt 10 Ch 11 (ss 372AK–372AV) which codified, with effect from 1 January 2002, reliefs for lessors and owner-

occupiers in respect of expenditure incurred on the provision of certain residential accommodation, and in particular s 372AU which provides a saver for relief due, and for a clawback of relief given, under old schemes.

335 Rented residential accommodation: deduction for certain expenditure on conversion

Amendments

1 Section 335 repealed by FA 2002 s 24(3)(*b*) with effect from 1 January 2002; but see now TCA 1997 Pt 10 Ch 11 (ss 372AK–372AV) which codified, with effect from 1 January 2002, reliefs for lessors and owner-occupiers in respect of expenditure incurred on the provision of certain residential accommodation, and in particular s 372AU which provides a saver for relief due, and for a clawback of relief given, under old schemes.

336 Rented residential accommodation: deduction for certain expenditure on refurbishment

Amendments

1 Section 336 repealed by FA 2002 s 24(3)(*b*) with effect from 1 January 2002; but see now TCA 1997 Pt 10 Ch 11 (ss 372AK–372AV) which codified, with effect from 1 January 2002, reliefs for lessors and owner-occupiers in respect of expenditure incurred on the provision of certain residential accommodation, and in particular s 372AU which provides a saver for relief due, and for a clawback of relief given, under old schemes.

337 Residential accommodation: allowance to owner-occupiers in respect of certain expenditure on construction or refurbishment

Amendments

1 Section 337 repealed by FA 2002 s 24(3)(*b*) with effect from 1 January 2002; but see now TCA 1997 Pt 10 Ch 11 (ss 372AK–372AV) which codified, with effect from 1 January 2002, reliefs for lessors and owner-occupiers in respect of expenditure incurred on the provision of certain residential accommodation, and in particular s 372AU which provides a saver for relief due, and for a clawback of relief given, under old schemes.

338 Provisions supplementary to sections 334 to 337

Amendments

1 Section 338 repealed by FA 2002 s 24(3)(*b*) with effect from 1 January 2002; but see now TCA 1997 Pt 10 Ch 11 (ss 372AK–372AV) which codified, with effect from 1 January 2002, reliefs for lessors and owner-occupiers in respect of expenditure incurred on the provision of certain residential accommodation, and in particular s 372AU which provides a saver for relief due, and for a clawback of relief given, under old schemes.

CHAPTER 3

Designated Areas, Designated Streets, Enterprise Areas and Multi-Storey Car Parks in Certain Urban Areas

Tax Briefing

TB24 Dec 1996 p 10 — Incentives in Enterprise Areas.

339 Interpretation (Chapter 3)

(1) In this Chapter—

"designated area" and **"designated street"** mean respectively an area or areas or a street or streets specified as a designated area or a designated street, as the case may be, by order under section 340;

"enterprise area" means—

(*a*) an area or areas specified as an enterprise area by order under section 340, or
(*b*) an area or area described in Schedule 7;

"lease", **"lessee"**, **"lessor"**, **"premium"** and **"rent"** have the same meanings respectively as in Chapter 8 of Part 4;

"market value", in relation to a building, structure or house, means the price which the unencumbered fee simple of the building, structure or house would fetch if sold in the open market in such manner and subject to such conditions as might reasonably be calculated to obtain for the vendor the best price for the building, structure or house, less the part of that price which would be attributable to the acquisition of, or of rights in or over, the land on which the building, structure or house is constructed;

"qualifying period" means—

(*a*) subject to subsection (2) and section 340 and other than for the purposes of section 344, the period commencing on the 1st day of August, 1994, and ending on the 31st day of July, 1997, or
(*b*) in respect of an area or areas described in Schedule 7, the period commencing on the 1st day of July, 1997, and ending on the [31st day of December, 1999];[1]

"refurbishment", in relation to a building or structure and other than for the purposes of sections 348 and 349, means any work of construction, reconstruction, repair or renewal, including the provision or improvement of water, sewerage or heating facilities, carried out in the course of the repair or restoration, or maintenance in the nature of repair or restoration, of the building or structure;

"the relevant local authority", in relation to the construction of, conversion into, refurbishment of, or, as the case may be, construction or refurbishment of a building or structure to which [paragraph (*a*) or (*e*) of subsection (2)][2] applies, means the council of a county or the corporation of a county or other borough or, where appropriate, the urban district council, in whose functional area the qualifying premises is situated;

"street" includes part of a street and the whole or part of any road, square, quay or lane.

(2) (*a*) Where in relation to the construction of, conversion into, refurbishment of, or, as the case may be, construction or refurbishment of a building or structure which is—

(i) to be an industrial building or structure to which section 341 applies,
(ii) a qualifying premises within the respective meanings assigned in sections 342, 345 (other than a building or structure to which paragraph (*a*)(v) of that meaning in that section applies), 346, 347, 348 and 349, or
(iii) a qualifying building within the meaning of section 343,

the relevant local authority gives a certificate in writing, on or before the 30th day of September, 1997, to the person constructing, converting or refurbishing, as the case may be, such a building or structure stating that it is satisfied that not less than 15 per cent of the total cost of the building or structure had been incurred before the 31st day of July, 1997, then, [the reference in paragraph (*a*) of the definition of **"qualifying period"** in subsection (1) to the period ending on the 31st day of July, 1997, shall be construed as a reference to the period ending on the 31st day of July, 1998.][3]

(*b*) In considering whether to give a certificate referred to in paragraph (*a*), the relevant local authority shall have regard only to the guidelines in relation to the giving of such certificates entitled **"Extension from 31 July, 1997, to 31 July, 1998, of the time limit for qualifying expenditure on developments"** issued by the Department of the Environment on the 28th day of January, 1997.

[(*c*) Where in relation to the construction of, conversion into, refurbishment of, or, as the case may be, construction or refurbishment of a building or structure to which paragraph (*a*) relates—

(i) the relevant local authority has given to the person constructing, converting or refurbishing, as the case may be, that building or structure, a certificate in writing to which that paragraph refers certifying that not less than 15 per cent of the total cost of the building or structure had been incurred before the 31st day of July, 1997, and

(ii) an application for planning permission for the work represented by the expenditure incurred or to be incurred on the building or structure had (in so far as such permission is required) been received by a planning authority not later than the 1st day of March, 1998, and

(iii) where the expenditure to be incurred on a building or structure has not been fully incurred by the 31st day of July, 1998, the relevant local authority gives a certificate in writing to the person referred to in subparagraph (i) stating that in its opinion—

(I) that person had, on the 31st day of July, 1997, a reasonable expectation that the expenditure to be incurred on the building or structure would have been incurred in full on or before the 31st day of July, 1998, and

(II) the failure to incur that expenditure in full on or before the 31st day of July, 1998, was, on the basis of reasons of a bona fide character stated to it, due, to a significant extent, to a delay outside the direct control of that person, including an unanticipated delay in obtaining the grant of planning permission or a fire certificate, an unanticipated delay due to legal proceedings or unanticipated difficulties in completing the acquisition of a site or involving the failure of a building contractor to fulfil his or her obligations or the need to respect any archaeological site or remains,

then, the reference in paragraph (*a*) of the definition of **"qualifying period"** to the period ending on the 31st day of July, 1997, shall be construed as a reference to the period ending on the 31st day of December, 1998.][4]

[(*d*) Where, in relation to the construction of, conversion into, refurbishment of, or, as the case may be, construction or refurbishment of a building or structure which complies with the requirements of subparagraphs (i), (ii) and (iii) of paragraph (*c*), being a qualifying premises within the meaning of section 346, 347, 348 or 349, where—

(i) the expenditure to be incurred on the house has not been fully incurred by the 31st day of December, 1998, and

(ii) the relevant local authority gives a certificate in writing on or before the 28th day of February, 1999, to the person constructing, converting or refurbishing, as the case may be, the house stating that it is satisfied that not less than 50 per cent of the total cost of the house and the site thereof had been incurred on or before the 31st day of December, 1998,

then, the reference in paragraph (*a*) of the definition of "qualifying period" in subsection (1) to the period ending on the 31st day of July, 1997, shall be construed as a reference to the period ending on the 30th day of April, 1999.][5]

[(*e*) (i) Where, in relation to the construction or refurbishment of a qualifying building within the meaning of section 343, the relevant local authority gives a certificate in writing on or before 31 May 2000 to the person constructing or refurbishing the qualifying building stating that it is satisfied that not less than 50 per cent of the total cost of the qualifying building and the site thereof had been incurred on or before 31 December 1999, then the reference in paragraph (*b*) of the definition of "qualifying period" in subsection (1) to the period ending on the 31st day of December, 1999, shall be construed as a reference to the period ending on 31 December 2000.

(ii) In considering whether to give such a certificate, the relevant local authority shall have regard only to guidelines in relation to the giving of such certificates issued by the Department of the Environment and Local Government.][6]

(3) Schedule 7 shall apply for the purposes of supplementing this Chapter.

Amendments

1 Substituted by FA 1998 s 24(1)(*a*)(i) with effect from 6 April 1998; previously "30th day of June, 2000".

2 Substituted by FA 2000 s 42(1)(*a*)(i) with effect from 1 July 1999; previously "subsection (2)(*a*)".

3 Substituted by FA 1998 s 24(1)(*a*)(ii)(I) with effect from 6 April 1998; previously "the reference in paragraph (*a*) of the definition of "qualifying period" to ending on the 31st day of July, 1997, shall be construed as a reference to ending on the 31st day of July, 1998.

4 Subs (2)(*c*) inserted by FA 1998 s 24(1)(*a*)(ii)(II) with effect from 6 April 1998.

5 Subs (2)(*d*) inserted by FA 1999 s 44(*a*) with effect from 6 April 1999.

6 Subs (2)(*e*) inserted by FA 2000 s 42(1)(*a*)(ii) with effect from 1 July 1999.

Cross-references

Ministerial power: s 340(1)(*a*), (2)(ii).

Double rent allowance, qualifying lease, subs (2)(*a*): s 345(1).

Revenue precedents

Issue: A developer receives a certificate from a relevant local authority certifying that not less than 15% of the total project costs have been incurred before 31/7/97. The developer sells on the site. Is the vendor entitled to be regarded as the person constructing the building for the purposes of TCA 1997 s 339(2)(*a*)?

Decision: In the event of a development site being sold, the person constructing, converting or refurbishing the building may be regarded as the person to whom the relevant local authority has given a certificate under s 339(2)(*a*) if no change occurs in the project as submitted by the vendors.

Issue: Is it Revenue practice to accept that site costs may be included in the computation of the cost of construction of a building for the purposes of s 339(2)(*a*)?

Decision: The reference to 15% of the total cost of the building in the section may be construed as 15% of the total project costs including site costs.

Definitions

person: IA 1937 s 11(*c*); writing: IA 1937 Sch.

Former enactments

FA 1994 s 38(1); FA 1995 s 35(1)(*a*); FA 1997 s 26(*a*).

340 Designated areas, designated streets and enterprise areas

(1) The Minister for Finance may, after consultation with the Minister for the Environment and Local Government, by order direct that—

(*a*) the area or areas, or street or streets, described in the order shall be a designated area, a designated street or, as the case may be, an enterprise area for the purposes of this Chapter, and

(*b*) as respects any such area or any such street so described, the definition of **"qualifying period"** in section 339 shall be construed as a reference to such period as shall be specified in the order in relation to that area or, as the case may be, that street; but no such period specified in the order shall commence before the 1st day of August, 1994, or end after the 31st day of July, 1997 [, or, as the case may be, after the day to which the reference to the 31st day of July, 1997, is, by virtue of section 339(2), to be construed].[1]

(2) The Minister for Finance may, after consultation with the Minister for Public Enterprise and following receipt of a proposal from or on behalf of a company intending to carry on qualifying trading operations (within the meaning of section 343) in an area or areas immediately adjacent to any of the airports commonly known as—

(*a*) Cork Airport,

(*b*) Donegal Airport,

(*c*) Galway Airport,

(*d*) Kerry Airport,

(*e*) Knock International Airport,

(*f*) Sligo Airport, or

(*g*) Waterford Airport,

being a company which, if those trading operations were to be carried on in an area which apart from this subsection would be an enterprise area, would be a qualifying company (within the meaning of section 343), by order direct that—

(i) the area or areas described in the order shall be an enterprise area for the purposes of this Chapter, and

[(ii) as respects any such area so described in the order, the reference in paragraph (*a*) of the definition of "qualifying period" in section 339(1) to the period commencing on the 1st day of August, 1994, and ending on the 31st day of July, 1997, shall be construed as a reference to such period as shall be specified in the order in relation to that area, but no such period specified in the order shall commence before 1 August 1994 or end after—

(I) 31 December 1999, or

(II) 31 December 2000, where in relation to the construction or refurbishment of a qualifying building within the meaning of section 343, the relevant local authority gives a certificate in writing on or before 31 May 2000 to the person constructing or refurbishing the qualifying building stating that it is satisfied that not less than 50 per cent of the total cost of the qualifying building and the site thereof had been incurred on or before 31 December 1999 and, in considering whether to give such a certificate, the relevant local authority shall have regard only to guidelines in relation to the giving of such certificates issued by the Department of the Environment and Local Government.][2]

(3) Every order made by the Minister for Finance under subsection (1) or (2) shall be laid before Dáil Éireann as soon as may be after it is made and, if a resolution annulling the order is passed by Dáil Éireann within the next 21 days on which Dáil Éireann has sat after the order is laid before it, the order shall be annulled accordingly, but without prejudice to the validity of anything previously done thereunder.

Amendments

1 Inserted by FA 1999 s 44(*b*) with effect from 6 April 1999.

2 Subs (2)(ii) substituted by FA 2000 s 42(1)(*b*) with effect from 1 July 1999.

Cross-references

Capital allowances for buildings in enterprise areas, subs (2): s 343(1) (qualifying trading operations), (8)(*a*)(iv), (11).

Double rent allowance, subss (1)(*a*), (2)(i): s 345(1)(qualifying lease).

Interpretation (Chapter 3), meanings of "designated area", "designated street" and "enterprise area": s 339(1).

Ministerial Orders

Taxes Consolidation Act 1997 (Designation of Urban Renewal Areas) Order 2000 (SI No 260 of 2000).

Definitions

Dáil Éireann: IA 1937 Sch.

Former enactments

FA 1994 s 39; FA 1995 s 35(1)(*b*); FA 1997 s 26(*b*).

341 Accelerated capital allowances in relation to construction or refurbishment of certain industrial buildings or structures

(1) This section shall apply to a building or structure the site of which is wholly within a designated area, or which fronts on to a designated street, and which is to be an industrial building or structure by reason of its use for a purpose specified in section 268(1)(*a*).

(2) Subject to subsection (4), section 271 shall apply in relation to capital expenditure incurred in the qualifying period on the construction or refurbishment of a building or structure to which this section applies as if—

(*a*) in subsection (1) of that section the definition of "industrial development agency" were deleted,

(*b*) in subsection (2)(*a*)(i) of that section "to which subsection (3) applies" were deleted,

(*c*) subsection (3) of that section were deleted,

(*d*) the following subsection were substituted for subsection (4) of that section:

"(4) An industrial building allowance shall be of an amount equal to 25 per cent of the capital expenditure mentioned in subsection (2).",

and

(*e*) in subsection (5) of that section "to which subsection (3)(*c*) applies" were deleted.

(3) Subject to subsection (4), section 273 shall apply in relation to capital expenditure incurred in the qualifying period on the construction or refurbishment of a building or structure to which this section applies as if—

(*a*) in subsection (1) of that section the definition of "industrial development agency" were deleted,

(*b*) the following paragraph were substituted for paragraph (*b*) of subsection (2) of that section:

"(*b*) As respects any qualifying expenditure, any allowance made under section 272 and increased under paragraph (*a*) in respect of that expenditure, whether claimed for one chargeable period or more than one such period, shall not in the aggregate exceed 50 per cent of the amount of that qualifying expenditure.",

and

(*c*) subsections (3) to (7) of that section were deleted.

(4) (*a*) In the case of an industrial building or structure which fronts on to a designated street, subsections (2) and (3) shall apply only in relation to capital expenditure incurred in the qualifying period on the refurbishment of the industrial building or structure and only if the following conditions are satisfied—

(i) that the industrial building or structure was comprised in an existing building or structure (in this subsection referred to as **"the existing building"**) on the 1st day of August, 1994, which fronts on to the designated street, and

(ii) that, apart from the capital expenditure incurred in the qualifying period on the refurbishment of the industrial building or structure, expenditure is incurred on the existing building which is—

(I) conversion expenditure within the meaning of section 347,

(II) relevant expenditure within the meaning of section 348, or

(III) qualifying expenditure within the meaning of section 349 (being qualifying expenditure on refurbishment within the meaning of that section),

and in respect of which a deduction has been given, or would on due claim being made be given, under section 347, 348 or 349, as the case may be.

(*b*) Notwithstanding paragraph (*a*), subsections (2) and (3) shall not apply in relation to so much (if any) of the capital expenditure incurred in the qualifying period on the refurbishment of the industrial building or structure as exceeds the amount of the deduction, or the aggregate amount of the deductions, which has been given, or which would on due claim being made be given, under section 347, 348 or 349, as the case may be, in respect of the conversion expenditure, the relevant expenditure or, as the case may be, the qualifying expenditure.

(5) Notwithstanding section 274(1), no balancing charge shall be made in relation to a building or structure to which this section applies by reason of any of the events specified in that section which occurs—

(*a*) more than 13 years after the building or structure was first used, or

(*b*) in a case where section 276 applies, more than 13 years after the capital expenditure on refurbishment of the building or structure was incurred.

(6) For the purposes only of determining, in relation to a claim for an allowance under section 271 or 273 as applied by this section, whether and to what extent capital expenditure incurred on the construction or refurbishment of an industrial building or structure is incurred or not incurred in the qualifying period, only such an amount of that capital expenditure as is properly attributable to work on the construction or, as the case may be, the refurbishment of the building or structure actually carried out during the qualifying period shall (notwithstanding any other provision of the Tax Acts as to the time when any capital expenditure is or is to be treated as incurred) be treated as having been incurred in that period.

Cross-references

Commercial building: s 342(2)(*a*).
Double rent allowance: s 345(1) (qualifying premises).
Enterprise area building: s 343(7)(*a*).
Local authority certificate stating 15% of building cost incurred before 31 July 1997: s 339(2)(*a*)(i).
Multi-storey car parks: s 344(2).

Definitions

Tax Acts: s 1(2).

Former enactments

FA 1994 s 40; FA 1995 s 35(1)(*c*).

342 Capital allowances in relation to construction or refurbishment of certain commercial premises

(1) (*a*) In this section, **"qualifying premises"** means a building or structure the site of which is wholly within a designated area, or which fronts on to a designated street, and which—

(i) apart from this section is not an industrial building or structure within the meaning of section 268, and

(ii) (I) is in use for the purposes of a trade or profession, or

(II) whether or not it is so used, is let on bona fide commercial terms for such consideration as might be expected to be paid in a letting of the building or structure negotiated on an arm's length basis,

but does not include any part of a building or structure in use as or as part of a dwelling house or an office.

(*b*) Notwithstanding paragraph (*a*)—

(i) in relation to a building or structure no part of the site of which is within any one of the county boroughs of Dublin, Cork, Limerick, Galway or Waterford, paragraph (*a*) shall be construed as if **"or an office"** were deleted;

(ii) where, in relation to a building or structure any part of the site of which is within any one of the county boroughs of Dublin, Cork, Limerick, Galway or Waterford, any part (in this paragraph referred to as **"the specified part"**) of the building or structure is not a qualifying premises and—

(I) the specified part is in use as, or as part of, an office, and

(II) the capital expenditure incurred in the qualifying period on the construction or refurbishment of the specified part is not more than 10 per cent of the total capital expenditure incurred in that period on the construction or refurbishment of the building or structure,

then, the specified part shall be treated as a qualifying premises.

(2) (*a*) Subject to subsections (3) to (6), the provisions of the Tax Acts (other than section 341) relating to the making of allowances or charges in respect of capital expenditure incurred on the construction or refurbishment of an industrial building or structure shall, notwithstanding anything to the contrary in those provisions, apply—

(i) as if a qualifying premises were, at all times at which it is a qualifying premises, a building or structure in respect of which an allowance is to be made for the purposes of income tax or corporation tax, as the case may be, under Chapter 1 of Part 9 by reason of its use for a purpose specified in section 268(1)(*a*), and

(ii) where any activity carried on in the qualifying premises is not a trade, as if it were a trade.

(*b*) An allowance shall be given by virtue of this subsection in respect of any capital expenditure incurred on the construction or refurbishment of a qualifying premises only in so far as that expenditure is incurred in the qualifying period.

(3) (*a*) In the case of a qualifying premises which fronts on to a designated street, subsection (2) shall apply only in relation to capital expenditure incurred in the qualifying period on the refurbishment of the qualifying premises and only if the following conditions are satisfied—

(i) that the qualifying premises were comprised in an existing building or structure (in this subsection referred to as **"the existing building"**) on the 1st day of August, 1994, which fronts on to the designated street, and

(ii) that, apart from the capital expenditure incurred in the qualifying period on the refurbishment of the qualifying premises, expenditure is incurred on the existing building which is—

(I) conversion expenditure within the meaning of section 347,

(II) relevant expenditure within the meaning of section 348, or

(III) qualifying expenditure within the meaning of section 349 (being qualifying expenditure on refurbishment within the meaning of that section),

and in respect of which a deduction has been given, or would on due claim being made be given, under section 347, 348 or 349, as the case may be.

(*b*) Notwithstanding paragraph (*a*), subsection (2) shall not apply in relation to so much (if any) of the capital expenditure incurred in the qualifying period on the refurbishment of the qualifying premises as exceeds the amount of the deduction, or the aggregate amount of the deductions, which has been given, or which would on due claim being made be given, under section 347, 348 or 349, as the case may be, in respect of the conversion expenditure, the relevant expenditure or, as the case may be, the qualifying expenditure.

(4) For the purposes of the application, by subsection (2), of sections 271 and 273 in relation to capital expenditure incurred in the qualifying period on the construction or refurbishment of a qualifying premises—

(*a*) section 271 shall apply as if—

(i) in subsection (1) of that section the definition of "industrial development agency" were deleted,

(ii) in subsection (2)(*a*)(i) of that section "to which subsection (3) applies" were deleted,

(iii) subsection (3) of that section were deleted,

(iv) the following subsection were substituted for subsection (4) of that section:

"(4) An industrial building allowance shall be of an amount equal to 50 per cent of the capital expenditure mentioned in subsection (2).",

and

(v) in subsection (5) of that section "to which subsection (3)(*c*) applies" were deleted,

and

(*b*) section 273 shall apply as if—

(i) in subsection (1) of that section the definition of "industrial development agency" were deleted, and

(ii) subsections (2)(*b*) and (3) to (7) of that section were deleted.

(5) Notwithstanding section 274(1), no balancing charge shall be made in relation to a qualifying premises by reason of any of the events specified in that section which occurs—

(*a*) more than 13 years after the qualifying premises was first used, or

(*b*) in a case where section 276 applies, more than 13 years after the capital expenditure on refurbishment of the qualifying premises was incurred.

(6) (*a*) Notwithstanding subsections (2) to (5), any allowance or charge which apart from this subsection would be made by virtue of subsection (2) in respect of capital expenditure incurred on the construction or refurbishment of a qualifying premises shall be reduced to one-half of the amount which apart from this subsection would be the amount of that allowance or charge.

(*b*) For the purposes of paragraph (*a*), the amount of an allowance or charge to be reduced to one-half shall be computed as if—

(i) this subsection had not been enacted, and

(ii) effect had been given to all allowances taken into account in so computing that amount.

(*c*) Nothing in this subsection shall affect the operation of section 274(8).

(7) For the purposes only of determining, in relation to a claim for an allowance by virtue of subsection (2), whether and to what extent capital expenditure incurred on the construction or refurbishment of a qualifying premises is incurred or not incurred in the qualifying period, only such an amount of that capital expenditure as is properly attributable to work on the construction or refurbishment of the premises actually carried out during the qualifying period shall (notwithstanding any other provision of the Tax Acts as to the time when any capital expenditure is or is to be treated as incurred) be treated as having been incurred in that period.

Cross-references

Double rent allowance: s 345(1) (qualifying premises).

Local authority certificate stating 15% of building cost incurred before 31 July 1997: s 339(2)(*a*)(ii).

Revenue precedents

Issue: Where there is a mix of residential and commercial units in a building, in an Urban Renewal Area, does the 10% rule in relation to offices apply to the total expenditure on commercial premises only or to the whole building, including the residential units?

Decision: Where the capital expenditure incurred on the provision of office accommodation in the qualifying period is not more than 10% of the capital expenditure incurred in that period on the entirety of the building or structure housing the office accommodation, the office will be regarded as a qualifying premises for the purposes of TCA 1997 s 342(1).

Issue: Is the beneficiary of a Settlement Trust entitled to capital allowances on a property situated in an Urban Renewal area if the expenditure is incurred by the Trust?

Decision: Expenditure incurred by trustees of a Settlement Trust is not construed as expenditure incurred by beneficiaries of the Trust for the purpose of TCA 1997 Pt 10, Ch 3.

Definitions

profession: s 2(1); tax: s 3(1); trade: ss 3(1), 4(1), 5(1); year: IA 1937 Sch.

Former enactments

FA 1994 s 41; FA 1995 s 35(1)(*d*).

343 Capital allowances in relation to construction or refurbishment of certain buildings or structures in enterprise areas

(1) In this section—

[**"property developer"** means a person carrying on a trade which consists wholly or mainly of the construction or refurbishment of buildings or structures with a view to their sale;][1]

"the Minister", except where the context otherwise requires, means the Minister for Enterprise, Trade and Employment;

"qualifying building" means a building or structure the site of which is wholly within an enterprise area and which is in use for the purposes of the carrying on of qualifying trading operations by a qualifying company, but does not include any part of a building or structure in use as or as part of a dwelling house;

[**"qualifying company"** means a company—

(*a*) (i) which has been approved for financial assistance under a scheme administered by Forfás, Enterprise Ireland, the Industrial Development Agency (Ireland) or Udarás na Gaeltachta, or

(ii) which is engaged in a qualifying trading operation within the meaning of paragraph (*c*) of the definition of "qualifying trading operations",

and

(*b*) to which the Minister has given a certificate under subsection (2) which has not been withdrawn in accordance with subsection (5) or (6);][2]

"qualifying trading operations" means—

[(*a*) the manufacture of goods within the meaning of Part 14,

(*b*) the rendering of services in the course of a service industry (within the meaning of the Industrial Development Act, 1986), or

(*c*) the rendering of services in the course or furtherance of a business of freight forwarding or the provision of logistical services in relation to such business where the rendering or provision of those services is carried on in an area or areas immediately adjacent to any of the airports to which section 340(2) refers.][3]

(2) Subject to subsection (4), the Minister may—

[(*a*) on the recommendation of Forfás (in conjunction with Enterprise Ireland, the Industrial Development Agency (Ireland) or Udarás na Gaeltachta, as may be appropriate, or the Minister for Public Enterprise in the case of a company to which paragraph (*a*)(ii) of the definition of "qualifying company" refers) in accordance with guidelines laid down by the Minister, and][4]

(*b*) following consultation with the Minister for Finance,

give a certificate to a company certifying that the company is, with effect from a date to be specified in the certificate, to be treated as a qualifying company for the purposes of this section.

(3) A certificate under subsection (2) may be given either without conditions or subject to such conditions as the Minister considers proper and specifies in the certificate.

(4) The Minister shall not certify under subsection (2) that a company is a qualifying company for the purposes of this section unless—

(*a*) the company is carrying on or intends to carry on qualifying trading operations in an enterprise area, and

(*b*) the Minister is satisfied that the carrying on by the company of such trading operations will contribute to the balanced development of the enterprise area.

(5) Where, in the case of a company in relation to which a certificate under subsection (2) has been given—

(*a*) the company ceases to carry on or, as the case may be, fails to commence to carry on qualifying trading operations in the enterprise area, or

(*b*) the Minister is satisfied that the company has failed to comply with any condition subject to which the certificate was given, the Minister may, by notice in writing served by registered post on the company, revoke the certificate with effect from such date as may be specified in the notice.

(6) Where, in the case of a company in relation to which a certificate under subsection (2) has been given, the Minister is of the opinion that any activity of the company has had or may have an adverse effect on the use or development of the enterprise area or is otherwise inimical to the balanced development of the enterprise area, then—

(*a*) the Minister may, by notice in writing served by registered post on the company, require the company to desist from such activity with effect from such date as may be specified in the notice, and

(*b*) if the Minister is not satisfied that the company has complied with the requirements of the notice, the Minister may, by a further notice in writing served by registered post on the company, revoke the certificate with effect from such date as may be specified in the further notice.

(7) (*a*) Subject to [subsections (8), (9) and (11)],[5] the provisions of the Tax Acts (other than section 341) relating to the making of allowances or charges in respect of capital expenditure incurred on the construction or refurbishment of an industrial building or structure shall, notwithstanding anything to the contrary in those provisions, apply as if a qualifying building were, at all times at which it is a qualifying building, a building or structure in respect of which an allowance is to be made for the purposes of income tax or corporation tax, as the case may be, under Chapter 1 of Part 9 by reason of its use for a purpose specified in section 268(1)(*a*).

(*b*) An allowance shall be given by virtue of this subsection in respect of any capital expenditure incurred on the construction or refurbishment of a qualifying building only in so far as that expenditure is incurred in the qualifying period.

(8) For the purposes of the application, by subsection (7), of sections 271 and 273 in relation to capital expenditure incurred in the qualifying period on the construction or refurbishment of a qualifying building—

(*a*) section 271 shall apply as if—

(i) in subsection (1) of that section the definition of "industrial development agency" were deleted,

(ii) in subsection (2)(*a*)(i) of that section "to which subsection (3) applies" were deleted,

(iii) subsection (3) of that section were deleted,

[(iv) the following subsection were substituted for subsection (4) of that section:

"(4) An industrial building allowance, in the case of a qualifying building (within the meaning of section 343(1)), shall be of an amount equal to—

(*a*) 25 per cent, or

(*b*) in the case of such a building the site of which is wholly within an area described in an order referred to in section 340(2)(i), 50 per cent,

of the capital expenditure mentioned in subsection (2)."][6]

and

(v) in subsection (5) of that section "to which subsection (3)(*c*) applies" were deleted,

and

(*b*) section 273 shall apply as if—

(i) in subsection (1) of that section the definition of "industrial development agency" were deleted,

(ii) the following paragraph were substituted for paragraph (*b*) of subsection (2) of that section:

"(*b*) As respects any qualifying expenditure, any allowance made under section 272 and increased under paragraph (*a*) in respect of that expenditure, whether claimed for one chargeable period or more than one such period, shall not in the aggregate exceed 50 per cent of the amount of that qualifying expenditure.",

and

(iii) subsections (3) to (7) of that section were deleted.

(9) Notwithstanding section 274(1), no balancing charge shall be made in relation to a qualifying building by reason of any of the events specified in that section which occurs—

(*a*) more than 13 years after the qualifying building was first used, or

(*b*) in a case where section 276 applies, more than 13 years after the capital expenditure on refurbishment of the qualifying building was incurred.

(10) For the purposes only of determining, in relation to a claim for an allowance by virtue of subsection (7), whether and to what extent capital expenditure incurred on the construction or refurbishment of a qualifying building is incurred or not incurred in the qualifying period, only such an amount of that capital expenditure as is properly attributable to work on the construction or refurbishment of the building actually carried out during the qualifying period shall (notwithstanding any other provision of the Tax Acts as to the time when any capital expenditure is or is to be treated as incurred) be treated as having been incurred in that period.

[(11) Notwithstanding the preceding provisions of this section, this section shall not apply in respect of expenditure incurred on the construction or refurbishment of a qualifying building, the site of which is wholly within an area described in an order referred to in section 340(2)(i)—

(*a*) where a property developer is entitled to the relevant interest, within the meaning of section 269, in relation to that expenditure, and

(*b*) either the person referred to in paragraph (*a*) or a person connected (within the meaning of section 10) with that person incurred the expenditure on the construction or refurbishment of the qualifying building concerned.][7]

Amendments

1 Definition of "property developer" inserted by FA 2000 s 42(1)(*c*)(i) with effect from 1 July 1999.

2 Definition of "qualifying company" substituted by FA 1999 s 44(*c*)(i) with effect from 6 April 1999.

3 Definition of "qualifying trading operations" paras (*a*)–(*b*) substituted by FA 1998 s 24(1)(*c*)(ii) from such date as the Minister for Finance may appoint by order.

4 Subs (2)(*a*) substituted by FA 1999 s 44(*c*)(ii) with effect from 6 April 1999.

5 Substituted by FA 2000 s 42(1)(*c*)(ii) with effect from 1 July 1999; previously "subsections (8) and (9)".

6 Subs (8)(*a*)(iv) substituted by FA 1999 s 44(*c*)(iii) with effect from 1 January 1998.

7 Subs (11) inserted by FA 2000 s 42(1)(*c*)(iii) with effect from 1 July 1999.

Cross-references

Double rent allowance: s 345(1) (qualifying premises).
Interpretation: s 339(2)(*a*)(iii), (*e*)(i).
Ministerial power: s 340(2)(ii)(II).

Tax Briefing

TB41 Sept 2000 pp 16–18 — Industrial and Commercial Buildings Capital Allowances — Finance Act 2000 Restrictions.

Definitions

company: s 4(1); Tax Acts: s 1(2).

Former enactments

FA 1994 s 41A; FA 1995 s 35(1)(*e*).

---

344 Capital allowances in relation to construction or refurbishment of certain multi-storey car parks

(1) In this section—

"multi-storey car park" means a building or structure consisting of 2 or more storeys wholly in use for the purpose of providing, for members of the public generally without preference for any particular class of person, on payment of an appropriate charge, parking space for mechanically propelled vehicles;

"qualifying multi-storey car park" means a multi-storey car park in respect of which the relevant local authority gives a certificate in writing to the person providing the multi-storey car park stating that it is satisfied that the multi-storey car park has been developed in accordance with criteria laid down by the Minister for the Environment and Local Government following consultation with the Minister for Finance;

[**"qualifying period"** means the period commencing on the 1st day of July, 1995, and ending on—

(*a*) the 30th day of June, 1998, or

(*b*) [30 September 1999],[1] where, in relation to the construction or refurbishment of the qualifying multi-storey car park concerned, the relevant local authority gives a certificate in writing on or before the 30th day of September, 1998, to the person constructing or refurbishing the qualifying multi-storey car park stating that it is satisfied that not less than 15 per cent of the total cost of the qualifying multi-storey car park and the site thereof had been incurred prior to the 1st day of July, 1998, and, in considering whether to give such a certificate, the relevant local authority shall have regard only to guidelines in relation to the giving of such certificates issued by the Department of the Environment and Local Government for the purposes [of this definition, or][2]

[(*c*) [31 July 2006][3], where, in relation to the construction or refurbishment of the qualifying multi-storey car park concerned (not being a qualifying multi-storey car park any part of the site of which is within either of the county boroughs of Cork or Dublin), the relevant local authority gives a certificate in writing on or before [31 December 2003][4] to the person constructing or refurbishing the qualifying multi-storey car park stating that it is satisfied that not less than 15 per cent of the total cost of the qualifying multi-storey car park and the site thereof had been incurred on or before [30 September 2003][5] and, in considering whether to give such a certificate, the relevant local authority shall have regard only to guidelines in relation to the giving of such certificates issued by the Department of the Environment and Local Government for the purposes of this definition;][6]

"the relevant local authority", in relation to the construction or refurbishment of a multi-storey car park, means—

(*a*) the corporation of a county or other borough or, where appropriate, the urban district council, or

[(*b*) in respect of the administrative county, the council of the county concerned,][7]

in whose functional area the multi-storey car park is situated.

(2) (*a*) Subject to [subsections (3) to (6A)],[8] the provisions of the Tax Acts (other than section 341) relating to the making of allowances or charges in respect of capital expenditure incurred on the construction or refurbishment of an industrial building or structure shall, notwithstanding anything to the contrary in those provisions, apply as if a qualifying multi-storey car park were, at all times at which it is a qualifying multi-storey car park, a building or structure in respect of which an allowance is to be made for the purposes of income tax or corporation tax, as the case may be, under Chapter 1 of Part 9 by reason of its use for a purpose specified in section 268(1)(*a*).

(*b*) An allowance shall be given by virtue of this subsection in respect of any capital expenditure incurred on the construction or refurbishment of a qualifying multi-storey car park only in so far as that expenditure is incurred in the qualifying period.

(3) In a case where capital expenditure is incurred in the qualifying period on the refurbishment of a qualifying multi-storey car park, subsection (2) shall apply only if the total amount of the capital expenditure so incurred is not less than an amount equal to 20 per cent of the market value of the qualifying multi-storey car park immediately before that expenditure is incurred.

(4) For the purposes of the application, by subsection (2), of sections 271 and 273 in relation to capital expenditure incurred in the qualifying period on the construction or refurbishment of a qualifying multi-storey car park—

(*a*) section 271 shall apply as if—

(i) in subsection (1) of that section the definition of "industrial development agency" were deleted,

(ii) in subsection (2)(*a*)(i) of that section "to which subsection (3) applies" were deleted,

(iii) subsection (3) of that section were deleted,

(iv) the following subsection were substituted for subsection (4) of that section:

"(4) An industrial building allowance shall be of an amount equal to 50 per cent of the capital expenditure mentioned in subsection (2).",

and

(v) in subsection (5) of that section "to which subsection (3)(*c*) applies" were deleted,

and

(*b*) section 273 shall apply as if—

(i) in subsection (1) of that section, the definition of "industrial development agency" were deleted, and

(ii) subsections (2)(*b*) and (3) to (7) of that section were deleted.

(5) Notwithstanding section 274(1), no balancing charge shall be made in relation to a qualifying multi-storey car park by reason of any of the events specified in that section which occurs—

(*a*) more than 13 years after the qualifying multi-storey car park was first used, or

(*b*) in a case where section 276 applies, more than 13 years after the capital expenditure on refurbishment of the multi-storey car park was incurred.

(6) (*a*) Notwithstanding subsections (2) to (5), any allowance or charge which apart from this subsection would be made by virtue of subsection (2) in respect of capital expenditure incurred on the construction or refurbishment of a qualifying multi-storey car park shall be reduced to one-half of the amount which apart from this subsection would be the amount of that allowance or charge.

(*b*) For the purposes of paragraph (*a*), the amount of an allowance or charge to be reduced to one-half shall be computed as if—

(i) this subsection had not been enacted, and

(ii) effect had been given to all allowances taken into account in so computing that amount.

(*c*) Nothing in this subsection shall affect the operation of section 274(8).

[(6A) Subsection (6) shall apply and have effect as respects capital expenditure referred to in subsection (2)(*b*), which is incurred after the 31st day of July, 1998, only if a qualifying lease, within the meaning of section 345, is granted in respect of the qualifying multi-storey car park in respect of which that expenditure is incurred.][9]

(7) For the purposes only of determining, in relation to a claim for an allowance by virtue of subsection (2), whether and to what extent capital expenditure incurred on the construction or refurbishment of a qualifying multi-storey car park is incurred or not incurred in the qualifying period, only such an amount of that capital expenditure as is properly attributable to work on the construction or refurbishment of the qualifying multi-storey car park actually carried out during the qualifying period shall (notwithstanding any other provision of the Tax Acts as to the time when any capital expenditure is or is to be treated as incurred) be treated as having been incurred in that period.

(8) Where by virtue of subsection (2) an allowance is given under Chapter 1 of Part 9 in respect of capital expenditure incurred on the construction or refurbishment of a qualifying multi-storey car park, no allowance shall be given in respect of that expenditure under that Chapter by virtue of any other provision of the Tax Acts.

Note

In regard to the definition of "local authority", it should be noted that, by virtue of Local Government Act 2001 s 3(2) and Sch 2, reference in any other enactment to "county borough corporation", "borough corporation" (not being a county borough corporation), "council of a county" and "council of an urban district", and to similar or analagous expressions, are now to be construed as references to "City council", "Borough council of a borough mentioned in Chapter 1 of Part 1 of Schedule 6 to the Local Government Act 2001", "County council" and "Town council of a town mentioned in Chapter 2 of Part 1 of Schedule 6 to the Local Government Act 2001", respectively.

Amendments

1 Substituted by FA 2000 s 42(1)(*d*)(i)(I) with effect from 1 July 1999; previously "the 30th day of June, 1999".

2 Substituted by FA 1999 s 44(*d*)(i)(I) with effect from 6 April 1999; previously "of this definition;".

3 Substituted by FA 2004 s 26(1)(*a*) with effect from 1 January 2004; previously "31 December 2004".

4 Substituted by FA 2002 s 23(1)(*a*)(ii) with effect from 1 January 2002; previously "31 December 2001".

5 Substituted by FA 2002 s 23(1)(*a*)(iii) with effect from 1 January 2002; previously "30 September 2001".

6 Definition of "qualifying period" para (*c*) substituted by FA 2000 s 42(1)(*d*)(i)(II) with effect from 1 July 1999.

7 Definition of "the relevant local authority" para (*b*) substituted by FA 2000 s 42(1)(*d*)(ii) with effect from 1 July 1999.

8 Substituted by FA 1999 s 44(*d*)(ii) with effect from 6 April 1999; previously "subsections (3) to (6)".

9 Subs (6A) inserted by FA 1999 s 44(*d*)(iii) with effect from 6 April 1999.

Cross-references

Double rent allowance: s 345(1) (qualifying premises), (1A).
Qualifying period: s 339(1) (qualifying period).

Tax Briefing

TB18 No 2 of 1995 par2.5 p 11 — Capital Allowances for Multi-storey Car Parks.
TB21 Mar 1996 p 9 — Urban Renewal Relief — Multi-storey Car Parks.

Definitions

person: IA 1937 s 11(*c*); Tax Acts: s 1(2); writing: IA 1937 Sch.

Former enactments

FA 1994 s 41B; FA 1995 s 35(1)(*f*); FA 1996 s 26(1).

345 Double rent allowance in respect of rent paid for certain business premises

(1) In this section—

[**"qualifying lease"** means, subject to subsections (1A) and (8), a lease in respect of a qualifying premises granted in the qualifying period, or within the period of one year from the day next after the end of the qualifying period, on bona fide commercial terms by a lessor to a lessee not connected with the lessor, or with any other person entitled to a rent in respect of the qualifying premises, whether under that lease or any other lease but, notwithstanding the foregoing, a lease which would otherwise be a qualifying lease shall not be such a lease if granted in respect of a building or structure within the meaning of paragraph (*a*)(iii) of the definition of "qualifying premises" the site of which is wholly within an area—

(*a*) described in an order referred to in section 340(1)(*a*), if the lease is granted on or after the 31st day of July, 1999, or

(*b*) described in Schedule 7, if the lease is granted on or after the 31st day of December, 1999, or

(*c*) described in an order referred to in section 340(2)(i), irrespective of the date of the granting of the lease;][1]

"qualifying premises" means, subject to subsection (5)(*a*), a building or structure—

(*a*) (i) the site of which is wholly within a designated area and which is a building or structure in use for a purpose specified in section 268(1)(*a*), and in respect of which capital expenditure is incurred in the qualifying period for which an allowance is to be made, or will by virtue of section 279 be made, for the purposes of income tax or corporation tax, as the case may be, under section 271 or 273, as applied by section 341,

(ii) the site of which is wholly within a designated area and in respect of which an allowance is to be made, or will by virtue of section 279 be made, for the purposes of income tax or corporation tax, as the case may be, under Chapter 1 of Part 9 by virtue of section 342,

(iii) the site of which is wholly within an enterprise area and in respect of which an allowance is to be made, or will by virtue of section 279 be made, for the purposes of income tax or corporation tax, as the case may be, under Chapter 1 of Part 9 by virtue of section 343,

(iv) the site of which is wholly within a designated area and which is a building or structure in use for the purposes specified in section 268(1)(*d*), and in respect of the construction or refurbishment of which capital expenditure is incurred in the qualifying period for which an allowance would but for subsection (6) be made for the purposes of income tax or corporation tax, as the case may be, under Chapter 1 of Part 9, or

(v) in respect of which an allowance is to be made, or will by virtue of section 279 be made, for the purposes of income tax or corporation tax, as the case may be, under Chapter 1 of Part 9 by virtue of section 344,

and

(*b*) which is let on bona fide commercial terms for such consideration as might be expected to be paid in a letting of the building or structure negotiated on an arm's length basis,

but, where capital expenditure is incurred in the qualifying period on the refurbishment of a building or structure in respect of which an allowance is to be made, or will by virtue of section 279 be made, or in respect of which an allowance would but for subsection (6) be made, for the purposes of income tax or corporation tax, as the case may be, under any of the provisions referred to in paragraph (*a*), the building or structure shall not be regarded as a qualifying premises unless the total amount of the expenditure so incurred is not less than an amount equal to 10 per cent of the market value of the building or structure immediately before that expenditure is incurred.

[(1A) Notwithstanding any other provision of this Chapter, including this section, "qualifying period" for the purposes of this section in the case of a building or structure within the meaning of paragraph (*a*)(v) of the definition of "qualifying premises" in subsection (1) means the period commencing on the 1st day of August, 1994, and ending on—

(*a*) the 31st day of July, 1997, or

(*b*) [30 September 1998],[2] where, in relation to the construction or refurbishment of the qualifying multi-storey car park concerned, the relevant local authority has certified in accordance with the requirements of paragraph (*b*) of the definition of "qualifying period" in section 344(1).][3]

(2) For the purposes of this section, so much of a period, being a period when rent is payable by a person in relation to a qualifying premises under a qualifying lease, shall be a relevant rental period as does not exceed—

(*a*) 10 years, or

(*b*) the period by which 10 years exceeds—

(i) any preceding period, or

(ii) if there is more than one preceding period, the aggregate of those periods,

for which rent was payable by that person or any other person in relation to that premises under a qualifying lease.

(3) Subject to subsection (4), where in the computation of the amount of the profits or gains of a trade or profession a person is apart from this section entitled to any deduction (in this subsection referred to as **"the first-mentioned deduction"**) on account of rent in respect of a qualifying premises occupied by such person for the purposes of that trade or profession which is payable by such person for a relevant rental period in relation to that qualifying premises under a qualifying lease, such person shall be entitled in that computation to a further deduction (in this subsection referred to as **"the second-mentioned deduction"**) equal to the amount of the first-mentioned deduction but, as respects a qualifying lease granted on or after the 21st day of April, 1997, where the first-mentioned deduction is on account of rent payable by such person to a connected person, such person shall not be entitled in that computation to the second-mentioned deduction.

(4) Where a person holds an interest in a qualifying premises out of which interest a qualifying lease is created directly or indirectly in respect of the qualifying premises and in respect of rent payable under the qualifying lease a claim for a further deduction under this section is made, and either such person or another person connected with such person—

(*a*) takes under a qualifying lease a qualifying premises (in this subsection referred to as **"the second-mentioned premises"**) occupied by such person or such other person, as the case may be, for the purposes of a trade or profession, and

(*b*) is apart from this section entitled, in the computation of the amount of the profits or gains of that trade or profession, to a deduction on account of rent in respect of the second-mentioned premises,

then, unless such person or such other person, as the case may be, shows that the taking on lease of the second-mentioned premises was not undertaken for the sole or main benefit of obtaining a further deduction on account of rent under this section, such person or such other person, as the case may be, shall not be entitled in the computation of the amount of the profits or gains of that trade or profession to any further deduction on account of rent in respect of the second-mentioned premises.

(5) (*a*) A building or structure in use for the purposes specified in section 268(1)(*d*) shall not be a qualifying premises for the purposes of this section unless the person to whom an allowance under Chapter 1 of Part 9 would but for

subsection (6) be made for the purposes of income tax or corporation tax, as the case may be, in respect of the capital expenditure incurred in the qualifying period on the construction or refurbishment of the building or structure elects by notice in writing to the appropriate inspector (within the meaning of section 950) to disclaim all allowances under that Chapter in respect of that capital expenditure.

(*b*) An election under paragraph (*a*) shall be included in the return required to be made by the person concerned under section 951 for the first year of assessment or the first accounting period, as the case may be, for which an allowance would but for subsection (6) have been made to that person under Chapter 1 of Part 9 in respect of that capital expenditure.

(*c*) An election under paragraph (*a*) shall be irrevocable.

(*d*) A person who has made an election under paragraph (*a*) shall furnish a copy of that election to any person (in this paragraph referred to as **"the second-mentioned person"**) to whom the person grants a qualifying lease in respect of the qualifying premises, and the second-mentioned person shall include the copy in the return required to be made by the second-mentioned person under section 951 for the year of assessment or accounting period, as the case may be, in which rent is first payable by the second-mentioned person under the qualifying lease in respect of the qualifying premises.

(6) Where a person who has incurred capital expenditure in the qualifying period on the construction or refurbishment of a building or structure in use for the purposes specified in section 268(1)(*d*) makes an election under subsection (5)(*a*), then, notwithstanding any other provision of the Tax Acts—

(*a*) no allowance under Chapter 1 of Part 9 shall be made to the person in respect of that capital expenditure,

(*b*) on the occurrence, in relation to the building or structure, of any of the events referred to in section 274(1), the residue of expenditure (within the meaning of section 277) in relation to that capital expenditure shall be deemed to be nil, and

(*c*) section 279 shall not apply in the case of any person who buys the relevant interest (within the meaning of section 269) in the building or structure.

(7) For the purposes of determining, in relation to paragraph (*a*)(iv) of the definition of **"qualifying premises"** and subsections (5) and (6), whether and to what extent capital expenditure incurred on the construction or refurbishment of a building or structure is incurred or not incurred in the qualifying period, only such an amount of that capital expenditure as is properly attributable to work on the construction or refurbishment of the building or structure actually carried out in the qualifying period shall (notwithstanding any other provision of the Tax Acts as to the time when any capital expenditure is or is to be treated as incurred) be treated as having been incurred in that period.

(8) (*a*) In this subsection—

"current value", in relation to minimum lease payments, means the value of those payments discounted to their present value at a rate which, when applied at the inception of the lease to—

(i) those payments, including any initial payment but excluding any payment or part of any payment for which the lessor will be accountable to the lessee, and

(ii) any unguaranteed residual value of the qualifying premises, excluding any part of such value for which the lessor will be accountable to the lessee,

produces discounted present values the aggregate amount of which equals the amount of the fair value of the qualifying premises;

"fair value", in relation to a qualifying premises, means an amount equal to such consideration as might be expected to be paid for the premises on a sale negotiated on an arm's length basis less any grants receivable towards the purchase of the qualifying premises;

"inception of the lease" means the earlier of the time the qualifying premises is brought into use or the date from which rentals under the lease first accrue;

"minimum lease payments" means the minimum payments over the remaining part of the term of the lease to be paid to the lessor, and includes any residual amount to be paid to the lessor at the end of the term of the lease and guaranteed by the lessee or by a person connected with the lessee;

"unguaranteed residual value", in relation to a qualifying premises, means that part of the residual value of that premises at the end of a term of a lease, as estimated at the inception of the lease, the realisation of which by the lessor is not assured or is guaranteed solely by a person connected with the lessor.

(*b*) A finance lease, that is—

(i) a lease in respect of a qualifying premises where, at the inception of the lease, the aggregate of the current value of the minimum lease payments (including any initial payment but excluding any payment or part of any payment for which the lessor will be accountable to the lessee) payable by the lessee in relation to the lease amounts to 90 per cent or more of the fair value of the qualifying premises, or

(ii) a lease which in all the circumstances is considered to provide in substance for the lessee the risks and benefits associated with ownership of the qualifying premises other than legal title to that premises,

shall not be a qualifying lease for the purposes of this section.

Amendments

1 Definition of "qualifying lease" substituted by FA 1999 s 44(*e*)(i) with effect from 6 April 1999.

2 Substituted by FA 2000 s 42(1)(*e*) with effect from 1 July 1999; previously "the 30th day of June, 1998".

3 Subs (1A) inserted by FA 1999 s 44(*e*)(ii) with effect from 6 April 1999.

Cross-references

Capital allowances for multi-storey car parks, meaning of "qualifying lease" applied: s 344(6A).

Life assurance companies, acquisition expenses: s 708(1).

Local authority certificate stating 15% of building cost incurred before 31 July 1997: s 339(2)(*a*)(ii).

Restriction on use by certain partnerships of certain losses, etc, transitional arrangements, subs (3): s 1017(2C)(*a*)("specified deduction").

Revenue precedents

Issue: Can a person claim the double deduction in circumstances where the property is owned and developed by charitable or religious institutions which are exempt from tax and as a result do not claim the capital allowances?

Decision: Yes, provided that all other aspects of the legislation are complied with.

Issue: The taxpayer paid rent under a qualifying lease and was entitled to the double deduction. A connected company was to purchase the property. Would the taxpayer still be entitled to the double deduction even though it would be connected with the new owner?

Decision: Yes - provided that the rent was still payable under the original lease. [Note: this position no longer applies in respect of leases granted on or after 21 April 1997.].

Issue: This case involves a company group. Trading is conducted through numerous retail outlets. All property is managed through one property investment company. If this company takes a lease of four qualifying units and sub-lets them to connected trading entities on the same terms and conditions as the head lease can the trading entities claim the double deduction?

Decision: Yes. In the circumstances of this case the trading entities may claim the double deduction. The intermediary lease appears to be for practical purposes only.

Issue: Where an assignment of a qualifying lease takes place can the person to whom the lease is assigned claim the double deduction, regardless of whether the assignment takes place within the qualifying period?

Decision: Yes, provided the normal conditions to qualify are satisfied.

Issue: Is it possible for a lessee to claim the double deduction in circumstances where the refurbishment expenditure on the premises is incurred by the lessee rather than the lessor?

Decision: In order for the double deduction to be due the rent in respect of which the double deduction is claimed would need to be paid under a lease which is granted after the necessary amount of refurbishment expenditure has been incurred.

Issue: Can the lessee of a premises which is owned by a local authority claim the double deduction in circumstances where the local authority is exempt from tax and does not claim capital allowances in respect of the premises?

Decision: Yes - provided all other conditions are satisfied.

Issue: Do payments for off-site storage of documents qualify for a double deduction in computing trading profits?

Decision: No — not unless rent is paid under a qualifying lease. Rent must be paid and a leasehold interest must be held by the claimant. Article published in Tax Briefing No 25 set out the conditions which must be satisfied.

Issue: A lessee enters into a qualifying lease with effect from the date the main contractor completes the landlord's works. Rent commences to be payable one month after the grant of the lease. Is the lessee regarded as occupying the qualifying premises during a fitting out period which may last several months?

Decision: The lessee would be regarded as occupying the premises for the purposes of the trade or profession during the fitting-out period provided that during the period they hold a qualifying lease on the premises.

Issue: If part of the capital expenditure incurred on a building in a designated area qualifies for capital allowances and part does not due to the expenditure falling outside the qualifying period, is there an apportionment of the double rent allowance?

Decision: The double rent deduction which is available by virtue of TCA 1997 s 345 is given where an allowance falls to be made by reason of s 342 of that Act. Once an allowance is given, and all the other conditions of the section are met, double rent deduction will be given, even where part of the capital expenditure does not qualify for capital allowances because it was incurred prior to designation.

Issue: A lease is granted in respect of a premises in a designated area in the qualifying period. The lessor subsequently incurs capital expenditure and qualifies for allowances under TCA 1997 s 343. Is the lease a qualifying lease within the meaning of s 345?

Decision: The double rent allowance is granted under TCA 1997 s 345 in respect of a letting under a qualifying lease which is defined as "a lease in respect of a qualifying premises granted in the qualifying period on bona fide commercial terms". The Commissioners interpret this to mean that a lease must be granted in respect of a qualifying premises before it can be a "qualifying lease" within the meaning of the section. A lease granted in respect of a premises in a designated area which is not a qualifying premises is not a qualifying lease. The subsequent incurring by the lessor of capital expenditure in respect of the premises will not alter the position.

Issue: Pension schemes are exempt from income tax on investment income, by virtue of TCA 1997 s 774. Please confirm that a premises in a designated area which is owned by a pension scheme will be a qualifying premises for the purposes of a double rent allowance.

Decision: It is accepted that for the purposes of s 45, Finance Act 1986, a building which is owned by a pension scheme which is exempt by virtue of s 16, Finance Act 1972, will be regarded as a qualifying premises. A lessee of such a building will not be denied the double rent allowance on the grounds that a capital allowance has not fallen to be made to the lessor where the lessor is such a pension scheme.

Issue: A company and its wholly owned subsidiary, as joint tenants, will enter into a 35 year lease agreement in respect of a premises situated in a designated area. Part of the building will be used as an industrial building by the parent. The other part used by the subsidiary will also be a qualifying premises. The lease payments will be apportioned between both companies and each company will make its own lease payments to the landlord. Please confirm that a double rent allowance is available.

Decision: Provided that both companies enter into a "qualifying lease" in respect of a "qualifying premises" (both terms within the meaning of TCA 1997 s 345) the fact that both companies will have equal tenancy rights in respect of the entire premises will not prevent them from claiming the double rent allowance under the said s 345.

Issue: Is a double rent allowance available in Urban Renewal areas for car spaces let on long leases to traders and professionals?

Decision: TCA 1997 s 345 provides that a Double Rent Allowance will be available to a person who is entitled to a deduction on account of rent in respect of a qualifying premises (as defined) occupied by him for the purposes of that trade or profession, and who otherwise meets the conditions laid down in that section. Provided therefore that the car park spaces are in use for the purposes of the trade or profession of the lessee, and subject to all other conditions being met, the provisions of the aforesaid s 345 would apply.

Issue: Instruction [10.1.3] Urban Renewal Relief on the issue of finance leases states that the question as to whether a lease is a finance lease should be considered primarily by reference to subparagraph (1)(b) of section 33(1) Finance Act 1990, i.e. is it a lease which provides for the lessee the risks and benefits of ownership. Is there further guidance as to when a lease provides for such risks and benefits?

Decision: Decision: A lease is considered in substance to provide for the lessee the benefits associated with ownership where the lessee has the benefit of any expected increase in the value of the property. Conversely, a lease is considered in substance to provide for the lessee the risks associated with ownership where the lessee has the risk of any expected decrease in the value of the property. This Office is of the view that the lessee is exposed to this variation if the property is acquired, in substance, through the lease payments. In the case of sale and leaseback arrangements, a lessee may have a call option to repurchase the property and the lessor may have a put option to transfer the property to the lessee. If the price at which the option can be exercised is equal to providing for the lessee the risks and benefits associated with ownership and accordingly the lease will not come within the definition of a finance lease for the purposes of double rent allowance.

Statement of practice

Off site document storage: ***Tax Briefing 25***, February 1997.

Definitions

lessee: s 5(1); lessee: s 5(1); lessor: s 5(1); person: IA 1937 s 11(*c*). profession: ss 2(1), 5(1); rent: s 5(1); tax: s 3(1); trade: ss 3(1), 4(1), 5(1); year of assessment: ss 2(1), 5(1); year: IA 1937 Sch.

Former enactments

FA 1990 s 33(1)–(2)(*a*); FA 1994 s 42; FA 1995 s 35(1)(g); FA 1997 s 26(*c*) and 27; FA 1997 s 150(4).

346 Rented residential accommodation: deduction for certain expenditure on construction

Amendments

1 Section 346 repealed by FA 2002 s 24(3)(*c*) with effect from 1 January 2002; but see now TCA 1997 Pt 10 Ch 11 (ss 372AK–372AV) which codified, with effect from 1 January 2002, reliefs for lessors and owner-occupiers in respect of expenditure incurred on the provision of certain residential accommodation, and in particular s 372AU which provides a saver for relief due, and for a clawback of relief given, under old schemes.

347 Rented residential accommodation: deduction for certain expenditure on conversion

Amendments

1 Section 347 repealed by FA 2002 s 24(3)(*c*) with effect from 1 January 2002; but see now TCA 1997 Pt 10 Ch 11 (ss 372AK–372AV) which codified, with effect from 1 January 2002, reliefs for lessors and owner-occupiers in respect of expenditure incurred on the provision of certain residential accommodation, and in particular s 372AU which provides a saver for relief due, and for a clawback of relief given, under old schemes.

348 Rented residential accommodation: deduction for certain expenditure on refurbishment

Amendments

1 Section 348 repealed by FA 2002 s 24(3)(*c*) with effect from 1 January 2002; but see now TCA 1997 Pt 10 Ch 11 (ss 372AK–372AV) which codified, with effect from 1 January 2002, reliefs for lessors and owner-occupiers in respect of expenditure incurred on the provision of certain residential accommodation, and in particular s 372AU which provides a saver for relief due, and for a clawback of relief given, under old schemes.

349 Residential accommodation: allowance to owner-occupiers in respect of certain expenditure on construction or refurbishment

Amendments

1 Section 349 repealed by FA 2002 s 24(3)(*c*) with effect from 1 January 2002; but see now TCA 1997 Pt 10 Ch 11 (ss 372AK–372AV) which codified, with effect from 1 January 2002, reliefs for lessors and owner-occupiers in respect of expenditure incurred on the provision of certain residential accommodation, and in particular s 372AU which provides a saver for relief due, and for a clawback of relief given, under old schemes.

350 Provisions supplementary to sections 346 to 349

Amendments

1 Section 350 repealed by FA 2002 s 24(3)(*c*) with effect from 1 January 2002; but see now TCA 1997 Pt 10 Ch 11 (ss 372AK–372AV) which codified, with effect from 1 January 2002, reliefs for lessors and owner-occupiers in respect of expenditure incurred on the provision of certain residential accommodation, and in particular s 372AU which provides a saver for relief due, and for a clawback of relief given, under old schemes.

350A Provision against double relief

[Where relief is given by virtue of any provision of this Chapter in relation to capital expenditure or other expenditure incurred on, or rent payable in respect of, any building or structure, premises or multi-storey car park, relief shall not be given in respect of that expenditure or that rent under any other provision of the Tax Acts.][1]

Amendments

1 Section 350A inserted by FA 1998 s 24(1)(*e*) with effect from 6 April 1998.

CHAPTER 4
Qualifying Resort Areas

Cross-references

Restriction on use of capital allowances on certain hotels, meaning of "qualifying resort area" applied: s 409B(1) (specified building).

Revenue information

Information leaflet IT29 — Tax Reliefs for Renewal and Improvement of Certain Resort Areas.

Tax Briefing

TB26 Apr 1997 p 15 — Capital allowances in respect of holiday cottages, holiday apartments and other self-catering accommodation.

TB43 April 2001 p 38 — Resort Areas — Timing of Claim for Capital Allowances.

TB47 Apr 2002 pp 20–21 — Qualifying Resort Areas: Treatment of income arising from the letting of holiday cottages.

351 Interpretation (Chapter 4)

In this Chapter—

"lease", **"lessee"**, **"lessor"** and **"rent"** have the same meanings respectively as in Chapter 8 of Part 4;

"market value", in relation to a building or structure, means the price which the unencumbered fee simple of the building or structure would fetch if sold in the open market in such manner and subject to such conditions as might reasonably be calculated to obtain for the vendor the best price for the building or structure, less the part of that price which would be attributable to the acquisition of, or of rights in or over, the land on which the building or structure is constructed;

[**"qualifying period"** means the period commencing on the 1st day of July, 1995, and ending on—

(*a*) the 30th day of June, 1998, or

(*b*) the 31st day of December, 1999, where, in relation to the construction of, conversion into, refurbishment of, or, as the case may be, construction or refurbishment of the building or structure concerned, being—

(i) a building or structure to which section 352 applies, or

(ii) a qualifying premises within the meaning of section 353, 354, 356, 357 or 358,

the relevant local authority gives a certificate in writing, on or before the 30th day of September, 1999, to the person constructing, converting or refurbishing, as the case may be, the building or structure stating that it is satisfied that not less than 50 per cent of the total cost of the building or structure and the site thereof had been incurred on or before the 30th day of June, 1999, and, in considering whether to give such a certificate, the relevant local authority shall have regard only to guidelines in relation to the giving of such certificates issued by the Department of the Environment and Local Government for the purposes of this definition;][1]

"qualifying resort area" means any area described in Schedule 8;

"refurbishment", in relation to a building or structure and other than for the purposes of section 358, means any work of construction, reconstruction, repair or renewal, including the provision or improvement of water, sewerage or heating facilities, carried out in the course of the repair or restoration, or maintenance in the nature of repair or restoration, of the building or structure.

[**"the relevant local authority"**, in relation to the construction of, conversion into, refurbishment of, or, as the case may be, construction or refurbishment of a building or structure of the kind referred to in paragraph (*b*) of the definition of "qualifying period", means the council of a county or the corporation of a county or other borough or, where appropriate, the urban district council, in whose functional area the building or structure is situated.][2]

Amendments

1 Definition of "qualifying period" substituted by FA 1999 s 45 with effect from 6 April 1999.

2 Definition of "the relevant local authority" inserted by FA 1998 s 27(*b*) with effect from 6 April 1998.

Cross-references

An "eligible town" for the purposes of the Town Renewal Act 2000, as amended by FA 2002, (and consequently for the purposes of relief under TCA 1997 Pt 10 Chs 10 and 11) cannot be within a "qualifying rural area" within the meaning of this section — Town Renewal Act 2000 s 1, definition of "eligible town", refers.

Definitions

land: IA 1937 Sch; person: IA 1937 s 11(*c*); writing: IA 1937 Sch.

Former enactments

FA 1995 s 46(1).

352 Accelerated capital allowances in relation to construction or refurbishment of certain industrial buildings or structures

(1) This section shall apply to a building or structure the site of which is wholly within a qualifying resort area and which is to be an industrial building or structure by reason of its use for the purposes specified in section 268(1)(*d*).

(2) Subject to subsection (5), section 271 shall apply in relation to capital expenditure incurred in the qualifying period on the construction or refurbishment of a building or structure to which this section applies as if—

(*a*) in subsection (1) of that section the definition of "industrial development agency" were deleted,

(*b*) in subsection (2)(*a*)(i) of that section "to which subsection (3) applies" were deleted,

(*c*) subsection (3) of that section were deleted,

(*d*) the following subsection were substituted for subsection (4) of that section:

"(4) An industrial building allowance shall be of an amount equal to 50 per cent of the capital expenditure mentioned in subsection (2).",

and

(*e*) in subsection (5) of that section "to which subsection (3)(*c*) applies" were deleted.

(3) Subject to subsection (5), section 272 shall apply in relation to capital expenditure incurred in the qualifying period on the construction or refurbishment of a building or structure to which this section applies as if the following subsection were substituted for subsection (3) of that section:

"(3) A writing down allowance shall be of an amount equal to 5 per cent of the expenditure referred to in subsection (2)(*c*).".

(4) Subject to subsection (5), section 273 shall apply in relation to capital expenditure incurred in the qualifying period on the construction or refurbishment of a building or structure to which this section applies as if—

(*a*) in subsection (1) of that section the definition of "industrial development agency" were deleted,

(*b*) the following paragraph were substituted for paragraph (*b*) of subsection (2) of that section:

"(*b*) As respects any qualifying expenditure, any allowance made under section 272 and increased under paragraph (*a*) in respect of that expenditure, whether claimed for one chargeable period or more than one such period, shall not in the aggregate exceed 75 per cent of the amount of that qualifying expenditure.",

and

(*c*) subsections (3) to (7) of that section were deleted.

(5) In the case where capital expenditure is incurred in the qualifying period on the refurbishment of a building or structure to which this section applies, subsections (2) to (4) shall apply only if the total amount of the capital expenditure so incurred is not less than an amount which is equal to 20 per cent of the market value of the building or structure immediately before that expenditure is incurred.

(6) For the purposes only of determining, in relation to a claim for an allowance under section 271, 272 or 273, as applied by this section, whether and to what extent capital expenditure incurred on the construction or refurbishment of an industrial building or structure is incurred or not incurred in the qualifying period, only such an amount of that capital expenditure as is properly attributable to work on the construction or, as the case may be, the refurbishment of the building or structure actually carried out during the qualifying period shall (notwithstanding any other provision of the Tax Acts as to the time when any capital expenditure is or is to be treated as incurred) be treated as having been incurred in that period.

Cross-references

Case V, Schedule D, computational rules and allowable deductions: s 97(2B)(*c*)(i).
Holiday cottages, disclaimer of capital allowances: s 355(1)(*a*).
Interpretation: s 351(qualifying period).

Definitions

market value: s 351; qualifying period: s 351; qualifying resort area: s 351; refurbishment: s 351.

Former enactments

FA 1995 s 47.

353 Capital allowances in relation to construction or refurbishment of certain commercial premises

(1) In this section—

"qualifying premises" means a building or structure the site of which is wholly within a qualifying resort area and which—

(*a*) apart from this section is not an industrial building or structure within the meaning of section 268, and
(*b*) is in use for the purposes of the operation of one or more qualifying tourism facilities,

but does not include any part of a building or structure in use as or as part of a dwelling house, other than a tourist accommodation facility of the type referred to in the definition of **"qualifying tourism facilities"**;

"qualifying tourism facilities" means—

(*a*) tourist accommodation facilities registered by Bord Fáilte Éireann under Part III of the Tourist Traffic Act, 1939, or specified in a list published under section 9 of the Tourist Traffic Act, 1957, and (*b*) such other classes of facilities as may be approved of for the purposes of this section by the Minister for Tourism, Sport and Recreation in consultation with the Minister for Finance.

(2) (*a*) Subject to subsections (3) to (6), the provisions of the Tax Acts relating to the making of allowances or charges in respect of capital expenditure incurred on the construction or refurbishment of an industrial building or structure shall, notwithstanding anything to the contrary in those provisions, apply—

(i) as if a qualifying premises were, at all times at which it is a qualifying premises, a building or structure in respect of which an allowance is to be made for the purposes of income tax or corporation tax, as the case may be, under Chapter 1 of Part 9 by reason of its use for a purpose specified in section 268(1)(*a*), and

(ii) where any activity carried on in the qualifying premises is not a trade, as if it were a trade.

(*b*) An allowance shall be given by virtue of this subsection in respect of any capital expenditure incurred on the construction or refurbishment of a qualifying premises only in so far as that expenditure is incurred in the qualifying period.

(3) In the case where capital expenditure is incurred in the qualifying period on the refurbishment of a qualifying premises, subsection (2) shall apply only if the total amount of the capital expenditure so incurred is not less than an amount which is equal to 20 per cent of the market value of the qualifying premises immediately before that expenditure is incurred.

(4) For the purposes of the application, by subsection (2), of sections 271, 272 and 273 in relation to capital expenditure incurred in the qualifying period on the construction or refurbishment of a qualifying premises—

(*a*) section 271 shall apply as if—

(i) in subsection (1) of that section the definition of "industrial development agency" were deleted,

(ii) in subsection (2)(*a*)(i) of that section "to which subsection (3) applies" were deleted,

(iii) subsection (3) of that section were deleted,

(iv) the following subsection were substituted for subsection (4) of that section:

"(4) An industrial building allowance shall be of an amount equal to 50 per cent of the capital expenditure mentioned in subsection (2).",

and

(v) in subsection (5) of that section "to which subsection (3)(*c*) applies" were deleted,

(*b*) section 272 shall apply as if the following subsection were substituted for subsection (3) of that section:

"(3) The writing down allowance shall be of an amount equal to 5 per cent of the expenditure referred to in subsection (2)(*c*).",

and

(*c*) section 273 shall apply as if—

(i) in subsection (1) of that section the definition of "industrial development agency" were deleted,

(ii) the following paragraph were substituted for paragraph (*b*) of subsection (2) of that subsection:

"(*b*) As respects any qualifying expenditure, any allowance made under section 272 and increased under paragraph (*a*) in respect of that expenditure, whether claimed in one chargeable period or more than one such period, shall not in the aggregate exceed 75 per cent of the amount of that qualifying expenditure.",

and

(iii) subsections (3) to (7) of that section were deleted.

(5) In the case of a qualifying premises which is such a premises by virtue of being a tourist accommodation facility of a type referred to in paragraph (*a*) of the definition of **"qualifying tourism facilities"**—

(*a*) the event of the premises ceasing to be registered or specified in the manner referred to in that paragraph of that definition shall be treated as if it were an event specified in section 274(1), and

(*b*) for the purposes of the application of section 274 on the occurrence of any such event, there shall, notwithstanding anything to the contrary in section 318, be treated as arising in relation to that event sale, insurance, salvage or compensation moneys in an amount equal to the aggregate of—

(i) the residue of the expenditure (within the meaning of section 277) incurred on the construction or refurbishment of the premises immediately before that event, and

(ii) the allowances made under Chapter 1 of Part 9 by virtue of subsection (2) in respect of the expenditure incurred on the construction or refurbishment of the premises.

(6) Notwithstanding section 274(1), no balancing charge shall be made in relation to any qualifying premises by reason of any of the events specified, or by virtue of subsection (5) treated as specified, in section 274(1) which occurs—

(*a*) more than 11 years after the qualifying premises was first used, or

(*b*) in a case where section 276 applies, more than 11 years after the capital expenditure on refurbishment of the qualifying premises was incurred.

(7) For the purposes only of determining, in relation to a claim for an allowance by virtue of subsection (2), whether and to what extent capital expenditure incurred on the construction or refurbishment of a qualifying premises is incurred or not incurred in the qualifying period, only such an amount of that capital expenditure as is properly attributable to work on the construction or refurbishment of the premises actually carried out during the qualifying period shall (notwithstanding any other provision of the Tax Acts as to the time when any capital expenditure is or is to be treated as incurred) be treated as having been incurred in that period.

(8) Where by virtue of subsection (2) an allowance is given under Chapter 1 of Part 9 in respect of any capital expenditure incurred on the construction or refurbishment of a qualifying premises, relief shall not be given in respect of that expenditure under any provision of the Tax Acts other than that Chapter.

Cross-references

Case V, Schedule D, computational rules and allowable deductions: s 97(2B)(*c*)(ii).

Double rent allowance: s 354(1) (qualifying premises).

Holiday cottages, disclaimer of capital allowances: s 355(1)(*b*).

Interpretation: s 351(qualifying period).

Restriction on use of capital allowances on holiday cottages: s 405(3)(*a*).

Revenue precedents

Issue: Qualifying premises for the purposes of TCA 1997 s 353 means, inter alia, a building in use for the purposes of the operation of one or more qualifying tourism facilities. Qualifying tourism facilities means tourist accommodation facilities specified in a list published under s 9 of the Tourist Traffic Act, 1957. Where the premises are only partly in use for letting to tourists or where they are let to persons other than tourists will the amount of the allowances be restricted?

Decision: Once the conditions for listing continue to be satisfied and the premises continues to be listed, the allowances will continue to be available. Non-tourist lettings during the months not advertised in the Self-Catering Guide will not debar the premises once none of the lettings are for more than two consecutive calendar months at any one time or for more than six months in any calendar year. The quantum of the available allowance is not restricted where there are any such non-tourist lettings.

Issue: The Department of Environment and Local Government has issued guidelines on residential development in urban renewal designated areas requiring a certain floor area. Bord Fáilte have their own separate requirements for floor area for tourist accommodation facilities. Which of the above guidelines should be followed in deciding floor area for residential properties in the Scheme for Renewal and Improvement of Certain Resort Areas?

Decision: The question of the floor area of a particular unit is dependent on the nature of the claim in respect of that unit. If capital allowances are being claimed by virtue of TCA 1997 s 353, it is the floor area requirement of Bord Fáilte for listing which must be complied with. If rented residential accommodation reliefs under TCA 1997 s 356, 357 or 358 (whichever section is appropriate) are being claimed, it is the floor area requirements of those sections which must be complied with.

Issue: Is it possible to claim capital allowances in respect of listed holiday homes whether these are single holiday homes or a group of holiday homes even where the holiday homes are not registered as a holiday cottage scheme with Bord Fáilte?

Decision: Tourist accommodation facilities listed under s 9, Tourist Traffic Act 1957 come within the definition of "qualifying tourism facilities" in TCA 1997 s 353. Single homes or groups of houses which are not registered under Part Ill of the Tourist Traffic Act 1939 are capable of being listed, provided that they meet with the necessary standards and criteria laid down by the Bord Fáilte. The question of what is, or is not, listed is of course a matter for Bord Fáilte.

Issue: In the case of qualifying tourism facilities which are B+Bs, is expenditure incurred on the private element disallowed?

Decision: No.

Issue: What type of retail units qualify under this scheme?

Decision: Retail outlets located in the same building as a holiday complex and with access only from within the complex (ie no street access) are considered eligible. In other words, a shop which is only accessible from within the holiday complex and presumably frequented predominately by the users of the holiday complex will qualify.

Issue: Are non-residents entitled to claim capital allowances under section 353 Taxes Consolidation Act 1997? Are they entitled to claim industrial buildings allowances under the Seaside Resort Scheme?

Decision: Non-residents are entitled to claim both types of allowances.

Tax Briefing

TB38 Dec 1999 p 7 — Tourist accommodation facilities: registration or listing with Bord Fáilte must be maintained for all years; it is not sufficient to be so registered or listed only for the initial year in which capital allowances are claimed. In the event of premises ceasing to be so registered or listed a balancing charge will apply.

Definitions

market value: s 351; qualifying period: s 351; qualifying resort area: s 351; refurbishment: s 351; Tax Acts: s 1(2); year: IA 1937 Sch.

Former enactments

FA 1995 s 48; FA 1997 s 146(1) and Sch 9 Pt I para 19.

354 Double rent allowance in respect of rent paid for certain business premises

(1) In this section—

"qualifying lease" means, subject to subsection (5), a lease in respect of a qualifying premises granted in the qualifying period on bona fide commercial terms by a lessor to a lessee not connected with the lessor, or with any other person who is entitled to a rent in respect of the qualifying premises, whether under that lease or any other lease;

"qualifying premises" means, subject to section 355(2), a building or structure the site of which is wholly within a qualifying resort area and—

(*a*) (i) which is a building or structure in use for the purposes specified in section 268(1)(*d*), and in respect of which capital expenditure is incurred in the qualifying period for which an allowance is to be made, or will by virtue of section 279 be made, for the purposes of income tax or corporation tax, as the case may be, under section 271, 272 or 273, as applied by section 352, or

(ii) in respect of which an allowance is to be made, or will by virtue of section 279 be made, for the purposes of income tax or corporation tax, as the case may be, under Chapter 1 of Part 9 by virtue of section 353,

and

(*b*) which is let on bona fide commercial terms for such consideration as might be expected to be paid in a letting of the building or structure negotiated on an arm's length basis,

but, where capital expenditure is incurred in the qualifying period on the refurbishment of a building or structure in respect of which an allowance is to be made, or will by virtue of section 279 be made, for the purposes of income tax or corporation tax, as the case may be, under any of the provisions referred to in paragraph (*a*), the building or structure shall not be regarded as a qualifying premises unless the total amount of the expenditure so incurred is not less than an amount equal to 20 per cent of the market value of the building or structure immediately before that expenditure is incurred.

(2) For the purposes of this section, so much of a period, being a period when rent is payable by a person in relation to a qualifying premises under a qualifying lease, shall be a relevant rental period as does not exceed—

(*a*) 10 years, or

(*b*) the period by which 10 years exceeds—

(i) any preceding period, or

(ii) if there is more than one preceding period, the aggregate of those periods,

for which rent was payable by that person or any other person in relation to that premises under a qualifying lease.

(3) Subject to subsection (4), where in the computation of the amount of the profits or gains of a trade or profession a person is apart from this section entitled to any deduction (in this subsection referred to as **"the first-mentioned deduction"**) on account of rent in respect of a qualifying premises occupied by such person for the purposes of that trade or profession which is payable by such person for a relevant rental period in relation to that qualifying premises under a qualifying lease, such person shall be entitled in that computation to a further deduction (in this subsection referred to as **"the second-mentioned deduction"**) equal to the amount of the first-mentioned deduction but, as respects a qualifying lease granted on or after the 21st day of April, 1997, where the first-mentioned deduction is on account of rent payable by such person to a connected person, such person shall not be entitled in that computation to the second-mentioned deduction.

(4) Where a person holds an interest in a qualifying premises out of which interest a qualifying lease is created directly or indirectly in respect of the qualifying premises and in respect of rent payable under the qualifying lease a claim for a further deduction under this section is made, and either such person or another person connected with such person—

(*a*) takes under a qualifying lease a qualifying premises (in this subsection referred to as **"the second-mentioned premises"**) occupied by such person or such other person, as the case may be, for the purposes of a trade or profession, and

(*b*) is apart from this section entitled, in the computation of the amount of the profits or gains of that trade or profession, to a deduction on account of rent in respect of the second-mentioned premises,

then, unless such person or such other person, as the case may be, shows that the taking on lease of the second-mentioned premises was not undertaken for the sole or main benefit of obtaining a further deduction on account of rent under this section, such person or such other person, as the case may be, shall not be entitled in the computation of the amount of the profits or gains of that trade or profession to any further deduction on account of rent in respect of the second-mentioned premises.

(5) (*a*) In this subsection—

"current value", in relation to minimum lease payments, means the value of those payments discounted to their present value at a rate which, when applied at the inception of the lease to—

(i) those payments, including any initial payment but excluding any payment or part of any payment for which the lessor will be accountable to the lessee, and

(ii) any unguaranteed residual value of the qualifying premises, excluding any part of such value for which the lessor will be accountable to the lessee,

produces discounted present values the aggregate amount of which equals the amount of the fair value of the qualifying premises;

"fair value", in relation to a qualifying premises, means an amount equal to such consideration as might be expected to be paid for the premises on a sale negotiated on an arm's length basis less any grants receivable towards the purchase of the qualifying premises;

"inception of the lease" means the earlier of the time the qualifying premises is brought into use or the date from which rentals under the lease first accrue;

"minimum lease payments" means the minimum payments over the remaining part of the term of the lease to be paid to the lessor, and includes any residual amount to be paid to the lessor at the end of the term of the lease and guaranteed by the lessee or by a person connected with the lessee;

"unguaranteed residual value", in relation to a qualifying premises, means that part of the residual value of that premises at the end of a term of a lease, as estimated at the inception of the lease, the realisation of which by the lessor is not assured or is guaranteed solely by a person connected with the lessor.

(*b*) A finance lease, that is—

(i) a lease in respect of a qualifying premises where, at the inception of the lease, the aggregate of the current value of the minimum lease payments (including any initial payment but excluding any payment or part of any payment for which the lessor will be accountable to the lessee) payable by the lessee in relation to the lease amounts to 90 per cent or more of the fair value of the qualifying premises, or

(ii) a lease which in all the circumstances is considered to provide in substance for the lessee the risks and benefits associated with ownership of the qualifying premises other than legal title to that premises,

shall not be a qualifying lease for the purposes of this section.

Cross-references

Holiday cottages, disclaimer of capital allowances: s 355(2)(*a*), (*d*).

Interpretation: s 351 (qualifying period).

Restriction on use by certain partnerships of certain losses, etc, transitional arrangements, subs (3): s 1017(2C)(*a*), (*e*)(II).

Restriction on use of capital allowances on holiday cottages, subs (4), (5): s 403(3)(*b*).

Revenue precedents

Issue: Where a partnership takes a lease of a scheme of registered holiday cottages and lets them to tourists will the partnership be entitled to a double deduction for the rent which it pays under the lease?

Decision: If the partnership is occupying qualifying premises for the purposes of a trade and there is no connection between the lessor and the lessee it will be entitled to the double deduction. However it will be a question of fact whether the income arising from the cottages is chargeable Case I or Case V and whether the cottages will be occupied by the partnership. Prima facie, property which is let would appear not to be occupied by the lessor.

Definitions

lease: s 351; lessee: s 351; lessor: s 351; market value: s 351; person: IA 1937 s 11(*c*); profession: s 2(1); qualifying period: s 351; qualifying resort area: s 351; refurbishment: s 351; rent: s 351; trade: s 3(1), 4(1), 5(1); year: IA 1937 Sch.

Former enactments

FA 1990 s 33(1)–(2)(*a*); FA 1995 s 49; FA 1997 ss 27, 150(4).

---

355 Disclaimer of capital allowances on holiday cottages, holiday apartments, etc

(1) This section shall apply to—

(*a*) a building or structure to which section 352 applies by virtue of the building or structure being a holiday cottage of the type referred to in section 268(3), and (*b*) a building or structure which is a qualifying premises within the meaning of section 353 by virtue of the building or structure being—

(i) a holiday apartment registered under Part III of the Tourist Traffic Act, 1939, or

(ii) other self-catering accommodation specified in a list published under section 9 of the Tourist Traffic Act, 1957.

(2) (*a*) Subject to subsection (5), a building or structure to which this section applies shall not be a qualifying premises for the purposes of section 354 unless the person to whom an allowance under Chapter 1 of Part 9 would but for subsection (3) be made for the purposes of income tax or corporation tax, as the case may be, in respect of the capital expenditure incurred in the qualifying period on the construction or refurbishment of the building or structure elects by notice in writing to the appropriate inspector (within the meaning of section 950) to disclaim all allowances under that Chapter in respect of that capital expenditure.

(*b*) An election under paragraph (*a*) shall be included in the return required to be made by the person concerned under section 951 for the first year of assessment or the first accounting period, as the case may be, for which an allowance would but for subsection (3) have been made to that person under Chapter 1 of Part 9 in respect of that capital expenditure.

(*c*) An election under paragraph (*a*) shall be irrevocable.

(*d*) A person who has made an election under paragraph (*a*) shall furnish a copy of that election to any person (in this paragraph referred to as **"the second-mentioned person"**) to whom the person grants a qualifying lease (within the meaning of section 354) in respect of a building or structure to which this section applies, and the second-mentioned person shall include the copy in the return required to be made by the second-mentioned person under section 951 for the year of assessment or accounting period, as the case may be, in which rent is first payable by the second-mentioned person under the qualifying lease in respect of such a building or structure.

(3) Subject to subsection (5), where a person who has incurred capital expenditure in the qualifying period on the construction or refurbishment of a building or structure to which this section applies makes an election under subsection (2)(*a*), then, notwithstanding any other provision of the Tax Acts—

(*a*) no allowance under Chapter 1 of Part 9 shall be made to the person in respect of that capital expenditure,

(*b*) on the occurrence, in relation to the building or structure, of any of the events referred to in section 274(1), the residue of expenditure (within the meaning of section 277) in relation to that capital expenditure shall be deemed to be nil, and

(*c*) section 279 shall not apply in the case of any person who buys the relevant interest (within the meaning of section 269) in the building or structure.

(4) Subject to subsection (5), where in the qualifying period a person incurs capital expenditure on the acquisition, construction or refurbishment of a building or structure

which is or is to be a building or structure to which subsection (1)(*b*) applies and an allowance is to be made in respect of that expenditure under section 271 or 272, then—

(*a*) neither section 305(1)(*b*) nor section 308(4) shall apply as respects that allowance, and

(*b*) neither section 381 nor section 396(2) shall apply as respects the whole or part, as the case may be, of any loss which would not have arisen but for the making of that allowance.

(5) This section shall not apply—

(*a*) to expenditure incurred in the qualifying period on the acquisition, construction or refurbishment of a building or structure (in this subsection referred to as **"the holiday cottage or apartment"**) which is or is to be a building or structure to which this section applies where before the 5th day of April, 1996—

(i) a binding contract in writing was entered into for the acquisition or construction of the holiday cottage or apartment,

(ii) an application for planning permission for the construction of the holiday cottage or apartment was received by a planning authority, or

(iii) in relation to the holiday cottage or apartment, an opinion in writing was issued by the Revenue Commissioners to the effect that an allowance to be made in respect of expenditure on the holiday cottage or apartment would not be restricted by virtue of section 408,

or

(*b*) where before the 5th day of April, 1996—

(i) expenditure was incurred on the acquisition of land on which the holiday cottage or apartment is to be constructed or refurbished, by the person who incurred the expenditure on that construction or refurbishment, or

(ii) a binding contract in writing was entered into for the acquisition of that land by that person,

and that person can prove to the satisfaction of the Revenue Commissioners that a detailed plan had been prepared and that detailed discussions had taken place with a planning authority in relation to the holiday cottage or apartment on or after the 8th day of February, 1995, but before the 5th day of April, 1996, and that this can be supported by means of an affidavit from the planning authority.

Cross-references

Double rent allowance, subs (2): s 354(1).

Restriction on use of capital allowances on certain industrial buildings or other premises, subs (1)(*b*): s 409A(1) (specified building).

Tax Briefing

TB31 Apr 1998 p 10-Subs (5) — Transitional arrangements.

Definitions

lease: s 351; person: IA 1937 s 11(*c*).

Former enactments

FA 1995 s 49A; FA 1996 s 30.

356 Rented residential accommodation: deduction for certain expenditure on construction

Amendments

1 Section 356 repealed by FA 2002 s 24(3)(*d*) with effect from 1 January 2002; but see now TCA 1997 Pt 10 Ch 11 (ss 372AK–372AV) which codified, with effect from 1 January 2002, reliefs for lessors and owner-occupiers in respect of expenditure incurred on the provision of certain residential accommodation, and in particular s 372AU which provides a saver for relief due, and for a clawback of relief given, under old schemes.

357 Rented residential accommodation: deduction for certain expenditure on conversion

Amendments

1 Section 357 repealed by FA 2002 s 24(3)(*d*) with effect from 1 January 2002; but see now TCA 1997 Pt 10 Ch 11 (ss 372AK–372AV) which codified, with effect from 1 January 2002, reliefs for lessors and owner-occupiers in respect of expenditure incurred on the provision of certain residential accommodation, and in particular s 372AU which provides a saver for relief due, and for a clawback of relief given, under old schemes.

358 Rented residential accommodation: deduction for certain expenditure on refurbishment

Amendments

1 Section 358 repealed by FA 2002 s 24(3)(*d*) with effect from 1 January 2002; but see now TCA 1997 Pt 10 Ch 11 (ss 372AK–372AV) which codified, with effect from 1 January 2002, reliefs for lessors and owner-occupiers in respect of expenditure incurred on the provision of certain residential accommodation, and in particular s 372AU which provides a saver for relief due, and for a clawback of relief given, under old schemes.

359 Provisions supplementary to sections 356 to 358

Amendments

1 Section 359 repealed by FA 2002 s 24(3)(*d*) with effect from 1 January 2002; but see now TCA 1997 Pt 10 Ch 11 (ss 372AK–372AV) which codified, with effect from 1 January 2002, reliefs for lessors and owner-occupiers in respect of expenditure incurred on the provision of certain residential accommodation, and in particular s 372AU which provides a saver for relief due, and for a clawback of relief given, under old schemes.

CHAPTER 5

Designated Islands

Amendments

1 Chapter 5 repealed by FA 2002 s 24(3)(*e*) with effect from 1 January 2002; but see now TCA 1997 Pt 10 Ch 11 (ss 372AK–372AV) which codified, with effect from 1 January 2002, reliefs for lessors and owner-occupiers in respect of expenditure incurred on the provision of certain residential accommodation, and in particular s 372AU which provides a saver for relief due, and for a clawback of relief given, under old schemes.

360 Interpretation (Chapter 5)

Amendments

1 Section 360 repealed by FA 2002 s 24(3)(*e*) with effect from 1 January 2002; but see now TCA 1997 Pt 10 Ch 11 (ss 372AK–372AV) which codified, with effect from 1 January 2002, reliefs for lessors and owner-occupiers in respect of expenditure incurred on the provision of certain residential accommodation, and in particular s 372AU which provides a saver for relief due, and for a clawback of relief given, under old schemes.

361 Rented residential accommodation: deduction for certain expenditure on construction

Amendments

1 Section 361 repealed by FA 2002 s 24(3)(*e*) with effect from 1 January 2002; but see now TCA 1997 Pt 10 Ch 11 (ss 372AK–372AV) which codified, with effect from 1 January 2002, reliefs for lessors and owner-occupiers in respect of expenditure incurred on the provision of certain residential accommodation, and in particular s 372AU which provides a saver for relief due, and for a clawback of relief given, under old schemes.

362 Rented residential accommodation: deduction for certain expenditure on conversion

Amendments

1 Section 362 repealed by FA 2002 s 24(3)(*e*) with effect from 1 January 2002; but see now TCA 1997 Pt 10 Ch 11 (ss 372AK–372AV) which codified, with effect from 1 January 2002, reliefs for lessors and owner-occupiers in respect of expenditure incurred on the provision of certain residential accommodation, and in particular s 372AU which provides a saver for relief due, and for a clawback of relief given, under old schemes.

363 Rented residential accommodation: deduction for certain expenditure on refurbishment

Amendments

1 Section 363 repealed by FA 2002 s 24(3)(*e*) with effect from 1 January 2002; but see now TCA 1997 Pt 10 Ch 11 (ss 372AK–372AV) which codified, with effect from 1 January 2002, reliefs for lessors and owner-occupiers in respect of expenditure incurred on the provision of certain residential accommodation, and in particular s 372AU which provides a saver for relief due, and for a clawback of relief given, under old schemes.

364 Residential accommodation: allowance to owner-occupiers in respect of certain expenditure on construction or refurbishment

Amendments

1 Section 364 repealed by FA 2002 s 24(3)(*e*) with effect from 1 January 2002; but see now TCA 1997 Pt 10 Ch 11 (ss 372AK–372AV) which codified, with effect from 1 January 2002, reliefs for lessors and owner-occupiers in respect of expenditure incurred on the provision of certain residential accommodation, and in particular s 372AU which provides a saver for relief due, and for a clawback of relief given, under old schemes.

365 Provisions supplementary to sections 360 to 364

Amendments

1 Section 365 repealed by FA 2002 s 24(3)(*e*) with effect from 1 January 2002; but see now TCA 1997 Pt 10 Ch 11 (ss 372AK–372AV) which codified, with effect from 1 January 2002, reliefs for lessors and owner-occupiers in respect of expenditure incurred on the provision of certain residential accommodation, and in particular s 372AU which provides a saver for relief due, and for a clawback of relief given, under old schemes.

CHAPTER 6
Dublin Docklands Area

Amendments

1 Chapter 6 repealed by FA 2002 s 24(3)(*e*) with effect from 1 January 2002.

366 Interpretation (Chapter 6)

Amendments

1 Section 366 repealed by FA 2002 s 24(3)(*e*) with effect from 1 January 2002.

367 Qualifying areas

Amendments

1 Section 367 repealed by FA 2002 s 24(3)(*e*) with effect from 1 January 2002.

368 Accelerated capital allowances in relation to construction or refurbishment of certain industrial buildings or structures

Amendments

1 Section 368 repealed by FA 2002 s 24(3)(*e*) with effect from 1 January 2002.

369 Capital allowances in relation to construction or refurbishment of certain commercial premises

Amendments

1 Section 369 repealed by FA 2002 s 24(3)(*e*) with effect from 1 January 2002.

370 Double rent allowance in respect of rent paid for certain business premises

Amendments

1 Section 370 repealed by FA 2002 s 24(3)(*e*) with effect from 1 January 2002.

371 Residential accommodation: allowance to owner-occupiers in respect of certain expenditure on construction or refurbishment

Amendments

1 Section 371 repealed by FA 2002 s 24(3)(*e*) with effect from 1 January 2002.

372 Provisions supplementary to section 371

Amendments

1 Section 372 repealed by FA 2002 s 24(3)(*e*) with effect from 1 January 2002.

[CHAPTER 7
Qualifying Areas][1]

Amendments

1 Chapter 7 title inserted by FA 1998 s 76 with effect from 6 April 1998.

Notes

By virtue of the Urban Renewal Act 1998 (as amended by FA 2002) s 5(3), a reference in Chapter 7 to a company established by a local authority is to be construed as including a reference to an authorised company, being a company appointed by a local authority under section 5(1) of that Act to be an authorised company for the purposes of that Act.

By virtue of the Urban Renewal Act 1998 (as amended by FA 2002) s 11(1), no relief may be granted under Chapter 7 in respect of the construction, refurbishment or conversion of a building, structure or house unless the local authority or authorised company which prepared the integrated area plan concerned has certified in writing, in a manner specified by the Minister for the Environment and Local Government, that such construction, refurbishment or conversion is consistent with the objectives of that plan.

Cross-references

See Urban Renewal Act 1998 (as amended by FA 2002) ss 5 (authorised companies), 8 (recommendations in respect of qualifying areas for the purposes of urban renewal reliefs), 11 (certain reliefs conditional on buildings, etc being consistent with integrated area plan) and 12 (monitoring of implementation of integrated area plan).

Revenue Information

Information Leaflet IT26A — Integrated Area Urban Renewal Scheme.

372A Interpretation and application (Chapter 7)

[(1) In this Chapter—

[**"existing building"** means a building or structure which—

(*a*) fronts on to a qualifying street, and

(*b*) existed on 13 September 2000;][1]

[**"facade"**, in relation to a building or structure or part of a building or structure, means the exterior wall of the building or structure or, as the case may be, the part of the building or structure which fronts on to a street;][2]

"lease", **"lessee"**, **"lessor"**, **"premium"** and **"rent"** have the same meanings respectively as in Chapter 8 of Part 4;

"market value", in relation to a building, structure or house, means the price which the unencumbered fee simple of the building, structure or house would fetch if sold in the open market in such manner and subject to such conditions as might reasonably be calculated to obtain for the vendor the best price for the building, structure or house, less the part of that price which would be attributable to the acquisition of, or of rights in or over, the land on which the building, structure or house is constructed;

"multi-storey car park" means a building or structure consisting of 2 or more storeys wholly or mainly in use for the purpose of providing, for members of the public generally without preference for any particular class of person, on payment of an appropriate charge, parking space for mechanically propelled vehicles;

[**"necessary construction"**, in relation to an existing building, means one or more of the following:

(*a*) construction of an extension to the building which does not exceed 30 per cent of the floor area of the building immediately before expenditure on the construction, conversion or refurbishment of the building was incurred, where such extension is necessary for the purposes of facilitating access to, or providing essential facilities in, one or more qualifying premises within the meaning of [Chapter 11 of this Part][3], (*b*) construction of an additional storey or additional storeys to the building which was or were, as the case may be, necessary for the restoration or enhancement of the streetscape, or

(*c*) construction of a replacement building;][4]

[**"property developer"** means a person carrying on a trade which consists wholly or mainly of the construction or refurbishment of buildings or structures with a view to their sale;][5]

"qualifying area" means an area or areas specified as a qualifying area under section 372B;

[**"qualifying period"** means—

[(*a*) subject to section 372B and in relation to a qualifying area, the period commencing on 1 August 1998 and ending on—

(i) 31 December 2002, or

(ii) where subsection (1A) applies, [31 July 2006][6],

and][7]

[(*b*) subject to section 372BA and in relation to a qualifying street, the period commencing on 6 April 2001 and ending on—

(i) 31 December 2004, or

(ii) where subsection (1B) applies, 31 July 2006;][8]][9]

[**"qualifying street"** means a street specified as a qualifying street under section 372BA;][10]

"refurbishment", in relation to a building or structure ...[11], means any work of construction, reconstruction, repair or renewal, including the provision or improvement of water, sewerage or heating facilities, carried out in the course of the repair or restoration, or maintenance in the nature of repair or restoration, of the [building or structure;][12]

[**"replacement building"**, in relation to a building or structure which fronts on to a qualifying street, means a building or structure or part of a building or structure, as the case may be, which is constructed to replace an existing building, where—

(*a*) (i) a notice under subsection (1) of section 3 or an order under subsection (5) of that section, of the Local Government (Sanitary Services) Act, 1964, which required the demolition of the existing building or part of that building, was given or made, as the case may be, on or after 13 September 2000 and before 31 March 2001, and

(ii) the replacement building is consistent with the character and size of the existing building,

or

(*b*) the demolition of the existing building (being a single storey building) was required for structural reasons, in order to facilitate the construction of an additional storey or additional storeys to the building which was or were, as the case may be, necessary for the restoration or enhancement of the streetscape;][13]

[**"relevant local authority"** means—

[(*a*) in relation to a qualifying area—

(i) the county council or the city council or the borough council or, where appropriate, the town council, within the meaning of the Local Government Act 2001, in whose functional area the area is situated, or

(ii) the authorised company (within the meaning of section 3(1) of the Urban Renewal Act 1998) which prepared the integrated area plan (within the meaning of that section) in respect of the area,

and][14]

(*b*) in relation to a qualifying street, in respect of the cities of Cork, Dublin, Galway, Limerick or Waterford, the city council of the city in whose functional area the street is situated;][15]

[**"street"** includes part of a street and the whole or part of any road, square, quay or lane.][13]

[(1A)[(*a*)This subsection shall apply where—

(i) the relevant local authority gives a certificate in writing on or before 30 September 2003, to the person constructing or refurbishing a building or structure or part of a building or structure, the site of which is wholly within a qualifying area, stating that it is satisfied that not less than 15 per cent of the total cost of constructing or refurbishing the building or structure or the part of the building or structure, as the case may be, and the acquisition of the site thereof had been incurred on or before 30 June 2003, and

(ii) the application for such a certificate is received by the relevant local authority on or before 31 July 2003.][16]

(*b*) In considering whether to give a certificate referred to in paragraph *(a)*, the relevant local authority shall have regard only to guidelines issued by the Department of the Environment and Local Government in relation to the giving of such certificates.][17]

[(1B) This subsection shall apply in relation to a qualifying street, as respects capital expenditure incurred on the construction or refurbishment of a building or structure, if—

(*a*) (i) a planning application (not being an application for outline permission within the meaning of section 36 of the Planning and Development Act 2000), in so far as planning permission is required, in respect of the construction or refurbishment work on the building or structure represented by that expenditure, is made in accordance with the Planning and Development Regulations 2001 to 2003,

(ii) an acknowledgement of the application, which confirms that the application was received on or before 31 December 2004, is issued by the planning authority in accordance with article 26(2) of the Planning and Development Regulations 2001 (SI No 600 of 2001), and

(iii) the application is not an invalid application in respect of which a notice is issued by the planning authority in accordance with article 26(5) of those regulations,

(*b*) (i) a planning application, in so far as planning permission was required, in respect of the construction or refurbishment work on the building or structure represented by that expenditure, was made in accordance with the Local Government (Planning and Development) Regulations 1994 (SI No 86 of 1994), not being an application for outline permission within the meaning of article 3 of those regulations,

(ii) an acknowledgement of the application, which confirms that the application was received on or before 10 March 2002, was issued by the planning authority in accordance with article 29(2)(*a*) of the regulations referred to in subparagraph (i), and

(iii) the application was not an invalid application in respect of which a notice was issued by the planning authority in accordance with article 29(2)(*b*)(i) of those regulations,

or

(*c*) where the construction or refurbishment work on the building or structure represented by that expenditure is exempted development for the purposes of the Planning and Development Act 2000 by virtue of section 4 of that Act or by virtue of Part 2 of the Planning and Development Regulations 2001 (SI No 600 of 2001) and—

(i) a detailed plan in relation to the development work is prepared,

(ii) a binding contract in writing, under which the expenditure on the development is incurred, is in existence, and

(iii) work to the value of 5 per cent of the development costs is carried out,

not later than 31 December 2004.][18]

(2) [This Chapter and Chapter 11 of this Part][19] shall apply [in relation to qualifying areas][20] if the Oireachtas passes an Act which refers to this Chapter and provides for the renewal of certain urban areas and the submission of plans (to be known as **"Integrated Area Plans"**) to the Minister for the Environment and Local Government which have been drawn up by local authorities or companies established by local authorities (being local authorities as referred to in such Act) in respect of an area or areas identified by such an authority or company on the basis of criteria prepared by that Minister, including physical and socio-economic renewal of such an area or areas.][21]

Amendments

1 Definition of "existing building" inserted by FA 2001 s 60(*a*)(i)(I) with effect from 6 April 2001.

2 Definition of "facade" inserted by FA 2003 s 27(1)(*a*) with effect from 1 March 1999.

3 Substituted by FA 2002 s 24(1) and Sch 2 Pt 1 para 2(*a*)(i)(I) with effect from 1 January 2002; previously "section 372F or 372I".

4 Definition of "necessary construction" inserted by FA 2001 s 60(*a*)(i)(II) with effect from 6 April 2001.

5 Definition of "property developer" inserted by FA 2000 s 44(1)(*a*)(i) with effect from 1 July 1999.

6 Substituted by FA 2004 s 26(1)(*b*)(i)(I) and shall come into operation on the making of an order to that effect by the Minister for Finance; previously "31 December 2004".

7 Definition of "qualifying period" para (*a*) substituted by FA 2002 s 23(1)(*b*)(i)(I) with effect from such day or days as the Minister for Finance may by order or orders appoint and different days may be appointed for

different provisions. By virtue of the Finance Act 2002 (Commencement of Paragraphs (*b*), (*c*)(i) and (*d*) of section 23(1)) Order 2002, SI No 459 of 2002, this amendment comes into operation on 10 September 2002.

8 Subs (1)(definition of "qualifying period")(*b*) substituted by FA 2004 s 26(1)(*b*)(i)(II) and shall come into operation on the making of an order to that effect by the Minister for Finance.

9 Definition of "qualifying period" substituted by FA 2001 s 60(*a*)(i)(III) with effect from 6 April 2001.

10 Definition of "qualifying street" inserted by FA 2001 s 60(*a*)(i)(IV) with effect from 6 April 2001.

11 Deleted by FA 2002 s 24(1) and Sch 2 Pt 1 para 2 (*a*)(i)(II) with effect from 1 January 2002; previously "and other than for the purposes of sections 372H and 372I".

12 Substituted by FA 2001 s 60(*a*)(i)(V) with effect from 6 April 2001; previously "the building or structure.".

13 Definitions of "replacement building" and "street" inserted by FA 2001 s 60(*a*)(i)(VI) with effect from 6 April 2001.

14 Definition of "relevant local authority" para (*a*) substituted by FA 2003 s 26(*a*)(i) with effect from 1 January 2003.

15 Definition of "relevant local authority" substituted by FA 2002 s 23(1)(*b*)(i)(II) with effect from such day or days as the Minister for Finance may by order or orders appoint and different days may be appointed for different provisions. By virtue of the Finance Act 2002 (Commencement of Paragraphs (*b*), (*c*)(i) and (*d*) of section 23(1)) Order 2002, SI No 459 of 2002, this amendment comes into operation on 10 September 2002.

16 Subs (1A)(*a*) substituted by FA 2003 s 26(*a*)(ii) with effect from 1 January 2003.

17 Subs (1A) inserted by FA 2002 s 23(1)(*b*)(ii) with effect from such day or days as the Minister for Finance may by order or orders appoint and different days may be appointed for different provisions. By virtue of the Finance Act 2002 (Commencement of Paragraphs (*b*), (*c*)(i) and (*d*) of section 23(1)) Order 2002, SI No 459 of 2002, this amendment comes into operation on 10 September 2002.

18 Subs (1B) inserted by FA 2004 s 26(1)(*b*)(ii) and shall come into operation on the making of an order to that effect by the Minister for Finance.

19 Substituted by FA 2002 s 24(1) and Sch 2 Pt 1 para 2 (*a*)(ii) with effect from 1 January 2002; previously "This Chapter".

20 Inserted by FA 2001 s 60(*a*)(ii) with effect from 6 April 2001.

21 Section 372A inserted by FA 1998 s 76 with effect from 6 April 1998.

Notes

By virtue of the Urban Renewal Act 1998 (as amended by FA 2002) s 4, the Act of the Oireachtas referred to in subs (2) is the Urban Renewal Act, 1998.

Cross-references

Industrial building or structure, meaning of "property developer" applied: s 268(1A), (1B).
Qualifying areas: s 372B(1)(*c*), (4).
Qualifying streets: s 372BA(1)(*bb*), (*c*).
Reliefs for lessors and owner-occupiers in respect of expenditure incurred on the provision of certain residential accommodation, interpretation, meanings of "existing building", "necessary construction" and "replacement building" applied: s 372AK(1).

Definitions

company: s 4(1); land: IA 1937 Sch; local authority: s 2(1); Oireachtas: IA 1937 Sch; person: IA 1937 s 11(*c*); writing: IA Sch 1937 Sch.

372B Qualifying areas

[(1) The Minister for Finance may, on the recommendation of the Minister for the Environment and Local Government (which recommendation shall take into consideration an Integrated Area Plan submitted by a local authority or a company established by a local authority to that Minister in respect of an area identified by it), by order direct that—

(*a*) the area or areas described (being wholly located within the boundaries of the area to which the Integrated Area Plan relates) in the order shall be a qualifying area for the purposes of one or more sections of [this Chapter or Chapter 11 of this Part][1],

[(*b*) where such an area or areas is or are to be a qualifying area—

(i) for the purposes of section 372D—

(I) one or more of the categories of building or structure mentioned in subsection (2) shall or shall not be a qualifying premises within the meaning of that section, and

(II) that area or those areas shall be a qualifying area for the purposes of either or both the construction of, and the refurbishment of, a qualifying premises within the meaning of that section;

(ii) for the purposes of section 372AR, that area or those areas shall be a qualifying area for the purposes of one or more of the following:

(I) the construction of,

(II) the conversion into, and

(III) the refurbishment (within the meaning of Chapter 11 of this Part) of,

a qualifying premises (within the meaning of that Chapter),][2]

[(*ba*) where such an area or areas is or are to be a qualifying area for the purposes of section 372AP, that section shall apply in relation to that area or those areas in so far as that section relates to one or more of the following:

(i) expenditure incurred on the construction of a house,

(ii) conversion expenditure incurred in relation to a house, and

(iii) refurbishment expenditure incurred in relation to a house,][3]

[(*c*) as respects any such area so described in the order and in so far as this Chapter is concerned, the definition of "qualifying period" in section 372A shall be construed as a reference to such period as shall be specified in the order in relation to that area; but no such period specified in the order shall commence before 1 August 1998 or end after—

(i) 31 December 2002, or

(ii) where section 372A(1A) applies, [31 July 2006][4],][5]

[(*d*) as respects any such area so described in the order and in so far as Chapter 11 of this Part is concerned, the definition of "qualifying period" in section 372AL shall be construed as a reference to such period as shall be specified in the order in relation to that area; but no such period specified in the order shall commence before 1 August 1998 or end after—

(i) 31 December 2002, or

(ii) where section 372AL(2) applies, [31 July 2006][6] .][7]

[(2) The categories of building or structure referred to in subsection (1)(*b*)(i)(I) shall be—

(*a*) buildings or structures which consist of office accommodation,

(*b*) multi-storey car parks,

(*c*) any other buildings or structures and in respect of which not more than 10 per cent of the capital expenditure incurred in the qualifying period on their construction or refurbishment relates to the construction or refurbishment of office accommodation,

(*d*) the facade of a building or structure or part of a building or structure referred to in paragraph (*a*),

(*e*) the facade of a building or structure or part of a building or structure referred to in paragraph (*c*).][8]

[(2A) The power to make an order under subsection (1) includes the power to amend or revoke the order.][9]

(3) Every order made by the Minister for Finance under subsection (1) shall be laid before Dáil Éireann as soon as may be after it is made and, if a resolution annulling the order is passed by Dáil Éireann within the next 21 days on which Dáil Éireann has sat after the order is laid before it, the order shall be annulled accordingly, but without prejudice to the validity of anything previously done thereunder.

(4) Notwithstanding an order under subsection (1), the granting of relief by virtue of any provision of [this Chapter or Chapter 11 of this Part][10] [in respect of the construction, refurbishment or conversion of a building, structure or house, the site of which is wholly within a qualifying area,][11] shall be subject to such other requirements as may be specified in or under the Act referred to in section 372A(2).][12]

Amendments

1 Substituted by FA 2002 s 24(1) and Sch 2 Pt 1 para 2(*b*)(i)(I) with effect from 1 January 2002; previously "this Chapter".

2 Subs (1)(*b*) substituted by FA 2003 s 27(1)(*b*)(i) with effect from 1 March 1999.

3 Subs (1)(*ba*) inserted by FA 2002 s 24(1) and Sch 2 Pt 1 para 2(*b*)(i)(II) with effect from 1 January 2002.

4 Substituted by FA 2004 s 26(1)(*c*)(i) and shall come into operation on the making of an order to that effect by the Minister for Finance; previously "31 December 2004".

5 Subs (1)(*c*) substituted by FA 2002 s 23(1)(*c*)(i) with effect from such day or days as the Minister for Finance may by order or orders appoint and different days may be appointed for different provisions. By virtue of the Finance Act 2002 (Commencement of Paragraphs (*b*), (*c*)(i) and (*d*) of section 23(1)) Order 2002, SI No 459 of 2002, this amendment comes into operation on 10 September 2002.

6 Substituted by FA 2004 s 26(1)(*c*)(ii) with effect from 1 January 2004; previously "31 December 2004".

7 Subs (1)(*d*) inserted by FA 2002 s 23(1)(*c*)(ii) with effect from 1 January 2002.

8 Subs (2) substituted by FA 2003 s 27(1)(*b*)(ii) with effect from 1 March 1999.

9 Subs (2A) inserted by FA 2003 s 27(1)(*b*)(iii) with effect from 1 March 1999.

10 Substituted by FA 2002 s 24(1) and Sch 2 Pt 1 para 2(*b*)(ii) with effect from 1 January 2002.

11 Inserted by FA 2001 s 60(*b*) with effect from 6 April 2001.

12 Section 372B inserted by FA 1998 s 76 with effect from 6 April 1998.

Cross-references

An "eligible town" for the purposes of the Town Renewal Act 2000, as amended by FA 2002 (and consequently for purposes of relief under TCA 1997 Pt 10 Chs 10 and 11) cannot be within an area described as a qualifying area in an order made under this section — Town Renewal Act 2000 s 1, definition of "eligible town", refers.

Interpretation and application: s 372A (qualifying area, qualifying period).

Reliefs for lessors and owner-occupiers in respect of expenditure incurred on the provision of certain residential accommodation, interpretation: s 372AK(1)("qualifying urban area"); qualifying period: s 372AL(1)(*a*); continuity, subs (1): s 372AV(7).

See also Urban Renewal Act 1998 (as amended by FA 2002), ss 9 (qualifying areas for urban renewal tax reliefs), 9A (designation of certain areas for rented residential reliefs), 11 (certain reliefs conditional on buildings etc being consistent with integrated area plan) and 12 (monitoring of implementation of integrated area plan).

Definitions

company: s 4(1); Dáil Éireann: IA 1937 Sch; local authority: s 2(1); refurbishment: s 372A(1).

372BA Qualifying streets

[(1) The Minister for Finance may, on the recommendation of the Minister for the Environment and Local Government (which recommendation shall take into consideration proposals submitted by a relevant local authority to that Minister in respect of a street identified by it), by order direct that—

(*a*) a street described (being a street situated in the functional area of the relevant local authority) in the order shall be a qualifying street for the purposes of one or more sections of [this Chapter or Chapter 11 of this Part][1],

(*b*) where such a street is to be a qualifying street for the purposes of section 372D, the categories of building or structure mentioned in subsection (2) shall not be a qualifying premises within the meaning of that section, and

[(*ba*) [where such a street is to be a qualifying street for the purposes of section 372AP, that section shall apply in relation to that street][2] in so far as that section relates to one or more of the following:

(i) expenditure incurred on the construction of a house,

(ii) conversion expenditure incurred in relation to a house, and

(iii) refurbishment expenditure incurred in relation to a house,][3]

[(*bb*) as respects any such street so described in the order and in so far as this Chapter is concerned, the definition of qualifying period in section 372A shall be construed as a reference to such period as shall be specified in the order in relation to that street; but no such period specified in the order shall commence before 6 April 2001 or end after—

(i) 31 December 2004, or

(ii) where section 372A(1B) applies, 31 July 2006,][4]

[(*c*) as respects any such street so described in the order and in so far as Chapter 11 of this Part is concerned, the definition of qualifying period in section 372A shall be construed as a reference to such period as shall be specified in the order in relation to that street; but no such period specified in the order shall commence before 6 April 2001 or end after—

(i) 31 December 2004, or

(ii) where section 372AL(1A) applies, 31 July 2006.][5]

(2) The categories of building or structure referred to in subsection (1)(*b*) shall be buildings or structures—

(*a*) other than those in use for the purposes of the retailing of goods or the provision of services only within the State,

(*b*) in use as offices, and

(*c*) in use for the provision of mail order or financial services.

[(2A) The power to made an order under subsection (1) includes the power to amend or revoke the order.][6]

(3) Every order made by the Minister for Finance under subsection (1) shall be laid before Dáil Éireann as soon as may be after it is made and, if a resolution annulling the order is passed by Dáil Éireann within the next 21 days on which Dáil Éireann has sat after the order is laid before it, the order shall be annulled accordingly, but without prejudice to the validity of anything previously done thereunder.

(4) Notwithstanding an order under subsection (1), no relief from income tax or corporation tax, as the case may be, may be granted [under this Chapter or Chapter 11 of this Part][7] in respect of the construction, refurbishment or conversion of a building, structure or house which fronts on to a qualifying street unless the relevant local authority has certified in writing that such construction, refurbishment or conversion is consistent with the aims, objectives and criteria for the Living over the Shop Scheme, as outlined in a circular of the Department of the Environment and Local Government entitled "Living Over The Shop Scheme", reference numbered UR 43A and dated 13 September 2000, or in any further circular of that Department amending paragraph 6 of the first-mentioned circular for the purposes of increasing the aggregate length of street allowable, to the manager of the relevant local authority concerned.][8]

Amendments

1 Substituted by FA 2002 s 24(1) and Sch 2 Pt 1 para 2(*c*)(i)(I) with effect from 1 January 2002; previously "this Chapter".

2 Substituted by FA 2004 s 26(1)(*d*)(i) with effect from 1 January 2002; previously "where such an area or areas is or are to be a qualifying area for the purposes of section 372AP, that section shall apply in relation to that area or those areas".

3 Subs (1)(*ba*) inserted by FA 2002 s 24(1) and Sch 2 Pt 1 para 2(*c*)(i)(II) with effect from 1 January 2002.

4 Subs (1)(*bb*) inserted by FA 2004 s 26(1)(*d*)(ii) and shall come into operation on the making of an order to that effect by the Minister for Finance.

5 Subs (1)(*c*) substituted by FA 2004 s 26(1)(*d*)(iii) with effect from 1 January 2004.

6 Subs (2A) inserted by FA 2003 s 27(1)(*c*) with effect from 6 April 2001.

7 Inserted by FA 2002 s 24(1) and Sch 2 Pt 1 para 2(*c*)(ii) with effect from 1 January 2002.

8 Section 372BA inserted by FA 2001 s 60(*c*) with effect from 6 April 2001.

Cross-references

Interpretation and application ("qualifying period", "qualifying street"): s 372A(1).

Reliefs for lessors and owner-occupiers in respect of expenditure incurred on the provision of certain residential accommodation, interpretation: s 372AK(1)("qualifying street"); qualifying period: s 372AL(1)(*b*); continuity, subs (1): s 372AV(7).

Definitions

Dáil Éireann: IA 1937 Sch; refurbishment: s 372A(1); relevant local authority: s 372A(1); street: s 372A(1); writing: IA 1937 Sch.

372C Accelerated capital allowances in relation to construction or refurbishment of certain industrial buildings or structures

[[(1) In this section "building or structure to which this section applies" means a building or structure or part of a building or structure the site of which is wholly within a qualifying area and which is to be an industrial building or structure by reason of its use for a purpose specified in section 268(1)(*a*).][1]

(2) Subject to subsection (4), section 271 shall apply in relation to capital expenditure incurred in the qualifying period on the construction or refurbishment of a building or structure to which this section applies as if—

(*a*) in subsection (1) of that section the definition of "industrial development agency" were deleted,

(*b*) in subsection (2)(*a*)(i) of that section "to which subsection (3) applies" were deleted,

(*c*) subsection (3) of that section were deleted,

(*d*) the following subsection were substituted for subsection (4) of that section:

"(4) An industrial building allowance shall be of an amount equal to [50 per cent][2] of the capital expenditure mentioned in subsection (2)."

and

(*e*) in subsection (5) of that section "to which subsection (3)(*c*) applies" were deleted.

(3) Subject to subsection (4), section 273 shall apply in relation to capital expenditure incurred in the qualifying period on the construction or refurbishment of a building or structure to which this section applies as if—

(*a*) in subsection (1) of that section the definition of "industrial development agency" were deleted,

(*b*) the following paragraph were substituted for paragraph (*b*) of subsection (2) of that section:

"(*b*) As respects any qualifying expenditure, any allowance made under section 272 and increased under paragraph (*a*) in respect of that expenditure, whether claimed for one chargeable period or more than one such period, shall not in the aggregate exceed 50 per cent of the amount of that qualifying expenditure."

and

(*c*) subsections (3) to (7) of that section were deleted.

(4) In the case where capital expenditure is incurred in the qualifying period on the refurbishment of a building or structure to which this section applies, subsections (2) and (3) shall apply only if the total amount of the capital expenditure so incurred is not less than an amount equal to 10 per cent of the market value of the building or structure immediately before that expenditure was incurred.

(5) Notwithstanding section 274(1), no balancing charge shall be made in relation to a building or structure to which this section applies by reason of any of the events specified in that section which occurs—

(*a*) more than 13 years after the building or structure was first used, or

(*b*) in a case where section 276 applies, more than 13 years after the capital expenditure on refurbishment of the building or structure was incurred.

(6) For the purposes only of determining, in relation to a claim for an allowance under section 271 or 273 as applied by this section, whether and to what extent capital expenditure incurred on the construction or refurbishment of an industrial building or structure is incurred or not incurred in the qualifying period, only such an amount of that capital expenditure as is properly attributable to work on the construction or, as the case may be, the refurbishment of the building or structure actually carried out during the

qualifying period shall (notwithstanding any other provision of the Tax Acts as to the time when any capital expenditure is or is to be treated as incurred) be treated as having been incurred in that period.][3]

Amendments

1 Subs (1) substituted by FA 2000 s 44(1)(*c*)(i) with effect from 1 July 1999.
2 Substituted by FA 2000 s 44(1)(*c*)(ii) with effect from 1 July 1999; previously "25 per cent".
3 Section 372C inserted by FA 1998 s 76 with effect from 6 April 1998.

Cross-references

Non-application of relief in certain cases and provision against double relief: s 372K(1), (2).

Definitions

market value: s 372A(1); qualifying area: s 372A(1); qualifying period: s 372A(1); refurbishment: s 372A(1).

372D Capital allowances in relation to construction or refurbishment of certain commercial premises

[(1) In this section, **"qualifying premises"** means a building or structure [or part of a building or structure][1] the site of which is wholly within a qualifying area [, or which fronts on to a qualifying street,][2] and which—

(*a*) apart from this section is not an industrial building or structure within the meaning of section 268, and

(*b*) (i) is in use for the purposes of a trade or profession, or

(ii) whether or not it is so used, is let on bona fide commercial terms for such consideration as might be expected to be paid in a letting of the building or structure negotiated on an arm's length basis,

but does not include any part of a building or structure in use as or as part of a dwelling house.

(2) (*a*) Subject to paragraph (*b*) and [subsections (3) to (5)],[3] the provisions of the Tax Acts (other than section 372C) relating to the making of allowances or charges in respect of capital expenditure incurred on the construction or refurbishment of an industrial building or structure shall, notwithstanding anything to the contrary in those provisions, apply—

(i) as if a qualifying premises were, at all times at which it is a qualifying premises, a building or structure in respect of which an allowance is to be made for the purposes of income tax or corporation tax, as the case may be, under Chapter 1 of Part 9 by reason of its use for a purpose specified in section 268(1)(*a*), and

[(ii) where any activity—

(I) carried on in the qualifying premises, or

(II) in a case where the facade of a building or structure or part of a building or structure is a qualifying premises, carried on in the building or structure or the part of the building or structure,

is not a trade, as if it were a trade.][4]

(*b*) An allowance shall be given by virtue of this subsection in respect of any capital expenditure incurred on the construction or refurbishment of a qualifying premises only in so far as that expenditure is incurred in the qualifying period.

(3) In the case where capital expenditure is incurred in the qualifying period on the refurbishment of a qualifying premises, subsection (2) shall apply only if the total amount of the capital expenditure so incurred is not less than an amount equal to 10 per cent of the market value of the qualifying premises immediately before that expenditure was incurred.

[(3A)(*a*) In the case of a qualifying premises which fronts on to a [qualifying street][5], subsection (2) shall apply in relation to capital expenditure incurred in the qualifying period on the construction or refurbishment of the qualifying premises, only if—

(i) the qualifying premises are comprised in the ground floor of—

(I) an existing building, or

(II) a replacement building,

and

[(ii) apart from the capital expenditure incurred in the qualifying period on the construction or refurbishment of the qualifying premises, expenditure is incurred on the upper floor or floors of the existing building or the replacement building, as the case may be, which is—

(I) eligible expenditure within the meaning of Chapter 11 of this Part (being eligible expenditure on necessary construction, or conversion expenditure or refurbishment expenditure within the meaning of that Chapter), or

(II) qualifying expenditure within the meaning of Chapter 11 of this Part (being qualifying expenditure on necessary construction, on conversion or on refurbishment within the meaning of that Chapter),

and in respect of which a deduction has been given, or would on due claim being made be given, under section 372AP or 372AR.][6]

[(*b*) Notwithstanding paragraph (*a*), subsection (2) shall not apply in relation to so much (if any) of the capital expenditure incurred in the qualifying period on the construction or refurbishment of the qualifying premises as exceeds the amount of the deduction, or the aggregate amount of the deductions, which has been given, or which would on due claim being made be given, under section 372AP or 372AR in respect of the eligible expenditure referred to in paragraph (*a*)(ii)(I) or the qualifying expenditure referred to in paragraph (*a*)(ii)(II).][7][8]

(4) For the purposes of the application, by subsection (2), of sections 271 and 273 in relation to capital expenditure incurred in the qualifying period on the construction or refurbishment of a qualifying premises—

(*a*) section 271 shall apply as if—

(i) in subsection (1) of that section the definition of "industrial development agency" were deleted,

(ii) in subsection (2)(*a*)(i) of that section "to which subsection (3) applies" were deleted,

(iii) subsection (3) of that section were deleted,

(iv) the following subsection were substituted for subsection (4) of that section:

"(4) An industrial building allowance shall be of an amount equal to 50 per cent of the capital expenditure mentioned in subsection (2)."

and

(v) in subsection (5) of that section "to which subsection (3)(*c*) applies" were deleted,

and

(*b*) section 273 shall apply as if—

(i) in subsection (1) of that section the definition of "industrial development agency" were deleted, ...[9]

[(ii) the following paragraph were substituted for paragraph (*b*) of subsection (2) of that section:

"(*b*) As respects any qualifying expenditure, any allowance made under section 272 and increased under paragraph (*a*) in respect of that expenditure, whether claimed for one chargeable period or more than one such period, shall not in the aggregate exceed 50 per cent of the amount of that qualifying expenditure."

and

(iii) subsections (3) to (7) of that section were deleted.][10]

(5) Notwithstanding section 274(1), no balancing charge shall be made in relation to a qualifying premises by reason of any of the events specified in that section which occur—

(*a*) more than 13 years after the qualifying premises was first used, or

(*b*) in a case where section 276 applies, more than 13 years after the capital expenditure on refurbishment of the qualifying premises was incurred.

...[11]

(7) For the purposes only of determining, in relation to a claim for an allowance by virtue of subsection (2), whether and to what extent capital expenditure incurred on the construction or refurbishment of a qualifying premises is incurred or not incurred in the qualifying period, only such an amount of that capital expenditure as is properly attributable to work on the construction or refurbishment of the premises actually carried out during the qualifying period shall (notwithstanding any other provision of the Tax Acts as to the time when any capital expenditure is or is to be treated as incurred) be treated as having been incurred in that period.][12]

Amendments

1 Inserted by FA 2000 s 44(1)(*d*)(i) with effect from 1 July 1999.

2 Inserted by FA 2001 s 60(*d*)(i) with effect from 6 April 2001.

3 Substituted by FA 2000 s 44(1)(*d*)(ii) with effect from 1 July 1999; previously "subsections (3) to (6A)".

4 Subs (2)(*a*)(ii) substituted by FA 2003 s 27(1)(*d*)(i) with effect from 1 March 1999.

5 Substituted by FA 2002 s 138 and Sch 6 paras 3(*f*) and 6(*c*)(ii) with effect from 6 April 2001; previously "designated street".

6 Subs (3A)(*a*)(ii) substituted by FA 2003 s 27(1)(*d*)(ii)(I) with effect from 1 January 2002.

7 Subs (3A)(*b*) substituted by FA 2003 s 27(1)(*d*)(ii)(II) with effect from 1 January 2002.

8 Subs (3A) inserted by FA 2001 s 60(*d*)(ii) with effect from 6 April 2001.

9 Deleted by FA 2000 s 44(1)(*d*)(iii)(I) with effect from 1 July 1999; previously "and".

10 Subs (4)(*b*)(ii) substituted by FA 2000 s 44(1)(*d*)(iii)(II) with effect from 1 July 1999.

11 Subss (6)–(6A) deleted by FA 2000 s 44(1)(*d*)(iv) with effect from 1 July 1999.

12 Section 372D inserted by FA 1998 s 76 with effect from 6 April 1998.

Cross-references

Non-application of relief in certain cases and provision against double relief: s 372K(1), (2).
Qualifying areas: s 372B(1)(*b*)(i).

Definitions

existing building: s 372A(1); facade: s 372A(1); market value: s 372A(1); necessary construction: s 372A(1); qualifying area: s 372A(1); qualifying period: s 372A(1); qualifying street: s 372A(1); refurbishment: s 372A(1); replacement building: s 372A(1); Tax Acts: s 1(2); trade: ss 2(1), 3(1).

372E Double rent allowance in respect of rent paid for certain business premises

Amendments

1 Section 372E repealed by FA 2002 s 24(3)(*f*) with effect from 1 January 2002.

372F Rented residential accommodation: deduction for certain expenditure on construction

Amendments

1 Section 372F repealed by FA 2002 s 24(3)(*f*) with effect from 1 January 2002; but see now TCA 1997 Pt 10 Ch 11 (ss 372AK–372AV) which codified, with effect from 1 January 2002, reliefs for lessors and owner-occupiers in respect of expenditure incurred on the provision of certain residential accommodation, and in particular s 372AV which provides for the continuity of the operation of the law relating to income tax, corporation tax and capital gains tax in that respect.

372G Rented residential accommodation: deduction for certain expenditure on conversion

Amendments

1 Section 372G repealed by FA 2002 s 24(3)(*f*) with effect from 1 January 2002; but see now TCA 1997 Pt 10 Ch 11 (ss 372AK–372AV) which codified, with effect from 1 January 2002, reliefs for lessors and owner-occupiers in respect of expenditure incurred on the provision of certain residential accommodation, and in particular s 372AV which provides for the continuity of the operation of the law relating to income tax, corporation tax and capital gains tax in that respect.

372H Rented residential accommodation: deduction for certain expenditure on refurbishment

Amendments

1 Section 372H repealed by FA 2002 s 24(3)(*f*) with effect from 1 January 2002; but see now TCA 1997 Pt 10 Ch 11 (ss 372AK–372AV) which codified, with effect from 1 January 2002, reliefs for lessors and owner-occupiers in respect of expenditure incurred on the provision of certain residential accommodation, and in particular s 372AV which provides for the continuity of the operation of the law relating to income tax, corporation tax and capital gains tax in that respect.

372I Residential accommodation: allowance to owner-occupiers in respect of certain expenditure on construction or refurbishment

Amendments

1 Section 372I repealed by FA 2002 s 24(3)(*f*) with effect from 1 January 2002; but see now TCA 1997 Pt 10 Ch 11 (ss 372AK–372AV) which codified, with effect from 1 January 2002, reliefs for lessors and

owner-occupiers in respect of expenditure incurred on the provision of certain residential accommodation, and in particular s 372AV which provides for the continuity of the operation of the law relating to income tax, corporation tax and capital gains tax in that respect.

372J Provisions supplementary to sections 372F to 372I

Amendments

1 Section 372J repealed by FA 2002 s 24(3)(*f*) with effect from 1 January 2002; but see now TCA 1997 Pt 10 Ch 11 (ss 372AK–372AV) which codified, with effect from 1 January 2002, reliefs for lessors and owner-occupiers in respect of expenditure incurred on the provision of certain residential accommodation, and in particular s 372AV which provides for the continuity of the operation of the law relating to income tax, corporation tax and capital gains tax in that respect.

372K Non-application of relief in certain cases and provision against double relief

[(1) Notwithstanding any other provision of this Chapter, sections 372C and 372D shall not apply—

(*a*) in respect of expenditure incurred on the construction or refurbishment of a building or structure or a qualifying premises—

(i) where a property developer is entitled to the relevant interest, within the meaning of section 269, in relation to that expenditure, and

(ii) either the person referred to in subparagraph (i) or a person connected (within the meaning of section 10) with that person incurred the expenditure on the construction or refurbishment of the building, structure or premises concerned,

[(*aa*) in respect of expenditure incurred on or after 6 April 2001 on the construction or refurbishment of a building or structure or a qualifying premises the site of which is wholly within a qualifying area where any part of such expenditure has been or is to be met, directly or indirectly, by [grant assistance or any other assistance which is granted by or through the State, any board established by statute, any public or local authority or any other agency of the State][1],][2]

(*b*) in respect of expenditure incurred on the construction or refurbishment of a building or structure or a qualifying premises where such building or structure or premises is in use for the purposes of a trade, or any activity treated as a trade, carried on by the person who is entitled to the relevant interest, within the meaning of section 269, in relation to that expenditure and such trade or activity is carried on wholly or mainly—

(i) in the sector of agriculture, including the production, processing and marketing of agricultural products,

(ii) in the coal industry, fishing industry or motor vehicle industry, or

(iii) in the transport, steel, shipbuilding, synthetic fibres or financial services sectors,

or

[(*c*) in respect of expenditure incurred on or after 1 January 2003 on the construction or refurbishment of any building or structure or qualifying premises provided for the purposes of a project which is subject to the notification requirements of—

(i) the "Multisectoral framework on regional aid for large investment projects" (OJ No C 107, 7.4.1998, p.7) prepared by the Commission of the European Communities and dated 7 April 1998, or

(ii) the "Multisectoral framework on regional aid for large investment projects" (OJ No C 70, 19.3.2002, p.8) prepared by the Commission of the European Communities and dated 19 March 2002,

as the case may be, unless approval of the potential capital allowances involved has been received from that Commission by the Minister for Finance, or by such other Minister of the Government, agency or body as may be nominated for that purpose by the Minister for Finance.][3]

(2) For the purposes of sections [sections 372C and 372D][4], where the site of any part of a building or structure is situate outside the boundary of a qualifying area and where expenditure incurred or treated as having been incurred in the qualifying period is attributable to the building or structure in general, such an amount of that expenditure shall be deemed to be attributable to the part which is situate outside the boundary of the qualifying area as bears to the whole of that expenditure the same proportion as the floor area of the part situate outside the boundary of the qualifying area bears to the total floor area of the building or structure.

(3) Where relief is given by virtue of any provision of this Chapter in relation to capital expenditure or other expenditure incurred on, or rent payable in respect of, any building, structure or premises, relief shall not be given in respect of that expenditure or that rent under any other provision of the Tax Acts.][5]

Amendments

1 Substituted by FA 2002 s 26(1)(*a*) as respects expenditure incurred on or after 7 February 2002; previously "grant assistance from the State or from any other person".

2 Subs (1)(*aa*) inserted by FA 2001 s 60(*j*) with effect from 6 April 2001.

3 Subs (1)(*c*) substituted by FA 2003 s 27(1)(*e*)(i) with effect from 1 January 2003.

4 Substituted by FA 2003 s 27(1)(*e*)(ii) with effect from 1 January 2003; previously "sections 372C, 372D, 372G and 372H".

5 Section 372K substituted by FA 2000 s 44(1)(*h*) with effect from 1 July 1999.

Tax Briefing

TB41 Sept 2000 pp 16–18 — Industrial and Commercial Buildings Capital Allowances — Finance Act 2000 Restrictions.

Definitions

person: IA 1937 s 11(*c*); property developer, qualifying area, qualifying period, refurbishment, rent: s 372A(1); Tax Acts: s 1(2).

[CHAPTER 8
Qualifying Rural Areas][1]

Amendments

1 Chapter 8 title inserted by FA 1998 s 77(*a*) with effect from 6 April 1998.

Cross-references

Case V, Schedule D, computational rules and allowable deductions: s 97(2B)(*d*).

Revenue information

Information leaflet IT65 — Rural Renewal Scheme.

372L Interpretation (Chapter 8)

[(1)][1] In this Chapter—

"lease", **"lessee"**, **"lessor"**, **"premium"** and **"rent"** have the same meanings respectively as in Chapter 8 of Part 4;

"market value", in relation to a building, structure or house, means the price which the unencumbered fee simple of the building, structure or house would fetch if sold in the open market in such manner and subject to such conditions as might reasonably be calculated to obtain for the vendor the best price for the building, structure or house, less the part of that price which would be attributable to the acquisition of, or of rights in or over, the land on which the building, structure or house is constructed;

[**"property developer"** means a person carrying on a trade which consists wholly or mainly of the construction or refurbishment of buildings or structures with a view to their sale;][2]

[**"qualifying period"** means—

(*a*) for the purposes of sections 372M, 372N and 372O, the period commencing on such day as the Minister for Finance may by order appoint [and ending on—

(i) 31 December 2004, or

(ii) where subsection (2) applies, 31 July 2006,][3]

...[4]][5]

"qualifying rural area" means any area described in Schedule 8A;

"refurbishment", in relation to a building or structure ...[6], means any work of construction, reconstruction, repair or renewal, including the provision or improvement of water, sewerage or heating facilities, carried out in the course of the repair or restoration, or maintenance in the nature of repair or restoration, of the building or structure.][7]

[(2) This subsection shall apply, as respects capital expenditure incurred on the construction or refurbishment of a building or structure, if—

(*a*) (i) a planning application (not being an application for outline permission within the meaning of section 36 of the Planning and Development Act 2000), in so far as planning permission is required, in respect of the construction or refurbishment work on the building or structure represented by that expenditure, is made in accordance with the Planning and Development Regulations 2001 to 2003,

(ii) an acknowledgement of the application, which confirms that the application was received on or before 31 December 2004, is issued by the planning authority in accordance with article 26(2) of the Planning and Development Regulations 2001 (SI No 600 of 2001), and

(iii) the application is not an invalid application in respect of which a notice is issued by the planning authority in accordance with article 26(5) of those regulations,

(*b*) (i) a planning application, in so far as planning permission was required, in respect of the construction or refurbishment work on the building or structure represented by that expenditure, was made in accordance with the Local Government (Planning and Development) Regulations 1994 (SI No 86 of 1994), not being an application for outline permission within the meaning of article 3 of those regulations,

(ii) an acknowledgement of the application, which confirms that the application was received on or before 10 March 2002, was issued by the planning authority in accordance with article 29(2)(*a*) of the regulations referred to in subparagraph (i), and

(iii) the application was not an invalid application in respect of which a notice was issued by the planning authority in accordance with article 29(2)(*b*)(i) of those regulations,

or

(*c*) where the construction or refurbishment work on the building or structure represented by that expenditure is exempted development for the purposes of the Planning and Development Act 2000 by virtue of section 4 of that Act or by virtue of Part 2 of the Planning and Development Regulations 2001 (SI No 600 of 2001) and—

(i) a detailed plan in relation to the development work is prepared,

(ii) a binding contract in writing, under which the expenditure on the development is incurred, is in existence, and

(iii) work to the value of 5 per cent of the development costs is carried out,

not later than 31 December 2004.][8]

Notes

By virtue of the Taxes Consolidation Act 1997 (Section 372L) (Commencement) Order 1999, SI No 205 of 1999, the commencement date referred to in para (*a*) of the definition of "qualifying period" is, for the purposes of sections 372M and 372N, 1 July 1999.

Amendments

1 Renumbered as (1) by FA 2004 s 26(1)(*e*)(i) and shall come into operation on the making of an order to that effect by the Minister for Finance.

2 Definition of "property developer" inserted by FA 2000 s 45(1)(*a*)(i) with effect from 1 July 1999.

3 Substituted by FA 2004 s 26(1)(*e*)(ii) and shall come into operation on the making of an order to that effect by the Minister for Finance; previously "and ending on 31 December 2004".

4 Definition of "qualifying period" paras (*b*) and (*c*) deleted by FA 2002 s 24(1) and Sch 2 Pt 1 para 2(*d*)(i) with effect from 1 January 2002.

5 Definition of "qualifying period" substituted by F(No 2)A 1998 s 4 with effect from 20 May 1998.

6 Deleted by FA 2002 s 24(1) and Sch 2 Pt 1 para 2(*d*)(ii) with effect from 1 January 2002; previously "and other than for the purposes of sections 372R and 372RA".

7 Section 372L inserted by FA 1998 s 77(*a*) with effect from 6 April 1998.

8 Subs (2) inserted by FA 2004 s 26(1)(*e*)(iii) and shall come into operation on the making of an order to that effect by the Minister for Finance

Cross-references

An "eligible town" for the purposes of the Town Renewal Act 2000, as amended by FA 2002 (and consequently for the purposes of relief under TCA 1997 Pt 10 Chs 10 and 11) cannot be within a "qualifying rural area" within the meaning of this section — Town Renewal Act 2000 s 1, definition of "eligible town", refers.

Definitions

land: IA 1937 Sch; writing: IA 1937 Sch.

372M Accelerated capital allowances in relation to construction or refurbishment of certain industrial buildings or structures

[(1) This section shall apply to a building or structure the site of which is wholly within a qualifying rural area and which is to be an industrial building or structure by reason of its use for a purpose specified in [paragraph (*a*) or (*b*) of section 268(1)].[1]

(2) Subject to subsection (4), section 271 shall apply in relation to capital expenditure incurred in the qualifying period on the construction or refurbishment of a building or structure to which this section applies as if—

(*a*) in subsection (1) of that section the definition of "industrial development agency" were deleted,

(*b*) in subsection (2)(*a*)(i) of that section "to which subsection (3) applies" were deleted,

(*c*) subsection (3) of that section were deleted,

(*d*) the following subsection were substituted for subsection (4) of that section:

"(4) An industrial building allowance shall be of an amount equal to [50 per cent][2] of the capital expenditure mentioned in subsection (2)."

and

(*e*) in subsection (5) of that section "to which subsection (3)(*c*) applies" were deleted.

(3) Subject to subsection (4), section 273 shall apply in relation to capital expenditure incurred in the qualifying period on the construction or refurbishment of a building or structure to which this section applies as if—

(*a*) in subsection (1) of that section the definition of "industrial development agency" were deleted,

(*b*) the following paragraph were substituted for [paragraph (*b*)][3] of subsection (2) of that section:

"(*b*) As respects any qualifying expenditure, any allowance made under section 272 and increased under paragraph (*a*) in respect of that expenditure, whether claimed for one chargeable period or more than one such period, shall not in the aggregate exceed 50 per cent of the amount of that qualifying expenditure."

and

(*c*) subsections (3) to (7) of that section were deleted.

(4) In the case where capital expenditure is incurred in the qualifying period on the refurbishment of a building or structure to which this section applies, subsections (2) and (3) shall apply only if the total amount of the capital expenditure so incurred is not less than an amount equal to 10 per cent of the market value of the building or structure immediately before that expenditure was incurred.

(5) Notwithstanding section 274(1), no balancing charge shall be made in relation to a building or structure to which this section applies by reason of any of the events specified in that section which occurs—

(*a*) more than 13 years after the building or structure was first used, or (*b*) in a case where section 276 applies, more than 13 years after the capital expenditure on refurbishment of the building or structure was incurred.

(6) For the purposes only of determining, in relation to a claim for an allowance under section 271 or 273 as applied by this section, whether and to what extent capital expenditure incurred on the construction or refurbishment of an industrial building or structure is incurred or not incurred in the qualifying period, only such an amount of that capital expenditure as is properly attributable to work on the construction or, as the case may be, the refurbishment of the building or structure actually carried out during the qualifying period shall (notwithstanding any other provision of the Tax Acts as to the time when any capital expenditure is or is to be treated as incurred) be treated as having been incurred in that period.][4]

Amendments

1 Substituted by FA 1999 s 47(1)(*b*) with effect from 6 April 1999; previously "section 268(1)(*a*)".

2 Substituted by FA 2000 s 45(1)(*b*) with effect from 1 July 1999; previously "25 per cent".

3 Substituted by FA 2001 s 59(1)(*b*)(i) with effect from 6 April 2001; previously "paragraph (*i*)".

4 Section 372M inserted by FA 1998 s 77(*a*) with effect from 6 April 1998.

Cross-references

Capital allowances in relation to commercial buildings: s 372N(2)(*a*).

Interpretation: s 372L (qualifying period).

Non-application of relief in certain cases and provision against double relief: s 372T(1).

Definitions

market value: s 372L; qualifying period: s 372L; qualifying rural area: s 372L; refurbishment: s 372L; Tax Acts: s 1(2).

372N Capital allowances in relation to construction or refurbishment of certain commercial buildings or structures

[(1) In this section—

"approved scheme" means a scheme undertaken with the approval of a local authority which has as its object, or amongst its objects, the provision of sewerage facilities, water supplies or roads for public purposes;

"qualifying premises" means a building or structure the site of which is wholly within a qualifying rural area, and which—

(*a*) apart from this section is not an industrial building or structure within the meaning of section 268, and

(*b*) (i) is in use for the purposes of a trade or profession or for the purposes of an approved scheme, or

(ii) whether or not it is so used, is let on bona fide commercial terms for such consideration as might be expected to be paid in a letting of the building or structure negotiated on an arm's length basis,

but does not include any part of a building or structure in use as or as part of a dwelling house.

(2) (*a*) Subject to paragraph (*b*) and [subsections (3) to (5)],[1] the provisions of the Tax Acts (other than section 372M) relating to the making of allowances or charges in respect of capital expenditure incurred on the construction or refurbishment

of an industrial building or structure shall, notwithstanding anything to the contrary in those provisions, apply—

(i) as if a qualifying premises were, at all times at which it is a qualifying premises, a building or structure in respect of which an allowance is to be made for the purposes of income tax or corporation tax, as the case may be, under Chapter 1 of Part 9 by reason of its use for a purpose specified in section 268(1)(*a*), and

(ii) where any activity carried on in the qualifying premises is not a trade, as if it were a trade.

(*b*) An allowance shall be given by virtue of this subsection in respect of any capital expenditure incurred on the construction or refurbishment of a qualifying premises only in so far as that expenditure is incurred in the qualifying period.

(3) In the case where capital expenditure is incurred in the qualifying period on the refurbishment of a qualifying premises, subsection (2) shall apply only if the total amount of the capital expenditure so incurred is not less than an amount equal to 10 per cent of the market value of the qualifying premises immediately before that expenditure was incurred.

(4) For the purposes of the application, by subsection (2), of sections 271 and 273 in relation to capital expenditure incurred in the qualifying period on the construction or refurbishment of a qualifying premises—

(*a*) section 271 shall apply as if—

(i) in subsection (1) of that section the definition of "industrial development agency" were deleted,

(ii) in subsection (2)(*a*)(i) of that section "to which subsection (3) applies" were deleted,

(iii) subsection (3) of that section were deleted,

(iv) the following subsection were substituted for subsection (4) of that section:

"(4) An industrial building allowance shall be of an amount equal to 50 per cent of the capital expenditure mentioned in subsection (2).",

and

(v) in subsection (5) of that section "to which subsection (3)(*c*) applies" were deleted,

and

(*b*) section 273 shall apply as if—

(i) in subsection (1) of that section the definition of "industrial development agency" were deleted, ...[2]

[(ii) the following paragraph were substituted for paragraph (*b*) of subsection (2) of that section:

"(*b*) As respects any qualifying expenditure, any allowance made under section 272 and increased under paragraph (*a*) in respect of that expenditure, whether claimed for one chargeable period or more than one such period, shall not in the aggregate exceed 50 per cent of the amount of that qualifying expenditure.",

and

(iii) subsections (3) to (7) of that section were deleted.][3]

(5) Notwithstanding section 274(1), no balancing charge shall be made in relation to a qualifying premises by reason of any of the events specified in that section which occurs—

(*a*) more than 13 years after the qualifying premises was first used, or
(*b*) in a case where section 276 applies, more than 13 years after the capital expenditure on refurbishment of the qualifying premises was incurred.

...[4]

(7) For the purposes only of determining, in relation to a claim for an allowance by virtue of subsection (2), whether and to what extent capital expenditure incurred on the construction or refurbishment of a qualifying premises is incurred or not incurred in the qualifying period, only such an amount of that capital expenditure as is properly attributable to work on the construction or refurbishment of the premises actually carried out during the qualifying period shall (notwithstanding any other provision of the Tax Acts as to the time when any capital expenditure is or is to be treated as incurred) be treated as having been incurred in that period.][5]

Amendments

1 Substituted by FA 2000 s 45(1)(*c*)(i) with effect from 1 July 1999; previously "subsections (3) to (6B)".
2 Deleted by FA 2000 s 45(1)(*c*)(ii)(I) with effect from 1 July 1999; previously "and".
3 Subs (4)(*b*)(ii) substituted by FA 2000 s 45(1)(*c*)(ii)(II) with effect from 1 July 1999.
4 Subs (6)–(6B) deleted by FA 2000 s 45(1)(*c*)(iii) with effect from 1 July 1999.
5 Section 372N inserted by FA 1998 s 77(*a*) with effect from 6 April 1998.

Cross-references

Interpretation: s 372L (qualifying period).
Non-application of relief in certain cases and provision against double relief: s 372T(1).

Definitions

market value: s 372L; qualifying period: s 372L; qualifying rural area: s 372L; refurbishment: s 372L; Tax Acts: s 1(2); trade: ss 3(1), 4(1).

372O Double rent allowance in respect of rent paid for certain business premises

Amendments

1 Section 372O repealed by FA 2002 s 24(3)(*g*) with effect from 1 January 2002.

372P Rented residential accommodation: deduction for certain expenditure on construction

Amendments

1 Section 372P repealed by FA 2002 s 24(3)(*g*) with effect from 1 January 2002; but see now TCA 1997 Pt 10 Ch 11 (ss 372AK–372AV) which codified, with effect from 1 January 2002, reliefs for lessors and owner-occupiers in respect of expenditure incurred on the provision of certain residential accommodation, and in particular s 372AV which provides for the continuity of the operation of the law relating to income tax, corporation tax and capital gains tax in that respect.

372Q Rented residential accommodation: deduction for certain expenditure on conversion

Amendments

1 Section 372Q repealed by FA 2002 s 24(3)(*g*) with effect from 1 January 2002; but see now TCA 1997 Pt 10 Ch 11 (ss 372AK–372AV) which codified, with effect from 1 January 2002, reliefs for lessors and owner-occupiers in respect of expenditure incurred on the provision of certain residential accommodation, and in particular s 372AV which provides for the continuity of the operation of the law relating to income tax, corporation tax and capital gains tax in that respect.

372R Rented residential accommodation: deduction for certain expenditure on refurbishment

Amendments

1 Section 372R repealed by FA 2002 s 24(3)(*g*) with effect from 1 January 2002; but see now TCA 1997 Pt 10 Ch 11 (ss 372AK–372AV) which codified, with effect from 1 January 2002, reliefs for lessors and owner-occupiers in respect of expenditure incurred on the provision of certain residential accommodation, and in particular s 372AV which provides for the continuity of the operation of the law relating to income tax, corporation tax and capital gains tax in that respect.

372RA Residential accommodation: allowance to owner-occupiers in respect of certain expenditure on construction or refurbishment

Amendments

1 Section 372RA repealed by FA 2002 s 24(3)(*g*) with effect from 1 January 2002; but see now TCA 1997 Pt 10 Ch 11 (ss 372AK–372AV) which codified, with effect from 1 January 2002, reliefs for lessors and owner-occupiers in respect of expenditure incurred on the provision of certain residential accommodation, and in particular s 372AV which provides for the continuity of the operation of the law relating to income tax, corporation tax and capital gains tax in that respect.

372S Provisions supplementary to sections 372P to 372R

Amendments

1 Section 372S repealed by FA 2002 s 24(3)(*g*) with effect from 1 January 2002; but see now TCA 1997 Pt 10 Ch 11 (ss 372AK–372AV) which codified, with effect from 1 January 2002, reliefs for lessors and owner-occupiers in respect of expenditure incurred on the provision of certain residential accommodation, and in particular s 372AV which provides for the continuity of the operation of the law relating to income tax, corporation tax and capital gains tax in that respect.

372T Non-application of relief in certain cases and provision against double relief

[(1) Notwithstanding any other provision of this Chapter sections 372M and 372N shall not apply—

(*a*) in respect of expenditure incurred on the construction or refurbishment of a building or structure or a qualifying premises—

(i) where a property developer is entitled to the relevant interest, within the meaning of section 269, in relation to that expenditure, and

(ii) either the person referred to in subparagraph (i) or a person connected (within the meaning of section 10) with that person incurred the expenditure on the construction or refurbishment of the building, structure or premises concerned, [(*aa*) in respect of expenditure incurred on or after 6 April 2001 on the construction or refurbishment of a building or structure or a qualifying premises where any part of such expenditure has been or is to be met, directly or indirectly, by [grant assistance or any other assistance which is granted by or through the State, any board established by statute, any public or local authority or any other agency of the State][1],][2]

[(*ab*) in respect of expenditure incurred on or after 1 January 2003 on the construction or refurbishment of any building or structure or qualifying premises provided for the purposes of a project which is subject to the notification requirements of—

(i) the "Multisectoral framework on regional aid for large investment projects" (OJ No C 107, 7.4.1998, p.7) prepared by the Commission of the European Communities and dated 7 April 1998, or

(ii) the "Multisectoral framework on regional aid for large investment projects" (OJ No C 70, 19.3.2002, p.8) prepared by the Commission of the European Communities and dated 19 March 2002,

as the case may be, unless approval of the potential capital allowances involved has been received from that Commission by the Minister for Finance, or by such other Minister of the Government, agency or body as may be nominated for that purpose by the Minister for Finance,][3]

(*b*) in respect of expenditure incurred on the construction or refurbishment of a building or structure or qualifying premises where such building or structure or premises is in use for the purposes of a trade, or any activity treated as a trade, carried on by the person who is entitled to the relevant interest, within the meaning of section 269, in relation to that expenditure and such trade or activity is carried on wholly or mainly—

(i) in the sector of agriculture, including the production, processing and marketing of agricultural products,

(ii) in the coal industry, fishing industry or motor vehicle industry, or

(iii) in the transport, steel, shipbuilding, synthetic fibres or financial services sectors,

or

(*c*) in relation to any building or structure or qualifying premises which is in use for the purposes of a trade, or any activity treated as a trade, where the number of the individuals employed or engaged in the carrying on of the trade or activity amounts to or exceeds 250.

(2) Where relief is given by virtue of any provision of this Chapter in relation to capital expenditure or other expenditure incurred on, or rent payable in respect of, any building, structure or premises, relief shall not be given in respect of that expenditure or that rent under any other provision of the Tax Acts.][4]][5]

Amendments

1 Substituted by FA 2002 s 26(1)(*b*) as respects expenditure incurred on or after 7 February 2002; previously "grant assistance from the State or from any other person".

2 Subs (1)(*aa*) inserted by FA 2001 s 59(1)(*b*)(v) with effect from 6 April 2001.

3 Subs (1)(*ab*) inserted by FA 2003 s 28 with effect from 1 January 2003.

[4] Section 372T substituted by FA 2000 s 45(1)(*e*) with effect from 1 July 1999.

[5] Section 372T inserted by FA 1998 s 77(*a*) with effect from 6 April 1998.

Tax Briefing

TB41 Sept 2000 pp 16–18 — Industrial and Commercial Buildings Capital Allowances — Finance Act 2000 Restrictions.

Definitions

person: IA 1937 s 11(*c*), property developer, qualifying rural area, rent: s 372L; Tax Acts: s 1(2).

[CHAPTER 9
Park and Ride Facilities and Certain Related Developments][1]

372U Interpretation (Chapter 9)

[(1) In this Chapter—

"guidelines" means, subject to subsection (2), guidelines in relation to—

(*a*) the location, development and operation of park and ride facilities,

(*b*) the development of commercial activities located at qualifying park and ride facilities, and

(*c*) the development of certain residential accommodation located at certain qualifying park and ride facilities,

issued by the Minister for the Environment and Local Government following consultation with the Minister for Public Enterprise and with the consent of the Minister for Finance;

"park and ride facility" means—

(*a*) a building or structure served by a bus or train service, in use for the purpose of providing, for members of the public generally, intending to continue a journey by bus or train and without preference for any particular class of person and on payment of an appropriate charge, parking space for mechanically propelled vehicles, and

(*b*) any area under, over or immediately adjoining the building or structure to which paragraph (*a*) refers on which a qualifying premises (within the meaning of [section 372W or 372AK][1]) is or is to be situated;

[**"property developer"** means a person carrying on a trade which consists wholly or mainly of the construction or refurbishment of buildings or structures with a view to their sale;][2]

"qualifying park and ride facility" means a park and ride facility in respect of which the relevant local authority, in consultation with such other agencies as may be specified in the guidelines, gives a certificate in writing to the person constructing or refurbishing such a facility stating that it is satisfied that the facility complies with the criteria and requirements laid down in the guidelines;

[**"qualifying period"** means the period commencing on 1 July 1999 and ending on—

(*a*) 31 December 2004, or

(*b*) where subsection (1A) applies, 31 July 2006;][3]

"the relevant local authority", in relation to the construction or refurbishment of a park and ride facility or a qualifying premises within the meaning of section 372W …[4], means—

(*a*) in respect of the county boroughs of Cork, Dublin, Galway, Limerick and Waterford, the corporation of the borough concerned,

(*b*) in respect of the administrative counties of Clare, Cork, Dún Laoghaire-Rathdown, Fingal, Galway, Kildare, Kilkenny, Limerick, Meath, South Dublin, Waterford and Wicklow, the council of the county concerned,

(*c*) an urban district council situated in the administrative county of Kildare, Meath or Wicklow,

in whose functional area the park and ride facility is situated.

[(1A) This subsection shall apply, as respects capital expenditure incurred on the construction or refurbishment of a building or structure, if—

(*a*) (i) a planning application (not being an application for outline permission within the meaning of section 36 of the Planning and Development Act 2000), in so far as planning permission is required, in respect of the construction or refurbishment work on the building or structure represented by that expenditure, is made in accordance with the Planning and Development Regulations 2001 to 2003,

(ii) an acknowledgement of the application, which confirms that the application was received on or before 31 December 2004, is issued by the planning authority in accordance with article 26(2) of the Planning and Development Regulations 2001 (SI No 600 of 2001), and

(iii) the application is not an invalid application in respect of which a notice is issued by the planning authority in accordance with article 26(5) of those regulations,

(*b*) (i) a planning application, in so far as planning permission was required, in respect of the construction or refurbishment work on the building or structure represented by that expenditure, was made in accordance with the Local Government (Planning and Development) Regulations 1994 (SI No 86 of 1994), not being an application for outline permission within the meaning of article 3 of those regulations,

(ii) an acknowledgement of the application, which confirms that the application was received on or before 10 March 2002, was issued by the planning authority in accordance with article 29(2)(*a*) of the regulations referred to in subparagraph (i), and

(iii) the application was not an invalid application in respect of which a notice was issued by the planning authority in accordance with article 29(2)(*b*)(i) of those regulations,

or

(*c*) where the construction or refurbishment work on the building or structure represented by that expenditure is exempted development for the purposes of the Planning and Development Act 2000 by virtue of section 4 of that Act or by virtue of Part 2 of the Planning and Development Regulations 2001 (SI No 600 of 2001) and—

(i) a detailed plan in relation to the development work is prepared,

(ii) a binding contract in writing, under which the expenditure on the development is incurred, is in existence, and

(iii) work to the value of 5 per cent of the development costs is carried out,

not later than 31 December 2004.][5]

(2) For the purposes of this Chapter, and without prejudice to the generality of the meaning of the guidelines referred to in subsection (1), the guidelines may include provisions in relation to all or any one or more of the following:

(*a*) the criteria for determining the suitability of a site as a location for a park and ride facility,

(*b*) the conditions to apply in relation to the provision of transport services to and from a park and ride facility, including provision for a formal agreement between a transport service provider and a park and ride facility operator where these functions are discharged by separate persons,

(*c*) the hours of operation of a park and ride facility and the level and structure of charges to be borne by members of the public in respect of parking and the use of transport services to or from a park and ride facility,

(*d*) the minimum number of vehicle parking spaces to be provided in a park and ride facility,

(*e*) the proportion of parking space, if any, in a park and ride facility which may, subject to any necessary conditions, be allocated for purposes connected with any commercial or residential development at a park and ride facility,

(*f*) the requirements to apply in relation to the development and operation of commercial activities, if any, at a park and ride facility, including requirements necessary to ensure that those activities do not have an adverse effect on the development and operation of the park and ride facility, and

(*g*) the requirements to apply in relation to the provision of residential accommodation, if any, at a park and ride facility, including requirements necessary to ensure that such accommodation does not have an adverse effect on the development and operation of the park and ride facility.][6]

Note

In regard to the definition of "relevant local authority", it should be noted that, by virtue of Local Government Act 2001 s 3(2) and Sch 2, reference in any other enactment to "county borough corporation", "borough corporation" (not being a county borough corporation), "council of a county" and "council of an urban district", and to similar or analagous expressions, are now to be construed as references to "City council", "Borough council of a borough mentioned in Chapter 1 of Part 1 of Schedule 6 to the Local Government Act 2001", "County council" and "Town council of a town mentioned in Chapter 2 of Part 1 of Schedule 6 to the Local Government Act 2001", respectively.

Amendments

1 Substituted by FA 2002 s 24(1) and Sch 2 Pt 1 para 2(*e*)(i) with effect from 1 January 2002; previously "section 372W, 372X or 372Y".

2 Definition of "property developer" inserted by FA 2002 s 23(1)(*e*)(i)(I) as respects expenditure incurred on or after 7 February 2002.

3 Subs (1)(definition of "qualifying period") substituted by FA 2004 s 26(1)(*f*)(i) with effect from 1 January 2004

4 Deleted by FA 2002 s 24(1) and Sch 2 Pt 1 para 2(*e*)(ii) with effect from 1 January 2002; previously "or the construction of a qualifying premises within the respective meanings assigned in sections 372X and 372Y".

5 Subs (1A) inserted by FA 2004 s 26(1)(*f*)(ii) with effect from 1 January 2004.

6 Section 382U inserted by FA 1999 s 70(1) with effect from 6 April 1999.

Cross-references

Capital allowances in relating to construction or refurbishment of certain park and ride facilities, definition of "qualifying park and ride facility" in subs (1): s 372V(4A).

Reliefs for lessors and owner-occupiers in respect of expenditure incurred on the provision of certain residential accommodation, interpretation, meanings of "guidelines", "qualifying park and ride facility" and "relevant local authority" applied: s 372AK(1).

Definitions

person: IA 1937 s 11(c); writing: IA 1937 Sch.

372V Capital allowances in relation to construction or refurbishment of certain park and ride facilities

[(1) (*a*) Subject to [subsections (2) to (4A)],[1] the provisions of the Tax Acts relating to the making of allowances or charges in respect of capital expenditure incurred on the construction or refurbishment of an industrial building or structure shall, notwithstanding anything to the contrary in those provisions, apply as if a qualifying park and ride facility were, at all times at which it is a qualifying park and ride facility, a building or structure in respect of which an allowance is to be made for the purposes of income tax or corporation tax, as the case may be, under Chapter 1 of Part 9 by reason of its use for a purpose specified in section 268(1)(*a*).

(*b*) An allowance shall be given by virtue of this subsection in respect of any capital expenditure incurred on the construction or refurbishment of a qualifying park and ride facility only in so far as that expenditure is incurred in the qualifying period.

(2) In a case where capital expenditure is incurred in the qualifying period on the refurbishment of a qualifying park and ride facility, subsection (1) shall apply only if the total amount of the capital expenditure so incurred is not less than an amount equal to 10 per cent of the market value of the qualifying park and ride facility immediately before that expenditure is incurred.

[(2A) This section shall not apply in respect of expenditure incurred on the construction or refurbishment of a qualifying park and ride facility—

(*a*) where a property developer is entitled to the relevant interest, within the meaning of section 269, in relation to that expenditure, and

(*b*) either the person referred to in paragraph *(a)* or a person connected (within the meaning of section 10) with that person incurred the expenditure on the construction or refurbishment of the qualifying park and ride facility concerned.][2]

(3) For the purposes of the application, by subsection (1), of sections 271 and 273 in relation to capital expenditure incurred in the qualifying period on the construction or refurbishment of a qualifying park and ride facility—

(*a*) section 271 shall apply—

(i) as if in subsection (1) of that section the definition of "industrial development agency" were deleted,

(ii) as if in subsection (2)(*a*)(i) of that section "to which subsection (3) applies" were deleted,

(iii) as if subsection (3) of that section were deleted,

(iv) as if the following subsection were substituted for subsection (4) of that section:

"(4) An industrial building allowance shall be of an amount equal to 50 per cent of the capital expenditure mentioned in subsection (2).",

and

(v) as if in subsection (5) of that section "to which subsection (3)(*c*) applies" were deleted,

and

(*b*) section 273 shall apply—

(i) as if in subsection (1) of that section, the definition of "industrial development agency" were deleted, and

(ii) as if subsections (2)(*b*) and (3) to (7) of that section were deleted.

(4) Notwithstanding section 274(1), no balancing charge shall be made in relation to a qualifying park and ride facility by reason of any of the events specified in that section which occurs—

(*a*) more than 13 years after the qualifying park and ride facility was first used [or, where subsection (4A) applies, first used as a qualifying park and ride facility,][3] or

(*b*) in a case where section 276 applies, more than 13 years after the capital expenditure on refurbishment of the [qualifying park and ride facility][4] was incurred.

[(4A) Notwithstanding subsections (1), (3)(*a*) and (4), where it is shown in respect of a building or structure which is to be a qualifying park and ride facility that the relevant local authority is unable to give the certificate in writing referred to in the definition of "qualifying park and ride facility" in section 372U(1) due to a delay in the provision of a train service to serve the building or structure, then, in relation to capital expenditure incurred in the qualifying period on the construction or refurbishment of that building or structure—

(*a*) section 271 shall apply—

(i) as if in the definition of "appropriate chargeable period" in subsection (1) of that section "the chargeable period in which the building or structure becomes an industrial building or structure" were substituted for "the chargeable period related to the expenditure", and

(ii) as if in subsection (6) of that section "if, within 5 years of the building or structure coming to be used, it is not an industrial building or structure" were substituted for "if the building or structure, when it comes to be used, is not an industrial building or structure",

(*b*) section 272 shall apply as if in subsection (4)(*a*)(ii) of that section "beginning with the time when the building or structure was first used as an industrial building or structure" were substituted for "beginning with the time when the building or structure was first used",

(*c*) section 274 shall apply—

(i) as if in subsection (1)(*b*)(i)(II) of that section "after the building or structure was first used as an industrial building or structure" were substituted for "after the building or structure was first used", and

(ii) as if in subsection (5)(*a*) of that section "when the building or structure was first used as an industrial building or structure" were substituted for "when the building or structure was first used for any purpose",

(*d*) section 277 shall apply—

(i) as if in subsection (2) of that section "when the building or structure is first used as an industrial building or structure" were substituted for "when the building or structure is first used", and

(ii) as if in subsection (4)(*a*) of that section "when the building or structure was first used as an industrial building or structure" were substituted for "when the building or structure was first used for any purpose",

(*e*) section 278 shall apply as if in subsection (2) of that section "before the building or structure is first used as an industrial building or structure" were substituted for "before the building or structure is first used for any purpose", and

(*f*) section 279 shall apply as if in subsections (2) and (3) of that section "before the building or structure is used as an industrial building or structure or within the period of one year after it commences to be so used" were substituted for "before the building or structure is used or within the period of one year after it commences to be used" (in each place where it occurs in those subsections).][5]

(5) For the purposes only of determining, in relation to a claim for an allowance by virtue of subsection (1), whether and to what extent capital expenditure incurred on the construction or refurbishment of a qualifying park and ride facility is incurred or not incurred in the qualifying period, only such an amount of that capital expenditure as is properly attributable to work on the construction or refurbishment of the qualifying park and ride facility actually carried out during the qualifying period shall (notwithstanding any other provision of the Tax Acts as to the time when any capital expenditure is or is to be treated as incurred) be treated as having been incurred in that period.

(6) Where an allowance is given under this section in respect of capital expenditure incurred on the construction or refurbishment of a qualifying park and ride facility, no allowance shall be given in respect of that expenditure by virtue of any other provision of the Tax Acts.][6]

Amendments

1 Substituted by FA 2001 s 58(*a*)(i) with effect from 6 April 2001; previously "subsections (2) to (4)".

2 Subs (2A) inserted by FA 2002 s 23(1)(*e*)(ii) as respects expenditure incurred on or after 7 February 2002.

3 Inserted by FA 2001 s 58(*a*)(ii)(I) with effect from 6 April 2001.

4 Substituted by FA 2001 s 58(*a*)(ii)(II) with effect from 6 April 2001; previously "park and ride facility".

5 Subs (4A) inserted by FA 2001 s 58(*a*)(iii) with effect from 6 April 2001.

6 Section 372V inserted by FA 1999 s 70(1) with effect from 6 April 1999.

Cross-references

Capital allowances in relation to construction or refurbishment of certain commercial premises at certain park and ride facilities, subs (4A): s 372W(5A).

Definitions

person: IA 1937 s 11(*c*); qualifying park and ride facility: s 372U(1); qualifying period: s 372U(1); Tax Acts: s 1(2); writing: IA 1937 Sch; year: IA 1937 Sch.

372W Capital allowances in relation to construction or refurbishment of certain commercial premises

[(1) In this section **"qualifying premises"** means a building or structure the site of which is wholly within the site of a qualifying park and ride facility and

(*a*) in respect of which the relevant local authority gives to the person constructing or refurbishing the premises a certificate in writing stating that it is satisfied that the premises and the activity to be carried on in the premises complies with the requirements laid down in the guidelines in relation to the development of commercial activity at a qualifying park and ride facility, ...[1]

(*b*) which apart from this section is not an industrial building or structure within the meaning of section 268(1), and

[(*c*) (i) is in use for thc purposes of the retailing of goods or the provision of services only within the State but excluding any building or structure in use—

(I) as offices, or

(II) for the provision of mail order or financial services,

or

(ii) is let on bona fide commercial terms for such use as is referred to in subparagraph (i) and for such consideration as might be expected to be paid in a letting of the building or structure negotiated on an arm's length basis,][2]

but does not include any part of a building or structure in use as or as part of a dwelling house.

(2) (*a*) Subject to paragraphs (*b*) and (*c*) and [subsections (3) to (5A)],[3] the provisions of the Tax Acts relating to the making of allowances or charges in respect of capital expenditure incurred on the construction or refurbishment of an industrial building or structure shall, notwithstanding anything to the contrary in those provisions, apply—

(i) as if a qualifying premises were, at all times at which it is a qualifying premises, a building or structure in respect of which an allowance is to be made for the purposes of income tax or corporation tax, as the case may be, under Chapter 1 of Part 9 by reason of its use for a purpose specified in section 268(1)(*a*), and

(ii) where any activity carried on in the qualifying premises is not a trade, as if it were a trade.

(*b*) An allowance shall be given by virtue of this subsection in respect of any capital expenditure incurred on the construction or refurbishment of a qualifying premises only in so far as that expenditure is incurred in the qualifying period.

(*c*) (i) An allowance shall be given by virtue of this subsection in respect of any capital expenditure incurred on the construction or refurbishment of a qualifying premises at a park and ride facility only in so far as that expenditure when aggregated with—

(I) other capital expenditure, if any, incurred on the construction or refurbishment of other qualifying premises and in respect of which an allowance would or would but for this paragraph be given, and

(II) other expenditure, if any, in respect of which there is provision for a deduction to be made by virtue of [section 372AP or 372AR][4],

incurred at that park and ride facility, does not exceed one-half of the total capital expenditure incurred at that park and ride facility in respect of which an allowance or deduction is to be made or would, but for this paragraph or [section 372AP(5) or 372AR(5)][5], be made by virtue of any provision of [this Chapter or Chapter 11][6].

(ii) A person who has incurred capital expenditure on the construction or refurbishment of a qualifying premises at a park and ride facility and who claims to have complied with the requirements of subparagraph (i) in relation to that expenditure, shall be deemed not to have so complied unless the person has received from the relevant local authority a certificate in writing issued by it stating that it is satisfied that those requirements have been met.

(3) In the case where capital expenditure is incurred in the qualifying period on the refurbishment of a qualifying premises, subsection (2) shall apply only if the total amount of the capital expenditure so incurred is not less than an amount equal to 10 per cent of the market value of the qualifying premises immediately before that expenditure was incurred.

[(3A) This section shall not apply in respect of expenditure incurred on the construction or refurbishment of a qualifying premises—

(*a*) where a property developer is entitled to the relevant interest, within the meaning of section 269, in relation to that expenditure, and

(*b*) either the person referred to in paragraph *(a)* or a person connected (within the meaning of section 10) with that person incurred the expenditure on the construction or refurbishment of the qualifying premises concerned.][7]

(4) For the purposes of the application, by subsection (2), of sections 271 and 273 in relation to capital expenditure incurred in the qualifying period on the construction or refurbishment of a qualifying premises—

(*a*) section 271 shall apply—

(i) as if in subsection (1) of that section the definition of "industrial development agency" were deleted,

(ii) as if in subsection (2)(*a*)(i) of that section "to which subsection (3) applies" were deleted,

(iii) as if subsection (3) of that section were deleted,

(iv) as if the following subsection were substituted for subsection (4) of that section:

"(4) An industrial building allowance shall be of an amount equal to 50 per cent of the capital expenditure mentioned in subsection (2).",

and

(v) as if in subsection (5) of that section "to which subsection (3)(*c*) applies" were deleted,

and

(*b*) section 273 shall apply—

(i) as if in subsection (1) of that section the definition of "industrial development agency" were deleted, and

(ii) as if subsections (2)(*b*) and (3) to (7) of that section were deleted.

(5) Notwithstanding section 274(1), no balancing charge shall be made in relation to a qualifying premises by reason of any of the events specified in that section which occur—

(*a*) more than 13 years after the qualifying premises was first used [or, where subsection (5A) applies, first used as a qualifying premises],[8] or

(*b*) in a case where section 276 applies, more than 13 years after the capital expenditure on refurbishment of the qualifying premises was incurred.

[(5A) Notwithstanding subsections (2)(*a*), (4)(*a*) and (5), where it is shown in respect of a building or structure which is to be a qualifying premises that the relevant local authority is unable to give the certificate in writing referred to in subsection (1)(*a*) relating to compliance with certain requirements at a park and ride facility which would be a qualifying park and ride facility but for the delay referred to in section 372V(4A), then, in relation to capital expenditure incurred in the qualifying period on the construction or refurbishment of the building or structure—

(*a*) section 271 shall apply—

(i) as if in the definition of "appropriate chargeable period" in subsection (1) of that section "the chargeable period in which the building or structure becomes an industrial building or structure" were substituted for "the chargeable period related to the expenditure", and

(ii) as if in subsection (6) of that section "if, within 5 years of the building or structure coming to be used, it is not an industrial building or structure" were substituted for "if the building or structure, when it comes to be used, is not an industrial building or structure",

(*b*) section 272 shall apply as if in subsection (4)(*a*)(ii) of that section "beginning with the time when the building or structure was first used as an industrial building or structure" were substituted for "beginning with the time when the building or structure was first used",

(*c*) section 274 shall apply—

(i) as if in subsection (1)(*b*)(i)(II) of that section "after the building or structure was first used as an industrial building or structure" were substituted for "after the building or structure was first used", and

(ii) as if in subsection (5)(*a*) of that section "when the building or structure was first used as an industrial building or structure" were substituted for "when the building or structure was first used for any purpose",

(*d*) section 277 shall apply—

(i) as if in subsection (2) of that section "when the building or structure is first used as an industrial building or structure" were substituted for "when the building or structure is first used", and

(ii) as if in subsection (4)(*a*) of that section "when the building or structure was first used as an industrial building or structure" were substituted for "when the building or structure was first used for any purpose".

(*e*) section 278 shall apply as if in subsection (2) of that section "before the building or structure is first used as an industrial building or structure" were substituted for "before the building or structure is first used for any purpose", and

(*f*) section 279 shall apply as if in subsections (2) and (3) of that section "before the building or structure is used as an industrial building or structure or within the period of one year after it commences to be so used" were substituted for "before the building or structure is used or within the period of one year after it commences to be used" (in each place where it occurs in those subsections).][9]

(6) For the purposes only of determining, in relation to a claim for an allowance by virtue of subsection (2), whether and to what extent capital expenditure incurred on the construction or refurbishment of a qualifying premises is incurred or not incurred in the qualifying period, only such an amount of that capital expenditure as is properly attributable to work on the construction or refurbishment of the premises actually carried out during the qualifying period shall (notwithstanding any other provision of the Tax Acts as to the time when any capital expenditure is or is to be treated as incurred) be treated as having been incurred in that period.

(7) Where an allowance is given under this section in respect of capital expenditure incurred on the construction or refurbishment of a qualifying premises, no allowance shall be given in respect of that expenditure by virtue of any other provision of the Tax Acts.][10]

Amendments

1 Deleted by FA 2001 s 58(*b*)(i)(I) with effect from 6 April 2001; previously "and".

2 Subs (1)(*c*) substituted by FA 2001 s 58(*b*)(i)(II) with effect from 6 April 2001.

3 Substituted by FA 2001 s 58(*b*)(ii) with effect from 6 April 2001; previously "subsections (3) to (5)".

4 Substituted by FA 2002 s 24(1) and Sch 2 Pt 1 para 2(*f*) with effect from 1 January 2002; previously "section 372X or 372Y".

5 Substituted by FA 2002 s 24(1) and Sch 2 Pt 1 para 2(*f*) with effect from 1 January 2002; previously "section 372X(4) or 372Y(2)(*c*)".

6 Substituted by FA 2004 s 26(1)(*g*) with effect from 1 January 2002; previously "this Chapter".

7 Subs (3A) inserted by FA 2002 s 23(1)(*e*)(iii) as respects expenditure incurred on or after 7 February 2002.

8 Inserted by FA 2001 s 58(*b*)(iii) with effect from 6 April 2001.

9 Sub (5A) inserted by FA 2001 s 58(*b*)(iv) with effect from 6 April 2001.

10 Section 372W inserted by FA 1999 s 70(1) with effect from 6 April 1999.

Cross-references

Interpretation, meaning of "qualifying premises" applied: s 372V(1) (park and ride facility, the relevant local authority).

Reliefs for lessors and owner-occupiers in respect of expenditure incurred on provision of certain residential accommodation, interpretation, meaning of "qualifying premises" applied: s 372AK(1)("relevant local authority", para (*b*)); relief for lessors, subs (2)(*c*): s 372AP(5)(*a*); relief for owner-occupiers, subs (2)(*c*): s 372AR(5)(*a*).

Definitions

guidelines: s 372U(1); house: s 372Z(1); person: IA 1937 s 11(*c*); profession: s 2(1); qualifying park and ride facility: s 372U(1); qualifying period: s 372U(1); relevant local authority: s 372U(1); Tax Acts: s 1(2); total floor area: s 372Z(1); trade: ss 3(1), 4(1); writing: IA 1937 Sch.

372X Rented residential accommodation: deduction for certain expenditure on construction

Amendments

1 Section 372X repealed by FA 2002 s 24(3)(*h*) with effect from 1 January 2002; but see now TCA 1997 Pt 10 Ch 11 (ss 372AK–372AV) which codified, with effect from 1 January 2002, reliefs for lessors and owner-occupiers in respect of expenditure incurred on the provision of certain residential accommodation, and in particular s 372AV which provides for the continuity of the operation of the law relating to income tax, corporation tax and capital gains tax in that respect.

372Y Residential accommodation: allowance to owner-occupiers in respect of certain expenditure on construction

Amendments

1 Section 372Y repealed by FA 2002 s 24(3)(*h*) with effect from 1 January 2002; but see now TCA 1997 Pt 10 Ch 11 (ss 372AK–372AV) which codified, with effect from 1 January 2002, reliefs for lessors and owner-occupiers in respect of expenditure incurred on the provision of certain residential accommodation, and in particular s 372AV which provides for the continuity of the operation of the law relating to income tax, corporation tax and capital gains tax in that respect.

372Z Provisions supplementary to sections 372X and 272Y

Amendments

1 Section 372Z repealed by FA 2002 s 24(3)(*h*) with effect from 1 January 2002; but see now TCA 1997 Pt 10 Ch 11 (ss 372AK–372AV) which codified, with effect from 1 January 2002, reliefs for lessors and owner-occupiers in respect of expenditure incurred on the provision of certain residential accommodation, and in particular s 372AV which provides for the continuity of the operation of the law relating to income tax, corporation tax and capital gains tax in that respect.

[CHAPTER 10
Designated areas of certain towns][1]

Amendments

1 Chapter 10 inserted by FA 2000 s 89(*a*) with effect from 6 April 2000.

Notes

By virtue of Town Renewal Act 2000 (as amended by FA 2002) s 7 no relief may be granted under Ch 10 in respect of the construction, refurbishment or conversion of a building, structure or house unless the county council which prepared the town renewal plan concerned has certified in writing, in a manner specified by the Minister for the Environment and Local Government, that such construction, refurbishment or conversion is consistent with the objectives of that town renewal plan, being the particular plan concerned that was taken into consideration by that Minister in the making by him to the Minister for Finance of the recommendations referred to in the Town Renewal Act 2000 s 6.

Some 100 towns around the country have now been designated as areas for tax incentives. Details of the designated towns are available from the Department of the Environment and Local Government's website at WWW.ENVIRON.IE.

Cross-references

See Town Renewal Act 2000 (as amended by FA 2002) ss 3 (town renewal plans), 5 (recommendations in respect of qualifying areas for purposes of town renewal tax reliefs), 7 (certain reliefs conditional on buildings etc being consistent with town renewal plan) and 8 (monitoring of implementation of town renewal plans).

Tax Briefing

TB42 Dec 2000 pp 24–27 — Town Renewal Scheme.

372AA Interpretation and application (Chapter 10)

[(1) In this Chapter—

[**"facade"**, in relation to a building or structure, part of a building or structure, or a house, means the exterior wall of the building or structure, the part of the building or structure or, as the case may be, the house which fronts on to a street;][1]

"lease", **"lessee"**, **"lessor"**, **"premium"** and **"rent"** have the same meanings respectively as in Chapter 8 of Part 4;

"market value", in relation to a building, structure or house, means the price which the unencumbered fee simple of the building, structure or house would fetch if sold in the open market in such manner and subject to such conditions as might reasonably be calculated to obtain for the vendor the best price for the building, structure or house, less the part of that price which would be attributable to the acquisition of, or of rights in or over, the land on which the building, structure or house is constructed;

"property developer" means a person carrying on a trade which consists wholly or mainly of the construction or refurbishment of buildings or structures with a view to their sale;

"qualifying area" means an area or areas specified as a qualifying area under section 372AB;

[**"qualifying period"** means, subject to section 372AB, the period commencing on 6 April 2001 and ending on—

(*a*) 31 December 2004, or

(*b*) where subsection (1A) applies, 31 July 2006;][2]

"refurbishment", in relation to a building or structure …[3], means any work of construction, reconstruction, repair or renewal, including the provision or improvement of water, sewerage or heating facilities, carried out in the course of the repair or restoration, or maintenance in the nature of repair or restoration, of the building or [structure;][4]

[**"street"**, includes part of a street and the whole or part of any road, square, quay or lane.][5]

[(1A) This subsection shall apply, as respects capital expenditure incurred on the construction or refurbishment of a building or structure, if—

(*a*) (i) a planning application (not being an application for outline permission within the meaning of section 36 of the Planning and Development Act 2000), in so far as planning permission is required, in respect of the construction or refurbishment work on the building or structure represented by that expenditure, is made in accordance with the Planning and Development Regulations 2001 to 2003,

(ii) an acknowledgement of the application, which confirms that the application was received on or before 31 December 2004, is issued by the planning authority in accordance with article 26(2) of the Planning and Development Regulations 2001 (SI No 600 of 2001), and

(iii) the application is not an invalid application in respect of which a notice is issued by the planning authority in accordance with article 26(5) of those regulations,

(*b*) (i) a planning application, in so far as planning permission was required, in respect of the construction or refurbishment work on the building or structure represented by that expenditure, was made in accordance with the Local Government (Planning and Development) Regulations 1994 (SI No 86 of 1994), not being an application for outline permission within the meaning of article 3 of those regulations,

(ii) an acknowledgement of the application, which confirms that the application was received on or before 10 March 2002, was issued by the planning authority in accordance with article 29(2)(*a*) of the regulations referred to in subparagraph (i), and

(iii) the application was not an invalid application in respect of which a notice was issued by the planning authority in accordance with article 29(2)(*b*)(i) of those regulations,

or

(*c*) where the construction or refurbishment work on the building or structure represented by that expenditure is exempted development for the purposes of the Planning and Development Act 2000 by virtue of section 4 of that Act or by virtue of Part 2 of the Planning and Development Regulations 2001 (SI No 600 of 2001) and—

(i) a detailed plan in relation to the development work is prepared,

(ii) a binding contract in writing, under which the expenditure on the development is incurred, is in existence, and

(iii) work to the value of 5 per cent of the development costs is carried out,

not later than 31 December 2004.][6]

(2) [This Chapter and Chapter 11 of this Part][7] shall apply if the Oireachtas passes an Act which refers to this Chapter and provides for the renewal of certain urban areas and the submission of plans (to be known as "Town Renewal Plans") to the Minister for the Environment and Local Government which have been drawn up by county councils (being county councils as referred to in such Act) in respect of an area or areas

identified by such an authority on the basis of criteria prepared by that Minister, including physical and socio-economic renewal of such an area or areas.][8]

Amendments

1 Definition of "facade" inserted by FA 2003 s 29(1)(*a*)(i) with effect from 6 April 2000.
2 Subs (1)(definition of "qualifying period") substituted by FA 2004 s 26(1)(*h*)(i) with effect from 1 January 2004.
3 Deleted by FA 2002 s 24(1) and Sch 2 Pt 1 para 2(*g*)(i)(II) with effect from 1 January 2002; previously "and other than for the purposes of sections 372AG and 372AH".
4 Substituted by FA 2003 s 29(1)(*a*)(ii) with effect from 6 April 2000; previously "structure.".
5 Definition of "street" inserted by FA 2003 s 29(1)(*a*)(iii) with effect from 6 April 2000.
6 Subs (1A) inserted by FA 2004 s 26(1)(*h*)(ii) with effect from 1 January 2004.
7 Substituted by FA 2002 s 24(1) and Sch 2 Pt 1 para 2(*g*)(ii) with effect from 1 January 2002; previously "This Chapter".
8 Section 372AA inserted by FA 2000 s 89(*a*) with effect from 6 April 2000.

Notes

By virtue of the Town Renewal Act 2000 (as amended by FA 2002) s 2, the Act of the Oireachtas referred to in subs (2) is the Town Renewal Act 2000.

Cross-references

qualifying areas: s 372AB(1)(*c*), (4).

See also the Town Renewal Act 2000 s 1 (interpretation), meaning of "qualifying area" in this section applied.

Definitions

land: IA 1937 Sch; the Oireachtas: IA 1937 Sch; trade: ss 3(1), 4(1); writing: IA 1937 Sch.

372AB Qualifying areas

[(1) The Minister for Finance may, on the recommendation of the Minister for the Environment and Local Government (which recommendation shall take into consideration a Town Renewal Plan submitted by a local authority to that Minister in respect of an area identified by it), by order direct that—

(*a*) the area or areas described (being wholly located within the boundaries of the area to which the Town Renewal Plan relates) in the order shall be a qualifying area for the purposes of one or more sections of [this Chapter or Chapter 11 of this Part][1],

[(*b*) where such an area or areas is or are to be a qualifying area—

(i) for the purposes of section 372AC, that area or those areas shall be a qualifying area for the purposes of one or more of the following—

(I) the construction,

(II) the refurbishment, and

(III) the refurbishment of the facade,

of a building or structure to which that section applies,

(ii) for the purposes of section 372AD—

(I) one or more of the categories of building or structure mentioned in subsection (2) shall or shall not be a qualifying premises within the meaning of that section, and

(II) that area or those areas shall be a qualifying area for the purposes of either or both the construction of, and the refurbishment of, a qualifying premises within the meaning of that section,

and

(iii) for the purposes of section 372AR, that area or those areas may be a qualifying area for the purposes of one or more of the following—

(I) the construction of,

(II) the conversion into,

(III) the refurbishment (within the meaning of Chapter 11 of this Part) of, and

(IV) the refurbishment (within the meaning of Chapter 11 of this Part) of the facade of,

a qualifying premises (within the meaning of that Chapter),][2]

[(*ba*) where such an area or areas is or are to be a qualifying area for the purposes of section 372AP, that section shall apply in relation to that area or those areas in so far as that section relates to one or more of the following:

(i) expenditure incurred on the construction of a house,

[(ii) conversion expenditure incurred in relation to a house,

(iii) refurbishment expenditure incurred in relation to a house, and

(iv) refurbishment expenditure incurred in relation to the facade of a house,][3]][4]

(*c*) as respects any such area so described in the order, the definition of "qualifying period" in section 372AA [and section 372AL][5] shall be construed as a reference to such period as shall be specified in the order in relation to that area; but no such period specified in the order shall commence before—

(i) in the case of sections 372AC and 372AD, [6 April 2001][6], and

(ii) in the case of [any provision of Chapter 11 of this Part][7], 1 April 2000,

[or end after 31 December 2004, or—

(I) in the case of sections 372AC and 372AD where section 372AA(1A) applies, end after 31 July 2006, and

(II) in the case of any provision of Chapter 11 of this Part where section 372AL(1A) applies, end after 31 July 2006.][8]

[(2) The categories of building or structure referred to in subsection (1)(*b*)(ii)(I) shall be—

(*a*) buildings or structures in use as offices,

(*b*) any other buildings or structures and in respect of which not more than 10 per cent of the capital expenditure incurred in the qualifying period on their construction or refurbishment relates to the construction or refurbishment of buildings or structures in use as offices,

(*c*) the facade of a building or structure or part of a building or structure referred to in paragraph (*a*), and

(*d*) the facade of a building or structure or part of a building or structure referred to in paragraph (*b*).][9]

[(2A) The power to make an order under subsection (1) includes the power to amend or revoke the order.][10]

(3) Every order made by the Minister for Finance under subsection (1) shall be laid before Dáil Éireann as soon as may be after it is made and, if a resolution annulling the

order is passed by Dáil Éireann within the next 21 days on which Dáil Éireann has sat after the order is laid before it, the order shall be annulled accordingly, but without prejudice to the validity of anything previously done thereunder.

(4) Notwithstanding an order under subsection (1), the granting of relief by virtue of any provision of [this Chapter or Chapter 11 of this Part][11] shall be subject to such other requirements as may be specified in or under the Act referred to in section 372AA(2).][12]

Amendments

1 Substituted by FA 2002 s 24(1) and Sch 2 Pt 1 para 2(*h*)(i)(I) with effect from 1 January 2002; previously "this Chapter".

2 Subs (1)(*b*) substituted by FA 2003 s 29(1)(*b*)(i) with effect from 6 April 2000.

3 Subs (1)(*ba*)(ii)–(iii) substituted by FA 2003 s 29(1)(*b*)(ii) with effect from 6 April 2000.

4 Subs (1)(*ba*) inserted by FA 2002 s 24(1) and Sch 2 Pt 1 para 2(*h*)(i)(III) with effect from 1 January 2002.

5 Inserted by FA 2002 s 24(1) and Sch 2 Pt 1 para 2(*h*)(i)(IV)(A) with effect from 1 January 2002.

6 Substituted by FA 2004 s 26(1)(*i*)(i) with effect from 1 January 2002; previously "the day referred to in paragraph (*a*) of the definition of 'qualifying period' in section 372AA".

7 Substituted by FA 2002 s 24(1) and Sch 2 Pt 1 para 2(*h*)(i)(IV)(B) with effect from 1 January 2002; previously "sections 372AE, 372AF, 372AG, 372AH and 372AI".

8 Substituted by FA 2004 s 26(1)(*i*)(ii) with effect from 1 January 2004; previously "or end after 31 December 2003".

9 Subs (2) substituted by FA 2003 s 29(1)(*b*)(iii) with effect from 6 April 2000.

10 Subs (2A) inserted by FA 2003 s 29(1)(*b*)(iv) with effect from 6 April 2000.

11 Substituted by FA 2002 s 24(1) and Sch 2 Pt 1 para 2(*h*)(ii) with effect from 1 January 2002; previously "this Chapter".

12 Section 372AB inserted by FA 2000 s 89(*a*) with effect from 6 April 2000.

Cross-references

Interpretation and application: s 372AA(1)("qualifying area", "qualifying period").

Reliefs for lessors and owner-occupiers in respect of expenditure incurred on the provision of certain residential accommodation, interpretation: s 372AK(1)("qualifying town area"); qualifying period: s 372AL(1)(*e*); continuity, subs (1); s 372AV(7).

See also Town Renewal Act 2000 (as amended by FA 2002), ss 6 (qualifying areas for town renewal tax reliefs), 6A (designation of certain areas for rented residential reliefs), and 8 (monitoring of implementation of town renewal plans).

List of Statutory Instruments designating certain areas as qualifying areas under the Town Renewal Scheme for certain periods and certain reliefs

SI No	SI Title
272	Taxes Consolidation Act 1997 (Qualifying Town — Renewal Areas) (Hacketstown, County Carlow) Order 2004
273	Taxes Consolidation Act 1997 (Qualifying Town — Renewal Areas) (Muinebheag (Bagenalstown), County Carlow) Order 2004
274	Taxes Consolidation Act 1997 (Qualifying Town — Renewal Areas) (Tullow, County Carlow) Order 2004
275	Taxes Consolidation Act 1997 (Qualifying Town — Renewal Areas) (Graiguenamanagh, County Kilkenny and Tinnahinch, County Carlow) Order 2004
276	Taxes Consolidation Act 1997 (Qualifying Town — Renewal Areas) (Baileborough, County Cavan) Order 2004
277	Taxes Consolidation Act 1997 (Qualifying Town — Renewal Areas) (Ballyjamesduff, County Cavan) Order 2004
278	Taxes Consolidation Act 1997 (Qualifying Town — Renewal Areas) (Cavan, County Cavan) Order 2004
279	Taxes Consolidation Act 1997 (Qualifying Town — Renewal Areas) (Cootehill, County Cavan) Order 2004

280 Taxes Consolidation Act 1997 (Qualifying Town — Renewal Areas) (Ennistymon, County Clare) Order 2004

281 Taxes Consolidation Act 1997 (Qualifying Town — Renewal Areas) (Kilrush, County Clare) Order 2004

282 Taxes Consolidation Act 1997 (Qualifying Town — Renewal Areas) (Miltown-Malbay, County Clare) Order 2004

283 Taxes Consolidation Act 1997 (Qualifying Town — Renewal Areas) (Scarriff, County Clare) Order 2004

284 Taxes Consolidation Act 1997 (Qualifying Town — Renewal Areas) (Sixmilebridge, County Clare) Order 2004

285 Taxes Consolidation Act 1997 (Qualifying Town — Renewal Areas) (Bantry, County Cork) Order 2004

286 Taxes Consolidation Act 1997 (Qualifying Town — Renewal Areas) (Cloyne, County Cork) Order 2004

287 Taxes Consolidation Act 1997 (Qualifying Town — Renewal Areas) (Charleville, County Cork) Order 2004

288 Taxes Consolidation Act 1997 (Qualifying Town — Renewal Areas) (Doneraile, County Cork) Order 2004

289 Taxes Consolidation Act 1997 (Qualifying Town — Renewal Areas) (Fermoy, County Cork) Order 2004

290 Taxes Consolidation Act 1997 (Qualifying Town — Renewal Areas) (Kanturk, County Cork) Order 2004

291 Taxes Consolidation Act 1997 (Qualifying Town — Renewal Areas) (Skibbereen, County Cork) Order 2004

292 Taxes Consolidation Act 1997 (Qualifying Town — Renewal Areas) (Ardara, County Donegal) Order 2004

293 Taxes Consolidation Act 1997 (Qualifying Town — Renewal Areas) (Ballybofey-Stranorlar, County Donegal) Order 2004

294 Taxes Consolidation Act 1997 (Qualifying Town — Renewal Areas) (Ballyshannon, County Donegal) Order 2004

295 Taxes Consolidation Act 1997 (Qualifying Town — Renewal Areas) (Moville, County Donegal) Order 2004

296 Taxes Consolidation Act 1997 (Qualifying Town — Renewal Areas) (Ramelton, County Donegal) Order 2004

297 Taxes Consolidation Act 1997 (Qualifying Town — Renewal Areas) (Ballygar, County Galway) Order 2004

298 Taxes Consolidation Act 1997 (Qualifying Town — Renewal Areas) (Clifden, County Galway) Order 2004

299 Taxes Consolidation Act 1997 (Qualifying Town — Renewal Areas) (Headford, County Galway) Order 2004

300 Taxes Consolidation Act 1997 (Qualifying Town — Renewal Areas) (Loughrea, County Galway) Order 2004

301 Taxes Consolidation Act 1997 (Qualifying Town — Renewal Areas) (Portumna, County Galway) Order 2004

302 Taxes Consolidation Act 1997 (Qualifying Town — Renewal Areas) (Caherciveen, County Kerry) Order 2004

303 Taxes Consolidation Act 1997 (Qualifying Town — Renewal Areas) (Castleisland, County Kerry) Order 2004

304 Taxes Consolidation Act 1997 (Qualifying Town — Renewal Areas) (Killorglin, County Kerry) Order 2004

305 Taxes Consolidation Act 1997 (Qualifying Town — Renewal Areas) (Listowel, County Kerry) Order 2004

306 Taxes Consolidation Act 1997 (Qualifying Town — Renewal Areas) (Castledermot, County Kildare) Order 2004

307 Taxes Consolidation Act 1997 (Qualifying Town — Renewal Areas) (Kilcock, County Kildare) Order 2004

308 Taxes Consolidation Act 1997 (Qualifying Town — Renewal Areas) (Kilcullen, County Kildare) Order 2004

309 Taxes Consolidation Act 1997 (Qualifying Town — Renewal Areas) (Monasterevan, County Kildare) Order 2004

310 Taxes Consolidation Act 1997 (Qualifying Town — Renewal Areas) (Rathangan, County Kildare) Order 2004

311 Taxes Consolidation Act 1997 (Qualifying Town — Renewal Areas) (Callan, County Kilkenny) Order 2004

312 Taxes Consolidation Act 1997 (Qualifying Town — Renewal Areas) (Castlecomer, County Kilkenny) Order 2004

313 Taxes Consolidation Act 1997 (Qualifying Town — Renewal Areas) (Pilltown, County Kilkenny) Order 2004

314 Taxes Consolidation Act 1997 (Qualifying Town — Renewal Areas) (Thomastown, County Kilkenny) Order 2004

315 Taxes Consolidation Act 1997 (Qualifying Town — Renewal Areas) (Urlingford, County Kilkenny) Order 2004

316 Taxes Consolidation Act 1997 (Qualifying Town — Renewal Areas) (Mountmellick, County Laois) Order 2004

317 Taxes Consolidation Act 1997 (Qualifying Town — Renewal Areas) (Mountrath, County Laois) Order 2004

318 Taxes Consolidation Act 1997 (Qualifying Town — Renewal Areas) (Portarlington, County Laois) Order 2004

319 Taxes Consolidation Act 1997 (Qualifying Town — Renewal Areas) (Rathdowney, County Laois) Order 2004

320 Taxes Consolidation Act 1997 (Qualifying Town — Renewal Areas) (Abbeyfeale, County Limerick) Order 2004

321 Taxes Consolidation Act 1997 (Qualifying Town — Renewal Areas) (Castleconnell, County Limerick) Order 2004

322 Taxes Consolidation Act 1997 (Qualifying Town — Renewal Areas) (Croom, County Limerick) Order 2004

323 Taxes Consolidation Act 1997 (Qualifying Town — Renewal Areas) (Kilmallock, County Limerick) Order 2004

324 Taxes Consolidation Act 1997 (Qualifying Town — Renewal Areas) (Rathkeale, County Limerick) Order 2004

325 Taxes Consolidation Act 1997 (Qualifying Town — Renewal Areas) (Ardee, County Louth) Order 2004

326 Taxes Consolidation Act 1997 (Qualifying Town — Renewal Areas) (Carlingford, County Louth) Order 2004

327 Taxes Consolidation Act 1997 (Qualifying Town — Renewal Areas) (Castlebellingham, County Louth) Order 2004

328 Taxes Consolidation Act 1997 (Qualifying Town — Renewal Areas) (Dunleer, County Louth) Order 2004

329 Taxes Consolidation Act 1997 (Qualifying Town — Renewal Areas) (Ballinrobe, County Mayo) Order 2004

330 Taxes Consolidation Act 1997 (Qualifying Town — Renewal Areas) (Belmullet, County Mayo) Order 2004

331 Taxes Consolidation Act 1997 (Qualifying Town — Renewal Areas) (Claremorris, County Mayo) Order 2004

332 Taxes Consolidation Act 1997 (Qualifying Town — Renewal Areas) (Foxford, County Mayo) Order 2004

333 Taxes Consolidation Act 1997 (Qualifying Town — Renewal Areas) (Newport, County Mayo) Order 2004

334 Taxes Consolidation Act 1997 (Qualifying Town — Renewal Areas) (Duleek, County Meath) Order 2004

335 Taxes Consolidation Act 1997 (Qualifying Town — Renewal Areas) (Kells, County Meath) Order 2004

336 Taxes Consolidation Act 1997 (Qualifying Town — Renewal Areas) (Oldcastle, County Meath) Order 2004

337 Taxes Consolidation Act 1997 (Qualifying Town — Renewal Areas) (Trim, County Meath) Order 2004

338 Taxes Consolidation Act 1997 (Qualifying Town — Renewal Areas) (Ballybay, County Monaghan) Order 2004

339 Taxes Consolidation Act 1997 (Qualifying Town — Renewal Areas) (Castleblayney, County Monaghan) Order 2004

340 Taxes Consolidation Act 1997 (Qualifying Town — Renewal Areas) (Clones, County Monaghan) Order 2004

341 Taxes Consolidation Act 1997 (Qualifying Town — Renewal Areas) (Banagher, County Offaly) Order 2004

342 Taxes Consolidation Act 1997 (Qualifying Town — Renewal Areas) (Clara, County Offaly) Order 2004

343 Taxes Consolidation Act 1997 (Qualifying Town — Renewal Areas) (Edenderry, County Offaly) Order 2004

344 Taxes Consolidation Act 1997 (Qualifying Town — Renewal Areas) (Ferbane, County Offaly) Order 2004

345 Taxes Consolidation Act 1997 (Qualifying Town — Renewal Areas) (Roscommon, County Rosscommon) Order 2004

346 Taxes Consolidation Act 1997 (Qualifying Town — Renewal Areas) (Bellaghy-Charlestown, County Sligo) Order 2004

347 Taxes Consolidation Act 1997 (Qualifying Town — Renewal Areas) (Rosses Point, County Sligo) Order 2004

348 Taxes Consolidation Act 1997 (Qualifying Town — Renewal Areas) (Borrisokane, County Tipperary) Order 2004

349 Taxes Consolidation Act 1997 (Qualifying Town — Renewal Areas) (Littleton, County Tipperary) Order 2004

350 Taxes Consolidation Act 1997 (Qualifying Town — Renewal Areas) (Nenagh, County Tipperary) Order 2004

351 Taxes Consolidation Act 1997 (Qualifying Town — Renewal Areas) (Templemore, County Tipperary) Order 2004

352 Taxes Consolidation Act 1997 (Qualifying Town — Renewal Areas) (Cahir, County Tipperary) Order 2004

353 Taxes Consolidation Act 1997 (Qualifying Town — Renewal Areas) (Cashel, County Tipperary) Order 2004

354 Taxes Consolidation Act 1997 (Qualifying Town — Renewal Areas) (Fethard, County Tipperary) Order 2004

355	Taxes Consolidation Act 1997 (Qualifying Town — Renewal Areas) (Killenaule, County Tipperary) Order 2004
356	Taxes Consolidation Act 1997 (Qualifying Town — Renewal Areas) (Cappaquin, County Waterford) Order 2004
357	Taxes Consolidation Act 1997 (Qualifying Town — Renewal Areas) (Kilmacthomas County Waterford) Order 2004
358	Taxes Consolidation Act 1997 (Qualifying Town — Renewal Areas) (Portlaw, County Waterford) Order 2004
359	Taxes Consolidation Act 1997 (Qualifying Town — Renewal Areas) (Tallow, County Waterford) Order 2004
360	Taxes Consolidation Act 1997 (Qualifying Town — Renewal Areas) (Castlepollard, County Westmeath) Order 2004
361	Taxes Consolidation Act 1997 (Qualifying Town — Renewal Areas) (Kilbeggan, County Westmeath) Order 2004
362	Taxes Consolidation Act 1997 (Qualifying Town — Renewal Areas) (Moate, County Westmeath) Order 2004
363	Taxes Consolidation Act 1997 (Qualifying Town — Renewal Areas) (Bunclody, County Wexford) Order 2004
364	Taxes Consolidation Act 1997 (Qualifying Town — Renewal Areas) (Ferns, County Wexford) Order 2004
365	Taxes Consolidation Act 1997 (Qualifying Town — Renewal Areas) (Gorey, County Wexford) Order 2004
366	Taxes Consolidation Act 1997 (Qualifying Town — Renewal Areas) (Taghmon, County Wexford) Order 2004
367	Taxes Consolidation Act 1997 (Qualifying Town — Renewal Areas) (Baltinglass, County Wicklow) Order 2004
368	Taxes Consolidation Act 1997 (Qualifying Town — Renewal Areas) (Carnew, County Wicklow) Order 2004
369	Taxes Consolidation Act 1997 (Qualifying Town — Renewal Areas) (Dunlavin, County Wicklow) Order 2004
370	Taxes Consolidation Act 1997 (Qualifying Town — Renewal Areas) (Rathdrum, County Wicklow) Order 2004
371	Taxes Consolidation Act 1997 (Qualifying Town — Renewal Areas) (Tinahely, County Wicklow) Order 2004

Definitions

Dáil Éireann: IA 1937 Sch; qualifying area: s 372AA(1); refurbishment: s 372AA(1).

372AC Accelerated capital allowances in relation to construction or refurbishment of certain industrial buildings or structures

[(1) In this section, **"building or structure to which this section applies"** means a building or structure or part of a building or structure the site of which is wholly within a qualifying area and which is to be an industrial building or structure by reason of its use for a purpose specified in section 268(1)(*a*).

(2) Subject to section 372AJ, section 271 shall apply in relation to capital expenditure incurred in the qualifying period on the construction or refurbishment of a building or structure to which this section applies as if—

(*a*) in subsection (1) of that section the definition of "industrial development agency" were deleted,

(*b*) in subsection (2)(*a*)(i) of that section "to which subsection (3) applies" were deleted,

(*c*) subsection (3) of that section were deleted,

(*d*) the following subsection were substituted for subsection (4) of that section:

"(4) An industrial building allowance shall be of an amount equal to 50 per cent of the capital expenditure mentioned in subsection (2)."

and

(*e*) in subsection (5) of that section "to which subsection (3)(*c*) applies" were deleted.

(3) Subject to section 372AJ, section 273 shall apply in relation to capital expenditure incurred in the qualifying period on the construction or refurbishment of a building or structure to which this section applies as if—

(*a*) in subsection (l) of that section the definition of "industrial development agency" were deleted,

(*b*) the following paragraph were substituted for paragraph (*b*) of subsection (2) of that section:

"(*b*) As respects any qualifying expenditure, any allowance made under section 272 and increased under paragraph (*a*) in respect of that expenditure, whether claimed for one chargeable period or more than one such period, shall not in the aggregate exceed 50 per cent of the amount of that qualifying expenditure.",

and

(*c*) subsections (3) to (7) of that section were deleted.

(4) Notwithstanding section 274(1), no balancing charge shall be made in relation to a building or structure to which this section applies by reason of any of the events specified in that section which occurs—

(*a*) more than 13 years after the building or structure was first used, or

(*b*) in a case where section 276 applies, more than 13 years after the capital expenditure on refurbishment of the building or structure was incurred.

(5) For the purposes only of determining, in relation to a claim for an allowance under section 271 or 273 as applied by this section, whether and to what extent capital expenditure incurred on the construction or refurbishment of an industrial building or structure is incurred or not incurred in the qualifying period, only such an amount of that capital expenditure as is properly attributable to work on the construction or, as the case may be, the refurbishment of the building or structure actually carried out during the qualifying period shall (notwithstanding any other provision of the Tax Acts as to the time when any capital expenditure is or is to be treated as incurred) be treated as having been incurred in that period.][1]

Amendments

1 Section 372AC inserted by FA 2000 s 89(*a*) with effect from 6 April 2000.

Cross-references

Capital allowances for commercial premises: s 372AD(2).

Non-application of relief in certain cases and provision against double relief: s 372AJ(1), (2).

Qualifying areas: s 372AB(1)(*b*)(i), (*c*).

Definitions

qualifying area, qualifying period, refurbishment: s 372AA(1); Tax Acts: s 1(2).

372AD Capital allowances in relation to construction or refurbishment of certain commercial premises

[(1) In this section, **"qualifying premises"** means a building or structure or part of a building or structure the site of which is wholly within a qualifying area and which—

(*a*) apart from this section is not an industrial building or structure within the meaning of section 268, and

(*b*) (i) is in use for the purposes of a trade or profession, or

(ii) whether or not it is so used, is let on bona fide commercial terms for such consideration as might be expected to be paid in a letting of the building or structure negotiated on an arm's length basis,

but does not include any part of a building or structure in use as or as part of a dwelling house.

(2) (*a*) Subject to paragraph (*b*), subsections (3) and (4) and section 372AJ, the provisions of the Tax Acts (other than section 372AC) relating to the making of allowances or charges in respect of capital expenditure incurred on the construction or refurbishment of an industrial building or structure shall, notwithstanding anything to the contrary in those provisions, apply—

(i) as if a qualifying premises were, at all times at which it is a qualifying premises, a building or structure in respect of which an allowance is to be made for the purposes of income tax or corporation tax, as the case may be, under Chapter 1 of Part 9 by reason of its use for a purpose specified in section 268(1)(*a*), and

[(ii) where any activity—

(I) carried on in the qualifying premises, or

(II) in a case where the facade of a building or structure or part of a building or structure is a qualifying premises, carried on in the building or structure or the part of the building or structure,

is not a trade, as if it were a trade.][1]

(*b*) An allowance shall be given by virtue of this subsection in respect of any capital expenditure incurred on the construction or refurbishment of a qualifying premises only in so far as that expenditure is incurred in the qualifying period.

(3) For the purposes of the application, by subsection (2), of sections 271 and 273 in relation to capital expenditure incurred in the qualifying period on the construction or refurbishment of a qualifying premises—

(*a*) section 271 shall apply as if—

(i) in subsection (1) of that section the definition of "industrial development agency" were deleted,

(ii) in subsection (2)(*a*)(i) of that section "to which subsection (3) applies" were deleted,

(iii) subsection (3) of that section were deleted,

(iv) the following subsection were substituted for subsection (4) of that section:

"(4) An industrial building allowance shall be of an amount equal to 50 per cent of the capital expenditure mentioned in subsection (2).",

and

(v) in subsection (5) of that section "to which subsection (3)(*c*) applies" were deleted,

and

(*b*) section 273 shall apply as if—

(i) in subsection (1) of that section the definition of "industrial development agency" were deleted,

(ii) the following paragraph were substituted for paragraph (*b*) of subsection (2) of that section:

"(*b*) As respects any qualifying expenditure, any allowance made under section 272 and increased under paragraph (*a*) in respect of that expenditure, whether claimed for one chargeable period or more than one such period, shall not in the aggregate exceed 50 per cent of the amount of that qualifying expenditure.",

and

(iii) subsections (3) to (7) of that section were deleted.

(4) Notwithstanding section 274(1), no balancing charge shall be made in relation to a qualifying premises by reason of any of the events specified in that section which occur—

(*a*) more than 13 years after the qualifying premises was first used, or

(*b*) in a case where section 276 applies, more than 13 years after the capital expenditure on refurbishment of the qualifying premises was incurred.

(5) For the purposes only of determining, in relation to a claim for an allowance by virtue of subsection (2), whether and to what extent capital expenditure incurred on the construction or refurbishment of a qualifying premises is incurred or not incurred in the qualifying period, only such an amount of that capital expenditure as is properly attributable to work on the construction or refurbishment of the premises actually carried out during the qualifying period shall (notwithstanding any other provision of the Tax Acts as to the time when any capital expenditure is or is to be treated as incurred) be treated as having been incurred in that period.][2]

Amendments

1 Subs (2)(*a*)(ii) substituted by FA 2003 s 29(1)(*c*) with effect from 6 April 2000.

2 Section 372AD inserted by FA 2000 s 89(*a*) with effect from 6 April 2000.

Cross-references

Qualifying areas: s 372AB(1)(*b*)(ii), (*c*).

Non-application of relief in certain cases and provision against double relief: s 372AJ(1), (2).

Definitions

qualifying area, qualifying period, refurbishment: s 372AA(1); Tax Acts: s 1(2); trade: ss 3(1), 4(1).

372AE Rented residential accommodation: deduction for certain expenditure on construction

Amendments

[1] Section 372AE repealed by FA 2002 s 24(3)(*i*) with effect from 1 January 2002; but see now TCA 1997 Pt 10 Ch 11 (ss 372AK–372AV) which codified, with effect from 1 January 2002, reliefs for lessors and owner-occupiers in respect of expenditure incurred on the provision of certain residential accommodation, and in particular s 372AV which provides for the continuity of the operation of the law relating to income tax, corporation tax and capital gains tax in that respect.

372AF Rented residential accommodation: deduction for certain expenditure on conversion

Amendments

[1] Section 372AF repealed by FA 2002 s 24(3)(*i*) with effect from 1 January 2002; but see now TCA 1997 Pt 10 Ch 11 (ss 372AK–372AV) which codified, with effect from 1 January 2002, reliefs for lessors and owner-occupiers in respect of expenditure incurred on the provision of certain residential accommodation, and in particular s 372AV which provides for the continuity of the operation of the law relating to income tax, corporation tax and capital gains tax in that respect.

372AG Rented residential accommodation: deduction for certain expenditure on refurbishment

Amendments

[1] Section 372AG repealed by FA 2002 s 24(3)(*i*) with effect from 1 January 2002; but see now TCA 1997 Pt 10 Ch 11 (ss 372AK–372AV) which codified, with effect from 1 January 2002, reliefs for lessors and owner-occupiers in respect of expenditure incurred on the provision of certain residential accommodation, and in particular s 372AV which provides for the continuity of the operation of the law relating to income tax, corporation tax and capital gains tax in that respect.

372AH Residential accommodation: allowance to owner-occupiers in respect of certain expenditure on construction of refurbishment

Amendments

[1] Section 372AH repealed by FA 2002 s 24(3)(*i*) with effect from 1 January 2002; but see now TCA 1997 Pt 10 Ch 11 (ss 372AK–372AV) which codified, with effect from 1 January 2002, reliefs for lessors and owner-occupiers in respect of expenditure incurred on the provision of certain residential accommodation, and in particular s 372AV which provides for the continuity of the operation of the law relating to income tax, corporation tax and capital gains tax in that respect.

372AI Provisions supplementary to sections 372AE to 372AH

Amendments

[1] Section 372AI repealed by FA 2002 s 24(3)(*i*) with effect from 1 January 2002; but see now TCA 1997 Pt 10 Ch 11 (ss 372AK–372AV) which codified, with effect from 1 January 2002, reliefs for lessors and owner-occupiers in respect of expenditure incurred on the provision of certain residential accommodation, and in particular s 372AV which provides for the continuity of the operation of the law relating to income tax, corporation tax and capital gains tax in that respect.

372AJ Non-application of relief in certain cases and provision against double relief

[(1) Notwithstanding any other provision of this Chapter, sections 372AC and 372AD shall not apply—

(*a*) in respect of expenditure incurred on the construction or refurbishment of a building or structure or a qualifying premises—

(i) where a property developer is entitled to the relevant interest, within the meaning of section 269, in relation to that expenditure, and

(ii) either the person referred to in subparagraph (i) or a person connected (within the meaning of section 10) with that person incurred the expenditure on the construction or refurbishment of the building, structure or premises concerned,

[(*aa*) in respect of expenditure incurred on or after 6 April 2001 on the construction or refurbishment of a building or structure or a qualifying premises where any part of such expenditure has been or is to be met, directly or indirectly, by [grant assistance or any other assistance which is granted by or through the State, any board established by statute, any public or local authority or any other agency of the State][1],

(*ab*) in respect of expenditure incurred on or after 6 April 2001 on the construction or refurbishment of a building or structure or a qualifying premises unless the relevant interest, within the meaning of section 269, in such expenditure is held by a small or medium-sized enterprise within the meaning of Annex 1 to Commission Regulation (EC) No 70/2001 of 12 January 2001(OJ No L10 of 13 January 2001, p 33), [or, as the case may be, by a micro, small or medium-sized enterprise within the meaning of the Annex to Commission Recommendation of 6 May 2003 concerning the definition of micro, small and medium-sized enterprises (OJ No L124 of 20 May 2003, p 36)][2]

...[3]][4]

(*b*) in respect of expenditure incurred on the construction or refurbishment of a building or structure or a qualifying premises where such building or structure or premises is in use for the purposes of a trade, or any activity treated as a trade, carried on by the person who is entitled to the relevant interest, within the meaning of section 269, in relation to that expenditure and such trade or activity is carried on wholly or mainly—

(i) in the sector of agriculture, including the production, processing and marketing of agricultural products,

(ii) in the coal industry, fishing industry or motor vehicle industry, or

(iii) in the transport, steel, shipbuilding, synthetic fibres or financial services sectors,

or

[(*c*) in respect of expenditure incurred on or after 1 January 2003 on the construction or refurbishment of any building or structure or qualifying premises provided for the purposes of a project which is subject to the notification requirements of—

(i) the "Multisectoral framework on regional aid for large investment projects" (OJ No C 107, 7.4.1998, p.7) prepared by the Commission of the European Communities and dated 7 April 1998, or

(ii) the "Multisectoral framework on regional aid for large investment projects" (OJ No C 70, 19.3.2002, p.8) prepared by the Commission of the European Communities and dated 19 March 2002,

as the case may be, unless approval of the potential capital allowances involved has been received from that Commission by the Minister for Finance, or by such other Minister of the Government, agency or body as may be nominated for that purpose by the Minister for Finance.][5]

(2) For the purposes of [sections 372AC and 372AD][6], where the site of any part of a building or structure is situated outside the boundary of a qualifying area and where expenditure incurred or treated as having been incurred in the qualifying period is attributable to the building or structure in general, such an amount of that expenditure shall be deemed to be attributable to the part which is situated outside the boundary of the qualifying area as bears to the whole of that expenditure the same proportion as the floor area of the part situated outside the boundary of the qualifying area bears to the total floor area of the building or structure.

(3) Where relief is given by virtue of any provision of this Chapter in relation to capital expenditure or other expenditure incurred on any building, structure or premises, relief shall not be given in respect of that expenditure under any other provision of the Tax Acts.][7]

Amendments

1 Substituted by FA 2002 s 26(1)(*c*) as respects expenditure incurred on or after 7 February 2002; previously "grant assistance from the State or from any other person".

2 Inserted by FA 2005 s 35 with effect from 1 January 2005.

3 Subs (1)(*ac*) deleted by FA 2002 s 27(1) with effect from 6 April 2001.

4 Subs (1)(*aa*)–(*ac*) inserted by FA 2001 s 80(1)(*f*) with effect from 6 April 2001.

5 Subs (1)(*c*) substituted by FA 2003 s 29(1)(*d*)(i) with effect from 1 January 2003.

6 Substituted by FA 2003 s 29(1)(*d*)(ii) with effect from 1 January 2002; previously "sections 372AC, 372AD, 372AF and 372AG".

7 Section 372AJ inserted by FA 2000 s 89(*a*) with effect from 6 April 2000.

Cross-references

Accelerated capital allowances for industrial buildings or structures: s 372AC(2).

Capital allowances for commercial premises: s 372AD(2)(*a*).

Tax Briefing

TB41 Sept 2000 pp 16–18 — Industrial and Commercial Buildings Capital Allowances — Finance Act 2000 Restrictions.

Definitions

market value: s 372AA(1); person: IA 1937 s 11(*c*); property developer, qualifying area, qualifying period: s 372AA(1); qualifying premises: s 372AD(1); refurbishment: ss 372AA(1), 372AG(1), 372AH(1); Tax Acts: s 1(2); trade: ss 3(1), 4(1).

[Chapter 11

Reliefs for lessors and owner-occupiers in respect of expenditure incurred on the provision of certain residential accommodation][1]

Amendments

1 Pt 10 Ch 11 (ss 372AK–372AV) inserted by FA 2002 s 24(1) and Sch 2 Pt 1 para 1 with effect from 1 January 2002.

Notes

By virtue of the Urban Renewal Act 1998 (as amended by FA 2002), s 11(1), no relief may be granted under Ch 11 in respect of the construction, refurbishment or conversion of a building, structure or house in a qualifying urban area unless the local authority or authorised company which prepared the integrated area plan concerned has certified in writing, in a manner specified by the Minister for the Environment and Local Government, that such construction, refurbishment or conversion is consistent with the objectives of that plan.

By virtue of the Town Renewal Act 2000 (as amended by FA 2002), s 7, no relief may be granted under Ch 11 in respect of the construction, refurbishment or conversion of a building, structure or house in a qualifying town area unless the county council which prepared the town renewal plan concerned has certified in writing, in a manner specified by the Minister for the Environment and Local Government, that such construction, refurbishment or conversion is consistent with the objectives of that town renewal plan, being the particular plan concerned that was taken into consideration by that Minister in the making by him to the Minister for Finance of the recommendations referred to in the Town Renewal Act 2000 s 6.

Some 100 towns around the country have been designated as areas for tax incentives. Details of the designated towns are available from the Department of the Environment and Local Government's Website at www.environ.ie.

Cross-references

Designated areas of certain towns, interpretation and application: s 372AA(2); qualifying areas: s 372AB(1)(*a*), (*b*)(iii), (*c*)(ii), (4).

Qualifying urban areas and qualifying streets, interpretation and application: s 372A(1)("necessary construction"), (2); qualifying areas: s 372B(1)(*a*), (*b*)(ii), (*d*), (4); qualifying streets: s 372BA(1)(*a*), (4); capital allowances in relation to construction or refurbishment of certain commercial premises: s 372D(3A)(*a*)(ii).

See also Urban Renewal Act 1998 (as amended by FA 2002), ss 8 (recommendation in respect of qualifying areas for purposes of urban renewal tax reliefs), 11 (certain reliefs conditional on buildings etc being consistent with integrated area plan) and 12 (monitoring of implementation of integrated area plan).

See also Town Renewal Act 2000 (as amended by FA 2002), ss 3 (town renewal plans), 5 (recommendations in respect of qualifying areas for purposes of town renewal tax reliefs), 7 (certain reliefs conditional on buildings etc being consistent with town renewal plan) and 8 (monitoring of implementation of town renewal plans).

Revenue precedents

Issue: Is the allowance available outside the 10 year period if it is not used up within that time? Can the allowance be set against rental income from other investment properties?

Decision: Yes.

Issue: A bona fide company reconstruction takes place whereby a new company is formed and the assets of an existing company are transferred to it. The shareholders and the number of shares held are the same in both companies. One of the assets transferred is a property on which rented residential relief has been claimed. Will a clawback arise in such circumstances?

Decision: It has been decided not to allow the concessional treatment sought. This is on the basis that 1) there is no hardship involved 2) the properties are to be transferred between two separate legal entities.

Issue: Does the use of a house by a builder as a show house prevent it from being a qualifying premises for the purposes of s 23 relief?

Decision: No.

Issue: Can a deduction allowable under s 23 be carried forward for more than 10 years if it exceeds the Case V profits in those 10 years?

Decision: Yes.

Issue: Where a qualifying premises is purchased by a bare trust on behalf of more than one partner, is each partner entitled to his/her proportionate share of the relief under s 23?

Decision: Yes.

Issue: Where two or more units of two or more storeys have a common or shared external entrance, are the units regarded as a maisonette?

Decision: Such units are regarded as a maisonette.

Issue: Where a property is purchased in joint names, how is relief apportioned.

Decision: Each party is entitled to treat his/her share of the expenditure as a deduction under s 97. Where a party has a life interest in the income from the property, that person's deduction is still confined to his/her share of the qualifying expenditure.

Issue: Statement of costs provided by builders to purchasers.

Decision: Figures provided in respect of site costs, site development and construction costs should always be the costs of the builder - not what is being charged to the purchaser under those headings.

Issue: The taxpayer paid a sum of money to a member of the public who was injured on a site where the taxpayer was constructing a rented residential premises. The taxpayer also incurred legal fees in connection with the claim. Can these amounts be claimed as part of the costs of the construction of the premises?

Decision: No. These are not direct costs associated with the construction of the premises in question.

Issue: Three artisan dwellings stand side by side and front onto a designated street. The developer wishes to demolish two and retain the facade of the remaining house. On completion of the development two or more houses will exist. Having regard to the fact that the meaning of refurbishment includes the carrying out of any works of construction would the development qualify for rented residential relief under TCA 1997 s 348(1)?

Decision: With regard to the first two buildings, refurbishment in TCA 1997 s 348(1) is defined in relation to a building, not in relation to a proposed building. If the two buildings are demolished refurbishment cannot be regarded as being carried out in relation to those buildings as they no longer exist. The building referred to in the definition of a specified building in s 348 is either of the three buildings and not the aggregate of those buildings. In order for either of the buildings to be regarded as a specified building it must contain two or more residential units prior to refurbishment. As the dwellings did not contain two or more such units rented residential relief is not available.

Issue: Should the grant received by an owner occupier be deducted from the purchase price of the property or from the amount of construction expenditure which the purchaser is deemed to have incurred?

Decision: From the latter.

Issue: Is Urban Renewal Relief available in respect of car park spaces in a multi-storey carpark which are sold with and apportioned to residential units which are part of the same development?

Decision: Where a car space belongs to or is necessarily or usually enjoyed with a residential unit the car space will be regarded as included in the definition of a house in TCA 1997 s 350(1).

Issue: If a deduction is available under either TCA 1997 s 356, 357 or 358 can it be set against all rental income of the claimant in computing liability to tax under Case V of Schedule D? The Explanatory Memorandum accompanying the Finance Act 1995 appears to distinguish the way the deduction in respect of expenditure incurred can be used.

Decision: Subss (2) of TCA 1997 s 356, (4) of 357 and (2) of 358 all regard the qualifying expenditure as if it were a deduction authorised by the provisions of TCA 1997 s 97(2). Section 75(2) of that act states: "Profits or gains chargeable under Case V of Schedule D shall, for all the purposes of ascertaining liability to income tax, be deemed to issue from a single source ......". The effect of all Case V income being deemed to issue from a single source is that only one Case V figure is chargeable, this being the sum of all Case V income less the deductions authorised by TCA 1997 s 97(2), including any amounts regarded as a Case V deduction by virtue of ss 356, 357 or 358.

Revenue information

A Revenue Explanatory Note on the operation of the provisions of TCA 1997 in relation to the Student Accommodation Scheme is available on Revenue's website (www.revenue.ie) under Publications/Technical Guidelines. Section 6 (Rent Pooling) of this note was amended in June 2004 to reinforce the prohibition on rent pooling outside the academic year and to clarify that houses or apartments that have not yet been sold to investors should not be included in a rent pooling arrangement. The amended note is available on Revenue's website www.revenue.ie under Whats New/Archive/June 2004.

Tax Briefing

TB23 Sept 1996 p 16 — Clawback of "section 23 type relief" in death cases.

TB29 Dec 1997 p 6 — Owner-occupier relief in respect of conversion expenditure and where property purchased from builder/developer.

TB33 Sept 1998 p 14 — Conversion/Refurbishment of residential properties: calculation of relief for lessors and owner-occupiers.

TB37 Oct 1999 p 9 — Owner-occupier relief — property in joint names (married couples).

372AK Interpretation (Chapter 11)

[In this Chapter—

"certificate of compliance" and **"certificate of reasonable cost"** shall be construed, respectively, in accordance with section 372AM;

"conversion expenditure" shall be construed in accordance with section 372AN;

"eligible expenditure" shall be construed in accordance with section 372AN;

"existing building" has the same meaning as in section 372A;

"facade", in relation to a house, means the exterior wall of the house which fronts on to a street;

"guidelines", in relation to a house the site of which is wholly within the site of a qualifying park and ride facility, has the same meaning as in section 372U;

"house" includes any building or part of a building used or suitable for use as a dwelling and any outoffice, yard, garden or other land appurtenant to or usually enjoyed with that building or part of a building;

"lease", **"lessee"** and **"lessor"** have the same meanings, respectively, as in Chapter 8 of Part 4;

"Minister", except where the context otherwise requires, means the Minister for the Environment and Local Government;

"necessary construction" has the same meaning as in section 372A and any reference in this Chapter (other than in section 372AR(1)*(a)*) to construction shall, in the case of a house which fronts on to a qualifying street or is comprised in a building or part of a building which fronts on to a qualifying street, apply as if it were a reference to necessary construction, unless the context requires otherwise;

"premium" has the same meaning as in Chapter 8 of Part 4;

"qualifying expenditure" shall be construed in accordance with section 372AQ;

"qualifying lease" shall be construed in accordance with section 372AO;

"qualifying period" shall be construed in accordance with section 372AL;

"qualifying park and ride facility" has the same meaning as in section 372U(1);

"qualifying premises" shall be construed in accordance with section 372AM;

"qualifying rural area" means any area described in Schedule 8A;

"qualifying street" means a street specified as a qualifying street under section 372BA;

"qualifying student accommodation area" means an area or areas specified as a qualifying area in the relevant guidelines;

"qualifying town area" means an area or areas specified as a qualifying area under section 372AB;

"qualifying urban area" means an area or areas specified as a qualifying area under section 372B;

"refurbishment" means—

(*a*) in relation to a building or a part of a building other than a special specified building, either or both of the following—

(i) the carrying out of any works of construction, reconstruction, repair or renewal, and

(ii) the provision or improvement of water, sewerage or heating facilities, where the carrying out of such works or the provision of such facilities is certified by the Minister, in any certificate of reasonable cost or certificate of compliance, as the case may be, granted by the Minister under section 372AM,

(*b*) in relation to a facade, any works of construction, reconstruction, repair or renewal [carried out][1] in the course of the repair or restoration, or maintenance in the nature of repair or restoration, of a facade, and

(*c*) in relation to a special specified building, any works of construction, reconstruction, repair or renewal, including the provision or improvement of water, sewerage or heating facilities, carried out in the course of the repair or restoration, or maintenance in the nature of repair or restoration, of the building or for the purposes of compliance with the requirements of the Housing (Standards for Rented Houses) Regulations 1993 (SI No 147 of 1993),

but paragraph (*c*) shall not apply for the purposes of sections 372AQ and 372AR;

"refurbishment expenditure" shall be construed in accordance with section 372AN;

"relevant cost" has the same meaning as in section 372AP;

"relevant guidelines", in relation to a house or building the site of which is wholly within a qualifying student accommodation area, means guidelines entitled "Guidelines on Residential Developments for 3rd Level Students" issued by the Minister for Education and Science in consultation with the Minister and with the consent of the Minister for Finance, or such other guidelines amending or replacing those guidelines issued in accordance with section 372AM(1)(*c*);

[**"relevant local authority"**,—

(*a*) in relation to a qualifying urban area, means—

(i) the county council or the city council or the borough council or, where appropriate, the town council, within the meaning of the Local Government Act 2001, in whose functional area the area is situated, or

(ii) the authorised company (within the meaning of section 3(1) of the Urban Renewal Act 1998) which prepared the integrated area plan (within the meaning of that section) in respect of the area,

and

(*b*) in relation to the construction of a house the site of which is wholly within the site of a qualifying park and ride facility and which is a qualifying premises for the purposes of this Chapter, has the same meaning as it has in section 372U(1) in relation to the construction or refurbishment of a park and ride facility or a qualifying premises within the meaning of section 372W;][2]

"relevant period" has the meaning assigned to it in section 372AP;

"rent" has the same meaning as in Chapter 8 of Part 4;

"replacement building" has the same meaning as in section 372A;

"special qualifying premises" shall be construed in accordance with section 372AM;

"special specified building" and **"specified building"** have the same meanings, respectively, as in section 372AN(6);

"street" includes part of a street and the whole or part of any road, square, quay or lane;

"tax incentive area" means—

(*a*) a qualifying urban area,

(*b*) a qualifying rural area,

(*c*) the site of a qualifying park and ride facility,

(*d*) a qualifying town area, or

(*e*) a qualifying student accommodation area;

"total floor area" means the total floor area of a house measured in the manner referred to in section 4(2)(*b*) of the Housing (Miscellaneous Provisions) Act, 1979.][3]

Amendments

1 Inserted by FA 2003 s 30(1)(*a*) with effect from 1 January 2002.

2 Definition of "relevant local authority" substituted by FA 2003 s 26(*d*) with effect from 1 January 2003.

3 Section 372AK inserted by FA 2002 s 24(1) and Sch 2 Pt 1 para 1 with effect from 1 January 2002.

Cross-references

Capital gains tax, deduction from consideration on disposal of certain assets, meaning of "house" applied: s 980(4)(*c*).

Park and ride facilities and certain related developments, interpretation: s 372V(1)("park and ride facility" para (*b*)).

Definitions

land: IA 1937 Sch.

372AL Qualifying period

[(1) For the purposes of this Chapter, **"qualifying period"**, in relation to—

(*a*) a qualifying urban area, means, subject to section 372B, the period commencing on 1 August 1998 and ending on—

(i) 31 December 2002, or

(ii) where subsection (2) applies, [31 July 2006][1],

(*b*) a qualifying street, means, subject to section 372BA, the period commencing on 6 April 2001 [and ending on 31 December 2004 or, where subsection (1A) applies, ending on 31 July 2006][2],

(*c*) a qualifying rural area, means—

(i) for the purposes of sections 372AP and (in so far as it relates to that section) section 372AS, the period commencing on 1 June 1998 [and ending on 31 December 2004 or, where subsection (1A) applies, ending on 31 July 2006][3], and

(ii) for the purposes of section 372AR and (in so far as it relates to that section) section 372AS, the period commencing on 6 April 1999 [and ending on 31 December 2004 or, where subsection (1A) applies, ending on 31 July 2006][3], (*d*) the site of a qualifying park and ride facility, means the period commencing on 1 July 1999 [and ending on 31 December 2004 or, where subsection (1A) applies, ending on 31 July 2006][4],

(*e*) a qualifying town area, means, subject to section 372AB, the period commencing on 1 April 2000 [and ending on 31 December 2004 or, where subsection (1A) applies, ending on 31 July 2006][5],

(*f*) a qualifying student accommodation area, means the period commencing on 1 April 1999 and ending on—

(i) 31 March 2003, or

[(ii) where subsection (1A) applies, 31 July 2006.][6]

and

(*g*) a special specified building, means the period commencing on 6 April 2001.

[(1A) This subsection shall apply, as respects expenditure incurred on the construction, conversion or, as the case may be, refurbishment of a building or structure, if—

(*a*) (i) a planning application (not being an application for outline permission within the meaning of section 36 of the Planning and Development Act 2000), in so far as planning permission is required, in respect of the construction, conversion or refurbishment work on the building or structure represented by that expenditure, is made in accordance with the Planning and Development Regulations 2001 to 2003,

(ii) an acknowledgement of the application, which confirms that the application was received on or before 31 December 2004, is issued by the planning authority in accordance with article 26(2) of the Planning and Development Regulations 2001 (SI No 600 of 2001), and

(iii) the application is not an invalid application in respect of which a notice is issued by the planning authority in accordance with article 26(5) of those regulations,

(*b*) (i) a planning application, in so far as planning permission was required, in respect of the construction, conversion or refurbishment work on the building or structure represented by that expenditure, was made in accordance with the Local Government (Planning and Development) Regulations 1994 (SI No 86 of 1994), not being an application for outline permission within the meaning of article 3 of those regulations,

(ii) an acknowledgement of the application, which confirms that the application was received on or before 10 March 2002, was issued by the planning authority in accordance with article 29(2)(*a*) of the regulations referred to in subparagraph (i), and

(iii) the application was not an invalid application in respect of which a notice was issued by the planning authority in accordance with article 29(2)(*b*)(i) of those regulations,

or

(*c*) where the construction, conversion or refurbishment work on the building or structure represented by that expenditure is exempted development for the purposes of the Planning and Development Act 2000 by virtue of section 4 of that Act or by virtue of Part 2 of the Planning and Development Regulations 2001 (SI No 600 of 2001) and—

(i) a detailed plan in relation to the development work is prepared,

(ii) a binding contract in writing, under which the expenditure on the development is incurred, is in existence, and

(iii) work to the value of 5 per cent of the development costs is carried out,

not later than 31 December 2004.][7]

(2) [(*a*) This subsection shall apply where—

(i) the relevant local authority gives a certificate in writing on or before September 2003, to the person constructing, converting or, as the case may be, refurbishing a building or part of a building, the site of which is wholly within a qualifying urban area, stating that it is satisfied that not less than 15 per cent of the total cost of constructing, converting or refurbishing the building or the part of the building, as the case may be, and the acquisition of the site thereof had been incurred on or before 30 June 2003, and

(ii) the application for such a certificate is received by the relevant local authority on or before 31 July 2003.][8]

(*b*) In considering whether to give a certificate referred to in paragraph (*a*), the relevant local authority shall have regard only to guidelines issued by the Department of the Environment and Local Government in relation to the giving of such certificates.][9]

Amendments

1 Substituted by FA 2004 s 26(1)(*j*)(i)(I) with effect from 1 January 2004; previously "31 December 2004".

2 Substituted by FA 2004 s 26(1)(*j*)(i)(II) with effect from 1 January 2004; previously "and ending on 31 December 2004".

3 Substituted by FA 2004 s 26(1)(*j*)(i)(III) with effect from 1 January 2004; previously "and ending on 31 December 2004".

4 Substituted by FA 2004 s 26(1)(*j*)(i)(IV) with effect from 1 January 2004; previously "and ending on 31 December 2004".

5 Substituted by FA 2004 s 26(1)(*j*)(i)(V) with effect from 1 January 2004; previously "and ending on 31 December 2004".

6 Subs (1)(*f*)(ii) substituted by FA 2004 s 26(1)(*j*)(i)(VI) with effect from 1 January 2004.

7 Subs (1A) inserted by FA 2004 s 26(1)(*j*)(ii) with effect from 1 January 2004.

8 Subs (2)(*a*) substituted by FA 2003 s 26(*e*)(ii) with effect from 1 January 2003.

9 Section 372AL inserted by FA 2002 s 24(1) and Sch 2 Pt 1 para 1 with effect from 1 January 2002.

Cross-references

Interpretation: s 372AK(1)("qualifying period").

Designated areas of certain towns, qualifying areas: s 372AB(1)(*c*).

Qualifying streets: s 372BA(1)(*c*).

Qualifying urban areas, making of Ministerial orders designating such areas: s 372B(1)(*d*).

Definitions

conversion: s 372AN(2); person: IA 1937 s 11(*c*); qualifying park and ride facility, qualifying rural area, qualifying street, qualifying student accommodation area, qualifying town area, qualifying urban area, refurbishment, relevant local authority, special specified building: s 372AK(1); writing: IA 1937 Sch.

372AM Grant of certain certificates and guidelines, qualifying and special qualifying premises

[(1) (*a*) The Minister may grant a certificate (in this Chapter referred to as a "certificate of compliance") for the purposes of section 372AP or 372AR, as the case may be, certifying that, at the time of granting the certificate and on the basis of the information available to the Minister at that time—

(i) the house to which the certificate relates complies—

(I) in the case of construction, with such conditions, if any, as may be determined by the Minister from time to time for the purposes of section 4 of the Housing (Miscellaneous Provisions) Act, 1979, in relation to standards of construction of houses and the provision of water, sewerage and other services in houses,

(II) in the case of conversion or refurbishment, with such conditions, if any, as may be determined by the Minister from time to time for the purposes of section 5 of the Housing (Miscellaneous Provisions) Act, 1979, in relation to standards for improvement of houses and the provision of water, sewerage and other services in houses,

(ii) the total floor area of that house is within the relevant floor area limits as specified in subsection (4), and

(iii) in the case of refurbishment, the refurbishment work was necessary for the purposes of ensuring the suitability as a dwelling of any house in the building or the part of the building and whether or not the number of houses in the building or the part of the building, or the shape or size of any such house, is altered in the course of such refurbishment,

but—

(A) in the case of a house the site of which is wholly within a qualifying town area, such certificate shall be granted only where an application has been received by the Minister within a period of one year from the day next after the end of the qualifying period, and

(B) in the case of a house, the site of which is wholly within a qualifying student accommodation area, such certificate shall be granted having regard to the relevant guidelines.

(*b*) (i) The Minister may grant a certificate (in this Chapter referred to as a "certificate of reasonable cost") for the purposes of section 372AP or 372AR, as the case may be, certifying that, at the time of granting the certificate and on the basis of the information available to the Minister at that time—

(I) the house to which the certificate relates complies—

(A) in the case of construction, with such conditions, if any, as may be determined by the Minister from time to time for the purposes of section 4 of the Housing (Miscellaneous Provisions) Act, 1979, in relation to standards of construction of houses and the provision of water, sewerage and other services in houses,

(B) in the case of conversion or refurbishment, with such conditions, if any, as may be determined by the Minister from time to time for the purposes of section 5 of the Housing (Miscellaneous Provisions) Act, 1979, in relation to standards for improvement of houses and the provision of water, sewerage and other services in houses,

(II) the amount specified in the certificate in relation to the cost of construction of, conversion into, or, as the case may be, refurbishment of, the house to which the certificate relates appears to the Minister to be reasonable,

(III) the total floor area of that house is within the relevant floor area limits as specified in subsection (4), and

(IV) in the case of refurbishment, the refurbishment work was necessary for the purposes of ensuring the suitability as a dwelling of any house in the building or the part of the building and whether or not the number of houses in the building or the part of the building, or the shape or size of any such house, is altered in the course of such refurbishment,

but—

(A) in the case of a house, the site of which is wholly within a qualifying town area, such certificate shall be granted only where an application has been received by the Minister within a period of one year from the day next after the end of the qualifying period, and

(B) in the case of a house, the site of which is wholly within a qualifying student accommodation area, such certificate shall be granted having regard to the relevant guidelines.

(ii) Section 18 of the Housing (Miscellaneous Provisions) Act, 1979, applies, with any necessary modifications, to a certificate of reasonable cost as if it were a certificate of reasonable value within the meaning of that section.

(*c*) The Minister for Education and Science may, in relation to a house or building the site of which is wholly within a qualifying student accommodation area, in consultation with the Minister and with the consent of the Minister for Finance—

(i) issue guidelines for the purposes of this Chapter and, without prejudice to the generality of the foregoing, such guidelines may include provisions in relation to all or any one or more of the following—

(I) the design and the construction of, conversion into, or refurbishment of, houses,

(II) the total floor area and dimensions of rooms within houses, measured in such manner as may be determined by the Minister,

(III) the provision of ancillary facilities and amenities in relation to houses,

(IV) the granting of certificates of reasonable cost and of certificates of compliance,

(V) the designation of qualifying areas,

(VI) the terms and conditions relating to qualifying leases, and

(VII) the educational institutions and the students attending those institutions for whom the accommodation is provided,

and

(ii) amend or replace relevant guidelines in like manner.

(2) Subject to this section, a house is a qualifying premises for the purposes of section 372AP or 372AR, as the case may be, where—

(*a*) the house fronts on to a qualifying street or is comprised in a building or part of a building which fronts on to a qualifying street, or the site of the house is wholly within a tax incentive area,

(*b*) the house is used solely as a dwelling,

(*c*) the house complies with the requirements of subsection (4) in respect of its total floor area,

(*d*) there is in force in respect of the house—

(i) a certificate of compliance or,

(ii) if it is not a house provided for sale, a certificate of reasonable cost the amount specified in which in respect of the cost of construction of the house, the cost of conversion in relation to the house or the cost of the refurbishment in relation to the house is not less than the expenditure actually incurred on such construction, conversion, or, as the case may be, refurbishment,

but where, in the case of section 372AP, the refurbishment expenditure or, in the case of section 372AR, the qualifying expenditure relates solely to the refurbishment of a facade, this paragraph shall not apply,

(*e*) in the case of a house the site of which is wholly within the site of a qualifying park and ride facility, the relevant local authority gives to the person constructing the house a certificate in writing stating that it is satisfied that the house or, in a case where the house is one of a number of houses in a single development, the development of which it is part complies with the requirements laid down in the guidelines in relation to the development of certain residential accommodation at a park and ride facility, and

(*f*) in so far as section 372AP is concerned, the house—

(i) where the eligible expenditure has been incurred on the construction of the house, without having been used is first let in its entirety under a qualifying lease,

(ii) where the eligible expenditure incurred is conversion expenditure in relation to the house, without having been used subsequent to the incurring of the expenditure on the conversion is first let in its entirety under a qualifying lease, and

(iii) where the eligible expenditure incurred is refurbishment expenditure in relation to the house, on the date of completion of the refurbishment to which the expenditure relates is let (or, if not let on that date, is, without having been used after that date, first let) in its entirety under a qualifying lease, and thereafter throughout the remainder of the relevant period (except for reasonable periods of temporary disuse between the ending of one qualifying lease and the commencement of another such lease) continues to be let under such a lease.

(3) Subject to this section, a house is a special qualifying premises for the purposes of section 372AP where—

(*a*) the house is comprised in a special specified building,

(*b*) the house is used solely as a dwelling,

(*c*) on the date of completion of the refurbishment to which the refurbishment expenditure in relation to the house relates, the house is let (or, if not let on that date, the house is, without having been used after that date, first let) in its entirety under a qualifying lease and thereafter throughout the remainder of the relevant period (except for reasonable periods of temporary disuse between the ending of one qualifying lease and the commencement of another such lease) continues to be let under such a lease, and

(*d*) the house is not a house on which expenditure has been incurred which qualified, or on due claim being made would qualify, for relief under—

(i) section 372AP on the basis that the house is a qualifying premises, or

(ii) any other provision of this Part.

(4) A house is not a qualifying premises for the purposes of section 372AP or 372AR unless—

(*a*) where the house fronts on to a qualifying street or is comprised in a building or part of a building which fronts on to a qualifying street, or where its site is wholly within—

(i) a qualifying urban area, or

(ii) the site of a qualifying park and ride facility,

the total floor area of the house is not less than 38 square metres and not more than 125 square metres,

(*b*) where the site of the house is wholly within a qualifying rural area, the total floor area of the house is not less than 38 square metres and—

(i) in the case of section 372AP—

(I) not more than 140 square metres, if the eligible expenditure incurred was incurred on the construction of the house before 6 December 2000,

(II) not more than 150 square metres, if the eligible expenditure incurred on or in relation to the house was conversion expenditure or refurbishment expenditure incurred before 6 December 2000, or

(III) not more than 175 square metres if the eligible expenditure incurred on or in relation to that house was or is incurred on or after 6 December 2000,

and

(ii) in the case of section 372AR, not more than 210 square metres, (*c*) where the site of the house is wholly within a qualifying town area, the total floor area of the house is not less than 38 square metres and—

(i) in the case of section 372AP—

(I) not more than 125 square metres, or

(II) not more than 150 square metres, if the eligible expenditure incurred on or in relation to the house is conversion expenditure or refurbishment expenditure incurred on or after 6 April 2001,

and

(ii) in the case of section 372AR—

(I) not more than 125 square metres, or

(II) not more than 210 square metres, if the qualifying expenditure incurred on or in relation to the house is incurred on or after 6 April 2001 on [the conversion or the refurbishment of the house][1],

and

(*d*) where the site of the house is wholly within a qualifying student accommodation area, the total floor area of the house complies with the requirements of the relevant guidelines.

(5) A house is not a qualifying premises or a special qualifying premises for the purposes of section 372AP if—

(*a*) it is occupied as a dwelling by any person connected with the person entitled to a deduction under that section in respect of the eligible expenditure incurred on or in relation to the house, and

(*b*) the terms of the qualifying lease in relation to the house are not such as might have been expected to be included in the lease if the negotiations for the lease had been at arm's length.

(6) (*a*) A house—

(i) which fronts on to a qualifying street or is comprised in a building or part of a building which fronts on to a qualifying street, or

(ii) the site of which is wholly within a qualifying urban area or a qualifying town area,

is not a qualifying premises for the purposes of section 372AP or 372AR unless the house or, in a case where the house is one of a number of houses in a single development, the development of which it is a part complies with such guidelines as may from time to time be issued by the Minister, with the consent of the Minister for Finance, for the purposes of furthering the objectives of urban renewal.

(*b*) Without prejudice to the generality of paragraph (*a*), guidelines issued for the purposes of that paragraph may include provisions in relation to all or any one or more of the following—

(i) the design and the construction of, conversion into, or, as the case may be, refurbishment of, houses,

(ii) the total floor area and dimensions of rooms within houses, measured in such manner as may be determined by the Minister,

(iii) the provision of ancillary facilities and amenities in relation to houses, and

(iv) the balance to be achieved between houses of different types and sizes within a single development of 2 or more houses or within such a development and its general vicinity having regard to the housing existing or proposed in that vicinity.

(7) A house, the site of which is wholly within a qualifying rural area, is not a qualifying premises for the purposes of section 372AP unless throughout the period of any qualifying lease related to that house, the house is used as the sole or main residence of the lessee in relation to that qualifying lease.

(8) A house which fronts on to a qualifying street or is comprised in a building or part of a building which fronts on to a qualifying street is not a qualifying premises for the purposes of section 372AP or 372AR unless—

(*a*) the house is comprised in the upper floor or floors of an existing building or a replacement building, and

(*b*) the ground floor of such building is in use for commercial purposes or, where it is temporarily vacant, it is subsequently so used.

(9) A house, the site of which is wholly within a qualifying student accommodation area, is not a qualifying premises for the purposes of section 372AP unless throughout the relevant period it is used for letting to and occupation by students in accordance with the relevant guidelines.

[(9A) A house, the site of which is wholly within a qualifying student accommodation area, is not a qualifying premises or a special qualifying premises for the purposes of section 372AP—

(*a*) (i) if any person, other than the person (in this subsection referred to as the **"investor"**) who incurred or, by virtue of subsection (8), (9) or (10) of that section, is treated as having incurred eligible expenditure on or in relation to the house, receives or is entitled to receive the rent, or any part of the rent, from the letting of the house during the relevant period in relation to the house, or

(ii) where two or more investors have incurred or, by virtue of subsection (8), (9) or (10) of that section, are treated as having incurred eligible expenditure on or in relation to the house, unless that part of the gross rent received or receivable from the letting of the house during the relevant period in relation to the house which is received or receivable by each investor bears the same proportion to that gross rent as the amount of the eligible expenditure which is incurred, or is so treated as having been incurred, on or in relation to the house by that investor bears to the total amount of the eligible expenditure which is incurred, or is so treated as having been incurred, on or in relation to the house by all such investors;

(*b*) where borrowed money is employed by an investor in the construction of, conversion into, refurbishment of, or, as the case may be, purchase of, the house, unless—

(i) that borrowed money is borrowed directly by the investor from a financial institution (within the meaning of section 906A),

(ii) the investor is personally responsible for the repayment of, the payment of interest on, and the provision of any security required in relation to, that borrowed money, and

(iii) there is no arrangement or agreement, whether in writing or otherwise and whether or not the person providing that borrowed money is aware of such agreement or arrangement, whereby any other person agrees to be responsible for any of the investor's obligations referred to in subparagraph (ii);

(*c*) where management or letting fees payable to a person in relation to the letting of the house are claimed by the investor as a deduction under section 97(2) for any chargeable period (within the meaning of section 321) ending in the relevant period in relation to the house, unless—

(i) such fees are shown by the claimant to be bona fide fees which reflect the level and extent of the services rendered by the person, and

(ii) the aggregate amount of such fees for that chargeable period is not more than an amount which is equal to 15 per cent of the gross amount of the rent received or receivable by the investor from the letting of the house for that chargeable period.

(9B) Subject to subsection (9C), subsection (9A) applies

(*a*) as respects eligible expenditure incurred on or in relation to a house on or after 18 July 2002, unless a binding contract for the construction of, conversion into or, as the case may be, refurbishment of the house was evidenced in writing before that date, and

(*b*) where subsection (9) or (10) of section 372AP applies, as respects expenditure incurred on the purchase of a house on or after 18 July 2002, unless a binding contract for the purchase of the house was evidenced in writing before that date.

(9C) Paragraphs (*a*) and (*c*) of subsection (9A) shall not apply as respects eligible expenditure incurred on or in relation to a house or, where subsection (9) or (10) of section 372AP applies, as respects expenditure incurred on the purchase of a house where, before 6 February 2003, the Revenue Commissioners have given an opinion in writing to the effect that the lease of the house between an investor and an educational institution referred to in the relevant guidelines, or a subsidiary (within the meaning of section 155 of the Companies Act 1963) of such an institution, would be a qualifying lease.][2]

(10)(*a*) A house is not a special qualifying premises for the purposes of section 372AP if the lessor has not complied with all the requirements of—

(i) the Housing (Standards for Rented Houses) Regulations 1993 (SI No 147 of 1993),

(ii) the Housing (Rent Books) Regulations 1993 (SI No 146 of 1993), and

(iii) the Housing (Registration of Rented Houses) Regulations 1996 (SI No 30 of 1996), as amended by the Housing (Registration of Rented Houses) (Amendment) Regulations 2000 (SI No 12 of 2000).

(*b*) A house is not a special qualifying premises for the purposes of section 372AP unless the house or, in a case where the house is one of a number of houses in a single development, the development of which it is a part complies with such guidelines as may from time to time be issued by the Minister, with the consent of the Minister for Finance, in relation to the refurbishment of houses as special qualifying premises.

(*c*) Without prejudice to the generality of paragraph (*b*), guidelines issued for the purposes of that paragraph may include provisions in relation to refurbishment of houses and the provision of ancillary facilities and amenities in relation to houses.

(11) A house is not a qualifying premises for the purposes of section 372AP or 372AR, or a special qualifying premises for the purposes of section 372AP, unless any person authorised in writing by the Minister for the purposes of those sections is permitted to inspect the house at all reasonable times on production, if so requested by a person affected, of his or her authorisation.][3]

Amendments

1 Substituted by FA 2003 s 30(1)(*b*) with effect from 1 January 2002; previously "the refurbishment of the house".

2 Subss (9A)–(9C) inserted by FA 2003 s 32(1) with effect from 18 July 2002.

3 Section 372AM inserted by FA 2002 s 24(1) and Sch 2 Pt 1 para 1 with effect from 1 January 2002.

Cross-references

Interpretation: s 372AK(1)("certificate of compliance", "certificate of reasonable cost", "qualifying premises", "refurbishment", "relevant guidelines" and "special qualifying premises").

Definitions

connected: s 10; conversion: s 372AN(2); conversion expenditure, eligible expenditure, guidelines, house, lease, lessee, lessor, qualifying lease, Minister: s 372AK(1); person: IA 1937 s 11(c); qualifying expenditure, qualifying lease, qualifying park and ride facility, qualifying period, qualifying rural area, qualifying street, qualifying student accommodation area, qualifying town area, qualifying urban area, refurbishment, refurbishment expenditure, relevant guidelines, relevant local authority, relevant period, replacement building, special specified building, tax incentive area, total floor area: s 372AK(1); writing: IA 1937 Sch.

372AN Eligible expenditure: lessors

[(1) Expenditure is eligible expenditure for the purposes of this Chapter where it is—

(*a*) expenditure incurred on—

(i) the construction of a house, other than a house referred to in subparagraph (ii), or

(ii) the necessary construction of a house which fronts on to a qualifying street or is comprised in a building or part of a building which fronts on to a qualifying street,

(*b*) conversion expenditure, or

(*c*) refurbishment expenditure.

(2) In this Chapter **"conversion expenditure"** means, subject to subsection (3), expenditure incurred on—

(*a*) the conversion into a house of—

(i) a building which fronts on to a qualifying street or the site of which is wholly within a tax incentive area other than the site of a qualifying park and ride facility, or

(ii) a part of a building which fronts on to a qualifying street or the site of which is wholly within a qualifying urban area or a qualifying town area,

where the building or, as the case may be, the part of the building has not been previously in use as a dwelling, and

(*b*) the conversion into 2 or more houses of—

(i) a building which fronts on to a qualifying street or the site of which is wholly within a tax incentive area other than the site of a qualifying park and ride facility, or

(ii) a part of a building which fronts on to a qualifying street or the site of which is wholly within a qualifying urban area or a qualifying town area,

where before the conversion the building or, as the case may be, the part of the building had not been in use as a dwelling or had been in use as a single dwelling,

and references in this Chapter to **"conversion"**, **"conversion into a house"** and **"expenditure incurred on conversion"** shall be construed accordingly;

(3) For the purposes of subsection (2), expenditure incurred on the conversion of a building or a part of a building includes expenditure incurred in the course of the conversion on either or both of the following—

(*a*) the carrying out of any works of construction, reconstruction, repair or renewal, and

(*b*) the provision or improvement of water, sewerage or heating facilities,

in relation to the building or the part of the building, as the case may be, or any outoffice appurtenant to or usually enjoyed with that building or part, but does not include—

(i) any expenditure in respect of which any person is entitled to a deduction, relief or allowance under any other provision of the Tax Acts, or

(ii) any expenditure attributable to any part (in this subsection referred to as a "non-residential unit") of the building or, as the case may be, the part of the building which on completion of the conversion is not a house.

(4) For the purposes of subsection (3)(ii), where expenditure is attributable to a building or a part of a building in general and not directly to any particular house or non-residential unit (within the meaning given by that subsection) comprised in the building or the part of the building on completion of the conversion, then such an amount of that expenditure shall be deemed to be attributable to a non-residential unit as bears to the whole of that expenditure the same proportion as the total floor area of the non-residential unit bears to the total floor area of the building or the part of the building, as the case may be.

(5) (*a*) For the purposes of this Chapter **"refurbishment expenditure"** means expenditure incurred on—

(i) (I) the refurbishment of a specified building, and

(II) in the case of a specified building the site of which is wholly within a qualifying town area, the refurbishment of a facade,

or

(ii) the refurbishment of a special specified building,

other than expenditure attributable to any part (in this subsection and in subsection (6) referred to as a "non-residential unit") of the building which on completion of the refurbishment is not a house.

(*b*) For the purposes of paragraph (*a*), where expenditure is attributable to—

(i) the specified building, or

(ii) the special specified building,

as the case may be, in general and not directly to any particular house or non-residential unit comprised in the building on completion of the refurbishment, then such an amount of that expenditure shall be deemed to be attributable to a non-residential unit as bears to the whole of that expenditure the same proportion as the total floor area of the non-residential unit bears to the total floor area of the building.

(6) For the purposes of subsection (5)—

"special specified building" means a building or part of a building—

(*a*) in which before the refurbishment to which the refurbishment expenditure relates there is one or more than one house, and

(*b*) which on completion of that refurbishment contains, whether in addition to any non-residential unit or not, one or more than one house;

"specified building" means—

(*a*) a building which fronts on to a qualifying street or the site of which is wholly within a tax incentive area other than the site of a qualifying park and ride facility, or

(*b*) a part of a building which fronts on to a qualifying street or the site of which is wholly within a qualifying urban area or a qualifying town area,

and in which before the refurbishment to which the refurbishment expenditure relates—

(i) there is one or more than one house—

(I) in the case of a building, the site of which is wholly within a qualifying rural area, or

(II) in the case of a building or part of a building, the site of which is wholly within a qualifying town area,

and

(ii) there are 2 or more houses—

(I) in the case of a building or part of a building which fronts on to a qualifying street or the site of which is wholly within a qualifying urban area, or

(II) in the case of a building the site of which is wholly within a qualifying student accommodation area,

and which on completion of that refurbishment contains, whether in addition to any non-residential unit or not—

(A) in the case of a building or part of a building to which paragraph (i) applies, one or more than one house,

(B) in the case of a building or part of a building to which paragraph (ii) applies, 2 or more houses.

(7) Other than in relation to a special qualifying premises, references in this section to the construction of, conversion into, or, as the case may be, refurbishment of, any premises shall be construed as including references to the development of the land on which the premises is situated or which is used in the provision of gardens, grounds, access or amenities in relation to the premises and, without prejudice to the generality of the foregoing, as including in particular—

(*a*) demolition or dismantling of any building on the land,

(*b*) site clearance, earth moving, excavation, tunnelling and boring, laying of foundations, erection of scaffolding, site restoration, landscaping and the provision of roadways and other access works,

(*c*) walls, power supply, drainage, sanitation and water supply, and

(*d*) the construction of any outhouses or other buildings or structures for use by the occupants of the premises or for use in the provision of amenities for the occupants.][1]

Amendments

[1] Section 372AN inserted by FA 2002 s 24(1) and Sch 2 Pt 1 para 1 with effect from 1 January 2002.

Cross-references

Interpretation: s 372AK(1)("conversion expenditure", "eligible expenditure" and "refurbishment expenditure"); subs (6): s 372AK(1)("special specified building" and "specified building").

Qualifying expenditure, owner-occupiers, subs (4): s 372AQ(4).

Determination of expenditure incurred in qualifying period, and date expenditure treated as incurred for relief purposes: subs (7): s 372AS(2).

Definitions

facade, house, necessary construction: s 372AK(1); land: IA 1937 Sch; person: IA 1937 s 11(*c*); qualifying park and ride facility, qualifying rural area, qualifying street, qualifying student accommodation area, qualifying town area, qualifying urban area, refurbishment: s 372K(1); Tax Acts: s 1(2); tax incentive area, total floor area: s 372AK(1).

372AO Qualifying lease

[(1) In this section **"market value"**, in relation to a building, structure or house, means the price which the unencumbered fee simple of the building, structure or house would fetch if sold in the open market in such manner and subject to such conditions as might reasonably be calculated to obtain for the vendor the best price for the building, structure or house, less the part of that price which would be attributable to the acquisition of, or of rights in or over, the land on which the building, structure or house is constructed.

(2) Subject to subsection (4), a lease of a house is a qualifying lease for the purposes of this Chapter where the consideration for the grant of the lease consists—

(*a*) solely of periodic payments all of which are or are to be treated as rent for the purposes of Chapter 8 of Part 4, or

(*b*) of payments of the kind mentioned in paragraph (*a*), together with a payment by means of a premium which—

(i) in the case of the construction of a house, does not exceed 10 per cent of the relevant cost of the house,

(ii) in the case of the conversion of a building into a house, does not exceed 10 per cent of the market value of the house at the time the conversion is completed, and

(iii) in the case of the refurbishment of a house—

(I) is payable on or subsequent to the date of the completion of the refurbishment to which the refurbishment expenditure relates or which, if payable before that date, is so payable by reason of or otherwise in connection with the carrying out of the refurbishment, and

(II) does not exceed 10 per cent of the market value of the house at the time of the completion of the refurbishment to which the refurbishment expenditure relates.

(3) For the purposes of subparagraph (ii) or (iii) of subsection (2)(*b*), as the case may be, where a house is a part of a building and is not saleable apart from the building of which it is a part, the market value of the house at the time the conversion is completed or, as the case may be, at the time of the completion of the refurbishment to which the refurbishment expenditure relates shall be taken to be an amount which bears to the market value of the building at that time the same proportion as the total floor area of the house bears to the total floor area of the building.

(4) A lease is not a qualifying lease for the purposes of this Chapter—

(*a*) if the terms of the lease contain any provision enabling the lessee or any other person, directly or indirectly, at any time to acquire any interest in the house to which the lease relates for a consideration less than that which might be expected to be given at that time for the acquisition of the interest if the negotiations for that acquisition were conducted in the open market at arm's length,

(*b*) where the lease relates to a qualifying rural area, if the duration of the lease is for a period of less than 3 months, or

(*c*) where the lease relates to a qualifying student accommodation area, if the lease does not comply with the requirements of the relevant guidelines.][1]

Amendments

1 Section 372AO inserted by FA 2002 s 24(1) and Sch 2 Pt 1 para 1 with effect from 1 January 2002.

Cross-references

Interpretation: s 372AK(1)("qualifying lease").

Definitions

conversion: s 372AN(2); house: s 372AK(1); land: IA 1937 Sch; lease, lessee, premium, qualifying rural area, qualifying student accommodation area, refurbishment, refurbishment expenditure, relevant cost, relevant guidelines, rent, total floor area: s 372AK(1).

372AP Relief for lessors

[(1) In this section—

"chargeable period" means an accounting period of a company or a year of assessment;

"relevant cost", in relation to a house, means, subject to subsection (6), an amount equal to the aggregate of—

(*a*) (i) where the eligible expenditure is on the construction of the house, the expenditure incurred on the acquisition of, or of rights in or over, any land on which the house is situated, or

(ii) where the eligible expenditure is conversion expenditure or refurbishment expenditure, the expenditure incurred on the acquisition of, or of rights in or over—

(I) any land on which the house is situated, and

(II) any building in which the house is comprised,

and

(*b*) the expenditure actually incurred on the construction of, conversion into, or, as the case may be, refurbishment of the house;

"relevant period", in relation to the incurring of eligible expenditure on or in relation to a qualifying premises or a special qualifying premises, means—

(*a*) where the eligible expenditure is incurred on the construction of, or in relation to the conversion of a building into, a qualifying premises, the period of 10 years beginning on the date of the first letting of the qualifying premises under a qualifying lease, and—

(*b*) where—

(i) the eligible expenditure incurred is refurbishment expenditure in relation to a qualifying premises or a special qualifying premises, the period of 10 years beginning on the date of the completion of the refurbishment to which the refurbishment expenditure relates, or

(ii) where the qualifying premises or, as the case may be, the special qualifying premises was not let under a qualifying lease on the date referred to in subparagraph (i), the period of 10 years beginning on the date of the first such letting after the date of such completion;

"relevant price paid", in relation to the purchase by a person of a house, means the amount which bears to the net price paid by such person on that purchase the same proportion as the amount of the eligible expenditure actually incurred on or in relation to the house, which is to be treated under section 372AS(1) as having been incurred in the qualifying period, bears to the relevant cost in relation to that house.

(2) Subject to subsections (3), (4) and (5), where a person, having made a claim in that behalf, proves to have incurred eligible expenditure on or in relation to a house which is a qualifying premises or a special qualifying premises—

(*a*) such person is entitled, in computing for the purposes of section 97(1) the amount of a surplus or deficiency in respect of the rent from the qualifying premises or, as the case may be, the special qualifying premises, to a deduction of so much (if any) of that expenditure as is to be treated under section 372AS(1) or under this section as having been incurred by such person in the qualifying period, and

(*b*) Chapter 8 of Part 4 shall apply as if that deduction were a deduction authorised by section 97(2).

(3) (*a*) Where the eligible expenditure incurred is refurbishment expenditure in relation to a house which is a special qualifying premises—

(i) the deduction to be given under subsection (2)*(a)* shall be given—

(I) for the chargeable period in which the expenditure is incurred or, if the special qualifying premises was not let under a qualifying lease during that chargeable period, the chargeable period in which occurs the date of the first such letting after the expenditure is incurred, and

(II) for any subsequent chargeable period in which that premises continues to be a special qualifying premises,

and

(ii) the deduction for each such chargeable period shall be of an amount equal to 15 per cent of the expenditure to which subsection (2)*(a)* refers.

(*b*) For the purposes of paragraph *(a)*—

(i) the aggregate amount to be deducted by virtue of that paragraph shall not exceed 100 per cent of the expenditure to which subsection (2)*(a)* refers, and

(ii) where a chargeable period consists of a period less than one year in length, the amount of the deduction to be given for the chargeable period shall be proportionately reduced.

(4) (*a*) This subsection applies to any premium or other sum which—

(i) is payable, directly or indirectly, under a qualifying lease or otherwise under the terms subject to which the lease is granted, to or for the benefit of the lessor or to or for the benefit of any person connected with the lessor, and

(ii) where the eligible expenditure incurred is refurbishment expenditure in relation to a qualifying premises or a special qualifying premises—

(I) is payable on or subsequent to the date of completion of the refurbishment to which the refurbishment expenditure relates, or

(II) if payable before that date, is so payable by reason of or otherwise in connection with the carrying out of the refurbishment.

(*b*) Where any premium or other sum to which this subsection applies, or any part of such premium or such other sum, is not or is not treated as rent for the purposes of section 97, the eligible expenditure to be treated as having been incurred in the qualifying period on or in relation to the qualifying premises or the special qualifying premises to which the qualifying lease relates shall be deemed for the purposes of subsection (2) to be reduced by the lesser of—

(i) the amount of such premium or such other sum or, as the case may be, that part of such premium or such other sum, and

(ii) the amount which bears to the amount mentioned in subparagraph (i) the same proportion as the amount of the eligible expenditure actually incurred on or in relation to the qualifying premises or, as the case may be, the special qualifying premises and which is to be treated under section 372AS(1) as having been incurred in the qualifying period bears to the whole of the eligible expenditure incurred on or in relation to the qualifying premises or the special qualifying premises, as the case may be.

(5) (*a*) A person is entitled to a deduction by virtue of subsection (2) in respect of eligible expenditure incurred on a qualifying premises at a park and ride facility only in so far as that expenditure when aggregated with—

(i) other eligible expenditure, if any, incurred on other qualifying premises at the park and ride facility and in respect of which a deduction is to be made or would, but for this subsection, be made, and

(ii) other expenditure, if any, incurred at the park and ride facility, in respect of which there is provision for a deduction under section 372AR,

does not exceed 25 per cent of the total expenditure incurred at the park and ride facility in respect of which an allowance or deduction is to be made or would, but for this subsection or section 372W(2)(*c*) or 372AR(5), be made by virtue of any provision of this Chapter or Chapter 9.

(*b*) A person who has incurred eligible expenditure on a qualifying premises at a park and ride facility and who claims to have complied with the requirements of paragraph (*a*) in relation to that expenditure, shall be deemed not to have so complied unless the person has received from the relevant local authority a certificate in writing issued by that authority stating that it is satisfied that those requirements have been met.

(6) Where a qualifying premises or a special qualifying premises forms a part of a building or is one of a number of buildings in a single development, or forms a part of a building which is itself one of a number of buildings in a single development, there shall be made such apportionment as is necessary—

(*a*) of the eligible expenditure incurred on the construction, conversion or, as the case may be, refurbishment of that building or those buildings, and

(*b*) of the amount which would be the relevant cost in relation to that building or those buildings if the building or buildings, as the case may be, were a single qualifying premises,

for the purposes of determining the eligible expenditure incurred on or in relation to the qualifying premises or the special qualifying premises, as the case may be, and the relevant cost in relation to the qualifying premises or the special qualifying premises, as the case may be.

(7) Where a house is a qualifying premises or a special qualifying premises and at any time during the relevant period in relation to the premises either of the following events occurs—

(*a*) the house ceases to be a qualifying premises or a special qualifying premises, as the case may be, or

(*b*) the ownership of the lessor's interest in the house passes to any other person but the house does not cease to be a qualifying premises or a special qualifying premises, as the case may be,

then, the person who before the occurrence of the event received or was entitled to receive a deduction or, as the case may be, deductions under subsection (2) in respect of eligible expenditure incurred on or in relation to that premises shall be deemed to have received on the day before the day of the occurrence of the event an amount as rent from that premises equal to the amount of that deduction or, as the case may be, the aggregate amount of those deductions.

(8) (*a*) Where the event mentioned in subsection (7)(*b*) occurs in the relevant period in relation to a house which is a qualifying premises or a special qualifying premises, the person to whom the ownership of the lessor's interest in the house passes shall be treated for the purposes of this section as having incurred in the qualifying period an amount of eligible expenditure on or in relation to the house equal to the amount which under section 372AS(1) or under this section (apart from subsection (4)(*b*)) the lessor was treated as having incurred in the qualifying period on or in relation to the house.

(*b*) Where a person purchases a house to which paragraph *(a)* applies, the amount treated under that paragraph as having been incurred by such person shall not exceed the relevant price paid by such person on the purchase.

(9) Subject to subsection (10), where eligible expenditure is incurred on or in relation to a house and—

(*a*) where the eligible expenditure was expenditure on the construction of the house, before the house is used it is sold, or

(*b*) where the eligible expenditure was conversion expenditure or refurbishment expenditure, before the house is used subsequent to the incurring of that expenditure it is sold,

then, the person who purchases the house shall be treated for the purposes of this section as having incurred in the qualifying period eligible expenditure on or in relation to the house equal to the lesser of—

(i) the amount of such expenditure which is to be treated under section 372AS(1) as having been incurred in the qualifying period, and

(ii) the relevant price paid by such person on the purchase,

but, where the house is sold more than once before it is used, or, as the case may be, before the house is used subsequent to the incurring of the expenditure, this subsection shall apply only in relation to the last of those sales.

(10) Where eligible expenditure is incurred on or in relation to a house by a person carrying on a trade or part of a trade which consists, as to the whole or any part of that trade, of the construction, conversion or refurbishment of buildings with a view to their sale and the house is sold in the course of that trade or, as the case may be, that part of that trade—

(*a*) where the eligible expenditure was expenditure on the construction of the house—

(i) before the house is used, or

(ii) where a house, the site of which is wholly within a qualifying student accommodation area, is sold on or after 5 December 2001, within a period of one year after it commences to be used,

and

(*b*) where the eligible expenditure was conversion expenditure or refurbishment expenditure—

(i) before the house is used subsequent to the incurring of that expenditure, or

(ii) where a house, the site of which is wholly within a qualifying student accommodation area, is sold on or after 5 December 2001, within a period of one year after it commences to be used subsequent to the incurring of that expenditure,

then—

(I) the person (in this subsection referred to as the "purchaser") who purchases the house shall be treated for the purposes of this section as having incurred in the qualifying period eligible expenditure on or in relation to the house equal to the relevant price paid by the purchaser on the purchase (in this subsection referred to as the "first purchase"), and

(II) in relation to any subsequent sale or sales of the house before the house is used, or, as the case may be, before the house is used subsequent to the incurring of the expenditure, subsection (9) shall apply as if the reference to the amount of eligible expenditure which is to be treated as having been incurred in the qualifying period were a reference to the relevant price paid on the first purchase.

(11) Expenditure in respect of which a person is entitled to relief under this section shall not include any expenditure in respect of which any person is entitled to a deduction, relief or allowance under any other provision of the Tax Acts.

(12) For the purposes of this section, expenditure shall not be regarded as incurred by a person in so far as it has been or is to be met, directly or indirectly, by the State, by any board established by statute or by any public or local authority.

(13) Section 555 shall apply as if a deduction under this section were a capital allowance and as if any rent deemed to have been received by a person under this section were a balancing charge.

(14) This section shall not apply in the case of any conversion or refurbishment unless planning permission, in so far as it is required, in respect of the conversion or, as the case may be, the work carried out in the course of the refurbishment has been granted under the Local Government (Planning and Development) Acts 1963 to 1999 or the Planning and Development Act, 2000.

(15) Section 372AS shall apply for the purposes of supplementing this section.][1]

Amendments

1 Section 372AP inserted by FA 2002 s 24(1) and Sch 2 Pt 1 para 1 with effect from 1 January 2002.

Cross-references

Continuity: s 372AV(7)(*a*), (*b*), (*c*), (8)(*a*), (*b*), (*c*).

Designated areas of certain towns, qualifying areas: s 372AB(1)(*ba*).

Determination of expenditure incurred in qualifying period, and date expenditure incurred for relief purposes: s 372AS(3)(*a*), (*b*); subs (2): s 372AS(1)(*a*), (1)(i).

Grant of certain certificates, guidelines, qualifying and special qualifying premises: s 372AM(1)(*a*), (*b*)(i), (2), (2)(*d*), (*f*), (3), (3)(*d*)(i), (4), (4)(*b*)(i), (*c*)(i), (5), (6)(*a*), (7), (8), (9), (9A), (9B), (9C), (10)(*a*), (*b*), (11).

Interpretation: s 372AK(1)("relevant cost", "relevant period").

Park and ride facilities and certain related developments, capital allowances in relation to construction or refurbishment of certain commercial premises: s 372W(2)(*c*)(i); subs (5): s 372W(2)(*c*)(i).
Qualifying period: s 372AL(1)(*c*)(i).
Qualifying streets: s 372BA(1)(*ba*).
Qualifying urban areas, qualifying areas: s 372B(1)(*ba*); capital allowances in relation to construction or refurbishment of certain commercial premises: s 372D(3A)(*a*)(ii), (*b*).
Relief for owner-occupiers: s 372AR(5)(*a*)(ii); subs (5): s 372AR(5)(*a*); subss (6)(*a*) and (10): s 372AR(7).
See also Urban Renewal Act 1998 (as amended by FA 2002), ss 8 (recommendations in respect of qualifying areas for purposes of urban renewal tax reliefs), 9A (designation of certain areas for rented residential reliefs) and 11 (certain reliefs conditional on buildings etc being consistent with integrated area plan).
See also Town Renewal Act 2000 (as amended by FA 2002), ss 5 (recommendations in respect of qualifying areas for purposes of town renewal tax reliefs), 6A (designation of certain areas for rented residential reliefs) and 7 (certain reliefs conditional on buildings etc being consistent with town renewal plan).

Revenue precedents

Issue: An individual incurs expenditure on refurbishment of a building to be used for student accommodation in a certain tax year. However, a Certificate of Reasonable Cost is not issued until the following tax year. Will the individual get relief for the year in which the expenditure was incurred?
Decision: Section 380D(2) now (section 372AP(2)) provides that where a person, having made a claim in that behalf, proves to have incurred relevant expenditure in relation to a house which is a qualifying premises such a person is entitled to a deduction. A house cannot be a qualifying premises unless a CRC has been issued in relation to refurbishment expenditure.

Definitions

capital allowance: s 2(1); connected: s 10; conversion: s 372AN(2); conversion expenditure, eligible expenditure, house: s 372AK(1); land: IA 1937 Sch; lease, lessor: s 372AK(1); local authority: s 2(1); person: IA 1937 s 11(*c*); premium, qualifying lease, qualifying period, qualifying premises, qualifying student accommodation area, refurbishment, refurbishment expenditure, relevant local authority, relevant period: s 372AK(1); statute: IA 1937 s 3; special qualifying premises: s 372K(1); Tax Acts: s 1(2); trade: ss 3(1), 4(1); writing: IA 1937 Sch; year of assessment: s 2(1).

372AQ Qualifying expenditure: owner-occupiers

[(1) For the purposes of this Chapter, but subject to subsection (3), "qualifying expenditure" means expenditure incurred by an individual on—

(*a*) the construction of, conversion into, or, as the case may be, refurbishment of a qualifying premises, and

(*b*) in the case of a qualifying premises the site of which is wholly within a qualifying town area, the refurbishment of a facade,

where the qualifying premises is a qualifying owner occupied dwelling in relation to the individual, after deducting from that amount of expenditure any sum in respect of or by reference to—

(i) that expenditure,

(ii) the qualifying premises, or

(iii) the construction, conversion or, as the case may be, refurbishment work in respect of which that expenditure was incurred,

which the individual has received or is entitled to receive, directly or indirectly, from the State, any board established by statute or any public or local authority.

(2) For the purposes of this section, "qualifying owner-occupied dwelling", in relation to an individual, means a qualifying premises which is first used, after the qualifying expenditure has been incurred, by the individual as his or her only or main residence.

(3) Subsection (1) applies—

(*a*) in the case of a qualifying premises which fronts on to a qualifying street or is comprised in a building or part of a building which fronts on to a qualifying street, as if the reference in that subsection to "construction" were a reference to "necessary construction", and

(*b*) in the case of a qualifying premises the site of which is wholly within the site of a qualifying park and ride facility, as if the reference in that subsection to "construction of, conversion into, or, as the case may be, refurbishment of" were a reference to "construction of".

(4) Subsection (7) of section 372AN, which relates to the construing of references in that section to the construction of, conversion into, or, as the case may be, refurbishment of, any premises, shall apply with any necessary modifications in construing references in this section to the construction of, conversion into, or, as the case may be, refurbishment of any premises.][1]

Amendments

[1] Section 372AQ inserted by FA 2002 s 24(1) and Sch 2 Pt 1 para 1 with effect from 1 January 2002.

Cross-references

Determination of expenditure incurred in qualifying period, and date expenditure treated as incurred for relief purposes, subs (4): s 372AS(2).

Interpretation: s 372AK(1)("qualifying expenditure", "refurbishment").

Definition

conversion: s 372AN(2); facade: s 372AK(1); local authority: s 2(1); necessary construction, qualifying park and ride facility, qualifying premises, qualifying street, qualifying town area, refurbishment: s 372AK(1); statute: IA 1937 s 3.

372AR Relief for owner-occupiers

[(1) Subject to this section, where an individual, having duly made a claim, proves to have incurred qualifying expenditure in a year of assessment, the individual is entitled, for that year of assessment and for any of the 9 subsequent years of assessment in which the qualifying premises in respect of which the individual incurred the qualifying expenditure is the only or main residence of the individual, to have a deduction made from his or her total income of an amount equal to—

(*a*) 5 per cent of the amount of that expenditure, where the qualifying expenditure has been incurred on the construction of the qualifying premises,

(*b*) 10 per cent of the amount of that expenditure, where the qualifying expenditure has been incurred on the necessary construction of a qualifying premises which fronts on to a qualifying street or is comprised in a building or part of a building which fronts on to a qualifying street, or

(*c*) 10 per cent of the amount of that expenditure, where the qualifying expenditure has been incurred on the conversion into or the refurbishment of the qualifying premises.

(2) Where the year of assessment first mentioned in subsection (1) or any of the 9 subsequent years of assessment is the year of assessment 2001, that subsection applies—

(*a*) as if for "any of the 9 subsequent years of assessment" there were substituted "any of the 10 subsequent years of assessment", (*b*) as respects the year of assessment 2001, as if "3.7 per cent" and "7.4 per cent" were substituted for "5 per cent" and "10 per cent", respectively, and

(*c*) as respects the year of assessment which is the 10th year of assessment subsequent to the year of assessment first mentioned in that subsection, as if "1.3 per cent" and "2.6 per cent" were substituted for "5 per cent" and "10 per cent", respectively.

(3) Notwithstanding subsection (1), where the individual or, being a husband or wife, the individual's spouse, is assessed to tax in accordance with section 1017, then, except where section 1023 applies, the individual shall be entitled to have the deduction, to which he or she is entitled under that subsection, made from his or her total income and the total income of his or her spouse, if any.

(4) A deduction shall be given under this section in respect of qualifying expenditure only in so far as that expenditure is to be treated under section 372AS(1) as having been incurred in the qualifying period.

(5) (*a*) A person is entitled to a deduction by virtue of subsection (1) in respect of qualifying expenditure incurred at a park and ride facility only in so far as that expenditure when aggregated with—

(i) other qualifying expenditure, if any, incurred at that park and ride facility in respect of which a deduction is to be made or would, but for this subsection, be made, and

(ii) other expenditure, if any, incurred at that park and ride facility in respect of which there is provision for a deduction under section 372AP,

does not exceed 25 per cent of the total expenditure incurred at that park and ride facility in respect of which an allowance or deduction is to be made or would, but for this subsection or section 372W(2)(*c*) or 372AP(5), be made by virtue of any provision of this Chapter or Chapter 9.

(*b*) A person who has incurred qualifying expenditure at a park and ride facility and who claims to have complied with the requirements of paragraph *(a)* in relation to that expenditure, shall be deemed not to have so complied unless the person has received from the relevant local authority a certificate in writing issued by that authority stating that it is satisfied that those requirements have been met.

(6) Where qualifying expenditure in relation to a qualifying premises is incurred by 2 or more persons, each of those persons shall be treated as having incurred the expenditure in the proportions in which they actually bore the expenditure, and the expenditure shall be apportioned accordingly.

(7) Subsections (6), (9) and (10) of section 372AP, in relation to—

(*a*) the apportionment of eligible expenditure incurred on or in relation to a qualifying premises and of the relevant cost in relation to that premises, and

(*b*) the amount of eligible expenditure to be treated as incurred in the qualifying period, apply, with any necessary modifications, for the purposes of this section, in determining—

(i) the amount of qualifying expenditure incurred on or in relation to a qualifying premises, and

(ii) the amount of qualifying expenditure to be treated as incurred in the qualifying period,

as they apply for the purposes of section 372AP.

(8) Expenditure in respect of which an individual is entitled to relief under this section shall not include any expenditure in respect of which any person is entitled to a deduction, relief or allowance under any other provision of the Tax Acts.

(9) This section shall not apply in the case of any conversion or refurbishment unless planning permission, in so far as it is required, in respect of the conversion or, as the case may be, the work carried out in the course of the refurbishment has been granted under the Local Government (Planning and Development) Acts 1963 to 1999 or the Planning and Development Act, 2000.

(10) Section 372AS applies for the purposes of supplementing this section.][1]

Amendments

1 Section 372AR inserted by FA 2002 s 24(1) and Sch 2 Pt 1 para 1 with effect from 1 January 2002.

Cross-references

Continuity: s 372AV(7)(*d*), (8)(*d*).

Designated areas of certain towns, qualifying areas: s 372AB(1)(*b*).

Determination of expenditure incurred in qualifying period, and date expenditure treated as incurred for relief purposes: s 372AS(3)(*c*); subs (1): s 372AS(1)(*b*), (1)(ii).

Grant of certain certificates, guidelines, qualifying and special qualifying premises: s 372AM(1)(*a*), (*b*)(i), (2), (2)(*d*), (4), (4)(*b*)(ii), (*c*)(ii), (6)(*a*), (8), (11).

Interpretation, subs (1)(*a*): s 372AK(1)("necessary construction", "refurbishment").

Park and ride facilities and certain related developments, capital allowances in relation to construction or refurbishment of certain commercial premises: s 372W(2)(*c*)(i); subs (5): s 372W(2)(*c*)(i).

Qualifying period: s 372AL(1)(*c*)(ii).

Qualifying town areas, qualifying areas: s 372AB(1)(*b*)(iii).

Qualfying urban areas, capital allowances in relation to construction or refurbishment of certain commercial premises: s 372D(3A)(*a*)(ii), (*b*).

Relief for lessors: s 372AP(5)(*a*)(ii); subs (5): s 372AP(5)(*a*).

See also Urban Renewal Act 1998 (as amended by FA 2002), ss 8 (recommendations in respect of qualifying areas for the purposes of urban renewal tax reliefs) and 9A (designation of certain areas for rented residential reliefs).

See also Town Renewal Act 2000 (as amended by FA 2002), ss 5 (recommendations in respect of qualifying areas for purposes of town renewal tax reliefs) and 6A (designation of certain areas for rented residential reliefs).

Definition

conversion: s 372AN(2); qualifying period, eligible expenditure, necessary construction, qualifying expenditure, qualifying period, qualifying premises, qualifying street, refurbishment, relevant cost, relevant local authority: s 372AK(1); Tax Acts: s 1(2); total income: s 3(1); writing: IA 1937 Sch; year of assessment s 2(1).

372AS Determination of expenditure incurred in qualifying period, and date expenditure treated as incurred for relief purposes

[(1) For the purposes of determining whether and to what extent—

(*a*) in relation to any claim under section 372AP(2), eligible expenditure incurred on or in relation to a qualifying premises or a special qualifying premises, and

(*b*) in relation to any claim under section 372AR(1), qualifying expenditure incurred on or in relation to a qualifying premises,

is incurred or not incurred during the qualifying period, only such an amount of that expenditure as is properly attributable to work on—

(i) in the case of a claim under section 372AP(2), the construction of, conversion into, or refurbishment of, the qualifying premises or, as the case may be, the refurbishment of the special qualifying premises, and

(ii) in the case of a claim under section 372AR(1), the construction of, conversion into, or refurbishment of the qualifying premises,

actually carried out during the qualifying period shall be treated as having been incurred during that period.

(2) Where, by virtue of section 372AN(7) or 372AQ(4), expenditure on the construction of, conversion into, or, as the case may be, refurbishment of, a qualifying premises includes expenditure on the development of any land, subsection (1) applies with any necessary modifications as if the references in that subsection to the construction of, conversion into, or, as the case may be, refurbishment of, the qualifying premises were references to the development of such land.

[(2A) For the purposes of determining the amount of eligible expenditure or qualifying expenditure incurred on or in relation to a building, the site of which—

(*a*) is situated partly inside and partly outside the boundary of a qualifying urban area, or

(*b*) is situated partly inside and partly outside the boundary of a qualifying town area,

and where expenditure incurred or treated as having been incurred in the qualifying period is attributable to the building in general, such an amount of that expenditure shall be deemed to be attributable to the part which is situated outside the boundary of the qualifying area as bears to the whole of that expenditure the same proportion as the floor area of the part situated outside the boundary of the qualifying area bears to the total floor area of the building.][1]

(3) (*a*) For the purposes of section 372AP other than those to which subsection (1) relates, expenditure incurred on the construction of, or, as the case may be, conversion into, a qualifying premises shall be deemed to have been incurred on the date of the first letting of the premises under a qualifying lease.

(*b*) For the purposes of section 372AP other than those to which subsection (1) relates, refurbishment expenditure incurred in relation to the refurbishment of a qualifying premises or a special qualifying premises shall be deemed to have been incurred on the date of the commencement of the relevant period, in relation to the premises, determined as respects the refurbishment to which the refurbishment expenditure relates.

(*c*) For the purposes of section 372AR other than those to which subsection (1) relates, expenditure incurred on the construction of, conversion into, or, as the case may be, refurbishment of a qualifying premises shall be deemed to have been incurred on the earliest date after the expenditure was actually incurred on which the premises is in use as a dwelling.][2]

Amendments

1 Subs (2A) inserted by FA 2003 s 30(1)(*c*) with effect from 1 January 2002.

2 Section 372AS inserted by FA 2002 s 24(1) and Sch 2 Pt 1 para 1 with effect from 1 January 2002.

Cross-references

Qualifying period: s 372AL(1)(c).

Relief for lessors, subs (1): s 372AP(1)("relevant price paid"), (2)(*a*), (4)(*b*)(ii), (8)(*a*), (9)(i); s 372AP(15).

Relief for owner-occupiers, subs (1): s 372AR(4); s 372AR(10).

Definitions

conversion: s 372AN(2); eligible expenditure: s 372AK(1); land: IA 1937 Sch; qualifying expenditure, qualifying lease, qualifying period, qualifying premises, refurbishment, refurbishment expenditure, relevant period: s 372AK(1).

372AT Appeals

[An appeal to the Appeal Commissioners lies on any question arising under this Chapter (other than a question on which an appeal lies under section 18 of the Housing (Miscellaneous Provisions) Act, 1979) in the like manner as an appeal would lie against an assessment to income tax or corporation tax, and the provisions of the Tax Acts relating to appeals apply accordingly.][1]

Amendments

1 Section 372AT inserted by FA 2002 s 24(1) and Sch 2 Pt 1 para 1 with effect from 1 January 2002.

Definitions

Appeal Commissioners: s 2(1); Tax Acts: s 1(2).

372AU Saver for relief due, and for clawback of relief given under, old schemes

[(1) Where, but for the repeal by section 24(3) of the Finance Act, 2002, of the provision concerned, a person would, in computing the amount of a surplus or deficiency in respect of rent from any premises—

(*a*) be entitled to a deduction, or

(*b*) be deemed to have received an amount as rent,

under—

(i) section 325, 326 or 327,

(ii) section 334, 335 or 336,

(iii) section 346, 347 or 348,

(iv) section 356, 357 or 358, or

(v) section 361, 362, or 363,

then, notwithstanding that repeal, the person is entitled to that deduction or is deemed to have received that amount as rent, as the case may be, under this Chapter, and accordingly this Chapter applies with any modifications necessary to give effect to this subsection.

(2) Where, but for the repeal by section 24(3) of the Finance Act, 2002, of the provision concerned, a person would, in the computation of his or her total income for any year of assessment, be entitled to a deduction under—

(*a*) section 328,
(*b*) section 337,
(*c*) section 349, or
(*d*) section 364,

then, notwithstanding that repeal, the person is entitled to that deduction for that year of assessment under this Chapter, and accordingly this Chapter applies with any modifications necessary to give effect to this subsection.][1]

Amendments

1 Section 372AU inserted by FA 2002 s 24(1) and Sch 2 Pt 1 para 1 with effect from 1 January 2002.

Definitions

rent: s 372AK(1); total income: s 3(1); year of assessment: s 2(1).

372AV Continuity

[(1) In this section, the "old enactments" means sections 372F, 372G, 372H, 372I, 372J, 372P, 372Q, 372R, 372RA, 372S, 372X, 372Y, 372Z, 372AE, 372AF, 372AG, 372AH and 372AI, and Parts 11A and 11B, being enactments repealed under section 24(3) of the Finance Act 2002.

(2) The continuity of the operation of the law relating to income tax, corporation tax and capital gains tax is not affected by the substitution of this Chapter for the old enactments.

(3) Any reference, whether express or implied, in any enactment or document, including this Chapter—

(*a*) to any provision of this Chapter, or
(*b*) to things done or to be done under or for the purposes of any provision of this Chapter,

shall, if and in so far as the nature of the reference permits, be construed as including, in relation to the times, years or periods, circumstances or purposes in relation to which the corresponding provision in the old enactments applied or had applied, a reference to, or, as the case may be, to things done or to be done under or for the purposes of, that corresponding provision.

(4) Any reference, whether express or implied, in any enactment or document, including the old enactments—

(*a*) to any provision of the old enactments, or
(*b*) to things done or to be done under or for the purposes of any provision of the old enactments,

shall, if and in so far as the nature of the reference permits, be construed as including, in relation to the times, years or periods, circumstances or purposes in relation to which the corresponding provision of this Chapter applies, a reference to, or as the case may be, to things done or deemed to be done or to be done under or for the purposes of, that corresponding provision.

(5) If and in so far as a provision of this Chapter operates, as on and from the date of the passing of the Finance Act, 2002, in substitution for a provision of the old enactments, anything done or having effect as if done under the provision of the old enactments before that date shall be treated on and from that date as if it were a thing done under the provision of this Chapter which so operates.

(6) Without prejudice to the generality of subsections (2) to (5), this Chapter applies as if a deduction given to a person under the old enactments were a deduction given to such person under this Chapter in respect of, as may be appropriate—

(*a*) eligible expenditure incurred in the qualifying period, on or in relation to a qualifying premises or a special qualifying premises, as the case may be, or

(*b*) qualifying expenditure incurred in the qualifying period on or in relation to a qualifying premises.

(7) Without prejudice to the generality of subsections (2) to (5), any reference in an order made under section 372B(1) or 372BA(1) to section 372F, 372G, 372H or 372I shall, as on and from the date of the passing of the Finance Act, 2002, be construed respectively as if it were a reference to—

(*a*) section 372AP, in so far as it relates to expenditure on construction,

(*b*) section 372AP, in so far as it relates to conversion expenditure,

(*c*) section 372AP, in so far as it relates to refurbishment expenditure, and

(*d*) section 372AR.

(8) Without prejudice to the generality of subsections (2) to (5), any reference in an order made under section 372AB(1) to section 372AE, 372AF, 372AG or 372AH shall, as on and from the date of the passing of the Finance Act, 2002, be construed respectively as if it were a reference to—

(*a*) section 372AP, in so far as it relates to expenditure on construction,

(*b*) section 372AP, in so far as it relates to conversion expenditure,

(*c*) section 372AP, in so far as it relates to refurbishment expenditure, and

(*d*) section 372AR.

(9) All officers who immediately before the date of the passing of the Finance Act, 2002, stood authorised or nominated for the purposes of any provision of the old enactments shall be deemed to be authorised or nominated, as the case may be, for the purposes of the corresponding provision of this Chapter.

(10) All instruments, documents, authorisations and letters or notices of appointment made or issued under the old enactments and in force immediately before the date of the passing of the Finance Act, 2002, shall continue in force as if made or issued under this Chapter.][1]

Amendments

1 Section 372AV inserted by FA 2002 s 24(1) and Sch 2 Pt 1 para 1 with effect from 1 January 2002.

Definitions

conversions expenditure, eligible expenditure, qualifying expenditure, qualifying period, qualifying premises, refurbishment expenditure, special qualifying premises: s 372AK(1).

PART 11
CAPITAL ALLOWANCES AND EXPENSES FOR CERTAIN ROAD VEHICLES

373 Interpretation (Part 11)

(1) Subject to section 380(1), this Part shall apply to a vehicle which is a mechanically propelled road vehicle constructed or adapted for the carriage of passengers, other than a vehicle of a type not commonly used as a private vehicle and unsuitable to be so used.

(2) In this Part, **"the specified amount"**, in relation to expenditure incurred on the provision or hiring of a vehicle to which this Part applies, means—

(*a*) [€3,174.35][1], where the expenditure was incurred on or after the 16th day of May, 1973, but such expenditure does not include—

(i) as respects sections 374, 375 and 377, expenditure incurred under a contract entered into before that day where either—

(I) the expenditure was incurred within 12 months after that day, or

(II) the contract was one of hire-purchase or for purchase by instalments, and

(ii) as respects subsections (2) and (3) of section 378 and section 379, expenditure where the contract of hire-purchase or for purchase by instalments was entered into before that day;

(*b*) [€4,444.08][2], where the expenditure was incurred after the 28th day of January, 1976, but such expenditure does not include—

(i) as respects sections 374, 375 and 377, expenditure incurred within 12 months after that day under a contract entered into before that day, and

(ii) as respects subsections (2) and (3) of section 378 and section 379, expenditure under a contract entered into on or before that day;

(*c*) [€5,078.95][3], where the expenditure was incurred on or after the 6th day of April, 1986, but such expenditure does not include—

(i) as respects sections 374, 375 and 377, expenditure incurred within 12 months after that day under a contract entered into before that day, and

(ii) as respects subsections (2) and (3) of section 378 and section 379, expenditure under a contract entered into before that day;

(*d*) [€7,618.43][4], where the expenditure was incurred on or after the 28th day of January, 1988, but such expenditure does not include—

(i) as respects sections 374, 375 and 377, expenditure incurred within 12 months after that day under a contract entered into before that day, and

(ii) as respects subsections (2) and (3) of section 378 and section 379, expenditure under a contract entered into before that day;

(*e*) [€8,888.17][5], where the expenditure was incurred on or after the 26th day of January, 1989, but such expenditure does not include—

(i) as respects sections 374, 375 and 377, expenditure incurred within 12 months after that day under a contract entered into before that day, and

(ii) as respects subsections (2) and (3) of section 378 and section 379, expenditure under a contract entered into before that day;

(*f*) [€12,697.38][6], where the expenditure was incurred on or after the 30th day of January, 1992, but such expenditure does not include—

(i) as respects sections 374, 375 and 377, expenditure incurred within 12 months after that day under a contract entered into before that day, and

(ii) as respects subsections (2) and (3) of section 378 and section 379, expenditure under a contract entered into before that day;

(*g*) [€16,506.60][7], where the expenditure was incurred on or after the 27th day of January, 1994, on the provision or hiring of a vehicle which on or after that day was first registered in the State under section 131 of the Finance Act, 1992, without having been previously registered in any other State which provides for the registration of a mechanically propelled vehicle, but such expenditure does not include—

(i) as respects sections 374, 375 and 377, expenditure incurred within 12 months after that day under a contract entered into before that day, and

(ii) as respects subsections (2) and (3) of section 378 and section 379, expenditure incurred under a contract entered into before that day;

(*h*) [€17,776.33][8], where the expenditure was incurred on or after the 9th day of February, 1995, on the provision or hiring of a vehicle which on or after that day was not a used or secondhand vehicle and was first registered in the State under section 131 of the Finance Act, 1992, without having been previously registered in any other State which provides for the registration of a mechanically propelled vehicle, but such expenditure does not include—

(i) as respects sections 374, 375 and 377, expenditure incurred within 12 months after that day under a contract entered into before that day, and

(ii) as respects subsections (2) and (3) of section 378 and section 379, expenditure incurred under a contract entered into before that day;

(*i*) [€19,046.07][9], where the expenditure was incurred on or after the 23rd day of January, 1997, on the provision or hiring of a vehicle which on or after that date was not a used or secondhand vehicle and was first registered in the State under section 131 of the Finance Act, 1992, without having been previously registered in any other State which duly provides for the registration of a [mechanically propelled vehicle;][10]

[(*j*) [€19,680.94][11], where the expenditure was incurred on or after the 3rd day of December, 1997, on the provision or hiring of a vehicle which, on or after that date was not a used or secondhand vehicle and was first registered in the State under section 131 of the Finance Act, 1992, without having been previously registered in any other state which duly provides for the registration of a [mechanically propelled vehicle;][12]][13]

[(*k*) [€20,315.81][14], where the expenditure was incurred on or after the 2nd day of December, 1998, on the provision or hiring of a vehicle which, on or after that date was not a used or secondhand vehicle and was first registered in the State under section 131 of the Finance Act, 1992, without having been previously registered in any other state which duly provides for the registration of a [mechanically propelled vehicle;][15,16]

[(*l*) [€20,950.68][17], where the expenditure was incurred on or after 1 December 1999 on the provision or hiring of a vehicle which, on or after that date was not a used or secondhand vehicle and was first registered in the State under section 131 of the Finance Act, 1992, without having been previously registered in any other state which duly provides for the registration of a [mechanically propelled vehicle;[18]][19]

[(*m*) [€21,585.55],[20] where the expenditure was incurred—

(i) in an accounting period ending on or after 1 January 2001, or

(ii) in a basis period for the year of assessment 2000–2001 or for a subsequent year of assessment, where that basis period ends on or after [1 January 2001;][21]][22]

[(*n*) €22,000, where the expenditure was incurred—

(i) in an accounting period ending on or after 1 January 2002, or

(ii) in a basis period for a year of assessment, where that basis period ends on or after 1 January 2002.][23]

(3) This Part (other than section 376) shall be construed as one with Part 9, except that in section 375 **"capital expenditure"** shall be construed without regard to section 316(1).

Amendments

1 Substituted by FA 2001 s 240(1), (2)(*a*), (*c*) and Sch 5 Pt 1 for 2002 and later tax years in the case of income tax and for accounting periods ending on or after 1 January 2002 in the case of corporation tax; previously "£2,500".

2 Substituted by FA 2001 s 240(1), (2)(*a*), (*c*) and Sch 5 Pt 1 for 2002 and later tax years in the case of income tax and for accounting periods ending on or after 1 January 2002 in the case of corporation tax; previously "£3,500".

3 Substituted by FA 2001 s 240(1), (2)(*a*), (*c*) and Sch 5 Pt 1 for 2002 and later tax years in the case of income tax and for accounting periods ending on or after 1 January 2002 in the case of corporation tax; previously "£4,000".

4 Substituted by FA 2001 s 240(1), (2)(*a*), (*c*) and Sch 5 Pt 1 for 2002 and later tax years in the case of income tax and for accounting periods ending on or after 1 January 2002 in the case of corporation tax; previously "£6,000".

5 Substituted by FA 2001 s 240(1), (2)(*a*), (*c*) and Sch 5 Pt 1 for 2002 and later tax years in the case of income tax and for accounting periods ending on or after 1 January 2002 in the case of corporation tax; previously "£7,000".

6 Substituted by FA 2001 s 240(1), (2)(*a*), (*c*) and Sch 5 Pt 1 for 2002 and later tax years in the case of income tax and for accounting periods ending on or after 1 January 2002 in the case of corporation tax; previously "£10,000".

7 Substituted by FA 2001 s 240(1), (2)(*a*), (*c*) and Sch 5 Pt 1 for 2002 and later tax years in the case of income tax and for accounting periods ending on or after 1 January 2002 in the case of corporation tax; previously "£13,000".

8 Substituted by FA 2001 s 240(1), (2)(*a*), (*c*) and Sch 5 Pt 1 for 2002 and later tax years in the case of income tax and for accounting periods ending on or after 1 January 2002 in the case of corporation tax; previously "£14,000".

9 Substituted by FA 2001 s 240(1), (2)(*a*), (*c*) and Sch 5 Pt 1 for 2002 and later tax years in the case of income tax and for accounting periods ending on or after 1 January 2002 in the case of corporation tax; previously "£15,000".

10 Substituted by FA 1998 s 29(*a*)(i) with effect from 6 April 1998; previously "mechanically propelled vehicle.".

[11] Substituted by FA 2001 s 240(1), (2)(*a*), (*c*) and Sch 5 Pt 1 for 2002 and later tax years; previously "£15,500" in the case of income tax and for accounting periods ending on or after 1 January 2002 in the case of corporation tax.

[12] Substituted by FA 1999 s 53(*a*)(i) with effect from 6 April 1999; previously "mechanically propelled vehicle.".

[13] Subs (2)(*j*) inserted by FA 1998 s 29(*a*)(ii) with effect from 6 April 1998.

[14] Substituted by FA 2001 s 240(1), (2)(*a*), (*c*) and Sch 5 Pt 1 for 2002 and later tax years; previously "£16,000" in the case of income tax and for accounting periods ending on or after 1 January 2002 in the case of corporation tax.

[15] Substituted by FA 2000 s 35(a)(i) with effect from 6 April 2000; previously "mechanically propelled vehicle.".

[16] Subs (2)(*k*) inserted by FA 1999 s 53(*a*)(ii) with effect from 6 April 1999.

[17] Substituted by FA 2001 s 240(1), (2)(*a*), (*c*) and Sch 5 Pt 1 for 2002 and later tax years; previously "£16,500" in the case of income tax and for accounting periods ending on or after 1 January 2002 in the case of corporation tax.

[18] Substituted by FA 2001 s 61(1)(*a*)(i) with effect from 6 April 2001; previously "mechanically propelled vehicle.".

[19] Subs (2)(*l*) inserted by FA 2000 s 35(*a*)(ii) with effect from 6 April 2000.

[20] Substituted by FA 2001 s 61(1)(*a*)(iii) for 2002 and later tax years; previously "£17,000".

[21] Substituted by FA 2002 s 28(1)(*a*)(i) with effect from 1 January 2002; previously "January 2001.".

[22] Subs (2)(*m*) inserted by FA 2001 s 61(1)(*a*)(ii) with effect from 6 April 2001.

[23] Subs (2)(*n*) inserted by FA 2002 s 28(1)(*a*)(ii) with effect from 1 January 2002.

Revenue precedents

Issue: Where a rebate of rentals arises in respect of leasing charges which have been restricted under TCA 1997 s 373, whether Revenue assesses the full amount of the rebate.

Decision: The amount of a rebate of rentals represents a return of leasing charges already allowed for tax purposes. Where a rebate of rentals arises in respect of leasing charges which have been restricted under s 373, Revenue will seek to assess only the proportion of the rebate which has been allowed for tax purposes to the lessee.

Former enactments

FA 1973 s 30(1), (5)–(6); FA 1976 s 31; FA 1986 s 50(1); FA 1988 s 24(1); FA 1989 s 12(1); FA 1992 s 21(1); FA 1994 s 21(1); FA 1995 s 23(1); FA 1997 s 21(1).

Corresponding UK tax provision

Capital Allowances Act 2001 ss 74 and 81.

374 Capital allowances for cars costing over certain amount

(1) In relation to a vehicle to which this Part applies, section 284 shall apply as if, for [the purposes of that section][1], the actual cost of the vehicle were taken to be the specified amount where the expenditure incurred on the provision of the vehicle exceeded that amount and, where an allowance which apart from this subsection would be made under section 284 is to be reduced by virtue of this subsection, any reference in the Tax Acts to an allowance made under section 284 shall be construed as a reference to that allowance as reduced under this subsection.

(2) In relation to a vehicle to which this Part applies, the allowances under section 284 to be taken into account for the purposes of Chapter 2 of Part 9 in computing the amount of expenditure still unallowed at any time shall be limited to those computed in accordance with subsection (1), and the expenditure incurred on the provision of the vehicle to be taken into account for the purposes of that Chapter shall be limited to the specified amount.

(3) Where the expenditure incurred on the provision of a vehicle to which this Part applies exceeds the specified amount, any balancing allowance or balancing charge shall be computed, in a case where there are sale, insurance, salvage or compensation moneys, as if the amount of those moneys (or, where in consequence of any provision of the Tax Acts other than this subsection some other amount is to be treated as the amount of those moneys, that other amount) were reduced in the proportion which the specified amount bears to the actual amount of that expenditure.

(4) (*a*) Where the expenditure incurred on the provision of a vehicle to which this Part applies exceeds the specified amount and—

(i) the person providing the vehicle (in this section referred to as **"the prior owner"**) sells the vehicle or gives it away so that subsection (5) of section 289, or that subsection as applied by subsection (6) of that section, applies in relation to the purchaser or donee,

(ii) the prior owner sells the vehicle and the sale is a sale to which section 312 applies, or

(iii) in consequence of a succession to the trade or profession of the prior owner, section 313(1) applies,

then, in relation to the purchaser, donee or successor, the price which the vehicle would have fetched if sold in the open market or the expenditure incurred by the prior owner on the provision of the vehicle shall be treated for the purposes of section 289, 312 or 313 as reduced in the proportion which the specified amount bears to the actual amount of that expenditure, and, in the application of subsection (3) to the purchaser, donee or successor, references to the expenditure incurred on the provision of the vehicle shall be construed as references to the expenditure so incurred by the prior owner.

(*b*) Where paragraph (*a*) has applied on any occasion in relation to a vehicle, and no sale or gift of the vehicle has since occurred other than one to which either section 289 or 312 applies, then, in relation to all persons concerned, the like consequences under paragraph (*a*) shall ensue as respects a gift, sale or succession within subparagraphs (i) to (iii) of that paragraph which occurs on any subsequent occasion as would ensue if the person who in relation to that sale, gift or succession is the prior owner had incurred expenditure on the provision of the vehicle of an amount equal to the expenditure so incurred by the person who was the prior owner on the first-mentioned occasion.

(5) In the application of section 290 to a case where the vehicle is the new machinery or plant referred to in that subsection, the expenditure shall be disregarded in so far as it exceeds the specified amount, but without prejudice to the application of subsections (1) to (4) to the vehicle.

(6) Where the capital expenditure incurred on the provision of a vehicle exceeds the specified amount but under section 317(2) any part of that expenditure is to be treated as not having been incurred by a person, the amount which (subject to subsections (1) to (5)) is to be treated for the purposes of Part 9 as having been incurred by that person shall be reduced in the proportion which the specified amount bears to the capital expenditure incurred on the provision of the vehicle.

Amendments

[1] Substituted by FA 2002 s 28(1)(*b*) as respects capital expenditure incurred on or after 1 January 2001; previously "the purpose of subsection (3) of that section".

Cross-references

Amount of allowance: s 373(2).
Chargeable period, and general provisions: s 321(*b*).
Non-resident company within the charge to corporation tax in respect of one source and income tax in respect of another: s 309(*b*).
Supplementary provisions: s 380.
Where hirer becomes owner: s 379.

Definitions

Income Tax Acts: s 1(2); person: IA 1937 s 11(*c*); profession: s 2(1); trade: s 3(1).

Former enactments

FA 1973 s 25; CTA 1976 s 21(1) and Sch 1 para 62; FA 1997 s 146(1) and Sch 9 Pt I para 6(1).

Corresponding UK tax provision

Capital Allowances Act 2001 ss 75–78.

375 Limit on renewals allowance for cars

In determining what amount (if any) is allowable—

(*a*) to be deducted in computing profits or gains chargeable to tax under Schedule D,

(*b*) to be deducted from emoluments chargeable to tax under Schedule E, or

(*c*) to be taken into account for the purposes of a management expenses claim under section 83 or under that section as applied by section 707,

in respect of capital expenditure incurred on the provision of a vehicle to which this Part applies, being expenditure exceeding the specified amount, the excess over the specified amount shall be disregarded; but, if on the replacement of the vehicle any amount becomes so allowable in respect of capital expenditure on any other vehicle, any deduction to be made, in determining the last-mentioned amount, for the value or proceeds of sale of the replaced vehicle or otherwise in respect of the replaced vehicle shall be reduced in the proportion which the specified amount bears to the cost of the replaced vehicle.

Cross-references

Amount of allowance: s 373(2).
Car hire, limit on deduction: s 377.
Hire purchase: s 378(2).
Supplementary provisions: s 380.

Definitions

month: IA 1937 Sch.

Former enactments

FA 1973 s 26; CTA 1976 s 164 and Sch 2 Pt I para 33 and Sch 3 Pt I.

376 Restriction of deduction in respect of running expenses of cars

Amendments

[1] Section 376 deleted by FA 2002 s 28(1)(*c*) as respects expenditure incurred in an accounting period ending on or after 1 January 2002, or in a basis period for a year of assessment, where that basis period ends on or after 1 January 2002.

377 Limit on deductions, etc for hiring cars

Where apart from this section the amount of any expenditure on the hiring (otherwise than by means of hire-purchase) of a vehicle to which this Part applies would be allowed to be deducted or taken into account as mentioned in section 375, and the retail price of the vehicle at the time it was made exceeded the specified amount, the amount of that expenditure shall be reduced in the proportion which the specified amount bears to that price.

Cross-references

Amount of allowance: s 373(2).
Hire purchase: s 378(3).
Supplementary provisions: s 380.
Where hirer becomes owner: s 379.

Former enactments

FA 1973 s 27.

Corresponding UK tax provision

Capital Allowances Act 2001 s 82.

378 Cars: provisions as to hire-purchase, etc

(1) In the case of a vehicle to which this Part applies, being a vehicle the retail price of which at the time of the contract in question exceeds the specified amount, subsections (2) to (4) shall apply.

(2) Where a person, having incurred capital expenditure on the provision of a vehicle to which this Part applies under a contract providing that such person shall or may become the owner of the vehicle on the performance of the contract, ceases to be entitled to the benefit of the contract without becoming the owner of the vehicle, that expenditure shall, in so far as it relates to the vehicle, be disregarded for the purposes of Chapter 2 of Part 9 and in determining what amount (if any) is allowable as mentioned in section 375.

(3) Where subsection (2) applies, all payments made under the contract shall be treated for tax purposes (including in particular for the purposes of section 377) as expenditure incurred on the hiring of the vehicle otherwise than by means of hire-purchase.

(4) Where the person providing the vehicle takes it under a hire-purchase contract, then, in apportioning the payments under the contract between capital expenditure incurred on the provision of the vehicle and other expenditure, so much of those payments shall be treated as such capital expenditure as is equal to the price which would be chargeable, at the time the contract is entered into, to the person providing the vehicle if that person were acquiring it on a sale outright.

Cross-references

Amount of allowance, subss (2)–(3): s 373(2).
Supplementary provisions, subss (2)–(3): s 380.

Definitions

person: IA 1937 s 11(*c*).

Former enactments

FA 1973 s 28.

Corresponding UK tax provision

Capital Allowances Act 2001 s 67.

379 Cars: provisions where hirer becomes owner

Where, having hired (otherwise than by means of hire-purchase) a vehicle to which this Part applies, a person subsequently becomes the owner of the vehicle and the retail price of the vehicle at the time it was made exceeded the specified amount, then, for the purposes of the Tax Acts (and in particular sections 374 and 377)—

(*a*) so much of the aggregate of the payments for the hire of the vehicle and of any payment for the acquisition of the vehicle as does not exceed the retail price of the vehicle at the time it was made shall be treated as capital expenditure incurred on the provision of the vehicle, and as having been incurred when the hiring began, and

(*b*) the payments to be treated as expenditure on the hiring of the vehicle shall be rateably reduced so as to amount in the aggregate to the balance.

Cross-references

Amount of allowance: s 373(2).

Supplementary provisions: s 380.

Definitions

Income Tax Acts: s 1(2); person: IA 1937 s 11(*c*).

Former enactments

FA 1973 s 29.

380 Provisions supplementary to sections 374 to 379

(1) Sections 374, 375 and 377, subsections (2) and (3) of section 378 and section 379 shall not apply where a vehicle is provided or hired, wholly or mainly, for the purpose of hire to or the carriage of members of the public in the ordinary course of trade.

(2) Sections 374 and 375, subsections (2) and (3) of section 378 and section 379 shall not apply in relation to a vehicle provided by a person who is a manufacturer of a vehicle to which this Part applies, or of parts or accessories for such a vehicle, if the person shows that the vehicle was provided solely for the purpose of testing the vehicle or parts or accessories for such vehicle; but, if during the period of 5 years beginning with the time when the vehicle was provided, such person puts it to any substantial extent to a use which does not serve that purpose only, this subsection shall be deemed not to have applied in relation to the vehicle.

(3) (*a*) There shall be made all such additional assessments and adjustments of assessments as may be necessary for the purpose of applying subsections (2) and (3) of section 378, section 379 and subsection (2), and any such additional assessments or adjustments of assessments may be made at any time.

(*b*) In the case of the death of a person who, if he or she had not died, would under subsections (2) and (3) of section 378, section 379 and subsection (2) have become chargeable to tax for any year, the tax which would have been so chargeable shall be assessed and charged on his or her executors or administrators and shall be a debt due from and payable out of his or her estate.

Cross-references

Non-commercial vehicles, subs (1): s 373(1).

Definitions

month: IA 1937 Sch; person: IA 1937 s 11(*c*); trade: s 3(1).

Former enactments

FA 1973 s 30(2)–(4); CTA 1976 s 164 and Sch 3 Pt II.

[PART 11A
INCOME TAX AND CORPORATION TAX: DEDUCTION FOR EXPENDITURE ON CONSTRUCTION, CONVERSION AND REFURBISHMENT OF CERTAIN RESIDENTIAL ACCOMMODATION FOR CERTAIN STUDENTS][1]

Amendments

1 Part 11A repealed by FA 2002 s 24(3)(*j*) with effect from 1 January 2002; but see now TCA 1997 Pt 10 Ch 11 (ss 372AK–372AV) which codified, with effect from 1 January 2002, reliefs for lessors and owner-occupiers in respect of expenditure incurred on the provision of certain residential accommodation, and in particular s 372AV which provides for the continuity of the operation of the law relating to income tax, corporation tax and capital gains tax in that respect.

380A Interpretation (Part 11A)

Amendments

1 Section 380A repealed by FA 2002 s 24(3)(*j*) with effect from 1 January 2002; but see now TCA 1997 Pt 10 Ch 11 (ss 372AK–372AV) which codified, with effect from 1 January 2002, reliefs for lessors and owner-occupiers in respect of expenditure incurred on the provision of certain residential accommodation, and in particular s 372AV which provides for the continuity of the operation of the law relating to income tax, corporation tax and capital gains tax in that respect.

380B Rented residential accommodation: deduction for certain expenditure on construction

Amendments

1 Section 380B repealed by FA 2002 s 24(3)(*j*) with effect from 1 January 2002; but see now TCA 1997 Pt 10 Ch 11 (ss 372AK–372AV) which codified, with effect from 1 January 2002, reliefs for lessors and owner-occupiers in respect of expenditure incurred on the provision of certain residential accommodation, and in particular s 372AV which provides for the continuity of the operation of the law relating to income tax, corporation tax and capital gains tax in that respect.

Cross-references

Residential Tenancies Act 2004, s 25 (non-application of Part 4) Security of Tenure — references in subs (4)(*a*) of that section to TCA 1997 s 380B(2).

380C Rented residential accommodation: deduction for certain expenditure on conversion

Amendments

1 Section 380C repealed by FA 2002 s 24(3)(*j*) with effect from 1 January 2002; but see now TCA 1997 Pt 10 Ch 11 (ss 372AK–372AV) which codified, with effect from 1 January 2002, reliefs for lessors and owner-occupiers in respect of expenditure incurred on the provision of certain residential accommodation, and in particular s 372AV which provides for the continuity of the operation of the law relating to income tax, corporation tax and capital gains tax in that respect.

Cross-references

Residential Tenancies Act 2004, s 25 (non-application of Part 4) Security of Tenure — references in subs (4)(*a*) of that section to TCA 1997 s 380C(4).

380D Rented residential accommodation: deduction for certain expenditure on refurbishment

Amendments

1 Section 380D repealed by FA 2002 s 24(3)(*j*) with effect from 1 January 2002; but see now TCA 1997 Pt 10 Ch 11 (ss 372AK–372AV) which codified, with effect from 1 January 2002, reliefs for lessors and owner-occupiers in respect of expenditure incurred on the provision of certain residential accommodation, and in particular s 372AV which provides for the continuity of the operation of the law relating to income tax, corporation tax and capital gains tax in that respect.

Cross-references

Residential Tenancies Act 2004, s 25 (non-application of Part 4) Security of Tenure — references in subs (4)(*a*) of that section to TCA 1997 s 380D(2).

380E Provisions supplementary to sections 380B to 380D

Amendments

1 Section 380E repealed by FA 2002 s 24(3)(*j*) with effect from 1 January 2002; but see now TCA 1997 Pt 10 Ch 11 (ss 372AK–372AV) which codified, with effect from 1 January 2002, reliefs for lessors and owner-occupiers in respect of expenditure incurred on the provision of certain residential accommodation, and in particular s 372AV which provides for the continuity of the operation of the law relating to income tax, corporation tax and capital gains tax in that respect.

380F Provision against double relief

Amendments

1 Section 380F repealed by FA 2002 s 24(3)(*j*) with effect from 1 January 2002; but see now TCA 1997 Pt 10 Ch 11 (ss 372AK–372AV) which codified, with effect from 1 January 2002, reliefs for lessors and owner-occupiers in respect of expenditure incurred on the provision of certain residential accommodation, and in particular s 372AV which provides for the continuity of the operation of the law relating to income tax, corporation tax and capital gains tax in that respect.

[PART 11B INCOME TAX AND CORPORATION TAX: DEDUCTION FOR EXPENDITURE ON REFURBISHMENT OF CERTAIN RESIDENTIAL ACCOMMODATION][1]

Amendments

1 Part 11B repealed by FA 2002 s 24(3)(*k*) with effect from 1 January 2002; but see now TCA 1997 Pt 10 Ch 11 (ss 372AK–372AV) which codified, with effect from 1 January 2002, reliefs for lessors and owner-occupiers in respect of expenditure incurred on the provision of certain residential accommodation, and in particular s 372AV which provides for the continuity of the operation of the law relating to income tax, corporation tax and capital gains tax in that respect.

380G Interpretation (Part 11B)

Amendments

1 Section 380G repealed by FA 2002 s 24(3)(*k*) with effect from 1 January 2002; but see now TCA 1997 Pt 10 Ch 11 (ss 372AK–372AV) which codified, with effect from 1 January 2002, reliefs for lessors and owner-occupiers in respect of expenditure incurred on the provision of certain residential accommodation, and in particular s 372AV which provides for the continuity of the operation of the law relating to income tax, corporation tax and capital gains tax in that respect.

380H Rented residential accommodation: deduction for certain expenditure on refurbishment

Amendments

1 Section 380H repealed by FA 2002 s 24(3)(*k*) with effect from 1 January 2002; but see now TCA 1997 Pt 10 Ch 11 (ss 372AK–372AV) which codified, with effect from 1 January 2002, reliefs for lessors and owner-occupiers in respect of expenditure incurred on the provision of certain residential accommodation, and in particular s 372AV which provides for the continuity of the operation of the law relating to income tax, corporation tax and capital gains tax in that respect.

380I Provisions supplementary to section 380H

Amendments

1 Section 380I repealed by FA 2002 s 24(3)(*k*) with effect from 1 January 2002; but see now TCA 1997 Pt 10 Ch 11 (ss 372AK–372AV) which codified, with effect from 1 January 2002, reliefs for lessors and owner-occupiers in respect of expenditure incurred on the provision of certain residential accommodation, and in particular s 372AV which provides for the continuity of the operation of the law relating to income tax, corporation tax and capital gains tax in that respect.

380J Provision against double relief

Amendments

1 Section 380J repealed by FA 2002 s 24(3)(*k*) with effect from 1 January 2002; but see now TCA 1997 Pt 10 Ch 11 (ss 372AK–372AV) which codified, with effect from 1 January 2002, reliefs for lessors and owner-occupiers in respect of expenditure incurred on the provision of certain residential accommodation, and in particular s 372AV which provides for the continuity of the operation of the law relating to income tax, corporation tax and capital gains tax in that respect.

PART 12
PRINCIPAL PROVISIONS RELATING TO LOSS RELIEF, TREATMENT OF CERTAIN LOSSES AND CAPITAL ALLOWANCES, AND GROUP RELIEF

Cross-references

Tonnage tax, transactions between associated persons and between tonnage tax trade and other activities of same company: s 697LA(1)("losses").

CHAPTER 1
Income Tax: Loss Relief

Cross-references

Farming, averaging of farming profits: s 657(11).
Relief on retirement for certain income of certain sportspersons: s 480A(8)(*c*).

381 Right to repayment of tax by reference to losses

(1) Subject to this section, where in any year of assessment any person has sustained a loss in any trade, profession or employment carried on by that person either solely or in partnership, that person shall be entitled, on making a claim in that behalf, to such repayment of income tax as is necessary to secure that the aggregate amount of income tax for the year ultimately borne by that person will not exceed the amount which would

have been borne by that person if the income of that person had been reduced by the amount of the loss.

(2) This section shall not apply to any loss sustained in any year of assessment by the owner of a stallion from the sale of services of mares by the stallion or of rights to such services or by the part-owner of a stallion from the sale of such services or such rights.

(3) (*a*) In this subsection, **"appropriate income"** means either earned or unearned income according as income arising during the same period as the loss to the person sustaining the loss from the same activity would have been that person's earned or unearned income.

(*b*) For the purposes of subsection (1), the amount of income tax which would have been borne if income had been reduced by the amount of a loss shall be computed—

(i) where the loss has been sustained by an individual, on the basis of treating the loss as reducing—

(I) firstly, the appropriate income of the individual,

(II) secondly, the other income of the individual,

(III) thirdly, in a case where the individual, or, being a husband or wife, the individual's spouse, is assessed to tax in accordance with section 1017, the appropriate income of the individual's wife or husband, as the case may be, and

(IV) finally, the other income of the individual's wife or husband, as the case may be, and

(ii) where the loss has been sustained in a trade carried on by a body corporate, on the basis of treating the loss as reducing—

(I) firstly, the income of the body corporate from profits or gains of the trade in which the loss was sustained, and

(II) then, the other income of the body corporate.

(4) The amount of a loss sustained in an activity shall for the purposes of this section be computed in the like manner as profits or gains arising or accruing from the activity would be computed under the relevant provisions of the Income Tax Acts.

(5) Where repayment has been made to a person for any year under this section—

(*a*) no portion of the loss which in the computation of the repayment was treated as reducing the person's income shall be taken into account in computing the amount of an assessment for any subsequent year, and

(*b*) so much of the loss as was required by subsection (3) to be treated as reducing income of a particular class or income from a particular source shall for the purposes of the Income Tax Acts be regarded as a deduction to be made from income of that class or from income from that source, as the case may be, in computing the person's total income for the year.

(6) Any claim to repayment under this section shall be made, in a form prescribed by the Revenue Commissioners, not later than 2 years after the end of the year of assessment and shall be made to and determined by the inspector; but any person aggrieved by any determination of the inspector on any such claim may, on giving notice in writing to the inspector within 21 days after notification to that person of the determination, appeal to the Appeal Commissioners.

(7) The Appeal Commissioners shall hear and determine an appeal to them under subsection (6) as if it were an appeal to them against an assessment to income tax, and the provisions of the Income Tax Acts relating to the rehearing of an appeal and to the statement of a case for the opinion of the High Court on a point of law shall, with the necessary modifications, apply accordingly.

Cross-references

Capital allowances used to create or augment a loss: s 392.
Effect of giving relief: s 394.
Farming or market gardening, restriction of losses: s 662(2)(*a*), (*b*).
Foreign life policies, disposals of certain policies: s 730K(4)(*a*).
Holiday cottages, disclaimer of capital allowance: s 355(4)(*b*); restriction on use of allowances: s 405(1)(*b*).
Leased assets, restriction on use of allowances: s 403(3).
Leased plant and machinery, restriction on use of allowances: s 404(4)(*c*)(i)(III).
Limited partnerships, specified provisions: s 1013(1).
Offshore funds, disposal of an interest in certain offshore funds: s 747E(4)(*a*).
Petroleum trade, abandonment expenditure and loss relief, subss (1), (3)–(7): s 695(3)(*b*).
Petroleum trade, treatment of losses: s 687(1).
Pre-trading expenditure, no double relief: s 82(3).
Purchase and sale of securities, traders other than dealers in securities: s 751(1)(*a*).
Restriction of reliefs where individual is not actively participating in certain trades: s 409D(1)("specified provisions").
Restriction on relief for losses by repayment of tax in case of dividend paid out of accumulated profits: s 753(*a*).
Restriction on use of losses on approved buildings: s 409C(3)(*c*); subs (1): s 409C(4).
Wear and tear allowances for licences for public hire (taxis) vehicles, subss (1) and (3)(*b*): s 286A(5)(*b*).

Case law

Irish

Subss (1)–(2)(*a*)(iii): Income for the determination of "loss relief" is the gross and not the net statutory income: *Navan Carpets Ltd v O'Culacháin* ITR Vol III p 403.

UK

Where the period in which the loss occurred forms the basis period for more than one year of assessment, the loss claimed cannot exceed the actual loss suffered: *IRC v Scott Adamson* (1933) 17 TC 679; *Westward Television Ltd v Hart* (1969) 45 TC 1.

Tax Briefing

TB47 April 2002 pp 26–28 — Income Tax Losses, Case I and II.

Definitions

Appeal Commissioners: s 2(1); High Court: IA 1937 Sch; inspector: ss 2(1), 5(1), 852; person: IA 1937 s 11(*c*); profession: s 2(1); total income: s 3(1); trade: s 3(1); writing: IA 1937 Sch; year of assessment: s 3(1).

Former enactments

ITA 1967 s 307(1), (1AAA) and (2)–(6); F(MP)A 1968 s 3(2) and Sch Pt I; FA 1974 s 26; FA 1979 s 17; FA 1980 s 19 and Sch 3 Pt III; FA 1983 s 14; FA 1997 s 146(2) and Sch 9 Pt II.

Corresponding UK tax provision

Income and Corporation Taxes Act 1988 ss 380 and 382.

382 Right to carry forward losses to future years

(1) Where, in any trade or profession carried on by a person, either solely or in partnership, such person has sustained a loss (to be computed in the like manner as profits or gains under the provisions of the Income Tax Acts applicable to Cases I and II of Schedule D) in respect of which relief has not been wholly given under section 381 or under any other provision of the Income Tax Acts, such person may claim that any portion of the loss for which relief has not been so given shall be carried forward and, in so far as may be, deducted from or set off against the amount of profits or gains on

which such person is assessed under Schedule D in respect of that trade or profession for any subsequent year of assessment, except that, if and in so far as relief in respect of any loss has been given to any person under this section, that person shall not be entitled to claim relief in respect of that loss under any other provision of the Income Tax Acts.

(2) Any relief under this section shall be given as far as possible from the assessment for the first subsequent year of assessment and, in so far as it cannot be so given, from the assessment for the next year of assessment and so on.

Cross-references

Amount of s 238 assessment to be allowed as a loss: s 390.

Farming, averaging of farm profits: s 657(11A).

Farming, restriction of losses: s 661(2).

Farming stock relief: s 666(3)(*a*)(i).

Revenue precedents

Issue: Are losses of farming partnership trade available for carry forward against profits of farming sole trade which farmer commences subsequently?

Decision: No.

Tax Briefing

TB47 April 2002 pp 26–28 — Income Tax Losses, Case I and II.

Definitions

person: IA 1937 s 11(*c*); profession: s 2(1); trade: s 3(1); year of assessment: s 3(1).

Former enactments

ITA 1967 s 309(1)–(2); FA 1996 s 132(2) and Sch 5 Pt II; FA 1997 s 146(1) and Sch 9 Pt I para 1(21).

Corresponding UK tax provision

Income and Corporation Taxes Act 1988 s 385.

---

383 Relief under Case IV for losses

(1) Where in any year of assessment a person sustains a loss in any transaction (being a transaction of such kind that, if any profits had arisen from the transaction, such person would have been liable to be assessed in respect of those profits under Case IV of Schedule D) in which such person engages, whether solely or in partnership, such person may claim for the purposes of the Income Tax Acts that the amount of that loss shall, as far as may be, be deducted from or set off against the amount of profits or gains on which such person is assessed under Case IV of Schedule D for that year and that any portion of the loss for which relief is not so given shall be carried forward and, in so far as may be, deducted from or set off against the amount of profits or gains on which such person is assessed under that Case for any subsequent year of assessment.

(2) In the application of this section to a loss sustained by a partner in a partnership, **"the amount of profits or gains on which such person is assessed"** shall, in respect of any year, be taken to mean such portion of the amount on which the partnership is assessed under Case IV of Schedule D as the partner would be required under the Income Tax Acts to include in a return of the partner's total income for that year.

(3) Any relief under this section by means of carrying forward any portion of a loss shall be given as far as possible from the assessment for the first subsequent year of assessment and, in so far as it cannot be so given, from the assessment for the next year of assessment and so on.

Cross-references

Foreign life policies, disposals of certain policies: s 730K(4)(*a*).

Offshore funds, disposal of an interest in certain offshore funds: s 747E(4)(*a*).

Petroleum trade, treatment of losses: s 687(2).

Transactions in certificates of deposit: s 814(5).

Definitions

person: IA 1937 s 11(*c*); total income: s 3(1); year of assessment: s 3(1).

Former enactments

ITA 1967 s 310; FA 1997 s 146(1) and Sch 9 Pt I para 1(22).

Corresponding UK tax provision

Income and Corporation Taxes Act 1988 s 392.

384 Relief under Case V for losses

(1) In this section, **"the person chargeable"** has the same meaning as in Chapter 8 of Part 4.

(2) Where in any year of assessment the aggregate amount of the deficiencies computed in accordance with section 97(1) exceeds the aggregate of the surpluses as so computed, the excess shall be carried forward and, in so far as may be, deducted from or set off against the amount of profits or gains on which the person chargeable is assessed under Case V of Schedule D for any subsequent year of assessment, and if income tax has been overpaid the amount overpaid shall be repaid.

(3) Any relief under this section shall be given as far as possible from the assessment for the first subsequent year of assessment and, in so far as it cannot be so given, from the assessment for the next year of assessment and so on.

Definitions

person: IA 1937 s 11(*c*); year of assessment: s 3(1).

Former enactments

ITA 1967 s 89; FA 1969 s 24; FA 1990 s 18(1)(*b*) and (*c*); FA 1997 s 146(1) and Sch 9 Pt I para 1(7).

Corresponding UK tax provision

Income and Corporation Taxes Act 1988 s 379A.

385 Terminal loss

(1) Where a trade or profession is permanently discontinued, and any person carrying on the trade or profession either solely or in partnership immediately before the time of the discontinuance has sustained in the trade or profession a loss to which this section applies (in this Chapter referred to as a **"terminal loss"**), then, subject to sections 386 to 389, that person may claim for the purposes of the Income Tax Acts that the amount of the terminal loss shall, as far as may be, be deducted from or set off against the amount of profits or gains on which that person has been charged to income tax under Schedule D in respect of the trade or profession for the 3 years of assessment last preceding that in which the discontinuance occurs, and there shall be made all such amendments of assessments or repayments of tax as may be necessary to give effect to the claim.

(2) Relief shall not be given in respect of the same matter both under this section and under any other provision of the Income Tax Acts.

(3) Any relief under this section shall be given as far as possible from the assessment for a later rather than an earlier year.

Cross-references

Amount of s 238 assessment to be allowed as a loss: s 390.
Determination of terminal loss: s 386(2).
Determination of claims for terminal loss to be made by inspector: s 389(1).
Calculation of profits or gains for the purposes of terminal loss: s 387.
Permanently discontinued, meaning: s 388.
Farming stock relief: s 666(3)(*a*)(ii).

Definitions

person: IA 1937 s 11(*c*); profession: s 2(1); trade: s 3(1).

Former enactments

ITA 1967 s 311.

Corresponding UK tax provision

Income and Corporation Taxes Act 1988 s 388.

386 Determination of terminal loss

(1) In this section, **"the relevant capital allowances"**, in relation to any year of assessment, means the capital allowances to be made in charging the profits or gains of the trade or profession for that year, excluding amounts carried forward from an earlier year, and for the purposes of paragraphs (*a*) and (*c*) of subsection (2) the amount of a loss shall be computed in the like manner as profits or gains are computed under the provisions of the Income Tax Acts applicable to Cases I and II of Schedule D.

(2) The question whether a person has sustained any, and if so what, terminal loss in a trade or profession shall for the purposes of section 385 be determined by taking the amounts, if any, of the following (in so far as they have not been otherwise taken into account so as to reduce or relieve any charge to income tax)—

(*a*) the loss sustained by the person in the trade or profession in the year of assessment in which it is permanently discontinued;

(*b*) the relevant capital allowances for that year of assessment;

(*c*) the loss sustained by the person in the trade or profession in the part of the preceding year of assessment beginning 12 months before the date of the discontinuance;

(*d*) the same fraction of the relevant capital allowances for that preceding year of assessment as the part beginning 12 months before the date of the discontinuance is of a year.

Cross-references

Amount of s 238 assessment to be allowed as a loss: s 390.
Permanently discontinued, meaning: s 388.
Terminal loss: s 385(1).

Definitions

month: IA 1937 Sch; person: IA 1937 s 11(*c*); profession: s 2(1); trade: s 3(1); year of assessment: s 3(1).

Former enactments

ITA 1967 s 312; FA 1996 s 131(2) and Sch 5 Pt I para 1(16).

Corresponding UK tax provision

Income and Corporation Taxes Act 1988 s 388.

387 Calculation of amount of profits or gains for purposes of terminal loss

(1) The amount of the profits or gains on which a person has been charged to income tax for any year of assessment in respect of the profits or gains of a trade or profession shall, for the purposes of relief under section 385 from the assessment for that year, be taken to be the full amount of the profits or gains on which the person was assessable for that year reduced by—

(*a*) a sum equal to the total amount of the deductions, if any, in respect of capital allowances made in charging the profits or gains,

(*b*) a sum equal to the amount of the deductions, if any, in respect of payments made or losses sustained, which were to be made from the profits or gains in computing for income tax purposes the person's total income for the year, or would have been so made if the person were an individual, and

(*c*) in the case of a body of persons, a sum equal to so much of the profits or gains as was applied in payment of dividends;

but, where any deduction mentioned in paragraph (*b*) may be treated in whole or in part either as having been made from the profits or gains or as having been made from other income, the deduction shall, as far as may be, be treated for the purposes of this subsection as made from the other income.

(2) Where under subsection (1)(*b*) the amount of the profits or gains on which a person was assessable for any year is reduced by reference to a payment made by the person, a like reduction shall be made in the amount of the terminal loss for which relief may be given under section 385 for earlier years unless the payment was made wholly and exclusively for the purposes of the trade or profession.

Cross-references

Amount of s 238 assessment to be allowed as a loss: s 390.
Permanently discontinued, meaning: s 388.
Terminal loss: s 385(1).

Definitions

body of persons: s 2(1); person: IA 1937 s 11(*c*); profession: s 2(1); total income: s 3(1); trade: s 3(1); year of assessment: s 3(1).

Former enactments

ITA 1967 s 313(1)–(2).

Corresponding UK tax provision

Income and Corporation Taxes Act 1988 s 388.

388 Meaning of "permanently discontinued" for purposes of terminal loss

For the purposes of sections 385 to 389, a trade or profession shall be treated as permanently discontinued and a new trade or profession set up or commenced when it is so treated for the purposes of section 69, or where by reference to section 1008(1)(*a*)(ii) a several trade of a partner has been deemed to have been permanently discontinued; but—

(*a*) a person who continues to be engaged in carrying on the trade or profession immediately after such a discontinuance shall not be entitled to relief in respect of any terminal loss on that discontinuance, and (*b*) on any discontinuance, a person not continuing to be so engaged may be given relief in respect of a terminal loss against profits or gains on which the person was charged in respect of the same trade or profession for a period before a previous discontinuance, if the person has been continuously engaged in carrying on the trade or profession between the 2 discontinuances, and, in the person's case, if the previous discontinuance occurred within 12 months before the others, it shall be disregarded for the purposes of section 386(2).

Cross-references

Amount of s 238 assessment to be allowed as a loss: s 390.
Terminal loss: s 385(1).

Case Law

Distinction between permanent and temporary discontinuance – *Cronin v Lunham Brothers Ltd* 3 ITR 363.

Definitions

month: IA 1937 Sch; person: IA 1937 s 11(*c*); profession: s 2(1); trade: s 3(1).

Former enactments

ITA 1967 s 314(1).

Corresponding UK tax provision

Income and Corporation Taxes Act 1988 s 389.

389 Determination of claim for terminal loss

(1) Any claim under section 385 shall be made to and determined by the inspector, but any person aggrieved by any decision of the inspector on any such claim may, on giving notice in writing to the inspector within 21 days after the notification to that person of the decision, appeal to the Appeal Commissioners.

(2) The Appeal Commissioners shall hear and determine an appeal to them under subsection (1) as if it were an appeal against an assessment to income tax, and the provisions of the Income Tax Acts relating to the rehearing of an appeal and to the statement of a case for the opinion of the High Court on a point of law shall, with the necessary modifications, apply accordingly.

Cross-references

Amount of s 238 assessment to be allowed as a loss: s 390.
Permanently discontinued, meaning: s 388.
Terminal loss: s 385(1).

Definitions

Appeal Commissioners: s 2(1); High Court: IA 1937 Sch; inspector: ss 2(1), 5(1), 852; person: IA 1937 s 11(*c*); writing: IA 1937 Sch.

Former enactments

ITA 1967 s 315; F(MP)A 1968 s 3(2) and Sch Pt I.

390 Amount of assessment made under section 238 to be allowed as a loss for certain purposes

(1) Subject to this section, where a person has been assessed to income tax for a year of assessment under section 238 in respect of a payment made wholly and exclusively for the purposes of a trade or profession, the amount on which income tax has been paid under that assessment shall for the purposes of sections 382 and 385 to 389 be treated as if it were a loss sustained in that trade or profession and relief in respect of such loss

shall be allowed accordingly; but no relief shall be allowed under this section in respect of any such payment or any part of such payment which is not ultimately borne by the person assessed or which is charged to capital.

(2) (*a*) This subsection shall apply to expenditure incurred for the purposes of a trade or profession which is set up and commenced on or after the 22nd day of January, 1997.

(*b*) Where an individual who has set up and commenced a trade or profession has been assessed to tax for any year of assessment under section 238 in respect of a payment made—

(i) before the time the trade or profession has been set up and commenced, and

(ii) wholly and exclusively for the purposes of the trade or profession,

then, this section shall apply in relation to the payment as it would apply if the payment were made at that time.

(*c*) An allowance or deduction shall not be made under any provision of the Tax Acts, other than this section, in respect of any expenditure or payment which is treated under this section as incurred on the day on which a trade or profession is set up and commenced.

(3) This section shall not apply to any sum assessed under section 238 by virtue of section 246(2), 757 or 1041(1).

Cross-references

Petroleum trade, interest and charges on income: s 690(5)(*b*).

Definitions

person: IA 1937 s 11(*c*); profession: s 2(1); trade: s 3(1); year of assessment: s 3(1).

Former enactments

ITA 1967 s 316; FA 1969 s 33(1) and Sch 4 Pt I; CTA 1976 s 164 and Sch 3 Pt I; FA 1976 s 5; FA 1997 s 29(3), (5)–(6).

Corresponding UK tax provision

Income and Corporation Taxes Act 1988 s 387

CHAPTER 2
Income Tax: Loss Relief — Treatment of Capital Allowances

391 Interpretation (Chapter 2)

(1) In this Chapter—

"balancing charges" means balancing charges under Part 9 or Chapter 1 of Part 29;

"year of claim", in relation to any claim under section 381, means the year of assessment for which the claim is made.

(2) For the purposes of this Chapter—

(*a*) any reference to capital allowances or balancing charges for a year of assessment shall be construed as a reference to those to be made in charging the profits or gains of the trade for that year, excluding, in the case of allowances, amounts carried forward from an earlier year, (*b*) effect shall be deemed to be given in charging the profits or gains of the trade for a year of assessment to allowances carried forward from an earlier year before it is given to allowances for the year of assessment, and

(*c*) any reference to an amount of capital allowances non-effective in a year of assessment shall be construed as referring to the amount to which effect cannot be given in charging the profits or gains of the trade for that year by reason of an insufficiency of profits or gains.

(3) This Chapter shall apply, with any necessary modifications, in relation to a profession or employment as it applies in relation to a trade.

Definitions

trade: s 3(1); year of assessment: s 3(1). profession: s 2(1).

Former enactments

ITA 1967 s 317(1), (2)(*b*), (*c*) and (*d*) and s 322; FA 1969 s 65(1) and Sch 5 Pt I; FA 1975 s 33(2) and Sch 1 Pt II; FA 1997 s 146(2) and Sch 9 Pt II.

392 Option to treat capital allowances as creating or augmenting a loss

(1) Subject to this Chapter, any claim made under section 381 for relief in respect of a loss sustained in any trade in any year of assessment (in this Chapter referred to as **"the year of the loss"**) may require the amount of the loss to be determined as if an amount equal to the capital allowances for the year of the loss were to be deducted in computing the profits or gains or losses of the trade in the year of the loss, and a claim may be so made notwithstanding that apart from those allowances a loss had not been sustained in the trade in the year of the loss.

(2) Where on any claim made by virtue of this Chapter relief is not given under section 381 for the full amount of the loss determined under subsection (1), the relief shall be referred, as far as may be, to the loss sustained in the trade rather than to the capital allowances in respect of the trade.

Cross-references

Capital allowances, extent to which taken into account, subs (1): s 393.
Farming or market gardening, restriction of losses: s 662(2)(*a*), (*b*).
Farming stock relief: s 666(3)(*c*).
Leased assets, restriction on use of allowances: s 403(3).
Petroleum trade, abandonment expenditure and loss relief: s 695(3)(*b*).
Restriction on use by certain partnerships of certain losses, etc, transitional arrangements, subs (1): s 1017(2C)(*b*)(ii)(II), (*d*)(iii).
Restriction on use of capital allowances on certain hotels, subs (1): s 409B(3).
Restriction on use of capital allowances on certain industrial buildings and other premises, subs (1): s 409A(3).
Wear and tear allowances for licences for public hire (taxis) vehicles: s 286A(5)(*b*).

Definitions

trade: s 3(1); year of assessment: s 3(1).

Former enactments

ITA 1967 s 318; FA 1979 s 19; FA 1997 s 146(1) and Sch 9 Pt I para 1(23).

393 Extent to which capital allowances to be taken into account for purposes of section 392

(1) The capital allowances for any year of assessment shall be taken into account under section 392(1) only if and in so far as such capital allowances are not required to offset

balancing charges for the year, and relief shall not be given by reference to the capital allowances so taken into account in respect of an amount greater than the amount non-effective in the year of assessment for which the claim is made.

(2) For the purposes of subsection (1), the capital allowances for any year of assessment shall be treated as required to offset balancing charges for the year up to the amount on which the balancing charges are to be made after deducting from that amount the amount, if any, of capital allowances for earlier years which is carried forward to that year and would, without the balancing charges, be non-effective in that year.

Cross-references

Leased assets, restriction on use of allowances: s 403(3).

Definitions

year of assessment: s 3(1).

Former enactments

ITA 1967 s 319; FA 1979 s 20; FA 1997 s 146(1) and Sch 9 Pt I para 1(24).

394 Effect of giving relief under section 381 by reference to capital allowances

Where for any year of claim relief is given under section 381 by reference to any capital allowances, then, for all the purposes of the Income Tax Acts, effect shall be deemed to have been given to those allowances up to the amount in respect of which relief is so given, and any relief previously given for a subsequent year on the basis that effect had not been so given to those allowances shall be adjusted, where necessary, by additional assessment.

Cross-references

Leased assets, restriction on use of allowances: s 403(3).

Former enactments

ITA 1967 s 320.

395 Relief affected by subsequent changes of law, etc

(1) Where relief given to a person by virtue of section 392(1) for any year of claim is affected by a subsequent alteration of the law, or by any discontinuance of the trade or other event occurring after the end of the year, any necessary adjustment may be made, and so much of any repayment of tax as exceeded the amount repayable in the events that happened shall, if not otherwise made good, be recovered from the person by assessment under Case IV of Schedule D.

(2) For the purpose of an assessment mentioned in subsection (1), the amount of capital allowances by reference to which the repayment was made, or an appropriate part of that amount, shall be deemed to be income chargeable under the said Case IV of Schedule D for the year of claim and shall be included in the return of income which the person is required to make under the provisions of the Income Tax Acts for that year.

Definitions

person: IA 1937 s 11(*c*); trade: s 3(1); year of assessment: s 3(1).

Former enactments

ITA 1967 s 321; FA 1996 s 132(1) and Sch 5 Pt I para 1(18).

CHAPTER 3
Corporation Tax: Loss Relief

Cross-references

Profits of life business, new basis: s 730A(6).

396 Relief for trading losses other than terminal losses

(1) Where in any accounting period a company carrying on a trade incurs a loss in the trade, the company may make a claim requiring that the loss be set off for the purposes of corporation tax against any trading income from the trade in succeeding accounting periods, and (so long as the company continues to carry on the trade) its trading income from the trade in any succeeding accounting period shall then be treated as reduced by the amount of the loss, or by so much of that amount as cannot, on that claim or on a claim (if made) under [subsection (2) or section 396A(3), 396B(2) or 455(3)][1], be relieved against income or profits of an earlier accounting period.

(2) Where in any accounting period a company carrying on a trade incurs a loss in the trade, then, subject to subsection (4), the company may make a claim requiring that the loss be set off for the purposes of corporation tax against profits (of whatever description) of that accounting period and, if the company was then carrying on the trade and the claim so requires, of preceding accounting periods ending within the time specified in subsection (3), and, subject to that subsection and to any relief for an earlier loss, the profits of any of those periods shall then be treated as reduced by the amount of the loss, or by so much of that amount as cannot be relieved under this subsection against profits of a later accounting period.

(3) The time referred to in subsection (2) shall be a time immediately preceding the accounting period first mentioned in subsection (2) equal in length to the accounting period in which the loss is incurred; but the amount of the reduction which may be made under that subsection in the profits of an accounting period falling partly before that time shall not exceed a part of those profits proportionate to the part of the period falling within that time.

(4) Subsection (2) shall not apply to trades within Case III of Schedule D.

(5) (*a*) Subject to paragraph (*b*), the amount of a loss incurred in a trade in an accounting period shall be computed for the purposes of this section in the like manner as trading income from the trade in that period would have been computed.

(*b*) Where expenses of management of an assurance company (within the meaning of section 706) are deductible under section 83 from the profits of the accounting period in which they were incurred, or of any accounting period subsequent to that period, those expenses shall not be taken into account in computing a loss incurred in a trade of the company.

(6) For the purposes of this section, **"trading income"**, in relation to any trade, means the income which is to be, or would be, included in respect of the trade in the total profits of the company; but where in an accounting period a company incurs a loss in a trade in respect of which it is within the charge to corporation tax under Case I or III of Schedule D, and in any later accounting period to which the loss or any part of the loss is

carried forward under subsection (1) relief in respect of the loss or that part of the loss cannot be given, or cannot wholly be given, because the amount of the trading income of the trade is insufficient, any interest or dividends on investments which would be taken into account as trading receipts in computing that trading income but for the fact that they have been subjected to tax under other provisions shall be treated for the purposes of subsection (1) as if they were trading income of the trade.

(7) Where in an accounting period the charges on income paid by a company [net of any part of those charges relieved under section 243B][2]—

(*a*) exceed the amount of the profits against which they are deductible, and

(*b*) include payments made wholly and exclusively for the purposes of a trade carried on by the company,

then, up to the amount of that excess or of those payments, whichever is the less, the charges on income so paid shall in computing a loss for the purposes of subsection (1) be deductible as if they were trading expenses of the trade.

(8) In this section, references to a company carrying on a trade are references to the company carrying on the trade so as to be within the charge to corporation tax in respect of the trade.

(9) A claim under subsection (2) shall be made within 2 years from the end of the accounting period in which the loss is incurred.

Amendments

1 Substituted by FA 2002 s 54(1)(*b*)(i)(I) as respects an accounting period ending on or after 6 March 2001 (for the purposes of computing the amount of charges on income paid for the purposes of the sale of goods (within the meaning of TCA 1997 s 454), a loss from the sale of goods (within the meaning of TCA 1997 s 455), relevant trading charges on income (within the meaning of TCA 1997 s 243A), and relevant trading losses (within the meaning of TCA 1997 s 396A), in respect of which relief may be claimed by virtue of FA 2002 s 54, where an accounting period of a company begins before 6 March 2001 and ends on or after that date, it shall be divided into 2 parts, one beginning on the date on which the accounting period begins and ending on 5 March 2001 and the other beginning on 6 March 2001 and ending on the date on which the accounting period ends, and both parts shall be treated as if they were separate accounting periods of the company); previously "subsection (2) or section 455(3)".

2 Inserted by FA 2002 s 54(1)(*b*)(i)(II) as respects an accounting period ending on or after 6 March 2001 (for the purposes of computing the amount of charges on income paid for the purposes of the sale of goods (within the meaning of TCA 1997 s 454), a loss from the sale of goods (within the meaning of TCA 1997 s 455), relevant trading charges on income (within the meaning of TCA 1997 s 243A), and relevant trading losses (within the meaning of TCA 1997 s 396A), in respect of which relief may be claimed by virtue of FA 2002s 54, where an accounting period of a company begins before 6 March 2001 and ends on or after that date, it shall be divided into 2 parts, one beginning on the date on which the accounting period begins and ending on 5 March 2001 and the other beginning on 6 March 2001 and ending on the date on which the accounting period ends, and both parts shall be treated as if they were separate accounting periods of the company.

Cross-references

Companies carrying on life business: s 709(2).

Company reconstructions without change of ownership, subss (1)–(2): s 400(7).

Corporation tax — late returns, restriction of relief, subs (2): s 1085(2)(*a*).

Corporation tax, manufacturing (10%) relief, subs (2): s 448(1)(*b*).

Corporation tax, relief for terminal losses, subss (1), (5)–(8): s 397(3); computation of losses attributable to income from certain securities, subs (5): s 398(1).

Exploration expenditure, subss (1)–(3) applied, for "trading income from the trade" or "trading income" read "profits (of whatever description)": s 679(3)(*a*); subs (1): s 679(4)(*b*)(ii).

Farming or market gardening, restriction of losses, subs (2): s 663(2)(*b*)(ii).

Farming stock relief: s 666(2)(*a*), (*b*)(ii).

Foreign currency, tax treatment of capital allowances and trading losses: s 402(3)(*a*).
Foreign life policies, disposal of certain policies: s 730K(4)(*b*).
Franked investment income, set off of losses, subs (2): s 157(2)(*c*), (4), (7)(*b*); financial concerns (set off of losses), subss (1), (6): s 158(1), (4).
Furnished lettings, restriction on use of allowances, subs (2): s 406.
Gifts to third level institutions, subs (2): s 485(7)(*b*).
Group relief, losses that may be surrendered, subss (2), (4): s 420(1).
Group relief, relation to other relief, subs (2): s 421(1)(*b*), (3).
Group relief, relevant losses and charges, subs (2): s 420A(3)(*a*), (*b*)(i); subs (4): s 420A(3)(*b*)(i); s 420A(4)(*b*).
Group relief, relief for certain losses on a value basis: s 420B(2).
Holiday cottages, disclaimer of capital allowance, subs (2): s 355(4)(*b*); restriction on use of allowances, subs (2): s 405(1)(*b*).
Leased assets, restriction on use of allowances, subs (2): s 403(4)(*a*).
Leased plant and machinery, restriction on use of allowances: s 404(4)(*a*), (*c*)(i)(II).
Leasing contracts, company reconstructions, subss (1)–(2): s 425(1)(*b*).
Limited partnerships, specified provisions, subs (2): s 1013(1).
Offshore funds, disposal of an interest in certain offshore funds: s 747E(4)(*b*).
Profit sharing schemes, payments to trustees: s 517(3)(*a*).
Petroleum trade, treatment of losses, subs (2): s 687(1).
Petroleum trade, interest and charges on income, subs (7): s 690(5)(*a*).
Petroleum trade, abandonment expenditure and loss relief, subss (2)–(3): s 695(3)(*c*).
Pre-trading expenditure, no double relief, subs (2): s 82(3).
Purchase and sale of securities, traders other than dealers in securities: s 751(1)(*b*).
Qualifying shipping trade, restriction on use of allowances: s 407(3)(*b*), (4)(*b*)(i).
Reduction of corporation tax liability in respect of certain trading income, subs (1): s 22A(1)("trading income").
Research and development expenditure, subs (1): s 766(2)(*c*)(ii)(II).
Restriction of group relief: s 456(2A)(*b*)(ii).
Restriction of loss relief, subs (2): s 455(1), (2).
Restriction on relief for losses by repayment of tax in case of dividend paid out of accumulated profits: s 753(*b*).
Voluntary Health Insurance Board, restriction of certain losses and deemed disposal of certain assets: s 841(2).

Case law

Irish

Subs (1): A change of ownership of a meat factory not a permanent cessation: *Cronin v Lunham Bros Ltd (In liquidation)* ITR Vol III p 363.

A company engaged in the business of milling and also trading in other bakery activities refused relief for discontinuance when its milling activities ceased for a period: *Boland's Ltd v Davis* ITR Vol I p 86.

UK

Subs (1): For a claim for loss relief to be valid, an irreducible minimum of information should be included: *R v IRC, ex parte Unilever* [1994] STC 841, [1996] STI 320.

Subs (6): Held investment income used to fund potential future liabilities to individuals other than customers was not trading income: *Nuclear Electric v Bradley* [1996] STC 405.

Subs (9): Where the Revenue accepted informal claims for loss relief over a period of 20 years, it would be unfair and an abuse of power to insist on a formal claim within the time limit: *R v IRC, ex parte Unilever* [1994] STC 841, [1996] STC 320.

Revenue information

Tax certificates issued by the Minister for Finance under section 445(2) and 446(2) of the Taxes Consolidation Act 1997 to IFSC/Shannon companies contain a condition restricting the offset of losses to the trading activities referred to in the certificate. The Department of Finance has confirmed that s 54 of the Finance Act 2002 may be applied to these companies on the same basis as it applies to non-certified companies.

Tax Briefing

TB44 June 2001 pp 39–40 — CT Losses, Charges and Group Relief Offset (following enactment of FA 2001 s 90).

Definitions

charges on income: ss 4(1), 243(1); company: ss 4(1), 5(1); franked investment income: ss 4(1), 156; franked payment: ss 4(1), 156; interest: s 4(1); month: IA 1937 Sch; profits: s 4(1); tax credit: ss 2(1), 136; trade: ss 3(1), 4(1), 5(1); within the charge to (tax): s 2(1).

Former enactments

CTA 1976 s 16(1)–(8) and (10); FA 1992 s 46(1)(b); FA 1993 s 22.

Corresponding UK tax provision

Income and Corporation Taxes Act 1988 ss 393 and 393A.

396A Relief for relevant trading losses

[(1) In this section—

"relevant trading income" has the same meaning as in section 243A;

[**"relevant trading loss"**, in relation to an accounting period of a company, means a loss incurred in the accounting period in a trade carried on by the company, other than—

(*a*) so much of the loss as is a loss incurred in an excepted trade within the meaning of section 21A, and

(*b*) any amount which is or would, if subsection (8) of section 403 had not been enacted, be the relevant amount of the loss for the purposes of subsection (4) of that section.][1]

(2) Notwithstanding subsection (2) of section 396, for the purposes of that subsection the amount of a loss in a trade incurred by a company in an accounting period shall be deemed to be reduced by the amount of a relevant trading loss incurred by the company in the accounting period.

(3) Subject to section 455, where in an accounting period a company carrying on a trade incurs a relevant trading loss, the company may make a claim requiring that the loss be set off for the purposes of corporation tax against income of the company, being—

(*a*) income specified in section 21A(4)(*b*), and

(*b*) relevant trading income,

of that accounting period and, if the company was then carrying on the trade and if the claim so requires, of preceding accounting periods ending within the time specified in subsection (4), and subject to that subsection and any relief for an earlier relevant trading loss, to the extent that the income of any of those accounting periods consists of or includes income specified in section 21A(4)(*b*) or relevant trading income, that income shall then be reduced by the amount of the relevant trading loss or by so much of that amount as cannot be relieved against income of a later accounting period.

(4) For the purposes of subsection (3), the time referred to in paragraph (*b*) of that subsection shall be the time immediately preceding the accounting period first mentioned in subsection (3) equal in length to that accounting period; but the amount of the reduction which may be made under subsection (3) in the relevant trading income of an accounting period falling partly before that time shall not exceed such part of that relevant trading income as bears to the whole of the relevant trading income the same proportion as the part of the accounting period falling within that time bears to the whole of that accounting period.][2]

[(5) A claim under subsection (3) shall be made within 2 years from the end of the accounting period in which the loss is incurred.][3]

Amendments

1 Definition of "relevant trading loss" substituted by FA 2005 s 45(1)(*a*) as respects any claim made by a company on or after 3 February 2005 for relief for a loss.

2 Section 396A inserted by FA 2001 s 90(1)(*b*)(i) as respects an accounting period ending on or after 6 March 2001.

3 Subs (5) substituted by FA 2003 s 59(1)(*b*) as respects accounting periods ending on or after 6 February 2003.

Note

For the purposes of computing the amount of relevant trading losses within the meaning of TCA 1997 s 396A, where an accounting period of a company begins before 6 March 2001 and ends on or after that date, it shall be divided into 2 parts, one beginning on the date on which the accounting period begins and ending on 5 March 2001 and the other beginning on 6 March 2001 and ending on the date on which the accounting period ends, and both parts shall be treated as if they were separate accounting periods of the company — see FA 2001 s 90(4), as substituted by FA 2002 s 55.

Cross-references

Corporation tax, late returns, restriction of certain claims for relief, subs (3): s 1085(2)(*a*).
Group relief, relief for certain losses on a value basis, meaning of "relevant trading loss" applied: s 420B(1); s 420B(2)(*a*); relevant losses and charges, meaning of "relevant trading loss" applied: s 420A(1); s 420A(3)(*a*).
Manufacturing relief: s 448(4).
Relief for certain gifts (to apply as if TCA 1997 ss 396A and 420A had not been enacted): s 483(5).
Relief for expenditure on significant buildings and gardens: s 482(11).
Relief for trading losses other than terminal losses, subs (3): s 396(1).
Relief for certain trading losses on a value basis, meaning of "relevant trading loss" applied: s 396B(1); subs (3): s 396B(2)(*a*).
Restriction of certain losses: s 455(2).
Restriction of relevant charges on income: s 243A(3).

Tax Briefing

TB44 June 2001 pp 39–40 — CT Losses, Charges and Group Relief Offset (following enactment of FA 2001 s 90).

Definitions

company: s 4(1); trade: s 4(1).

396B Relief for certain trading losses on a value basis

[(1) In this section—

[**"relevant corporation tax"**, in relation to an accounting period of a company, means the corporation tax which would be chargeable on the company for the accounting period apart from—

(*a*) this section and sections 239, 241, 420B, 440 and 441, and

(*b*) where the company carries on a life business (within the meaning of section 706 of the Principal Act), any corporation tax which would be attributable to policyholders' profits;][1]

"relevant trading loss" has the same meaning as in section 396A ...[2].

(2) Where in any accounting period a company carrying on a trade incurs a relevant trading loss and the amount of the loss exceeds an amount equal to the aggregate of the [amounts which could, if a timely claim for such set off had been made by the company, have been set off][3] in respect of that loss for the purposes of corporation tax against—

(*a*) income of the company of that accounting period and any preceding accounting period in accordance with section 396A(3), and (*b*) income of the company from the sale of goods of that accounting period and any preceding accounting period in accordance with section 455(3),

the company may claim relief under this section in respect of the excess.

(3) Where for any accounting period a company claims relief under this section in respect of the excess, the relevant corporation tax of the company for that accounting period and, if the company was then carrying on the trade and the claim so requires, for preceding accounting periods ending within the time specified in subsection (4), shall be reduced—

(*a*) in so far as the excess consists of a loss from the sale of goods (within the meaning of section 455), by an amount equal to 10 per cent of the loss from the sale of goods, and

(*b*) in so far as the excess consists of a loss (in this section referred to as the "remainder of the relevant trading loss") which is not a loss from the sale of goods (within the meaning of section 455), by an amount determined by the formula—

$$L \times \frac{R}{100}$$

where—

L is the amount of the remainder of the relevant trading loss, and

R is the rate per cent of corporation tax which, by virtue of section 21, applies in relation to the accounting period.

(4) For the purposes of subsection (3), the time referred to in that subsection shall be the time immediately preceding the accounting period first mentioned in subsection (3) equal in length to that accounting period; but the amount of the reduction which may be made under subsection (3) in the relevant corporation tax for an accounting period falling partly before that time shall not exceed such part of that relevant corporation tax as bears to the whole of that relevant corporation tax the same proportion as the part of the accounting period falling within that time bears to the whole of that accounting period.

(5) (*a*) Where a company makes a claim for relief for any accounting period under this section in respect of any relevant trading loss incurred in a trade in an accounting period, an amount (which shall not exceed the amount of the excess in respect of which a claim under this section may be made), determined in accordance with paragraph (*b*), shall be treated for the purposes of the Tax Acts as an amount of loss relieved against profits of that accounting period.

(*b*) Subject to paragraph (*c*), the amount determined in accordance with this paragraph in relation to an accounting period is an amount equal to the aggregate of the following amounts:

(i) where relief is given under paragraph (*a*) of subsection (3) for the accounting period, an amount equal to 10 times the amount by which the relevant corporation tax payable for the accounting period is reduced by virtue of that paragraph, and

(ii) where relief is given under paragraph (*b*) of subsection (3) for the accounting period, an amount determined by the formula—

$$T \times \frac{100}{R}$$

where—

T is the amount by which the relevant corporation tax payable is reduced by virtue of subsection (3)(*b*), and

R is the rate per cent of corporation tax which, by virtue of section 21, applies in relation to the accounting period.

(*c*) (i) In this paragraph **"relevant amount"** means an amount (not being an amount incurred by a company for the purposes of a trade carried on by it) of charges on income, expenses of management or other amount (not being an allowance to which effect is given under section 308(4)) which is deductible from, or may be treated as reducing, profits of more than one description.

(ii) For the purposes of paragraph (*b*), where as respects an accounting period of a company a relevant amount is deductible from, or may be treated as reducing, profits of more than one description, the amount by which corporation tax is reduced by virtue of subsection (3) shall be deemed to be the amount by which it would have been reduced if no relevant amount were so deductible or so treated.

[(6) A claim under subsection (2) shall be made within 2 years from the end of the accounting period in which the loss is incurred.][4][5]

Amendments

1 Subs (1)(definition of "relevant corporation tax") substituted by FA 2004 s 37(1) as respects any claim for relief made on or after 4 February 2004.

2 Deleted by FA 2005 s 45(1)(*b*) in respect of any claim made by a company on or after 3 February 2005 for relief for a loss.

3 Substituted by FA 2003 s 59(1)(*c*)(i) as respects a claim under TCA 1997 s 396B made on or after 6 February 2003; previously "amounts set off".

4 Subs (6) inserted by FA 2003 s 59(1)(*c*)(ii) as respects accounting periods ending on or after 6 February 2003.

5 Section 396B inserted by FA 2002 s 54(1)(*b*)(ii) as respects an accounting period ending on or after 6 March 2001 (for the purposes of computing the amount of charges on income paid for the purposes of the sale of goods (within the meaning of TCA 1997 s 454), a loss from the sale of goods (within the meaning of TCA 1997 s 455), relevant trading charges on income (within the meaning of TCA 1997 s 243A), and relevant trading losses (within the meaning of TCA 1997 s 396A), in respect of which relief may be claimed by virtue of FA 2002 s 54, where an accounting period of a company begins before 6 March 2001 and ends on or after that date, it shall be divided into 2 parts, one beginning on the date on which the accounting period begins and ending on 5 March 2001 and the other beginning on 6 March 2001 and ending on the date on which the accounting period ends, and both parts shall be treated as if they were separate accounting periods of the company).

Cross-references

Corporation tax, late returns, restriction of certain claims for relief, subs (2): s 1085(2)(*ba*).

Offshore funds, disposal of an interest in: s 747E(4)(*b*).

Relief for certain charges on income on a value basis: s 243B(1)("relevant corporation tax").

Relief for trading losses other than terminal losses, subs (2): s 396(1).

Revenue information

Tax certificates issued by the Minister for Finance under section 445(2) and 446(2) of the Taxes Consolidation Act 1997 to IFSC/Shannon companies contain a condition restricting the offset of losses to the trading activities referred to in the certificate. The Department of Finance has confirmed that s 54 of the Finance Act 2002 may be applied to these companies on the same basis as it applies to non-certified companies.

Tax Briefing

TB51 Jan 2003 pp 14–18 — Losses, Charges and Group Relief — Relief for certain losses on a value basis (FA 2002 s 54).

Definitions

company: s 4(1); profits: s 4(1); Tax Acts: s 1(2); trade: ss 3(1), 4(1).

397 Relief for terminal loss in a trade

(1) (*a*) Where a company ceasing to carry on a trade has, in any accounting period falling wholly or partly within the previous 12 months, incurred a loss in the trade, the company may claim to set the loss off for the purposes of corporation tax against trading income from the trade in accounting periods falling wholly or partly within the 3 years preceding those 12 months (or within any shorter period throughout which the company has carried on the trade) and, subject to subsections (2) and (3) and to any relief for earlier losses, the trading income of any of those accounting periods shall then be treated as reduced by the amount of the loss, or by so much of that amount as cannot be relieved under this subsection against income of a later accounting period.

(*b*) Relief shall not be given under this subsection in respect of any loss in so far as the loss has been or can be otherwise taken into account so as to reduce or relieve any charge to tax.

(2) Where a loss is incurred in an accounting period falling partly outside the 12 months mentioned in subsection (1), relief shall be given under that subsection in respect of a part only of that loss proportionate to the part of the period falling within those 12 months, and the amount of the reduction which may be made under that subsection in the trading income of an accounting period falling partly outside the 3 years mentioned in that subsection shall not exceed a part of that income proportionate to the part of the period falling within those 3 years.

(3) Subsections (5) to (8) of section 396 shall apply for the purposes of this section as they apply for the purposes of section 396(1), and relief shall not be given under this section in respect of a loss incurred in a trade so as to interfere with any relief under [section 243 or 243A][1] in respect of payments made wholly and exclusively for the purposes of that trade.

Amendments

1 Substituted by FA 2005 s 147 and Sch 6 para 1(*f*) as respects accounting periods ending on or after 3 February 2005; previously "section 243".

Cross-references

Companies carrying on life business: s 709(2).

Company reconstructions without change of ownership, subs (3): s 400(9).

Corporation tax, computation of losses attributable to income from certain securities, subs (3): s 398(1).

Exploration expenditure, subss (1)–(2) applied, for "trading income from the trade" or "trading income" read "profits (of whatever description)": s 679(3)(*a*).

Farming stock relief: s 666(2)(*b*)(iii).

Foreign currency, tax treatment of capital allowances and trading losses: s 402(3)(*a*).

Franked investment income in the case of financial concerns, set off of losses (subs (1)): s 158(1), (3)(*b*), (6).
Group relief, relation to other relief: s 421(1)(*c*).
Group relief, relevant losses and charges: s 420A(4)(*a*).
Profit sharing schemes, payments to trustees: s 517(3)(*a*).
Restriction of group relief: s 456(2A)(*b*)(i).

Definitions

company: ss 4(1), 5(1); month: IA 1937 Sch; trade: ss 3(1), 4(1), 5(1).

Former enactments

CTA 1976 s 18(1)–(3).

Corresponding UK tax provision

Income and Corporation Taxes Act 1988 s 397 [repealed].

398 Computation of losses attributable to exemption of income from certain securities

(1) Notwithstanding subsection (5) of section 396 or subsection (3) of section 397, in ascertaining for the purposes of those sections whether and to what extent a company has incurred a loss in carrying on a trade in the State through a branch or agency, the interest on, and other profits or gains from, a security held by or for the branch or agency shall be treated as a trading receipt of the trade if such interest or other profits or gains would, if sections 43, 49 and 50 had not been enacted, have been so treated, or have been included in an amount so treated.

(2) Subsection (1) shall apply for the purposes of ascertaining whether and to what extent a company has incurred a loss where apart from that subsection the company would be treated as having incurred a loss and that loss would be—

(*a*) set-off against the trading income or profits (whether of that company or any other company) of, or

(*b*) incurred in,

an accounting period.

Definitions

branch or agency: ss 4(1), 5(1); company: ss 4(1), 5(1); profits: s 4(1).

Former enactments

FA 1992 s 42(2)–(3)(*b*) (apart from proviso thereto).

399 Losses in transactions from which income would be chargeable under Case IV or V of Schedule D

(1) (*a*) Where in any accounting period a company incurs a loss in a transaction in respect of which the company is within the charge to corporation tax under Case IV of Schedule D, the company may claim to set the loss off against the amount of any income arising from such transactions in respect of which the company is assessed to corporation tax under that Case for the same or any subsequent accounting period, and the company's income in any accounting period from such transactions shall then be treated as reduced by the amount of the loss, or by so much of that amount as cannot be relieved under this section against income of an earlier accounting period.

(*b*) Where a company sustains a loss in a transaction which, if profit had arisen from it, would be chargeable to tax by virtue of subsection (3) or (4) of section 814, then, if the company is chargeable to tax in respect of the interest payable on the amount of money the right to which has been disposed of, the amount of that interest shall be included in the amounts against which the company may claim to set off the amount of its loss under this subsection.

(2) (*a*) Where in any accounting period a company is within the charge to corporation tax under Case V of Schedule D and the aggregate of the deficiencies, computed in accordance with section 97(1), exceeds the aggregate of the surpluses as so computed, the excess may, on a claim being made in that behalf, be deducted from or set off, as far as may be, against the amount of any income in respect of which the company is assessed to corporation tax under Case V of Schedule D for previous accounting periods ending within the time specified in subsection (3), and, subject to that subsection and to any relief for an earlier excess of deficiencies, that income of any of those periods shall then be treated as reduced, as far as may be, by the amount of the excess, and any portion of the excess for which relief is not so given shall be set off against the income in respect of which the company is assessed to corporation tax under Case V of Schedule D for any subsequent accounting period.

(*b*) Any relief under this subsection by means of carrying forward any portion of the excess referred to in paragraph (*a*) shall be given as far as possible from the first subsequent assessment and, in so far as it cannot be so given, then from the next assessment and so on.

(3) The time referred to in subsection (2) shall be a time immediately preceding the accounting period first mentioned in subsection (2) equal in length to the accounting period in which the excess of deficiencies occurred; but the amount of the reduction which may be made under that subsection in the income of an accounting period falling partly before that time shall not exceed a part of that income proportionate to the part of the period falling within that time.

(4) A claim under subsection (2) shall be made within 2 years from the end of the accounting period in which the excess of deficiencies was incurred.

Cross-references

Corporation tax — late returns, restriction of relief, subs (2): s 1085(2)(*a*).

Foreign life policies, disposal of certain policies: s 730K(4)(*b*).

Life assurance companies, annuity business, separate charge on profits: s 715(3).

Offshore funds, disposal of an interest in certain offshore funds: s 747E(4)(*b*).

Petroleum trade, treatment of losses, subs (1): s 687(2).

Transactions in certificates of deposit: s 814(5).

Definitions

company: ss 4(1), 5(1); interest: s 4(1); within the charge to (tax): s 2(1).

Former enactments

CTA 1976 s 19.

Corresponding UK tax provision

Income and Corporation Taxes Act 1988 s 396.

400 Company reconstructions without change of ownership

(1) For the purposes of this section—

(*a*) a trade carried on by 2 or more persons shall be treated as belonging to them in the shares in which they are entitled to the profits of the trade;

(*b*) a trade or interest in a trade belonging to any person as trustee (otherwise than for charitable or public purposes) shall be treated as belonging to the persons for the time being entitled to the income under the trust;

(*c*) a trade or interest in a trade belonging to a company shall, where the result of so doing is that subsection (5) or (10) applies in relation to an event, be treated in any of the ways permitted by subsection (2).

(2) For the purposes of this section, a trade or interest in a trade which belongs to a company engaged in carrying on the trade may be regarded—

(*a*) as belonging to the persons owning the ordinary share capital of the company and as belonging to those persons in proportion to the amount of their holdings of that capital, or

(*b*) in the case of a company which is a subsidiary company, as belonging to a company which is its parent company, or as belonging to the persons owning the ordinary share capital of that parent company, and as belonging to those persons in proportion to the amount of their holdings of that capital,

and any ordinary share capital owned by a company may, if any person or body of persons has the power to secure by means of the holding of shares or the possession of voting power in or in relation to any company, or by virtue of any power conferred by the articles of association or other document regulating any company, that the affairs of the company owning the share capital are conducted in accordance with that person's or that body of persons' wishes, be regarded as owned by that person or body of persons having that power.

(3) For the purposes of subsection (2)—

(*a*) references to ownership shall be construed as references to beneficial ownership;

(*b*) a company shall be deemed to be a subsidiary of another company if and so long as not less than 75 per cent of its ordinary share capital is owned by that other company, whether directly or through another company or other companies, or partly directly and partly through another company or other companies;

(*c*) the amount of ordinary share capital of one company owned by a second company through another company or other companies, or partly directly and partly through another company or other companies, shall be determined in accordance with subsections (5) to (10) of section 9;

(*d*) where any company is a subsidiary of another company, that other company shall be considered as its parent company unless both are subsidiaries of a third company.

(4) In determining for the purposes of this section whether or to what extent a trade belongs at different times to the same persons, persons who are relatives of one another and the persons from time to time entitled to the income under any trust shall

respectively be treated as a single person, and for this purpose **"relative"** means husband, wife, ancestor, lineal descendant, brother or sister.

(5) (*a*) Where, on a company (in this section referred to as **"the predecessor"**) ceasing to carry on a trade, another company (in this section referred to as **"the successor"**) begins to carry on the trade and—

(i) on or at any time within 2 years after that event, the trade or an interest amounting to not less than a 75 per cent share in the trade belongs to the same persons as the trade or such an interest belonged to at some time within a year before that event, and

(ii) the trade is not, within the period taken for the comparison under subparagraph (i), carried on otherwise than by a company within the charge to tax in respect of the trade,

then, the Corporation Tax Acts shall apply subject to subsections (6) to (9).

(*b*) In subparagraphs (i) and (ii) of paragraph (*a*), references to the trade shall apply also to any other trade of which the activities comprise the activities of the first-mentioned trade.

(6) The trade shall not be treated as permanently discontinued nor a new trade as set up and commenced for the purpose of the allowances and charges provided for by sections 307 and 308; but there shall be made to or on the successor in accordance with those sections all such allowances and charges as would, if the predecessor had continued to carry on the trade, have been made to or on the predecessor, and the amount of any such allowance or charge shall be computed as if the successor had been carrying on the trade since the predecessor began to do so and as if everything done to or by the predecessor had been done to or by the successor (but so that no sale or transfer which on the transfer of the trade is made to the successor by the predecessor of any assets in use for the purpose of the trade shall be treated as giving rise to any such allowance or charge).

(7) The predecessor shall not be entitled to relief under section 397 except as provided by subsection (9) and, subject to any claim made by the predecessor under section 396(2), the successor shall be entitled to relief under section 396(1), as for a loss sustained by the successor in carrying on the trade, for any amount for which the predecessor would have been entitled to claim relief if the predecessor had continued to carry on the trade.

(8) Any securities within the meaning of section 748 which, at the time when the predecessor ceases to carry on the trade, form part of the trading stock belonging to the trade shall be treated for the purposes of that section as having been sold at that time in the open market by the predecessor and as having been purchased at that time in the open market by the successor.

(9) On the successor ceasing to carry on the trade—

(*a*) if the successor does so within 4 years of succeeding to the trade, any relief which might be given to the successor under section 397 on the successor ceasing to carry on the trade may, in so far as that relief cannot be given to the successor, be given to the predecessor as if the predecessor had incurred the loss (including any amount treated as a loss under section 397(3)), and (*b*) if the successor ceases to carry on the trade within one year of succeeding to the trade, relief may be given to the predecessor under section 397 in respect of any loss incurred by the predecessor (or any amount treated as such a loss under section 397(3));

but, for the purposes of section 397 as it applies by virtue of this subsection to the giving of relief to the predecessor, the predecessor shall be treated as ceasing to carry on the trade when the successor does so.

(10) Where the successor ceases to carry on the trade within the period taken for the comparison under subsection (5)(*a*)(i) and, on its doing so, a third company begins to carry on the trade, then, no relief shall be given to the predecessor by virtue of subsection (9) by reference to that event; but, subject to that, subsections (6) to (9) shall apply both in relation to that event (together with the new predecessor and successor) and to the earlier event (together with the original predecessor and successor), but so that—

(*a*) in relation to the earlier event, **"successor"** shall include the successor at either event, and

(*b*) in relation to the later event, **"predecessor"** shall include the predecessor at either event,

and, if the conditions of this subsection are thereafter again satisfied, this subsection shall apply again in the like manner.

(11) Where, on a company ceasing to carry on a trade, another company begins to carry on the activities of the trade as part of its trade, that part of the trade carried on by the successor shall for the purposes of this subsection be treated as a separate trade, if the effect of so treating it is that subsection (5) or (10) applies to that event in relation to that separate trade, and where, on a company ceasing to carry on part of a trade, another company begins to carry on the activities of that part as its trade or part of its trade, the predecessor shall for the purposes of this section be treated as having carried on that part of its trade as a separate trade, if the effect of so treating it is that subsection (5) or (10) applies to that event in relation to that separate trade.

(12) Where under subsection (11) any activities of a company's trade are to be treated as a separate trade on the company ceasing or beginning to carry them on, any necessary apportionment shall be made of receipts or expenses.

(13) Where by virtue of subsection (12) any sum is to be apportioned and, at the time of the apportionment, it appears that it is material as respects the liability to tax (for whatever period) of 2 or more companies, any question which arises as to the manner in which the sum is to be apportioned shall, for the purposes of the tax of all those companies, be determined by the Appeal Commissioners who shall determine the question in the like manner as if it were an appeal against an assessment, and the provisions of the Income Tax Acts relating to the rehearing of an appeal and to the statement of a case for the opinion of the High Court on a point of law shall apply accordingly with any necessary modifications, and all those companies shall be entitled to appear before and be heard by the Appeal Commissioners or to make representations to them in writing.

(14) Any relief to be given under this section by means of discharge or repayment of tax shall be given on the making of a claim.

Cross-references

BES relief, qualifying company, subs (2): s 495(12)(*a*)(iii).

BES relief, replacement capital, subss (1)(*a*)–(*b*), (2)–(3): s 500(5).

EU Council Directive 90/434/EEC, mergers, divisions, subss (6)–(9): s 631(2)(*c*).

Farming or market gardening, restriction of losses, subs (6): s 663(3).

Group, transfer of company to another: s 424(2)(*a*).

Leasing contracts, company reconstructions: s 425(2)(*a*).

Case law

Where company took over part only of another company's business, it was held that the relative scale of activities indicated the trade of the two companies was not the same: *Rolls Royce Motors Ltd v Bamford* [1976] STC 162.

Where a company took over the trade of its supplier, even though the profits of that trade were no longer being separately realised, claim for losses was allowed: *Falmer Jeans Ltd v Rodin* [1990] STC 270.

Revenue precedents

Issue: Whether a transfer of plant is necessary for s 400(6) to apply.
Decision: A transfer of the plant used in the trade is not necessary for the section to apply.

Definitions

Appeal Commissioners: s 2(1); body of persons: s 2(1); company: ss 4(1), 5(1); Income Tax Acts: s 1(2); ordinary share capital: s 2(1); person: IA 1937 s 11(*c*); relative: s 3(1); profits: s 4(1); trade: ss 3(1), 4(1), 5(1); trading stock: s 5(1); within the charge to (tax): s 2(1); writing: IA 1937 Sch.

Former enactments

CTA 1976 s 20.

Corresponding UK tax provision

Income and Corporation Taxes Act 1988 ss 343 and 344.

401 Change in ownership of company: disallowance of trading losses

(1) In this section, **"major change in the nature or conduct of a trade"** includes—

(*a*) a major change in the type of property dealt in, or services or facilities provided, in the trade, or

(*b*) a major change in customers, outlets or markets of the trade,

and this section shall apply even if the change is the result of a gradual process which began outside the period of 3 years mentioned in subsection (2)(*a*).

(2) Where—

(*a*) within any period of 3 years, there is both a change in the ownership of a company and (whether earlier or later in that period or at the same time) a major change in the nature or conduct of a trade carried on by the company, or

(*b*) at any time after the scale of the activities in a trade carried on by a company has become small or negligible and before any considerable revival of the trade, there is a change in the ownership of the company,

relief shall not be given—

(i) under section 396 by setting a loss incurred by the company in an accounting period beginning before the change of ownership against any income or other profits of an accounting period ending after the change of ownership, or

(ii) under paragraph 16 or 18 of Schedule 32 against corporation tax payable for any accounting period ending after the change of ownership.

(3) (*a*) In applying this section to the accounting period in which the change of ownership occurs, the part ending with the change of ownership and the part after that change shall be treated as 2 separate accounting periods, and the profits or losses of the accounting period shall be apportioned to the 2 parts.

(*b*) The apportionment under paragraph (*a*) shall be on a time basis according to the respective lengths of the 2 parts except that, if it appears that that method would operate unreasonably or unjustly, such other method shall be used as appears just and reasonable.

(4) In relation to any relief available under section 400, subsection (2) shall apply as if any loss sustained by a predecessor company had been sustained by a successor company and as if the references to a trade included references to the trade as carried on by a predecessor company.

(5) (*a*) Where relief in respect of a company's losses has been restricted under this section, then, notwithstanding section 320(6), in applying the provisions of Part 9 and of Chapter 1 of Part 29 relating to balancing charges to the company by reference to any event after the change of ownership of the company, any allowance or deduction to be made in taxing the company's trade for any chargeable period before the change of ownership shall be disregarded unless the profits or gains of that chargeable period, or of any subsequent chargeable period before the change of ownership, were sufficient to give effect to the allowance or deduction.

(*b*) In applying this subsection, it shall be assumed that any profits or gains are applied in giving effect to any such allowance or deduction in preference to being set off against any loss which is not attributable to such an allowance or deduction.

(6) Where the operation of this section depends on circumstances or events at a time after the change of ownership (but not more than 3 years after that change), an assessment to give effect to this section shall not be out of time if made within [4 years][1] from that time or the latest of those times.

(7) Schedule 9 shall apply for the purpose of supplementing this section.

Amendments

1 Substituted by FA 2003 s 17(*f*) with effect from: (*a*) such day or days as the Minister for Finance may by order or orders appoint either generally or with reference to any particular purpose or provision and different days may be so appointed for different purposes or different provisions and (*b*) notwithstanding the generality of (*a*), any order made by the Minister for Finance in accordance with the provisions of that paragraph may contain, and be subject to, such conditions as the Minister considers appropriate and which are specified in the order; previously "10 years". By virtue of Finance Act 2003 (Commencement of Section 17) Order 2003, SI No 508 of 2003, this amendment comes into operation in relation to the making, on or after 1 January 2005, of an assessment referred to in section 401(6).

Cross-references

Advance corporation tax subss (6), (7) applied by s 167(7).

Penalties for failure to furnish certain information and for incorrect information: s 1075(1), (2).

Supplementary: Sch 9 paras 1, 2(*d*), 3–6, 8.

Case law

A major change in the conduct of the trade was held not to have occurred where the company sold its products through a distribution company rather than direct to customers: *Willis v Peeters Picture Frame Ltd* [1983] STC 453.

The effect of the change on the taxpayers trade is one of the factors to be taken into account in determining whether the change is major or not: *Purchase v Tesco Stores* [1984] STC 304. See also *Pobjoy Mint Ltd v Lane* [1984] STC 327.

Tax Briefing

TB56 July 2004 pp 6–11 — Repayments, Interest and Time Limits — Section 17 FA 2003 changes.

TB57 Oct 2004 pp 7–9 — New Time Limits - Section 17 FA 2003 changes.

TB57 Oct 2004 p 15 — Repayments, Interest and Time Limits - correction to TB56 p 8.

Definitions

company: ss 4(1), 5(1); profits: s 4(1); trade: ss 3(1), 4(1), 5(1).

Former enactments

CTA 1976 s 27(1)–(7).

Corresponding UK tax provision

Income and Corporation Taxes Act 1988 s 768.

CHAPTER 4

Income Tax and Corporation Tax: Treatment of Certain Losses and Certain Capital Allowances

402 Foreign currency: tax treatment of capital allowances and trading losses of a company

(1) (*a*) In this section—

"functional currency" means—

(i) in relation to a company resident in the State, the currency of the primary economic environment in which the company operates, and

(ii) in relation to a company not resident in the State, the currency of the primary economic environment in which the company carries on trading activities in the State,

but, where the profit and loss account of a company for any period of account has been prepared in terms of the currency of the State, that currency shall be the functional currency of the company for that period;

"profit and loss account" and **"rate of exchange"** have the same meanings respectively as in section 79;

"representative rate of exchange" means a rate of exchange of a currency for another currency equal to the mid-market rate at close of business recorded by the Central Bank of Ireland, or by a similar institution of another State, for those 2 currencies.

(*b*) For the purposes of this section, the currency of the primary economic environment of a company shall be determined—

(i) in the case of a company resident in the State, with reference to the currency in which—

(I) revenues and expenses of the company are primarily generated, and

(II) the company primarily borrows and lends, and

(ii) in the case of a company not so resident which carries on trading activities in the State, with reference to the currency in which—

(I) revenues and expenses of those activities are primarily generated, and

(II) the company primarily borrows and lends for the purposes of those activities.

(*c*) For the purposes of this section, the day on which any expenditure is incurred shall be taken to be the day on which the sum in question becomes payable.

[(*d*) In this section references to an amount having been incurred in, or computed in terms of, a currency other than the functional currency of a company shall not include a reference to an amount having been incurred in, or computed in terms of, the currency of a state, which currency has been substituted by another currency of that state, where that other currency is the functional currency of the company.

(*e*) For the purposes of this section where at any time, in relation to a state, the currency (hereafter in this paragraph referred to as **"the old currency"**) is substituted by another currency, the representative rate of exchange of the currency of that state for the currency of another state at any previous time shall mean the representative rate of exchange of the old currency of that state for the currency of that other state.]

(2) (*a*) Subject to paragraph (*b*), the amount (which may be nil) of any allowance or charge to be made for any accounting period—

(i) in taxing a trade of a company, and

(ii) by reference to capital expenditure incurred by the company on or after the 1st day of January, 1994,

shall be—

(I) computed in terms of the functional currency of the company by reference to amounts expressed in that currency, and

(II) given effect, in accordance with section 307(2)(*a*), by being treated as a trading expense or receipt, as the case may be, of the trade in computing the trading income or loss, expressed in that functional currency, of the trade for that accounting period.

(*b*) (i) For the purposes of the computation of an allowance or charge to be made for an accounting period (in this paragraph referred to as **"the first-mentioned period"**) by reference to capital expenditure incurred by a company on or after the 1st day of January, 1994, and

(ii) without prejudice to any allowance made by reference to that expenditure for an accounting period earlier than the first-mentioned period,

where that expenditure was incurred, or an allowance referable to that expenditure was computed, in terms of a currency other than the functional currency of the company for the first-mentioned period, then, that expenditure or allowance, as the case may be, shall be expressed in terms of that functional currency by reference to a representative rate of exchange of that functional currency for the other currency for the day on which that expenditure was incurred.

(3) (*a*) Subject to paragraph (*b*), for the purposes of sections 396 and 397, the amount (which may be nil) of any set-off due to a company against income or profits of an accounting period in respect of a loss from a trade incurred by the company in an accounting period shall—

(i) be computed in terms of the company's functional currency by reference to amounts expressed in that currency, and

(ii) then be expressed in terms of the currency of the State by reference to the rate of exchange which—

(I) is used to express in terms of the currency of the State the amount of the income from the trade for the accounting period in which the loss is to be set off, or

(II) would be so used if there were such income.

(*b*) (i) For the purposes of the computation of any set-off due to a company against income or profits of an accounting period (in this paragraph referred to as **"the first-mentioned period"**) in respect of a loss from a trade incurred by the company in an accounting period, and

(ii) without prejudice to any set-off made against the income or profits of an accounting period earlier than the first-mentioned period by reference to that loss,

where that loss, or any set-off referable to that loss, was computed in terms of a currency other than the functional currency of the company for the first-mentioned period, then, that loss or set-off, as the case may be, shall be expressed in terms of that functional currency by reference to a rate of exchange of that functional currency for the other currency, being an average of representative rates of exchange of that functional currency for the other currency during the accounting period in which the loss was incurred.

Amendments

1 Subs (1)(*d*)–(*e*) inserted by FA 1998 s 47 and Sch 2 para 5 with effect from such date as the Minister for Finance may appoint by order. The subsections come into operation from 31 December 1998 — Finance Act, 1998 (Section 47) (Commencement) Order, 1998, SI No 502 of 1998, refers.

Cross-references

Foreign currency: computation of income and chargeable gains, meaning of "functional currency" applied: s 79(1)(*c*).

Tax Briefing

TB31 Apr 1998 p 5 — The Euro and Tax: companies with non-IR£ functional currency.

Definitions

company: ss 4(1), 5(1); profits: s 4(1); trade: s 3(1).

Former enactments

CTA 1976 s 14A; FA 1994 s 56(*b*).

403 Restriction on use of capital allowances for certain leased assets

(1) (*a*) In this section—

"chargeable period or its basis period" has the same meaning as in section 321(2);

"lessee" and **"lessor"**, in relation to machinery or plant provided for leasing, mean respectively the person to whom the machinery or plant is or is to be leased and the person providing the machinery or plant for leasing, and **"lessee"** and **"lessor"** include respectively the successors in title of a lessee or a lessor;

"the relevant period" has the meaning assigned to it by subsection (9)(*b*);

"the specified capital allowances" means capital allowances in respect of—

(i) expenditure incurred on machinery or plant provided on or after the 25th day of January, 1984, for leasing in the course of a trade of leasing, or

(ii) the diminished value of such machinery or plant by reason of wear and tear,

other than capital allowances in respect of machinery or plant to which subsection (6), (7), (8) or (9) applies;

"trade of leasing" means—

(i) a trade which consists wholly of the leasing of machinery or plant, or

(ii) any part of a trade treated as a separate trade by virtue of subsection (2).

(*b*) For the purposes of this section—

(i) letting on charter a ship or aircraft which has been provided for such letting, and

(ii) letting any item of machinery or plant on hire,

shall be regarded as leasing of machinery or plant if apart from this paragraph it would not be so regarded.

(*c*) Where a company carries on a trade of operating ships in the course of which a ship is let on charter, paragraph (*b*) shall not apply so as to treat the letting on charter as the leasing of machinery or plant if apart from this section the letting would be regarded for the purposes of Case I of Schedule D as part of the activities of the trade.

(2) Where in any chargeable period or its basis period a person carries on as part of a trade any leasing of machinery or plant, that leasing shall be treated for the purposes of the Tax Acts, other than any provision of those Acts relating to the commencement or cessation of a trade, as a separate trade distinct from all other activities carried on by such person as part of the trade, and any necessary apportionment shall be made of receipts or expenses.

(3) (*a*) Notwithstanding section 381, where relief is claimed under that section in respect of a loss sustained in a trade of leasing, the amount of that loss, in so far as by virtue of section 392 it is referable to the specified capital allowances, shall be treated for the purposes of subsections (1) and (3)(*b*) of section 381 as reducing profits or gains of that trade of leasing only and shall not be treated as reducing any other income.

(*b*) Where paragraph (*a*) applies in the case of any claimant to relief under section 381—

(i) any limitation imposed by section 393 on the amount of capital allowances which may be taken into account under section 392 shall be referred, as far as may be, to the specified capital allowances rather than to any other capital allowances, and

(ii) notwithstanding section 392(2) (but without prejudice to paragraph (*a*) and to the order in which income is to be treated as reduced under section 381(3)(*b*)), the claimant may specify the extent to which any reduction of income treated as occurring by virtue of section 381 is to be referred to so much of the loss as is attributable to the loss, if any, actually sustained in the trade of leasing, the specified capital allowances or any other capital allowances, and, where the claimant so specifies, section 394 shall apply in accordance with the claimant's specification and not in accordance with section 392(2).

(4) (*a*) Where in an accounting period a company carrying on a trade of leasing incurs a loss in that trade and any specified capital allowances have been treated by virtue of section 307 or 308 as trading expenses in arriving at the amount of the loss, the relevant amount of the loss shall not be available—

(i) for relief under section 396(2), except to the extent that it can be set off under that section against the company's income from the trade of leasing only, or

(ii) to be surrendered by means of [group relief except to the extent that it could be set off under section 420A against income of a trade of leasing carried on by the claimant company if paragraph (*b*) of the definition of relevant trading loss in section 420A were deleted][1].

(*b*) For the purposes of paragraph (*a*), the relevant amount of the loss shall be the full amount of the loss or, if it is less, an amount equal to—

(i) where no capital allowances, other than the specified capital allowances, have been treated by virtue of section 307 or 308 as trading expenses in arriving at the amount of the loss, the amount of the specified capital allowances, or

(ii) where, in addition to the specified capital allowances, other capital allowances have been so treated by virtue of section 307 or 308, the lesser of—

(I) the amount of the specified capital allowances, and

(II) the amount by which the loss exceeds the amount of the other capital allowances;

but, where the amount of the loss does not exceed the amount of the other capital allowances, the relevant amount of the loss shall be nil.

(5) Sections 305(1)(*b*), 308(4) and 420(2) shall not apply in relation to capital allowances—

(*a*) in respect of expenditure incurred on or after the 25th day of January, 1984, on the provision of machinery or plant, or

(*b*) in respect of the diminished value of machinery or plant by reason of wear and tear, if that machinery or plant was first acquired on or after the 25th day of January, 1984, by the person to whom the capital allowances are to be or have been made,

other than capital allowances in respect of machinery or plant to which subsection (6) or (7) applies.

[(5A)(*a*) In this subsection **"appointed day"** has the same meaning as in section 284(3A).

(*b*) In relation to capital allowances in respect of machinery or plant to which section 284(3A) applies—

(i) notwithstanding subsections (3) and (5)—

(I) subsection (3) shall not apply, and

(II) section 305(1)(*b*) shall apply,

where the capital expenditure on that machinery or plant is incurred in the period of 2 years commencing on the appointed day, and

(ii) notwithstanding subsections (4) and (5)—

(I) subsection (4) shall not apply, and

(II) sections 308(4) and 420(2) shall apply,

where the capital expenditure on that machinery or plant is incurred in the period of [6 years][2] commencing on the appointed day.

(*c*) This subsection shall come into operation on the appointed day.][3]

(6) References in this section to machinery or plant to which this subsection applies are references to machinery or plant provided on or after the 25th day of January, 1984, for leasing where the expenditure incurred on the provision of the machinery or plant was incurred under an obligation entered into by the lessor and the lessee before—

(*a*) the 25th day of January, 1984, or

(*b*) the 1st day of March, 1984, pursuant to negotiations which were in progress between the lessor and the lessee before the 25th day of January, 1984.

(7) References in this section to machinery or plant to which this subsection applies are references to machinery or plant provided on or after the 25th day of January, 1984, for leasing where the expenditure incurred on the provision of the machinery or plant (or, in the case of a film to which section 6 or 7 of the Irish Film Board Act, 1980, applies, the cost of the making of the film) has been or is to be met directly or indirectly, wholly or partly, by the Industrial Development Authority, the Irish Film Board, the Shannon Free Airport Development Company Limited, or Údarás na Gaeltachta; but this subsection shall not apply to machinery or plant provided for leasing on or after the 13th day of May, 1986, unless—

(*a*) the machinery or plant is a film to which section 6 or 7 of the Irish Film Board Act, 1980, applies, or

(*b*) the expenditure incurred on the provision of the machinery or plant (not being a film of the kind mentioned in paragraph (*a*)) was incurred under an obligation entered into by the lessor and the lessee before—

(i) the 13th day of May, 1986, or

(ii) the 1st day of September, 1986, pursuant to negotiations which were in progress between the lessor and the lessee before the 13th day of May, 1986.

(8) The reference in the definition of **"the specified capital allowances"** to machinery or plant to which this subsection applies is a reference to machinery or plant provided

for leasing by a lessor to a lessee in the course of the carrying on by the lessor of relevant trading operations within the meaning of section 445 or 446, and—

(*a*) in respect of the expenditure on which no allowance has been or will be made under section 283, or

(*b*) in respect of which no allowance on account of wear and tear to be made under section 284 has been or will be increased under section 285.

(9) (*a*) (i) In this subsection, **"specified trade"**, in relation to a [lessee or lessor],[4] means a trade which throughout the relevant period consists wholly or mainly of the manufacture of goods (including activities which, if the [lessee or lessor][4] were to make a claim for relief in respect of the trade under Part 14, would be regarded for the purposes of that Part as the manufacture of goods).

(ii) For the purposes of subparagraph (i), a trade shall be regarded, as respects the relevant period, as consisting wholly or mainly of particular activities only if the total amount receivable by the [lessee or lessor][3] from sales made or, as the case may be, in payment for services rendered in the course of those activities in the relevant period is not less than 75 per cent of the total amount receivable by the [lessee or lessor][4] from all sales made or, as the case may be, in payment for all services rendered in the course of the trade in the relevant period.

(iii) As respects a person who carries on a trade of leasing and who incurred expenditure on the provision before the 20th day of April, 1990, of machinery or plant for leasing under an obligation entered into before that date by the lessor and a lessee who carries on a trade which but for section 443(6) would be a specified trade, this subsection shall apply as if the trade carried on by the lessee were a specified trade.

(iv) For the purposes of subparagraph (iii), an obligation shall be treated as entered into before the 20th day of April, 1990, only if before that date there were in existence a binding contract in writing under which that obligation arose.

[(*b*) The reference in the definition of **"the specified capital allowances"** to machinery or plant to which this subsection applies is a reference to machinery or plant (not being a film of the kind mentioned in subsection (7)(*a*)) provided on or after the 13th day of May, 1986, for leasing by a lessor to a lessee (who is not a person connected with the lessor) under a lease the terms of which include an undertaking given by the lessee that, during a period (in this section referred to as **"the relevant period"**) which is not less than 3 years and which commences on the day on which the machinery or plant is first brought into use by the lessee, the machinery or plant so provided will—

(i) where it is so provided before the 4th day of March, 1998, be used by the lessee for the purposes only of a specified trade carried on in the State by the lessee, and

[(ii) where it is so provided on or after that day, be used by the lessee for the purposes only of a specified trade carried on in the State by the lessee and, except where the lessor provides the machinery or plant for leasing in the course of a specified trade carried on by the lessor, that it will not be used for the purposes of any other trade, or business or activity other than the lessor's trade.][5][6]

(*c*) Any machinery or plant in respect of which an undertaking mentioned in paragraph (*b*) has been given by a lessee, and which at any time has been treated as machinery or plant to which this subsection applies, shall at any later time cease to be machinery or plant to which this subsection applies if at that later time it appears to the inspector (or on appeal to the Appeal Commissioners) that the undertaking has not been fulfilled by the lessee.

(*d*) Where any machinery or plant ceases in accordance with paragraph (*c*) to be machinery or plant to which this subsection applies, such assessments or adjustments of assessments shall be made to recover from the lessor any relief from tax given to the lessor because the machinery or plant was treated as machinery or plant to which this subsection applies.

(*e*) This subsection shall not apply to machinery or plant provided for leasing on or after the 13th day of May, 1986, if the expenditure incurred on the provision of the machinery or plant was incurred under an obligation entered into by the lessor and the lessee before—

(i) the 13th day of May, 1986, or

(ii) the 1st day of September, 1986, pursuant to negotiations which were in progress between the lessor and the lessee before the 13th day of May, 1986.

(10) For the purposes of subsections (6), (7) and (9)—

(*a*) an obligation shall be treated as having been entered into before a particular date only if before that date there was in existence a binding contract in writing under which that obligation arose, and

(*b*) negotiations pursuant to which an obligation was entered into shall not be regarded as having been in progress between a lessor and a lessee before a particular date unless on or before that date preliminary commitments or agreements in relation to that obligation had been entered into between the lessor and the lessee.

Amendments

1 Substituted by FA 2005 s 45(1)(*c*) as respects an accounting period ending on or after 3 February 2005; previously "group relief".

2 Substituted by FA 2001 s 52(2) from such date as the Minister may by order appoint; previously "3 years". By virtue of Finance Act 2001 (Commencement of Section 52) Order 2004, SI No 124 of 2004, this amendment came into operation on 24 March 2004.

3 Subs (5A) inserted by FA 1998 s 23(*b*) with effect from the "appointed day", the date which the Minister for Finance appoints by order for the commencement of s 284(3A), namely, 4 September 1998 — Taxes Consolidation Act, 1997 (Section 284(3A)) (Commencement) Order 1998, SI No 321 of 1998 refers.

4 Substituted by FA 1999 s 52(1)(*a*) with effect from 4 March 1998; previously "lessee".

5 Subs (9)(*b*)(ii) substituted by FA 1999 s 52(1)(*b*) with effect from 4 March 1998.

6 Subs (9)(*b*) substituted by FA 1998 s 31 with effect from 6 April 1998.

Cross-references

Group relief, relevant losses and charges, subss (4) and (8): s 420A(1) ("relevant trading loss").

Leased machinery or plant, restriction of on use of allowances, meanings of "lessee" and "lessor" applied: s 404(1)(*a*); specified leasing trade, this section, apart from subss (5)–(9) applies: s 404(2)(*a*).

Qualifying shipping trade, restriction on use of allowances: s 407(4)(*c*), (6).

Petroleum trade, development expenditure: s 692(5)(*a*)(ii).

Relief for relevant trading losses, subss (4) and (8): s 396A(1) ("relevant trading loss").

Restriction on use by certain partnerships of certain losses, etc, transitional arrangements, meaning of "lessor" and "lessee" applied: s 1017(2C)(*c*)(ii).

Shipping tonnage tax, capital allowances, general: s 697O(2).

Taxation of certain short-term leases of plant and machinery, meaning of "lessee" and "lessor" applied: s 80A(1); s 80A(2)(*c*).

Revenue precedents

Issue: Where some unexpected event occurs so that plant and equipment provided for use in a specified trade is destroyed or otherwise cannot be used necessitating its replacement before the 3 year period required by s 403(9) has expired will this be regarded as a breach of the undertaking given for the purposes of that section?

Decision: In the circumstances it is agreed that such an occurrence will not be treated as a breach of this undertaking. The key issue is that the machinery is not used for any non-qualifying purpose.

Issue: If a racecourse stand, which qualifies for capital allowances as plant, is leased can excess allowances be set against other income?

Decision: No. It appears such allowances are restricted by the provisions of TCA 1997 s 403(5).

Definitions

Appeal Commissioners: s 2(1); capital allowance: ss 2(1), 5(1); company: ss 4(1), 5(1); group relief: ss 4(1), 411; inspector: ss 2(1), 5(1), 852; lessee: s 5(1); lessor: s 5(1); person: IA 1937 s 11(*c*); profits: s 4(1); Tax Acts: s 1(2); trade: s 3(1); writing: IA 1937 Sch.

Former enactments

FA 1984 s 40(1)–(10); FA 1986 s 53; FA 1987 s 26; FA 1990 s 41(5)(*a*) and (*c*); FA 1994 s 61(1).

404 Restriction on use of capital allowances for certain leased machinery or plant

(1) (*a*) In this section—

"agricultural machinery" means machinery or plant used or intended to be used for the purposes of a trade of farming (within the meaning of section 654) or machinery or plant of a type commonly used for such a trade which is used or intended to be used for the purposes of a trade which consists of supplying services which normally play a part in agricultural production;

"asset" means machinery or plant;

"chargeable period", "chargeable period related to", and **"chargeable period or its basis period"** have the same meanings respectively as in section 321(2);

"fair value", in relation to a leased asset, means an amount equal to such consideration as might be expected to be paid for the asset at the inception of the lease on a sale negotiated on an arm's length basis, less any grants receivable by the lessor towards the purchase of the asset;

"inception of the lease" means the date on which the leased asset is brought into use by the lessee or the date from which lease payments under the lease first accrue, whichever is the earlier;

"lease payments" means the lease payments over the term of the lease to be paid to the lessor in relation to the leased asset, and includes any residual amount to be paid to the lessor at or after the end of the term of the lease and guaranteed by the lessee or by a person connected with the lessee or under the terms of any scheme or arrangement between the lessee and any other person;

"lessee" and **"lessor"** have the same meanings respectively as in section 403;

"predictable useful life", in relation to an asset, means the useful life of the asset estimated at the inception of the lease, having regard to the purpose for which the asset was acquired and on the assumption that—

(i) its life will end when it ceases to be useful for the purpose for which it was acquired, and

(ii) it will be used in the normal manner and to the normal extent throughout its life;

"relevant lease payment" means—

(i) the amount of any lease payment as provided under the terms of the lease, or

(ii) where the lease provides for the amount of any lease payment to be determined by reference to [a rate known as the European Interbank Offered Rate][1], or a similar rate, the amount calculated by reference to that rate if the rate per cent at the inception of the lease were the rate per cent at the time of the payment;

"relevant lease payments related to a chargeable period or its basis period" means relevant lease payments under the lease or the amounts which are treated as the relevant lease payments and which, if they were the actual amounts payable under the lease, would be taken into account in computing the income of the lessor for that chargeable period or its basis period or any earlier such period;

"relevant period" means the period—

(i) beginning at the inception of the lease, and

(ii) ending at—

(I) the earliest time at which the aggregate of amounts of the discounted present value at the inception of the lease of relevant lease payments which are payable at or before that time amounts to 90 per cent or more of the fair value of the leased asset, or

(II) if it is earlier, at the end of the predictable useful life of the asset,

and, for the purposes of this definition, relevant lease payments shall be discounted at a rate which, when applied at the inception of the lease to the amount of the relevant lease payments, produces discounted present values the aggregate of which equals the amount of the fair value of the leased asset at the inception of the lease, but where the duration of the relevant period determined in accordance with the preceding provisions of this definition is more than 7 years, the relevant period shall not be the period so determined but shall be the period which would be determined in accordance with this definition if for "90 per cent" there were substituted "95 per cent".

(*b*) For the purposes of this section—

(i) a lease of an asset shall be a relevant lease unless—

(I) as respects any chargeable period or its basis period of the lessor which falls wholly or partly in the relevant period, the aggregate of the amounts of relevant lease payments related to the chargeable period or its basis period and the amounts of relevant lease payments related to any earlier chargeable period or its basis period is not less than an amount determined by the formula—

$$W \times P \times \frac{90 + (10 \times W)}{100}$$

where—

P is the aggregate of the amounts of relevant lease payments payable by the lessee in relation to the leased asset in the relevant period, and

W is an amount determined by the formula—

$$\frac{E}{R}$$

where—

E is the length of the part of the relevant period which has expired at the end of the chargeable period or its basis period, and

R is the length of the relevant period, and

(II) except for an amount of relevant lease payments which is inconsequential, the excess of the total relevant lease payments under the lease over the aggregate of the relevant lease payments in the relevant period is payable to the lessor, or would be so payable if the relevant lease payments were the actual amounts payable under the lease, within a period the duration of which does not exceed—

(A) where the exception to the definition of **"relevant period"** does not apply, one-seventh of the duration of the relevant period, and

(B) where that exception does apply, one-ninth of the duration of the relevant period,

or one year, whichever is the greater, and which commences immediately after the end of the relevant period,

(ii) a lease, the duration of the relevant period in respect of which exceeds 10 years and which apart from this subparagraph would be a relevant lease, shall not be a relevant lease if it is a lease of an asset, being an asset—

(I) provided for the purposes of a project, specified in the list referred to in section 133(8)(*c*)(iv), which has been approved for grant aid by the Industrial Development Authority, the Shannon Free Airport Development Company Limited or Údarás na Gaeltachta, and

(II) to which section 283(5) or 285(7)(*a*)(i) applies,

and it would not be a relevant lease if for clauses (I) and (II) of subparagraph (i) there were substituted the following:

"(I) the aggregate of the relevant lease payments related to a chargeable period or its basis period of the lessor which falls wholly or partly in the period (in this subsection referred to as 'the first period') of 3 years beginning at the inception of the lease is not less than an amount determined by the formula—

$$V \times \frac{D}{100} \times \frac{80}{100} \times \frac{M}{12}$$

where—

D is the rate per cent at the inception of the lease of the rate known as the [the rate known as the 6 month European Interbank Offered Rate],[2] expressed as a rate per annum,

M is the number of months in the chargeable period or its basis period, and

V is the fair value of the asset at the inception of the lease,

(II) as respects any chargeable period or its basis period of the lessor which falls wholly or partly in the period (in this subsection referred to as **'the second period'**) commencing immediately after the first period and ending at the end of the relevant period, the aggregate of the amounts of relevant lease payments related to the chargeable period or its basis period and the amounts of relevant lease payments related to any earlier chargeable period or its basis period falling wholly or partly in the second period is not less than an amount determined by the formula—

$$\frac{E}{R} \times P$$

where—

E is the length of the part of the second period which has expired at the end of the chargeable period or its basis period,

P is the aggregate of the amounts of relevant lease payments payable by the lessee in relation to the leased asset in the second period, and

R is the length of the second period, and

(III) except for an amount of relevant lease payments which is inconsequential, the excess of the total relevant lease payments under the lease over the aggregate of the relevant lease payments in the relevant period is payable to the lessor, or would be so payable if the relevant lease payments were the actual amounts payable under the lease, within a period of one year after the end of the relevant period.",

(iii) an amount of relevant lease payments shall be treated as inconsequential if the aggregate of amounts, estimated at the inception of the lease, of discounted value, at the end of the period specified in clause (II) of subparagraph (i) or clause (III) of that subparagraph (construed in accordance with subparagraph (ii)), as the case may be, of the relevant lease payments after that time does not exceed 5 per cent of the fair value of the leased asset or [€2,540][3], whichever is the lesser, and, for the purposes of this subparagraph, relevant lease payments shall be discounted at the rate specified in the definition of **"relevant period"**, and

(iv) where a chargeable period or its basis period, being an accounting period of a company, begins before and ends after a date, being the commencement of the relevant period, the first period or the second period or the end of such a period, as the case may be, it shall be divided into one part beginning on the day on which the accounting period begins and ending at the beginning or the end, as the case may be, of the relevant period, the first period or the second period, and another part beginning immediately after that time and ending on the day on which the accounting period ends, and both parts shall be treated as if they were separate accounting periods.

(2) (*a*) Where in the course of a trade an asset is provided by a person for leasing under a relevant lease, the letting of the asset under that relevant lease shall be treated as a separate trade of leasing (in this subsection referred to as a **"specified leasing trade"**) distinct from all other activities, including other leasing activities, of the person, and section 403, apart from subsections (5) to (9) of that section, shall apply in relation to a specified leasing trade as it applies in relation to a trade of leasing within the meaning of that section.

(*b*) Sections 305(1)(*b*), 308(4) and 420(2) shall not apply in relation to capital allowances—

(i) in respect of expenditure incurred on the provision of an asset, or

(ii) on account of the wear and tear of an asset,

which is provided by a person for leasing under a relevant lease.

(3) Notwithstanding subsection (1)(*b*), a lease of an asset which consists of agricultural machinery or plant shall not be a relevant lease unless it would be such a lease if the amounts of relevant lease payments related to any chargeable period or its basis period were taken to be an amount equal to 50 per cent of the aggregate of the amounts of relevant lease payments related to that chargeable period or its basis period and the amounts of relevant lease payments related to a period equal in length to, and ending immediately before the commencement of, that period.

(4) (*a*) Where at any time after the 11th day of April, 1994, either of the following events occurs—

(i) the terms of a lease of an asset entered into before that day are altered, or

(ii) a lessor and a lessee agree to terminate a lease of an asset and, at or about that time, a further agreement to lease the asset is entered into by the lessor and the lessee or an agreement is entered into by the lessor and a person connected with the lessee, by the lessee and a person connected with the lessor or by a person connected with the lessor and a person connected with the lessee,

such that the aggregate of the amounts of the lease payments which are payable, or which would be payable if the relevant lease payments were the actual amounts payable under the lease, after any time exceeds the aggregate of the amounts of such relevant lease payments which would have been payable after that time if the events in subparagraph (i) or (ii) had not taken place, then, notwithstanding subsection (6)(*a*), unless it is shown that the change or the termination was effected for bona fide commercial reasons, the lease (including the terminated lease) shall be treated as if it were at all times a relevant lease, and relief given under Part 9, Chapter 1 or 2 of this Part, or section 396 or 420, which would not have been given if the lease was a relevant lease, shall be withdrawn.

(*b*) The withdrawal of an allowance or relief under paragraph (*a*) shall be made—

(i) for the chargeable period related to the event giving rise to the withdrawal of the relief, and

(ii) in accordance with paragraph (*c*),

and both—

(I) details of the event giving rise to the withdrawal of the allowance or relief, and

(II) the amount to be treated as income under paragraph (*c*),

shall be included in the return required to be made by the lessor under section 951 for that chargeable period.

(*c*) (i) Notwithstanding any other provision of the Tax Acts, where relief is to be withdrawn under paragraph (*a*) in respect of—

(I) any amount which was set off against income under section 305,

(II) the amount of any loss which was set off under section 307, 308, 396 or 420 against profits, or

(III) the amount of any loss which was treated by virtue of a claim under section 381 as reducing income,

and which would not have been so set off or treated if the lease were a relevant lease, such amount (in this subsection referred to as **"the relevant amount"**) as would not have been so set off or treated, increased in accordance with subparagraph (ii), shall be treated as income arising in the chargeable period specified in paragraph (*b*)(i).

(ii) The amount by which the relevant amount is to be increased under subparagraph (i) shall be an amount determined by the formula—

$$A \times \frac{R}{100} \times M$$

where—

A is the relevant amount,

M is the number of [days][4] in the period beginning on the date on which tax for the chargeable period in which the losses were treated as reducing income, or set off against profits, as the case may be, was due and payable and ending on the date on which tax for the chargeable period for which the withdrawal of relief is to be made is due and payable, and

R [is 0.0273.][5]

(5) Notwithstanding subsection (1)(*b*), where at any time on or after the 11th day of April, 1994, a person (in this subsection referred to as **"the lessor"**) acquires an asset from another person who before that date was the owner of the asset and at or about that

time the lessor or a person connected with the lessor leases the asset to the other person or a person connected with the other person, then, unless—

(*a*) the asset is new and unused, or

(*b*) the lease would not be a relevant lease if—

(i) for the first formula in subsection (1)(*b*)(i)(I) there were substituted "W x P", and

(ii) subsection (1)(*b*)(ii) had not been enacted,

the lease shall be a relevant lease for the purposes of this section.

(6) This section shall apply as on and from the 23rd day of December, 1993; but a lease of an asset shall not be a relevant lease if—

(*a*) a binding contract in writing for the letting of the asset was concluded before that day,

(*b*) [it is a lease of machinery or plant provided for leasing by a lessor to a lessee][6] in the course of relevant trading operations within the meaning of section 445 or 446, or

(*c*) subject to subsections (4) and (5)—

(i) the relevant period does not exceed 5 years,

(ii) the fair value of the asset does not exceed [€63,500][7] and, except where the assets are separate and distinct assets used independently of each other and the use of one is not an integral part of the use of the other, the fair value of an asset which is leased by a lessor to a lessee shall for the purposes of this subparagraph be treated as exceeding [€63,500][7] if the aggregate of the fair value of such an asset and the fair value of any other asset leased by the lessor to the lessee in the period of 12 months ending at the inception of the lease of such an asset exceeds [€63,500][7], and

(iii) the lease provides for lease payments to be made at annual or more frequent regular intervals throughout the period of the lease such that none of those payments, other than a payment which consists of the consideration for the disposal of the asset for an amount equal to its market value (being its market value if it were not subject to any lease) at the time of disposal, is significantly greater than any of the lease payments payable before it.

Amendments

1 Substituted by FA 1998 s 47 and Sch 2 para 6(*a*) from such date as the Minister for Finance may appoint by order; previously "a rate known as the Dublin Interbank Offered Rate and a record of which is kept by the Central Bank of Ireland".

2 Substituted by FA 1998 s 47 and Sch 2 para 6(*b*) from such date as the Minister for Finance may appoint by order; previously "the rate known as the 6 month Dublin Interbank Offered Rate and a record of which is maintained by the Central Bank of Ireland".

3 Substituted by FA 2001 s 240(1) and (2)(*c*) and Sch 5 Pt 1 for accounting periods ending on or after 1 January 2002; previously "£2,000".

4 Substituted by FA 2005 s 147 and Sch 6 para 1(*g*)(i) with effect from 3 February 2005; previously "months".

5 Substituted by FA 2005 s 147 and Sch 6 para 1(*g*)(ii) with effect from 3 February 2005; previously "is the rate per cent specified in section 1080(1).".

6 Substituted by FA 2003 s 39 with effect from 1 January 2003; previously "the leasing of the asset is carried on".

7 Substituted by FA 2001 s 240(1) and (2)(*l*)(iii) and Sch 5 Pt 1 as respects a lease entered into on or after 1 January 2002; previously "£50,000".

Amendments 1 and 2 came into operation from 1 January 1999 — Finance Act, 1998 (Section 47) (Commencement) Order, 1998, SI No 502 of 1998, refers.

Cross-references

Qualifying shipping trade, restriction on use of allowances, subs (1)(*b*)(I)–(II): s 407(5).

Definitions

lease: s 5(1); lessor: s 5(1); month: IA 1937 Sch; person: IA 1937 s 11(*c*); profits: s 4(1); tax: s 3(1); Tax Acts: s 1(2); trade: s 3(1); year: IA 1937 Sch.

Former enactments

FA 1994 s 30(1)–(5) and (7).

405 Restriction on use of capital allowances on holiday cottages

(1) [Subject to subsections (2) and (3)],[1] where on or after the 24th day of April, 1992, a person incurs capital expenditure on the acquisition or construction of a building or structure which is or is to be an industrial building or structure by virtue of being a holiday cottage within the meaning of section 268, and an allowance is to be made in respect of that expenditure under section 271 or 272—

[(*a*) sections 305(1)(*b*), 308(4) and 420(2) shall not apply as respects that allowance, and][2]

(*b*) neither section 381 nor section 396(2) shall apply as respects the whole or part (as the case may be) of any loss which would not have arisen but for the making of that allowance.

(2) This section shall not apply to expenditure incurred before the 6th day of April, 1993, on the acquisition or construction of a building or structure (in this subsection referred to as **"the holiday cottage"**) which is or is to be an industrial building or structure by virtue of being a holiday cottage within the meaning of section 268 if before the 24th day of April, 1992—

(*a*) a binding contract in writing for the construction of the holiday cottage was entered into, or

(*b*) (i) a binding contract in writing for the purchase or lease of land for the construction of the holiday cottage was entered into, and

(ii) an application for planning permission for the construction of the holiday cottage was received by a planning authority.

[(3) This section shall not apply to a building or structure which is in use as a holiday cottage and comprised in premises first registered on or after 6 April 2001 in a register of approved holiday cottages established by Bord Fáilte Éireann under Part Ill of the Tourist Traffic Act, 1939, where, prior to such premises becoming so registered—

(*a*) the building or structure was a qualifying premises within the meaning of section 353, by virtue of being in use for the purposes of the operation of a tourist accommodation facility specified in a list published under section 9 of the Tourist Traffic Act, 1957, and

(*b*) the provisions of section 355(4) did not apply to expenditure incurred on the acquisition, construction or refurbishment of that building or structure, by virtue of the provisions of section 355(5).][3]

Amendments

1 Substituted by FA 2001 s 62(1)(*a*)(i)(I) with effect from 6 April 2001; previously "Subject to subsection (2)".

2 Subs (1)(*a*) substituted by FA 2001 s 62(1)(*a*)(i)(II) with effect from 6 April 2001.

3 Subs (3) inserted by FA 2001 s 62(1)(*a*)(ii) with effect from 6 April 2001.

Revenue precedents

Issue: Is an application for outline planning permission regarded as an application for planning permission for the purposes of TCA 1997 s 405?

Decision: An application for outline planning permission satisfies the requirement of s 405(2)(*b*) (ii).

Issue: Do the ring-fence provisions in the section apply to the purchaser of a holiday cottage, in respect of which allowances have been claimed, where the original construction expenditure was incurred before the cut-off date?

Decision: No - the purchaser is claiming in respect of the residue of the original expenditure not in respect of the expenditure incurred on the purchase of the property.

Definitions

capital allowance: ss 2(1), 5(1); land: s 5(1), IA 1937 Sch; lease: s 5(1); person: IA 1937 s 11(*c*); writing: IA 1937 Sch.

Former enactments

FA 1992 s 25.

406 Restriction on use of capital allowances on fixtures and fittings for furnished residential accommodation

[Where a person incurs capital expenditure of the type to which subsection (7) of section 284 applies and an allowance is to be made in respect of that expenditure under that section, sections 305(1)(*b*), 308(4) and 420(2) shall not apply as respects that allowance.][1]

Amendments

1 Section 406 substituted by FA 2001 s 62(1)(*b*) with effect from 6 April 2001.

Former enactments

ITA 1967 s 241(11)(*b*); FA 1997 s 22.

407 Restriction on use of losses and capital allowances for qualifying shipping trade

(1) In this section—

"lessee", in relation to a ship provided for leasing, means the person to whom the ship is or is to be leased and includes the successors in title of a lessee;

"qualifying ship" means a seagoing vessel which—

(*a*) (i) is owned to the extent of not less than 51 per cent by a person or persons resident in the State, or

(ii) is the subject of a letting on charter without crew by a lessor not resident in the State,

(*b*) in the case of a vessel to which paragraph (*a*)(i) applies, is registered in the State under Part II of the Mercantile Marine Act, 1955, and, in the case of a vessel to which paragraph (*a*)(ii) applies, is a vessel in respect of which it can be shown that the requirements of the Merchant Shipping Acts, 1894 to 1993, have been complied with as if it had been a vessel registered under that Part, (*c*) is of not less than 100 tons gross tonnage, and

(*d*) is self-propelled,

but, notwithstanding anything in paragraph (*a*), (*b*), (*c*) or (*d*), does not include—

(i) a fishing vessel, other than a vessel normally used for the purposes of an activity mentioned in paragraph (*d*) of the definition of **"qualifying shipping activities"**,

(ii) a tug, other than a tug in respect of which a certificate has been given by the Minister for the Marine and Natural Resources certifying that in the opinion of the Minister the tug is capable of operating in seas outside the portion of the seas which are, for the purposes of the Maritime Jurisdiction Act, 1959 (as amended by the Maritime Jurisdiction (Amendment) Act, 1988), the territorial seas of the State,

(iii) a vessel (including a dredger) used primarily as a floating platform for working machinery or as a diving platform, and

(iv) any other vessel of a type not normally used for the purposes of qualifying shipping activities;

"qualifying shipping activities" means activities carried on by a company in the course of a trade and which consist of—

(*a*) the use of a qualifying ship for the purpose of carrying by sea passengers or cargo for reward,

(*b*) the provision on board the qualifying ship of services ancillary to that use of the qualifying ship,

(*c*) the granting of rights by virtue of which another person provides or will provide those services on board that qualifying ship,

(*d*) the subjecting of fish to a manufacturing process on board a qualifying ship,

(*e*) the letting on charter of a qualifying ship for use for those purposes where the operation of the ship and the crew of the ship remain under the direction and control of the company, or

(*f*) the use of a qualifying ship for the purposes of transporting supplies or personnel to, or providing services in respect of, a mobile or fixed rig, platform, vessel or installation of any kind at sea;

"qualifying shipping trade" means a trade, the income from which is within the charge to corporation tax, carried on in the relevant period, which consists solely of the carrying on of qualifying shipping activities or, in the case of a trade consisting partly of the carrying on of such activities and partly of the carrying on of other activities, that part of the trade consisting solely of the carrying on of qualifying shipping activities and which is treated by virtue of subsection (3) as a separate trade;

"relevant certificate" means a certificate issued with the consent of the Minister for Finance by the Minister for the Marine and Natural Resources in relation to the letting on charter of a ship certifying, on the basis of a business plan and any other information supplied by the lessee to the Minister for the Marine and Natural Resources, that that Minister is satisfied that the lease is in respect of a ship which—

(*a*) will result in an upgrading and enhancement of the lessee's fleet leading to improved efficiency and the maintenance of competitiveness, (*b*) (i) has the potential to create a reasonable level of additional sustainable employment and other socio-economic benefits in the State, or

(ii) will assist in maintaining or promoting the lessee's trade in the carrying on of a qualifying shipping activity and the maintenance of a reasonable level of sustainable employment and other socio-economic benefits in the State,

and

(*c*) will result in the leasing of a ship which complies with current environmental and safety standards;

"the relevant period" means the period from [1 January 1987 to [31 December 2006][1]];[2]

"specified capital allowances" means capital allowances in respect of—

(*a*) expenditure incurred by any person in the relevant period on the provision of a qualifying ship which is in use in or is intended to be used in a qualifying shipping trade, or

(*b*) the diminished value by reason of wear and tear during the relevant period of a qualifying ship in use for the purposes of a qualifying shipping trade,

notwithstanding that any such capital allowances are not treated as trading expenses of the qualifying shipping trade.

(2) Before issuing a relevant certificate, the Minister for the Marine and Natural Resources shall be satisfied that the lease concerned is for bona fide commercial purposes and not part of a scheme or arrangement the main purpose or one of the main purposes of which is the avoidance of tax.

(3) (*a*) Subject to paragraph (*b*), where during the relevant period a company carries on qualifying shipping activities as part of a trade, those activities shall be treated for the purposes of the Tax Acts, other than any provision of those Acts relating to the commencement or cessation of a trade, as a separate trade distinct from all other activities carried on by the company as part of the trade, and any necessary apportionment shall be made of receipts or expenses.

(*b*) This subsection shall not apply in relation to a claim by the company for the set-off under section 396(1)—

(i) against income arising during the relevant period, of a loss incurred before the commencement of the relevant period, and

(ii) against income arising after the end of the relevant period, of a loss incurred during the relevant period.

(4) Notwithstanding any other provision of the Tax Acts apart from subsection (5), for the purposes of granting relief from tax in respect of any income or profits arising in the relevant period or for the purposes of determining the amount of such income or profits which is chargeable to tax—

(*a*) specified capital allowances shall be allowed only—

(i) in computing the income from a qualifying shipping trade, or

(ii) in computing or charging to tax any income arising from the letting on charter of the qualifying ship to which the specified capital allowances refer, other than letting on charter which is a qualifying shipping activity,

and shall not be allowed in computing any other income or profits or in taxing any other trade or in charging any other income to tax,

(*b*) a loss incurred in the relevant period in a qualifying shipping trade shall not be set off—

(i) against any profits under section 396(2), except to the extent of the amount of income from a qualifying shipping trade included in those profits, or

(ii) against the total profits of a claimant company under section 420(1), except to the extent of the amount of income from a qualifying shipping trade included in those total profits,

and

(*c*) the letting on charter of a ship referred to in paragraph (*a*)(ii) in the course of a trade shall be deemed, notwithstanding subsection (1)(*c*) of section 403, to be a trade of leasing for the purposes of that section and to be a separate trade as provided for in subsection (2) of that section.

(5) As respects a ship a binding contract in writing for the acquisition or construction of which was concluded on or after the 1st day of July, 1996, subsection (4)(*c*) shall not apply in the case of a letting on charter of a ship referred to in that subsection where the lease in respect of the ship is a lease the terms of which comply with clauses (I) and (II) of section 404(1)(*b*)(i), and where the lessee produces to the Revenue Commissioners a relevant certificate.

(6) A qualifying shipping trade shall not be regarded as a specified trade for the purposes of section 403.

Amendments

1 Substituted by FA 2003 s 40 with effect from 1 January 2003; previously "31 December 2002".

2 Substituted by FA 2001 s 82(1)(*b*) with effect from 1 January 2001; previously "the 1st day of January, 1987, to the 31st day of December, 2000".

Cross-references

Charge to corporation tax at 12½ per cent, meaning of "qualifying shipping activities" and "qualifying shipping trade" applied: s 21(1A).

Corporation tax, manufacturing (10%) relief, subs (4)(*b*): s 448(1)(*b*).

Interest treated as a distribution, qualifying shipping trade not treated as a specified trade: ss 133(1)(*d*), 134(1)(*d*).

"Qualifying shipping activities" and "qualifying shipping trade", manufacturing (10%) rate, meanings applied: s 443(11)(*a*).

Restriction of loss relief, subs (4)(*b*): s 455(1).

Definitions

capital allowance: ss 2(1), 5(1); company: ss 4(1), 5(1); person: IA 1937 s 11(*c*); profits: s 4(1); Tax Acts: s 1(2); trade: s 3(1); within the charge to (tax): s 2(1);

Former enactments

FA 1987 s 28(1)–(2), (4)–(5)(*a*); FA 1988 s 40(1) and (3); FA 1990 s 42(1); FA 1994 s 62; FA 1996 s 54.

408 Restriction on tax incentives on property investment

(1) In this section—

"property investment scheme" means any scheme or arrangement made for the purpose, or having the effect, of providing facilities, whether promoted by means of public advertisement or otherwise, for the public or a section of the public to share, either directly or indirectly and whether as beneficiaries under a trust or by any other means, in income or gains arising or deriving from the acquisition, holding or disposal of, or of an interest in, a building or structure or a part of a building or structure, but does not include a scheme or arrangement as respects which the Revenue Commissioners or, on appeal, the Appeal Commissioners, having regard to such information as may be produced to them, are of the opinion that—

(*a*) the manner in which persons share in the income or gains, and

(*b*) the number of persons who so share,

are in accordance with a practice which commonly prevailed in the State during the period of 5 years ending immediately before the 30th day of January, 1991, for the sharing of such income or gains by persons resident in the State and such that the persons so sharing qualified for relief under section 305(1)(*b*) or 308(4);

"specified interest" means an interest in or deriving from a building or structure held by a person pursuant to a property investment scheme.

(2) Where a person holds a specified interest, then, as respects expenditure incurred or deemed to be incurred on or after the 30th day of January, 1991, sections 305(1)(*b*) and 308(4) shall not apply as respects an allowance under section 271 or 272 which is to be made to the person by reason of the holding by the person of the specified interest.

(3) The Appeal Commissioners shall hear and determine an appeal made to them under this section as if it were an appeal against an assessment to income tax, and the provisions of the Income Tax Acts relating to the rehearing of an appeal and to the statement of a case for the opinion of the High Court on a point of law shall apply accordingly with any necessary modifications.

Revenue Precedents

Issue: Two groups of investors propose to buy one floor each of a two storey building in an Enterprise Area. The building as a whole is to be let to the same tenant. The two groups have engaged separate tax agents. Does the number of persons referred to in Section 408(1) relate to the whole building or each floor?

Decision: The number 13 referred to in instruction 12.4.3 relates to the whole of a building and not to a particular floor of a building.

Definitions

Appeal Commissioners: s 2(1); High Court: IA 1937 Sch; person: IA 1937 s 11(*c*).

Former enactments

FA 1991 s 24.

409 Capital allowances: room ownership schemes

(1) In this section—

"hotel investment" means capital expenditure incurred either on the construction of, or the acquisition of a relevant interest in, a building or structure which is to be regarded as an industrial building or structure within the meaning of subsection (1)(*d*) of section 268, other than a building or structure to which subsection (3) of that section relates;

"hotel partnership" includes any syndicate, group or pool of persons, whether or not a partnership, through or by means of which a hotel investment is made;

"market value" shall be construed in accordance with section 548;

"member", in relation to a hotel partnership, includes every person who participates in that partnership or who has contributed capital, directly or indirectly, to that partnership;

"preferential terms", in relation to the acquisition of an interest referred to in subsection (3)(*a*)(i), means terms under which such interest is acquired for a consideration which, at the time of the acquisition, is or may be other than its market value.

(2) This section is for the purpose of counteracting any room ownership scheme entered into in connection with a hotel investment by a hotel partnership.

(3) For the purposes of this section—

(*a*) a scheme shall be a room ownership scheme in connection with a hotel investment if, at the time a hotel investment is made by a hotel partnership, there exists any agreement, arrangement, understanding, promise or undertaking (whether express or implied and whether or not enforceable or intended to be enforceable by legal proceedings) under or by virtue of which any member of that hotel partnership, or a person connected with such member, may—

(i) acquire on preferential terms an interest in, or

(ii) retain for use other than for the purposes of the trade of hotel-keeping,

any room or rooms in, or any particular part of, the building or structure which is the subject of the hotel investment, and

(*b*) where a hotel investment is made by one or more than one member of a hotel partnership, it shall be deemed to be made by the hotel partnership.

(4) Subject to subsection (5), no allowance shall be made under Chapter 1 of Part 9 in respect of a hotel investment by a hotel partnership where, in connection with any such investment, there exists a room ownership scheme.

(5) (*a*) Except where provided for in paragraph (*b*), this section shall apply to a hotel investment the capital expenditure in respect of which is incurred on or after the 26th day of March, 1997.

(*b*) This section shall not apply to a hotel investment if, before the 26th day of March, 1997, in respect of a building or structure which is the subject of such investment—

(i) a binding contract in writing was entered into for the construction of, or the acquisition of a relevant interest in, the building or structure, or

(ii) an application for planning permission for the construction of the building or structure was received by a planning authority.

Former enactments

FA 1997 s 24(1)–(3), (4)(*a*)–(*b*), (5).

409A Income tax: restriction on use of capital allowances on certain industrial buildings and other premises

[(1) In this section—

"active partner", in relation to a partnership trade, means a partner who works for the greater part of his or her time on the day-to-day management or conduct of the partnership trade;

"industrial development agency" means the Industrial Development Agency (Ireland);

"partnership trade" and **"several trade"** have the same meanings, respectively, as in Part 43;

"specified building" means—

(*a*) a building or structure which is or is to be an industrial building or structure by reason of its use or its deemed use for a purpose specified in section 268(1), and

(*b*) any other building or structure in respect of which an allowance is to be made, or will by virtue of section 279 be made, for the purposes of income tax under Chapter 1 of Part 9 by virtue of Part 10 or section 843 [or 843A],[1]

but does not include a building or structure—

(i) which is or is deemed to be an industrial building or structure by reason of its use for the purposes specified in section 268(1)(*d*), or

(ii) to which section 355(1)(*b*) applies.

[(2) Subject to subsection (5), in relation to any allowance to be made to an individual under Chapter 1 of Part 9 for any year of assessment in respect of capital expenditure incurred on or after 3 December 1997, on a specified building, section 305 shall apply as if the following were substituted for subsection (1)(*b*) of that section:

"(*b*) (i) Notwithstanding paragraph (*a*), where an allowance referred to in that paragraph is available primarily against income of the specified class and the amount of the allowance is greater than the amount of the person's income of that class for the first-mentioned year of assessment (after deducting or setting off any allowances for earlier years), then the person may, by notice in writing given to the inspector not later than 2 years after the end of the year of assessment, elect that the excess or [€31,750],[2] whichever is the lower, shall be deducted from or set off—

(I) against the individual's other income for that year of assessment, or

(II) where the individual, or, being a husband or wife, the individual's spouse, is assessed to tax in accordance with section 1017, firstly, against the individual's other income for that year of assessment and, subsequently, against the income of the individual's husband or wife, as the case may be, for that year of assessment.

(ii) Where an election is made in accordance with subparagraph (i), the excess or [€31,750],[2] whichever is the lower, shall be deducted from or set off against the income referred to in clause (I) or (II) of that subparagraph, as the case may be, and tax shall be discharged or repaid accordingly and only the balance, if any, of the amount of the allowance referred to in paragraph (*a*) over all the income referred to in the said clause (I) or (II), as the case may be, for that year of assessment shall be deducted from or set off against the person's income of the specified class for succeeding years.][3]

(3) Subject to subsection (5), where—

(*a*) any allowance or allowances under Chapter 1 of Part 9 is or are to be made for a year of assessment to an individual, being an individual who is a partner in a partnership trade, in respect of capital expenditure incurred on or after the 3rd day of December, 1997, on a specified building, and

(*b*) that allowance or those allowances is or are to be made in taxing the individual's several trade,

then, unless in the basis period for the year of assessment in respect of which that allowance or those allowances is or are to be made the individual is an active partner in relation to the partnership trade, the amount of any such allowance or allowances which is to be taken into account for the purposes of section 392(1) shall not exceed an amount determined by the formula—

A + [€31,750][4]

where A is the amount of the profits or gains of the individual's several trade in the year of loss before section 392(1) is applied.

(4) Where an individual is a partner in 2 or more partnership trades, then, for the purposes of subsection (3), those partnership trades in relation to which the individual is not an active partner shall, in relation to that individual, be deemed to be a single partnership trade and the individual's several trades in relation to those partnership trades shall be deemed to be a single several trade.

(5) This section shall not apply to an allowance to be made to an individual under Chapter 1 of Part 9 in respect of capital expenditure incurred on or after the 3rd day of December, 1997, on a specified building where before that date—

(*a*) (i) in the case of construction, the foundation for the specified building was laid in its entirety,

(ii) in the case of a refurbishment project, work to the value of 5 per cent of the total cost of that refurbishment project was carried out, or

(iii) a project for which the specified building is to be provided had been approved for grant assistance by an industrial development agency but only where that approval was given within a period of 2 years preceding that date,

or

(*b*) (i) an application for planning permission for the work represented by that expenditure on the specified building had (in so far as such permission is required) been received by a planning authority before the 3rd day of December, 1997, or

(ii) the individual can prove, to the satisfaction of the Revenue Commissioners, that a detailed plan had been prepared for the work represented by that expenditure and that detailed discussions had taken place with a planning authority in relation to the specified building before the 3rd day of December, 1997, and that this can be supported by means of an affidavit or statutory declaration duly made on behalf of the planning authority concerned,

and that expenditure is incurred under an obligation entered into by the individual in relation to the specified building before—

(i) the 3rd day of December, 1997, or

(ii) [the 1st day of May, 1998, pursuant to negotiations which were in progress before the 3rd day of December, 1997.][5]

(6) For the purposes of subsection (5)—

(*a*) an obligation shall be treated as having been entered into before a particular date only if, before that date, there was in existence a binding contract in writing under which that obligation arose, and

(*b*) negotiations pursuant to which an obligation was entered into shall not be regarded as having been in progress before a particular date unless preliminary commitments or agreements in writing in relation to that obligation had been entered into before that date.

(7) Where an individual has entered into an obligation to which subsection (5) relates to incur capital expenditure on a specified building on or after the 3rd day of December, 1997, and that individual dies before any part of that expenditure has been incurred, another individual who—

(*a*) undertakes in writing to honour the obligation entered into by the deceased individual, and

(*b*) incurs that part of the capital expenditure on the specified building which would otherwise have been incurred by the deceased individual,

shall be deemed to have complied with the requirements of subsection (5) in relation to that expenditure.

(8) This section shall, with any necessary modifications, apply in relation to a profession as it applies in relation to a trade.][6]

Amendments

1 Inserted by FA 1999 s 49(*a*) with effect from 6 April 1999.

2 Substituted by FA 2001 s 62(1)(*c*)(i)(II) as respects an allowance to be made for 2002 and later tax years; previously "£18,500".

3 Subs (2) substituted by FA 2001 s 62(1)(*c*)(i)(I) as respects an allowance to be made for the short tax "year" 2001 and later tax years.

4 Substituted by FA 2001 s 62(1)(*c*)(ii)(II) as respects an allowance to be made for 2002 and later tax years; previously "£25,000" (short tax "year" 2001: £18,500 (FA 2001 s 62(1)(*c*)(ii)(I)).

5 This wording was due to be substituted by Urban Renewal Act 1998 s 20(1)(*c*) with effect from such date as the Minister for Finance may appoint by order — Urban Renewal Act, 1998 s 2(5), as substituted by FA

1999 s 42, refers. No such order was made and Urban Renewal Act s 20(1)(*c*) was repealed by FA 2000 s 38 with effect from 6 April 2000.

[6] Section 409A inserted by FA 1998 s 30 with effect from 6 April 1998.

Cross-references

References to profits or gains (subs (3)) in the Income Tax Acts do not include chargeable gains within meaning of Capital Gains Tax Acts: s 3(4).

Restriction on use by certain partnerships of certain losses, etc, transitional arrangements: s 1017(2C)(*a*) ("excepted expenditure").

Restriction on use of capital allowances on certain hotels, meaning of "active partner" applied: s 409B(1).

Tax Briefing

TB31 Apr 1998 p 17 — Clarification and guidance on transitional arrangements provided for under subsection (5).

Definitions

affidavit: IA 1937 Sch; inspector: s 2(1); person: IA 1937 s 11(*c*); writing: IA 1937 Sch; year of assessment: s 2(1).

409B Income tax: restriction on use of capital allowances on certain hotels, etc

[(1) In this section—

"active partner", in relation to a partnership trade, has the same meaning as in section 409A;

"partnership trade" and **"several trade"** have the same meanings, respectively, as in Part 43;

"specified building" means a building or structure which is or is deemed to be an industrial building or structure by reason of its use for a purpose specified in section 268(1)(*d*) but does not include—

(*a*) any such building or structure (not being a building or structure in use as a holiday camp referred to in section 268(3))—

(i) the site of which is wholly within any of the administrative counties of Cavan, Donegal, Leitrim, Mayo, Monaghan, Roscommon and Sligo but not within a qualifying resort area within the meaning of Chapter 4 of Part 10, and

(ii) in which the accommodation and other facilities provided meet a standard specified in guidelines issued by the Minister for Tourism, Sport and Recreation with the consent of the Minister for Finance,

and

(*b*) a building or structure which is deemed to be such a building or structure by reason of its use as a holiday cottage of the type referred to in section 268(3).

(2) Subject to subsection (4), section 305(1)(*b*) shall not apply in relation to any allowance to be made to an individual for a year of assessment under Chapter 1 of Part 9 in respect of capital expenditure incurred on or after the 3rd day of December, 1997, on a specified building.

(3) Subject to subsection (4), where—

(*a*) any allowance or allowances under Chapter 1 of Part 9 is or are to be made for a year of assessment to an individual, being an individual who is a partner in a partnership trade, in respect of capital expenditure incurred on or after the 3rd day of December, 1997, on a specified building, and

(*b*) that allowance or those allowances is or are to be made in taxing the individual's several trade,

then, unless in the basis period for the year of assessment in respect of which that allowance or those allowances is or are to be made the individual is an active partner in relation to the partnership trade, the amount of any such allowance or allowances which is to be taken into account for the purposes of section 392(1) shall not exceed the amount of the profits or gains of the individual's several trade in the year of loss before that section is applied.

(4) This section shall not apply to an allowance to be made to an individual under Chapter 1 of Part 9 in respect of capital expenditure incurred on or after the 3rd day of December, 1997, on a specified building where before that date—

(*a*) (i) in the case of construction, the foundation for the specified building was laid in its entirety, or

(ii) in the case of a refurbishment project, work to the value of 5 per cent of the total cost of that refurbishment project was carried out,

or

(*b*) (i) an application for planning permission for the work represented by that expenditure on the specified building had (in so far as such permission is required) been received by a planning authority before the 3rd day of December, 1997, or

(ii) the individual can prove, to the satisfaction of the Revenue Commissioners, that a detailed plan had been prepared for the work represented by that expenditure and that detailed discussions had taken place with a planning authority in relation to the specified building before the 3rd day of December, 1997, and that this can be supported by means of an affidavit or statutory declaration duly made on behalf of the planning authority concerned,

and that expenditure is incurred under an obligation entered into by the individual in relation to the specified building before—

(i) the 3rd day of December, 1997, or

(ii) the 1st day of May, 1998, pursuant to negotiations which were in progress before the 3rd day of December, 1997.

(5) For the purposes of subsection (4)—

(*a*) an obligation shall be treated as having been entered into before a particular date only if, before that date, there was in existence a binding contract in writing under which that obligation arose, and

(*b*) negotiations pursuant to which an obligation was entered into shall not be regarded as having been in progress before a particular date unless preliminary commitments or agreements in writing in relation to that obligation had been entered into before that date.

(6) Where an individual has entered into an obligation to which subsection (4) relates to incur capital expenditure on a specified building on or after the 3rd day of December, 1997, and that individual dies before any part of that expenditure has been incurred, another individual who—

(*a*) undertakes in writing to honour the obligation entered into by the deceased individual, and

(*b*) incurs that part of the capital expenditure on the specified building which would otherwise have been incurred by the deceased individual,

shall be deemed to have complied with the requirements of subsection (4) in relation to that expenditure.

(7) This section shall, with any necessary modifications, apply in relation to a profession as it applies in relation to a trade.][1]

Amendments

1 Section 409B inserted by FA 1998 s 30 with effect from 6 April 1998.

Cross-references

References to profits or gains (subs (3)) in the Income Tax Acts do not include chargeable gains within meaning of Capital Gains Tax Acts: s 3(4).

Restriction on use by certain partnerships of certain allowances, etc: s 1017(2C)(*a*) ("excepted expenditure").

Tax Briefing

TB31 Apr 1998 p 17 — Clarification and guidance on transitional arrangements provided for under subsection (4).

Definitions

affidavit: IA 1937 Sch; person: IA 1937 s 11(*c*); writing: IA 1937 Sch; year of assessment: s 2(1).

409C Income tax: restriction on use of losses on approved buildings

[(1) In this section—

"approved building", **"the Minister"** and **"qualifying expenditure"** have, respectively, the meaning assigned to each of them by section 482(1)*(a)*;

"the claimant" has the meaning assigned to it by section 482(2)*(a)*;

"eligible charity" has the meaning assigned to it by paragraph 1 of Part 3 of Schedule 26A;

"ownership interest", in relation to a building, means an estate or interest in a building which would entitle the person who holds it, to make a claim under section 482 as owner of the building;

"relevant determinations", in relation to a building, means the determinations made by the Minister and the Revenue Commissioners, respectively, in accordance with section 482(5)*(a)*.

(2) For purposes of this section, a scheme shall be a passive investment scheme, in relation to a building, in any case where—

(*a*) an ownership interest, in relation to the building, is transferred by one person (in this section referred to as the "transferor") to another person (in this section referred to as the "transferee"),

(*b*) at the time of the transfer, or at any time in the period of 5 years commencing at that time, the building is an approved building, and (*c*) (i) at the time of the transfer, arrangements subsist (whether express or implied and whether or not enforceable by legal proceedings) under or by virtue of which the transferor, or any person connected with the transferor (within the meaning of section 10)—

(I) may retain the right to determine how any qualifying expenditure in relation to the building is to be incurred,

(II) may obtain, whether directly or indirectly, a payment or other benefit representing any part of the value to the transferee of relief under the Tax Acts by virtue of a claim under section 482(2) in respect of qualifying expenditure in relation to the building, or

(III) may re-acquire the transferee's ownership interest (referred to in paragraph *(a)*),

or

(ii) the transfer is made for the sole or main purpose of facilitating a claim by the transferee under section 482(2).

(3) This section applies where—

(*a*) by virtue of subsection (2) of section 482, qualifying expenditure in relation to an approved building is treated as a loss sustained in a trade carried on by a claimant, as owner of the building, in a chargeable period (referred to in paragraph (*b*)(i) of that subsection),

(*b*) the claimant is an individual who is a transferee [under a passive investment scheme],[1] and

(*c*) relief is claimed under section 381 in respect of the loss referred to in paragraph *(a)*.

(4) Where this section applies, the amount of the loss referred to in subsection (3)*(a)* which can be treated as reducing income for a year of assessment under section 381(1) shall be—

(*a*) the full amount of the loss, or

(*b*) €31,750,

whichever is the lesser.

(5) Where by virtue of subsection (4) relief cannot be given for a year of assessment for part of the loss referred to in subsection (3)*(a)*, then for the purposes of section 482(3) such relief shall be treated as not being given owing to an insufficiency of income.

(6) This section shall not apply—

(*a*) to qualifying expenditure, in relation to an approved building, incurred before 5 December 2001,

(*b*) to qualifying expenditure, in relation to an approved building, incurred on or after 5 December 2001 and before 31 December 2003, where the relevant determinations have been made in relation to that building before 5 December 2001, (*c*) to qualifying expenditure, incurred before 31 December 2003, in relation to a building, in respect of which—

(i) the Revenue Commissioners have, before 5 December 2001, indicated in writing, that proposals made to them are broadly acceptable, so as to enable them to make a determination under section 482(5)*(a)*, and

(ii) an officer of the Department of Arts, Heritage, Gaeltacht and the Islands has, before 5 December 2001, indicated in writing that, having inspected the building, the officer is satisfied that, if required, the officer would recommend to the Minister that a determination under section 482(5)*(a)* be made by the Minister, or

(*d*) to qualifying expenditure, incurred before 31 December 2003, in relation to a building where—

(i) the Minister has made a determination under section 482(5)*(a)* before 5 December 2001, in relation to the building, and

(ii) the claimant has undertaken to gift, whether directly or indirectly, to the transferor, who is an eligible charity, the full value of the relief to which the individual is entitled under the Tax Acts by virtue of making a claim under section 482(2), and the individual does so.][2]

Amendments

[1] Inserted by FA 2003 s 163 and Sch 6 para 1(*a*) with effect from 1 January 2002.

[2] Section 409C inserted by FA 2002 s 14 with effect from 1 January 2002.

Tax Briefing

TB47 April 2002 pp 10–11 — Restriction on use of losses on approved buildings.

Definitions

person: IA 1937 s 11(*c*); Tax Acts: s 1(2); trade: s 3(1); writing: IA 1937 Sch; year of assessment: s 2(1).

409D Restriction of reliefs where individual is not actively participating in certain trades

[(1) In this section—

"active trader", in relation to a trade, means an individual who works for the greater part of his or her time on the day-to-day management or conduct of the trade;

"electronic" includes electrical, digital, magnetic, optical, electromagnetic, biometric, photonic and any other form of related technology;

"specified provisions" means sections 305 and 381;

"specified trade" means a trade consisting of or including—

(*a*) the generation of electricity,

(*b*) trading operations which are petroleum activities (within the meaning of section 21A),

(*c*) the development or production of—

(i) films,

(ii) film projects,

(iii) film properties, or

(iv) music properties,

(*d*) the acquisition of rights to participate in the revenues of—

(i) film properties, or

(ii) music properties,

or

(*e*) the production of, the distribution of, or the holding of an interest in—

(i) either or both a film negative and its associated soundtrack, a film tape or a film disc,

(ii) an audio tape or audio disc, or

(iii) a film property produced by electronic means or a music property produced by electronic means;

"relevant year of assessment" means—

(*a*) in relation to a trade consisting of or including the generation of electricity, the year of assessment 2002 or any subsequent year during which the individual carried on such trade otherwise than as an active trader, and

(*b*) in relation to any other specified trade, the year of assessment 2003 or any subsequent year during which the individual carried on that trade otherwise than as an active trader.

(2) Where, in the case of an individual who carries on a specified trade otherwise than as an active trader, an amount may apart from this section be given or allowed under any of the specified provisions—

(*a*) in respect of a loss sustained by the individual in the specified trade in a relevant year of assessment, including a loss which is computed taking account of interest laid out or expended by the individual in respect of a loan where the proceeds of the loan were used to incur expenditure on machinery or plant used for the purposes of the specified trade concerned, or

(*b*) as an allowance to be made to the individual for a relevant year of assessment either in taxing the specified trade or by means of discharge or repayment of tax to which he or she is entitled by reason of the individual carrying on the specified trade concerned,

then, notwithstanding any other provision of the Tax Acts, such an amount may be given or allowed only against income from the specified trade concerned and shall not be allowed in computing any other income or profits or in taxing any other trade or in charging any other income to tax.][1]

Amendments

1 Section 409D inserted by FA 2003 s 12(1) as respects an allowance under TCA 1997 Part 9 in respect of machinery or plant to be made for 2002 or later tax year in relation to a trade consisting of or including the generation of electricity, and for 2003 or later tax year in relation to any other trade, and any loss sustained in a trade consisting of or including the generation of electricity in 2002 or later tax year, and any other trade in 2003 or later tax year.

Definitions

tax: s 3(1), Tax Acts: s 1(2); trade: s 3(1); year of assessment: s 2(1).

409E Income tax: ring-fence on use of certain capital allowances on certain industrial buildings and other premises

[(1) In this section—

"company" has the same meaning as in section 4;

"rent" has the same meaning as in Chapter 8 of Part 4;

"relevant interest" has the same meaning as in section 269;

"residue of expenditure" shall be construed in accordance with section 277;

"specified amount of rent", in relation to a specified building and an individual for a year of assessment, means the amount of the surplus in respect of the rent from the specified building to which the individual becomes entitled for the year of assessment, as computed in accordance with section 97(1);

"specified building" means—

(*a*) a building or structure, or a part of a building or structure, which is or is to be an industrial building or structure by reason of its use or deemed use for a purpose specified in section 268(1) and in relation to which an allowance has been, or is to be, made to a company under Chapter 1 of Part 9, or

(*b*) any other building or structure, or a part of any other building or structure, in relation to which an allowance has been, or is to be, so made to a company by virtue of Part 10 or section 843 or 843A,

in respect of

(i) the capital expenditure incurred or deemed to be incurred on the construction or refurbishment of the building or structure or, as the case may be, the part of the building or structure, or

(ii) the residue of that expenditure.

(2) This section applies where—

(*a*) at any time beginning on or after 1 January 2003 a company is entitled to the relevant interest in relation to any capital expenditure incurred or deemed to be incurred on the construction or refurbishment of a specified building,

(*b*) subsequent to the time referred to in paragraph (*a*) an individual becomes entitled to that relevant interest or any part of that relevant interest, whether or not subsequent to that time any other person or persons had previously become so entitled, and

(*c*) the individual is entitled, in charging income under Case V of Schedule D, to an allowance under Chapter 1 of Part 9 in respect of the capital expenditure referred to in paragraph (*a*) or the residue of that expenditure.

(3) Where this section applies, then, notwithstanding any other provision of the Income Tax Acts—

(*a*) any allowance to be made to the individual for any year of assessment (being the year of assessment 2003 or any subsequent year of assessment) under Chapter 1 of Part 9, in respect of the capital expenditure referred to in subsection (2)(*a*) or the residue of that expenditure, shall—

(i) not exceed the specified amount of rent for that year of assessment,

(ii) be made in charging the specified amount of rent under Case V of Schedule D for that year of assessment, and

(iii) be available only in charging the specified amount of rent, (*b*) section 278 shall apply with any modifications necessary to give effect to paragraph (*a*), and

(*c*) section 305(1)(*c*) shall apply in relation to an allowance to be made in accordance with paragraph (*a*).][1]

Amendments

1 Section 409E inserted by FA 2003 s 13(1).

Cross-references

Income tax, manner of granting, and effect of, allowances made in chargeing income under Case V of Schedule D, subs (3): s 305(1)(*c*); meaning of "specified amount of rent", "specified building" and "residue of expenditure" applied: s 305(1)(*c*).

Definitions

Income Tax Acts: s 1(2); year of assessment: s 2(1).

CHAPTER 5
Group Relief

Cross-references

Bank levy credit, ss 412–418 applied: s 487(1)(*b*)(ii).
Companies' chargeable gains, ss 413–419 applied: s 616(1)(*b*).
Company residence, ss 412 to 418 applied as if "50 per cent" substituted for "75 per cent" in each place it occurs and as if subpara (iii) of s 411(1)(*c*) were deleted: s 23A(1)(*b*)(i)(III).
Corporation tax — late returns, restriction of relief: s 1085(2)(*c*), (*ca*), (*cb*).
Distributions to certain non-residents, ss 412–418 applied as if s 411(1)(*c*) were deleted: s 153(3); and as if section 411(1)(*c*) were deleted and a revised subsection were substituted for subsection (1) of section 412: s 153(3A)(*b*).
Dividends regarded as paid out of profits accumulated before given date: Sch 22 para 5(3)(*b*).
Dividend withholding tax, exemption for certain non-resident persons, ss 412–418 applied as if s 411(1)(*c*) were deleted: s 172D(5); and as if s 411(1)(*c*) were deleted and a revised subsection were substituted for subsection (1) of section 412: s 172D(6)(*b*).
Double tax relief, ss 413–415 and 418 (without regard to s 411(1)(*c*)) applied: s 450(1)(*c*).
Exemption from tax in the case of gains on certain disposals of shares: s 626B(1)(*b*)(i)(B).
Manufacturing (10%) rate, ss 412–417 applied by: s 443(1)(*c*).
Particulars to be supplied by new companies, ss 412–418 apply as if s 411(1)(*c*) were deleted: s 882(5)(*a*).
Patent income distributions, ss 412–418 applied: s 141(5)(*b*)(iii).
Schemes to avoid liability to tax under Sch F, ss 413–415 and 418 apply as if s 411(1)(*c*) were deleted: s 817(1)(*c*).
Securitisation of assets: s 110(3)(*a*).
Subsidiaries, 90 per cent, 75 per cent, 51 per cent, meaning of: s 9.
Tax relief for branch profits, ss 412–418 apply as if s 411(1)(*c*) were deleted: s 847(1)(*b*)(ii).

410 Group payments

(1) (*a*) In this section—

[**"EEA Agreement"** means the Agreement on the European Economic Area signed at Oporto on 2 May 1992, as adjusted by the Protocol signed at Brussels on 17 March 1993;

"EEA State" means a state which is a contracting party to the EEA Agreement;

"relevant Member State" means—

(i) a Member State of the European Communities, or

(ii) not being such a Member State, an EEA State which is a territory with the government of which arrangements having the force of law by virtue of [section 826(1)(*a*)][1] have been made;][2]

[**"tax"**, in relation to a [relevant Member State][3] other than the State, means any tax imposed in the Member State which corresponds to corporation tax in the State;][4]

"trading or holding company" means a trading company or a company whose business consists wholly or mainly in the holding of shares or securities of trading companies which are its 90 per cent subsidiaries;

"trading company" means a company whose business consists wholly or mainly of the carrying on of a trade or trades.

[(*b*) For the purposes of this section—

(i) a company shall be owned by a consortium if 75 per cent or more of the ordinary share capital of the company is beneficially owned between them by 5 or fewer companies resident in one or more than one [relevant Member State][5] of which none of these companies beneficially owns less than 5 per cent of that capital, and those companies shall be called the members of the consortium, and

[(ii) references to a company resident in a relevant Member State shall be construed as references to a company which, by virtue of the law of a relevant Member State, is resident for the purposes of tax in such a relevant Member State.][6]][7]

(2) References in this section to payments received by a company shall apply to any payments received by another person on behalf of or in trust for the company, but shall not apply to any payments received by the company on behalf of or in trust for another person.

(3) In determining for the purposes of this section whether one company is a 51 per cent subsidiary of another company, that other company shall be treated as not being the owner of—

(*a*) any share capital which it owns directly or indirectly in a company not resident [in a [relevant Member State][8]],[9] or

(*b*) any share capital which it owns indirectly and which is owned directly by a company for which a profit on the sale of the shares would be a trading receipt.

(4) Where a company receives from another company (both being companies resident in [a relevant Member State][10]) any payments to which this section applies, and either—

(*a*) the company making the payment is—

(i) a 51 per cent subsidiary of the other company or of a company [resident in a [relevant Member State][11]][12] of which the other company is a 51 per cent subsidiary, or

(ii) a trading or holding company owned by a consortium the members of which include the company receiving the payment, or

(*b*) the company receiving the payment is a 51 per cent subsidiary of the company making the payment, then, subject to subsections (5) to (7), the payment shall be made without deduction of income tax and neither section 238 nor section 246 shall apply to the payment.

[(5) This section shall apply to any payments which—

(*a*) for the purposes of corporation tax, are charges on income of the company making them or would be so if they were not deductible in computing profits or any description of profits or if section 243(7) did not apply to them, and

(*b*) where the company receiving the payments is not resident in the State, are taken into account in computing income of that company chargeable to tax in a relevant Member State,

but shall not apply to payments received by a company on any investments if a profit on the sale of those investments would be treated as a trading receipt of that company.][13]

(6) Where a company purports by virtue of subsection (4) to make any payment without deduction of income tax and income tax ought to have been deducted, the inspector may make such assessments, adjustments or set-offs as may be required for securing that the resulting liabilities to tax (including interest on unpaid tax) of the company making and the company receiving the payment are, in so far as possible, the same as they would have been if the income tax had been duly deducted.

(7) Where tax assessed under subsection (6) on the company which made the payment is not paid by that company before the expiry of 3 months from the date on which that tax is payable, that tax shall, without prejudice to the right to recover it from that company, be recoverable from the company which received the payment.

Amendments

1 Substituted by FA 2004 s 89 and Sch 3 para 1(*j*) with effect from 25 March 2004; previously "section 826".

2 Definitions of "EEA Agreement", "EEA State" and "relevant Member State" inserted by FA 2002 s 37(*a*)(i)(I) with effect from 1 January 2002.

3 Substituted by FA 2002 s 37(*a*)(i)(II) with effect from 1 January 2002; previously "Member State of the European Communities".

4 Definition of "tax" inserted by FA 1999 s 78(1)(*a*)(i) for accounting periods ending on or after 1 July 1998.

5 Substituted by FA 2002 s 37(*a*)(ii)(I) with effect from 1 January 2002; previously "Member State of the European Communities".

6 Subs (1)(*b*)(ii) substituted by FA 2002 s 37(*a*)(ii)(II) with effect from 1 January 2002.

7 Subs (1)(*b*) substituted by FA 1999 s 78(1)(*a*)(ii) for accounting periods ending on or after 1 July 1998.

8 Substituted by FA 1999 s 78(1)(*a*)(iii) for accounting periods ending on or after 1 July 1998; previously "in the State".

9 Substituted by FA 2002 s 37(*a*)(iii) with effect from 1 January 2002; previously "Member State of the European Communities".

10 Substituted by FA 2005 s 52(1)(*a*) as respects accounting periods ending on or after 1 March 2005.

11 Substituted by FA 1999 s 78(1)(*a*)(iv) for accounting periods ending on or after 1 July 1998; previously "so resident".

12 Substituted by FA 2002 s 37(*a*)(iv) with effect from 1 January 2002; previously "Member State of the European Communities".

13 Subs (5) substituted by FA 2005 s 52(1)(*b*) as respects accounting periods ending on or after 1 March 2005.

Definitions

charges on income: ss 4(1), 243(1); company: ss 4(1), 5(1); inspector: ss 2(1), 5(1), 852; month: IA 1937 Sch; ordinary share capital: s 2(1); person: IA 1937 s 11(*c*); profits: s 4(1); trade: ss 3(1), 4(1), 5(1).

Former enactments

CTA 1976 s 105; FA 1992 s 50(1).

Corresponding UK tax provision

Income and Corporation Taxes Act 1988 s 247(4).

411 Surrender of relief between members of groups and consortia

(1) (*a*) For the purposes of this section and the following sections of this Chapter—

["**EEA Agreement**" means the Agreement on the European Economic Area signed at Oporto on 2 May 1992, as adjusted by the Protocol signed at Brussels on 17 March 1993;

"**EEA State**" means a state which is a contracting party to the EEA Agreement;][1]

"**holding company**" means a company whose business consists wholly or mainly in the holding of shares or securities of companies which are its 90 per cent subsidiaries and are trading companies;

["**relevant Member State**" means—

(i) a Member State of the European Communities, or

(ii) not being such a Member State, an EEA State which is a territory with the government of which arrangements having the force of law by virtue of [section 826(1)(*a*)][2] have been made.][3]

["**tax**", in relation to a [relevant Member State][4] other than the State, means any tax imposed in the Member State which corresponds to corporation tax in the State;][5]

"**trading company**" means a company whose business consists wholly or mainly of the carrying on of a trade or trades;

[a company shall be owned by a consortium if 75 per cent or more of the ordinary share capital][6] of the company is directly and beneficially owned between them by 5 or fewer companies, and those companies shall be called the members of the consortium;

2 companies shall be deemed to be members of a group of companies if one company is the 75 per cent subsidiary of the other company or both companies are 75 per cent subsidiaries of a third company.

(*b*) In applying for the purposes of this section and the following sections of this Chapter the definition of "**75 per cent subsidiary**" in section 9, any share capital of a registered industrial and provident society shall be treated as ordinary share capital.

(*c*) References in this section and in the following sections of this Chapter to a company shall apply only to [a company which, by virtue of the law of a [relevant Member State][7], is resident for the purposes of tax in such a Member State],[8] and in determining for the purposes of this section and the following sections of this Chapter whether one company is a 75 per cent subsidiary of another company, the other company shall be treated as not being the owner of—

(i) any share capital which it owns directly in a company if a profit on a sale of the shares would be treated as a trading receipt of its trade,

(ii) any share capital which it owns indirectly and which is owned directly by a company for which a profit on the sale of the shares would be a trading receipt, or

(iii) any share capital which it owns directly or indirectly in a [company, not being a company which, by virtue of the law of a [relevant Member State][7], is resident for the purposes of tax in such a Member State].[9]

(2) Relief for trading losses and other amounts eligible for relief from corporation tax may in accordance with this Chapter be surrendered by a company (called the **"surrendering company"**) which is a member of a group of companies and, on the making of a claim by another company (called the **"claimant company"**) which is a member of the same group, may be allowed to the claimant company by means of a relief from corporation tax called **"group relief"**.

(3) Group relief shall also be available in accordance with the following provisions of this Chapter—

(*a*) where the surrendering company is a trading company owned by a consortium and is not a 75 per cent subsidiary of any company, and the claimant company is a member of the consortium,

(*b*) where the surrendering company is a trading company which—

(i) is a 90 per cent subsidiary of a holding company owned by a consortium, and

(ii) is not a 75 per cent subsidiary of a company other than the holding company,

and the claimant company is a member of the consortium, or

(*c*) where the surrendering company is a holding company owned by a consortium and is not a 75 per cent subsidiary of any company, and the claimant company is a member of the consortium;

but no claim may be made by a member of a consortium if a profit on a sale of the share capital of the surrendering company or holding company which that member owns would be treated as a trading receipt of that member nor if the member's share in the consortium in the relevant accounting period of the surrendering company or holding company is nil.

(4) Subject to the following provisions of this Chapter, 2 or more claimant companies may make claims relating to the same surrendering company and to the same accounting period of that surrendering company.

(5) A payment for group relief shall not—

(*a*) be taken into account in computing profits or losses of either company for corporation tax purposes, and

(*b*) be regarded as a distribution or a charge on income for any of the purposes of the Corporation Tax Acts,

and, in this subsection, **"payment for group relief"** means a payment made by the claimant company to the surrendering company in pursuance of an agreement between them as respects an amount surrendered by means of group relief, being a payment not exceeding that amount.

Amendments

1 Definitions of "EEA Agreement" and "EEA State" inserted by FA 2002 s 37(*b*)(i)(I) with effect from 1 January 2002.

2 Substituted by FA 2004 s 89 and Sch 3 para 1(*k*) with effect from 25 March 2004; previously "section 826".

3 Definition of "relevant Member State" inserted by FA 2002 s 37(*b*)(i)(II) with effect from 1 January 2002.

4 Substituted by FA 2002 s 37(*b*)(i)(III) with effect from 1 January 2002; previously "Member State of the European Communities".

5 Definition of "tax" inserted by FA 1999 s 78(1)(*b*)(i) for accounting periods ending on or after 1 July 1998.

6 Substituted by FA 2000 s 79 with effect from 6 April 2000; previously "a company shall be owned by a consortium if all of the ordinary share capital".

7 Substituted by FA 2002 s 37(*b*)(ii) with effect from 1 January 2002; previously "Member State of the European Communities".

8 Substituted by FA 1999 s 78(1)(*b*)(ii)(I) for accounting periods ending on or after 1 July 1998; previously "companies resident in the State".

9 Substituted by FA 1999 s 78(1)(*b*)(ii)(II) for accounting periods ending on or after 1 July 1998; previously "company not resident in the State".

Cross-references

Company residence, subs (1)(*c*) treated as deleted: s 23A(1)(*b*)(i)(III).
Corporation tax — late returns, restriction of relief, meaning of "group relief" applied: s 1085(1)(*a*).
Distributions to certain non-resident persons, subs (1)(*c*) treated as deleted: s 153(3), (3A)(*b*)(i).
Dividend withholding tax, exemption for certain non-resident persons, subs (1)(*c*) treated as deleted: s 172D(5), (6)(*b*)(i).
Double tax relief, subs (1)(*c*) treated as deleted: s 450(1)(*c*).
Employee loan to acquire an interest in employing company, meaning of "holding company" applied: s 250(1).
Group, transfer of company to another, subss (2), (3)(*a*)–(*c*): s 424(3), (4).
Petroleum trade, group relief, meanings of "claimant company" and "surrendering company": s 688(1).
Restriction of relief for payments of interest, subs (2), meaning of "claimant company" and "surrendering company" applied: s 817A(2).
Schemes to avoid liability to tax under Sch F, subs (1)(*c*) treated as deleted: s 817(1)(*c*).
Tax credit for research and development expenditure subs (1)(*c*) treated as deleted: s 766(1)(*b*)(ii)(II).
Tax relief for branch profits, subs (1)(*c*): s 847(1)(*b*)(ii).

Case law

UK

Restriction of relief to UK companies held contrary to Community law: *IRC v Colmer* [1998] STC 874.

Definitions

company: ss 4(1), 5(1); Corporation Tax Acts: s 1(2); distribution: ss 4(1), 436, 437; ordinary share capital: s 2(1); profits: s 4(1); trade: ss 3(1), 4(1), 5(1).

Former enactments

CTA 1976 s 107.

Corresponding UK tax provision

Income and Corporation Taxes Act 1988 s 402.

412 Qualification for entitlement to group relief

(1) Notwithstanding that at any time a company (in this subsection referred to as **"the subsidiary company"**) is a 75 per cent subsidiary or a 90 per cent subsidiary, within the meaning of section 9, of another company (in this section referred to as **"the parent company"**), it shall not be treated at that time as such a subsidiary for the purposes of group relief unless additionally at that time—

(*a*) the parent company is beneficially entitled to not less than 75 per cent or, as the case may be, 90 per cent of any profits available for distribution to equity holders of the subsidiary company, and (*b*) the parent company would be beneficially entitled to not less than 75 per cent or, as the case may be, 90 per cent of any assets of the subsidiary company available for distribution to its equity holders on a winding up.

(2) Subject to subsection (3), for the purposes of group relief a member's share in a consortium, in relation to an accounting period of the surrendering company, shall be whichever is the lowest in that period of the following percentages—

(*a*) the percentage of the ordinary share capital of the surrendering company beneficially owned by that member,

(*b*) the percentage to which that member is beneficially entitled of any profits available for distribution to equity holders of the surrendering company, and

(*c*) the percentage to which that member would be beneficially entitled of any assets of the surrendering company available for distribution to its equity holders on a winding up,

and, if any of those percentages have fluctuated in that accounting period, the average percentage over the period shall be taken for the purposes of this subsection.

(3) In any case where the surrendering company is a subsidiary of a holding company owned by a consortium, for references in subsection (2) to the surrendering company there shall be substituted references to the holding company.

Cross-references

Bank levy credit, this section applied: s 487(1)(*b*)(ii).
Beneficial percentage, meaning: s 418.
Company residence, this section applied: s 23(1)(*b*)(i)(III).
Distributions to certain non-residents, this section applied: s 153(3), and this section applied with revised subsection (1): s 153(3A)(*b*).
Dividend withholding tax, exemption for certain non-resident persons, this section applied: s 172D(5), and this section applied with revised subsection (1): s 172D(6)(*b*).
Limited rights to profits or assets: s 416(4).
Loan treated as security: s 419(1).
Manufacturing (10%) rate, this section applied by: s 443(1)(*c*).
Notional winding up, meaning: s 415(1).
Patent income distributions, this section applied: s 141(5)(*b*).
Profit distribution, meaning: s 414(1).
Tax credit for research and development expenditure, this section applied (with modifications): s 766(1)(*b*)(ii).
Tax relief for branch profits, this section applied: s 847(1)(*b*)(iii).

Case law

Held a 75% parent company which granted an option to another shareholder to purchase 5% of its 75% shareholding remained a 75% parent: *Sainsbury plc v O'Connor* [1991] STC 318.

Definitions

company: ss 4(1), 5(1); distribution: ss 4(1), 436, 437; group relief: ss 4(1), 411; ordinary share capital: s 2(1); profits: s 4(1).

Former enactments

CTA 1976 s 108.

Corresponding UK tax provision

Income and Corporation Taxes Act 1988 s 413.

413 Profits or assets available for distribution

(1) In this Chapter, **"fixed-rate preference shares"** means shares which—

(*a*) are issued for consideration which is or includes new consideration, (*b*) do not carry any right either to conversion into shares or securities of any other description or to the acquisition of any additional shares or securities,

(*c*) do not carry any right to dividends other than dividends which—

(i) are of a fixed amount or at a fixed rate per cent of the nominal value of the shares, and

(ii) represent no more than a reasonable commercial return on the new consideration received by the company in respect of the issue of the shares,

and

(*d*) on repayment do not carry any rights to an amount exceeding that new consideration except in so far as those rights are reasonably comparable with those general for fixed dividend shares quoted on a stock exchange in the State.

(2) In this section, **"new consideration"** has the same meaning as in section 135.

(3) (*a*) In this subsection—

"normal commercial loan" means a loan of or including new consideration and—

(i) which does not carry any right either to conversion into shares or securities of any other description or to the acquisition of additional shares or securities,

(ii) which does not entitle the loan creditor to any amount by means of interest which depends to any extent on the results of the company's business or any part of it or on the value of any of the company's assets or which exceeds a reasonable commercial return on the new consideration loaned, and

(iii) in respect of which the loan creditor is entitled on repayment to an amount which either does not exceed the new consideration loaned or is reasonably comparable with the amount generally repayable (in respect of an equal amount of new consideration) under the terms of issue of securities quoted on a stock exchange in the State;

"ordinary shares" means all shares other than fixed-rate preference shares.

(*b*) For the purposes of this Chapter, an equity holder of a company shall be any person who—

(i) holds ordinary shares in the company, or

(ii) is a loan creditor of the company in respect of a loan which is not a normal commercial loan,

and any reference in this Chapter to profits or assets available for distribution to a company's equity holders shall not include a reference to any profits or assets available for distribution to any equity holder otherwise than as an equity holder.

(4) Subsection (6) of section 433 apart from paragraph (*b*) of that subsection shall apply for the purposes of subsection (3)(*b*)(ii) as it applies for the purposes of Part 13.

(5) Notwithstanding anything in subsections (1) to (4) but subject to subsection (6), where—

(*a*) any person has directly or indirectly provided new consideration for any shares or securities in the company, and

(*b*) that person or any person connected with that person uses for the purposes of such person's trade assets which belong to the company and in respect of which there is made to the company any of the allowances specified in Chapter 2 of Part 9 or section 670, 673, 674, 677, 680 or 765,

then, for the purposes of this Chapter, that person and no other person shall be treated as being an equity holder in respect of those shares or securities and as being beneficially entitled to any distribution of profits or assets attributable to those shares or securities.

(6) In any case where subsection (5) applies in relation to a bank in such circumstances that—

(*a*) the only new consideration provided by the bank as mentioned in subsection (5)(*a*) is provided in the normal course of its banking business by means of a normal commercial loan within the meaning of subsection (3), and

(*b*) the cost to the company concerned of the assets within subsection (5)(*b*) which are used as mentioned in that subsection by the bank or a person connected with the bank is less than the amount of that new consideration,

references in subsection (5), other than the reference in subsection (5)(*a*), to shares or securities in the company shall be construed as a reference to so much only of the loan referred to in paragraph (*a*) as is equal to the cost referred to in paragraph (*b*).

Cross-references

Bank levy credit, this section applied: s 487(1)(*b*)(ii).
Companies' chargeable gains, this section applied: s 616(1)(*b*).
Company residence, this section applied: s 23A(1)(*b*)(i)(III).
Distributions to certain non-resident persons, this section applied: s 153(3), (3A)(*b*).
Dividend withholding tax, exemption for certain non-resident persons, this section applied: s 172D(5), (6)(*b*).
Double tax relief, this section applied: s 450(1)(*c*).
Exemption from tax in the case of gains on certain disposals of shares, this section applied (with modifications): s 626B(1)(*b*)(i)(B).
Individuals qualifying for BES relief: s 493(6).
Loan treated as security: s 419(2).
Manufacturing (10%) rate, this section applied by: s 443(1)(*c*).
Particulars to be supplied by new companies: s 882(5)(*a*).
Patent income distribution, this section applied: s 141(5)(*b*)(iii).
Schemes to avoid liability to tax under Sch F, this section applied: s 817(1)(*c*).
Tax credit for research and development expenditure, this section applied (with modifications): s 766(1)(*b*)(ii).
Tax relief for branch profits, this section applied: s 847(1)(*b*)(ii).

Definitions

company: ss 4(1), 5(1); distribution: ss 4(1), 436, 437; group relief: ss 4(1), 411; interest: s 4(1); person: IA 1937 s 11(*c*); profits: s 4(1); trade: ss 3(1), 4(1), 5(1).

Former enactments

CTA 1976 s 109; FA 1977 s 42 and Sch 1 Pt IV para 1(*b*).

Corresponding UK tax provision

Income and Corporation Taxes Act 1988 Sch 18.

414 Meaning of "the profit distribution"

(1) Subject to the following provisions of this Chapter, for the purposes of section 412 the percentage to which one company is beneficially entitled of any profits available for distribution to the equity holders of another company means the percentage to which the first company would be so entitled in the relevant accounting period on a distribution in money to those equity holders of—

(*a*) an amount of profits equal to the total profits of the other company which arise in that accounting period (whether or not any of those profits are in fact distributed), or

(*b*) if there are no profits of the other company in that accounting period, profits of [€100][1],

and in the following provisions of this Chapter that distribution is referred to as **"the profit distribution"**.

(2) For the purposes of the profit distribution, it shall be assumed that no payment is made by means of repayment of share capital or of the principal secured by any loan unless that payment is a distribution.

(3) Subject to subsection (2), where an equity holder is entitled as such to a payment of any description which apart from this subsection would not be treated as a distribution, it shall nevertheless be treated as an amount to which the equity holder is entitled on the profit distribution.

Amendments

1 Substituted by FA 2001 s 240(1) and (2)(*c*) and Sch 5 Pt 1 for accounting periods ending on or after 1 January 2002; previously "£100".

Cross-references

Bank levy credit, this section applied: s 487(1)(*b*)(ii).
Beneficial percentage, meaning: s 418.
Companies' chargeable gains, this section applied: s 616(1)(*b*).
Company residence, this section applied: s 23A(1)(*b*)(i)(III).
Diminished share of profits or assets, subs (1): s 417(2)(*a*).
Distributions to certain non-resident persons, this section applied: s 153(3), (3A)(*b*).
Dividend withholding tax, exemption for certain non-resident persons, this section applied: s 172D(5), (6)(*b*).
Double tax relief, this section applied: s 450(1)(*c*).
Exemption from tax in the case of gains on certain disposals of shares, this section applied (with modifications): s 626B(1)(*b*)(i)(B).
Individuals qualifying for BES relief: s 493(6).
Limited rights to profits or assets, subs (1): s 416(2), (3).
Loan treated as security: s 419(2).
Manufacturing (10%) rate, this section applied: s 443(1)(*c*).
Patent income distributions, this section applied: s 141(5)(*b*)(iii).
Schemes to avoid liability to tax under Sch F, this section applied by: s 817(1)(*c*).
Tax credit for research and development expenditure, this section applied (with modifications): s 766(1)(*b*)(ii).
Tax relief for branch profits, this section applied: s 847(1)(*b*)(ii).

Definitions

company: ss 4(1), 5(1); distribution: ss 4(1), 436, 437; group relief: ss 4(1), 411; profits: s 4(1).

Former enactments

CTA 1976 s 110.

Corresponding UK tax provision

Income and Corporation Taxes Act 1988 Sch 18.

415 Meaning of "the notional winding up"

(1) Subject to the following provisions of this Chapter, for the purposes of section 412 the percentage to which one company would be beneficially entitled of any assets of another company available for distribution to its equity holders on a winding up means the percentage to which the first company would be so entitled if the other company were to be wound up and on that winding up the value of the assets available for distribution to its equity holders (after deducting any liabilities to other persons) were equal to—

(*a*) the excess, if any, of the total amount of the assets of the company, as shown in the balance sheet relating to its affairs as at the end of the relevant accounting period, over the total amount of those of its liabilities as so shown which are not liabilities to equity holders as such, or

(*b*) if there is no such excess or if the company's balance sheet is prepared to a date other than the end of the relevant accounting period, [€100][1].

(2) In the following provisions of this Chapter, a winding up on the basis specified in subsection (1) is referred to as **"the notional winding up"**.

(3) If on the notional winding up an equity holder would be entitled as such to an amount of assets of any description which apart from this subsection would not be treated as a distribution of assets, it shall nevertheless be treated, subject to subsection (4), as an amount to which the equity holder is entitled on the distribution of assets on the notional winding up.

(4) (*a*) In this subsection, **"new consideration"** has the same meaning as in section 135.

(*b*) Where an amount (in this subsection referred to as **"the returned amount"**), which corresponds to the whole or any part of the new consideration provided by a person who is an equity holder of a company for any shares or securities in respect of which such person is an equity holder, is applied by the company directly or indirectly in the making of a loan to, or in the acquisition of any shares or securities in, the equity holder or any person connected with the equity holder, then, for the purposes of this Chapter—

(i) the total amount of the assets referred to in subsection (1)(*a*) shall be taken to be reduced by a sum equal to the returned amount, and

(ii) the amount of assets to which the equity holder is beneficially entitled on the notional winding up shall be taken to be reduced by a sum equal to the returned amount.

Amendments

1 Substituted by FA 2001 s 240(1) and (2)(*c*) and Sch 5 Pt 1 for accounting periods ending on or after 1 January 2002; previously "£100".

Cross-references

Bank levy credit, this section applied: s 487(1)(*b*)(ii).
Beneficial percentage, meaning: s 418.
Companies' chargeable gains, this section applied: s 616(1)(*b*).
Company residence, this section applied: s 23A(1)(*b*)(i)(III).
Diminished share of profits or assets, subs (1): s 417(2)(*b*).
Distributions to certain non-resident persons, this section applied: s 153(3), (3A)(*b*).
Dividend withholding tax, exemption for certain non-resident persons, this section applied: s 172D(5), (6)(*b*).

Double tax relief, this section applied: s 450(1)(*c*).
Exemption from tax in the case of gains on certain disposals of shares, this section applied (with modifications): s 626B(1)(*b*)(i)(B).
Individuals qualifying for BES relief: s 493(6).
Limited rights to profits or assets, subs (1): s 416(2), (4).
Loan treated as security: s 419(2).
Manufacturing (10%) rate, this section applied: s 443(1)(*c*).
Patent income distributions, this section applied: s 141(5)(*b*)(iii).
Schemes to avoid liability to tax under Sch F, this section applied: s 817(1)(*c*).
Tax credit for research and development expenditure, this section applied (with modifications): s 766(1)(*b*)(ii).
Tax relief for branch profits, this section applied: s 847(1)(*b*)(ii).

Definitions

company: ss 4(1), 5(1); group relief: ss 4(1), 411; person: IA 1937 s 11(*c*).

Former enactments

CTA 1976 s 111.

Corresponding UK tax provision

Income and Corporation Taxes Act 1988 Sch 18.

416 Limited right to profits or assets

(1) This section shall apply if any of the equity holders—

(*a*) to whom the profit distribution is made, or

(*b*) who is entitled to participate in the notional winding up,

holds as such equity holder any shares or securities which carry rights in respect of dividend or interest or assets on a winding up which are wholly or partly limited by reference to a specified amount or amounts (whether the limitation takes the form of the capital by reference to which a distribution is calculated or operates by reference to an amount of profits or assets or otherwise).

(2) Where this section applies, there shall be determined—

(*a*) the percentage of profits to which on the profit distribution the first company referred to in section 414(1) would be entitled, and

(*b*) the percentage of assets to which on the notional winding up the first company referred to in section 415(1) would be entitled,

if, to the extent that they are limited as mentioned in subsection (1), the rights of every equity holder within that subsection (including the first company concerned if it is such an equity holder) had been waived.

(3) Where on the profit distribution the percentage of profits determined as mentioned in subsection (2)(*a*) is less than the percentage of profits determined under section 414(1) without regard to subsection (2)(*a*), the lesser percentage shall be taken for the purposes of section 412 to be the percentage of profits to which on the profit distribution the first company referred to in section 414(1) would be entitled as mentioned in that section.

(4) Where on the notional winding up the percentage of assets determined as mentioned in subsection (2)(*b*) is less than the percentage of assets determined under section 415(1) without regard to subsection (2)(*b*), the lesser percentage shall be taken for the purposes of section 412 to be the percentage to which on the notional winding up the first

company referred to in section 415(1) would be entitled of any assets of the other company available for distribution to its equity holders on a winding up.

Cross-references

Bank levy credit, this section applied: s 487(1)(*b*)(ii).
Beneficial percentage, meaning: s 418.
Companies' chargeable gains, this section applied: s 616(1)(*b*).
Company residence, this section applied: s 23A(1)(*b*)(i)(III).
Diminished share of profits or assets, subss (3), (4): s 417(4), (5).
Distributions to certain non-resident persons, this section applied: s 153(3), (3A)(*b*).
Dividend withholding tax, exemption for certain non-resident persons, this section applied: s 172D(5), (6)(*b*).
Exemption from tax in the case of gains on certain disposals of shares, this section applied (with modifications): s 626B(1)(*b*)(i)(B).
Loan treated as security: s 419(2).
Manufacturing (10%) rate, this section applied by: s 443(1)(*c*).
Patent income distributions, this section applied: s 141(5)(*b*)(iii).
Tax credit for research and development expenditure, this section applied (with modifications): s 766(1)(*b*)(ii).
Tax relief for branch profits, this section applied: s 847(1)(*b*)(ii).

Definitions

company: ss 4(1), 5(1); distribution: ss 4(1), 436, 437; group relief: ss 4(1), 411; interest: s 4(1); profits: s 4(1).

Former enactments

CTA 1976 s 112.

Corresponding UK tax provision

Income and Corporation Taxes Act 1988 Sch 18.

417 Diminished share of profits or assets

(1) This section shall apply if at any time in the relevant accounting period any of the equity holders—

(*a*) to whom the profit distribution is made, or

(*b*) who is entitled to participate in the notional winding up,

holds as such an equity holder any shares or securities which carry rights in respect of dividend or interest or assets on a winding up which are of such a nature (as, for example, if any shares will cease to carry a right to a dividend at a future time) that, if the profit distribution or the notional winding up were to take place in a different accounting period, the percentage to which, in accordance with the preceding provisions of this Chapter, that equity holder would be entitled of profits on the profit distribution or of assets on the notional winding up would be different from the percentage determined in the relevant accounting period.

(2) Where this section applies, there shall be determined—

(*a*) the percentage of profits to which on the profit distribution the first company referred to in section 414(1) would be entitled, and

(*b*) the percentage of assets to which on the notional winding up the first company referred to in section 415(1) would be entitled,

if the rights of the equity holders in the relevant accounting period were the same as they would be in the different accounting period referred to in subsection (1).

(3) Where in the relevant accounting period an equity holder holds as such any shares or securities in respect of which arrangements exist by virtue of which, in that or any

subsequent accounting period, the equity holder's entitlement to profits on the profit distribution or to assets on the notional winding up could be different as compared with the equity holder's entitlement if effect were not given to the arrangements, then, for the purposes of this section—

(*a*) it shall be assumed that effect would be given to those arrangements in a later accounting period, and

(*b*) those shares or securities shall be treated as though any variation in the equity holder's entitlement to profits or assets resulting from giving effect to the arrangements were the result of the operation of such rights attaching to the shares or securities as are referred to in subsection (1).

(4) Subsections (3) and (4) of section 416 shall apply for the purposes of this section as they apply for the purposes of that section, and accordingly references in those subsections to subsection (2)(*a*) and subsection (2)(*b*) of that section shall be construed respectively as references to subsection (2)(*a*) and subsection (2)(*b*) of this section.

(5) In any case where section 416 applies as well as this section, section 416 shall be applied separately (in relation to the profit distribution and the notional winding up)—

(*a*) on the basis specified in subsection (2), and

(*b*) without regard to that subsection,

and subsections (3) and (4) of section 416 shall apply accordingly in relation to the percentages so determined as if for **"lesser"** there were substituted **"lowest"**.

Cross-references

Bank levy credit, this section applied: s 487(1)(*b*)(ii).

Beneficial percentage, meaning: s 418.

Companies' chargeable gains, this section applied: s 616(1)(*b*).

Company residence, this section applied: s 23A(1)(*b*)(i)(III).

Distribution to certain non-resident persons, this section applied: s 153(3), (3A)(*b*).

Dividend withholding tax, exemption for certain non-resident persons, this section applied: s 172D(5), (6)(*b*).

Information as to arrangements for transferring relief, subs (3): s 427(1), (3)(*a*).

Exemption from tax in the case of gains on certain disposals of shares, this section applied (with modifications): s 626B(1)(*b*)(i)(B).

Loan treated as security: s 419(2).

Manufacturing (10%) rate, this section applied by: s 443(1)(*c*).

Patent income distributions, this section applied: s 141(5)(*b*)(iii).

Tax credit for research and development expenditure, this section applied (with modifications): s 766(1)(*b*)(ii).

Tax relief for branch profits, this section applied: s 847(1)(*b*)(ii).

Case law

An option to purchase 5% of shares granted by a 75% shareholder to another shareholder held not to be an arrangement affecting the rights attaching to the shares: *Sainsbury plc v O'Connor* [1991] STC 318.

Definitions

company: ss 4(1), 5(1); group relief: ss 4(1), 411; interest: s 4(1); profits: s 4(1).

Former enactments

CTA 1976 s 113.

Corresponding UK tax provision

Income and Corporation Taxes Act 1988 Sch 18.

418 Beneficial percentage

For the purposes of section 412 and sections 414 to 417—

(*a*) the percentage to which one company is beneficially entitled of any profits available for distribution to the equity holders of another company, and

(*b*) the percentage to which one company would be beneficially entitled of any assets of another company on a winding up,

means the percentage to which the first company is or would be so entitled either directly or through another company or other companies or partly directly and partly through another company or other companies.

Cross-references

Bank levy credit, this section applied: s 487(1)(*b*)(ii).
Companies' chargeable gains, this section applied: s 616(1)(*b*).
Company residence, this section applied: s 23A(1)(*b*)(III).
Distribution to certain non-resident persons, this section applied: s 153(3), (3A)(*b*).
Dividend withholding tax, exemption for certain non-resident persons, this section applied: s 172D(5), (6)(*b*).
Double tax relief, this section applied by: s 450(1)(*c*).
Exemption from tax in the case of gains on certain disposals of shares, this section applied (with modifications): s 626B(1)(*b*)(i)(B).
Loan treated as security: s 419(2).
Patent income distributions, this section applied: s 141(5)(*b*)(iii).
Schemes to avoid liability to tax under Sch F, this section applied: s 817(1)(*c*).
Tax credit for research and development expenditure, this section applied (with modifications): s 766(1)(*b*)(ii).
Tax relief for branch profits, this section applied: s 847(1)(*b*)(ii).

Definitions

company: ss 4(1), 5(1); group relief: ss 4(1), 411; profits: s 4(1).

Former enactments

CTA 1976 s 114.

Corresponding UK tax provision

Income and Corporation Taxes Act 1988 Sch 18.

419 The relevant accounting period, etc

(1) In this Chapter, **"the relevant accounting period"** means—

(*a*) in a case within section 412(1), the accounting period current at the time in question, and

(*b*) in a case within section 412(2), the accounting period in relation to which the share in the consortium is to be determined.

(2) For the purposes of sections 413 to 418, a loan to a company shall be treated as a security whether or not it is a secured loan and, if it is a secured loan, regardless of the nature of the security.

Cross-references

Companies' chargeable gains, this section applied: s 616(1)(*b*).
Exemption from tax in the case of gains on certain disposals of shares, this section applied (with modifications): s 626B(1)(*b*)(i)(B).

Definitions

company: ss 4(1), 5(1); group relief: ss 4(1), 403.

Former enactments

CTA 1976 s 115.

Corresponding UK tax provision

Income and Corporation Taxes Act 1988 Sch 18.

420 Losses, etc which may be surrendered by means of group relief

[(1) Where in any accounting period the surrendering company has incurred a loss, computed as for the purposes of section 396(2), in carrying on a trade in respect of which the company is within the charge to corporation tax, the amount of the loss may be set off for the purposes of corporation tax against the total profits of the claimant company for its corresponding accounting period; but this subsection shall not apply—

(*a*) to so much of a loss as is excluded from section 396(2) by section 396(4) or 663, or

(*b*) so as to reduce the profits of a claimant company which carries on life business (within the meaning of section 706) by an amount greater that the amount of such profits (before a set off under this subsection) computed in accordance with Case I of Schedule D and section 710(1).][1]

(2) Where for any accounting period any capital allowances are to be made to the surrendering company which are to be given by discharge or repayment of tax or in charging its income under Case V of Schedule D and are to be available primarily against a specified class of income, so much of the amount of those capital allowances (exclusive of any carried forward from an earlier period) as exceeds its income of the relevant class arising in that accounting period (before deduction of any losses of any other period or of any capital allowances) may be set off for the purposes of corporation tax against the total profits of the claimant company for its corresponding accounting period.

(3) Where for any accounting period the surrendering company (being an investment company) may under section 83(2) deduct any amount as expenses of management disbursed for that accounting period, so much of that amount (exclusive of any amount deductible only by virtue of section 83(3)) as exceeds the company's profits of that accounting period may be set off for the purposes of corporation tax against the total profits of the claimant company (whether an investment company or not) for its corresponding accounting period.

(4) The surrendering company's profits of the period shall be determined for the purposes of subsection (3) without any deduction under section 83 and without regard to any deduction to be made in respect of losses or allowances of any other period.

(5) References in subsections (3) and (4) to section 83 shall not include references to that section as applied by section 707 to companies carrying on life business.

(6) Where in any accounting period the surrendering company has paid any amount by means of charges on income, so much of that amount as exceeds its profits of the period may be set off for the purposes of corporation tax against the total profits of the claimant company for its corresponding accounting period.

(7) The surrendering company's profits of the period shall be determined for the purposes of subsection (6) without regard to any deduction to be made in respect of losses or allowances of any other period or to expenses of management deductible only by virtue of section 83(3).

(8) In applying any of the preceding subsections in the case of a claim made by a company as a member of a consortium, only a fraction of the loss referred to in subsection (1), or of the excess referred to in subsection (2), (3) or (6), as the case may be, may be set off under the subsection in question, and that fraction shall be equal to that member's share in the consortium, subject to any further reduction under section 422(2).

[(9) (*a*) References in the preceding subsections to a surrendering company shall not include references to a company carrying on life business except to the extent that such life business is new basis business within the meaning of section 730A (inserted by the Finance Act, 2000).

(*b*) For the purposes of this section "life business" shall be construed in accordance with section 706(1).][2]

Amendments

1 Inserted by FA 2001 s 65(1) as respects accounting periods commencing on or after 1 January 1999.

2 Subs (9) substituted by FA 2000 s 54 with effect from 6 April 2000.

Cross-references

Allowance of charges on income: s 243(2).
Corporation tax — late returns, restriction of relief, subs (1), (2), (3), (6): s 1085(2)(*c*).
Corporation tax, manufacturing (10%) relief, subs (6): s 448(1)(*c*).
Exploration expenditure, subs (1): s 679(3)(*b*).
Gifts to third level institutions, subs (1): s 485(7)(*b*).
Group or consortium, company joining or leaving: s 423(3)(*a*).
Group relief, relevant losses and charges, subs (1) and (6): s 420A(2).
Leased assets, restriction on use of allowances, subs (2): s 403(5), (5A).
Leased plant and machinery, restriction on use of allowances, subs (2): s 404(2)(*b*), (4)(*a*), (*c*)(i)(II).
Limited partnerships, specified provisions, subss (1), (2), (6): s 1013(1).
Petroleum trade, interest and charges on income, subs (6): s 690(6).
Pre-trading expenditure deduction, no double relief: s 82(3).
Qualifying shipping trade, restriction on use of allowances: s 407(4)(*b*)(ii).
Restriction of group relief, subss (1), (6): s 456(2).
Restriction of relief for payments of interest, subs (6): s 817A(2).
Restriction on use of capital allowances for fixtures and fittings for furnished residential accommodation, subs (2): s 406.
Restriction on use of capital allowances on holiday cottages, subs (2): s 405(1)(*a*).

Tax Briefing

TB41 Sept 2000 p 21 — Life Assurance Companies Group Relief and New Basis Business.
TB44 June 2001 p 39–40 — CT Losses, Charges and Group Relief Offset (following enactment of FA 2001 s 90).

Revenue precedents

Issue: TCA 1997 s 342(2)(*a*) states that all the provisions of the Tax Acts relating to the making of allowances or charges in respect of capital expenditure incurred shall apply. Does TCA 1997 s 420(2) relate to the making of allowances and thereby permitting the set off of allowances against the profits of a group company?
Decision: If capital allowances are available to the lessor, the provisions of TCA 1997 s 420(2) will apply.

Definitions

capital allowance: s 2(1); charges on income: ss 4(1), 243(1); company: ss 4(1), 5(1); group relief: ss 4(1), 411; profits: s 4(1); trade: ss 3(1), 4(1), 5(1).

Former enactments

CTA 1976 s 116(1)–(8) and (10).

Corresponding UK tax provision

Income and Corporation Taxes Act 1988 s 403.

420A Group relief: relevant losses and charges

[(1) In this section—

"relevant trading charges on income" and **"relevant trading income"** have the same meanings, respectively, as in section 243A;

[**"relevant trading loss"**, in relation to an accounting period of a company, means a loss incurred in the accounting period in a trade carried on by the company, other than—

(*a*) so much of the loss as is a loss incurred in an excepted trade within the meaning of section 21A, and

(*b*) any amount which is or would, if subsection (8) of section 403 had not been enacted, be the relevant amount of the loss for the purposes of subsection (4) of that section.][1]

(2) Notwithstanding subsections (1) and (6) of section 420 and section 421, where in any accounting period the surrendering company incurs a relevant trading loss or an excess of relevant trading charges on income, that loss or excess may not be set off for the purposes of corporation tax against the total profits of the claimant company for its corresponding accounting period.

(3) (*a*) Subject to section 456, where in any accounting period the surrendering company incurs a relevant trading loss, computed as for the purposes of section 396(2), or an excess of relevant trading charges on income in carrying on a trade in respect of which the company is within the charge to corporation tax, that loss or excess may be set off for the purposes of corporation tax against—

(i) income specified in section 21A(4)(*b*), and

(ii) relevant trading income,

of the claimant company for its corresponding accounting period as reduced by any amounts allowed as deductions against that income under section 243A or set off against that income under section 396A.

(*b*) Paragraph (*a*) shall not apply—

(i) to so much of a loss as is excluded from section 396(2) by section 396(4) or 663, or

(ii) so as to reduce the profits of a claimant company which carries on life business (within the meaning of section 706) by an amount greater than the amount of such profits (before a set off under this subsection) computed in accordance with Case 1 of Schedule D and section 710(1).

(4) Group relief allowed under subsection (3) shall reduce the income from a trade of the claimant company for an accounting period—

(*a*) before relief granted under section 397 in respect of a loss incurred in a succeeding accounting period or periods, and (*b*) after the relief granted under section 396 in respect of a loss incurred in a preceding accounting period or periods.

(5) For the purposes of this section in the case of a claim made by a company as a member of a consortium, only a fraction of a relevant trading loss or an excess of relevant trading charges on income may be set off, and that fraction shall be equal to that member's share in the consortium, subject to any further reduction under section 422(2).][2]

Amendments

1 Definition of "relevant trading loss" substituted by FA 2005 s 45(1)(*d*) as respects any claim made by a company on or after 3 February 2005 for relief for a loss.

2 Section 420A inserted by FA 2001 s 90(1)(*b*)(ii) as respects an accounting period ending on or after 6 March 2001.

Note

For the purposes of computing relevant trading charges on income within the meaning of TCA 1997 s 243A and relevant trading losses within the meaning of TCA 1997 s 396A, where an accounting period of a company begins before 6 March 2001 and ends on or after that date, it shall be divided into 2 parts, one beginning on the date on which the accounting period begins and ending on 5 March 2001 and the other beginning on 6 March 2001 and ending on the date on which the accounting period ends, and both parts shall be treated as if they were separate accounting periods of the company — see FA 2001 s 90(4), as substituted by FA 2002 s 55.

Cross-references

Corporation tax, late returns, restriction of certain claims for relief, subs (3): s 1085(2)(*ca*).
Group relief, relief for certain losses on a value basis: s 420B(2)(*c*).
Relief for certain gifts (to apply as if TCA 1997 ss 396A and 420A had not been enacted): s 483(5).
Relief for expenditure on significant buildings and gardens: s 482(11).
Restriction on use of capital allowances for certain leased assets: s 403(4)(*a*)(ii).
Manufacturing (10%) relief: s 448(3)(*b*)(iii), (4)(iii).
Restriction of group relief, subs (3): s 456(2).

Revenue information

Tax certificates issued by the Minister for Finance under sections 445(2) and 446(2) of the Taxes Consolidation Act 1997 to IFSC/Shannon companies contain a condition restricting the offset of losses to the trading activities referred to in the certificate. The Department of Finance has confirmed that s 54 of the Finance Act 2002 may be applied to these companies on the same basis as it applies to non-certified companies.

Tax Briefing

TB44 June 2001 pp 39–40 — CT Losses, Charges and Group Relief Offset (following enactment of FA 2001 s 90).

Definitions

company: s 4(1); profits: s 4(1); trade: s 4(1).

420B Group relief: Relief for certain losses on a value basis

[(1) In this section—

[**"relevant corporation tax"**, in relation to an accounting period of a company, means the corporation tax which would be chargeable on the company for the accounting period apart from—

(*a*) this section and sections 239, 241, 440 and 441, and

(*b*) where the company carries on a life business (within the meaning of section 706 of the Principal Act), any corporation tax which would be attributable to policyholders' profits;][1]

"relevant trading charges on income" has the same meaning as in section 243A;

"relevant trading loss" has the same meaning as in section 396A ...[2].

[(2) Where in any accounting period the surrendering company has incurred a relevant trading loss, computed as for the purposes of section 396(2), or an excess of relevant trading charges on income, in carrying on a trade in respect of which the company is within the charge to corporation tax, and the amount of the loss or excess is greater than an amount equal to the aggregate of the amounts which could, if timely claims had been made for such set off, have been set off in respect of that loss or excess for the purposes of corporation tax against—

(*a*) the income of the company in accordance with section 243A or section 396A,

(*b*) the income of the company from the sale of goods in accordance with section 454 or 455, and

(*c*) income of any other company in accordance with section 420A or 456,

the claimant company may claim relief under this section for its corresponding accounting period in respect of the amount (in this section referred to as the **"relievable loss"**) by which the loss or excess is greater that that aggregate.][3]

(3) Where for any accounting period a company claims relief under this section in respect of a relievable loss, the relevant corporation tax of the company for the accounting period shall be reduced—

(*a*) in so far as the relievable loss consists of a loss from the sale of goods (within the meaning of section 455) or charges on income paid for the sale of goods (within the meaning of section 454), by an amount equal to 10 per cent of that loss from the sale of goods or those charges on income from the sale of goods, and

(*b*) in so far as the relievable loss consists of a loss or charges on income (in this section referred to as the "remainder of the loss or charges") which is not a loss or charge on income of the type mentioned in paragraph (*a*), by an amount determined by the formula—

$$L \times \frac{R}{100}$$

where—

L is an amount equal to the remainder of the loss or charges, and

R is the rate per cent specified in section 21 in relation to the accounting period.

(4) (*a*) Where for any accounting period a company claims relief under this section in respect of any relevant trading loss or excess of relevant trading charges on income, the surrendering company shall be treated as having surrendered, and the claimant company shall be treated as having claimed relief for, trading losses and charges on income of an amount determined in accordance with paragraph (*b*).

(*b*) The amount determined in accordance with this paragraph is an amount equal to the aggregate of the following amounts:

(i) where relief is given under paragraph (*a*) of subsection (3) for the accounting period, an amount equal to 10 times the amount by which the relevant corporation tax payable for the accounting period is reduced by virtue of that paragraph, and

(ii) where relief is given under paragraph (*b*) of subsection (3) for the accounting period, an amount determined by the formula—

$$T \times \frac{100}{R}$$

where—

T is the amount by which the relevant corporation tax payable for the accounting period is reduced by virtue of subsection (3)(*b*), and

R is the rate per cent of corporation tax which, by virtue of section 21, applies in relation to the accounting period.][4]

Amendments

1 Subs (1)(definition of "relevant corporation tax") substituted by FA 2004 s 38(1) as respects any claim for relief made on or after 4 February 2004.

2 Deleted by FA 2005 s 45(1)(*e*) with effect from 1 January 2005.

3 Subs (2) substituted by FA 2003 s 59(1)(*d*) as respects a claim under TCA 1997 s 420B made on or after 6 February 2003.

4 Section 420B inserted by FA 2002 s 54(1)(*b*)(iii) as respects an accounting period ending on or after 6 March 2001 (for the purposes of computing the amount of charges on income paid for the purposes of the sale of goods (within the meaning of TCA 1997 s 454), a loss from the sale of goods (within the meaning of TCA 1997 s 455), relevant trading charges on income (within the meaning of TCA 1997 s 243A), and relevant trading losses (within the meaning of TCA 1997 s 396A), in respect of which relief may be claimed by virtue of FA 2002 s 54, where an accounting period of a company begins before 6 March 2001 and ends on or after that date, it shall be divided into 2 parts, one beginning on the date on which the accounting period begins and ending on 5 March 2001 and the other beginning on 6 March 2001 and ending on the date on which the accounting period ends, and both parts shall be treated as if they were separate accounting periods of the company).

Cross-references

Corporation tax, late returns, restriction of certain claims for relief, subs (2): s 1085(2)(*cb*).

Relief for certain charges on income on a value basis: s 243B(1)("relevant corporation tax").

Relief for certain trading losses on a value basis: s 396B(1)("relevant corporation tax").

Tax Briefing

TB51 Jan 2003 pp 14–18 — Losses, Charges and Group Relief — Relief for certain losses on a value basis [FA 2002 s 54].

Definitions

company: s 4(1); trade: ss 3(1), 4(1).

421 Relation of group relief to other relief

(1) In this section, **"relief derived from a subsequent accounting period"** means—

(*a*) relief under section 308(4) in respect of capital allowances to be made for an accounting period after the accounting period the profits of which are being computed,

(*b*) relief under section 396(2) in respect of a loss incurred in an accounting period after the accounting period the profits of which are being computed, and (*c*) relief under section 397 in respect of a loss incurred in an accounting period after the end of the accounting period the profits of which are being computed.

(2) Group relief for an accounting period shall be allowed as a deduction against the claimant company's total profits for the period before reduction by any relief derived from a subsequent accounting period, but as reduced by any other relief from tax (including relief in respect of charges on income under section 243(2)).

(3) That other relief shall be determined on the assumption that the company makes all relevant claims under section 308(4) or 396(2).

(4) The reductions to be made in total profits of an accounting period against which any relief derived from a subsequent accounting period is to be set off shall include any group relief for the first-mentioned accounting period.

Cross-references

Group or consortium, company joining or leaving, subs (2): s 423(2)(*b*).
Group relief, relevant losses and charges: s 420A(2).
Restriction of group relief: s 456(2).

Definitions

capital allowance: s 2(1); charges on income: ss 4(1), 243(1); company: ss 4(1), 5(1); group relief: ss 4(1), 411; profits: s 4(1).

Former enactments

CTA 1976 s 117(1), (2), (3)(*a*), (*b*) and (*d*) and (4).

Corresponding UK tax provision

Income and Corporation Taxes Act 1988 s 407.

422 Corresponding accounting periods

(1) For the purposes of group relief, any accounting period of the claimant company which falls wholly or partly within an accounting period of the surrendering company shall correspond to that accounting period.

(2) Where an accounting period of the surrendering company and a corresponding accounting period of the claimant company do not coincide—

(*a*) the amount which may be set off against the total profits of the claimant company for the corresponding accounting period shall be reduced by applying the fraction—

$$\frac{A}{B}$$

(if that fraction is less than unity), and

(*b*) those profits against which the amount mentioned in paragraph (*a*) (as reduced where so required) may be set off shall be reduced by applying the fraction—

$$\frac{A}{C}$$

(if that fraction is less than unity),

where—

A is the length of the period common to the 2 accounting periods,

B is the length of the accounting period of the surrendering company, and

C is the length of the corresponding accounting period of the claimant company.

Cross-references

Group relief, losses that may be surrendered, subs (2): s 420(8).
Group relief, relevant losses and charges, subs (2): s 420A(5).
Group or consortium, company joining or leaving: s 423(3)(*b*), (*c*).
Restriction of charges on income: s 454(1)(*a*).
Restriction of group relief, subs (2): s 456(5)(*a*).

Definitions

company: ss 4(1), 5(1); group relief: ss 4(1), 411; profits: s 4(1).

Former enactments

CTA 1976 s 118.

Corresponding UK tax provision

Income and Corporation Taxes Act 1988 s 408 [repealed].

423 Company joining or leaving group or consortium

(1) Subject to this section, group relief shall be given only if the surrendering company and the claimant company are members of the same group, or fulfil the conditions for relief for a consortium, throughout the whole of the surrendering company's accounting period to which the claim relates and throughout the whole of the corresponding accounting period of the claimant company.

(2) Where on any occasion 2 companies become or cease to be members of the same group, then, for the purposes specified in subsection (3), it shall be assumed as respects each company that on that occasion (unless a true accounting period of the company begins or ends then) an accounting period of the company ends and a new one begins, the new accounting period to end with the end of the true accounting period (unless before then there is a further break under this subsection) and—

(*a*) that the losses or other amounts of the true accounting period are apportioned to the component accounting periods on a time basis according to their lengths, and

(*b*) that the amount of total profits for the true accounting period of the company against which group relief may be allowed in accordance with section 421(2) is also so apportioned to the component accounting periods.

(3) Where the one company is the surrendering company and the other company is the claimant company—

(*a*) references in section 420 to accounting periods, to profits, and to losses, allowances, expenses of management or charges on income of the surrendering company, shall be construed in accordance with subsection (2);

(*b*) references in subsection (1) and in section 422 to accounting periods shall be so construed that if the 2 companies are members of the same group in the surrendering company's accounting period they shall under section 422 also be members of the same group in any corresponding accounting period of the claimant company;

(*c*) references in section 422 to profits, and amounts to be set off against the profits, shall be so construed that an amount apportioned under subsection (2) to a component accounting period may fall to be reduced under section 422(2).

(4) Subsections (2) and (3) shall apply with the necessary modifications where a company begins or ceases to fulfil the conditions for relief for a consortium, either as a surrendering company or as a claimant company, as they apply where 2 companies become or cease to be members of the same group.

Cross-references

Double allowances etc, exclusion of, subss (2), (3): s 428(3)(*a*), (4)(*a*), (5)(*a*).

Definitions

charges on income: ss 4(1), 243(1); company: ss 4(1), 5(1); group relief: ss 4(1), 411; profits: s 4(1).

Former enactments

CTA 1976 s 119.

Corresponding UK tax provision

Income and Corporation Taxes Act 1988 s 409 [repealed].

424 Effect of arrangements for transfer of company to another group, etc

(1) In this section—

"control" has the meaning assigned to it by section 11;

"third company" means a company which, apart from any provision made by or under any arrangements specified in subsection (3)(*b*) or (4)(*b*), is not a member of the same group of companies as the first company (within the meaning of subsection (3)) or, as the case may be, the trading company or holding company to which subsection (4) applies.

(2) For the purposes of this section, a company shall be a successor of another company if it carries on a trade which in whole or in part the other company has ceased to carry on and the circumstances are such that—

(*a*) section 400 applies in relation to the 2 companies as the predecessor and the successor within the meaning of that section, or

(*b*) the 2 companies are connected with each other.

(3) Where apart from this section 2 companies (in this subsection referred to respectively as **"the first company"** and **"the second company"**) would be treated as members of the same group of companies and—

(*a*) in an accounting period one of the 2 companies has trading losses or other amounts eligible for relief from corporation tax which apart from this section it would be entitled to surrender as mentioned in section 411(2), and (*b*) arrangements are in existence by virtue of which, at some time during or after the expiry of that accounting period—

(i) the first company or any successor of the first company could cease to be a member of the same group of companies as the second company and could become a member of the same group of companies as a third company,

(ii) any person has or could obtain, or any persons together have or could obtain, control of the first company but not of the second company, or

(iii) a third company could begin to carry on the whole or any part of a trade which at any time in that accounting period is carried on by the first company, and could do so either as a successor of the first company or as a successor of another company which is not a third company but which, at some time during or after the expiry of that accounting period, has begun to carry on the whole or any part of that trade,

then, for the purposes of this Chapter, the first company shall be treated as not being a member of the same group of companies as the second company.

(4) Where a trading company is owned by a consortium or is a 90 per cent subsidiary of a holding company owned by a consortium and—

(*a*) in any accounting period the trading company had trading losses or other amounts eligible for relief from corporation tax which apart from this section it would be entitled to surrender as mentioned in section 411(2), and

(*b*) arrangements are in existence by virtue of which—

(i) the trading company or any successor of the trading company could, at some time during or after the expiry of that accounting period, become a 75 per cent subsidiary of a third company,

(ii) any person who owns, or any persons who together own, less than 50 per cent of the ordinary share capital of the trading company has or together have, or could at some time during or after the expiry of that accounting period obtain, control of the trading company,

(iii) any person, other than a holding company of which the trading company is a 90 per cent subsidiary, either alone or together with connected persons, holds or could obtain, or controls or could control, the exercise of not less than 75 per cent of the votes which may be cast on a poll taken at a general meeting of the trading company in that accounting period or in any subsequent accounting period, or

(iv) a third company could begin to carry on, at some time during or after the expiry of that accounting period, the whole or any part of a trade which at any time in that accounting period is carried on by the trading company, and could do so either as a successor of the trading company or as a successor of another company which is not a third company but which, at some time during or after the expiry of that accounting period, has begun to carry on the whole or any part of that trade, then, for the purposes of this Chapter, the trading company shall be treated as though it were not (as the surrendering company) within paragraph (*a*), (*b*) or (*c*) of section 411(3).

(5) In any case where a trading company is a 90 per cent subsidiary of a holding company owned by a consortium, any reference in subsection (4) to the trading company, other than a reference in paragraph (*b*)(iv) of that subsection, shall be construed as including a reference to the holding company.

Cross-references

Information as to arrangements for transferring relief: s 427(1).

Case law

Subs (3): Held companies not members of the same group only for the duration of the arrangements in question: *Shepherd v Land Law plc* [1990] STC 795.

Definitions

company: ss 4(1), 5(1); group relief: ss 4(1), 411; ordinary share capital: s 2(1); person: IA 1937 s 11(*c*); trade: ss 3(1), 4(1), 5(1).

Former enactments

CTA 1976 s 120.

Corresponding UK tax provision

Income and Corporation Taxes Act 1988 s 410.

425 Leasing contracts: effect on claims for losses of company reconstructions

(1) Subject to this section, where—

(*a*) under a contract entered into after the 27th day of November, 1975, a company (in this section referred to as **"the first company"**) incurs capital expenditure on the provision of machinery or plant which the first company lets to another person by another contract (in this section referred to as a **"leasing contract"**),

(*b*) apart from this subsection the first company would be entitled to claim relief under subsection (1) or (2) of section 396 in respect of losses incurred on the leasing contract, and

(*c*) in the accounting period for which an allowance under section 283 or 285 in respect of the expenditure referred to in paragraph (*a*) is made to the first company, arrangements are in existence by virtue of which, at some time during or after the expiry of that accounting period, a successor company will be able to carry on any part of the first company's trade which consists of or includes the performance of all or any of the obligations which apart from the arrangements would be the first company's obligations under the leasing contract,

then, in the accounting period specified in paragraph (*c*) and in any subsequent accounting period, the first company shall not be entitled to claim relief as mentioned in paragraph (*b*) except in computing its profits (if any) arising under the leasing contract.

(2) For the purposes of this section, a company shall be a successor of the first company if the circumstances are such that—

(*a*) section 400 applies in relation to the first company and the other company as the predecessor and the successor respectively within the meaning of that section, or

(*b*) the 2 companies are connected with each other.

(3) For the purposes of this section, losses incurred on a leasing contract and profits arising under such a contract shall be computed as if the performance of the leasing contract were a trade begun to be carried on by the first company, separately from any other trade which it may carry on, at the commencement of the letting under the leasing contract.

(4) In determining whether the first company would be entitled to claim relief as mentioned in subsection (1)(*b*), any losses incurred on the leasing contract shall be treated as incurred in a trade carried on by that company separately from any other trade which it may carry on.

Cross-references

Information as to arrangements for transferring relief: s 427(1), (2)(*b*), (3)(*b*).

Definitions

company: ss 4(1), 5(1); person: IA 1937 s 11(*c*); profits: s 4(1); trade: ss 3(1), 4(1), 5(1).

Former enactments

CTA 1976 s 121.

Corresponding UK tax provision

Income and Corporation Taxes Act 1988 s 395.

426 Partnerships involving companies: effect of arrangements for transferring relief

(1) For the purposes of this section, the amount of a company's share in the profits or loss of any accounting period of a partnership shall be such amount as is determined in accordance with section 1009.

(2) Subsection (3) shall apply in relation to a company (in this section referred to as **"the partner company"**) which is a member of a partnership carrying on a trade if arrangements are in existence (whether as part of the terms of the partnership or otherwise) whereby—

(*a*) in respect of the whole or any part of the value of, or of any portion of, the partner company's share in the profits or loss of any accounting period of the partnership, another member of the partnership or any person connected with another member of the partnership receives any payment or acquires or enjoys, directly or indirectly, any other benefit in money's worth, or

(*b*) in respect of the whole or any part of the cost of, or any portion of, the partner company's share in the loss of any accounting period of the partnership, the partner company, or any person connected with that company, receives any payment or acquires or enjoys, directly or indirectly, any other benefit in money's worth, other than a payment in respect of group relief to the partner company by a company which is a member of the same group as the partner company for the purposes of group relief.

(3) (*a*) In this subsection, **"relevant accounting period of the partnership"** means any accounting period of the partnership in which any arrangements specified in subsection (2) are in existence or to which any such arrangements apply.

(*b*) In any case where this subsection applies in relation to the partner company—

(i) the company's share in the loss of the relevant accounting period of the partnership and its share in any charges on income (within the meaning of section 243) paid by the partnership in that accounting period shall not be available for set-off for the purposes of corporation tax except against its profits of the several trade,

(ii) except in accordance with subparagraph (i), no trading losses shall be available for set-off for the purposes of corporation tax against the profits of the company's several trade for the relevant accounting period of the partnership, and

(iii) except in accordance with subparagraphs (i) and (ii), no amount which apart from this subsection would be available for relief against profits shall be available for set-off for the purposes of corporation tax against so much of the company's total profits as consists of profits of its several trade for the relevant accounting period of the partnership.

(4) Where a company is a member of a partnership and tax in respect of any profits of the partnership is chargeable under Case IV or V of Schedule D, this section shall apply in relation to the company's share in the profits or loss of the partnership as if—

(*a*) the profits or loss to which the company's share is attributable were the profits of, or the loss incurred in, a several trade carried on by the company, and

(*b*) any allowance to be made by discharge or repayment of tax or in charging income under Case V of Schedule D were an allowance made in taxing that trade.

Cross-references

Information as to arrangements for transferring relief: s 427(1), (2)(*c*), (3)(*c*).

Definitions

charges on income: ss 4(1), 243(1); company: ss 4(1), 5(1); group relief: ss 4(1), 411; person: IA 1937 s 11(*c*); profits: s 4(1); trade: ss 3(1), 4(1), 5(1).

Former enactments

CTA 1976 s 122(1)–(5).

Corresponding UK tax provision

Income and Corporation Taxes Act 1988 s 116.

427 Information as to arrangements for transferring relief, etc

(1) In this section, section 417(3) and sections 424 to 426, **"arrangements"** means arrangements of any kind, whether in writing or not.

(2) Where a company—

(*a*) makes a claim for group relief,

(*b*) being a party to a leasing contract (within the meaning of section 425) claims relief as mentioned in subsection (1)(*b*) of that section, or

(*c*) being a member of a partnership, claims any relief which, if section 426(3) applied in relation to it, it would not be entitled to claim, and the inspector has reason to believe that any relevant arrangements may exist, or may have existed at any time material to the claim, then, at any time after the claim is made, the inspector may serve notice in writing on the company requiring it to furnish the inspector, within such time, being not less than 30 days, from the giving of the notice as the inspector may direct, with—

(i) a declaration in writing stating whether or not any such arrangements exist or existed at any material time,

(ii) such information as the inspector may reasonably require for the purpose of satisfying the inspector whether or not any such arrangements exist or existed at any material time, or

(iii) both such a declaration and such information.

(3) In this section, **"relevant arrangements"**, in relation to a claim within any of paragraphs (*a*) to (*c*) of subsection (2), means arrangements referred to in the provision specified in the corresponding paragraph below—

(*a*) section 417(3) or subsection (3) or (4) of section 424,

(*b*) section 425(1)(*c*), or

(*c*) section 426(2).

(4) In a case within paragraph (*a*) of subsection (2), a notice under that subsection may be served on the surrendering company (within the meaning of section 411) instead of or as well as on the company claiming relief.

(5) In a case within paragraph (*c*) of subsection (2), a notice under that subsection may be served on the partners instead of or as well as on the company, and accordingly may require the partners, instead of or as well as the company, to furnish the declaration, information or declaration and information concerned.

Cross-references

Penalties for failure to furnish certain information and for incorrect information: s 1075(1), (2).

Definitions

company: ss 4(1), 5(1); group relief: ss 4(1), 411; inspector: ss 2(1), 5(1), 852; writing: IA 1937 Sch.

Former enactments

CTA 1976 s 123.

---

428 Exclusion of double allowances, etc

(1) Relief shall not be given more than once in respect of the same amount, whether by giving group relief and by giving some other relief (in any accounting period) to the surrendering company or by giving group relief more than once.

(2) In accordance with subsection (1), 2 or more claimant companies shall not, in respect of any one loss or other amount for which group relief may be given, and whatever their accounting periods corresponding to that of the surrendering company, obtain in aggregate more relief than could be obtained by a single claimant company whose corresponding accounting period coincided with the accounting period of the surrendering company.

(3) Where claims for group relief are made by more than one claimant company which relate to the same accounting period of the same surrendering company, and—

(*a*) all the claims so made are admissible only by virtue of subsection (2) or (3) of section 423, and

(*b*) there is a part of the surrendering company's accounting period during which none of those claimant companies is a member of the same group as the surrendering company,

then, those claimant companies shall not obtain in all more relief than could be obtained by a single claimant company which was not a member of the same group as the surrendering company during that part of the surrendering company's accounting period (but was a member during the remainder of that accounting period).

(4) Where claims for group relief are made by a claimant company as respects more than one surrendering company for group relief to be set off against its total profits for any one accounting period, and—

(*a*) all the claims so made are admissible only by virtue of subsection (2) or (3) of section 423, and

(*b*) there is a part of the claimant company's accounting period during which none of the surrendering companies by reference to which the claims are made is a member of the same group as the claimant company,

then, the claimant company shall not obtain in all more relief to be set off against its profits for the accounting period than it could obtain on a claim as respects a single surrendering company (with unlimited losses and other amounts eligible for relief) which was not a member of the same group as the claimant company during that part of the claimant company's accounting period (but was a member during the remainder of that accounting period).

(5) The following provisions shall apply as respects a claim (in this subsection referred to as a **"consortium claim"**) for group relief made by a company as a member of a consortium:

(*a*) a consortium claim, and a claim other than a consortium claim, shall not both have effect as respects the loss or other amount of the same accounting period of the same surrendering company unless each of the 2 claims is as respects a loss or other amount apportioned under section 423(2)(*a*) to a component of that accounting period, and the 2 components do not overlap;

(*b*) in subsections (3) and (4) consortium claims shall be disregarded;

(*c*) paragraph (*a*) shall apply according to the order in which claims are made.

(6) Without prejudice to section 320(6), any reference in Part 9, Chapter 1 of Part 24, Chapter 1 of Part 29 and section 765 to an allowance made shall include a reference to an allowance which would be made but for the granting of group relief or but for that and but for an insufficiency of profits or other income against which to make it.

Definitions

company: ss 4(1), 5(1); group relief: ss 4(1), 411; profits: s 4(1).

Former enactments

CTA 1976 s 124; FA 1997 s 146(1) and Sch 9 Pt I para 10(6).

Corresponding UK tax provision

Income and Corporation Taxes Act 1988 s 411.

429 Claims and adjustments

(1) A claim for group relief—

(*a*) need not be for the full amount available,

(*b*) shall require the consent of the surrendering company notified to the inspector in such form as the Revenue Commissioners may require, and

(*c*) shall be made within 2 years from the end of the surrendering company's accounting period to which the claim relates.

(2) A claim for group relief by a company as a member of a consortium shall require the consent of each other member of the consortium, notified to the inspector in such form as the Revenue Commissioners may require, in addition to the consent of the surrendering company.

(3) Where the inspector ascertains that any group relief which has been given is or has become excessive, he or she may make an assessment to corporation tax under Case IV of Schedule D in the amount which in his or her opinion ought to be charged.

(4) Subsection (3) is without prejudice to the making of an assessment under section 919(5)(*b*)(iii) and to the making of all such other adjustments by means of discharge or repayment of tax or otherwise as may be required where a claimant company has obtained too much relief, or a surrendering company has foregone relief in respect of a corresponding amount.

Case law

Held company could not, outside the two year time limit, withdraw its earlier claim for group relief and substitute a new one: *Farmer v Bankers Trust* [1990] STC 564.

Held claim for group relief valid even though amount of relief not made available within the two year period. Held also there is no time limit within which the surrendering company must notify the Revenue of its consent: *Gallic Leasing Ltd v Coburn* [1991] STC 699.

Held claim may be made after a company left the group: *AW Chapman Ltd v Hennessy* [1982] STC 214.

Definitions

company: ss 4(1), 5(1); group relief: ss 4(1), 411; inspector: ss 2(1), 5(1), 852.

Former enactments

CTA 1976 s 125.

Corresponding UK tax provision

Income and Corporation Taxes Act 1988 s 412.

PART 13
CLOSE COMPANIES

Cross-references

Penalties for failure to furnish certain information and for incorrect information: s 1075(1), (2).
Profits or assets available for distribution: s 413(4).
Section 12B(4) (inserted by Health Insurance (Amendment) Act 2001 s 10) of the Health Insurance Act 1994.

CHAPTER 1
Interpretation and General

Cross-references

Approved share option schemes, eligibility, meaning of close company applied: Sch 12C para 7(*b*).

430 Meaning of "close company"

(1) For the purposes of the Corporation Tax Acts, **"close company"** means a company under the control of 5 or fewer participators, or of participators who are directors, but does not include—

(*a*) a company not resident in the State,
(*b*) a registered industrial and provident society, being a society within the meaning of section 698,
(*c*) a building society within the meaning of section 702,
(*d*) a company controlled by or on behalf of the State and not otherwise a close company, ...[1]
[(*da*) a company controlled by or on behalf of—
  (i) a Member State of the European Communities (other than the State) or,
  (ii) the government of a territory, with which government, arrangements having the force of law by virtue of [section 826(1)(*a*)][2] have been made,

and which company is not otherwise a close company, or][3]
(*e*) a company within subsection (4) or section 431.

(2) For the purposes of this section—

(*a*) a company shall be treated as controlled by or on behalf of the State only if it is under the control of the State, or of persons acting on behalf of the State, independently of any other person, and
(*b*) where a company is so controlled, it shall not be treated as being otherwise a close company unless it can be treated as a close company by virtue of being under the control of persons acting independently of the State.

[(2A) For the purposes of this section—

(*a*) a company shall be treated as controlled by or on behalf of a Member State of the European Communities (other than the State) or the government of a territory with which arrangements having the force of law by virtue of [section 826(1)(*a*)][4] have been made only if it is under the control of that Member State or the government of that territory, or of persons acting on behalf of that Member State or the government of that territory, independently of any other person, and (*b*) where a company is so controlled, it shall not be treated as being otherwise a close company unless it can be treated as a close company by virtue of being under the control of persons acting independently of that Member State or the government of that territory.][5]

(3) A company resident in the State (but not within paragraph (*b*) or (*c*) of subsection (1)) shall also be a close company if, on a full distribution of its distributable income, more than 50 per cent of that income would be paid directly or indirectly to 5 or fewer participators, or to participators who are directors.

(4) A company shall not be treated as a close company—

(*a*) if—

(i) it is controlled by a company which is not a close company, or by 2 or more companies none of which is a close company, and

(ii) it cannot be treated as a close company except by taking as one of the 5 or fewer participators requisite for its being so treated a company which is not a close company,

or

(*b*) if it cannot be treated as a close company except by virtue of paragraph (*c*) of section 432(2) and would not be a close company if the reference in that paragraph to participators did not include loan creditors who are companies other than close companies.

(5) References in subsection (4) to a close company shall be treated as including a company which if resident in the State would be a close company.

(6) Where shares in any company (in this subsection referred to as **"the first company"**) are at any time after the 5th day of April, 1976, held on trust for an exempt approved scheme (within the meaning of Chapter 1 of Part 30), then, unless the scheme is established wholly or mainly for the benefit of persons who are, or are dependants of, employees or directors or past employees or directors of—

(*a*) the first company,

(*b*) an associated company of the first company,

(*c*) a company under the control of any director, or associate of a director, of the first company or of 2 or more persons each of whom is such a director or associate, or

(*d*) a close company,

the persons holding the shares shall for the purposes of subsection (4) be deemed to be the beneficial owners of the shares and in that capacity to be a company which is not a close company.

Amendments

1 Deleted by FA 2003 s 63(*a*)(i) with effect from 1 January 2003; previously "or".

2 Substituted by FA 2004 s 89 and Sch 3 para 1(*l*)(i) with effect from 25 March 2004; previously "section 826".

3 Subs (1)(*da*) inserted by FA 2003 s 63(*a*)(ii) with effect from 1 January 2003.

4 Substituted by FA 2004 s 89 and Sch 3 para 1(*l*)(ii) with effect from 25 March 2004; previously "section 826".

5 Subs (2A) inserted by FA 2003 s 63(*b*) with effect from 1 January 2003.

Cross-references

Approved savings-related share option schemes, meaning of "close company" applied: Sch 12A paras 8(3)(*a*), 12(*c*); subs (1)(*a*): Sch 12A para 8(2).

Approved share option scheme, meaning of "close company" applied: Sch 12C para 13(*c*); subs (1)(*a*): Sch 12C para 10(*a*).

Bonus issue following repayment of share capital: s 131(4).

Connected persons, meaning of "close company" applied: s 10(1).

Loans to participators on or after 23 May 1983, subs (1)(*b*) to be regarded as deleted: s 438(8).

Profit sharing schemes, conditions as to the shares, meaning of "close company" applied: Sch 11 paras 9(*c*), 11A(2)(*b*); individuals ineligible to participate: Sch 11 paras 14(2), (3)(*a*).

Repayment of share capital following bonus issue: s 132(5).

Retirement annuities, interpretation, meaning of "close company" applied: s 783(1)(*a*).

Schemes to avoid liability to tax under Sch F, meaning of "close company" applied: s 817(1)(*a*).

Transfer of assets abroad, Revenue power to obtain information: s 808(5).

Definitions

associated company: s 432(1); company: ss 4(1), 5(1); distribution: ss 4(1), 436, 437; person: IA 1937 s 11(*c*).

Former enactments

CTA 1976 s 94.

Corresponding UK tax provision

Income and Corporation Taxes Act 1988 s 414.

431 Certain companies with quoted shares not to be close companies

(1) In this section, **"share"** includes **"stock"**.

(2) For the purposes of this section—

(*a*) a person shall be a principal member of a company—

(i) if such person possesses a percentage of the voting power in the company of more than 5 per cent and, where there are more than 5 such persons, if such person is one of the 5 persons who possess the greatest percentages, or

(ii) if (because 2 or more persons possess equal percentages of the voting power in the company) there are no such 5 persons, such person is one of the 6 or more persons (so as to include those 2 or more who possess equal percentages) who possess the greatest percentages,

(*b*) a principal member's holding shall consist of the shares which carry the voting power possessed by the principal member, and

(*c*) in determining the voting power which a person possesses, there shall be attributed to such person any voting power which for the purposes of section 432 would be attributed to such person under subsection (5) or (6) of that section.

(3) Subject to this section, a company shall not be treated as being at any time a close company if—

(*a*) shares in the company carrying not less than 35 per cent of the voting power in the company (not being shares entitled to a fixed rate of dividend, whether with or without a further right to participate in profits) have been allotted unconditionally to, or acquired unconditionally by, and are at that time beneficially held by, the public, and (*b*) any such shares have within the preceding 12 months been the subject of dealings on a recognised stock exchange, and the shares have within those 12 months been quoted in the official list of a recognised stock exchange.

(4) Subsection (3) shall not apply to a company at any time when the total percentage of the voting power in the company possessed by all of the company's principal members exceeds 85 per cent.

(5) For the purposes of subsection (3), shares in a company shall be deemed to be beneficially held by the public only if the shares—

(*a*) are within subsection (6), and

(*b*) are not within the exceptions in subsection (7),

and the reference to shares which have been allotted unconditionally to, or acquired unconditionally by, the public shall be construed accordingly.

(6) Shares are within this subsection (as being beneficially held by the public) if the shares—

(*a*) are beneficially held by a company resident in the State which is not a close company, or by a company not so resident which would not be a close company if it were so resident,

(*b*) are held on trust for an exempt approved scheme (within the meaning of Chapter 1 of Part 30), or

(*c*) are not comprised in a principal member's holding.

(7) (*a*) Shares shall be deemed not to be held by the public if the shares are held—

(i) by any director, or associate of a director, of the company,

(ii) by any company under the control of any such director or associate, or of 2 or more persons each of whom is such a director or associate,

(iii) by an associated company of the company, or

(iv) as part of any fund the capital or income of which is applicable or applied wholly or mainly for the benefit of, or of the dependants of, the employees or directors, or past employees or directors, of the company, or of any company within subparagraph (ii) or (iii).

(*b*) References in this subsection to shares held by any person include references to any shares the rights or powers attached to which could for the purposes of section 432 be attributed to that person under subsection (5) of that section.

Cross-references

Approved savings-related share option schemes: Sch 12A para 8(2).

Approved share option schemes, subss (3) to (7) disregarded: Sch 12C para 10(*a*).

Capital acquisitions tax, market value of certain shares in private companies: CATCA 2003 s 27(1)("private company").

Close company, meaning: s 430(1)(*e*).

Connected persons, meaning of "close company" applied: s 10(1).

Profit sharing schemes, individuals ineligible to participate, meaning of "close company" applied: Sch 11 para 14(2).

Schemes to avoid liability to tax under Sch F, meaning of "close company" applied: s 817(1)(*a*).

Transfer of assets abroad, Revenue power to obtain information: s 808(5).

Definitions

associated company: s 432(1); company: ss 4(1), 5(1); month: IA 1937 Sch; person: IA 1937 s 11(*c*); profits: s 4(1).

Former enactments

CTA 1976 s 95.

Corresponding UK tax provision

Income and Corporation Taxes Act 1988 s 415.

432 Meaning of "associated company" and "control"

(1) For the purposes of this Part, a company shall be treated as another company's associated company at a particular time if, at that time or at any time within one year previously, one of the 2 companies has control of the other company, or both companies are under the control of the same person or persons.

(2) For the purposes of this Part, a person shall be taken to have control of a company if such person exercises, or is able to exercise or is entitled to acquire, control, whether direct or indirect, over the company's affairs, and in particular, but without prejudice to the generality of the foregoing, if such person possesses or is entitled to acquire—

(*a*) the greater part of the share capital or issued share capital of the company or of the voting power in the company,

(*b*) such part of the issued share capital of the company as would, if the whole of the income of the company were distributed among the participators (without regard to any rights which such person or any other person has as a loan creditor), entitle such person to receive the greater part of the amount so distributed, or

(*c*) such rights as would, in the event of the winding up of the company or in any other circumstances, entitle such person to receive the greater part of the assets of the company which would then be available for distribution among the participators.

(3) Where 2 or more persons together satisfy any of the conditions of subsection (2), they shall be taken to have control of the company.

(4) For the purposes of subsection (2), a person shall be treated as entitled to acquire anything which such person is entitled to acquire at a future date or will at a future date be entitled to acquire.

(5) For the purposes of subsections (2) and (3), there shall be attributed to any person any rights or powers of a nominee for such person, that is, any rights or powers which another person possesses on such person's behalf or may be required to exercise on such person's direction or behalf.

(6) For the purposes of subsections (2) and (3), there may also be attributed to any person all the rights and powers of—

(*a*) any company of which such person has, or such person and associates of such person have, control,

(*b*) any 2 or more companies of which such person has, or such person and associates of such person have, control,

(*c*) any associate of such person, or
(*d*) any 2 or more associates of such person,

including the rights and powers attributed to a company or associate under subsection (5), but excluding those attributed to an associate under this subsection, and such attributions shall be made under this subsection as will result in the company being treated as under the control of 5 or fewer participators if it can be so treated.

Cross-references

Close company, meaning, subs (2)(*c*): s 430(4)(*b*).
Quoted company not close: s 431(2)(*c*), (7)(*b*).

Control, definition applied for:

application of PAYE to certain perquisites: s 985A(1A)(*b*);
application to High Court seeking order requiring information, associated institutions: s 908B(1)("associated institution");
approved savings-related share option schemes, interpretation: Sch 12A para 1(1), (4);
approved share option schemes, interpretation: Sch 12C para 1(1), (4)(*b*);
business expansion scheme, subss (2)–(6): s 488(1);
company ceasing to be resident in the State, deemed disposal of assets, meaning of "control" (subss (2)–(6)) applied, but in subs (6) for "5 or fewer participators" read "persons resident in a relevant territory": s 627(2)(*a*);
company residence, meaning of "control" (subss(2)–(6)) applied but in subs (6) for "5 or fewer participators" read "persons who, by virtue of the law of a relevant territory (within the meaning of section 23A) are resident for the purposes of tax in a relevant territory or relevant territories" or, as may be appropriate, "persons not resident for the purposes of tax in a relevant territory (within the meaning of section 23A): s 23A(1)(*b*)(ii);
connected person: s 10(1);
credit in respect of tax deducted from emoluments of certain directors: s 997A(1)(*a*).
distributions to certain non-residents, meaning of "control" (subss (2)–(6) applied, but in subs (6) for "5 or fewer participators" read "persons resident in the State": s 153(1A);
distributions to certain non-residents, meaning of "control" (subss (2)–(6)) applied, but in subs (6) for "5 or fewer participators" read "persons who, by virtue of the law of a relevant territory (within the meaning assigned by section 153), are resident for the purposes of tax in such a relevant territory (within that meaning)" or, as may be appropriate, "persons who are not resident for the purposes of tax in a relevant territory (within that meaning)": s 153(2)(*a*), (*b*);
dividend withholding tax, exemption for certain non-resident persons, meaning of "control" (subss (2)–(6)) applied, but in subs (6) for "5 or fewer participators" read "persons resident in the State": s 172D(3A);
dividend withholding tax, exemption for certain non-resident persons, meaning of "control" (subss (2)–(6)) applied, but in subs (6) for "5 or fewer participators" read "persons who, by virtue of the law of a relevant territory (within the meaning assigned by section 172A), are resident for the purpose of tax in such a relevant territory (within that meaning)" or, as may be appropriate, "persons who are not resident for the purposes of tax in a relevant territory (within that meaning)": s 172D(4)(*a*), (*b*);
employee share ownership trusts: Sch 12A para 1(4)(*a*);
industrial and provident societies, transfer of shares to members: s 701(1);
material interest in offshore funds: s 743(7);
non-resident trusts, attribution of gains to beneficiaries, whether company is controlled by a person or persons is to be construed in accordance with TCA 1997 s 432 without regard to subs (6) thereof: s 579A(2)(*e*)(iii);
particulars to be supplied by new companies: s 882(1)(*b*);
power of inspection: returns and collection of appropriate tax (DIRT), meaning of associated company applied: s 904A(1);
profit sharing schemes: Sch 11 para 1;
reduction of corporation tax liability in respect of certain trading income: s 22A(4)(*a*);
restriction on deductibility of certain interest, meaning of "control" (subss (2)–(6)) applied, but in subs (6) for "5 or fewer participators" as if there were substituted "persons resident in the State": s 817C(2A)(*b*)(i);
Schedule 2, para 13(9) of the Valuation Act 2001;
securities issued by the Minister for Finance (subss (2)–(6)), but in subs (6) substitute "persons resident in a relevant territory" for "5 or fewer participators": s 44(1);
shipping tonnage tax, meaning of control (subss (2)–(6)) applied: s 697A(1);
subcontractors' withholding tax: s 531(13)(*a*)(iv), (14)(*c*)(vi);
tax on non-resident company recoverable from another group member or controlling director: s 629(1);

Associated company, definition (subs (1)) applied for:

approved savings-related share option schemes, interpretation: Sch 12A para 1(1); conditions as to shares: Sch 12A para 15(*c*);
approved share option schemes, interpretation: Sch 12C para 1(1);
implementation of Council Directive 2003/48/EC of 3 June 2003 on Taxation of Savings Income in the form of Interest Payments, audit: s 898N(1);
non-resident trusts, attribution of gains to beneficiaries, whether a company is associated with another company is to be construed in accordance with TCA 1997 s 432 without regard to subs (6) thereof: s 539A(2)(*e*)(iv);
profit sharing schemes, conditions as to the shares: Sch 11 para 11(*c*);
section 12B (inserted by Health Insurance (Amendment) Act 2001 s 10) of the Health Insurance Act 1994.
use of different accounting policies within a group of companies: s 76C(2)(*b*).

Definitions

company: ss 4(1), 5(1); distribution: ss 4(1), 436, 437; person: IA 1937 s 11(*c*).

Former enactments

CTA 1976 s 102; FA 1996 s 132(1) and Sch 5 Pt I para 10(4).

Corresponding UK tax provision

Income and Corporation Taxes Act 1988 s 416.

433 Meaning of "participator", "associate", "director" and "loan creditor"

(1) For the purposes of this Part, **"participator"**, in relation to any company, means a person having a share or interest in the capital or income of the company and, without prejudice to the generality of the preceding words, includes—

(*a*) any person who possesses, or is entitled to acquire, share capital or voting rights in the company,

(*b*) any loan creditor of the company,

(*c*) any person who possesses, or is entitled to acquire, a right to receive or participate in distributions of the company (construing **"distributions"** without regard to section 436 or 437) or any amounts payable by the company (in cash or in kind) to loan creditors by means of premium on redemption, and

(*d*) any person entitled to secure that income or assets (whether present or future) of the company will be applied directly or indirectly for such person's benefit.

(2) (*a*) References in subsection (1) to being entitled to do anything apply where a person is entitled to do it at a future date or will at a future date be entitled to do it.

(*b*) Subsection (1) is without prejudice to any particular provision of this Part requiring a participator in one company to be treated as being also a participator in another company.

(3) (*a*) In this subsection, **"relative"** means husband, wife, ancestor, lineal descendant, brother or sister.

(*b*) For the purposes of this Part but subject to paragraph (*c*), **"associate"**, in relation to a participator, means—

(i) any relative or partner of the participator,

(ii) the trustee or trustees of any settlement in relation to which the participator is, or any relative (living or dead) of the participator is or was, a settlor (**"settlement"** and **"settlor"** having the same meanings respectively as in section 10), and

(iii) where the participator is interested in any shares or obligations of the company which are subject to any trust or are part of the estate of a deceased person, any other person interested in those shares or obligations,

and has a corresponding meaning in relation to a person other than a participator.

(*c*) Paragraph (*b*)(iii) shall not apply so as to make an individual an associate as being entitled or eligible to benefit under a trust—

(i) if the trust relates exclusively to an exempt approved scheme (within the meaning of Chapter 1 of Part 30), or

(ii) if the trust is exclusively for the benefit of the employees, or the employees and directors, of the company or their dependants (and not wholly or mainly for the benefit of the directors or their relatives) and the individual in question is not (and could not as a result of the operation of the trust become), either on his or her own or with his or her relatives, the beneficial owner of more than 5 per cent of the ordinary share capital of the company,

and, in applying subparagraph (ii), any charitable trusts which may arise on the failure or determination of other trusts shall be disregarded.

(4) For the purposes of this Part, **"director"** includes any person—

(*a*) occupying the position of director by whatever name called,

(*b*) in accordance with whose directions or instructions the directors are accustomed to act,

(*c*) who is a manager of the company or otherwise concerned in the management of the company's trade or business, and

(*d*) who is, either on his or her own or with one or more associates, the beneficial owner of, or able, directly or through the medium of other companies or by any other indirect means, to control, 20 per cent or more of the ordinary share capital of the company.

(5) In subsection (4)(*d*), **"either on his or her own or with one or more associates"** requires a person to be treated as owning or, as the case may be, controlling what any associate owns or controls, even if he or she does not own or control share capital on his or her own and, in subsection (3)(*c*)(ii), **"either on his or her own or with his or her relatives"** has a corresponding meaning.

(6) (*a*) For the purposes of this Part but subject to paragraph (*b*), **"loan creditor"**, in relation to a company, means a creditor in respect of—

(i) any debt incurred by the company for—

(I) any money borrowed or capital assets acquired by the company,

(II) any right to receive income created in favour of the company, or

(III) consideration the value of which to the company was (at the time when the debt was incurred) substantially less than the amount of the debt (including any premium on the debt),

or

(ii) any redeemable loan capital issued by the company.

(*b*) A person carrying on a business of banking shall not be deemed to be a loan creditor in respect of any loan capital issued or debt incurred by the company for money loaned by such person to the company in the ordinary course of that business.

(7) A person who is not the creditor in respect of any debt or loan capital to which subsection (6) applies but nevertheless has a beneficial interest in that debt or loan capital shall to the extent of that interest be treated for the purposes of this Part as a loan creditor in respect of that debt or loan capital.

Cross-references

Attribution to participators of chargeable gains accruing to non-resident company, meaning of "participator" applied: s 590(1).
Profits or assets available for distribution, subs (6): s 413(4).
Retirement annuities, interpretation, meaning of "participator" applied: s 783(1)(*a*).
Returns by nominee holders of securities, meaning of "loan creditor" applied, subs (6): s 892(1)(*a*).

Associate, subs (3), definition applied for:

approved savings-related share option schemes: Sch 12A para 8(3)(*b*);
approved share option schemes: Sch 12C paras 1(3), 10(*b*);
business expansion scheme: s 488(1);
employee share ownership trusts, interpretation: Sch 12 para 1(4)(*a*);
profit sharing schemes, conditions as to the shares: Sch 11 para 11(3)(*b*).

Director, subs (4), definition applied for:

Income Tax (Relevant Contracts) Regulations 2000, SI No 71 of 2000: ITRCR 2000 Reg 2;
business expansion scheme: s 488(1).

Case law

Subs (3)(*b*): Held a testator of a will is not a settlor: *IRC v Buchanan* (1958) 37 TC 365.
Subs (3)(*b*): Held 'interested' includes both fiduciary and beneficial interests: *Willingale v Islington Green Investment Co* (1972) 38 TC 460.
For observations on distinction between legal and beneficial interest – *J Bibby & Sons Ltd v CIR* 29 TC 167.

Definitions

company: ss 4(1), 5(1); distribution: ss 4(1), 436, 437; interest: s 4(1); ordinary share capital: s 2(1); person: IA 1937 s 11(*c*); relative: s 3(1); settlement: ss 5(1), 10; trade: ss 3(1), 4(1), 5(1).

Former enactments

CTA 1976 s 103; FA 1997 s 146(1) and Sch 9 Pt I para 10(5).

Corresponding UK tax provision

Income and Corporation Taxes Act 1988 s 417.

434 Distributions to be taken into account and meaning of "distributable income", "investment income", "estate income", etc

(1) In this section—

...[1]

"estate income" means income (other than yearly or other interest) chargeable to tax under Case III, IV or V of Schedule D, and arising from the ownership of land (including any interest in or right over land) or from the letting furnished of any building or part of a building;

[**"franked investment income"** excludes—

(*a*) a distribution made out of exempt profits within the meaning of section 140, (*b*) a distribution made out of disregarded income within the meaning of section 141 and to which subsection (3)(*a*) of that section applies, and

(*c*) a distribution made out of exempted income within the meaning of section 142;][2]

[**"income"** of a company for an accounting period means the income as computed in accordance with subsection (4);][2]

[**"investment income"** of a company means income other than estate income which, if the company were an individual, would not be earned income within the meaning of section 3, but, without prejudice to the meaning of **"franked investment income"** in this section, does not include—

(*a*) any interest or dividends on investments which, having regard to the nature of the company's trade, would be taken into account as trading receipts in computing trading income but for the fact that they have been subjected to tax otherwise than as trading receipts, or but for the fact that by virtue of section 129 they are not to be taken into account in computing income for corporation tax, and

(*b*) any dividends or other distributions received by the company in respect of shares at a time when any gain on a disposal of the shares would not have been a chargeable gain by virtue of section 626B or would not have been a chargeable gain by virtue of section 626B if paragraphs (*a*) and (*b*) of subsection (3) of that section were deleted.][3]

[**"relevant charges"**, in relation to an accounting period of a company, means charges on income paid in the accounting period by the company and which are allowed as deductions under section 243, other than so much of those charges as is paid for the purposes of an excepted trade within the meaning of section 21A;][4]

...[1]

"trading company" means any company which exists wholly or mainly for the purpose of carrying on a trade and any other company whose income does not consist wholly or mainly of investment or estate income.

(2) For the purposes of section 440, the distributions of a company for an accounting period shall be taken to be the aggregate of—

(*a*) any dividends which are declared for or in respect of the accounting period and are paid or payable during the accounting period or within 18 months after the end of the accounting period, and

(*b*) all distributions, other than dividends, made in the accounting period.

(3) Where—

(*a*) a period of account for or in respect of which a company declares a dividend is not an accounting period,

(*b*) the dividend is paid or payable during the period of account or within 18 months after the end of the period of account, and

(*c*) part of the period of account falls within an accounting period, then, the proportion of the amount of the dividend to be treated for the purposes of subsection (2) as being for or in respect of the accounting period shall be the same as the proportion which that part of the period of account bears to the whole of that period.

(4) [The income][5] of a company for an accounting period shall be the income for the accounting period, computed in accordance with the Corporation Tax Acts, exclusive of franked investment income, before deducting—

(*a*) any loss incurred in any trade or profession carried on by the company which is carried forward from an earlier, or carried back from a later, accounting period,

(*b*) any loss which if it were a profit would be chargeable to corporation tax on the company under Case III or IV of Schedule D and which is carried forward from an earlier accounting period or any expenses of management or any charges on income which are so carried forward, and

(*c*) any excess of deficiencies over surpluses which if such excess were an excess of surpluses over deficiencies would be chargeable to corporation tax on the company under Case V of Schedule D and which is carried forward from an earlier, or carried back from a later, accounting period,

and after deducting—

(*d*) any loss incurred in the accounting period in any trade or profession carried on by the company,

(*e*) any loss incurred in the accounting period which if it were a profit would be chargeable to corporation tax on the company under Case III or IV of Schedule D,

(*f*) any excess of deficiencies over surpluses which if such excess were an excess of surpluses over deficiencies would be chargeable to corporation tax on the company for the accounting period under Case V of Schedule D,

[(*g*) any amount which is an allowable deduction against relevant trading income by virtue of section 243A.][6]

[(5) (*a*) The estate and investment income of a company for an accounting period shall be the amount by which the sum of—

(i) the amount of franked investment income for the accounting period, and

[(ii) an amount determined by applying to the amount of the income of the company for the accounting period the fraction—

$$\frac{A}{B}$$

where—

A is the aggregate of the amounts of estate income and investment income taken into account in computing the income of the company for the accounting period, and

B is the amount of the company's income before taking account of any amount specified in paragraphs (*d*) to (*g*) of subsection (4),][7]

exceeds the aggregate of—

(I) the amount of relevant charges, and

(II) the amount which is an allowable deduction in computing the total profits for the accounting period in respect of expenses of management by virtue of section 83(2).

(*b*) The trading income of a company for an accounting period shall be the income of the company for the accounting period after deducting—

[(i) an amount equal to the sum of the amounts specified in subparagraphs (i) and (ii) of paragraph (*a*),][8]

(ii) where the aggregate of the amounts specified in clauses (I) and (II) of paragraph (*a*) exceeds the sum of the amounts specified in subparagraphs (i) and (ii) of that paragraph, the amount of the excess, and

(iii) charges on income paid for the purposes of an excepted trade within the meaning of section 21A.

(5A)(*a*) For the purposes of sections 440 and 441, but subject to paragraph (*b*)—

"distributable estate and investment income" of a company for an accounting period means the estate and investment income of the company for the accounting period after deducting the amount of corporation tax which would be payable by the company for the accounting period if the tax were computed on the basis of that income;

"distributable trading income" of a company for an accounting period means the trading income of the company for the accounting period after deducting the amount of corporation tax which, apart from sections 22A(2) and 448(2), would be payable by the company for the accounting period if the tax were computed on the basis of that income.

(*b*) In the case of a trading company, the distributable estate and investment income for an accounting period shall be the amount determined in accordance with paragraph (*a*) reduced by 7.5 per cent.][9]

(6) The amount for part of an accounting period of any description of income referred to in this section shall be a proportionate part of the amount for the whole period.

(7) Where a company is subject to any restriction imposed by law as regards the making of distributions, regard shall be had to this restriction in determining the amount of income on which a surcharge shall be imposed under section 440.

Amendments

1 Definitions of "distributable income" and "trading income" deleted by FA 2003 s 163 and Sch 6 para 1(*b*)(i) as respects accounting periods ending on or after 14 March 2001.

2 Definitions of "franked investment income" and "income" inserted by FA 2001 s 91(1)(*a*)(ii) as respects an accounting period ending on or after 14 March 2001.

3 Subs (1)(definition of "investment income") substituted by FA 2004 s 36 with effect from 1 January 2004.

4 Definition of "relevant charges" inserted by FA 2001 s 91(1)(*a*)(iii) as respects an accounting period ending on or after 14 March 2001.

5 Substituted by FA 2001 s 91(1)(*b*)(i) as respects an accounting period ending on or after 14 March 2001; previously "For the purposes of subsection (1), the income".

6 Subs (4)(*g*) and (*h*) substituted by FA 2001 s 91(1)(*b*)(ii) as respects an accounting period ending on or after 14 March 2001.

7 Subs (5)(*a*)(ii) substituted by FA 2003 s 163 and Sch 6 para 1(*b*)(ii) as respects accounting periods ending on or after 14 March 2001.

8 Subs (5)(*b*)(i) substituted by FA 2002 s 138 and Sch 6 paras 3(*g*)(ii) and 6(*c*)(iii) as respects an accounting period ending on or after 14 March 2001.

9 Subs (5) substituted and subs (5A) inserted by FA 2001 s 91(1)(*c*) as respects an accounting period ending on or after 14 March 2001.

Cross-references

Service companies, undistributed income surcharge, subss (2), (3), (6), (7): s 441(6)(*a*); subss (1)–(5): s 441(6)(*b*).

Definitions

chargeable gain: ss 5(1); 545; charges on income: ss 4(1), 243(1); company: ss 4(1), 5(1); distribution: ss 4(1), 436, 437; franked investment income: ss 4(1), 156; interest: s 4(1); land: s 5(1), IA 1937 Sch; month: IA 1937 Sch; profession: ss 2(1), 5(1); profits: s 4(1); shares: s 5(1); trade: ss 3(1), 4(1), 5(1).

Former enactments

CTA 1976 s 100; FA 1989 s 27(1).

Corresponding UK tax provision

Income and Corporation Taxes Act 1988 Sch 19 [repealed].

435 Information

(1) The inspector may by notice in writing require any company which is, or appears to the inspector to be, a close company to furnish him or her within such time (not being less than 30 days) as may be specified in the notice with such particulars as he or she thinks necessary for the purposes of this Part.

(2) Where for the purposes of this Part any person in whose name any shares are registered is so required by notice in writing by the inspector, such person—

(*a*) shall state whether or not such person is the beneficial owner of the shares, and

(*b*) if not the beneficial owner of the shares or any of them, shall furnish the name and address of the person or persons on whose behalf the shares are registered in such person's name.

(3) Subsection (2) shall apply in relation to loan capital as it applies in relation to shares.

(4) (*a*) In this subsection, **"securities"** includes shares, stocks, bonds, debentures and debenture stock and any promissory note or other instrument evidencing indebtedness issued to a loan creditor of the company.

(*b*) For the purposes of this Part, the inspector may by notice in writing require—

(i) any company which appears to the inspector to be a close company to furnish him or her with particulars of any bearer securities issued by the company and the names and addresses of the persons to whom the securities were issued and the respective amounts issued to each person, and

(ii) any person to whom securities were so issued, or any person to whom or through whom such securities were subsequently sold or transferred, to furnish the inspector with such further information as he or she may require with a view to enabling him or her to ascertain the names and addresses of the persons beneficially interested in the securities.

Definitions

close company: ss 4(1), 430, 431; company: ss 4(1), 5(1); inspector: ss 2(1), 5(1), 852; person: IA 1937 s 11(*c*); writing: IA 1937 Sch.

Former enactments

CTA 1976 s 104.

CHAPTER 2
Additional Matters to be Treated as Distributions, Charges to Tax in Respect of Certain Loans and Surcharges on Certain Undistributed Income

436 Certain expenses for participators and associates

(1) Subject to the exceptions mentioned in section 130, **"distribution"**, in relation to a close company, includes, unless otherwise stated, any such amount as is required to be treated as a distribution by subsection (3).

(2) For the purposes of this section, any reference to a participator includes an associate of a participator, and any participator in a company which controls another company shall be treated as being also a participator in that other company.

(3) (*a*) Subject to paragraph (*b*), where a close company incurs expense in or in connection with the provision for any participator of living or other accommodation, entertainment, domestic or other services, or other benefits or facilities of whatever nature, the company shall be treated as making a distribution to such participator of an amount equal to so much of that expense as is not made good to the company by such participator.

(*b*) Paragraph (*a*) shall not apply to expense incurred in or in connection with the provision of benefits or facilities for a person to whom section 118 applies as a director or employee of the company, or the provision for the spouse, children or dependants of any such person of any pension, annuity, lump sum, gratuity or other like benefit to be given on his or her death or retirement.

(4) Any reference in subsection (3) to expense incurred in or in connection with any matter shall include a reference to a proper proportion of any expense incurred partly in or in connection with that matter, and section 119 shall apply for the purposes of subsection (3) as it applies for the purposes of section 118, references to subsection (3) being substituted for references to section 118(1).

(5) Subsection (3) shall not apply if the company and the participator are both resident in the State and—

(*a*) one is a subsidiary of the other or both are subsidiaries of a third company also so resident, and

(*b*) the benefit to the participator arises on or in connection with the transfer of assets or liabilities by the company to the participator, or to the company by the participator.

(6) The question whether one company is a subsidiary of another company for the purpose of subsection (5) shall be determined as if it were a question whether it is a 51 per cent subsidiary of the other company, except that the other company shall be treated as not being the owner of—

(*a*) any share capital which it owns directly in a company if a profit on a sale of the shares would be treated as a trading receipt of its trade,

(*b*) any share capital which it owns indirectly and which is owned directly by a company for which a profit on the sale of the shares would be a trading receipt, or

(*c*) any share capital which it owns directly or indirectly in a company not resident in the State.

(7) (*a*) Where each of 2 or more close companies makes a payment to a person (in this paragraph referred to as **"the first-mentioned person"**) who is not a participator in that company, but is a participator in another of those companies, and the companies are acting in concert or under arrangements made by any person, then, each of those companies and any participator in it shall be treated as if the payment made to the first-mentioned person had been made by that company.

(*b*) This subsection shall apply with any necessary modifications in relation to the giving of any consideration and to the provision of any facilities as it applies in relation to the making of a payment.

Cross-references

Distribution, meaning: s 130(1).

Interest paid to directors, directors' associates, subs (7): s 437(7).

Loans of art objects, subs (3) not to apply to expenses: s 236(3).

Participator, associate, director, loan creditor, meanings: s 433(1)(*c*).

Schedule F, meaning of "distribution" applied: s 20(1)("1").

Definitions

close company: ss 4(1), 430, 431; company: ss 4(1), 5(1); distribution: ss 4(1), 436, 437; person: IA 1937 s 11(*c*); trade: ss 3(1), 4(1), 5(1).

Former enactments

CTA 1976 s 96.

Corresponding UK tax provision

Income and Corporation Taxes Act 1988 s 418.

437 Interest paid to directors and directors' associates

(1) In this section, **"interest"** includes any other consideration paid or given by the close company for the use of money advanced, or credit given, by any person, and references to interest paid shall be construed accordingly.

(2) For the purposes of this section, a person shall have a material interest in a company if the person, either on the person's own or with any one or more of the person's associates, or if any associate of the person with or without any such other associates, is the beneficial owner of, or is able, directly or through the medium of other companies or by any other indirect means, to control, more than 5 per cent of the ordinary share capital of the company.

(3) Subject to the exceptions mentioned in section 130(1), this section shall apply where in any accounting period any interest is paid by a close company to, or to an associate of, a person—

(*a*) who is a director of the close company, or of any company which controls or is controlled by the close company, and

(*b*) who has a material interest—

(i) in the close company, or

(ii) where the close company is controlled by another company, in that other company.

(4) Where the total amount so paid to any person in the accounting period exceeds the limit imposed in that person's case, the excess shall be deemed to be a distribution made by the close company to that person.

(5) The limit shall be calculated in the first instance as an overall limit applying to the aggregate of all interest which is within subsection (3) and which was paid by the close company in the accounting period and, where there are 2 or more different recipients, that overall limit shall be apportioned between them according to the amounts of interest paid to them respectively.

(6) The overall limit shall be a sum equal to interest at 13 per cent per annum or such other rate of interest as the Minister for Finance may from time to time prescribe on whichever is the lesser of—

(*a*) the total of the loans, advances and credits on which the interest within subsection (3) was paid by the close company in the accounting period or, if the total was different at different times in the accounting period, the average total over the accounting period, and

(*b*) the nominal amount of the issued share capital of the close company plus the amount of any share premium account (or other comparable account by whatever name called) of the company, taking both amounts as at the beginning of the accounting period.

(7) This section shall apply subject to section 436(7).

Cross-references

Approved savings-related share option schemes, subs (2): Sch 12A paras 8(3)(*b*)(ii), 27(1), (2).
Approved share option schemes, subs (2): Sch 12C paras 10(*b*), 21(1), (2).
Distribution, meaning: s 130(1).
Interest paid by companies and to non-residents: s 246(3)(*g*).
Loans to participators etc, subss (2)–(3): s 438(7).
Participator, associate, director, loan creditor, meanings: s 433(1)(*c*).
Profit sharing schemes, individuals ineligible to participate, subs (2): Sch 11 para 14(3)(*b*)(ii).
Schedule F, meaning of "distribution" applied: s 20(1)("1").

Definitions

close company: ss 4(1), 430, 431; company: ss 4(1), 5(1); distribution: ss 4(1), 436, 437; interest: s 4(1); ordinary share capital: s 2(1); person: IA 1937 s 11(*c*).

Former enactments

CTA 1976 s 97.

438 Loans to participators, etc

(1) (*a*) Subject to this section, where a close company, otherwise than in the ordinary course of a business carried on by it which includes the lending of money, makes any loan or advances any money to an individual who is a participator in the company or an associate of a participator, the company shall be deemed for the purposes of this section to have paid in the year of assessment in which the loan or advance is made an annual payment of an amount which, after deduction of income tax at the standard rate for the year of assessment in which the loan or advance is made, is equal to the amount of the loan or advance.

(*b*) Section 239 shall apply for the purposes of the charge, assessment and recovery of the tax referred to in paragraph (*a*).

(*c*) The annual payment referred to in paragraph (*a*) shall not be a charge on the company's income within the meaning of section 243.

(2) For the purposes of this section, the cases in which a close company is to be regarded as making a loan to any person shall include a case where—

(*a*) that person incurs a debt to the close company, or

(*b*) a debt due from that person to a third person is assigned to the close company,

and in such a case the close company shall be regarded as making a loan of an amount equal to the debt; but paragraph (*a*) shall not apply to a debt incurred for the supply by the close company of goods or services in the ordinary course of its trade or business unless the period of credit given exceeds 6 months or is longer than that normally given to the company's customers.

(3) Subsection (1) shall not apply to a loan made to a director or employee of a close company, or of an associated company of the close company, if—

(*a*) the amount of the loan, or that amount when taken together with any other outstanding loans which were made by the close company or any of its associated companies to the borrower, or to the spouse of the borrower, does not exceed [€19,050][1],

(*b*) the borrower works full-time for the close company or any of its associated companies, and

(*c*) the borrower does not have a material interest in the close company or in any associated company of the close company but, if the borrower acquires such a material interest at a time when the whole or part of any such loan remains outstanding, the close company shall be regarded as making to the borrower at that time a loan of an amount equal to the sum outstanding.

(4) (*a*) Where, after a company has been assessed to tax under this section in respect of any loan or advance, the loan or advance or any part of it is repaid to the company, relief shall be given from that tax or a proportionate part of that tax by discharge or repayment.

(*b*) Relief under this subsection shall be given on a claim which shall be made within 10 years from the end of the year of assessment in which the repayment is made.

(5) Where under arrangements made by any person otherwise than in the ordinary course of a business carried on by that person—

(*a*) a close company makes a loan or advance which apart from this subsection does not give rise to any charge on the company under subsection (1), and

(*b*) some person other than the close company makes a payment or transfers property to, or releases or satisfies (in whole or in part) a liability of, an individual who is a participator in the company or an associate of a participator,

then, unless in respect of the matter referred to in paragraph (*b*) there is to be included in the total income of the participator or associate an amount not less than the loan or advance, this section shall apply as if the loan or advance had been made to the participator or associate.

(6) In subsections (1) and (5)(*b*), the references to an individual shall apply also to a company receiving the loan or advance in a fiduciary or representative capacity and [to a company not resident in a Member State of the European Communities and, for the purposes of this subsection, a company is a resident of a Member State of the European Communities if the company is by virtue of the law of that Member State resident for the purposes of tax (being, in the case of the State, corporation tax and, in any other case, being any tax imposed in the Member State which corresponds to corporation tax in the State) in such Member State][2].

(7) For the purposes of this section, any participator in a company which controls another company shall be treated as being also a participator in that other company, and section 437(2) shall apply for the purpose of determining whether a person has for the purpose of subsection (3) a material interest in a company.

(8) For the purposes of this section and in relation to any loan or advance made on or after the 23rd day of May, 1983, section 430(1) shall apply as if paragraph (*b*) of that section were deleted.

Amendments

1 Substituted by FA 2001 s 240(1) and (2)(*a*) and Sch 5 Pt 1 for 2002 and later tax years; previously "£15,000".

2 Substituted by FA 2003 s 45(1)(*a*) with effect from 6 February 2003 as respects the making of a loan, the advance of any money, the incurring of any debt, or the assignment of any debt; previously "to a company not resident in the State".

Cross-references

Debt, release of: s 439(3).
Extension of TCA 1997 s 438 to loans by companies controlled by close companies, subs (1): s 438A(2), (3); subs (2): s 438A(7); s 438A(6), (8).
Income tax on payments by resident companies, "relevant payment" includes annual payments under this section: s 239(1)(*b*).
Returns of profits: s 884(2)(*e*).
Self-assessment, notices of preliminary tax, subs (4): s 953(7)(*a*)(ii).
Wear and tear allowances for licences for public hire (taxi) vehicles, subs (4): s 286A(6).

Case law

UK

A sum of money misappropriated by a participator is not a loan: *Stephens v T Pittas Ltd* [1983] STC 576.
Company obliged to give notification of its liability under this section and failure to do so constituted neglect: *Earlspring Properties v Guest* [1995] STC 479.
Overdrawn director's account held to constitute a loan to a participator: *Joint v Bracken Developments Ltd* [1994] STC 300.
Participator incurred a debt when company provided services, payment for which was made at year end: *Grant v Watton* [1999] STC 330.

Definitions

charges on income: ss 4(1), 243(1); close company: ss 4(1), 430, 431; company: ss 4(1), 5(1); interest: s 4(1); month: IA 1937 Sch; person: IA 1937 s 11(*c*); total income: s 3(1); trade: ss 3(1), 4(1), 5(1); year of assessment: ss 2(1), 5(1).

Former enactments

CTA 1976 s 98(1)–(7) and (9); FA 1983 s 35.

Corresponding UK tax provision

Income and Corporation Taxes Act 1988 s 419.

438A Extension of section 438 to loans by companies controlled by close companies

[(1) In this section **"loan"** includes advance.

(2) Subject to subsection (5), where a company which is controlled by a close company makes a loan which, apart from this section, does not give rise to a charge under subsection (1) of section 438, that section applies as if the loan had been made by the close company.

(3) Subject to subsection (5), where a company which is not controlled by a close company makes a loan which, apart from this section, does not give rise to a charge under subsection (1) of section 438 and a close company subsequently acquires control of it, that section applies as if thc loan had bccn madc by the close company immediately after the time when it acquired control.

(4) Where 2 or more close companies together control the company that makes or has made the loan, subsections (2) and (3) apply—

(*a*) as if each of them controlled that company, and

(*b*) as if the loan had been made by each of those close companies,

but the loan shall be apportioned between those close companies in such proportion as may be appropriate having regard to the nature and amount of their respective interests in the company that makes or has made the loan.

(5) Subsections (2) and (3) do not apply if it is shown that no person has made any arrangements (otherwise than in the ordinary course of a business carried on by that person) as a result of which there is a connection—

(*a*) between the making of the loan and the acquisition of control, or

(*b*) between the making of the loan and the provision by the close company of funds for the company making the loan,

and the close company shall be regarded as providing funds for the company making the loan if it directly or indirectly makes any payment or transfers any property to, or releases or satisfies (in whole or in part) a liability of, the company making the loan.

(6) Where, by virtue of this section, section 438 applies as if a loan made by one company had been made by another company, any question under that section whether—

(*a*) the company making the loan did so otherwise than in the ordinary course of a business carried on by it which includes the lending of money,

(*b*) the loan or any part of it has been repaid to the company,

(*c*) the company has released or written off the whole or part of the debt in respect of the loan,

shall be determined by reference to the company that makes the loan.

(7) References to a company making a loan include references to cases in which the company is, or if it were a close company would be, regarded as making a loan by virtue of section 438(2).

(8) This section shall be construed together with section 438.][1]

Amendments

1 Section 438A inserted by FA 2003 s 45(1)(*b*) as respects the making of a loan, the advance of any money, the incurring of any debt, or the assignment of any debt, on or after 6 February 2003.

Definitions

close company: ss 4(1), 430, 431; company: s 4(1); control: s 432.

439 Effect of release, etc of debt in respect of loan under section 438

(1) Subject to this section, where a company is assessed or liable to be assessed under section 438 in respect of a loan or advance and releases or writes off the whole or part of the debt in respect of the loan or advance, then—

(*a*) for the purpose of computing the total income of the person to whom the loan or advance was made, a sum equal to the amount so released or written off shall be treated as income received by such person after deduction of income tax by virtue of section 238 (at the standard rate for the year of assessment in which the whole or part of the debt was released or written off) from a corresponding gross amount,

(*b*) no repayment of income tax shall be made in respect of that income,

(*c*) notwithstanding paragraph (*a*), the income included by virtue of that paragraph in the total income of that person shall be treated for the purposes of sections 237 and 238 as not brought into charge to income tax, and

(*d*) for the purposes of section 59(ii), any amount to be treated as income by virtue of paragraph (*a*) shall be treated as if income tax had been deducted from that amount at the standard rate for the year of assessment in which the whole or part of the debt was released or written off; but, where such amount (or the aggregate of such amounts if more than one) exceeds the amount of the individual's taxable income charged at the standard rate or the higher rate, the amount of the credit under section 59(ii) in respect of the excess shall not, notwithstanding anything in section 59, exceed the amount of the income tax, if any, charged on that excess.

(2) If the loan or advance referred to in subsection (1) was made to a person who has since died, or to trustees of a trust which has come to an end, this section, instead of applying to the person to whom it was made, shall apply to the person from whom the debt is due at the time of release or writing off (and accordingly, if it is due from such person as personal representative within the meaning of Chapter 1 of Part 32, the amount treated as received by such person shall be, as regards the higher rate of tax, included for the purposes of that Chapter in the aggregate income of the estate), and subsection (1) shall apply accordingly with the necessary modifications.

(3) This section shall be construed together with section 438.

Cross-references

Administration of estates of deceased persons, subs (2): s 799(1)(*b*)(i).

Case law

A release held to exist although the company's assets were not depleted: *Collins v Addies; Greenfield v Bains* [1992] STC 746.

Definitions

company: ss 4(1), 5(1); higher rate: ss 3(1), 15; person: IA 1937 s 11(*c*); taxable income: ss 3(1), 458; total income: s 3(1); year of assessment: ss 2(1), 5(1).

Former enactments

CTA 1976 s 99(1), (2) and (4).

Corresponding UK tax provision

Income and Corporation Taxes Act 1988 s 421.

440 Surcharge on undistributed investment and estate income

(1) (*a*) Where for an accounting period of a close company the [distributable estate and investment income][1] exceeds the distributions of the company for the accounting period, there shall be charged on the company an additional duty of corporation tax (in this section referred to as a **"surcharge"**) amounting to 20 per cent of the excess.

(*b*) Notwithstanding paragraph (*a*)—

(i) a surcharge shall not be made on a company where the excess is equal to or less than the lesser of the following amounts—

(I) [€635][2] or, if the accounting period is less than 12 months, [€635][2] proportionately reduced, and

(II) where the company has one or more associated companies, [€635][2] divided by one plus the number of those associated companies or, if the accounting period is less than 12 months, [€635][2] proportionately reduced divided by one plus the number of those associated companies;

(ii) where the excess is greater than the lesser amount on which by virtue of subparagraph (i) a surcharge would not be made, the amount of the surcharge shall not be greater than a sum equal to 80 per cent of the amount by which the excess is greater than that lesser amount.

(2) Where the aggregate of—

(*a*) the accumulated undistributed income of the company at the end of the accounting period, and

(*b*) any amount which, on or after the 27th day of November, 1975, was transferred to capital reserves or was used to issue shares, stock or securities as paid up otherwise than for new consideration (within the meaning of section 135) or was otherwise used so as to reduce the amount referred to in paragraph (*a*),

is less than the excess referred to in subsection (1), that subsection shall apply as if the amount of that aggregate were substituted for the excess.

...[3]

(3) In applying subsection (1) to any accounting period of a company, an associated company which has not carried on any trade or business at any time in that accounting period (or, if an associated company during part only of that accounting period, at any time in that part of that accounting period) shall be disregarded.

(4) In determining how many associated companies a company has in an accounting period or whether a company has an associated company in an accounting period, an

associated company shall be counted even if it was an associated company for part only of the accounting period, and 2 or more associated companies shall be counted even if they were associated companies for different parts of the accounting period.

...[4]

(6) A surcharge made under this section on a company in respect of an accounting period (in this subsection referred to as **"the first-mentioned accounting period"**)—

(*a*) shall be charged on the company for the earliest accounting period which ends on or after a day which is 12 months after the end of the first-mentioned accounting period, and

(*b*) shall be treated as corporation tax chargeable for that accounting period;

but where there is no such accounting period so ending, the surcharge shall be charged for, and treated as corporation tax of, the accounting period in respect of which it is made.

(7) The provisions of the Corporation Tax Acts relating to—

(*a*) assessments to corporation tax,

(*b*) appeals against such assessments (including the rehearing of appeals and the statement of a case for the opinion of the High Court), and

(*c*) the collection and recovery of corporation tax,

shall apply in relation to a surcharge made under this section as they apply to corporation tax charged otherwise than under this section.

Amendments

1 Substituted by FA 2001 s 91(2)(*a*) as respects an accounting period ending on or after 14 March 2001; previously "aggregate of the distributable investment income and distributable estate income".

2 Substituted by FA 2001 s 240(1) and (2)(*c*) and Sch 5 Pt 1 for accounting periods ending on or after 1 January 2002; previously "£500".

3 Subs (2A) deleted by FA 2003 s 163 and Sch 6 para 1(*c*) as respects accounting periods ending on or after 14 March 2001.

4 Subs (5) repealed by FA 2000 s 69(2) and Sch 2 Part 2 with effect from 6 April 1999 in the case of income tax and as respects accounting periods commencing on or after that date in the case of corporation tax.

Cross-references

Close company surcharges, distributable estate and investment income, distributable trading income, meanings: s 434(2) and (5A).

Dividends regarded as paid out of profits accumulated before given date: Sch 22 para 4(2)(*c*).

Group relief, relief for certain losses on a value basis: s 420B(1)("relevant corporation tax").

Manufacturing (10%) rate, meaning of "relevant corporation tax": s 448(1)(*d*).

Relief for certain charges on income on a value basis: s 243B(1)("relevant corporation tax").

Relief for certain trading losses on a value basis: s 396B(1)("relevant corporation tax").

Relief in respect of unrelieved losses and capital allowances carried forward from 1975–76: Sch 32 para 16(1).

Service companies, undistributed income, surcharge, subs (1) does not apply, but subss (2)–(7) do: s 441(5).

Taxation of collective investment undertakings: s 734(9)(*b*).

Unquoted company buying its own shares: s 176.

Tax Briefing

TB25 Feb 1997 p 12 — Estate income and distributable income are calculated, net of "section 23" type relief (TCA 1997 ss 325–327; 334–336; 346–348; 356–358; 361–363; 372F–372H; 372P–372R; 372X; 380B–380D) carried forward.

TB34 Dec 1998 p 23 — Advance corporation tax may be set off against surcharge.

Case law

Subs (1): Payments made during a liquidation held not to be distributions within s 84 which effected a surcharge on a close company's investment income: *Rahinstown Estate Co Ltd (In liquidation) v Hughes* ITR Vol III, p 517.

Definitions

company: ss 4(1), 5(1); close company: ss 4(1), 430, 431; distribution: ss 4(1), 436, 437; month: IA 1937 Sch; tax credit: ss 2(1), 136.

Former enactments

CTA 1976 s 28(4)–(5) and s 101; FA 1990 s 47; FA 1997 s 146(1) and Sch 9 Pt I para 10(4).

441 Surcharge on undistributed income of service companies

(1) In this section, **"service company"** means, subject to subsection (2)—

(*a*) a close company whose business consists of or includes the carrying on of a profession or the provision of professional services,

(*b*) a close company having or exercising an office or employment, or

(*c*) a close company whose business consists of or includes the provision of services or facilities of whatever nature to or for—

(i) a company within either of the categories referred to in paragraphs (*a*) and (*b*),

(ii) an individual who carries on a profession,

(iii) a partnership which carries on a profession,

(iv) a person who has or exercises an office or employment, or

(v) a person or partnership connected with any person or partnership referred to in subparagraphs (i) to (iv);

but the provision by a close company of services or facilities to or for a person or partnership not connected with the company shall be disregarded for the purposes of this paragraph.

(2) Where the principal part of a company's income which is chargeable to corporation tax under Cases I and II of Schedule D and Schedule E is not derived from—

(*a*) carrying on a profession,

(*b*) providing professional services,

(*c*) having or exercising an office or employment,

(*d*) providing services or facilities (other than providing services or facilities to or for a person or partnership not connected with the company) to or for any person or partnership referred to in subparagraphs (i) to (v) of subsection (1)(*c*), or

(*e*) any 2 or more of the activities specified in paragraphs (*a*) to (*d*),

the company shall be deemed not to be a service company.

(3) For the purposes of this section—

(*a*) a partnership shall be treated as connected with a company or individual (and a company or individual shall be treated as connected with a partnership) if any one of the partners in the partnership is connected with the company or individual, and

(b) a partnership shall be treated as connected with another partnership if any one of the partners in the partnership is connected with any one of the partners in the other partnership.

(4) (a) Where for an accounting period of a service company the aggregate of—

[(i) the distributable estate and investment income, and

(ii) 50 per cent of the distributable trading income,][1]

exceeds the distributions of the company for the accounting period, there shall be charged on the company an additional duty of corporation tax (in this section referred to as a **"surcharge"**) amounting to 15 per cent of the excess.

(b) Notwithstanding paragraph (a)—

(i) a surcharge shall not be made on a company where the excess is equal to or less than the lesser of the following amounts—

(I) [€635][2] or, if the accounting period is less than 12 months, [€635][2] proportionately reduced, and

(II) where the company has one or more associated companies, [€635][2] divided by one plus the number of those associated companies or, if the accounting period is less than 12 months, [€635][2] proportionately reduced divided by one plus the number of those associated companies;

(ii) where the excess is greater than the lesser amount on which by virtue of subparagraph (i) a surcharge would not be made, the amount of the surcharge shall not be greater than a sum equal to 80 per cent of the amount by which the excess is greater than that lesser amount;

(iii) the surcharge shall apply to so much of the excess calculated under this subsection in respect of an accounting period of a company as is not greater than the excess of the [distributable estate and investment income][3] of the accounting period over the distributions of the company for the accounting period as if the reference in this subsection apart from this subparagraph to 15 per cent were a reference to 20 per cent.

(5) Section 440(1) shall not apply in relation to a service company, but subsections (2) to (7) of section 440 shall apply in relation to a surcharge made under this section as they apply in relation to a surcharge made under section 440 with the substitution in subsections (2) and (3) of section 440 of a reference to subsection (4) of this section for the reference to subsection (1) of that section.

(6) (a) Subsections (2), (3), (6) and (7) of section 434 shall apply for the purposes of this section as they apply for the purposes of section 434 or 440, as the case may be.

(b) For the purposes of this section—

(i) the income of a company for an accounting period shall be its income computed for that period in accordance with section 434(4);

(ii) [**"distributable estate and investment income"** and **"distributable trading income"**][4] of a company for an accounting period have the same meanings respectively as in subsections (1) and (5) of section 434 with the substitution for the reference to a trading company in each place where it occurs in subsection (5) of that section of a reference to a service company.

Amendments

1 Subs (4)(*a*)(i)–(ii) substituted by FA 2001 s 91(3)(*a*)(i) as respects an accounting period ending on or after 14 March 2001.

2 Substituted by FA 2001 s 240(1) and (2)(*c*) and Sch 5 Pt 1 for accounting periods ending on or after 1 January 2002; previously "£500".

3 Substituted by FA 2001 s 91(3)(*a*)(ii) as respects an accounting period ending on or after 14 March 2001; previously "aggregate of the distributable investment income and distributable estate income".

4 Substituted by FA 2001 s 91(3)(*b*) as respects an accounting period ending on or after 14 March 2001; previously "'distributable income', 'distributable investment income' and 'distributable estate income'".

Cross-references

Dividends regarded as paid out of profits accumulated before given date: Sch 22 para 4(2)(*c*).

Group relief, relief for certain losses on a value basis: s 420B(1).

Manufacturing (10%) rate, meaning of "relevant corporation tax": s 448(1)(*d*).

Relief for certain charges on income on a value basis: s 243B(1) ("relevant corporation tax").

Relief for certain trading losses on a value basis: s 396B(1) ("relevant corporation tax").

Relief in respect of unrelieved losses and capital allowances carried forward from 1975–76: Sch 32 para 16(1).

Unquoted company buying its own shares: s 176.

Case law

Irish

Subs (1): An advertising company was not considered to be a business consisting of carrying on a profession for surcharge purposes: *MacGiolla Mhaith v Brian Cronin and Associates Ltd* ITR Vol III p 211.

UK

Held to be exercising a profession:

Actress: *Davies v Braithwaite* (1931) 18 TC 198.

Barrister: *Seldon v Croom-Johnston* (1932) 16 TC 740.

Journalist: *CIR v Maxse* (1919) 12 TC 41.

Optician: *CIR v North and Ingram* (1918) 2 KB 705.

Held not to be exercising a profession:

Dance band leader: *Loss v CIR* (1945) 2 All ER 683.

Insurance broker: *Durant v CIR* (1921) 12 TC 245.

Professional gambler: *Graham v Green* (1925) 2 TC 309.

The surcharge position of a company for any accounting period should be decided by reference to the company's status at balance sheet date – *CHW (Huddersfield) Ltd v CIR* 41 TC 92.

Revenue precedents

Issue: Whether the activities of each of the following were carrying on a profession: 1) Public Relations co.; 2) Insurance broker; 3) Livestock auctioneering in a cattle mart; 4) Auctioneers/estate agents; 5) Quantity surveyors.

Decision: Whether professional services were provided was a question of fact but in the cases in question it was decided as follows: 1), 2), 3) were not; and 4) and 5) were.

Tax Briefing

TB25 Feb 1997 p 12 — Estate income and distributable income are calculated net of "section 23" type relief (TCA 1997 ss 325–327; 334–336; 346–348; 356–358; 361–363; 372F–372H; 372P — 372R; 372X; 380B–380D) carried forward.

TB34 Dec 1998 p 23 — Advance corporation tax may be set off against surcharge.

TB48 June 2002 p 19 — Professional Service Company Surcharge — what activities constitute the carrying on of a profession.

Definitions

close company: ss 4(1), 430, 431; company: s 4(1); distribution: ss 4(1), 436, 437; month: IA 1937 Sch; person: IA 1937 s 11(*c*).

Former enactments

CTA 1976 s 162(1)–(6); FA 1990 s 48; FA 1995 s 55(1); FA 1996 s 52(1); FA 1997 s 146(1) and Sch 9 Pt I para 10(9).

PART 14
TAXATION OF COMPANIES ENGAGED IN MANUFACTURING TRADES, CERTAIN TRADING OPERATIONS CARRIED ON IN SHANNON AIRPORT AND CERTAIN TRADING OPERATIONS CARRIED ON IN THE CUSTOM HOUSE DOCKS AREA

Cross-references

Bank levy credit: s 487(1)(*a*)(iii)("T").
BES relief, qualifying trades: s 496(2)(*a*)(i).
Dealers in securities: s 749(2A)(*a*)(ii), (2B)(*a*).
Enterprise area buildings: s 343(1) (qualifying trading operations).
Relief from corporation tax by means of credit in respect of foreign tax, unilateral relief: Sch 24 para 9D(3)(*b*).

CHAPTER 1
Interpretation and General

442 Interpretation (Part 14)

(1) In this Part—

[**"expansion operations"**, in relation to a company, includes—

(*a*) increases in production capacity for existing or directly related product lines of the company, and

(*b*) the addition of support functions directly related to the existing trading operations of the company;

"industrial development agency" means—

(*a*) the Industrial Development Authority in Ireland,
(*b*) the Shannon Free Airport Development Company,
(*c*) Údarás na Gaeltachta,
(*d*) the Industrial Development Agency, Ireland,
(*e*) Forbairt,
(*f*) Forfás, or
(*g*) Enterprise Ireland;][1]

"merchandise" means goods other than goods within the meaning of section 443;

[**"relevant accounting period"**, in relation to a trade carried on by a company which consists of or includes the manufacture of goods, means an accounting period or part of an accounting period of a company ending on or before—

(*a*) where subsection (11) or (12) of section 443 applies, the 31st day of December, 2000, (*b*) in the case of a trade, other than a specified trade, which is set up and commenced on or after the 23rd day of July, 1998, the 31st day of December, 2002, and

(*c*) in any other case, the 31st day of December, 2010;

"relief under this Part" means the reduction of corporation tax provided for in section 448(2);][2]

[**"specified trade"**, in relation to a company—

(*a*) means a trade which consists of or includes trading operations specified in a grant agreement (in this definition referred to as "the relevant grant agreement") entered into between the company and an industrial development agency on foot of an approval of grant assistance for the company made by the industrial development agency on or before the 31st day of July, 1998, but—

(*b*) does not include such part of the trade as consists of expansion operations which commenced to be carried on on or after the 23rd day of July, 1998, other than such of those operations as would fall within the terms of the relevant grant agreement;][3]

(2) For the purposes of this Part, where a part only of an accounting period of a company is a relevant accounting period, all amounts referable to the accounting period shall be apportioned, on the basis of the proportion which the length of the relevant accounting period bears to the length of the accounting period of the company, for the purpose of ascertaining any amount required to be taken into account in respect of the relevant accounting period.

[(3) Where, by virtue of the application of the definition of "specified trade", an accounting period or part of an accounting period—

(*a*) would be a relevant accounting period in relation to a part (in this subsection referred to as "the first-mentioned part") of a trade carried on by a company, and

(*b*) would not be a relevant accounting period in relation to another part (in this subsection referred to as "the second-mentioned part") of that trade,

then, for the purposes of this Part—

(i) the first-mentioned part and the second-mentioned part shall each be treated as a separate trade, and

(ii) there shall be apportioned to the first-mentioned part and the second-mentioned part such proportion of the total amount receivable from sales made and services rendered in the course of the trade, and of expenses incurred in the course of the trade, in the accounting period or part of the accounting period, as the case may be, as is just and reasonable.

(4) Where—

(*a*) on or after the 23rd day of July, 1998, a company (in this subsection referred to as "the successor company") succeeds to a trade or part of a trade which was carried on by another company (in this subsection referred to as "the original company"), and (*b*) the original company has or could have made a claim to relief under this Part in relation to the trade or part of the trade,

then, subject to sections 445 and 446, relief, in so far as such relief relates to the trade or part of the trade in question, shall be granted to the successor company as respects the remaining relevant accounting periods for which such relief might have been claimed by the original company if it had continued to carry on the trade or part of the trade in question.][4]

Amendments

1 Definitions of "expansion operations" and "industrial development agency" inserted by FA 1999 s 74(*a*)(i)(I) with effect from 6 April 1999.

2 Definitions of "relevant accounting period" and "relief under this Part" substituted by FA 1999 s 74(*a*)(i)(II) with effect from 6 April 1999.

3 Definition of "specified trade" inserted by FA 1999 s 74(*a*)(i)(III) with effect from 6 April 1999.

4 Subs (3)–(4) inserted by FA 1999 s 74(*a*)(ii) with effect from 6 April 1999.

Cross-references

Relief from corporation tax by means of credit in respect of foreign tax, unilateral relief: Sch 24 para 9D(3)(*a*); subs (2): Sch 24 para 9D(3)(*b*).

Tax Briefing

TB55 April 2004 p 18 — Manufacturing Relief — where company commenced trading on or after 23 July 1998.

Definitions

company: s 4(1); trade: ss 3(1), 4(1).

Former enactments

FA 1980 s 38 and s 40; FA 1990 s 40 and s 41(6); FA 1991 s 35.

443 Meaning of "goods"

(1) (*a*) In this Part, **"goods"** means, subject to this section, goods manufactured in the State in the course of a trade by the company which, in relation to the relevant accounting period, is the company claiming relief under this Part in relation to the trade.

(*b*) Where—

(i) there are 2 companies one of which manufactures goods and the other of which sells the goods in the course of its trade, and

(ii) one of the companies is a 90 per cent subsidiary of the other company or both companies are 90 per cent subsidiaries of a third company,

any goods manufactured in the State by one of the companies shall, when sold in the course of its trade by the other company, be deemed to have been manufactured in the State by that other company.

(*c*) Sections 412 to 417 shall apply for the purposes of paragraph (*b*)(ii) as they apply for the purposes of Chapter 5 of Part 12.

(2) The definition of **"goods"** shall include fish produced in the State on a fish farm in the course of a trade by the company which, in relation to the relevant accounting period, is the company claiming relief under this Part in relation to the trade, and references in this Part to manufactured shall be construed, in relation to fish, as including references to produced and cognate words shall be construed accordingly.

(3) The definition of **"goods"** shall include plants cultivated in the State, by the process of plant biotechnology known as **"micro-propagation"** or **"plant cloning"**, in the course of a trade by the company which, in relation to the relevant accounting period, is the company claiming relief under this Part in relation to the trade, and references in this Part to manufactured shall be construed, in relation to such plants, as including references to cultivated and cognate words shall be construed accordingly.

(4) The definition of **"goods"** shall include—

(*a*) meat processed in the State in an establishment approved and inspected in accordance with the European Communities (Fresh Meat) Regulations, 1987 (SI No 284 of 1987), and

(*b*) subject to subsections (5) and (6)(*a*)(iii), fish which has been subjected to a process of manufacture in the State,

in the course of a trade by the company which, in the relevant accounting period, is the company claiming relief under this Part in relation to the trade, and references in this Part to manufactured and cognate words shall be construed accordingly.

(5) (*a*) The definition of **"goods"** shall not include goods sold by retail by the company claiming relief under this Part.

(*b*) For the purposes of paragraph (*a*), goods shall be deemed not to be sold by retail if they are sold—

(i) to a person who carries on a trade of selling goods of the class to which the goods so sold to such person belong,

(ii) to a person who uses goods of that class for the purposes of a trade carried on by such person, or

(iii) to a person, other than an individual, who uses goods of that class for the purposes of an undertaking carried on by such person.

(6) Without prejudice to the generality of subsection (1) and subject to subsections (2) to (4) and (8) to (15), goods shall not for the purposes of this section be regarded as manufactured if they are goods which result from a process—

(*a*) which consists primarily of any one of the following—

(i) dividing (including cutting), purifying, drying, mixing, sorting, packaging, branding, testing or applying any other similar process to a product, produce or material that is acquired in bulk so as to prepare that product, produce or material for sale or distribution, or any combination of such processes,

(ii) applying methods of preservation, pasteurisation or maturation or other similar treatment to any foodstuffs, or any combination of such processes,

(iii) cooking, baking or otherwise preparing food or drink for human consumption which is intended to be consumed, at or about the time it is prepared, whether or not in the building or structure in which it is prepared or whether or not in the building to which it is delivered after being prepared,

(iv) improving or altering any articles or materials without imposing on them a change in their character, or

(v) repairing, refurbishing, reconditioning, restoring or other similar processing of any articles or materials, or any combination of such processes,

or

(*b*) which, subject to subsection (1)(*b*), is not carried out by the company claiming relief under this Part.

(7) (*a*) In this subsection, **"the intervention agency"** means the Minister for Agriculture and Food, when exercising or performing any power or function conferred on that Minister by regulation 3 of the European Communities (Common Agricultural Policy) (Market Intervention) Regulations, 1973 (SI No 24 of 1973), and any other person when exercising or performing any corresponding power or function in any Member State of the European Communities.

(*b*) Notwithstanding any other provision of the Tax Acts, the definition of **"goods"** shall not include goods sold to the intervention agency.

(*c*) For the purposes of paragraph (*b*), the sale of goods to a person other than the intervention agency shall be deemed to be a sale to the intervention agency if and to the extent that those goods are ultimately sold to the intervention agency; but the rendering to the intervention agency of services consisting of the subjecting of meat belonging to the agency to a process of manufacture carried out in an establishment specified in subsection (4)(*a*) shall not be regarded as a sale of goods to the agency.

(8) For the purpose of relief under this Part, in relation to a company that carries on a trade which consists of or includes the repairing of ships—

(*a*) repairs carried out in the State to a ship shall be regarded as the manufacture in the State of goods, and

(*b*) any amount receivable in payment for such repairs so carried out shall be regarded as an amount receivable from the sale of goods.

(9) (*a*) In this subsection, **"engineering services"** means design and planning services the work on the rendering of which is carried out in the State in connection with chemical, civil, electrical or mechanical engineering works executed outside the territories of the Member States of the European Communities.

(*b*) For the purpose of relief under this Part, in relation to a company which carries on a trade which consists of or includes the rendering of engineering services—

(i) the rendering in the State of such services shall be regarded as the manufacture in the State of goods, and

(ii) any amount receivable in payment for such services so rendered shall be regarded as an amount receivable from the sale of goods.

(10)(*a*) In this subsection, **"computer services"** means one or more of the following—

(i) data processing services,

(ii) software development services, and

(iii) technical or consultancy services relating to either or both services specified in subparagraphs (i) and (ii), the work on the rendering of which is carried out in the State in the course of a service undertaking in respect of which—

(I) (A) an employment grant was made by the Industrial Development Authority under section 25 of the Industrial Development Act, 1986, or

(B) an employment grant was made by the Industrial Development Agency (Ireland) or Forbairt, as may be appropriate, under section 12(2) of the Industrial Development Act, 1993,

(II) a grant under section 3, or financial assistance under section 4, of the Shannon Free Airport Development Company Limited (Amendment) Act, 1970, was made available by the Shannon Free Airport Development Company Limited, or

(III) financial assistance was made available by Údarás na Gaeltachta under section 10 of the Údarás na Gaeltachta Act, 1979.

(*b*) For the purposes of relief under this Part, in relation to a company carrying on a trade which consists of or includes the rendering of computer services—

(i) the rendering of the computer services shall be regarded as the manufacture in the State of goods, and

(ii) any amount receivable in payment for the rendering of the computer services shall be regarded as an amount receivable from the sale of goods.

(11)(*a*) In this subsection, **"qualifying shipping activities"** and **"qualifying shipping trade"** have the same meanings respectively as in section 407.

(*b*) For the purposes of relief under this Part, in relation to a company carrying on a qualifying shipping trade—

(i) qualifying shipping activities carried on in the course of the qualifying shipping trade shall be regarded as the manufacture in the State of goods, and

(ii) any amount receivable from the carrying on of qualifying shipping activities shall be regarded as an amount receivable from the sale of goods.

(12)(*a*) In this subsection—

"export goods" means goods which, in relation to the manufacturer of those goods, are goods for the purposes of this Part and which are exported by a Special Trading House which is not the manufacturer of the goods but which, in relation to the relevant accounting period, is the company claiming relief from tax by virtue of this subsection, where the selling by the Special Trading House of the goods so exported is selling by wholesale;

"selling by wholesale" means selling goods of any class to a person who carries on a business of selling goods of that class or who uses goods of that class for the purposes of a trade or undertaking carried on by such person;

"Special Trading House" means a company which exists solely for the purpose of carrying on a trade consisting solely of the selling of export goods manufactured by a firm which employs less than 200 persons.

(*b*) For the purposes of this subsection, goods shall be deemed to be exported when they are transported out of the State in the course of the selling by wholesale of those goods and are not subsequently transported into the State in the course of the selling by wholesale of those goods.

(*c*) For the purposes of relief under this Part, in relation to a Special Trading House—

(i) export goods when exported in the course of its trade by a Special Trading House shall be deemed to have been manufactured by the Special Trading House, notwithstanding that the manufacturer has claimed, or is entitled to claim, relief under this Part in respect of the sale by it of those goods, and

(ii) any amount receivable by the Special Trading House in payment for the sale of export goods shall be regarded as an amount receivable from the sale of goods.

(*d*) This subsection shall apply subject to the Export Promotion (Amendment) Act, 1987.

(13) For the purposes of relief under this Part, in relation to a company which carries on a trade, not being a relevant trading operation within the meaning of section 445(7)(*a*), which consists of or includes the repair or maintenance of aircraft, aircraft engines or components—

(*a*) such repair or maintenance carried out in the State shall be regarded as the manufacture in the State of goods, and

(*b*) any amount receivable in payment for such repair or maintenance so carried out shall be regarded as an amount receivable from the sale of goods.

(14)(*a*) In this subsection, **"film"** means a film which is produced—

(i) on a commercial basis with a view to the realisation of profit, and

(ii) wholly or principally for exhibition to the public in cinemas or by means of television broadcasting or for training or documentary purposes,

and in respect of which not less than 75 per cent of the work on the production is carried out in the State.

(*b*) For the purposes of relief under this Part, in relation to a company carrying on a trade which consists of or includes the production of a film—

(i) the production of the film by the company claiming the relief shall be regarded as the manufacture in the State of goods, and

(ii) any amount receivable for that production shall be regarded as an amount receivable from the sale of goods.

(15) For the purposes of relief under this Part, in relation to a company which carries on a trade which consists of or includes the remanufacture and repair of computer equipment or of subassemblies where such equipment or subassemblies were originally manufactured by that company or a connected company—

(*a*) such remanufacture or repair carried out in the State shall be regarded as the manufacture in the State of goods, and

(*b*) any amount receivable in payment for such remanufacture or repair so carried out shall be regarded as an amount receivable from the sale of goods.

(16)(*a*) In this subsection—

"agricultural society" means a society—

(i) in relation to which both the following conditions are satisfied:

(I) the number of the society's members is not less than 50, and

(II) all or a majority of the society's members are persons who are mainly engaged in and derive the principal part of their income from husbandry,

or

(ii) to which a certificate under paragraph (*b*) relates;

"fishery society" means a society—

(i) in relation to which both the following conditions are satisfied:

(I) the number of the society's members is not less than 20, and

(II) all or a majority of the society's members are persons who are mainly engaged in and derive the principal part of their income from fishing,

or

(ii) to which a certificate under paragraph (*c*) relates;

"qualifying goods" means goods purchased by a society from its members where such goods, in relation to those members, are or would but for subsection (7) be goods for the purposes of this Part;

"qualifying society" means an agricultural society or a fishery society—

(i) which carries on a trade which consists wholly or mainly of the selling by wholesale of qualifying goods, and

(ii) all or a majority of the members of which are agricultural societies or fishery societies;

"selling by wholesale" means selling goods of any class to a person who carries on a business of selling goods of that class or who uses goods of that class for the purposes of a trade or undertaking carried on by such person;

"society" means a society registered under the Industrial and Provident Societies Acts, 1893 to 1978.

(*b*) The Minister for Finance may, on the recommendation of the Minister for Agriculture and Food, give a certificate entitling a society to be treated for the purposes of this subsection as an agricultural society notwithstanding that one or both of the conditions in paragraph (i) of the definition of **"agricultural society"** is or are not complied with in relation to the society.

(*c*) The Minister for Finance may, on the recommendation of the Minister for the Marine and Natural Resources, give a certificate entitling a society to be treated for the purposes of this subsection as a fishery society notwithstanding that one or both of the conditions in paragraph (i) of the definition of **"fishery society"** is or are not complied with in relation to the society.

(*d*) A certificate given under—

(i) paragraph (*a*) or (*b*) of section 70(2) of the Finance Act, 1963,

(ii) paragraph (*a*) or (*b*) of section 220(2) of the Income Tax Act, 1967, or

(iii) paragraph (*a*) or (*b*) of section 18(2) of the Finance Act, 1978,

shall, unless it has been revoked, be deemed to be a certificate given under paragraph (*b*) or (*c*), as the case may be.

(*e*) A certificate given under paragraph (*b*) or (*c*)—

(i) shall have effect as from such date, whether before or after the date on which it is given, as may be stated in the certificate, and

(ii) shall be published in Iris Oifigiúil as soon as may be after the certificate is given.

(*f*) A certificate given under paragraph (*b*) or (*c*) may be revoked by the Minister for Finance at any time and notice of any such revocation shall be published as soon as may be in Iris Oifigiúil.

(*g*) For the purposes of relief under this Part, in relation to a qualifying society—

(i) qualifying goods sold by wholesale in the course of its trade by the qualifying society shall be deemed to have been manufactured by the qualifying society, notwithstanding that the society which manufactured those goods has claimed, or is entitled to claim, relief under this Part in respect of the sale by it of those goods, and

(ii) any amount receivable from the sale of qualifying goods by the qualifying society shall be regarded as an amount receivable from the sale of goods.

(17)(*a*) In this subsection—

"agricultural society" and **"society"** have the same meanings respectively as in subsection (16);

"milk product" means butter, whey-butter, cream, cheese, condensed milk, dried or powdered milk, dried or powdered skim-milk, dried or powdered whey, chocolate crumb, casein, butter-oil, lactose, and any other product made wholly or mainly from milk or from a by-product of milk and approved for the purposes of this section by the Minister for Finance after consultation with the Minister for Agriculture and Food;

"qualifying company" means a company to which a certificate under paragraph (*c*) relates;

"qualifying trade" means a trade carried on by a company which consists wholly or mainly of the manufacture of milk products;

"relevant product" means milk purchased by an agricultural society from its members, being milk sold by the agricultural society to a qualifying company.

(*b*) For the purposes of this subsection (other than this paragraph), where a trade consists partly of the manufacture of milk products, then, unless the trade consists mainly of the application of a process of pasteurisation to milk, the part of the trade which consists of the manufacture of milk products shall be treated as a separate trade.

(*c*) Where the Minister for Agriculture and Food is satisfied that a company—

(i) carried on a qualifying trade during the whole of the period of 3 years ending immediately before the day from which the certificate specified subsequently in this paragraph has effect,

(ii) is carrying on a qualifying trade and intends to continue to carry it on for a period which when added to the period for which it has been carrying it on will amount to not less than 3 years, or

(iii) intends to carry on a qualifying trade for a period of not less than 3 years, that Minister may, after consultation with the Minister for Finance, give a certificate to the company stating that the company may be treated as a qualifying company for the purposes of this subsection, and, whenever such a certificate is given to a company, the company shall be so treated during the period for which the certificate has effect.

(*d*) A certificate given under paragraph (*c*)—

(i) shall have effect for the period beginning on such day, whether before or after the day on which it is given, as may be specified in the certificate and ending on the day which is 2 years after that day, and

(ii) may be revoked by the Minister for Agriculture and Food after consultation with the Minister for Finance.

(*e*) Notice of a revocation under paragraph (*d*) shall be published as soon as may be in Iris Oifigiúil and the revocation shall have effect as on and from the thirtieth day after the day on which it is so published.

(*f*) For the purposes of relief under this Part, in relation to the sale by an agricultural society of relevant products—

(i) relevant products shall be deemed to have been manufactured by the agricultural society, and

(ii) any amount receivable from the sale of relevant products by the agricultural society shall be regarded as an amount receivable from the sale of goods.

(18) For the purposes of relief under this Part, in relation to a company to which a profit or loss specified in section 80 arises, the amount of any profit which is deemed by that section to be a profit or gain of the trade carried on by the company shall be regarded as an amount receivable from the sale of goods.

(19)(*a*) In this subsection, **"newspaper"** means a newspaper—

(i) the contents of each issue of which consist wholly or mainly, as regards the quantity of printed matter contained in the newspaper, of information on the principal current events and topics of general public interest,

(ii) the format of which is commonly regarded as newspaper format, and

(iii) which is—

(I) printed on newsprint,

(II) intended to be sold to the public, and

(III) normally published at least fortnightly.

(*b*) For the purposes of relief under this Part, in relation to a company which carries on a trade which consists of or includes the production in the State of a newspaper—

(i) the production of the newspaper (including the rendering of advertising services in the course of the production of the newspaper) by the company shall be regarded as the manufacture in the State of goods, and

(ii) any amount receivable—

(I) from the sale of copies of the newspaper, or

(II) from the rendering by the company of advertising services in the course of the production of the newspaper,

shall be regarded as an amount receivable from the sale of goods.

(20) Subject to subsection (19), for the purposes of this Part, where in a relevant accounting period a company renders advertising services in the course of a trade carried on by it which consists wholly or partly of the production of a newspaper, magazine or other similar product, then—

(*a*) any amount receivable in payment for the rendering of such services shall not be regarded as an amount receivable from the sale of goods, and

(*b*) for the purposes of section 448, the company's income from the trade for a relevant accounting period shall be regarded as not derived solely from the sale of goods and merchandise.

(21) For the purpose of relief under this Part, in relation to a company which carries on a trade which consists of or includes the rendering to another person of services by means of subjecting commodities or materials belonging to that person to any process of manufacturing—

(*a*) the rendering in the State of such services shall be regarded as the manufacture in the State of goods, and

(*b*) any amount receivable in payment for services so rendered shall be regarded as an amount receivable from the sale of goods.

(22) The inspector may by notice in writing require a company, a Special Trading House (within the meaning of subsection (12)), a qualifying society (within the meaning of subsection (16)) or an agricultural society (within the meaning of subsection (17)), as the case may be, claiming relief from tax by virtue of subsection (8), (9), (10), (11), (12), (13), (14), (15), (16), (17), (18), (19) or (21), as the case may be, to furnish him or her with such information or particulars as may be necessary for the purpose of giving effect to that subsection, and subsection (2) of section 448 shall apply as if the matters of which proof is required by that subsection included the information or particulars specified in a notice under this subsection.

Cross-references

BES relief, qualifying trades, subs (10): s 496(2)(*a*)(i)(III); subs (12): s 496(2)(*a*)(xiv).

BES relief, qualifying trades, subs (3): s 496(2)(*a*)(viii).

BES relief, qualifying trades (subss (3), (11)–(12), (16), (17), (19)): s 496(2)(*a*)(i)(I).

Foreign tax credit (subs (10)(*b*)(ii)): s 449(1)(*b*).

Industrial and provident societies, transfer of shares to members, meaning of society applied, subs (16): s 701(1).

Interest treated as a distribution, meanings of "agricultural society" and "fishery society" (subs (16)) applied: ss 133(1)(*a*), 134(1)(*a*).

Merchandise, meaning: s 442(1).

Relevant accounting period, meaning, subss (11)–(12): s 442(1).

Shannon airport, trading operation, meaning, subs (13): s 445(1).

Case law

Irish

Subs (1): Held the Court would not make an order under the Companies Act 1963 s 89 to perfect an invalid issue of shares to enable the company to claim retrospectively manufacturing relief: *In the matter of Sugar Distributors Ltd* [1996] 1 ILRM 339.

Regarded as "manufacture"

Assembly of agricultural machinery: *Irish Agricultural Machinery Ltd v O'Culacháin* ITR Vol III, 611.

Newspaper advertising revenue held to be receivable "in respect of" sales of manufactured goods (newspapers): *McGurrin v The Champion Publications Ltd* ITR Vol IV p 466. See subs (20) above which now disallows such relief.

Production of nappy liners and "J cloths" from bales of fabric: *O'Laochdha v Johnson and Johnson (Ireland) Ltd* ITR Vol IV p 361.

Production of day-old chicks: *Kelly (J K) v Cobb Straffan IR Ltd* ITR Vol IV p 526.

Conditioning (adding carbon dioxide and increasing alcohol level) of bottled Guinness: *Hussey v Gleeson (M J) & Co Ltd* ITR Vol IV p 533.

The production of road markings from chemical mixture in heated vat, subsequently poured onto the road, held not to be "construction operations" but manufacturing: *Inspector of Taxes v Highway Markings Ltd*, Appeal Commissioners, 1994 (not further appealed). See ***Tax Briefing 25***, February 1997.

Pasteurisation of milk: *Cronin v Strand Dairy Ltd* ITR Vol III p 411.

Ripening of bananas: *McCann v O'Culacháin* ITR Vol III p 304.

NB: Subs (6) now excludes milk pasteurisation and banana ripening. In this regard, see *Saatchi and Saatchi Advertising Ltd v Kevin McGarry* [1998] ITR 99.

Recycling wastepaper, sufficient change in raw materials to constitute manufacturing – *P O'Muircheasa (IOT) v Bailey Wastepaper Ltd* 2003 ITR 111.

Not regarded as "manufacture"

Irish

Production of TV films by an advertising company where the processing was done abroad: *O'Culacháin v Hunter Advertising Ltd* ITR Vol IV p 35.

Production of out of season dwarfed chrysanthemums: *Brosnan v Leeside Nurseries* ITR Vol II, I [1998] 2 IR 311.

UK

Processing of rye grass seed held to be manufacture of goods: *Samuel McCausland v Ministry of Commerce* [1955] NILR 36. This activity would not now be regarded as "manufacture" in Ireland by virtue of subs (6).

Revenue precedents

Issue: Whether the process of anodising aluminium qualifies.

Decision: Yes.

Issue: Where animal feed is manufactured in a feed mill and supplied, including delivery, by pumping directly into farmers' silos for which delivery no separate charge is made: whether all qualifies.

Decision: Yes.

Issue: Whether the assembly of components – from the one source – into motorbikes qualified as a manufacturing process.

Decision: Disallowed by Revenue – not sufficient degree of change – may be appealed.

Issue: Whether the assembly of component parts ordered from suppliers in different countries and from different sources and used in a process to produce agricultural machinery qualified for manufacturing relief.

Decision: Accepted. The degree of processing resulted in machines which were more than an aggregation of individual components. *Irish Agricultural Machinery Limited* – High Court – Unreported – 6 February 1987. Supreme Court – Irish Tax Report [Volume III Page 611–16 March 1989].

Issue: Does the blending of tea qualify for manufacturing relief? The process involves sophisticated blending by which precise quantities of tea leaves are blended by machine to produce specific blends.

Decision: Allowed. A new product results from the process.

Issue: Design and processing bromides of advertising material to newspaper and magazine publishers where design cost is greater than the processing cost: amount of the relief.

Decision: Relief confined to the nominal value of the bromide: essentially a design rather than a printing process.

Issue: Production of straws containing diluted bulls' semen for use in AI: whether qualifying.

Decision: No.

Issue: Whether the three types of product, still water, unflavoured water and flavoured water would qualify for manufacturing relief. The process involves ozonation, granular activated carbon filtration, chilling, bottling and carbonation.

Decision: Accepted.

Issue: Producing ready-cooked, chilled, vacuum packed meals for the travel industry: whether qualifies.

Decision: Yes.

Issue: Where software development qualifies under subs (10) and some of the development is the subject of a co-development agreement with another company, whether that operates to deprive the company of relief by virtue of subs (6)(*b*).

Decision: No, provided co-development does not exceed 15% of the total.

Issue: Whether commercial photographer is producing "goods" for the purposes of the relief.

Decision: No, income arises from the photographer's skill rather than from "goods".

Issue: Sale of industrial information compiled and placed on magnetic tape or as a printed report; whether qualifying.
Decision: No, sale of information essentially.
Issue: (1) Whether computer assembly and upgrade qualify; (2) Whether qualifies if the replacement component will have the same capabilities as the item replaced.
Decision: (1) Yes. (2) No, repair only.
Issue: Does the customisation of systems - not always made in Ireland, but where integration takes place in Ireland — qualify for the 10% rate?
Decision: Allowed - only a small element of turnover arose from non-Irish systems.
Issue: Does a 90% subsidiary selling the goods of a resident manufacturing company have to be resident in the state to qualify for manufacturing relief?
Decision: No.
Issue: Does manufacturing relief apply to the sale of software developed by a software developer and sold embedded in bought in hardware? In the particular case the provision of the hardware is ancillary to the sale of the software package and by far the greater portion of the income derives from the software.
Decision: Allowed.
Issue: Do the following qualify for manufacturing relief: 1. Assembly of PCs from bought in components? 2. Bought in peripherals ie printers and monitors?
Decision: 1. Yes. 2. Allow provided (*a*) they are built in to the manufactured product, or (*b*) sold as part of an integrated package and tested by the 10% company.
Issue: Does manufacturing relief apply to the verification of integrated circuits (the process results in a Classification which is encoded onto each component)? The equipment used in the process resembles an automated assembly line.
Decision: Allowed.
Issue: (1) Development and production of computer programmes in the form of magnetic disks or tapes: whether qualifying; (2) Whether the repair of computer programmes qualifies under subs (15).
Decision: (1) Yes. (2) No - this applies to repair of physical hardware rather than software.
Issue: Whether writing and installing software qualifies where company is not in receipt of IDA employment grant.
Decision: No.
Issue: Will manufacturing relief apply to income generated by a software developer, charging a monthly fee for the use of the software?
Decision: Allowed, in the particular circumstances of the computer industry.
Issue: Whether localisation, where some of the process is subcontracted out, would qualify for manufacturing relief. The Irish company engages in a process whereby a computer program is broken down into various codes, and those requiring amendment are identified. Part of the localisation is done by the company and the localisation of other codes is sub-contracted out under instructions. The Irish company then re-engineers the program.
Decision: Allowed. In this instance the job was controlled by the company seeking relief and there was significant amount of Software development done by the company itself.
Issue: Whether graphic design sold in diskette format or in the form of a hard copy such as slides would qualify for manufacturing relief?
Decision: Disallowed. The income earned would result from the graphic design and not from the sale of the diskette or slides.
Issue: If two companies manufacture a product in partnership, can both companies avail of manufacturing relief.
Decision: Yes. Format of partnership is important.
Issue: Would software developed by companies which are not in receipt of employment grants qualify for manufacturing relief? The company manufactures specific software applications for banks and financial institutions which are sold to the client in disk format.
Decision: Allowed provided there is a sale of a tangible product such as a disk.
Issue: 1. Whether the sale of software (manufactured by the company) by perpetual licence would qualify for manufacturing relief. 2. Whether the sale of software (manufactured by the company) on disc accompanied by a licence allowing multiple use would qualify.
Decision: 1 and 2 Allowed. Both 1 & 2 in the circumstances of the computer industry accepted as a outright sale.
Issue: (1) Localisation of Master programme; encoding revised software on to physical medium and sale either outright or by perpetual licence; (2) Conversion, training and maintenance related to the software.
Decision: (1) All qualify. (2) Not qualifying.

Issue: 1. Whether the duplication of computer discs would qualify for the 10% rate. 2 Would the subcontracting of some of the duplication, to meet production requirements qualify for 10%?
Decision: 1. Allowed. 2 Allowed provided income from the subcontracted element represents not more than 5% of total income.
Issue: Would the sale of software on a term basis qualify for manufacturing relief? Life of software not expected to extend beyond three years. Value at end of three years of little significance.
Decision: Allowed. Software considered to be in a different category to other manufactured products, where leasing arrangements do not qualify.
Issue: Whether the manufacture, on site of a new pipe inside an old one, qualifies for manufacturing relief.
Decision: Disallowed. As the work was carried out on site it was considered to be construction.
Issue: Production of data labels by cutting acrylic rolls to size and laser printing data including bar codes onto the labels: whether qualifies.
Decision: Yes.
Issue: Whether a service provided for a parent or unconnected company would be regarded as data processing where the operations are grant aided by the IDA, or other appropriate agencies, as a computer service. Types of activities include 1. Telephone calls for hotel reservations or airplane tickets are taken, data processed and that data passed on to another company (no sale of hotel rooms or airline tickets takes place.) 2. Technical support for computer services is provided over the phone. 3 Invoices, accounts and other data are processed for third parties.
Decision: 1, 2, 3 Allowed.
Issue: Whether the operation of a VAT refund scheme by means of computer processing qualifies.
Decision: No, due to retail basis of service and the nature of the service which is not a data processing service; notwithstanding receipt by the company of an IDA employment grant.
Issue: Whether the production of day-old chicks in a controlled environment qualified for manufacturing relief.
Decision: Claim accepted by the High Court. Irish Tax Report [Volume IV] Page 526. Decision called into question by comments by Supreme Court in Leeside Nurseries case.
Issue: Whether the making of bridges, crowns and dental prostheses by dental technicians qualifies.
Decision: Yes.
Issue: Construction of designs and layouts for packaging, brochures etc. and the design sold on computer disk: whether qualifying.
Decision: No: design service.
Issue: (1) Whether design and programming diskette qualifies; (2) Whether installation satisfied of and tuition in respect of software qualifies.
Decision: (1) Yes, provided subs (10) re grant; (2) No.
Issue: Whether production of a journal/magazine using desktop publishing software qualifies.
Decision: No.
Issue: Whether production of disc controller for computer systems qualifies.
Decision: Yes.
Issue: Whether the drying of grass seeds and the drying and spraying of cereal is excluded from relief by subs (6).
Decision: Yes.
Issue: Whether the duplication of video cassettes qualifies for manufacturing relief.
Decision: Allowed.
Issue: Whether a process whereby plants are held in a controlled environment subject to specified amounts of light, heat and water, and the addition of chemicals qualify for manufacturing.
Decision: Claim rejected by the Supreme Court. Leeside Nurseries case. A key issue was whether the end product is capable of being manufactured.
Issue: Whether a monthly fee for the supply of electricity generated by a company would be regarded as income from the sale of goods. The fee consisting of two elements, representing a charge for the facility being on stand by on the grid (ie a payment of account of electricity produced) and a charge to cover the fuel and variable production costs for the electricity supplied to the grid.
Decision: Allowed.
Issue: Whether the production of electricity by means of wind power would qualify for manufacturing relief.
Decision: Accepted.
Issue: Will manufacturing relief apply to a process whereby a logo or design is embroidered on a garment which is bought in by the company?
Decision: Disallowed.
Issue: Whether the following processes qualify for manufacturing relief: embryo transfer with some level of processing; laboratory production of embryos; freezing of embryos.

Decision: Disallowed.
Issue: Whether re-processing and re-manufacture of whole engines or parts thereof for which a warranty is then given is excluded by subs (6)(v).
Decision: Yes.
Issue: Whether the Isle of Man is outside the EC for subs (9)(*a*).
Decision: Yes.
Issue: Whether the trade of showing films on a ferry qualifies as a shipping activity for the purposes of manufacturing relief.
Decision: Allowed.
Issue: Whether the process of post production of a film would qualify for manufacturing relief. In this case the process was more advanced than usual and included the addition of sound, colour and special effects which resulted in the production of a product which was significantly different to the one worked on.
Decision: Allowed. Where post production involves only subtitling, editing or adaptation of a film, the process would not qualify for the relief.
Issue: Whether a film set consisting of backgrounds, windows and doors, painted and decorated would qualify. The set is made in a factory.
Decision: Allowed. The assembly of the sets on site would not qualify.
Issue: What is the definition of fish farming for the purposes of manufacturing relief? Does the production of ornamental fish qualify?
Decision: Allowed. The EU has adopted the FAO definition. Farming implies some form of intervention in the rearing process to enhance production such as regular stocking, feeding and protection from predators. Advice of Bord lascaigh Mara sought in each case.
Issue: Whether the processing of prawns in the following manner would qualify for manufacturing relief, addition of chemicals, freezing and glazing.
Decision: Refused by Revenue, granted by Appeal Commissioner and not appealed further by Revenue.
Issue: (1) Whether subs (6) applies to subs (4) generally; (2) whether blast freezing fish is a process of manufacture.
Decision: (1) No, only as to the extent specified in subs 4(*b*) ; (2) Yes.
Issue: Whether fish which is subject to a process of manufacture qualifies for the reduced rate of corporation tax.
Decision: Allowed.
Issue: Whether the rearing of young fowl to marketable age, their killing, bleeding, scalding, plucking, evisceration, grading, bagging, freezing and boxing qualifies.
Decision: Yes.
Issue: Bulk fruit broken down, cleaned and edible oils added:- (1) whether qualifies. (2) whether excluded by subs (6).
Decision: (1) No. (2) Yes.
Issue: Whether processing which includes variations of moisture, blending to specific specifications and the addition of stenching agent to various gases, qualify for manufacturing relief.
Decision: Allowed.
Issue: (1) Grain drying: whether excluded by subs (6); (2) whether excluded when grain milled into meal by third party and sold on; (3) when grain dried, milled and sold in bulk meal form by one company.
Decision: (1) Yes. (2) Yes. (3) No.
Issue: Company providing "design for print": whether qualifying.
Decision: No, it is a non-qualifying service rather than a manufacturing process irrespective of the medium in which the design is sold.
Issue: (1) Interest relating to the late payment of sales proceeds qualifies even where it is intergroup companies; (2) Whether interest on inter-company balances arising from the transfer of sale proceeds from one company to another for financing qualifies.
Decision: (1) Yes. (2) No.
Issue: Is interest earned on short term deposits income from the sale of goods?
Decision: Disallowed.
Issue: Company produces a by software developer master diskette, the duplication of which is sub-contracted; its income is a licence fee which is a percentage of the end price of the software. Whether qualifies for the relief.
Decision: Yes.
Issue: (1) Whether the assembly of life rafts is manufacturing; (2) whether the repair of life rafts is "ship" repairs for the purposes of subs (8).
Decision: (1) No. (2) No.

Issue: Whether lobsters kept in an artificially induced state of suspended animation for sale live during the off-season qualify.
Decision: No.
Issue: Whether activities carried out in an EU approved plant qualifies for manufacturing relief. Livestock purchased and slaughtered, waste offal removed, meat deboned, treated with preservatives, carved and stored in refridgerated unit.
Decision: Allowed. The slaughter of animals and their further processing, in an EU approved establishment in accordance with European Union (Fresh Meat) regulations 1987 is allowed for the purposes of the 10% scheme. Outside of these establishments the process will qualify only if it meets the general test for manufacturing. Qualifying categories of processing would include the manufacture of sausages, puddings, cooked meats, rashers, pork etc. Processes where cutting only is involved would not qualify. The slaughter of animals and processing into cuts of meat would qualify.
Issue: Production of low-fat milk with vitamins added; fortified skim milk; buttermilk and flavoured school milk: (1) whether manufacture; (2) whether excluded by subs (6).
Decision: (1) Yes; (2) no; greater degree of change to end products.
Issue: Whether rewinding of motor engines fails within subs (6)(v).
Decision: Yes.
Issue: Whether the exploitation by a record company of sound recordings by way of licence arrangements would qualify for manufacturing relief.
Decision: Allowed for usual form of licencing by independent record production companies. Payment based on each record sold. Does not relate to the copyright in the material featured. Arises from the copyright in the recording.
Issue: Whether the duplication of sound recording master tapes qualifies for manufacturing relief.
Decision: Allowed. Sound recordings also qualify.
Issue: Whether a mussel farm is a "fish farm" for subs (2).
Decision: Yes.
Issue: Whether the production of a newspaper which does not come within s 443 would qualify if a company leases a printing facility, and undertakes the printing itself.
Decision: Allowed. Provided the company has control of the printing and bears the employees costs. The company must print itself to qualify outside s 443(19).
Issue: Would a freesheet newspaper with a circulation of 35,000 copies qualify for manufacturing relief.
Decision: Disallowed. TCA 1997s 443(19)(*a*)(ii) requires that a newspaper is intended to be sold to the public.
Issue: Would a paper dealing with greyhound racing, coursing and greyhounds generally, be regarded as coming within the definition of a newspaper as outlined in TCA 1997 s 443(19)(*a*)(i) for the purposes of manufacturing relief?
Decision: Disallowed.
Issue: Nut processing to remove skin and shell followed by roasting: whether qualifies.
Decision: Yes.
Issue: Offals produced by meat factories whether "goods".
Decision: Yes.
Issue: (1) Whether printing letters and brochures etc. qualifies; (2) whether office support ie copying, design and communication qualifies.
Decision: (1) Yes, provided sold wholesale; (2) No.
Issue: Whether the following qualify for manufacturing relief: 1. Machine processing of peat and the addition of fertiliser, lime and sand to produce horticultural products. 2. Processing and blending to affect moisture content and screening to remove debris to produce a consistent product.
Decision: 1. Allowed. 2. Disallowed. Not sufficient change in character of the product.
Issue: Does validation of pharmaceutical products qualify for manufacturing relief? Pharmaceutical products are subjected to a process by qualified chemists who ensure that the stringent requirements of the Drugs and Medicines regulatory authorities are met. A company involved in the validation process would take full legal responsibility for the finished product.
Decision: Allowed.
Issue: Does the subcontracting out of the granulation process disqualify a process from manufacturing relief? The remaining process involves the sampling, testing and mixing of specified quantities of ingredients to produce a homogeneous mixture. The mixture is a new product distinguishable from the individual ingredients. (Contrast with the mixing of fruit where the character of the individual ingredients remain).
Decision: Allowed. The remaining activities constitute manufacture in their own right.
Issue: Would manufacturing relief apply to the packaging and bottling of tablets in the 12 month period, while full manufacturing was being set up? The delay was outside the company's control.

Decision: Allowed.
Issue: Would the sale of goods not manufactured by a company qualify in the period prior to full manufacture?
Decision: Yes; provided full manufacture was not possible due to circumstances outsides the company's control.
Issue: Whether commercial photo developing carried on in a processing laboratory qualifies.
Decision: Yes.
Issue: Whether the printing of a newspaper may be contracted-out by the company claiming relief under subs (19) without loss of the relief.
Decision: Yes.
Issue: Would the process whereby information is transferred to a printing plate or film positive qualify for the 10% rate?
Decision: Allowed.
Issue: (1) Whether printing and re-printing textbooks qualifies; (2) whether sales to schools are "retail sales".
Decision: (1) Yes. (2) No.
Issue: Subsidiary of consulting engineering firm trading only with the parent: printing and binding reports and developing photos of maps etc: whether qualifying.
Decision: No, ancillary to engineering practice.
Issue: 1. Does printing which includes, design of layout and typeset, preparation of plates and printing qualify for manufacturing relief? 2. Will manufacturing relief apply to the production of a magazine or newspaper which does not conform to the definition in TCA 1997 s 443(19), where the actual printing is subcontracted out?
Decision: 1. Allowed. 2. Disallowed. To qualify outside of 443(19) a company would have to print the newspaper itself.
Issue: Whether cutting, levelling and polishing bought-in marble and slate slabs into fireplace hearths and risers qualifies.
Decision: Yes.
Issue: (1) Whether the design and construction on magnetic media of computer software qualifies when sold on a physical medium; (2) Whether feasibility studies related to the appropriate hardware for the resultant software qualifies;
Decision: (1) Yes. (2) No.
Issue: Programming of bought in programmable calculators and sale as one unit: whether qualifying.
Decision: No.
Issue: Whether the processing of waste paper to remove contaminants, metal extracts etc, and to compress the paper into bales would be a manufacturing process. The end product is referred to as substitute wood pulp fibre.
Decision: Disallowed. Appeal Commissioners ruled in favour of the company. Revenue is appealing to the High Court.
Issue: Whether a process to convert wastewater sludge to a granular fertiliser would constitute a manufacturing Process. The process involves the addition of lime and cement kiln dust and the subjecting of it to various temperature and drying procedures. The sludge is bought from local authorities, processed and sold to the horticultural/agricultural industry.
Decision: Allowed.
Issue: Whether a service company which subjects waste to various treatments to make it safe for disposal or re-use would qualify for manufacturing relief.
Decision: Disallowed.
Issue: Can a company remanufacturing computer equipment not originally manufactured by it qualify for manufacturing relief? In the case of this process the products are upgraded by the addition of software upgrades.
Decision: Allowed. Exceptional case - the degree of upgrade is sufficient to have the product come within the general understanding of manufacture.
Issue: Does the remanufacture of laser printer cartridges qualify for manufacturing relief? In the particular case key parts were manufactured in house and added so effectively a new product was produced.
Decision: Allowed. We are distinguishing this case from cartridges that are remanufactured by assembling used parts only, with the addition of some minor upgrading.
Issue: Whether goods sold to social organisations and residents organisations would be regarded as goods sold by retail for the purposes of s 443(5)(*a*).
Decision: No.
Issue: Whether the following items are to be treated as income from the sale of "goods" for the purposes of the section i) foreign exchange gains/losses arising on trading balances; ii) balancing charges on the disposal of trading assets.
Decision: Yes.

Issue: Where a company is engaged in crushing stone; and grading and washing sand as a whole process: whether all qualifies.
Decision: Yes.
Issue: Whether the production sileage additives of these is excluded by subs (6).
Decision: Yes.
Issue: (1) Whether the production of pickled skin pelts from sheepskins qualifies; (2) Whether the production of unscoured graded skin wool qualifies.
Decision: (1) Yes. (2) No.
Issue: Would the production of sound recordings to the stage of a master tape qualify for manufacturing relief?
Decision: Allowed
Issue: Would a company who subjects materials (gowns, drapes, etc) belonging to another company to a process of resterilisation qualify for manufacturing relief? The same goods are subjected to the same process a number of times.
Decision: Disallowed. There is no sale of goods, more akin to a laundry service.
Issue: Design and planning the installation of food processing/pasteurisation systems the installation of which was carried out by the employees of other companies; whether the first company was carrying out a manufacturing process.
Decision: No.
Issue: Production of large refrigeration system using contracted-in labour: whether qualifying.
Decision: Yes.
Issue: Manufacture of mail bags in which some of the finishing was contracted-out; whether qualifying.
Decision: Yes, provided sub-contracting does not exceed 3% of total.
Issue: The production of television programmes: whether qualifying given the use of sub-contractors to do some ot the production work.
Decision: Yes.
Issue: Whether the testing of dairy, meat and feed products and accreditation for export is a manufacturing process.
Decision: No, testing is not a manufacturing process.
Issue: Whether the manufacture of Garden Sheds, Gates, Pallets etc, from boards which are converted from trees growing in a forest would qualify for manufacturing relief.
Decision: Allowed.
Issue: Whether manufacturing relief would apply to: 1. Rough timber bought in, sawn into different lengths, planed and moulded, grooved into various products, door frames etc. 2. Rough timber bought in and put through treatment mill where it is treated with preservative.
Decision: 1. Allowed. 2. Disallowed. Note: Cutting into different sizes without producing a product or moulding the timber would not qualify.
Issue: Whether the production of standard quality eggs from turkeys in a controlled environment qualified for manufacturing relief.
Decision: Refused by Revenue.
Issue: (1) Potatoes cleaned, peeled, dipped in preservatives and packed: whether qualifying; (2) Vegetables peeled, sliced or diced and packed: whether qualifying.
Decision: (1) No. (2) No.
Issue: Whether company making bumpers, side barriers, grilles etc. and using them to replace damaged parts of customers' vehicles qualifies;
Decision: No, subs (6)(v) applies.
Issue: Production of premium vodka from uncut spirit: whether qualifies.
Decision: Yes.
Issue: Whether using waste plastic to make virgin quality PVC granules is a manufacturing process.
Decision: Yes.

Statement of Practice

Manufacturing relief — SP — CT/3/90

Tax Briefing

TB11 July 1993 para 2–3 — Outline of Revenue practice in relation to insurance proceeds and companies qualifying for 10% rate of corporation tax.

TB17 No 1 of 1995 para 2.1 — Quarry industry: company engaged solely in crushing of stone qualifies for 10% rate of corporation tax; washing and grading of sand and gravel excluded from qualification for 10% rate of corporation tax.

TB25 Feb 1997 p 12 — "Road marking" companies: Revenue accept 55% of overall turnover arises from "manufacturing" and remaining 45% arises from "construction operations".
TB33 Sept 1998 p 12 — Revenue accept that provision of blast freezing and cold storage facilities to the food industry qualifies for the 10% rate of corporation tax where the premises in which the process is carried out is approved as required by s.443(4)(a).

Definitions

company: ss 4(1), 5(1); distribution: ss 4(1), 436, 437; person: IA 1937 s 11(*c*); Tax Acts: s 1(2); trade: ss 3(1), 4(1), 5(1); writing: IA 1937 Sch.

Former enactments

FA 1980 s 39; FA 1981 s 17(*a*); FA 1984 s 45(*b*); FA 1987 s 28(3), s 29 and s 31; SI 61/1988; FA 1990 s 41(1); FA 1991 s 32(1); FA 1992 s 47; FA 1993 s 44(1) and s 47(3); FA 1994 s 48(1); FA 1997 s 146(1) and Sch 9 Pt I para 11(1).

444 Exclusion of mining and construction operations

(1) For the purposes of relief under this Part, income from the sale of goods shall not include income from—

(*a*) any mining operations for the purpose of obtaining, whether by underground or surface working, any scheduled mineral, mineral compound or mineral substance (within the meaning of section 2 of the Minerals Development Act, 1940), or

(*b*) any construction operations (within the meaning of Chapter 2 of Part 18).

(2) Where a company carries on a trade which consists of or includes the manufacture of goods and—

(*a*) in the course of the trade, it carries on any mining operations (within the meaning of subsection (1)(*a*)) from which it obtains any scheduled mineral, mineral compound or mineral substance of the kind referred to in that subsection, and

(*b*) any such mineral, mineral compound or mineral substance is not sold by the company in the course of the trade but forms the whole or part of the materials used in the manufacture of such goods or is to any extent incorporated in the goods in the course of their manufacture,

then, part of the income which apart from this subsection would be income from the sale of goods for the purposes of section 448 shall be deemed for the purposes of subsection (1) to be income from such mining operations, and that part shall be such amount as appears to the inspector or on appeal to the Appeal Commissioners to be just and reasonable.

(3) Where the amount receivable from a sale of goods includes consideration for the carrying out in relation to those goods of any construction operations (within the meaning of Chapter 2 of Part 18), then, part of the income which apart from this subsection would be income from the sale of goods for the purposes of section 448 shall be deemed for the purposes of subsection (1) to be income from such construction operations, and that part shall be such amount as appears to the inspector or on appeal to the Appeal Commissioners to be just and reasonable.

Case Law

Whether operation is mining or manufacturing – *Patrick J O'Connell (IOT) v Tara Mines Ltd* 2001 ITR p 79 and 2002 ITR p 143.

Revenue precedents

Issue: Making and erection of aluminium gutters: whether qualifies:

Decision: Manufacture is a question of fact to be determined by the Inspector; "erection" is "ancillary" construction operation.

Issue: (1) Whether the manufacture of doors, window frames, stairs, kitchen and bar units and similar items qualify s 443; (2) Whether installation is construction s 444.

Decision: (1) Yes. (2) Yes.

Issue: Manufacture and installation of refrigeration and ventilation units for industry: whether qualifying; s 443. whether "construction" for s 444; when "construction" begins.

Decision: Manufacture qualifies; installation is "construction"; "construction" begins when materials are brought on site.

Issue: Whether portable cabins including floor coverings, blinds, plumbing and delivery qualify; s 443; whether s 444 applies.

Decision: Cabins qualify; floor coverings and blinds can be included on "de minimus" basis; delivery can be included as "goods" if not separately charged; plumbing is a construction operation.

Issue: Manufacture supply and laying of tarmacadam: whether qualifies: s 443.

Decision: Apportion to exclude laying which is a "construction" operation; otherwise qualifies.

Definitions

Appeal Commissioners: s 2(1); company: ss 4(1), 5(1); inspector: ss 2(1), 5(1), 852; minerals: s 5(1); mining: s 5(1); trade: s 3(1).

Former enactments

FA 1980 s 50.

445 Certain trading operations carried on in Shannon Airport

(1) In this section—

"the airport" has the same meaning as in the Customs-Free Airport Act, 1947;

"company" means any company carrying on a trade;

"the Minister" means the Minister for Finance;

"qualified company" means a company the whole or part of the trade of which is carried on in the airport;

"relevant trading operations" means trading operations specified in a certificate given by the Minister under subsection (2);

"trading operation" means any trading operation which apart from this section and section 443(13) is not the manufacture of goods for the purpose of this Part but is carried on by a qualified company.

(2) Subject to subsections (7) and (8), the Minister may give a certificate certifying that such trading operations of a qualified company as are specified in the certificate are, with effect from a date specified in the certificate, relevant trading operations for the purpose of this section, and any certificate so given shall, unless it is revoked under subsection (4), (5) or (6), remain in force [until—

(*a*) in the case of those operations which, on or before the 31st day of May, 1998, were approved by the Minister for carry on in the airport, the 31st day of December, 2005, and

(*b*) in the case of those operations which are so approved after the 31st day of May, 1998, the 31st day of December, 2002].[1]

[(2A) An operation which would fall within any class or kind of operation specified in a certificate under subsection (2) to be a relevant trading operation but for the fact that it involves the currency of the State shall, with effect from the commencement of section 47 of the Finance Act, 1998, in relation to paragraph 7 of Schedule 2 to that Act, be deemed to fall within that class or kind of operation and to have been specified in that certificate as a relevant trading operation.][2]

(3) A certificate given under subsection (2) may be given either without conditions or subject to such conditions as the Minister considers proper and specifies in the certificate.

(4) Where in the case of a company in relation to which a certificate under subsection (2) has been given—

(*a*) the trade of the company ceases or becomes carried on wholly outside the airport, or

(*b*) the Minister is satisfied that the company has failed to comply with any condition subject to which the certificate was given,

the Minister may, by notice in writing served by registered post on the company, revoke the certificate with effect from such date as may be specified in the notice.

(5) Where, in the case of a company in relation to which a certificate under subsection (2) has been given, the Minister is of the opinion that any activity of the company has had, or may have, an adverse effect on the use or development of the airport or is otherwise inimical to the development of the airport, then—

(*a*) the Minister may, by notice in writing served by registered post on the company, require the company to desist from such activity with effect from such date as may be specified in the notice, and

(*b*) if the Minister is not satisfied that the company has complied with the requirements of that notice, the Minister may, by a further notice in writing served by registered post on the company, revoke the certificate with effect from such date as may be specified in the further notice.

[(6) Where the Minister and a company in relation to which a certificate under subsection (2) has been given—

(*a*) agree to the revocation of that certificate, or

(*b*) agree to the revocation of that certificate and its replacement by another certificate to be given to the company under subsection (2),

the Minister may by notice in writing served by registered post on the company, revoke the first-mentioned certificate with effect from such date as may be specified in the notice; but this subsection shall not affect the operation of subsection (4) or (5).][3]

(7) The Minister shall not certify under subsection (2) that a trading operation is a relevant trading operation unless it is carried on in the airport and is within one or more of the following classes of trading operations—

(*a*) the repair or maintenance of aircraft,

(*b*) trading operations in relation to which the Minister is of the opinion, after consultation with the Minister for Public Enterprise, that they contribute to the use or development of the airport, or

(*c*) trading operations ancillary to any of those operations described in paragraph (*a*) or (*b*) or to any operations consisting apart from this section of the manufacture of goods.

(8) The Minister shall not certify under subsection (2) that any of the following trading operations is a relevant trading operation—

(*a*) the rendering of—

(i) services to embarking or disembarking aircraft passengers, including hotel, catering, money-changing or transport (other than air transport) services, or

(ii) services in connection with the landing, departure, loading or unloading of aircraft,

(*b*) the operation of a scheduled air transport service,

(*c*) selling by retail, otherwise than by mail order or other distance selling, which satisfies the requirement of subsection (7)(*b*),

(*d*) the sale of consumable commodities for the fuelling of aircraft or for shipment as aircraft stores.

(9) For the purposes of relief under this Part, in the case of a qualified company carrying on relevant trading operations—

(*a*) the relevant trading operations shall be regarded as the manufacture in the State of goods, and

(*b*) any amount receivable in payment for anything sold, or any services rendered, in the course of the relevant trading operations shall be regarded as an amount receivable from the sale of goods.

(10) The inspector may by notice in writing require a company claiming relief from tax by virtue of this section to furnish him or her with such information or particulars as may be necessary for the purpose of giving effect to this section, and subsection (2) of section 448 shall apply as if the matters of which proof is required by that subsection included the information or particulars specified in a notice under this section.

Amendments

1 Substituted by FA 1999 s 74(*b*) with effect from 6 April 1999.

2 Subs (2A) inserted by FA 1998 s 47 and Sch 2 para 7 from such date as the Minister for Finance may appoint by order. The subsection came into operation from 1 January 1999 — Finance Act, 1998 (Section 47) (Commencement) Order, 1998, SI No 502 of 1998 refers.

3 Subs (6) substituted by FA 2000 s 83(1)(*a*) with effect from 1 January 2000.

Cross-references

Appeals: s 447.

Application of s 130 to certain interest, meaning of "qualified company", "relevant trading operations" and "the airport" applied: s 452(1)(*a*).

Attribution of distributions to accounting periods, subs (1): s 154(5)(*a*).

Double tax relief, meaning of "relevant trading operations" applied: s 450(1)(*e*).

Foreign tax credit, subs (9)(*b*): s 449(1) (an amount receivable from the sale of goods).

Industrial building accelerated annual allowance, continued for certain approved projects: s 273(5)(*a*).

Industrial building allowance, continued for certain approved projects: s 271(3)(*a*).

Interest (certain) not to be chargeable, meaning of relevant trading operations applied: s 198(1)(*c*); s 198(1) to apply in relation to interest paid on relevant securities as if the following subsection were substituted for subsection (2) of this section ... "(2) Subject to subsections (7) and (8), the Minister may give a certificate certifying that such trading operations of a qualified company as are specified in the certificate are, with effect from a date specified in the certificate, relevant trading operations for the purposes of this section"...: s 198(2).
Interest payments by companies and to non-residents, meaning of "relevant trading operations" applied: s 246(3)(*c*)(i); s 246(3)(*c*) to apply as if the following subsection were substituted for subsection (2) of this section... "(2) Subject to subsections (7) and (8), the Minister may give a certificate certifying that such trading operations of a qualified company as are specified in the certificate are, with effect from a date specified in the certificate, relevant trading operations for the purposes of this section."...: s 246(4)(*a*).
Interest treated as a distribution, "specified trade" does not include Shannon activities: s 133(1)(*a*); restriction of relief: s 133(9)(*b*)(ii), (13)(*c*)(iv).
Interpretation: s 442(4).
Leased assets, restriction on use of allowances: s 403(8).
Leased plant and machinery, restriction on use of allowances: s 404(6)(*b*).
Manufacturing (10%) rate, aircraft maintenance, subs (7)(*a*): s 443(13).
Patent royalty, income exemption, applies to 10% activities other than those mentioned in subs (7)(*b*)–(*c*): s 234(1).
Plant and machinery accelerated wear and tear allowance, continued for certain approved projects: s 285(5)(*a*).
Plant and machinery initial allowance, continued for certain approved projects: s 283(4)(*a*).
Preference share dividends, no tax credit: s 138(1).
Taxation of collective investment undertakings: meanings of "relevant trading operations", "specified company": s 734(1)(*a*); for the definition of "specified collective investment undertaking", references to qualifying management company in subs (2), to be construed as if this following subsection were substituted for subsection (2) of this section: ... "(2) Subject to subsections (7) and (8), the Minister may give a certificate certifying that such trading operations of a qualifying company as are specified in the certificate are, with effect from a date specified in the certificate, relevant trading operations for the purposes of this section: s 734(1)(*c*)(i).

Tax Briefing

TB51 Jan 2003 p 18 — The provision of FA 2002 s 54 providing for relief for certain losses, etc on a value basis may be applied to Shannon companies certified under TCA 1997 s 445(2) on the same basis as they apply to non-certified companies.

Definitions

company: ss 4(1), 5(1); inspector: ss 2(1), 5(1), 852; trade: ss 3(1), 4(1), 5(1); writing: IA 1937 Sch.

Former enactments

FA 1980 s 39A(1)–(7) and (10); FA 1981 s 17(*b*); FA 1986 s 56(2); FA 1988 s 35; FA 1991 s 33; FA 1992 s 52; FA 1996 s 53.

446 Certain trading operations carried on in Custom House Docks Area

(1) In this section—

"the Area" means, subject to subsection (12), the Custom House Docks Area within the meaning of section 322;

"company" means any company carrying on a trade;

"the Minister" means the Minister for Finance;

"qualified company" means a company to which the Minister has given a certificate under subsection (2);

"relevant trading operations" means trading operations specified in a certificate given by the Minister under subsection (2);

"trading operation" means any trading operation which apart from this section is not the manufacture of goods for the purposes of this Part.

(2) Subject to subsections (7) and (9), the Minister may give a certificate certifying that such trading operations of a company as are specified in the certificate are, with effect from a date specified in the certificate, relevant trading operations for the purposes of this section, and any certificate so given shall, unless it is revoked under [subsection (4), (5), (5A) or (6)],[1] remain in force [until—

(*a*) in the case of those operations which, on or before the 31st day of July, 1998, were approved by the Minister for carry on in the Area, the 31st day of December, 2005, and

(*b*) in the case of those operations which are so approved after the 31st day of July, 1998, the 31st day of December, 2002].[2]

[(2A) An operation which would fall within any class or kind of operation specified in a certificate under subsection (2) to be a relevant trading operation but for the fact that it involves the currency of the State shall, with effect from the commencement of section 47 of the Finance Act, 1998, in relation to paragraph 8 of Schedule 2 to that Act, be deemed to fall within that class or kind of operation and to have been specified in that certificate as a relevant trading operation.][3]

[(2B) Where—

(*a*) on 31 March 2000 the relevant trading operations of a qualified company are the carrying on of a business of managing the activities or the whole or part of the assets of a specified collective investment undertaking (within the meaning of section 734(1)), and

(*b*) at any time after 31 March 2000 the specified collective investment undertaking ceases to be a specified collective investment undertaking but is an investment undertaking (within the meaning of section 739B),

then that business at that time, to the extent that the management can be directly attributed to be for the benefit of unit holders (within the meaning of section 739B) in the investment undertaking who are persons resident outside the State, shall be deemed to be relevant trading operations and to have been specified as relevant trading operations in the certificate given to the qualified company under subsection (2); and for the purposes of the Tax Acts, such apportionment as is just and reasonable may be made of any profits arising to the qualified company.

(2C) Where—

(*a*) on 31 December 2000 the relevant trading operations of a qualified company are the carrying on of a life business (within the meaning of section 706(1)), and

(*b*) at any time after 31 December 2000 the qualified company would be in breach of the conditions under which a certificate was given to the qualified company under subsection (2), solely by virtue of the qualified company commencing policies or contracts with persons who reside in the State,

then the trading operations of the qualified company at that time, to the extent that they are trading operations carried on with persons resident outside the State, shall be deemed to be relevant trading operations and the conditions under which the certificate was given shall be deemed not to have been breached; and for the purposes of the Tax

Acts, such apportionment as is just and reasonable may be made of any profits arising to the qualified company.

(2D) Where on 31 March 2000 the trading operations of a qualified company are the carrying on of a business of managing the activities or the whole or part of the assets of a qualifying company (within the meaning of section 110), then such management shall, at any time after 31 March 2000 and to the extent referred to in subsection (7)(*c*)(ii)(V)(C) (inserted by the *Finance Act, 2000*), be deemed to be relevant trading operations and to have been specified as relevant trading operations in the certificate given to the qualified company under subsection (2); and for the purposes of the Tax Acts such apportionment as is just and reasonable may be made of any profits arising to the qualified company.][4]

(3) A certificate given under subsection (2) may be given either without conditions or subject to such conditions as the Minister considers proper and specifies in the certificate.

(4) Where in the case of a company in relation to which a certificate under subsection (2) has been given—

(*a*) the trade of the company ceases or, except in the case of a company in relation to which the Minister has, in accordance with subsection (9), given a certificate under subsection (2) and which has not yet commenced to carry on in the Area the trading operation or trading operations specified in the certificate, becomes carried on wholly outside the Area, or

(*b*) the Minister is satisfied that the company has failed to comply with any condition subject to which the certificate was given,

the Minister may, by notice in writing served by registered post on the company, revoke the certificate with effect from such date as may be specified in the notice.

(5) Where, in the case of a company in relation to which a certificate under subsection (2) has been given, the Minister is of the opinion that any activity of the company has had, or may have, an adverse effect on the use or development of the Area or is otherwise inimical to the development of the Area, then—

(*a*) the Minister may, by notice in writing served by registered post on the company, require the company to desist from such activity with effect from such date as may be specified in the notice, and

(*b*) if the Minister is not satisfied that the company has complied with the requirements of that notice, the Minister may, by a further notice in writing served by registered post on the company, revoke the certificate with effect from such date as may be specified in the further notice.

[(5A) Notwithstanding subsection (5), where, in the case of a company in relation to which a certificate under subsection (2) has been given, the Minister receives a notification from the Central Bank of Ireland in accordance with section 96 of the Central Bank Act, 1989, as to the non-compliance by the company with any obligation imposed on it by the Central Bank of Ireland under Chapter VII of the Central Bank Act, 1989, the Minister shall, by notice in writing served by registered post on the company, revoke the certificate with effect from such date as may be specified in the notice.][5]

[(6) Where the Minister and a company in relation to which a certificate under subsection (2) has been given—

(*a*) agree to the revocation of that certificate, or

(*b*) agree to the revocation of that certificate and its replacement by another certificate to be given to the company under subsection (2),

the Minister may by notice in writing served by registered post on the company, revoke the first-mentioned certificate with effect from such date as may be specified in the notice; but this subsection shall not affect the operation of subsection (4), (5) or (5A).][6]

(7) Subject to subsection (9), the Minister shall not certify under subsection (2) that a trading operation is a relevant trading operation unless—

(*a*) it is carried on in the Area,

(*b*) the Minister is satisfied that it will contribute to the development of the Area as an International Financial Services Centre, and

(*c*) it is within one or more of the following classes of trading operations—

[(i) the provision for persons not ordinarily resident in the State of services which are of a type normally provided by a bank in the ordinary course of its trade,][7]

(ii) the carrying on on behalf of persons not ordinarily resident in the State of international financial activities, including in particular—

(I) global money-management,

[(II) international dealings in currencies and in futures, options and similar financial assets,][8]

[(III) dealings in bonds, equities and similar instruments,][9]

(IV) insurance and related activities, or

[(V) the management of the activities or the whole or part of the assets of—

(A) a specified collective investment undertaking (within the meaning of section 734),

(B) an investment undertaking (within the meaning of section 739B) to the extent that the management can be directly attributed to be for the benefit of unit holders (within the said meaning) in the investment undertaking who are persons resident outside the State; and for the purposes of the Tax Acts, such apportionment as is just and reasonable may be made of any profits arising to a qualified company,

(C) a qualifying company (within the meaning of section 110), to the extent that the management directly relates to assets of the qualifying company which the qualifying company acquired directly or indirectly from an originator (within the said meaning) not being assets which were created, acquired or held by or in connection with a branch or agency through which the originator carries on a trade in the State.][10]

(iii) the provision for persons not ordinarily resident in the State of services of, or facilities for, processing, control, accounting, communication, clearing, settlement or information storage in relation to financial activities,

(iv) dealing by a company in commodity futures or commodity options on behalf of persons not ordinarily resident in the State—

(I) other than on behalf of persons who—

(A) carry on a trade in which commodities of a type which are the subject of the futures or options, as the case may be, are used in the course of the carrying on of the trade, or

(B) would be regarded as connected with a person who carries on such a trade,

or

(II) where dealing in futures and options, some or all of which are commodity futures or commodity options, as the case may be, is the principal relevant trading operation carried on by the company,

(v) the development or supply of computer software for use in the provision of services or facilities of a type referred to in subparagraph (iii) or for the reprocessing, analysing or similar treatment of information in relation to financial activities, or

(vi) trading operations similar to or ancillary to any of those operations described in the preceding provisions of this section in relation to which the Minister is of the opinion that they contribute to the use of the Area as an International Financial Services Centre.

(8) References in subsection (7) to any service or facility provided for, or any activity carried on on behalf of, a person not ordinarily resident in the State shall not include any such service or facility provided for, or any activity carried on on behalf of, the whole or any part of a trade carried on by that person in the State.

[(8A) Where the trading operations of a qualified company, for the purposes of carrying on its relevant trading operations, include the procurement of services from a person who is resident in the State and, in the opinion of the Minister such procurement will contribute to the development of the Area as an International Financial Services Centre, the procurement shall be regarded for the purposes of the Tax Acts as part of the relevant trading operations of the qualified company and to have been specified as relevant trading operations in the certificate given to the qualified company under subsection (2) where they are not so specified.][11]

(9) Where the Minister would have certified a trading operation under subsection (2) but for the fact that the condition specified in subsection (7)(*a*) was not satisfied as respects the trading operation, the Minister may, notwithstanding that such condition is not satisfied, certify the trading operation under subsection (2) if the Minister is satisfied that—

(*a*) the trading operation is not carried on in the Area due to circumstances outside the control of the company carrying on the trading operation, and

(*b*) such company intends to carry on, and will commence to carry on, the trading operation in the Area within such period of time as the Minister may specify under subsection (3) as a condition subject to which the Minister gives the certificate under subsection (2) in respect of the trading operation.

(10) For the purpose of relief under this Part, in the case of a qualified company carrying on relevant trading operations—

(*a*) the relevant trading operations shall be regarded as the manufacture in the State of goods, and

(*b*) any amount receivable in payment for anything sold, or any services rendered, in the course of the relevant trading operations shall be regarded as an amount receivable from the sale of goods.

(11) The inspector may by notice in writing require a company claiming relief from tax by virtue of this section to furnish him or her with such information or particulars as may be necessary for the purpose of giving effect to this section, and subsection (2) of section 448 shall apply as if the matters of which proof is required by that subsection included the information or particulars specified in a notice under this section.

(12)(*a*) For the purposes of this section, the Minister for Finance, after consultation with the Minister for the Environment and Local Government, may, by order direct that the definition of **"the Custom House Docks Area"** in section 322 shall include such area or areas described in the order which but for the order would not be included in that definition and, where the Minister for Finance so orders, the definition of **"the Custom House Docks Area"** in that section shall for the purposes of this section be deemed to include that area or those areas.

(*b*) The Minister for Finance may, for the purposes of making an order under this section and an order under section 322, exercise the powers to make those orders by making one order for the purposes of both of those sections.

(*c*) The Minister for Finance may make orders for the purpose of this section and any order made under this section shall be laid before Dáil Éireann as soon as may be after it is made and, if a resolution annulling the order is passed by Dáil Éireann within the next 21 days on which Dáil Éireann has sat after the order is laid before it, the order shall be annulled accordingly, but without prejudice to the validity of anything previously done thereunder.

Amendments

1 Substituted by FA 2000 s 83(1)(*b*)(i) with effect from 23 March 2000; previously "subsection (4), (5) or (6)".

2 Substituted by FA 1999 s 74(*c*) with effect from 6 April 1999.

3 Inserted by FA 1998 s 47 and Sch 2 para 8(*a*) from such date as the Minister for Finance may appoint by order. The Amendment came into operation from 1 January 1999 — Finance Act, 1998 (Section 47) (Commencement) Order, 1998, SI No 502 of 1998, refers.

4 Subss (2B)–(2D) inserted by FA 2000 s 80(a) with effect from 6 April 2000.

5 Subs (5A) inserted by FA 2000 s 83(1)(*b*)(ii) with effect from 23 March 2000.

6 Subs (6) substituted by FA 2000 s 83(1)(*b*)(iii) with effect from 1 January 2000.

7 Substituted by FA 1998 s 47 and Sch 2 para 8(*b*)(i) from such date as the Minister for Finance may appoint by order; previously:

"(i) the provision for persons not ordinarily resident in the State of services, in relation to transactions in foreign currencies, which are of a type normally provided by a bank in the ordinary course of its trade,".

The Amendment came into operation from 1 January 1999 — Finance Act, 1998 (Section 47) (Commencement) Order, 1998, SI No 502 of 1998, refers.

8 Substituted by FA 1998 s 47 and Sch 2 para 8(*b*)(ii)(I) from such date as the Minister for Finance may appoint by order; previously:

"(II) international dealings in foreign currencies and in futures, options and similar financial assets which are denominated in foreign currencies,".

The Amendment came into operation from 1 January 1999 — Finance Act, 1998 (Section 47) (Commencement) Order, 1998, SI No 502 of 1998, refers.

9 Substituted by FA 1998 s 47 and Sch 2 para 8(*b*)(ii)(II) from such date as the Minister for Finance may appoint by order; previously:

"(III) dealings in bonds, equities and similar instruments which are denominated in foreign currencies,".

The Amendment came into operation from 1 January 1999 — Finance Act, 1998 (Section 47) (Commencement) Order, 1998, SI No 502 of 1998, refers.

10 Subs (7)(*c*)(ii)(V) substituted by FA 2000 s 80(*b*) with effect from 6 April 2000.

11 Subs (8A) inserted by FA 2000 s 80(*c*) with effect from 6 April 2000.

Cross-references

Appeals: s 447.

Application of s 130 to certain interest, meaning of "qualified company", "relevant trading operations" and "the area" applied: s 452(1)(*a*).

Attribution of distributions to accounting periods, subs (1): s 154(5)(*a*).

Bank levy credit: s 487(1)(*a*) (accounting profit) (ii)(III).

BES relief, qualifying trades: s 496(2)(*a*)(i)(I); subs (2)(*b*): s 496(2)(*a*)(iv).

Double tax relief, meanings of "qualified company", and "relevant payment" applied: s 450(1)(*a*); meaning of "relevant trading operations" applied: s 450(1)(*e*).

Foreign tax credit, subs (10)(*b*): s 449(1) (an amount receivable from the sale of goods).

IFSC operations, investment income from outside the State: s 451(1).

Industrial building accelerated annual allowance, continued for certain approved projects: s 273(5)(*a*).

Industrial building allowance, continued for certain approved projects: s 273(3)(*a*).

Interest (certain) not to be chargeable, meaning of relevant trading operations applied: s 198(1)(*c*); s 198(1) to apply in relation to interest paid on relevant securities as if the following subsection were substituted for subsection (2) of this section ... "(2) Subject to subsections (7) and (9), the Minister may give a certificate certifying that such trading operations of a company as are specified in the certificate are, with effect from a date specified in the certificate, relevant trading operations for the purpose of this section: s 198(2).

Interest paid to company resident in a treaty country not a distribution: s 452(1)(*a*).

Interest payments by companies and to non-residents, meaning of "relevant trading operations" applied: s 246(3)(*c*)(i); s 246(3)(*c*) to apply as if the following subsection were substituted for subsection (2) of this section .. "(2) Subject to subsections (7) and (9), the Minister may give a certificate certifying that such trading operations of a company as are specified in the certificate are, with effect from a date specified in the certificate, relevant trading operations for the purposes of this section." ...: s 246(4)(*b*).

Interest treated as a distribution, restriction of relief: s 133(9)(*c*)(iii), (10)(*b*)(iii).

Interpretation: s 442(4).

Leased assets, restriction on use of allowances: s 403(8).

Leased plant and machinery, restriction on use of allowances: s 404(6)(*b*).

Patent royalty, income exemption, applies to 10% activities other than those mentioned in this section: s 234(1).

Plant and machinery accelerated wear and tear allowance, continued for certain approved projects: s 285(5)(*a*).

Plant and machinery initial allowance, continued for certain approved projects: s 283(4)(*a*).

Preference share dividends, no tax credit: s 138(1).

Profits of life business, in applying the definition of "foreign life assurance business" in s 451(1) for purposes of s 710(2)(*a*) this section applied as if the following subsection were substituted for subs (2): ... "(2) Subject to subsections (7) and (9), the Minister may give a certificate certifying that such trading operations of a company as are specified in the certificate are, with effect from a date specified in the certificate, relevant trading operations for the purpose of this section."...: s 710(2)(*b*).

Restriction of loss relief: s 455(7).

Taxation of collective investment undertakings: meanings of "the Area", "relevant trading operations" and "specified company": s 734(1)(*a*); for the definition of "specified collective investment undertaking", references to qualifying management company in subs (2), to be construed as if the following subsection were substituted for subsection (2) of this section: ... "(2) Subject to subsections (7) and (8), the Minister may give a certificate certifying that such trading operations of a company as are specified in the certificate are, with effect from a date specified in the certificate, relevant trading operations for the purpose of this section.": s 734(1)(*c*)(ii).

Tax Briefing

TB51 Jan 2003 s 18 — The provisions of FA 2002 s 54 providing for relief for certain losses on a value basis may be applied to IFSC companies certified under TCA 1997 s s 446(2) on the same basis as they apply to non-certified companies.

Definitions

company: ss 4(1), 5(1); Corporation Tax Acts: s 1(2); inspector: ss 2(1), 5(1), 852; person: IA 1937 s 11(*c*); profits: s 4(1); Tax Acts: s 1(2); trade: ss 3(1), 4(1), 5(1); writing: IA 1937 Sch.

Former enactments

FA 1980 s 39B(1)–(6), (7)(*a*) and (*b*), (8) and (9); FA 1987 s 30; FA 1991 s 34; FA 1992 s 53; FA 1994 s 53; FA 1995 s 65; FA 1997 s 28.

447 Appeals

[An appeal to the Appeal Commissioners shall lie on any question arising under this Part (apart from any question arising under section 445 or 446) in the like manner as an appeal would lie against an assessment to corporation tax, and the provisions of the Tax Acts relating to appeals shall apply accordingly.][1]

Amendments

[1] Section 477 substituted by FA 2000 s 83(1)(*c*) with effect from 23 March 2000.

Definitions

Appeal Commissioners: s 2(1); Tax Acts: s 1(2).

Former enactments

FA 1980 s 51.

CHAPTER 2
Principal Provisions

448 Relief from corporation tax

[(1) (*a*) For the purposes of this section, references to **"charges on income paid for the purposes of the sale of goods"**, where they are in the course of a trade in an accounting period, shall be taken to be such amount as would be the amount of the income from the sale of goods in that period if, notwithstanding subsection (4), the reference to "the company's income for the relevant accounting period from the sale in the course of the trade mentioned in that subsection of goods and merchandise" for the purposes of subsection (3), were to the amount of so much of the charges on income paid wholly and exclusively for the purposes of the trade in that period as appears to the inspector or on appeal to the Appeal Commissioners to be referable to charges on income paid for the purpose of the sale of goods and merchandise.

(*b*) For the purposes of this section, references to a **"loss from the sale of goods"**, where they are in the course of a trade in an accounting period, shall be such amount as would be the amount of the income from the sale of goods in that period if, notwithstanding subsection (4), the reference to "the company's income for the relevant accounting period from the sale in the course of the trade mentioned in that subsection of goods and merchandise" for the purposes of subsection (3), were to the amount of so much of the loss, computed as for the purposes of section 396(2), from the trade in the period as appears to the inspector or on appeal to the Appeal Commissioners to be referable to a loss incurred in the sale of goods and merchandise, but a loss such as is mentioned in section 407(4)(*b*) shall not be a loss from the sale of goods.

(*c*) For the purposes of this section references to an **"excess of charges on income paid for the purpose of the sale of goods"**, where they are in the course of the trade in an accounting period, shall be so much of an amount, being the amount by which the charges on income paid by a company for the purpose of the sale of goods in the course of the trade in that period exceed the income from the sale of goods in the course of the trade in that period, as does not exceed the excess referred to in section 420(6) as computed for the company for that period.

(*d*) (i) For the purposes of this section, **"relevant corporation tax"** means the corporation tax which, apart from this section, sections 22A, 239, 241, 440, 441, 449, 644B and 827 and paragraphs 16 and 18 of Schedule 32, would be chargeable for the relevant accounting period exclusive of the corporation tax chargeable on the part of the company's profits attributable to chargeable gains for that period.

(ii) For the purpose of subparagraph (i), the part of the company's profits attributable to chargeable gains for the relevant accounting period shall be taken to be the amount brought into the company's profits for that period for the purposes of corporation tax in respect of chargeable gains before any deduction for charges on income, expenses of management or other amounts which can be deducted from or set against or treated as reducing profits of more than one description.][1]

[(2) Where a company which carries on a trade which consists of or includes the manufacture of goods claims and proves as respects a relevant accounting period that during that period any amount was receivable in respect of the sale in the course of the trade of goods, corporation tax payable by the company for that period, in so far as it is referable to the income from the sale of those goods, shall be reduced—

(*a*) by eleven-sixteenths, in so far as it is corporation tax charged on profits which under section 26(3) are apportioned to the financial year 1998,

(*b*) by nine-fourteenths, in so far as it is corporation tax charged on profits which under section 26(3) are apportioned to the financial year 1999,

(*c*) by seven-twelfths, in so far as it is corporation tax charged on profits which under section 26(3) are apportioned to the financial year 2000,

(*d*) by one-half, in so far as it is corporation tax charged on profits which under section 26(3) are apportioned to the financial year 2001,

(*e*) by three-eighths, in so far as it is corporation tax charged on profits which under section 26(3) are apportioned to the financial year 2002, and

(*f*) by one-fifth, in so far as it is corporation tax charged on profits which under section 26(3) are apportioned to the financial year 2003 or any subsequent financial year,

and the corporation tax referable to the income from the sale of those goods shall be such an amount as bears to the part of the relevant corporation tax charged on profits which under section 26(3) are apportioned to the financial year in question the same proportion as the income from the sale of those goods bears to the total income brought into charge to corporation tax for the relevant accounting period.][2]

[(3) For the purposes of subsection (2), the **"income from the sale of those goods"** shall be the amount determined by—

(*a*) firstly, calculating such sum (in this subsection referred to as the **"relevant sum"**) as bears to the amount of the company's income for the relevant accounting period from the sale in the course of the trade mentioned in that subsection of goods and merchandise the same proportion as the amount receivable by the company in the relevant accounting period from the sale in the course of the trade of goods bears to the total amount receivable by the company in the relevant accounting period from the sale in the course of the trade of goods and merchandise, and

[(*b*) then, deducting from the relevant sum—

(i) the amount of any charges on income paid for the purposes of the sale of goods in the relevant accounting period,

(ii) the amount of any loss from the sale of goods incurred by the company in the relevant accounting period, and

(iii) the amount of any excess of charges on income paid for the purpose of the sale of goods or the amount of any loss from the sale of goods, incurred by a surrendering company and allowed under section 420A,

allowed against income of the trade in the relevant accounting period.][3]

(4) For the purposes of subsection (3), the **"company's income for the relevant accounting period from the sale in the course of the trade mentioned in that subsection of goods and merchandise"** shall be determined as an amount equal to—

(*a*) in any case where the income from the trade is derived solely from sales of goods and merchandise, the amount of the company's income from the trade, and

(*b*) in any other case, such amount of the income from the trade as appears to the inspector or on appeal to the Appeal Commissioners to be just and reasonable,

but shall be so determined as if—

(i) no relief for charges had been claimed under section 243A ...[4],

(ii) no relief for a loss in a trade had been claimed under section 396A ...[5], and

(iii) no group relief had been allowed under section 420A ...[6],

for the relevant accounting period.][7]

(5) (*a*) For the purposes of this Part, the amount receivable by a company in a relevant accounting period from the sale of goods or merchandise—

(i) shall be deemed to be reduced by the amount of any duty paid or payable by the company in respect of the goods or merchandise or in respect of the materials used in their manufacture, and

(ii) shall not include any amount in respect of value-added tax chargeable on the sale of the goods or merchandise.

(*b*) The inspector may by notice in writing require a company making a claim for relief under this Part to furnish him or her with such information or particulars as may be necessary for the purposes of giving effect to this subsection, and subsection (2) shall apply as if the matters of which proof is required by that subsection included the information or particulars specified in a notice under this subsection.

[(5A) Where any part of the profits of an accounting period of a company is charged to corporation tax in accordance with section 21A, then—

(*a*) for the purposes of this section, the relevant corporation tax in relation to the accounting period shall be reduced by an amount determined by the formula—

$$\frac{R}{100} \times S$$

where—

R is the rate per cent specified in section 21A(3) in relation to the accounting period, and

S is an amount equal to so much of the profits of the company for the accounting period as are charged to tax in accordance with section 21A,

and

(*b*) notwithstanding section 4(4)(*b*), the income of a company, referred to in the expression "total income brought into charge to corporation tax", for the accounting period for the purposes of subsection (2) shall be the sum determined by section 4(4)(*b*) for that period reduced—

...[8]

(ii) by an amount equal to so much of the profits of the company for the accounting period as are charged to tax in accordance with section 21A.][9]

(6) A company shall not be entitled to relief under this Part in relation to a trade as respects a relevant accounting period unless it makes a claim for the relief under subsection (2) before the date on which the assessment for the accounting period which coincides with or includes that relevant accounting period becomes final and conclusive.

....[10]

Amendments

1 Subs (1) substituted by FA 2005 s 53(1)(*a*) as respects accounting periods ending on or after 3 February 2005.

2 Subs (2) substituted by FA 1999 s 71 and Sch 1 para 1(*a*) with effect from 6 April 1999.

3 Subs (3)(*b*) substituted by FA 2005 s 53(1)(*b*) as respects accounting periods ending on or after 3 February 2005.

4 Deleted by FA 2005 s 53(1)(*c*)(i) as respects accounting periods ending on or after 3 February 2005; previously "or 454".

5 Deleted by FA 2005 s 53(1)(*c*)(ii) as respects accounting periods ending on or after 3 February 2005; previously "or 455".

6 Deleted by FA 2005 s 53(1)(*c*)(iii) as respects accounting periods ending on or after 3 February 2005; previously "or 456".

7 Subs (3)–(4) substituted by FA 2001 s 90(1)(*c*)(i)(I) as respects an accounting period ending on or after 6 March 2001.

8 Subs (5A)(*b*)(i) deleted by FA 2005 s 53(1)(*d*) as respects accounting periods ending on or after 3 February 2005.

9 Subs (5A) inserted by FA 1999 s 71 and Sch 1 para 1(*b*) with effect from 6 April 1999.

10 Subs (7) deleted by FA 2000 s 83(1)(*d*)(ii) as respects accounting periods beginning after 1 April 2000.

Note

As regards the amendments effected by FA 2001 s 90, for the purposes of computing the amount of relevant trading charges on income within the meaning of TCA 1997 s 243A and relevant trading losses within the meaning of TCA 1997 s 396A, and those amendments as they apply to TCA 1997 ss 454 and 456, where an accounting period of a company begins before 6 March 2001 and ends on or after that date, it shall be divided into 2 parts, one beginning on the date on which the accounting period begins and ending on 5 March 2001 and the other beginning on 6 March 2001 and ending on the date on which the accounting period ends, and both parts shall be treated as if they were separate accounting periods of the company, and for the purposes of computing the amount of charges on income paid for the purposes of the sale of goods within the meaning of TCA 1997 s 454 and a loss from the sale of goods within the meaning of TCA 1997 s 455, where an accounting period of a company begins before 1 January 2003 and ends on or after that date, it shall be divided into 2 parts, one beginning on the date on which the accounting period begins and ending on 31 December 2002 and the other beginning on 1 January 2003 and ending on the date on which the accounting period ends, and both parts shall be treated as if they were separate accounting periods of the company — see FA 2001 s 90(4), as substituted by FA 2002 s 55.

Cross-references

Associated persons, subs (2), transactions between, information: s 453(5).

Close company surcharges, distributions to be taken into account and meaning of distributable and estate income: s 434(5A)(*a*)("distributable trading income").

Distributions out of profits from trading in Shannon Airport: s 144(8)("S").

Double tax relief: s 450(4).

Foreign tax credit: s 449(2)(*c*).

Manufacturing (10%) rate, exclusion of mining and construction operations: s 444(1), (3).

Manufacturing (10%) rate, information required, subs (2): s 443(22).

Manufacturing (10%) rate, International Financial Services Centre, subs (2): s 446(11).

Newspaper advertising revenue: s 443(20).

Provisions as to relief from income tax and corporation tax by means of credit in respect of foreign tax, limit on total credit — corporation tax: Sch 24 para 4(4)(*b*).

Reduction of corporation tax liability in respect of certain trading income: s 22A(1)("income from sale of goods"): s 22A(2)(*a*)(ii).

Relief in respect of corporation profits tax losses: Sch 32 para 18(4)(*bb*).

Relief in respect of unrelieved losses and capital allowances carried forward from 1975–76: Sch 32 para 16(1), (3).

Relief under this Part, meaning, subs (2): s 442(1).

Restriction of certain charges on income: s 454(1).

Restriction of loss relief: s 455(1).

Case law

Subs (2): Newspaper advertising revenue held to be receivable "in respect of" sales of manufactured goods (newspapers): *McGurrin v The Champion Publications Ltd* ITR Vol IV p 466.

Subs (6): Held taxpayer cannot reopen final assessments to backdate claim for manufacturing relief: *Saatchi & Saatchi v McGarry* [1998] ITR 99.

Definitions

accounting period: s 27; Appeal Commissioners: s 2(1); chargeable gain: ss 4(1), 5(1), 534; charges on income: ss 4(1), 243(1); company: ss 4(1), 5(1); inspector: ss 2(1), 852; profits: s 4(1); trade: ss 3(1); 4(1); writing: IA 1937 Sch.

Former enactments

FA 1980 s 41(1)–(5) and (8)–(9); FA 1992 s 54; F(No 2)A 1992 s 1; FA 1994 s 54(*b*); FA 1995 s 54(2) and Sch 4 Pt II para 1(2) and s 61; FA 1997 s 59(2) and Sch 4 Pt II para 1(1)–(2).

449 Credit for foreign tax not otherwise credited

(1) In this section—

"an amount receivable from the sale of goods" means an amount which—

(*a*) being an amount receivable from the sale of computer software, or

(*b*) by virtue of section 443(10)(*b*)(ii), 445(9)(*b*) or 446(10)(*b*),

is regarded as receivable from the sale of goods for the purposes of relief under this Part;

"relevant foreign tax", where borne by a company in respect of an amount receivable from the sale of goods, means tax—

(*a*) which under the laws of any foreign territory has been deducted from that amount,

(*b*) which corresponds to income tax or corporation tax,

(*c*) which has not been repaid to the company, ...[1]

(*d*) for which credit is not allowable under arrangements within the meaning of [Schedule 24, and][2]

[(*e*) which is not treated under Schedule 24 as reducing the amount of any income;][3]

"the total amount receivable from the sale of goods", in relation to a company in the course of a trade in a relevant accounting period, means the aggregate of amounts, receivable by the company in the course of the trade in the relevant accounting period, which are regarded by virtue of this Part as receivable from the sale of goods for the purposes of relief under this Part.

(2) For the purposes of this section—

(*a*) the amount of the corporation tax which apart from subsection (3) would be payable by a company and which is attributable to an amount receivable from the sale of goods shall be an amount equal to 10 per cent of the amount of the income of the company referable to the amount so receivable [reduced by the relevant foreign tax][4];

(*b*) the amount of any income of a company referable to an amount receivable from the sale of goods in the course of a trade in a relevant accounting period shall, subject to paragraph 4(5) of Schedule 24, be taken to be such sum as bears to the total amount of the income of the company from the sale of goods in the course of the trade for the relevant accounting period [increased by the amount of the relevant foreign tax,][5] the same proportion as the amount receivable from the sale of goods bears to the total amount receivable by the company from the sale of goods in the course of the trade in the relevant accounting period;

(*c*) the total amount of income of a company from the sale of goods in the course of a trade in a relevant accounting period shall be taken to be the sum referred to in subsection (3) of section 448, which for the purposes of subsection (2) of that section is to be taken to be the income of the trade for the relevant accounting period referred to in the expression **"the income from the sale of those goods"** in subsection (2) of that section.

(3) The amount of corporation tax which apart from this subsection would be payable by a company for a relevant accounting period shall be reduced by so much of nine-tenths of any relevant foreign tax borne by the company in respect of an amount receivable from the sale of goods in that period in the course of a trade as does not exceed the corporation tax which would be so payable and which is attributable to the amount receivable from the sale of goods.

...[6]

Amendments

1 Deleted by FA 1998 s 59(*a*) with effect from 6 April 1998; previously "and".

2 Substituted by FA 1998 s 59(*b*) with effect from 6 April 1998; previously "Schedule 24;".

3 Definition of "relevant foreign tax" para (*e*) inserted by FA 1998 s 59(*c*) with effect from 6 April 1998.

4 Inserted by FA 2003 s 60(1)(*a*) as respects accounting periods ending on or after 6 February 2003.

5 Inserted by FA 2003 s 60(1)(*b*) as respects accounting periods ending on or after 6 February 2003.

6 Subs (4) deleted by FA 2000 s 83(1)(*d*)(ii) as respects accounting periods beginning after 1 April 2000.

Cross-references

Corporation tax, manufacturing (10%) relief: s 448(1)(*d*).

Provisions as to relief from income tax and corporation tax by means of credit in respect of foreign tax, limit on total credit — corporation tax: Sch 24 para 4(3), (5); unilateral relief: Sch 24 para 9A(5).

Definitions

charges: s 243; company: ss 4(1), 5(1); Corporation Tax Acts: s 1(2); trade: ss 3(1), 4(1), 5(1).

Former enactments

FA 1980 s 39C; FA 1994 s 54(*a*); FA 1995 s 63.

450 Double taxation relief

(1) (*a*) In this section—

"appropriate inspector", **"chargeable period"** and **"specified return date for the chargeable period"** have the same meanings respectively as in Part 41;

"arrangements" and **"foreign tax"** have the same meanings respectively as in paragraph 1(1) of Schedule 24;

"credit institution" means an undertaking whose business it is to receive deposits or other repayable funds from the public and to grant credit on its own account;

"group relevant payment" means a relevant payment made to a relevant company by a company related to the relevant company;

"qualified company" and **"relevant trading operations"** have, subject to paragraph (*e*), the same meanings respectively as in section 446;

"relevant company" means a qualified company, other than a credit institution or a 25 per cent subsidiary of a credit institution, the relevant trading operations of which—

(i) are wholly carried on by persons—

(I) who are employees of the qualified company or a company related to it and who are not employees of any employer other than the qualified company or the company related to it, as the case may be, and

(II) in respect of whom there does not exist any understanding or arrangement the purpose of which, or one of the purposes of which, is to provide for the engagement of the services of those persons, whether as employees or otherwise, should they cease to be employed by the qualified company or the company related to it, as the case may be,

and

(ii) are not managed or directed, whether directly or indirectly, by another qualified company other than a company related to the first-mentioned qualified company;

"relevant foreign tax" means so much of the amount of foreign tax as—

(i) has been deducted from relevant payments,

(ii) would have been so deducted if the laws of the territory under which the tax was deducted prohibited the deduction of tax from such payments at a rate in excess of 10 per cent, and

(iii) has not been repaid;

"relevant payment" means a payment of interest which—

(i) arises from a source within a territory in regard to which arrangements have the force of law, and

(ii) is regarded, subject to paragraph (*e*), by virtue of section 446(10)(*b*) as receivable by a relevant company from the sale of goods for the purposes of relief under this Part.

(*b*) For the purposes of this section, a company shall be treated as related to another company at any relevant time if at that time one of the 2 companies is a 25 per cent subsidiary of the other company, or both companies are 25 per cent subsidiaries of the same company.

(*c*) For the purposes of paragraph (*b*), a company (in this paragraph referred to as **"the subsidiary company"**) shall not be deemed to be a 25 per cent subsidiary of another company (in this paragraph referred to as **"the parent company"**) at any time if the percentage—

(i) of any profits, which are available for distribution to equity holders, of the subsidiary company at such time to which the parent company is beneficially entitled at such time, or

(ii) of any assets, which are available for distribution to equity holders on a winding up, of the subsidiary company at such time to which the parent company would be beneficially entitled at such time on a winding up of the subsidiary company,

is less than 25 per cent of such profits or assets, as the case may be, of the subsidiary company at such time, and sections 413, 414, 415 and 418 shall, with any necessary modifications but without regard to section 411(1)(*c*) in so far as it relates to those sections, apply to the determination of the percentage of those profits or assets, as the case may be, to which a company is beneficially entitled as they apply to the determination for the purposes of Chapter 5 of Part 12 of the percentage of any such profits or assets to which a company is so entitled.

(*d*) For the purposes of this section, a company shall be deemed to be a 25 per cent subsidiary of another company if and so long as not less than 25 per cent of its ordinary share capital would be treated as owned directly or indirectly by that other company if section 9 (other than subsection (1) of that section) were to apply for the purposes of this paragraph, and, where a company (in this paragraph referred to as **"that company"**) would be treated for the purposes of this section as a 25 per cent subsidiary of a credit institution which is not a company, if the credit institution were a company, that company shall be so treated for those purposes.

(*e*) For the purpose of this section apart from this paragraph—

(i) a payment made to a company in the course of relevant trading operations (within the meaning of section 445), being a payment which is regarded by virtue of section 445(9)(*b*) as receivable from the sale of goods for the purposes of relief under this Part, shall be treated as so regarded by virtue of section 446(10)(*b*), and

(ii) if the company is a qualified company carrying on relevant trading operations (within the meaning of section 445), it shall be treated as being a qualified company carrying on relevant trading operations (within the meaning of section 446),

so long as the relevant trading operations (within the meaning of section 445) could be certified by the Minister for Finance as relevant trading operations for the purposes of section 446 if they were carried on in the Area (within the meaning of section 446) rather than in the airport (within the meaning of section 445).

(2) Notwithstanding paragraph 4 of Schedule 24 but subject to subsection (3), where a relevant company elects to have the amount of the credit, which is to be allowed to the company in respect of foreign tax deducted from group relevant payments made to the company in a relevant accounting period, computed as if, for the purposes of paragraph 4 of Schedule 24, the amount of the corporation tax attributable to the income attributable to those group relevant payments were deemed to be increased by an amount which—

(*a*) shall be allocated by the company in such amounts and to such part of that income as the company thinks fit, and

(*b*) shall not exceed 35 per cent of the amount of corporation tax which—

(i) apart from this section would be payable by the company, and

(ii) is attributable to all relevant payments made to the company in the course of the trade in the accounting period,

the amount of that credit shall be so computed for those purposes.

(3) Where an election is made by a company under subsection (2) in respect of a relevant accounting period—

(*a*) any credit for foreign tax deducted from group relevant payments made to the company in the accounting period shall be computed as if the amount of foreign tax deducted from those group relevant payments were the amount of relevant foreign tax comprised in that amount, and

(*b*) so much of that credit as would not have been allowed to the company apart from this section shall be disregarded for the purposes of paragraph 7(3)(*c*) of Schedule 24.

(4) (*a*) For the purposes of subsection (2), the amount of corporation tax which apart from this section would be payable by a company and which is attributable to

relevant payments made to the company shall be an amount determined by the formula—

$$A - B$$

where—

A is an amount equal to 10 per cent of the amount of the income of the company attributable to relevant payments, and

B is the credit which apart from this section would be allowed to the company in respect of foreign tax deducted from those payments.

(*b*) For the purposes of paragraph (*a*)—

(i) the amount of the income of a company attributable to relevant payments made to the company in the course of a trade in a relevant accounting period shall, subject to paragraph 4(5) of Schedule 24, be taken to be such sum as bears to the total amount of the income of the company from the sale of goods in the course of the trade in the relevant accounting period the same proportion as those relevant payments bear to the total amount receivable by the company from the sale of goods in the course of the trade in the accounting period, and

(ii) the total amount of income of a company from the sale of goods in the course of a trade in a relevant accounting period shall be taken to be the sum referred to in subsection (3) of section 448 which, for the purposes of subsection (2) of that section, is to be taken to be the income of the trade for the relevant accounting period referred to in the expression **"the income from the sale of those goods"** in subsection (2) of that section.

...[1]

(6) An election referred to in subsection (2) shall be made in writing to the appropriate inspector in relation to the company making the election on or before that company's specified return date for the chargeable period in respect of which it is making the election.

Amendments

1 Subs (5) deleted by FA 2000 s 83(1)(*e*)(ii) as respects accounting periods beginning after 1 April 2000.

Cross-references

Provisions as to relief from income tax and corporation tax by means of credit in respect of foreign tax, limit on total credit — corporation tax: Sch 24 para 4(5).

Definitions

charges: s 243; person: IA 1937 s 11(*c*); trade: ss 3(1), 4(1), 5(1); writing: IA 1937 Sch; year: IA 1937 Sch.

Former enactments

FA 1980 s 39D; FA 1995 s 62.

451 Treatment of income and gains of certain trading operations carried on in Custom House Docks Area from investments held outside the State

(1) In this section—

"the Area" has the same meaning as it has for the purposes of section 446;

"foreign life assurance business" means relevant trading operations within the meaning of section 446 consisting of life assurance business with policy holders and annuitants who at the time such business is contracted reside outside the State and, as regards any policy issued or contract made, as the case may be, with such policy holders or annuitants in the course of such business, such policy or contract does not provide for—

(*a*) the granting of any additional contractual rights, or

(*b*) an option to have another policy or contract substituted for it,

at a time when the policy holder or annuitant, as the case may be, resides in the State;

"foreign unit trust business" means relevant trading operations within the meaning of section 446 consisting of the management of the investments of one or more qualifying unit trusts;

"qualifying unit trust" means a unit trust scheme—

(*a*) which is a registered unit trust scheme within the meaning of the Unit Trusts Act, 1972,

(*b*) the business of which—

(i) is carried on in the Area, or

(ii) is not so carried on but is carried on in the State and would be carried on in the Area but for circumstances outside the control of the person or persons carrying on the business,

and

(*c*) as respects which all holders of units in the scheme are persons resident outside the State;

"tax" means income tax, corporation tax or capital gains tax, as may be appropriate.

(2) Notwithstanding any other provision of the Tax Acts, the rate at which any tax is chargeable (before any credit is allowed for foreign tax) in respect of income arising or chargeable gains accruing from securities or possessions in any place outside the State that are investments of a foreign life assurance business or investments managed by a foreign unit trust business shall not exceed 10 per cent.

Cross-references

Capital acquisitions tax, exemption of certain policies of assurance, meaning of "foreign life assurance business" applied: CATCA 2003 s 74(1)("old policy").

Profits of life business, subs (1), the definition of "foreign life assurance business" applies for the purposes of s 446 as if "and any certificate so given shall, unless it is revoked under subsection (4), (5) or (6), remain in force until the 31st day of December, 2005" were deleted from s 446(2): s 710(2)(*b*).

Profits of life business: new basis, meaning of "foreign life assurance business" applied: s 730A(1)("new basis business").

Definitions

chargeable gain: ss 4(1), 5(1), 534; company: ss 4(1), 5(1); person: IA 1937 s 11(*c*); Tax Acts: s 1(2); unit trust: s 5(1); units: s 5(1).

Former enactments

FA 1988 s 36(4); FA 1997 s 66(1).

452 Application of section 130 to certain interest

[(1) (*a*) In this section—

"arrangements" means arrangements having the force of law by virtue of [section 826(1)(*a*)][1];

"relevant territory" means—

(i) a Member State of the European Communities other than the State, or

(ii) not being such a Member State, a territory with the government of which arrangements have been made;

"qualified company" and **"relevant trading operations"** have the same meanings as they have for the purposes of sections 445 and 446, but trading operations shall not be treated as relevant trading operations (within the meaning of section 445) if they are not trading operations which could be certified by the Minister for Finance as relevant trading operations for the purposes of section 446 if they were carried on in the area (within the meaning of section 446) rather than the airport (within the meaning of section 445);

"tax", in relation to a relevant territory, means any tax imposed in that territory which corresponds to corporation tax in the State.

(*b*) For the purposes of this section, a company shall be regarded as being a resident of a relevant territory if—

(i) in a case where the relevant territory is a territory with the government of which arrangements have been made, the company is regarded as being a resident of that territory under those arrangements, and

(ii) in any other case, the company is by virtue of the law of the relevant territory resident for the purposes of tax in that territory.

(2) (*a*) This paragraph shall apply to so much of any interest as—

(i) is a distribution by virtue only of section 130(2)(*d*)(iv),

(ii) is payable by a company in the ordinary course of a trade carried on by that company and would, but for section 130(2)(*d*)(iv), be deductible as a trading expense in computing the amount of the company's income from the trade, and

(iii) is interest payable to a company which is a resident of a relevant territory.

(*b*) Where a company proves that paragraph (*a*) applies to any interest payable by it for an accounting period and elects to have that interest treated as not being a distribution for the purposes of section 130(2)(*d*)(iv), then, section 130(2)(*d*)(iv) shall not apply to that interest.

(3) (*a*) This paragraph shall apply to so much of any interest as—

(i) is a distribution by virtue only of section 130(2)(*d*)(iv),

(ii) is payable by a qualified company in the course of carrying on relevant trading operations and would but for section 130(2)(*d*)(iv) be deductible as a trading expense in computing the amount of the company's income from the relevant trading operations, and

(iii) represents no more than a reasonable commercial return for the use of the principal in respect of which the interest is paid by the qualified company.

(*b*) Where a qualified company proves that paragraph (*a*) applies to any interest payable by it for an accounting period and elects to have that interest treated as not being a distribution for the purposes of section 130(2)(*d*)(iv), then, section 130(2)(*d*)(iv) shall not apply to that interest.

(4) An election under subsection (2)(*b*) or (3)(*b*) in relation to interest payable by a company for an accounting period shall be made in writing to the inspector and furnished together with the company's return of its profits for the period.][2]

Amendments

1 Substituted by FA 2004 s 89 and Sch 3 para 1(*m*) with effect from 25 March 2004; previously "section 826".

2 Section 452 substituted by FA 2001 s 87 with effect from 6 April 2001.

Cross-references

Matters to be treated as distributions: s 130(2B).

Definitions

company: ss 4(1), 5(1); distribution: ss 4(1), 436, 437; inspector: ss 2(1), 852; interest: s 4(1); profits: s 4(1); writing: IA 1937 Sch.

Former enactments

FA 1988 s 37; FA 1994 s 49.

453 Transactions between associated persons

(1) In this section, **"control"** has the same meaning as in section 11.

(2) Where a company making a claim for relief under this Part (in this subsection referred to as **"the buyer"**) buys from another person (in this subsection referred to as **"the seller"**), and—

(*a*) the seller has control over the buyer or, the seller being a body corporate or partnership, the buyer has control over the seller or some other person has control over both the seller and the buyer, and

(*b*) the price in the transaction is less than that which might have been expected to obtain if the parties to the transaction had been independent parties dealing at arm's length,

then, the income or losses of the buyer and the seller shall be computed for any purpose of the Tax Acts as if the price in the transaction had been that which would have obtained if the transaction had been a transaction between independent persons dealing at arm's length.

(3) Where a company making a claim for relief under this Part (in this subsection referred to as **"the seller"**) sells goods to another person (in this subsection referred to as **"the buyer"**) and—

(*a*) the buyer has control over the seller or, the buyer being a body corporate or partnership, the seller has control over the buyer or some other person has control over both the seller and the buyer, and

(*b*) the goods are sold at a price greater than the price which they might have been expected to fetch if the parties to the transaction had been independent parties dealing at arm's length,

then, the income or losses of the buyer and the seller shall be computed for any purpose of the Tax Acts as if the goods had been sold by the seller to the buyer for the price which the goods would have fetched if the transaction had been a transaction between independent persons dealing at arm's length.

(4) For the purposes of subsection (3), a company shall be deemed to sell goods where and to the extent that for the purposes of this Part any amount receivable by it in payment for any trading activity is regarded as an amount receivable from the sale of goods, and **"seller"** and **"buyer"** shall be construed accordingly.

(5) The inspector may by notice in writing require a company making a claim for relief under this Part to furnish him or her with such information or particulars as may be necessary for the purposes of this section, and subsection (2) of section 448 shall apply as if the matters of which proof is required by that subsection included the information or particulars specified in a notice under this section.

Definitions

company: ss 4(1), 5(1); inspector: ss 2(1), 5(1), 852; person: IA 1937 s 11(*c*); Tax Acts: s 1(2); writing: IA 1937 Sch.

Former enactments

FA 1980 s 44.

454 Restriction of certain charges on income

(1) (*a*) In this section—

"trade" means a trade carried on by a company which consists of or includes the manufacture of goods (including activities carried on in an accounting period which, if the company had sufficient profits in that period and made a claim for relief in respect of the trade under this Part for that period, would be regarded for the purposes of this Part as the manufacture of goods);

"income from the sale of goods" in an accounting period in the course of a trade carried on by a company shall, subject to section 422 as applied for the purposes of relief under section 456, be such income as would be **"the income from the sale of those goods"** in that period in the course of the trade for the purposes of a claim under section 448(2), if—

(i) no group relief under section 456 or loss relief under section 455(3) were allowed against income from the trade in that period,

(ii) the company had sufficient profits, and

(iii) the company made a claim for relief under this Part;

"charges on income paid for the purpose of the sale of goods" in the course of a trade in an accounting period shall be such amount as would be the amount of the income from the sale of goods in that period if, notwithstanding section 448(4), **"the company's income for the relevant accounting period from the sale in the course of the trade mentioned in that subsection of goods and merchandise"** for the purposes of section 448(3) were the amount of so much of the charges on income paid wholly and exclusively for the purposes of the trade in that period as appears to the inspector or on appeal to the Appeal Commissioners to be referable to charges on income paid for the purpose of the sale of goods and merchandise;

"the sale of goods and merchandise" in the course of a trade carried on by a company means the sale of such goods and merchandise as would respectively be treated as goods and merchandise for the purposes of a claim under this Part, if the company had a sufficiency of profits and had made such a claim.

[(*b*) For the purposes of this section, where a part only of an accounting period of a company is a relevant accounting period, the accounting period shall be divided into 2 parts, one beginning on the day on which the accounting period begins and ending on the last day of the accounting period which is within the relevant accounting period, and the other beginning on the day after that last-mentioned day and ending on the day on which the accounting period ends, and both parts shall be treated as if they were separate accounting periods of the company.][1]

[(2) Notwithstanding sections 243 and 243A, charges on income paid for the purposes of the sale of goods by a company in a relevant accounting period in the course of a trade or trades, as the case may be, shall not be allowed as deductions against the total profits, or against the relevant trading income [(within the meaning of section 243A)][2], of the company for the relevant accounting period.

(3) Charges on income paid for the purposes of the sale of goods by a company in a relevant accounting period which charges on income would, apart from subsection (2) and section 243A(2), be allowed as deductions against the total profits of the company for the accounting period, shall be allowed as deductions against the company's income from the sale of goods, as reduced by any amount set off under section 455, for the accounting period.][3]

Amendments

1 Subs (1)(*b*) substituted by FA 1999 s 74(*d*)(i) with effect from 6 April 1999.

2 Inserted by FA 2002 s 54(1)(*c*) as respects an accounting period ending on or after 6 March 2001 (for the purposes of computing the amount of charges on income paid for the purposes of the sale of goods (within the meaning of TCA 1997 s 454), a loss from the sale of goods (within the meaning of TCA 1997 s 455), relevant trading charges on income (within the meaning of TCA 1997 s 243A), and relevant trading losses (within the meaning of TCA 1997 s 396A), in respect of which relief may be claimed by virtue of FA 2002 s 54, where an accounting period of a company begins before 6 March 2001 and ends on or after that date, it shall be divided into 2 parts, one beginning on the date on which the accounting period begins and ending on 5 March 2001 and the other beginning on 6 March 2001 and ending on the date on which the accounting period ends, and both parts shall be treated as if they were separate accounting periods of the company).

3 Subs (2)–(3) substituted by FA 2001 s 90(1)(*c*)(ii) as respects an accounting period ending on or after 6 March 2001.

Note

Section 454 ceased to have effect from 1 January 2003 (FA 2001 s 90(3)).

For the purposes of the amendments to this section effected by FA 2001 s 90 where an accounting period of a company begins before 6 March 2001 and ends on or after that date, it shall be divided into 2 parts, one beginning on the date on which the accounting period begins and ending on 5 March 2001 and the other beginning on 6 March 2001 and ending on the date on which the accounting period ends, and both parts shall be treated as if they were separate accounting periods of the company, and for the purposes of computing the amount of charges on income paid for the purposes of the sale of goods within the meaning of TCA 1997 s 454, where an accounting period of a company begins before 1 January 2003 and ends on or after that date, it shall be divided into 2 parts, one beginning on the date on which the accounting period begins and ending on 31 December 2002 and the other beginning on 1 January 2003 and ending on the date on which the accounting period ends, and both parts shall be treated as if they were separate accounting periods of the company — see FA 2001 s 90(4), as substituted by FA 2002 s 55.

Cross-references

Group relief, relief for certain losses on a value basis: s 420B(2)(b); meaning of "charges on income paid for the sale of goods" applied: s 420B(3)(*a*).
Higher rate of corporation tax, meaning of "income from sale of goods" applied: s 21A(4)(*a*).
Reduction of corporation tax liability in respect of certain trading income: s 22A(1)("relevant charges in income").
Relief for certain charges on income on a value basis, meaning of "charges on income paid for the purposes of the sale of goods" applied: s 243B(1), (3); s 243(2)(*b*).
Restriction of loss relief: s 455(1).
Restriction of group relief, meaning of "trade", "income from the sale of goods", "charges on income paid for the purposes of the sale of goods" and "the sale of goods and merchandise" applied: s 456(1); s 456(2A)(*a*)(i).
Restriction of relevant charges on income: s 243A(3).

Revenue information

Tax certificates issued by the Minister for Finance under sections 445(2) and 446(2) of the Taxes Consolidation Act 1997 to IFSC/Shannon companies contain a condition restricting the offset of losses to the trading activities referred to in the certificate. The Department of Finance has confirmed that s 54 of the Finance Act 2002 may be applied to these companies on the same basis as it applies to non-certified companies.

Statement of practice

Surcharge and other penalties or restriction for late submission of tax returns: SP GEN/1/93, January 1993.

Tax Briefing

TB44 June 2001 pp 39–40 — CT Losses, Charges and Group Relief Offset (following enactment of FA 2001 s 90).

Definitions

charges on income: ss 4(1), 243(1); company: ss 4(1), 5(1); profits: s 4(1); relevant accounting period: s 442(1); trade: ss 3(1), 4(1).

Former enactments

CTA 1976 s 10A(1)(*a*) and (*b*)(ii), (2)–(3); FA 1992 s 46(1)(*a*); FA 1993 s 50.

455 Restriction of certain losses

(1) (*a*) In this section—

"trade", **"income from the sale of goods"** and **"the sale of goods and merchandise"** have the same meanings respectively as in section 454;

"a loss from the sale of goods" in the course of a trade in an accounting period shall be such amount as would be the amount of the income from the sale of goods in that period if, notwithstanding section 448(4), "the company's income for the relevant accounting period from the sale in the course of the trade mentioned in that subsection of goods and merchandise" for the purposes of section 448(3) were the amount of so much of the loss, computed as for the purposes of section 396(2), from the trade in the period as appears to the inspector or on appeal to the Appeal Commissioners to be referable to a loss incurred in the sale of goods and merchandise, but a loss such as is mentioned in section 407(4)(*b*) shall not be a loss from the sale of goods.

(*b*) Section 454(1)(*b*) shall apply for the purposes of this section as it applies for the purposes of section 454.

(2) [Notwithstanding sections 396(2) and 396A(2) but subject to subsections (6) and (7), for the purposes of those sections][1] the amount of a loss in a trade incurred by a company in [a relevant accounting period][2] shall be deemed to be reduced by the amount of a loss from the sale of goods, if any, incurred in the trade by the company in [the relevant accounting period][3].

(3) Subject to subsections (6) and (7), where in [a relevant accounting period][4] a company carrying on a trade incurs a loss from the sale of goods, the company may make a claim requiring that the loss be set off for the purposes of corporation tax against its income from the sale of goods—

(*a*) of [that relevant accounting period],[5] and

(*b*) if it was then carrying on the trade and if the claim so requires, of preceding accounting periods ending within the time specified in subsection (4),

and, subject to any relief for an earlier loss, to the extent that the trading income of any of those accounting periods consists of or includes income from the sale of goods, that trading income shall then be reduced by so much of the loss as cannot be relieved against trading income of a later accounting period.

(4) For the purposes of subsection (3), the time referred to in paragraph (*b*) of that subsection shall be the time immediately preceding the accounting period first-mentioned in subsection (3) equal in length to that accounting period; but the amount of the reduction which may be made under subsection (3) in the trading income of an accounting period falling partly before that time shall not exceed such part of the income from the sale of goods included in that trading income as bears to the income from the sale of goods the same proportion as the part of the accounting period falling within that time bears to the whole of that accounting period.

...[6]

(6) This section shall not apply to so much of a company's loss from the sale of goods in the course of a trade in an accounting period as does not exceed the amount of the capital allowances under Part 9 or Chapter 1 of Part 29 which are to be made for the accounting period in taxing the trade, and for the purposes of this subsection no account shall be taken of capital allowances other than capital allowances in respect of machinery or plant or an industrial building or structure—

(*a*) provided for the purposes of a project approved within the period of 2 years ending on the 31st day of December, 1988, by the Industrial Development Authority,

(*b*) the expenditure on the provision of which was incurred on or before the 31st day of March, 1995, and

(*c*) more than 50 per cent of the expenditure on the provision of which was incurred, or was the subject of a binding contract entered into, before the 1st day of April, 1992.

(7) This section shall not apply to so much of a company's loss from the sale of goods in the course of a trade in an accounting period as does not exceed the amount of the capital allowances under section 323(2) deducted by the company in computing the loss which the company has incurred in that period in carrying on trading operations specified in a certificate given to it, and not subsequently revoked, by the Minister for Finance under section 446.

Amendments

1 Substituted by FA 2001 s 90(1)(*c*)(iii)(I) as respects an accounting period ending on or after 6 March 2001; previously "Notwithstanding section 396(2) but subject to subsections (6) and (7), for the purposes of that section".

2 Substituted by FA 1999 s 74(*e*)(i) with effect from 6 April 1999; previously "an accounting period".
3 Substituted by FA 1999 s 74(*e*)(i) with effect from 6 April 1999; previously "the accounting period".
4 Substituted by FA 1999 s 74(*e*)(ii) with effect from 6 April 1999; previously "an accounting period".
5 Substituted by FA 1999 s 74(*e*)(ii) with effect from 6 April 1999; previously "that accounting period".
6 Subs (5) deleted by FA 2001 s 90(1)(*c*)(iii)(II) as respects an accounting period ending on or after 6 March 2001.

Note

Section 455 will cease to have effect from 1 January 2003 (FA 2001 s 90(3)).
For the purposes of computing the amount of a loss from the sale of goods within the meaning of TCA 1997 s 455, where an accounting period of a company begins before 1 January 2003 and ends on or after that date, it shall be divided into 2 parts, one beginning on the date on which the accounting period begins and ending on 31 December 2002 and the other beginning on 1 January 2003 and ending on the date on which the accounting period ends, and both parts shall be treated as if they were separate accounting periods of the company — see FA 2001 s 90(4), as substituted by FA 2002 s 55.

Cross-references

Corporation tax, relief for trading losses other than terminal losses, subs (3): s 396(1).
Group relief, relief for certain losses on a value basis: s 420B(2)(*b*); meaning of "loss from the sale of goods" applied: s 420B(3)(*a*).
Pre-trading expenditure, no double relief, subs (3): s 82(3).
Reduction of corporation tax liability in respect of certain trading income: s 22A(1)("relevant trading loss").
Relief for certain trading losses on a value basis, subs (3): s 396B(2)(*b*); meaning of "a loss from the sale of goods" applied: s 396B(3)(*a*), (*b*).
Relief for trading losses other than terminal losses, subs (3): s 396(1).
Relief for relevant trading losses: s 396A(3).
Restriction of certain charges on income, subs (3): s 454(1); s 454(3).
Restriction of group relief, meaning of "a loss from the sale of goods" applied: s 456(1); s 456(2A)(*a*)(ii).

Statement of practice

Surcharge and other penalties or restriction for late submission of tax returns: SP GEN/1/93, January 1993.

Tax Briefing

TB44 June 2001 pp 30–40 — CT Losses, Charges and Group Relief Offset (following enactment of FA 2001 s 90).

Definitions

capital allowance: ss 2(1), 5(1); company: ss 4(1), 5(1); profits: s 4(1); relevant accounting period: s 442(1); trade: ss 3(1), 4(1).

Former enactments

CTA 1976 s 16A; FA 1992 s 46(1)(*c*).

456 Restriction of group relief

(1) (*a*) In this section—

"trade", **"income from the sale of goods"**, **"charges on income paid for the purposes of the sale of goods"** and **"the sale of goods and merchandise"** have the same meanings respectively as in section 454;

"a loss from the sale of goods" has the same meaning as in section 455;

"an excess of charges on income paid for the purpose of the sale of goods" in the course of the trade in an accounting period shall be so much of an amount, being the amount by which the charges on income paid by a company for the purpose of the sale of goods in the course of the trade in that period exceed the income from the sale of goods in the course of the trade in that period, as does not exceed the excess referred to in section 420(6) as computed for the company for that period.

(*b*) Section 454(1)(*b*) shall apply for the purposes of this section as it applies for the purposes of section 454.

[(2) Notwithstanding subsections (1) and (6) of section 420 and sections 420A(3) and 421, where in any relevant accounting period the surrendering company incurs a loss from the sale of goods or an excess of charges on income paid for the sale of goods, that loss or excess may not be set off for the purposes of corporation tax against the total profits, or against the relevant trading income, of the claimant company for its corresponding accounting period.

(2A)(*a*) Where in any relevant accounting period the surrendering company incurs a loss from the sale of goods or an excess of charges on income paid for the sale of goods, that loss or excess may be set off for the purposes of corporation tax against the income from the sale of goods of the claimant company for its corresponding accounting period, as reduced by any amounts—

(i) allowed as deductions against that income under section 454, or

(ii) set off against that income under section 455.

(*b*) Group relief allowed under paragraph (*a*) shall reduce the income from a trade of the claimant company for an accounting period—

(i) before relief granted under section 397 in respect of a loss incurred in a succeeding accounting period or periods, and

(ii) after the relief granted under section 396 in respect of a loss incurred in a preceding accounting period or periods.][1]

(4) This section shall not apply to so much of a loss from the sale of goods in the course of a trade in an accounting period as does not exceed the amount of the capital allowances under section 323(2) deducted by the surrendering company in computing the loss which the company has incurred in that period in carrying on trading operations specified in a certificate given to it, and not subsequently revoked, by the Minister for Finance under section 446.

(5) For the purposes of this section—

(*a*) in the case of a claim made by a company as a member of a consortium, only a fraction of a loss from the sale of goods or an excess of charges on income paid for the purpose of the sale of goods may be set off, and that fraction shall be equal to that member's share in the consortium, subject to any further reduction under section 422(2), and

...[2]

Amendments

1 Subs (2)–(3) substituted by FA 2001 s 90(1)(*c*)(iv)(I) as respects an accounting period ending on or after 6 March 2001.

2 Subs (5)(*b*) deleted by FA 2001 s 90(1)(*c*)(iv)(II) as respects an accounting period ending on or after 6 March 2001.

Note

Section 456 will cease to have effect from 1 January 2003 (FA 2001 s 90(3)).

For the purposes of the amendments to this section effected by FA 2001 s 90, where an accounting period of a company begins before 6 March 2001 and ends on or after that date, it shall be divided into 2 parts, one beginning on the date on which the accounting period begins and ending on 5 March 2001 and the other beginning on 6 March 2001 and ending on the date on which the accounting period ends, and both parts shall be treated as if they were separate accounting periods of the company, and for the purposes of computing the amount of charges on income paid for the purposes of the sale of goods within the meaning of TCA 1997 s 454 and a loss from the sale of goods within the meaning of TCA 1997 s 455, where an accounting period of a company begins before 1 January 2003 and ends on or after that date, it shall be divided into 2 parts, one beginning on the date on which the accounting period begins and ending on 31 December 2002 and the other beginning on 1 January 2003 and ending on the date on which the accounting period ends, and both parts shall be treated as if they were separate accounting periods of the company — see FA 2001 s 94(4), as substituted by FA 2002 s 55.

Cross-references

Group relief, relevant losses and charges: s 420A(3)(*a*); relief for certain losses on a value basis: s 420B(2)(*c*).
Pre-trading expenditure, no double relief: s 82(3).
Restriction of charges on income: s 454(1).

Tax Briefing

TB44 June 2001 pp 39–40 — CT Losses, Charges and Group Relief Offset (following enactment of FA 2001 s 90).

Definitions

Appeal Commissioners: s 2(1); capital allowance: s 2(1); charges on income: ss 4(1), 243(1); company: ss 4(1), 5(1); group relief: ss 4(1), 411; inspector: ss 2(1), 5(1), 852; relevant accounting period: s 442(1); profits: s 4(1); trade: ss 3(1), 4(1), 5(1).

Former enactments

CTA 1976 s 116A(1)(*a*) and (*b*)(ii), (2)–(3), (4)(*b*) and (5); FA 1988 s 34; FA 1992 s 46(2).

457 Application of section 448 where profits are charged to corporation tax at the reduced rate

Amendments

Section 457 deleted by FA 2001 s 90(1)(*c*)(v) as respects an accounting period ending on or after 6 March 2001.

Note

As regards the amendments effected by FA 2001 s 90, for the purposes of computing the amount of relevant trading charges on income within the meaning of TCA 1997 s 243A and relevant trading losses within the meaning of TCA 1997 s 396A and in so far as those amendments apply to TCA 1997 ss 454 and 456, where an accounting period of a company begins before 6 March 2001 and ends on or after that date, it shall be divided into 2 parts, one beginning on the date on which the accounting period begins and ending on 5 March 2001 and the other beginning on 6 March 2001 and ending on the date on which the accounting period ends, and both parts shall be treated as if they were separate accounting periods of the company, and for the purposes of computing the amount of charges on income paid for the purposes of the sale of goods within the meaning of TCA 1997 s 454 and a loss from the sale of goods within the meaning of TCA 1997 s 455, where an accounting period of a company begins before 1 January 2003 and ends on or after that date, it shall be divided into 2 parts, one beginning on the date on which the accounting period begins and ending on 31 December 2002 and the other beginning on 1 January 2003 and ending on the date on which the accounting period ends, and both parts shall be treated as if they were separate accounting periods of the company — see FA 2001 s 90(4), as substituted by FA 2002 s 55.

PART 15
PERSONAL ALLOWANCES AND RELIEFS AND CERTAIN OTHER INCOME TAX AND CORPORATION TAX RELIEFS

CHAPTER 1
Personal Allowances and Reliefs

Revenue information

Information leaflet IT1 — Allowances, Reliefs & Tax Rates.
Information leaflet IT3 — Tax-Free Allowances.
Information leaflet IT12 — Disabled Persons & Income Tax.

Tax Briefing

TB35 Mar 1999 p 1–5 — Standard rating of allowances.
TB41 Sept 2000 p 5 — Tax Credit System from 6 April 2001.
TB42 Dec 2000 pp 1–13 — Tax Credit System.

458 Deductions allowed in ascertaining taxable income and provisions relating to reductions in tax

(1) An individual who, in the manner prescribed by the Income Tax Acts, makes a claim in that behalf and[, subject to subsection (1B),][1] makes a return in the prescribed form of the individual's total income shall be entitled—

(*a*) for the purpose of ascertaining the amount of the income on which he or she is to be charged to income tax (in the Income Tax Acts referred to as **"the taxable income"**) to have such deductions as are specified in the provisions referred to in Part 1 of the Table to this section, but subject to those provisions, made from the individual's total income, and

[(*b*) to have the income tax to be charged on the individual reduced by such tax credits and other reductions as are specified in the provisions referred to in Part 2 of that Table, but subject to subsection (1A) and those provisions.][2]

[(1A) Where an individual is entitled to a tax credit specified in a provision referred to in Part 2 of the Table to this section, the income tax to be charged on the individual for the year of assessment, other than in accordance with section 16(2), shall be reduced by the lesser of—

(*a*) the amount of the tax credit, or

(*b*) the amount which reduces that income tax to nil.][3]

[(1B) The requirement in subsection (1) to make a return in the prescribed form of the individual's total income shall not apply, except where the Revenue Commissioners otherwise direct, where the claim falls to be taken into account—

(*a*) in the making of deductions or repayments of tax under Chapter 4 of Part 42 and the regulations made under that Chapter, or

(*b*) except in the case of a chargeable person (within the meaning of section 950), in relation to a repayment of tax deducted under that Chapter and those regulations.][4]

(2) Subsections (3) and (4) of section 459 and paragraph 8 of Schedule 28 shall apply for the purposes of claims for—

(*a*) any such deductions from total income as are specified in the provisions referred to in Part 1 of the Table to this section, and

[(*b*) any such tax credits or reductions in tax as are specified in the provisions referred to in Part 2 of the Table to this section.][5]

TABLE

Part 1

[Section 372AR][6]

...[7]

...[8]

...[9]

...[10]

...[11]

...[12]

Section 467

...[13]

Section 469

Section 471

...[14]

[Section 472A][15]

[Section 472B][16]

...[17]

Section 479

Section 481

Section 489

Paragraphs 12 and 20 of Schedule 32

Part 2

Section 244

[Section 461][18]

[Section 461A][19]

[Section 462][20]

[Section 463][21]

[Section 464][22]

[Section 465][23]

[Section 466][24]

[Section 466A][25]

[Section 468][26]

Section 470

[Section 470A][27]

[Section 472][28]

[Section 472C][29]

[Section 473][30]

[Section 473A][31]

...[32]

Section 476

Section 477

Section 478

[Section 848A(7)][33]

Amendments

1 Inserted by FA 2005 s 24(1)(*a*)(i) with effect from 25 March 2005.

2 Subs (1)(*b*) substituted by FA 2001 s 2(3) and Sch 1 para 1(*e*)(i) for short tax "year" 2001 and later tax years.

3 Subs (1A) inserted by FA 2001 s 2(3) and Sch 1 para 1(*e*)(ii) for short tax "year" 2001 and later tax years.

4 Subs (1B) inserted by FA 2005 s 24(1)(*a*)(ii) with effect from 25 March 2005.

5 Subs (2)(*b*) substituted by FA 2001 s 2(3) and Sch 1 para 1(*e*)(iii) for short tax "year" 2001 and later tax years.

6 Substituted by FA 2002 s 24(1) and Sch 2 Pt 1 para 2(*i*) with effect from 1 January 2002; previously "Section 328", "Section 337", "Section 349", "Section 364", "Section 371", "Section 372I", "Section 372RA", "Section 372Y" and "Section 372AH".

7 Deleted by FA 2000 s 5(*b*)(i) for 2000–2001 and later tax years; previously "Section 461A".

8 Deleted by FA 2000 s 6(*c*) for 2000–2001 and later tax years; previously "Section 462A".

9 Deleted by FA 2000 s 7(*b*)(i) for 2000–2001 and later tax years; previously "Section 463".

10 Deleted by FA 2000 s 8(*b*)(i) for 2000–2001 and later tax years; previously "Section 464".

11 Deleted by FA 2000 s 9(*b*)(i) for 2000–2001 and later tax years; previously "Section 465".

12 Deleted by FA 2000 s 10(*b*)(i) for 2000–2001 and later tax years; previously "Section 466".

13 Deleted by FA 2000 s 11(*b*)(i) for 2000–2001 and later tax years; previously "Section 468".

14 Deleted by FA 1999 s 7(*a*)(i) for 1999–2000 and later tax years; previously "Section 472".

15 Inserted by FA 1998 s 16(*b*)(i) with effect from 6 April 1998.

16 Inserted by FA 1998 s 14(1)(*a*) with effect from 6 April 1998, previously "Section 472".

17 Deleted by FA 2000 s 13(*e*)(i) for 2000–2001 and later tax years; previously "Section 473(2)".

18 Substituted by FA 2001 s 2(3) and Sch 1 para 1(*e*)(iv) for short tax "year" 2001 and later tax years; previously "Section 461(2)".

19 Inserted by FA 2000 s 5(*b*)(ii) for 2000–2001 and later tax years.

20 Inserted by FA 1999 s 5(*b*)(ii) for 1999–2000 and later tax years.

21 Inserted by FA 2000 s 7(*b*)(ii) for 2000–2001 and later tax years.

22 Inserted by FA 2000 s 8(*b*)(ii) for 2000–2001 and later tax years.

23 Inserted by FA 2000 s 9(*b*)(ii) for 2000–2001 and later tax years.

24 Inserted by FA 2000 s 10(*b*)(ii) for 2000–2001 and later tax years.

25 Inserted by FA 2000 s 12(*b*) for 2000–2001 and later tax years.

26 Inserted by FA 2000 s 11(*b*)(ii) for 2000–2001 and later tax years.

27 Inserted by FA 2001 s 20(*a*)(i) with effect from 6 April 2001.

28 Inserted by FA 1999 s 7(*a*)(ii) for 1999–2000 and later tax years.

29 Inserted by FA 2001 s 11(1)(*a*) for short tax "year" 2001 and later tax years.

30 Substituted by FA 2000 s 13(*e*)(ii) for 2000–2001 and later tax years; previously "Section 473(3)".

31 Inserted by FA 2001 s 29(2) with effect from 6 April 2001.

32 Deleted by FA 2001 s 29(2) with effect from 6 April 2001; previously "Section 474", "Section 474A", "Section 475" and "Section 475A".

33 Substituted by FA 2001 s 45(2) with effect from 6 April 2001; previously "Section 485A(4)".

Cross-references

Age exemption: s 188(6)(*a*).

Aggregation of assessments, meaning of "personal reliefs" applied: s 921(1).

Application for separate assessment, meaning of "personal reliefs": s 1023(1).

Charging and assessing of non-residents, entitlement to tax credit in respect of distributions: s 1033.

Charging and assessing of non-residents, restrictions on certain reliefs: s 1032(1).

Leased farm land exemption: s 664(6)(*a*).

Reduction in income tax for certain income earned outside the State: s 825A(1).

Relief for health expenses, subs (2): s 469(6).

Relief for trade union subscriptions: s 472C(4).

Relief from income tax in respect of income from dealing in residential development land: s 644(3)(*b*).

Definitions

total income: s 3(1).

Former enactments

ITA 1967 s 137; FA 1996 s 132(1) and Sch 5 para 1(3); FA 1997 ss 8(8), 57(4) and 146(1) and Sch 9 Pt I para 1(8).

Corresponding UK tax provision

Income and Corporation Taxes Act 1988 s 256.

459 General provisions relating to allowances, deductions and reliefs

(1) A claimant shall not be entitled to an allowance, deduction or relief under the provisions specified in the Table to section 458 in respect of any income the tax on which the claimant is entitled to charge against any other person, or to deduct, retain or satisfy out of any payment which the claimant is liable to make to any other person.

(2) Except where otherwise provided, any allowance, deduction or relief under the provisions specified in the Table to section 458 shall be given either by discharge or reduction of the assessment, or by repayment of the excess which has been paid, or by all of those means, as the case may require.

(3) Any claim shall be accompanied by a declaration and statement in the prescribed form signed by the claimant setting out—

(*a*) all the particular sources from which the claimant's income arises and the particular amount arising from each source,

(*b*) all particulars of any yearly interest or other annual payments reserved or charged on the claimant's income, whereby the claimant's income is or may be diminished, and

(*c*) all particulars of sums which the claimant has charged or may be entitled to charge on account of tax against any other person, or which the claimant has deducted, or may be entitled to deduct, out of any payment to which the claimant is or may be liable.

(4) (*a*) The claim shall be made and proved in accordance with the powers and provisions under which tax under Schedule D is ascertained and charged.

(*b*) Where a claimant is not in the State, an affidavit stating the particulars required by the Income Tax Acts, and taken before any person who has authority to administer in the place where the claimant resides an oath with regard to any matter relating to the public revenue of the State, may be received by the Revenue Commissioners.

(*c*) Where satisfactory proof is given that a claimant is unable to attend in person, a claim on the claimant's behalf may be made by any guardian, trustee, attorney, agent or factor acting for the claimant.

(*d*) Where a person is assessable on behalf of any other person, such person may make a claim on behalf of that other person.

[(5) Subsections (3) and (4) shall not apply, except where the Revenue Commissioners otherwise direct, in relation to a claim which falls to be taken into account—

(*a*) in the making of deductions or repayments of tax under Chapter 4 of Part 42 and the regulations made under that Chapter, or

(*b*) except in the case of a chargeable person (within the meaning of section 950), in relation to a repayment of tax deducted under that Chapter and those regulations.][1]

Amendments

1 Subs (5) inserted by FA 2005 s 24(1)(*b*) with effect from 25 March 2005.

Cross-references

Age exemption, subss (1)–(2) applied s 188(6)(*a*); subs (3)–(4) applied: s 188(6)(*b*).

Leased farm land exemption, subss (1)–(2) applied: s 664(6)(*a*); subss (3)–(4) applied: s 664(6)(*b*).

Maintenance in the case of separated spouses, subss (1)–(2) applied: s 1025(5)(*a*); subss (3)–(4) applied: s 1025(5)(*b*).

Patent royalty income exemption, subss (3)–(4) applied: s 234(8).

Relief for health expenses, subs (2): s 469(6).

Special provisions relating to year of marriage, subss (1)–(2) applied: s 1020(6)(*a*); subss (3)–(4) applied: s 1020(6)(*b*).

Definitions

affidavit: IA 1937 Sch; oath: IA 1937 Sch; person: IA 1937 s 11(*c*).

Former enactments

ITA 1967 s 146, s 149 and Sch 4 para 1(1) and para 2(1) and (3)–(5); F(MP)A 1968 s 3(4)–(5) and Sch Pt III and Pt IV; FA 1996 s 132(1) and Sch 5 Pt I para 1(5)–(6).

460 Rate of tax at which repayments are to be made

(1) Subject to subsections (2) and (3), any repayment of income tax for any year of assessment to which any person may be entitled in respect of any allowance, deduction, relief or reduction under the provisions specified in the Table to section 458 shall, except where otherwise provided by the Income Tax Acts, be made at the standard rate of tax or at the higher rate, as the case may be.

(2) In the case of any person who proves as regards any year that, by reason of the allowances, deductions or reliefs to which that person is entitled, he or she has no taxable income for that year, any repayment to be made shall be a repayment of the whole amount of the tax paid by him or her, whether by deduction or otherwise, in respect of his or her income for that year.

(3) In relation to repayments of tax, the amount of tax to be repaid under this section to any person for any year shall not exceed a sum equal to the difference between the amount of tax paid by that person, whether by deduction or otherwise, in respect of his or her income for that year and the amount of tax which would be payable by him or her for that year if his or her total income had been charged to tax in accordance with the Income Tax Acts.

Cross-references

Age exemption, this section applied by s 188(6)(*a*).

Leased farm land exemption: s 664(6)(*a*).

Maintenance in the case of separated spouses: s 1025(5)(*a*).

Special provisions relating to year of marriage: s 1020(6)(*a*).

Definitions

person: IA 1937 s 11(*c*); standard rate: s 3(1); taxable income: ss 3(1), 458; total income: s 3(1); year of assessment: s 3(1).

Former enactments

ITA 1967 s 497; FA 1976 s 7; FA 1996 s 132(2) and Sch 5 para 1(23).

461 Basic personal tax credit

[In relation to any year of assessment, an individual shall be entitled to a tax credit (to be known as the **"basic personal tax credit"**) of—

(*a*) [€3,160],[1] in a case in which the claimant is a married person who—

(i) is assessed to tax for the year of assessment in accordance with section 1017, or

(ii) proves that his or her spouse is not living with him or her but is wholly or mainly maintained by him or her for the year of assessment and that the claimant is not entitled, in computing his or her income for tax purposes for that year, to make any deduction in respect of the sums paid by him or her for the maintenance of his or her spouse,

(*b*) [€3,160],[1] in a case in which the claimant in the year of assessment is a widowed person, other than a person to whom paragraph (*a*) applies, whose spouse has died in the year of assessment, and

(*c*) [€1,580],[2] in the case of any other claimant.][3]

Amendments

1 Substituted by FA 2005 s 3(1) and Sch 1 para (*a*) for 2005 and subsequent years of assessment; previously "€3,040".

2 Substituted by FA 2005 s 3(1) and Sch 1 para (*a*) for 2005 and subsequent years of assessment; previously "€1,520".

3 Section 461 substituted by FA 2001 s 2(3) and Sch 1 para 1(*f*) for short tax "year" 2001 and later tax years.

Cross-references

Additional tax credit for certain widowed persons, paras (*a*), (*b*) and (*c*): s 461A.

Age exemption, para (*a*): s 188(2)(*a*), (3).

Age tax credit: s 464.

Deductions allowed in ascertaining taxable income and provisions relating to reductions in tax: s 458(1), (2); s 459(1), (2).

Exemption from income tax and associated marginal relief, para (*a*): s 187(1)(*a*).

Interpretation of Income Tax Acts: s 3(1)("personal tax credit").

Method of apportioning reliefs and charging tax in cases of separate assessment: s 1024(2)(*a*)(ii).

One parent family tax credit, paras (*a*) and (*b*): s 462(1)(*b*).

Rate of tax at which repayments are to be made: s 460.

Case law

Mere difference in treatment of different categories of person was not in itself unconstitutional: *Mac Mathúna v Ireland and the Attorney General* (Supreme Court, 14 July 1994) (a social welfare case).

Definitions

year of assessment: s 3(1).

Former enactments

ITA 1967 s 138; FA 1980 s 3; FA 1982 s 2(3) and Sch 1 para 1(*a*)(i); FA 1988 s 3(3) and Sch 1 para (*a*); FA 1996 s 3 and Sch 1 para 1(*a*).

Corresponding UK tax provision

Income and Corporation Taxes Act 1988 ss 257 and 257A.

461A Additional tax credit for certain widowed persons

[A widowed person, other than a person to whom paragraph (*a*) or (*b*) of section 461, or to whom section 462, applies, shall, in addition to the basic personal tax credit referred to in section 461(*c*), be entitled to a tax credit (to be known as the **"widowed person tax credit"**) of [€400].[1]][2]

Amendments

1 Substituted by FA 2005 s 3(1) and Sch 1 para (*b*) for 2005 and subsequent years of assessment; previously "€300".

2 Section 461A substituted by FA 2001 s 2(3) and Sch 1 para 1(*g*) for short tax "year" 2001 and later tax years.

Cross-references

Application for separate assessment, relief under this section is not a "personal relief": s 1023(1).

Deductions allowed in ascertaining taxable income and provisions relating to reductions in tax: s 458(1), (2); s 459(1), (2).

Interpretation of Income Tax Acts: s 3(1)("personal tax credit").

Rate of tax at which repayments are to be made: s 460.

462 One-parent family tax credit

[(1) (*a*) In this section, **"qualifying child"**, in relation to any claimant and year of assessment, means—

(i) a child—

(I) born in the year of assessment,

(II) who, at the commencement of the year of assessment, is under the age of 18 years, or

(III) who, if over the age of 18 years at the commencement of the year of assessment—

(A) is receiving full-time instruction at any university, college, school or other educational establishment, or

(B) is permanently incapacitated by reason of mental or physical infirmity from maintaining himself or herself and had become so permanently incapacitated before he or she had attained the age of 21 years or had become so permanently incapacitated after attaining the age of 21 years but while he or she had been in receipt of such full-time instruction,

and

(ii) a child who is a child of the claimant or, not being such a child, is in the custody of the claimant and is maintained by the claimant at the claimant's own expense for the whole or part of the year of assessment.

(*b*) This section shall apply to an individual who is not entitled to a basic personal tax credit mentioned in paragraph (*a*) or paragraph (*b*) of section 461.

(2) Subject to subsection (3), where a claimant, being an individual to whom this section applies, proves for a year of assessment that a qualifying child is resident with him or her for the whole or part of the year, the claimant shall be entitled to a tax credit (to be known as the **"one-parent family tax credit"**) of [€1,580],[1] but this section shall not apply for any year of assessment in the case of a husband or a wife where the wife is living with her husband, or in the case of a man and woman living together as man and wife.

(3) A claimant shall be entitled to only one tax credit under subsection (2) for any year of assessment irrespective of the number of qualifying children resident with the claimant in that year.

(4) (*a*) The references in subsection (1)(*a*) to a child receiving full-time instruction at an educational establishment shall include references to a child undergoing training by any person (in this subsection referred to as **"the employer"**) for any trade or profession in such circumstances that the child is required to devote the whole of his or her time to the training for a period of not less than 2 years.

(*b*) For the purpose of a claim in respect of a child undergoing training, the inspector may require the employer to furnish particulars with respect to the training of the child in such form as may be prescribed by the Revenue Commissioners.

(5) Where any question arises as to whether any person is entitled to a tax credit under this section in respect of a child over the age of 18 years as being a child who is receiving full-time instruction referred to in this section, the Revenue Commissioners may consult the Minister for Education and Science.][2]

Amendments

1 Substituted by FA 2005 s 3(1) and Sch 1 para (*c*) for 2005 and subsequent years of assessment; previously "€1,520"

2 Section 462 substituted by FA 2001 s 2(3) and Sch 1 para 1(*h*) for short tax "year" 2001 and later tax years.

Cross-references

Additional tax credit for certain widowed persons: s 461A.
Age exemption and low income exemption, qualifying child: s 187(2)(*b*).
Application for separate assessment, relief under this section is not a "personal relief": s 1023(1).
Deductions allowed in ascertaining taxable income and provisions relating to reductions in tax: s 458(1), (2); s 459(1), (2).
Interpretation of Income Tax Acts: s 3(1)("personal tax credit").
Rate of charge: s 15(2)(*b*).
Rate of tax at which repayments are to be made: s 460.
Reduction in age of majority from 21 to 18 will not affect entitlements: s 7(2).
Relief for the long term unemployed: s 472A(1)(*a*)("qualifying child").
Widowed parent tax credit: s 463(1)("qualifying child").

Case law

A challenge to the constitutionality of this provision by married parents with dependent children was defeated: *Mhicmhathúna v Ireland* [1995] ILRM 69.

Revenue information

Information leaflet IT9 — One-Parent Family Tax Credit.

Definitions

inspector: ss 2(1), 5(1), 852; profession: s 2(1); trade: s 3(1); year: IA 1937 Sch; year of assessment: s 3(1).

Former enactments

ITA 1967 s 138A(1)–(6); FA 1985 s 4; FA 1996 s 3 and Sch 1 para 1(*b*).

462A Additional allowance for widowed parents and other single parents

Amendments

1 Section 462A deleted by FA 2000 s 6(*b*) for 2000–2001 and later tax years.

463 Widowed parent tax credit

[(1) In this section—

"claimant" means an individual whose spouse dies in a year of assessment;

"qualifying child", in relation to a claimant and a year of assessment, has the same meaning as in section 462, and the question of whether a child is a qualifying child shall be determined on the same basis as it would be for the purposes of section 462, and subsections (3), (4) and (5) of that section shall apply accordingly.

(2) Where a claimant proves, in relation to any of the 5 years of assessment immediately following the year of assessment in which the claimant's spouse dies, that—

(*a*) he or she has not remarried before the commencement of the year, and

(*b*) a qualifying child is resident with him or her for the whole or part of the year,

the claimant shall, in respect of each of the years in relation to which the claimant so proves, be entitled to a tax credit (to be known as **"the widowed parent tax credit"**) as follows—

(i) for the first of those 5 years, [€2,800],[1]

(ii) for the second of those 5 years, [€2,300],[2]

(iii) for the third of those 5 years, [€1,800],[3]

(iv) for the fourth of those 5 years, [€1,300],[4] and

(v) for the fifth of those 5 years, [€800],[5]

but this section shall not apply for any year of assessment in the case of a man and woman living together as man and wife.][6]

Amendments

1 Substituted by FA 2005 s 3(1) and Sch 1 para (*d*) for 2005 and subsequent years of assessment; previously "€2,600".

2 Substituted by FA 2005 s 3(1) and Sch 1 para (*d*) for 2005 and subsequent years of assessment; previously "€2,100".

3 Substituted by FA 2005 s 3(1) and Sch 1 para (*d*) for 2005 and subsequent years of assessment; previously "€1,600".

4 Substituted by FA 2005 s 3(1) and Sch 1 para (*d*) for 2005 and subsequent years of assessment; previously "€1,100".

5 Substituted by FA 2005 s 3(1) and Sch 1 para (*d*) for 2005 and subsequent years of assessment; previously "€600".

6 Section 463 substituted by FA 2001 s 2(3) and Sch 1 para 1(*i*) for short tax "year" 2001 and later tax years.

Cross-references

Application for separate assessment, relief under this section is not a "personal relief": s 1023(1).

Deductions allowed in ascertaining taxable income and provisions relating to reductions in tax: s 458(2); s 459(1), (2).

Interpretation of Income Tax Acts: s 3(1)("personal tax credit").

Rate of tax at which repayments are to be made: s 460.

Definitions

year of assessment: s 2(1).

Former enactments

FA 1991 s 4(1)–(2); FA 1996 s 132(1) and Sch 5 Pt I para 17.

Corresponding UK tax provision

Income and Corporation Taxes Act 1988 s 262 [repealed].

464 Age tax credit

[Where for any year of assessment an individual is entitled to a basic personal tax credit under section 461 and proves that at any time during that year of assessment—

(*a*) the individual, or

(*b*) in the case of a married person whose spouse is living with him or her and who is assessed to tax in accordance with section 1017, either the individual or the individual's spouse,

was of the age of 65 years or over, the individual shall, in addition to the tax credit to which the individual is entitled under section 461 for that year of assessment, be entitled to an additional tax credit (to be known as the **"age tax credit"**) of—

(i) in a case where the individual is a married person whose spouse is living with him or her and the individual is assessed to tax in accordance with section 1017, [€410],[1] and

(ii) in any other case, [€205].[2]][3]

Amendments

1 Substituted by FA 2002 s 3 and Sch 1 para 1(*e*) for 2002 and later tax years; previously "€408" (short tax "year" 2001 "£238").

2 Substituted by FA 2002 s 3 and Sch 1 para 1(*e*) for 2002 and later tax years; previously "€204" (short tax "year" 2001 "£119").

3 Section 464 substituted by FA 2001 s 2(3) and Sch 1 para 1(*j*) for short tax "year" 2001 and later tax years.

Cross-references

Deductions allowed in ascertaining taxable income and provisions relating to reductions in tax: s 458(1), (2); s 459(1), (2).

Interpretation of Income Tax Acts: s 3(1)("personal tax credit").

Method of apportioning reliefs and charging tax in cases of separate assessment: s 1024(2)(*a*)(ii).

Rate of tax at which repayments are to be made: s 460.

Revenue information

Information leaflet IT45 — Allowances for Over 65's

Definitions

year of assessment: s 2(1).

Former enactments

FA 1974 s 8(1); FA 1980 s 19 and Sch 1 Pt III para 4; FA 1986 s 3 and Sch 1; FA 1997 s 3(1) and (3) and Sch 1 para 2.

Corresponding UK tax provision

Income and Corporation Taxes Act 1988 s 257.

465 Incapacitated child tax credit

[(1) Where a claimant proves that he or she has living at any time during a year of assessment any child who—

(*a*) is under the age of 18 years and is permanently incapacitated by reason of mental or physical infirmity, or (*b*) if over the age of 18 years at the commencement of the year, is permanently incapacitated by reason of mental or physical infirmity from maintaining himself or herself and had become so permanently incapacitated before he or she had attained the age of 21 years or had become so permanently incapacitated after attaining the age of 21 years but while he or she had been in receipt of full-time instruction at any university, college, school or other educational establishment,

the claimant shall, subject to this section, be entitled in respect of each such child to a tax credit (to be known as the **"incapacitated child tax credit"**) of [€1,000].[1]

(2) (*a*) A child under the age of 18 years shall be regarded as permanently incapacitated by reason of mental or physical infirmity only if the infirmity is such that there would be a reasonable expectation that if the child were over the age of 18 years the child would be incapacitated from maintaining himself or herself.

(*b*) A tax credit under this section shall be in substitution for and not in addition to any tax credit to which the individual might be entitled in respect of the same child under section 466.

(3) Where the claimant proves for the year of assessment—

(*a*) that the claimant has the custody of and maintains at his or her own expense any child who, but for the fact that that child is not a child of the claimant, would be a child referred to in subsection (1), and

(*b*) that neither the claimant nor any other individual is entitled to a tax credit in respect of the same child under subsection (1) or under any other provision of this Part (other than section 466A), or, if any other individual is entitled to such a tax credit, that such other individual has relinquished his or her claim to that tax credit,

the claimant shall be entitled to the same tax credit in respect of the child as if the child were a child of the claimant.

(4) (*a*) The reference in subsection (1) to a child receiving full-time instruction at an educational establishment shall include a reference to a child undergoing training by any person (in this subsection referred to as **"the employer"**) for any trade or profession in such circumstances that the child is required to devote the whole of his or her time to the training for a period of not less than 2 years.

(*b*) For the purpose of a claim in respect of a child undergoing training, the inspector may require the employer to furnish particulars with respect to the training of the child in such form as may be prescribed by the Revenue Commissioners.

(5) Where any question arises as to whether any person is entitled to a tax credit under this section in respect of a child over the age of 21 years as being a child who had become permanently incapacitated by reason of mental or physical infirmity from maintaining himself or herself after attaining that age but while in receipt of full-time instruction referred to in this section, the Revenue Commissioners may consult the Minister for Education and Science.

(6) Where for any year of assessment 2 or more individuals are or would but for this subsection be entitled under this section to relief in respect of the same child, the following provisions shall apply:

(*a*) only one tax credit under this section shall be allowed in respect of the child;

(*b*) where the child is maintained by one individual only, that individual only shall be entitled to claim such tax credit;

(*c*) where the child is maintained jointly by two or more individuals, each of those individuals shall be entitled to claim such part of such tax credit as is proportionate to the amount expended by him or her on the maintenance of the child;

(*d*) in ascertaining for the purposes of this subsection whether an individual maintains a child and, if so, to what extent, any payment made by the individual for or towards the maintenance of the child which the individual is entitled to deduct in computing his or her total income for the purposes of the Income Tax Acts shall be deemed not to be a payment for or towards the maintenance of the child.][1]

Amendments

1 Substituted by FA 2005 s 3(1) and Sch 1 para (*e*) for 2005 and subsequent years of assessment; previously "€500".

2 Section 465 substituted by FA 2001 s 2(3) and Sch 1 para 1(*k*) for short tax "year" 2001 and later tax years.

Cross-references

Deductions allowed in ascertaining taxable income and provisions relating to reductions in tax: s 458(1), (2); s 459(1), (2).

Employed person taking care of incapacitated individual: s 467(4).

Interpretation of Income Tax Acts: s 3(1)("personal tax credit").

Maintenance in the case of separated spouses: s 1025(1), (4)(*d*).

Method of apportioning reliefs and charging tax in cases of separate assessment (this section other than subs (3)): s 1024(2)(*a*)(ii).

Method of apportioning reliefs and charging tax in cases of separate assessment, subs (3): s 1024(2)(*a*)(iii).

Rate of tax at which repayments are to be made: s 460.

Reduction in age of majority from 21 to 18 will not affect entitlements: s 7(2).

Case law

Restriction of allowance for dependent children to incapacitated children held not unconstitutional: *Mhicmhathúna v Ireland* [1995] ILRM 69.

Revenue precedents

Issue: Is a child suffering from Dyslexia regarded as permanently incapacitated from maintaining him/herself? *Decision:* Generally, it is taken that there is a reasonable expectation that, if the child was over the age of 16 years, it would not prevent him/her from maintaining him/herself.

Revenue information

Information leaflet IT18 — Incapacitated Child Tax Credit.

Definitions

Income Tax Acts: s 1(2); inspector: ss 2(1), 5(1), 852; person: IA 1937 s 11(*c*); profession: s 2(1); trade: s 3(1); year: IA 1937 Sch; year of assessment: s 2(1).

Former enactments

ITA 1967 s 141(1)–(6); FA 1986 s 4; FA 1991 s 126; FA 1996 s 3 and Sch 1 para 1(*c*).

466 Dependent relative tax credit

[(1) In this section **"specified amount"** means an amount which does not exceed by more than [€280][1] the aggregate of the payments to which an individual is entitled in a year of assessment in respect of an old age (contributory) pension at the maximum rate under the Social Welfare (Consolidation) Act, 1993, if throughout that year of assessment such individual were entitled to such a pension and—

(*a*) has no adult dependant or qualified children (within the meaning, in each case, of that Act),

(*b*) is over the age of 80 years (or such other age as may be specified in that Act for the time being in place of 80 years),

(*c*) is living alone, and

(*d*) is ordinarily resident on an island.

(2) Where for any year of assessment a claimant proves that he or she maintains at his or her own expense any person, being—

(*a*) a relative of the claimant, or of the claimant's spouse, incapacitated by old age or infirmity from maintaining himself or herself,

(*b*) the widowed father or widowed mother of the claimant or of the claimant's spouse, whether incapacitated or not, or

(*c*) a son or daughter of the claimant who resides with the claimant and on whose services the claimant, by reason of old age or infirmity, is compelled to depend,

and being an individual whose total income from all sources for that year of assessment does not exceed a sum equal to the specified amount, the claimant shall be entitled in respect of each individual whom the claimant so maintains to a tax credit (to be known as the **"dependent relative tax credit"**) of [€60][2] for the year of assessment.

(3) Where 2 or more individuals jointly maintain any individual referred to in paragraphs (*a*) to (*c*) of subsection (2), the tax credit to be granted under this section in respect of that individual shall be apportioned between them in proportion to the amount or value of their respective contributions towards the maintenance of that individual.][3]

Amendments

1 Substituted by FA 2001 s 2(3) and Sch 1 para 2(*h*)(i) for 2002 and later tax years; previously "£163".

2 Substituted by FA 2002 s 3 and Sch 1 para 1(*g*) for 2002 and later tax years; previously "€56" (short tax "year" 2001 "£33").

3 Section 466 substituted by FA 2001 s 2(3) and Sch 1 para 1(*l*) for short tax "year" 2001 and later tax years.

Cross-references

Capital acquisitions tax, exemption of certain receipts: CATCA 2003 s 82(2)(*b*).

Deductions allowed in ascertaining taxable income and provisions relating to reductions in tax: s 458(1), (2); s 459(1), (2).

Employed person taking care of incapacitated individual: s 467(4).

Incapacitated child credit: s 465(2)(*b*).

Interpretation of Income Tax Acts: s 3(1)("personal tax credit").

Method of apportioning reliefs and charging tax in cases of separate assessment: s 1024(2)(*a*)(iii).

Rate of tax at which repayments are to be made: s 460.

Relief for interest paid on certain home loans, subs (2)(*a*) and (*b*): s 244(1)(*a*) ("dependent relative").

Revenue precedents

Issue: Whether or not a person is incapacitated by reason of infirmity from maintaining himself/herself for purposes of section 466.

Decision: Any claim that is supported by a certificate signed by a medical practitioner to the effect that the relative was incapacitated by infirmity from maintaining himself/herself during the tax year to which the claim relates will be allowed.

Revenue information

Information leaflet IT46 — Dependent Relative Tax Credit.

Definitions

person: IA 1937 s 11(*c*); relative: s 3(1); total income: s 3(1); year of assessment: s 3(1).

Former enactments

ITA 1967 s 142; FA 1977 s 1; FA 1979 s 1; FA 1982 s 2 and Sch 1 para 1; FA 1997 s 146(1) and Sch 9 Pt I para 1(10).

Corresponding UK tax provision

Income and Corporation Taxes Act 1988 s 263 [repealed].

466A Home carer tax credit

[(1) In this section—

"dependent person", in relation to a qualifying claimant, means a person (other than the spouse of the qualifying claimant) who, subject to subsection (3), resides with that qualifying claimant and who is—

(*a*) a child in respect of whom either the qualifying claimant or his or her spouse is, at any time in a year of assessment, in receipt of child benefit under Part IV of the Social Welfare (Consolidation) Act, 1993, or

(*b*) an individual who, at any time during a year of assessment, is of the age of 65 years or over, or

(*c*) an individual who is permanently incapacitated by reason of mental or physical infirmity;

"qualifying claimant", in relation to a year of assessment, means an individual—

(*a*) who is assessed to tax for that year in accordance with section 1017, and

(*b*) who, or whose spouse (in this section referred to as the **"carer spouse"**) is engaged during that year in caring for one or more dependent persons;

"relative", in relation to a qualifying claimant, includes a relation by marriage and a person in respect of whom the qualifying claimant is or was the legal guardian.

(2) Where for any year of assessment an individual proves that he or she is a qualifying claimant he or she shall be entitled to a tax credit (to be known as the **"home carer tax credit"**) of [€770].[1]

(3) For the purposes of this section—

(*a*) a dependent person in relation to a qualifying claimant who is a relative of that claimant or the claimant's spouse shall be regarded as residing with the qualifying claimant if—

(i) the relative lives in close proximity to the qualifying claimant, and

(ii) a direct system of communication exists between the qualifying claimant's residence and the residence of the relative,

and

(*b*) a qualifying claimant and a relative shall be regarded as living in close proximity if they reside—

(i) next door in adjacent residences, or

(ii) on the same property, or

(iii) within 2 kilometres of each other.

(4) A qualifying claimant shall be entitled to only one tax credit under subsection (2) for any year of assessment irrespective of the number of dependent persons resident with the qualifying claimant in that year.

(5) A tax credit under this section in respect of a dependent person shall be granted to one and only one qualifying claimant being the person with whom that dependent person normally resides or, where subsection (3) applies, the person who, or whose spouse, normally cares for the dependent person.

(6) (*a*) Where in any year of assessment the carer spouse is entitled in his or her own right to [total income][2] exceeding [€5,080][3] in that year, the tax credit shall be reduced by one-half of the amount of that excess.

(*b*) For the purposes of paragraph (*a*), no account shall be taken of—

(i) any Carer's Benefit payable under Chapter 11A (inserted by the Social Welfare Act, 2000) of Part II of the Social Welfare (Consolidation) Act, 1993, or

(ii) any Carer's Allowance payable under Chapter 10 of Part III of that Act.

(7) (*a*) Notwithstanding subsection (6) but subject to the other provisions of this section including this subsection, a tax credit may be granted for a year of assessment where the claimant was entitled to a tax credit under this section for the immediately preceding year of assessment.

(*b*) Where a tax credit is to be granted for a year of assessment by virtue of paragraph (*a*), it shall not exceed the amount of the tax credit granted in the immediately preceding year of assessment.

(*c*) A tax credit shall not be granted for a year of assessment by virtue of paragraph (*a*) if it was so granted for the immediately preceding year of assessment.

(8) Where for any year of assessment a tax credit is granted to an individual under this section, the individual shall not also be entitled to the benefit of the provision contained in section 15 (3) but the individual may elect by notice in writing to the inspector to have the benefit under the said section granted instead of the tax credit granted under this section.][4]

Amendments

1 Substituted by FA 2002 s 3 and Sch 1 para 1(*h*)(i) for 2002 and later tax years; previously "€762" (short tax "year" 2001 "£444").

2 Substituted by FA 2002 s 3 and Sch 1 para 1(*h*)(ii) for 2002 and later tax years; previously "an income".

3 Substituted by FA 2001 s 2(3) and Sch 1 para 2(*i*)(ii) for 2002 and later tax years; previously "£2,960".

4 Section 466A substituted by FA 2001 s 2(3) and Sch 1 para 1(*m*) for short tax "year" 2001 and later tax years.

Cross-references

Deductions allowed in ascertaining taxable income and provisions relating to reductions in tax: ss 458(1), (2), 459(1), (2).

Incapacitated child tax credit: s 465(3)(*b*).

Interpretation of Income Tax Acts: s 3(1)("personal tax credit").

Rate of tax at which repayments are to be made: s 460.

Revenue information

Information leaflet IT66 Home Carer's Tax Credit.

Tax Briefing

TB51 Jan 2003 p 20 — Can employees working in Ireland on short term assignments claim the home carer tax credit in respect of a dependant child where the claimant is not in receipt of child benefit in the State? Yes, if the claimant is in receipt of a similar type payment in his/her home country. The other conditions as set out in TCA 1997 s 466A, eg child residing with qualifying claimant etc, must be met.

Definitions

inspector: ss 2(1), 852; total income: s 3(1); writing: IA 1937 Sch; year of assessment: s 2(1).

467 Employed person taking care of incapacitated individual

[(1) In this section **"relative"**, in relation to an individual, includes a relation by marriage and a person in respect of whom the individual is or was the legal guardian.

(2) Subject to this section, where an individual for a year of assessment proves—

(*a*) that throughout the year of assessment either he or she or a relative of the individual was totally incapacitated by physical or mental infirmity, and

(*b*) that for the year of assessment the individual, or in a case to which section 1017 applies, the individual's spouse, has employed a person (including a person whose services are provided by or through an agency) for the purpose of having care of the individual (being the individual or the individual's relative) who is so incapacitated,

the individual shall, in computing the amount of his or her taxable income, be entitled to a deduction from his or her total income of the lesser of—

(i) the amount ultimately borne by him or her or the individual's spouse in the year of assessment in employing the employed person, and

(ii) [€30,000][1] in respect of each such incapacitated individual.

(3) Where 2 or more individuals are entitled for a year of assessment to a deduction under this section in respect of the same incapacitated individual, the following provisions shall apply:

(*a*) the aggregate of the deductions to be granted to those individuals shall not exceed [€30,000][1], and

(*b*) the relief to be granted under this section in relation to the incapacitated individual shall be apportioned between them in proportion to the amount ultimately borne by each of them in employing the employed person.

(4) Where for any year of assessment a deduction is allowed to an individual under this section, the individual shall not be [entitled to relief][2] in respect of the employed person (including a person whose services are provided by or through an agency) under section 465 or section 466.][3]

Amendments

1 Substituted by FA 2002 s 5 for 2002 and later tax years; previously "€12,700" (and for short tax "year" 2001 "£7,400").

2 Substituted by FA 2000 s 14 and Sch 14 para 4 with effect from 6 April 2000; previously "entitled to a deduction".

3 Section 467 substituted by FA 1999 s 9 for 1999–2000 and later tax years.

Cross-references

Deductions allowed in ascertaining taxable income: ss 458(1), (2), 459(1)–(2).
Method of apportioning reliefs and charging tax in cases of separate assessment, subs (3): s 1024(2)(*a*)(iv).
Rate of tax at which repayments are to be made: s 460.

Revenue information

Information leaflet IT47 — Employed Person Taking Care of Incapacitated Individual.

Definitions

person: IA 1937 s 11(*c*); taxable income: ss 3(1), 458; total income: s 3(1); year of assessment: ss 2(1), 5(1).

Former enactments

FA 1969 s 3(1), (2) and (4); FA 1980 s 19 and Sch 1 Pt III para 2; FA 1996 s 3 and Sch 1 para 2.

468 Blind person's tax credit

[(1) In this section, **"blind person"** means a person whose central visual acuity does not exceed 6/60 in the better eye with correcting lenses, or whose central visual acuity exceeds 6/60 in the better eye or in both eyes but is accompanied by a limitation in the fields of vision that is such that the widest diameter of the visual field subtends an angle no greater than 20 degrees.

(2) Where an individual proves for a year of assessment that—

(*a*) he or she was for the whole or any part of the year of assessment a blind person, or

(*b*) where he or she is assessed to tax in accordance with section 1017, either or both he or she and his or her spouse was for the whole or any part of the year of assessment a blind person,

the individual shall be entitled to a tax credit (to be known as the **"blind person's tax credit"**) of [€1,000],[1] or where the individual and his or her spouse are both blind, [€2,000].[2]][3]

Amendments

1 Substituted by FA 2005 s 3(1) and Sch 1 para (*f*) for 2005 and subsequent years of assessment; previously "€800".

2 Substituted by FA 2005 s 3(1) and Sch 1 para (*f*) for 2005 and subsequent years of assessment; previously "€1,600".

3 Section 468 substituted by FA 2001 s 2(3) and Sch 1 para 1(*n*) for short tax "year" 2001 and later tax years.

Cross-references

Deductions allowed in ascertaining taxable income and provisions relating to reductions in tax: s 458(1), (2); s 459(1), (2).
Intepretation of Income Tax Acts: s 3(1)("personal tax credit").
Method of apportioning reliefs and charging tax in cases of separate assessment: s 1024(2)(*a*)(ii).
Rate of tax at which repayments are to be made: s 460.

Revenue information

Information leaflet IT35 — Blind Persons Tax Credits and Reliefs.

Definitions

year of assessment: s 2(1).

Former enactments

FA 1971 s 11(1)–(2); FA 1985 s 3 and Sch 1; FA 1996 s 3 and Sch 1 para 3.

Corresponding UK tax provision

Income and Corporation Taxes Act 1988 s 265.

469 Relief for health expenses

(1) In this section—

[**"dependant"** in relation to an individual, means—

(*a*) a relative of the individual, and

(*b*) any other person being—

(i) an individual who, at any time during the year of assessment, is of the age of 65 years or over, or

(ii) an individual who is permanently incapacitated by reason of mental or physical infirmity,][1]

[**"educational psychologist"** means a person who is entered on a register maintained by the Minister for Education and Science for the purposes of this section in accordance with guidelines set down by that Minister with the consent of the Minister for Finance;][2]

"health care" means prevention, diagnosis, alleviation or treatment of an ailment, injury, infirmity, defect or disability, and includes care received by a woman in respect of a pregnancy ...[3], but does not include routine ophthalmic treatment or routine dental treatment;

"health expenses" means expenses in respect of the provision of health care, being expenses representing the cost of—

(*a*) the services of a practitioner,

(*b*) diagnostic procedures carried out on the advice of a practitioner,

(*c*) maintenance or treatment in a hospital,

(*d*) drugs or medicines supplied on the prescription of a practitioner,

(*e*) the supply, maintenance or repair of any medical, surgical, dental or nursing appliance used on the advice of a practitioner,

(*f*) physiotherapy or similar treatment prescribed by a practitioner,

(*g*) orthoptic or similar treatment prescribed by a practitioner, ...[4]

(*h*) transport by [ambulance, or][5]

[(*i*) as respects a dependant of the individual referred to in paragraphs (*a*) and (*b*)(ii) of the definition of "dependant" who for the year of assessment—

(*a*) is under the age of 18 years, or

(*b*) if over the age of 18 years, at the commencement of the year of assessment, is receiving full-time instruction at any university, college, school or other educational establishment,

either or both—

(i) educational psychological assessment carried out by an educational psychologist, and

(ii) speech and language therapy carried out by a speech and language therapist;][6]

"hospital" means—

(*a*) any institution which is provided and maintained by [the Health Service Executive][7] for the provision of services pursuant to the [Health Acts 1947 to 2004][8], (*b*) any institution in which services are provided on behalf of [the Health Service Executive][7] pursuant to the [Health Acts 1947 to 2004][8],

(*c*) any hospital, nursing home, maternity home or other institution approved of for the purposes of this section by the Minister for Finance after consultation with the Minister for Health and Children;

"practitioner" means any person who is—

(*a*) registered in the register established under section 26 of the Medical Practitioners Act, 1978,

(*b*) registered in the register established under section 26 of the Dentists Act, 1985, or

(*c*) in relation to health care provided outside the State, entitled under the laws of the country in which the care is provided to [practice][9] medicine or dentistry there;

"qualified person", in relation to an individual, means the individual personally or any dependant of the individual;

[**"relative"**, in relation to an individual, means—

(*a*) husband, wife, ancestor, lineal descendant, brother or sister,

(*b*) mother or father of the individual's spouse,

(*c*) brother or sister of the individual's spouse,

(*d*) spouse of the individual's son or daughter, and

(*e*) a child, not being a child of the individual, who for the year of assessment—

(i) is in the custody of the individual and is maintained by the individual at the individual's own expense for the whole or part of the year of assessment, and

(ii) (I) is under the age of 18 years, or

(II) if over the age of 18 years, at the commencement of the year of assessment, is receiving full-time instruction at any university, college, school or other educational establishment;][10]

"routine dental treatment" means the extraction, scaling and filling of teeth and the provision and repairing of artificial teeth or dentures;

...[11]

"routine ophthalmic treatment" means sight testing and advice as to the use of spectacles or contact lenses and the provision and repairing of spectacles or [contact lenses;][12]

[**"speech and language therapist"** means a person approved of for the purposes of this section by the Minister for Health and Children in accordance with guidelines set down by that Minister with the consent of the Minister for Finance.][13]

(2) (*a*) Subject to this section, where an individual for a year of assessment proves that in the year of assessment he or she defrayed health expenses incurred for the provision of health care for any one qualified person and the amount of which in the aggregate exceeds [€125][14], the individual shall be entitled, for the purpose of ascertaining the amount of the income on which he or she is to be

charged to income tax, to have a deduction of the amount of the excess made from his or her total income.

(*b*) Where an individual proves that in the year of assessment he or she defrayed health expenses incurred for the provision of health care for qualified persons and which amount in the aggregate to more than [€250][15], the individual shall be entitled, for the purpose of ascertaining the amount of the income on which he or she is to be charged to income tax, to have a deduction of the amount by which the aggregate of the health expenses so computed exceeds [€250][15] made from his or her total income, and such deduction shall be in substitution for and not in addition to a deduction under paragraph (*a*).

(3) For the purposes of this section—

(*a*) (i) any expenses defrayed by a married man in a year of assessment shall be deemed to have been defrayed by his wife if for the year of assessment she is to be treated under the Income Tax Acts as living with him and she is assessed to tax in accordance with section 1017, or

(ii) any expenses defrayed by a married woman in a year of assessment shall be deemed to have been defrayed by her husband if for the year of assessment she is to be treated under the Income Tax Acts as living with him and he is assessed to tax in accordance with section 1017,

(*b*) any expenses defrayed out of the estate of a deceased person by his or her executor or administrator shall be deemed to have been defrayed by the deceased person immediately before his or her death, and

(*c*) expenses shall be regarded as not having been defrayed in so far as any sum in respect of, or by reference to, the health care to which they relate has been, or is to be, received, directly or indirectly, by the individual or the individual's estate, or by any dependant of the individual or such dependant's estate, from any public or local authority or under any contract of insurance or by means of compensation or otherwise.

...[16]

(5) In making a claim for a deduction under this section, an individual who, after the end of the year of assessment for which the claim is made, has defrayed or is deemed to have defrayed any expenses relating to health care provided in that year may elect that all deductions to be allowed to him or her under this section for that year and for subsequent years of assessment shall be determined as if those expenses had been defrayed at the time when the health care to which they relate was provided.

(6) Notwithstanding sections 458(2) and 459(2)—

(*a*) any claim for a deduction under this section—

(i) shall be made in such form as the Revenue Commissioners may from time to time prescribe, and

(ii) shall be accompanied by such statements in writing as regards any class of expenses by reference to which the deduction is claimed, including statements by persons to whom payments were made, as may be indicated by the prescribed form as being required as regard expenses of that class, and (*b*) in all cases relief from tax consequent on the allowance of a deduction under this section shall be given by means of repayment.

Amendments

1 Definition of "dependant" substituted by FA 2002 s 9(*a*)(i) for 2002 and later tax years.

2 Definition of "educational psychologist" inserted by FA 2001 s 8(*b*) for short tax "year" 2001 and later tax years.

3 Deleted by FA 2001 s 8(*c*) for short tax "year" 2001 and later tax years; previously "other than routine maternity care".

4 Deleted by FA 2002 s 9(*a*)(ii)(I) for 2002 and later tax years; previously "or".

5 Substituted by FA 2002 s 9(*a*)(ii)(II) for 2002 and later tax years; previously "ambulance".

6 Subs (1) definition of "health expenses" para (*i*) substituted by FA 2003 s 163 and Sch 6 para 1(*d*) with effect from 28 March 2003.

7 Substituted by FA 2005 s 147 and Sch 6 para 1(*h*)(i)(I) with effect from 25 March 2005; previously "a health board".

8 Substituted by FA 2005 s 147 and Sch 6 para 1(*h*)(i)(II) with effect from 25 March 2005; previously "Health Acts, 1947 to 1996".

9 Substituted by FA 2005 s 147 and Sch 6 para 1(*h*)(ii) with effect from 25 March 2005; previously "practise".

10 Definition of "relative" inserted by FA 2002 s 9(*a*)(iv) for 2002 and later tax years.

11 Definition of "routine maternity care" deleted by FA 2001 s 8(*e*) for short tax "year" 2001 and later tax years.

12 Substituted by FA 2002 s 9(*a*)(iii) for 2002 and later tax years: previously "contact lenses.".

13 Definition of "speech and language therapist" inserted by FA 2001 s 8(*f*) for short tax "year" 2001 and later tax years.

14 Substituted by FA 2001 s 24(1), (2)(*a*) and Sch 5 Pt 1 for 2002 and later tax years; previously "£100" (and for short tax "year" 2001 £74).

15 Substituted by FA 2001 s 240(1), (2)(*a*) and Sch 5 Pt 1 for 2002 and later tax years; previously "£200" (and for short tax "year" 2001 £148).

16 Subs (4) deleted by FA 2002 s 9(*b*) for 2002 and later tax years.

Cross-references

Deductions allowed in ascertaining taxable income: s 458(2); s 459(1), (2).
Method of apportioning reliefs and charging tax in cases of separate assessment: s 1024(2)(*a*)(v).
Professional services withholding tax, meaning of "practitioner" applied: s 520(1).
Rate of tax at which repayments are to be made: s 460.
Relief for insurance against expenses of illness, meaning of "health expenses" and "routine dental treatment" applied: s 470(1)("relevant contract").
An updated list of approved hospitals and nursing homes for the purposes of TCA 1997 s 469 is available on Revenue's website (www.revenue.ie) under Publications/Lists. A hard copy of the list can be ordered from Revenue Forms and Leaflets Service at 01–8780100.

Revenue precedents

Issue: Is tax relief allowed on medical expenses incurred prior to the 2001 tax year in relation to caesarian sections?
Decision: Yes. Tax relief is available on expenses not reimbursed by private medical insurance schemes.

Revenue information

Information leaflet IT6 — Medical Expenses Relief.
An information note on tax relief for nursing home care is available on Revenue's website — www.revenue.ie — under Whats New/Archive/November 2004.

Tax Briefing

TB17 No 1 of 1995 par1.2 p 5 Health Expenses — Dependent Relative.
TB27 Aug 1997 p 4 Health Expenses — Kidney Patients and Children with Cancer.
TB33 Sept 1998 p 7 Health Expenses — Guidelines & Procedures on Claims.
TB37 Oct 1999 p 13 — dental implants are not regarded as "routine dental treatment" (ie the provision of artificial teeth) and therefore qualify for relief.
TB41 Sept 2000 p 30 — Health Expenses — Kidney Patients — Update on Reliefs available.

TB43 Apr 2001 p 15 — Health Expenses Relief — Finance Act 2001 Changes.

TB50 Oct 2002 p 15 — Revenue treat expenditure on the removal of impacted wisdom teeth by a dentist in a dentist's surgery as not constituting "routine dental treatment". Consequently, tax relief will be given in respect of such expenditure.

TB55 April 2004 p 12 — Health Expenses: Kidney Patients, Child Oncology Patients and Children with Permanent Disabilities.

Definitions

Income Tax Acts: s 1(2); local authority: s 2(1); relative: s 3(1); total income: s 3(1); person: IA 1937 s 11(*c*); writing: IA 1937 Sch; year of assessment: s 2(1).

Former enactments

ITA 1967 s 195B(3) and (6); FA 1967 s 12(1), (2)(*a*) and (*c*), (3), (4)–(5)(*a*) and (*b*); FA 1969 s 7; FA 1972 s 9; FA 1980 s 19 and Sch 1 Pt III para 2; FA 1986 s 5; FA 1993 s 10(1); FA 1994 s 8; FA 1997 s 146(1) and Sch 9 Pt I para 2.

470 Relief for insurance against expenses of illness

(1) In this section—

"appropriate percentage", in relation to a year of assessment, means a percentage equal to the standard rate of tax for that year;

[**"authorised insurer"** means—

(*a*) any undertaking entered in the Register of Health Benefits Undertakings, lawfully carrying on such business of medical insurance referred to in paragraph (*a*) of the definition of **"relevant contract"** but, in relation to an individual, also means any undertaking authorised pursuant to Council Directive No 73/239/EEC of 24 July 1973 (OJ No L228, 16.8.1973, p 3), Council Directive No 88/357/EEC of 22 June 1988 (OJ No L172, 4.7.1988, p 1), and Council Directive No 92/49/EEC of 18 June 1992 (OJ No L228, 11.8.1992, p 1), where such a contract was effected with the individual when the individual was not resident in the State but was resident in another Member State of the European Communities, or

(*b*) (i) any undertaking standing authorised under—

(I) the European Communities (Non-Life Insurance) Framework Regulations 1994 (SI No 359 of 1994),

(II) the European Communities (Non-Life Insurance) Regulations 1976 (SI No 115 of 1976), or

(III) the European Communities (Non-Life Insurance) (Amendment) (No 2) Regulations 1991 (SI No 142 of 1991),

or

(ii) any undertaking authorised by the authority charged by law with the duty of supervising the activities of insurance undertakings in a Member State of the European Communities other than the State in accordance with Article 6 of Council Directive No 73/239/EEC of 24 July 1973 as inserted by Article 4 of Council Directive No 92/49/EEC of 18 June 1992,

lawfully carrying on such business of dental insurance referred to in paragraph (*b*) of the definition of **"relevant contract"**;][1]

[**"relevant contract"** means a contract of insurance which, in relation to an individual, the spouse of the individual, or the children or other dependants of the individual or of the spouse of the individual, provides specifically, whether in conjuction with other benefits or not, for the reimbursement or discharge, in whole or in part, of—

(*a*) actual health expenses (within the meaning of section 469), being a contract of medical insurance, or

(*b*) dental expenses other than expenses in respect of routine dental treatment (within the meaning of section 469), being a contract of dental insurance;][2]

[**"relievable amount"**, in relation to a payment to an authorised insurer under a relevant contract, means—

(*a*) where the payment covers no benefits other than such reimbursement or discharge as is referred to in the definition of **"relevant contract"**, an amount equal to the full amount of the payment, or

(*b*) where the payment covers benefits other than such reimbursement or discharge as is referred to in that definition, an amount equal to so much of the payment as is referable to such reimbursement or discharge.][3]

[(2) Subject to subsection (3), where for a year of assessment—

(*a*) an individual, or

(*b*) if the individual is a married person assessed to tax in accordance with section 1017, the individual's spouse,

has made a payment to an authorised insurer under a relevant contract, then, the income tax to be charged on the individual for the year of assessment, other than in accordance with section 16(2), shall be reduced by an amount which is the lesser of—

(i) an amount equal to the appropriate percentage of the relievable amount in relation to the payment, and

(ii) the amount which reduces that income tax to nil.

(3) (*a*) Where, on or after 6 April 2001, an individual makes a payment to an authorised insurer in respect of a premium due on or after that date under a relevant contract for which relief is due under subsection (2), the individual shall be entitled to deduct and retain out of it an amount equal to the appropriate percentage, for the year of assessment in which the payment is due, of the relievable amount in relation to the payment.

(*b*) An authorised insurer to which a payment referred to in paragraph (*a*) is made—

(i) shall accept the amount paid after deduction in discharge of the individual's liability to the same extent as if the deduction had not been made, and

(ii) may, on making a claim in accordance with regulations, recover from the Revenue Commissioners an amount equal to the amount deducted.][4]

(4) Where relief is given under this section, no relief or deduction under any other provision of the Income Tax Acts shall be given or allowed in respect of the payment or part of a payment, as the case may be.

[(5) (*a*) The Revenue Commissioners shall make regulations providing generally as to administration of this section and those regulations may, in particular and without prejudice to the generality of the foregoing, include provision—

(i) that a claim under subsection (3)(*b*)(ii) by an authorised insurer, which has registered with the Revenue Commissioners for the purposes of making such a claim, shall—

(I) be made in such form and manner,

(II) be made at such time, and

(III) be accompanied by such documents,

as provided for in the regulations;

(ii) for the making of annual information returns by authorised insurers, in such form (including electronic form) and manner as may be prescribed, and containing specified details in relation to—

(I) each individual making payments to such insurers under relevant contracts in a year of assessment,

(II) the total amount of premiums paid under a relevant contract by that individual in the year of assessment, and

(III) the total amount deducted by that individual under subsection (3)(*a*);

and

(iii) for the furnishing of information to the Revenue Commissioners for the purposes of the regulations.

(*b*) Every regulation made under this section shall be laid before Dáil Éireann as soon as may be after it is made and, if a resolution annulling the regulation is passed by Dáil Éireann within the next 21 days on which Dáil Éireann has sat after the regulation is laid before it, the regulation shall be annulled accordingly, but without prejudice to the validity of anything previously done thereunder.

(6) (*a*) Where any amount is paid to an authorised insurer by the Revenue Commissioners as an amount recoverable by virtue of subsection (3)(*b*)(ii) but is an amount to which that authorised insurer is not entitled, that amount shall be repaid by the authorised insurer.

(*b*) There shall be made such assessments, adjustments or set-offs as may be required for securing repayment of the amount referred to in paragraph (*a*) and the provisions of this Act relating to the assessment, collection and recovery of income tax shall, in so far as they are applicable and with necessary modification, apply in relation to the recovery of such amount.][5]

Note

In relation to the short tax "year" 2001 an individual is entitled to relief under TCA 1997 s 470 in respect of premiums paid to an authorised insurer under a relevant contract both in that "year" and in the preceding tax year (2000–2001), notwithstanding any other provision to the contrary.

Amendments

1 Definition of "authorised insurer" substituted by FA 2004 s 11(*a*) with effect from 25 March 2004.

2 Definition of "relevant contract" substituted by FA 2004 s 11(*b*) with effect from 25 March 2004.

3 Definition of "relievable amount" inserted by FA 2001 s 19(1)(*a*)(ii) for short tax "year" 2001 and later tax years.

4 Subss (2)–(3) substituted by FA 2001 s 19(1)(*b*) for short tax "year" 2001 and later tax years.

5 Subss (5)–(6) inserted by FA 2001 s 19(1)(*c*) for short tax "year" 2001 and later tax years.

Cross-references

Deductions allowed in ascertaining taxable income and provisions relating to reductions in tax: s 458(2); s 459(1), (2).

Method of apportioning reliefs and charging tax in cases of separate assessment: s 1024(2)(*a*)(vi).

Penalties: Sch 29, column 1.

Power of inspection, claims by authorised insurers, meaning of "authorised insurer" applied: s 904E(1); subs (3)(*b*)(ii): s 904E(2).

Professional services withholding tax, meanings of "authorised insurer" and "contract of insurance" applied: s 520(1).

Rate of tax at which repayments are to be made: s 460.

Taxation of certain perquisites, definitions of "appropriate percentage", "authorised insurer", "relevant contract" and "relieveable amount" applied: s 112A(1); subs (3)(*a*): s 112A(2)(i), (3)(*b*)(i).

Regulations

Medical Insurance (Relief at Source) Regulations 2001 (SI No 129 of 2001).

Tax Briefing

TB26 Apr 1997 p 12 — Medical insurance relief.

TB43 April 2001 pp 23–24 — Medical Insurance Relief — Tax Relief at Source.

TB Supplement May 2004 p 30 — List of authorised insurers.

Revenue information

A list of Authorised Insurers entered on the Register of Health Benefit Undertakings for the purpose of this section is available on Revenue's website — www.revenue.ie — under Publications/Lists.

Information Leaflet (CG11 — Medical Insurance — Tax Relief at Source).

Definitions

Income Tax Acts: s 1(2); Dáil Éireann: IA 1937 Sch; year of assessment: s 2(1).

Former enactments

ITA 1967 s 145(1)–(4); FA 1980 s 19 and Sch 1 Pt III para 1; FA 1996 s 7 and s 132(1) and Sch 5 Pt I para 1(4).

470A Relief for premiums under qualifying long-term care policies

[(1) In this section—

"activities of daily living" means one or more of the following, that is to say, washing, dressing, feeding, toileting, mobility and transferring;

"appropriate percentage", in relation to a year of assessment, means a percentage equal to the standard rate of tax for that year;

"long-term care services" means necessary diagnostic, preventive, therapeutic, curing, treating, mitigating and rehabilitative services and maintenance or personal care services carried out by or on the advice of a practitioner;

"maintenance or personal care services" means any care the primary purpose of which is the provision of needed assistance with any of the disabilities as a result of which an individual is a relevant individual (including protection from threats to health and safety due to severe cognitive impairment);

"mobility" means the ability to move indoors from room to room on level surfaces;

"policy" means a policy of insurance;

"PPS Number", in relation to an individual, means that individual's Personal Public Service Number within the meaning of section 223 of the Social Welfare (Consolidation) Act, 1993;

"practitioner" means any person who is registered in the register established under section 26 of the Medical Practitioners Act, 1978, or, in relation to long-term care services provided outside the State, is entitled under the laws of the territory in which such services are provided to practice medicine there;

"qualifying individual" in relation to an individual and a qualifying long-term care policy, means—

(*a*) the individual,

(*b*) the spouse or a child of the individual, or

(*c*) a relative of the individual or of the spouse of the individual;

"qualifying insurer" means, subject to subsection (2), the holder of—

(i) an authorisation issued by the Minister for Enterprise, Trade and Employment under the European Communities (Life Assurance) Regulations of 1984 (SI No. 57 of 1984) as amended, or

(ii) an authorisation granted by the authority charged by law with the duty of supervising the activities of insurance undertakings in a Member State of the European Communities, other than the State, in accordance with Article 6 of Directive No. 79/267/EEC (OJ No L 63 of 13 March, 1979, p 1), who is carrying on the business of life assurance in the State, or

(iii) an official authorisation to undertake insurance in Iceland, Liechtenstein and Norway pursuant to the EEA Agreement within the meaning of the European Communities (Amendment) Act, 1993, and who is carrying on the business of life assurance in the State;

"qualifying long-term care policy" means a policy which provides for the discharge or reimbursement of expenses of long-term care services for a relevant individual and which, in accordance with the provisions of this section, is approved of by the Revenue Commissioners for the purposes of this section;

"relative", in relation to an individual or the spouse of the individual, includes a relation by marriage and a person in respect of whom the individual is or was the legal guardian;

"relevant individual", in relation to a qualifying long-term care policy, means a qualifying individual in relation to that policy in respect of whom a practitioner has certified that the individual is—

(*a*) unable to perform (without substantial assistance from another individual) at least 2 of the activities of daily living for a period of at least 90 days due to a loss of functional capacity, or

(*b*) requires substantial supervision to protect such individual from threats to health and safety due to severe cognitive impairment;

"transferring" means the ability to move from a bed to an upright chair or a wheelchair and vice versa.

(2) (*a*) A person shall not be a qualifying insurer until such time as the person has been entered in a register maintained by the Revenue Commissioners for the purposes of this section and any regulations made thereunder.

(*b*) Where at any time a qualifying insurer—

(i) is not resident in the State, or

(ii) is not carrying on business in the State through a fixed place of business,

the qualifying insurer shall ensure that there is a person resident in the State and appointed by the qualifying insurer to be responsible for the discharge of all the duties and obligations imposed on the qualifying insurer by this section and any regulations made thereunder.

(*c*) Where a qualifying insurer appoints a person in accordance with paragraph (*b*), that insurer shall advise the Revenue Commissioners of the identity of that person and the fact of the person's appointment.

(3) (*a*) The Revenue Commissioners shall not approve a policy for the purposes of this section unless they are satisfied that—

(i) the only benefits provided under the policy are the discharge or reimbursement of expenses of long-term care services in respect of an individual who is a relevant individual in relation to the policy,

(ii) the policy is either not expressed to be terminable by the insurer under the terms of the policy, or is expressed to be so terminable only in special circumstances mentioned in the policy,

(iii) the policy secures that for the purposes of the policy the question of whether an individual is a relevant individual shall be determined by reference to at least 5 activities of daily living,

(iv) subject to paragraph (*b*), the policy does not provide for—

(I) a lump sum payment on termination,

(II) a cash surrender value, or

(III) any other money,

that can be paid or assigned to any person, borrowed, or pledged as collateral for a loan, and

(v) the policy is not connected with any other policy.

(*b*) A policy shall not fail to meet the requirements of paragraph (*a*)(iv) merely because it provides for the payment of periodic amounts of money without regard to the expenses incurred on the services provided during the period to which the payments relate.

(*c*) A policy is connected with another policy, whether held by the same person or another person, if—

(i) either policy was issued in respect of an assurance made with reference to the other, or with a view to enabling the other to be made on particular terms, or with a view to facilitating the making of the other on particular terms, and

(ii) the terms on which either policy was issued would have been different if the other policy had not been issued.

(4) (*a*) A long-term care policy shall be a qualifying long-term care policy within the meaning of this section if it conforms with a form which at the time it is issued is either—

(i) a standard form approved by the Revenue Commissioners as a standard form of qualifying long-term care policy, or

(ii) a form varying from a standard form so approved in no other respects than by making such alterations to that standard form as are, at the time the policy is issued, approved by the Revenue Commissioners as being compatible with a qualifying long-term care policy when made to that standard form and satisfying any conditions subject to which the alterations are so approved.

(*b*) In approving a policy, or a standard form of a policy, as a qualifying long-term care policy for the purposes of this section, the Revenue Commissioners may disregard any provision of the policy which appears to them insignificant.

(5) Where, for any year of assessment, an individual, who is resident in the State, makes a payment to a qualifying insurer in respect of a premium under a qualifying long-term care policy, the beneficiary of which is a qualifying individual in relation to the individual, the individual making the payment shall, subject to the condition specified in subsection (6), be entitled to relief under this section in accordance with subsection (8).

(6) The condition specified in this subsection is that, at the time the long-term care policy is entered into, the individual (in this subsection referred to as the **"declarer"**) furnishes to the qualifying insurer a declaration in writing which—

(*a*) is made and signed by the declarer,

(*b*) is made in such form as may be prescribed or authorised by the Revenue Commissioners,

(*c*) contains the declarer's full name, the address of his or her permanent residence and his or her PPS Number,

(*d*) declares that—

(i) at the time the declaration is made that he or she is resident in the State, and

(ii) the beneficiary under the policy is a qualifying individual in relation to the declarer,

and

(*e*) contains an undertaking that if, at any time while the long-term care policy is in force, the declarer ceases to be resident in the State he or she will notify the qualifying insurer accordingly.

(7) (*a*) A qualifying insurer shall—

(i) keep and retain for the longer of the following periods—

(I) a period of 6 years, and

(II) a period which, in relation to the long-term care policy in respect of which the declaration is made, ends not [earlier][1] than 3 years after the date on which premiums have ceased to be paid or payable in respect of the policy,

all declarations of the kind mentioned in subsection (6) which have been made in respect of qualifying long-term care policies issued by the qualifying insurer, and

(ii) on being so required by notice given to that insurer in writing by an inspector, make available within the State to the inspector, within the time specified in the notice, all or any of the declarations of the kind mentioned in subsection (6).

(*b*) The inspector may examine or take extracts from or copies of any declarations made available to him or her under paragraph (*a*).

(8) (*a*) Where an individual makes a payment to a qualifying insurer in respect of which he or she is entitled to relief under this section, the individual shall be entitled to deduct and retain out of the payment an amount equal to the appropriate percentage for the year of assessment in which payment of the premium falls due.

(*b*) The qualifying insurer to whom a payment referred to in paragraph (*a*) is made—

(i) shall accept the amount paid after deduction in discharge of the individual's liability to the same extent as if the deduction had not been made, and

(ii) may, on making a claim in accordance with regulations, recover from the Revenue Commissioners an amount equal to the amount deducted.

(9) (*a*) The Revenue Commissioners shall make regulations providing generally as to administration of this section and those regulations may, in particular and without prejudice to the generality of the foregoing, include provision

(i) for the registration of persons as qualifying insurers for the purposes of this section and those regulations,

(ii) that a claim under subsection (8)(*b*)(ii) by a qualifying insurer shall—

(I) be made in such form and manner,

(II) be made at such time, and

(III) be accompanied by such documents,

as provided for in the regulations,

(iii) for the making of annual information returns by qualifying insurers, in such form (including electronic form) and manner as may be prescribed, and containing specified details in relation to—

(I) each individual making payments to such insurers under qualifying long-term care policies in a year of assessment,

(II) the total amount of premiums paid under a qualifying long-term care policy by that individual in the year of assessment, and

(III) the total amount deducted by that individual under subsection (8)(*a*),

and

(iv) for the furnishing of information to the Revenue Commissioners for the purposes of the regulations.

(*b*) Every regulation made under this section shall be laid before Dáil Éireann as soon as may be after it is made and, if a resolution annulling the regulation is passed by Dáil Éireann within the next 21 days on which Dáil Éireann has sat after the regulation is laid before it, the regulation shall be annulled accordingly, but without prejudice to the validity of anything previously done thereunder.

(10)(*a*) Where any amount is paid to a qualifying insurer by the Revenue Commissioners as an amount recoverable by virtue of subsection (8)(*b*)(ii) but is an amount to which that qualifying insurer is not entitled, that amount shall be repaid by the qualifying insurer.

(*b*) There shall be made such assessments, adjustments or set-offs as may be required for securing repayment of the amount referred to in paragraph (*a*) and the provisions of this Act relating to the assessment, collection and recovery of income tax shall, in so far as they are applicable and with necessary modification, apply in relation to the recovery of such amount.

(11) Where relief is given under this section in respect of a payment, relief shall not be given under any other provision of the Income Tax Acts in respect of that payment.

(12) The Revenue Commissioners may nominate any of their officers, including an inspector, to perform any acts and discharge any functions authorised by this section, other than those specified in subsection (9), to be performed or discharged by them.][2]

Amendments

1 Substituted by FA 2002 s 138 and Sch 6 paras 3(*h*) and 6(*c*)(ii) with effect from 6 April 2001; previously "later".

2 Section 470A inserted by FA 2001 s 20(*a*)(ii) with effect from 6 April 2001.

Cross-references

Deductions allowed in ascertaining taxable income and provisions relating to repayments of tax: s 458(2), s 459(1), (2).

Method of apportioning reliefs and charging tax in cases of separate assessment: s 1024(2)(*a*)(vi).

Penalties: Sch 29, column 1.

Power of inspection, claims by qualifying insurers, meaning of "qualifying insurer" and "qualifying long-term care policy" applied: s 904G(1); subs (8)(*b*)(ii): s 924G(2).

Rate of tax at which repayments are to be made: s 460.

Taxation of certain perquisites, definitions of "qualifying insurer" and "qualifying long-term care policy" applied: s 112A(1); subs (8)(*a*): s 112A(2)(ii), (3)(*b*)(ii).

Regulations

Long-Term Care Insurance (Relief at Source) Regulations 2001 (SI No 130 of 2001).

Tax Briefing

TB43 April 2001 p 16 — Relief for premiums under qualifying long-term care policies.

Definitions

Dáil Éireann: IA 1937 Sch; Income Tax Acts: s 1(2); inspector: ss 2(1), 852; person: IA 1937 s 11(*c*); standard rate: s 3(1); tax: s 3(1); writing: IA 1937 Sch; year: IA 1937 Sch; year of assessment: s 2(1).

471 Relief for contributions to permanent health benefit schemes

(1) In this section—

"benefit" and **"permanent health benefit scheme"** have the same meanings respectively as in section 125;

"contribution", in relation to a permanent health benefit scheme, means any premium paid or other periodic payment made to the scheme in consideration of the right to benefit under it, being a premium or payment which bears a reasonable relationship to the benefits secured by it.

(2) Where an individual for a year of assessment proves that in that year of assessment he or she made a contribution or contributions to a bona fide permanent health benefit

scheme or schemes, the individual shall be entitled, for the purpose of ascertaining the amount of the income on which he or she is to be charged to income tax, to have a deduction of so much of the contributions as does not exceed 10 per cent of his or her total income for that year of assessment made from his or her total income.

(3) In a case where the amount of a contribution made by an employer to a permanent health benefit scheme is charged to income tax under Chapter 3 of Part 5 as a perquisite of the office or employment of a director or employee, that amount shall be deemed for the purposes of subsection (2) to be a contribution made by the director or employee to the scheme in the year in respect of which it is so charged to income tax.

Notes

The manner of granting relief for approved permanent health insurance policies changes from 6 April 2001. From this date, employers should deduct the premiums on such policies from the gross pay of employees for tax and PRSI purposes. This grants income tax relief automatically to the employees and it mirrors the treatment of contributions to approved superannuation schemes — Revenue Tax Briefing, Issue 43, April 2001 p 35.

Cross-references

Deductions allowed in ascertaining taxable income: ss 458(2), 459(1)–(2).

Income Tax (Employments) (Consolidated) Regulations 2001, SI No 559 of 2001: reg 41 (interpretation — Pt 7).

Method of apportioning reliefs and charging tax in cases of separate assessment: s 1024(2)(*a*)(vii).

Rate of tax at which repayments are to be made: s 460.

Former enactments

FA 1979 s 8(1), (2)(*a*) and (3).

472 Employee tax credit

[(1) (*a*) In this section—

"appropriate percentage", in relation to a year of assessment, means a percentage equal to the standard rate of tax for that year;

"emoluments" means emoluments to which Chapter 4 of Part 42 applies or is applied, but does not include—

(i) emoluments paid directly or indirectly by a body corporate (or by any person who would be regarded as connected with the body corporate) to a proprietary director of the body corporate or to the spouse or child of such a proprietary director, and

(ii) emoluments paid directly or indirectly by an individual (or by a partnership in which the individual is a partner) to the spouse or child of the individual;

"director" means—

(i) in relation to a body corporate the affairs of which are managed by a board of directors or similar body, a member of that board or body,

(ii) in relation to a body corporate the affairs of which are managed by a single director or similar person, that director or person, and

(iii) in relation to a body corporate the affairs of which are managed by the members themselves, a member of the body corporate,

and includes any person who is or has been a director;

"proprietary director" means a director of a company who is either the beneficial owner of, or able, either directly or through the medium of other companies or by any other indirect means, to control, more than 15 per cent of the ordinary share capital of the company;

"specified employed contributor" means a person who is an employed contributor for the purposes of the Social Welfare (Consolidation) Act, 1993, but does not include a person—

(i) who is an employed contributor for those purposes by reason only of section 9(1)(*b*) of that Act, or

(ii) to whom Article 81, 82 or 83 of the Social Welfare (Consolidated Contributions and Insurability) Regulations, 1996 (SI No 312 of 1996), applies.

(*b*) For the purposes of the definition of **"proprietary director"**, ordinary share capital which is owned or controlled as referred to in that definition by a person, being a spouse or a minor child of a director, or by a trustee of a trust for the benefit of a person or persons, being or including any such person or such director, shall be deemed to be owned or controlled by such director and not by any other person.

(2) The exclusion from the definition of **"emoluments"** of the emoluments referred to in subparagraphs (i) and (ii) of that definition shall not apply for any year of assessment to any such emoluments paid to an individual, being a child (other than a child who is a proprietary director) to whom subparagraph (i) or (ii) of that definition relates, if for that year—

(*a*) (i) the individual is a specified employed contributor, or

(ii) the [Income Tax (Employments) (Consolidated) Regulations 2001 (SI No 559 of 2001)][1], in so far as they apply, have, in relation to any such emoluments paid to the individual in the year of assessment, been complied with by the person by whom the emoluments are paid,

(*b*) the conditions of the office or employment, in respect of which any such emoluments are paid, are such that the individual is required to devote, throughout the year of assessment, substantially the whole of the individual's time to the duties of the office or employment and the individual does in fact do so, and

(*c*) the amount of any such emoluments paid to the individual in the year of assessment are not less than [€4,572].[2]

(3) Where an individual is in receipt of profits or gains from an office or employment held or exercised outside the State, such profits or gains shall be deemed to be emoluments within the meaning of subsection (1) if such profits or gains—

(*a*) are chargeable to tax in the country in which they arise,

(*b*) on payment by the person making such payment, are subject to a system of tax deduction similar in form to that provided for in Chapter 4 of Part 42,

(*c*) are chargeable to tax in the State on the full amount of such profits or gains under Schedule D, and

(*d*) if the office or employment was held or exercised in the State and the person was resident in the State, would be emoluments within the meaning of that subsection.

(4) Where, for any year of assessment, a claimant proves that his or her total income for the year consists in whole or in part of emoluments (including, in a case where the claimant is a married person assessed to tax in accordance with section 1017, any emoluments of the claimant's spouse deemed to be income of the claimant by that section for the purposes referred to in that section) the claimant shall be entitled to a tax credit (to be known as the **"employee tax credit"**) of—

(*a*) where the emoluments (but not including, in the case where the claimant is a married person so assessed, the emoluments, if any, of the claimant's spouse) arise to the claimant, the lesser of an amount equal to the appropriate percentage of the emoluments and [€1,270],[3] and

(*b*) where, in a case where the claimant is a married person so assessed, the emoluments arise to the claimant's spouse, the lesser of an amount equal to the appropriate percentage of the emoluments and [€1,270].[3]

(5) Where a tax credit is due under this section by virtue of subsection (2), it shall be given by means of repayment of tax.][4]

Amendments

1 Substituted by FA 2002 s 138 and Sch 6 paras 3(*i*) and 6(*c*)(i) with effect from 1 January 2002; previously "Income Tax (Employments) Regulations, 1960 (SI No 28 of 1960)".

2 Substituted by FA 2001 s 2(3) and Sch 1 para 2(*k*)(i) for 2002 and later tax years; previously "£2,664".

3 Substituted by FA 2005 s 3(1) and Sch 1 para (*g*) for 2005 and subsequent years of assessment; previously "€1,040".

4 Section 472 substituted by FA 2001 s 2(3) and Sch 1 para 1(*o*) for short tax "year" 2001 and later tax years.

Cross-references

Agreed pay restructuring, meaning of "emoluments" applied: s 202(1)(*a*).

Deductions allowed in ascertaining taxable income and provisions relating to reductions in tax: ss 458(1), (2), 459(1),(2).

Disturbance and compensation payments, meanings of "director" and "proprietary director" applied: s 480(1)(*a*).

Employer preferential loan, chargeable amount is not emoluments for the purposes of this section: s 122(6).

Interpretation of Income Tax Acts: s 3(1)("personal tax credit").

Method of apportioning reliefs and charging tax in cases of separate assessment: s 1024(2)(*a*)(viii).

Profits or gains do not include chargeable gains within the meaning of the Capital Gains Tax Acts: s 3(4).

Rate of tax at which repayments are to be made: s 460.

Reduction in income tax for certain income earned outside the State, meaning of "proprietary director" applied: s 825A(1).

Relief for the long term unemployed, meaning of "director" and "proprietary director" applied: s 472A(1)(*a*); meaning of "emoluments" and subs (2) applied: s 472A(1)(*a*).

Definitions

person: IA 1937 s 11(*c*); standard rate: s 3(1); total income: s 3(1); year of assessment: s 3(1).

Former enactments

ITA 1967 s 138B, s 195B(3) and (6); FA 1972 Sch 1 Pt III para 4; FA 1974 s 64(2); FA 1980 s 3; FA 1988 s 3 and Sch 1; FA 1991 s 7; FA 1993 s 10(1); FA 1994 s 4; FA 1997 s 146(1) and Sch 9 Pt I paras 1(9), 5(3).

472A Relief for the long-term unemployed

[(1) (*a*) In this section—

[**"the Act of 1993"** means the Social Welfare (Consolidation) Act, 1993;

"continuous period of unemployment" has the meaning assigned in section 120(3) of the Act of 1993;][1]

"director" and **"proprietary director"** have the same meanings, respectively, as in section 472;

"emoluments" has the same meaning as in subsection (1)(*a*) of section 472 and, in relation to the exclusions from that definition, subsection (2) of that section shall apply accordingly;

"employment" means an office or employment of profit such that any emoluments of the office or employment of profit are to be charged to tax under Schedule E;

"employment scheme" means a scheme or programme which provides for the payment in respect of an employment to an employer or an employee of a grant, subsidy or other such payment funded wholly or mainly, directly or indirectly, by the State or by any board established by statute or by any public or local authority;

"qualifying child", in relation to a claimant and a year of assessment, has the same meaning as in section 462, and the question of whether a child is a qualifying child shall be determined on the same basis as it would be for the purposes of section 462, and [subsections (4) and (5)][2] of that section shall apply accordingly;

"qualifying employment" means an employment which—

(i) commences on or after the 6th day of April, 1998,

(ii) is of at least 30 hours duration per week, and

(iii) is capable of lasting at least 12 months,

but does not include—

(I) an employment from which the previous holder was unfairly dismissed,

(II) an employment with a person who, in the 26 weeks immediately prior to the commencement of an employment by a qualifying individual, has reduced, by way of redundancy, the number of employees in such person's trade or profession, or

(III) an employment in respect of which more than 75 per cent of the emoluments therefrom arise from commissions;

[**"qualifying individual"** means an individual who commences a qualifying employment and who—

(i) (I) immediately prior to the commencement of that qualifying employment has been unemployed throughout the period of 12 months immediately preceding the commencement of the employment and has, in respect of that period of unemployment, been in receipt of—

(A) unemployment benefit under Chapter 9 of Part II of the Act of 1993, in respect of a continuous period of unemployment of not less than 312 days, or

(B) unemployment assistance under Chapter 2 of Part III of the Act of 1993, in respect of a continuous period of unemployment of not less than 312 days, or

(C) one-parent family payment under Chapter 9 of Part III of the Act of 1993, in respect of a continuous period of unemployment of not less than 312 days, or

(II) is in any other separate category of persons approved of for the purposes of this section by the Minister for Social, Community and Family Affairs with the consent of the Minister for Finance,

and

(ii) was not previously a qualifying individual for the purposes of this section;][3]

"unemployment payment" means a payment of unemployment benefit or unemployment assistance payable under the Social Welfare Acts.

(*b*) For the purposes of the definition of **"qualifying individual"**—

(i) any period of—

(I) attendance at a non-craft training course provided or approved of by An Foras Áiseanna Saothair,

(II) participation in a programme administered by An Foras Áiseanna Saothair and known as the Community Employment Scheme,

(III) participation in a programme administered by An Foras Áiseanna Saothair and known as the Job Initiative,

(IV) participation in, or participation in or attendance at, an activity to which paragraph (*g*) or (*h*), respectively, of section 120(5) of the Social Welfare (Consolidation) Act, 1993, relates,

shall be deemed to be a period of unemployment for the purposes of this section, and

(ii) any payment in respect of a period of attendance at, or participation in, an activity, programme or scheme mentioned in subparagraph (i) shall be deemed to be an unemployment payment for the purposes of this section if the qualifying individual concerned was in receipt of an unemployment payment immediately prior to the commencement [of such period, and][4]

[(iii) every Sunday in any period of consecutive days shall not be treated as a day of unemployment and shall be disregarded in computing any such period.][5]

(2) Subject to the provisions of this section, where an individual proves that he or she is a qualifying individual, he or she shall, in relation to the 3 years of assessment commencing with either—

(*a*) the year of assessment in which a qualifying employment commences, or

(*b*) by election made by him or her in writing to the inspector, the year of assessment following the year of assessment in which the qualifying employment commences,

be entitled, in computing the amount of his or her taxable income, to have a deduction made from so much of his or her total income as is attributable to emoluments from that qualifying employment as follows:

(i) for the first of those 3 years, [€3,810][6],

(ii) for the second of those 3 years, [€2,540][7], and

(iii) for the third of those 3 years, [€1,270][8].

(3) (*a*) Subject to the provisions of paragraphs (*b*) and (*c*), where a qualifying individual who is entitled to a deduction under subsection (2) for one or more of the 3 years of assessment referred to in that subsection proves that, for one or more of those years, a qualifying child is resident with him or her for the whole or part of the year, he or she shall, in respect of each of the 3 years referred to in subsection (2) in relation to which he or she so proves, be entitled, in computing the amount of his or her taxable income, to have a deduction made from so much of his or her total income as is attributable to emoluments from the qualifying employment as follows:

(i) for the first of those 3 years, [€1,270][9] in respect of each qualifying child,

(ii) for the second of those 3 years, [€850][10] in respect of each qualifying child, and

(iii) for the third of those 3 years, [€425][11] in respect of each qualifying child.

(*b*) Only one deduction of [€1,270][9], [€850][10] and [€425][11] shall be allowed in respect of each qualifying child.

(*c*) Where for a year of assessment, 2 or more qualifying individuals would but for this paragraph be entitled under this section to relief in respect of the same qualifying child, the following provisions shall apply:

(i) the amount of the deduction to be granted for that year in respect of the qualifying child will be the amount due under paragraph (*a*) subject to the provisions of paragraph (*b*),

(ii) where the qualifying child is maintained by only one of the qualifying individuals concerned, that individual shall be entitled to claim the deduction,

(iii) where the qualifying child is maintained jointly by one or more qualifying individuals, the deduction due for the year of assessment in respect of the child shall be apportioned between the qualifying individuals who contribute to the maintenance of the child—

(I) in the same proportion as each maintains the child, or

(II) in such manner as they jointly notify in writing to the inspector;

(iv) in ascertaining for the purposes of this subsection whether a qualifying individual maintains a qualifying child, any payment made by that individual for or towards the maintenance of the child which the individual is entitled to deduct in computing his or her total income for the purposes of the Income Tax Acts shall be deemed not to be a payment for or towards the maintenance of the child.

(4)Where, within the 3 years mentioned in subsection (3), the qualifying employment (in this subsection referred to as **"the first-mentioned employment"**) in respect of which the qualifying individual is entitled to a deduction under subsection (2) ceases, the qualifying individual shall be entitled to have so much of the deductions mentioned in subsections (2) and (3) as cannot be set against his or her emoluments from the first-mentioned employment carried forward and set against the emoluments from his or her next, and only next, qualifying employment, but the deduction for any year of assessment to be set against the emoluments from either or both qualifying employments shall not exceed the deductions due under subsections (2) and (3) for that year.

(5) (*a*) The deductions mentioned in subsections (2) and (3) shall not be due if the qualifying individual, or his or her employer, is benefiting, or has benefited, in respect of the qualifying employment in respect of which a claim under this section is made, under an employment scheme, whether statutory or otherwise.

(*b*) For the purposes of the definition of an employment scheme, an activity, programme or course mentioned in [subsection (1)(*b*)(i)][12] shall be deemed not to be an employment scheme.

(6) Any claim for relief under this section—

(*a*) shall be made in such form as the Revenue Commissioners may from time to time provide, and

(*b*) shall contain such information and be accompanied by such statement in writing as may be indicated in the said form as the Revenue Commissioners may reasonably require for the purposes of the section.][13]

Amendments

1 Definitions of "the Act of 1993" and "continuous period of unemployment" inserted by FA 1999 s 35(*a*)(i) with effect from 6 April 1999.

2 Substituted by FA 2002 s 138 and Sch 6 paras 3(*j*) and 6(*c*)(i) with effect from 6 April 2001; previously "subsections (4) and (6)".

3 Definition of "qualifying individual" substituted by FA 1999 s 35(1)(*a*)(ii) with effect from 6 April 1999.

4 Substituted by FA 1999 s 35(*b*)(i) with effect from 6 April 1999; previously "of such period.".

5 Subs (1)(*b*)(iii) inserted by FA 1999 s 35(*b*)(ii) with effect from 6 April 1999.

6 Substituted by FA 2001 s 240(1) and (2)(*a*) and Sch 5 Pt 1 for 2002 and later tax years; previously "£3,000".

7 Substituted by FA 2001 s 240(1) and (2)(*a*) and Sch 5 Pt 1 for 2002 and later tax years; previously "£2,000".

8 Substituted by FA 2001 s 240(1) and (2)(*a*) and Sch 5 Pt 1 for 2002 and later tax years; previously "£1,000".

9 Substituted by FA 2001 s 240(1) and (2)(*a*) and Sch 5 Pt 1 for 2002 and later tax years; previously "£1,000".

10 Substituted by FA 2001 s 240(1) and (2)(*a*) and Sch 5 Pt 1 for 2002 and later tax years; previously "£666".

11 Substituted by FA 2001 s 240(1) and (2)(*a*) and Sch 5 Pt 1 for 2002 and later tax years; previously "£334".

12 Substituted by FA 1999 s 35(*c*) with effect from 6 April 1999; previously "subsection (2)".

13 Section 472A inserted by FA 1998 s 16(*b*)(ii).

Cross-references

Deductions allowed in ascertaining taxable income: ss 458(2), 459(1), (2).

Double deduction in respect of certain emoluments, meaning of "emoluments", "employment", "employment scheme", "qualifying employment" and "qualifying individual" applied: s 88A(1); subs (1)(*b*)(i): s 88A(2)(*c*).

Method of apportioning reliefs and charging tax in cases of separate assessment: s 1024(2)(*a*)(viii).

Revenue information

Information leaflet IT58 — Revenue Job Assist Information for Employees.

Tax Briefing

TB31 Apr 1998 p 14 — Revenue Job Assist.

TB35 Mar 1999 p 21 — People in receipt of Disability Allowance or Blind Persons Pension for a period of at least 12 months; this category of persons has been approved for the purposes of the relief from 1 January 1999 by the Minister for Social, Community and Family Affairs.

Definitions

Income Tax Acts: s 1(1); inspector: s 2(1); month: IA 1937 Sch; profession: s 2(1); taxable income: s 3(1); total income: s 3(1); trade: ss 3(1), 4(1); year of assessment: s 2(1).

472B Seafarer allowance, etc

[(1) In this section—

"authorised officer" has the same meaning as in section 818;

"employment" means an office or employment of profit such that any emoluments of the office or employment of profit are to be charged to tax under Schedule D or Schedule E;

"international voyage" means a voyage beginning or ending in a port outside the State;

"Member State" means a member state of the European Communities;

"Member State's Register" shall be construed in accordance with the Annex to the Official Journal of the European Communities (No C205) of the 5th day of July, 1997;

"qualifying employment" means an employment, being an employment to which this section applies, the duties of which are performed wholly on board a sea-going ship on an international voyage;

"qualifying individual" means an individual who—

(*a*) holds a qualifying employment, and

(*b*) has entered into an agreement (known as "articles of agreement") with the master of that ship;

"sea-going ship" means a ship which—

(*a*) is registered in a Member State's Register, and

(*b*) is used solely for the trade of carrying by sea passengers or cargo for reward,

but does not include a fishing vessel.

(2) For the purposes of this section—

(*a*) an individual shall be deemed to be absent from the State for a day if the individual is absent from the State at the end of the day, and

[(*b*) a port outside the State shall be deemed to include a mobile or fixed rig, platform or installation of any kind in any maritime area.][1]

(3) (*a*) Subject to paragraph (*b*), this section shall apply to an employment other than—

(i) an employment the emoluments of which are paid out of the revenue of the State, or

(ii) an employment with any board, authority or other similar body established in the State by or under statute.

(*b*) This section shall not apply in any case where the income from an employment—

(i) is chargeable to tax in accordance with section 71(3), or

(ii) is income to which section 822 applies.

(4) Where for any year of assessment an individual resident in the State makes a claim in that behalf to an authorised officer and satisfies that officer that he or she is a qualifying individual and that he or she was absent from the State for at least [125 days][2] [169

days][2], or such greater number of days as the Minister for Finance, after consultation with the Minister for the Marine and Natural Resources, may from time to time, by order made for the purposes of this subsection, substitute for that number of days (or, as the case may be, for the number of days substituted by the last previous order under this subsection), in that year for the purposes of performing the duties of a qualifying employment, he or she shall be entitled, in computing the amount of his or her taxable income, to have a deduction of [€6,350][3] made from so much, if any, of his or her total income as is attributable to the income, profits or gains from the qualifying employment.

[(4A)(*a*) Notwithstanding subsection (4), but subject to paragraph (*b*)—

(i) as respects the year of assessment 2001, the reference in that subsection to "125 days" shall be construed as a reference to "119 days", and

(ii) as respects the year of assessment 2002 and subsequent years of assessment, the reference in that subsection to "169 days" shall be construed as a reference to "161 days".

(*b*) Paragraph (*a*) shall come into operation on such day as the Minister for Finance may by order appoint.][4]

(5) Where, for a year of assessment, an individual claims a deduction under this section, he or she shall not be entitled to a deduction under section 823.

(6) For the purposes of the definition of **"qualifying employment"** in this section, any duties of the employment not performed on board a sea-going ship on an international voyage, the performance of which is merely incidental to the performance of the duties of the employment on board a sea-going ship on an international voyage, shall be treated for the purposes of that definition as having been performed on board the sea- going ship.][5]

Amendments

1 Subs (2)(*b*) substituted by FA 1999 s 15 with effect from 6 April 1999.

2 Substituted by FA 2001 s 30(*a*)(i) for short tax "year" 2001; previously "169 days" and reverts to "169 days" for 2002 and later tax years.

3 Substituted by FA 2001 s 30(*a*)(ii) for 2002 and later tax years; previously "£5,000" (short tax "year" 2001: £3,700 (FA 2001 s 30(*a*)(i)).

4 Subs (4A) inserted by FA 2001 s 30(*b*). By virtue of the Finance Act 2001 (Section 30) (Commencement) Order 2003, SI No 126 of 2003 made on 7 April 2003, subs (4A) comes into operation on 6 April 2001.

5 Section 472B inserted by FA 1998 s 14(1)(*b*) from such date as the Minister for Finance may appoint by order. The section came into operation on 17 February 1999 — Taxes Consolidation Act, 1997 (Section 472B) (Commencement) Order 1999, SI No 48 of 1999 refers.

Cross-references

Deduction for income earned outside the State, meaning of "qualifying employment", "qualifying individual" and "sea-going ship" applied: s 823(2A)(*a*).

Method of apportioning reliefs and charging tax in cases of separate assessment: s 1024(2)(*a*)(viii).

Reduction in income tax for certain income earned outside the State: s 825A(5).

Residence of individuals, subs (4): s 819.

Tax Briefing

TB36 June 1999 pp 18–19 — Seafarer's allowance.

TB43 April 2001 p 16 — Seafarer's allowance — Finance Act 2001 changes.

Definitions

Income Tax Acts: s 1(1); inspector: s 2(1); profession: s 2(1); taxable income: s 3(1); total income: s 3(1); trade: ss 3(1), 4(1); year of assessment: s 2(1).

472C Relief for trade union subscriptions

[(1) In this section—

"appropriate percentage", in relation to a year of assessment, means a percentage equal to the standard rate of tax for that year;

"specified amount", in relation to an individual for a year of assessment, means [€200][1];

"trade union" means a body which is either—

(*a*) the holder of a negotiation licence under the Trade Union Act, 1941,

(*b*) an excepted body within the meaning of section 6 of that Act as amended by the Trade Union Act, 1942,

(*c*) a garda representative body established under the Garda Síochána Act, 1977, namely—

(i) the association known as the Association of Garda Sergeants and Inspectors established under regulation 5(1) of the Garda Síochána (Associations) Regulations, 1978 (SI No 135 of 1978),

(ii) the association known as the Garda Representative Association established under regulation 4(1) of the Garda Síochána (Associations) Regulations, 1978,

(iii) the association known as the Association of Garda Superintendents established under regulation 4(1) of the Garda Síochána (Associations) (Superintendents and Chief Superintendents) Regulations, 1987 (SI No 200 of 1987),

or

(*d*) a Defence Forces representative body established under section 2 of the Defence (Amendment) Act, 1990, and regulations pursuant to that Act.

(2) Where an individual is a member of a trade union at any time in a year of assessment (being the year of assessment 2001 or a subsequent year of assessment), the income tax to be charged on the individual or, in the case of an individual whose spouse is assessed to tax in accordance with the provisions of section 1017, the individual's spouse, for the year of assessment, other than in accordance with section 16(2), shall, subject to the following provisions of this section, be reduced by the lesser of—

(*a*) the appropriate percentage of the specified amount, or

(*b*) the amount which reduces that income tax to nil.

(3) Notwithstanding subsection (2), the relief (if any) to which an individual is entitled under this section for the year of assessment 2001 shall, in addition to the relief (if any) to which the individual is entitled for the year of assessment 2002, be allowed to the individual in accordance with the provisions of subsection (2), in respect of the income tax to be charged on the individual for the year of assessment 2002.

(4) Relief under this section shall be allowed in priority to relief under any of the other provisions mentioned in the Table to section 458.

(5) Where the relief (if any) to which an individual is entitled under this section in respect of income tax to be charged on the individual for the year of assessment 2001 is not wholly allowed to the individual in respect of the income tax to be charged on the individual for the year of assessment 2002 owing to an insufficiency of total income of the individual in that year of assessment, the portion of the relief not so allowed shall be allowed to the individual in respect of the income tax to be charged on the individual for the year of assessment 2001 such relief being limited to the lesser of—

(*a*) the portion of the relief not so allowed, and

(*b*) the relief which reduces that income tax to nil.

(6) If an individual is a member of more than one trade union, either at the same time or at different times in a year of assessment, the individual shall be treated, for the purposes of the relief under this section, as if the individual were a member of one trade union only in that year of assessment.

(7) (*a*) Notwithstanding the provisions of any other enactment—

(i) an employer of individuals entitled to relief under this section, or

(ii) a trade union of which such individuals are or were members,

shall on receipt of a request from the Revenue Commissioners furnish to them either directly or indirectly the following information, to the extent that such information is in their possession, in relation to any such individual—

(I) the name and address of the individual,

(II) the name of the trade union of which the individual is a member,

(III) the Personal Public Service Number of the individual, and

(IV) the name and address of the employer of the individual.

(*b*) A return by an employer or a trade union under paragraph (*a*) shall, unless the Revenue Commissioners otherwise direct, be in an electronic format approved by the Revenue Commissioners.

(8) (*a*) The information referred to in subsection (7)(*a*) shall be used by the Revenue Commissioners for the purposes of facilitating the granting of relief under this section and shall be used for no other purpose.

(*b*) The provisions of section 872 shall not apply or have effect in relation to such information.][1]

Amendments

1 Substituted by FA 2004 s 4 for 2004 and subsequent years of assessment; previously "€130".

2 Section 472C inserted by FA 2001 s 11(1)(*b*) for short tax "year" 2001 and later tax years.

Cross-references

Deductions allowed in ascertaining taxable income and provisions relating to reductions in tax: s 458(1), (2), s 459(1), (2).

Method of apportioning reliefs and charging tax in cases of separate assessment: s 1024(2)(*a*)(viii*a*).

Definitions

standard rate: s 3(1); tax: s 3(1); total income: s 3(1); year of assessment: s 3(1).

473 Allowance for rent paid by certain tenants

(1) In this section—

[**"appropriate percentage"**, in relation to a year of assessment, means a percentage equal to the standard rate of tax for that year;][1]

"residential premises" means property held under a tenancy, being—

(*a*) a building or part of a building used or suitable for use as a dwelling, and

(*b*) land which the occupier of a building or part of a building used as a dwelling has for his or her own occupation and enjoyment with the building or part of a building as its garden or grounds of an ornamental nature;

"rent" includes any periodical payment in the nature of rent made in return for a special possession of residential premises or for the use, occupation or enjoyment of residential premises, but does not include so much of any rent or payment as—

(*a*) is paid or made to defray the cost of maintenance of or repairs to residential premises for which in the absence of agreement to the contrary the tenant would be liable,

(*b*) relates to the provision of goods or services,

(*c*) relates to any right or benefit other than the bare right to use, occupy and enjoy residential premises, or

(*d*) is the subject of a right of reimbursement or a subsidy from any source enjoyed by the person making the payment, unless such reimbursement or subsidy cannot be obtained;

[**"specified limit"**, in relation to an individual for a year of assessment, means—

(*a*) in the case of—

(i) a married person assessed to tax in accordance with section 1017, or

(ii) a widowed person,

€3,000; but, if at any time during the year of assessment the individual was of the age of 55 years or over, "specified limit" means €6,000, and

(*b*) in any other case, €1,500; but, if at any time during the year of assessment the individual was of the age of 55 years or over, "specified limit" means €3,000;][2]

"tenancy" includes any contract, agreement or licence under or in respect of which rent is paid, but does not include—

(*a*) a tenancy which apart from any statutory extension is a tenancy for a freehold estate or interest or for a definite period of 50 years or more,

(*b*) a tenancy in relation to which the person beneficially entitled to the rent is a Minister of the Government, the Commissioners of Public Works in Ireland or a housing authority for the purposes of the Housing Act, 1966, or

(*c*) a tenancy in relation to which an agreement or provision exists under which the rent paid or part of it is or may be treated as consideration or part consideration, in whatever form, for the creation of a further or greater estate, tenancy or interest in the residential premises concerned or in any other property.

[(2) Where an individual (in this section referred to as the "claimant") proves that in the year of assessment he or she has made a payment on account of rent in respect of residential premises which, during the period in respect of which the payment was made, was his or her main residence, the income tax to be charged on the claimant, other than in accordance with section 16(2), for that year of assessment shall be reduced by an amount which is the least of—

(*a*) the amount equal to the appropriate percentage of the aggregate of such payments proved to be so made,

(*b*) the appropriate percentage of the specified limit in relation to the claimant for the year of assessment, and

(*c*) the amount that reduces that income tax to nil.][3]

[(3) For the purposes of this section, where a claimant is a married person assessed to tax for the year of assessment in accordance with section 1017, any payments made by the claimant's spouse, in respect of which that spouse would have been entitled to relief under this section if he or she were assessed to tax for the year of assessment in accordance with section 1016 (apart from subsection (2) of that section), shall be deemed to have been made by the claimant.][4]

(4) (*a*) Where a payment is made partly on account of rent and partly on account of anything which is not rent, such apportionment of the payment shall be made as is necessary in order to determine for the purposes of this section the amount paid on account of rent.

(*b*) Any apportionment required by this subsection shall be made by the inspector according to the best of his or her knowledge and judgment.

(5) Where a payment on account of rent is made in respect of any period, that payment shall be deemed for the purposes of this section to be made in the year in which the period falls; but, if the period falls partly in one year and partly in another year, the amount of the payment made in respect of that period shall be apportioned to each year in the proportion which the part of the period falling in that year bears to the whole of the period, and the amount so apportioned to a year shall be deemed for the purposes of this section to be paid in that year.

(6) (*a*) Any claim for relief under this section in respect of rent paid in a year of assessment shall be accompanied by—

(i) a certificate and statement, in a form prescribed by the Revenue Commissioners, signed by the claimant setting out—

(I) the name, address and income tax reference number of the claimant,

(II) the name, address and, as may be appropriate, the income tax or corporation tax reference number of the person or body of persons beneficially entitled to the rent under the tenancy under which the rent was paid,

(III) the postal address of the premises in respect of which the rent was paid, and

(IV) full particulars of the tenancy under which the rent was paid,

and

(ii) a receipt or acknowledgement in respect of such rent given in accordance with subsection (8).

(*b*) Failure to furnish any of the particulars mentioned in paragraph (*a*)(i) or failure to furnish a receipt or acknowledgement mentioned in paragraph (*a*)(ii) shall be grounds for refusal of the claim; but—

(i) the inspector may waive the requirement at paragraph (*a*)(i)(II) on receipt of satisfactory proof that the claimant's inability to comply with that requirement is bona fide, and

(ii) the inspector may waive the requirements at paragraph (*a*)(ii) on receipt of satisfactory proof of the total rent paid in the relevant period and on being furnished with the name and address of the person or body of persons to whom it was paid.

(7) (*a*) Any person aggrieved by a decision of the inspector on any question arising under subsection (4) or (6) may, by notice in writing to that effect given to the inspector within 30 days from the date on which notice of the decision is given to that person, make an application to have his or her claim for relief heard and determined by the Appeal Commissioners.

(*b*) Where an application is made under paragraph (*a*), the Appeal Commissioners shall hear and determine the claim in the like manner as an appeal made to them against an assessment to income tax, and the provisions of the Income Tax Acts relating to such an appeal (including the provisions relating to the rehearing of an appeal and to the statement of a case for the opinion of the High Court on a point of law) shall apply accordingly with any necessary modifications.

(8) (*a*) Where a person (in this subsection referred to as **"the tenant"**) who is entitled to relief under this section for a year of assessment, or who has reason to believe that he or she may be so entitled, requests a receipt or acknowledgement of the rent paid by him or her in that year, the person or body of persons beneficially entitled to the rent shall, within 7 days from the date of the request, give to the tenant a receipt or acknowledgement of the rent paid by the tenant in that year of assessment.

(*b*) Any receipt or acknowledgement given in accordance with this subsection shall be in writing and shall contain—

(i) the name and address of the tenant,

(ii) the name, address and, as may be appropriate, the income tax or corporation tax reference number of the person or body of persons giving the receipt or acknowledgement, and

(iii) the amount of the rent paid in the year of assessment and the period within that year in respect of which it is paid.

(9) (*a*) The Revenue Commissioners may make regulations, for the purpose of giving effect to this section, with respect to the allowance granted by this section, or to any matter ancillary or incidental thereto, or, in particular and without prejudice to the generality of the foregoing, to provide for—

(i) the proof by a claimant of a payment on account of rent,

(ii) the disclosure of information by a person in receipt of a payment on account of rent,

(iii) the maintenance of records and the production to and inspection by persons authorised by the Revenue Commissioners of such records and the taking by such persons of copies of or of extracts from such records, and

(iv) appeals with respect to matters arising under the regulations which would not otherwise be the subject of an appeal.

(*b*) Every regulation made under this section shall be laid before Dáil Éireann as soon as may be after it is made and, if a resolution annulling the regulation is passed by Dáil Éireann within the next 21 days on which Dáil Éireann has sat after the regulation is laid before it, the regulation shall be annulled accordingly, but without prejudice to the validity of anything previously done thereunder.

[(10) Any relief under this section shall be in substitution for and not in addition to any relief to which the claimant might be entitled in respect of the same payment under any other provision of the Income Tax Acts.][5]

Amendments

1 Definition of "appropriate percentage" inserted by FA 2000 s 13(*a*)(i) for 2000–2001 and later tax years.

2 Definition of "specified limit" substituted by FA 2005 s 6 for 2005 and subsequent years of assessment.

3 Subs (2) substituted by FA 2000 s 13(*b*) for 2000–2001 and later tax years.

4 Subs (3) substituted by FA 2000 s 13(*c*) for 2000–2001 and later tax years.

5 Subs (10) substituted by FA 2000 s 13(*d*) for 2000–2001 and later tax years.

Cross-references

Deductions allowed in ascertaining taxable income and provisions relating to reductions in tax: s 458(1), (2); s 459(1), (2).

Method of apportioning reliefs and charging tax in cases of separate assessment: s 1024(2)(*a*)(vi).

Penalty: Sch 29 column 1.

Rate of tax at which repayments are to be made: s 460.

Revenue precedents

Issue: Whether property for which rent paid must be situated in the State; whether land lord must be resident in the State.

Decision: No requirement that property must be in the State or that landlord must be resident in the State.

Issue: A housing authority for the purposes of the Housing Act 1966.

Decision: A county council, a county borough corporation, a borough corporation, an urban district council or Town commissioners.

Statutory instrument

Subs (9): Income Tax (Rent Relief) Regulations 1982 (SI 318/1982).

Definitions

Appeal Commissioners: s 2(1); body of persons: s 2(1); High Court: IA 1937 Sch; Minister of the Government: IA 1937 Sch; Income Tax Acts: s 1(2); inspector: ss 2(1), 5(1), 852; person: IA 1937 s 11(*c*); rent: s 5(1); standard rate: ss 3(1), 15; writing: IA 1937 Sch; year of assessment: s 3(1).

Former enactments

ITA 1967 s 142A and 195B(3) and (6); FA 1982 s 5(1); FA 1985 s 7(*a*); FA 1991 s 8; FA 1993 s 10(1); FA 1995 s 5.

473A Relief for fees paid for third level education, etc

[(1) In this section—

"academic year", in relation to an approved course, means a year of study commencing on a date not earlier than the 1st day of August in a year of assessment;

"appropriate percentage", in relation to a year of assessment, means a percentage equal to the standard rate of tax for that year;

"approved college", in relation to a year of assessment, means—

(*a*) a college or institution of higher education in the State which—

(i) provides courses to which a scheme approved by the Minister under the Local Authorities (Higher Education) Grants Acts, 1968 to 1992, applies, or

(ii) operates in accordance with a code of standards which from time to time may, with the consent of the Minister for Finance, be laid down by the Minister, and which the Minister approves for the purposes of this section;

(*b*) any university or similar institution of higher education in a Member State of the European Union (other than the State) which—

(i) is maintained or assisted by recurrent grants from public funds of that or any other Member State of the European Union (including the State), or

(ii) is a duly accredited university or institution of higher education in the Member State in which it is situated;

(*c*) a college or institution in another Member State of the European Union providing distance education in the State, which—

(i) provides courses to which a scheme approved by the Minister under the Local Authority (Higher Education) Grants Acts, 1968 to 1992, applies, or

(ii) operates in accordance with a code of standards which from time to time may, with the consent of the Minister for Finance, be laid down by the Minister, and which the Minister approves for the purposes of this section;

(*d*) any university or similar institution of higher education in any country, other than the State or a Member State of the European Union which—

(i) is maintained or assisted by recurrent grants from public funds of that country, or

(ii) is a duly accredited university or institution of higher education in the country in which it is situated;

"approved course" means—

(*a*) a full-time or part-time undergraduate course of study provided by a college to which paragraph (*a*), (*b*) or (*c*) of the definition of **"approved college"** relates which—

(i) is of at least 2 academic years' duration, and

(ii) in the case of a course provided by a college to which paragraph (*a*)(ii) or (*c*)(ii) of the definition of **"approved college"** relates, the Minister, having regard to a code of standards which from time to time may, with the consent of the Minister for Finance, be laid down by the Minister in relation to the quality of education to be offered on such approved course, approves of for the purposes of this section;

(*b*) a postgraduate course of study leading to a postgraduate award, based on a thesis or on the results of an examination or both, in an approved college—

(i) of not less than one academic year, but not more than 4 academic years, in duration,

(ii) that requires an individual, undertaking the course, to have been conferred with a degree or an equivalent qualification, and

(iii) that, in the case of a course provided by a college to which paragraph (*a*)(ii) of the definition of **"approved college"** relates, the Minister, having regard to any code of standards which from time to time may, with the consent of the Minister for Finance, be laid down by the Minister in relation to the quality of education to be offered on such approved course, approves for the purposes of this section;

"dependant", in relation to an individual, means a spouse or child of the individual or a person in respect of whom the individual is or was the legal guardian;

"the Minister" means the Minister for Education and Science;

"qualifying fees", in relation to an approved course and an academic year, means the amount of fees chargeable in respect of tuition to be provided in relation to that course in that year which, with the consent of the Minister for Finance, the Minister approves of for the purposes of this section.

(2) Subject to this section, where an individual for a year of assessment proves that he or she has, on his or her own behalf or on behalf of his or her dependant, made a payment in respect of qualifying fees in respect of an approved course for the academic year in relation to that course commencing in that year of assessment, the income tax to be charged on the individual for that year of assessment, other than in accordance with section 16(2), shall be reduced by an amount which is the lesser of—

(*a*) the amount equal to the appropriate percentage of the aggregate of all such payments proved to be so made, and

(*b*) the amount which reduces that income tax to nil.

(3) In the case of an individual who is a married person assessed to tax for a year of assessment in accordance with section 1017, any payment in respect of qualifying fees made by the individual's spouse shall, except where section 1023 applies, be deemed to have been made by the individual.

(4) For the purposes of this section, a payment in respect of qualifying fees shall be regarded as not having been made in so far as any sum in respect of, or by reference to, such fees has been or is to be received, directly or indirectly, by the individual, or, as the case may be, his or her dependant, from any source whatever by means of grant, scholarship or otherwise.

(5) (*a*) Where the Minister is satisfied that an approved college, within the meaning of paragraph (*a*)(ii) or (*c*)(ii) of the definition of **"approved college"**, or an approved course in that college, no longer meets the appropriate code of

standards laid down, the Minister may by notice in writing given to the approved college withdraw, with effect from the year of assessment following the year of assessment in which the notice is given, the approval of that college or course, as the case may be, for the purposes of this section.

(*b*) Where the Minister withdraws the approval of any college or course for the purposes of this section, notice of its withdrawal shall be published as soon as may be in Iris Oifigiúil.

(6) Any claim for relief under this section made by an individual in respect of fees paid to an approved college shall be accompanied by a statement in writing made by the approved college concerned stating each of the following, namely—

(*a*) that the college is an approved college for the purposes of this section,
(*b*) the details of the course undertaken by the individual or his or her dependant,
(*c*) the duration of the course, and
(*d*) the amount of the fees paid in respect of the course.

(7) Where for the purposes of this section any question arises as to whether—

(*a*) a college is an approved college, or
(*b*) a course of study is an approved course,

the Revenue Commissioners may consult with the Minister.

(8) On or before 1 July in each year of assessment, the Minister shall furnish the Revenue Commissioners with full details of—

(*a*) all colleges and courses in respect of which approval has been granted and not withdrawn for the purposes of this section, and
(*b*) the amount of the qualifying fees in respect of each such course for the academic year commencing in that year of assessment.][1]

Amendments

1 Section 473A inserted by FA 2001 s 29(1) with effect from 6 April 2001.

Cross-references

Method of apportioning reliefs and charging tax in cases of separate assessment: s 1024(2)(*a*)(ix).

Revenue information

A list of approved colleges and courses for the purposes of this section is available on Revenue's website www.revenue.ie under the headings Publications/Lists.

Definitions

standard rate: ss 3(1), 15; tax: s 3(1); writing: IA 1937 Sch; year of assessment: s 2(1).

474 Relief for fees paid to private colleges for full-time third level education

Amendments

1 Section 474 repealed by FA 2001 s 29(3) with effect from 6 April 2001.

474A Relief for fees paid to publicly funded colleges in the European Union for full-time third level education

Amendments

1 Section 474A repealed by FA 2001 s 29(3) with effect from 6 April 2001.

475 Relief for fees paid for part-time third level education

Amendments

1 Section 475 repealed by FA 2001 s 29(3) with effect from 6 April 2001.

475A Relief for postgraduate fees

Amendments

1 Section 475A repealed by FA 2001 s 29(3) with effect from 6 April 2001.

476 Relief for fees paid for training courses

(1) In this section—

"An Foras" means An Foras Áiseanna Saothair;

[**"appropriate percentage"** means, in relation to a year of assessment, a percentage equal to the standard rate of tax for that year;][1]

"approved course provider" means a person providing approved courses who—

(*a*) operates in accordance with a code of standards which from time to time may, with the consent of the Minister for Finance, be agreed between An Foras and the Minister, and

(*b*) is approved of by An Foras for the purposes of this section;

"approved course" means a course of study or training, other than a postgraduate course, provided by an approved course provider which—

(*a*) is confined to—

(i) such aspects of information technology, or

(ii) such foreign languages,

as are approved of by the Minister, with the consent of the Minister for Finance, for the purposes of this section,

(*b*) is of less than 2 years' duration,

(*c*) results in the awarding of a certificate of competence, and

(*d*) having regard to a code of standards which from time to time may, with the consent of the Minister for Finance, be agreed between An Foras and the Minister in relation to—

(i) the quality and standard of training to be provided on the approved course, and

(ii) the methods and facilities to be used by the course provider in delivering the course and in assessing competence,

is approved of by An Foras for the purposes of this section;

"certificate of competence", in relation to an approved course, means a certificate awarded in accordance with the standards set out in the code of standards referred to in paragraph (*d*) of the definition of **"approved course"** and certifying that a minimum level of competence has been achieved by the individual to whom the certificate is awarded;

[**"dependant"** means, in relation to an individual, a spouse or child of the individual or a person in respect of whom the individual is or was the legal guardian;][2]

"foreign language" means a language other than an official language of the State;

"the Minister" means the Minister for Enterprise, Trade and Employment;

"qualifying fees", in relation to an approved course, means the amount of fees chargeable in respect of tuition to be provided in relation to such course where the net amount of such fees are not less than [€315][3] and to the extent that they do not exceed [€1,270][4].

[(2) Subject to this section, where an individual proves that—

(*a*) he or she has, on his or her own behalf or on behalf of his or her dependant, made a payment in respect of qualifying fees in respect of an approved course, and

(*b*) the individual in respect of whom the fees are paid has been awarded a certificate of competence in respect of that course,

the income tax to be charged on the individual, other than in accordance with section 16(2), for the year of assessment in which that certificate of competence is awarded shall be reduced by an amount which is the lesser of—

(i) the amount equal to the appropriate percentage of the aggregate of all such payments proved to be so made, and

(ii) the amount which reduces that income tax to nil.

(3) In the case of an individual who is a married person assessed to tax for a year of assessment in accordance with section 1017, any payment in respect of qualifying fees made by the individual's spouse shall, except where section 1023 applies, be deemed to have been made by the individual.][5]

(4) Relief under this section shall not be given in respect of an individual for a year of assessment in respect of more than one approved course.

(5) For the purposes of this section, a payment in respect of qualifying fees shall be regarded as not having been made in so far as any sum, in respect of or by reference to such fees, has been or is to be received either directly or indirectly by an individual from any source whatever by means of grant, scholarship or otherwise.

(6) An Foras, where it is satisfied that an approved course provider, or an approved course provided by an approved course provider, no longer meets the appropriate code of standards laid down, may by notice in writing given to the approved course provider withdraw the approval of that course provider or approved course, as the case may be, from such date as it considers appropriate, and this section shall cease to apply to that course provider or that course, as the case may be, with effect from that date.

(7) (*a*) As soon as may be practicable after An Foras has—

(i) approved a course provider or a course for the purposes of this section, or

(ii) withdrawn such approval,

An Foras shall notify the Revenue Commissioners in writing of such approval or withdrawal of approval.

(*b*) Where any question arises as to whether for the purposes of this section—

(i) a course provider is an approved course provider, or

(ii) a training course is an approved course,

the Revenue Commissioners may consult with An Foras.

(8) Any relief under this section shall be in substitution for and not in addition to any relief to which the individual might be entitled to in respect of the same payment under any other provision of the Income Tax Acts.

(9) This section shall come into operation on such date as may be fixed by order of the Minister for Finance.

Amendments

1 Definition of "appropriate percentage" inserted by FA 2000 s 21(1)(*e*)(i)(I) for 2000–2001 and later tax years.

2 Definition of "dependant" inserted by FA 2000 s 21(*e*)(i)(II) for 2000–2001 and later tax years.

3 Substituted by FA 2001 s 240(1) and (2)(*a*) and Sch 5 Pt 1 for 2002 and later tax years; previously "£250".

4 Substituted by FA 2001 s 240(1) and (2)(*a*) and Sch 5 Pt 1 for 2002 and later tax years; previously "£1,000".

5 Subss (2)–(3) substituted by FA 2000 s 21(*e*)(ii) for 2000–2001 and later tax years.

Operative Date

The section comes into operation with effect from 31 March. 1998 — Taxes Consolidation Act. 1997 (Section 476) (Commencement) Order, SI No 87 of 1998 refers.

Cross-references

Deductions allowed in ascertaining taxable income and provisions relating to reductions in tax: s 458(1), (2); s 459(1), (2).

Method of apportioning reliefs and charging tax in cases of separate assessment: s 1024(2)(*a*)(ix).

Tax Briefing

TB34 Dec 1998 p 7 — Training Courses IT and Foreign Languages.

List of approved courses and approved course providers are available from any tax office or from the *Revenue Forms and Leaflets Service* at 01–8780100. The list is also available on Revenue's website www.revenue.ie under the headings Publications/Lists.

Definitions

Income Tax Acts: s 1(2).

standard rate: ss 3(1), 15, year of assessment: s 2(1).

Former enactments

FA 1997 s 8(1)–(7) and (10)–(11).

---

477 Relief for service charges

(1) (*a*) In this section—

"appropriate percentage", in relation to a year of assessment, means a percentage equal to the standard rate of tax for that year;

"claimant" has the meaning assigned to it by subsection (2);

"financial year" means the period of 12 months ending on the 31st day of December in that year;

"group water supply scheme" means a scheme referred to in the Housing (Improvement Grants) Regulations, 1983 (SI No 330 of 1983);

"service" means the provision by or on behalf of a local authority of—

(i) a supply of water for domestic purposes,

(ii) domestic refuse collection or disposal, or

(iii) domestic sewage disposal facilities;

"service charge" means a charge imposed under—

(i) the Local Government (Financial Provisions)(No 2) Act, 1983, or

(ii) section 65A (inserted by the Local Government (Sanitary Services) Act, 1962, and amended by the Local Government (Financial Provisions)(No 2) Act, 1983) of the Public Health (Ireland) Act, 1878,

in respect of the provision by a local authority of any service or services, and **"service charges"** shall be construed accordingly;

...[1].

(*b*) References in this section to an amount paid on time shall mean payment of that amount by such date or dates as a local authority shall decide.

(2) Where in relation to income tax for a year of assessment an individual (in this section referred to as a **"claimant"**) proves that in the financial year immediately before the year of assessment the amount which he or she was liable to pay in respect of service charges for that financial year has been paid in full and on time, the income tax to be charged on the claimant for that year of assessment, other than in accordance with section 16(2), shall, subject to subsections (3) and (5), be reduced by an amount which is the least of—

(*a*) the amount equal to the appropriate percentage of the amount proved to be so paid,

...[2]

(*c*) the amount which reduces that income tax to nil.

(3) (*a*) In the case of a claimant assessed to tax for the year of assessment in accordance with section 1017, any payments made by the spouse of the claimant, in respect of which that spouse would have been entitled to relief under this section if the spouse were assessed to tax for the year of assessment in accordance with section 1016 (apart from subsection (2) of that section), shall be deemed to have been made by the claimant.

(*b*) In the case of an individual who resides on a full-time basis in the premises to which the service charges relate and pays such service charges in accordance with the requirements of this section on behalf of the claimant, that claimant may disclaim the relief provided by this section in favour of the individual, and such disclaimer shall be in such form as the Revenue Commissioners may require.

(4) A claimant who wishes to claim relief under this section shall furnish to the local authority to which a payment in respect of the service charges referred to in subsection (2) is made the claimant's identifying number, known as the Revenue and Social Insurance (RSI) Number.

(5) (*a*) Any claim for relief under this section shall, unless the details referred to in subsection (6) in respect of a claimant are provided on the basis set out in paragraph (*c*) of that subsection, be accompanied by a certificate given in accordance with subsection (6) or, in a case to which ...[3] subsection (7)

applies, a receipt or acknowledgement referred to in [paragraph (*c*) of that subsection][4].

(*b*) Failure to furnish a certificate or receipt or acknowledgement mentioned in paragraph (*a*), or to be included in the return referred to in subsection (6)(*c*), shall be grounds for refusal of the claim.

(6) (*a*) Where in a financial year—

(i) a claimant has furnished his or her identifying number in accordance with subsection (4),

(ii) the total amount which he or she was liable to pay in respect of service charges for that year has been paid on time, and

(iii) arrears, if any, of service charges have been paid in accordance with guidelines in relation to the payment of arrears of service charges entitled **"Finance Act, 1995 — Payment of Service Charges Arrears"** issued to local authorities by the Department of the Environment,

the local authority to which payment was made shall, [subject to paragraph (*d*),][5] give to the claimant a certificate in respect of such payment.

(*b*) A certificate given in accordance with this subsection shall contain—

(i) the name, address and the identifying number, known as the Revenue and Social Insurance (RSI) Number, of the claimant,

(ii) the name and address of the local authority giving the certificate,

(iii) the amount paid and the financial year in respect of which it was paid, and

(iv) confirmation that the payment referred to in subparagraph (iii) was paid on time and represents the full amount of the service charges which the claimant was liable to pay for the financial year for which the certificate was given.

[(*c*) Each local authority shall, on or before 1 November each year, provide the Revenue Commissioners with a return in such computerised format as the Revenue Commissioners may require for the purposes of giving effect to the relief provided for in this section and containing, in respect of every claimant who has furnished an identifying number mentioned in subsection (4), the details specified in subparagraphs (i), (iii) and (iv) of paragraph (*b*).][6]

(*d*) Where a local authority makes a return in accordance with paragraph (*c*), the certificate mentioned in paragraph (*a*) need not be given to any claimant referred to in such return.

[(7) Where the service consists of the provision of domestic refuse collection or disposal, is provided and charged for by a person or body of persons other than a local authority, and where such person or body of persons has—

(*a*) notified its provision to the local authority in whose functional area such service is provided,

(*b*) furnished to that local authority such information as the local authority may from time to time request concerning that person or body of persons or the service provided by that person or body of persons, and

(*c*) given a receipt or acknowledgement to a claimant containing—

(i) the name, address and, as may be appropriate, the income tax or corporation tax reference number of the person or body of persons,

(ii) the claimant's name and address,

(iii) the amount paid, and

(iv) the financial year in respect of which the payment for the service was paid,

a claimant shall be entitled to relief, subject to this section other than subsection (6), in respect of the amount paid.

(7A) Where the service consists of the provision of domestic refuse collection or disposal, is provided by a local authority or a person or body of persons referred to in subsection (7)(*a*), is charged for other than by means of a specified annual charge in respect of that service, and a claimant is not entitled to make a claim for relief either under subsection (2), in respect of the provision of domestic refuse collection or disposal, or subsection (7), the claimant shall for the purposes of this section be taken to have made a payment of €195 in respect of that service and shall be entitled to relief, subject to this section other than subsections (5) and (6), in respect of such an amount.

(7B) Where a service charge is imposed in respect of the provision of a service other than a service referred to in subsections (7) and (7A), those subsections shall apply only where the claimant also qualifies for relief under this section in respect of the service charge.][7]

(8) The provision of a supply of water for domestic purposes effected by a group water supply scheme shall be treated for the purposes of this section as if it were provided by a local authority, and a payment by an individual member of such a scheme in respect of such provision shall be deemed to be a payment in respect of service charges.

(9) Any deduction made under this section shall be in substitution for and not in addition to any deduction to which the individual might be entitled in respect of the same payment under any other provision of the Income Tax Acts.

Amendments

1 Definition of "specified limit" deleted by FA 2002 s 6(*a*) with effect from 1 January 2002.

2 Subs (2)(*b*) deleted by FA 2002 s 6(*b*) with effect from 1 January 2002.

3 Deleted by FA 2002 s 6(*c*) with effect from 1 January 2002; previously "paragraph (*a*)(i) of".

4 Substituted by FA 2002 s 6(*c*) with effect from 1 January 2002; previously "clause (III) of that paragraph"

5 Substituted by FA 2001 s 10(*a*) for short tax "year" 2001 and later tax years; previously "subject to paragraph (*c*),"

6 Subs (6)(*c*) substituted by FA 2002 s 6(*d*) with effect from 1 January 2002.

7 Subs (7) substituted and subss (7A)–(7B) inserted by FA 2002 s 6(*e*) with effect from 1 January 2002.

Cross-references

Deductions allowed in ascertaining taxable income: ss 458(2), 459(1)–(2).

Method of apportioning reliefs and charging tax in cases of separate assessment: s 1024(2)(*a*)(ix).

Penalty: Sch 29 column 1.

Rate of tax at which repayments are to be made: s 460.

Revenue information

Information leaflet IT27 — Tax Relief for Service Charges.

Tax Briefing

TB21 Mar 1996 p 4 — Relief for Service Charges.

Definitions

body of persons: s 2(1); local authority: s 2(1); year of assessment: s 2(1).

Former enactments

FA 1995 s 7(1)–(8).

478 Relief for payments made by certain persons in respect of alarm systems

(1) In this section—

“appropriate percentage”, in relation to a year of assessment, means a percentage equal to the standard rate of tax for that year;

“installation” means the placing in position, including any necessary wiring, drilling, plastering or similar work, of a relevant alarm system;

“qualifying expenditure”, in relation to a qualifying individual, means expenditure incurred in the qualifying period in connection with either or both the provision and installation of a relevant alarm system in a premises which is the qualifying individual’s sole or main residence, but does not include any expenditure in so far as it is in respect of the repair, maintenance or monitoring of such an alarm system;

“qualifying individual”, in relation to qualifying expenditure, means an individual who at the time the expenditure is incurred has attained the age of 65 years and who for the greater part of the year of assessment in which the expenditure is incurred lives alone;

“qualifying period” means the period beginning on the 23rd day of January, 1996, and ending on the 5th day of April, 1998;

“relative”, in relation to a qualifying individual, includes a relation by marriage and a person in respect of whom the individual is or was the legal guardian;

“relevant alarm system” means an electrical apparatus which when activated is designed to give notice to the effect that there is an intruder present or attempting to enter the premises in which it is installed.

(2) Where a claimant, being a qualifying individual or a relative of that individual, having made a claim in that behalf, proves that he or she has incurred qualifying expenditure in relation to the qualifying individual, the income tax to be charged on the claimant, other than in accordance with section 16(2), for the year of assessment in which the expenditure is incurred shall be reduced by an amount which is the least of—

(*a*) the appropriate percentage of the qualifying expenditure,

(*b*) the appropriate percentage of [€1,015.79][1], and

(*c*) the amount which reduces that income tax to nil.

(3) Any claim for relief under this section shall be in such form as may be prescribed by the Revenue Commissioners for the purpose and shall be accompanied by a receipt or receipts, as may be appropriate, for the amount of qualifying expenditure incurred; but, where the qualifying expenditure includes expenditure in respect of installation, the receipt in respect of such expenditure shall contain the installer’s name and address and the installer’s value-added tax registration number or income tax reference number.

(4) Any deduction made under this section shall be in substitution for and not in addition to any deduction to which the individual might be entitled in respect of the same payment under any other provision of the Income Tax Acts.

Amendments

[1] Substituted by FA 2001 s 240(1) and (2)(*a*) and Sch 5 Pt 1 for 2002 and later tax years; previously "£800".

Cross-references

Deductions allowed in ascertaining taxable income: ss 458(2), 459(1)- (2).
Method of apportioning reliefs and charging tax in cases of separate assessment: s 1024(2)(*a*)(ix).
Rate of tax at which repayments are to be made: s 460.

Revenue precedents

Issue: Whether the provisions in TCA 1997 s 478 could be extended, by concession, to an elderly married couple, living together.
Decision: Relief may only be allowed to individuals aged 65 and up, who live alone.

Revenue information

Information leaflet IT33 — Tax Relief for Home Alarms.

Definitions

Income Tax Acts: s 1(2); person: IA 1937 s 11(*c*); year of assessment: ss 2(1), 5(1); standard rate: ss 3(1), 15; tax: s 3(1).

Former enactments

FA 1996 s 5.

479 Relief for new shares purchased on issue by employees

(1) (*a*) In this section—

"director" has the same meaning as in Chapter 3 of Part 5;

"eligible employee", in relation to a qualifying company, means—

(i) where the company is a trading company, a director or an employee of the company, or

(ii) where the company is a holding company, a director or an employee of the company or of a company which is its 75 per cent subsidiary;

"eligible shares", in relation to a qualifying company, means new shares forming part of the ordinary share capital of the company which—

(i) are fully paid up,

(ii) throughout [the period of 3 years][1] beginning with the date on which they are issued, carry no present or future preferential right to dividends or to the company's assets on its winding up and no present or future preferential right to be redeemed,

(iii) are not subject to any restrictions other than restrictions which attach to all shares of the same class, and

(iv) are issued to and acquired by an eligible employee in relation to the company at not less than their market value at the time of issue;

"holding company" means a company whose business consists wholly or mainly of the holding of shares or securities of trading companies which are its 75 per cent subsidiaries;

"market value" shall be construed in accordance with section 548;

"qualifying company" means a company which at the time the eligible shares are issued is—

(i) incorporated in the State,

(ii) resident in the State and not resident elsewhere, and

(iii) (I) a trading company, or

(II) a holding company;

"trading company" means a company whose business consists wholly or mainly of the carrying on wholly or mainly in the State of a trade or trades;

"75 per cent subsidiary", in relation to a company, has the meaning assigned to it for the purposes of the Corporation Tax Acts by section 9, as applied for the purposes of section 411 by paragraphs (*b*) and (*c*) of subsection (1) of that section.

(*b*) References in this section to a disposal of shares include references to a disposal of an interest or right in or over the shares, and an individual shall be treated for the purposes of this section as disposing of any shares which he or she is treated by virtue of section 587 as exchanging for other shares.

(*c*) Shares in a company shall not be treated for the purposes of this section as being of the same class unless they would be so treated if dealt in on a stock exchange in the State.

(2) Subject to this section, where an eligible employee in relation to a qualifying company subscribes for eligible shares in the qualifying company, the eligible employee shall be entitled to have a deduction made from his or her total income for the year of assessment in which the shares are issued of an amount equal to the amount of the subscription; but a deduction shall not be given to the extent to which the amount subscribed by an eligible employee for eligible shares issued to him or her in all years of assessment exceeds [€6,350][2].

(3) Subsection (2) shall not apply as respects any amount subscribed for eligible shares if within [the period of 3 years][3] from the date of their acquisition—

(*a*) those shares are disposed of, or

(*b*) the eligible employee who made the subscription receives in respect of those shares any money or money's worth which does not constitute income in his or her hands for the purpose of income tax,

and there shall be made all such assessments, additional assessments or adjustments of assessments as are necessary to withdraw any relief from income tax already given under subsection (2) in respect of the amount subscribed ...[4].

(4) Except where the shares are in a company whose ordinary share capital, at the time of acquisition of the shares by the eligible employee, consists of shares of one class only, the majority of the issued shares of the same class as the eligible shares shall be shares other than—

(*a*) eligible shares, and

(*b*) shares held by persons who acquired their shares in pursuance of a right conferred on them or an opportunity afforded to them as a director or employee of the qualifying company or any of its 75 per cent subsidiaries.

[(5) In relation to shares in respect of which relief has been given under subsection (2) and not withdrawn, any question—

(*a*) as to which (if any) such shares issued to an eligible employee at different times a disposal relates, or

(*b*) as to whether a disposal relates to such shares or to other shares,

shall for the purposes of this section be determined as it would be determined for the purposes of section 498 but without regard to the reference in subsection (4) (as amended by the Finance Act, 1998) of that section to subsection (3) of this section.][5]

(6) Where there occurs in relation to any of the eligible shares of an eligible employee (in this subsection referred to as **"the original holding"**) a transaction which results in a new holding (within the meaning of section 584) being equated with the original holding for the purposes of capital gains tax, then, for the purposes of subsection (3)—

(*a*) the new holding shall be treated as shares in respect of which relief under this section has been given,

(*b*) the transaction shall not be treated as involving a disposal of the original holding,

(*c*) the consideration for the disposal of the original holding to the extent that it consists of the new holding shall not be treated as money or money's worth, and

(*d*) a disposal of the whole or a part of the new holding shall be treated as a disposal of the whole or a corresponding part of the shares in respect of which relief has been given under this section.

(7) Any amount in respect of which relief is allowed under subsection (2) and not withdrawn shall be treated as a sum which by virtue of section 554 is to be excluded from the sums allowable under section 552.

(8) An eligible employee shall not be entitled to relief under subsection (2) in respect of any shares unless the shares are subscribed for and issued for bona fide commercial reasons and not as part of a scheme or arrangement the main purpose or one of the main purposes of which is the avoidance of tax.

Amendments

1 Substituted by FA 1998 s 11(1)(*a*) as on and from 12 February 1998; previously "the period of 5 years".

2 Substituted by FA 2001 s 240(1) and (2)(*a*) and Sch 5 Pt 1 for 2002 and later tax years; previously "£5,000".

3 Substituted by FA 1998 s 11(1)(*b*)(i) as on and from 12 February 1998; previously "the period of 5 years".

4 Deleted by FA 1998 s 11(1)(*b*)(ii) as on and from 12 February 1998.

5 Subs (5) substituted by FA 1998 s 11(1)(*c*) as and from 12 February 1998.

Cross-references

BES relief, disposal of shares, subs (3): s 498(4).
BES relief, no double relief: s 489(13).
Deductions allowed in ascertaining taxable income: ss 458(2), 459(1)–(2).
Method of apportioning reliefs and charging tax in cases of separate assessment: s 1024(2)(*a*)(ix).
Rate of tax at which repayments are to be made: s 460.

Definitions

company: ss 4(1), 5(1); Corporation Tax Acts: s 1(2); Income Tax Acts: s 1(2); ordinary share capital: s 2(1); person: IA 1937 s 11(*c*); shares: s 5(1); total income: s 3(1); trade: s 3(1); year of assessment: ss 2(1), 5(1).

Former enactments

FA 1986 s 12(1)–(8); FA 1996 s 12 and s 132(1) and Sch 5 Pt I para 15.

480 Relief for certain sums chargeable under Schedule E

(1) (*a*) In this section—

"director" and **"proprietary director"** have the same meanings respectively as in section 472;

"employee", in relation to a body corporate, includes any person taking part in the management of the affairs of the body corporate who is not a director, and includes a person who is to be or has been an employee;

"part-time director", in relation to a body corporate, means a director who is not required to devote substantially the whole of his or her time to the service of the body corporate;

"proprietary employee", in relation to a company, means an employee who is the beneficial owner of, or able, either directly or through the medium of other companies or by any other indirect means, to control, more than 15 per cent of the ordinary share capital of the company.

(*b*) For the purposes of the definitions of **"proprietary director"** and **"proprietary employee"**, ordinary share capital which is owned or controlled as referred to in those definitions by a person, being a spouse or a minor child of a director or employee, or by a trustee of a trust for the benefit of a person or persons, being or including any such person or such director or employee, shall be deemed to be owned or controlled by such director or employee and not by any other person.

(2) (*a*) Subject to paragraph (*b*), this section shall apply to any payment which is chargeable to tax under Schedule E and made to the holder of an office or employment to compensate for—

(i) a reduction or a possible reduction of future remuneration arising from a reorganisation of the business of the employer under whom the office or employment is held or a change in the working procedures, working methods, duties or rates of remuneration of such office or employment, or

(ii) a change in the place where the duties of the office or employment are performed.

(*b*) This section shall not apply to—

(i) a payment to which section 123 applies, or

(ii) a payment to—

(I) a proprietary director,

(II) a part-time director,

(III) a proprietary employee, or

(IV) a person who is a part-time employee by reason of not being required to devote substantially the whole of his or her time to the service of his or her employer.

(3) Where an individual has received a payment to which this section applies, the individual shall be entitled, on making a claim in that behalf and on proof of the relevant facts to the satisfaction of the inspector, to have the total amount of income tax payable

by the individual for the year of assessment for which the payment is chargeable reduced to the total of the following amounts—

(*a*) the amount of income tax which would have been payable by him or her for that year if he or she had not received the payment, and

(*b*) income tax on the whole of the payment at the rate ascertained in the manner specified in subsection (4).

(4) There shall be ascertained the additional income tax, over and above the amount referred to in subsection (3)(*a*), which would have been payable by the holder of the office or employment if his or her total income for the year of assessment referred to in subsection (3) had included one-third only of the payment, and the rate of income tax for the purposes of subsection (3)(*b*) shall then be ascertained by dividing the additional income tax computed in accordance with this subsection by an amount equal to one-third of the payment.

(5) (*a*) Relief from tax under this section shall in all cases be given by means of repayment.

(*b*) A claimant shall not be entitled to relief under this section in respect of any income the tax on which he or she is entitled to charge against any other person, or to deduct, retain or satisfy out of any payment which he or she is liable to make to any other person.

Cross-references

Exemption in respect of certain payments under employment law, subs (2)(*a*): s 192A(5)(*b*).

Definitions

inspector: ss 2(1), 5(1), 852; person: IA 1937 s 11(*c*); total income: s 3(1); year of assessment: ss 2(1), 5(1).

Former enactments

FA 1968 s 3; FA 1974 ss 11, 64(2) and Sch 1 Pt II; FA 1997 s 146(1) and Sch 9 Pt I para 5(3).

480A Relief on retirement for certain income of certain sportspersons

[(1) In this section "basis period", in relation to a year of assessment, means the period on the profits or gains of which income tax for the year of assessment is to be finally computed under the Income Tax Acts.

(2) Notwithstanding any other provision of the Income Tax Acts other than section 1006A, this section applies where in the year of assessment 2002 or any subsequent year of assessment an individual (in this section referred to as the "relevant individual") who is resident in the State for that year of assessment and engaged in an occupation (in this section referred to as the "specified occupation"), or carries on a profession (in this section referred to as the "specified profession"), specified in Schedule 23A proves to the satisfaction of the Revenue Commissioners that he or she has in that year of assessment ceased permanently to be engaged in the specified occupation or to carry on the specified profession, as the case may be.

(3) Where this section applies, the relevant individual shall, on the making of a claim in that behalf, be entitled to have a deduction made from his or her total income for up to any 10 of the years of assessment mentioned in subsection (4).

(4) The years of assessment referred to in subsection (3) are the year of assessment in which the relevant individual ceases permanently to be engaged in the specified occupation or to carry on the specified profession, as the case may be, and any previous

year of assessment not being earlier than the year of assessment 1990–91, for which the relevant individual was resident in the State.

(5) The amount of the deduction to be made under subsection (3) for any year of assessment shall be an amount equal to 40 per cent of the receipts, before deducting expenses, of the relevant individual for the basis period for that year of assessment which arose wholly and exclusively from the engagement of the relevant individual in the specified occupation or from the carrying on by the relevant individual of the specified profession, as the case may be.

(6) For the purposes of subsection (5), receipts shall be regarded as deriving wholly and exclusively from the engagement of the relevant individual in the specified occupation or from the carrying on by the relevant individual of the specified profession, as the case may be, only to the extent that such receipts derive directly from the actual participation by the relevant individual in the sport associated with the specified occupation or the specified profession, and accordingly—

(*a*) include—

(i) where the relevant individual is an employee, so much of all salaries, fees, wages, bonuses or perquisites paid to the relevant individual by his or her employer as a direct consequence of the participation by the relevant individual in the sport associated with the specified occupation, and

(ii) where the relevant individual carries on the specified profession, all match or performance fees, prize moneys and appearance moneys paid to the relevant individual by any other person as a direct consequence of the participation of the relevant individual in the sport associated with the specified profession,

but

(*b*) do not include—

(i) sponsorship moneys received by the relevant individual, or

(ii) receipts received by the relevant individual for participation in advertisements, promotions, videos or television or radio programmes, or for personal appearances or interviews, newspaper or magazine articles, or for the right to use the individual's image or name to promote or endorse products or services or in any other manner.

(7) A claim under this section shall be included in the return of income to be made by the relevant individual for the year of assessment in which the relevant individual ceases permanently to be engaged in the specified occupation, or to carry on the specified profession, as the case may be.

(8) (*a*) Relief from income tax under this section shall in all cases be given by means of repayment.

(*b*) Any repayment of income tax due under this section shall not carry interest.

(*c*) Relief under this section for any year of assessment shall not create or augment a loss for that year of assessment for the purposes of Chapter 1 of Part 12.

(9) A deduction given under this section for any year of assessment shall not be taken into account in determining the net relevant earnings (within the meaning of section 787) of the relevant individual for that year of assessment.

(10) Where any relief has been given to a relevant individual under this section and the relevant individual subsequently recommences to be engaged in the specified occupation or to carry on the specified profession, as the case may be, that relief shall be withdrawn by making an assessment to income tax under Case IV of Schedule D for the year of assessment for which that relief was given and, notwithstanding anything in the Income Tax Acts, such an assessment may be made at any time.][1]

Amendments

[1] Section 480A inserted by FA 2002 s 12 with effect from 1 January 2002.

Tax Briefing

TB47 April 2002 p 9 — Relief from Income Tax in respect of certain earnings of sportspersons.

Definitions

Income Tax Acts: s 1(2); profession: s 2(1); resident: s 2(1); total income: s 3(1); year of assessment: s 2(1).

CHAPTER 2

Income Tax and Corporation Tax: Reliefs Applicable to Both

481 Relief for investment in films

(1) In this section—

"allowable investor company", in relation to a qualifying company, means a company which is not connected with the qualifying company;

"authorised officer" means an officer of the Revenue Commissioners authorised by them in writing for the purposes of this section;

[**"eligible individual"** means an individual who is a citizen of Ireland or of another Member State of the European Communities, or an individual domiciled, resident or ordinarily resident in the State or in another Member State of the European Communities;][1]

"film" means—

[(*a*) a film of a kind which is included within the categories of films eligible for certification by the Revenue Commissioners under subsection (2A), as specified in regulations made under subsection (2E), and][2]

(*b*) [as respects every film],[3] a film which is produced—

(i) on a commercial basis with a view to the realisation of profit, and

(ii) wholly or principally for exhibition to the public in cinemas or by means of television broadcasting,

but does not include a film made for exhibition as an advertising programme or as a commercial;

"the Minister" means the Minister for [Arts, Sport and Tourism][4];

[**"qualifying company"** means a company which—

(*a*) (i) is incorporated and resident in the State, or

(ii) is carrying on a trade in the State through a branch or agency,

(*b*) exists solely for the purposes of the production and distribution of only one qualifying film, and (*c*) does not contain in its name—

(i) registered under either or both the Companies Acts, 1963 to 1999, and the Registration of Business Names Act, 1963, or

(ii) registered under the law of the territory in which it is incorporated,

the words "Ireland", "Irish", "Éireann", "Éire" or "National";][5]

[**"qualifying film"** means a film in respect of which the Revenue Commissioners have issued a certificate under subsection (2A), which has not been revoked under subsection (2D);][6]

"qualifying individual", in relation to a qualifying company, means an individual who is not connected with the company;

[**"qualifying period"**, in relation to an allowable investor company and a qualifying individual, means the period commencing on 23 January 1996, and ending on [31 December 2008][7];][8]

"relevant deduction" means a deduction of an amount equal to 80 per cent of a relevant investment;

"relevant investment" means a sum of money which is—

(*a*) paid in the qualifying period to a qualifying company in respect of shares in the company by an allowable investor company on its own behalf or by a qualifying individual on that individual's own behalf, and is paid by the allowable investor company or by the qualifying individual, as the case may be, directly to the qualifying company,

[(*b*) paid by the allowable investor company or the qualifying individual, as the case may be, for the purposes of enabling the qualifying company to produce a film in respect of which, at the time such sum of money is paid, the authorised officer has given notice in writing to the qualifying company that the Revenue Commissioners are satisfied for the time being that an application in writing, in the form prescribed by the Revenue Commissioners and containing such information as may be specified in regulations made under subsection (2E), has been made to enable the Revenue Commissioners to consider whether a certificate should be issued to that company under subsection (2A), and][9]

(*c*) used by the qualifying company within 2 years of the receipt of that sum for those purposes,

but does not include a sum of money paid to the qualifying company on terms which provide that it will be repaid, [other than a provision for its repayment in the event of the Revenue Commissioners not giving a certificate under subsection (2A)][10], and a reference to the making of a relevant investment shall be construed as a reference to the payment of such a sum to a qualifying company.

(2) [(*a*) The Minister, on request from the Revenue Commissioners following an application to them by a qualifying company for a certificate under subsection (2A) in relation to a film to be produced by the company, may subject to paragraph (*b*) and in accordance with regulations made under subsection (2E), give authorisation to the Revenue Commissioners that they may, subject to subsection (2A), issue a certificate under that subsection to the qualifying company in relation to that film.

(*b*) In considering whether to give the authorisation referred to in paragraph (*a*), the Minister, in accordance with regulations made under subsection (2E), shall have regard to—

(i) the categories of films eligible for certification by the Revenue Commissioners under subsection (2A), as specified in those regulations, and

(ii) any contribution which the production of the film is expected to make to either or both the development of the film industry in the State and the promotion and expression of Irish culture,

and where such authorisation is given, the Minister, having regard to those matters, shall specify in the authorisation such conditions, as the Minister may consider proper, including a condition—

...][11]

(II) in relation to—

(A) the employment and responsibility of the producer, and the producer company, of a film for the production of that film, and

(B) the employment of personnel, including trainees, (other than the producer) for the production of that film.][12]

[(*c*) The specified percentage shall not exceed—

(i) where the total cost of production of the film does not exceed [€5,080,000][13], 66 per cent,

(ii) where the total cost of production of the film exceeds [€5,080,000][13] and does not exceed [€6,350,000][14], the amount per cent (in this subparagraph referred to as the "allowable percentage") where the amount of the allowable percentage is determined by the formula—

$$[66 - \frac{(11 \times E)}{€1,270,000]^{15}}$$

where E is the excess of the total cost of production of the film over [€5,080,000][13], and

(iii) where the total cost of production of the film exceeds [€6,350,000][14], 55 per cent;

but, in any case to which subparagraph (i), (ii) or (iii) relates, the total cost of production of the film which is met by relevant investments shall not exceed [€15,000,000][16].][17]

...[18]

[(2A)(*a*) Subject to the provisions of this subsection, the Revenue Commissioners, on the making of an application by a qualifying company, may, in accordance with regulations made under subsection (2E), issue a certificate to a qualifying company stating, in relation to a film to be produced by the company, that the film may be treated as a qualifying film for the purpose of this section.

(*b*) The Revenue Commissioners shall not issue a certificate under paragraph (*a*) unless given authorisation that they may do so by the Minister under subsection (2)(*a*).

(*c*) Nothing in this section shall be construed as obliging the Revenue Commissioners to issue a certificate under paragraph (*a*) and in any case where, in relation to a film, the principal photography has commenced, the first animation drawings have commenced or the first model movement has commenced, as the case may be, before application is made by a qualifying company, the Revenue Commissioners shall not issue a certificate under that paragraph.

(*d*) An application for a certificate under paragraph (*a*) shall be in the form prescribed by the Revenue Commissioners and shall contain such information as may be specified in regulations made under subsection (2E).

(*e*) In considering whether to issue a certificate under paragraph (*a*) the Revenue Commissioners shall, in respect of the proposed production of the film, examine all aspects of the qualifying company's proposal.

(*f*) The Revenue Commissioners may refuse to issue a certificate under paragraph (*a*) if they are not satisfied with any aspect of the qualifying company's application and, in particular, the Revenue Commissioners may refuse to issue a certificate—

(i) if they have reason to believe that the budget or any particular item of proposed expenditure in the budget is inflated, or

(ii) where—

(I) they are not satisfied that there is a commercial rationale for the corporate structure proposed—

(A) for the production, financing, distribution or sale of the film, or

(B) for all of those purposes,

or

(II) they are of the opinion that the corporate structure proposed would hinder the Revenue Commissioners in verifying compliance with any of the provisions governing the relief.

(*g*) A certificate issued by the Revenue Commissioners under paragraph (*a*) shall be subject to such conditions specified in the certificate as the Revenue Commissioners may consider proper, having regard, in particular, to the examination referred to in paragraph (*e*) and any conditions specified in the authorisation given by the Minister under subsection (2)(*a*), and in particular the Revenue Commissioners shall specify in the certificate a condition—

...[19]

(ii) in relation to the matters specified by the Minister in the authorisation by virtue of subsection (2)(*b*)(II),

(iii) subject to subsection (2)(*c*), that the amount per cent of the total cost of production of the film which may be met by relevant investments shall not exceed [the amount per cent (in subsection (2)(*c*) referred to as "the specified percentage") specified in the certificate][20],

[(iv) in relation to the minimum amount of money to be expended on the production of the qualifying film–

(I) directly by the qualifying company on the employment, by the company, of eligible individuals, in so far as those individuals exercise their employment in the State in the production of the qualifying film, and

(II) directly or indirectly by the qualifying company, on the provision of certain goods, services and facilities, as set out in regulations made under subsection (2E),][21]

[(v) where financial arrangements have been approved by the Revenue Commissioners in accordance with subsection (2C)(*ba*), in relation to any matter pertaining to those arrangements.][22]

(*h*) The Revenue Commissioners, having consulted with the Minister as appropriate, may amend or revoke any condition (including a condition added by virtue of this paragraph) specified in the certificate, or add to such conditions, by giving notice in writing to the qualifying company concerned of the amendment, revocation or addition, and this section shall apply as if—

(i) a condition so amended or added by the notice was specified in the certificate, and

(ii) a condition so revoked was not specified in the certificate.

(2B) In carrying out their functions under this section the Revenue Commissioners may—

(*a*) consult with any person, agency or body of persons, as in their opinion may be of assistance to them, and

(*b*) notwithstanding any obligation as to secrecy or other restriction on the disclosure of information imposed by, or under, the Tax Acts or any other statute or otherwise, disclose any detail in a qualifying company's application which they consider necessary for the purposes of such consultation.

(2C) A company shall not be regarded as a qualifying company for the purposes of this section—

(*a*) unless the company, in relation to a qualifying film, notifies the Revenue Commissioners in writing immediately when the principal photography has commenced, the first animation drawings have commenced or the first model movement has commenced, as appropriate,

(*b*) [subject to paragraph (*ba*),][23] if the financial arrangements which the company enters into in relation to the qualifying film are—

(i) financial arrangements of any type with a person resident, registered or operating in a territory other than—

(I) a Member State of the European Communities, or

(II) a territory with the government of which, arrangements having the force of law by virtue of section 826(1)(*a*), have been made,

or

(ii) financial arrangements under which funds are channelled, directly or indirectly, to, or through, a territory other than a territory referred to in clause (I) or (II) of subparagraph (i), [(*ba*) (i) Paragraph (*b*) shall not apply to financial arrangements in relation to a transaction or series of transactions, where such arrangements have been approved by the Revenue Commissioners.

(ii) The Revenue Commissioners shall not approve financial arrangements, to which paragraph (*b*) would, but for this paragraph, apply unless:

(I) the arrangements relate to either or both—

(A) an investment made in a qualifying film, and

(B) the filming of part of a film in a territory other than a territory referred to in clause (I) or (II) of paragraph (*b*)(i),

(II) a request for approval is made by the qualifying company to the Revenue Commissioners before such arrangements are effected,

(III) the qualifying company demonstrates to the satisfaction of the Revenue Commissioners that it can provide, if requested, sufficient records to enable the Revenue Commissioners to verify—

(A) in the case of an investment, the amount of the investment made in the qualifying company and the person who made the investment, and

(B) in the case of filming in a territory, the amount of each item of expenditure on the production of the qualifying film expended in the territory, whether expended by the qualifying company or by any other person, and

(IV) they are satisfied that it is appropriate to grant such approval.

(iii) In considering whether to grant an approval under this paragraph in relation to financial arrangements, the Revenue Commissioners may seek any information they consider appropriate in relation to the arrangements or in relation to any person who is, directly or indirectly, a party to the arrangements.

(iv) Where the Revenue Commissioners have approved financial arrangements in accordance with this paragraph, no amount of money expended, either directly or indirectly, as part of the arrangements may be regarded, for the purposes of subsection (2A)(*g*)(iv), as an amount of money expended on either the employment of eligible individuals or on the provision of goods, services and facilities as referred to in that subsection.][24]

(*c*) unless the company provides, when requested to do so by the Revenue Commissioners, for the purposes of verifying compliance with the provisions governing the relief or with any condition specified in a certificate issued by them under subsection (2A)(*a*), evidence to vouch each item of expenditure in the State or elsewhere on the production and distribution of the qualifying film, whether expended by the qualifying company or by any other person engaged, directly or indirectly, by the qualifying company to provide goods, services or facilities in relation to such production or distribution and, in particular, such evidence shall include—

(i) records required to be kept or retained by the company by virtue of section 886, and

(ii) records, in relation to the production and distribution of the qualifying film, required to be kept or retained by that other person by virtue of section 886, or which would be so required if that other person were subject to the provisions of that section,

and

(*d*) unless the company, within such time as is specified in the regulations made under subsection (2E)—

(i) notifies the Revenue Commissioners in writing of the date of completion of the production of the qualifying film,

(ii) provides to the Revenue Commissioners and to the Minister, such number of copies of the film in such format and manner as may be specified in those regulations, and

(iii) provides to the Revenue Commissioners, a compliance report, in such format and manner specified in those regulations, which proves to the satisfaction of the Revenue Commissioners that—

(I) the provisions of this section in so far as they apply in relation to the company and a qualifying film have been met, and

(II) any conditions attaching to a certificate issued to the company in relation to a qualifying film under subsection (2A)(*a*) have been fulfilled.

(2D) Where a company fails—

(*a*) to comply with any of the provisions of subsection (2C) or any other provision governing the relief, or

(*b*) to fulfil any of the conditions to which a certificate issued to it under paragraph (*a*) of subsection (2A) is subject, by virtue of paragraph (*g*) or (*h*) of that subsection,

that failure shall constitute the failure of an event to happen by reason of which relief may be withdrawn under subsection (11) and the Revenue Commissioners may, by notice in writing served by registered post on the company, revoke the certificate.

(2E) The Revenue Commissioners with the consent of the Minister for Finance, and with the consent of the Minister in relation to the matters to be considered regarding the issue of an authorisation under subsection (2), shall make regulations with respect to the administration by them of the relief under this section and with respect to the matters to be considered by the Minister for the purposes of that subsection and, without prejudice to the generality of the foregoing, regulations under this subsection may include provision—

(*a*) governing the application for certification pursuant to subsection (2A) and the information and documents to be provided in or with such application,

(*b*) specifying the categories of films eligible for certification by the Revenue Commissioners under subsection (2A),

(*c*) prescribing the form of such application,

(*d*) governing the records that a qualifying company shall maintain or provide to the Revenue Commissioners,

(*e*) governing the period for which, and the place at which, such records shall be maintained, (*f*) specifying the time within which a qualifying company shall notify the Revenue Commissioners of the completion of the production of a qualifying film,

(*g*) specifying the time within which, and the format, number and manner in which, copies of a qualifying film shall be provided to the Revenue Commissioners and to the Minister,

(*h*) specifying the form and content of the compliance report to be provided to the Revenue Commissioners, the manner in which such report shall be made and verified, the documents to accompany the report and the time within which such report shall be provided,

(*i*) governing the type of expenditure which may be accepted by the Revenue Commissioners as expenditure on the production of a qualifying film,

(*j*) governing the provision of the goods, services and facilities referred to in subsection (2A)(*g*)(iv)(II), including the place of origin of those goods, services and facilities, the place in which they are provided and the location of the supplier,

(*k*) specifying the currency exchange rate to be applied to expenditure on the production of a qualifying film, ...[25]

(*l*) specifying the criteria to be considered by the Minister, in relation to the matters referred to in subsections (2)(*b*)(i) and (ii)—

(i) in deciding whether to give authorisation to the Revenue Commissioners under subsection (2)(*a*), and

(ii) in specifying conditions in such authorisation, as provided for in subsection (2)(*b*),

and the information required for those purposes to be included in the application made to the Revenue Commissioners under subsection (2A) by a qualifying company.][26]

[(*m*) governing the approval of financial arrangements in accordance with subsection (2C)(*ba*), and

(*n*) governing the employment of eligible individuals, as referred to in subsection (2A)(*g*)(iv), and the circumstances in which expenditure by a qualifying company would be regarded as expenditure on the employment of those individuals in the production of a qualifying film.][27]

(3) Subject to this section, where in an accounting period an allowable investor company makes a relevant investment, it shall, on making a claim in that behalf, be given a relevant deduction from its total profits for the accounting period; but, where the amount of the relevant deduction to which the allowable investor company is entitled under this section in an accounting period exceeds its profits for that accounting period, an amount equal to 125 per cent of the amount of that excess shall be carried forward to the succeeding accounting period and the amount so carried forward shall be treated for the purposes of this section as if it were a relevant investment made in that succeeding accounting period.

(4) (*a*) [Subject to paragraph (*b*), where in the period—

(I) being a period of 12 months (in paragraph (*b*) referred to as a "12 month period") ending on an anniversary of the 22nd day of January, 1996, or

(II) commencing on the 23rd day of January, 1999, and ending on the 5th day of April, 2000 (in paragraph (*b*) referred to as the "specified period"),

the amount or the aggregate amount of the relevant investments made,][28] by an allowable investor company, or by such company and all companies (which other companies are referred to in paragraph (*b*) as **"connected companies"**) which at any time in that period would be regarded as connected with such company, exceeds [€10,160,000][29]—

(i) no relief shall be given under this section in respect of the amount of the excess, and

(ii) where there is more than one relevant investment, the inspector or, on appeal, the Appeal Commissioners shall make such apportionment of the relief available as shall be just and reasonable to allocate to each relevant investment a due proportion of the relief available and, where necessary, to grant to each allowable investor company concerned an amount of relief proportionate to the amount of the relevant investment or the aggregate amount of the relevant investments made by it in the period.

(*b*) No relief shall be given under this section in respect of the amount or the aggregate amount of the relevant investments (in this paragraph referred to as **"the total amount"**) made by an allowable investor company and its connected companies—

(i) to the extent that the amount of the relevant investment, or the total amount made in any one qualifying company, exceeds [€3,810,000][30], and

(ii) where in any 12 month period [, or in the specified period,][31] the total amount exceeds [€3,810,000][30], to the extent that the excess comprises a relevant investment or relevant investments made in a qualifying company to enable the company to produce a film, the total cost of production of which exceeds [€5,080,000][32].

(5) Subject to this section, where in any year of assessment a qualifying individual makes a relevant investment, the individual shall, on making a claim in that behalf, be given a relevant deduction from his or her total income for that year of assessment.

(6) A relevant deduction shall not be given under this section in respect of any relevant investment made by a qualifying individual in a qualifying company in any year of assessment unless the amount of that relevant investment or the total amount of the relevant investments made by the individual in the qualifying company in that year is [€250][33] or more and, for the purposes of this section in the case of a qualifying individual who is married and is assessed to tax for a year of assessment in accordance with section 1017, any relevant investment made by the qualifying individual's spouse in the qualifying company in that year of assessment shall be deemed to have been made by the qualifying individual.

(7) A relevant deduction shall not be given to a qualifying individual under this section for a year of assessment to the extent to which the amount of the relevant investment or the total amount of the relevant investments (whether or not made in the same qualifying company) made or treated as made by the individual in that year of assessment exceeds [€31,750][34].

(8) Where for any year of assessment a greater relevant deduction would be given to a qualifying individual under this section but for either or both of the following reasons—

(*a*) an insufficiency of total income, or

(*b*) the operation of subsection (7),

then, 125 per cent of the relevant deduction which cannot be given to the individual under this section for either or both of those reasons shall be carried forward to the next year of assessment and shall be treated for the purposes of this section as a relevant investment made by the individual in that next year; but an amount shall not be carried forward to any year of assessment after [the year of assessment 2008].[35]

(9) To the extent that an amount once carried forward to a year of assessment under subsection (8) (and treated as a relevant investment made by a qualifying individual in that year of assessment) gives rise to a relevant deduction which is not deducted from the qualifying individual's total income for that year of assessment, the amount shall to that extent be carried forward again to the next year of assessment (and treated as a relevant investment made by the individual in that next year), and so on for succeeding years of assessment; but an amount shall not be carried forward to any year of assessment after [the year of assessment 2008].[36]

(10) A relevant deduction under this section shall be given to a qualifying individual for any year of assessment as follows—

(*a*) in the first instance, in respect of an amount of relevant investment carried forward from an earlier year of assessment in accordance with subsection (8) or (9), and, in respect of such an amount so carried forward, for an earlier year of assessment in priority to a later year of assessment, and

(*b*) only thereafter, in respect of any other amount of relevant investment in respect of which a relevant deduction is to be given in that year of assessment.

(11)(*a*) A claim to relief under this section may be allowed at any time after the time specified in paragraph (*b*) in respect of the payment of a sum to a qualifying company, which, if it is used, within 2 years of its being paid, by the qualifying company for the production of a qualifying film, will be a relevant investment, if all the conditions for relief are or will be satisfied; but the relief shall be withdrawn if, by reason of the happening of any subsequent event including [the revocation, under subsection (2D), by the Revenue Commissioners of a certificate issued by them under subsection (2A)][37] or the failure of an event to happen which at the time the relief was given was expected to happen, the company or the individual, as the case may be, making the claim was not entitled to the relief allowed.

(*b*) The time referred to in paragraph (*a*) is the time when all of the following events have occurred—

(i) the payment in respect of which relief is claimed has been made, and

(ii) in relation to the qualifying film the principal photography has commenced, the first animation drawings have commenced or the first model movement has commenced, as appropriate.

(12) A claim for relief in respect of a relevant investment in a company shall not be allowed unless it is accompanied by a certificate issued by the company in such form as

the Revenue Commissioners may direct and certifying that the conditions for the relief, in so far as they apply to the company and the qualifying film, are or will be satisfied in relation to that investment.

(13) Before issuing a certificate for the purposes of subsection (12), a company shall furnish the authorised officer with—

(*a*) a statement to the effect that it satisfies or will satisfy the conditions for the relief in so far as they apply in relation to the company and a film,

...[38]

(*d*) such other information as the Revenue Commissioners may reasonably require.

[(14)(*a*) A certificate referred to in subsection (12) shall not be issued without the approval in writing of the authorised officer and where the authorised officer has not received the information sought under subsection (13)(*d*), or has reason to believe that the conditions for the relief are not, or will not be, satisfied, the authorised officer shall not give such approval.

(*b*) Where, in accordance with paragraph (*a*), the authorised officer does not give the approval referred to in that paragraph, the officer shall issue a determination to that effect and the provisions of section 949 shall apply to such determination as if it were a determination made on a matter referred to in section 864.][39]

(15) Any statement under subsection (13) shall—

(*a*) contain such information as the Revenue Commissioners may reasonably require,

(*b*) be in such form as the Revenue Commissioners may direct, and

(*c*) contain a declaration that it is correct to the best of the company's knowledge and belief.

(16) Where a company has issued a certificate for the purposes of subsection (12) or furnished a statement under subsection (13) and either—

(*a*) the certificate or statement was made fraudulently or negligently, or

(*b*) the certificate was issued in contravention of subsection (14),

then—

(i) the company shall be liable to a penalty not exceeding [€630][40] or, in the case of fraud, not exceeding [€1,265][41], and such penalty may, without prejudice to any other method of recovery, be proceeded for and recovered summarily in the like manner as in summary proceedings for the recovery of any fine or penalty under any Act relating to the excise, and

(ii) no relief shall be given under this section and, if any such relief has been given, it shall be withdrawn.

(17) For the purpose of regulations made under section 986, no regard shall be had to the relief unless a claim for it has been duly made and admitted.

(18) An allowable investor company or a qualifying individual shall not be entitled to relief in respect of a relevant investment unless the relevant investment—

(*a*) has been made for bona fide commercial reasons and not as part of a scheme or arrangement the main purpose or one of the main purposes of which is the avoidance of tax,

(*b*) has been or will be used in the production of a qualifying film, and

(*c*) is made at the risk of the allowable investor company or the qualifying individual, as the case may be, and—

(i) in a case where it is made by an allowable investor company, neither the company nor any person who would be regarded as connected with the company, or

(ii) in a case where it is made by a qualifying individual, neither the individual nor any person who would be regarded as connected with the individual,

is entitled to receive any payment in money or money's worth or other benefit directly or indirectly borne by or attributable to the qualifying company, other than a payment made on an arm's length basis for goods or services supplied or a payment out of the proceeds of exploiting the film to which the allowable investor company or the qualifying individual, as the case may be, is entitled under the terms subject to which the relevant investment is made.

(19) Where any relief has been given under this section which is subsequently found not to have been due or is to be withdrawn by virtue of subsection (11) or (16), that relief shall be withdrawn by making an assessment to corporation tax or income tax, as the case may be, under Case IV of Schedule D for the accounting period or accounting periods, or the year of assessment or years of assessment, as the case may be, in which relief was given and, notwithstanding anything in the Tax Acts, such an assessment may be made at any time.

(20)(*a*) In this subsection, **"new ordinary shares"** means new ordinary shares forming part of the ordinary share capital of a qualifying company which, throughout the period of one year commencing on the date such shares are issued, carry no present or future preferential right to dividends, or to a company's assets on its winding up, and no present or future preferential right to be redeemed.

(*b*) Subject to paragraph (*d*), where an allowable investor company is entitled to relief under this section in respect of any sum or any part of a sum, or would be so entitled on making due claim, as a relevant deduction from its total profits for any accounting period, it shall not be entitled to any relief for that sum or that part of a sum, in computing its income or profits, or as a deduction from its income or profits, for any accounting period under any other provision of the Corporation Tax Acts or the Capital Gains Tax Acts.

(*c*) Subject to paragraph (*d*), where a qualifying individual is entitled to relief under this section in respect of any sum or any part of a sum, or would be so entitled on making due claim, as a relevant deduction from his or her total income for any year of assessment—

(i) the individual shall not be entitled to any relief for that sum or that part of a sum in computing his or her total income, or as a deduction from his or her total income, for any year of assessment under any other provision of the Income Tax Acts, and

(ii) so much of that sum or that part of a sum as is equal to the amount of the relevant deduction given in relation thereto shall be treated as a sum which by virtue of section 554 is to be excluded from the sums allowable as a deduction in the computation of gains and losses for the purposes of the Capital Gains Tax Acts.

(*d*) Where an allowable investor company or a qualifying individual has made a relevant investment by means of a subscription for new ordinary shares of a qualifying company and none of those shares is disposed of by the allowable investor company or the qualifying individual, as the case may be, within one year of their acquisition by that company or that individual, as the case may be, then, the sums allowable as deductions from the consideration in the computation for the purpose of capital gains tax of the gain or loss accruing to the company or the individual, as the case may be, on the disposal of those shares shall be determined without regard to any relief under this section which the company or the individual, as the case may be, has obtained, or would be entitled on due claim to obtain, except that where those sums exceed the consideration they shall be reduced by an amount equal to the lesser of—

(i) the amount of the relevant deduction allowed to the allowable investor company or the qualifying individual, as the case may be, under this section in respect of the subscription for those shares, and

(ii) the amount of the excess;

but, if the disposal of shares is by a qualifying individual and the disposal is within section 1028(5), this paragraph shall not apply.

(21) This section shall apply subject to paragraph 22 of Schedule 32, which contains certain transitional provisions in relation to relief under this section.

[(22) The Revenue Commissioners shall be responsible for verifying compliance with conditions specified in any certificate issued by the Minister prior to [1 January 2005][42], where the qualifying company has not, prior to [1 January 2005][43], submitted the items, statements, reports or other matters required to be submitted to the Minister under the terms of such certificate to enable the Minister to verify such compliance.

(23) Every regulation made under this section shall be laid before Dáil Éireann as soon as may be after it is made and, if a resolution annulling the regulation is passed by Dáil Éireann within the next 21 days on which Dáil Éireann has sat after the regulation is laid before it, the regulation shall be annulled accordingly, but without prejudice to the validity of anything previously done thereunder.][44]

Amendments

1 Definition of "eligible individual" inserted by FA 2004 s 28(1)(*a*)(i) with effect from such day or days as the Minister for Finance may by order or orders appoint and different days may be appointed for different purposes or different provisions. By virtue of the Finance Act 2004 (Commencement of Section 28) Order 2004, SI No 814 of 2004, FA 2004 s 28 comes into operation on 1 January 2005 and this amendment applies as respects an application made on or after 1 January 2005 by a qualifying company (within the meaning of TCA 1997 s 481) for a certificate under TCA 1997 s 481 in relation to a film to which that section relates.

2 Subs (1)(definition of "film")(*a*) substituted by FA 2004 s 28(1)(*a*)(ii) with effect from such day or days as the Minister for Finance may by order or orders appoint and different days may be appointed for different purposes or different provisions. By virtue of the Finance Act 2004 (Commencement of Section 28) Order 2004, SI No 814 of 2004, FA 2004 s 28 comes into operation on 1 January 2005 and this amendment applies as respects an application made on or after 1 January 2005 by a qualifying company (within the meaning of TCA 1997 s 481) for a certificate under TCA 1997 s 481 in relation to a film to which that section relates.

3 Substituted by FA 1998 s 32(1)(*b*) with effect as on and from 6 April 1997; previously "as respects any other film".

4 Substituted by FA 2004 s 28(1)(*a*)(iii) with effect from such day or days as the Minister for Finance may by order or orders appoint and different days may be appointed for different purposes or different provisions; previously "Arts, Heritage, Gaeltacht and the Islands". By virtue of the Finance Act 2004 (Commencement of Section 28) Order 2004, SI No 814 of 2004, FA 2004 s 28 comes into operation on 1 January 2005 and this amendment applies as respects an application made on or after 1 January 2005 by a qualifying company (within the meaning of TCA 1997 s 481) for a certificate under TCA 1997 s 481 in relation to a film to which that section relates.

5 Definition of "qualifying company" substituted by FA 2000 s 48(1)(*a*)(i) with effect from such date as the Minister for Finance may appoint by order (viz with effect from 20 July 2000 by virtue of Finance Act, 2000 (Section 48) (Commencement) Order 2000 (SI No 258 of 2000 refers); previously "**'qualifying company'** means a company which—

(*a*) is incorporated in the State,

(*b*) is resident in the State and not resident elsewhere,

(*c*) exists solely for the purposes of the production and distribution of only one qualifying film, and

(*d*) does not contain in its name registered under either or both the Companies Acts, 1963 to 1990, or the Registration of Business Names Act, 1963, the words **'Ireland'**, **'Irish'**, **'Éireann'**, **'Éire'** or **'National'**,".

6 Definition of "qualifying film" substituted by FA 2004 s 28(1)(*a*)(iv) with effect from such day or days as the Minister for Finance may by order or orders appoint and different days may be appointed for different purposes or different provisions. By virtue of the Finance Act 2004 (Commencement of Section 28) Order 2004, SI No 814 of 2004, FA 2004 s 28 comes into operation on 1 January 2005 and this amendment applies as respects an application made on or after 1 January 2005 by a qualifying company (within the meaning of TCA 1997 s 481) for a certificate under TCA 1997 s 481 in relation to a film to which that section relates.

7 Substituted by FA 2004 s 28(1)(*a*)(v) with effect from such day or days as the Minister for Finance may by order or orders appoint and different days may be appointed for different purposes or different provisions; previously "31 December 2004". By virtue of the Finance Act 2004 (Commencement of Section 28) Order 2004, SI No 814 of 2004, FA 2004 s 28 comes into operation on 1 January 2005 and this amendment applies as respects an application made on or after 1 January 2005 by a qualifying company (within the meaning of TCA 1997 s 481) for a certificate under TCA 1997 s 481 in relation to a film to which that section relates.

8 Definition of "qualifying period" substituted by FA 2000 s 48(1)(*a*)(ii) with effect from such date as the Minister for Finance may appoint by order (viz with effect from 20 July 2000 by virtue of Finance Act, 2000 (Section 48) (Commencement) Order 2000 (SI No 258 of 2000 refers); previously "**'qualifying period'**—

(*a*) in relation to an allowable investor company, means the period commencing on the 23rd day of January, 1996, and ending on the 5th day of April, 2000, and

(*b*) in relation to a qualifying individual, means the period commencing on the 23rd day of January, 1996, and ending on the 5th day of April, 2000;

9 Subs (1)(definition of "relevant investment")(*b*) substituted by FA 2004 s 28(1)(*a*)(vi)(I) with effect from such day or days as the Minister for Finance may by order or orders appoint and different days may be appointed for different purposes or different provisions. By virtue of the Finance Act 2004 (Commencement of Section 28) Order 2004, SI No 814 of 2004, FA 2004 s 28 comes into operation on 1 January 2005 and this amendment applies as respects an application made on or after 1 January 2005 by a qualifying company (within the meaning of TCA 1997 s 481) for a certificate under TCA 1997 s 481 in relation to a film to which that section relates.

10 Substituted by FA 2004 s 28(1)(*a*)(vi)(II) with effect from such day or days as the Minister for Finance may by order or orders appoint and different days may be appointed for different purposes or different provisions; previously "other than a provision for its repayment in the event of the Minister not giving a certificate under subsection (2)". By virtue of the Finance Act 2004 (Commencement of Section 28) Order 2004, SI No 814 of 2004, FA 2004 s 28 comes into operation on 1 January 2005 and this amendment applies as respects an application made on or after 1 January 2005 by a qualifying company (within the meaning of TCA 1997 s 481) for a certificate under TCA 1997 s 481 in relation to a film to which that section relates.

11 Subs (2)(*b*)(I) deleted by FA 2005 s 36(*a*) with effect from 1 January 2005.

12 Subs (2)(*a*) and (*b*) substituted by FA 2004 s 28(1)(*b*)(i) with effect from such day or days as the Minister for Finance may by order or orders appoint and different days may be appointed for different purposes or different provisions. By virtue of the Finance Act 2004 (Commencement of Section 28) Order 2004, SI No 814 of 2004, FA 2004 s 28 comes into operation on 1 January 2005 and this amendment applies as respects an application made on or after 1 January 2005 by a qualifying company (within the meaning of TCA 1997 s 481) for a certificate under TCA 1997 s 481 in relation to a film to which that section relates.

13 Substituted by FA 2001 s 240(1), (2)(*l*)(iv) and Sch 5 Pt 1 as respects a certificate issued under subsection (2)(*a*)(i) of this section on or after 1 January 2002; previously "£4,000,000".

14 Substituted by FA 2001 s 240(1), (2)(*l*)(iv) and Sch 5 Pt 1 as respects a certificate issued under subsection (2)(*a*)(i) of this section on or after 1 January 2002; previously "£5,000,000".

15 Formula substituted by FA 2003 s 58(1)(*b*) with effect from 1 January 2002.

16 Substituted by FA 2004 s 28(1)(*b*)(ii) with effect from such day or days as the Minister for Finance may by order or orders appoint and different days may be appointed for different purposes or different provisions; previously "€10,480,000". By virtue of the Finance Act 2004 (Commencement of Section 28) Order 2004, SI No 814 of 2004, FA 2004 s 28 comes into operation on 1 January 2005 and this amendment applies as respects an application made on or after 1 January 2005 by a qualifying company (within the meaning of TCA 1997 s 481) for a certificate under TCA 1997 s 481 in relation to a film to which that section relates.

17 Subs (2)(*c*) substituted by FA 2000 s 48(1)(*b*) with effect from such date as the Minister for Finance may appoint by order (viz with effect from 20 July 2000 by virtue of Finance Act, 2000 (Section 48) (Commencement) Order 2000 (SI No 258 of 2000 refers); previously

"(*c*) (i) Subject to subparagraphs (ii) and (iii), the specified percentage shall not exceed—

(I) where the total cost of production of the film does not exceed £4,000,000, 60 per cent,

(II) where the total cost of production of the film exceeds £4,000,000 and does not exceed £5,000,000, the amount per cent (in this subparagraph referred to as **'the allowable percentage'**) where the amount of the allowable percentage is determined by the formula—

$$66 - \frac{(11 \times E)}{£1,000,000}$$

where E is the excess of the total cost of production of the film over £4,000,000, and

(III) where the total cost of production of the film exceeds £5,000,000, 50 per cent;

but, in any case to which clause (I), (II) or (III) relates, the total cost of production of the film which is met by relevant investments shall not exceed £7,500,000, and where the percentage of the work on the production of the film carried out in the State (in this paragraph referred to as the **"lower percentage"**) is less than 50 per cent, this paragraph shall be construed as if the reference to 60 per cent, the reference to the allowable percentage and the reference to 50 per cent were a reference to the lower percentage.

(ii) (I) In relation to a film (other than an animation film) in respect of which the principal photography commences at any time during the months of October, November, December and January, and the production of the film continues to completion without unreasonable delay from that time, or

(II) in relation to a film in respect of which post production work is to be carried out wholly or mainly in the State,

the references in subparagraph (i) to—

(A) 60 per cent shall be construed as a reference to 66 per cent,

(B) 50 per cent shall be construed as a reference to 55 per cent, and

(C) £7,500,000 shall be construed as a reference to £8,250,000.

(iii) In relation to a film in respect of which not less than one-half of the amount of the total cost of production met by relevant investments has been met by relevant investments paid by allowable investor companies, the references in this paragraph (apart from this subparagraph) to—

(I) £7,500,000 shall be treated as a reference to £15,000,000 and

(II) £8,250,000 shall be treated as a reference to £16,500,000."

18 Subs (2)(*d*) and (*e*) deleted by FA 2004 s 28(1)(*b*)(iii) with effect from such day or days as the Minister for Finance may by order or orders appoint and different days may be appointed for different purposes or different provisions. By virtue of the Finance Act 2004 (Commencement of Section 28) Order 2004, SI No 814 of 2004, FA 2004 s 28 comes into operation on 1 January 2005 and this amendment applies as respects an application made on or after 1 January 2005 by a qualifying company (within the meaning of TCA 1997 s 481) for a certificate under TCA 1997 s 481 in relation to a film to which that section relates.

19 Subs (2A)(*g*)(i) deleted by FA 2005 s 36(*b*)(i) with effect from 1 January 2005.

20 Substituted by FA 2005 s 36(*b*)(ii) with effect from 1 January 2005; previously "the specified percentage, as referred to in that subsection".

21 Subs (2A)(*g*)(iv) substituted by FA 2005 s 36(*b*)(iii) with effect from 1 January 2005.

22 Subs (2A)(*g*)(v) inserted by FA 2005 s 36(*b*)(iv) with effect from 1 January 2005.

23 Inserted by FA 2005 s 36(*c*)(i) with effect from 1 January 2005.

24 Subs (2C)(*ba*) inserted by FA 2005 s 36(*c*)(ii) with effect from 1 January 2005.

25 Deleted by FA 2005 s 36(*d*)(i) with effect from 1 January 2005; previously "and".

26 Subs (2A)–(2E) inserted by FA 2004 s 28(1)(*c*) with effect from such day or days as the Minister for Finance may by order or orders appoint and different days may be appointed for different purposes or different provisions. By virtue of the Finance Act 2004 (Commencement of Section 28) Order 2004, SI No 814 of 2004, FA 2004 s 28 comes into operation on 1 January 2005 and this amendment applies as respects an application made on or after 1 January 2005 by a qualifying company (within the meaning of TCA 1997 s 481) for a certificate under TCA 1997 s 481 in relation to a film to which that section relates. But, in so far as it relates to the insertion of subs (2E), 1 January 2005 in the day on which the amendment comes into operation.

27 Subs (2E)(*m*)–(*n*) inserted by FA 2005 s 36(*d*)(ii) with effect from 1 January 2005.

28 Substituted by FA 1999 s 61(*b*)(i) with effect from 6 April 1999.

29 Substituted by FA 2001 s 240(1) and (2)(*c*) and Sch 5 Pt 1 for accounting periods ending on or after 1 January 2002; previously "£8,000,000".

30 Substituted by FA 2001 s 240(1) and (2)(*c*) and Sch 5 Pt 1 for accounting periods ending on or after 1 January 2002; previously "£3,000,000".

31 Inserted by FA 1999 s 61(*b*)(ii) with effect from 6 April 1999.

32 Substituted by FA 2001 s 240(1) and (2)(*c*) and Sch 5 Pt 1 for accounting periods ending on or after 1 January 2002; previously "£4,000,000".

33 Substituted by FA 2002 s 138 and Sch 6 paras 3(*k*) and 6(*c*)(i) with effect from 1 January 2002; previously "£200" (short tax "year"2001: £148" (FA 2001 s 77(2) and Sch 2 paras 23(*a*) and 61(*a*))).

34 Substituted by FA 2001 s 240(1) and (2)(*a*) and Sch 5 Pt 1 for 2002 and later tax years; previously "£25,000" (short tax "year" 2001:£18,500 (FA 2001 s 77(2) and Sch 2 paras 23(*b*) and 61(*a*))).

35 Substituted by FA 2004 s 28(1)(*d*) with effect from such day or days as the Minister for Finance may by order or orders appoint and different days may be appointed for different purposes or different provisions; previously "the year of assessment 2004". By virtue of the Finance Act 2004 (Commencement of Section 28) Order 2004, SI No 814 of 2004, FA 2004 s 28 comes into operation on 1 January 2005 and this amendment applies as respects an application made on or after 1 January 2005 by a qualifying company (within the meaning of TCA 1997 s 481) for a certificate under TCA 1997 s 481 in relation to a film to which that section relates.

36 Substituted by FA 2004 s 28(1)(*e*) with effect from such day or days as the Minister for Finance may by order or orders appoint and different days may be appointed for different purposes or different provisions; previously "the year of assessment 2004". By virtue of the Finance Act 2004 (Commencement of Section 28) Order 2004, SI No 814 of 2004, FA 2004 s 28 comes into operation on 1 January 2005 and this amendment applies as respects an application made on or after 1 January 2005 by a qualifying company (within the meaning of TCA 1997 s 481) for a certificate under TCA 1997 s 481 in relation to a film to which that section relates.

37 Substituted by FA 2004 s 28(1)(*f*) with effect from such day or days as the Minister for Finance may by order or orders appoint and different days may be appointed for different purposes or different provisions; previously "the revocation by the Minister of a certificate under subsection (2)". By virtue of the Finance Act 2004 (Commencement of Section 28) Order 2004, SI No 814 of 2004, FA 2004 s 28 comes into operation on 1 January 2005 and this amendment applies as respects an application made on or after 1 January 2005 by a qualifying company (within the meaning of TCA 1997 s 481) for a certificate under TCA 1997 s 481 in relation to a film to which that section relates.

38 Subs (13)(*b*) and (*c*) deleted by FA 2004 s 28(1)(*g*) with effect from such day or days as the Minister for Finance may by order or orders appoint and different days may be appointed for different purposes or different provisions; previously "(*b*) a copy of any notification required to be given to the Minister under subsection (2)(*b*)(iii), (*c*) a copy of the certificate, including a copy of any notice given by the Minister amending, revoking or adding a condition to that certificate, under subsection (2) in respect of the film, and". By virtue of the Finance Act 2004 (Commencement of Section 28) Order 2004, SI No 814 of 2004, FA 2004 s 28 comes into operation on 1 January 2005 and this amendment applies as respects an application made on or after 1 January 2005 by a qualifying company (within the meaning of TCA 1997 s 481) for a certificate under TCA 1997 s 481 in relation to a film to which that section relates.

39 Subs (14) substituted by FA 2003 s 58(1)(*e*) with effect from 28 March 2003.

40 Substituted by FA 2001 s 240(1) and (2)(*k*) and Sch 5 Pt 1 as respects any act or omission which takes place or begins on or after 1 January 2002; previously "£500".

41 Substituted by FA 2001 s 240(1) and (2)(*k*) and Sch 5 Pt 1 as respects any act or omission which takes place or begins on or after 1 January 2002; previously "£1,000".

42 Substituted by FA 2005 s 36(*e*) with effect from 1 January 2005; previously "the day appointed by order made by the Minister for Finance for the coming into operation of this subsection".

43 Substituted by FA 2005 s 36(*e*) with effect from 1 January 2005; previously "the day so appointed".

44 Subss (22) and (23) inserted by FA 2004 s 28(1)(*h*) with effect from such day or days as the Minister for Finance may by order or orders appoint and different days may be appointed for different purposes or different provisions. By virtue of the Finance Act 2004 (Commencement of Section 28) Order 2004, SI No 814 of 2004, FA 2004 s 28 comes into operation on 1 January 2005 and this amendment applies as respects an application made on or after 1 January 2005 by a qualifying company (within the meaning of TCA 1997 s 481) for a certificate under TCA 1997 s 481 in relation to a film to which that section relates.

Cross-references

BES relief, qualifying trades: s 496(2)(*a*)(i)(II).
Deductions allowed in ascertaining taxable income: s 458(2); s 459(1), (2).
Rate of tax at which repayments are to be made: s 460.
Film relief claim, no interest relief: s 251(*b*).
Method of apportioning reliefs and charging tax in cases of separate assessment: s 1024(2)(*a*)(x).
Self assessment, date for payment of tax: s 958(6)(*b*).
Transitional, subss (2), (4): Sch 32 para 22(1), (6)–(8).

Regulations

Film Regulations 2004 (SI No 869 of 2004).

Tax Briefing

TB53 Aug 2003 p 14 — Proposals for Investments under Section 481: Advance Opinions.

Revenue information

Information leaflet IT57 — Relief for Investment in Films.

Guidelines on the administration of the scheme of tax relief for investment in films may be downloaded from the Revenue website (www.revenue.ie) under Publications/Technical Guidelines.

Proposals for Investments under Section 481: Advance Opinions — Guidelines may be downloaded from the Revenue website (www.revenue.ie) under Publications/Technical Guidelines.

A Guidance Note for Film Producers and Promoters on the certification of qualifying films under section 481, which was published on 23 December 2004, may be downloaded from Revenue's website www.revenue.ie under Whats New/Archive/ December 2004.

A Guidance Note for Film Producers and Promoters on post-certification requirements for qualifying companies under section 481, which was published on 23 December 2004, may be downloaded from Revenue's website www.revenue.ie under Whats New/Archive/December 2004.

Definitions

Appeal Commissioners: s 2(1); body of persons: s 2(1); Capital Gains Tax Acts: s 1(2); company: ss 4(1), 5(1); Corporation Tax Acts: s 1(2); Dáil Éireann: IA 1937 Sch; inspector: ss 2(1), 852; month: IA 1937 Sch; ordinary share capital: s 2(1); person: IA 1937 s 11(*c*); profits: s 4(1); shares: s 5(1); Tax Acts: s 1(2); writing: IA 1937 Sch; year of assessment: s 2(1).

Former enactments

FA 1987 s 35(1)–(20); FA 1996 s 31(1); FA 1997 s 30.

482 Relief for expenditure on significant buildings and gardens

(1) (*a*) In this section—

"approved building" means a building to which subsection (5) applies;

"approved garden" means a garden (other than a garden, being land occupied or enjoyed with an approved building as part of its garden or grounds of an ornamental nature) which, on application to the Minister and the Revenue Commissioners in that behalf by a person who owns or occupies the garden, is determined—

(i) by the Minister to be a garden which is intrinsically of significant horticultural, scientific, historical, architectural or aesthetic interest, and

(ii) by the Revenue Commissioners to be a garden to which reasonable access is afforded to the public;

"approved object", in relation to an approved building, has the meaning assigned to it by subsection (6);

"authorised person" means—

(i) an inspector or other officer of the Revenue Commissioners authorised by them in writing for the purposes of this section, or

(ii) a person authorised by the Minister in writing for the purposes of this section;

"chargeable period" has the same meaning as in section 321(2);

"the Minister" means the Minister for Arts, Heritage, Gaeltacht and the Islands;

"public place", in relation to an approved building in use as a tourist accommodation facility, means a part of the building to which all patrons of the facility have access;

"qualifying expenditure", in relation to an approved building, means expenditure incurred by the person who owns or occupies the approved building on one or more of the following—

(i) the repair, maintenance or restoration of the approved building or the maintenance or restoration of any land occupied or enjoyed with the approved building as part of its garden or grounds of an ornamental nature, and

(ii) to the extent that the aggregate expenditure in a chargeable period, being the year 1997–98 and any subsequent year of assessment, or an accounting period of a company beginning on or after the 6th day of April, 1997, does not exceed [€6,350][1]—

(I) the repair, maintenance or restoration of an approved object in the approved building,

(II) the installation, maintenance or replacement of a security alarm system in the approved building, and

(III) public liability insurance for the approved building;

"relevant expenditure", in relation to an approved garden, means—

(i) in the case of expenditure incurred in a chargeable period, being the year 1997–98 and any subsequent year of assessment, or an accounting period of a company beginning on or after the 6th day of April, 1997, expenditure incurred by the person who owns or occupies the approved garden on one or more of the following—

(I) the maintenance or restoration of the approved garden, and

(II) to the extent that the aggregate expenditure in a chargeable period does not exceed [€6,350][1]—

(A) the repair, maintenance or restoration of an approved object in the approved garden,

(B) the installation, maintenance or replacement of a security alarm system in the approved garden, and

(C) public liability insurance for the approved garden, and

[(ii) in the case of expenditure incurred in a chargeable period earlier than that referred to in subparagraph (i), expenditure incurred by the person who owned or occupied the approved garden on the maintenance or restoration of the garden;][2]

"security alarm system" means an electrical apparatus installed as a fixture in the approved building or in the approved garden which when activated is designed to give notice to the effect that there is an intruder present or attempting to enter the approved building or the approved garden, as the case may be, in which it is installed;

"tourist accommodation facility" means an accommodation facility—

(i) registered in the register of guest houses maintained and kept by Bord Fáilte Éireann under Part III of the Tourist Traffic Act, 1939, or

(ii) listed in the list published or caused to be published by Bord Fáilte Éireann under section 9 of the Tourist Traffic Act, [1957;][3]

[**"weekend day"** means a Saturday or a Sunday.][4]

(*b*) For the purposes of this section, expenditure shall not be regarded as having been incurred in so far as any sum in respect of or by reference to the work to which the expenditure relates has been or is to be received directly or indirectly by the person making a claim in respect of the expenditure under subsection (2) from the State, from any public or local authority, from any other person or under any contract of insurance or by means of compensation or otherwise.

(*c*) For the purposes of this section, references to an approved building, unless the contrary intention is expressed, shall be construed as including a reference to any land occupied or enjoyed with an approved building as part of its garden or grounds of an ornamental nature.

(2) (*a*) Subject to this section, where a person (in this section referred to as **"the claimant"**), having made a claim in that behalf, proves that the conditions specified in paragraph (*b*) have been met, then, the Tax Acts shall apply as if the amount of the qualifying expenditure referred to in subparagraph (i) of paragraph (*b*) were a loss sustained in the chargeable period referred to in that subparagraph in a trade carried on by the claimant separate from any trade actually carried on by the claimant.

(*b*) The conditions referred to in paragraph (*a*) are—

(i) that the claimant has incurred in a chargeable period qualifying expenditure in relation to an approved building,

(ii) that the claimant has [on or before the 1st day of November][5] in the chargeable period in respect of which the claim is made and in each of the chargeable periods comprising whichever is the shortest of the following periods—

(I) the period consisting of the chargeable periods since the 23rd day of May, 1994,

(II) the period consisting of the chargeable periods since a determination under subsection (5)(*a*)(ii) was made in relation to the building,

(III) the period consisting of the chargeable periods since the approved building was purchased or occupied by the claimant,

(IV) the period consisting of the 5 chargeable periods immediately preceding the chargeable period for which the claim is made,

provided Bord Fáilte Éireann (in this paragraph referred to as **"the Board"**) with particulars of—

(A) the name, if any, and address of the approved building, and

(B) the days and times during the year when access to the approved building is afforded to the public or the period or periods during the year when the approved building is in use as a tourist accommodation facility, as the case may be,

such particulars being provided to the Board on the understanding by the person and the Board that they may be published by the Board or by another body concerned with the promotion of tourism, and

(iii) where the approved building was in use as a tourist accommodation facility in any of the chargeable periods applicable for the purposes of subparagraph (ii), that the approved building was registered in the register of guest houses maintained and kept by the Board under Part III of the Tourist Traffic Act, 1939, or listed in the list published or caused to be published by the Board under section 9 of the Tourist Traffic Act, 1957, in those chargeable periods.

(*c*) Relief authorised by this subsection shall not apply for any chargeable period before the chargeable period in which the application concerned is made to the Revenue Commissioners under subsection (5)(*a*).

[(*d*) For the purpose only of determining, in relation to a claim referred to in paragraph (*a*), whether and to what extent qualifying expenditure incurred in relation to an approved building is incurred or not incurred in a chargeable period, only such an amount of that qualifying expenditure as is properly attributable to work which was actually carried out during the chargeable period shall (notwithstanding any other provision of the Tax Acts as to the time when any expenditure is or is to be treated as incurred) be treated as having been incurred in that period.][6]

(3) (*a*) Where—

(i) by virtue of subsection (2), qualifying expenditure in a chargeable period is treated as if it were a loss sustained in the chargeable period in a trade carried on by the person separate from any trade actually carried on by that person, and

(ii) owing to an insufficiency of income, relief under the Tax Acts cannot be given for any part of the qualifying expenditure so treated (in this subsection referred to as **"the unrelieved amount"**),

then, the Tax Acts shall apply as if the unrelieved amount were a loss sustained in the following chargeable period in a trade carried on by the person separate from any trade actually carried on by that person.

(*b*) Where owing to an insufficiency of income relief under the Tax Acts cannot be given by virtue of paragraph (*a*) for any part of the unrelieved amount, then, the Tax Acts shall apply as if that part of the unrelieved amount were a loss sustained in the chargeable period following the period referred to in paragraph (*a*) in a trade carried on by the person separate from any trade actually carried on by that person.

(*c*) Where in any chargeable period relief under the Tax Acts is due by virtue of 2 or more of the following provisions, that is, subsection (2) and paragraphs (*a*) and (*b*), then, the following provisions shall apply:

(i) any relief due under those Acts by virtue of paragraph (*b*) shall be given in priority to any relief due under those Acts by virtue of subsection (2) or paragraph (*a*), and

(ii) where relief has been given in accordance with subparagraph (i) or where no such relief is due, any relief due under those Acts by virtue of paragraph (*a*) shall be given in priority to relief due under those Acts by virtue of subsection (2).

(4) No relief shall be allowed under this section for expenditure in respect of which relief may be claimed under any other provision of the Tax Acts.

(5) (*a*) This subsection shall apply to a building in the State which, on application to the Minister and the Revenue Commissioners in that behalf by a person who owns or occupies the building, is determined—

(i) by the Minister to be a building which is intrinsically of significant scientific, historical, architectural or aesthetic interest, and

(ii) by the Revenue Commissioners to be a building either—

(I) to which reasonable access is afforded to the public, or

(II) which is in use as a tourist accommodation facility for at least 6 months in any calendar year (in this subsection referred to as **"the required period"**) including not less than 4 months in the period commencing on the 1st day of May and ending on the 30th day of September in any such year.

(*b*) Without prejudice to the generality of the requirement that reasonable access be afforded to the public, access to a building shall not be regarded as being reasonable access afforded to the public unless—

(i) access to the whole or a substantial part of the building is afforded at the same time,

[(ii) subject to temporary closure necessary for the purposes of the repair, maintenance or restoration of the building, access is so afforded for a period of not less than 60 days in any year, and—

(I) such period shall include, as respects determinations made by the Revenue Commissioners in accordance with paragraph (*a*)(ii)—

(A) before the passing of the Finance Act, 2000, not less than 40 days, and

(B) on or after the passing of the Finance Act, 2000, not less than 40 days, of which not less than 10 are weekend days,

during the period commencing on 1 May and ending on 30 September, and

(II) in respect of each such period, on each day concerned access is afforded in a reasonable manner and at reasonable times for a period, or periods in the aggregate, of not less than [4 hours,][7]][8]

(iii) the price, if any, paid by the public in return for that access is in the opinion of the Revenue Commissioners reasonable in amount and does not operate to preclude the public from seeking [access to the building, and][9]

[(iv) the Revenue Commissioners are satisfied that—

(I) details relating to that access are publicised or drawn to the attention of the public by way of advertisement, leaflet, press notice or similar means annually,

(II) a notice containing the details of the dates and times at which access is afforded to the public—

(A) is displayed on the days on which such access is so afforded and in a conspicuous location at or near the place where the public can gain entrance to the building concerned, and

(B) is so displayed so as to be easily visible and legible by the public,

and

(III) conditions, if any, in regard to that access are such that they would not act as a disincentive to the public from seeking such access.][10]

(*c*) Where under paragraph (*a*) the Minister makes a determination in relation to a building and, by reason of any alteration made to the building or any deterioration of the building subsequent to the determination being made, the Minister considers that the building is no longer a building which is intrinsically of significant scientific, historical, architectural or aesthetic interest, the Minister may, by notice in writing given to the owner or occupier of the building, revoke the determination with effect from the date on which the Minister considers that the building ceased to be a building which is intrinsically of significant scientific, historical, architectural or aesthetic interest, and this subsection shall cease to apply to the building from that date.

(*d*) Where under paragraph (*a*) the Revenue Commissioners make a determination in relation to a building, and reasonable access to the building ceases to be afforded to the public or the building ceases to be used as a tourist accommodation facility for the required period, as the case may be, the Revenue Commissioners may, by notice in writing given to the owner or occupier of the building, revoke the determination with effect from the date on which they consider that such access or such use, as the case may be, so ceased, and—

(i) this subsection shall cease to apply to the building from that date, and

(ii) if relief has been given under this section in respect of qualifying expenditure incurred in relation to that building in the period of 5 years ending on the date from which the revocation has effect, that relief shall be withdrawn and there shall be made all such assessments or additional assessments as are necessary to give effect to this subsection.

(*e*) Where—

(i) the Revenue Commissioners make a determination (in this paragraph referred to as the **"first-mentioned determination"**) that a building is either a building to which reasonable access is afforded to the public or a building which is in use as a tourist accommodation facility for the required period,

(ii) such access ceases to be so afforded or such building ceases to be so used, as the case may be, in a chargeable period subsequent to the chargeable period in which the first-mentioned determination was made, and

(iii) on application to them in that chargeable period in that behalf by the person who owns or occupies the building, the Revenue Commissioners revoke the first-mentioned determination and make a further determination (in this paragraph referred to as the **"second-mentioned determination"**) with effect from the date of revocation of the first- mentioned determination—

(I) in the case of a building in respect of which a determination was made that it is a building to which reasonable access is afforded to the public, that the building is a building which is in use as a tourist accommodation facility for the required period, or

(II) in the case of a building in respect of which a determination was made that it is a building which is in use as a tourist accommodation facility for the required period, that the building is a building to which reasonable access is afforded to the public,

then, paragraph (*d*) shall not apply on the revocation of the first-mentioned determination and for the purposes of that paragraph the second-mentioned determination shall be treated as having been made at the time of the making of the first-mentioned determination.

(6) (*a*) In this subsection, **"approved object"**, in relation to an approved building, means an object (including a picture, sculpture, print, book, manuscript, piece

of jewellery, furniture, or other similar object) or a scientific collection which is owned by the owner or occupier of the approved building and which, on application to them in that behalf by that person, is determined—

(i) by the Minister, after consideration of any evidence in relation to the matter which such owner or occupier submits to the Minister and after such consultation (if any) as may seem to the Minister to be necessary with such person or body of persons as in the opinion of the Minister may be of assistance to the Minister, to be an object which is intrinsically of significant national, scientific, historical or aesthetic interest, and

(ii) by the Revenue Commissioners, to be an object reasonable access to which is afforded, and in respect of which reasonable facilities for viewing are provided, in the building to the public.

(*b*) Without prejudice to the generality of the requirement that reasonable access be afforded, and that reasonable facilities for viewing be provided, to the public, access to and facilities for the viewing of an object shall not be regarded as being reasonable access afforded, or the provision of reasonable facilities for viewing, to the public unless, subject to such temporary removal as is necessary for the purposes of the repair, maintenance or restoration of the object as is reasonable—

(i) in a case where the approved building is a tourist accommodation facility, the object is displayed in a public place in the building, or

(ii) in the case of any other approved building—

(I) access to the object is afforded and such facilities for viewing the object are provided to the public on the same days and at the same times as access is afforded to the public to the approved building in which the object is kept, and

(II) the price, if any, paid by the public in return for such access is in the opinion of the Revenue Commissioners reasonable in amount and does not operate to preclude the public from seeking access to the object.

(*c*) Where under paragraph (*a*) the Minister makes a determination in relation to an object and, by reason of any alteration made to the object, or any deterioration of the object, subsequent to the determination being made, the Minister considers that the object is no longer an object which is intrinsically of significant national, scientific, historical or aesthetic interest, the Minister may, by notice in writing given to the owner or occupier of the building, revoke the determination with effect from the date on which the Minister considers that the object ceased to be an object which is intrinsically of significant national, scientific, historical or aesthetic interest, and this subsection shall cease to apply to the object from that date.

(*d*) Where under paragraph (*a*) the Revenue Commissioners make a determination in relation to an object and—

(i) reasonable access to the object ceases to be afforded, or reasonable facilities for the viewing of the object cease to be provided, to the public, or

(ii) the object ceases to be owned by the person to whom relief in respect of that qualifying expenditure has been granted under this section,

the Revenue Commissioners may, by notice in writing given to the owner or occupier of the approved building in which the object is or was kept, revoke that determination with effect from the date on which they consider that such access, such facilities for viewing or such ownership, as the case may be, so ceased, and—

(I) this subsection shall cease to apply to the object from that date, and

(II) if relief has been given under this section in respect of qualifying expenditure incurred in relation to that object in the period of 2 years ending on the date from which the revocation has effect, that relief shall be withdrawn and there shall be made all such assessments or additional assessments as are necessary to give effect to this subsection.

(7) [(*a*) Where a person makes a claim under subsection (2), an authorised person may at any reasonable time enter the building in respect of which the qualifying expenditure has been incurred for the purpose of—

(i) inspecting, as the case may be, the building or an object or of examining any work in respect of which the expenditure to which the claim relates was incurred, or

(ii) ensuring that the requirements in relation to reasonable access set out in subsection (5) are being complied with.][11]

(*b*) Whenever an authorised person exercises any power conferred on him or her by this subsection, the authorised person shall on request produce his or her authorisation for the purposes of this section to any person concerned.

(*c*) Any person who obstructs or interferes with an authorised person in the course of exercising a power conferred on the authorised person by this subsection shall be guilty of an offence and shall be liable on summary conviction to a fine not exceeding [€630][12].

[(8) Notwithstanding that the Revenue Commissioners have before the passing of the Finance Act, 2000, made a determination in accordance with subsection (5)(*a*)(ii) that a building is a building to which reasonable access is afforded to the public, relief under subsection (2), in relation to qualifying expenditure incurred in a chargeable period beginning on or after 1 January 1995, in respect of the building shall not be given unless the person who owns or occupies the building satisfies the Revenue Commissioners [on or before 1 November][13] in the chargeable period that it is a building to which reasonable access is afforded to the public having regard to—

(*a*) in a case where the qualifying expenditure is incurred in a chargeable period beginning before 1 October 2000, subsection (5)(*b*)(ii)(I)(A), and

(*b*) in a case where the qualifying expenditure is incurred in a chargeable period beginning on or after 1 October 2000, subsection (5)(*b*)(ii)(I)(B).][14]

(9) In respect of relevant expenditure incurred on or after the 6th day of April, 1993, this section shall, with any necessary modifications, apply in relation to an approved garden as it applies in relation to qualifying expenditure incurred in relation to an approved building.

(10) Any claim for relief under this section—

(*a*) shall be made in such form as the Revenue Commissioners may from time to time prescribe, and

(*b*) shall be accompanied by such statements in writing as regards the expenditure for which relief is claimed, including statements by persons to whom payments were made, as may be indicated by the prescribed form.

[(11) The Tax Acts shall apply to a loss referred to in subsection (2) as they would apply if sections 396A and 420A had not been enacted.][15]

Amendments

1 Substituted by FA 2001 s 240(1), (2)(*a*), (*c*) and Sch 5 Pt 1 for 2002 and later tax years in the case of income tax and accounting periods ending on or after 1 January 2002 in the case of corporation tax; previously "£5,000" (short tax "year" 2001: £3,700 (FA 2001 s 77(2) and Sch 2 paras 24(*a*), (*b*)).

2 Definition of "relevant expenditure" subpara (ii) substituted by FA 2002 s 42(1)(*a*) with effect from 30 November 1997.

3 Substituted by FA 2000 s 49(*a*) with effect from 23 March 2000; previously "1957.".

4 Definition of "weekend day" inserted by FA 2000 s 49(*a*) with effect from 23 March 2000.

5 Substituted by FA 2002 s 42(1)(*b*) as respects a chargeable period, being the year of assessment 2002 and any subsequent year of assessment or an accounting period of a company beginning on or after 1 January 2002; previously "on or before the 1st day of January"

6 Subs (2)(*d*) inserted by FA 1998 s 33 as respects qualifying expenditure incurred on or after 12 February 1998.

7 Substituted by FA 2005 s 28(*a*)(i) with effect from 1 January 2005; previously "4 hours, and".

8 Subs (5)(*b*)(ii) substituted by FA 2000 s 49(*b*) were effect from 23 March 2000.

9 Substituted by FA 2005 s 28(*a*)(ii) with effect from 1 January 2005; previously "access to the building.".

10 Subs (5)(*b*)(iv) substituted by FA 2005 s 28(*a*)(iii) with effect from 1 January 2005.

11 Subs (7)(*a*) substituted by FA 2005 s 28(*b*) with effect from 1 January 2005.

12 Substituted by FA 2001 s 240(1) and (2)(*k*) and Sch 5 Pt 1 as respects acts or omissions which take place or begin on or after 1 January 2002; previously "£500".

13 Substituted by FA 2002 s 42(1)(*c*) as respects a chargeable period, being the year of assessment 2002 and any subsequent year of assessment or an accounting period of a company beginning on or after 1 January 2002; previously "on or before 1 January".

14 Subs (8) substituted by FA 2000 s 49(*c*) with effect from 23 March 2000.

15 Subs (11) inserted by FA 2002 s 42(1)(*d*) with effect from 6 March 2001.

Cross-references

Loans of art objects, meanings of "relevant building" and "relevant garden" applied: s 236(1).

Restriction on use of losses on approved buildings, subs (1), meanings of "approved building", "the Minister" and "qualifying expenditure" applied: s 409C(1); s 409C(1) ("ownership interest"); subs (2): s 409C(2)(*c*)(i)(II), (ii), (3)(*a*), (5)(*a*)(ii); subs (2)(*a*), meaning of "claimant" applied: s 409C(1); subs (3): s 409C(5); subs (5)(*a*): s 409C(1) ("relevant determinations"), (6)(*c*)(i), (ii), (*d*).

Revenue information

Information leaflet IT30 — Relief for Expenditure on Approved Buildings and Gardens in the State.

Information leaflet IT56 — Relief for Expenditure on Approved Objects in Approved Buildings and Gardens.

Properties of Significant Horticulture, Scientific, Historical, Architectural or Aesthetic Interest in Ireland — this booklet, which contains a list of those properties that are open to the public under section 482 TCA 1997 is available on Revenue's website: www.revenue.ie under Publications/Lists.

Definitions

inspector: ss 2(1), 5(1), 852; land: s 5(1), IA 1937 Sch; local authority: ss 2(1), 5(1); month: IA 1937 Sch; person: IA 1937 s 11(*c*); Tax Acts: s 1(2); trade: s 3(1); year: IA 1937 Sch.

Former enactments

FA 1982 s 19; FA 1993 s 29; FA 1994 s 18; FA 1995 s 20; FA 1997 s 17.

483 Relief for certain gifts

(1) (*a*) In this subsection, **"public moneys"** means moneys charged on or issued out of the Central Fund or provided by the Oireachtas.

(*b*) This section shall apply to a gift of money made to the Minister for Finance for use for any purpose for or towards the cost of which public moneys are provided and which is accepted by that Minister.

(2) Where a person who has made a gift to which this section applies claims relief from income tax or corporation tax by reference to the gift, subsection (3) or, as the case may be, subsection (4) shall apply.

(3) For the purposes of income tax for the year of assessment in which the person makes the gift, the amount of the gift shall be deducted from or set off against any income of the person chargeable to income tax for that year and income tax shall, where necessary, be discharged or repaid accordingly, and the total income of the person or, where the person is a married person whose income is deemed to be the income of his or her spouse, the total income of his or her spouse shall be calculated accordingly.

(4) For the purposes of corporation tax, where the person making the gift is a company, the amount of the gift shall be deemed to be a loss incurred by the company in a separate trade in the accounting period in which the gift is made.

[(5) The Tax Acts shall apply to a loss referred to in subsection (4) as they would apply if sections 396A and 420A had not been enacted.][1]

Amendments

1 Subs (5) inserted by FA 2002 s 56(1) with effect from 6 March 2001.

Definitions

the Oireachtas: IA 1937 Sch; person: IA 1937 s 11(*c*); Tax Acts: s 1(2); total income: s 3(1); year of assessment: s 3(1).

Former enactments

ITA 1967 s 195B(3) and (6) and s 547(1)–(3); CTA 1976 s 147(1)–(2) and Sch 2 Pt I para 27; FA 1993 s 10(1).

484 Relief for gifts for education in the arts

Amendments

Section 484 repealed by TCA 1997 s 848A(13) (inserted by FA 2001 s 45) with effect from 6 April 2001.

485 Relief for gifts to third-level institutions

Amendments

Section 485 repealed by TCA 1997 s 848A(13) (inserted by FA 2001 s 45) with effect from 6 April 2001.

485A Relief for gifts made to designated schools

Amendments

Section 485A repealed by TCA 1997 s 848A(13) (inserted by FA 2001 s 45) with effect from 6 April 2001.

485B Relief for gifts to the Scientific and Technological Education (Investment) Fund

Amendments

Section 485B repealed by TCA 1997 s 848A(13) (inserted by FA 2001 s 45) with effect from 6 April 2001.

CHAPTER 3

Corporation Tax Reliefs

486 Corporation tax: relief for gifts to First Step

Amendments

Section 486 repealed by TCA 1997 s 848A(13) (inserted by FA 2001 s 45) with effect from 6 April 2001.

486A Corporate donations to eligible charities

Amendments

Section 486A repealed by TCA 1997 s 848A(13) (inserted by FA 2001 s 45) with effect from 6 April 2001.

486B Relief for investment in renewable energy generation

[(1) In this section—

"authorised officer" means an officer of the Revenue Commissioners authorised by them in writing for the purposes of this section;

"commencement date" means the day on which section 62 of the Finance Act, 1998, comes into operation;

"the Minister" means the Minister for Public Enterprise;

"new ordinary shares" means new ordinary shares forming part of the ordinary share capital of a qualifying company which, throughout the period of five years commencing on the date such shares are issued, carry no present or future preferential right to dividends, or to a company's assets on its winding up, and no present or future preferential right to be redeemed;

"qualifying company" means a company which—

(*a*) is incorporated in the State,
(*b*) is resident in the State and not resident elsewhere, and
(*c*) exists solely for the purposes of undertaking a qualifying energy project;

"qualifying energy project" means a renewable energy project in respect of which the Minister has given a certificate under subsection (2) which has not been revoked under that subsection;

[**"qualifying period"** means the period commencing on the commencement date and ending on [31 December 2006][1];][2]

"relevant cost" in relation to a qualifying energy project means the amount of the capital expenditure incurred or to be incurred by the qualifying company for the purposes of undertaking the qualifying energy project reduced by an amount equal to such part of that expenditure as—

(*a*) is attributable to the acquisition of, or of rights in or over, land, and

(*b*) has been or is to be met directly or indirectly by the State or by any person other than the qualifying company;

"relevant deduction" means, subject to subsections (4) and (5), a deduction of an amount equal to a relevant investment;

"relevant investment" means a sum of money which is—

(*a*) paid in the qualifying period by a company on its own behalf to a qualifying company in respect of new ordinary shares in the qualifying company and is paid by the company directly to the qualifying company,

(*b*) paid by the company for the purposes of enabling the qualifying company to undertake a qualifying energy project, and

(*c*) used by the qualifying company within 2 years of the receipt of that sum for those purposes,

but does not include a sum of money paid to the qualifying company on terms which provide that it will be repaid, and a reference to the making of a relevant investment shall be construed as a reference to the payment of such a sum to a qualifying company;

"renewable energy project" means a renewable energy project (including a project successful in the Third Alternative Energy Requirement Competition (AER III — 1997) initiated by the Minister) in one or more of the following categories of technology—

(*a*) solar power,

(*b*) windpower,

(*c*) hydropower, and

(*d*) biomass.

(2) (*a*) (i) The Minister, on the making of an application by a qualifying company, may give a certificate to the qualifying company stating, in relation to a renewable energy project to be undertaken by the company, that the renewable energy project is a qualifying energy project for the purposes of this section.

(ii) An application under this section shall be in such form, and shall contain such information, as the Minister may direct.

(*b*) A certificate given by the Minister under paragraph (*a*) shall be subject to such conditions as the Minister may consider proper and specifies in the certificate.

(*c*) The Minister may amend or revoke any condition (including a condition amended by virtue of this paragraph) specified in such a certificate; the Minister shall give notice in writing to the qualifying company concerned of the amendment or revocation and, on such notice being given, this section shall apply as if—

(i) a condition so amended and the amendment of which is specified in the notice was specified in the certificate, and

(ii) a condition so revoked and the revocation of which is specified in the notice was not specified in the certificate.

(*d*) A reference in paragraph (*c*) to the amendment of a condition specified in a certificate includes a reference to the addition of any matter, by way of a further condition, to the terms of the certificate.

(*e*) Where a company fails to comply with any of the conditions specified in a certificate issued to it under paragraph (*a*)—

(i) that failure shall constitute the failure of an event to happen by reason of which relief is to be withdrawn under subsection (6), and

(ii) the Minister may, by notice in writing served by registered post on the company, revoke the certificate.

(3) Subject to this section, where in an accounting period a company makes a relevant investment, it shall, on making a claim in that behalf, be given a relevant deduction from its total profits for the accounting period; but, where the amount of the relevant deduction to which the company is entitled under this section in an accounting period exceeds its profits for that accounting period, an amount equal to that excess shall be carried forward to the succeeding accounting period and the amount so carried forward shall be treated for the purposes of this section as if it were a relevant investment made in that succeeding accounting period.

(4) Where in any period of 12 months ending on the day before an anniversary of the commencement date, the amount or the aggregate amount of the relevant investments made, or treated as made, by a company, or by the company and all companies which at any time in that period would be regarded as connected with the company, exceeds [€12,700,000][3]—

(*a*) no relief shall be given under this section in respect of the amount of the excess, and

(*b*) where there is more than one relevant investment, the inspector or, on appeal, the Appeal Commissioners shall make such apportionment of the relief available as shall be just and reasonable to allocate to each relevant investment a due proportion of the relief available and, where necessary, to grant to each company concerned an amount of relief proportionate to the amount of the relevant investment or the aggregate amount of the relevant investments made by it in the period.

(5) Relief under this section shall not be given in respect of a relevant investment which is made at any time in a qualifying company if, at that time, the aggregate of the amounts of that relevant investment and all other relevant investments made in the qualifying company at or before that time exceeds an amount equal to—

(*a*) 50 per cent of the relevant cost of the project, or

(*b*) [€9,525,000][4],

whichever is the lesser.

(6) (*a*) A claim to relief under this section may be allowed at any time after the time specified in paragraph (*c*) in respect of the payment of a sum to a qualifying company if—

(i) that payment, if it is used, within 2 years of its being paid, by the qualifying company for the purposes of a qualifying energy project, will be a relevant investment, and

(ii) all the conditions specified in this section for the giving of the relief are or will be satisfied,

but the relief shall be withdrawn if, by reason of the happening of any subsequent event including the revocation by the Minister of a certificate under subsection (2) or the failure of an event to happen which at the time the relief was given was expected to happen, the company making the claim was not entitled to the relief allowed.

(*b*) Where a company has made a relevant investment by means of a subscription for new ordinary shares of a qualifying company and any of those shares are disposed of at any time within 5 years after the time specified in paragraph (*c*), a claim to relief under this section shall not be allowed in respect of the amount subscribed for those shares, and if any such relief has been given, it shall be withdrawn.

(*c*) The time referred to in paragraph (*a*) and paragraph (*b*) is the time when the payment in respect of which relief is claimed has been made.

(7) A claim for relief in respect of a relevant investment in a company shall not be allowed unless it is accompanied by a certificate issued by the company in such form as the Revenue Commissioners may direct and certifying that the conditions for the relief, in so far as they apply to the company and the qualifying energy project, are or will be satisfied in relation to that relevant investment.

(8) Before issuing a certificate for the purposes of subsection (7), a qualifying company shall furnish the authorised officer with—

(*a*) a statement to the effect that it satisfies or will satisfy the conditions for the relief in so far as they apply in relation to the company and the qualifying energy project,

(*b*) a copy of the certificate, including a copy of any notice given by the Minister specifying the amendment or revocation of a condition specified in that certificate, under subsection (2) in respect of the qualifying energy project, and

(*c*) such other information as the Revenue Commissioners may reasonably require,

(9) A certificate to which subsection (7) relates shall not be issued—

(*a*) without the authority of the authorised officer, or

(*b*) in relation to a relevant investment in respect of which relief may not be given by virtue of subsection (5).

(10) Any statement under subsection (8) shall—

(*a*) contain such information as the Revenue Commissioners may reasonably require,

(*b*) be in such form as the Revenue Commissioners may direct, and

(*c*) contain a declaration that it is correct to the best of the company's knowledge and belief.

(11) Where a qualifying company has issued a certificate for the purposes of subsection (7) or furnished a statement under subsection (8) and either—

(*a*) the certificate or statement is false or misleading in a material respect and is so false or misleading due to fraud or neglect, or

(*b*) the certificate was issued in contravention of subsection (9),

then—

(i) the company shall be liable to a penalty not exceeding [€630][5] or, in the case of fraud, not exceeding [€1,265][6], and such penalty may, without prejudice to any other method of recovery, be proceeded for and recovered summarily in the like manner as in summary proceedings for the recovery of any fine or penalty under any Act relating to the excise, and

(ii) no relief shall be given under this section in respect of the matter to which the certificate or statement relates and, if any such relief has been given, it shall be withdrawn.

(12) A company shall not be entitled to relief in respect of a relevant investment unless the relevant investment—

(*a*) has been made for bona fide commercial reasons and not as part of a scheme or arrangement the main purpose or one of the main purposes of which is the avoidance of tax,

(*b*) has been or will be used for the purposes of undertaking a qualifying energy project, and

(*c*) is made at the risk of the company and neither the company nor any person who would be regarded as connected with the company is entitled to receive any payment in money or money's worth or other benefit directly or indirectly borne by or attributable to the qualifying company, other than a payment made on an arm's length basis for goods or services supplied or a payment out of the proceeds of exploiting the qualifying energy project to which the company is entitled under the terms subject to which the relevant investment is made.

(13) Where any relief has been given under this section which is subsequently found not to have been due or is to be withdrawn by virtue of subsection (6) or (11), that relief shall be withdrawn by making an assessment to corporation tax, under Case IV of Schedule D, for the accounting period or accounting periods in which relief was given and, notwithstanding anything in the Tax Acts, such an assessment may be made at any time.

(14)(*a*) Subject to paragraph (*b*), where a company is entitled to relief under this section in respect of any sum or any part of a sum, or would be so entitled on duly making a claim in that behalf, as a relevant deduction from its total profits for any accounting period, it shall not be entitled to any relief for that sum or that part of a sum, in computing its income or profits, or as a deduction from its income or profits, for any accounting period under any other provision of the Tax Acts or the Capital Gains Tax Acts.

(*b*) Where a company has made a relevant investment by means of a subscription for new ordinary shares of a qualifying company and none of those shares is disposed of by the company within five years of their acquisition by that company, then, the sums allowable as deductions from the consideration ("the consideration concerned") in the computation for the purpose of capital gains tax of the gain or loss accruing to the company on the disposal of those shares shall be determined without regard to any relief under this section which the company has obtained, or would be entitled, on duly making a claim in that behalf, to obtain, except that, where those sums exceed the consideration concerned, they shall be reduced by an amount equal to the lesser of—

(i) the amount of the relevant deduction allowed to the company under this section in respect of the subscription for those shares, and

(ii) the amount of the excess.][7]

Amendments

1 Substituted by FA 2004 s 39(1) with effect from such day as the Minister for Finance may appoint by order; previously "31 December 2004". By virtue of the Finance Act 2004 (Section 39) (Commencement) Order 2004, SI No 645 of 2004, this amendment comes into operation on 27 September 2004.

2 Definition of "qualifying period" substituted by FA 2002 s 43(1) from such day as the Minister for Finance may by order appoint: previously "'qualifying period' means the period commencing on the commencement date and ending on the day before the third anniversary of that date;". By virtue of the Finance Act 2002 (Section 43) Commencement Order 2004, SI No 646 of 2004, this amendment comes into operation on 24 September 2004.

3 Substituted by FA 2001 s 240(1) and (2)(*c*) and Sch 5 Pt 1 for accounting periods ending on or after 1 January 2002; previously "£10,000,000".

4 Substituted by FA 2001 s 240(1) and (2)(*c*) and Sch 5 Pt 1 for accounting periods ending on or after 1 January 2002; previously "£7,500,000".

5 Substituted by FA 2001 s 240(1) and (2)(*k*) and Sch 5 Pt 1 for acts or omissions which take place or begin on or after 1 January 2002; previously "£500".

6 Substituted by FA 2001 s 240(1) and (2)(*k*) and Sch 5 Pt 1 for acts or omissions which take place or begin on or after 1 January 2002; previously "£1,000".

7 Section 486B inserted by FA 1998 s 62 from such date as the Minister for Finance may appoint by order. The section came into operation from 18 March 1999—Finance Act, 1998 (Section 62) (Commencement) Order, 1999 SI No 65 of 1999 refers.

Definitions

Appeal Commissioners: s 2(1); Capital Gains Tax Acts: s 1(2); company: ss 4(1), 5(1); inspector: s 2(1); month: IA 1937 Sch; ordinary share capital: s 2(1); person: IA 1937 s 11(*c*); profits: s 4(1); tax: s 2(2); writing: IA 1937 Sch.

487 Corporation tax: credit for bank levy

(1) (*a*) In this section—

"accounting profit" means the amount of profit, after taxation and before extraordinary items—

(i) shown in the profit and loss account—

(I) in the case of a company resident in the State, which is required under section 148 of the Companies Act, 1963, to be laid before the annual general meeting of the company, or which would be so shown but for subsection (4) of section 149 of that Act, and

(II) in the case of a company not resident in the State and carrying on a trade in the State through a branch or agency, of that branch or agency and which is certified by the auditor appointed under section 160 of the Companies Act, 1963, or under the law of the state in which the company is incorporated and which corresponds to that section, as presenting a true and fair view of the profit or loss attributable to that branch or agency,

(ii) reduced by the amount of such profit as is attributable to—

(I) dividends received from companies resident in the State which are members of the group of which that company is a member,

(II) gains on disposal of capital assets,

(III) relevant trading operations within the meaning of section 446,

(IV) trading operations carried on outside of the State and in respect of which the company is chargeable to corporation tax in the State and to tax on income in another state, and

(V) dividends received from companies not resident in the State,

and

(iii) increased—

(I) as respects income from sources specified in subparagraphs (III), (IV) and (V) of paragraph (ii), by an amount determined by the formula—

$$\frac{100 \times T}{R}$$

where—

T is the corporation tax chargeable in respect of that income computed in accordance with the provisions of the Corporation Tax Acts and after allowing relief under Parts 14 and 35, and

R is the rate of corporation tax for the accounting period concerned and to which section 21 relates, but where part of the accounting period falls in one financial year and the other part falls in the financial year succeeding the first-mentioned financial year, R shall be determined by applying the formula specified in section 78(3)(*b*), and

(II) by the amount of stamp duty charged under section 64 of the Finance Act, 1989, section 108 of the Finance Act, 1990, section 200 of the Finance Act, 1992, or section 142 of the Finance Act, 1995, and under [section 126 of the Stamp Duties Consolidation Act, 1999],[1] as has been taken into account in computing that amount of profit, after taxation and before extraordinary items;

"adjusted group base tax", in relation to a relevant period, means—

(i) an amount determined by the formula—

$$\frac{T \times P}{B}$$

where—

T is the group base tax,

P is the group profit of the relevant period, and

B is the group base profit,

or

(ii) if it is greater, the group advance corporation tax of the relevant period;

"advance corporation tax", in relation to a relevant period, means the aggregate of the amounts of advance corporation tax paid or treated as paid by a company, and not repaid, under Chapter 8 of Part 6, in respect of distributions made in accounting periods falling wholly or partly within the relevant period and, where an accounting period falls partly within a relevant period, the aggregate shall include a part of the advance corporation tax so paid proportionate to the part of the accounting period falling within the relevant period;

"base profit", in relation to a company, means 50 per cent of the aggregate of the amounts of accounting profit of a company for accounting periods falling wholly or partly in the period beginning on the 1st day of April, 1989, and ending on the 31st day of March, 1991, and, where an accounting period falls partly within that period, the aggregate shall include a part of the accounting profit of the accounting period proportionate to the part of the accounting period falling within that period;

"base tax" means 50 per cent of the aggregate of the corporation tax chargeable on a company, exclusive of the corporation tax on the part of the company's profits attributable to chargeable gains and before the set-off of advance corporation tax under Chapter 8 of Part 6, for accounting periods falling wholly or partly in the period beginning on the 1st day of April, 1989, and ending on the 31st day of March, 1991, and, where an accounting period falls partly within that period, the aggregate shall include a part of the corporation tax so chargeable for the accounting period proportionate to the part of the accounting period falling within that period;

"group advance corporation tax", in relation to a relevant period, means the aggregate of the amounts of advance corporation tax in relation to the relevant period of companies which throughout the relevant period are members of the group;

"group base profit" means the aggregate of the amounts of base profit of companies which throughout the relevant period are members of the group;

"group base tax" means the aggregate of the amounts of base tax of companies which throughout the relevant period are members of the group, but where the amount of the group base tax is an amount which is—

(i) greater than 43 per cent, or

(ii) lower than 10 per cent,

of the group base profit, computed in accordance with this section but without regard to subparagraphs (III), (IV) and (V) of paragraph (ii), or subparagraph (I) of paragraph (iii), of the definition of **"accounting profit"**, the group base tax shall be deemed to be an amount equal to 25 per cent of the group base profit as so computed;

"group profit", in relation to a relevant period, means the aggregate of the amounts of profit of the relevant period of companies which throughout that period are members of the group;

"group tax liability", in relation to a relevant period, means the aggregate of the amounts of tax liability of the relevant period of companies which throughout that period are members of the group;

"levy payment" means the aggregate of the amounts charged in the year 1992 or in any later year under section 200 of the Finance Act, 1992, or section 142 of the Finance Act, 1995, and which have been paid, on or before the date by which the amounts are payable, by companies which are members of a group;

"profit", in relation to a relevant period, means the aggregate of the accounting profit, computed on the same basis as that on which the base profit of the company is computed, of a company for accounting periods falling wholly or partly within the relevant period and, where an accounting period falls partly within a relevant period, the aggregate shall include a part of the accounting profit of the accounting period proportionate to the part of the accounting period falling within that relevant period;

"relevant period", in relation to a levy payment, means a period beginning on the 1st day of April preceding the date on or before which the levy payment is to be made and ending on the 31st day of March next after that date;

"tax liability", in relation to a relevant period, means the aggregate of the corporation tax which apart from this section would be chargeable on a company, exclusive of the corporation tax on the part of the company's profits attributable to chargeable gains and before the set-off of advance corporation tax under Chapter 8 of Part 6, for accounting periods falling wholly or partly within the relevant period and, where an accounting period falls partly within that period, the aggregate shall include a part of the corporation tax so chargeable for the accounting period proportionate to the part of the accounting period falling within that period.

(*b*) For the purposes of this section—

(i) 2 companies shall be deemed to be members of a group if one company is a 75 per cent subsidiary of the other company or both companies are 75 per cent subsidiaries of a third company; but—

(I) in determining whether one company is a 75 per cent subsidiary of another company, the other company shall be treated as not being the owner of—

(A) any share capital which it owns directly in a company if a profit on a sale of the shares would be treated as a trading receipt of its trade, or

(B) any share capital which it owns indirectly, and which is owned directly by a company for which a profit on a sale of the shares would be a trading receipt,

and

(II) a company which is an assurance company within the meaning of section 706 shall not be a member of a group,

(ii) sections 412 to 418 shall apply for the purposes of this paragraph as they apply for the purposes of Chapter 5 of Part 12,

(iii) a company and all its 75 per cent subsidiaries shall form a group and, where that company is a member of a group as being itself a 75 per cent subsidiary, that group shall comprise all its 75 per cent subsidiaries and the first-mentioned group shall be deemed not to be a group; but a company which is not a member of a group shall be treated as if it were a member of a group which consists of that company, and accordingly references to group advance corporation tax, group base profit, group base tax, group profit and group tax liability shall be construed as if they were respectively references to advance corporation tax, base profit, base tax, profit and tax liability of that company,

(iv) the part of a company's profits attributable to chargeable gains for an accounting period shall be taken to be the amount brought into the company's profits for that period for the purposes of corporation tax in respect of chargeable gains before any deduction for charges on income, expenses of management or other amounts which can be deducted from or set against or treated as reducing profits of more than one description,

(v) the income or profit attributable to any trading operations or dividends shall be such amount of the income or profit as appears to the inspector or on appeal to the Appeal Commissioners to be just and reasonable, and

(vi) corporation tax chargeable in respect of any income shall be the corporation tax which would not have been chargeable but for that income.

(2) Where for a relevant period in relation to a levy payment the group tax liability exceeds the adjusted group base tax of that relevant period, all or part of the levy payment, not being greater than the excess of the group tax liability over the adjusted group base tax, may be set against the group tax liability of the relevant period in accordance with this section.

(3) (*a*) In this subsection, **"appropriate inspector"** has the same meaning as in section 950.

(*b*) Where under subsection (2) an amount of levy payment may be set against the group tax liability of a relevant period, so much (in this paragraph referred to as **"the apportionable part"**) of the amount as bears to that amount the same proportion as the tax liability of the relevant period of a company which is a member of the group bears to the group tax liability of the relevant period shall be apportioned to the company, and the companies which are members of the group may, by giving notice in writing to the appropriate inspector within a period of 9 months after the end of the relevant period, elect to have the apportionable part apportioned in such manner as is specified in the notice.

(4) Where an amount is apportioned to a company under subsection (3), that amount shall be set against the tax liability of the relevant period of the company and, to the extent that an amount is so set off, it shall be treated for the purposes of the Corporation Tax Acts as if it were a payment of corporation tax made on the day on which that

corporation tax is to be paid; but an amount or part of an amount which is to be treated as if it were a payment of corporation tax may not be repaid to a company by virtue of a claim to relief under the Corporation Tax Acts or for any other reason.

(5) Where under subsection (4) an amount is to be set against the tax liability of a relevant period of a company and the tax liability of the relevant period consists of the aggregate of corporation tax chargeable for more accounting periods than one, the amount shall be set against the corporation tax of each of those accounting periods in the proportion which the corporation tax of the accounting period or the part of the accounting period, as the case may be, and which is included in the tax liability of the relevant period bears to the tax liability of the relevant period.

(6) Where—

(*a*) the end of an accounting period (in this subsection referred to as **"the first-mentioned accounting period"**) of a company which is a member of a group does not coincide with the end of the relevant period,

(*b*) the tax liability of—

(i) one or more accounting periods of the company ending after the end of the first-mentioned accounting period, or

(ii) one or more accounting periods of any other member of the group ending after the end of the first-mentioned accounting period,

is to be taken into account in determining the amount of the levy payment which may be set off under this section against the corporation tax of—

(I) the first-mentioned accounting period, or one or more accounting periods ending before the end of that period, of the company, or

(II) one or more accounting periods of any other member of the group ending on or before the end of the first-mentioned accounting period,

and

(*c*) on the specified return date (within the meaning of section 950) it is not possible—

(i) for the first-mentioned accounting period, or any other accounting period ending before the end of that period, of the company, or

(ii) for one or more accounting periods of any other member of the group ending on or before the end of the first-mentioned accounting period,

to determine the amount of the levy payment which may be so set off,

then, the amount of levy payment which may be set off under this section against the corporation tax of an accounting period shall be taken to be the amount which would have been so set off if a period of 12 months ending on the last day of the most recent accounting period of the parent company (being a member of the group which is not a subsidiary of any other member of the group) which ends in the relevant period were the relevant period; but, where a part only of that period of 12 months falls after the 31st day of March, 1992, the amount to be set off under this subsection shall be reduced to an amount proportionate to the part of that period of 12 months falling after that day.

(7) (*a*) A company shall deliver, as soon as they become available, such particulars as are required to determine the amount of levy payment which apart from subsection (6) is to be set off against the corporation tax of an accounting period.

(*b*) Where an amount of levy payment has been set off against corporation tax of an accounting period under subsection (6) and the company delivers such particulars as are required to be delivered in accordance with paragraph (*a*), the inspector shall adjust any computation or assessment by reference to the difference between these amounts and any amount of corporation tax overpaid shall be repaid and any amount of corporation tax underpaid shall be paid.

(8) (*a*) An amount of tax to be repaid under subsection (7) shall be repaid with interest in all respects as if it were a repayment of preliminary tax under section 953(7).

(*b*) Interest shall not be charged under section 1080 on any amount of tax underpaid under this subsection unless the amount is not paid within one month of the date on which the amount of the underpayment is notified to the chargeable person by the inspector, and the amount of tax so unpaid shall not be treated as part of the tax payable for the chargeable period for the purposes of section 958(4)(*b*).

Amendments

1 Substituted by SDCA 1999 s 162 and Sch 4 with effect from 15 December 1999; previously "section 94 of the Finance Act, 1986".

Definitions

Appeal Commissioners: s 2(1); branch or agency: s 4(1); charges on income: ss 4(1), 243(1); company: ss 4(1), 5(1); Corporation Tax Acts: s 1(2); month: IA 1937 Sch; person: IA 1937 s 11(*c*); profits: s 4(1); shares: s 5(1); trade: ss 3(1), 4(1), 5(1); writing: IA 1937 Sch.

Former enactments

FA 1992 s 45; FA 1995 s 56; FA 1997 s 146(1) and Sch 9 Pt I para 16(1).

PART 16
INCOME TAX RELIEF FOR INVESTMENT IN CORPORATE TRADES—BUSINESS EXPANSION SCHEME AND SEED CAPITAL SCHEME

Cross-references

Method of apportioning reliefs and charging tax in cases of separate assessment: s 1024(2)(*a*)(xi).

Self assessment, date for payment of tax: s 958(6)(*a*).

Special investment schemes: s 737(8)(*a*)(iv), (9)(*a*).

Special portfolio investment accounts: s 838(7).

Transitional arrangements in relation to FA 1998 s 34: FA 1998 s 35(1) (the principal provisions) and (3).

Transitional arrangements in relation to FA 2004 s 18(1)(*a*)(ii): FA 2004 s 19(1)(the principal provisions).

Revenue information

Information leaflet IT15 — The Seed Capital Scheme: Tax Refunds for New Enterprises.

Information leaflet IT55 — The Business Expansion Scheme: Relief for Investment in Corporate Trades.

Tax Briefing

TB47 April 2002 p 10 — Business Expansion and Seed Capital Schemes — Finance Act 2002 amendments.

TB47 April 2002 p 21 — Extension of limits for Business Expansion Scheme and possible application of s 501 TCA 1997.

488 Interpretation (Part 16)

(1) In this Part—

"advance factory building" means a factory building the construction of which is—

(*a*) promoted by a local community group the objective of which, or one of the main objectives of which, is to promote the development of, and the creation of opportunities for employment in, its locality, and

(*b*) undertaken without any prior commitment, either direct or indirect, in writing or otherwise, by a person that either the person or any other person will enter into a lease for its use;

"associate" has the same meaning in relation to a person as it has by virtue of subsection (3) of section 433 in relation to a participator, except that the reference in paragraph (*b*) of that subsection to any relative of a participator shall be excluded from such meaning;

"certifying agency" means an industrial development agency, Bord Fáilte Éireann, An Bord Iascaigh Mhara or An Bord Tráchtála— The Irish Trade Board (as may be appropriate);

"certifying Minister" means the Minister for Agriculture and Food, the Minister for Arts, Heritage, Gaeltacht and the Islands or the Minister for the Marine and Natural Resources (as may be appropriate);

"control", except in sections 493(7) and 507(2)(*b*), shall be construed in accordance with subsections (2) to (6) of section 432;

"debenture" has the same meaning as in section 2 of the Companies Act, 1963;

"director" shall be construed in accordance with section 433(4);

"eligible shares" means new ordinary shares which, throughout the period of 5 years beginning on the date on which they are issued, carry no present or future preferential right to dividends or to a company's assets on its winding up and no present or future preferential right to be redeemed;

[**"Exchange Axess"** means the company incorporated under the Companies Acts, 1963 to 1999, on 19 July 1999 as Exchange Axess Limited;][1]

"factory building" has the same meaning as in section 2 of the Industrial Development Act, 1986;

"full-time employee" and **"full-time director"** have the same meanings respectively as in section 250;

"industrial development agency" means Forbairt, the Industrial Development Agency (Ireland), the Shannon Free Airport Development Company Limited or Údarás na Gaeltachta (as may be appropriate);

"market value" shall be construed in accordance with section 548;

"ordinary shares" means shares forming part of a company's ordinary share capital;

"qualifying company" has the meaning assigned to it by section 495;

"qualifying trading operations" has the meaning assigned to it by section 496(2);

"relevant employment", in relation to a specified individual, means employment throughout the relevant period by the company in which the specified individual makes a relevant investment (being that individual's first such investment in that company) and where the specified individual is a full-time employee or full-time director of the company;

"relevant investment", in relation to a specified individual, means the amount or the aggregate of the amounts subscribed in a year of assessment by the specified individual for eligible shares in a qualifying company which carries on or intends to carry on relevant trading operations;

"relevant period", in relation to relief in respect of any eligible shares issued by a company, means—

(*a*) as respects sections 493 and 498 to 501, the period beginning on the incorporation of the company (or, if the company was incorporated more than 2 years before the date on which the shares were issued, beginning 2 years before that date) and ending 5 years after the issue of the shares,

(*b*) as respects sections 495, 496, 503 and 507, the period beginning on the date on which the shares were issued and ending either 3 years after that date or, where the company was not at that date carrying on a qualifying trade, 3 years after the date on which it subsequently began to carry on such a trade,

(*c*) as respects a relevant employment, the period beginning on the date on which the shares are issued or, if later, the date on which the employment commences and ending 12 months after that date, and

(*d*) as respects a specified individual, the period beginning on the date on which the shares are issued and ending either 2 years after that date or, where the company was not at that date carrying on relevant trading operations, 2 years after the date on which it subsequently began to carry on such operations;

"relevant trading operations" has the meaning assigned to it by section 497;

"specified individual" has the meaning assigned to it by section 494;

"the relief" and **"relief"** mean relief under section 489, and references to the amount of the relief shall be construed in accordance with subsection (6) of that section;

"unquoted company" means a company none of whose shares, stocks or debentures are—

(*a*) listed in the official list of a stock exchange, or

[(*b*) quoted on an unlisted securities market of a stock exchange other than—

(i) on the market known, and referred to in this definition, as the Developing Companies Market of the Irish Stock Exchange, or

(ii) on the Developing Companies Market of the Irish Stock Exchange and on any similar or corresponding market of the stock exchange of one or more Member States of the European Communities; but this subparagraph shall not apply unless the shares, stocks or debentures are quoted on the Developing Companies Market of the Irish Stock Exchange before or at the same time as they are firstly quoted on an unlisted securities market of a stock exchange of another Member State of the European Communities.][2]

(2) References in this Part to a disposal of shares include references to a disposal of an interest or right in or over the shares, and an individual shall be treated for the purposes of this Part as disposing of any shares which the individual is treated by virtue of section 587 as exchanging for other shares.

(3) References in this Part to the reduction of any amount include references to its reduction to nil.

(4) References in this Part to a trade shall be construed—

(*a*) without regard to so much of the definition of **"trade"** in section 3 as relates to adventures or concerns in the nature of trade, and

(*b*) as including—

(i) the construction and leasing of an advance factory building,

(ii) the research and development or other similar activity referred to in section 496(2)(*a*)(x), and

(iii) the production, publication, marketing and promotion of a qualifying recording or qualifying recordings referred to in section 496(2)(*a*)(xii);

but for the other purposes of the Tax Acts the question of whether a trade is being carried on shall be determined without regard to this subsection.

Amendments

1 Definition of "Exchange Axess" inserted by FA 2000 s 19(1)(*a*) with effect from 1 May 1998.

2 Definition of "unquoted company" para (*b*) substituted by FA 1999 s 16(*a*) with effect from 6 April 1997.

Cross-references

Capital gains tax share reinvestment relief, meanings of "eligible shares" and "ordinary shares" applied: s 591(1).

Finance for trade of subsidiary, para (*b*) of definition of "relevant period", subs (1), applied by: Sch 10 para 1.

Special portfolio investment accounts, meaning of "eligible shares" applied: s 838(5)(*a*).

Transitional arrangements in relation to FA 1998 s 34, meaning of "certifying agency", "certifying Minister" and "eligible shares" applied: FA 1998 s 35(1).

Transitional arrangements in relation to FA 2004 s 18(1)(*a*)(ii), meaning of "certifying agency", "certifying Minister", "eligible shares" and "industrial development agency" applied: FA 2004 s 19(1).

Definitions

company: ss 4(1), 5(1); interest: s 4(1); lease: s 5(1); ordinary share capital: s 2(1); person: IA 1937 s 11(*c*); relative: s 3(1); shares: s 5(1); trade: ss 3(1), 4(1), 5(1); writing: IA 1937 Sch.

Former enactments

FA 1984 s 11(1), (3) and (4), s 12(2) and (7) and s 16(4); FA 1985 s 13(*a*); FA 1990 s 10(*a*); FA 1993 s 25(*a*) and (*b*)(v); FA 1994 s 16(1)(*a*)(i); FA 1995 s 17(1)(*a*); FA 1996 s 16 and s 131; FA 1997 s 9(*a*); FA 1997 s 146(1) and Sch 9 Pt I para 13(1).

Corresponding UK tax provision

Income and Corporation Taxes Act 1988 s 312.

489 The relief

(1) This Part shall apply for affording relief from income tax where, subject to subsection (2)—

(*a*) an individual who qualifies for the relief subscribes for eligible shares in a qualifying company, (*b*) those shares are issued to the individual for the purpose of raising money for a qualifying trade being carried on by the company or which the company intends to carry on, and

(*c*) the company provides satisfactory evidence, and it appears to the Revenue Commissioners after such consultation, if any, as may seem to them to be necessary with such person or body of persons as in their opinion may be of assistance to them, that the money was used, is being used or is intended to be used—

(i) for the purposes of—

(I) enabling the company, or enlarging its capacity, to undertake qualifying trading operations,

(II) enabling the company to engage in, or assisting the company in—

(A) research and development,

(B) the acquisition of technological information and data,

(C) the development of new or existing products or services, or

(D) the provision of new products or services,

(III) enabling the company to identify new markets, and to develop new and existing markets, for its products and services, or

(IV) enabling the company to increase its sales of products or provision of services,

and

(ii) with a view to the creation or maintenance of employment—

(I) in the company, or

(II) in the case of qualifying trading operations referred to in section 496(2)(*a*)(ix), in either or both a company contracted to construct the advance factory building concerned and a company which enters into a lease for its use.

(2) Where the money raised for the purpose specified in subsection (1)(*b*) was used, is being used or is intended to be used—

(*a*) for the purposes of qualifying trading operations referred to in section 496(2)(*a*)(iv) and in respect of which money is raised or intended to be raised under this Part by virtue of section 496(2)(*a*)(iv)(II), the evidence referred to in subsection (1)(*c*) shall include the certificate referred to in section 496(5),

(*b*) for the purposes of qualifying trading operations referred to in section 496(2)(*a*)(vii), the evidence referred to in subsection (1)(*c*) shall include the certificate referred to in section 496(7),

(*c*) for the purposes of qualifying trading operations referred to in section 496(2)(*a*)(x) (in this paragraph referred to as **"the operations"**), the evidence referred to in subsection (1)(*c*) shall include a certificate by an industrial development agency certifying that it is satisfied that the operations—

(i) have the potential to result in the commencement of qualifying trading operations referred to in subparagraphs (i), (ii) and (viii) of section 496(2)(*a*), and

(ii) have commenced,

(*d*) for the purposes of qualifying trading operations referred to in section 496(2)(*a*)(xii), the evidence referred to in subsection (1)(*c*) shall include the certificate referred to in section 496(8),

(*e*) for the purpose of the construction and the leasing of an advance factory building, the evidence referred to in subsection (1)(*c*) shall include a certificate by an industrial development agency certifying that it has satisfied itself that—

(i) the building is or will be an advance factory building, and

(ii) (I) the advance factory building is or will be situated in an area which, on the basis of guidelines agreed with the consent of the Minister for Finance between the industrial development agency and the Minister for Enterprise, Trade and Employment or the Minister for Arts, Heritage, Gaeltacht and the Islands (as may be appropriate in the circumstances), was or is in particular need of development and of the creation of opportunities for employment, and

(II) the construction of the advance factory building contributes or will contribute significantly to meeting those needs, and

(*f*) for the purposes of relevant trading operations, the evidence referred to in subsection (1)(*c*) shall include a certificate under section 497(2).

(3) Subject to subsections (4) and (5), relief in respect of the amount subscribed by an individual for any eligible shares shall be given as a deduction of that amount from his or her total income for the year of assessment in which the shares are issued.

(4) Where—

(*a*) in accordance with section 508 relief is due in respect of an amount subscribed as nominee for a qualifying individual by the managers of a designated fund, and

(*b*) the eligible shares in respect of which the amount is subscribed are issued in the year of assessment following the year of assessment in which that amount was subscribed to the designated fund,

the individual may elect by notice in writing to the inspector to have the relief due given as a deduction from his or her total income for the year of assessment in which the amount was subscribed to the designated fund, instead of (as provided for in subsection (3)) as a deduction from his or her total income for the year of assessment in which the shares are issued.

[(4A) Notwithstanding any other provision of this section, where—

(*a*) (i) in accordance with section 508 relief is due in respect of an amount subscribed as nominee for a qualifying individual by the managers of a designated fund,

(ii) the amount so subscribed was subscribed to the designated fund in the period beginning on 1 January 2002 and ending on 31 January 2002, and

(iii) the eligible shares in respect of which the amount is subscribed by the managers of the designated fund are issued on or before 31 December 2002,

or

(*b*) eligible shares are issued by a qualifying company to a qualifying individual in the period beginning on 1 January 2002 and ending on 31 January 2002,

the qualifying individual may elect by notice in writing to the inspector to have the relief due given as a deduction from his or her total income for the year of assessment 2001 instead of (as provided for in subsection (3)) as a deduction from his or her total income for the year of assessment 2002.][1]

[(4B) Notwithstanding any other provision of this section, where—

(*a*) (i) in accordance with section 508 relief is due in respect of an amount subscribed as nominee for a qualifying individual by the managers of a designated fund,

(ii) the amount so subscribed was subscribed to the designated fund in the period beginning on 1 January 2004 and ending on 4 February 2004, and

(iii) the eligible shares in respect of which the amount is subscribed by the managers of the designated fund are issued on or before 31 December 2004,

or

(*b*) eligible shares are issued by a qualifying company to a qualifying individual in the period beginning on 1 January 2004 and ending on 4 February 2004,

then the qualifying individual may elect, by notice in writing to the inspector, to have the relief due given as a deduction from his or her total income for the year of assessment 2003 instead of (as provided for in subsection (3)) as a deduction from his or her total income for the year of assessment 2004.][2]

(5) (*a*) Subject to this subsection, a specified individual may, in relation to a relevant investment made by such individual (being that individual's first such investment), elect by notice in writing to the inspector to have the relief due given as a deduction from such individual's total income for any one of the [6 years][2] of assessment immediately before the year of assessment in which the eligible shares in respect of that investment are issued which such individual nominates for the purpose, instead of (as provided for in subsection (3)) as a deduction from the specified individual's total income for the year of assessment in which the shares are issued, and accordingly, subject to section 490 and paragraphs (*c*) and (*d*), for the purpose of granting such relief (but for no other purpose of this Part) the shares shall be deemed to have been issued in the year of assessment so nominated.

(*b*) Where the specified individual makes a subsequent relevant investment (being that individual's second such investment)—

(i) in the same company as such individual's first such investment, and

(ii) within either the year of assessment following the end of the year of assessment in which such individual's first such investment was made or the year of assessment subsequent to that year,

then, the specified individual may, in relation to such individual's second such investment, elect by notice in writing to the inspector to have the relief due given as a deduction from such individual's total income for any one of the [6 years][3] of assessment immediately before the year of assessment in which the eligible shares in respect of such individual's first such investment were issued which such individual nominates for the purpose, instead of (as provided for in subsection (3)) as a deduction from such individual's total income for the year of assessment in which the eligible shares in respect of such individual's second such investment are issued, and accordingly, subject to section 490 and paragraphs (*c*) and (*d*), for the purpose of granting such relief (but for no other purpose of this Part) the shares issued in respect of the second such investment shall be deemed to have been issued in the year of assessment so nominated.

(*c*) Where any of the years of assessment following the year of assessment nominated under paragraph (*a*) or (*b*), as the case may be, precede the year of assessment in which the eligible shares in respect of the specified individual's first relevant investment are in fact issued, subsections (3) to (5) of section 490 shall operate to give relief in such years of assessment as may be nominated by such individual for that purpose.

(*d*) To the extent that the amount of the relief which would be due in respect of the specified individual's first relevant investment or second relevant investment, as the case may be, has not been given in accordance with paragraphs (*a*) to (*c*), it shall, subject to subsections (3) to (5) of section 490, be given for the year of assessment in which the eligible shares in respect of the first such investment or the second such investment, as the case may be, are in fact issued or, if appropriate, a subsequent year of assessment.

(*e*) This subsection shall apply in respect of not more than 2 relevant investments made by a specified individual on or after the 2nd day of June, 1995.

(6) References in this Part to the amount of the relief are references to the amount of the deduction given under subsection (3), (4) or (5) (as may be appropriate).

(7) (*a*) Subject to paragraphs (*b*) and (*c*), the relief shall be given on a claim and shall not be allowed—

(i) (I) in the case of a relevant investment, unless and until the company commences to carry on the relevant trading operations, and

(II) in any other case, unless and until the company has carried on the trade for 4 months, and

(ii) if the company is not carrying on that trade at the time when the shares are issued, unless the company—

(I) expends not less than 80 per cent of the money subscribed for the shares on research and development work which is connected with and undertaken with a view to the carrying on of the trade, and begins to carry on the trade within 3 years after that time,

or

(II) otherwise begins to carry on the trade within 2 years after that time.

(*b*) In the case of qualifying trading operations referred to in section 496(2)(*a*)(ix), for the purposes of paragraph (*a*), the trade shall be deemed to have commenced on the date on which the construction of the advance factory building commenced.

(*c*) In the case of qualifying trading operations referred to in section 496(2)(*a*)(x), for the purposes of paragraph (*a*), the trade shall be deemed to have commenced on the date on which the certificate referred to in subsection (2)(*c*) was issued.

(8) Subject to subsection (7)(*a*)(i), a claim for relief may be allowed at any time if the conditions for the relief are then satisfied.

(9) In the case of a claim allowed before the end of the relevant period, the relief shall be withdrawn if by reason of any subsequent event it appears that the claimant was not entitled to the relief allowed.

(10) In the case of a claim allowed before a specified individual commences a relevant employment with the company in which that individual has made a relevant investment (being that individual's first such investment), the relief shall be withdrawn if the specified individual fails to commence such employment—

(*a*) within the year of assessment in which the investment is made, or

(*b*) if later, within 6 months of the date of—

(i) where the investment consists of the subscription of only one amount for eligible shares, that subscription, or

(ii) where the investment consists of the subscription of more than one amount for eligible shares, the last such subscription.

(11) Where by reason of its being wound up, or dissolved without winding up, the company carries on the qualifying trade for a period shorter than 4 months, subsection (7)(*a*)(i) shall apply as if it referred to that shorter period but only if it is shown that the winding up or dissolution was for bona fide commercial reasons and not as part of a scheme or arrangement the main purpose or one of the main purposes of which was the avoidance of tax.

(12) Subject to section 506, no account shall be taken of the relief, in so far as it is not withdrawn, in determining whether any sums are excluded by virtue of section 554 from the sums allowable as a deduction in the computation of gains and losses for the purposes of the Capital Gains Tax Acts.

(13) Where an individual is entitled to relief under this section in respect of a subscription by him or her for eligible shares in a company, he or she shall not be entitled to relief in respect of that subscription under section 479.

(14)(*a*) In this subsection, **"distribution"** has the same meaning as in the Corporation Tax Acts.

(*b*) For the purposes of this subsection, an amount specified or implied shall include an amount specified or implied in a foreign currency.

(*c*) This subsection shall apply to shares in a company where any agreement, arrangement or understanding exists which could reasonably be considered to eliminate the risk that the person beneficially owning those shares—

(i) might, at or after a time specified in or implied by that agreement, arrangement or understanding, be unable to realise directly or indirectly in money or money's worth an amount so specified or implied, other than a distribution, in respect of those shares, or

(ii) might not receive an amount so specified or implied of distributions in respect of those shares.

(*d*) The reference in this subsection to the person beneficially owning shares shall be deemed to be a reference to both that person and any person connected with that person.

(*e*) Relief from income tax shall not be allowed under this Part in respect of the amount subscribed for any shares to which this subsection applies.

(15) This section shall apply only where the shares concerned are issued in the period [commencing on 6 April 1984 and ending on [31 December 2006][4]][5].

Amendments

1 Subs (4A) inserted by FA 2002 s 16(*a*)(i) with effect from 1 January 2002.

2 Subs (4B) inserted by FA 2004 s 18(1)(*a*)(i) with effect from 1 January 2004.

3 Substituted by FA 2002 s 16(*a*)(ii) with effect from 1 January 2002; previously "5 years".

4 Substituted by FA 2004 s 18(2)(*a*) and (3)(*b*)(i) (as amended by FA 2005 s 27(*b*)(i)) with effect from 5 February 2004 (FA 2005 s 27(*b*)(i)); previously "4 February 2004" by virtue of FA 2004 s 18(1)(*a*)(ii), but to be read as "31 December 2004" under certain transitional arrangements where certain conditions are met — see FA 2004 s 19(3)). The amendment was to come into operation on the making of an order to that effect by the Minister for Finance. By virtue of the Finance Act 2004 (Commencement of Section 18(2)) Order 2004 (SI No 758 of 2004) the amendment comes into operation on 29 November 2004.

5 Substituted by FA 2001 s 12(*a*) with effect from 6 April 2001; previously "commencing on the 6th day of April, 1984, and ending on the 5th day of April, 2001".

Cross-references

Certification where aggregate amount raised exceeds £250,000 (subs (1)(*c*)(i)): s 492(1)(*a*), (*b*)(II); combined certificate (subs (2)(*c*)): s 492(2)(*a*)(i)).
Claims (subs (7)(*a*)(i)(II)): s 503(1).
Deductions allowed in ascertaining taxable income: s 458(2); s 459(1), (2).
Finance for trade of subsidiary, subs (1)(*b*): Sch 10 para 1; subss (1)(*c*), (7), (8), (11) applied by: Sch 10 para 1.
Limits on the relief, subss (4), (4A) and (4B): s 490(3)(*a*).
Rate of tax at which repayments are to be made: s 460.
Relief, meaning applied: s 488(1).
Seed capital investors qualifying for BES relief: s 493(8)(*a*)(ii).
Transitional arrangements in relation to FA 1998 s 34, subs (2)(*e*): FA 1998 s 35(7)(*b*)(iii).
Transitional arrangements in relation to FA 2004 s 18(1)(*a*)(ii), subs (2)(*b*): FA 2004 s 19(5)(*b*)(ii).
Value received from company, sub (1)(*c*): s 499(3A)(*a*)(iii).

Case law

Held shares "issued" when registered: *National Westminster Bank plc v IRC* [1994] STC 580.

Revenue precedents

Issue: Whether relief should be allowed for part shares if and when bonus share issue takes place that will eliminate any part shares being held by investors.
Decision: Relief allowed as the bonus issue would ensure that each investor would be registered as the owner of full shares.
Issue: When did shares actually issue?
Decision: Issue of shares occurred when the legal transaction was completed by way of registration.
Issue: Would an individual working 37 hours with the seed capital company and 37 hours with another company satisfy the requirement that full time employment must be taken up in the seed capital company?
Decision: No.
Issue: Can BES money be used to repay bank borrowings which are financing a company's trade?
Decision: Yes.
Issue: Would the existence of a Patent Royalty Company which resulted in a return of patent income to the BES investor, offend this section?
Decision: No, if the patent company is engaged in licensing arrangements with the manufacturing company and if distributable reserves are eliminated prior to BES investment.
Issue: Whether a promise to investors of an asset in lieu of investment after the five year relevant investment period contravenes s 489(14).
Decision: S 489(14) was contravened.

Issue: (1) Whether promoters be allowed by way of agreement with fund, to withhold some of their money until it was required by the company, and they would then subscribe for the agreed number of shares. (2) Would an agreed investment by promoters (which is required by a designated fund) offend the risk provisions?
Decision: (1) Agreed this would not eliminate risk. (2) No. It just demonstrates the commitment of the promoters to the project.
Issue: Does BES relief apply where assets are used as payment for shares?
Decision: No, the shares must be issued for the purposes of raising money for the qualifying trade.

Definitions

body of persons: s 2(1); company: ss 4(1), 5(1); Income Tax Acts: s 1(2); inspector: ss 2(1), 852; lease: s 5(1); month: IA 1937 Sch; person: IA 1937 s 11(*c*); shares: s 5(1); total income: s 3(1); trade: s 3(1); writing: IA 1937 Sch; year of assessment: ss 2(1), 5(1).

Former enactments

FA 1984 s 12(1), (3)–(6A) and (8)–(11); FA 1985 s 13(*b*); FA 1987 s 8(*b*); FA 1990 s 10(*b*) and s34(1)(*a*) and (*b*)(ii), (2) and (4); FA 1991 s 15(1)(*a*); FA 1993 s 25(*b*)(i), (iii), (iv), (v) and (vi); FA 1995 s 17(*b*); FA 1996 s 17.

Corresponding UK tax provision

Income and Corporation Taxes Act 1988 ss 289 and 289A.

490 Limits on the relief

(1) (*a*) Subject to section 508 and paragraph (*b*), the relief shall not be given in respect of any amount subscribed by an individual for eligible shares issued to the individual by any company in any year of assessment unless the amount or total amount subscribed by the individual for the eligible shares issued to the individual by the company in that year is [€250][1] or more.

(*b*) In the case of an individual who is a married person assessed to tax for a year of assessment in accordance with section 1017, any amount subscribed by the individual's spouse for eligible shares issued to that spouse in that year of assessment by the company shall be deemed to have been subscribed by the individual for eligible shares issued to the individual by the company.

(2) The relief shall not be given to the extent to which the amount or total amount subscribed by an individual for eligible shares issued to the individual in any year of assessment (whether or not by the same company) exceeds [€31,750][2].

(3) (*a*) Where in any year of assessment a greater amount of relief would be given to an individual in respect of the amount or the total amount subscribed by the individual for eligible shares (in this subsection referred to as **"the relevant subscription"**) issued to the individual in that year or, where [subsection (4), (4A) or (4B) of section 489][3] applies, in the following year of assessment but for either or both of the following reasons—

(i) an insufficiency of total income, or

(ii) the operation of subsection (2),

the amount of the relief which would be given but for those reasons less the amount or the aggregate amount of any relief in respect of the relevant subscription which is given in that year of assessment shall be carried forward to the next year of assessment, and shall be treated for the purposes of the relief as an amount subscribed directly by the individual for eligible shares issued to the individual in that next year.

(*b*) This subsection shall not apply for any year of assessment subsequent to [the year of assessment [2006][4]].[5]

(4) (*a*) If and in so far as an amount once carried forward to a year of assessment under subsection (3) (and treated as an amount subscribed directly by an individual for eligible shares issued to the individual in that year of assessment) is not deducted from his or her total income for that year of assessment, it shall be carried forward again to the next year of assessment (and treated as an amount subscribed directly by the individual for eligible shares issued to the individual in that next year), and so on for succeeding years of assessment.

(*b*) This subsection shall not apply for any year of assessment subsequent to [the year of assessment [2006][4]].[5]

(5) The relief shall be given to an individual for any year of assessment in the following order—

(*a*) in the first instance, in respect of an amount carried forward from an earlier year of assessment in accordance with subsection (3) or (4) and, in respect of such an amount so carried forward, for an earlier year of assessment in priority to a later year of assessment, and

(*b*) only thereafter, in respect of any other amount for which relief is to be given in that year of assessment.

Amendments

1 Substituted by FA 2001 s 240(1) and (2)(*a*) and Sch 5 Pt 1 for 2002 and later tax years; previously "£200" (short tax "year" 2001: £148 (FA 2001 s 77(2) and Sch 2 paras 25(*a*) and 61(*a*))).

2 Substituted by FA 2001 s 240(1) and (2)(*a*) and Sch 5 Pt 1 for 2002 and later tax years; previously "£25,000" (short tax "year" 2001: £18,500 (FA 2001 s 77(2) and Sch 2 paras 25(*b*) and 61(*a*))).

3 Substituted by FA 2004 s 18(1)(*b*)(i) with effect from 1 January 2004; previously "section 489(4) or (4A)".

4 Substituted by FA 2004 s 18(1)(*b*)(ii) with effect from 1 January 2004; previously "2003".

5 Substituted by FA 2001 s 12(*b*) with effect from 6 April 2001; previously "the year 2000–01".

Cross-references

Designated funds, subs (1)(*a*): s 508(2)(*a*).
Relief, specified individual: s 489(5)(*c*)–(*d*).
Restriction of relief: s 491(5)(*b*).

Revenue precedents

Issue: Whether TCA 1997 s 490(1)(*b*) means that a subscription for shares by a non-assessable spouse is regarded for all purposes as a subscription by the assessable spouse.
Decision: No; the paragraphs applies only as regards the minimum subscription required for a husband and wife, a subscription of £200 by either or both will fulfil the minimum subscription rule.
Issue: Whether relief is transferable in the case of a married couple jointly assessed for tax.
Decision: No. The maximum allowable subscription of £25,000 applies to each spouse separately.

Definitions

company: ss 4(1), 5(1); shares: s 5(1); total income: s 3(1); year: IA 1937 Sch; year of assessment: ss 2(1), 5(1).

Former enactments

ITA 1967 s 195B(3) and (6); FA 1984 s 13(1)–(2C); FA 1987 s 9; FA 1993 s 10(1) and s 25(*c*)(i); FA 1996 s 18.

Corresponding UK tax provision

Income and Corporation Taxes Act 1988 s 290.

491 Restriction on relief where amounts raised exceed permitted maximum

(1) In this section, **"qualifying subsidiary"**, in relation to a company, means a subsidiary of that company of a kind which a company may have by virtue of section 507.

[(2)[(*a*) Subject to this section, where a company raises any amount through the issue of eligible shares on or after 1 January 2002 (in this section referred to as "the relevant issue"), relief shall not be given in respect of the excess of the amount so raised over the amount determined by the formula—

$$A - B$$

where—

A is—

(i) in the case of a company which, or whose qualifying subsidiary, raises the amount by virtue of section 496(2)(*a*)(iv)(II), €127,000,

(ii) in the case where the money raised was used, is being used or is intended to be used solely for qualifying trading operations referred to in section 496(2)(*a*)(ix) carried on or to be carried on by the company or its qualifying subsidiary, €1,270,000,

or

(iii) in any other case, [€1,000,000][1],

and

B is the lesser of—

(i) the appropriate amount represented by A in the formula, and

(ii) an amount equal to the aggregate of all amounts raised by the company through the issue of eligible shares at any time before the relevant issue.][2]

(*b*) (i) Where a company raises any amount through a relevant issue which amount consists of a relevant investment and any other amount, the relevant issue shall be deemed for the purposes of this subsection (but for no other purpose of this Part) to consist of 2 separate issues of eligible shares one of which shall be in respect of the relevant investment (in this paragraph referred to as "the first issue") and the other in respect of the other amount raised (in this paragraph referred to as "the second issue").

(ii) Where subparagraph (i) applies, the first issue shall be deemed for the purposes of this subsection (but for no other purpose of this Part) to have been made on the day before the date of the relevant issue and the second issue shall be deemed for the purposes of this subsection (but for no other purpose of this Part) to have been made on the date of the relevant issue and paragraph (*a*) shall apply accordingly.

(3) [(*a*) Where, on or after 1 January 2002, a company raises any amount through a relevant issue and that company is associated (within the meaning of this section) with one or more other companies, then, as respects that company, relief shall not be given in respect of the excess of the amount so raised over the amount determined by the formula—

$$A - B$$

where—

A is—

(i) in the case of a company which, or whose qualifying subsidiary, raises the amount by virtue of section 496(2)*(a)*(iv)(II), €127,000,

(ii) in the case where the money raised was used, is being used or is intended to be used solely for qualifying trading operations referred to in section 496(2)*(a)*(ix) carried on or to be carried on by the company or its qualifying subsidiary, €1,270,000, or

(iii) in any other case, [€1,000,000][1],

and

B is the lesser of—

(i) the appropriate amount represented by A in the formula, and

(ii) the aggregate of all amounts raised through the issue of eligible shares at any time before or on the date of the relevant issue by all of the companies (including that company) which are associated within the meaning of this section.][3]

(b) (i) Where a company raises any amount through a relevant issue which amount consists of a relevant investment and any other amount, the relevant issue shall be deemed for the purposes of this subsection (but for no other purpose of this Part) to consist of 2 separate issues of eligible shares one of which shall be in respect of the relevant investment (in this paragraph referred to as "the first issue") and the other in respect of the other amount raised (in this paragraph referred to as "the second issue").

(ii) Where subparagraph (i) applies, the first issue shall be deemed for the purposes of this subsection (but for no other purpose of this Part) to have been made on the day before the date of the relevant issue and the second issue shall be deemed for the purposes of this subsection (but for no other purpose of this Part) to have been made on the date of the relevant issue and paragraph *(a)* shall apply accordingly.][4]

[(3A) Notwithstanding anything in subsections (2) and (3), relief shall not be given in respect of a relevant issue to the extent that—

(a) the amount raised by the relevant issue, or

(b) the aggregate of—

(i) the amount to be raised through the relevant issue, and

(ii) the amount or amounts, if any, raised through the issue of eligible shares other than the relevant issue, within the period of 6 months ending with the date of that relevant issue, by the company or by all of the companies (including the company making the relevant issue) which are associated within the meaning of this section, as the case may be,

exceeds €750,000.][5]

(4) For the purposes of this section, a company shall be associated with another company where—

(a) in the case of that company, or a company which is, or was at any time, its qualifying subsidiary, and

(b) that other company, or a company which is, or was at any time, its qualifying subsidiary,

it could reasonably be considered that—

(i) both companies act in pursuit of a common purpose,

(ii) any person or any group of persons or groups of persons having a reasonable commonality of identity have or had the means or power, either directly or indirectly, to determine the trading operations carried on or to be carried on by both companies, or

(iii) both companies are under the control of any person or group of persons or groups of persons having a reasonable commonality of identity;

but for the purposes of this section a company shall not be considered as associated with another company by reason only of the fact [that—

(I) a subscription for eligible shares in both companies is made by a person or persons having the management of an investment fund designated under section 508 as nominee for any person or group or groups of persons, or

(II) both companies hold shares or securities in, or have made loans to, Exchange Axess or carry on in limited partnership with Exchange Axess such qualifying trading operations as are referred to in section 496(2)(*a*)(iv).][6]

[(5) In determining for the purposes of the formula in subsection (2)(*a*) or, as the case may be, the formula in subsection (3)(*a*) the amount to which paragraph (ii) of the definition of "B" in those formulas relates, account shall not be taken of any amount—

(*a*) which is subscribed by a person other than an individual who qualifies for relief, or

(*b*) in respect of which relief is precluded by virtue of section 490.][7]

(6) Where as a consequence of subsection (2) or (3) the giving of relief would be precluded on claims in respect of shares issued to 2 or more individuals, the available relief shall be divided between them respectively in proportion to the amounts which have been subscribed by them for the shares to which their claims relate and which apart from this section would be eligible for relief.

Amendments

1 Substituted by FA 2004 s 18(2)(*b*)(i) (as amended by FA 2005 s 27(*a*)(i)) and FA 2004 s 18(3)(*b*)(ii) (as amended by FA 2005 s 27(*b*)(ii)) in relation to eligible shares issued on or after 1 January 2004; previously "€750,000". The amendment was to come into operation on the making of an order to that effect by the Minister for Finance. By virtue of the Finance Act 2004 (Commencement of Section 18(2)) Order 2004 (SI No 758 of 2004) the amendment comes into operation on 29 November 2004.

2 Subs (2)(*a*) substituted by FA 2002 s 16(*c*)(i) with effect from 1 January 2002.

3 Subs (3)(*a*) substituted by FA 2002 s 16(*c*)(ii) with effect from 1 January 2002.

4 Subs (2)–(3) substituted by FA 1998 s 34(*a*)(i)(I), subject to FA 1998 s 35 (which provides for certain transitional arrangements), as respects eligible shares issued on or after 3 December 1997.

5 Subs (3A) inserted by FA 2004 s 18(2)(*b*)(ii) (as amended by FA 2005 s 27(*a*)(i)) and FA 2004 s 18(3)(*b*)(ii) (as amended by FA 2005 s 27(*b*)(ii)) in relation to eligible shares issued on or after 5 February 2004. The amendment was to come into operation on the making of an order to that effect by the Minister for Finance. By virtue of the Finance Act 2004 (Commencement of Section 18(2)) Order 2004 (SI No 758 of 2004) the amendment comes into operation on 29 November 2004.

6 Substituted by FA 2000 s 19(*b*) with effect from 1 May 1998; previously "that a subscription for eligible shares in both companies is made by a person or persons having the management of an investment fund designated under section 508 as nominee for any person or group or groups of persons."

7 Subs (5) substituted by FA 1998 s 34(*a*)(i)(II), subject to FA 1998 s 35 (which provides for certain transitional arrangements), as respects eligible shares issued on or after 3 December 1997.

Cross-references

Certification where aggregate amount raised exceeds £250,000, subss (5)–(6) apply with any necessary modifications: s 492(6).

Revenue precedents

Issue: A manufacturer was having difficulty obtaining raw materials. The company organised a BES scheme for an entirely independent raw materials supplier. There were certain agreements between the companies including the sharing of manufacturing facilities and obligations in relation to the sale of outputs. The supplier raised BES funds up to the limit. A BES scheme was proposed for a second supplier controlled by entirely different parties. Were the companies associated for the purposes of this section?

Decision: Yes. The company shared a common purpose with the first supplier.

Issue: An individual set up a number of companies and raised BES funds to the limit. His daughter set up a new venture to produce a completely different product. She was qualified in her own right. Were the companies associated for the purposes of this section?

Decision: No, because there were no business or financial transactions between the companies, nor agreements, arrangements or understandings under which the person with the existing companies or an associated person would take over the venture at a future date.

Issue: A company had raised up to its limit in respect of its trade. The daughter of the family controlling the original company proposed to raise money for a complimentary trade. Were the companies associated for the purposes of this section?

Decision: Yes. The companies were pursuing a common purpose and a group of persons with a reasonable commonality of identity had determined the trading operations to be carried on.

Issue: Whether s 493(1) precludes the shares of a married couple being registered in joint names.

Decision: No, provided the shares are subscribed for by one spouse and the inspector of taxes is issued with a letter signed by both parties confirming the amount invested by each spouse.

Definitions

company: ss 4(1), 5(1); person: IA 1937 s 11(*c*); shares: s 5(1); writing: IA 1937 Sch.

Former enactments

FA 1984 s 13A; FA 1989 s 9; FA 1991 s 15(1)(*c*) and s17(1)(*b*) and (*c*); FA 1993 s 25(*d*)(i)(II) and FA 1996 s 19(1)–(2); FA 1997 s 146(1) and Sch 9 Pt I para 13(2).

492 Certification in respect of an issue of eligible shares where aggregate of amounts raised by a company exceeds £250,000

Amendments

Section 492 deleted by FA 1998 s 34(*a*)(ii), subject to FA 1998 s 35 (which provides for certain transitional arrangements), as respects eligible shares issued on or after 3 December 1997.

Former enactments

FA 1984 s 13B; FA 1996 s 20; FA 1997 s 146(1) and Sch 9 Pt I para 13(3).

493 Individuals qualifying for relief

(1) (*a*) An individual shall qualify for relief if he or she subscribes on his or her own behalf for eligible shares in a qualifying company and is not at any time in the relevant period connected with the company.

(*b*) For the purposes of this section and paragraph 2 of Schedule 10, any question whether an individual is connected with a company shall be determined in accordance with this section.

(2) An individual shall be connected with a company if the individual or an associate of the individual is—

(*a*) a partner of the company, or

(*b*) subject to subsection (3), a director or employee of the company or of another company which is a partner of that company.

(3) An individual shall not be connected with a company by reason only that the individual or an associate of the individual is a director or employee of the company or of another company which is a partner of that company unless the individual or the individual's associate (or a partnership of which the individual or the individual's associate is a member) receives a payment from either company during the period of 5 years beginning on the date on which the shares are issued or is entitled to receive such a payment in respect of that period or any part of it; but for that purpose there shall be disregarded—

(*a*) any payment or reimbursement of travelling or other expenses wholly, exclusively and necessarily incurred by the individual or the individual's associate in the performance of the duties of the individual or of the associate, as the case may be, as such director or employee,

(*b*) any interest which represents no more than a reasonable commercial return on money lent to either company,

(*c*) any dividend or other distribution paid or made by either company which does not exceed a normal return on the investment,

(*d*) any payment for the supply of goods to either company which does not exceed their market value, and

(*e*) any reasonable and necessary remuneration which—

(i) (I) is paid for services rendered to either company in the course of a trade or profession (not being secretarial or managerial services or services of a kind provided by the company itself), and

(II) is taken into account in computing the profits or gains of the trade or profession under Case I or II of Schedule D or would be so taken into account if it fell in a period on the basis of which those profits or gains are assessed under that Schedule,

or

(ii) in a case where the individual is a director or an employee of either company and is not otherwise connected with either company, is paid for service rendered to the company of which the individual is a director or an employee in the course of the directorship or the employment.

(4) An individual shall be connected with a company if he or she directly or indirectly possesses or is entitled to acquire more than 30 per cent of—

(*a*) the issued ordinary share capital of the company,

(*b*) the loan capital and issued share capital of the company, or

(*c*) the voting power in the company.

(5) For the purposes of subsection (4)(*b*), the loan capital of a company shall be treated as including any debt incurred by the company—

(*a*) for any money borrowed or capital assets acquired by the company,

(*b*) for any right to receive income created in favour of the company, or

(*c*) for consideration the value of which to the company was (at the time when the debt was incurred) substantially less than the amount of the debt (including any premium on the debt).

(6) An individual shall be connected with a company if he or she directly or indirectly possesses or is entitled to acquire such rights as would, in the event of the winding up of the company or in other circumstances, entitle the individual to receive more than 30 per cent of the assets of the company which would at that time be available for distribution to equity holders of the company, and for the purposes of this subsection—

(*a*) the persons who are equity holders of the company, and

(*b*) the percentage of the assets of the company to which the individual would be entitled,

shall be determined in accordance with sections 413 and 415, references in section 415 to the first company being construed as references to an equity holder and references to a winding up being construed as including references to any other circumstances in which assets of the company are available for distribution to its equity holders.

(7) An individual shall be connected with a company if he or she has control of it within the meaning of section 11.

(8) (*a*) An individual shall not be connected with a company by reason only of subsection (4), (6) or (7)—

(i) if throughout the relevant period the aggregate of all amounts subscribed for the issued share capital and the loan capital (within the meaning of subsection (5)) of the company does not exceed [€317,500][1], or

(ii) in the case of a specified individual, by virtue only of a relevant investment in respect of which he or she has been given relief in accordance with section 489(5).

(*b*) Notwithstanding paragraph (*a*), relief granted to an individual in respect of a subscription for eligible shares at a time when by virtue of this subsection the individual was not connected with the company shall not be withdrawn by reason only that the individual subsequently becomes connected with the company by virtue of subsection (4), (6) or (7).

(9) For the purposes of this section, an individual shall be treated as entitled to acquire anything which he or she is entitled to acquire at a future date or will at a future date be entitled to acquire, and there shall be attributed to any person any rights or powers of any other person who is an associate of that person.

(10) In determining for the purposes of this section whether an individual is connected with a company, no debt incurred by the company by overdrawing an account with a person carrying on a business of banking shall be treated as loan capital of the company if the debt arose in the ordinary course of that business.

(11) Where an individual subscribes for shares in a company with which the individual is not connected (either within the meaning of this section or by virtue of paragraph 2(2)(*b*) of Schedule 10), he or she shall nevertheless be treated as connected with it if he or she subscribes for the shares as part of any arrangement which provides for another person to subscribe for shares in another company with which the individual or any other individual who is a party to the arrangement is connected (within the meaning of this section or by virtue of that paragraph).

Amendments

1 Substituted by FA 2001 s 240(1) and (2)(*a*) and Sch 5 Pt 1 for 2002 and later tax years; previously "£250,000".

Cross-references

Finance for trade of subsidiary, subss (2), (4), (6) applied by: Sch 10 para 2(1); subss (5), (9) applied by: Sch 10 para 2(3).

Information that would disqualify a claimant to be sent to inspector: s 505(1); subs (11): (4), (5).

Meaning of "control", subs (7): s 488(1).

Relevant period, meaning: s 488(1).

Seed capital investors, definition of "loan capital" used: s 494(4)(*b*)(ii).

Value received by persons other than claimants, subs (4): s 501(5), (7).

Value received from company: s 499(3)(*c*)(i), (5).

Withdrawal of BES relief: s 504(7)(*a*).

Case law

Held an individual had to establish he was not connected with the company at any time during the relevant period and not simply at the date the application was made to issue BES certificate: *Wild v Cannavan* [1997] STC 966.

Revenue precedents

Issue: Would the holding of more than 30% of the shareholdings, on a temporary basis, in a new company, by promoters, disqualify them from BES relief?

Decision: No. Provided their shareholding was reduced below 30% when the BES shares are issued.

Definitions

company: ss 4(1), 5(1); distribution: ss 4(1), 436, 437; interest: s 4(1); ordinary share capital: s 2(1); person: IA 1937 s 11(*c*); profession: ss 2(1), 5(1); profits: s 4(1); shares: s 5(1); trade: s 3(1).

Former enactments

FA 1984 s 14; FA 1993 s 25(*e*); FA 1994 s 16(1)(*b*); FA 1997 s 146(1) and Sch 9 Pt I para 13(4).

Corresponding UK tax provision

Income and Corporation Taxes Act 1988 s 291.

494 Specified individuals

(1) An individual shall be a specified individual if he or she qualifies for relief in respect of a relevant investment and complies with this section.

(2) (*a*) Subject to paragraph (*b*), the individual, in each of the 3 years of assessment preceding the year of assessment which precedes the year of assessment in which that individual makes a relevant investment (being that individual's first such investment), shall not have been in receipt of income chargeable to tax otherwise than under—

(i) Schedule E, or

(ii) Case III of Schedule D in respect of profits or gains from an office or employment held or exercised outside the State,

in excess of the lesser of—

(I) the aggregate of the amounts, if any, of that individual's income chargeable to tax under Schedule E and under Case III of Schedule D in respect of the profits or gains referred to in subparagraph (ii), and

[(II) €25,000 or, in the case of the year of assessment 2001, €18,500.][1]

(*b*) Paragraph (*a*) shall not apply to an individual who makes a subscription for eligible shares in a qualifying company which carries on or intends to carry on qualifying trading operations referred to in [sections 496(2)(*a*)(iv) and 496(2)(*a*)(xv)].[2]

(3) The individual shall throughout the relevant period possess at least 15 per cent of—

(*a*) as respects a subscription for eligible shares made before the 2nd day of June, 1995, the issued share capital, or

(*b*) as respects a subscription for eligible shares made on or after that date, the issued ordinary share capital,

of the company in which that individual makes a relevant investment.

(4) (*a*) For the purposes of paragraph (*b*) and subsections (5) and (6), **"specified date"**, in relation to a relevant investment in a company, means—

(i) where the investment consists of the subscription of only one amount for eligible shares, the date of that subscription, or

(ii) where that investment consists of the subscription of more than one amount for eligible shares, the date of the last such subscription.

(*b*) Subject to subsections (5) and (6), the individual at the specified date, in relation to that individual's first relevant investment in a company, or within the period of 12 months immediately preceding that date, either directly or indirectly, shall not possess or have possessed, or shall not be or have been entitled to acquire, more than 15 per cent of—

(i) the issued ordinary share capital,

(ii) the loan capital (within the meaning of section 493(5)) and the issued share capital, or

(iii) the voting power,

of any company other than—

(I) the company in which that individual makes that relevant investment, or

(II) a company to which subsection (5) applies.

(5) This subsection shall apply to a company which during a period of 5 years ending on the specified date in relation to an individual's first relevant investment in a company—

(*a*) was not entitled to any assets, other than cash on hands or a sum of money on deposit (within the meaning of section 895) not exceeding [€130][3],

(*b*) did not carry on a trade, profession, business or other activity including the making of investments, and

(*c*) did not pay charges on income within the meaning of section 243.

(6) (*a*) For the purposes of paragraph (*b*)—

(i) **"accounting period"** means an accounting period determined in accordance with section 27, and

(ii) a company shall be regarded as a company which carries on wholly or mainly trading operations referred to in paragraph (*b*)(i) only if in each of the 3 accounting periods referred to in paragraph (*b*)(ii) the total amount receivable from sales made or services rendered in the course of such trading operations is not less than 75 per cent of the total amount receivable by the company from all sales made and services rendered in the course of the trade.

(*b*) An individual shall not be regarded as failing to satisfy the requirements of subsection (4) merely by reason of the fact that the individual does not satisfy those requirements in relation to only one company (other than the company in which the individual makes his or her first relevant investment or a company to which subsection (5) applies)—

(i) which exists wholly or mainly for the purpose of carrying on trading operations other than trading operations consisting of dealing in shares, securities, land, currencies, futures or traded options, and

(ii) where the total amount receivable by that company from sales made and services rendered in the course of that company's trading operations did not exceed [€127,000][4] in each of that company's 3 accounting periods immediately preceding the accounting period of that company in which the specified date occurs in relation to that individual's first relevant investment.

(7) An individual shall not be regarded as ceasing to comply with subsection (3) merely by reason of the fact that the company in which the individual makes a relevant investment is wound up, or dissolved without winding up, before the end of the relevant period but only if it is shown that the winding up or dissolution is for bona fide commercial reasons and is not part of a scheme or arrangement the main purpose or one of the main purposes of which was the avoidance of tax.

Amendments

1 Subs (2)(*a*)(ii) substituted by FA 2004 s 18(2)(*c*) and FA 2004 s 18(3)(*b*)(iii) (as amended by FA 2005 s 27(*b*)(iii)) in relation to relevant investments made on or after 5 February 2004. The amendment was to come into operation on the making of an order to that effect by the Minister for Finance. By virtue of the Finance Act 2004 (Commencement of Section 18(2)) Order 2004 (SI No 758 of 2004) the amendment comes into operation on 29 November 2004.

2 Substituted by FA 2002 s 15(*a*) with effect from 1 January 2003; previously "section 496(2)(*a*)(iv)".

3 Substituted by FA 2001 s 240(1) and (2)(*l*)(vi) and Sch 5 Pt 1 as respects a subscription for eligible shares (within the meaning of s 488) where the specified date (within the meaning of s 494) in relation to that subscription is a date on or after 1 January 2002; previously "£100".

4 Substituted by FA 2001 s 240(1) and (2)(*l*)(vi) and Sch 5 Pt 1 as respects a subscription for eligible shares (within the meaning of s 488) where the specified date (within the meaning of s 494) in relation to that subscription is a date on or after 1 January 2002; previously "£100,000".

Cross-references

Meaning applied: s 488(1).

Revenue precedents

Issue: Would a 9 month period at a course abroad, during which the individual was not employed, disqualify the individual from seed capital relief? The period abroad was within the three year period during which the individual was required to be in PAYE type employment.

Decision: No.

Issue: Would a period spent on a contract basis during which withholding tax was deducted and the same conditions as other workers applied, satisfy the requirements in relation to PAYE type employment?

Decision: Yes.

Issue: Would PAYE type employment in the US satisfy the PAYE type employment requirement to qualify for the scheme?

Decision: Yes.

Definitions

month: IA 1937 Sch; profession: ss 2(1), 5(1); shares: s 5(1); tax: s 3(1); trade: s 3(1); year: IA 1937 Sch; year of assessment: ss 2(1), 5(1).

Former enactments

FA 1984 s 14A; FA 1995 s 17(1)(*d*); FA 1997 s 9(*b*).

Corresponding UK tax provision

Income and Corporation Taxes Act 1988 s 291B.

495 Qualifying companies

[(1) In this section—

"EEA Agreement" means the Agreement on the European Economic Area signed at Oporto on 2 May 1992, as adjusted by the Protocol signed at Brussels on 17 March 1993;

"EEA State" means a state which is a contracting party to the EEA Agreement;

"qualifying subsidiary", in relation to a company, means a subsidiary of that company of a kind which a company may have by virtue of section 507.

(2) A company shall be a qualifying company if it is incorporated in the State or in an EEA State other than the State and complies with this section.][1]

(3) (*a*) The company shall throughout the relevant period be an unquoted company [which is resident in the State, or is resident in an EEA State other than the State and carries on business in the State through a branch or agency,][2] and be—

(i) a company which exists wholly for the purpose of carrying on wholly or mainly in the State one or more qualifying trades, or

(ii) a company whose business consists wholly of—

(I) the holding of shares or securities of, or the making of loans to, one or more qualifying subsidiaries of the [company,][3]

(II) both the holding of such shares or securities, or the making of such loans and the carrying on wholly or mainly in the State of one or more qualifying [trades, or][4]

[(III) both the holding of shares or securities in, or the making of loans to, Exchange Axess, and the carrying on in limited partnership with Exchange Axess of such qualifying trading operations as are referred to in section 496(2)(*a*)(iv) [and, in the case of a company to which this clause applies, its business shall be regarded as having complied with the conditions of this clause throughout the relevant period (where, otherwise, it would not have done so) if it so complied for that part of the relevant period up to and including 31 December 2002][5].][6]

(*b*) Where a company raises any amount through the issue of eligible shares for the purposes of raising money for a qualifying trade which is being carried on by a qualifying subsidiary or which such a qualifying subsidiary intends to carry on, the amount so raised shall be used for the purpose of acquiring eligible shares in the qualifying subsidiary and for no other purpose.

[(3A) The company shall—

(*a*) as respects the period 5 February 2004 to 31 December 2004 be a small or medium-sized enterprise within the meaning of Annex 1 to Commission

Regulation (EC) No 70/2001 of 12 January 2001 (OJ No L10 of 13 January 2001, p 33), and

(*b*) as respects the period commencing on 1 January 2005 be a micro, small or medium-sized enterprise within the meaning of Annex 1 to Commission Regulation (EC) No 364/2004 of 25 February 2004 (OJ No L63 of 28 February 2004, p 22).][7]

(4) (*a*) A company whose trade consists of the cultivation of horticultural produce within the meaning of section 496(7) shall not be a qualifying company unless and until it has shown to the satisfaction of the Revenue Commissioners that it has submitted to, and has had approved of by, the Minister for Agriculture and Food (in this subsection referred to as **"the Minister"**) a 3 year development and marketing plan in respect of the company's trade, being a plan primarily designed and formulated to increase the exportation of such produce or to displace the importation of such produce.

(*b*) In considering whether to approve of such a plan, the Minister shall have regard only to such guidelines in relation to such approval as may from time to time be agreed between the Minister and the Minister for Finance, and those guidelines may, without prejudice to the generality of the foregoing, set out—

(i) the extent to which the company's interest in land and buildings (other than greenhouses) may form part of its total assets,

(ii) specific requirements which have to be met in order to comply with either of the objectives mentioned in paragraph (*a*), and

(iii) the extent to which the money raised through the issue of eligible shares should be used to identify new markets and to develop new or existing markets for the company's produce.

(5) A company whose trade consists of the production, publication, marketing and promotion of a qualifying recording within the meaning of section 496(8) shall not be a qualifying company—

(*a*) unless it exists solely for the purposes of the production, publication, marketing and promotion of a qualifying recording or qualifying recordings by only one new artist, and

(*b*) unless and until it shows to the satisfaction of the Revenue Commissioners that a certificate referred to in section 496(8) has been given and not revoked by the Minister for Arts, Heritage, Gaeltacht and the Islands to the company in relation to such qualifying recording or qualifying recordings;

but, where a certificate referred to in section 496(8) is revoked by the Minister for Arts, Heritage, Gaeltacht and the Islands, the company shall not be a qualifying company.

(6) (*a*) A company whose trade includes one or more tourist traffic undertakings within the meaning of section 496(9) shall not be a qualifying company unless and until it has shown to the satisfaction of the Revenue Commissioners that it has submitted to, and has had approved of by, Bord Fáilte Éireann a 3 year development and marketing plan in respect of that undertaking or those undertakings, as the case may be, being a plan primarily designed and formulated to increase tourist traffic and revenue from outside the State.

(*b*) In considering whether to approve of such a plan, Bord Fáilte Éireann shall have regard only to such guidelines in relation to such approval as may from time to time be agreed, with the consent of the Minister for Finance, between it and the Minister for Tourism, Sport and Recreation, and those guidelines may, without prejudice to the generality of the foregoing, set out—

(i) the extent to which the company's interests in land and buildings may form part of its total assets,

(ii) specific requirements which have to be met in order to comply with the objective mentioned in paragraph (*a*), and

(iii) the extent to which the money raised through the issue of eligible shares should be used in promoting outside the State the undertaking or undertakings, as the case may be.

(7) Without prejudice to the generality of subsection (3) but subject to subsection (8), a company shall cease to comply with subsection (3) if before the end of the relevant period a resolution is passed, or an order is made, for the winding up of the company (or, in the case of a winding up otherwise than under the Companies Act, 1963, any other act is done for the like purpose) or the company is dissolved without winding up.

(8) A company shall not be regarded as ceasing to comply with subsection (3) by reason only of the fact that it is wound up or dissolved without winding up if—

(*a*) it is shown that the winding up or dissolution is for bona fide commercial reasons and not part of a scheme or arrangement the main purpose or one of the main purposes of which is the avoidance of tax, and

(*b*) the company's net assets, if any, are distributed to its members before the end of the relevant period or, in the case of a winding up, the end (if later) of 3 years from the commencement of the winding up.

(9) The company's share capital shall not at any time in the relevant period include any issued shares not fully paid up.

(10) Subject to section 507, the company shall not at any time in the relevant period—

(*a*) control (or together with any person connected with it control) another company or be under the control of another company (or of another company and any person connected with that other company), or

(*b*) be a 51 per cent subsidiary of another company or itself have a 51 per cent subsidiary,

and no arrangements shall be in existence at any time in that period by virtue of which the company could fall within paragraph (*a*) or (*b*).

(11) A company shall not be a qualifying company if, in the case of a company in which a relevant investment is made by a specified individual (being that individual's first such investment in that company), any transaction in the relevant period between the company and another company (being the immediate former employer of the individual), or a company which controls or is under the control of that other company, is otherwise than by means of a transaction at arm's length, or if—

(*a*) (i) an individual has acquired a controlling interest in the company's trade after the 5th day of April, 1984, and

(ii) at any time in the period mentioned in subsection (14) the individual has or has had a controlling interest in another trade,

and

(*b*) the trade carried on by the company or a substantial part of that trade—

(i) is concerned with the same or similar types of property or parts of property or provides the same or similar services or facilities as the other trade, or

(ii) serves substantially the same or similar outlets or markets as the other trade.

(12) For the purposes of this section, a person shall have a controlling interest in a trade—

(*a*) in the case of a trade carried on by a company, if—

(i) such person controls the company,

(ii) the company is a close company for the purposes of the Corporation Tax Acts and such person or an associate of such person is a director of the company and the beneficial owner of, or able directly or through the medium of other companies or by any other indirect means to control, more than 30 per cent of the ordinary share capital of the company, or

(iii) not less than 50 per cent of the trade could, in accordance with section 400(2), be regarded as belonging to such person,

or

(*b*) in any other case, if such person is entitled to not less than 50 per cent of the assets used for, or the income arising from, the trade.

(13) For the purposes of subsection (12), there shall be attributed to any person any rights or powers of any other person who is an associate of that person.

(14) The period referred to in subsection (11)(*a*)(ii) shall be the period beginning 2 years before and ending 3 years after—

(*a*) the date on which the shares were issued, or

(*b*) if later, the date on which the company began to carry on the trade.

(15) In subsections (11) and (14), references to a company's trade shall include references to the trade of any of its subsidiaries.

[(16) Notwithstanding the foregoing provisions of this section, a company shall not be a qualifying company while the company is regarded as a firm in difficulty for the purposes of the Community Guidelines on State Aid for rescuing and restructuring firms in difficulty ((*a*) OJ No C288 of 9 October 1999, p 2 up to and including 9 October 2004, and (*b*) OJ No C244 of 1 October 2004, p 2 as on and from 10 October 2004).][8]

Amendments

1 Subss (1) and (2) substituted by FA 2004 s 18(2)(*cc*)(i) (inserted by FA 2005 s 27(*a*)(ii)) and FA 2004 s 18(3)(*b*)(iii*a*) (inserted by FA 2005 s 27(*b*)(iv) with effect from 5 February 2004. The amendment was to come into operation on the making of an order to that effect by the Minister for Finance. By virtue of the Finance Act 2004 (Commencement of Section 18(2)) Order 2004 (SI No 758 of 2004) the amendment comes into operation on 29 November 2004.

2 Substituted by FA 2004 s 18(2)(*cc*)(ii) (inserted by FA 2005 s 27(*a*)(ii)) and FA 2004 s 18(3)(*b*)(iii*a*) (inserted by FA 2005 s 27(*b*)(iv)) with effect from 5 February 2004; previously "which is resident in the

State and not resident elsewhere,". The amendment was to come into operation on the making of an order to that effect by the Minister for Finance. By virtue of the Finance Act 2004 (Commencement of Section 18(2)) Order 2004 (SI No 758 of 2004) the amendment comes into operation on 29 November 2004.

3 Substituted by FA 2000 s 19(1)(*c*)(i) with effect from 1 May 1998; previously "company, or".

4 Substituted by FA 2000 s 19(1)(*c*)(ii) with effect from 1 May 1998; previously "trades.".

5 Inserted by FA 2003 s 15(*b*) with effect from 1 January 2003.

6 Subs (3)(*a*)(iv)(III) inserted by FA 2000 s 19(1)(*c*)(iii) with effect from 1 May 1998.

7 Subs (3A) inserted by FA 2004 s 18(2)(*cc*)(iii) (inserted by FA 2005 s 27(*a*)(ii)) with effect from 5 February 2004.

7 Subs (16) inserted by FA 2004 s 18(2)(*cc*)(iv) (inserted by FA 2005 s 27(*a*)(ii))with effect from 5 February 2004.

Cross-references

Certification where aggregate amount raised exceeds £250,000, combined certificate (subss (4)(*a*), (6)(*a*)): s 492(2)(*a*)(ii), (iii)(I).

Information that would disqualify a claimant to be sent to inspector: s 505(2); subs (10): s 505(4), (5).

Relevant period, meaning: s 488(1).

Subsidiaries, application to, subs (3)(*a*)(i): s 507(1)(*b*)(i).

Transitional arrangements in relation to FA 1998 s 34, meaning of "qualifying subsidiary" applied: FA 1998 s 35(1).

Transitional arrangements in relation to FA 2004 s 18(1)(*a*)(ii), meaning of "qualifying subsidiary" applied: FA 2004 s 19(1).

Value received from company, subs (8): s 499(4).

Withdrawal of BES relief: s 504(7)(*a*).

Revenue precedents

Issue: Would a company carrying on a qualifying trade in partnership be precluded per se from being considered to be a qualifying company?

Decision: No, provided that the company carrying on a trade in partnership invests the monies raised in ITSELF, then that company can be regarded as a qualifying company (provided the other conditions are met). If, however, the BES monies raised are used to invest in a partnership trade then the company would not qualify, ie the BES money must be used for the BES company's trade.

Issue: Where it is not technically possible to organise a BES scheme because a company is a member of a group, would a hive-down of certain activities be allowed?

Decision: Yes, provided the Revenue Commissioners are satisfied that the hive-down is necessary because of technical difficulties with the BES and for no other reason and the company is a stand alone company after the BES share issue, and also provided there is no attempt to breach s 491.

Issue: A qualifying company can only have qualifying subsidiaries. Would the existence of non-qualifying subsidiaries, which are now dormant, disqualify the company?

Decision: No, provided the subsidiaries remained dormant.

Issue: If Udaras na Gaeltachta owns a majority of the shares in the company, mainly for the purpose of injecting capital into the company, would this offend this rule?

Decision: No. Udaras shares are akin to a loan.

Issue: Where part of a trade is transferred from an existing company to a new company, can the original company retain control of the second company until a BES investment is made?

Decision: No.

Issue: Would companies serving different markets although the same industry, offend this section?

Decision: No. If there was a good commercial reason for establishing the second company and if there would be no transfer of business from one to the other or winding down of one business.

Issue: Would a sound recording company controlled by individuals who had control of other sound recording companies breach this section?

Decision: No – it is necessary for the purposes of the law to set up a separate company and this is acceptable provided that there is no attempt to breach s 491.

Issue: If two relatives have 25% each of the shares in the BES company and they also hold 60% and 20% respectively in a company carrying on a similar trade, would this offend the provisions of this rule?

Decision: No. As "associate" for the purposes of s 495(11) excludes relatives, no individual has control.

Issue: (1) Whether non-trading activities or income which arises as an incidental to the carrying on of the trade eg interest on cash flow, rents from letting part of the company's trading premises etc.... or (2) whether incidental shareholdings in other companies, be they subsidiaries, suppliers, or customers; would be regarded as diluting the companies 100% existence for trading purposes or (3) whether the holding of lands and buildings

by a holding company, which are used by its subsidiary companies, would be regarded as affecting the "wholly" provision of this section.
Decision: (1) No. (2) No, provided such holdings are part of the natural trading environment in which the company operates and provided the holdings are for the purposes related to the trade. (3) No, so long as the holding company retains ownership and the land and buildings were used by the subsidiary companies throughout the relevant period.
Issue: Can assets be used as payment of shares?
Decision: Yes, provided there is no transfer of trade involved.

Definitions

close company: ss 4(1), 430, 431; company: ss 4(1), 5(1); Corporation Tax Acts: s 1(2); land: s 5(1), IA 1937 Sch; ordinary share capital: s 2(1); person: IA 1937 s 11(*c*); shares: s 5(1); trade: s 3(1).

Former enactments

FA 1984 s 15(1)–(12); FA 1985 s 13(*c*); FA 1987 s 10(*a*); FA 1991 s 17(2); FA 1993 s 25(*f*); FA 1995 s 17(1)(*e*); FA 1996 s 22; FA 1997 s 146(1) and Sch 9 Pt I para 13(5).

Corresponding UK tax provision

Income and Corporation Taxes Act 1988 s 293.

---

496 Qualifying trades

(1) A trade shall be a qualifying trade if it complies with the requirements of this section.

(2) The trade shall throughout the relevant period—

(*a*) consist wholly or mainly of one or more of the following trading operations (in this Part referred to as **"qualifying trading operations"**)—

(i) the manufacture of goods within the meaning of Part 14; but—

(I) those trading operations or activities included in the definition, or regarded as the manufacture in the State, of **"goods"** for the purpose of Part 14 by virtue of subsections (3), (11), (12), (16), (17) and (19) of section 443 and of section 446 shall not, subject to the following provisions of this paragraph, be regarded as qualifying trading operations for the purposes of [this Part,][1]

(II) the production of a film (within the meaning of section 481) shall not be regarded as qualifying trading operations for the purposes of [this Part, and][2]

[(III) as respects a subscription for eligible shares issued on or after 5 February 2004, trading operations consisting of software development services referred to in subparagraph (ii) of paragraph (*a*) of section 443(10) and which would be qualifying trading operations if the employment grants referred to in subparagraph (I) of that paragraph were made, shall, notwithstanding anything in subparagraph (ii), be regarded as qualifying trading operations if approval for the making of such grant is obtained,][3]

(ii) the rendering of services (other than relevant trading operations within the meaning of section 446) in the course of a service industry (within the meaning of the Industrial Development Act, 1986) in respect of which—

(I) (A) a grant towards the employment of persons was made by Forbairt or the Industrial Development Agency (Ireland) under section 12(2) of the Industrial Development Act, 1993, or

(B) shares in the qualifying company concerned were purchased or taken by Forbairt or the Industrial Development Agency (Ireland) in accordance with section 31 of the Industrial Development Act, 1986,

(II) a grant under section 3, or financial assistance under section 4 of the Shannon Free Airport Development Company Limited (Amendment) Act, 1970, was made available by the [Shannon Free Airport Development Company Limited,][4]

(III) financial assistance was made available by Údarás na Gaeltachta under section 10 of the [Údarás na Gaeltachta Act, [1979,][5]][6]

[(IV) as respects a subscription for eligible shares issued on or after 6 April 2001 [and before the passing of the Finance Act 2003][7], a County Enterprise Board (being a board referred to in the Schedule to the Industrial Development Act, 1995) has, in accordance with the provisions of that Act, made a loan or grant to, or made an equity investment in, the qualifying company [concerned, or][8]][9]

[(V) as respects a subscription for eligible shares issued on or after the passing of the Finance Act 2003, a County Enterprise Board (being a board referred to in the Schedule to the Industrial Development Act 1995) has, in accordance with guidelines agreed between the board and the Minister for Enterprise, Trade and Employment, with the consent of the Minister for Finance, given a certificate certifying that the service industry is a qualifying service industry for the purposes of this section,][10]

(iii) in respect of a relevant investment, the rendering of services referred to in subparagraph (ii) in respect of which an employment grant would have been made or a grant or financial assistance would have been made available, as the case may be, by an industrial development agency under one of the provisions referred to in that subparagraph only for the fact that the industrial development agency concerned was or is precluded from making such an employment grant or making available such a grant or financial assistance, as the case may be, by reason of the fact that a grant or financial assistance had already been made by some other person,

(iv) in respect of—

(I) a relevant investment, or

(II) a subscription for eligible shares, other than such a subscription consisting of a relevant investment, made on or before the 5th day of April, 1998, and in respect of which a certificate for the purposes of this Part has been issued in accordance with subsection (5),

and notwithstanding subparagraph (ii), the rendering of relevant trading operations (within the meaning of section 446) carried on for the purposes of or in connection with trading operations on an exchange facility established in the Custom House Docks Area (within the meaning of section 322) [and in the case of a relevant investment made on or before 31 December 2002, trading operations undertaken [on or after 1 January 2003 and on or before 31 December 2004][11] on an exchange facility established in the Custom House Docks Area will be deemed to be relevant trading operations for the purposes of this section notwithstanding the expiry, in accordance with the provisions of section 446(2)(*b*), of the certificate given by the Minister for Finance under that subsection],[12]

(v) in respect of a relevant investment, the rendering of services referred to in subparagraph (ii) in respect of which an industrial development agency or, as respects a relevant investment made on or after the 10th day of May, 1997, a County Enterprise Board (being a board referred to in the Schedule to the Industrial Development Act, 1995) has provided financial support of not less than [€2,540][13] towards the undertaking of a feasibility study by a person approved of by the agency or the County Enterprise Board into the potential commercial viability of the services to be rendered,

(vi) research and development activities within the meaning of subsection (6),

(vii) the cultivation of horticultural produce within the meaning of subsection (7),

(viii) the cultivation of plants referred to in section 443(3),

(ix) the construction and the leasing of an advance factory building,

(x) the research and development or other similar activity undertaken with a view to the carrying on of trading operations referred to in subparagraphs (i), (ii) and (viii),

(xi) the cultivation of mushrooms in the State,

(xii) the production, publication, marketing and promotion of a qualifying recording, or qualifying recordings, within the meaning of subsection (8),

(xiii) the operation of one or more tourist traffic undertakings within the meaning of subsection (9), and

(xiv) the sales of export goods by a Special Trading House within the meaning of section 443(12),

[(xv) in respect of a relevant investment made [on or after 1 January 2003 and on or before 31 December 2004],[11] the rendering of trading operations carried on for the purposes of or in connection with trading operations on an exchange facility established in the Custom House Docks Area (within the meaning of section 322),][14]

and

...[15]

(3) Notwithstanding subsection (2), a trade which during the relevant period consists partly of qualifying trading operations and partly of other trading operations shall be regarded for the purposes of that subsection as a trade which consists wholly or mainly of qualifying trading operations only if the total amount receivable in the relevant period from sales made and services rendered in the course of qualifying trading operations is not less than 75 per cent of the total amount receivable by the company from all sales made and services rendered in the course of the trade in the relevant period.

(4) (*a*) In this subsection—

"financial activities" means the provision of, and all matters relating to the provision of, financing or refinancing facilities by any means which involves, or has an effect equivalent to, the extension of credit;

"financing or refinancing facilities" includes—

(i) loans, mortgages, leasing, lease rental and hire-purchase, and all similar arrangements,

(ii) equity investment,

(iii) the factoring of debts and the discounting of bills, invoices and promissory notes, and all similar instruments,

(iv) the underwriting of debt instruments and all other kinds of financial securities, and

(v) the purchase or sale of financial assets;

"financial assets" includes shares, gilts, bonds, foreign currencies and all kinds of futures, options and currency and interest rate swaps, and similar instruments, including commodity futures and commodity options, invoices and all types of receivables, obligations evidencing debt (including loans and deposits), leases and loan and lease portfolios, bills of exchange, acceptance credits and all other documents of title relating to the movement of goods, commercial paper, promissory notes and all other kinds of negotiable or transferable instruments.

(*b*) For the purposes of this section—

(I) the leasing of machinery or plant,

(II) the leasing of land or buildings (other than the leasing of an advance factory building), or

(III) the carrying on of financial activities (other than such financial activities as are included in the activities referred to in [subsections (2)(*a*)(iv) and (2)(*a*)(xv)][16]),

shall not be regarded as qualifying trading operations.

[(4A) Notwithstanding the provisions of this section, trading operations carried on in the coal industry or in the steel and shipbuilding sectors shall not be regarded as qualifying trading operations for the purposes of this Part.][17]

(5) (*a*) In this subsection, **"certification committee"** means the committee consisting of a chairperson and 4 other members who from time to time may be appointed by the Minister for Finance for the purposes of this section.

(*b*) Subject to paragraph (*c*), the certification committee may, subject to such conditions as the committee considers proper and specifies in a certificate under this subsection, including a condition as to the maximum amount of money which may be raised by the company under this Part, issue a certificate for the purposes of this Part to a company which carries on or intends to carry on qualifying trading operations referred to in subsection (2)(*a*)(iv) and in respect of which money is raised or intended to be raised by the company under this Part by virtue of subsection (2)(*a*)(iv)(II), where—

(i) on the basis of such information as is supplied to the committee by the company or which the committee may reasonably request the company to furnish to it, and

(ii) such guidelines for the purpose as may be agreed from time to time between the committee and the Minister for Finance, the committee is satisfied that—

(I) the qualifying trading operations carried on or to be carried on by the company will contribute to the development of the exchange facility on which those operations will be carried on, and

(II) the money raised or to be raised by the company under this Part has the potential to maintain or create a reasonable level of sustainable employment.

(*c*) The certification committee shall not give a certificate under this subsection to a company—

(i) after the 5th day of April, 1998, and

(ii) to the extent that the aggregate of all subscriptions made or to be made for eligible shares arising out of the issue of such certificates exceeds [€2,539,476.16][18].

(6) (*a*) For the purposes of subsection (2)(*a*)(vi), **"research and development activities"** means systematic, investigative or experimental activities which—

(i) are carried on wholly or mainly in the State,

(ii) involve innovation or technical risk, and

(iii) are carried on for the purpose of—

(I) acquiring new knowledge with a view to that knowledge having a specific commercial application, or

(II) creating new or improved materials, products, devices, processes or services,

and other activities that are carried on wholly or mainly in the State for a purpose directly related to the carrying on of activities of the kind referred to in subparagraph (iii).

(*b*) Notwithstanding paragraph (*a*), activities that are carried on by means of—

(i) market research, market testing, market development, sales promotion or consumer surveys,

(ii) quality control,

(iii) prospecting, exploring or drilling for minerals, petroleum or natural gas for the purpose of determining the size or quality of any deposits,

(iv) the making of cosmetic modifications or stylistic changes to products, processes or production methods,

(v) management studies or efficiency surveys, or

(vi) research in social sciences, arts or humanities,

shall not be **"research and development activities"** for the purposes of subsection (2)(*a*)(vi).

(*c*) For the purposes of paragraph (*a*), systematic, investigative or experimental activities or other activities shall be regarded as carried on wholly or mainly in the State only if not less than 75 per cent of the total amount expended in the course of such activities in the relevant period is expended in the State.

(7) For the purposes of subsection (2)(*a*)(vii), **"the cultivation of horticultural produce"** means the cultivation in a greenhouse or greenhouses in the State of plants used for food or for the production of food or ornament or of herbaceous plants, and

includes the technical procedures in relation to such cultivation necessary for the production and preparation for market of flowers, decorative foliage, fruit, nursery stock, herbs and vegetable crops (including potatoes and seed potatoes), being a greenhouse or greenhouses in respect of which a certificate has been issued by the Minister for Agriculture and Food certifying that—

(*a*) the construction, improvement or repair of the greenhouse or greenhouses concerned, or

(*b*) the installation or improvement of irrigation or heating facilities in the greenhouse or greenhouses concerned,

may be eligible to be grant-aided under a scheme of assistance administered by that Minister.

(8) (*a*) For the purposes of subsection (2)(*a*)(xii), **"qualifying recording"** means a recording in any recording format in any musical style, including any associated video directly related to such recording, by a new artist, produced in a studio in the State, in respect of which the Minister for Arts, Heritage, Gaeltacht and the Islands (in this subsection referred to as **"the Minister"**) has, subject to such conditions as the Minister may consider proper and specifies in a certificate under this subsection, including a condition as to the maximum amount of money which may be raised under this Part in relation to a qualifying recording, given a certificate to the company which intends to produce the qualifying recording, stating that the recording and any such associated video may be treated as a qualifying recording for the purposes of this Part.

(*b*) In considering whether to give a certificate under this subsection, the Minister shall have regard only to such guidelines as the Minister may from time to time lay down with the consent of the Minister for Finance, and those guidelines may, without prejudice to the generality of the foregoing, include provision for—

(i) the circumstances in which an artist is to be, and continues to be, regarded as a new artist, and

(ii) the manner, extent and timing in which the money to be raised under this Part by a company for the production, publication, marketing and promotion of a qualifying recording is to be used.

(*c*) A certificate under this subsection or any condition of such certificate may be amended, revoked or added to by the Minister by giving notice in writing to the qualifying company concerned of such amendment, revocation or addition, and this section shall apply as if—

(i) a condition so amended or added to by the notice was specified in the certificate, and

(ii) a condition so revoked was not specified in the certificate.

(9) For the purposes of subsection (2)(*a*)(xiii), **"tourist traffic undertakings"** means—

(*a*) the operation of tourist accommodation facilities for which Bord Fáilte Éireann maintains a register in accordance with the Tourist Traffic Acts, 1939 to 1995, other than hotels, guest houses and self-catering accommodation,

(*b*) the operation of such other classes of facilities as may be approved of for the purposes of the relief by the Minister for Finance, in consultation with the

Minister for Tourism, Sport and Recreation, on the recommendation of Bord Fáilte Éireann in accordance with specific codes of standards laid down by it, or

(*c*) the promotion outside the State of—

(i) one or more tourist accommodation facilities for which Bord Fáilte Éireann maintains a register in accordance with the Tourist Traffic Acts, 1939 to 1995, or

(ii) any of the facilities mentioned in paragraph (*b*).

(10) The trade shall during the relevant period be conducted on a commercial basis and with a view to the realisation of profits.

Amendments

1 Substituted by FA 2004 s 18(2)(*d*)(i)(I)(A) (substituted by FA 2005 s 27(*a*)(iii)) and FA 2004 s 18(3)(*b*)(iv) (as amended by FA 2005 s 27(*b*)(v)), as respects subscriptions for eligible shares made on or after 5 February 2004; previously "this Part, and". The amendment was to come into operation on the making of an order to that effect by the Minister for Finance. By virtue of the Finance Act 2004 (Commencement of Section 18(2)) Order 2004 (SI No 758 of 2004) the amendment comes into operation on 29 November 2004.

2 Substituted by FA 2004 s 18(2)(*d*)(i)(I)(B) (substituted by FA 2005 s 27(*a*)(iii)) and FA 2005 s 18(3)(*b*)(iv) (as amended by FA 2005 s 27(*b*)(v)), as respects subscriptions for eligible shares made on or after 5 February 2004; previously "this Part,". The amendment was to come into operation on the making of an order to that effect by the Minister for Finance. By virtue of the Finance Act 2004 (Commencement of Section 18(2)) Order 2004 (SI No 758 of 2004) the amendment comes into operation on 29 November 2004.

3 Subs (2)(*a*)(i)(III) inserted by FA 2004 s 18(2)(*d*)(i)(I)(C) (substituted by FA 2005 s 27(*a*)(iii)) and FA 2005 s 18(3)(*b*)(iv) (as amended by FA 2005 s 27(*b*)(v)), as respects subscriptions for eligible shares made on or after 5 February 2004. The amendment was to come into operation on the making of an order to that effect by the Minister for Finance. By virtue of the Finance Act 2004 (Commencement of Section 18(2)) Order 2004 (SI No 758 of 2004) the amendment comes into operation on 29 November 2004.

4 Substituted by FA 2001 s 12(*c*)(i) with effect from 6 April 2001; previously "Shannon Free Airport Development Company Limited, or".

5 Substituted by FA 2003 s 15(*c*)(i) with effect from 1 January 2003; previously "1979, or".

6 Substituted by FA 2001 s 12(*c*)(ii) with effect from 6 April 2001; previously "Udarás na Gaeltachta Act, 1979,".

7 Inserted by FA 2003 s 15(*c*)(ii)(I) with effect from 1 January 2003.

8 Substituted by FA 2003 s 15(*c*)(ii)(II) with effect from 1 January 2003; previously "concerned".

9 Subs (2)(*a*)(ii)(IV) inserted by FA 2001 s 12(*c*)(iii) with effect from 6 April 2001.

10 Subs (2)(*a*)(ii)(V) inserted by FA 2003 s 15(*c*)(iii) with effect from 1 January 2003.

11 Substituted by FA 2004 s 18(2)(*d*)(i)(II) (substituted by FA 2005 s 27(*a*)(iii)) and FA 2004 s 18(3)(*b*)(iv) (as amended by FA 2005 s 27(*b*)(v)), as respects subscriptions for eligible shares made on or after 5 February 2004; previously "on or after 1 January 2003". The amendment was to come into operation on the making of an order to that effect by the Minister for Finance. By virtue of the Finance Act 2004 (Commencement of Section 18(2)) Order 2004 (SI No 758 of 2004) the amendment comes into operation on 29 November 2004.

12 Inserted by FA 2003 s 15(*c*)(iv) with effect from 1 January 2003.

13 Substituted by FA 2003 s 163 and Sch 6 para 1(*e*) with effect from 1 January 2002; previously "£2,000".

14 Inserted by FA 2003 s 15(*c*)(v) with effect from 1 January 2003.

15 Subs (2)(*b*) deleted by FA 2003 s 15(*c*)(vi) with effect from 1 January 2003.

16 Substituted by FA 2003 s 15(*c*)(vii) with effect from 1 January 2003; previously "subsection (2)(*a*)(iv)".

17 Subs (4A) inserted by FA 2004 s 18(2)(*d*)(ii) (substituted by FA 2005 s 27(*a*)(iii)) and FA 2004 s 18(3)(*b*)(iv) (as amended by FA 2005 s 27(*b*)(v)), as respects subscriptions for eligible shares made on or after 5 February 2004. The amendment was to come into operation on the making of an order to that effect by the Minister for Finance. By virtue of the Finance Act 2004 (Commencement of Section 18(2)) Order 2004 (SI No 758 of 2004) the amendment comes into operation on 29 November 2004.

18 Substituted by FA 2001 s 240(1) and (2)(*a*) and Sch 5 Pt 1 for 2002 and later tax years; previously "£2,000,000".

Cross-references

Certification where aggregate amount raised exceeds £250,000, combined certificate (subss (7), (8)): s 492(2)(*a*)(iii)(II), (iv)); meaning of "authority", subs (2)(*a*): s 492(3).
Financial asset (subs (4)(*a*)), meaning applied: Asset Covered Securities Act 2001 s 3 (interpretation).
Information that would disqualify a claimant to be sent to inspector: s 505(2).
Qualifying company, subs (2)(*a*)(iv): s 495(3)(*a*)(ii)(III); subss (7), (8), (9): s 495(4)(*a*), (5), (6)(*a*).
Qualifying trading operations, meaning applied, subs (2): s 488(1).
References to a trade, subs (2)(*a*)(x), (xii): s 488(4).
Relevant period, meaning: s 488(1).
Relevant trading operations, subs (2)(*a*)(ix): s 497(1); subs (2)(*a*)(ii), (v): s 497(2); subs (2)(*a*)(iv), (viii), (xii) and (xv): s 497(4).
Relief, specified individual, subs (2)(*a*)(ix), (x): s 489(7)(*b*), (*c*).
Restriction on relief where amounts raised exceed permitted maximum, subss (2)(*a*)(iv)(II), (ix): s 491(2), (3); subs (2)(*a*)(iv): s 491(4).
Seed capital investors, subs (2)(*a*)(iv), (xv): s 494(2)(*b*).
Transitional arrangements in relation to FA 1998 s 34, meaning of "qualifying trading operations" applied: FA 1998 s 35(1); subs (2)(*a*)(i), (ii), (iii), (v), (viii), (ix), (xi), (xiii): FA 1998 s 35(7)(*c*)(i); subs (2)(*a*)(vii): FA 1998 s 35(7)(*c*)(ii); subs (2)(*a*)(xii): FA 1998 s 35(7)(*c*)(iii).
Transitional arrangements in relation to FA 2004 s 18(1)(a)(ii), meaning of "qualifying trading operations" applied: FA 2004 s 19(1); subs (2)(*a*)(i), (ii), (iii), (v), (viii), (ix), (xi), (xiii): FA 2004 s 19(5)(*c*)(i); subs (2)(*a*)(vii): FA 2004 s 19(5)(*c*)(ii); subs (2)(*a*)(xii): FA 2004 s 19(5)(iii).
Withdrawal of BES relief: s 504(7)(*a*).

Certificates

subs (2)(*a*)(iv): s 489(2)(*a*).
subs (2)(*a*)(vii): s 489(2)(*b*).
subs (2)(*a*)(x): s 489(2)(*c*).
subs (2)(*a*)(i): s 489(2)(*c*)(i).
subs (2)(*a*)(ii): s 489(2)(*c*)(i).
subs (2)(*a*)(viii): s 489(2)(*c*)(i).

Case law

UK

Castleton Management Services Ltd v Kirkwood (Inspector of Taxes) (2001) STC 95.

Revenue precedents

Issue: Where IDA employment grant given to Co. A re: certain services, such services subsequently taken over by Co. B, would this be regarded as a "qualifying trade" within meaning of s 496?
Decision: It would be regarded as a "qualifying trade" within meaning of s 496.

Definitions

company: ss 4(1), 5(1); land: s 5(1), IA 1937 Sch; person: IA 1937 s 11(*c*); profits: s 4(1); shares: s 5(1); Tax Acts: s 1(2); trade: s 3(1).

Former enactments

FA 1984 s 16(1)–(3); FA 1987 s 11; FA 1988 s 7; FA 1989 s 9(*c*)(i); FA 1990 s 10(*c*); FA 1991 s 15(1)(*c*)(ii) and (iii); FA 1993 s 25(*g*)(i); FA 1994 s 16(1)(*c*); FA 1995 s 17(1)(*f*); FA 1996 s 23; FA 1997 s 9(*c*).

Corresponding UK tax provision

Income and Corporation Taxes Act 1988 s 297.

---

497 Relevant trading operations

(1) For the purposes of this Part, **"relevant trading operations"** means qualifying trading operations (other than those operations referred to in section 496(2)(*a*)(ix)) in respect of which a certifying agency or a certifying Minister, as the case may be (in this section referred to as **"the authority"**), has given a certificate under subsection (2).

(2) Subject to this section, the authority may, in respect of qualifying trading operations carried on or to be carried on by a company, give a certificate to the company certifying that the authority is satisfied, on the basis of such information as is supplied to the

authority by the company or which the authority may reasonably require the company to furnish, that the carrying on of such qualifying trading operations by the company is or will be a bona fide new venture which, having regard to—

(*a*) the potential for the creation of additional sustainable employment, and

(*b*) the desirability of minimising the displacement of existing employment,

may be eligible—

(i) in the case of qualifying trading operations referred to in section 496(2)(*a*)(v), based on guidelines agreed, with the consent of the Minister for Finance, between the certifying agency and the Minister for Arts, Heritage, Gaeltacht and the Islands or the Minister for Enterprise, Trade and Employment (as may be appropriate in the circumstances), for the payment of the grants or the financial assistance referred to in section 496(2)(*a*)(ii) within a reasonable period after the completion of the feasibility study carried out in relation to the trading operations concerned in accordance with section 496(2)(*a*)(v), and

(ii) in any other case but subject to subsection (4), based on guidelines agreed—

(I) with the consent of the Minister for Finance, between the certifying agency and the Minister for Arts, Heritage, Gaeltacht and the Islands or the Minister for Enterprise, Trade and Employment or the Minister for the Marine and Natural Resources or the Minister for Tourism, Sport and Recreation (as may be appropriate in the circumstances), or

(II) between the certifying Minister and the Minister for Finance,

to be grant aided under a scheme of assistance administered by the authority.

(3) The carrying on of qualifying trading operations referred to in subsection (2) by a company shall not be regarded as not being a bona fide new venture by reason only that they were carried on as or as part of a trade by another person at any time before the issue of the eligible shares in respect of which relief is claimed.

(4) A certificate to which subsection (2) relates may be given by—

(*a*) the Industrial Development Agency (Ireland) in respect of qualifying trading operations referred to in [sections 496(2)(*a*)(iv) and 496(2)(*a*)(xv)][1],

(*b*) the Minister for Agriculture and Food in respect of qualifying trading operations referred to in section 496(2)(*a*)(viii), or

(*c*) the Minister for Arts, Heritage, Gaeltacht and the Islands in respect of qualifying trading operations referred to in section 496(2)(*a*)(xii),

without regard to whether such operations are eligible to be grant-aided but, in considering whether to give such a certificate, the agency or the Minister, as the case may be, shall have regard to such guidelines in relation to the giving of such a certificate as may be agreed—

(i) with the consent of the Minister for Finance, between the agency and the Minister for Enterprise and Employment, or

(ii) between the Minister for Agriculture and Food or the Minister for Arts, Heritage, Gaeltacht and the Islands (as may be appropriate) and the Minister for Finance.

(5) Bord Fáilte Éireann shall not give a certificate under subsection (2) in a case where the value of a company's interests in land and buildings (excluding fixtures and fittings) is or is intended to be greater than 50 per cent of the value of its assets as a whole.

(6) An authority shall not give a certificate under subsection (2) unless the company concerned undertakes in writing to furnish the authority when requested to do so with such details in relation to the carrying on of the qualifying trading operations as the authority may specify.

(7) (*a*) For the purposes of this Chapter, as respects a relevant investment made on or after the 10th day of May, 1997, a certificate under subsection (2) may, instead of being given by the authority, be given by a County Enterprise Board (being a board referred to in the Schedule to the Industrial Development Act, 1995) to a company carrying on or intending to carry on one or more qualifying trading operations mentioned in subparagraphs (i), (ii) and (v) of section 496(2)(*a*), and subsections (2) and (6) shall, subject to the modification specified in paragraph (*b*) and any other necessary modification, apply accordingly.

(*b*) The modification referred to in paragraph (*a*) is that for the purposes of this subsection, the guidelines of the kind mentioned in paragraphs (i) and (ii) of subsection (2) shall be agreed between the Minister for Finance and the Minister for Arts, Heritage, Gaeltacht and the Islands or the Minister for Enterprise, Trade and Employment, as may be appropriate in the circumstances.

Amendments

[1] Substituted by FA 2003 s 15(*d*) with effect from 1 January 2003; previously "section 496(2)(*a*)(iv)".

Cross-references

Meaning applied: s 488(1).

Transitional arrangements in relation to FA 1998 s 34: FA 1998 s 35(7)(*b*)(iv).

Transitional arrangements in relation to FA 2004 s 18(1)(*a*)(ii): FA 2004 s 19(5)(*b*)(iii).

Former enactments

FA 1984 s 16A; FA 1995 s 17(1)(*g*); FA 1996 s 24; FA 1997 s 9(*d*).

498 Disposals of shares

(1) Where an individual disposes of any eligible shares before the end of the relevant period, then—

(*a*) in a case where the disposal is otherwise than by means of a bargain made at arm's length, the individual shall not be entitled to any relief in respect of those shares, and

(*b*) in any other case, the amount of relief to which the individual is entitled in respect of those shares shall be reduced by the amount or value of the consideration which the individual receives for those shares.

(2) Subsection (1) shall not apply to a disposal made by a wife to her husband at a time when she is treated as living with him for income tax purposes in accordance with section 1015 or to a disposal made at such a time by him to her; but where shares issued to one of them have been transferred to the other by a transaction inter vivos—

(*a*) that subsection shall apply on the disposal of the shares by the transferee to a third person, and (*b*) if at any time the wife ceases to be treated as living with her husband for income tax purposes in accordance with section 1015 and any of those shares have not been disposed of by the transferee before that time, any assessment for withdrawing relief in respect of those shares shall be made on the transferee.

(3) (*a*) For the purposes of this subsection, references to an option or an agreement shall include references to a right or obligation to acquire or grant an option or enter into an agreement, and references to the exercise of an option shall include references to the exercise of an option which may be acquired or granted by the exercise of such a right or under such an obligation.

(*b*) Where in the relevant period an individual, either directly or indirectly—

(i) (I) acquires an option where the exercise of the option, either under the terms of the option or under the terms of any arrangement or undertaking subject to which or otherwise in connection with which the option is acquired, would—

(A) bind the person from whom the option was acquired or any other person, or

(B) cause that person or such other person,

to purchase or otherwise acquire any eligible shares for a price which, having regard to the terms of the option or the terms of such arrangement or undertaking and the net effect of those terms considered as a whole, is other than the market value of the eligible shares at the time the purchase or acquisition is made, or

(II) enters into an agreement where, either under the terms of the agreement or under the terms of any arrangement or understanding subject to which or otherwise in connection with which the agreement is made, it would—

(A) bind the person with whom the agreement is made or any other person, or

(B) cause that person or such other person,

to purchase or otherwise acquire any eligible shares in the manner described in clause (I),

or

(ii) (I) grants to any person an option where the exercise of the option, either under the terms of the option or under the terms of any arrangement or understanding subject to which or otherwise in connection with which the option is granted, would bind the individual to dispose, or cause the individual to dispose, of any eligible shares to the person to whom the individual granted the option or any other person for a price which, having regard to the terms of the option or the terms of such arrangement or understanding and the net effect of those terms considered as a whole, is other than the market value of the eligible shares at the time the disposal is made, or

(II) enters into an agreement where, either under the terms of the agreement or under the terms of any arrangement or understanding subject to which or otherwise in connection with which the agreement is made, it would bind the individual to dispose, or cause the individual to dispose, of any eligible shares to the person with whom the agreement is made or any other person in the manner described in clause (I),

the individual shall not be entitled to any relief in respect of the shares to which the option or the agreement relates.

[(4) Where an individual holds ordinary shares of any class in a company and the relief has been given in respect of some shares of that class but not others, any disposal by the individual of ordinary shares of that class in the company, not being a disposal to which section 479(3) or 512(2) applies, shall be treated for the purposes of this section as relating to those in respect of which relief has been given under this Part rather than to others.][1]

(5) Where the relief has been given to an individual in respect of shares of any class in a company which have been issued to the individual at different times, any disposal by the individual of shares of that class shall be treated for the purposes of this section as relating to those issued earlier rather than to those issued later.

(6) Where shares in respect of which the relief was given have by virtue of any such allotment mentioned in subsection (1) of section 584 (not being an allotment for payment) been treated under subsection (3) of that section as the same asset as a new holding—

(*a*) the new holding shall be treated for the purposes of subsection (4) as shares in respect of which the relief has been given, and

(*b*) a disposal of the whole or part of the new holding shall be treated for the purposes of this section as a disposal of the whole or a corresponding part of those shares.

(7) Shares in a company shall not be treated for the purposes of this section as being of the same class unless they would be so treated if dealt in on a stock exchange in the State.

Amendments

1 Subs (4) substituted by FA 1998 s 34(*b*) with effect from 12 February 1998.

Cross-references

Capital gains tax: s 506(2).
Employee share purchase schemes: s 479(5).
Information that would disqualify a claimant to be sent to inspector: s 505(1).
Relevant period, meaning: s 488(1)(*a*).
Withdrawal of BES relief, subs (1)(*b*): s 504(5), (7)(*a*)–(*b*).

Revenue precedents

Issue: Does the death of an individual constitute a disposal of shares for the purposes of this section?
Decision: No.
Issue: Would the exchange of shares in a RICT company for equal shares in a new holding company (also a qualifying company) lead to a loss of RICT relief?
Decision: No - where the restructuring is essential to ensure that the existing employment is safeguarded and future job creation is facilitated.

Issue: If investors swap their shares in a subsidiary for shares in a holding company, it would normally be referred to as disposal. However, because s 498(1)(*b*) applies, there is no clawback of the relief because no consideration was received by the shareholders. Is this true?
Decision: No. Revenue would not accept this interpretation of the section. However, they would be prepared to consider allowing investors to retain relief if the existing investors in the qualifying subsidiary were given shares in the qualifying company on a share for share basis.
Issue: Where an individual disposes of shares in a company on the take-over of that company within the three year "relevant period", would the relief be withdrawn by virtue of this section?
Decision: Yes.
Issue: Would the existence of a cap on dividends and assets on a winding up, and a put-call option offend this rule?
Decision: No. The existence of a cap would not necessarily preclude the granting of approval but its bearing on other aspects of the case would need to be examined.

Definitions

company: ss 4(1), 5(1); person: IA 1937 s 11(*c*); shares: s 5(1).

Former enactments

FA 1984 s 17; FA 1989 s 9(*d*).

499 Value received from company

(1) In this section, **"ordinary trade debt"** means any debt for goods or services supplied in the ordinary course of a trade or business where the credit period given does not exceed 6 months and is not longer than that normally given to the customers of the person carrying on the trade or business.

(2) In this section—

(*a*) any reference to a payment or transfer to an individual includes a reference to a payment or transfer made to the individual indirectly or to his or her order or for his or her benefit, and

(*b*) any reference to an individual includes a reference to an associate of the individual and any reference to the company includes a reference to any person connected with the company.

(3) For the purposes of this section, an individual shall receive value from a company where the company—

(*a*) repays, redeems or repurchases any of its share capital or securities which belong to the individual or makes any payment to the individual for giving up his or her right to any of the company's share capital or any security on its cancellation or extinguishment,

(*b*) repays any debt owed to the individual other than—

(i) an ordinary trade debt incurred by the company, or

(ii) any other debt incurred by the company—

(I) on or after the earliest date on which the individual subscribed for the shares in respect of which the relief is claimed, and

(II) otherwise than in consideration of the extinguishment of a debt incurred before that date,

(*c*) makes to the individual any payment for giving up his or her right to any debt on its extinguishment other than—

(i) a debt in respect of a payment of the kind mentioned in paragraph (*d*) or (*e*) of section 493(3), or

(ii) a debt of the kind mentioned in subparagraph (i) or (ii) of paragraph (*b*), (*d*) releases or waives any liability of the individual to the company or discharges, or undertakes to discharge, any liability of the individual to a third person,

(*e*) makes a loan or advance to the individual,

(*f*) provides a benefit or facility for the individual,

(*g*) transfers an asset to the individual for no consideration or for consideration less than its market value or acquires an asset from the individual for consideration exceeding its market value, or

(*h*) makes to the individual any other payment except a payment of the kind mentioned in paragraph (*a*), (*b*), (*c*), (*d*) or (*e*) of section 493(3) or a payment in discharge of an ordinary trade debt.

[(3A)(*a*) A specified individual shall not have received value from a company by virtue of subsection (3)(*b*) where—

(i) the specified individual has made an investment in the company by way of a loan,

(ii) the loan is converted into eligible shares within one year of the making of the loan, and

(iii) the specified individual provides a statement by the auditor of the company certifying that, in his or her opinion, the money raised by the company by way of the loan was used, and only used, by it in accordance with the provisions of section 489(1)(*c*).

(*b*) Where paragraph (*a*) applies, conversion of the loan into eligible shares shall, notwithstanding any other provision of this Part, be treated as the making of a relevant investment by the specified individual on the date of the making of the loan.

(*c*) For the purposes of this subsection **"auditor"**, in relation to a company, means the person or persons appointed as auditor of the company for all the purposes of the Companies Acts 1963 to 2003.][1]

(4) For the purposes of this section, an individual shall also receive value from the company where the individual receives in respect of ordinary shares held by the individual any payment or asset in a winding up or in connection with a dissolution of the company, being a winding up or dissolution within section 495(8).

(5) For the purposes of this section, an individual shall also receive value from the company where any person who for the purposes of section 493 would be treated as connected with the company—

(*a*) purchases any of its share capital or securities which belong to the individual, or

(*b*) makes any payment to the individual for giving up any right in relation to any of the company's share capital or securities.

(6) The value received by an individual shall be—

(*a*) in a case within paragraph (*a*), (*b*) or (*c*) of subsection (3), the amount receivable by the individual or, if greater, the market value of the shares, securities or debt in question,

(*b*) in a case within subsection (3)(*d*), the amount of the liability,

(*c*) in a case within subsection (3)(*e*), the amount of the loan or advance, (*d*) in a case within subsection (3)(*f*), the cost to the company of providing the benefit or facility less any consideration given for it by the individual,

(*e*) in a case within subsection (3)(*g*), the difference between the market value of the asset and the consideration (if any) given for it,

(*f*) in a case within subsection (3)(*h*), the amount of the payment,

(*g*) in a case within subsection (4), the amount of the payment or, as the case may be, the market value of the asset, and

(*h*) in a case within subsection (5), the amount receivable by the individual or, if greater, the market value of the shares or securities in question.

(7) For the purposes of subsection (3)(*d*), a company shall be treated as having released or waived a liability where the liability is not discharged by payment within 12 months of the time when it ought to have been discharged by payment.

(8) For the purposes of subsection (3)(*e*), there shall be treated as if it were a loan made by the company to the individual—

(*a*) the amount of any debt (other than an ordinary trade debt) incurred by the individual to the company, and

(*b*) the amount of any debt due from the individual to a third person which has been assigned to the company.

(9) Where an individual who subscribes for eligible shares in a company—

(*a*) has, before the issue of the shares but within the relevant period, received any value from the company, or

(*b*) on or after their issue but before the end of the relevant period, receives any such value,

then, the amount of the relief to which the individual is entitled in respect of the shares shall be reduced by the value so received.

(10) Where by virtue of this section any relief is withheld or withdrawn in the case of an individual to whom ordinary shares in a company have been issued at different times, the relief shall be withheld or withdrawn in respect of shares issued earlier rather than in respect of shares issued later.

Amendments

1 Subs (3A) inserted by FA 2004 s 18(2)(*e*) and FA 2004 s 18(3)(*b*)(i) (as amended by FA 2005 s 27(*b*)(i)) with effect from 5 February 2004. The amendment was to come into operation on the making of an order to that effect by the Minister for Finance. By virtue of the Finance Act 2004 (Commencement of Section 18(2)) Order 2004 (SI No 758 of 2004) the amendment comes into operation on 29 November 2004.

Cross-references

Finance for trade of subsidiary, subs (9): Sch 10 para 3(1).
Information that would disqualify a claimant to be sent to inspector: s 505(1), (2), (6)(*a*).
Relevant period, meaning: s 488(1)(*a*).
Value received by persons other than claimants, subs (3): s 501(1), (8).
Withdrawal of BES relief: s 504(7)(*c*).

Revenue precedents

Issue: Whether value received for the purposes of subs (3)(*b*) where a director's loan is repaid.
Decision: Yes.
Issue: Would a payment of "hello money" which is not outside of the industry norm, be regarded as value received as provided for in this section?
Decision: No.

Issue: Does the provision of company cars for directors as part of the remuneration package, where the directors are assessable to tax under Schedule E in respect of the benefit, constitute value received from the company?
Decision: No, provided the level of benefit does not exceed the generally accepted levels.
Issue: Would the issue of bonus shares be regarded as value received?
Decision: No, where the overall value of the individual shareholding is not increased.

Definitions

company: ss 4(1), 5(1); month: IA 1937 Sch; person: IA 1937 s 11(*c*); shares: s 5(1); trade: s 3(1).

Former enactments

FA 1984 s 18.

Corresponding UK tax provision

Income and Corporation Taxes Act 1988 s 300.

500 Replacement capital

(1) In this section—

"subsidiary" means a subsidiary of a kind which a qualifying company may have by virtue of section 507;

"trade" includes any business, profession or vocation, and references to a trade previously carried on include references to part of such a trade.

(2) An individual to whom subsection (3) applies shall not be entitled to relief in respect of any shares in a company where at any time in the relevant period the company or any of its subsidiaries—

(*a*) begins to carry on, as its trade or as a part of its trade, a trade previously carried on at any time in that period otherwise than by the company or any of its subsidiaries, or

(*b*) acquires the whole or greater part of the assets used for the purposes of a trade previously so carried on.

(3) This subsection shall apply to an individual where—

(*a*) any person or group of persons to whom an interest amounting in the aggregate to more than a 50 per cent share in the trade (as previously carried on) belonged at any time in the relevant period is a person or a group of persons to whom such an interest in the trade carried on by the company, or any of its subsidiaries, belongs or has at any such time belonged, or

(*b*) any person or group of persons who controls or at any such time has controlled the company is a person or a group of persons who at any such time controlled another company which previously carried on the trade,

and the individual is that person or one of those persons.

(4) An individual shall not be entitled to relief in respect of any shares in a company where—

(*a*) the company comes to acquire all of the issued share capital of another company at any time in the relevant period, and

(*b*) any person or group of persons who controls or has at any such time controlled the company is a person or a group of persons who at any such time controlled that other company, and the individual is that person or one of those persons.

(5) For the purposes of subsection (3)—

(*a*) the person or persons to whom a trade belongs and, where a trade belongs to 2 or more persons, their respective shares in that trade shall be determined in accordance with paragraphs (*a*) and (*b*) of subsection (1), and subsections (2) and (3), of section 400, and

(*b*) any interest, rights or powers of a person who is an associate of another person shall be treated as those of that other person.

Cross-references

Assessment for withdrawing relief: s 504(7)(*a*).

Information that would disqualify a claimant to be sent to inspector: s 505(2).

Relevant period, meaning: s 488(1)(*a*).

Definitions

company: ss 4(1), 5(1); person: IA 1937 s 11(*c*); profession: ss 2(1), 5(1); shares: s 5(1); trade: s 3(1).

Former enactments

FA 1984 s 19.

Corresponding UK tax provision

Income and Corporation Taxes Act 1988 s 302.

501 Value received by persons other than claimants

(1) The relief to which an individual is entitled in respect of any shares in a company shall be reduced in accordance with subsection (4) if at any time in the relevant period the company repays, redeems or repurchases any of its share capital which belongs to any member other than—

(*a*) that individual, or

(*b*) another individual whose relief is thereby reduced by virtue of section 499(3),

or makes any payment to any such member for giving up such member's right to any of the company's share capital on its cancellation or extinguishment.

(2) Subsection (1) shall not apply in relation to the redemption of any share capital for which the redemption date was fixed before the 26th day of January, 1984.

(3) Where—

(*a*) after the 5th day of April, 1984, a company issues share capital (in this subsection referred to as **"the original shares"**) of nominal value equal to the authorised minimum (within the meaning of the Companies (Amendment) Act, 1983) for the purposes of complying with the requirements of section 6 of that Act, and

(*b*) after the registrar of companies has issued the company with a certificate under section 6 of that Act the company issues eligible shares,

subsection (1) shall not apply in relation to any redemption of any of the original shares within 12 months of the date on which those shares were issued.

(4) Where subsection (1) applies, the amount of relief to which an individual is entitled shall be reduced by the amount receivable by the member or, if greater, the nominal value of the share capital in question and, where apart from this subsection 2 or more

individuals would be entitled to relief, the reduction shall be made in proportion to the amounts of relief to which those individuals would have been entitled apart from this subsection.

(5) Where at any time in the relevant period a member of a company receives or is entitled to receive any value from the company within the meaning of this subsection, then, for the purposes of section 493(4) in its application to any subsequent time—

(*a*) the amount of the company's issued ordinary share capital, and

(*b*) the amount of the part of that capital which consists of the shares relevant to section 493(4) and the amount of the part consisting of the remainder,

shall each be treated as reduced in accordance with subsection (6).

(6) The amount of each of the parts mentioned in subsection (5)(*b*) shall be treated as equal to such proportion of that amount as the amount subscribed for that part less the relevant value bears to the amount subscribed, and the amount of the issued share capital shall be treated as equal to the sum of the amounts treated under this subsection as the amount of those parts respectively.

(7) In subsection (5)(*b*), the reference to the part of the capital which consists of the shares relevant to section 493(4) is a reference to the part consisting of shares which (within the meaning of that section) the individual directly or indirectly possesses or is entitled to acquire, and in subsection (6) **"the relevant value"**, in relation to each of the parts mentioned in that subsection, means the value received by the member or members entitled to the shares of which that part consists.

(8) For the purposes of subsection (5), a member of a company receives or is entitled to receive value from the company within the meaning of that subsection in any case in which an individual would receive value from the company by virtue of paragraph (*d*), (*e*), (*f*), (*g*) or (*h*) of section 499(3) (but treating as excepted from paragraph (*h*) all payments made for full consideration), and the value received shall be determined as for the purposes of that section.

(9) For the purposes of subsection (8), a person shall be treated as entitled to receive anything which the person is entitled to receive at a future date or will at a future date be entitled to receive.

(10) Where by virtue of this section any relief is withheld or withdrawn in the case of an individual to whom ordinary shares in the company have been issued at different times, the relief shall be withheld or withdrawn in respect of shares issued earlier rather than in respect of shares issued later.

Cross-references

Finance for trade of subsidiary, subs (1): Sch 10 para 3(2); subss (5) and (8): Sch 10 para 3(1).

Information that would disqualify a claimant to be sent to inspector: s 505(2), (6).

Relevant period, meaning: s 488(1).

Withdrawal of BES relief, subs (1): s 504(7)(*a*).

Revenue precedents

Issue: Would capitalisation of the reserves affect BES applications?

Decision: No, as long as market value of the shareholders capital remains the same and the company does not repay, redeem, or repurchase any of the share capital.

Issue: Would a bank backed management buy-out (after the three years relevant period), where the bank insists on being given security over the assets of the company, constitute a receipt of value received by non-BES members?
Decision: No, where the BES money has long since been dissipated.
Issue: Would the repurchase by a company of shares held by Foir Teo disqualify the BES shareholders?
Decision: No, provided the shares are temporary redeemable shares.

Tax Briefing

TB47 April 2002 p 21 — Extension of limits for the Business Expansion Scheme (FA 2002) — possible application of s 501 TCA 1997.

Definitions

company: ss 4(1), 5(1); month: IA 1937 Sch; ordinary share capital: s 2(1); person: IA 1937 s 11(*c*); shares: s 5(1).

Former enactments

FA 1984 s 20.

Corresponding UK tax provision

Income and Corporation Taxes Act 1988 s 303.

502 Prevention of misuse

An individual shall not be entitled to relief in respect of any shares unless the shares are subscribed and issued for bona fide commercial purposes and not as part of a scheme or arrangement the main purpose or one of the main purposes of which is the avoidance of tax.

Cross-references

Finance for trade of subsidiary: Sch 10 para 4.
Information that would disqualify a claimant to be sent to inspector: s 505(2), (4), (5).
Withdrawal of BES relief: s 504(7)(*d*).

Definitions

shares: s 5(1).

Former enactments

FA 1984 s 21.

503 Claims

(1) A claim for the relief in respect of eligible shares issued by a company in any year of assessment shall be made—

(*a*) not earlier than—

(i) in the case of a relevant investment, the date on which the company commences to carry on the relevant trading operations, and

(ii) in any other case, the end of the period of 4 months mentioned in section 489(7)(*a*)(i)(II),

and

(*b*) not later than 2 years after the end of that year of assessment or, if that period of 4 months ended after the end of that year, not later than 2 years after the end of that period.

(2) A claim for relief in respect of eligible shares in a company shall not be allowed unless it is accompanied by a certificate issued by the company in such form as the Revenue Commissioners may direct and certifying that the conditions for the relief, in so far as they apply to the company and the trade, are satisfied in relation to those shares.

(3) Before issuing a certificate under subsection (2), a company shall furnish the inspector with a statement to the effect that it satisfies the conditions for the relief, in so far as they apply in relation to the company and the trade, and has done so at all times since the beginning of the relevant period.

(4) No such certificate shall be issued without the authority of the inspector or where the company or a person connected with the company has given notice to the inspector under section 505(2).

(5) Any statement under subsection (3) shall—

(*a*) contain such information as the Revenue Commissioners may reasonably require,

(*b*) be in such form as the Revenue Commissioners may direct, and

(*c*) contain a declaration that it is correct to the best of the company's knowledge and belief.

(6) Where a company has issued a certificate under subsection (2) or furnished a statement under subsection (3), and—

(*a*) the certificate or statement is made fraudulently or negligently, or

(*b*) the certificate was issued in contravention of subsection (4),

the company shall be liable to a penalty not exceeding [€630][1] or, in the case of fraud, [€1,265][2], and such penalty may, without prejudice to any other method of recovery, be proceeded for and recovered summarily in the like manner as in summary proceedings for the recovery of any fine or penalty under any Act relating to the excise.

(7) For the purpose of regulations made under section 986, no regard shall be had to the relief unless a claim for it has been duly made and admitted.

(8) For the purposes of section 1080, [income tax][3]—

(*a*) shall be regarded as due and payable notwithstanding that relief from the tax (whether by discharge or repayment) is subsequently given on a claim for the relief, but

(*b*) shall, unless paid earlier or due and payable later, be regarded as paid, to the extent that relief from tax is due under this Part, on the date of the making of the claim on which the relief is given,

and section 1081 shall not apply in consequence of any discharge or repayment for giving effect to the relief.

Amendments

1 Substituted by FA 2001 s 240(1) and (2)(*k*) and Sch 5 Pt 1 as respects acts or omissions which take place or begin on or after 1 January 2002; previously "£500".

2 Substituted by FA 2001 s 2401) and (2)(*k*) and Sch 5 Pt 1 as respects acts or omissions which take place or begin on or after 1 January 2002; previously "£1,000".

3 Substituted by FA 2005 s 145(7)(*a*) and Sch 5 Pt 1 in relation to any unpaid income tax, corporation tax or capital gains tax, as the case may be, that has not been paid before 1 April 2005 regardless of when that tax became due and payable and notwithstanding anything to the contrary in any other enactment other than TCA 1997 s 1082; previously "income tax charged by an assessment".

Cross-references

Designated funds, subs (2): s 508(5); subs (6): s 508(7).

Relevant period, meaning: s 488(1).

Definitions

company: ss 4(1), 5(1); inspector: ss 2(1), 852; month: IA 1937 Sch; person: IA 1937 s 11(*c*); shares: s 5(1); trade: s 3(1); year of assessment: ss 2(1), 5(1).

Former enactments

FA 1984 s 22; FA 1993 s 25(*h*); FA 1995 s 17(1)(*h*)(i).

Corresponding UK tax provision

Income and Corporation Taxes Act 1988 s 306.

504 Assessments for withdrawing relief

(1) Where any relief has been given which is subsequently found not to have been due, that relief shall be withdrawn by the making of an assessment to income tax under Case IV of Schedule D for the year of assessment for which the relief was given.

(2) Where any relief given in respect of shares for which either a married person or his or her spouse has subscribed, and which were issued while the married person was assessed in accordance with section 1017, is to be withdrawn by virtue of a subsequent disposal of those shares by the person who subscribed for them and at the time of the disposal the married person is not so assessable, any assessment for withdrawing that relief shall be made on the person making the disposal and shall be made by reference to the reduction of tax flowing from the amount of the relief regardless of any allocation of that reduction under subsections (2) and (3) of section 1024 or of any allocation of a repayment of income tax under section 1020.

(3) Subject to this section, any assessment for withdrawing relief which is made by reason of an event occurring after the date of the claim may be made within [4 years][1] after the end of the year of assessment in which that event occurs.

(4) No assessment for withdrawing relief in respect of shares issued to any person shall be made by reason of any event occurring after his or her death.

(5) Where a person has, by a disposal or disposals to which section 498(1)(*b*) applies, disposed of all the ordinary shares issued to the person by a company, no assessment for withdrawing relief in respect of any of those shares shall be made by reason of any subsequent event unless it occurs at a time when the person is connected with the company within the meaning of section 493.

(6) Subsection (3) is without prejudice to section 924(2)(*c*).

(7) In its application to an assessment made by virtue of this section, section 1080 shall apply as if the date on which the income tax charged by the assessment becomes due and payable were—

(*a*) in the case of relief withdrawn by virtue of section 493, 495, 496, [500][2] or 501(1) in consequence of any event after the grant of the relief, the date of that event;

(*b*) in the case of relief withdrawn by virtue of section 498(1) in consequence of a disposal after the grant of the relief, the date of the disposal;

(*c*) in the case of relief withdrawn by virtue of section 499 in consequence of a receipt of value after the grant of the relief, the date of the receipt;

(*d*) in the case of relief withdrawn by virtue of section 502—

(i) in so far as effect has been given to the relief in accordance with regulations under section 986, the 5th day of April in the year of assessment in which effect was so given, and

(ii) in so far as effect has not been so given, the date on which the relief was granted;

(*e*) in the case of relief withdrawn by virtue of—

(i) a specified individual failing or ceasing to hold a relevant employment, or

(ii) an individual ceasing to be a specified individual,

the date of the failure or the cessation, as the case may be.

(8) For the purposes of subsection (7), the date on which the relief shall be granted is the date on which a repayment of tax for giving effect to the relief was made or, if there was no such repayment, the date on which the inspector issued a notice to the claimant showing the amount of tax payable after giving effect to the relief.

Amendments

1 Substituted by FA 2003 s 17(*f*) with effect from: (*a*) such day or days as the Minister for Finance may by order or orders appoint either generally or with reference to any particular purpose or provision and different days may be so appointed for different purposes or different provisions and (*b*) notwithstanding the generality of (*a*), any order made by the Minister for Finance in accordance with the provisions of that paragraph may contain, and be subject to, such conditions as the Minister considers appropriate and which are specified in the order; previously "10 years". By virtue of Finance Act 2003 (Commencement of Section 17) Order 2003, SI No 508 of 2003, this amendment comes into operation in relation to the making, on or after 1 January 2005, of an assessment under section 504.

2 Substituted by FA 1998 s 34(*c*) with effect from 6 April 1998.

Tax Briefing

TB56 July 2004 pp 6–11 — Repayments, Interest and Time Limits — Section 17 FA 2003 changes.

TB57 Oct 2004 pp 7–9 — New Time Limits — Section 17 FA 2003 changes.

TB57 Oct 2004 p 15 — Repayments, Interest and Time Limits - correction to TB56 p 8.

Definitions

company: ss 4(1), 5(1); inspector: ss 2(1), 852; person: IA 1937 s 11(*c*); shares: s 5(1); year of assessment: ss 2(1), 5(1).

Former enactments

FA 1984 s 23; FA 1993 s 25(*i*)(i); FA 1995 s 17(1)(i).

Corresponding UK tax provision

Income and Corporation Taxes Act 1988 s 307.

505 Information

(1) Where an event occurs by reason of which any relief given to an individual is to be withdrawn by virtue of section 493, 498 or 499, the individual shall within 60 days of coming to know of the event give a notice in writing to the inspector containing particulars of the event.

(2) Where an event occurs by reason of which any relief in respect of any shares in a company is to be withdrawn by virtue of section 495, 496, 499, 500, 501 or 502—

(*a*) the company, and

(*b*) any person connected with the company who has knowledge of that matter, shall within 60 days of the event or, in the case of a person within paragraph (*b*), of that person coming to know of it, give a notice in writing to the inspector containing particulars of the event or payment.

(3) Where the inspector has reason to believe that a person has not given a notice which the person is required to give under subsection (1) or (2) in respect of any event, the inspector may by notice in writing require that person to furnish him or her within such time (not being less than 60 days) as may be specified in the notice with such information relating to the event as the inspector may reasonably require for the purposes of this Part.

(4) Where relief is claimed in respect of shares in a company and the inspector has reason to believe that it may not be due by reason of any arrangement or scheme mentioned in section 493(11), 495(10) or 502, the inspector may by notice in writing require any person concerned to furnish him or her within such time (not being less than 60 days) as may be specified in the notice with—

(*a*) a declaration in writing stating whether or not, according to the information which that person has or can reasonably obtain, any such arrangement or scheme exists or has existed, and

(*b*) such other information as the inspector may reasonably require for the purposes of the provision in question and as that person has or can reasonably obtain.

(5) References in subsection (4) to the person concerned are, in relation to sections 493(11) and 502, references to the claimant and, in relation to sections 495(10) and 502, references to the company and any person controlling the company.

(6) Where relief has been given in respect of shares in a company—

(*a*) any person who receives from the company any payment or asset which may constitute value received (by that person or another) for the purposes of section 499 or 501(5), and

(*b*) any person on whose behalf such a payment or asset is received,

shall, if so required by the inspector, state whether the payment or asset received by that person or on that person's behalf is received on behalf of any person other than that person and if so the name and address of that other person.

(7) Where relief has been claimed in respect of shares in a company, any person who holds or has held shares in the company and any person on whose behalf any such shares are or were held shall, if so required by the inspector, state whether the shares which are or were held by that person or on that person's behalf are or were held on behalf of any person other than that person and if so the name and address of that other person.

(8) No obligation as to secrecy imposed by statute or otherwise shall preclude the inspector from disclosing to a company that relief has been given or claimed in respect of a particular number or proportion of its shares.

Cross-references

Claims, subs (2): s 503(4).

Finance for trade of subsidiary, subss (4), (5): Sch 10 para 4.

Penalty, subss (3), (4): Sch 29 column 2.

Penalty, subss (1), (2): Sch 29 column 3.

Definitions

company: ss 4(1), 5(1); inspector: ss 2(1), 5(1), 852; person: IA 1937 s 11(*c*); shares: s 5(1); statute: IA 1937 s 3; writing: IA 1937 Sch.

Former enactments

FA 1984 s 24(1)–(8).

Corresponding UK tax provision

Income and Corporation Taxes Act 1988 s 310.

506 Capital gains tax

(1) The sums allowable as deductions from the consideration in the computation for the purposes of capital gains tax of the gain or loss accruing to an individual on the disposal of shares in respect of which any relief has been given and not withdrawn shall be determined without regard to that relief, except that where those sums exceed the consideration they shall be reduced by an amount equal to the lesser of—

(*a*) the amount of that relief, and

(*b*) the excess;

but this subsection shall not apply to a disposal within section 1028(5).

(2) In relation to shares in respect of which relief has been given and not withdrawn, any question—

(*a*) as to which of any such shares issued to a person at different times a disposal relates, or

(*b*) whether a disposal relates to such shares or to other shares,

shall for the purposes of capital gains tax be determined as for the purposes of section 498.

(3) Where an individual holds ordinary shares in a company and the relief has been given in respect of some of the shares but not others, then, if there is a reorganisation (within the meaning of section 584) affecting those shares, section 584(3) shall apply separately to the shares in respect of which the relief has been given and to the other shares (so that the shares of each kind shall be treated as a separate holding of original shares and identified with a separate new holding).

(4) There shall be made all such adjustments of capital gains tax, whether by means of assessment or by means of discharge or repayment of tax, as may be required in consequence of the relief being given or withdrawn.

Cross-references

Relief: s 489(12).

Tax Briefing

TB21 Mar 1996 p 12 — Losses arising on disposal of BES shares.

Definitions

company: ss 4(1), 5(1); person: IA 1937 s 11(*c*); shares: s 5(1).

Former enactments

FA 1984 s 25.

507 Application to subsidiaries

(1) A qualifying company may in the relevant period have one or more subsidiaries if—

(*a*) the conditions in subsection (2) are satisfied in respect of the subsidiary or each subsidiary and, except where provided in subsection (3), continue to be so satisfied until the end of the relevant period, and

(*b*) the subsidiary or each subsidiary is a company—

(i) within section 495(3)(*a*)(i), or

(ii) which exists solely for the purpose of carrying on any trade which consists solely of any one or more of the following trading operations—

(I) the purchase of goods or materials for use by the qualifying company or its subsidiaries,

(II) the sale of goods or materials produced by the qualifying company or its subsidiaries, or

(III) the rendering of services to or on behalf of the qualifying company or its subsidiaries.

(2) The conditions referred to in subsection (1)(*a*) are—

(*a*) that the subsidiary is a 51 per cent subsidiary of the qualifying company,

(*b*) that no other person has control of the subsidiary within the meaning of section 11, and

(*c*) that no arrangements are in existence by virtue of which the conditions in paragraphs (*a*) and (*b*) could cease to be satisfied.

(3) The conditions referred to in subsection (1)(*a*) shall not be regarded as ceasing to be satisfied by reason only of the fact that the subsidiary or the qualifying company is wound up or dissolved without winding up if—

(*a*) it is shown that the winding up or dissolution is for bona fide commercial reasons and not part of a scheme or arrangement the main purpose or one of the main purposes of which is the avoidance of tax, and

(*b*) the net assets, if any, of the subsidiary or, as the case may be, the qualifying company are distributed to its members before the end of the relevant period or, in the case of a winding up, the end (if later) of 3 years from the commencement of the winding up.

(4) Where a qualifying company has one or more subsidiaries in the relevant period, this Part shall apply subject to Schedule 10.

Cross-references

Finance for trade of subsidiary, subs (2)(*c*): Sch 10 para 4.
Meaning of "control", subs (2)(*b*): s 488(1).
Qualifying company: s 495(1), (10).
Relevant period, meaning: s 488(1).
Replacement capital, meaning of "qualifying subsidiary" applied: s 500(1).
Restrictions on relief, meaning of "qualifying subsidiary" applied: s 491(1).

Revenue precedents

Issue: Would a situation where a subsidiary takes title to the goods manufactured by the qualifying company and then sells them on or "lease-on" to customers, be regarded as rendering of services to ensure that the subsidiary would be a qualifying one?
Decision: Yes.

Definitions

company: ss 4(1), 5(1); person: IA 1937 s 11(*c*); trade: s 3(1).

Former enactments

FA 1984 s 26; FA 1985 s 13(*d*); FA 1991 s 15(1)(*f*).

Corresponding UK tax provision

Income and Corporation Taxes Act 1988 s 308.

508 Nominees and designated funds

(1) Shares subscribed for, issued to, held by or disposed of for an individual by a nominee shall be treated for the purposes of this Part as subscribed for, issued to, held by or disposed of by that individual.

(2) (*a*) Relief shall be given, and section 490(1)(*a*) shall not apply, in respect of an amount subscribed as nominee for an individual by a person or persons having the management of an investment fund designated by the Revenue Commissioners for the purposes of this section (in this Part referred to as **"the managers of a designated fund"**) where the amount so subscribed forms part of the fund.

(*b*) Except where provided by paragraph (*a*), relief shall not be given in respect of an amount subscribed as nominee for an individual by a person or persons having the management of an investment fund where the amount so subscribed forms part of the fund.

(3) The Revenue Commissioners may, if they think fit, having regard to the facts of the particular case and after such consultation, if any, as may seem to them to be necessary with such person or body of persons as in their opinion may be of assistance to them, and subject to such conditions, if any, as they think proper to attach to the designation, designate an investment fund for the purposes of this Part.

(4) (*a*) The Revenue Commissioners may, by notice in writing given to the managers of a designated investment fund, withdraw the designation given for the purposes of this section to the fund in accordance with subsection (3) and, on the giving of the notice, the fund shall cease to be a designated fund as respects any subscriptions made after the date of the notice referred to in paragraph (*b*).

(*b*) Where the Revenue Commissioners withdraw the designation of any fund for the purposes of this section, notice of the withdrawal shall be published as soon as may be in Iris Oifigiúil.

(5) Where an individual claims relief in respect of eligible shares in a company which have been issued to the managers of a designated fund as nominee for the individual, section 503(2) shall apply as if it required—

(*a*) the certificate referred to in that section to be issued by the company to the managers, and

(*b*) the claim for relief to be accompanied by a certificate issued by the managers, in such form as the Revenue Commissioners may authorise, furnishing such information as the Revenue Commissioners may require and certifying that the managers hold certificates issued to them by the companies concerned, for the purposes of section 503(2) in respect of the holdings of eligible shares shown on the managers' certificate.

(6) The managers of a designated fund may be required by a notice given to them by an inspector or other officer of the Revenue Commissioners to deliver to the officer within the time limited by the notice a return of the holdings of eligible shares shown on certificates issued by them in accordance with subsection (5) in the year of assessment to which the return relates.

(7) Section 503(6) shall not apply in relation to any certificate issued by the managers of a designated fund for the purposes of subsection (5).

(8) Without prejudice to the generality of subsection (3), the Revenue Commissioners shall designate a fund for the purposes of this Part only if they are satisfied that—

- (*a*) the fund is established under irrevocable trusts for the sole purpose of enabling individuals who qualify for the relief (in this subsection referred to as **"qualifying individuals"**) to invest in eligible shares of a qualifying company, and
- (*b*) under the terms of the trusts it is provided that—
  - (i) the entire fund is to be invested without undue delay in eligible shares,
  - (ii) the fund is to subscribe only for shares which, subject to the circumstances of the qualifying individuals participating in the fund (in this subsection referred to as "participants"), qualify those participants for relief,
  - (iii) pending investment in eligible shares, any moneys subscribed for the purchase of shares are to be placed on deposit in a separate account with a bank licensed to transact business in the State,
  - (iv) any amounts received by means of dividends or interest are, subject to a commission in respect of management expenses at a rate not exceeding a rate which shall be specified in the deed of trust under which the fund has been established, to be paid without undue delay to the participants,
  - (v) any charges to be made by means of management or other expenses in connection with the establishment, the running, the winding down or the termination of the fund shall be at a rate not exceeding a rate which shall be specified in the deed of trust under which the fund is established,
  - (vi) audited accounts of the fund are submitted annually to the Revenue Commissioners as soon as may be after the end of each period for which accounts of the fund are made up,
  - (vii) the managers, the trustees of the fund and any of their associates are not for the time being connected either directly or indirectly with any company whose shares comprise part of the fund,
  - (viii) any discounts on eligible shares received by the trustees or managers of the fund are accepted solely for the benefit of the participants,
  - (ix) the fund is a closed fund and the closing date for participation precedes the making of the first investment,
  - (x) if a limit is placed on the size of the fund or a minimum amount for investment is stipulated, any subscriptions not accepted are to be returned without undue delay, and
  - (xi) no participant is allowed to have any shares in any company in which the fund has invested transferred into his or her name until 5 years have elapsed from the date of the issue of the shares to the fund.

Cross-references

Limits on relief: s 490(1).
Relief: s 489(4)(*a*), (4A)(*a*), (4B)(*a*).
Restriction of relief: s 491(4), (4A)(*a*)(i).
Special investment schemes: s 737(9)(*c*).
Transitional arrangements in relation to FA1998 s 34: FA 1998 s 35(1)(specified designated fund).
Transitional arrangements in relation to FA 2004 s 18(1)(*a*)(ii): FA 2004 s 19(1)(specified designated fund).

Definitions

body of persons: s 2(1); company: ss 4(1), 5(1); inspector: ss 2(1), 5(1), 852; interest: s 4(1); person: IA 1937 s 11(*c*); shares: s 5(1); writing: IA 1937 Sch; year of assessment: ss 2(1), 5(1).

Former enactments

FA 1984 s 27 and FA 1985 s 13(*e*).

Corresponding UK tax provision

Income and Corporation Taxes Act 1988 s 311.

PART 17
PROFIT SHARING SCHEMES AND EMPLOYEE SHARE OWNERSHIP TRUSTS

Cross-references

Electricity (Supply) (Amendment) Act 2001 s 1 ("approved scheme").
Restriction of deductions for employee benefit contributions, restriction does not apply to any deduction that is allowable under Part 17: s 81A(7)(*c*).

CHAPTER 1
Profit Sharing Schemes

Cross-references

Approval of profit sharing schemes: Sch 11 paras 4(1A)(*a*)(i) and 5(1)(*b*).
Provisions as to the trust instrument: Sch 11 para 18(*a*).
Taxation of acquisition by a company of its own shares, conditions as to residence and period of ownership: s 177(6).

Revenue information

A Guide to Profit Sharing Schemes, Oct 1998.

Tax Briefing

TB20 No 4 of 1995 par1.1 — Approved Profit Sharing Schemes — Guidelines on Certain Schemes.
TB38 Dec 1999 p 17 — The value of any rights arising to an employee under an approved profit sharing scheme may be regarded as emoluments for the purposes of Schedule 3 for the purposes of calculating standard capital superannuation benefit.
TB40 June 2000 p 29 — Profit Sharing Schemes (Finance Act 2000 amendments).
TB46 Dec 2001 s 34 — Approved Profit Sharing Scheme — Salary foregone/contributory element for short tax "year" 2001.
TB47 April 2002 — Approved Profit Sharing Schemes (APSS's) and Employee Share Ownership Trusts (ESOT's) — Finance Act 2002 changes.
TB54 Dec 2003 p 13 — Approved Profit Sharing Schemes — Interaction with a Direct Demerger.
TB56 July 2004 pp 20–22 — Approved Profit Sharing Schemes.

509 Interpretation (Chapter 1)

(1) In this Chapter and in Schedule 11—

"the appropriate percentage", in relation to any shares, shall be construed in accordance with section 511(3);

"approved scheme" shall be construed in accordance with section 510(1);

"the company concerned" has the meaning assigned to it by paragraph 3(1) of Schedule 11;

"group scheme" and, in relation to such a scheme, **"participating company"** have the meanings respectively assigned to them by paragraph 3(2) of Schedule 11;

"initial market value", in relation to any shares, shall be construed in accordance with section 510(2);

"locked-in value", in relation to any shares, shall be construed in accordance with section 512(1);

"market value", in relation to any shares, shall be construed in accordance with section 548;

"participant" shall be construed in accordance with section 510(1)(*a*);

"the period of retention" has the meaning assigned to it by section 511(1)(*a*);

"the release date" has the meaning assigned to it by section 511(2);

[**"shares"** includes stock and specified securities;

"specified securities" means securities (within the meaning of Schedule 12), other than ordinary shares, which—

(*a*) were transferred to the trustees of an approved scheme by the trustees of an employee share ownership trust to which section 519 applies, and

(*b*) were—

(i) securities issued to the trustees of the employee share ownership trust referred to in paragraph (*a*) in an exchange to which section 586 applies,

(ii) securities (in this subparagraph referred to as "similar securities") similar to the securities referred to in subparagraph (i) and which were acquired by those trustees using dividends received in respect of the securities so referred to or in respect of similar securities so acquired,

(iii) securities issued to those trustees as a result of a reorganisation or reduction of share capital (in accordance with section 584) which occurred subsequent to the exchange referred to in subparagraph (i) and which securities represent the securities issued in that exchange and the similar securities (if any) referred to in subparagraph (ii), or

(iv) securities (in this subparagraph referred to as 'similar securities') similar to the securities first-mentioned in subparagraph (iii) and which were acquired by those trustees using dividends received in respect of the securities so mentioned in subparagraph (iii) or in respect of similar securities so acquired,

but subject to the condition that, where the company which issued the securities in the exchange referred to in paragraph (*b*) is a company limited by shares (within the meaning of section 5 of the Companies Act, 1963), the trustees of the employee share ownership trust have, as a result of the exchange, acquired such percentage of the ordinary share capital of the company which issued the securities that is not less than the percentage of the ordinary share capital of the company which the trustees held immediately prior to the exchange;][1]

"the trust instrument", in relation to an approved scheme, means the instrument referred to in paragraph 3(3)(*c*) of Schedule 11;

"the trustees", in relation to an approved scheme or a participant's shares, means the body of persons for the establishment of which the scheme shall provide as mentioned in paragraph 3(3) of Schedule 11.

(2) Any provision of this Chapter with respect to—

(*a*) the order in which any of a participant's shares are to be treated as disposed of for the purposes of this Chapter, or

(*b*) the shares in relation to which an event is to be treated as occurring for any such purpose,

shall apply notwithstanding any direction given to the trustees with respect to shares of a particular description or to shares appropriated to the participant at a particular time.

(3) For the purposes of capital gains tax—

(*a*) no deduction shall be made from the consideration for the disposal of any shares by reason only that an amount determined under this Chapter is chargeable to income tax,

(*b*) any charge to income tax by virtue of section 513 shall be disregarded in determining whether a distribution is a capital distribution within the meaning of section 583, and

(*c*) nothing in any provision referred to in subsection (2) shall affect the rules applicable to the computation of a gain accruing on a part disposal of a holding of shares or other securities which were acquired at different times.

[(4) The Revenue Commissioners may nominate any of their officers to perform any acts and discharge any functions authorised by this Chapter or by Schedule 11 to be performed or discharged by them.][2]

Amendments

1 Definition of "shares" substituted and definition of "specified securities" inserted by FA 2002 s 13(1)(*a*)(i) with effect from 16 April 2001.

2 Subs (4) inserted by FA 2002 s 13(1)(*a*)(ii) with effect from 16 April 2001.

Cross-references

Employee share ownership trusts, subparas (ii) and (iv) of para (*b*) of definition of "specified securities": Sch 12 para 13(3)(*a*).

Profit sharing schemes, conditions as to shares, para (*b*) of definition of "specified securities": Sch 11 para 8A(*b*).

Definitions

body of persons: s 2(1); company: ss 4(1), 5(1); distribution: ss 4(1), 436, 437; person: IA 1937 s 11(*c*); part disposal: ss 5(1), 534.

Former enactments

FA 1982 s 50.

Corresponding UK tax provision

Income and Corporation Taxes Act 1988 s 187.

510 Approved profit sharing schemes: appropriated shares

(1) In this Chapter, references to an approved scheme are references to a scheme approved of as is mentioned in subsection (3) and, in relation to such a scheme—

(*a*) any reference to a participant is a reference to an individual to whom the trustees of the scheme have appropriated shares, and

(*b*) subject to section 514, any reference to a participant's shares is a reference to the shares which have been appropriated to the participant by the trustees of an approved scheme.

(2) Any reference in this Chapter to the initial market value of any of a participant's shares is a reference to the market value of those shares determined—

(*a*) except where paragraph (*b*) applies, on the date on which the shares were appropriated to the participant, and

(*b*) if the Revenue Commissioners and the trustees of the scheme agree in writing, on or by reference to such earlier date or dates as may be provided for in the agreement.

(3) This section shall apply where the trustees of a profit sharing scheme approved of in accordance with Part 2 of Schedule 11 appropriate shares—

(*a*) which have previously been acquired by the trustees, and

(*b*) as to which the conditions in Part 3 of that Schedule are fulfilled,

to an individual who participates in the scheme.

(4) Notwithstanding anything in the Income Tax Acts, a charge to tax shall not be made on any individual in respect of the receipt of a right to receive the beneficial interest in shares passing or to be passed to that individual by virtue of such an appropriation of shares as is mentioned in subsection (3).

(5) Notwithstanding anything in the approved scheme concerned or in the trust instrument or in section 511, for the purposes of capital gains tax a participant shall be treated as absolutely entitled to his or her shares as against the trustees.

[(5A)(*a*) This subsection shall apply where—

(i) the trustees of an approved profit sharing scheme make an appropriation of shares, to which section 510(3) applies, to a participant,

(ii) the shares concerned were transferred to the trustees of the approved scheme concerned by the trustees of an employee share ownership trust to which section 519 applies, and

(iii) the shares were transferred at a date later than that on which the shares could have first been transferred in accordance with the terms of the employee share ownership trust deed or any other document but, for whatever reason, were not transferred on that earlier date.

(*b*) Where this subsection applies, the appropriation to the participant concerned shall, for the purposes of capital gains tax, be deemed to have taken place on the day following the day on which those shares could have first been transferred by the trustees of the employee share ownership trust concerned, in accordance with the terms of the trust deed under which that trust was established or any other document.][1]

(6) Where the trustees of an approved scheme acquire any shares as to which the conditions in Part 3 of Schedule 11 are fulfilled and, within the period of 18 months beginning with the date of their acquisition, those shares are appropriated in accordance with the scheme—

(*a*) section 805 shall not apply to income consisting of dividends on those shares received by the trustees, and

(*b*) any gain accruing to the trustees on the appropriation of those shares shall not be a chargeable gain,

and, for the purpose of determining whether any shares are appropriated within that period of 18 months, shares which were acquired at an earlier time shall be taken to be appropriated before shares of the same class which were acquired at a later time.

(7) The Revenue Commissioners may by notice in writing require any person to furnish to them, within such time as they may direct (but not being less than 30 days), such information as they think necessary for the purposes of their functions under this Chapter, including in particular information to enable them—

(*a*) to determine whether to approve of a scheme or withdraw an approval already given, and

(*b*) to determine the liability to tax, including capital gains tax, of any participant in an approved scheme.

Amendments

1 Subs (5A) inserted by FA 1999 s 69(1)(*a*)(i) in respect of an appropriation of shares made by the trustees of an approved scheme on or after 25 March 1999.

Cross-references

"approved scheme" (subs (1)), "initial market value" (subs (2)), "participant" (subs (1)(*a*)), are construed in accordance with this section: s 509(1).
Individuals ineligible to participate, subs (1): Sch 11 para 13A(3).
Penalty, subs (7): Sch 29 column 2.
Shares acquired from an employee share ownership trust, subs (3): s 511A(1)(*a*).

Revenue precedents

Issue: Where shares are purchased by Trustees over a period of time can the average purchase price be used as the initial market value of the shares at the date of appropriation?
Decision: Yes, provided the purchase period does not exceed 30 days.

Definitions

chargeable gain: ss 4(1), 5(1), 534; Income Tax Acts: s 1(2); month: IA 1937 Sch; person: IA 1937 s 11(*c*).

Former enactments

FA 1982 s 51(1)–(7).

Corresponding UK tax provision

Income and Corporation Taxes Act 1988 s 186.

511 The period of retention, release date and appropriate percentage

(1) (*a*) In this Chapter, **"the period of retention"**, in relation to any of a participant's shares, means the period beginning on the date on which those shares are appropriated to the participant and ending on the second anniversary of that date or, if it is earlier—

(i) the date on which the participant ceases to be an employee or director of a relevant company by reason of injury or disability or on account of his or her being dismissed by reason of redundancy (within the meaning of the Redundancy Payments Acts, 1967 to 1991),

(ii) the date on which the participant reaches pensionable age (within the meaning of section 2 of the Social Welfare (Consolidation) Act, 1993), or

(iii) the date of the participant's death.

(*b*) In paragraph (*a*), **"relevant company"** means the company concerned or, if the scheme in question is a group scheme, a participating company and, in the application of paragraph (*a*) to a participant in a group scheme, the participant shall not be treated as ceasing to be an employee or director of a relevant company until such time as he or she is no longer an employee or director of any of the participating companies.

(2) In this Chapter, **"the release date"**, in relation to any of a participant's shares, means—

(*a*) as on and from the 10th day of May, 1997, the third anniversary of the date on which the shares were appropriated to the participant, and

(*b*) before the 10th day of May, 1997, the fifth anniversary of the date on which the shares were appropriated to the participant.

(3) Subject to section 515(4), for the purposes of the provisions of this Chapter charging an individual to income tax under Schedule E by reason of the occurrence of an event relating to any of the individual's shares, any reference to the appropriate percentage in relation to those shares shall be determined according to the time of that event, as follows—

(*a*) as respects such an occurrence as on and from the 10th day of May, 1997—

(i) if the event occurs before the third anniversary of the date on which the shares were appropriated to the participant and subparagraph (ii) does not apply, the appropriate percentage shall be 100 per cent, and

(ii) if, in a case where at the time of the event the participant—

(I) has ceased to be an employee or director of a relevant company as mentioned in subsection (1)(*a*)(i), or

(II) has reached pensionable age (within the meaning of section 2 of the Social Welfare (Consolidation) Act, 1993),

the event occurs before the third anniversary of the date on which the shares were appropriated to the participant, the appropriate percentage shall be 50 per cent, and

(*b*) as respects such an occurrence before the 10th day of May, 1997—

(i) if the event occurs before the fourth anniversary of the date on which the shares were appropriated to the participant and subparagraph (iii) does not apply, the appropriate percentage shall be 100 per cent,

(ii) if the event occurs on or after the fourth anniversary and before the fifth anniversary of the date on which the shares were appropriated to the participant and subparagraph (iii) does not apply, the appropriate percentage shall be 75 per cent, and

(iii) if, in a case where at the time of the event the participant—

(I) has ceased to be an employee or director of a relevant company as mentioned in subsection (1)(*a*)(i), or

(II) has reached pensionable age (within the meaning of section 2 of the Social Welfare (Consolidation) Act, 1993),

the event occurs before the fifth anniversary of the date on which the shares were appropriated to the participant, the appropriate percentage shall be 50 per cent.

(4) No scheme shall be approved of as is mentioned in section 510(3) unless the Revenue Commissioners are satisfied that, whether under the terms of the scheme or otherwise, every participant in the scheme is bound in contract with the company concerned—

(*a*) to permit his or her shares to remain in the hands of the trustees throughout the period of retention,

(*b*) not to assign, charge or otherwise dispose of his or her beneficial interest in his or her shares during that period,

(*c*) if he or she directs the trustees to transfer the ownership of his or her shares to him or her at any time before the release date, to pay to the trustees before the transfer takes place a sum equal to income tax at the standard rate on the appropriate percentage of the locked-in value of the shares at the time of the direction, and

(*d*) not to direct the trustees to dispose of his or her shares at any time before the release date in any other way except by sale for the best consideration in money that can reasonably be obtained at the time of the sale.

(5) No obligation placed on the participant by virtue of subsection (4)(*c*) shall be construed as binding his or her personal representatives to pay any sum to the trustees.

(6) Any obligation imposed on a participant by virtue of subsection (4) shall not prevent the participant from—

(*a*) directing the trustees to accept an offer for any of his or her shares (in this paragraph referred to as **"the original shares"**) if the acceptance or agreement will result in a new holding (within the meaning of section 584) being equated with the original shares for the purposes of capital gains tax,

(*b*) directing the trustees to agree to a transaction affecting his or her shares or such of those shares as are of a particular class if the transaction would be entered into pursuant to a compromise, arrangement or scheme applicable to or affecting—

(i) all the ordinary share capital of the company in question or, as the case may be, all the shares of the class in question, or

(ii) all the shares, or shares of the class in question, held by a class of shareholders identified otherwise than by reference to their employment or their participation in an approved scheme,

(*c*) directing the trustees to accept an offer of cash, with or without other assets, for his or her shares if the offer forms part of a general offer made to holders of shares of the same class as his or her shares or of shares in the same company and made in the first instance on a condition such that if it is satisfied the person making the offer will have control (within the meaning of section 11) of that company, or

(*d*) agreeing, after the expiry of the period of retention, to sell the beneficial interest in his or her shares to the trustees for the same consideration as in accordance with subsection (4)(*d*) would be required to be obtained for the shares themselves.

(7) If in breach of his or her obligation under subsection (4)(*b*) a participant assigns, charges or otherwise disposes of the beneficial interest in any of his or her shares, the participant shall as respects those shares be treated for the purposes of this Chapter as if, at the time they were appropriated to him or her, he or she was ineligible to participate in the scheme, and section 515 shall apply accordingly.

Cross-references

Appropriated shares: s 510(5).
Approval of profit sharing schemes: Sch 11 para 3(1); subs (4)(*a*), (*c*), (*d*): Sch 11 para 5(1)(*a*).
Assessment of trustees in respect of sums received, subs (4)(*c*): s 516.
Disposal of scheme shares: s 512(8)(*a*).
In this Part and Sch 11, "the appropriate percentage" is construed in accordance with subs (3): s 509(1).
Profit sharing schemes, provisions as to the trust instrument, subs (4)(*c*)–(*d*): Sch 11 para 16(2)(*b*); subs (6)(*a*)-(*c*): Sch 11 para 16(1).
Shares acquired from an employee share ownership trust: s 511A(2); subs (11)(*a*): s 511A(2)(*a*)(ii).

Definitions

company: ss 4(1), 5(1); ordinary share capital: s 2(1); person: IA 1937 s 11(*c*); personal representatives: ss 5(1), 799; standard rate: ss 3(1), 15.

Former enactments

FA 1982 s 52; FA 1986 s 11; FA 1997 s 50(*a*).

Corresponding UK tax provision

Income and Corporation Taxes Act 1988 s 187.

511A Shares acquired from an employee share ownership trust

[(1) This section applies where, on or after the passing of the Finance Act, 1998—

(*a*) the trustees of an approved scheme make an appropriation of shares to which section 510(3) applies to a participant,

(*b*) the shares concerned had been transferred to the trustees of the approved scheme by the trustees of an employee share ownership trust to which section 519 applies, and

(*c*) the participant concerned was a beneficiary (within the meaning of paragraph 11 or 11A, as the case may be, of Schedule 12) under the employee share ownership trust concerned at all times (other than any period which forms part of the 30 day period referred to in paragraph 12A(b) of Schedule 11) during the period (in this section referred to as the "holding period")—

(i) beginning on—

(I) the day the shares concerned were acquired by that employee share ownership trust, or

(II) if later, the day that participant last became such a beneficiary, and

(ii) ending on the day those shares were appropriated to that participant.

(2) Where this section applies, then, notwithstanding section 511—

(*a*) the period of retention, in relation to the participant and the shares concerned, ends—

(i) in the case where the holding period is 2 years or more, on the day following the end of the holding period, and

(ii) in any other case, on the day following the end of a period which, when added to the holding period, forms a period of 2 years, or, if it is earlier, on the date referred to in subparagraph (i), (ii) or (iii), as the case may be, of section 511(1)(*a*),

and

(*b*) the release date, in relation to the participant and the shares concerned, means—

(i) in the case where the holding period is 3 years or more, the day following the end of the holding period, and

(ii) in any other case, the day following the end of a period which, when added to the holding period, forms a period of 3 years.][1]

Amendments

1 Section 511A substituted by FA 2002 s 13(1)(*b*) with effect from 16 April 2001.

Corresponding UK tax provision

Taxation of Chargeable Gains Act 1992 ss 227 and 228.

512 Disposals of scheme shares

(1) Subject to sections 514 and 515(6), any reference in this Chapter to the locked-in value of any of a participant's shares at any time shall be construed as follows:

(*a*) if before that time the participant has become chargeable to income tax by virtue of section 513 on a percentage of the amount or value of any capital receipt (within the meaning of that section) which is referable to those shares, the locked-in value of the shares shall be the amount by which their initial market value exceeds the amount or value of that capital receipt or, if there has been more than one such receipt, the aggregate of those receipts, and

(*b*) in any other case, the locked-in value of the shares shall be their initial market value.

(2) Where the trustees dispose of any of a participant's shares at any time before the release date or, if it is earlier, the date of the participant's death, the participant shall, subject to subsections (3) and (4), be chargeable to income tax under Schedule E for the year of assessment in which the disposal takes place on the appropriate percentage of the locked-in value of the shares at the time of the disposal.

(3) Subject to subsection (4), if on a disposal of shares within subsection (2) the proceeds of the disposal are less than the locked-in value of the shares at the time of the disposal, subsection (2) shall apply as if that locked-in value were reduced to an amount equal to the proceeds of the disposal.

(4) Where at any time before the disposal of any of a participant's shares a payment was made to the trustees to enable them to exercise rights arising under a rights issue,

subsections (2) and (3) shall, subject to subsection (5)(*b*), apply as if the proceeds of the disposal were reduced by an amount equal to that proportion of that payment or, if there was more than one such payment, of the aggregate of those payments which, immediately before the disposal, the market value of the shares disposed of bore to the market value of all the participant's shares held by the trustees at that time.

(5) (*a*) In this subsection, **"shares"**, in relation to shares allotted or to be allotted on a rights issue, includes securities and rights of any description.

(*b*) For the purposes of subsection (4)—

(i) no account shall be taken of any payment to the trustees if or to the extent that it consists of the proceeds of a disposal of rights arising under a rights issue, and

(ii) in relation to a particular disposal, the amount of the payment or, as the case may be, of the aggregate of the payments referred to in that subsection shall be taken to be reduced by an amount equal to the total of the reduction (if any) previously made under that subsection in relation to earlier disposals,

and any reference in subsection (4) or subparagraph (i) to the rights arising under a rights issue is a reference to rights conferred in respect of a participant's shares, being rights to be allotted, on payment, other shares in the same company.

(6) Where the disposal referred to in subsection (2) is made from a holding of shares appropriated to the participant at different times, then, in determining for the purposes of this Chapter—

(*a*) the initial market value and the locked-in value of each of those shares, and

(*b*) the percentage which is the appropriate percentage in relation to each of those shares,

the disposal shall be treated as being of shares appropriated earlier before those appropriated later.

(7) Where at any time the participant's beneficial interest in any of his or her shares is disposed of, the shares in question shall be treated for the purposes of this Chapter as having been disposed of at that time by the trustees for (subject to subsection (8)) the like consideration as was obtained for the disposal of the beneficial interest, and for the purpose of this subsection there shall be no disposal of the participant's beneficial interest if and at the time when that interest becomes vested in any person on the insolvency of the participant or otherwise by operation of the law of the State.

(8) Where—

(*a*) a disposal of shares within subsection (2) is a transfer to which section 511(4)(*c*) applies,

(*b*) the Revenue Commissioners are of the opinion that any other disposal within that subsection is not at arm's length and accordingly direct that this subsection shall apply, or

(*c*) a disposal of shares within that subsection is one which is treated as taking place by virtue of subsection (7) and takes place within the period of retention, the proceeds of the disposal for the purposes of this Chapter shall be taken to be equal to the market value of the shares at the time of the disposal.

Cross-references

"locked-in value" for purposes of this Part and Sch 11 shall be construed in accordance with subs (1): s 510(1).
BES relief, disposal of shares, subs (2): s 498(4).
Capital receipts in respect of scheme shares: s 513(2)(*b*); subs (5)(*b*): s 513(3)(*a*).
Company reconstructions etc, subs (1)(*a*): s 514(5)(*b*).
Excess or unauthorised shares, subs (6): s 515(4)(*b*).

Definitions

company: ss 4(1), 5(1); person: IA 1937 s 11(*c*); year of assessment: ss 2(1), 5(1).

Former enactments

FA 1982 s 53.

Corresponding UK tax provision

Income and Corporation Taxes Act 1988 s 186.

---

513 Capital receipts in respect of scheme shares

(1) Subject to this section, where, in respect of or by reference to any of a participant's shares, the trustees become or the participant becomes entitled, before the release date, to receive any money or money's worth (in this section referred to as a **"capital receipt"**), the participant shall be chargeable to income tax under Schedule E for the year of assessment in which the entitlement arises on the appropriate percentage (determined as at the time when the trustees become or the participant becomes so entitled) of the amount or value of the receipt.

(2) Money or money's worth shall not be a capital receipt for the purposes of this section if or, as the case may be, to the extent that—

(*a*) it constitutes income in the hands of the recipient for the purposes of income tax,

(*b*) it consists of the proceeds of a disposal within section 512, or

(*c*) it consists of new shares within the meaning of section 514.

(3) Where, pursuant to a direction given by or on behalf of the participant or any person in whom the beneficial interest in the participant's shares is for the time being vested, the trustees—

(*a*) dispose of some of the rights arising under a rights issue within the meaning of section 512(5)(*b*), and

(*b*) use the proceeds of that disposal to exercise other such rights,

the money or money's worth which constitutes the proceeds of that disposal shall not be a capital receipt for the purposes of this section.

(4) Where apart from this subsection the amount or value of a capital receipt would exceed the sum which, immediately before the entitlement to the receipt arose, was the locked-in value of the shares to which the receipt is referable, subsection (1) shall apply as if the amount or value of the receipt were equal to that locked-in value.

(5) Subsection (1) shall not apply in relation to a receipt if the entitlement to it arises after the death of the participant to whose shares it is referable.

(6) Subsection (1) shall not apply in relation to any receipt the amount or value of which (after any reduction under subsection (4)) does not exceed [€13][1].

Amendments

[1] Substituted by FA 2001 s 240(1) and (2)(*a*) and Sch 5 Pt 1 for 2002 and later tax years; previously "£10".

Cross-references

Capital distribution: s 509(3)(*b*).

Company reconstructions etc, meaning of "capital receipt" applied: s 514(6).

Disposal of scheme shares: s 512(1)(*a*).

Profit sharing schemes, provisions as to the trust instrument, subs (3): Sch 11 para 17(*a*).

Definitions

person: IA 1937 s 11(*c*); year of assessment: ss 2(1), 5(1).

Former enactments

FA 1982 s 54.

Corresponding UK tax provision

Income and Corporation Taxes Act 1988 Sch 10(4).

514 Company reconstructions, amalgamations, etc

(1) In this section—

"new shares" means shares comprised in the new holding which were issued in respect of, or otherwise represent, shares comprised in the original holding;

"the corresponding shares", in relation to any new shares, means those shares in respect of which the new shares were issued or which the new shares otherwise represent.

(2) This section shall apply where there occurs in relation to any of a participant's shares (in this section referred to as **"the original holding"**) a transaction (in this section referred to as a **"company reconstruction"**) which results in a new holding (within the meaning of section 584) being equated with the original holding for the purposes of capital gains tax.

(3) (*a*) Where shares are issued as part of a company reconstruction in circumstances such that section 131(2) applies, those shares shall be treated for the purposes of this section as not forming part of the new holding.

(*b*) Nothing in this Chapter shall affect the application of section 130(2)(*c*) or 132(2).

(4) Subject to this section, references in this Chapter to a participant's shares shall be construed, after the time of the company reconstruction, as being or, as the case may be, as including, references to any new shares, and for the purposes of this Chapter—

(*a*) a company reconstruction shall be treated as not involving a disposal of shares comprised in the original holding,

(*b*) the date on which any new shares are to be treated as having been appropriated to the participant shall be the date on which the corresponding shares were appropriated, and

(*c*) the conditions in Part 3 of Schedule 11 shall be treated as fulfilled with respect to any new shares if those conditions were (or were treated as) fulfilled with respect to the corresponding shares.

(5) In relation to shares comprised in the new holding, section 512(1) shall apply as if the references in that section to the initial market value of the shares were references to their locked-in value immediately after the company reconstruction, which shall be determined by—

(*a*) ascertaining the aggregate amount of locked-in value immediately before the reconstruction of those shares comprised in the original holding which had at that time the same locked-in value, and

(*b*) distributing that amount proportionately among—

(i) such of those shares as remain in the new holding, and

(ii) any new shares in relation to which those shares are the corresponding shares,

according to their market value immediately after the date of the reconstruction, and section 512(1)(*a*) shall apply only to capital receipts after the date of the reconstruction.

(6) For the purposes of this Chapter, where as part of a company reconstruction the trustees become entitled to a capital receipt (within the meaning of section 513), their entitlement to the capital receipt shall be taken to arise before the new holding comes into being and, for the purposes of subsection (5), before the date on which the locked-in value of any shares comprised in the original holding falls to be ascertained.

(7) In relation to a new holding, any reference in this section to shares includes securities and rights of any description which form part of the new holding for the purposes of section 584.

Cross-references

Appropriated shares: s 510(1)(*b*).
Capital receipts in respect of scheme shares: s 513(2)(*c*).
Disposal of scheme shares: s 512(1).
Excess or unauthorised shares: s 515(7).
Profit sharing schemes, provisions as to the trust instrument: Sch 11 para 17(*a*).

Revenue precedents

Issue: Will relief under TCA 1997 s 514 be allowed in a company reconstruction where only cash is on offer to employees for their shares?

Decision: The relief will be applied where: (1) under the terms of the reconstruction shares can be exchanged for cash only, (2) the scheme will be continued by the new company, (3) all the cash is retained by the Trustees and not passed to the participants, and, (4) the total sums are reinvested by the Trustees in shares in the new company, without delay.

Definitions

company: ss 4(1), 5(1).

Former enactments

FA 1982 s 55.

Corresponding UK tax provision

Income and Corporation Taxes Act 1988 Sch 10(5) and 10(5A).

515 Excess or unauthorised shares

[(1) Subject to subsection (2B), where the total of the initial market values of all the shares appropriated to an individual in any one year of assessment (whether under a single approved scheme or under 2 or more such schemes) exceeds—

(*a*) [€12,700][1], or

(*b*) [€38,100][2] where the conditions in subsection (2A) are satisfied,

subsections (4) to (7) shall apply to any excess shares, that is, any share which caused the applicable limit to be exceeded and any share appropriated after the applicable limit was exceeded.

(2) For the purposes of subsection (1), where a number of shares is appropriated to an individual at the same time under 2 or more approved schemes, the same proportion of the shares appropriated at that time under each scheme shall be regarded as being appropriated before the limit of [€12,700][1] or the limit of [€38,100][2], as the case may be, is exceeded.

(2A) The conditions referred to in paragraph (*b*) of subsection (1) are—

(*a*) the shares appropriated to such individual have been transferred to the trustees of the approved scheme concerned by the trustees of an employee share ownership trust to which section 519 applies,

(*b*) at each given time in the [period of 5 years, or such lesser period as the Minister for Finance may by order prescribe,][3] commencing with the date of the establishment of the employee share ownership trust 50 per cent, or such lesser percentage as the Minister for Finance may by order prescribe, of the securities retained by the trustees at the time were pledged by them as security for borrowings,

(*c*) at the time of transfer referred to in paragraph (*a*) a period of at least 10 years commencing on the date the employee share ownership trust was established and ending at the time when all the shares pledged as security for borrowings by the trustees of the employee share ownership trust became unpledged (hereafter in this section referred to as the "encumbered period") has elapsed, and

(*d*) no shares which were pledged, at any time since the trust was established, as security for borrowings by the trustees of the employee share ownership trust were previously transferred to the trustees of the approved scheme because they remained so pledged during the encumbered period.

(2B) The limit of [€38,100][2] in paragraph (*b*) of subsection (1) may only be applied in the first year of assessment during which the encumbered period has elapsed and then only in respect of shares appropriated after that period has so elapsed.][4]

(3) Where the trustees of an approved scheme appropriate shares to an individual at a time when the individual is ineligible to participate in the scheme by virtue of Part 4 of Schedule 11, subsections (4) to (7) shall apply in relation to those shares, and in those subsections those shares are referred to as **"unauthorised shares"**.

(4) For the purposes of any provision of this Chapter charging an individual to income tax under Schedule E by reason of the occurrence of an event relating to any of the individual's shares—

(*a*) the appropriate percentage in relation to excess shares or unauthorised shares shall in every case be 100 per cent, and (*b*) without prejudice to section 512(6), the event shall be treated as relating to shares which are not excess shares or unauthorised shares before shares which are.

(5) Excess shares or unauthorised shares which have not been disposed of before the release date, or if it is earlier, the date of the death of the participant whose shares they are, shall be treated for the purposes of this Chapter as having been disposed of by the trustees immediately before the release date or, as the case may require, the date of the participant's death, for a consideration equal to their market value at that time.

(6) The locked-in value at any time of any excess shares or unauthorised shares shall be their market value at that time.

(7) Where there has been a company reconstruction to which section 514 applies, a new share (within the meaning of that section) shall be treated as an excess share or unauthorised share if the corresponding share (within the meaning of that section) or, if there was more than one corresponding share, each of them was an excess share or an unauthorised share.

[(8) Where an order is proposed to be made under subsection (2A)(*b*), a draft of the order shall be laid before Dáil Éireann, and the order shall not be made until a resolution approving of the draft has been passed by Dáil Éireann.][5]

Amendments

1 Substituted by FA 2001 s 240(1) and (2)(*a*) and Sch 5 Pt 1 for 2002 and later tax years; previously "£10,000" (short tax "year" 2001:£7,400 (FA 2001 s 77(2) and Sch 2 paras 27 and 61(*a*))).

2 Substituted by FA 2001 s 240(1) and (2)(*a*) and Sch 5 Pt 1 for 2002 and later tax years; previously "£30,000".

3 Substituted by FA 2000 s 24(*a*) with effect from 6 April 2000; previously "5 years".

4 Subs (1)–(2) substituted by FA 1999 s 69(1)(*a*)(iii) with effect from 6 April 1999.

5 Subs (8) inserted by FA 2000 s 24(*b*) with effect from 6 April 2000.

Cross-references

Approval of schemes: Sch 11 para 3(4).

Disposal of scheme shares, subs (6): s 512(1).

Individuals ineligible to participate: Sch 11 paras 13A(2) and 13B(2).

Period of retention, release date, appropriate percentage, subs (4): s 511(3), (7).

Taxation of acquisition by a company of its own shares, conditions as to residence and period of ownership, subs (4) to (7): s 177(6).

Definitions

company: ss 4(1), 5(1); year of assessment: ss 2(1), 5(1).

Former enactments

FA 1982 s 56; FA 1995 s 16.

Corresponding UK tax provision

Income and Corporation Taxes Act 1988 Sch 10(6).

516 Assessment of trustees in respect of sums received

Where in connection with a direction to transfer the ownership of a participant's shares to which paragraph (*c*) of section 511(4) applies the trustees receive such a sum as is referred to in that paragraph—

(*a*) the trustees shall be chargeable to income tax under Case IV of Schedule D on an amount equal to the appropriate percentage of the locked-in value of the shares at the time of the direction, and

(*b*) the amount on which the participant is to be charged to income tax as a result of the transfer shall be deemed to be an amount from which income tax has been deducted at the standard rate pursuant to section 238.

Definitions

standard rate: ss 3(1), 15.

Former enactments

FA 1982 s 57.

Corresponding UK tax provision

Income and Corporation Taxes Act 1988 Sch 10(7).

517 Payments to trustees of approved profit sharing scheme

(1) Subject to subsections (3) and (4), as respects any accounting period, any sum expended in that accounting period by the company concerned or, in the case of a group scheme, by a participating company in making a payment or payments to the trustees of an approved scheme shall be included—

(*a*) in the sums to be deducted in computing for the purposes of Schedule D the profits or gains for that accounting period of a trade carried on by that company, or

(*b*) if that company is an investment company within the meaning of section 83 or a company in the case of which that section applies by virtue of section 707, in the sums to be deducted under section 83(2) as expenses of management in computing the profits of the company for that accounting period for the purposes of corporation tax,

only if one of the conditions in subsection (2)(*b*) is fulfilled.

(2) (*a*) In this subsection, **"the relevant period"** means the period of 9 months beginning on the day following the end of the period of account in which the sum mentioned in subsection (1) is charged as an expense of the company incurring the expenditure or such longer period as the Revenue Commissioners may allow by notice in writing given to that company.

(*b*) The conditions referred to in subsection (1) are —

(i) that before the expiry of the relevant period the sum mentioned in subsection (1) is applied by the trustees in the acquisition of shares for appropriation to individuals who are eligible to participate in the scheme by virtue of their being or having been employees or directors of the company making the payment, and

(ii) that the sum is necessary to meet the reasonable expenses of the trustees in administering the scheme.

(3) (*a*) In this subsection, **"trading income"**, in relating to any trade, means the income from the trade computed in accordance with the rules applicable to Case I of Schedule D before any deduction under this Chapter and after any set-off or reduction of income by virtue of section 396 or 397, and after any

deduction or addition by virtue of section 307 or 308, and after any deduction by virtue of section 666.

(*b*) No deduction shall be allowed under this section or under any other provision of the Tax Acts in respect of so much of any sum or the aggregate amount of any sums expended by a participating company in an accounting period in the manner referred to in subsection (1) as exceeds the company's—

(i) trading income for that accounting period, in the case of a company to which paragraph (*a*) of that subsection applies, or

(ii) income for that accounting period, in the case of a company to which paragraph (*b*) of that subsection applies, after taking into account any sums which apart from this section are to be deducted under section 83(2) as expenses of management in computing the profits of the company for the purposes of corporation tax.

(4) The deduction to be allowed under this section or under any other provision of the Tax Acts in respect of any sum or the aggregate amount of any sums expended by a participating company in an accounting period in the manner referred to in subsection (1) shall not exceed such sum as is in the opinion of the Revenue Commissioners reasonable, having regard to the number of employees or directors of the company making the payment who have agreed to participate in the scheme, the services rendered by them to that company, the levels of their remuneration, the length of their service or similar factors.

(5) For the purposes of this section, the trustees of an approved scheme shall be taken to apply sums paid to them in the order in which the sums are received by them.

Definitions

company: ss 4(1), 5(1); month: IA 1937 Sch; profits: s 4(1); Tax Acts: s 1(2); trade: s 3(1).

Former enactments

FA 1982 s 58; FA 1983 s 24; FA 1984 s 31(*b*); FA 1997 s 146(1) and Sch 9 Pt I para 12(3).

Corresponding UK tax provision

Income and Corporation Taxes Act 1988 s 85.

518 Costs of establishing profit sharing schemes

(1) This section shall apply to a sum expended on or after the 10th day of May, 1997, by a company in establishing a profit sharing scheme which the Revenue Commissioners approve of in accordance with Part 2 of Schedule 11 and under which the trustees acquire no shares before such approval is given.

(2) A sum to which this section applies shall be included—

(*a*) in the sums to be deducted in computing for the purposes of Schedule D the profits or gains of a trade carried on by the company, or

(*b*) if the company is an investment company within the meaning of section 83 or a company in the case of which that section applies by virtue of section 707, in the sums to be deducted under section 83(2) as expenses of management in computing the profits of the company for the purposes of corporation tax.

(3) In a case where—

(*a*) subsection (2) applies, and

(*b*) the approval is given after the end of the period of 9 months beginning on the day following the end of the accounting period in which the sum is expended,

then, for the purpose of subsection (2), the sum shall be treated as expended in the accounting period in which the approval is given and not in the accounting period mentioned in paragraph (*b*).

Former enactments

FA 1982 s 58A; FA 1997 s 50(*b*).

Corresponding UK tax provision

Income and Corporation Taxes Act 1988 s 84A.

CHAPTER 2
Employee Share Ownership Trusts

Tax Briefing

TB40 June 2000 p 29 — Employee Share Ownership Trusts — Finance Act 2000 amendments.
TB47 April 2002 p 10 — Employee Share Ownership Trusts — Finance Act 2002 amendments.

519 Employee share ownership trusts

(1) (*a*) This section shall apply to an employee share ownership trust which the Revenue Commissioners have approved of as a qualifying employee share ownership trust in accordance with Schedule 12 and which approval has not been withdrawn.

(*b*) This section shall be construed together with Schedule 12.

(2) Where, in an accounting period of a company, the company expends a sum—

(*a*) in establishing a trust to which this section applies, or

(*b*) in making a payment by means of contribution to the trustees of a trust which at the time the sum is expended is a trust to which this section applies, and—

(i) at that time the company or a company which it then controls has employees who are eligible to benefit under the terms of the trust deed, and

(ii) before the expiry of the expenditure period the sum is expended by the trustees for one or more of the qualifying purposes,

then, the sum shall be included—

(I) in the sums to be deducted in computing for the purposes of Schedule D the profits or gains for that accounting period of a trade carried on by that company, or

(II) if the company is an investment company within the meaning of section 83 or a company in the case of which that section applies by virtue of section 707, in the sums to be deducted under section 83(2) as expenses of management in computing the profits of the company for that accounting period for the purposes of corporation tax.

(3) Where—

(*a*) subsection (2)(*a*) applies, and

(*b*) the trust is established after the end of the period of 9 months beginning on the day following the end of the accounting period in which the sum is expended by the company,

then, for the purposes of subsection (2), the sum shall be treated as expended in the accounting period in which the trust is established and not in the accounting period mentioned in paragraph (*b*).

(4) For the purposes of subsection (2)(*b*)(i), the question whether one company is controlled by another shall be construed in accordance with section 432.

(5) For the purposes of subsection (2)(*b*)(ii)—

(*a*) each of the following shall be a qualifying purpose—

(i) the acquisition of shares in the company which established the trust,

(ii) the repayment of sums borrowed,

(iii) the payment of interest on sums borrowed,

(iv) the payment of any sum to a person who is a beneficiary under the terms of [the trust deed,][1]

[(iv*a*) the payment of any sum or the transfer of securities to the personal representatives of a deceased beneficiary under the terms of the trust deed, and][2]

(v) the meeting of expenses,

and

(*b*) the expenditure period shall be the period of 9 months beginning on the day following the end of the accounting period in which the sum is expended by the company or such longer period as the Revenue Commissioners may allow by notice given to the company.

(6) For the purposes of this section, the trustees of an employee share ownership trust shall be taken to expend sums paid to them in the order in which the sums are received by them, irrespective of the number of companies making payments.

[(7) The trustees of a trust to which this section applies shall not be chargeable to income tax in respect of income consisting of dividends in respect of securities held by the trust if, and to the extent that, the income is expended within the expenditure period (within the meaning of paragraph 13 of Schedule 12) by the trustees for one or more of the qualifying purposes referred to in that paragraph...[3].][4]

[(7A) Where the trustees of a trust to which this section applies—

(*a*) sell securities on the open market, or

(*b*) receive a sum on the redemption of securities,

any gain accruing to such trustees shall not be a chargeable gain if, and to the extent that the proceeds of such sale or redemption, as the case may be, are used—

(i) to repay moneys borrowed by those trustees,

(ii) to pay interest on such borrowings, or

(iii) to pay a sum to the personal representatives of a deceased beneficiary.][5]

(8) Where the trustees of a trust to which this section applies transfer securities to the trustees of a profit sharing scheme approved under Part 2 of Schedule 11, any gain accruing to those first-mentioned trustees on that transfer shall not be a chargeable gain.

[(8A) Where the trustees of a trust to which this section applies transfer securities to the personal representatives of a deceased beneficiary, any gain accruing to the trustees on that transfer shall not be a chargeable gain.

(8B) The payment of any sum as is referred to in [subsection (7A)(iii)][6] or the transfer of any securities to which subsection (8A) applies shall, notwithstanding any other provision of the Income Tax Acts, be exempt from income tax.][7]

(9) Notwithstanding anything in [subsections (1) to (8B)][8], where the Revenue Commissioners in accordance with Schedule 12 withdraw approval of an employee share ownership trust as a qualifying employee share ownership trust, then, as on and from the date from which that withdrawal has effect, this section shall not apply in relation to—

(*a*) any sum expended by a company in making a payment to that trust,

[(*b*) income consisting of dividends in respect of securities held by that trust,

(*c*) the transfer of securities to a profit sharing scheme approved under Part 2 of [Schedule 11,][9]

[(*ca*) the payment of any sum or the transfer of securities to the personal representatives of a deceased beneficiary of the trust, or][10]

[(*d*) the gain accruing to the trustees of that trust from—

(i) the sale on the open market, or

(ii) the redemption,

of securities.][11]][12]

[(10) For the purposes of this section—

"deceased beneficiary" means a person who on the date of such person's death—

(*a*) would have been eligible to have [securities][13] appropriated to him or her, had such [securities][13] been available for appropriation, under a scheme approved of by the Revenue Commissioners under Schedule 11 and for which approval has not been withdrawn, and

(*b*) was a beneficiary under the terms of a trust deed of an employee share ownership trust approved of by the Revenue Commissioners under Schedule 12 and for which approval has not been withdrawn and which trust deed contained provision for the transfer of securities to the trustees of the scheme referred to in paragraph (*a*) and for the payment of sums and for the transfer of securities to the personal representatives of deceased beneficiaries.][14]

Amendments

1 Substituted by FA 2001 s 13(*a*)(i)(I) from 6 April 2001; previously "the trust deed, and".

2 Subs (5)(*a*)(iv*a*) inserted by FA 2001 s 13(*a*)(i)(II) from 6 April 2001.

3 Repealed by FA 2000 s 69(2) and Sch 2 Part 2 with effect from 6 April 1999 in the case of income tax and as respects accounting periods commencing on or after that date in the case of corporation tax; previously ", but the trustees shall not be entitled to the set-off or payment of a tax credit under section 136 in respect of those dividends".

4 Subs (7) substituted by FA 1998 s 36(*b*) with effect from 27 March 1998.

5 Subs (7A) substituted by FA 2002 s 13(1)(*c*)(i) with effect from 16 April 2001.

6 Substituted by FA 2004 s 89 and Sch 3 para 1(*n*) with effect from 25 March 2004; previously "subsection (7A)(*c*)".

7 Subss (8A)–(8B) inserted by FA 2001 s 13(*a*)(iii) from 6 April 2001.

8 Substituted by FA 2001 s 13(*a*)(iv)(I) from 6 April 2001; previously "subsections (1) to (8)".

9 Substituted by FA 2001 s 13(*a*)(iv)(II) from 6 April 2001; previously "Schedule 11, or".

10 Subs (9)(*ca*) inserted by FA 2001 s 13(*a*)(iv)(III) from 6 April 2001.

11 Subs (9)(*d*) substituted by FA 2002 s 13(1)(*c*)(ii) with effect from 16 April 2001.

12 Subs (9)(*b*)–(*c*) substituted by FA 1999 s 69(1)(*b*)(ii) in respect of employee share ownership trusts approved under TCA 1997 Sch 12 para 2 on or after 25 March 1999.

13 Substituted by FA 2002 s 13(1)(*c*)(iii) with effect from 16 April 2001; previously "shares".

14 Subs (10) inserted by FA 2001 s 13(*a*)(v) from 6 April 2001.

Cross-references

ACC Bank Act 2001 s 1, "trust" is an employee share ownership trust to which TCA 1997 s 519 applies and which is a trust to acquire and hold shares, or shares in a holding company, for the benefit of employees of ACC Bank or a subsidiary.

Distributions, matters to be treated as, subs (6): s 130(2C).

Irish National Petroleum Corporation may establish one or more trusts to which TCA 1997 s 519 relates: Irish National Petroleum Corporation Limited Act 2001 s 5(1).

Profit sharing schemes, appropriated shares: s 510(5A)(*a*)(ii); conditions as to shares: Sch 11 para 8(*d*); excess or unauthorised shares: s 515(2A)(*a*); individuals ineligible to participate: Sch 11 para 12A(*a*); interpretation: s 509(1) ("specified securities"); shares acquired from an employee share ownership trust: s 511A(1)(*b*).

Trustee Savings Bank Act 1989 s 57(1) (as substituted by Trustees Savings Bank (Amendment) Act 2001 s 1), "trust" means an employee share ownership trust to which TCA 1997 s 519 applies.

Definitions

chargeable gain: ss 5(1), 545; company: ss 4(1), 5(1); Income Tax Acts: s 1(2); personal representative: s 5(1).

Former enactments

FA 1997 s 51.

Corresponding UK tax provision

Income and Corporation Taxes Act 1988 s 85A.

[CHAPTER 3][1]
Savings-Related Share Option Schemes

Amendments

1 Inserted by FA 1999 s 68(*a*) with effect from 6 April 1999.

Revenue information

A Guide to Savings-Related Share Option Schemes may be downloaded from Revenue's website (www.revenue.ie) under Publications/Technical Guidelines.

Tax Briefing

TB42 Dec 2000 pp 29–34 — Savings-Related Share Option Schemes.

TB48 June 2002 p 18 — Revenue are prepared to accept that if, during a period of an unpaid leave, an employee directs his or her contributions through the company's payroll, then, paragraph 6(d) of the Dept. of Finance specification for Certified Contractual Savings Schemes will continue to be complied with. This procedure will only apply so long as the participant remains an employee of the company which established the scheme or of a participating company.

519A Approved savings-related share option schemes

[(1) (*a*) The provisions of this section shall apply where an individual obtains a right to acquire shares in a body corporate—

(i) by reason of the individual's office or employment as a director or employee of that or any other body corporate, and

(ii) that individual obtains that right in accordance with the provisions of a savings-related share option scheme approved under Schedule 12A on or after the 6th day of April, 1999, and in respect of which approval has not been withdrawn.

(*b*) This section shall he construed together with Schedule 12A.

(2) Tax shall not be chargeable under any provision of the Tax Acts in respect of the receipt of the right referred to in subsection (1).

(3) Subject to subsection (4) if the individual exercises the right in accordance with the provisions of the scheme at a time when it is approved tax shall not be chargeable under any provision of the Tax Acts in respect of any gain realised by the exercise of the right.

[(3A)(*a*) Where, in exercising a right in accordance with the provisions of the scheme at a time when it is approved, the individual acquires scheme shares from a relevant body, neither a chargeable gain nor an allowable loss shall accrue to the relevant body on the disposal of the scheme shares, and the individual shall, notwithstanding section 547(1)(*a*), be deemed for the purposes of the Capital Gains Tax Acts to have acquired the scheme shares for a consideration equal to the amount paid for their acquisition.

(*b*) In this subsection and in section 519B—

"relevant body" means a trust or a company which exists for the purpose of acquiring and holding scheme shares;

"schemes shares" has the meaning assigned to it by paragraph 10 of Schedule 12A.][1]

(4) Subsection (3) shall not apply in respect of a right obtained by a person under a scheme which is exercised within 3 years of its being obtained by virtue of a provision included in a scheme pursuant to paragraph 22 of Schedule 12A.

(5) In this section "savings-related share option scheme" has the meaning assigned to it by Schedule 12A.][2]

Amendments

1 Subs (3A) inserted by FA 2000 s 51(*a*)(i) with effect from 6 April 2000.

2 Section 519A inserted by FA 1999 s 68(*a*) with effect from 6 April 1999.

Cross-references

Approval of schemes, subs (3): Sch 12A para 4(1).

Exchange provisions: Sch 12A para 16(4).

Definitions

allowable loss: ss 5(1), 546; Capital Gains Tax Acts: s 1(2); chargeable gain: ss 5(1); 545; Tax Acts: s 1(2).

Corresponding UK tax provision

Income and Corporation Taxes Act 1988 s 135.

519B Costs of establishing savings-related share option schemes

[(1) [Subject to subsection (2A) this section shall apply][1] to a sum expended on or after the 6th day of April, 1999, by a company in establishing a savings-related share option scheme which the Revenue Commissioners approve of in accordance with the provisions of Schedule 12A and under which no employee or director obtains rights before such approval is given.

(2) A sum to which this section applies shall be included—

(*a*) in the sums to be deducted in computing for the purposes of Schedule D the profits or gains of a trade carried on by the company, or

(*b*) if the company is an investment company within the meaning of section 83 or a company in the case of which that section applies by virtue of section 707, in the sums to be deducted under section 83(2) as expenses of management in computing the profits of the company for the purposes of corporation tax.

[(2A) Notwithstanding any provision of the Tax Acts, any sum expended by the company, either directly or indirectly, to enable a relevant body to acquire scheme shares shall not be included—

(*a*) in the sums to be deducted in computing for the purposes of Schedule D the profits or gains of a trade carried on by the company, or

(*b*) if the company is an investment company within the meaning of section 83 or a company in the case of which that section applies by virtue of section 707, in the sums to be deducted under section 83(2) as expenses of management in computing the profits of the company for the purposes of corporation tax.][2]

(3) In a case where—

(*a*) subsection (2) applies, and

(*b*) the approval is given after the end of the period of 9 months beginning on the day following the end of the accounting period in which the sum is expended,

then, for the purpose of subsection (2), the sum shall be treated as expended in the accounting period in which the approval is given and not the accounting period mentioned in paragraph (*b*).][3]

Amendments

1 Substituted by FA 2000 s 51(*a*)(ii)(I) with effect from 6 April 2000; previously "This section shall apply".

2 Subs (2A) inserted by FA 2000 s 51(*a*)(ii)(II) with effect from 6 April 2000.

3 Section 519B inserted by FA 1999 s 68(*a*) with effect from 6 April 1999.

Definitions

company: ss 4(1), 5(1); month: IA 1937 Sch; profits: s 4(1); Tax Acts: s 1(2); trade: ss 3(1), 4(1), 5(1).

Corresponding UK tax provision

Income and Corporation Taxes Act 1988 s 84A.

519C Interest, etc under certified contractual savings schemes

[(1) In this section—

"qualifying savings institution" means any of the following persons—

(*a*) a person who is a holder of a licence granted under section 9 of the Central Bank Act, 1971, or a person who holds a licence or other similar authorisation under the law of any other Member State of the European Communities which corresponds to a licence granted under that section,

(*b*) a building society within the meaning of section 256,

(*c*) a trustee savings bank within the meaning of the Trustee Savings Banks Act, 1989,

...[1]

...[2]

...[2]

(*g*) the Post Office Savings Bank,

(*h*) a credit union within the meaning of the Credit Union Act, 1997, or

(*i*) such other person as the Minister for Finance may by order prescribe.

(2) Any terminal bonus or interest paid by a qualifying savings institution to an individual under a certified contractual savings scheme shall be exempt from income tax and shall not be reckoned in computing total income for the purposes of the Income Tax Acts.

(3) Any terminal bonus or interest paid by a qualifying savings institution under a certified contractual savings scheme shall not, where the qualifying savings institution is a relevant deposit taker within the meaning of section 256, be relevant interest for the purposes of that section and accordingly shall not be subject to deduction of appropriate tax under section 257.

(4) In this section "certified contractual savings scheme" means a scheme—

(*a*) which provides for periodical contributions to be made by individuals for a specified period to a qualifying savings institution where the deposit represented by such contributions would, but for subsection (3), constitute a relevant deposit within the meaning of section 256 if the qualifying savings institution were a relevant deposit taker within the meaning of that section,

(*b*) where the individuals referred to in paragraph (*a*)—

(i) are eligible to participate in, that is to say, to obtain and exercise rights under, an approved savings-related share option scheme, and

(ii) whose contributions under the scheme are to be used in accordance with paragraph 17 of Schedule 12A,

and

(*c*) which is certified by the Revenue Commissioners as qualifying for exemption under this section by reference to requirements specified by the Minister for Finance in accordance with Schedule 12B.

(5) Schedule 12B to this Act which contains provisions supplementing this section shall have effect.

(6) This section shall apply in relation to any terminal bonus or interest paid by a qualifying savings institution on or after the 6th day of April, 1999, under a certified contractual savings scheme.][3]

Amendments

1 Definition of "qualifying savings institution", para (*d*) repealed by ACC Bank Act 2001 s 12(1) and Sch with effect from such date as the Minister for Finance may appoint by order. By virtue of the ACC Bank Act 2001 (Sections 6, 8, 10, 11(2) and 12) (Commencement) Order, 2002, SI No 69 of 2002, this amendment came into operation with effect from 28 February 2002.

2 Definition of "qualifying savings institution", paras (*e*) and (*f*) repealed with effect from 12 February 2001 by ICC Bank Act 2000 s 7 and the ICC Bank Act 2000 (Sections 5 and 7) (Commencement) Order 2000 (SI No 396 of 2001); previously "(*e*) ICC Bank plc," and "(*f*) ICC Investment Bank Limited,".

3 Section 519C inserted by FA 1999 s 68(*a*) with effect from 6 April 1999.

Cross-references

Approved savings-related share option schemes, exercise of rights: Sch 12A para 17.

Certified contractual savings schemes, specifications by Minister for Finance: Sch 12B para 1; subs (4)(*c*): Sch 12B paras 2(1), 3(1), 4(1).

Definitions

Income Tax Acts: s 1(2); person: IA 1937 s 11(*c*); total income: s 3(1).

Corresponding UK tax provision

Income and Corporation Taxes Act 1988 s 326.

[CHAPTER 4

Approved Share Option Schemes][1]

Amendments

1 TCA 1997 Pt 17 Ch 4 inserted by FA 2001 s 15(*a*) with effect from 30 March 2001.

Revenue information

A guide to Approved Share Option Schemes is available on Revenue's website (www.revenue.ie) under Publications/Technical Guidelines.

Tax Briefing

TB43 April 2001 pp 15–16 — Approved Share Option Schemes.

519D Approved share option schemes

[(1) The provisions of this section shall apply where an individual obtains a right to acquire shares in a body corporate—

(*a*) by reason of the individual's office or employment as a director or employee of that or any other body corporate, and

(*b*) that individual obtains the right in accordance with the provisions of a share option scheme approved under Schedule 12C and in respect of which approval has not been withdrawn.

(2) Tax shall not be chargeable under any provision of the Tax Acts in respect of the receipt of the right referred to in subsection (1).

(3) Subject to subsection (4) (except where paragraph 18(2) of Schedule 12C applies), if the individual exercises the right in accordance with the provisions of the scheme at a time when it is approved—

(*a*) tax shall not be chargeable under any provision of the Tax Acts in respect of any gain realised by the exercise of the right, and

(*b*) notwithstanding section 547(1)(*a*), the individual shall be deemed for the purposes of the Capital Gains Tax Acts to have acquired the shares, acquired by the exercise of the right, for a consideration equal to the amount paid for their acquisition.

(4) Subsection (3) shall not apply in relation to the exercise by any individual of a right in accordance with the provisions of a scheme if the period beginning with his or her obtaining the right and ending with his or her disposal of any of—

(*a*) the shares acquired by the exercise of the right, or

(*b*) in a case where section 584, 586 or 587 applies, the shares received in exchange for the shares so acquired,

is less than 3 years.

(5) (*a*) Where, in exercising a right in accordance with the provisions of the scheme at a time when it is approved, the individual acquires scheme shares from a relevant body, neither a chargeable gain nor an allowable loss shall accrue to the relevant body on the disposal of the scheme shares, and the individual shall, notwithstanding section 547(1)(*a*), be deemed for the purposes of the Capital Gains Tax Acts to have acquired the scheme shares for a consideration equal to the amount paid for their acquisition.

(*b*) In this subsection and in subsection (6)—

"relevant body" means a trust or a company which exists for the purpose of acquiring and holding scheme shares;

"scheme shares" has the meaning assigned to it by paragraph 11 of Schedule 12C.

(6) (*a*) Subject to paragraph (*c*), this subsection applies to a sum expended by a company in establishing a share option scheme which the Revenue Commissioners approve of in accordance with the provisions of Schedule 12C and under which, subject to subsection (7), no employee or director obtains rights before such approval is given.

(*b*) A sum to which this subsection applies shall be included—

(i) in the sums to be deducted in computing for the purposes of Schedule D the profits or gains of a trade carried on by the company, or

(ii) if a company is an investment company within the meaning of section 83 or a company in the case of which that section applies by virtue of section 707, in the sums to be deducted under section 83(2) as expenses of management in computing the profits of the company for the purposes of corporation tax.

(*c*) Notwithstanding paragraph (*b*) or any other provision of the Tax Acts, any sum expended by a company, either directly or indirectly, to enable a relevant body to acquire scheme shares shall not be included—

(i) in the sums to be deducted in computing for the purposes of Schedule D the profits or gains of a trade carried on by the company, or

(ii) if the company is an investment company within the meaning of section 83 or a company in the case of which that section applies by virtue of section 707, in the sums to be deducted under section 83(2) as expenses of management in computing the profits of the company for the purposes of corporation tax.

(*d*) In a case where—

(i) paragraph (*b*) applies, and

(ii) the approval is given after the end of the period of 9 months beginning on the day following the end of the accounting period in which the sum is expended,

then, for the purposes of paragraph (*b*), the sum shall be treated as expended in the accounting period in which approval is given and not the accounting period mentioned in subparagraph (ii).

(7) (*a*) Where a share option scheme is approved by the Revenue Commissioners under Schedule 12C and, prior to such approval, an individual had obtained

under the scheme a right which meets the conditions of paragraph (*b*), that right shall be treated for all the purposes of this section and Schedule 12C as if it had been obtained under an approved scheme.

(*b*) The conditions of this paragraph are—

(i) the right was exercised on or after 15 February 2001,

(ii) the scheme is approved by the Revenue Commissioners under Schedule 12C on or before 31 December 2001, and

(iii) at the time—

(I) the right was obtained, and

(II) the right was exercised, if such exercise occurred before the scheme was approved under Schedule 12C,

the scheme would, at each of those times, have been capable of approval under Schedule 12C if that Schedule had been in force from the time the right was obtained.][1]

Amendments

1 Section 519D inserted by FA 2001 s 15(*a*) with effect from 30 March 2001.

Cross-references

Exchange provisions, Sch 12C para 17(4)(*a*).

Information, subs (7)(*b*): Sch 12C para 20(2)(*b*).

Transfer of rights, subss (3), (4): Sch 12C para 18(2).

Definitions

allowable loss: ss 4(1), 5(1); Capital Gains Tax Acts: s 1(2); chargeable gain: ss 4(1), 5(1); company: ss 4(1), 5(1); profits: s 4(1); tax: ss 2(1), 3(1); Tax Acts: s 1(2); trade: ss 3(1), 4(1).

PART 18

PAYMENTS IN RESPECT OF PROFESSIONAL SERVICES BY CERTAIN PERSONS AND PAYMENTS TO SUBCONTRACTORS IN CERTAIN INDUSTRIES

CHAPTER 1

Payments in Respect of Professional Services by Certain Persons

Cross-references

Power of inspection: tax deduction from payments in respect of professional services by certain persons: s 904J(3)(*a*).

Revenue information

Information leaflet IT19 — Professional Services Withholding Tax (PSWT).

Information leaflet IT61 — A Revenue Guide to Professional Services Withholding Tax for Accountable Persons and Specified Persons.

Statements of Practice

Professional Services Withholding Tax IT/01/95, Sept 1995.

Professional Services Withholding Tax — Interim Refunds — IT/03/90, Dec 1990.

Tax Briefing

TB15 July 1994 par4.1 — Professional Services Withholding Tax (PSWT) — Contracts performed abroad by non- residents.

TB22 June 1996 p 15 — PSWT — Commencement & Cessations, Partnerships.

TB23 Sept 1996 p 15 — PSWT — Apportionment of credit.

TB28 Oct 1997 p 3 — Documentation used for PSWT.

TB44 June 2002 pp 26–27 — Professional Services Withholding Tax: Changes consequent on the changeover to the calendar tax year.
TB47 Apr 2002 p 19 — PSWT — Calendar Tax Year: accounting periods ending 31 March 2002; change of accounting period.
TB52 May 2003 p 25 — PSWT and treatment of interest paid under the Late Payment in Commercial Transactions Regulations 2002, SI No 388 of 2002.
TB53 Aug 2003 p 20 — PSWT (Finance Act 2003 Changes).
TB56 July 2004 p 12 — When claiming credit for PSWT on either Form 11 or Form CT1, the full amount of PSWT credit due for the year should be entered, even if any interim refunds/claims has already been made. The amount of any interim refund will automatically be deducted from the amount claimed. If you only enter the amount of credit now due (i.e. the amount less the interim refund/claim) the assessment will show a reduced credit, if any.

520 Interpretation (Chapter 1)

(1) In this Chapter—

"accountable person" has the meaning assigned to it by section 521;

"appropriate tax", in relation to a relevant payment, means—

(*a*) where such payment does not include value-added tax, a sum representing income tax on the amount of that payment at the standard rate in force at the time of payment, and

(*b*) where such payment includes value-added tax, a sum representing income tax at the standard rate in force at the time of payment on the amount of that payment exclusive of the value-added tax;

"authorised insurer" has the same meaning as in section 470;

"basis period for a year of assessment", in relation to a specified person, means—

(*a*) where a relevant payment is to be included in a computation of profits or gains of that person for the purposes of Case I or II of Schedule D, the period on the profits or gains of which income tax for that year is to be finally computed for the purposes of Case I or II of Schedule D, and—

[(i) where 2 basis periods overlap, then, subject to subsection (3), the period common to both shall be deemed for the purposes of this Chapter to fall in the second basis period only,][1]

(ii) where there is an interval between the end of the basis period for one year of assessment and the basis period for the next year of assessment, the interval shall be deemed to be part of the second basis period, and

(iii) the reference in subparagraph (i) to the overlapping of 2 periods shall be construed as including a reference to the coincidence of 2 periods or to the inclusion of one period in another, and the reference to the period common to both shall be construed accordingly,

and

(*b*) in any other case, the year of assessment;

"contract of insurance" means a contract between an authorised insurer and a subscriber in respect of such insurance as is referred to in the definition of **"relevant contract"** in section 470(1);

[**"income tax month"** means—

(*a*) in relation to a period prior to 6 December 2001, a month beginning on the 6th day of a month and ending on the 5th day of the next month,

(*b*) the period beginning on 6 December 2001 and ending on 31 December 2001, and

(*c*) thereafter, a calendar month;][2]

"member", in relation to a contract of insurance, means a person who is named in the relevant policy of insurance and who has been accepted for insurance by an authorised insurer;

"practitioner" has the same meaning as in section 469;

"professional services" includes—

(*a*) services of a medical, dental, pharmaceutical, optical, aural or veterinary nature,

(*b*) services of an architectural, engineering, quantity surveying or surveying nature, and related services,

(*c*) services of accountancy, auditing or finance and services of financial, economic, marketing, advertising or other consultancies,

(*d*) services of a solicitor or barrister and other legal services,

(*e*) geological services, and

(*f*) training services provided on behalf of An Foras Áiseanna Saothair;

"relevant medical expenses" means expenses incurred in respect of professional services provided by a practitioner, being expenses that are or may become the subject of a claim for their reimbursement or discharge in whole or in part under a contract of insurance but not including any such expenses that—

(*a*) under the terms of the contract of insurance may (except in the case of certain expenses that in the opinion of the authorised insurer concerned are unusually large) be the subject of a claim for their discharge or reimbursement only—

(i) after the expiry of a stated period of 12 months in which the expenses are incurred, and

(ii) to the extent that the aggregate of the expenses and any other expenses incurred in that period exceeds a stated amount,

or

(*b*) are incurred in respect of professional services provided by a practitioner outside the State;

"relevant payment" means a payment made by—

(*a*) an accountable person in respect of professional services whether or not such services are provided to the accountable person making the payment, or

(*b*) an authorised insurer to a practitioner in accordance with section 522, or otherwise, in the discharge of a claim in respect of relevant medical expenses under a contract of insurance, but excludes—

(i) emoluments within the scope of Chapter 4 of Part 42 to which that Chapter [applies,][3]

(ii) payments under a relevant contract (within the meaning of section 530) from which tax has been deducted in accordance with subsection (1) of section 531, or would have been so deducted but for subsection (12) of that [section,][4]

[(iii) a payment by one accountable person to another in reimbursement of a relevant [payment, and][5]][6]

[(iv) a payment by one accountable person to—

(I) another accountable person being a person whose income is exempt from corporation tax or is disregarded for the purposes of the Tax Acts, or

(II) a body which has been granted an exemption from tax for the purposes of section 207;][7]

"specified person", in relation to a relevant payment, means the person to whom that payment is made;

"subscriber", in relation to a contract of insurance, means a person (other than an authorised insurer) who is a party to the contract and in whose name the relevant policy of insurance is registered.

(2) For the purposes of this Chapter—

(*a*) any reference in this Chapter to the amount of a relevant payment shall be construed as a reference to the amount which would be the amount of that payment if no appropriate tax were to be deducted from that payment, and

(*b*) in relation to a specified person, appropriate tax referable to—

(i) an accounting period, or

(ii) a basis period for a year of assessment,

means the appropriate tax deducted from a relevant payment which is taken into account in computing the specified person's profits or gains for that period and where there is more than one such relevant payment in that period the aggregate of the appropriate tax deducted from such payments.

[(3) Where, by virtue of the application of subsections (2)(*a*) and (3B) of section 65, a specified person's basis period for the year of assessment 2002, being a 12 month period ending in the period from 1 January 2002 to 5 April 2002, is also treated as the specified person's basis period for the year of assessment 2001, that basis period shall be deemed for the purposes of this Chapter to be the basis period for the year of assessment 2001 only.][8]

Amendments

1 Definition of "basis period for a year of assessment" para (*a*)(i) substituted by FA 2001 s 77(2) and Sch 2 para 28(*a*)(i) with effect from 6 April 2001.

2 Definition of "income tax month" substituted by FA 2001 s 77(2) and Sch 2 para 28(*a*)(ii) with effect from 6 April 2001.

3 Substituted by FA 2003 s 10(1)(*a*)(i) with effect from 1 January 2003; previously "applies, and".

4 Substituted by FA 2005 s 15(1)(*a*) with effect from 25 March 2005; previously "section, and".

5 Substituted by FA 2005 s 15(1)(*b*) with effect from 25 March 2005; previously "payment;".

[6] Definition of "relevant payment" subpara (iii) inserted by FA 2003 s 10(1)(*a*)(iii) with effect from 1 January 2003.

[7] Definition of "relevant payment" para (iv) inserted by FA 2005 s 15(1)(*c*) with effect from 25 March 2005.

[8] Subs (3) inserted by FA 2001 s 77(2) and Sch 2 para 28(*b*) with effect from 6 April 2001.

Cross-references

Power of inspection: tax deduction from payments in respect of professional services by certain persons, meaning of "specified person" applied: s 904J(1).

Case Law

Provisions giving relief for PSWT on a preceding year basis held to be unconstitutional – *Michael Daly v Revenue Commissioners & the Attorney General* [1995] ITR 185.

Revenue precedents

Issue: What is the treatment of grants paid by accountable persons?

Decision: General grants are not subject to PSWT. Grants for specific professional services are subject to PSWT.

Definitions

month: IA 1937 Sch; person: IA 1937 s 11(*c*); standard rate: ss 3(1), 15; Tax Acts: s 1(2); year of assessment: ss 2(1), 5(1).

Former enactments

FA 1987 s 13; FA 1988 s 8(*a*)(i) and (ii); FA 1992 s 10.

521 Accountable persons

(1) In this Chapter, **"accountable person"** means, subject to subsection (2), a person specified in Schedule 13.

(2) Where any of the persons specified in Schedule 13 is a body corporate, **"accountable person"** includes any subsidiary of that body corporate where such subsidiary is resident in the State and, for the purposes of this subsection, **"subsidiary"** has the meaning assigned to it by section 155 of the Companies Act, 1963.

(3) For the purposes of this Chapter, the Minister for Finance may by regulations extend or restrict the meaning of **"accountable person"** by adding or deleting one or more persons to or from, as the case may be, the list of persons specified in Schedule 13.

(4) Where regulations are proposed to be made under subsection (3), a draft of the regulations shall be laid before Dáil Éireann and the regulations shall not be made until a resolution approving of the draft has been passed by Dáil Éireann.

Note

Aer Lingus Act 2004 — subs (3) of section 12 (certain Acts not to apply to company) provides that TCA 1997 s 521 will cease to apply to Aer Lingus Group public limited company on the coming into operation of that subsection.

Cross-references

Meaning of "accountable person" applied: s 520.

Power of inspection: tax deduction from payments in respect of professional services by certain persons, meaning of "accountable person" applied: s 904J(1).

Definitions

Dáil Éireann: IA 1937 Sch; Minister of the Government: IA 1937 Sch; local authority: s 2(1); person: IA 1937 s 11(*c*); year of assessment: ss 2(1), 5(1).

Former enactments

FA 1987 s 14; FA 1992 s 11(1).

522 Obligation on authorised insurers

Subject to section 523(1), where under a contract of insurance a claim is made to an authorised insurer in respect of relevant medical expenses—

(*a*) the insurer shall discharge the claim by making payment to the extent of the amount of the benefit, if any, due under the contract, to the practitioner who provided the professional services to the subscriber or member concerned to whom the relevant medical expenses relate, and

(*b*) the subscriber or member, as the case may be, shall be acquitted and discharged of such amount as is represented by the payment as if the subscriber or member had made such payment.

Cross-references

Deduction of tax: s 523(2)(*a*).

Relevant payment: s 520(1).

Former enactments

FA 1987 s 14A; FA 1988 s 8(*c*).

523 Deduction of tax from relevant payments

(1) (*a*) An accountable person making a relevant payment shall deduct from the amount of the payment the appropriate tax in relation to the payment.

(*b*) The specified person to whom the amount is payable shall allow such deduction on receipt of the residue of the payment.

(*c*) The accountable person making the deduction and, if the accountable person is an authorised insurer, any subscriber or member on whose behalf the accountable person is making the relevant payment shall be acquitted and discharged of such amount as is represented by the deduction, as if the amount had actually been paid.

(2) Where—

(*a*) in accordance with section 522, a relevant payment has been made to a practitioner by an authorised insurer, and

(*b*) in accordance with subsection (1), the practitioner has allowed a deduction of appropriate tax in respect of that payment and a subscriber or member has been acquitted and discharged of so much money as is represented by the deduction,

the practitioner shall, if any amount in respect of the relevant medical expenses to which the relevant payment relates has been paid by the subscriber or member, pay to the subscriber or member, as the case may be, an amount equal to the amount by which the aggregate of the amount paid by the subscriber or member and the amount of the relevant payment exceeds the relevant medical expenses.

(3) (*a*) The Minister for Finance may make such regulations as that Minister considers necessary or expedient for the purpose of giving full effect to this Chapter in so far as it relates to authorised insurers and the making of payments under contracts of insurance in respect of relevant medical expenses, and, in particular but without prejudice to the generality of the foregoing, regulations under this subsection may—

(i) specify the circumstances and the manner in which a payment (other than a relevant payment) may be made or claimed in respect of relevant medical expenses, and

(ii) provide for the indemnification of an individual against claims in respect of relevant medical expenses, or any other claims arising out of acts done or omitted to be done by the individual pursuant to this Chapter or regulations made under this subsection in so far as this Chapter relates or those regulations relate to authorised insurers and the making of payments under contracts of insurance in respect of relevant medical expenses.

(*b*) Every regulation made under this subsection shall be laid before Dáil Éireann as soon as may be after it is made and, if a resolution annulling the regulation is passed by Dáil Éireann within the next 21 days on which Dáil Éireann has sat after the regulation is laid before it, the regulation shall be annulled accordingly, but without prejudice to the validity of anything previously done thereunder.

(4) The provisions of the Tax Acts relating to the computation of profits or gains shall not be affected by the deduction of appropriate tax from relevant payments in accordance with subsection (1), and accordingly the amount of such relevant payments shall be taken into account in computing the profits or gains of the specified person for tax purposes.

Cross-references

Obligation on authorised insurers, subs (1): s 522.

Tax Briefing

TB31 Apr 1998 p 13 — Professional services withholding tax should not be deducted from interest paid under the Prompt Payment of Accounts Act, 1997 on foot of payments for professional services.

Definitions

Dáil Éireann: IA 1937 Sch; person: IA 1937 s 11(*c*); Tax Acts: s 1(2).

Former enactments

FA 1987 s 15; FA 1988 s 8(*d*).

524 Identification of, and issue of documents to, specified persons

(1) The specified person shall furnish to the accountable person concerned—

(*a*) in the case of a specified person resident in the State or a person having a permanent establishment or fixed base in the State—

(i) details of the specified person's income tax or corporation tax number, as may be appropriate, and

(ii) if the relevant payment includes an amount in respect of value-added tax, the specified person's value-added tax registration number, and

(*b*) in the case of a specified person other than a person mentioned in paragraph (*a*), details of the specified person's country of residence and the specified person's tax reference in that country.

(2) Where the specified person has complied with subsection (1), the accountable person, on making a relevant payment, shall give to such person in a form prescribed by the Revenue Commissioners particulars of—

(*a*) the name and address of the specified person,

(*b*) the specified person's tax reference as furnished in accordance with paragraph (*a*)(i) or (*b*) of subsection (1),

(*c*) the amount of the relevant payment,

(*d*) the amount of the appropriate tax deducted from that payment, and

(*e*) the date on which the payment is made.

Cross-references

Credit for appropriate tax borne, subs (2): s 526(3).

Interim refunds, subs (2): s 527(2)(*c*).

Definitions

person: IA 1937 s 11(*c*).

Former enactments

FA 1987 s 16.

525 Returns and collection of appropriate tax

(1) Within [14 days][1] from the end of every income tax month, an accountable person shall remit to the Collector-General all amounts of appropriate tax which the accountable person is liable under this Chapter to deduct from relevant payments made by the accountable person during that income tax month.

(2) Each remittance under subsection (1) shall be accompanied by a return containing, in relation to each specified person to whom a relevant payment has been made in the income tax month concerned, the particulars required by the return.

(3) A return shall be required to be made by an accountable person for an income tax month notwithstanding that no relevant payments were made by the accountable person in that income tax month.

(4) Every return shall be in a form prescribed by the Revenue Commissioners and shall include a declaration to the effect that the return is correct and complete.

(5) The Collector-General shall give the accountable person a receipt for the total amount so remitted.

[(6) The provisions of Chapter 2 relating to the assessment, collection and recovery of tax deductible under section 531(1) shall apply to the assessment, collection and recovery of appropriate tax.][2]

Amendments

1 Substituted by FA 2001 s 77(2) and Sch 2 paras 29 and 61(*d*) with effect from 1 January 2002; previously "10 days".

2 Subs (6) substituted by FA 2003 s 10(1)(*b*) with effect from 1 January 2003.

Cross-references

Power of inspection, tax deduction from payments in respect of professional services by certain persons: s 904J(2).

Definitions

Income Tax Acts: s 1(2); person: IA 1937 s 11(*c*).

Former enactments

FA 1987 s 17.

526 Credit for appropriate tax borne

(1) Where in relation to an accounting period a specified person is within the charge to corporation tax and has borne appropriate tax referable to that accounting period, the specified person may, subject to section 529, claim to have the amount of appropriate tax specified in subsection (4) set against corporation tax chargeable for that accounting period and, where such appropriate tax exceeds such corporation tax, to have the excess refunded to the specified person.

(2) Where in relation to a year of assessment a specified person is within the charge to income tax and has borne appropriate tax referable to the basis period for that year of assessment, the specified person may, subject to section 529, claim to have the amount of appropriate tax specified in subsection (4) set against the income tax chargeable for the year of assessment and, where such appropriate tax exceeds such income tax, to have the excess refunded to the specified person.

(3) The specified person shall, in respect of each claim under subsection (1) or (2), furnish, in respect of each amount of appropriate tax included in the claim, the form given to the specified person by an accountable person in accordance with section 524(2).

(4) The amount of the appropriate tax to be set against corporation tax for an accounting period or against income tax for a year of assessment in accordance with subsection (1) or (2) shall be the total of the appropriate tax referable to the accounting period or to the basis period for the year of assessment, as the case may be, which is included in the forms furnished in accordance with subsection (3) and not repaid under this Chapter.

Cross-references

Apportionment of credits or interim refunds, subs (3): s 528; limitation on: s 529.

Statement of practice

Credit for professional service withholding tax is available on a current year basis: SP IT/1/95 — Professional services withholding tax.

Tax Briefing

TB56 July 2004 p 12 — When claiming credit for PSWT on either Form 11 or Form CT1, the full amount of PSWT credit due for the year should be entered, even if any interim refunds/claims has already been made. The amount of any interim refund will automatically be deducted from the amount claimed. If you only enter the amount of credit now due (i.e. the amount less the interim refund/claim) the assessment will show a reduced credit, if any.

Definitions

person: IA 1937 s 11(*c*); profits: s 4(1); within the charge to (tax): s 2(1); year of assessment: ss 2(1), 5(1).

Former enactments

FA 1987 s 18.

---

527 Interim refunds of appropriate tax

(1) A specified person may make a claim for an interim refund of the whole or part of the appropriate tax referable to an accounting period or to a basis period for a year of assessment, as the case may be (in this section referred to as **"the first-mentioned period"**), and the inspector shall, if he or she is satisfied that the specified person making the claim has complied with the requirements of subsection (2), make such

refund as is specified in subsection (3) and, subject to those requirements as modified by subsection (4)(*a*), make such refund as is specified in that subsection.

(2) The requirements of this subsection are—

(*a*) that the profits or gains for the accounting period or for the basis period for the year of assessment, as the case may be, immediately preceding the first-mentioned period have been finally determined for tax purposes,

(*b*) that the amount of tax which was payable for that accounting period or year of assessment corresponding to that basis period has been paid (whether by credit for appropriate tax or otherwise), and

(*c*) that the specified person shall, in respect of each relevant payment included in the claim, furnish to the inspector the form given to the specified person by an accountable person in accordance with section 524(2).

(3) The amount of the tax to be refunded shall be the excess of the total of the appropriate tax included in the forms furnished in accordance with subsection (2)(*c*) (and not already repaid under the provisions of this section) over the amount of tax referred to in subsection (2)(*b*) less the amount which the specified person is liable to pay or remit—

(*a*) under the Value-Added Tax Act, 1972, and the regulations made under that Act,

(*b*) under Chapter 4 of Part 42 and the regulations made under that Chapter, and

(*c*) in respect of employment contributions under the Social Welfare (Consolidation) Act, 1993, and the regulations made under that Act.

[(3A) Where a specified person makes a claim for an interim refund of the whole or part of the appropriate tax referable to the basis period for the year of assessment 2001 or the year of assessment 2002, subsection (3) shall apply as if the reference in that subsection to the amount of tax referred to in subsection (2)(*b*) were a reference to—

(*a*) in the case where the claim relates to the basis period for the year of assessment 2001, 74 per cent, and

(*b*) in the case where the claim relates to the basis period for the year of assessment 2002, 135 per cent,

of the amount of tax referred to in subsection (2)(*b*).][1]

(4) (*a*) Where the first-mentioned period is the period in which the trade or profession of the specified person has been set up and commenced, paragraphs (*a*) and (*b*) of subsection (2) shall not apply and the inspector shall, in accordance with this subsection, make an interim refund to the specified person in respect of appropriate tax deducted from relevant payments taken, or to be taken, into account in computing the profits or gains of the trade or profession.

(*b*) For the purposes of determining the amount of the interim refund, the inspector shall determine—

(i) an amount equal to the amount of tax at the standard rate on an amount determined by the formula—

$$E \times \frac{A}{B} \times \frac{C}{P}$$

where—

A is the estimated total amount of the relevant payments to be taken into account as income in computing for tax purposes the profits or gains of the first-mentioned period,

B is the estimated total sum of all amounts to be so taken into account as income in computing those profits or gains,

C is the estimated number of months or fractions of months comprised in the period in respect of which the claim to the refund is made,

E is the estimated amount to be laid out or expended wholly and exclusively by the specified person in the first-mentioned period for the purposes of the trade or profession, and

P is the estimated number of months or fractions of months comprised in the first-mentioned period,

and the inspector shall make the estimates referred to in this formula to the best of his or her knowledge and belief and in accordance with the information available to him or her, and

(ii) the amount of appropriate tax deducted from the relevant payments in respect of which forms have been furnished in accordance with subsection (2)(*c*) after deducting from that amount any amount of such tax already refunded for the period in respect of which the claim to a refund is made.

(*c*) The inspector shall refund an amount of appropriate tax equal to the lesser of the amounts determined at subparagraphs (i) and (ii) of paragraph (*b*).

(5) Where the specified person claims and proves the presence of particular hardship, the Revenue Commissioners may waive (in whole or in part) one or more of the conditions for the making of a refund specified in this section and, where they so waive such a condition or conditions, they shall determine, having regard to all the circumstances and taking into account the objects and intentions of subsections (1) to (4), an amount of a refund or a further refund which they consider to be just and reasonable and they shall authorise the inspector to make such refund or such further refund, as the case may be, accordingly.

(6) For the purposes of this section, the income of a specified person for an accounting period or a basis period for a year of assessment shall be the total of all amounts received or receivable by the specified person which are taken into account in computing the profits or gains of the specified person's trade or profession for that period.

Amendments

1 Subs (3A) inserted by FA 2001 s 77(2) and Sch 2 para 30 with effect from 6 April 2001.

Cross-references

Apportionment of credits or interim refunds, subs (2)(*c*): s 528; limitation on: s 529.

Definitions

inspector: ss 2(1), 5(1), 852; month: IA 1937 Sch; person: IA 1937 s 11(*c*); profession: s 2(1); profits: s 4(1); standard rate: ss 3(1), 15; trade: s 3(1); year of assessment: ss 2(1), 5(1).

Statement of practice

Interim refunds, circumstances regarded as constituting "particular hardship" (subs (5)): SP IT/3/90, December 1990.

Former enactments

FA 1987 s 19.

528 Apportionment of credits or interim refunds of appropriate tax

Where the form referred to in either section 526(3) or 527(2)(*c*) relates to 2 or more specified persons, any necessary apportionment shall be made for the purposes of giving effect to sections 526 and 527.

Definitions

person: IA 1937 s 11(*c*).

Former enactments

FA 1987 s 20.

529 Limitation on credits or interim refunds of appropriate tax

No amount of appropriate tax shall be set off or refunded more than once under this Chapter, and any amount of appropriate tax refunded in accordance with section 527 shall not be available for set-off under section 526.

Cross-references

Credit for appropriate tax borne: s 526(1), (2).

Former enactments

FA 1987 s 21.

CHAPTER 2
Payments to Subcontractors in Certain Industries

Cross references

Manufacturing (10%) rate, exclusion of mining and construction operations: s 444(1)(*b*), (3).

Payment of tax by donation of heritage items, meaning of "Tax Acts" excludes this Chapter: s 1003(1)(*a*).

Power of inspection, tax deduction from payments to certain subcontractors, meanings of "principal", "relevant contract", "relevant operations" and "subcontractor" applied: s 904(1).

Professional services withholding tax (PSWT), the provisions of this Chapter relating to assessment, collection and recovery of tax deductible under s 531(1) apply to the assessment, collection and recovery of PSWT: s 525(6).

Taxes (Offset of Repayments) Regulations 2002, SI No 471 of 2002, regs 2(1) (interpretation — "taxhead" para (*a*)), 3(*a*)(iv) (order of priority of offset against liabilities) and 4(*a*)(vii) (special arrangements regarding corporation tax, income tax and capital gains tax).

Revenue information

Information leaflet IT25 — Employees and Contractors in the Construction Industry.

Information leaflet IT63 — Relevant Contracts Tax (Construction, Forestry and Meat Processing Industries) — Guide for Principal Contractors.

Information leaflet IT64 — Relevant Contracts Tax (Construction, Forestry and Meat Processing Industries) — Guide for Sub-Contractors.

eBriefing

eBrief no 12–2004 From 5 April 2004, applications for C2s or payment cards from traders in Counties Dublin, Wicklow, Meath and Kildare should be directed to the local Revenue District (previously dealt with in Tallaght).

Tax Briefing

TB22 June 1996 p 1 — Relevant Contracts Tax (RCT).

TB26 Apr 1997 p 16 — Form RCT1 Requirements.

TB27 Aug 1997 p 3 — RCT — Finance Act 1997 changes.

TB33 Sept 1998 p 15 — Employed or Self-Employed — Guidelines.
TB37 Oct 1999 pp 8–9 — Relevant Contracts Tax — Finance Act 1999 Changes.
TB49 Aug 2002 p 14 — Relevant Contracts Tax — Revenue will accept that RCT does not apply where relevant operations are performed wholly abroad. RCT will be regarded as applying where the relevant operations are performed or partly performed in the State. For this purpose, the State is taken to include the territory of Ireland, its territorial waters and any area outside the territorial waters of Ireland over which Ireland has exploration or exploitation rights.
Contracts are sometimes performed partly in the State and partly outside. Where the performance abroad is merely incidental to the performance in the State, RCT will be regarded as appying to the full contract.
In all other cases, RCT need only be applied to the part of the contract that is performed in the State. Where there is a single price for the entire contract, payments may be apportioned on a basis agreed in advance with the Inspector of Taxes. For example, payment for construction of a gas pipeline to the UK might be apportioned on the basis of the respective lengths of the pipeline in the State and in the UK.
TB51 Jan 2003 pp 11–12 — Relevant Contracts Tax and Integrated Taxation Processing.
TB52 May 2003 p 11–12 — Relevant Contracts Tax — Finance Act 2003 changes.
TB52 May 2003 p 25 — RCT and the treatment of interest paid under the Late Payment in Commercial Transactions Regulations, SI No 388 of 2002.
TB54 Dec 2003 p 5 — Only new 8 digit RCTDC/C45 form should be used from 1 February 2004 when principal contractors are making payments to uncertified subcontractors.
TB58 Dec 2004 pp 1–2 — New Registration Procedures for Principal Contractors.

530 Interpretation (Chapter 2)

(1) In this Chapter—

"certificate of authorisation" means a certificate issued under section 531(11);

"certificates of deduction" has the meaning assigned to it by section 531(6)(*f*);

[**"certified subcontractor"**, in relation to a principal, means a subcontractor—

(*a*) in respect of whom the principal holds, at the time of making a payment under a relevant contract to the subcontractor, a relevant payments card for the year in which the payment is made, and

(*b*) in respect of whom the principal has not received a notice under paragraph (*a*) of subsection 13 of section 531;][1]

"construction operations" means operations of any of the following descriptions—

(*a*) the construction, alteration, repair, extension, demolition or dismantling of buildings or structures,

(*b*) the construction, alteration, repair, extension or demolition of any works forming, or to form, part of the land, including walls, roadworks, power lines, [telecommunication apparatus,][2] aircraft runways, docks and harbours, railways, inland waterways, pipelines, reservoirs, water mains, wells, sewers, industrial plant and installations for purposes of land drainage,

(*c*) the installation in any building or structure of systems of heating, lighting, air-conditioning, soundproofing, ventilation, power supply, drainage, sanitation, water supply, burglar or fire protection,

(*d*) the external cleaning of buildings (other than cleaning of any part of a building in the course of normal maintenance) or the internal cleaning of buildings and structures, in so far as carried out in the course of their construction, alteration, extension, repair or restoration,

(*e*) operations which form an integral part of, or are preparatory to, or are for rendering complete such operations as are described in paragraphs (*a*) to (*d*), including site clearance, earth-moving, excavation, tunnelling and boring, laying of foundations, erection of scaffolding, site restoration, landscaping and the provision of roadways and other access works,

(*f*) operations which form an integral part of, or are preparatory to, or are for rendering complete, the drilling for or extraction of minerals, oil, natural gas or the exploration for, or exploitation of, natural resources,

(*g*) the haulage for hire of materials, machinery or plant for use, whether used or not, in any of the construction operations referred to in paragraphs (*a*) to (*f*);

"the contractor" has the meaning assigned to it by the definition of **"relevant contract"**;

"director" means—

(*a*) in relation to a body corporate the affairs of which are managed by a board of directors or similar body, a member of that board or body,

(*b*) in relation to a body corporate the affairs of which are managed by a single director or similar person, that director or person,

(*c*) in relation to a body corporate the affairs of which are managed by the members themselves, a member of the body corporate,

and includes any person who is or has been a director;

"employee", in relation to a body corporate, includes any person taking part in the management of the affairs of the body corporate who is not a director, and includes a person who is to be or has been an employee;

"forestry operations" means operations of any of the following descriptions—

(*a*) the thinning, lopping or felling of trees in woods, forests or other plantations,

(*b*) with effect from the 6th day of October, 1997, the planting of trees in woods, forests or other plantations,

(*c*) with effect from the 6th day of October, 1997, the maintenance of woods, forests and plantations and the preparation of land, including woods or forests which have been harvested, for planting,

(*d*) the haulage or removal of thinned, lopped or felled trees,

(*e*) the processing (including cutting or preserving) of wood from thinned, lopped or felled trees in sawmills or other like premises,

(*f*) the haulage for hire of materials, machinery or plant for use, whether used or not, in any of the operations referred to in paragraphs (*a*) to (*e*);

[**"income tax month"** means—

(*a*) in relation to a period prior to 6 December 2001, a month beginning on the 6th day of a month and ending on the 5th day of the next month,

(*b*) the period beginning on 6 December 2001 and ending on 31 December 2001, and

(*c*) thereafter, a calendar month;][3]

[**"meat processing operations"** means operations of any of the following descriptions—

(*a*) the slaughter of cattle, sheep, pigs, domestic fowl, turkeys, guinea-fowl, ducks or geese, (*b*) the catching of domestic fowl, turkeys, guinea-fowl, ducks or geese,

(*c*) the division (including cutting or boning) sorting, packaging (including vacuum packaging), rewrapping or branding of, or the application of any other similar process to, the carcasses or any part of the carcasses (including meat) of slaughtered cattle, sheep, pigs, domestic fowl, turkeys, guinea-fowl, ducks or geese,

(*d*) the application of methods of preservation (including cold storage) to the carcasses or any part of the carcasses (including meat) of slaughtered cattle, sheep, pigs, domestic fowl, turkeys, guinea-fowl, ducks or geese,

(*e*) the loading or unloading of the carcasses or part of the carcasses (including meat) of slaughtered cattle, sheep, pigs, domestic fowl, turkeys, guinea-fowl, ducks or geese at any establishment where any of the operations referred to in paragraphs (*a*), (*c*) and (*d*) are carried on,

(*f*) the haulage of the carcasses or any part of the carcasses (including meat) of slaughtered cattle, sheep, pigs, domestic fowl, turkeys, guinea-fowl, ducks or geese from any establishment where any of the operations referred to in paragraphs (*a*), (*c*) and (*d*) are carried on,

[(*fa*) the rendering of the carcasses or any part of the carcasses of slaughtered cattle, sheep, pigs, domestic fowl, turkeys, guinea-fowl, ducks or geese,][4]

(*g*) the cleaning down of any establishment where any of the operations referred to in paragraphs (*a*), (*c*) and (*d*) are carried on,

(*h*) the grading, sexing and transport of day-old chicks of domestic fowl, turkeys, guineafowl, ducks or geese,

(*i*) the haulage for hire of cattle, sheep, pigs, domestic fowl, turkeys, guinea-fowl, ducks or geese or of any of the materials, machinery or plant for use, whether used or not, in any of the operations referred to in paragraphs (*a*) *to* (*h*).][5]

"the principal" has the meaning assigned to it by the definition of **"relevant contract"**;

"proprietary director", means a director of a company who is either the beneficial owner of, or able, either directly or through the medium of other companies or by any other indirect means, to control, more than 15 per cent of the ordinary share capital of the company;

"proprietary employee" means an employee who is either the beneficial owner of, or able, either directly or through the medium of other companies or by any other indirect means, to control, more than 15 per cent of the ordinary share capital of the company;

[**"qualifying period"** means the period of 3 years, or such shorter period as the inspector may allow, ending on [31 December][6] in the year preceding the year of assessment which is the first year of assessment of the period, in respect of which a certificate of authorisation is sought together with the period, if any, from [1 January][7] in the said first year of assessment to the date on which the application for the said certificate is received by the Revenue Commissioners;][8]

"relevant contract" means a contract (not being a contract of employment) whereby a person (in this Chapter referred to as **"the contractor"**) is liable to another person (in this Chapter referred to as **"the principal"**)—

(*a*) to carry out relevant operations,

(*b*) to be answerable for the carrying out of such operations by others, whether under a contract with the contractor or under other arrangements made or to be made by the contractor, or

[(*c*) to furnish the contractor's own labour or the labour of others in the carrying out of relevant operations or to arrange for the labour of others to be furnished for the carrying out of such operations,][9]

but, as respects relevant contracts entered into on or after the 15th day of May, 1996, a separate relevant contract shall be deemed to exist between the principal and each individual member of a gang or group of persons, including a partnership in respect of which the principal has not received a relevant payments card, where relevant operations are performed collectively by the gang or group, notwithstanding that any payment or part of a payment in respect of such relevant operations is made by the principal to one or more of the gang or group or to some other person;

"relevant operations" means construction operations, forestry operations or meat processing operations, as the case may be;

"relevant payments card" has the meaning assigned to it by section 531(12);

"relevant tax deduction card" has the meaning assigned to it by section 531(6)(*c*)(iii);

"subcontractor" has the meaning assigned to it by section 531(1).

[**"uncertified subcontractor"** means a subcontractor who is not a certified subcontractor.][10]

(2) In relation to a case where a subcontractor is chargeable to corporation tax, unless the context otherwise requires, references in this Chapter to tax shall include references to corporation tax and references to a year of assessment shall include references to an accounting period.

(3) For the purposes of the definition of **"proprietary director"** and **"proprietary employee"**, ordinary share capital which is owned or controlled as referred to in those definitions by a person, being a spouse or a minor child of a director or employee, or by a trustee of a trust for the benefit of a person or persons, being or including any such person or such director or employee, shall be deemed to be owned or controlled by such director or employee and not by any other person.

Amendments

1 Definition of "certified subcontractor" inserted by FA 2001 s 28(*a*) with effect from 6 April 2001.

2 Inserted by FA 2002 s 51(1)(*a*)(i) with effect from 1 April 2002.

3 Definition of "income tax month" substituted by FA 2001 s 77(2) and Sch 2 para 31(*a*) with effect from 6 April 2001.

4 Definition of "meat processing operations" para (*fa*) inserted by FA 2002 s 51(1)(*a*)(ii) with effect from 1 April 2002.

5 Definition of "meat processing operations" substituted by FA 1998 s 37(1)(*a*) with effect from 6 October 1998; prior to that the following definition applies:

"'**meat processing operations**' means operations of any of the following descriptions—

(*a*) the slaughter of cattle, sheep or pigs,

(*b*) the division (including cutting or boning), sorting, packaging (including vacuum packaging) or branding of, or the application of any other similar process to, the carcasses or any part of the carcasses of slaughtered cattle, sheep or pigs, (*c*) the application of methods of preservation (including cold storage) to the carcasses or any part of the carcasses of slaughtered cattle, sheep or pigs,

(*d*) the loading or unloading of the carcasses or any part of the carcasses of slaughtered cattle, sheep or pigs at any establishment where any of the operations referred to in paragraphs (*a*) to (*c*) are carried on;"

6 Substituted by FA 2001 s 77(2) and Sch 2 paras 31(*b*) and 61(*d*) with effect from 1 January 2002; previously "the 5th day of April".

7 Substituted by FA 2001 s 77(2) and Sch 2 paras 31(*b*) and 61(*d*) with effect from 1 January 2002; previously "the 6th day of April".

8 Definition of "qualifying period" substituted by FA 1999 s 18(1)(*a*)(ii) for 1999–2000 and later tax years.

9 Definition of "relevant contract" para (*c*) substituted by FA 1999 s 18(1)(*a*)(iii) for 1999–2000 and later tax years.

10 Definition of "uncertified subcontractor" inserted by FA 2001 s 28(*b*) with effect from 6 April 2001.

Cross-references

Higher rate of corporation tax: s 21A(1) (construction operations).

Income Tax (Relevant Contracts) Regulations 2000, SI No 71 of 2000, meanings of "principal", "proprietary director", "relevant contract" and "relevant operations" applied: ITRCR 2000 Reg 2.

Payment to subcontractors in certain industries, meaning of "principal" applied: s 531(6)(*ba*)(i).

Professional services withholding tax, relevant payment: s 520(1).

Relief from income tax in respect of income from dealing in residential development land: s 644A(1)(construction operations).

Case law

Subs (1): Two sister companies arranged that quarrying material should be sold by the excavating company to hauliers who would, in turn, sell it to the other company and also arrange to have the material delivered to customers of the second company. Arrangement held not to involve a "construction operations" contract: *O'Grady v Laragan Quarries Ltd* ITR Vol IV p 269.

Processes involved in the operation of road marking companies include processes which are construction operations – *Judge v Highway Markings Ltd* [Appeal Commissioners 1994].

Revenue precedents

Issue: Whether payments for cold storage facilities in respect of meat products fall within the RCT scheme.

Decision: Such payments do fall within the RCT scheme. The activity comes within the definition of meat processing operations.

Former enactments

FA 1970 s 17(1) and (13); FA 1972 Sch 1 Pt III para 4; FA 1974 s 64(2); FA 1976 s 21; FA 1992 s 28(*a*); FA 1995 s 18(1)(*a*); FA 1996 s 41(*a*); FA 1997 s 13(1)(*a*), 146(1) and Sch 9 Pt I para 5(3).

Corresponding UK tax provision

Income and Corporation Taxes Act 1988 s 567.

---

531 Payments to subcontractors in certain industries

(1) Subject to this section, where in the performance of a relevant contract in the case of which the principal is—

(*a*) a person who, in respect of the whole or any part of the relevant operations to which the contract relates, is the contractor under another relevant contract,

(*b*) a person—

(i) carrying on a business which includes the erection of buildings or the manufacture, treatment or extraction of materials for use, whether used or not, in construction operations,

[(ii) carrying on a business of meat processing operations in an establishment approved and inspected in accordance with the European Communities (Fresh Meat) Regulations, 1997 (SI No 434 of 1997) or, as the case may be, the European Communities (Fresh Poultry-meat) Regulations, 1996 (SI No 3 of 1996), or][1]

(iii) carrying on a business which includes the processing (including cutting and preserving) of wood from thinned or felled trees in sawmills or other like premises or the supply of thinned or felled trees for such processing,

(*c*) a person connected with a company carrying on a business mentioned in paragraph (*b*),

(*d*) a local authority, a public utility society (within the meaning of section 2 of the Housing Act, 1966) or a body referred to in subparagraph (i) or (ii) of section 12(2)(*a*) or section 19 or 45 of that Act,

(*e*) a Minister of the Government,

(*f*) any board established by or under statute, or

(*g*) a person who carries on any gas, water, electricity, hydraulic power, dock, canal or railway undertaking,

the principal makes a payment, or as respects relevant contracts entered into on or after the 15th day of May, 1996, is deemed to make a payment pursuant to subsection (3), to another person (whether the contractor or not and in this section referred to as **"the subcontractor"**), the principal shall deduct from the payment and pay to the Collector-General tax at the rate of 35 per cent of the amount of such payment.

(2) A person carrying on a business shall not be deemed to be a person of a kind specified in subsection (1)(*b*) by reason only of the fact that in the course of that business such person erects buildings for the use or occupation of such person or employees of such person.

(3) As respects relevant contracts entered into on or after the 15th day of May, 1996, where relevant operations are performed by a gang or group of persons, including a partnership in respect of which the principal has not received a relevant payments card, and notwithstanding that any payment or part of a payment in respect of such relevant operations is made by the principal to one or more of the gang or group or to some other person, then, for the purposes of this section and any regulations made under this section, such payment or part of a payment shall be deemed to have been made by the principal to the individual members of that gang or group in the proportions in which the payment or any amount in respect of the payment is to be divided amongst them.

[(3A)(*a*) [Not later than the 14th day of an income tax month],[2] a principal or any person who was previously a principal and who has been required to do so by notice in writing from the Revenue Commissioners, shall—

(i) make a return to the Collector-General, on the prescribed form, of the amount, if any, of tax which that person was liable under this section to deduct from payments made to uncertified sub-contractors during [the previous income tax month],[3] and

(ii) remit to the Collector the amount of the tax, if any, which the person was so liable to deduct.

(*b*) The Collector-General shall furnish the person concerned with a receipt in respect of the payment; such a receipt shall consist of whichever of the following the Collector-General considers appropriate, namely—

(i) a separate receipt on the prescribed form in respect of each such payment, or

(ii) a receipt on the prescribed form in respect of all such payments that have been made within a period specified in the receipt.][4]

[(3B)(*a*) Subject to paragraph (*b*), where a principal or any person who was previously a principal makes a remittance of tax in respect of a year of assessment or a period comprised in a year of assessment and details of the remittance are not included in a return required to be made under subsection (3A), the amount comprised in the remittance shall be deemed to be a remittance in respect of the first income tax month of the year of assessment.

(*b*) Where, within 1 month of interest being demanded of a person by the Collector-General under subsection (9) by virtue of the application of paragraph (*a*), the person makes a return to the Collector-General under subsection (3A) for the income tax month or months to which the remittance of tax relates and of the amount comprised in the remittance for each of those income tax months, paragraph (*a*) shall be deemed not to have applied and the remittance shall be treated for the purposes of this section as a remittance or, as the case may be, remittances of tax for the respective income tax month or months.][5]

(4) In computing for the purposes of Schedule D the profits or gains arising or accruing to a subcontractor who receives a payment from which tax has been deducted in accordance with subsection (1), the payment shall be treated as being of an amount equal to the aggregate of the net amount received after deduction of the tax and the amount of the tax deducted.

(5) In so far as a subcontractor is chargeable to tax in respect of any profits or gains arising or accruing to the subcontractor from a trade or vocation, the subcontractor shall be treated as having paid on account of tax so chargeable any tax which was deducted from payments taken into account in the computation of those profits or gains and which has not been repaid or for which a set-off has not been made, and the Revenue Commissioners shall make regulations for giving effect to this subsection and those regulations shall, in particular, include provision—

(*a*) as to the manner in which, and the periods for which, tax deducted under this section is to be taken into account as a sum paid on account of the liability to tax of a subcontractor,

(*b*) for repayment, on due claim made for a period (in this paragraph referred to as **"the repayment period"**) [commencing on the 1st day of a year of assessment and ending on the last day of the income tax month in which the payment was made],[6] of such portion of the tax deducted from payments received by a subcontractor during the repayment period (reduced by any amount of such tax repaid or set off) as appears to the Revenue Commissioners to exceed the proportionate part of the amount of tax for which the subcontractor is liable or is estimated to be liable for that year of assessment, and

(*c*) for repayment in cases where the total of the tax deducted from payments received by a subcontractor and not repaid to the subcontractor exceeds the aggregate of—

(i) the amount of tax for which the subcontractor is liable, and

(ii) any amount which the subcontractor is liable to remit—

(I) under the Value-Added Tax Act, 1972,

(II) under the Capital Gains Tax Acts,

(III) under Chapter 4 of Part 42, and

(IV) in respect of—

(A) employment contributions and self-employment contributions under the Social Welfare Acts,

(B) health contributions under the Health Contributions Act, 1979, and

(C) Employment and Training Levy under the Youth Employment Agency Act, 1981, as amended by the Labour Services Act, 1987.

(6) The Revenue Commissioners shall make regulations with respect to the [assessment (including estimated assessment), estimation, charge, collection and recovery of tax deductible under subsection (1)][7] and the regulations may, in relation to such tax, include any matters which might be included in regulations under section 986 in relation to tax deductible under Chapter 4 of Part 42 and, without prejudice to the generality of the foregoing, regulations under this subsection may include provision for—

(*a*) (i) the issue for a year of assessment, or, in relation to such class or classes of subcontractor as may be specified in the regulations, for such longer period as may be so specified, of certificates of authorisation,

(ii) the refusal to issue, appeal against refusal to issue, recall or cancellation of certificates of authorisation and the surrender of such certificates, and

(iii) the production of documents or other material, including a photograph of the subcontractor or, in a case where the subcontractor is not an individual, a photograph of the individual by whom the certificate of authorisation will be produced in accordance with subsection (12)(*a*), in support of an application for a certificate of authorisation;

(*b*) (i) the making, before the entering into of a relevant contract, by the persons who intend to enter into such a contract of a declaration, in a specified form, to the effect that, having regard to guidelines published by the Revenue Commissioners for the information of such persons as to the distinctions between contracts of employment and relevant contracts and without prejudice to the question of whether a particular contract is a contract of employment or a relevant contract, they have satisfied themselves that in their opinion the contract which they propose to enter into is not a contract of employment,

(ii) the publication of guidelines by the Revenue Commissioners for the purposes of subparagraph (i), and

(iii) the keeping by principals of every such declaration and the inspection of any or all such declarations;

[(*ba*) (i) the setting up by the Revenue Commissioners and the maintenance by them of a register containing details of every person who is a principal within the meaning of section 530(1), and

(ii) requiring every such person as is specified in the regulations, to notify the Revenue Commissioners within the period and in such manner as is provided for in the said regulations, that that person is a principal for the purposes of this Chapter;][8]

(*c*) the keeping by principals of—

(i) such records as may be specified in the regulations,

(ii) relevant payments cards and the entry on those cards of such particulars as may be specified in the regulations,

(iii) cards (in this Chapter referred to as **"relevant tax deduction cards"**) in such form as may be prescribed by the regulations and containing particulars of any deductions under subsection (1) and the entry on those cards of such other particulars as may be specified in the regulations;

(*d*) the making to the Revenue Commissioners of such returns relating to the payments made by principals as may be specified in the regulations and the inspection of the records referred to in paragraph (*c*) (including the cards referred to in that paragraph);

(*e*) the keeping by subcontractors of such records as may be specified in the regulations containing particulars of payments received by them, and the inspection of such records;

(*f*) the completion by principals of certificates of tax deducted (in this Chapter referred to as **"certificates of deduction"**) from payments made to subcontractors and, as respects relevant contracts entered into on or after the 15th day of May, 1996, the entry on certificates of deduction of such particulars as may be specified in the regulations;

(*g*) the furnishing by subcontractors to principals of all such information or particulars as are required by principals to enable principals to comply with any provision of regulations made under this section;

(*h*) the sending to subcontractors, in cases where tax was deducted under subsection (1) from payments made to them, of statements containing particulars of their liability (if any) to tax for a year of assessment.

(7) Every regulation made under this section shall be laid before Dáil Éireann as soon as may be after it is made and, if a resolution annulling the regulation is passed by Dáil Éireann within the next 21 days on which Dáil Éireann has sat after the regulation is laid before it, the regulation shall be annulled accordingly, but without prejudice to the validity of anything previously done thereunder.

(8) The provisions of every enactment and of [the Income Tax (Relevant Contracts) Regulations 2000 (SI No 71 of 2000)][9], which apply to the recovery of any amount of tax which a principal of the kind referred to in subsection (1) is liable under this section and those Regulations to pay to the Collector-General shall apply to the recovery of any amount of interest payable on that tax as if that amount of interest were a part of that tax.

(9) Where an amount of tax which a person who is or is deemed to be a principal of the kind referred to in subsection (1) is liable under this section and any regulations under subsection (6) to pay to the Collector-General is not so paid, simple interest on the amount shall be paid by the person to the Collector-General and shall be calculated from

the date on which the amount became due for payment at a rate of [0.0322 per cent for each day or part of a day][10] which the amount remains unpaid.

[(10) Subsection (9) shall apply to tax recoverable from a person by virtue of a notice issued under [the Income Tax (Relevant Contracts) Regulations 2000][11], as if the tax were tax which the person was liable under subsection (3A) to remit—

(i) where the notice relates to an income tax month or months, for the respective income tax month or months referred to in the notice, and

[(ii) where the notice relates to a year of assessment, for the first income tax month in the year of assessment to which the notice relates, but where the inspector determines, or, on appeal against the notice, the Appeal Commissioners determine, the amount of tax which the person was liable to remit, but had not remitted, for each income tax month comprised in the year of assessment, interest shall be calculated and payable in respect of each amount so determined in accordance with subsection (9) as if that amount were included in a notice in respect of the income tax month in question.][12]][13]

(11)(*a*) The Revenue Commissioners shall, on application to them in that behalf by a person, issue to the person a certificate (in this section referred to as a **"certificate of authorisation"**) if they are satisfied—

(i) that the person is or is about to become a subcontractor engaged in the business of carrying out relevant contracts,

(ii) that the business is or will be carried on from a fixed place of business established in a permanent building and has or will have such equipment, stock and other facilities as in the opinion of the Revenue Commissioners are required for the purposes of the business,

(iii) that in connection with the business records to which section 886(2) refers are being or will be kept, and any other records normally kept in connection with such a business are being or will be kept properly and accurately,

(iv) that—

(I) the person, any partnership in which the person is or was a partner and any company (within the meaning of the Companies Act, 1963) of which the person is or was a proprietary director or proprietary employee,

(II) in a case where the person is a partnership, each partner, and

(III) in a case where the person is a company, each director of the company and any person who is either the beneficial owner of, or able, directly or indirectly, to control, more than 15 per cent of the ordinary share capital of the company,

has throughout the qualifying period complied with all the obligations imposed by the Tax Acts, the Capital Gains Tax Acts or the Value-Added Tax Act, 1972, in relation to—

(A) the payment or remittance of the [taxes, interest and penalties][14] required to be paid or remitted under those Acts,

(B) the delivery of returns, and

(C) requests to supply to an inspector accounts of, or other information about, any business carried on, by that individual, partnership or company, as the case may be, ...[15]

(v) that there is good reason to expect that that person, partnership or company will comply with the obligations referred to in subparagraph (iii) in relation to periods ending after the date of termination of the [qualifying period, and][16]

[(vi) in the case of a person who was resident outside the State at some time during the qualifying period, that the person has throughout the qualifying period complied with all the obligations comparable to those mentioned in subparagraph (iv) imposed by the laws of the country in which that person was resident at any time during the qualifying period.][17]

(*b*) A person in respect of whom the Revenue Commissioners are not satisfied in relation to any one or more of the matters specified in [subparagraphs (i) to (iv) and (vi)][18] of paragraph (*a*) shall nevertheless, for the purposes of the issue of a certificate of authorisation, be treated as a person in respect of whom they are so satisfied if the Revenue Commissioners are of the opinion that in all the circumstances such person's failure to satisfy them in relation to such matter or matters ought to be disregarded for those purposes.

[(*ba*) Notwithstanding paragraph (*a*), where the Revenue Commissioners have issued a certificate of authorisation to a person under the provisions of that paragraph or paragraph (*b*), the Revenue Commissioners may issue a further certificate of authorisation to that person without a requirement that the person make a further application to them in that behalf, where they are satisfied, in respect of that person, in relation to the matters specified in subparagraphs (i) to (vi) of paragraph (*a*), or, as the case may be, where the provisions of paragraph (*b*) apply.][19]

(*c*) A certificate of authorisation issued under this subsection shall be valid for such period as the Revenue Commissioners may provide by regulations made pursuant to subsection (6).

[(12)(*a*) Where a subcontractor to whom a certificate of authorisation has been issued produces it to a principal, the principal shall apply to the Revenue Commissioners for a card (in this Chapter referred to as a "relevant payments card") in respect of the subcontractor.

(*b*) Notwithstanding paragraph (*a*), where—

(i) a subcontractor has notified the Revenue Commissioners of details of the bank account, held in the State in the name of the subcontractor or in the case of a subcontractor who is not resident in the State, held either in the State or in the State in which the subcontractor is resident, into which payments in respect of relevant contracts are to be made (hereafter in this subsection referred to as "the nominated bank account"), and

(ii) the principal undertakes to make all payments to the subcontractor in question directly to the nominated bank account,

the principal may apply to the Revenue Commissioners for a relevant payments card where the subcontractor has provided details of the certificate of authorisation to the principal together with details of the nominated bank account into which payments are to be made by the principal.

[(*c*) Notwithstanding paragraphs (*a*) and (*b*), a principal may apply for a relevant payments card in respect of a subcontractor for a year of assessment where—

(i) the principal has been issued with a relevant payments card in respect of the subcontractor for the immediately preceding year of assessment,

(ii) the relevant contract between the principal and the subcontractor in relation to which the relevant payments card is required is likely to be ongoing at the end of that preceding year, and

(iii) the principal has obtained from the subcontractor details of the subcontractor's certificate of authorisation for the year of assessment to which the application for the relevant payments card relates.][20]

(*d*) Where on [the making of an application under paragraph (*a*), (*b*) or (*c*)][21] the Revenue Commissioners are satisfied that a relevant payments card in respect of the subcontractor ought to be issued to the principal, they shall issue such a card to the principal who, on receiving the card shall, subject to subsection (13), be entitled during the [year of assessment][22] (or the unexpired portion of the [year of assessment][22]) to which the relevant payments card relates to make payment without deduction of tax to the subcontractor named on the card but, in the case of an application to which paragraph (*b*) applies or an application to which paragraph (*c*) applies where the relevant payments card mentioned in subparagraph (i) of that paragraph was issued following an application made under and in accordance with paragraph (*b*), any such payments shall be made by the principal directly to the nominated bank account.][23]

(13)(*a*) Where it appears to the Revenue Commissioners that—

(i) a certificate of authorisation was issued on the basis of false or misleading information,

(ii) a certificate of authorisation would not have been issued if information obtained subsequent to its issue had been available at the date of its issue,

(iii) a person to whom a certificate of authorisation was issued has permitted it to be misused,

(iv) in the case of a certificate issued to a company, there has been a change in control (within the meaning of section 432) of the company,

(v) a person to whom a certificate of authorisation was issued has failed to comply with any of the obligations imposed on such person by the Tax Acts, the Capital Gains Tax Acts, the Value-Added Tax Act, 1972, or by any regulations made thereunder in relation to—

(I) the payment or remittance of the taxes required to be paid or remitted under any of those Acts,

(II) the delivery of returns, and

(III) requests to supply to an inspector accounts of, or other information about, any business carried on by such person,

or

(vi) the business of carrying out relevant contracts in relation to which the certificate of authorisation was issued has ceased to be carried on by the person to whom the certificate was issued, the Revenue Commissioners may at any time cancel the certificate and give notice in writing to that effect to any principal.

(*b*) Where a principal receives a notice under paragraph (*a*), the principal shall—

(i) deduct tax in accordance with subsection (1) from any payments made to the person to whom the notice relates on or after the date of receipt of the notice, and

(ii) return to the Revenue Commissioners any relevant payments cards issued to the principal in relation to that person and any relevant tax deduction card kept by the principal in relation to that person.

(*c*) The Revenue Commissioners shall advise a person in relation to whom a notice under paragraph (*a*) was issued of the issue of such notice and shall require such person to return to them forthwith the certificate of authorisation issued to such person.

(14)(*a*) Where any person—

(i) for the purpose of obtaining a certificate of authorisation or a relevant payments card makes any false statement or furnishes any document which is false in a material particular,

(ii) disposes of a certificate of authorisation otherwise than by the return of the certificate to the Revenue Commissioners,

(iii) fails to return a certificate of authorisation to the Revenue Commissioners when required to do so in accordance with subsection (13)(*c*),

(iv) is in possession of a certificate of authorisation that was not issued to such person by the Revenue Commissioners, or

(v) produces to a principal a certificate of authorisation after such person has been advised by the Revenue Commissioners of the issue of a notice under subsection (13)(*c*),

such person shall be guilty of an offence and shall be liable on summary conviction to a fine of [€1,265][24] or, at the discretion of the court, to imprisonment for a term not exceeding 6 months or to both the fine and the imprisonment.

(*b*) Any person who aids, abets, counsels or procures—

(i) the obtaining of a certificate of authorisation by means of a false statement,

(ii) the use by any person, other than the person to whom it was issued by the Revenue Commissioners, of a certificate of authorisation, or

(iii) the production to a principal of a document that is not a certificate of authorisation but purports to be such a certificate,

shall be guilty of an offence and shall be liable on summary conviction to a fine of [€1,265][24] or, at the discretion of the court, to imprisonment for a term not exceeding 6 months or to both the fine and the imprisonment.

(*c*) Any person who—

(i) fails to enter on a relevant payments card or relevant tax deduction card such particulars as are required to be entered on that card by virtue of this section and any regulations made under this section,

(ii) fails to return to the Revenue Commissioners the relevant payments card or relevant tax deduction card in accordance with subsection (13)(*b*),

(iii) returns to the Revenue Commissioners any such card on which are entered particulars which are incorrect in any material particular,

(iv) fails to comply with any provision of regulations made under this section requiring such person—

(I) to make any declaration,

(II) to provide any information or particulars to principals, or

(III) to keep or produce any records, documents or declarations,

(v) fails to give a subcontractor from whom tax has been deducted under subsection (1) a certificate of deduction in the prescribed form containing such particulars as are required to be entered in that certificate by virtue of any regulations made under this section, or

(vi) being a company to which a certificate of authorisation has been issued under subsection (11), fails to notify the Revenue Commissioners of a change in control (within the meaning of section 432) of the company,

shall be guilty of an offence and shall be liable on summary conviction to a fine of [€1,265][24].

(15) Notwithstanding any other enactment, summary proceedings in respect of offences under this section may be instituted within 10 years of the commission of the offence.

(16) Section 987(4), subsection (4) of section 1052 (other than as that subsection applies in relation to proceedings for the recovery of a penalty in relation to a return referred to in sections 879 and 880), subsections (3) and (7) of section 1053 and sections 1068 and 1069 shall, with any necessary modifications, apply for the purposes of this section and any regulations made under this section as they apply for the purposes of those provisions.

(17) Any person who is aggrieved by a refusal by the Revenue Commissioners to issue a certificate of authorisation under this section may, by notice in writing to that effect given to the Revenue Commissioners within 30 days from the date of such refusal, apply to have such person's application heard and determined by the Appeal Commissioners.

[(17A) Any person who is aggrieved by the cancellation of a certificate of authorisation by the Revenue Commissioners in accordance with subsection (13) may, by notice in writing to that effect given to the Revenue Commissioners within 30 days from the date of such cancellation, appeal against such cancellation to the Appeal Commissioners but, pending the decision of the Appeal Commissioners in the matter, unless the Revenue Commissioners, on application to them, reinstate the certificate of authorisation pending the making of that decision, the certificate shall remain cancelled.][25]

(18) The Appeal Commissioners shall hear and determine an appeal made to them under subsection (17) [or subsection (17A)][26] as if it were an appeal against an assessment to income tax and, subject to subsection (19), the provisions of the Income Tax Acts relating to such an appeal (including the provisions relating to the rehearing of an appeal and to the statement of a case for the opinion of the High Court on a point of law) shall apply accordingly with any necessary modifications.

(19) On the hearing of an appeal made under subsection (17), the Appeal Commissioners shall have regard to all matters to which the Revenue Commissioners may or are required to have regard under this section.

(20) For the purposes of the hearing or rehearing of an appeal under [subsection (17) or subsection (17A)][27], the Revenue Commissioners may nominate any of their officers to act on their behalf.

Amendments

1 Subs (1)(*b*)(ii) substituted by FA 1998 s 37(1)(*b*) with effect from 6 October 1998; previously it read:

"(ii) carrying on a business of meat processing operations in an establishment approved and inspected in accordance with the European Communities (Fresh Meat) Regulations, 1987 (SI No 284 of 1987), or".

2 Substituted by FA 2001 s 77(2) and Sch 2 paras 32(*a*) and 61(*d*) as on and from 1 January 2002; previously "Within 9 days from the end of an income tax month".

3 Substituted by FA 2001 s 77(2) and Sch 2 paras 32(*a*) and 61(*d*) as on and from 1 January 2002; previously "that income tax month".

4 Subs (3A) inserted by FA 1999 s 18(1)(*b*)(i) for 1999–2000 and later tax years.

5 Subs (3B) inserted by FA 2003 s 33(1)(*a*) with effect for 2003 and later tax years.

6 Substituted by FA 2001 s 77(2) and Sch 2 paras 32(*a*) and 61(*d*) as on and from 1 January 2002; previously "commencing on the 6th day of April in a year of assessment and ending on the 5th day of the month following the date of the payment or, if the payment was made on or before the 5th day of a month, ending on the 5th day of that month".

7 Substituted by FA 1999 s 18(1)(*b*)(ii) for 1999–2000 and later tax years; previously "assessment (including estimated assessment), charge, collection and recovery of tax deductible under subsection (1)".

8 Subs (6)(*ba*) inserted by FA 2004 s 20(1)(*a*) with effect from 25 March 2004.

9 Substituted by FA 2002 s 51(1)(*b*)(i) with effect from 6 April 2000; previously "the Income Tax (Construction Contracts) Regulations, 1971 (SI No 1 of 1971),".

10 Substituted by FA 2002 s 129(1)(*b*) with effect from 1 September 2002 as regards interest chargeable in respect of an amount due to be paid or remitted, whether before, on, or after that date; previously "1 per cent for each month or part of a month during".

11 Substituted by FA 2002 s 51(1)(*b*)(ii) with effect from 6 April 2000; previously "the Income Tax (Construction Contracts) Regulations, 1971 (SI No 1 of 1971),".

12 Subs (10)(ii) substituted by FA 2003 s 33(1)(*b*) with effect for 2003 and later tax years.

13 Subs (10) substituted by FA 1999 s 18(1)(*b*)(iii) for 1999–2000 and later tax years.

14 Substituted by FA 2002 s 51(1)(*b*)(iii)(I) with effect from 1 April 2002; previously "taxes".

15 Deleted by FA 1999 s 18(1)(*b*)(iv)(I) for 1999–2000 and later tax years; previously "and".

16 Substituted by FA 1999 s 18(1)(*b*)(iv)(II) for 1999–2000 and later tax years; previously "qualifying period.".

17 Subs (11)(*a*)(vi) inserted by FA 1999 s 18(1)(*b*)(iv)(III) for 1999–2000 and later tax years.

18 Substituted by FA 2002 s 51(1)(*b*)(iii)(II) with effect from 1 January 2002; previously "subparagraphs (i) to (iv)".

19 Subs (11)(*ba*) inserted by FA 2004 s 20(1)(*b*) with effect from 1 January 2004.

20 Subs (12)(*c*) substituted by FA 2003 s 33(1)(*c*)(i) as respects applications made under TCA 1997 s 531(12)(*c*) on or after 28 March 2003.

21 Substituted by FA 2003 s 33(1)(*c*)(ii) as respects applications made under TCA 1997 s 531(12)(*c*) on or after 28 March 2003; previously "such application".

22 Substituted by FA 2001 s 77(2) and Sch 2 para 32(*c*) with effect from 6 April 2001; previously "income tax year".

23 Subs (12) substituted by FA 1999 s 18(1)(*b*)(v) in respect of applications for relevant payments cards made on or after 6 October 1999.

24 Substituted by FA 2001 s 240(1) and (2)(*k*) and Sch 5 Pt 1 as respects any act or omission which takes place or begins on or after 1 January 2002; previously "£1,000".

25 Subs (17A) inserted by FA 1999 s 18(1)(*b*)(vi) for 1999–2000 and later tax years.

26 Inserted by FA 1999 s 18(1)(*b*)(vii) for 1999–2000 and later tax years.

27 Substituted by FA 2004 s 20(1)(*c*) with effect for 1999–2000 and later years of assessment; previously "subsection (17)".

Cross-references

Certified subcontractor, subs 13(*a*): s 530(1).

Deduction from consideration on disposal of certain assets, meaning of "certificate of authorisation" applied: s 980(8A)(*a*)(i).

Income Tax (Relevant Contracts) Regulations 2000 ITRCR 2000, SI No 71 of 2000; Regs 2 ("principal"), 12(1)(*a*), 13(1)(*a*), (*b*)(ii), 14(1), (3)(*b*); subs (1): Regs 2("sub-contractor"), 6, 16(1); subs (3A): Reg 13(1), (2)(*c*); subs (5): Regs 2 ("repayment period"), 16(3)(*c*)(ii); subs (6)(*a*)(i): Reg 11(*b*); subs (11): Reg 2 ("sub-contractor's certificate"); subs 11(*a*): Reg 11(2)(*a*)(ii); subs (11)(*b*): Reg 11(2)(*c*); subs (12)(*a*): Regs 9(1), 10(4), 18(2); subs (12)(*b*): Reg 18(3); subs (12)(*c*): Reg 18(4); subs (12)(*a*), (*b*), (*c*): Regs 8(2)(*a*), 18(1); subs 13(*a*): Regs 2, 19(*c*), (*d*).

Penalty: Sch 29 column 1.

Penalty: Sch 29 column 3.

Power of inspection, tax deduction from payments to certain subcontractors, meaning of "records" applied: s 904(1).

Priority in winding up, subs (1): s 1000(*a*).

Professional services withholding tax, "relevant payment" excludes payments subject to relevant contracts withholding tax: s 520(1); s 525(6).

Relevant payments card, subs (12), meaning applied for this Chapter: s 530(1).

Relevant tax deduction card, subs (6)(*c*)(ii), meaning applied for this Chapter: s 530(1).

Revenue offences, subss (1), (3A): s 1078(2)(ii).

Status of interest on unpaid taxes and duties, subs (9): s 1089(1)(*c*).

Subcontractor, subs (1), meaning applied for this Chapter: s 530(1).

Regulations

Income Tax (Relevant Contracts) Regulations, 2000 (SI No 71 of 2000).

Income Tax (Relevant Contracts) Regulations, 2001 (SI No 131 of 2001).

Income Tax (Relevant Contracts) Regulations 2004 (SI No 761 of 2004).

Revenue precedents

Issue: Whether Inspector is entitled to be present at a hearing in accordance with Regulation 17 of the 1971 RCT regulations.

Decision: The Inspector is not entitled to be present at such a hearing.

Issue: Whether a supplier of Liquefied Petroleum Gas is a person carrying on a gas undertaking for the purposes of TCA 1997 s 531(1)(g).

Decision: Yes.

Issue: Whether a principal contractor who makes a payment in kind rather than a payment of money to subcontractor is obliged to operate RCT on the payment in kind.

Decision: RCT applies to payments in kind in the same way as it applies to payments of money. "Payment" in TCA 1997 s 531 (1) can include payment other than in money form. The value of the payment in kind is the market value. This can be determined at appeal, if necessary.

Definitions

Appeal Commissioners: s 2(1); Collector-General: s 2(1); Dáil Éireann: IA 1937 Sch; High Court: IA 1937 Sch; Income Tax Acts: s 1(2); inspector: ss 2(1), 5(1), 852; land: IA 1937 Sch; local authority: s 2(1); month: IA 1937 Sch; person: IA 1937 s 11(*c*); statute: IA 1937 s 3; trade: s 3(1); writing: IA 1937 Sch; year of assessment: ss 2(1), 5(1).

Former enactments

FA 1970 s 17(2)–(12) and (14)–(17); FA 1976 s 21; FA 1978 s 46; FA 1981 s 7; FA 1990 s 131; FA 1992 s 28(*b*)–(*h*); FA 1995 s 18(1)(*b*) and (*c*); FA 1996 s 41(*b*), (*c*) and (*d*); FA 1970 s 17(10A); FA 1997 s 13(1)(*b*)–(*c*).

Corresponding UK tax provision

Income and Corporation Taxes Act 1988 ss 559–567.

THE TAXATION OF CHARGEABLE GAINS

PART 19
PRINCIPAL PROVISIONS RELATING TO TAXATION OF CHARGEABLE GAINS

Cross-references

Petroleum trade, exploration expenditure: s 693(14).

CHAPTER 1
Assets and Acquisitions and Disposals of Assets

532 Assets

All forms of property shall be assets for the purposes of the Capital Gains Tax Acts whether situated in the State or not, including—

(*a*) options, debts and incorporeal property generally,

(*b*) any currency other than Irish currency, and

(*c*) any form of property created by the person disposing of it, or otherwise becoming owned without being acquired.

Case law

An asset has been held to include the right of a company under a contract of employment to a lump sum on premature termination of the contract by the employee: *O'Brien v Benson's Hosiery (Holdings) Ltd* [1979] STC 735.

The right to payments under a royalty agreement is an asset: *Rank Xerox v Lane* [1979] STC 740.

Where an asset was sold for an lump sum plus an unquantifiable future amount held the right to this future amount was a separate asset: *Marren v Ingles* [1980] STC 500.

The right to a new lease under Landlord and Tenant legislation held to be a separate asset from the original lease: *Bayley v Rogers* [1980] STC 544.

A mere hope is not an asset but a right to share in a designated fund is: *Davenport v Chilver* [1983] STC 426.

The right to sue for negligence is a chose in action and is an asset: *Zim Properties Ltd v Proctor* [1985] STC 90.

The unfettered right to trade freely is not an asset: *Kirby v Thorn EMI plc* [1987] STC 621.

Definitions

allowable loss: ss 4(1), 5(1), 546; chargeable gain: ss 5(1), 545; person: IA 1937 s 11(*c*).

Former enactments

CGTA 1975 s 7(1); FA 1980 s 62(*a*).

Corresponding UK tax provision

Taxation of Chargeable Gains Act 1992 s 21.

533 Location of assets

The situation of assets specified in this section shall, except where otherwise provided by section 29, be determined for the purposes of the Capital Gains Tax Acts in accordance with the following provisions:

(*a*) the situation of rights or interests (otherwise than by means of security) in or over immovable property shall be that of the immovable property;

(*b*) subject to this section, the situation of rights or interests (otherwise than by means of security) in or over tangible movable property shall be that of the tangible movable property;

(*c*) subject to this section, a debt, secured or unsecured, shall be situated in the State only if the creditor is resident in the State;

(*d*) shares or securities issued by any municipal or governmental authority, or by any body created by such an authority, shall be situated in the country of that authority;

(*e*) subject to paragraph (*d*), registered shares or securities shall be situated where they are registered and, if registered in more than one register, where the principal register is situated;

(*f*) a ship or aircraft shall be situated in the State only if the owner is resident in the State, and an interest or right in or over a ship or aircraft shall be situated in the State only if the person entitled to the interest or right is resident in the State;

(*g*) the situation of goodwill as a trade, business or professional asset shall be at the place where the trade, business or profession is carried on;

(*h*) patents, trade marks and designs shall be situated where they are registered and, if registered in more than one register, where each register is situated, and copyright, franchises, rights and licences to use any copyright material, patent, trade mark or design shall be situated in the State if they, or any rights derived from them, are exercisable in the State;

(*i*) a judgment debt shall be situated where the judgment is recorded.

Definitions

person: IA 1937 s 11(*c*); profession: ss 2(1), 5(1); resident: s 5(1); shares: s 5(1); trade: s 5(1), ITA 1967 s 1(1).

Former enactments

CGTA 1975 s 48.

Corresponding UK tax provision

Taxation of Chargeable Gains Act 1992 s 275.

534 Disposals of assets

For the purposes of the Capital Gains Tax Acts—

(*a*) references to a disposal of an asset include, except where the context otherwise requires, references to a part disposal of an asset, and

(*b*) there shall be a part disposal of an asset where an interest or right in or over the asset is created by the disposal, as well as where it subsists before the disposal, and, generally, there shall be a part disposal of an asset where, on a person making a disposal, any description of property derived from the asset remains undisposed of.

Cross-references

Disposals where assets lost or destroyed or become of negligible value: s 538(2A)(*c*)(i).

Options and forfeited deposits: s 540(2).

Tax Briefing

TB41 Sept 2000 p 34 — The partition of a joint tenancy or tenancy in common is a disposal for capital gains tax purposes.

Case law

Subs (1): When a company issues shares it is not disposing of any asset: *Stanton v Drayton Commercial Investments Co Ltd* [1981] STC 525.

Former enactments

CGTA 1975 s 8(1).

Corresponding UK tax provision

Taxation of Chargeable Gains Act 1992 s 21.

535 Disposals where capital sums derived from assets

(1) In this section, **"capital sum"** means any money or money's worth not excluded from the consideration taken into account in the computation of the gain under Chapter 2 of this Part.

(2) (*a*) Subject to sections 536 and 537(1) and to any other exceptions in the Capital Gains Tax Acts, there shall be for the purposes of those Acts a disposal of an asset by its owner where any capital sum is derived from the asset notwithstanding that no asset is acquired by the person paying the capital sum, and this paragraph shall apply in particular to—

(i) capital sums received by means of compensation for any kind of damage or injury to an asset or for the loss, destruction or dissipation of an asset or for any depreciation or risk of depreciation of an asset,

(ii) capital sums received under a policy of insurance of the risk of any kind of damage or injury to, or the loss or depreciation of, an asset,

(iii) capital sums received in return for forfeiture or surrender of a right or for refraining from exercising a right, and

(iv) capital sums received as consideration for use or exploitation of an asset.

(*b*) Without prejudice to paragraph (*a*)(ii) but subject to paragraph (*c*), neither the rights of the insurer nor the rights of the insured under any policy of insurance, whether the risks insured relate to property or not, shall constitute an asset on the disposal of which a gain may accrue, and in this paragraph **"policy of insurance"** does not include a policy of assurance on human life.

(*c*) Paragraph (*b*) shall not apply where the right to any capital sum within paragraph (*a*)(ii) is assigned after the event giving rise to the damage or injury to, or the loss or depreciation of, an asset has occurred, and for the purposes of the Capital Gains Tax Acts such an assignment shall be deemed to be a disposal of an interest in the asset concerned.

Cross-references

Compensation and insurance money, subs (2)(*a*)(i)–(iv): s 536(1)(*a*).

Options and forfeited deposits: s 540(2).

Time of disposal, subs (2)(*a*)(i)–(iv): s 542(2).

Woodlands, subs (2): s 564(1)(*b*).

Case law

Irish

Subs (2): No basis for withholding 15% tax as the taxpayer was ordinarily resident in the State: *Pine Valley Developments Ltd and others v Minister for the Environment and others* ITR Vol IV p 543.

Subs (2)(*a*)(iii): Sum received for abandonment of an option held to be a disposal of an asset: *Dilleen v Kearns* ITR Vol IV p 547. See also *Golding v Kaufmann* [1985] STC 152; *Welbeck Securities Ltd v Powlson* [1987] STC 468.

UK

Subs (2): Compensation payment for loss of mining rights held to be a capital payment derived from an asset: *Glenboig Union Fireclay Company Ltd* (1921) 12 TC 427.

Compensation payment for consequential loss on negligent damage to jetty held to be an income receipt: *London and Thames Haven Oil Wharves Ltd v Attwooll* (1967) 24 TC 491.

Compensation paid to tenant farmer on service of notice to quit held not a capital sum derived from an asset: *Davis v Powell* [1977] STC 32; *Drummond v Austin Brown* [1983] STC 506.
Payment under a statutory compensation fund held to be a capital sum derived from an asset: *Davenport v Chilver* [1983] STC 426.
Compensation payment for loss of stock and consequential loss held not a capital but income receipt: *Lang v Rice* [1984] STC 172.
Where solicitors were negligent in the sale of property, compensation paid was a capital sum derived from an asset: *Zim Properties Ltd v Proctor* [1985] STC 90.
A payment made under a covenant to protect a company from competition held to be a capital sum derived from an asset: *Kirby v Thorn EMI plc* [1987] STC 621.
Held this provision did not apply where consideration was received for a grant of the owner's title to assets and the part disposal rules applied: *Chaloner v Pellipar Investments* [1996] STC 234.

Revenue precedents

Issue: Is a premium payable by the EC in respect of grubbing up of orchards an income or capital receipt?
Decision: It is a capital receipt.
Issue: Liability where policies are cross-assigned by business partners and company directors.
Decision: Where such policies are cross-assigned by partners/directors, no liability to CGT will arise on a disposal of an interest in the policy or on the occasion of sums becoming payable under the policy.

Definitions

person: IA 1937 s 11(*c*).

Former enactments

CGTA 1975 s 8(2) and (7).

Corresponding UK tax provision

Taxation of Chargeable Gains Act 1992 s 22.

536 Capital sums: receipt of compensation and insurance moneys not treated as a disposal in certain cases

(1) (*a*) Subject to paragraph (*b*), where the recipient so claims, receipt of a capital sum within subparagraph (i), (ii), (iii) or (iv) of section 535(2)(*a*) derived from an asset which is not lost or destroyed shall not be treated as a disposal of the asset if—

(i) the capital sum is wholly applied in restoring the asset, or

(ii) the capital sum is applied in restoring the asset except for a part of the capital sum which is not reasonably required for the purpose and which is small as compared with the whole capital sum;

but, if the receipt is not treated as a disposal, all sums which, if the receipt had been so treated, would have been taken into account as consideration for that disposal in the computation of a gain accruing on the disposal shall be deducted from any expenditure allowable under Chapter 2 of this Part as a deduction in computing a gain on the subsequent disposal of the asset.

(*b*) Paragraph (*a*) shall not apply to cases within subparagraph (ii) of that paragraph if immediately before the receipt of the capital sum there is no expenditure attributable to the asset under paragraphs (*a*) and (*b*) of section 552(1) or if the consideration for the part disposal deemed to be effected on receipt of the capital sum exceeds that expenditure.

(2) Where an asset is lost or destroyed and a capital sum received as compensation for the loss or destruction, or under a policy of insurance of the risk of the loss or destruction, is, within one year of receipt or such longer period as the inspector may allow, applied in acquiring an asset in replacement of the asset lost or destroyed, the

owner shall on due claim be treated for the purposes of the Capital Gains Tax Acts as if—

(*a*) the consideration for the disposal of the old asset were (if otherwise of a greater amount) of such amount as would secure that on the disposal neither a loss nor a gain accrued to such owner, and

(*b*) the amount of the consideration for the acquisition of the new asset were reduced by the excess of the amount of the capital sum received as compensation or under the policy of insurance, together with any residual or scrap value, over the amount of the consideration which such owner is treated as receiving under paragraph (*a*).

(3) A claim shall not be made under subsection (2) if part only of the capital sum is applied in acquiring the new asset; but, if all of that capital sum except for a part which is less than the amount of the gain (whether all chargeable gain or not) accruing on the disposal of the old asset is so applied, the owner shall on due claim be treated for the purposes of the Capital Gains Tax Acts as if—

(*a*) the amount of the gain so accruing were reduced to the amount of that part of the capital sum not applied in acquiring the new asset (and, if not all chargeable gain, with a proportionate reduction in the amount of the chargeable gain), and

(*b*) the amount of the consideration for the acquisition of the new asset were reduced by the amount by which the gain is reduced under paragraph (*a*).

(4) This section shall not apply in relation to a wasting asset.

Cross-references

Disposal where capital sum derived from asset: s 535(2)(*a*).
Indexation of expenditure, subs (1)(*a*): s 556(8).

Revenue precedents

Issue: Allowability of relief under s 536(2) where a building has been destroyed.
Decision: In strictness, no relief is due as in law, the building and the land on which it stands are one asset. However, in practice, the "old" and the "new" buildings may be treated as distinct assets separate from the land on which they stand and relief may be allowed under s 536(2). This practice does not apply to a leasehold with less than 50 years to run.

Definitions

chargeable gain: ss 5(1), 545; inspector: ss 2(1), 5(1), 852; part disposal: ss 5(1), 534; wasting asset: ss 5(1), 560, Sch 14 para 2.

Former enactments

CGTA 1975 s 29(1)–(3) and (5).

Corresponding UK tax provision

Taxation of Chargeable Gains Act 1992 s 23.

537 Mortgages and charges not to be treated as disposals

(1) The conveyance or transfer as security of an asset or of an interest or right in or over an asset, or the transfer of a subsisting interest or right as security in or over an asset (including a retransfer on redemption of the security), shall not be treated for the purposes of the Capital Gains Tax Acts as involving any acquisition or disposal of the asset.

(2) Where a person entitled to an asset as security or to the benefit of a charge or incumbrance on an asset deals with the asset for the purpose of enforcing or giving effect to the security, charge or incumbrance, such person's dealings with the asset shall

be treated for the purposes of the Capital Gains Tax Acts as if they were done through such person as nominee by the person entitled to the asset subject to the security, charge or incumbrance, and this subsection shall apply to the dealings of any person appointed to enforce or give effect to the security, charge or incumbrance as receiver and manager or judicial factor as it applies to the dealings of the person so entitled.

(3) An asset shall be treated as having been acquired free of any interest or right as security subsisting at the time of any acquisition of the asset, and as being disposed of free of any such interest or right subsisting at the time of the disposal and, where an asset is acquired subject to any such interest or right, the full amount of the liability thereby assumed by the person acquiring the asset shall form part of the consideration for the acquisition and disposal in addition to any other consideration.

Cross-references

Disposals by liquidators and other persons, subs (2): s 571(5), (6).
Disposal where capital sum derived from asset, subs (1): s 535(2).

Case law

Irish

Subs (2): Under a High Court order a bank obtained authorisation to sell property held on mortgage against a defaulting company. On the disposal the purchaser retained 15% of the consideration in the absence of a clearance certificate. Held that the bank was not entitled to a refund of the payment: *Bank of Ireland Finance Ltd v Revenue Commissioners* ITR Vol IV p 547.

UK

Subs (1): The conveyance of an asset by way of security is not a disposal only where the conveyance is to secure compliance with an obligation on the performance of which the property reverts to the transferor: *Aspden v Hildesley* [1982] STC 206.

Former enactments

CGTA 1975 s 8(4)–(6).

Corresponding UK tax provision

Taxation of Chargeable Gains Act 1992 s 26.

538 Disposals where assets lost or destroyed or become of negligible value

(1) Subject to the Capital Gains Tax Acts and in particular to section 540, the occasion of the entire loss, destruction, dissipation or extinction of an asset shall for the purposes of those Acts constitute a disposal of the asset whether or not any capital sum as compensation or otherwise is received in respect of the destruction, dissipation or extinction of the asset.

(2) Where on a claim by the owner of an asset the inspector is satisfied that the value of an asset has become negligible, the inspector may allow the claim, and thereupon the Capital Gains Tax Acts shall apply as if the claimant had sold and immediately reacquired the asset for a consideration of an amount equal to the value specified in the claim.

[(2A)(*a*) Where as a result of the dissolution of a body corporate, property of the body corporate becomes property of the State by virtue of Part III of the State Property Act, 1954, and the Minister for Finance, in accordance with that Part of that Act, waives the right of the State to that property in favour of a person who holds or has held shares in the body corporate, then, notwithstanding section 31 and subject to paragraph (*c*), any allowable loss (in this subsection referred to as a **"claimed loss"**) accruing to the person by virtue of a claim made under subsection (2) in respect of those shares shall not be allowable as a deduction from chargeable gains in any year of assessment earlier than the year of assessment in which the property is disposed of by the person and any necessary adjustments may be made by way of assessment or additional assessment to give effect to this paragraph.

(*b*) Paragraph (*a*) shall apply in relation to a body corporate which has no share capital as if references to shares included references to any interest in the body corporate possessed by members of the body corporate.

(*c*) For the purposes of paragraph (*a*)—

(i) where in a year of assessment there is a part disposal (within the meaning of section 534) of property, only so much of the claimed loss shall be allowable as a deduction from chargeable gains in that year of assessment as bears to the amount of the claimed loss the same proportion as the market value, when acquired, of the part of the property which is disposed of bears to the market value of the whole of that property when acquired,

(ii) the year of assessment in which property is disposed of by a person, where the disposal, being a disposal to the husband or wife of the person, is a disposal to which section 1028(5) applies, shall mean the year of assessment in which the property is subsequently disposed of by the person's wife or husband, as the case may be, where the subsequent disposal is a disposal to which section 1028(5) does not apply.][1]

(3) For the purposes of subsections (1) and (2), a building and any permanent or semi-permanent structure in the nature of a building may be regarded as an asset separate from the land on which it is situated; but, where either of those subsections applies in accordance with this subsection, the person deemed to make the disposal of the building shall be treated as if such person had also sold and immediately reacquired the site of the building or structure (including in the site any land occupied for purposes ancillary to the use of the building or structure) for a consideration equal to its market value at that time.

Amendments

1 Subs (2A) inserted by FA 1998 s 67 as respects a waiver of the right of the State to property on or after 12 February 1998.

Cross-references

Disposal within four weeks of acquisition: s 581(3).

Exemption from tax in the case of gains on certain disposals of shares, subs (2): Sch 25A para 6.

Companies' chargeable gains, depreciatory transactions within a group, subs (2): s 621(2).

Foreign life policies, disposals of certain policies: s 730K(3).

Offshore funds, disposal of interests in non-qualifying funds, calculation of unindexed gain: Sch 20 par 3(2).

Offshore funds, disposal of an interest in certain offshore funds: s 747E(3).

Case law

Subs (2): The loss is deemed to arise in the tax year in which the claim is lodged: *Williams v Bullivant* [1983] STC 107; *Larner v Warrington* [1985] STC 442.

Little v George Little Sebire & Co (2001) STC 1065.

Revenue precedents

Issue: Assets of negligible value - when is a loss [under s 538(2)] allowed?

Decision: On a strict interpretation a loss arising on a deemed disposal under s 538(2) is allowable only in the year of claim. However, in practice, a claim made within twelve months of the end of the year of assessment or accounting period for which relief is sought will be admitted, provided that the asset was of negligible value in the year of assessment or account period concerned.

Issue: Allowability of losses in respect of goodwill written down to nil in balance sheet.

Decision: Where a partnership has written off goodwill in the balance sheet and a partner makes a subsequent disposal of his share in partnership assets, including goodwill, the partner is treated as realising a loss on the goodwill if he has a cost greater than nil.

Tax Briefing

TB52 May 2003 p 19 — Losses — assets with negligible value.

Definitions

allowable loss: ss 5(1), 546; chargeable gain: ss 5(1), 545; Income Tax Acts: s 1(2); inspector: ss 2(1), 5(1), 852; land: s 5(1), IA 1937 Sch; person: IA 1937 s 11(*c*); resident: s 5(1); shares: s 5(1); year of assessment: ss 2(1), 5(1).

Former enactments

CGTA 1975 s 12(3)–(5).

Corresponding UK tax provision

Taxation of Chargeable Gains Act 1992 s 24.

539 Disposals in cases of hire purchase and similar transactions

A hire purchase or other transaction under which the use and enjoyment of an asset is obtained by a person for a period at the end of which the property in the asset will or may pass to such person shall be treated for the purposes of the Capital Gains Tax Acts, both in relation to such person and in relation to the person from whom the use and enjoyment of the asset is obtained, as if it amounted to an entire disposal of the asset to such person at the beginning of the period for which such person obtains the use and enjoyment of the asset, but subject to such adjustments of tax, whether by means of repayment or discharge of tax or otherwise, as may be required where the period for which such person has the use and enjoyment of the asset terminates without the property in the asset passing to such person.

Definitions

land: s 5(1), IA 1937 Sch; person: IA 1937 s 11(*c*).

Former enactments

CGTA 1975 s 10(2).

Corresponding UK tax provision

Taxation of Chargeable Gains Act 1992 s 27.

540 Options and forfeited deposits

(1) In this section—

"quoted option" means an option which at the time of abandonment or other disposal is quoted and dealt in on a stock exchange in the State or elsewhere in the same manner as shares;

"traded option" means an option which at the time of abandonment or other disposal is quoted on a stock exchange or a futures exchange in the State or elsewhere;

references to an option include references to an option binding the grantor to grant a lease for a premium or to enter into any other transaction which is not a sale, and references to buying and selling in pursuance of an option shall be construed accordingly.

(2) Without prejudice to sections 534 and 535, the grant of an option, including—

(*a*) the grant of an option binding the grantor to sell an asset the grantor does not own and, because the option is abandoned, never has occasion to own, and

(*b*) the grant of an option binding the grantor to buy an asset which, because the option is abandoned, the grantor does not acquire,

shall constitute the disposal of an asset (being the option) for the purposes of the Capital Gains Tax Acts, but subject to the following provisions of this section as to treating the grant of an option as part of a larger transaction.

(3) Where an option is exercised, the grant of the option and the transaction entered into by the grantor in fulfilment of the grantor's obligations under the option shall be treated as a single transaction, and accordingly for the purposes of the Capital Gains Tax Acts—

(*a*) if the option binds the grantor to sell, the consideration for the option shall be part of the consideration for the sale, and

(*b*) if the option binds the grantor to buy, the consideration for the option shall be deducted from the cost of acquisition incurred by the grantor in buying in pursuance of the grantor's obligations under the option.

(4) The exercise of an option by the person for the time being entitled to exercise it shall not constitute the disposal of an asset for the purposes of the Capital Gains Tax Acts by that person; but, if an option is exercised, the acquisition of the option (whether directly from the grantor or not) and the transaction entered into by the person exercising the option in exercise of that person's rights under the option shall be treated as a single transaction, and accordingly for the purposes of the Capital Gains Tax Acts—

(*a*) if the option binds the grantor to sell, the cost of acquiring the option shall be part of the cost of acquiring the asset which is sold, and

(*b*) if the option binds the grantor to buy, the cost of the option shall be treated as a cost incidental to the disposal of the asset which is bought by the grantor of the option.

(5) (*a*) The abandonment of an option by the person for the time being entitled to exercise it shall constitute the disposal of an asset (being the option) for the purposes of the Capital Gains Tax Acts by that person.

(*b*) Subject to subsections (7) and (8)(*a*), the abandonment of an option by the person for the time being entitled to exercise it shall not for the purposes of the Capital Gains Tax Acts give rise to an allowable loss.

(6) In relation to the disposal by means of transfer of an option binding the grantor to sell or buy shares or securities which have a quoted market value on a stock exchange in the State or elsewhere, the option shall be regarded for the purposes of the Capital Gains Tax Acts as a wasting asset the life of which ends when the right to exercise the option ends, or when the option becomes valueless, whichever is the earlier, but without prejudice to the application of the provisions of Chapter 2 of this Part relating to wasting assets to other descriptions of options.

(7) Where an option, being an option to acquire assets exercisable by a person intending to use the assets, if acquired, for the purposes of a trade carried on by that person or which that person commences to carry on within 2 years of that person's acquisition of the option, is disposed of or abandoned, then—

(*a*) if the option is abandoned, subsection (5)(*b*) shall not apply, and

(*b*) section 560(3) shall not apply.

(8) (*a*) Where—

(i) a quoted option to subscribe for shares in a company, or

(ii) a traded option,

is disposed of or abandoned, then—

(I) if the option is abandoned, subsection (5)(*b*) shall not apply, and

(II) section 560(3) and subsection (6) shall not apply.

(*b*) Where a quoted option to subscribe for shares in a company is dealt in within 3 months after the taking effect, with respect to the company granting the option, of any reorganisation, reduction, conversion or amalgamation to which section 584, 585, 586 or 587 applies (or within such longer period as the Revenue Commissioners may by notice in writing allow), the option shall for the purposes of section 584, 585, 586 or 587 be regarded as the shares which could be acquired by exercising the option, and section 548(3) shall apply for determining its market value.

(9) This section shall apply in relation to an option binding the grantor both to sell and to buy as if it were 2 separate options with 50 per cent of the consideration attributed to each option.

(10) This section shall apply in relation to a forfeited deposit of purchase money or other consideration money for a prospective purchase or other transaction which is abandoned as it applies in relation to the consideration for an option which binds the grantor to sell and which is not exercised.

Cross-references

Building societies, change of status, rights to shares in a successor company: Sch 16 para 4(2).

Demutualisation of assurance companies, meaning of "option" applied: s 588(3).

Case law

Sum received for abandonment of an option held to be a disposal of an asset: *Dilleen v Kearns* ITR Vol IV p 547. See also *Golding v Kaufmann* [1985] STC 152; *Welbeck Securities Ltd v Powlson* [1987] STC 468.

Payment for release from restrictive covenant not deductible in calculating consideration for grant of option: *Garner v Pounds* [1999] STC 18.

Definitions

company: s 5(1); lease: s 5(1); month: IA 1937 Sch; person: IA 1937 s 11(*c*); shares: s 5(1); trade: s 5(1), ITA 1967 s 1(1); wasting asset: ss 5(1), 560, Sch 14 para 2; writing: IA 1937 Sch.

Former enactments

CGTA 1975 s 47(1)–(6) and (8)–(11); FA 1992 s 63.

Corresponding UK tax provision

Taxation of Chargeable Gains Act 1992 s 144.

541 Debts

(1) (*a*) For the purposes of the Capital Gains Tax Acts but subject to paragraph (*b*), where a person incurs a debt to another person (being the original creditor), whether in Irish currency or in some other currency, no chargeable gain shall accrue to that creditor or to that creditor's personal representative or legatee on a disposal of the debt.

(*b*) Paragraph (*a*) shall not apply in the case of a debt on a security within the meaning of section 585.

(2) Subject to subsection (1) and sections 585 and 586, the satisfaction of a debt or part of a debt (including a debt on a security within the meaning of section 585) shall be treated for the purposes of the Capital Gains Tax Acts as a disposal of the debt or of that part by the creditor made at the time when the debt or that part is satisfied.

(3) Where property is acquired by a creditor in satisfaction of the creditor's debt or part of that debt, then, subject to sections 585 and 586, the property shall not be treated for the purposes of the Capital Gains Tax Acts as disposed of by the debtor or acquired by the creditor for a consideration greater than its market value at the time of the creditor's acquisition of it; but, if under subsection (1) (and in a case not within either section 585 or 586) no chargeable gain is to accrue on a disposal of the debt by the original creditor and a chargeable gain accrues to that creditor on a disposal by that creditor of the property, the amount of the chargeable gain shall (where necessary) be reduced so as not to exceed the chargeable gain which would have accrued if that creditor had acquired the property for a consideration equal to the amount of the debt or that part of the debt.

(4) For the purposes of the Capital Gains Tax Acts, a loss accruing on the disposal of a debt acquired by the person making the disposal from the original creditor or the original creditor's personal representative or legatee at a time when the creditor or the creditor's personal representative or legatee is a person connected with the person making the disposal, and so acquired either directly or by one or more than one purchase through persons all of whom are connected with the person making the disposal, shall not be an allowable loss.

(5) Where the original creditor is a trustee and the debt when created is settled property, subsections (1) and (4) shall apply as if for the references to the original creditor's personal representative or legatee there were substituted references to any person becoming absolutely entitled as against the trustee to the debt on its ceasing to be settled property and to that person's personal representative or legatee.

(6) This section shall not apply to a debt owed by a bank which is not in Irish currency and which is represented by a sum standing to the credit of a person in an account in the bank, unless it represents currency acquired by the holder for the personal expenditure outside the State of the holder or his or her family or dependants (including expenditure on the maintenance of any residence outside the State).

(7) For the purposes of this section, a debenture issued by any company shall be deemed to be a security (within the meaning of section 585) if it is issued—

(*a*) on a reorganisation referred to in section 584(2) or in pursuance of the debenture's allotment on any such reorganisation,

(*b*) in exchange for shares in or debentures of another company where the requirements of section 586(2) are satisfied in relation to the exchange,

(*c*) under any arrangements referred to in section 587(2),

(*d*) in connection with any transfer of assets referred to in section 631,

(*e*) in connection with any disposal of assets referred to in section 632,

(*f*) in the course of a transaction which is the subject of an application under section 637, or

(*g*) in pursuance of rights attached to any debenture within paragraph (*a*), (*b*), (*c*), (*d*), (*e*) or (*f*)

(8) Paragraphs (*d*), (*e*) and (*f*), and (in so far as it relates to debentures within those paragraphs) paragraph (*g*), of subsection (7) shall apply as respects the disposal of a debenture on or after the 26th day of March, 1997.

Cross-references

Attribution to shareholders of chargeable gains accruing to non-resident company, subs (6): s 590(7)(*b*).
Reorganisation of companies into Trustee Savings Banks, capital gains: Sch 17 para 5(6).
Treatment of debts on a change in currency: s 541A(1).

Case law

What loans are to be regarded as a debt on a security, see *Mooney v McSweeney* [1997] ITR 163.
Subs (1): A right to an unquantifiable contingent future amount is not a debt: *Marren v Ingles* [1980] STC 500; *Marson v Marriage* [1980] STC 177.
"Debt on a security" is not a synonym for a secured debt: *Cleveleys Investment Trust Co v IRC* [1975] STC 457.
Debt on a security must be capable of being dealt in: *Taylor Clark International v Lewis* [1998] STC 1253.
A debt on a security must be marketable and be capable of conversion into shares or other securities: *Aberdeen Construction Group Ltd v IRC* [1978] STC 127; *WT Ramsay v IRC* [1981] STC 174.
Whether gain realised on forward contract a disposal of a debt: *Whittles v Uniholdings Ltd (No 3)* [1996] STC 914.
The redemption of a loan note, which had been acquired for shares in a "paper for paper" exchange was held to be in law, as it was in fact, a disposition of the loan note. The loan note was found not to be a "debt on a security": Supreme Court, *O'Connell v Keleghan.*

Definitions

allowable loss: ss 4(1), 5(1), 546; Capital Gains Tax Acts: s 1(2); chargeable gain: ss 5(1), 545; legatee: s 5(1); person: IA 1937 s 11(*c*); personal representative: ss 5(1), 799; settled property: s 5(1).

Former enactments

CGTA 1975 s 46; FA 1980 s 62(*b*); FA 1996 s 61(1); FA 1997 s 78.

Corresponding UK tax provision

Taxation of Chargeable Gains Act 1992 s 251.

541A Treatment of debts on a change in currency

[(1) Where on any day a debt (to which section 541 does not apply by virtue of subsection (6) of that section) owed to a person in a currency other than Irish currency, becomes a debt in Irish currency as a result of the currency of a State being substituted by another currency, which other currency also on that day becomes Irish currency, then, subject to subsection (2), that debt shall be deemed, for the purposes of the Capital Gains Tax Acts, on the day preceding that day, to be disposed of by the person and immediately reacquired by the person at its market value.

(2) [Subject to subsection (4) and notwithstanding any other provision of the Capital Gains Tax Acts],[1] where in respect of a debt a chargeable gain accrues to a person by virtue of subsection (1), that chargeable gain shall be assessed and charged as if it were a chargeable gain which accrued to the person at the time of the disposal of the debt and shall not be assessed and charged otherwise.

(3) For the purposes of subsection (2), in relation to a debt owed to a person, the satisfaction of the debt or part of the debt shall be treated as a disposal of the debt or of that part at the time when the debt or that part is satisfied.][2]

[(4) (*a*) In this subsection—

"assurance company" has the meaning assigned to it in section 706;

"life business fund" has the meaning assigned to it in section 719;

"special investment fund" has the meaning assigned to it in section 723;

"special investment scheme" has the meaning assigned to it in section 737;

"undertaking for collective investment" has the meaning assigned to it in section 738.

(*b*) Where the person referred to in subsection (1) is a company and either—

(i) the company is an assurance company and the debt referred to in that subsection is an asset of the company's life business fund, or

(ii) the company is an undertaking for collective investment and the debt referred to in that subsection is an asset of the undertaking,

subsection (1) shall not apply and where the day (in this paragraph referred to as **"the deemed disposal day"**) on which, but for this paragraph, the debt would be deemed to be disposed of and reacquired in accordance with subsection (1), is not the day on which an accounting period of the company ends—

(I) in case of an assurance company, section 719(2) shall apply in respect of the debt as if, for this purpose only, the deemed disposal day was the day on which an accounting period of the company ends and the chargeable gain or allowable loss thereby accruing shall be included in the net amount (within the meaning of section 720) in respect of the accounting period in which the deemed disposal day falls, and

(II) in case of an undertaking for collective investment, section 738(4)(*a*) shall apply in respect of the debt as if, for this purpose only, the deemed disposal day was the day on which an accounting period of the company ends and the chargeable gain or allowable loss thereby accruing shall be included in the net amount (within the meaning of section 738(4)(*b*)) in respect of the accounting period in which the deemed disposal day falls.

(*c*) Where the person referred to in subsection (1) is an undertaking for collective investment and is not a company, subsection (2) shall not apply but the chargeable gain or allowable loss which accrues to the undertaking by virtue of subsection (1) shall be treated as accruing to the undertaking by virtue of paragraph (*a*) of section 738(4) and the provisions of that section shall apply accordingly.

(*d*) Subsection (2) shall not apply to a debt which is—

(i) an asset of a special investment fund of an assurance company, or

(ii) an asset which is subject to any trust created pursuant to a special investment scheme.][3]

Amendments

1 Substituted by FA 1999 s 87(1)(*a*) with effect from 31 December 1998; previously "Notwithstanding any other provision of the Capital Gains Tax Acts".

2 Section 541A inserted by FA 1998 s 47 and Sch 2 para 9 with effect from such date as the Minister for Finance may appoint by order. The section came into operation from 31 December 1998 — Finance Act, 1998 (Section 47) (Commencement) Order, 1998, SI No 502 of 1998, refers.

3 Subs (4) inserted by FA 1999 s 87(1)(*b*) with effect from 31 December 1998.

Tax Briefing

TB31 Apr 1998 p 6 — The Euro and Tax: Capital Gains Tax — Foreign Currency Gains/Losses arising otherwise than in the course of a trade.

Definitions

allowable loss: ss 5(1), 546; Capital Gains Tax Acts: s 1(2); chargeable gain: ss 5(1), 545; company: ss 4(1), 5(1); person: IA 1937 s 11(*c*).

541B Restrictive covenants

[(1) Where—

(*a*) a person gives an undertaking (whether absolute or qualified and whether legally valid or not), the tenor or effect of which is to restrict the person as to the person's conduct or activities,

(*b*) in respect of the giving of that undertaking by the person, or of the total or partial fulfilment of that undertaking by the person, any sum is paid either to the person or to any other person, and

(*c*) that sum is neither—

(i) treated, for the purposes of the Tax Acts, as profits or gains chargeable to tax under Schedule D or Schedule E, nor

(ii) treated as consideration for the disposal of an asset for the purposes of the Capital Gains Tax Acts,

the amount of the sum shall be deemed for the purposes of the Capital Gains Tax Acts to be the amount of a chargeable gain accruing to the person to whom it is paid (for the year of assessment in which it is paid) on the disposal of a chargeable asset.

(2) Where valuable consideration otherwise than in the form of money is given in respect of the giving of, or the total or partial fulfilment of, any undertaking, subsection (1) applies as if a sum had instead been paid equal to the value of that consideration.][1]

Amendments

1 Section 541B inserted by FA 2003 s 70(1) as respects the giving of an undertaking by a person on or after 6 February 2003, the tenor or effect of which is to restrict the person as to the person's conduct or activities.

Definitions

Capital Gains Tax Acts: s 1(2); chargeable gain: s 5(1); person: IA 1937 s 11(*c*); Tax Acts: s 1(2); year of assessment: ss 2(1), 5(1).

542 Time of disposal and acquisition

(1) (*a*) Subject to paragraph (*b*) and subsection (2), for the purposes of the Capital Gains Tax Acts, where an asset is disposed of and acquired under a contract, the time at which the disposal and acquisition is made shall be the time at which the contract is made (and not, if different, the time at which the asset is conveyed or transferred).

(*b*) Where the contract is conditional (and in particular where it is conditional on the exercise of an option), the time at which the disposal and acquisition is made shall be the time at which the condition is satisfied.

(*c*) For the purposes of the Capital Gains Tax Acts, where an interest in land is acquired, otherwise than under a contract, by an authority possessing compulsory purchase powers, the time at which the disposal and acquisition is made shall be the time at which the compensation for the acquisition is agreed or otherwise determined (variations on appeal being disregarded for this purpose) or, if earlier, the time at which the authority enters on the land in pursuance of its powers.

[(*d*) Notwithstanding paragraph (*c*), for the purposes of the Capital Gains Tax Acts where a person who is engaged in farming (within the meaning of section 654) disposes of an interest in land to an authority possessing compulsory purchase powers, for the purposes mentioned in section 652(5)*(a)*, and immediately before the disposal the land was used for the purposes of farming, the chargeable gain (if any) on the disposal shall be deemed to accrue in the year of assessment in which the person receives the consideration for the disposal.][1]

(2) For the purposes of subparagraphs (i) to (iv) of section 535(2)(*a*), the time of disposal shall be the time at which any capital sum is received.

Amendments

1 Subs (1)(*d*) inserted by FA 2002 s 62 with effect from 1 January 2002.

Case law

Subs (1)(*b*): Contract for sale of fleet of taxis held not conditional where licence passed only on payment of last instalment: *Lyon v Pettigrew* [1985] STC 369.

Revenue information

eBrief no. 4–2004

Having considered the High Court judgment in the case of *O'Connor v Coady* reported in December 2003 (a non-tax case concerning planning permission and the rescission of contract), Revenue considers that no change is required to the existing treatment of conditional contracts. The time of disposal, in the case of such contracts, will continue to be the time when the condition is satisfied. Consequently, if a contract is stated to be conditional on the grant of planning permission, the time of disposal will be when such planning permission is granted.

Tax Briefing

TB36 June 1999 p 14 — Time of disposal.

TB41 Sept 2000 p 32 — A contract expressed as being subject to loan approval is a conditional contract.

TB47 April 2002 p 15 — Finance Act 2002 changes.

Definitions

Capital Gains Tax Acts: s 1(2); land: s 5(1), IA 1937 Sch; person: IA 1937 s 11(*c*); year of assessment: s 2(1).

Former enactments

CGTA 1975 s 10(1) and (3).

Corresponding UK tax provision

Taxation of Chargeable Gains Act 1992 s 28.

543 Transfers of value derived from assets

(1) Without prejudice to the generality of the provisions of the Capital Gains Tax Acts as to the transactions which are disposals of assets, any transaction which under this section is to be treated as a disposal of an asset—

(*a*) shall be so treated (with a corresponding acquisition of an interest in the asset) notwithstanding that there is no consideration, and

(*b*) in so far as, on the assumption that the parties to the transaction were at arm's length, the party making the disposal could have obtained consideration or additional consideration for the disposal, shall be treated as not being at arm's length, and the consideration so obtainable, added to the consideration actually passing, shall be treated as the market value of what is acquired.

(2) (*a*) Where a person having control of a company exercises that control so that value passes out of shares in the company owned by such person or a person with whom such person is connected, or out of rights over the company exercisable by such person or by a person with whom such person is connected, and passes into other shares in or rights over the company, that exercise of such person's control shall be a disposal of the shares or rights out of which the value passes by the person by whom they were owned or exercisable.

(*b*) References in paragraph (*a*) to a person include references to 2 or more persons connected with one another.

(3) Where, after a transaction which results in the owner of land or of any other description of property becoming the lessee of the property, there is any adjustment of the rights and liabilities under the lease (whether or not involving the grant of a new lease) which as a whole is favourable to the lessor, that shall constitute a disposal by the lessee of an interest in the property.

(4) Where an asset is subject to any description of right or restriction, the extinction or abrogation in whole or in part of the right or restriction by the person entitled to enforce it shall constitute a disposal by that person of the right or restriction.

Case law

UK

Subs (2)(*a*): Taxpayers held to exercise control where a resolution was passed as a result of which value passed out of their shares even though they were absent and consequently did not vote in favour of the resolution: *Floor v Davis* [1979] STC 379.

Definitions

company: s 5(1); land: s 5(1), IA 1937 Sch; lease: s 5(1); lessee: s 5(1); lessor: s 5(1); person: IA 1937 s 11(*c*); shares: s 5(1).

Former enactments

CGTA 1975 s 45.

Corresponding UK tax provision

Taxation of Chargeable Gains Act 1992 s 29.

CHAPTER 2
Computation of Chargeable Gains and Allowable Losses

Cross-references

Double taxation relief: s 828(4).

Exclusion of premiums taxed under Sch D Case V: Sch 14 para 6(1), (3)(*a*), (5).

Leases of land as wasting assets, restriction of allowable expenditure: Sch 14 para 2(4).

Sub-leases out of short leases: Sch 14 para 5(2).

---

544 Interpretation and general (Chapter 2)

(1) In this Chapter, **"renewals allowance"** means a deduction allowable in computing profits, gains or losses for the purposes of the Income Tax Acts by reference to the cost of acquiring an asset in replacement of another asset, and for the purposes of this Chapter a renewals allowance shall be regarded as a deduction allowable in respect of the expenditure incurred on the asset which is being replaced.

(2) References in this Chapter to sums taken into account as receipts or as expenditure in computing profits, gains or losses for the purposes of the Income Tax Acts shall include references to sums which would be so taken into account but for the fact that any profits or gains of a trade, profession or employment are not chargeable to income tax or that losses are not allowable for those purposes.

(3) References in this Chapter to income or profits charged or chargeable to tax include references to income or profits taxed or, as the case may be, taxable by deduction at source.

(4) No deduction shall be allowable in a computation under the Capital Gains Tax Acts more than once from any sum or from more than one sum.

(5) For the purposes of any computation under this Chapter of a gain accruing on a disposal, any necessary apportionment shall be made of any consideration or of any expenditure, and the method of apportionment adopted shall, subject to this Chapter, be such method as appears to the inspector or on appeal the Appeal Commissioners to be just and reasonable.

(6) Section 557 and the other provisions of the Capital Gains Tax Acts for apportioning on a part disposal expenditure which is deductible in computing a gain shall be operated before the operation of and without regard to—

- (*a*) section 1028(5),
- (*b*) section 597, and
- (*c*) any other provision making an adjustment to secure that neither a gain nor a loss accrues on a disposal.

(7) Any assessment to income tax or any decision on a claim under the Income Tax Acts, and any decision on an appeal under the Income Tax Acts against such an assessment or decision, shall be conclusive in so far as under any provision of the Capital Gains Tax Acts liability to tax depends on the provisions of the Income Tax Acts.

(8) In so far as the provisions of the Capital Gains Tax Acts require the computation of a gain by reference to events before the 6th day of April, 1974, all those provisions, including the provisions fixing the amount of the consideration deemed to be given on a disposal or an acquisition, shall apply except in so far as expressly excluded.

Definitions

chargeable gain: ss 5(1), 545; Income Tax Acts: s 1(2); person: IA 1937 s 11(*c*); personal representatives: ss 5(1), 799; settlement: ss 5(1), 10.

Former enactments

CGTA 1975 s 51(2), Sch 1 paras 1 and 5(3) and Sch 4 para 13; CGT(A)A 1978 s 17 and Sch 2.

Corresponding UK tax provision

Taxation of Chargeable Gains Act 1992 s 41.

545 Chargeable gains

(1) Where under the Capital Gains Tax Acts an asset is not a chargeable asset, no chargeable gain shall accrue on its disposal.

(2) The amount of the gain accruing on the disposal of an asset shall be computed in accordance with this Chapter, and subject to the other provisions of the Capital Gains Tax Acts.

(3) Except where otherwise expressly provided by the Capital Gains Tax Acts, every gain shall be a chargeable gain.

Cross-references

Chargeable gain, this meaning applied: s 5(1).

Self assessment, meaning of "chargeable gain" applied, subs (3): s 950(1).

Former enactments

CGTA 1975 s 7(2) and s 11; CGT(A)A 1978 s 17 and Sch 2.

546 Allowable losses

(1) Where under the Capital Gains Tax Acts an asset is not a chargeable asset, no allowable loss shall accrue on its disposal.

(2) Except where otherwise expressly provided, the amount of a loss accruing on a disposal of an asset shall be computed in the same way as the amount of a gain accruing on a disposal is computed.

(3) Except where otherwise expressly provided, the provisions of the Capital Gains Tax Acts which distinguish gains which are chargeable gains from those which are not, or which make part of a gain a chargeable gain and part not, shall apply also to distinguish losses which are allowable losses from those which are not, and to make part of a loss an allowable loss and part not, and references in the Capital Gains Tax Acts to an allowable loss shall be construed accordingly.

(4) A loss accruing to a person in a year of assessment for which the person is neither resident nor ordinarily resident in the State shall not be an allowable loss for the purposes of the Capital Gains Tax Acts unless under section 29(3) the person would be chargeable to capital gains tax in respect of a chargeable gain if there had been a gain instead of a loss on that occasion.

(5) Except where provided by section 573, an allowable loss accruing in a year of assessment shall not be allowable as a deduction from chargeable gains in any earlier year of assessment, and relief shall not be given under the Capital Gains Tax Acts—

(*a*) more than once in respect of any loss or part of a loss, and

(*b*) if and in so far as relief has been or may be given in respect of that loss or part of a loss under the Income Tax Acts.

(6) For the purposes of section 31, where, on the assumption that there were no allowable losses to be deducted under that section, a person would be chargeable under the Capital Gains Tax Acts at more than one rate of tax for a year of assessment, any allowable losses to be deducted under that section shall be deducted—

(*a*) if the person would be so chargeable at 2 different rates, from the chargeable gains which would be so chargeable at the higher of those rates and, in so far as they cannot be so deducted, from the chargeable gains which would be so chargeable at the lower of those rates, and (*b*) if the person would be so chargeable at 3 or more rates, from the chargeable gains which would be so chargeable at the highest of those rates and, in so far as they cannot be so deducted, from the chargeable gains which would be so chargeable at the next highest of those rates, and so on.

Cross-references

Disposals by liquidators and other persons, meaning of "referable gains tax", subs (6): s 571(2)(*c*)(ii); meaning of "referable corporation tax", subs (6): s 571(3)(*c*)(i)(II).

Disposal within four weeks of acquisition: s 581(3).

Foreign life assurance and deferred annuities, subs (2): s 595(3)(*b*).

Foreign life policies, disposal of certain policies: s 730K(3).

Offshore funds, disposal of interests in non-qualifying funds, calculation of unindexed gain: Sch 20 par 3(2).

Offshore funds, disposal of an interest in certain offshore funds: s 747E(3).

Undertaking for collective investment, taxation of unit holders, subs (2): s 739(4)(*c*).

Case law

Irish

Subs (2): A technical loss arising from a pre-ordained series of transactions held to be allowable for capital gains tax purposes: *McGrath and others v MacDermott* ITR Vol III p 683; see also s 811.

Definitions

chargeable gain: ss 4(1), 5(1), 545; person: IA 1937 s 11(*c*).

Former enactments

CGTA 1975 s 7(2) and s12(1), (2), (6)–(7); CGT(A)A 1978 s 16 and Sch 1 para 7.

Corresponding UK tax provision

Taxation of Chargeable Gains Act 1992 s 16.

547 Disposals and acquisitions treated as made at market value

(1) Subject to the Capital Gains Tax Acts, a person's acquisition of an asset shall for the purposes of those Acts be deemed to be for a consideration equal to the market value of the asset where—

(*a*) the person acquires the asset otherwise than by means of a bargain made at arm's length (including in particular where the person acquires it by means of a gift),

(*b*) the person acquires the asset by means of a distribution from a company in respect of shares in the company, or

(*c*) the person acquires the asset wholly or partly—

(i) for a consideration that cannot be valued,

(ii) in connection with the person's own or another person's loss of office or employment or diminution of emoluments, or

(iii) otherwise in consideration for or in recognition of the person's or another person's services or past services in any office or employment or of any other service rendered or to be rendered by the person or another person.

[(1A)(*a*) Notwithstanding subsection (1), where, by virtue of section 31 of the State Property Act, 1954, the Minister for Finance waives, in favour of a person, the right of the State to property, the person's acquisition of the property shall for the purposes of the Capital Gains Tax Acts be deemed to be for a consideration equal to the amount (including a nil amount) of the payment of money made by the person as one of the terms of that waiver.][1]

(2) (*a*) In this subsection, **"shares"** includes stock, debentures and any interests to which section 587(3) applies and any option in relation to such shares, and references in this subsection to an allotment of shares shall be construed accordingly.

(*b*) Notwithstanding subsection (1) and section 584(3), where a company, otherwise than by means of a bargain made at arm's length, allots shares in the company (in this subsection referred to as **"the new shares"**) to a person connected with the company, the consideration which the person gives or becomes liable to give for the new shares shall for the purposes of the Capital Gains Tax Acts be deemed to be an amount (including a nil amount) equal to the lesser of—

(i) the amount or value of the consideration given by the person for the new shares, and

(ii) the amount by which the market value of the shares in the company which the person held immediately after the allotment of the new shares exceeds the market value of the shares in the company which the person held immediately before the allotment or, if the person held no such shares immediately before the allotment, the market value of the new shares immediately after the allotment.

(3) Subsection (1) shall not apply to the acquisition of an asset where—

(*a*) there is no corresponding disposal of the asset, and

(*b*) (i) there is no consideration in money or money's worth for the asset, or

(ii) the consideration for the asset is of an amount or value which is lower than the market value of the asset.

(4) (*a*) Subject to the Capital Gains Tax Acts, a person's disposal of an asset shall for the purposes of those Acts be deemed to be for a consideration equal to the market value of the asset where—

(i) the person disposes of the asset otherwise than by means of a bargain made at arm's length (including in particular where the person disposes of it by means of a gift), or

(ii) the person disposes of the asset wholly or partly for a consideration that cannot be valued.

(*b*) Paragraph (*a*) shall not apply to a disposal by means of a gift made before the 20th day of December, 1974, and any loss incurred on a disposal by means of a gift made before that date shall not be an allowable loss.

Amendments

1 Subs (1A) inserted by FA 1998 s 68 as respects the acquisition of an asset on or after 12 February 1998.

Cross-references

Approved savings-related share option schemes, subs (1)(*a*): s 519A(3A)(*a*).

Approved share option schemes, subs (1)(*a*): s 519D(3)(*b*), (5)(*a*).

Approved share option schemes, transitional: Sch 32 para 7(2)(*b*).

Disposals to State, public bodies and charities: s 611(1)(*a*).

Special investment policies, consideration given for fund's assets: s 723(2).

Special investment schemes, consideration given for assets subject to trust created under the scheme: s 737(2)(*b*).

Transactions between connected persons: s 549(2).

Undertaking for collective investment, meaning of consideration: s 738(1)(*a*), (9)(*b*).

Case law

Whether sum of money paid to discharge subsidiary's debt formed part of consideration for disposal of subsidiary: *Spectros International plc v Madden* [1997] STC 114

Taxpayer who purchased a debt due to their company by a company with which they had no connection for a fraction of its value could not substitute the value of the debt as their acquisition cost: *Whitehouse v Ellam* [1995] STC 503.

Subs (3): inserted to defeat avoidance arrangements arising out of the decision in *Harrison v Nairn Williamson* [1978] STC 67.

Fact that shares sold at undervalue did not necessarily mean the bargain was otherwise than arm's-length: *Bullivant Holdings v IRC* [1998] STC 905.

Definitions

allowable loss: ss 4(1), 5(1), 546; company: s 5(1); person: IA 1937 s 11(*c*); shares: s 5(1).

Former enactments

CGTA 1975 s 9; FA 1982 s 62; FA 1992 s 62.

Corresponding UK tax provision

Taxation of Chargeable Gains Act 1992 s 17.

548 Valuation of assets

(1) Subject to this section, in the Capital Gains Tax Acts, **"market value"**, in relation to any assets, means the price which those assets might reasonably be expected to fetch on a sale in the open market.

(2) In estimating the market value of any assets, no reduction shall be made in the estimate on account of the estimate being made on the assumption that the whole of the assets is to be placed on the market at the same time.

(3) (*a*) The market value of shares or securities quoted on a stock exchange in the State or in the United Kingdom shall, except where in consequence of special circumstances the prices quoted are by themselves not a proper measure of market value, be as follows—

(i) in relation to shares or securities listed in the Stock Exchange Official List — Irish—

(I) the price shown in that list at which bargains in the shares or securities were last recorded (the previous price), or

(II) where bargains other than bargains done at special prices were recorded in that list for the relevant date, the price at which the bargains were so recorded or, if more than one such price was so recorded, a price halfway between the highest and the lowest of such prices,

taking the amount under clause (I) if less than under clause (II) or if no such business was recorded on the relevant date, and taking the amount under clause (II) if less than under clause (I), and

(ii) in relation to shares or securities listed in the Stock Exchange Daily Official List—

(I) the lower of the 2 prices shown in the quotations for the shares or securities on the relevant date plus 25 per cent of the difference between those 2 figures, or

(II) where bargains other than bargains done at special prices were recorded in that list for the relevant date, the price at which the bargains were so recorded or, if more than one such price was so recorded, a price halfway between the highest and the lowest of such prices,

taking the amount under clause (I) if less than under clause (II) or if no such bargains were recorded for the relevant date, and taking the amount under clause (II) if less than under clause (I).

(*b*) Notwithstanding paragraph (*a*)—

(i) where the shares or securities are listed in both of the Official Lists referred to in that paragraph for the relevant date, the lower of the 2 amounts as ascertained under subparagraphs (i) and (ii) of that paragraph shall be taken,

(ii) this subsection shall not apply to shares or securities for which some other stock exchange affords a more active market, and

(iii) if the stock exchange concerned, or one of the stock exchanges concerned, is closed on the relevant date, the market value shall be ascertained by reference to the latest previous date or earliest subsequent date on which it is open, whichever affords the lower market value.

(4) Where shares and securities are not quoted on a stock exchange at the time at which their market value is to be determined by virtue of subsection (1), it shall be assumed for the purposes of such determination that in the open market which is postulated for the purposes of subsection (1) there is available to any prospective purchaser of the asset in question all the information which a prudent prospective purchaser of the asset might reasonably require if such prospective purchaser were proposing to purchase it from a willing vendor by private treaty and at arm's length.

(5) In the Capital Gains Tax Acts, **"market value"**, in relation to any rights of unit holders in any unit trust (including any unit trust legally established outside the State) the buying and selling prices of which are published regularly by the managers of the trust, means an amount equal to the buying price (that is, the lower price) so published on the relevant date or, if none was published on that date, on the latest date before that date.

(6) If and in so far as any appeal against an assessment to capital gains tax or against a decision on a claim under the Capital Gains Tax Acts involves the question of the value of any shares or securities in a company resident in the State, other than shares or securities quoted on a stock exchange, that question shall be determined in the like manner as an appeal against an assessment made on the company.

(7) Subsection (6) shall apply for the purposes of corporation tax as it applies for the purposes of capital gains tax.

Cross-references

Approved retirement fund, meaning of "market value" applied: s 784A(1E).

Approved savings-related share option schemes, interpretation, meaning of "market value" applied: Sch 12A para 1(1).

Approved share option schemes, interpretation, meaning of "market value" applied: Sch 12C para 1(1).

Certain unit trusts not to be collective investment undertakings: s 735; option for non-application of s 735, meaning of "market value" applied: s 736(3).

Charge to income tax of offshore income gain, meaning of "market value" applied: s 745(5)(*a*).

Company ceasing to be resident in the State, deemed disposal of assets, meaning of "market value" applied: s 627(1)(*a*).
Deferral of payment of tax under section 128 (tax treatment of share options), meaning of "market value" applied: s 128A(4A)(*k*).
Distributions, matters treated as, meaning of "market value" applied: s 130(2C)(*e*).
Employee share options schemes, meaning of "market value" applied: s 128(1)(*a*).
Employee share purchase schemes, meaning of "market value" applied: s 479(1)(*a*).
Material interest in offshore funds, meaning of "market value" applied, subs (5): s 743(9).
Notional loans relating to shares, etc, meaning of "market value" applied: s 122A(1).
Options and forfeited deposits, subs (3): s 540(8)(*b*).
Personal Retirement Savings Accounts (PRSAs), interpretation, "market value" to be construed in accordance with this section: s 787A(1).
Profit sharing schemes, market value, meaning applied: s 509(1).
Room ownership schemes, market value, meaning applied: s 409(1).
Schemes to avoid liability to tax under Sch F, meaning of "market value" applied: s 817(1)(*a*).
Special investment schemes, meaning of "market value" applied: s 737(1)(*a*).
Special portfolio investment accounts, meaning of "market value" applied: s 838(1)(*a*).
Undertakings for collective investment, taxation of unit holders, meaning of "market value" applied: s 739(2)(*e*)(iv).
Valuation of benefits in kind, meaning of "market value" applied: s 119(4)(*b*).
Voluntary Health Insurance Board, restriction of certain losses and deemed disposal of certain assets, meaning of "market value" applied: s 841(1).

Case law

Irish

Circuit Court judge's findings of fact that land was to be valued at £3,000 per acre upheld: *McMahon v Murphy* ITR Vol IV p 125.

UK

Held the Crown may give evidence of share transactions in the same company and previous agreements between the company and the Revenue regarding share valuation: *IRC v Stenhouse Trustees* [1992] STC 103.

Tax Briefing

TB46 Dec 2001 p 26 — Calculation of Base Cost of Eircom shares and Vodafone shares.

Definitions

company, resident, shares, unit trust, unit holder: s 5(1).

Former enactments

CGTA 1975 s 49(1)–(6); CTA 1976 Sch 2 Pt II para 7.

Corresponding UK tax provision

Taxation of Chargeable Gains Act 1992 s 272.

549 Transactions between connected persons

(1) This section shall apply for the purposes of the Capital Gains Tax Acts where a person acquires an asset and the person making the disposal is connected with the person acquiring the asset.

(2) Without prejudice to the generality of section 547, the person acquiring the asset and the person making the disposal shall be treated as parties to a transaction otherwise than by means of a bargain made at arm's length.

(3) Where on the disposal a loss accrues to the person making the disposal, the loss shall not be deductible except from a chargeable gain accruing to that person on some other disposal of an asset to the person acquiring the asset mentioned in subsection (1), being a disposal made at a time when they are connected persons.

(4) Subsection (3) shall not apply to a disposal by means of a gift in settlement if the gift and the income from it are wholly or primarily applicable for educational, cultural or

recreational purposes, and the persons benefiting from the application for those purposes are confined to members of an association of persons for whose benefit the gift was made, not being persons all or most of whom are connected persons.

(5) Where the asset mentioned in subsection (1) is an option to enter into a sale or other transaction given by the person making the disposal, a loss accruing to a person acquiring the asset shall not be an allowable loss unless it accrues on a disposal of the option at arm's length to a person not connected with the person acquiring the asset.

(6) Where the asset mentioned in subsection (1) is subject to any right or restriction enforceable by the person making the disposal or by a person connected with that person, then (where the amount of the consideration for the acquisition is in accordance with subsection (2) deemed to be equal to the market value of the asset), that market value shall be what its market value would be if not subject to the right or restriction, reduced by the lesser of—

(*a*) the market value of the right or restriction, and

(*b*) the amount by which its extinction would enhance the value of the asset to its owner.

(7) Where the right or restriction referred to in subsection (6)—

(*a*) is of such a nature that its enforcement would or might effectively destroy or substantially impair the value of the asset without bringing any countervailing advantage either to the person making the disposal or a person connected with that person,

(*b*) is an option or other right to acquire the asset, or

(*c*) in the case of incorporeal property, is a right to extinguish the asset in the hands of the person giving the consideration by forfeiture or merger or otherwise,

then, the market value of the asset shall be determined, and the amount of the gain accruing on the disposal shall be computed, as if the right or restriction did not exist.

(8) (*a*) Where a person disposes of an asset to another person in such circumstances that—

(i) subsection (7) would but for this subsection apply in determining the market value of the asset, and

(ii) the person is not chargeable to capital gains tax under section 29 or 30 in respect of any gain accruing on the person's disposal of the asset,

then, as respects any subsequent disposal of the asset by the other person, that other person's acquisition of the asset shall for the purposes of the Capital Gains Tax Acts be deemed to be for an amount equal to the market value of the asset determined as if subsection (7) had not been enacted.

(*b*) This subsection shall apply—

(i) to disposals made on or after the 25th day of January, 1989, and

(ii) for the purposes of the determination of any deduction to be made from a chargeable gain accruing on or after the 25th day of January, 1989, in respect of an allowable loss, notwithstanding that the loss accrued or but for this section would have accrued on a disposal made before that day.

(9) Subsections (6) and (7) shall not apply to a right of forfeiture or other right exercisable on breach of a covenant contained in a lease of land or other property, or to any right or restriction under a mortgage or other charge.

Revenue precedents

Issue: Treatment of gains arising on changes in partnership asset sharing ratios.

Decision: Occasions of charge arise on disposals between partners. A change in asset-sharing ratios involves a disposal/acquisition, most commonly on retirement of a partner or admission of a new partner. Where (1) no consideration is involved, (2) there is no revaluation of assets, (3) other than as Partners, the individuals are not connected persons within the meaning of TCA 1997 s 10(4) the transaction is a bona fide commercial arrangement not forming part of a tax avoidance scheme - no gain is triggered and a re-allocation of balance sheet values is acceptable.

Definitions

allowable loss: ss 4(1), 5(1), 546; chargeable gain: ss 5(1), 545; close company ss 5(1), 430; control: s 432; company: s 5(1); land: s 5(1), IA 1937 Sch; lease: s 5(1); person: IA 1937 s 11(*c*); relative: s 3(1); resident: s 5(1); settlement s 5(1).

Former enactments

CGTA 1975 s 33(1)–(6); FA 1989 s 87.

Corresponding UK tax provision

Taxation of Chargeable Gains Act 1992 s 18.

550 Assets disposed of in series of transactions

Where a person is given, or acquires from one or more persons with whom such person is connected, by means of 2 or more transactions, assets of which the aggregate market value, when considered separately in relation to the separate other transactions, is less than the aggregate market value of those assets when considered together, then, for the purposes of the Capital Gains Tax Acts, the market value of the assets where relevant shall be taken to be the larger market value and that value shall be apportioned rateably to the respective disposals.

Former enactments

CGTA 1975 s 34.

Corresponding UK tax provision

Taxation of Chargeable Gains Act 1992 s 19.

551 Exclusion from consideration for disposals of sums chargeable to income tax

(1) In this section, **"rent"** includes any rent charge, fee farm rent and any payment in the nature of a rent.

(2) There shall be excluded from the consideration for a disposal of an asset taken into account in the computation under this Chapter of the gain accruing on that disposal any money or money's worth charged to income tax as income of, or taken into account as a receipt in computing income, profits, gains or losses for the purposes of the Income Tax Acts of, the person making the disposal; but the exclusion from consideration under this subsection shall not be taken as applying to a computation in accordance with Case I of Schedule D for the purpose of restricting relief in respect of expenses of management under section 707.

(3) Subsection (2) shall not be taken as excluding from the consideration so taken into account any money or money's worth taken into account in the making of a balancing charge under Part 9 or under Chapter 1 of Part 29.

(4) This section shall not preclude the taking into account in a computation under this Chapter of the gain, as consideration for the disposal of an asset, of the capitalised value of a rent (as in a case where rent is exchanged for some other asset), or of a right of any other description to income or to payments in the nature of income over a period, or to a series of payments in the nature of income.

Cross-references

Deduction of offshore income gain in calculating capital gain, subs (2): s 747(2).
Disallowance of premiums treated as rent under superior lease: Sch 14 para 7(2).
Exclusion of premiums taxed under Sch D Case V: Sch 14 para 6(5).
Life assurance companies, management expenses deduction, subs (2): s 707(5)(*b*).
Overseas life assurance companies, investment income: s 726(6)(*a*)(ii).
Petroleum trade, exploration expenditure, subs (3): s 693(14)(*a*).
Transactions in land, Schedule D Case IV: s 644(5).

Definitions

Appeal Commissioners: ss 2(1), 5(1); Income Tax Acts: s 1(2); inspector: ss 2(1), 5(1), 852; part disposal: ss 5(1), 534; person: IA 1937 s 11(*c*); profession: ss 2(1), 5(1); rent: s 5(1); trade: s 5(1).

Former enactments

CGTA 1975 s 51(1) and Sch 1 para 2; CTA 1976 s 140(2) and Sch 2 Pt II para 8.

Corresponding UK tax provision

Taxation of Chargeable Gains Act 1992 s 37.

552 Acquisition, enhancement and disposal costs

(1) Subject to the Capital Gains Tax Acts, the sums allowable as a deduction from the consideration in the computation under this Chapter of the gain accruing to a person on the disposal of an asset shall be restricted to—

(*a*) the amount or value of the consideration in money or money's worth given by the person or on the person's behalf wholly and exclusively for the acquisition of the asset, together with the incidental costs to the person of the acquisition or, if the asset was not acquired by the person, any expenditure wholly and exclusively incurred by the person in providing the asset,

(*b*) the amount of any expenditure wholly and exclusively incurred on the asset by the person or on the person's behalf for the purpose of enhancing the value of the asset, being expenditure reflected in the state or nature of the asset at the time of the disposal, and any expenditure wholly and exclusively incurred by the person in establishing, preserving or defending the person's title to, or to a right over, the asset, and

(*c*) the incidental costs to the person of making the disposal.

[(1A)(*a*) In this subsection "rate of exchange" means a rate at which 2 currencies might reasonably be expected to be exchanged for each other by persons dealing at arm's length.

(*b*) For the purposes of subsection (1) where a sum allowable as a deduction was incurred in a currency other than the currency of the State, it shall be expressed in terms of the currency of the State by reference to the rate of exchange of the currency of the State for the other currency at the time that the sum was incurred.][1]

(2) For the purposes of the Capital Gains Tax Acts as respects the person making the disposal, the incidental costs to the person of the acquisition of the asset or of its disposal shall consist of expenditure wholly and exclusively incurred by that person for the purposes of the acquisition or, as the case may be, the disposal, being fees, commission or remuneration paid for the professional services of any surveyor, valuer, auctioneer, accountant, agent or legal advisor and costs of transfer or conveyance (including stamp duty), together with—

(*a*) in the case of the acquisition of an asset, costs of advertising to find a seller, and

(*b*) in the case of a disposal, costs of advertising to find a buyer and costs reasonably incurred in making any valuation or apportionment required for the purposes of the computation under this Chapter of the gain, including in particular expenses reasonably incurred in ascertaining market value where required by the Capital Gains Tax Acts.

(3) (*a*) Where—

(i) a company incurs expenditure on the construction of any building, structure or works, being expenditure allowable as a deduction under subsection (1) in computing a gain accruing to the company on the disposal of the building, structure or works, or of any asset comprising the building, structure or works,

(ii) that expenditure was defrayed out of borrowed money,

(iii) the company charged to capital all or any part of the interest on that borrowed money referable to a period ending on or before the disposal, and

(iv) the company is chargeable to capital gains tax in respect of the gain,

then, the sums so allowable under subsection (1) shall include the amount of that interest charged to capital except in so far as such interest has been taken into account for the purposes of relief under the Income Tax Acts, or could have been so taken into account but for an insufficiency of income or profits or gains.

(*b*) Subject to paragraph (*a*), no payment of interest shall be allowable as a deduction under this section.

(4) Without prejudice to section 554, there shall be excluded from the sums allowable as a deduction under this section any premium or other payment made under a policy of insurance of the risk of any kind of damage or injury to, or loss or depreciation of, the asset.

(5) In the case of a gain accruing to a person on the disposal of, or of a right or interest in or over, an asset to which the person became absolutely entitled as legatee or as against the trustees of settled property—

(*a*) any expenditure within subsection (2) incurred by the person in relation to the transfer of the asset to the person by the personal representatives or trustees, and

(*b*) any such expenditure incurred in relation to the transfer of the asset by the personal representatives or trustees,

shall be allowable as a deduction under this section.

Amendments

1 Subs (1A) inserted by FA 1998 s 47 and Sch 2 para 10 with effect from such date as the Minister for Finance may appoint by order. The subsection came into operation from 31 December 1998 — Finance Act, 1998 (Section 47) (Commencement) Order, 1998, SI No 502 of 1998, refers.

Cross-references

Assets derived from other assets, subs (1): s 559(1).
Compensation and insurance money, subs (1): s 536(1)(*b*).
Contingent liabilities: s 562(1).
Demutualisation of assurance companies, subs (1): s 588(4).
Disposals to State, public bodies and charities: s 611(1)(*a*).
Employee share option schemes: s 128(10).
Employee share purchase schemes: s 479(7).
EU Council Directive 90/434/EEC, mergers, divisions, subs (1)(*a*): s 631(4)(*b*).
Exclusion of expenditure that is deductible for income tax: s 554.
Expenditure by lessee under terms of lease, subs (1)(*b*): Sch 14 para 8.
Foreign life assurance and deferred annuities: s 594(4)(*e*).
Indexation of expenditure, subs (1): s 556(2)(*a*).
Interest charged to capital: s 553.
Leases of land as wasting assets, restriction of allowable expenditure, subs (1)(*a*): Sch 14 para 2(2); subs (1)(*b*): Sch 14 para 2(4)(*b*).
Part disposals, subs (1): s 557(1).
Premiums for leases, subs (1)(*b*): Sch 14 para 4(3)(*b*)(ii).
Relinquishing of life interest by the person entitled: s 577A(*b*).
Restriction of losses by reference to capital allowances: s 555(1).
Shares and securities, identification, subs (1)(*a*)–(*b*): s 580(5)(*b*)(ii)–(iii).
Shares in close company transferring assets at undervalue, subs (1)(*a*): s 589(2).
Sub-leases out of short leases, subs (1)(*a*), (*b*): Sch 14 para 5(2)–(4).
Transfer of business to a company, subs (1)(*a*): s 600(4)(*b*), (5)(*a*).
Wasting assets qualifying for capital allowances, subs (1)(*a*)–(*b*): s 561(1)(*a*).
Wasting assets: s 560(3)–(5).
Wasting chattels, subs (1)(*a*), (*b*): s 603(2)(*a*), (3)(*a*).

Case law

Arrears of rent paid by a liquidator not allowed as enhancement expenditure: *Emmerson v Computer Time International Ltd* [1977] STC 170.
Costs incurred by trustees in varying the terms of a settlement allowed as incidental cost of disposal: *IRC v Chubbs' Trustee* (1979) 47 TC 353.
Notional cost of taxpayer's own labour not allowed: *Oram v Johnson* [1980] STC 222.
Where asset bought and sold in foreign currency, amount deductible from the sterling value of the sale proceeds is the sterling value of the cost of acquisition calculated at the date of the acquisition: *Bentley v Pike* [1981] STC 360; *Capcount Trading v Evans* [1993] STC 11.
Costs incurred by taxpayer in valuing shares allowed as a deduction but costs incurred in negotiating share valuation with the Revenue and appealing assessment were not: *Caton's administrators v Couch* [1997] STC 970.

Tax Briefing

TB31 Apr 1998 p 6 — The Euro and Tax: Capital Gains Tax — Computational Rules.

Definitions

company: s 5(1); Income Tax Acts: s 1(2); legatee: s 5(1); local authority: s 2(1); person: IA 1937 s 11(*c*); personal representatives: s 5(1), 799; settled property: s 5(1); statute: s 2(1), IA 1937 s 3.
Expenditure on obtaining release of restrictive covenant subsequent to grant of option not allowable: *Garner v Pounds Shipowners* [1999] STC 18.

Former enactments

CGTA 1975 s 51(1) and Sch 1 para 3(1)–(5); CTA 1976 s 140 and Sch 2 Pt II para 9.

Corresponding UK tax provision

Taxation of Chargeable Gains Act 1992 s 38.

553 Interest charged to capital

Where—

(*a*) a company incurs expenditure on the construction of any building, structure or works, being expenditure allowable as a deduction under section 552 in computing a gain accruing to the company on the disposal of the building, structure or works, or of any asset comprising the building, structure or works,

(*b*) that expenditure was defrayed out of borrowed money, and

(*c*) the company charged to capital all or any of the interest on that borrowed money referable to a period or part of a period ending on or before the disposal,

then, the sums so allowable shall, notwithstanding section 552(3)(*b*), include the amount of that interest charged to capital.

Definitions

company: ss 4(1), 5(1); interest: s 4(1).

Former enactments

CTA 1976 s 128.

Corresponding UK tax provision

Taxation of Chargeable Gains Act 1992 s 40.

554 Exclusion of expenditure by reference to income tax

(1) There shall be excluded from the sums allowable under section 552 as a deduction any expenditure allowable as a deduction in computing the profits or gains or losses of a trade or profession for the purposes of income tax or allowable as a deduction in computing any other income or profits or gains or losses for the purposes of the Income Tax Acts and any expenditure which, although not so allowable as a deduction in computing any losses, would be so allowable but for an insufficiency of income or profits or gains, and this subsection shall apply irrespective of whether effect is or would be given to the deduction in computing the amount of tax chargeable or by discharge or repayment of tax or in any other way.

(2) Without prejudice to subsection (1), there shall be excluded from the sums allowable under section 552 as a deduction any expenditure which, if the assets or all the assets to which the computation relates were, and had at all times been, held or used as part of the fixed capital of a trade the profits or gains of which were chargeable to income tax, would be allowable as a deduction in computing the profits or gains or losses of the trade for the purposes of the Income Tax Acts.

Cross-references

Acquisition, enhancement and disposal costs: s 552(4).

BES investments: s 489(12).

Employee share purchase schemes: s 479(7).

Film investments: s 481(20)(*c*)(ii).

Restriction of losses by reference to capital allowances: s 555(1).

Transactions in land, Schedule D Case IV: s 644(5).

Definitions

Income Tax Acts: s 1(2); profession: ss 2(1), 5(1); trade: s 5(1).

Former enactments

CGTA 1975 s 51(1) and Sch 1 para 4.

Corresponding UK tax provision

Taxation of Chargeable Gains Act 1992 s 39.

555 Restriction of losses by reference to capital allowances and renewals allowances

(1) Section 554 shall not require the exclusion from the sums allowable as a deduction under section 552 of any expenditure as being expenditure in respect of which a capital allowance or renewals allowance is made but, in the computation of the amount of a loss accruing to the person making the disposal, there shall be excluded from the sums allowable as a deduction any expenditure to the extent to which any capital allowance or renewals allowance has been or may be made in respect of that expenditure.

(2) Where the person making the disposal acquired the asset—

(*a*) by a transfer to which section 289(6) or 295 applies, or

(*b*) by a transfer by means of a sale in relation to which an election under section 312(5) was made,

then, this section shall apply as if any capital allowance made to the transferor in respect of the asset had (except in so far as any loss to the transferor was restricted under those sections) been made to the person making the disposal (being the transferee) and, where the transferor acquired the asset by such a transfer, capital allowances which by virtue of this subsection may be taken into account in relation to the transferor shall also be taken into account in relation to the transferee, and so on for any series of transfers before the disposal.

(3) The amount of capital allowances to be taken into account under this section in relation to a disposal includes any allowances to be made by reference to the event which is the disposal, and there shall be deducted from the amount of the allowances the amount of any balancing charge to which effect has been or is to be given by reference to the event which is the disposal, or any earlier event, and of any balancing charge to which effect might have been so given but for the making of an election under section 290.

Cross-references

Companies' chargeable gains, disposals or acquisitions outside a group: s 619(1).

Part disposals: s 557(3).

Petroleum trade, exploration expenditure: s 693(14)(*b*).

Reliefs for lessors and owner-occupiers in respect of expenditure incurred on the provision of certain residential accommodation, relief for lessors: s 372AP(13).

Definitions

capital allowance: ss 2(1), 5(1); Income Tax Acts: s 1(2).

Former enactments

CGTA 1975 s 51(1) and Sch 1 para 5(1)–(2) and (4).

Corresponding UK tax provision

Taxation of Chargeable Gains Act 1992 s 41.

556 Adjustment of allowable expenditure by reference to consumer price index

(1) In this section—

"the consumer price index number" means the All Items Consumer Price Index Number compiled by the Central Statistics Office;

"the consumer price index number relevant to any year of assessment" means the consumer price index number at the [mid-November][1] before the commencement of that year expressed on the basis that the consumer price index at mid-November, 1968, was 100.

(2) (*a*) For the purposes of computing the chargeable gain accruing to a person on the disposal of an asset, each sum (in this section referred to as **"deductible expenditure"**) allowable as a deduction from the consideration for the disposal under paragraphs (*a*) and (*b*) of section 552(1) shall be adjusted by multiplying it by the figure (in this section referred to as **"the multiplier"**) [specified in subsection (5), determined under subsection (6) or specified in subsection (6A), as the case may be.][2]

(*b*) This subsection shall not apply in relation to deductible expenditure where the person making the disposal had incurred the expenditure in the period of 12 months ending on the date of the disposal.

(3) For the purposes of the Capital Gains Tax Acts, it shall be assumed that an asset held by a person on the 6th day of April, 1974, was sold and immediately reacquired by such person on that date, and there shall be deemed to have been given by such person as consideration for the reacquisition an amount equal to the market value of the asset at that date.

(4) Subsections (2) and (3) shall not apply in relation to the disposal of an asset if as a consequence of the application of those subsections—

(*a*) a gain would accrue on that disposal to the person making the disposal and either a smaller gain or a loss would so accrue if those subsections did not apply, or

(*b*) a loss would so accrue and either a smaller loss or a gain would accrue if those subsections did not apply,

and accordingly, in a case to which paragraph (*a*) or (*b*) applies, the amount of the gain or loss accruing on the disposal shall be computed without regard to subsections (2) and (3); but, in a case where this subsection would otherwise substitute a loss for a gain or a gain for a loss, it shall be assumed in relation to the disposal that the relevant asset was acquired by the owner for a consideration such that neither a gain nor a loss accrued to the owner on making the disposal.

(5) In relation to the disposal of an asset made in the year 1997–98, the multiplier shall be the figure mentioned in column (2) of the Table to this subsection opposite the mention in column (1) of that Table of the year of assessment in which the deductible expenditure was incurred.

TABLE

Year of assessment in which deductible expenditure incurred	Multiplier
(1)	(2)
1974–75	6.112
1975–76	4.936
1976–77	4.253
1977–78	3.646
1978–79	3.368
1979–80	3.039
1980–81	2.631
1981–82	2.174
1982–83	1.829
1983–84	1.627
1984–85	1.477
1985–86	1.390
1986–87	1.330
1987–88	1.285
1988–89	1.261
1989–90	1.221
1990–91	1.171
1991–92	1.142
1992–93	1.101
1993–94	1.081
1994–95	1.063
1995–96	1.037
1996–97	1.016

(6) (*a*) The Revenue Commissioners shall make regulations specifying the multipliers, determined in accordance with paragraph (*b*), in relation to the disposal of an asset made in the year 1998–99 and shall make corresponding regulations in relation to the disposal of an asset made [in each subsequent year][3] of assessment up to and including the year of assessment 2003.][4]

(*b*) The multiplier, in relation to the disposal of an asset made in the year 1998–99 or [any subsequent year of assessment up to and including the year of assessment 2003,][5] shall be the quotient, rounded up to 3 decimal places, obtainable by dividing the consumer price index number relevant to the year of assessment in which the disposal is made by the consumer price index number relevant to the year of assessment in which the deductible expenditure was incurred.

[(6A) In relation to the disposal of an asset made in the year 2004 or any subsequent year of assessment, the multiplier shall be the figure mentioned in column (2) of the Table to this subsection opposite the mention in column (1) of that Table of the year of assessment in which the deductible expenditure was incurred.

TABLE

Year of assessment in which deductible expenditure incurred	Multiplier
(1)	(2)
1974–75	7.528
1975–76	6.080
1976–77	5.238
1977–78	4.490
1978–79	4.148
1979–80	3.742
1980–81	3.240
1981–82	2.678
1982–83	2.253
1983–84	2.003
1984–85	1.819
1985–86	1.713
1986–87	1.637
1987–88	1.583
1988–89	1.553
1989–90	1.503
1990–91	1.442
1991–92	1.406
1992–93	1.356
1993–94	1.331

1994–95	1.309
1995–96	1.277
1996–97	1.251
1997–98	1.232
1998–99	1.212
1999–00	1.193
2000–01	1.144
2001	1.087
2002	1.049
2003 and subsequent years	1.000][6]

(7) Every regulation made under this section shall be laid before Dáil Éireann as soon as may be after it is made and, if a resolution annulling the regulation is passed by Dáil Éireann within the next 21 days on which Dáil Éireann has sat after the regulation is laid before it, the regulation shall be annulled accordingly, but without prejudice to the validity of anything previously done thereunder.

(8) A capital sum which under section 536(1)(*a*) is to be deducted from any expenditure allowable as a deduction in computing a gain on the disposal of an asset shall be deducted from the sum applied in restoring the asset before subsection (2) is applied to the residue, if any, of that sum.

(9) An amount determined in accordance with subsection (3) in respect of an asset shall be reduced by any expenditure within section 565 which relates to the asset and which was incurred before the 6th day of April, 1974, and subsection (2) shall apply to the residue of that amount.

Amendments

1 Substituted by FA 2001 s 77(2) and Sch 2 paras 33 and 61(*d*) with effect from 1 January 2002; previously "mid-February".

2 Substituted by FA 2003 s 65(*a*) with effect from 1 January 2003; previously "specified in subsection (5) or determined under subsection (6), as the case may be.".

3 Substituted by FA 2005 s 147 and Sch 6 para 1(*i*) with effect from 25 March 2005; previously "in in each subsequent year".

4 Substituted by FA 2003 s 65(*b*) with effect from 1 January 2003; previously "each subsequent year of assessment.".

5 Substituted by FA 2003 s 65(*c*) with effect from 1 January 2003; previously "any subsequent year of assessment,".

6 Subs (6A) and Table inserted by FA 2003 s 65(*d*) with effect from 1 January 2003.

Cross-references

Calls on shares: s 582.
Capital gains tax share reinvestment, withdrawal of relief: s 591(12).
Chargeable gains of life business: s 711(1)(*a*)(i).
Companies' chargeable gains, company reconstruction or amalgamation, transfer of assets: s 615(2).
Disposals or acquisitions outside a group: s 619(2)(*a*).
Development land chargeable gains, restriction of indexation relief, subs (2): s 651.

Disposal of interests in non-qualifying funds, calculation of unindexed gain, subs (2): Sch 20 par 2(2)(*b*); gains since 6 April 1990, subs (4): Sch 20 para 4(3)(*b*).
Disposals involving an equalisation element, subs (4): Sch 20 para 8(3).
EU Council Directive 90/434/EEC, transfer of development land: s 633.
Foreign life assurance and deferred annuities, no indexation: s 594(2)(*c*).
Offshore funds, disposal of an interest in certain offshore funds, subs (2): s 747E(2)(*b*).
Replacement of business or other assets: s 597(6).
Replacement of qualifying premises: s 600A(4).
Special investment schemes: s 737(8)(*a*)(ii).
Special portfolio investment accounts: s 838(4)(*c*).
Undertaking for collective investment: s 738(5)(*a*)(i); taxation of unit holders: s 739(3)(*a*)(ii)(II): subs (4): s 739(5)(*a*)(ii).

Definitions

chargeable gain: ss 4(1), 5(1), 534; Dáil Éireann: IA 1937 Sch; month: IA 1937 Sch; person: IA 1937 s 11(*c*); year of assessment: ss 2(1), 5(1).

Statutory instrument

Year expenditure incurred	Multiplier for disposal in tax year					
	2003	2002	2001	2001–01	1999–00	1998–99	1997–98
2002	1.049						
2001	1.087	1.037					
2000–01	1.144	1.091	1.053				
1999–00	1.193	1.138	1.098	1.043			
1998–99	1.212	1.156	1.115	1.059	1.016		
1997–98	1.232	1.175	1.134	1.077	1.033	1.017	
1996–97	1.251	1.194	1.152	1.094	1.050	1.033	1.016
1995–96	1.277	1.218	1.175	1.116	1.071	1.054	1.037
1994–95	1.309	1.248	1.205	1.144	1.098	1.081	1.063
1993–94	1.331	1.270	1.226	1.164	1.117	1.099	1.081
1992–93	1.356	1.294	1.249	1.186	1.138	1.120	1.101
1991–92	1.406	1.341	1.294	1.229	1.179	1.161	1.142
1990–91	1.442	1.376	1.328	1.261	1.210	1.191	1.171
1989–90	1.503	1.434	1.384	1.314	1.261	1.241	1.221
1988–89	1.553	1.481	1.430	1.358	1.303	1.282	1.261
1987–88	1.583	1.510	1.457	1.384	1.328	1.307	1.285
1986–87	1.637	1.562	1.507	1.432	1.373	1.352	1.330
1985–86	1.713	1.633	1.577	1.497	1.436	1.414	1.390
1984–85	1.819	1.735	1.674	1.590	1.525	1.502	1.477
1983–84	2.003	1.911	1.844	1.752	1.680	1.654	1.627
1982–83	2.253	2.149	2.074	1.970	1.890	1.860	1.829
1981–82	2.678	2.554	2.465	2.342	2.246	2.211	2.174
1980–81	3.240	3.091	2.983	2.833	2.718	2.675	2.631
1979–80	3.742	3.570	3.445	3.272	3.139	3.090	3.039
1978–79	4.148	3.956	3.819	3.627	3.479	3.425	3.368
1977–78	4.490	4.283	4.133	3.926	3.766	3.707	3.646
1976–77	5.238	4.996	4.822	4.580	4.393	4.325	4.253
1975–76	6.080	5.799	5.597	5.316	5.099	5.020	4.936

1974–75	7.528	7.180	6.930	6.582	6.313	6.215	6.112
	1	2	3	4	5	6	7

1 Capital Gains Tax (Multipliers) (2003) Regulations (SI 12/2003).
2 Capital Gains Tax (Multipliers) (2002) Regulations (SI 1/2002).
3 Capital Gains Tax (Multipliers) (2001) Regulations (SI 125/2001).
4 Capital Gains Tax (Multipliers) (2000–2001) Regulations (SI 76/2000).
5 Capital Gains Tax (Multipliers) (1999–2000) Regulations (SI 111/1999).
6 Capital Gains Tax (Multipliers) (1998–99) Regulations, 1998 (SI 110/1998).
7 See subsection (5).

Former enactments

CGT(A)A 1978 ss 3, 16 and Sch 1 para 1; SI 157/1997.

Corresponding UK tax provision

Taxation of Chargeable Gains Act 1992 ss 53–57.

557 Part disposals

(1) Where a person disposes of an interest or rights in or over an asset and, generally wherever on the disposal of an asset, any description of property derived from that asset remains undisposed of, the sums which under paragraphs (*a*) and (*b*) of section 552(1) are attributable to the asset shall be apportioned both for the purposes of the computation under this Chapter of the gain accruing on the disposal and for the purpose of applying this Chapter in relation to the property which remains undisposed of.

(2) Such portion of the expenditure shall be allowable as a deduction in computing under this Chapter the amount of the gain accruing on the disposal as bears the same proportion to the total of those sums as the value of the consideration for the disposal bears to the aggregate of that value and the market value of the property which remains, and the balance of the expenditure shall be attributed to the property which remains undisposed of.

(3) Any apportionment to be made in pursuance of this section shall be made before the operation of section 555 and, if after a part disposal there is a subsequent disposal of an asset, the capital allowances or renewals allowances to be taken into account in pursuance of that section in relation to the subsequent disposal shall, subject to subsection (4), be those referable to the sums which under paragraphs (*a*) and (*b*) of section 552(1) are attributable to the asset whether before or after the part disposal, but those allowances shall be reduced by the amount (if any) by which the loss on the earlier disposal was restricted under that section.

(4) This section shall not be taken as requiring the apportionment of any expenditure which on the facts is wholly attributable to the asset or part of the asset which is disposed of or wholly attributable to the asset or part of the asset which remains undisposed of.

Cross-references

Apportionment of expenditure: s 544(6).
Companies' chargeable gains, groups of companies: s 616(6)(*a*).
Deduction of offshore income gain in calculating capital gain, subs (2): s 747(4).
Foreign life assurance funds, deemed disposal and reacquisition of certain assets: s 719(6).
Premiums for leases: Sch 14 para 3(2).
Sub-leases out of short leases: Sch 14 para 5(2).

Exclusion of premiums taxed under Sch D Case V: Sch 14 para 6(1).
Part disposal pre 6 April 1978: s 558(2).

Tax Briefing

TB41 Sept 2000 p 34 — A partition of a joint tenancy or tenancy in common is a disposal for capital gains tax purposes.
TB42 Dec 2000 p 48 — CGT treatment of capital sums derived from shares (part disposal).

Definitions

capital allowance: ss 2(1), 5(1); part disposal: ss 5(1), 534; person: IA 1937 s 11(*c*).

Former enactments

CGTA 1975 s 51(1) and Sch 1 para 6.

Corresponding UK tax provision

Taxation of Chargeable Gains Act 1992 s 21.

558 Part disposals before 6th day of April, 1978

(1) Where on or after the 6th day of April, 1974, but before the 6th day of April, 1978, a person made a disposal (to which paragraph 6 of Schedule 1 to the Capital Gains Tax Act, 1975, applied) of an asset held by such person on the 6th day of April, 1974, and—

(*a*) the amount of the chargeable gain which accrued on that disposal was determined under paragraph 18 of Schedule 1 to the Capital Gains Tax Act, 1975, and

(*b*) any property derived from that asset remained undisposed of on the 6th day of April, 1978,

then, for the purpose of determining the balance of the expenditure which under section 557 is to be attributed to the property which remains undisposed of, it shall be assumed that on the disposal the amount of the chargeable gain referred to in paragraph (*a*) had been determined, not under paragraph 18 of Schedule 1 to the Capital Gains Tax Act, 1975, but on the assumption that the asset was disposed of and immediately reacquired by the person on the 6th day of April, 1974.

(2) Where on or after the 6th day of April, 1974, but before the 6th day of April, 1978, a person made a disposal (to which paragraph 6 of Schedule 1 to the Capital Gains Tax Act, 1975, applied) of an asset acquired by such person on a death which occurred on or after the 6th day of April, 1974, and—

(*a*) the amount of the chargeable gain which accrued on that disposal was determined on the basis that the asset had been acquired by such person on a date earlier than the date of that death, and

(*b*) any property derived from that asset remained undisposed of on the 6th day of April, 1978,

then, notwithstanding subsection (1), for the purpose of determining the balance of the expenditure which under section 557 is to be attributed to the property which remains undisposed of, it shall be assumed that on the disposal the amount of the chargeable gain referred to in paragraph (*a*) had been determined as if section 14(1) of the Capital Gains Tax Act, 1975 (as amended by section 6 of the Capital Gains Tax (Amendment) Act, 1978) or, as the case may be, section 15(4)(*b*) of the Capital Gains Tax Act, 1975 (as amended by section 7 of the Capital Gains Tax (Amendment) Act, 1978) had applied at the date of that disposal.

Definitions

chargeable gain: ss 4(1), 5(1), 534; part disposal: ss 5(1), 534; person: IA 1937 s 11(*c*).

Former enactments

CGT(A)A 1978 s 16 and Sch 1 para 10(1)–(2).

Corresponding UK tax provision

Taxation of Chargeable Gains Act 1992 s 55.

559 Assets derived from other assets

(1) If and in so far as, in a case where assets have been merged or divided or have changed their nature, or rights or interests in or over assets have been created or extinguished, the value of an asset is derived from any other asset in the same ownership, an appropriate proportion of the sums allowable as a deduction in respect of the other asset under paragraphs (*a*) and (*b*) of section 552(1) shall, both for the purpose of the computation of a gain accruing on the disposal of the first-mentioned asset and, if the other asset remains in existence, on a disposal of that other asset, be attributed to the first-mentioned asset.

(2) The appropriate proportion shall be computed by reference to the market value at the time of disposal of the assets (including rights or interests in or over the assets) which have not been disposed of and the consideration received in respect of the assets (including rights or interests in or over the assets) disposed of.

Former enactments

CGTA 1975 s 51(1) and Sch 1 para 7.

Corresponding UK tax provision

Taxation of Chargeable Gains Act 1992 s 43.

560 Wasting assets

(1) In this Chapter—

"the residual or scrap value", in relation to a wasting asset, means the predictable value, if any, which the wasting asset will have at the end of its predictable life as estimated in accordance with this section;

"wasting asset" means an asset with a predictable life not exceeding 50 years, but so that—

(*a*) freehold land shall not be a wasting asset whatever its nature and whatever the nature of the buildings or works on that land,

(*b*) **"life"**, in relation to any tangible movable property, means useful life, having regard to the purpose for which the tangible assets were acquired or provided by the person making the disposal,

(*c*) plant and machinery shall in every case be regarded as having a predictable life of less than 50 years, and in estimating that life it shall be assumed that its life will end when it is finally put out of use as being unfit for further use and that it will be used in the normal manner and to the normal extent and will be so used throughout its life as so estimated, and

(*d*) a life interest in settled property shall not be a wasting asset until the predictable expectation of life of the life tenant is 50 years or less, and the predictable life of life interests in settled property and of annuities shall be ascertained from actuarial tables approved by the Revenue Commissioners.

(2) The question as to what is the predictable life of an asset, and the question as to what is its predictable residual or scrap value, if any, at the end of that life, shall, in so far as those questions are not immediately answered by the nature of the asset, be taken in relation to any disposal of the asset as they were known or ascertainable at the time when the asset was acquired or provided by the person making the disposal.

(3) In the computation under this Chapter of the gain accruing on the disposal of a wasting asset, it shall be assumed—

(*a*) that any expenditure attributable to the asset under section 552(1)(*a*), after deducting the residual or scrap value, if any, of the asset, is written off at a uniform rate from its full amount at the time when the asset is acquired or provided to nil at the end of its life, and

(*b*) that any expenditure attributable to the asset under section 552(1)(*b*) is written off at a uniform rate from the full amount of that expenditure at the time when that expenditure is first reflected in the state or nature of the asset to nil at the end of its life.

(4) Where any expenditure attributable to the asset under section 552(1)(*b*) creates or increases a residual or scrap value of the asset, the residual or scrap value to be deducted under subsection (3)(*a*) shall be the residual or scrap value so created or increased.

(5) Any expenditure written off under this section shall not be allowable as a deduction under section 552.

Cross-references

Chattel exemption: s 602(1).

Leases of land as wasting assets, restriction of allowable expenditure, subss (3)–(5): Sch 14 para 2(6).

Options and forfeited deposits, subs (3): s 540(7)(*b*), (8)(*a*).

Wasting assets qualifying for capital allowances, subss (3)–(5): s 561(1), (2)(*c*).

Definitions

land: s 5(1), IA 1937 Sch; person: IA 1937 s 11(*c*); settled property: s 5(1); wasting asset: ss 5(1), 560, Sch 14 para 2; year: IA 1937 Sch.

Former enactments

CGTA 1975 s 51(1) and Sch 1 paras 8 and 9.

Corresponding UK tax provision

Taxation of Chargeable Gains Act 1992 s 44.

561 Wasting assets qualifying for capital allowances

(1) Subsections (3) to (5) of section 560 shall not apply in relation to a disposal of an asset—

(*a*) which, from the beginning of the period of ownership of the person making the disposal to the time when the disposal is made, is used solely for the purposes of a trade or profession and in respect of which that person has claimed or could have claimed any capital allowance in respect of any expenditure attributable to the asset under paragraph (*a*) or (*b*) of section 552(1), or

(*b*) on which the person making the disposal has incurred any expenditure which has otherwise qualified in full for any capital allowance.

(2) In the case of the disposal of an asset which in the period of ownership of the person making the disposal has been used partly for the purposes of a trade or profession and partly for other purposes, or has been used for the purposes of a trade or profession for part of that period, or which has otherwise qualified in part only for capital allowances—

(*a*) the consideration for the disposal and any expenditure attributable to the asset under paragraph (*a*) or (*b*) of section 552(1) shall be apportioned by reference to the extent to which that expenditure qualified for capital allowances,

(*b*) the computation under this Chapter of the gain on the disposal shall be made separately in relation to the apportioned parts of the expenditure and consideration,

(*c*) subsections (3) to (5) of section 560 shall not apply for the purposes of the computation in relation to the part of the consideration apportioned to use for the purposes of the trade or profession or to the expenditure qualifying for capital allowances,

(*d*) if an apportionment of the consideration for the disposal has been made for the purposes of making any capital allowance to the person making the disposal or for the purpose of making any balancing charge on that person, that apportionment shall be employed for the purposes of this section, and

(*e*) subject to paragraph (*d*), the consideration for the disposal shall be apportioned for the purposes of this section in the same proportions as the expenditure attributable to the asset is apportioned under paragraph (*a*).

Cross-references

Leases of land as wasting assets, restriction of allowable expenditure: Sch 14 para 2(6).

Definitions

capital allowance: ss 2(1), 5(1); person: IA 1937 s 11(*c*); profession: ss 2(1), 5(1); trade: s 5(1); wasting asset: ss 5(1), 560, Sch 14 para 2.

Former enactments

CGTA 1975 s 51(1) and Sch 1 para 10.

Corresponding UK tax provision

Taxation of Chargeable Gains Act 1992 s 47.

562 Contingent liabilities

(1) No allowance shall be made under section 552—

(*a*) in the case of a disposal by means of assigning a lease of land or other property, for any liability remaining with or assumed by the person making the disposal by means of assigning the lease which is contingent on a default in respect of liabilities thereby or subsequently assumed by the assignee under the terms and conditions of the lease;

(*b*) for any contingent liability of the person making the disposal in respect of any covenant for quiet enjoyment or other obligation assumed—

(i) as vendor of land or of any estate or interest in land,

(ii) as a lessor, or

(iii) as grantor of an option binding that person to sell land or an interest in land or to grant a lease of land;

(*c*) for any contingent liability in respect of a warranty or representation made on a disposal by means of a sale or lease of any property other than land.

(2) Where it is shown to the satisfaction of the inspector that any contingent liability mentioned in subsection (1) has become enforceable and is being or has been enforced, such adjustment, whether by means of discharge or repayment of tax or otherwise, shall be made as may be necessary.

Case law

Immediate binding obligation held not a contingent liability: *Garner v Pounds Shipowners* [1999] STC 18.

Definitions

inspector: ss 2(1), 5(1), 852; land: s 5(1), IA 1937 Sch; lease: s 5(1); lessor: s 5(1); person: IA 1937 s 11(*c*).

Former enactments

CGTA 1975 s 51(1) and Sch 1 para 11.

563 Consideration due after time of disposal

(1) (*a*) In the computation of a chargeable gain, consideration for the disposal shall be taken into account without any discount for postponement of the right to receive any part of the consideration and without regard to a risk of any part of the consideration being irrecoverable or to the right to receive any part of the consideration being contingent.

(*b*) Where any part of the consideration taken into account in accordance with paragraph (*a*) is shown to the satisfaction of the inspector to be irrecoverable, such adjustment, whether by means of discharge or repayment of tax or otherwise, shall be made as the case may require.

(2) Subsection (1) shall apply for the purposes of corporation tax as it applies for the purposes of capital gains tax.

Case law

Held did not apply where consideration was wholly uncertain in amount: *Marren v Ingles* [1979] STC 637; *Marson v Marriage* [1980] STC 177.

Loss on exchange to sterling held not irrecoverable consideration: *Goodbrand v Loffland Bros North Sea* [1998] STC 930.

Definitions

chargeable gain: ss 5(1), 545; inspector: ss 2(1), 5(1), 852; month: IA 1937 Sch; person: IA 1937 s 11(*c*).

Former enactments

CGTA 1975 s 44(2); CTA 1976 s 140(2) and Sch 2 Pt II para 6.

Corresponding UK tax provision

Taxation of Chargeable Gains Act 1992 s 49.

564 Woodlands

(1) In the computation under this Chapter of the gain accruing on the disposal by an individual of woodland, there shall be excluded—

(*a*) consideration for the disposal of trees growing on the land, and

(*b*) notwithstanding section 535(2), capital sums received under a policy of insurance in respect of the destruction of or damage or injury to trees by fire or other hazard on such land.

(2) In the computation under this Chapter of the gain, so much of the cost of woodland as is attributable to trees growing on the land shall be disregarded.

(3) References in this section to trees include references to saleable underwood.

Definitions

land: s 5(1), IA 1937 Sch.

Former enactments

CGTA 1975 s 51(1) and Sch 1 para 12.

Corresponding UK tax provision

Taxation of Chargeable Gains Act 1992 s 250.

565 Expenditure reimbursed out of public money

There shall be excluded from the computation under this Chapter of a gain accruing on a disposal any expenditure which has been or is to be met directly or indirectly by any government, by any board established by statute or by any public or local authority whether in the State or elsewhere.

Cross-references

Indexation of expenditure: s 556(9).

Former enactments

CGTA 1975 s 51(1) and Sch 1 para 3(7).

Corresponding UK tax provision

Taxation of Chargeable Gains Act 1992 s 50.

566 Leases

Schedule 14 shall apply for the purposes of the Capital Gains Tax Acts.

Former enactments

CGTA 1975 s 51(1).

Corresponding UK tax provision

Taxation of Chargeable Gains Act 1992 s 240.

CHAPTER 3

Assets Held in a Fiduciary or Representative Capacity, Inheritances and Settlements

Revenue information

Information leaflet REV1 — What to do about tax when someone dies.

567 Nominees, bare trustees and agents

(1) References in the Capital Gains Tax Acts to any asset held by a person as trustee for another person absolutely entitled as against the trustee are references to a case where that other person has the exclusive right, or would have such a right if that other person were not an infant or other person under disability, subject only to satisfying any outstanding charge, lien or right of the trustees to resort to the asset for payment of duty, taxes, costs or other outgoings, to direct how that asset shall be dealt with.

(2) In relation to assets held by a person (in this subsection referred to as **"the first-mentioned person"**) as nominee for another person, or as trustee for another person absolutely entitled as against the trustee, or for any person who would be so entitled but for being an infant or other person under disability (or for 2 or more persons who are or would be jointly so entitled), the Capital Gains Tax Acts shall apply as if the property were vested in, and the acts of the first-mentioned person in relation to the assets were

the acts of, the person or persons for whom the first-mentioned person is the nominee or trustee (acquisitions from or disposals to the first-mentioned person by that person or those persons being disregarded accordingly).

[(3) Where exploration or exploitation activities are carried on by a person on behalf of the holder of a licence or lease granted under the Petroleum and Other Minerals Development Act, 1960, such holder shall for the purpose of an assessment to capital gains tax be deemed to be the agent of that person.][1]

(4) Schedule 1 shall apply for the purpose of supplementing subsection (3).

Amendments

[1] Subs (3) substituted by FA 2001 s 44(*b*) with effect from 6 April 2001.

Cross-references

Attribution of gains to beneficiaries: s 579A(1)(*b*).

Building societies, change of status, rights to shares in a successor company, subs (2): Sch 16 para 4(5)(*c*).

Chargeable gains accruing to unit trusts: s 731(2).

Funds in court, subs (2): s 572(2).

Person becoming absolutely entitled to settled property, subs (2): s 576(1).

Settled property, meaning: s 5(1).

Case law

Subs (1): Settlor held absolutely entitled to the trust property as against the trustees, where the trustees bound by the trust to carry out his instructions in relation to the property: *Boothe v Ellard* [1980] 1 WLR 1443.

"Absolutely entitled" is not necessarily restricted to beneficial entitlement: *Hart v Briscoe; Hoare Trustees v Gardner* [1978] STC 89; [1978] 1 All ER 781; *Bond v Pickford* [1983] STC 517.

Subs (2): Beneficiaries held not to be absolutely entitled as against the trustees as they had not a vested and indefeasible interest in possession: *Tomlinson v Glynns Executor & Trustee Company Limited* (1969) 45 TC 600.

Sole residuary legatee held not absolutely entitled as against the trustees to the testator's assets which had been sold to pay testator's debts and to provide for a legacy: *Cochrane v IRC* (1974) 49 TC 299.

Beneficiaries who could not call for immediate payment of their shares held not absolutely entitled as against the trustees: *Crowe v Appleby* [1975] STC 502; *Stephenson v Barclay's Bank Trust Co Ltd* [1975] STC 151; *Prest v Bettinson* [1980] STC 607.

The word "jointly" means common to two or more and is not confined to joint tenants: *Kidson v MacDonald & Another* [1974] STC 54; *Harthan v Mason* [1980] STC 94.

"Person" includes an unincorporated association: *Frampton and another (Trustees of the Worthing Rugby Football Club) v IRC* [1985] STC 186.

Former enactments

CGTA 1975 s 8(3) and s 15(10) and Sch 4 para 2; FA 1973 s 33(4) and (7).

Corresponding UK tax provision

Taxation of Chargeable Gains Act 1992 s 60.

568 Liability of trustees, etc

(1) Capital gains tax chargeable in respect of chargeable gains accruing to the trustees of a settlement or capital gains tax due from the personal representatives of a deceased person may be assessed and charged on and in the name of one or more of those trustees or personal representatives.

(2) Subject to section 567(2), chargeable gains accruing to the trustees of a settlement or to the personal representatives of a deceased person, and capital gains tax chargeable on or in the name of such trustees or personal representatives, shall not be regarded for the purposes of the Capital Gains Tax Acts as accruing to or chargeable on any other person,

nor shall any trustee or personal representative be regarded for the purposes of those Acts as an individual.

Definitions

chargeable gain: ss 5(1), 545; Income Tax Acts: s 1(2); person: IA 1937 s 11(*c*); personal representatives: s 5(1), 799; settlement: ss 5(1), 10.

Former enactments

CGTA 1975 s 51(1) and Sch 4 para 12.

Corresponding UK tax provision

Taxation of Chargeable Gains Act 1992 s 65.

569 Assets of insolvent person

(1) In this section, **"deed of arrangement"** means a deed of arrangement to which the Deeds of Arrangement Act, 1887, applies.

(2) In relation to assets held by a person as trustee or assignee in bankruptcy or under a deed of arrangement, the Capital Gains Tax Acts shall apply as if the assets were vested in, and the acts of the trustee or assignee in relation to the assets were the acts of, the bankrupt or debtor (acquisitions from or disposals to such person by the bankrupt or debtor being disregarded accordingly), and tax in respect of any chargeable gains which accrue to any such trustee or assignee shall be assessable on and recoverable from such trustee or assignee.

(3) Assets held by a trustee or assignee in bankruptcy or under a deed of arrangement at the death of the bankrupt or debtor shall for the purposes of the Capital Gains Tax Acts be regarded as held by a personal representative of the deceased, and—

(*a*) subsection (2) shall not apply after the death, and

(*b*) section 573(2) shall apply as if any assets held by a trustee or assignee in bankruptcy or under a deed of arrangement at the death of the bankrupt or debtor were assets of which the deceased was competent to dispose and which then devolved on the trustee or assignee as if the trustee or assignee were a personal representative.

(4) Assets vesting in a trustee in bankruptcy after the death of the bankrupt or debtor shall for the purposes of the Capital Gains Tax Acts be regarded as held by a personal representative of the deceased, and subsection (2) shall not apply.

Case law

Subs (2): Tax on disposal by trustee or assignee falls on him to discharge and is part of the costs of the administration of the bankruptcy which must be discharged in priority to all debts: *Re McMeekin* [1974] STC 429.

Definitions

chargeable gain: ss 5(1), 545; person: IA 1937 s 11(*c*); personal representative: ss 5(1), 799.

Former enactments

CGTA 1975 s 40.

Corresponding UK tax provision

Taxation of Chargeable Gains Act 1992 s 66.

570 Company in liquidation

Where assets of a company are vested in a liquidator under section 230 of the Companies Act, 1963, or otherwise, the Capital Gains Tax Acts shall apply as if the assets were vested in, and the acts of the liquidator in relation to the assets were acts of, the company (acquisitions from or disposals to the liquidator by the company being disregarded accordingly).

Cross-references

Disposals by liquidators and other persons: s 571(5).

Definitions

company: s 5(1).

Former enactments

CGTA 1975 s 41.

Corresponding UK tax provision

Taxation of Chargeable Gains Act 1992 s 8(6).

571 Chargeable gains accruing on disposals by liquidators and certain other persons

(1) In this section

"accountable person" means—

(*a*) a liquidator of a company, or

(*b*) any person entitled to an asset by means of security or to the benefit of a charge or encumbrance on an asset or, as the case may be, any person appointed to enforce or give effect to the security, charge or encumbrance;

"the company" has the meaning assigned to it by subsection (6);

"the debtor" has the meaning assigned to it by subsection (5);

"referable capital gains tax" has the meaning assigned to it by subsection (2);

"referable corporation tax" has the meaning assigned to it by subsection (3);

"relevant disposal" has the same meaning as in section 648.

(2) In this section—

(*a*) in a case where no chargeable gains other than the chargeable gains mentioned in subsection (5)(*a*) (in this subsection referred to as **"the referable gains"**) accrued to the debtor in the year of assessment, **"referable capital gains tax"** means the amount of capital gains tax which apart from subsection (5) would be assessable on the debtor in respect of the referable gains;

(*b*) in a case where, in addition to the referable gains, other chargeable gains accrued to the debtor in the year of assessment and, in charging all of those gains to capital gains tax without regard to subsection (5), the same rate of tax would apply, and either—

(i) none of the disposals on which the chargeable gains accrued is a relevant disposal, or

(ii) each of the disposals is a relevant disposal,

"referable capital gains tax" means an amount of tax determined by the formula—

$$\frac{A}{B} \times C$$

where—

A is the amount of capital gains tax which apart from subsection (5) would be assessable on the debtor in respect of the referable gains if no other chargeable gains accrued to the debtor in the year of assessment and if no deductions or reliefs were to be allowed against the referable gains,

B is the amount of capital gains tax which apart from subsection (5) would be assessable on the debtor in respect of all chargeable gains, including the referable gains, which accrued to the debtor in the year of assessment, if no deductions or reliefs were to be allowed against those chargeable gains, and

C is the amount of capital gains tax which apart from subsection (5) would be assessable on the debtor in respect of the total amount of chargeable gains, including the referable gains, which accrued to the debtor in the year of assessment;

(*c*) in any other case, **"referable capital gains tax"** means the amount of capital gains tax which apart from subsection (5) and taking into account—

(i) all other chargeable gains accruing to the debtor in the year of assessment, and

(ii) where appropriate, sections 546(6), 601(3) and 653,

would be the amount of capital gains tax appropriate to the referable gains.

(3) In this section—

(*a*) in a case where no chargeable gains other than—

(i) the chargeable gains mentioned in subsection (6)(*a*) (in this subsection referred to as **"the referable gains"**), or

(ii) any chargeable gains accruing on a relevant disposal,

accrued to the company in the accounting period, **"referable corporation tax"** means the amount of capital gains tax which apart from subsection (6) would be assessable on the company in respect of the referable gains on the assumptions that—

(I) notwithstanding any provision to the contrary in the Corporation Tax Acts, capital gains tax was to be charged in respect of the referable gains in accordance with the Capital Gains Tax Acts, and

(II) accounting periods were years of assessment,

or, if it is less, the amount of corporation tax which apart from subsection (6) would be assessable on the company for the accounting period;

(*b*) in a case where, in addition to the referable gains, other chargeable gains (not being chargeable gains accruing on a relevant disposal) accrued to the company in the accounting period and, on the assumptions made in paragraph (*a*), in charging all of those gains to capital gains tax without regard to subsection (6), the same rate of tax would apply, **"referable corporation tax"** means an amount of tax determined by the formula—

$$\frac{D}{E} \times F$$

where—

D is the amount of capital gains tax which, apart from subsection (6) and on the assumptions made in paragraph (*a*), would be assessable on the company in respect of the referable gains if no other chargeable gains accrued to the company in the accounting period and if no deductions or reliefs were to be allowed against the referable gains,

E is the amount of capital gains tax which, apart from subsection (6) and on the assumptions made in paragraph (*a*), would be assessable on the company in respect of all chargeable gains including the referable gains (but not including chargeable gains accruing on a relevant disposal) which accrued to the company in the accounting period, if no deductions or reliefs were to be allowed against those chargeable gains, and

F is the amount (in this subsection referred to as **"the notional amount"**) of capital gains tax which apart from subsection (6) would in accordance with section 78(2) be calculated in relation to the company for the accounting period in respect of all chargeable gains including the referable gains or, if it is less, the amount of corporation tax which apart from subsection (6) would be assessable on the company for the accounting period;

(*c*) (i) in any other case, **"referable corporation tax"** means, subject to subparagraph (ii), the amount of capital gains tax which, apart from subsection (6) and on the assumptions made in paragraph (*a*), and taking into account—

(I) all other chargeable gains (not being chargeable gains accruing on a relevant disposal) accruing to the company in the accounting period, and

(II) where appropriate, sections 546(6) and 653,

would be the amount of capital gains tax appropriate to the referable gains;

(ii) in any case in which subparagraph (i) applies, if the notional amount is greater than the amount of corporation tax which apart from subsection (6) would be assessable on the company for the accounting period, **"referable corporation tax"** shall mean an amount determined by the formula—

$$\frac{G}{H} \times K$$

where—

G is the amount which under subparagraph (i) would be the referable corporation tax,

H is the notional amount, and

K is the amount of corporation tax which apart from subsection (6) would be assessable on the company for the accounting period.

(4) (*a*) In any case where, in calculating an amount of referable capital gains tax or referable corporation tax under subsection (2)(*c*) or (3)(*c*), deductions or reliefs were to be allowed against chargeable gains accruing in a year of assessment or in an accounting period and apart from this subsection those deductions or reliefs (or part of them) would be set against 2 or more chargeable gains chargeable at the same rate of capital gains tax, then, those deductions or reliefs (or, as the case may be, that part of them) shall, in so far as is necessary to calculate the amount of referable capital gains tax or referable corporation tax, be apportioned between the chargeable gains chargeable at the same rate in proportion to the amounts of those chargeable gains.

(*b*) In the case of chargeable gains accruing to a company (not being chargeable gains accruing on a relevant disposal), any reference in paragraph (*a*) to a rate of tax shall be construed as a reference to the rate of capital gains tax which would be applicable to those gains on the assumptions made in subsection (3)(*a*).

(5) Where section 537(2) or 570 applies in respect of the disposal of an asset in a year of assessment by an accountable person, then, notwithstanding any provision of the Capital Gains Tax Acts—

(*a*) any referable capital gains tax in respect of any chargeable gains which accrue on the disposal shall be assessable on and recoverable from the accountable person,

(*b*) the referable capital gains tax shall be treated as a necessary disbursement out of the proceeds of the disposal and shall be paid by the accountable person out of those proceeds, and

(*c*) referable capital gains tax paid by the accountable person shall discharge a corresponding amount of the liability to capital gains tax, for the year of assessment in which the disposal is made, of the person (in this section referred to as **"the debtor"**) who apart from this subsection is the chargeable person in relation to the disposal.

(6) Where section 78(8) or 537(2) applies in respect of the disposal (not being a relevant disposal) of an asset in an accounting period of a company by an accountable person, then, notwithstanding any provision of the Corporation Tax Acts—

(*a*) any referable corporation tax in respect of any chargeable gains which accrue on the disposal shall be assessable on and recoverable from the accountable person,

(*b*) the referable corporation tax shall be treated as a necessary disbursement out of the proceeds of the disposal and shall be paid by the accountable person out of those proceeds, and

(*c*) referable corporation tax paid by the accountable person shall discharge a corresponding amount of the liability to corporation tax, for the accounting period in which the disposal is made, of the company (in this section referred to as **"the company"**) which apart from this subsection is the chargeable person in relation to the disposal.

(7) Notwithstanding any provision of the Capital Gains Tax Acts or of the Corporation Tax Acts, the amount of referable capital gains tax or referable corporation tax, as the case may be, which under this section is assessable on an accountable person in relation

to a disposal, shall be recoverable by an assessment on the accountable person to income tax under Case IV of Schedule D for the year of assessment in which the disposal occurred on an amount the income tax on which at the standard rate for that year of assessment is equal to the amount of the referable capital gains tax or referable corporation tax, as the case may be.

(8) Where tax is paid by an accountable person under this section and it is established that the amount of tax paid is excessive, appropriate relief by means of repayment or otherwise shall be given to the accountable person.

(9) Subject to subsections (5)(*c*) and (6)(*c*), nothing in this section shall affect the amount of chargeable gains on which—

(*a*) the debtor is chargeable to capital gains tax, or

(*b*) the company is chargeable to corporation tax.

Definitions

chargeable gain: ss 4(1), 5(1), 534; company: ss 4(1), 5(1); Corporation Tax Acts: s 1(2); standard rate: ss 3(1), 15; year of assessment: ss 2(1), 5(1).

Former enactments

FA 1983 s 56.

572 Funds in court

(1) In this section—

"the Accountant" means the Accountant attached to the court or a deputy appointed by the Minister for Justice, Equality and Law Reform;

"court" means the High Court except where the reference is to the Circuit Court;

"funds in court" means any moneys (and investments representing such moneys), annuities, stocks, shares or other securities standing or to be placed to the account of the Accountant in the books of the Bank of Ireland or any company, and includes boxes and other effects.

(2) For the purposes of section 567(2), funds in court shall be regarded as held by the Accountant as nominee for the persons entitled to or interested in the funds or, as the case may be, for their trustees.

(3) Where funds in court standing to an account in the books of the Accountant are invested or after investment are realised, the method by which the Accountant effects the investment or the realisation of investments shall not affect the question as to whether there is for the purposes of the Capital Gains Tax Acts an acquisition or, as the case may be, a disposal of an asset representing funds in court standing to that account, and in particular there shall for those purposes be an acquisition or disposal of assets notwithstanding that the investment of funds in court standing to an account in the books of the Accountant, or the realisation of funds which have been so invested, is effected by setting off in the Accountant's accounts investment in one account against realisation of investments in another.

(4) This section shall apply with any necessary modifications to funds in the Circuit Court as it applies to funds in court.

Definitions

Bank of Ireland: IA 1937 Sch; Circuit Court: IA 1937 Sch; company: s 5(1); High Court: IA 1937 Sch; person: IA 1937 s 11(*c*); shares: s 5(1).

Former enactments

CGTA 1975 s 42.

Corresponding UK tax provision

Taxation of Chargeable Gains Act 1992 s 61.

573 Death

(1) In this section, references to assets of which a deceased person was competent to dispose are references to assets of the deceased which the deceased could if of full age and capacity have disposed of by will, assuming that all the assets were situated in the State and that the deceased was domiciled in the State, and include references to the deceased's severable share in any assets to which immediately before his or her death he or she was beneficially entitled as a joint tenant.

(2) For the purposes of the Capital Gains Tax Acts, the assets of which a deceased person was competent to dispose—

(*a*) shall be deemed to be acquired on his or her death by the personal representatives or other person on whom they devolve for a consideration equal to their market value at the date of the death; but

(*b*) shall not be deemed to be disposed of by him or her on his or her death (whether or not they were the subject of a testamentary disposition).

(3) Allowable losses sustained by an individual in the year of assessment in which he or she dies may, in so far as they cannot be deducted from chargeable gains accruing in that year, be deducted from chargeable gains accruing to the deceased in the 3 years of assessment preceding the year of assessment in which the death occurs, taking chargeable gains accruing in a later year before those accruing in an earlier year, and there shall be made all such amendments of assessments or repayments of tax as may be necessary to give effect to this subsection.

(4) In relation to property forming part of the estate of a deceased person, the personal representatives shall for the purposes of the Capital Gains Tax Acts be treated as being a single and continuing body of persons (distinct from the persons who may from time to time be the personal representatives), and that body shall be treated as having the deceased's residence, ordinary residence and domicile at the date of death.

(5) Where any asset is acquired by a person as legatee no chargeable gain shall accrue to the personal representatives, but the legatee shall be treated as if the personal representatives' acquisition of the asset had been the legatee's acquisition of the asset.

(6) Where not more than 2 years, or such longer period as the Revenue Commissioners may by notice in writing allow, after a death any of the dispositions of the property of which the deceased was competent to dispose, whether effected by will or under the law relating to intestacies or otherwise, are varied by a deed of family arrangement or similar instrument, this section shall apply as if the variations made by the deed or other instrument were effected by the deceased, and no disposition made by the deed or other instrument shall constitute a disposal for the purposes of the Capital Gains Tax Acts.

Cross-references

Allowable losses: s 546(5).

Assets of insolvent persons, subs (2): s 569(3)(*b*).

Disposal of material interest in offshore fund, subs (2): s 741(3), (4).

Foreign funds, taxation and returns of certain funds, interpretation and application, subs (2)(*b*): s 747B(3).

Foreign life assurance and deferred annuities, taxation and returns, s 594(2) to apply as if subs (2)(*b*) of this section had not been enacted: s 594(1)(*c*)(iii).

Offshore funds, taxation and returns of certain funds, interpretation and application, subs (2)(*b*): s 747B(3).

Case law

Subs (6): Where words were omitted from a deed of family arrangement, the court could order that the missing words be read in so as to give effect to the obvious intention of the deed: *Schneider v Mills* [1993] STC 430.

Where will varied by deed of family arrangement which resulted in property passing to a discretionary trust, the settlor to the trust is the testator and not the beneficiary executing the deed: *Marshall v Kerr* [1993] STC 360.

Definitions

allowable loss: ss 4(1), 5(1), 546; body of persons: s 2(1); chargeable gain: ss 5(1), 545; legatee: s 5(1); person: IA 1937 s 11(*c*); personal representative: ss 5(1), 799; writing: IA 1937 Sch; year of assessment: ss 2(1), 5(1).

Former enactments

CGTA 1975 s 14; CGT(A)A 1978 s 6(1).

Corresponding UK tax provision

Taxation of Chargeable Gains Act 1992 s 62.

574 Trustees of settlement

(1) (*a*) In relation to settled property, the trustees of a settlement shall for the purposes of the Capital Gains Tax Acts be treated as being a single and continuing body of persons (distinct from the persons who may from time to time be the trustees) and, subject to paragraph (*b*), that body shall be treated as being resident and ordinarily resident in the State unless the general administration of the trusts is ordinarily carried on outside the State and the trustees or a majority of them for the time being are not resident or not ordinarily resident in the State.

(*b*) A person carrying on a business which consists of or includes the management of trusts, and acting as trustees of a trust in the course of that business, shall be treated in relation to that trust as not resident in the State if the whole of the settled property consists of or derives from property provided by a person not at the time (or, in the case of a trust arising under a testamentary disposition or on an intestacy or partial intestacy, at his or her death) domiciled, resident or ordinarily resident in the State and, if in such a case the trustees or a majority of them are or are treated in relation to that trust as not resident in the State, the general administration of the trust shall be treated as ordinarily carried on outside the State.

(2) Where any amount of capital gains tax assessed on the trustees or any one trustee of a settlement in respect of a chargeable gain accruing to the trustee is not paid within 6 months from the date when it becomes payable by the trustees or trustee and, before or after the expiration of that period of 6 months, the asset in respect of which the chargeable gain accrued, or any part of the proceeds of sale of that asset, is transferred by the trustees to a person who as against the trustees is absolutely entitled to it, then, that person may, at any time within 2 years from the time when that amount of tax

became payable, be assessed and charged (in the name of the trustees) to an amount of capital gains tax not exceeding the amount of capital gains tax chargeable on an amount equal to the amount of the chargeable gain and, where part only of the asset or of the proceeds was transferred, not exceeding a proportionate part of that amount.

(3) For the purposes of this section, where part of the property comprised in a settlement is vested in one trustee or set of trustees and part in another trustee or set of trustees (and in particular where settled land within the meaning of the Settled Land Act, 1882, is vested in the tenant for life and investments representing capital money are vested in the trustees of the settlement), they shall be treated as together constituting and, in so far as they act separately, as acting on behalf of a single body of trustees.

Cross-references

Chargeable gains accruing to unit trusts: s 731(2).

Company buying its own shares, residence of trustees: s 177(3).

Case law

A number of transaction which had no bona fide commercial purpose were held to constitute a settlement: *Copeman v Coleman* (1939) 22 TC 594; *Chinn v Collins* [1981] STC 1.

Commercial transactions with no element of bounty cannot constitute a settlement: *Bulmer v CIR* (1966) 44 TC 1; *IRC v Plummer* [1979] STC 793; *Berry v Warnett* [1980] STC 504; *IRC v Levy* [1982] STC 442.

There is a deemed disposal where trustees transfer trust assets so as to take them out of the original settlement and subject them to new trusts: *Hart v Briscoe* [1978] STC 89; *Hoare Trustees v Gardner* [1978] STC 89.

Held an appointment of trust property by trustees did not create a separate settlement: *Roome v Edwards* [1981] STC 96; *Bond v Pickford* [1983] STC 517; *Swires v Renton* [1991] STC 490.

Definitions

allowable loss: ss 4(1), 5(1), 546; body of persons: s 2(1); chargeable gain: ss 5(1), 545; land: s 5(1), IA 1937 Sch; month: IA 1937 Sch; person: IA 1937 s 11(*c*); resident: s 5(1); settled property: s 5(1); settlement s 5(1); shares: s 5(1); year of assessment: ss 2(1), 5(1).

Former enactments

CGTA 1975 s 15(1), (9) and (11).

Corresponding UK tax provision

Taxation of Chargeable Gains Act 1992 s 69.

575 Gifts in settlement

A gift in settlement, whether revocable or irrevocable, shall be a disposal of the entire property thereby becoming settled property notwithstanding that the donor has some interest as a beneficiary under the settlement and notwithstanding that the donor is a trustee or the sole trustee of the settlement.

Cross-references

Chargeable gains accruing to unit trusts: s 731(2).

Former enactments

CGTA 1975 s 15(2).

Corresponding UK tax provision

Taxation of Chargeable Gains Act 1992 s 70.

576 Person becoming absolutely entitled to settled property

(1) On the occasion when a person becomes absolutely entitled to any settled property as against the trustee, all the assets forming part of the settled property to which the person becomes so entitled shall be deemed for the purposes of the Capital Gains Tax Acts to

have been disposed of by the trustee, and immediately reacquired by the trustee in the trustee's capacity as a trustee within section 567(2), for a consideration equal to their market value.

(2) On the occasion when a person becomes absolutely entitled to any settled property as against the trustee, any allowable loss which has accrued to the trustee in respect of property which is, or is represented by, the property to which that person becomes so entitled (including any allowable loss carried forward to the year of assessment in which that occasion falls), being a loss which cannot be deducted from chargeable gains accruing to the trustee in that year, but before that occasion, shall be treated for the purposes of the Capital Gains Tax Acts as if it were an allowable loss accruing at that time to the person becoming so entitled, instead of to the trustee.

Cross-references

Chargeable gains accruing to unit trusts: s 731(2).

Death of annuitant, subs (1): s 578.

Disposals to State, public bodies and charities, subs (1): s 611(2).

Miscellaneous exemptions, subs (1): s 613(4)(*b*).

Relinquishing of life interest by the person entitled, subs (1): s 577A(1).

Termination of life interest on death of person entitled, subs (1): s 577(2).

Case law

Subs (1): Children became absolutely entitled as against the trustees as class of beneficiaries closed when their father died and not when he became paralysed and incapable of having more children: *Figg v Clarke* [1997] STC 247.

Time of becoming absolutely entitled: *Begg MacBrearty v Stilwell (Trustee of the Coke Settlement)* [1996] STC 413.

Former enactments

CGTA 1975 s 15(3) and (8).

Corresponding UK tax provision

Taxation of Chargeable Gains Act 1992 s 71.

577 Termination of life interest on death of person entitled

(1) (*a*) In this section, **"life interest"**, in relation to a settlement—

(i) includes a right under the settlement to the income of, or the use or occupation of, settled property for the life of a person (or for the lives of persons) other than the person entitled to the right,

(ii) does not include any right which is contingent on the exercise of the discretion of the trustee or the discretion of some other person, and

(iii) does not include an annuity, notwithstanding that the annuity is payable out of or charged on settled property or the income of settled property except where some or all of the settled property is appropriated by the trustees as a fund out of which the annuity is payable and there is no right of recourse to settled property not so appropriated, or to the income of settled property not so appropriated.

(*b*) Without prejudice to subsection (4)(*b*), where under paragraph (*a*)(iii) an annuity is to be treated as a life interest in relation to a settlement, the settled property or the part of the settled property appropriated by the trustees as a fund out of which the annuity is payable shall, while the annuity is payable and on the occasion of the death of the annuitant, be treated for the purposes of subsection (3) as being settled property under a separate settlement.

(2) Where by virtue of section 576(1) the assets forming part of any settled property are deemed to be disposed of and reacquired by the trustee on the occasion when a person becomes absolutely entitled to the assets as against the trustee, then, if that occasion is the termination of a life interest by the death of the person entitled to that interest—

(*a*) no chargeable gain shall accrue on the disposal, and

(*b*) the reacquisition under that section shall be deemed to be for a consideration equal to the market value of the assets at the date of the death.

(3) On the termination of a life interest in possession in all or any part of settled property, the whole or a corresponding part of each of the assets forming part of the settled property and not ceasing at that time to be settled property shall be deemed for the purposes of the Capital Gains Tax Acts at that time to be disposed of by the trustee, and immediately reacquired by the trustee, for a consideration equal to the whole or a corresponding part of the market value of the asset.

(4) For the purposes of subsection (3)—

(*a*) a life interest which is a right to part of the income of settled property shall be treated as a life interest in a corresponding part of the settled property, and

(*b*) if there is a life interest in a part of the settled property and, where that interest is a life interest in income, there is no right of recourse to, or to the income of, the remainder of the settled property, the part of the settled property in which the life interest subsists shall while it subsists be treated for the purposes of this subsection as being settled property under a separate settlement.

(5) (*a*) Subject to paragraph (*b*), where—

(i) as a consequence of a termination, on the death of the person entitled to it, of a life interest in settled property, subsection (3) applies, and

(ii) an asset which forms the whole or any part of that settled property—

(I) is comprised in an inheritance (within the meaning of the [Capital Acquisitions Tax Consolidation Act 2003][1]) taken on the death, and

(II) is exempt from tax in relation to the inheritance under [section 77][2] of that Act, or that section as applied by [section 77(6) and (7) of the Capital Acquisitions Tax Consolidation Act 2003],[3]

that asset shall for the purposes of subsection (3), be excluded from the assets deemed to be disposed of and immediately reacquired.

(*b*) Where, in a year of assessment, in respect of an asset an exemption from tax in relation to an inheritance referred to in paragraph (*a*) ceases to apply, then, the chargeable gain which but for paragraph (*a*) would have accrued to the trustee on the termination of the life interest in accordance with subsection (3) shall be deemed to accrue to the trustee in that year of assessment and shall accordingly be included in the return required to be made by the trustee concerned under section 951, for that year of assessment.

Amendments

[1] Substituted by CATCA 2003 s 119 and Sch 3 with effect from 21 February 2003; previously "Capital Acquisitions Tax Act 1976".

[2] Substituted by CATCA 2003 s 119 and Sch 3 with effect from 21 February 2003; previously "section 55".

[3] Substituted by CATCA 2003 s 119 and Sch 3 with effect from 21 February 2003; previously "section 39 of the Finance Act 1978".

Cross-references

Chargeable gains accruing to unit trusts: s 731(2).

Death of annuitant, subs (3): s 578.

Disposals to State, public bodies and charities, subs (3): s 611(2).

Relinquishing of life interest by the person entitled, meaning of "life interest" applied: s 577A.

Former enactments

CGTA 1975 s 15(4)–(6) and (12); CGT(A)A 1978 s 7(1); FA 1997 s 73(1).

Corresponding UK tax provision

Taxation of Chargeable Gains Act 1992 s 72.

577A Relinquishing of a life interest by the person entitled

[Where by virtue of section 576(1) the assets forming part of any settled property are deemed to be disposed of and immediately reacquired by the trustee on the occasion when a person becomes absolutely entitled to the assets as against the trustee, then, in case that occasion is the relinquishing of a life interest (within the meaning of section 577) by the person entitled to that interest, the trustee shall be given such relief as would be given under sections 598 and 599 to the person who relinquished the life interest—

(*a*) if the person had become absolutely entitled to the assets as against the trustee at the commencement of the life interest and had continued to be so entitled throughout the period (in this section referred to as the **"life interest period"**) that the life interest subsisted, and

(*b*) as if any expenditure of the kind referred to in paragraph (*b*) of section 552(1) that was incurred on the assets during the life interest period by the trustee had been incurred by the person.][1]

Amendments

[1] Section 577A inserted by FA 1998 s 69 as respects disposals deemed to be made on or after 12 February 1998.

Definitions

person: IA 1937 s 11(*c*); settled property: s 5(1).

578 Death of annuitant

Sections 576(1) and 577(3) shall apply where an annuity which is not a life interest within the meaning of section 577 is terminated by the death of the annuitant as they apply on the termination of a life interest (within the meaning of that section) by the death of the person entitled to that life interest.

Cross-references

Chargeable gains accruing to unit trusts: s 731(2).

Former enactments

CGTA 1975 s 15(7).

Corresponding UK tax provision

Taxation of Chargeable Gains Act 1992 s 75.

579 Non-resident trusts

(1) This section shall apply as respects chargeable gains accruing to the trustees of a settlement where the trustees are not resident and not ordinarily resident in the State, and where the settlor or one of the settlors is domiciled and either resident or ordinarily resident in the State, or was domiciled and either resident or ordinarily resident in the State when such settlor made the settlement.

(2) (*a*) Any beneficiary under the settlement who is domiciled and either resident or ordinarily resident in the State in any year of assessment shall be treated for the purposes of the Capital Gains Tax Acts as if an apportioned part of the amount, if any, on which the trustees would have been chargeable to capital gains tax under section 31, if domiciled and either resident or ordinarily resident in the State in that year of assessment, had been chargeable gains accruing to the beneficiary in that year of assessment.

(*b*) For the purposes of this section, any amount referred to in paragraph (*a*) shall be apportioned in such manner as is just and reasonable between persons having interests in the settled property, whether the interest is a life interest or an interest in reversion, and so that the chargeable gain is apportioned as near as may be according to the respective values of those interests, disregarding in the case of a defeasible interest the possibility of defeasance.

(3) For the purposes of this section—

(*a*) where in any of the 5 years ending with that in which the chargeable gain accrues a person has received a payment or payments out of the income of the settled property made in exercise of a discretion, such person shall be regarded, in relation to that chargeable gain, as having an interest in the settled property of a value equal to that of an annuity of a yearly amount equal to 20 per cent of the total of the payments so received by such person in those 5 years, and

(*b*) where a person (in this paragraph referred to as **"the recipient"**) receives at any time after the chargeable gain accrues a capital payment made out of the settled property in exercise of a discretion, being a payment which represents the chargeable gain in whole or in part, then, except in so far as any part of the gain has been attributed under this section to some other person who is domiciled and resident or ordinarily resident in the State, the recipient shall, if domiciled and resident or ordinarily resident in the State, be treated as if the chargeable gain or, as the case may be, the part of the chargeable gain represented by the capital payment, had accrued to the recipient at the time when the recipient received the capital payment.

(4) In the case of a settlement made before the 28th day of February, 1974—

(*a*) subsection (2) shall not apply to a beneficiary whose interest is solely in the income of the settled property and who cannot, by means of the exercise of any power of appointment or power of revocation or otherwise, obtain for himself or herself, whether with or without the consent of any other person, any part of the capital represented by the settled property, and

(*b*) payment of capital gains tax chargeable on a gain apportioned to a beneficiary in respect of an interest in reversion in any part of the capital represented by the settled property may be postponed until that person becomes absolutely entitled to that part of the settled property, or disposes of the whole or any part of his or her interest, unless he or she can, by any means described in paragraph (*a*), obtain for himself or herself any of it at any earlier time,

and, for the purposes of this subsection, property added to a settlement after the settlement is made shall be regarded as property under a separate settlement made at the time when the property is so added.

(5) In any case in which the amount of any capital gains tax payable by a beneficiary under a settlement in accordance with this section is paid by the trustees of the settlement, such amount shall not for the purposes of income tax or capital gains tax be regarded as a payment to such beneficiary.

(6) This section shall not apply in relation to a loss accruing to the trustees of the settlement.

Cross-references

Attribution of gains to beneficiaries: s 579A(2)(*b*), (*f*).

Offshore income gains accruing to persons resident or domiciled abroad, for any reference to a chargeable gain substitute a reference to an offshore income gain: s 746(1)(*a*); in subs (2) for "the Capital Gains Tax Acts" substitute "the Tax Acts": s 746(1)(*b*); in subs (2) for "capital gains tax under section 31" read "income tax by virtue of section 745": s 746(1)(*c*); in subs (5) for "any capital gains tax payable" read "any income tax or corporation tax payable" and for "for the purposes of income tax" read "for the purposes of income tax, corporation tax": s 746(1)(*d*); subs (3): s 746(2); s 746(4).

Capital gains tax, returns relating to non-resident companies and trusts: s 917.

Self assessment, due dates for payment, subs (4)(*b*): s 959(5).

Case law

Potential beneficiaries under a discretionary settlement have "interests in the settled property" and the entire gain must be apportioned among them: *Leedale v Lewis* [1982] STC 169; *Bayley v Garrod* [1983] STC 287.

Where gains ought to have been attributed to beneficiaries in the year in which they arose but were not, the Revenue cannot seek to tax payments made out of the gains in a later tax year: *Ewart v Taylor* [1983] STC 721.

Where beneficiaries assigned their interest in the settlement prior to the sale of trust property by the trustees, they could not be assessed on the gain arising to the trustees: *Jones v Lincoln-Lewis* [1991] STC 307.

Gains are computed as if the trustees were UK resident or ordinarily resident and the gain so computed is treated as a chargeable gain accruing to the beneficiary — the provision does not make the trustees themselves chargeable to tax: *Rothschild v Lawrenson* [1994] STC 8.

Definitions

chargeable gain: ss 5(1), 545; person: IA 1937 s 11(*c*); resident: s 5(1); settled property: s 5(1); settlement s 5(1); year of assessment: ss 2(1), 5(1).

Former enactments

CGTA 1975 s 37.

Corresponding UK tax provision

Taxation of Chargeable Gains Act 1992 s 83 and Sch 11(18).

579A Attribution of gains to beneficiaries

[(1) (*a*) For the purposes of this section and the following sections of this Chapter, **"capital payments"** means any payment which is not chargeable to income tax on the recipient or, in the case of a recipient who is neither resident nor ordinarily resident in the State, any payment received otherwise than as income, but does not include a payment under a transaction entered into at arm's length.

(*b*) In paragraph (*a*) references to a payment include references to the transfer of an asset and the conferring of any benefit, and to any occasion on which settled property becomes property to which section 567(2) applies.

(*c*) The amount of a capital payment made by way of loan, and of any other capital payment which is not an outright payment of money, shall be taken to be equal to the value of the benefit conferred by it.

(*d*) A capital payment shall be treated as received by a beneficiary from the trustees of a settlement if—

(i) the beneficiary receives it from the trustees directly or indirectly,

(ii) it is directly or indirectly applied by the trustees in payment of any debt of the beneficiary or is otherwise paid for the benefit of the beneficiary, or

(iii) it is received by a third party at the beneficiary's direction.

[(2) (*a*) This section shall apply to a settlement for any year of assessment (beginning on or after 6 April 1999) during which the trustees are at no time resident or ordinarily resident in the State and—

(i) the settlor does not have an interest in the settlement at any time in that year of assessment, or

(ii) the settlor does have an interest in the settlement but—

(I) was not domiciled in the State, and

(II) was neither resident nor ordinarily resident in the State,

in that year of assessment, or when the settlor made the settlement.

(*b*) Section 579 shall not apply as respects chargeable gains accruing after 5 April 1999 to trustees of a settlement to which this section applies; and references in subsections (4) and (5) to capital payments received by beneficiaries do not include references to any payments received before 11 February 1999 or any payments received on or after that date so far as they represent a chargeable gain which accrued to the trustees in respect of a disposal by the trustees before 11 February 1999.

(*c*) For the purposes of this subsection a settlor has an interest in a settlement if—

(i) any relevant property which is, or may at any time become, comprised in the settlement is, or will or may become, applicable for the benefit of or payable in any circumstances to, a relevant beneficiary,

(ii) any relevant income which arises, or may arise, under the settlement is, or will or may become, applicable for the benefit of or payable in any circumstances to, a relevant beneficiary, or

(iii) a relevant beneficiary enjoys a benefit directly or indirectly from any relevant property which is comprised in the settlement or any relevant income arising under the settlement.

(*d*) In this subsection—

"relevant beneficiary" means—

(i) the settlor,

(ii) the spouse of the settlor,

(iii) a company controlled by either or both the settlor and the spouse of the settlor, or

(iv) a company associated with a company referred to in paragraph (iii) of this definition;

"relevant income" means income originating from the settlor;

"relevant property" means property originating from the settlor.

(*e*) For the purposes of this subsection—

(i) references to property originating from a person are references to property provided by that person, and property representing that property,

(ii) references to income originating from a person are references to income from property originating from that person and income provided by that person,

(iii) whether a company is controlled by a person or persons shall be construed in accordance with section 432 without regard to subsection (6) of that section,

(iv) whether a company is associated with another company shall be construed in accordance with section 432 without regard to subsection (6) of that section, and

(v) references to relevant property comprised in a settlement being, or becoming, applicable for the benefit of or payable in any circumstances to, a relevant beneficiary, do not include references to the repayment of, or obligation to repay, a loan to a settlor which loan was provided by the settlor to the trustees of the settlement on terms that it would be repaid.

(*f*) Where, for the year of assessment 2002 or any subsequent year of assessment, chargeable gains are treated as accruing to a beneficiary under a settlement by virtue of section 579, then notwithstanding that section such chargeable gains, in so far as they are in respect of a disposal made on or after 7 March 2002 by the trustees of the settlement, shall be treated as accruing to the settlor in relation to the settlement and not to any other person, if the settlor is resident or ordinarily resident in the State, whether or not the settlor is the beneficiary.][1]

(3) There shall be computed in respect of every year of assessment for which this section applies the amount on which the trustees would have been chargeable to capital gains tax under section 31 if they had been resident and ordinarily resident in the State in the year of assessment and that amount, together with the corresponding amount in respect of any earlier such year of assessment, so far as not already treated under subsection (4) or section 579F(2) as chargeable gains accruing to beneficiaries under the settlement, is in this section referred to as **"the trust gains for the year of assessment"**.

(4) Subject to this section, the trust gains for a year of assessment shall be treated for the purposes of the Capital Gains Tax Acts as chargeable gains accruing in the year of assessment to beneficiaries of the settlement who receive capital payments from the trustees in the year of assessment or have received such payments in any earlier year of assessment.

(5) The attribution of chargeable gains to beneficiaries under subsection (4) shall be made in proportion to, but shall not exceed, the amounts of capital payments received by them.

(6) A capital payment shall be left out of account for the purposes of subsections (4) and (5) to the extent that chargeable gains have, by reason of the payment, been treated as accruing to the recipient in an earlier year of assessment.

(7) A beneficiary shall not be charged to tax on chargeable gains treated by virtue of subsection (4) as accruing to him or her in any year of assessment unless he or she is domiciled in the State at some time in that year of assessment.

(8) For the purposes of this section a settlement arising under a will or intestacy shall be treated as made by the testator or, as the case may be, intestate at the time of death.

(9) In any case in which the amount of any capital gains tax payable by a beneficiary under a settlement in accordance with this section is paid by the trustees of the settlement, such amount shall not for the purposes of income tax or capital gains tax be regarded as a payment to the beneficiary.

...[2]][3]

Amendments

1 Subs (2) substituted by FA 2002 s 47(1)(*a*) with effect from 11 February 1999.

2 Subss (10) and (11) deleted by FA 2002 s 47(1)(*b*) with effect from 11 February 1999.

3 Section 579A inserted by FA 1999 s 88(1) with effect from 11 February 1999.

Cross-references

Migrant settlement: s 579F(1), (3).

Offshore income gains accruing to persons resident or domiciled abroad, for any reference to a chargeable gain substitute a reference to an offshore income gain: s 746(1)(*a*); in subs (4) for "the Capital Gains Tax Acts" read "the Tax Acts": s 746(1)(*b*); in subs (3) for "capital gains tax under section 31" read "income tax by virtue of section 745": s 746(1)(*c*); in subs (9) for "any capital gains tax payable" read "any income tax or corporation tax payable" and for "for the purposes of income tax" read "for the purposes of income tax, corporation tax": s 746(1)(*d*); subs (4): s 746(2A); s 746(4)(*b*).

Returns relating to non-resident companies and trusts: s 917.

Transfer of assets abroad, liability of non-transferors: s 807A(6).

Definitions

Capital Gains Tax Acts: s 1(2); chargeable gain: ss 5(1); 545; ordinarily resident: s 5(1); person: IA 1937 s 11(*c*); resident: s 5(1); settlement: s 5(1); year of assessment: s 5(1).

Corresponding UK tax provision

Taxation of Chargeable Gains Act 1992 s 87.

579B Trustees ceasing to be resident in the State

[(1) In this section and in the following sections of this Chapter—

"arrangements" means arrangements having the force of law by virtue of [section 826(1)(*a*)][1] (as extended to capital gains tax by section 828);

"the new assets" and **"the old assets"** have the meaning assigned, respectively, to them by section 597(4).

(2) This section shall apply where the trustees of a settlement become at any time (hereafter in this section referred to as the **"relevant time"**) neither resident nor ordinarily resident in the State.

(3) The trustees to whom this section applies shall, for the purposes of the Capital Gains Tax Acts, be deemed—

(*a*) to have disposed of the defined assets immediately before the relevant time, and

(*b*) immediately to have reacquired them,

at their market value at that time.

(4) Subject to subsections (5) and (6), the defined assets are all assets constituting settled property of the settlement immediately before the relevant time.

(5) If immediately after the relevant time—

(*a*) the trustees carry on a trade in the State through a branch or agency, and

(*b*) any assets are situated in the State and either used in or for the purposes of the trade or used or held for the purposes of the branch or agency,

the assets falling within paragraph (*b*) shall not be defined assets.

(6) Assets shall not be defined assets if—

(*a*) they are of a description specified in any arrangements, and

(*b*) the trustees would, were they to dispose of them immediately before the relevant time, fall to be regarded for the purposes of the arrangements as not being liable in the State to tax on gains accruing to them on the disposal.

(7) Notwithstanding anything in that section—

(*a*) section 597 shall not apply where the trustees—

(i) have disposed of the old assets, or their interest in them, before the relevant time, and

(ii) acquire the new assets, or their interest in them, after the relevant time, and

(*b*) where under section 597 a chargeable gain accruing on a disposal of old assets is treated as not accruing until a time later (being the time that the new assets cease to be used for the purposes of a trade or other purposes as referred to in subsection (2) of that section) than the time of the disposal, and, but for this subsection, the later time would fall after the relevant time, the chargeable gain shall be treated as accruing immediately before the relevant time,

unless the new assets are excepted from the application of this subsection by subsection (8).

(8) If at the time when the new assets are acquired—

(*a*) the trustees carry on a trade in the State through a branch or agency, and

(*b*) any new assets, which immediately after the relevant time, are situated in the State and either used in or for the purposes of the trade or used or held for the purposes of the branch or agency,

the assets falling within paragraph (*b*) shall be excepted from the application of subsection (7).][2]

Amendments

1 Substituted by FA 2004 s 89 and Sch 3 para 1(*o*) with effect from 25 March 2004; previously "section 826".

2 Section 579B inserted by FA 1999 s 88(1) with effect from 11 February 1999.

Cross-references

Death of trustee: special rules: s 579C(1)(*a*), (2), (4)(*b*).
Miscellaneous exemptions for certain kind of property: s 613(4)(a).
Offshore income gain accruing to persons resident or domiciled abroad: s 746(4)(b).
Past trustees: liability for tax: s 579D(2)(a), (3).
Returns relating to non-resident companies and trusts: s 917.
Supplementary provisions: s 613A(1).

Definitions

branch or agency: s 5(1); Capital Gains Tax Acts: s 1(2); chargeable gain: ss 5(1), 545; market value: ss 5(1), 548; ordinarily resident: s 5(1); resident: s 5(1); settled property: s 5(1); settlement: s 5(1); trade: ss 3(1), 4(1), 5(1).

Corresponding UK tax provision

Taxation of Chargeable Gains Act 1992 s 80.

579C Death of trustee: special rules

[(1) Subsection (2) applies where—

(*a*) section 579B applies as a result of the death of a trustee of a settlement, and
(*b*) within the period of 6 months beginning with the death, the trustees of the settlement become resident and ordinarily resident in the State.

(2) Section 579B shall apply as if the defined assets were restricted to such assets (if any) as—

(*a*) would be defined assets apart from this section, and
(*b*) fall within subsection (3).

(3) Assets fall within this subsection if they were disposed of by the trustees in the period which—

(*a*) begins with the death, and
(*b*) ends when the trustees become resident and ordinarily resident in the State.

(4) Where—

(*a*) at any time the trustees of a settlement become resident and ordinarily resident in the State as a result of the death of a trustee of the settlement, and
(*b*) section 579B applies as regards the trustees of the settlement in circumstances where the relevant time (within the meaning of that section) falls within the period of 6 months beginning with the death,

that section shall apply as if the defined assets were restricted to such assets (if any)—

(i) as would be defined assets but for this section, and
(ii) which the trustees acquired in the period beginning with the death and ending with the relevant time.][1]

Amendments

1 Section 579C inserted by FA 1999 s 88(1) with effect from 11 February 1999.

Cross-references

Offshore income gains accruing to persons resident or domiciled abroad: s 746(4)(*b*).
Returns relating to non-resident companies and trusts: s 917.

Definitions

month: IA 1937 Sch; ordinarily resident: s 5(1); resident: s 5(1); settlement: s 5(1).

Corresponding UK tax provision

Taxation of Chargeable Gains Act 1992 s 81.

579D Past trustees: liability for tax

[(1) In this section **"specified period"**, in relation to a year of assessment, means the period beginning with the specified return date for the year of assessment (within the meaning of section 950) and ending 3 years after the time [when a return under section 951 for the chargeable period is delivered to the Collector-General].[1]

(2) For the purposes of this section—

(*a*) where the relevant time (within the meaning of section 579B) falls within the period of 12 months beginning with the 11th day of February, 1999, the relevant period is the period beginning with that day and ending with the relevant time, and

(*b*) in any other case, the relevant period is the period of 12 months ending with the relevant time.

(3) This section shall apply at any time on or after the 11th day of February, 1999, where—

(*a*) section 579B applies as regards the trustees (in this section referred to as **"migrating trustees"**) of a settlement, and

(*b*) any tax, which is payable by the migrating trustees in respect of a chargeable gain accruing to them for a year of assessment (in this section referred to as **"the year of assessment concerned"**) by virtue of section 579B(3), is not paid within 6 months after the date on or before which the tax is due and payable.

(4) The Revenue Commissioners may, at any time before the end of the specified period in relation to the year of assessment concerned, serve on any person to whom subsection (5) applies, a notice—

(*a*) stating the amount which remains unpaid of the tax payable by the migrating trustees for the year of assessment concerned, and

(*b*) requiring that person to pay that amount within 30 days of the service of the notice.

(5) This subsection applies to any person who, at any time within the relevant period, was a trustee of the settlement, other than such a person who—

(*a*) ceased to be a trustee of the settlement before the end of the relevant period, and

(*b*) shows that, when he or she (or in the case of a company, the company) ceased to be a trustee of the settlement, there was no proposal that the trustees might become neither resident nor ordinarily resident in the State.

(6) Any amount which a person is required to pay by a notice under this section—

(*a*) may be recovered by that person from the migrating trustees,

(*b*) shall not be allowed as a deduction in computing income, profits, gains or losses for any tax purposes, and

(*c*) may be recovered from that person as if it were tax due by such person.][2]

Amendments

1 Substituted by FA 2001 s 78(2)(*b*) for the short tax "year" 2001 and later tax years (income tax and capital gains tax) and as respects accounting periods of companies ending on or after 1 April 2001; previously "when a return under section 951 for the chargeable period is delivered to the appropriate inspector (within the meaning of section 950)".

2 Section 579D inserted by FA 1999 s 88(1) with effect from 11 February 1999.

Cross-references

Offshore income gain accruing to persons resident or domiciled abroad: s 746(4)(*b*).
Returns relating to non-resident companies and trusts: s 917.

Definitions

Collector-General: ss 2(1), 851; company: ss 4(1), 5(1); month: IA 1937 Sch; ordinarily resident: s 5(1); resident: s 5(1); settlement: s 5(1); year: IA 1937 Sch; year of assessment: s 5(1).

Corresponding UK tax provision

Taxation of Chargeable Gains Act 1992 s 82.

579E Trustees ceasing to be liable to Irish tax

[(1) This section shall apply where the trustees of a settlement, while continuing to be resident and ordinarily resident in the State, become at any time (in this section referred to as **"the time concerned"**) on or after the 11th day of February, 1999, trustees who fall to be regarded for the purposes of any arrangements—

(*a*) as resident in a territory outside the State, and

(*b*) as not liable in the State to tax on gains accruing on disposals of assets (in this section referred to as **"relevant assets"**) which constitute settled property of the settlement and fall within descriptions specified in the arrangements.

(2) The trustees shall be deemed for all the purposes of the Capital Gains Tax Acts—

(*a*) to have disposed of their relevant assets immediately before the time concerned, and

(*b*) immediately to have reacquired them,

at their market value at that time.

(3) Notwithstanding anything in that section—

(*a*) section 597 shall not apply where—

(i) the new assets are, or an interest in them is, acquired by the trustees of a settlement,

(ii) at the time of the acquisition the trustees are resident and ordinarily resident in the State and fall to be regarded for the purposes of any arrangements as resident in a territory outside the State,

(iii) the assets are of a description specified in those arrangements, and

(iv) the trustees would, were they to dispose of the assets immediately after the acquisition, fall to be regarded for the purposes of the arrangements as not being liable in the State to tax on gains accruing to them on the disposal,

and

(*b*) where under section 597 a chargeable gain accruing on a disposal of the old assets is treated as not accruing until a time later (being the time that the new assets cease to be used for the purposes of a trade or other purposes as set out in subsection (2) of that section) than the time of the disposal, and but for this paragraph, the latter time would fall after the time concerned, the chargeable gain shall be treated as accruing immediately before the time concerned, if—

(i) the new assets are of a description specified in any arrangements, and

(ii) the trustees would, were they to dispose of the new assets immediately after the time concerned, fall to be regarded for the purposes of those arrangements as not being liable in the State to tax on gains accruing to them on the disposal.][1]

Amendments

1 Section 579E inserted by FA 1999 s 88 with effect from 11 February 1999.

Cross-references

Offshore income gain accruing to persons resident or domiciled abroad: s 746(4)(*b*).
Returns relating to non-resident companies and trusts: s 917.
Supplementary provisions: s 613A(3), (4)(*a*), (7)(*b*).

Definitions

arrangements: s 579(1); Capital Gains Tax Acts: s 1(2); chargeable gains: ss 5(1), 545; market value: ss 5(1), 548; new assets: s 579B(1); old assets: s 579B(1); ordinarily resident: s 5(1); resident: s 5(1); settled property: s 5(1); settlement: s 5(1); trade: ss 3(1); 4(1), 5(1).

579F Migrant settlements

[(1) Where a period (in this section referred to as **"a non-resident period"**) of one or more years of assessment for which section 579A applies to a settlement, succeeds a period (in this section referred to as **"a resident period"**) of one or more years of assessment for each of which section 579A does not apply to the settlement, a capital payment received by a beneficiary in the resident period shall be disregarded for the purposes of section 579A if it was not made in anticipation of a disposal made by the trustees in the non-resident period.

(2) Where—

(*a*) a non-resident period is succeeded by a resident period, and

(*b*) the trust gains for the last year of assessment of the non-resident period are not, or not wholly, treated as chargeable gains accruing to beneficiaries, then, subject to subsection (3), those trust gains, or the outstanding part of them, shall be treated as chargeable gains accruing in the first year of assessment of the resident period, to beneficiaries of the settlement who receive capital payments from the trustees in that year of assessment, and so on for the second and subsequent years until the amount treated as accruing to the beneficiaries is equal to the amount of the trust gains for the last year of assessment of the non- resident period.

(3) Subsections (5) and (7) of section 579A shall apply in relation to subsection (2) as they apply in relation to subsection (4) of that section.][1]

Amendments

1 Section 579F inserted by FA 1999 s 88(1) with effect from 11 February 1999.

Cross-references

Attribution of gains to beneficiaries: subs (2): s 579A(3).
Offshore income gain accruing to persons resident or domiciled abroad: s 746(4)(*b*).
Returns relating to non-resident companies and trusts: s 917.
Transfer of assets abroad, liability of non-transferors, subs (2): s 807A(6).

Definitions

capital payments: s 579A(1); chargeable gain: ss 5(1), 545; settlement: s 5(1); year of assessment: s 5(1).

Corresponding UK tax provision

Taxation of Chargeable Gains Act 1992 s 89.

CHAPTER 4
Shares and Securities

Tax Briefing

TB45 June 2000 pp 17–20 — CGT and Disposal of Shares (calculation of gain, first in first out rules, disposal of shares within 4 weeks of acquisition, bonus issues, rights issues).

580 Shares, securities, etc: identification

(1) For the purposes of identifying shares acquired with shares subsequently disposed of, in so far as the shares are of the same class, shares acquired at an earlier time shall for the purposes of the Capital Gains Tax Acts be deemed to have been disposed of before shares acquired at a later time.

(2) Shares shall not be treated for the purposes of this section as being of the same class unless, if dealt with on a stock exchange, they would be so treated, but shall be treated in accordance with this section notwithstanding that they are identified in a different way by a disposal or by the transfer or delivery giving effect to the disposal.

(3) This section shall apply to securities as it applies to shares.

(4) This section apart from subsection (2) shall apply in relation to any assets as it applies in relation to shares where the assets are of a nature to be dealt in without identifying the particular assets disposed of or acquired.

(5) (*a*) This subsection shall apply in relation to the disposal of any assets to which paragraph 13 of Schedule 1 to the Capital Gains Tax Act, 1975, applied, where—

(i) any such assets were on the 6th day of April, 1978, comprised in a holding of the kind referred to in that paragraph,

(ii) the holding consisted of assets acquired on different dates, and

(iii) before the 6th day of April, 1978, there had been a disposal of assets which if that disposal had not taken place would have been comprised in the holding on that date.

(*b*) For the purposes of applying subsection (1) in relation to each disposal to which this subsection applies—

(i) shares acquired on different dates shall be treated as if they were distinguishable parts of a single asset (in this subsection referred to as **"the holding"**) acquired respectively on the separate dates on which they were acquired and for the consideration for which they were acquired, and

(ii) it shall be assumed that, on each occasion before the 6th day of April, 1978, on which a disposal was made of shares in the holding, each of the distinguishable parts of the holding as it existed immediately before the disposal was reduced, both as regards the number of shares comprised in that part and the expenditure attributable to that part under paragraphs (*a*) and (*b*) of section 552(1), in the same proportion as the number of shares so disposed of bears to the number of shares comprised in the holding immediately before that disposal, and

(iii) the number of shares comprised in each such part on the 6th day of April, 1978, and the expenditure attributable (apart from section 556) to that part under paragraphs (*a*) and (*b*) of section 552(1) shall, in relation to a disposal made on or after that date, be the number and expenditure respectively determined in accordance with this subsection.

(*c*) Nothing in this subsection shall affect the computation of any chargeable gain or allowable loss in relation to any disposal of assets made before the 6th day of April, 1978.

(6) This section shall apply subject to section 581.

Cross-references

Special investment policies, consideration given for fund's assets: s 723(2).

Special investment schemes, consideration given for assets subject to trust created under the scheme: s 737(2)(*b*).

Undertakings for collective investment, taxation of unit holders: s 739(2)(*e*)(v).

Definitions

allowable loss: ss 4(1), 5(1), 535; chargeable gain: ss 4(1), 5(1), 534; shares: s 5(1).

Former enactments

CGT(A)A 1978 s 16 and Sch 1 para 4.

Corresponding UK tax provision

Taxation of Chargeable Gains Act 1992 Pt VI.

581 Disposals of shares or securities within 4 weeks of acquisition

(1) For the purposes of the Capital Gains Tax Acts, where the same person in the same capacity disposes of shares of the same class as shares which such person acquired within 4 weeks preceding the disposal, the shares disposed of shall be identified with the shares so acquired within those 4 weeks.

(2) For the purposes of the Capital Gains Tax Acts, where the quantity of shares of the same class disposed of exceeds the quantity of shares of the same class acquired within the period of 4 weeks preceding the disposal, the excess shall be identified with shares of the same class acquired otherwise than within the period of 4 weeks.

(3) Where a loss accrues to a person on the disposal of shares and such person reacquires shares of the same class within 4 weeks after the disposal, that loss shall not be allowable under section 538 or 546 otherwise than by deduction from a chargeable gain accruing to such person on the disposal of the shares reacquired; but, if the quantity of shares so reacquired is less than the quantity so disposed of, such proportion of the loss shall be allowable under section 538 or 546 as bears the same proportion to the loss on the disposal as the quantity not reacquired bears to the quantity disposed of.

(4) In the case of a man and his wife living with him—

(*a*) subsections (1) and (2) shall, with the necessary modifications, apply where shares are acquired by one of them and shares of the same class are disposed of within 4 weeks by the other, and (*b*) subsection (3) shall, with the necessary modifications, apply also where a loss on the disposal accrues to one of them and the acquisition after the disposal is made by the other.

(5) This section shall apply to securities as it applies to shares.

Cross-references

Chargeable gains of life business: subss (1), (2)–(3) (in so far as a chargeable gain is not thereby disregarded for the purposes of that subsection) apply as if ss 719, 723(7)(*a*), s 711(1)(*a*)(ii) and Sch 32 para 24 had not been enacted: s 711(1)(*b*).

Shares and securities, identification: s 580(6).

Special investment schemes: subss (1), (2)–(3) (in so far as a chargeable gain is not thereby disregarded for the purposes of that subsection) apply as if s 737(8)(*a*)(i) and (iii) had not been enacted: s 737(8)(*a*)(v).

Undertakings for collective investment: subss (1), (2)–(3) (in so far as a chargeable gain is not thereby disregarded for the purposes of that subsection) apply as if s 737(4), (5)(*a*)(ii) and (*c*) had not been enacted: s 738(5)(*b*).

Definitions

capital allowance: ss 2(1), 5(1); chargeable gain: ss 5(1), 545; class (of shares): s 5(1); person: IA 1937 s 11(*c*); shares: s 5(1); week: IA 1937 Sch.

Former enactments

CGTA 1975 s 51(1) and Sch 1 para 14(1)–(5).

Corresponding UK tax provision

Taxation of Chargeable Gains Tax Act 1992 s 106.

582 Calls on shares

Where, as respects an issue of shares in or debentures of a company, a person gives any consideration on a date which is more than 12 months after the date on which the shares or debentures were allotted, the consideration shall, in the computation of a gain accruing to such person on a disposal of the shares or debentures, be deemed for the purposes of section 556 to be expenditure incurred on the date on which the consideration was given.

Definitions

company: ss 4(1), 5(1); month: IA 1937 Sch; person: IA 1937 s 11(*c*); shares: s 5(1).

Former enactments

CGT(A)A 1978 s 16 and Sch 1 para 3.

Corresponding UK tax provision

Taxation of Chargeable Gains Tax Act 1992 s 113.

583 Capital distributions by companies

(1) In this section, **"capital distribution"** means any distribution from a company (including a distribution in the course of dissolving or winding up the company) in money or money's worth except a distribution which in the hands of the recipient constitutes income for the purposes of income tax.

(2) Where a person receives or becomes entitled to receive in respect of shares in a company any capital distribution from the company (other than a new holding within the meaning of section 584), such person shall be treated for the purposes of the Capital Gains Tax Acts as if such person had in consideration of that capital distribution disposed of an interest in the shares.

Cross-references

Disposal of business or farm on "retirement": s 598(7).
Profit sharing schemes: s 509(3)(*b*).
Reorganisation or reduction of share capital: s 584(5)(*a*), (8).
Recovery of capital gains tax from shareholder, meaning of "capital distribution" applied: s 977(1).

Revenue precedents

Issue: Does a charge under TCA 1997 s 583 arise in the case of a capital distribution on a group restructuring?
Decision: Where a capital distribution is generated purely by an internal group restructuring undertaken for bona fide purposes, no charge under TCA 1997 s 583 will be imposed.

Definitions

company: s 5(1); person: IA 1937 s 11(*c*); shares: s 5(1).

Former enactments

CGTA 1975 s 51(1) and Sch 2 para 1.

Corresponding UK tax provision

Taxation of Chargeable Gains Act 1992 s 122.

584 Reorganisation or reduction of share capital

(1) In this section—

"new holding", in relation to any original shares, means the shares in and debentures of the company which as a result of the reorganisation or reduction of capital represent the original shares (including such, if any, of the original shares as remain);

"original shares" means shares held before and concerned in the reorganisation or reduction of capital;

references to a reorganisation of a company's share capital include—

(*a*) any case where persons are, whether for payment or not, allotted shares in or debentures of the company in respect of and in proportion to (or as nearly as may be in proportion to) their holdings of shares in the company or of any class of shares in the company, and

(*b*) any case where there is more than one class of shares and the rights attached to shares of any class are altered;

references to a reduction of share capital do not include the paying off of redeemable share capital and, where shares in a company are redeemable by the company otherwise than by the issue of shares or debentures (with or without other consideration) and otherwise than in a liquidation, the shareholder shall be treated as disposing of the shares at the time of the redemption.

(2) This section shall apply for the purposes of the Capital Gains Tax Acts in relation to any reorganisation or reduction of a company's share capital.

(3) [Subject to subsections (4) to (9)],[1] a reorganisation or reduction of a company's share capital shall not be treated as involving any disposal of the original shares or any acquisition of the new holding or any part of it; but the original shares (taken as a single asset) and the new holding (taken as a single asset) shall be treated as the same asset acquired as the original shares were acquired.

(4) (*a*) Where on a reorganisation or reduction of a company's share capital a person gives or becomes liable to give any consideration for such person's new

holding or any part of it, that consideration shall, in the computation of a gain accruing to such person on a disposal of the new holding or any part of it, be deemed for the purposes of section 556 to be expenditure incurred on the date the consideration was given and, if the new holding or part of it is disposed of with a liability attaching to it in respect of that consideration, the consideration given for the disposal shall be adjusted accordingly.

(*b*) Notwithstanding paragraph (*a*), there shall not be treated as consideration given for the acquisition of the new holding—

(i) any surrender, cancellation or other alteration of the original shares or of the rights attached to the original shares, or

(ii) any consideration consisting of any application, in paying up the shares or debentures or any part of them, of any assets of the company, or of any dividend or other distribution declared out of those assets but not made;

but, if section 816 applies in relation to the issue of any of the shares, the sum in cash which the person would have received if the person had not exercised the option to receive additional share capital instead of a sum in cash shall be treated for the purposes of this subsection as consideration given for those shares.

(5) Where on a reorganisation or reduction of a company's share capital a person receives (or is deemed to receive), or becomes entitled to receive, any consideration other than the new holding for the disposal of an interest in the original shares, and in particular—

(*a*) where under section 583 such person is to be treated as if such person had in consideration of a capital distribution disposed of an interest in the original shares, or

(*b*) where such person receives (or is deemed to receive) a consideration from other shareholders in respect of a surrender of rights derived from the original shares,

such person shall be treated as if the new holding resulted from such person having for that consideration disposed of an interest in the original shares (but without prejudice to the original shares and the new holding being treated in accordance with subsection (3) as the same asset).

(6) Where, for the purpose of computing the gain or loss accruing to a person from the acquisition and disposal of any part of the new holding, it is necessary to apportion the cost of acquisition of any of the original shares between the part which is disposed of and the part which is retained, the apportionment shall be made by reference to market value at the date of the disposal (with such adjustment of the market value of any part of the new holding as may be required to offset any liability attaching to the new holding but forming part of the cost to be apportioned), and any corresponding apportionment for the purposes of subsection (5) shall be made in the like manner.

(7) Notwithstanding subsection (6)—

(*a*) where a new holding—

(i) consists of more than one class of shares in or debentures of the company and one or more of those classes is of shares or debentures which, at any time not later than the end of the period of 3 months beginning on the date on which the reorganisation or reduction of capital took effect, or of such longer period as the Revenue Commissioners may by notice in writing allow, had quoted market values on a recognised stock exchange in the State or elsewhere, or

(ii) consists of more than one class of rights of unit holders and one or more of those classes is of rights the prices of which were published regularly by the managers of the scheme at any time not later than the end of that period of 3 months (or longer if so allowed), and

(*b*) where, for the purpose of computing the gain or loss accruing to a person from the acquisition and disposal of the whole or any part of any class of shares or securities or rights of unit holders forming part of a new holding of the kind referred to in paragraph (*a*), it is necessary to apportion costs of acquisition between the part that is disposed of and the part that is retained,

then, the cost of acquisition of the new holding shall first be apportioned between the entire classes of shares or debentures or rights of which it consists by reference to market value on the first day (whether that day fell before the reorganisation or reduction of capital took effect or later) on which market values or prices were quoted or published for the shares, debentures or rights mentioned in paragraph (*a*) or (*b*) (with such adjustment of the market value of any class as may be required to offset any liability attaching thereto but forming part of the cost to be apportioned) and, for the purposes of this subsection, the day on which a reorganisation of share capital involving the allotment of shares or debentures or unit holders' rights takes effect shall be the day following the day on which the right to renounce any allotment expires.

(8) Where a person receives or becomes entitled to receive in respect of any shares in or debentures of a company a provisional allotment of shares in or debentures of the company and such person disposes of such person's rights, section 583 shall apply as if the amount of the consideration for the disposal were a capital distribution received by such person from the company in respect of the first-mentioned shares, and as if such person had, instead of disposing of the rights, disposed of an interest in those shares.

[(9) Subsection (3) shall not apply to the extent that the new holding comprises debentures, loan stock or other similar securities issued or allotted on or after 4 December 2002, unless—

(*a*) they were so issued or allotted pursuant to a binding written agreement made before that date, or

(*b*) this section has application by virtue of section 586.][2]

Amendments

1 Substituted by FA 2003 s 66(*a*)(i) with effect from 1 January 2003; previously "Subject to subsections (4) to (8)".

2 Subs (9) inserted by FA 2003 s 66(*a*)(ii) with effect from 1 January 2003.

Cross-references

Approved share option schemes: s 519D(4)(*b*).

BES relief, disposal of shares: s 498(6); capital gains tax: s 506(3).

Capital distributions by companies: s 583(2).

Capital gains tax, deduction from consideration on disposal of certain assets, meaning of "shares": s 980(2)(*e*).
Capital gains tax, returns and information, subs (3): s 913(5).
Company amalgamation by exchange of shares: s 586(1).
Company buying its own shares, residence conditions and ownership period: s 177(10).
Company reconstructions and amalgamations: s 587(2).
Conversion of securities: s 585(2).
Debts, subs (2): s 541(7)(*a*).
Deduction of offshore income gain in calculating capital gain, meaning of "new holding" applied, subs (1): s 747(6).
Demutualisation of assurance companies: s 588(4).
Disposal of material interest in offshore fund, subs (3): s 741(1).
Disposals and acquisitions treated as made at market value, subs (3): s 547(2)(*b*).
Employee share ownership trusts: Sch 12, paras 15(*a*), 18(2)(*a*).
Employee share purchase schemes: s 479(6).
Exchange of shares held as trading stock, meaning of "new holding" and "original shares" applied: s 715A(1); s 715A(3), (6).
Exemption from tax in the case of gains on certain disposals of shares: s 626B(1)(*b*)(iii); Sch 25A, paras 1(*a*), 5(1), (2).
Non-qualifying offshore funds: s 744(4).
Offshore fund operating equalisation arrangements, subs (3): s 742(5), (6).
Options and forfeited deposits: s 540(8)(*b*).
Profit sharing schemes, conditions as to shares: Sch 11 para 8A; interpretation: s 509(1) ("specified securities").
Reduced rate of capital gains tax on disposal by individuals of shares in unquoted companies, subs (4): s 592(7).
Returns of profits, subs (3): s 884(3).
Unit trusts, reorganisation of units in unit trust scheme: s 733(2), (3).

Case law

Subs (1): does not define exhaustively all increases in share capital which constitute a reorganisation of share capital: *Young Austen v Dunstan* [1989] STC 69.

Tax Briefing

TB42 Dec 2000 p 48 — CGT treatment in relation to "paper for paper" transaction.
TB46 Dec 2001 p 26 — Calculation of Base Cost of Eircom shares and Vodafone shares.
TB52 May 2003 p 13 — Finance Act 2003 changes.
TB53 Aug 2003 p 3 — First Active plc, CGT treatment for repayment of share capital to its shareholders in June 2003.
TB53 Aug 2003 pp 21–23 — Jefferson Smurfit shares CGT implications on takeover of company by MDCP Acquisitions Limited.

Definitions

control: s 432; class (of shares): s 5(1); company: s 5(1); month: IA 1937 Sch; person: IA 1937 s 11(*c*); shares: s 5(1); unit holder: s 5(1); writing: IA 1937 Sch.

Former enactments

CGTA 1975 s 51(1) and Sch 2 para 2(1)–(7) and (9); CGT(A)A 1978 s 16 and Sch 1 para 5.

---

585 Conversion of securities

(1) In this section—

"conversion of securities" includes—

(*a*) a conversion of securities of a company into shares in the company,

[(*b*) a conversion at the option of the holder of the securities converted as an alternative to the redemption of those securities for cash where the conversion takes place before 4 December 2002, or where the conversion takes place after that date pursuant to a binding written agreement made before that date, and][1] (*c*) any exchange of securities effected in pursuance of any enactment which provides for the compulsory acquisition of any shares or securities and the issue of securities or other securities instead;

"security" includes any loan stock or similar security, whether of any government or of any public or local authority or of any company and whether secured or unsecured but excluding securities within section 607.

(2) Section 584 shall apply with any necessary modifications in relation to the conversion of securities as it applies in relation to the reorganisation or reduction of a company's share capital.

Amendments

[1] Definition of "conversion of securities" para (*b*) substituted by FA 2003 s 66(*b*) with effect from 1 January 2003.

Cross-references

Company buying its own shares, residence conditions and ownership period: s 177(10).
Debts: s 541(1)–(3).
Non-qualifying offshore funds: s 744(4)(*a*).
Exchange of shares held as trading stock: s 751A(3), (6).
Offshore fund operating equalisation arrangements: s 742(6).
Options and forfeited deposits: s 540(8)(*b*).
Reduced rate of capital gains tax on disposal by individuals of shares in unquoted companies: s 592(7)(*b*).
Unit trusts, reorganisation of units in unit trust scheme: s 733(3).

Case law

The redemption of a loan note, which had been acquired for shares in a "paper for paper" exchange was held to be, in law as it is in fact, a disposition of the loan note. The loan note was found not to be a "debt on a security": Supreme Court: *MacAongusa v Ringmahon Company.*

Tax Briefing

TB52 May 2003 p 13 — Finance Act 2003 changes.

Definitions

company: s 5(1); local authority: s 2(1); shares: s 5(1); writing: IA 1937 Sch.

Former enactments

CGTA 1975 s 51(1) and Sch 2 para 3.

Corresponding UK tax provision

Taxation of Chargeable Gains Act 1992 s 132.

586 Company amalgamations by exchange of shares

(1) Subject to section 587, where a company issues shares or debentures to a person in exchange for shares in or debentures of another company, section 584 shall apply with any necessary modifications as if the 2 companies were the same company and the exchange were a reorganisation of its share capital.

(2) This section shall apply only where—

(*a*) the company issuing the shares or debentures has, or in consequence of the exchange will have, control of the other company, or

(*b*) the first-mentioned company issues the shares or debentures in exchange for shares as the result of a general offer made to members of the other company or any class of them (with or without exceptions for persons connected with the first-mentioned company), the offer being made in the first instance on a condition such that if it were satisfied the first-mentioned company would have control of the other company.

(3) (*a*) In this subsection, **"shares"** includes stock, debentures and any interests to which section 587(3) applies and also includes any option in relation to such shares.

(*b*) This section shall not apply to the issue by a company of shares in the company by means of an exchange referred to in subsection (1) unless it is shown that the exchange is effected for bona fide commercial reasons and does not form part of any arrangement or scheme of which the main purpose or one of the main purposes is avoidance of liability to tax.

[(*c*) This section shall not apply where, on or after 4 December 2002, a company issues debentures, loan stock or other similar securities to a person in exchange for shares of another company unless—

(i) such issue is pursuant to a binding written agreement made before that date, or

(ii) the company issuing the debentures, loan stock or other similar securities and the person to whom they are issued are members of the same group (within the meaning of section 616) throughout the period commencing one year before and ending one year after the day the debentures, loan stock or other similar securities are issued, or

(iii) the other company is a company quoted on a recognised stock exchange and its board of directors had, before 4 December 2002, made a public announcement that they had agreed the terms of a recommended offer to be made for the company's entire issued, and to be issued, ordinary share capital.][1]

Amendments

1 Subs (3)(*c*) inserted by FA 2003 s 66(*c*) with effect from 1 January 2003.

Cross-references

Approved share option schemes: s 519D(4)(*b*).

Capital gains tax, returns and information: s 913(5).

Companies' chargeable gains, shares in subsidiary member of group: s 625(6)(*a*).

Company buying its own shares, residence conditions and ownership period: s 177(10).

Company reconstructions and amalgamations: s 587(3); subs (1): 587(2); meaning of "shares" applied: s 587(4)(*a*).

Debts: s 541(2)–(3); subs (2): (7)(*b*).

Disposal of business or farm on "retirement": s 598(1)(*d*)(ii*a*)(I).

Disposal of material interest in offshore fund, subs (1): s 741(5).

Employee share ownership trusts: Sch 12, paras 15(*b*), 18(2)(*b*).

Exchange of shares held as trading stock: s 751A(3), (6).

Exemption from tax in the case of gains on certain disposals of shares: Sch 25A, para 5(1), (2).

Non-qualifying offshore funds: s 744(4)(*a*).

Offshore fund operating equalisation arrangements: s 742(6).

Options and forfeited deposits: s 540(8)(*b*).

Profit sharing schemes, conditions as to shares: Sch 11 para 8(*d*); interpretation: s 509(1) ("specified securities").

Reduced rate of capital gains tax on disposal by individuals of shares in unquoted companies: s 592(7)(*b*).

Reorganisation or reduction of share capital: s 584(9)(*b*).

Return of profits: s 884(3).

Unit trusts, reorganisation of units in unit trust scheme: s 733(2), (3).

Caselaw relating to the corresponding UK provision

This legislation was enacted to outlaw the kind of schemes involved in: *Floor v Davis* [1979] STC 379 and *Furniss v Dawson* [1982] STC 267.

Westcott v Woolcombers Ltd (1987) STC 600.

Revenue precedents

Issue: Does an earn-out which consists of shares qualify for relief under s 586?

Decision: Where part of the consideration for a take-over consists of shares or securities to be issued at a future date if a contingency is satisfied, the earn out element will be treated as a security and relief under s 586 may be due. This will apply only insofar as the earnout element does not or could not take the form of cash.

Tax Briefing

TB48 June 2002 p 15 — Company amalgamations by exchange of shares.

TB52 May 2003 p 13 — Finance Act 2003 changes.

Definitions

class (of shares): s 5(1); company: s 5(1); person: IA 1937 s 11(*c*); shares: s 5(1); writing: IA 1937 Sch.

Former enactments

CGTA 1975 s 51(1) and Sch 2 para 4; FA 1982 s 63(1)(*a*) and (2).

Corresponding UK tax provision

Taxation of Chargeable Gains Tax Act 1992 s 135.

587 Company reconstructions and amalgamations

(1) In this section, **"scheme of reconstruction or amalgamation"** means a scheme for the reconstruction of any company or companies or the amalgamation of any 2 or more companies, and references to shares or debentures being retained include their being retained with altered rights or in an altered form, whether as the result of reduction, consolidation, division or otherwise.

(2) Where under any arrangement between a company and the persons holding shares in or debentures of the company or any class of such shares or debentures, being an arrangement entered into for the purposes of or in connection with a scheme of reconstruction or amalgamation, another company issues shares or debentures to those persons in respect of and in proportion to (or as nearly as may be in proportion to) their holdings of the first-mentioned shares or debentures, but the first-mentioned shares or debentures are either retained by those persons or cancelled, then, those persons shall be treated as exchanging the first-mentioned shares or debentures for those held by them in consequence of the arrangement (any shares or debentures retained being for this purpose regarded as if they had been cancelled and replaced by a new issue), and accordingly section 586(1) shall apply to such exchange of shares or debentures.

(3) Subsection (2) shall apply in relation to a company which has no share capital as if references to shares in or debentures of a company included references to any interests in the company possessed by members of the company, and sections 584 and 586 shall apply accordingly.

(4) (*a*) In this subsection, **"shares"** has the same meaning as in section 586(3).

(*b*) This section shall not apply to the issue by a company of shares in the company under a scheme of reconstruction or amalgamation referred to in subsection (2) unless it is shown that the reconstruction or amalgamation is effected for bona fide commercial reasons and does not form part of any arrangement or scheme of which the main purpose or one of the main purposes is avoidance of liability to tax.

[(*c*) This section shall not apply to any person to whom, under a scheme of reconstruction or amalgamation, a company issues debentures, loan stock or other similar securities on or after 4 December 2002, unless—

(i) they were issued pursuant to a binding written agreement made before that date, or

(ii) that person and the company are members of the same group (within the meaning of section 616) throughout the period commencing one year before and ending one year after the day the debentures, loan stock or other similar securities were issued, or

(iii) they were issued pursuant to a scheme or arrangement, the principal terms of which had been brought to the attention of the Revenue Commissioners and the Revenue Commissioners had acknowledged in writing before 4 December 2002, to the effect that the scheme or arrangement was a scheme of reconstruction and amalgamation.][1]

Amendments

1 Subs (4)(*c*) inserted by FA 2003 s 66(*d*) with effect from 1 January 2003.

Cross-references

Approved share option schemes: s 519D(4)(*b*).

Capital gains tax, returns and information: s 913(5).

Companies' chargeable gains, shares in subsidiary member of group: s 625(6)(*a*), (7).

Company amalgamation by exchange of shares: s 586(1); subs (3): s 586(3)(*a*).

Company buying its own shares, residence conditions and ownership period: s 177(10).

Demutualisation of assurance companies: s 588(4); subss (2)–(3): s 588(2).

Disposal of business or farm on "retirement": s 598(1)(*d*)(ii*a*)(II).

Disposal of material interest in offshore fund: s 741(5).

Disposals and acquisitions treated as made at market value, subs (3): s 547(2)(*a*).

Employee share purchase schemes, disposal of shares: s 479(1)(*b*).

Exchange of shares held as trading stock: s 751A(3), (6).

Exemption from tax in the case of gains on certain disposals of shares: Sch 25A, para 5(1), (2).

Options and forfeited deposits: s 540(8)(*b*).

Profit sharing schemes, individuals ineligible to participate: Sch 11 para 13A(1).

Return of profits: s 884(3).

Reduced rate of capital gains tax on disposal by individuals of shares in unquoted companies: s 592(7)(*b*).

Case law

Where a share for share swap occurs within a group, the section only applies to the shareholder exchanging its holding for a new holding and does not apply to the company the subject of the reorganisation: *Westcott v Woolcombers Ltd* [1987] STC 600; *Nap Holdings UK Ltd v Whittles* [1994] STC 979.

Revenue Precedents

Issue: Break up of family trading company (or group of companies).

Decision: Where a family trading company (or group of companies) is broken up into separate individual trading companies, such an event will not be regarded as a disposal for CGT purposes provided that the value of each individual's holding in the company remains strictly unaltered and also provided certain other conditions are met.

Tax Briefing

TB44 June 2001 pp 34–35 — Partition of Family Trading Companies — CGT.

TB47 April 2002 p 17 — Retirement Relief and Reconstructions.

TB48 June 2002 pp 15–17 — Company reconstructions and amalgamations.

TB52 May 2002 p 13 — Finance Act 2003 changes.

Definitions

class (of shares): s 5(1); company: s 5(1); person: IA 1937 s 11(*c*); shares: s 5(1); writing: IA 1937 Sch.

Former enactments

CGTA 1975 s 51(1) and Sch 2 para 5; FA 1982 s 63(1)(*b*) and (2).

Corresponding UK tax provision

Taxation of Chargeable Gains Act 1992 s 135.

---

588 Demutualisation of assurance companies

(1) In this section—

"assurance company" has the same meaning as in section 3 of the Insurance Act, 1936;

"free shares", in relation to a member of the assurance company, means any shares issued by the successor company to that member in connection with the arrangement but for no new consideration;

"member", in relation to the assurance company, means a person who is or has been a member of it, in that capacity, and any reference to a member includes a reference to a member of any particular class or description;

"new consideration" means consideration other than—

(*a*) consideration provided directly or indirectly out of the assets of the assurance company or the successor company, or

(*b*) consideration derived from a member's shares or other rights in the assurance company or the successor company.

(2) This section shall apply as on and from the 21st day of April, 1997, in respect of an arrangement between a company and its members, being an arrangement to which subsection (2) of section 587 applies by virtue of subsection (3) of that section, and where the company is an assurance company which carries on a mutual life business.

(3) Where in connection with the arrangement there is conferred on a member of the assurance company concerned any rights—

(*a*) to acquire shares in another company (in this section referred to as the **"successor company"**) in priority to other persons,

(*b*) to acquire shares in the successor company for consideration of an amount or value lower than the market value of the shares, or

(*c*) to free shares in the successor company,

then, any such rights so conferred on a member shall be regarded for the purposes of capital gains tax as an option (within the meaning of section 540) granted to and acquired by such member for no consideration and having no value at the time of that grant and acquisition.

(4) Where in connection with the arrangement shares in the successor company are issued to a member of the assurance company concerned, and such shares are treated under section 587 as having been exchanged by the member for the interest in the company possessed by the member, those shares shall, notwithstanding section 584, be regarded for the purposes of section 552(1)—

(*a*) as having been issued to the member for a consideration given by the member of an amount or value equal to the amount or value of any new consideration given by the member for the shares or, if no new consideration is given, as having been issued for no consideration, and

(*b*) as having, at the time of their issue to the member, a value equal to the amount or value of the new consideration so given or, if no new consideration is given, as having no value;

but this subsection is without prejudice to the operation where applicable of subsection (3).

(5) Subsection (6) shall apply in any case where—

(*a*) in connection with the arrangement, shares in the successor company are issued by that company to trustees on terms which provide for the transfer of those shares to members of the assurance company concerned for no new consideration, and

(*b*) the circumstances are such that in the hands of the trustees the shares constitute settled property.

(6) (*a*) Where this subsection applies, then, for the purposes of capital gains tax—

(i) the shares shall be regarded as acquired by the trustees for no consideration,

(ii) the interest of any member in the settled property constituted by the shares shall be regarded as acquired by the member for no consideration and as having no value at the time of its acquisition, and

(iii) where on the occasion of a member becoming absolutely entitled as against the trustees to any of the settled property, both the trustees and the member shall be treated as if, on the member becoming so entitled, the shares in question had been disposed of and immediately reacquired by the trustees, in their capacity as trustees within section 567(2), for a consideration of such an amount as would secure that on the disposal neither a gain nor a loss would accrue to the trustees, and accordingly section 576(1) shall not apply in relation to that occasion.

(*b*) Reference in paragraph (*a*) to the case where a member becomes absolutely entitled to settled property as against the trustees shall be taken to include reference to the case where the member would become so entitled but for being a minor or otherwise under a legal disability.

Tax Briefing

TB30 Feb 1998 p 14 — Persons who acquired "free" and "discounted" shares as part of the Norwich Union Flotation may nominate the block of shares from which a disposal of shares is made.
TB47 April 2002 p 17 — Demutualisation of Scottish Provident.

Former enactments

CGTA 1975 s 51(1) and Sch 2 para 5A; FA 1997 s 70.

Corresponding UK tax provision

Taxation of Chargeable Gains Act 1992 s 211.

589 Shares in close company transferring assets at undervalue

(1) Where a close company transfers an asset to any person otherwise than by means of a bargain made at arm's length and for a consideration of an amount or value less than the market value of the asset, an amount equal to the difference shall be apportioned among the issued shares of the company, and the holders of those shares shall be treated in accordance with subsections (2) and (3).

(2) For the purposes of the computation of a chargeable gain accruing on the disposal of any of those shares by the person owning them on the date of transfer, an amount equal

to the amount so apportioned to that share shall be excluded from the expenditure allowable as a deduction under section 552(1)(*a*) from the consideration for the disposal.

(3) Where the person owning any of those shares at the date of transfer is itself a close company, an amount equal to the amount apportioned to the shares so owned under subsection (1) to that close company shall be apportioned among the issued shares of that close company, and the holders of those shares shall be treated in accordance with subsection (2), and so on through any number of close companies.

(4) This section shall apply to a company within section 590 as it applies to a close company.

Cross-references

Companies' chargeable gains, groups of companies: s 616(6)(*b*).
Companies' chargeable gains, transfer of trading stock within a group: s 618.

Definitions

chargeable gain: ss 5(1), 545; close company: ss 5(1), 430; company: s 5(1); person: IA 1937 s 11(*c*); shares: s 5(1).

Former enactments

CGTA 1975 s 35(1)–(3) and (5); CTA 1976 s 140 and Sch 2 Pt II para 3(1).

Corresponding UK tax provision

Taxation of Chargeable Gains Act 1992 s 125.

590 Attribution to participators of chargeable gains accruing to non-resident company

[(1) In this section—

(*a*) **"participator"**, in relation to a company, has the meaning assigned to it by section 433(1);

(*b*) references to a person's interest as a participator in a company are references to the interest in the company which is represented by all the factors by reference to which the person falls to be treated as such a participator; and

(*c*) references to the extent of such an interest are references to the proportion of the interests as participators of all the participators in the company (including any who are not resident or ordinarily resident in the State) which on a just and reasonable apportionment is represented by that interest.

(2) For the purposes of this section, where—

(*a*) the interest of any person in a company is wholly or partly represented by an interest (in this subsection referred to as the **"person's beneficial interest"**) which the person has under any settlement, and

(*b*) the person's beneficial interest is the factor, or one of the factors, by reference to which the person would be treated, apart from this subsection, as having an interest as a participator in the company,

the interest as a participator in the company which would be that person's shall be deemed, to the extent that it is represented by the person's beneficial interest, to be an interest of the trustees of the settlement, and not an interest of the person's, and references in this section, in relation to a company, to a participator shall be construed accordingly.

(3) This section shall apply as respects chargeable gains accruing to a company—

(*a*) which is not resident in the State, and

(*b*) which would be a close company if it were resident in the State.

(4) Subject to this section, every person who at the time when the chargeable gain accrues to the company is resident or ordinarily resident in the State, who, if an individual, is domiciled in the State, and who is a participator in the company, shall be treated for the purposes of the Capital Gains Tax Acts as if a part of the chargeable gain had accrued to that person.

(5) The part of the chargeable gain referred to in subsection (4) shall be equal to the proportion of that gain that corresponds to the extent of the participator's interest as a participator in the company.

(6) Subsection (4) shall not apply in the case of any participator in the company to which the gain accrues where the aggregate amount falling under that subsection to be apportioned to the participator and to persons connected with the participator does not exceed one-twentieth of the gain.

(7) This section shall not apply in relation to—

(*a*) a chargeable gain accruing on the disposal of assets, being tangible property, whether movable or immovable, or a lease of such property, where the property was used, and used only, for the purposes of a trade carried on by the company wholly outside the State,

(*b*) a chargeable gain accruing on the disposal of currency or of a debt within section 541(6), where the currency or debt is or represents money in use for the purposes of a trade carried on by the company wholly outside the State, or

(*c*) a chargeable gain in respect of which the company is chargeable to capital gains tax by virtue of section 29 or to corporation tax by virtue of section 25 (2) (*b*).

(8) Where—

(*a*) any amount of capital gains tax is paid by a person in pursuance of subsection (4), and

(*b*) an amount in respect of the chargeable gain is distributed, whether by way of dividend or distribution of capital or on the dissolution of the company, within 2 years from the time when the chargeable gain accrued to the company,

that amount of tax, so far as neither reimbursed by the company nor applied as a deduction under subsection (9), shall be applied for reducing or extinguishing any liability of the person to income tax in respect of the distribution or (in the case of a distribution falling to be treated as a disposal on which a chargeable gain accrues to the person), to any capital gains tax in respect of the distribution.

(9) The amount of capital gains tax paid by a person in pursuance of subsection (4), so far as neither reimbursed by the company nor applied under subsection (8) for reducing any liability to tax, shall be allowable as a deduction in the computation under the Capital Gains Tax Acts of a gain accruing on the disposal by the person of any asset representing the person's interest as a participator in the company.

(10) In ascertaining for the purposes of subsection (8) the amount of income tax chargeable on any person for any year of assessment on or in respect of a distribution, any such distribution mentioned in that subsection which falls to be treated as income of that person for that year of assessment shall be regarded as forming the highest part of the income on which the person is charged to tax for the year of assessment.

(11) To the extent that it would reduce or extinguish chargeable gains accruing by virtue of this section to a person in a year of assessment, this section shall apply in relation to a loss accruing to the company on the disposal of an asset in that year of assessment as it would apply if a gain instead of a loss had accrued to the company on the disposal, but shall only apply in relation to that person; and, subject to the preceding provisions of this subsection, this section shall not apply in relation to a loss accruing to the company.

(12) Where the person who is a participator in the company at the time when the chargeable gain accrued to the company is itself a company which is not resident in the State but which would be a close company if it were resident in the State, an amount equal to the amount apportioned under subsection (5) out of the chargeable gain to the participating company's interest as a participator in the company to which the gain accrues shall be further apportioned among the participators in the participating company according to the extent of their respective interests as participators, and subsection (4) shall apply to them accordingly in relation to the amounts further apportioned, and so on through any number of companies.

(13) The persons treated by this section as if a part of a chargeable gain accruing to a company had accrued to them shall include trustees who are participators in the company, or in any company amongst the participators in which the gain is apportioned under subsection (12), if when the gain accrued to the company the trustees are neither resident nor ordinarily resident in the State.

(14) Where any tax payable by any person by virtue of subsection (4) is paid by the company to which the chargeable gain accrues, or in a case under subsection (12) is paid by any such other company, the amount so paid shall not, for the purposes of income tax, capital gains tax or corporation tax, be regarded as a payment to the person by whom the tax was originally payable.

(15) For the purposes of this section, the amount of the gain or loss accruing at any time to a company which is not resident in the State shall be computed (where it is not the case) as if the company were within the charge to corporation tax on capital gains.

(16)(*a*) In this subsection—

"group" shall be construed in accordance with subsections (1) (excluding paragraph (*a*)), (3) and (4) of section 616;

"non-resident group" of companies—

(i) in the case of a group none of the members of which is resident in the State, means that group, and

(ii) in the case of a group 2 or more members of which are not resident in the State, means the members not resident in the State.

(*b*) For the purposes of this section—

(i) [section 617 (other than paragraphs (*b*) and (*c*) of subsection (1)), section 618 (with the omission of the words "to which this section applies" in subsections (1)(*a*) and (2), of "such" in subsection (1)(*c*) and of subsection (3)), section 619(2) (with the substitution for "in the course of a disposal to which section 617 applies" of "at a time when both were members of the group") and section 620(2) (with the omission of the words "to which this section applies")][1] shall apply in relation to non-resident companies which are members of a non-resident group of companies as they apply in relation to companies resident in the State which are members of a group of companies, and

(ii) sections 623 [(apart from paragraphs (*c*) and (*d*) of subsection (2))][2] and 625 shall apply as if for any reference in those sections to a group of companies there were substituted a reference to a non-resident group of companies, and as if references to companies were references to companies not resident in the State.][3]

Amendments

1 Substituted by FA 2001 s 39(1)(*a*) in respect of cases in which s 617, 618, 619(2) or 620(2) have effect as amended by FA 2001; previously "sections 617 to 620".

2 Inserted by FA 2001 s 39(1)(*b*) in respect of cases in which s 617, 618, 619(2) or 620(2) have effect as amended by FA 2001.

3 Section 590 substituted by FA 1999 s 89(1) in respect of chargeable gains accruing to a company on or after 11 February 1999.

Cross-references

Capital gains tax, returns and information: s 917.

Offshore income gains accruing to persons resident or domiciled abroad, for any reference to "chargeable gain" read "offshore income gain"; for the reference in subs (9) to "capital gains tax" read "income tax or corporation tax" and treat subss (7)(*a*)–(*b*) and (11) as deleted: s 746(3).

Shares in close company transferring assets at undervalue: s 589(4).

Definitions

chargeable gain: ss 5(1), 545; close company: ss 5(1), 430; company: s 5(1); lease: s 5(1); ordinarily resident: s 5(1); person: IA 1937 s 11(*c*); resident: s 5(1); shares: s 5(1); trade: s 5(1); year of assessment: ss 2(1), 5(1).

Former enactments

CGTA 1975 s 36; CTA 1976 s 129(6)(*c*) and (7), s140(2) and s 159 and Sch 2 Pt II paras 4 and 5.

Corresponding UK tax provision

Taxation of Chargeable Gains Act 1992 ss 13 and 191 [repealed].

591 Relief for individuals on certain reinvestment

(1) In this section—

"director" has the same meaning as in section 116;

"eligible shares" and **"ordinary shares"** have the same meanings respectively as in section 488;

"full-time director", **"full-time employee"**, **"part-time director"** and **"part-time employee"** have the same meanings respectively as in section 250;

"holding company" means a company whose business consists wholly or mainly in the holding of shares in, or securities of, one or more companies which are trading companies and which are its 51 per cent subsidiaries;

"material disposal" has the meaning assigned to it by subsection (5);

"ordinary share capital" has the same meaning as in section 2;

"the original holding" has the meaning assigned to it by subsection (2);

"qualifying company" has the meaning assigned to it by subsection (7);

"qualifying investment" has the meaning assigned to it by subsection (6);

"the reinvestor" has the meaning assigned to it by subsection (2);

"the specified period" has the meaning assigned to it by subsection (6)(*b*);

"trade" includes a profession, and **"trading company"**, **"trading group"**, **"qualifying trade"** (within the meaning of subsection (8)) and **"qualifying trading operations"** (within the meaning of that subsection) shall be construed accordingly;

"trading company" means a company whose business consists wholly or mainly of the carrying on of a trade or trades;

"trading group" means a holding company and one or more trading companies which are 51 per cent subsidiaries of the holding company;

"unquoted company" means a company none of whose shares, stocks or debentures are listed in the official list of a stock exchange or quoted on an unlisted securities market of a stock exchange;

"51 per cent subsidiary" has the meaning assigned to it by section 9.

(2) (*a*) Subject to this section, where the consideration which an individual (in this section referred to as **"the reinvestor"**) [obtains for any material disposal, before 4 December 2002, by][1] him or her of shares in or securities of any company (in this section referred to as **"the original holding"**) is applied by him or her within the period of 3 years from the date of that disposal in acquiring a qualifying investment, the reinvestor shall, on making a claim in that behalf, be treated for the purposes of the Capital Gains Tax Acts as if the chargeable gain accruing on the disposal of the original holding did not accrue until he or she disposes of the qualifying investment.

(*b*) Notwithstanding paragraph (*a*), where—

(i) the disposal of the qualifying investment is a material disposal for the purposes of this section, and

(ii) the consideration for that disposal is applied by the reinvestor within the period of 3 years from the date of that disposal in acquiring another qualifying investment,

the reinvestor shall be treated as if the chargeable gain accruing on the disposal of the original holding did not accrue until he or she disposes of the other qualifying investment and any further qualifying investment which is acquired in a similar manner.

(3) (*a*) Where an individual is not entitled to be treated in accordance with subsection (2) solely by reason of not having satisfied the requirements of either or both paragraphs (*a*) and (*e*) of subsection (6), and—

(i) all the other requirements of this section have been satisfied,

(ii) the capital gains tax on the disposal of the original holding has been paid in full, and

(iii) the individual has, throughout a period of 2 years beginning within the specified period, been a full-time employee or a full-time director of the qualifying company,

then, the individual—

(I) shall be entitled on making a claim in that behalf to such repayment of capital gains tax as would secure that the tax which is ultimately borne by the individual does not exceed the tax which would have been borne by the individual if he or she had been entitled to be treated in accordance with subsection (2), and

(II) shall be treated for the purposes of the Capital Gains Tax Acts as if the chargeable gain accruing on the disposal of the original holding did not accrue until the individual disposes of the qualifying investment, and subsection (2)(*b*) shall apply for the purposes of this subsection as it applies for the purposes of subsection (2).

(*b*) No repayment of tax under this subsection shall carry interest.

(4) Subsection (2) shall not apply if part only of the amount or value of the consideration for the material disposal of the original holding is applied, within the period of 3 years from the date of that disposal, in acquiring a qualifying investment but, if all of the amount of that consideration except for a part which is less than the amount of the gain accruing on the disposal is so applied, the reinvestor shall, on making a claim in that behalf, be treated for the purposes of the Capital Gains Tax Acts as if the amount of the gain accruing on the disposal were reduced to the amount of the consideration not applied in acquiring a qualifying investment, and the balance of the gain shall be treated as if it did not accrue until the reinvestor disposes of the qualifying investment.

(5) For the purposes of this section, the disposal of shares in or securities of a company shall be a material disposal if—

(*a*) throughout the period of 3 years ending with the date of the disposal, or

(*b*) in a case where the company commenced to trade at any time in the period mentioned in paragraph (*a*), throughout the period beginning at that time and ending with the date of the disposal,

the following conditions are satisfied—

(i) the company has been a trading company or a holding company, and

(ii) the reinvestor has been a full-time employee, part-time employee, full-time director or part-time director of the company or, if that company is a member of a trading group, of one or more companies which are members of the trading group.

(6) For the purposes of this section, an individual shall be regarded as acquiring a qualifying investment where he or she acquires any eligible shares in a qualifying company if—

(*a*) he or she holds not less than 5 per cent of the ordinary share capital of the company at any time in the period (in this subsection referred to as **"the initial period"**) beginning on the date of the acquisition of the eligible shares and ending on the date which is one year after the date of the disposal of the original holding,

(*b*) he or she holds not less than 15 per cent of the ordinary share capital of the company at any time in the period (in this section referred to as **"the specified period"**) beginning on the date of the acquisition of the eligible shares and ending on the date which is 3 years after the date of the disposal of the original holding,

(*c*) within the specified period, the company uses the money raised through the issue of the eligible shares for the purposes of enabling it, or enlarging its capacity, to undertake qualifying trading operations (within the meaning of subsection (8)),

(*d*) the company is not—

(i) the company in which the original holding has subsisted, or

(ii) a company that was a member of the same trading group as that company,

and

(*e*) he or she becomes at any time within the initial period, and is throughout the period beginning at that time and—

(i) ending at the end of the specified period, or

(ii) in a case where the company is wound up or dissolved without winding up and the conditions mentioned in subsection (7)(*d*) are satisfied, ending at the time of the commencement of the winding up or dissolution of the company,

a full-time employee or a full-time director of the company.

(7) (*a*) For the purposes of this section and subject to paragraphs (*b*) to (*d*), a company shall be a qualifying company if it is incorporated in the State and if—

(i) it is throughout the specified period—

(I) an unquoted company resident in the State and not resident elsewhere, and

(II) a company which exists wholly for the purposes of carrying on wholly or mainly in the State of one or more qualifying trades,

and

(ii) it is not at any time in the specified period—

(I) under the control of another company (or of another company and any person connected with that other company), or

(II) without being under the control of another company, a 51 per cent subsidiary of that other company.

(*b*) A company shall be deemed not to have ceased to be a qualifying company solely by virtue of shares in the company commencing, at any time in the specified period, to be quoted on the market known as the Developing Companies Market of the Irish Stock Exchange.

(*c*) A company shall cease to be a qualifying company if at any time in the specified period a resolution is passed, or an order is made, for the winding up of the company (or in the case of a winding up otherwise than under the Companies Act, 1963, any other act is done for the like purpose) or the company is dissolved without winding up.

(*d*) Notwithstanding paragraph (*c*), a company shall be deemed not to have ceased to be a qualifying company solely by virtue of the application of that paragraph where—

(i) it is shown that the winding up or dissolution is for bona fide commercial reasons and does not form part of a scheme or arrangement the main purpose or one of the main purposes of which is the avoidance of income tax, corporation tax or capital gains tax, and

(ii) the company's net assets, if any, are distributed to its members within 3 years from the commencement of the dissolution or the winding up.

(8) (*a*) In this subsection, **"qualifying trading operations"**, in relation to a trade, means all the operations of the trade excluding those of dealing in shares, securities, land, currencies, futures or traded options.

(*b*) A trade shall be a qualifying trade for the purposes of subsection (7) if throughout the specified period the trade—

(i) is conducted on a commercial basis and with a view to the realisation of profits, and

(ii) consists wholly or mainly of qualifying trading operations,

and a trade which during the specified period consists partly of qualifying trading operations and partly of other trading operations shall be regarded for the purposes of this subsection as a trade which consists wholly or mainly of qualifying trading operations only if the total amount receivable in the specified period by the company carrying on the trade from sales made and services rendered in the course of qualifying trading operations is not less than 75 per cent of the total amount receivable by the company from all sales made and services rendered in the course of the trade in the specified period.

(9) A claim for relief under this section may be made after the making of a material disposal and the acquisition of eligible shares in a qualifying company if all the conditions for the relief are or will be satisfied, but the relief shall be withdrawn if, by reason of the subsequent happening of any event or failure of an event to happen which at the time the relief was claimed was expected to happen, the individual by whom the relief was claimed is not entitled to the relief so claimed.

(10) The withdrawal of relief under subsection (9) shall be made—

(*a*) for the year of assessment in which the happening or failure to happen, as the case may be, of the event giving rise to the withdrawal of the relief occurred, and

(*b*) in accordance with subsection (11),

and both—

(i) details of the happening or the failure to happen, as the case may be, of the event giving rise to the withdrawal of relief, and

(ii) the amount to be treated as a gain under subsection (11),

shall be included in the return required to be made by the individual concerned under section 951 for that year of assessment.

(11)(*a*) Notwithstanding any other provision of the Capital Gains Tax Acts, where relief is to be withdrawn under subsection (9) for any year of assessment, such amount (in this subsection referred to as **"the relevant amount"**) of the chargeable gain which accrued to the reinvestor on the disposal of the original holding as was treated under subsection (2) or (4) as not accruing at that time—

(i) reduced in accordance with paragraph (*b*), and

(ii) increased in accordance with paragraph (*c*),

shall be treated as a gain which accrued in that year of assessment.

(*b*) The amount by which the relevant amount is to be reduced under paragraph (*a*)(i) is an amount equal to the aggregate of—

(i) to the extent that such excess has not been deducted in years of assessment subsequent to the year of assessment in which the disposal of the original holding occurred, the excess of the amount of the losses which would have been deducted under section 31 in the year of assessment in which the disposal of the original holding occurred, if relief under this section had not been claimed, over the amount of such losses which were so deducted in that year, and

(ii) any amount of chargeable gains in the year of assessment in which the disposal of the original holding occurred in respect of which the reinvestor would not by virtue of section 601 have been charged to capital gains tax if relief under this section had not been claimed.

(*c*) The amount by which the relevant amount is to be increased under paragraph (*a*)(ii) is an amount determined by the formula—

$$G \times \frac{R}{100} \times M$$

where—

G is the relevant amount reduced in accordance with paragraph (*b*),

[R is 0.083][2], and

M is the number of months in the period beginning on the date on which capital gains tax for the year of assessment in which the disposal of the original holding occurred was due and payable and ending on the date on which capital gains tax for the year of assessment for which the withdrawal of relief is to be made is due and payable.

(12) A chargeable gain or the balance of a chargeable gain which under subsection (2) or (4), as may be appropriate, is treated as accruing at a date later than the date of the disposal on which it accrued shall not be so treated for the purposes of section 556.

(13) Without prejudice to the provisions of the Capital Gains Tax Acts providing generally for apportionments, where consideration is given for the acquisition or disposal of any assets some or part of which are shares or other securities to the acquisition or disposal of which a claim under this section relates and some or part of which are not, the consideration shall be apportioned in such manner as is just and reasonable.

(14) This section shall not apply unless the acquisition of a qualifying investment was made for bona fide commercial reasons and not wholly or partly for the purposes of realising a gain from the disposal of the qualifying investment.

Amendments

1 Substituted by FA 2003 s 67(1)(*a*) with effect from 1 January 2003; previously "obtains for any material disposal by".

2 Substituted by FA 2005 s 145(7)(*a*) and Sch 5 Pt 1 in relation to any unpaid income tax, corporation tax or capital gains tax, as the case may be, that has not been paid before 1 April 2005 regardless of when that tax became due and payable and notwithstanding anything to the contrary in any other enactment other than TCA 1997 s 1082; previously "R is the rate per cent specified in section 1080(1)".

Revenue information

Information leaflet CGT3 — Roll-over Relief for Individuals on disposal of Certain Shares.

Revenue precedents

Issue: The term "qualifying trading operations" means all trading operations except dealing in shares, securities, land, currencies, futures or traded options.

Decision: For the purpose of relief under section 591, investment in a property development company will not be excluded provided: 1. The land is acquired with a view to the development and disposal of the completed development: and 2. Most of the profit is derived from the enhanced property resulting from the development (as opposed to increases in the value of land from the obtaining of planning permission or a general rise in land values). The type of operation that would be excluded would include situations where land is simply bought and sold without actually being developed. Revenue would not seek to exclude genuine building and construction companies from the relief.

Tax Briefing

TB52 May 2003 p 13 — Capital Gains Tax — Finance Act 2003.

Definitions

chargeable gain: ss 4(1), 5(1), 534; company: ss 4(1), 5(1); land: s 5(1), IA 1937 Sch; month: IA 1937 Sch; ordinary share capital: s 2(1); person: IA 1937 s 11(*c*); shares: s 5(1); trade: s 3(1); year of assessment: ss 2(1), 5(1); year: IA 1937 Sch.

Former enactments

FA 1993 s 27(1)–(5) (apart from proviso to subs (5)) and subss (6)–(13); FA 1994 s 65(*b*); FA 1995 s 74(1);FA 1996 s 62(1); FA 1997 s 75(1).

Corresponding UK tax provision

Taxation of Chargeable Gains Act 1992 s 164.

---

592 Reduced rate of capital gains tax on certain disposals of shares by individuals

---

Amendments

Repealed by FA 1998 s 70 as respects disposals made on or after 3 December 1997.

CHAPTER 5
Life Assurance and Deferred Annuities

593 Life assurance and deferred annuities

(1) This section shall apply for the purposes of the Capital Gains Tax Acts as respects any policy of assurance or contract for a deferred annuity on the life of any person.

(2) No chargeable gain shall accrue on the disposal of or of an interest in the rights under any such policy of assurance or contract except where the person making the disposal is not the original beneficial owner and acquired the rights or interests for a consideration in money or money's worth.

(3) Subject to subsection (2), the occasion of the payment of the sum or sums assured by a policy of assurance or of the first instalment of a deferred annuity, and the occasion of the surrender of a policy of assurance or of the rights under a contract for a deferred annuity, shall be the occasion of a disposal of the rights under the policy of assurance or contract for a deferred annuity, and the amount of the consideration for the disposal of a contract for a deferred annuity shall be the market value at that time of the right to the first and further instalments of the annuity.

(4) In subsection (3), the reference to payment of the sum assured shall include a reference to the transfer of investments or other assets to the owner of the policy in accordance with the policy.

Cross-references

Foreign life assurance and deferred annuities, subs (2): s 594(2)(*b*), (4)(*d*); s 594 to be construed with: subs (3)–(4) as if subs (3) were not subject to subs (2): s 594(1)(*b*).

Life policy or deferred annuity contract entered into or acquired by company, subs (2): s 595(2); s 595 to be construed with subss (3)–(4) as if subs (3) were not subject to subs (2): s 595(1)(*c*).

Definitions

chargeable gain: ss 5(1), 545; person: IA 1937 s 11(*c*).

Former enactments

CGTA 1975 s 20.

Corresponding UK tax provision

Taxation of Chargeable Gains Act 1992 s 210.

594 Foreign life assurance and deferred annuities: taxation and returns

(1) (*a*) (i) For the purposes of this section, a policy of assurance or contract for a deferred annuity on the life of any person, being a policy issued or a contract made before the 20th day of May, 1993, shall be treated as a policy issued or contract made, as the case may be, after that date if there is a variation of the policy or contract on or after that date which directly or indirectly increases the benefits secured by, or extends the term of, the policy or contract, as the case may be.

(ii) For the purposes of subparagraph (i), where a policy of assurance issued or a contract made before the 20th day of May, 1993, provides an option to have another policy or contract substituted for it or to have any of its terms changed, any change in the terms of the policy or contract made in pursuance of the option shall be deemed to be a variation of the policy or contract, as the case may be.

(*b*) Subject to subsection (2), this section shall be construed together with subsections (3) and (4) of section 593 as if subsection (3) of that section were not subject to subsection (2) of that section.

(*c*) (i) In this paragraph and in subsection (3)—

"assurance company" has the same meaning as in section 3 of the Insurance Act, 1936;

"excluded policy" means a policy of assurance or contract for a deferred annuity on the life of any person where the policy is issued to or the contract is made with, as the case may be, a person who did not continuously reside outside the State throughout the period of 6 months commencing on the date of issue or the date of contract, as the case may be;

"life assurance fund" has the same meaning as in the Insurance Acts 1909 to 1969;

"relevant company" means a company which is—

(I) resident in the State, or

(II) chargeable under Case III of Schedule D by virtue of section 726 in respect of its income from the investment of its life assurance fund.

(ii) Subsection (2) shall apply to any policy of assurance or contract for a deferred annuity on the life of any person which is a policy issued or a contract made, as the case may be ...[1]—

(I) otherwise than by an assurance company which is a relevant company, or

(II) being a policy or contract which is an excluded policy issued or made, as the case may be, by a relevant company to which section 710(2) applies.

[(iii) Subsection (2) shall apply as if section 573(2)(*b*) had not been enacted.

(iv) For the purposes of subsection (2)—

(I) there shall be a disposal of or of an interest in the rights of a policy of assurance, where benefits are payable under the policy, and

(II) where at any time, a policy of assurance, or an interest therein, gives rise to benefits in respect of death or disability, either on or before maturity of the policy, the amount or value of such benefits which shall be taken into account for the purposes of determining the amount of a gain under that subsection shall be the excess of the value of the policy or, as the case may be, the interest therein, immediately before that time, over the value of the policy or, as the case may be, the interest therein, immediately after that time.

(v) For the purposes of subparagraph (iv), the value of a policy or of an interest therein at any time means—

(I) in the case of a policy which has a surrender value, the surrender value, of the policy or, as the case may be, of the interest therein, at that time, and,

(II) in the case of a policy which does not have a surrender value, the market value of the rights or other benefits conferred by the policy or, as the case may be, the interest therein, at that time.][2]

(2) (*a*) In this subsection, **"relevant gain"** means a chargeable gain arising on a disposal of or of an interest in the rights under any policy of assurance or contract for a deferred annuity to which this subsection applies, including a disposal by a person who is not the original beneficial owner of those rights and who acquired them or an interest in them for a consideration in money or money's worth.

(*b*) Section 593(2) shall not apply in respect of any disposal of or of any interest in the rights under any policy of assurance or contract for a deferred annuity to which this subsection applies.

(*c*) A relevant gain shall be computed as if section 556 had not been enacted.

(*d*) Notwithstanding section 31, the total amount of chargeable gains accruing to a person chargeable in a year of assessment after deducting any allowable losses shall not be less than the total amount of any relevant gains accruing to the person in that year, and accordingly any deduction for allowable losses made in computing the total amount of chargeable gains so accruing shall not exceed the total amount of chargeable gains so accruing which are not relevant gains.

(*e*) Notwithstanding section 601 or 1028(4), an individual shall be charged to capital gains tax on the amount of any relevant gains accruing to the individual.

[(*f*) Notwithstanding subsection (3) of section 28, the rate of capital gains tax in respect of a relevant gain accruing to a person shall be 40 per cent.][3]

[(*g*) Where a policy was issued or a contract made before 20 May 1993, only so much of the gain on disposal as accrued on or after 20 March 2001 shall be a chargeable gain.][4]

...[5]

(4) [(*a*) in this subsection, **"reinsurance contract"** means any contract or other agreement for reassurance or reinsurance in respect of—

(i) any policy of assurance on the life of any person, or

(ii) any class of such policies,

not being new basis business within the meaning of section 730A.][6]

(*b*) Where apart from this paragraph a reinsurance contract would not be a policy of assurance on the life of any person for the purposes of the Capital Gains Tax Acts, it shall be deemed to be such a policy for those purposes.

(*c*) Subsections (2) and (3) shall not apply to, and shall be deemed never to have applied to, reinsurance contracts; but, where apart from this paragraph a reinsurance contract would not be a relevant policy within the meaning of section 595 for the purposes of that section, it shall be deemed not to be such a policy for those purposes.

(*d*) (i) Subject to paragraph (*e*), where subsection (2) would (apart from paragraph (*c*)) apply to a reinsurance contract in respect of any policy of assurance on the life of any person, being a policy issued on or after the 1st day of January, 1995, section 593(2) shall not apply in respect of any disposal or deemed disposal on or after the 1st day of January, 1995, of, or of any interest in, rights of the insured company under the reinsurance contract to the extent that—

(I) those rights refer to that policy, and

(II) the insured company could receive, otherwise than on the death, disablement or disease of any person or one of a class of persons to whom that policy refers, payment on a disposal of those rights the aggregate amount of which would exceed the aggregate amount of payment made by it in respect of those rights.

(ii) Subparagraph (i) shall apply as if—

(I) as respects any reinsurance contract made before the 20th day of May, 1993, that contract were made on that day, and

(II) as respects any reinsurance contract made or modified on or after the 1st day of January, 1995, there were deleted from subparagraph (i) "being a policy issued on or after the 1st day of January, 1995,".

(iii) Subparagraphs (i) and (ii) of subsection (1)(*a*) shall apply for the purposes of this paragraph as if for "the 20th day of May, 1993" there were substituted "the 1st day of January, 1995".

(*e*) Paragraph (*d*) shall not apply to any disposal of or of any interest in rights under a reinsurance contract, being a disposal resulting directly from the death, disablement or disease of a person or one of a class of persons to whom the reinsurance contract refers; but in computing any gain or loss in respect of a disposal or deemed disposal of or of any interest in rights of the insured company under a reinsurance contract—

(i) there shall be excluded from the sums allowable under section 552 so much of any payment made by the insured company under the reinsurance contract as is paid in respect of an entitlement to a payment on the death, disablement or disease of a person, or one of a class of persons, and

(ii) there shall be added to the consideration taken into account under Chapter 2 of this Part the market value of an entitlement for any period, commencing on or after the most recent acquisition or deemed acquisition by the insured company of those rights, to a payment on the death, disablement or disease of a person, or one of a class of persons, to the extent that the insured company held the entitlement for that period in place of any return which would otherwise have accrued under the reinsurance contract and increased that consideration.

Amendments

1 Deleted by FA 2001 s 66(1)(*a*)(i) with effect from 20 March 2001; previously ", on or after the 20th day of May, 1993".

2 Subs (1)(*c*)(iii)–(v) inserted by FA 2001 s 66(1)(*a*)(ii) with effect from 20 March 2001.

3 Subs (2)(*f*) inserted by FA 1998 s 65(1)(*b*) in relation to disposals made on or after 12 February 1998.

[4] Subs (2)(g) inserted by FA 2001 s 66(1)(*a*)(iii) with effect from 20 March 2001.
[5] Subs (3) deleted by FA 2001 s 66(1)(*b*) in respect of any chargeable period (within the meaning of s 321(2)) commencing on or after 15 February 2001.
[6] Subs (4)(*a*) substituted by FA 2001 s 66(1)(*c*) with effect from 1 January 2001.

Cross-references

Foreign life assurance fund, deemed disposal and reacquisition of certain assets, gains or losses arising, subs (4): s 720(2).
Foreign life policies, disposal of certain policies: s 730K(1); subs (2): s 730K(2).
Life policy or deferred annuity contract entered into or acquired by company: s 595(1)(*a*) (relevant policy).

Tax Briefing

TB23 Sept 1996 p 14 — Returns to be made by Intermediaries in the Financial Services Area.
TB49 Aug 2002 pp 18–20 — Returns to be made by Intermediaries in relation to certain offshore products.

Definitions

allowable loss: ss 4(1), 5(1), 546; chargeable gain: ss 5(1), 545; CTA 1976 ss 1(5)(*c*), 155(5); person: IA 1937 s 11(*c*); year of assessment: ss 2(1), 5(1).

Former enactments

CGTA 1975 s 20A; FA 1993 s 24; FA 1995 s 68; FA 1997 s 74(1).

595 Life assurance policy or deferred annuity contract entered into or acquired by company

(1) (*a*) In this section—

"relevant disposal" means a disposal of or an interest in the rights under any relevant policy, other than—

(i) a disposal by a person who is not the original beneficial owner of those rights and who acquired them or an interest in them for a consideration in money or money's worth, or

(ii) a disposal resulting directly from the death, disablement or disease of a person, or one of a class of persons, specified in the terms of the policy;

"relevant gain" means a chargeable gain arising on a relevant disposal;

[**"relevant policy"** means a policy of life assurance or a contract for a deferred annuity on the life of a person, entered into or acquired by a company on or after 11 April 1994, which is not—

(*a*) a policy to which section 594 applies, or

(*b*) new basis business within the meaning of section 730A (inserted by the Finance Act, 2000).][1]

(*b*) (i) For the purposes of this section, a policy of assurance or a contract for a deferred annuity on the life of any person, entered into by a company before the 11th day of April, 1994, shall be treated as a policy or contract, as the case may be, entered into on or after that date if there is a variation of the policy or contract on or after that date which directly or indirectly increases the benefits secured by, or extends the term of, the policy or contract, as the case may be.

(ii) For the purposes of subparagraph (i), where a policy or contract entered into by a company before the 11th day of April, 1994, provides an option to have another policy or contract substituted for it or to have any of its terms changed, any change in the terms of the policy or contract which is made in pursuance of the option shall be deemed to be a variation of the policy or contract, as the case may be.

(*c*) Subject to subsection (2), this section shall be construed together with subsections (3) and (4) of section 593, as if subsection (3) of that section were not subject to subsection (2) of that section.

(2) Section 593(2) shall not apply in respect of any relevant disposal.

(3) (*a*) For the purposes of the Corporation Tax Acts—

(i) any relevant gain arising to a company shall be treated as if it were the net amount of a gain from the gross amount of which corporation tax has been deducted at the standard rate (within the meaning of section 3) of income tax,

(ii) the amount to be taken into account in respect of the relevant gain in computing in accordance with section 78 the company's chargeable gains, for the accounting period in which the relevant gain arises, shall be that gross amount, and

(iii) the corporation tax treated as deducted from that gross amount shall—

(I) be set off against the corporation tax assessable on the company for that accounting period, or

(II) in so far as it cannot be set off in accordance with clause (I), be repaid to the company.

(*b*) Paragraph (*a*) shall be disregarded for the purposes of section 546(2).

(*c*) This subsection shall be construed together with the Corporation Tax Acts.

(4) For the purposes of this section, a contract, being a policy of life assurance or a contract for a deferred annuity on the life of any person, shall be treated as having been entered into by a company before the 11th day of April, 1994, if—

(*a*) (i) a document referable to the contract was served on the company in pursuance of section 52 of the Insurance Act, 1989, before the 11th day of April, 1994, and

(ii) the company entered into the contract on or before the 22nd day of April, 1994,

or

(*b*) (i) the contract was entered into before the 30th day of June, 1994, by the company,

(ii) before the 11th day of April, 1994—

(I) there was in existence a binding agreement in writing under which the company was obliged to acquire land, and

(II) preliminary commitments or agreements had been entered into by the company—

(A) to obtain a loan, which was to be secured on the land, to defray money applied in acquiring the land, and

(B) to enter into the contract primarily for the purpose of repaying the loan,

and

(iii) the agreement under which the loan was advanced obliges the company to apply any payment made to it under the contract to the repayment of the loan before any other application by it of such payment.

Amendments

1 Definition of "relevant policy" substituted by FA 2000 s 55 with effect from 6 April 2000.

Cross-references

Foreign life assurance and deferred annuities: s 594(4)(*c*).

Tax Briefing

TB41 Sept 2000 p 21 — Life Assurance Companies — New Regime — Basis of Taxation.

Definitions

chargeable gain: ss 4(1), 5(1), 534; company: ss 4(1), 5(1); interest: s 4(1); land: s 5(1), IA 1937 Sch; person: IA 1937 s 11(*c*). tax: s 3(1); Corporation Tax Acts: s 1(2); writing: IA 1937 Sch.

Former enactments

CGTA 1975 s 20B; FA 1994 s 58.

CHAPTER 6
Transfers of Business Assets

596 Appropriations to and from stock in trade

(1) Where an asset acquired by a person otherwise than as trading stock of a trade carried on by the person is appropriated by that person for the purposes of the trade as trading stock (whether on the commencement of the trade or otherwise) and, if that person had then sold the asset for its market value, a chargeable gain or allowable loss would have accrued to that person, that person shall be treated for the purposes of the Capital Gains Tax Acts as having by such appropriation disposed of the asset by selling it for its then market value.

(2) Where at any time an asset forming part of the trading stock of a person's trade is appropriated by the person for any other purpose or is retained by the person on that person ceasing to carry on the trade, that person shall be treated for the purposes of the Capital Gains Tax Acts as having acquired the asset at that time for a consideration equal to the amount brought into the accounts of the trade in respect of the asset for the purposes of income tax on the appropriation or on that person ceasing to carry on the trade, as the case may be.

(3) Subsection (1) shall not apply in relation to a person's appropriation of an asset for the purposes of a trade if the person is chargeable to income tax in respect of the profits of the trade under Case I of Schedule D, and instead elects that the market value of the asset at the time of the appropriation shall, in computing the profits of the trade for the purposes of income tax, be treated as reduced by the amount of the chargeable gain or increased by the amount of the allowable loss referred to in that subsection and, where that subsection does not apply by reason of such an election, the profits of the trade shall be computed accordingly; but—

(*a*) if a person making an election under this subsection is at the time of the appropriation carrying on the trade in partnership with others, the election shall not have effect unless concurred in by the others, and (*b*) an election under this subsection shall not be made in any case where the application of subsection (1) would give rise to an allowable loss.

Cross-references

Companies' chargeable gains, transfer of trading stock within group: s 618(1), (2).

Exemption from tax in the case of gains on certain disposals of shares: Sch 25A, para 8(2).

Married persons: s 1028(6).

Transactions in land, Schedule D Case IV: s 644(4).

Case law

To qualify as trading stock, an asset should be of a kind normally dealt in by the company in the course of its trade and be acquired with a view to resale at a profit: *Reed v Nova Securities Ltd* [1984] STC 124; *Coates v Arndale Properties Ltd* [1984] STC 637.

Tax Briefing

TB35 Mar 1999 p 25 — Subs (1) does apply where an asset already held as a capital asset in one trade is appropriated to a new trade.

Definitions

allowable loss: ss 4(1), 5(1), 546; chargeable gain: ss 5(1), 545; person: IA 1937 s 11(*c*); trade: s 5(1); trading stock: ss 5(1), 89.

Former enactments

CGTA 1975 s 51(1) and Sch 1 para 15; FA 1990 s 86.

Corresponding UK tax provision

Taxation of Chargeable Gains Act 1992 s 161.

597 Replacement of business and other assets

(1) In this section, **"farming"**, **"trade"**, **"profession"**, **"office"** and **"employment"** have the same meanings respectively as in the Income Tax Acts, but not so as to apply the provisions of those Acts as to the circumstances in which, on a change in the persons carrying on a trade, a trade is to be regarded as discontinued or as set up and commenced, and **"a trade of dealing in or developing land"** shall include a business of dealing in or developing land regarded as a trade under those Acts.

(2) This section shall apply with the necessary modifications in relation to—

(*a*) the discharge of the functions of a public authority,

(*b*) the occupation of woodlands where the woodlands are managed by the occupier on a commercial basis and with a view to the realisation of profits,

(*c*) a profession, office or employment,

(*d*) such of the activities of a body of persons whose activities are carried on otherwise than for profit and are wholly or mainly directed to the protection or promotion of the interests of its members in the carrying on of their trade or profession as are so directed,

(*e*) the activities of a body of persons, being a body not established for profit whose activities are wholly or mainly carried on otherwise than for profit, but in the case of assets within subsection (3)(*b*) only if they are both occupied and used by the body and in the case of other specified assets only if they are used by the body,

(*f*) such of the activities of a body of persons established for the sole purpose of promoting athletic or amateur games or sports as are directed to that purpose, and

(*g*) farming,

as it applies in relation to a trade.

(3) The following shall be assets for the purpose of this section—

(*a*) plant or machinery;

(*b*) except where the trade is a trade of dealing in or developing land, or of providing services for the occupier of land in which the person carrying on the trade has an estate or interest—

(i) any building or part of a building and any permanent or semi-permanent structure in the nature of a building occupied (as well as used) only for the purposes of the trade,

(ii) any land occupied (as well as used) only for the purposes of the trade, provided that where the trade is a trade of dealing in or developing land, but a profit on the sale of any land held for the purposes of the trade would not form part of the trading profits, the trade shall be treated for the purposes of this subsection as if it were not a trade of dealing in or developing land;

[(*c*) goodwill,

(*d*) any financial assets owned by a body of persons referred to in paragraph (*f*) of subsection (2); for the purposes of this paragraph **"financial assets"** means shares of any company and stocks, bonds and obligations of any government, municipal corporation, company or other body corporate.][1]

(4) (*a*) Where—

(i) the consideration which a person carrying on a trade [obtains for the disposal, before 4 December 2002, of,][2] or of that person's interest in, assets (in this section referred to as **"the old assets"**) used only for the purposes of the trade throughout the period of ownership is applied by that person in acquiring other assets, or an interest in other assets (in this section referred to as **"the new assets"**),

(ii) the new assets on their acquisition are taken into use and used only for the purposes of the trade, and

(iii) the old assets and the new assets are assets of a kind specified in subsection (3),

then, the person carrying on the trade shall on making a claim in that behalf be treated for the purposes of the Capital Gains Tax Acts as if the chargeable gain accruing on the old assets did not accrue until that person ceases to use the new assets for the purposes of the trade.

(*b*) Where the consideration for the disposal of the new assets is applied in acquiring other new assets which on the acquisition are taken into use and used only for the purposes of the trade and are assets specified in subsection (3), then, the person carrying on the trade shall be treated as if the chargeable gain accruing on the disposal of the old assets did not accrue until that person ceases to use the other new assets for the purposes of the trade and any further new assets which are acquired in a similar manner, taken into use, and used only, for the purposes of the trade and are assets specified in subsection (3).

(5) Subsection (4) shall not apply if part only of the amount or value of the consideration for the disposal of or of the interest in the old assets is applied as described in that subsection, but if all of the amount or value of the consideration except for a part which is less than the amount of the gain (whether all chargeable gain or not) accruing on the

disposal of or of the interest in the old assets is so applied, then, the person carrying on the trade shall on making a claim in that behalf be treated for the purposes of the Capital Gains Tax Acts as if the amount of the gain accruing on the disposal of the old assets were reduced to the amount of consideration not applied in the acquisition of the new assets (and if not all chargeable gain with a proportionate reduction in the amount of the chargeable gain) and the balance of the gain (or chargeable gain) shall be treated as if it did not accrue until that person ceases to use the new assets for the purposes of the trade.

(6) A chargeable gain or the balance of a chargeable gain which under subsection (4) or (5), as may be appropriate, is treated as accruing on a date later than the date of the disposal on which it accrued shall not be so treated for the purposes of section 556.

(7) This section shall apply only if the acquisition of or of the interest in the new assets takes place, or an unconditional contract for the acquisition is entered into, in the period beginning 12 months before and ending 3 years after the disposal of or of the interest in the old assets, or at such earlier or later time as the Revenue Commissioners may by notice in writing allow; but, where an unconditional contract for the acquisition is so entered into, this section may be applied on a provisional basis without waiting to ascertain whether the new assets are, or the interest in the new assets is, acquired in pursuance of the contract, and when that fact is ascertained all necessary adjustments shall be made by making assessments or by repayment or discharge of tax, and shall be so made notwithstanding any limitation in the Capital Gains Tax Acts on the time within which assessments may be made.

(8) This section shall not apply unless the acquisition of or of the interest in the new assets was made for the purpose of their use in the trade, and not wholly or partly for the purpose of realising a gain from the disposal of or of the interest in the new assets.

(9) Where over the period of ownership or any substantial part of the period of ownership part of a building or structure is, and part is not, used for the purposes of a trade, this section shall apply as if the part so used, together with any land occupied for purposes ancillary to the occupation and use of that part of the building or structure, were a separate asset, and subject to any necessary apportionments of consideration for an acquisition or disposal of or of an interest in the building or structure and other land.

(10) Where the old assets were not used for the purposes of the trade throughout the period of ownership, this section shall apply as if a part of the asset representing its use for the purposes of the trade, having regard to the time and extent to which it was and was not used for those purposes, were a separate asset which had been wholly used for the purposes of the trade, and this subsection shall apply in relation to that part subject to any necessary apportionment of consideration for an acquisition or disposal of or of the interest in the asset.

(11)(*a*) This section shall apply in relation to a person who carries on 2 or more trades which are in different localities, but which are concerned wholly or mainly with goods or services of the same kind, as if, in relation to the assets used for the purposes of the trades, the trades were the same trade.

(*b*) This section shall apply in relation to a person who ceases to carry on a trade or trades (in this paragraph referred to as **"the old trade or trades"**) which the person has carried on for a period of 10 years or more and commences to carry on another trade or trades (in this paragraph referred to as **"the new trade or trades"**) within a period of 2 years from the date on which the person ceased to carry on the old trade or trades as if, in relation to the old assets used for the purposes of one of the old trades and the new assets used for the purposes of the new trade, the 2 trades were the same trade.

(12) Without prejudice to the provisions of the Capital Gains Tax Acts providing generally for apportionments, where consideration is given for the acquisition or disposal of assets some or part of which are assets in relation to which a claim under subsection (4) or (5) applies, and some or part of which are not, the consideration shall be apportioned in such manner as is just and reasonable.

Amendments

[1] Subs (3)(*c*) substituted by FA 1998 s 71(1) as respects disposals made on or after 27 March 1998.

[2] Substituted by FA 2003 s 67(1)(*b*) with effect from 1 January 2003 but does not apply to a disposal made by a person, on or after 4 December 2002 and on or before 31 December 2003, of an asset used for the purposes of the person's trade (or any other activity of the person as is referred to in TCA 1997 s 597(2)), where the person claims that, but for the amendment made by FA 2003 s 67(1)(*b*), the person would have been entitled to claim that the chargeable gain accruing on that disposal could not accrue to the person until assets, which were acquired by the person before 4 December 2002 or acquired under an unconditional contract entered into by the person before that date, ceased to be used for the purposes of that trade of the person, or, as the case may be, that other activity of the person; previously "obtains for the disposal of,".

Cross-references

Companies' chargeable gains, company ceasing to be member of a group: s 623(1)(*b*); deemed disposal in certain circumstances: s 620A(1)(*b*)(ii).

Company ceasing to be resident in the State, deemed disposal of assets, meaning of "the new assets" and "the old assets" applied: s 627(1)(*a*).

Development land disposals, no relief: s 652(1); relief for assets of authorised racecourse and authorised greyhound race track: s 652(3) and (3A).

Disposal of business or farm on "retirement", qualifying assets: s 598(1)(*d*).

Gifts, recovery of capital gains tax from donee, meanings of "old asset" and "new asset" applied: s 978(1).

Petroleum trade, restriction of loss relief, subs (11): s 689(2).

Reorganisation into companies of Trustee Savings Banks, capital gains: Sch 17 para 5(5).

Replacement of business assets by group members, meaning of "old assets" and "new assets" applied: s 620(1); s 620(2).

Trustees ceasing to be resident in the State, meaning of "the new assets" and "the old assets" applied: s 579B(1); s 579B(7).

Trustees ceasing to be liable to Irish tax: s 579E(3)(*a*), (*b*).

Case law

Irish

Subs (4): Roll-over relief refused where non-resident owners let land on conacre as they were not carrying on a trade: *O'Coindealbháin v Price* ITR Vol IV p 1.

UK

Subs (4): The asset must have been used for the purposes of the trade and mere visits to a site and an application for planning permission does not constitute use: *Temperley v Visibell Ltd* [1974] STC 64.

The new asset must be actually taken into use on its acquisition: *Campbell Connelly & Co Ltd v Barnett* [1994] STC 50.

Held a taxpayer who purchased land and buildings as single asset and within 12 months sold part of the same land and buildings could not roll over the gain into the acquisition cost of the land and buildings retained: *Watton v Tippett* [1997] STC 893.

Subs (10): Where the old asset was used for trade purposes for part only of the period of ownership, the period when no chargeable gain accrued prior to the enactment of the Act is ignored: *Richart v J Lyons & Co Ltd* [1989] STC 665.

Revenue precedents

Issue: Cessation of trade carried on for less than 10 years and commencement of similar trade.

Decision: Strictly, relief is not due as s 597(ii)(*b*) requires that the old trade be carried on for at least 10 years. However, s 597(ii)(*a*) allows relief where two trades, wholly or mainly concerned with goods or services of the same kind are carried on. This is read as applying where the trades are carried on simultaneously or successively, thus covering a cessation of one trade and the commencement of a similar trade.

Tax Briefing

TB35 Mar 1999 p 25 — Rollover relief not available where an asset owned personally by an individual and used for trade purposes by a company in which individual is a major shareholder is sold by the individual who re-invests the proceeds in another asset which is also used for the purposes of the trade carried on by the company — the legislation provides that for relief to apply the assets must be disposed of by the person carrying on the trade.

TB52 May 2003 p 13 — Capital Gains Tax — Finance Act 2003 changes.

TB52 May 2003 p 24 — In calculating tax on a deferred gain, the rate of tax to be charged on the gain is the rate pertaining on the date of the event which gives rise to the crystallisation of the gain and not the date of the original disposal, the gain on which was deferred. However, indexation only applies to the date of the original disposal.

Definitions

body of persons: s 2(1); chargeable gain: ss 5(1), 545; Income Tax Acts: s 1(2); land: s 5(1), IA 1937 Sch; month: IA 1937 Sch; person: IA 1937 s 11(*c*); profession: ss 2(1), 5(1); trade: s 5(1); writing: IA 1937 Sch.

Former enactments

CGTA 1975 s 28; CGT(A)A 1978 s 9.

Corresponding UK tax provision

Taxation of Chargeable Gains Act 1992 s 152.

598 Disposals of business or farm on "retirement"

(1) (*a*) In this section and in section 599—

"chargeable business asset" means an asset (including goodwill but not including shares or securities or other assets held as investments) which is, or is an interest in, an asset used for the purposes of farming, or a trade, profession, office or employment, carried on by—

(i) the individual,

(ii) the individual's family company, or

(iii) a company which is a member of a trading group of which the holding company is the individual's family company,

other than an asset on the disposal of which no gain accruing would be a chargeable gain;

"family company", in relation to an individual, means, subject to paragraph (*b*), a company the voting rights in which are—

(i) as to not less than 25 per cent, exercised by the individual, or

(ii) as to not less than 75 per cent, exercisable by the individual or a member of his or her family and, as to not less than 10 per cent, exercisable by the individual himself or herself;

"family", in relation to an individual, means the husband or wife of the individual, and a relative of the individual or of the individual's husband or wife, and **"relative"** means brother, sister, ancestor or lineal descendant;

"full-time working director" means a director required to devote substantially the whole of his or her time to the service of the company in a managerial or technical capacity;

"holding company" means a company whose business (disregarding any trade carried on by it) consists wholly or mainly of the holding of shares or securities of one or more companies which are its 75 per cent subsidiaries;

"qualifying assets", in relation to a disposal, includes—

[(i) the chargeable business assets of the individual which apart from tangible moveable property he or she has owned for a period of not less than 10 years ending with the disposal and which have been his or her chargeable business assets throughout the period of 10 years ending with that disposal,][1]

[(ii) (I) the shares or securities, which the individual has owned for a period of not less than 10 years ending with the disposal, being shares or securities of a relevant company that is a company—

(A) which has been a trading company, or a farming company, and the individual's family company, or

(B) which has been a member of a trading group, of which the holding company is the individual's family company,

during a period of not less than 10 years ending with the disposal and the individual has been a working director of the relevant company for a period of not less than 10 years during which period he or she has been a full-time working director of the relevant company for a period of not less than 5 years, and

(II) land, machinery or plant (if any) which the individual has owned for a period of not less than 10 years ending with the disposal, and which—

(A) was used throughout that period for the purposes of the relevant company, and

(B) is disposed of at the same time and to the same person as the shares or securities referred to in subparagraph (I),

(iii) land used for the purposes of farming carried on by the individual which he or she has owned and used for that purpose for a period of not less than 10 years ending with the transfer of an interest in that land for the purposes of complying with the terms of the Scheme, and

(iv) land which has been let by the individual at any time in the period of 5 years ending with the disposal, where—

(I) immediately before the time the land was first let in that period, the land was owned by the individual and used for the purposes of farming carried on by the individual for a period of not less than 10 years ending at that time, and

(II) the disposal is a disposal referred to in section 652(5)*(a)*;][2]

[**"the Scheme"** means the scheme known as—

(i) the Scheme of Early Retirement From Farming introduced by the Minister for Agriculture and Food for the purpose of implementing Council Regulation (EEC) No 2079/92 of 30 June 1992 (OJ No L.215, of 30.7.92, p 91), or

(ii) the Scheme of Early Retirement From Farming introduced by the Minister for Agriculture, Food and Rural Development for the purpose of implementing Council Regulation (EC) No 1257/1999 of 17 May 1999 (OJ No L.160, of 26.6.99, p 80),][3]

"trade", **"farming"**, **"profession"**, **"office"** and **"employment"** have the same meanings respectively as in the Income Tax Acts;

"trading company" means a company whose business consists wholly or mainly of the carrying on of one or more trades or professions;

"trading group" means a group of companies consisting of the holding company and its 75 per cent subsidiaries, the business of whose members taken together consists wholly or mainly of the carrying on of one or more trades or professions;

"75 per cent subsidiary" has the meaning assigned to it by section 9.

(*b*) For the purposes of the definition of **"family company"**, where a company which is a holding company would not but for this paragraph be an individual's family company, but would be such a company if the individual had not at any time on or after the 6th day of April, 1987, and before the 6th day of April, 1990, disposed of shares in the company to a child (within the meaning of section 599) of the individual, the company shall be deemed to be the individual's family company.

(*c*) In this section, references to the disposal of the whole or part of an individual's qualifying assets include references to the disposal of the whole or part of the assets provided or held for the purposes of an office or employment by the individual exercising that office or employment.

(*d*) For the purposes of the definition of **"qualifying assets"**, there shall be taken into account—

[(i) (I) the period of ownership of an asset by a spouse of an individual as if it were a period of ownership of the asset by the individual, and

(II) where a spouse of an individual has died, the period of use of an asset by the spouse as if it were a period of use of the asset by the individual,][4]

(ii) where the chargeable business assets are new assets within the meaning of section 597, the period of ownership of the old assets as if it were a period of ownership of the new assets,

[(ii*a*) the period for which an individual was a director or, as the case may be, a full-time working director of the following companies as if it were a period for which the individual was a director of a **"relevant company"** (which, for the purposes of this subparagraph, means a company referred to in paragraph (ii) of the definition of qualifying assets in subsection (1)(*a*)):

(I) a company that was treated as being the same company as the relevant company for the purposes of section 586,

(II) a company involved in the same scheme of reconstruction or amalgamation under section 587 with the relevant company,][5]

(iii) where the qualifying assets are shares or securities in a family company to which section 600 applies, the period immediately before the transfer to the company of chargeable business assets during which those assets were owned by the individual as if it were a period of ownership of the individual of the qualifying assets or a period throughout which he or she was a full-time working director, as may be appropriate, and

(iv) a period immediately before the death of the spouse of the individual throughout which the deceased was a full-time working director as if it were a period throughout which the individual was a full-time working director.

(2) (*a*) Subject to this section, where an individual who has attained the age of 55 years disposes of the whole or part of his or her qualifying assets, then—

(i) if the amount or value of the consideration for the disposal does not exceed [€500,000][6], relief shall be given in respect of the full amount of capital gains tax chargeable on any gain accruing on the disposal;

(ii) if the amount or value of the consideration for the disposal exceeds [€500,000][6], the amount of capital gains tax chargeable on the gain accruing on the disposal shall not exceed 50 per cent of the difference between the amount of that consideration and [€500,000][6].

(*b*) For the purposes of paragraph (*a*), the amount of capital gains tax chargeable in respect of the gain shall be the amount of tax which would not have been chargeable but for that gain.

(3) For the purposes of subsection (2), the consideration on the disposal of qualifying assets by the individual shall be aggregated, and nothing in this section shall affect the computation of gains accruing on the disposal of assets other than qualifying assets.

(4) Where a disposal of qualifying assets includes a disposal of shares or securities of the individual's family company, the amount of the consideration to be taken into account for the purposes of subsection (2) in respect of those shares or securities shall be the proportion of the consideration for those shares or securities which is equal to—

(*a*) in a case where the individual's family company is not a holding company, the proportion which the part of the value of the company's chargeable assets at the time of the disposal which is attributable to the value of the company's chargeable business assets bears to the whole of that value, and

(*b*) in a case where the individual's family company is a holding company, the proportion which the part of the value of the chargeable assets of the trading group (excluding shares or securities of one member of the group held by another member of the group) at the time of the disposal which is attributable to the value of the chargeable business assets of the trading group bears to the whole of that value;

but nothing in this section shall affect liability on any gains calculated by reference to the balance of the consideration for the disposal of those shares or securities.

(5) For the purposes of subsection (4), every asset shall be a chargeable asset except one on the disposal of which by the company or a member of the trading group, as the case may be, at the time of the disposal of the shares or securities, no gain accruing to the company or member of the trading group, as the case may be, would be a chargeable gain.

(6) (*a*) The total of the amounts of relief given under this section for any year of assessment and all years of assessment before such year shall not exceed such amount as would reduce the total amount of capital gains tax chargeable for all those years of assessment below the amount which would be chargeable if the disposals of qualifying assets had all been made in the year of assessment.

(*b*) Where at any time the relief given under this section exceeds the amount of relief which would be given if the disposals of qualifying assets for the year of assessment and all years of assessment before such year had been made in the year of assessment, any necessary adjustment may be made by means of assessment or additional assessment and such assessment may be made at any time not more than 10 years after the end of the year of assessment in which the last of such disposals is made.

(*c*) For the purposes of this subsection, a disposal of qualifying assets other than a disposal of the whole of such assets, by a husband to a wife or by a wife to a husband shall, notwithstanding section 1028(5), be taken into account at the market value of the assets.

(7) Subsection (2) shall apply where under section 583 an individual is treated as disposing of interests in shares or securities of his or her family company in consideration of a capital distribution from the company (not being a distribution consisting of chargeable business assets) in the course of dissolving or winding up the company as it applies where he or she disposes of shares or securities of the company.

Amendments

1 Definition of "qualifying assets" para (i) substituted by FA 1998 s 72(1)(*a*)(i) as respects a disposal of an asset on or after 6 April 1998.

2 Definition of "qualifying assets" paras (ii) and (iii) substituted and para (iv) inserted by FA 2002 s 59 with effect from 1 January 2002.

3 Definition of "the Scheme" substituted by FA 2003 s 68(1)(*a*) as respects a disposal of an asset on or after 27 November 2000.

4 Subs (1)(*d*)(i) substituted by FA 2003 s 68(1)(*b*) as respects a disposal of a asset on or after 6 February 2003.

5 Subs (1)(*d*)(ii*a*) inserted by FA 2003 s 68(1)(*c*) as respects a disposal of a asset on or after 6 February 2003.

6 Substituted by FA 2003 s 68(1)(*d*) as respects a disposal of a asset on or after 6 February 2003; previously "€476,250".

Cross-references

Annual exempt amount: s 601(5).

Disposal within the family of business or farm, subss (2), (4): s 599(3); subs (3): s 599(5).

Relinquishing of life interest by the person entitled: s 577A.

Case law

In the definition of family company, it was held the voting rights of a company were "exercisable" even though it had appointed no representative to exercise the rights: *Hepworth v Smith* [1981] STC 354.

Held a disposal by a taxpayer of a milk quota nearly one year after he had sold his farm and given up farming did not constitute a disposal of the whole or part of a business: *Wase v Bourke* [1996] STC 18.

Held that the words "his time" in the phrase "substantially the whole of his time" in the definition of "full-time working officer or employer" in the UK equivalent legislation referred to working time and were to be read as meaning his time being that of a "full-time" working employee. "Full-time" has to be used in the appropriate capacity — in general that would be the normal hours worked by full-time managerial and technical employees. If work done for the relevant company qualified, it was irrelevant that the person carried out non-qualifying work for another company. Plaintiff worked 50 hours per week of which 42.5 were spend working for the company in a managerial company. The fact that he worked 7.5 hours in another capacity was irrelevant. He devoted the whole of his time amounting to full working time to the services of the company in a managerial capacity, and was therefore entitled to retirement relief on a capital distribution by that company: *Palmer v Moloney* 1999 [STC890].

Held a company must be a family company throughout the whole period of ten years: *Davenport v Hasslacher* [1997] STC 254.

Revenue precedents

Issue: Must ten year requirement be absolute with regard to terminally ill?

Decision: Where individual is terminally ill and a sufficient percentage of the time limit has expired Revenue accepts requirements of s 598 are met.

Issue: Where a holding company is interposed or removed during the 10 years prior to disposal the taxpayer will not satisfy the requirements that he have held the shares for ten years and have been a working director for five years.

Decision: A "look through" approach may be taken and the taxpayer will be treated as satisfying both conditions.

Issue: Transfer of trade to subsidiary in 10 years prior to disposal.

Decision: In strictness, relief is not due, as the holding company has not been a holding company throughout the 10 years ending with the disposal. In practice, relief will be allowed where all other requirements of the section are met.

Issue: Where a lease expires and a new lease is granted, can the period of ownership of the old lease be aggregated with that of the new lease for the purpose of the ten year ownership requirement?

Decision: Whilst the old lease and the new lease are separate assets, in practice the periods of ownership may be aggregated.

Issue: Where a company would be a holding company within the meaning of Section 598(1) Taxes Consolidation Act , 1997 except for shares held in its subsidiary company by a limited liability company funded by the International Fund for Ireland with the object of creating employment in a disadvantaged area.

Decision: The shares held by a limited company funded by the International Fund for Ireland with the object of creating employment in a disadvantaged area should be ignored in the determination of whether or not a company is a holding company within the meaning of Section 598(1) Taxes Consolidation Act, 1997.

Tax Briefing

TB26 Apr 1997 p 10 — Retirement relief and liquidations.

TB36 June 1999 pp 14–15 — Disposal of a taxi plate; Land let on conacre.

TB47 Apr 2002 pp 15–16 — Finance Act 2002 changes.

TB52 May 2003 p 13 — Finance Act 2003 changes.

Definitions

company: s 5(1); profession: s 2(1), shares: s 5(1); trade: s 5(1); year of assessment: ss 2(1), 5(1).

Former enactments

CGTA 1975 s 26(1)–(6); FA 1990 s 84(*c*)(iii); FA 1991 s 42(*b*); FA 1995 s 71(1); FA 1996 s 60(1).

Corresponding UK tax provision

Taxation of Chargeable Gains Act 1992 s 163.

599 Disposals within family of business or farm

(1) (*a*) In this section, **"child"**, in relation to a disposal, includes a nephew or a niece who has worked substantially on a full-time basis for the period of 5 years ending with the disposal in carrying on, or assisting in the carrying on of, the trade, business or profession concerned or the work of, or connected with, the office or employment concerned.

(*b*) Subject to this section, where an individual who has attained the age of 55 years disposes of the whole or part of his or her qualifying assets to his or her child, relief shall be given in respect of the capital gains tax chargeable on any gain accruing on the disposal.

(*c*) For the purposes of paragraph (*b*), the capital gains tax chargeable in respect of the gain shall be the amount of tax which would not have been chargeable but for that gain.

(2) Nothing in this section shall affect the computation of gains accruing on the disposal of assets other than qualifying assets by an individual who makes a disposal within subsection (1).

(3) Section 598(4) shall apply to a disposal within subsection (1) as it applies to a disposal within section 598(2).

(4) (*a*) Where assets comprised in a disposal to a child in respect of which relief has been granted under this section are, within 6 years of the disposal by the individual concerned, disposed of by the child, the capital gains tax which if subsection (1) had not applied would have been charged on the individual on his or her disposal of those assets to the child shall be assessed and charged on the child, in addition to any capital gains tax chargeable in respect of the gain accruing to the child on the child's disposal of those assets.

(*b*) An assessment to give effect to this subsection shall not be out of time if made within [4 years][1] after the end of the year of assessment in which the assets are disposed of by the child.

(5) The consideration on a disposal within subsection (1) shall not be taken into account for the purposes of aggregation under section 598(3).

Amendments

1 Substituted by FA 2003 s 17(*f*) with effect from: (*a*) such day or days as the Minister for Finance may by order or orders appoint either generally or with reference to any particular purpose or provision and different days may be so appointed for different purposes or different provisions and (*b*) notwithstanding the generality of (*a*), any order made by the Minister for Finance in accordance with the provisions of that paragraph may contain, and be subject to, such conditions as the Minister considers appropriate and which are specified in the order; previously "10 years". By virtue of Finance Act 2003 (Commencement of Section 17) Order 2003, SI No 508 of 2003, this amendment comes into operation in relation to the making, on or after 1 January 2005, of an assessment referred to in section 599(4)(*b*).

Cross-references

Annual exempt amount: s 601(5).

Disposal of business or farm on "retirement", meaning of "child": s 598(1)(*b*); meanings of "chargeable business asset", "family company", "family", "full-time working director", "holding company", "qualifying assets", "trading company" and "trading group": s 598(1)(*a*).

Relinquishing of life interest by the person entitled: s 577A.

Revenue precedents

Issue: Is relief clawed back where the child disposes of the shares within 6 years in a "share for share" transaction?

Decision: If the "share for share" reorganisation comes within TCA 1997 s 584, it will not constitute a disposal for the purposes of s 599(4).

Tax Briefing

TB56 July 2004 pp 6–11 — Repayments, Interest and Time Limits — Section 17 FA 2003 changes.

TB57 Oct 2004 pp 7–9 — New Time Limits - Section 17 FA 2003 changes.

TB57 Oct 2004 p 15 — Repayments, Interest and Time Limits - correction to TB56 p 8.

Definitions

commencement: IA 1937 Sch; profession: s 2(1); trade: s 5(1); year of assessment: s 5(1).

Former enactments

CGTA 1975 s 27; CGT(A)A 1978 s 8; FA 1990 s 85; FA 1995 s 72; FA 1996 s 132(2) and Sch 5 Pt II.

Corresponding UK tax provision

Taxation of Chargeable Gains Act 1992 s 163.

600 Transfer of business to company

(1) In this section—

"net chargeable gains" means chargeable gains less allowable losses;

references to the business, in relation to shares or consideration received in exchange for the business, include references to assets of the business referred to in subsection (2).

(2) This section shall apply for the purposes of the Capital Gains Tax Acts where a person who is not a company transfers to a company a business as a going concern, together with the whole of the assets of the business or together with the whole of those assets other than cash, and the business is so transferred wholly or partly in exchange for shares (in this section referred to as **"the new assets"**) issued by the company to the person transferring the business.

(3) The amount determined under subsection (5) shall be deducted from the aggregate (in this section referred to as **"the gain on the old assets"**) of the net chargeable gains.

(4) For the purpose of computing any chargeable gain accruing on the disposal of any new asset—

(*a*) the amount determined under subsection (5) shall be apportioned between the new assets as a whole, and

(*b*) the sums allowable as a deduction under section 552(1)(*a*) shall be reduced by the amount apportioned to the new asset under paragraph (*a*),

and, if the shares which comprise the new assets are not all of the same class, the apportionment between the shares under paragraph (*a*) shall be in accordance with their market values at the time they were acquired by the transferor.

(5) (*a*) In this subsection, **"the cost of the new assets"** means any sums which would be allowable as a deduction under section 552(1)(*a*) if the new assets were disposed of as a whole in circumstances giving rise to a chargeable gain.

(*b*) The amount referred to in subsections (3) and (4)(*a*) shall be such portion of the gain on the old assets as bears the same proportion to the total of such gains as the cost of the new assets bears to the value of the whole of the consideration received by the transferor in exchange for the business.

(6) This section shall not apply to the transfer by a person of a business to a company wholly or partly in exchange for shares issued by the company, unless it is shown that the transfer is effected for bona fide commercial reasons and does not form part of any arrangement or scheme of which the main purpose or one of the main purposes is avoidance of liability to tax.

Cross-references

Company buying its own shares, residence conditions and ownership period: s 177(10).

Disposal of business or farm on "retirement": s 598(1)(*d*)(iii).

Deduction of offshore income gain in calculating capital gain, subs (5)(*b*): s 747(5).

Offshore funds, disposal of interests in non-qualifying funds, calculation of unindexed gain: Sch 20 para 3(1).

Revenue precedents

Issue: Liabilities taken over — do they represent consideration?

Decision: Liabilities of the business included in the transfer rank as consideration for the transfer because the discharge of liabilities of the transferor by the transferee is equivalent to the payment of cash by the transferee to the transferor. In practice, however, where an individual transfers a business to a company, in exchange for shares only and assets exceed liabilites, bona fide trade creditors taken over will not be treated as consideration.

Case law

Transfer of a farming business held to be transferred as a going concern although the business was conveyed shortly afterwards to a smaller farm located elsewhere: *Gordon v IRC* [1991] STC 174.

Definitions

allowable loss: ss 4(1), 5(1), 546; chargeable gain: ss 5(1), 545; class (of shares): s 5(1); company: s 5(1); person: IA 1937 s 11(*c*); shares: s 5(1).

Former enactments

CGTA 1975 s 51(1) and Sch 2 para 6; FA 1992 s 61.

Corresponding UK tax provision

Taxation of Chargeable Gains Act 1992 s 162.

600A Replacement of qualifying premises

[(1) In this section—

"qualifying premises", in relation to a person, means a building or part of a building, or an interest in a building or a part of a building—

[(*a*) in which there is one or more residential units,][1]

(*b*) in respect of which the person is entitled to a rent or to receipts from any easement, and

(*c*) in respect of which all the requirements of the Regulations are complied with;

"Regulations" means—

(i) the Housing (Standards for Rented Houses) Regulations, 1993 (SI No 147 of 1993),

(ii) the Housing (Rent Books) Regulations, 1993 (SI No 146 of 1993), and

(iii) the Housing (Registration of Rented Houses) Regulations, 1996, as amended by the Housing (Registration of Rented Houses) (Amendment) Regulations, 2000 (SI No 12 of 2000);

"replacement premises", in relation to a person, means a building or part of a building, or an interest in a building or a part of a building—

(*a*) which the person acquires with the consideration obtained by the person from the disposal of a qualifying premises,

[(*b*) in which the number of residential units is—

(i) not less than 3, and

(ii) not less than the number of residential units in the qualifying premises,][2]

(*c*) in respect of which the person is entitled to a rent or to receipts from any easement, and

(*d*) in respect of which all the requirements of the Regulations are complied with;

"residential unit" means a separately contained part of a residential premises used or suitable for use as a dwelling.

(2) (*a*) Where the consideration which a person obtains [for the disposal, before 4 December 2002, of][3] a qualifying premises, which was a qualifying premises throughout the period of its ownership by the person, is applied by that person in acquiring a replacement premises, then the person shall, subject to paragraph (*b*), be treated for the purposes of the Capital Gains Tax Acts as if the chargeable gain accruing on the disposal of the qualifying premises did not accrue until—

(i) that person disposes of the replacement premises, or

(ii) the replacement premises ceases to be a replacement premises.

(*b*) Where the consideration for the disposal of the replacement premises is applied by a person in acquiring a further replacement premises then, the person shall be treated as if the chargeable gain accruing on the disposal of the qualifying premises did not accrue until that person disposes of the further replacement premises or any other further replacement premises which are acquired in a similar manner, or that further replacement premises or any other further replacement premises which are acquired in a similar manner, cease to be a replacement premises.

(3) Subsection (2) shall not apply if part only of the amount or value of the consideration for the disposal of the qualifying premises is applied as described in that subsection; but if all of the amount or value of the consideration except for a part which is less than the amount of the gain (whether all chargeable or not) accruing on the disposal of the qualifying premises is so applied, then, the person shall on making a claim in that behalf be treated for the purposes of the Capital Gains Tax Acts—

(*a*) as if the amount of the gain accruing on the disposal of the qualifying premises were reduced to the amount of consideration not applied in the acquisition of the replacement premises (and if not all chargeable gain with a proportionate reduction in the amount of the chargeable gain), and

(*b*) in respect of the balance of the gain or chargeable gain as if it did not accrue until that person disposes of the replacement premises or the replacement premises ceases to be a replacement premises.

(4) A chargeable gain or the balance of a chargeable gain which under subsection (2) or (3), as may be appropriate, is treated as accruing on a date later than the date of the disposal on which it accrued shall not be so treated for the purposes of section 556.

(5) This section shall apply only if the acquisition of the replacement premises takes place, or an unconditional contract for the acquisition is entered into, in the period beginning 12 months before and ending 3 years after the disposal of the qualifying premises, or at such earlier or later time as the Revenue Commissioners may by notice in writing allow; but, where an unconditional contract for the acquisition is so entered into, this section may be applied on a provisional basis without waiting to ascertain whether the replacement premises is acquired in pursuance of the contract, and when that fact is ascertained all necessary adjustments shall be made by making assessments or by repayment or discharge of tax, and shall be so made notwithstanding any limitation in the Capital Gains Tax Acts on the time within which assessments may be made.

(6) This section shall not apply if the acquisition of the replacement premises was wholly or partly for the purpose of realising a gain from the disposal of the replacement premises.

(7) Where the qualifying premises was not a qualifying premises throughout the period of ownership of a person making a claim under this section, the section shall apply as if a part of the qualifying premises representing the period for which it was a qualifying premises was a separate asset, and this section shall apply in relation to that part subject to any necessary apportionments of consideration for an acquisition or disposal of the interest in the premises.

(8) Without prejudice to the provisions of the Capital Gains Tax Acts providing generally for apportionments, where consideration is given for the acquisition or disposal of assets some or part of which are assets in relation to which a claim under subsection (2) or (3) applies, and some or part of which are not, the consideration shall be apportioned in such manner as is just and reasonable.][4]

Amendments

1 Definition of "qualifying premises" para (*a*) substituted by FA 2002 s 60(*a*) with effect from 1 January 2002.

2 Definition of "replacement premises" para (*b*) substituted by FA 2002 s 60(*b*) with effect from 1 January 2002.

3 Substituted by FA 2003 s 67(1)(*c*) with effect from 1 January 2003 but does not apply to a disposal made by a person, on or after 4 December 2002 and on or before 31 December 2003, of a qualifying premises (within the meaning of TCA 1997 s 600A) where the person claims that, but for the amendment made by FA 2003 s 67(1)(*c*), the person would have been entitled to claim that the chargeable gain accruing on that disposal could not accrue to the person until a replacement premises (within that meaning) which were acquired by the person before 4 December 2002, or acquired by the person under an unconditional contract entered into before that date was disposed of by the person, or ceased to be a replacement premises; previously "for the disposal of".

4 Section 600A inserted by FA 2001 s 92(1) for disposals on or after 5 January 2001.

Tax Briefing

TB43 April 2001 p 19 — Rollover relief on certain investment property.
TB47 April 2002 p 15 — Finance Act 2002 changes.
TB52 May 2003 p 13 — Finance Act 2003 changes.

Definitions

Capital Gains Tax Acts: s 1(2); chargeable gain: ss 5(1), 545; person: IA 1937 s 11(*c*); writing: IA 1937 Sch.

CHAPTER 7
Other Reliefs and Exemptions

601 Annual exempt amount

(1) An individual shall not be chargeable to capital gains tax for a year of assessment if the amount on which he or she is chargeable to capital gains tax under section 31 for that year does not exceed [€1,270][1].

(2) Where the amount on which an individual is chargeable to capital gains tax under section 31 for a year of assessment exceeds [€1,270][1], only the excess of that amount over [€1,270][1] shall be charged to capital gains tax for that year.

(3) Where, on the assumption that subsection (2) did not apply, an individual would be chargeable under the Capital Gains Tax Acts at more than one rate of tax for a year of assessment, the relief to be given under that subsection in respect of the first [€1,270][1] of chargeable gains shall be given—

(*a*) if the individual would be so chargeable at 2 different rates, in respect of the chargeable gains which would be so chargeable at the higher of those rates and, in so far as relief cannot be so given, in respect of the chargeable gains which would be so chargeable at the lower of those rates, and

(*b*) if the individual would be so chargeable at 3 or more rates, in respect of the chargeable gains which would be so chargeable at the highest of those rates and, in so far as relief cannot be so given, in respect of the chargeable gains which would be so chargeable at the next highest of those rates, and so on.

(4) In the case of an individual who dies in the year of assessment, this section shall apply with the substitution for the reference to the individual of a reference to his or her personal representatives, and the amount of chargeable gains shall be that on which the personal representatives are chargeable in respect of gains accruing before death.

(5) Relief shall not be given under this section where relief is allowed under section 598 or 599.

Amendments

1 Substituted by FA 2001 s 240(1) and (2)(*b*) and Sch 5 Pt 1 for 2002 and later tax years; previously "£1,000" (short tax "year" 2001: £740 (FA 2001 s 77(2) and Sch 2 paras 34 and 61(*a*))).

Cross-references

Capital gains tax share reinvestment, withdrawal of relief: s 591(11)(*b*)(ii).
Disposals by liquidators and other persons, meaning of "referable capital gains tax", subs (3): s 571(2)(*c*).
Foreign life assurance and deferred annuities: s 594(2)(*e*).
Married persons, subs (1): s 1028(4).
Special portfolio investment accounts: s 838(4)(*c*).

Tax Briefing

A non-resident individual (who is liable to capital gains tax in Ireland on the disposal of specified assets, e.g. land, buildings, etc, by virtue of TCA 1997 s 28(3)) is entitled to the £1,000 annual exemption.

Definitions

chargeable gain: ss 5(1), 545; personal representatives: s 5(1), 799; year of assessment: ss 2(1), 5(1).

Former enactments

CGTA 1975 s 16; CGT(A)A 1978, ss 16, 17, Sch 1 para 8 and Sch 2; FA 1992 s 59.

Corresponding UK tax provision

Taxation of Chargeable Gains Act 1992 s 3.

602 Chattel exemption

(1) In this section, tangible movable property shall not include a wasting asset within the meaning of section 560.

(2) Subject to this section, a gain accruing on a disposal by an individual of an asset which is tangible movable property shall not be a chargeable gain if the amount or value of the consideration for the disposal does not exceed [€2,540][1].

(3) (*a*) The amount of capital gains tax chargeable in respect of a gain accruing on a disposal within subsection (2) for a consideration the amount or value of which

exceeds [€2,540][1] shall not exceed 50 per cent of the difference between the amount of that consideration and [€2,540][1].

(*b*) For the purposes of this subsection, the capital gains tax chargeable in respect of the gain shall be the amount of tax which would not have been chargeable but for that gain.

(4) Subsections (2) and (3) shall not affect the amount of an allowable loss accruing on the disposal of an asset, but for the purposes of computing under the Capital Gains Tax Acts the amount of a loss accruing on the disposal by an individual of tangible movable property the consideration for the disposal shall, if less than [€2,540][1], be deemed to be [€2,540][1] and the losses which are allowable losses shall be restricted accordingly.

(5) Where 2 or more assets which have formed part of a set of articles of any description all owned at one time by one person are disposed of by that person—

(*a*) to the same person, or

(*b*) to persons who are acting in concert or who are connected persons,

whether on the same or different occasions, the 2 or more transactions shall be treated as a single transaction disposing of a single asset, but with any necessary apportionments of the reductions in tax and in allowable losses under subsections (3) and (4), and this subsection shall also apply where the assets or some of the assets are disposed of on different occasions, and one of those occasions falls after the 28th day of February, 1974, but before the 6th day of April, 1974, but not so as to make any gain accruing on a disposal before the 6th day of April, 1974, a chargeable gain.

(6) Where the disposal is of a right or interest in or over tangible movable property, then—

(*a*) in the first instance, subsections (2) to (4) shall be applied in relation to the asset as a whole, taking the consideration as including, in addition to the consideration for the disposal (in this subsection referred to as **"the actual consideration"**), the market value of what remains undisposed of,

(*b*) if the sum of the actual consideration and that market value exceeds [€2,540][1], the limitation on the amount of tax in subsection (3) shall be to 50 per cent of the difference between that sum and [€2,540][1] multiplied by the fraction equal to the actual consideration divided by that sum, and

(*c*) if that sum is less than [€2,540][1], any loss shall be restricted under subsection (4) by deeming the consideration to be the actual consideration plus that fraction of the difference between that sum and [€2,540][1].

(7) This section shall not apply—

(*a*) in relation to a disposal of commodities of any description by a person dealing on a terminal market or dealing with or through a person ordinarily engaged in dealing on a terminal market, or

(*b*) in relation to a disposal of currency of any description.

Amendments

1 Substituted by FA 2001s 240(1) and (2)(*l*)(vii) and Sch 5 Pt 1 as respects disposals made on or after 1 January 2002; previously "£2,000".

Definitions

allowable loss: ss 4(1), 5(1), 546; chargeable gain: ss 5(1), 545; person: IA 1937 s 11(*c*); wasting asset: ss 5(1), 560, Sch 14 para 2.

Former enactments

CGTA 1975 s 17.

Corresponding UK tax provision

Taxation of Chargeable Gains Act 1992 s 262.

603 Wasting chattels

(1) Subject to this section, no chargeable gain shall accrue on the disposal of or of an interest in an asset which is tangible movable property and a wasting asset.

(2) Subsection (1) shall not apply to a disposal of or of an interest in an asset where—

(*a*) from the beginning of the period of ownership of the person making the disposal to the time when the disposal is made, the asset has been used and used solely for the purposes of a trade or profession and that person has claimed or could have claimed any capital allowance in respect of any expenditure attributable to the asset or interest under paragraph (*a*) or (*b*) of section 552(1), or

(*b*) the person making the disposal has incurred any expenditure on the asset or interest which has otherwise qualified in full for any capital allowance.

(3) In the case of the disposal of or of an interest in an asset which, in the period of ownership of the person making the disposal, has been used partly for the purposes of a trade or profession and partly for other purposes, or has been used for the purposes of a trade or profession for part of that period, or which has otherwise qualified in part only for capital allowances—

(*a*) the consideration for the disposal and any expenditure attributable to the asset or interest under paragraph (*a*) or (*b*) of section 552(1) shall be apportioned by reference to the extent to which that expenditure qualified for capital allowances,

(*b*) the computation of the gain shall be made separately in relation to the apportioned parts of the expenditure and consideration, and

(*c*) subsection (1) shall not apply to any gain accruing by reference to the computation in relation to the part of the consideration apportioned to use for the purposes of the trade or profession, or to the expenditure qualifying for capital allowances.

(4) Subsection (1) shall not apply to a disposal of commodities of any description by a person dealing on a terminal market or dealing with or through a person ordinarily engaged in dealing on a terminal market.

Definitions

capital allowance: ss 2(1), 5(1); chargeable gain: ss 5(1), 545; person: IA 1937 s 11(*c*); profession: ss 2(1), 5(1); trade: s 5(1), ITA 1967 s 1(1); wasting asset: ss 5(1), 560, Sch 14 para 2.

Former enactments

CGTA 1975 s 18.

603A Disposal of site to child

[(1) This section applies to the disposal of land which at the date of disposal has a market value which does not exceed [€254,000].[1]

(2) Subject to this section, a chargeable gain shall not accrue on a disposal of land to which this section applies where the disposal—

(*a*) is by a parent to a child of the parent, and

(*b*) is for the purpose of enabling the child to construct a dwelling house on the land which dwelling house is to be occupied by the child as his or her only or main residence.

(3) Where a child—

(*a*) at any time disposes of the land or a part of the land referred to in subsection (2), other than to his or her spouse, and

(*b*) the land being disposed of does not contain a dwelling house which—

(i) was constructed by the child since the time of acquisition of the land, and

(ii) has been occupied by the child as his or her only or main residence for a period of 3 years,

the chargeable gain which, but for subsection (2), would have accrued on the disposal of that land to the child, shall be treated as accruing to the child at the time of the disposal referred to in paragraph (*a*).

(4) Where subsection (2) applies to a disposal of land by a parent to a child, it shall not apply to any such subsequent disposal to that child unless, by virtue of subsection (3), the full amount of the chargeable gain which, but for subsection (2) would have accrued to the parent, is treated as accruing to the child.][2]

Amendments

1 Substituted by FA 2001 s 93(2) with effect from 1 January 2002; previously "£200,000".

2 Section 603A inserted by FA 2001 s 93(1)(*a*) for disposals on or after 6 December 2000.

Tax Briefing

TB43 April 2001 p 19 — Transfer of site from parent to child.

Definitions

chargeable gain: ss 5(1), 545; land: IA 1937 Sch; market value: ss 5(1); 548; year: IA 1937 Sch.

604 Disposals of principal private residence

(1) In this section, **"the period of ownership"**—

(*a*) where the individual has had different interests at different times, shall be taken to begin from the first acquisition taken into account in determining the expenditure which under the Capital Gains Tax Acts is allowable as a deduction in computing the amount of the gain to which this section applies, and

(*b*) for the purposes of subsections (3) to (5), shall not include any period before the 6th day of April, 1974.

(2) This section shall apply to a gain accruing to an individual on the disposal of or of an interest in—

(*a*) a dwelling house or part of a dwelling house which is or has been occupied by the individual as his or her only or main residence, or

(*b*) land which the individual has for his or her own occupation and enjoyment with that residence as its garden or grounds up to an area (exclusive of the site of the dwelling house) not exceeding one acre;

but, where part of the land occupied with a residence is and part is not within this subsection, then, that part shall be taken to be within this subsection which, if the remainder were separately occupied, would be the most suitable for occupation and enjoyment with the residence.

(3) The gain shall not be a chargeable gain if the dwelling house or the part of a dwelling house has been occupied by the individual as his or her only or main residence throughout the period of ownership or throughout the period of ownership except for all or any part of the last 12 months of that period.

(4) Where subsection (3) does not apply, such portion of the gain shall not be a chargeable gain as represents the same proportion of the gain as the length of the part or parts of the period of ownership during which the dwelling house or the part of a dwelling house was occupied by the individual as his or her only or main residence, but inclusive of the last 12 months of the period of ownership in any event, bears to the length of the period of ownership.

(5) (*a*) In this subsection, **"period of absence"** means a period during which the dwelling house or part of a dwelling house was not the individual's only or main residence and throughout which he or she had no residence or main residence eligible for relief under this section.

(*b*) For the purposes of subsections (3) and (4)—

(i) any period of absence throughout which the individual worked in an employment or office all the duties of which were performed outside the State, and

(ii) in addition, any period of absence not exceeding 4 years (or periods of absence which together did not exceed 4 years) throughout which the individual was prevented from residing in the dwelling house or the part of a dwelling house in consequence of the situation of the individual's place of work or in consequence of any condition imposed by the individual's employer requiring the individual to reside elsewhere, being a condition reasonably imposed to secure the effective performance by the employee of the employee's duties,

shall be treated as if in that period of absence the dwelling house or the part of a dwelling house was occupied by the individual as his or her only or main residence if both before and after the period the dwelling house (or the part in question) was occupied by the individual as his or her only or main residence.

(6) Where the gain accrues from the disposal of a dwelling house or part of a dwelling house part of which is used exclusively for the purposes of a trade, business or profession, the gain shall be apportioned and subsections (2) to (5) shall apply in

relation to the part of the gain apportioned to the part which is not exclusively used for those purposes.

(7) Where at any time in the period of ownership there is a change in the dwelling house or the part of it which is occupied as the individual's residence, whether on account of a reconstruction or conversion of a building or for any other reason, or there have been changes as regards the use of part of the dwelling house for the purpose of a trade, business or profession or for any other purpose, the relief given by this section may be adjusted in such manner as the inspector and the individual may agree, or as the Appeal Commissioners may on an appeal consider to be just and reasonable.

(8) For the purposes of this section, an individual shall not be treated as having more than one main residence at any one time and in so far as it is necessary to determine which of 2 or more residences is an individual's main residence for any period—

(*a*) that question may be determined by agreement between the inspector and the individual on the latter giving notice in writing to the inspector by the end of the year 1975–76 or within 2 years from the beginning of that period if that is later, and

(*b*) failing such agreement, the question shall be determined by the inspector, whose determination may be as respects either the whole or specified parts of the period of ownership in question,

and notice of any determination by the inspector under paragraph (*b*) shall be given to the individual who may appeal to the Appeal Commissioners against that determination within 21 days of service of the notice.

(9) In the case of a man and his wife living with him—

(*a*) there may be for the purposes of this section only one residence or main residence for both so long as they are living together and, where a notice under subsection (8)(*a*) affects both the husband and his wife, it must be made by both,

(*b*) if the one disposes of, or of his or her interest in, the dwelling house or part of a dwelling house which is their only or main residence to the other, or if it passes on death to the other as legatee, the other's period of ownership shall begin with the beginning of the period of ownership of the one making the disposal or from whom it passes on death,

(*c*) if paragraph (*b*) applies but the dwelling house or part of a dwelling house was not the only or main residence of both throughout the period of ownership of the one making the disposal, account shall be taken of any part of that period during which it was the only or main residence of the one as if it was also the only or main residence of the other, and

(*d*) any notice under subsection (8)(*b*) which affects a residence owned by the husband and a residence owned by the wife shall be given to each and either may appeal under that subsection.

(10) This section shall also apply in relation to a gain accruing to a trustee on a disposal of settled property, being an asset within subsection (2), where during the period of ownership of the trustee the dwelling house or the part of a dwelling house mentioned in

that subsection has been the only or main residence of an individual entitled to occupy it under the terms of the settlement, and in this section as so applied—

(*a*) references to the individual shall be taken as references to the trustee except in relation to the occupation of the dwelling house or the part of a dwelling house, and

(*b*) the notice which may be given to the inspector under subsection (8)(*a*) shall be a joint notice by the trustee and the person entitled to occupy the dwelling house or the part of a dwelling house.

(11)(*a*) In this subsection, **"dependent relative"**, in relation to an individual, means a relative of the individual, or of the wife or husband of the individual, who is incapacitated by old age or infirmity from maintaining himself or herself, or the widowed father or widowed mother (whether or not he or she is so incapacitated) of the individual or of the wife or husband of the individual.

(*b*) Where as respects a gain accruing to an individual on the disposal of, or of an interest in, a dwelling house or part of a dwelling house which is, or has at any time in his or her period of ownership been, the sole residence of a dependent relative of the individual, provided rent-free and without any other consideration, the individual so claims, such relief shall be given in respect of it and of its garden or grounds as would be given under this section if the dwelling house (or part of the dwelling house) had been the individual's only or main residence in the period of residence by the dependent relative, and shall be so given in addition to any relief available under this section apart from this subsection; but no more than one dwelling house (or part of a dwelling house) may qualify for relief as being the residence of a dependent relative of the claimant at any one time.

(12)(*a*) In this subsection—

"base date", in relation to an asset disposed of by an individual, means the date of acquisition by the individual of the asset or, if the asset was held by the individual on the 6th day of April, 1974, that date;

"base value", in relation to an asset disposed of by an individual, means the amount or value of the consideration, in money or money's worth, given by the individual or on his or her behalf wholly and exclusively for the acquisition of the asset exclusive of the incidental costs to the individual of the acquisition or, if the asset was held by the individual on the 6th day of April, 1974, the market value of the asset on that date;

"current use value" and **"development land"** have the same meanings respectively as in section 648.

(*b*) Where—

(i) a gain accrues to an individual on the disposal of or of an interest in an asset which is development land, and

(ii) apart from this subsection relief would be given under this section in respect of the disposal of that asset (being an asset within subsection (2) or (11)),

then, subject to paragraph (*c*), that relief shall be given in respect of the gain (or where appropriate in respect of a portion of the gain) only to the extent (if any) to which such relief would be given if, in computing the chargeable gain accruing on the disposal (notwithstanding that the disposal was a disposal of development land), there were excluded from the computation—

(I) the amount (if any) by which the base value of the asset exceeds the current use value of the asset on the base date,

(II) the amount by which the consideration for the disposal of the asset exceeds the current use value of the asset on the date of the disposal,

(III) if the asset was not held by the individual on the 6th day of April, 1974, such proportion (if any) of the incidental costs to the individual of the acquisition of the asset as would be referable to the amount (if any) referred to in subparagraph (I), and

(IV) such proportion of the incidental costs to the individual of the disposal of the asset as would be referable to the amount referred to in subparagraph (II).

(*c*) Paragraph (*b*) shall not apply to a disposal made by an individual in any year of assessment if the total consideration in respect of all disposals made by that individual in that year and to which that paragraph would otherwise apply does not exceed [€19,050][1].

(13) Apportionments of consideration shall be made wherever required by this section and in particular where a person disposes of a dwelling house only part of which is the person's only or main residence.

(14) This section shall not apply in relation to a gain if the acquisition of or of the interest in the dwelling house or the part of the dwelling house was made wholly or mainly for the purpose of realising a gain from the disposal of it, and shall not apply in relation to a gain in so far as the gain is attributable to any expenditure which was incurred after the beginning of the period of ownership and wholly or mainly for the purpose of realising a gain from the disposal.

Amendments

[1] Substituted by FA 2001 s 240(1) and (2)(*b*) and Sch 5 Pt 1 for 2002 and later tax years; previously "£15,000" (short tax "year" 2001: £11,100 (FA 2001 s 77(2) and Sch 2 paras 35 and 61(*a*))).

Cross-references

Disposal to authority possessing compulsory purchase powers: s 605(5).
Rent a room (income tax) relief: s 216A(8).
Transactions in land, Schedule D Case IV: s 643(2).

Case law

Subs (2): The grounds of a house sold some time after the sale of the house cannot qualify for relief: *Varty v Lynes* [1976] STC 508.

Held a caravan qualified for relief: *Makins v Elson* [1977] STC 46; but where caravan used for periodic visits only, no relief available: *Moore v Thompson* [1986] STC 170.

A caretaker's lodge was treated as part of the dwelling house and qualified for relief: *Batey v Wakefield* [1981] STC 326; *Williams v Merrylees* [1987] STC 445; but a bungalow built a considerable distance from the main house did not: *Markey v Sanders* [1987] STC 256; *Lewis v Rook* [1992] STC 171.

Held separate flats not to constitute one residence: *Honour v Norris* [1992] STC 304.

Held temporary occupation did not qualify as residence: *Goodwin v Curtis* [1998] STC 475.

Subs (8): The two year period runs from the time when it first becomes necessary to elect between two residences: *Griffin v Craig-Harvey* [1994] STC 54.

Subs (10): A beneficiary under a discretionary trust occupying a house at the discretion of trustees held "entitled to occupy" and accordingly, the house qualified for relief: *Sansom v Peay* [1976] STC 494.

Definitions

Appeal Commissioners: ss 2(1), 5(1); chargeable gain: ss 5(1), 545; inspector: ss 2(1), 5(1), 852; land: s 5(1), IA 1937 Sch; legatee: s 5(1); month: IA 1937 Sch; person: IA 1937 s 11(*c*); profession: ss 2(1), 5(1); rent: s 5(1); settled property: s 5(1); settlement: s 5(1); trade: s 5(1); writing: IA 1937 Sch; year of assessment: ss 2(1), 5(1).

Former enactments

CGTA 1975 s 25; FA 1979 s 35; FA 1980 s 61(*c*); FA 1984 s 67; FA 1997 s 146(1) and Sch 9 Pt I para 9(2).

Corresponding UK tax provision

Taxation of Chargeable Gains Act 1992 ss 222–226.

605 Disposals to authority possessing compulsory purchase powers

(1) [Where a person makes a disposal, before 4 December 2002, of][1] or of an interest in property situate in the State (in this section referred to as **"the original assets"**) to an authority possessing compulsory purchase powers and claims and proves to the satisfaction of the Revenue Commissioners that—

(*a*) the disposal would not have been made but for—

(i) the exercise of those powers, or

(ii) the giving by the authority of formal notice of its intention to exercise those powers,

(*b*) the whole of the consideration for the disposal and no more is applied in acquiring other property situate in the State or an interest in such other property (in this section referred to as **"the replacement assets"**), and

[(*c*) subject to subsection (4A), the original assets and the replacement assets are within one, and the same one, of the classes of assets specified in subsection (5),][2]

then, for the purposes of the Capital Gains Tax Acts, the disposal shall not be treated as involving any disposal of the original assets and the acquisition shall not be treated as involving any acquisition of the replacement assets or any part of those assets, but the original assets and the replacement assets shall be treated as the same assets acquired as the original assets were acquired.

(2) In a case where subsection (1) would apply but for the fact that an amount in excess of the amount or value of the consideration for the disposal concerned is applied as described in paragraph (*b*) of that subsection—

(*a*) the person making the disposal shall be treated for the purposes of the Capital Gains Tax Acts as if, in consideration of that excess, that person had acquired at the time of the acquisition of the replacement assets a portion of those assets which bears to the whole the same proportion as the amount of the excess bears to the amount or value of the consideration applied in acquiring the replacement assets, and

(*b*) subsection (1) shall apply to the remainder of those assets and to the original assets.

(3) In a case where subsection (1) would apply but for the fact that part of the amount or value of the consideration for the disposal concerned is not applied as described in paragraph (*b*) of that subsection—

(*a*) the person making the disposal shall be treated for the purposes of the Capital Gains Tax Acts as if, in consideration of that part, that person had disposed of an interest in the original assets, and

(*b*) subsection (1) shall apply to the remainder of those assets and to the replacement assets.

(4) This section shall apply only if the acquisition of the replacement assets takes place, or an unconditional contract for the acquisition is entered into, in the period beginning 12 months before and ending 3 years after the disposal of the original assets, or at such earlier or later time as the Revenue Commissioners may by notice in writing allow; but, where an unconditional contract for the acquisition is so entered into, this section may be applied on a provisional basis without ascertaining whether the replacement assets are acquired in pursuance of the contract, and when that fact is ascertained all necessary adjustments shall be made by making assessments or by repayment or discharge of tax, and shall be so made notwithstanding any limitation in the Capital Gains Tax Acts on the time within which assessments may be made.

[(4A) Where the original assets is land which has been let by the person making the disposal at any time in the period of 5 years ending with the disposal and, immediately before the time the land was first let in that period, the land was owned by that person and used by that person for farming (within the meaning of section 654) for a period of not less than 10 years ending with the time the land was first so let, the land may be treated as being within Class 1, which is referred to in subsection (5).][3]

(5) The classes of assets referred to in subsection (1) shall be as follows:

Class 1

Assets of a trade carried on by the person making the disposal which consist of—

(*a*) plant or machinery;

(*b*) except where the trade is a trade of dealing in or developing land, or of providing services for the occupier of land in which the person carrying on the trade has an estate or interest—

(i) any building or part of a building and any permanent or semi-permanent structure in the nature of a building occupied (as well as used) only for the purposes of the trade,

(ii) any land occupied (as well as used) only for the purposes of the trade, provided that where the trade is a trade of dealing in or developing land, but a profit on the sale of any land held for the purposes of the trade would not form part of the trading profits, the trade shall be treated for the purposes of this subsection as if it were not a trade of dealing in or developing land;

(*c*) goodwill.

Class 2

Any land or buildings, not being land or buildings within Class 1, but excluding a dwelling house or part of a dwelling house in relation to which the person making the disposal would be entitled to claim relief under section 604.

Amendments

[1] Substituted by FA 2003 s 67(1)(*d*) with effect from 1 January 2003 but does **not** apply to a disposal made by a person, on or after 4 December 2002 and on or before 31 December 2003, of original assets (within the meaning of TCA 1997 s 605), where the person claims and proves to the satisfaction of the Revenue Commissioners that, but for the amendment made by FA 2003 s 67(1)(*d*), the person would have been entitled to claim that that disposal would not be treated as a disposal for the purposes of the Capital Gains Tax Acts by virtue of the person having, before 4 December 2002, acquired, or entered into an unconditional contract to acquire, new assets (within that meaning); previously "Where a person makes a disposal of".

[2] Subs (1)(*c*) substituted by FA 2002 s 61(*a*) with effect from 1 January 2002.

[3] Subs (4A) inserted by FA 2002 s 61(*b*) with effect from 1 January 2002.

Cross-references

Development land disposals, this section does not apply: s 652(4); development land disposal to authority with compulsory purchase power for "road building", this section does apply with acquisition of replacement assets to take place within the period beginning 2 years before and ending 8 years after the disposal: s 652(5).

Tax Briefing

TB47 April 2002 p 15 — Finance Act 2002 changes.
TB52 May 2003 p 13 — Finance Act 2003 changes.

Definitions

land: s 5(1), IA 1937 Sch; month: IA 1937 Sch; person: IA 1937 s 11(*c*); profits: s 4(1); trade: s 3(1); writing: IA 1937 Sch.

Former enactments

CGT(A)A 1978 s 5.

Corresponding UK tax provision

Taxation of Chargeable Gains Act 1992 s 247.

606 Disposals of work of art, etc, loaned for public display

(1) This section shall apply to an object, being any picture, print, book, manuscript, sculpture, piece of jewellery or work of art which—

(*a*) in the opinion of the Revenue Commissioners, after such consultation (if any) as may seem to them to be necessary with such person or body of persons as in their opinion may be of assistance to them, has a market value of not less than [€31,740][1] at the date when the object is loaned to a gallery or museum in the State, being a gallery or museum approved of by the Revenue Commissioners for the purposes of this section, and

(*b*) is the subject of or included in a display to which the public is afforded reasonable access in the gallery or museum to which it has been loaned for a period (in this section referred to as **"the qualifying period"**) of not less than 6 years from the date the object is so loaned.

(2) Where after the end of the qualifying period a disposal of an object to which this section applies is made by the person who had loaned the object in the circumstances described in subsection (1), the disposal shall be treated for the purposes of the Capital Gains Tax Acts as being made for such consideration as to secure that neither a gain nor a loss accrues on the disposal.

Amendments

[1] Substituted by FA 2001 s 240(1) and (2)(*b*) and Sch 5 Pt 1 for 2002 and later tax years; previously "£25,000".

Cross-references

Loans of art objects, benefit in kind exemption, this section does not apply: s 236(6).

Definitions

body of persons: s 2(1); person: IA 1937 s 11(*c*).

Former enactments

FA 1991 s 43(1)–(2).

607 Government and certain other securities

(1) The following shall not be chargeable assets—

(*a*) securities (including savings certificates) issued under the authority of the Minister for Finance,

(*b*) stock issued by—

(i) a local authority, or

(ii) a harbour authority mentioned in the First Schedule to the Harbours Act, 1946,

(*c*) land bonds issued under the Land Purchase Acts,

(*d*) debentures, debenture stock, certificates of charge or other forms of security issued by the Electricity Supply Board, Bord Gáis Éireann, Radio Telefís Éireann, ...[1] , ...[2] Córas Iompair Éireann, ...[3] Bord na Móna, Aerlínte Éireann, Teoranta, Aer Lingus, Teoranta or Aer Rianta, Teoranta,

(*e*) securities issued by the Housing Finance Agency under section 10 of the Housing Finance Agency Act, 1981,

(*f*) securities issued by a body designated under section 4(1) of the Securitisation (Proceeds of Certain Mortgages) Act, 1995,

[(*fa*) securities issued by the National Development Finance Agency under section 6 of the National Development Finance Agency Act 2002,][4]

(*g*) securities issued in the State, with the approval of the Minister for Finance, by the European Community, the European Coal and Steel Community, the International Bank for Reconstruction and Development, the European Atomic Energy Community or the European Investment Bank, and

(*h*) securities issued by An Post and guaranteed by the Minister for Finance.

(2) (*a*) All futures contracts which—

(i) are unconditional contracts for the acquisition or disposal of any of the instruments referred to in subsection (1) or any other instruments to which this section applies by virtue of any other enactment (whenever enacted), and

(ii) require delivery of the instruments in respect of which the contracts are made,

shall not be chargeable assets.

(*b*) The requirement in paragraph (*a*) that the instrument be delivered shall be treated as satisfied where a person who has entered into a futures contract dealt in or quoted on a futures exchange or stock exchange closes out the futures contract by entering into another futures contract, so dealt in or quoted, with obligations which are reciprocal to those of the contract so closed out and are thereafter settled in respect of both futures contracts by means (if any) of a single cash payment or receipt.

Amendments

1 Repealed by ICC Bank Act 2000 s 7 and the ICC Bank Act 2000 (Commencement) (Sections 5 and 7) Order 2001 (SI No 396 of 2001) as respects debentures, debenture stock, certificates of charge or other forms of security issued on or after 12 February 2001; previously "ICC Bank plc".

2 Deleted by FA 2001 s 241(*b*) as respects any securities issued by Bord Telecom Éireann or Irish Telecommunications Investments plc on or after 15 February 2001; previously "Bord Telecom Éireann, Irish Telecommunications Investments plc,".

3 Repealed by ACC Bank Act 2002 s 12(1) and Sch, other than as respects debentures, debenture stock, certificates of charge or other forms of security issued before the commencement of this repeal. By virtue of the ACC Bank Act 2001 (Sections 6, 8, 10, 11(2) and 12) (Commencement) Order 2002, SI No 69 of 2002, the commencement date is 28 February 2002.

4 Subs (1)(*fa*) inserted by FA 2003 s 43(1)(*d*) with effect from 6 February 2003.

Cross-references

Capital gains tax, returns and information: s 913(3)(*a*).
Chargeable gains of life business: s 711(1)(*a*)(ii).
Dealers in securities: s 749(2C).
Foreign life assurance funds, deemed disposal and reacquisition of certain assets: s 719(3)(*a*).
Implementation of Council Directive 2003/48/EC of 3 June 2003 on Taxation of Savings Income in the Form of Interest Payments, interpretation: s 898B(1)("securities").
Overseas life assurance companies, investment income: s 726(6)(*a*)(ii).
Special investment schemes: s 737(8)(*a*)(iii).
Special portfolio investment accounts, meaning of "gains": s 838(1)(*a*); relevant investment: s 838(4)(*c*).
Taxation of income deemed to arise from certain sales of securities, meaning of "securities": s 815(1).
Unit trusts, special arrangements for qualifying unit trusts: s 732(1).
Undertaking for collective investment: s 738(4)(*a*)(ii), (5)(*a*)(ii).

Cross-references

See also ss 784A(2) and 784C(7) regarding exemption from capital gains tax of chargeable gains arising in respect of assets held in approved retirement funds and approved minimum retirement funds.

Definitions

local authority: s 2(1); person: IA 1937 s 11(*c*).

Former enactments

CGTA 1975 s 19; FA 1982 s 41(*a*); FA 1984 s 66; FA 1988 s 70(2); FA 1989 s 32 and s 95(2); FA 1992 s 24(2); FA 1996 s 39(1) and (5).

Corresponding UK tax provision

Taxation of Chargeable Gains Act 1992 s 115.

608 Superannuation funds

(1) (*a*) In this subsection, **"financial futures"** and **"traded options"** mean respectively financial futures and traded options for the time being dealt in or quoted on any futures exchange or any stock exchange, whether or not that exchange is situated in the State.

(*b*) For the purposes of subsection (2), a contract entered into in the course of dealing in financial futures or traded options shall be regarded as an investment.

[(2) A gain shall not be a chargeable gain if accruing to a person from the person's disposal of assets held by that person as part of a fund approved under section 774, 784(4) or 785(5) or held by that person as PRSA assets (within the meaning of section 787A).][1]

[(2A) A gain shall not be a chargeable gain if accruing to a person who is exempt from income tax under section 790B.][2]

(3) Where part only of a fund is approved under a section referred to in subsection (2), the gain shall be exempt from being a chargeable gain to the same extent only as income derived from the assets would be exempt under that section.

(4) For the purposes of this section, the fund set up under section 6A of the Oireachtas (Allowances to Members) Act, 1938 (inserted by the Oireachtas (Allowances to Members) and Ministerial and Parliamentary Offices (Amendment) Act, 1960), shall be deemed to be a fund approved under section 774.

Amendments

1 Subs (2) substituted by FA 2003 s 14(1)(*a*) with effect from 28 March 2003.

2 Subs (2A) inserted by FA 2005 s 58 with effect from 25 March 2005.

Cross-references

See also ss 784A(2) and 784C(7) regarding exemption from capital gains tax of chargeable gains arising in respect of assets held in approved retirement funds and approved minimum retirement funds.

Definitions

chargeable gain: ss 5(1), 545; person: IA 1937 s 11(*c*).

Former enactments

CGTA 1975 s 21; FA 1988 s 30(1)–(2)(*b*); FA 1991 s 38.

Corresponding UK tax provision

Taxation of Chargeable Gains Act 1992 s 237.

609 Charities

(1) Subject to subsection (2), a gain shall not be a chargeable gain if it accrues to a charity and is applicable and applied for charitable purposes.

(2) Where property held on charitable trusts ceases to be subject to charitable trusts—

(*a*) the trustees shall be treated as if they had disposed of and immediately reacquired the property for a consideration equal to its market value, any gain on the disposal being treated as not accruing to a charity, and

(*b*) if and in so far as any of that property represents directly or indirectly the consideration for the disposal of assets by the trustees, any gain accruing on that disposal shall be treated as not having accrued to a charity,

and an assessment to capital gains tax chargeable by virtue of paragraph (*b*) may be made at any time not more than 10 years after the end of the year of assessment in which the property ceases to be subject to charitable trusts.

Revenue information

Information leaflet CHY1 — Applying for relief from Tax on the Income and Property of Charities

Definitions

chargeable gain: ss 5(1), 545; charity: ss 5(1), 208; year of assessment: ss 2(1), 5(1).

Former enactments

CGTA 1975 s 22.

Corresponding UK tax provision

Taxation of Chargeable Gains Act 1992 s 256.

610 Other bodies

(1) A gain shall not be a chargeable gain if it accrues to a body specified in Part 1 of Schedule 15.

(2) A gain shall not be a chargeable gain if it accrues to a body specified in Part 2 of Schedule 15 in respect of a disposal by that body of an asset to the Interim Board established under the Milk (Regulation of Supply) (Establishment of Interim Board) Order, 1994 (SI No 408 of 1994).

Definitions

chargeable gain: ss 5(1), 545; Corporation Tax Acts: s 1(2); local authority: s 2(1); tax: s 3(1).

Former enactments

CGTA 1975 s 23; FA 1989 s 33; FA 1991 s 20(2); FA 1994 s 32(5); FA 1995 s 44(1) and (3); FA 1996 s 39(1) and (6) and s 64; FA 1997 s 49(1) and (3).

611 Disposals to State, public bodies and charities

(1) (*a*) Where a disposal of an asset is made otherwise than under a bargain at arm's length—

(i) to the State,

(ii) to a charity, or

(iii) to any of the bodies within section 28(3) of the Finance Act, 1931,

section 547 shall not apply but, if the disposal is for no consideration or for a consideration not exceeding the sums which would be allowable as a deduction under sections 552 and 828(4) for the purposes of computing a chargeable gain, then—

(I) the disposal and acquisition shall be treated for the purposes of the Capital Gains Tax Acts as being made for such consideration as to secure that neither a gain nor a loss accrues on the disposal, and

(II) where the disposal is to a person within subparagraph (ii) or (iii) and the asset is later disposed of by that person in such circumstances that if a gain accrued on the later disposal it would be a chargeable gain, the capital gains tax which would have been chargeable in respect of the gain accruing on the earlier disposal if section 547 had applied in relation to it shall be assessed and charged on the person making the later disposal in addition to any capital gains tax chargeable in respect of the gain accruing to that person on the later disposal.

(*b*) Where relief was given under this subsection in respect of a disposal to a person of an asset, being a disposal made before the 20th day of December, 1978, and there is a later disposal of the asset by the person on or after that date, paragraph (*a*)(II) shall apply as if the first-mentioned disposal were the earlier disposal referred to in that paragraph.

(*c*) An assessment to give effect to paragraph (*a*)(II) shall not be out of time if made within [4 years][1] after the end of the year of assessment in which the asset concerned is disposed of by the person making the later disposal.

(*d*) For the purposes of paragraph (*a*)(II), the amount of the capital gains tax which would have been chargeable in respect of the gain accruing on the earlier disposal shall be the amount of tax which would not have been chargeable but for that gain.

(2) Where under section 576(1) or 577(3) any assets or parts of any assets forming part of settled property are deemed to be disposed of and reacquired by the trustee, and—

(*a*) where the assets deemed to be disposed of under section 576(1) are reacquired on behalf of the State, a charity or a body within section 28(3) of the Finance Act, 1931, or

(*b*) the assets which or parts of which are deemed to be disposed of and reacquired under section 577(3) are held for the purposes of the State, a charity or a body within section 28(3) of the Finance Act, 1931,

then, if no consideration is received by any person for or in connection with any transaction by virtue of which the State, the charity or other body becomes so entitled or the assets are so held, the disposal and acquisition of the assets to which the State, the charity or other body becomes so entitled or of the assets which are held as mentioned in paragraph (*b*) shall be treated for the purposes of the Capital Gains Tax Acts as made for such consideration as to secure that neither a gain nor a loss accrues on the disposal.

Amendments

1 Substituted by FA 2003 s 17(*f*) with effect from: (*a*) such day or days as the Minister for Finance may by order or orders appoint either generally or with reference to any particular purpose or provision and different days may be so appointed for different purposes or different provisions and (*b*) notwithstanding the generality of (*a*), any order made by the Minister for Finance in accordance with the provisions of that paragraph may contain, and be subject to, such conditions as the Minister considers appropriate and which are specified in the order; previously "10 years". By virtue of Finance Act 2003 (Commencement of Section 17) Order 2003, SI No 508 of 2003, this amendment comes into operation in relation to the making, on or after 1 January 2005, of an assessment referred to in section 611(1)(*c*).

Tax Briefing

TB56 July 2004 pp 6–11 — Repayments, Interest and Time Limits — Section 17 FA 2003 changes.

TB57 Oct 2004 pp 7–9 — New Time Limits - Section 17 FA 2003 changes.

TB57 Oct 2004 p 15 — Repayments, Interest and Time Limits - correction to TB56 p 8.

Definitions

chargeable gain: ss 5(1), 545; charity: ss 5(1), 208; commencement: IA 1937 Sch; person: IA 1937 s 11(*c*); settled property: s 5(1); year of assessment: ss 2(1), 5(1).

Former enactments

CGTA 1975 s 39; CGT(A)A 1978 s 10.

Corresponding UK tax provision

Taxation of Chargeable Gains Act 1992 s 257.

612 Scheme for retirement of farmers

For the purposes of the Capital Gains Tax Acts, an amount by means of capital sum or premium provided under the European Communities (Retirement of Farmers) Regulations, 1974 (SI No 116 of 1974), whether or not an annuity is granted in place of such capital sum or premium, shall not be deemed to form part of the consideration for the disposal in relation to which such capital sum or premium is provided.

Former enactments

CGTA 1975 s 30.

613 Miscellaneous exemptions for certain kinds of property

(1) The following shall not be chargeable gains—

(*a*) any bonus payable under an instalment saving scheme within the meaning of section 53 of the Finance Act, 1970;

(*b*) any prize under section 22 of the Finance (Miscellaneous Provisions) Act, 1956;

(*c*) any sum obtained by means of compensation or damages for any wrong or injury suffered by an individual in his or her person or in his or her profession.

(2) Winnings from betting (including pool betting), lotteries, sweepstakes or games with prizes shall not be chargeable gains, and rights to winnings obtained by participating in any pool betting, lottery, sweepstake or game with prizes shall not be chargeable assets.

(3) No chargeable gain shall accrue on the disposal of a right to or to any part of—

(*a*) any allowance, annuity or capital sum payable out of any superannuation fund, or under any superannuation scheme, established solely or mainly for persons employed in a profession, trade, undertaking or employment, and their dependants,

(*b*) an annuity granted otherwise than under a contract for a deferred annuity by a company as part of its business of granting annuities on human life, whether or not including instalments of capital, or

(*c*) annual payments due under a covenant made by any person and not secured on any property.

(4) (*a*) [Subject to subsection (5), no chargeable gain][1] shall accrue on the disposal of an interest created by or arising under a settlement (including in particular an annuity or life interest and the reversion to an annuity or life interest)—

(i) by the person for whose benefit the interest was created by the terms of the settlement, or

(ii) by any other person except one who acquired, or derives that person's title from one who acquired, the interest for a consideration in money or money's worth, other than consideration consisting of another interest under the settlement.

(*b*) Subject to paragraph (*a*), where a person who has acquired an interest in settled property (including in particular the reversion to an annuity or life interest) becomes as the holder of that interest absolutely entitled as against the trustee to any settled property, the person shall be treated as disposing of the interest in consideration of obtaining that settled property, but without prejudice to any gain accruing to the trustee on the disposal of that property deemed to be effected by the trustee under section 576(1).

[(5) Subsection (4)(*a*) shall not apply—

(*a*) to the disposal of an interest in settled property, other than such a disposal treated under subsection (4)(*b*) as made in consideration of obtaining the settled property, if at the time of the disposal the trustees are neither resident nor ordinarily resident in the State, (*b*) if the settlement falls within subsection (6), or

(*c*) the property comprised in the settlement is or includes property that is derived directly or indirectly from a settlement falling within subsection (6).

(6) (*a*) In this subsection **"arrangements"** means arrangements having the force of law by virtue of [section 826(1)(*a*)][2] (as extended to capital gains tax by section 828).

(*b*) A settlement falls within this subsection if there has been a time when the trustees of the settlement—

(i) were neither resident nor ordinarily resident in the State, or

(ii) fell to be regarded for the purposes of any arrangements as resident in a territory outside the State.][3]

Amendments

1 Substituted by FA 1999 s 90(1)(*a*)(i) for disposals on or after 11 February 1999 of an interest created by or arising under a settlement; previously "No chargeable gain".

2 Substituted by FA 2004 s 89 and Sch 3 para 1(*p*) with effect from 25 March 2004; previously "section 826".

3 Subs (5)–(6) inserted by FA 1999 s 90(1)(*a*)(ii) for disposals on or after 11 February 1999 of an interest created by or arising under a settlement.

Cross-references

Overseas life assurance companies, investment income: s 726(6)(*a*)(ii).

Capital gains tax, returns and information: s 913(3)(*a*).

Supplementary provisions: subss (4)(*a*), (5)(*a*): s 613A(1)(*b*), (4)(*b*).

Definitions

chargeable gain: ss 5(1), 545; company: s 5(1); ordinarily resident: s 5(1); person: IA 1937 s 11(*c*); profession: ss 2(1), 5(1); resident: s 5(1); settled property: s 5(1); settlement: s 2(1); trade: s 5(1).

Former enactments

CGTA 1975 s 24.

613A Supplementary provisions

[(1) Subject to this section, subsection (2) shall apply where—

(*a*) section 579B applies as regards the trustees of a settlement,

(*b*) after the relevant time (within the meaning of that section) a person disposes of an interest created by or arising under the settlement and the circumstances are such that subsection (4)(*a*) of section 613 does not apply by virtue of subsection (5)(*a*) of that section, and

(*c*) the interest was created for the benefit of the person making the disposal or that person otherwise acquired it, before the relevant time.

(2) For the purposes of calculating any chargeable gain accruing on the disposal of the interest, the person disposing of it shall be treated as having—

(*a*) disposed of it immediately before the relevant time, and

(*b*) immediately reacquired it,

at its market value at that time.

(3) Subsection (2) shall not apply if section 579E applied as regards the trustees in circumstances where the time concerned (within the meaning of that section) fell before

the time when the interest was created for the benefit of the person disposing of it or when the person otherwise acquired it.

(4) Subsection (6) applies where—

(*a*) section 579B applies as regards the trustees of a settlement,

(*b*) after the relevant time (within the meaning of that section) a person disposes of an interest created by or arising under the settlement and the circumstances are such that subsection (4)(*a*) of section 613 does not apply by virtue of subsection (5)(*a*) of that section,

(*c*) the interest was created for the person's benefit, or the person otherwise acquired it, before the relevant time, and

(*d*) section 579E applied as regards the trustees in circumstances where the time concerned (within the meaning of that section) fell in the relevant period.

(5) The relevant period is the period which—

(*a*) begins when the interest was created for the benefit of the person disposing of it or when the person otherwise acquired it, and

(*b*) ends with the relevant time.

(6) For the purposes of calculating any chargeable gain accruing on the disposal of the interest, the person disposing of it shall be treated as having—

(*a*) disposed of it immediately before the time determined in accordance with subsection (7), and

(*b*) immediately reacquired it,

at its market value at that time.

(7) The time mentioned in subsection (6) is—

(*a*) where there is only one such time, the time concerned, or

(*b*) where there is more than one time concerned, because section 579E applied more than once, the earliest time concerned.

(8) Where subsection (2) applies, subsection (6) shall not apply.][1]

Amendments

1 Section 613A inserted by FA 1999 s 90(1)(*b*) for disposals on or after 11 February 1999 of an interest created by or arising under a settlement.

Definitions

chargeable gain: ss 5(1), 545; market value: ss 5(1), 548; person: IA 1937 s 11(*c*); settlement: s 5(1).

Corresponding UK tax provision

Taxation of Chargeable Gains Act 1992 s 85.

PART 20
COMPANIES' CHARGEABLE GAINS

Cross-references

75 per cent subsidiary, meaning of: s 9.

CHAPTER 1
General

614 Capital distribution derived from chargeable gain of company: recovery of tax from shareholder

(1) In this section, **"capital distribution"** has the same meaning as in section 583.

(2) This section shall apply where a person connected with a company resident in the State receives or becomes entitled to receive in respect of shares in the company any capital distribution from the company, other than a capital distribution representing a reduction of capital, and—

(*a*) the capital so distributed derives from the disposal after the 5th day of April, 1976, of assets in respect of which a chargeable gain accrues to the company, or

(*b*) the distribution constitutes such a disposal of assets.

(3) Where the corporation tax assessed on the company for the accounting period in which the chargeable gain accrues included any amount in respect of chargeable gains, and any of the tax assessed on the company for that period is not paid within 6 months from the date when it becomes payable by the company, the person referred to in subsection (2) may by an assessment made within 2 years from that date be assessed and charged (in the name of the company) to an amount of that corporation tax—

(*a*) not exceeding the amount or value of the capital distribution which that person has received or became entitled to receive, and

(*b*) not exceeding a proportion equal to that person's share of the capital distribution made by the company of corporation tax on the amount and at the rate charged in respect of that gain in the assessment in which that tax was charged.

(4) A person paying any amount of tax under this section shall be entitled to recover a sum equal to that amount from the company.

(5) This section is without prejudice to any liability of the person receiving or becoming entitled to receive the capital distribution in respect of a chargeable gain accruing to such person by reference to the capital distribution as constituting a disposal of an interest in shares in the company.

Definitions

chargeable gain: ss 5(1), 545; company: ss 4(1), 5(1); distribution: ss 4(1), 436, 437; month: IA 1937 Sch; person: IA 1937 s 11(*c*).

Former enactments

CTA 1976 s 126.

Corresponding UK tax provision

Taxation of Chargeable Gains Act 1992 s 189.

615 Company reconstruction or amalgamation: transfer of assets

(1) In this section—

"scheme of reconstruction or amalgamation" means a scheme for the reconstruction of any company or companies or the amalgamation of any 2 or more companies;

"trading stock" has the same meaning as in section 89.

[(2) (*a*) Subject to this section, where—

(i) any scheme of reconstruction or amalgamation involves the transfer of the whole or part of a company's business to another company,

(ii) (I) the company acquiring the assets is resident in the State at the time of the acquisition, or the assets are chargeable assets in relation to that company immediately after that time, and

(II) the company from which the assets are acquired is resident in the State at the time of the acquisition, or the assets are chargeable assets in relation to that company immediately before that time,

and

(iii) the first-mentioned company receives no part of the consideration for the transfer (otherwise than by the other company taking over the whole or part of the liabilities of the business),

then, in so far as relates to corporation tax on chargeable gains, both companies shall be treated as if any assets included in the transfer were acquired by the one company from the other company for a consideration of such amount as would secure that on the disposal by means of the transfer neither a gain nor a loss would accrue to the company making the disposal, and for the purposes of section 556 the acquiring company shall be treated as if the respective acquisitions of the assets by the other company had been the acquiring company's acquisition of the assets.

(*b*) For the purposes of paragraph (*a*)—

(i) an asset is a **"chargeable asset"** in relation to a company at any time if, were the asset to be disposed of by the company at that time, any gain accruing to the company would be a chargeable gain, and

(ii) a reference to a company shall apply only to a company which, by virtue of the law of a [relevant Member State][2], is resident for the purposes of tax in such a Member State, and for this purpose **"tax"**, in relation to a [relevant Member State][2] other than the State, means any tax imposed in the Member State which corresponds to corporation tax in the State.][1]

(3) This section shall not apply in relation to an asset which until the transfer formed part of trading stock of a trade carried on by the company making the disposal, or in relation to an asset acquired as trading stock for the purposes of a trade carried on by the company acquiring the asset.

Amendments

1 Subs (2) substituted by FA 2001 s 38(1)(*a*) in respect of a disposal on or after 15 February 2001.

2 Substituted by FA 2002 s 36(*a*) with effect from 1 January 2002; previously "Member State of the European Communities".

Cross-references

Companies' chargeable gains, deemed disposal in certain circumstances: s 620A(1)(*b*)(i)(I).
EU Council Directive 90/434/EEC, transfer of development land, subs (2): s 633.

Revenue Precedents

Issue: Break up of family trading company (or group of companies).
Decision: Where a family trading company (or group of companies) is broken up into separate individual trading companies, such an event will not be regarded as a disposal for CGT purposes provided that the value of each individual's holding in the company remains strictly unaltered and also provided certain other conditions are met.

Tax Briefing

TB44 June 2001 pp 34–35 — Partition of Family Trading Companies — CGT (application of above precedent).
TB47 April 2002 p 17 — Retirement Relief and Reconstructions.
TB48 June 2002 pp 16–17 — Company Reconstructions and Amalgamations.
TB51 Jan 2003 p 6 — Revenue will accept that where partition is achieved by means of a capital reduction resolved and passed at an extraordinary general meeting and confirmed by the High Court pursuant to section 72 of the Companies Act 1963, the above precedent may have application. For the relief to be granted, all other conditions as outlined in TB44 must be satisfied.

Definitions

chargeable gain: ss 5(1), 545; company: ss 4(1), 5(1); trade: ss 3(1), 4(1), 5(1); trading stock: ss (1), 89.

Former enactments

CTA 1976 s 127; CGT(A)A 1978 s 13.

Corresponding UK tax provision

Taxation of Chargeable Gains Act 1992 s 139.

616 Groups of companies: interpretation

(1) For the purposes of this section and of the following sections [of this Chapter][1]—

[(*a*) subject to section 621(1), a reference to a company or companies shall apply only to a company or companies, as limited by subsection (2), being a company or, as the case may be, companies which, by virtue of the law of a [relevant Member State][2], is or are resident for the purposes of tax in such a Member State, and for this purpose **"tax"**, in relation to a [relevant Member State][2] other than the State, means any tax imposed in the Member State which corresponds to corporation tax in the State, and references to a member or members of a group of companies shall be construed accordingly;][3]

(*b*) a company is an effective 75 per cent subsidiary of another company (in this paragraph referred to as "the parent") at any time if at that time—

(i) the company is a 75 per cent subsidiary (within the meaning of section 9) of the parent,

(ii) the parent is beneficially entitled to not less than 75 per cent of any profits available for distribution to equity holders of the company, and

(iii) the parent would be beneficially entitled to not less than 75 per cent of the assets of the company available for distribution to its equity holders on a winding up,

and sections 413 to 419 shall apply for the purposes of this paragraph as they apply for the purposes of Chapter 5 of Part 12;

(*bb*) a principal company and all its effective 75 per cent subsidiaries shall form a group, and where a principal company is a member of a group as being itself an effective 75 per cent subsidiary that group shall comprise all its effective 75 per cent subsidiaries;

(*c*) "principal company" means a company of which another company is an effective 75 per cent subsidiary;][4]

(*d*) in applying the definition of **"75 per cent subsidiary"** in section 9, any share capital of a registered industrial and provident society shall be treated as ordinary share capital;

(*e*) **"group"** and **"subsidiary"** shall be construed with any necessary modifications where applied to a company incorporated under the law of a country outside the [State;][5]

[(*f*) an asset is a **"chargeable asset"** in relation to a company at any time if, were the asset to be disposed of by the company at that time, any gain accruing to the company would be a chargeable gain.][6]

(2) For the purposes of this section and of the following sections of this Part, references to a company shall apply only to—

(*a*) a company within the meaning of the Companies Act, 1963,

(*b*) a company constituted under any other Act or a charter or letters patent or ...[7] formed under the law of a country or territory outside the State,

(*c*) a registered industrial and provident society, being a society within the meaning of section 698, and

(*d*) a building society incorporated or deemed by virtue of section 124(2) of the Building Societies Act, 1989, to be incorporated under that Act.

(3) For the purposes of this section and of the following sections of this Part, a group shall remain the same group so long as the same company remains the principal company of the group and, if at any time the principal company of a group becomes [an effective 75 per cent subsidiary][8] of another company, the group of which it was the principal company before that time shall be regarded as the same as the group of which that other company is the principal company or [an effective 75 per cent subsidiary],[8] and the question whether or not a company has ceased to be a member of a group shall be determined accordingly.

(4) For the purposes of this section and of the following sections of this Part, the passing of a resolution or the making of an order or any other act for the winding up of a company shall not be regarded as the occasion of that company or of any [effective 75 per cent subsidiary][9] of that company ceasing to be a member of a group of companies.

(5) (*a*) The following sections of this Part, except in so far as they relate to the recovery of tax, shall also apply in relation to bodies from time to time established by or under any enactment for the carrying on of any industry or part of an industry, or of any undertaking, under national ownership or control as if—

(i) such bodies were companies within the meaning of those sections,

(ii) any such bodies charged with related functions and subsidiaries of any of them formed a group, and

(iii) any 2 or more such bodies charged at different times with the same or related functions were members of a group.

(*b*) Paragraph (*a*) shall apply subject to any enactment by virtue of which property, rights, liabilities or activities of one such body mentioned in that paragraph are to be treated for corporation tax as those of another such body.

(6) For the purposes of this Part—

(*a*) section 557 and all other provisions for apportioning on a part disposal expenditure which is deductible in computing a gain shall be operated before the operation of and without regard to—

(i) section 617(1), and

(ii) any other enactment making an adjustment to secure that neither a gain nor a loss occurs on a disposal;

(*b*) section 589 shall not apply where the transfer is a disposal to which section 617(1) applies.

[(7) For the purposes of this Part—

"EEA Agreement" means the Agreement on the European Economic Area signed at Oporto on 2 May 1992, as adjusted by the Protocol signed at Brussels on 17 March 1993;

"EEA State" means a state which is a contracting party to the EEA Agreement;

"relevant Member State" means—

(*a*) a Member State of the European Communities, or

(*b*) not being such a Member State, an EEA State which is a territory with the government of which arrangements having the force of law by virtue of [section 826(1)(*a*)][10] have been made;][11]

Amendments

1 Substituted by FA 1999 s 56(1)(*a*)(i) for accounting periods ending on or after 1 July 1998 where it relates to TCA 1997 s 616(1)(*a*), in any other case with effect from 11 February 1999; previously "of this Part".

2 Substituted by FA 2002 s 36(*b*)(i) with effect from 1 January 2002; previously "Member State of the European Communities".

3 Subs (1)(*a*) substituted by FA 2001 s 38(1)(*b*)(i)(I) with effect from 15 February 2001.

4 Subs (1)(*a*)–(*c*) substituted by FA 1999 s 56(1)(*a*)(ii) for accounting periods ending on or after 1 July 1998 where it relates to TCA 1997 s 616(1)(*a*), in any other case with effect from 11 February 1999.

5 Substituted by FA 2001 s 38(1)(*b*)(i)(II) with effect from 15 February 2001; previously "State.".

6 Subs (1)(*f*) inserted by FA 2001 s 38(1)(*b*)(i)(III) with effect from 15 February 2001.

7 Deleted by FA 2001 s 38(1)(*b*)(ii) with effect from 15 February 2001; previously "(although resident in the State)".

8 Substituted by FA 1999 s 56(1)(*b*)(i) with effect from 11 February 1999; previously "a 75 percent subsidiary".

9 Substituted by FA 1999 s 56(1)(*b*)(ii) with effect from 11 February 1999; previously "75 per cent subsidiary".

10 Substituted by FA 2005 s 147 and Sch 6 para 1(*j*) with effect from 25 March 2005; previously "section 826".

11 Subs (7) inserted by FA 2002 s 36(*b*)(ii) with effect from 1 January 2002.

Cross-references

Attribution to shareholders of chargeable gains accruing to non-resident company, "group" to be construed in accordance with subss (1)(excluding para (*a*)), (3)–(4): s 590(16)(*a*).

Companies chargeable gains, exemptions in case of certain mergers, subs (1)(*a*): s 624(5).

Company amalgamation by exchange of shares, meaning of "group" applied: s 586(3)(*c*).

Company reconstructions and amalgamations, meaning of "group" applied: s 587(4)(*c*).
Development land chargeable gains: s 649(3)(*a*).
Exemption from tax in the case of gains on certain disposals of shares, this section does not apply: s 626B(1)(*b*)(v).
Restriction on set-off of pre-entry losses, subs (3): Sch 18A para 1(6).
Tax on non-resident company recoverable from another member of group or from controlling director, "group" to be construed in accordance with this section as if references to resident in a Member State of the European Communities were omitted and as if 51 per cent subsidiaries substituted for 75 per cent subsidiaries: s 629(1)("group").
Transitional provisions in respect of section 623: s 623A(1), (2)(*a*).
Transitional provisions in respect of section 625: s 625A(1) (the new definition), (2)(*a*).

Case law

Advantage was taken of this provision and the definition of "ordinary share capital" in s 2 to effect a tax free sale: *Burman v Hedges and Butler Ltd* [1979] STC 136.

Definitions

chargeable gain: ss 5(1), 545; company: ss 4(1), 5(1); ordinary share capital: s 2(1); part disposal: ss 5(1), 534.

Former enactments

CTA 1976 s 129(1)–(6)(*b*); FA 1990 s 58.

Corresponding UK tax provision

Taxation of Chargeable Gains Act 1992 s 170.

617 Transfers of assets, other than trading stock, within group

[(1) Notwithstanding any provision in the Capital Gains Tax Acts fixing the amount of the consideration deemed to be received on a disposal or given on an acquisition, where—

(*a*) a member of a group of companies disposes of an asset to another member of the group,

(*b*) the company making the disposal is resident in the State at the time of the disposal or the asset is a chargeable asset in relation to that company immediately before that time, and

(*c*) the other company is resident in the State at the time of the disposal or the asset is a chargeable asset in relation to that company immediately after that time,

both members shall, except where provided by subsections (2) and (3), be treated, in so far as relates to corporation tax on chargeable gains, as if the asset acquired by the member to whom the disposal is made were acquired for a consideration of such amount as would secure that on the other member's disposal neither a gain nor a loss would accrue to that other member; but, where it is assumed for any purpose that a member of a group of companies has sold or acquired an asset, it shall be assumed also that it was not a sale to or acquisition from another member of the group.][1]

(2) Subsection (1) shall not apply where the disposal is—

(*a*) a disposal of a debt from a member of a group of companies effected by satisfying the debt or part of it, or

(*b*) a disposal of redeemable shares in a company on the occasion of their redemption,

and the reference in that subsection to a member of a group of companies disposing of an asset shall not apply to anything which under section 583 is to be treated as a disposal of an interest in shares in a company in consideration for a capital distribution (within the meaning of that section) from that company, whether or not involving a reduction of capital.

(3) For the purposes of subsection (1), in so far as the consideration for the disposal consists of money or money's worth by means of compensation for any kind of damage or injury to assets, or for the destruction or dissipation of assets or for anything which depreciates or might depreciate an asset, the disposal shall be treated as being to the person who, whether as an insurer or otherwise, ultimately bears the burden of furnishing that consideration.

Amendments

1 Subs (1) substituted by FA 2001 s 38(1)(*c*) as respects a disposal on or after 15 February 2001.

Cross-references

Attribution to shareholders of chargeable gains accruing to non-resident company, s 617 (other than paras (*b*) and (*c*) of subs (1)) applied by: s 590(16)(*b*)(i).

Companies' chargeable gains, deemed disposal in certain circumstances: s 620A(1)(*b*)(i)(II).

Companies' chargeable gains, groups of companies, subs (1): s 616(6).

Companies' chargeable gains, disposals or acquisitions outside a group, subs (1): s 619(1).

Companies' chargeable gains, dividend stripping: s 622(2)(*a*).

EU Council Directive 90/434/EEC, transfer of assets to parent, ss 617–619 applied by: s 632(1).

Development land chargeable gains, ss 617 and 621–626 applied by: s 649(2).

Restriction on set-off of pre-entry losses: Sch 18A para 1(4).

Case law

Subs (1): Held subsection applies to the transferee company where there is a share for share exchange between two companies in a group: *Westcott v Woolcombers Ltd* [1987] STC 600; *Nap Holdings UK Ltd v Whittles* [1994] STC 979.

Subs (2): Held subsection did not apply where parent company acquired quoted shares in satisfaction of its interest in its subsidiary on liquidation and, accordingly, the parent company was held to have acquired the shares at the cost to the subsidiary: *Innocent v Whaddon Estates Ltd* [1982] STC 115.

Revenue precedents

Issue: Transfers within a group involving a non-resident company.

Decision: Under s 617 certain assets can be transferred within a capital gains tax group without a chargeable gain arising. Instead, the transferee company takes the asset at the same time and cost at which it was originally acquired by the transferor company. The definition of a capital gains tax group in s 616 confines this relief to such group companies where both companies are resident in the State. In practice Revenue will allow similar relief in circumstances involving transfers within a non-resident CGT group where assets are transferred as part of a transfer of a trade carried on in the State where profits of the trade, including chargeable gains, are chargeable to Corporation Tax. The assets must be in use for the purpose of the trade and there must be no discontinuance of the trade ie the transferee will continue to carry on the trade. The transfer must also be for bona fide commercial reasons and not to avoid tax. To avail of this treatment a formal submission must be made to the Technical Services (CGT) area of the Office of the Chief Inspector of Taxes. This will involve formal undertakings from the transferee and the group parent in relation to the asset transferred.

Definitions

Capital Gains Tax Acts: s 1(2); chargeable gain: ss 5(1), 545; company: ss 4(1), 5(1); distribution: ss 4(1), 436, 437; person: IA 1937 s 11(*c*).

Former enactments

CTA 1976 s 130.

Corresponding UK tax provision

Taxation of Chargeable Gains Act 1992 s 171.

---

618 Transfers of trading stock within group

[(1) Where—

(*a*) a company which is a member of a group of companies acquires an asset as trading stock of a trade to which this section applies,

(*b*) the acquisition is from another company which is a member of the group, and

(*c*) the asset did not form part of the trading stock of any such trade carried on by the other company,

the company acquiring the asset shall be treated for the purposes of section 596 as having acquired the asset otherwise than as trading stock and immediately appropriated it for the purposes of the trade as trading stock.][1]

(2) Where a member of a group of companies disposes of an asset to another member of the group and the asset formed part of the trading stock of a trade [to which this section applies][2] carried on by the member disposing of the asset but is acquired by the other member otherwise than as trading stock of a trade carried on by that other member, the member disposing of the asset shall be treated for the purposes of section 596 as having immediately before the disposal appropriated the asset for some purpose other than the purpose of use as trading stock.

[(3) This section applies to—

(*a*) a trade carried on by a company which is resident in the State, and

(*b*) a trade carried on in the State through a branch or agency by a company which is not so resident.][3]

Amendments

1 Subs (1) substituted by FA 2001 s 38(1)(*d*)(i) as respects an acquisition or disposal on or after 15 February 2001.

2 Inserted by FA 2001 s 38(1)(*d*)(ii) as respects an acquisition or disposal on or after 15 February 2001.

3 Subs (3) inserted by FA 2001 s 38(1)(*d*)(iii) as respects an acquisition or disposal on or after 15 February 2001.

Cross-references

Attribution to shareholders of chargeable gains accruing to non-resident company, s 618 (with the omission of the words "to which this section applies" in subs (1)(*a*) and (2), of "such" in subs (1)(*c*) and of subs (3)) applied by: s 590(16)(*b*)(i).

EU Council Directive 90/434/EEC, transfer of assets to parent, ss 617–619 applied by: s 632(1).

Exemption from tax in the case of gains on certain disposals of shares: Sch 25A, para 8(2).

Development land chargeable gains, subs (2): s 649(3)(*b*).

Case law

Irish

A sum received by a merchant bank from the liquidation of a subsidiary which had earlier been held by the courts not to be trading, was also to be excluded from the trading receipts of the parent: *Guinness and Mahon v Browne* ITR Vol III, pp 373, 644.

UK

To qualify as trading stock, an asset should be of a kind normally dealt in by the company in the course of its trade and be acquired with a view to resale at a profit: *Reed v Nova Securities* [1984] STC 124; *Coates v Arndale Properties Ltd* [1984] STC 637.

Definitions

company: ss 4(1), 5(1); trade: ss 3(1), 4(1), 5(1); trading stock: ss 5(1), 89.

Former enactments

CTA 1976 s 131.

Corresponding UK tax provision

Taxation of Chargeable Gains Act 1992 s 173.

619 Disposals or acquisitions outside group

(1) Where a company which is or has been a member of a group of companies disposes of an asset which it acquired from another member of the group [in the course of a disposal to which section 617 applies][1], section 555 shall apply in relation to any capital allowances made to the other member (in so far as not taken into account in relation to a disposal of the asset by that other member), and so on as respects previous transfers of the asset between members of the group, but this shall not be taken as affecting the consideration for which an asset is deemed under section 617(1) to be acquired.

(2) (*a*) Section 556 shall apply in relation to a disposal of an asset by a company which is or has been a member of a group of companies, and which acquired the asset from another member of the group [in the course of a disposal to which section 617 applies][1], as if all members of the group for the time being were the same person, and as if the acquisition or provision of the asset by the group, so taken as a single person, had been the acquisition or provision of the asset by the member disposing of the asset.

(*b*) Notwithstanding paragraph (*a*), where at any time after the asset was acquired or provided by the group so taken as a single person and before the 24th day of April, 1992, there was an acquisition (in this paragraph referred to as **"the later acquisition"**) of the asset by a member of the group from another member of the group as a result of a relevant disposal (within the meaning of section 648), this subsection shall apply as if the reference in paragraph (*a*) to the acquisition or provision of the asset by the group were a reference to the later acquisition or, where there was more than one, the last such acquisition.

Amendments

1 Substituted by FA 2001 s 38(1)(*e*) as respects an acquisition on or after 15 February 2001; previously "at a time when both were members of the group".

Cross-references

Attribution to shareholders of chargeable gains accruing to non-resident company, s 619(2) (with the substitution for "in the course of a disposal to which section 617 applies" of "at a time when both were members of the group") applied by: s 590(16)(*b*)(i).

EU Council Directive 90/434/EEC, transfer of assets to parent, ss 617–619 applied by: s 632(1).

Definitions

capital allowance: s 2(1); company: ss 4(1), 5(1); person: IA 1937 s 11(*c*).

Former enactments

CTA 1976 s 132; CGT(A)A 1978 s 14; FA 1992 s 73.

Corresponding UK tax provision

Taxation of Chargeable Gains Act 1992 s 174.

620 Replacement of business assets by members of group

[(1) For the purposes of this section **"old assets"** and **"new assets"** have the same meanings as in section 597.

(2) Subject to subsection (4), for the purposes of section 597 all the trades to which this section applies carried on by members of a group of companies shall be treated as a single trade (except in a case of one member of the group acquiring, or acquiring the interest in, the new assets from another member or disposing of, or disposing of the interest in, the old assets to another member).

(3) This section applies to—

(*a*) any trade carried on by a company which is resident in the State, and

(*b*) any trade carried on in the State through a branch or agency of a company which is not so resident.

(4) This section shall not apply unless—

(*a*) the company disposing of the old assets is resident in the State at the time of the disposal, or the assets are chargeable assets in relation to that company immediately before that time, and

(*b*) the company acquiring the new assets is resident in the State at the time of acquisition, or the assets are chargeable assets in relation to that company immediately after that time.][1]

Amendments

1 Section 620 substituted by FA 2001 s 38(1)(*f*) as respects either a disposal or acquisition on or after 15 February 2001 (whether a company is a member of a group at the time of the acquisition or disposal corresponding to such a disposal or acquisition will be determined in accordance with s 616 as amended by FA 2001 s 38(1)(*b*)), or both a disposal and acquisition on or after 15 February 2001.

Cross-references

Attribution to shareholders of chargeable gains accruing to non-resident company, s 620(2) (with the omission of the words "to which this section applies" applied by: s 590(16)(*b*)(i).

Companies' chargeable gains, deemed disposal in certain circumstances: s 620A(1)(*b*)(ii).

Definitions

company: ss 4(1), 5(1); trade: ss 3(1), 4(1), 5(1).

Former enactments

CTA 1976 s 133.

620A Deemed disposal in certain circumstances

[(1) This section applies in relation to a company where—

(*a*) at any time on or after 15 February 2001 an asset ceases to be a chargeable asset in relation to the company—

(i) where at the time of the acquisition of the asset by the company the asset consisted of shares deriving their value or the greater part of their value from assets specified in paragraph (*a*) or (*b*) of section 29(3), by virtue of the assets ceasing to so derive their value or the greater part of their value, or

(ii) by virtue of the asset becoming situated outside the State, and

(*b*) (i) the company acquired the asset in the course of—

(I) a transfer to which section 615 applies, or

(II) a disposal to which section 617 applies,

or

(ii) by virtue of section 620 the asset constitutes new assets for the purposes of section 597.

(2) Where this section applies in relation to a company, the company shall be deemed for the purposes of the Capital Gains Tax Acts and the Corporation Tax Acts—

(*a*) to have disposed of the asset immediately before the time when it ceased to be a chargeable asset in relation to the company, and

(*b*) immediately to have reacquired it,

at its market value at that time.][1]

Amendments

1 Section 620A inserted by FA 2001 s 38(1)(g) with effect from 15 February 2001.

Definitions

Capital Gains Tax Acts: s 1(2); company: ss 4(1), 5(1); Corporation Tax Acts: s 1(2); market value: ss 5(1), 548.

621 Depreciatory transactions in group

(1) For the purposes of this section—

"securities" includes any loan stock or similar security whether secured or unsecured;

references to the disposal of assets include references to any method by which one company which is a member of a group appropriates the goodwill of another member of the group;

[a **"group of companies"** may consist of companies some or all of which are not resident for the purposes of tax in a [relevant Member State][1].][2]

(2) References in this section to the disposal of shares or securities include references to the occasion of the making of a claim under section 538(2) that the value of shares or securities has become negligible, and references to a person making a disposal shall be construed accordingly.

(3) This section shall apply as respects a disposal of shares in or securities of a company (in this section referred to as an **"ultimate disposal"**) if the value of the shares or securities has been materially reduced by a depreciatory transaction effected on or after the 6th day of April, 1974, and for this purpose **"depreciatory transaction"** means—

(*a*) any disposal of assets at other than market value by one member of a group of companies to another, or

(*b*) any other transaction satisfying the conditions of subsection (4);

but a transaction shall not be treated as a depreciatory transaction to the extent that it consists of a payment which is required to be or has been taken into account, for the purposes of corporation tax on chargeable gains, in computing a chargeable gain or allowable loss accruing to the person making the ultimate disposal.

(4) The conditions referred to in subsection (3)(*b*) are—

(*a*) that the company, the shares in which or securities of which are the subject of the ultimate disposal, or any [effective 75 per cent subsidiary][3] of that company, was a party to the transaction, and

(*b*) that the parties to the transaction were or included 2 or more companies which at the time of the transaction were members of the same group of companies.

(5) Without prejudice to the generality of subsection (3), the cancellation of any shares in or securities of one member of a group of companies under section 72 of the

Companies Act, 1963, shall, to the extent that immediately before the cancellation those shares or securities were the property of another member of the group, be taken to be a transaction fulfilling the conditions in subsection (4).

(6) Where the person making the ultimate disposal is or has at any time been a member of the group of companies referred to in subsection (3) or (4), any allowable loss accruing on the disposal shall be reduced to such extent as appears to the inspector, or on appeal the Appeal Commissioners, or on a rehearing by a judge of the Circuit Court, that judge, to be just and reasonable having regard to the depreciatory transaction; but, if the person making the ultimate disposal is not a member of that group when disposing of the shares or securities, no reduction of the loss shall be made by reference to a depreciatory transaction which took place when that person was not a member of that group.

(7) The inspector, Appeal Commissioners or the judge of the Circuit Court shall make the decision under subsection (6) on the basis that the allowable loss ought not to reflect any diminution in the value of the company's assets attributable to a depreciatory transaction, but allowance may be made for any other transaction on or after the 6th day of April, 1974, which has enhanced the value of the company's assets and depreciated the value of the assets of any other member of the group.

(8) (*a*) Where under subsection (6) a reduction is made in an allowable loss, any chargeable gain accruing on a disposal of the shares in or securities of any other company which was a party to the depreciatory transaction by reference to which the reduction was made, being a disposal not later than 10 years after the depreciatory transaction, shall be reduced to such extent as appears to the inspector, or on appeal to the Appeal Commissioners, or on a rehearing by a judge of the Circuit Court, that judge, to be just and reasonable having regard to the effect of the depreciatory transaction on the value of those shares or securities at the time of their disposal.

(*b*) Notwithstanding paragraph (*a*), the total amount of any one or more reductions in chargeable gains made by reference to a depreciatory transaction shall not exceed the amount of the reductions in allowable losses made by reference to that depreciatory transaction.

(*c*) All such adjustments, whether by means of discharge or repayment of tax or otherwise, as are required to give effect to this subsection may be made at any time.

Amendments

1 Substituted by FA 2002 s 36(*c*) with effect from 1 January 2002; previously "Member State of the European Communities".

2 Definition of "a group of companies" substituted by FA 2001 s 38(1)(*h*) as respects a case in which the depreciatory transaction (within the meaning of s 621) is on or after 15 February 2001.

3 Substituted by FA 1999 s 56(1)(*c*) with effect from 11 February 1999; previously "75 per cent subsidiary".

Cross-references

Companies' chargeable gains, groups of companies, subs (1): s 616(1)(*a*).
Companies' chargeable gains, dividend stripping: s 622(2)(*a*), (3).
Development land chargeable gains, ss 617 and 621–626 applied by: s 649(2).

Definitions

allowable loss: ss 4(1), 5(1), 546; Appeal Commissioners: s 2(1); chargeable gain: ss 5(1), 545; Circuit Court: IA 1937 Sch; company: ss 4(1), 5(1); inspector: ss 2(1), 5(1), 852; person: IA 1937 s 11(*c*).

Former enactments

CTA 1976 s 138.

Corresponding UK tax provision

Taxation of Chargeable Gains Act 1992 s 176.

622 Dividend stripping

(1) This section shall apply where one company (in this section referred to as **"the first company"**) has a holding in another company (in this section referred to as **"the second company"**) and the following conditions are fulfilled—

(*a*) that the holding amounts to, or is an ingredient in a holding amounting to, 10 per cent of all holdings of the same class in the second company,

(*b*) that the first company is not a dealing company in relation to the holding,

(*c*) that a distribution is or has been made on or after the 6th day of April, 1974, to the first company in respect of the holding, and

(*d*) that the effect of the distribution is that the value of the holding is or has been materially reduced.

(2) (*a*) Where this section applies in relation to a holding, section 621 shall apply in relation to any disposal of any shares or securities comprised in the holding, whether the disposal is by the first company or by any other company to which the holding is transferred by a transfer to which section 617 applies, as if the distribution were a depreciatory transaction and, if the companies concerned are not members of a group of companies, as if they were.

(*b*) Notwithstanding paragraph (*a*), the distribution shall not be treated as a depreciatory transaction to the extent that it consists of a payment which is required to be or has been taken into account, for the purposes of corporation tax on chargeable gains, in computing a chargeable gain or allowable loss accruing to the person making the ultimate disposal.

(3) This section shall be construed together with section 621.

(4) For the purposes of this section, a company shall be a dealing company in relation to a holding if a profit on the sale of the holding would be taken into account in computing the company's trading profits.

(5) References in this section to a holding in a company are references to a holding of shares or securities by virtue of which the holder may receive distributions made by the company, but so that—

(*a*) a company's holdings of different classes in another company shall be treated as separate holdings, and

(*b*) holdings of shares or securities which differ in the entitlements or obligations they confer or impose shall be regarded as holdings of different classes.

(6) For the purposes of subsection (1)—

(*a*) all a company's holdings of the same class in another company shall be treated as ingredients constituting a single holding, and

(*b*) a company's holding of a particular class shall be treated as an ingredient in a holding amounting to 10 per cent of all holdings of that class if the aggregate of that holding and other holdings of that class held by connected persons amounts to 10 per cent of all holdings of that class.

Cross-references

Development land chargeable gains, ss 617 and 621–626 applied by: s 649(2).

Definitions

allowable loss: ss 4(1), 5(1), 546; chargeable gain: ss 5(1), 545; company: ss 4(1), 5(1); distribution: ss 4(1), 436, 437; person: IA 1937 s 11(*c*); profits: s 4(1).

Former enactments

CTA 1976 s 139.

623 Company ceasing to be member of group

(1) For the purposes of this section—

(*a*) 2 or more companies shall be associated companies if by themselves they would form a group of companies;

(*b*) a chargeable gain shall be deferred on a replacement of business assets if, by one or more claims under section 597, a chargeable gain on the disposal of those assets is treated as not accruing until the new assets within the meaning of that section cease to be used for the purpose of a trade carried on by the company making the claim;

(*c*) an asset acquired by the chargeable company shall be treated as the same as an asset owned at a later time by that company or an associated company if the value of the second asset is derived in whole or in part from the first asset, and in particular where the second asset is a freehold, and the first asset was a leasehold and the lessee has acquired the reversion;

(*d*) references to a company ceasing to be a member of a group of companies shall not apply to cases where a company ceases to be a member of a group by being wound up or dissolved or in consequence of another member of the group being wound up or dissolved where the winding up or dissolution of the member or the other member, as the case may be, is for bona fide commercial reasons and is not part of a scheme or arrangement the main purpose or one of the main purposes of which is the avoidance of tax.

[(2) This section applies where—

(*a*) a company (in this section referred to as the **"chargeable company"**) which is a member of a group of companies acquires an asset from another company which at the time of acquisition was a member of the group,

(*b*) the chargeable company ceases to be a member of the group within the period of 10 years after the time of the acquisition,

(*c*) the chargeable company is resident in the State at the time of acquisition of the asset, or the asset is a chargeable asset in relation to that company immediately after that time, and

(*d*) the other company is resident in the State at the time of that acquisition, or the asset is a chargeable asset in relation to that company immediately before that time.][1]

(3) (*a*) Where 2 or more associated companies (in this subsection referred to as **"the associated companies"**) cease to be members of a group at the same time—

(i) subsection (2) shall not apply as respects an acquisition by one from another of the associated companies, and

(ii) where—

(I) a dividend has been paid or a distribution has been made by one of the associated companies to a company which is not one of the associated companies, and

(II) the dividend so paid or the distribution so made has been paid or made, as the case may be, wholly or partly out of profits which derive from the disposal of any asset by one to another of the associated companies,

the amount of the dividend paid or the amount or value of the distribution made, to the extent that it is paid or made, as the case may be, out of those profits, shall be deemed for the purposes of the Capital Gains Tax Acts to be consideration (in addition to any other consideration) received by the member of the group or former member of the group in respect of a disposal, being a disposal which gave rise to or was caused by the associated companies ceasing to be members of the group.

(*b*) Paragraph (*a*)(ii) shall not apply to a distribution other than a dividend where a company ceases to be a member of a group of companies before the 23rd day of April, 1996.

(4) If when the chargeable company ceases to be a member of the group the chargeable company, or an associated company also leaving the group, owns otherwise than as trading stock—

(*a*) the asset referred to in subsection (2), or

(*b*) property on the acquisition of which a chargeable gain in relation to the asset has been deferred on a replacement of business assets,

the chargeable company shall be treated for the purposes of the Capital Gains Tax Acts as if immediately after its acquisition of the asset it had sold and immediately reacquired the asset at market value at that time.

(5) Where any of the corporation tax assessed on a company in consequence of this section is not paid within 6 months from the date when it becomes payable, then—

(*a*) a company which on that date, or immediately after the chargeable company ceased to be a member of the group, was the principal company of the group, and

(*b*) a company which owned the asset on that date or when the chargeable company ceased to a member of the group,

may, at any time within 2 years from the time when the tax became payable, be assessed and charged (in the name of the chargeable company) to all or any part of that tax, and a company paying any amount of tax under this subsection shall be entitled to recover a sum of that amount from the chargeable company.

(6) Notwithstanding any limitation on the time for making assessments, an assessment to corporation tax chargeable in consequence of this section may be made at any time within 10 years from the time when the chargeable company ceased to be a member of the group, and where under this section the chargeable company is to be treated as having disposed of and reacquired an asset, all such recomputations of liability in respect of other disposals, and all such adjustments of tax, whether by means of assessment or by means of discharge or repayment of tax, as may be required in consequence of this section shall be made.

Amendments

1 Subs (2) substituted by FA 2001 s 38(1)(*i*) as respects an asset acquired on or after 15 February 2001.

Cross-references

Attribution to shareholders of chargeable gains accruing to non-resident company, s 623 (apart from paras (*c*) and (*d*) of subs (2)) applied by: s 590(16)(*b*)(ii).

Exemptions in case of certain mergers: s 624(1).

Exemption from tax in the case of gains on disposals of certain shares, subs (4): Sch 25A, para 7.

Development land chargeable gains, ss 617 and 621–626 applied by: s 649(2).

Development land chargeable gains: s 649(3)(*b*).

Transitional provisions in respect of section 623: s 623A(3)(*a*); subs (4): s 623A(2)(*b*); subs (2): s 623A(3)(*c*).

Case law

UK

Loss of residence of a company did not prevent the company being a chargeable company: *Dunlop v Pardoe* [1998] STC 479.

Definitions

chargeable gain: ss 5(1), 545; company: ss 4(1), 5(1); month: IA 1937 Sch; trade: ss 3(1), 4(1), 5(1); trading stock: ss 5(1), 89.

Former enactments

CTA 1976 s 135 and FA 1996 s 51.

Corresponding UK tax provision

Taxation of Chargeable Gains Act 1992 ss 178–181.

623A Transitional provisions in respect of section 623

[(1) In this section **"the new definition"** means section 616 as amended by section 56 of the Finance Act, 1999, and **"the old definition"** means that section as it had effect on the 10th day of February, 1999.

(2) Where—

(*a*) on the 11th day of February, 1999, a company ceases, for the purposes of section 616 and the provisions of this Part subsequent to that section, to be a member of a group by reason only of the substitution for the old definition of the new definition, and

(*b*) in consequence of ceasing to be such a member the company would, apart from this section, be treated by virtue of section 623(4) as selling an asset at any time,

the company shall not be treated as selling the asset at that time unless the conditions in subsection (3) become satisfied, assuming for that purpose that the old definition applies.

(3) The conditions referred to in subsection (2) are—

(*a*) that for the purposes of section 623, the company ceases at any time (in this subsection referred to as the "relevant time") to be a member of the group referred to in subsection (2)(*a*),

(*b*) that, at the relevant time, the company (or an associated company also ceasing to be a member of that group at that time) owns, otherwise than as trading stock, the asset, or property on the acquisition of which a chargeable gain in relation to the asset has been deferred on a replacement of business assets, and

(*c*) that the time of acquisition of the asset referred to in section 623(2) fell within the period of 10 years ending with the relevant time.][1]

Amendments

1 Section 623A inserted by FA 1999 s 56(1)(*d*) with effect from 11 February 1999.

Case law

UK

Loss of residence of a company did not prevent the company being a chargeable company: *Dunlop v Pardoe* [1998] STC 479.

Definitions

chargeable gain: ss 5(1), 545; company: ss 4(1), 5(1); trading stock: ss 5(1),89; year: IA 1937 Sch.

624 Exemption from charge under section 623 in case of certain mergers

(1) Section 623 shall not apply in a case where—

(*a*) as part of a merger a company (in this section referred to as **"company A"**) ceases to be a member of a group of companies (in this section referred to as **"the A group"**), and

(*b*) it is shown that the merger was carried out for bona fide commercial reasons and that the avoidance of liability to tax was not the main or one of the main purposes of the merger.

(2) In this section, **"merger"** means an arrangement (including a series of arrangements)—

(*a*) whereby one or more companies (in this section referred to as **"the acquiring company"** or, as the case may be, **"the acquiring companies"**) none of which is a member of the A group acquires or acquire, otherwise than with a view to their disposal, one or more interests in the whole or part of the business which, before the arrangement took effect, was carried on by company A,

(*b*) whereby one or more members of the A group acquires or acquire, otherwise than with a view to their disposal, one or more interests in the whole or part of the business or each of the businesses which, before the arrangement took effect, was carried on either by the acquiring company or acquiring companies or by a company at least 90 per cent of the ordinary share capital of which was then beneficially owned by 2 or more of the acquiring companies, and

(*c*) in respect of which the conditions in subsection (4) are fulfilled.

(3) For the purposes of subsection (2), a member of a group of companies shall be treated as carrying on as one business the activities of that group.

(4) The conditions referred to in subsection (2)(*c*) are—

(*a*) that not less than 25 per cent by value of each of the interests acquired as mentioned in paragraphs (*a*) and (*b*) of subsection (2) consists of a holding of ordinary share capital, and the remainder of the interest or, as the case may be, of each of the interests acquired as mentioned in paragraph (*b*) of that subsection consists of a holding of share capital (of any description) or debentures or both,

(*b*) that the value or, as the case may be, the aggregate value of the interest or interests acquired as mentioned in subsection (2)(*a*) is substantially the same as the value or, as the case may be, the aggregate value of the interest or interests acquired as mentioned in subsection (2)(*b*), and

(*c*) that the consideration for the acquisition of the interest or interests acquired by the acquiring company or acquiring companies as mentioned in subsection (2)(*a*), disregarding any part of that consideration which is small by comparison with the total, either consists of, or is applied in the acquisition of, or consists partly of and as to the balance is applied in the acquisition of, the interest or interests acquired by members of the A group as mentioned in subsection (2)(*b*),

and for the purposes of this subsection the value of an interest shall be determined as at the date of its acquisition.

(5) Notwithstanding section 616(1)(*a*), references in this section to a company shall include references to [a company which is not resident in a [relevant Member State][1]][2].

Amendments

1 Substituted by FA 2002 s 36(*d*) with effect from 1 January 2002; previously "Member State of the European Communities".

2 Substituted by FA 2001 s 38(1)(*j*) with effect from 15 February 2001; previously "a company resident outside the State".

Cross-references

Attribution to participators of chargeable gains accruing to non-resident company, s 624 applied by: s 590(16)(*b*)(ii).

Development land chargeable gains, ss 617 and 621–626 applied by: s 649(2).

Tax Briefing

TB48 June 2002 p 17 — Exemption from section 623 TCA 1997 for certain mergers (section 624 TCA 1997).

Definitions

company: ss 4(1), 5(1); ordinary share capital: s 2(1).

Former enactments

CTA 1976 s 136.

Corresponding UK tax provision

Taxation of Chargeable Gains Act 1992 s 181.

625 Shares in subsidiary member of group

(1) (*a*) This section shall apply if a company (in this section referred to as **"the subsidiary"**) ceases to be a member of a group of companies, and on an earlier occasion shares in the subsidiary were disposed of by another company (in this section referred to as **"the chargeable company"**) which was then a member of that group in the course of an amalgamation or reconstruction in the group,

but only if that earlier occasion fell within the period of 10 years ending on the date on which the subsidiary ceases to be a member of the group.

(*b*) References in this section to a company ceasing to be a member of a group of companies shall not apply to cases where a company ceases to be a member of a group by being wound up or dissolved or in consequence of another member of the group being wound up or dissolved.

(2) The chargeable company shall be treated for the purposes of the Capital Gains Tax Acts as if immediately before the earlier occasion it had sold and immediately reacquired the shares referred to in subsection (1)(*a*) at market value at that time.

(3) Where before the subsidiary ceases to be a member of the group the chargeable company has ceased to exist, or a resolution has been passed, or an order made, for the winding up of the company, or any other act has been done for the like purpose, any corporation tax to which, if the chargeable company had continued in existence, it would have been chargeable in consequence of this section may be assessed and charged (in the name of the chargeable company) on the company which is, at the time when the subsidiary ceases to be a member of the group, the principal company of the group.

(4) Where any of the corporation tax assessed on a company in consequence of this section, or in pursuance of subsection (3), is not paid within 6 months from the date when it becomes payable, then—

(*a*) a company which is on that date, or was on the earlier occasion, the principal company of the group, and

(*b*) any company taking an interest in the subsidiary as part of the amalgamation or reconstruction in the group,

may at any time within 2 years from the time when the tax became payable, be assessed and charged (in the name of the chargeable company) to all or any part of that tax, and a company paying any amount of tax under this subsection shall be entitled to recover a sum of that amount from the chargeable company or, as the case may be, from the company assessed under subsection (3).

(5) Notwithstanding any limitation on the time for making assessments, an assessment to corporation tax chargeable in consequence of this section may be made at any time within 10 years from the time when the subsidiary ceased to be a member of the group and, in relation to any disposal of the property after the earlier occasion, there shall be made all such adjustments of tax, whether by means of assessment or by means of discharge or repayment of tax, as may be required in consequence of this section.

(6) For the purposes of this section, there shall be a disposal of shares in the course of an amalgamation or reconstruction in a group of companies if—

(*a*) section 586 or 587 applies to shares in a company so as to equate them with shares in or debentures of another company, and

(*b*) the companies are members of the same group or become members of the same group as a result of the amalgamation or reconstruction.

(7) Where by virtue of section 587 shares are to be treated as cancelled and replaced by a new issue, references in this section to a disposal of shares include references to the occasion of the shares being so treated.

Cross-references

Attribution to shareholders of chargeable gains accruing to non-resident company, s 625 applied by: s 590(16)(*b*).

Development land chargeable gains, ss 617 and 621–626 applied by: s 649(2).

Transitional provisions in respect of section 625, meaning of "the subsidiary" and "the chargeable company" applied: s 625A(1); subs (2): s 625A(2)(*b*); subs (1)(*a*): s 625A(3)(*b*); s 625A(3)(*a*).

Definitions

company: ss 4(1), 5(1); month: IA 1937 Sch.

Former enactments

CTA 1976 s 137.

625A Transitional provisions in respect of section 625

[(1) In this section—

"the subsidiary" and **"the chargeable company"** have the same meanings, respectively, assigned to them by 625(1);

"the new definition" means section 616 as amended by section 56 of the Finance Act, 1999, and **"the old definition"** means that section as it had effect on the 10th day of February, 1999.

(2) Where—

(*a*) on the 11th day of February, 1999, the subsidiary company ceases, for the purposes of section 616 and the provisions of this Part subsequent to that section, to be a member of a group by reason only of the substitution for the old definition of the new definition, and

(*b*) in consequence of ceasing to be such a member the chargeable company would, apart from this section, be treated by virtue of section 625(2) as selling shares in the subsidiary at any time,

the chargeable company shall not be treated as selling the shares at that time unless the conditions in subsection (3) become satisfied assuming for that purpose that the old definition applies.

(3) The conditions referred to in subsection (2) are—

(*a*) that for the purposes of section 625 the subsidiary ceases at any time (in this subsection referred to as "the relevant time") to be a member of the group referred to in subsection (2)(*a*), and

(*b*) that the time of the earlier occasion referred to in section 625(1)(*a*) fell within the period of 10 years ending with the relevant time.][1]

Amendments

1 Section 625A inserted by FA 1999 s 57(1)(*e*) with effect from 11 February 1999.

Definitions

company: ss 4(1), 5(1); year: IA 1937 Sch.

626 Tax on company recoverable from other members of group

(1) Where at any time a chargeable gain accrues to a company which at that time is a member of a group of companies and any of the corporation tax assessed on the

company for the accounting period in which the chargeable gain accrues is not paid within 6 months from the date when it becomes payable by the company, then, if the tax so assessed included any amount in respect of chargeable gains—

(*a*) a company which at the time when the gain accrued was the principal company of the group, and

(*b*) any other company which in any part of the period of 2 years ending with that time was a member of that group of companies and owned the asset disposed of or any part of it or, where the asset is an interest or right in or over another asset, owned either asset or any part of either asset,

may at any time within 2 years from the time when the tax became payable be assessed and charged (in the name of the company to whom the chargeable gain accrued) to an amount of that corporation tax not exceeding corporation tax on the amount and at the rate charged in respect of that gain in the assessment on the company to which the chargeable gain accrued.

(2) A company paying any amount of tax under subsection (1) shall be entitled to recover a sum of that amount—

(*a*) from the company to which the chargeable gain accrued, or

(*b*) if that company is not the company which was the principal company of the group at the time when the chargeable gain accrued, from that principal company,

and a company paying any amount under paragraph (*b*) shall be entitled to recover a sum of that amount from the company to which the chargeable gain accrued and, in so far as it is not so recovered, to recover from any company which is for the time being a member of the group and which has while a member of the group owned the asset disposed of or any part of that asset (or, where that asset is an interest or right in or over another asset, owned either asset or any part of either asset) such proportion of the amount unrecovered as is just having regard to the value of the asset at the time when the asset, or an interest or right in or over that asset, was disposed of by that company.

Cross-references

Development land chargeable gains, ss 617 and 621–626 applied by: s 649(2).

Definitions

chargeable gain: ss 5(1), 545; company: ss 4(1), 5(1); month: IA 1937 Sch.

Former enactments

CTA 1976 s 134.

Corresponding UK tax provision

Taxation of Chargeable Gains Act 1992 s 190.

626A Restriction on set-off of pre-entry losses

[For the purposes of Part 20, Schedule 18A (which makes provision in relation to losses accruing to a company before the time when it becomes a member of a group of companies and losses accruing on assets held by any company at such a time) shall apply.][1]

Amendments

[1] Section 626A inserted by FA 1999 s 56(1)(*f*) with effect from 11 February 1999.

Definitions

company: ss 4(1), 5(1).

Corresponding UK tax provision

Taxation of Chargeable Gains Act 1992 s 177A.

626B Exemption from tax in the case of gains on certain disposals of shares

[(1) (*a*) In this section, section 626C and Schedule 25A—

"investor company" and **"investee company"** have the meanings assigned by subsection (2);

"relevant territory" means—

(i) a Member State of the European Communities, or

(ii) not being such a Member State, a territory with the government of which arrangements having the force of law by virtue of section 826(1)(*a*) have been made;

...[1]

"tax" in relation to a relevant territory other than the State means any tax imposed in that territory which corresponds to income tax or corporation tax in the State;

"2 year period" means a period ending on the day before the second anniversary of the day on which the period began.

(*b*) For the purposes of this section, section 626C and Schedule 25A—

(i) a company shall only be a parent company in relation to another company at any time if that time falls within an uninterrupted period of not less than 12 months throughout which it directly or indirectly holds shares in that company by virtue of which—

(I) it holds not less than [5 per cent][2] of the company's ordinary share capital,

(II) it is beneficially entitled to not less than [5 per cent][2] of the profits available for distribution to equity holders of the company, and

(III) it would be beneficially entitled on a winding up to not less than [5 per cent][2] of the assets of the company available for distribution to equity holders,

and for the purposes of this subparagraph—

(A) subsections (2) to (10) of section 9 shall apply with any necessary modifications, and

(B) sections 413 to 419 shall apply as they apply for the purposes of Chapter 5 of Part 12 but as if "in a relevant territory" were substituted for "in the State" in subparagraph (iii) of section 413(3)(*a*) and as if paragraph (*c*) of section 411(1), other than that paragraph as it applies by virtue of subparagraphs (i) and (ii), were disregarded,

(ii) in determining whether the conditions in paragraph (*a*) of subsection (2) are satisfied, a company that is a member of a group shall be treated as holding so much of any shares held by any other company in the group and as having so much of the entitlement of any such company to any rights enjoyed by virtue of holding shares—

(I) as the company would not, apart from this paragraph, hold or have, and

(II) as are not part of a life business fund within the meaning of section 719,

and, for the purposes of this subparagraph, **"group"** means a company which has one or more 51 per cent subsidiaries together with those subsidiaries,

(iii) in determining whether the treatment provided for in subsection (2) applies, the question of whether there is a disposal shall be determined without regard to section 584 or that section as applied by any other section: and, to the extent to which an exemption under subsection (2) does apply in relation to a disposal, section 584 shall not apply in relation to the disposal,

(iv) where assets of a company are vested in a liquidator under section 230 of the Companies Act 1963 or otherwise, the assets shall be deemed to be vested in, and the acts of liquidation in relation to the assets shall be deemed to be the acts of, the company (and acquisitions from, and disposals to, the liquidator shall be disregarded accordingly),

(v) section 616 shall not apply.

(2) A gain accruing to a company (in this section referred to as the **"investor company"**) on a disposal of shares in another company (in this section referred to as the **"investee company"**) is not a chargeable gain if—

[(*a*) the disposal by the investor company is at a time—

(i) when the investor company is a parent company of the investee company, or

(ii) within the 2 year period beginning on the most recent day on which the investor company was a parent company of the investee company,][3]

(*b*) the investee company is, by virtue of the law of a relevant territory, resident for the purposes of tax in the relevant territory at the time of the disposal, and

(*c*) at the time of the disposal—

(i) the investee company is a company whose business consists wholly or mainly of the carrying on of a trade or trades, or

(ii) the business of—

(I) the investor company,

(II) each company of which the investor company is the parent company, and

(III) the investee company, if it is not a company referred to in clause (II), and any company of which the investee company is the parent company, taken together consists wholly or mainly of the carrying on of a trade or trades.

(3) The treatment of a gain, as not being a chargeable gain, provided by this section and section 626C shall not apply—

(*a*) to a disposal that by virtue of any provision relating to chargeable gains is deemed to be for a consideration such that no gain or loss accrues to the person making the disposal,

(*b*) to a disposal a gain on which would, by virtue of any provision other than this section or section 626C, not be a chargeable gain,

(*c*) to disposals, including deemed disposals, of shares which are part of a life business fund within the meaning of section 719,

(*d*) to a disposal of shares deriving their value or the greater part of this value directly or indirectly from assets specified in paragraphs (*a*) and (*b*) of section 29(3).

(4) Schedule 25A shall have effect for the purposes of supplementing this section and section 626C.][4]

Amendments

1 Definition of "relevant time" deleted by FA 2005 s 54(1)(*a*) with effect from 2 February 2004.

2 Substituted by FA 2005 s 54(1)(*b*) with effect from 2 February 2004; previously "10 per cent".

3 Subs (2)(*a*) substituted by FA 2005 s 54(1)(*c*) with effect from 2 February 2004.

4 Section 626B inserted by FA 2004 s 42(1)(*a*) with effect from such day as the Minister for Finance may appoint by order. By virtue of the Finance Act 2004 (Commencement of Sections 31 and 42) Order 2004, SI No 551 of 2004, this amendment comes into operation with effect from 2 February 2004.

Cross-references

Meaning of "investment income": s 434(1).

Treatment of assets related to shares: s 626C(2)(*a*)(ii), (b)(ii).

Tax Briefing

TB55 April 2004 pp 8–9 — Note on TCA 1997 ss 626B and 626C and Sch 25A.

Definitions

chargeable gain: s 5(1); company: ss 4(1), 5(1); market value: ss 5(1), 548; ordinary share capital: s 2(1); shares: s 5(1); trade: ss 3(1), 4(1), 5(1); 51 per cent subsidiary: s 9.

626C Treatment of assets related to shares

[(1) For the purposes of this section—

(*a*) an asset is related to shares in a company if it is—

(i) an option to acquire or dispose of shares in that company,

(ii) a security to which are attached rights by virtue of which the holder is or may become entitled, whether by conversion or exchange or otherwise, to acquire or dispose of—

(I) shares in that company,

(II) an option to acquire or dispose of shares in that company, or

(III) another security falling within this paragraph, or

(iii) an option to acquire or dispose of any security within subparagraph (ii) or an interest in any such security, (*b*) in determining whether a security is within paragraph (*a*)(ii), no account shall be taken—

(i) of any rights attached to the security other than rights relating, directly or indirectly, to shares of the company in question, or

(ii) of rights as regards which, at the time the security came into existence, there was no more than a negligible likelihood that they would in due course be exercised to a significant extent.

(2) A gain accruing to a company (in this subsection referred to as the **"first-mentioned company"**) on the disposal of an asset related to shares in another company is not a chargeable gain if—

(*a*) (i) immediately before the disposal the first-mentioned company holds shares in the other company, and

(ii) any gain accruing to the first-mentioned company on a disposal at that time of the shares would, by virtue of section 626B, not be a chargeable gain,

or

(*b*) (i) immediately before the disposal the first-mentioned company does not hold shares in the other company but is a member of a group and another member of that group does hold shares in the other company, and

(ii) if the first-mentioned company, rather than the other member of the group, held the shares, any gain accruing to the first-mentioned company on a disposal at that time of the shares would, by virtue of section 626B, not be a chargeable gain;

and for the purposes of this paragraph **"group"** means a company which has one or more 51 per cent subsidiaries together with those subsidiaries.][1]

Amendments

[1] Section 626C inserted by FA 2004 s 42(1)(*a*) with effect from such day as the Minister for Finance may appoint by order. By virtue of the Finance Act 2004 (Commencement of Sections 31 and 42) Order 2004, SI No 551 of 2004, this amendment comes into operation with effect from 2 February 2004.

Cross-references

Exemption from tax in the case of gains on certain disposals of shares: s 626B(1)(*a*), (b), (3), (4).

Tax Briefing

TB55 April 2004 pp 8–9 — Note on TCA 1997 ss 626B and 626C and Sch 25A.

Definitions

chargeable gain: s 5(1); company: ss 4(1), 5(1); shares: s 5(1); 51 per cent subsidiary: s 9.

CHAPTER 2

Provisions Where Companies Cease to be Resident in the State

627 Deemed disposal of assets

(1) (*a*) In this section and in section 628—

"designated area", **"exploration or exploitation activities"** and **"exploration or exploitation rights"** have the same meanings respectively as in section 13;

"exploration or exploitation assets" means assets used or intended for use in connection with exploration or exploitation activities carried on in the State or in a designated area;

"market value" shall be construed in accordance with section 548;

"the new assets" and **"the old assets"** have the meanings assigned respectively to them by section 597.

(*b*) For the purposes of this section and section 628, a company shall not be regarded as ceasing to be resident in the State by reason only that it ceases to exist.

(2) (*a*) In this subsection—

"control" shall be construed in accordance with subsections (2) to (6) of section 432 as if in subsection (6) of that section for **"5 or fewer participators"** there were substituted **"persons resident in a relevant territory"**;

"excluded company" means a company of which not less than 90 per cent of its issued share capital is held by a foreign company or foreign companies, or by a person or persons directly or indirectly controlled by a foreign company or foreign companies;

"foreign company" means a company which—

(i) is not resident in the State,

(ii) is under the control of a person or persons resident in a relevant territory, and

(iii) is not under the control of a person or persons resident in the State;

[**"relevant territory"** means a territory with the government of which arrangements having the force of law by virtue of [section 826(1)(*a*)][1] have been made.][2]

(*b*) Subject to paragraph (*c*), this section and section 628 shall apply to a company (in this section referred to as a **"relevant company"**) if at any time (in this section and in section 628 referred to as **"the relevant time"**) on or after the 21st day of April, 1997, the company ceases to be resident in the State.

(*c*) This section and section 628 shall not apply to a company which is an excluded company.

(3) A relevant company shall be deemed for the purposes of the Capital Gains Tax Acts—

(*a*) to have disposed of all its assets, other than assets excepted from this subsection by subsection (5), immediately before the relevant time, and

(*b*) to have immediately reacquired them,

at the market value of the assets at that time.

(4) Section 597 shall not apply where a relevant company—

(*a*) has disposed of the old assets, or of its interest in those assets, before the relevant time, and

(*b*) acquires the new assets, or its interest in those assets, after the relevant time,

unless the new assets are excepted from this subsection by subsection (5).

(5) Where at any time after the relevant time a relevant company carries on a trade in the State through a branch or agency—

(*a*) any assets which, immediately after the relevant time, are situated in the State and are used in or for the purposes of the trade, or are used or held for the purposes of the branch or agency, shall be excepted from subsection (3), and

(*b*) any new assets which, after that time, are so situated and are so used or so held shall be excepted from subsection (4),

and references in this subsection to assets situated in the State include references to exploration or exploitation assets and to exploration or exploitation rights.

Amendments

1 Substituted by FA 2004 s 89 and Sch 3 para 1(*q*) with effect from 25 March 2004; previously "section 826".

2 Definition of "relevant territory" substituted by FA 1998 s 48 and Sch 3 para 5 with effect from 1 January 1998 for corporation tax and 6 April 1998 for capital gains tax; previously:

"'relevant territory' means—

(i) the United States of America, or

(ii) a territory with the government of which arrangements having the force of law by virtue of section 826 have been made.'

Cross-references

Postponement of charge, meaning of "deemed disposal", subs (3) applied: s 628(1).

75% subsidiary: s 627(2)(*a*).

Tax on non-resident company recoverable from another group member or controlling director: s 629(2).

Former enactments

FA 1997 s 42.

Corresponding UK tax provision

Taxation of Chargeable Gains Act 1992 ss 185 and 186.

628 Postponement of charge on deemed disposal under section 627

(1) (*a*) In this section—

"deemed disposal" means a disposal which by virtue of section 627(3) is deemed to have been made;

"foreign assets" of a company means any assets of the company which immediately after the relevant time are situated outside the State and are used in or for the purposes of a trade carried on by the company outside the State.

(*b*) For the purposes of this section, a company shall be a 75 per cent subsidiary of another company if and so long as not less than 75 per cent of its ordinary share capital (within the meaning of section 2) is owned directly by that other company.

(2) Where—

(*a*) immediately after the relevant time a company (in this section referred to as **"the company"**) to which this section applies by virtue of section 627 is a 75 per cent subsidiary of another company (in this section referred to as **"the principal company"**) which is resident in the State, and

(*b*) the principal company and the company jointly so elect by notice in writing given to the inspector within 2 years after the relevant time,

the Capital Gains Tax Acts shall apply subject to subsections (3) to (6).

(3) Any allowable losses accruing to the company on a deemed disposal of foreign assets shall be set off against the chargeable gains so accruing and—

(*a*) that deemed disposal shall be treated as giving rise to a single chargeable gain equal to the aggregate of those gains after deducting the aggregate of those losses, and

(*b*) the whole of that single chargeable gain shall be treated as not accruing to the company on that disposal but an equivalent amount (in this section referred to as **"the postponed gain"**) shall be taken into account in accordance with subsections (4) and (5).

(4) (*a*) In this subsection, **"the appropriate proportion"** means the proportion which the chargeable gain taken into account in determining the postponed gain in respect of the part of the relevant assets disposed of bears to the aggregate of the chargeable gains so taken into account in respect of the relevant assets held immediately before the time of the disposal.

(*b*) Where at any time within 10 years after the relevant time the company disposes of any assets (in this subsection referred to as **"relevant assets"**) the chargeable gains on which were taken into account in determining the postponed gain, there shall be deemed to accrue to the principal company as a chargeable gain at that time the whole or the appropriate proportion of the postponed gain in so far as not already taken into account under this subsection or subsection (5).

(5) Where at any time within 10 years after the relevant time—

(*a*) the company ceases to be a 75 per cent subsidiary of the principal company, or

(*b*) the principal company ceases to be resident in the State,

there shall be deemed to accrue to the principal company as a chargeable gain—

(i) where paragraph (*a*) applies, at that time, and

(ii) where paragraph (*b*) applies, immediately before that time,

the whole of the postponed gain in so far as not already taken into account under this subsection or subsection (4).

(6) Where at any time—

(*a*) the company has allowable losses which have not been allowed as a deduction from chargeable gains, and (*b*) a chargeable gain accrues to the principal company under subsection (4) or (5),

then, if and to the extent that the principal company and the company jointly so elect by notice in writing given to the inspector within 2 years after that time, those losses shall be allowed as a deduction from that gain.

Cross-references

Company ceasing to be resident: s 627(1)(*b*).

Relevant territory: s 627(2).

Former enactments

FA 1997 s 43.

Corresponding UK tax provision

Taxation of Chargeable Gains Act 1992 s 187.

629 Tax on non-resident company recoverable from another member of group or from controlling director

(1) In this section—

"chargeable period" means a year of assessment or an accounting period, as the case may be;

"controlling director", in relation to a company, means a director of the company who has control of the company (construing control in accordance with section 432);

"director", in relation to a company, has the same meaning as in section 116, and includes any person within section 433(4);

"group" has the meaning which would be given by section 616 if in that section references to residence in [a [relevant Member State][1]][2] were omitted and for references to **"75 per cent subsidiaries"** there were substituted references to **"51 per cent subsidiaries"**, and references to a company being a member of a group shall be construed accordingly;

"specified period", in relation to a chargeable period, means the period beginning with the specified return date for the chargeable period (within the meaning of section 950) and ending 3 years after the time [when a return under section 951 for the chargeable period is delivered to the Collector-General];[3]

"tax" means corporation tax or capital gains tax, as the case may be.

(2) This section shall apply at any time on or after the 21st day of April, 1997, where tax payable (being tax which but for section 627 or 628 would not be payable) by a company (in this section referred to as **"the taxpayer company"**) for a chargeable period (in this section referred to as **"the chargeable period concerned"**) is not paid within 6 months after the date on or before which the tax is due and payable.

(3) The Revenue Commissioners may, at any time before the end of the specified period in relation to the chargeable period concerned, serve on any person to whom subsection (4) applies a notice—

(*a*) stating the amount which remains unpaid of the tax payable by the taxpayer company for the chargeable period concerned and the date on or before which the tax became due and payable, and

(*b*) requiring that person to pay that amount within 30 days of the service of the notice.

(4) (*a*) This subsection shall apply to any person, being—

(i) a company which is, or during the period of 12 months ending with the time when the gain accrued was, a member of the same group as the taxpayer company, and

(ii) a person who is, or during that period was, a controlling director of the taxpayer company or of a company which has, or within that period had, control over the taxpayer company.

(*b*) This subsection shall apply in any case where the gain accrued before the 21st day of April, 1998, with the substitution in paragraph (*a*)(i) of "beginning with the 21st day of April, 1997, and" for "of 12 months".

(5) Any amount which a person is required to pay by a notice under this section may be recovered from the person as if it were tax due by such person, and such person may recover any such amount paid on foot of a notice under this section from the taxpayer company.

(6) A payment in pursuance of a notice under this section shall not be allowed as a deduction in computing any income, profits or losses for any tax purposes.

Amendments

1 Substituted by FA 2002 s 36(*e*) with effect from 1 January 2002; previously "Member State of the European Communities".

2 Substituted by FA 2001 s 38(1)(*k*) with effect from 15 February 2001; previously "the State".

3 Substituted by FA 2001 s 78(2)(*b*) for the short tax "year" 2001 and later tax years (income tax and capital gains tax) and as respects accounting periods of companies ending on or after 1 April 2001; previously "when a return under section 951 for the chargeable period is delivered to the appropriate inspector (within the meaning of section 950)".

Definitions

Collector-General: ss 2(1), 851; person: IA 1937 s 11(*c*).

Former enactments

FA 1997 s 44.

Corresponding UK tax provision

Taxation of Chargeable Gains Act 1992 s 191.

PART 21
MERGERS, DIVISIONS, TRANSFERS OF ASSETS AND EXCHANGES OF SHARES CONCERNING COMPANIES OF DIFFERENT MEMBER STATES

Tax Briefing

TB32 June 1998 p 10 — Separate return required where relief from CGT is sought on transfer of assets within EU group — see article concerned for requirements of the return.

630 Interpretation (Part 21)

In this Part—

“bilateral agreement” means arrangements having the force of law by virtue of section 826;

“company” means a company from a Member State;

“company from a Member State” has the meaning assigned to it by Article 3 of the Directive;

“the Directive” means Council Directive No 90/434/EEC of 23 July, 1990 (OJ No L225, 20.8.1990, p 1) on the common system of taxation applicable to mergers, divisions, transfers of assets and exchanges of shares concerning companies of different Member States;

“Member State” means a Member State of the European Communities;

“receiving company” means the company to which the whole or part of a trade is transferred in the course of a transfer;

“securities” means shares and debentures;

“shares” includes stock;

“transfer” means the transfer by a company of the whole or part of its trade in the circumstances set out in section 631(1) or 634(2), as the case may be;

“transferring company” means the company by which the whole or part of a trade is transferred in the course of a transfer.

Cross-references

“the Directive”: OJ No L225. 20 August 1990, page 1.

Former enactments

FA 1992 s 64.

631 Transfer of assets generally

(1) (*a*) This section shall apply where a company transfers the whole of a trade carried on by it in the State to another company and the consideration for the transfer consists solely of the issue to the transferring company of securities (in this section referred to as **“the new assets”**) in the receiving company.

(*b*) A company which transfers part of a trade to another company shall be treated for the purposes of this section as having carried on that part of its trade as a separate trade.

(2) (*a*) The transfer shall not be treated as giving rise to any allowance or charge provided for by section 307 or 308.

(*b*) There shall be made to or on the receiving company in accordance with sections 307 and 308 all such allowances and charges as would, if the transferring company had continued to carry on the trade and had continued to use the transferred assets for the purposes of the trade, have been made to or on the transferring company in respect of any assets transferred in the course of the transfer, and the amount of any such allowance or charge shall be computed as if the receiving company had been carrying on the trade since the transferring company began to do so and as if everything done to or by the transferring company had been done to or by the receiving company.

(*c*) This subsection shall not apply as respects assets transferred in the course of a transfer if in consequence of the transfer, or a transaction of which the transfer is a part, the Corporation Tax Acts are to apply subject to subsections (6) to (9) of section 400.

(3) For the purposes of the Capital Gains Tax Acts and, in so far as they apply to chargeable gains, the Corporation Tax Acts—

(*a*) the transfer shall not be treated as involving any disposal by the transferring company, and

(*b*) the receiving company shall be treated as if the assets transferred to it in the course of the transfer were acquired by it at the same time and for the same consideration at which they were acquired by the transferring company and as if all things done by the transferring company relating to the assets transferred in the course of the transfer had been done by the receiving company.

(4) Where, at any time within a period of 6 years commencing on the day on which the assets were transferred in the course of the transfer, the transferring company disposes of the new assets then, for the purposes of the Capital Gains Tax Acts and, in so far as they apply to chargeable gains, the Corporation Tax Acts, in computing any chargeable gain on the disposal of any new assets—

(*a*) the aggregate of the chargeable gains less allowable losses which but for subsection (3)(*a*) would have been chargeable on the transferring company shall be apportioned between the new assets as a whole, and

(*b*) the sums allowable as a deduction under section 552(1)(*a*) shall be reduced by the amount apportioned to the new asset under paragraph (*a*),

and, if the securities which comprise the new assets are not all of the same type, the apportionment between the securities under paragraph (*a*) shall be in accordance with their market value at the time they were acquired by the transferring company.

(5) Subsections (2) to (4) shall not apply if—

(*a*) immediately after the time of the transfer—

(i) the assets transferred in the course of the transfer are not used for the purposes of a trade carried on by the receiving company in the State,

(ii) the receiving company would not be chargeable to corporation tax or capital gains tax in respect of any chargeable gains accruing to it on a disposal, if it were to make such a disposal, of any assets (other than cash) acquired in the course of the transfer, or

(iii) any of the assets are assets in respect of which, by virtue of being of a description specified in a bilateral agreement, the receiving company is to be regarded as not liable in the State to corporation tax or capital gains tax on gains accruing to it on a disposal,

or

(*b*) the transferring company and the receiving company jointly so elect by notice in writing to the inspector, and such notice shall be made by the time by which a return is to be made by the transferring company under section 951 for the accounting period in which the transfer takes place.

Cross-references

Debts: s 541(7)(*d*).

EU Council Directive 90/434/EEC, mergers, divisions, meaning of "transfer" applied, subs (1): s 630.

EU Council Directive 90/434/EEC, transfer of assets to parent: s 632(1)(*b*); subs (5): s 632(2).

EU Council Directive 90/434/EEC, avoidance of tax, ss 631–634 do not apply: s 635.

EU Council Directive 90/434/EEC, returns: s 636(2).

Definitions

allowable loss: ss 4(1), 5(1), 546; company: ss 4(1), 5(1); Corporation Tax Acts: s 1(2); inspector: ss 2(1), 5(1), 852; trade: s 3(1); writing: IA 1937 Sch.

Former enactments

FA 1992 s 65.

632 Transfer of assets by company to its parent company

(1) Where a company disposes of an asset used for the purposes of a trade carried on by it in the State to another company which holds all of the securities representing the company's capital and but for this section the companies would not be treated in accordance with section 617 in respect of the asset, then, if—

(*a*) immediately after the disposal the company acquiring the asset commences to use the asset for the purposes of a trade carried on by it in the State, and

(*b*) the disposal is not, or does not form part of, a transfer to which section 631 applies,

sections 617 to 619 shall apply as if the companies were resident in the State.

(2) Subsection (5) of section 631 shall apply with any necessary modification for the purposes of this section as if references in that subsection to subsections (2) to (4) of that section were references to subsection (1) of this section.

Cross-references

Debts: s 541(7)(*e*).

EU Council Directive 90/434/EEC, avoidance of tax, ss 631–634 do not apply: s 635.

EU Council Directive 90/434/EEC, returns: s 636(2).

Definitions

company: ss 4(1), 5(1); resident: s 5(1); trade: s 3(1).

Former enactments

FA 1992 s 66.

633 Company reconstruction or amalgamation: transfer of development land

Where a company, for the purposes of or in connection with a scheme of reconstruction or amalgamation (within the meaning of section 615), disposes of an asset which consists of development land (within the meaning of section 648) to another company and—

(*a*) the disposal is not made in the course of a transfer to which section 631 applies, and

(*b*) the company disposing of the asset and the company acquiring the asset would, if—

(i) the definition of **"chargeable gains"** in section 78(4), and

(ii) section 649(1),

were deleted, be treated in accordance with section 615(2) in respect of that asset,

then, the companies shall be treated for the purposes of the Capital Gains Tax Acts as if the asset was acquired by the one company from the other company for a consideration of such amount as would secure that on the disposal neither a gain nor a loss would accrue to the company making the disposal, and for the purposes of section 556 the acquiring company shall be treated as if the acquisition of the asset by the other company had been the acquiring company's acquisition of the asset.

Cross-references

EU Council Directive 90/434/EEC, avoidance of tax, ss 631–634 do not apply: s 635.

EU Council Directive 90/434/EEC, returns: s 636(2).

Definitions

company: ss 4(1), 5(1); land: s 5(1), IA 1937 Sch.

Former enactments

FA 1992 s 67.

634 Credit for tax

(1) In this section—

"law of the Member State which has the effect of deferring a charge to tax on a gain" means any law of the Member State concerned which provides—

(*a*) that the gain accruing to the transferring company on the disposal of the assets in the course of the transfer is to be treated as not accruing until the disposal of the assets by the receiving company,

(*b*) that the receiving company is to be treated as having acquired the assets for a consideration of such amount as would secure that, for the purposes of charging the gain on the disposal to tax in that Member State, neither a gain nor a loss would accrue to the transferring company on the transfer and the receiving company is to be treated as if the acquisition of the assets by the transferring company had been the receiving company's acquisition of the assets, or

(*c*) such other deferral of a charge to tax as corresponds to paragraph (*a*) or (*b*);

"relevant certificate given by the tax authorities of a Member State" means a certificate so given and which states—

(*a*) whether gains accruing to the transferring company on the transfer would have been chargeable to tax under the law of the Member State but for—

(i) the Directive, or

(ii) any provision of the law of the Member State which has the effect of deferring a charge to tax on a gain in the case of such a transfer,

(*b*) if those gains accruing would have been so chargeable, the amount of tax which would have been payable under that law if, in so far as is permitted under that law, any losses arising on the transfer are set against any gains so arising and any deductions and reliefs available to the transferring company under that law other than the provisions mentioned in paragraph (*a*) had been claimed.

(2) Where—

(*a*) a company resident in the State transfers the whole or part of a trade which immediately before the time of the transfer it carried on in a Member State (other than the State) through a branch or agency to a company not resident in the State,

(*b*) the transfer includes the whole of the assets of the transferring company used for the purposes of the trade or the part of the trade or the whole of those assets other than cash, and

(*c*) the consideration for the transfer consists wholly or partly of the issue to the transferring company of securities in the receiving company,

then, tax specified in a relevant certificate given by the tax authorities of the Member State in which the trade was so carried on shall be treated for the purposes of Chapter 1 of Part 35 as tax—

(i) payable under the law of that Member State, and

(ii) in respect of which credit may be allowed under a bilateral agreement.

Cross-references

EU Council Directive 90/434/EEC, mergers, divisions, meaning of "transfer" applied, subs (2): s 630.

EU Council Directive 90/434/EEC, avoidance of tax, ss 631–634 do not apply: s 635.

EU Council Directive 90/434/EEC, returns: s 636(2), (3).

Definitions

branch or agency: ss 4(1), 5(1); company: ss 4(1), 5(1); land: s 5(1), IA 1937 Sch; resident: s 5(1); trade: s 3(1).

Former enactments

FA 1992 s 69.

635 Avoidance of tax

Notwithstanding any other provision of the Tax Acts or the Capital Gains Tax Acts, sections 631 to 634 shall not apply as respects a transfer or disposal unless it is shown that the transfer or disposal, as the case may be, is effected for bona fide commercial reasons and does not form part of any arrangement or scheme of which the main purpose or one of the main purposes is avoidance of liability to income tax, corporation tax or capital gains tax.

Definitions

Tax Acts: s 1(2).

Former enactments

FA 1992 s 70.

636 Returns

(1) In this section, **"appropriate inspector"** has the same meaning as in section 950.

(2) Where section 631, 632, 633 or 634 applies in relation to a transfer or disposal, the transferring company shall make a return of the transfer or disposal, as the case may be, to the appropriate inspector in such form as the Revenue Commissioners may require.

(3) Where corporation tax or capital gains tax payable by a company is to be reduced by virtue of section 634, a return under this section shall include a relevant certificate given by the tax authorities of the Member State in which the trade was carried on immediately before the time of the transfer.

(4) A company shall make a return under this section within 9 months from the end of the accounting period in which the transfer occurs.

Definitions

company: ss 4(1), 5(1); inspector: ss 2(1), 5(1), 852; trade: s 3(1).

Former enactments

FA 1992 s 71.

637 Other transactions

(1) The Revenue Commissioners may, on an application being made to them in writing in respect of a transaction—

(*a*) of a type specified in the Directive, and

(*b*) to which this Part does not apply,

give such relief as appears to them to be just and reasonable for the purposes of giving effect to the Directive.

(2) An application under this section shall be made in such form as the Revenue Commissioners may require.

Cross-references

Debts: s 541(7)(*f*).

Definitions

writing: IA 1937 Sch.

Former enactments

FA 1992 s 72.

638 Apportionment of amounts

Where for the purposes of this Part any sum is to be apportioned and at the time of the apportionment it appears that it is material as respects the liability to tax (for whatever period) of 2 or more companies, any question which arises as to the manner in which the sum is to be apportioned shall be determined for the purposes of the tax of all those companies by the Appeal Commissioners who shall determine the question in the like manner as if it were an appeal against an assessment, and the provisions of the Income Tax Acts relating to the rehearing of an appeal and to the statement of a case for the opinion of the High Court on a point of law shall apply accordingly with any necessary modifications, and all those companies shall be entitled to appear and be heard by the Appeal Commissioners or to make representations to them in writing.

Definitions

Appeal Commissioners: s 2(1); High Court: IA 1937 Sch; Income Tax Acts: s 1(2).

Former enactments

FA 1992 s 74.

TRANSACTIONS IN LAND

PART 22
PROVISIONS RELATING TO DEALING IN OR DEVELOPING LAND AND DISPOSALS OF DEVELOPMENT LAND

CHAPTER 1

Income Tax and Corporation Tax: Profits or Gains from Dealing in or Developing Land

Cross-references

Higher rate of corporation tax: s 21A(1) (dealing in or developing land).

639 Interpretation (Chapter 1)

(1) In this Chapter, except where the context otherwise requires—

"company" includes any body corporate;

"development", in relation to any land, means—

(*a*) the construction, demolition, extension, alteration or reconstruction of any building on the land, or

(*b*) the carrying out of any engineering or other operation in, on, over or under the land to adapt it for materially altered use,

and **"developing"** and **"developed"** shall be construed accordingly;

"market value", in relation to any property, means the price which that property might reasonably be expected to fetch if sold in the open market;

"trading stock" has the same meaning as in section 89;

any reference to the disposal of an interest in land includes a reference to the creation of an interest, and any reference to the acquisition of an interest in land includes a reference to the acquisition of an interest which ceases on the acquisition.

(2) For the purposes of this Chapter—

(*a*) a person shall not be regarded as disposing of an interest in land by reason of the person conveying or transferring the interest by means of security or of the person granting a lease of the land on terms which do not require the payment of any fine, premium or like sum, and

(*b*) an option or other right to acquire or dispose of any interest in any land shall be deemed to be an interest in the land.

(3) This Chapter shall apply notwithstanding Chapter 8 of Part 4.

Cross-references

Higher rate of corporation tax, meaning of "development" applied: s 21A(1)(qualifying land).

Definitions

land: IA 1937; person: IA 1937 s 11(*c*).

Former enactments

F(MP)A 1968 s 16(1), (2) and (4).

640 Extension of charge under Case I of Schedule D to certain profits from dealing in or developing land

(1) For the purposes of subsection (2)—

(*a*) a dealing in land shall be regarded as taking place where a person having an interest in any land disposes, as regards the whole or any part of the land, of that interest or of an interest which derives from that interest, and``

(*b*) a person who secures the development of any land shall be regarded as developing that land.

(2) (*a*) Where apart from this section all or some of the activities of a business of dealing in or developing land would not be regarded as activities carried on in the course of a trade within Schedule D but would be so regarded if every disposal of an interest in land included among such activities (including a disposal of an interest in land which apart from this section is a disposal of the full interest in the land which the person carrying on the business had acquired) were treated as fulfilling the conditions specified in paragraph (*b*), the business shall be deemed to be wholly a trade within Schedule D or, as the case may be, part of such a trade, and the profits or gains of that business shall be charged to tax under Case I of Schedule D accordingly

(*b*) The conditions referred to in paragraph (*a*) are—

(i) that the disposal was a disposal of the full interest in the land which the person carrying on the business had acquired, and

(ii) that the interest disposed of had been acquired by such person in the course of the business.

(3) Where an interest in land is disposed of in the course of the winding up of a company, the company shall for the purposes of this section be deemed not to have ceased to carry on the trade or business which it carried on before the commencement of the winding up until the completion of the disposal, or of the last such disposal where there is more than one, and the question whether any such disposal was made in the course of a business of dealing in or developing land which is, or is to be deemed to be, a trade or part of a trade shall accordingly be determined without regard to the fact that the company is being wound up.

Case law

Subs (2)(*a*): A company which acquired farm land held to have appropriated it to trading stock (ie development land) following an official report recommending the building of a satellite town in the area: *O'hArgáin v B Ltd (In voluntary liquidation)* ITR Vol III p 9.

Definitions

company: s 639(1); land: IA 1937 Sch; person: IA 1937 s 11(*c*); trade: s 3(1).

Former enactments

F(MP)A 1968 s 17; FA 1981 s 28.

---

641 Computation under Case I of Schedule D of profits or gains from dealing in or developing land

(1) Where a business of dealing in or developing land is, or is to be regarded as, a trade within Schedule D or a part of such a trade, the provisions applicable to Case I of that

Schedule shall, as respects the computation of the profits or gains of the business, apply subjcct to subsections (2) to (4).

(2) (*a*) Any consideration (other than rent or an amount treated as rent under section 98) for the disposal of an interest in any land or in a part of any land shall be treated as a consideration for the disposal of trading stock and accordingly shall be taken into account as a trading receipt.

(*b*) Any interest in any land which is held by a person carrying on a trade (in this section referred to as **"the trader"**) and which has become trading stock of the trade shall thereafter, until the discontinuance of the trade, continue to be such trading stock.

(*c*) Where the trader has acquired an interest in any land otherwise than for consideration in money or money's worth, the trader shall, subject to paragraph (*d*), be deemed to have purchased the interest for a consideration equal to its market value at the time of acquisition.

(*d*) Where at the time of acquisition of an interest in any land the trade had not been commenced or the interest was not then appropriated as trading stock, the trader shall be deemed to have purchased the interest for a consideration equal to its market value at the time of its appropriation as trading stock.

(*e*) Any consideration (other than receipts within section 75(1)(*b*) the profits or gains arising from which are by virtue of that section chargeable to tax under Case V of Schedule D) for the granting by the trader of any right in relation to the development of any land shall be taken into account as a trading receipt.

(3) Account shall not be taken of any sum (in this subsection referred to as **"the relevant sum"**) which is paid or is payable at any time by the trader as consideration for the forfeiture or surrender of the right of any person to an annuity or other annual payment unless—

(*a*) the annuity or other annual payment arises under—

(i) a testamentary disposition, or

(ii) a liability incurred for—

(I) valuable and sufficient consideration all of which is required to be taken into account in computing for the purposes of income tax or corporation tax the income of the person to whom that consideration is given, or

(II) consideration given to a person who—

(A) has not at any time carried on a business of dealing in or developing land which is, or is to be regarded as, a trade or a part of a trade, and

(B) is not and was not at any time connected with any of the following persons—

(*aa)* the trader,

(*bb*) a person who is or was at any time connected with the trader, and

(*cc*) any other person who, in the course of a business of dealing in or developing land which is, or is to be regarded as, a trade or a part of a trade, holds or held an interest in land on which the annuity or other annual payment was charged or reserved,

or

(*b*) the relevant sum is required to be taken into account in computing for the purposes of income tax or corporation tax the profits or gains of a trade of dealing in or developing land carried on by the person to whom the relevant sum is payable.

(4) (*a*) Paragraph (*b*) shall apply where—

(i) a sum (in this subsection referred to as **"the relevant sum"**) is payable—

(I) by a person (in this subsection referred to as **"the relevant person"**) who is not the trader, and

(II) as consideration for the forfeiture or surrender of the right (in this subsection referred to as **"the right"**) of any person to an annuity or other annual payment,

(ii) the relevant sum is not required to be taken into account in computing for the purposes of income tax or corporation tax the profits or gains of a trade of dealing in or developing land carried on by the person to whom the relevant sum is payable, and

(iii) the trader incurs expenditure (in this subsection referred to as **"the cost"**) in acquiring any interest (in this subsection referred to as **"the interest"**) in land on which the annuity or other annual payment had been reserved or charged.

(*b*) Where this paragraph applies—

(i) the trader shall be treated as having expended in acquiring the interest an amount equal to the amount which would have been expended if the right had not been forfeited or surrendered, and

(ii) the excess of the cost over the amount determined in accordance with subparagraph (i) shall be treated for the purposes of subsection (3) as having been payable by the trader as consideration for the forfeiture or surrender of the right.

(*c*) For the purposes of this subsection, all such apportionments and valuations shall be made as appear to the inspector or on appeal to the Appeal Commissioners to be just and reasonable.

(*d*) This subsection shall not apply where the relevant person carries on a trade of dealing in or developing land and pays the relevant sum in the course of carrying on that trade.

Case law

Subs (2)(*a*): Argument that profit arising on the disposal of property to be determined on the capitalised value of lease rents payable rather than actual expenditure incurred rejected by the Courts: *Cronin v Cork and County Property Co Ltd* ITR Vol III p 198; *Belvedere Estates Ltd v O'Connláin* ITR Vol III p 271.

Definitions

Appeal Commissioners: s 2(1); development: s 639(1); inspector: ss 2(1), 5(1), 852; land: IA 1937 Sch; market value: s 639(1); person: IA 1937 s 11(*c*); trade: s 3(1); trading stock: s 639(1).

Former enactments

F(MP)A 1968 s 18; FA 1981 s 29(2)(*a*).

642 Transfers of interests in land between certain associated persons

(1) Where an interest in land is disposed of by any person (in this subsection referred to as **"the disponer"**) to a person connected with the disponer (in this subsection referred to as **"the transferee"**) and—

(*a*) the interest is disposed of at a price greater than its market value, and

(*b*) the price—

(i) is not to be taken into account in relation to the disponer in computing for tax purposes the profits or gains of a trade which is or includes a business of dealing in or developing land, but

(ii) is to be so taken into account in relation to the transferee,

the transferee shall for tax purposes be deemed to have acquired the interest at a price equal to the market value of the interest at the time of its acquisition by the transferee.

(2) (*a*) Where an interest in land is disposed of by any person (in this subsection referred to as **"the disponer"**) to a person connected with the disponer (in this subsection referred to as **"the transferee"**) and—

(i) the interest is disposed of at a price less than its market value, and

(ii) the price—

(I) is not to be taken into account in relation to the transferee in computing for tax purposes the profits or gains of a trade which is or includes a business of dealing in or developing land, but

(II) is to be so taken into account in relation to the disponer,

the disponer shall for tax purposes be deemed to have disposed of the interest at a price equal to the market value of the interest at the time of the disposal by the disponer.

(*b*) A disposal by means of gift shall be regarded for the purposes of this subsection as being a disposal at a nominal price.

(3) In the application of this section to a case in which a lease is granted, any reference to price shall be construed as a reference to the fine, premium or like sum payable for the grant of the lease.

Definitions

land: IA 1937 Sch; market value: s 639(1); person: IA 1937 s 11(*c*); trade: s 3(1).

Former enactments

F(MP)A 1968 s 19.

643 Tax to be charged under Case IV on gains from certain disposals of land

(1) In this section and in section 644—

"capital amount" means any amount in money or money's worth which apart from this section is not to be included in any computation of income for the purposes of the Tax

Acts, and other expressions which include the word **"capital"** shall be construed accordingly;

"chargeable period" means an accounting period of a company or a year of assessment;

"land" includes any interest in land, and references to the land include references to all or any part of the land;

"share" includes stock;

references to property deriving its value from land include references to—

(*a*) any shareholding in a company, or any partnership interest, or any interest in settled property, deriving its value or the greater part of its value directly or indirectly from land, and

(*b*) any option, consent or embargo affecting the disposition of land.

(2) This section shall not apply to a gain accruing to an individual which by virtue of section 604 is exempt from capital gains tax or which would be so exempt but for subsection (14) of that section.

(3) This section shall apply in any case where—

(*a*) land or any property deriving its value from land is acquired with the sole or main object of realising a gain from disposing of the land,

(*b*) land is held as trading stock, or

(*c*) land is developed by a company with the sole or main object of realising a gain from disposing of the land when developed,

and any gain of a capital nature is obtained from disposing of the land—

(i) by the person acquiring, holding or developing the land, or by a person connected with that person, or

(ii) where any arrangement or scheme is effected as respects the land which enables the gain to be realised directly or indirectly by any transaction, or by any series of transactions, by any person who is a party to or concerned in the arrangement or scheme,

and this subsection shall apply whether that gain is obtained by any such person for that person's benefit or for the benefit of any other person.

(4) Where this section applies, the whole of any gain mentioned in subsection (3) shall for the purposes of the Tax Acts be treated—

(*a*) as being income which arises at the time when the gain is realised and which constitutes profits or gains chargeable to tax under Case IV of Schedule D for the chargeable period in which the gain is realised, and

(*b*) subject to subsections (5) to (17), as being income of the person by whom the gain is realised.

(5) For the purposes of this section, land shall be treated as disposed of if, by any one or more transactions or by any arrangement or scheme, whether concerning the land or property deriving its value from the land, the property in the land or control over the land is effectively disposed of, and references in subsection (3) to the acquisition or

development of land or property with the sole or main object of realising a gain from disposing of the land shall be construed accordingly.

(6) For the purposes of this section—

(*a*) where, whether by a premature sale or otherwise, a person directly or indirectly makes available to another person the opportunity of realising a gain, the gain of that other person shall be treated as having been obtained for that other person by the first-mentioned person, and

(*b*) any number of transactions may be regarded as constituting a single arrangement or scheme if a common purpose is discerned in those transactions or if there is other sufficient evidence of a common purpose.

(7) In applying this section, account shall be taken of any method, direct or indirect, by which—

(*a*) any property or right is transferred or transmitted to another person, or

(*b*) the value of any property or right is enhanced or diminished,

and accordingly the occasion of the transfer or transmission of any property or right by whatever method and the occasion when the value of any property or right is enhanced may be treated as an occasion on which tax becomes chargeable under this section.

(8) Subsection (7) shall apply in particular to—

(*a*) sales, contracts and other transactions made otherwise than for full consideration or for more than full consideration,

(*b*) any method by which any property or right, or the control of any property or right, is transferred or transmitted to any person by assigning—

(i) share capital or other rights in a company,

(ii) rights in a partnership, or

(iii) an interest in settled property,

(*c*) the creation of any option or consent or embargo affecting the disposition of any property or right, and to the consideration given for the option, or for the giving of the consent or the release of the embargo, and

(*d*) the disposal of any property or right on the winding up, dissolution or termination of any company, partnership or trust.

(9) For the purposes of this section, such method of computing a gain shall be adopted as is just and reasonable in the circumstances, taking into account the value of what is obtained for disposing of the land and allowing only such expenses as are attributable to the land disposed of, and in applying this subsection—

(*a*) where an interest in land is acquired and the reversion is retained on disposal, account may be taken of the way in which the profits or gains under Case I of Schedule D of a person dealing in land are computed in such a case, and

(*b*) account may be taken of the adjustments to be made in computing such profits or gains under sections 99(2) and 100(4).

(10) Paragraph (*c*) of subsection (3) shall not apply to so much of any gain as is fairly attributable to the period, if any, before the intention to develop that land was formed, and which would not be within paragraph (*a*) or (*b*) of that subsection, and in applying

this subsection account shall be taken of the treatment under Case I of Schedule D of a person who appropriates land as trading stock.

(11) If all or any part of the gain accruing to any person is derived from value, or an opportunity of realising a gain, provided directly or indirectly by some other person (whether or not put at the disposal of the first-mentioned person), subsection (4)(*b*) shall apply to the gain or that part of the gain with the substitution of that other person for the person by whom the gain was realised.

(12) Where there is a disposal of shares in—

(*a*) a company which holds land as trading stock, or

(*b*) a company which owns directly or indirectly 90 per cent or more of the ordinary share capital of another company which holds land as trading stock,

and all the land so held is disposed of in the normal course of its trade by the company which held the land, and so as to procure that all opportunity of profit in respect of the land arises to that company, then, notwithstanding subsection (3)(i), this section shall not apply to any gain accruing to the holder of shares as being a gain on property deriving value from that land (but without prejudice to any liability under subsection (3)(ii)).

(13) In ascertaining for the purposes of this section the intentions of any person, the objects and powers of any company, partners or trustees, as set out in any memorandum or articles of association or other document, shall not be conclusive.

(14) For the purposes of ascertaining whether and to what extent the value of any property or right is derived from any other property or right, value may be traced through any number of companies, partnerships and trusts, and the property held by any company, partnership or trust shall be attributed to the shareholders, partners or beneficiaries at each stage in such manner as is just and reasonable.

(15) In applying this section—

(*a*) any expenditure, receipt, consideration or other amount may be apportioned by such method as is just and reasonable, and

(*b*) all such valuations shall be made as may be necessary to give effect to this section.

(16) For the purposes of this section, partners, trustees of settled property or personal representatives may be regarded as persons distinct from the individuals or other persons who are for the time being partners, trustees or personal representatives.

(17) This section shall apply to a person, whether resident in the State or not, if all or any part of the land in question is situated in the State.

Cross-references

Power to obtain information: s 645(1), (2)(*b*).

Relief from income tax in respect of income from dealing in residential development land: s 644A(2)(*b*).

Relief from corporation tax in respect of income from dealing in residential development land: s 644B(3)(*a*), (*b*)(i), (ii).

Supplementary provisions: s 644(1)–(3); subss (3)(*c*), (10): s 644(4); subs (11): s 644(5).

Definitions

company, control, development: s 639(1); land: IA 1937 Sch; person: IA 1937 s 11(*c*); trade: s 3(1); trading stock: s 639(1); year of assessment: s 5(1).

Former enactments

F(MP)A 1968 s 20; FA 1981 s 29(3).

Corresponding UK tax provision

Income and Corporation Taxes Act 1988 s 776.

644 Provisions supplementary to section 643

(1) (*a*) Where a person (in this subsection referred to as **"the first-mentioned person"**) is assessed to tax under section 643 and that assessment to tax arises in consequence of and in respect of consideration receivable by another person (in this subsection referred to as **"the second-mentioned person"**)—

(i) the first-mentioned person shall be entitled to recover from the second-mentioned person any part of that tax which the first-mentioned person has paid,

(ii) if any part of that tax remains unpaid at the expiration of 6 months from the date when it became due and payable, it shall be recoverable from the second-mentioned person as though the second-mentioned person were the person so assessed, but without prejudice to the right to recover the tax from the first-mentioned person, and

(iii) for the purposes of subparagraph (i), the inspector shall on request furnish a certificate specifying the amount of income in respect of which tax has been paid and the amount of tax so paid, and the certificate shall be evidence until the contrary is proved of any facts stated in the certificate.

(*b*) For the purposes of this subsection, any amount which by virtue of section 643 is treated as the income of a person shall, notwithstanding any other provision of the Tax Acts, be treated as the highest part of the person's income.

(2) Where it appears to the Revenue Commissioners that any person entitled to any consideration or other amount chargeable to tax under section 643 is not resident in the State, they may direct that section 238 shall apply to any payment forming part of that amount as if the payment were an annual payment charged with tax under Schedule D, but without prejudice to the final determination of the liability of that person, including any liability under subsection (1)(*a*)(ii).

(3) Section 643 shall apply subject to any provision of the Tax Acts deeming income to be income of a particular person.

(4) Where by virtue of section 643(3)(*c*) any person is charged to tax on the realisation of a gain, and by virtue of section 643(10) the computation of the gain proceeded on the basis that the land or some other property was appropriated at any time as trading stock, that land or other property shall also be treated on that basis for the purposes of section 596.

(5) Where by virtue of section 643(11) the person charged to tax is a person other than the person for whom the capital amount was obtained or the person by whom the gain was realised and the tax has been paid, then, for the purposes of sections 551 and 554,

the person for whom the capital amount was obtained or the person by whom the gain was realised, as may be appropriate, shall be regarded as having been charged to the tax so paid.

Cross-references

Power to obtain information: s 645(1), (2)(*b*).

Same meanings apply to supplementary provisions: s 643(1).

Definitions

capital amount, chargeable period: s 644; inspector: ss 2(1), 5(1), 852; month: IA 1937 Sch; person: IA 1937 s 11(*c*); trade: s 3(1); trading stock: s 639(1); land: s 644, IA 1937 Sch; share: s 644.

Former enactments

F(MP)A 1968 s 21; FA 1981 s 29(3).

Corresponding UK tax provision

Income and Corporation Taxes Act 1988 s 777.

644A Relief from income tax in respect of income from dealing in residential development land

[(1) In this section—

"basis period" has the same meaning as in section 127(1);

"construction operations", in relation to residential development land, means operations of any of the descriptions referred to in the definition of "construction operations" in section 530(1) other than such operations as consist of—

(*a*) the demolition or dismantling of any building or structure on the land,

(*b*) the construction or demolition of any works forming part of the land, being roadworks, water mains, wells, sewers or installations for the purposes of land drainage, or

(*c*) any other operations which are preparatory to residential development on the land other than the laying of foundations for such development;

"residential development" includes any development which is ancillary to the development and which is necessary for the proper planning and development of the area in question;

"residential development land" means land—

(*a*) disposed of to—

(i) a housing authority (within the meaning of section 23 of the Housing (Miscellaneous Provisions) Act, 1992),

(ii) the National Building Agency Limited (being the company referred to in section 1 of the National Building Agency Limited Act, 1963), or

(iii) a body standing approved of for the purposes of section 6 of the Housing (Miscellaneous Provisions) Act, 1992,

which land is specified in a certificate in writing given by a housing authority or the National Building Agency Limited, as appropriate, as land being required for the purposes of the Housing Acts, 1966 to 1998,

(*b*) in respect of which permission for residential development has been granted under [the Local Government (Planning and Development) Acts 1963 to 1999 or the Planning and Development Act 2000,][1] and such permission has not ceased to exist, or

(*c*) which is, in accordance with a development objective (as indicated in the development plan of the planning authority concerned), for use solely or primarily for residential purposes.

(2) This section applies to profits or gains being—

(*a*) profits or gains arising from dealing in or developing residential development land in the course of a business consisting of or including dealing in or developing land which is, or is regarded as, a trade within Schedule D or a part of such a trade, or

(*b*) any gain of a capital nature arising from the disposing of residential development land which, by virtue of section 643, constitutes profits or gains chargeable to tax under Case IV of Schedule D.

(3) Notwithstanding any other provision of the Tax Acts and subject to subsections (4) and (5)—

(*a*) to the extent to which profits or gains of a basis period for a year of assessment consist of profits or gains to which this section applies, those profits or gains—

(i) shall be chargeable to income tax for that year at the rate of 20 per cent, and

(ii) shall not be reckoned in computing total income for that year for the purposes of the Income Tax Acts, and

(*b*) the provisions of sections 187 and 188, and the reductions specified in Part 2 of the Table to section 458 shall not apply as regards income tax so charged.

(4) For the purposes of this section—

(*a*) where a trade consists partly of dealing in residential development land and partly of other operations or activities, the part of the trade consisting of dealing in residential development land and the part of the trade consisting of other operations or activities shall each be treated as a separate trade, and the total amount receivable from sales made and services rendered in the course of the trade, and of expenses incurred in the trade, shall be apportioned to each such part,

(*b*) in computing the profits or gains to which this section applies, no account shall be taken, in determining those profits or gains, of that part, if any, of profits or gains which are attributable to construction operations on the land, and

(*c*) where, in order to give effect to the provisions of this section, an apportionment of profits and gains, amounts receivable or expenses incurred is required to be made, such apportionment shall be made in a manner that is just and reasonable.

(5) This section shall not apply to profits or gains arising to a person in a year of assessment if that person so elects by notice in writing to the inspector on or before the specified return date for the chargeable period (within the meaning of section 950).][2]

Amendments

1 Substituted by FA 2004 s 83(1)(*a*) with effect from 11 March 2002; previously "section 26 of the Local Government (Planning and Development) Act, 1963,".

2 Section 644A inserted by FA 2000 s 52 in relation to profits or gains arising on or after 1 December 1999.

Cross-references

Higher rate of corporation tax, meaning of "residential development land" applied: s 21A(5)(*a*).

Relief from corporation tax in respect of income from dealing in residential land, meaning of "residential development" and "residential development land" applied: s 644B(1); meaning of "construction operations" applied: s 644B(3)(*b*)(i).

Tax Briefing

TB40 June 2000 pp 1–2 — Residential Development Land — Income Tax.

TB45 Oct 2001 p 11 — Revenue will not charge PRSI or the Health Contribution on profits or gains chargeable under TCA 1997 s 644A.

Definitions

Income Tax Acts: s 1(2); land: IA 1937 Sch; Tax Acts: s 1(2); total income: s 3(1); writing: IA 1937 Sch.

644B Relief from corporation tax in respect of income from dealing in residential development land

[(1) In this section—

"excepted trade" has the same meaning as in section 21A;

"residential development" and **"residential development land"** have the same meaning as each has in section 644A.

(2) (*a*) Where in an accounting period a company carries on an excepted trade the operations or activities of which consist of or include dealing in land which, at the time at which it is disposed of by the company, is residential development land, the corporation tax payable by the company for the accounting period, in so far as it is referable to trading income from dealing in residential development land, shall be reduced by one-fifth.

(*b*) For the purposes of paragraph (*a*)—

(i) the corporation tax payable by a company for an accounting period which is referable to trading income from dealing in residential development land shall be such amount as bears to the amount of corporation tax for the period referable to income of an excepted trade the same proportion as—

(I) the amount receivable by the company in the accounting period from the disposal in the course of the excepted trade of residential development land, exclusive of so much of that amount as is attributable to construction operations (within the meaning of section 21A) carried out by or for the company on the land, bears to

(II) the total amount receivable by the company in the accounting period, exclusive of so much of that amount as is attributable to construction operations (within the meaning of section 21A) carried out by or for the company on land disposed of by it, in the course of the excepted trade,

and

(ii) corporation tax referable to income from an excepted trade for an accounting period shall be such sum as bears to the amount of corporation tax charged for the period in accordance with section 21A at the rate of 25 per cent the same proportion as the amount of the company's profits treated under section 21A as consisting of income from the excepted trade bears to the total amount of the profits of the company for the period so charged at the rate of 25 per cent.

(3) (*a*) Where in an accounting period income of a company which is chargeable under Case IV of Schedule D by virtue of section 643 consists of or includes an amount in respect of a gain obtained from disposing of land which, at the time of its disposal, is residential development land, the corporation tax payable by the company for the accounting period, in so far as it is referable to that gain, shall be reduced by one-fifth.

(*b*) For the purposes of paragraph (*a*)—

(i) the corporation tax payable by a company for an accounting period which is referable to a gain from disposing of residential development land shall be such amount as bears to the amount of corporation tax for the accounting period referable to a gain charged to tax in accordance with section 643 the same proportion as so much of the amount (in this subparagraph referred to as the "specified amount") of the last-mentioned gain as is attributable to the disposal of residential development land (exclusive of any part of the gain as is referable to construction operations, within the meaning of section 644A, carried out by the company) bears to the specified amount, and

(ii) corporation tax referable to a gain from disposing of land which is treated by virtue of section 643 as income chargeable under Case IV of Schedule D shall be such sum as bears to the amount of corporation tax charged for the accounting period in accordance with section 21A at the rate of 25 per cent the same proportion as the amount of the company's profits which consists of income chargeable under Case IV of Schedule D by virtue of section 643 bears to the total amount of the profits of the company for the period so charged at the rate of 25 per cent.

(4) (*a*) Where a company makes a claim in that behalf, the corporation tax payable by the company for an accounting period ending before 1 January 2001 shall be computed as if subparagraph (ii) of paragraph (*a*) of the definition of excepted operations in section 21A did not have effect in relation to residential development land.

(*b*) For the purposes of this subsection where an accounting period of a company begins before 1 January 2001 and ends on or after that day, it shall be divided into two parts, one beginning on the day on which the accounting period begins and ending on 31 December 2000 and the other beginning on 1 January 2001 and ending on the day on which the accounting period ends, and both parts shall be treated for the purpose of this section as if they were separate accounting periods of the company.

Amendments

1 Section 644B inserted by FA 2000 s 52 in relation to accounting periods ending on or after 1 January 2000. For the purposes of this section where an accounting period of a company begins before 1 January 2000 and ends on or after that day, it shall be divided into two parts, one beginning on the day on which the accounting period begins and ending on 31 December 1999 and the other beginning on 1 January 2000 and ending on the day on which the accounting period ends, and both parts shall be treated for the purpose of this section as if they were separate accounting periods of the company.

Cross-references

Corporation tax, manufacturing (10%) relief: s 448(1)(*d*).

Relief from income tax and corporation tax by means of credit in respect of foreign tax: Sch 24 para 4(4)(*e*).

Tax Briefing

TB40 June 2000 pp 4–5 — Residential Development Land — Corporation Tax.

Definitions

company: ss 4(1), 5(1); land: IA 1937 Sch; profits: s 4(1).

645 Power to obtain information

(1) The inspector may by notice in writing require any person to furnish him or her within such time as may be specified in the notice (not being less than 30 days) with such particulars as the inspector thinks necessary for the purposes of sections 643 and 644.

(2) The particulars which a person is obliged to furnish under this section, if required by notice to do so, shall include particulars as to—

(*a*) transactions or arrangements with respect to which the person is or was acting on behalf of others,

(*b*) transactions or arrangements which in the opinion of the inspector should properly be examined for the purposes of sections 643 and 644, notwithstanding that in the opinion of the person to whom the notice is given no liability to tax arises under those sections, and

(*c*) whether the person to whom the notice is given has taken or is taking any transactions or arrangements of a description specified in the notice and, if so, what transactions or arrangements, and what part the person has taken or is taking in those transactions or arrangements.

(3) Notwithstanding anything in subsection (2), a solicitor shall not be deemed for the purposes of subsection (2)(*c*) to have taken part in any transaction or arrangements by reason only that he or she has given professional advice to a client in connection with the transaction or arrangements, and shall not, in relation to anything done by him or her on behalf of a client, be compellable under this section, except with the consent of the client, to do more than state that he or she is or was acting on behalf of a client, and give the name and address of the client.

Cross-references

Penalty: Sch 29, column 2.

Definitions

inspector: ss 2(1), 5(1), 852; person: IA 1937 s 11(*c*); writing: IA 1937 Sch.

Former enactments

F(MP)A 1968 s 22; FA 1981 s 29(3).

Corresponding UK tax provision

Income and Corporation Taxes Act 1988 s 778.

646 Postponement of payment of income tax to be permitted in certain cases

(1) In this section, **"basis period"**, in relation to any year of assessment, means the period on the profits or gains of which income tax for that year is finally computed under Case I of Schedule D in respect of the trade or, where by virtue of the Income Tax

Acts the profits or gains of any other period are taken to be the profits or gains of that period, that other period.

(2) Where—

(*a*) a person (in this section referred to as **"the vendor"**) carrying on a trade of dealing in or developing land (in this section referred to as **"the trade"**) disposes in the course of the trade of the full interest acquired by the person in any land,

(*b*) the person to whom the disposition is made (in this section referred to as **"the purchaser"**) is not connected with the vendor,

(*c*) the terms subject to which the disposition is made provide for the grant of a lease of the land by the purchaser to the vendor,

(*d*) a sum representing the value of the vendor's right to be granted a lease is to be taken into account as a consideration for the disposal in computing the profits or gains of the trade, and

(*e*) within 6 months after the time of the disposition, a lease of the land in accordance with those terms is granted by the purchaser to the vendor,

subsections (3) and (4) shall apply in relation to income tax for a year of assessment in the basis period for which the disposition is made.

(3) Where, at the time when any amount of income tax charged by an assessment in respect of the profits or gains of the trade would but for this subsection become due and payable, the vendor—

(*a*) retains the leasehold interest acquired by the vendor from the purchaser, and

(*b*) has not disposed, as regards the whole or any part of the land, of an interest derived from that leasehold interest,

then, a part of that amount of income tax equal to 90 per cent of so much of such tax as would not have been chargeable if no sum had to be taken into account as mentioned in subsection (2)(*d*) shall be payable in 9 equal instalments at yearly intervals the first of which is payable on the 1st day of January in the year following that in which but for this subsection that amount of income tax would have been payable.

(4) Where, in a case in which the postponement of payment of any amount of income tax has been authorised by subsection (3), the vendor—

(*a*) ceases to retain the leasehold interest acquired by the vendor from the purchaser,

(*b*) disposes, as regards the whole or any part of the land, of an interest derived from that leasehold interest,

(*c*) being an individual, dies, or

(*d*) being a company, commences to be wound up,

then, that amount of income tax or, as the case may be, so much of that amount of income tax as has not already become due and payable shall become due and payable forthwith.

Cross-references

Corporation tax, postponement of tax, subs (2)(*b*)–(*e*): s 647(1)(*b*).

Definitions

company: s 639(1); Income Tax Acts: s 1(2); land: IA 1937 Sch; month: IA 1937 Sch; person: IA 1937 s 11(*c*); trade: s 3(1); year of assessment: ss 2(1), 5(1).

Former enactments

F(MP)A 1968 s 23(1)–(3) and (5).

647 Postponement of payment of corporation tax to be permitted in certain cases

(1) Where—

(*a*) for any accounting period the profits of a company consist of or include income from a trade of dealing in or developing land in the course of which the company disposes of the full interest acquired by it in any land,

(*b*) in relation to that disposal, the conditions specified in paragraphs (*b*) to (*e*) of section 646(2) are satisfied, and

(*c*) at the time when any amount of corporation tax charged by an assessment for that accounting period would but for this section become due and payable the company—

(i) retains the leasehold interest acquired by it from the person to whom the disposition is made, and

(ii) has not disposed, as regards the whole or any part of the land, of an interest derived from that leasehold interest,

then, a part of that amount of corporation tax equal to 90 per cent of so much of that amount as would not have been chargeable if no sum had to be taken into account as mentioned in section 646(2)(*d*) shall be payable in 9 equal instalments at yearly intervals the first of which shall be payable on the expiration of 12 months from the date on which but for this section that amount of corporation tax would have been payable.

(2) Where, in a case in which the postponement of payment of any amount of corporation tax has been authorised by subsection (1), the company—

(*a*) ceases to retain the leasehold interest acquired by it,

(*b*) disposes, as regards the whole or any part of the land, of an interest derived from that leasehold interest, or

(*c*) commences to be wound up,

then, that amount of corporation tax or, as the case may be, so much of that amount of corporation tax as has not already become due and payable shall become due and payable forthwith.

Definitions

company: ss 4(1), 5(1); land: s 5(1), IA 1937 Sch; month: IA 1937 Sch; person: IA 1937 s 11(*c*); profits: s 4(1); trade: ss 3(1), 4(1), 5(1).

Former enactments

CTA 1976 s 150.

CHAPTER 2
Capital Gains Tax: Disposals of Development Land

648 Interpretation (Chapter 2)

In this Chapter—

"the Act of 1963" means the Local Government (Planning and Development) Act, 1963;

[**"the Act of 2000"** means the Planning and Development Act 2000;][1]

"compulsory disposal" means a disposal to an authority possessing compulsory purchase powers, which is made pursuant to the exercise of those powers or the giving of formal notice of intention to exercise those powers, other than a disposal to which section 29 of the Act of 1963 applies;

"current use value"—

(*a*) in relation to land at any particular time, means the amount which would be the market value of the land at that time if the market value were calculated on the assumption that it was at that time and would remain unlawful to carry out any development [(within the meaning of section 3 of the Act of 1963, or, on or after 21 January 2002, within the meaning of section 3 of the Act of 2000)][2] in relation to the land other than development of a minor nature, and

(*b*) in relation to shares in a company (being shares deriving their value or the greater part of their value directly or indirectly from land, other than shares quoted on a stock exchange) at any particular time, means the amount which would be the market value of the shares at that time if the market value were calculated on the same assumption, in relation to the land from which the shares so derive value, as is mentioned in paragraph (*a*);

"development land" means land in the State the consideration for the disposal of which, or the market value of which at the time at which the disposal is made, exceeds the current use value of that land at the time at which the disposal is made, and includes shares deriving their value or the greater part of their value directly or indirectly from such land, other than shares quoted on a Stock Exchange;

[**"development of a minor nature"** means development (not being development by a local authority or a statutory undertaker within the meaning of section 2 of the Act of 1963, or, on or after 11 March 2002, within the meaning of section 2 of the Act of 2000) which, under or by virtue of section 4 of the Act of 1963, or, on or after 11 March 2002, under or by virtue of section 4 of the Act of 2000, is exempted development for the purposes of the Local Government (Planning and Development) Acts 1963 to 1999 or the Act of 2000;][3]

"relevant disposal" means a disposal of development land made on or after the 28th day of January, 1982.

Amendments

1 Definition of "the Act of 2002" inserted by FA 2004 s 83(1)(*b*)(i) with effect from 21 January 2002.

2 Substituted by FA 2004 s 83(1)(*b*)(ii) with effect from 21 January 2002; previously "(within the meaning of section 3 of the Act of 1963)".

3 Definition of "development of a minor nature" substituted by FA 2004 s 83(1)(*b*)(iii) with effect from 11 March 2002.

Cross-references

Companies' chargeable gains, disposals or acquisitions outside a group: s 619(2)(*b*).

Computation of companies' chargeable gains: s 78(4).

Disposals by liquidators and other persons, meaning of "relevant disposal" applied: s 571(1).

EU Council Directive 90/434/EEC, transfer of development land: s 633.

Reduced rate of capital gains tax on share disposals: s 592(1).

Definitions

chargeable gain: ss 4(1), 5(1), 534; company: ss 4(1), 5(1); Corporation Tax Acts: s 1(2); land: s 5(1), IA 1937 Sch; local authority: ss 2(1), 5(1); person: IA 1937 s 11(*c*); profits: s 4(1).

Former enactments

FA 1982 s 36(1).

649 Companies chargeable to capital gains tax in respect of chargeable gains accruing on relevant disposals

(1) Notwithstanding any provision to the contrary in the Corporation Tax Acts, a company shall not be chargeable to corporation tax in respect of chargeable gains accruing to it on relevant disposals, and accordingly—

(*a*) such gains shall not be regarded as profits of the company for the purposes of corporation tax, and

(*b*) the company shall be chargeable to capital gains tax under the Capital Gains Tax Acts in respect of those gains.

(2) Sections 617 and 621 to 626 shall apply with any necessary modifications in relation to capital gains tax to which a company is chargeable on chargeable gains accruing to the company on a relevant disposal as they apply in relation to corporation tax on chargeable gains, and references in those sections to corporation tax shall be construed as including references to capital gains tax.

(3) (*a*) Where a company which is or has been a member of a group of companies (within the meaning of section 616) makes a relevant disposal of an asset which, as a result of a disposal which was not a relevant disposal, the company had acquired from another member of that group at a time when both were members of the group, the amount of the chargeable gain accruing on the relevant disposal and the capital gains tax on that gain shall be computed as if all members of the group for the time being were the same person and as if the acquisition or provision of the asset by the group, so taken as a single person, had been the acquisition or provision of the asset by the member disposing of the asset.

(*b*) Notwithstanding paragraph (*a*), where under section 618(2) or 623 a member of the group (in this paragraph referred to as **"the first-mentioned member"**) had been treated as having acquired or reacquired the asset at a time later than the original acquisition or provision of the asset by the first-mentioned member or by another member of the group, as the case may be, paragraph (*a*) shall apply as if the reference in that paragraph to the acquisition or provision of the asset by the group were a reference to its acquisition or reacquisition so treated as having been made by the first-mentioned member.

Cross-references

EU Council Directive 90/434/EEC, transfer of development land, subs (1): s 633(*b*).

Definitions

chargeable gain: s 5(1); person: IA 1937 s 11(*c*); relevant disposal: s 648.

Former enactments

FA 1982 s 36(4)–(6); FA 1992 s 68(*a*).

649A Relevant disposals: rate of charge

[(1) Notwithstanding section 28(3) and subject to subsection (2), the rate of capital gains tax in respect of a chargeable gain accruing to a person on a relevant disposal shall be—

[(*a*) in the case of a relevant disposal made in the period from 3 December 1997 to 30 November 1999, 40 per cent, and

(*b*) in the case of a relevant disposal made on or after 1 December 1999, 20 per cent.][1]

...[2]

(2) (*a*) Subsection (1) shall not apply to a relevant disposal to which this subsection applies and, accordingly, the rate of capital gains tax in respect of a chargeable gain on such a relevant disposal shall be 20 per cent.

(*b*) This subsection shall apply to the following:

(i) a relevant disposal to which section 650 refers;

(ii) a relevant disposal made in the period from 23 April 1998 to 30 November 1999, being a disposal of land to a housing authority (within the meaning of section 23 of the Housing (Miscellaneous Provisions) Act, 1992) which land is specified in a certificate given by the housing authority as land required for the purposes of the Housing Acts, 1966 to 1998;

(iii) a relevant disposal made in the period from 10 March 1999 to 30 November 1999, being a disposal of land to the National Building Agency Limited or to a body approved for the purposes of section 6 of the Housing (Miscellaneous Provisions) Act, 1992, which land is specified in a certificate given by a housing authority or the National Building Agency Limited, as appropriate, as land required for the purposes of the Housing Acts, 1966 to 1998;

(iv) a relevant disposal made in the period from 23 April 1998 to 30 November 1999, being a disposal of land in respect of the whole of which, at the time at which the disposal is made, permission for residential development has been granted under section 26 of the Local Government (Planning and Development) Act, 1963, and such permission has not ceased to exist, other than a disposal to which paragraph (*c*) applies;

(v) a relevant disposal made in the period from 10 March 1999 to 30 November 1999, being a disposal of land in respect of the whole of which, at the time at which the disposal is made, is, in accordance with a development objective (as indicated in the development plan of the planning authority concerned), for use solely or primarily for residential purposes other than a disposal to which paragraph (*c*) applies.

(*c*) This paragraph shall apply to a relevant disposal being a disposal—

(i) by a person (in this paragraph referred to as the "disponer") to a person who is connected with the disponer, or

(ii) of land under a relevant contract in relation to the disposal.][3]

(3) In this section—

"development plan" has the meaning assigned to it by the Local Government (Planning and Development) Act, 1963;

"planning authority" has the meaning assigned to it by section 2(2) of the Local Government (Planning and Development) Act, 1963;

"relevant contract", in relation to a disposal of land, means a contract or other arrangement under which the land is disposed of which is conditional on permission for development, other than permission for residential development, being granted under section 26 of the Local Government (Planning and Development) Act, 1963, in respect of the land;

"residential development" includes any development which is ancillary to the development and which is necessary for the proper planning and development of the area in question.][4]

Amendments

1 Subs (1)(*a*)–(*b*) substituted by FA 2001 s 94(*a*) with effect from 6 April 2001.

2 Subs (1)(*c*) deleted by FA 2001 s 94(*b*) with effect from 6 April 2001.

3 Subs (1) and (2) substituted by FA 2000 s 86 with effect from 6 April 2000.

4 Section 649A (inserted by FA 1998 s 65(*c*) in relation to disposals made on or after 3 December 1997) substituted by F(No2)A 1998 s 3 with effect from 20 May 1998.

Tax Briefing

TB35 Mar 1999 p 15 — Gain on the grant of a right of way over development land which has planning permission for residential development is chargeable at 40 per cent.

TB39 Mar 2000 p 17 — Development Land — CGT Treatment; relevant disposal: s 648.

TB52 May 2003 p 18 — Part disposal of development land.

Definitions

chargeable gain: s 5(1); land: IA 1937 Sch; person: IA 1937 s 11(*c*).

650 Exclusion of certain disposals

Sections 651 to 653 shall not apply to a relevant disposal made by an individual in any year of assessment if the total consideration in respect of all relevant disposals made by that individual in that year does not exceed [€19,050][1].

Amendments

1 Substituted by FA 2001 s 240(1) and (2)(*b*) and Sch 5 Pt 1 for 2002 and later tax years; previously "£15,000" (short tax "year" 2001: £11,100 (FA 2001 s 77(2) and Sch 2 paras 36 and 61(*a*))).

Cross-references

Rate of charge: s 649A(2)(*b*).

Definitions

relevant disposal: s 648; year of assessment: ss 2(1), 5(1).

Former enactments

FA 1982 s 37.

651 Restriction of indexation relief in relation to relevant disposals

For the purposes of computing the chargeable gain accruing to a person on a relevant disposal, the adjustment of sums allowable as deductions from the consideration for the disposal which under section 556(2) would otherwise be made shall be made only to—

(*a*) such part of the amount or value of the consideration in money or money's worth given by the person or on the person's behalf wholly and exclusively for the acquisition of the asset, together with the incidental costs to the person of the acquisition, as is equal to the current use value of the asset at the date of the acquisition together with such proportion of the incidental costs to the person of the acquisition as would be referable to such value, or

(*b*) in the case of an asset to which section 556(3) applies, such part of the market value of the asset on the 6th day of April, 1974, as is equal to the current use value of the asset on that date.

Cross-references

Development land chargeable gains, £15,000 limit for disposals by individuals: s 650.

Revenue precedents

Issue: Compensation for suspension of milk quota.
Decision: Regarded as a capital receipt.

Definitions

chargeable gain: ss 4(1), 5(1), 534; person: IA 1937 s 11(*c*); relevant disposal: s 648.

Former enactments

FA 1982 s 38.

652 Non-application of reliefs on replacement of assets in case of relevant disposals

(1) Consideration obtained for a relevant disposal shall not be regarded for the purposes of relief under section 597 as having been obtained for the disposal of old assets within the meaning of that section.

(2) (*a*) In this subsection, **"the relevant local authority"**, in relation to a relevant disposal, means the council of a county or the corporation of a county or other borough or, where appropriate, the urban district council, in whose functional area the land being disposed of is situated.

(*b*) Subsection (1) shall not apply to a relevant disposal where the relevant local authority gives a certificate in writing to the person making the disposal stating that the land being disposed of is subject to a use which, on the basis of guidelines issued by the Minister for the Environment and Local Government, is inconsistent with the protection and improvement of the amenities of the general area within which that land is situated or is otherwise damaging to the local environment.

(3) (*a*) In this subsection—

"assets of an authorised racecourse" means assets of a racecourse which is an authorised racecourse where the assets are used for the provision of appropriate facilities or services to carry on horseracing at race meetings or to accommodate persons associated with horseracing, including members of the public;

"authorised racecourse" has the same meaning as in section 2 of the Irish Horseracing Industry Act, 1994.

(*b*) Subject to paragraph (*c*), subsection (1) shall not apply to consideration obtained for a relevant disposal where—

(i) throughout a period of 5 years ending with the time of disposal the old assets, and

(ii) the new assets within the meaning of section 597,

are assets of an authorised racecourse.

(*c*) Section 597 shall apply in relation to assets of an authorised racecourse as if—

(i) references in subsections (4) and (5) of that section to new assets ceasing to be used for the purposes of a trade included a reference to new assets ceasing to be assets of an authorised racecourse, and

(ii) subsection (11)(*b*) had not been enacted.

[(3A)(*a*) In this subsection—

"greyhound race", **"greyhound race track"** and **"greyhound race track licence"** have the same meanings respectively as in section 2 of the Greyhound Industry Act, 1958,

"assets of an authorised greyhound race track" means assets of a greyhound race track which is an authorised greyhound race track where the assets are used for the provision of appropriate facilities or services to hold greyhound races or to accommodate persons associated with greyhound racing, including members of the public;

"authorised greyhound race track" means a greyhound race track in respect of which a greyhound race track licence has been granted, and that licence has not been revoked.

(*b*) Subject to paragraph (*c*), subsection (1) shall not apply to consideration obtained for a relevant disposal where—

(i) throughout a period of 5 years ending with the time of disposal the old assets, and

(ii) the new assets within the meaning of section 597,

are assets of an authorised greyhound race track.

(*c*) Section 597 shall apply in relation to assets of an authorised greyhound race track as if—

(i) references in subsections (4) and (5) of that section to new assets ceasing to be used for the purposes of a trade included a reference to new assets ceasing to be assets of an authorised greyhound race track, and

(ii) subsection (11)(*b*) had not been enacted.

(3B) Subsection (1) shall not apply to consideration obtained for a relevant disposal effected by an order made under section 28(1) of the Dublin Docklands Development Authority Act, 1997.][1]

(4) Section 605 shall not apply to a relevant disposal.

[(5) (*a*) Subsection (4) shall not apply to a relevant disposal made to an authority possessing compulsory purchase powers where the disposal is made—

(i) for the purposes of enabling the authority to construct, widen or extend a road or part of a road, or

(ii) for a purpose connected with or ancillary to the construction, widening or extension of a road or part of a road by the authority.

(*b*) Where section 605 applies to a relevant disposal by virtue of this subsection that section shall be construed as if for subsection (4) of that section the following were substituted:

"(4) This section shall apply only if the acquisition of the replacement assets takes place, or an unconditional contract for the acquisition is entered into, in the period beginning 2 years before and ending 8 years after the disposal of the original assets, or at such earlier or later time as the Revenue Commissioners may by notice in writing allow; but, where an unconditional contract for the acquisition is so entered into, this section may be applied on a provisional basis without ascertaining whether the replacement assets are acquired in pursuance of the contract, and when that fact is ascertained all necessary adjustments shall be made by making assessments or by repayment or discharge of tax, and shall be so made notwithstanding any limitation in the Capital Gains Tax Acts on the time within which assessments may be made.".][2]

(6) Subsections (1) and (4) shall not apply to a relevant disposal made by a body of persons established for the sole purpose of promoting athletic or amateur games or sports, being a disposal which is made in relation to such of the activities of that body as are directed to that purpose.

Amendments

1 Subs (3A) and (3B) inserted by FA 1998 s 73 as respects relevant disposals made on or after 6 April 1998.

2 Subs (5) substituted by FA 2001 s 95(1) as respects relevant disposals made on or after 6 December 2000.

Cross-references

Development land chargeable gains, exclusion of certain disposals by individuals: s 650.

Disposals within family business or farm, subs (5)(*a*): s 598(1)(*a*) ("qualifying assets", para (iv)).

Time of disposal and acquisition, subs (5)(*a*): s 542(1)(*d*).

Revenue precedents

Issue: Does land let and used for farming qualify for relief under TCA 1997 s 605?

Decision: S 652(5) effectively allows relief under s 605 on the disposal of development land to a local authority possessing compulsory purchase powers in certain circumstances. The land in question must be land occupied and used only for the purpose of farming. There is no requirement that the person making the disposal has to have farmed the land him/herself and thus, let land can qualify as long as it has been occupied and used by the lessor for the purposes of farming.

Tax Briefing

TB43 April 2001 p 19 — Disposal of farmland under compulsory purchase order.

Definitions

body of persons: s 2(1); Capital Gains Tax Acts: s 1(2); person: IA 1937 s 11(*c*); relevant disposal: s 648; writing: IA 1937 Sch.

Former enactments

FA 1982 s 39; FA 1995 s 73(1); FA 1997 s 77(1).

653 Restriction of relief for losses, etc in relation to relevant disposals

(1) Notwithstanding any provision to the contrary in the Capital Gains Tax Acts, any losses accruing on disposals which are not relevant disposals shall not, in the computation of a person's liability to capital gains tax in respect of chargeable gains accruing on relevant disposals, be deducted from the amount of those chargeable gains.

(2) In the computation of the amount on which under section 31 capital gains tax is to be charged on chargeable gains accruing on relevant disposals, any allowable losses accruing on relevant disposals may be deducted in accordance with that section but, in so far as they are so deducted, they shall not be treated as relevant allowable losses within the meaning of section 78(4) for the purposes of the calculation required to be made under section 78(2), and for the purposes of this subsection any necessary assessments or additional assessments, as may be appropriate, may be made.

Cross-references

Disposals by liquidators and other persons, meaning of "referable gains tax": s 571(2)(*c*)(ii); meaning of "referable corporation tax": s 571(3)(*c*)(i)(II).

Development land chargeable gains, £15,000 limit for disposals by individuals: s 650.

Definitions

allowable loss: ss 4(1), 5(1), 546; chargeable gain: ss 4(1), 5(1), 534; person: IA 1937 s 11(*c*); relevant disposal: s 648.

Former enactments

FA 1982 s 40(1)–(2).

OTHER SPECIAL PROVISIONS

PART 23
FARMING AND MARKET GARDENING

Cross-reference

Interpretation of Tax Acts: s 2(1)("capital allowance").

Revenue Information

Information Leaflet on Taxation Issues for Milk Production Partnerships.

CHAPTER 1
Interpretation and General

654 Interpretation (Part 23)

In this Part other than in section 664—

"farming" means farming farm land, that is, land in the State wholly or mainly occupied for the purposes of husbandry, other than market garden land;

"market garden land" means land in the State occupied as a nursery or garden for the sale of the produce (other than land used for the growth of hops), and **"market gardening"** shall be construed accordingly;

"occupation", in relation to any land other than market garden land, means having the use of that land or having the right by virtue of any easement (within the meaning of section 96) to graze livestock on that land.

Cross-references

Cattle and milk dealers, meaning of "market garden land" applied: s 53(1).
Disclosure of information to rating authorities, meaning of "occupation" applied: s 1092(3).
Disposals to authority possessing compulsory purchase powers, meaning of "farming" applied: s 605(4A).
Industrial building or structure, includes buildings for the intensive production of cattle, sheep, pigs, poultry or eggs: s 268(1)(*e*).
Industrial building or structure, includes market gardening structures: s 268(1)(*c*).
Leased plant and machinery, restriction on use of allowances: s 404(1)(*a*) (agricultural machinery).
Time of disposal and acquisition, meaning of "farming" applied: s 542(1)(*d*).

Revenue precedents

Issue: Whether bee-keeping fails within the definition of husbandry.
Decision: Revenue accept CCJ decision that bee-keeping is to be regarded as husbandry.
Issue: Is mushroom growing in tunnels regarded as farming within the meaning of Section 654 Taxes Consolidation Act 1997?
Decision: Mushroom growing in tunnels is not regarded as farming within the meaning of Section 654 Taxes Consolidation Act 1997. It is regarded as market gardening. As a consequence, farm buildings allowance, income averaging and stock relief is not available. An industrial buildings allowance is available at the rate of 10%.

Definitions

land: IA 1937 Sch; person: IA 1937 s 11(*c*); trade: s 3(1).

Former enactments

ITA 1967 s 54(1); FA 1974 s 13; FA 1975 s 12; FA 1978 s 12(1); FA 1983 s 120 and Sch 4.

655 Farming and market gardening profits to be charged to tax under Schedule D

(1) For the purposes of the Tax Acts, farming shall be treated as the carrying on of a trade or, as the case may be, of part of a trade, and the profits or gains of farming shall be charged to tax under Case I of Schedule D.

(2) Notwithstanding anything to the contrary in Part 43, farming carried on by any person, whether solely or in partnership, shall be treated as the carrying on of a single trade; but this subsection shall not prejudice or restrict the operation of Chapter 3 of Part 4 where a partnership trade of farming is set up and commenced or is permanently discontinued.

(3) Market gardening shall, for the purposes of the Tax Acts in relation to the person by whom it is carried on, be treated as a trade, and the profits or gains of market gardening shall be charged to tax under Case I of Schedule D.

Cross-references

Farming buildings expenditure: s 658(1).
Farming pollution control capital expenditure: s 659(1)(*a*).

Revenue precedents

Issue: Where compensation is paid for the non-allocation of a milk quota to a partnership can each of the partners claim the reduction outlined in article 1.3 of Tax Briefing No 14?
Decision: No. The reductions outlined in the article should be applied to the compensation amount received by the partnership with the reduced amount forming part of the trading income of the partnership for the year of receipt.
Issue: Are payments from the Department of agriculture under the Flood Damage Relief Scheme 1995 chargeable to Income Tax?
Decision: Yes. It is the Revenue view that these payments, which are in respect of the loss of livestock or fodder, are income receipts liable to income tax in the hands of the recipient.
Issue: What is the taxation treatment of sheep headage and ewe premium payments?
Decision: All headage payments and ewe premia are trading receipts for tax purposes.

Issue: How are the payments received under the EEC Scheme of Installation Aid for Young Farmers taxed?
Decision: The scheme, which was introduced by EEC Council Regulation No. 797/85 provides for the payment to farmers of a single premium. Such a payment may be treated as a capital sum which will not give rise to a charge to Capital Gains Tax as there is no disposal of an asset.
Issue: Whether EU installation grant paid to suitably qualified farmers a capital grant.
Decision: Yes.
Issue: What is the commencement date for the review procedure for the valuation of brood mares?
Decision: The review procedure outlined in the article titled "Book value of Brood Mares" in issue 25 of Tax Briefing operates in respect of accounting periods ending on or after 1 December 1994.

Definitions

person: IA 1937 s 11(*c*); trade: s 3(1).

Former enactments

ITA 1967 s 54(2)(*a*); FA 1969 s 65(1) and Sch 5 Pt I; FA 1974 s 15; FA 1983 s 11.

Corresponding UK tax provision

Income and Corporation Taxes Act 1988 s 53.

656 Farming: trading stock of discontinued trade

(1) In this section, **"specified return date for the chargeable period"** has the same meaning as in section 950.

(2) Where trading stock of a trade of farming is transferred by a farmer (in this subsection referred to as **"the transferor"**) to another farmer (in this subsection referred to as **"the transferee"**), the transferor and the transferee may jointly elect that—

(*a*) section 89(2)(*b*) shall not apply, and

(*b*) in computing their respective profits or gains from farming, the transferor and the transferee shall include such stock at the value at which the stock is included in the accounts of the transferor at the date of discontinuance,

and such election shall be made in writing on or before the specified return date for the chargeable period in which the stock is transferred.

Former enactments

ITA 1967 s 62(1)(proviso); FA 1996 s 11.

657 Averaging of farm profits

(1) In this section—

"an individual to whom subsection (1) applies" means an individual carrying on farming in a year of assessment and—

(*a*) who at any time in the year of assessment is also carrying on either solely or in partnership another trade or profession,

(*b*) whose spouse, in a case where the individual is a married person, is at any time in the year of assessment also carrying on either solely or in partnership another trade or profession, other than a trade consisting solely of the provision of accommodation in buildings on the farm land occupied by the individual, the provision of such accommodation being ancillary to the farming of that farm land,

(*c*) who at any time in the year of assessment is a director of a company carrying on a trade or profession and is either the beneficial owner of, or able, either directly or through the medium of other companies or by any other means, to control, more than 25 per cent of the ordinary share capital of the company, or

(*d*) whose spouse, in a case where the individual is a married person, is at any time in the year of assessment a director of a company carrying on a trade or profession and is either the beneficial owner of, or able, either directly or through the medium of other companies or by any other means, to control, more than 25 per cent of the ordinary share capital of the company,

but paragraphs (*b*) and (*d*) shall not apply in a case where the wife of an individual is treated for tax purposes as not living with her husband;

"company" means a company within the meaning of the Companies Act, 1963;

"director" includes a person holding any office or employment under a company.

(2) The definition of **"an individual to whom subsection (1) applies"** shall apply in the case of a married person whose wife is carrying on farming, and shall apply in such a case as if the references to the individual were references to the individual's wife.

(3) For the purposes of paragraphs (*c*) and (*d*) of the definition of **"an individual to whom subsection (1) applies"**, ordinary share capital which is owned or controlled in the manner referred to in those paragraphs by a person, being the spouse or a minor child of a director, or by the trustee of a trust for the benefit of a person or persons, being or including any such person or such director, shall be deemed to be owned or controlled by such director and not by any other person.

(4) (*a*) Subject to paragraph (*b*), where an assessment in respect of profits or gains from farming is made for any year of assessment on an individual, other than an individual to whom subsection (1) applies, the individual may on giving notice in writing to that effect to the inspector within 30 days after the date of the notice of assessment elect to be charged to income tax for that year in respect of those profits or gains in accordance with subsection (5), and—

(i) the Income Tax Acts shall apply in relation to the assessment as if the notice given to the inspector were a notice of appeal against the assessment under section 933, and

(ii) the assessment shall be amended as necessary so as to give effect to the election so made by the individual.

(*b*) This subsection shall not apply as respects any year of assessment where for either of the 2 immediately preceding years of assessment the individual was not charged to tax in respect of profits or gains from farming in accordance with section 65(1).

(5) (*a*) An individual who is to be charged to income tax for a year of assessment in respect of profits or gains from farming in accordance with this subsection shall be so charged under Case I of Schedule D on the full amount of those profits or gains determined on a fair and just average of the profits or gains from farming of the individual in each of the 3 years ending on the date in the year of assessment to which it has been customary to make up accounts or, where it has not been customary to make up accounts, on [31 December][1] in the year of assessment.

[(*aa*) As respects the year of assessment 2001, this subsection shall apply as if in paragraph (*a*) "74 per cent of the full amount of those profits or gains" were substituted for "the full amount of those profits or gains".

(*ab*) For the purposes of paragraph (*a*), where an individual makes up annual accounts to a date in the period from 1 January 2002 to 5 April 2002, those accounts shall, in addition to being accounts made up to a date in the year of assessment 2002, be treated as accounts made up to a date in the year of assessment 2001.][2]

(*b*) Any profits or gains arising to, and any loss sustained by, the individual in the 3 years referred to in paragraph (*a*) in the carrying on of farming shall be aggregated for the purposes of this subsection.

(6) (*a*) Subject to paragraph (*b*) and subsection (7), where as respects a year of assessment an individual duly elects in accordance with subsection (4), the individual shall be charged to income tax for that year and for each subsequent year of assessment in respect of profits or gains from farming in accordance with subsection (5).

(*b*) This subsection shall not apply for any year of assessment in which the individual—

(i) is an individual to whom subsection (1) applies, or

(ii) is not chargeable to tax on profits or gains from farming.

(7) Where for a year of assessment an individual is by virtue of subsection (6) chargeable to income tax in respect of profits or gains from farming in accordance with subsection (5) and the individual was so chargeable for each of the 3 years of assessment immediately preceding the year of assessment, he or she may, [on including a claim in that behalf with the return required under section 951 for the year of assessment],[3] elect to be charged to tax for that year of assessment in accordance with Chapter 3 of Part 4; but, where in the case of an individual subsection (6) does not apply for any year of assessment by reason of paragraph (*b*)(i) of that subsection, the individual shall be deemed to be entitled to elect and to have duly elected, as respects that year of assessment, in accordance with this subsection.

(8) Where as respects a year of assessment an individual duly elects or is deemed to have elected in accordance with subsection (7)—

(*a*) the individual shall be charged to income tax for that year and for each subsequent year of assessment in accordance with Chapter 3 of Part 4, and

(*b*) there shall be made such assessment or assessments, if any, as may be necessary to secure that the amount of profits or gains from farming on which the individual is charged for each of the 2 years of assessment immediately preceding the year preceding the year of assessment, as respects which the individual elects or is deemed to have elected in accordance with subsection (7), shall be not less than the amount on which the individual is charged by virtue of subsection (6) in accordance with subsection (5) for the year preceding the year of assessment.

[(8A) Where as respects the year of assessment 2002 an individual duly elects or is deemed to have elected in accordance with subsection (7), subsection (8) shall apply as if the following were substituted for paragraph (*b*) of that subsection:

" (*b*) there shall be made such assessment or assessments, if any, as may be necessary to secure that the amount of the profits or gains from farming on which the individual is charged for each of the years of assessment 1999–2000 and 2000–2001 shall be not less than 135 per cent of the amount on which the individual is charged by virtue of subsection (6) in accordance with subsection (5) for the year of assessment 2001.".

(8B) Where as respects the year of assessment 2003 an individual duly elects or is deemed to have elected in accordance with subsection (7), subsection (8) shall apply as if the following were substituted for paragraph (*b*) of that subsection:

"(*b*) there shall be made such assessment or assessments, if any, as may be necessary to secure that the amount of the profits or gains from farming on which the individual is charged for the year of assessment 2000–2001 and the year of assessment 2001 shall be—

(i) in the case of the year of assessment 2000–2001, not less than, and

(ii) in the case of the year of assessment 2001, not less than 74 per cent of,

the amount on which the individual is charged by virtue of subsection (6) in accordance with subsection (5) for the year of assessment 2002.".

(8C) Where as respects the year of assessment 2004 an individual duly elects or is deemed to have elected in accordance with subsection (7), subsection (8) shall apply as if the following were substituted for paragraph (*b*) of that subsection:

"(*b*) there shall be made such assessment or assessments, if any, as may be necessary to secure that the amount of the profits or gains from farming on which the individual is charged for each of the years of assessment 2001 and 2002 shall be—

(i) in the case of the year of assessment 2001, not less than 74 per cent of, and

(ii) in the case of the year of assessment 2002, not less than,

the amount on which the individual is charged by virtue of subsection (6) in accordance with subsection (5) for the year of assessment 2003.".][4]

(9) In determining for any year of assessment what capital allowances, balancing allowances or balancing charges are to be made to or on an individual in taxing a trade of farming in accordance with subsection (5), the individual shall be deemed to be chargeable for that year of assessment in respect of the profits or gains of the trade in accordance with section 65(1).

(10) Nothing in this section shall prejudice or restrict the operation of section 67 in any case where a trade of farming is permanently discontinued.

(11) Where for any year of assessment a loss is aggregated with profits or gains in accordance with subsection (5)(*b*) and the amount of the loss is in excess of the profits or gains, one-third of the amount of such excess shall be deemed for the purposes of Chapter 1 of Part 12 to be a loss sustained in the trade of farming in the final year of the

3 years on the average of the profits or gains of which the individual is to be charged to tax for that year of assessment, and any loss so aggregated shall not be eligible for relief under any provision of the Income Tax Acts apart from this subsection.

[(11A) As respects the year of assessment 2001, subsection (11) shall apply as if in that subsection "74 per cent of one-third of the amount of such excess" were substituted for "one-third of the amount of such excess" and, where this subsection applies, the individual may claim that 26 per cent of one-third of the amount of the excess referred to in subsection (11) shall, notwithstanding anything to the contrary in that subsection, be carried forward under section 382 for deduction from or set-off against the profits or gains of the individual from farming for any subsequent year of assessment.][5]

(12) The profits or gains from farming on which an individual is to be charged to tax for any year of assessment by virtue of subsection (6) in accordance with subsection (5) shall be deemed to be the profits or gains from farming of that individual in determining his or her total income for that year for the purposes of the Income Tax Acts apart from this section, and any provision of those Acts relating to the delivery of any return, account (including balance sheet), statement, declaration, book, list or other document or the furnishing of any particulars shall apply as if this section had not been enacted.

Amendments

1 Substituted by FA 2001 s 77(2) and Sch 2 para 37(*a*)(i) with effect from 6 April 2001; previously "the 5th day of April".

2 Subs (5)(*aa*)–(*ab*) inserted by FA 2001 s 77(2) and Sch 2 para 37(*a*)(ii) with effect from 6 April 2001.

3 Substituted by FA 2001 s 78(2)(*c*) for the short tax "year" 2001 and later tax years (income tax and capital gains tax) and as respects accounting periods of companies ending on or after 1 April 2001; previously "by notice in writing given to the inspector with the return required under section 951 for the year of assessment".

4 Subss (8A)–(8C) inserted by FA 2001 s 77(2) and Sch 2 para 37(*b*) with effect from 6 April 2001.

5 Subs (11A) inserted by FA 2001 s 77(2) and Sch 2 para 37(*c*) with effect from 6 April 2001.

Cross-references

Taxation of certain farm payments, subs (5): s 657A(1) ("relevant individual").

Revenue precedents

Issue: Where there is a farming loss but a balancing charge arises is the taxpayer "charged to tax in respect of profits or gains from farming" for that year for the purposes of s 657(4)(*b*)?
Decision: No.

Issue: What is the position regarding averaging in situations where a farmer is a sole trader and also farming in partnership?
Decision: Where a taxpayer has farming income as a sole trader and also income from a farming partnership, on an ongoing basis, the income averaging rules should be applied to both businesses in view of the fact that under s 655 all farming carried on by any person whether solely or in partnership is treated as the carrying on of a single trade.

Issue: Can the taxable amount of "Mulder compensation", as computed in accordance with Article 1.3 of Tax Briefing No. 14, be averaged in the normal way?
Decision: Yes.

Issue: Qualification for income averaging - (i) losses incurred (ii) commencement of farming in partnership.
Decision: (i) The fact that a farmer incurs a loss while on income averaging does not affect his entitlement to be on income averaging. (ii) Where a farmer trading as a sole trader on income averaging starts trading as a partner, Revenue would be prepared to allow income averaging to continue for existing farming activities; once the partnership trade had been in existence for sufficiently long to be assessed for two years in accordance with TCA 1997 s 65(1), the farmer could opt for averaging in respect of this trade.

Issue: A father and son farm in partnership. If the father decides to retire and the son continues to farm as a sole trader, is the son entitled to continue on income averaging. What review procedure applies in these circumstances?

Decision: The cessation of a partnership trade and the commencement of a sole trade will not affect an individual's entitlement to income averaging. TCA 1997 s 657(6))(*a*) provides that once an individual elects for income averaging he is charged to tax for each year of assessment in respect of profits based on a 3 year average. He will continue to be charged in this manner until either of the following applies: (*a*) he is an individual to whom subs (1) applies, in which case he is deemed to elect to opt out of averaging (*b*) he is not chargeable to tax on farming profits (*c*) he elects to opt out of averaging (*d*) he is deemed to elect to opt out of average. This only applies in the case of (*a*). A review, for the purposes of s 657(8)(*b*) , will therefore not be required in these circumstances as the individual has not elected or deemed to have elected out of averaging. A review will however be necessary under TCA 1997 s 67 of both the father's and son's assessments.

Issue: Where a farmer, who is on income averaging in respect of a sole trade of farming, commences to carry on farming in partnership, will he be entitled to elect for averaging in respect of the partnership trade?

Decision: An individual who, in addition to carrying on a sole trade of farming, the profits of which are charged to tax by virtue of TCA 1997 s 657, commences to carry on farming in partnership so that part of his profits from the single trade of farming are charged to tax under income averaging and part are charged in accordance with the provisions of TCA 1997 s 66(1), might not, strictly speaking, be entitled to elect for income averaging. In practice, however, each part of the overall trade would be looked at separately, so that the income averaging could continue to be allowed in respect of the sole trade, and income averaging could be claimed as soon as the partnership had been assessed in accordance with s 65(1), TCA 1997, for the requisite two preceding years.

Issue: Will a surviving spouse be entitled to continue on income averaging where the deceased spouse had formerly been on such income averaging?

Decision: Where, on the death of a spouse, who was on income averaging, the farming trade passes in its entirety to the person's surviving spouse, that spouse will be regarded as continuing on income averaging.

Issue: A farmer availed of income averaging for a number of years and then ceased to trade. On the discontinuance of the trade a review of the penultimate year is required. Is the revision based on a comparison of the actual profits and the current year profits or with the "averaged" profits?

Decision: Subs (10) of TCA 1997 s 657 ensures that the provisions of TCA 1997 s 67 will operate, even where an election has been made for income averaging. If the actual profits of the penultimate year exceed the "averaged" profit on which the person has been charged, the person will instead be charged on the actual profits or gains of that year.

Issue: A farmer elects for income averaging for a year of assessment. The following year he commences to carry on another trade. A review is therefore required under TCA 1997 s 657(8)(*b*). Given that averaging was only in operation for one year would the revision apply to the averaged year only?

Decision: TCA 1997 s 657(8)(*b*) provides that where an individual is deemed to have elected out of income averaging, the amount of profits or gains from farming upon which he is charged for each of the two years of assessment immediately preceding the year preceding the year of assessment in which he is deemed to have elected out will be reviewed. The Act makes no provision for a lesser review period where the person was not charged to tax by virtue of the provisions of s 657 for three or more years.

Issue: A farmer, by notice in writing, elected to be charged to tax for a year of assessment in accordance with the provisions of TCA 1997 s 657. Is there any concession by which he may be regarded as not having made the election?

Decision: TCA 1997 s 657 does not provide for the reversal of an election. There is no non-statutory practice whereby this election may be regarded as not having been made.

Issue: A farmer's trading profits for a year of assessment are nil due to stock relief. Profits arose in the two years prior to that year. Is the farmer entitled to claim income averaging for the year subsequent to the year in which the stock relief was claimed?

Decision: An individual is not entitled to elect to be charged to tax, for a year of assessment, in respect of farming profits, under TCA 1997 s 657, where the individual was not charged to tax in either of the two immediately preceding years in respect of profits from farming on the current year basis (ie in accordance with TCA 1997 s 65(1)). Stock relief is given as a deduction in computing an individual's trading profits. An individual cannot be regarded as being charged to tax in respect of profits if no trading profits arise.

Definitions

Income Tax Acts: s 1(2); inspector: ss 2(1), 5(1), 852; person: IA 1937 s 11(*c*); profession: s 2(1); profits or gains: s 3(4); standard rate: ss 3(1), 15; total income: s 3(1); trade: s 3(1); year of assessment: ss 2(1), 5(1).

Former enactments

FA 1974 s 16(1)–(2) and (4)–(5) and s 20B (apart from proviso to subs (2)(*b*)); FA 1975 s 14(1)(*a*) and (*b*); FA 1977 s 10; FA 1981 s 10; FA 1983 s 120 and Sch 4; FA 1990 s 20(2); FA 1997 s 146(2) and Sch 9 Pt II.

657A Taxation of certain farm payments

[(1) In this section—

"relevant individual" means an individual who is in receipt of—

(*a*) a relevant payment or relevant payments, and

(*b*) a payment under the EU Single Payment Scheme operated by the Department of Agriculture and Food under Council Regulation No 1782/2003 of 29 September 2003 (OJ No L270 of 21.10.2003, p 1),

in respect of both of which the individual would be, apart from this section, chargeable to income tax on the profits or gains from farming for the year of assessment 2005, but does not include an individual who in the year of assessment 2005 is chargeable to income tax in respect of profits or gains from farming in accordance with subsection (5) of section 657;

"relevant payment" means a payment made at any time in the calendar year 2005 to an individual under any of the EU schemes specified in the Table to this section.

(2) A relevant individual may elect to have the aggregate of all relevant payments made to the individual treated in accordance with subsections (3) to (6), and each such election shall be made in such form and contain such information as the Revenue Commissioners may require.

(3) Notwithstanding any other provision of the Income Tax Acts apart from subsection (4), where an individual elects in accordance with subsection (2), the relevant payment or relevant payments shall be disregarded as respects the year of assessment 2005 and shall instead be treated for the purposes of the Income Tax Acts as arising in equal instalments in the year of assessment 2005 and in the 2 immediately succeeding years of assessment.

(4) Where a trade of farming is permanently discontinued, tax shall be charged under Case IV of Schedule D for the year of assessment in which such discontinuation takes place in respect of the amount of any relevant payment which would, but for such discontinuance, be treated by virtue of subsection (3) as arising in a year of assessment or years of assessment ending after such discontinuance.

(5) An election under subsection (2) by a person to whom this section applies, shall be made by notice in writing on or before 31 October 2006 and shall be included in the annual statement required to be delivered on or before that date under the Income Tax Acts of the profits or gains from farming for the year of assessment 2005.

(6) Subject to subsection (4) an election made under subsection (2) cannot be altered or varied during the period to which it refers.

TABLE

1.	Special Beef Premium Schemes.
2.	Suckler Cow Premium Scheme.
3.	Ewe Premium Schemes.
4.	Extensification Payments Scheme.
5.	Slaughter Premium Scheme.

6. Arable Aid Schemes.
7. National Envelope Top-Ups.][1]

Amendments

1 Section 657A inserted by FA 2005 s 29 with effect from 1 January 2005.

Definitions

Income Tax Acts: s 1(2); profits or gains: s 3(4); writing: IA 1937 Sch; year of assessment: s 2(1).

658 Farming: allowances for capital expenditure on construction of buildings and other works

(1) This section shall apply to any person carrying on farming, the profits or gains of which are chargeable to tax in accordance with section 655.

(2) (*a*) Where a person to whom this section applies incurs, for the purpose of a trade of farming land occupied by such person, any capital expenditure on the construction of farm buildings (excluding a building or part of a building used as a dwelling), fences, roadways, holding yards, drains or land reclamation or other works, there shall be made to such person during a writing-down period of 7 years beginning with the chargeable period related to that expenditure, writing-down allowances (in this section referred to as **"farm buildings allowances"**) in respect of that expenditure and such allowances shall be made in taxing the trade.

(*b*) As respects each of the first 6 years of the writing-down period, the farm buildings allowance to be made under this subsection shall be 15 per cent of the capital expenditure referred to in paragraph (*a*) and, as respects the last year of the writing-down period, the farm buildings allowance to be made under this subsection shall be 10 per cent of that expenditure.

(*c*) Where the capital expenditure referred to in paragraph (*a*) was incurred before the 27th day of January, 1994, this section shall apply subject to paragraph 23 of Schedule 32.

(3) For the purposes of the application to this section of section 321, **"basis period"** has the meaning assigned to it by section 306.

(4) Where for any year of assessment an individual is not chargeable to income tax in respect of profits or gains from farming in accordance with Chapter 3 of Part 4, and that year is a year of assessment in respect of which, if the individual had been so chargeable, he or she could have claimed a farm buildings allowance under this section, that allowance shall for the purposes of this section be deemed to have been made for that year of assessment and shall not be carried forward and set off against profits or gains chargeable for any subsequent year of assessment.

(5) Any capital expenditure incurred by a person about to carry on farming but before commencing farming shall for the purposes of this section be treated as if it had been incurred on the first day on which the person commences farming.

(6) Any claim for a farm buildings allowance to be made to a person under this section shall be included in the annual statement required to be delivered by the person under the Income Tax Acts of the profits or gains from farming, and section 304(4) shall apply

in relation to the allowance as it applies in relation to allowances to be made under Part 9.

(7) Any claim for a farm buildings allowance under this section shall be made to and determined by the inspector, but any person aggrieved by any decision of the inspector on any such claim may, on giving notice in writing to the inspector within 21 days after the notification to that person of the decision, appeal to the Appeal Commissioners.

(8) The Appeal Commissioners shall hear and determine an appeal to them made under subsection (7) as if it were an appeal against an assessment to tax, and the provisions of the Income Tax Acts relating to the rehearing of an appeal and to the statement of a case for the opinion of the High Court on a point of law shall apply accordingly with any necessary modifications.

(9) Subject to subsection (10), where a person who is entitled to a farm buildings allowance under this section in respect of capital expenditure incurred for the purpose of farming farm land transfers such person's interest in that farm land or any part of that farm land to another person, that other person shall, to the exclusion of the first-mentioned person, be entitled to the allowances under this section for the chargeable periods following the chargeable period in which the transfer of interest took place.

(10) Where the transfer of interest to which subsection (9) refers takes place in relation to part of the farm land, subsection (9) shall apply to so much of the allowance as is properly referable to that part of the land as if it were a separate allowance.

(11) Where expenditure is incurred partly for the purposes of farming and partly for other purposes, subsection (2) shall apply to so much only of that expenditure as on a just apportionment ought fairly to be treated as incurred for the purposes of farming.

(12) No farm buildings allowance shall be made by virtue of this section in respect of any expenditure if for the same or any other chargeable period an allowance is or has been made in respect of that expenditure under Chapter 1 of Part 9.

(13) Expenditure shall not be regarded for the purposes of this section as having been incurred by a person in so far as it has been or is to be met directly or indirectly by the State or by any person other than the first-mentioned person.

Cross-references

Capital allowance is given on VAT exclusive expenditure: s 319(1)(*b*).

Chargeable period and general provisions: s 321(*c*).

Expenditure incurred before 27 January 1994: Sch 32 para 23(1)(*a*).

Farming pollution control capital expenditure: s 659(11).

Non-resident company within the charge to corporation tax in respect of one source and income tax in respect of another: s 309(*c*).

Revenue precedents

Issue: If a farmer retires and leases his buildings to another farmer can he continue to claim the remaining farm buildings allowances in respect of the buildings?

Decision: No. In order to qualify for the farm buildings allowances he must be carrying on farming, the profits or gains of which are chargeable in accordance with s 655.

Issue: Farmer lets farm building to partnership in which he is a partner; is Farm Buildings allowance due?

Decision: Yes, provided the building is let at market value and the payment is not in respect of services to the partnership. If the farmer introduces the buildings into the partnership, the capital allowances would go to the partnership.

Issue: A farmer proposes to transfer his farm to a trust under which he would retain a life interest with remainder interests to a discretionary settlement in favour of his children. The issue arising is whether the person would not be regarded as having transferred his interest to another person for the purposes of TCA 1997 s 658(9), having regard to the retention of a life interest in that asset and to the fact that it is he, rather than the trust, which will be continuing the trade of farming on the land.

Decision: Where a person transfers a farm to a trust, with the retention of a life interest, there will be a transfer for the purposes of TCA 1997 s 658(9).

Issue: If a Local Authority carries out accommodation works such as fencing as part of the compensation given for land acquired under a compulsory purchase order is the farmer entitled to farm buildings allowance in respect of that expenditure?

Decision: Section 658 Taxes Consolidation Act 1997 provides that a farm buildings allowance will be made where a farmer incurs any capital expenditure on the construction of farm buildings. The agreement of the compensation terms arising under the Compulsory Purchase Order does not amount to a contract under which a farmer may be regarded as having incurred expenditure. Accordingly, such allowances are not available.

Tax Briefing

TB20 No.4 of 1995 par1.2 — Race Horse Trainers and Title to Farm Buildings Allowances.

Definitions

Appeal Commissioners: s 2(1); High Court: IA 1937 Sch; Income Tax Acts: s 1(2); inspector: ss 2(1), 5(1), 852; local authority: s 2(1); person: IA 1937 s 11(*c*); statute: IA 1937 s 3; trade: s 3(1); writing: IA 1937 Sch; year of assessment: ss 2(1), 5(1).

Former enactments

FA 1974 s 22(1)–(3) and (5)–(11); CTA 1976 s 21(1) and Sch 1 para 70; FA 1983 s 15; FA 1993 s 34(2); FA 1994 s 23.

659 Farming: allowances for capital expenditure on the construction of farm buildings, etc for control of pollution

(1) This section shall apply to any person—

(*a*) carrying on farming, the profits or gains of which are charge able to tax in accordance with section 655,

(*b*) for whom, in respect of capital expenditure to which paragraph (*c*) refers and in respect of farm land occupied by him or her, a farm nutrient management plan has been drawn up by an agency or planner approved to draw up such plans by the Department of Agriculture and Food, and drawn up in accordance with—

(i) the guidelines in relation to such plans entitled **"Farm Nutrient Management Plan"** issued by the Department of Agriculture, Food and Forestry on the 21st day of March, 1997, or

(ii) a plan drawn up under the scheme known as the Rural Environment Protection Scheme (REPS) or the scheme known as the Erne Catchment Nutrient Management Scheme, both being schemes administered by the Department of Agriculture and Food,

and

(*c*) who incurs capital expenditure on or after the 6th day of April, 1997, and before [1 January 2009][1] on the construction of those farm buildings (excluding a building or part of a building used as a dwelling) or structures specified in the Table to this section in the course of a trade of farming land occupied by such person where such building or structures are constructed in accordance with that farm nutrient management plan and are certified as being necessary by that agency or planner for the purpose of securing a reduction in or the elimination of any pollution arising from the trade of farming.

[(2) (*a*) Subject to the provisions of Article 6 of Council Regulation (EEC) No. 2328/91 of 15 July 1991 (OJ No L218, 6.8.1991, p 1), on improving the efficiency of agricultural structures, as amended, and subject to subsections (3) and (3A), where a person to whom this section applies—

(i) has delivered to the Department of Agriculture, Food and Rural Development a farm nutrient management plan referred to in subsection (1)(*b*), and

(ii) incurs capital expenditure to which subsection (1) applies,

there shall be made to such person during the writing-down periods, specified in paragraph (*b*), writing-down allowances (in this section referred to as "farm pollution control allowances") in respect of that expenditure and such allowances shall be made in taxing the trade.

(*b*) The writing-down periods referred to in paragraph (*a*) shall be—

(i) 8 years beginning with the chargeable period related to the capital expenditure, where that expenditure is incurred before [6 April 2000,][2]

(ii) 7 years beginning with the chargeable period related to the capital expenditure, where that expenditure is incurred on or after [6 April 2000 but before 1 January 2005, or][3][4]

[(iii) 3 years beginning with the chargeable period related to the capital expenditure, where that expenditure is incurred on or after 1 January 2005.][5]

(3) The farm pollution control allowances to be made in accordance with subsection (2) in respects of capital expenditure incurred in a chargeable period shall be—

[(*a*) as respects the first year of the writing-down period referred to in subsection (2)(*b*)(i), where the capital expenditure was incurred—

(i) before 6 April 1998, an amount equal to 50 per cent of that expenditure or [€12,700][6], whichever is the lesser,

(ii) on or after 6 April 1998 and before 6 April 2000, an amount equal to 50 per cent of that expenditure or [€19,050][7], whichever is the lesser,][8]

(*b*) as respects the next 6 years of that writing-down period, an amount equal to 15 per cent of the balance of that expenditure after deducting the amount of any allowance made by virtue of paragraph (*a*), and

(*c*) as respects the last year of that writing-down period, an amount equal to 10 per cent of the balance of that expenditure after deducting the amount of any allowance made by virtue of paragraph (*a*).

[(3A) The farm pollution control allowances to be made in accordance with subsection (2) during the writing-down period referred to in subsection (2)(*b*)(ii), in respect of capital expenditure incurred in a chargeable period, where that expenditure is incurred [on or after 6 April 2000 but before 1 January 2005 shall,][9] subject to subsection (3B), be an amount equal to—

(*a*) 15 per cent of that expenditure incurred for each of the first 6 years of the writing-down period, and (*b*) 10 per cent of that expenditure for the last year of the writing-down period.

[(3AA) The farm pollution control allowances to be made in accordance with subsection (2) during the writing-down period referred to in subsection (2)(*b*)(iii) in respect of capital expenditure incurred in a chargeable period, shall where that expenditure is incurred on or after 1 January 2005, and subject to subsection (3BA), be an amount equal to 33$\frac{1}{3}$ per cent of that expenditure incurred for each of the 3 years of the writing-down period.][10]

(3B)(*a*) [In this subsection and subsection (3BA)][11]—

"residual amount", in relation to capital expenditure incurred in a chargeable period, means an amount equal to 50 per cent of that expenditure or [€31,750][12] whichever is the lesser;

"specified amount", in relation to capital expenditure incurred in a chargeable period, means the balance of that expenditure after deducting the [residual amount.][13]

...[14]

(*b*) Notwithstanding subsection (3A), where farm pollution control allowances are to be made to a person in accordance with that subsection during the writing-down period referred to in subsection (2)(*b*)(ii), such person may elect to have those allowances made in accordance with this subsection and, where such person so elects, the allowances shall be made in accordance with this subsection only.

(*c*) Where paragraph (*b*) applies to a person, the farm pollution control allowance to be made to such person during the writing-down period referred to in subsection (2)(*b*)(ii) shall be an amount equal to—

(i) 15 per cent of the specified amount for each of the first 6 years of the writing-down period, and

(ii) 10 per cent of the specified amount for the last year of the writing-down period, and

(iii) subject to paragraph (*d*), the whole or any part of the residual amount, as is specified by the person to whom the allowances are to be made, in any year of the writing-down period.

(*d*) The allowances to be made in accordance with subparagraphs (i) and (iii) of paragraph (*c*) or subparagraphs (ii) and (iii) of that paragraph, as the case may be, for any year of the writing-down period, shall not in the aggregate exceed the residual amount.

[(3BA)(*a*)Notwithstanding subsection (3AA), where farm pollution control allowances are to be made to a person in accordance with that subsection during the writing-down period referred to in subsection (2)(*b*)(iii), such person may elect to have those allowances made in accordance with this subsection and, where such person so elects, the allowances shall be made in accordance with this subsection only.

(*b*) Where paragraph (*a*) applies to a person, the farm pollution control allowance to be made to such person during the writing-down period referred to in subsection (2)(*b*)(iii) shall be an amount equal to—

(i) $33\frac{1}{3}$ per cent of the specified amount for each of the 3 years of the writing-down period, and

(ii) subject to paragraph (*c*), the whole or any part of the residual amount, as is specified by the person to whom the allowances are to be made, in any year of the writing-down period.

(*c*) The allowances to be made in accordance with paragraph (*b*) for any year of the writing-down period, shall not in the aggregate exceed the residual amount.][15]

[(3C)(*a*) An election by a person to whom this section applies in relation to the farm pollution control allowances claimed in subsection (3B) or (3BA), as the case may be, shall be made in writing on or before the specified return date for the chargeable period (within the meaning of section 950) in which the expenditure is incurred and shall be included in the annual statement required to be delivered under the Income Tax Acts of the profits or gains from farming as set out in subsection (5).][16]

(*b*) An election made under the provision of paragraph (*a*) cannot be altered or varied during the writing-down period to which it refers.][17]

(4) For the purposes of the application to this section of section 321, **"basis period"** has the meaning assigned to it by section 306.

(5) Any claim by a person for a farm pollution control allowance to be made to such person shall be included in the annual statement required to be delivered under the Income Tax Acts of the profits or gains from farming, and section 304(4) shall apply in relation to the allowance as it applies in relation to allowances to be made under Part 9.

(6) Any claim for a farm pollution control allowance shall be made to and determined by the inspector, but any person aggrieved by any decision of the inspector on any such claim may, on giving notice in writing to the inspector within 21 days after the notification to the person of the decision, appeal to the Appeal Commissioners.

(7) The Appeal Commissioners shall hear and determine an appeal to them made under subsection (6) as if it were an appeal against an assessment to tax, and the provisions of the Income Tax Acts relating to the rehearing of an appeal and to the statement of a case for the opinion of the High Court on a point of law shall apply accordingly with any necessary modifications.

(8) Subject to subsection (9), where a person who is entitled to farm pollution control allowances in respect of farm land occupied by the person transfers his or her interest in that farm land or any part of that farm land to another person, that other person shall, to the exclusion of the first-mentioned person, be entitled to the allowances under this section for the chargeable periods following the chargeable period in which the transfer of interest took place.

(9) Where the transfer of interest to which subsection (8) refers took place in relation to part of the farm land, subsection (8) shall apply to so much of the farm pollution control allowance as is properly referable to that part of the land as if it were a separate allowance.

(10) Where expenditure is incurred partly for a purpose for which a farm pollution control allowance is to be made and partly for another purpose, subsection (2) shall

apply to so much only of that expenditure as on a just apportionment ought fairly to be treated as incurred for the first-mentioned purpose.

(11) No farm pollution control allowance shall be made in respect of any expenditure if for the same or any other chargeable period an allowance is or has been made in respect of that expenditure under [Chapter 1 or Chapter 2][18] of Part 9 or section 658.

(12) Expenditure shall not be regarded for the purposes of this section as having been incurred by a person in so far as it has been or is to be met directly or indirectly by the State or by any person other than the first-mentioned person.

(13) For the purposes only of determining, in relation to a claim for a farm pollution control allowance, whether and to what extent capital expenditure incurred on the construction of a building or structure to which this section applies is incurred or not incurred in the period specified in subsection (1)(*c*), only such an amount of that capital expenditure as is properly attributable to work on the construction of the building or structure actually carried out during that period shall (notwithstanding any other provision of the Tax Acts as to the time when any capital expenditure is or is to be treated as incurred) be treated as having been incurred in that period.

TABLE

Farm Buildings and Structures to Which Allowances for the Control of Pollution Apply

1. Waste storage facilities including slurry tanks.
2. Soiled water tanks.
3. Effluent tanks.
4. Tank fences and covers.
5. Dungsteads and manure pits.
6. Yard drains for storm and soiled water removal.
7. Walled silos, silage bases and silo aprons.
8. Housing for cattle, including drystock accommodation, byres, loose houses, slatted houses, sloped floor houses and kennels, roofed feed or exercise yards where such houses or structures eliminate soiled water.
9. Housing for sheep and unroofed wintering structures for sheep and sheep dipping tanks.

Amendments

1 Substituted by FA 2005 s 30(*a*) with effect from 1 January 2005; previously "1 January 2007".

2 Substituted by FA 2005 s 30(*b*)(i) with effect from 1 January 2005; previously "6 April 2000, or".

3 Substituted by FA 2005 s 30(*b*)(ii) with effect from 1 January 2005; previously "6 April 2000,".

4 Subs (2) substituted by FA 2000 s 60(*b*)(i) with effect from 6 April 2000.

5 Subs (2)(*b*)(iii) inserted by FA 2005 s 30(*b*)(iii) with effect from 1 January 2005.

6 Substituted by FA 2001 s 240(1) and (2)(*a*) and (*c*) and Sch 5 Pt 1 for 2002 and later tax years in the case of income tax and for accounting periods ending on or after 1 January 2002 in the case of corporation tax; previously "£10,000".

7 Substituted by FA 2001 s 240(1) and (2)(*a*) and (*c*) and Sch 5 Pt 1 for 2002 and later tax years in the case of income tax and for accounting periods ending on or after 1 January 2002 in the case of corporation tax; previously "£15,000".

8 Subs (3)(*a*) substituted by FA 2000 s 60(*b*)(ii) with effect from 6 April 2000.
9 Substituted by FA 2005 s 30(*c*) with effect from 1 January 2005; previously "6 April 2000,".
10 Subs (3AA) inserted by FA 2005 s 30(*d*) with effect from 1 January 2005.
11 Substituted by FA 2005 s 30(*e*)(i) with effect from 1 January 2005; previously "In this subsection".
12 Substituted by FA 2001 s 240(1) and (2)(*a*) and (*c*) and Sch 5 Pt 1 for 2002 and later tax years in the case of income tax and for accounting periods ending on or after 1 January 2002 in the case of corporation tax; previously "£25,000".
13 Substituted by FA 2005 s 30(*e*)(ii) with effect from 1 January 2005; previously "residual amount;".
14 Deleted by FA 2005 s 30(*e*)(iii) with effect from 1 January 2005; previously "'specified return date for the chargeable period' has the same meaning as in section 950.".
15 Subs (3BA) inserted by FA 2005 s 30(*f*) with effect from 1 January 2005.
16 Subs (3C)(*a*) substituted by FA 2005 s 30(*g*) with effect from 1 January 2005.
17 Subs (3A)–(3C) inserted by FA 2000 s 60(*b*)(iii) with effect from 6 April 2000.
18 Substituted by FA 2005 s 30(*h*) with effect from 1 January 2005; previously "Chapter 1".

Cross-references

Capital allowance is given on VAT-exclusive expenditure: s 319(1)(*b*).
Chargeable period and general provisions: s 321(1)(*c*).

Definitions

Appeal Commissioners: ss 2(1), 850; High Court: IA 1937 Sch; Income Tax Acts: s 1(2); person: IA 1937 s 11(*c*); profits or gains: s 3(4); writing: IA 1937 Sch.

Former enactments

FA 1997 s 20(1)–(13).

---

660 Farming: wear and tear allowances deemed to have been made in certain cases

(1) In this section—

"balancing allowance" and **"balancing charge"** have the same meanings respectively as in Chapter 2 of Part 9;

"wear and tear allowance" means an allowance made under section 284.

(2) In determining whether any, and if so what, wear and tear allowance, balancing allowance or balancing charge in respect of machinery or plant is to be made to or on any person for any chargeable period in taxing a trade of farming, there shall be deemed to have been made to that person, for every previous chargeable period in which the machinery or plant belonged to that person and which is a chargeable period to be taken into account for the purpose of this section, such wear and tear allowance or greater wear and tear allowance, if any, in respect of the machinery or plant as would have been made to that person if, in relation to every such previous chargeable period—

(*a*) the profits or gains from farming had been chargeable to tax under Case I of Schedule D,

(*b*) those profits or gains had been charged to tax in accordance with section 58 of the Income Tax Act, 1967, and not in an amount determined under section 21 of the Finance Act, 1974,

(*c*) farming had been carried on by that person since the date on which that person acquired the machinery or plant,

(*d*) the machinery or plant had been used by that person solely for the purposes of farming since that date, and

(*e*) a proper claim had been duly made by that person for wear and tear allowance in respect of the machinery or plant for every relevant chargeable period.

(3) There shall be taken into account for the purposes of this section every previous chargeable period in which the machinery or plant concerned belonged to the person and—

(*a*) during which the machinery or plant was not used by the person for the purposes of farming,

(*b*) in respect of which the person was charged to tax on an amount determined in accordance with section 21 of the Finance Act, 1974,

(*c*) during which farming was not carried on by the person, or

(*d*) during which farming was carried on by the person in such circumstances that the full amount of the profits or gains of farming was not liable to be charged to tax under Case I of Schedule D.

(4) In the case of a company (within the meaning of section 4(1)), subsection (2)(*c*) shall not alter the periods which are to be taken as chargeable periods but, if during any period after the 5th day of April, 1976, and after the company acquired the machinery or plant, the company has not been within the charge to corporation tax, any year of assessment or part of a year of assessment falling within that period shall be taken as a chargeable period as if it had been an accounting period of the company.

(5) Nothing in this section shall affect section 288(4).

Cross-references

Chargeable period and general provisions: s 321(1)(*c*).

Non-resident company within the charge to corporation tax in respect of one source and income tax in respect of another: s 309(*c*).

Definitions

person: IA 1937 s 11(*c*); profits or gains: s 3(4); trade: s 3(1); year of assessment: ss 2(1), 5(1).

Former enactments

FA 1974 s 25; CTA 1976 s 21(1) and Sch 1 para 71; FA 1978 s 14(*c*).

661 Farming: restriction of relief in respect of certain losses

(1) This section shall apply to a loss sustained by a person in the carrying on of farming in any year of assessment, being a year for which such person was not chargeable to tax in respect of profits or gains from farming.

(2) No relief shall be given under section 382 in respect of a loss to which this section applies by deducting such loss from or setting it off against the amount of the profits or gains from farming assessed for any year of assessment.

Definitions

person: IA 1937 s 11(*c*); profits or gains: s 3(4); year of assessment: ss 2(1), 5(1).

Former enactments

FA 1978 s 15(1)–(2); FA 1983 s 120 and Sch 4.

662 Income tax: restriction of relief for losses in farming or market gardening

(1) In this section—

"prior 3 years", in relation to a loss incurred in a year of assessment, means the last 3 years of assessment before that year;

"prior period of loss" means the prior 3 years or, if losses were incurred in successive years of assessment amounting in the aggregate to a period longer than 3 years (and ending when the prior 3 years end), that longer period.

(2) (*a*) Any loss (including any amount in respect of allowances which by virtue of section 392 is to be treated as a loss) incurred in a trade of farming or market gardening shall not be available for relief under section 381 unless it is shown that, for the year of assessment in which the loss is claimed to have been incurred, the trade was being carried on on a commercial basis and with a view to the realisation of profits in the trade.

(*b*) Without prejudice to paragraph (*a*), any loss (including any amount in respect of allowances which by virtue of section 392 is to be treated as a loss) incurred in any year of assessment in a trade of farming or market gardening shall not be available for relief under section 381 if in each of the prior 3 years a loss was incurred in carrying on that trade.

(*c*) For the purposes of this section, the fact that a trade of farming or market gardening was being carried on at any time so as to afford a reasonable expectation of profit shall be conclusive evidence that it was then being carried on with a view to the realisation of profits.

(*d*) This subsection shall not restrict relief for any loss or any capital allowance where it is shown by the claimant—

(i) that the whole of the claimant's farming or market gardening activities in the year following the prior 3 years are of such a nature, and carried on in such a way, as would have justified a reasonable expectation of the realisation of profits in the future if those activities had been undertaken by a competent farmer or market gardener, and

(ii) that if such farmer or market gardener had undertaken those activities at the beginning of the prior period of loss, such farmer or market gardener could not reasonably have expected those activities to become profitable until after the end of the year following the prior period of loss.

(*e*) This subsection shall not restrict relief where the carrying on of the trade forms part of and is ancillary to a larger trading undertaking.

(3) In ascertaining for the purposes of this section whether a loss was incurred in any year, the rules applicable to Case I of Schedule D shall be applied.

(4) Where a trade of farming or market gardening is or is to be treated as being carried on for a part only of a year of assessment by reason of its being set up and commenced, or discontinued, or both, in that year, subsection (2) shall apply in relation to that trade as regards that part of that year.

(5) Subsection (2) shall not restrict relief for any loss or capital allowance if the trade was set up and commenced within the prior 3 years, and for the purposes of this subsection a trade shall be treated as discontinued and a new trade set up in any event which under the Income Tax Acts is to be treated as equivalent to the permanent discontinuance or setting up of a trade.

(6) Notwithstanding subsection (5), where at any time there has been a change in the persons engaged in carrying on a trade of farming or market gardening, this section shall apply to any person who was engaged in carrying on the trade immediately before

and immediately after the change as if the trade were the same before and after the change without any discontinuance and as if a person and another person with whom such person is connected were the same person.

Revenue precedents

Issue: Can losses be claimed in the fourth year in a commencement situation?

Decision: Yes, s 662(5) indicates that the restriction on relief for losses does not apply for a year of assessment if the trade was set up and commenced within the last three years of assessment before that year.

Issue: An individual carries on the trade of farming and the trade of dealing in land. The farming trade is not as great, in monetary terms, as the trade of dealing in land. Will the trade of farming be regarded as forming part of and being ancillary to the larger trade of dealing in land for the purposes of claiming relief for farm losses in the fourth consecutive year?

Decision: TCA 1997 s 662(2)(*e*) provides that relief is not to be denied where the loss making farm is part of and ancillary to a larger undertaking. The subsection is designed to meet cases such as that of a butcher who makes a practice of fattening bullocks for his business, or a manufacturer who grows his own raw materials or a seedsman, a chemical manufacturer or a fertiliser manufacturer who runs a farm for testing or improving his products. The phrase "part of and ancillary to" is interpreted strictly. Ancillary means subservient and annexed to (Croom-Johnson J in *Cross v Emery* at 31 TC 198). It implies a close operating link with and contribution to the larger undertaking. The question of whether the carrying on of the trade of farming forms part of the trade of dealing in land is a matter of fact. Prima facie, it is highly unlikely that it could form such a part. The farming operations are not sufficiently linked to the trade of dealing in land nor do they contribute to that trade. The trade of farming cannot therefore be regarded as being ancillary to the trade of dealing in land.

Definitions

Income Tax Acts: s 1(2); person: IA 1937 s 11(*c*); trade: s 3(1); year of assessment: ss 2(1), 5(1).

Former enactments

FA 1974 s 27(1)–(6); FA 1975 s 33(2) and Sch 1 Pt II; FA 1996 s 132(2) and Sch 5 Pt II.

663 Corporation tax: restriction of relief for losses in farming or market gardening

(1) In this section—

"prior 3 years", in relation to a loss incurred in an accounting period, means the last 3 years before the beginning of the accounting period.

"prior period of loss" means the prior 3 years or, if losses were incurred in successive accounting periods amounting in all to a period longer than 3 years (and ending when the prior 3 years end), that longer period.

(2) (*a*) Any loss incurred in a trade of farming or market gardening shall not be available for relief under section 396(2) unless it is shown that, for the accounting period in which the loss is claimed to have been incurred, the trade was being carried on on a commercial basis and with a view to the realisation of profits in the trade.

(*b*) (i) In this paragraph, **"loss computed without regard to capital allowances"** means a loss ascertained in accordance with the rules of Case I of Schedule D but so that, notwithstanding sections 307 and 308, no account shall be taken of any allowance or charge which otherwise would be taken into account under those sections.

(ii) Without prejudice to paragraph (*a*), any loss incurred in any accounting period in a trade of farming or market gardening shall not be available for relief under section 396(2) if a loss computed without regard to capital allowances was incurred in carrying on that trade in that accounting period and in each of the accounting periods wholly or partly comprised in the prior 3 years.

(*c*) For the purposes of this section, the fact that a trade of farming or market gardening was being carried on at any time so as to afford a reasonable expectation of profit shall be conclusive evidence that it was then being carried on with a view to the realisation of profits.

(*d*) This subsection shall not restrict relief for any loss where it is shown by the claimant company—

(i) that the whole of its farming or market gardening activities in the year following the prior 3 years are of such a nature, and carried on in such a way, as would have justified a reasonable expectation of the realisation of profits in the future if those activities had been undertaken by a competent farmer or market gardener, and

(ii) that if such farmer or market gardener had undertaken those activities at the beginning of the prior period of loss, such farmer or market gardener could not reasonably have expected those activities to become profitable until after the end of the year following the prior period of loss.

(*e*) This subsection shall not restrict relief where the carrying on of the trade forms part of and is ancillary to a larger trading undertaking.

(3) Subsection (2) shall not restrict relief for any loss if the trade was set up and commenced within the prior 3 years, and for the purposes of this subsection a trade shall be treated as discontinued and a new trade set up in any event which under the Tax Acts is to be treated as equivalent to the permanent discontinuance or setting up of a trade; but a trade shall not be treated as discontinued if under section 400(6) it is not to be treated as discontinued for the purpose of capital allowances and charges.

(4) Where a trade of farming or market gardening is or is to be treated as being carried on for a part only of an accounting period by reason of its being set up and commenced, or discontinued, or both, in that accounting period, subsection (2) shall apply in relation to that trade as regards that part of that accounting period.

(5) Notwithstanding subsection (3), where at any time there has been a change in the persons engaged in carrying on a trade of farming or market gardening, this section shall apply to any person, who was engaged in carrying on the trade immediately before and immediately after the change as if the trade were the same before and after the change without any discontinuance and as if a person and another person with whom such person is connected were the same person, and accordingly relief from corporation tax may be restricted under this section by reference to losses some of which are incurred in years of assessment and some, computed without regard to capital allowances, are incurred in a company's accounting periods.

Cross-references

Group relief, losses that may be surrendered: s 420(1).

Group relief, relevant losses and charges: s 420A(3)(*b*).

Definitions

capital allowance: s 2(1); company: ss 4(1), 5(1); person: IA 1937 s 11(*c*); profits: s 4(1); Tax Acts: s 1(2); trade: ss 3(1), 4(1), 5(1).

Former enactments

CTA 1976 s 17.

664 Relief for certain income from leasing of farm land

(1) (*a*) In this section—

"farm land" means land in the State wholly or mainly occupied for the purposes of husbandry and includes a building (other than a building or part of a building used as a dwelling) situated on the land and used for the purposes of farming that land;

"lease", **"lessee"**, **"lessor"** and **"rent"** have the same meanings respectively as in Chapter 8 of Part 4;

"qualifying lease" means a lease of farm land which is—

(i) in writing or evidenced in writing,

(ii) for a definite term of 5 years or more, and

(iii) made on an arm's length basis between a qualifying lessor or qualifying lessors and a lessee or lessees who is, or each of whom is, a qualifying lessee in relation to the qualifying lessor or the qualifying lessors;

"qualifying lessee", in relation to a qualifying lessor or qualifying lessors, means an individual—

(i) who is not connected with the qualifying lessor or with any of the qualifying lessors, and

(ii) who uses any farm land leased by him or her from the qualifying lessor or the qualifying lessors for the purposes of a trade of farming carried on by him or her solely or in partnership;

"qualifying lessor" means an individual who—

(i) is aged [40 years][1] or over or is permanently incapacitated by reason of mental or physical infirmity from carrying on a trade of farming, and

(ii) has not after the 30th day of January, 1985, leased the farm land which is the subject of the qualifying lease from a person or persons, who is or are, or one of whom is, connected with him or her, on terms which are not such as might have been expected to be included in a lease if the negotiations for the lease had been at arm's length;

"the specified amount", in relation to any surplus or surpluses (within the meaning of section 97(1)) arising in respect of the rent or the rents from any farm land let under a qualifying lease or qualifying leases, means, subject to paragraph (*b*), the lesser of—

(i) the amount of that surplus or the aggregate amount of those surpluses,

(ii) as respects a qualifying lease or qualifying leases made—

(I) in the period beginning on the 6th day of April, 1985, and ending on the 19th day of January, 1987, [€2,539.48][2],

(II) in the period beginning on the 20th day of January, 1987, and ending on the 31st day of December, 1987, [€3,555.27][3],

(III) in the period beginning on the 1st day of January, 1988, and ending on the 29th day of January, 1991, [€2,539.48][2],

(IV) in the period beginning on the 30th day of January, 1991, and ending on the 22nd day of January, 1996—

(A) [€5,078.95][4], in a case where the qualifying lease or qualifying leases is or are for a definite term of 7 years or more, and

(B) [€3,809.21][5], [in any other case,][6]

[(V) in the period beginning on 23 January 1996, and ending on 31 December 2003—

(A) €7,618.43, in a case where the qualifying lease or qualifying leases is or are for a definite term of 7 years or more, and

(B) €5,078.95, in any other case,

or

(VI) on or after 1 January 2004—

(A) €10,000, in a case where the qualifying lease or qualifying leases is or are for a definite term of 7 years or more, and

(B) €7,500, in any other case,][7]

and

(iii) where the rent or rents was or were not receivable in respect of a full year's letting or lettings, such amount as bears to the amount determined in accordance with clause (I), (II), (III), (IV) or (V), as may be appropriate, of subparagraph (ii) the same proportion as the amount of the rent or the aggregate amount of the rents bears to the amount of the rent or the aggregate amount of the rents which would be receivable for a full year's letting or lettings.

(*b*) Where the income of a qualifying lessor consists of or includes rent or rents—

(i) from a qualifying lease or qualifying leases made in the period beginning on the 20th day of January, 1987, and ending on the 31st day of December, 1987, and from a qualifying lease made—

(I) in the period beginning on the 6th day of April, 1985, and ending on the 19th day of January, 1987, or

(II) in the period beginning on the 1st day of January, 1988, and ending on the 29th day of January, 1991,

the specified amount shall not exceed [€3,555.27][3];

(ii) from a qualifying lease or qualifying leases made in the period beginning on the 30th day of January, 1991, and ending on the 22nd day of January, 1996, and from a qualifying lease made before the 30th day of January, 1991, the specified amount shall not exceed—

(I) [€5,078.95][4], in a case where the qualifying lease or qualifying leases is or are for a definite term of 7 years or more, and

(II) [€3,809.21][5], in any other case;

[(iii) from a qualifying lease or qualifying leases made in the period beginning on 23 January 1996, and ending on 31 December 2003, and from a qualifying lease made before 23 January 1996, the specified amount shall not exceed—

(I) €7,618.43, in a case where the qualifying lease or qualifying leases is or are for a definite term of 7 years or more, and

(II) €5,078.95, in any other case;

(iv) from a qualifying lease or qualifying leases made on or after 1 January 2004, and from a qualifying lease made at any other time, the specified amount shall not exceed—

(I) €10,000, in a case where the qualifying lease or qualifying leases is or are for a definite term of 7 years or more, and

(II) €7,500, in any other case.][8]

(2) Where for any year of assessment—

(*a*) the total income of a qualifying lessor consists of or includes any profits or gains chargeable to tax under Case V of Schedule D, and

(*b*) any surplus or surpluses (within the meaning of section 97(1)) arising in respect of the rent or rents from any farm land let under a qualifying lease or qualifying leases has been or have been taken into account in computing the amount of those profits or gains,

the qualifying lessor shall in determining that total income be entitled to a deduction of the lesser of—

(i) the specified amount in relation to the surplus or surpluses, and

(ii) the amount of the profits or gains.

(3) The amount of any deduction due under subsection (2) shall—

(*a*) where by virtue of section 1017 a woman's income is deemed to be her husband's income, be determined separately as regards the part of his income which is his by virtue of that section and the part which is his apart from that section, or

(*b*) where by virtue of section 1017 a man's income is deemed to be his wife's income, be determined separately as regards the part of her income which is hers by virtue of that section and the part which is hers apart from that section,

and where section 1023 applies any deduction allowed by virtue of subsection (2) shall be allocated to the person and to his or her spouse as if they were not married.

(4) (*a*) For the purposes of subsection (2), where a single qualifying lease relates to both farm land and other property, goods or services, only such amount, if any, of the surplus arising in respect of the rent payable under the lease as is determined by the inspector and after such apportionments of rent, expenses and other deductions as are necessary, according to the best of the inspector's knowledge and judgment, to be properly attributable to the lease of the farm land shall be treated as a surplus arising in respect of a rent from farm land let under a qualifying lease.

(*b*) Any amount which by virtue of paragraph (*a*) is determined by the inspector may be amended by the Appeal Commissioners or by the Circuit Court on the hearing or the rehearing of an appeal against that determination.

(5) For the purposes of determining the amount of any relief to be granted under this section, the inspector may by notice in writing require the lessor to furnish such information as the inspector considers necessary.

(6) (*a*) Subsections (1) and (2) of section 459 and section 460 shall apply to a deduction under this section as they apply to any allowance, deduction, relief or reduction under the provisions specified in the Table to section 458.

(*b*) Subsections (3) and (4) of section 459 and paragraph 8 of Schedule 28 shall, with any necessary modifications, apply in relation to a deduction under this section.

Amendments

1 Substituted by FA 2004 s 14(1)(*a*)(i) with effect from 1 January 2004; previously "55 years".

2 Substituted by FA 2001 s 240(1) and (2)(*a*) and Sch 5 Pt 1 for 2002 and later tax years; previously "£2,000".

3 Substituted by FA 2001 s 240(1) and (2)(*a*) and Sch 5 Pt 1 for 2002 and later tax years; previously "£2,800".

4 Substituted by FA 2001 s 240(1) and (2)(*a*) and Sch 5 Pt 1 for 2002 and later tax years; previously "£4,000".

5 Substituted by FA 2001 s 240(1) and (2)(*a*) and Sch 5 Pt 1 for 2002 and later tax years; previously "£3,000".

6 Substituted by FA 2004 s 14(1)(*a*)(ii)(I) with effect from 1 January 2004; previously "in any other case, or".

7 Definition of "the specified amount" (ii)(V) substituted by FA 2004 s 14(1)(*a*)(ii)(II) with effect from 1 January 2004.

8 Subs (1)(*b*)(iii) substituted by FA 2004 s 14(1)(*b*) with effect from 1 January 2004.

Cross-references

Meanings of "farming", "market garden land" and "occupation": s 654.

Revenue precedents

Issue: Is a niece or nephew connected with an uncle or aunt for the purposes of this section?
Decision: No.
Issue: A verbal agreement was made to lease land for a five year period. A written agreement evidencing the verbal agreement was drawn up at the commencement of the final year of the lease. The issue is whether relief can be claimed for all years since the commencement of the verbal agreement.
Decision: The Commissioners would consider granting relief under TCA 1997 s 664 if (*a*) the lessor could prove to the satisfaction of the Inspector of Taxes that the farmland had actually been leased in the period and that he had received rental income from the leasing and had returned same for income tax purposes, and (*b*) all the other conditions provided for in s 664 TCA, 1997 had been met.

Definitions

Appeal Commissioners: s 2(1); Circuit Court: IA 1937 Sch; Income Tax Acts: s 1(2); inspector: ss 2(1), 5(1), 852; land: s 5(1), IA 1937 Sch; lease: s 5(1); person: IA 1937 s 11(*c*); profits: s 4(1); profits or gains: s 3(4); rent: s 5(1); total income: s 3(1); trade: s 3(1); writing: IA 1937 Sch; year of assessment: ss 2(1), 5(1).

Former enactments

ITA 1967 s 195B(3) and (6); FA 1985 s 10, FA 1987 s 2, FA 1991 s 10; FA 1993 s 10(1); FA 1996 s 10, s 132(1) and Sch 5 Pt I para 14.

CHAPTER 2

Farming: Relief for Increase in Stock Values

665 Interpretation (Chapter 2)

In this Chapter—

"accounting period", in relation to a person, means—

(*a*) where the person is a company, an accounting period determined in accordance with section 27, or

(*b*) where the person is not a company, a period of one year ending on the date to which the accounts of the person are usually made up, but, where accounts have not been made up or where accounts have been made up for a greater or lesser period than one year, the accounting period shall be such period not exceeding one year as the Revenue Commissioners may determine;

"chargeable period" has the same meaning as in section 321(2);

"company" has the same meaning as in section 4;

"period of account", in relation to a person, means a period for which the accounts of the person have been made up;

...[1]

"specified return date for the chargeable period" has the same meaning as in section 950;

"trading income", in relation to the trade of farming, means—

(*a*) where the person is a company, the income from the trade computed in accordance with the rules applicable to Case I of Schedule D, or

(*b*) in the case of any other person, the profits or gains of the trade computed in accordance with the rules applicable to Case I of Schedule D;

"trading stock", in relation to the trade of farming, has the same meaning as in section 89 and, in determining the value of a person's trading stock at any time for the purposes of a deduction under section 666, to the extent that at or before that time any payments on account have been received by the person in respect of any trading stock, the value of that stock shall be reduced accordingly.

Amendments

1 Definition of "person" deleted by FA 2001 s 46 with effect from 6 April 2001.

Revenue precedents

Issue: Does the definition of trading stock for the purposes of stock relief include such items as fertilisers, pesticides, purchased feeds, home produced feeds, diesel and machinery parts?

Decision: The definition of trading stock in TCA 1997 s 89 includes "materials such as are used in the manufacture, preparation, or construction of property such as is sold in the ordinary course of that trade". Stock relief should therefore be allowed on items which are inputs to the property which is sold in the ordinary course of the business (eg feed, fertiliser, seeds, etc). It should not be allowed on expense stocks such as machine parts, diesel etc.

Issue: Is deer farming regarded as a separate trade from farming? Are deer regarded as trading stock for the purposes of stock relief?

Decision: A person involved in deer farming is regarded as carrying on the trade of farming. Where deer farming is carried on in conjunction with another farming enterprise, the two enterprises are regarded as one trade for the purposes of tax. Deer are regarded as trading stock for the purposes of stock relief.

Definitions

company: ss 4(1), 5(1); person: IA 1937 s 11(*c*); trade: s 3(1); trading stock: ss 5(1), 89.

Former enactments

FA 1996 s 133.

666 Deduction for increase in stock values

(1) Subject to this Chapter, where—

(*a*) a person carries on in an accounting period the trade of farming in respect of which the person is within the charge to tax under Case I of Schedule D, and (*b*) the value of the person's trading stock of that trade at the end of the accounting period (in this Chapter referred to as its **"closing stock value"**) exceeds the value of the trading stock of that trade at the beginning of the accounting period (in this Chapter referred to as its **"opening stock value"**),

the person shall, in the computation for the purposes of tax of the trading income of that trade, be entitled to a deduction under this section equal to 25 per cent of the amount of that excess as if the deduction were a trading expense incurred in the accounting period, and the amount of that excess is referred to in this Chapter as the person's **"increase in stock value"**.

(2) In the case of a company—

(*a*) the amount of the deduction under this section in an accounting period shall not exceed the amount of the company's trading income for that period after all reductions of income for that period by virtue of sections 396 and 397 and after all deductions and additions for that period by virtue of sections 307 and 308 and before any deduction allowed by virtue of this section, and

(*b*) where a deduction allowed by virtue of this section in computing the company's income from the trade of farming for an accounting period applies for an accounting period (in this subsection referred to as **"the relevant period"**), the company shall not be entitled to—

(i) a deduction under section 307 or 308 for any accounting period later than the relevant period in respect of any allowance treated as a trading loss of the trade before the commencement of the relevant period,

(ii) a set-off of a loss under section 396 for any accounting period later than the relevant period in respect of a loss sustained in the trade before the commencement of the relevant period, or

(iii) a set-off of a loss under section 397 for any accounting period earlier than the relevant period in respect of a loss sustained in the trade.

(3) In the case of a person other than a company, where a deduction allowed by virtue of this section in computing the person's trading profits of the trade of farming for an accounting period applies for a year of assessment (in this subsection referred to as **"the relevant year"**)—

(*a*) the person shall not be entitled to relief—

(i) under section 382 for any year of assessment later than the relevant year in respect of a loss sustained in the trade before the commencement of the relevant year, or

(ii) under section 385 for any year of assessment earlier than the relevant year in respect of a loss sustained in the trade,

(*b*) section 304(4) or that section as applied by any other provision of the Income Tax Acts shall not apply as respects a capital allowance or part of a capital allowance which is or is deemed to be all or part of a capital allowance for the relevant year and to which full effect has not been given in that year because there were no profits or gains chargeable for that year or there was an insufficiency of profits or gains chargeable for that year, (*c*) section 392 shall not apply to the capital allowances or any part of such allowances for the relevant year, and

(*d*) the amount of any deduction given under this section shall not exceed the amount of the person's trading income from the trade of farming for the relevant year before any deduction allowed by virtue of this section.

[(4) (*a*) A deduction shall not be allowed under this section in computing a company's trading income for any accounting period which ends after 31 December 2006.

(*b*) Any deduction allowed by virtue of this section in computing the profits or gains of the trade of farming for an accounting period of a person other than a company shall not apply for any purpose of the Income Tax Acts for any year of assessment later than the year 2006.][1]

(5) A person shall not be entitled to a deduction under this section for any chargeable period unless a written claim for such a deduction is made on or before the specified return date for that chargeable period.

(6) This section shall apply to a trade of farming carried on by a partnership as it applies to a trade of farming carried on by a person.

Amendments

1 Subs (4) substituted by FA 2005 s 31(1) with effect from 3 February 2005.

Cross-references

Compulsory disposals of livestock: s 668(4), (4A).
Farming stock relief: s 665 (trading stock).
Profit sharing schemes, payments to trustees: s 517(3)(*a*).
Supplementary provisions: s 669(2)(*a*), (3)(*a*), (3)(*b*), (4)(*a*), (5)(*a*).
Young trained farmers, subs (1), for "100 per cent" read "25 per cent": s 667(2)(*a*); s 667A(6)(*a*).

Definitions

company: ss 4(1), 5(1); Income Tax Acts: s 1(2); person: IA 1937 s 11(*c*); profits or gains: s 3(4); tax: s 3(1); trade: s 3(1); trading stock: ss 5(1), 89; year of assessment: ss 2(1), 5(1).

Former enactments

FA 1996 s 134; FA 1997 s 18.

667 Special provisions for qualifying farmers

(1) [In this section, but subject to section 667A,][1] **"qualifying farmer"** means an individual who—

(*a*) in the year 1993–94 or any subsequent year of assessment first qualifies for grant aid under the Scheme of Installation Aid for Young Farmers operated by the Department of Agriculture and Food under Council Regulation (EEC) No 797/85 of 12 March 1985 (OJ No L93 of 30.3.1985, p 6) or that Regulation as may be revised from time to time, or

(*b*) (i) first becomes chargeable to income tax under Case I of Schedule D in respect of profits or gains from the trade of farming for the year 1993–94 or any subsequent year of assessment,

(ii) has not attained the age of 35 years at the commencement of the year of assessment referred to in subparagraph (i), and

(iii) at any time in the year of assessment so referred to—

(I) is the holder of a qualification set out in the Table to this section (in this subparagraph referred to as **"the Table"**) and, in the case of a qualification set out in subparagraph (*c*), (*d*), (*e*), (*f*) or (*g*) of paragraph 3, or in paragraph 4, of the Table, is also the holder of a certificate issued by Teagasc— The Agricultural and Food Development Authority (in this section referred to as **"Teagasc"**) certifying that such person has satisfactorily attended a course of training in farm management the aggregate duration of which exceeded 80 hours; but, where Teagasc certifies that any other qualification corresponds to a qualification set out in the Table, that other qualification shall for the purposes of this subsection be treated as if it were the corresponding qualification so set out, [or][2]

(II) (A) has satisfactorily attended full-time a course at a third-level institution in any discipline for a period of not less than 2 years' duration, and

(B) is the holder of a certificate issued by Teagasc certifying satisfactory attendance at a course of training in either or both agriculture and horticulture the aggregate duration of which exceeded [180 hours.][3]

...[4]

...[5]

(2) In the case of a qualifying farmer—

(*a*) section 666(1) shall apply as if "100 per cent" were substituted for "25 per cent";

(*b*) paragraph (*a*) shall apply in computing a person's trading profits for an accounting period in the case of an individual who becomes a qualifying farmer—

(i) on or after the 6th day of April, 1993, and before the 6th day of April, 1995, for the year of assessment 1995–96 and for each of the 3 immediately succeeding [years of assessment, or][6]

[(ii) on or after 6 April 1995 and on or before 31 December 2004, for the year of assessment in which the individual becomes a qualifying farmer and for each of the 3 immediately succeeding years of assessment.][7]][8]

TABLE

1. Qualifications awarded by Teagasc:
   (*a*) Certificate in Farming;
   (*b*) Diploma in Commercial Horticulture;
   (*c*) Diploma in Amenity Horticulture;
   (*d*) Diploma in Pig Production;
   (*e*) Diploma in Poultry Production.
2. Qualifications awarded by the Farm Apprenticeship Board:

(*a*) Certificate in Farm Management;

(*b*) Certificate in Farm Husbandry;

(*c*) Trainee Farmer Certificate.

3. Qualifications awarded by a third-level institution:

(*a*) Degree in Agricultural Science awarded by the National University of Ireland through the National University of Ireland, Dublin;

(*b*) Degree in Horticultural Science awarded by the National University of Ireland through the National University of Ireland, Dublin;

(*c*) Degree in Veterinary Science awarded by the National University of Ireland through the National University of Ireland, Dublin;

(*d*) Degree in Rural Science awarded by the National University of Ireland through the National University of Ireland, Cork or by the University of Limerick;

(*e*) Diploma in Rural Science awarded by the National University of Ireland through the National University of Ireland, Cork;

(*f*) Degree in Dairy Science awarded by the National University of Ireland through the National University of Ireland, Cork;

(*g*) Diploma in Dairy Science awarded by the National University of Ireland through the National University of Ireland, Cork.

4. Certificates awarded by the National Council for Educational Awards:

(*a*) National Certificate in Agricultural Science studied through Kildalton Agricultural College and Waterford Regional Technical College;

(*b*) National Certificate in Business Studies (Agribusiness) studied through the Franciscan Brothers Agricultural College, Mountbellew, and Galway Regional Technical College.

Amendments

1 Substituted by FA 2004 s 13(1)(*a*)(i) with effect from 1 January 2004; previously "In this section,".

2 Inserted by FA 2004 s 13(1)(*a*)(ii)(I) with effect from 1 January 2004.

3 Substituted by FA 2004 s 13(1)(*a*)(ii)(II) with effect from 1 January 2004; previously "180 hours,".

4 Deleted by FA 2004 s 13(1)(*a*)(ii)(II) with effect from 1 January 2004; previously "or".

5 Definition of "qualifying farmer"(*b*)(iii)(III) deleted by FA 2004 s 13(1)(*a*)(ii)(III) with effect from 1 January 2004.

6 Substituted by FA 1998 s 39(*a*) with effect from 6 April 1998; previously "years of assessment,".

7 Subs (2)(*b*)(ii) substituted by FA 2003 s 19(1) with effect from such day as the Minister for Finance may by order appoint; pending the making of such an order, to qualify for relief under this section it is necessary to become a "qualifying farmer" before 31 December 2002.

8 Subs (2)(*b*)(ii), (iii) substituted by FA 1998 s 39(*b*) with effect from 6 April 1998.

Cross-references

Further provisions for qualifying farmers: s 667A(7)(*a*), (*b*).

Revenue precedents

Issue: Is a young farmer regarded as being a holder of a qualification in the year he completes his Teagasc course or in the year he receives his certificate?

Decision: An individual would be regarded as holding a qualification once he has been conferred with a degree/diploma or presented with a certificate. The Certificate in Farming qualification is presented in September or October each year.

Definitions

person: IA 1937 s 11(*c*); year of assessment: ss 2(1).

Former enactments

FA 1994 Sch 6; FA 1996 s 135; FA 1997 s 19.

667A Further provisions for qualifying farmers

[(1) In this section **"qualifying farmer"** means an individual who—

(*a*) in the year 2004 or any subsequent year of assessment first qualifies for grant aid under the Scheme of Installation Aid for Young Farmers operated by the Department of Agriculture and Food under Council Regulation (EEC) No 797/85 of 12 March 1985 (OJ No L93, 30.3.1985, p 6) or that Regulation as may be revised from time to time, or

(*b*) (i) first becomes chargeable to income tax under Case I of Schedule D in respect of profits or gains from the trade of farming for the year 2004 or any subsequent year of assessment,

(ii) has not attained the age of 35 years at the commencement of the year of assessment referred to in subparagraph (i), and

(iii) at any time in the year of assessment so referred to satisfies the conditions set out in subsection (2), (3) or (4).

(2) The conditions required by this subsection are that the individual, referred to in the definition of **"qualifying farmer"** in subsection (1), is the holder of a qualification set out in the Table to this section (in this Section referred to as the **"Table"**), and—

(*a*) in the case of a qualification set out in paragraph 1(*f*) or paragraph 2(*h*) of the Table, is also the holder of a certificate awarded by the Further Education and Training Awards Council for achieving the minimum stipulated standard in assessments completed in a course of training, approved by Teagasc—

(i) in either or both agriculture and horticulture, the aggregate duration of which exceeded 100 hours, and

(ii) in farm management, the aggregate duration of which exceeded 80 hours,

or

(*b*) in the case of a qualification set out in subparagraph (*b*), (*c*) or (*d*) of paragraph 3 of the Table, is also the holder of a certificate awarded by the Further Education and Training Awards Council for achieving the minimum stipulated standard in assessments completed in a course of training, approved by Teagasc, in farm management, the aggregate duration of which exceeded 80 hours.

(3) The conditions required by this subsection are that the individual, referred to in the definition of **"qualifying farmer"** in subsection (1)—

(*a*) has achieved the required standard for entry into the third year of a full-time course of 3 or more years' duration in any discipline at a third-level institution and that has been confirmed by that institution, and

(*b*) is the holder of a certificate awarded by the Further Education and Training Awards Council for achieving a minimum stipulated standard in assessments completed in a course of training, approved by Teagasc—

(i) in either or both agriculture and horticulture, the aggregate duration of which exceeded 100 hours, and

(ii) in farm management, the aggregate duration of which exceeded 80 hours.

(4) The conditions required by this subsection are that the individual, referred to in the definition of **"qualifying farmer"** in subsection (1), is the holder of a letter of confirmation from Teagasc confirming satisfactory completion of a course of training, approved by Teagasc, for persons who in the opinion of Teagasc are restricted in their learning capacity due to physical, sensory, mental health or intellectual disability.

(5) For the purposes of subsection (2) where Teagasc certifies that—

(*a*) any other qualification corresponds to a qualification set out in the Table, and

(*b*) that other qualification is deemed by the National Qualifications Authority of Ireland to be at least at a standard equivalent to that of the qualification set out in the Table,

then that other qualification shall be treated as if it were the qualification set out in the Table.

(6) In the case of a qualifying farmer—

(*a*) section 666(1) shall apply as if "100 per cent" were substituted for 25 "per cent", and

(*b*) paragraph (*a*) shall apply in computing a person's trading profits for an accounting period in the case of an individual who becomes a qualifying farmer at any time in the period beginning on or after 1 January 2004 and ending on or before [31 December 2006][1], for the year of assessment in which the individual becomes a qualifying farmer and for each of the 3 immediately succeeding years of assessment.

(7) For the purposes of this section, an individual who, before 1 January 2004—

(*a*) is the holder of a qualification set out in the Table to section 667 or a qualification certified by Teagasc as corresponding to such a qualification so set out, in respect of which—

(i) satisfactory attendance at a course of training in farm management, the aggregate duration of which exceeded 80 hours, is required in order for the conditions of paragraph (*b*)(iii) of the definition of "qualifying farmer" in section 667(1) to be satisfied, shall be deemed to be the holder of a qualification corresponding to that set out in paragraph 3(*b*) of the Table, or

(ii) satisfactory attendance at a course of training is not required in order for the conditions of paragraph (*b*)(iii) of the definition of "qualifying farmer" in section 667(1) to be satisfied, shall be deemed to be the holder of a qualification corresponding to that set out in paragraph 2(*a*) of the Table,

(*b*) satisfies the requirements set out in paragraph (*b*)(iii)(II)(A) of the definition of "qualifying farmer" in section 667(1), shall be deemed to satisfy the requirements set out in subsection (3)(*a*), and (*c*) is the holder of a certificate issued by Teagasc certifying satisfactory attendance at a course of training—

(i) in farm management, the aggregate duration of which exceeded 80 hours, shall be deemed to be the holder of a certificate referred to in subsection (2)(*b*), or

(ii) in either or both agriculture and horticulture, the aggregate duration of which exceeded 180 hours, shall be deemed to be the holder of a certificate referred to in subsection (2)(*a*).

TABLE

1. Qualifications awarded by the Further Education and Training Awards Council:

(*a*) Vocational Certificate in Agriculture — Level 3;

(*b*) Advanced Certificate in Agriculture;

(*c*) Vocational Certificate in Horticulture — Level 3;

(*d*) Vocational Certificate in Horse Breeding and Training — Level 3;

(*e*) Vocational Certificate in Forestry — Level 3;

(*f*) Awards other than those referred to in subparagraphs (*a*) to (*e*) which are, at least, at a standard equivalent to that of the award referred to in subparagraph (*a*).

2. Qualifications awarded by the Higher Education and Training Awards Council:

(*a*) National Certificate in Agriculture;

(*b*) National Diploma in Agriculture;

(*c*) National Certificate in Science in Agricultural Science;

(*d*) National Certificate in Business Studies in Agri-Business;

(*e*) National Certificate in Technology in Agricultural Mechanisation;

(*f*) National Diploma in Horticulture;

(*g*) National Certificate in Business Studies in Equine Studies;

(*h*) National Certificate or Diploma awards other than those referred to in subparagraphs (*a*) to (*g*).

3. Qualifications awarded by other third-level institutions:

(*a*) Primary degrees awarded by the faculties of General Agriculture and Veterinary Medicine at University College Dublin;

(*b*) Bachelor of Science (Education) in Biological Sciences awarded by the University of Limerick;

(*c*) Bachelor of Science in Equine Science awarded by the University of Limerick;

(*d*) Diploma or Certificate in Science (Equine Science) awarded by the University of Limerick.][2]

Amendments

1 Substituted by FA 2005 s 32(1) with effect from such day as the Minister for Finance may by order appoint; previously "31 December 2004".

2 Section 667A inserted by FA 2004 s 13(1)(*b*) with effect from 1 January 2004.

Definitions

year of assessment: s 2(1).

668 Compulsory disposals of livestock

(1) In this section—

"excess" means the excess of the relevant amount over the value of the stock to which this section applies at the beginning of the accounting period in which the disposal takes place;

"relevant amount" means the amount of any income received by a person as a result or in consequence of a disposal of stock to which this section applies;

[**"stock to which this section applies"** means—

(*a*) all cattle forming part of the trading stock of the trade of farming, where such cattle are compulsorily disposed of on or after 6 April 1993, under any statute relating to the eradication or control of diseases in livestock, and for the purposes of this section all cattle shall be regarded as compulsorily disposed of where, in the case of any disease eradication scheme relating to the eradication or control of brucellosis in livestock, all eligible cattle for the purposes of any such scheme, together with such other cattle as are required to be disposed of, are disposed of, or

(*b*) animals and poultry of a kind specified in Parts I and II, respectively, of the First Schedule to the Diseases of Animals Act, 1966, forming part of the trading stock of the trade of farming, where all animals or poultry of the particular kind forming part of that trade of farming are disposed of on or after 6 December 2000, in such circumstances that compensation is paid by the Minister for Agriculture, Food and Rural Development in respect of that disposal.][1]

(2) Where stock to which this section applies is disposed of in an accounting period by a person carrying on the trade of farming, the person may elect to have the excess treated in accordance with subsections (3) to (5), and such election shall be made in such form and contain such information as the Revenue Commissioners may require.

(3) (*a*) Notwithstanding any other provision of the Tax Acts apart from [paragraph (*b*) and subsection (3A)][2], where a person elects in accordance with subsection (2), the excess shall be disregarded as respects the accounting period in which it arises and shall instead be treated for the purposes of the Tax Acts as arising in equal instalments in each of [the 4 immediately succeeding accounting periods][3].

(*b*) [Notwithstanding paragraph (*a*) but subject to subsection (3A)][4], where the person further elects, the excess shall be treated as arising in such equal instalments in the accounting period in which it arises and in [the 3 immediately succeeding accounting periods][5].

[(3A) Where a trade of farming is permanently discontinued, tax shall be charged under Case IV of Schedule D for the chargeable period in which such discontinuation takes place in respect of the amount of the excess which would, but for such discontinuance, be treated by virtue of subsection (3) as arising in an accounting period or accounting periods ending after such discontinuance.][6]

[(4) Subject to subsection (4A), where, not later than the end of the period over which the excess is treated as arising under subsection (3), the person incurs or intends to incur expenditure on the replacement of stock to which this section applies in an amount not less than the relevant amount, then the person shall, in substitution for any deduction to which the person might otherwise be entitled under section 666 as a result of incurring an amount of expenditure equal to the relevant amount, be deemed to be entitled to a deduction under that section—

(*a*) where subsection (3)*(a)* applies, for each of the 4 immediately succeeding accounting periods referred to in that subsection, and

(*b*) where subsection (3)(*b*) applies, for the accounting period in which the excess arises and each of the 3 immediately succeeding accounting periods referred to in that subsection,

and the amount of that deduction shall be an amount equal to the amount treated as arising in each accounting period under subsection (3)*(a)* or (3)(*b*), as the case may be, and section 666 shall apply with any necessary modifications in order to give effect to this subsection.

(4A) Where it subsequently transpires that the expenditure actually incurred, on the replacement of stock to which this section applies, by the end of the period over which the excess is treated as arising under subsection (3), was less than the relevant amount, then—

(*a*) the aggregate deduction to which the person is deemed by subsection (4) to be entitled under section 666 in respect of the 4 accounting periods referred to in paragraph *(a)* or (*b*), as the case may be, of that subsection shall be reduced to an amount that bears the same proportion to that aggregate deduction as the expenditure actually incurred in those 4 accounting periods bears to the relevant amount, and

(*b*) the reduction to be made in accordance with paragraph *(a)* shall, as far as possible, be made in a later accounting period in priority to an earlier accounting period.][7]

(5) An election under this section shall be made by notice in writing made on or before the specified return date for the chargeable period in which the stock to which this section applies is compulsorily disposed of.

[(6) Where—

(*a*) by virtue of the operation of section 65, the profits or gains of both the year of assessment 2001 and the year of assessment 2002 are computed on the basis of an accounting period of one year ending in the period from 1 January 2002 to 5 April 2002, and

(*b*) an instalment referred to in subsection (3) is treated as arising in that accounting period,

then, notwithstanding any other provision of the Tax Acts—

(i) an amount equal to 74 per cent of that instalment shall be taken to be part of the profits or gains of the trade of farming for the year of assessment 2001, and

(ii) an amount equal to 26 per cent of that instalment shall be taken to be part of the profits or gains of the trade of farming for the year of assessment 2002.

(7) Where, by virtue of subsection (4), a person is deemed to be entitled to a deduction under section 666 in respect of the accounting period referred to in subsection (6), then—

(*a*) 74 per cent of such deduction shall be granted for the year of assessment 2001, and

(*b*) 26 per cent of such deduction shall be granted for the year of assessment 2002.][8]

Amendments

1 Definition of "stock to which this section applies" substituted by FA 2001 s 49 with effect from 6 April 2001.

2 Substituted by FA 2002 s 29(1)(*a*)(i) as respects disposals made on or after 21 February 2001; previously "paragraph (*b*)".

3 Substituted by FA 2002 s 29(1)(*a*)(i) as respects disposals made on or after 21 February 2001; previously "the 2 immediately succeeding accounting periods".

4 Substituted by FA 2002 s 29(1)(*a*)(ii) as respects disposals made on or after 21 February 2001; previously "Notwithstanding paragraph *(a)*".

5 Substituted by FA 2002 s 29(1)(*a*)(ii) as respects disposals made on or after 21 February 2001; previously "the immediately succeeding accounting period".

6 Subs (3A) inserted by FA 2002 s 29(1)(*b*) as respects disposals made on or after 21 February 2001.

7 Subs (4) substituted and subs (4A) inserted by FA 2002 s 29(1)(*c*) as respects disposals made on or after 21 February 2001.

8 Subss (6) and (7) inserted by FA 2002 s 29(1)(*d*) with effect from 6 April 2001.

Revenue precedents

Issue: The section defines "relevant amount" as the amount of income received as a result of a disposal of stock. In the context of this definition to what does the word income refer?

Decision: The reference to income in the definition is a reference to the total proceeds received in respect of the cattle which are compulsorily disposed of.

Issue: Do the provisions of the section apply if a partial disposal of cattle held by a farmer takes place?

Decision: No - partial disposals do not come within the provisions of the section, apart from those in relation to brucellosis as outlined in the section.

Issue: If a loss arises in a year as a result of an election made under this section is the loss available for set off against income?

Decision: Yes - subject to the usual restrictions in s 662.

Issue: Does the 100% stock relief apply to stock which has been disposed of due to BSE?

Decision: Cattle which have been disposed of due to Bovine Spongiform Encephalopathy (BSE) are regarded as cattle compulsorily disposed of under a statute relating to the eradication or control of diseases in livestock for the purposes of the definition of "stock to which this section applies" in s 668(1) TCA.

Issue: Under the Brucellosis Eradication Scheme all female cattle and certain male cattle are required to be disposed of. A person may elect to avail of the 100% compulsory disposal stock relief in respect of them. Is the ordinary 25% stock relief available in respect of an increase in the stock which is not required to be disposed of?

Decision: If a person elects to claim a 100% stock relief deduction under section 668 in respect of cattle compulsory disposed of, they are not entitled to a further deduction in respect of those cattle under section 666 for that year.

Issue: Taxpayer received BSE compensation and elected under section 668 of the Taxes Consolidation Act, 1997 to have the excess treated as arising in each of the 2 immediately succeeding accounting periods on a 50/50 basis for the years ended 31 March 2000 and 31 March 2001. Taxpayer successfully restocked during the year ended 31 March 2000 but was prevented from doing so during the year ending 31 March 2001 due to the onset of foot and mouth disease.

Decision: As the difficulties which prevented the taxpayer restocking were due to foot and mouth disease and could not have been provided for under the provisions of Section 668. The taxpayer was allowed to concessionally: have the second installment of the profit on disposal of cattle from BSE compensation normally taxable in the year ending 31 March 2001 to be deferred and taxed in the following year ending 31 March 2002. The taxpayer was entitled to the balance of the stock releif in respect of his accounts to year ending 31 March 2002.

Tax Briefing

TB47 Apr 2002 p 11 — Disposal of livestock due to disease eradication measures — Finance Act 2002 changes.
TB50 Oct 2002 pp 3–4 — Compulsory Disposals of Livestock.

Definitions

person: IA 1937 s 11(*c*); profits or gains: s 3(4); trading stock: ss 5(1), 89; writing: IA 1937 Sch.

Former enactments

FA 1996 s 136.

669 Supplementary provisions (Chapter 2)

(1) (*a*) Where a person has acquired or disposed of trading stock otherwise than in the normal conduct of the trade of farming, the person shall be treated for the purposes of this Chapter as having, at the beginning or end of the relevant period of account, trading stock of such value as appears to the inspector (or on appeal to the Appeal Commissioners) to be just and reasonable having regard to all the circumstances of the case.

(*b*) Where the value of a person's trading stock at the beginning of a period of account is not calculated on the basis used for the calculation of the value of the trading stock at the end of that period, the value of the trading stock at the beginning of that period shall for the purposes of this Chapter be treated as being what it would have been if it had been calculated on that basis.

(2) (*a*) In any case where a person's accounting period does not coincide with a period of account or with 2 or more consecutive periods of account, the person's increase in stock value in the accounting period shall be determined for the purposes of section 666 not in accordance with subsection (1) of that section but by reference to a period (in this section referred to as **"the reference period"**) determined in accordance with this subsection.

(*b*) In any case where the beginning of a person's accounting period does not coincide with the beginning of a period of account, the reference period shall begin at the beginning of the period of account which is current at the beginning of the person's accounting period.

(*c*) In any case where the end of the person's accounting period does not coincide with the end of a period of account, the reference period shall end at the end of the period of account which is current at the end of the person's accounting period.

(*d*) In any case where paragraph (*b*) does not apply, the reference period shall begin at the beginning of the person's accounting period and, in any case where paragraph (*c*) does not apply, the reference period shall end at the end of the person's accounting period.

(3) (*a*) In any case where subsection (2)(*a*) applies, a person's increase in stock value in the accounting period shall be determined for the purposes of section 666 by the formula—

$$\frac{A \times (C - O)}{N}$$

where—

A is the number of months in the person's accounting period,

C is the value of the person's trading stock at the end of the reference period,

O is the value of the person's trading stock at the beginning of the reference period, and

N is the number of months in the reference period.

(*b*) In any case where a person's increase in stock value in an accounting period is to be determined in accordance with paragraph (*a*), then, in section 666 and subsections (4) to (6), any reference to the person's closing stock value shall be construed as a reference to the value of the person's trading stock at the end of the reference period.

(4) (*a*) A person shall not be entitled to a deduction under section 666 for an accounting period if that accounting period ends by virtue of the person ceasing to—

(i) carry on the trade of farming,

(ii) be resident in the State, or

(iii) be within the charge to tax under Case I of Schedule D in respect of that trade.

(*b*) In any case where a person's increase in stock value in an accounting period is to be determined in accordance with subsection (3)(*a*), paragraph (*a*) shall apply as if the reference in that paragraph to the person's accounting period were a reference to any of the accounting periods comprised in the person's reference period.

(5) (*a*) Subject to paragraphs (*b*) to (*d*), where a person claims a deduction under section 666 and, immediately before the beginning of an accounting period, the person was not carrying on the trade to which the claim relates, then, unless—

(i) the person acquired the initial trading stock of that trade on a sale or transfer from another person on that person's ceasing to carry on that trade, and

(ii) the stock so acquired is or is included in the person's trading stock as valued at the beginning of the accounting period,

the person shall be treated for the purposes of section 666 and subsections (1) to (4) as having at the beginning of the accounting period trading stock of such value as appears to the inspector to be just and reasonable.

(*b*) In determining for the purposes specified in paragraph (*a*) the value of trading stock to be attributed to a person at the beginning of the accounting period, the inspector shall have regard to all the relevant circumstances of the case and in particular to—

(i) movements during the person's accounting period in the costs of items of a kind comprised in the person's trading stock during that period, and

(ii) changes during that period in the volume of the trade in question carried on by the person.

(*c*) The Appeal Commissioners dealing with an appeal from the decision of an inspector on a claim in a case where in accordance with paragraph (*a*) the inspector has attributed to a person at the beginning of an accounting period trading stock of a particular value shall, in hearing and determining the appeal in so far as it relates to the value of the trading stock to be so attributed, determine such value as appears to the Appeal Commissioners to be just and reasonable, having regard to those factors to which the inspector is required to have regard by virtue of paragraph (*b*).

(*d*) In any case where subsection (2)(*a*) applies to a person's accounting period, for any reference in paragraphs (*a*) to (*c*) to that accounting period there shall be substituted a reference to the reference period.

(6) In any case where a person's accounting period or reference period consists of a number of complete months and a fraction of a month, any reference in this section to the number of months in the period shall be construed as including that fraction of a month (and in any case where any such period is less than one month any such reference shall be construed as a reference to that fraction of a month of which the period consists).

Definitions

inspector: ss 2(1), 5(1), 852; month: IA 1937 Sch; person: IA 1937 s 11(*c*); trading stock: ss 5(1), 89.

Former enactments

FA 1996 s 137.

[CHAPTER 3
Milk Quotas][1]

Amendments

1 Chapter 3 inserted by FA 2000 s 61(*b*) and is to come into operation on such day as the Minister for Finance, with the consent of the Minister for Agriculture, Food and Rural Development, may appoint by order. By virtue of Taxes Consolidation Act 1997 (Commencement of Chapter 3 of Part 23) Order 2001, SI No 505 of 2001, this Chapter came into operation on 1 November 2001.

669A Interpretation

[In this Chapter—

...[1]

"levy" means the levy referred to in Council Regulation (EEC) No 3950 of 28 December 1992 (OJ NO L405, 31.12.92, p 1), as amended;

"milk" means the produce of the milking of one or more cows and "other milk products" includes cream, butter and cheese;

"milk quota" means—

(*a*) the quantity of a milk or other milk products which may be supplied by a person carrying on farming, in the course of a trade of farming land occupied by such person to a purchaser in a milk quota year without that person being liable to pay a levy, or

(*b*) the quantity of a milk or other milk products which may be sold or transferred free for direct consumption by a person carrying on farming, in the course of a trade of farming land occupied by such person in a milk quota year without that person being liable to pay a levy;

"milk quota restructuring scheme" means a scheme introduced by the Minister for Agriculture, Food and Rural Development under the provisions of Article 8(*b*) of Council Regulation (EEC) No. 3950 of 28 December 1992, as amended;

"milk quota year" means a twelve month period beginning on 1 April and ending on the following 31 March;

"purchaser" has the meaning assigned to it under Council Regulation (EEC) No. 3950 of 28 December 1992;

"qualifying expenditure" means—

(*a*) in the case of milk quota to which paragraph (*a*) of the definition of "qualifying quota" refers, the amount of the capital expenditure incurred on the purchase of that qualifying quota, and

(*b*) in the case of milk quota to which paragraph (*b*) of the definition of "qualifying quota" refers, the lesser of—

(i) the amount of capital expenditure incurred on the purchase of that qualifying quota, or

(ii) the amount of capital expenditure which would have been incurred on the purchase of that qualifying quota if the price paid were the maximum price for the milk quota year in which the purchase took place as set by the Minister for Agriculture, Food and Rural Development for the purposes of a Milk Quota Restructuring Scheme;

"qualifying quota" means—

(*a*) a milk quota purchased by a person on or after 1 April 2000 under a Milk Quota Restructuring Scheme, or

[(*b*) any other milk quota purchased on or after 1 April 2000;][2]

"writing-down period" has the meaning assigned to it by section 669B(2).][3]

Amendments

1 Definition of "lessee" deleted by FA 2002 s 30(1)(*a*) with effect from 6 April 2000.

2 Definition of "qualifying quota" para (*b*) substituted by FA 2002 s 30(1)(*b*) with effect from 6 April 2000.

3 Section 669A inserted by FA 2000 s 61(*b*) and is to come into operation on such day as the Minister for Finance, with the consent of the Minister for Agriculture, Food and Rural Development, may appoint by order. By virtue of Taxes Consolidation Act 1997 (Commencement of Chapter 3 of Part 23) Order 2001, SI No 505 of 2001, this section came into operation on 1 November 2001.

Definitions

land: IA 1937 Sch; person: IA 1937 s 11(*c*); trade: ss 3(1), 4(1).

669B Annual allowances for capital expenditure on purchase of milk quota

[(1) Where, on or after 6 April 2000, a person incurs qualifying expenditure on the purchase of a qualifying quota, there shall, subject to and in accordance with this Chapter, be made to that person writing-down allowances during the writing-down period as specified in subsection (2); but no writing-down allowance shall be made to a person in respect of any qualifying expenditure unless the allowance is to be made to the person in taxing the person's trade of farming.

(2) The writing-down period referred to in subsection (1) shall be 7 years commencing with the beginning of the chargeable period related to the qualifying expenditure.

(3) The writing-down allowances to be made during the writing-down period referred to in subsection (2) in respect of qualifying expenditure shall be determined by the formula—

$$A \times \frac{B}{C}$$

where—

[A is the amount of the qualifying expenditure incurred on the purchase of the milk quota,][1]

B is the length of the part of the chargeable period falling within the writing-down period, and

C is the length of the writing-down period.][2]

Amendments

1 Substituted by FA 2003 s 163 and Sch 6 para 1(*f*) with effect from 1 November 2001; previously "A is the amount of the capital expenditure incurred on the purchase of the milk quota,".

2 Section 669B inserted by FA 2000 s 61(*b*) and is to come into operation on such day as the Minister for Finance, with the consent of the Minister for Agriculture, Food and Rural Development, may appoint by order. By virtue of Taxes Consolidation Act 1997 (Commencement of Chapter 3 of Part 23) Order 2001, SI No 505 of 2001, this section came into operation on 1 November 2001.

Definitions

chargeable period: s 321(2); chargeable period related to expenditure: s 321(2); milk quota: s 669A; person: IA 1937 s 11(*c*); qualifying expenditure: s 669A; qualifying quota: s 669A.

669C Effect of sale of quota

[(1) Where a person incurs qualifying expenditure on the purchase of a qualifying quota and, before the end of the writing-down period, any of the following events occurs—

(*a*) the person sells the qualifying quota or so much of the quota as the person still owns;

(*b*) the qualifying quota comes to an end or ceases altogether to be used;

(*c*) the person sells part of the qualifying quota and the net proceeds of the sale (in so far as they consist of capital sums) are not less than the amount of the qualifying expenditure remaining unallowed;

no writing-down allowance shall be made to that person for the chargeable period related to the event or any subsequent chargeable period.

(2) Where a person incurs qualifying expenditure on the purchase of a qualifying quota and, before the end of the writing-down period, either of the following events occurs—

(*a*) the qualifying quota comes to an end or ceases altogether to be used;

(*b*) the person sells all of the qualifying quota or so much of that quota as the person still owns, and the net proceeds of the sale (in so far as they consist of capital sums) are less that the amount of the qualifying expenditure remaining unallowed;

there shall, subject to and in accordance with this Chapter, be made to that person for the [chargeable period][1] related to the event an allowance (in this Chapter referred to as a **"balancing allowance"**) equal to—

(i) if the event is the qualifying quota coming to an end or ceasing altogether to be used, the amount of the qualifying expenditure remaining unallowed, and

(ii) if the event is a sale, the amount of the qualifying expenditure remaining unallowed less the net proceeds of the sale.

(3) Where a person who has incurred qualifying expenditure on the purchase of a qualifying quota sells all or any part of that quota and the net proceeds of the sale (in so far as they consist of capital sums) exceed the amount of the qualifying expenditure remaining unallowed, if any, there shall, subject to and in accordance with this Chapter, be made on that person for the chargeable period related to the sale a charge (in this Chapter referred to as a **"balancing charge"**) on an amount equal to—

(*a*) the excess, or

(*b*) where the amount of the qualifying expenditure remaining unallowed is nil, the net proceeds of the sale.

(4) Where a person who has incurred qualifying expenditure on the purchase of a qualifying quota sells a part of that quota and subsection (3) does not apply, the amount of any writing-down allowance made in respect of that expenditure for the chargeable period related to the sale or any subsequent chargeable period shall be the amount determined by—

(*a*) subtracting the net proceeds of the sale (in so far as they consist of capital sums) from the amount of the expenditure remaining unallowed at the time of the sale, and

(*b*) dividing the result by the number of complete years of the writing-down period which remained at the beginning of the chargeable period related to the sale,

and so on for any subsequent sales.

(5) References in this section to the amount of any qualifying expenditure remaining unallowed shall in relation to any event be construed as references to the amount of that expenditure less any writing-down allowances made in respect of that expenditure for chargeable periods before the chargeable period related to that event, and less also the net proceeds of any previous sale by the person who incurred the expenditure of any part of the qualifying quota acquired by the expenditure, in so far as those proceeds consist of capital sums.

(6) Notwithstanding subsection (1) to (5)—

(*a*) no balancing allowance shall be made in respect of any expenditure unless a writing-down allowance has been, or, but for the happening of the event giving rise to the balancing allowance, could have been, made in respect of that expenditure, and

(*b*) the total amount on which a balancing charge is made in respect of any expenditure shall not exceed the total writing-down allowances actually made in respect of that expenditure less, if a balancing charge has previously been made in respect of that expenditure, the amount on which that charge was made.][2]

Amendments

1 Substituted by FA 2001 s 27 with effect from 6 April 2001; previously "accounting period".

2 Section 669C inserted by FA 2000 s 61(*b*) and is to come into operation on such day as the Minister for Finance, with the consent of the Minister for Agriculture, Food and Rural Development, may appoint by order. By virtue of Taxes Consolidation Act 1997 (Commencement of Chapter 3 of Part 23) Order 2001, SI No 505 of 2001, this section came into operation on 1 November 2001.

Cross-references

Application of Chapter 4 of Part 9: s 669E(2).

Definitions

chargeable period: s 321(2); chargeable period related to event: s 321(2); person: IA 1937 s 11(*c*); qualifying expenditure: s 669A; qualifying quota: s 669A; writing-down period: s 669A.

669D Manner of making allowances and charges

[An allowance or charge under this Chapter shall be made to or on a person in taxing the profits or gains from farming but only if at any time in the chargeable period or its basis period the qualifying quota in question was used for the purposes of that trade.][1]

Amendments

1 Section 669D inserted by FA 2000 s 61(*b*) and is to come into operation on such day as the Minister for Finance, with the consent of the Minister for Agriculture, Food and Rural Development, may appoint by order. By virtue of Taxes Consolidation Act 1997 (Commencement of Chapter 3 of Part 23) Order 2001, SI No 505 of 2001, this section came into operation on 1 November 2001.

Definitions

chargeable period or its basis period: s 321(2); person: IA 1937 s 11(*c*); qualifying quota: s 669A; trade: ss 3(1), 4(1).

669E Application of Chapter 4 of Part 9

[(1) Subject to subsection (2), Chapter 4 of Part 9 shall apply as if this Chapter were contained in that Part.

(2) In Chapter 4 of Part 9, as applied by virtue of subsection (1) to a qualifying quota, the reference in section 312(5)(*a*)(i) to the sum mentioned in paragraph (*b*) shall in the case of a qualifying quota be construed as a reference to the amount of the qualifying expenditure on the acquisition of the qualifying quota remaining unallowed, computed in accordance with section 669C.][1]

Amendments

1 Section 669E inserted by FA 2000 s 61(*b*) and is to come into operation on such day as the Minister for Finance, with the consent of the Minister for Agriculture, Food and Rural Development, may appoint by order. By virtue of Taxes Consolidation Act 1997 (Commencement of Chapter 3 of Part 23) Order 2001, SI No 505 of 2001, this section came into operation on 1 November 2001.

Definitions

qualifying expenditure: s 669A; qualifying quota: s 669A.

669F Commencement (Chapter 3)

[This Chapter shall come into operation on such day as the Minister for Finance, with the consent of the Minister for Agriculture, Food and Rural Development, may, by order, appoint.]

Amendments

1 Section 669F inserted by FA 2000 s 61(*b*). By virtue of Taxes Consolidation Act 1997 (Commencement of Chapter 3 of Part 23) Order 2001, SI No 505 of 2001, this Chapter came into operation on 1 November 2001.

PART 24
TAXATION OF PROFITS OF CERTAIN MINES AND PETROLEUM TAXATION

CHAPTER 1
Taxation of Profits of Certain Mines

Cross-references

Apportionment of consideration and exchanges and surrenders of leasehold interests: s 311(4).

Capital allowance is given on VAT exclusive expenditure: s 319(*c*).

"Capital allowance" includes an allowance under this Chapter: s 2(1).

Chargeable period, and general provisions: s 321(*d*).

Special provisions as to certain sales: s 312(2)(*a*)(ii).

670 Mine development allowance

(1) In this section—

"mine" means a mine operated for the purpose of obtaining, whether by underground or surface working, any scheduled mineral, mineral compound or mineral substance within the meaning of section 2 of the Minerals Development Act, 1940, but, in relation to capital expenditure incurred before the 6th day of April, 1960, **"mine"** means an underground excavation made for the purpose of getting minerals;

references to capital expenditure incurred in connection with a mine shall be construed as references to capital expenditure incurred—

(*a*) in the development of the mine on searching for, or on discovering and testing, mineral deposits or winning access to such deposits, or

(*b*) on the construction of any works which are of such a nature that when the mine has ceased to be operated they are likely to have so diminished in value that their value will be nil or almost nil,

but as excluding references to—

(i) any expenditure on the acquisition of the site of the mine or of the site of any such works or of rights in or over any such site,

(ii) any expenditure on the acquisition of, or of rights over, the deposits, or

(iii) any expenditure on works constructed wholly or mainly for subjecting the raw product of the mine to any process except a process designed for preparing the raw product for use as such;

references to assets representing capital expenditure incurred in connection with a mine shall be construed as including—

(*a*) in relation to expenditure on searching for, discovering and testing deposits, references to any information or other results obtained from any search, exploration or enquiry on which the expenditure was incurred,

(*b*) references to any part of such assets, and

(*c*) in the case of any such assets destroyed or damaged, references to any insurance moneys or other compensation moneys in respect of such destruction or damage.

(2) Expenditure shall not for the purposes of this section be regarded as having been incurred by a person carrying on the trade of working a mine in so far as the expenditure has been or is to be met directly or indirectly out of moneys provided by the Oireachtas or by any other person (not being a person who has carried on the trade of working that mine).

(3) Any person who carries on the trade of working a mine and who has on or after the 6th day of April, 1946, incurred any capital expenditure in connection with the mine may apply for an allowance (in this section referred to as a **"mine development allowance"**) in respect of that capital expenditure.

(4) Application for a mine development allowance for any chargeable period may be made to the inspector not later than 24 months after the end of that period.

(5) (*a*) Subject to paragraph (*b*), the following provisions shall apply in relation to the amount of a mine development allowance for any chargeable period in respect of any capital expenditure incurred in connection with a mine:

(i) the inspector shall estimate to the best of his or her judgment the life (in this subsection referred to as **"the estimated life"**) of the deposits, but shall not estimate such life at more than 20 years;

(ii) the inspector shall then estimate the amount of the difference (in this subsection referred to as **"the estimated difference"**) between the capital expenditure incurred in connection with the mine and the amount which in his or her opinion the assets representing that capital expenditure are likely to be worth at the end of the estimated life;

(iii) the inspector shall, subject to this section, allow as the mine development allowance for that chargeable period an amount equal to a sum which bears to the estimated difference the same proportion as the length of that chargeable period bears to the length of the estimated life;

(iv) if capital expenditure incurred in connection with the mine was incurred during that chargeable period, then, that chargeable period shall for the purposes of subparagraph (iii) be taken to comprise so much only of that chargeable period as is subsequent to the date on which the capital expenditure was incurred.

(*b*) The total of the mine development allowances shall not exceed the estimated difference.

(6) A mine development allowance to any person carrying on the trade of working a mine shall be made in taxing that trade, and section 304(4) shall apply in relation to the allowance as it applies in relation to allowances to be made under Part 9.

(7) A mine development allowance shall not be made in respect of any capital expenditure incurred in connection with a mine in any case where the asset representing that capital expenditure is an asset in respect of which an allowance may be made under section 284.

(8) Where a mine development allowance for any chargeable period has been made in respect of capital expenditure incurred in connection with a mine, then, for that chargeable period section 85 shall not apply as respects any such asset.

(9) Any capital expenditure incurred on or after the 6th day of April, 1946, in connection with a mine by a person about to carry on the trade of working the mine but before commencing such trade shall be treated for the purposes of this section as if it had been incurred on the first day of the commencement of such trade.

(10) Where mine development allowances in respect of any capital expenditure incurred in connection with a mine have been made and the mine has finally ceased to be operated, the following provisions shall apply:

(*a*) the inspector shall review the mine development allowances;

(*b*) if on such review it appears that the amount of the difference (in this subsection referred to as **"the difference"**) between the capital expenditure incurred in connection with the mine and the amount which the assets representing that capital expenditure at such cessation were worth at such cessation exceeds the total of the mine development allowances, then, further mine development allowances equal to the excess may be made for any chargeable period (being the chargeable period in which the mine has finally ceased to be operated or any previous chargeable period), but the total of such further mine development allowances shall not amount to more than the excess and if necessary effect may be given to this paragraph by means of repayment;

(*c*) if on such review it appears that the difference is less than the total of the mine development allowances, then, the deficiency or the total of the mine development allowances, whichever is the less, shall be treated as a trading receipt of the trade of working the mine accruing immediately before such cessation.

(11) Where the person (in this subsection referred to as **"the vendor"**) carrying on the trade of working a mine sells to any other person (not being a person who succeeds the vendor in that trade) any asset representing capital expenditure incurred in connection with the mine and by reference to which mine development allowances have been made, the following provisions shall apply:

(*a*) if the total of the mine development allowances when added to the sum realised on the sale of that asset is less than that capital expenditure by any amount (in this subsection referred to as **"the unexhausted allowance"**), then, further mine development allowances may be granted to the vendor in respect of any chargeable period (being the chargeable period of such sale or any previous chargeable period), but the total of such further mine development allowances shall not exceed the unexhausted allowance;

(*b*) if the total of the mine development allowances when added to the sum realised on the sale of that asset exceeds that capital expenditure, then, the amount of such excess or the total of the mine development allowances, whichever is the less, shall be treated as a trading receipt of the trade accruing immediately before the sale.

(12) Where—

(*a*) mine development allowances in respect of any capital expenditure incurred in connection with a mine have been made to a person (in this subsection referred to as **"the original trader"**) carrying on the trade of working the mine, and

(*b*) another person (in this subsection referred to as **"the successor"**) succeeds to that trade,

mine development allowances may continue to be made in respect of that capital expenditure to the successor, but in no case shall the amount of such allowances exceed the amount to which the original trader would have been entitled if the original trader had continued to carry on that trade.

(13) Where for any chargeable period a company was entitled to relief from tax by virtue of Chapter II or Chapter III of Part XXV of the Income Tax Act, 1967, then, for the purposes of subsections (5) and (10) to (12), there shall be deemed to have been made for that chargeable period in respect of any expenditure the full mine development allowance which on due claim could have been made for that chargeable period in respect of that expenditure, unless that allowance has in fact been made.

(14) An appeal to the Appeal Commissioners shall lie on any question arising under this section in the like manner as an appeal would lie against an assessment, and the provisions of the Income Tax Acts relating to appeals shall apply accordingly.

Cross-references

Discontinuance of trade: s 321(9)(*b*).

Dividends regarded as paid out of profits accumulated before given date: Sch 22 para 5(3)(*e*).

Exploration expenditure, subs (11): s 679(4)(*a*).

Industrial building construction or refurbishment expenditure does not include expenditure under this section: s 270(2)(*c*).

Investment allowance in respect of exploration expenditure, subs (6): s 677(1).

Mine development allowance, meaning applied: s 672(1).

Mineral depletion allowance: s 680(1).

Mining development and exploration expenditure: s 673(1).

Non-resident company within the charge to corporation tax in respect of one source and income tax in respect of another: s 309(*d*).

Petroleum trade, abandonment expenditure and loss relief: s 695(8).

Petroleum trade, development expenditure: s 692(4)(*c*).

Petroleum trade, exploration expenditure: s 693(12).

Profits or assets available for distribution: s 413(5)(*b*).

Reorganisation into companies of Trustee Savings Banks, capital allowances: Sch 17 para 2(1)(*a*).

Taxation of certain short-term leases of plant and machinery: s 80A(2)(*b*).

Definitions

Appeal Commissioners: s 2(1); inspector: ss 2(1), 5(1), 852; month: IA 1937 Sch; the Oireachtas: IA 1937 Sch; person: IA 1937 s 11(*c*); trade: s 3(1).

Former enactments

ITA 1967 s 245; CTA 1976 s 21(1) and Sch 1 para 10; FA 1980 s 17(3); FA 1996 s 132(2) and Sch 5 Pt II.

671 Marginal coal mine allowance

(1) In this section, **"marginal coal mine"** means a coal mine in the State being worked for the purpose of the production of coal and in respect of which the Minister for the Marine and Natural Resources gives a certificate stating that that Minister is satisfied that the profits derived or to be derived from the working of that mine are such that, if tax is to be charged on those profits in accordance with the Income Tax Acts, other than this section, the mine is unlikely to continue to be worked.

(2) The Minister for Finance, after consultation with the Minister for the Marine and Natural Resources, may direct in respect of a marginal coal mine that for any particular year of assessment the tax chargeable on the profits of that mine shall be reduced to such amount (including nil) as may be specified by the Minister for Finance.

(3) Where a person is carrying on the trade of working a coal mine in respect of which the Minister for Finance gives a direction under subsection (2) in respect of a year of assessment, an allowance shall be made as a deduction in charging the profits of that trade to tax for that year of assessment of such amount as will ensure that the tax charged in respect of the profits of that trade shall equal the amount specified by that Minister.

(4) This section shall apply for corporation tax as it applies for income tax, and references to the Income Tax Acts, to years of assessment and to a deduction in charging the profits of a trade shall apply as if they were or included respectively references to the Corporation Tax Acts, to accounting periods and to a deduction made in computing the trading income for corporation tax.

Definitions

Income Tax Acts: s 1(2); person: IA 1937 s 11(*c*); trade: s 3(1); year of assessment: ss 2(1), 5(1).

Former enactments

FA 1974 s 74; CTA 1976 s 140(1), s164, Sch 2 Pt I para 48 and Sch 3 Pt II.

672 Interpretation (sections 672 to 683)

(1) In this section and in sections 673 to 683, except where otherwise provided or the context otherwise requires—

"development expenditure" means capital expenditure—

(*a*) on the development of a qualifying mine, or

(*b*) on the construction of any works in connection with a qualifying mine which are of such a nature that, when the mine ceases to be operated, they are likely to have so diminished in value that their value will be nil or almost nil, and includes interest on money borrowed to meet such capital expenditure, but does not include expenditure on—

(i) the acquisition of the site of the mine or the site of any such works or of rights in or over any such site,

(ii) the acquisition of a scheduled mineral asset, or

(iii) works constructed wholly or mainly for subjecting the raw product of the mine to any process except a process designed for preparing the raw product for use as such;

"exploration expenditure" means capital expenditure on searching in the State for deposits of scheduled minerals or on testing such deposits or winning access to such deposits, and includes capital expenditure on systematic searching for areas containing scheduled minerals and searching by drilling or other means for scheduled minerals in those areas, but does not include expenditure on operations in the course of working a qualifying mine or expenditure which is development expenditure;

"mine development allowance" has the same meaning as in section 670;

"qualifying mine" means a mine being worked for the purpose of obtaining scheduled minerals;

"scheduled mineral asset" means a deposit of scheduled minerals or land comprising such a deposit or an interest in or right over such deposit or land;

"scheduled minerals" means minerals specified in the Table to this section occurring in non-bedded deposits of such minerals.

(2) Except where provided for in sections 674 to 676, expenditure shall not be regarded for the purposes of this section and sections 673 to 683 as having been incurred by a person carrying on the trade of working a qualifying mine in so far as the expenditure has been or is to be met directly or indirectly out of moneys provided by the Oireachtas or by any other person (not being a person who has carried on the trade of working that mine).

(3) The Minister for Finance may by regulations add minerals occurring in non-bedded deposits of such minerals to the Table to this section.

(4) Every regulation made under subsection (3) shall be laid before Dáil Éireann as soon as may be after it is made and, if a resolution annulling the regulation is passed by Dáil Éireann within the next 21 days on which Dáil Éireann has sat after the regulation is laid before it, the regulation shall be annulled accordingly, but without prejudice to the validity of anything previously done thereunder.

TABLE

SCHEDULED MINERALS

Barytes

Felspar

Serpentinous marble

Quartz rock

Soapstone

Ores of copper

Ores of gold

Ores of iron

Ores of lead

Ores of manganese

Ores of molybdenum

Ores of silver Ores of sulphur

Ores of zinc.

Cross-references

Exploration expenditure incurred by person not engaged in trade of mining: s 676(1)(*b*).

Exploration expenditure: s 679(2).

Non-resident company within the charge to corporation tax in respect of one source and income tax in respect of another: s 309(*d*).

Petroleum taxation, meaning of "qualifying mine" applied: s 684(1).

Definitions

land: IA 1937 Sch; the Oireachtas: IA 1937 Sch; person: IA 1937 s 11(*c*); trade: s 3(1).

Former enactments

F(TPCM)A 1974 s 1(1)–(2) and (6)–(7); CTA 1976 s 21(1) and Sch 1 para 63; FA 1996 s 132(1) and Sch 5 Pt I para 8.

673 Allowance in respect of development expenditure and exploration expenditure

(1) Subject to subsections (2) and (3), where a person carrying on the trade of working a qualifying mine incurs on or after the 6th day of April, 1974, any development expenditure or exploration expenditure and makes application under section 670 for a mine development allowance for a chargeable period in respect of such expenditure—

(*a*) that expenditure shall be deemed to be expenditure in respect of which that allowance may be granted, whether or not in the case of exploration expenditure a deposit of scheduled minerals is found as a result of the expenditure,

(*b*) the amount of such allowance for that chargeable period shall be equal to the total amount of—

(i) the exploration expenditure, and

(ii) in the case of development expenditure, the amount of the difference between that expenditure and the amount which in the opinion of the inspector the assets representing that expenditure are likely to be worth at the end of the estimated life of the qualifying mine, and

(*c*) in relation to a case in which this section has applied, any reference in the Tax Acts to an allowance made under section 670 shall be construed as including a reference to an allowance made under that section by virtue of this section.

(2) For the purposes of this section, no account shall be taken of exploration expenditure incurred before the 1st day of April, 1990, as a result of which a deposit of scheduled minerals is not found if the expenditure was incurred more than 10 years before the date

on which the person carrying on the trade of working a qualifying mine commenced to carry on that trade.

(3) No allowance shall be made under subsection (1) in respect of expenditure incurred before the 6th day of April, 1974, whether or not such expenditure is by virtue of any provision of the Tax Acts deemed to have been incurred on or after that date.

Cross-references

Expenditure on abortive exploration: s 674(3).

Exploration expenditure incurred by bodies corporate: s 675(1).

Exploration expenditure incurred by person not engaged in trade of mining: s 676(1)(*b*).

Exploration expenditure: s 679(2), (4)(*a*).

Grants and subsidies: s 672(2).

Investment allowance in respect of exploration expenditure: s 677(1).

Meanings of "development expenditure", "exploration expenditure", "mine development allowance", "qualifying mine", "scheduled mineral asset", "scheduled minerals": s 672(1).

Mineral depletion allowance: s 680(1).

Non-resident company within the charge to corporation tax in respect of one source and income tax in respect of another: s 309(*d*).

Profits or assets available for distribution: s 413(5)(*b*).

Definitions

Income Tax Acts: s 1(2); inspector: ss 2(1), 5(1), 852; person: IA 1937 s 11(*c*); trade: s 3(1); year of assessment: ss 2(1), 5(1).

Former enactments

F(TPCM)A 1974 s 2(1) and (4); CTA 1976 s 21(1) and Sch 1 para 64; FA 1990 s 39(*a*).

Corresponding UK tax provision

Income and Corporation Taxes Act 1988 s 91C.

674 Expenditure on abortive exploration

(1) (*a*) Where a person who commences to carry on a trade of working a qualifying mine has incurred exploration expenditure and that expenditure was not incurred in connection with the qualifying mine, then, subject to paragraph (*b*), in taxing the trade for the chargeable period in which the person commences to carry on the trade, there shall be made an allowance of an amount equal to the amount of that expenditure.

(*b*) For the purposes of paragraph (*a*), no account shall be taken of exploration expenditure incurred before the 1st day of April, 1990, if the expenditure was incurred more than 10 years before the date on which the person commences to carry on the trade of working the qualifying mine.

(2) Where in a case referred to in subsection (1) the person concerned is a body corporate and there was or is, after all or part of the expenditure referred to in that subsection had been incurred by the body corporate, a change in ownership (within the meaning of Schedule 9) of the body corporate or of a body corporate that is a parent body or a wholly-owned subsidiary (within the meaning of section 675) of the first-mentioned body corporate, no allowance shall be made under this section in respect of any part of that expenditure incurred before the date of the change in ownership; but, in any case where part of the ordinary share capital of any body corporate is acquired by a Minister of the Government, such acquisition shall be disregarded in determining whether or not there was or is such a change in ownership.

(3) Where a person commences to carry on the trade of working a qualifying mine but has not incurred the exploration expenditure incurred in connection with that mine, no allowance shall be made under this section or by virtue of section 673 in respect of exploration expenditure incurred by that person before the date on which that person commences to carry on that trade.

(4) Subject to paragraphs 16 and 18 of Schedule 32, a person shall not be entitled to an allowance in respect of the same expenditure both under this section and under some other provision of the Tax Acts.

Cross-references

Exploration expenditure incurred by bodies corporate: s 675(1).
Exploration expenditure incurred by person not engaged in trade of mining: s 676(1)(*b*).
Exploration expenditure, subs (3): s 679(2).
Grants and subsidies: s 672(2).
Meanings of "development expenditure", "exploration expenditure", "mine development allowance", "qualifying mine", "scheduled mineral asset", "scheduled minerals": s 672(1).
Non-resident company within the charge to corporation tax in respect of one source and income tax in respect of another: s 309(*d*).
Profits or assets available for distribution: s 413(5)(*b*).

Definitions

Income Tax Acts: s 1(2); person: IA 1937 s 11(*c*); trade: s 3(1); year of assessment: ss 2(1), 5(1).

Former enactments

F(TPCM)A 1974 s 3(2)–(5); CTA 1976 s 21(1) and Sch 1 para 65; FA 1990 s 39(*b*).

Corresponding UK tax provision

Capital Allowances Act 2001 s 401.

675 Exploration expenditure incurred by certain bodies corporate

(1) Subject to subsection (2), where exploration expenditure, in respect of which an allowance may be claimed by virtue of section 673 or 674, or (as respects expenditure incurred on or after the 1st day of April, 1990) by virtue of section 673 as applied by section 679, is or has been incurred by a body corporate (in this section referred to as **"the exploration company"**) and—

(*a*) another body corporate is or is deemed to be a wholly-owned subsidiary of the exploration company, or

(*b*) the exploration company is or is deemed to be a wholly-owned subsidiary of another body corporate,

then, the expenditure or so much of it as the exploration company specifies—

(i) in the case referred to in paragraph (*a*), may at the election of the exploration company be deemed to have been incurred by such other body corporate (being a body corporate which is or is deemed to be a wholly-owned subsidiary of the exploration company) as the exploration company specifies,

(ii) in the case referred to in paragraph (*b*), may at the election of the exploration company be deemed to have been incurred by the body corporate (in this paragraph referred to as **"the parent body"**) of which the exploration company was, at the time the expenditure was incurred, a wholly-owned subsidiary or by such other body corporate (being a body corporate which is or is deemed to be a wholly-owned subsidiary of the parent body) as the exploration company specifies, and, in a case where that expenditure was incurred on a date before the incorporation of the body corporate so specified, sections 672 to 683 shall apply in relation to the granting of any allowance in respect of that expenditure as if that body corporate had been in existence at the time the expenditure was incurred and had incurred the expenditure at that time.

(2) (*a*) The same expenditure shall not be taken into account in relation to more than one trade by virtue of this section.

(*b*) Subject to paragraphs 16 and 18 of Schedule 32, an allowance shall not be granted in respect of the same expenditure both by virtue of this section and under some other provision of the Tax Acts.

(3) A body corporate shall for the purposes of subsection (1) be deemed to be a wholly-owned subsidiary of another body corporate if and so long as all of its ordinary share capital is owned by that other body corporate, whether directly or through another body corporate or other bodies corporate or partly directly and partly through another body corporate or other bodies corporate; but, where part of the ordinary share capital of any body corporate is held by a Minister of the Government and the remainder of the ordinary share capital of that body corporate is held by another body corporate, the first-mentioned body corporate shall for the purposes of subsection (1) be deemed to be a wholly owned subsidiary of the last mentioned body corporate.

(4) Subsections (5) to (10) of section 9 shall apply for the purpose of determining the amount of ordinary share capital held in a body corporate through other bodies corporate.

Cross-references

Expenditure on abortive exploration: s 674(2).
Exploration expenditure incurred by person not engaged in trade of mining: s 676(1)(*b*).
Exploration expenditure: s 679(2).
Grants and subsidies: s 672(2).
Investment allowance in respect of exploration expenditure: s 677(2)(*b*).
Meanings of "development expenditure", "exploration expenditure", "mine development allowance", "qualifying mine", "scheduled mineral asset", "scheduled minerals": s 672(1).
Non-resident company within the charge to corporation tax in respect of one source and income tax in respect of another: s 309(*d*).

Definitions

Income Tax Acts: s 1(2); trade: s 3(1).

Former enactments

F(TPCM)A 1974 s 4; CTA 1976 s 21(1) and Sch 1 para 66; FA 1990 s 39(*c*).

676 Expenditure incurred by person not engaged in trade of mining

(1) Where—

(*a*) a person incurs exploration expenditure which results in the finding of a deposit of scheduled minerals, and

(*b*) without having carried on any trade which consists of or includes the working of that deposit and without any allowance or deduction under or by virtue of sections 672 to 683 having been made to the person in respect of that expenditure, the person sells any assets representing that expenditure to another person, then, if that other person carries on such a trade in connection with that deposit, that other person shall for the purposes of sections 672 to 683 be deemed to have incurred, for the purposes of the trade and in connection with the deposit, exploration expenditure equal to the lesser of—

(i) the amount of the exploration expenditure represented by the assets, and

(ii) the price paid by that other person for the assets,

and that expenditure shall be deemed to have been incurred by that other person on the date on which that other person commences to carry on that trade.

(2) A person who by virtue of subsection (1) is deemed to have incurred an amount of exploration expenditure shall be deemed not to have incurred that amount of expenditure unless the working of the deposit results in the production of scheduled minerals in reasonable commercial quantities.

(3) Subject to paragraphs 16 and 18 of Schedule 32, a deduction or allowance in respect of the same expenditure shall not be made both under this section and under some other provision of the Tax Acts.

(4) Section 677 shall not apply to expenditure in respect of which an allowance is made by virtue of this section.

Cross-references

Exploration expenditure incurred by person not engaged in trade of mining: s 676(1)(*b*).

Exploration expenditure: s 679(2).

Grants and subsidies: s 672(2).

Meanings of "development expenditure", "exploration expenditure", "mine development allowance", "qualifying mine", "scheduled mineral asset", "scheduled minerals": s 672(1).

Non-resident company within the charge to corporation tax in respect of one source and income tax in respect of another: s 309(*d*).

Definitions

Income Tax Acts: s 1(2); person: IA 1937 s 11(*c*); trade: s 3(1).

Former enactments

F(TPCM)A 1974 s 5; CTA 1976 s 21(1) and Sch 1 para 67.

677 Investment allowance in respect of exploration expenditure

(1) Where a person carrying on the trade of working a qualifying mine incurs on or after the 6th day of April, 1974, exploration expenditure in relation to which section 673 applies, there shall, in addition to any mine development allowance made in respect of such expenditure, be made to the person in taxing the trade for the chargeable period for which such mine development allowance is made an allowance (which shall be known as an **"exploration investment allowance"**) equal to 20 per cent of such expenditure, and section 670(6) shall apply to an exploration investment allowance as it applies to a mine development allowance.

(2) (*a*) No allowance shall be made under this section in respect of exploration expenditure—

(i) incurred before the 6th day of April, 1974, whether or not such expenditure is by virtue of any provision of the Tax Acts deemed to have been incurred on or after that date, or

(ii) which is deemed to be incurred by a person other than the person who incurred the expenditure.

(*b*) Paragraph (*a*) shall not apply in respect of expenditure deemed under section 675 to have been incurred by a body corporate other than the body corporate which incurred the expenditure.

Cross-references

Exploration expenditure incurred by person not engaged in trade of mining: s 676(1)(*b*), (4).
Exploration expenditure: s 679(2).
Grants and subsidies: s 672(2).
Meanings of "development expenditure", "exploration expenditure", "mine development allowance", "qualifying mine", "scheduled mineral asset", "scheduled minerals": s 672(1).
Non-resident company within the charge to corporation tax in respect of one source and income tax in respect of another: s 309(*d*).
Profits or assets available for distribution: s 413(5)(*b*).

Definitions

person: IA 1937 s 11(*c*); trade: s 3(1).

Former enactments

F(TPCM)A 1974 s 6; CTA 1976 s 21(1) and Sch 1 para 68.

678 Allowance for machinery and plant

(1) Where on or after the 6th day of April, 1974, new machinery or new plant (other than vehicles suitable for the conveyance by road of persons or goods or the haulage by road of other vehicles) is provided for use for the purposes of the trade of working a qualifying mine, that machinery or plant shall, if it is not qualifying machinery or plant, be deemed for the purpose of section 285 to be qualifying machinery or plant.

(2) Where on or after the 6th day of April, 1974, a person carrying on the trade of working a qualifying mine incurs capital expenditure on the provision of new machinery or new plant (other than vehicles suitable for the conveyance by road of persons or goods or the haulage by road of other vehicles) for the purposes of that trade, there shall be made to the person for the chargeable period related to the expenditure an allowance equal to 20 per cent of the expenditure, and such allowance shall be made in taxing the trade.

(3) For the purposes of ascertaining the amount of any allowance to be made to any person under section 284 in respect of expenditure incurred during a chargeable period on any qualifying machinery or plant, no account shall be taken of an allowance under subsection (2) in respect of that expenditure, and in section 284(4) **"the allowances on that account"** and **"the allowances"** where it occurs before **"exceed"** shall each be construed as not including a reference to any allowance made under subsection (2) to the person by whom the trade of working a qualifying mine is carried on.

(4) Where an allowance under subsection (2) has been made to any person in respect of expenditure incurred on the provision of qualifying machinery or plant and the machinery or plant is sold by that person without the machinery or plant having been used by that person for the purposes of the trade of working a qualifying mine or before the expiration of the period of 2 years from the day on which the machinery or plant began to be so used, the allowance shall be withdrawn and all such additional assessments and adjustments of assessments shall be made as may be necessary for or in consequence of the withdrawal of the allowance.

(5) For the purposes of this section—

(*a*) the day on which any expenditure is incurred shall be taken to be the day when the sum in question becomes payable,

(*b*) expenditure shall not be regarded as having been incurred by a person in so far as it has been or is to be met directly or indirectly by the State, by any board established by statute or by any public or local authority,

(*c*) any expenditure incurred for the purposes of a trade by a person about to carry on the trade shall be treated as if that expenditure had been incurred by that person on the first day on which that person carries on the trade,

(*d*) capital expenditure shall not include any expenditure which is allowed to be deducted in computing for the purposes of tax the profits or gains of a trade carried on by the person incurring the expenditure, and

(*e*) subsections (2) and (3) of section 306 shall apply in determining the chargeable period (being a year of assessment) for which an allowance is to be made under this section.

(6) For the purposes of the Income Tax Acts, any claim by a person for an allowance under this section in taxing the person's trade shall be included in the annual statement required to be delivered under those Acts of the profits or gains of the person's trade and shall be accompanied by a certificate signed by the claimant (which shall be deemed to form part of the claim) stating that the expenditure was incurred on the provision of qualifying machinery or plant and giving such particulars as show that the allowance is to be made.

(7) Section 304(4) shall apply in relation to an allowance under subsection (2) as it applies in relation to allowances to be made under Part 9.

Cross-references

Exploration expenditure incurred by person not engaged in trade of mining: s 676(1)(*b*).

Exploration expenditure: s 679(2).

Grants and subsidies: s 672(2).

Meanings of "development expenditure", "exploration expenditure", "mine development allowance", "qualifying mine", "scheduled mineral asset", "scheduled minerals": s 672(1).

Non-resident company within the charge to corporation tax in respect of one source and income tax in respect of another: s 309(*d*).

Case law

Contractor allowed full investment allowance even though the plant had been used to a small extent outside the designated area: *McNally v O'Maoldomhnaigh* ITR Vol IV p 22.

Definitions

person: IA 1937 s 11(*c*); trade: s 3(1); year of assessment: ss 2(1), 5(1).

Former enactments

F(TPCM)A 1974 s 7(1), (3)–(4); CTA 1976 s 21 and Sch 1 paras 57, 58, 59 and 69; FA 1971 s 22(3)–(4), s 23, s 24 and s 25; FA 1997 s 146(1) and Sch 9 Pt I para 7(1).

679 Exploration expenditure

(1) (*a*) In this section—

"exploration company" means a company, the business of which for the time being consists primarily of exploring for scheduled minerals;

"exploring for scheduled minerals" means searching in the State for deposits of scheduled minerals or testing such deposits or winning access to such deposits, and includes the systematic searching for areas containing scheduled minerals and searching by drilling or other means for scheduled minerals within those areas, but does not include operations which are operations in the course of developing or working a qualifying mine.

(*b*) This section shall apply as respects expenditure incurred on or after the 1st day of April, 1990.

(2) Subject to subsections (3) to (5), for as long as a company—

(*a*) is an exploration company,

(*b*) does not carry on a trade of working a qualifying mine, and

(*c*) incurs capital expenditure (including such expenditure incurred on the provision of plant and machinery) for the purposes of exploring for scheduled minerals,

the company shall be deemed for the purposes of sections 673, 674(3), 677 and 678 and the other provisions of the Tax Acts, apart from section 672, subsections (1), (2) and (4) of section 674 and sections 675, 676, 680, 681, 682 and 683—

(i) to be carrying on a trade of working a qualifying mine,

(ii) to come within the charge to corporation tax in respect of that trade when it first incurs the capital expenditure referred to in paragraph (*c*), and

(iii) to incur for the purposes of that trade that expenditure incurred on the provision of plant and machinery,

so that all allowances or charges to be made for an accounting period by virtue of this subsection and section 673, 677 or 678 shall be given effect by treating the amount of any allowance as a trading expense of that trade in the period and by treating the amount on which any such charge is to be made as a trading receipt of that trade in the period.

(3) Where by virtue of subsection (2) a company is to be treated as incurring a loss in a trade in an accounting period, the company—

(*a*) shall be entitled to relief in respect of the loss under ...[1] subsections (1) to (3) of section 396 and subsections (1) and (2) of section 397 as if for **"trading income from the trade"** or **"trading income"**, wherever occurring in sections 396 and 397, there were substituted **"profits (of whatever description)"**, and

(*b*) subject to subsection (4)(*b*)(ii), shall not otherwise be entitled to relief in respect of the loss or to surrender relief under section 420(1) in respect of the loss.

(4) (*a*) Any asset representing exploration expenditure in respect of which an allowance or deduction has been made to a company by virtue of subsection (2) and section 673 shall for the purposes of section 670(11) be treated as an asset representing capital expenditure incurred in connection with the mine which the company is deemed to be working by virtue of subsection (2), and the company shall not cease to be deemed to be carrying on the trade of working that mine, so as to be within the charge to corporation tax in respect of that trade, before any sale of such an asset in the event of such a sale.

(*b*) Subject to paragraph (*c*), where a company begins at any time (in this paragraph and in paragraph (*c*) referred to as **"the relevant time"**) to carry on a trade of working a qualifying mine and accordingly ceases to be deemed to carry on such a trade, the company shall be treated as carrying on the same trade before and after that time for the purposes of—

(i) any allowance, charge or trade receipt treated as arising by reference to any capital expenditure incurred before the relevant time, and

(ii) relief, other than by virtue of subsection (3), under section 396(1) for any losses arising before the relevant time, in so far as relief has not already been given for those losses by virtue of this section.

(*c*) Paragraph (*b*) shall not apply where there is a change in the ownership of the company within a period of—

(i) 12 months ending at the relevant time, or

(ii) 24 months beginning at the relevant time.

(*d*) Schedule 9 shall apply for the purposes of supplementing this subsection.

(5) (*a*) Notwithstanding any other provision of the Tax Acts, where an allowance or deduction has been given by virtue of this section in respect of any expenditure, no other allowance or deduction shall be given by virtue of any provision of the Tax Acts, including this section, in respect of that expenditure.

(*b*) Paragraph (*b*) of section 261 shall apply to a company for as long as it is deemed by virtue of subsection (2) to be carrying on a trade of working a qualifying mine as if "who is not a company within the charge to corporation tax in respect of the payment" were deleted from that paragraph.

Amendments

1 Deleted by FA 2003 s 41(1)(*i*) as respects accounting periods ending on or after 6 February 2003; previously "157,".

Cross-references

Exploration expenditure incurred by bodies corporate: s 675(1).

Exploration expenditure incurred by person not engaged in trade of mining: s 676(1)(*b*).

Grants and subsidies: s 672(4).

Meanings of "development expenditure", "exploration expenditure", "mine development allowance", "qualifying mine", "scheduled mineral asset", "scheduled minerals": s 672(1).

Supplementary, subs (4): Sch 9 paras 1, 2(*d*), 3–6, 8.

Definitions

company: ss 4(1), 5(1); month: IA 1937 Sch; person: IA 1937 s 11(*c*); Tax Acts: s 1(2); trade: s 3(1).

Former enactments

F(TPCM)A 4 s 7A; FA 1990 s 39(*d*).

680 Annual allowance for mineral depletion

(1) Where a person carrying on the trade of working a qualifying mine incurs after the 31st day of March, 1974, capital expenditure on the acquisition of a scheduled mineral asset entitling such person to work deposits of scheduled minerals and in connection with that trade commences to work those deposits, such person shall be entitled to mine development allowances under section 670 in respect of that capital expenditure to the extent that such person would have been entitled to such allowances if that capital expenditure had been capital expenditure incurred in the development of the mine, but section 673 shall not apply in respect of any such expenditure.

(2) Where a person who commences to carry on the trade of working a qualifying mine [at any time][1] on or after the 6th day of April, 1974, incurred capital expenditure before that [time][2] on the acquisition of a scheduled mineral asset in connection with that mine, such person shall for the purposes of this section be deemed to have incurred that expenditure on the day on which such person commences to carry on that trade, and subsection (1) shall apply accordingly.

Amendments

1 Inserted by FA 1998 s 40(*a*) with effect from 6 April 1998.

2 Substituted by FA 1998 s 40(*b*); previously "date" with effect from 6 April 1998.

Cross-references

Exploration expenditure incurred by person not engaged in trade of mining: s 676(1)(*b*).

Exploration expenditure: s 679(2).

Grants and subsidies: s 672(2).

Meanings of "development expenditure", "exploration expenditure", "mine development allowance", "qualifying mine", "scheduled mineral asset", "scheduled minerals": s 672(1).

Profits or assets available for distribution: s 413(5)(*b*).

Definitions

person: IA 1937 s 11(*c*); trade: s 3(1).

Former enactments

F(TPCM)A 1974 s 8; CTA 1976 s 140 and Sch 2 Pt I para 37.

Corresponding UK tax provision

Capital Allowances Act 2001 s 395.

681 Allowance for mine rehabilitation expenditure

(1) (*a*) In this section—

"integrated pollution control licence" means a licence granted under section 83 of the Environmental Protection Agency Act, 1992;

"mine rehabilitation fund", in relation to a qualifying mine, means a fund—

(i) which consists of amounts paid by a person carrying on the trade of working a qualifying mine to another person (in this section referred to as **"the fund holder"**) not connected with the first-mentioned person,

(ii) which is obliged to be maintained under the terms—

(I) of a State mining facility, or

(II) of any other agreement in writing to which the Minister is a party and to which the State mining facility is subject,

(iii) the sole purpose of which is to have available at the time a qualifying mine ceases to be worked such amount as is specified in a certificate given by the Minister under subsection (2) as being the amount which in the Minister's opinion could reasonably be expected to be necessary to meet rehabilitation expenditure in relation to the qualifying mine, and

(iv) no part of which may be paid to the person, or a person connected with that person, who is working or has worked the qualifying mine except where—

(I) the fund holder has been authorised in writing by the Minister, and by either or both the relevant local authority and the Environmental Protection Agency, to make a payment to the person or the connected person, as the case may be, for the purposes of incurring rehabilitation expenditure in relation to the qualifying mine, or

(II) an amount may be paid to the person or the connected person, as the case may be, after a certificate of completion of rehabilitation in relation to the qualifying mine has been submitted to and approved by—

(A) the Minister, and

(B) either or both the relevant local authority and the Environmental Protection Agency;

"the Minister" means the Minister for the Marine and Natural Resources;

"qualifying mine" means a mine being worked for the purpose of obtaining scheduled minerals, dolomite and dolomitic limestone, [fireclay, coal,][1] calcite and gypsum, or any of those minerals;

"rehabilitation expenditure" means expenditure incurred in connection with the rehabilitation of the site of a mine or part of a mine, being expenditure incurred by a person who has ceased to work the mine in order to comply with any condition—

(i) of a State mining facility,

(ii) subject to which planning permission for development consisting of the mining and working of minerals was granted, or

(iii) subject to which an integrated pollution control licence for an activity specified in the First Schedule to the Environmental Protection Agency Act, 1992, was granted;

"rehabilitation" includes landscaping and the carrying out of any activities which take place after the mine ceases to be worked and which are required by a condition subject to which planning permission for development consisting of the mining and working of minerals, or an integrated pollution control licence, was granted;

"relevant local authority", in relation to a qualifying mine, means the council of a county or the corporation of a county or other borough or, where appropriate, the urban district council, in whose functional area the mine is situated;

"relevant payments" means payments specified in accordance with paragraph (*b*)(iii) of subsection (2) in a certificate given under that subsection and which are paid at or about the time specified in the certificate;

"State mining facility", in relation to a mine, means a State mining lease, a State mining licence or a State mining permission granted by the Minister in relation to the mine.

(*b*) For the purposes of this section—

(i) any reference to the site of a mine includes a reference to land used in connection with the working of the mine, and

(ii) the net cost to any person of the rehabilitation of the site of a mine shall be the excess, if any, of rehabilitation expenditure over any receipts attributable to the rehabilitation (whether for spoil or other assets removed from the site or for tipping rights or otherwise).

(*c*) For the purposes of this section, subsections (2) and (3) of section 306 shall apply in determining the chargeable period (being a year of assessment) for which an allowance is to be made under this section.

(2) (*a*) Where in relation to a fund the Minister is of the opinion that—

(i) the matters set out in paragraphs (i), (ii) and (iv) of the definition of **"mine rehabilitation fund"** are satisfied, and

(ii) the sole purpose of the fund is to have available at the time a qualifying mine ceases to be worked such amount as could reasonably be expected to be necessary to meet rehabilitation expenditure in relation to the qualifying mine,

the Minister may give a certificate to that effect.

(*b*) A certificate given under paragraph (*a*) shall, in addition to the information specified in that paragraph, specify—

(i) the number of years, being the Minister's opinion of the life (in this section referred to as **"the estimated life"**) of the mine remaining at the time the certificate is given,

(ii) the amount which in the Minister's opinion could reasonably be expected to be necessary to meet rehabilitation expenditure in relation to the qualifying mine, and

(iii) the amounts (in this section referred to as **"the scheduled payments"**) required to be paid to the fund holder, and the times at which such amounts are to be paid, so as to achieve the purpose specified in paragraph (*a*)(ii).

(*c*) The Minister may, by notice in writing given to a person to whom a certificate has been given under this section, amend the certificate.

(3) (*a*) An allowance equal to so much of any rehabilitation expenditure in relation to a qualifying mine as does not exceed the net cost of the rehabilitation of the site of the mine shall be made to a person under this section for the chargeable period related to the expenditure.

(*b*) Expenditure incurred by a person after the person ceases to carry on the trade of working a qualifying mine shall be treated as having been incurred on the last day on which the person carried on the trade.

(4) (*a*) Subject to paragraphs (*b*) and (*c*), where the Minister has issued a certificate under subsection (2) in respect of a mine rehabilitation fund related to a qualifying mine, an allowance shall be made to the person who—

(i) is working the qualifying mine, and

(ii) is obliged to make relevant payments to the fund holder in relation to the fund,

for any chargeable period which falls wholly or partly in the period (in this subsection referred to as **"the funding period"**) commencing on the date on which the Minister gives the certificate and ending at the end of the estimated life of the mine, and the amount of the allowance shall be an amount determined by the formula—

$$E \times \frac{N}{12} \times \frac{1}{L}$$

where—

E is the aggregate of the scheduled payments,

N is the number of months in the chargeable period, or the part of the chargeable period falling in the funding period, and

L is the number of years in the estimated life of the mine.

(*b*) The aggregate of the amounts of allowances under this subsection for a chargeable period and all preceding chargeable periods shall not exceed the aggregate of the amounts of relevant payments made in the chargeable period or its basis period and in all preceding chargeable periods or their basis periods.

(*c*) Where effect cannot be given to an allowance or part of an allowance under this subsection for a chargeable period by virtue of paragraph (*b*), the allowance or the part of the allowance, as the case may be, shall be added to the amount of an allowance under this subsection for the following chargeable period and, subject to paragraph (*b*), shall be deemed to be part of the allowance for that period or, if there is no such allowance for that period, shall be deemed to be the allowance for that period, and so on for succeeding periods.

(5) Where the Minister by notice in writing amends a certificate under subsection (2)(*c*) in a chargeable period or its basis period—

(*a*) if the aggregate of the amounts of allowances made under subsection (4) for the chargeable period and all preceding chargeable periods exceeds the aggregate of the amounts of allowances which would have been made under that subsection for those chargeable periods if the certificate had been amended in accordance with the notice at the time the certificate was given, an amount equal to the amount of the excess shall be treated as a trading receipt of the chargeable period in which, or in the basis period for which, the certificate was amended, and

(*b*) if the aggregate of the amounts of allowances which would have been made under subsection (4) for the chargeable period and all preceding chargeable periods if the certificate had been amended in accordance with the notice at the time the certificate was given exceeds the aggregate of the amounts of allowances made under that subsection for those chargeable periods, the allowance under subsection (4) for the chargeable period shall, subject to subsection (4)(*b*), be increased by an amount equal to the excess.

(6) (*a*) Subject to paragraph (*b*), an amount received by a person who is working or has worked a qualifying mine, or by a person connected with such a person, from the fund holder of a mine rehabilitation fund in relation to the qualifying mine, or otherwise in connection with the mine rehabilitation fund, shall be treated as trading income of the person in accordance with this section.

(*b*) The amount to be treated as trading income for a chargeable period shall not exceed the excess of the aggregate of the amounts of allowances made under subsections (4) and (5) in that chargeable period and in any preceding chargeable periods over the aggregate amounts treated under this subsection or subsection (5) as trading income for all preceding chargeable periods.

(*c*) An amount to be treated under this subsection as trading income of a person shall be treated as income of—

(i) where the amount is received at any time when the person is working the qualifying mine, the chargeable period in which, or in the basis period for which, the amount is received, and

(ii) in any other case, the chargeable period in which the mine ceases to be worked.

(*d*) Notwithstanding paragraph (*c*), where an amount is to be treated as income of a chargeable period in accordance with subparagraph (ii) of that paragraph, the amount shall be assessed for the chargeable period in which, or in the basis period for which, the amount is received, and details of the receipt of the amount shall be included in the return required to be made by the person under section 951 for that chargeable period.

(7) Where a person (in this subsection referred to as **"the first-mentioned person"**) ceases to work a qualifying mine and any obligations of the first-mentioned person to rehabilitate the site of the mine are transferred to any other person, that other person shall be treated for the purposes of this section as if that other person had worked the qualifying mine and as if everything done to or by the first-mentioned person had been done to or by that other person.

(8) As respects any person who incurs rehabilitation expenditure in respect of which an allowance is made under subsection (3)—

(*a*) rehabilitation expenditure shall not otherwise be deductible in computing income of the person for any purpose of income tax or corporation tax,

(*b*) an allowance shall not be made in respect of the expenditure under any provision of the Tax Acts other than this section, and

(*c*) to the extent that any receipts are taken into account under subsection (1)(*b*)(ii) to determine the net cost of the rehabilitation of the site of a mine, those receipts shall not constitute income of the person for any purpose of income tax or corporation tax.

(9) An allowance under this section made to a person who is carrying on a trade of working a mine shall be made in taxing that trade, and section 304(4) shall apply in relation to an allowance under subsection (4) as it applies in relation to allowances to be made under Part 9.

Amendments

[1] Inserted by FA 1998 s 41 with effect from 6 April 1998.

Cross-references

Exploration expenditure incurred by person not engaged in trade of mining: s 676(1)(*b*).

Exploration expenditure: s 679(2).

Grants and subsidies: s 672(2).

Meanings of "development expenditure", "exploration expenditure", "mine development allowance", "qualifying mine", "scheduled mineral asset", "scheduled minerals": s 672(1).

Definitions

person: IA 1937 s 11(*c*); trade: s 3(1).

Former enactments

F(TPCM)A 1974 s 8A(1)–(9); FA 1996 s 34; FA 1997 s 146(1) and Sch 9 Pt I para 7(2).

682 Marginal mine allowance

(1) In this section, **"marginal mine"** means a qualifying mine in respect of which the Minister for the Marine and Natural Resources gives a certificate stating that that Minister is satisfied that the profits derived or to be derived from the working of that mine are such that, if tax is to be charged on those profits in accordance with the Income Tax Acts, other than this section, the mine is unlikely to be worked or to continue to be worked.

(2) The Minister for Finance, after consultation with the Minister for the Marine and Natural Resources, may direct in respect of a marginal mine that for any particular year of assessment the tax chargeable on the profits of that qualifying mine shall be reduced to such amount (including nil) as may be specified by the Minister for Finance.

(3) Where a person is carrying on the trade of working a qualifying mine in respect of which the Minister for Finance gives a direction under subsection (2) in respect of a year of assessment, an allowance (which shall be known as a **"marginal mine allowance"**) shall be made as a deduction in charging the profits of that trade to income tax for that year of assessment of such amount or amounts as will ensure that the tax charged in respect of the profits of that trade shall equal the amount specified by that Minister.

(4) This section shall apply for corporation tax as it applies for income tax, and the references to the Income Tax Acts, to a year of assessment and to charging the profits of that trade to income tax shall apply as if they were respectively references to the Corporation Tax Acts, to an accounting period and to computing the profits of that trade for the purposes of corporation tax.

Cross-references

Exploration expenditure incurred by person not engaged in trade of mining: s 676(1)(*b*).
Exploration expenditure: s 679(2).
Grants and subsidies: s 672(2).
Meanings of "development expenditure", "exploration expenditure", "mine development allowance", "qualifying mine", "scheduled mineral asset", "scheduled minerals": s 672(1).

Definitions

Income Tax Acts: s 1(2); person: IA 1937 s 11(*c*); trade: s 3(1); year of assessment: ss 2(1), 5(1).

Former enactments

F(TPCM)A 1974 s 10; CTA 1976 s 140(1), s 164, Sch 2 Pt I para 38 and Sch 3 Pt II.

683 Charge to tax on sums received from sale of scheduled mineral assets

(1) In this section—

"chargeable period" means an accounting period of a company or a year of assessment;

any reference to the sale of a right to a scheduled mineral asset includes a reference to the grant of a licence to work scheduled minerals.

(2) Where a person resident in the State sells any scheduled mineral asset and the net proceeds of the sale consist wholly or partly of a capital sum, the person shall, subject to this section, be charged to tax under Case IV of Schedule D for the chargeable period in which the sum is received by the person on an amount equal to that sum; but where the

person is an individual who, not later than 24 months after the end of the year of assessment in which the sum is paid, elects by notice in writing to the inspector to be charged to tax for that year of assessment and for each of the 5 succeeding years of assessment on an amount equal to one-sixth of that sum, the person shall be so charged.

(3) (*a*) In this subsection, **"tax"** shall mean income tax, unless the seller of the scheduled mineral asset, being a company, would be within the charge to corporation tax in respect of any proceeds of the sale not consisting of a capital sum.

(*b*) Subject to paragraph (*c*), where a person not resident in the State sells any scheduled mineral asset and the net proceeds of the sale consist wholly or partly of a capital sum, then—

(i) the person shall be charged to tax in respect of that sum under Case IV of Schedule D for the chargeable period in which the sum is received by the person, and

(ii) section 238 shall apply to that sum as if it were an annual payment payable otherwise than out of profits or gains brought into charge to tax.

(*c*) Where the person referred to in paragraph (*b*) is an individual who, not later than 24 months after the end of the year of assessment in which the sum is paid elects by notice in writing to the Revenue Commissioners that the sum shall be treated for the purpose of tax for that year and for each of the 5 succeeding years as if one-sixth of that sum were included in his or her income chargeable to tax for each of those years respectively, it shall be so treated, and all such repayments and assessments of tax for each of those years shall be made as are necessary to give effect to the election; but—

(i) the election shall not affect the amount of tax to be deducted and accounted for under section 238,

(ii) where any sum is deducted under section 238, any adjustments necessary to give effect to the election shall be made by means of repayment of tax, and

(iii) those adjustments shall be made year by year and as if one-sixth of the sum deducted had been deducted in respect of tax for each year, and no repayment of, or of any part of, that portion of the tax deducted which is to be treated as deducted in respect of tax for any year shall be made unless and until it is ascertained that the tax ultimately to be paid for that year is less than the amount of tax paid for that year.

(4) Where the scheduled mineral asset sold by a person was acquired by the person by purchase and the price paid consisted wholly or partly of a capital sum, subsections (2) and (3) shall apply as if any capital sum received by the person when the person sells the asset were reduced by the amount of that sum; but nothing in this subsection shall affect the amount of tax to be deducted and accounted for under section 238 by virtue of subsection (3), and where any sum is deducted under section 238 any adjustment necessary to give effect to this subsection shall be made by means of repayment of tax.

(5) Where by virtue of an order made by the Minister for the Marine and Natural Resources under section 14 of the Minerals Development Act, 1940, scheduled minerals or rights to work such minerals are acquired and that Minister pays compensation to any

person in respect of such acquisition, that person shall be deemed for the purposes of this section to have sold a scheduled mineral asset for a capital sum equal to the amount of compensation paid to that person, and subsections (2) to (4) shall apply to the compensation as they apply to a capital sum received in respect of a sale of a scheduled mineral asset.

Cross-references

Exploration expenditure incurred by person not engaged in trade of mining: s 676(1)(*b*).

Exploration expenditure: s 679(2).

Grants and subsidies: s 672(2).

Meanings of "development expenditure", "exploration expenditure", "mine development allowance", "qualifying mine", "scheduled mineral asset", "scheduled minerals": s 672(1).

Revenue precedents

Issue: If an individual disposes of mineral rights in land but retains ownership of the land how are the proceeds to be taxed?

Decision: The proceeds are liable to Income Tax under Schedule D, Case IV.

Definitions

inspector: ss 2(1), 5(1), 852; month: IA 1937 Sch; person: IA 1937 s 11(*c*); writing: IA 1937 Sch; year of assessment: ss 2(1), 5(1).

Former enactments

F(TPCM)A 1974 s 11; CTA 1976 s 140 and Sch 2 Pt I para 39; FA 1981 s 9(*e*).

CHAPTER 2
Petroleum Taxation

Cross-references

Shipping tonnage tax, meaning of "petroleum extraction activities" applied: s 697A(1) ("qualifying ship", para (*e*)).

684 Interpretation (Chapter 2)

(1) In this Chapter—

"abandonment activities", in relation to a relevant field or any part of it, means those activities of a person, whether carried on by the person or on behalf of the person, which comply with the requirements of a petroleum lease held by the person, or, if the person is a company, held by the company or a company associated with it, in respect of—

(*a*) the closing down, decommissioning or abandonment of the relevant field or the part of it, as the case may be, or

(*b*) the dismantlement or removal of the whole or a part of any structure, plant or machinery which is not situated on dry land and which has been brought into use for the purposes of transporting as far as dry land petroleum won from the relevant field or from the part of it, as the case may be;

"abandonment expenditure", in relation to a relevant field or any part of it, means expenditure incurred on abandonment activities in relation to the field or the part of it, as the case may be;

"chargeable period" means an accounting period of a company or a year of assessment;

"designated area" means an area designated by order under section 2 of the Continental Shelf Act, 1968;

"development expenditure" means capital expenditure incurred in connection with a relevant field on the provision for use in carrying on petroleum extraction activities of—

(*a*) machinery or plant,

(*b*) any works, buildings or structures, or

(*c*) any other assets,

which are of such a nature that when the relevant field ceases to be worked they are likely to be so diminished in value that their value will be nil or almost nil, but does not include—

(i) expenditure on any vehicle suitable for the conveyance by road of persons or goods or the haulage by road of other vehicles,

(ii) expenditure on any building or structure for use as a dwelling house, shop or office or for any purpose ancillary to the purposes of a dwelling house, shop or office,

(iii) (I) expenditure incurred on petroleum exploration activities, and

(II) payments made to the Minister for the Marine and Natural Resources on the application for, or in consideration of the granting of, a licence (other than a petroleum lease) or other payments made to that Minister in respect of the holding of the licence,

(iv) expenditure on the acquisition of the site of a relevant field, or of the site of any works, buildings or structures or of rights in or over any such site,

(v) expenditure on the acquisition of, or of rights in or over, deposits of petroleum,

(vi) expenditure on—

(I) machinery or plant, or

(II) works, buildings or structures,

provided for the processing or storing of petroleum won in the course of carrying on petroleum extraction activities, other than the initial treatment and storage of such petroleum,

or

(vii) any interest payment,

and **"assets representing development expenditure"** shall be construed accordingly and shall include any results obtained from any search or enquiry on which the expenditure was incurred;

"dry land" means land not permanently covered by water;

"exploration expenditure" means—

(*a*) capital expenditure incurred on petroleum exploration activities, and

(*b*) payments made to the Minister for the Marine and Natural Resources on the application for, or in consideration of the granting of, a licence (other than a petroleum lease) or other payments made to that Minister in respect of the holding of the licence, but does not include any interest payment, and **"assets representing exploration expenditure"** shall be construed accordingly and shall include any results obtained from any search, exploration or enquiry on which the expenditure was incurred;

"initial treatment and storage", in relation to petroleum won from a relevant field, means the doing of any of the following—

(*a*) subjecting petroleum so won to any process of which the sole purpose is to enable the petroleum to be safely stored, safely loaded into a tanker or safely accepted for refining,

(*b*) separating petroleum so won and consisting of gas from other petroleum so won,

(*c*) separating petroleum won and consisting of gas of a kind that is transported and sold in normal commercial practice from other petroleum so won and consisting of gas,

(*d*) liquefying petroleum so won and consisting of gas of such a kind as is mentioned in paragraph (*c*) for the purpose of transporting such petroleum,

(*e*) subjecting petroleum so won to any process so as to secure that petroleum disposed of without having been refined has the quality that is normal for petroleum so disposed of from the relevant field, or

(*f*) storing petroleum so won before its disposal or its appropriation to refining or to any use, except use in—

(i) winning petroleum from a relevant field, including searching in that field for and winning access to such petroleum, or

(ii) transporting as far as dry land petroleum that is won from a place not on dry land,

but does not include any activity carried on as part of or in association with the refining of petroleum;

"licence" means—

(*a*) an exploration licence,

(*b*) a lease undertaking,

(*c*) a licensing option,

(*d*) a petroleum prospecting licence,

(*e*) a petroleum lease, or

(*f*) a reserved area licence,

granted in respect of an area in the State or a designated area under the Petroleum and Other Minerals Development Act, 1960, and which was granted subject to—

(i) the licensing terms set out in the Notice entitled **"Ireland Exclusive Offshore Licensing Terms"** presented to each House of the Oireachtas on the 29th day of April, 1975,

(ii) licensing terms presented to each House of the Oireachtas on a day or days which fall after the 29th day of April, 1975, or

(iii) licensing terms to which paragraph (i) or (ii) relates, as amended or varied from time to time;

"licensed area" means an area in respect of which a licence is in force;

"mining trade" means a trade consisting only of working a mine which is a qualifying mine or, in the case of a trade consisting partly of such an activity and partly of one or more other activities, the part of the trade consisting only of working such a mine which is treated by virtue of section 685 as a separate trade;

"petroleum" means petroleum (within the meaning of section 2(1) of the Petroleum and Other Minerals Development Act, 1960) won or capable of being won under the authority of a licence;

"petroleum activities" means any one or more of the following activities—

(*a*) petroleum exploration activities,

(*b*) petroleum extraction activities, and

(*c*) the acquisition, enjoyment or exploitation of petroleum rights;

"petroleum exploration activities" means activities of a person carried on by the person or on behalf of the person in searching for deposits of petroleum in a licensed area, in testing or appraising such deposits or in winning access to such deposits for the purposes of such searching, testing or appraising, where such activities are carried on under a licence (other than a petroleum lease) authorising the activities and held by the person or, if the person is a company, held by the company or a company associated with it;

"petroleum extraction activities" means activities of a person carried on by the person or on behalf of the person under a petroleum lease authorising the activities and held by the person or, if the person is a company, held by the company or a company associated with it in—

(*a*) winning petroleum from a relevant field, including searching in that field for and winning access to such petroleum,

(*b*) transporting as far as dry land petroleum so won from a place not on dry land, or

(*c*) effecting the initial treatment and storage of petroleum so won from the relevant field;

"petroleum profits", in relation to a company which is chargeable to corporation tax on its profits, means the income of the company from petroleum activities and any amount to be included in its total profits in respect of chargeable gains accruing to the company from disposals of petroleum-related assets;

"petroleum-related asset" means any of the following assets or any part of such an asset—

(*a*) any petroleum rights,

(*b*) any asset representing exploration expenditure or development expenditure,

(*c*) shares deriving their value or the greater part of their value, whether directly or indirectly, from petroleum activities, other than shares dealt in on a stock exchange;

"petroleum rights" means rights to petroleum to be extracted or to interests in, or to the benefit of, petroleum, and includes an interest in a licence;

"petroleum trade" means a trade consisting only of trading activities which are petroleum activities or, in the case of a trade consisting partly of such activities and partly of other activities, the part of the trade consisting only of trading activities which are petroleum activities which is treated by virtue of section 685 as a separate trade;

"qualifying mine" has the same meaning as in section 672;

"relevant field" means an area in respect of which a licence, being a petroleum lease, is in force.

(2) For the purposes of this Chapter, 2 companies shall be associated with one another if—

(*a*) one company is a 51 per cent subsidiary of the other company,

(*b*) each company is a 51 per cent subsidiary of a third company, or

(*c*) one company is owned by a consortium of which the other company is a member,

and for the purposes of paragraph (*c*) a company shall be owned by a consortium if all the ordinary share capital of that company is directly and beneficially owned between them by 5 or fewer companies, which companies are in this Chapter referred to as **"the members of the consortium"**.

Definitions

company: ss 4(1), 5(1); land: s 5(1), IA 1937 Sch; lease: s 5(1); minerals: s 5(1); the Oireachtas: IA 1937 Sch; ordinary share capital: s 2(1); person: IA 1937 s 11(*c*); profits: s 4(1); shares: s 5(1); trade: s 3(1).

Former enactments

FA 1992 s 75; FA 1995 s 42(*a*).

685 Separation of trading activities

(1) Where a person carries on any petroleum activities as part of a trade and those activities apart from any other activity would constitute a trade, those activities shall be treated for the purposes of the Tax Acts and the Capital Gains Tax Acts as a separate trade distinct from all other activities carried on by the person as part of the trade, and any necessary apportionment shall be made of receipts and expenses.

(2) Where a person works a qualifying mine as part of a trade, that activity shall be treated for the purposes of this Chapter as a separate trade distinct from all other activity carried on by the person as part of the trade, and any necessary apportionment shall be made of receipts and expenses.

Cross-references

Mining trade, petroleum trade, meanings: s 684(1).

Definitions

person: IA 1937 s 11(*c*); Tax Acts: s 1(2); trade: s 3(1).

Former enactments

FA 1992 s 76.

686 Reduction of corporation tax

(1) In this section—

"petroleum profits on which corporation tax falls finally to be borne", in relation to a company, means the amount of the petroleum profits of the company after making all deductions and giving or allowing all reliefs that for the purposes of corporation tax are made from, or given or allowed against, or are treated as reducing—

(*a*) those profits, or

(*b*) income or chargeable gains, if any, included in those profits;

"relevant petroleum lease" means a petroleum lease in respect of a relevant field, being a field discovered by petroleum exploration activities carried on under a licence (other than a petroleum lease) which authorises the carrying on of those activities for a period which, apart from any extension of the period or revision or renewal of the licence—

(*a*) is not longer than 10 years, where the petroleum lease is granted by the Minister for the Marine and Natural Resources before the 1st day of June, 2003,

(*b*) is longer than 10 years but not longer than 15 years, where the petroleum lease is granted by the Minister for the Marine and Natural Resources before the 1st day of June, 2007, or

(*c*) is longer than 15 years, where the petroleum lease is granted by the Minister for the Marine and Natural Resources before the 1st day of June, 2013,

but a petroleum lease in respect of a relevant field shall be a relevant petroleum lease where—

(i) the field was discovered under a lease which is not a licence,

(ii) the lease under which the field was discovered expired before the petroleum lease is granted, and

(iii) the petroleum lease is granted by the Minister for the Marine and Natural Resources before the 1st day of June, 2003.

(2) (*a*) Subject to paragraph (*b*), corporation tax payable by a company for an accounting period shall be reduced by the amount, if any, determined by the formula—

$$I \times \frac{R - 25}{100}$$

where—

I is the amount for the accounting period of the income to which this section applies, and

R is the rate per cent of corporation tax specified in section 21(1) for the financial year or years in which the accounting period falls.

(*b*) Notwithstanding paragraph (*a*), where part of the accounting period falls in one financial year (in this paragraph referred to as **"the first-mentioned financial year"**) and the other part falls in the financial year succeeding the first-mentioned financial year and different rates of corporation tax are in force under section 21(1) for each of those years, then, R in paragraph (*a*) shall be the rate per cent determined by the formula—

$$\frac{(A \times C)}{E} + \frac{(B \times D)}{E}$$

where—

A is the rate per cent in force for the first-mentioned financial year,

B is the rate per cent in force for the financial year succeeding the first-mentioned financial year,

C is the length of that part of the accounting period falling in the first-mentioned financial year,

D is the length of that part of the accounting period falling in the financial year succeeding the first-mentioned financial year, and

E is the length of the accounting period.

(3) The income to which this section applies shall be the income of a company for an accounting period determined by the formula—

$$(F - G) \times \frac{S}{T}$$

where—

F is the amount for the accounting period of the company's petroleum profits on which corporation tax falls finally to be borne,

G is the amount to be included in the company's profits brought into charge to corporation tax for the accounting period in respect of chargeable gains accruing to the company from disposals of petroleum-related assets,

S is the aggregate of the income of the company for the accounting period which is—

(*a*) trading income attributable to sales of petroleum won by the company, or

(*b*) income, other than trading income, from the enjoyment or exploitation of petroleum rights,

under a relevant petroleum lease granted to the company or a company associated with the company, and

T is the aggregate of the income of the company for the accounting period from its petroleum trade or other petroleum activities.

(4) For the purposes of subsection (3), the income of a company for an accounting period which is trading income attributable to sales of petroleum won by the company under a relevant petroleum lease shall be the income, if any, determined by the formula—

$$O \times \frac{P}{Q}$$

where—

O is the income of the company for the accounting period from its petroleum trade,

P is the aggregate of money or money's worth receivable by the company from sales in the accounting period of petroleum won by it under the relevant petroleum lease, and

Q is the aggregate of money or money's worth receivable by the company from sales of petroleum in the accounting period in the course of carrying on its petroleum trade.

Amendments

1 By virtue of FA 2005 s 55, section 686 ceases to have effect as respects accounting periods ending on or after 3 February 2005.

Definitions

company: ss 4(1), 5(1); lease: s 5(1); profits: s 4(1); trade: s 3(1).

Former enactments

FA 1992 s 77; FA 1995 s 42(*b*).

687 Treatment of losses

(1) Notwithstanding sections 381 and 396(2)—

(*a*) as respects a loss incurred by a person in a petroleum trade, relief shall not be given—

(i) under section 381 against any income other than income arising from petroleum activities, or

(ii) under section 396(2) against any profits other than petroleum profits, and

(*b*) as respects any loss, other than a loss incurred in a petroleum or a mining trade, incurred by a person, relief shall not be given—

(i) under section 381 against income arising from petroleum activities, or

(ii) under section 396(2) against petroleum profits.

(2) Notwithstanding sections 383 and 399(1), the amount of any income of a person which is within the charge to tax under Case IV of Schedule D, and which is income arising from petroleum activities, shall not be reduced by the amount of any loss which may be relieved under section 383 or 399(1), other than a loss incurred in petroleum activities, and the amount of any loss so incurred shall not be treated under either of those sections as reducing the amount of any income other than income arising from petroleum activities.

(3) Notwithstanding sections 305(1)(*b*) and 308(4), a capital allowance which is to be given by discharge or repayment of tax, or in charging income under Case V of Schedule D, shall not to any extent be given effect—

(*a*) under section 305 against income arising from petroleum activities, or

(*b*) under section 308(4) against petroleum profits.

Definitions

mining: s 5(1); person: IA 1937 s 11(*c*); profits: s 4(1); within the charge to (tax): s 2(1).

Former enactments

FA 1992 s 78.

688 Treatment of group relief

(1) In this section, **"claimant company"** and **"surrendering company"** have the meanings respectively assigned to them by section 411.

(2) On a claim for group relief made by a claimant company in relation to a surrendering company, group relief shall not be allowed against any petroleum profits of the claimant company except to the extent that the claim relates to—

(*a*) a loss incurred by the surrendering company in a petroleum or mining trade, or

(*b*) charges on income paid, other than to a connected person, by the surrendering company which consist of payments made wholly and exclusively for the purposes of such a trade,

and group relief in respect of any such loss incurred by the surrendering company, or in respect of any charge on income paid by the surrendering company which is a payment made wholly and exclusively for the purposes of the petroleum or mining trade, shall not be allowed against any profits of the claimant company other than its petroleum profits.

Definitions

company: ss 4(1), 5(1); group relief: ss 4(1), 411; mining: s 5(1); profits: s 4(1).

Former enactments

FA 1992 s 79.

689 Restriction of relief for losses on certain disposals

(1) Notwithstanding any provision of the Capital Gains Tax Acts or of the Corporation Tax Acts relating to the deduction of allowable losses for the purposes of capital gains tax or of corporation tax on chargeable gains—

(*a*) an allowable loss accruing on a disposal of an asset other than a petroleum-related asset shall not be deducted from the amount of a chargeable gain accruing on a disposal of a petroleum-related asset, and

(*b*) an allowable loss accruing on a disposal of a petroleum-related asset shall not be deducted from the amount of a chargeable gain accruing on a disposal of an asset other than a petroleum-related asset.

(2) Subsection (11) of section 597 shall apply as respects the application of that section to a disposal of assets which have been used by the person disposing of them for the purposes of a petroleum trade as if each reference in that subsection to a **"trade"** or **"trades"** were respectively a reference to a **"petroleum trade"** or **"petroleum trades"** within the meaning of this Chapter.

Definitions

allowable loss: ss 4(1), 5(1), 546; Corporation Tax Acts: s 1(2); person: IA 1937 s 11(*c*); trade: s 3(1).

Former enactments

FA 1992 s 80(1)–(2).

690 Interest and charges on income

(1) In computing the amount of—

(*a*) a person's profits or gains for the purposes of income tax, or
(*b*) a person's income for the purposes of corporation tax,

arising from a petroleum trade, no deduction shall be made in respect of—

(i) any interest payable by the person to a connected person to the extent that the amount of the interest exceeds for whatever reason the amount which, having regard to all the terms on which the money in respect of which it is payable was borrowed and the standing of the borrower, might have been expected to be payable if the lender and the borrower had been independent parties dealing at arm's length,
(ii) interest payable by the person on any money borrowed to meet expenditure incurred on petroleum exploration activities, or
(iii) interest payable by the person on any money borrowed to meet expenditure incurred in acquiring petroleum rights from a connected person.

(2) Section 130(2)(*d*)(iv) shall not apply to so much of any interest as—

(*a*) would but for section 130(2)(*d*)(iv) be deductible in computing the amount of a company's income from a petroleum trade,
(*b*) would not be precluded by subsection (1) from being so deducted, and
(*c*) is interest payable to a company which is a resident ...[1] of a territory with the government of which arrangements having the force of law by virtue of [section 826(1)(*a*)][2] have been made,

and for the purposes of paragraph (*c*) ...[3] a company shall be regarded as being a resident of a territory ...[4] if it is so regarded under arrangements made with the government of that territory and having the force of law by virtue of [section 826(1)(*a*)][2].

(3) Notwithstanding section 243—

(*a*) no deduction shall be allowed from that part of a company's profits which consists of petroleum profits in respect of—

(i) a charge on income paid by the company to a connected person, or
(ii) any other charge on income paid by the company unless it is a payment made wholly and exclusively for the purposes of a petroleum or mining trade carried on by the company,

and

(*b*) no deduction shall be allowed from that part of a company's profits which consists of profits other than petroleum profits in respect of any charge on income paid by the company which is a payment made wholly and exclusively for the purposes of a petroleum trade carried on by the company.

(4) In applying section 237 to any annual payment made by a person whose profits or gains for the purposes of income tax arise wholly or partly from petroleum activities—

(*a*) the profits or gains arising from those activities shall not be treated as profits or gains which have been brought into charge to income tax—

(i) where the annual payment is made to a connected person, or

(ii) unless (but subject to subparagraph (i)) the payment is made wholly and exclusively for the purposes of a petroleum or mining trade carried on by the person making the payment,

and

(*b*) profits or gains, other than profits or gains arising from petroleum activities, shall not be treated as profits or gains which have been brought into charge to income tax where the annual payment is made wholly and exclusively for the purposes of a petroleum trade carried on by the person making the payment.

(5) Relief shall not be allowed—

(*a*) under section 396(7) in respect of a payment to which subsection (3)(*a*)(i) applies, or

(*b*) under section 390 in respect of a payment to which subsection (4)(*a*)(i) applies,

where the payment is made wholly and exclusively for the purposes of a petroleum trade.

(6) In any case where for an accounting period of a company charges on income paid by the company are allowable under section 243—

(*a*) such amount of those charges as, by virtue of subsection (3)—

(i) is not allowable against a part of the company's profits, but

(ii) is allowable against the remaining part (in this subsection referred to as **"other profits"**) of its profits,

exceeds the other profits, and

(*b*) the amount of that excess is greater than the amount, if any, by which the total of the charges on income which, subject to subsection (3), are allowable to the company under section 243 exceeds the total of the company's profits,

then, for the purpose of enabling the company to surrender the excess referred to in paragraph (*a*) by means of group relief, section 420(6) shall apply as if—

(I) the reference in that section to the amount paid by the surrendering company by means of charges on income were a reference to so much of that amount as by virtue of subsection (3) is allowable only against the company's other profits, and

(II) the reference in that section to the surrendering company's profits were a reference to its other profits only.

Amendments

1 Deleted by FA 1998 s 48 and Sch 3 para 6(*a*) with effect from 1 January 1998 for corporation tax and 6 April 1998 for income tax; previously "of the United States of America or".

2 Substituted by FA 2004 s 89 and Sch 3 para 1(*r*) with effect from 25 March 2004; previously "section 826".

3 Deleted by FA 1998 s 48 and Sch 3 para 6(*b*) with effect from 1 January 1998 for corporation tax and 6 April 1998 for income tax; previously "'resident of the United States of America' has the meaning assigned to it by the Convention set out in Schedule 25, and".

4 Deleted by FA 1998 s 48 and Sch 3 para 6(*c*) with effect from 1 January 1998 for corporation tax and 6 April 1998 for income tax; previously ", other than the United States of America,".

Definitions

charges on income: ss 4(1), 243(1); company: ss 4(1), 5(1); the Government: IA 1937 Sch; group relief: ss 4(1), 411; mining: s 5(1); person: IA 1937 s 11(*c*); profits: s 4(1); resident: s 5(1); trade: s 3(1).

Former enactments

FA 1992 s 81(1)–(5) and (7).

691 Restriction of set-off of advance corporation tax

Amendments

Section 691 deleted by FA 2003 s 41(1)(*q*) as respects accounting periods ending on or after 6 February 2003.

692 Development expenditure: allowances and charges

(1) Subject to subsection (4), the provisions of the Tax Acts relating to allowances and charges in respect of capital expenditure shall apply in relation to a petroleum trade as if each reference in those provisions to machinery or plant included a reference to assets, not being machinery or plant, representing development expenditure.

(2) In relation to assets representing development expenditure, section 284(2) shall, subject to subsection (3), apply [as if the references in paragraphs (*a*)(i), (*aa*) and (*ad*) of that section to 15 per cent, 20 per cent and 12.5 per cent, respectively, were each a reference to 100 per cent][1].

(3) Assets representing development expenditure shall not be treated for the purposes of section 284(1) as being in use for the purposes of a petroleum trade at the end of any chargeable period or its basis period which ends before the commencement of production of petroleum in commercial quantities from the relevant field in connection with which the assets were provided.

(4) The following provisions shall not apply as respects development expenditure—

(*a*) Chapters 1 and 3 of Part 9,
(*b*) section 283,
(*c*) section 670,
(*d*) Chapter 1 of Part 29,
(*e*) sections 763 to 765, and
(*f*) section 768.

(5) (*a*) For the purposes of this section, assets representing development expenditure shall be deemed to include assets (in this subsection referred to as **"leased assets"**) provided for leasing to a person carrying on a petroleum trade where such leased assets would, if they had been provided by that person, be assets representing development expenditure, and where this paragraph applies—

(i) section 284 shall apply as if the trade for the purposes of which the leased assets are (or would under section 298(1) be regarded as being) in use were a petroleum trade carried on by the lessor, and

(ii) section 403 shall apply as if each reference in that section to machinery or plant included a reference to assets, not being machinery or plant, representing development expenditure.

(*b*) For the purposes of subsection (4), capital expenditure on the provision of leased assets shall be deemed to be development expenditure.

Amendments

1 Substituted by FA 2003 s 23(1)(*c*) with effect from 4 December 2002; previously "as if the reference to paragraph (*a*)(i) of that section to 15 per cent were a reference to 100 per cent".

Definitions

capital allowance: ss 2(1), 5(1); lease: s 5(1); lessor: s 5(1); person: IA 1937 s 11(*c*); Tax Acts: s 1(2); trade: s 3(1).

Former enactments

FA 1992 s 83; FA 1996 s 132(1) and Sch 5 Pt I para 18.

693 Exploration expenditure: allowances and charges

(1) Subject to subsections (5) and (16), where a person carrying on a petroleum trade has incurred any exploration expenditure (not being expenditure which has been or is to be met directly or indirectly by any other person) there shall be made to the person for the chargeable period related to the expenditure an allowance equal to the amount of the expenditure.

(2) (*a*) Subject to paragraph (*b*), where a person carrying on a petroleum trade has incurred any exploration expenditure in respect of which an allowance has been made to the person under subsection (1) and disposes of assets representing any amount of that expenditure, a charge (in this section referred to as a **"balancing charge"**) equal to the net amount or value of the consideration in money or money's worth received by the person on the disposal shall be made on the person for the chargeable period related to the disposal or, if the disposal occurs after the date on which the trade is permanently discontinued, for the chargeable period related to the discontinuance.

(*b*) The amount on which a balancing charge is made shall not exceed the amount of the allowance made to the person under subsection (1) in respect of the amount of exploration expenditure represented by the assets disposed of.

(3) Where any assets representing exploration expenditure are destroyed, those assets shall for the purposes of subsection (2) be treated as if they had been disposed of immediately before their destruction, and any sale, insurance, salvage or compensation moneys received in respect of the assets by the person carrying on the petroleum trade shall be treated as if those moneys were consideration received on that disposal.

(4) Where a person disposes of any assets representing exploration expenditure incurred by the person in connection with an area which at the time of the disposal is, or which subsequently becomes, a relevant field (or part of such a field), the person who acquires the assets shall, if that person carries on a petroleum trade which consists of or includes the working of the relevant field (or, as the case may be, the part of the relevant field), be deemed for the purposes of this section to have incurred—

(*a*) on the day on which that person acquires the assets, or

(*b*) if later, on the day on which that person commences to work the area connected with the assets as a relevant field (or, as the case may be, as part of the relevant field), an amount of exploration expenditure equal to the lesser of—

(i) the amount of the exploration expenditure represented by the assets, and

(ii) the amount or value of the consideration given by that person on the acquisition of the assets.

(5) (*a*) Any exploration expenditure incurred by a person before the person commences to carry on a petroleum trade shall be treated for the purposes of subsection (1) as if that expenditure had been incurred by that person on the first day on which that person carries on the petroleum trade.

(*b*) Notwithstanding paragraph (*a*), no account shall be taken for the purposes of this subsection of expenditure incurred in connection with an area which is not a relevant field, or part of such a field, being worked in the course of carrying on the petroleum trade, if the expenditure was incurred more than 25 years before that first day.

(6) Where a person incurs exploration expenditure before commencing to carry on a petroleum trade and subsection (5) applies as respects that expenditure and, before the person commences to carry on that trade, the person disposes of assets representing any amount of that expenditure, the allowance to be made to the person under this section in respect of that expenditure shall be reduced by the net amount or value of any consideration in money or money's worth received by the person on that disposal.

(7) For the purposes of this section other than for the purposes of subsections (4) and (5)(*a*), the day on which any expenditure is incurred shall be taken to be the day on which the sum in question becomes payable.

(8) Any allowance or balancing charge made to or on a person under this section shall be made to or on the person in taxing the person's petroleum trade but, subject to subsection (4), such allowance shall not be made in respect of the same expenditure in taxing more than one such trade.

(9) Section 304(4) shall apply in relation to an allowance under this section as it applies in relation to an allowance to be made under Part 9.

(10) Section 307(2)(*a*) shall apply for the purposes of this section, and subsections (2) to (7) of section 321 shall apply for the interpretation of this section.

(11) Subsections (2) and (3) of section 306 shall apply in determining the chargeable period (being a year of assessment) for which an allowance or a balancing charge is to be made under this section.

(12) References to capital expenditure in Part 9 and in section 670, Chapter 1 of Part 29 and sections 763 to 765 shall be deemed not to include references to expenditure which is exploration expenditure, and exploration expenditure shall be deemed not to be expenditure on know-how for the purposes of section 768.

(13) Notwithstanding subsection (12), the following provisions—

(*a*) section 312,

(*b*) subsections (1) and (2) of section 316,

(*c*) section 317(2),

(*d*) section 318, and
(*e*) subsections (4) and (5) of section 320,

shall, with any necessary modifications, apply for the purposes of this section as they apply for the purposes of Part 9 and Chapter 1 of Part 29.

(14) Part 19 shall apply as if—

(*a*) the reference in section 551(3) to a balancing charge included a reference to a balancing charge under this section, and
(*b*) references in section 555 to a capital allowance (or capital allowances) and to a balancing charge included references respectively to an allowance (or allowances) and a balancing charge under this section.

(15) Section 319 shall apply as if subsections (1) and (2) of that section included references to this section.

(16) For the purposes of this section, a person shall be deemed not to be carrying on a petroleum trade unless and until the person is carrying on in the course of that trade trading activities which are petroleum extraction activities.

(17) Any reference in this section to assets representing any exploration expenditure shall be construed as including a reference to a part of or share in any such assets, and any reference in this section to a disposal or acquisition of any such assets shall be construed as including a reference to a disposal or acquisition of a part of or share in any such assets.

Cross-references

Petroleum trade, abandonment expenditure and loss relief, subss (9)–(11) and (15): s 695(9).
Petroleum trade, exploration expenditure incurred by certain companies: s 694(1), (2)(*c*).

Definitions

capital allowance: ss 2(1), 5(1); person: IA 1937 s 11(*c*); trade: s 3(1).

Former enactments

FA 1992 s 84; FA 1997 s 146(1) and Sch 9 Pt I para 16(2).

694 Exploration expenditure incurred by certain companies

(1) For the purposes of section 693, where exploration expenditure (not being expenditure which has been or is to be met directly or indirectly by any other person) is incurred by a company (in this section referred to as an **"exploration company"**) and—

(*a*) another company is a wholly-owned subsidiary of the exploration company, or
(*b*) the exploration company is at the time the exploration expenditure is incurred a wholly-owned subsidiary of another company (in this section referred to as **"the parent company"**),

then, the expenditure or so much of it as the exploration company specifies—

(i) in the case referred to in paragraph (*a*), may at the election of the exploration company be deemed to have been incurred by such other company (being a wholly-owned subsidiary of the exploration company) as the exploration company specifies, and
(ii) in the case referred to in paragraph (*b*), may at the election of the exploration company be deemed to have been incurred by the parent company or by such

other company (being a wholly-owned subsidiary of the parent company) as the exploration company specifies.

(2) Where under subsection (1) exploration expenditure incurred by an exploration company is deemed to have been incurred by another company (in this subsection referred to as **"the other company"**)—

(*a*) the expenditure shall be deemed to have been incurred by the other company at the time at which the expenditure was actually incurred by the exploration company,

(*b*) in a case where the expenditure was incurred at a time before the incorporation of the other company, that company shall be deemed to have been in existence at the time the expenditure was incurred, and

(*c*) in the application of section 693 to a petroleum trade carried on by the other company, the expenditure shall be deemed—

(i) to have been incurred by the other company for the purposes of that trade, and

(ii) not to have been met directly or indirectly by the exploration company.

(3) The same expenditure shall not be taken into account in relation to more than one trade by virtue of this section.

(4) A deduction or allowance shall not be made in respect of the same expenditure both by virtue of this section and under some other provision of the Tax Acts.

(5) A company shall for the purposes of subsection (1) be deemed to be a wholly-owned subsidiary of another company if and so long as all of its ordinary share capital is owned by that other company, whether directly or through another company or other companies, or partly directly and partly through another company or other companies, and paragraph 6 of Schedule 9 shall apply for the purposes of supplementing this subsection as if the reference in that paragraph to that Schedule were a reference to this subsection.

Definitions

company: ss 4(1), 5(1); ordinary share capital: s 2(1); trade: s 3(1).

Former enactments

FA 1992 s 85.

695 Abandonment expenditure: allowances and loss relief

(1) In this section, **"abandonment losses"** means so much of a loss in a petroleum trade incurred by a person in a chargeable period as does not exceed the total amount of allowances which—

(*a*) are to be made to the person for that chargeable period under this section, and

(*b*) have been taken into account in determining the amount of that loss in the petroleum trade.

(2) Subject to subsections (5) to (9), where in a chargeable period a person, who is or has been carrying on in relation to a relevant field or a part of it petroleum extraction activities other than effecting the initial treatment and storage of petroleum that is won from the relevant field, incurs abandonment expenditure (not being expenditure which

has been or is to be met directly or indirectly by any other person) in relation to the field or the part of it, as the case may be, there shall be made to the person for the chargeable period an allowance equal to the amount of the expenditure.

(3) (*a*) Subject to paragraph (*b*), as respects so much of a loss in a petroleum trade incurred by a person in a chargeable period as is an abandonment loss, the person shall be entitled on making a claim in that behalf to such repayment of income tax as is necessary to secure that the aggregate amount of income tax for the chargeable period and the 3 chargeable periods immediately preceding it will not exceed the amount which would have been borne by the person if the person's income arising from petroleum activities for each of those chargeable periods had been reduced by the lesser of—

(i) the abandonment loss, and

(ii) so much of the abandonment loss as could not on that claim be treated as reducing such income of a later chargeable period.

(*b*) Relief under paragraph (*a*) in respect of a loss shall be deemed for the purposes of the Tax Acts to be relief given under section 381(1) such that—

(i) no further relief shall be given under section 381(1) in respect of so much of an abandonment loss as is an amount in respect of which relief has been given under paragraph (*a*), and

(ii) subsections (3) to (7) of section 381 and section 392 shall apply to relief under paragraph (*a*) as they apply to relief under section 381.

(*c*) As respects so much of a loss in a petroleum trade incurred by a person in a chargeable period as is an abandonment loss, subsections (2) and (3) of section 396 shall apply as if the time specified in subsection (3) of that section were a period of 3 years ending immediately before the chargeable period in which the loss is incurred.

(4) So much of the abandonment losses, if any, incurred by a person on or before the day on which the person permanently discontinues to carry on a petroleum trade (in this subsection referred to as **"the first-mentioned trade"**) as would not apart from this subsection be allowed against or treated as reducing the person's or any other person's income or profits, shall be treated as incurred by the person in the first chargeable period of the first petroleum trade (in this section referred to as **"the new trade"**) to be carried on by the person after the permanent discontinuance of the first-mentioned trade as a trading expense of the new trade.

(5) Where a petroleum trade carried on by a person has been permanently discontinued, any abandonment expenditure incurred by the person after the discontinuance shall be treated for the purposes of subsection (2) as if that expenditure had been incurred by the person on the last day on which the person carries on the petroleum trade.

(6) For the purposes of this section other than subsections (4) and (5), the day on which any expenditure is incurred shall be taken to be the day on which the sum in question becomes payable.

(7) Any allowance made to a person under this section shall be made in taxing the person's petroleum trade, but such allowance shall not be made in respect of the same expenditure in taxing more than one trade.

(8) References to capital expenditure in Part 9 and in section 670, Chapter 1 of Part 29 and sections 763 to 765 shall be deemed not to include references to expenditure which is abandonment expenditure; but subsections (1) and (2) of section 316 and sections 317(2) and 320(5) shall, with any necessary modifications, apply for the purposes of this section as they apply for the purposes of Part 9 and Chapter 1 of Part 29.

(9) Subsections (9) to (11) and (15) of section 693 shall apply for the purposes of this section as they apply for the purposes of that section.

Definitions

person: IA 1937 s 11(*c*); Tax Acts: s 1(2); trade: s 3(1).

Former enactments

FA 1992 s 86.

696 Valuation of petroleum in certain circumstances

(1) Where a person disposes, otherwise than by means of a sale at arm's length, of petroleum acquired by the person by virtue of petroleum activities carried on by the person, then, for the purposes of the Tax Acts the disposal of the petroleum and its acquisition by the person to whom the disposal was made shall be treated as having been for a consideration equal to the market value of the petroleum at the time the disposal was made.

(2) (*a*) In this subsection, **"relevant appropriation"**, in relation to any petroleum won or otherwise acquired in the course of the carrying on by a person of petroleum activities, means the appropriation of that petroleum to refining or to any use except use for petroleum extraction activities carried on by the person, and **"relevantly appropriated"** shall be construed accordingly.

(*b*) Where a person who carries on in the course of a trade petroleum activities and other activities makes a relevant appropriation of any petroleum won or otherwise acquired by the person in the course of the petroleum activities without disposing of the petroleum, then, for the purposes of the Tax Acts the person shall be treated as having at the time of the appropriation—

(i) sold the petroleum in the course of the petroleum trade carried on by the person, and

(ii) bought the petroleum in the course of a separate trade consisting of the activities other than the petroleum activities,

and as having so sold and bought the petroleum at a price equal to its market value at the time the petroleum was relevantly appropriated.

(3) For the purposes of this section, the market value at any time of any petroleum shall be the price which that petroleum might reasonably be expected to fetch on a sale of that petroleum at that time if the parties to the transaction were independent parties dealing at arm's length.

Definitions

person: IA 1937 s 11(*c*); trade: s 3(1).

Former enactments

FA 1992 s 87.

697 Treatment of certain disposals

(1) In this section, **"relevant period"**, as respects a disposal, means the period beginning 12 months before and ending 3 years after the disposal, or such longer period as the Minister for the Marine and Natural Resources may, on the application of the person making the disposal, certify to be in that Minister's opinion reasonable having regard to the proper exploration, delineation or development of any licensed area.

(2) This section shall apply where on or after the 14th day of January, 1985, a person, with the consent of the Minister for the Marine and Natural Resources, makes a disposal of an interest in a licensed area (including the part disposal of such an interest or the exchange of an interest owned by the person in one licensed area for an interest in another licensed area) and the disposal is shown to the satisfaction of that Minister to have been made for the sole purpose of ensuring the proper exploration, delineation or development of any licensed area.

(3) Where this section applies as respects a disposal by a person (neither being nor including an exchange referred to in subsection (2)) and the consideration received by the person is in the relevant period wholly and exclusively applied (whether by the person, or on that person's behalf by the person acquiring the asset disposed of) for the purposes of either or both of the following—

(*a*) petroleum exploration activities, and

(*b*) searching for or winning access to petroleum in a relevant field,

then, for the purposes of the Capital Gains Tax Acts, if the person making the disposal makes a claim in that behalf, the disposal shall not be treated as involving any disposal of an asset but the consideration shall not, as respects any subsequent disposal of any asset acquired or brought into being or enhanced in value by the application of that consideration, be deductible from the consideration for that subsequent disposal in the computation of the chargeable gain accruing on that disposal.

(4) (*a*) Where this section applies as respects an exchange referred to in subsection (2), then, for the purposes of the Capital Gains Tax Acts, if the person making such an exchange makes a claim in that behalf, the exchange shall not be treated as involving any disposal or acquisition by that person of an asset, but the asset given by that person and the asset acquired by that person in the exchange shall be treated as the same asset acquired as the asset given by that person was acquired.

(*b*) Notwithstanding paragraph (*a*)—

(i) where the person receives for the exchange any consideration in addition to the interest in the other licensed area, this subsection shall not apply as respects the claim made by that person unless the additional consideration is applied in the relevant period in the manner referred to in subsection (3) but, where that additional consideration is so applied and the person makes a claim that this subsection should apply, it shall so apply as if the asset given by that person in exchange were such portion only of that asset as is equal in value to the interest in the other licensed area taken by that person in the exchange, and subsection (3) shall apply as if the remaining portion of the asset so given by that person were disposed of by that person for that additional consideration, and

(ii) where the person gives for the exchange any consideration in addition to the interest in a licensed area given by that person in the exchange, this subsection shall apply as respects the claim made by that person as if the interest in the other licensed area taken by that person in the exchange were such portion only of that interest as is equal in value to the interest in the licensed area given by that person in the exchange.

Former enactments

FA 1992 s 88.

[PART 24A
SHIPPING: TONNAGE TAX][1]

Amendments

1 Part 24A (ss 697A–697Q) inserted by FA 2002 s 53(1) with effect from 28 March 2003.

Cross-references

Rate of corporation tax: s 21(3)(*c*).

Tonnage tax, appeals: Sch 18B para 33; arrangements for dealing with group matters: Sch 18B para 22(1), (3)(*a*), (*b*); company not to be treated as member of more than one group: Sch 18B para 21(2); company temporarily ceasing to operate qualifying ships: Sch 18B para 7(3); delegation of powers and functions of Revenue Commissioners: Sch 18B para 34; measurement of tonnage of ship: Sch 18B para 31(1); renewal election: Sch 18B para 6(1).

Tax Briefing

TB52 May 2003 pp 12–13 — Tonnage Tax (Finance Act 2003 changes).

697A Interpretation (Part 24A)

[(1) In this Part and in Schedule 18B—

"bareboat charter terms", in relation to the charter of a ship, means the letting on charter of a ship for a stipulated period on terms which give the charterer possession and control of the ship, including the right to appoint the master and crew;

"chartered in" means—

(*a*) in relation to a single company, the letting on charter of a ship to the company otherwise than on bareboat charter terms, and

(*b*) in relation to a group of companies, the letting on charter of a ship otherwise than on bareboat charter terms to a qualifying company that is a member of the group by a person who is not a qualifying company that is a member of the group;

"company election" and **"group election"** have the meanings respectively assigned to them by section 697D(1);

[**"commencement date"** means the date of the passing of the Finance Act 2003;][1]

"control" shall be construed in accordance with subsections (2) to (6) of section 432;

"initial period" has the meaning assigned to it by paragraph 2 of Schedule 18B;

"group of companies" means—

(*a*) all the companies of which an individual has control, or

(*b*) where a company that is not controlled by another person controls one or more other companies, that company and all the companies of which that company has control,

and references to membership of a group and group shall be construed accordingly;

"Member State" means a Member State of the European Communities;

"qualifying company" means a company—

(*a*) within the charge to corporation tax,

(*b*) that operates qualifying ships, and

(*c*) which carries on the strategic and commercial management of those ships in the State;

"qualifying group" means a group of companies of which one or more members are qualifying companies;

"qualifying ship" means, subject to subsection (2), a self-propelled seagoing vessel (including a hovercraft) of 100 tons or more gross tonnage which is certificated for navigation at sea by the competent authority of any country or territory, but does not include a vessel (in this Part and in Schedule 18B referred to as a "vessel of an excluded kind") which is—

(*a*) a fishing vessel or a vessel used for subjecting fish to a manufacturing or other process on board the vessel,

(*b*) a vessel of a kind whose primary use is for the purposes of sport or recreation,

(*c*) a harbour, estuary or river ferry,

(*d*) an offshore installation, including a mobile or fixed rig, a platform or other installation of any kind at sea,

(*e*) a tanker used for petroleum extraction activities (within the meaning of Chapter 2 of Part 24),

(*f*) a dredger, including a vessel used primarily as a floating platform for working machinery or as a diving platform,

(*g*) a tug in respect of which a certificate has not been given by the Minister for the Marine and Natural Resources certifying that in the opinion of the Minister the tug is capable of operating in seas outside the portion of the seas which are, for the purposes of the Maritime Jurisdiction Act, 1959, the territorial seas of the State;

"tonnage tax" has the meaning assigned to it in section 697B;

"tonnage tax activities", in relation to a tonnage tax company, means activities carried on by the company in the course of a trade which consists of one or more than one of the activities described in paragraphs *(a)* to (*j*) and paragraph (*m*) of the definition of "relevant shipping income";

"tonnage tax asset" means an asset used wholly and exclusively for the purposes of the tonnage tax activities of a tonnage tax company;

"tonnage tax company" and **"tonnage tax group"** mean, respectively, a company or group in relation to which a tonnage tax election has effect;

"tonnage tax election" has the meaning assigned to it in section 697D(1);

"tonnage tax profits", in relation to a tonnage tax company, means the company's profits for an accounting period calculated in accordance with section 697C;

"tonnage tax trade", in relation to a tonnage tax company, means a trade carried on by the company the income from which is within the charge to corporation tax and which consists solely of the carrying on of tonnage tax activities or, in the case of a trade consisting partly of the carrying on of such activities and partly of other activities, that part of the trade consisting solely of the carrying on of tonnage tax activities and which is treated under section 697L as a separate trade carried on by the company;

"relevant shipping income", in relation to a tonnage tax company, means the company's income from—

(*a*) the carrying of passengers by sea in a qualifying ship operated by the company ...[2],

(*b*) the carriage of cargo by sea in a qualifying ship operated by the company...[3],

[(*c*) towage, salvage or other marine assistance by a qualifying ship operated by the company, but does not include income from any such work undertaken in a port or an area under the jurisdiction of a port authority,][4]

(*d*) transport in connection with other services of a kind necessarily provided at sea by a qualifying ship operated by the company,

[(*e*) the provision on board a qualifying ship operated by the company of goods or services ancillary to the carriage of passengers or cargo, but only to the extent that such goods or services are provided for consumption on board the qualifying ship,][5]

(*f*) the granting of rights by virtue of which another person provides or will provide such ancillary services on board a qualifying ship operated by the company,

(*g*) other ship-related activities that are a necessary and integral part of the business of operating the company's qualifying ships,

...[6]

(*i*) the letting on charter of a qualifying ship for use for the carriage by sea of passengers and cargo where the operation of the ship and the crew of the ship remain under the direction and control of the company,

(*j*) the provision of ship management services for qualifying ships operated by the company,

(*k*) a dividend or other distribution of a company not resident in the State (in this Part referred to as the "overseas company") in respect of which the conditions set out in section 697H(1) are met,

(*l*) gains treated as income by virtue of section 697J,

...[6]

"relevant shipping profits", in relation to a tonnage tax company, means—

(*a*) the company's relevant shipping income, and

(*b*) so much of the company's chargeable gains as are excluded from the charge to tax by section 697N;

"renewal election" has the meaning assigned to it in paragraph 6 of Schedule 18B;

"75 per cent limit" has the meaning assigned to it by section 697E.

(2) A vessel is not a qualifying ship for the purposes of this Part if the main purpose for which it is used is the provision of goods or services of a kind normally provided on land.

(3) (*a*) References in this Part and in Schedule 18B to a company or group entering or leaving tonnage tax are references to its becoming or ceasing to be a tonnage tax company or group.

(*b*) References in this Part and in Schedule 18B to a company or group of companies being subject to tonnage tax are references to the company or group being entitled to calculate its profits in accordance with the provisions of this Part and that Schedule.

(4) Schedule 18B shall apply for the purposes of this Part.][7]

Amendments

1 Definition of "commencement date" substituted by FA 2003 s 62(1)(*a*)(i) with effect from 28 March 2003.

2 Deleted by FA 2003 s 62(1)(*a*)(ii)(I) with effect from 28 March 2003; previously . ", including income in respect of which the conditions set out in section 697I are met".

3 Deleted by FA 2003 s 62(1)(*a*)(ii)(II) with effect from 28 March 2003; previously: ", including income in respect of which the conditions set out in section 697I are met".

4 Definition of "relevant shipping income" para (*c*) substituted by FA 2003 s 62(1)(*a*)(ii)(III) with effect from 28 March 2003.

5 Definition of "relevant shipping income" para (*e*) substituted by FA 2003 s 62(1)(*a*)(ii)(IV) with effect from 28 March 2003.

6 Definition of "relevant shipping income" paras (*h*) and (*m*) deleted by FA 2003 s 62(1)(*a*)(ii)(V) with effect from 28 March 2003.

7 Section 697A inserted by FA 2002 s 53(1) with effect from 28 March 2003.

Cross-references

Tonnage tax, meaning of operating a ship, para (*j*) of definition of "relevant shipping income": Sch 18B para 8(6); relevant shipping income, cargo and passengers, paras (*a*) and (*b*) of definition of "relevant shipping income": s 697I; relevant shipping income, foreign currency gains, definition of "relevant shipping income": s 697J(2); relevant shipping income, distributions of overseas shipping companies, para (*k*) of definition of "relevant shipping income": s 697H(1).

Definitions

chargeable gain: s 4(1); company; s 4(1); person: IA 1937 s 11(*c*); profits: s 4(1); trade: ss 3(1), 4(1).

697B Application

[Notwithstanding any other provision of the Tax Acts or the Capital Gains Tax Acts, this Part and Schedule 18B shall apply to provide an alternative method (in this Part referred to as "tonnage tax") for computing the profits of a qualifying company for the purposes of corporation tax.][1]

Amendments

1 Section 697B inserted by FA 2002 s 53(1) with effect from 28 March 2003.

Cross-references

Interpretation (Pt 24A): s 697A(1) ("tonnage tax").

Definitions

Capital Gains Tax Acts: s 1(2); company: s 4(1); profits: s 4(1); qualifying company: s 697A(1).

697C Calculation of profits of tonnage tax company

[(1) The tonnage tax profits of a tonnage tax company shall be charged to corporation tax in place of the company's relevant shipping profits.

(2) Where the profits of a tonnage tax company would be relevant shipping income, any loss accruing to the company in respect of its tonnage tax activities or any loss which would, but for this subsection, be taken into account by virtue of section 79 in computing the trading income of the company shall not be brought into account for the purposes of corporation tax.

(3) A company's tonnage tax profits for an accounting period in respect of each qualifying ship operated by the company shall be calculated in accordance with this section by reference to the net tonnage of each qualifying ship operated by the company and, for this purpose, the net tonnage of a ship shall be rounded down (if necessary) to the nearest multiple of 100 tons.

(4) The daily profit to be attributed to each qualifying ship operated by the company shall be determined by reference to the net tonnage of the ship as follows:

(*a*) for each 100 tons up to 1,000 tons, €1.00,
(*b*) for each 100 tons between 1,000 and 10,000 tons, €0.75,
(*c*) for each 100 tons between 10,000 and 25,000 tons, €0.50, and
(*d*) for each 100 tons above 25,000 tons, €0.25.

(5) The profit to be attributed to each qualifying ship for the accounting period shall be determined by multiplying the daily profit as determined under subsection (4) by—

(*a*) the number of days in the accounting period, or
(*b*) if the ship was operated by the company as a qualifying ship for only part of the period, by the number of days in that part of the accounting period.

(6) The amount of the company's tonnage tax profits for the accounting period shall be the aggregate of the profit determined in respect of each qualifying ship operated by the company in accordance with subsection (5).

(7) If 2 or more companies are to be regarded as operators of a ship by virtue of a joint interest in the ship, or in an agreement for the use of the ship, the tonnage tax profits of each company shall be calculated as if each were entitled to a share of the profits proportionate to its share of that interest.

(8) If 2 or more companies are to be treated as the operator of a ship otherwise than as mentioned in subsection (7), the tonnage tax profits of each shall be computed as if each were the only operator.][1]

Amendments

1 Section 697C inserted by FA 2002 s 53(1) with effect from 28 March 2003.

Cross-references

Interpretation (Pt 24A): s 697A(1) ("tonnage tax profits").

Definitions

company: s 4(1); qualifying ship, tonnage tax company, tonnage tax profits, relevant shipping income, relevant shipping profits: s 697A(1).

697D Election for tonnage tax

[(1) Tonnage tax shall apply only if an election (in this Part and Schedule 18B referred to as a "tonnage tax election") under this Part to that effect is made by a qualifying single company (in this Part and in Schedule 18B referred to as a "company election") or by a qualifying group of companies (in this Part and in Schedule 18B referred to as a "group election").

(2) (*a*) Tonnage tax shall only apply to a company which is a member of a group of companies if the company joins in a group election which shall be made jointly by all the qualifying companies in the group.

(*b*) A group election shall have effect in relation to all qualifying companies in the group.

(3) A tonnage tax election shall be made only if the requirements of section 697E and 697F are met.

(4) Part 1 of Schedule 18B shall apply for the purposes of making and giving effect to an election under this Part.][1]

Amendments

1 Section 697D inserted by FA 2002 s 53(1) with effect from 28 March 2003.

Cross-references

Interpretation (Pt 24A): s 697A(1) ("company election", "group election", "tonnage tax election"); renewal election: Sch 18B para 6(2).

Definitions

company: s 4(1); group of companies, qualifying company, qualifying group, tonnage tax: s 697A(1).

697E Requirement that not more than 75 per cent of fleet tonnage is chartered in

[(1) It shall be a requirement (in this Part and Schedule 18B referred to as the "75 per cent limit") of entering or remaining within tonnage tax—

(*a*) in the case of a single company, that not more than 75 per cent of the net tonnage of the qualifying ships operated by it is chartered in,

(*b*) in the case of a group of companies, that not more than 75 per cent of the aggregate net tonnage of the qualifying ships operated by the members of the group that are qualifying companies is chartered in.

(2) A ship shall not be counted more than once in determining for the purposes of subsection (1)(*b*) the aggregate net tonnage of the qualifying ships operated by the members of a group that are qualifying companies.

(3) Where a tonnage tax election (not being a renewal election) is made before the end of the initial period and the 75 per cent limit is exceeded in the first relevant accounting period, the election shall be treated as never having been of any effect.

(4) Where a tonnage tax election (not being a renewal election) is made after the end of the initial period, then—

(*a*) if the 75 per cent limit is exceeded in the first relevant accounting period, the election shall not have effect in relation to that period,

(*b*) if the 75 per cent limit is exceeded in the first and second relevant accounting periods, the election shall not have effect in relation to either of those periods, and

(*c*) if the 75 per cent limit is exceeded in the first, second and third relevant accounting periods, the election shall be treated as never having been of any effect.

(5) For the purposes of subsections (3) and (4) the first, second or third relevant accounting period means—

(*a*) in relation to a single company, the accounting period that, if the election had been effective, would have been the first, second or third accounting period of the company after its entry into tonnage tax, and

(*b*) in relation to a group of companies, the accounting period that, if the election had been effective, would have been the first, second or third accounting period of a member of the group that would have been a tonnage tax company.

(6) References in this section to the 75 per cent limit being exceeded in an accounting period are to the limit being exceeded on average over the accounting period in question.

(7) (*a*) If the 75 per cent limit is exceeded in 2 or more consecutive accounting periods of a tonnage tax company (in this subsection referred to as the "relevant company") the Revenue Commissioners may give notice excluding the relevant company or the group of companies of which the relevant company is a member from tonnage tax.

(*b*) The effect of any such notice is that the relevant company's tonnage tax election or the tonnage tax election of the group of which the relevant company is a member shall cease to be in force from such date as may be specified in the notice.

(*c*) The specified date shall not be earlier than the beginning of the accounting period of the relevant company that follows the second consecutive accounting period of that company in which the limit is exceeded.

(*d*) Subject to any arrangements under paragraph 22 of Schedule 18B, a notice under this subsection need only be given to the relevant company.][1]

Amendments

1 Section 697E inserted by FA 2002 s 53(1) with effect from 28 March 2003.

Cross-references

Appeals: s 697G; election for tonnage tax: 697D(3); interpretation (Pt 24A): s 697A(1) ("75 per cent limit"); when election takes effect: Sch 18B para 3(6).

Definitions

company: s 4(1); group of companies, initial period, qualifying ship, tonnage tax, tonnage tax company, tonnage tax election: s 697A(1).

697F Requirement not to enter into tax avoidance arrangements

[(1) It shall be a condition of remaining within tonnage tax that a company is not a party to any transaction or arrangement that is an abuse of the tonnage tax regime.

(2) A transaction or arrangement shall be such an abuse as is referred to in subsection (1) if in consequence of its being, or having been, entered into the provisions of this Part and Schedule 18B may be applied in a way that results (or would but for this subsection result) in—

(*a*) a tax advantage (within the meaning of section 811) being obtained for—

(i) a company other than a tonnage tax company, or

(ii) a tonnage tax company in respect of its non-tonnage tax activities, or

(*b*) the amount of the tonnage tax profits of a tonnage tax company being artificially reduced.

(3) If a tonnage tax company is a party to any such transaction or arrangement as is referred to in subsection (1), the Revenue Commissioners may—

(*a*) if it is a single company, give notice excluding it from tonnage tax;

(*b*) if it is a member of a group, subject to paragraph 22 of Schedule 18B, give notice to the tonnage tax company excluding the group from tonnage tax.

(4) The effect of such a notice as is referred to in subsection (3)—

(*a*) in the case of a single company, is that the company's tonnage tax election shall cease to be in force from the beginning of the accounting period in which the transaction or arrangement was entered into, and

(*b*) in the case of a group, is that the group's tonnage tax election shall cease to be in force from such date as may be specified in the notice, but the date so specified shall not be earlier than the beginning of the earliest accounting period in which any member of the group entered into the transaction or arrangement in question.

(5) The provisions of sections 697P apply where a company ceases to be a tonnage tax company by virtue of this section.][1]

Amendments

1 Section 697F inserted by FA 2002 s 53(1) with effect from 28 March 2003.

Cross-references

Appeals: s 697G; election for tonnage tax: s 697D(3); withdrawal of relief on company leaving tonnage tax: s 697P(1)(*b*).

Definitions

company: s 4(1); tonnage tax, tonnage tax activities, tonnage tax company, tonnage tax election, tonnage tax profits: s 697A(1).

697G Appeals

[Any person aggrieved by the giving of such a notice as is referred to in section 697E or 697F may by notice in writing to that effect made to the Revenue Commissioners within 30 days from the date of the giving of the first-mentioned notice appeal to the Appeal Commissioners. In the case of a notice given to a tonnage tax company which is a member of a group of companies only one appeal may be brought, but it may be brought jointly by 2 or more members of the group concerned.][1]

Amendments

1 Section 697G inserted by FA 2002 s 53(1) with effect from 28 March 2003.

Definitions

Appeal Commissioners: s 2(1); group of companies: s 697A(1); person: IA 1937 s 11(*c*); tonnage tax company: s 697A(1); writing: IA 1937 Sch.

697H Relevant shipping income: distributions of overseas shipping companies

[(1) The conditions referred to in paragraph (*k*) of the definition of "relevant shipping income" in section 697A are—

(*a*) that the overseas company operates qualifying ships;

(*b*) that more than 50 per cent of the voting power in the overseas company is held by a company resident in a Member State, or that 2 or more companies each of which is resident in a Member State hold in aggregate more than 50 per cent of that voting power;

(*c*) that the 75 per cent limit is not exceeded in relation to the overseas company in any accounting period in respect of which the distribution is paid;

(*d*) that all the income of the overseas company is such that, if it were a tonnage tax company, it would be relevant shipping income;

(*e*) that the distribution is paid entirely out of profits arising at a time when—

(i) the conditions in paragraphs (*a*) to (*d*) were met, and

(ii) the tonnage tax company was subject to tonnage tax;

and

(*f*) the profits of the overseas company out of which the distribution is paid are subject to a tax on profits (in the country of residence of the company or elsewhere, or partly in that country and partly elsewhere).

(2) A dividend or other distribution of an overseas company which is made out of profits which are referable to a dividend or other distribution in relation to which the conditions of subsection (1) are met shall be deemed for the purposes of this Part to be a dividend or other distribution in respect of which the conditions in subsection (1) are met.

(3) Section 440 shall not apply to dividends and other distributions of an overseas company which is relevant shipping income of a tonnage tax company.][1]

Amendments

1 Section 697H inserted by FA 2002 s 53(1) with effect from 28 March 2003.

Cross-references

Interpretation (Pt 24A): s 697A(1) ("relevant shipping income" para (*k*)); general exclusion of investment income: s 697K(3).

Definitions

company: s 4(1); qualifying ship, relevant shipping income tonnage tax, tonnage tax company, 75 per cent limit: s 697A(1).

697I Relevant shipping income: cargo and passengers

Amendments

Section 697I deleted by FA 2003 s 62(1)(*b*) with effect from 28 March 2003.

697J Relevant shipping income: foreign currency gains

[(1) This section shall apply to—

(*a*) any gain, whether realised or unrealised, attributable to a relevant monetary item (within the meaning of section 79) which would but for this Part be taken into account in computing the trading income of a company's tonnage tax trade in accordance with section 79, and

(*b*) any gain, whether realised or unrealised, attributable to a relevant contract (within the meaning of section 79) which would but for this Part be taken into account in computing the trading income of a company's tonnage tax trade in accordance with section 79.

(2) Where this section applies to any gain, the gain shall be treated as income for the purposes of the definition of "relevant shipping income" in section 697A.][1]

Amendments

1 Section 697J inserted by FA 2002 s 53(1) with effect from 28 March 2003

Cross-references

Interpretation (Pt 24A): s 697A(1) ("relevant shipping income" para (*e*)).

Definitions

company: s 4(1); tonnage tax trade: s 697A(1).

697K General exclusion of investment income

[(1) Income from investments shall not be relevant shipping income, and for this purpose "income from investments" includes any income chargeable to tax under Case III, IV or V of Schedule D or under Schedule F.

(2) To the extent that an activity gives rise to income from investments it shall not be regarded as part of a company's tonnage tax activities.

(3) Subsection (1) shall not apply to income that is relevant shipping income under sections 697H and 697I or to income that is relevant shipping income by virtue of paragraph (*m*) of the definition of "relevant shipping income".][1]

Amendments

1 Section 697K inserted by FA 2002 s 53(1) with effect from 28 March 2003.

Definitions

company: s 4(1); relevant shipping income, tonnage, tax activities: s 697A(1).

697L Tonnage tax trade

[(1) Subject to section 697M, where in an accounting period a tonnage tax company carries on as part of a trade tonnage tax activities, those activities shall be treated for the purposes of the Corporation Tax Acts (other than any provision of those Acts relating to the commencement or cessation of a trade) as a separate trade distinct from all other activities carried on by the company as part of the trade.

(2) An accounting period of a company shall end (if it would not otherwise do so) when the company enters or leaves tonnage tax.

[(3) A company to which subsection (1) applies shall, as respects any activities which are treated by virtue of that subsection as a separate trade distinct from all other activities carried on by that company as part of its trade, comply with all the requirements of the Tax Acts and the Capital Gains Tax Acts as respects those activities regarding the computation of tax and the keeping of records separate from any other activity carried on by that company.][1]][2]

Amendments

[1] Subs (3) inserted by FA 2003 s 62(1)(*c*) with effect from 28 March 2003.

[2] Section 697L inserted by FA 2002 s 53(1) with effect from 28 March 2003.

Cross-references

Interpretation (Pt 24A): s 697A(1) ("tonnage tax trade").

Definitions

Capital Gains Tax Acts: s 1(2); company: s 4(1); Corporation Tax Acts: s 1(2); tonnage tax, tonnage tax activities, tonnage tax company; s 697A(1); Tax Acts: s 1(2); trade: ss 3(1), 4(1).

697LA Transactions between associated persons and between tonnage tax trade and other activities of same company

[(1) In this section—

"control" shall be construed in accordance with section 11;

"losses" includes amounts in respect of which relief may be given in accordance with section 83(3) and Part 12;

"transaction" includes any agreement, arrangement or understanding of any kind (whether or not it is, or is intended to be, legally enforceable).

(2) Where—

(*a*) provision is made or imposed as between a tonnage tax company and another company by means of a transaction,

(*b*) the results of the transaction are taken into account in computing the tonnage tax company's relevant shipping income,

(*c*) at the time of the transaction—

(i) one of the companies is directly or indirectly under the control of the other, or

(ii) both of the companies are, directly or indirectly, under the control of the same person or persons,

and

(*d*) the relevant shipping income of the tonnage tax company is greater than it would be if the parties to the transaction had been independent parties dealing at arm's length,

then, the income or losses of both companies shall be computed for any purpose of the Tax Acts as if the consideration in the transaction had been that which would have obtained if the transaction had been a transaction between independent persons dealing at arm's length.

(3) Subsection (2) shall apply in relation to a tonnage tax company where provision is made or imposed as between the company's tonnage tax trade and other activities carried on by the company as if—

(*a*) that trade and those other activities were carried on by two different persons,

(*b*) those persons had entered into a transaction, and

(*c*) the two persons were both controlled by the same person at the time of the making or imposition of the provision.

(4) A company to which subsection (2) or (3) applies shall keep for a period not less than 6 years sufficient documentation to prove how prices and terms have been determined in a transaction to which that subsection applies, including a written and detailed explanation of the pricing principles it has applied in relation to any such business transaction.

(5) An officer of the Revenue Commissioners may by notice in writing require a company to which subsection (2) or (3) applies to furnish him or her with such information, particulars or documentation as may be necessary for that officer to establish whether or not the company has complied with this section.

(6) Section 1052 shall apply to a failure to comply with subsection (5) as it applies to a failure to deliver a return referred to in that section.

(7) Sections 900 and 901 shall apply to records under this section as if they were books, records or documents within the meaning of section 900.

(8) Nothing in this section is to be construed as affecting the computation of a company's tonnage tax profits.][1]

Amendments

1 Section 697LA inserted by FA 2003 s 62(1)(*d*) with effect from 28 March 2003.

Definitions

company: s 4(1); person: IA 1937 s 11(*c*); Tax Acts: s 1(2); relevant shipping income, tonnage tax activities, tonnage tax company, tonnage tax profits, tonnage tax trade: s 697A(1); writing: IA 1937 Sch.

697LB Treatment of finance costs

[(1) (*a*) In this section—

"deductible finance costs outside the tonnage tax trade" means—

(i) in relation to a tonnage tax company, the total of the amounts that may be taken into account in respect of finance costs in calculating for the purpose of corporation tax the company's profits other than relevant shipping profits, and

(ii) in relation to a group of companies, so much of the group's finance costs as may be taken into account in calculating for the purposes of corporation tax—

(I) in the case of a group member which is a tonnage tax company, the company's profits other than relevant shipping profits, and

(II) in the case of a group member which is not a tonnage tax company, the company's profits;

"finance costs", in relation to a company, means the cost of debt finance for that company, including—

(i) any interest expense which gives rise to a deduction under section 81 or relief under Part 8,

(ii) any gain or loss referred to in section 79 in relation to debt finance,

(iii) the finance cost implicit in a payment under a finance lease,

(iv) the finance cost payable on debt factoring or on any similar transaction, and

(v) any other costs arising from what would be considered on generally accepted accounting practice to be a financing transaction;

"finance lease", in relation to finance costs, means any arrangements that provide for machinery or plant to be leased or otherwise made available by a person (in this definition referred to as the **"lessor"**) to another person such that, in cases where the lessor and persons connected with the lessor are all companies resident in the State—

(i) the arrangements, or

(ii) the arrangements in which they are comprised,

fall, in accordance with generally accepted accounting practice, to be treated in the accounts, including any consolidated group accounts relating to two or more companies of which that company is one, of one or more of those companies as a finance lease or as a loan;

"total finance costs" means—

(i) in relation to a tonnage tax company, so much of the company's finance costs as could, if there were no tonnage tax election, be taken into account in calculating the company's profits for the purposes of corporation tax, and

(ii) in relation to a group of companies, so much of the group's finance costs as could, if there were no tonnage tax election, be taken into account in calculating for the purposes of corporation tax the profits of any group member.

(*b*) For the purposes of this section, where, in the case of a group of companies, an accounting period of a company does not coincide with the corresponding accounting period of another group company or companies, then the periods shall be matched on whatever basis appears to be just and reasonable.

(2) Where it appears, in relation to an accounting period of a tonnage tax company (not being a member of a group of companies) which carries on tonnage tax activities and which also carries on other activities, that the company's deductible finance costs outside the tonnage tax trade exceed a fair proportion of the company's total finance costs, then an adjustment as determined in accordance with subsection (3) shall be made in computing the company's profits for corporation tax purposes for that accounting period.

(3) (*a*) The proportion of the company's deductible finance costs outside the tonnage tax trade which are to be treated as exceeding a fair proportion of the company's total finance costs shall be determined on a just and reasonable basis.

(*b*) The just and reasonable determination referred to in paragraph (*a*) shall be made by reference to the extent to which the debt finance of the company, in respect of which the company's total finance costs are incurred, is applied in such a way that any profits arising, directly or indirectly, would be relevant shipping profits.

(4) Where an adjustment is to be made under subsection (2), an amount equal to the excess determined in accordance with subsection (3) shall be taken into account in computing the trading income of the company's non-tonnage tax activities for the accounting period in respect of which the adjustment arises.

(5) Where it appears, in relation to an accounting period of a tonnage tax company (being a member of a tonnage tax group) where the activities carried on by the members of the group include activities other than the carrying on of a tonnage tax trade or tonnage tax trades, that the group's deductible finance costs outside the tonnage tax trade exceed a fair proportion of the group's total finance costs, then an adjustment as determined in accordance with subsection (6) shall be made in computing the company's profits for corporation tax purposes for that accounting period.

(6) (*a*) The proportion of the group's deductible finance costs outside the tonnage tax trade which are to be treated as exceeding a fair proportion of the company's total finance costs shall be determined on a just and reasonable basis.

(*b*) The just and reasonable determination referred to in paragraph (*a*) shall be made by reference to the extent to which the debt finance of the group, in respect of which the group's total finance costs are incurred, is applied in such a way that any profits arising, directly or indirectly, would be relevant shipping profits.

(7) Where an adjustment is to be made under subsection (5), an amount equal to the proportion of the excess determined in accordance with subsection (6) which the company's tonnage tax profits bears to the tonnage tax profits of all the members of the group shall be taken into account in computing the trading income of the company's non-tonnage tax activities for the accounting period in respect of which the adjustment arises.

(8) No adjustment shall be made under this section if—

(*a*) in calculating for a period a company's deductible finance costs outside the tonnage tax trade of the company, or

(*b*) in calculating for a period a group's deductible finance costs outside the tonnage tax trades of the group,

the amount taken into account in respect of costs and losses is exceeded by the amount taken into account in respect of profits and gains.][1]

Amendments

1 Section 697LB inserted by FA 2003 s 62(1)(*d*) with effect from 28 March 2003.

Definitions

company: 4(1); connected: s 10; person: IA 1937 s 11(*c*); group of companies, relevant shipping profits, tonnage tax activities, tonnage tax company, tonnage tax election, tonnage tax group, tonnage tax profits, tonnage tax trade: s 697A(1).

697M Exclusion of reliefs, deductions and set-offs

[(1) No relief, deduction or set-off of any description is allowed against the amount of a company's tonnage tax profits.

(2) (*a*) When a company enters tonnage tax, any losses that have accrued to it before entry and are attributable—

(i) to activities that under tonnage tax become part of the company's tonnage tax trade, or

(ii) to a source of income that under tonnage tax becomes relevant shipping income,

shall not be available for loss relief in any accounting period beginning on or after the company's entry into tonnage tax.

(*b*) Any apportionment necessary to determine the losses so attributable shall be made on a just and reasonable basis.

(*c*) In paragraph (*a*) "loss relief" includes any means by which a loss might be used to reduce the amount in respect of which that company, or any other company, is chargeable to tax.

(3) (*a*) Any relief or set off against a company's tax liability for an accounting period shall not apply in relation to so much of that tax liability as is attributable to the company's tonnage tax profits.

(*b*) Relief to which this subsection applies includes, but is not limited to, any relief or set-off under section 826, 828 or Part 2 of Schedule 24.

(*c*) This subsection shall not apply to any set-off under section 24(2) or 25(3).][1]

Amendments

1 Section 697M inserted by FA 2002 s 53(1) with effect from 28 March 2003.

Cross-references

Tonnage tax trade: s 697L(1).

Definitions

company: s 4(1); relevant shipping income, tonnage tax, tonnage tax profits, tonnage tax trade: s 697A(1).

697N Chargeable gains

[(1) Where for one or more continuous periods of at least 12 months part of an asset has been used wholly and exclusively for the purposes of the tonnage tax activities of a tonnage tax company and part has not, this section shall apply as if the part so used were a separate asset.

(2) Where subsection (1) applies, any necessary apportionment of the gain or loss on the disposal of the whole asset shall be made on a just and reasonable basis.

(3) (*a*) When an asset is disposed of that is or has been a tonnage tax asset—

(i) any gain or loss on the disposal, which but for this paragraph would have been the amount of the chargeable gain or the allowable loss, shall be a chargeable gain or allowable loss only to the extent (if any) to which it is referable to periods during which the asset was not a tonnage tax asset, and

(ii) any such chargeable gain or allowable loss on a disposal by a tonnage tax company shall be treated as arising otherwise than in the course of the company's tonnage tax trade.

(*b*) For the purposes of paragraph *(a)*, the proportion of the gain or loss referable to periods during which the asset was not a tonnage tax asset shall be determined by the formula:

$$\frac{(P - T)}{P}$$

where

P is the total length of the period since the asset was created or, if later, the last third-party disposal, and

T is the length of the period (or the aggregate length of the periods) since—

(I) the asset was created, or

(II) if later, the last third-party disposal,

during which the asset was a tonnage tax asset.

(*c*) In paragraph (*b*) a "third-party disposal" means a disposal (or deemed disposal) that is not treated as one on which neither a gain nor a loss accrues to the person making the disposal.

(4) A tonnage tax election shall not affect the deduction under section 31 as applied by section 78(2) of relevant allowable losses (within the meaning of section 78) that accrued to a company before it became a tonnage tax company.

Amendments

1 Section 697N inserted by FA 2002 s 53(1) with effect from 28 March 2003.

Cross-references

Interpretation (Pt 24A): s 697A(1) ("relevant shipping profits" para (*b*)).

Definitions

allowable loss, chargeable gain: s 5(1); company: s 4(1); person: IA 1937 s 11(*c*); tonnage tax activities, tonnage tax asset, tonnage tax company, tonnage tax trade: s 697A(1).

697O Capital allowances: general

[(1) A company's tonnage tax trade shall not be treated as a trade for the purposes of determining the company's entitlement to capital allowances under Part 9 or under any other provision which is to be construed as one with that Part, but nothing in this subsection shall be taken as preventing the making of a balancing charge under those provisions as applied by Schedule 18B.

(2) Notwithstanding any other provision of the Tax Acts, Part 9 insofar as it relates to machinery or plant shall not apply to machinery or plant provided for leasing by a lessor (within the meaning of section 403) who is an individual to a lessee (within the meaning of section 403) for use in a tonnage tax trade carried on or to be carried on by the lessee.

(3) Part 3 of Schedule 18B shall apply for the purposes of applying the provisions of Part 9 or any other provision which is to be construed as one with that Part for the purposes of a tonnage tax trade of a tonnage tax company.][1]

Amendments

1 Section 697O inserted by FA 2002 s 53(1) with effect from 28 March 2003.

Cross-references

Tonnage tax exit, plant and machinery: Sch 18B para 19(3)(*b*).

Definitions

company: s 4(1); Tax Acts: s 1(2); tonnage tax company, tonnage tax trade: s 697A(1).

697P Withdrawal of relief etc on company leaving tonnage tax

[(1) This section shall apply where a company ceases to be a tonnage tax company—

(*a*) on ceasing to be a qualifying company for reasons relating wholly or mainly to tax, or

(*b*) under section 697F.

(2) Where this section applies, section 697N shall apply in relation to chargeable gains (within the meaning of the Capital Gains Tax Acts), but not losses, on all relevant disposals as if the company had never been a tonnage tax company and for this purpose a "relevant disposal" means a disposal—

(*a*) on or after the day on which the company ceases to be a tonnage tax company, or

(*b*) at any time during the period of 6 years immediately preceding that day when the company was a tonnage tax company.

(3) Where subsection (2) operates to increase the amount of the chargeable gain on a disposal made at a time within the period mentioned in subparagraph (2)(*b*), the gain is treated to the extent of the increase—

(*a*) as arising immediately before the company ceased to be a tonnage tax company, and

(*b*) as not being relevant shipping profits of the company.

(4) No relief, deduction or set-off of any description shall be allowed against the amount of that increase or the corporation tax charged on that amount.

(5) Where this section applies and in a relevant accounting period during which the company was a tonnage tax company the company was liable to a balancing charge in relation to which paragraph 16 or 17, as appropriate, of Schedule 18B applied to reduce the amount of the charge, then the company shall be treated as having received an additional amount of profits chargeable to corporation tax equal to the aggregate of the amounts by which those balancing charges were reduced.

(6) For the purposes of subsection (5) a "relevant accounting period" means an accounting period ending not more than 6 years before the day on which the company ceased to be a tonnage tax company.

(7) The additional profits referred to in subsection (5) shall be treated—

(*a*) as arising immediately before the company ceased to be a tonnage tax company, and

(*b*) as not being relevant shipping profits of the company.

(8) No relief, deduction or set-off of any description shall be allowed against those profits or against the corporation tax charged on them.][1]

Amendments

[1] Section 697P inserted by FA 2002 s 53(1) with effect from 28 March 2003.

Cross-references

Miscellaneous and supplemental: Sch 18B para 32.

Definitions

Capital Gains Tax Acts: s 1(2); chargeable gain: s 5(1); company: s 4(1); profits: s 4(1); qualifying company, relevant shipping profits, tonnage tax company: s 697A(1).

697Q Ten year disqualification from re-entry into tonnage tax

[(1) This section shall apply in every case where a company ceases to be a tonnage tax company otherwise than on the expiry of a tonnage tax election.

(2) Where this section applies—

(*a*) a company election made by a former tonnage tax company shall be ineffective if made before the end of the period of 10 years beginning with the date on which the company ceased to be a tonnage tax company, and

(*b*) a group election that—

(i) is made in respect of a group whose members include a former tonnage tax company, and

(ii) would result in that company becoming a tonnage tax company,

shall be ineffective if made before the end of the period of 10 years beginning with the date on which that company ceased to be a tonnage tax company.

(3) This section shall not prevent a company becoming a tonnage tax company under and in accordance with the rules in Part 4 of Schedule 18B.

(4) In this section **"former tonnage tax company"** means a company that is not a tonnage tax company but has previously been a tonnage tax company.][1]

Amendments

[1] Section 697Q inserted by FA 2002 s 53(1) with effect from 28 March 2003.

Cross-references

Miscellaneous and supplemental: Sch 18B para 32.

Definitions

company: s 4(1); company election, group election, tonnage tax company, tonnage tax election: s 697A(1).

PART 25
INDUSTRIAL AND PROVIDENT SOCIETIES, BUILDING SOCIETIES, AND TRUSTEE SAVINGS BANKS

CHAPTER 1
Industrial and Provident Societies

698 Interpretation (Chapter 1)

In this Chapter, except where the context otherwise requires—

"loan interest", in relation to a society, means any interest payable by the society in respect of any mortgage, loan, loan stock or deposit;

"share interest", in relation to a society, means any interest, dividend, bonus or other sum payable to a shareholder of the society by reference to the amount of the shareholder's holding in the share capital of the society;

"society" means a society registered under the Industrial and Provident Societies Acts, 1893 to 1978;

references to the payment of share interest or loan interest include references to the crediting of such interest.

Cross-references

Close company, meaning: s 430(1)(*b*).

Companies' chargeable gains, groups of companies, meaning of "society" applied: s 616(2)(*c*).

Former enactments

ITA 1967 s 218; FA 1975 s 33(2) and Sch 1 Pt II.

699 Deduction as expenses of certain sums, etc

(1) In computing for the purposes of Case I of Schedule D the profits or gains of a society, there shall be deducted as expenses any sums which—

(*a*) represent a discount, rebate, dividend or bonus granted by the society to members of the society or other persons in respect of amounts paid or payable by or to them on account of their transactions with the society, being transactions taken into account in that computation and calculated by reference to those amounts or to the magnitude of those transactions and not by reference to the amount of any share or interest in the capital of the society;

(*b*) are share interest or loan interest paid by the society, being interest wholly and exclusively laid out or expended for the purposes of the trade.

(2) (*a*) Where for the year 1962–63 or any previous year of assessment an annual allowance, balancing allowance or balancing charge in respect of capital expenditure on the construction of a building or structure might have been made to or on a society under Part V of the Finance Act, 1959, but for the circumstance that the society was exempt from tax under Schedule D, any writing down allowance, balancing allowance or balancing charge to be made in respect of the expenditure under Part 9 for any chargeable period shall be computed as if every annual allowance, balancing allowance and balancing charge which might have been so made had been made; but nothing in this paragraph shall affect section 274(8).

(*b*) Where for the year 1962–63 or any previous year of assessment an annual allowance in respect of capital expenditure on the purchase of patent rights might have been made to or on a society under Part V of the Finance Act, 1959, but for the circumstance that the society was exempt from tax under Schedule D, the amount of the expenditure remaining unallowed (within the meaning of section 756) shall, in relation to any balancing allowance or balancing charge under Chapter 1 of Part 29 to be made to or on the society in respect of the expenditure for any chargeable period, be computed as if every annual allowance which might have been so made had been made.

Cross-references

Industrial and provident societies, computation, subs (1): s 700(3).

Definitions

trade: s 3(1); person: IA 1937 s 11(*c*); writing: IA 1937 Sch; year of assessment: s 3(1).

Former enactments

ITA 1967 s 219(1) and (4)(*b*)–(*c*); FA 1974 s 47; CTA 1976 s 30(5)(*a*).

700 Special computational provisions

(1) Notwithstanding anything in the Tax Acts, [other than Chapter 5 of Part 8,][1] any share or loan interest paid by a society—

(*a*) shall be paid without deduction of income tax and shall be charged under Case III of Schedule D, and

(*b*) shall not be treated as a distribution;

but paragraph (*a*) shall not apply to any share interest or loan interest payable to a person whose usual place of abode is not in the State.

[(1A) For the purposes of subsection (1), **"society"** shall include a credit union which is—

(*a*) registered as such under the Credit Union Act, 1997, or

(*b*) deemed to be so registered by virtue of section 5(3) of that Act.][2]

(2) In computing the corporation tax payable for any accounting period of a society, section 243 shall apply subject to the deletion of **"yearly"** in subsection (4)(*a*) of that section.

(3) On or before [31 January][3] in each year, every society shall deliver to the inspector a return in such form as the Revenue Commissioners may prescribe specifying—

(*a*) the name and place of residence of every person to whom share interest or loan interest amounting to the sum of [€90][4] or more has been paid by the society in the year of assessment which ended before that date, and

(*b*) the amount of such share interest or loan interest paid in that year to each of those persons,

and, if such a return is not fully made as respects any year of assessment, the society shall not be entitled to any deduction under section 97(2)(*e*), 243 or 699(1) in respect of any payments of share interest or loan interest which it was required to include in the return, and all such assessments and additional assessments shall be made as may be necessary to give effect to this subsection.

Amendments

1 Inserted by FA 2001 s 57(1)(*b*) with effect from such date as the Minister for Finance may by order or orders appoint. This amendment came into operation with effect from 1 January 2002 — Finance Act 2001 (Section 57) (Commencement) Order 2001, SI No 596 of 2001, refers.

2 Subs (1A) inserted by FA 2000 s 32(1) with effect from 6 April 1999.

3 Substituted by FA 2001 s 77(2) and Sch 2 paras 39(*a*) and 61(*f*) in relation to a return due under TCA 1997 s 700(3) in respect of the short tax "year" 2001 or later tax year; previously "the 1st day of May".

4 Substituted by FA 2001 s 240 (1) and (2)(*a*) and Sch 5 Pt 1 for 2002 and later tax years; previously "£70" (short tax "year" 2001: £52 (FA 2001 s 77(2) and Sch 2 paras 39(*b*) and 61(*a*))).

Cross-references

Interest payments by companies and to non-residents: s 246(3)(*f*).

Definitions

charges on income: ss 4(1), 243(1); distribution: ss 4(1), 436, 437; inspector: ss 2(1), 5(1), 852; interest: s 4(1); person: IA 1937 s 11(*c*); Tax Acts: s 1(2); year of assessment: ss 2(1), 5(1).

Former enactments

CTA 1976 s 30(2)–(4); FA 1978 s 19.

701 Transfer of shares held by certain societies to members of society

(1) In this section—

"company" has the meaning assigned to it by section 5(1);

"consideration" means consideration in money or money's worth;

"control", in relation to a company, shall be construed in accordance with section 432;

"society" means a society registered under the Industrial and Provident Societies Acts, 1893 to 1978, which is an agricultural society or a fishery society within the meaning of section 443(16).

(2) (*a*) In this subsection and in subsection (4), **"the appropriate number"**, in relation to a member's original shares, means such portion (or as near as may be to such portion) of the total number of the referable shares owned by the member at the time of the transfer as bears to that number the same proportion as the total number of shares in the company which are subject to the transfer bears to the total number of shares in the company owned by the society immediately before the transfer, and the number of the referable shares owned by a member shall be an amount determined by the formula—

$$\frac{A \times B}{C} \times \frac{D}{B}$$

where—

A is the market value of the shares in the company owned by the society immediately before the transfer,

B is the total number of the shares in the society in issue immediately before the transfer,

C is the market value of the total assets (including the shares in the company) of the society immediately before the transfer, and

D is the number of shares in the society owned by the member immediately before the transfer.

(*b*) Where on or after the 6th day of April, 1993, a society, being a society which at any time on or after that date controls or has had control of a company, transfers to the members of the society shares owned by it in the company (in this section referred to as **"the transfer"**) and—

(i) the transfer, in so far as it relates to any member, is in respect of and in proportion to, or as nearly as may be in proportion to, that member's holding of shares (in this section referred to as **"the original shares"**) in the society immediately before the transfer,

(ii) no consideration (apart from the consideration given by the members represented by the cancellation of the original shares referred to in subparagraph (iii)) for, or in connection with, the transfer is given to or received from any member (or any person connected with that member) by the society (or any person connected with the society), and

(iii) on the transfer or as soon as possible after the transfer, the original shares (or the appropriate number of those shares) of each member are cancelled without any consideration (apart from the consideration given to the members represented by the transfer to the members of the shares in the company) for or in connection with such cancellation being given to or received from any member (or any person connected with that member) by the society (or any person connected with the society) and, where the original shares (or the appropriate number of those shares) have been issued to a member at different times, any cancellation of such shares shall involve those issued earlier rather than those issued later,

then, subject to subsection (5), subsections (3) and (4) shall apply.

(3) For the purposes of the Corporation Tax Acts, the transfer shall be treated as —

(*a*) not being a distribution within the meaning of Part 6, and

(*b*) being for a consideration of such amount as would secure that, for the purposes of charging the gain on the disposal by the society of the shares owned by it in the company, neither a gain nor a loss would accrue to the society.

(4) For the purposes of the Capital Gains Tax Acts—

(*a*) the cancellation of the original shares (or the appropriate number of those shares) shall not be treated as involving any disposal of those shares, and

(*b*) each member shall be treated as if the shares transferred to that member in the course of the transfer were acquired by that member at the same time and for the same consideration at which the original shares (or the appropriate number of those shares) were acquired by that member and, for the purposes of giving effect to this paragraph, where the original shares (or the appropriate number of those shares) have been issued to a member at different times, there shall be made all such apportionments as are in the circumstances just and reasonable.

(5) This section shall not apply unless it is shown that the transfer is effected for bona fide commercial reasons and does not form part of any arrangement or scheme of which the main purpose or one of the main purposes is avoidance of liability to corporation tax or capital gains tax.

(6) In a case where this section applies, the society concerned shall include in the return required to be made by it under section 884 a statement of the total number of shares cancelled in accordance with subsection (2)(*b*)(iii).

Definitions

company: ss 4(1), 5(1); Capital Gains Tax Acts: s 1(2); Corporation Tax Acts: s 1(2);distribution: ss 4(1), 436, 437; person: IA 1937 s 11(*c*); shares: s 5(1).

Former enactments

FA 1993 s 35(1)(*a*) and (2)–(6); FA 1997 s 146(1) and Sch 9 Pt I para 17(2).

CHAPTER 2
Building Societies

702 Union or amalgamation of, transfer of engagement between, societies

(1) In this section, **"building society"** means a building society within the meaning of the Building Societies Acts, 1874 to 1989.

(2) Where in the course of or as part of a union or amalgamation of 2 or more building societies or a transfer of engagements from one building society to another building society there is a disposal of an asset by one society to another society, both societies shall be treated for the purposes of corporation tax in respect of chargeable gains as if the asset were acquired from the society making the disposal for a consideration of such amount as would secure that on the disposal neither a gain nor a loss would accrue to the society making the disposal.

Cross-references

Close company, meaning: s 430(1)(*c*).

Case law

Subs (1): A company whose business consisted of the advancement of loans not regarded as a building society by virtue of housing loans granted to employees: *Property Loan and Investment Co Ltd v Revenue Commissioners* ITR Vol II p 25.

Definitions

chargeable gain: ss 5(1), 545; distribution: ss 4(1), 436, 437; interest: s 4(1); profits: s 4(1); Tax Acts: s 1(2); within the charge to (tax): s 2(1); year of assessment: ss 2(1), 5(1).

Former enactments

CTA 1976 s 31(5) and (8).

703 Change of status of society

(1) In this section and in Schedule 16—

"building society" means a building society incorporated or deemed by section 124(2) of the Building Societies Act, 1989, to be incorporated under that Act, and references to **"society"** shall be construed accordingly;

"successor company" means a successor company within the meaning of Part XI of the Building Societies Act, 1989.

(2) Schedule 16 shall apply where a society converts into a successor company in accordance with Part XI of the Building Societies Act, 1989.

Definitions

company: ss 4(1), 5(1).

Former enactments

FA 1990 s 57.

CHAPTER 3
Trustee Savings Banks

704 Amalgamation of trustee savings banks

(1) In this Chapter and in Schedule 17, **"trustee savings bank"** has the same meaning as in the Trustee Savings Banks Act, 1989.

(2) Where any assets or liabilities of a trustee savings bank are transferred or deemed to be transferred to another trustee savings bank in accordance with Part IV of the Trustee Savings Banks Act, 1989, those banks shall be treated for the purposes of the Tax Acts and the Capital Gains Tax Acts as if they were the same person.

Definitions

person: IA 1937 s 11(*c*); Tax Acts: s 1(2).

Former enactments

FA 1990 s 59.

705 Reorganisation of trustee savings banks into companies

Schedule 17 shall apply to the reorganisation in accordance with section 57 of the Trustee Savings Banks Act, 1989, of—

(*a*) one or more trustee savings banks into a company, or

(*b*) a company referred to in subparagraph (i) of subsection (3)(*c*) of that section into a company referred to in subparagraph (ii) of that subsection.

Definitions

company: ss 4(1), 5(1).

Former enactments

FA 1990 s 60.

PART 26
LIFE ASSURANCE COMPANIES

Cross-references

UK double taxation agreement: s 832(4)(*c*).

CHAPTER 1
General Provisions

Cross-references

Approved retirement fund, for purposes of s 784A this Chapter is to apply as if references therein to pension business were references to moneys held in an approved retirement fund: s 784A(5).

706 Interpretation and general (Part 26)

(1) In this Part, unless the context otherwise requires—

"actuary" has the same meaning as in section 3 of the Insurance Act, 1936;

"annuity business" means the business of granting annuities on human life;

"annuity fund" means, where an annuity fund is not kept separately from the life assurance fund of an assurance company, such part of the life assurance fund as represents the liability of the company under its annuity contracts, as stated in its periodical returns;

"assurance company" has the same meaning as in section 3 of the Insurance Act, 1936;

"excluded annuity business", in relation to an assurance company, means annuity business which—

(*a*) is not pension business, or the liability of the company in respect of which is not taken into account in determining the foreign life assurance fund (within the meaning of section 718(1)) of the company, and

(*b*) arises out of a contract for the granting of an annuity on human life, being a contract effected, extended or varied on or after the 6th day of May, 1986, and which fails to satisfy any one or more of the following conditions—

(i) that the annuity shall be payable (whether or not its commencement is deferred for any period) until the end of a human life or for a period ascertainable only by reference to the end of a human life (whether or not continuing after the end of a human life),

(ii) that the amount of the annuity shall be reduced only on the death of a person who is an annuitant under the contract or by reference to a bona fide index of prices or investment values, and

(iii) that the policy document evidencing the contract shall expressly and irrevocably prohibit the company from agreeing to commutation in whole or in part of any annuity arising under the contract;

"general annuity business" means any annuity business which is not—

(*a*) excluded annuity business, or

(*b*) pension business,

and **"pension business"** shall be construed in accordance with subsections (2) and (3);

"life business" includes **"life assurance business"** and **"industrial assurance business"**, which have the same meanings respectively as in section 3 of the Insurance Act, 1936, and where a company carries on both businesses may mean either;

"life assurance fund" and **"industrial assurance fund"** have the same meanings respectively as in the Insurance Acts, 1909 to 1969, and **"life assurance fund"**, in relation to industrial assurance business, means the industrial assurance fund;

"market value" shall be construed in accordance with section 548;

"overseas life assurance company" means an assurance company having its head office outside the State but carrying on life assurance business through a branch or agency in the State;

"pension fund" and **"general annuity fund"** shall be construed in accordance with subsection (2);

"periodical return", in relation to an assurance company, means a return deposited with the Minister for Enterprise, Trade and Employment under the Assurance Companies Act, 1909, and the Insurance Act, 1936;

"policy" and **"premium"** have the same meanings respectively as in section 3 of the Insurance Act, 1936;

"special investment business", **"special investment fund"** and **"special investment policy"** have the meanings respectively assigned to them by section 723;

"valuation period" means the period in respect of which an actuarial report is made under section 5 of the Assurance Companies Act, 1909, as extended by section 55 of the Insurance Act, 1936.

(2) Any division to be made between general annuity business, pension business and other life assurance business shall be made on the principle of—

(*a*) referring to pension business any premiums within subsection (3), together with the incomings, outgoings and liabilities referable to those premiums, and the policies and contracts under which they are or have been paid, and

(*b*) allocating to general annuity business all other annuity business except excluded annuity business,

and references to **"pension fund"** and **"general annuity fund"** shall be construed accordingly, whether or not such funds are kept separately from the assurance company's life assurance fund.

(3) The premiums to be referred to pension business shall be those payable under contracts which are (at the time when the premium is payable) within one or other of the following descriptions—

(*a*) any contract with [an individual who, at the time the contract is made, is][1] , or but for an insufficiency of profits or gains would be, chargeable to income tax in respect of relevant earnings (within the meaning of section 783) from a trade, profession, office or employment carried on or held by him or her, being a contract approved by the Revenue Commissioners under section 784 or 785 or any contract under which there is payable an annuity in relation to which section 786(3) applies;

(*b*) any contract (including a contract of assurance) entered into for the purposes of, and made with the persons having the management of, an exempt approved scheme (within the meaning of Chapter 1 of Part 30), being a contract so framed that the liabilities undertaken by the assurance company under the contract correspond with liabilities against which the contract is intended to secure the scheme;

(*c*) any contract with the trustees or other persons having the management of a scheme approved under section 784 or 785 or under both of those sections, being a contract which—

(i) was entered into for the purposes only of that scheme, and

(ii) in the case of a contract entered into or varied on or after the 6th day of April, 1958, is so framed that the liabilities undertaken by the assurance company under the contract correspond with liabilities against which the contract is intended to secure the scheme;

[(*d*) (i) any PRSA contract (within the meaning of Chapter 2A of Part 30), and

(ii) any contract with a PRSA provider (within that meaning) being a contract which was entered into for the purposes only of the PRSA concerned;][2,3]

and, in this subsection and in subsection (2), **"premium"** includes any consideration for an annuity.

(4) (*a*) In this subsection, **"deduction"** means any deduction, relief or set-off which may be treated for the purposes of corporation tax as reducing profits of more than one description.

(*b*) For the purposes of the Corporation Tax Acts, any deduction from the profits of an assurance company, being profits of more than one class of life assurance business referred to in section 707(2), shall be treated as reducing the amount of the profits of each such class of business by an amount which bears the same proportion to the amount of the deduction as the amount of the profits of that class of business, before any deduction, bears to the amount of the profits of the company brought into charge to corporation tax.

Amendments

1 Substituted by FA 2003 s 54(*a*) with effect from 1 January 2003; previously "an individual who is".

2 Subs (3)(*d*) inserted by Pensions (Amendment) Act 2002 s 4(1)(*b*)(i) with effect from such date or dates as the Minister for Social, Community and Family Affairs may appoint by order. By virtue of Pensions (Amendment) Act, 2002 (Commencement) Order 2002, SI No 502 of 2002, this amendment came into operation on 7 November 2002.

3 Subs (3)(*d*) substituted by FA 2003 s 54(*b*) with effect from 1 January 2003.

Cross-references

Bank levy credit: s 487(1)(*b*)(i)(II).

Capital acquistions tax, exemption of certain policies of assurance, meaning of "assurance company" applied: CATCA 2003 s 74(1).

Capital gains tax, persons chargeable, meaning of "overseas life assurance company" and "life business" applied: s 29(3)(*d*).

Certain trading operations carried on in Custom House Docks Area, meaning of "life business" applied: s 446(2C)(*a*).

Corporation tax, relief for trading losses other than terminal losses, meaning of "assurance company" applied: s 396(5).

Corporation tax: treatment of tax free income of non resident banks, insurance businesses etc: s 845(5).

Foreign currency, computation of income and chargeable gains, meaning of "life business" applied, subs (1): s 79(3).

Group relief, losses that may be surrendered, meaning of "life business" applied: s 420(1)(*b*), (9)(*b*).

Group relief, relevant losses and charges, meaning of "life business" applied: s 420A(3)(*b*)(ii).

Group relief, relief for certain losses on a value basis, meaning of "life business" applied: s 420B(1)("relevant corporation tax").

Investment undertakings (declarations), meaning of "life business" applied: Sch 2B para 3(*d*).

Investment undertakings (gain arising on a chargeable event), meaning of "life business" applied: s 739D(6)(*b*).

Power of inspection (returns and collection of appropriate tax) — assurance companies, meaning of "assurance company" and "life business" applied: s 904C(1).

Relief for certain trading losses on a value basis, meaning of "life business" applied: s 396B(1)("relevant corporation tax").

Special savings incentive accounts, meaning of "annuity business", "pension business" applied: s 848B(3)(*c*).

Taxation of reverse premiums, meaning of "assurance company" and "life business" applied: s 98A(6).

Treatment of debts on a change in currency, meaning of "assurance company" applied: s 541A(4)(*a*).

Definitions

branch or agency: ss 4(1), 5(1); company: ss 4(1), 5(1); person: IA 1937 s 11(*c*); profession: ss 2(1), 5(1); profits: s 4(1); trade: ss 3(1), 4(1), 5(1).

Former enactments

CTA 1976 ss 36A(7) and 50(2)–(4); FA 1979 s 28(5); FA 1986 s 59(*d*); FA 1993 s 11(*f*) and (*k*); FA 1996 s 132(1) and Sch 5 Pt I para 10(2)–(3).

Corresponding UK tax provision

Income and Corporation Taxes Act 1988 s 431.

707 Management expenses

(1) Subject to sections 709 and 710, section 83 shall apply for computing the profits of a company carrying on life business, whether mutual or proprietary (and not charged to corporation tax in respect of it under Case I of Schedule D), whether or not the company

is resident in the State, as that section applies in relation to an investment company, except that—

(*a*) there shall be deducted from the amount treated as expenses of management for any accounting period—

(i) any repayment or refund receivable in the period of the whole or part of a sum disbursed by the company for that period or any earlier period as expenses of management, including commissions (in whatever manner described),

(ii) reinsurance commissions earned by the company in the period, and

(iii) the amount of any fines or fees receivable in the period or profits arising from reversions in the period,

and in calculating profits arising from reversions the company may set off against those profits any losses arising from reversions in any previous accounting period during which any enactment granting this relief was in operation in so far as they have not already been so set off, and

[(*b*) no deduction shall be made under section 83(2)(*b*) other than in respect of the amount of any income (other than receipts from premiums) which, if the profits of the company were chargeable to corporation tax under Case I of Schedule D, would be taken into account in computing those profits and any such deduction from the amount treated as expenses of management under that section shall not be regarded as reducing acquisition expenses within the meaning of section 708.][1]

(2) [(*a*) Where the life assurance business of an assurance company includes more than one of the following classes of business—

(i) pension business,

(ii) general annuity business, and

(iii) life assurance business (excluding such pension business and general annuity business),

then, for the purposes of the Corporation Tax Acts, the business of each such class shall be treated as though it were a separate business, and subsection (1) shall apply separately to each such class of business as if it were the only business of the company.][2]

(*b*) Any amount of an excess referred to in section 83(3) which is carried forward from an accounting period ending before the 27th day of May, 1986, may for the purposes of section 83(2) be deducted in computing the profits of the company for a later accounting period in respect of such of the classes of business referred to in paragraph (*a*) as the company may elect; but any amount so deducted in computing the profits from one of those classes of business shall not be deducted in computing the profits of the company from another of those classes of business.

[(*c*) Any amount of excess referred to in section 83(3) in relation to special investment business, which is available to be carried forward from an accounting period ending in 2002, may for the purposes of that section, be carried forward to the succeeding accounting period and treated as relating to life assurance business, other than new basis business (within the meaning of section 730A(1)).][3]

(3) ...[4]

(4) Relief under subsection (1) shall not be given to any such company in so far as it would, if given in addition to all other reliefs to which the company is entitled, reduce the corporation tax borne by the company on the income and gains of its life business for any accounting period to less than would have been paid if the company had been charged to tax at the rate specified in section 21(1) in respect of that business under Case I of Schedule D and, where relief has been withheld in respect of any accounting period by virtue of this subsection, the excess to be carried forward by virtue of section 83(3) shall be increased accordingly.

(5) (*a*) For the purposes of subsection (4)—

...[5]

...[6]

(iv) sections 709(2), 710 and 714 shall, and section 396(5)(*b*) shall not, apply for the purposes of computing the profits of the life assurance business or the industrial assurance business, as the case may be, which would have been charged to tax under Case I of Schedule D.

(*b*) The reference in section 551(2) to computing income or profits or gains or losses shall not be taken as applying to a computation of a company's income for the purposes of subsection (4).

Amendments

1 Subs (1)(*b*) substituted by FA 1999 s 86(1) for income accruing for accounting periods commencing on or after 1 January 1999.

2 Subs (2)(*a*) substituted by FA 2003 s 52(1)(*a*)(i)(I) as respects accounting periods ending in 2003 and later years.

3 Subs (2)(*c*) inserted by FA 2003 s 52(1)(*a*)(i)(II) as respects accounting periods ending in 2003 and later years.

4 Subs (3) repealed by FA 1999 s 197 and Sch 6 with effect from 25 March 1999.

5 Subs (5)(*a*)(i)–(ii) repealed by FA 2000 s 69(2) and Sch 2 Part 2 with effect from 6 April 1999 in the case of income tax and as respects accounting periods commencing on or after that date in the case of corporation tax.

6 Subs (5)(*a*)(iii) deleted by FA 2003 s 52(1)(*a*)(ii) as respects accounting periods ending in 2003 and later years.

Cross-references

Approved pension schemes, exemptions and reliefs, subs (4): s 774(6)(*b*).
Approved share option schemes: s 519D(6)(*b*)(ii), (*c*)(ii).
Business entertainment expenses: s 840(2)(*b*).
Capital gains tax, exclusion of sums chargeable to income tax: s 551(2).
Cars, limit on renewals allowance: s 375(*c*); restriction of deduction in respect of running expenses: s 376(1) (qualifying expenditure).
Chargeable gains of life business, subs (2)(*a*)(iii)–(iv): s 711(3).
Costs of establishing profit sharing schemes: s 518(1).
Costs of establishing savings-related share option schemes: s 519B(2)(*b*), (2A)(*b*).
Employee share ownership trusts: s 519(2).
Foreign life assurance funds: s 718(5)(*a*).
Group relief, losses that may be surrendered: s 420(5).
Life assurance companies, acquisition expenses: s 708(4)(*b*), (6).
Life assurance companies, annuity business, separate charge on profits: s 715(2)(*b*).
Life assurance companies, chargeable gains: s 713(1)(*d*).

Life assurance companies, management expenses deduction, subs (2): s 706(4)(*b*).
Overseas life assurance companies, management expenses: s 728.
Personal Retirement Savings Accounts (PRSAs), allowance to employer, subs (4): s 787J(2).
Profit sharing schemes, payments to trustees: s 517(1)(*b*).
Profits of life business: s 710(4), (5)(*b*).
Redundancy payments, deduction: s 109(3).
Restrictive covenants, management expense deduction: s 127(5).
Transactions in certificates of deposit: s 814(6).
UK double taxation agreement: s 832(4)(*a*).

Definitions

company: s 4(1); Corporation Tax Acts: s 1(2); distribution: ss 4(1), 436, 437; profits: s 4(1).

Former enactments

CTA 1976 s 33(1)–(2); FA 1986 s 59(*a*); FA 1992 s 44(*a*).

Corresponding UK tax provision

Income and Corporation Taxes Act 1988 s 76.

708 Acquisition expenses

(1) For the purposes of this section and subject to subsections (2) to (4), the acquisition expenses for any period of an assurance company carrying on life assurance business shall be such of the following expenses of management, including commissions (in whatever manner described) and excluding any payment of rent in respect of which a deduction is to be made twice by virtue of section 324, 333 or 345 in the computation of profits or gains, as are for that period attributable to the company's life assurance business (excluding pension business and general annuity business)—

(*a*) expenses of management which are disbursed solely for the purpose of the acquisition of business, and

(*b*) so much of any other expenses of management which are disbursed partly for the purpose of the acquisition of business and partly for other purposes as are properly attributable to the acquisition of business,

reduced by—

(i) any repayment or refund receivable in the period of the whole or part of management expenses within paragraph (*a*) or (*b*) and disbursed by the company for that period or any earlier period, and

(ii) reinsurance commission earned by the company in that period which is referable to life assurance business (excluding pension business and general annuity business).

(2) Subsection (1) shall not apply to acquisition expenses in respect of policies of life assurance issued before the 1st day of April, 1992, but without prejudice to the application of that subsection to any commission (in whatever manner described) attributable to a variation on or after that date in a policy of life assurance issued before that date, and for this purpose the exercise of any rights conferred by a policy shall be regarded as a variation of the policy.

(3) In subsection (1), **"the acquisition of business"** includes the securing on or after the 1st day of April, 1992, of the payment of increased or additional premiums in respect of a policy of assurance which has already been issued before, on or after that date.

(4) For the purposes of subsection (1) and in relation to any period, the expenses of management attributable to a company's life assurance business (excluding pension business and general annuity business) shall be expenses—

(*a*) which are disbursed for that period (disregarding any treated as so disbursed by section 83(3)), and

(*b*) which, disregarding subsection (5), are deductible as expenses of management of such life assurance business in accordance with section 707.

(5) Notwithstanding anything in section 707, only one-seventh of the acquisition expenses for any accounting period (in this section referred to as **"the base period"**) shall be treated as deductible under that section for the base period, and in subsections (6) and (7) any reference to the full amount of the acquisition expenses for the base period is a reference to the amount of those expenses which would be deductible for that period apart from this subsection.

(6) Where by virtue of subsection (5) only a fraction of the full amount of the acquisition expenses for the base period is deductible under section 707 for that period, then, subject to subsection (7), a further one-seventh of the full amount shall be so deductible for each succeeding accounting period after the base period until the whole of the full amount has become so deductible, except that for any accounting period of less than a year the fraction of one-seventh shall be proportionately reduced.

[(6A) Acquisition expenses for any accounting period ending on or before 31 December 2002 which relate to special investment business shall, for the purposes of subsection (6), be treated as acquisition expenses which relate to life assurance business (excluding pension business and general annuity business).][1]

(7) For any accounting period for which the fraction of the full amount of the acquisition expenses for the base period which would otherwise be deductible in accordance with subsection (6) exceeds the balance of those expenses which has not become deductible for earlier accounting periods, only that balance shall be deductible.

Amendments

[1] Subs (6A) inserted by FA 2003 s 52(1)(*b*) as respects accounting periods ending in 2003 and later years.

Cross-references

Chargeable gains of life business: s 711(3)(*b*).
Management expenses: s 707(1)(*b*).

Definitions

company: s 4(1); profits: s 4(1).

Former enactments

CTA 1976 s 33A(1)–(5) and (7)–(8); FA 1992 s 44(*c*); FA 1993 s 23; FA 1996 s 46; FA 1997 s 156(3).

709 Companies carrying on life business

(1) Where an assurance company carries on life business in conjunction with insurance business of any other class, the life business shall for the purposes of corporation tax be treated as a separate business from any other class of business carried on by the company.

(2) In ascertaining for the purposes of section 396 or 397 whether and to what extent a company has incurred a loss on its life business, any profits derived from the

investments of its life assurance fund (including franked investment income of a company resident in the State) shall be treated as part of the profits of that business.

Cross-references

Life assurance companies, management expenses deduction: s 707(1); subs (2): s 707(5)(*a*)(iv).

Definitions

franked investment income: ss 4(1), 156; profits: s 4(1).

Former enactments

CTA 1976 s 34.

710 Profits of life business

(1) Where the profits of an assurance company in respect of its life business are for the purposes of the Corporation Tax Acts computed in accordance with the provisions applicable to Case I of Schedule D, the following provisions shall apply:

(*a*) such part of those profits as belongs or is allocated to, or is expended on behalf of, policyholders or annuitants shall be excluded in making the computation;

(*b*) such part of those profits as is reserved for policyholders or annuitants shall also be excluded in making the computation but, if any profits so excluded as being so reserved cease at any time to be so reserved and are not allocated to, or expended on behalf of, policyholders or annuitants, those profits shall be treated as profits of the company for the accounting period in which they ceased to be so reserved.

(2) (*a*) Subject to paragraph (*b*), [where a company's trading operations on 31 December 2000 consisted solely of foreign life assurance business][1] (within the meaning of section 451(1)) the following provisions shall apply:

(i) subject to this subsection, the company shall be chargeable to corporation tax in respect of the profits of that business under Case I of Schedule D;

(ii) notwithstanding subsection (1)(*b*), where apart from this subparagraph any part of those profits would be excluded in computing the income chargeable under Case I of Schedule D solely by virtue of that part being reserved for policyholders or annuitants, that part shall not be excluded in computing the income so chargeable;

...[2]

[(*b*) In applying the definition of **"foreign life assurance business"** in section 451(1) for the purposes of paragraph (*a*), section 446 shall apply as if the following subsection were substituted for subsection (2) of that section:

"(2) Subject to subsections (7) and (9), the Minister may give a certificate certifying that such trading operations of a company as are specified in the certificate are, with effect from a date specified in the certificate, relevant trading operations for the purpose of this section.".][3]

(3) (*a*) In this subsection—

"policy of assurance" means—

(i) a policy of assurance issued by a company (to which subsection (2) applies) to an individual who on the date the policy is issued resides outside the State and who continuously so resides throughout a period of not less than 6 months commencing on that date, or

(ii) a policy issued or a contract made which is not a retirement benefits policy solely by virtue of the age condition not being complied with;

"relevant amount"—

(i) in relation to a policy of assurance, means the amount determined by the formula—

$$V - P$$

and

(ii) in relation to a retirement benefits policy, means the amount determined by the formula—

$$(V - P) \times \frac{75}{100}$$

where—

V is the amount or the aggregate of amounts by which the market value of all the entitlements under the policy of assurance or the retirement benefits policy, as the case may be, increased during any period or periods in which the policyholder was residing in the State, and

P is the amount of premiums or like sums paid in respect of the policy of assurance or the retirement benefits policy, as the case may be, during any period or periods in which the policyholder was residing in the State;

"retirement benefits policy" means a policy issued or a contract made by a company (to which subsection (2) applies)—

(i) to or with, as the case may be, an individual who, on the date the policy is issued or the contract is made, resides outside the State and who continuously so resides throughout a period of not less than 6 months commencing on that date, and

(ii) on terms which include the condition (in this subsection referred to as **"the age condition"**) that the main benefit secured by the policy or contract is the payment by the company (otherwise than on the death or disability of the individual) of a sum to the individual on or after the individual attains the age of 60 years and before the individual attains the age of 70 years and that condition is complied with.

(*b*) Where, in respect of a policy of assurance or a retirement benefits policy, a sum is payable by a company (otherwise than by reason of death or disability of the policyholder) to a policyholder who is resident or ordinarily resident in the State (within the meaning of Part 34), then—

(i) the company shall be deemed for the purposes of the Corporation Tax Acts to have made, in the year of assessment in which the sum is payable, an annual payment of an amount equal to the relevant amount in relation to the policy of assurance or the retirement benefits policy, as the case may be, and section 239 shall apply for the purposes of the charge, assessment and recovery of such tax,

(ii) the company shall be entitled to deduct the tax out of the sum otherwise payable,

(iii) the recipient of the sum payable shall not be entitled to repayment of, or credit for, such tax so deducted, and

(iv) the sum paid, or any part of the sum paid, shall not be reckoned in computing total income of the recipient of the sum paid for the purposes of the Income Tax Acts.

(4) Where an assurance company carries on both life assurance business and industrial assurance business, the business of each such class shall for the purposes of the Corporation Tax Acts be treated as though it were a separate business, and section 707 shall apply separately to each such class of business.

(5) (*a*) Where under section 25(1) of the Insurance Act, 1989, an assurance company amalgamates its industrial assurance and life assurance funds, subsection (4) shall not apply to that company for any accounting period ending on or after the completion of the amalgamation and before the recommencement, if any, of a separate industrial assurance or life assurance fund.

(*b*) For the purposes of applying section 707, in so far as it is affected by—

(i) management expenses or charges on income which apart from section 83(3) would be treated as respectively incurred for or paid in an accounting period ending before the day on which the amalgamation is completed, or

(ii) any loss incurred in such a period,

to a company which has amalgamated its industrial assurance and life assurance funds, subsection (4) shall apply as if the company had not amalgamated its funds.

(6) For the purposes of subsections (2) and (5), where an accounting period of an assurance company begins before the day (in this subsection referred to as **"the day of amalgamation"**) on which the company completes the amalgamation of its industrial assurance and life assurance funds and ends on or after the day of amalgamation, that period shall be divided into one part beginning on the day on which the accounting period begins and ending on the day before the day of amalgamation and another part beginning on the day of amalgamation and ending on the day on which the accounting period ends, and both parts of the accounting period shall be treated as if they were separate accounting periods.

Amendments

1 Substituted by FA 2000 s 56(1)(*a*) for 2001 and later financial years; previously "where a company's trading operations consist solely of a foreign life assurance business".

2 Subs (2)(*a*)(iii)–(iv) deleted by FA 2000 s 56(1)(*b*) for 2001 and later financial years; previously

"(iii) the charge to corporation tax under Schedule D of income from investments (in this subsection referred to as **"shareholders' investments"**) which are not investments of any fund representing the amount of the liability of the company in respect of its business with policyholders and annuitants shall not be under Case I of that Schedule;

(iv) notwithstanding section 707, section 83 shall apply for computing the profits of the company as respects expenses of management, including commissions, to the extent that those expenses—

(I) are disbursed for the purposes of managing shareholders' investments, and

(II) would not apart from this subparagraph be deductible in computing the profits, or any description of profits, of the company for the purposes of corporation tax."

3 Subs (2)(*b*) substituted by FA 1999 s 85(*b*) with effect from 6 April 1999.

Cross-references

Foreign life assurance and deferred annuities, subs (2): s 594(1)(*c*)(ii)(II).

Group relief, losses which may be surrendered, subs (1): s 420(1)(*b*).

Group relief, relevant losses and charges, subs (1): s 420A(3)(*b*)(ii).

Life assurance companies, annuity business, separate charge on profits, subs (1): s 715(2)(*a*).

Life assurance companies, investment income reserved for policy holders, subs (1): s 713(5), (6)(*a*).

Life assurance companies, management expenses deduction: s 707(1), (5)(*a*)(iv).

Life assurance companies, profits of life business, new basis: s 730A(6).

Case law

Distribution management expenses: *Johnson v Prudential Assurance Co Ltd* [1996] STC 647.

Life assurance policy: *Fuji Finance Inc v Aetna Life Assurance*, UK High Court [1994] STI 1544.

Definitions

charges on income: ss 4(1), 243(1); company: s 4(1); profits: s 4(1).

Former enactments

CTA 1976 s 35; FA 1991 s 30; FA 1994 s 60; FA 1997 s 67.

711 Chargeable gains of life business

[(1) For the purposes of computing corporation tax on chargeable gains accruing to a fund or funds maintained by an assurance company in respect of its life business—

(*a*) (i) section 556, and

(ii) section 607,

shall not apply,

(*b*) section 581 shall, as respects—

(i) subsections (1) and (2) of that section, and

(ii) subsection (3) of that section, in so far as a chargeable gain is not thereby disregarded for the purposes of that subsection,

apply as if paragraph 24 of Schedule 32, section 719, section 723(7)(*a*) and paragraph (*a*)(ii) had not been enacted,

(*c*) the amount of capital gains tax computed for the purposes of section 78(2) ...[1] is the amount so computed as if, notwithstanding section 28(3), the rate of capital gains tax were—

(i) throughout the financial year 1999, subject to paragraph (*d*), 40 per cent, and

(ii) throughout each subsequent financial year, the rate of corporation tax specified in section 21(1) for that financial year,

and

(*d*) where for an accounting period the expenses of management (within the meaning of section 83 as applied by section 707), deductible exceeds the amount of profits from which they are deductible, the reference in paragraph (*c*)(i) to 40 per cent shall be a reference to the rate of corporation tax referred to in section 21(1) for the financial year 1999.][2]

(2) (*a*) In this subsection—

"the appropriate amount in respect of the interest" means the appropriate amount in respect of the interest which would be determined in accordance with Schedule 21 if a company were the first buyer and carried on a trade to which section 749(1) applies but, in so determining the appropriate amount in respect of the interest in accordance with Schedule 21, paragraph 3(4) of that Schedule shall apply as if **"in the opinion of the Appeal Commissioners"** were deleted;

"securities" has the same meaning as in section 815.

(*b*) Where in an accounting period a company disposes of any securities and in the following accounting period interest becoming payable in respect of the securities is receivable by the company, the gain or loss accruing on the disposal shall be computed as if the price paid by the company for the securities was reduced by the appropriate amount in respect of the interest; but where for an accounting period this paragraph applies so as to reduce the price paid for securities, the amount by which the price paid for the securities is reduced shall be treated as a loss arising in the following accounting period from the disposal of the securities.

(3) Subject to section 720, where an assurance company, in the course of carrying on a class of life assurance business mentioned in subparagraph (iii) or (iv) of section 707(2)(*a*), disposes of or is deemed to dispose of assets in an accounting period, the amount, if any, for each such class of business by which the aggregate of allowable losses exceeds the aggregate of chargeable gains on the disposals or deemed disposals in the course of that class of business in the accounting period shall be—

(*a*) disregarded for the purposes of section 31, and

(*b*) treated for the purposes of the Corporation Tax Acts as a sum disbursed by the company in the accounting period as an expense of management, other than an acquisition expense (within the meaning of section 708), incurred in the course of carrying on that class of business.

(4) For the purposes of subsection (3), any amount which apart from paragraph 24 of Schedule 32 would be treated as a chargeable gain or an allowable loss of an accounting period of a company by virtue of section 720 shall also be treated as arising on a disposal of assets by the company in the accounting period so that each such amount shall be taken into account in determining the amount, if any, by which the aggregate of allowable losses exceeds the aggregate of chargeable gains on disposals of assets by the company in the course of carrying on life assurance business [(excluding pension business and general annuity business)][3] in the accounting period.

Amendments

1 Deleted by FA 2003 s 52(1)(*c*)(i) as respects accounting periods ending in 2003 and later years; previously ", otherwise than in respect of the special investment fund,".

2 Subs (1) substituted by FA 2000 s 81(1)(*a*) with effect for 1999 and later financial years.

3 Substituted by FA 2003 s 52(1)(*c*)(ii) as respects accounting periods ending in 2003 and later years; previously "(excluding pension business, general annuity business and special investment business)".

Definitions

allowable loss: ss 4(1), 5(1), 546; chargeable gain: ss 5(1), 545; company: s 4(1); profits: s 4(1).

Former enactments

CTA 1976 s 35A; FA 1993 s 11(*d*); FA 1996 s 47(1).

712 Distributions received from Irish resident companies

(1) [Section 129 and subsections (4) and (5) of section 153][1] shall not apply as respects a distribution received by an assurance company in connection with that part of its life business the profits of which are charged to corporation tax otherwise than under Case I or IV of Schedule D...[2].

...[3]

Amendments

[1] Substituted by FA 1999 s 28(2) in respect of distributions made on or after 6 April 1999; previously "Sections 129 and 153(1)".

[2] Repealed by FA 2000 s 69(2) and Sch 2 Part 2 with effect from 6 April 1999 in the case of income tax and as respects accounting periods commencing on or after that date in the case of corporation tax; previously ", and the income represented by the distribution shall be equal to the aggregate of the amount of the distribution and the amount of the tax credit in respect of the distribution".

[3] Subs (2) repealed by FA 2000 s 69(2) and Sch 2 Part 2 with effect from 6 April 1999 in the case of income tax and as respects accounting periods commencing on or after that date in the case of corporation tax.

Definitions

company: s 4(1); distribution: ss 4(1), 436, 437; franked investment income: ss 4(1), 156; profits: s 4(1); tax credit: ss 2(1), 136.

Former enactments

CTA 1976 s 33B; FA 1993 s 11(*c*).

713 Investment income reserved for policyholders

(1) For the purposes of this section—

(*a*) **"unrelieved profits"** means the amount of profits on which corporation tax falls finally to be borne;

(*b*) the amount of tax which is or would be chargeable on a company shall be taken to be the amount of tax which is or would be so chargeable after allowance of any relief to which the company is or would be entitled otherwise than under this section ...[1].

...[2]

[(3) Notwithstanding sections 21(1) and 21A and subject to subsection (6)(*b*), corporation tax shall be charged in respect of the part specified in subsection (6)(*a*) of unrelieved profits of an accounting period of an assurance company from investments referable to life business ...[3] at the rate determined by the formula—

$$\frac{(N2 \times SR1) + (N3 \times SR2)}{N1}$$

where—

N1 is the number of months in the accounting period,

N2 is the number of months from the day of the commencement of the accounting period to the earlier of—

(*a*) the end of the year of assessment (in this subsection referred to as the "first year of assessment") in which that day falls, and

(*b*) the end of the accounting period,

N3 is N1 reduced by N2,

SR1 is the standard rate for the first year of assessment, and

SR2 is the standard rate for the year of assessment immediately subsequent to the first year of assessment.][4]

...[5]

(5) (*a*) Subject to paragraph (*b*), the franked investment income from investments held in connection with a company's life business shall be apportioned between—

(i) policyholders or annuitants, and

(ii) shareholders,

by attributing to policyholders or annuitants such fraction of that income as the fraction (in this subsection referred to as **"the appropriate fraction"**) of the profits of the company's life business which, on a computation of such profits in accordance with the provisions applicable to Case I of Schedule D (whether or not the company is in fact charged to tax under that Case for the relevant accounting period or periods), would be excluded under section 710(1).

(*b*) Where the franked investment income referred to in paragraph (*a*) exceeds the profits of the company's life business as computed in accordance with the provisions applicable to Case I of Schedule D other than section 710, the part of the franked investment income attributable to policy holders or annuitants shall be the aggregate of—

(i) the appropriate fraction of the franked investment income in so far as not exceeding those profits, and

(ii) the amount of the excess of the franked investment income over those profits.

(6) (*a*) Where the aggregate of the unrelieved profits and the shareholders' part of the franked investment income exceeds the profits of the company in respect of its life business for the relevant accounting periods computed in accordance with the provisions of Case I of Schedule D as extended by sections 710 and 714 (whether or not the company is charged to tax under that Case), the part referred to in subsection (3) shall be the lesser of—

(i) the amount of that excess, and

(ii) the unrelieved profits,

and

(*b*) where the aggregate referred to in paragraph (*a*) is less than the profits of the company's life business as so computed, subsection (3) shall not apply.

(7) This section shall apply subject to paragraph 24 of Schedule 32.

Amendments

1 Repealed by FA 2000 s 69(2) and Sch 2 Part 2 with effect from 6 April 1999 in the case of income tax and as respects accounting periods commencing on or after that date in the case of corporation tax; previously "or under section 136, 712(2) or 730".

2 Deleted by FA 2000 s 81(1)(*b*)(i) with effect for 2000 and later financial years.

3 Deleted by FA 2003 s 52(1)(*d*) as respects accounting periods ending in 2003 and later years; previously ", other than special investment business,".

4 Subs (3) substituted by FA 2000 s 81(1)(*b*)(ii) with effect for 2000 and later financial years.

5 Subs (4) deleted by FA 2000 s 81(1)(*b*)(iii) with effect for 2000 and later financial years.

Cross-references

Life assurance companies, computation of profits: s 714(1).

Provisions as to relief from income tax and corporation tax by means of credit in respect of foreign tax, limit on total credit — corporation tax, subs (3): Sch 24 para 4(4)(*c*).

Transitional: Sch 32 para 24.

Definitions

chargeable gain: ss 5(1), 545; company: s 4(1); the financial year: s 4(1); franked investment income: ss 4(1), 156; profits: s 4(1); standard rate: ss 3(1), 15; year of assessment: s 2(1).

Former enactments

CTA 1976 s 36; FA 1993 s 11(*e*); FA 1996 s 48(1); FA 1997 s 68.

Corresponding UK tax provision

Income and Corporation Taxes Act 1988 s 433 [repealed].

714 Life business: computation of profits

(1) For the purposes of [section 713],[1] the exclusion by section 129 from the charge to corporation tax of franked investment income shall not prevent such income of a company resident in the State attributable to the investments of the company's life assurance fund from being taken into account as part of the profits in computing trading income in accordance with the provisions applicable to Case I of Schedule D.

...[2]

Amendments

1 Substituted by FA 2000 s 69(1) and Sch 2 Part 1 para (*n*) with effect from 6 April 1999 in the case of income tax and as respects accounting periods commencing on or after that date in the case of corporation tax.

2 Subs (2) repealed by FA 2000 s 69(2) and Sch 2 Part 2 with effect from 6 April 1999 in the case of income tax and as respects accounting periods commencing on or after that date in the case of corporation tax.

Cross-references

Life assurance companies, investment income reserved for policy holders: s 713(6)(*b*).

Life assurance companies, management expenses deduction: s 707(5)(*a*)(iv).

Definitions

company: s 4(1); franked investment income: ss 4(1), 156; profits: s 4(1).

Former enactments

CTA 1976 s 38; FA 1993 s 11(*g*).

715 Annuity business: separate charge on profits

(1) Except in the case of an assurance company charged to tax in accordance with the provisions applicable to Case I of Schedule D in respect of the profits of its life assurance business, profits arising to an assurance company from pension business or general annuity business shall be treated as annual profits or gains within Schedule D and shall be chargeable to corporation tax under Case IV of that Schedule, and for that purpose—

(*a*) the business of each such class shall be treated separately, and

(*b*) subject to paragraph (*a*) and subsection (2), the profits from each such class of business shall be computed in accordance with the provisions applicable to Case I of Schedule D.

(2) In making the computation in accordance with the provisions applicable to Case I of Schedule D—

[(*a*) (i) subject to subparagraphs (ii), (iii) and (iv), subsection (1) of section 710 shall apply with the necessary modifications and in particular shall apply as if there were deleted from that subsection all references to policyholders other than holders of policies referable to pension business,

(ii) where apart from this subparagraph any profits would be excluded in making the computation solely by virtue of that part being reserved for holders of policies referable to pension business, that part shall not be so excluded,

(iii) in relation to investments of any fund representing the amount of the liabilities of the company to policyholders in respect of its pension business or general annuity business, as the case may be,

(I) any increase in value of those investments (whether realised or unrealised) shall be taken into account as a receipt, and

(II) any decrease in value of those investments (whether realised or unrealised) shall be taken into account as an expense,

to the extent that the increase or decrease, as the case may be, is included in the value of those liabilities as valued by the actuary to the company, and

(iv) where the profits of an assurance company for an accounting period (in this subparagraph referred to as "the first accounting period") are computed in accordance with subparagraph (iii) and the profits of the most recent preceding accounting period are not so computed, the increase or decrease in the value of investments referred to in subparagraph (iii) shall as respects the first accounting period be computed by reference to the cost of the investments at the time they were acquired by the company and such increase or decrease shall be treated as a receipt or as an expense, as the case may be.][1]

(*b*) no deduction shall be allowed in respect of any expense, being an expense of management referred to in section 707, and

(*c*) there may be set off against the profits of pension business or general annuity business any loss, to be computed on the same basis as the profits, which was sustained in the same class of business in any previous accounting period while the company was within the charge to corporation tax in respect of that class of business in so far as that loss not already been so set off.

(3) Section 399 shall not be taken as applying to a loss sustained by a company on its general annuity business or pension business.

(4) The treatment of an annuity as containing a capital element for the purposes of section 788 shall not prevent the full amount of the annuity from being deductible in computing profits or from being treated as a charge on income for the purposes of the Corporation Tax Acts.

(5) Notwithstanding any other provision of the Corporation Tax Acts, any annuity paid by a company and referable to its excluded annuity business—

(*a*) shall not be treated as a charge on income for the purposes of the Corporation Tax Acts, and

(*b*) shall be deductible in computing for the purposes of Case I of Schedule D the profits of the company in respect of its life assurance business.

Amendments

1 Subs (2)(*a*) substituted by FA 1998 s 64 as respects an accounting period of a company ending on or after 4 March 1998.

Cross-references

Corporation tax: treatment of tax free income of non resident banks, insurance businesses etc: s 845(3(*b*)(ii).

Foreign life assurance funds: s 718(5)(*b*).

Life assurance companies, general annuity business: s 716(1), (4).

Life assurance companies, pension business: s 717(4), (5)(*a*), (6).

Overseas life assurance companies, general annuity and pension business: s 727(1), (2).

Overseas life assurance companies, income tax, foreign tax and tax credit: s 729(1).

Definitions

company: s 4(1); Corporation Tax Acts: s 1(2); profits: s 4(1); within the charge to (tax): s 2(1).

Former enactments

CTA 1976 s 39; FA 1986 s 59(*b*); FA 1996 s 132(2) and Sch 5 Pt II.

Corresponding UK tax provision

Income and Corporation Taxes Act 1988 s 436.

716 General annuity business

(1) In this section, **"taxed income"** means income charged to corporation tax, otherwise than under section 715, and franked investment income.

(2) In the case of a company carrying on general annuity business, the annuities paid by the company, in so far as referable to that business and in so far as they do not exceed the taxed income of the part of the annuity fund so referable, shall be treated as charges on income.

(3) Notwithstanding any other provision of the Corporation Tax Acts, any annuities which under subsection (2) are treated as charges on income of a company (in this subsection referred to as **"the first-mentioned company"**) for an accounting period shall not be allowed as deductions against any profits (whether of the first-mentioned company or of any other company) other than against that part of the total profits ...[1] arising in that accounting period to the first-mentioned company from its general annuity business.

(4) In computing under section 715 the profits arising to an assurance company from general annuity business—

(*a*) taxed income shall not be taken into account as part of those profits, and

(*b*) of the annuities paid by the company and referable to general annuity business—

(i) those which under subsection (2) are treated as charges on income shall not be deductible, and

(ii) those which are not so treated shall, notwithstanding section 76, be deductible.

(5) A company not resident in the State which carries on through a branch or agency in the State any general annuity business shall not be entitled to treat any part of the annuities paid by it which are referable to that business as paid out of profits or gains brought into charge to income tax.

Amendments

1 Deleted by FA 2003 s 41(1)(*i*) as respects accounting periods ending on or after 6 February 2003; previously "(including, where a claim is made under section 157 for the purposes mentioned in subsection (2)(*a*) of that section, any franked investment income)".

Definitions

branch or agency: ss 4(1), 5(1); charges on income: ss 4(1), 243(1); company: s 4(1); Corporation Tax Acts: s 1(2); franked investment income: ss 4(1), 156; profits: s 4(1).

Former enactments

CTA 1976 s 40; FA 1986 s 59(*c*).

---

717 Pension business

(1) Exemption from corporation tax shall be allowed in respect of income from, and chargeable gains in respect of, investments and deposits of so much of an assurance company's life assurance fund and separate annuity fund, if any, as is referable to pension business.

(2) (*a*) In this subsection, **"financial futures"** and **"traded options"** mean respectively financial futures and traded options which are for the time being dealt in or quoted on any futures exchange or any stock exchange, whether or not that exchange is situated in the State.

(*b*) For the purposes of subsection (1), a contract entered into in the course of dealing in financial futures or traded options shall be regarded as an investment.

(3) The exemption from tax conferred by subsection (1) shall not exclude any sums from being taken into account as receipts in computing profits or losses for any purpose of the Corporation Tax Acts.

(4) Subject to subsection (5), the exclusion by section 129 from the charge to corporation tax of franked investment income shall not prevent such income being taken into account as part of the profits in computing under section 715 income from pension business.

(5) (*a*) Where for any accounting period there is apart from this subsection a profit arising to an assurance company from pension business (computed in accordance with section 715) and the company so elects as respects all or any part of its franked investment income arising in that period, being an amount of franked investment income not exceeding the amount of the profit arising from pension business, subsections (1) and (4) shall not apply to the franked investment income to which the election relates.

(*b*) An election under paragraph (*a*) shall be made by notice in writing given to the inspector not later than 2 years after the end of the accounting period to which the election relates or within such longer period as the Revenue Commissioners may by notice in writing allow.

(6) In computing under section 715 the profits from pension business, annuities shall be deductible notwithstanding section 76(5), and a company shall not be entitled to treat as paid out of profits or gains brought into charge to income tax any part of the annuities paid by the company which is referable to pension business.

Cross-references

Overseas life assurance companies, income tax, foreign tax and tax credit: s 729(1).

Definitions

chargeable gain: ss 5(1), 545; company: ss 4(1), 5(1); Corporation Tax Acts: s 1(2); franked investment income: ss 4(1), 156; inspector: ss 2(1), 5(1), 852; profits: s 4(1); writing: IA 1937 Sch.

Former enactments

CTA 1976 s 41; FA 1988 s 30(1)–(2)(*c*); FA 1991 s 38.

Corresponding UK tax provision

Income and Corporation Taxes Act 1988 ss 437–438C.

718 Foreign life assurance funds

(1) In this section, **"foreign life assurance fund"** means—

(*a*) any fund representing the amount of the liability of an assurance company in respect of its life business with policy holders and annuitants residing outside the State whose proposals were made to, or whose annuity contracts were granted by, the company at or through a branch or agency outside the State, and

(*b*) where such a fund is not kept separately from the life assurance fund of the company, such part of the life assurance fund as represents the liability of the company under such policies and annuity contracts, such liability being estimated in the same manner as it is estimated for the purposes of the periodical returns of the company.

(2) Corporation tax under Case III of Schedule D on income arising from securities and possessions in any place outside the State which form part of the investments of the foreign life assurance fund of an assurance company shall be computed on the full amount of the actual sums received in the State from remittances payable in the State, or from property imported, or from money or value arising from property not imported, or from money or value so received on credit or on account in respect of such remittances, property, money or value brought into the State without any deduction or abatement.

(3) Where—

(*a*) any securities issued by the Minister for Finance with a condition in the terms specified in section 43, or

(*b*) any stocks or other securities to which section 49 applies and which are issued with either or both of the conditions specified in subsection (2) of that section,

for the time being form part of the investments of the foreign life assurance fund of an assurance company, the income arising from any of those stocks or securities, if applied for the purposes of that fund or reinvested so as to form part of that fund, shall not be liable to corporation tax.

(4) Where the Revenue Commissioners are satisfied that any income arising from the investments of the foreign life assurance fund of an assurance company has been remitted to the State and invested as part of the investments of that fund in any stocks or securities of a type referred to in subsection (3), that income shall not be liable to corporation tax and any such tax paid on that income shall if necessary be repaid to the company on the making of a claim.

(5) Where income from investments of the foreign life assurance fund of an assurance company has been relieved from corporation tax in accordance with this section, a corresponding reduction shall be made—

(*a*) in the relief granted under section 707 in respect of expenses of management, and

(*b*) in any amount on which the company is chargeable to corporation tax by virtue of section 715—

(i) in respect of general annuity business, or

(ii) in respect of pension business,

in so far as the investment income relieved is referable to general annuity business or pension business, as the case may be.

(6) Where this section applies in relation to income arising from investments of any part of an assurance company's life assurance fund, it shall apply in the like manner in relation to chargeable gains accruing from the disposal of any such investments, and losses so accruing shall not be allowable losses.

Cross-references

Interpretation: s 705(1) (excluded annuity business).

Deemed disposal and reacquisition of certain assets, meaning of "foreign life assurance fund" applied: s 719(1).

Definitions

allowable loss: ss 4(1), 5(1), 546; branch or agency: ss 4(1), 5(1); chargeable gain: ss 5(1), 545; company: s 4(1).

Former enactments

CTA 1976 s 42(1)–(5) and (8).

Corresponding UK tax provisions

Income and Corporation Taxes Act 1988 s 441.

719 Deemed disposal and reacquisition of certain assets

(1) In this section and in section 720—

"average", in relation to 2 amounts, means 50 per cent of the aggregate of those 2 amounts;

"closing", in relation to an accounting period, means the position at the end of the valuation period which coincides with that accounting period or in which that accounting period falls;

"foreign life assurance fund" has the same meaning as in section 718;

"investment reserve", in relation to an assurance company, means the excess of the value of the assets of the company's life business fund over the liabilities of the life business;

"life business fund" means the fund or funds maintained by an assurance company in respect of its life business ...[1];

"linked assets" means assets of an assurance company identified in its records as assets by reference to the value of which benefits provided for under a policy or contract are to be determined;

"linked liabilities" means liabilities in respect of benefits to be determined by reference to the value of linked assets;

"opening", in relation to an accounting period, means the position at the beginning of the valuation period which coincides with that accounting period or in which that accounting period falls;

"with-profits liabilities" means liabilities in respect of policies or contracts under which the policy holders or annuitants are eligible to participate in surplus.

(2) Each asset of the life business fund of an assurance company on the day on which an accounting period of the company ends shall, subject to this section, be deemed to have been disposed of and immediately reacquired by the company on that day at the asset's market value on that day.

(3) Subsection (2) shall not apply to—

(*a*) (i) assets to which section 607 applies, other than, with effect as on and from the 26th day of March, 1997, where such assets are held in connection with a contract or other arrangement which secures the future exchange of the assets for other assets to which that section does not apply, or

(ii) assets which are strips within the meaning of section 55.

(*b*) assets linked solely to pension business ...[2], or

(*c*) assets of the foreign life assurance fund,

and, in relation to other assets which are not assets linked solely to life assurance business [(excluding pension business and general annuity business)][3], shall apply only to the relevant chargeable fraction for an accounting period of each class of asset.

(4) In subsection (3), **"the relevant chargeable fraction for an accounting period"**—

(*a*) in relation to linked assets, means the fraction of which—

(i) the denominator is the average of such of the opening and closing life business liabilities as are liabilities in respect of benefits to be determined by reference to the value of linked assets other than—

[(I) assets linked solely to life assurance business (excluding pension business and general annuity business), or pension business, and][4]

(II) assets of the foreign life assurance fund, and

(ii) the numerator is the average of such of the opening and closing liabilities within subparagraph (i) as are liabilities of business the profits of which are not charged to tax under Case I or IV of Schedule D, and (*b*) in relation to assets other than linked assets, means the fraction of which—

(i) the denominator is the aggregate of—

(I) the average of the opening and closing life business liabilities, other than liabilities in respect of benefits to be determined by reference to the value of linked assets and liabilities of the foreign life assurance business ...[5], and

(II) the average of the opening and closing amounts of the investment reserve, and

(ii) the numerator is the aggregate of—

(I) the average of such of the opening and closing liabilities within subparagraph (i) as are liabilities of business the profits of which are not charged to tax under Case I or IV of Schedule D, and

(II) the average of the appropriate parts of the opening and closing amounts of the investment reserve.

(5) (*a*) In this subsection, **"liabilities"** does not include the liabilities of the foreign life assurance business ...[6].

(*b*) In subsection (4), **"appropriate part"**, in relation to the investment reserve, means—

(i) where none, or only an insignificant proportion, of the liabilities of the life business are with-profits liabilities, the part of that reserve which bears to the whole the same proportion as the amount of the liabilities of business, the profits of which are not charged to tax under Case I or IV of Schedule D, which are not linked liabilities bears to the whole amount of the liabilities of the life business which are not linked liabilities, and

(ii) in any other case, the part of that reserve which bears to the whole the same proportion as the amount of the with-profits liabilities of business, the profits of which are not charged to tax under Case I or IV of Schedule D, bears to the whole amount of the with-profits liabilities of the life business.

(6) For the purposes of this section, in applying section 557 to the computation of gains accruing to an assurance company on the disposal, on the day on which an accounting period of the company ends, of assets which are not linked solely to life assurance business [(excluding pension business or general annuity business)],[7] the company shall be deemed to have acquired all of the assets of its life business fund, other than the assets it acquired in that accounting period, at their respective market values on the day immediately before the day on which that period began.

[(7) For the purposes of this section, assets of the foreign life assurance fund and liabilities of the foreign life assurance business shall be disregarded in determining the investment reserve.][8]

Amendments

1 Deleted by FA 2003 s 52(1)(*e*)(i) as respects accounting periods ending in 2003 and later years; previously "other than its special investment business".

2 Deleted by FA 2003 s 52(1)(*e*)(ii)(I) as respects accounting periods ending in 2003 and later years; previously "or special investment business".

3 Substituted by FA 2003 s 52(1)(*e*)(ii)(II) as respects accounting periods ending in 2003 and later years; previously "(excluding pension business, general annuity business and special investment business)".

[4] Subs (4)(*a*)(i)(I) substituted by FA 2003 s 52(1)(*e*)(iii)(I) as respects accounting periods ending in 2003 and later years.

[5] Deleted by FA 2003 s 52(1)(*e*)(iii)(II) as respects accounting periods ending in 2003 and later years; previously "or special investment business".

[6] Deleted by FA 2003 s 52(1)(*e*)(iv) as respects accounting periods ending in 2003 and later years; previously "or special investment business".

[7] Substituted by FA 2003 s 52(1)(*e*)(v) as respects accounting periods ending in 2003 and later years; previously "(excluding pension business, general annuity business or special investment business)".

[8] Subs (7) substituted by FA 2003 s 52(1)(*e*)(vi) as respects accounting periods ending in 2003 and later years.

Cross-references

Chargeable gains of life business: s 581(1), (2)–(3) (in so far as a chargeable gain is not thereby disregarded for the purposes of that subsection) apply as if: ss 719, 723(7)(*a*), (*a*)(ii) and Sch 32 para 24 had not been enacted: s 711(1)(*b*).

Exemption from tax in the case of gains on certain disposals of shares, meaning of "life business fund" applied: s 626B(1)(*b*)(ii)(II), (3)(*c*).

Gains or losses arising under this section: s 720(1), (2), (5).

Restriction on set-off of pre-entry losses: Sch 18A para 1(9).

Treatment of debts on a change in currency, meaning of "life business fund" applied: s 541A(4)(*a*); subs (2): s 541A(4)(*b*)(I).

Definitions

company: s 4(1); profits: s 4(1)

Former enactments

CTA 1976 s 46A; FA 1992 s 44(*d*); FA 1993 s 11(*j*); FA 1997 s 69.

720 Gains or losses arising by virtue of section 719

(1) Subject to subsections (2) to (4), chargeable gains or allowable losses which would otherwise accrue on disposals deemed by virtue of section 719 to have been made in a company's accounting period (other than a period in which the company ceased to carry on life business) shall be treated, subject to paragraphs (*b*) and (*c*), as not accruing to the company, but instead—

(*a*) there shall be ascertained the difference (in this section referred to as **"the net amount"**) between the aggregate of those gains and the aggregate of those losses,

(*b*) one-seventh of the net amount shall be treated as a chargeable gain or, where it represents an excess of losses over gains, as an allowable loss accruing to the company in the accounting period, and

(*c*) a further one-seventh shall be treated as a chargeable gain or, as the case may be, as an allowable loss accruing in each succeeding accounting period until the whole amount has been accounted for.

(2) As respects chargeable gains or allowable losses accruing on disposals of rights under reinsurance contracts (within the meaning of section 594(4)) deemed by virtue of section 719 to have been made in the accounting period or part of an accounting period falling wholly within the year ending on—

(*a*) the 31st day of December, 1997, this section shall not apply to three-sevenths,

(*b*) the 31st day of December, 1998, this section shall not apply to two-sevenths, or

(*c*) the 31st day of December, 1999, this section shall not apply to one-seventh,

of those chargeable gains and allowable losses.

(3) For any accounting period of less than one year, the fraction of one-seventh referred to in subsection (1)(*c*) shall be proportionately reduced and, where this subsection has applied in relation to any accounting period before the last for which subsection (1)(*c*) applies, the fraction treated as accruing in that last accounting period shall be reduced so as to secure that no more than the whole of the net amount has been accounted for.

(4) Where a company ceases to carry on life business before the beginning of the last of the accounting periods for which subsection (1)(*c*) would apply in relation to a net amount, the fraction of that amount which is treated as accruing in the accounting period in which the company ceases to carry on life business shall be such as to secure that the whole of the net amount has been accounted for.

(5) Where in an accounting period a company incurs a loss on the disposal (in this subsection referred to as the **"first-mentioned disposal"**) of an asset the gain or loss in respect of a deemed disposal of which was included in a net amount to which subsection (1)(*b*) applied for any preceding accounting period, then, so much of the allowable loss on the first-mentioned disposal as is equal to the excess of the amount of the loss over the amount which, if section 719 had not been enacted, would have been the allowable loss on the first-mentioned disposal shall be treated for the purposes of this section as an allowable loss which would otherwise accrue on disposals deemed by virtue of section 719 to have been made in the company's accounting period.

Cross-references

Chargeable gains of life business: s 711(3), (4).
Foreign life assurance funds, deemed disposal and reacquisition of certain assets: s 719(1).
Restriction on set-off of pre-entry losses: Sch 18A para 1(9).
Treatment of debts on a change in currency, meaning of "the net amount" applied: s 541A(4)(*b*)(I).

Definitions

allowable loss: ss 4(1), 5(1), 546; chargeable gain: ss 4(1), 5(1), 545; company: s 4(1); year: IA 1937 Sch.

Former enactments

CTA 1976 s 46B; FA 1992 s 44(*d*); FA 1995 s 69; FA 1996 s 50.

721 Life policies carrying rights not in money

Where any investments or other assets are, in accordance with a policy issued in the course of life business carried on by an assurance company, transferred to the policyholder, the policyholder's acquisition of the assets and the disposal of the assets to the policyholder shall be deemed to be for a consideration equal to the market value of the assets—

(*a*) for the purposes of the Capital Gains Tax Acts, and

(*b*) for the purposes of computing income in accordance with Case I or IV of Schedule D.

Definitions

company: s 4(1).

Former enactments

CTA 1976 s 48.

Corresponding UK tax provision

Income and Corporation Taxes Act 1988 s 443.

722 Benefits from life policies issued before 6th April, 1974

(1) This section shall apply in relation to policies of life assurance issued before the 6th day of April, 1974, by a company carrying on life business, being policies which—

(*a*) provide for benefits consisting to any extent of investments of a specified description or of a sum of money to be determined by reference to the value of such investments, but

(*b*) do not provide for the deduction from those benefits of any amount by reference to tax chargeable in respect of chargeable gains.

(2) Where—

(*a*) the investments of the company's life assurance fund, in so far as referable to those policies, consist wholly or mainly of investments of the description so specified, and

(*b*) on the company becoming liable under any of those policies for any such benefits (including benefits to be provided on the surrender of a policy), a chargeable gain accrues to the company from the disposal, in meeting or for the purpose of meeting that liability, of investments of that description forming part of its life assurance fund, or would so accrue if the liability were met by or from the proceeds of such a disposal,

then, the company shall be entitled as against the person receiving the benefits to retain out of the benefits a part of the benefits not exceeding in amount or value corporation tax at the full rate in respect of the chargeable gain referred to in paragraph (*b*) computed without regard to any amount retained under this subsection and reduced in accordance with section 78(1).

Definitions

chargeable gain: ss 5(1), 545; company: ss 4(1), 5(1); person: IA 1937 s 11(*c*).

Former enactments

CTA 1976 s 49.

Corresponding UK tax provision

Income and Corporation Taxes Act 1988 s 444.

CHAPTER 2

Special Investment Policies

723 Special investment policies

(1) In this section—

"excluded shares" means—

(*a*) shares in an investment company within the meaning of Part XIII of the Companies Act, 1990,

(*b*) shares in an undertaking for collective investment in transferable securities within the meaning of the European Communities (Undertakings for Collective Investment in Transferable Securities) Regulations, 1989 (SI No 78 of 1989), or (*c*) shares in a company, being shares the market value of which may be expected to approximate at all times to the market value of the proportion of the assets of the company which they represent;

"inspector", in relation to any matter, means an inspector of taxes appointed under section 852, and includes such other officers as the Revenue Commissioners shall appoint in that behalf;

"mortality cover" means any amount payable under a policy of life assurance in the event of the death of a person specified in the terms of that policy;

"ordinary shares" means shares forming part of a company's ordinary share capital;

"qualifying shares" means ordinary shares—

(*a*) in a company resident in the State, or

(*b*) (i) listed in the official list of the Irish Stock Exchange, or

(ii) dealt in on the smaller companies market, or the unlisted securities market, of the Irish Stock Exchange,

other than excluded shares;

...[1]

"special investment business" means so much of the life business of an assurance company as is connected with special investment policies;

[**"special investment fund"** means a fund in respect of which the conditions specified in subsection (2) are satisfied as respects accounting periods ending on or before 31 December 2002, of the assurance company concerned;][2]

[**"special investment policy"** means a policy of life assurance issued by an assurance company to an individual on or after 1 February 1993 and before 1 January 2001, in respect of which—

[(*a*) the conditions specified in subsection (3) are satisfied as respects accounting periods ending on or before 31 December 2002, of the assurance company concerned, and][3]

(*b*) a declaration of the kind specified in subsection (4) has been made to the assurance company;][4]

"specified qualifying shares", in relation to a special investment fund, means qualifying shares in a company the issued share capital of which has a market value of less than [€255,000,000][5] when the shares are acquired for the fund.

(2) The conditions referred to in the definition of **"special investment fund"** are as follows:

(*a*) the fund shall be owned by an assurance company;

(*b*) the fund shall be kept separately from its other funds, if any, by the assurance company;

(*c*) the fund shall represent only the liabilities of the assurance company in respect of its special investment business, and accordingly there shall not be any arrangements whereby any asset of the fund is connected directly or indirectly with any business of the company other than its special investment business;

(*d*) the aggregate of the consideration given for shares which are at any time before the 1st day of February, 1994, assets of the fund shall not be less than—

(i) as respects qualifying shares, 40 per cent, and

(ii) as respects specified qualifying shares, 6 per cent,

of the aggregate of the consideration given for the assets which are assets of the fund at that time;

(*e*) the aggregate of the consideration given for shares which are at any time within the year ending on the 31st day of January, 1995, assets of the fund shall not be less than—

(i) as respects qualifying shares, 45 per cent, and

(ii) as respects specified qualifying shares, 9 per cent,

of the aggregate of the consideration given for the assets which are assets of the fund at that time;

(*f*) the aggregate of the consideration given for shares which are at any time within the year ending on the 31st day of January, 1996, assets of the fund shall not be less than—

(i) as respects qualifying shares, 50 per cent, and

(ii) as respects specified qualifying shares, 10 per cent,

of the aggregate of the consideration given for the assets which are assets of the fund at that time;

[(*g*) the aggregate of consideration given for shares which are, at any time on or after 1 February 1996 and before 31 December 2000, assets of the fund shall not be less than—

(i) as respects qualifying shares, 55 per cent, and

(ii) as respects specified qualifying shares, 10 per cent,

of the aggregate of the consideration given for the assets which are assets of the fund at that time,][6]

and for the purposes of paragraphs (*d*) to (*g*) the amount of the consideration given for assets of the fund shall be determined in accordance with sections 547, 580 and 724.

(3) The conditions referred to in the definition of **"special investment policy"** are as follows:

(*a*) the policy of life assurance concerned shall be designated by the assurance company concerned as a special investment policy;

(*b*) any payments received by the company in respect of the policy shall not, or shall not in the aggregate if there is more than one such payment, exceed [€63,500][7];

...[8]

(*d*) the policy shall not be issued to or owned by an individual who is not of full age;

(*e*) the policy shall be issued to an individual—

(i) who is beneficially entitled to, and

(ii) to whom there shall be paid,

all amounts, other than mortality cover, payable under the policy by the company;

(*f*) except in the case of a policy issued to and owned jointly only by a couple married to each other, the policy shall not be a joint policy;

(*g*) unless the policy is issued to and owned jointly only by a couple married to each other, the policy shall be the only such policy owned by the individual;

(*h*) if the policy is to be issued to and owned jointly only by a couple married to each other, it shall be the only such policy, or one of 2 only such policies, owned only by them;

and for the purposes of paragraphs (*d*) to (*h*) references to ownership of a policy shall be construed as references to beneficial ownership of the policy.

(4) The declaration referred to in paragraph (*b*) of the definition of **"special investment policy"** shall be a declaration in writing to an assurance company which—

(*a*) (i) is made by the individual (in this section referred to as **"the declarer"**) to whom any amounts, other than mortality cover, are payable by the assurance company in respect of the policy in respect of which the declaration is made, and

(ii) is signed by the declarer,

(*b*) is made in such form as may be prescribed or authorised by the Revenue Commissioners,

(*c*) declares that at the time when the declaration is made the conditions referred to in paragraphs (*d*) to (*h*) of subsection (3) are satisfied in relation to the policy in respect of which the declaration is made,

(*d*) contains the full name and address of the individual beneficially entitled to any amounts, other than mortality cover, payable in respect of the policy in respect of which the declaration is made,

(*e*) contains an undertaking by the declarer that, if any of the conditions specified in paragraphs (*d*) to (*h*) of subsection (3) cease to be satisfied in respect of the policy in respect of which the declaration is made, the declarer will notify the assurance company accordingly, and

(*f*) contains such other information as the Revenue Commissioners may reasonably require for the purposes of this section.

(5) (*a*) An assurance company shall—

(i) keep and retain for not less than the longer of the following periods—

(I) a period of 6 years, and

(II) a period which, in relation to the policy in respect of which the declaration is made, ends not earlier than 3 years after the date on which the company ceases to have any liability in respect of the policy, and

(ii) on being so required by notice given to it in writing by an inspector, make available to the inspector within the time specified in the notice,

all declarations of the kind specified in subsection (4) which have been made to the company.

(*b*) The inspector may examine and take copies of or of extracts from a declaration made available to him or her under paragraph (*a*).

...[9]

Amendments

1 Definition of "relevant period" deleted by FA 2001 s 68(1)(*a*) with effect from 1 January 2001.

2 Definition of "special investment fund" substituted by FA 2003 s 52(1)(*f*)(i)(I) as respects accounting periods ending in 2003 and later years.

3 Definition of "special investment policy" para (*a*) substituted by FA 2003 s 52(1)(*f*)(i)(II) as respects accounting periods ending in 2003 and later years.

4 Definition of "special investment policy" substituted by FA 2000 s 62 with effect from 6 April 2000.

5 Substituted by FA 2001 s 240(1) and (2)(*c*) and Sch 5 Pt 1 for accounting periods ending on or after 1 January 2002; previously "£200,000,000"; previously "£100,000,000" (FA 1998 s 53: 6 April 1998).

6 Subs (2)(g) substituted by FA 2001 s 68(1)(*b*) with effect from 1 January 2001.

7 Substituted by FA 2001 s 240(1) and (2)(*c*) and Sch 5 Pt 1 for accounting periods ending on or after 1 January 2002: previously "£50,000".

8 Subs (3)(*c*) deleted by FA 2001 s 68(1)(*c*) with effect from 1 January 2001.

9 Subss (6) and (7) deleted by FA 2003 s 52(1)(*f*)(i)(III) as respects accounting periods ending in 2003 and later years.

Cross-references

Chargeable gains of life business: s 581(1), (2)–(3) (in so far as a chargeable gain is not thereby disregarded for the purposes of that subsection) apply as if: ss 719, 723(7)(*a*), (*a*)(ii) and Sch 32 para 24 had not been enacted: s 711(1)(*b*).

Interpretation: s 705(1) (excluded annuity business).

Limits to special investments, subs (1): s 839(5)(*b*).

Provisions as to relief from income tax and corporation tax by means of credit in respect of foreign tax, limit on total credit — corporation tax, subs (6): Sch 24 para 4(4)(*d*).

Special investment policies, breach of conditions, subs (2)(*c*): s 725(2)(*a*); subss (3), (4): s 725(1)(*a*).

Special investment schemes, meanings of "inspector", "ordinary shares" and "qualifying shares" applied: s 737(1)(*a*).

Treatment of debts on a change in currency, meaning of "special investment fund" applied: s 541A(4)(*a*).

Revenue information

Information leaflet IT17 — Special Savings Accounts and other Special Investment Products.

Definitions

allowable loss: ss 4(1), 5(1), 546; chargeable gain: ss 5(1), 545; company: s 4(1); profits: s 4(1).

Former enactments

CTA 1976 s 36A(1)–(6) and (8); FA 1993 s 11(*f*); FA 1994 s 33; FA 1996 s 49.

724 Transfer of assets into or out of special investment fund

[Where, in an accounting period ending on or before 31 December 2002, an assurance company transfers][1] the whole or part of an asset (any interest in or rights over an asset being regarded for the purposes of this section as part of the asset)—

(*a*) which it owned before the transfer, or which was created by the transfer, into, or

(*b*) which it owns after the transfer, out of,

its special investment fund, the company shall be deemed to have disposed of and immediately reacquired the asset or the part of the asset, as the case may be, at the market value of the asset or the part of the asset, as the case may be, at the time of the transfer.

Amendments

1 Substituted by FA 2003 s 52(1)(*g*) as respects accounting periods ending in 2003 and later years; previously "Where an assurance company transfers".

Cross-references

Special investment policies, consideration given for fund's assets: s 723(2).

Definitions

company: s 4(1).

Former enactments

CTA 1976 s 36B; FA 1993 s 11(*f*).

725 Special investment policies: breaches of conditions

(1) For the purposes of this section, a policy of life assurance held by an individual, whether married or not, shall not be a special investment policy [at any particular time on or before 31 December 2002,][1] if—

(*a*) as respects the policy—

(i) a declaration of the kind specified in section 723(4) has not been made, or

(ii) any of the conditions referred to in section 723(3) is not satisfied at that time,

or

(*b*) as respects the individual, he or she has at that time a beneficial interest prohibited by section 839 in classes of investment mentioned in paragraphs (*a*) to (*d*) of subsection (1) of that section.

(2) Where an assurance company becomes aware [at any time on or before 31 December 2002,][2] that a policy of life assurance which it has treated as a special investment policy is not such a policy—

(*a*) the assurance company shall ensure that in accordance with section 723(2)(*c*) its special investment fund does not after that time represent its liability in respect of the policy, and

(*b*) for the purposes of the Tax Acts other than section 958(4), the liability to corporation tax of the company for the accounting period in which it became aware that the policy was not a special investment policy shall be increased by an amount determined by the formula—

$$(A - B) \times \frac{10}{9} \times \frac{S - 10}{100}$$

where—

A is the amount which was the assumed liability, other than the liability, if any, in respect of mortality cover, of the company in respect of the policy immediately before it became aware that the policy was not a special investment policy,

B is—

(i) the amount which was the liability, other than the liability, if any, in respect of mortality cover, of the company in respect of the policy when the policy ceased to be a special investment policy, or

(ii) if the policy was never a special investment policy, the amount of the aggregate of the payments received and not repaid by the company in respect of the policy, and

S is the standard rate per cent for the year of assessment in which that accounting period ends.

Amendments

1 Substituted by FA 2003 s 52(1)(*h*)(i) as respects accounting periods ending in 2003 and later years; previously "at any particular time".

2 Substituted by FA 2003 s 52(1)(*h*)(ii) as respects accounting periods ending in 2003 and later years; previously "at any time".

Definitions

standard rate per cent: s 4(1); year of assessment: ss 2(1), 5(1).

Former enactments

CTA 1976 s 36C; FA 1993 s 11(*f*).

CHAPTER 3

Provisions Applying to Overseas Life Assurance Companies

726 Investment income

(1) Any income of an overseas life assurance company from the investments of its life assurance fund (excluding the pension fund, general annuity fund and special investment fund, if any), wherever received, shall, to the extent provided in this section, be deemed to be profits comprised in Schedule D, and shall be charged to corporation tax under Case III of Schedule D.

(2) Distributions received from companies resident in the State shall be taken into account under this section notwithstanding their exclusion from the charge to corporation tax.

(3) Where an overseas life assurance company is entitled to an amount (in this subsection referred to as **"the first amount"**), being an amount which corresponds to a tax credit, by virtue of having received a distribution from a company not resident in the State, the distribution shall be treated for the purposes of this section as representing income equal to the aggregate of the amount or value of that distribution and the first amount.

(4) A portion only of the income from the investments of the life assurance fund (excluding the pension fund, general annuity fund and special investment fund, if any) shall be charged in accordance with subsection (1), and for any accounting period that portion shall be determined by the formula—

$$\frac{A \times B}{C}$$

where—

A is the total income from those investments for that period,

B is the average of the liabilities for that period to policyholders resident in the State and to policyholders resident outside the State whose proposals were made to the company at or through its branch or agency in the State, and

C is the average of the liabilities for that period to all the company's policyholders,

but any reference in this subsection to liabilities does not include liabilities in respect of special investment, general annuity or pension business.

(5) For the purposes of this section—

(*a*) the liabilities of an assurance company attributable to any business at any time shall be ascertained by reference to the net liabilities of the company as valued by an actuary for the purposes of the relevant periodical return, and

(*b*) the average of any liabilities for an accounting period shall be taken as 50 per cent of the aggregate of the liabilities at the beginning and end of the valuation period which coincides with that accounting period or in which that accounting period falls.

(6) (*a*) For the purposes of this subsection—

(i) **"the average of branch liabilities for an accounting period"** means the aggregate of the amounts represented by B in subsection (4), B in section 727(2) and the average of the liabilities attributable to pension business for the accounting period, and

(ii) **"the assets to which this subsection applies"** are assets the gains from the disposal of which are chargeable to corporation tax by virtue of subsections (3) and (6) of section 29 together with assets the gains from the disposal of which would be so chargeable but for sections 551, 607 and 613.

(*b*) Where the average of branch liabilities for an accounting period exceeds the mean value for the accounting period of the assets to which this subsection applies, the amount to be included in profits under section 78(1) shall be an amount determined by the formula—

$$\frac{A \times B}{C}$$

where—

A is the amount which apart from this subsection would be so included in profits,

B is the average of branch liabilities for the accounting period, and

C is the mean value for the accounting period of the assets to which this subsection applies.

(7) Section 70(1) as applied to corporation tax shall not apply to income to which subsection (1) applies.

Cross-references

Corporation tax: treatment of tax free income of non resident banks, insurance businesses etc: s 845(5).

Local authority securities authorised by the Minister for Finance (and beneficially held by non-residents) to be issued tax free, are tax free, but this exemption is ignored in the case of a company chargeable under this section: s 50(2)(*b*).

Overseas life assurance companies, income tax, foreign tax and tax credit: s 729(1), (3).

Securities authorised by Minister for Finance (and beneficially held by non-residents) are tax free, but this exemption is ignored in the case of a company chargeable under this section: s 49(3)(*a*).

UK double taxation agreement, subs (4): s 832(4)(*b*).

Definitions

branch or agency: ss 4(1), 5(1); company: ss 4(1), 5(1); distribution: ss 4(1), 436, 437; profits: s 4(1); tax credit: ss 2(1), 136; total income: s 3(1).

Former enactments

CTA 1976 s 43; FA 1993 s 11(*h*); FA 1995 s 64; FA 1996 s 132(2) and Sch 5 Pt II.

727 General annuity and pension business

(1) Nothing in the Corporation Tax Acts shall prevent the distributions of companies resident in the State from being taken into account as part of the profits in computing under section 715 the profits arising from pension business and general annuity business to an overseas life assurance company.

(2) Any charge to tax under section 715 for any accounting period on profits arising to an overseas life assurance company from general annuity business shall extend only to a portion of the profits arising from that business, and that portion shall be determined by the formula—

$$\frac{A \times B}{C}$$

where—

A is the total amount of those profits,

B is the average of the liabilities attributable to that business for the relevant accounting period in respect of contracts with persons resident in the State or contracts with persons resident outside the State whose proposals were made to the company at or through its branch or agency in the State, and

C is the average of the liabilities attributable to that business for that accounting period in respect of all contracts.

(3) For the purposes of this section—

(*a*) the liabilities of an assurance company attributable to general annuity business at any time shall be ascertained by reference to the net liabilities of the company as valued by an actuary for the purposes of the relevant periodical return, and

(*b*) the average of any liabilities for an accounting period shall be taken as 50 per cent of the aggregate of the liabilities at the beginning and end of the valuation period which coincides with that accounting period or in which that accounting period falls.

Cross-references

Overseas life assurance companies, income tax, foreign tax and tax credit: s 729(4).
Overseas life assurance companies, investment income, subs (2): s 726(6)(*a*)(i).

Definitions

branch or agency: ss 4(1), 5(1); company: ss 4(1), 5(1); Corporation Tax Acts: s 1(2); distribution: ss 4(1), 436, 437; person: IA 1937 s 11(*c*); profits: s 4(1).

Former enactments

CTA 1976 s 44.

728 Expenses of management

The relief under section 707 available to an overseas life assurance company in respect of its expenses of management shall be limited to expenses attributable to the life assurance business carried on by the company at or through its branch or agency in the State.

Former enactments

CTA 1976 s 33(3); FA 1992 s 44(*b*).

729 Income tax, foreign tax and tax credit

(1) Section 77(6) shall not affect the liability to tax of an overseas life assurance company in respect of the investment income of its life assurance fund under section 726 or in respect of the profits of its annuity business under sections 715, 717 and 727.

(2) For the purposes of section 25(3) as it applies to life business, the amount of the income tax referred to in that section which shall be available for set-off under that section in an accounting period shall be limited in accordance with subsections (3) and (4).

(3) Where the company is chargeable to corporation tax for an accounting period in accordance with section 726 in respect of the income from the investments of its life assurance fund, the amount of income tax available for set-off against any corporation tax assessed for that period on that income shall not exceed an amount equal to income tax at the standard rate on the portion of income from investments which is chargeable to corporation tax by virtue of subsection (4) of that section.

(4) Where the company is chargeable to corporation tax for an accounting period in accordance with section 727 on a proportion of the total amount of the profits arising from its general annuity business, the amount of income tax available for set-off against any corporation tax assessed for that period on those profits shall not exceed an amount equal to income tax at the standard rate on the like proportion of the income from investments included in computing those profits.

...[1]

(6) Section 828(4) shall not affect the liability to tax under section 726 of an overseas life assurance company in respect of gains from the disposal of investments held in connection with its life business.

...[2]

Amendments

1 Subs (5) repealed by FA 2000 s 69(2) and Sch 2 Part 2 with effect from 6 April 1999 in the case of income tax and as respects accounting periods commencing on or after that date in the case of corporation tax.

2 Subs (7) repealed by FA 2000 s 69(2) and Sch 2 Part 2 with effect from 6 April 1999 in the case of income tax and as respects accounting periods commencing on or after that date in the case of corporation tax.

Cross-references

Life assurance companies, distributions received from Irish resident companies, subs (5): s 712(2)(*a*).
Non-resident company trading through a branch or agency in the State: s 25(3).

Definitions

company: s 4(1); distribution: ss 4(1), 436, 437; profits: s 4(1); standard rate per cent: s 4(1); tax credit: ss 2(1), 136; year of assessment: ss 2(1), 5(1).

Former enactments

CTA 1976 s 45; FA 1988 s 31(2) and Sch 2 Pt I para 2(2); FA 1997 s 37 and Sch 2 paras 1–2.

730 Tax credit in respect of distributions

Amendments

Section 730 repealed by FA 2000 s 69(2) and Sch 2 Part 2 with effect from 6 April 1999 in the case of income tax and as respects accounting periods commencing on or after that date in the case of corporation tax.

[CHAPTER 4

Taxation of Assurance Companies — New Basis][1]

Amendments

1 Chapter 4 inserted by FA 2000 s 53 with effect from 6 April 2000.

Revenue information

General Guidelines for calculating tax due and for completing declarations under the "gross roll-up" taxation regime are available on Revenue's website: www.revenue.ie under "Publications" and "Technical Guidelines".

Tax Briefing

TB41 Sept 2000 p 19 — Life Assurance Companies — New Taxation Regime.
TB43 Apr 2001 pp 8–10 — Life Assurance Companies — Tax Computations — New Basis Business.

730A Profits of life business: new basis

[(1) In this Chapter and Chapter 5 of this Part—

"assurance company" means an assurance company chargeable to corporation tax;

[**"credit union"** has the meaning assigned to it in section 2 of the Credit Union Act 1997;

"financial institution" means—

(*a*) a person who holds a licence under section 9 of the Central Bank Act 1971,

(*b*) a person referred to in section 7(4) of the Central Bank Act 1971, or

(*c*) a credit institution duly authorised by virtue of Directive No 2000/12/EC of 20 March 2000 (OJ No L.126, of 26 May 2000, p 1);][1]

"new basis business" means—

(*a*) where an assurance company was carrying on life business on 1 April 2000, other than where the assurance company's trading operations at that time consisted solely of foreign life assurance business within the meaning of section 451(1)—

[(i) all policies and contracts commenced by the assurance company on or after 1 January 2001 except those which refer to industrial assurance business, and][2]

(ii) all policies and contracts commenced by the assurance company before that date in so far as they relate to—

(I) pension business and general annuity business, and

(II) permanent health insurance, in respect of which the profits arising to the assurance company were before 1 January 2001 charged to tax under Case I of Schedule D,

(*b*) where an assurance company was carrying on life business on 1 April 2000, and the assurance company's trading operations at that time consisted solely of foreign life assurance business within the meaning of section 451(1), all policies and contracts commenced by the assurance company on or after 1 January 2001, and

(*c*) where an assurance company was not carrying on life business on 1 April 2000, subject to subsection (2), all policies and contracts commenced by the assurance company [from the time it began to carry on life business;][3]

[**"Service"** means the Courts Service;][4]

[**"sinking fund or capital redemption business"** has the same meaning as in section 3 of the Insurance Act, 1936.][5]

(2) Where an assurance company begins to carry on life business after 1 April 2000 and before 31 December 2000, the assurance company may elect that all policies and contracts commenced by it before 31 December 2000 be treated as not being new basis business in so far as they relate to life business (other than pension business and general annuity business).

(3) Life business of an assurance company, in so far as it comprises new basis business, shall for the purposes of the Corporation Tax Acts be treated as though it were a separate business, that is a business separate from other business (if any) carried on by the assurance company.

(4) Notwithstanding Chapters 1 and 3 of this Part, an assurance company shall be charged to corporation tax in respect of the profits of new basis business under Case I of Schedule D and those profits shall, subject to subsection (5), be computed in accordance with the provisions applicable to that Case of that Schedule.

(5) Where all or part of the profits of an assurance company are, under this Chapter, to be computed in accordance with the provisions applicable to Case I of Schedule D, the following provisions shall also apply—

(*a*) such part of those profits as belongs or is allocated to, or is expended on behalf of, policyholders or annuitants shall be excluded in making the computation, and

(*b*) there shall not be excluded in making the computation any remaining part of those profits reserved for policyholders or annuitants.

[(6) Notwithstanding the provisions of Chapter 3 of Part 12, where an assurance company incurs a loss in respect of new basis business, the amount of the loss which may be set off against profits of any other business of the company shall not exceed such amount of those profits computed under the provisions of Case I of Schedule D and section 710.

(7) (*a*) This subsection applies to a company carrying on any mutual life assurance business.

(*b*) Subject to paragraph (*c*), in respect of each accounting period of a company to which this subsection applies, one-twentieth of the amount determined under subsection (8)(*c*) shall be treated as annual profits or gains within Schedule D and shall be chargeable to corporation tax under Case III of that Schedule.

(*c*) Where for an accounting period the value referred to in subsection (8)(*c*)(ii) is not less than such value at 31 December 2000, but exceeds the value referred to in subsection (8)(*c*)(i), an amount equal to one-twentieth of the excess may be deducted from annual profits or gains chargeable to corporation tax by virtue of paragraph (*b*), of the previous accounting period (so long as it commences on or after 1 January 2001) or a subsequent accounting period.

(8) (*a*) In this subsection **"statutory accounts"**, in relation to a company means—

(i) in the case of a company (in this definition referred to as the **"resident company"**) resident in the State, the profit and loss account and balance sheet of that company, and

(ii) in the case of a company (in this definition referred to as the **"non-resident company"**) not resident in the State but carrying on a trade in the State through a branch or agency, the profit and loss account and balance sheet of the company,

a report in respect of which is required to be made to the members of the company by an auditor appointed under section 160 of the Companies Act, 1963, or under the law of the State in which the resident company or non-resident company is incorporated and which corresponds to that section.

(*b*) For the purposes of this subsection the liabilities of an assurance company attributable to any business at any time shall be ascertained by reference to the net liabilities of the company as valued by an actuary for the purposes of the statutory accounts in relation to the company.

(*c*) The amount referred to in subsection (7)(*b*) is—

(i) the total value at the end of the accounting period,

less—

(ii) the total value at the beginning of the accounting period,

of all funds the allocation of which to policyholders has not been determined; but in the case of an overseas life assurance company, the values referred to in subparagraphs (i) and (ii) at a time shall be multiplied by the following fraction—

$$\frac{A}{B}$$

where—

A is the liabilities at that time to policyholders whose proposals were made to the company at or through its branch or agency in the State, and

B is the liabilities at that time to all the company's policyholders.][6]][7]

Amendments

1 Definitions of "credit union" and "financial institution" inserted by FA 2003 s 57(*a*)(i) with effect from 1 January 2003.

2 Definition of "new business" para (*a*)(i) substituted by FA 2001 s 69(1)(*a*)(i) as respects accounting periods commencing on or after 1 January 2001.

3 Substituted by FA 2001 s 69(1)(*a*)(ii) as respects accounting periods commencing on or after 1 January 2001; previously "from the time it began to carry on life business.".

4 Definition of "Service" inserted by FA 2003 s 57(*a*)(ii) with effect from 1 January 2003.

5 Definition of "sinking fund or capital redemption business" inserted by FA 2001 s 69(1)(*b*) as respects accounting periods commencing on or after 1 January 2001.

6 Subss (6)–(8) inserted by FA 2001 s 69(1)(*c*) as respects accounting periods commencing on or after 1 January 2001.

7 Section 730A inserted by FA 2000 s 53 with effect from 6 April 2000.

Cross-references

Chargeable event, subs (2): s 730C(1)(para (*b*) of definition of "chargeable event").

Foreign life assurance and deferred annuities, taxation and returns, meaning of "new basis business" applied: s 594(4)(*a*).

Life assurance company, management expenses, meaning of "new basis business" applies: s 707(2)(*c*).

Life assurance policy or deferred annuity contract entered into or acquired by company, meaning of "new basis business" applied: s 595(1)(*a*)("relevant policy").

Losses, etc, which may be surrendered by means of group relief, meaning of "new basis business" applied: s 420(9)(*a*).

Definitions

assurance company: s 706(1); branch or agency: ss 4(1), 5(1); company: ss 4(1), 5(1); general annuity business: s 706(1); industrial assurance business: s 706(1); life business: s 706(1); overseas life assurance company: s 706(1); pension business: s 706(1); policy: s 706(1); profits: s 4(1).

[CHAPTER 5
Policyholders — New Basis][1]

Amendments

1 Chapter 5 inserted by FA 2000 s 53 with effect from 6 April 2000.

Cross-references

Power of inspection (returns and collection of appropriate tax), assurance companies: s 904C(3)(*a*).

Termination of special savings incentive account: s 848H(3)(*b*)(ii).

Revenue information

General Guidelines for calculating tax due and for completing declarations under the "gross roll-up" taxation regime are available on Revenue's website: www.revenue.ie under "Publications" and "Technical Guidelines".

Tax Briefing

TB41 Sept 2000 pp 19–20 — Life Assurance Companies — Policyholders — New Basis.

730B Taxation of policyholders

[(1) In this Chapter **"return"** means a return under section 730G.

[(2) Subject to subsection (3), this Chapter applies for the purpose of imposing certain charges to tax in respect of a policy (in this Chapter referred to as a **"life policy"**) which is—

(*a*) a policy of assurance on the life of any person, or

(*b*) a policy in respect of sinking fund or capital redemption business,

where the life policy is new basis business of the assurance company which commenced the life policy.][1]

(3) This Chapter does not apply to a life policy which relates to pension business, general annuity business or permanent health insurance business, of an assurance company.][2]

[(4) For the purposes of this Chapter—

(*a*) where a policyholder is a person entrusted to pay all premiums (in this subsection referred to as **"group premiums"**) in respect of a life policy (in this subsection referred to as a **"group policy"**), out of money under the control or subject to the order of any Court, this Chapter shall apply as if the group policy comprised separate life policies (in this subsection referred to as **"separate life policies"**),

(*b*) each person beneficially entitled to any part of the rights conferred by the group policy shall be treated as being the policyholder of a separate life policy,

(*c*) the premiums paid in respect of each separate life policy shall be such amount of the said money included in group premiums paid, which is beneficially owned by the policyholder of the separate life policy,

(*d*) a gain which, but for the provisions of section 730D(2), would have arisen on the happening of a chargeable event in relation to the group policy shall be treated as if it were a gain arising on a chargeable event in relation to any separate policy where, and to the extent that, the gain is beneficially owned by the policyholder of that separate policy,

(*e*) subsections (2), (3) and (4) of section 730F, sections 730G and 730GA and section 904C apply as if references in those subsections and sections to an assurance company were to read as references to the Service, and

(*f*) the Service shall in respect of each year of assessment, on or before 28 February in the year following the year of assessment, make a return (including where it is the case, a nil return) to the Revenue Commissioners in electronic format approved by them, which in respect of each year of assessment—

(i) specifies the total amount of gains (in this section referred to as the **"total gains"**) arising in respect of the group policy, and

(ii) specifies in respect of each policyholder of a separate policy—

(I) where available, the name and address of the policyholder,

(II) the amount of the total gains to which the person has beneficial entitlement, and

(III) such other information as the Revenue Commissioners may require.][3]

Amendments

1 Subs (2) substituted by FA 2001 s 70(1)(*a*) with effect from 1 January 2001.

2 Section 730B inserted by FA 2000 s 53 with effect from 6 April 2000.

3 Subs (4) inserted by FA 2003 s 57(*b*) with effect from 1 January 2003.

Cross-references

Power of inspection (returns and collection of appropriate tax), assurance companies, meaning of "life policy" applied: s 904C(1).

Definitions

assurance company: s 730A(1); company: ss 4(1), 5(1); general annuity business: s 706(1); new basis business: s 730A(1); pension business: s 706(1); person: IA 1937 s 11(*c*); policy: s 706(1); premium: s 706(1); sinking fund or capital redemption business: s 730A(1); year of assessment: ss 2(1), 5(1).

730BA Personal portfolio life policy

[(1) In this section—

"building society" has the same meaning as in section 256;

"foreign life policy" has the same meaning as in section 730H;

"internal linked fund", in relation to an assurance company, means a fund maintained by the assurance company to which fund the assurance company appropriates certain linked assets and which fund may be subdivided into subdivisions the value of each of which is determined by the assurance company by reference to the value of such linked assets;

"investment undertaking" has the same meaning as in section 739B;

"land" includes an interest in land and also includes shares deriving their value or the greater part of their value directly or indirectly from land other than shares quoted on a recognised stock exchange;

"linked asset", in relation to an assurance company, means an asset of the assurance company which is identified in the records of the assurance company as an asset by reference to the value of which asset the benefits provided for under a life policy are to be determined;

"policyholder" has the same meaning as it has for the purposes of section 730E;

"prices' index" means—

(*a*) the all items consumer price index compiled by the Central Statistics Office,

(*b*) any general index of prices corresponding to such consumer price index and duly published by or on behalf of any state other than the State, or

(*c*) any published index of prices of shares listed on a recognised stock exchange;

"public" means individuals generally, companies generally, or a combination of these, as the case may be;

"units" has the same meaning as in section 739B.

(2) In this Chapter and in Chapter 6 of this Part "personal portfolio life policy" means, subject to subsection (4), a life policy or a foreign life policy, as the case may be, under whose terms—

(*a*) (i) some or all of the benefits conferred by the policy are or were determined by reference to the value of, or the income from, property of any description (whether or not specified in the policy), or

(ii) some or all of the benefits conferred by the policy are or were determined by reference to fluctuations in, or fluctuations in an index of, the value of property of any description (whether or not specified in the policy),

and

(*b*) some or all of the property or the index may be or was selected by or the selection of some or all of the property or index may be or was influenced by—

(i) the policyholder,

(ii) a person acting on behalf of the policyholder,

(iii) a person connected (within the meaning of section 10) with the policyholder,

(iv) a person connected (within that meaning) with a person acting on behalf of the policyholder,

(v) the policyholder and a person connected (within that meaning) with the policyholder, or

(vi) a person acting on behalf of both the policyholder and a person connected (within that meaning) with the policyholder.

(3) For the purposes of paragraph (*b*) of subsection (2) and without prejudice to the application of that provision, the terms of a life policy or a foreign life policy shall be treated as permitting the selection referred to in that paragraph where—

(*a*) the terms of the policy or any other agreement between any person referred to in that paragraph and the assurance company concerned—

(i) allow the exercise of an option by any person referred to in that paragraph to make the selection referred to in that paragraph,

(ii) give the assurance company discretion to offer any person referred to in that paragraph the right to make the selection referred to in that paragraph, or

(iii) allow any of the persons referred to in that paragraph the right to request, subject to the agreement of the assurance company, a change in the terms of the policy such that the selection referred to in that paragraph may be made by any of those persons,

or

(*b*) the policyholder is unable under the terms of the policy to select any of the property so as to determine the benefits under the policy, but any of the persons referred to in that paragraph has or had the option of requiring the assurance company to appoint an investment advisor (no matter how such a person is described) in relation to the selection of the property which is to determine the benefits under the policy.

(4) A life policy or a foreign life policy is not a personal portfolio life policy if—

(*a*) (i) the only property which may be or has been selected is—

(I) property which the assurance company concerned has appropriated to an internal linked fund,

(II) property consisting of any of the following—

(A) units in an investment undertaking, or

(B) cash, including cash deposited in a bank account or similar account (including cash deposited in a share account with a building society) except where the acquisition of the cash was made wholly or partly for the purpose of realising a gain from the disposal of the cash, or

(III) property consisting of a combination of the property specified in clauses (I) and (II),

and the property satisfies the condition specified in subsection (5), or

(ii) the only index which may be or has been selected is of a description specified in subsection (6),

and

(*b*) as respects a life policy or a foreign life policy commenced on or after 5 December 2001 (other than a policy in respect of which the only property which may be selected is property described in paragraph *(a)*(i)(II)(B) or a policy in respect of which marketing or other promotional literature was published before that date) the terms under which the policy is offered meet the requirements of subsection (7).

(5) The condition specified in this subsection is that at the time when the property is or was available to be selected the opportunity to select—

(*a*) in the case of land, that property, and

(*b*) in any other case, property of the same description as the first-mentioned property,

is or was available to the public on terms which provide or provided that the opportunity to select the property is or was available to any person falling within the terms of the opportunity and that opportunity is or was clearly identified to the public, in marketing or other promotional literature published at that time by the assurance company concerned, as available generally to any person falling within the terms of the opportunity.

(6) The description of index specified by this subsection is an index consisting of a prices' index or a combination of prices' indices where at the time the index is or was available to be selected the opportunity to select the same index is or was available to the public on terms which provide or provided that the opportunity to select the index is or was available to any person falling within the terms of the opportunity and that opportunity is or was clearly identified to the public, in marketing or other promotional literature published at that time by the assurance company concerned, as available generally to any person falling within the terms of the opportunity.

(7) The requirements of this subsection are that—

(*a*) the assurance company concerned does not subject any person to any treatment in connection with the opportunity which is different or more burdensome than any treatment to which any other person is or may be subject, and

(*b*) where the terms of the opportunity referred to in subsection (5) include terms—

(i) which set out the capital requirement of the opportunity and this requirement is identified to the public in the marketing or other promotional material published by the assurance company at the time the property is available to be selected, and

(ii) indicating that 50 per cent or more by value of the property referred to in that subsection is or is to be land, the amount any one person may invest in the policy shall not represent more than 1 per cent of the capital requirement (exclusive of any borrowings) of the opportunity as so identified.][1]

Amendments

1 Section 730BA inserted by FA 2002 s 40(1)(*a*) as respects the happening of a chargeable event in relation to a life policy (within the meaning of Pt 26 Ch 5), or the receipt by a person of a payment in respect of a foreign life policy (within the meaning of Pt 26 Ch 6) or the disposal in whole or in part of a foreign life policy (within that meaning), on or after 26 September 2001.

Definitions

assurance company: s 730A(1); company: ss 4(1), 5(1); land: IA 1937 Sch; life policy: s 730B(2); person: IA 1937 s 11(*c*); policy: s 706(1).

730C Chargeable event

[(1) Subject to the provisions of this section, in this Chapter—

(*a*) **"chargeable event"**, in relation to a life policy, means—

(i) the maturity of the life policy (including where payments are made on death or disability, which payments result in the termination of the life policy),

(ii) the surrender in whole or in part of the rights conferred by the life policy (including where payments are made on death or disability, which payments do not result in the termination of the life policy),

(iii) the assignment in whole or in part, of those rights, and

[(iv) the ending of a relevant period, where such ending is not otherwise a chargeable event within the meaning of this section, and for the purposes of this subparagraph "relevant period" in relation to a life policy means a period of 7 years beginning with the inception of the policy and each subsequent period of 7 years beginning immediately after the preceding relevant period,][1]

(*b*) in the case of a life policy issued by an assurance company which could have made an election under section 730A(2), but did not so do, a chargeable event shall be deemed to happen on 31 December 2000, where the life policy was commenced before that date.

(2) No account shall be taken for the purposes of subsection (1) of an assignment in whole or in part effected—

(*a*) by way of security for a debt, or the discharge of a debt secured by the rights concerned, where the debt is a debt due to a financial institution ...[2],

(*b*) between a husband and wife,

(*c*) between the spouses or former spouses concerned (as the case may be), by virtue or in consequence of an order made under Part III of the Family Law (Divorce) Act, 1996, on or following the granting of a decree of divorce,

(*d*) between the spouses concerned, by virtue or in consequence of an order made under Part II of the Family Law Act, 1995, on or following the granting of a decree of judicial separation within the meaning of that Act, or

(*e*) between the spouses or former spouses concerned (as the case may be), by virtue of an order or other determination of like effect, which is analogous to an order referred to in paragraph (*c*) or (*d*), of a court under the law of a territory other than the State made under or in consequence of the dissolution of a marriage or the legal separation of the spouses, being a dissolution or legal separation that is entitled to be recognised as valid in the State.

(3) (*a*) Where at any time a life policy, or an interest therein, gives rise to benefits in respect of death or disability, the amount or value of such benefits which shall be taken into account for the purposes of determining the amount of a gain under section 730D shall be the excess of the value of the policy or, as the case may be, the interest therein, immediately before that time, over the value of the policy or, as the case may be, the interest therein, immediately after that time.

(*b*) For the purposes of paragraph (*a*), the value of an interest therein at a time means—

(i) in the case of a policy which has a surrender value, the surrender value of the policy or, as the case may be, of the interest therein, at that time, and,

(ii) in the case of a policy which does not have a surrender value, the market value of the rights or other benefits conferred by the policy or, as the case may be, the interest therein, at that time.

(*c*) In determining the amount or value of benefits payable under a life policy for the purposes of paragraph (*a*) or (*b*), no account shall be taken of any amount of appropriate tax which may be required by this Chapter to be deducted from such benefits.][3]

Amendments

1 Subs (1)(*a*)(iv) inserted by FA 2005 s 42(1)(*a*) with effect from such day or days as the Minister for Finance may by order appoint either generally or with reference to any particular provision of FA 2005 s 42 or class of policy and different days may be so appointed for different provisions of FA 2005 s 42 or for different classes of policies.

2 Deleted by FA 2003 s 57(*c*) with effect from 1 January 2003; previously "(within the meaning of section 906A)".

3 Section 730C substituted by FA 2001 s 70(1)(*b*) with effect from 15 February 2001.

Cross-references

Deduction of tax on the happening of a chargeable event, subs (1)(*b*): s 730F(3)(*a*)(ii)(II); subs (1)(*a*)(iv): s 730F(3)(a)(ii)(Ia).

Gain arising on a chargeable event, subs (1)(*b*): s 730D(1)(*e*); subs (1)(*c*)(*a*)(iv): s 730D(1)(*da*), (4)(*ba*), (5)(*a*)(i).

Power of inspection (return and collection of appropriate tax), assurance companies, meaning of "chargeable event" applied: s 904C(1).

Definitions

life policy: s 703B(2); policy: s 706(1).

730D Gains arising on a chargeable event

[(1) On the happening of a chargeable event in relation to a life policy, there shall, subject to subsection (2), be treated as arising—

(*a*) if the chargeable event is the maturity of the life policy or the surrender in whole of the rights thereby conferred, a gain in the amount determined under subsection (3)(*a*),

(*b*) if the chargeable event is an assignment of the whole of the rights conferred by the life policy, a gain in the amount determined under subsection (3)(*b*), (*c*) if the chargeable event is the surrender of part of the rights conferred by the life policy, a gain in the amount determined under subsection (3)(*c*),

(*d*) if the chargeable event is the assignment of part of the rights conferred by the life policy, a gain in the amount determined under subsection (3)(*d*), ...[1]

[(*da*) if the chargeable event is the ending of a relevant period in accordance with section 730C(1)(*a*)(iv), a gain in the amount determined under subsection (3)(*da*), and][2]

(*e*) if the chargeable event is deemed to happen on 31 December 2000 under section 730C(1)(*b*), a gain in the amount determined under subsection (3)(*e*).

[(2) A gain shall not be treated as arising on the happening of a chargeable event in relation to a life policy where—

(*a*) immediately before the chargeable event, the assurance company which commenced the life policy—

(i) is in possession of a declaration, in relation to the life policy, of a kind referred in section 730E(2), and

(ii) is not in possession of any information which would reasonably suggest that—

(I) the information contained in that declaration is not, or is no longer, materially correct,

(II) the policyholder (within the meaning of section 730E) failed to comply with the undertaking referred to in section 730E(2)(*f*), or

(III) immediately before the chargeable event the policyholder (within the said meaning) is resident or ordinarily resident in the State,

[(*b*) immediately before the chargeable event, the policyholder is—

(i) a company carrying on life business,

(ii) an investment undertaking (within the meaning of section 739B),

(iii) (I) a person who is entitled to exemption from income tax under Schedule D by virtue of section 207(1)(*b*), or

(II) a person who is entitled to exemption from corporation tax by virtue of section 207(1)(*b*) as it applies for the purposes of corporation tax under section 76(6),

(iv) a PRSA provider (which has the same meaning as that assigned to it in Chapter 2A (inserted by the Pensions (Amendment) Act 2002) of Part 30),

(v) a credit union, or

(vi) a person entrusted to pay all premiums payable, in respect of the life policy, out of money under the control or subject to the order of any Court,

and the assurance company which commenced the life policy is in possession of a declaration, in relation to the life policy, of a kind referred to in section 730E(3), or][3]

(*c*) where the life policy is an asset held in a special savings incentive account within the meaning of section 848B (inserted by the Finance Act, 2001) and the assurance company which commenced the life policy is in possession of a declaration of a kind referred to in section 730E(3A).][4]

[(2A)(*a*) In this subsection—

"EEA Agreement" means the Agreement on the European Economic Area signed at Oporto on 2 May 1992, as adjusted by the Protocol signed at Brussels on 17 March 1993;

"EEA state" means a State, other than the State, which is a Contracting Party to the EEA Agreement;

"offshore state" means a State, other than the State, which is—

(*a*) a Member State of the European Communities, or

(*b*) a State which is an EEA state.

(*b*) A gain shall not be treated as arising on the happening of a chargeable event in relation to a life policy where—

(i) the assurance company which commenced the life policy has established a branch in an offshore state,

(ii) the commitment represented by that life policy is covered through that branch, and

(iii) the assurance company has received written approval from the Revenue Commissioners, to the effect that the provisions of subsection (2)*(a)* need not apply to the life policy, and that approval has not been withdrawn.

(*c*) The Revenue Commissioners may give the approval referred to in paragraph (*b*)(iii) subject to such conditions as they consider necessary.

(*d*) The Revenue Commissioners may nominate in writing an inspector or other officer to perform any acts and discharge any functions authorised by this subsection to be performed or discharged by the Revenue Commissioners.][5]

(3) The amount referred to—

(*a*) in subsection (1)(*a*) is the amount determined by the formula—

$$B - P,$$

(*b*) in subsection (1)(*b*) is the amount determined by the formula—

$$V - P,$$

(*c*) in subsection (1)(*c*) is the amount determined by the formula—

$$B - \frac{(P \times B)}{V},$$

(*d*) in subsection (1)(*d*) is the amount determined by the formula—

$$A - \frac{(P \times A)}{V},$$

...[6]

[(*da*) in subsection (1)(*da*) is the amount determined by the formula—

$$V - P$$

and][7]

(*e*) in subsection (1)(*e*) is the amount determined by the formula—

$$V - P,$$

where

B is the amount or value of the sum payable and other benefits arising by reason of the chargeable event,

P is subject to subsection (4), an amount of premiums (in this section referred to as "allowable premiums") being the total of all premiums paid in respect of the life policy immediately before the chargeable event, to the extent that they have not been taken into account in determining a gain on the previous happening of a chargeable event,

V is the value of the rights and other benefits conferred by the life policy immediately before the chargeable event, and

A is the value of the part of the rights and other benefits conferred by the life policy, which has been assigned,

without having regard to any amount of appropriate tax (within the meaning of section 730F) in connection with the chargeable event.

(4) [(*a*) For the purposes of subsection (3), the amount of premiums taken into account in determining a gain on the happening of a chargeable event, is where the gain is, or would but for subsection (2) be determined—

(i) under paragraph (*c*) of subsection (3), an amount equal to the lesser of B and—

$$\frac{(P \times B)}{V},$$

and

(ii) under paragraph (*d*) of subsection (3), an amount equal to the lesser of A and—

$$\frac{(P \times A)}{V},$$][8]

(*b*) Where a chargeable event in relation to a life policy is deemed to happen on 31 December 2000 then, for the purposes of determining a gain arising on the happening of a subsequent chargeable event, the allowable premiums immediately after 31 December 2000 shall be deemed to be the greater of—

(i) an amount equal to the value of the policy immediately after 31 December 2000, and

(ii) the allowable premiums immediately before 31 December 2000.

[(*ba*) Where a chargeable event in relation to a life policy is the ending of a relevant period in accordance with section 730C(1)(*a*)(iv) then, for the purposes of determining a gain arising on the happening of a subsequent chargeable event, the allowable premiums immediately after the time of such ending shall be deemed to be the greater of—

(i) an amount equal to the value of the policy immediately after the time of such ending, and

(ii) the allowable premiums immediately before such ending.][9]

(*c*) Where a chargeable event in relation to a life policy is an assignment of the whole of the rights conferred by the life policy then, for the purposes of determining a gain arising on the happening of a subsequent chargeable event, the allowable premiums immediately after the time of assignment shall be deemed to be the greater of—

(i) an amount equal to the value of the policy immediately after the time of the assignment, and

(ii) the allowable premiums immediately before the assignment.

(*d*) Where a chargeable event in relation to a life policy is the assignment of part of the rights conferred by the life policy then the policy shall, for the purposes of determining a gain arising on the happening of any subsequent chargeable event, be treated as if it were comprised of 2 policies, that is—

(i) one policy conferring the part of the rights assigned, the allowable premiums in respect of which immediately after the assignment are an amount equal to the value of the policy immediately after the assignment, and

(ii) the other policy conferring the rights which were not assigned, the allowable premiums in respect of which immediately after the assignment are the amount of the allowable premiums immediately before the assignment reduced by the amount of premiums taken into account in determining a gain on the assignment.][10]

[(5) (*a*) Where at any time—

(i) a chargeable event, being a chargeable event (in this subsection referred to as a "relevant event") within the meaning of section 730C(1)(*a*)(iv), occurs in relation to a life policy which commenced before 1 May 2005,

(ii) immediately before that time the assurance company that commenced the life policy does not have in its possession a declaration in relation to the policy of the kind referred to in subsection (2), and

(iii) the permanent address of the policyholder, as stated in the policy, is not in the State and the assurance company does not have reasonable grounds to believe that the policyholder is resident in the State,

then the assurance company may elect to be treated in relation to that chargeable event for the purposes of subsection (2) as if, immediately before that time, the assurance company was in possession of a declaration in relation to the policy of the kind referred to in that subsection.

(*b*) Where at any time—

(i) a relevant event occurred in relation to a life policy and a chargeable event, not being a relevant event, subsequently occurs in relation to the policy,

(ii) this subsection applied to the relevant event in accordance with paragraph (*a*), and

(iii) immediately before that time the assurance company that commenced the life policy does not have in its possession a declaration in relation to the policy of the kind referred to in subsection (2), then paragraph (*a*) shall be deemed not to have applied to the relevant event and any appropriate tax payable by virtue of a gain arising under this section shall be due and payable as if paragraph (*a*) had not been enacted.][11]

Amendments

1 Deleted by FA 2005 s 42(1)(*b*)(i)(I) with effect from such day or days as the Minister for Finance may by order appoint either generally or with reference to any particular provision of FA 2005 s 42 or class of policy and different days may be so appointed for different provisions of FA 2005 s 42 or for different classes of policies; previously "and".

2 Subs (1)(*da*) inserted by FA 2005 s 42(1)(*b*)(i)(II) with effect from such day or days as the Minister for Finance may by order appoint either generally or with reference to any particular provision of FA 2005 s 42 or class of policy and different days may be so appointed for different provisions of FA 2005 s 42 or for different classes of policies.

3 Subs (2)(*b*) substituted by FA 2003 s 57(*d*)(i) with effect from 1 January 2003.

4 Subs (2) substituted by FA 2001 s 70(1)(*c*)(i) with effect from 1 January 2001.

5 Subs (2A) inserted by FA 2002 s 48(1)(*b*) with effect from 1 January 2002.

6 Deleted by FA 2005 s 41(1)(*b*)(ii)(I) with effect from such day or days as the Minister for Finance may by order appoint either generally or with reference to any particular provision of FA 2005 s 42 or class of policy and different days may be so appointed for different provisions of FA 2005 s 42 or for different classes of policies; previously "and".

7 Subs (3)(*da*) inserted by FA 2005 s 42(1)(*b*)(ii)(II) with effect from such day or days as the Minister for Finance may by order appoint either generally or with reference to any particular provision of FA 2005 s 42 or class of policy and different days may be so appointed for different provisions of FA 2005 s 42 or for different classes of policies.

8 Subs (4)(*a*) substituted by FA 2001 s 70(1)(*c*)(ii) with effect from 1 January 2001.

9 Subs (4)(*ba*) inserted by FA 2005 s 42(1)(*b*)(iii) with effect from such day or days as the Minister for Finance may by order appoint either generally or with reference to any particular provision of FA 2005 s 42 or class of policy and different days may be so appointed for different provisions of FA 2005 s 42 or for different classes of policies.

10 Section 730D inserted by FA 2000 s 53 with effect from 6 April 2000.

11 Subs (5) inserted by FA 2005 s 42(1)(*b*)(iv) with effect from such day or days as the Minister for Finance may by order appoint either generally or with reference to any particular provision of FA 2005 s 42 or class of policy and different days may be so appointed for different provisions of FA 2005 s 42 or for different classes of policies.

Cross-references

Assessment of appropriate tax where tax not deducted under section 730F, subs (3) and (4); s 730FA(2)(ii).
Chargeable event: s 730C(3)(*a*).
Declarations, subs (2)(*a*): s 730E(2); subs (2)(*b*): s 730E(3); subs (2)(*c*): s 730E(3A); s 730E(4).
Deduction of tax on the happening of a chargeable event: s 730F(1)(definition of "appropriate tax").
Taxation of policyholders, subs (2): s 730B(4)(*d*).

Definitions

assurance company: s 730A(1); chargeable event: s 730C(1); company: ss 4(1), 5(1); credit union: s 730A(1); inspector: s 2(1); life policy: s 730B(2); ordinarily resident: ss 2(1), 5(1), 820; person; IA 1937 s 11(*c*); policy: s 706(1); premium: s 706(1); resident: ss 2(1), 5(1), 819; writing: IA 1937 Sch.

730E Declarations

[(1) In this section and in section 730F, **"policyholder"**, in relation to a life policy, at any time means—

(*a*) where the rights conferred by the life policy are vested at that time in a person as beneficial owner, such person,

(*b*) where the rights conferred by the life policy are held at that time on trusts created by a person, such person, and (*c*) where the rights conferred by the life policy are held at that time as security for a debt owed by a person, such person.

(2) The declaration referred to in [section 730D(2)(*a*)][1] in relation to a life policy is, subject to subsection (4), a declaration in writing to the assurance company which—

[(*a*) is made by the policyholder [at or about the time of the inception of the life policy][2],][3]

(*b*) is signed by the policyholder,

(*c*) is made in such form as may be prescribed or authorised by the Revenue Commissioners,

[(*d*) declares that the policyholder is not resident and not ordinarily resident in the State at the time of making the declaration,][4]

(*e*) contains—

(i) the name of the policyholder,

(ii) the address of the principal place of residence of the policyholder,

(*f*) contains an undertaking by the policyholder that if the policyholder becomes resident in the State, the policyholder will notify the assurance company accordingly, and

(*g*) contains such other information as the Revenue Commissioners may reasonably require for the purposes of this Chapter.

[(3) The declaration referred to in section 730D(2)(*b*) in relation to a life policy is, subject to subsection (4), a declaration in writing to the assurance company which—

(*a*) is made by the policyholder,

(*b*) is signed by the policyholder,

(*c*) is made in such form as may be prescribed or authorised by the Revenue Commissioners,

(*d*) contains the name and address of the policyholder,

[(*e*) declares that the policyholder, at the time the declaration is made, is—

(i) a company carrying on life business,

(ii) an investment undertaking (which has the same meaning as that assigned to it in section 739B),

(iii) (I) a person who is entitled to exemption from income tax under Schedule D by virtue of section 207(1)(*b*), or

(II) a person who is entitled to exemption from corporation tax by virtue of section 207(1)(*b*) as it applies for the purposes of corporation tax under section 76(6),

(iv) a PRSA provider (which has the same meaning as that assigned to it in Chapter 2A (inserted by the Pensions (Amendment) Act 2002) of Part 30),

(v) a credit union, or

(vi) a person entrusted to pay all premiums payable, in respect of the life policy, out of money under the control or subject to the order of any Court,

(*f*) contains an undertaking that should the policyholder cease to be a person referred to in subparagraph (i) to (v), or (vi) of paragraph (*e*), the assurance company will be advised accordingly, and][5] (*g*) contains such other information as the Revenue Commissioners may reasonably require for the purposes of this Chapter.

(3A) The declaration referred to in section 730D(2)(*c*) in relation to a life policy is a declaration in writing to the assurance company which—

(*a*) is made by a qualifying savings manager (in this paragraph referred to as the **"declarer**') within the meaning of section 848B (inserted by the Finance Act, 2001), in respect of the life policy which is an asset held in a special savings incentive account,

(*b*) is signed by the declarer,

(*c*) is made in such form as may be prescribed or authorised by the Revenue Commissioners,

(*d*) declares that, at the time the declaration is made, the life policy in respect of which the declaration is made—

(i) is an asset held in a special savings investment account, and

(ii) is managed by the declarer for the individual who is beneficially entitled to the life policy,

(*e*) contains the name and the address, and the PPS Number (within the meaning of section 223 of the Social Welfare (Consolidation) Act, 1993), of the individual referred to in paragraph (*d*),

(*f*) contains an undertaking by the declarer that if the life policy ceases to be an asset held in the special savings incentive account, the declarer will notify the assurance company accordingly, and

(*g*) contains such other information as the Revenue Commissioners may reasonably require for the purposes of this Chapter.][6]

(4) Where, immediately before the happening of a chargeable event, the rights conferred by a life policy were vested beneficially in 2 or more persons, or were held on trusts created, or as security for a debt owed, by 2 or more persons, this section and section 730D shall have effect in relation to each of those persons as if he or she had been the sole owner, settlor or, as the case may be, debtor, but with references to the amount of the gain construed as references to the part of it proportionate to his or her share in the rights at the time of the event, or, as the case may require, when the trusts were created.][7]

[(5) An insurance company shall keep and retain declarations referred to in this section for a period of 6 years from the time the life policy in respect of which the declaration was made ceases.][8]

Amendments

1 Substituted by FA 2001 s 70(1)(*d*)(i)(I) with effect from 1 January 2001; previously "section 730D(2)(*a*)(i)".

2 Inserted by FA 2005 s 42(1)(*c*) with effect from such day or days as the Minister for Finance may by order appoint either generally or with reference to any particular provision of FA 2005 s 42 or class of policy and different days may be so appointed for different provisions of FA 2005 s 42 or for different classes of policies.

3 Subs (2)(*a*) substituted by FA 2001 s 70(1)(*d*)(i)(II) with effect from 1 January 2001.

4 Subs (2)(*d*) substituted by FA 2001 s 70(1)(*d*)(i)(III) with effect from 1 January 2001.

5 Subs (3)(*e*) and (*f*) substituted by FA 2003 s 57(*e*)(i) with effect from 1 January 2003.

6 Subs (3) substituted and subs (3A) inserted by FA 2001 s 70(1)(*d*)(ii) with effect from 1 January 2001.

7 Section 730E inserted by FA 2000 s 53 with effect from 6 April 2000.

8 Subs (5) inserted by FA 2003 s 57(*e*)(ii) with effect from 1 January 2003.

Cross-references

Gain arising on a chargeable event: s 730D(2)(*a*)(i), (ii), (*b*), (*c*).
Personal portfolio life policy, meaning of "policyholder" applied: s 730BA(1).
Power of inspection (returns and collection of appropriate tax), assurance companies, meaning of "policyholder" applied: s 904C(1); s 904C(1)("declarations").

Definitions

assurance company: s 730A(1); chargeable event: s 730C(1); company: ss 4(1), 5(1); credit union: s 730A(1); life business: s 706(1); life policy: s 730B(2); ordinarily resident: ss 2(1), 5(1), 820; person: IA 1937 s 11(*c*); policy: s 706(1); resident: ss 2(1), 5(1), 819.

730F Deduction of tax on the happening of a chargeable event

[(1) In this section and in section 730G, **"appropriate tax"**, in connection with a chargeable event in relation to a life policy, means a sum representing income tax on the amount of the gain treated in accordance with section 730D as thereby arising—

[(*a*) subject to paragraph (*b*), where the chargeable event falls on or after 1 January 2001, at a rate determined by the formula—

$$(S+3) \text{ per cent}$$

where S is the standard rate per cent (within the meaning of section 4),

(*b*) where, in the case of a personal portfolio life policy, the chargeable event falls on or after 26 September 2001, at a rate determined by the formula—

$$(S+23) \text{ per cent}$$

where S is the standard rate per cent (within the meaning of section 4), and

(*c*) where the chargeable event falls on or before 31 December 2000, at a rate of 40 per cent.][1]

(2) An assurance company shall account for appropriate tax in accordance with section 730G.

(3) (*a*) An assurance company which is liable to account for appropriate tax in connection with a chargeable event in relation to a life policy shall, at the time of the chargeable event, be entitled—

(i) where the chargeable event is the maturity or surrender whether in whole or in part of the rights conferred by the life policy, to deduct from the proceeds payable to the policyholder on maturity, or as the case may be, surrender in whole or in part, an amount equal to the appropriate tax,

(ii) where the chargeable event—

(I) is the assignment, in whole or in part, of the rights conferred by the life policy, or

[(I*a*) is the ending of a relevant period in accordance with section 730C(1)(*a*)(iv), or][2]

(II) is deemed to happen on 31 December 2000 under section 730C(1)(*b*),

to appropriate and realise sufficient assets underlying the life policy, to meet the amount of appropriate tax for which the assurance company is liable to account, (*b*) the policyholder shall allow such deduction or, as the case may be, such appropriation, and

(*c*) the assurance company shall be acquitted and discharged of so much as is represented by the deduction or, as the case may be, the appropriation as if the amount of the deduction or the value of the appropriation had been paid to the policyholder.

[(4) Where in the period commencing on 26 September 2001 and ending on 5 December 2001 in connection with a chargeable event in relation to a personal portfolio life policy—

(*a*) an assurance company which is entitled to deduct an amount equal to the appropriate tax in accordance with subsection (3)(*a*)(i), or to appropriate and realise sufficient assets to meet the amount of appropriate tax for which the assurance company is liable to account for in accordance with subsection (3)(*a*)(ii), and

(*b*) the assurance company fails to deduct an amount equal to the appropriate tax due or fails to appropriate and realise sufficient assets to account for the amount of appropriate tax due,

then, for the purposes of regulating the time and manner in which any appropriate tax, which has not been accounted for or paid, shall be accounted for and paid, section 730FA shall apply to the exclusion of section 730G (apart from subsection (7)) and section 730GA.][3][4]

Amendments

1 Subs (1)(*a*)–(*b*) substituted and subs (1)(*c*) inserted by FA 2002 s 40(1)(*b*)(i) as respects the happening of a chargeable event in relation to a life policy (within the meaning of Pt 26 Ch 5) on or after 26 September 2001.

2 Subs (3)(*a*)(ii)(I*a*) substituted by FA 2005 s 42(1)(*d*) with effect from such day or days as the Minister for Finance may by order appoint either generally or with reference to any particular provision of FA 2005 s 42 or class of policy and different days may be so appointed for different provisions of FA 2005 s 42 or for different classes of policies.

3 Subs (4) inserted by FA 2002 s 40(1)(*b*)(ii) as respects the happening of a chargeable event in relation to a life policy (within the meaning of Pt 26 Ch 5) on or after 26 September 2001.

4 Section 730F inserted by FA 2000 s 53 with effect from 6 April 2000.

Cross-references

Assessment of appropriate tax where tax not deducted under s 730F, subs (3)(*a*)(i): s 730FA(2)(*a*), (2)(iii), (4)(*a*); subs (3)(*a*)(ii): s 730FA(2)(*b*), (2)(iii), (4)(*b*); subs (4)(*b*): s 730FA(1).

Capital acquisitions tax, set off, subs (1): s 730GB.

Declarations: s 730D(3).

Gain arising on a chargeable event, meaning of "appropriate tax" applied: s 730D(3).

Power of inspection (returns and collection of appropriate tax), assurance companies, meaning of "appropriate tax" applied: s 904C(1).

Taxation of policyholders, subss (2)–(4): s 730B(4)(*e*).

Definitions

assurance company: s 730A(1); chargeable event: s 730C(1); company: ss 4(1), 5(1); life policy: s 730B(2); policy: s 706(1); policyholder: s 730E(1).

730FA Assessment of appropriate tax where tax not deducted under section 730F

[(1) Where section 730F(4)(*b*) applies then, notwithstanding any other provision of the Tax Acts or the Capital Gains Tax Acts, this section shall apply for the purposes of regulating the time and manner in which any appropriate tax which remains to be accounted for and paid in connection with a chargeable event, which happened in the period commencing on 26 September 2001 and ending on 5 December 2001, in relation to a personal portfolio life policy shall be assessed, accounted for and paid.

(2) An assurance company shall for each personal portfolio life policy in respect of which it has not—

(*a*) deducted an amount equal to the amount of appropriate tax, for which the assurance company is liable to account, in accordance with subsection (3)*(a)*(i) of section 730F, or

(*b*) appropriated and realised sufficient assets to meet the amount of appropriate tax, for which the assurance company is liable to account, in accordance with subsection (3)*(a)*(ii) of section 730F,

make and deliver to the inspector to whom it is customary for the assurance company to make a return under section 951 a return on or before 31 December 2001 containing in each case—

(i) the name, address and, if appropriate, the registered office, of the policyholder,

(ii) the amount of the gain arising on the happening of the chargeable event in relation to the policy, including details of all amounts referred to in subsections (3) and (4) of section 730D which are relevant to the determination of the gain arising on the chargeable event in question,

(iii) the amount actually deducted in accordance with section 730F(3)*(a)*(i) or the amount actually realised in accordance with section 730F(3)*(a)*(ii),

(iv) the method of payment of the benefits under the policy,

(v) if payment was made to a person other than the policyholder, details of the name and address of that person, and

(vi) details of the property which is a linked asset in relation to the personal portfolio life policy.

(3) An assurance company which fails to deliver, within the time specified in subsection (2), the return referred to in that subsection or which fails to deliver such a return which is correct may, in addition to any penalty to which it may be liable, be made liable for the payment of any appropriate tax due in respect of a personal portfolio life policy to which that subsection applies which remains unpaid. An inspector may make an assessment on the assurance company to the best of his or her judgement of the appropriate tax so unpaid.

(4) Where, in connection with a chargeable event in relation to a personal portfolio life policy, an assurance company—

(*a*) fails to deduct an amount equal to the appropriate tax which should have been deducted in accordance with subsection (3)*(a)*(i) of section 730F, or

(*b*) fails to appropriate and realise sufficient assets to meet the full amount of appropriate tax for which the assurance company is liable to account for in accordance with subsection (3)*(a)*(ii) of section 730F,

then the policyholder or the person to whom the payment referred to in subsection (2) was made shall be liable for the payment of any appropriate tax due in relation to the personal portfolio life policy which remains unpaid. An inspector may make an assessment on the policyholder or the person concerned to the best of his or her judgement of the appropriate tax so unpaid.

(5) Where an inspector makes an assessment under subsection (3) or (4) it shall not be necessary to set out in the notice of assessment any particulars other than particulars as to the amount of appropriate tax to be paid by the assurance company or the policyholder, as appropriate.

(6) (*a*) An inspector may at any time amend or further amend an assessment made on a person under subsection (3) or (4) by making such alterations in or additions to the assessment as he or she considers necessary and the inspector shall give notice to the person of the assessment so amended or so further amended.

(*b*) After the end of a period of 6 years starting from 31 December 2001, no assessment shall be made under subsection (3) or (4) or no assessment made under either of those subsections shall be amended or further amended.

(7) For the purposes of making an assessment under subsection (3) or (4) or for the purposes of amending or further amending such an assessment an inspector may make such enquiries or take such action within his or her powers as he or she considers necessary—

(*a*) to satisfy himself or herself as to the accuracy or otherwise of the return referred to in subsection (2), or

(*b*) where no such return is made or an incorrect return is made, for the purposes of ascertaining the information which should have been included in such a return.

(8) Appropriate tax specified in an assessment made under subsection (3) or (4) or in an amended assessment made under subsection (6) shall be due and payable within one month after the issue of the notice of assessment or the amended assessment, as appropriate, subject to any appeal against the assessment.][1]

Amendments

1 Section 730FA inserted by FA 2002 s 40(1)(*c*) as respects the happening of a chargeable event in relation to a life policy (within the meaning of Pt 26 Ch 5) on or after 26 September 2001.

Cross-references

Deduction of tax on the happening of a chargeable event: s 730F(4).

Penalties, subs (2): Sch 29 column 1.

Power of inspection (returns and collection of appropriate tax), assurance companies: s 904C(1) ("return").

Definitions

appropriate tax: s 730F(1); assurance company: s 730A(1); Capital Gains Tax Acts: s 1(2); chargeable event: s 730C(1); inspector: s 2(1); linked asset: s 730BA(1); person: IA 1937 s 11(*c*); policyholder: s 730E(1); Tax Acts: s 1(2).

730G Returns and collection of appropriate tax

[(1) Notwithstanding any other provision of the Tax Acts, this section shall apply for the purposes of regulating the time and manner in which appropriate tax in connection with a chargeable event in relation to a life policy shall be accounted for and paid.

(2) An assurance company shall for each financial year make to the Collector-General—

(*a*) a return of the appropriate tax in connection with chargeable events happening on or prior to 30 June, within 30 days of that date, and

(*b*) a return of appropriate tax in connection with chargeable events happening between 1 July and 31 December, within 30 days of that later date, and

where it is the case, the return shall specify that there is no appropriate tax for the period in question.

(3) The appropriate tax in connection with a chargeable event which is required to be included in a return shall be due at the time by which the return is to be made and shall be paid by the assurance company to the Collector-General, and the appropriate tax so due shall be payable by the assurance company without the making of an assessment; but appropriate tax which has become so due may be assessed on the assurance company (whether or not it has been paid when the assessment is made) if that tax or any part of it is not paid on or before the due date.

(4) Where it appears to the inspector that there is an amount of appropriate tax in relation to a chargeable event which ought to have been but has not been included in a return, or where the inspector is dissatisfied with any return, the inspector may make an assessment on the assurance company to the best of his or her judgement, and any amount of appropriate tax in connection with a chargeable event due under an assessment made by virtue of this subsection shall be treated for the purposes of interest on unpaid tax as having been payable at the time when it would have been payable if a correct return had been made.

(5) Where any item has been incorrectly included in a return as appropriate tax, the inspector may make such assessments, adjustments or set-offs as may in his or her judgement be required for securing that the resulting liabilities to tax, including interest on unpaid tax, whether of the assurance company making the return or of any other person, are in so far as possible the same as they would have been if the item had not been included.

(6) (*a*) Any appropriate tax assessed on an assurance company shall be due within one month after the issue of the notice of assessment (unless that tax is due earlier under subsection (3)) subject to any appeal against the assessment, but no appeal shall affect the date when any amount is due under subsection (3).

(*b*) On determination of the appeal against an assessment under this Chapter, any appropriate tax overpaid shall be repaid.

(7) (*a*) The provisions of the Income Tax Acts relating to—

(i) assessments to income tax,

(ii) appeals against such assessments (including the rehearing of appeals and the statement of a case for the opinion of the High Court), and

(iii) the collection and recovery of income tax,

shall, in so far as they are applicable, apply to the assessment, collection and recovery of appropriate tax.

(*b*) Any amount of appropriate tax shall carry interest at the rate of [0.0322 per cent for each day or part of a day][1] from the date when the amount becomes due and payable until payment.

(*c*) [Subsections (3) to (5) of section 1080][2] shall apply in relation to interest payable under paragraph (*b*) as they apply in relation to interest payable under section 1080.

(*d*) In its application to any appropriate tax charged by any assessment made in accordance with this Chapter, section 1080 shall apply as if [subsection (2)(*b*)][3] of that section were deleted.

(8) Every return shall be in a form prescribed by the Revenue Commissioners and shall include a declaration to the effect that the return is correct and complete.][4]

Amendments

1 Substituted by FA 2002 s 129(1)(*a*) with effect from 1 September 2002 as regards interest chargeable in respect of an amount due to be paid or remitted, whether before, on, or after that date; previously "1 per cent for each month or part of a month".

2 Substituted by FA 2005 s 145(7)(*a*) and Sch 5 Pt 1 in relation to any unpaid income tax, corporation tax or capital gains tax, as the case may be, that has not been paid before 1 April 2005 regardless of when that tax became due and payable and notwithstanding anything to the contrary in any other enactment other than TCA 1997 s 1082; previously "Subsections (2) to (4) of section 1080".

3 Substituted by FA 2005 s 145(7)(*a*) and Sch 5 Pt 1 in relation to any unpaid income tax, corporation tax or capital gains tax, as the case may be, that has not been paid before 1 April 2005 regardless of when that tax became due and payable and notwithstanding anything to the contrary in any other enactment other than TCA 1997 s 1082; previously "subsection (1)(*b*)".

4 Section 730G inserted by FA 2000 s 53 with effect from 6 April 2000.

Cross-references

Deduction of tax on the happening of a chargeable event: s 730F(1), (2), (4).
Penalty: Sch 29, column 1.
Power of inspection (returns and collection of appropriate tax), assurance companies: s 904C(1)("return").
Repayment of appropriate tax: s 730GA.
Taxation of policyholders: s 730B(1)("return"); s 730B(4)(*e*).

Definitions

appropriate tax: s 730F(1); assurance company: s 730A(1); chargeable event: s 730C(1); Collector-General: ss 2(1), 851; High Court: IA 1937 Sch; Income Tax Acts: s 1(2); inspector: ss 2(1), 852; life policy: s 730B(2); person: IA 1937 s 11(*c*); policy: s 706(1); Tax Acts: s 1(2).

730GA Repayment of appropriate tax

[For the purposes of a claim to relief, under section 189, 189A or 192, or a repayment of income tax in consequence thereof, the amount of a payment made to a policyholder by an assurance company shall be treated as a net amount of income from the gross amount of which has been deducted income tax, of an amount equal to the amount of appropriate tax (within the meaning of section 730F) deducted from the payment, and such amount of gross income shall be treated as chargeable to tax under Case III of Schedule D.][1]

Amendments

1 Section 730GA inserted by FA 2001 s 70(1)(*f*) with effect from 1 January 2001.

Cross-references

Deduction of tax on the happening of a chargeable event: s 730F(4).
Taxation of policyholders: s 730B(4)(*e*).

Definitions

assurance company: s 730A(1).

730GB Capital acquisitions tax: set-off

[Where on the death of a person, an assurance company is liable to account for appropriate tax (within the meaning of section 730F(1)) in connection with a gain arising on a chargeable event in relation to a life policy, the amount of such tax, in so far as it does not exceed the amount of appropriate tax to which the assurance company would be liable if that tax was calculated in accordance with section 730F(1)(*a*), shall be treated as an amount of capital gains tax paid for the purposes of [section 104 of the Capital Acquisitions Tax Act 2003][1].][2]

Amendments

1 Substituted by CATCA 2003 s 119 and Sch 3 with effect from 21 February 2003; previously "section 63 of the Finance Act 1985".

2 Section 730GB substituted by FA 2003 s 57(*f*) with effect from 1 January 2003 (originally inserted by FA 2001 s 70(1)(*f*) with effect from 1 January 2001).

Definitions

assurance company: s 730A(1); chargeable event: s 730C(1); life policy: s 730B(2); policy: s 706(1).

[CHAPTER 6
Certain Foreign Life Policies — Taxation and Returns][1]

Amendments

1 Part 26 Ch 6 inserted by FA 2001 s 67(1) with effect from 1 January 2001.

Cross-references

Personal portfolio life policy, meaning of applied for purposes of this Chapter: s 730BA(2).

730H Interpretation and application

[(1) In this Chapter—

"chargeable period" has the same meaning as in section 321(2);

"EEA Agreement" means the Agreement on the European Economic Area signed at Oporto on 2 May 1992, as adjusted by the Protocol signed at Brussels on 17 March 1993;

"EEA state" means a State, other than the State, which is a Contracting Party to the EEA Agreement;

"foreign life policy" means a policy of assurance on the life of a person commenced—

(*a*) by a branch or agency, carrying on business in an offshore state, of an assurance company, or

(*b*) by an assurance company carrying on business in an offshore state, other than by its branch or agency carrying on business in the State;

"OECD" means the organisation known as the Organisation for Economic Co-operation and Development;

"offshore state" means a State other than the State which is—

(i) a Member State of the European Communities,

(ii) a State which is an EEA state, or

(iii) a State which is a member of the OECD, the government of which have entered into arrangements having the force of law by virtue of [section 826(1)(*a*)][1];

"relevant payment" means any payment made to a person in respect of a foreign life policy where such payments are made annually or at more frequent intervals, other than a payment made in consideration of the disposal, in whole or in part, of the foreign life policy;

"return of income" has the meaning assigned to it by section 1084;

"specified return date for the chargeable period" has the meaning assigned to it by section 950;

"standard rate per cent" has the meaning assigned to it by section 4.

(2) For the purposes of this Chapter—

(*a*) there shall be a disposal of an asset if there would be such a disposal for the purposes of the Capital Gains Tax Acts,

(*b*) an income shall be correctly included in a return made by a person, only where that income is included in a return of income made by the person on or before the specified return date for the chargeable period in which the income arises, and

(*c*) details of a disposal shall be correctly included in a return made by a person, only where details of the disposal are included in a return of income made by the person or, where the person has died, his or her executor or administrator, on or before the specified return date for the chargeable period in which the disposal is made.][2]

Amendments

1 Substituted by FA 2004 s 89 and Sch 3 para 1(*s*) with effect from 25 March 2004; previously "section 826".

2 Section 730H inserted by FA 2001 s 67(1) with effect from 1 January 2001.

Cross-references

Personal portfolio life policy, meaning of "foreign life policy" applied: s 730BA(1).

Definitions

assurance company: s 706(1); branch or agency: ss 4(1); 5(1); Capital Gains Tax Acts: s 1(2); person: IA 1937 s 11(*c*).

730I Returns on acquisition of foreign policy

[Where in any chargeable period a person acquires a foreign life policy, the person shall, notwithstanding anything to the contrary in section 950 or 1084, be deemed for that chargeable period to be a chargeable person for the purposes of sections 951 and 1084, and the return of income to be delivered by the person for that chargeable period shall include the following particulars—

(*a*) the name and address of the person who commenced the foreign life policy,

(*b*) a description of the terms of the foreign life policy including premiums payable, and

(*c*) the name and address of the person through whom the foreign life policy was acquired.][1]

Amendments

1 Section 730I inserted by FA 2001 s 67(1) with effect from 1 January 2001.

Definitions

chargeable period: s 730H(1); foreign life policy: s 730H(1); person: IA 1937 s 11(*c*); return of income: s 730H(1).

730J Payment in respect of foreign life policy

[(1) Where on or after 1 January 2001 a person who has a foreign life policy is in receipt of a payment in respect of the foreign life policy, then—

[(*a*) where the person is not a company, and—

(i) income represented by the payment is correctly included in a return made by the person, then, notwithstanding section 15, the rate of income tax to be charged on the income shall be—

(I) where the payment is a relevant payment, the standard rate (within the meaning of section 3) of income tax in force at the time of the payment, and

(II) where the payment is not a relevant payment and is not made in consideration of the disposal, in whole or in part, of the foreign life policy—

(A) in the case of a foreign life policy which is a personal portfolio life policy, at the rate determined by the formula—

$$(S + 23) \text{ per cent}$$

where S is the standard rate per cent for the year of assessment in which the payment is made, and

(B) in any other case, at the rate determined by the formula—

$$(S + 3) \text{ per cent}$$

where S is the standard rate per cent for the year of assessment in which the payment is made,

and

(ii) where the income represented by the payment is not correctly included in a return made by the person, the income shall be charged to income tax—

(I) in the case of a foreign life policy which is a personal portfolio life policy, at the rate determined by the formula—

$$(H + 20) \text{ per cent}$$

where H is a rate per cent determined in relation to the person by section 15 for the year of assessment in which the payment is made, and

(II) in any other case, at a rate determined in relation to the person by section 15 for the year of assessment in which the payment is made][1]

(*b*) where the person is a company, the income represented by the payment shall be charged to tax under Case III of Schedule D.][2]

Amendments

[1] Subs (1)(*a*) substituted by FA 2002 s 40(2)(*a*) as respects the receipt by a person of a payment in respect of a foreign life policy (within the meaning of Pt 26 Ch 6) or the disposal in whole or in part of a foreign life policy (within that meaning) on or after 26 September 2001.

[2] Section 730J inserted by FA 2001 s 67(1) with effect from 1 January 2001.

Definitions

company: ss 4(1), 5(1); foreign life policy: s 730H(1); person: IA 1937 s 11(*c*); relevant payment: s 730H(1); standard rate per cent: s 730H(1); year of assessment: s 2(1).

730K Disposal of foreign life policy

[(1) Where on or after 1 January 2001 a person disposes, in whole or in part, of a foreign life policy, and the disposal gives rise to a gain computed in accordance with subsection (2), and details of the disposal have been correctly included in a return made by the person, then notwithstanding section 594, the amount of the gain shall be treated as an amount of income chargeable to tax under Case IV of Schedule D, and where the person is not a company, the rate of income tax to be charged on that income shall be the rate determined by the formula—

[(*a*) in the case of a foreign life policy which is a personal portfolio life policy, at the rate determined by the formula—

$$(S+23) \text{ per cent}$$

where S is the standard rate per cent for the year of assessment in which the payment is made, and

(*b*) in any other case, at the rate determined by the formula—

$$(S+3) \text{ per cent}$$

where S is the standard rate per cent for the year of assessment in which the payment is made,][1]

(2) The amount of the gain accruing on a disposal referred to in subsection (1) is the amount of the relevant gain (within the meaning of section 594(2)) which would be computed if the gain accruing on the disposal were computed for the purposes of that section.

(3) Notwithstanding sections 538 and 546, where apart from this subsection the effect of any computation under subsection (2) would be to produce a loss, the gain on the disposal referred to in subsection (1) shall be treated as nil and accordingly for the purposes of this Chapter no loss shall be treated as accruing on such disposal.

(4) Where, as a result of a disposal by a person, an amount of income is chargeable to tax under Case IV of Schedule D in accordance with subsection (1), that amount shall not be reduced by a claim made by the person—

(*a*) where the person is not a company, under section 381 or 383, or

(*b*) where the person is a company, under section 396 or 399.

(5) Where an individual is chargeable to tax in accordance with subsection (1) in respect of an amount of income—

(*a*) the tax thereby payable, in so far as it is paid, shall be treated as an amount of capital gains tax paid for the purposes of [section 104 of the Capital Acquisitions Tax Consolidation Act 2003][2], and

(*b*) that amount of income shall not be included in reckonable income (within the meaning of the Health Contributions Regulations, 1979 (SI No 107 of 1979)) for the purposes of those Regulations.][3]

Amendments

1 Formula substituted by FA 2002 s 40(2)(*b*) as respects the receipt by a person of a payment in respect of a foreign life policy (within the meaning of Pt 26 Ch 6) or the disposal in whole or in part of a foreign life policy (within that meaning) on or after 26 September 2001.

2 Substituted by FA 2005 s 147 and Sch 6 para 1(*k*) with effect from 21 February 2003; previously "section 63 of the Finance Act, 1985".

3 Section 730K inserted by FA 2001 s 67(1) with effect from 1 January 2001.

Definitions

company: ss 4(1), 5(1); foreign life policy: s 730H(1); person: IA 1937 s 11(*c*); standard rate per cent: s 730H(1); year of assessment: s 2(1).

PART 27
UNIT TRUSTS AND OFFSHORE FUNDS

CHAPTER 1
Unit Trusts

731 Chargeable gains accruing to unit trusts

(1) In this section, **"capital distribution"** means any distribution from a unit trust, including a distribution in the course of terminating the unit trust, in money or money's worth except a distribution which in the hands of the recipient constitutes income for the purposes of income tax.

(2) For the purposes of the Capital Gains Tax Acts and without prejudice to section 567 and sections 574 to 578, chargeable gains accruing to a unit trust in any year of assessment shall be assessed and charged on the trustees of the unit trust.

(3) The trustees of a unit trust shall for the purposes of the Capital Gains Tax Acts be treated as being a single and continuing body of persons (distinct from the persons who may from time to time be the trustees), and that body shall be treated as being resident and ordinarily resident in the State unless the general administration of the unit trust is ordinarily carried on outside the State and the trustees or a majority of them for the time being are not resident or not ordinarily resident in the State.

(4) Where a person receives or becomes entitled to receive in respect of units in a unit trust any capital distribution from the unit trust, such person shall be treated as having in consideration of that capital distribution disposed of an interest in the units.

(5) (*a*) Where throughout a year of assessment [all the issued units in a unit trust which neither is, nor is deemed to be, an authorised unit trust scheme (within the meaning of the Unit Trusts Act, 1990)][1] are assets such that if those units

were disposed of by the unit holder any gain accruing would be wholly exempt from capital gains tax (otherwise than by reason of residence or by virtue of section 739(3)), gains accruing to the unit trust in that year shall not be chargeable gains.

(*b*) For the purposes of any assessment to capital gains tax, paragraph (*a*) shall not apply as respects a unit trust to which subsection (6) applies.

[(*c*) Where, by virtue of paragraph (*a*), gains accruing to a unit trust in a year of assessment are not chargeable gains, then—

(i) the unit trust shall not be chargeable to income tax for that year of assessment, and

(ii) a deposit (within the meaning of section 256(1)), which is an asset of the unit trust, shall not be a relevant deposit (within the meaning of that section) for the purposes of Chapter 4 of Part 8, for that year of assessment.][2]

(6) Gains accruing on the disposal of units in a unit trust shall not be chargeable gains for the purposes of the Capital Gains Tax Acts where—

(*a*) the trustees of the unit trust have at all times (but not taking into account any time before the 6th day of April, 1974) been resident and ordinarily resident in the State, and

(*b*) the unit trust is a scheme which is established for the purpose or has the effect, solely or mainly, of providing facilities for the participation by the public as beneficiaries under a trust in profits or income arising from the acquisition, holding, management or disposal of securities or any other property whatever and which is administered by the holder of a licence under the Insurance Act, 1936, and for participation in which, in respect of units first issued after the 14th day of June, 1973, a policy of assurance on human life is required to be effected (but so that the units do not become the property of the owner of the policy either as benefits or otherwise).

(7) (*a*) Subject to paragraph (*b*), where there is a disposal in any year of assessment of units in a unit trust—

(i) not being an undertaking for collective investment (within the meaning of section 738) which began carrying on business on or after the 25th day of May, 1993,

(ii) all the assets of which were throughout the year of assessment 1993–94 assets, whether mentioned in section 19 of the Capital Gains Tax Act, 1975, or in any other provision of the Capital Gains Tax Acts, to which that section applied, and

(iii) the person disposing of the units acquired the units before the 6th day of April, 1994,

then, the chargeable gain on the disposal shall be computed as if the units had been sold and immediately reacquired by that person on the 5th day of April, 1994, at their market value at that date.

(*b*) Paragraph (*a*) shall not apply in relation to the disposal of units—

(i) if as a consequence of the application of that paragraph a gain would accrue on that disposal to the person making the disposal and either a smaller gain or a loss would so accrue if that paragraph did not apply, or

(ii) if as a consequence of the application of that paragraph a loss would so accrue and either a smaller loss or a gain would accrue if that paragraph did not apply,

and accordingly in a case to which subparagraph (i) or (ii) applies, the amount of the gain or loss accruing on the disposal shall be computed without regard to this subsection (other than this paragraph) but, in a case where this paragraph would otherwise substitute a loss for a gain or a gain for a loss, it shall be assumed in relation to the disposal that the units were acquired by the person disposing of them for a consideration such that neither a gain nor a loss accrued to that person on making the disposal.

Amendments

1 Substituted by FA 2001 s 71(1)(*a*) with effect from 1 January 2001.

1 Subs (5)(*c*) inserted by FA 2001 s 71(1)(*b*) for 2000–01 and later tax years.

Cross-references

Dividend withholding tax, exemption from for certain persons, subs (5)(*a*): s 172C(2)(*db*), (3)(*cb*) and Sch 2A para 11(*f*).

Interest payments by companies and to non-residents, subs (5)(*a*): s 246(1)("investment undertaking").

Investment undertakings (declarations), subs (5)(a): Sch 2B para 6(d).

Investment undertakings (gain arising on a chargeable event), subs (5)(*a*): s 739D(6)(*e*), (8B)(*a*), (8C)(*a*), (*b*)(i).

Investment undertakings (interpretation and application), subs (5)(*a*): s 739B(1)("investment undertaking"); ss 739B(3)(*c*); 739B(6)(*c*).

Option for non-application of s 731(6): s 736(2)(*b*).

Taxation of collective investment undertakings: s 734(4)(*b*).

Undertaking for collective investment, meaning, subs (5)(*a*): s 738(1)(*a*) (undertaking for collective investment).

Definitions

body of persons: s 2(1); chargeable gain: ss 5(1), 545; person: IA 1937 s 11(*c*); resident: s 5(1); settled property: s 5(1); unit trust: s 5(1); units: s 5(1); unit holder: s 5(1); year: IA 1937 Sch; year of assessment: ss 2(1), 5(1).

Former enactments

CGTA 1975 s 31; FA 1977 s 34; FA 1979 s 37(1); FA 1993 s 19; FA 1994 s 64.

732 Special arrangements for qualifying unit trusts

(1) In this section—

"securities" includes securities within section 607 and stocks, shares, bonds and obligations of any government, municipal corporation, company or other body corporate;

"quoted securities" means securities which, at any time at which they are to be taken into account for the purposes of this section, or at any time in the period of 6 years immediately before such time, have or have had quoted market values on a stock exchange in the State or elsewhere.

(2) This section shall apply—

(*a*) to a unit trust (in this section referred to as a **"qualifying unit trust"**)—

(i) which is a registered unit trust scheme (within the meaning of section 3 of the Unit Trusts Act, 1972),

(ii) the trustees of which are resident and ordinarily resident in the State,

(iii) the prices of units in which are published regularly by the managers,

(iv) all the units in which are of equal value and carry the same rights, and

(v) which, at all times since it was registered in the register established under the Unit Trusts Act, 1972, but subject to subsection (7), satisfied the conditions specified in subsection (6), and

(*b*) to disposals of assets which are units in a qualifying unit trust (in this section referred to as **"qualifying units"**).

(3) Chargeable gains accruing to a qualifying unit trust in any year of assessment shall be chargeable to capital gains tax at one-half of the rate specified in section 28(3).

(4) Chargeable gains which derive from the disposal of qualifying units and accrue to a person chargeable to capital gains tax shall be chargeable to tax at one-half of the rate at which those gains would be chargeable under the Capital Gains Tax Acts apart from this subsection.

(5) For any accounting period of a company, being an accounting period for which the company is chargeable to corporation tax in respect of chargeable gains—

(*a*) where the total amount of chargeable gains accruing to the company for the accounting period derives from the disposal of qualifying units, the amount which apart from this section would be included in respect of chargeable gains in the company's total profits for the accounting period under section 78(1) shall be reduced by 50 per cent,

(*b*) where the total amount of chargeable gains accruing to the company for the accounting period includes—

(i) an amount in respect of such chargeable gains on the disposal of qualifying units, and

(ii) an amount in respect of such chargeable gains on the disposal of assets other than qualifying units,

the amount which apart from this section would be included in respect of chargeable gains in the company's total profits for the accounting period under section 78(1) shall be reduced by such amount as bears to the amount to be so included the same proportion as one-half of the amount referred to in subparagraph (i) bears to the total of the amounts referred to in subparagraphs (i) and (ii).

(6) The conditions referred to in subsection (2)(*a*)(v) are that—

(*a*) not less than 80 per cent of the units were held by persons who acquired them pursuant to an offer made to the general public,

(*b*) the number of unit holders was not less than 50 and no one unit holder was the beneficial owner of more than 5 per cent of the units in issue at any time, and for the purposes of this paragraph a person and any persons with whom such person is connected shall be treated as one unit holder,

(*c*) the value of quoted securities held by the trustees on behalf of the unit trust was not less than 80 per cent by value of the assets so held by the trustees, and

(*d*) the securities held by the trustees on behalf of the unit trust in any one company did not exceed 15 per cent by value of the total securities so held by the trustees.

(7) The Revenue Commissioners may treat a unit trust as a qualifying unit trust for the purposes of this section notwithstanding that one or more of the conditions specified in subsection (6) was or were not complied with in relation to the unit trust—

(*a*) for the period ending on the 5th day of April, 1978, in the case where the unit trust became registered in the register established under the Unit Trusts Act, 1972, before the 6th day of April, 1976, and

(*b*) for the period ending on a date not more than 2 years after the date on which the unit trust became registered in that register, in the case where the unit trust became so registered on or after the 6th day of April, 1976.

Cross-references

Taxation of collective investment undertakings: s 734(7).

Definitions

chargeable gain: ss 5(1), 545; company: s 5(1); person: IA 1937 s 11(*c*); resident: s 5(1); shares: s 5(1); unit trust: s 5(1); units: s 5(1); unit holder: s 5(1); year of assessment: ss 2(1), 5(1).

Former enactments

CGTA 1975 s 32; FA 1977 s 35; CGTA(A) 1978 s 16 and Sch 1 para 9; FA 1997 s 146(2) and Sch 9 Pt II.

733 Reorganisation of units in unit trust scheme

(1) In this section, references to a reorganisation of units in a trust scheme include—

(*a*) any case where persons are, whether for payment or not, allotted units in the scheme in respect of and in proportion to (or as nearly as may be in proportion to) their holdings of units in the scheme or of any class of units in the scheme, and

(*b*) any case where there is more than one class of units and the rights attached to units of any class are altered.

(2) (*a*) Subject to paragraph (*b*), section 584 shall apply with any necessary modification in relation to a reorganisation or reduction of units in any unit trust scheme registered under the Unit Trusts Act, 1972, or authorised under the European Communities (Undertakings for Collective Investment in Transferable Securities) Regulations, 1989 (SI No 78 of 1989), as if (except as respects subsection (7) of that section)—

(i) that scheme were a company, and

(ii) the units in that scheme were shares in the company.

(*b*) Where but for this paragraph this section would apply to any reorganisation or reduction of units in a unit trust scheme in a year of assessment so that units which are deemed not to be chargeable assets for that year for the purposes of the Capital Gains Tax Acts would be treated as **"original shares"** or a **"new holding"** within the meaning of section 584, that section shall not apply to that reorganisation or reduction of units in the unit trust scheme.

(3) The references in subsection (2) to section 584 do not include references to that section as applied by section 585 or 586.

Cross-references

Offshore fund operating equalisation arrangements: s 742(6).

Definitions

class (of shares): s 5(1); company: s 5(1); person: IA 1937 s 11(*c*); shares: s 5(1); unit trust: s 5(1); units: s 5(1); year of assessment: ss 2(1), 5(1).

Former enactments

CGTA 1975 s 51(1) and Sch 2 para 2A; FA 1990 s 87.

734 Taxation of collective investment undertakings

(1) (*a*) In this section and in Schedule 18—

"accounting period", in relation to a collective investment undertaking, means the chargeable period or its basis period (within the meaning of section 321(2)) on the income or profits of which the undertaking is chargeable to income tax or corporation tax, as the case may be, for any chargeable period (within the meaning of that section), or would be so chargeable but for an insufficiency of income or profits, and—

(i) where 2 basis periods overlap, the period common to both shall be deemed to fall in the first basis period only,

(ii) where there is an interval between the end of the basis period for one chargeable period and the basis period for the next chargeable period, the interval shall be deemed to be part of the second basis period, and

(iii) the reference in paragraph (i) to the overlapping of 2 periods shall be construed as including a reference to the coincidence of 2 periods or to the inclusion of one period in another, and the reference to the period common to both shall be construed accordingly;

"the Acts" means the Tax Acts and the Capital Gains Tax Acts;

"the airport" has the same meaning as in the Customs-Free Airport Act, 1947;

"appropriate tax", in relation to the amount of any relevant payment made by a collective investment undertaking or in relation to any amount of undistributed relevant income of such an undertaking, as the case may be, means a sum representing tax on the amount of the payment or the amount of the undistributed relevant income, as appropriate, at a rate equal to the standard rate of income tax in force at the time of the payment or at the end of the accounting period to which the undistributed relevant income relates, as the case may be, after making a deduction from that sum of an amount equal to, or to the aggregate of—

(i) in the case of a relevant payment—

(I) in so far as it is made wholly or partly out of relevant income which at a previous date had been or formed part of the undistributed relevant income of the undertaking, the amount of any appropriate tax deducted—

(A) from the relevant income, or

(B) where the payment, or that part of the payment which is made out of relevant income, is less than the relevant income, from such part of the relevant income as is represented by the payment, or that part of the payment, as the case may be, and

(II) any other amount or amounts of tax deducted—

(A) from the relevant profits out of which the relevant payment is made, or

(B) where the payment is less than the profits, from such part of the profits as is represented by the payment,

under any of the provisions of the Acts apart from this section and which is or are not repayable to the collective investment undertaking,

or

(ii) in the case of an amount of undistributed relevant income, any amount or amounts of tax deducted from the income under any of the provisions of the Acts apart from this section and which is or are not repayable to the collective investment undertaking,

but the amount of the deduction shall not exceed the amount of the sum;

"the Area" has the same meaning as it has for the purposes of section 446;

"chargeable gain" has the same meaning as in the Capital Gains Tax Acts;

"collective investor", in relation to an authorised investment company (within the meaning of Part XIII of the Companies Act, 1990), means an investor, being a life assurance company, pension fund or other investor—

(i) who invests in securities or any other property whatever with moneys contributed by 50 or more persons—

(I) none of whom has at any time directly or indirectly contributed more than 5 per cent of such moneys, and

(II) each of a majority of whom has contributed moneys to the investor with the intention of being entitled, otherwise than on the death of any person or by reference to a risk of any kind to any person or property, to receive from the investor—

(A) a payment which, or

(B) payments the aggregate of which,

exceeds those moneys by a part of the profits or income arising to the investor,

and

(ii) who invests in the authorised investment company primarily for the benefit of those persons;

"collective investment undertaking" means, subject to paragraph (*b*)—

(i) a unit trust scheme which is or is deemed to be an authorised unit trust scheme (within the meaning of the Unit Trusts Act, 1990) and which has not had its authorisation under that Act revoked,

(ii) any other undertaking which is an undertaking for collective investment in transferable securities within the meaning of the relevant Regulations, being an undertaking which holds an authorisation, which has not been revoked, issued pursuant to the relevant Regulations,

(iii) a limited partnership which—

(I) has as its principal business, as expressed in the partnership agreement establishing the limited partnership, the investment of its funds in property, and

(II) has been authorised to carry on that business, under any enactment which provides for such authorisation, by the Central Bank of Ireland,

and where, in addition to being a collective investment undertaking, it is also a specified collective investment undertaking, and

(iv) any authorised investment company (within the meaning of Part XIII of the Companies Act, 1990)—

(I) which has not had its authorisation under that Part of that Act revoked, and

(II) (A) which has been designated in that authorisation as an investment company which may raise capital by promoting the sale of its shares to the public and has not ceased to be so designated, or

(B) (*aa*) which is not a qualified company,

(*bb*) which in addition to being a collective investment undertaking is also a specified collective investment undertaking, and

(*cc*) where all the holders of units who must be resident outside the State, for the company to be a specified collective investment undertaking, are collective investors;

"distribution" has the same meaning as in the Corporation Tax Acts;

"qualified company" has, in relation to any business of a collective investment undertaking carried on in—

(i) the airport, the same meaning as it has for the purposes of section 445, or

(ii) the Area, the same meaning as it has for the purposes of section 446;

"qualifying management company", in relation to a collective investment undertaking, means a qualified company which in the course of relevant trading operations carried on by the qualified company manages the whole or any part of the investments and other activities of the business of the undertaking;

"relevant gains", in relation to a collective investment undertaking, means gains accruing to the undertaking, being gains which would constitute chargeable gains in the hands of a person resident in the State;

"relevant income", in relation to a collective investment undertaking, means any amounts of income, profits or gains which arise to or are receivable by the collective investment undertaking, being amounts of income, profits or gains—

(i) which are or are to be paid to unit holders as relevant payments,

(ii) out of which relevant payments are or are to be made to unit holders, or

(iii) which are or are to be accumulated for the benefit of, or invested in transferable securities for the benefit of, unit holders,

and which if they arose to an individual resident in the State would in the hands of the individual constitute income for the purposes of income tax;

"relevant payment" means a payment made to a unit holder by a collective investment undertaking by reason of rights conferred on the unit holder as a result of holding a unit or units in the collective investment undertaking, other than a payment made in respect of the cancellation, redemption or repurchase of a unit;

"relevant profits", in relation to a collective investment undertaking, means the relevant income and relevant gains of the undertaking;

"relevant Regulations" means the European Communities (Undertakings for Collective Investment in Transferable Securities) Regulations, 1989 (SI No 78 of 1989);

"relevant trading operations" has, in relation to any business of a collective investment undertaking carried on by a qualified company in—

(i) the airport, the same meaning as it has for the purposes of section 445, or

(ii) the Area, the same meaning as it has for the purposes of section 446;

"return" means a return under paragraph 1(2) of Schedule 18;

"specified collective investment undertaking" means, subject to paragraph (*c*), a collective investment undertaking—

(i) most of the business of which, to the extent that it is carried on in the State—

(I) (A) is carried on in the Area by the undertaking or by a qualifying management company of the undertaking or by the undertaking and the qualifying management company of the undertaking, or

(B) is not so carried on in the Area but—

(*aa*) is so carried on in the State,

(*bb*) would be so carried on in the Area but for circumstances outside the control of the person or persons carrying on the business, and

(*cc*) is so carried on in the Area when those circumstances cease to exist,

or

(II) is carried on in the airport by the undertaking or by a qualifying management company of the undertaking or by the undertaking and the qualifying management company of the undertaking,

and

(ii) in which, except to the extent that such units are held by the undertaking itself, the qualifying management company of the undertaking, a company referred to in section 710(2), a specified company or another specified collective investment undertaking, all the holders of units in the undertaking are persons resident outside the State,

and includes any company limited by shares or guarantee which—

(iii) is wholly owned by such a collective investment undertaking or its trustees, if any, for the benefit of the holders of units in that undertaking,

(iv) is so owned solely for the purpose of limiting the liability of that undertaking or its trustees, as the case may be, in respect of futures contracts, options contracts or other financial instruments with similar risk characteristics, by enabling it or its trustees, as the case may be, to invest or deal in such investments through the company, and

(v) would, if references to an undertaking in paragraph (i) were to be construed as including references to a company limited by shares or guarantee, satisfy the condition set out in paragraph (i);

"specified company" means a company—

(i) which is—

(I) a qualified company carrying on relevant trading operations (within the meaning of section 446), or

(II) a qualified company carrying on relevant trading operations (within the meaning of section 445) so long as those relevant trading operations could be certified by the Minister for Finance as relevant trading operations for the purposes of section 446 if they were carried on in the Area rather than in the airport,

and

[(ii) (I) not more than 25 per cent of the share capital of which is owned directly or indirectly by persons resident in the State, or

(II) all of the share capital of which is owned directly by another company resident in the State and not more than 25 per cent of the share capital of that other company is owned directly or indirectly by persons resident in the State,][1]

"tax" means income tax, corporation tax or capital gains tax, as may be appropriate;

"transferable securities" has the same meaning as in the relevant Regulations;

"undistributed relevant income", in relation to a collective investment undertaking, means any relevant income arising to or receivable by the undertaking in an accounting period of the undertaking and which at the end of the accounting period has not been paid to the unit holders and from which appropriate tax has not previously been deducted;

"unit" includes any investment, such as a subscription for shares or a contribution of capital, in a collective investment undertaking, being an investment which entitles the investor—

(i) to a share of the investments or relevant profits of, or

(ii) to receive a distribution from,

the collective investment undertaking;

"unit holder", in relation to a collective investment undertaking, means any person who by reason of the holding of a unit, or under the terms of a unit, in the undertaking is entitled to a share of any of the investments or relevant profits of, or to receive a distribution from, the undertaking.

(*b*) References in this section to a collective investment undertaking, apart from such references in the definition of **"specified collective investment undertaking"**, shall include references to a company limited by shares or guarantee which is a specified collective investment undertaking.

(*c*) For the purposes of the definition of **"specified collective investment undertaking"**, a reference to a qualifying management company shall be construed as if—

[(i) in section 445 the following subsection were substituted for subsection (2) of that section:

"(2) Subject to subsections (7) and (8), the Minister may give a certificate certifying that such trading operations of a qualified company as are specified in the certificate are, with effect from a date specified in the certificate, relevant trading operations for the purpose of this section.",

and

(ii) in section 446 the following subsection were substituted for subsection (2) of that section:

"(2) Subject to subsections (7) and (9), the Minister may give a certificate certifying that such trading operations of a company as are specified in the certificate are, with effect from a date specified in the certificate, relevant trading operations for the purpose of this section.".][2]

(2) For the purposes of this section—

(*a*) where any payment is made out of relevant profits or out of any part of such profits from which any tax including appropriate tax has been deducted and the payment is less than the relevant profits or that part of such profits, the amount of the tax so deducted which is referable to the part of the profits represented by the payment shall be the amount which bears to the total amount of the tax deducted from the relevant profits or the part of such profits, the same proportion as the amount of the payment bears to the amount of the relevant profits or the part of such profits, as the case may be, and

(*b*) any reference in this section to the amount of a relevant payment shall be construed as a reference to the amount which would be the amount of the relevant payment if the appropriate tax were not to be deducted from the relevant payment or from any undistributed relevant income out of which the relevant payment or any part of such payment is made.

(3) Notwithstanding anything in the Acts but subject to subsection (5), a collective investment undertaking shall not be chargeable to tax in respect of relevant profits, but the relevant profits shall be chargeable to tax in the hands of any unit holder, including the undertaking, to whom a relevant payment of or out of the relevant profits is made if

and to the extent that the unit holder would be chargeable to tax in the State on such relevant profits, or on such part of the relevant profits as is represented by the payment, on the basis that and in all respects as if, subject to subsections (4) and (6), the relevant profits or that part of the relevant profits had arisen or accrued to the unit holder without passing through the hands of the undertaking.

(4) Where in accordance with subsection (3) a unit holder is to be charged to tax on a relevant payment made by a collective investment undertaking which is not a specified collective investment undertaking—

(*a*) in so far as any amount of the relevant payment on which the unit holder is to be so charged is or is made out of relevant income, the unit holder shall be charged to tax on that amount under Case IV of Schedule D as if it were an amount of income arising to the unit holder at the time the payment is made, and

(*b*) in so far as any amount of the relevant payment on which the unit holder is to be so charged is or is made out of relevant gains, it shall be treated as a capital distribution within the meaning of section 731 and, if it is not already the case, the Capital Gains Tax Acts shall apply in all respects as if the amount of the relevant payment were a capital distribution made by a unit trust and the unit or units in respect of which it is paid were a unit or units in a unit trust.

(5) (*a*) Where a collective investment undertaking which is not a specified collective investment undertaking—

(i) makes a relevant payment of or out of relevant profits to a unit holder resident in the State, or

(ii) has at the end of an accounting period of the undertaking any undistributed relevant income,

it shall deduct out of the amount of the relevant payment or the amount of the undistributed relevant income, as the case may be, the appropriate tax.

(*b*) Where appropriate tax is deducted in accordance with paragraph (*a*)—

(i) the unit holder to whom the relevant payment is made or the unit holder or unit holders entitled to the relevant income, as the case may be, shall allow the deduction, and

(ii) the collective investment undertaking shall, on the making of the relevant payment to the unit holder or on the making of any relevant payment out of the undistributed relevant income to any unit holder, as the case may be, be acquitted and discharged of so much money as is represented—

(I) by the deduction, or

(II) where the relevant payment is less than the amount of the undistributed relevant income, by so much of the deduction as is referable to the relevant payment,

as if the amount of money had actually been paid to the unit holder.

(*c*) Schedule 18 shall apply for the purposes of supplementing this subsection.

(6) (*a*) Where a unit holder receives a relevant payment from a collective investment undertaking which is not a specified collective investment undertaking and appropriate tax has been deducted from the payment, or from the relevant

profits or part of those profits out of which the payment is made, then, the unit holder shall—

(i) if the unit holder is not resident in the State for tax purposes at the time the payment is made, be entitled, on due claim and on proof of the facts, to repayment of the appropriate tax, or so much of it as is referable to the relevant payment, as the case may be, or

(ii) in any other case, be entitled—

(I) to have the unit holder's liability to tax under any assessment made in respect of the relevant payment or any part of the relevant payment reduced by a sum equal to so much, if any, of the appropriate tax as is referable to the amount of the relevant payment contained in the assessment, and

(II) where the appropriate tax so referable exceeds the unit holder's liability to tax in respect of the relevant payment, or in respect of that part of the relevant payment contained in the assessment, to repayment of the excess.

(*b*) For the purposes of paragraph (*a*)(ii), the inspector or on appeal the Appeal Commissioners shall make such apportionment of the appropriate tax deducted from a relevant payment, or from the relevant profits out of which the relevant payment or any part of the relevant payment is made, as is just and reasonable to determine the amount of the appropriate tax, if any, referable to any part of the relevant payment contained in an assessment.

(7) Section 732 shall not apply as on and from—

(*a*) the 24th day of May, 1989, to—

(i) a qualifying unit trust (within the meaning of section 732), and

(ii) the disposal of qualifying units (within the meaning of that section) in such a qualifying unit trust,

where the qualifying unit trust is also a specified collective investment undertaking, and

(*b*) (i) the 6th day of April, 1990, or

(ii) where this section applies by virtue of subsection (12)(*b*) on an earlier day to a qualifying unit trust which is a collective investment undertaking, such earlier day in respect of the qualifying unit trust,

to such a qualifying unit trust or to the disposal of such qualifying units in the qualifying unit trust, where the qualifying unit trust is a collective investment undertaking without also being a specified collective investment undertaking.

(8) Section 805 shall not apply to a collective investment undertaking if but for this subsection it would otherwise apply.

(9) As respects any collective investment undertaking which is a company (within the meaning of the Corporation Tax Acts)—

(*a*) a relevant payment made out of the relevant profits of the undertaking or a payment made in respect of the cancellation, redemption or repurchase of a unit in the undertaking shall not be treated as a distribution for any of the purposes of the Tax Acts, and

(*b*) if but for this subsection section 440 would otherwise apply, it shall not apply to the collective investment undertaking.

(10) Notwithstanding section 1034, a person not resident in the State shall not by virtue of that section be assessable and chargeable in the name of an agent in respect of a relevant payment made out of the relevant profits of a collective investment undertaking.

(11) For the purposes of the Tax Acts, a unit holder other than a qualifying management company shall not be treated as carrying on a trade in the State through a branch or agency or otherwise where that unit holder would not be so treated if the unit holder did not hold any units in a specified collective investment undertaking.

(12) This section shall apply as on and from—

(*a*) in the case of a specified collective investment undertaking, the 24th day of May, 1989, and

(*b*) in the case of any other collective investment undertaking, the 6th day of April, 1990, or such earlier day, not being earlier than the 6th day of April, 1989, as the Revenue Commissioners may agree to in writing with any such other collective investment undertaking in respect of that undertaking.

Amendments

1 Definition of "specified company" para (ii) substituted by FA 1998 s 42 with effect from 6 April 1998.

2 Subs (1)(*c*)(i)–(ii) substituted by FA 1999 s 85(*c*) with effect from 6 April 1999.

Cross-references

Accounting for and payment of tax deducted from relevant payments and undistributed relevant income, time and manner of payment, subs (5): Sch 18 para 1(1), (2); statement to be given on making of relevant payment, subss (1)(*a*), (5): Sch 18 para 2.

Capital acquisitions tax, exemption of specified collective investment undertakings, meaning of "specified collective investment undertaking" and "unit" applied: CATCA 2003 s 75.

Certain interest not to be chargeable, meaning of "specified collective investment undertaking" applied: s 198(1)(*c*)(i)(II).

Certain trading operations carried on in Custom House Docks Area, meaning of "specified collective investment undertaking" applied: s 446(2B)(*a*), (7)(*c*)(ii)(V)(A).

Certain unit trusts not to be collective investment undertakings: s 735(2); option for non-application of s 735: s 736(1).

Dividend withholding tax, meaning of collective investment undertaking applied: s 172A(1)(*a*) ("collective investment undertaking").

Interest payments by companies and to non-residents, meaning of "specified collective investment undertaking" applied: s 246(3)(*c*)(ii).

Investment undertakings (gain arising on a chargeable event), meaning of "unit" and "unit holder" applied: s 739D(1)(*c*), (8)(*a*).

Investment undertakings (interpretation and application), meanings of "qualifying management company", "specified collective investment undertaking" and "specified company" applied: s 739B(1); s 739B(4).

Penalty, subs (5): Sch 29 column 3.

Special investment scheme is not a collective investment undertaking (within the meaning of this section): s 737(6)(*a*).

Revenue precedents

Issue: Would investment by Lloyds syndicates, some of whose members are resident in Ireland for tax purposes, prejudice the tax exempt status of the fund?

Decision: No, Lloyds syndicates are regarded as non-resident investors and there is no look through to the individual Lloyds "names".

Issue: Would the take-over of a foreign fund, with Irish resident investors, by an SCIU prejudice the tax exempt status of the SCIU?
Decision: No, provided the Irish investors are removed from the fund within 3 months of the date of the take-over.
Issue: Would the holding of units by an Irish resident nominee company on behalf of non-residents prejudice the exempt status of the SCIU?
Decision: No, provided the nominee company is in the business of holding shares in a nominee capacity and advance approval is received from the Revenue Commissioners.

Statement of practice

Revenue powers: SP GEN/1/94, May 1994.

Definitions

Appeal Commissioners: ss 2(1), 5(1); branch or agency: s 5(1); chargeable gain: ss 4(1), 5(1), 534; company: ss 4(1), 5(1); Corporation Tax Acts: s 1(2); distribution: s 4(1); inspector: ss 2(1), 5(1), 852; person: IA 1937 s 11(*c*); profits: s 4(1); resident: s 5(1); shares: s 5(1); standard rate: ss 3(1), 15; Tax Acts: s 1(2); trade: s 3(1); unit trust: s 5(1); units: s 5(1); unit holder: s 5(1); writing: IA 1937 Sch.

Former enactments

FA 1989 s 18(1)–(9) and (11)–(12); FA 1991 s 19(1)–(2); FA 1993 s 20(*a*); FA 1994 s 25(1); SI 227/1994; FA 1995 s 38; FA 1996 s 35(1); FA 1997 s 32.

735 Certain unit trusts not to be collective investment undertakings

(1) This section shall apply to any unit trust scheme (within the meaning of the Unit Trusts Act, 1972) where there is or was at any time in respect of any or all units issued after the 14th day of June, 1973, a requirement for participation in that unit trust scheme that a policy of assurance on human life be effected (but without those units becoming the property of the owner of the policy either as benefits or otherwise).

(2) Notwithstanding section 734, a unit trust scheme to which this section applies shall be deemed not to be a collective investment undertaking for the purposes of that section and Schedule 18.

Cross-references

Option for non-application of s 735: s 736(1).

Definitions

unit trust: s 5(1).

Former enactments

FA 1990 s 35(1)–(2).

736 Option for non-application of section 735

(1) Where the trustees of a unit trust scheme (within the meaning of the Unit Trusts Act, 1990), which apart from section 735 would be a collective investment undertaking for the purposes of section 734 and Schedule 18, have not later than the 1st day of November, 1992—

(*a*) paid the capital gains tax which would have been chargeable on them if—

(i) on the 31st day of March, 1992, they had disposed of all the assets of the unit trust scheme, and

(ii) the resulting chargeable gains were chargeable to tax at one-half of the rate at which they would have been chargeable under the Capital Gains Tax Acts apart from this subparagraph,

and

(*b*) given notice in writing to the Revenue Commissioners that they have paid that tax in accordance with paragraph (*a*),

then, notwithstanding section 735, the unit trust scheme (in this section referred to as **"the relevant unit trust"**) shall be deemed to be and to have been a collective investment undertaking for the purposes of section 734 and Schedule 18 with effect from the 1st day of April, 1992.

(2) (*a*) Where units in a relevant unit trust were held by a person on the 31st day of March, 1992, they shall be treated, for the purposes of computing chargeable gains accruing to the person on or after the 1st day of April, 1992, as having been acquired by the person on the 31st day of March, 1992.

(*b*) Section 731(6) shall not apply to disposals on or after the 1st day of April, 1992, of units in a relevant unit trust.

(3) Where the consideration received for a disposal, or given for an acquisition, of an asset on the 31st day of March, 1992, is to be determined as a result of this section, it shall be deemed to be an amount equal to the market value of the asset on that day, and for this purpose **"market value"**, in relation to any asset, shall be construed in accordance with section 548.

Definitions

chargeable gain: ss 4(1), 5(1), 534; unit trust: s 5(1); writing: IA 1937 Sch.

Former enactments

FA 1992 s 36.

737 Special investment schemes

(1) (*a*) In this section—

"inspector", **"ordinary shares"**, and **"qualifying shares"** have the same meanings respectively as in section 723;

"authorised unit trust scheme" means a unit trust scheme which is or is deemed to be an authorised unit trust scheme (within the meaning of the Unit Trusts Act, 1990) and which has not had its authorisation under that Act revoked;

"market value" shall be construed in accordance with section 548;

...[1]

"special investment scheme" means an authorised unit trust scheme in respect of which the conditions specified in subsection (2) are satisfied;

[**"special investment units"** means units sold to an individual on or after 1 February 1993 and before 1 January 2001 by the management company or trustee under an authorised unit trust scheme in respect of which—

(*a*) the conditions specified in subsection (3) are satisfied, and

(*b*) a declaration of the kind specified in subsection (4) has been made to the management company or trustee;][2]

"specified qualifying shares", in relation to a special investment scheme, means qualifying shares in a company which, when the shares are acquired for the scheme, has an issued share capital the market value of which is less than [€255,000,000][3];

"units", in relation to an authorised unit trust scheme, means any units (whether described as units or otherwise) into which are divided the beneficial interests in the assets subject to any trust created under the scheme.

(*b*) A reference in this section to the management company or trustee under an authorised unit trust scheme shall be construed as a reference to the person in whom are vested the powers of management relating to property for the time being subject to any trust created pursuant to the scheme or, as the case may be, to the person in whom such property is or may be vested in accordance with the terms of the trust.

(2) (*a*) The conditions referred to in the definition of **"special investment scheme"** are as follows:

(i) the beneficial interests in the assets subject to any trust created under the authorised unit trust scheme concerned shall be divided into special investment units;

(ii) the aggregate of the consideration given for shares which are at any time before the 1st day of February, 1994, assets subject to any trust created under the scheme shall not be less than—

(I) as respects qualifying shares, 40 per cent, and

(II) as respects specified qualifying shares, 6 per cent,

of the aggregate of the consideration given for the assets which are at that time subject to any such trust;

(iii) the aggregate of the consideration given for shares which are at any time within the year ending on the 31st day of January, 1995, assets subject to any trust created under the scheme shall not be less than—

(I) as respects qualifying shares, 45 per cent, and

(II) as respects specified qualifying shares, 9 per cent,

of the aggregate of the consideration given for the assets which are at that time subject to any such trust;

(iv) the aggregate of the consideration given for shares which are at any time within the year ending on the 31st day of January, 1996, assets subject to any trust created under the scheme shall not be less than—

(I) as respects qualifying shares, 50 per cent, and

(II) as respects specified qualifying shares, 10 per cent,

of the aggregate of the consideration given for the assets which are at that time subject to any such trust;

[(v) the aggregate of consideration given for shares which are, at any time on or after 1 February 1996 and before 31 December 2000, assets subject to any trust created under the scheme shall not be less than—

(I) as respects qualifying shares, 55 per cent, and

(II) as respects specified qualifying shares, 10 per cent,

of the aggregate of the consideration given for the assets which are at that time subject to any such trust.][4]

(*b*) For the purposes of subparagraphs (ii) to (v) of paragraph (*a*), the amount of the consideration given for assets subject to any trust created under the scheme shall be determined in accordance with sections 547 and 580.

(3) (*a*) The conditions referred to in the definition of **"special investment units"** are as follows:

(i) the special investment units shall be so designated in the trusts created under the authorised unit trust scheme concerned;

(ii) the aggregate of payments made on or before any day to the management company or trustee under the scheme by or on behalf of an individual in respect of special investment units owned, whether jointly or otherwise, by the individual on that day shall not exceed [€63,500][5];

...[6]

(iv) special investment units shall not be sold to or owned by an individual who is not of full age;

(v) special investment units shall only be sold to an individual—

(I) who shall be beneficially entitled to, and

(II) to whom there shall be paid,

all amounts payable in respect of those units by the management company or trustee under the scheme;

(vi) except in the case of special investment units sold to and owned jointly only by a couple married to each other, units shall not be jointly owned;

(vii) except in the case of special investment units bought by and owned jointly only by a couple married to each other, an individual who owns such units of an authorised unit trust scheme shall not buy or own such units of another authorised unit trust scheme;

(viii) where a couple married to each other buy and jointly own special investment units of an authorised unit trust scheme, they shall not buy or own such units in any other such scheme either individually or jointly, other than units which they buy and jointly own in one other such scheme.

(*b*) For the purposes of subparagraphs (ii) to (iv) and (vi) to (viii) of paragraph (*a*), references to ownership of special investment units shall be construed as references to beneficial ownership of the units.

(*c*) For the purposes of subparagraphs (ii) and (iii) of paragraph (*a*), a disposal of special investment units of an authorised unit trust scheme acquired by an individual at different times shall be assumed to be a disposal of units acquired later, rather than of units acquired earlier, by the individual.

(4) The declaration referred to in the definition of **"special investment units"** is a declaration in writing to the management company or trustee under an authorised unit trust scheme which—

(*a*) (i) is made by the individual (in this section referred to as **"the declarer"**) to whom any amounts are payable by the management company or trustee in respect of units in respect of which the declaration is made, and

(ii) is signed by the declarer,

(*b*) is made in such form as may be prescribed or authorised by the Revenue Commissioners,

(*c*) declares that at the time when the declaration is made the conditions specified in subparagraphs (iv) to (viii) of subsection (3)(*a*) are satisfied in relation to the units in respect of which the declaration is made,

(*d*) contains the full name and address of the individual beneficially entitled to any amounts payable in respect of the units in respect of which the declaration is made,

(*e*) contains an undertaking by the declarer that, if any of the conditions referred to in subparagraphs (iv) to (viii) of subsection (3)(*a*) ceases to be satisfied in respect of the units in respect of which the declaration is made, the declarer will notify the management company or trustee accordingly, and

(*f*) contains such other information as the Revenue Commissioners may reasonably require for the purposes of this section.

(5) (*a*) The management company or trustee under an authorised unit trust scheme shall—

(i) keep and retain for not less than the longer of the following periods—

(I) a period of 6 years, and

(II) a period which, in relation to the units in respect of which the declaration is made, ends 3 years after the earliest date on which all of those units stand cancelled, redeemed or bought by the management company or trustee, and

(ii) on being so required by notice given to it in writing by an inspector, make available to the inspector within the time specified in the notice,

all declarations of the kind specified in subsection (4) which have been made to it.

(*b*) The inspector may examine and take copies of or of extracts from a declaration made available to him or her under paragraph (*a*).

(6) (*a*) Notwithstanding section 734, a special investment scheme shall not be a collective investment undertaking for the purposes of that section and Schedule 18; but a special investment scheme shall continue to be treated as a collective investment undertaking (within the meaning of section 734) for the purposes of section 206(*a*) of the Finance Act, 1992.

(*b*) Notwithstanding any other provision of the Tax Acts or the Capital Gains Tax Acts but subject to paragraphs (*c*) and (*d*)—

(i) income tax in respect of income arising to a special investment scheme shall be chargeable at the standard rate, and such income shall not be charged to an additional duty of income tax under section 805, and

(ii) capital gains tax in respect of chargeable gains accruing to a special investment scheme shall be chargeable at the rate specified in section 28(3).

[(*c*) Any income tax or capital gains tax chargeable in accordance with paragraph (*b*) shall be the amount of such tax, before it is reduced by any credit, relief or other deduction under the Tax Acts or the Capital Gains Tax Acts apart from this section, which is 20 per cent of income arising or chargeable gains accruing, as the case may be, to the scheme.][7]

(*d*) Only so much of income arising or gains accruing to the scheme shall be chargeable to income tax or capital gains tax, as the case may be, in accordance with paragraph (*b*) as is or is to be—

(i) paid to, or

(ii) accumulated or invested for the benefit of,

holders of special investment units or as would be so paid, accumulated or invested if any gains accruing to the scheme by virtue of subsection (8) were gains on an actual disposal of the assets concerned.

(7) ...[8]

(*c*) Notwithstanding Chapter 4 of Part 8, that Chapter shall apply to a deposit (within the meaning of that Chapter) for the time being subject to any trust created pursuant to a special investment scheme as if such a deposit were not a relevant deposit (within the meaning of that Chapter).

(8) (*a*) Notwithstanding the Capital Gains Tax Acts, for the purposes of computing chargeable gains arising to a special investment scheme—

(i) each asset which on [31 December][9] is subject to any trust created pursuant to the scheme shall be deemed to have been disposed of and immediately reacquired by the management company or trustee under the scheme on that day at the asset's market value on that day,

(ii) section 556 shall not apply,

(iii) section 607 shall not apply,

(iv) without prejudice to the treatment of losses on such shares as allowable losses, gains accruing on the disposal or deemed disposal of eligible shares (within the meaning of Part 16) in a qualifying company (within the meaning of that Part) shall not be chargeable gains, and

(v) as respects section 581—

(I) subsections (1) and (2) of that section, and

(II) subsection (3) of that section, in so far as a chargeable gain is not thereby disregarded for the purposes of that subsection,

shall apply as if subparagraphs (i) and (iii) had not been enacted.

(*b*) Where in a year of assessment the management company or trustee under a special investment scheme incurs allowable losses on disposals or deemed disposals of assets subject to any trust created pursuant to the scheme, the amount, if any, by which the aggregate of such allowable losses exceeds the aggregate of chargeable gains on such disposals in the year of assessment shall be—

(i) disregarded for the purposes of section 31,

(ii) treated as reducing the income chargeable to income tax arising to the scheme in that year of assessment, and

(iii) to the extent that it is not treated as reducing income arising to the scheme in that year of assessment, treated for the purposes of the Capital Gains Tax Acts and this paragraph as an allowable loss incurred in the next year of assessment on a disposal of an asset subject to a trust created pursuant to the scheme.

[(*bb*) Where in a year of assessment (in this section referred to as the **"year of cessation"**) the business of a special investment scheme ceases and an amount, but for that cessation, would under paragraph (*b*)(iii) be treated as an amount of allowable loss incurred in the next year of assessment, that amount may be deducted from chargeable gains accruing to the special investment scheme in the 3 years of assessment preceding the year of cessation taking chargeable gains accruing in a later year before those accruing in an earlier year, and there shall be made all such amendments of assessments or repayments as may be necessary to give effect to this paragraph.][10]

(*c*) (i) In this paragraph—

"the appropriate amount in respect of the interest" means the appropriate amount in respect of the interest which would be determined in accordance with Schedule 21 if the management company or the trustee was the first buyer and the management company or the trustee carried on a trade to which section 749(1) applies but, in determining the appropriate amount in respect of the interest in accordance with Schedule 21, paragraph 3(4) of that Schedule shall apply as if "in the opinion of the Appeal Commissioners" were deleted;

"securities" has the same meaning as in section 815.

(ii) Where in a year of assessment (in this paragraph referred to as **"the first year of assessment"**) any securities which are assets subject to any trust created pursuant to a special investment scheme are disposed of and in the following year of assessment interest becoming payable in respect of the securities is receivable by the special investment scheme, then, for the purposes of computing the chargeable gains for the first year of assessment, the price paid by the management company or the trustee for the securities shall be treated as reduced by the appropriate amount in respect of the interest.

(iii) Where for a year of assessment subparagraph (ii) applies so as to reduce the price paid for securities, the amount by which the price paid for the securities is reduced shall be treated as a loss arising in the following year of assessment from the disposal of the securities.

(9) (*a*) In this subsection, **"eligible shares"** means eligible shares within the meaning of Part 16 in a qualifying company within the meaning of that Part.

(*b*) Distributions received by the management company or trustee under a special investment scheme in respect of eligible shares which are subject to any trust created in pursuance of the scheme shall not be chargeable to income tax ...[11].

(*c*) Notwithstanding section 508, the Revenue Commissioners shall not designate a special investment scheme for the purposes of Part 16.

(10)(*a*) Any payment made to a holder of special investment units by the management company or trustee under the special investment scheme concerned by reason of rights conferred on the holder as a result of holding such units shall not be reckoned in computing total income for the purposes of the Income Tax Acts.

(*b*) Section 732 shall not apply to a special investment scheme or the disposal of special investment units.

(*c*) No chargeable gain shall accrue on the disposal of, or of an interest in, special investment units.

(*d*) Notwithstanding any other provision of the Income Tax Acts or the Capital Gains Tax Acts, the holder of special investment units of a special investment scheme shall not be entitled to any credit for or payment of any income tax or capital gains tax paid in respect of income arising to, or capital gains accruing to, the scheme.

Amendments

1 Definition of "relevant period" deleted by FA 2001 s 73(1)(*a*) with effect from 1 January 2001.

2 Definition of "special investment units" substituted by FA 2000 s 57(*a*) with effect from 6 April 2000.

3 Substituted by FA 2001 s 240(1) and (2)(*c*) and Sch 5 Pt 1 for accounting periods ending on or after 1 January 2002; previously "£200,000,000"; previously "£100,000,000 (FA 1998 s 53: 6 April 1998).

4 Subs (2)(*a*)(v) substituted by FA 2001 s 73(1)(*b*) with effect from 1 January 2001.

5 Substituted by FA 2001 s 240(1) and (2)(*a*) and Sch 5 Pt 1 for 2002 and later tax years; previously "£50,000".

6 Subs (3)(*a*)(iii) deleted by FA 2001 s 73(1)(*c*) with effect from 1 January 2001.

7 Subs (6)(*c*) substituted by FA 1999 s 63(1)(*c*) with effect from 6 April 1999.

8 Subs (7)(*a*)–(*b*) repealed by FA 2000 s 69(2) and Sch 2 Part 2 with effect from 6 April 1999 in the case of income tax and as respects accounting periods commencing on or after that date in the case of corporation tax

9 Substituted by FA 2001 s 77(2) and Sch 2 paras 40 and 61(*c*) for the short tax "year" 2001 and later tax years; previously "the 5th day of April".

10 Subs (8)(*bb*) inserted by FA 2003 s 50 with effect from 1 January 2003.

11 Repealed by FA 2000 s 69(2) and Sch 2 Part 2 with effect from 6 April 1999 in the case of income tax and as respects accounting periods commencing on or after that date in the case of corporation tax; previously "; but, notwithstanding subsection (7) or section 136, the tax credit in respect of a distribution to which this paragraph applies shall be disregarded for the purposes of the Tax Acts and the Capital Gains Tax Acts".

Cross-references

Interest payments by companies and to non-residents, meaning of "special investment scheme" applied: s 246(1)("investment undertaking").

Investment undertakings (interpretation and application), meaning of "special investment scheme" applied: s 739B(1).

Limits to special investments: s 839(1)(*c*); subs (3)(*a*)(ii): s 839(2)(*a*)(ii), (*b*)(ii)(II); subs (1): (definition of "special investment units", para (*b*)), information regarding beneficial interest: s 839(5)(*c*).

Treatment of debts on a change in currency; meaning of "special investment scheme" applied: s 541A(4)(*a*).

Undertaking for collective investment does not include a unit trust scheme which is a special investment scheme within the meaning of this section: s 738(1)(*a*).

Revenue precedents

Issue: Whether an investor can invest more than £75,000 in one SIP if amounts are held under different account numbers and no amount in one account exceeds £75,000.

Decision: An investor cannot invest more than £75,000 in one SIP. The legislation provides that the aggregate of payments made under the scheme shall not exceed £75,000.

Revenue information

Information leaflet IT17 — Special Savings Accounts and other Special Investment Products.

Definitions

allowable loss: ss 4(1), 5(1), 546; Capital Gains Tax Acts: s 1(2); chargeable gain: ss 4(1), 5(1), 534; company: ss 4(1), 5(1); distribution: ss 4(1), 436, 437; Income Tax Acts: s 1(2); inspector: ss 2(1), 5(1), 852; person: IA 1937 s 11(*c*); shares: s 5(1); standard rate: ss 3(1), 15; tax credit: ss 2(1), 136; Tax Acts: s 1(2); total income: s 3(1); unit trust: s 5(1); writing: IA 1937 Sch; year of assessment: ss 2(1), 5(1); year: IA 1937 Sch.

Former enactments

FA 1993 s 13; FA 1994 s 34(*a*); FA 1996 s 36.

738 Undertakings for collective investment

(1) (*a*) In this section and in section 739—

"chargeable period" means an accounting period of an undertaking for collective investment which is a company or, as respects such an undertaking which is not a company, a year of assessment;

"designated assets" means—

(i) land, or

(ii) shares in a company resident in the State which are not shares—

(I) listed in the official list, or

(II) dealt in on the smaller companies market or the unlisted securities market,

of the Irish Stock Exchange;

"designated undertaking for collective investment" means an undertaking for collective investment which, on the 25th day of May, 1993, owned designated assets for which that undertaking gave consideration (determined in accordance with section 547) the aggregate of which is not less than 80 per cent of the aggregate of the consideration (as so determined) which that undertaking gave for the total assets it owned at that date;

"distribution" has the same meaning as in the Corporation Tax Acts;

"guaranteed undertaking for collective investment" means an undertaking for collective investment all of the issued units of which, on the 25th day of May, 1993, are units in respect of each of which the undertaking will make one payment only, being a payment—

(i) to be made on a specified date in cancellation of those units, and

(ii) which is the aggregate of—

(I) a fixed amount, and

(II) an amount, which may be nil, determined by a stock exchange index or indices;

"relevant Regulations" means the European Communities (Undertakings for Collective Investment in Transferable Securities) Regulations, 1989 (SI No 78 of 1989);

"undertaking for collective investment" means, subject to paragraph (*b*)—

(i) a unit trust scheme, other than—

(I) a unit trust mentioned in section 731(5)(*a*), or

(II) a special investment scheme (within the meaning of section 737),

which is or is deemed to be an authorised unit trust scheme (within the meaning of the Unit Trusts Act, 1990) and has not had its authorisation under that Act revoked,

(ii) any other undertaking which is an undertaking for collective investment in transferable securities within the meaning of the relevant Regulations, being an undertaking which holds an authorisation, which has not been revoked, issued pursuant to the relevant Regulations, or

(iii) any authorised investment company (within the meaning of Part XIII of the Companies Act, 1990) which—

(I) has not had its authorisation under that Part of that Act revoked, and

(II) has been designated in that authorisation as an investment company which may raise capital by promoting the sale of its shares to the public and has not ceased to be so designated,

which is neither a specified collective investment undertaking (within the meaning of section 734(1)) nor an offshore fund (within the meaning of section 743);

"unit" includes a share and any other instrument granting an entitlement—

(i) to a share of the investments or relevant profits of, or

(ii) to receive a distribution from,

an undertaking for collective investment;

"unit holder", in relation to an undertaking for collective investment, means any person who by reason of the holding of a unit, or under the terms of a unit, in the undertaking is entitled to a share of any of the investments or relevant profits of, or to receive a distribution from, the undertaking;

"standard rate" has the same meaning as in section 3(1);

"standard rate per cent" has the same meaning as in section 4(1).

(*b*) For the purposes of this section and section 739, references to an undertaking for collective investment (other than in this paragraph) shall be construed so as to include a reference to a trustee, management company or other such person who—

(i) is authorised to act on behalf, or for the purposes, of the undertaking, and

(ii) habitually does so,

to the extent that such construction brings into account for the purposes of this section and section 739 any matter relating to the undertaking, being a matter which would not otherwise be brought into account for those purposes.

(*c*) For the purposes of this section—

(i) as respects an undertaking for collective investment which is a company, where an accounting period of the company begins before the 6th day of April, 1994, and ends on or after that day, it shall be divided into 2 parts, one beginning on the day on which the accounting period begins and ending on the 5th day of April, 1994, and the other beginning on the 6th day of April, 1994, and ending on the day on which the accounting period ends, and both parts shall be treated as if they were separate accounting periods of the company, and

(ii) without prejudice to section 815(2), any attribution of income or chargeable gains of such an undertaking to periods treated as separate accounting periods by virtue of subparagraph (i) shall be made—

(I) as respects such income, on the basis of the time that income arises to the undertaking, and

(II) as respects such capital gains, on the basis of the time of disposal of the assets concerned,

and section 4(6) shall not apply for the purpose of such attribution.

(2) (*a*) Other than in the case of subsections (7) to (9) of section 734, that section shall not apply, and the following provisions of this section shall apply, to an undertaking for collective investment as respects the chargeable periods of the undertaking ending on or after—

(i) the 6th day of April, 1994, if the undertaking was carrying on a collective investment business on the 25th day of May, 1993, or

(ii) the 25th day of May, 1993, if the undertaking was not carrying on such a business at that date.

[(*b*) (i) As respects an undertaking for collective investment which is a company, the corporation tax which is chargeable on its profits on which corporation tax falls finally to be borne for a chargeable period shall, for the purposes of the Tax Acts, be such tax before it is reduced by any credit, relief or other reduction under those Acts, computed as if the rate of corporation tax were equal to the standard rate for the year of assessment in which the chargeable period falls.][1]

(ii) For the purposes of this paragraph, where part of the chargeable period falls in one year of assessment (in this subparagraph referred to as **"the first-mentioned year"**) and the other part falls in the year of assessment succeeding the first-mentioned year and different standard rates are in force for each of those years, **"the standard rate"** shall be deemed to be a rate per cent determined by the formula—

$$\frac{(A - C)}{E} + \frac{(B \times D)}{E}$$

where—

A is the standard rate per cent in force for the first-mentioned year,

B is the standard rate per cent in force for the year of assessment succeeding the first-mentioned year,

C is the length of that part of the chargeable period falling in the first-mentioned year,

D is the length of that part of the chargeable period falling in the year of assessment succeeding the first-mentioned year, and

E is the length of the chargeable period.

(*c*) In computing profits for the purposes of paragraph (*b*), section 78(2) shall apply as if the rate per cent of capital gains tax specified in section 28(3), were [the rate per cent of corporation tax specified in section 21(1)].[2]

(*d*) As respects an undertaking for collective investment which is not a company—

[(i) the capital gains tax which is chargeable on the chargeable gains accruing in a year of assessment to the undertaking shall be the amount of such tax, before it is reduced by any credit, relief or other deduction under any provision, other than under this section, of the Tax Acts or the Capital Gains Tax Acts, which is the standard rate, for the year of assessment, of the chargeable gains accruing to the undertaking, and][3]

(ii) only so much of income arising or gains accruing to the undertaking shall be chargeable to income tax or capital gains tax, as the case may be, as is or is to be—

(I) paid to, or

(II) accumulated or invested for the benefit of,

unit holders in the undertaking or as would be so paid, accumulated or invested if any gains accruing to the scheme by virtue of subsection (4) were gains on an actual disposal of the assets concerned.

(3) (*a*) (i) Section 129 shall not apply as respects a distribution received by an undertaking for collective investment which is a company...[4].

...[5]

(*c*) Notwithstanding Chapter 4 of Part 8, that Chapter shall apply to a deposit (within the meaning of that Chapter) which is for the time being beneficially owned by an undertaking for collective investment which is not a company as if such a deposit were not a relevant deposit (within the meaning of that Chapter).

(4) (*a*) (i) Every asset of an undertaking for collective investment on the day on which a chargeable period of the undertaking ends shall, subject to subparagraph (ii) and paragraphs (*b*) to (*e*), be deemed to have been disposed of and immediately reacquired by the undertaking at the asset's market value on that day.

(ii) Subparagraph (i) shall not apply to—

(I) assets to which section 607 applies other than where such assets are held in connection with a contract or other arrangement which secures the future exchange of the assets for other assets to which that section does not apply, and

(II) assets which are strips within the meaning of section 55.

(*b*) Subject to paragraphs (*c*) and (*d*), chargeable gains or allowable losses, which would otherwise accrue to an undertaking for collective investment on disposals deemed by virtue of paragraph (*a*) to have been made in a chargeable period (other than a period in which the collective investment business of the undertaking concerned ceases) of the undertaking, shall be treated, subject to subparagraphs (ii) and (iii), as not accruing to it, and instead—

(i) there shall be ascertained the difference (in this subsection referred to as **"the net amount"**) between the aggregate of those gains and the aggregate of those losses,

(ii) one-seventh of the net amount shall be treated as a chargeable gain or, where it represents an excess of losses over gains, as an allowable loss accruing to the undertaking on disposals of assets deemed to be made in the chargeable period, and

(iii) a further one-seventh shall be treated as a chargeable gain or, as the case may be, as an allowable loss accruing on disposals of assets deemed to be made in each succeeding chargeable period until the whole amount has been accounted for.

(*c*) For any chargeable period of less than one year, the fraction of one-seventh referred to in paragraph (*b*)(iii) shall be proportionately reduced and, where this paragraph has applied in relation to any chargeable period before the last such period for which paragraph (*b*)(iii) applies, the fraction treated as accruing in that last chargeable period shall be reduced so as to secure that no more than the whole of the net amount has been accounted for.

(*d*) Where the collective investment business of the undertaking concerned ceases before the beginning of the last of the chargeable periods for which paragraph (*b*)(iii) would apply in relation to a net amount, the fraction of that amount that is treated as accruing in the chargeable period in which the business ceases shall be such as to secure that the whole of the net amount has been accounted for.

(*e*) Where in a chargeable period an undertaking for collective investment incurs a loss on the disposal (in this paragraph referred to as **"the first-mentioned disposal"**) of an asset the gain or loss in respect of a deemed disposal of which was included in a net amount to which paragraph (*b*)(ii) applied for any preceding chargeable period, so much of the allowable loss on the first-mentioned disposal as is equal to the excess of the amount of the loss over the amount which but for paragraph (*a*) would have been the allowable loss on the first-mentioned disposal shall be treated for the purposes of paragraph (*b*) as an allowable loss which would otherwise accrue to the undertaking for collective investment on disposals deemed by virtue of paragraph (*a*) to have been made in the chargeable period.

(5) Notwithstanding the Capital Gains Tax Acts, for the purposes of computing chargeable gains accruing to an undertaking for collective investment—

(*a*) (i) section 556, and

(ii) section 607,

shall not apply,

(*b*) section 581 shall as respects—

(i) subsections (1) and (2) of that section, and

(ii) subsection (3) of that section, in so far as a chargeable gain is not thereby disregarded for the purposes of that subsection,

apply as if subsection (4), paragraph (*a*)(ii) and paragraph (*c*) had not been enacted, and

(*c*) if the undertaking was carrying on a collective investment business on the 25th day of May, 1993, it shall be deemed to have acquired each of the assets it holds on the 5th day of April, 1994, apart from assets to which section 607 applies, at the asset's market value on that date.

(6) Subject to subsection (4)(*b*), where an undertaking for collective investment incurs allowable losses on disposals or deemed disposals of assets in a chargeable period, the

amount (if any) by which the aggregate of such allowable losses exceeds the aggregate of chargeable gains on such disposals in the chargeable period shall—

(*a*) be disregarded for the purposes of section 31,

(*b*) be treated as reducing the income chargeable to income tax or corporation tax arising to the undertaking in that chargeable period, and

(*c*) to the extent that it is not treated as reducing income arising to the undertaking in that chargeable period, be treated for the purposes of the Capital Gains Tax Acts and this subsection as an allowable loss incurred on a disposal of an asset deemed to be made in the next chargeable period.

(7) (*a*) In this subsection—

"the appropriate amount in respect of the interest" means the appropriate amount in respect of the interest which would be determined in accordance with Schedule 21 if the undertaking for collective investment was the first buyer and it carried on a trade to which section 749(1) applies but, in determining the appropriate amount in respect of the interest in accordance with Schedule 21, paragraph 3(4) of that Schedule shall apply as if **"in the opinion of the Appeal Commissioners"** were deleted;

"securities" has the same meaning as in section 815.

(*b*) Where in a chargeable period an undertaking for collective investment disposes of any securities and in the following chargeable period or its basis period interest becoming payable in respect of the securities is receivable by the undertaking for collective investment, then, the gain or loss accruing on the disposal shall be computed as if the price paid by the undertaking for collective investment for the securities was reduced by the appropriate amount in respect of the interest.

(*c*) Where for a chargeable period paragraph (*b*) applies so as to reduce the price paid for securities, the amount by which the price paid for the securities is reduced shall be treated as a loss arising in the following chargeable period from the disposal of the securities.

(8) Notwithstanding any provision of the Tax Acts or the Capital Gains Tax Acts other than section 739, unit holders in an undertaking for collective investment shall not be entitled to any credit for or repayment of any income tax, capital gains tax or corporation tax paid in respect of income arising to, capital gains accruing to or profits of the undertaking.

(9) (*a*) Notwithstanding subsection (2) but subject to paragraph (*b*), subsections (1) to (8) and section 739 shall be construed as respects designated undertakings for collective investment and guaranteed undertakings for collective investment as if every reference in those subsections and in that section—

(i) to the 5th day of April, 1994, were a reference to the 5th day of April, 1998, and

(ii) to the 6th day of April, 1994, were a reference to the 6th day of April, 1998,

and, as respects such an undertaking, those subsections and section 739 shall not apply except as so construed.

(*b*) Where—

(i) the aggregate of the consideration (determined in accordance with section 547) given for the designated assets owned at any time after the 25th day of May, 1993, and before the 5th day of April, 1997, by a designated undertaking for collective investment is less than 80 per cent of the aggregate of the consideration (as so determined) given for the total assets owned by the undertaking at that time, or

(ii) at any time before the 5th day of April, 1997, a guaranteed undertaking for collective investment makes any payment to unit holders in the undertaking which is not a payment in cancellation of those units,

paragraph (*a*) shall be construed as respects that undertaking as if each reference in that paragraph—

(I) to the 5th day of April, 1998, were a reference to the 5th day of April, and

(II) to the 6th day of April, 1998, were a reference to the 6th day of April,

subsequent to the time referred to in subparagraph (i) or (ii), as the case may be.

Amendments

1 Subs (2)(*b*)(i) substituted by FA 2000 s 57(*b*) with effect from 6 April 2000.

2 Substituted by FA 1998 s 49 with effect from 6 April 1997; previously "the rate per cent of corporation tax specified in section 21(1)(*b*)".

3 Subs (2)(*d*)(i) substituted by FA 1999 s 64(1) for 1998–99 and later tax years.

4 Repealed by FA 2000 s 69(2) and Sch 2 Part 2 with effect from 6 April 1999 in the case of income tax and as respects accounting periods commencing on or after that date in the case of corporation tax; previously ", and the income represented by the distribution shall be equal to the aggregate of the distribution and the amount of the tax credit in respect of the distribution".

5 Subs (3)(*a*)(ii)–(*b*) repealed by FA 2000 s 69(2) and Sch 2 Part 2 with effect from 6 April 1999 in the case of income tax and as respects accounting periods commencing on or after that date in the case of corporation tax.

Cross-references

Chargeable gains accruing to unit trusts: s 731(7)(*a*).

Dividend withholding tax, meaning of "undertaking for collective investment applied": s 172A(1)(*a*) ("collective investment undertaking").

Investment undertakings (interpretation and application): s 739B(4).

Provisions as to relief from income tax and corporation tax by means of credit in respect of foreign tax, limit on total credit — corporation tax, subs (2): Sch 24 para 4(4)(*c*).

Reorganisation of undertakings for collective investment, meaning of "undertaking for collective investment applied": s 739A(1)(*a*); subs (4)(*a*)(i): s 739A(2).

Restriction on set-off of pre-entry losses, subs (4)(*a*), (*b*): Sch 18A para 1(9).

Taxation of income deemed to arise from certain sales of securities, meaning of "undertaking for collective investment": s 815(3)(*c*)(i).

Treatment of debts on a change in currency, meaning of "undertaking for collective investment" applied: s 541A(4)(*a*); subss (4)(*a*), (*b*): s 541A(4)(*b*)(II), (*c*).

Definitions

allowable loss: ss 4(1), 5(1), 546; Capital Gains Tax Acts: s 1(2); chargeable gain: ss 4(1), 5(1), 534; company: ss 4(1), 5(1); Corporation Tax Acts: s 1(2);distribution: ss 4(1), 436, 437; franked investment income: ss 4(1), 156; land: s 5(1), IA 1937 Sch; person: IA 1937 s 11(*c*); profits: s 4(1); shares: s 5(1); standard credit rate per cent: s 4(1); standard rate: ss 3(1), 15; tax credit: ss 2(1), 136; Tax Acts: s 1(2); unit trust: s 5(1); year of assessment: ss 2(1), 5(1); year: IA 1937 Sch.

Former enactments

FA 1993 s 17; FA 1994 s 57(*a*); FA 1996 s 38(1); FA 1997 s 35.

---

739 Taxation of unit holders in undertakings for collective investment

(1) Subject to this section, as respects a payment made on or after the 6th day of April, 1994, in money or money's worth to a unit holder by reason of rights conferred on the holder as a result of holding units in an undertaking for collective investment—

(*a*) where the holder is not a company, the payment shall not be reckoned in computing the total income of the holder for the purposes of the Income Tax Acts, and

(*b*) where apart from this paragraph the payment would be taken into account for the purposes of computing income chargeable to corporation tax, such payment shall be treated as if it were the net amount of an annual payment chargeable to tax under Case IV of Schedule D from the gross amount of which income tax has been deducted at the standard rate.

(2) (*a*) This subsection shall apply to a payment which—

(i) is made on or after the 6th day of April, 1994, in money or money's worth, by reason of rights conferred on a unit holder as a result of holding units in an undertaking for collective investment, and

(ii) apart from subsection (1) would be charged to corporation tax under Case I of Schedule D.

(*b*) Subsection (1) shall not apply to a payment to which this subsection applies.

(*c*) For the purposes of the Tax Acts other than paragraphs (*d*) and (*e*)—

(i) the income for a chargeable period attributable to a payment to which this subsection applies shall be increased by an amount determined by reference to paragraph (*d*), and

(ii) the amount so determined shall be deemed to be an amount of income tax which shall—

(I) be set off against corporation tax assessable on the unit holder for the chargeable period, or

(II) in so far as it cannot be set off in accordance with clause (I), be repaid to the unit holder.

(*d*) The amount referred to in paragraph (*c*), by which the income attributable to a payment to which this subsection applies is to be increased, shall be determined by the formula—

$$I \times \frac{A}{100 - A}$$

where—

I is the income attributable to a payment to which this subsection applies, and

A is the standard rate per cent for the year of assessment in which the payment is made.

(*e*) For the purposes of this subsection, in computing income attributable to a payment—

(i) an amount shall be deducted from the payment if the payment arises on a sale or other transfer of ownership, or on a cancellation, redemption or repurchase by the undertaking for collective investment, of units or an interest in units, and an amount shall not be deducted otherwise,

(ii) subject to subparagraphs (iii) to (v), the amount of the consideration in money or money's worth given by or on behalf of the unit holder for the acquisition of units or an interest in units for which the payment is made, and not any other amount, shall be deducted from the payment,

(iii) where units are acquired by the unit holder before the 6th day of April, 1994, in an undertaking for collective investment carrying on business on the 25th day of May, 1993, the consideration for the acquisition of the units shall be deemed to be the amount of their market value (within the meaning of section 548) on the 6th day of April, 1994, if that amount is greater than the consideration given, or deemed by virtue of subparagraph (iv) to be given, by the unit holder for their acquisition,

(iv) where units are acquired by a unit holder for a consideration which is less than the market value (within the meaning of section 548) of the units on the day the unit holder acquired them, the consideration given by the unit holder for those units shall be deemed to be that market value, and

(v) the amount of consideration given for units shall be determined in accordance with section 580.

(3) (*a*) Subject to paragraph (*b*) and subsections (5) and (6), as respects a disposal on or after the 6th day of April, 1994, of units in an undertaking for collective investment by a person other than a company—

(i) no chargeable gain shall accrue on the disposal if the person disposing of the units acquired them on or after that date, and

(ii) if the person disposing of the units acquired them before that date, the chargeable gains on the disposal shall be computed as if—

(I) the consideration for the disposal were the market value of the units on the 5th day of April, 1994, and

(II) for the purposes of selecting the appropriate multiplier (within the meaning of section 556) and of applying paragraph 25 of Schedule 32 the disposal were made in the year 1993–94,

and for the purposes of this subsection and subsection (4) references to units shall be construed as including a reference to an interest in units, and accordingly this subsection and subsection (4) shall apply with any necessary modifications.

(*b*) Clause (I) of paragraph (*a*)(ii) shall not apply in relation to the disposal of units if as a consequence of the application of that clause—

(i) a gain would accrue on that disposal to the person making the disposal and either a smaller gain or loss would so accrue if that clause did not apply, or

(ii) a loss would so accrue and either a smaller loss or a gain would accrue if that clause did not apply,

and accordingly, in a case to which subparagraph (i) or (ii) applies, the amount of the gain or loss accruing on the disposal shall be computed without regard to clause (I) of paragraph (*a*)(ii) but, in a case where this paragraph would otherwise substitute a loss for a gain or a gain for a loss, it shall be assumed in relation to the disposal that the units were acquired by the person disposing of them for a consideration such that neither a gain nor a loss accrued to that person on making the disposal.

(4) (*a*) Subject to paragraph (*b*) and subsections (5) and (6), as respects a disposal by a company on or after the 6th day of April, 1994, of units in an undertaking for collective investment, for the purposes of the Corporation Tax Acts—

(i) any chargeable gain accruing on the disposal shall, notwithstanding section 21(3), be treated as if it were the net amount of a gain from the gross amount of which capital gains tax has been deducted at the standard rate of income tax,

(ii) the amount to be taken into account in respect of the chargeable gain in computing in accordance with section 78 the company's chargeable gains for the accounting period in which the company disposes of the units shall be the gross amount of the chargeable gain, and

(iii) the capital gains tax treated as deducted from the gross amount of the chargeable gain shall—

(I) be set off against the corporation tax assessable on the company for the accounting period, or

(II) in so far as it cannot be set off in accordance with clause (I), be repaid to the company.

(*b*) As respects a disposal by a company of units which it acquired before the 6th day of April, 1994, in an undertaking for collective investment carrying on business on the 25th day of May, 1993, paragraph (*a*) shall apply only to so much of the chargeable gain accruing to the company on that disposal of units as does not exceed the chargeable gain which would have accrued on that disposal had the company sold and immediately reacquired those units on the 5th day of April, 1994, at their market value on that day.

(*c*) This subsection shall be disregarded for the purposes of section 546(2).

(5) (*a*) Where a person (in this subsection referred to as **"the disponer"**) disposing of units in an undertaking for collective investment acquired them—

(i) on or after the 6th day of April, 1994, and

(ii) in such circumstances that by virtue of any enactment other than section 556(4) the disponer and the person from whom the disponer acquired them (in this subsection referred to as **"the previous owner"**) were to be treated for the purposes of the Capital Gains Tax Acts as if the disponer's acquisition were for a consideration of such an amount as would secure that, on the disposal under which the disponer acquired them, neither a gain nor a loss accrued to the previous owner,

then, the previous owner's acquisition of the interest shall be treated as the disponer's acquisition of the interest.

(*b*) Where the previous owner acquired the units disposed of on or after the 6th day of April, 1994, and in circumstances similar to those referred to in paragraph (*a*), the acquisition of the units by the previous owner's predecessor shall be treated for the purposes of this section as the previous owner's acquisition, and so on back through previous acquisitions in similar circumstances until the first such acquisition before the 6th day of April, 1994, or, as the case may be, until an acquisition on a disposal on or after that date.

(6) Where an undertaking for collective investment was not carrying on a collective investment business on the 25th day of May, 1993, this section shall apply as respects payments by, or disposals of units in, that undertaking as if—

(*a*) **"on or after the 6th day of April, 1994,"** were deleted from subsections (1), (2), (3) and (4), and

(*b*) paragraphs (*a*)(ii) and (*b*) were deleted from subsection (3).

Cross-references

Chargeable gains accruing to unit trusts, subs (3): s 731(5)(*a*).
Investment undertakings (interpretation and application): s 739B(4).
Tax credits: s 738(8), (9)(*a*).
Undertaking for collective investment, meanings of "chargeable period", designated assets", designated undertaking for collective investment", "distribution", "guaranteed undertaking for collective investment", "relevant Regulations", "undertaking for collective investment", "unit", "unit holder", standard rate", "standard rate per cent": s 738(1)(*a*); references to include references to a trustee, management company or other person authorised to act on behalf of the undertaking: s 738(1)(*b*).

Definitions

chargeable gain: ss 4(1), 5(1), 534; chargeable period: s 738(1)(*a*); Corporation Tax Acts: s 1(2); designated assets: s 738(1)(*a*); designated undertaking for collective investment: s 738(1)(*a*); distribution: s 738(1)(*a*); guaranteed undertaking for collective investment: s 738(1)(*a*); interest: s 4(1); Income Tax Acts: s 1(2); person: IA 1937 s 11(*c*); relevant Regulations: s 738(1)(*a*); undertaking for collective investment: s 738(1)(*a*); unit: s 738(1)(*a*); unit holder: s 738(1)(*a*); standard rate: s 738(1)(*a*); standard rate per cent: s 738(1)(*a*); tax: s 3(1); Tax Acts: s 1(2); total income: s 3(1); year of assessment: ss 2(1), 5(1).

Former enactments

FA 1993 s 18; FA 1994 s 57(*b*).

739A Reorganisation of undertakings for collective investment

(1) (*a*) In this section **"undertaking for collective investment"** has the meaning assigned to it in section 738(1).

(*b*) Where an undertaking for collective investment (in this section referred to as the "first undertaking") disposes of assets (in this section referred to as "transferred assets") to another undertaking for collective investment in exchange for the issue of units to the first undertaking by that other undertaking for collective investment, no chargeable gains shall accrue to the first undertaking on that disposal.

(2) For the purposes of computing a gain accruing to the first undertaking on a disposal or first deemed disposal, under section 738(4)(*a*)(i), of the units referred to in subsection (1), notwithstanding any other provision of the Capital Gains Tax Acts, the amount or value of the consideration in money or moneys worth given by the first undertaking for the acquisition of the units is—

(*a*) where the transferred assets fell within section 738(4)(*a*)(i), the value of the transferred assets on their latest deemed disposal by the first undertaking under that section, and

(*b*) where the transferred assets did not fall within section 738(4)(*a*)(i), the cost incurred by the first mentioned undertaking in acquiring the transferred assets.][1]

Amendments

[1] Section 739A inserted by FA 2000 s 57(*c*) with effect from 6 April 2000.

Definitions

Capital Gains Tax Acts: s 1(2); chargeable gains: ss 5(1), 545.

[CHAPTER 1A
Investment Undertakings][1]

Amendments

[1] Chapter 1A inserted by FA 2000 s 58(*a*) with effect from 6 April 2000.

Cross-references

Investment undertakings declarations: Sch 2B paras 2(*g*), 3(*f*), 4(*f*), 5(*f*), 6(*f*), 7(*h*), 8(*f*), 9(*g*), 9A(*g*), 10(*h*), 11(*g*), 13(*f*) and 14(*f*).

Power of inspection (returns and collection of appropriate tax), investment undertakings: s 904D(3)(*a*).

Termination of special savings incentive accounts: s 848H(3)(*b*)(iii).

Revenue information

Investment undertakings — General guidelines for calculating tax due and for completing declarations forms can be downloaded from the Revenue Website at www.revenue.ie under "Publications" and "Technical Guidelines". A list of the clearing systems designated by Revenue as recognised clearing systems for the purposes of s 739B is available on the Revenue website www.revenue.ie under Publications/Lists.

Tax Briefing

TB42 Dec 2000 p 29 — Investment Undertakings — Overview of new tax regime.

739B Interpretation and application

[(1) In this Chapter and in Schedule 2B—

"the Acts" means the Tax Acts and the Capital Gains Tax Acts;

"approved minimum retirement fund" has the meaning assigned to it in section 784C;

"approved retirement fund" has the meaning assigned to it in section 784A;

"chargeable event", in relation to an investment undertaking in respect of a unit holder, means—

(*a*) the making of a relevant payment by the investment undertaking,

(*b*) the making of any other payment by the investment undertaking to a person, by virtue of that person being a unit holder (whether or not in respect of the cancellation, redemption or repurchase of a unit) ...,[1]

(*c*) the transfer by a unit holder, by way of sale or otherwise ...,[2] of entitlement to a unit in the investment undertaking, ...[3]

[(*cc*) the appropriation or cancellation of units of a unit holder by an investment undertaking for the purposes of meeting the amount of appropriate tax payable on any gain arising by virtue of paragraph (*c*), and][4]

(*d*) a chargeable event shall be deemed to happen on 31 December 2000 in respect of all unit holders (if any) at that date in relation to an investment undertaking—

(i) which commenced on or after 1 April 2000, or

(ii) which was on 31 March 2000 a specified collective investment undertaking, but does not include—

[(I) any exchange by a unit holder, effected by way of a bargain made at arm's length by an investment undertaking which is an umbrella scheme, of units in a sub-fund of the investment undertaking, for units in another sub-fund of the investment undertaking,

(II) any exchange by a unit holder, effected by way of a bargain made at arm's length by an investment undertaking, of units in the investment undertaking for other units in the investment undertaking,

[(II*a*) any transaction in relation to, or in respect of, relevant units (within the meaning of subsection (2A)(*a*)) in an investment undertaking which transaction arises only by virtue of a change of court funds manager for that undertaking,][5]

(III) any transaction in relation to, or in respect of, units which are held in a recognised clearing system, and

(IV) the transfer by a unit holder of entitlement to a unit where the transfer is—

(A) between a husband and wife,

(B) between the spouses or former spouses concerned (as the case may be), by virtue or in consequence of an order made under Part Ill of the Family Law (Divorce) Act, 1996, on or following the granting of a decree of divorce,

(C) between the spouses concerned, by virtue or in consequence of an order made under Part II of the Family Law Act, 1995, on or following the granting of a decree of judicial separation within the meaning of that Act, or

(D) between the spouses or former spouses concerned (as the case may be), by virtue of an order or other determination of like effect, which is analogous to an order referred to in subparagraph (B) or (C), of a court under the law of a territory other than the State made under or in consequence of the dissolution of a marriage or the legal separation of the spouses, being a dissolution or legal separation that is entitled to be recognised as valid in the State,

but on the happening of a chargeable event following such a transfer, the then unit holder shall be treated as having acquired the unit transferred at the same cost as the person who transferred the unit;][6]

"collective investor", in relation to an authorised investment company (within the meaning of Part XIII of the Companies Act, 1990), means an investor, being a life assurance company, pension fund or other investor—

(*a*) who invests in securities or any other property whatever with moneys contributed by 50 or more persons

(i) none of whom has at any time directly or indirectly contributed more than 5 per cent of such moneys, and

(ii) each of a majority of whom has contributed moneys to the investor with the intention of being entitled, otherwise than on death of any person or by reference to a risk of any kind to any person or property, to receive from the investor—

(I) a payment which, or

(II) payments the aggregate of which,

exceeds those moneys by a part of the profits or income arising to the investor,

and

(*b*) who invests in the authorised investment company primarily for the benefit of those persons;

[**"court funds manager"** means a person appointed by the Service to set up and administer an investment undertaking with money under the control or subject to the order of any Court;][7]

[**"credit union"** has the meaning assigned to it in section 2 of the Credit Union Act 1997;][8]

"distribution" has the same meaning as in the Corporation Tax Acts;

"intermediary" means a person who—

(*a*) carries on a business which consists of, or includes, the receipt of payments from an investment undertaking on behalf of other persons, or

(*b*) holds units in an investment undertaking on behalf of other persons;

"investment undertaking" means—

(*a*) a unit trust scheme, other than—

(i) a unit trust mentioned in section 731(5)(*a*), or

(ii) a special investment scheme,

which is or is deemed to be an authorised unit trust scheme (within the meaning of the Unit Trusts Act, 1990) and has not had its authorisation under that Act revoked,

(*b*) any other undertaking which is an undertaking for collective investment in transferable securities within the meaning of the relevant Regulations, being an undertaking which holds an authorisation, which has not been revoked, issued pursuant to the relevant Regulations,

(*c*) any authorised investment company (within the meaning of Part XIII of the Companies Act, 1990)—

(i) which has not had its authorisation under that Part of that Act revoked, and

(ii) (I) which has been designated in that authorisation as an investment company which may raise capital by promoting the sale of its shares to the public and has not ceased to be so designated, or

(II) each of the shareholders of which is a collective investor,

and

(*d*) an investment limited partnership (within the meaning of the Investment Limited Partnerships Act, 1994),

which is not an offshore fund (within the meaning of section 743); but includes any company limited by shares or guarantee which—

(A) is wholly owned by such an investment undertaking or its trustees, if any, for the benefit of the holders of units in that undertaking, and

(B) is so owned solely for the purpose of limiting the liability of that undertaking or its trustees, as the case may be, in respect of futures contracts, options contracts or other financial instruments with similar risk characteristics, by enabling it or its trustees, as the case may be, to invest or deal in such investments through the company,

which is not an offshore fund (within the meaning of section 743);

[**"money market fund"** has the same meaning as it has in Regulation (EC) No 2423/2001 of the European Central Bank of 22 November 2001 (OJ No L333 of 17 December 2001, p 1);][9]

"pension scheme" means an exempt approved scheme within the meaning of section 774 or a retirement annuity contract or a trust scheme to which section 784 or 785 applies;

"qualifying fund manager" has the meaning assigned to it in section 784A;

"qualifying management company" has the meaning assigned to it in section 734(1);

[**"qualifying savings manager"** has the meaning assigned to it in section 848B (inserted by the Finance Act, 2001);][10]

...[11]

"relevant gains", in relation to an investment undertaking, means gains accruing to the investment undertaking, being gains which would constitute chargeable gains in the hands of a person resident in the State including gains which would so constitute chargeable gains if all assets concerned were chargeable assets and no exemption from capital gains tax applied;

"relevant income", in relation to an investment undertaking, means any amounts of income, profits or gains which arise to or are receivable by the investment undertaking, being amounts of income, profits or gains—

(*a*) which are or are to be paid to unit holders as relevant payments,

(*b*) out of which relevant payments are or are to be made to unit holders, or

(*c*) which are or are to be accumulated for the benefit of, or invested for the benefit of, unit holders,

and which if they arose to an individual resident in the State would in the hands of the individual constitute income for the purposes of income tax;

"relevant payment" means a payment including a distribution made to a unit holder by an investment undertaking by reason of rights conferred on the unit holder as a result of holding a unit or units in the investment undertaking, where such payments are made annually or at more frequent intervals, other than a payment made in respect of the cancellation, redemption or repurchase of a unit;

"relevant profits", in relation to an investment undertaking, means the relevant income and relevant gains of the investment undertaking;

[**"relevant Regulations"** means the European Communities (Undertaking for Collective Investment in Transferable Securities) Regulations 1989 (SI No 78 of 1989) as amended or extended from time to time and any other regulations that may be construed as one with those Regulations;][12]

"return" means a return under section 739F;

[**"Service"** means the Courts Service;][13]

"specified collective investment undertaking" and **"specified company"** have, respectively, the meanings assigned to them in section 734(1);

"special investment scheme" has the same meaning as in section 737;

[**"special savings incentive account"** has the meaning assigned to it by section 848B (inserted by the Finance Act, 2001);][14]

"standard rate" has the same meaning as in section 3(1);

"umbrella scheme" means an investment undertaking—

(*a*) which is divided into a number of sub-funds, and

(*b*) in which the unit holders are entitled to exchange units in one sub-fund for units in another;

"unit" includes any investment made by a unit holder, such as a subscription for shares or a contribution of capital, in an investment undertaking, being an investment which entitles the investor—

(*a*) to a share of the investments or relevant profits of, or

(*b*) to receive a relevant payment from,

the investment undertaking;

"unit holder", in relation to an investment undertaking, means any person who by reason of the holding of a unit, or under the terms of a unit, in the investment undertaking is entitled to a share of any of the investments or relevant profits of, or to receive a relevant payment from, the investment undertaking.

[(1A) The definition of **"recognised clearing system"** in section 246A(2) applies for the purposes of this Chapter as it applies for the purposes of section 246A.][15]

(2) For the purposes of this Chapter, Schedule 2B and section 904D, references to an investment undertaking (other than in this subsection) shall be construed so as to include a reference to a trustee, management company or other such person who—

(*a*) is authorised to act on behalf, or for the purposes, of the investment undertaking, and

(*b*) habitually does so,

to the extent that such construction brings into account for the purposes of this Chapter, Schedule 2B and section 904D any matter relating to the investment undertaking, being a matter which would not otherwise be brought into account for those purposes; but such construction shall not render the trustee, management company or other such person liable in a personal capacity to any tax imposed by this Chapter on an investment undertaking.

[(2A)(*a*) Where money under the control or subject to the order of any Court is applied to acquire units (in this section referred to as **"relevant units"**) in an investment undertaking, subsections (2) and (3) of section 739E, section 739F and section 904D shall apply as if references in those sections and subsections to the investment undertaking were to read as references to the Service.

(*b*) The Service shall in respect of each year of assessment, on or before 28 February in the year following the year of assessment, make a return (including where it is the case, a nil return) to the Revenue Commissioners in electronic format approved by them, which in respect of each year of assessment—

(i) specifies the total amount of gains (in this section referred to as the **"total gains"**) arising to the investment undertaking in respect of relevant units, and

(ii) specifies in respect of each person who is or was beneficially entitled to those units—

(I) where available, the name and address of the person,

(II) the amount of the total gains to which the person has beneficial entitlement, and

(III) such other information as the Revenue Commissioners may require.][16]

[(3) This Chapter applies to an investment undertaking and the unit holders in relation to that investment undertaking where the investment undertaking—

(*a*) is on 31 March 2000 a specified collective investment undertaking, from 1 April 2000,

(*b*) first issued units on or after 1 April 2000, from the day of such first issue, or

(*c*) was a unit trust mentioned in section 731(5)(*a*), from the day on which the unit trust became an investment undertaking.][17]

(4) Where this Chapter applies to an investment undertaking, sections 734, 738 and 739 shall not apply to that investment undertaking or to unit holders in relation to that investment undertaking.

(5) Schedule 2B has effect for the purposes of supplementing this Chapter.

(6) For the purposes of this Chapter and Schedule 2B, where a holder of units in an investment undertaking is—

(*a*) an investment undertaking,

(*b*) a special investment scheme, or

(*c*) a unit trust to which section 731(5)(*a*) applies,

the unit holder shall be treated as being entitled to the units so held.][18]

Amendments

1 Deleted by FA 2001 s 74(1)(*a*)(i)(I)(A) with effect from 15 February 2001; previously "other than a payment made on the death of a unit holder".

2 Deleted by FA 2001 s 74(1)(*a*)(i)(I)(B) with effect from 15 February 2001; previously "(other than as a result of the death of the unit holder)".

3 Deleted by FA 2004 s 29(1)(*a*)(i) as respects the appropriation or cancellation of a unit (within the meaning of TCA 1997 s 739B) on or after 4 February 2004; previously "and".

4 Subs (1)(*cc*) inserted by FA 2004 s 29(1)(*a*)(ii) as respects the appropriation or cancellation of a unit (within the meaning of TCA 1997 s 739B) on or after 4 February 2004.

5 Definition of "chargable event" para (II*a*) inserted by FA 2005 s 40(*a*)(i) with effect from 1 January 2005.

6 Definition of "chargeable event" paras (A) — (B) substituted by FA 2001 s 74(1)(*a*)(i)(I)(C) with effect from 15 February 2001.

7 Definition of "court funds manager" inserted by FA 2005 s 40(*a*)(ii) with effect from 1 January 2005.

8 Definition of "credit union" inserted by FA 2003 s 53(*a*)(i)(I) with effect from 1 January 2003.

9 Definition of "money market fund" inserted by FA 2003 s 53(*a*)(i)(II) with effect from 1 January 2003.

10 Definition of "qualifying savings manager" inserted by FA 2001 s 74(1)(*a*)(i)(II) with effect from 15 February 2001.

11 Definition of "recognised clearing system" deleted by FA 2003 s 49(3)(*c*)(i) with effect from 28 March 2003.

12 Definition of "relevant Regulations" inserted by FA 2003 s 53(*a*)(i)(III) with effect from 1 January 2003.

13 Definition of "Service" inserted by FA 2003 s 53(*a*)(i)(IV) with effect from 1 January 2003.

14 Definition of "special savings incentive account" inserted by FA 2001 s 74(1)(*a*)(i)(III) with effect from 15 February 2001.

15 Subs (1A) inserted by FA 2003 s 49(3)(*c*)(ii) with effect from 28 March 2003.

16 Subs (2A) inserted by FA 2003 s 53(*a*)(ii) with effect from 1 January 2003.

17 Subs (3) substituted by FA 2001 s 74(1)(*a*)(ii) with effect from 1 April 2000.

18 Section 739B inserted by FA 2000 s 58(*a*) with effect from 6 April 2000.

Cross-references

Capital acquisitions tax, exemption of specified collective investment undertakings, meanings of "investment undertaking" and "unit" applied: CATCA 2003 s 75.

Certain trading operations carried on in Custom House Docks Area, meaning of "investment undertaking" and "unit holder" applied: s 446(2B), (7)(*c*)(II)(B).

Cross-border pension schemes, exemption of — for the purposes of section 739B(1), the reference to "an exempt approved scheme within the meaning of section 774" in the definition of "pension scheme" in s 739B(1) is deemed to include a reference to a scheme referred to in s 790B(2): s 790B(4).

Dividend withholding tax, interpretation, meaning of "investment undertaking" applied: s 172A(1)("collective investment undertaking").

Gain arising on a chargeable event, subs (1)(para (II*a*) of definition of "chargeable event"): s 739D(1)(*bb*).

Interest in respect of wholesale debt instruments, Revenue may designate by order one or more clearing systems to be a "recognised clearing system" for the purposes of TCA 1997 ss 64 and 246A and this section: s 246A(1)(*b*).

Life assurance companies, taxation of policyholders — new basis, personal portfolio life policy, meaning of "investment undertaking" and "units" applied: s 730BA(1); personal portfolio life policy, meaning of "investment undertaking" and "units" applied: s 730BA(1); gains arising on a chargeable event, meaning of "investment undertaking" applied: s 730D(2)(*b*)(ii); declarations: s 730E(3)(*e*)(ii).

Interest payments by companies and to non-residents, meaning of "investments undertaking" applied: s 246(1)("investment undertaking").

Power of inspection (returns and collection of appropriate tax), investment undertakings, meaning of "investment undertaking" and "unit holder" applied: s 904D(1).

Special savings incentive accounts, interpretation, meaning of "investment undertaking" applied: s 848B(1).

Stamp duties, certain stocks and marketable securities, meaning of "investment undertaking" applied: SDCA 1999 s 88(1)(*b*), (2)(*b*); certain financial services instruments, meaning of "investment undertaking" applied: SDCA 1999 s 90(3)(*b*).

Revenue information

A list of the clearing systems designated by Revenue as recognised clearing systems for the purposes of this section is available on the Revenue website www.revenue.ie under Publications/Lists.

Definitions

Capital Gains Tax Acts: s 1(2); chargeable gain: ss 4(1), 5(1); company: ss 4(1), 5(1); Corporation Tax Acts: s 1(2); distribution: s 4(1); person: IA 1937 s 11(*c*); Tax Acts: s 1(2); year of assessment: ss 2(1); 5(1).

739C Charge to tax

[[(1) Notwithstanding anything in the Acts, an investment undertaking shall ...[1] not be chargeable to tax in respect of relevant profits otherwise than to the extent provided for in this Chapter.

...[2]][3]

(2) Notwithstanding Chapter 4 of Part 8, that Chapter shall apply to a deposit (within the meaning of that Chapter) to which an investment undertaking is for the time being entitled as if such deposit were not a relevant deposit within the meaning of that Chapter.][4]

Amendments

1 Deleted by FA 2005 s 44(*c*)(i) with effect from 1 January 2005; previously ", subject to subsection (1A),".

2 Subs (1A) deleted by FA 2005 s 44(*c*)(ii) with effect from 1 January 2005.

3 Subs (1) substituted and subs (1A) inserted by FA 2003 s 53(*b*) with effect from 1 January 2003.

4 Section 739C inserted by FA 2000 s 58(*a*) with effect from 6 April 2000.

Definitions

the Acts, investment undertaking: s 739B(1).

739D Gain arising on a chargeable event

[(1) [In this Chapter and Schedule 2B][1]—

[(*a*) references to an investment undertaking being associated with another investment undertaking are references to both investment undertakings being set up and promoted by the same person,][2]

(*b*) references to an amount invested by a unit holder in an investment undertaking for the acquisition of a unit (in this paragraph referred to as the "original unit"), where the original unit is a unit in a sub-fund of an umbrella scheme and the original unit has been exchanged for a unit or units of another sub-fund of the umbrella scheme, are references to the amount invested by the unit holder for the acquisition of the original unit, ...[3]

[(*bb*) references to an amount invested by a unit holder in an investment undertaking for the acquisition of a unit (in this paragraph referred to as the "original unit"), where the original unit has been exchanged for a unit or units in a transaction of the type referred to in paragraph (II*a*) of the definition of "chargeable event" in section 739B(1), are references to the amount invested by the unit holder for the acquisition of the original unit, and][4]

(*c*) references to an amount invested by a unit holder in an investment undertaking for the acquisition of a unit shall, where the investment undertaking was on 31 March 2000 a specified collective investment undertaking and the unit was at that time a unit (within the meaning of section 734(1)) held by the unit holder as a unit holder (within the meaning of the said section) in relation to the specified collective investment undertaking, be references to the amount invested by the unit holder for the acquisition of the unit (within the said meaning) of the specified collective investment undertaking, or where that unit was otherwise acquired by the unit holder, the value of that unit at its date of acquisition by the unit holder.

(2) On the happening of a chargeable event in relation to an investment undertaking in respect of a unit holder, there shall, subject to this section, be treated as arising to the investment undertaking a gain in the amount of—

(*a*) where the chargeable event is the making of a relevant payment, the amount of the relevant payment, (*b*) where the chargeable event is the making of any other payment by the investment undertaking to a person, by virtue of that person being a unit holder, otherwise than on the cancellation, redemption or repurchase of a unit, the amount of the payment,

(*c*) where the chargeable event is the making of a payment by the investment undertaking to a unit holder, on the cancellation, redemption or repurchase of a unit—

(i) the amount determined under subsection (3), or

(ii) where the investment undertaking has made an election under subsection (5), the amount of the payment reduced by the amount invested by the unit holder in the investment undertaking in acquiring the unit, and where the unit was otherwise acquired by the unit holder, the amount so invested shall be the value of the unit at the time of its acquisition by the unit holder,

(*d*) where the chargeable event is the transfer by a unit holder of entitlement to a unit,

(i) the amount determined under subsection (4), or

(ii) where the investment undertaking has made an election under subsection (5), the value of the unit transferred at the time of transfer reduced by the amount invested by the unit holder in the investment undertaking in acquiring the unit, and where the unit was otherwise acquired by the unit holder, the amount so invested shall be the value of the unit at the time of its acquisition by the unit holder, ...[5]

(*e*) where the chargeable event is deemed to happen on 31 December 2000, the excess (if any) of the value of the units held by the unit holder on that day over the total amount invested in the investment undertaking by the unit holder for the acquisition of the units, and where any unit was otherwise acquired by the unit holder, the amount so invested to acquire that unit shall be the value of the unit at the time of its acquisition by the unit holder.

[(*dd*) where the chargeable event is the appropriation or cancellation of units by an investment undertaking as a consequence of the transfer by a unit holder of entitlement to a unit, the amount determined under subsection (5A), and][6]

[(3) The amount referred to in subsection (2)(*c*) is the amount determined by the formula—

$$P - \frac{(C \times P)}{V}$$

where—

P is the amount in money or money's worth payable to the unit holder on the cancellation, redemption or repurchase of units, without having regard to any amount of appropriate tax (within the meaning of section 739E) thereby arising,

C is the total amount invested by the unit holder in the investment undertaking to acquire the units held by the unit holder immediately before the chargeable event and—

(*a*) where any unit was otherwise acquired by the unit holder, or (*b*) where a chargeable event was deemed to happen on 31 December 2000 in respect of the unit holder of that unit,

the amount so invested to acquire the unit is—

(i) where paragraph (*a*) applies, the value of the unit at the time of its acquisition by the unit holder, and

(ii) where paragraph (*b*) applies, the greater of the cost of first acquisition of the unit by the unit holder and the value of the unit on 31 December 2000, without having regard to any amount of appropriate tax (within the meaning of section 739E) thereby arising,

and

V is the total value of the units held by the unit holder immediately before the chargeable event.

(4) The amount referred to in subsection (2)(*d*) is the amount determined by the formula—

$$V1 - \frac{(C \times V1)}{V2}$$

where—

V1 is the value of the units transferred, at the time of transfer, without having regard to any amount of appropriate tax (within the meaning of section 739E) thereby arising,

C is the total amount invested by the unit holder in the investment undertaking to acquire the units held by the unit holder immediately before the chargeable event and—

(*a*) where any unit was otherwise acquired by the unit holder, or

(*b*) a chargeable event was deemed to happen on 31 December 2000 in respect of the unit holder of that unit,

the amount so invested to acquire the unit is—

(i) where paragraph (*a*) applies, the value of the unit at the time of its acquisition by the unit holder, and

(ii) where paragraph (*b*) applies, the greater of the cost of first acquisition of the unit by the unit holder and the value of the unit on 31 December 2000, without having regard to any amount of appropriate tax (within the meaning of section 739E) thereby arising,

and

V2 is the total value of the units held by the unit holder immediately before the chargeable event.

(5) (*a*) The election referred to in paragraphs (*c*) and (*d*) of subsection (2) is an irrevocable election made by an investment undertaking in respect of all its unit holders at the time of the election or at any other time, so that, for the purposes of identifying units acquired with units subsequently disposed of by a unit holder, units acquired at an earlier time are deemed to have been disposed of before units acquired at a later time.

(*b*) On the first occasion that an investment undertaking is required to compute a gain on the happening of a chargeable event in respect of a unit holder on the cancellation, redemption, repurchase or transfer of a unit, and—

(i) the gain is computed in accordance with paragraph (*a*), the investment undertaking will be deemed to have made the election specified in that paragraph, or

(ii) the gain is not computed in accordance with paragraph (*a*), an election under paragraph (*a*) shall not be made.][7]

[(5A) The amount referred to in subsection (2)(*dd*) is the amount determined by the formula—

$$A \times G \times \frac{100}{100 - (G \times (S + 3))}$$

where—

A is the appropriate tax payable on the transfer by a unit holder of entitlement to a unit in accordance with subsection (2)(*d*),

G is the amount of the gain on that transfer of that unit divided by the value of that unit, and

S is the standard rate per cent (within the meaning of section 4).][8]

(6) A gain shall not be treated as arising to an investment undertaking on the happening of a chargeable event in respect of a unit holder where, immediately before the chargeable event, the unit holder—

(*a*) is a pension scheme which has made a declaration to the investment undertaking in accordance with paragraph 2 of Schedule 2B,

(*b*) is a company carrying on life business within the meaning of section 706, and which company has made a declaration to the investment undertaking in accordance with paragraph 3 of Schedule 2B,

(*c*) is another investment undertaking which has made a declaration to the investment undertaking in accordance with paragraph 4 of Schedule 2B,

(*d*) is a special investment scheme which has made a declaration to the investment undertaking in accordance with paragraph 5 of Schedule 2B,

(*e*) is a unit trust to which section 731(5)(*a*) applies, and the unit trust has made a declaration to the investment undertaking in accordance with paragraph 6 of Schedule 2B,

[(*f*) (i) is a person who—

(I) is exempt from income tax under Schedule D by virtue of section 207(1)(*b*), or

(II) is exempt from corporation tax by virtue of section 207(1)(*b*) as it applies for the purposes of corporation tax under section 76(6),

and

(ii) has made a declaration to the investment undertaking in accordance with paragraph 7 of Schedule 2B,][9] (*g*) is a qualifying management company or a specified company and has made a declaration to the investment undertaking in accordance with paragraph 8 of [Schedule 2B,][10]

[(*h*) is a person who is entitled to exemption from income tax and capital gains tax by virtue of section 784A(2) (as amended by the Finance Act 2000) or by virtue of section 848E (inserted by the Finance Act, 2001) and the units held are assets of an approved retirement fund, an approved minimum retirement fund or, as the case may be, a special savings incentive account, and the qualifying fund manager, or, as the case may be, the qualifying savings manager has made a declaration to the investment undertaking in accordance with paragraph 9 of [Schedule 2B,][11]][12]

[(*i*) is a person who is entitled to exemption from income tax and capital gains tax by virtue of section 787I (as inserted by section 4 of the Pensions (Amendment) Act, 2002) and the units held are assets of a PRSA (within the meaning of Chapter 2A of Part 30) and the PRSA administrator (within the meaning of that Chapter 2A) has made a declaration to the investment undertaking in accordance with paragraph 9A of Schedule 2B,][13]

[(*j*) is a credit union that has made a declaration to the investment undertaking in accordance with paragraph 9B of Schedule 2B, or

(*k*) (I) is a company that—

(A) is or will be within the charge to corporation tax in accordance with section 739G(2), in respect of payments made to it by the investment undertaking,

(B) has made a declaration to that effect and has provided the investment undertaking with the company's tax reference number (within the meaning of section 885), and

(II) the investment undertaking is a money market fund,][14]

and the investment undertaking is in the possession of the declaration immediately before the chargeable event.

(7) Subject to subsection (8), a gain shall not be treated as arising to an investment undertaking on the happening of a chargeable event in respect of a unit holder where, immediately before the chargeable event, the investment undertaking—

(*a*) is in possession of a declaration of a kind referred to in—

(i) paragraph 10 of Schedule 2B, or

(ii) where the unit holder is not a company, paragraph 11 of that Schedule, and

(*b*) is not in possession of any information which would reasonably suggest that—

(i) the information contained in that declaration is not, or is no longer, materially correct,

(ii) the unit holder failed to comply with the undertaking referred to in paragraph 10(*g*) or 11(*f*), as the case may be, of Schedule 2B, or

(iii) immediately before the chargeable event the unit holder is resident or ordinarily resident in the State.

[(7A) Where an investment undertaking is in possession of—

(*a*) a declaration made by a unit holder who is a person referred to in subsection (6), or

(*b*) a declaration made by a unit holder of the kind referred to in subsection (7) and paragraph (*b*) of that subsection is satisfied,

which unit holder is entitled to the units in respect of which the declaration was made, a gain shall not be treated as arising—

(i) to the investment undertaking on the happening of a chargeable event in respect of the unit holder in relation to any other units in the investment undertaking to which the unit holder becomes entitled, or

(ii) to another investment undertaking which is associated with the investment undertaking referred to in paragraph (i), on the happening of a chargeable event in respect of the unit holder in relation to units in that other investment undertaking to which the unit holder becomes entitled.][15]

[(8) (*a*) A gain shall not be treated as arising to an investment undertaking on the happening of a chargeable event in respect of a unit holder where the investment undertaking was on 31 March 2000 a specified collective investment undertaking and—

(i) the unit holder was a unit holder (within the meaning of section 734(1)) in relation to that specified collective investment undertaking at that time and the investment undertaking on or before 30 June 2000 makes to the Collector-General a declaration in accordance with paragraph 12 of Schedule 2B, or

(ii) the unit holder otherwise became a unit holder on or before 30 September 2000 and the investment undertaking forwarded to the Collector-General, on or before 1 November 2000, a list containing the name and address of each such unit holder who is resident in the State,

otherwise than, subject to paragraph (*b*), in respect of a unit holder (in this subsection and in section 739G referred to as an **"excepted unit holder"**)—

(I) whose name is included in the schedule to the declaration referred to in paragraph 12(*d*) of Schedule 2B or the list referred to in paragraph (ii), and

(II) who has not made a declaration of a kind referred to in subsection (6) to the investment undertaking.

(*b*) A gain shall not be treated as arising to an investment undertaking on the happening of a chargeable event in respect of an excepted unit holder where a chargeable event is deemed to happen on 31 December 2000.

(8A) Where under subsection (8)(*a*) a gain is not treated as arising to an investment undertaking on the happening of a chargeable event in respect of a unit holder who acquired units on or before 30 September 2000, a gain shall not be treated as arising—

(*a*) to the investment undertaking on the happening of a chargeable event in respect of the unit holder in relation to any other units in the investment undertaking to which the unit holder becomes entitled, or

(*b*) to another investment undertaking which is associated with the investment undertaking referred to in paragraph (*a*), on the happening of a chargeable event in respect of the unit holder in relation to units in that other investment undertaking to which the unit holder becomes entitled.

(8B) A gain shall not be treated as arising to an investment undertaking on the happening of a chargeable event in respect of a unit holder where—

(*a*) the investment undertaking was a unit trust mentioned in section 731(5)(*a*),

(*b*) the unit holder held units in that unit trust at the time that it became an investment undertaking, and

(*c*) within 30 days of that time, the investment undertaking forwards to the Collector-General a list containing the name and address of each such unit holder and such other information as the Revenue Commissioners reasonably require.

[(8C)(*a*) In this section a **"scheme of amalgamation"** means an arrangement whereby a unit holder in a unit trust referred to in section 731(5)(*a*) exchanges units so held, for units in an investment undertaking.

(*b*) A gain shall not be treated as arising to an investment undertaking on the happening of a chargeable event in respect of a unit holder where—

(i) the unit holder acquires units in the investment undertaking in exchange for units held in a unit trust referred to in section 731(5)(*a*), under a scheme of amalgamation, and

(ii) within 30 days of the scheme of amalgamation taking place, the investment undertaking forwards to the Collector-General a list containing, in respect of each unit holder who so acquired units in the investment undertaking, the name and address and such other information as the Revenue Commissioners may reasonably require.

(8D)[(*a*) In this subsection—

"offshore fund" means any of the following—

(i) a company not resident in the State,

(ii) a unit trust scheme, the trustees of which are neither resident nor ordinarily resident in the State, and

(iii) any arrangements not within subparagraphs (i) or (ii) which take effect by virtue of the law of a territory outside the State and which under that law create rights in the nature of co-ownership (without restricting that expression to its meaning in the law of the State),

in which persons have an interest and which is established for the purposes of collective investment by such persons and references in this subsection to an offshore fund shall be construed as a reference to any such company, unit trust scheme or arrangements, in which such persons have an interest;

"scheme of migration and amalgamation" means an arrangement whereby the assets of an offshore fund are transferred to an investment undertaking in exchange for the issue by the investment undertaking of units to each of the persons who have an interest in the offshore fund, in proportion to the value of that interest, and as a result of which the value of that interest becomes negligible.

(*b*) A gain shall not be treated as arising to an investment undertaking on the happening of a chargeable event in respect of a unit holder where—

(i) under a scheme of migration and amalgamation the unit holder acquires units in the investment undertaking in exchange for the unit holder's interest in an off-shore fund, and

(ii) within 30 days of the scheme of migration and amalgamation taking place, the investment undertaking forwards to the Collector-General a declaration of a kind referred to in paragraph (*c*),

otherwise than in respect of a unit holder whose name is included in the schedule referred to in paragraph (*c*)(ii).][16]

(*c*) The declaration referred to in paragraph (*b*) is a declaration in writing made and signed by the investment undertaking which—

(i) declares to the best of the investment undertaking's knowledge and belief that at the time of the scheme of migration and amalgamation it did not issue units to a person who was resident in the State at that time, other than such persons whose names and addresses are set out on the schedule to the declaration, and

(ii) contains a schedule which sets out the name and address of each person who was resident in the State at the time that the person was issued units by the investment undertaking under the scheme of migration and amalgamation.][17]

[(9) A gain shall not be treated as arising to an investment undertaking on the happening of a chargeable event in respect of a unit holder, where immediately before the chargeable event the investment undertaking or an investment undertaking associated with the first-mentioned investment undertaking—

(*a*) is, in relation to the units concerned, in possession of a declaration of a kind referred to in paragraph 13 of Schedule 2B, and

(*b*) is not in possession of any information which would reasonably suggest that—

(i) the information contained in that declaration is not, or is no longer, materially correct,

(ii) the intermediary failed to comply with the undertaking referred to in paragraph 13(*e*) of Schedule 2B, or

(iii) any of the persons, on whose behalf the intermediary holds units of, or receives payments from, the investment undertaking, is resident or ordinarily resident in the State.

(9A) A gain shall not be treated as arising to an investment undertaking on the happening of a chargeable event in respect of a unit holder where immediately before the chargeable event the investment undertaking or an investment undertaking associated with the first-mentioned investment undertaking—

(*a*) is, in relation to the units concerned, in possession of a declaration of a kind referred to in paragraph 14 of Schedule 2B, and

(*b*) is not in possession of any information which would reasonably suggest that—

(i) the information contained in that declaration is not, or is no longer, materially correct,

(ii) the intermediary failed to comply with the undertaking referred to in paragraph 14(*e*) of Schedule 2B, or

(iii) any of the persons, on whose behalf the intermediary holds units of, or receives payment from, the investment undertaking, is not a person referred to in [paragraphs (*a*) to (*k*)][18] of section 739D(6).][19]

[(10) An investment undertaking shall keep and retain declarations made to it in accordance with Schedule 2B for a period of 6 years from the time the unit holder of the units in respect of which the declaration was made, ceases to be both such a unit holder and a unit holder in all investment undertakings which are associated with the investment undertaking.][20]][21]

Amendments

1 Substituted by FA 2002 s 44(*a*) with effect from 1 January 2002; previously "In this Chapter".

2 Subs (1)(*a*) substituted by FA 2001 s 74(1)(*b*)(i) with effect from 1 April 2000.

3 Deleted by FA 2005 s 40(*b*)(i) with effect from 1 January 2005; previously "and".

4 Subs (1)(*bb*) inserted by FA 2005 s 40(*b*)(ii) with effect from 1 January 2005.

5 Deleted by FA 2004 s 29(1)(*b*)(i) as respects the appropriation or cancellation of a unit (within the meaning of TCA 1997 s 739B) on or after 4 February 2004; previously "and".

6 Subs (1)(*dd*) inserted by FA 2004 s 29(1)(*b*)(ii) as respects the appropriation or cancellation of a unit (within the meaning of TCA 1997 s 739B) on or after 4 February 2004.

7 Subss (3)–(5) substituted by FA 2001 s 74(1)(*b*)(ii) with effect from 1 April 2000.

8 Subs (5A) inserted by FA 2004 s 29(1)(*b*)(iii) as respects the appropriation or cancellation of a unit (within the meaning of TCA 1997 s 739B) on or after 4 February 2004.

9 Subs (6)(*f*) substituted by FA 2002 s 44(*b*) with effect from 1 January 2002.

10 Substituted by Pensions (Amendment) Act 2002 s 4(1)(*c*)(i) with effect from such date as the Minister for Social, Community and Family Affairs may appoint by order; previously "Schedule 2B, or". By virtue of Pensions (Amendment) Act, 2002 (Commencement) Order 2002, SI No 502 of 2002, this amendment comes into operation on 7 November 2002.

11 Substituted by FA 2003 s 53(*c*)(i) with effect from 1 January 2003; previously "Schedule 2B, or".

12 Subs (6)(*h*) substituted by FA 2001 s 74(1)(*b*)(iii) with effect from 1 April 2000.

13 Subs(6)(*i*) inserted by Pensions (Amendment) Act 2002 s 4(1)(*c*)(iii) with effect from such date or dates as the Minister for Social, Community and Family Affairs may appoint by order. By virtue of Pensions (Amendment) Act, 2002 (Commencement) Order 2002, SI No 502 of 2002, this amendment comes into operation on 7 November 2002.

14 Subss (6)(*j*) and (6)(*k*) inserted by FA 2003 s 53(*c*)(ii) with effect from 1 January 2003.

15 Subs (7A) inserted by FA 2001 s 74(1)(*b*)(iv) with effect from 1 April 2000.

16 Subs (8D)(*a*)–(*b*) substituted by FA 2002 s 44(*c*) with effect from 1 January 2002.

17 Subs (8) substituted and subs (8A)–(8D) inserted by FA 2001 s 74(1)(*b*)(v) with effect from 1 April 2000.

18 Substituted by FA 2003 s 53(*d*) with effect from 1 January 2003; previously "paragraphs (*a*) to (*h*)".

19 Subs (9) substituted and (9A) inserted by FA 2002 s 44(*d*) with effect from 1 January 2002.

20 Subs (10) substituted by FA 2001 s 74(1)(*b*)(vii) with effect from 1 April 2000.

21 Section 739D inserted by FA 2000 s 58(*a*) with effect from 6 April 2000.

Cross-references

Declarations, subs (6)(*a*): Sch 2B para 2; subs (6)(*b*): Sch 2B para 3; subs (6)(*c*): Sch 2B para 4; subs (6)(*d*): Sch 2B para 5; subs (6)(*e*): Sch 2B para 6; subs (6)(*f*): Sch 2B para 7; subs (6)(*g*): Sch 2B para 8; subs (6)(*h*): Sch 2B para 9; subs (6)(i): Sch 2B para 9A; subs (7)(*a*)(i): Sch 2B para 10; subs (7)(*a*)(ii): Sch 2B para 11; subs (8)(*a*): Sch 2B para 12; subs (9)(*a*): Sch 2B para 13.

Deduction of tax on occurrence of a chargeable event, subs (2): s 739E(1)(*a*), (*b*), (*c*).

Taxation of unit holders in investment undertakings, subs (8): s 739G(1).

Definitions

chargeable event: s 739B(1); Collector-General: ss 2(1), 851; company: ss 4(1), 5(1); intermediary, investment undertaking, pension scheme, qualifying management company, relevant payment, special investment scheme, specified collective investment undertaking, specified company, umbrella fund, unit, unit holder: s 739B(1); ordinarily resident: ss 2(1), 5(1), 820; resident: ss 2(1), 5(1), 819; unit trust: s 5(1); writing: IA 1937 Sch.

739E Deduction of tax on the occurrence of a chargeable event

[(1) In this section and sections 739F and 739G, **"appropriate tax"**, in connection with a chargeable event in relation to an investment undertaking in respect of a unit holder, means a sum representing income tax on the amount of the gain arising to an investment undertaking—

(*a*) where the amount of the gain is provided by section 739D(2)(*a*), at the standard rate for the year of assessment in which the gain arises,

(*b*) where the chargeable event happens on or after 1 January 2001 and the amount of the gain is provided by [paragraph (*b*), (*c*), (*d*) or (*dd*)][1] of section 739D(2), at a rate determined by the formula—

$$(S+3) \text{ per cent}$$

where S is the standard rate per cent (within the meaning of section 4), and

(*c*) where the chargeable event happens in the period commencing on 1 April 2000 and ending on 31 December 2000 and the amount of the gain is provided by paragraph (*b*), (*c*), (*d*) or (*e*) of section 739D(2), at a rate of 40 per cent.

(2) An investment undertaking shall account for the appropriate tax in connection with a chargeable event in relation to a unit holder in accordance with section 739F.

(3) An investment undertaking which is liable to account for appropriate tax in connection with a chargeable event in relation to a unit holder shall, at the time of the chargeable event, where the chargeable event is—

(*a*) the making of a payment to a unit holder, be entitled to deduct from the payment an amount equal to the appropriate tax,

(*b*) (i) the transfer by a unit holder of entitlement to a unit, ...[2]

[(*ia*) the appropriation or cancellation of units as a consequence of the transfer by a unit holder of entitlement to a unit, or][3]

(ii) deemed to happen on 31 December 2000,

be entitled to appropriate or cancel such units of the unit holder as are required to meet the amount of appropriate tax,

and the investment undertaking shall be acquitted and discharged of such deduction or, as the case may be, such appropriation or cancellation as if the amount of appropriate tax had been paid to the unit holder and the unit holder shall allow such deduction or, as the case may be, such appropriation or cancellation.][4]

Amendments

1 Substituted by FA 2004 s 29(1)(*c*)(i) as respects the appropriation or cancellation of a unit (within the meaning of TCA 1997 s 739B) on or after 4 February 2004; previously "paragraph (*b*), (*c*) or (*d*)".

2 Deleted by FA 2004 s 29(1)(*c*)(ii)(I) as respects the appropriation or cancellation of a unit (within the meaning of TCA 1997 s 739B) on or after 4 February 2004; previously "or".

3 Subs (3)(*b*)(*ia*) inserted by FA 2004 s 29(1)(*c*)(ii)(II) as respects the appropriation or cancellation of a unit (within the meaning of TCA 1997 s 739B) on or after 4 February 2004.

4 Section 739E inserted by FA 2000 s 58(*a*) with effect from 6 April 2000.

Cross-references

Gain arising on a chargeable event, meaning of "appropriate tax" applied: s 739D(3), (4).

Power of inspection (returns and collection of appropriate tax), investment undertaking, meaning of "appropriate tax" applied: s 904D(1).

Interpretation and application, subs (2) and (3): s 739B(2A)(*a*).

Revenue offences: s 1078(2)(*f*).

Definitions

chargeable event, investment undertaking, unit, unit holder: s 739B(1).

739F Returns and collection of appropriate tax

[(1) Notwithstanding any other provision of the Tax Acts, this section shall apply for the purposes of regulating the time and manner in which appropriate tax in connection with a chargeable event in relation to a unit holder shall be accounted for and paid.

(2) An investment undertaking shall for each financial year make to the Collector-General—

(*a*) a return of the appropriate tax in connection with chargeable events happening on or prior to 30 June, within 30 days of that date, and

(*b*) a return of appropriate tax in connection with chargeable events happening between 1 July and 31 December, within 30 days of that later date,

and where it is the case, the return shall specify that there is no appropriate tax for the period in question.

(3) The appropriate tax in connection with a chargeable event which is required to be included in a return shall be due at the time by which the return is to be made and shall be paid by the investment undertaking to the Collector- General, and the appropriate tax so due shall be payable by the investment undertaking without the making of an assessment; but appropriate tax which has become so due may be assessed on the investment undertaking (whether or not it has been paid when the assessment is made) if that tax or any part of it is not paid on or before the due date.

(4) Where it appears to the inspector that there is an amount of appropriate tax in relation to a chargeable event which ought to have been but has not been included in a return, or where the inspector is dissatisfied with any return, the inspector may make an assessment on the investment undertaking to the best of his or her judgement, and any amount of appropriate tax in connection with a chargeable event due under an assessment made by virtue of this subsection shall be treated for the purposes of interest on unpaid tax as having been payable at the time when it would have been payable if a correct return had been made.

[(5) Where—

(*a*) any item has been incorrectly included in a return as appropriate tax, the inspector may make such assessments, adjustments or set-offs as may in his or her judgement be required for securing that the resulting liabilities, including interest on unpaid tax, whether of the investment undertaking making the return or of any other person, are in so far as possible the same as they would have been if the item had not been included, or

(*b*) any item has been correctly included in a return, but within one year of the making of the return the investment undertaking proves to the satisfaction of the Revenue Commissioners that it is just and reasonable that an amount of appropriate tax (included in the return) which has been paid, should be repaid to the investment undertaking, such amount may be repaid to the investment undertaking.][1]

(6) (*a*) Any appropriate tax assessed on an investment undertaking shall be due within one month after the issue of the notice of assessment (unless that tax is due earlier under subsection (3)) subject to any appeal against the assessment, but no appeal shall affect the date when any amount is due under subsection (3).

(*b*) On determination of the appeal against an assessment under this Chapter, any appropriate tax overpaid shall be repaid.

(7) (*a*) The provisions of the Income Tax Acts relating to—

(i) assessments to income tax,

(ii) appeals against such assessments (including the rehearing of appeals and the statement of a case for the opinion of the High Court), and

(iii) the collection and recovery of income tax,

shall, in so far as they are applicable, apply to the assessment, collection and recovery of appropriate tax.

(*b*) Any amount of appropriate tax shall carry interest at the rate of [0.0322 per cent for each day or part of a day][2] from the date when the amount becomes due and payable until payment.

[(*c*) [Subsections (3) to (5) of section 1080][3] shall apply in relation to interest payable under paragraph (*b*) as they apply in relation to interest payable under section 1080.][4]

(*d*) In its application to any appropriate tax charged by any assessment made in accordance with this Chapter, section 1080 shall apply as if [subsection (2)(*b*)][5] of that section were deleted.

(8) Every return shall be in a form prescribed by the Revenue Commissioners and shall include a declaration to the effect that the return is correct and complete.][6]

Amendments

1 Subs (5) substituted by FA 2001 s 74(1)(*c*) with effect from 1 April 2000.

2 Substituted by FA 2002 s 129(1)(*a*) with effect from 1 September 2002 as regards interest chargeable in respect of an amount due to be paid or remitted, whether before, on, or after that date; previously "1 per cent for each month or part of a month".

3 Substituted by FA 2005 s 145(7)(*a*) and Sch 5 Pt 1 in relation to any unpaid income tax, corporation tax or capital gains tax, as the case may be, that has not been paid before 1 April 2005 regardless of when that tax became due and payable and notwithstanding anything to the contrary in any other enactment other than TCA 1997 s 1082; previously "Subsections (2) to (4) of section 1080".

4 Subs (7)(*c*) substituted by FA 2001 s 74(1)(*d*) with effect from 1 April 2000.

5 Substituted by FA 2005 s 145(7)(*a*) and Sch 5 Pt 1 in relation to any unpaid income tax, corporation tax or capital gains tax, as the case may be, that has not been paid before 1 April 2005 regardless of when that tax became due and payable and notwithstanding anything to the contrary in any other enactment other than TCA 1997 s 1082; previously "subsection (1)(*b*)".

6 Section 739F inserted by FA 2000 s 58(*a*) with effect from 6 April 2000.

Cross-references

Deduction of tax on the occurrence of a chargeable event: s 739E(1), (2).
Interpretation and application: s 739B(1)("return"), (2A)(*a*).
Penalties: Sch 29 column 1.
Power of inspection, investment undertakings: s 904D(1)("return").

Revenue offences: s 1078(2)(*f*).
Taxation of unit holders in investment undertakings, subs (5): s 739G(2)(i).

Definitions

appropriate tax; s 739E(1); chargeable event: s 739B(1); Collector-General: ss 2(1), 851; High Court: IA 1937 Sch; Income Tax Acts: s 1(2); inspector: ss 2(1), 852; investment undertaking: s 739B(1); month: IA 1937 Sch; person: IA 1937 s 11(*c*); unit holder: s 739B(1).

739G Taxation of unit holders in investment undertakings

[(1) Where a chargeable event in relation to an investment undertaking in respect of a unit holder is deemed to happen on 31 December 2000 and the unit holder is an excepted unit holder referred to in section 739D(8), the unit holder shall be treated for all the purposes of the Capital Gains Tax Acts as if the amount of the gain which, but for section 739D(8)(*b*), would have arisen to the investment undertaking on the happening of the chargeable event, were a chargeable gain accruing to the unit holder at that time and notwithstanding section 28, the rate of capital gains tax in respect of that chargeable gain shall be 40 per cent.

(2) As respects a payment in money or money's worth to a unit holder by reason of rights conferred on the unit holder as a result of holding units in an investment undertaking to which this Chapter applies—

(*a*) where the unit holder is not a company and the payment is a payment from which appropriate tax has been deducted, the payment shall not be reckoned in computing the total income of the unit holder for the purposes of the Income Tax Act and shall not be treated as giving rise to a chargeable gain under the Capital Gains Tax Acts,

[(*b*) where the unit holder is not a company and the payment is a payment from which appropriate tax has not been deducted, the payment shall be treated as if it were a payment from an offshore fund to which the provisions of Chapter 4 of this Part apply, and the provisions of section 747D, or section 747E apply as appropriate,][1]

(*c*) where the unit holder is a company, the payment is a relevant payment and appropriate tax has been deducted from the payment, the amount received by the unit holder shall, subject to paragraph (*g*), be treated for the purposes of the Tax Acts as the net amount of an annual payment chargeable to tax under Case IV of Schedule D from the gross amount of which income tax has been deducted at the standard rate,

(*d*) where the unit holder is a company, the payment is a relevant payment and appropriate tax has not been deducted from the payment, the amount of the payment shall, subject to paragraph (*g*), be treated for the purposes of the Tax Acts as income arising to the unit holder, constituting profits or gains chargeable to tax under Case IV of Schedule D,

[(*e*) where the unit holder is a company, the payment is not a relevant payment and appropriate tax has been deducted therefrom, such payment shall, subject to paragraph (*g*), not otherwise be taken into account for the purposes of the Tax Acts,

(*f*) where the unit holder is a company, the payment is not a relevant payment and appropriate tax has not been deducted from the payment, the amount of such payment shall, subject to paragraph (*g*), be treated for the purposes of the Tax

Acts as income arising to the unit holder, constituting profits or gains chargeable to tax under Case IV of Schedule D; but where the payment is in respect of the cancellation, redemption, repurchase or transfer of units, such income shall be reduced by the amount of the consideration in money or money's worth given by the unit holder for the acquisition of those units,][2]

(*g*) where the unit holder is a company chargeable to tax on the payment under Case I of Schedule D—

(i) subject to subparagraph (ii), the amount received by the unit holder increased by the amount (if any) of appropriate tax so deducted shall be income of the unit holder for the chargeable period in which the payment is made,

(ii) where the payment is made on the cancellation, redemption or repurchase of units by the investment undertaking, such income shall be reduced by the amount of the consideration in money or money's worth given by the unit holder for the acquisition of those units, and

(iii) the amount (if any) of appropriate tax deducted shall be set off against corporation tax assessable on the unit holder for the chargeable period in which the payment is made,

(*h*) the amount of a payment made to a unit holder by an investment undertaking, where the unit holder is a company which is not resident in the State or the unit holder, not being a company, is neither resident nor ordinarily resident in the State, shall not be [chargeable to income tax,][3]

[(*i*) otherwise than by virtue of section 739F(5) or paragraph (*j*), no repayment of appropriate tax shall be made to any person who is not a company within the charge to corporation tax, and

(*j*) notwithstanding paragraph (*a*), for the purposes of a claim to relief, under section 189, 189A or 192, or a repayment of income tax in consequence thereof, the amount of a payment made to a unit holder shall be treated as a net amount of income from the gross amount of which has been deducted income tax (of an amount equal to the amount of appropriate tax deducted in making the payment), and such gross amount of income shall be treated as chargeable to tax under Case III of Schedule D.][4]

[(3) References in subsection (2) to payments, from which appropriate tax has not been deducted, made to a unit holder by an investment undertaking, include references to payments made to a unit holder who holds units which are held in a recognised clearing system.

(4) Where the units of an investment undertaking are denominated in a currency other than the currency of the State (in this subsection referred to as **"foreign currency"**), then for the purposes of the Capital Gains Tax Acts the amount of foreign currency given by a unit holder to the investment undertaking for the acquisition of a unit in the investment undertaking shall be deemed to have been disposed of and reacquired by the unit holder—

(*a*) immediately before it was so given, and

(*b*) immediately after the unit holder receives payment for the cancellation, redemption or repurchase of, or as the case may be, transfer of, his or her units.

(5) Where appropriate tax is payable as a result of the death of a person, the amount of such tax, in so far as it has been paid, shall be treated as an amount of capital gains tax paid, for the purposes of [section 104 of the Capital Acquisitions Tax Consolidation Act 2003][5].][6]][7]

Amendments

1 Subs (2)(*b*) substituted by FA 2003 s 53(*e*) with effect from 1 January 2003.

2 Subs (2)(*e*)–(*f*) substituted by FA 2001 s 74(1)(*e*)(i)(II) with effect from 1 April 2000.

3 Substituted by FA 2001 s 74(1)(*e*)(i)(III) with effect from 1 April 2000; previously "chargeable to income tax, and".

4 Subs (2)(*i*) substituted by FA 2001 s 74(1)(*e*)(i)(IV) with effect from 1 April 2000.

5 Substituted by CATCA 2003 s 119 and Sch 3 with effect from 21 February 2003; previously "section 63 of the Finance Act 1985".

6 Subs (3)–(5) inserted by FA 2001 s 74(1)(*e*)(ii) with effect from 1 April 2000.

7 Section 739G inserted by FA 2000 s 58(*a*) with effect from 6 April 2000.

Cross-references

Deduction of tax on occurrence of a chargeable event: s 739E(1).

Gain arising on a chargeable event, subs (2): s 739D(6)(*k*)(I)(A).

Definitions

appropriate tax: s 739E(1); Capital Gains Tax Acts: s 1(2); chargeable event: s 739B(1); company: ss 4(1), 5(1); Income Tax Acts: s 1(2); investment undertaking, relevant payment: s 739B(1); Tax Acts: s 1(2); total income: s 3(1); unit, unit holder: s 739B(1).

739H Investment undertakings: reconstructions and amalgamations

[(1) In this section—

"exchange", in relation to a scheme of reconstruction or amalgamation, means the issue of units (in this section referred to as "new units") by an investment undertaking (in this section referred to as the "new undertaking") to the unit holders of another investment undertaking (in this section referred to as the "old undertaking") in respect of and in proportion to (or as nearly as may be in proportion to) their holdings of units (in this section referred to as "old units") in the old undertaking in exchange for the transfer by the old undertaking of all its assets and liabilities to the new undertaking where the exchange is entered into for the purposes of or in connection with a scheme of reconstruction or amalgamation;

"scheme of reconstruction or amalgamation" means a scheme for the reconstruction of any investment undertaking or investment undertakings or the amalgamation of any 2 or more investment undertakings.

(2) The cancellation of old units arising from an exchange in relation to a scheme of reconstruction or amalgamation shall not be a chargeable event and the amount invested by a unit holder for the acquisition of the new units shall for the purposes of this Chapter be the amount invested by the unit holder for the acquisition of the old units.][1]

Amendments

1 Section 739H inserted by FA 2000 s 58(*a*) with effect from 6 April 2000.

Definitions

investment undertaking, unit, unit holder: s 739B(1).

739I Common contractual funds

(1) (*a*) In this section **"common contractual fund"** means—

(i) a collective investment undertaking being an unincorporated body established by a management company under which the participants by contractual arrangement participate and share in the property of the collective investment undertaking as co-owners, where it is expressly stated under its deed of constitution to be established pursuant to an Act of the Oireachtas and which holds an authorisation issued in accordance with such Act and which is not established pursuant to Council Directive No 85/611/EEC of 20 December 1985 (OJ No L375/3, 31.12.1985), as amended by Council Directive No 88/220/EEC of 22 March 1988 (OJ No L100/31, 19.4.1988) and Directive No 95/26/EC of the Council and of the European Parliament of 29 June 1995 (OJ No L168/7, 18.7.1995), or

(ii) an investment undertaking within the meaning of paragraph (*b*) of the definition of **"investment undertaking"** which is constituted otherwise than under trust law or statute law.

(*b*) For the purposes of this section the definitions of **"relevant gains"**, **"relevant income"**, **"relevant payment"**, **"relevant profits"**, **"unit"** and **"unit holder"** shall apply, with any necessary modifications, to a collective investment undertaking within the meaning of paragraph (i) of the definition of **"common contractual fund"** as they apply to an investment undertaking within the meaning of paragraph (*b*) of the definition of **"investment undertaking"**.

(2) (*a*) Notwithstanding anything in the Tax Acts and subject to subsections (3) and (4), a common contractual fund shall not be chargeable to tax in respect of relevant profits.

(*b*) For the purposes of the Tax Acts, relevant income and relevant gains in relation to a common contractual fund shall be treated as arising, or as the case may be, accruing, to each unit holder of the common contractual fund in proportion to the value of the units beneficially owned by the unit holder, as if the relevant income and relevant gains had arisen or, as the case may be, accrued, to the unit holders in the common contractual fund without passing through the hands of the common contractual fund.

(3) Subsection (2) shall only apply where each of the units of the common contractual fund—

(*a*) is an asset of a pension fund or beneficially owned by a person other than an individual, or

(*b*) is held by a custodian or trustee for the benefit of a person other than an individual.

(4) Every common contractual fund shall in respect of each year of assessment, on or before 28 February in the year following the year of assessment, make a statement (including where it is the case, a statement with a nil amount) to the Revenue Commissioners in electronic format approved by them, which in respect of each year of assessment—

(*a*) specifies the total amount of relevant profits arising to the common contractual fund in respect of units in that fund, and (*b*) specifies in respect of each person who is a unit holder—

(i) the name and address of the person,

(ii) the amount of the relevant profits to which the person is entitled, and

(iii) such other information as the Revenue Commissioners may require.

(5) Notwithstanding Chapter 4 of Part 8, that Chapter shall apply to a deposit (within the meaning of that Chapter) to which a common contractual fund is for the time being entitled as if such deposit were not a relevant deposit within the meaning of that Chapter.][1]

Amendments

1 Section 739I inserted by FA 2005 s 44(*d*) with effect from 1 January 2005.

Cross-references

Capital acquisitions tax, exemption of specified collective investment undertakings, meaning of "investment undertaking and "unit" applied: CATCA 2003, s 75(1).

Dividend withholding tax, interpretation, meaning of "common contractual fund" applied: s 172A(1)(*a*) ("collective investment undertaking").

Interest payments to companies and to non-residents, meaning of "common contractual fund" applied: s 246(1) ("investment undertaking").

Stamp duties, certain stocks and marketable securities, meaning of "common contractual fund" applied: SDCA s 88(1)(*b*)(i).

Definitions

investment undertaking: s 739B(1); person: IA 1937 s 11(*c*); relevant gains, relevant income, relevant payment, relevant profits: s 739B(1); Tax Acts: s 1(2); unit, unit holder: s 739B(1); year of assessment: s 2(1).

CHAPTER 2
Offshore Funds

Cross-references

Capital gains tax: rate of charge, meaning of "material interest", "non-qualifying fund" and "offshore fund" applied: s 747A(1).

Distributing funds, the distribution test: Sch 19 para 1(1).

Funds operating equalisation arrangements: Sch 19 para 2(2)(*b*).

Disposal of interests in non-qualifying funds: Sch 20 para 1.

Disposals involving an equalisation element, subs (3): Sch 20 para 6(1).

740 Interpretation (Chapter 2 and Schedules 19 and 20)

In this Chapter and in Schedules 19 and 20—

"account period" shall be construed in accordance with subsections (8) to (10) of section 744;

"disposal" shall be construed in accordance with section 741(2);

"distributing fund" shall be construed in accordance with subsections (2) and (3) of section 744;

"the equalisation account" has the meaning assigned to it by section 742(1);

"Irish equivalent profits" has the meaning assigned to it by paragraph 5 of Schedule 19;

"material interest" shall be construed in accordance with section 743(2);

"non-qualifying fund" has the meaning assigned to it by section 744(1);

"offshore fund" has the meaning assigned to it by section 743(1);

"offshore income gain" shall be construed in accordance with paragraphs 5 and 6(1) of Schedule 20.

Definitions

material interest: s 743(2); profits: s 4(1).

Former enactments

FA 1990 s 62.

741 Disposals of material interests in non-qualifying offshore funds

(1) This Chapter shall apply to a disposal by any person of an asset if at the time of the disposal—

(*a*) the asset constitutes a material interest in an offshore fund which is or has at any material time been a non-qualifying offshore fund, or

(*b*) the asset constitutes an interest in a company resident in the State or in a unit trust scheme, the trustees of which are at that time resident in the State and at a material time on or after the 1st day of January, 1991, the company or unit trust scheme was a non-qualifying offshore fund and the asset constituted a material interest in that fund,

and, for the purpose of determining whether the asset disposed of is within paragraph (*b*), subsection (3) of section 584 shall apply as it applies for the purposes of the Capital Gains Tax Acts.

(2) Subject to subsections (3) to (7) and section 742, there shall be a disposal of an asset for the purposes of this Chapter if there would be such a disposal for the purposes of the Capital Gains Tax Acts.

(3) Notwithstanding anything in paragraph (*b*) of section 573(2), where a person dies and the assets of which he or she was competent to dispose include an asset which is or has at any time been a material interest in a non-qualifying offshore fund, then, for the purposes of this Chapter (other than section 742) that interest shall, immediately before the acquisition referred to in paragraph (*a*) of section 573(2), be deemed to be disposed of by the deceased for such a consideration as is mentioned in that paragraph; but nothing in this subsection shall affect the determination in accordance with subsection (1) of the question whether that deemed disposal is one to which this Chapter applies.

(4) Subject to subsection (3), section 573 shall apply for the purposes of this Chapter as it applies for the purposes of the Capital Gains Tax Acts, and the reference in that subsection to the assets of which a deceased person was competent to dispose shall be construed in accordance with subsection (1) of that section.

(5) Notwithstanding anything in section 586 or 587, in any case where—

(*a*) a company (in this subsection referred to as **"the acquiring company"**) issues shares or debentures in exchange for shares in or debentures of another company (in this subsection referred to as **"the acquired company"**) and the acquired company is or was at a material time a non-qualifying offshore fund and the acquiring company is not such a fund, or (*b*) persons are to be treated in consequence of an arrangement as exchanging shares, debentures or other interests in or of an entity which is or was at a material time a non-qualifying offshore fund for assets which do not constitute interests in such a fund,

then, section 586(1) shall not apply for the purposes of this Chapter.

(6) In any case where (apart from subsection (5)) section 586(1) would apply, the exchange concerned of shares, debentures or other interests in or of a non-qualifying fund shall for the purposes of this Chapter constitute a disposal of interests in the offshore fund for a consideration equal to their market value at the time of the exchange.

(7) (*a*) In this subsection, **"relevant consideration"** means consideration which, assuming the application to the disposal of the Capital Gains Tax Acts, would be taken into account in determining the amount of the gain or loss accruing on the disposal, whether that consideration was given by or on behalf of the person making the disposal or by or on behalf of a predecessor in title of the person making the disposal whose acquisition cost represents directly or indirectly the whole or any part of the acquisition cost of the person making the disposal.

(*b*) For the purposes of this section, a material time in relation to the disposal of an asset shall be any time on or after—

(i) the 6th day of April, 1990, where the asset was acquired on or before that date, or

(ii) where the asset was not so acquired, the earliest date on which any relevant consideration was given for the acquisition of the asset.

Cross-references

Capital gains tax: rate of charge, subss (2) to (7): s 747A(3).

Deduction of offshore income gain in calculating capital gain, subs (6): s 747(6).

Disposal of interests in non-qualifying funds, calculation of unindexed gain, subss (2)–(6): Sch 20 par 2(2).

Disposal, subs (2) applied: s 740.

Offshore fund operating equalisation arrangements, subss (1), (7): s 742(3).

Revenue precedents

Issue: Whether gains arising from the disposal of a material interest in an offshore fund held under a trust are assessable on the trustee or on the beneficiary.

Decision: Under general law, such gains form part of the capital of the trust and accordingly are not available for distribution to the beneficiary. Therefore, they are assessable on the trustee.

Definitions

company: ss 4(1), 5(1); material interest: s 743(2); non-qualifying fund: s 744(1); offshore funds: s 743(1); person: IA 1937 s 11(*c*); shares: s 5(1).

Former enactments

FA 1990 s 63.

Corresponding UK tax provision

Income and Corporation Taxes Act 1988 s 757.

---

742 Offshore funds operating equalisation arrangements

(1) For the purposes of this Chapter, an offshore fund operates equalisation arrangements if and at a time when arrangements are in existence which have the result that where—

(*a*) a person acquires by means of initial purchase a material interest in the fund at some time during a period relevant to the arrangements, and

(*b*) the fund makes a distribution for a period which begins before the date of the acquisition of that interest,

the amount of that distribution paid to the person (assuming the person is still retaining that interest) will include a payment of capital debited to an account (in this Chapter and in Schedules 19 and 20 referred to as **"the equalisation account"**) maintained under the arrangements and determined by reference to the income which had accrued to the fund at the date of the person's acquisition.

(2) For the purposes of this section, a person shall acquire an interest in an offshore fund by means of initial purchase if the person's acquisition is by—

(*a*) subscription for or allotment of new shares, units or other interests issued or created by the fund, or

(*b*) direct purchase from the persons concerned with the management of the fund and their sale to that person is made in their capacity as managers of the fund.

(3) Without prejudice to section 741(1), this Chapter shall apply, subject to subsections (4) to (6), to a disposal by any person of an asset if—

(*a*) at the time of the disposal the asset constitutes a material interest in an offshore fund which at that time is operating equalisation arrangements,

(*b*) the fund is not and has not at any material time (within the meaning of section 741(7)) been a non-qualifying offshore fund, and

(*c*) the proceeds of the disposal are not to be taken into account as a trading receipt.

(4) This Chapter shall not by virtue of subsection (3) apply to a disposal if—

(*a*) the disposal takes place during the period mentioned in subsection (1)(*a*), and

(*b*) throughout so much of that period as precedes the disposal the income of the offshore fund concerned has been of the nature referred to in paragraph 3(1) of Schedule 19.

(5) An event which apart from section 584(3) would constitute a disposal of an asset shall constitute such a disposal for the purpose of determining whether by virtue of subsection (3) there is a disposal to which this Chapter applies.

(6) The reference in subsection (5) to section 584(3) shall be deemed to include a reference to that section as applied by section 586 or 733 but not as applied by section 585.

Cross-references

Deduction of offshore income gain in calculating capital gain, subss (2)(*b*), (3): s 747(7)(*a*); subs (5): s 747(6).
Disposal of material interest in offshore fund: s 741(2), (3); Sch 20 para 1.
Disposals involving an equalisation element, subss (5)–(6): Sch 20 para 8(2).
Equalisation account, meaning applied, subs (1): s 740.
Funds operating equalisation arrangements, subss (3), (5)–(6): Sch 19 para 2(2)(*b*); subs (4): Sch 19 para 2(2)(*c*); subs (2): Sch 19 para 2(7).

Definitions

disposal: s 741(2); distribution: ss 4(1), 436, 437; material interest: s 743(2); offshore funds: s 743(1); person: IA 1937 s 11(*c*); shares: s 5(1); units: s 5(1).

Former enactments

FA 1990 s 64.

Corresponding UK tax provision

Income and Corporation Taxes Act 1988 s 758.

743 Material interest in offshore funds

(1) In this Chapter, references to a material interest in an offshore fund shall be construed as references to such an interest in any of the following—

(*a*) a company resident outside the State,

(*b*) a unit trust scheme the trustees of which are not resident in the State, and

(*c*) any arrangements not within paragraph (*a*) or (*b*) which take effect by virtue of the law of a territory outside the State and which under that law create rights in the nature of co-ownership (without restricting that expression to its meaning in the law of the State),

and any reference in this Chapter to an offshore fund shall be construed as a reference to any such company, unit trust scheme or arrangements in which any person has an interest which is a material interest.

(2) Subject to subsections (3) to (9), a person's interest in a company, unit trust scheme or arrangements shall be a material interest if at the time when the person acquired the interest it could be reasonably expected that at some time during the period of 7 years beginning at the time of the acquisition the person would be able to realise the value of the interest (whether by transfer, surrender or in any other manner).

(3) For the purposes of subsection (2), a person shall be deemed to be able to realise the value of an interest if the person can realise an amount which is reasonably approximate to that portion which the interest represents (directly or indirectly) of the market value of the assets of the company or, as the case may be, of the assets subject to the scheme or arrangements.

(4) For the purposes of subsections (2) and (3)—

(*a*) a person shall be deemed to be able to realise a particular amount if the person is able to obtain that amount either in money or in the form of assets to the value of that amount, and

(*b*) if at any time an interest in an offshore fund has a market value which is substantially greater than the portion which the interest represents, as mentioned in subsection (3), of the market value at that time of the assets concerned, the ability to realise such a market value of the interest shall not be regarded as an ability to realise such an amount as is referred to in that subsection.

(5) An interest in a company, scheme or arrangements shall be deemed not to be a material interest if it is either—

(*a*) an interest in respect of any loan capital or debt issued or incurred for money which in the ordinary course of business of banking is loaned by a person carrying on that business, or

(*b*) a right arising under a policy of insurance.

(6) Shares in a company within subsection (1)(*a*) (in this section referred to as **"the overseas company"**) shall not constitute a material interest if—

(*a*) the shares are held by a company and the holding of them is necessary or desirable for the maintenance and development of a trade carried on by the company or a company associated with it,

(*b*) the shares confer at least 10 per cent of the total voting rights in the overseas company and a right in the event of a winding up to at least 10 per cent of the assets of that company remaining after the discharge of all liabilities having priority over the shares,

(*c*) not more than 10 persons hold shares in the overseas company and all the shares in that company confer both voting rights and a right to participate in the assets on a winding up, and

(*d*) at the time of its acquisition of the shares the company had such a reasonable expectation as is referred to in subsection (2) by reason only of the existence of either or both—

(i) an arrangement under which, at some time within the period of 7 years beginning at the time of acquisition, that company may require the other participators to purchase its shares, and

(ii) provisions of either an agreement between the participators or the constitution of the overseas company under which the company will be wound up within a period which is or is reasonably expected to be shorter than the period referred to in subsection (2),

and in this paragraph **"participators"** means the persons holding shares which are within paragraph (*c*).

(7) For the purposes of subsection (6)(*a*), a company shall be associated with another company if one company has control (within the meaning of section 432) of the other company or both companies are under the control (within the meaning of that section) of the same person or persons.

(8) An interest in a company within subsection (1)(*a*) shall be deemed not to be a material interest at any time when the following conditions are satisfied—

(*a*) that the holder of the interest has the right to have the company wound up, and

(*b*) that in the event of a winding up the holder is, by virtue of the interest and any other interest which the holder then holds in the same capacity, entitled to more than 50 per cent of the assets remaining after the discharge of all liabilities having priority over the interest or interests concerned.

(9) The market value of any asset for the purposes of this Chapter shall be determined in the like manner as it would be determined for the purposes of the Capital Gains Tax Acts except that, in the case of an interest in an offshore fund for which there are separate published buying and selling prices, section 548(5) shall apply with any necessary modifications for determining the market value of the interest for the purposes of this Chapter.

Cross-references

Dividend withholding tax (interpretation), "collective investment undertaking" does not include an offshore fund within meaning of this section: s 172A(1)(*a*).

Income taxable under Case III of Schedule D, subs (1): Sch 19 para 3(1).
Investment undertakings, interpretation and application, "investment undertaking" does not include an offshore fund within the meaning of this section: s 739B(1).
Non-qualifying offshore funds, subs (1): s 744(10).
Offshore fund, meaning applied, subs (1): s 740.
Offshore funds with wholly-owned subsidiaries, subs (3): Sch 19 para 11(1)–(4); subs (1): Sch 19 para 11(2).
Returns in relation to material interests in offshore funds, meaning of "material interest" applied, subs (2): s 896(1); meaning of "offshore fund" applied, subs (1): s 896(1).
Taxation and returns of certain offshore funds, interpretation and application, meaning of "material interest" and "offshore fund" applied: s 747B(1).
Undertaking for collective investment, meaning: s 738(1)(*a*).

Definitions

company: ss 4(1), 5(1); material interest: s 743(2); offshore funds: s 743(1); person: IA 1937 s 11(*c*); shares: s 5(1); trade: s 3(1); unit trust: s 5(1).

Former enactments

FA 1990 s 65.

Corresponding UK tax provision

Income and Corporation Taxes Act 1988 s 759.

744 Non-qualifying offshore funds

(1) For the purposes of this Chapter, an offshore fund shall be a non-qualifying fund except during an account period of the fund in respect of which the fund is certified by the Revenue Commissioners as a distributing fund.

(2) An offshore fund shall not be certified as a distributing fund in respect of an account period unless with respect to that period the fund pursues a full distribution policy within the meaning of Part 1 of Schedule 19.

(3) Subject to Part 2 of Schedule 19, an offshore fund shall not be certified as a distributing fund in respect of any account period if at any time during that period—

(*a*) more than 5 per cent by value of the assets of the fund consists of interests in other offshore funds,

(*b*) subject to subsections (4) and (5), more than 10 per cent by value of the assets of the fund consists of interests in a single company,

(*c*) the assets of the fund include more than 10 per cent of the issued share capital of any company or of any class of that share capital, or

(*d*) subject to subsection (6), there is more than one class of material interest in the offshore fund and they do not all receive proper distribution benefits within the meaning of subsection (7).

(4) For the purposes of subsection (3)(*b*), in any account period the value, expressed as a percentage of the value of all the assets of an offshore fund, of that portion of the assets of the fund which consists of an interest in a single company shall be determined as at the most recent occasion (whether in that account period or an earlier one) on which the fund acquired an interest in that company for consideration in money or in money's worth; but for this purpose there shall be disregarded any occasion—

(*a*) on which the interest acquired constituted the new holding for the purposes of section 584, including that section as applied by section 585 or 586, and (*b*) on which no consideration fell to be given for the interest acquired, other than the interest which constituted the original shares for the purposes of section 584, including that section as so applied.

(5) Except for the purpose of determining the total value of the assets of an offshore fund, an interest in a company shall be disregarded for the purposes of subsection (3)(*b*) if—

(*a*) the company carries on a banking business in the State or elsewhere which provides current or deposit account facilities in any currency for members of the public and bodies corporate, and

(*b*) the interest consists of a current or deposit account provided in the normal course of the company's banking business.

(6) There shall be disregarded for the purposes of subsection (3)(*d*) any interests in an offshore fund which—

(*a*) are held solely by persons employed or engaged in or about the management of the assets of the fund,

(*b*) carry no right or expectation to participate directly or indirectly in any of the profits of the fund, and

(*c*) on a winding up or on redemption carry no right to receive anything other than the return of the price paid for the interests.

(7) Where in any account period of an offshore fund there is more than one class of material interests in the fund, the classes of interests shall not (for the purposes of subsection (3)(*d*)) all receive proper distribution benefits unless, were each class of interests and the assets which that class represents interests in and assets of a separate offshore fund, each of those separate funds would (with respect to that period) pursue a full distribution policy within the meaning of Part 1 of Schedule 19.

(8) For the purposes of this Chapter and Schedule 19, an account period of an offshore fund shall begin—

(*a*) on the 6th day of April, 1990, or, if it is later, whenever the fund begins to carry on its activities, and

(*b*) whenever an account period of the fund ends without the fund then ceasing to carry on its activities.

(9) For the purposes of this Chapter and Schedule 19, an account period of an offshore fund shall end on the first occurrence of any of the following—

(*a*) the expiration of 12 months from the beginning of the period;

(*b*) an accounting date of the fund or, if there is a period for which the fund does not make up accounts, the end of that period;

(*c*) the fund ceasing to carry on its activities.

(10) For the purposes of this Chapter and Schedule 19—

(*a*) an account period of an offshore fund which is a company within section 743(1)(*a*) shall end if and at the time when the company ceases to be resident outside the State, and (*b*) an account period of an offshore fund which is a unit trust scheme within section 743(1)(*b*) shall end if and at the time when the trustees of the scheme become resident in the State.

(11) Parts 3 and 4 of Schedule 19 shall apply with respect to the procedure for and in connection with the certification of an offshore fund as a distributing fund.

Cross-references

Account period, subss (8)–(10) applied: s 740.
Certification procedure, application for certification, subss (2)–(3): Sch 19 para 15(1)(*d*).
Disposal of interests in non-qualifying funds, calculation of unindexed gain: Sch 20 par 2(2)(*a*).
Disregarding of investments forming less than 5% of a fund, subs (3)(*c*): Sch 19 para 13(2).
Distributing fund, subss (2)–(3) applied: s 740.
Non-qualifying fund, subs (1): s 740.
Offshore funds investing in trading companies, subs (3): Sch 19 para 10(2)–(4).
Offshore funds with interests in dealing and management companies, subs (3)(*c*): Sch 19 para 12(1).
Offshore funds with wholly-owned subsidiaries, subs (3): Sch 19 para 11(1), (4).
Offshore funds, modifications of conditions for certification in certain cases, subs (3): Sch 19 para 6(2)(*b*), (3)(*a*) and para 7(*b*).
Power of Revenue Commissioners to disregard certain breaches of conditions, subs (3): Sch 19 para 14.

Revenue information

A list of Distributing Offshore Funds approved by Revenue in accordance with this section is available on Revenue's website www.revenue.ie under Publications/Lists.

Definitions

company: ss 4(1), 5(1); material interest: s 743(2); month: IA 1937 Sch; offshore funds: s 743(1); person: IA 1937 s 11(*c*); profits: s 4(1); shares: s 5(1).

Former enactments

FA 1990 s 66.

Corresponding UK tax provision

Income and Corporation Taxes Act 1988 s 760.

745 Charge to income tax or corporation tax of offshore income gain

(1) Where a disposal to which this Chapter applies gives rise, in accordance with Schedule 20, to an offshore income gain, then, subject to this section, the amount of that gain shall be treated for the purposes of the Tax Acts as—

(*a*) income arising at the time of the disposal to the person making the disposal, and

(*b*) constituting profits or gains chargeable to tax under Case IV of Schedule D for the chargeable period (within the meaning of section 321(2)) in which the disposal is made.

(2) Subject to subsection (3), sections 25(2)(*b*), 29 and 30 shall apply in relation to income tax or corporation tax in respect of offshore income gains as they apply in relation to capital gains tax or corporation tax in respect of chargeable gains.

(3) In the application of sections 29 and 30 in accordance with subsection (2), section 29(3)(*c*) shall apply with the deletion of **"situated in the State"**.

(4) In the case of individuals resident or ordinarily resident but not domiciled in the State, subsections (4) and (5) of section 29 shall apply in relation to income tax chargeable by virtue of subsection (1) on an offshore income gain as they apply in

relation to capital gains tax in respect of gains accruing to such individuals from the disposal of assets situated outside the State.

(5) (*a*) In this subsection, **"charity"** has the same meaning as in section 208, and **"market value"** shall be construed in accordance with section 548.

(*b*) A charity shall be exempt from tax in respect of an offshore income gain if the gain is applicable and applied for charitable purposes; but, if the property held on charitable trusts ceases to be subject to charitable trusts and that property represents directly or indirectly an offshore income gain, the trustees shall be treated as if they had disposed of and immediately reacquired that property for a consideration equal to its market value, any gain (calculated in accordance with Schedule 20) accruing being treated as an offshore income gain not accruing to a charity.

(6) In any case where—

(*a*) a disposal to which this Chapter applies is a disposal of settled property within the meaning of the Capital Gains Tax Acts, and

(*b*) for the purposes of the Capital Gains Tax Acts, the general administration of the trusts is ordinarily carried on outside the State and the trustees or a majority of them for the time being are not resident or not ordinarily resident in the State,

then, subsection (1) shall not apply in relation to any offshore income gain to which the disposal gives rise.

Cross-references

Payments in respect of personal injuries: s 189(2)(a)("relevant income").

Payments in respect of thalidomide children: s 192(2).

Special trusts for permanently incapacitated individuals: s 189A(2), (4)(*a*)("relevant income").

Taxation and returns of certain offshore funds, disposal of an interest in an offshore fund: s 747E(1).

Definitions

chargeable gain: ss 4(1), 5(1), 534; charity: ss 5(1), 208; disposal: s 741(2); offshore income gain: Sch 20 paras 5–6(1); person: IA 1937 s 11(*c*); profits: s 4(1); resident: s 5(1); settled property: s 5(1); Tax Acts: s 1(2).

Former enactments

FA 1990 s 67.

Corresponding UK tax provision

Income and Corporation Taxes Act 1988 s 761.

746 Offshore income gains accruing to persons resident or domiciled abroad

[(1) Subject to subsection (2), sections 579 and 579A shall apply in relation to their application to offshore income gains as if—

(*a*) for any references to a chargeable gain there were substituted a reference to an offshore income gain,

(*b*) in subsection (2) of section 579 and subsection (4) of section 579A for "the Capital Gains Tax Acts" there were substituted "the Tax Acts",

(*c*) in subsection (2) of section 579 and subsection (3) of section 579A for "capital gains tax under section 31" there were substituted "income tax by virtue of section 745", and (*d*) in subsection (5) of section 579 and subsection (9) of section 579A—

(i) for "any capital gains tax payable" there were substituted "any income tax or corporation tax payable", and

(ii) for "for the purposes of income tax" there were substituted "for the purposes of income tax, corporation tax".][1]

(2) Where in any year of assessment—

(*a*) under section 579(3), as it applies apart from subsection (1), a chargeable gain is to be attributed to a beneficiary, and

(*b*) under section 579(3), as applied by subsection (1), an offshore income gain is also to be attributed to the beneficiary,

section 579 shall apply as if it required offshore income gains to be attributed before chargeable gains.

[(2A) Where in any year of assessment—

(*a*) under section 579A(4), as it applies apart from subsection (1), a chargeable gain is to be attributed to a beneficiary, and

(*b*) under section 579A(4), as applied by subsection (1), an offshore income gain is also to be attributed to the beneficiary,

section 579A shall apply as if it required offshore income gains to be attributed before chargeable gains.][2]

(3) Section 590 shall apply in relation to its application to offshore income gains as if—

(*a*) for any reference to a chargeable gain there were substituted a reference to an offshore income gain,

[(*b*) for the reference in subsection (9) of that section to capital gains tax there were substituted a reference to income tax or corporation tax, and

(*c*) paragraphs (*a*) and (*b*) of subsection (7), and subsection (11), of that section were deleted.][3]

(4) Section 917 shall apply in relation to offshore income gains as if—

(*a*) for "chargeable gains" there were substituted "offshore income gains", and

[(*b*) for "capital gains tax under sections 579 to 579F or section 590" there were substituted "income tax or corporation tax under sections 579 to 579F or section 590, as applied by section 746.][4]

(5) Subject to subsection (6), for the purpose of determining whether an individual ordinarily resident in the State has a liability for income tax in respect of an offshore income gain arising on a disposal to which this Chapter applies where the disposal is made by a person resident or domiciled out of the State—

(*a*) [sections 806, 807 and 807A][5] shall apply as if the offshore income gain arising to the person resident or domiciled out of the State constituted income becoming payable to such person, and

(*b*) accordingly any reference in [sections 806, 807 and 807A][5] to income of, or payable or arising to, such person shall include a reference to the offshore income gain arising to such person by reason of the disposal to which this Chapter applies.

(6) To the extent that an offshore income gain is treated by virtue of subsection (1) or (3) as having accrued to any person resident or ordinarily resident in the State, that gain shall not be deemed to be the income of any individual for the purposes of [sections 806, 807 and 807A][5] or Part 31.

Amendments

1 Subs (1) substituted by FA 1999 s 58(1)(*a*) with effect from 11 February 1999.

2 Subs (2A) inserted by FA 1999 s 58(1)(*b*) with effect from 11 February 1999.

3 Subs (3)(*b*)–(*c*) substituted by FA 1999 s 58(1)(*c*) with effect from 11 February 1999.

4 Subs (4)(*b*) substituted by FA 1999 s 58(1)(*d*) with effect from 11 February 1999.

5 Substituted by FA 1999 s 58(1)(*e*) with effect from 11 February 1999; previously "sections 806 and 807".

Definitions

chargeable gain: ss 4(1), 5(1), 534; disposal: s 741(2); offshore income gain: Sch 20 paras 5–6(1); person: IA 1937 s 11(*c*); resident: s 5(1); year of assessment: ss 2(1), 5(1).

Former enactments

FA 1990 s 68.

Corresponding UK tax provision

Income and Corporation Taxes Act 1988 s 762.

---

747 Deduction of offshore income gain in determining capital gain

(1) This section shall apply where a disposal (being a disposal to which this Chapter applies) gives rise to an offshore income gain and, if that disposal also constitutes the disposal of the interest concerned for the purposes of the Capital Gains Tax Acts, that disposal is referred to in this section as **"the disposal for the purposes of the Capital Gains Tax Acts"**.

(2) So far as relates to an offshore income gain which arises on a material disposal (within the meaning of Part 1 of Schedule 20), subsections (3) and (4) shall apply in relation to the disposal for the purposes of the Capital Gains Tax Acts in substitution for section 551(2).

(3) Subject to subsections (4) to (7), in the computation in accordance with the Capital Gains Tax Acts of any gain accruing on the disposal for the purposes of those Acts, a sum equal to the offshore income gain shall be deducted from the sum which would otherwise constitute the amount or value of the consideration for the disposal.

(4) Where the disposal for the purposes of the Capital Gains Tax Acts is of such a nature that by virtue of section 557 an apportionment is to be made of certain expenditure, no deduction shall be made by virtue of subsection (3) in determining for the purposes of the apportionment in section 557(2) the amount or value of the consideration for the disposal.

(5) Where the disposal for the purposes of the Capital Gains Tax Acts forms part of a transfer to which section 600 applies, then, for the purposes of subsection (5)(*b*) of that section, the value of the whole of the consideration received by the transferor in exchange for the business shall be taken to be what it would be if the value of the consideration (other than shares so received by the transferor) were reduced by a sum equal to the offshore income gain.

(6) Where the disposal to which this Chapter applies constitutes such a disposal by virtue of section 741(6) or 742(5), the Capital Gains Tax Acts shall apply as if an amount equal to the offshore income gain to which the disposal gives rise were given (by the person making the exchange concerned) as consideration for the new holding (within the meaning of section 584(1)).

(7) In any case where —

(*a*) a disposal to which this Chapter applies by virtue of subsection (3) of section 742 is made otherwise than to the offshore fund concerned or to the persons referred to in subsection (2)(*b*) of that section,

(*b*) subsequently a distribution referable to the asset disposed of is paid either to the person who made the disposal or to a person connected with such person, and

(*c*) the disposal gives rise (in accordance with Part 2 of Schedule 20) to an offshore income gain,

then, for the purposes of the Tax Acts, the amount of the first distribution within paragraph (*b*) shall be taken to be reduced or, as the case may be, extinguished by deducting from such amount an amount equal to the offshore income gain referred to in paragraph (*c*) and, if that amount exceeds the amount of that first distribution, the balance shall be set against the second and, where necessary, any subsequent distribution within paragraph (*b*) until the balance is exhausted.

Cross-references

Taxation and returns of certain offshore funds, disposal of an interest in an offshore fund: s 747E(1).

Definitions

disposal: s 741(2); distribution: ss 4(1), 436, 437; offshore income gain: Sch 20 paras 5–6(1); person: IA 1937 s 11(*c*); Tax Acts: s 1(2).

Former enactments

FA 1990 s 69(1)–(7).

Corresponding UK tax provision

Income and Corporation Taxes Act 1988 s 763.

[CHAPTER 3
Offshore Funds: Supplementary Provisions][1]

Amendments

1 Chapter 3 title inserted by FA 1998 s 66.

747A Capital gains tax: rate of charge

[(1) In this section **"material interest"**, **"non-qualifying fund"** and **"offshore fund"** shall have the same meaning as is assigned to them in Chapter 2 of this Part.

(2) This section shall apply to a disposal, on or after the 12th day of February, 1998, by a person of an asset, if at the time of the disposal—

(*a*) the asset constitutes a material interest in an offshore fund which is not nor was at any material time a non-qualifying offshore fund, or

(*b*) the asset constitutes an interest in a company resident in the State or in a unit trust scheme, the trustees of which are at that time resident in the State and at a material time on or after the 1st day of January, 1991, the company or unit trust scheme was an offshore fund other than a non-qualifying offshore fund and the asset constituted a material interest in that fund.

(3) Subsections (2) to (7) of section 741 shall apply for the purposes of this section as if references in those subsections to a non-qualifying offshore fund were references to an offshore fund.

(4) Notwithstanding subsection (3) of section 28, the rate of capital gains tax in respect of chargeable gains accruing to a person on the disposal of an asset to which this section applies shall be 40 per cent.][1]

Amendments

1 Section 747A inserted by FA 1998 s 66 as respects disposals on or after 12 February 1998.

Definitions

chargeable gain: s 5(1); person: IA 1937 s 11(*c*).

[CHAPTER 4

Certain Offshore Funds — Taxation and Returns][1]

Amendments

1 Part 27 Ch 4 inserted by FA 2001 s 72(1) with effect from 1 January 2001.

Cross-references

Taxation of unit holders in investment undertakings: s 739G(2)(*b*).

747B Interpretation and application

[(1) In this Chapter—

"chargeable period" has the same meaning as in section 321(2);

"EEA Agreement" means the Agreement on the European Economic Area signed at Oporto on 2 May 1992, as adjusted by the Protocol signed at Brussels on 17 March 1993;

"EEA state" means a State, other than the State, which is a Contracting Party to the EEA Agreement;

"material interest" shall be construed in accordance with section 743;

"OECD" means the organisation known as the Organisation for Economic Co-operation and Development;

"offshore fund" has the meaning assigned to it by section 743;

"offshore state" means a State, other than the State, which is—

(i) a Member State of the European Communities,

(ii) a State which is an EEA state, or

(iii) a State which is a member of the OECD, the government of which have entered into arrangements having the force of law by virtue of [section 826(1)(*a*)][1];

"relevant payment" means any payment including a distribution made to a person in respect of a material interest in an offshore fund, where such payments are made annually or at more frequent intervals, other than a payment made in consideration of the disposal of an interest in the offshore fund;

"return of income" has the meaning assigned to it by section 1084;

"specified return date for the chargeable period" has the meaning assigned to it by section 950;

"standard rate per cent" has the meaning assigned to it by section 4;

(2) This Chapter applies to an offshore fund which—

(*a*) being a company, the company is resident in,

(*b*) being a unit trust scheme, the trustees of the unit trust scheme are resident in, or

(*c*) being any arrangements referred to in section 743(1), those arrangements take effect by virtue of the law of,

an offshore state.

(3) For the purposes of this Chapter—

(*a*) (i) there shall be a disposal of an asset if there would be such a disposal for the purposes of the Capital Gains Tax Acts, and

(ii) where, on the death of a person, an asset which the person was competent to dispose, is a material interest in an offshore fund to which this Chapter applies, then, notwithstanding section 573(2)(*b*), such material interest shall be deemed to be disposed of and reacquired by the person immediately before the death of the person for a consideration equal to its then market value,

(*b*) an income shall be correctly included in a return made by a person, only where that income is included in a return of income made by the person on or before the specified return date for the chargeable period in which the income arises, and

(*c*) details of a disposal shall be correctly included in a return made by a person, only where details of the disposal are included in a return of income made by the person or, where the person has died, his or her executor or administrator, on or before the specified return date for the chargeable period in which the disposal is made.][2]

Amendments

1 Substituted by FA 2004 s 89 and Sch 3 para 1(*t*) with effect from 25 March 2004; previously "section 826".

2 Section 747B inserted by FA 2001 s 72(1) with effect from 1 January 2001.

Definitions

Capital Gains Tax Acts: s 1(2); company: ss 4(1), 5(1); market value: ss 5(1), 548; person: IA 1937 s 11(*c*); unit trust: s 5(1).

747C Return on acquisition of material interest

[Where in any chargeable period a person acquires a material interest in an offshore fund, the person shall, notwithstanding anything to the contrary in section 950 or 1084, be deemed for that chargeable period to be a chargeable person for the purposes of sections 951 and 1084, and the return of income to be delivered by the person for that chargeable period shall include the following particulars—

(*a*) the name and address of the offshore fund,

(*b*) a description, including the cost to the person, of the material interest acquired, and

(*c*) the name and address of the person through whom the material interest was acquired.][1]

Amendments

1 Section 747C inserted by FA 2001 s 72(1) with effect from 1 January 2001.

Definitions

chargeable period, material interest, offshore fund: s 747B(1); person: IA 1937 s 11(*c*); return of income: s 747B(1).

747D Payment in respect of offshore funds

[Where on or after 1 January 2001 a person who has a material interest in an offshore fund, is in receipt of a payment from the offshore fund, then—

(*a*) where the person is not a company, and

(i) the income represented by the payment is correctly included in a return made by the person, then notwithstanding section 15, the rate of income tax to be charged on the income shall be—

(I) where the payment is a relevant payment, the standard rate per cent, and

(II) where the payment is not a relevant payment and is not made in consideration of the disposal of an interest in the offshore fund, at the rate determined by the formula—

$$(S + 3) \text{ per cent,}$$

where S is the standard rate per cent, and

(ii) where the income represented by the payment is not correctly included in a return made by the person, the income shall be charged to income tax at a rate determined by section 15,

and

[(*b*) where the person is a company and the payment is not taken into account as a receipt of a trade carried on by the company, the income represented by the payment shall be charged to tax under Case III of Schedule D.][1]][2]

Amendments

1 Para (*b*) substituted by FA 2002 s 46(1)(*a*) with effect from 1 January 2001.

2 Section 747D inserted by FA 2001 s 72(1) with effect from 1 January 2001.

Cross-references

Taxation of unit holders in investment undertakings: s 739G(2)(*b*).

Definitions

company: ss 4(1), 5(1); material interest, offshore fund: s 747B(1); person: IA 1937 s 11(*c*); relevant payment, standard rate per cent: s 747B(1); trade: ss 3(1), 4(1).

747E Disposal of an interest in offshore funds

[(1) Where on or after 1 January 2001 a person who has a material interest in an offshore fund, disposes of an interest in the offshore fund and the disposal gives rise to a gain computed in accordance with subsection (2) then, notwithstanding sections 745 and 747, where the gain is not taken into account in computing the profits or gains of a trade carried on by a company, the amount of that gain shall—

[(*a*) be treated as an amount of income chargeable to tax under Case IV of Schedule D, and the rate of corporation tax to be charged on that income shall, notwithstanding section 21A(3), be the rate of income tax chargeable on income referred to in paragraph (*b*), and][1]

(*b*) where the person is not a company, and the person has correctly included details of the disposal in a return made by the person, the rate of income tax to be charged on that income shall, notwithstanding section 15, be the rate determined by the formula—

$$(S+3) \text{ per cent}$$

where S is the standard rate per cent.][2]

(2) The amount of the gain accruing on a disposal referred to in subsection (1) is the amount which would be the amount of a gain accruing on the disposal for the purposes of the Capital Gains Tax Acts, if it were computed without regard to—

(*a*) any charge to tax by virtue of this section, and

(*b*) section 556(2).

(3) Notwithstanding sections 538 and 546, where apart from this subsection the effect of any computation under subsection (2) would be to produce a loss, the gain on the disposal referred to in subsection (1) shall be treated as nil and [for the purposes of the Tax Acts and the Capital Gains Tax Acts][3] no loss shall be treated as accruing on such disposal.

(4) Where, as a result of a disposal by a person, an amount of income is chargeable to tax under Case IV of Schedule D, that amount shall not be reduced by a claim made by the person—

(*a*) where the person is not a company, under section 381 or 383, or

(*b*) where the person is a company, under [section 396, 396B][4] or 399.

(5) Where an individual is chargeable to tax in accordance with subsection (1) in respect of an amount of income—

(*a*) the tax thereby payable, in so far as it is paid, shall be treated as an amount of capital gains tax paid, for the purposes of [section 104 of the Capital Acquisitions Tax Consolidation Act 2003],[5] and

(*b*) that amount of income shall not be included in reckonable income (within the meaning of the Health Contributions Regulations, 1979 (SI No 107 of 1979)) for the purposes of those Regulations.][6]

Amendments

1 Subs (1)(*a*) substituted by FA 2003 s 55(1) with effect from 1 January 2001.

2 Subs (1) substituted by FA 2002 s 46(1)(*b*) with effect from 1 January 2001.

3 Substituted by FA 2005 s 43(1) as respects the disposal of an interest in an offshore fund on or after 3 February 2005.

4 Substituted by FA 2004 s 30(*a*) with effect from 1 January 2004; previously "section 396".

5 Substituted by CATCA 2003 s 119 and Sch 3 with effect from 21 February 2003; previously "section 63 of the Finance Act 1985".

6 Section 747E inserted by FA 2001 s 72(1) with effect from 1 January 2001.

Cross-references

Reconstructions and amalgamations in offshore funds, subs (2): s 747(2).
Taxation of unit holders in investment undertakings: s 739G(2)(*b*).

Definitions

Capital Gains Tax Acts: s 1(2); company: ss 4(1), 5(1); material interest, offshore fund: s 747B(1); person: IA 1937 s 11(*c*); standard rate per cent: s 747B(1); Tax Acts: s 1(2).

747F Reconstructions and amalgamations in offshore funds

[(1) In this section **"scheme of reconstruction or amalgamation"** means an arrangement under which each person who has a material interest in an offshore fund (in this section referred to as an **"old interest"**) receives in place of that old interest a material interest in another offshore fund (in this section referred to as the **"new interest"**) in respect of or in proportion to, or as nearly as may be in proportion to, the value of the old interest and as a result of which the value of that old interest becomes negligible.

(2) Where, in connection with a scheme of reconstruction or amalgamation, a person disposes of an old interest and receives in place of that old interest a new interest, the disposal of the old interest shall not give rise to a gain but the new interest shall for the purposes of section 747E(2) be treated as acquired at the same time and at the same cost as the old interest.][1]

Amendments

1 Section 747F inserted by FA 2004 s 30(*b*) with effect from 1 January 2004.

Definitions

offshore fund: s 747B(1); person: IA 1937 s 11(*c*).

PART 28
PURCHASE AND SALE OF SECURITIES

CHAPTER 1
Purchase and Sale of Securities

748 Interpretation and application (Chapter 1)

(1) In this Chapter and in Schedule 21—

"distribution" has the same meaning as in the Corporation Tax Acts;

"interest" includes a distribution and any dividend which is not such a distribution and, in applying references to interest in relation to such a distribution, **"gross interest"** or **"gross amount"** means the distribution together with the tax credit to which the recipient of the distribution is entitled in respect of it and **"net interest"** means the distribution exclusive of any such tax credit;

"person" includes any body of persons, and references to a person entitled to any exemption from income tax include, in a case of an exemption expressed to apply to income of a trust or fund, references to the persons entitled to make claims for the granting of that exemption;

"securities" includes stocks and shares;

securities shall be deemed to be similar if they entitle their holders to the same rights against the same persons as to capital and interest and the same remedies for the enforcement of those rights, notwithstanding any difference in the total nominal amounts of the respective securities or in the form in which they are held or the manner in which they can be transferred.

(2) Subject to this section, this Chapter shall apply in the case of a purchase by a person (in this Chapter referred to as **"the first buyer"**) of any securities and their subsequent sale by the first buyer, where the result of the transaction is that interest becoming payable in respect of the securities (in this Chapter referred to as **"the interest"**) is receivable by the first buyer.

(3) This Chapter shall not apply in the case where—

(*a*) the time elapsing between the purchase by the first buyer and the first buyer's taking steps to dispose of the securities exceeds 6 months, or

(*b*) that time exceeds one month and in the opinion of the Revenue Commissioners the purchase and sale were each effected at the current market price and the sale was not effected in pursuance of an agreement or arrangement made before or at the time of the purchase.

(4) An appeal shall lie to the Appeal Commissioners with respect to any opinion of the Revenue Commissioners under subsection (3)(*b*) in the like manner as an appeal would lie against an assessment to income tax, and the provisions of the Income Tax Acts relating to appeals shall apply accordingly.

(5) The reference in subsection (3) to the first buyer taking steps to dispose of the securities shall be construed—

(*a*) if the first buyer sold the securities in the exercise of an option the first buyer had acquired, as a reference to the first buyer's acquisition of the option, and

(*b*) in any other case, as a reference to the first buyer selling the securities.

(6) (*a*) For the purposes of this Chapter but subject to paragraph (*b*), a sale of securities similar to, and of the like nominal amount as, securities previously bought (in this subsection referred to as **"the original securities"**) shall be equivalent to a sale of the original securities and subsection (5) shall apply accordingly, and, where the first buyer bought parcels of similar securities at different times, a subsequent sale of any of the securities shall, in so far as may be, be related to the last of the parcels to be bought, and then to the last but one, and so on.

(*b*) A person shall be under no greater liability to tax by virtue of this subsection than would have been the case if instead of selling the similar securities the person had sold the original securities.

(7) Where, at the time when a trade is or is deemed to be set up and commenced, any securities form part of the trading stock belonging to the trade, those securities shall be treated for the purposes of this section as having been sold at that time in the open market by the person to whom they belonged immediately before that time and as having been purchased at that time in the open market by the person thereafter engaged in carrying on the trade, and, subject to this subsection, where there is a change in the persons engaged in carrying on a trade which is not a change on which the trade is deemed to be discontinued, this section shall apply in relation to the person so engaged after the change as if anything done to or by that person's predecessor had been done to or by that person.

Cross-references

Company reconstructions without change of ownership: s 400(8).

Definitions

Appeal Commissioners: s 2(1); body of persons: s 2(1); month: IA 1937 Sch; person: IA 1937 s 11(*c*); trade: s 3(1).

Former enactments

ITA 1967 s 367; F(MP)A 1968 s 3(2) and Sch Pt I; CTA 1976 s 140(1) and Sch 2 Pt I para 17.

749 Dealers in securities

(1) Subject to this section, where the first buyer is engaged in carrying on a trade which consists of or comprises dealings in securities, then, in computing for any of the purposes of the Tax Acts the profits arising from or loss sustained in the trade, the price paid by the first buyer for the securities shall be reduced by the appropriate amount in respect of the interest determined in accordance with Schedule 21.

(2) Where in the opinion of the Revenue Commissioners the first buyer is bona fide carrying on the business of a discount house in the State, or where the first buyer is a member of a stock exchange in the State who is recognised by the committee of that stock exchange as carrying on the business of a dealer, subsection (1) shall not apply in relation to securities bought in the ordinary course of such business.

[(2A)(*a*) Subsection (1) shall not apply for a chargeable period if the securities are overseas securities purchased by the first buyer in the ordinary course of the first buyer's trade as a dealer in securities and the following conditions are satisfied—

(i) that the interest payable in respect of all such overseas securities to which this Chapter applies is brought into account in computing, for the purposes of the Tax Acts, the profits or gains arising from, or losses sustained in, the trade for the chargeable period, and

(ii) where credit against tax would, but for this section, fall to be allowed for the chargeable period in respect of that interest by virtue of Part 14 or 35 or Schedule 24, that the first buyer elects by notice in writing, on or before the specified return date for the chargeable period, that such credit shall not be so allowed.

(*b*) In this subsection—

"foreign local authority" means an authority, corresponding in substance to a local authority for the purposes of the Local Government Act 2001, which is established outside the State and whose functions are carried on primarily outside the State;

"foreign local government" means any local or regional government in any jurisdiction outside the State;

"foreign public authority" means an authority, corresponding in substance to a public authority for the purposes of the Local Government Act 2001, which is established outside the State and whose functions are carried on primarily outside the State;

"overseas securities" means securities issued—

(i) by a government of a territory outside of the State,

(ii) by a foreign local authority, foreign local government or foreign public authority, or

(iii) by any other body of persons not resident in the State;

"specified return date for the chargeable period" has the same meaning as in section 950.

(2B) Where an election is made in accordance with subsection (2A)(*a*)(ii)—

(*a*) then, notwithstanding Parts 14 and 35 and Schedule 24, credit against tax in respect of the interest shall not be allowed by virtue of either of those Parts or, as the case may be, that Schedule,

(*b*) that election shall be included in the return, required to be made by the first buyer under section 951, for the chargeable period, and

(*c*) that election shall have effect only for the chargeable period for which it is made.

(2C) Subsection (1) shall not apply for a chargeable period if the securities are securities, which are not chargeable assets for the purposes of the Capital Gains Tax Acts by virtue of section 607, purchased by the first buyer in the ordinary course of the first buyer's trade as a dealer in securities and the interest payable in respect of all such securities to which this Chapter applies is brought into account in computing, for the purposes of the Tax Acts, the profits or gains arising from, or losses sustained in, the trade for the chargeable period.][1]

(3) Subsection (1) shall not apply if the interest is to any extent required to be taken into account under section 752 as if it were a trading receipt which had not borne tax or would to any extent be so required to be taken into account but for paragraph 2 of Schedule 22.

Amendments

[1] Subss (2A), (2B) and (2C) inserted by FA 2003 s 31(1) with effect from 1 January 2003.

Cross-references

Chargeable gains of life business, subs (1): s 711(2)(*a*).

Dividends regarded as paid out of profits accumulated before given date, subs (3): Sch 22 para 5(3)(*h*).

Purchase and sale of securities, appropriate amount in respect of the interest: Sch 21 para 1, 4.

Purchase and sale of securities, traders other than dealers in securities: s 751(2).

Special portfolio investment accounts, subs (1): s 838(4)(*d*)(i).

Definitions

Capital Gains Tax Acts: s 1(2); person: IA 1937 s 11(*c*); Tax Acts: s 1(2); trade: ss 3(1), 4(1); writing: IA 1937 Sch.

Former enactments

ITA 1967 s 368.

Corresponding UK tax provision

Income and Corporation Taxes Act 1988 s 732.

750 Persons entitled to exemption

Where the first buyer is entitled under any enactment to an exemption from tax which apart from this section would extend to the interest, then, subject to this section, the exemption shall not extend to an amount equal to the appropriate amount in respect of the interest determined in accordance with Schedule 21; but, if the first buyer is so entitled and any annual payment is payable by the first buyer out of the interest, the annual payment shall be deemed as to the whole of that payment—

(*a*) to be paid out of profits or gains not brought into charge to tax and section 238 shall apply accordingly, and

(*b*) for the purposes of corporation tax, not to be a payment which is a charge on income.

Cross-references

Purchase and sale of securities, appropriate amount in respect of the interest: Sch 21 paras 2, 4.

Definitions

trade: s 3(1); year of assessment: s 3(1).

Former enactments

ITA 1967 s 370; CTA 1976 Sch 2 Pt 1 para 19.

Corresponding UK tax provision

Income and Corporation Taxes Act 1988 s 733.

751 Traders other than dealers in securities

(1) Where the first buyer carries on a trade not within section 749, then, in ascertaining—

(*a*) for the purposes of income tax, whether any, and if so what, repayment of tax is to be made to the first buyer under section 381 by reference to any loss sustained in the trade for the year of assessment the first buyer's income for which includes the interest, there shall be disregarded—

(i) the appropriate amount in respect of the interest determined in accordance with Schedule 21, and

(ii) any tax paid on that amount;

(*b*) for the purposes of corporation tax, the income or profits against which the loss may be set off under section ...[1] 396, there shall be disregarded the appropriate amount in respect of the interest determined in accordance with Schedule 21.

(2) Where the first buyer is a body corporate and carries on a trade not within section 749 or a business consisting mainly in the making of investments, then, if any annual

payment payable by the body corporate is to any extent payable out of the interest, that annual payment shall be deemed to that extent—

(*a*) for the purposes of income tax, not to be payable out of profits or gains brought into charge to tax and section 238 shall apply accordingly, and

(*b*) for the purposes of corporation tax, not to be a payment which is a charge on income.

Amendments

1 Deleted by FA 2003 s 41(1)(*k*) as respects accounting periods ending on or after 6 February 2003; previously "157 or".

Cross-references

Purchase and sale of securities, appropriate amount in respect of the interest: Sch 21 paras 2, 4.

Definitions

trade: s 3(1); year of assessment: s 3(1).

Former enactments

ITA 1967 s 370; CTA 1976 Sch 2 Pt 1 para 19.

Corresponding UK tax provision

Income and Corporation Taxes Act 1988 s 734.

751A Exchange of shares held as trading stock

[(1) In this section—

"new holding", in relation to original shares, and "original shares" have, respectively, the same meanings as in section 584(1).

(2) Subsections (4) and (5) shall apply where a transaction to which this section applies occurs in relation to any original shares—

(*a*) to which a person carrying on a business consisting wholly or partly of dealing in securities is beneficially entitled, and

(*b*) which are such that a profit on their sale would form part of the trading profits of that business.

(3) This section applies to any transaction, being a disposal of original shares which, if the original shares were not such as are mentioned in subsection (2) would result in the disposal not being treated as a disposal by virtue of sections 584 to 587; but does not apply to any transaction in relation to which section 751B applies.

(4) Subject to subsection (5), in making any computation in accordance with the provisions of the Tax Acts applicable to trading profits chargeable to tax under Case I of Schedule D—

(*a*) the transaction to which this section applies shall be treated as not involving any disposal of the original shares, and

(*b*) the new holding shall be treated as the same asset as the original shares.

(5) Where, under a transaction to which this section applies, the person concerned receives or becomes entitled to receive any consideration in addition to the new holding, subsection (4) shall have effect as if the references to the original shares were references to the proportion of them which the market value of the new holding at the time of the transaction bears to the aggregate of that value and the market value at that time (or, if it is cash, the amount) of that consideration.

(6) Subsections (4) and (5) shall have effect with the necessary modifications in relation to any computation made for the purposes of section 707(4) in a case where the original shares held by the company concerned and the new holding are treated as the same asset by virtue of any of sections 584 to 587.][1]

Amendments

1 Section 751A inserted by FA 1999 s 59(1) with effect from 11 February 1999.

Definitions

company: ss 4(1), 5(1); market value: s 548; person: IA 1937 s 11(*c*); Tax Acts: s 1(2).

751B Exchange of Irish Government bonds

[(1) In this section—

"chargeable period" has the same meaning as in section 321(2);

"the exchange" in relation to an investor, means the exchange of old securities for new securities under the Exchange Programme in Irish Government bonds as designated by the National Treasury Management Agency;

"investor" means any person who as beneficial owner of securities exchanges them for new securities under the exchange;

"last payment day" in relation to old securities, means the last day, before the day on which the exchange takes place, on which interest is payable in respect of the old securities; and in a case where a payment of such interest may be made on a number of days, that interest shall be treated as payable on the first of those days; but if there has not been any day upon which interest in respect of old securities has been payable before the day on which the exchange takes place, the last payment day means the day of issue of the old securities;

"old securities" means the first-mentioned securities in the definition of "investor";

"new securities" means the securities issued to an investor in exchange for old securities under the exchange;

"securities" means securities to which section 36 applies.

(2) (*a*) Subsections (3) and (5) shall apply as respects an investor who is a person carrying on a trade or business which consists wholly or partly of dealing in securities in respect of which any profits or gains are chargeable to tax under Case I of Schedule D.

(*b*) Subsection (6) shall apply as respects any investor other than an investor referred to in paragraph (*a*).

(3) There shall be computed for the chargeable period in which the exchange by an investor to whom this subsection applies takes place, an amount of tax (in this section referred to as **"the deferred tax"**) where the deferred tax is found by the formula—

(*a*) in a case where the investor is chargeable to tax in the chargeable period in respect of interest received in the chargeable period—

A - B - C, and

(*b*) in any other case—

$$A - B$$

where—

A is the amount of tax which, apart from this section, would finally fall to be borne by the investor for that chargeable period;

B is the amount of tax which, apart from this section, would finally fall to be borne by the investor for that chargeable period if the exchange were not taken into account in computing that tax, but, in a case to which paragraph (*b*) applies, includes the tax on interest which has accrued in respect of old securities from the beginning of that chargeable period, or the day on which the old securities were acquired by the investor, whichever is later, to the day on which the exchange took place; and

C is the amount representing the tax on accrued interest for that chargeable period in respect of old securities which is included in A.

(4) For the purposes of subsection (3) the accrued interest in respect of old securities is the interest accrued on such securities from—

(*a*) the last payment day in respect of the old securities, or
(*b*) the day on which the old securities were acquired by an investor,

whichever is later.

(5) Where an investor to whom this section applies so elects, the amount of tax which, apart from this subsection, finally falls to be borne for the chargeable period in which the exchange takes place, shall be reduced by the amount of the deferred tax and the amount of the deferred tax shall be deemed to be an amount of tax which finally falls to be borne for the chargeable period (in this subsection referred to as the "later chargeable period") in which the new securities are disposed of in addition to any tax, which apart from this subsection, finally falls to be borne for the later chargeable period and the provisions of Part 41 shall apply accordingly.

(6) (*a*) Subject to paragraph (*b*), the amount of capital gains tax, which apart from this subsection, would be chargeable on chargeable gains accruing to an investor to whom this subsection applies, on the disposal of old securities, after such chargeable gains have been reduced by any allowable losses under section 31, shall, if the investor so elects, be deemed to be an amount of capital gains tax chargeable on chargeable gains which are deemed to accrue to the investor in the chargeable period (in this subsection referred to as the "later chargeable period") in which the new securities are disposed of (and not in any other chargeable period) in addition to any capital gains tax chargeable on chargeable gains accruing to the investor in the later chargeable period and the provisions of Part 41 shall apply accordingly.

(*b*) Section 815 shall apply to the disposal of the old securities to which paragraph (*a*) applies as if—

(i) there were inserted, in subsection (3)(*b*) of that section after "profits of the trade", "unless the trade consists wholly or partly of a life business the profits of which are not assessed to corporation tax under Case I of Schedule D for that accounting period", and

(ii) subsection (3)(*c*) of that section were deleted.

(7) The election referred to in subsections (5) and (6) shall be made within a period of two years after the end of the chargeable period in which the disposal of the old securities takes place.][1]

Amendments

1 Section 751B inserted by FA 1999 s 59(1) in respect of an exchange of old securities for new securities in the period beginning on 11 February 1999, and ending before 1 January 2000.

Cross-references

Exchange of shares held as trading stock: s 751A(3).

Definitions

allowable loss: ss 5(1), 546; chargeable gain: ss 5(1), 545; person: IA 1937 s 11(*c*); trading stock: ss 5(1),89; year: IA 1937 Sch.

CHAPTER 2

Purchases of Shares by Financial Concerns and Persons Exempted from Tax, and Restriction on Relief for Losses by Repayment of Tax in Case of Dividends Paid Out of Accumulated Profits

752 Purchases of shares by financial concerns and persons exempted from tax

(1) For the purposes of this Chapter and Schedule 22—

(*a*) references to a dividend shall, except where the context otherwise requires, be construed as including references to a distribution, and to an amount which under any enactment is to be treated as a distribution, made on or after the 6th day of April, 1976,

(*b*) in relation to such a distribution, including an amount to be so treated as a distribution, references to a dividend being paid or becoming payable or being received or becoming receivable on shares shall be construed as references to a distribution or an amount to be so treated as a distribution being made or received in respect of shares or securities, and

(*c*) in applying references to a dividend in relation to a distribution, **"gross amount"** or **"gross dividend"** means the distribution together with the tax credit to which the recipient of the distribution is entitled in respect of it, and **"net amount"** or **"net dividend"** means the distribution exclusive of any such tax credit,

and in this subsection **"distribution"** has the same meaning as in the Corporation Tax Acts.

(2) (*a*) In this section and in Schedule 22—

"company" includes any body corporate, but does not include a company not resident in the State;

"control", in relation to a body corporate, means the power of a person to secure—

(i) by means of the holding of shares or the possession of voting power in or in relation to that or any other body corporate, or

(ii) by virtue of any powers conferred by the articles of association or other document regulating that or any other body corporate, that the affairs of the first-mentioned body corporate are conducted in accordance with the wishes of that person and, in relation to a partnership, means the right to a share of more than 50 per cent of the assets, or of more than 50 per cent of the income, of the partnership;

"person" includes any body of persons, and references to a person entitled to any exemption from tax include, in a case of an exemption expressed to apply to income of a trust or fund, references to the persons entitled to make claims for the granting of that exemption;

"share" includes stock other than debenture or loan stock;

"shares of a class to which this section applies" means shares of any class forming part of a company's share capital, other than a class of fully-paid preference shares carrying only a right to dividends at a rate per cent of the nominal value of the shares which is fixed and which in the opinion of the Appeal Commissioners does not substantially exceed the yield generally obtainable on preference shares the prices of which are quoted on stock exchanges in the State.

(*b*) For the purposes of this section and Schedule 22—

(i) shares shall be regarded as of different classes if the rights and obligations respectively attached to them are distinguishable as regards the payment of dividends or the amount paid up or in any other respect;

(ii) any reference to shares acquired in right of other shares includes a reference to shares acquired in pursuance of an offer or invitation which was restricted to holders of those other shares;

(iii) 2 trades shall be regarded as under the same control if they are carried on by persons one of whom is a body of persons over whom the other has control or both of whom are bodies of persons under the control of a third person, and several trades shall be regarded as under the same control if each is under the same control as all of the others, and in this subparagraph **"body of persons"** includes a partnership.

(3) Where a person engaged in carrying on a trade which consists of or comprises dealings in shares or other investments becomes entitled to receive a dividend on a holding of shares of a class to which this section applies, being shares sold or issued to that person or otherwise acquired by that person not more than 10 years before the date on which the dividend becomes payable, and the dividend is to any extent paid out of profits accumulated before the date on which the shares were so acquired, then, if those shares, or those shares together with—

(*a*) any other shares the dividend on which is payable to that person and which were sold or issued to that person or otherwise acquired by that person not more than 10 years before the date on which the dividend becomes payable,

(*b*) in a case where the trade is under the same control as another trade which consists of or comprises dealings in shares or other investments, any shares the dividend on which is payable to the person engaged in carrying on that other trade and which were sold or issued to that person or otherwise acquired by that person not more than 10 years before the date on which the dividend becomes payable, and

(*c*) any shares to be taken into account under subsection (5), amount to 10 per cent or more of the issued shares of that class, the net amount of the dividend received on the shares in the holding shall, to the extent to which it was paid out of profits accumulated before the shares were acquired, be taken into account in computing for the purposes of the Tax Acts the profits or gains or losses of the trade as if it were a trading receipt which had not borne tax.

(4) Where a person entitled under the Tax Acts to an exemption from tax which extends to dividends on shares becomes entitled to receive a dividend on a holding of shares of a class to which this section applies, being shares sold or issued to that person or otherwise acquired by that person not more than 10 years before the date on which the dividend becomes payable, and the dividend is to any extent paid out of the profits accumulated before the date on which the shares were so acquired, then, if those shares, or those shares together with—

(*a*) any other shares the dividend on which is payable to that person and which were sold or issued to that person or otherwise acquired by that person not more than 10 years before the date on which the dividend becomes payable, and

(*b*) any shares to be taken into account under subsection (5),

amount to 10 per cent or more of the issued shares of that class, the exemption shall, to an extent proportionate to the extent to which the dividend is paid out of profits accumulated before the date on which the shares were acquired, not apply to the dividend; but, if any annual payment is payable by that person out of the dividend, that annual payment shall be deemed as to the whole of that payment—

(i) to be paid out of profits or gains not brought into charge to tax and section 238 shall apply accordingly, and

(ii) for the purposes of corporation tax, not to be a payment which is a charge on income.

(5) Where 2 or more persons, being persons engaged in carrying on trades of the kind mentioned in subsection (3) or entitled to an exemption of the kind mentioned in subsection (4), have each acquired shares in a company and the transactions in pursuance of which the acquisition was made were either transactions entered into by those persons acting in concert or transactions together comprised in any arrangements made by any person, then, in the application of either of those subsections in relation to a dividend payable to one of those persons on shares which include shares so acquired (or shares acquired in right of those shares), there shall be taken into account under subsection (3)(*c*) or, as the case may be, subsection (4)(*b*) any shares the dividend on which is payable to any other of those persons, being shares so acquired by that other person (or shares acquired in right of those shares).

(6) Where any shares have been sold or otherwise disposed of by a person who held shares of that kind acquired at different times, it shall be assumed for the purposes of this section that shares which have been held for a longer time have been disposed of before shares which have been held for a shorter time.

(7) Where, at the time when a trade is or is deemed to be set up and commenced, any shares form part of the trading stock belonging to the trade, those shares shall be regarded for the purposes of this section as having been acquired at that time by the

person then engaged in carrying on the trade, and, subject to this subsection, where there is a change in the persons engaged in carrying on a trade which is not a change on which the trade is deemed to be discontinued, this section shall apply in relation to the person so engaged after the change as if anything done to or by that person's predecessor had been done to or by that person.

(8) Schedule 22 shall apply for the purpose of ascertaining whether a dividend is to be regarded as paid to any extent out of profits accumulated before a particular date.

Cross-references

Dealers in securities, provisions regarding interest: s749(3).

Dividends regarded as paid out of profits accumulated before given date: Sch 22 para 1(1), (2); subs (3): Sch 22 para 5(3)(*g*)–(*h*).

Restriction on relief for losses by repayment of tax in case of dividend paid out of accumulated profits, subs (3): s 753.

Definitions

body of persons: s 2(1); person: IA 1937 s 11(*c*); trade: s 3(1).

Former enactments

ITA 1967 s 371; F(MP)A 1968 s 3(2) and Sch Pt I; CTA 1976 s 140(1) and s164 and Sch 2 Pt 1 para 20 and Sch 3 Pt I.

753 Restriction on relief for losses by repayment of tax in case of dividends paid out of accumulated profits

Where a person or a body of persons carries on a trade, other than a trade mentioned in section 752(3), and the person's or the body of persons' income for any year of assessment or, as the case may be, accounting period includes a dividend the net amount of which would, if the trade were a trade mentioned in section 752(3), be required to any extent to be taken into account as a trading receipt which has not borne tax, then, in ascertaining—

(*a*) for the purposes of income tax, whether any or what repayment of tax is to be made to that person or body of persons under section 381 by reference to any loss sustained in the trade for that year of assessment, there shall be disregarded—

(i) the gross amount corresponding to so much of that net amount as would have been required to be taken into account as a trading receipt which has not borne tax, and

(ii) any tax credit in respect of the amount required to be disregarded under subparagraph (i);

(*b*) for the purposes of corporation tax, the income or profits against which the loss may be set off under section ...[1] 396, there shall be disregarded the gross amount corresponding to so much of that net amount as would have been required to be taken into account as a trading receipt which has not borne tax.

Amendments

[1] Deleted by FA 2003 s 41(1)(*l*) as respects accounting periods ending on or after 6 February 2003; previously "157 or".

Definitions

body of persons: s 2(1); person: IA 1937 s 11(*c*); trade: s 3(1); year of assessment: s 3(1).

Former enactments

ITA 1967 s 372; CTA 1976 s 140(1) and Sch 2 Pt 1 para 21(1).

PART 29
PATENTS, SCIENTIFIC AND CERTAIN OTHER RESEARCH, KNOW-HOW AND CERTAIN TRAINING

Cross-references

"Capital allowance" includes an allowance under this Part: s 2(1).

CHAPTER 1
Patents

Cross-references

Capital gains tax, exclusion of sums chargeable to income tax: s 551(3).
Change in ownership of a company, disallowance of trading losses: s 401(5).
Dividends regarded as paid out of profits accumulated before given date: Sch 22 para 5(3)(*e*).
Group relief, exclusion of double allowances etc: s 428(6).
Industrial and provident societies, expenses: s 699(2)(*b*).
Loss relief, meaning of "balancing charges" applied: s 391(1).
Partnerships and European Economic Interest Groupings, meaning of "balancing charge" applied: s 1007(1).
Petroleum trade, abandonment expenditure and loss relief: s 695(8).
Petroleum trade, development expenditure: s 692(4).
Petroleum trade, exploration expenditure: s 693(12), (13).
Reorganisation into companies of Trustee Savings Banks, capital allowances: Sch 17 para 2(1)(*a*).
Restriction of loss relief: s 455(6).
Taxation of certain short-term leases of plant and machinery: s 80A(2)(*b*).

754 Interpretation (Chapter 1)

(1) In this Chapter—

"the commencement of the patent", in relation to a patent, means the date from which the patent rights become effective;

"income from patents" means—

(*a*) any royalty or other sum paid in respect of the user of a patent, and

(*b*) any amount on which tax is payable for any chargeable period by virtue of this Chapter;

"Irish patent" means a patent granted under the laws of the State;

"patent rights" means the right to do or to authorise the doing of anything which but for that right would be an infringement of a patent;

"the writing-down period" has the meaning assigned to it by section 755(2).

(2) In this Chapter, any reference to the sale of part of patent rights includes a reference to the grant of a licence in respect of the patent in question, and any reference to the purchase of patent rights includes a reference to the acquisition of a licence in respect of a patent; but, if a licence granted by a person entitled to any patent rights is a licence to

exercise those rights to the exclusion of the grantor and all other persons for the whole of the remainder of the term for which the rights subsist, the grantor shall be treated for the purposes of this Chapter as thereby selling the whole of the rights.

(3) Where, under section 77 of the Patents Act, 1992, or any corresponding provisions of the law of any country outside the State, an invention which is the subject of a patent is made, used, exercised or vended by or for the service of the State or the government of the country concerned, this Chapter shall apply as if the making, user, exercise or vending of the invention had taken place in pursuance of a licence, and any sums paid in respect thereof shall be treated accordingly.

Definitions

person: IA 1937 s 11(*c*).

Former enactments

ITA 1967 s 284; CTA 1976 s 21(1) and Sch 1 para 35; FA 1997 s 146(1) and Sch 9 Pt I para 1(19).

Corresponding UK tax provision

Income and Corporation Taxes Act 1988 s 533.

755 Annual allowances for capital expenditure on purchase of patent rights

(1) Where a person incurs capital expenditure on the purchase of patent rights, there shall, subject to and in accordance with this Chapter, be made to that person writing-down allowances in respect of that expenditure during the writing-down period; but no writing-down allowance shall be made to a person in respect of any expenditure unless—

(*a*) the allowance is to be made to the person in taxing the person's trade, or

(*b*) any income receivable by the person in respect of the rights would be liable to tax.

(2) (*a*) Subject to paragraphs (*b*) to (*d*), the writing-down period shall be the 17 years beginning with the chargeable period related to the expenditure.

(*b*) Where the patent rights are purchased for a specified period, paragraph (*a*) shall apply with the substitution for the reference to 17 years of a reference to 17 years or the number of years comprised within that period, whichever is the less.

(*c*) Where the patent rights purchased begin one complete year or more after the commencement of the patent and paragraph (*b*) does not apply, paragraph (*a*) shall apply with the substitution for the reference to 17 years of a reference to 17 years less the number of complete years which, when the rights begin, have elapsed since the commencement of the patent or, if 17 complete years have so elapsed, of a reference to one year.

(*d*) For the purposes of this subsection, any expenditure incurred for the purposes of a trade by a person about to carry on the trade shall be treated as if that expenditure had been incurred by that person on the first day on which that person carries on the trade unless before that first day that person has sold all the patent rights on the purchase of which the expenditure was incurred.

Cross-references

"the writing down period", meaning applied, subs (2): s 754(1).

Definitions

person: IA 1937 s 11(*c*); trade: s 3(1).

Former enactments

ITA 1967 s 285; CTA 1976 s 21(1) and Sch 1 para 36.

Corresponding UK tax provision

Income and Corporation Taxes Act 1988 s 520 [repealed].

756 Effect of lapse of patent rights

(1) Where a person incurs capital expenditure on the purchase of patent rights and, before the end of the writing-down period, any of the following events occurs—

(*a*) the rights come to an end without being subsequently revived;

(*b*) the person sells all those rights or so much of those rights as the person still owns;

(*c*) the person sells part of those rights and the net proceeds of the sale (in so far as they consist of capital sums) are not less than the amount of the capital expenditure remaining unallowed;

no writing-down allowance shall be made to that person for the chargeable period related to the event or for any subsequent chargeable period.

(2) Where a person incurs capital expenditure on the purchase of patent rights and, before the end of the writing-down period, either of the following events occurs—

(*a*) the rights come to an end without being subsequently revived;

(*b*) the person sells all those rights or so much of those rights as the person still owns, and the net proceeds of the sale (in so far as they consist of capital sums) are less than the amount of the capital expenditure remaining unallowed;

there shall, subject to and in accordance with this Chapter, be made to that person for the chargeable period related to the event an allowance (in this Chapter referred to as a **"balancing allowance"**) equal to—

(i) if the event is the rights coming to an end, the amount of the capital expenditure remaining unallowed, and

(ii) if the event is a sale, the amount of the capital expenditure remaining unallowed less the net proceeds of the sale.

(3) Where a person who has incurred capital expenditure on the purchase of patent rights sells all or any part of those rights and the net proceeds of the sale (in so far as they consist of capital sums) exceed the amount of the capital expenditure remaining unallowed, if any, there shall, subject to and in accordance with this Chapter, be made on that person for the chargeable period related to the sale a charge (in this Chapter referred to as a **"balancing charge"**) on an amount equal to—

(*a*) the excess, or

(*b*) where the amount of the capital expenditure remaining unallowed is nil, the net proceeds of the sale.

(4) Where a person who has incurred capital expenditure on the purchase of patent rights sells a part of those rights and subsection (3) does not apply, the amount of any writing-down allowance made in respect of that expenditure for the chargeable period related to the sale or any subsequent chargeable period shall be the amount determined by—

(*a*) subtracting the net proceeds of the sale (in so far as they consist of capital sums) from the amount of the expenditure remaining unallowed at the time of the sale, and

(*b*) dividing the result by the number of complete years of the writing-down period which remained at the beginning of the chargeable period related to the sale,

and so on for any subsequent sales.

(5) References in this section to the amount of any capital expenditure remaining unallowed shall in relation to any event be construed as references to the amount of that expenditure less any writing-down allowances made in respect of that expenditure for chargeable periods before the chargeable period related to that event, and less also the net proceeds of any previous sale by the person who incurred the expenditure of any part of the rights acquired by the expenditure, in so far as those proceeds consist of capital sums.

(6) Notwithstanding subsections (1) to (5)—

(*a*) no balancing allowance shall be made in respect of any expenditure unless a writing-down allowance has been, or, but for the happening of the event giving rise to the balancing allowance, could have been, made in respect of that expenditure, and

(*b*) the total amount on which a balancing charge is made in respect of any expenditure shall not exceed the total writing-down allowances actually made in respect of that expenditure less, if a balancing charge has previously been made in respect of that expenditure, the amount on which that charge was made.

Cross-references

Industrial and provident societies, expenses: s 699(2)(*b*).

Patents, in s 312(5)(*a*)(i), the reference to the sum mentioned in para (*b*) in the case of patents rights is to be construed as a reference to the amount of capital expenditure on the acquisition of the patent rights remaining unallowed, computed in accordance with this section: s 762(2)(*a*).

Definitions

income from patents, the commencement of the patent, patent rights, Irish patent: s 755(1); person: IA 1937 s 11(*c*).

Former enactments

ITA 1967 s 286; CTA 1976 s 21(1) and Sch 1 para 37.

Corresponding UK tax provision

Income and Corporation Taxes Act 1988 s 523.

757 Charges on capital sums received for sale of patent rights

(1) (*a*) Subject to paragraphs (*b*) and (*c*), where a person resident in the State sells any patent rights and the net proceeds of the sale consist wholly or partly of a capital sum, that person shall, subject to this Chapter, be charged to tax under Case IV of Schedule D for the chargeable period in which the sum is received

by that person and for successive chargeable periods, being charged in each period on the same fraction of the sum as the period is of 6 years (or such less fraction as has not already been charged).

(*b*) Where the person by notice in writing served on the inspector not later than 12 months after the end of the chargeable period in which the capital sum was received elects that the whole of that sum shall be charged to tax for the chargeable period in which the sum is received, it shall be charged to tax accordingly.

(*c*) Where the person by notice in writing served on the inspector not later than 12 months after the end of the chargeable period in which the capital sum was received applies to have the fraction referred to in paragraph (*a*) determined as being other than the same fraction as the chargeable period is of 6 years, then, if it appears to the Revenue Commissioners that hardship is likely to arise having regard to all the circumstances of the case unless a direction is given under this paragraph, they may direct that the fraction shall be the same fraction of the sum as the chargeable period is of a number of years other than 6 years, and that the charge shall be spread accordingly.

(2) (*a*) Where a person not resident in the State sells any patent rights and the net proceeds of the sale consist wholly or partly of a capital sum, and the patent is an Irish patent, then, subject to this Chapter—

(i) the person shall be chargeable to tax in respect of that sum under Case IV of Schedule D, and

(ii) section 238 shall apply to that sum as if it were an annual payment payable otherwise than out of profits or gains brought into charge to tax.

(*b*) Where, not later than 12 months after the end of the year of assessment in which the sum referred to in paragraph (*a*) is paid, the person to whom it is paid, by notice in writing to the Revenue Commissioners, elects that the sum shall be treated for the purpose of income tax for that year and for each of the 5 succeeding years as if one-sixth of that sum were included in that person's income chargeable to tax for all those years respectively, it shall be so treated, and all such repayments and assessments of tax for each of those years shall be made as are necessary to give effect to the election; but—

(i) the election shall not affect the amount of tax to be deducted and accounted for under section 238,

(ii) where any sum is deducted under section 238, any adjustments necessary to give effect to the election shall be made by means of repayment of tax, and

(iii) those adjustments shall be made year by year and as if one-sixth of the sum deducted had been deducted in respect of tax for each year, and no repayment of or of any part of that portion of the tax deducted which is to be treated as deducted in respect of tax for any year shall be made unless and until it is ascertained that the tax ultimately to be paid for that year is less than the amount of tax paid for that year.

(3) (*a*) In subsection (2), **"tax"** shall mean income tax, unless the seller of the patent rights, being a company, would be within the charge to corporation tax in respect of any proceeds of the sale not consisting of a capital sum.

(b) Where paragraph (a) of subsection (2) applies to charge a company to corporation tax in respect of a sum paid to it, paragraph (b) of that subsection shall not apply; but—

(i) the company may, by notice in writing given to the Revenue Commissioners not later than 12 months after the end of the accounting period in which the sum is paid, elect that the sum shall be treated as arising rateably in the accounting periods ending not later than 6 years from the beginning of the accounting period in which the sum is paid (being accounting periods during which the company remains within the charge to corporation tax by virtue of subsection (2)(a)), and

(ii) there shall be made all such repayments of tax and assessments to tax as are necessary to give effect to any such election.

(4) Where the patent rights sold by a person, or the rights out of which the patent rights sold by a person were granted, were acquired by the person by purchase and the price paid consisted wholly or partly of a capital sum, subsections (1) to (3) shall apply as if any capital sum received by the person on the sale of the rights were reduced by the amount of that sum; but—

(a) where between the purchase and the sale the person has sold part of the patent rights acquired by the person and the net proceeds of that sale consist wholly or partly of a capital sum, the amount of the reduction to be made under this subsection in respect of the subsequent sale shall itself be reduced by the amount of that sum, and

(b) nothing in this subsection shall affect the amount of tax to be deducted and accounted for under section 238 by virtue of subsection (2) and, where any sum is deducted under section 238, any adjustment necessary to give effect to this subsection shall be made by means of repayment of tax.

(5) This section shall apply in relation to any sale of part of any patent rights as it applies in relation to sales of patent rights.

Cross-references

Amount of s 238 assessment to be allowed as a loss: s 390(3).

Capital sums: effect of death, winding up and partnership changes: s 760(2), (3)(b), (4)(b).

Partnerships: s 1011(1).

Patents, in s 316(1), the reference to any expenditure or sum in the case of which a deduction to of tax is to be or may be, made under s 237 or s 238 shall not include a sum in the case of which such a deduction is to be or may be so made by virtue of this section: s 762(2)(b).

Patents, spreading revenue payments over several years: s 759(4).

Definitions

the commencement of the patent, Irish patent, income from patents: s 755(1); inspector: ss 2(1), 5(1), 852; month: IA 1937 Sch; the operative date, patent rights: s 755(1); person: IA 1937 s 11(c); writing: IA 1937 Sch; year of assessment: s 3(1).

Former enactments

ITA 1967 s 288; CTA 1976 s 21(1) and Sch 1 para 38.

Corresponding UK tax provision

Income and Corporation Taxes Act 1988 s 524.

758 Relief for expenses

(1) Notwithstanding section 81, in computing the profits or gains of any trade, there shall be allowed to be deducted as expenses any fees paid or expenses incurred in obtaining for the purposes of the trade the grant of a patent or an extension of the term of a patent.

(2) Where—

(*a*) a person, otherwise than for the purposes of a trade carried on by the person, pays any fees or incurs any expenses in connection with the grant or maintenance of a patent or the obtaining of an extension of a term of a patent, and

(*b*) those fees or expenses would, if they had been paid or incurred for the purposes of a trade, have been allowable as a deduction in estimating the profits or gains of the trade,

there shall be made to the person for the chargeable period in which those fees or expenses were paid or incurred an allowance equal to the amount of those fees or expenses.

(3) Where a patent is granted in respect of any invention, an allowance equal to so much of the net amount of any expenses incurred by an individual who, whether alone or in conjunction with any other person, actually devised the invention as is properly ascribable to the devising of that invention (not being expenses in respect of which, or of assets representing which, an allowance is to be made under any other provision of the Tax Acts) shall be made to that individual for the year of assessment in which the expenses were incurred.

Definitions

person: IA 1937 s 11(*c*); trade: s 3(1); year of assessment: s 3(1).

Former enactments

ITA 1967 s 290(1)–(3); CTA 1976 s 21(1) and Sch 1 para 39.

Corresponding UK tax provision

Income and Corporation Taxes Act 1988 s 526.

759 Spreading of revenue payments over several years

(1) In this section, any reference to the tax payable by a person includes, in cases where the income of an individual's spouse is deemed to be the income of the individual, references to the income tax payable by the individual's spouse.

(2) Where a royalty or other sum to which section 237 or 238 applies is paid in respect of the user of a patent and that user extended over a period of 6 complete years or more, the person receiving the payment may require that the tax payable by that person by reason of the receipt of that sum shall be reduced so as not to exceed the total amount of tax which would have been payable by that person if that royalty or sum had been paid in 6 equal instalments at yearly intervals, the last of which was paid on the date on which the payment was in fact made.

(3) Subsection (2) shall apply in relation to a royalty or other sum where the period of the user is 2 complete years or more but less than 6 complete years as it applies to the

royalties and sums mentioned in that subsection, but with the substitution for the reference to 6 equal instalments of a reference to so many equal instalments as there are complete years comprised in that period.

(4) Nothing in this section shall apply to any sum to which section 238 applies by virtue of section 757.

Definitions

person: IA 1937 s 11(*c*).

Former enactments

ITA 1967 s 195B(3) and (6) and s 291; CTA 1976 s 21(1) and Sch 1 para 40; FA 1993 s 10(1).

Corresponding UK tax provision

Income and Corporation Taxes Act 1988 s 527.

760 Capital sums: effect of death, winding up and partnership changes

(1) In this section, any references to tax paid or borne or payable or to be paid or borne by a person include, in cases where the income of an individual's spouse is deemed to be income of the individual, references to the income tax paid or borne, or payable or to be paid or borne, by the individual's spouse.

(2) Where a person on whom, by reason of the receipt of a capital sum, a charge is to be, or would otherwise be, made under section 757 dies or, being a body corporate, commences to be wound up—

(*a*) no sums shall be charged under that section on that person for any chargeable period subsequent to that in which the death takes place or the winding up commences, and

(*b*) the amount to be charged for the chargeable period in which the death occurs or the winding up commences shall be increased by the total amounts which but for the death or winding up would have been charged for subsequent chargeable periods.

(3) (*a*) In the case of a death, the personal representatives may, by notice in writing served on the inspector not later than 21 days after notice has been served on them of the charge to be made by virtue of this section, require that the tax payable out of the estate of the deceased by reason of the increase provided for by this section shall be reduced so as not to exceed the amount determined in accordance with paragraph (*b*).

(*b*) The amount referred to in paragraph (*a*) shall be the total amount of tax which would have been payable by the deceased or out of his or her estate by reason of the operation of section 757 in relation to the capital sum if, instead of the amount to be charged for the year in which the death occurs being increased by the whole amount of the sums charged for subsequent years, the several amounts to be charged for the years beginning with that in which the capital sum was received and ending with that in which the death occurred had each been increased by that whole amount divided by the number of those years.

(4) (*a*) In this subsection, **"the relevant period"** has the same meaning as in Part 43.

(*b*) Where, under Chapter 4 of Part 9 as modified by Part 43, charges under section 757 are to be made on 2 or more persons as being the persons for the time being carrying on a trade, and the relevant period comes to an end, subsection (2) shall apply in relation to the ending of the relevant period as it applies where a body corporate commences to be wound up.

(*c*) Where paragraph (*b*) applies—

(i) the additional sums which under subsection (2) are to be charged for the year in which the relevant period ends shall be aggregated and apportioned among the members of the partnership immediately before the ending of the relevant period according to their respective interests in the partnership profits at that time and each partner (or, if that partner is dead, his or her personal representatives) charged for his or her proportion, and

(ii) each partner (or, if that partner is dead, his or her personal representatives) shall have the same right to require a reduction of the total tax payable by him or her or out of his or her estate by reason of the increase provided for by this section as would have been exercisable by the personal representatives under subsection (3) in the case of a death, and that subsection shall apply accordingly but as if the reference to the amount of tax which would have been payable by the deceased or out of his or her estate in the event mentioned in that subsection were a reference to the amount of tax which would in that event have been paid or borne by the partner in question or out of his or her estate.

Definitions

inspector: ss 2(1), 5(1), 852; person: IA 1937 s 11(*c*); trade: s 3(1); writing: IA 1937 Sch.

Former enactments

ITA 1967 s 195B(3) and (6) and s 293; CTA 1976 s 21(1) and Sch 1 para 42; FA 1993 s 10(1).

Corresponding UK tax provision

Income and Corporation Taxes Act 1988 s 525.

761 Manner of making allowances and charges

(1) An allowance or charge under this Chapter shall be made to or on a person in taxing the person's trade if—

(*a*) the person is carrying on a trade the profits or gains of which are, or, if there were any, would be, chargeable to tax under Case I of Schedule D for the chargeable period for which the allowance or charge is made, and

(*b*) at any time in the chargeable period or its basis period the patent rights in question, or other rights out of which they were granted, were or were to be used for the purposes of that trade;

but nothing in this subsection shall affect the preceding provisions of this Chapter allowing a deduction as expenses in computing the profits or gains of a trade or requiring a charge to be made under Case IV of Schedule D.

(2) Except where provided for in subsection (1), an allowance under this Chapter shall be made by means of discharge or repayment of tax and shall be available against income from patents, and a charge under this Chapter shall be made under Case IV of Schedule D.

Cross-references

Application of Part 9 Chapter 4, subs (2): s 762(1).

Definitions

Income from patents, patent rights: s 755(1); person: IA 1937 s 11(*c*); trade: s 3(1).

Former enactments

ITA 1967 s 292; CTA 1976 s 21(1) and Sch 1 para 41.

Corresponding UK tax provision

Income and Corporation Taxes Act 1988 s 528.

762 Application of Chapter 4 of Part 9

(1) Subject to subsection (2), Chapter 4 of Part 9 shall apply as if this Chapter were contained in that Part, and any reference in the Tax Acts to any capital allowance to be given by means of discharge or repayment of tax and to be available or available primarily against a specified class of income shall include a reference to any capital allowance given in accordance with section 761(2).

(2) In Chapter 4 of Part 9, as applied by virtue of subsection (1) to patent rights—

(*a*) the reference in section 312(5)(*a*)(i) to the sum mentioned in paragraph (*b*) shall in the case of patent rights be construed as a reference to the amount of the capital expenditure on the acquisition of the patent rights remaining unallowed, computed in accordance with section 756, and

(*b*) the reference in section 316(1) to any expenditure or sum in the case of which a deduction of tax is to be or may be made under section 237 or 238 shall not include a sum in the case of which such a deduction is to be or may be so made by virtue of section 757.

Former enactments

ITA 1967 s 299(4)(*b*)(iii) and s 303(1); CTA 1976 s 21(1) and Sch 1 para 46 and para 49.

Corresponding UK tax provision

Income and Corporation Taxes Act 1988 s 532.

CHAPTER 2

Scientific and Certain Other Research

763 Interpretation (sections 764 and 765)

(1) In this section—

"designated area" means an area designated by order under section 2 of the Continental Shelf Act, 1968;

"exploring for specified minerals" means searching in the State for deposits of specified minerals or testing such deposits or winning access to such deposits, and includes the systematic searching for areas containing specified minerals and searching by drilling or other means for specified minerals within those areas, but does not include operations in the course of developing or working a mine;

"licence" means—

(*a*) an exploration licence,

(*b*) a petroleum prospecting licence,

(*c*) a petroleum lease, or

(*d*) a reserved area licence, duly granted before the 11th day of June, 1968, in respect of an area in the State, or on or after the 11th day of June, 1968, in respect of either or both a designated area and an area in the State, and which was or may be so granted subject to such licensing terms as were presented to each House of the Oireachtas, and includes any such licence the terms of which have been duly amended or varied from time to time;

"licensed area" means an area in respect of which a licence is in force;

"mine" means an underground excavation for the purpose of getting specified minerals;

"petroleum" includes—

(*a*) any mineral oil or relative hydrocarbon and natural gas and other liquid or gaseous hydrocarbons and their derivatives or constituent substances existing in its natural condition in strata (including, without limitation, distillate, condensate, casinghead gasoline and such other substances as are ordinarily produced from oil and gas wells), and

(*b*) any other mineral substance contained in oil or natural gas brought to the surface with them in the normal process of extraction, but does not include coal and bituminous shales and other stratified deposits from which oil can be extracted by distillation,

won or capable of being won under the authority of a licence;

"petroleum exploration activities" means activities of a person carried on by the person or on behalf of the person in searching for deposits in a licensed area, in testing or appraising such deposits or in winning access to such deposits for the purposes of such searching, testing and appraising, where such activities are carried on under a licence (other than a petroleum lease) authorising the activities and held by the person or, if the person is a company, held by the company or a company associated with it;

"petroleum extraction activities" means activities of a person carried on by the person or on behalf of the person under a petroleum lease authorising the activities and held by the person or, if the person is a company, held by the company or a company associated with it in—

(*a*) winning petroleum from a relevant field, including searching in that field for, and winning access to, such petroleum,

(*b*) transporting as far as dry land petroleum so won from a place not on dry land, or

(*c*) effecting the initial treatment and storage of petroleum so won from the relevant field;

"relevant field" means an area in respect of which a licence, being a petroleum lease, is in force;

"specified minerals" means the following minerals occurring in non-bedded deposits of such minerals, that is, barytes, felspar, serpentinous marble, quartz rock, soapstone, ores of copper, ores of gold, ores of iron, ores of lead, ores of manganese, ores of molybdenum, ores of silver, ores of sulphur and ores of zinc.

(2) In sections 764 and 765—

"asset" includes part of an asset;

"expenditure on scientific research" does not include any expenditure incurred in the acquisition of rights in or arising out of scientific research;

"scientific research" means, subject to subsections (3) and (4), any activities in the fields of natural or applied science for the extension of knowledge.

(3) For the purposes of the definition of **"scientific research"**, that definition shall, subject to subsection (4), be construed as including and be deemed always to have included a provision excluding from that definition the following activities—

(*a*) exploring for specified minerals,

(*b*) petroleum exploration activities, and

(*c*) petroleum extraction activities.

(4) As respects activities carried on before the 29th day of January, 1992, subsection (3) shall not apply for the purpose of computing any charge to income tax or corporation tax on a person who has before the 3rd day of December, 1991, made a claim in respect of expenditure incurred in exploring for specified minerals or in respect of petroleum exploration activities or in respect of petroleum extraction activities.

(5) For the purposes of sections 764 and 765, expenditure shall not be regarded as incurred by a person in so far as it is or is to be met directly or indirectly out of moneys provided by the Oireachtas or by any person other than the first-mentioned person.

(6) The same expenditure shall not be taken into account for any of the purposes of section 764 or 765 in relation to more than one trade.

Cross-references

Petroleum trade, abandonment expenditure and loss relief: s 695(8).

Petroleum trade, development expenditure: s 692(4)(*e*).

Petroleum trade, exploration expenditure: s 693(12).

Definitions

company: ss 4(1), 5(1); land: s 5(1), IA 1937 Sch; lease: s 5(1); minerals: s 5(1); the Oireachtas: IA 1937 Sch; person: IA 1937 s 11(*c*).

Case law

Subs (2): Expenditure on unsuccessful oil and gas exploration regarded as qualifying expenditure: *Texaco (Ireland) Ltd v Murphy* ITR Vol IV p 91. Other than for persons who had claimed under ITA 1967 s 244 in respect of such expenditure, "scientific research" is deemed always to have excluded exploration for specified minerals (or petroleum) or petroleum extraction (subs (3)).

Former enactments

ITA 1967 s 244(1), (8)–(9); CTA 1976 s 21(1) and Sch 1 para 9; FA 1992 s 39.

764 Deduction for revenue expenditure on scientific research

(1) Where a person carrying on a trade—

(*a*) incurs non-capital expenditure on scientific research relating to the trade, or

(*b*) pays any sum to—

(i) a body carrying on scientific research and approved for the purposes of this section by the Minister for Finance, or

(ii) an Irish university,

in order that such body or university may undertake scientific research, then, the expenditure so incurred or the sum so paid shall be deducted as an expense in computing the profits or gains of the trade.

(2) Where a person carrying on a trade—

(*a*) incurs non-capital expenditure on scientific research or pays any sum to a body or university referred to in subsection (1)(*b*) in order that the body or university may undertake scientific research, and

(*b*) the expenditure so incurred or the sum so paid is not deductible as an expense under subsection (1) because the scientific research is not related to any trade being carried on by the person,

then, the expenditure so incurred or the sum so paid shall be deducted as an expense in computing the profits or gains of the person's trade.

Notes

This section is to apply (with effect from 6 April 2001) as if subsection (1)(*b*) were deleted and subsection (2) is to be construed accordingly — see TCA 1997 s 848A(13) (inserted by FA 2001 s 45).

Cross-references

Apportionment of consideration and exchanges and surrenders of leasehold interests: s 311(4).

Capital allowance is given on VAT exclusive expenditure: s 319(*d*).

Chargeable period, and general provisions: s 321(1)(*e*).

Donations to approved bodies, relief for, this section to apply as if subs (1)(*b*) were deleted and subs (2) to be construed accordingly: s 848A(12).

Discontinuance of trade: s 321(9)(*c*).

Expenditure not to be taken in to account in relation to more than one trade: s 763(6).

Grants and subsidies: s 763(5).

Meanings of "asset", "expenditure on scientific research", "scientific research": s 763(2), (3).

Non-resident company within the charge to corporation tax in respect of one source and income tax in respect of another: s 309(*e*).

Petroleum trade, abandonment expenditure and loss relief: s 695(8).

Petroleum trade, development expenditure: s 692(4)(*e*).

Petroleum trade, exploration expenditure: s 693(12).

Special provisions as to certain sales: s 312(2)(*a*)(ii).

Tax credit for research and development expenditure: s 766(1)(*a*)("expenditure on research and development").

Former enactments

ITA 1967 s 244(2) and (2A); CTA 1976 s 21(1) and Sch 1 para 9.

Corresponding UK tax provision

Capital Allowances Act 2001 s 439.

765 Allowances for capital expenditure on scientific research

(1) Where a person—

(*a*) incurs capital expenditure on scientific research,

(*b*) (i) is then carrying on a trade to which such expenditure relates, or

(ii) subsequently sets up and commences a trade which is related to such research,

(*c*) applies to the inspector for an allowance under this subsection in respect of such expenditure, and (*d*) so applies—

(i) in the case where the expenditure was incurred while carrying on the trade, within 24 months after the end of the chargeable period in which it was incurred, or

(ii) in the case where the expenditure was incurred before the setting up and commencement of the trade, within 24 months after the end of the chargeable period in which the trade was set up and commenced,

then, subject to this section, there shall be made in taxing the trade for the chargeable period mentioned in whichever of subparagraphs (i) and (ii) of paragraph (*d*) is applicable an allowance equal to the amount of the expenditure.

(2) Where a person carrying on a trade incurs capital expenditure on scientific research in respect of which an allowance may not be made under subsection (1) because the scientific research is not related to any trade being carried on by that person, there shall be made in taxing that person's trade for the chargeable period in which the expenditure was incurred an allowance equal to the amount of the expenditure.

(3) Where an asset representing capital expenditure on scientific research ceases at any time from any cause whatever to be used for such research, relating to the trade carried on by the person who incurred the expenditure, then —

(*a*) an amount equal to the allowance made under this section in respect of that expenditure, or, if the value of the asset immediately before the cessation is less than that allowance, equal to that value, shall be treated as a trading receipt of the trade accruing immediately before the cessation, and

(*b*) in the application of section 284 to an allowance made in respect of the asset for any chargeable period after that in which the cessation takes place, the actual cost of the asset shall be treated as being reduced by the amount of the allowance effectively made.

(4) Where an allowance under this section is made to a person for any chargeable period in respect of expenditure represented wholly or partly by assets, no allowance in respect of those assets shall be made to that person under section 85 or 284 for that chargeable period.

(5) Section 304(4) shall apply in relation to an allowance under subsection (1) or (2) as it applies in relation to allowances to be made under Part 9.

Cross-references

Apportionment of consideration and exchanges and surrenders of leasehold interests: s 311(4).

Balancing allowances and charges, meaning of scientific research allowance: s 288(4)(*a*).

Capital allowance is given on VAT exclusive expenditure: s 319(*d*).

Chargeable period and general provisions: s 321(1)(*e*).

Discontinuance of trade: s 321(9)(*c*).

Dividends regarded as paid out of profits accumulated before given date, subss (1), (2): Sch 22 para 5(3)(*e*).

Expenditure not to be taken into account in relation to more than one trade: s 763(6).

Grants and subsidies: s 763(5).

Industrial building construction or refurbishment expenditure does not include expenditure under this section: s 270(2)(*c*).

Meanings of "asset", "expenditure on scientific research", "scientific research": s 763(2), (3).

Non-resident company within the charge to corporation tax in respect of one source and income tax in respect of another: s 309(*e*).

Petroleum trade, abandonment expenditure and loss relief: s 695(8).
Petroleum trade, development expenditure: s 692(4)(*e*).
Petroleum trade, exploration expenditure: s 693(12).
Profits or assets available for distribution: s 413(5).
Reorganisation into companies of Trustee Savings Banks, capital allowances: Sch 17 para 2(1)(*a*).
Special provisions as to certain sales: s 312(2)(*a*)(ii).

Definitions

inspector: ss 2(1), 5(1), 852; month: IA 1937 Sch; the Oireachtas: IA 1937 Sch; person: IA 1937 s 11(*c*); trade: s 3(1).

Former enactments

ITA 1967 s 244(3)–(7); CTA 1976 s 21(1) and Sch 1 para 9; FA 1980 s 17(3); FA 1996 s 132(2) and Sch 5 Pt II.

766 Tax credit for research and development expenditure

[(1) (*a*) In this section—

"appropriate inspector" has the same meaning as in section 950;

"EEA Agreement" means the Agreement on the European Economic Area signed at Oporto on 2 May 1992 as adjusted by the Protocol signed at Brussels on 17 March 1993;

"expenditure on research and development", in relation to a company, means expenditure, other than expenditure on a building or structure, incurred by the company in the carrying on by it of research and development activities in a relevant Member State, being expenditure—

[(i) which—

(I) is allowable for the purposes of tax in the State as a deduction in computing income from a trade (otherwise than by virtue of section 307), or would be so allowable but for the fact that for accounting purposes it is brought into account in determining the value of an intangible asset, or

(II) is relieved under Part 8,][1]

(ii) on machinery or plant which qualifies for any allowance under Part 9 or this Chapter, or

(iii) which qualifies for an allowance under section 764,

but—

(I) expenditure on research and development shall not include a royalty or other sum paid by a company in respect of the user of an invention—

(A) if the royalty or other sum is paid to a person who is connected with the company within the meaning of section 10 and is income from a qualifying patent within the meaning of section 234, or

(B) to the extent to which the royalty or other sum exceeds the royalty or other sum which would have been paid if the payer of the royalty or other sum and the beneficial recipient of the royalty or other sum were independent persons acting at arm's length,

...[2]

[(IA) expenditure by a company on research and development shall not include any amount of interest notwithstanding that such interest is brought into account by the company in determining the value of an asset, and][3]

(II) expenditure incurred by a company which is resident in the State shall not be expenditure on research and development if it—

(A) may be taken into account as an expense in computing income of the company,

(B) is expenditure in respect of which an allowance for capital expenditure may be made to the company, or

(C) may otherwise be allowed or relieved in relation to the company,

for the purposes of tax in a territory other than the State;

"group expenditure on research and development", in relation to a relevant period of a group of companies, means the aggregate of the amounts of expenditure on research and development incurred in the relevant period by qualified companies which for the relevant period are members of the group: but—

(i) expenditure incurred by a company which is a member of a group for a part of a relevant period shall only be included in group expenditure on research and development if the expenditure is incurred at a time when the company is a member of the group, and

(ii) expenditure on research and development incurred by a company which has been included in group expenditure on research and development in relation to a group shall not be included in group expenditure on research and development in relation to any other group;

"qualified company", in relation to a relevant period, means a company which—

(i) throughout the relevant period—

(I) carries on a trade,

(II) is a 51 per cent subsidiary of a company which carries on a trade, or

(III) is a 51 per cent subsidiary of a company whose business consists wholly or mainly of the holding of stocks, shares or securities of a company which carries on a trade or more than one such company,

(ii) carries out research and development activities in the relevant period, and

(iii) maintains a record of expenditure incurred by it in the carrying out by it of those activities;

"qualifying group expenditure on research and development", in relation to a relevant period, means an amount equal to the excess of the amount of group expenditure on research and development in relation to the relevant period over the threshold amount in relation to the relevant period;

"relevant Member State" means a state which is a Member State of the European Communities or, not being such a Member State, a state which is a contracting party to the EEA Agreement;

"relevant period" means—

(i) in the case of companies which are members of a group the respective ends of the accounting periods of the members of which coincide, the period of 12 months throughout which one or more members of the group carries on a trade and ending at the end of the first accounting period which commences on or after 1 January 2004, and

(ii) in the case of companies which are members of a group the respective ends of the accounting periods of which do not coincide, the period specified in a notice in writing made jointly by companies which are members of the group and given to the appropriate inspector within a period of 9 months after the end of the period so specified, being a period of 12 months throughout which one or more members of the group carries on a trade and ending at the end of the first accounting period of a company which is a member of the group which accounting period commences on or after 1 January 2004,

and each subsequent period of 12 months commencing immediately after the end of the preceding relevant period;

"research and development activities" means systematic, investigative or experimental activities in a field of science or technology, being one or more of the following—

(i) basic research, namely, experimental or theoretical work undertaken primarily to acquire new scientific or technical knowledge without a specific practical application in view,

(ii) applied research, namely, work undertaken in order to gain scientific or technical knowledge and directed towards a specific practical application, or

(iii) experimental development, namely, work undertaken which draws on scientific or technical knowledge or practical experience for the purpose of achieving technological advancement and which is directed at producing new, or improving existing, materials, products, devices, processes, systems or services including incremental improvements thereto:

but activities will not be research and development activities unless they—

(I) seek to achieve scientific or technological advancement, and

(II) involve the resolution of scientific or technological uncertainty;

"threshold amount", in relation to a relevant period of a group of companies, means—

(i) where the relevant period is a period commencing at any time after 31 December 2003 and before 1 January 2007, the aggregate of the amounts of expenditure on research and development incurred in the period of one year ending on a date in the year 2003 which corresponds with the date on which the relevant period ends,

(ii) in any other case, the aggregate of the amounts of expenditure on research and development incurred in the period of one year ending on a date which is 3 years before the end of the relevant period, by all companies which are members of the group in the threshold period in relation to the relevant period concerned: but expenditure incurred by a company which is a member of the group for a part of the threshold period shall only be included in the threshold amount if the expenditure is incurred at a time when the company is a member of the group;

"threshold period", in relation to a relevant period, means the period of one year referred to in the definition of "threshold amount";—

"university or institute of higher education" means—

(i) a college or institution of higher education in the State which—

(I) provides courses to which a scheme approved by the Minister for Education and Science under the Local Authorities (Higher Education Grants) Acts 1968 to 1992 applies, or

(II) operates in accordance with a code of standards which from time to time may, with the consent of the Minister for Finance, be laid down by the Minister for Education and Science, and which the Minister for Education and Science approves for the purposes of section 473A;

(ii) any university or similar institution of higher education in a relevant Member State (other than the State) which—

(I) is maintained or assisted by recurrent grants from public funds of that or any other relevant Member State (including the State), or

(II) is a duly accredited university or institution of higher education in the Member State in which it is situated.

(*b*) For the purposes of this section—

(i) 2 companies shall be deemed to be members of a group if one company is a 51 per cent subsidiary of the other company or both companies are 51 per cent subsidiaries of a third company: but in determining whether one company is a 51 per cent subsidiary of another company, the other company shall be treated as not being the owner of—

(I) any share capital which it owns directly in a company if a profit on a sale of the shares would be treated as a trading receipt of its trade, or

(II) any share capital which it owns indirectly, and which is owned directly by a company for which a profit on a sale of the shares would be a trading receipt;

(ii) sections 412 to 418 shall apply for the purposes of this paragraph as they would apply for the purposes of Chapter 5 of Part 12 if—

(I) "51 per cent subsidiary" were substituted for "75 per cent subsidiary" in each place where it occurs in that Chapter, and

(II) paragraph (*c*) of section 411(1) were deleted;

(iii) a company and all its 51 per cent subsidiaries shall form a group and, where that company is a member of a group as being itself a 51 per cent subsidiary, that group shall comprise all its 51 per cent subsidiaries and the first-mentioned group shall be deemed not to be a group: but a company which is not a member of a group shall be treated as if it were a member of a group which consists of that company;

(iv) in determining whether a company was a member of a group of companies (in this subparagraph referred to as the **"threshold group"**) for the purposes of determining the threshold amount in relation to a relevant period of a group of companies (in this subparagraph referred to as the **"relevant group"**), the threshold group shall be treated as the same group as the relevant group notwithstanding that one or more of the companies in the threshold group is not in the relevant group, or vice versa, where any person or group of persons which controlled the threshold group is the same as, or has a reasonable commonality of identity with, the person or group of persons which controls the relevant group;".

(v) expenditure shall not be regarded as having been incurred by a company if it has been or is to be met directly or indirectly by grant assistance or any other assistance which is granted by or through the State, any board established by statute, any public or local authority or any other agency of the State;

(vi) where a company—

(I) incurs expenditure on research and development at a time when the company is not carrying on a trade, being expenditure which, apart from this subparagraph, is not included in group expenditure on research and development, and

(II) the company begins to carry on a trade after that time,

the expenditure shall be treated as it would if the company had commenced to carry on the trade at the time the expenditure was incurred;

(vii) where in any period a company—

(I) incurs expenditure on research and development, and

(II) pays a sum to a university or institute of higher education in order for that university or institute to carry on research and development activities in a relevant Member State,

so much of the sum so paid as does not exceed 5 per cent of that expenditure shall be treated as if it were expenditure incurred by the company on the carrying on by it of research and development activities.

(2) Where for any accounting period a company makes a claim in that behalf to the appropriate inspector, the corporation tax of the company for that accounting period shall be reduced by an amount equal to 20 per cent of qualifying expenditure attributable to the company as is referable to the accounting period.

(3) For the purposes of subsection (2)—

(*a*) qualifying expenditure attributable to a company in relation to a relevant period shall be so much of the amount of qualifying group expenditure on research and development in the relevant period as is attributed to the company in the manner specified in a notice made jointly in writing to the appropriate inspector by the qualified companies that are members of the group: but where no such notice is given means an amount determined by the formula—

$$Q \times \frac{C}{G}$$

where—

Q is the qualifying group expenditure on research and development in the relevant period,

C is the amount of expenditure on research and development incurred by the company in the relevant period at a time when the company is a member of the group, and

G is the group expenditure on research and development in the relevant period,

(*b*) where a relevant period coincides with an accounting period of a company, the amount of qualifying expenditure on research and development attributable to the company as is referable to the accounting period of the company shall be the full amount of that expenditure, and

(*c*) where the relevant period does not coincide with an accounting period of the company—

(i) the qualifying expenditure on research and development attributable to the company shall be apportioned to the accounting periods which fall wholly or partly in the relevant period, and

(ii) the amount so apportioned to an accounting period shall be treated as the amount of qualifying expenditure on research and development attributable to the company as is referable to the accounting period of the company.

(4) Where as respects any accounting period of a company the amount by which the company is entitled to reduce corporation tax of the accounting period exceeds the corporation tax of the company for the accounting period, the excess shall be carried forward and treated as an amount by which corporation tax for the next succeeding accounting period may be reduced, and so on for succeeding accounting periods.

(5) Where a company claims relief under this section in respect of any accounting period, it shall specify the amount of relief claimed in its return under section 951 for that accounting period.

(6) (*a*) The Minister for Enterprise, Trade and Employment, in consultation with the Minister for Finance, may make regulations for the purposes of this section providing—

(i) that such categories of activities as may be specified in the regulations are not research and development activities, and

(ii) that such other categories of activities as may be specified in the regulations are research and development activities.

(*b*) Where regulations are to be made under this subsection, a draft of the regulations shall be laid before Dáil Éireann and the regulations shall not be made until a resolution approving the draft has been passed by Dáil Éireann.][4]

Amendments

1 Definition of "expenditure on research and development" subpara (i) substituted by FA 2005 s 48(1)(*f*)(i) as respects any period of account beginning on or after 1 January 2005.

2 Deleted by FA 2005 s 48(1)(*f*)(ii) as respects any period of account beginning on or after 1 January 2005; previously "and".

3 Definition of "expenditure on research and development" clause (IA) inserted by FA 2005 s 48(1)(*f*)(ii) as respects any period of account beginning on or after 1 January 2005.

4 Section 766 substituted by FA 2004 s 33(1)(*a*) with effect from such day as the Minister for Finance may appoint by order and has effect as respects expenditure incurred on or after that day. By virtue of the Finance Act 2004 (Section 33) (Commencement) Order 2004, SI No 425 of 2004, this amendment comes into operation with effect from 1 January 2004.

Cross-references

Distributions out of income from patent royalties, meaning of "research and development activities" applied: s 141(5)(*a*).

Tax credit on expenditure on buildings or structures used for research and development, meanings of "qualified company", "relevant Member State" and "research and development activities applied: s 766A(1)(*a*); meaning of "research and development" applied: s 766A(1)(*b*)(ii)(III); subs (1)(*b*)(i) to (iii) applied: s 766A(1)(*b*)(iv).

Regulations

Taxes Consolidation Act 1997 (Prescribed Research and Development Activities) Regulations 2004 (SI No 434 of 2004).

Revenue Information

Revenue Guidelines for the Research and Development Tax Credit can be downloaded from Revenue's website — **www.revenue.ie** — under Publications/Technical Guidelines.

For the purposes of determining the amounts of expenditure on plant and machinery to be included in any computation of tax credit due under TCA 1997 s 766, Revenue are prepared to accept that expenditure on plant and machinery may be treated as incurred on either (1) the date the plant and machinery is first brought into use for the purposes of a trade or (2) the date the expenditure becomes payable. This latter option is subject to a condition that the credit will be clawed back, if the plant or machinery is not brought into use for the purpose of a trade within two years of the expenditure becoming payable.

Tax Briefing

TB55 April 2004 pp 6–7 — Research and Development Credit.

Definitions

company: s 4(1); inspector: ss 2(1), 5(1), 852; month: IA 1937 Sch; writing: IA 1937 Sch; trade: ss 3(1), 4(1), 5(1); year: IA 1937 Sch; 51 per cent subsidiary: s 9.

Former enactments

FA 1995 s 59(1)–(4); FA 1996 s 57(1).

766A Tax credit on expenditure on buildings or structures used for research and development

[(1) (*a*) In this section—

"qualified company", **"relevant member State"** and **"research and development activities"** have the same meanings as in section 766;

"refurbishment", in relation to a building or structure, means any work of construction, reconstruction, repair or renewal including the provision of water, sewerage or heating facilities carried out in the course of the repair or restoration, or maintenance in the nature of repair or restoration, of the building or structure;

"relevant expenditure" on a building or structure, in relation to a company, means expenditure incurred by the company on the construction of a building or structure which is to be used wholly and exclusively for the purposes of the carrying on by the company of research and development activities in a relevant Member State, being expenditure which qualifies for an allowance under Part 9 or this Part: but expenditure incurred by a company which is resident in the State shall not be relevant expenditure if it—

(i) may be taken into account as an expense in computing income of the company,

(ii) is expenditure in respect of which an allowance for capital expenditure may be made to the company, or

(iii) may otherwise be allowed or relieved in relation to the company,

for the purposes of tax in a territory other than the State.

(*b*) For the purposes of this section—

(i) expenditure shall not be regarded as having been incurred by a company if it has been or is to be met directly or indirectly by the State;

(ii) a reference to expenditure incurred on the construction of a building or structure includes expenditure on the refurbishment of the building or structure, but does not include—

(I) any expenditure incurred on the acquisition of, or of rights in or over, any land,

(II) any expenditure on the provision of machinery or plant or on any asset treated for any chargeable period as machinery or plant, or

(III) any expenditure on research and development within the meaning of section 766;

(iii) where a building or structure which is to be used for the purposes of the carrying on of research and development activities forms part of a building or is one of a number of buildings in a single development, or forms a part of a building which is itself one of a number of buildings in a single development, there shall be made such apportionment as is necessary of the expenditure incurred on the construction of the whole building or number of buildings, as the case may be, for the purpose of determining the expenditure incurred on the construction of the building or structure which is to be used for the purposes of carrying on of research and development activities,

(iv) paragraphs (i) to (iii) of section 766(1)(*b*) shall apply.

(2) Where in an accounting period a qualified company incurs relevant expenditure on a building or structure, the corporation tax of the company for each accounting period falling wholly or partly into the period of 4 years commencing at the beginning of that accounting period shall be reduced by an amount determined by the formula—

$$E \times \frac{M}{1460}$$

where—

E is an amount equal to 20 per cent of the amount of the relevant expenditure on the building or structure, and

M is the number of days in the accounting period which fall into that period of 4 years.

(3) Where—

(i) in an accounting period a company incurs relevant expenditure on a building or structure,

(ii) in relation to that expenditure the corporation tax of the company is reduced under subsection (2), and

(iii) at any time in the period of 10 years commencing at the beginning of that accounting period the building or structure is sold or commences to be used for purposes other than the carrying on by the company of research and development activities,

then the company—

(I) shall not be entitled to reduce corporation tax under subsection (2) for any accounting period ending after the time specified in paragraph (iii), and

(II) shall be charged to tax under Case IV of Schedule D for the accounting period in which the building or structure is sold, or as the case may be commences to be used for purposes other than the carrying on by the company of research and development activities, in an amount equal to 4 times the aggregate amount by which corporation tax of the company or another company was reduced under subsection (2) or (4) in relation to that expenditure.

(4) (*a*) Subject to paragraphs (*b*) and (*c*) where as respects any accounting period of a company the amount by which the company is entitled under this section to reduce corporation tax of the accounting period exceeds the relevant corporation tax of the company for the accounting period, the excess shall be carried forward and treated as an amount by which corporation tax for the next succeeding accounting period may be reduced, and so on for succeeding accounting periods.

(*b*) Where the company referred to in paragraph (*a*) is a member of a group of companies, the company may specify that the excess specified in paragraph (*a*), or any part of that excess, is to be treated as an amount by which corporation tax payable by another company which is a member of that group for that other company's corresponding accounting period is to be reduced.

(*c*) So much of the excess specified under paragraph (*a*) as is treated under paragraph (*b*) as an amount by which tax payable by another company is to be reduced shall not be carried forward under paragraph (*a*).

(5) Where a company claims relief under this section in respect of any accounting period, it shall specify the amount of relief claimed in its return under section 951 for that accounting period.][1]

Amendments

1 Section 766A inserted by FA 2004 s 33(1)(*a*) with effect from such day as the Minister for Finance may appoint by order and has effect as respects expenditure incurred on or after that day. By virtue of the Finance Act 2004 (Section 33) (Commencement) Order 2004, SI No 425 of 2004, this amendment comes into operation with effect from 1 January 2004.

Revenue Information

Revenue Guidelines for the Research and Development Tax Credit can be downloaded from Revenue's website — **www.revenue.ie** — under Publications/Technical Guidelines.

Definitions

company: s 4(1).

Tax Briefing

TB55 April 2004 pp 6–7 — Research and Development Credit.

767 Payment to universities and other approved bodies for research in, or teaching of, approved subjects

Amendments

This section repealed by TCA 1997 s 848A(13) (inserted by FA 2001 s 45) with effect from 6 April 2001.

CHAPTER 3
Know-How and Certain Training

768 Allowance for know-how

(1) In this section—

"control" has the same meaning as in section 312;

"know-how" means industrial information and techniques likely to assist in the manufacture or processing of goods or materials, or in the carrying out of any agricultural, forestry, fishing, mining or other extractive operations;

references to a body of persons include references to a partnership.

(2) (*a*) For the purposes of this subsection, a person incurring expenditure on know-how before the setting up and commencement of the trade in which it is used shall be treated as incurring it on that setting up and commencement.

(*b*) Where a person incurs expenditure on know-how for use in a trade carried on by the person or, having incurred expenditure on know-how, sets up and commences a trade in which it is used, there shall, subject to this section, be allowed to be deducted as expenses, in computing for the purposes of Case I of Schedule D the profits or gains of the trade, such part of the expenditure as would but for this section not be allowed to be so deducted.

(3) Where a person acquires a trade or part of a trade and, together with the trade or the part of the trade, know-how used in the trade or part of the trade, no amount shall be allowed to be deducted under this section in respect of expenditure incurred on the acquisition of the know-how.

(4) Subsection (2) shall not apply on any sale of know-how where the buyer is a body of persons over whom the seller has control, or the seller is a body of persons over whom the buyer has control, or both the seller and the buyer are bodies of persons and some other person has control over both of them.

Cross-references

Petroleum trade, development expenditure: s 692(4)(*f*).

Petroleum trade, exploration expenditure: s 693(12).

Definitions

body of persons: s 2(1); person: IA 1937 s 11(*c*); trade: s 3(1).

Former enactments

FA 1968 s 2.

Corresponding UK tax provision

Income and Corporation Taxes Act 1988 s 530 [repealed].

769 Relief for training of local staff before commencement of trading

(1) Where, before the day of the setting up or commencement of a trade consisting of the production for sale of manufactured goods, a person who is about to carry on the trade incurs or has incurred expenditure on the recruitment and training, with a view to their employment in the trade, of persons all or a majority of whom are Irish citizens, there shall be made to such person allowances in respect of that expenditure during a writing-down period of 3 years beginning on that day, and such allowances shall be made in taxing the trade.

(2) For the purposes of this section—

(*a*) expenditure shall not include any expenditure incurred by a person in respect of which no deduction would have been allowable to the person, in computing the profits or gains of the trade under the provisions of the Tax Acts applicable to Case I of Schedule D, if it had been incurred on or after the day of the setting up or commencement of the trade;

(*b*) expenditure shall not be regarded as having been incurred by a person in so far as it has been or is to be met directly or indirectly by the State or by any person other than the first-mentioned person;

(*c*) the date on which any expenditure is incurred shall be taken to be the date on which the sum in question becomes payable.

(3) Section 304(4) shall apply in relation to an allowance under subsection (1) as it applies in relation to an allowance to be made under Part 9.

(4) For the purposes of the Income Tax Acts, any claim by a person for an allowance under this section shall be included in the annual statement required to be delivered under those Acts of the profits or gains of the person's trade and shall be accompanied by a certificate signed by the claimant (which shall be deemed to form part of the claim) stating that the expenditure was incurred on the recruitment and training, with a view to their employment in the trade, of persons all or a majority of whom are Irish citizens and giving such particulars as show that the allowance is to be made.

Cross-references

Capital allowance is given on VAT exclusive expenditure: s 319(*d*).

Chargeable period, and general provisions: s 321(1)(*f*).

Discontinuance of trade: s 321(9)(*d*).

Non-resident company within the charge to corporation tax in respect of one source and income tax in respect of another: s 309(*e*).

Reorganisation into companies of Trustee Savings Banks, capital allowances: Sch 17 para 2(1)(*a*).

Definitions

person: IA 1937 s 11(*c*); statute: IA 1937 s 3; s 1(1); trade: s 3(1).

Former enactments

ITA 1967 s 305; CTA 1976 s 21(1) and Sch 1 para 51; FA 1993 s 34(1)(*c*).

[CHAPTER 4
Transmission Capacity Rights][1]

Amendments

1 Chapter 4 inserted by FA 2000 s 64 and, by virtue of FA 2003 s 20, comes into operation with effect from the date of the passing of the Finance Act 2003, ie 28 March 2003.

769A Interpretation (Chapter 4)

[(1) In this Chapter—

"capacity rights" means the right to use wired, radio or optical transmission paths for the transfer of voice, data or information;

[**"control"** shall be construed in accordance with section 432;

"qualifying expenditure" means capital expenditure incurred on the purchase of capacity rights, but does not include expenditure incurred on or after 6 February 2003 which consists of a licence fee or other payment paid to the Commission for Communications Regulation in respect of a licence or permission granted by that Commission on or after that date under—

(*a*) the Wireless Telegraphy Acts 1926 to 1988, or

(*b*) the Postal and Telecommunications Services Act 1983;][1]

"writing-down period" has the meaning assigned to it by section 769B(2).

(2) In this Chapter, any reference to the sale of part of capacity rights includes a reference to the grant of a licence in respect of the capacity rights in question, and any reference to the purchase of capacity rights includes a reference to the acquisition of a licence in respect of capacity rights; but, if a licence granted by a company entitled to any capacity rights is a licence to exercise those rights to the exclusion of the grantor and all other persons for the whole of the remainder of the term for which the rights subsist, the grantor shall be treated for the purposes of this Chapter as thereby selling the whole of the rights.][2]

Amendments

1 Definitions of "control" and "qualifying expenditure" inserted by FA 2003 s 20(1)(*a*) with effect from 28 March 2003.

2 Section 769A inserted by FA 2000 s 64 and by virtue of FA 2003 s 20 comes into operation with effect from the date of the passing of the Finance Act 2003, ie 28 March 2003.

Definitions

person: IA 1937 s 11(*c*).

769B Annual allowances for capital expenditure on purchase of capacity rights

[(1) Where, on or after 1 April 2000, a company incurs [qualifying expenditure][1] on the purchase of capacity rights, there shall, subject to and in accordance with this Chapter, be made to that company writing-down allowances, in respect of that expenditure during the writing-down period; but no writing-down allowance shall be made to a company in respect of any expenditure unless—

(*a*) the allowance is to be made to the company in taxing the company's trade, or (*b*) any income receivable by the company in respect of the rights would be liable to tax.

(2) (*a*) Subject to paragraph (*c*), the writing-down period shall be—

(i) a period of 7 years, or

(ii) where the capacity rights are purchased for a specified period which exceeds 7 years, the number of years for which the capacity rights are purchased,

commencing with the beginning of the accounting period related to the expenditure.

(*b*) For the purposes of this section, writing-down allowances shall be determined by the formula—

$$A \times \frac{B}{C}$$

where—

A is the amount of the [qualifying expenditure][1] incurred on the purchase of the capacity rights,

B is the length of the part of the chargeable period falling within the writing-down period, and

C is the length of the writing-down period.

(*c*) For the purposes of this subsection, any expenditure incurred for the purposes of a trade by a company about to carry on the trade shall be treated as if that expenditure had been incurred by that company on the first day on which that company carries on the trade unless before that day the company has sold all the capacity rights on the purchase of which the expenditure was incurred.

[(3) (*a*) Notwithstanding any other provisions of this Chapter, where a company (in this paragraph referred to as the "buyer") incurs qualifying expenditure on the purchase from another company (in this paragraph referred to as the "seller") of capacity rights, no allowances shall be made under this Chapter to the buyer in respect of that expenditure if both companies are companies within a group of companies, unless an allowance had been made under this Chapter to the seller (or would have been made to the seller if it had not sold those rights) in respect of the capital expenditure it incurred on the purchase of those rights.

(*b*) For the purposes of this subsection—

(i) a **"group of companies"** means a company and any other companies of which it has control or with which it is associated, and

(ii) a company is associated with another company where it could reasonably be considered that—

(I) any person or any group of persons or groups of persons having a reasonable commonality of identity has or have, as the case may be, or had the means or power, either directly or indirectly, to determine the trading operations carried on or to be carried on by both companies, or

(II) both companies are under the control of any person or any group of persons or groups of persons having a reasonable commonality of identity.][2]][3]

Amendments

1 Substituted by FA 2003 s 20(1)(*b*)(i) with effect from 28 March 2003; previously "capital expenditure".
2 Subs (3) inserted by FA 2003 s 20(1)(*b*)(ii) with effect from 28 March 2003.
3 Section 769B inserted by FA 2000 s 64 and by virtue of FA 2003 s 20 comes operation with effect from the date of the passing of the Finance Act 2003, ie 28 March 2003.

Definitions

capacity rights: s 769A(1); chargeable period: s 321(2); chargeable period related to the expenditure: s 321(2); company: ss 4(1), 5(1); trade: ss 4(1), 5(1).

769C Effect of lapse of capacity rights

[(1) Where a company incurs [qualifying expenditure][1] on the purchase of capacity rights and, before the end of the writing-down period, any of the following events occurs—

(*a*) the rights come to an end without provision for their subsequent renewal or the rights cease altogether to be exercised;
(*b*) the company sells all those rights or so much of them as it still owns;
(*c*) the company sells part of those rights and the amount of net proceeds of the sale (in so far as they consist of capital sums) are not less than the amount of the [qualifying expenditure][1] remaining unallowed;

no writing-down allowance shall be made to that company for the chargeable period related to the event or for any subsequent chargeable period.

(2) Where a company incurs [qualifying expenditure][1] on the purchase of capacity rights and, before the end of the writing-down period, either of the following events occurs—

(*a*) the rights come to an end without provision for their subsequent renewal or the rights cease altogether to be exercised;
(*b*) the company sells all those rights or so much of them as it still owns, and the amount of the net proceeds of the sale (in so far as they consist of capital sums) are less than the amount of the [qualifying expenditure][1] remaining unallowed;

there shall, subject to and in accordance with this Chapter, be made to that company for the accounting period related to the event an allowance (in this Chapter referred to as a "balancing allowance") equal to—

(i) if the event is one referred to in paragraph (*a*), the amount of the [qualifying expenditure][1] remaining unallowed, and
(ii) if the event is one referred to in paragraph (*b*), the amount of the [qualifying expenditure][1] remaining unallowed less the amount of the net proceeds of the sale.

(3) Where a company which has incurred [qualifying expenditure][1] on the purchase of capacity rights sells all or any part of those rights and the amount of the net proceeds of the sale (in so far as they consist of capital sums) exceeds the amount of the [qualifying expenditure][1] remaining unallowed, if any, there shall, subject to and in accordance with

this Chapter, be made on that company for the chargeable period related to the sale a charge (in this Chapter referred to as a "balancing charge") on an amount equal to—

(*a*) the excess, or

(*b*) where the amount of the [qualifying expenditure][1] remaining unallowed is nil, the amount of the net proceeds of the sale.

(4) Where a company which has incurred [qualifying expenditure][1] on the purchase of capacity rights sells a part of those rights and subsection (3) does not apply, the amount of any writing-down allowance made in respect of that expenditure for the chargeable period related to the sale or any subsequent chargeable period shall be the amount determined by—

(*a*) subtracting the amount of the net proceeds of the sale (in so far as they consist of capital sums) from the amount of the expenditure remaining unallowed at the time of the sale, and

(*b*) dividing the result by the number of complete years of the writing-down period which remained at the beginning of the chargeable period related to the sale,

and so on for any subsequent sales.

(5) References in this section to the amount of any [qualifying expenditure][1] remaining unallowed shall in relation to any event aforesaid be construed as references to the amount of that expenditure less any writing-down allowances made in respect of that expenditure for chargeable periods before the chargeable period related to that event, and less also the amount of the net proceeds of any previous sale by the company which incurred the expenditure of any part of the rights acquired by the expenditure, in so far as those proceeds consist of capital sums.

(6) Notwithstanding subsections (1) to (5)—

(*a*) no balancing allowance shall be made in respect of any expenditure unless a writing-down allowance has been, or, but for the happening of the event giving rise to the balancing allowance, could have been, made in respect of that expenditure, and

(*b*) the total amount on which a balancing charge is made in respect of any expenditure shall not exceed the total writing-down allowances actually made in respect of that expenditure less, if a balancing charge has previously been made in respect of that expenditure, the amount on which that charge was made.][2]

Amendments

1 Substituted by FA 2003 s 20(1)(*c*) with effect from 28 March 2003; previously "capital expenditure".

2 Section 769C inserted by FA 2000 s 64 and by virtue of FA 2003 s 20 comes into operation with effect from the date of the passing of the Finance Act 2003, ie 28 March 2003.

Cross-references

Application of Chapter 4 of Part 9: s 769E(2).

Definitions

capacity rights: s 769A(1); chargeable period: s 321(2); chargeable period related to the expenditure: s 321(2); company: ss 4(1), 5(1); writing-down period: s 769A(1).

769D Manner of making allowances and charges

[(1) An allowance or charge under this Chapter shall be made to or on a company in taxing the company's trade if—

(*a*) the company is carrying on a trade the profits or gains of which are or, if there were any, would be, chargeable to corporation tax for the chargeable period for which the allowance or charge is made, and

(*b*) at any time in the chargeable period or its basis period the capacity rights in question, or other rights out of which they were granted, were used for the purposes of that trade.

(2) Except where provided for in subsection (1), an allowance under this Chapter shall be made by means of discharge or repayment of tax and shall be available against income from capacity rights, and a charge under this Chapter shall be made under Case IV of Schedule D.][1]

Amendments

1 Section 769D inserted by FA 2000 s 64 and by virtue of FA 2003 s 20 comes into operation with effect from the date of the passing of the Finance Act 2003, ie 28 March 2003.

Cross-references

Application of Chapter 4 of Part 9: s 769E(1).

Definitions

capacity rights: s 769A(1); chargeable period or its basis period: s 321(2); company: ss 4(1), 5(1); trade: ss 3(1), 4(1).

769E Application of Chapter 4 of Part 9

[(1) Subject to subsection (2), Chapter 4 of Part 9 shall apply as if this Chapter were contained in that Part, and any reference in the Tax Acts to any capital allowance to be given by means of discharge or repayment of tax and to be available or available primarily against a specified class of income shall include a reference to any capital allowance given in accordance with section 769D(2).

(2) In Chapter 4 of Part 9, as applied by virtue of subsection (1) to capacity rights, the reference in section 312(5)(*a*)(i) to the sum mentioned in paragraph (*b*) shall in the case of capacity rights be construed as a reference to the amount of the [qualifying expenditure][1] on the acquisition of the capacity rights remaining unallowed, computed in accordance with section 769C.][2]

Amendments

1 Substituted by FA 2003 s 20(1)(*d*) with effect from 28 March 2003; previously "capital expenditure".

2 Section 769E inserted by FA 2000 s 64 and by virtue of FA 2003 s 20 comes into operation with effect from the date of the passing of the Finance Act 2003, ie 28 March 2003.

Definitions

capacity rights: s 769A(1); Tax Acts: s 1(2).

769F Commencement (Chapter 4)

[This Chapter shall come into operation [on the date of the passing of the Finance Act 2003][1].][2]

Amendments

1 Substituted by FA 2003 s 20(1)(*e*) with effect from 28 March 2003; previously "on such day as the Minister for Finance may, by order, appoint".

2 Section 769F inserted by FA 2000 s 64.

PART 30
OCCUPATIONAL PENSION SCHEMES, RETIREMENT ANNUITIES, PURCHASED LIFE ANNUITIES AND CERTAIN PENSIONS

Cross-references

Restriction of deductions for employee benefit contributions, restriction does not apply to any deduction that is allowable under Part 30: s 81A(7)(*d*).
Special arrangements in relation to schemes approved before 6 April 1999 in context of changes effected to Part 30 by FA 1999 s 19(1): FA 1999 s 19(2)(*d*).
Special arrangements in relation to schemes approved before 6 April 2000 in context of changes effected to Part 30 by FA 2000 s 23(1): FA 2000 s 23(2)(*d*).

Revenue information

Information leaflet IT 14 — New Pension Options for the Self-Employed and Directors of Family Companies — April, 1999.

Tax Briefing

TB41 Sept 2000 — New Pension Options — Finance Act 2000 Changes.

CHAPTER 1
Occupational Pension Schemes

Cross-references

Application for approval of a scheme: Sch 23 para 1.
Capital acquisitions tax, exemption relating to retirement benefits: CATCA 2003 s 85(1)(*a*).
Close company, meaning: s 430(6).
Company buying its own shares: s 185(2)(*a*).
Life assurance companies: s 706(3)(*b*).
Limit on remuneration for purposes of relief under this Chapter: s 790A.
Non exempt retirement benefits: s 201(3)(*d*).
Overseas pension plans, migrant member relief, interpretation and general: s 787M(1) ("qualifying overseas pension plan").
Participator, associate, director, loan creditor, meanings: s 433(3)(*c*)(i).
PAYE system, regulations: s 986(1)(*g*).
Pensions Act 1990 (as amended by Pensions (Amendment) Act 2002) ss 4, 46(1)(*b*)(ii), 48(3)(*b*), 49(4) and 122(1).
Personal Retirement Savings Accounts (PRSAs), interpretation and supplemental, meaing of "approved scheme", "retirement benefits scheme" and "statutory scheme" applied: s 787A(1).
Qualifying overseas pension plans, relief for contributions, meaning of "employer" applied: s 787N(1).
Quoted company not close: s 431(6)(*b*).
Returns by employers in relation to pension products: s 897A(1)("employee", "employer").
Unclaimed Life Assurance Policies Act 2003, interpretation, s 2(1) ("approved policy"); unclaimed policies, s 6(3)(*a*).

Revenue Information

Revenue Pensions Manual — New Edition (April 2005) — requests for copies may be made via the Revenue website. The contact address is: lcdretirebens@revenue.ie.

Tax Briefing

TB22 June 1996 p 4 — Transfer of Pension rights between Irish and UK Schemes.
TB24 Dec 1996 p 6 — Small Self-Administered Pension Schemes.
TB52 May 2003 pp 9–10 — Pension Products and Retirement Funds (Finance Act 2003 changes).

770 Interpretation and supplemental (Chapter 1)

(1) In this Chapter, except where the context otherwise requires—

[**"additional voluntary contributions"** means voluntary contributions made to a scheme by an employee which are—

(i) contributions made under a rule or part of a rule, as the case may be, of a retirement benefits scheme (in this definition referred to as the "main scheme") which provides specifically for the payment of members' voluntary contributions, other than contributions made at the rate or rates specified for members' contributions in the rules of the main scheme, or

(ii) contributions made under a separately arranged scheme for members' voluntary contributions which is associated with the main scheme;][1]

[**"administrator"**, in relation to a retirement benefits scheme, means the person or persons, established in a Member State of the European Communities, having the management of the scheme, and references to the administrator of a scheme shall be deemed to include the person mentioned in section 772(2)(*c*)(ii);][2]

"approved scheme" means a retirement benefits scheme for the time being approved by the Revenue Commissioners for the purposes of this Chapter;

[**"approved retirement fund"** has the meaning assigned to it by section 784A;

"approved minimum retirement fund" has the meaning assigned to it by section 784C;][3]

"company" includes any body corporate or unincorporated body of persons other than a partnership;

"director", in relation to a company, includes—

(*a*) in the case of a company the affairs of which are managed by a board of directors or similar body, a member of that board or body,

(*b*) in the case of a company the affairs of which are managed by a single director or similar person, that director or person,

(*c*) in the case of a company the affairs of which are managed by the members themselves, a member of that company,

and includes a person who is to be or has been a director;

"employee"—

(*a*) in relation to a company, includes an officer of the company, any director of the company and any other person taking part in the management of the affairs of the company, and

(*b*) in relation to any employer, includes a person who is to be or has been an employee,

and **"employer"** and other cognate expressions shall be construed accordingly;

"exempt approved scheme" has the meaning assigned to it by section 774;

"final remuneration" means the average annual remuneration of the last 3 years' service;

[**"overseas pension scheme"** means a retirement benefits scheme, other than a state social security scheme, which is—

(*a*) operated or managed by an Institution for Occupational Retirement Provision as defined by Article 6(*a*) of Directive 2003/41/EC of the European Parliament and of the Council of 3 June 2003 (OJ No L235, 23.9.2003, p 10), and

(*b*) established in a Member State of the European Communities, other than the State, which has given effect to that Directive in its national law;][4]

"pension" includes annuity;

[**"pension adjustment order"** means an order made in accordance with either section 12 of the Family Law Act, 1995, or section 17 of the Family Law (Divorce) Act, 1996;][5]

[**"proprietary director"** means a director who, either alone or together with his or her spouse and minor children is or was, at any time within 3 years of the date of—

(i) the specified normal retirement date,

(ii) an earlier retirement date, where applicable,

(iii) leaving service, or

(iv) in the case of a pension or part of a pension payable in accordance with a pension adjustment order, the relevant date in relation to that order,

the beneficial owner of shares which, when added to any shares held by the trustees of any settlement to which the director or his or her spouse had transferred assets, carry more than 5 per cent of the voting rights in the company providing the benefits or in a company which controls that company;][6]

[**"Personal Retirement Savings Account"** or **"PRSA"** has the same meaning as in Chapter 2A of this Part;][7]

"relevant benefits" means any pension, lump sum, gratuity or other like benefit—

(*a*) given or to be given on retirement or on death or in anticipation of retirement, or, in connection with past service, after retirement or death, or

(*b*) to be given on or in anticipation of or in connection with any change in the nature of the service of the employee in question,

but does not include any benefit which is to be afforded solely by reason of the death or disability of a person resulting from an accident arising out of or in the course of his or her office or employment and for no other reason;

[**"relevant date"** means, in relation to a pension adjustment order, the date on which the decree of separation or the decree of divorce, as the case may be, was granted, by reference to which the pension adjustment order in question was made;][8]

[**"retirement benefits scheme"** has the meaning assigned to it by section 771;][9]

"service" means service as an employee of the employer in question and other expressions, including **"retirement"**, shall be construed accordingly;

[**"state social security scheme"** means a system of mandatory protection put in place by the Government of a country or territory, other than the State, to provide a minimum level of retirement income or other benefits, the level of which is determined by that Government;][10]

"statutory scheme" means a retirement benefits scheme established by or under any enactment.

(2) Any reference in this Chapter to the provision of relevant benefits, or of a pension, for employees of an employer includes a reference to the provision of those benefits or that pension by means of a contract between the administrator or the employer and a third person.

(3) Schedule 23 shall apply for the purposes of supplementing this Chapter and shall be construed as one with this Chapter.

Amendments

1 Definition of "additional voluntary contributions" inserted by FA 2000 s 23(1)(*a*)(i) with effect from 6 April 2000.

2 Definition of "administrator" substituted by FA 2005 s 21(1)(*a*)(i)(I) as respects any retirement benefits scheme approved on or after 1 January 2005.

3 Definitions of "approved retirement fund" and "approved minimum retirement fund" inserted by FA 1999 s 19(1)(*a*)(i)(I) in respect of any retirement benefits scheme approved on or after 6 April 1999.

4 Definition of "overseas pension scheme" inserted by FA 2005 s 21(1)(*a*)(i)(II) as respects any retirement benefits scheme approved on or after 1 January 2005.

5 Definition of "pension adjustment order" inserted by FA 2001 s 18(*a*)(i)(I) with effect from 6 April 2001.

6 Definition of "proprietary director" substituted by FA 2001 s 18(*a*)(i)(II) with effect from 6 April 2001.

7 Definition of "Personal Retirement Savings Account" inserted by Pensions (Amendment) Act 2002 s 4(1)(*d*)(i) with effect from such date or dates as the Minister for Social, Community and Family Affairs may appoint by order. By virtue of Pensions (Amendment) Act, 2002 (Commencement) Order 2002, SI No 502 of 2002, this amendment comes into operation on 7 November 2002.

8 Definition of "relevant date" inserted by FA 2001 s 18(*a*)(i)(III) with effect from 6 April 2001.

9 Definition of "retirement benefits scheme" inserted by FA 2005 s 21(1)(*a*)(i)(III) as respects any retirement benefits scheme approved on or after 1 January 2005.

10 Definition of "state security scheme" inserted by FA 2005 s 21(1)(*a*)(i)(IV) as respects any retirement benefits scheme approved on or after 1 January 2005.

Cross-references

Dividend withholding tax, declarations of exemption, meaning of "administrator" applied: Sch 2A, para 1 (appropriate person).

Employee share options schemes, meaning of "director" and "employee" applied: s 128(1)(*a*).

Investment undertakings, declarations, meaning of "administrator" applied: Sch 2B para 1.

Surcharge on certain income of trustees: s 805(2)(*c*).

Definitions

body of persons: s 2(1); person: IA 1937 s 11(*c*).

Former enactments

FA 1972 s 13(1), (2) and (4); FA 1974 s 86 and Sch 2 Pt II.

Corresponding UK tax provision

Income and Corporation Taxes Act 1988 s 612.

771 Meaning of "retirement benefits scheme"

(1) In this Chapter, **"retirement benefits scheme"** means, subject to this section, a scheme for the provision of benefits consisting of or including relevant benefits, but does not include any scheme under the Social Welfare (Consolidation) Act, 1993, providing such benefits.

(2) References in this Chapter to a scheme include references to a [contract,][1] deed, agreement, series of agreements or other arrangements providing for relevant benefits, notwithstanding that it relates or they relate only to—

(*a*) a small number of employees or to a single employee, or

(*b*) the payment of a pension starting immediately on the making of the arrangements.

(3) The Revenue Commissioners may if they think fit treat a retirement benefits scheme relating to employees of 2 or more different classes or descriptions as being for the purposes of this Chapter 2 or more separate retirement benefits schemes relating respectively to such one or more of those classes or descriptions of those employees as the Revenue Commissioners think fit.

(4) For the purposes of this Chapter—

(*a*) employees may be regarded as belonging to different classes or descriptions if they are employed by different employers, and

(*b*) a particular class or description of employee may consist of a single employee or any number of employees.

Amendments

[1] Inserted by FA 2005 s 21(1)(*a*)(ii) as respects any retirement benefits scheme approved on or after 1 January 2005.

Definitions

employee: s 770(1); employer: s 770(1); pension: s 770(1); relevant benefits: s 770(1).

Former enactments

FA 1972 s 14.

772 Conditions for approval of schemes and discretionary approval

(1) Subject to this section, the Revenue Commissioners shall approve any retirement benefits scheme for the purposes of this Chapter if it satisfies all of the prescribed conditions, namely—

(*a*) the conditions set out in subsection (2), and

(*b*) the conditions as respects benefits set out in subsection (3).

(2) The conditions referred to in subsection (1)(*a*) are—

(*a*) that the scheme is bona fide established for the sole purpose of providing relevant benefits in respect of service as an employee, being benefits payable to, or to the widow or widower, children or dependants or personal representatives of, the employee;

(*b*) that the scheme is recognised by the employer and employees to whom it relates, and that every employee who is or has a right to be a member of the scheme has been given written particulars of all essential features of the scheme which concern the employee;

[(*c*) that in relation to the discharge of all duties and obligations imposed on the administrator of a scheme by this Chapter—

(i) the administrator of an overseas pension scheme has entered into a contract with the Revenue Commissioners enforceable in a Member State of the European Communities in relation to the discharge of those duties and obligations and in entering into such a contract the parties to the contract have acknowledged and agreed in writing that—

(I) it is governed solely by the laws of the State, and

(II) that the courts of the State have exclusive jurisdiction in determining any dispute arising under it,

or

(ii) there is a person resident in the State, appointed by the administrator, who will be responsible for the discharge of all of those duties and obligations and the administrator shall notify the Revenue Commissioners of the appointment of that person and the identity of that person;][1]

(*d*) that the employer is a contributor to the scheme;

(*e*) that the scheme is established in connection with some trade or undertaking carried on in the State by a person resident in the State;

(*f*) no amount can be paid, whether during the subsistence of the scheme or later, by means of repayment of an employee's contributions under the scheme.

(3) The conditions as respects benefits referred to in subsection (1)(*b*) are—

(*a*) that any benefit for an employee is a pension on retirement at a specified age not earlier than 60 years and not later than 70 years, or on earlier retirement through incapacity, which does not exceed one-sixtieth of the employee's final remuneration for each year of service up to a maximum of 40 years;

[(*b*) that any pension for any widow, widower, children or dependants of an employee who dies before retirement shall be a pension or pensions payable on the employee's death of an amount that does not or, as the case may be, do not in aggregate exceed any pension or pensions which, consonant with the condition in paragraph *(a),* could have been provided for the employee on retirement on attaining the specified age, if the employee had continued to serve until the employee attained that age at an annual rate of remuneration equal to the employee's final remuneration;][2]

(*c*) that any lump sums provided for any widow or widower, children, dependants or personal representatives of an employee who dies before retirement shall not exceed in the aggregate 4 times the employee's final remuneration;

[(*d*) that any benefit for any widow, widower, children or dependants of an employee payable on the employee's death after retirement is a pension or pensions such that the aggregate amount of such pension or, as the case may be, pensions so payable does not exceed any pension or pensions payable to the employee;][3]

...[4]

(*f*) [that, subject to subsection (3A),][5] no pension is capable in whole or in part of surrender, commutation or assignment, except in so far as the scheme allows an employee on retirement to obtain by commutation of the employee's pension a lump sum or sums not exceeding in all three-eightieths of the employee's final remuneration for each year of service up to a maximum of 40 years;

(*g*) that no other benefits are payable under the scheme.

[(3A)[(*a*)The Revenue Commissioners shall not approve a retirement benefits scheme for the purposes of this Chapter unless it appears to them that the scheme provides for any individual entitled to a pension under the scheme who is—

[(i) a proprietary director of, or where a pension or part of a pension is payable in accordance with a pension adjustment order, the spouse or former spouse to whom the pension or part of the pension is so payable, of a proprietary director of, a company to which the scheme relates, or][6]

(ii) an individual entitled to rights arising from additional voluntary contributions to the scheme,

to opt, on or before the date on which that pension would otherwise become payable, for the transfer, on or after that date, to—

(I) the individual, or

(II) an approved retirement fund,

of an amount equivalent to the amount determined by the formula—

$$A - B$$

where—

A is—

(i) in the case of a proprietary director, the amount equal to the value of the individual's accrued rights under the scheme exclusive of any lump sum paid in accordance with subsection (3)(*f*), and

(ii) in the case of any other individual, the amount equal to the value of the individual's accrued rights under the scheme which relate to additional voluntary contributions paid by that individual exclusive of any part of that amount paid by way of lump sum in accordance with subsection (3)(*f*) in conjunction with the scheme rules, and

B is the amount or value of assets which the trustees, administrators or other person charged with the management of the scheme (in this section referred to as "the trustees") would, if the assumptions in paragraph (*b*) were made, be required, in accordance with section 784C, to transfer to an approved minimum retirement fund held in the name of the individual or to apply in purchasing an annuity payable to the individual with effect from the date of the exercise of the said option.][7]

(*b*) The assumptions in this paragraph are—

[(i) that the retirement benefits scheme or, as the case may be, the relevant part of the scheme was an annuity contract approved in accordance with section 784,][8]

(ii) that the trustees of the retirement benefit scheme were a person lawfully carrying on the business in the State of providing annuities on human life with whom the said contract had been made, and

(iii) that the individual had opted in accordance with subsection (2A) of section 784.

(3B) Where an individual opts in accordance with subsection (3A) then—

(*a*) the provisions of subsection (2B) of section 784 and of sections 784A, 784B, 784C, 784D and 784E shall, with any necessary modifications, apply as if—

(i) any reference in those sections to the person lawfully carrying on in the State the business of granting annuities on human life were a reference to the trustees of the retirement benefit scheme,

(ii) any reference in those sections to the annuity contract were references to the retirement benefit scheme, and

...[9]

(*b*) [in the case of a proprietary director,][10] paragraph (*f*) of subsection (3) shall apply as if the reference to "a lump sum or sums not exceeding in all three-eightieths of the employee's final remuneration for each year of service up to a maximum of 40 years" were a reference to "a lump sum not exceeding 25 per cent of the value of the pension which would otherwise be payable".][11]

[(3C) Where the rules of a retirement benefits scheme provide for the purchase of an annuity from a company carrying on the business of granting annuities on human life, references in subsection (3A) to the date on which a pension would otherwise become payable shall, in relation to that retirement benefits scheme, be construed as references to the latest date on which such an annuity must be purchased in accordance with those rules.][12]

[(3D) A retirement benefits scheme shall not cease to be an approved scheme because of any provision in the rules of the scheme whereby, either or both—

(*a*) a member's entitlements under the scheme, other than an amount referred to in paragraph (*b*), may, either on the member's changing employment or on the scheme being wound up, be transferred to one or more than one PRSA to which that member is the contributor if the following conditions are satisfied, that is to say—

(i) benefits have not become payable to the member under the scheme, and

(ii) the period or the aggregate of the periods for which the individual has been a member of the scheme or of any other scheme related to that individual's employment with, or with any person connected with, the employer immediately before the said transfer is 15 years or less,

(*b*) an amount equal to the accumulated value of a member's contributions to the scheme, which consist of additional voluntary contributions made by the member, may be transferred to one or more than one PRSA to which that member is the contributor.][13]

[(3E) A retirement benefits scheme shall neither cease to be an approved scheme nor shall the Revenue Commissioners be prevented from approving a retirement benefits scheme for the purposes of this Chapter because of any provision in the rules of the scheme which makes provision for borrowing by the scheme.][14]

(4) (*a*) The Revenue Commissioners may if they think fit having regard to the facts of a particular case and subject to such conditions, if any, as they think proper to attach to the approval, approve a retirement benefits scheme for the purposes of this Chapter, notwithstanding that it does not satisfy one or more of the prescribed conditions.

(*b*) The Revenue Commissioners may in particular approve by virtue of this subsection a scheme which—

(i) exceeds the limits imposed by the prescribed conditions as respects benefits for less than 40 years' service,

(ii) allows benefits to be payable on retirement within 10 years of the specified age or on earlier incapacity,

(iii) provides for the return in certain contingencies of employees' contributions and payment of interest (if any) on the contributions, or

(iv) relates to a trade or undertaking carried on only partly in the State and by a person not resident in the State.

[(*c*) Notwithstanding paragraphs (*a*) and (*b*), the Revenue Commissioners shall not approve a scheme unless it appears to them that the scheme complies with the provisions of subsection (3A).][15]

(5) Where in the opinion of the Revenue Commissioners the facts concerning any scheme or its administration cease to warrant the continuance of their approval of the scheme, they may at any time, by notice in writing to the administrator, withdraw their approval on such grounds, and from such date, as may be specified in the notice.

(6) Where an alteration has been made in a retirement benefits scheme, no approval given as regards the scheme before the alteration shall apply after the date of the alteration unless the alteration has been approved by the Revenue Commissioners.

(7) For the purpose of determining whether a retirement benefits scheme, in so far as it relates to a particular class or description of employees, satisfies or continues to satisfy the prescribed conditions, that scheme shall be considered in conjunction with any other retirement benefits scheme or schemes relating to employees of that class or description, and, if those conditions are satisfied in the case of both or all of those schemes taken together, they shall be taken to be satisfied in the case of each of them but otherwise those conditions shall be taken to be satisfied in the case of none of them.

Amendments

1 Subs (2)(*c*) substituted by FA 2005 s 21(1)(*a*)(iii) as respects any retirement benefits scheme approved on or after 1 January 2005.

2 Subs (3)(*b*) substituted by FA 2002 s 10(1)(*a*)(i)(I) with effect from 25 March 2002.

3 Subs (3)(*d*) substituted by FA 2002 s 10(1)(*a*)(i)(II) with effect from 25 March 2002.

4 Subs (3)(*e*) deleted by FA 2002 s 10(1)(*a*)(i)(III) with effect from 25 March 2002.

5 Substituted by FA 1999 s 19(1)(*a*)(ii)(I) in respect of any retirement benefits scheme approved on or after 6 April 1999; previously "that".

6 Subs (3A)(*a*)(i) substituted by FA 2001 s 18(1)(*a*)(ii) with effect from 6 April 2001.

7 Subs (3A)(*a*) substituted by FA 2000 s 23(1)(*b*)(i) with effect from 6 April 2000.

8 Subs (3A)(*b*)(i) substituted by FA 2000 s 23(1)(*b*)(ii) with effect from 6 April 2000.

9 Subs (3B)(*a*)(iii) deleted by FA 2000 s 23(1)(*b*)(iii)(I) as regards an approved retirement fund or an approved minimum retirement fund, as the case may be, where the assets in the fund were first accepted into the fund by the qualifying fund manager on or after 6 April 2000; previously "(iii) any reference in those sections to Case IV of Schedule D were a reference to Schedule E, and"

10 Inserted by FA 2000 s 23(1)(*b*)(iii)(II) with effect from 6 April 2000.

11 Subs (3A)–(3B) inserted by FA 1999 s 19(1)(*a*)(ii)(II) in respect of any retirement benefits scheme approved on or after 6 April 1999.

12 Subs (3C) inserted by FA 2000 s 23(1)(*b*)(iv) with effect from 6 April 1999.

13 Subs (3D) inserted by Pensions (Amendment) Act 2002 s 4(1)(*d*)(ii) with effect from such date as the Minister for Social, Community and Family Affairs may appoint by order. By virtue of Pensions (Amendment) Act, 2002 (Commencement) Order 2002, SI No 502 of 2002, this amendment comes into operation on 7 November 2002.

14 Subs (3E) inserted by FA 2004 s 16(1) with effect from 25 March 2004.

15 Subs (4)(*c*) inserted by FA 1999 s 19(1)(*a*)(ii)(III) in respect of any retirement benefits scheme approved on or after 6 April 1999.

Cross-references

Administrator, meaning, subs (2)(*c*)(ii): s 770(1).
Approved schemes, exemptions and reliefs, subs (3)(*b*), (*f*): s 774(7)(*ba*)(i).
Charge to income tax, commutation of entire pension: s 781(4)(*a*).
General medical services scheme, subss (2), (3): s 773(1).
Personal Retirement Savings Accounts (PRSAs), extent of relief, subs (3)(*b*), (*c*): s 787(3); s 787E(3)(*d*); taxation of payments from a PRSA, subs (3)(*f*): s 787G(3)(*a*).
Responsibility of administrator of scheme, subs (2)(*c*)(ii): Sch 23 para 4(2).
Retirement annuities, interpretation, subs (3)(*b*), (c): s 783(2)(*a*).
Special arrangements in relation to schemes approved before 6 April 1999 in context of changes effected to Part 30 by FA 1999 s 19(1), subs (3A): FA 1999 s 19(2)(*d*), (*e*).
Special arrangements in relation to schemes approved before 6 April 2000 in context of changes effected to Part 30 by FA 2000, s 23(1), subs (3A): FA 2000 s 23(2)(*d*).

Case law

Tax avoidance, assets from approved scheme transferred to unapproved scheme: *R v IRC (ex parte Roux Waterside Inn Ltd)* [1997] STC 781.

Revenue precedents

Issue: Can a residual Widows/Widowers/Dependant pension be commuted, if trivial?
Decision: No. They can only be commuted when they come into payment.
Issue: Normal retirement age firemen.
Decision: Normal retirement ages from age 55 are acceptable.
Issue: Normal retirement age Moneybroker/Dealers.
Decision: In the case of Directors engaged as moneybroker/dealers or as managers responsible for such dealers, NRA of 55 and upwards acceptable.
Issue: Normal retirement age later than 70?
Decision: Only where it is customary for employees in a particular occupation to retire at an age later than 70.
Issue: Split transfer values.
Decision: Revenue Practice would not permit the splitting of a member's total benefits so that part of such benefits would be dealt with by a transfer payment and a part held by the trustees of the scheme as a deferred benefit.
Issue: Calculation of remuneration for pension benefit purposes. Is remuneration for pension purposes reduced by virtue of the deduction for income earned outside the State (Sec 823 TCA)?
Decision: No. The remuneration figure on which benefits are based is the remuneration before the deduction for income earned abroad (excluding the United Kingdom).
Issue: Fluctuating Emoluments. What may be included for Final Remuneration purposes?
Decision: The following may be included: Benefits in Kind chargeable under Sec 118 TCA, Expenses Allowances chargeable under Sec 117 TCA, Preferential Loans chargeable under Sec 112 TCA (net amount after interest relief), Share Options Share Participation Schemes chargeable under Sec 128 TCA (only the amount actually charged).
Issue: Do the restrictions outlined in Practice Notes 9.3 and 9.4 apply in cases where benefits are deferred to Normal Retirement Age?
Decision: No.
Issue: Can an employer make further contributions to a scheme after benefits for ex-employee have been transferred to a buy out bond?
Decision: Yes, if within approvable limits and as it is likely that maximum approvable lump sum element of benefits would be taken from the buy out bond, the further benefits arising would need to be in pension form only.
Issue: Can a scheme capable of approval be established after the point of retirement?
Decision: Yes, but only to the extent that it provides for benefits for the ex employee in a non-commutable form.
Issue: Can Employees in receipt of long term disability benefits remain in an occupational pension scheme?
Decision: Where an insurance company has undertaken to continue to pay long term disability payments in cases where employments have been effectively terminated then there will be no Revenue objection to the continuation of those members in the employers pension scheme, and for the continuation of appropriate funding through the relevant amounts received for such purposes under the disability scheme.
Issue: Do the provisions of Practice Note 4.4 apply to one member schemes?
Decision: No the provisions in Practice Note 4.4 apply to one man insured arrangements only.

Issue: How should advance payments of contributions which are due and payable in subsequent accounting periods be treated?
Decision: They should be disallowed. Neither can they be treated as special contributions and spread forward as such special contributions are only allowable to fund for past service, or to augment benefits already secured, or to make up an actuarial deficiency.
Issue: In what circumstances can funds be transferred to a UK buy out bond?
Decision: Only if the individual would be resident in the UK subsequent to termination of service.
Issue: Is it permissible for an employer to make payments to employees to compensate for changes in the benefit structure of a pension scheme, free of tax?
Decision: If the situation is a bone fide one, for example arising out of Labour Relations recommendation and ultimately a Labour Court ruling then it may be possible for the employer to pay the compensation free of tax. Each case would have to be judged on its merits.
Issue: How to allow relief on contributions paid periodically while the individual is on a career break?
Decision: Amounts paid during absence on career break to be treated as "special contributions" and allowable on a spread forward basis. Thus, relief becomes available when the individual re-commences the employment.
Issue: Do all employee contributions qualify for PRSI relief?
Decision: No. Purely as a consequence of the operation of the net pay arrangement the ordinary annual contribution is relieved from PRSI Special Contributions (those paid directly by the employee to the scheme) do not qualify for PRSI relief.
Issue: Can Irish Insurance Companies appoint foreign fund managers?
Decision: Yes, but only fund managers resident in EU States.
Issue: Can a non-Irish national seconded to work in Ireland remain in his home country scheme and get relief from Irish tax on his contributions to that scheme?
Decision: Yes, provided that the secondment here is for a period of less than 10 years, the scheme is a trust scheme, and the benefits to be provided by the overseas scheme are within Irish approval limits.
Issue: Salary Sacrifice.
Decision: While the question of taxation of the emoluments is a matter for the appropriate Tax District dealing with the employees it is the opinion of this Office that any arrangement under which an employee waived an entitlement to remuneration or accepted a reduction in remuneration in return for a corresponding payment by the employer into the pension scheme to enhance the employee's pension benefits would be regarded as an application of the employee's income.
Issue: Are tax free lump sums in commutation of foreign pensions taxable in Ireland should the individual come to reside in this country following their retirement?
Decision: No.
Issue: Will tax relief be allowed on contributions made by employees who have left service?
Decision: Relief may be granted on contributions made on or shortly after leaving service. This is intended to cater for special circumstances where there might be an unavoidable delay in the employee making a special contribution, for example, in many public sector schemes retiring employees have deductions made from lump sums to pay for spouse's benefits which qualify for relief. Strictly speaking contributions should only be paid by "employees" and not ex-employees.

Definitions

administrator: s 770(1); approved retirement fund: s 770(1); approved minimum retirement fund: s 770(1); connected: s 10; employee: s 770(1); employer: s 770(1); final remuneration: s 770(1); overseas pension scheme: 770(1); person: IA 1937 s 11(*c*); pension: s 770(1); proprietary director: s 770(1); PRSA: s 770(1); relevant benefits: s 770(1); retirement benefits scheme: s 771; service: s 770(1); trade: s 3(1); writing: IA 1937 Sch.

Former enactments

FA 1972 s 15(1)–(7); FA 1974 s 64(1); FA 1992 s 6(*a*); FA 1996 s 131(2) and Sch 5 Pt II; FA 1997 s 146(1) and Sch 9 Pt I para 5(1).

773 General Medical Services: scheme of superannuation

(1) The Revenue Commissioners may, if they think fit and subject to any undertakings and conditions that they think proper to attach to the approval, approve for the purposes of this Chapter a scheme of superannuation provided for under an agreement for the provision of services under section 58 of the Health Act, 1970 (in this section referred to as a **"relevant scheme"**) as if it were a retirement benefits scheme within the meaning

of this Chapter and notwithstanding that it does not satisfy one or more of the conditions set out in subsections (2) and (3) of section 772.

(2) As respects a relevant scheme approved under this section, this Chapter and Schedule 23 shall apply subject to any necessary modifications and in particular as if in this Chapter and in that Schedule—

(*a*) **"employee"** included a registered medical practitioner providing services under an agreement for the provision of services under section 58 of the Health Act, 1970 (in this section referred to as an **"agreement"**),

(*b*) **"service"** included services by a registered medical practitioner under an agreement and an **"office or employment"** included the provision of such services, and

(*c*) a reference to Schedule E were a reference to Case II of Schedule D except in section 779.

(3) Chapter 2 of this Part shall apply as if a member of a relevant scheme were the holder of a pensionable office or employment and such member's income assessable to tax under Case II of Schedule D arising from an agreement were remuneration from such an office or employment.

Definitions

retirement benefits scheme: s 771.

Former enactments

FA 1991 s 12.

774 Certain approved schemes: exemptions and reliefs

[(1) This section shall apply as respects—

(*a*) any approved scheme shown to the satisfaction of the Revenue Commissioners to be established under irrevocable trusts,

(*b*) any approved scheme which is an overseas pension scheme, or

(*c*) any other approved scheme as respects which the Revenue Commissioners, having regard to any special circumstance, direct that this section shall apply,

and any scheme which is for the time being within paragraph (*a*), (*b*) or (*c*) is in this Chapter referred to as an **"exempt approved scheme"**.][1]

(2) This section shall apply only as respects income arising or contributions paid at a time when a scheme is an exempt approved scheme.

(3) Exemption from income tax shall, on a claim being made in that behalf, be allowed in respect of income derived from investments or deposits of a scheme if, or to such extent as the Revenue Commissioners are satisfied that, it is income from investments or deposits held for the purposes of the scheme.

(4) (*a*) In this subsection, **"financial futures"** and **"traded options"** mean respectively financial futures and traded options for the time being dealt in or quoted on any futures exchange or any stock exchange, whether or not that exchange is situated in the State.

(*b*) For the purposes of subsection (3), a contract entered into in the course of dealing in financial futures or traded options shall be regarded as an investment.

(5) Exemption from income tax shall, on a claim being made in that behalf, be allowed in respect of underwriting commissions if, or to such extent as the Revenue Commissioners are satisfied that, the underwriting commissions are applied for the purposes of the scheme, and in respect of which the trustees of the scheme would but for this subsection be chargeable to tax under Case IV of Schedule D.

(6) (*a*) For the purposes of this section and section 775—

(i) a reference to a **"chargeable period"** shall be construed as a reference to a **"chargeable period or its basis period"** (within the meaning of section 321), and

(ii) in relation to an employer whose chargeable period is a year of assessment, **"basis period"** means the period on the profits or gains of which income tax for that year of assessment is to be finally computed for the purposes of Case I or II of Schedule D in respect of the trade, profession or vocation of the employer.

(*b*) Any sum paid by an employer by means of contribution under the scheme shall for the purposes of Case I or II of Schedule D and of sections 83 and 707(4) be allowed to be deducted as an expense, or expense of management, incurred in the chargeable period in which the sum is paid but no other sum shall for those purposes be allowed to be deducted as an expense, or expense of management, in respect of the making, or any provision for the making, of any contributions under the scheme.

(*c*) The amount of an employer's contributions which may be deducted under paragraph (*b*) shall not exceed the amount contributed by that employer under the scheme in respect of employees in a trade or undertaking in respect of the profits of which the employer is assessable to income tax or corporation tax, as the case may be.

(*d*) A sum not paid by means of an ordinary annual contribution shall for the purposes of paragraph (*b*) be treated, as the Revenue Commissioners may direct, either as an expense incurred in the chargeable period in which the sum is paid, or as an expense to be spread over such period of years as the Revenue Commissioners think proper.

(*e*) In the case of any employer for a chargeable period, being—

(i) where the chargeable period is an accounting period of a company, an accounting period ending on or before the 21st day of April, 1997, and

(ii) where the chargeable period is a year of assessment, any year of assessment the employer's basis period for which ends on or before that date,

this subsection shall apply subject to paragraph 26 of Schedule 32.

(7) (*a*) Any ordinary annual contribution paid under the scheme by an employee shall, in assessing income tax under Schedule E, be allowed to be deducted as an expense incurred in the year in which the contribution is paid.

(*b*) Any contribution, which is not an ordinary annual contribution, paid or borne by an employee under the scheme may, as the Revenue Commissioners think proper—

(i) be treated, as respects the year in which it is paid, as an ordinary annual contribution paid in that year, or

[(ii) in the case of—

(I) such a contribution made on retirement, following an application in writing made before 6 February 2003 by the employee in response to an invitation in writing under the scheme, pursuant to the rules of the scheme—

(A) to contribute towards the purchase for superannuation purposes of relevant benefits, consisting of only a pension on retirement not exceeding one-eightieth of the employee's final remuneration for each year of service up to a maximum of 40 years and a lump sum not exceeding three-eightieths of the employee's final remuneration for each year of service up to a maximum of 40 years, in respect of actual service by the employee before becoming a member of the scheme, and

(B) to make such purchase by way of such a contribution either on retirement or otherwise,

and as a consequence of which application the employee opted, or was treated by the scheme as opting, to make the contribution on retirement, for the purposes of receiving relevant benefits under the scheme in excess of the benefits which, if the application referred to had not been made, the employee would otherwise have been entitled to receive under those rules, or

(II) a contribution to which paragraph (*ba*) applies,

be apportioned among such years as the Revenue Commissioners direct, and the amount of the contribution attributed thereby to any year shall be treated as an ordinary annual contribution paid in that year.][2]

[(*ba*) This paragraph applies to a contribution, which is not an ordinary annual contribution, and which—

(i) is required by the rules of the scheme to be made, in respect of a benefit to which section 772(3)(*b*) applies, by way of deduction from a lump sum payable to the employee in accordance with section 772(3)(*f*), or

(ii) is, following resumption of or change of employment, made, on retirement, in connection with the repayment by the employee to the scheme of superannuation contributions previously refunded to the employee or of relevant benefits provided to the employee on the employee's leaving an employment in relation to service in which the superannuation contributions or, as the case may be, the relevant benefits related.][3]

[(*c*) The aggregate amount of annual contributions (whether ordinary annual contributions or contributions treated as ordinary annual contributions) allowed to be deducted in any year shall not exceed—

(i) in the case of an individual who at any time during the year of assessment was of the age of 30 years or over but had not attained the age of 40 years, 20 per cent,

(ii) in the case of an individual who at any time during the year of assessment was of the age of 40 years or over but had not attained the age of 50 years, 25 per cent,

(iii) in the case of an individual who at any time during the year of assessment was of the age of 50 years or over, 30 per cent, and

(iv) in any other case, 15 per cent,

of the remuneration for that year of the office or employment in respect of which the contributions are paid.][4]

[(*d*) Where in any year of assessment a reduction or a greater reduction would be made under this section in the remuneration of an individual but for an insufficiency of remuneration, the amount of the reduction which would have been made but for that reason, less the amount of the reduction which is made in that year, shall be carried forward to the next year of assessment, and shall be treated for the purposes of relief under this section as the amount of an annual contribution paid in the next year of assessment.

(*e*) In so far as an amount once carried forward under paragraph (*d*) (and treated as an amount of an annual contribution paid in the next year of assessment) is not deducted from or set off against the individual's remuneration for that year of assessment, it shall be carried forward again to the following year of assessment (and treated as the amount of an annual contribution paid in that year of assessment) and so on for succeeding years.][5]

[(8) Subject to paragraphs (*b*) and (*ba*) of subsection (7) where in relation to a year of assessment any contribution, which is not an ordinary annual contribution, is paid by an employee under the scheme after the end of the year of assessment but before the specified return date for the chargeable period (within the meaning of Part 41), the contribution may, if the individual so elects on or before that date, be treated for the purposes of this section as paid in the earlier year (and not in the year in which it is paid); but where the amount of that contribution, together with any other contribution to the scheme paid by the individual in the year to which the contribution relates (or treated as so paid by virtue of any previous election under this subsection), exceeds the maximum amount of contributions allowed to be deducted in that year, the election shall have no effect as respects the excess.][6]

Amendments

1 Subs (1) substituted by FA 2005 s 21(1)(*a*)(iv) as respects any retirement benefits scheme approved on or after 1 January 2005.

2 Subs (7)(*b*)(ii) substituted by FA 2004 s 16(2) with effect from 6 February 2003.

3 Subs (7)(*ba*) inserted by FA 2003 s 14(1)(*b*)(i)(II) with effect from 6 February 2003.

4 Subs (7)(*c*) substituted by FA 2002 s 10(1)(*a*)(ii) for 2002 and later tax years.

5 Subs (7)(*d*)–(*e*) inserted by FA 2003 s 14(1)(*b*)(i)(III) with effect from 6 February 2003.

6 Subs (8) inserted by FA 2003 s 14(1)(*b*)(i)(IV) with effect from 6 February 2003.

Cross-references

Capital gains tax, superannuation funds: s 608(2), (4).

Cross-border pension schemes, exemption of, exempt approved scheme meaning applied: s 790B(4).

Deduction for income earned outside the State, subs (7): s 823(1) ("the specified amount").

Dividend withholding tax, declarations of exemption, exempt approved scheme, meaning applied: Sch 2A, para (1) ("appropriate person").

Dividend withholding tax (interpretation), exempt approved scheme, meaning applied: s 172A(1)(*a*) ("pension scheme").

Exempt approved scheme, meaning applied, subs (1): s 770(1).

Exemption from and refund of health contributions, Health Contributions Act 1979 s 7A(3)(*c*) (inserted by Social Welfare (Miscellaneous Provisions) Act 2002 s 16 and Sch Pt 3).

Income Tax (Employments) (Consolidated) Regulations 2001, SI No 559 of 2001: reg 41 (interpretation — Pt 7).

Investment undertakings, declarations: Sch 2B para 1 ("appropriate person").

Investment undertakings, (interpretation and application), exempt approved scheme, meaning applied: s 739B(1)("pension scheme").

Qualifying overseas pension plans, relief for contributions: subss (6), (7): s 787N(1).

Return of contributions — payment to personal pensions, Social Welfare (Consolidation) Act 1993 s 29C(1)(*c*) (inserted by Social Welfare (Miscellaneous Provisions) Act 2002 s 11).

Returns by employers in relation to pension products: s 897A(1)("employee pension contribution", "employer pension contribution").

Supplementary provisions, subs (6): s 775(2)(*b*), (3).

Case law

Subs (7): Held the General Commissioners were not entitled to review the exercise of discretion of a pension board as to how pension contribution was to be treated as a deduction: *Kelsall v Investment Chartwork Ltd* [1994] STC 33.

Revenue precedents

Issue: Does "remuneration" under ss 774/776 include termination payments chargeable to tax under s 123?

Decision: For the purposes of ss 774/776 "remuneration" does not include payments which are chargeable to tax under s 123.

Definitions

approved scheme: s 770(1); employee: s 770(1); employer: s 770(1); exempt approved scheme: s 770(1); final remuneration: s 770(1); overseas pension scheme: s 770(1); relevant benefits: s 770(1); retirement: s 770(1); service: s 770(1); trade: s 3(1); writing: IA 1937 Sch; year of assessment: s 2(1).

Former enactments

FA 1972 s 16(1)–(5) and (7); CTA 1976 s 140(1), s 164, Sch 2 Pt I para 31 and Sch 3 Pt I; FA 1988 s 30(1)-(2)(*a*); FA 1991 s 38; FA 1997 s 41(1)(*a*) and (3).

Corresponding UK tax provision

Income and Corporation Taxes Act 1988 s 592.

775 Certain approved schemes: provisions supplementary to section 774(6)

(1) Where—

(*a*) after the 21st day of April, 1997, there is an actual payment by an employer of a contribution under an exempt approved scheme,

(*b*) apart from this section that payment would be allowed to be deducted as an expense, or expense of management, of the employer in relation to any chargeable period, and

(*c*) the total of previously allowed deductions exceeds the relevant maximum,

then, the amount allowed to be so deducted in respect of the payment mentioned in paragraph (*a*) and of any other actual payments of contributions under the scheme which, having been made after the 21st day of April, 1997, are within paragraph (*b*) in relation to the same chargeable period shall be reduced by whichever is the lesser of the excess and the amount which reduces the deduction to nil.

(2) In relation to any such actual payment by an employer of a contribution under an exempt approved scheme as would be allowed to be deducted as mentioned in subsection (1) in relation to any chargeable period—

(*a*) the reference in that subsection to the total of previously allowed deductions is a reference to the aggregate of every amount in respect of the making, or any provision for the making, of that or any other contribution under the scheme, which has been allowed to be deducted as an expense, or expense of management, of that person in relation to all previous chargeable periods, and

(*b*) the reference to the relevant maximum is a reference to the amount which would have been that aggregate if the restriction on deductions for sums other than actual payments imposed by virtue of section 774(6) had been applied in relation to every previous chargeable period,

and for the purposes of this subsection an amount the deduction of the whole or any part of which is to be taken into account as allowed in relation to more than one chargeable period shall be treated as if the amount allowed were a different amount in the case of each of those periods.

(3) For the purposes of this section, any payment which is treated under paragraph (*d*) of section 774(6) as spread over a period of years shall be treated as actually paid at the time when it is treated as paid in accordance with that paragraph.

Definitions

employee: s 770.

Former enactments

FA 1972 s 16A; FA 1997 s 41(1)(*b*).

Corresponding UK tax provision

Income and Corporation Taxes Act 1988 s 592.

776 Certain statutory schemes: exemptions and reliefs

(1) This section shall apply to any statutory scheme established under a public statute.

(2) (*a*) Any ordinary annual contribution paid under a scheme to which this section applies by any officer or employee shall, in assessing income tax under Schedule E, be allowed to be deducted as an expense incurred in the year in which the contribution is paid.

(*b*) Any contribution, which is not an ordinary annual contribution, paid or borne by an officer or employee under a scheme to which this section applies may, as the Revenue Commissioners think proper—

(i) be treated, as respects the year in which it is paid, as an ordinary annual contribution paid in that year, or

[(ii) in the case of—

(I) such a contribution made on retirement, following an application in writing made before 6 February 2003 by the employee in response to an invitation in writing under the scheme, pursuant to the rules of the scheme—

(A) to contribute towards the purchase for superannuation purposes of relevant benefits, consisting of only a pension on retirement not exceeding one-eightieth of the employee's final remuneration for each year of service up to a maximum of 40 years and a lump sum not exceeding three-eightieths of the employee's final remuneration for each year of service up to a maximum of 40 years, in respect of actual service by the employee before becoming a member of the scheme, and

(B) to make such purchase by way of such a contribution either on retirement or otherwise,

and as a consequence of which application the employee opted, or was treated by the scheme as opting, to make the contribution on retirement, for the purposes of receiving relevant benefits under the scheme in excess of the benefits which, if the application referred to had not been made, the employee would otherwise have been entitled to receive under those rules, or

(II) a contribution to which paragraph (*ba*) applies,

be apportioned among such years as the Revenue Commissioners direct, and the amount of the contribution attributed thereby to any year shall be treated as an ordinary annual contribution paid in that year.][1]

[(*ba*) This paragraph applies to a contribution, which is not an ordinary annual contribution, and which—

(i) is required by the statute under which the scheme is established or by any other statute or regulation to be made in respect of the provision of a pension for any widow, widower, children or dependants of the officer or employee by way of a deduction from a lump sum payable to the employee on retirement, or

(ii) is, following resumption of or on change of employment, made, on retirement, in connection with the repayment by the officer or employee to the scheme of superannuation contributions previously refunded to the officer or employee or of relevant benefits provided to the officer or employee on the officer or employee's leaving the office or employment in relation to service in which the superannuation contributions or, as the case may be, the relevant benefits related.][2]

[(*c*) The aggregate amount of annual contributions (whether ordinary annual contributions or contributions treated as ordinary annual contributions) allowed to be deducted in any year shall not exceed—

(i) in the case of an individual who at any time during the year of assessment was of the age of 30 years or over but had not attained the age of 40 years, 20 per cent,

(ii) in the case of an individual who at any time during the year of assessment was of the age of 40 years or over but had not attained the age of 50 years, 25 per cent,

(iii) in the case of an individual who at any time during the year of assessment was of the age of 50 years or over, 30 per cent, and

(iv) in any other case, 15 per cent,

of the remuneration for that year of the office or employment in respect of which the contributions are paid.][3]

[(*d*) Where in any year of assessment a reduction or a greater reduction would be made under this section in the remuneration of an individual but for an insufficiency of remuneration, the amount of the reduction which would have been made but for that reason, less the amount of the reduction which is made in that year, shall be carried forward to the next year of assessment, and shall be treated for the purposes of relief under this section as the amount of an annual contribution paid in the next year of assessment.

(*e*) In so far as an amount once carried forward under paragraph (*d*) (and treated as an amount of an annual contribution paid in the next year of assessment) is not deducted from or set off against the individual's remuneration for that year of assessment, it shall be carried forward again to the following year of assessment (and treated as the amount of an annual contribution paid in that year of assessment) and so on for succeeding years.][4]

[(3) Subject to paragraphs (*b*) and (*ba*) of subsection (2), where in relation to a year of assessment any contribution, which is not an ordinary annual contribution, is paid by an employee under the scheme after the end of the year of assessment but before the specified return date for the chargeable period (within the meaning of Part 41), the contribution may, if the individual so elects on or before that date, be treated for the purposes of this section as paid in the earlier year (and not in the year in which it is paid); but where the amount of that contribution, together with any other contribution to the scheme paid by the individual in the year to which the contribution relates (or treated as so paid by virtue of any previous election under this subsection), exceeds the maximum amount of contributions allowed to be deducted in that year, the election shall have no effect as respects the excess.][5]

Amendments

1 Subs (2)(*b*)(ii) substituted by FA 2004 s 16(3) with effect from 6 February 2003.

2 Subs (2)(*ba*) inserted by FA 2003 s 14(1)(*b*)(ii)(II) with effect from 6 February 2003.

3 Subs (2)(*c*) substituted by FA 2002 s 10(1)(*a*)(iii) for 2002 and later tax years.

4 Subs (2)(*d*)–(*e*) inserted by FA 2003 s 14(1)(*b*)(ii)(III) with effect from 6 February 2003.

5 Subs (3) inserted by FA 2003 s 14(1)(*b*)(ii)(IV) with effect from 6 February 2003.

Cross-references

Exemption from and refund of health contributions, Health Contributions Act 1979 s 7A(3)(c) (inserted by Social Welfare (Miscellaneous Provisions) Act 2002 s 16 and Sch Pt 3).

Income Tax (Employments) (Consolidated) Regulations 2001, SI No 559 of 2001; reg 41 (interpretation Pt 7).

Return of Contributions — payment to personal pensions, Social Welfare (Consolidation) Act 1993 s 29C(1)(c) (inserted by Social Welfare (Miscellaneous Provisions) Act 2002 s 11).

Returns by employers in relation to pension products: s 897A(1)("employee pension contribution").

Revenue precedents

Issue: Does "remuneration" under ss 774/776 include termination payments chargeable to tax under s 123?

Decision: For the purposes of ss 774/776 "remuneration" does not include payments which are chargeable to tax under s 123.

Issue: An individual who had previously taken a refund of superannuation contributions subsequently repays the refund. The individual is charged "interest" to restore the actuarial value of the refund received.

Decision: The "interest" is a superannuation contribution and qualifies for relief when paid.

Definitions

employee: s 770(1); final remuneration: s 770(1); relevant benefits: s 770(1); retirement: s 770(1); service: s 770(1); statutory scheme: s 770(1); statute: IA 1937 s 3; writing: IA 1937 Sch; year of assessment: s 2(1).

Former enactments

FA 1972 s 17(1)–(2).

Corresponding UK tax provision

Income and Corporation Taxes Act 1988 s 594.

777 Charge to income tax in respect of certain relevant benefits provided for employees

(1) Subject to this Chapter, where pursuant to a retirement benefits scheme the employer in any year of assessment pays a sum with a view to the provision of any relevant benefits for any employee of that employer, then (whether or not the accrual of the benefits is dependent on any contingency), the sum paid, if not otherwise chargeable to income tax as income of the employee, shall be deemed for the purposes of the Income Tax Acts to be income of that employee for that year of assessment and assessable to income tax under Schedule E.

(2) Subject to this Chapter, where—

(*a*) the circumstances in which any relevant benefits under a retirement benefits scheme are to accrue are not such as will render the benefits assessable to income tax as emoluments of the employee in respect of whom the benefits are paid, and

(*b*) the provision of those benefits is not, or is not fully, secured by the payment of sums by the employer with a view to the provision of those benefits,

then (whether or not the accrual of the benefits is dependent on any contingency), an amount equal to the cost, estimated in accordance with subsection (3), of securing the provision by a third person of the benefits or, as the case may be, of the benefits in so far as not already secured by the payment of sums mentioned in subsection (1) shall be deemed for the purposes of the Income Tax Acts to be income of the employee for the year or years of assessment specified in subsection (3) and assessable to income tax under Schedule E.

(3) The cost referred to in subsection (2) shall be estimated either—

(*a*) as an annual sum payable in each year of assessment in which the scheme in question is in force or the employee is serving, up to and including the year of assessment in which the benefits accrue or there ceases to be any possibility of the accrual of the benefits, or

(*b*) as a single sum payable in the year of assessment in which falls the date when the employee acquired the right to the relevant benefits or the date when the employee acquired the right to any increase in the relevant benefits,

as may be more appropriate in the circumstances of the case.

(4) Where the employer pays any sum mentioned in subsection (1) in relation to more than one employee, the sum so paid shall for the purpose of that subsection be apportioned among those employees by reference to the separate sums which would have had to be paid to secure the separate benefits to be provided for them respectively, and the part of the sum apportioned to each of them shall be deemed for that purpose to have been paid separately in relation to that one of them.

(5) Any reference in this section to the provision for an employee of relevant benefits shall include a reference to the provision of benefits payable to the employee's spouse, widow or widower, children, dependants or personal representatives.

Cross-references

Exempt benefits: s 201(2)(*c*).
Exemptions, subss (1), (2): s 778(1)–(3).

Definitions

employee, employer: s 770(1); Income Tax Acts: s 1(2); person: IA 1937 s 11(*c*); relevant benefits: s 770(1); retirement benefits scheme: s 771; year of assessment: ss 2(1), 5(1).

Former enactments

FA 1972 s 18(1)(*a*), (2)–(5); FA 1997 s 146(1) and Sch 9 Pt I para 5(2).

Corresponding UK tax provision

Income and Corporation Taxes Act 1988 s 595.

778 Exceptions to charge to tax under section 777

(1) Neither subsection (1) nor subsection (2) of section 777 shall apply where the retirement benefits scheme in question is—

(*a*) an approved scheme,

(*b*) a statutory scheme, or

(*c*) a scheme set up by a Government outside the State for the benefit, or primarily for the benefit, of its employees.

(2) Neither subsection (1) nor subsection (2) of section 777 shall apply for any year of assessment where apart from those subsections the employee is under the Income Tax Acts either not assessable to income tax in respect of the emoluments of his or her employment or is so assessable in respect of those emoluments on the basis of the amount received in the State.

(3) Where, in respect of the provision for an employee of any relevant benefits, a sum has been deemed to be income of the employee by virtue of subsection (1) or (2) of section 777, and subsequently the employee proves to the satisfaction of the Revenue Commissioners—

(*a*) that no payment in respect of or in substitution for the benefits has been made, and

(*b*) that some event has occurred by reason of which no such payment will be made,

and the employee makes application for relief under this subsection within 6 years from the time when that event occurred, the Revenue Commissioners shall give relief in respect of tax on that sum by repayment or otherwise as may be appropriate, and, if the employee satisfies the Revenue Commissioners in relation to some particular part of the benefits but not the whole of the benefits, the Revenue Commissioners may give such relief as may seem to them just and reasonable.

Cross-references

Exempt benefits: s 201(2)(*d*).
Qualifying overseas pension plans, relief for contributions, subs (1): s 787N(1).
Reliefs in respect of income tax charged on payments on retirement etc, subs (1): Sch 3 para 1(1), (2)(*b*).

Definitions

approved scheme, employee: s 770(1); Income Tax Acts: s 1(2); relevant benefits: s 770(1); retirement benefits scheme: s 771; statutory scheme: s 770(1); year of assessment: ss 2(1), 5(1).

Former enactments

FA 1972 s 19.

Corresponding UK tax provision

Income and Corporation Taxes Act 1988 s 596.

779 Charge to income tax of pensions under Schedule E

[(1) Subject to subsection (2), pensions paid under any scheme, including an overseas pension scheme, which is approved or is being considered for approval under this Chapter shall, notwithstanding anything in section 18 or 19, be charged to tax under Schedule E, and Chapter 4 of Part 42 shall apply accordingly.][1]

(2) In respect of any scheme which is approved or is being considered for approval under this Chapter, the Revenue Commissioners may direct that until such date as they may specify pensions under the scheme shall be charged to tax as annual payments under Case III of Schedule D, and tax shall be deductible under section 237 or 238 accordingly.

Amendments

1 Subs (1) substituted by FA 2005 s 21(1)(*a*)(v) as respects any retirement benefits scheme approved on or after 1 January 2005.

Cross-references

General medical services scheme: s 773(2)(*c*).

Definitions

overseas pension scheme: s 770(1); pension: s 770(1).

Former enactments

FA 1972 s 20.

780 Charge to income tax on repayment of employees' contributions

(1) In this section and in section 781, **"employee"**, in relation to a statutory scheme, includes an officer.

(2) Subject to this section, tax shall be charged under this section on any repayment to an employee during his or her lifetime of any contribution (including interest on contributions, if any) if the payment is made under—

(*a*) a scheme which is or has at any time been an exempt approved scheme, or

(*b*) a statutory scheme established under a public statute.

[(2A) This section shall not apply to the extent that any repayment of contributions is transferred by the administrator of the scheme to the administrator of a PRSA, by way of contribution to a PRSA to which the employee is the contributor.][1]

(3) This section shall not apply where the employee's employment was carried on outside the State.

(4) Subsection (2)(*a*) shall not apply in relation to a contribution made after the scheme ceases to be an exempt approved scheme unless it again becomes an exempt approved scheme.

(5) Where any payment is chargeable to tax under this section, the administrator of the scheme shall be charged to income tax under Case IV of Schedule D and, subject to subsection (7), the rate of the tax shall be [the standard rate in force at the time of payment][2]; but, in the case of any repayment under a statutory scheme established under a public statute, the administrator of the scheme shall be entitled to deduct the tax chargeable in respect of that repayment from the amount of that repayment.

(6) The tax shall be charged on the amount paid or, if the administrator is entitled under the rules of the relevant scheme or otherwise to deduct the tax before payment, on the amount before deduction of tax, and the amount so charged to tax shall not be treated as income for any other purpose of the Income Tax Acts.

(7) (*a*) The Minister for Finance may by order from time to time increase or decrease the rate of tax under subsection (5).

(*b*) Every order under paragraph (*a*) shall be laid before Dáil Éireann as soon as may be after it is made and, if a resolution annulling the order is passed by Dáil Éireann within the next 21 days on which Dáil Éireann has sat after the order is laid before it, the order shall be annulled accordingly, but without prejudice to the validity of anything previously done thereunder.

Amendments

[1] Subs (2A) inserted by Pensions (Amendment) Act 2002 s 4(1)(*d*)(iii) with effect from such date as the Minister for Social, Community and Family Affairs may appoint by order. By virtue of Pensions (Amendment) Act, 2002 (Commencement) Order 2002, SI No 502 of 2002, this amendment comes into operation on 7 November 2002.

[2] Substituted by FA 2002 s 10(1)(*a*)(iv) for any repayment of contributions referred to in TCA 1997 s 780 which is made on or after 5 December 2001; previously "25 per cent".

Cross-references

Charge to income tax, commutation of entire pension, subs (6): s 781(3).

Occupational pension schemes, charge to tax in respect of unauthorised and certain other payments: Sch 23 para 8.

Personal Retirement Savings Accounts (PRSAs), transfers to PRSAs, subss (2) and (2A): s 787F(*c*).

Definitions

administrator, approved scheme: s 770(1); Dáil Éireann: IA 1937 Sch; employee, exempt approved scheme: s 770(1); Income Tax Acts: s 1(2); PRSA: s 770(1); standard rate: ss 3(1), 15; statutory scheme: s 770(1); statute: IA 1937 s 3.

Former enactments

FA 1972 s 21(1)–(5)(*a*) and (6)–(7); FA 1973 s 18; FA 1992 s 6(*b*).

Corresponding UK tax provision

Income and Corporation Taxes Act 1988 s 598.

781 Charge to income tax: commutation of entire pension

(1) Where—

(*a*) a scheme which is or has at any time been an approved scheme, or

(*b*) a statutory scheme established under a public statute, contains a rule allowing in special circumstances a payment in commutation of an employee's entire pension, and any pension is commuted, whether wholly or not, under the rule, tax shall be charged on the amount by which the sum receivable exceeds—

(i) the largest sum which would have been receivable in commutation of any part of the pension if the scheme had contained a rule providing that the aggregate value of the relevant benefits payable to an employee on or after retirement, excluding any pension which was not commutable, should not exceed three-eightieths of the employee's final remuneration for each year of service up to a maximum of 40 years, or

(ii) the largest sum which would have been receivable in commutation of any part of the pension under any rule of the scheme authorising the commutation of part (but not the whole) of the pension, or which would have been so receivable but for those circumstances,

whichever gives the lesser amount chargeable to tax.

(2) This section shall not apply where the employee's employment was carried on outside the State.

(3) Where any amount is chargeable to tax under this section, the administrator of the scheme shall be charged to income tax under Case IV of Schedule D on that amount and, subject to subsection (6) of section 780 which shall apply as it applies to tax chargeable under that section, the rate of tax shall be 10 per cent.

(4) In applying paragraph (i) or (ii) of subsection (1)—

(*a*) the same considerations shall be taken into account, including the provisions of any other relevant scheme, as would have been taken into account by the Revenue Commissioners in applying section 772, and

(*b*) where the scheme has ceased to be an approved scheme, account shall only be taken of the rules of the scheme at the date of the cesser.

Cross-references

Charge to income tax on repayment of employees' contributions, meaning of "employee" applied: s 780(1).

Occupational pension schemes, charge to tax in respect of unauthorised and certain other payments: Sch 23 para 8.

Definitions

administrator: s 770(1); approved scheme: s 770(1); final remuneration: s 770(1); pension: s 770(1); relevant benefits: s 770(1); service: s 770(1); statutory scheme: s 770(1); statute: IA 1937 s 3.

Former enactments

FA 1972 s 22(1)–(4); FA 1992 s 6(*c*).

Corresponding UK tax provision

Income and Corporation Taxes Act 1988 s 599.

---

782 Charge to tax: repayments to employer

(1) Where any payment is made or becomes due to an employer out of funds which are or have been held for the purposes of a scheme which is or has at any time been an exempt approved scheme, then—

(*a*) if the scheme relates to a trade or profession carried on by the employer, the payment shall be treated for the purposes of the Tax Acts as a receipt of that trade or profession receivable when the payment is due or on the last day on which the trade or profession is carried on by the employer, whichever is the earlier;

(*b*) if the scheme does not relate to such a trade or profession, the employer shall be charged to tax on the amount of the payment under Case IV of Schedule D, but only in proportion to the extent that the payment represents contributions by the employer under the scheme which were allowable as deductions for tax purposes.

(2) This section shall not apply to a payment which was due before the scheme became an exempt approved scheme.

(3) References in this section to any payment include references to any transfer of assets or other transfer of money's worth.

Definitions

employer, exempt approved scheme: s 770(1); Income Tax Acts: s 1(2); profession: s 2(1); trade: s 3(1).

Former enactments

FA 1972 s 23.

Corresponding UK tax provision

Income and Corporation Taxes Act 1988 s 601.

CHAPTER 2
Retirement Annuities

Cross-references

Capital acquisitions tax, exemption relating to retirement benefits: CATCA 2003 s 85(1)(*a*).

Exemption from and refund of health contributions, Health Contribution Act 1979 s 7A(3)(b) (inserted by Social Welfare (Miscellaneous Provisions) Act 2002 s 16 and Sch Pt 3).

General medical services scheme: s 773(3).

Limit on net relevant earnings for purposes of relief under this Chapter: s 790A.

Overseas pension plans, migrant member relief, interpretation and general: s 787M(1) ("qualifying overseas pension plan").

PAYE Regulations: s 986(1)(*g*).

Personal Retirement Savings Accounts (PRSAs), interpretation and supplemental: s 787A(1)("retirement annuity contract"); extent of relief: s 787E(5); transfer to and from PRSA: s 787L(2)(*c*).

Qualifying overseas pension plans, relief for contributions: s 787N(1).

Return of contributions — payment to personal pensions, Social Welfare (Consolidation) Act 1993 s 29C(1)(*c*) (inserted by Social Welfare (Miscellaneous Provisions) Act 2002 s 11).

Unclaimed Life Assurance Policies Act 2003, unclaimed policies, s 6(3)(*c*) — meaning of "sponsored superannuation scheme" applied.

Tax Briefing

TB52 May 2003 pp 9–10 — Pension Products and Retirement Funds (Finance Act 2003 changes).

783 Interpretation and general (Chapter 2)

(1) (*a*) [In this Chapter][1]—

["**approved retirement fund**" has the meaning assigned to it by section 784A;

["**close company**" has the same meaning as in section 430;

"**connected person**" has the same meaning as in section 10;][2]

"approved minimum retirement fund" has the meaning assigned to it by section 784C;][3]

"director" means—

(i) in relation to a body corporate the affairs of which are managed by a board of directors or similar body, a member of that board or body,

(ii) in relation to a body corporate the affairs of which are managed by a single director or similar person, that director or person,

(iii) in relation to a body corporate the affairs of which are managed by the members themselves, a member of the body corporate,

and includes any person who is or has been a director;

"employee", in relation to a body corporate, includes any person taking part in the management of the affairs of the body corporate who is not a director, and includes a person who is or has been an employee;

"investment company" means a company the income of which consists mainly of investment income;

"investment income", in relation to a company, means income which, if the company were an individual, would not be earned income;

[**"participator"** has the same meaning as in section 433;][4]

"proprietary director" means a director of a company who is either the beneficial owner of, or able, either directly or through the medium of other companies or by any other indirect means, to control, more than 15 per cent of the ordinary share capital of the company;

"proprietary employee", in relation to a company, means an employee who is the beneficial owner of, or able, either directly or through the medium of other companies or by any other indirect means, to control, more than 15 per cent of the ordinary share capital of the company;

"sponsored superannuation scheme" means a scheme or arrangement relating to service in particular offices or employments and having for its object or one of its objects the making of provision in respect of persons serving in those offices or employments against—

(i) future retirement or partial retirement,

(ii) future termination of service through death or disability, or

(iii) similar matters,

being a scheme or arrangement under which any part of the cost of the provision so made is or has been borne otherwise than by those persons by reason of their service (whether it is the cost or part of the cost of the benefits provided, or of paying premiums or other sums in order to provide those benefits, or of administering or instituting the scheme or arrangement).

(*b*) For the purposes of the definitions of **"proprietary director"** and **"proprietary employee"**, ordinary share capital which is owned or controlled as is specified in those definitions by a person, being a spouse or an infant child of a director or employee, or by the trustee of a trust for the benefit of a person or persons, being or including any such person or such director or employee, shall be deemed to be owned or controlled by such director or employee and not by any other person.

(*c*) For the purposes of the definition of **"sponsored superannuation scheme"**, a person shall be treated as bearing by reason of his or her service the cost of any payment made or agreed to be made in respect of his or her service if that payment or the agreement to make it is treated under the Income Tax Acts as increasing the person's income or would be so treated if he or she were chargeable to tax under Schedule E in respect of his or her emoluments from that service.

(2) (*a*) For the purposes of this Chapter, an office or employment shall be a pensionable office or employment only if service in it is service to which a sponsored superannuation scheme relates (not being a scheme under which the benefits provided in respect of that service are limited to [benefits of a kind referred to in paragraphs (*b*) and (*c*) of section 772(3), including any similar benefit provided under a statutory scheme established under a public statute,][5]); but references to a pensionable office or employment apply whether or not the duties are performed wholly or partly in the State or the holder is chargeable to tax in respect of the office or employment.

(*b*) For the purposes of paragraph (*a*), service in an office or employment shall not be treated as service to which a sponsored superannuation scheme relates by reason only of the fact that the holder of the office or employment might (though he or she does not) participate in the scheme by exercising or refraining from exercising an option open to him or her by virtue of that service.

[(*c*) For the purposes of calculating the amount of any reduction in net relevant earnings in respect of any qualifying premium or of any PRSA contribution (within the meaning of Chapter 2A of this Part) this Chapter and Chapter 2A shall apply as if any contribution by an employee to a sponsored superannuation scheme relating to service in an office or employment, which is not a pensionable office or employment within the meaning of paragraph (*a*), were a payment of a qualifying premium for which relief had been given under this Chapter.][6]

(3) For the purposes of this Chapter but subject to subsection (4), **"relevant earnings"**, in relation to an individual, means any income of the individual chargeable to tax for the year of assessment in question, being either—

(*a*) income arising in respect of remuneration from an office or employment of profit held by the individual, other than a pensionable office or employment,

(*b*) income from any property which is attached to or forms part of the emoluments of any such office or employment of profit held by the individual, or

(*c*) income which is chargeable under Schedule D and is immediately derived by the individual from the carrying on or exercise by the individual of his or her trade or profession either as an individual or, in the case of a partnership, as a partner personally acting in the partnership;

but does not include any remuneration from an investment company of which the individual is a proprietary director or a proprietary employee.

(4) For the purposes of this Chapter, the relevant earnings of an individual shall not be treated as the relevant earnings of his or her spouse, notwithstanding that the individual's income chargeable to tax is treated as his or her spouse's income.

(5) The Revenue Commissioners may make regulations prescribing the procedure to be adopted in giving effect to this Chapter in so far as such procedure is not otherwise provided for and, without prejudice to the generality of the foregoing, may by such regulations—

(*a*) prescribe the manner and form in which claims for relief from or repayment of tax are to be made,

(*b*) prescribe the time limit for the making of any such claim,

(*c*) require the trustees or other persons having the management of an approved trust scheme to deliver from time to time such information and particulars as the Revenue Commissioners may reasonably require for the purposes of this Chapter, and

(*d*) apply for purposes of this Chapter or of the regulations any provision of the Income Tax Acts (with or without modifications).

(6) Where any person, for the purpose of obtaining for that person or for any other person any relief from or repayment of tax under this Chapter, knowingly makes any false statement or false representation, that person shall be liable to a penalty of [€630][7].

Amendments

1 Substituted by FA 2003 s 14(1)(*c*)(i)(I)(A) with effect from 6 February 2003; previously "In this section".

2 Definitions of "close company" and "connected person" inserted by FA 2003 s 14(1)(*c*)(i)(I)(B) with effect from 6 February 2003.

3 Definitions of "approved retirement fund" and "approved minimum retirement fund" inserted by FA 1999 s 19(1)(*b*)(i) in respect of any annuity contract for the time being approved by the Revenue Commissioners under s 784 entered into on or after 6 April 1999.

4 Definition of "participator" inserted by FA 2003 s 14(1)(*c*)(i)(I)(C) with effect from 6 February 2003.

5 Substituted by FA 2003 s 14(1)(*c*)(i)(II)(*a*) with effect from 1 January 2003; previously "a lump sum payable on the termination of the service through death before the age of 70 years or some lower age or disability before the age of 70 or some lower age".

6 Subs (2)(*c*) inserted by by FA 2003 s 14(1)(*c*)(i)(II)(*b*) with effect from 1 January 2003.

7 Substituted by FA 2001 s 240(1) and (2)(*k*) and Sch 5 Pt 1 as respects any act or omission which takes place on or begins on or after 1 January 2002; previously "£500".

Cross-references

Capital element in purchased annuities, subs (1): s 788(2)(*b*).

Income Tax (Employments) (Consolidated) Regulations 2001, interpretation (Part 7), meaning of "relevant earnings" applied: ITECR 2001 reg 41(*d*).

Life assurance companies, meaning of "relevant earnings" applied: s 706(3)(*a*).

Recovery of penalties: s 1061(1).

Case law

Subs (3): Held income received by external Name at Lloyds was not "derived by him from the carrying on or exercise by him of his trade as an individual": *Koenigsberger v Mellor* [1995] STC 547.

Revenue precedents

Issue: What is the earliest retirement age for Jockeys?

Decision: Age 50.

Issue: Is income payable under an approved Permanent Health Benefit policy regarded as relevant earnings for RAC purposes?

Decision: Yes, if the contributions to the scheme are not maintained by the policy.

Issue: What is the earliest retirement age for different classes of occupations under retirement annuity contracts?
Decision: Badminton Players, Boxers, Cricketers, Croupiers, Cyclists, Dancers, Divers, Footballers, Golfers (Tournament earnings), Jockeys Flat racing and National Hunt, Motor Cyclist (Competitive), Motor racing drivers, Off shore Riggers, Rugby players (professional), Speedway Riders, Squash players, Table Tennis Players, Tennis Players, Trapeze Artists, Wrestlers can retire at 50. Air Pilots, Brass Instrumentalists, Distant Water trawlermen, Firemen (Part-time), Inshore fishermen, Moneybroker dealers, Singers can retire at 55.
Issue: Can premiums continue to be paid after the individual becomes non-resident?
Decision: Only where the individual goes abroad on a temporary basis (for periods up to 3 years) and it must be clear that the intention is to return and resume in the occupation which constituted the source of relevant earnings. Individual cases to be submitted to Retirement Benefits Districts.
Issue: Is income which qualifies for the artists exemption regarded as relevant earnings for the purpose of an RAC?
Decision: Such income is "not chargeable to tax". As there is not a source of relevant earnings the individual is not entitled to effect an RAC.
Issue: Can an employer pay retirement annuity premiums on behalf of the employee?
Decision: Yes, but it is chargeable to PAYE, PRSI and Levies. Relief is due to the individual subject to the 15% limit.
Issue: Is the figure for relevant earnings reduced by virtue of the deduction for income earned outside the State (TCA 1997 s 823)?
Decision: No. Relevant earnings not reduced to take account of income earned outside the State.

Definitions

Income Tax Acts: s 1(2); qualifying premium: s 784(1)(*a*); year of assessment: s 2(1).

Former enactments

ITA 1967 s 195B(6), s 235(6)–(9) and s 238(3)–(4); FA 1969 s 65(1) and Sch 5 Pt I; FA 1972 Sch 1 Pt III para 4; FA 1993 s 10(1); FA 1996 s 132(2) and Sch 5 Pt II; FA 1997 s 146(1) and Sch 9 Pt I para 5(3).

784 Retirement annuities: relief for premiums

[(1) (*a*) Where an individual, being an individual referred to in paragraph *(b),* pays a premium or other consideration under an annuity contract for the time being approved by the Revenue Commissioners as being a contract by which the main benefit secured is, or would, but for the exercise of an option by the individual under subsection (2A), be a life annuity for the individual in his or her old age or under a contract for the time being approved under section 785 (in this Chapter referred to as a **"qualifying premium"**), relief from income tax may be given in respect of the qualifying premium under section 787.

(*b*) An individual referred to in this paragraph is an individual who is or was (or but for an insufficiency of profits or gains would be or would have been) for any year of assessment chargeable to tax in respect of relevant earnings from any trade, profession, office or employment carried on or held by him or her and who paid a qualifying premium in that year.][1]

(2) (*a*) [Subject to subsections (2A) and (3) and to section 786,][2] the Revenue Commissioners shall not approve a contract unless it appears to them to satisfy the following conditions—

[(i) that it is made by the individual with a person lawfully carrying on the business of granting annuities on human life, and, where that person—

(I) is not resident in the State, or

(II) is not trading in the State through a fixed place of business,

that person is an insurance undertaking authorised to transact insurance business in the State under Directive 2002/83/EC of the European

Parliament and of the Council of 5 November 2002 (OJ No L345, 19.12.2002, p 1),][3]

(ii) that it includes provision securing that no annuity payable under it shall be capable in whole or in part of surrender, commutation or assignment, and

(iii) that it does not—

(I) provide for the payment by that person during the life of the individual of any sum except sums payable by means of annuity to the individual,

(II) provide for the annuity payable to the individual to commence before the individual attains the age of 60 years or after he or she attains the age of [75 years],[4]

(III) provide for the payment by that person of any other sums except sums payable by means of annuity to the individual's widow or widower and any sums which, in the event of no annuity becoming payable either to the individual or to a widow or widower, are payable to the individual's personal representatives by means of return of premiums, reasonable interest on premiums or bonuses out of profits,

(IV) provide for the annuity, if any, payable to a widow or widower of the individual to be of a greater annual amount than that paid or payable to the individual, or

(V) provide for the payment of any annuity otherwise than for the life of the annuitant.

[(*b*) Notwithstanding paragraph (*a*)—

(i) the contract may provide for the payment to the individual, at the time the annuity commences to be payable or, where the individual opts in accordance with subsection (2A), at the time of the transfer referred to in that subsection, of a lump sum by means of commutation of part of the annuity where the individual elects, at or before the time when the annuity first becomes payable to him or her or before the date of such transfer, to be paid the lump sum, and

(ii) the amount payable under subparagraph (i) shall not exceed 25 per cent of the value of the annuity payable or the value of the annuity which would have been payable if the individual had not opted in accordance with subsection (2A).

(*c*) The reference in paragraph (*b*)(i) to the commutation of part of the annuity shall, in a case where the individual has opted in accordance with subsection (2A), be construed as a reference to the commutation of the annuity which would, but for such election, be payable if the individual opted to have the annuity paid with effect from the date of the transfer referred to in that subsection.][5]

[(2A) The Revenue Commissioners shall not approve a contract unless it appears to them that the contract provides for the individual entitled to an annuity under the contract to exercise, on or before the date on which that annuity would otherwise become payable, an option for the transfer by the person with whom the contract is made, on or after that date, to—

(*a*) the individual, or

(*b*) an approved retirement fund,

of an amount equivalent to the amount determined by the formula—

$$A - B$$

where—

A is the amount equal to the value of the individual's accrued rights under the contract exclusive of any lump sum paid in accordance with paragraph (*b*) of subsection (2), and

B is the amount or value of assets which the person with whom the contract is made is required, in accordance with section 784C, to transfer to an approved minimum retirement fund held in the name of the individual or to apply in purchasing an annuity payable to the individual with effect from the date of the exercise of the said option.

[(2B)(*a*) Where an individual opts in accordance with subsection (2A), any amount paid to the individual by virtue of that subsection, other than an amount payable by virtue of paragraph (*b*) of subsection (2), [shall, notwithstanding anything in section 18 or 19,][6] be regarded as a payment of emoluments to which Schedule E applies and, accordingly, the provisions of Chapter 4 of Part 42 shall, subject to paragraph (*b*), apply to any such payment.

(*b*) The person making a payment to which paragraph (*a*) refers shall deduct tax from the payment at the higher rate for the year of assessment in which the payment is made unless that person has received from the Revenue Commissioners a [certificate of tax credits and standard rate cut-off point][7] or a tax deduction card for that year in respect of the individual beneficially entitled to the payment.][8]][9]

[(2C) Notwithstanding anything contained in this Part, a retirement annuity contract shall not cease to be an approved contract because of any provision in law, whether or not contained in the contract, whereby the parties to the contract may cancel the contract and effect a transfer of assets into one or more than one PRSA of which the individual who is a party to that approved contract is the contributor.][10]

(3) The Revenue Commissioners may, if they think fit and subject to any conditions they think proper to impose, approve a contract otherwise satisfying the conditions referred to in subsection (2), notwithstanding that the contract provides for one or more of the following matters—

(*a*) the payment after the individual's death of an annuity to a dependant, not being the widow or widower of the individual;

(*b*) the payment to the individual of an annuity commencing before he or she attains the age of 60 years, where the annuity is payable on the individual becoming permanently incapable through infirmity of mind or body of carrying on his or her own occupation or any occupation of a similar nature for which he or she is trained or fitted;

(*c*) where the individual's occupation is one in which persons customarily retire before attaining the age of 60 years, the annuity to commence before the individual attains that age (but not before he or she attains the age of 50 years);

(*d*) ...[11]

(*e*) the annuity payable to any person to continue for a term certain (not exceeding 10 years) notwithstanding his or her death within that term, or the annuity payable to any person to terminate, or be suspended, on marriage (or remarriage) or in other circumstances;

(*f*) in the case of an annuity which is to continue for a term certain, the annuity to be assignable by will and, in the event of any person dying entitled to the annuity, the annuity to be assignable by his or her personal representatives in the distribution of the estate so as to give effect to a testamentary disposition, or to the rights of those entitled on intestacy or to an appropriation of the annuity to a legacy or to a share or interest in the estate.

(4) Subsections (1) to (3) shall apply in relation to a contribution under a trust scheme or part of a trust scheme approved by the Revenue Commissioners as they apply in relation to a premium under an annuity contract so approved, with the modification that for the condition in subsection (2)(*a*)(i) there shall be substituted a condition that the scheme (or the part of the scheme)—

(*a*) is established under the law of and administered in the State,

(*b*) is established for the benefit of individuals engaged in or connected with a particular occupation (or one or other of a group of occupations) and for the purpose of providing retirement annuities for those individuals with or without subsidiary benefits for their families or dependants, and

(*c*) is so established under irrevocable trusts by a body of persons comprising or representing the majority of the individuals so engaged in the State,

and with the necessary modifications of other references to the contract or the person with whom it is made, and exemption from income tax shall be allowed in respect of income derived from investments or deposits of any fund maintained for the purpose referred to in paragraph (*b*) under a scheme or part of a scheme for the time being approved under this subsection.

[(4A) At any time when the person referred to in subsection (2)(*a*)(i) or in section 785(1)—

(*a*) is not resident in the State, or

(*b*) is not trading in the State through a fixed place of business,

the person shall, in relation to the discharge of all duties and obligations imposed by this section or, as the case may be, by section 785—

(i) enter into a contract with the Revenue Commissioners enforceable in a Member State of the European Communities in relation to the discharge of those duties and obligations and in entering into such a contract the parties to the contract shall acknowledge and agree in writing that—

(I) it is governed solely by the laws of the State, and

(II) that the courts of the State shall have exclusive jurisdiction in determining any dispute arising under it,

or

(ii) ensure that there is a person resident in the State (referred to in this paragraph as the "appointed person"), appointed by the person, to be responsible for the discharge of those duties and obligations and the person shall notify the Revenue Commissioners of the appointment of the appointed person and the identity of the appointed person.

(4B) The Revenue Commissioners may by notice in writing require the person to whom premiums are payable under any contract for the time being approved under this section or under section 785, or the appointed person referred to in subsection (4A)(ii), as the case may be, to provide, within 30 days of the date of such notice, such information and particulars as may be specified in the notice as they may reasonably require for the purposes of this Chapter, and, without prejudice to the generality of the foregoing, such information and particulars may include—

(*a*) the name, address and PPS Number (within the meaning of section 787A(1)) of the individual with whom the contract has been made,

(*b*) the name, address and PPS Number (within that meaning) of the individual or individuals to whom any payment of an annuity in respect of the contract has been made, and

(*c*) the amount of the annuity payments referred to in paragraph (*b*).][12]

(5) The Revenue Commissioners may at any time, by notice in writing given to the persons by and to whom premiums are payable under any contract for the time being approved under this section or to the trustees or other persons having the management of any trust scheme so approved, withdraw that approval on such grounds and from such date (including a date before the date of the notice) as may be specified in the notice and, where any approval is so withdrawn, there shall be made such assessments as may be appropriate for the purpose of withdrawing any reliefs given under this Chapter consequent on the approval.

(6) Nothing in sections 4 and 6 of the Policies of Assurance Act, 1867, shall be taken to apply to any contract approved under this section.

[(7) Notwithstanding anything in section 18 or section 19, any payment of an annuity made on or after 1 January 2002 in respect of an annuity contract approved under this section or under section 785 shall be regarded as a pension chargeable to tax under Schedule E, and Chapter 4 of Part 42 shall apply accordingly.][13]

Amendments

1 Subs (1) substituted by FA 2002 s 10(1)(*b*) for 2002 and later tax years.

2 Substituted by FA 1999 s 19(1)(*b*)(ii)(II)(A) in respect of any annuity contract for the time being approved by the Revenue Commissioners under s 784 entered into on or after 6 April 1999; previously "Subject to subsection (3)".

3 Subs (2)(*a*)(i) substituted by FA 2005 s 21(1)(*b*)(i)(I) as respects any annuity contract approved by the Revenue Commissioners under TCA 1997 s 784 entered into on or after 1 January 2005.

4 Substituted by FA 1999 s 19(*b*)(ii)(II)(B) in respect of any annuity contract for the time being approved by the Revenue Commissioners under s 784 entered into on or after 6 April 1999; previously "70 years".

5 Subs (2)(*b*) substituted by FA 1999 s 19(*b*)(ii)(III) in respect of any annuity contract for the time being approved by the Revenue Commissioners under s 784 entered into on or after 6 April 1999.

6 Substituted by FA 2005 s 21(1)(*b*)(i)(II) as respects any annuity contract approved by the Revenue Commissioners under TCA 1997 s 784 entered into on or after 1 January 2005; previously "shall".

7 Substituted by FA 2003 s 163 and Sch 6 para 1(*g*) with effect from 6 April 2001; previously "certificate of tax free allowances".

8 Subs (2B) substituted by FA 2000 s 23(1)(*c*) with effect from 6 April 2000.

9 Subs (2A)–(2B) inserted by FA 1999 s 19(*b*)(ii)(IV) in respect of any annuity contract for the time being approved by the Revenue Commissioners under s 784 entered into on or after 6 April 1999.

10 Subs (2C) inserted by Pensions (Amendment) Act 2002 s 4(1)(*d*)(iv) with effect from such date as the Minister for Social, Community and Family Affairs may appoint by order. By virtue of Pensions

(Amendment) Act, 2002 (Commencement) Order, 2002, SI No 502 of 2002, this amendment comes into operation on 7 November 2002.

11 Subs (3)(*d*) deleted by FA 1999 s 19(*b*)(ii)(V) in respect of any annuity contract for the time being approved by the Revenue Commissioners under s 784 entered into on or after 6 April 1999.

12 Subss (4A) and (4B) inserted by FA 2005 s 21(1)(*b*)(i)(III) as respects any annuity contract approved by the Revenue Commissioners under TCA 1997 s 784 entered into on or after 1 January 2005.

13 Subs (7) inserted by FA 2001 s 18(*b*)(i) with effect from 6 April 2001.

Cross-references

Approval of certain other contracts: s 786(1).

Approval of contracts for dependants or for life assurance: s 785(6); subss (2)–(3): s 785(4); subs (4)(*a*)–(*c*): s 785(5).

Approved minimum retirement fund, subs (2A): s 784C(2), (3), (4)(*a*).

Capital acquisitions tax, relief in respect of certain policies of insurance, subs (4)(*c*): CATCA 2003 s 72(1) ("approved retirement fund tax").

Capital element in purchased annuities: s 788(2)(*b*).

Capital gains tax, superannuation funds, subs (4): s 608(2).

Conditions for approval of schemes and discretionary approval: s 772(3A)(*b*)(i); subs (2A): s 772(3A)(*b*)(iii); subs (2B): s 772(3B)(*a*).

Conditions relating to approved minimum retirement fund, subs (2A): s 784D(1)(*b*)(i), (*d*)(iv), (3)(*a*).

Conditions relating to approved retirement fund, subs (2A): s 784B(1)(*b*)(i), (3)(*a*).

Dividend withholding tax (interpretation): s 172A(1)(a) ("pension scheme").

Dividend withholding tax, declarations of exemption: Sch 2A para 1 ("appropriate person").

Investment undertakings (interpretation and application): s 739B(1)("pension scheme").

Investment undertakings, declarations: Sch 2B para 1 ("appropriate person").

Life assurance companies: s 706(3)(*a*), (*c*).

Personal Retirement Savings Accounts (PRSAs), approved retirement fund option, subs (2A): s 787H(3).

Qualifying overseas pension plans, relief for contributions; subs (1): s 787N(1).

Returns by employers in relation to pension products, meaning of "qualifying premium" applied: s 897A(1)("RAC premium").

Special arrangements in relation to annuity contract approved before 6 April in context of changes effected to Part 30 by FA 1999 s 19(1): FA 1999 s 19(2)(*d*), (*e*).

Unclaimed Life Assurance Policies Act 2003, interpretation, s 2(1)("approved policy").

Revenue precedents

Issue: Normal Retirement Age for Musicians.

Decision: Earliest age retirement is 60 with the exception of brass instrumentalists, who can retire from age 55.

Tax Briefing

TB26 Apr 1997 p 17 Lloyds Underwriters — Irish Names: from 1996/97 a name's underwriting profits and income arising from Funds at Lloyds treated as earned income for retirement annuity purposes without reference to the concept of a "working name".

Definitions

higher rate: ss 3(1), 15; person: IA 1937 s 11(*c*); profession: s 2(1); profits or gains: s 3(4); trade: s 3(1); writing: IA 1937 Sch; year of assessment: s 3(1).

Former enactments

ITA 1967 s 235(1)–(5) and (10); FA 1974 s 65.

Corresponding UK tax provision

Income and Corporation Taxes Act 1988 s 619.

784A Approved retirement fund

[(1) (*a*) In this section—

"approved retirement fund" means a fund which is managed by a qualifying fund manager and which complies with the conditions of section 784B;

"qualifying fund manager" means—

[(*a*) a person who is a holder of a licence granted under section 9 of the Central Bank Act, 1971, or a person who holds a licence or other similar authorisation under the law of any other Member State of the European Communities which corresponds to a licence granted under that section,][1]

(*b*) a building society within the meaning of section 256,

(*c*) a trustee savings bank within the meaning of the Trustee Savings Banks Act, 1989,

...[2]

...[3]

...[3]

(*g*) the Post Office Savings Bank,

(*h*) a credit union within the meaning of the Credit Union Act, 1997,

(*i*) a collective investment undertaking within the meaning of section 172A,

[(*j*) the holder of—

(i) an authorisation issued by the Minister for Enterprise, Trade and Employment under the European Communities (Life Assurance) Framework Regulations of 1984 (SI No 57 of 1984) as amended, or

(ii) an authorisation granted by the authority charged by law with the duty of supervising the activities of insurance undertakings in a Member State other than the State in accordance with Article 6 of Directive No 79/267/EEC (OJ No L63, 13.3.1979, p 1), who is carrying on the business of life assurance in the State, or

(iii) an official authorisation to undertake insurance in Iceland, Liechtenstein and Norway pursuant to the EEA Agreement within the meaning of the European Communities (Amendment) Act, 1993, and who is carrying on the business of life assurance in the State,][4]

(*k*) a person—

(i) which is an authorised member firm of the Irish Stock Exchange, within the meaning of the Stock Exchange Act, 1995, or a member firm (which carries on a trade in the State through a branch or agency) of a stock exchange of any other Member State of the European Communities, and

(ii) which has sent to the Revenue Commissioners a notification of its name and address and of its intention to act as a qualifying fund manager,

or

[(*l*) a firm approved under section 10 of the Investment Intermediaries Act, 1995, which is authorised to hold client money, other than a firm authorised as a Restricted Activity Investment Product Intermediary, where the firm's authorisation permits it to engage in the proposed activities, or a business firm which has been authorised to provide similar investment business services under the laws of a Member State of the European Communities which correspond to that Act;][5]

"tax reference number", in relation to an individual, has the meaning assigned to it by section 885 in relation to a specified person within the meaning of that section.

(*b*) For the purposes of this Chapter, references to an approved retirement fund shall be construed as a reference to assets in an approved retirement fund which are managed for an individual by a qualifying fund manager and which are beneficially owned by the individual.

[(*c*) Nothing in this Part shall be construed as authorising or permitting a person who is a qualifying fund manager to provide any services which that person would not otherwise be authorised or permitted to provide in the State.

(*d*) Any reference in this section to a distribution in relation to an approved retirement fund shall be construed as including any payment or transfer of assets out of the fund or any assignment of assets out of the fund, including a payment, transfer or assignment to the individual beneficially entitled to the assets, other than a payment, transfer or assignment to another approved retirement fund the beneficial owner of the assets in which is the individual who is beneficially entitled to the assets in the first-mentioned approved retirement fund, whether or not the payment, transfer or assignment is made to the said individual.][6]

[(1A) Without prejudice to the generality of subsection (1)(*d*), where assets of an approved retirement fund are used in connection with any of the transactions referred to in subsection (1B), the transaction shall be regarded as a distribution for the purposes of this section of the amount specified in that subsection.

(1B) The transactions referred to in subsection (1A) and the amount to be regarded as a distribution in relation to any such transaction are as follows—

(*a*) in the case of a loan made to the individual beneficially entitled to the assets in an approved retirement fund or to any person connected with that individual, the amount to be regarded as a distribution for the purposes of this section is an amount equal to the value of the assets of the approved retirement fund used to make such a loan or used as security for such a loan,

(*b*) in the case of the acquisition of property from the individual beneficially entitled to the assets in an approved retirement fund or from any person connected with that individual, the amount to be regarded as a distribution for the purposes of this section is an amount equal to the value of the assets in the approved retirement fund used in or in connection with that acquisition,

(*c*) in the case of the sale of any asset in an approved retirement fund to the individual beneficially entitled to the assets in an approved retirement fund or to any person connected with that individual, the amount to be regarded as a distribution for the purposes of this section is an amount equal to the value of the asset sold,

(*d*) in the case of the acquisition of—

(i) any property which is to be used as holiday property, or

(ii) property which is to be used as a residence,

by the individual beneficially entitled to the assets in the approved retirement fund or by any person connected with that individual, the amount to be regarded as a distribution for the purposes of this section is an amount equal to the value of the assets in the approved retirement fund used in or in connection with that acquisition, but where property is acquired, on or after 6 February 2003, in relation to the acquisition of which a distribution is not treated as arising under this Chapter and that property commences to be used for one of the purposes mentioned in subparagraphs (i) or (ii) of this paragraph, the distribution shall be treated as arising at the date such use commences and the amount to be regarded as a distribution for the purposes of this section is an amount equal to the value of the assets of the approved retirement fund used in or in connection with the acquisition together with any assets used in or in connection with any expenditure on the improvement or repair of the property in question,

(*e*) in the case of the acquisition of shares or any other interest in a company, which is a close company or which would be a close company but for the fact that the company is not resident in the State, in relation to which the individual beneficially entitled to the assets in the approved retirement fund or a person connected with that individual is a participator, the amount to be regarded as a distribution for the purposes of this section is an amount equal to the value of assets in the approved retirement fund used in or in connection with that acquisition, and

(*f*) in the case of the acquisition of tangible moveable property, the amount to be regarded as a distribution for the purposes of this section is an amount equal to the value of the assets in the approved retirement fund used in or in connection with that acquisition.

(1C) An amount which has been regarded as a distribution from an approved retirement fund, in accordance with this section, shall not be regarded as an asset in that approved retirement fund for any purpose.

(1D) Any property, the acquisition or sale of which is regarded as giving rise to a distribution of assets in an approved retirement fund, shall not be regarded as an asset in that approved retirement fund.

(1E) For the purposes of subsection (1B) references to the value of an asset in an approved retirement fund shall, except where the asset is cash, be construed as references to the market value of the asset, within the meaning of section 548.][7]

[(2) Subject to subsections (3) and (4), exemption from income tax and capital gains tax shall be allowed in respect of the income and chargeable gains arising in respect of assets held in an approved retirement fund.

(3) Subject to subsection (4)—

(*a*) the amount or value of any distribution by a qualifying fund manager in respect of assets held in an approved retirement fund [shall, notwithstanding anything in section 18 or 19,][8] be treated as a payment to the person beneficially entitled to the assets in the fund of emoluments to which Schedule E applies and, accordingly, the provisions of Chapter 4 of Part 42 shall apply to any such distribution, and (*b*) the qualifying fund manager shall deduct tax from the distribution at the higher rate for the year of assessment in which the distribution is made unless the qualifying fund manager has received from the Revenue Commissioners a [certificate of tax credits and standard rate cut-off point][9] or a tax deduction card for that year in respect of the person referred to in paragraph (*a*).

(4) (*a*) Where the distribution referred to in subsection (3) is made following the death of the individual who was prior to death beneficially entitled to the assets of the approved retirement fund, the amount or value of the distribution shall be treated as the income of that individual for the year of assessment in which that individual dies and, subject to paragraph (*b*), subsection (3) shall apply accordingly.

(*b*) Subsection (3) shall not apply to a distribution made following the death of the individual who was prior to death beneficially entitled to the assets in an approved retirement fund where the distribution is made—

(i) to another such fund (hereafter in this subsection referred to as "the second-mentioned fund") the beneficial owner of the assets in which is the spouse of the said individual, or

(ii) to, or for the sole benefit of, any child of the individual.

(*c*) Where, in a case referred to in paragraph (*b*), the distribution is made—

(i) to a person who had attained the age of 21 years at the date of death of the individual beneficially entitled to the assets in the approved retirement fund, or

(ii) following the death of the beneficial owner of the second-mentioned fund, not being a distribution to or for the sole benefit of a child of that owner who at the time of death of that person had not attained the age of 21 years,

the qualifying fund manager shall deduct tax from the distribution at the standard rate of income tax in force at the time of the making of such a distribution, and—

(I) notwithstanding anything contained in any provision of the Income Tax Acts, the amount so charged to tax shall not be treated as income for any other purpose of those Acts, and

(II) the provisions of Chapter 4 of Part 42 and Regulations made in accordance with that Chapter shall, with any necessary modifications, apply to any deduction made under this subsection as if such a deduction were made in accordance with [Regulation 22(2)(*b*)(ii) of the Income Tax (Employments) (Consolidated) Regulations 2001 (SI No 559 of 2001)][10].

(5) For the purposes of this section, Chapter 1 of Part 26 shall apply as if references in that Chapter to pension business were references to moneys held in an approved retirement fund.

(6) Notwithstanding Chapter 4 of Part 8, that Chapter shall apply to a deposit (within the meaning of that Chapter) where the deposit consists of money held by a qualifying fund manager in that capacity as if such a deposit were not a relevant deposit (within the meaning of that Chapter).

(7) [(*a*) At any time when the qualifying fund manager—

(i) is not resident in the State, or

(ii) is not trading in the State through a fixed place of business,

the qualifying fund manager shall, in relation to the discharge of all duties and obligations relating to approved retirement funds which are imposed on the qualifying fund manager by virtue of this Chapter—

(I) enter into a contract with the Revenue Commissioners enforceable in a Member State of the European Communities in relation to the discharge of those duties and obligations and in entering into such a contract the parties to the contract shall acknowledge and agree in writing that—

(A) it shall be governed solely by the laws of the State, and

(B) that the courts of the State shall have exclusive jurisdiction in determining any dispute arising under it,

or

(II) ensure that there is a person resident in the State, appointed by the qualifying fund manager, who will be responsible for the discharge of all of those duties and obligations and shall notify the Revenue Commissioners of the appointment of that person and the identity of that person.][11]

(*b*) A qualifying fund manager shall be liable to pay to the Collector-General income tax which the fund manager is required to deduct from any distribution by virtue of this Chapter and the individual beneficially entitled to assets held in an approved retirement fund, including the personal representatives of a deceased individual who was so entitled prior to that individual's death, shall allow such deduction; but where there are no funds or insufficient funds available out of which the qualifying fund manager may satisfy the tax required to be deducted, the amount of such tax for which there are insufficient funds available shall be a debt due to the qualifying fund manager from the individual beneficially entitled to the asset in the approved retirement fund or from the estate of the deceased individual, as the case may be.][12]][13]

[(8) (*a*) Within one month of commencing to act as manager of approved retirement funds, a qualifying fund manager shall give notice to that effect to the Revenue Commissioners.

(*b*) A qualifying fund manager who commenced to act as manager of an approved retirement fund prior to the passing of the Finance Act 2003 shall give notice to that effect to the Revenue Commissioners within three months of the passing of that Act.

(*c*) A notice under paragraph (*a*) or (*b*) shall specify the date the qualifying fund manager commenced to so act.] [14]

[(9) The Revenue Commissioners may by notice in writing require a qualifying fund manager or the person appointed under subsection (7)(*a*)(II), as the case may be, to provide within 30 days of the date of such notice, such information and particulars as may be specified in the notice as they may reasonably require for the purposes of this Chapter, and without prejudice to the generality of the foregoing, such information and particulars may include—

(*a*) the name, address and tax reference number of the individual in whose name the approved retirement fund is or was held,

(*b*) the name, address and tax reference number of any individual to whom any distribution has been made, and

(*c*) the amount of any distributions referred to in paragraph (*b*).][15]

Amendments

1 Definition of "qualifying fund manager" para (*a*) substituted by FA 2000 s 23(1)(*d*)(i)(I) with effect from 6 April 2000.

2 Definition of "qualifying fund manager" para (*d*) repealed by ACC Bank Act 2001 s 12(1) and Sch with effect from such date as the Minister for Finance may appoint by order. By virtue of the ACC Bank Act 2001 (Sections 6, 8, 10, 11(2) and 12) (Commencement) Order 2002, SI No 69 of 2002, this amendment came into operation with effect from 28 February 2002.

3 Definition of "qualifying fund manager" paras (*e*) and (*f*) repealed with effect from 12 February 2001 by ICC Bank Act 2000 s 7 and the ICC Bank Act 2000 (Sections 5 and 7) (Commencement) Order 2001 (SI No 396 of 2001); previously "(*e*) ICC Bank plc," and "(*f*) ICC Investment Bank Limited,".

4 Definition of "qualifying fund manager" para (*j*) substituted by FA 2000 s 23(1)(*d*)(i)(II) with effect from 6 April 2000.

5 Definition of "qualifying fund manager" para (*l*) substituted by FA 2000 s 23(1)(*d*)(i)(III) with effect from 6 April 2000.

6 Subs (1)(*c*)–(*d*) inserted by FA 2000 s 23(1)(*d*)(ii) with effect from 6 April 2000.

7 Subss (1A)–(1E) inserted by by FA 2003 s 14(1)(*c*)(ii) with effect from 6 February 2003.

8 Substituted by FA 2005 s 21(1)(*b*)(ii)(I) as respects any annuity contract approved by the Revenue Commissioners under TCA 1997 s 784 entered into on or after 1 January 2005; previously "shall".

9 Substituted by FA 2001 s 2 and Sch 1 para 1(*p*) (as amended by FA 2002 s 138 and Sch 6 paras 5(*h*)(i) and 6(*e*)(i)) for short tax "year" 2001 and later tax years; previously "certificate of tax-free allowances".

10 Substituted by FA 2002 s 138 and Sch 6 paras 3(*l*) and 6(*c*)(i) with effect from 1 January 2002; previously "Regulation 25(2)(*b*) of the Income Tax (Employments) Regulations, 1960 (SI No 28 of 1960)".

11 Subs (7)(*a*) substituted by FA 2005 s 21(1)(*b*)(ii)(II) as respects any annuity contract approved by the Revenue Commissioners under TCA 1997 s 784 entered into on or after 1 January 2005.

12 Subs (2)–7) substituted by FA 2000 s 23(1)(d)(iii) as regards an approved retirement fund or an approved minimum retirement fund, as the case may be, where the assets in the fund were first accepted into the fund by the qualifying fund manager on or after 6 April 2000.

13 Section 784A inserted by FA 1999 s 19(1)(*b*)(iii) in respect of any annuity contract for the time being approved by the Revenue Commissioners under s 784 entered into on or after 6 April 1999.

14 Subs (8) inserted by FA 2003 s 14(1)(*c*)(iii) with effect from 28 March 2003.

15 Subs (9) substituted by FA 2005 s 21(1)(*b*)(ii)(III) as respects any annuity contract approved by the Revenue Commissioners under TCA 1997 s 784 entered into on or after 1 January 2005.

Cross-references

Approved minimum retirement fund, meaning of "qualifying fund manager" applied: s 784C(1); s 784C(6), (7).

Capital acquisitions tax, exemption relating to retirement benefits, meaning of approved retirement fund applied: CATCA 2003 s 85(1).

Conditions for approval of schemes and discretionary approval: s 772(3B)(*a*).

Dividend withholding tax, interpretation, meaning of "approved retirement fund", "qualifying fund manager" applied: s 172A(1)(*a*).

Interpretation and supplemental (Chapter 1), meaning of "approved retirement fund" applied: s 770(1).

Interpretation and general, meaning of "approved retirement fund" applied: s 783(1)(*a*).

Investment undertakings (gain arising on a chargeable event), subs (2): s 739D(6)(*h*).

Investment undertakings (interpretation and application), meaning of "approved retirement fund" and "qualifying fund manager" applied: s 739B(1).

Penalties, subs (8): Sch 29, column 1.

Personal Retirement Savings Accounts (PRSAs), interpretation and supplemental, meaning of "approved retirement fund" applied: s 787A(1); approved retirement fund option: s 787H(2)(*b*), (3); taxation of payments from a PRSA, subs (4): s 787G(6); s 787G(4A).

Purchased life annuities, meaning of "approved retirement fund" applied: s 788(2)(*f*).

Definitions

chargeable gain: ss 5(1), 545; close company: s 783(1)(*a*); Collector-General: ss 2(1), 851; connected person: s 783(1)(*a*); higher rate: ss 3(1), 15; Income Tax Acts: s 1(2); month: IA 1937 Sch; participator: s 783(1)(*a*); person: IA 1937 s 11(*c*); standard rate: ss 3(1), 15; writing: IA 1937 Sch; year of assessment: s 2(1).

784B Conditions relating to an approved retirement fund

[(1) The conditions of this section are—

(*a*) an approved retirement fund shall be held by a qualifying fund manager in the name of the individual who is beneficially entitled to the assets in the fund,

(*b*) assets held in an approved retirement fund shall consist of and only of one or more of—

(i) assets transferred to the fund by virtue of an option exercised by the individual in accordance with section 784(2A),

(ii) assets which were previously held in another approved retirement fund held in the name of the individual or the individual's deceased spouse, and

(iii) assets derived from such assets as are referred to in subparagraphs (i) and (ii),

(*c*) the individual referred to in paragraph (*a*) shall, on the opening of an approved retirement fund, make a declaration of the kind mentioned in paragraph (*d*) to the qualifying fund manager, and

(*d*) the declaration referred to in paragraph (*c*) shall be a declaration, in writing, to the qualifying fund manager which—

(i) is made by the individual who is beneficially entitled to the assets in the approved retirement fund,

(ii) is made in such form as may be prescribed or authorised by the Revenue Commissioners,

(iii) contains the full name, address and tax reference number of the individual referred to in subparagraph (i),

(iv) declares that the assets included in the fund consist only of assets referred to in paragraph (*b*) to which the individual was beneficially entitled, and

(v) contains such other information as the Revenue Commissioners may reasonably require for the purposes of this Act.

(2) A qualifying fund manager shall not accept any assets into an approved retirement fund unless the fund manager receives a certificate to which subsection (3) applies in relation to those assets from a person lawfully carrying on in the State the business of granting annuities on human life or from another qualifying fund manager.

(3) A certificate to which this subsection applies is a certificate stating—

(*a*) that the assets in relation to which the certificate refers are assets to which the individual named on the certificate is beneficially entitled and which are being transferred to the approved retirement fund, or have previously been transferred to an approved retirement fund, in accordance with subsection (2A) of section 784,

(*b*) that the assets in relation to which the certificate is given do not form part of an approved minimum retirement fund within the meaning of section 784C, and (*c*) the amount of the balance on the income and gains account, and the residue in relation to the approved retirement fund, the assets of which are being transferred or assigned to the qualifying fund manager.

(4) Subsection (2) of section 263 shall apply to a declaration made in accordance with subsection (1)(*c*) or a certificate to which subsection (3) applies as it applies in relation to declarations of a kind mentioned in that section.

(5) The Minister for Finance may by order specify requirements regarding the operation of approved retirement funds.][1]

Amendments

1 Section 784B inserted by FA 1999 s 19(1)(*b*)(iii) in respect of any annuity contract for the time being approved by the Revenue Commissioners under s 784 entered into on or after 6 April 1999.

Cross-references

Approved minimum retirement fund, subs (1) and (5): s 784C(6).
Approved retirement fund, definition of "approved retirement fund": s 784A(1)(*a*).
Conditions for approval of schemes and discretionary approval: s 772(3B)(*a*).
Personal Retirement Savings Accounts (PRSAs), approved retirement fund option: s 787H(3).

Definitions

approved retirement fund: s 784A(1)(*a*); person: IA 1937 s 11(*c*); qualifying fund manager: s 784A(1)(*a*); residue: s 784A(3)(*b*); tax reference number: s 784A(1)(*a*); writing: IA 1937 Sch.

784C Approved minimum retirement fund

[(1) In this section, **"an approved minimum retirement fund"** means a fund managed by a qualifying fund manager (within the meaning of section 784A) and which complies with the conditions of section 784D.

(2) Subject to subsections (3) and (4), where an individual, who has not attained the age of 75 years, exercises an option in accordance with subsection (2A) of section 784, the amount referred to as B in the formula in the said subsection which the person with whom the annuity contract is made shall—

(*a*) transfer to an approved minimum retirement fund in respect of that individual, or

(*b*) apply in the purchase of an annuity payable to the individual, shall be the lesser of—

(i) the amount referred to as A in that formula, or

(ii) [€63,500][1].

(3) Where the individual has already exercised an option in accordance with subsection (2A) of section 784, the amount referred to as B in the formula in subsection (2A) shall be such amount as will result in the aggregate of the amount required in respect of all such options, in accordance with subsection (2A), to be transferred to an approved minimum retirement fund or applied in the purchase of an annuity payable to the individual being the lesser of—

(*a*) the aggregate of the amount referred to as A in that formula in relation to each contract, or

(*b*) [€63,500][1].

(4) (*a*) Where, at the date of exercise of an option under subsection (2A) of section 784, the individual by whom the option is exercised [is in receipt of][2] specified income amounting to [€12,700][3] per annum, the amount referred to as B in the formula in the said section 784(2A) shall be nil.

(*b*) For the purposes of this subsection, "specified income" means a pension or annuity which is payable for the life of the individual, including a pension payable under the Social Welfare (Consolidation) Act, 1993, and any pension to which the provisions of section 200 apply.

(5) Subject to subsection (6), the qualifying fund manager shall not make any payment or transfer of assets out of the approved minimum retirement fund [, including any distribution or amount regarded under this Chapter as a distribution, other than—][4]

(*a*) a transfer of all the assets of the fund to another qualifying fund manager to be held as an approved minimum retirement fund, or

(*b*) a payment or transfer of income, profits or gains, or gains on disposal of investments received by the qualifying fund manager in respect of assets held in the approved fund to the individual beneficially entitled to the assets in the fund.

(6) Where the individual referred to in subsection (2) attains the age of 75 years or dies, the approved minimum retirement fund shall, thereupon, become an approved retirement fund and the provisions of section 784A, subsections (1) and (5) of section 784B and section 784E shall apply accordingly.

[(7) The provisions of section 784A shall, with any necessary modifications, apply to income and chargeable gains arising from, and to distributions in respect of assets, held in an approved minimum retirement fund as they apply to assets held in an approved retirement fund.][5]

...[6]][7]

Amendments

1 Substituted by FA 2001 s 240(1) and (2)(*a*) and Sch 5 Pt 1 for 2002 and later tax years; previously "£50,000".

2 Substituted by FA 2005 s 21(1)(*b*)(iii) as respects any exercise of an option in accordance with TCA 1997 s 784(2A) on or after 3 February 2005; previously "is entitled to".

3 Substituted by FA 2001 s 240(1) and (2)(*a*) and Sch 5 Pt 1 for 2002 and later tax years; previously "£10,000".

4 Substituted by FA 2003 s 14(1)(*c*)(iv) with effect from 6 February 2003; previously "other than—".

5 Subs (7) substituted by FA 2000 s 23(1)(*e*)(i) as respects an approved retirement fund or an approved minimum retirement fund, as the case may be, where the assets in the fund were first accepted into the fund by the qualifying fund manager on or after 6 April 2000.

6 Subs (8)–(9) deleted by FA 2000 s 23(1)(*e*)(ii) as respects an approved retirement fund or an approved minimum retirement fund, as the case may be, where the assets in the fund were first accepted into the fund by the qualifying fund manager on or after 6 April 2000.

7 Section 784C inserted by FA 1999 s 19(1)(*b*)(iii) in respect of any annuity contract for the time being approved by the Revenue Commissioners under s 784 entered into on or after 6 April 1999.

Cross-references

Capital acquisitions tax, exemption relating to retirement benefits, meaning of approved minimum retirement fund applied: CATCA 2003 s 85(1).

Conditions for approval of schemes and discretionary approval: s 772(3A)(*a*), meaning of "B"; s 772(3B)(*a*).

Conditions relating to an approved minimum retirement fund, subs (3): s 784D(3)(*b*).

Conditions relating to an approved retirement fund: s 784B(3)(*b*).

Dividend withholding tax, interpretation, meaning of "approved minimum retirement fund" applied: s 172A(1)(*a*).

Interpretation and general (Chapter 2), meaning of "approved minimum retirement fund" applied: s 783(1)(*a*).

Interpretation and supplemental (Chapter 1), meaning of "approved minimum retirement fund" applied: s 770(1).

Investment undertakings, interpretation and application, meaning of "approved minimum retirement fund" applied: s 739B(1).

Personal Retirement Savings Accounts (PRSAs), interpretation and supplemental, meaning of "approved minimum retirement fund" applied: s 787A(1); approved retirement fund option: s 787H(2)(*b*), (3).

Purchased life annuities, meaning of "approved minimum retirement fund" applied: s 788(2)(*f*).

Retirement annuities, relief for premiums: s 784(2A), meaning of "B".

Definitions

chargeable gain: ss 5(1), 545; person: IA 1937 s 11(*c*).

784D Conditions relating to an approved minimum retirement fund

[(1) The conditions of this section are—

(*a*) an approved minimum retirement fund shall be held in the name of the individual who is beneficially entitled to the assets in the fund,

(*b*) assets held in an approved minimum retirement fund shall consist of one or more of the following—

(i) assets transferred to the fund by virtue of an option exercised by the individual in accordance with section 784(2A),

(ii) assets which were previously held in another approved minimum retirement fund held in the name of the individual, and

(iii) assets derived from such assets as are referred to in subparagraphs (i) and (ii),

(*c*) the individual referred to in paragraph (*a*) shall make a declaration of the kind mentioned in paragraph (*d*) to the qualifying fund manager,

(*d*) the declaration referred to in paragraph (*c*) shall be a declaration, in writing, to the qualifying fund manager which—

(i) is made by the individual who is beneficially entitled to the assets in the approved minimum retirement fund,

(ii) is made in such form as may be prescribed or authorised by the Revenue Commissioners,

(iii) contains the full name, address and tax reference number of the individual referred to in subparagraph (i),

(iv) declares that assets included in the fund consist only of assets referred to in paragraph (*b*) to which the individual was beneficially entitled in accordance with section 784(2A), and

(v) contains such other information as the Revenue Commissioners may reasonably require for the purposes of this Act.

(2) A qualifying fund manager shall not accept any assets into an approved minimum retirement fund unless the fund manager receives a certificate to which subsection (3) applies in relation to those assets from a person lawfully carrying on in the State the business of granting annuities on human life or from another qualifying fund manager.

(3) A certificate to which this subsection applies is a certificate stating—

(*a*) that the assets in relation to which the certificate is given are the assets of an approved minimum retirement fund to which the individual named on the certificate is beneficially entitled and which are being transferred to the approved minimum retirement fund or have previously been transferred to such a fund in accordance with subsection (2A) of section 784,

(*b*) in the case of assets transferred by another qualifying fund manager, the amount or value of assets transferred to the approved minimum retirement fund for the purposes of subsection (3) of section 784C.

(4) Subsection (2) of section 263 shall apply to a declaration made in accordance with subsection (1)(*c*) or a certificate to which subsection (3) applies as it applies in relation to declarations of a kind mentioned in that section.

(5) The Minister for Finance may specify requirements regarding the operation of approved minimum retirement funds.][1]

Amendments

1 Section 784D inserted by FA 1999 s 19(1)(*b*)(iii) in respect of any annuity contract for the time being approved by the Revenue Commissioners under s 784 entered into on or after 6 April 1999.

Cross-references

Approved minimum retirement fund: s 784C(1).

Conditions for approval of schemes and discretionary approval: s 772(3B)(*a*).

Personal Retirement Savings Accounts (PRSAs), approved retirement fund option: s 787H(3).

Definitions

approved minimum retirement fund: s 784C(1); person: IA 1937 s 11(*c*); qualifying fund manager: s 784A(1)(*a*); tax reference number: s 784A(1)(*a*); writing: IA 1937 Sch.

784E Returns, and payments of tax, by qualifying fund managers

[(1) A qualifying fund manager shall, within 14 days of the end of the month in which a distribution is made out of the residue of an approved retirement fund, make a return to the Collector-General which shall contain details of—

(*a*) the name and address of the person in whose name the approved retirement fund is or was held,

(*b*) the tax reference number of that person,

(*c*) the name and address of the person to whom the distribution was made,

(*d*) the amount of the distribution, and

(*e*) the tax which the qualifying fund manager is required to account for in relation to that distribution (hereafter in this section referred to as **"the appropriate tax"**).

(*e*) the tax which the qualifying fund manager is required to account for in relation to that distribution (hereafter in this section referred to as **"the appropriate tax"**).

(2) The appropriate tax in relation to a distribution which is required to be included in a return shall be due at the time by which the return is to be made and shall be paid by the qualifying fund manager to the Collector-General, and the appropriate tax so due shall be payable by the qualifying fund manager without the making of an assessment; but appropriate tax which has become so due may be assessed on the qualifying fund

manager (whether or not it has been paid when the assessment is made) if that tax or any part of it is not paid on or before the due date.

(3) Where it appears to the inspector that there is any amount of appropriate tax in relation to a distribution which ought to have been but has not been included in a return, or where the inspector is dissatisfied with any return, the inspector may make an assessment on the qualifying fund manager to the best of his or her judgement, and any amount of appropriate tax in relation to a distribution due under an assessment made by virtue of this subsection shall be treated for the purposes of interest on unpaid tax as having been payable at the time when it would have been payable if a correct return had been made.

(4) Where any item has been incorrectly included in a return as a distribution, the inspector may make such assessments, adjustments or set-offs as may in his or her judgement be required for securing that the resulting liabilities to tax, including interest on unpaid tax, whether of the qualifying fund manager or any other person, are in so far as possible the same as they would have been if the item had not been so included.

(5) (*a*) Any appropriate tax assessed on a qualifying fund manager under this Chapter shall be due within one month after the issue of the notice of assessment (unless that tax is due earlier under subsection (1)) subject to any appeal against the assessment, but no such appeal shall affect the date when any amount is due under subsection (1).

(*b*) On the determination of an appeal against an assessment under this section, any appropriate tax overpaid shall be repaid.

(6) (*a*) The provisions of the Income Tax Acts relating to—

(i) assessments to income tax,

(ii) appeals against such assessments (including the rehearing of appeals and the statement of a case for the opinion of the High Court), and

(iii) the collection and recovery of income tax,

shall, in so far as they are applicable, apply to the assessment, collection and recovery of appropriate tax.

(*b*) Any amount of appropriate tax payable in accordance with this Chapter without the making of an assessment shall carry interest at the rate of [0.0322 per cent for each day or part of a day][1] from the date when the amount becomes due and payable until payment.

(*c*) [Subsections (3) to (5) of section 1080][2] shall apply in relation to interest payable under paragraph (*b*) as they apply in relation to interest payable under section 1080.

(*d*) In its application to any appropriate tax charged by any assessment made in accordance with this section, section 1080 shall apply as if [subsection (2)(*b*)][3] of that section were deleted.

(7) Every return shall be in a form prescribed or authorised by the Revenue Commissioners and shall include a declaration to the effect that the return is correct and complete.

(8) (*a*) A qualifying fund manager shall, on or before the specified return date for the chargeable period, within the meaning of section 950, prepare and deliver to

the appropriate inspector, within the meaning of that section, a return in relation to each approved retirement fund held by that fund holder at any time during the year of assessment.

(*b*) The return under paragraph (*a*) shall, in relation to each approved retirement fund, contain—

(i) the name, address and tax reference number of the individual beneficially entitled to the assets in the fund,

(ii) details of any income, profits and gains, and any chargeable gains derived from assets held in the fund and of any tax deducted from income, profits or gains received,

(iii) details of any distributions made out of the assets held in the approved retirement fund, and

(iv) such further details as the Revenue Commissioners may reasonably require for the purposes of this section.][4, 5]

Amendments

1 Substituted by FA 2002 s 129(1)(*a*) with effect from 1 September 2002 as regards interest chargeable in respect of an amount due to be paid or remitted, whether before, on, or after that date; previously "1 per cent for each month or part of a month".

2 Substituted by FA 2005 s 145(7)(*a*) and Sch 5 Pt 1 in relation to any unpaid income tax, corporation tax or capital gains tax, as the case may be, that has not been paid before 1 April 2005 regardless of when that tax became due and payable and notwithstanding anything to the contrary in any other enactment other than TCA 1997 s 1082; previously "Subsections (2) to (4) of section 1080".

3 Substituted by FA 2005 s 145(7)(*a*) and Sch 5 Pt 1 in relation to any unpaid income tax, corporation tax or capital gains tax, as the case may be, that has not been paid before 1 April 2005 regardless of when that tax became due and payable and notwithstanding anything to the contrary in any other enactment other than TCA 1997 s 1082; previously "subsection (1)(*b*)".

4 Section 784E inserted by FA 1999 s 19(1)(*b*)(iii) in respect of any annuity contract for the time being approved by the Revenue Commissioners under s 784 entered into on or after 6 April 1999.

5 Section 784E deleted by FA 2000 s 23(1)(*f*) as respects an approved retirement fund or an approved minimum retirement fund, as the case may be, where the assets in the fund were first accepted into the fund by the qualifying fund manager on or after 6 April 2000.

Definitions

approved retirement fund: s 784A(1)(*a*); chargeable gain: ss 5(1), 545; Collector-General: ss 2(1); 851; High Court: IA 1937 Sch; Income Tax Acts: s 1(2); inspector: ss 2(1); 852; month: IA 1937 Sch; person: IA 1937 Sch; qualifying fund manager: s 784A(1)(*a*).

785 Approval of contracts for dependants or for life assurance

(1) The Revenue Commissioners may approve for the purposes of this Chapter a contract made by an individual with a person (in subsection (2) referred to as **"the insurer"**) lawfully carrying on in the State the business of granting annuities on human life if—

(*a*) the main benefit secured by the contract is the provision of an annuity for the wife or husband of the individual or for any one or more dependants of the individual, or

(*b*) the sole benefit secured by the contract is the provision of a lump sum on the death of the individual before he or she attains the age of [75 years],[1] being a lump sum payable to the individual's personal representatives.

[(1A) For the purposes of subsection (1), the reference in subsection (1) to a person lawfully carrying on in the State the business of granting annuities on human life shall include a reference to an insurance undertaking, authorised to transact insurance business in the State under Directive 2002/83/EC of the European Parliament and of the Council of 5 November 2002 (OJ No L345, 19.12.2002, p 1)—

(*a*) is not resident in the State, or

(*b*) is not trading in the State through a fixed place of business.][2]

(2) The Revenue Commissioners shall not approve a contract made by an individual with the insurer under subsection (1)(*a*) unless it appears to them to satisfy the following conditions—

(*a*) that any annuity payable to the wife or husband or dependant of the individual commences on the death of the individual;

(*b*) that any annuity payable under the contract to the individual commences at a time after the individual attains the age of 60 years and, unless the individual's annuity is one to commence on the death of a person to whom an annuity would be payable under the contract if that person survived the individual, cannot commence after the time when the individual attains the age of [75 years];[1]

(*c*) that the contract does not provide for the payment by the insurer of any sum, other than any annuity payable to the individual's wife or husband or dependant or to the individual except, in the event of no annuity becoming payable under the contract, any sums payable to the individual's personal representatives by means of return of premiums, reasonable interest on premiums or bonuses out of profits;

(*d*) that the contract does not provide for the payment of any annuity otherwise than for the life of the annuitant;

(*e*) that the contract provides that no annuity payable under it shall be capable in whole or in part of surrender, commutation or assignment.

(3) The Revenue Commissioners may, if they think fit and subject to any conditions they think proper to impose, approve a contract under subsection (1)(*a*), notwithstanding that in one or more respects it does not appear to them to satisfy the conditions specified in subsection (2).

(4) Subsections (2) and (3) of section 784 shall not apply to the approval of a contract under this section.

(5) The Revenue Commissioners may approve a trust scheme or part of a trust scheme otherwise satisfying the conditions specified in paragraphs (*a*) to (*c*) of section 784(4), notwithstanding that its main purpose is to provide annuities for the wives, husbands and dependants of the individuals, or lump sums payable to the individuals' personal representatives on death, and—

(*a*) subsections (1) to (4) shall apply with any necessary modifications in relation to such approval,

(*b*) this Chapter shall apply to the scheme or part of the scheme when so approved as it applies to a contract approved under this section, and

(*c*) the exemption from income tax provided in section 784(4) shall apply to the scheme or part of the scheme when so approved.

(6) Except where otherwise provided in this Chapter, any reference in the Income Tax Acts to a contract, scheme or part of a scheme approved under section 784 shall include a reference to a contract, scheme or part of a scheme approved under this section.

Amendments

1 Substituted by FA 1999 s 19(1)(*b*)(iv) in respect of any annuity contract for the time being approved by the Revenue Commissioners under s 784 entered into on or after 6 April 1999; previously "70 years (or any greater age approved under section 784(3)(*d*))".

2 Subs (1A) inserted by FA 2005 s 21(1)(*b*)(iv) as respects any annuity contract approved by the Revenue Commissioners under TCA 1997 s 784 entered into on or after 1 January 2005.

Cross-references

Approval of certain other contracts, subs (1)(*a*): s 786(3).
Capital gains tax, superannuation funds, subs (5): s 608(2).
Deposit interest retention tax, declarations, retirement annuity contract or trust scheme to which this section applies: s 265(1)(*b*).
Dividend withholding tax (interpretation): s 172A(1)(*a*) ("pension scheme").
Dividend withholding tax, declarations of exemption: Sch 2A para 1 ("appropriate person").
Investment undertakings (interpretation and application): s 739B(1)("pension scheme").
Investment undertakings, declarations: Sch 2B para 1 ("appropriate person").
Life assurance companies: s 706(3)(*a*), (*c*).
Nature and amount of relief for premiums: s 787(8), (10).
Retirement annuities, relief for premiums: s 784(1)(*a*), (1A), (1B), (7).
Unclaimed Life Assurance Policies Act 2003, interpretation, s 2(1)("approved policy").

Definitions

Income Tax Acts: s 1(2); person: IA 1937 s 11(*c*); year of assessment: s 3(1).

Former enactments

ITA 1967 s 235A(1)–(6); FA 1974 s 66.

Corresponding UK tax provision

Income and Corporation Taxes Act 1988 s 620.

786 Approval of certain other contracts

[(1) The Revenue Commissioners shall not approve an annuity contract under section 784 unless the contract provides that the individual by whom it is made may require a sum representing the value of his or her accrued rights under the contract—

(*a*) to be paid by the person with whom it is made to such other person as the individual may specify, and

(*b*) to be applied by such other person in payment of the premium or other consideration under an annuity contract made between the individual and that other person and approved by the Revenue Commissioners under that section,

if the first-mentioned contract is otherwise to be approved by the Revenue Commissioners under that section.][1]

(2) References in subsection (1) to the individual by whom a contract is made include references to any widow, widower or dependant having accrued rights under the contract.

(3) Where, in accordance with a provision of the kind referred to in subsection (1) of an annuity contract approved under section 784 or a corresponding provision of a contract approved under section 785(1)(*a*), a sum representing the value of accrued rights under one contract (in this subsection referred to as **"the original contract"**) is paid by means

of premium or other consideration under another contract (in this subsection referred to as **"the substituted contract"**), any annuity payable under the substituted contract shall be treated as earned income of the annuitant to the same extent that an annuity under the original contract would have been so treated.

Amendments

[1] Subs (1) substituted by FA 1999 s 19(1)(*b*)(v) in respect of any annuity contract for the time being approved by the Revenue Commissioners under s 784 entered into on or after 6 April 1999.

Cross-references

Capital element in purchased annuities, subs (3): s 788(2)(*c*).

Life assurance companies: s 706(3)(*a*).

Retirement annuities, relief for premiums: s 784(2)(*a*).

Definitions

person: IA 1937 s 11(*c*).

Former enactments

FA 1979 s 28(1)–(3).

Corresponding UK tax provision

Income and Corporation Taxes Act 1988 s 621.

---

787 Nature and amount of relief for qualifying premiums

(1) For the purposes of relief under this section, an individual's relevant earnings shall be those earnings before giving effect to any deduction to be made from those earnings in respect of a loss or in respect of a capital allowance (within the meaning of section 2), and references to income in this section (other than references to total income) shall be construed similarly.

(2) For the purposes of this section, **"net relevant earnings"**, in relation to an individual and subject to subsections (3) to (5), means the amount of the individual's relevant earnings for the year of assessment in question less the amount of any deductions to be made from the relevant earnings in computing the individual's total income for that year, being either—

(*a*) deductions in respect of payments made by the individual, or

(*b*) deductions in respect of losses or of such allowances mentioned in subsection (1), being losses or allowances arising from activities, profits or gains of which would be included in computing relevant earnings of the individual or of the individual's spouse for the year of assessment.

[(2A) Notwithstanding subsection (2), for the purposes of relief under this section an individual's net relevant earnings shall not exceed [€254,000][1] or such other amount as shall be specified in regulations made by the Minister for Finance.

(2B) Where regulations are proposed to be made under subsection (2A), a draft of the regulations shall be laid before Dáil Éireann and the regulations shall not be made until a resolution approving of the draft has been passed by Dáil Éireann.][2]

(3) Where in any year of assessment for which an individual claims and is allowed relief under this section there is to be made in computing the total income of the individual or of the individual's spouse a deduction in respect of any such loss or allowance of the individual referred to in subsection (2)(*b*), and the deduction or part of it is to be so

made from income other than relevant earnings, then, the amount of the deduction made from that other income shall be treated as reducing the individual's net relevant earnings for subsequent years of assessment and shall be deducted as far as may be from those of the following year, whether or not the individual claims or is entitled to claim relief under this section for that year, and in so far as it cannot be so deducted, then from those of the next year, and so on.

(4) Where an individual's income for any year of assessment consists partly of relevant earnings and partly of other income, then, as far as may be, any deductions to be made in computing the individual's total income, and which may be treated in whole or in part either as made from relevant earnings or as made from other income, shall be treated for the purposes of this section as being made from those relevant earnings in so far as they are deductions in respect of any such loss referred to in subsection (2)(*b*) and otherwise as being made from that other income.

(5) An individual's net relevant earnings for any year of assessment shall be computed without regard to any relief to be given for that year under this section either to the individual or to the individual's spouse.

(6) Where relief is to be given under this section in respect of any qualifying premium paid by an individual, the amount of that premium shall, subject to this section, be deducted from or set off against the individual's relevant earnings for the year of assessment in which the premium is paid.

(7) Where in relation to a year of assessment a qualifying premium is paid after the end of the year of assessment but [on or before the specified return date for the chargeable period (within the meaning of Part 41)][3] the premium may, if the individual so elects on or before that date, be treated for the purposes of this section as paid in the earlier year (and not in the year in which it is paid); but where—

(*a*) the amount of that premium, together with any qualifying premiums paid by the individual in the year to which the assessment relates (or treated as so paid by virtue of any previous election under this subsection), exceeds the maximum amount of the reduction which may be made under this section in the individual's relevant earnings for that year, or

(*b*) the amount of that premium itself exceeds the increase in that maximum amount which is due to taking into account the income on which the assessment is made,

the election shall have no effect as respects the excess.

[(8) Subject to this section, the amount which may be deducted or set off in any year of assessment (whether in respect of one or more qualifying premiums and whether or not including premiums in respect of a contract approved under section 785) shall not be more than—

(*a*) in the case of an individual who at any time during the year of assessment was of the age of 30 years or over but had not attained the age of 40 years, 20 per cent,

(*b*) in the case of an individual who at any time during the year of assessment was of the age of 40 years or over but had not attained the age of 50 years, 25 per cent, (*c*) in the case of an individual who at any time during the year of assessment was of the age of 50 years or over or who for the year of assessment was a specified individual, 30 per cent, and

(*d*) in any other case, 15 per cent,

of the individual's net relevant earnings for that year, and the amount to be deducted shall to the greatest extent possible include qualifying premiums in respect of contracts approved under section 785.

(8A) For the purposes of this section, "specified individual", in relation to a year of assessment, means an individual whose relevant earnings for the year of assessment were derived wholly or mainly from an occupation or profession specified in Schedule 23A.

(8B) The Minister for Finance may, after consultation with the Minister for Tourism, Sport and Recreation, by regulations extend or restrict the meaning of specified individual by adding or deleting one or more occupations or professions to or from, as the case may be, the list of occupations and professions specified in Schedule 23A.

(8C) Where regulations are proposed to be made under subsection (8B), a draft of the regulations shall be laid before Dáil Éireann and the regulations shall not be made until a resolution approving of the draft has been passed by Dáil Éireann.][4]

....[5]

[(10) Where in any year of assessment a reduction or a greater reduction would be made under this section in the relevant earnings of an individual but for an insufficiency of net relevant earnings, the amount of the reduction which would have been made but for that reason, less the amount of the reduction which is made in that year, shall be carried forward to the next year of assessment, and shall be treated for the purposes of relief under this section as the amount of a qualifying premium paid in the next year of assessment.][6]

(11) If and in so far as an amount once carried forward under subsection (10) (and treated as the amount of a qualifying premium paid in the next year of assessment) is not deducted from or set off against the individual's net relevant earnings for that year of assessment, it shall be carried forward again to the following year of assessment (and treated as the amount of a qualifying premium paid in that year of assessment), and so on for succeeding years.

....[7]

(13) Where relief under this section for any year of assessment is claimed and allowed (whether or not relief is then to be given for that year), and afterwards there is made any additional assessment, alteration of an assessment, or other adjustment of the claimant's liability to tax, there shall be made also such adjustments, if any, as are consequential thereon in the relief allowed or given under this section for that or any subsequent year of assessment.

(14) Where relief under this section is claimed and allowed for any year of assessment in respect of any payment, relief shall not be given in respect of that payment under any other provision of the Income Tax Acts for the same or a later year of assessment nor (in

the case of a payment under an annuity contract) in respect of any other premium or consideration for an annuity under the same contract.

(15) Relief shall not be given under this section in respect of a qualifying premium except on a claim made to and allowed by the inspector, but any person aggrieved by any decision of the inspector on any such claim may, on giving notice in writing to the inspector within 21 days after the notification to that person of the decision, appeal to the Appeal Commissioners.

(16) The Appeal Commissioners shall hear and determine an appeal to them under subsection (15) as if it were an appeal to them against an assessment to income tax, and the provisions of the Income Tax Acts relating to the rehearing of an appeal and to the statement of a case for the opinion of the High Court on a point of law shall, with the necessary modifications, apply accordingly.

Amendments

1 Substituted by FA 2001 s 240(1) and (2)(*a*) and Sch 5 Pt 1 for 2002 and later tax years; previously "£200,000" (short tax "year" 2001: £148,000: FA 2001 s 77(2) and Sch 2 paras 41 and 61(*a*)).

2 Subs (2A)–(2B) inserted by FA 1999 s 19(1)(*b*)(vi)(I) for 1999–2000 and later tax years.

3 Substituted by FA 1998 s 46 with effect from 6 April 1998; previously "on or before 31st day of January in the year following the year of assessment".

4 Subs (8) substituted by FA 1999 s 19(1)(*b*)(vi)(II) for 1999–2000 and later tax years.

5 Subs (9) deleted by FA 2001 s 18(*b*)(iii)(I) with effect from 6 April 2001.

6 Subs (10) substituted by FA 2001 s 18(*b*)(iii)(II) with effect from 6 April 2001.

7 Subs (12) deleted by FA 2001 s 18(*b*)(iii)(III) with effect from 6 April 2001.

Cross-references

Deduction for income earned outside the State: s 823(1) ("the specified amount").

Donations to approved bodies, relief for not to be taken into account in determining net relevant earnings if chargeable person within self assessment: s 848A(7).

Donations to certain sports bodies, relief for not to be taken into account in determining net relevant earnings if chargeable person within self assessment: s 847A(9).

"Earned income" includes an annuity payable under this Chapter, relieved under this section: s 3(3)(*a*).

Income Tax (Employments) (Consolidated) Regulations 2001, interpretation (Part 7): ITECR 2001 reg 41(*d*).

Qualifying overseas pension plans, relief for contributions: s 787N(1).

Relief on retirement for certain income of certain sportspersons, relief not to be taken into account in determining "net relevant earnings": s 480A(9).

Retirement annuities, relief for premiums: s 784(1)(*a*).

Capital element in purchased annuities: s 788(2)(*d*), (9).

Statement of practice

Subss (8)–(9), retirement annuity relief may be computed as 15% or 5% of "net relevant earnings" after deducting chargeable annual payments to "descendants" (as defined in s 792(2)): SP IT/2/90, October 1990.

Tax Briefing

TB28 Oct 1997 p 9 — GMS Superannuation Plan — Retirement Annuity Relief.

TB44 June 2001 p 27 — Under no circumstances will an election (under TCA 1997 s 787(7)) made outside the prescribed time limit be admitted.

Definitions

Appeal Commissioners: s 2(1); Dáil Éireann, High Court: IA 1937 Sch; inspector: ss 2(1), 5(1), 852; person: IA 1937 s 11(*c*); total income: s 3(1); writing: IA 1937 Sch.; year of assessment: s 3(1);

Former enactments

ITA 1967 s 236(1), and (2B)–(9) and (11), s 238(1)–(2); F(MP)A 1968 s 3(2) and Sch Pt I; FA 1974 s 67(1)–(2); FA 1975 s 33(2) and Sch 1 Pt II; FA 1978 s 4; FA 1990 s 27(1); FA 1996 s 13(*a*).

Corresponding UK tax provision

Income and Corporation Taxes Act 1988 s 623-.

[CHAPTER 2A
Personal Retirement Savings Accounts][1]

Amendments

[1] Chapter 2A (ss 787A–787L) inserted by Pensions (Amendment) Act 2002 s 4(1)(*d*)(v) with effect from such date as the Minister for Social, Community and Family Affairs may appoint by order. By virtue of Pensions Amendment Act, 2002 (Commencement) Order 2002, SI No 502 of 2002, this amendment comes into operation on 7 November 2002.

Cross-references

Application of section 985 (PAYE method of collection) to certain perquisites, etc, meaning of "PRSA" applied: s 985A(1)(*a*)(i).

Benefits in kind, general charging provision, meaning of "PRSA" applied: s 118(5).

Capital element in certain purchased annuities, meaning of "PRSA assets" applied: s 788(2)(*g*).

Investment undertakings, gain arising on a chargeable event, meaning of "PRSA" and "PRSA administrator" applied: s 739D(6)(i).

Life assurance companies, interpretation and general, meaning of "PRSA contract" and "PRSA provider" applied: s 706(3)(*d*).

Life assurance companies, policyholders — new basis, gains arising on a chargeable event, meaning of "PRSA provider" applied: s 730D(2)(*b*)(iv); declarations, meaning of "PRSA provider" applied: s 730E(3)(*e*)(iv).

Limit on net relevant earnings for purposes of relief under this Chapter: s 790A.

Occupational pension schemes, interpretation and supplemental, meaning of "Personal Retirement Savings Account" or "PRSA" applied: s 770(1).

Overseas pension plans, migrant member relief, interpretation and general: s 787M(1) ("qualifying overseas pension plan").

PAYE Regulations: s 986(1)(*g*)(ii).

Pensions Act 1990 (as amended by Pensions (Amendment) Act 2002) ss 94(3) and 109(1).

Qualifying overseas pension plans, relief for contributions: s 787N(1).

Retirement annuities, interpretation, meaning of "PRSA contribution" applied: s 783(2)(*c*).

Unclaimed Life Assurance Policies Act 2003, interpretation, s 2(1)("approved policy"), meaning of "Personal Retirement Savings Account" applied; s 2(1)("policyholder" para (*f*)) meaning of "contributor" applied.

Tax Briefing

TB47 April 2002 pp 29–31 — Tax Rules relating to Personal Retirement Savings Accounts (PRSA).

TB50 Oct 2002 pp 18–19 — PRSAs — PAYE Net Pay Arrangement.

TB52 May 2003 pp 9–10 — Pension Products and Retirement Funds (Finance Act 2003 changes).

787A Interpretation and supplemental

[(1) In this Chapter, unless the context otherwise requires—

"additional voluntary PRSA contributions" means contributions made to a PRSA by an employee, who is a member of an approved scheme or of a statutory scheme, which are—

(i) contributions made under a rule or part of a rule, as the case may be, of a retirement benefits scheme (in this definition referred to as the "main scheme") which provides specifically for the payment of voluntary contributions to a PRSA by members of the main scheme, or

(ii) contributions made under a separately arranged scheme approved by the Revenue Commissioners which is associated with the main scheme and which provides for voluntary contributions to a PRSA by members of the main scheme;

"approved scheme" has the same meaning as in Chapter 1 of this Part;

"approved retirement fund" has the meaning assigned to it by section 784A;

"approved minimum retirement fund" has the meaning assigned to it by section 784C;

"contract of employment" means—

(*a*) a contract of service or apprenticeship, or

(*b*) any other contract whereby an individual agrees with another person, who is carrying on the business of an employment agency (within the meaning of the Employment Agency Act, 1971) and is acting in the course of that business, to do or perform personally any work or service for a third person (whether or not the third person is party to the contract),

whether the contract is express or implied or if express, whether it is oral or in writing;

"contributor" means an individual who enters into a PRSA contract with a PRSA provider and an individual shall be regarded as a contributor to a PRSA notwithstanding that all contributions are made by that individual's employer;

"director", in relation to a company includes—

(*a*) in the case of a company the affairs of which are managed by a board of directors or similar body, a member of that board or body,

(*b*) in the case of a company the affairs of which are managed by a single director or similar person, that director or person,

(*c*) in the case of a company the affairs of which are managed by the members themselves, a member of that company,

and includes a person who is to be or has been a director;

"distribution" has the same meaning as in the Corporation Tax Acts;

"employee"—

(*a*) means a person of any age, who has entered into or works under (or where the employment has ceased, entered into or worked under) a contract of employment and references, in relation to an employer, to an employee shall be construed as references to an employee employed by that employer; and for the purposes of this Chapter, a person holding office under, or in the service of, the State (including a civil servant within the meaning of the Civil Service Regulation Act, 1956) shall be deemed to be an employee employed by the State or Government, as the case may be, and an officer or servant of a local authority for the purposes of the Local Government Act, 2001, or of a harbour authority, [the Health Service Executive][1] or vocational education committee shall be deemed to be an employee employed by the authority, [the Executive or the committee][2], as the case may be), and

(*b*) in relation to a company, includes a director or other officer of the company and any other person taking part in the management of the affairs of the company;

"employer" means, in relation to an employee, the person with whom the employee has entered into, or for whom the employee works under (or, where the employment has ceased, entered into or worked under), a contract of employment, subject to the qualification that the person, who under a contract of employment referred to in paragraph (*b*) of the definition of "contract of employment" is liable to pay the wages of the individual concerned, in respect of the work or service concerned shall be deemed to be the individual's employer;

"market value" shall be construed in accordance with section 548;

"PPS Number", in relation to an individual, means that individual's Personal Public Service Number within the meaning of section 223 of the Social Welfare (Consolidation) Act, 1993;

"Personal Retirement Savings Account" means a personal retirement savings account established by a contributor with a PRSA provider under the terms of a PRSA contract and the expression **"PRSA"** shall be construed accordingly;

"PRSA administrator" means the PRSA provider or a person to whom a PRSA provider delegates in pursuance of Part X of the Pensions Act, 1990, its administrative functions in relation to a PRSA, including a person appointed by the PRSA provider [in accordance with section 787G(5)(ii)][3];

"PRSA assets" means the assets held on behalf of a contributor in a PRSA and includes the value of any contributions made to that PRSA by any employer of the contributor;

"PRSA contract" means a contract entered into between a PRSA provider and a contributor in respect of a PRSA product;

"PRSA contribution" means a contribution within the meaning of Part X of the Pensions Act, 1990;

"PRSA product" means a PRSA product (within the meaning of Part X of the Pensions Act, 1990) that for the time being stands approved under section 94 of that Act;

"PRSA provider" has the same meaning as in Part X of the Pensions Act, 1990;

"relevant payment" in relation to a PRSA means any payment, including a distribution, made by reason of rights arising as a result of a PRSA contract and includes any annuity payable by reason of such rights;

"retirement annuity contract" means a contract approved by the Revenue Commissioners in accordance with Chapter 2 of this Part;

"retirement benefits scheme" has the same meaning as in Chapter 1 of this Part;

"specified individual", in relation to a year of assessment, means an individual whose relevant earnings for the year of assessment were derived wholly or mainly from an occupation or profession specified in Schedule 23A;

"statutory scheme" has the same meaning as in Chapter 1 of this Part.

(2) Subject to subsection (1), a word or expression that is used in this Chapter and is also used in Part X of the Pensions Act, 1990 has, except where the context otherwise requires, the same meaning in this Chapter as it has in that Part.][4]

Amendments

1 Substituted by FA 2005 s 147 and Sch 6 para 1(*l*)(i) with effect from 25 March 2005; previously "health board".

2 Substituted by FA 2005 s 147 and Sch 6 para 1(*l*)(ii) with effect from 25 March 2005; previously "board or committee".

3 Substituted by FA 2005 s 21(1)(*c*)(i) as respects any PRSA contract entered into on or after 1 January 2005 in respect of a PRSA product approved by the Revenue Commissioners under TCA 1997 s 787K; previously "in accordance with section 787G(5)".

4 Section 787A inserted by Pensions (Amendment) Act 2002 s 4(1)(*d*)(v) with effect from such date as the Minister for Social, Community and Family Affairs may appoint by order. By virtue of Pensions (Amendment) Act, 2002 (Commencement) Order 2002, SI No 502 of 2002, this amendment comes into operation on 7 November 2002.

Cross-references

Capital gains tax, superannuation funds, meaning of PRSA assets applied: s 608(2).

Dividend withholding tax, general, meaning of "PRSA administrator" and "PRSA assets" applied: s 172A(1)(*a*).

Retirement annuities, relief for premiums, meaning of "PPS Number" applied: s 784(4B).

Returns by employers in relation to pension products, meanings of "PRSA", "PRSA contribution", "employee" and "employer" applied: s 897A(1).

Definitions

company: s 4(1); Corporation Tax Acts: s 1(2); person: IA 1937 s 11(*c*); writing: IA 1937 Sch; year of assessment: s 2(1).

787B Relevant earnings and net relevant earnings

[(1) For the purposes of this Chapter but subject to subsection (2), **"relevant earnings"**, in relation to an individual, means any income of the individual chargeable to tax for the year of assessment in question, being any of the following—

(*a*) income arising in respect of remuneration from an office or employment of profit held by the individual,

(*b*) income from any property which is attached to or forms part of the emoluments of any such office or employment of profit held by the individual, or

(*c*) income which is chargeable under Schedule D and is immediately derived by the individual from the carrying on or exercise by the individual of his or her trade or profession either as an individual or, in the case of a partnership, as a partner personally acting in the partnership;

but does not include any remuneration from an investment company of which the individual is a proprietary director or a proprietary employee.

(2) For the purposes of this Chapter, the relevant earnings of an individual shall not be treated as the relevant earnings of his or her spouse, notwithstanding that the individual's income chargeable to tax is treated as his or her spouse's income.

(3) For the purposes of relief under this Chapter, an individual's relevant earnings shall be those earnings before giving effect to any deduction to be made from those earnings in respect of a loss or in respect of a capital allowance (within the meaning of section 2), and references to income in this Chapter (other than references to total income) shall be construed similarly.

(4) For the purposes of this Chapter, **"net relevant earnings"**, in relation to an individual and subject to subsections (5) to (7), means the amount of the individual's relevant earnings for the year of assessment in question less the amount of any deductions to be made from the relevant earnings in computing the individual's total income for that year, being either—

(*a*) deductions in respect of payments made by the individual, or

(*b*) deductions in respect of losses or of such allowances mentioned in subsection (3), being losses or allowances arising from activities, profits or gains of which would be included in computing relevant earnings of the individual or of the individual's spouse for the year of assessment.

(5) Where in any year of assessment for which an individual claims and is allowed relief under this Chapter there is to be made in computing the total income of the individual or of the individual's spouse a deduction in respect of any such loss or allowance of the individual referred to in subsection (4)(*b*), and the deduction or part of it is to be so made from income other than relevant earnings, then, the amount of the deduction made from that other income shall be treated as reducing the individual's net relevant earnings for subsequent years of assessment and shall be deducted as far as may be from those of the following year, whether or not the individual claims or is entitled to claim relief under this Chapter for that year, and in so far as it cannot be so deducted, then from those of the next year, and so on.

(6) Where an individual's income for any year of assessment consists partly of relevant earnings and partly of other income, then, as far as may be, any deductions to be made in computing the individual's total income, and which may be treated in whole or in part either as made from relevant earnings or as made from other income, shall be treated for the purposes of this section as being made from those relevant earnings in so far as they are deductions in respect of any such loss referred to in subsection (4)(*b*) and otherwise as being made from that other income.

(7) An individual's net relevant earnings for any year of assessment shall be computed without regard to any relief to be given for that year under this Chapter either to the individual or to the individual's spouse.

(8) Notwithstanding anything in this section, for the purposes of relief under this Chapter an individual's net relevant earnings shall not exceed €254,000 but this subsection shall not apply as regards relief for additional voluntary PRSA contributions.][1]

Amendments

[1] Section 787B inserted by Pensions (Amendment) Act 2002 s 4(1)(*d*)(v) with effect from such date as the Minister for Social, Community and Family Affairs may appoint by order. By virtue of Pensions (Amendment) Act, 2002 (Commencement) Order 2002, SI No 502 of 2002, this amendment comes into operation on 7 November 2002.

Definitions

additional voluntary PRSA contributions: s 787A(1); profession: s 2(1); profits or gains: s 3(4); total income: s 3(1); trade: ss 3(1), 4(1); year of assessment: s 2(1).

787C PRSAs — method of granting relief for PRSA contributions

[(1) Subject to the provisions of this Chapter, relief from income tax shall be given in respect of contributions to a PRSA by an individual chargeable to tax in respect of relevant earnings from any trade, profession, office or employment carried on or held by that individual.

(2) Where relief is to be given under this Chapter in respect of any contribution made by an individual, the amount of that contribution shall, subject to this section, be deducted from or set off against the individual's relevant earnings for the year of assessment in which the contribution is paid.

(3) Where in relation to a year of assessment a contribution to a PRSA is made after the end of the year of assessment but on or before the specified return date for the chargeable period (within the meaning of Part 41) the payment may, if the individual so elects on or before that date, be treated for the purposes of this section as paid in the earlier year (and not in the year in which it is paid); but where—

(*a*) the amount of that contribution, together with any contributions made by the individual in the year to which the assessment relates (or treated as so paid by virtue of any previous election under this subsection), exceeds the maximum amount of the reduction which may be made under this Chapter in the individual's relevant earnings for that year, or

(*b*) the amount of that PRSA contribution itself exceeds the increase in that maximum amount which is due to taking into account the income on which the assessment is made,

the election shall have no effect as respects the excess.

(4) Where in any year of assessment a reduction or a greater reduction would be made under this section in the relevant earnings of an individual but for an insufficiency of net relevant earnings, the amount of the reduction which would be made but for that reason, less the amount of any reduction which is made in that year, shall be carried forward to the next year of assessment, and shall be treated for the purposes of relief under this Chapter as the amount of a qualifying contribution paid in that next year of assessment.

(5) If and in so far as an amount once carried forward under subsection (4) (and treated as the amount of a qualifying payment made in the next year of assessment) is not deducted from or set off against the individual's net relevant earnings for that year of assessment, it shall be carried forward again to the following year of assessment (and treated as the amount of a qualifying payment made in that year of assessment), and so on for succeeding years.

(6) Where relief under this Chapter for any year of assessment is claimed and allowed (whether or not relief is then to be given for that year), and afterwards there is made any additional assessment, alteration of an assessment, or other adjustment of the claimant's liability to tax, there shall be made also such adjustments, if any, as are consequential thereon in the relief allowed or given under this Chapter for that or any subsequent year of assessment.

(7) Where relief under this Chapter is claimed and allowed for any year of assessment in respect of any contribution, relief shall not be given in respect of that contribution under any other provision of the Income Tax Acts for the same or a later year of assessment.][1]

Amendments

1 Section 787C inserted by Pensions (Amendment) Act 2002 s 4(1)(*d*)(v) with effect from such date as the Minister for Social, Community and Family Affairs may appoint by order. By virtue of Pensions (Amendment) Act, 2002 (Commencement) Order 2002, SI No 502 of 2002, this amendment comes into operation on 7 November 2002.

Cross-references

Qualifying overseas pension plans, relief for contributions: s 787N(1).

Definitions

Income Tax Acts: s 1(2); net relevant earnings: s 787B(4); profession: s 2(1); PRSA: s 787A(1); PRSA contribution: s 787A(1); relevant earnings: s 787B(1); trade: s 3(1); year of assessment: s 2(1).

787D Claims to relief

[(1) Relief shall not be given under this Chapter in respect of a contribution to a PRSA except on a claim made to and allowed by the inspector, but any person aggrieved by any decision of the inspector on any such claim may, on giving notice in writing to the inspector within 21 days after the notification to that person of the decision, appeal to the Appeal Commissioners.

(2) The Appeal Commissioners shall hear and determine an appeal to them under subsection (1) as if it were an appeal to them against an assessment to income tax, and the provisions of the Income Tax Acts relating to the rehearing of an appeal and to the statement of a case for the opinion of the High Court on a point of law shall, with the necessary modifications, apply accordingly.][1]

Amendments

[1] Section 787D inserted by Pensions (Amendment) Act 2002 s 4(1)(*d*)(v) with effect from such date as the Minister for Social, Community and Family Affairs may appoint by order. By virtue of Pensions (Amendment) Act, 2002 (Commencement) Order 2002, SI No 502 of 2002, this amendment comes into operation on 7 November 2002.

Definitions

Appeal Commissioners: s 2(1); High Court: IA 1937 Sch; Income Tax Acts: s 1(2); inspector: s 2(1); person: IA 1937 s 11(*c*); PRSA: s 787A(1); writing: IA 1937 Sch.

787E Extent of relief

[(1) Subject to this section, the amount which may be deducted or set off in any year in respect of contributions made by, or deemed in accordance with subsection (2) to have been made by, an individual to one or more PRSA products, hereafter in this section referred to as the maximum allowable contribution, shall not be more than—

[(*a*) in the case of an individual who at any time during the year of assessment was of the age 30 years or over but had not attained the age of 40 years, 20 per cent,

(*b*) in the case of an individual who at any time during the year of assessment was of the age 40 years or over but had not attained the age of 50 years, 25 per cent,

(*c*) in the case of an individual who at any time during the year of assessment was of the age 50 years or over or who for the year of assessment was a specified individual, 30 per cent,

and

(*d*) in any other case, 15 per cent,][1]

of the individual's net relevant earnings for that year of assessment.

(2) Where for a year of assessment a sum is chargeable to tax in accordance with section 118(5) in respect of a contribution by an employer to a PRSA, the employee shall, in addition to any contributions actually made by the employee, be deemed, for the

purposes of this section, to have made contributions to the said PRSA in that year of assessment equal to such sum.

(3) [Where during a year of assessment an individual is a member either of an approved scheme or of a statutory scheme (hereafter referred to as a "scheme") in relation to an office or employment, not being a scheme under which the benefits provided in respect of that service are limited to benefits of a kind referred to in paragraphs (*b*) and (*c*) of section 772(3), including any similar benefit provided under a statutory scheme established under a public statute,][2] the following provisions shall apply, that is to say—

(*a*) relief shall be allowed under this Chapter as regards relevant earnings from that office or employment only in respect of contributions that are additional voluntary PRSA contributions,

(*b*) notwithstanding subsection (1), the amount which may be deducted or set off in that year of assessment in respect of such contributions against the individual's net relevant earnings from that office or employment shall not be more than—

(i) in the case of an individual who at any time during the year of assessment was of the age of 30 years or over but had not attained the age of 40 years, 20 per cent,

(ii) in the case of an individual who at any time during the year of assessment was of the age of 40 years or over but had not attained the age of 50 years, 25 per cent,

(iii) in the case of an individual who at any time during the year of assessment was of the age of 50 years or over, 30 per cent, and

(iv) in any other case, 15 per cent,

of the remuneration for that year of the office or employment in respect of which the contributions are made, reduced by the amount of any contributions of the individual in the year to any scheme related to the office or employment of which he or she is a member,

(*c*) the amount of the net relevant earnings of the individual in respect of which any other PRSA contributions are to be deducted or set off shall be reduced by the amount of the remuneration from such office or employment, and

(*d*) notwithstanding sections 787K and 787L, the aggregate benefits under—

(i) all schemes, of which the individual is a member, related to the office or employment, and

(ii) all Personal Retirement Savings Accounts to which the individual is the contributor of additional voluntary PRSA contributions,

shall not exceed the maximum benefits that could be provided for the individual by reference to section 772.

(4) Notwithstanding subsection (1), where the maximum allowable contribution would but for this subsection be less than €1,525, subsection (1) shall apply as if the said maximum allowable contribution were €1,525.

(5) Where an individual is entitled to relief for a year of assessment under Chapter 2 of this Part in respect of a qualifying premium, the maximum allowable contribution for

that year of assessment, other than additional voluntary PRSA contributions, shall be reduced by the amount of such relief.][3]

Amendments

[1] Subs (1)(*a*)–(*c*) substituted by FA 2003 s 14(1)(*d*)(i) with effect from 1 January 2003.

[2] Substituted by FA 2003 s 14(1)(*d*)(ii) with effect from 1 January 2003; previously "Where during a year of assessment an individual is a member of either of an approved scheme or of a statutory scheme (hereafter referred to as a "scheme") in relation to an office or employment".

[3] Section 787E inserted by Pensions (Amendment) Act 2002 s 4(1)(*d*)(v) with effect from such date as the Minister for Social, Community and Family Affairs may appoint by order. By virtue of Pensions (Amendment) Act, 2002 (Commencement) Order 2002, SI No 502 of 2002, this amendment comes into operation on 7 November 2002.

Cross-references

Qualifying overseas pension plans, relief for contributions: s 787N(1).
Returns by employers in relation to pension products, subs (2): s 897A(1)("PRSA employer contribution").
Transfers to PRSAs: s 787F.

Definitions

additional voluntary PRSA contribution: s 787A(1); approved scheme: s 787A(1); employee: s 787A(1); employer: s 787A(1); net relevant earnings: s 787B(4); PRSA: s 787A(1); PRSA contribution: s 787A(1); relevant earnings: s 787B(1); statutory scheme: s 787A(1); year of assessment: s 2(1).

787F Transfers to PRSAs

[To the extent that any contribution to one or more than one PRSA is made from—

(*a*) the value of accrued rights under a retirement annuity contract,

(*b*) the value of accrued rights under an approved scheme or a statutory scheme, or

(*c*) a repayment of contributions to which section 780(2) would, but for subsection (2A) (inserted by the Pensions (Amendment) Act, 2002) of that section, otherwise apply,

it shall not be taken into account for the purposes of section 787E and no relief shall be allowed under this Chapter in respect of such a contribution.][1]

Amendments

[1] Section 787F inserted by Pensions (Amendment) Act 2002 s 4(1)(*d*)(v) with effect from such date as the Minister for Social, Community and Family Affairs may appoint by order. By virtue of Pensions (Amendment) Act, 2002 (Commencement) Order 2002, SI No 502 of 2002, this amendment comes into operation on 7 November 2002.

Cross-references

Qualifying overseas pension plans, relief for contributions: s 787N(1).

Definitions

approved scheme: s 787A(1); PRSA: s 787A(1); retirement annuity contract: s 787A(1); statutory scheme: s 787A(1).

787G Taxation of payments from a PRSA

[(1) Subject to subsections (2), (3) and (4)—

(*a*) the amount or value of any assets that a PRSA administrator makes available to, or pays to, a PRSA contributor or to any other person, including any annuity where the whole or part of the consideration for the grant of the annuity consisted of assets which, at the time of application of the said assets for the purchase of the annuity, were PRSA assets, [shall, notwithstanding anything in section 18 or 19,][1] be treated as a payment to the PRSA contributor of emoluments to which Schedule E applies and, accordingly, the provisions of Chapter 4 of Part 42 shall apply to any such payment or amount treated as a payment, and

(*b*) the PRSA administrator shall deduct tax from the assets at the higher rate for the year of assessment in which the assets are made available unless the PRSA administrator has received from the Revenue Commissioners a certificate of tax credits and standard rate cut-off point or a tax deduction card for that year in respect of the PRSA contributor.

(2) A PRSA administrator shall be liable to pay to the Collector-General the income tax which the PRSA administrator is required to deduct from any assets of a PRSA by virtue of this section and the individual beneficially entitled to assets held in a PRSA, including the personal representatives of a deceased individual who was so entitled prior to that individual's death, shall allow such deduction; but where there are no funds or insufficient funds available out of which the PRSA administrator may satisfy the tax required to be deducted, the amount of such tax for which there are insufficient funds available shall be a debt due to the PRSA administrator from the individual beneficially entitled to the assets in the PRSA or from the estate of the deceased individual, as the case may be.

(3) Subsection (1) shall not apply where the assets made available from a PRSA are—

(*a*) an amount made available, at the time assets of the PRSA are first made available to the PRSA contributor, by way of lump sum not exceeding 25 per cent of the value of the assets in the PRSA at that time or, in the case of a PRSA to which additional voluntary PRSA contributions were made, an amount not exceeding the amount that may be paid by way of lump sum in accordance with section 772(3)(*f*) in conjunction with the rules of the scheme,

(*b*) an amount transferred to an approved retirement fund or to an approved minimum retirement fund in accordance with section 787H,

(*c*) an amount made available to the personal representatives of the PRSA contributor in accordance with section 787K(1)(*c*)(iii),

(*d*) a transfer of assets from a PRSA to another PRSA, an approved scheme or a statutory scheme where—

(i) in relation to that other PRSA, approved scheme or statutory scheme the contributor to the first-mentioned PRSA is either a contributor or a member as the case may be, and

(ii) the first-mentioned PRSA is not a PRSA in respect of which a lump sum to which paragraph (*a*) applies has been paid or made available.

(4) For the purposes of this Chapter, the circumstances in which a PRSA administrator shall be treated as making assets of a PRSA available to an individual shall include—

(*a*) the making of a relevant payment by the PRSA administrator,

(*b*) any circumstances whereby assets cease to be assets of the PRSA, and

(*c*) any circumstances whereby assets cease to be beneficially owned by the contributor to the PRSA.

[(4A) Without prejudice to the generality of subsection (4), the circumstances in which a PRSA administrator shall, for the purposes of this Chapter, be treated as making assets of a PRSA available to an individual shall include the use of those assets in connection with any transaction which would, if the assets were assets of an approved retirement fund, be regarded under section 784A as giving rise to a distribution for the purposes of that section and the amount to be regarded as made available shall be calculated in accordance with that section.][2]

[(5) At any time when a PRSA administrator—

(*a*) is not resident in the State, or

(*b*) is not trading in the State through a fixed place of business,

the PRSA administrator shall, in relation to the discharge of all duties and obligations relating to Personal Retirement Savings Accounts which are imposed on the PRSA administrator by virtue of this Chapter—

(i) enter into a contract with the Revenue Commissioners enforceable in a Member State of the European Communities in relation to the discharge of those duties and obligations and in entering into such a contract the parties to the contract shall acknowledge and agree in writing that—

(I) it shall be governed solely by the laws of the State, and

(II) that the courts of the State shall have exclusive jurisdiction in determining any dispute arising under it,

or

(ii) ensure that there is a person resident in the State, appointed by the PRSA administrator, who will be responsible for the discharge of all of those duties and obligations and shall notify the Revenue Commissioners of the appointment of that person and the identity of that person.][3]

[(5A) The Revenue Commissioners may by notice in writing require a PRSA administrator, a PRSA provider or the person appointed under subsection (5)(ii), as the case may be, to provide, within 30 days of the date of such notice, such information and particulars as may be specified in the notice as they may reasonably require for the purposes of this Chapter, and, without prejudice to the generality of the foregoing, such information and particulars may include—

(*a*) the name, address and PPS Number of the PRSA contributor,

(*b*) the name, address and PPS Number of any person to whom any payments have been made, or to whom any assets have been made available, by the PRSA administrator or the PRSA provider, and

(*c*) the amount of any payments and the value of any assets referred to in paragraph (*b*).][4]

(6) Notwithstanding subsection (1), where assets of a PRSA are treated under subsection (4) as having been made available to an individual, the provisions of section 784A(4) shall apply as if assets of that PRSA at the time of death of that individual were assets of an approved retirement fund.][5]

Amendments

1 Substituted by FA 2005 s 21(1)(*c*)(ii)(I) as respects any PRSA contract entered into on or after 1 January 2005 in respect of a PRSA product approved by the Revenue Commissioners under TCA 1997 s 787K; previously "shall".

2 Subs (4A) inserted by FA 2003 s 14(1)(*d*)(iii) with effect from 1 January 2003.

3 Sub (5) substituted by FA 2005 s 21(1)(*c*)(ii)(II) as respects any PRSA contract entered into on or after 1 January 2005 in respect of a PRSA product approved by the Revenue Commissioners under TCA 1997 s 787K.

4 Sub (5A) inserted by FA 2005 s 21(1)(*c*)(ii)(III) as respects any PRSA contract entered into on or after 1 January 2005 in respect of a PRSA product approved by the Revenue Commissioners under TCA 1997 s 787K.

5 Section 787G inserted by Pensions (Amendment) Act 2002 s 4(1)(*d*)(v) with effect from such date as the Minister for Social, Community and Family Affairs may appoint by order. By virtue of Pensions (Amendment) Act, 2002 (Commencement) Order 2002, SI No 502 of 2002, this amendment comes into operation on 7 November 2002.

Cross-references

Approved Retirement Fund option, subs (3)(*a*): s 787H(2)(*a*).
Interpretation and supplemental, subs (5)(ii): s 787A(1)("PRSA administrator").
Revenue approval of PRSA products, subs (3)(*a*): s 787K(1)(*c*)(II).

Definitions

additional voluntary PRSA contributions, approved minimum retirement fund, approved retirement fund, approved scheme: s 787A(1); Collector-General: s 2(1); higher rate: s 3(1); person: IA 1937 s 11(*c*); PRSA, PRSA administrator, PRSA asset, PRSA provider: s 787A(1); resident: s 2(1); tax: s 3(1); writing: IA 1937 Sch; year of assessment: 2(1).

787H Approved Retirement Fund option

[(1) At any time assets of a PRSA are allowed to be made available to a beneficiary in accordance with section 787K, that individual may opt to have those assets transferred to an approved retirement fund and the PRSA administrator shall make that transfer.

(2) The assets that a PRSA administrator shall transfer to an approved retirement fund in accordance with subsection (1) shall be the assets available in the PRSA at the time the election under that subsection is made less—

- (*a*) any lump sum the PRSA administrator is permitted to pay without deduction of tax in accordance with section 787G(3)(*a*), and
- (*b*) any amount the PRSA administrator is required to transfer to an approved minimum retirement fund in accordance with section 784C, by virtue of subsection (3).

(3) Where an individual opts in accordance with subsection (1), sections 784A to 784D shall apply as if that option were an option in accordance with section 784(2A).][1]

Amendments

1 Section 787H inserted by Pensions (Amendment) Act 2002 s 4(1)(*d*)(v) with effect from such date as the Minister for Social, Community and Family Affairs may appoint by order. By virtue of Pensions (Amendment) Act, 2002 (Commencement) Order 2002, SI No 502 of 2002, this amendment comes into operation on 7 November 2002.

Cross-references

Revenue approval of PRSA products: s 787K(1); subs (1): s 787K(1)(*c*)(i)(III), (IV).
Taxation of payments from a PRSA: s 787G(3)(*b*).

Definitions

approved minimum retirement fund, approved retirement fund, PRSA, PRSA administrator: s 787A(1); tax: s 3(1).

787I Exemption of PRSA

[(1) Exemption from income tax shall, on a claim being made in that behalf, be allowed in respect of income derived from investments or deposits of a PRSA if, or to such extent as the Revenue Commissioners are satisfied that, it is income from investments or deposits held for the purposes of the PRSA.

(2) (*a*) In this subsection, **"financial futures"** and **"traded options"** mean respectively financial futures and traded options for the time being dealt in or quoted on any futures exchange or any stock exchange, whether or not that exchange is situated in the State.

(*b*) For the purposes of subsection (1), a contract entered into in the course of dealing in financial futures or traded options shall be regarded as an investment.

(3) Exemption from income tax shall, on a claim being made in that behalf, be allowed in respect of underwriting commissions if, or to such extent as the Revenue Commissioners are satisfied that, the underwriting commissions are applied for the purposes of the PRSA, and in respect of which the administrator of the PRSA would, but for this subsection, be chargeable to tax under Case IV of Schedule D.][1]

Amendments

1 Section 787I inserted by Pensions (Amendment) Act 2002 s 4(1)(*d*)(v) with effect from such date as the Minister for Social, Community and Family Affairs may appoint by order. By virtue of Pensions (Amendment) Act, 2002 (Commencement) Order 2002, SI No 502 of 2002, this amendment comes into operation on 7 November 2002.

Cross-references

Investment undertakings, gain arising on a chargeable event: s 739D(6)(i).

Cross-references

Qualifying overseas pension plans, relief for contributions: s 787N(1).

Definitions

PRSA, PRSA administrator: s 787A(1).

787J Allowance to employer

[(1) For the purposes of this section—

(*a*) a reference to a **"chargeable period"** shall be construed as a reference to a "chargeable period or its basis period" (within the meaning of section 321), and

(*b*) in relation to an employer whose chargeable period is a year of assessment, **"basis period"** means the period on the profits or gains of which income tax for that year of assessment is to be finally computed for the purposes of Case I or II of Schedule D in respect of the trade, profession or vocation of the employer.

(2) Subject to subsection (3), any sum paid by an employer by way of contribution under a PRSA contract of an employee shall for the purposes of Case I or II of Schedule D and of sections 83 and 707(4) be allowed to be deducted as an expense, or expense of management, incurred in the chargeable period in which the sum is paid but no other sum shall for those purposes be allowed to be deducted as an expense, or expense of

management, in respect of the making, or any provision for the making, of any contributions under the PRSA contract.

(3) The amount of an employer's contributions which may be deducted under subsection (2) shall not exceed the amount contributed by that employer to Personal Retirement Savings Accounts in respect of employees in a trade or undertaking in respect of the profits of which the employer is assessable to income tax or corporation tax, as the case may be.][1]

Amendments

1 Section 787J inserted by Pensions (Amendment) Act 2002 s 4(1)(*d*)(v) with effect from such date as the Minister for Social, Community and Family Affairs may appoint by order. By virtue of Pensions (Amendment) Act, 2002 (Commencement) Order 2002, SI No 502 of 2002, this amendment comes into operation on 7 November 2002.

Cross-references

Qualifying overseas pension plans, relief for contributions: s 787N(1).

Definitions

employee, employer, Personal Retirement Savings Account, PRSA contract: s 787A(1); profession: s 2(1); trade: ss 3(1), 4(1).

787K Revenue approval of PRSA products

[(1) Subject to subsection (2) and to sections 787H and 787L, the Revenue Commissioners shall not approve, for the purposes of section 94(3) of the Pensions Act, 1990, a PRSA product (within the meaning of Part X of that Act) unless it appears to them to satisfy the following conditions—

(*a*) that the arrangements in respect of that product will be entered into by an individual with a person lawfully carrying on in the State the business of a PRSA provider,

(*b*) that it includes provision securing that no annuity payable under it shall be capable in whole or in part of surrender, commutation or assignment, and

(*c*) that it does not—

(i) provide for the payment of any sum or the making available of PRSA assets, by that person during the life of the individual of any sum except—

(I) sums payable by means of annuity to the individual,

(II) a sum payable without deduction of tax by way of lump sum, in accordance with section 787G(3)(*a*),

(III) assets transferred to an approved retirement fund or to an approved minimum retirement fund, in accordance with section 787H(1), or

(IV) assets made available to the PRSA contributor by the PRSA administrator, where the PRSA administrator retains such assets as would be required to be transferred to an approved minimum retirement fund if the PRSA contributor opted in accordance with section 787H(1),

(ii) provide for the annuity or other sums payable to the individual to commence or for assets to be made available to the individual before the individual attains the age of 60 years or after he or she attains the age of 75 years,

(iii) provide for the payment by that person of any other sums except sums payable by means of annuity to the individual's widow or widower and any sums which, in the event of no annuity or other benefits becoming payable either to the individual or to a widow or widower, are payable to the individual's personal representatives by way of transfer of the PRSA assets to the estate of the PRSA contributor,

(iv) provide for the annuity, if any, payable to a widow or widower of the individual to be of a greater annual amount than that paid or payable to the individual, or

(v) provide for the payment of any annuity otherwise than for the life of the annuitant.

(2) The Revenue Commissioners may, if they think fit and subject to any conditions they think proper to attach to the approval under section 94 of the Pensions Act, 1990, approve, for the purposes of section 94(3) of that Act, a product otherwise satisfying the conditions referred to in subsection (1), notwithstanding that the product provides for one or more of the following matters—

(*a*) the payment to the individual of an annuity or other sums or the making available of assets of the PRSA to the individual commencing before he or she attains the age of 60 years, where the annuity or other sums are payable on the individual becoming permanently incapable through infirmity of mind or body of carrying on his or her own occupation or any occupation of a similar nature for which he or she is trained or fitted,

(*b*) in the case of an individual being an employee, the payment to the individual of an annuity or other sums or the making available of assets of the PRSA to the individual commencing on retirement at age 50 or over,

(*c*) where the individual's occupation is one in which persons customarily retire before attaining the age of 60 years, the payment of the annuity or other sums to commence or the making available of assets of the PRSA to commence before the individual attains that age (but not before he or she attains the age of 50 years),

(*d*) the annuity payable to any person to continue for a term certain (not exceeding 10 years) notwithstanding his or her death within that term, or the annuity payable to any person to terminate, or be suspended, on marriage (or remarriage) or in other circumstances,

(*e*) in the case of an annuity which is to continue for a term certain, the annuity to be assignable by will and, in the event of any person dying entitled to the annuity, the annuity to be assignable by his or her personal representatives in the distribution of the estate so as to give effect to a testamentary disposition, or to the rights of those entitled on intestacy or to an appropriation of the annuity to a legacy or to a share or interest in the estate.

(3) Where, having regard to the provisions of this Chapter, the Revenue Commissioners are, at any time, of the opinion that approval of a product under section 94 of the Pensions Act, 1990, ought to be withdrawn they shall give notice in writing to the Pensions Board of that opinion and such a notice shall specify the grounds on which they formed that opinion.

(4) Where approval of a product is withdrawn pursuant to section 97 of the Pensions Act, 1990, there shall be made such assessments or amendment of assessments as may be appropriate for the purpose of withdrawing any relief given under this Chapter consequent on the grant of the approval.][1]

Amendments

1 Section 787K inserted by Pensions (Amendment) Act 2002 s 4(1)(*d*)(v) with effect from such date or dates as the Minister for Social, Community and Family Affairs may appoint by order. By virtue of Pensions (Amendment) Act, 2002 (Commencement) Order 2002, SI No 502 of 2002, this amendment comes into operation on 7 November 2002.

Cross-references

Approved Retirement Fund option: s 787H(1).

Extent of relief: s 787E(3)(*d*).

Taxation of payments from a PRSA, subs (1)(*c*)(iii): s 787G(3)(*c*).

Transfers to and from PRSA: s 787L(1).

Definitions

approved minimum retirement fund, approved retirement fund, employee: s 787A(1); person: IA 1937 s 11(c); PRSA asset, PRSA contributor, PRSA product, PRSA provider: s 787A(1); tax: s 3(1).

787L Transfers to and from PRSA

[(1) In addition to the requirements imposed by section 787K for the granting of such approval, the Revenue Commissioners shall not approve, for the purposes of section 94(3) of the Pensions Act, 1990, a PRSA product (within the meaning of Part X of that Act) unless the product provides that the individual who has entered into the arrangements in respect of it may require a sum representing the value of his or her accrued rights under the product—

(*a*) to be paid by the person with whom the individual has entered into such arrangements to such other person as the individual may specify, and

(*b*) to be applied by such other person in payment either of a contribution under a PRSA contract made between the individual and that other person or a contribution under an approved scheme of which the individual is a member.

(2) Without prejudice to subsection (1), the Revenue Commissioners shall not approve, for the purposes of section 94(3) of the Pensions Act, 1990, a PRSA product (within the meaning of Part X of that Act) unless the product provides that the PRSA provider may receive contributions from—

(*a*) another PRSA in respect of which the contributor to the first-mentioned PRSA is the contributor,

(*b*) either an approved scheme or a statutory scheme in respect of which the contributor to the first-mentioned PRSA is a member, or

(*c*) a contract approved by the Revenue Commissioners in accordance with Chapter 2 of this Part to which the contributor to the first-mentioned PRSA is a party.

(3) References in subsection (1) to the individual by whom a contract is made include references to any widow, widower or dependant having accrued rights under the contract.][1]

Amendments

1 Section 787L inserted by Pensions (Amendment) Act 2002 s 4(1)(*d*)(v) with effect from such date as the Minister for Social, Community and Family Affairs may appoint by order. By virtue of Pensions (Amendment) Act, 2002 (Commencement) Order 2002, SI No 502 of 2002, this amendment comes into operation on 7 November 2002.

Cross-references

Extent of relief: s 787E(3)(*d*).

Revenue approval of PRSA products: s 787K(1).

Definitions

approved scheme: s 787A(1); person: IA 1937 s 11(*c*); PRSA, PRSA contract, PRSA product, PRSA provider, statutory scheme: s 787A(1).

[CHAPTER 2B
Overseas Pension Plans: Migrant Member Relief]1

Amendments

1 Chapter 2B (ss 787M–787N) inserted by FA 2005 s 21(1)(*d*) as respects contributions to a qualifying overseas pension plan made on or after 1 January 2005.

Cross-references

Limit on remuneration and net relevant earnings for purposes of relief under this Chapter: s 790A.

787M Interpretation and general (Chapter 2B)

[(1) In this Chapter, unless the context otherwise requires—

"administrator", in relation to an overseas pension plan, means the person or persons having the management of the plan;

"contributions" include premia;

"certificate of contributions" means a certificate obtained by the relevant migrant member from the administrator and provided to the Revenue Commissioners, in a form to be furnished by the Revenue Commissioners for that purpose, containing for each calendar year the following particulars in respect of the relevant migrant member of the plan—

(*a*) his or her name, address, PPS Number and policy reference number,

(*b*) the contributions paid by him or her under the plan in that year, and

(*c*) where relevant, the contributions, if any, paid under the plan in that year in respect of him or her by, or on behalf of, his or her employer;

"overseas pension plan" means a contract, an agreement, a series of agreements, a trust deed or other arrangements, other than a state social security scheme, which is established in, or entered into under the law of, a Member State of the European Communities, other than the State;

"national of a Member State of the European Communities" means any individual possessing the nationality or citizenship of a Member State of the European Communities;

"policy reference number" means the unique identifying number of a relevant migrant member in relation to an overseas pension plan;

"PPS Number" means a personal public service number within the meaning of section 223 of the Social Welfare (Consolidation) Act 1993;

"qualifying overseas pension plan" means an overseas pension plan—

(*a*) which is in good faith established for the sole purpose of providing benefits of a kind similar to those referred to in Chapters 1, 2, or 2A of this Part,

(*b*) in respect of which tax relief is available under the law of the Member State of the European Communities in which the plan is established in respect of any contributions paid under the plan, and

(*c*) in relation to which the relevant migrant member of the plan complies with the requirements of subsection (2);

"relevant migrant member" means an individual who is a resident of the State and who is a member of a qualifying overseas pension plan and who, in relation to any contributions paid under the plan—

(*a*) was, at the time the individual first became a member of the pension plan, a resident of a Member State of the European Communities, other than the State, and entitled to tax relief in respect of contributions paid under the plan under the law of that Member State of the European Communities,

(*b*) was a member of the pension plan at the beginning of the period in which the individual became a resident of the State,

(*c*) was, immediately before the beginning of that period, resident outside of the State for a continuous period of 3 years, and

(*d*) (i) is a national of a Member State of the European Communities, or

(ii) not being such an individual, was a resident of a Member State of the European Communities, other than the State, immediately before becoming a resident of the State;

"resident" means—

(*a*) in the case of a Member State of the European Communities with the Government of which arrangements having the force of law by virtue of section 826(1)(*a*) have been made, that the individual is regarded as being a resident of that State under those arrangements, and

(*b*) in any other case, that the individual is by virtue of the law of that State a resident of that State for the purposes of tax;

"state social security scheme" means a system of mandatory protection put in place by the Government of a country or territory, other than the State, to provide a minimum level of retirement income or other benefits, the level of which is determined by that Government;

"tax reference number" means, in relation to an institution operating or managing an overseas pension plan, the unique identification number allocated to the institution by a Member State of the European Communities, other than the State, for the purposes of taxation, and where more than one such number has been allocated, the reference number appropriate to the business in the course of which the overseas pension plan was issued.

(2) The requirements referred to in paragraph (*c*) of the definition of **"qualifying overseas pension plan"** in subsection (1) are that the relevant migrant member—

(*a*) obtains from the administrator of the plan and provides to the Revenue Commissioners in such form and manner as they may specify—

(i) such evidence as they may reasonably require to verify the position in relation to paragraphs (*a*) and (*b*) of the definition of "qualifying overseas pension plan" in subsection (1), and

(ii) the following particulars in relation to the plan—

(I) the name, address and tax reference number of the institution operating or managing the plan,

(II) the policy reference number of the relevant migrant member of the plan,

(III) the date on which the relevant migrant member became a member of the plan,

(IV) the date on which contributions under the plan first became payable,

(V) the date on which benefits under the plan first become payable,

and

(*b*) has irrevocably instructed the administrator of the plan to provide to the Revenue Commissioners such information as they may reasonably require in relation to any payments made under the plan.][1]

Amendments

1 Section 787M inserted by FA 2005 s 21(1)(*d*) as respects contributions to a qualifying overseas pension plan made on or after 1 January 2005.

Cross-references

Qualifying overseas pension plans; relief for contributions: s 787N(2); subs (2)(*b*): s 787N(3)(*a*).

Definitions

person: IA 1937 s 11(*c*); year: IA 1937 Sch.

787N Qualifying overseas pension plans: relief for contributions

[(1) Where in any year of assessment, contributions are paid to any qualifying overseas pension plan—

(*a*) by a relevant migrant member of that plan, or

(*b*) by, or on behalf of, an employer in respect of an employee (within the meaning of Chapter 1) who is a relevant migrant member of that plan,

then, where the relevant migrant member has provided a certificate of contributions, relief for that year of assessment under the provisions of section 774(6), 774(7) and 778(1) of Chapter 1 (which relates to occupational pension schemes), or, as the case may be, section 787 of Chapter 2 (which relates to retirement annuities), or sections 787C, 787E, 787F or 787J of Chapter 2A (which relates to personal retirement savings accounts), shall, with any necessary modifications, apply to those contributions as if—

(i) the qualifying overseas pension plan was an exempt approved scheme under Chapter 1 or an annuity contract for the time being approved by the Revenue Commissioners under Chapter 2, or a PRSA product approved under Chapter 2A for the purposes of section 94(3) of the Pensions Act 1990, and

(ii) the relevant migrant member of the qualifying overseas pension plan was—

(I) an employee within the meaning of Chapter 1,

(II) an individual referred to in section 784(1) of Chapter 2, or

(III) an individual referred to in Chapter 2A.

(2) An individual who would be a relevant migrant member of a qualifying overseas pension plan but for the fact that he or she fails to meet the requirement in paragraph (*c*) of the definition of "relevant migrant member" in section 787M shall, notwithstanding that, be treated as a relevant migrant member if the Revenue Commissioners are of the opinion that in all the circumstances the failure of the individual to meet the condition ought to be disregarded for that purpose.

(3) (*a*) The Revenue Commissioners may by notice in writing require the administrator of a qualifying overseas pension plan who has received an irrevocable instruction as provided for in section 787M(2)(*b*), to provide within 30 days of the date of such notice such information and particulars, in relation to payments under the plan, as the Revenue Commissioners may reasonably require for the purposes of this Chapter.

(*b*) The notice referred to in paragraph (*a*) shall specify—

(i) the information and particulars required by the Revenue Commissioners, and

(ii) the form and manner in which such information and particulars are to be provided.][1]

Amendments

1 Section 787N inserted by FA 2005 s 21(1)(*d*) as respects contributions to a qualifying overseas pension plan made on or after 1 January 2005.

Definitions

administrator: s 787M(1); certificate of contributions: s 787M(1); contributions: s 787M(1); qualifying overseas pension plan: s 787M(1); relevant migrant member: s 787M(1); writing: IA 1937 Sch; year of assessment: s 2(1).

CHAPTER 3
Purchased Life Annuities

788 Capital element in certain purchased annuities

(1) In this section—

"life annuity" means an annuity payable for a term ending with (or at a time ascertainable only by reference to) the end of a human life, whether or not there is provision for the annuity to end during the life on the expiration of a fixed term or on the happening of any event or otherwise, or to continue after the end of the life in particular circumstances;

"purchased life annuity" means a life annuity granted for a consideration in money or money's worth in the ordinary course of a business of granting annuities on human life.

(2) This section shall not apply to—

(*a*) any annuity which apart from this section would be treated for the purposes of the provisions of the Income Tax Acts relating to tax on annuities and other annual payments as consisting to any extent in the payment or repayment of a capital sum,

(*b*) any annuity purchased under or for the purposes of any sponsored superannuation scheme within the meaning of section 783(1), or any scheme approved under section 784, or in pursuance of any obligation imposed or offer or invitation made under or in connection with any such scheme, or any other annuity purchased by any person in recognition of another's services (or past services) in any office or employment,

(*c*) any annuity payable under a substituted contract within the meaning of section 786(3),

(*d*) any annuity where the whole or part of the consideration for the grant of the annuity consisted of sums satisfying the conditions for relief from tax under section 787, ...[1]

(*e*) any annuity purchased in pursuance of any direction in a will, or to provide for an annuity payable by virtue of a will or settlement out of income of property disposed of by the will or settlement (whether with or without resort to [capital),][2]

[(*f*) any annuity where the whole or part of the consideration for the grant of the annuity consisted of assets which, at the time of application of the said assets for the purchase of the annuity, were assets in an approved retirement fund, within the meaning of section 784A, or in an approved minimum retirement fund, within the meaning of section [784C, or][3]][4]

[(*g*) any annuity where the whole or part of the consideration for the grant of the annuity consisted of assets which, at the time of the application of the said assets for the purchase of the annuity, were PRSA assets, within the meaning of Chapter 2A of this Part.][5]

(3) A purchased life annuity (not being of a description excepted by subsection (2)) shall, for the purposes of the provisions of the Income Tax Acts relating to tax on annuities and other annual payments, be treated as containing a capital element and, to the extent of the capital element, as not being an annual payment or in the nature of an annual payment; but the capital element in such an annuity shall be taken into account in computing profits or gains or losses for other purposes of the Income Tax Acts in any circumstances in which a lump sum payment would be taken into account.

(4) In the case of any purchased life annuity to which this section applies—

(*a*) the capital element shall be determined by reference to the amount or value of the payments made or other consideration given for the grant of the annuity,

(*b*) the proportion which the capital element in any annuity payment bears to the total amount of that payment shall be constant for all payments on account of the annuity,

(*c*) where neither the term of the annuity nor the amount of any annuity payment depends on any contingency other than the duration of a human life or lives, that proportion shall be the same proportion which the total amount or value of the consideration for the grant of the annuity bears to the actuarial value of the annuity payments as determined in accordance with subsection (5), and

(*d*) where paragraph (*c*) does not apply, that proportion shall be such as may be just, having regard to that paragraph and to the contingencies affecting the annuity.

(5) For the purposes of subsection (4)—

(*a*) any entire consideration given for the grant of an annuity and for some other matter shall be apportioned as appears just (but so that a right to a return of premiums or other consideration for an annuity shall not be treated for this purpose as a distinct matter from the annuity), (*b*) where it appears that the amount or value of the consideration purporting to be given for the grant of an annuity has affected, or has been affected by, the consideration given for some other matter, the aggregate amount or value of those considerations shall be treated as one entire consideration given for both and shall be apportioned under paragraph (*a*) accordingly, and

(*c*) the actuarial value of any annuity payments shall be taken to be their value as at the date when the first of those payments begins to accrue, that value being determined by reference to the prescribed tables of mortality and without discounting any payment for the time to elapse between that date and the date it is to be made.

(6) Where a person making a payment on account of any life annuity has been notified in the prescribed manner of any decision as to its being or not being a purchased life annuity to which this section applies or as to the amount of the capital element, if any, and has not been notified of any alteration of that decision, the notice shall be evidence until the contrary is proved as to those matters for the purpose of determining the amount of income tax which the person is entitled or required to deduct from the payment, or for which the person is liable in respect of the payment.

(7) Where a person making a payment on account of a purchased life annuity to which this section applies has not been notified in the prescribed manner of the amount of the capital element, the amount of income tax which the person is entitled or required to deduct from the payment, or for which the person is liable in respect of it, shall be the same as if the annuity were not a purchased life annuity to which this section applies.

(8) Any person, other than a company which is within the charge to corporation tax, carrying on a business of granting annuities on human life shall be entitled to repayment of any income tax borne by that person by deduction or otherwise for any year of assessment up to the amount of income tax which, if this section had not been enacted, that person would have been entitled to deduct and retain on making payments due in that year of assessment on account of life annuities and which in accordance with this section that person has not deducted.

(9) This section shall apply to life annuities whenever purchased or commencing, and the reference to section 787 in subsection (2)(*d*) shall be construed accordingly.

Amendments

1 Deleted by FA 1999 s 20(1)(*a*) with effect from 6 April 1999; previously "or".

2 Substituted by Pensions (Amendment) Act 2002 s 4(1)(*d*)(vi)(I) with effect from such date as the Minister for Social, Community and Family Affairs may appoint by order; previously "capital),". By virtue of Pensions (Amendment) Act, 2002 (Commencement) Order 2002, SI No 502 of 2002, this amendment comes into operation on 7 November 2002.

3 Substituted by Pensions (Amendment) Act 2002 s 4(1)(*d*)(vi)(II) with effect from such date es as the Minister for Social, Community and Family Affairs may appoint by order; previously "784C.". By virtue of Pensions (Amendment) Act, 2002 (Commencement) Order 2002, SI No 502 of 2002, this amendment comes into operation on 7 November 2002.

4 Subs (2)(*f*) inserted by FA 1999 s 20(1)(*c*) with effect from 6 April 1999.

5 Subs (2)(*g*) substituted by Pensions (Amendment) Act 2002 s 4(1)(*d*)(vi)(III) with effect from such date as the Minister for Social, Community and Family Affairs may appoint by order. By virtue of Pensions (Amendment) Act, 2002 (Commencement) Order 2002, SI No 502 of 2002, this amendment comes into operation on 7 November 2002.

Cross-references

Life assurance companies, annuity business, separate charge on profits: s 715(4).
Supplementary provisions: s 789(1), (4)(*a*).

Definitions

person: IA 1937 s 11(*c*); year of assessment: s 3(1).

Former enactments

ITA 1967 s 239; CTA 1976 s 140(1) and Sch 2 Pt I para 9; FA 1979 s 28(4); FA 1996 s 132(1) and Sch 5 Pt I para 1(10) and (11); FA 1997 s 146(1) and Sch 9 Pt I para 1(15).

Corresponding UK tax provision

Income and Corporation Taxes Act 1988 ss 656 and 657.

789 Supplementary provisions (Chapter 3)

(1) Any question as to whether an annuity is a purchased life annuity to which section 788 applies, or what is the capital element in such an annuity, shall be determined by the inspector, but any person aggrieved by any decision of the inspector on any such question may appeal within the prescribed time to the Appeal Commissioners.

(2) Except where otherwise provided in this Chapter, the procedure to be adopted in giving effect to this Chapter shall be such as may be prescribed.

(3) The Revenue Commissioners may make regulations for prescribing anything which is to be prescribed under this Chapter, and the regulations may apply, for the purposes of this Chapter or of the regulations, any provision of the Income Tax Acts (with or without modifications), and in particular the provisions relating to the rehearing of an appeal and to the statement of a case for the opinion of the High Court on a point of law.

(4) Regulations under subsection (3) may in particular make provision as to the time limit for making any claim for relief from or repayment of tax under this Chapter and as to all or any of the following matters—

(*a*) the information to be given in connection with the determination of any question whether an annuity is a purchased life annuity to which section 788 applies, or what is the capital element in an annuity, and the persons who may be required to give any such information;

(*b*) the manner of giving effect to the decision on any such question, and the making of assessments for the purpose on the person entitled to the annuity (notwithstanding anything in section 237);

(*c*) the extent to which any decision on any such question is to be binding and the circumstances in which it may be reviewed.

(5) Where any person, for the purpose of obtaining for that person or for any other person any relief from or repayment of tax under this Chapter, knowingly makes any false statement or false representation, that person shall be liable to a penalty of [€630][1].

Amendments

1 Substituted by FA 2001 s 240(1) and (2)(*k*) and Sch 5 Pt 1 as respects any act or omission which takes place or begins on or after 1 January 2002; previously "£500".

Cross-references

Recovery of penalties: s 1061(1).

Statutory instrument

IT(PLA)R 1959 (SI 152/1959).

Definitions

Appeal Commissioners: s 2(1); High Court: IA 1937 Sch; inspector: ss 2(1), 5(1), 852; person: IA 1937 s 11(*c*).

Former enactments

ITA 1967 s 240; F(MP)A 1968 s 3(2) and Sch Pt I.

Corresponding UK tax provision

Income and Corporation Taxes Act 1988 s 658.

CHAPTER 4
Miscellaneous

790 Liability of certain pensions, etc to tax

Where an individual has ceased to hold an office or employment and a pension, annuity or other annual payment is paid to the individual or to the individual's widow or widower, or to the individual's child or any of the individual's relatives or dependants by the person or the heirs, executors, administrators or successors of the person under whom the individual held such office or by whom the individual was so employed, such pension, annuity or other annual payment shall, notwithstanding that it is paid voluntarily or is capable of being discontinued, be deemed to be income for the purpose of assessment of income tax and shall be assessed and charged under Schedule D or E, as the case may require.

Definitions

person: IA 1937 s 11(*c*); relative: s 3(1).

Former enactments

ITA 1967 s 225; FA 1997 s 146(1) and Sch 9 Pt I para 1(14).

790A Limit on earnings

[Notwithstanding anything in this Part, for the purposes of giving relief to an individual under—

(*a*) Chapter 1 in respect of an employee's contribution to a retirement benefits scheme,

(*b*) Chapter 2 in respect of a qualifying premium under an annuity contract,

(*c*) Chapter 2A in respect of a PRSA contribution, and

(*d*) Chapter 2B in respect of a contribution to an overseas pension plan,

the aggregate of the individual's remuneration, within the meaning of Chapter 1 and that Chapter as applied by Chapter 2B, and net relevant earnings, within the meaning of Chapters 2 and 2A and those Chapters as applied by Chapter 2B, shall not exceed €254,000.][1]

Amendments

1 Section 790A substituted by FA 2005 s 21(1)(*e*)(i) with effect from 1 January 2005.

Definitions

overseas pension plan: s 787M(1); PRSA contribution: s 787A(1); qualifying premium: s 784(1)(*a*); retirement benefits scheme: s 771(1).

790B Exemption of cross-border scheme

[(1) In this section—

"competent authority", in relation to the State , means the national authority designated to carry out the duties provided for in the Directive arising from the transposition of the Directive into the law of the State;

"Directive" means Directive 2003/41/EC of the European Council and of the Parliament of 3 June 2003 (OJ No L235, 23.9.2003, p 10) on the activities and supervision of institutions for occupational retirement provision;

"European undertaking", in relation to a scheme, means an undertaking located in a European State which makes or proposes to make contributions to a scheme in respect of European members;

"European members" means individuals who are or have been employed or self-employed in a European State and in respect of which employment or self employment the trustees of the scheme have accepted or propose to accept contributions from the European undertaking;

"European State" means a Member State of the European Communities other than the State;

"scheme" means an occupational pension scheme established in the State under irrevocable trusts which provides, or is capable of providing, retirement benefits (within the meaning of Article 6(*d*) of the Directive) in relation to European members;

"trustees", in relation to a scheme, means the trustees of the scheme;

"undertaking" means any undertaking or other body, regardless of whether it includes or consists of one or more persons, which acts as an employer or as an association, or other representative body, of self employed persons.

(2) Subsections (3) and (4) shall apply to any scheme in respect of which, arising from the transposition of the Directive into the law of the State, the trustees have received from the competent authority—

(*a*) an authorisation, and

(*b*) an approval,

to accept contributions from a European undertaking in respect of European members, which authorisation has not been revoked.

(3) (*a*) Exemption from income tax shall, on a claim being made in that behalf, be allowed in respect of income derived from investments or deposits of a scheme, if or to such extent as the Revenue Commissioners are satisfied that, it is income from investments or deposits held for the purposes of the scheme.

(*b*) (i) In this subsection **"financial futures"** and **"traded options"** mean respectively financial futures and traded options for the time being dealt in or quoted on any futures exchange or any stock exchange, whether or not that exchange is situated in the State.

(ii) For the purposes of paragraph (*a*), a contract entered into in the course of dealing in financial futures or traded options shall be regarded as an investment.

(*c*) Exemption from income tax shall, on a claim being made in that behalf, be allowed in respect of underwriting commissions if, or to such extent as the Revenue Commissioners are satisfied that, the underwriting commissions are applied for the purposes of the scheme, and in respect of which the trustees of the scheme would but for this subsection be chargeable to tax under Case IV of Schedule D.

(4) For the purposes of sections 172A(1), 256(1) and 739B(1), the reference to "an exempt approved scheme within the meaning of section 774" in the definition of **"pension scheme"** in those sections shall be deemed to include a reference to a scheme referred to in subsection (2).][1]

Amendments

1 Section 790B inserted by FA 2005 s 21(1)(*e*)(ii) with effect with effect from such day or days as the Minister for Finance may by order appoint and different days may be appointed for different purposes or different provisions.

Cross-references

Capital gains tax, exemption of superannuation funds: s 608(2A).

Definitions

person: IA 1937 s 11(*c*).

PART 31
TAXATION OF SETTLORS, ETC IN RESPECT OF SETTLED OR TRANSFERRED INCOME

CHAPTER 1

Revocable Dispositions for Short Periods and Certain Dispositions in Favour of Children

791 Income under revocable dispositions

(1) In this Chapter and in paragraph 27 of Schedule 32, except where the context otherwise requires, **"disposition"** includes any trust, covenant, agreement or arrangement.

(2) Any income of which any person (in this subsection referred to as **"the first-mentioned person"**) is able or has been able, without the consent of any other person by means of the exercise of any power of appointment, power of revocation or otherwise however by virtue or in consequence of a disposition made directly or indirectly by the first-mentioned person, to obtain for the first-mentioned person the beneficial enjoyment shall be deemed for the purposes of the Income Tax Acts to be the income of the person who is or was able to obtain such beneficial enjoyment, and not to be the income of any other person.

(3) Where any power referred to in subsection (2) may be exercised by a person with the consent of the wife or husband of the person, the power shall for the purposes of subsection (2) be deemed to be exercisable without the consent of another person, except where the husband and wife are living apart either by agreement or under an order of a court of competent jurisdiction.

(4) Where any power referred to in subsection (2) is exercisable by the wife or husband of the person who made the disposition, the power shall for the purposes of subsection (2) be deemed to be exercisable by the person who made the disposition.

Case law

Irish

Subs (2): A disposition by nun applying her income for the purposes of the Order while she remained a member held to be revocable: *Hughes v Smyth (Sister Mary Bernard)* ITR Vol I p 411.

UK

Settlor held properly assessable on trust income where the settlement provided that trustees were to advance him funds on request: *D'Ambrumenil v IRC* (1940) 23 TC 440.

Revenue precedents

Issue: Whether a covenant made in consideration of child minding services, where the parties are cohabiting, is an effective disposition of income.

Decision: No; the payment is not pure income profit in the hands of the recipient.

Issue: Whether deed of covenant for period which exceeds or may exceed 6 years, where payments made for period less than 6 years; whether UK case law relevant in deciding if covenant for a sufficient period.

Decision: The fact that payments under deed are made for less than 6 years does not render the deed ineffective; UK case law is relevant, although the wording is different.

Definitions

person: IA 1937 s 11(*c*).

Former enactments

ITA 1967 s 438 and s 442.

792 Income under dispositions for short periods

(1) (*a*) In this subsection, **"relevant individual"** means an individual who is—

(i) permanently incapacitated by reason of mental or physical infirmity, or

(ii) aged 65 years or over.

(*b*) Any income which, by virtue of or in consequence of any disposition made directly or indirectly by any person (other than a disposition made for valuable and sufficient consideration), is payable to or applicable for the benefit of any other person, but excluding any income which—

(i) arises from capital of which the disponer by the disposition has divested absolutely himself or herself in favour of or for the benefit of the other person,

...[1]

(iv) being payable to a relevant individual for the individual's own use, is so payable for a period which exceeds or may exceed 6 years, or

(v) being applicable for the benefit of a named relevant individual, is so applicable for a period which exceeds or may exceed 6 years,

shall be deemed for the purposes of the Income Tax Acts to be the income of the person, if living, by whom the disposition was made and not to be the income of any other person.

(2) (*a*) This subsection shall apply to a disposition or dispositions of a kind or kinds referred to in subparagraphs (ii) to (v) of subsection (1)(*b*) made directly or indirectly by a person being an individual (in this subsection referred to as **"the disponer"**) except in so far as, by virtue or in consequence of such disposition or dispositions, income is payable or applicable in a year of assessment, in the

manner referred to in subparagraph (iv) or (v) of that subsection, to or for the benefit of an individual referred to in subsection (1)(*a*)(i).

(*b*) Notwithstanding subsection (1), in relation to the disponer, any income which—

(i) is payable or applicable in a year of assessment by virtue or in consequence of a disposition or dispositions to which this subsection applies, and

(ii) is in excess of 5 per cent of the total income of the disponer for the year of assessment,

shall be deemed for the purposes of the Income Tax Acts to be the income of the disponer, if living, and not to be the income of any other person.

(*c*) Where paragraph (*b*) applies in relation to the disponer, for the purpose of determining for income tax purposes the amount of income which remains the income of persons other than the disponer for a year of assessment by virtue or in consequence of a disposition or dispositions to which this subsection applies, the aggregate of the income so remaining shall be apportioned amongst those other persons in proportion to their entitlements under such disposition or dispositions for that year.

...[1]

(4) As respects the year of assessment 1997–98, this section shall apply subject to paragraph 27 of Schedule 32 in respect of a disposition to which that paragraph applies by a person in so far as, by virtue or in consequence of such a disposition, income is payable in that year of assessment to or for the benefit of an individual to whom that paragraph applies.

Amendments

1 Subs (1)(*b*)(ii) and (iii) and subs (3) repealed by TCA 1997 s 848A(13) (inserted by FA 2001 s 45) with effect from 6 April 2001.

Cross-references

Recovery of tax from trustee and payment to trustee of excess tax recoupment: s 793(1), (2).

Case law

Irish

Vows of poverty did not prevent the making of valid dispositions of income by individual members of a religious order even though all the covenanted income was paid into a common fund: *Revenue Commissioners v HI*, TL 126.

UK

Subs (1): The required minimum period is measured from the date of the first payment to the date of the last payment as provided for in the investment: *IRC v St Lukes Hostel Trustee* (1930) 15 TC 682.

Payments made under a covenant for less than six years to a UK resident by a non-resident settlor not liable for UK tax, held properly assessable on the UK resident: *Becker v Wright* (1966) 42 TC 591.

Covenantee need not have a beneficial interest in the payments, but the money must be applied for his or her benefit: *Action Aid Ltd v Revenue Commissioners* (High Court, 1997).

Revenue precedents

Issue: Whether payment made before date of deed of covenant is an effective disposition of income for the purposes of s 792.

Decision: No; the payment is not made by virtue or in consequence of the disposition.

Issue: Whether pensions payable to former partners are paid for valuable and sufficient consideration.

Decision: In the circumstances of the case, it was held that s 792 did not apply to such pensions because they were paid for valuable and sufficient consideration. Neither did s 242 apply to such covenants.

Issue: (1) Whether covenants can be made to two or more individuals. (2) Whether references to "a person who is an individual" excludes companies.

Decision: (1) Covenants can be made to two or more individuals. (2) References to a "person who is an individual" excludes companies.
Issue: Whether a person suffering from chronic back pain is considered to be permanently incapacitated for the purposes of covenant relief.
Decision: A person suffering from chronic back pain will be considered to be permanently incapacitated for the purposes of covenant relief if there is evidence to show the person is in fact incapacitated and that the condition is permanent.
Issue: Whether a covenant to a college or university should be capable of lasting 4 years.
Decision: A covenant to a college or university should be capable of lasting four years.
Issue: Whether the 5% restriction, which applied in relation to covenants from parent to child, applied in the case of a covenant from a natural/biological parent to his/her child who had been given up for adoption.
Decision: The 5% restriction did apply in these circumstances. The adopted child remained the "child" of the natural parent for the purposes of covenant relief.
Issue: In calculating 5% of a covenantor's total income for the purposes of the covenant relief, whether income which qualifies for foreign earnings deduction under TCA 1997 s 823 is included in total income.
Decision: Income which qualifies for foreign earnings deduction is excluded from total income of the covenator for the purposes of calculating the 5% restriction for covenant relief.
Issue: Whether relief due for unwitnessed deed of covenant.
Decision: Yes; there appears to be no rule requiring a deed of covenant to be witnessed.
Issue: Covenants - When a Deed of Covenant is open-ended.
Decision: The Deed of Covenant in this case is void of uncertainty in that it does not set out the exact period for which the covenant is to last, nor does it set out the payment date.
Issue: Covenants - Period of Deed of Covenant varied.
Decision: A Deed which includes the wording "or for as long as I shall remain a member of Seanad Éireann" is effective per the office of the Revenue Solicitor given that it is capable of lasting four years.
Issue: Natural Sciences.
Decision: The percentage of time devoted to the teaching of natural sciences should be equal to the percentage of the general expenditure of the school attributed towards the teaching of natural sciences.

Revenue information

Information leaflet IT 7 — Covenants to Individuals.

Statement of practice

Retirement annuity relief may be computed as 15% or 5% of "net relevant earnings" (s 787(8)–(9)) after deducting chargeable annual payments to "descendants" (subs (2)): SP IT/2/90, October 1990.

Tax Briefing

TB5 Jan 1992 para 1.5 — Interaction of capital allowances, mortgage interest, BES relief, covenants, etc. with "net relevant earnings" and retirement annuity relief.

TB17 No.1 of 1995 para 1.1 — Covenant relief

TB31 Apr 1998 p 18 — Covenants for "research" or "teaching of the natural sciences": required 3 year minimum period measured from date of first payment to date of last payment; if no payment dates specified covenant has to be for a period of 4 years in order for Revenue to be satisfied as to 3 year minimum period between first and last payment.

TB31 Apr 1998 p 19 — Updated list of Natural Science subjects — March 1998 (copies available from Charities Section, Revenue Commissioners, Government Offices, Nenagh, Co. Tipperary).

Definitions

body of persons: s 2(1); person: IA 1937 s 11(*c*); total income: s 3(1); year: IA 1937 Sch; year of assessment: s 3(1).

Former enactments

ITA 1967 s 439; FA 1995 s 13(1)(*a*) and (2).

793 Recovery of tax from trustee and payment to trustee of excess tax recoupment

(1) Where by virtue of section 792 any income tax becomes chargeable on and is paid by the person by whom the disposition was made, that person shall be entitled—

(*a*) to recover from any trustee or other person to whom the income is payable by virtue or in consequence of the disposition the amount of the tax so paid, and (*b*) for that purpose to require the Revenue Commissioners to furnish to that person a certificate specifying the amount of the income in respect of which that person has so paid tax and the amount of the tax so paid, and any certificate so furnished shall be evidence until the contrary is proved of the matters of fact stated in that certificate.

(2) Where any person obtains in respect of any allowance or relief a repayment of income tax in excess of the amount of the repayment to which that person would but for section 792 have been entitled, an amount equal to the excess shall be paid by that person to the trustee or other person to whom the income is payable by virtue or in consequence of the disposition or, where there are 2 or more such persons, shall be apportioned among those persons as the case may require.

(3) Where any question arises as to the amount of any payment or as to any apportionment to be made under subsection (2), that question shall be decided by the Appeal Commissioners whose decision on that question shall be final.

(4) Any income which is deemed by virtue of this Chapter to be the income of any person shall be deemed to be the highest part of that person's income.

Definitions

Appeal Commissioners: s 2(1); person: IA 1937 s 11(*c*).

Former enactments

ITA 1967 s 441; F(MP)A 1968 s 3(2) and Sch Pt I; FA 1974 s 86 and Sch 2 Pt I; FA 1996 s 132(2) and Sch 5 Pt II; FA 1997 s 146(1) and Sch 9 Pt I para 1(28).

Corresponding UK tax provision

Income and Corporation Taxes Act 1988 s 689.

CHAPTER 2
Settlements on Children Generally

794 Interpretation and application (Chapter 2)

(1) In this Chapter—

"income" (except where in sections 795(1), 796(2)(*b*) and subsections (4) and (5) of section 797 it is immediately preceded by **"as"** or **"that person's"** and except also in section 798) includes any income chargeable to income tax by deduction or otherwise and any income which would have been so chargeable if it had been received in the State by a person resident or ordinarily resident in the State;

"settlement" includes any disposition, trust, covenant, agreement or arrangement, and any transfer of money or other property or of any right to money or other property.

(2) This Chapter shall apply to every settlement wherever and whenever made or entered into.

(3) This Chapter shall not apply in relation to any income arising under a settlement in any year of assessment for which the settlor is not chargeable to income tax as a resident in the State, and references in this Chapter to income shall be construed accordingly.

(4) This Chapter shall not apply to any income which, by virtue or in consequence of a settlement and during the life of the settlor, is in any year of assessment paid to or for the

benefit of a minor, not being a child of the settlor, if such minor is permanently incapacitated by reason of mental or physical infirmity.

(5) For the purposes of this Chapter, the following provisions shall apply in relation to the construction of **"irrevocable instrument"**:

(*a*) an instrument shall not be an irrevocable instrument if the trusts of the instrument provide for all or any one or more of the following matters—

(i) the payment or application to or for the settlor for the settlor's own benefit of any capital or income or accumulations of income in any circumstances whatever during the life of a person (in this paragraph referred to as a **"beneficiary"**) to or for the benefit of whom any income or accumulations of income is or are or may be payable or applicable under the trusts of the instrument,

(ii) the payment or application during the life of the settlor to or for the husband or wife of the settlor for his own or her own benefit of any capital or income or accumulations of income in any circumstances whatever during the life of any beneficiary,

(iii) the termination of the trusts of the instrument by the act or on the default of any person, and

(iv) the payment by the settlor of a penalty in the event of the settlor failing to comply with the instrument;

(*b*) an instrument shall not be prevented from being an irrevocable instrument by reason only that the trusts of the instrument include any one or more of the following provisions—

(i) a provision under which any capital or income or accumulations of income will or may become payable to or applicable for the benefit of the settlor or the husband or wife of the settlor, on the bankruptcy of a person (in this paragraph referred to as a **"beneficiary"**) to or for the benefit of whom any income or accumulations of income is or are or may be payable or applicable under the trusts of the instrument,

(ii) a provision under which any capital or income or accumulations of income will or may become payable to or applicable for the benefit of the settlor or the husband or wife of the settlor, in the event of any beneficiary making an assignment of or charge on such capital or income or accumulations of income, and

(iii) a provision for the termination of the trusts of the instrument in such circumstances or manner that such termination would not, during the life of any beneficiary, benefit any person other than that beneficiary or that beneficiary's husband, wife or issue;

(*c*) **"irrevocable instrument"** includes instruments whenever made.

Cross-references

Benefit in kind charge, meaning of "settlement" applied: s 118(8).

Power to require return of property, meaning of "settlement" applied: s 909(1).

Case law

A mother with a life interest in income of a settlement appointed by a revocable disposition part of her entitlement in favour of her infant daughter. It was held that the mother still retained her entitlement to the income: *EG v MacSamhrain* ITR Vol II p 352.

Definitions

person: IA 1937 s 11(*c*); year of assessment: s 3(1).

Former enactments

ITA 1967 s 443(2), (3) and (5), s 445 and s 447; FA 1995 s 12(1)(*a*)(ii), (*c*)(i) and (iv).

795 Income settled on children

(1) Where, by virtue or in consequence of a settlement and during the life of the settlor, any income is in any year of assessment paid to or for the benefit of a person, such income shall, if at the time of payment such person is a minor, be treated for the purposes of the Income Tax Acts as income of the settlor for that year and not as income of any other person.

(2) For the purposes of this Chapter, but subject to section 796—

(*a*) income which, by virtue or in consequence of a settlement to which this Chapter applies, is so dealt with that it or assets representing it will or may become payable or applicable to or for the benefit of a person in the future (whether on the fulfilment of a condition, or on the happening of a contingency, or as the result of the exercise of a power or discretion conferred on any person, or otherwise) shall be deemed to be paid to or for the benefit of that person, and

(*b*) any income dealt with in the manner referred to in paragraph (*a*) which is not required by the settlement to be allocated, at the time when it is so dealt with, to any particular person or persons shall be deemed to be paid in equal shares to or for the benefit of each of the persons to or for the benefit of whom or any of whom the income or assets representing it will or may become payable or applicable.

Cross-references

Income, meaning, subss (1): s 794(1).

Irrevocable instruments: s 796(2).

Former enactments

ITA 1967 s 443(1); FA 1995 s 12(1)(*a*)(i) and (*c*).

796 Irrevocable instruments

(1) In this section, **"property"** does not include any annual or other periodical payment secured by the covenant of the settlor, or by a charge made by the settlor on the whole or any part of the settlor's property or the whole or any part of the settlor's future income, or by both such covenant and such charge.

(2) Where by virtue of an irrevocable instrument property is vested in or held by trustees on such trusts that in any year of assessment section 795 would but for this section apply to the income of such property, the following provisions shall apply:

(*a*) section 795 shall not apply—

(i) in respect of any part of such income which is in that year of assessment accumulated for the benefit of a person, or

(ii) in respect of income arising in that year of assessment from accumulations of income referred to in subparagraph (i);

(*b*) whenever in any year of assessment any sum whatever is paid under the trusts of such irrevocable instrument out of—

(i) such property,

(ii) the accumulations of the income of such property,

(iii) the income of such property, or

(iv) the income of those accumulations,

to or for the benefit of a person who at the time of payment is a minor, such sum shall, subject to the limitation in paragraph (*c*), be deemed for the purposes of this Chapter to be paid as income;

(*c*) paragraph (*b*) shall not apply to so much of such sum as is equal to the amount by which the aggregate of such sum and all other sums (if any) paid after the 5th day of April, 1937, under the trusts of such irrevocable instrument to or for the benefit of that person or any other person (being a person who at the time of payment was a minor) exceeds the aggregate amount of the income arising after the 5th day of April, 1937, from such property together with the income arising after that date from those accumulations;

(*d*) for the purposes of paragraph (*c*), the reference in that paragraph to another sum paid to or for the benefit of a person who at the time of payment was a minor shall be construed, in relation to a payment to which this paragraph applies of any such sum, as a reference to a sum so paid to or for the benefit of a person who at the beginning of the year of assessment in which such other sum was paid was a minor;

(*e*) paragraph (*d*) shall apply to any payment of any such sum—

(i) made before the 6th day of April, 1971, or

(ii) in the case of a payment to or for the benefit of a child born after the 6th day of April, 1971, and so made by virtue or in consequence of a settlement made before the 28th day of April, 1971, made in the year 1971–72;

(*f*) for the purposes of paragraphs (*c*) and (*d*), references in those paragraphs to a person being at a particular time a minor shall, where that time is before the 6th day of April, 1986, be construed as references to a person who at that time was under the age of 21 years and was not or had not been married.

Cross-references

Income, meaning, subs (2)(*b*): s 794(1).
Income settled on children: s 795(2).

Case law

A settlement has been held to include:

a series of non-commercial transactions: *Copeman v Coleman* (1939) 22 TC 594; *Chinn v Collins* [1981] STC 1;

a gift of shares: *Hood Barrs v IRC* (1945) 27 TC 385;

a gift of money: *Thomas v Marshall* (1952) 34 TC 178;

the surrender of a life interest: *IRC v Buchanan* (1957) 37 TC 365.

Commercial transactions with no element of bounty cannot constitute a settlement: *IRC v Leiner* (1964) 41 TC 589; *Bulmer v IRC* (1966) 44 TC 1; *IRC v Plummer* [1979] STC 793; *Berry v Warnett* [1980] STC 504. Meaning of "settlement": *Young v Pearce* [1996] STC 743.

Revenue precedents

Issue: Whether a payment under a deed of transfer of property is a disposition of income or an instalment payment of a present debt.
Decision: On the facts of the case, where there was no present debt, but an undertaking to make a series of payments, the payments would be treated as annual payments which would reduce the income of the payer and be income in the hands of the recipient.

Definitions

disposition: s 791; person: IA 1937 s 11(*c*); year of assessment: s 3(1).

Former enactments

ITA 1967 s 444 and 447; FA 1971 s 16(2)–(3); FA 1995 s 12(1)(*b*).

797 Recovery of tax from trustee and payment to trustee of excess tax recoupment

(1) Where by virtue of this Chapter any income tax becomes chargeable on and is paid by a settlor, such settlor shall be entitled—

(*a*) to recover from any trustee or other person to whom the income is payable by virtue or in consequence of the settlement the amount of the tax so paid, and

(*b*) for that purpose to require the Revenue Commissioners to furnish to such settlor a certificate specifying the amount of the income in respect of which such settlor has so paid tax and the amount of the tax so paid, and every certificate so furnished shall be evidence until the contrary is proved of the matters of fact stated in the certificate.

(2) Where any person obtains in respect of any allowance or relief a repayment of income tax in excess of the amount of the repayment to which that person would but for this Chapter have been entitled, an amount equal to the excess shall be paid by that person to the trustee or other person to whom the income is payable by virtue or in consequence of the settlement and, where there are 2 or more such trustees or other persons, in such proportions as the circumstances may require.

(3) Where any question arises as to the amount of any payment or as to any apportionment to be made under subsection (2), that question shall be decided by the Appeal Commissioners whose decision on that question shall be final.

(4) Any income which by virtue of this Chapter is treated as income of any person shall be deemed to be the highest part of that person's income.

(5) No repayment shall be made under paragraph 21 of Schedule 32 on account of tax paid in respect of any income which has by virtue of this Chapter been treated as income of a settlor.

Cross-references

Income, meaning, subss (4), (5): s 794(1).

Definitions

Appeal Commissioners: s 2(1); disposition: s 791; person: IA 1937 s 11(*c*); settlement: s 796; income: s 796.

Former enactments

ITA 1967 s 446; F(MP)A 1968 s 3(2) and Sch Pt I; FA 1974 s 86 and Sch 2 Pt I; FA 1997 s 146(1) and Sch 9 Pt I para 1(29).

798 Transfer of interest in trade to children

(1) Where by any means whatever (including indirect means or means consisting of a series of operations and whenever adopted) a trade, which at any time before the adoption of such means was carried on by any person solely or in partnership, becomes a trade carried on by one or more than one child of such person or by means of a partnership in which such person and one or more than one child of such person are partners, the following provisions shall apply:

(*a*) such means shall for the purposes of this Chapter be deemed to constitute a settlement as respects which such person shall be deemed to be the settlor;

(*b*) the profits or gains arising from the trade after the adoption of such means, in so far as they arise to one or, as the case may be, more than one child of such person shall for the purposes of this Chapter be deemed to be the same income as would have arisen to such person had such means not been adopted;

(*c*) **"income"** where it first occurs in section 795 shall be deemed to include those profits or gains in so far as they arise to one or more than one child of such person.

(2) The amount of the income of a person from the profits or gains of a trade deemed by virtue of subsection (1) to be income of another person shall, if the first-mentioned person is engaged actively in the carrying on of the trade, be the full amount of that income reduced by a sum (in subsection (3) referred to as **"the appropriate sum"**) equal to the amount which would have been allowed in computing those profits or gains in respect of the first-mentioned person if that person, instead of being a person engaged in the carrying on of the trade, had been a person employed by a person or persons carrying on the trade.

(3) The appropriate sum shall be deemed to be profits or gains arising to the first-mentioned person referred to in subsection (2) from the exercise of an office or employment within the meaning of Schedule E.

Cross-references

Income, meaning: s 794(1).

The wording included in this section was introduced by FA 1948 following a Supreme Court decision in favour of a taxpayer that an arrangement to introduce a minor child as a partner into a business did not fall foul of the provisions as now included in s 443(1): *O'Dwyer v Cafolla and Co*, 2 ITC 374.

Definitions

disposition: s 791; person: IA 1937 s 11(*c*); settlement: s 796; income: s 796; trade: s 3(1).

Former enactments

ITA 1967 s 448(1), (3)–(4).

PART 32
ESTATES OF DECEASED PERSONS IN COURSE OF ADMINISTRATION AND SURCHARGE ON CERTAIN INCOME OF TRUSTEES

Cross-references

Loans to participators, effect of release of debt: s 439(2).

Revenue information

Information leaflet REV1 — What to do about tax when someone dies.

CHAPTER 1
Estates of Deceased Persons in Course of Administration

799 Interpretation (Chapter 1)

(1) (*a*) In this Chapter—

"administration period" has the meaning assigned to it by section 800(1);

"charges on residue", in relation to the estate of a deceased person, means the following liabilities properly payable out of the estate and interest payable in respect of those liabilities—

(i) funeral, testamentary, and administration expenses and debts,

(ii) general legacies, demonstrative legacies and annuities, and

(iii) any other liabilities of the deceased person's personal representatives as such,

but, in the case of any such liabilities which, as between persons interested under a specific disposition or in a legacy referred to in paragraph (ii) or in an annuity and persons interested in the residue of the estate, fall exclusively or primarily on the property that is the subject of the specific disposition or on the legacy or annuity, includes only such part (if any) of those liabilities as fall ultimately on the residue;

"foreign estate", as regards any year of assessment, means an estate other than an Irish estate;

"Irish estate", as regards any year of assessment, means an estate the income of which comprises only income which either has borne Irish income tax by deduction or in respect of which the personal representatives are directly assessable to Irish income tax, other than an estate any part of the income of which is income in respect of which the personal representatives are entitled to claim exemption from Irish income tax by reference to the fact that they are not resident or not ordinarily resident in the State;

"personal representative", in relation to the estate of a deceased person, means his or her personal representative within the meaning of section 3(1) of the Succession Act, 1965, and includes any person who takes possession of or intermeddles with the property of the deceased and also includes any person having, in relation to the deceased, under the law of another country any functions corresponding to the functions for administration purposes under the law of the State of a personal representative within the meaning of that section, and references to personal representatives as such shall be construed as references to personal representatives in their capacity as having such functions;

"specific disposition" means a specific devise or bequest made by a testator, and includes any disposition having, whether by virtue of any enactment or otherwise, under the law of the State or of another country an effect similar to that of a specific devise or bequest under the law of the State.

(*b*) For the purposes of this Chapter—

(i) references to the aggregate income of the estate of a deceased person for any year of assessment shall be construed, subject to *section 439(2)*, as references to the aggregate income from all sources for that year of the personal representatives of the deceased as such, treated as consisting of—

(I) any such income chargeable to Irish income tax by deduction or otherwise, such income being computed at the amount on which that tax falls to be borne for that year, and

(II) any such income which would have been so chargeable if it had arisen in the State to a person resident and ordinarily resident in the State, such income being computed at the full amount of that income actually arising during that year, less such deductions as would have been allowable if it had been charged to Irish income tax, but excluding any income from property devolving on the personal representatives otherwise than as assets for payment of the debts of the deceased;

(ii) references to sums paid include references to assets transferred or appropriated by a personal representative to himself or herself and to debts set off or released;

(iii) references to sums payable include references to assets as to which an obligation to transfer or a right of a personal representative to appropriate to himself or herself is subsisting on the completion of the administration and to debts as to which an obligation to release is set off, or a right of a personal representative so to do in his or her own favour, is then subsisting;

(iv) references to amount in relation to assets referred to in subparagraphs (ii) and (iii) shall be construed as references to the value of those assets at the date on which they were transferred or appropriated, or at the completion of the administration, as the case may require, and, in relation to such debts, as references to the amount of such debts.

(2) For the purposes of this Chapter—

(*a*) a person shall be deemed to have an absolute interest in the residue of the estate of a deceased person, or in a part of the residue of that estate, if and so long as the capital of the residue or of that part of the residue, as the case may be, would if the residue had been ascertained be properly payable to the person or to another in the person's right for the person's benefit, or is properly so payable, whether directly by the personal representatives, or indirectly through a trustee or other person;

(*b*) a person shall be deemed to have a limited interest in the residue of the estate of a deceased person, or in a part of the residue of that estate, during any period (other than a period during which the person has an absolute interest in the residue or in that part of the residue, as the case may be) where the income of the residue or of that part of the residue, as the case may be, for that period would, if the residue had been ascertained at the commencement of that period, be properly payable to the person, or to another person in the person's right, for the person's benefit, whether directly by the personal representatives, or indirectly through a trustee or other person;

(*c*) real estate included (either by a specific or a general description) in a residuary gift made by the will of a testator shall be deemed to be a part of the residue of the testator's estate and not to be the subject of a specific disposition.

(3) Where different parts of the estate of a deceased person are the subjects respectively of different residuary dispositions, this Chapter shall apply in relation to each such part with the substitution—

(*a*) for references to the estate of references to that part of the estate, and

(*b*) for references to the personal representatives of the deceased as such of references to those personal representatives in their capacity as having the functions referred to in the definition of **"personal representative"** in relation to that part of the estate.

Cross-references

Company acquiring its own shares, meaning of "personal representative" applied: s 173(1).

Home loan interest, meaning of "personal representative" applied: s 244(6)(*a*).

Surcharge on certain income of trustees, meaning of "personal representative" applied, subs (1): s 805(1)(*a*).

Revenue precedents

Issue: Whether, in view of the decision in *Lynch v Burke, Revenue* can overturn a transfer of assets made prior to death where there is insufficient assets in the deceased person's estate to meet tax liabilities.

Decision: It appears that Revenue would have a number of defences in cases where conveyances other than for good consideration were made to defeat Revenue claims, notwithstanding the Supreme Court decision in that case. In particular, in the case of a transferor who is still alive, it seems that resort to the Bankruptcy Act would enable such voluntary transfers to be overturned, where the transfer had been made in the previous five years. The Conveyancing Act 1634 could also be used to set aside such transfers.

Definitions

person: IA 1937 s 11(*c*); year of assessment: s 3(1).

Former enactments

ITA 1967 s 450; CTA 1976 s 140 and Sch 2 Pt I para 23; FA 1997 s 146(1) and Sch 9 Pt I para 1(30).

Corresponding UK tax provision

Income and Corporation Taxes Act 1988 s 701.

800 Limited interest in residue

(1) This section shall apply in relation to a person who, during the period commencing on the death of a deceased person and ending on the completion of the administration of the estate of the deceased person (in this Chapter referred to as **"the administration period"**) or during a part of that period, has a limited interest in the residue of that estate or in a part of the residue of that estate.

(2) When any sum has been paid during the administration period in respect of that limited interest, the amount of that sum shall, subject to subsection (3), be deemed for the purposes of the Income Tax Acts to have been paid to that person as income for the year of assessment in which that sum was paid or, in the case of a sum paid in respect of an interest that has ceased, for the last year of assessment in which that interest was subsisting.

(3) On the completion of the administration of the estate—

(*a*) the aggregate amount of all sums paid before or payable on the completion of the administration in respect of that limited interest shall be deemed to have accrued due to that person from day to day during the administration period or the part of that period during which that person had that interest, as the case may be, and to have been paid to that person as it accrued due,

(*b*) the amount deemed to have been paid to that person by virtue of paragraph (*a*) in any year of assessment shall be deemed for the purposes of the Income Tax Acts to have been paid to that person as income for that year, and

(*c*) where the amount deemed to have been paid to that person as income for any year by virtue of this subsection is less or greater than the amount deemed to have been paid to that person as income for that year by virtue of subsection (2), such adjustments shall be made as are provided in section 804.

(4) Any amount deemed to have been paid to that person as income for any year by virtue of this section shall—

(*a*) in the case of an Irish estate, be deemed to be income of such an amount as would after deduction of income tax at the standard rate of tax for that year be equal to the amount deemed to have been so paid and to be income that has borne income tax at that standard rate of tax;

(*b*) in the case of a foreign estate, be deemed to be income of the amount deemed to have been so paid, and shall be chargeable to income tax under Case III of Schedule D as if it were income arising from securities in a place outside the State.

(5) Where—

(*a*) a person has been charged to income tax for any year by virtue of this section in respect of an amount deemed to have been paid to that person as income in respect of an interest in a foreign estate, and

(*b*) any part of the aggregate income of that estate for that year has borne Irish income tax by deduction or otherwise,

the income in respect of which that person has been so charged to tax shall on proof of the facts be reduced by an amount bearing the same proportion thereto as the part of that aggregate income which has borne Irish income tax bears to the whole of that aggregate income.

(6) Where relief has been given in accordance with subsection (5), such part of the amount in respect of which the person has been charged to income tax as corresponds to the proportion referred to in that subsection shall for the purpose of computing the person's total income be deemed to represent income of such an amount as would after deduction of income tax at the standard rate of tax be equal to that part of the amount charged.

Cross-references

Administration period, subs (1), meaning applied: s 799(1)(*a*).

Special provisions as to certain interests, subss (4)–(6): s 803(3)(*b*).

Definitions

person: IA 1937 s 11(*c*); standard rate: s 3(1); total income: s 3(1); year of assessment: s 3(1).

Former enactments

ITA 1967 s 451; F(MP)A 1968 s 3(5) and Sch Pt IV; FA 1974 s 11 and Sch 1 Pt II.

Corresponding UK tax provision

Income and Corporation Taxes Act 1988 s 695.

801 Absolute interest in residue

(1) This section shall apply in relation to a person who during the administration period or a part of that period has an absolute interest in the residue of the estate of a deceased person or in a part of the residue of that estate.

(2) There shall be ascertained in accordance with section 802 the amount of the residuary income of the estate for each whole year of assessment, and for each part of a year of assessment, during which—

(*a*) the administration period was current, and

(*b*) that person had that interest,

and the amount so ascertained in respect of any year or part of a year, or, in the case of a person having an absolute interest in a part of a residue, a proportionate part of that amount, is in this Chapter referred to as the **"residuary income"** of that person for that year of assessment.

(3) When any sum has or any sums have been paid during the administration period in respect of that absolute interest, the amount of that sum or the aggregate amount of those sums shall, subject to subsection (4), be deemed for the purposes of the Income Tax Acts to have been paid to that person as income to the extent to which, and for the year or years of assessment for which, that person would have been treated for those purposes as having received income if—

(*a*) that person had had a right to receive in each year of assessment—

(i) in the case of an Irish estate, that person's residuary income for that year less income tax for that year at the standard rate of tax, or

(ii) in the case of a foreign estate, that person's residuary income for that year,

and

(*b*) that sum or the aggregate of those sums had been available for application primarily in or towards satisfaction of those rights as they accrued and had been so applied.

(4) In the case of an Irish estate, any amount deemed to have been paid to that person as income for any year by virtue of subsection (3) shall be deemed to be income of such an amount as would after deduction of income tax at the standard rate of tax for that year be equal to the amount deemed to have been so paid, and to be income which has borne income tax at the standard rate of tax.

(5) On the completion of the administration of the estate—

(*a*) the amount of the residuary income of that person for any year of assessment shall be deemed for the purposes of the Income Tax Acts to have been paid to that person as income for that year and, in the case of an Irish estate, shall be deemed to have borne tax by reference to the standard rate of tax, and (*b*) where the amount deemed to have been paid to that person as income for any year by virtue of this subsection is less or greater than the amount deemed to have been paid to that person as income for that year by virtue of subsection (3) or (4), such adjustments shall be made as are provided in section 804.

(6) In the case of a foreign estate, any amount deemed to have been paid to that person as income for any year by virtue of this section shall be deemed to be income of that amount, and shall be chargeable to income tax under Case III of Schedule D as if it were income arising from securities in a place outside the State.

(7) Where—

(*a*) a person has been charged to income tax for any year by virtue of this section in respect of an amount deemed to have been paid to that person as income in respect of an interest in a foreign estate, and

(*b*) any part of the aggregate income of that estate for that year has borne Irish income tax by deduction or otherwise,

the income in respect of which that person has been so charged to tax shall on proof of the facts be reduced by an amount bearing the same proportion thereto as the part of that aggregate income which has borne Irish income tax bears to the whole of that aggregate income.

(8) Where relief has been given in accordance with subsection (7), such part of the amount in respect of which the person has been charged to income tax as corresponds to the proportion referred to in that subsection shall for the purpose of computing the person's total income be deemed to represent income of such an amount as would after deduction of income tax at the standard rate of tax be equal to that part of the amount charged.

(9) For the purposes of any charge to corporation tax to which this section is applied, the residuary income of a company shall be computed in the first instance by reference to years of assessment, and the residuary income for any such year shall be apportioned between the accounting periods (if more than one) comprising that year.

Cross-references

Supplementary provisions: s 802(2)(*b*).

Definitions

person: IA 1937 s 11(*c*); standard rate: s 3(1); year of assessment: s 3(1).

Former enactments

ITA 1967 s 452; CTA 1976 Sch 2 Pt I para 24.

Corresponding UK tax provision

Income and Corporation Taxes Act 1988 s 696.

802 Supplementary provisions as to absolute interest in residue

(1) The amount of the residuary income of an estate for any year of assessment shall be ascertained by deducting from the aggregate income of the estate for that year—

(*a*) the amount of any annual interest, annuity or other annual payment for that year which is a charge on residue and the amount of any payment made in that year in respect of any such expenses incurred by the personal representatives as such in the management of the assets of the estate as, in the absence of any express provision in a will, would be properly chargeable to income, but excluding any such interest, annuity or payment allowed or allowable in computing the aggregate income of the estate, and

(*b*) the amount of any of the aggregate income of the estate for that year to which a person has on or after assent become entitled by virtue of a specific disposition either for a vested interest during the administration period or for a vested or contingent interest on the completion of the administration.

(2) (*a*) In this subsection, **"benefits received"**, in relation to an absolute interest, means the following amounts in respect of all sums paid before, or payable on, the completion of the administration in respect of that interest—

(i) as regards a sum paid before the completion of the administration in the case of an Irish estate, such an amount as would, after deduction of income tax at the standard rate of tax for the year of assessment in which that sum was paid, be equal to that sum or, in the case of a foreign estate, the amount of that sum, and

(ii) as regards a sum payable on the completion of the administration in the case of an Irish estate, such an amount as would, after deduction of income tax at the standard rate of tax for the year of assessment in which the administration is completed, be equal to that sum or, in the case of a foreign estate, the amount of that sum.

(*b*) In the event of its appearing, on the completion of the administration of an estate in the residue of which, or in a part of the residue of which, a person had an absolute interest at the completion of the administration, that the aggregate of the benefits received in respect of that interest does not amount to as much as the aggregate for all years of the residuary income of the person having that interest, that person's residuary income for each year shall be reduced for the purpose of section 801 by an amount bearing the same proportion thereto as the deficiency bears to the aggregate for all years of that person's residuary income.

(3) In the application of subsection (2) to a residue or a part of a residue in which a person, other than the person having an absolute interest at the completion of the administration, had an absolute interest at any time during the administration period, the aggregates mentioned in that subsection shall be computed in relation to those interests taken together, and the residuary income of that other person shall also be subject to reduction under that subsection.

Cross-references

Absolute interests in residue: s 801(2).

Revenue precedents

Issue: Extent of credit available to beneficiaries in respect of tax paid by executors.

Decision: The executor is liable to tax at the standard rate on the gross income of the estate but can make distributions only out of the net income ie gross income less expenses of management. Forms R185 issued by executors should reflect this ie executors should not issue certificates for the gross income received by them.

Definitions

person: IA 1937 s 11(*c*); standard rate: s 3(1); year of assessment: s 3(1).

Former enactments

ITA 1967 s 453.

Corresponding UK tax provision

Income and Corporation Taxes Act 1988 s 697.

---

803 Special provisions as to certain interests

(1) Where the personal representatives of a deceased person have as such a right in relation to the estate of another deceased person such that, if that right were vested in them for their own benefit, they would have an absolute interest or a limited interest in the residue of that estate or in part of the residue of that estate, the personal representatives shall be deemed to have that interest notwithstanding that that right is not vested in them for their own benefit, and any amount deemed to be paid to them as income by virtue of this Chapter shall be treated as part of the aggregate income of the estate of the person whose personal representatives they are.

(2) Where different persons have successively during the administration period absolute interests in the residue of the estate of a deceased person or in a part of the residue of that estate, sums paid during that period in respect of the residue or of that part of the residue, as the case may be, shall be treated for the purpose of this Chapter as having been paid in respect of the interest of the person who first had an absolute interest in that residue or that part of that residue up to the amount of—

(*a*) in the case of an Irish estate, the aggregate for all years of that person's residuary income less income tax at the standard rate of tax, or

(*b*) in the case of a foreign estate, the aggregate for all years of that person's residuary income,

and, as to any balance up to a corresponding amount, in respect of the interest of the person who next had an absolute interest in that residue or that part of that residue, as the case may be, and so on.

(3) Where on the exercise of a discretion any of the income of the residue of the estate of a deceased person for any period (being the administration period or a part of the administration period) would, if the residue had been ascertained at the commencement of that period, be properly payable to any person, or to another person in that person's right, for that person's benefit, whether directly by the personal representatives or indirectly through a trustee or other person—

(*a*) the amount of any sum paid pursuant to an exercise of the discretion in favour of that person shall be deemed for the purposes of the Income Tax Acts to have been paid to that person as income for the year of assessment in which it was paid, and

(*b*) subsections (4) to (6) of section 800 shall apply in relation to an amount deemed to have been paid as income by virtue of paragraph (*a*).

Definitions

person: IA 1937 s 11(*c*); standard rate: s 3(1).

Former enactments

ITA 1967 s 454.

Corresponding UK tax provision

Income and Corporation Taxes Act 1988 s 698.

804 Adjustments and information

(1) Where on the completion of the administration of an estate any amount is deemed by virtue of this Chapter to have been paid to any person as income for any year of assessment and—

(*a*) that amount is greater than the amount previously deemed to have been paid to that person as income for that year by virtue of this Chapter, or

(*b*) no amount has previously been so deemed to have been paid to that person as income for that year,

an assessment or additional assessment may be made on that person for that year and tax charged accordingly or, on a claim being made for the purpose, any relief or additional relief to which that person may be entitled shall be allowed accordingly.

(2) Where on the completion of the administration of an estate any amount is deemed by virtue of this Chapter to have been paid to any person as income for any year of assessment and that amount is less than the amount that has previously been so deemed to have been paid to that person, then—

(*a*) if an assessment has already been made on that person for that year, such adjustments shall be made in that assessment as may be necessary for the purpose of giving effect to the provisions of this Chapter which take effect on the completion of the administration, and any tax overpaid shall be repaid, and

(*b*) if—

(i) any relief has been allowed to that person by reference to the amount previously deemed by virtue of this Chapter to have been paid to that person as income for that year, and

(ii) the amount of that relief exceeds the amount of relief which could have been given by reference to the amount which, on the completion of the administration, is deemed to have been paid to that person as income for that year,

the relief so given in excess may, if not otherwise made good, be charged under Case IV of Schedule D and recovered from that person accordingly.

(3) Notwithstanding anything in the Income Tax Acts, the time within which—

(*a*) an assessment or additional assessment may be made for the purposes of this Chapter,

(*b*) an assessment may be adjusted for those purposes, or

(*c*) a claim for relief may be made by virtue of this Chapter,

shall not expire before the end of the third year following the year of assessment in which the administration of the estate in question was completed.

(4) The Revenue Commissioners may by notice in writing require any person, being or having been a personal representative of a deceased person, or having or having had an absolute interest or a limited interest in the residue of the estate of a deceased person or in a part of the residue of that estate, to furnish them within such time as they may direct (not being less than 28 days) with such particulars as they think necessary for the purposes of this Chapter.

Cross-references

Absolute interests in residue: s 801(5)(*b*).
Limited interest in residue: s 800(3)(*c*).
Self assessment, amendment of and time limit for assessments, subs (3): s 955(2)(*b*).
Penalty, subs (4): Sch 29 column 2.

Definitions

person: IA 1937 s 11(*c*); writing: IA 1937 Sch; year of assessment: s 3(1).

Former enactments

ITA 1967 s 455.

Corresponding UK tax provision

Income and Corporation Taxes Act 1988 s 700.

CHAPTER 2
Surcharge on Certain Income of Trustees

805 Surcharge on certain income of trustees

(1) (*a*) In this section—

"personal representative" has the same meaning as in section 799(1);

"trustees" does not include personal representatives, but where personal representatives, on or before the completion of the administration of the estate of a deceased person, pay to trustees any sum representing income which, if the personal representatives were trustees, would be income to which this section applies, that sum shall be deemed to be paid to the trustees as income and to have borne income tax at the standard rate.

(*b*) This subsection shall be construed together with Chapter 1 of this Part.

(2) This section shall apply to income arising to trustees in any year of assessment in so far as it—

(*a*) is income which is to be accumulated or which is payable at the discretion of the trustees or any other person, whether or not the trustees have power to accumulate the income,

(*b*) is neither, before being distributed, the income of any person other than the trustees nor treated for any purpose of the Income Tax Acts as the income of a settlor,

(*c*) is not income arising under a trust established for charitable purposes only or income from investments, deposits or other property held for the purposes of a fund or scheme established for the sole purpose of providing relevant benefits within the meaning of section 770,

(*d*) exceeds the income applied in defraying the expenses of the trustees in that year which are properly chargeable to income, or would be so chargeable but for any express provisions of the trust, and

(*e*) is not distributed to one or more persons within that year of assessment or within 18 months after the end of that year of assessment in such circumstances that the income distributed is to be treated for the purposes of the Income Tax Acts as the income of the person or persons to whom it is distributed.

(3) (*a*) Income to which this section applies shall, in addition to being chargeable to income tax at the standard rate for the year of assessment for which it is so chargeable, be charged to an additional duty of income tax (in this section referred to as a **"surcharge"**) at the rate of 20 per cent.

(*b*) A surcharge to be made on trustees under this section in respect of income arising in a year of assessment (in this subsection referred to as **"the first year of assessment"**) shall—

(i) be charged on the trustees for the year of assessment in which a period of 18 months beginning immediately after the end of the first year of assessment ends, and

(ii) be treated as income tax chargeable for the year of assessment for which it is so charged.

(*c*) Subject to subsection (4), the Income Tax Acts shall apply in relation to a surcharge made under this section as they apply to income tax charged otherwise than by virtue of this section.

(4) Where income in respect of which a surcharge is made is distributed, no relief from or repayment in respect of the surcharge shall be allowed or made to the person to whom the income is distributed.

(5) A notice given to trustees under any provision specified in column 1 or 2 of Schedule 29 may require that a return of the income arising to them shall include particulars of the manner in which the income has been applied, including particulars as to the exercise by them of any discretion and of the persons in whose favour that discretion has been so exercised.

Cross-references

Profit sharing schemes, appropriated shares: s 510(6)(*a*).
Special investment schemes, income arising to, no surcharge: s 737(6)(*b*)(i).
Taxation of collective investment undertakings: s 734(8).

Tax Briefing

TB33 Sept 1998 p 17 — Discretionary Trust Tax concessionally allowed as expense properly chargeable to income for the purposes of calculating the surcharge but Capital Gains Tax is **not** so allowed.

Definitions

Income Tax Acts: s 1(2); person: IA 1937 s 11(*c*); personal representatives: ss 5(1), 799; standard rate: ss 3(1), 15; year of assessment: ss 2(1), 5(1).

Former enactments

FA 1976 s 13; FA 1990 s 8.

PART 33
ANTI-AVOIDANCE

CHAPTER 1
Transfer of Assets Abroad

806 Charge to income tax on transfer of assets abroad

(1) [In this section and section 807A—][1]

"assets" includes property or rights of any kind;

“associated operation”, in relation to any transfer, means an operation of any kind effected by any person in relation to any of the assets transferred or any assets representing whether directly or indirectly any of the assets transferred, or to the income arising from any such assets, or to any assets representing whether directly or indirectly the accumulations of income arising from any such assets;

“benefit” includes a payment of any kind;

“company” means any body corporate or unincorporated association;

“transfer”, in relation to rights, includes the creation of those rights.

(2) [For the purposes of this section and section 807A—][2]

(*a*) any body corporate incorporated outside the State shall be treated as if it were resident out of the State whether it is so resident or not,

(*b*) a reference to an individual shall be deemed to include the husband or wife of the individual, and

(*c*) references to assets representing any assets, income or accumulations of income include references to shares in or obligations of any company to which, or obligations of any other person to whom, those assets, that income or those accumulations are or have been transferred.

(3) This section shall apply for the purpose of preventing the avoidance by [individuals resident or ordinarily resident in the State][3] of liability to income tax by means of transfers of assets by virtue or in consequence of which, either alone or in conjunction with associated operations, income becomes payable to persons resident or domiciled out of the State.

(4) Where by virtue or in consequence of any such transfer, either alone or in conjunction with associated operations, such an individual has power to enjoy (within the meaning of this section), whether forthwith or in the future, any income of a person resident or domiciled out of the State which, if it were income of that individual received by that individual in the State, would be chargeable to tax by deduction or otherwise, that income shall, whether it would or would not have been chargeable to tax apart from this section, be deemed to be income of that individual for the purposes of the Income Tax Acts.

(5) (*a*) In this subsection, **“capital sum”** means—

(i) any sum paid or payable by means of loan or repayment of a loan, and

(ii) any other sum paid or payable otherwise than as income, being a sum not paid or payable for full consideration in money or money’s worth.

(*b*) Where, whether before or after any such transfer, such an individual receives or is entitled to receive any capital sum the payment of which is in any way connected with the transfer or any associated operation, any income which, by virtue or in consequence of the transfer, either alone or in conjunction with associated operations, has become the income of a person resident or domiciled out of the State shall, whether it would or would not have been chargeable to tax apart from this section, be deemed to be the income of that individual for the purposes of the Income Tax Acts.

[(*c*) For the purposes of paragraph (*b*), there shall be treated as a capital sum which an individual receives or is entitled to receive any sum which a third person receives or is entitled to receive at the individual's direction or by virtue of the assignment by the individual of the individual's right to receive it.][4]

[(5A) Nothing in subsection (3) shall be taken to imply that the provisions of subsections (4) and (5) apply only if—

(*a*) the individual in question was resident or ordinarily resident in the State at the time when the transfer was made, or

(*b*) the avoidance of liability to income tax is the purpose, or one of the purposes, for which the transfer was effected.][5]

(6) An individual shall for the purposes of this section be deemed to have power to enjoy income of a person resident or domiciled out of the State where—

(*a*) the income is in fact so dealt with by any person as to be calculated, at some point of time and whether in the form of income or not, to enure for the benefit of the individual,

(*b*) the receipt or accrual of the income operates to increase the value to the individual of any assets held by the individual or for the individual's benefit,

(*c*) the individual receives or is entitled to receive at any time any benefit provided or to be provided out of that income or out of moneys which are or will be available for the purpose by reason of the effect or successive effects of the associated operations on that income and on any assets which directly or indirectly represent that income,

(*d*) the individual has power, by means of the exercise of any power of appointment or power of revocation or otherwise, to obtain for himself or herself, whether with or without the consent of any other person, the beneficial enjoyment of the income, or may in the event of the exercise of any power vested in any other person become entitled to the beneficial enjoyment of the income, or

(*e*) the individual is able, in any manner whatever and whether directly or indirectly, to control the application of the income.

(7) In determining whether an individual has power to enjoy income within the meaning of this section, regard shall be had to the substantial result and effect of the transfer and any associated operations, and all benefits which may at any time accrue to the individual (whether or not the individual has rights at law or in equity in or to those benefits) as a result of the transfer and any associated operations shall be taken into account irrespective of the nature or form of the benefits.

(8) Subsections (4) and (5) shall not apply where the individual shows in writing or otherwise to the satisfaction of the Revenue Commissioners—

(*a*) that the purpose of avoiding liability to taxation was not the purpose or one of the purposes for which the transfer or associated operations or any of them was effected, or

(*b*) that the transfer and any associated operations were bona fide commercial transactions and were not designed for the purpose of avoiding liability to taxation.

(9) In any case where a person is aggrieved by a decision taken by the Revenue Commissioners in exercise of their functions under subsection (8), the person shall be entitled to appeal to the Appeal Commissioners against the decision of the Revenue Commissioners and the Appeal Commissioners shall hear and determine the appeal as if it were an appeal against an assessment to tax, and the provisions of the Income Tax Acts relating to the rehearing of an appeal and to the statement of a case for the opinion of the High Court on a point of law shall apply accordingly with any necessary modifications.

Amendments

1 Substituted by FA 1999 s 60(1)(*a*)(i) with effect from 11 February 1999; previously "In this section-".

2 Substituted by FA 1999 s 60(1)(*a*)(ii) with effect from 11 February 1999; previously "For the purposes of this section-".

3 Substituted by FA 1998 s 12(1)(*a*)(i) as respects income arising on or after 12 February 1998 irrespective of when the transfer or associated operations took place; previously "individuals ordinarily resident in the State".

4 Subs (5)(*c*) inserted by FA 1999 s 60(1)(*a*)(iii) as respects any sum which a third person receives or becomes entitled to receive on or after 11 February 1999.

5 Subs (5A) inserted by FA 1998 s 12(1)(*a*)(ii) as respects income arising on or after 12 February 1998 irrespective of when the transfer or associated operations took place.

Cross-references

Application of provisions of Income Tax Acts: s 810.
Deductions and reliefs: s 807.
Income not exempted: s 809.
Liability of non-transferors: s 807A(1)(*b*), (7).
Offshore income gains accruing to persons resident or domiciled abroad: s 746(5), (6).
Revenue power to obtain information: s 808(2), (3)(*b*).

Case law

Subs (2): The word "wife" held not to include "widow": *Vestey v IRC* (1949) 31 TC 1.

Subs (4): Held equivalent section could not apply to tax on individual unconnected with the transfer of assets abroad even if he had power to enjoy the income: *Vestey v IRC* [1980] STC 10 (overruling *Congreve v IRC* (1946) 30 TC 163, *Bambridge v IRC* (1955) 36 TC 313, *Phillipi v IRC* (1971) 47 TC 75).

Held the section did not apply where a company, not under the taxpayer's control, transferred assets abroad: *IRC v Pratt* [1982] STC 756.

However, see *CIR v Shroder* [1983] STC 480 where it was held that individual who had power to appoint trustees could not control the application of the income.

Subs (3) Sum payable under a will trust towards the upkeep of a house jointly occupied by two taxpayers, allocation between the taxpayers was an issue of fact; thus the income of each consisted of a share of the total figure involved – *Shanks v IRC* 14 TC 249.

There is a view that apportionment is not possible even in the case of joint incomes, see dissenting judgment of McCarthy J in *Revenue Commissioners v ORMG* 3ITR 28.

Subs (6): Individual who had power to appoint and remove directors held to have power to enjoy the company's income: *Lee v IRC* (1941) 24 TC 207.

Held section applied where person resident outside the country received capital not income: *IRC v McGuckian* [1997] STC 908; but not where the transferor was not ordinarily resident in the UK at the time of the transfer: *IRC v Willoughby* [1997] STC 995.

Individual who transferred assets to a foreign company in return for shares and non-interest bearing debentures held to have power to enjoy company's income where company profits used to purchase her debenture: *Latilla v IRC* (1943) 25 TC 107.

An individual held not to have power to enjoy income where his control over the income could only be exercised jointly with another and in a capacity of trustee: *Vestey v IRC* (1949) 31 TC 1.

An individual who transferred investments to a foreign company increasing the value of a debt the company owed to him held to have power to enjoy company's income: *Ramsden v IRC* (1957) 37 TC 619.

Transferor had power to enjoy income where trustees had power to resettle trust funds and include him as a beneficiary: *IRC v Botnar* [1998] STC 38.

Subss (8)–(9): Bona fide commercial transactions were held to have been involved in: *IRC v Kleinwort Benson Ltd* (1969) 45 TC 369; *Clark v IRC* [1978] STC 614.

Definitions

Appeal Commissioners: s 2(1); commencement: IA 1937 Sch; High Court: IA 1937 Sch; Income Tax Acts: s 1(2); person: IA 1937 s 11(*c*); writing: IA 1937 Sch.

Former enactments

FA 1974 s 57(1)–(7) and (8)(*a*)–(*c*) and (*e*)–(*f*).

Corresponding UK tax provision

Income and Corporation Taxes Act 1988 s 739.

807 Deductions and reliefs in relation to income chargeable to income tax under section 806

(1) Income tax chargeable by virtue of section 806 shall be charged under Case IV of Schedule D.

(2) In computing the liability to income tax of an individual chargeable by virtue of section 806, the same deductions and reliefs shall be allowed as would have been allowed if the income deemed to be income of the individual by virtue of that section had actually been received by the individual.

(3) Where an individual has been charged to income tax on any income deemed to be income of the individual by virtue of section 806 and that income is subsequently received by the individual, it shall be deemed not to form part of the individual's income again for the purposes of the Income Tax Acts.

(4) In any case where an individual has for the purposes of section 806 power to enjoy income of a person abroad by reason of receiving any such benefit referred to in subsection (6)(*c*) of that section, the individual shall be chargeable to income tax by virtue of that section under Case IV of Schedule D for the year of assessment in which the benefit is received on the whole of the amount or value of that benefit, except in so far as it is shown that the benefit derives directly or indirectly from income on which the individual has already been charged to income tax for that or a previous year of assessment.

[(5) An individual who is domiciled out of the State shall not be chargeable to income tax in respect of any income deemed to be the individual's by virtue of section 806 if the individual would not, by reason of being so domiciled, have been chargeable to income tax in respect of it if it had in fact been the individual's income.][1]

Amendments

1 Subs (5) inserted by FA 1999 s 60(1)(*b*) with effect from 12 February 1998.

Cross-references

Offshore income gains accruing to persons resident or domiciled abroad: s 746(5), (6).

Revenue power to obtain information: s 808(2), (3)(*b*).

Case law

Subs (2): Held taxpayer's liability should be based on the full amount of the foreign dividends received by the company and no deduction should be allowed for company expenses: *Lord Chetwode v IRC* [1974] STC 474.

Definitions

Income Tax Acts: s 1(2); person: IA 1937 s 11(*c*); year of assessment: ss 2(1), 5(1).

Former enactments

FA 1974 s 58.

807A Liability of non-transferors

[(1) This section shall apply where—

(*a*) by virtue or in consequence of a transfer of assets, either alone or in conjunction with associated operations, income becomes payable to a person who is resident or domiciled out of the State, and

(*b*) an individual who is resident or ordinarily resident in the State and who is not liable to tax under section 806 by reference to the transfer, receives a benefit provided out of assets which are available for the purpose by virtue or in consequence of the transfer or of any associated operations.

(2) Subject to the provisions of this section, the amount or value of any such benefit as is mentioned in subsection (1), if not otherwise chargeable to income tax in the hands of the recipient, shall—

(*a*) to the extent to which it falls within the amount of relevant income of years of assessment up to and including the year of assessment in which the benefit is received, be treated for all the purposes of the Income Tax Acts as the income of the individual for that year of assessment,

(*b*) to the extent to which it is not by virtue of this subsection treated as the income of the individual for that year of assessment and falls within the amount of relevant income of the next following year of assessment, be treated for those purposes as the individual's income for the next following year of assessment,

and so on for subsequent years of assessment, taking the reference in paragraph (*b*) to the year of assessment mentioned in paragraph (*a*) as a reference to that year of assessment and any other year of assessment before the subsequent year of assessment in question.

(3) Subject to subsection (8), the relevant income of a year of assessment, in relation to an individual, is any income which arises in that year of assessment to a person resident or domiciled out of the State and which by virtue or in consequence of the transfer or associated operations referred to in subsection (1) can directly or indirectly be used for providing a benefit for the individual or for enabling a benefit to be provided for the individual.

(4) Income tax chargeable by virtue of this section shall be charged under Case IV of Schedule D.

(5) An individual who is domiciled out of the State shall not, in respect of any benefit not received in the State, be chargeable to tax under this section by reference to relevant income which is such that, if the individual had received it, the individual would not, by reason of the individual being so domiciled, have been chargeable to income tax in respect of it, and section 72 shall apply for the purposes of this subsection as it would apply for the purposes of section 71(3) if the benefit were income arising from securities and possessions in any place outside the State.

(6) Where—

(*a*) the whole or part of the benefit received by an individual in a year of assessment is a capital payment within the meaning of section 579A or

579F(2) (by virtue of not falling within the amount of relevant income referred to in subsection (2)(*a*)), and

(*b*) chargeable gains are by reason of that payment treated under either section 579A or 579F(2) as accruing to the individual in that or a subsequent year of assessment,

subsection (2)(*b*) shall apply in relation to any year of assessment (in this subsection referred to as "a year of charge") after one in which chargeable gains have been so treated as accruing to the individual, as if a part of the amount or value of the benefit corresponding to the amount of those gains had been treated under that subsection as income of the individual for a year of assessment before the year of charge.

(7) Subsections (8) and (9) of section 806 shall apply for the purposes of this section as they apply for the purposes of subsections (4) and (5) of that section.

(8) This section shall apply irrespective of when the transfer or associated operations referred to in subsection (1) took place, but shall apply only to relevant income arising on or after the 11th day of February, 1999.][1]

Amendments

1 Section 807A inserted by FA 1999 s 60(1)(*c*) with effect from 11 February 1999.

Cross-references

Application of Income Tax Acts: s 810.

Charge to income tax on transfers of assets abroad: s 806(1), (2).

Offshore income gain accruing to persons resident or domiciled abroad: s 746(5), (6).

Power to obtain information: s 808(2), (3)(*b*).

Saver: s 809.

Definitions

chargeable gain: ss 5(1), 545; Income Tax Acts: s 1(2); person: IA 1937 s 11(*c*); year of assessment: ss 2(1), 5(1).

Corresponding UK tax provision

Income and Corporation Taxes Act 1988 s 740.

808 Power to obtain information

(1) In this section, **"settlement"** and **"settlor"** have the same meanings respectively as in section 10.

(2) The Revenue Commissioners or such officer as the Revenue Commissioners may appoint may by notice in writing require any person to furnish them within such time as they may direct (not being less than 28 days) with such particulars as they think necessary for the purposes of sections 806, [807, 807A and 809].[1]

(3) The particulars which a person shall furnish under this section, if required by such a notice to do so, shall include particulars as to—

(*a*) transactions with respect to which the person is or was acting on behalf of others;

(*b*) transactions which in the opinion of the Revenue Commissioners, or of such officer as the Revenue Commissioners may appoint, it is proper that they should investigate for the purposes of sections 806, [807, 807A and 809],[1] notwithstanding that in the opinion of the person to whom the notice is given no liability to tax arises under those sections;

(*c*) whether the person to whom the notice is given has taken or is taking any (and if so what) part in any (and if so what) transactions of a description specified in the notice.

(4) Notwithstanding anything in subsection (3), a solicitor shall not be deemed for the purposes of paragraph (*c*) of that subsection to have taken part in a transaction by reason only that the solicitor has given professional advice to a client in connection with that transaction, and shall not, in relation to anything done by the solicitor on behalf of a client, be compellable under this section, except with the consent of the client, to do more than state that the solicitor is or was acting on behalf of a client, and specify the name and address of the client and also—

(*a*) in the case of anything done by the solicitor in connection with the transfer of any asset by or to [an individual resident or ordinarily resident in the State][2] to or by any body corporate mentioned in subsection (5), or in connection with any associated operation in relation to any such transfer, to specify the names and addresses of the transferor and the transferee or of the persons concerned in the associated operation, as the case may be;

(*b*) in the case of anything done by the solicitor in connection with the formation or management of any body corporate mentioned in subsection (5), to specify the name and address of the body corporate;

(*c*) in the case of anything done by the solicitor in connection with the creation, or with the execution of the trusts, of any settlement by virtue or in consequence of which income becomes payable to a person resident or domiciled out of the State, to specify the names and addresses of the settlor and of that person.

(5) The bodies corporate referred to in subsection (4) are bodies corporate resident or incorporated outside the State which are, or if resident in the State would be, close companies within the meaning of sections 430 and 431.

(6) Nothing in this section shall impose on any bank the obligation to furnish any particulars of any ordinary banking transactions between the bank and a customer carried out in the ordinary course of banking business, unless the bank has acted or is acting on behalf of the customer in connection with the formation or management of any body corporate mentioned in subsection (4)(*b*) or in connection with the creation, or with the execution of the trusts, of any settlement mentioned in subsection (4)(*c*).

Amendments

1 Substituted by FA 1999 s 60(1)(*d*) with effect from 11 February 1999; previously "807 and 809".

2 Substituted by FA 1998 s 12(1)(*b*) as respects income arising on or after 12 February 1998 irrespective of when the transfer or associated operations took place; previously "an individual ordinarily resident in the State".

Cross-references

Penalty: Sch 29 column 2.

Case law

Irish

Subs (6): Revenue powers do not extend to the supply of information concerning the transfer of funds abroad where a bank merely acts as a conduit for a transaction and where a loan against the security of the transferred funds is negotiated separately: *Royal Trust Co Ltd and others v Revenue Commissioners* [1982] ILRM 459.

A notice was not invalid despite the scope of the information requested by the Revenue concerning clients affairs and the cost of compliance: *Stokes Kennedy Crowley and Co v Revenue Commissioners* [1986] IR 663.

UK

Subs (6): Attempts by the bank to resist disclosure notices on the grounds that the transactions in question were ordinary banking transactions failed in: *Mankowitz v Special Commissioners* (1971) 46 TC 707; *Royal Bank of Canada v IRC* (1971) 47 TC 565; *Clinch v IRC* (1973) 49 TC 52.

Definitions

person: IA 1937 s 11(*c*); writing: IA 1937 Sch.

Former enactments

FA 1974 s 59(1)–(5); FA 1977 s 3; FA 1997 s 146(1) and Sch 9 Pt I para 8(2).

Corresponding UK tax provision

Income and Corporation Taxes Act 1988 s 745.

809 Saver

Where any income of any person is by virtue of the Income Tax Acts, and in particular, but without prejudice to the generality of the foregoing, by virtue of [sections 806 and 807A],[1] to be deemed to be income of any other person, that income shall not be exempt from tax either—

(*a*) as being derived from any stock or other security to which section 43, 47, 49 or 50 applies, or

(*b*) by virtue of section 35 or 63,

by reason of the first-mentioned person not being resident, or not being ordinarily resident, or being neither domiciled nor ordinarily resident, in the State.

Amendments

1 Substituted by FA 1999 s 60(1)(*e*) with effect from 11 February 1999; previously "section 806".

Cross-references

Revenue power to obtain information: s 808(2), (3)(*b*).

Definitions

Income Tax Acts: s 1(2); person: IA 1937 s 11(*c*).

Former enactments

FA 1974 s 60.

810 Application of Income Tax Acts

The provisions of the Income Tax Acts relating to the charge, assessment, collection and recovery of tax, to appeals against assessments and to cases to be stated for the opinion of the High Court shall apply to income tax chargeable by virtue of [sections 806 and 807A][1] subject to any necessary modifications.

Amendments

1 Substituted by FA 1999 s 60(1)(*e*) with effect from 11 February 1999; previously "section 806".

Definitions

High Court: IA 1937 Sch; Income Tax Acts: s 1(2).

Former enactments

FA 1974 s 61.

CHAPTER 2
Miscellaneous

811 Transactions to avoid liability to tax

(1) (*a*) In this section—

"the Acts" means—

(i) the Tax Acts,
(ii) the Capital Gains Tax Acts,
(iii) the Value-Added Tax Act, 1972, and the enactments amending or extending that Act,
(iv) the [Capital Acquisitions Tax Consolidation Act 2003],[1] and the enactments amending or extending that Act,
(v) Part VI of the Finance Act, 1983, and the enactments amending or extending that Part, and
(vi) the statutes relating to stamp duty,

and any instruments made thereunder;

"business" means any trade, profession or vocation;

"notice of opinion" means a notice given by the Revenue Commissioners under subsection (6);

"tax" means any tax, duty, levy or charge which in accordance with the Acts is placed under the care and management of the Revenue Commissioners and any interest, penalty or other amount payable pursuant to the Acts;

"tax advantage" means—

(i) a reduction, avoidance or deferral of any charge or assessment to tax, including any potential or prospective charge or assessment, or
(ii) a refund of or a payment of an amount of tax, or an increase in an amount of tax, refundable or otherwise payable to a person, including any potential or prospective amount so refundable or payable,

arising out of or by reason of a transaction, including a transaction where another transaction would not have been undertaken or arranged to achieve the results, or any part of the results, achieved or intended to be achieved by the transaction;

"tax avoidance transaction" has the meaning assigned to it by subsection (2);

"tax consequences", in relation to a tax avoidance transaction, means such adjustments and acts as may be made and done by the Revenue Commissioners pursuant to subsection (5) in order to withdraw or deny the tax advantage resulting from the tax avoidance transaction;

"transaction" means—

(i) any transaction, action, course of action, course of conduct, scheme, plan or proposal,
(ii) any agreement, arrangement, understanding, promise or undertaking, whether express or implied and whether or not enforceable or intended to be enforceable by legal proceedings, and

(iii) any series of or combination of the circumstances referred to in paragraphs (i) and (ii),

whether entered into or arranged by one person or by 2 or more persons—

(I) whether acting in concert or not,

(II) whether or not entered into or arranged wholly or partly outside the State, or

(III) whether or not entered into or arranged as part of a larger transaction or in conjunction with any other transaction or transactions.

(*b*) In subsections (2) and (3), for the purposes of the hearing or rehearing under subsection (8) of an appeal made under subsection (7) or for the purposes of the determination of a question of law arising on the statement of a case for the opinion of the High Court, the references to the Revenue Commissioners shall, subject to any necessary modifications, be construed as references to the Appeal Commissioners or to a judge of the Circuit Court or, to the extent necessary, to a judge of the High Court, as appropriate.

(2) For the purposes of this section and subject to subsection (3), a transaction shall be a **"tax avoidance transaction"** if having regard to any one or more of the following—

(*a*) the results of the transaction,

(*b*) its use as a means of achieving those results, and

(*c*) any other means by which the results or any part of the results could have been achieved,

the Revenue Commissioners form the opinion that—

(i) the transaction gives rise to, or but for this section would give rise to, a tax advantage, and

(ii) the transaction was not undertaken or arranged primarily for purposes other than to give rise to a tax advantage,

and references in this section to the Revenue Commissioners forming an opinion that a transaction is a tax avoidance transaction shall be construed as references to the Revenue Commissioners forming an opinion with regard to the transaction in accordance with this subsection.

(3) (*a*) Without prejudice to the generality of subsection (2), in forming an opinion in accordance with that subsection and subsection (4) as to whether or not a transaction is a tax avoidance transaction, the Revenue Commissioners shall not regard the transaction as being a tax avoidance transaction if they are satisfied that—

(i) notwithstanding that the purpose or purposes of the transaction could have been achieved by some other transaction which would have given rise to a greater amount of tax being payable by the person, the transaction—

(I) was undertaken or arranged by a person with a view, directly or indirectly, to the realisation of profits in the course of the business activities of a business carried on by the person, and

(II) was not undertaken or arranged primarily to give rise to a tax advantage,

or

(ii) the transaction was undertaken or arranged for the purpose of obtaining the benefit of any relief, allowance or other abatement provided by any provision of the Acts and that the transaction would not result directly or indirectly in a misuse of the provision or an abuse of the provision having regard to the purposes for which it was provided.

(*b*) In forming an opinion referred to in paragraph (*a*) in relation to any transaction, the Revenue Commissioners shall have regard to—

(i) the form of that transaction,

(ii) the substance of that transaction,

(iii) the substance of any other transaction or transactions which that transaction may reasonably be regarded as being directly or indirectly related to or connected with, and

(iv) the final outcome and result of that transaction and any combination of those other transactions which are so related or connected.

(4) Subject to this section, the Revenue Commissioners as respects any transaction may at any time—

(*a*) form the opinion that the transaction is a tax avoidance transaction,

(*b*) calculate the tax advantage which they consider arises, or which but for this section would arise, from the transaction,

(*c*) determine the tax consequences which they consider would arise in respect of the transaction if their opinion were to become final and conclusive in accordance with subsection (5)(*e*), and

(*d*) calculate the amount of any relief from double taxation which they would propose to give to any person in accordance with subsection (5)(*c*).

(5) (*a*) Where the opinion of the Revenue Commissioners that a transaction is a tax avoidance transaction becomes final and conclusive, they may, notwithstanding any other provision of the Acts, make all such adjustments and do all such acts as are just and reasonable (in so far as those adjustments and acts have been specified or described in a notice of opinion given under subsection (6) and subject to the manner in which any appeal made under subsection (7) against any matter specified or described in the notice of opinion has been finally determined, including any adjustments and acts not so specified or described in the notice of opinion but which form part of a final determination of any such appeal) in order that the tax advantage resulting from a tax avoidance transaction shall be withdrawn from or denied to any person concerned.

(*b*) Subject to but without prejudice to the generality of paragraph (*a*), the Revenue Commissioners may—

(i) allow or disallow in whole or in part any deduction or other amount which is relevant in computing tax payable, or any part of such deduction or other amount,

(ii) allocate or deny to any person any deduction, loss, abatement, relief, allowance, exemption, income or other amount, or any part thereof, or

(iii) recharacterize for tax purposes the nature of any payment or other amount.

(*c*) Where the Revenue Commissioners make any adjustment or do any act for the purposes of paragraph (*a*), they shall afford relief from any double taxation which they consider would but for this paragraph arise by virtue of any adjustment made or act done by them pursuant to paragraphs (*a*) and (*b*).

(*d*) Notwithstanding any other provision of the Acts, where—

(i) pursuant to subsection (4)(*c*), the Revenue Commissioners determine the tax consequences which they consider would arise in respect of a transaction if their opinion that the transaction is a tax avoidance transaction were to become final and conclusive, and

(ii) pursuant to that determination, they specify or describe in a notice of opinion any adjustment or act which they consider would be, or be part of, those tax consequences,

then, in so far as any right of appeal lay under subsection (7) against any such adjustment or act so specified or described, no right or further right of appeal shall lie under the Acts against that adjustment or act when it is made or done in accordance with this subsection, or against any adjustment or act so made or done that is not so specified or described in the notice of opinion but which forms part of the final determination of any appeal made under subsection (7) against any matter specified or described in the notice of opinion.

(*e*) For the purposes of this subsection, an opinion of the Revenue Commissioners that a transaction is a tax avoidance transaction shall be final and conclusive—

(i) if within the time limited no appeal is made under subsection (7) against any matter or matters specified or described in a notice or notices of opinion given pursuant to that opinion, or

(ii) as and when all appeals made under subsection (7) against any such matter or matters have been finally determined and none of the appeals has been so determined by an order directing that the opinion of the Revenue Commissioners to the effect that the transaction is a tax avoidance transaction is void.

(6) (*a*) Where pursuant to subsections (2) and (4) the Revenue Commissioners form the opinion that a transaction is a tax avoidance transaction, they shall immediately on forming such an opinion give notice in writing of the opinion to any person from whom a tax advantage would be withdrawn or to whom a tax advantage would be denied or to whom relief from double taxation would be given if the opinion became final and conclusive, and the notice shall specify or describe—

(i) the transaction which in the opinion of the Revenue Commissioners is a tax avoidance transaction,

(ii) the tax advantage or part of the tax advantage, calculated by the Revenue Commissioners which would be withdrawn from or denied to the person to whom the notice is given,

(iii) the tax consequences of the transaction determined by the Revenue Commissioners in so far as they would refer to the person, and

(iv) the amount of any relief from double taxation calculated by the Revenue Commissioners which they would propose to give to the person in accordance with subsection (5)(*c*).

(*b*) Section 869 shall, with any necessary modifications, apply for the purposes of a notice given under this subsection or subsection (10) as if it were a notice given under the Income Tax Acts.

(7) Any person aggrieved by an opinion formed or, in so far as it refers to the person, a calculation or determination made by the Revenue Commissioners pursuant to subsection (4) may, by notice in writing given to the Revenue Commissioners within 30 days of the date of the notice of opinion, appeal to the Appeal Commissioners on the grounds and, notwithstanding any other provision of the Acts, only on the grounds that, having regard to all of the circumstances, including any fact or matter which was not known to the Revenue Commissioners when they formed their opinion or made their calculation or determination, and to this section—

(*a*) the transaction specified or described in the notice of opinion is not a tax avoidance transaction,

(*b*) the amount of the tax advantage or the part of the tax advantage, specified or described in the notice of opinion which would be withdrawn from or denied to the person is incorrect,

(*c*) the tax consequences specified or described in the notice of opinion, or such part of those consequences as shall be specified or described by the appellant in the notice of appeal, would not be just and reasonable in order to withdraw or to deny the tax advantage or part of the tax advantage specified or described in the notice of opinion, or

(*d*) the amount of relief from double taxation which the Revenue Commissioners propose to give to the person is insufficient or incorrect.

(8) The Appeal Commissioners shall hear and determine an appeal made to them under subsection (7) as if it were an appeal against an assessment to income tax and, subject to subsection (9), the provisions of the Income Tax Acts relating to the rehearing of an appeal and to the statement of a case for the opinion of the High Court on a point of law shall apply accordingly with any necessary modifications; but on the hearing or rehearing of the appeal—

(*a*) it shall not be lawful to enquire into any grounds of appeal other than those specified in subsection (7), and

(*b*) at the request of the appellants, 2 or more appeals made by 2 or more persons pursuant to the same opinion, calculation or determination formed or made by the Revenue Commissioners pursuant to subsection (4) may be heard or reheard together.

(9) (*a*) On the hearing of an appeal made under subsection (7), the Appeal Commissioners shall have regard to all matters to which the Revenue Commissioners may or are required to have regard under this section, and—

(i) in relation to an appeal made on the grounds referred to in subsection (7)(*a*), the Appeal Commissioners shall determine the appeal, in so far as it is made on those grounds, by ordering, if they or a majority of them—

(I) consider that the transaction specified or described in the notice of opinion or any part of that transaction is a tax avoidance transaction, that the opinion or the opinion in so far as it relates to that part is to stand,

(II) consider that, subject to such amendment or addition thereto as the Appeal Commissioners or the majority of them deem necessary and as they shall specify or describe, the transaction, or any part of it, specified or described in the notice of opinion, is a tax avoidance transaction, that the transaction or that part of it be so amended or added to and that, subject to the amendment or addition, the opinion or the opinion in so far as it relates to that part is to stand, or

(III) do not so consider as referred to in clause (I) or (II), that the opinion is void,

(ii) in relation to an appeal made on the grounds referred to in subsection (7)(*b*), they shall determine the appeal, in so far as it is made on those grounds, by ordering that the amount of the tax advantage or the part of the tax advantage specified or described in the notice of opinion be increased or reduced by such amount as they shall direct or that it shall stand,

(iii) in relation to an appeal made on the grounds referred to in subsection (7)(*c*), they shall determine the appeal, in so far as it is made on those grounds, by ordering that the tax consequences specified or described in the notice of opinion shall be altered or added to in such manner as they shall direct or that they shall stand, or

(iv) in relation to an appeal made on the grounds referred to in subsection (7)(*d*), they shall determine the appeal, in so far as it is made on those grounds, by ordering that the amount of the relief from double taxation specified or described in the notice of opinion shall be increased or reduced by such amount as they shall direct or that it shall stand.

(*b*) This subsection shall, subject to any necessary modifications, apply to the rehearing of an appeal by a judge of the Circuit Court and, to the extent necessary, to the determination by the High Court of any question or questions of law arising on the statement of a case for the opinion of the High Court.

(10) The Revenue Commissioners may at any time amend, add to or withdraw any matter specified or described in a notice of opinion by giving notice (in this subsection referred to as **"the notice of amendment"**) in writing of the amendment, addition or withdrawal to each and every person affected thereby, in so far as the person is so affected, and subsections (1) to (9) shall apply in all respects as if the notice of amendment were a notice of opinion and any matter specified or described in the notice of amendment were specified or described in a notice of opinion; but no such amendment, addition or withdrawal may be made so as to set aside or alter any matter which has become final and conclusive on the determination of an appeal made with regard to that matter under subsection (7).

(11) Where pursuant to subsections (2) and (4) the Revenue Commissioners form the opinion that a transaction is a tax avoidance transaction and pursuant to that opinion notices are to be given under subsection (6) to 2 or more persons, any obligation on the Revenue Commissioners to maintain secrecy or any other restriction on the disclosure of

information by the Revenue Commissioners shall not apply with respect to the giving of those notices or to the performance of any acts or the discharge of any functions authorised by this section to be performed or discharged by them or to the performance of any act or the discharge of any functions, including any act or function in relation to an appeal made under subsection (7), which is directly or indirectly related to the acts or functions so authorised.

(12) The Revenue Commissioners may nominate any of their officers to perform any acts and discharge any functions, including the forming of an opinion, authorised by this section to be performed or discharged by the Revenue Commissioners, and references in this section to the Revenue Commissioners shall with any necessary modifications be construed as including references to an officer so nominated.

(13) This section shall apply as respects any transaction where the whole or any part of the transaction is undertaken or arranged on or after the 25th day of January, 1989, and as respects any transaction undertaken or arranged wholly before that date in so far as it gives rise to, or would but for this section give rise to—

(*a*) a reduction, avoidance or deferral of any charge or assessment to tax, or part thereof, where the charge or assessment arises by virtue of any other transaction carried out wholly on or after a date, or

(*b*) a refund or a payment of an amount, or of an increase in an amount, of tax, or part thereof, refundable or otherwise payable to a person where that amount or increase in the amount would otherwise become first so refundable or otherwise payable to the person on a date,

which could not fall earlier than the 25th day of January, 1989.

Amendments

1 Substituted by CATCA 2003 s 119 and Sch 3 with effect from 21 February 2003; previously "Capital Acquisitions Tax Act 1976".

Cross-references

Meaning of "the Acts" applied: Asset Covered Securities Act 2001 s 81(2).

Shipping tonnage tax, requirement not to enter into tax avoidance arrangements, meaning of "tax advantage" applied: s 697F(2)(*a*).

This section to be construed together with the Value Added Tax Acts 1972–1997, in so far as relating to value added tax: s 1104(3).

This section to be construed together with the Stamp Act 1891 and the enactments amending or extending that Act, in so far as relating to stamp duties: s 1104(4).

This section to be construed together with the Capital Acquisitions Tax Act 1976, and the enactments amending or extending that Act, in so far as relating to capital acquisitions tax: s 1104(5).

This section to be construed together with FA 1983 Pt VI and the enactments amending or extending that Part, in so far as relating to residential property tax: s 1104(6).

Caselaw relating to the corresponding UK provision

Bona fide commercial motives: *Marwood Homes Ltd v IRC* [1996] STI 51.

Expenditure on plant funded by non-recourse borrowings allowable: *Airspace Investments Ltd v Moore* (High Court, Lynch J, 15 April 1994) Contrast *Ensign Tankers (Leasing) Ltd v Stokes* [1992] STC 226.

Meaning of "tax advantage": *IRC v Universities Superannuation Scheme* [1997] STC 1.

Trustees of Omega Group Pension Scheme v IRC (2001) STC 121.

IRC v Trustees of the Sema Group Pension Scheme (2002) STC 276.

Definitions

Appeal Commissioners: ss 2(1), 5(1); Circuit Court: IA 1937 Sch; High Court: IA 1937 Sch; person: IA 1937 s 11(*c*); profession: ss 2(1), 5(1); profits: s 4(1); statute: s 2(1), IA 1937 s 3; Tax Acts: s 1(2); trade: s 3(1); writing: IA 1937 Sch.

Former enactments

FA 1989 s 86.

Corresponding UK tax provision

Income and Corporation Taxes Act 1988 s 703.

812 Taxation of income deemed to arise from transfers of right to receive interest from securities

(1) In this section—

"interest" includes dividends, annuities and shares of annuities;

"securities" include stocks and shares of all descriptions.

(2) Where in any year of assessment or accounting period an owner (in this section referred to as **"the owner"**) of any securities sells or transfers the right to receive any particular interest payable (whether before or after such sale or transfer) in respect of those securities without selling or transferring those securities, then, and in every such case, the following provisions shall apply:

(*a*) for the purposes of the Tax Acts that interest (whether it would or would not be chargeable to tax if this section had not been enacted)—

(i) shall be deemed to be the income of the owner or, where the owner is not the beneficial owner of the securities and some other person (in this section referred to as **"the beneficiary"**) is beneficially entitled to the income arising from the securities, the income of the beneficiary,

(ii) shall be deemed to be income of the owner or the beneficiary, as the case may be, for that year of assessment or accounting period, as the case may be,

(iii) shall not be deemed to be income of any other person, and

(iv) shall, where the proceeds of the sale or transfer are chargeable to tax under Schedule C or under Chapter 2 of Part 4, be deemed to be equal in amount to the amount of those proceeds;

(*b*) where the right to receive that particular interest is subsequently sold, transferred or otherwise realised, the proceeds of such subsequent sale, transfer or other realisation shall not be deemed for any of the purposes of the Tax Acts to be income of the person by or on whose behalf such subsequent sale, transfer or other realisation is made or effected;

(*c*) where the securities are of such character that the interest payable in respect of the securities may be paid without deduction of tax, then, unless the owner or beneficiary, as the case may be, shows that the proceeds of any sale or other realisation of the right to receive the interest, which is deemed to be income of the owner or of the beneficiary, as the case may be, by virtue of this section, have been charged to tax under Schedule C or under Chapter 2 of Part 4, the owner or beneficiary, as the case may be, shall be chargeable to tax under Case

IV of Schedule D in respect of that interest, but shall be entitled to credit for any tax which that interest is shown to have borne;

(*d*) where in any case to which paragraph (*c*) applies the computation of the tax in respect of the interest which is made chargeable under Case IV of Schedule D by that paragraph would, if that interest had been chargeable under Case III of Schedule D, have been made by reference to the amount received in the State, the tax chargeable pursuant to paragraph (*c*) shall be computed on the full amount of the sums received in the State in the year of assessment or in any subsequent year of assessment in which the owner remains the owner of the securities;

(*e*) nothing in this subsection shall affect any provision of the Tax Acts authorising or requiring the deduction of tax from any interest which is deemed by virtue of this subsection to be income of the owner or of the beneficiary or from the proceeds of any subsequent sale, transfer or other realisation mentioned in this subsection of the right to receive that particular interest.

(3) In relation to corporation tax—

(*a*) subsection (2)(*c*) shall apply (subject to the provisions of the Corporation Tax Acts relating to distributions) to any interest, whether or not the securities are of such character that the interest may be paid without deduction of tax, and as if ", but shall be entitled to credit for any tax which that interest is shown to have borne" were deleted, and

(*b*) subsection (2)(*d*) shall not apply.

(4) The Revenue Commissioners may by notice in writing require any person to furnish them, within such time (not being less than 28 days from the service of the notice) as shall be specified in the notice, with such particulars in relation to all securities of which such person was the owner at any time during the period specified in the notice as the Revenue Commissioners may consider to be necessary for the purposes of this section or for the purpose of discovering whether—

(*a*) tax has been borne in respect of the interest payable in respect of those securities, or

(*b*) the proceeds of any sale, transfer or other realisation of the right to receive the interest in respect of those securities has been charged to tax under Schedule C or under Chapter 2 of Part 4.

Cross-references

Penalty, subs (4): Sch 29 column 2.

Definitions

person: IA 1937 s 11(*c*); writing: IA 1937 Sch; year of assessment: s 3(1).

Former enactments

ITA 1967 s 449; CTA 1976 s 140(1) and Sch 2 Pt I para 22.

Corresponding UK tax provision

Income and Corporation Taxes Act 1988 s 730.

813 Taxation of transactions associated with loans or credit

(1) This section shall apply as respects any transaction effected with reference to the lending of money or the giving of credit, or the varying of the terms on which money is loaned or credit is given, or which is effected with a view to enabling or facilitating any such arrangement concerning the lending of money or the giving of credit.

(2) Subsection (1) shall apply whether the transaction is effected between the lender or creditor and the borrower or debtor, or between either of them and a person connected with the other or between a person connected with one and a person connected with the other.

(3) Where the transaction provides for the payment of any annuity or other annual payment, not being interest but being a payment chargeable to tax under Schedule D, the payment shall be treated for the purposes of the Tax Acts as if it were a payment of annual interest.

(4) Where the transaction is one by which an owner of any securities or other property carrying a right to income (in this subsection referred to as **"the owner"**) agrees to sell or transfer the property, and by the same or any collateral agreement—

(*a*) the purchaser or transferee (in this subsection referred to as **"the buyer"**) or a person connected with the buyer agrees to sell or transfer at a later date the same or any other property to the owner or a person connected with the owner, or

(*b*) the owner or a person connected with the owner acquires an option, which the owner or the person connected with the owner subsequently exercises, to buy or acquire the same or any other property from the buyer or a person connected with the buyer,

then, without prejudice to the liability of any other person, the owner shall be chargeable to tax under Case IV of Schedule D on an amount equal to any income which arises from the first-mentioned property at any time before the repayment of the loan or the termination of the credit.

(5) Where under the transaction a person assigns, surrenders or otherwise agrees to waive or forego income arising from any property (without a sale or transfer of the property), then, without prejudice to the liability of any other person, the first-mentioned person shall be chargeable to tax under Case IV of Schedule D on a sum equal to the amount of income assigned, surrendered, waived or foregone.

(6) Where credit is given for the purchase price of any property and the rights attaching to the property are such that during the subsistence of the debt the purchaser's rights to income from the property are suspended or restricted, the purchaser shall be treated for the purposes of subsection (5) as having surrendered a right to income of an amount equivalent to the income which the purchaser has in effect foregone by obtaining the credit.

(7) The amount of any income payable subject to deduction of tax at the standard rate shall be taken for the purposes of subsection (5) as the amount before deduction of that tax.

Definitions

Income Tax Acts: s 1(2); person: IA 1937 s 11(*c*); standard rate: ss 3(1), 15.

Former enactments

FA 1974 s 41(1)–(6); CTA 1976 s 140(1) and Sch 2 Pt I para 45, s 164 and Sch 3 Pt II.

Corresponding UK tax provision

Income and Corporation Taxes Act 1988 s 786.

814 Taxation of income deemed to arise from transactions in certificates of deposit and assignable deposits

(1) In this section—

"assignable deposit" means a deposit of money in any currency, which has been deposited with any person, whether it is to be repaid with or without interest and which at the direction of the depositor may be assigned with or without interest to another person;

"certificate of deposit" means a document relating to money in any currency, which has been deposited with the issuer or some other person, being a document which recognises an obligation to pay a stated amount to bearer or to order, with or without interest, and being a document by the delivery of which, with or without endorsement, the right to receive that stated amount, with or without interest, is transferable.

(2) This section shall apply to any right—

(*a*) to receive from any person an amount of money, with or without interest, which is stated in a certificate of deposit issued to the person who has deposited the money or to any other person, or

(*b*) to receive from any person an amount of money, with or without interest, being a right arising from an assignable deposit which may be assigned or transferred to another person by the person who has deposited the money or by any person who has acquired the right to do so.

(3) Where after the 3rd day of April, 1974, a person acquires a right to which this section applies, any gain arising to the person from the disposal of that right or, except in so far as it is a right to receive interest, from its exercise shall, if not to be taken into account as a trading receipt, be deemed for the purposes of the Tax Acts to be annual profits or gains chargeable to tax under Case IV of Schedule D and shall be charged to tax accordingly.

(4) Where on or before the 3rd day of April, 1974, a person acquired a right to which this section applies and disposes or disposed of, or exercises or exercised, the right after that date, so much of any gain arising to the person from that disposal, or, except in so far as it is a right to receive interest, from that exercise, as bears to the total amount of the gain the same proportion as the number of days from the 3rd day of April, 1974, to the date of the disposal or exercise bears to the total number of days from the date of the acquisition to the date of the disposal or exercise, shall, if not to be taken into account as a trading receipt, be deemed for the purposes of the Tax Acts to be annual profits or gains chargeable to tax under Case IV of Schedule D and shall be charged to tax accordingly.

(5) Where a person sustains a loss in a transaction which if profits had arisen from it would be chargeable to tax by virtue of subsection (3) or (4), then, if the person is chargeable to tax under Schedule C or D in respect of the interest payable on the amount of money the right to which has been disposed of, the amount of that interest shall be included in the amounts against which the person may claim to set off the amount of the loss under section 383 or 399, as the case may be.

(6) For the purposes of this section, profits or gains shall not be treated as falling to be taken into account as a trading receipt by reason only that they are included in the computation required by section 707.

Cross-references

Corporation tax, relief for Schedule D Case IV or V losses, subss (3)–(4): s 399(1)(*b*).

Definitions

person: IA 1937 s 11(*c*).

Former enactments

FA 1974 s 55; CTA 1976 s 140(1) and Sch 2 Pt I para 47; FA 1977 s 42 and Sch 1 Pt IV para 5.

Corresponding UK tax provision

Income and Corporation Taxes Act 1988 s 56.

815 Taxation of income deemed to arise on certain sales of securities

(1) In this section—

"owner", in relation to securities, means at any time the person who would be entitled, if the securities were redeemed at that time by the person who issued them, to the proceeds of the redemption;

"securities" includes—

(*a*) assets which are not chargeable assets for the purposes of capital gains tax by virtue of section 607, and

(*b*) stocks, bonds and obligations of any government, municipal corporation, company or other body corporate, whether creating or evidencing a charge on assets or not,

but does not include shares (within the meaning of the Companies Act, 1963) of a company (within the meaning of that Act) or similar body.

(2) (*a*) Subject to paragraphs (*b*) to (*d*) and subsection (3), where the owner of a security (in this subsection referred to as **"the owner"**) sells or transfers, or causes or authorises to be sold or transferred, the security and where any interest payable in respect of the security is receivable otherwise than by the owner, then, for the purposes of this section—

(i) interest payable in respect of the security shall be deemed for the purposes of the Tax Acts to have accrued on a day to day basis from the date on which the owner acquired the security, and

(ii) the owner shall be chargeable under Case IV of Schedule D on interest so deemed to have accrued from that date up to the date of the contract for sale or transfer of the security or the date of payment of the consideration in respect of the sale or transfer, whichever is the later.

(*b*) Where during the owner's period of ownership of the security the owner has received interest in respect of the security in respect of which the owner is chargeable to tax under any other provision of the Tax Acts, the amount of interest on which the owner is chargeable under this section shall be reduced by the amount in respect of which the owner is so chargeable under that other provision.

(*c*) Where under the terms of the sale or transfer of the security or an associated agreement, arrangement, understanding, promise or undertaking, whether express or implied, the owner—

(i) agrees to buy back or reacquire the security, or

(ii) acquires an option which the owner subsequently exercises to buy back or reacquire the security,

the charge to tax imposed under this section shall be based on the interest deemed to have accrued up to the next date after that sale or transfer on which interest is payable in respect of the security.

(*d*) Where the owner subsequently resells or retransfers, or causes or authorises to be resold or retransferred, the security, any further charge to tax under this section in respect of that subsequent resale or retransfer shall be based on interest deemed to have accrued from a date not earlier than that next payment date.

(3) This section shall not apply—

(*a*) where the security has been held by the same owner for a continuous period of at least 2 years immediately before the date of such contract for sale or transfer or the date of such payment of consideration, whichever is the later, as is referred to in subsection (2)(*a*), the personal representatives of a deceased person whose estate is in the course of administration and the deceased person being regarded for the purposes of this paragraph as being the same owner,

(*b*) where the owner is a person carrying on a trade which consists wholly or partly of dealing in securities, the profits of which are chargeable to income tax or corporation tax under Case I of Schedule D for the year of assessment or, as the case may be, the accounting period in respect of which the consideration for the sale is taken into account in computing for the purposes of assessment to income tax or corporation tax for that year or accounting period the profits of the trade,

(*c*) where—

(i) the owner is an undertaking for collective investment (within the meaning of section 738), and

(ii) any gain or loss accruing to the owner on the sale or transfer is a chargeable gain or an allowable loss, as the case may be,

(*d*) where the sale or transfer is a sale or transfer by a wife to her husband at a time when she is treated as living with him for income tax purposes as provided in section 1015, or a sale or transfer by a husband to a wife at such time, the husband and the wife being regarded for the purposes of paragraph (*a*), in the case of such a transaction or in the case of a sale or transfer by the husband or the wife to any other person after such a transaction or transactions, as being the same owner, or

(*e*) where the security is a security the interest on which is treated as a distribution for the purposes of the Corporation Tax Acts.

(4) The reference in subsection (2)(*c*) to buying back or reacquiring the security shall be deemed to include references to buying or acquiring a similar security, and securities shall be so deemed to be similar if they entitle their holders to the same rights against the

same persons as to capital and interest and the same remedies for the enforcement of those rights, notwithstanding any difference in the total nominal amounts of the respective securities or in the form in which they are held or the manner in which they can be transferred.

(5) (*a*) For the purposes of identifying securities acquired by an owner with securities included in a sale or transfer by the owner, in so far as the securities are of the same class, securities acquired at a later date shall be deemed to be so included before securities acquired at an earlier date.

(*b*) Securities shall be regarded as being of the same class where they entitle their owners to the same rights against the same person as to capital and interest and the same remedies for the enforcement of those rights.

(6) (*a*) Without prejudice to any other provision of the Tax Acts requiring the disclosure of information, an inspector may by notice in writing require any person to whom paragraph (*b*) applies to furnish within the time specified in the notice such particulars as the inspector considers necessary for the purposes of this section and for the purpose of determining whether a charge to tax arises under this section.

(*b*) This paragraph shall apply to—

(i) a person who issues a security,

(ii) any agent of such a person, and

(iii) an owner of a security.

Cross-references

Chargeable gains of life business, meaning of "securities" applied: s 711(2)(*a*).

Exchange of Irish Government bonds, s 815 to apply to disposal of old securities to which s 751B(6)(*a*) applies as if in subs (3)(*b*) "unless the trade consists wholly or partly of a life business the profits of which are not assessed to corporation tax under Case I of Schedule D for that accounting period" were inserted after "profits of the trade" and as if subs (3)(*c*) were deleted: s 751B(6)(*b*).

Penalty: Sch 29 column 2.

Special investment schemes, meaning of "securities" applied: s 737(8)(*c*).

Strips of securities, meaning of "securities" applied, subs (1): s 55(1).

Undertakings for collective investment, subs (2): s 738(1)(*c*); meaning of "securities" applied: s 738(7)(*a*).

Revenue precedents

Issue: Whether sub-paragraph (*b*) of subs (2) of s 815 can operate to reduce the Case IV chargeable figure to a figure less than nil so as to create a loss.

Decision: No.

Definitions

company: ss 4(1), 5(1); Corporation Tax Acts: s 1(2); distribution: ss 4(1), 436, 437; inspector: ss 2(1), 5(1), 852; person: IA 1937 s 11(*c*); personal representative: s 5(1), 784; profits: s 4(1); shares: s 5(1); Tax Acts: s 1(2); trade: s 3(1); writing: IA 1937 Sch.

Former enactments

FA 1984 s 29(1)–(3)(*a*) and (4)–(5); FA 1991 s 27; FA 1993 s 21; FA 1994 s 26.

Corresponding UK tax provision

Income and Corporation Taxes Act 1988 s 709.

816 Taxation of shares issued in place of cash dividends

[(1) In this section—

"company" means any body corporate;

"quoted company" means a company whose shares, or any class of whose shares—

(*a*) are listed in the official list of the Irish Stock Exchange or on any other stock exchange, or

(*b*) are quoted on the market known as the Developing Companies Market, or the market known as the Exploration Securities Market, of the Irish Stock Exchange or on any similar or corresponding market of any other stock exchange;

"share" means share in the share capital of a company and includes stock and any other interest in the company.

(2) Where any person as a consequence of the exercise (whether before, on or after the declaration of a distribution of profits by a company) of an option to receive in respect of shares in the company either a sum in cash or additional share capital of the company, receives such additional share capital, then, an amount equal to the amount which that person would have received if that person had received the distribution in cash instead of such share capital shall for the purposes of the Tax Acts—

(*a*) where the company is resident outside the State, be deemed to be income received by the person from the company, and such income shall be treated as income from securities and possessions outside the State and be assessed and charged to tax under Case III of Schedule D,

(*b*) where the company is resident in the State and is a quoted company—

(i) be treated as a distribution made by the company, and

(ii) be deemed to be a distribution received by the person,

and

(*c*) where the company is resident in the State and is not a quoted company, be deemed to be profits or gains of the person, being profits or gains not within any other Case of Schedule D and not charged by virtue of any other Schedule, and be assessed and charged to tax under Case IV of Schedule D.

(3) Where a company is treated under subsection (2)(*b*)(i) as making a distribution to a person, section 152 shall apply with any necessary modifications as if the distribution were a dividend to which subsection (1) of that section applies.][1]

(4) For the purposes of this section, an option to receive either a dividend in cash or additional share capital shall be conferred on a person not only where that person is required to choose one or the other, but also where that person is offered the one subject to a right, however expressed, to choose the other instead, and a person's abandonment of, or failure to exercise, such a right shall be treated for those purposes as an exercise of the option.

Amendments

1 Subs (1)–(3) substituted by FA 1998 s 43(1)(*a*) as respects shares issued by a company on or after 3 December 1997.

Cross-references

Capital gains tax, reorganisation or reduction of share capital: s 584(4)(*b*).
Dividend withholding tax (interpretation): s 172A(1)(*a*) ("relevant distribution"), (2)(*b*), (*c*).
Interpretation of Corporation Tax Acts, subs (2)(*b*): s 4(1) (distributions).
Matters to be treated as distributions, subs (2)(*b*): s 130(1) (distributions).
Schedule F, subs (2)(*b*): s 20(1) (distributions).

Definitions

distribution: ss 4(1), 20(1); person: IA 1937 s 11(*c*); Tax Acts: s 1(2).

Former enactments

FA 1974 s 56(1), (2), (3)(*b*) and (*c*) and (4); FA 1993 s 36.

Corresponding UK tax provision

Income and Corporation Taxes Act 1988 s 249.

817 Schemes to avoid liability to tax under Schedule F

(1) (*a*) In this section—

"appeal" means an appeal made in accordance with section 933;

"close company" has the same meaning as it has, by virtue of sections 430 and 431, for the purposes of the Corporation Tax Acts;

"market value" shall be construed in accordance with section 548;

"new consideration" has the same meaning as in section 135;

"shares" includes loan stock, debentures and any interest or rights in or over, or any option in relation to, shares, loan stock or debentures, and references to **"shareholder"** shall be construed accordingly.

(*b*) (i) For the purposes of this section, there shall be a disposal of shares by a shareholder where the shareholder disposes of shares or is treated under the Capital Gains Tax Acts as disposing of shares, and references to a disposal of shares shall include references to a part disposal of shares within the meaning of those Acts.

(ii) Where under any arrangement between a close company (in this subparagraph referred to as **"the first-mentioned company"**) and its, or some of its, shareholders (being any arrangement similar to an arrangement entered into for the purposes of or in connection with a scheme of reconstruction or amalgamation) another close company issues shares to those shareholders in respect of or in proportion to (or as nearly as may be in proportion to) their holdings of shares in the first-mentioned company, but the shares in the first-mentioned company are either retained by the shareholders or are cancelled, then, those shareholders shall for the purposes of this section be treated as making a disposal or a part disposal, as the case may be, of the shares in the first-mentioned company in exchange for those shares held by them in consequence of such arrangement.

(*c*) For the purposes of this section, the interest of a shareholder in a trade or business shall not be significantly reduced following a disposal of shares, or the carrying out of a scheme or arrangement of which the disposal of shares is a part, only if at any time after the disposal the percentage of—

(i) the ordinary share capital of the close company carrying on the trade or business at such time which is beneficially owned by the shareholder at such time,

(ii) any profits, which are available for distribution to equity holders, of the close company carrying on the trade or business at such time to which the shareholder is beneficially entitled at such time, or

(iii) any assets, available for distribution to equity holders on a winding up, of the close company carrying on the trade or business at such time to which the shareholder would be beneficially entitled at such time on a winding up of the close company,

is not significantly less than the percentage of that ordinary share capital or those profits or assets, as the case may be, of the close company carrying on the trade or business at any time before the disposal—

(I) which the shareholder beneficially owned, or

(II) to which the shareholder was beneficially entitled,

at such time before the disposal, and sections 413 to 415 and section 418 shall apply, but without regard to section 411(1)(*c*) in so far as it relates to those sections, with any necessary modifications, to the determination for the purposes of this paragraph of the percentage of share capital or other amount which a shareholder beneficially owns or is beneficially entitled to, as they apply to the determination for the purposes of Chapter 5 of Part 12 of the percentage of any such amount which a company so owns or is so entitled to.

[(*ca*) For the purposes of this section, following a disposal of shares in a close company by a shareholder or the carrying out of a scheme or arrangement of which the disposal is a part, the interest of the shareholder in any trade or business which was carried on by the close company shall be deemed—

(i) to include the interest, or interests as the case may be, in that trade or business of one or more persons connected with the shareholder, if increasing that interest of the shareholder by such interest, or interests as the case may be, would result in the interest of the shareholder in the trade or business not having been significantly reduced,

(ii) notwithstanding paragraph (*c*), not to have been significantly reduced where—

(I) the business carried on by the close company, taking account of any trade carried on by that company, consisted wholly or mainly of the holding of shares in another company carrying on a trade or business or in more than one such other company, and

(II) the interest of the shareholder in any such trade or business last-mentioned in clause (I), whether or not that trade or business continues to be carried on by such other company after the disposal, is not significantly reduced,

(iii) notwithstanding paragraph (*c*), not to have been significantly reduced where the gain realised by the shareholder on that disposal is wholly or mainly attributable to payments or other transfers of value from another company or companies, which is or are controlled by that shareholder or by that shareholder and persons connected with him or her, to the close company, and

(iv) not to have been significantly reduced where—

(I) it would not have been so reduced if the shareholder were to be treated as beneficially entitled to any shares to which he or she could, at any time, become so entitled by the exercise of a discretion by trustees,

(II) the acquisition of those shares by the trustees was directly or indirectly related to a disposal, including a prior or subsequent disposal, of such shares by the shareholder, and

(III) the shares were acquired by the trustees with the direct or indirect financial assistance of a company or companies, which is or are controlled by the shareholder or by the shareholder and persons connected with the shareholder.][1]

(*d*) The value of any amount received in money's worth shall for the purposes of this section be the market value of the money's worth at the time of its receipt.

(2) This section shall apply for the purposes of counteracting any scheme or arrangement undertaken or arranged by a close company, or to which the close company is a party, being a scheme or arrangement the purpose of which, or one of the purposes of which, is to secure that any shareholder in the close company avoids or reduces a charge or assessment to income tax under Schedule F by converting into a capital receipt of the shareholder any amount which would otherwise be available for distribution by the close company to the shareholder by means of a dividend.

(3) Subject to subsection (7), this section shall apply to a disposal of shares in a close company by a shareholder if, following the disposal or the carrying out of a scheme or arrangement of which the disposal is a part, the interest of the shareholder in any trade or business (in this section referred to as **"the specified business"**) which was carried on by the close company at the time of the disposal, whether or not the specified business continues to be carried on by the close company after the disposal, is not significantly reduced.

(4) Subject to subsection (5) and notwithstanding section 130(1) or any provision of the Capital Gains Tax Acts, the amount of—

(*a*) the proceeds in either or both money and money's worth received by a shareholder in respect of a disposal of shares in a close company to which this section applies, or

(*b*) if it is less than those proceeds, the excess of those proceeds over any consideration, being consideration which—

(i) is new consideration received by the close company for the issue of those shares, and

(ii) has not previously been taken into account for the purposes of this subsection,

shall be treated for the purposes of the Tax Acts as a distribution (within the meaning of the Corporation Tax Acts) made at the time of the disposal by the close company to the shareholder.

(5) (*a*) In this subsection, **"capital receipt"** means, as appropriate in the circumstances, any amount of either or both money and money's worth (other than shares issued by a close company carrying on the specified business) which—

(i) is received by a shareholder in respect of a disposal of shares or by reason of any act done pursuant to a scheme or arrangement of which the disposal is a part, and

(ii) apart from this section is not chargeable to income tax in the hands of the shareholder.

(*b*) The amount which at any time may be treated under subsection (4) as a distribution made by a close company to a shareholder in respect of any disposal of shares in the close company shall not exceed the amount of the capital receipt, or the aggregate of the amounts of the capital receipts, which at such time has or have been received by the shareholder—

(i) in respect of the disposal, or

(ii) by reason of any act done pursuant to a scheme or arrangement of which the disposal is a part.

(*c*) A capital receipt received by a shareholder at any time on or after the disposal shall in respect of such time result in so much of the amount mentioned in subsection (4) being treated as a distribution (which is made by the close company to the shareholder at the time of the disposal) as does not exceed the amount of the capital receipt, or the aggregate of the amounts of such capital receipts, which at such time on or after the disposal has or have been received by the shareholder.

(*d*) Where as a result of a shareholder having received a capital receipt a close company is treated as having made a distribution to the shareholder under subsection (4), any provision of the Income Tax Acts in respect of interest on unpaid tax shall apply for the purposes of tax due in respect of that distribution as if the tax were due and payable only from the day on which the shareholder received the capital receipt.

...[2]

(7) This section shall not apply as respects a disposal of shares in a close company by a shareholder where it is shown to the satisfaction of the inspector or, on the hearing or the rehearing of an appeal, to the satisfaction of the Appeal Commissioners or a judge of the Circuit Court, as the case may be, that the disposal was made for bona fide commercial reasons and not as part of a scheme or arrangement the purpose or one of the purposes of which was the avoidance of tax.

Amendments

1 Subs (1)(*ca*) inserted by FA 2005 s 38(1) as respects any disposal of shares made on or after 1 March 2005.

2 Subs (6) deleted by FA 2003 s 41(1)(*m*) as respects accounting periods ending on or after 6 February 2003.

Definitions

Appeal Commissioners: ss 2(1), 5(1); Circuit Court: IA 1937 Sch; close company: s 4(1), 430, 431; company: ss 4(1), 5(1); connected: s 10; distribution: ss 4(1), 436, 437; Income Tax Acts: s 1(2); inspector: ss 2(1), 5(1), 852; ordinary share capital: s 2(1); part disposal: ss 5(1), 534; profits: s 4(1); shares: s 5(1); Tax Acts: s 1(2); tax credit: ss 2(1), 136; trade: s 3(1).

Former enactments

FA 1989 s 88(1)–(7).

817A Restriction of relief for payments of interest

[(1) Relief shall not be given to any person under Part 8 in respect of any payment of interest, including interest treated as a charge on income, if a scheme has been effected or arrangements have been made such that the sole or main benefit that might be expected to accrue to that person from the transaction under which the interest is paid is the obtaining of a reduction in tax liability by means of any such relief.

(2) Where relief in respect of interest paid, being interest treated as a charge on income, is claimed by virtue of section 420(6), any question under this section as to what benefit might be expected to accrue from the transaction under which that interest is paid shall be determined by reference to the claimant company (within the meaning of section 411 (2)) and the surrendering company (within the meaning of that section) taken together.][1]

Amendments

1 Section 817A inserted by FA 2000 s 73(1) as respects interest paid on or after 29 February 2000.

Definitions

person: IA 1937 s 11(*c*).

817B Treatment of interest in certain circumstances

(1) (*a*) In this section—

"chargeable period" means an accounting period of a company or a year of assessment, and a reference to a chargeable period or its basis period is a reference to the chargeable period if it is an accounting period and to the basis period for it if it is a year of assessment;

"basis period" means the period on the profits or gains of which income tax is to be finally computed under Schedule D or, where by virtue of the Income Tax Acts the profits or gains of any other period are to be taken to be the profits or gains of that period, that other period.

(*b*) For the purposes of this section, in relation to interest which is to be taken into account in computing income chargeable to tax under Case I of Schedule D—

(i) where 2 basis periods overlap, the period common to both shall be deemed to fall in the first basis period only,

(ii) where there is an interval between the end of the basis period for one year of assessment and the basis period for the next year of assessment, the interval shall be deemed to be part of the first basis period, and

(iii) the reference in subparagraph (i) to the overlapping of 2 periods shall be construed as including a reference to the coincidence of 2 periods or to the inclusion of one period in another, and the reference to the period common to both shall be construed accordingly.

(2) Notwithstanding any other provision of the Tax Acts, where, in relation to a chargeable period (in this subsection referred to as the "earlier chargeable period"), a person receives interest in the chargeable period or its basis period, so much of the amount of the interest as, apart from this section—

(*a*) would not be taken into account in computing the person's income chargeable to tax under Schedule D for the earlier chargeable period, and

(*b*) would be so taken into account for a subsequent chargeable period or subsequent chargeable periods, shall be taken into account in computing the person's income so chargeable for the earlier chargeable period and shall not be so taken into account for the subsequent chargeable period or, as the case may be, the subsequent chargeable periods.][1]

Amendments

1 Section 817B inserted by FA 2000 s 73(1) as respects interest received on or after 29 February 2000.

Cross-references

Restriction on deductibility of certain interest, meaning of "chargeable period" and "basis period" applied: s 817C(1).

Definitions

Income Tax Acts: s 1(2); person: IA 1937 s 11(*c*); Tax Acts: s 1(2); year of assessment: s 2(1).

817C Restriction on deductibility of certain interest

[(1) In this section—

"chargeable period" and **"basis period"** have the same meanings as they have for the purposes of section 817B;

"relevant date", in relation to a chargeable period, means the date on which the basis period for the chargeable period ends;

"relevant liability" means a liability of one person to another person.

(2) [Subject to subsection (2A), this section applies where][1] —

(*a*) interest is payable by a person, directly or indirectly, to a connected person (being interest which, if it were paid, would be chargeable to tax under Schedule D),

(*b*) the interest would, apart from this section, be allowable in computing trading income of a trade carried on by the person, and

(*c*) (i) in a case where the connected person is chargeable to tax in respect of the interest, the interest does not fall to be taken into account, or

(ii) in any other case, if the connected person were resident in the State the interest would not fall to be taken into account,

in computing the trading income of a trade carried on by the connected person.

[(2A)(*a*) This section does not apply where the connected person referred to in subsection (2) is a company which—

(i) is not resident in the State, and

(ii) is not under the control, whether directly or indirectly, of a person who is, or persons who are, resident in the State.

(*b*) For the purposes of this subsection—

(i) **"control"** shall be construed in accordance with subsections (2) to (6) of section 432 as if in subsection (6) of that section for "5 or fewer participators" there were substituted "persons resident in the State", and

(ii) a company shall not be treated as under the control whether directly or indirectly, of a person or persons if that person is or those persons are, in turn under the control of another person or other persons.][2]

(3) Where this section applies, so much of any interest payable, or treated under subsection (4) as payable, by a person, directly or indirectly, to a connected person in respect of a relevant liability shall not be allowable in computing trading income chargeable on the person for a chargeable period (in this subsection referred to as the **"first-mentioned chargeable period"**) as is greater than the excess of A over B where—

A is the aggregate of amounts of interest on the relevant liability which are chargeable to tax as income of the connected person, or would be so chargeable but for the provisions of section 198 or of arrangements having the force of law by virtue of [section 826(1)(*a*),][3] for all chargeable periods the basis periods for which end on or before the relevant date in relation to the first-mentioned chargeable period, and

B is the aggregate of the amounts of interest on the relevant liability which have been allowed as deductions in computing trading income for the purposes of tax for, or have otherwise been allowed or relieved for the purposes of tax in, chargeable periods the basis periods for which end before the relevant date in relation to the first-mentioned chargeable period.

(4) Interest which, by virtue of subsection (3), is not allowable in computing trading income for a chargeable period shall be treated as being payable in the basis period for the following chargeable period.

(5) Where under arrangements made by any person (in this subsection referred to as the **"first person"**)—

(*a*) interest is payable by the first person to another person such that this section does not apply by virtue only of the fact that the persons concerned are not connected, and

(*b*) interest is payable by some other person to a person (in this subsection referred to as the **"second person"**) connected with the first person such that this section does not apply by virtue only of the fact that the other person and the second person are not connected,

then, subsections (3) and (4) shall apply as if the interest had been payable by the first person to the second person.][4]

Amendments

1 Substituted by FA 2004 s 32(1)(*a*) as respects any chargeable period ending on or after 6 February 2003.; previously "This section applies where".

2 Subs (2A) inserted by FA 2004 s 32(1)(*b*) as respects any chargeable period ending on or after 6 February 2003.

3 Substituted by FA 2004 s 89 and Sch 3 para 1(*u*) with effect from 25 March 2004; previously "section 826".

4 Section 817C inserted by FA 2003 s 44(1) as respects any chargeable period ending on or after 6 February 2003.

Definitions

company: s 4(1); connected, connected person: s 10; person: IA 1937 s 11(*c*); trade: ss 3(1), 4(1).

PART 34
PROVISIONS RELATING TO THE RESIDENCE OF INDIVIDUALS

Cross-references

Capital acquisitions tax, general interpretation: CATCA 2003 s 2(6).
Profits of life business: s 710(3)(*b*).

Revenue information

Information leaflet RES1 — Explanatory Leaflet on the Legislative Provisions relating to the Residence in Ireland of Individuals for Tax Purposes

818 Interpretation (Part 34)

In this Part other than in section 825—

"the Acts" means—

(*a*) the Tax Acts,

(*b*) the Capital Gains Tax Acts, and

(*c*) the [Capital Acquisitions Tax Consolidation Act 2003],[1] and the enactments amending or extending that Act,

and any instruments made thereunder;

"authorised officer" means an officer of the Revenue Commissioners authorised by them in writing for the purposes of this Part;

"present in the State", in relation to an individual, means the personal presence of the individual in the State;

"tax" means any tax payable in accordance with any provision of the Acts.

Amendments

1 Substituted by CATCA 2003 s 119 and Sch 3 with effect from 21 February 2003; previously "Capital Acquisitions Tax Act 1976".

Cross-references

Reduction on income tax for certain income earned outside the State, meaning of "authorised officer" applied: s 825A(1).
Seafarer allowance, meaning of "authorised officer" applied: s 472B(1).

Former enactments

FA 1994 s 149.

819 Residence

(1) For the purposes of the Acts, an individual shall be resident in the State for a year of assessment if the individual is present in the State—

(*a*) at any one time or several times in the year of assessment for a period in the whole amounting to 183 days or more, or

(*b*) at any one time or several times—

(i) in the year of assessment, and

(ii) in the preceding year of assessment,

for a period (being a period comprising in the aggregate the number of days on which the individual is present in the State in the year of assessment and the number of days on which the individual was present in the State in the preceding year of assessment) in the aggregate amounting to 280 days or more.

(2) Notwithstanding subsection (1)(*b*), where for a year of assessment an individual is present in the State at any one time or several times for a period in the aggregate amounting to not more than 30 days—

(*a*) the individual shall not be resident in the State for the year of assessment, and

(*b*) no account shall be taken of the period for the purposes of the aggregate mentioned in subsection (1)(*b*).

(3) (*a*) Notwithstanding subsections (1) and (2), an individual—

(i) who is not resident in the State for a year of assessment, and

(ii) to whom paragraph (*b*) applies,

may at any time elect to be treated as resident in the State for that year and, where an individual so elects, the individual shall for the purposes of the Acts be deemed to be resident in the State for that year.

(*b*) This paragraph shall apply to an individual who satisfies an authorised officer that the individual is in the State—

(i) with the intention, and

(ii) in such circumstances,

that the individual will be resident in the State for the following year of assessment.

(4) For the purposes of this section, an individual shall be deemed to be present in the State for a day if the individual is present in the State at the end of the day.

Tax Briefing

TB15 July 1994 par 3 — Residence of individuals.

TB17 No.1 of 1995 p 9 — Electing to be resident.

Definitions

resident: s 5(1); year: IA 1937 Sch; year of assessment: ss 2(1), 5(1).

Former enactments

FA 1994 s 150.

820 Ordinary residence

(1) For the purposes of the Acts, an individual shall be ordinarily resident in the State for a year of assessment if the individual has been resident in the State for each of the 3 years of assessment preceding that year.

(2) An individual ordinarily resident in the State shall not for the purposes of the Acts cease to be ordinarily resident in the State for a year of assessment unless the individual has not been resident in the State in each of the 3 years of assessment preceding that year.

Tax Briefing

TB15 July 1994 par3 — Residence of individuals — ordinary residence.

TB17 No. 1 of 1995 p 10 — Ordinary residence.

Definitions

resident: s 5(1); year: IA 1937 Sch; year of assessment: ss 2(1), 5(1).

Former enactments

FA 1994 s 151.

821 Application of sections 17 and 18(1) and Chapter 1 of Part 3

(1) Where an individual is not resident but is ordinarily resident in the State, sections 17 and 18(1) and Chapter 1 of Part 3 shall apply as if the individual were resident in the State; but this section shall not apply in respect of—

(*a*) the income of an individual derived from one or more of the following—

(i) a trade or profession, no part of which is carried on in the State, and

(ii) an office or employment, all the duties of which are performed outside the State, and

(*b*) other income of an individual which in any year of assessment does not exceed [€3,810][1].

(2) In determining for the purposes of subsection (1) whether the duties of an office or employment are performed outside the State, any duties performed in the State, the performance of which is merely incidental to the performance of the duties of the office or employment outside the State, shall be treated as having been performed outside the State.

Amendments

1 Substituted by FA 2001 s 240(1) and (1)(*a*) and Sch 5 Pt 1 for 2002 and later tax years; previously "£3,000" (short tax "year" 2001:£2,220 (FA 2001 s 77(2) and Sch 2 paras 43 and 61(*a*))).

Revenue precedents

Issue: Ordinary Residence and Fiscal Domicile Articles of DTA.
Decision: Where the individual is chargeable to Irish tax by virtue of his/her ordinary residence status in Ireland, he/she may be "fiscally domiciled" in Ireland, ie resident "of" Ireland, for the purposes of a Double Taxation Convention, subject to tie breaker rules provided there is a "fiscal domicile Article" within the relevant Double Taxation Convention.

Tax Briefing

TB17 No. 1 of 1995 p 10 — Ordinary residence.
TB25 Feb 1997 p 10 — "other income" which does not exceed "£3,000" means other foreign income.

Definitions

profession: s 2(1); resident: s 5(1); trade: s 3(1); year: IA 1937 Sch.

Former enactments

FA 1994 s 152; FA 1995 s 169(1).

822 Split year residence

(1) For the purposes of a charge to tax on any income, profits or gains from an employment, where during a year of assessment (in this section referred to as **"the relevant year"**)—

(*a*) (i) an individual who has not been resident in the State for the preceding year of assessment satisfies an authorised officer that the individual is in the State—

(I) with the intention, and

(II) in such circumstances,

that the individual will be resident in the State for the following year of assessment, or

(ii) an individual who is resident in the State satisfies an authorised officer that the individual is leaving the State, other than for a temporary purpose—

(I) with the intention, and

(II) in such circumstances,

that the individual will not be resident in the State for the following year of assessment,

and

(*b*) the individual would but for this section be resident in the State for the relevant year,

subsection (2) shall apply in relation to the individual.

(2) (*a*) An individual to whom paragraphs (*a*)(i) and (*b*) of subsection (1) apply shall be deemed to be resident in the State for the relevant year only from the date of his or her arrival in the State.

(*b*) An individual to whom paragraphs (*a*)(ii) and (*b*) of subsection (1) apply shall be deemed to be resident in the State for the relevant year only up to and including the date of his or her leaving the State.

(3) Where by virtue of this section an individual is resident in the State for part of a year of assessment, the Acts shall apply as if—

(*a*) income arising during that part of the year or, in a case to which section 71(3) applies, amounts received in the State during that part of the year were income arising or amounts received for a year of assessment in which the individual is resident in the State, and

(*b*) income arising or, as the case may be, amounts received in the remaining part of the year were income arising or amounts received in a year of assessment in which the individual is not resident in the State.

Cross references

Deduction for income earned outside the State: s 823(2)(*b*)(ii).

Reduction in income tax for certain income earned outside the State: s 825A(2)(*b*).

Seafarer allowance: s 472B(3)(*b*)(ii).

Revenue precedents

Issue: Split Year Treatment Date of arrival. From what date does residence in Ireland commence for split year treatment? An individual came to Ireland on 1 July, 1994 to take up employment with an Irish subsidiary of a German company. He worked here for 1 week and then spent the following 3 months in Germany, finally returning to Ireland in October, 1994.

Decision: It was decided that his date of arrival for split year purposes was 1 July as he arrived in the State to take up employment with the intention and in such circumstances as to become permanently resident.

Issue: Split Year Treatment holiday return visits.

Decision: Return visits to Ireland for holidays will not affect the application of split year treatment, assuming of course that all the other conditions of TCA 1997 s 822.

Tax Briefing

TB17 No.1 of 1995 p 6 — Split year treatment.

Definitions

profits: s 4(1); tax: s 3(1); year of assessment: ss 2(1), 5(1).

Former enactments

FA 1994 s 153.

823 Deduction for income earned outside the State

(1) In this section—

[**"qualifying day"**, in relation to an office or employment of an individual, means a day on or before 31 December 2003 which is one of at least 11 consecutive days throughout the whole of which the individual is absent from the State for the purposes of the performance of the duties of the office or employment or of those duties and the duties of other offices or employments of the individual outside the State and which (taken as a whole) are substantially devoted to the performance of such duties, but no day shall be counted more than once as a qualifying day;][1]

"relevant period", in relation to a year of assessment, means a continuous period of 12 months—

(*a*) part only of which is comprised in the year of assessment, and

(*b*) no part of which is comprised in another relevant period;

[**"the specified amount"** in relation to an office or employment means an amount determined by the formula—

$$\frac{D \times E}{365}$$

where—

D is the number of qualifying days in relation to the office or employment in the year of assessment concerned, and

E is all the income, profits or gains from any office, employment or pension whether chargeable under Schedule D or E (including income from offices or employments the duties of which are performed in the State) of an individual in that year after deducting any contribution or qualifying premium in respect of which there is provision for a deduction under section 774(7) or 787 but excluding—

(*a*) any expense to which 118 applies,

(*b*) any amount treated as emoluments of an employment under section 121(2)(*b*)(ii) by virtue of a car being made available by reason of the employment,

(*c*) any sum treated for the purposes of section 112 as a perquisite of an office or employment by virtue of section 122,

(*d*) any payment to which section 123 applies,

(*e*) any sum deemed to be profits or gains arising or accruing from an office or employment by virtue of section 127(2), or

(*f*) any gain to which section 128 applies.][2]

(2) (*a*) Subject to paragraph (*b*), this section shall apply to—

(i) an office of director of a company which is within the charge to corporation tax, or would be within the charge to corporation tax if it were resident in the State, and which carries on a trade or profession,

(ii) an employment other than—

(I) an employment the emoluments of which are paid out of the revenue of the State, or

(II) an employment with any board, authority or other similar body established by or under statute.

(*b*) This section shall not apply in any case where the income from an office or employment—

(i) is chargeable to tax in accordance with section 71(3),

(ii) is subject to section 73, or would be so subject if the employment were deemed to be property situated where the employment is exercised, or

(iii) is income to which section 822 applies.

[(2A)(*a*) In this subsection, "qualifying employment", "qualifying individual" and "sea-going ship" have the same meanings, respectively, as in section 472B.

(*b*) Where in any period of at least [11 consecutive days][3] in which a qualifying individual is absent from the State for the purposes of the performance of the duties of a qualifying employment, the sea-going ship on which he or she, in that period, performs those duties—

(i) visits a port in the United Kingdom, and

(ii) also visits a port other than a port in the State or in the United Kingdom,

then subparagraph (ii) of subsection (2)(*b*) shall not apply to the income, profits or gains from the qualifying employment for such period.][4]

(3) Where for any year of assessment an individual resident in the State makes a claim in that behalf to and satisfies an authorised officer that—

(*a*) the duties of an office or employment to which this section applies of the individual are performed wholly or partly outside the State, and

(*b*) either—

(i) the number of days in that year which are qualifying days in relation to the office or employment (together with any days which are qualifying days in relation to any other such office or employment of the individual), or

(ii) the number of such days referred to in subparagraph (i) in a relevant period in relation to that year,

amounts to at least 90 days [or, in the case where subparagraph (i) applies and the year of assessment concerned is the year of assessment 2001, 67 days][5],

there shall be deducted from the income, profits or gains from the office or employment to be assessed under Schedule D or E, as may be appropriate, an amount equal to the specified amount [in relation to that office or employment or the amount of the income, profits or gains [whichever is the lesser; but that amount, or the aggregate of those amounts where there is more than one such office or employment, shall not exceed [€31,750][6].][7][8]

(4) Notwithstanding anything in the Acts, the income, profits or gains from an office or employment shall for the purposes of this section be deemed not to include any amounts paid in respect of expenses incurred wholly, exclusively and necessarily in the performance of the duties of the office or employment.

Amendments

1 Definition of "qualifying day" substituted by FA 2001 s 31(1)(*a*)(i) with effect from 26 January 2001.

2 Definition of "the specified amount" substituted by FA 1999 s 21(1)(*a*) for 1999–2000 and later tax years and for 1998–99 to the extent that the income, profits or gains to be included in computing the specified amount accrues to an individual on or after 10 March 1999.

3 Substituted by FA 2000 s 47(1)(*b*) with effect from 29 February 2000; previously "14 consecutive days".

4 Subs (2A) inserted by FA 1998 s 14(1)(*c*) with effect from 6 April 1998.

5 Inserted by FA 2001 s 31(1)(*b*)(i) with effect from 6 April 2001.

6 Substituted by FA 2001 s 240(1) and (2)(*a*) and Sch 5 Pt 1 for 2002 and later tax years; previously "£25,000" (short tax "year" 2001: £18,500 (FA 2001 s 31(1)(*b*)(ii))).

7 Substituted by FA 2000 s 47(1)(*c*) with effect for 2000–2001 and later tax years; for 1999–2000, as if the reference to "that amount, or the aggregate of those amounts where there is more than one such office or employment" were a reference to "such portion of that amount, or such portion of the aggregate of those amounts where there is more than one such office or employment, which arises by virtue of income, profits or gains accruing or paid on or after 29 February 2000"; previously "whichever is the lesser".

8 Inserted by FA 1999 s 21(1)(*b*) for 1999–2000 and later tax years and for 1998–99 to the extent that the income, profits or gains to be included in computing the specified amount accrues to an individual on or after 10 March 1999.

Cross-references

Profits or gains do not include chargeable gains within meaning of Capital Gains Tax Acts: s 3(4).
Reduction in income tax for certain income earned outside the State: s 825A(5).
Seafarers allowance: s 472B(5).

Tax Briefing

TB17 No.1 of 1995 p 8 — Foreign earnings deduction.
TB31 Apr 1998 p 10 — Day of departure counts as "qualifying day" where it is followed by a continuous period of absence of at least 13 days.
TB36 June 1999 — Foreign earnings deduction: Finance Act 1999 amendments.
TB40 June 2000 pp 11–12 — Foreign earnings deduction: Finance Act 2000 amendments.
TB43 April 2001 pp 16–17 — Foreign earnings deduction: Finance Act 2001 amendments.

Definitions

month: IA 1937 Sch; profession: s 2(1); trade: s 3(1); year of assessment: ss 2(1), 5(1).

Former enactments

FA 1994 s 154; FA 1995 s 170(1).

Corresponding UK tax provision

Income and Corporation Taxes Act 1988 s 193.

824 Appeals

(1) An individual aggrieved by a decision of an authorised officer on any question arising under the provisions of this [Part][1] which require an individual to satisfy an authorised officer on such a question may, by notice in writing to that effect given to the authorised officer within 2 months from the date on which notice of the decision is given to the individual, make an application to have the question heard and determined by the Appeal Commissioners.

(2) Where an application is made under subsection (1), the Appeal Commissioners shall hear and determine the question concerned in the like manner as an appeal made to them against an assessment, and the provisions of the Acts relating to such an appeal (including the provisions relating to the rehearing of an appeal and to the statement of a case for the opinion of the High Court on a point of law) shall apply accordingly with any necessary modifications.

Amendments

[1] Substituted by FA 2000 s 160 with effect from 23 March 2000; previously "Chapter".

Definitions

Appeal Commissioners: ss 2(1), 850; writing: IA 1937 Sch.

Former enactments

FA 1994 s 156.

825 Residence treatment of donors of gifts to the State

(1) In this section—

"the Acts" means—

(*a*) the Tax Acts,
(*b*) the Capital Gains Tax Acts, and
(*c*) the [Capital Acquisitions Tax Consolidation Act 2003];[1]

"donor" means an individual who makes a gift to the State;

"gift" means a gift of property to the State which, on acceptance of the gift by the Government pursuant to the State Property Act, 1954, becomes vested pursuant to that Act in a State authority within the meaning of that Act;

"Irish tax" means any tax imposed by the Acts;

"property" includes interests and rights of any description;

"relevant date", in relation to an individual (being a donor or the spouse of a donor), means the date (not being earlier than the 1st day of September, 1974) on which the individual leaves the State for the purpose of residence (other than occasional residence) outside the State;

"tax in that country" means any tax imposed in that country which is identical with or substantially similar to Irish tax;

"visits" means—

(*a*) in relation to a donor, visits by the donor to the State after the relevant date for the purpose of advising on the management of the property which is the subject of the gift, being visits that are in the aggregate less than 182 days in any year of assessment in which they are made, and
(*b*) in relation to the spouse of a donor, visits by that spouse when accompanying the donor on visits of the kind referred to in paragraph (*a*).

(2) Where for any year of assessment a person (being a donor or the spouse of a donor) is resident in a country outside the State for the purposes of tax in that country and is chargeable to that tax without any limitation as to chargeability, then, notwithstanding anything to the contrary in the Tax Acts—

(*a*) as respects the year of assessment in which the relevant date occurs, that person shall not as from the relevant date be regarded as ordinarily resident in the State for the purposes of Irish tax, and
(*b*) as respects any subsequent year of assessment, in determining whether that person is resident or ordinarily resident in the State for the purposes of Irish tax, visits shall be disregarded.

Amendments

1 Substituted by CATCA 2003 s 119 and Sch 3 with effect from 21 February 2003; previously "Capital Acquisitions Tax Act 1976".

Definitions

the Government: IA 1937 Sch; person: IA 1937 s 11(*c*); resident: s 5(1); Tax Acts: s 1(2); year of assessment: ss 2(1), 5(1).

Former enactments

FA 1977 s 53.

825A Reduction in income tax for certain income earned outside the State

[(1) In this section—

"authorised officer" has the same meaning as in section 818;

"proprietary director" has the same meaning as in section 472;

"qualifying employment", in relation to a year of assessment, means an office (including an office of director of a company which would be within the charge to corporation tax if it were resident in the State, and which carries on a trade or profession) or employment which is held—

(*a*) outside the State in a territory with the Government of which arrangements are for the time being in force by virtue of [section 826(1)(*a*)][1], and

(*b*) for a continuous period of not less than 13 weeks, but excluding any such office or employment—

(i) the emoluments of which are paid out of the revenue of the State,

(ii) with any board, authority or other similar body established in the State by or under statute;

"the specified amount" in relation to an individual means, as respects the year of assessment concerned, the amount of tax for that year determined by the formula—

$$\frac{A \times B}{C}$$

where—

A is the amount of tax which, apart from this section, would be chargeable on the individual for that year of assessment, other than tax charged in accordance with section 16(2), and after taking account of any such reductions in tax as are specified in the provisions referred to in Part 2 of the Table to section 458 but before credit for any foreign tax paid on any income, profits or gains assessed for that year,

B is the total income of the individual for that year but excluding any income, profits or gains from a qualifying employment for that year,

C is the total income of the individual for that year.

(2) This section shall not apply in any case where the income, profits or gains from a qualifying employment are—

(*a*) chargeable to tax in accordance with section 71(3),

(*b*) income, profits or gains to which section 822 applies, or (*c*) income, profits or gains paid to a proprietary director or to the spouse of that person by a company of which that person is a proprietary director.

(3) Where for any year of assessment an individual resident in the State makes a claim in that behalf to an authorised officer and satisfies that officer that—

(*a*) he or she is in receipt of income, profits or gains from a qualifying employment,

(*b*) the duties of that qualifying employment are performed wholly outside the State in a territory, or territories, with the Government or Governments of which arrangements are for the time being in force by virtue of [section 826(1)(*a*)][2],

(*c*) the full amount of the income, profits or gains from that qualifying employment is, under the laws of the territory in which the qualifying employment is held or of the territory or territories in which the duties of the qualifying employment are performed, subject to, and not exempt or otherwise relieved from, the charge to tax,

(*d*) the foreign tax due on that income, profits or gains from that qualifying employment has been paid and not repaid or entitled to be repaid, and

(*e*) during any week in which he or she is absent from the State for the purposes of the performance of the duties of the qualifying employment, he or she is present in the State for at least one day in that week,

he or she shall, where the amount of tax payable in respect of his or her total income for that year would, but for this section, exceed the specified amount, be entitled to have the amount of tax payable reduced to the specified amount.

(4) In determining for the purposes of paragraph (*b*) of subsection (3) whether the duties of a qualifying employment are exercised outside the State, any duties performed in the State, the performance of which is merely incidental to the performance of the duties of the qualifying employment outside the State, shall be treated for the purposes of this section as having been performed outside the State.

(5) This section shall not apply in any case where the income, profits or gains of a qualifying employment are the subject of a claim for relief under—

(*a*) section 472B, or

(*b*) section 823.

(6) Where in any case an individual has the tax payable in respect of his or her total income for a year of assessment reduced in accordance with subsection (3), that individual shall, notwithstanding anything in Part 35, not be entitled to a credit for foreign tax paid on the income, profits or gains from a qualifying employment in that year.

(7) For the purposes of this section, an individual shall be deemed to be present in the State for a day if the individual is present in the State at the end of the day.

(8) Notwithstanding anything in the Tax Acts, the income, profits or gains from a qualifying employment shall for the purposes of this section be deemed not to include any amounts paid in respect of expenses incurred wholly, exclusively and necessarily in the performance of the duties of the qualifying employment.][3]

Amendments

1 Substituted by FA 2004 s 89 and Sch 3 para 1(*v*) with effect from 25 March 2004; previously "section 826".

2 Substituted by FA 2005 s 147 and Sch 6 para 1(*m*) with effect from 25 March 2005; previously "section 826".

3 Section 825A inserted by FA 1998 s 13 with effect from 6 April 1998.

Cross-references

Profits or gains does not include chargeable gains within the meaning of Capital Gains Tax Acts: s 3(4).
Residence of individuals, subs (3): s 819.

Tax Briefing

TB34 Dec 1998 p 18 — Trans-Border Workers

Definitions

profession: s 2(1); tax: s 3(1); Tax Acts: s 1(2); total income: s 3(1); trade: ss 3(1); 4(1): year of assessment: s 2(1).

PART 35
DOUBLE TAXATION RELIEF

CHAPTER 1
Principal Reliefs

Cross-references

Dealers in securities: s 749(2A)(*a*)(ii), (2B)(*a*).
EU Council Directive 90/434/EEC, credit for tax: s 634(2).
Reduction in income tax for certain income earned outside the State: s 825A(6).

826 Agreements for relief from double taxation

[(1) Where the Government by order declare that arrangements specified in the order have been made with the government of any territory outside the State in relation to—

(*a*) affording relief from double taxation in respect of—

(i) income tax;

(ii) corporation tax in respect of income and chargeable gains;

(iii) any taxes of a similar character imposed by the laws of the State or by the laws of that territory,

or

(*b*) exchanging information for the purposes of the prevention and detection of tax evasion in respect of the taxes specified in paragraph (*a*),

and that it is expedient that those arrangements should have the force of law, then, subject to this section and section 835, the arrangements shall, notwithstanding any enactment, have the force of law.][1]

(2) Schedule 24 shall apply where arrangements which have the force of law by virtue of this section provide that tax payable under the laws of the territory concerned shall be allowed as a credit against tax payable in the State.

(3) Any arrangements to which the force of law is given under this section may include provision for relief from tax for periods before the passing of this Act or before the

making of the arrangements and provisions as to income or chargeable gains which is or are not subject to double taxation, and subsections (1) and (2) shall apply accordingly.

(4) For the purposes of subsection (1), arrangements made with the head of a foreign state shall be regarded as made with the government of that state.

(5) Any order made under this section may be revoked by a subsequent order, and any such revoking order may contain such transitional provisions as appear to the Government to be necessary or expedient.

(6) Where an order is proposed to be made under this section, a draft of the order shall be laid before Dáil Éireann and the order shall not be made until a resolution approving of the draft has been passed by Dáil Éireann.

(7) Where any arrangements have the force of law by virtue of this section, the obligation as to secrecy imposed by any enactment shall not prevent the Revenue Commissioners or any authorised officer of the Revenue Commissioners from disclosing to any authorised officer of the government with which the arrangements are made such information as is required to be disclosed under the arrangements.

(8) The necessary apportionments as respects corporation tax shall be made where arrangements having the force of law by virtue of this section apply to the unexpired portion of an accounting period current at a date specified by the arrangements, and any such apportionment shall be made in proportion to the number of months or fractions of months in the part of the relevant accounting period before that date and in the remaining part of the relevant accounting period respectively.

(9) The Revenue Commissioners may from time to time make regulations generally for carrying out the provisions of this section or any arrangements having the force of law under this section and may in particular, but without prejudice to the generality of the foregoing, by those regulations provide—

(*a*) for securing that relief from taxation imposed by the laws of the territory to which any such arrangements relate does not enure to the benefit of persons not entitled to such relief, and

(*b*) for authorising, in cases where tax deductible from any periodical payment has, in order to comply with any such arrangements, not been deducted and it is discovered that the arrangements do not apply to that payment, the recovery of the tax by assessment on the person entitled to the payment or by deduction from subsequent payments.

Amendments

[1] Subs (1) substituted by FA 2003 s 38(*a*) with effect from 1 January 2003.

Cross-references

Application in relation to corporation profits tax under old law, subs (7): s 827.

Application of s 130 to certain interest, certain interest not to be treated as a distribution: s 452(1)(*a*)("arrangements").

Capital gains tax: s 828(1), (2); subs (7): s 828(3).

Capital gains tax, temporary non-residents, meaning of "arrangements" applied: s 29A(4).

Certain interest not to be chargeable, meaning of "arrangements" applied: s 198(1)(*a*)("relevant territory").

Companies' chargeable gains, groups of companies, interpretation, meaning of "arrangements" applied: s 616(7) ("relevant Member State").

Company residence, meaning of "arrangements" applied: s 23A(1)(*a*).

Corporation tax relief, dividends from a non-resident subsidiary: s 222(1)(*b*).
Deemed disposal of assets where company ceases to be resident in State, meaning of "arrangements" applied: s 627(2)(*b*)("relevant territory").
Distributions to certain non-residents, meaning of "arrangements" applied: s 153(1) ("relevant territory").
Dividends regarded as paid out of profits accumulated before given date: Sch 22 para 4(2).
Dividend withholding tax (interpretation), meaning of "arrangements" applied: s 172A(1)(*a*) ("relevant territory").
EU Council Directive 90/434/EEC, mergers, divisions, transfers of assets, meaning of bilateral agreement applied: s 630.
Exemption from tax in the case of gains on certain disposals of shares, meaning of "arrangements" applied: s 626B(1)(*a*)("relevant territory").
Foreign life policies, taxation and returns of certain policies, interpretation and application, meaning of "arrangements" applied: s 730H(1)("offshore state").
Foreign tax incentive reliefs: s 829(2), (3).
Group relief, group payments, meaning of "arrangements" applied: s 410(1)(*a*) ("relevant Member State").
Group relief, surrender of relief between members of groups and consortia, meaning of "arrangements" applied: s 411(1)(*a*) ("relevant Member State").
Implementation of Council Directive 90/435/EEC concerning the common system of taxation applicable in the case of parent companies and subsidiaries of different Member States, meaning of "arrangements" applied: s 831(1)(*a*).
Implementation of Council Directive 2003/49/EC of 3 June 2003 on a common system of taxation applicable to interest and royalty payments made between associated companies of different Member States, interpretation, meaning of "arrangements" applied: s 267G(1).
Implementation of Council Directive 2003/48/EC on Taxation of Savings Income in the Form of Interest Payments, credit for withholding tax: s 898M(3)(*a*), (*b*).
Information for tax authorities in other territories: s 912A(1).
Interest paid by companies and to non-residents, meaning of "arrangements" applied: s 246(1) ("relevant territory").
Interest paid to company resident in a treaty country not a distribution: s 452(1)(*b*).
Matters to be treated as distributions, meaning of "arrangements" applied: s 130(3)(*d*) ("relevant Member State").
Meaning of "close company", meaning of "arrangements" applied: s 430(1)(*da*)(ii), (2A)(*a*).
Miscellaneous exemptions for certain kinds of property, meaning of "arrangements" applied: s 613(6)(*a*).
Offshore funds, taxation and returns of certain offshore funds, interpretation and application, meaning of "arrangements" applied: s 747B(1).
Overseas pension plans, migrant member relief, interpretation and general, meaning of "arrangements" applied: s 787M(1) ("resident").
Petroleum trade, interest and charges on income: s 690(2)(*c*).
Provisions as to relief from income tax and corporation tax by means of credit in respect of foreign tax, meaning of "arrangements" applied: Sch 24 para 1(1) ("arrangements", "relevant Member State"); limit on total credit — income tax: Sch 24 para 5(2).
Reduction in income tax for certain income earned outside the State, subs (1)(*a*): s 825A(1), (3).
Relevant territory, securities issued by Minister for Finance: s 44(1).
Relief for investment in films, meaning of "arrangements" applied: s 481(2C)(*b*)(i)(II).
Repayment of tax: s 865(1)("correlative adjustment").
Restriction on deductibility of certain interest, meaning of "arrangements" applied: s 817C(3).
Return by settlor in relation to non-resident trustees, meaning of "arrangements" applied: s 917B(1).
Shipping tonnage tax, exclusion of reliefs, deductions and set-offs: s 697M(3)(*b*).
Treatment for double taxation relief purposes of foreign tax incentive reliefs: s 829(2), (3).
Trustees ceasing to be resident in the State, meaning of "arrangements" applied: s 579B(1).

Statutory instruments

Country	*Treaty signed*	*Treaty ratified*	*SI No*	*Effective date*		
				Income tax	*Corporation tax*	*Capital gains tax*
Australia	31 May 1983	21 Dec 1983	406/1983	6 April 1984	1 Jan 1984	6 April 1984
Austria	24 May 1966	5 Jan 1968	250/1967	6 April 1964	1 April 1964*	
(Protocol)	19 June 1987	9 Dec 1988	29/1988	6 April 1976	1 Jan 1974	6 April 1974
Belgium	24 June 1970	31 Dec 1973	66 /1973	6 April 1973	1 April 1973*	

Bulgaria	5 Oct 2000	5 Jan 2001	372/2000	1 Jan 2003	1 Jan 2002	1 Jan 2003
Canada	23 Nov 1966	6 Dec 1967	212/1967	6 April 1968	1 Jan 1968*	
Canada (re-negotiation)	8 Oct 2003 (not in force)		773/2004			
China	19 April 2000	28 Dec 2000	373/2000	6 April 2001	1 Jan 2001	6 April 2001
Croatia	21 June 2002	29 Oct 2003	574/2002	1 Jan 2004	1 Jan 2004	1 Jan 2004
Cyprus	24 Sept 1968	4 Dec 1970	79/1970	6 April 1962	1 April 1962*	
Czech Republic	14 Nov 1995	21 April 1996	321/1995	1 Jan 1997	1 Jan 1997	1 Jan 1997
Denmark	26 March 1993	8 Oct 1993	286/1993	6 April 1994	1 Jan 1994	6 April 1994
Estonia	16 Dec 1997	23 Dec 1998	496/1998	6 April 1999	1 Jan 1999	6 April 1999
Finland	27 March 1992	26 Nov 1993	289/1993	6 April 1990	1 Jan 1990	6 April 1990
France	21 March 1968	15 June 1971	162/1970	6 April 1966	1 April 1966*	
Germany	17 Oct 1962	2 April 1964	212/1962	6 April 1959	1 April 1959*	
Greece	24 Nov 2003	29 Dec 2004	774/2004	1 Jan 2005	1 Jan 2005	1 Jan 2005
Hungary	25 April 1995	5 Dec 1996	301/1995	6 April 1997	1 Jan 1997	6 April 1997
Iceland	17 Dec 2003	17 Dec 2004	775/2004	1 Jan 2005	1 Jan 2005	1 Jan 2005
India	6 Nov 2000	26 Dec 2001	521/2001	1 Jan 2002	1 Jan 2002	1 Jan 2002
Israel	20 Nov 1995	24 Dec 1995	323/1995	6 April 1996	1 Jan 1996	6 April 1996
Italy	11 June 1971	14 Feb 1975	61/1973	6 April 1967	1 April 1967*	
Japan	18 Jan 1974	4 Nov 1974	259/1974	6 April 1974	1 April 1974*	
Korea (Rep of)	18 July 1990	27 Nov 1991	290/1991	6 April 1992	1 Jan 1992	6 April 1992
Latvia	13 Nov 1997	28 Jan 1998	504/1997	6 April 1999	1 Jan 1999	6 April 1999
Luthuania	18 Nov 1997	19 Feb 1998	503/1997	6 April 1999	1 Jan 1999	6 April 1999
Luxembourg	14 Jan 1972	25 Feb 1975	65/1973	6 April 1968	1 April 1968*	
Malaysia	28 Nov 1998	11 Sept 1999	495/1998	6 April 2000	1 Jan 2000	6 April 2000
Mexico	22 Oct 1998	31 Dec 1998	497/1998	6 April 1999	1 Jan 1999	6 April 1999
Netherlands	11 Feb 1969	12 May 1970	22/1970	6 April 1965	1 April 1965*	
New Zealand	19 Sept 1986	26 Sept 1988	30/1988	6 April 1989	1 Jan 1989	6 April 1989
Norway (1969)	21 Oct 1969	21 Aug 1970	80/1970	6 April 1967	1 April 1967*	
Norway (2000)	22 Nov 2000	27 Nov 2001	520/2001	1 Jan 2002	1 Jan 2002	1 Jan 2002
Pakistan	13 April 1973	20 Dec 1974	260/1974	6 April 1968	April 1968*	
Poland	13 Nov 1995	22 Dec 1995	322/1995	6 April 1996	1 Jan 1996	6 April 1996
Portugal	1 June 1993	11 July 1994	102/1994	6 April 1995	1 Jan 1995	6 April 1995
Romania	21 Oct 1999	29 Dec 2000	427/1999	6 April 2001	1 Jan 2001	6 April 2001
Russia	29 April 1994	7 July 1995	428/1994	6 April 1996	1 Jan 1996	6 April 1996
Slovak Rep	8 June 1999	30 Dec 1999	426/1999	6 April 2000	1 Jan 2000	6 April 2000
Slovenia	12 Mar 2002	11 Dec 2002	73/2003	1 Jan 2003	1 Jan 2003	1 Jan 2003
South Africa	7 Oct 1997	5 Dec 1997	478/1997	6 April 1998	1 Jan 1998	6 April 1998
Spain	10 Feb 1994	21 Nov 1994	308/1994	6 April 1995	1 Jan 1995	6 April 1995
Sweden	8 Oct 1986	5 April 1988	348/1987	6 April 1988	1 Jan 1989	6 April 1988
(Protocol)	1 July 1993	21 Dec 1993	398/1993	20 Jan 1994	20 Jan 1994	20 Jan 1994
Switzerland	8 Nov 1966	16 Feb 1968	240/1967	6 April 1965	1 April 1965*	
(Protocol)	24 Oct 1980	25 April 1984	76/1984	6 April 1976	1 Jan 1974	6 April 1974
United Kingdom	2 June 1976	23 Dec 1976	319/1976	6 April 1976	1 Jan 1974	6 April 1976

(Protocol)	7 Nov 1994	21 Sept 1995	209/1995	6 April 1994	1 April 1994	
(Protocol)	4 Nov 1998	23 Dec 1998	494/1998	6 April 1999	1 Jan 1999	6 April 1999
USA	28 July 1997	17 Dec 1997	477/1997	6 April 1998	1 Jan 1998	6 April 1998
(Protocol)	24 Sept 1999	13 July 2000	425/1999	1 Sept 2000	1 Sept 2000	1 Sept 2000
Zambia	29 March 1971	31 July 1973	130/1973	6 April 1967	1 April 1967*	

* Corporation profits tax.

An agreement replacing the existing treaty with Canada was signed on 8 October 2003, and parliamentary procedures to bring the treaty into force were completed by Ireland in December 2004. Subject to the necessary parliamentary procedures being completed by Canada in 2005, it is expected that this treaty will become effective for tax periods in 2006. New treaties with Argentina, Chile, Egypt, Kuwait, Malta, Morocco, Singapore, Tunisia, Turkey and Ukraine are being negotiated. Existing treaties with Cyprus and France are in the process of re-negotiation.

Representations regarding proposed conventions may be made to: the International Section, Direct Taxes International & Administration Division, Office of the Revenue Commissioners, Dublin Castle, Dublin 2.

Case law

Subs (1): s 130(2)(*d*)(iv) concerning interest to be treated as distribution held to take precedence over the application of the wording in Article 12 of the Ireland/Japan Double Taxation Convention (SI 259/1974): *Murphy v Asahi Synthetic Fibres (Ireland) Ltd* [1986] IR 777. See s 690(2).

Revenue precedents

Issue: Is credit available in this country for UK composite rate tax which applied to interest payments on deposits from 6 April 1985 to 5 April 1991?

Decision: No credit available in this country.

Definitions

Dáil Éireann: IA 1937 Sch; the Government: IA 1937 Sch; person: IA 1937 s 11(*c*); month: IA 1937 Sch.

Former enactments

ITA 1967 s 361; FA 1974 s 86 and Sch 2 Pt I; CTA 1976 s 22(2), s 23(1) and s 166(1) and Sch 4 Pt I; FA 1983 s 47(4).

Corresponding UK tax provision

Income and Corporation Taxes Act 1988 s 788.

827 Application to corporation tax of arrangements made in relation to corporation profits tax under old law

Subject to any express amendments made by the Corporation Tax Acts and except in so far as arrangements made on or after the 31st day of March, 1976, provide otherwise, any arrangements made under section 361 of the Income Tax Act, 1967, or any earlier enactment corresponding to that section, in relation to corporation profits tax shall apply in relation to corporation tax and income and chargeable gains chargeable to corporation tax as they are expressed to apply in relation to corporation profits tax and profits chargeable to corporation profits tax, and not as they apply in relation to income tax; but this section shall not affect the operation, as they apply to corporation tax, of section 826(7) and paragraph 12 of Schedule 24.

Cross-references

Manufacturing (10%) rate, meaning of "relevant corporation tax": s 448(1)(*d*).

Former enactments

CTA 1976 ss 22(1), 23(1).

Corresponding UK tax provision

Income and Corporation Taxes Act 1988 s 789.

828 Capital gains tax: double taxation relief

(1) For the purposes of giving relief from double taxation in relation to capital gains tax charged under the law of any country outside the State, in section 826 and Schedule 24 as they apply for the purposes of income tax, for references to income there shall be substituted references to chargeable gains, for references to the Income Tax Acts there shall be substituted references to the Capital Gains Tax Acts and for references to income tax there shall be substituted references to capital gains tax meaning, as the context may require, tax charged under the law of the State or tax charged under the law of a country outside the State.

(2) In so far as capital gains tax charged under the law of a country outside the State may by virtue of this section be taken into account under section 826 and Schedule 24 as applied by this section, that tax, whether relief is given by virtue of this section in respect of it or not, shall not be taken into account for the purposes of those provisions as they apply apart from this section.

(3) Section 826(7) shall apply in relation to capital gains tax as it applies in relation to income tax.

(4) Subject to subsections (1) to (3) and the other provisions of the Capital Gains Tax Acts relating to double taxation, the tax chargeable under the law of any country outside the State on the disposal of an asset which is borne by the person making the disposal shall be allowable as a deduction in the computation under Chapter 2 of Part 19 of the gain accruing on the disposal.

Cross-references

Disposals to State, public bodies and charities, subs (4): s 611(1)(*a*).

Miscellaneous exemptions for certain kinds of property: s 613(6)(*a*).

Overseas life assurance companies, income tax, foreign tax and tax credit, subs (4): s 729(6).

Return by settlor in relation to non-resident trustees: s 917B(1).

Shipping tonnage tax, exclusion of reliefs, deductions and set-offs: s 697M(3)(*b*).

Trustees ceasing to be resident in the State: s 579B(1) (arrangements).

Former enactments

CGTA 1975 ss 38, 51(1) and Sch 1 Pt I para 3(6); FA 1997 s 146(1) and Sch 9 Pt I para 9(3).

Corresponding UK tax provision

Income and Corporation Taxes Act 1988 s 788.

---

829 Treatment for double taxation relief purposes of foreign tax incentive reliefs

(1) This section shall apply to any relief given with a view to promoting industrial, commercial, scientific, educational or other development in a territory outside the State.

(2) For the purposes of section 826 and Schedule 24, any amount of tax under the law of a territory outside the State which would have been payable but for a relief to which this section applies given under that law (being a relief with respect to which provision is made in arrangements for double taxation relief which are the subject of an order under section 826(1)) shall be treated as having been payable, and references in [section 826(1)(*a*)][1] and in Schedule 24 to double taxation, tax payable or chargeable or tax not chargeable directly or by deduction shall be construed accordingly.

(3) The Revenue Commissioners may make regulations generally for carrying out the provisions of this section or any arrangements having the force of law under section 826 and may in particular, but without prejudice to the generality of the foregoing, provide in the regulations—

(*a*) for the purposes of this section or of the regulations, for the application (with or without modifications) of any provision of the Tax Acts or any regulations made under those Acts, including the provisions relating to the rehearing of an appeal and to the statement of a case for the opinion of the High Court on a point of law, and

(*b*) that the whole or any part of a dividend paid out of profits or gains which consist of or include profits or gains in relation to which double taxation relief is given by virtue of this section is not to be regarded as income or profits for any purpose of the Tax Acts.

Amendments

1 Substituted by FA 2004 s 89 and Sch 3 para 1(*w*) with effect from 25 March 2004; previously "section 826".

Definitions

High Court: IA 1937 Sch; Income Tax Acts: s 1(2).

Former enactments

FA 1970 s 57(2)–(5); CTA 1976 s 166(1) and Sch 4 Pt I.

CHAPTER 2

Miscellaneous

830 Relief to certain companies liable to foreign tax

(1) In this section—

"accounting period" includes a part of an accounting period;

"external tax" means a tax chargeable and payable under the law of the territory in which the paying company is resident, being a territory to which this section applies, and which corresponds to Irish corporation tax or income tax or both of those taxes, but a tax payable under the law of a province, state or other part of a country, or which is levied by or on behalf of a municipality or other local body, shall for the purposes of this subsection be deemed not to correspond to those taxes.

[(2) This section shall apply to every territory other than a territory with the Government of which arrangements are for the time being in force by virtue of [section 826(1)(*a*)][1].][2]

(3) Where a company (in this section referred to as **"the investing company"**) has paid by deduction or otherwise, or is liable to pay, by reference to any part of its income arising in a territory to which this section applies, tax for any accounting period and it is shown to the satisfaction of the Revenue Commissioners that—

(*a*) that part of the investing company's income consists of a dividend or interest paid to it by a company resident in the territory (in this section referred to as **"the paying company"**) not less than 50 per cent of the voting power in which is controlled directly or indirectly by the investing company, (*b*) that dividend or interest arose from the investment in the paying company by the investing company, whether by means of loan or otherwise, of a sum or sums representing—

(i) profits the Irish tax referable to which was reduced to nil under—

(I) Part III of the Finance (Miscellaneous Provisions) Act, 1956,

(II) Chapter IV of Part XXV of the Income Tax Act, 1967, or

(III) Part IV of the Corporation Tax Act, 1976,

(ii) such proportion of profits the Irish tax referable to which was reduced otherwise than to nil under those provisions as is equal to the proportion by which that Irish tax has been so reduced, or

(iii) profits arising from exempted trading operations which by virtue of—

(I) Parts I and II of the Finance (Miscellaneous Provisions) Act, 1958,

(II) Chapter I of Part XXV of the Income Tax Act, 1967, or

(III) Part V of the Corporation Tax Act, 1976,

were not, in relation to the company by which such operations were carried on, taken into account for any purpose of—

(A) the Income Tax Acts,

(B) Part V of the Finance Act, 1920, and the enactments amending or extending that Part, or

(C) the Corporation Tax Acts,

and

(*c*) the investing company has paid external tax in the territory in respect of that part of its income,

then, the Revenue Commissioners may grant to the investing company in respect of that accounting period such relief as is just with a view to affording relief in respect of the double taxation of that part of the investing company's income, but not exceeding the lesser of—

(*aa*) 50 per cent of the total of the corporation tax which but for this section would be payable by the investing company in respect of that part of its income, and

(*bb*) the amount of the external tax paid or payable in the territory in respect of that part of its income after deduction of any relief to which the company may be entitled in that territory.

(4) (*a*) External tax paid by the paying company in respect of its profits shall be taken into account in considering whether any, and if so what, relief ought to be allowed in respect of a dividend paid by the paying company to the investing company, and for the purposes of this section (other than this subsection) such tax or the appropriate part of such tax shall be regarded as external tax paid by the investing company.

(*b*) Paragraph 8 of Schedule 24 shall apply for the purpose of ascertaining the amount of the external tax paid by the paying company which is to be taken into account in relation to any dividend paid by the paying company to the investing company as it applies to the computation of foreign tax to be taken into account for the purposes of that paragraph.

(5) (*a*) Nothing in this section shall authorise the granting of relief under this section to any company in respect of any accounting period to such an extent as would reduce the aggregate amount (computed after deduction of any relief to which the company may be entitled in the territory) of the corporation tax and external tax payable by such company in respect of any part of its income of the kind described in subsection (3)(*a*) arising in a territory to which this section applies below the amount of corporation tax which would be payable by the company in respect of that part of its income if that part of its income had arisen in the State and had been liable in the hands of the investing company to corporation tax.

(*b*) In computing for the purposes of paragraph (*a*) the amount of corporation tax which would be so payable by the company in respect of that part of its income if that part had arisen in the State—

(i) no deduction for external tax shall be made from that part of its income, and

(ii) where pursuant to subsection (4) external tax paid by the paying company is regarded as external tax paid by the investing company, that part of the investing company's income shall be treated as increased by the amount of the external tax which is so regarded.

(6) Relief under this section shall be given as a credit against corporation tax chargeable by reference to the part of the investing company's income referred to in subsection (3)(*a*).

(7) (*a*) Any claim for relief under this section shall be made in writing to the inspector not later than 6 years from the end of the accounting period to which it relates.

(*b*) An appeal to the Appeal Commissioners shall lie on any question arising under this section in the like manner as an appeal would lie against an assessment to corporation tax, and the provisions of the Tax Acts relating to appeals shall apply accordingly.

Amendments

1 Substituted by FA 2004 s 89 and Sch 3 para 1(*x*) with effect from 25 March 2004; previously "section 826".

2 Subs (2) substituted by FA 1998 s 48 and Sch 3 para 9 with effect from 1 January 1998 for corporation tax and 6 April 1998 for income tax; previously:

"(2) This section shall apply to every territory other than—

(*a*) Northern Ireland and Great Britain,

(*b*) the United States of America, and

(*c*) a territory with the Government of which arrangements are for the time being in force by virtue of section 826."

Cross-references

Provisions as to relief from income tax and corporation tax by means of credit in respect of foreign tax, limit on total credit — income tax: Sch 24 para 5(3).

Definitions

Appeal Commissioners: ss 2(1), 850; company: ss 4(1), 5(1); Great Britain: IA 1937 Sch; Income Tax Acts: s 1(2); inspector: ss 2(1), 5(1), 852; interest: s 4(1); Tax Acts: s 1(2); profits: s 4(1); writing: IA 1937 Sch.

Former enactments

CTA 1976 s 163.

Corresponding UK tax provision

Income and Corporation Taxes Act 1988 s 788.

831 Implementation of Council Directive No 90/435/EEC concerning the common system of taxation applicable in the case of parent companies and subsidiaries of different Member States

(1) (*a*) In this section—

"arrangements" means arrangements having the force of law by virtue of [section 826(1)(*a*)][1] ;

"bilateral agreement" means any arrangements, protocol or other agreement between the Government and the government of another Member State;

[**"company"** ...[2] means a company of a Member State;][3]

"company of a Member State" has the meaning assigned to it by Article 2 of the Directive;

"the Directive" means Council Directive No 90/435/EEC of 23 July 1990[, as amended by Council Directive No 2003/123/EC of 22 December 2003 (OJ No L. 7 of 13.1.2004, p. 41),][4] (OJ No L225 of 20.8.1990, p 6) on the common system of taxation applicable in the case of parent companies and subsidiaries of different Member States;

"distribution" means income from shares or from other rights, not being debt claims, to participate in a company's profits, and includes any amount assimilated to income from shares under the taxation laws of the State of which the company making the distribution is resident;

"foreign tax" means any tax which—

(i) is payable under the laws of a Member State other than the State, and

(ii) (I) is specified in paragraph (*c*) of Article 2 of the Directive, or

(II) is substituted for and is substantially similar to a tax so specified;

"Member State" means a Member State of the European Communities;

[**"parent company"** means a company (referred to in this definition as the "first-mentioned company") being—

[(i) a company which owns at least 5 per cent of the share capital of another company which is not resident in the State, or][5]

(ii) a company not resident in the State which owns at least [5 per cent][6] of the share capital of another company which is resident in the State,

but where a bilateral agreement contains a provision to the effect—

(I) that a company shall only be a parent company during any uninterrupted period of at least 2 years throughout which at least [5 per cent][6] of the share capital of the other company is owned by the first-mentioned company, or

(II) that—

(A) the requirement (being the requirement for the purposes of this definition) that a company own at least [5 per cent][6] of the share capital of another shall be treated as a requirement that the first-mentioned company holds at least [5 per cent][6] of the voting rights in the other company, or

(B) that requirement shall be so treated and a company shall only be a parent company during any uninterrupted period of at least 2 years throughout which at least [5 per cent][6] of the voting rights in the other company is held by the first-mentioned company,

then, in its application to a company to which the provision in the bilateral agreement applies, this definition shall apply subject to that provision and shall be construed accordingly;

"tax", in relation to a relevant territory, means any tax imposed in that territory which corresponds to income tax or corporation tax in the State.][7]

(*b*) For the purposes of this section, a company shall be a subsidiary of another company which owns shares or holds voting rights in it where the other company's ownership of those shares or holding of those rights is sufficient for that other company to be a parent company.

(*c*) A word or expression used in this section and in the Directive has, unless the contrary intention appears, the same meaning in this section as in the Directive.

(2) Subject to subsections (3) and (4), where a parent company ...[8] receives a distribution chargeable in the State to corporation tax, other than a distribution in a winding up, from its subsidiary [which is a company not resident in the State][9]—

(*a*) credit shall be allowed for—

[(i) any withholding tax charged on the distribution by a Member State pursuant to a derogation duly given from Article 5.1 of the Directive,][10]

(ii) any foreign tax, not chargeable directly or by deduction in respect of the distribution, which is borne by the company making the distribution, and is properly attributable to the proportion of its profits which is represented by the distribution, in so far as that foreign tax exceeds so much of any tax credit in respect of the distribution as is payable to the parent company by the Member State in which the company making the distribution is [resident, and][11]

[(iii) any foreign tax borne by a company that would be allowed under paragraph 9B of Schedule 24 if in subparagraphs (2) and (3) "and is connected with the relevant company" in each place where it occurs were deleted.][12]

against corporation tax in respect of the distribution to the extent that credit for such withholding tax and foreign tax would not otherwise be so allowed, and

(*b*) notwithstanding Chapter 2 of Part 4, the distribution shall not be a dividend to which that Chapter applies.

[(2A) Subject to subsections (3) and (4), where by virtue of the legal characteristics of a subsidiary (being a company which is not resident in the State) of a parent company, the parent company is chargeable to tax in the State on its share of the profits of the subsidiary company as they arise credit shall be allowed for so much of—

(*a*) any foreign tax borne by the subsidiary, and

(*b*) any foreign tax that would be treated as tax paid by the subsidiary company under paragraph 9B of Schedule 24 if—
(i) the subsidiary company were the foreign company for the purposes of that paragraph, and
(ii) in subparagraphs (2) and (3) of that paragraph "and is connected with the relevant company" in both places where it occurs were deleted,

as is properly attributable to the proportion of the subsidiary's profits which are chargeable on the parent company in the State against corporation tax in respect of the profits so chargeable on the parent company to the extent that credit for such foreign tax would not otherwise be so allowed.][13]

(3) Where by virtue of subsection (2)(*a*) [or (2A)][14] a company is to be allowed credit for tax payable under the laws of a Member State other than the State, Schedule 24 shall apply for the purposes of that subsection as if—

(*a*) the provisions of that subsection were arrangements providing that tax so payable shall be allowed as a credit against tax payable in the State, and
(*b*) references in Schedule 24 to a dividend were references to a distribution within the meaning of this section.

(4) Subsection (2) shall apply without prejudice to any provision of a bilateral agreement.

[(5) Chapter 8A of Part 6, other than section 172K, shall not apply to a distribution made to a parent company which is not resident in the State by its subsidiary which is a company resident in the State.

...[15]

(6) Subsection (5) shall not have effect in relation to a distribution made to a parent company if the majority of the voting rights in the parent company are controlled directly or indirectly by persons, other than persons who by virtue of the law of any relevant territory are resident for the purposes of tax in such a relevant territory (within the meaning assigned by section 172A), unless it is shown that the parent company exists for bona fide commercial reasons and does not form part of any arrangement or scheme of which the main purpose, or one of the main purposes, is the avoidance of liability to income tax (including dividend withholding tax under Chapter 8A of Part 6), corporation tax or capital gains tax.][16]

Amendments

1 Substituted by FA 2004 s 89 and Sch 3 para 1(*y*) with effect from 25 March 2004; previously "section 826".

2 Deleted by FA 2004 s 34(*a*)(i) with effect from 1 January 2004; previously ", other than in the expression 'unlimited company' in subsection (5A),".

3 Definition of "company" substituted by FA 2000 s 33(*a*) as respects distributions made on or after 6 April 2000.

4 Inserted by FA 2004 s 34(*a*)(ii) with effect from 1 January 2004.

5 Subs (1)(definition of "parent company")(i) substituted by FA 2004 s 34(*a*)(iii)(I) with effect from 1 January 2004.

6 Substituted by FA 2004 s 34(*a*)(iii)(II) with effect from 1 January 2004; previously "25 per cent".

7 Definition of "parent company" substituted by FA 1999 s 29(*a*) with effect from 6 April 1999.

8 Deleted by FA 2004 s 34(*b*)(i) with effect from 1 January 2004; previously "which is resident in this State".

9 Inserted by FA 1999 s 29(*b*)(ii) with effect from 6 April 1999.

[10] Subs (2)(*a*)(i) substituted by FA 2004 s 34(*b*)(ii)(I) with effect from 1 January 2004.
[11] Substituted by FA 2004 s 34(*b*)(ii)(II) with effect from 1 January 2004; previously "resident,".
[12] Subs (2)(*a*)(iii) inserted by FA 2004 s 34(*b*)(ii)(III) with effect from 1 January 2004.
[13] Subs (2A) inserted by FA 2004 s 34(*c*) with effect from 1 January 2004.
[14] Inserted by FA 2004 s 34(*d*) with effect from 1 January 2004.
[15] Subs (5A) deleted by FA 2004 s 34(*e*) with effect from 1 January 2004.
[16] Subss (5)–(6) inserted by FA 1999 s 29(*c*) with effect from 6 April 1999.

Cross-references

Distributions to certain non-residents: s 153(5).
Dividend withholding tax on relevant distributions: s 172B(6).
Double taxation relief, unilateral relief: Sch 24, para 9A(5).

Case law

Two year holding period for 25% share: *Denkavit International BV and ors v Bundemsamt fur Finanzen*, ECJ 291/94, 292/94 [1996] STC 1445.

Tax Briefing

TB55 April 2004 p 7 — Parent and Subsidiary Companies.

Definitions

company: ss 4(1), 5(1); distribution: ss 4(1), 436, 437; the Government: IA 1937 Sch; shares: s 5(1); tax credit: ss 2(1), 136; year: IA 1937 Sch.

Former enactments

FA 1991 s 36.

831A Treatment of distributions to certain parent companies

[(1) (*a*) In this section—

"company", in relation to a company that is resident for the purposes of tax in Switzerland, means a company which—

(i) takes one of the forms specified in Article 15 of the Agreement attached to the Council Decision (2004/911/EC) of 2 June 2004 on the signing and conclusion of the Agreement between the European Community and the Swiss Confederation providing for measures equivalent to those laid down in Council Directive 2003/48/EC of 3 June 2003 on taxation of savings income in the form of interest payments and the accompanying Memorandum of Understanding (OJ No L381, 28.12.2004, p 32), and

(ii) is subject to tax in Switzerland without being exempt;

"parent company" means a company which controls not less than 25 per cent of the voting power in another company;

"tax", in relation to Switzerland, means any tax imposed in Switzerland which corresponds to income tax or corporation tax in the State.

(*b*) For the purposes of this section a company shall be a subsidiary of another company which holds voting rights in it where the other company's holding of those rights is sufficient for that other company to be a parent company.

(2) Chapter 8A of Part 6, other than section 172K, shall not apply to a distribution made to a parent company which is, by virtue of the law of Switzerland, resident for the purposes of tax in Switzerland by its subsidiary which is a company resident in the State.][1]

Amendments

[1] Section 831A inserted by FA 2005 s 51(1) as respects a distribution made on or after 1 July 2005.

Definitions

company; ss 4(1), 5(1); distribution: ss 4(1), 436, 437.

832 Provisions in relation to Convention for reciprocal avoidance of double taxation in the State and the United Kingdom of income and capital gains

(1) In this section—

"the Convention" means the Convention between the Government of Ireland and the Government of the United Kingdom for the avoidance of double taxation and the prevention of fiscal evasion with respect to taxes on income and capital gains, and the Protocol amending the Convention, both of which are set out in the Schedule to the Double Taxation Relief (Taxes on Income and Capital Gains) (United Kingdom) Order, 1976 [(SI No 319 of 1976).][1]

...[2].

...[3].

(3) For the purpose of giving effect to the Convention, the Tax Acts shall, for any year for which the Convention is in force, apply subject to the modifications in section 73.

(4) (*a*) In applying section 707 in the case of a society registered under the enactments for the time being in force in the United Kingdom corresponding to the Friendly Societies Acts, 1896 to 1977, only expenses of management attributable to the life business referable to contracts of assurance made on or after the 6th day of April, 1976, shall be taken into account.

(*b*) In applying subsection (4) of section 726 in the case of a society referred to in paragraph (*a*), there shall be excluded from the liabilities of which B in that subsection is the average any liabilities to policy holders arising from contracts made before the 6th day of April, 1976.

(*c*) This subsection shall be construed as one with Part 26.

Amendments

1 Substituted by FA 1999 s 67(1)(*a*)(i) with effect from 6 April 1999 for income tax and 1 January 1999 for corporation tax; previously "(SI No 319 of 1976);".

2 Definition of "dividend" deleted by FA 1999 s 67(1)(*a*)(ii) with effect from 6 April 1999 for income tax and 1 January 1999 for corporation tax.

3 Subs (2) deleted by FA 1999 s 67(1)(*b*) with effect from 6 April 1999 for income tax and 1 January 1999 for corporation tax.

Definitions

the Government: IA 1937 Sch; person: IA 1937 s 11(*c*); Tax Acts: s 1(2); tax credit: ss 2(1), 136; year of assessment: ss 2(1), 5(1).

Former enactments

FA 1977 s 39(1) and (3)–(5); FA 1996 s 132(2) and Sch 5 Pt II.

833 Convention with United States of America

Amendments

Deleted by FA 1998 s 48 and Sch 3 para 10 with effect from 1 January 1998 for corporation tax and 6 April 1998 for income tax and capital gains tax.

834 Relief in respect of ships documented under laws of United States of America

Amendments

Deleted by FA 1998 s 48 and Sch 3 para 10 with effect from 1 January 1998 for corporation tax and 6 April 1998 for income tax and capital gains tax.

835 Saver for arrangements made under section 362 of Income Tax Act, 1967

Notwithstanding the repeal of section 362 of the Income Tax Act, 1967, by section 23(1) of the Finance Act, 1987, where before the 9th day of July, 1987, an order was made under section 362 of the Income Tax Act, 1967, the arrangement to which the order relates shall continue to have the force of law.

Statutory instruments

Double taxation agreements etc: s 826(1).

Sea or air transport agreements in force:

Territory outside the State	Relevant Statutory Instrument
South Africa	SI 210/1959
Spain	SI 26/1977

Former enactments

FA 1987 s 23(2).

PART 36
MISCELLANEOUS SPECIAL PROVISIONS

836 Allowances for expenses of members of Oireachtas

(1) An allowance payable under section 3 of the Oireachtas (Allowances to Members) and Ministerial and Parliamentary Offices (Amendment) Act, 1992, shall be exempt from income tax and shall not be reckoned in computing income for the purposes of the Income Tax Acts.

[(1A) Subsection (1) shall apply to—

(*a*) an allowance payable under section 2 of the Oireachtas (Allowances to Members) Act, 1938, and section 5 of the Oireachtas (Allowances to Members) and Ministerial and Parliamentary Offices (Amendment) Act, 1964, in respect of travelling facilities within the meaning of the first-mentioned Act, and

(*b*) an allowance payable under section 1 or 2 of the Oireachtas (Allowances to Members) Act, 1962,

as it applies to an allowance payable under section 3 of the Oireachtas (Allowances to Members) and Ministerial and Parliamentary Offices (Amendment) Act, 1992.][1]

(2) Sections 114 and 115 shall not apply in relation to expenses in full settlement of which an allowance is payable under section 3 of the Oireachtas (Allowances to Members) and Ministerial and Parliamentary Offices (Amendment) Act, 1992, and no claim shall lie under those sections in respect of those expenses; but where a Minister of the Government, the Attorney General or a Minister of State, being—

(*a*) a member of Dáil Éireann for a constituency outside the county borough and the administrative county of Dublin, or

(*b*) a member of Seanad Éireann whose main residence is situated outside that county borough and administrative county,

is, arising out of the performance of his or her duties as an office holder or as a member of the Oireachtas, obliged to maintain a second residence in addition to his or her main residence, he or she shall be granted a deduction under section 114 in respect of expenses incurred by him or her in maintaining that second residence.

Amendments

1 Subs (1A) inserted by section 21 of the Oireachtas (Allowance to Members) and Ministerial, Parliamentary, Judicial and Court Offices (Amendment) Act, 1998 with effect from 6 April, 1997.

Former enactments

Oireachtas (Allowances to Members) and Ministerial and Parliamentary Offices (Amendment) Act 1992 s 4.

Corresponding UK tax provision

Income and Corporation Taxes Act 1988 s 200.

837 Members of the clergy and ministers of religion

In assessing the income tax chargeable under any Schedule on a member of the clergy or minister of any religious denomination, the following deductions may be made from any profits, fees or emoluments of his or her profession—

(*a*) any sums of money paid or expenses incurred by him or her wholly, exclusively and necessarily in the performance of his or her duty as a member of the clergy or minister of any religious denomination;

(*b*) such part of the rent (not exceeding one-eighth), as the inspector by whom the assessment is made may allow, paid by him or her in respect of a dwelling house any part of which is used mainly and substantially for the purposes of his or her duty as a member of the clergy or minister of any religious denomination.

Definitions

inspector: ss 2(1), 5(1), 852; profession: s 2(1).

Former enactments

ITA 1967 s 544(1); FA 1969 s 65(1) and Sch 5 Pt I.

Corresponding UK tax provision

Income and Corporation Taxes Act 1988 s 332.

838 Special portfolio investment accounts

(1) (*a*) In this section—

“designated broker” means a person—

(i) which is a dealing member firm of the Irish Stock Exchange or a member firm (which carries on a trade in the State through a branch or agency) of a stock exchange of any other Member State of the European Communities, and

(ii) which has sent to the Revenue Commissioners a notification of its name and address and of its intention to accept specified deposits;

"gains" means chargeable gains within the meaning of the Capital Gains Tax Acts, including gains which but for section 607 would be chargeable gains;

"market value" shall be construed in accordance with section 548;

"ordinary shares" means shares forming part of a company's ordinary share capital;

"qualifying shares" means ordinary shares in a company which are—

(i) listed in the official list of the Irish Stock Exchange, or

(ii) quoted on the market known as the Developing Companies Market, or the market known as the Exploration Securities Market, of the Irish Stock Exchange,

other than—

(I) shares in an investment company within the meaning of Part XIII of the Companies Act, 1990,

(II) shares in an undertaking for collective investment in transferable securities within the meaning of the European Communities (Undertakings for Collective Investment in Transferable Securities) Regulations, 1989 (SI No 78 of 1989), or

(III) shares in a company, being shares the market value of which may be expected to approximate at all times to the market value of the proportion of the assets of the company which they represent;

"relevant income or gains" means the aggregate of the income and gains, including losses, arising from relevant investments, but only so much of income arising to or gains accruing to the special portfolio investment account shall be relevant income or gains as is or is to be—

(i) paid to, or

(ii) accumulated or invested for the benefit of,

the individual in whose name the special portfolio investment account is held, or would be so paid, accumulated or invested if any gains accruing to the account in accordance with subsection (4)(*e*) were gains on an actual disposal of the assets concerned;

"relevant investment" means an investment in [fully paid-up][1]—

(i) qualifying shares and specified qualifying shares, or

(ii) qualifying shares, specified qualifying shares and securities,

as the case may be, acquired by a designated broker [at market value][2] by the expenditure of money contributed by means of a specified deposit, and held by a designated broker in a special portfolio investment account;

...[3]

"securities" means securities—

(i) issued under the authority of the Minister for Finance, or

(ii) issued by the Electricity Supply Board, Radio Telefís Éireann, ...[4] , ...[5] Córas Iompair Éireann, ...[6] Bord na Móna, Aerlínte Éireann cuideachta phoiblí theoranta, Aer Lingus plc or Aer Rianta cuideachta phoiblí theoranta,

which are listed in the official list of the Irish Stock Exchange;

"special portfolio investment account" means an account opened [on or after 1 February 1993 and before 6 April 2001],[7] in which a relevant investment is held and in respect of which the conditions referred to in paragraph (*c*) are complied with;

"specified deposit" means a sum of money paid by an individual to a designated broker for the purpose of acquiring assets which will form part of a relevant investment;

"specified qualifying shares", in relation to a special portfolio investment account, means qualifying shares in a company which when the shares are acquired for the account has an issued share capital the market value of which is less than [€255,000,000][8].

(*b*) For the purposes of this section, Chapter 4 of Part 8 shall be construed as if—

(i) references to **"deposit"**, **"interest"**, **"relevant deposit"**, **"relevant deposit taker"**, **"relevant interest"** and **"special savings account"** were respectively references to **"specified deposit"**, **"income or gains"**, **"relevant investment"**, **"designated broker"**, **"relevant income or gains"** and **"special portfolio investment account"** within the meaning of this section, and

(ii) subsections (4) and (5) of section 258 and section 259 had not been enacted.

(*c*) Notwithstanding subsection (3), section 264 shall apply to a special portfolio investment account as if—

(i) paragraphs (*d*) to (i) of subsection (1) of that section had not been enacted, and

(ii) the conditions in subsection (2) of this section had been included in subsection (1) of that section.

(2) The conditions referred to in subsection (1)(*c*)(ii) are:

(*a*) each special portfolio investment account and all assets held in such an account shall be kept separately from all other investment accounts, if any, operated by a designated broker;

(*b*) the amount of a specified deposit or, if there is more than one, the aggregate of such amounts in respect of assets held at the same time as part of a special portfolio investment account shall not exceed—

(i) in the case of a special portfolio investment account in respect of which—

(I) the first specified deposit was made on or before the 5th day of April, 2000, and

(II) an amount (in this paragraph referred to as **"the particular amount"**) equal to the whole or a part of the specified deposit or specified deposits has been used to acquire shares in a company quoted on the market known as the Developing Companies Market of the Irish Stock

Exchange and those shares are at that time held as assets of the special portfolio investment account,

[€63,500][9] increased by the lesser of—

(A) the particular amount, and

(B) [€12,700][10],

and

(ii) in the case of any other special portfolio investment account, [€63,500][9];

...[11]

(*d*) the aggregate of the consideration given for shares which are at any time before the 1st day of February, 1994, assets of a special portfolio investment account shall not be less than—

(i) as respects qualifying shares, 40 per cent, and

(ii) as respects specified qualifying shares, 6 per cent,

of the aggregate of the consideration given for the assets of the account at that time;

(*e*) the aggregate of the consideration given for shares which are at any time within the year ending on the 31st day of January, 1995, assets of a special portfolio investment account shall not be less than—

(i) as respects qualifying shares, 45 per cent, and

(ii) as respects specified qualifying shares, 9 per cent,

of the aggregate of the consideration given for the assets of the account at that time;

(*f*) the aggregate of the consideration given for shares which are at any time within the year ending on the 31st day of January, 1996, assets of a special portfolio investment account shall not be less than—

(i) as respects qualifying shares, 50 per cent, and

(ii) as respects specified qualifying shares, 10 per cent,

of the aggregate of the consideration given for the assets of the account at that time;

(*g*) the aggregate of the consideration given for shares which are at any time [on or after 1 February 1996 and before 31 December 2000],[12] assets of a special portfolio investment account shall not be less than—

(i) as respects qualifying shares, 55 per cent, and

(ii) as respects specified qualifying shares, 10 per cent,

of the aggregate of the consideration given for the assets of the account at that time;

and for the purposes of—

(I) paragraphs (*b*) and (*c*), a disposal of shares or securities, being shares or securities, as the case may be, of the same class acquired for a special portfolio investment account at different times, shall be assumed to be a disposal of shares or securities, as the case may be, acquired later, rather than of shares or securities, as the case may be, acquired earlier for the special portfolio investment account, and

(II) paragraphs (*d*) to (*g*), the amount of the consideration given for shares shall be determined in accordance with sections 547 and 580.

(3) Chapter 4 of Part 8 (other than section 259) shall, subject to this section and with any other necessary modifications, apply to special portfolio investment accounts as it applies to special savings accounts[, and in particular the rate of appropriate tax specified in section 256(1) in relation to relevant interest payable in respect of a relevant deposit or relevant deposits held in a special savings account shall apply to special portfolio investment accounts].[13]

(4) (*a*) Paragraphs (*b*) to (*h*) shall apply notwithstanding any other provision of the Tax Acts and the Capital Gains Tax Acts.

(*b*) Where for any year of assessment a loss arises from the computation of relevant income or gains, that loss shall be included in the computation of the relevant income or gains of the special portfolio investment account for the next year of assessment and, in so far as relief for the loss cannot be so given, it shall be set against such relevant income or gains in the next year of assessment and, where appropriate, in each subsequent year of assessment in so far as it cannot be so relieved, and no further relief shall be allowed under any provision of the Tax Acts or the Capital Gains Tax Acts in respect of that loss.

[(*bb*) Notwithstanding paragraph (*b*), where, at the time a special portfolio investment account is closed, a loss has not been relieved under that paragraph because of an insufficiency of relevant income or gains at that time, that loss shall for the purposes of section 31 be treated as an allowable loss accruing at that time to the individual in whose name the special portfolio investment account was held.][14]

(*c*) Sections 556, 601, 607 and [1028(5)][15] shall not apply in relation to any gains referable to a relevant investment.

(*d*) (i) In this paragraph—

"the appropriate amount in respect of the interest" means the appropriate amount in respect of the interest which would be determined in accordance with Schedule 21 if the designated broker were the first buyer and the designated broker carried on a trade to which section 749(1) applies; but, in so determining the appropriate amount in respect of the interest in accordance with Schedule 21, paragraph 3(4) of that Schedule shall apply as if **"in the opinion of the Appeal Commissioners"** were deleted;

"securities" has the same meaning as in section 815.

(ii) Subject to subparagraph (iii), where—

(I) in a year of assessment (in this subparagraph referred to as **"the first year of assessment"**) securities which are assets of a special portfolio investment account are disposed of, and

(II) in the following year of assessment interest becoming payable in respect of the securities is receivable by the special portfolio investment account,

then, for the purposes of computing the relevant income or gains for the first year of assessment, the price paid by the designated broker for the securities shall be treated as reduced by the appropriate amount in respect of the interest.

(iii) Where for a year of assessment subparagraph (ii) applies so as to reduce the price paid for securities, the amount by which the price paid for the securities is reduced shall be treated as a loss arising in the following year of assessment from the disposal of the securities.

(*e*) For the purpose of computing relevant income or gains of a special portfolio investment account for a year of assessment, each asset of a special portfolio investment account on [31 December][16] in that year of assessment shall be deemed to have been disposed of and immediately reacquired by the designated broker on that day at the asset's market value on that day.

[(*f*) Subject to subsection (5), where in a year of assessment the relevant income or gains of a special portfolio investment account includes a distribution from a company resident in the State, the amount or value of that distribution shall be taken into account in computing the relevant income or gains for that year of assessment.][17]

...[18]

(*h*) Capital gains tax shall not be chargeable on the disposal of assets held as part of a relevant investment; but this paragraph shall not prevent any such disposals from being taken into account in computing the amount of relevant income or gains on which appropriate tax is payable.

(5) (*a*) In this subsection—

"eligible shares" has the same meaning as in section 488;

"qualifying company" has the meaning assigned to it by section 495.

(*b*) Without prejudice to the treatment of losses on eligible shares as allowable losses, gains accruing on the disposal or deemed disposal of eligible shares in a qualifying company shall not for the purposes of computing appropriate tax in accordance with subsection (6) be treated as gains.

(*c*) Distributions included in the relevant income or gains of a special portfolio investment account in respect of eligible shares in qualifying companies shall not be taken into account in computing appropriate tax in accordance with subsection (6) ...[19].

(6) (*a*) For the purposes of sections 257 and 258, a designated broker shall, in relation to each special portfolio investment account—

(i) be deemed to have made a payment on [31 December][20] in each year of assessment of the amount of relevant income or gains for that year of assessment, and

(ii) be liable to make a payment of appropriate tax in relation to such payment.

(*b*) The designated broker may deduct an amount on account of any such payment of appropriate tax and the individual beneficially entitled to the assets in the special portfolio investment account shall allow such deduction from any income or from the proceeds of the sale of any assets which the designated broker holds as part of the special portfolio investment account; but, where there are no such funds or insufficient funds available out of which the designated broker may satisfy the appropriate tax, the amount of such tax shall be an amount due to the designated broker from the person beneficially entitled to the relevant investment.

(*c*) For the purposes of this section, section 258 shall apply as if in subsection (2) of that section **"on or before [31 October]**[21] **following that year of assessment"** were substituted for **"within 15 days from the end of the year of assessment"**.

(7) Part 16 shall not apply in relation to any shares which form part of a relevant investment.

Amendments

1 Inserted by FA 1999 s 65(1)(*a*)(i)(I) with effect from 1 December 1998.

2 Inserted by FA 1999 s 65(1)(*a*)(i)(II) with effect from 1 December 1998.

3 Definition of "relevant period" deleted by FA 2001 s 56(*a*)(ii) with effect from 6 April 2001.

4 Repealed by ICC Bank Act 2000 s 7 and the ICC Bank Act 2000 (Sections 5 and 7) (Commencement) Order 2001 (SI No 396 of 2001) as respects securities issued on or after 12 February 2001; previously "ICC Bank plc".

5 Deleted by FA 2001 s 241(*c*) as respects any securities issued by Bord Telecom Éireann or Irish Telecommunications Investments plc on or after 15 February 2001; previously "Bord Telecom Éireann, Irish Telecommunications Investments plc,".

6 Repealed by ACC Bank Act 2001 s 12(1) and Sch, other than as respects securities issued before the commencement of this repeal. By virtue of the ACC Bank Act 2001 (Sections 6, 8, 10, 11(2) and 12) (Commencement) Order 2002, SI No 69 of 2002, the commencement date is 28 February 2002.

7 Substituted by FA 2001 s 56(*a*)(i) with effect from 6 April 2001; previously "on or after the 1st day of February, 1993".

8 Substituted by FA 2001 s 240(1) and (2)(*a*) and Sch 5 Pt 1 for 2002 and later tax years; previously "£200,000,000"; previously "£100,000,000": FA 1998 s 53.

9 Substituted by FA 2001 s 240(1) and (2)(*a*) and Sch 5 Pt 1 for 2002 and later tax years; previously "£50,000".

10 Substituted by FA 2001 s 240(1) and (2)(*a*) and Sch 5 Pt 1 for 2002 and later tax years; previously "£10,000".

11 Subs (2)(*c*) deleted by FA 2001 s 56(*b*)(i) with effect from 6 April 2001.

12 Substituted by FA 2001 s 56(*b*)(ii) with effect from 6 April 2001; previously "on or after the 1st day of February, 1996".

13 Substituted by FA 1999 s 65(1)(*c*) with effect from 6 April 1999; previously; "but that Chapter shall so apply as if, in relation to relevant interest payable in respect of a relevant deposit or relevant deposits held in a special savings account, the rate of appropriate tax were 10 per cent".

14 Subs (4)(*bb*) inserted by FA 2002 s 50 with effect from 1 January 2002.

15 Substituted by FA 1999 s 65(1)(*d*) with effect from 1 December 1998; previously "1028(4)".

16 Substituted by FA 2001 s 77(2) and Sch 2 paras 46(*a*) and 61(*c*) for short tax "year" 2001 and later tax years; previously "the 5th day of April".

17 Subs (4)(*f*) substituted by FA 2000 s 69(1) and Sch 2 Part 1 para (*o*) with effect from 6 April 1999 in the case of income tax and as respects accounting periods commencing on or after that date in the case of corporation tax.

18 Subs (4)(*g*) repealed by FA 2000 s 69(2) and Sch 2 Part 2 with effect from 6 April 1999 in the case of income tax and as respects accounting periods commencing on or after that date in the case of corporation tax.

19 Repealed by FA 2000 s 69(2) and Sch 2 Part 2 with effect from 6 April 1999 in the case of income tax and as respects accounting periods commencing on or after that date in the case of corporation tax; previously "; but notwithstanding" to "the Capital Gains Tax Acts".

20 Substituted by FA 2001 s 77(2) and Sch 2 paras 46(*b*)(i) and 61(*c*) for short tax "year" 2001 and later tax years; previously "the 5th day of April".

21 Substituted by FA 2001 s 77(2) and Sch 2 paras 46(*b*)(ii) and 61(*c*) for short tax "year" 2001 and later tax years; previously "the 1st day of November".

Cross-references

Dividend withholding tax, declaration by designated stockbroker, meaning of "the relevant income or gains" applied: Sch 2A para 7B(*f*).

Dividend withholding tax, interpretation, meaning of "designated broker" and "special portfolio investment account" applied: s 172A(1).

Dividend withholding tax, exemption for certain persons, meaning of "relevant income or gains" applied: s 172C(2)(*g*)(i), (3)(*b*).

Limits to special investments: s 839(1)(*d*), (3); subs (2)(*b*): s 839(2)(*a*)(ii), (*b*)(ii)(II).

Revenue precedents

Issue: If a SPIA holder gets income from the SPIA in the form of shares, can the shares be left in the SPIA without breaching the investment limit?

Decision: Yes, provided the income is not taken out of the SPIA. The investment limit is breached only if the cash given to the designated broker for investment exceeds the limit. After 5 years the balance in the SPIA must be reduced to the prescribed limit.

Issue: Whether the 10% limit for special qualifying shares applies only at the date of the original investment.

Decision: The aggregate of the consideration given for shares which are at any time held in a SPIA must be, as respects specified qualifying shares, at least 10% of the aggregate of the consideration given for the assets of the SPIA at that time.

Revenue information

Information leaflet IT17 — Special Savings Accounts and other Special Investment Products.

Definitions

allowable loss: ss 4(1), 5(1), 546; Capital Gains Tax Acts: s 1(2); chargeable gain: ss 4(1), 5(1), 534; class (of shares): s 5(1); company: ss 4(1), 5(1); distribution: ss 4(1), 436, 437; person: IA 1937 s 11(*c*); profits: s 4(1); shares: s 5(1); tax credit: ss 2(1), 136; Tax Acts: s 1(2); year of assessment: ss 2(1), 5(1); year: IA 1937 Sch.

Former enactments

FA 1993 s 14 (other than proviso to subs (4)(*c*) and subs (6)(*b*)); FA 1994 s 12(2) and s34(*b*); FA 1995 s 11(2); FA 1996 s 37(1); FA 1997 ss 37(1), 146(1) and Sch 9 Pt I para 17(1).

839 Limits to special investments

(1) Subject to subsection (2), an individual shall not at the same time have a beneficial interest in investments of more than one of the following classes of investment—

(*a*) special savings accounts within the meaning of section 256(1) (such an account being referred to subsequently in this section as a **"special savings account"**);

...[1]

(*c*) special investment units within the meaning of section 737;

(*d*) special portfolio investment accounts within the meaning of section 838.

(2) (*a*) An individual, whether married or not, who does not have a joint interest in an investment of a class mentioned in subsection (1) may have a beneficial interest, that is not a joint interest, in 2 such investments, being a special savings account and an investment of a class mentioned in [paragraph (*c*) or (*d*)][2] of that subsection, during a period throughout which—

(i) as respects the special savings account, the condition specified in section 264(1)(i) would be satisfied if [€31,750][3] were substituted for [€63,500][4] in that condition, or

(ii) as respects the other investment, the condition specified in [section 737(3)(*a*)(ii) or 838(2)(*b*)][5] relevant to that investment would be satisfied if [€31,750][3] were substituted for [€63,500][4] in those conditions.

(*b*) A couple married to each other, neither of whom has an interest, that is not a joint interest, in an investment of a class mentioned in subsection (1), may have a joint beneficial interest—

(i) in 2 or 3 such investments, so long as those investments include a special savings account and an investment of a class mentioned in [paragraph (*c*) or (*d*)][6] of that subsection, or

(ii) in 4 such investments, being 2 special savings accounts and 2 other investments of a class (which need not be the same class for the 2 investments) mentioned in [paragraph (*c*) or (*d*)][7] of that subsection, during a period throughout which—

(I) as respects the special savings accounts, the condition specified in section 264(1)(i) would be satisfied if [€31,750][3] were substituted for [€63,500][4] in that condition, or

(II) as respects the other investments, the condition specified in [section 737(3)(*a*)(ii) or 838(2)(*b*)][8] relevant to each of those investments would be satisfied if [€31,750][3] were substituted for [€63,500][4] in those conditions.

[(3) So long as an individual, whether married or not, does not have a beneficial interest in an investment of a class mentioned in subsection (1) other than—

(*a*) a beneficial interest, whether or not a joint interest, in one investment, or

(*b*) a joint beneficial interest in 2 investments of a class (which need not be the same class) mentioned in subsection (1),

then, sections 264, ...[9] 737 and 838 shall apply to that one investment or those 2 investments, as the case may be, as if every reference to [€63,500][4] in those sections were a reference to [€95,250][10].][11]

(4) Where an individual may hold a beneficial interest, whether jointly or otherwise, in an investment of a class mentioned in subsection (1) only for as long as a condition specified in the Tax Acts in respect of the investment would be satisfied if a reference to [€31,750][3] were substituted for a reference to [€63,500][4] in the condition so specified, then, any provision of those Acts which apart from this subsection would have the effect at any time of restricting that investment to an investment the value of which does not exceed [€63,500][4] shall apply to that investment as if the reference to [€63,500][4] in the provision were a reference to [€31,750][3].

(5) Any declaration referred to in—

(*a*) paragraph (*b*) of the definition of **"special savings account"** in section 256(1),

(*b*) paragraph (*b*) of the definition of **"special investment policy"** in section 723(1), or

(*c*) paragraph (*b*) of the definition of **"special investment units"** in section 737(1),

shall contain—

(i) such information in relation to the beneficial interest, which at the time the declaration is made the individual making the declaration holds, whether jointly or otherwise, in investments of a class mentioned in subsection (1), and

(ii) such undertakings, to the person to whom the declaration is made, to supply at any later time information in relation to such interests of that individual at that later time,

as the Revenue Commissioners may reasonably require for the purposes of this section.

Amendments

1 Subs (1)(*b*) deleted by FA 2003 s 52(1)(*i*)(i) as respects accounting periods ending in 2003 and later years.

2 Substituted by FA 2003 s 52(1)(*i*)(ii) as respects accounting periods ending in 2003 and later years; previously "paragraph (*b*), (*c*) or (*d*)".

3 Substituted by FA 2001 s 240(1) and (2)(*a*) and Sch 5 Pt 1 for 2002 and later tax years; previously "£25,000".

4 Substituted by FA 2001 s 240(1) and (2)(*a*) and Sch 5 Pt 1 for 2002 and later tax years; previously "£50,000".

5 Substituted by FA 2003 s 52(1)(*i*)(iii) as respects accounting periods ending in 2003 and later years; previously "section 723(3)(*b*), 737(3)(*a*)(ii) or 838(2)(*b*)".

6 Substituted by FA 2003 s 52(1)(*i*)(iv) as respects accounting periods ending in 2003 and later years; previously "paragraph (*b*), (*c*) or (*d*)".

7 Substituted by FA 2003 s 52(1)(*i*)(v) as respects accounting periods ending in 2003 and later years; previously "paragraph (*b*), (*c*) or (*d*)".

8 Substituted by FA 2003 s 52(1)(*i*)(vi) as respects accounting periods ending in 2003 and later years; previously "section 723(3)(*b*), 737(3)(*a*)(ii) or 838(2)(*b*)".

9 Deleted by FA 2003 s 52(1)(*i*)(vii) as respects accounting periods ending in 2003 and later years; previously "723".

10 Substituted by FA 2001 s 240(1) and (2)(*a*) and Sch 5 Pt 1 for 2002 and later tax years; previously "£75,000".

11 Subs (3) substituted by FA 1999 s 66 with effect from 6 April 1999.

Cross-references

Special investment policies, breach of conditions: s 725(1)(*b*).

Revenue information

Information leaflet IT17 — Special Savings Accounts and other Special Investment Products.

Definitions

class (of shares): s 5(1); interest: s 4(1); person: IA 1937 s 11(*c*); Tax Acts: s 1(2); writing: IA 1937 Sch.

Former enactments

FA 1993 s 16; FA 1994 s 34(*c*)–(*g*).

840 Business entertainment

(1) In this section—

"business entertainment" means entertainment (including the provision of accommodation, food and drink or any other form of hospitality in any circumstances whatever) provided directly or indirectly by—

(*a*) any person (in this definition referred to as **"the first-mentioned person"**),

(*b*) any person who is a member of the first-mentioned person's staff, or

(*c*) any person providing or performing any service for the first-mentioned person, the entertainment being entertainment that is provided in the course of, or is incidental to, the provision or performance of the service,

in connection with a trade carried on by the first-mentioned person, but does not include anything provided by that person for bona fide members of that person's staff unless its provision for them is incidental to its provision also for others;

a reference to expenses incurred in, or to the use of an asset for, providing entertainment includes a reference to expenses incurred in, or to the use of an asset for, providing anything incidental thereto;

a reference to a trade includes a reference to a business, profession or employment;

a reference to the members of a person's staff is a reference to persons employed by the person, directors of a company or persons engaged in the management of the company being for this purpose deemed to be persons employed by the company.

(2) In respect of any expenses incurred in providing business entertainment, no sum shall be—

(*a*) deducted in computing the amount of profits or gains chargeable to tax under Schedule D,

(*b*) included in computing any expenses of management in respect of which a deduction may be claimed under section 83 or 707, or

(*c*) allowed under section 114.

(3) (*a*) In this subsection, **"the specified provisions"** means the provisions of Part 9 relating to machinery or plant.

(*b*) Where any asset is used or is provided for use wholly or partly for the purpose of providing business entertainment, no allowance under any of the specified provisions shall be made for any year of assessment or for any accounting period of a company in respect of the use of the asset or the expenditure incurred in the provision of the asset to the extent that it is used or is to be used for that business entertainment.

(4) The expenses to which subsection (2) applies include in the case of any person any sum paid by that person to, on behalf of or placed by that person at the disposal of a member of that person's staff for the purpose of defraying expenses incurred or to be incurred by the member of the staff in providing business entertainment.

(5) This section shall apply in relation to the provision of a gift as it applies in relation to the provision of entertainment.

(6) (*a*) Where by reason of the provision or performance of a service an amount is paid or payable to a person referred to in paragraph (*c*) of the definition of **"business entertainment"**, so much of the amount as is equal to the cost of any business entertainment that is provided in the course of, or is incidental to the provision or performance of, the service shall be deemed to be incurred in providing business entertainment.

(*b*) The cost of any business entertainment shall be determined by the inspector according to the best of his or her knowledge and judgment.

(*c*) A determination made under paragraph (*b*) may be amended by the Appeal Commissioners or by the Circuit Court on the hearing or the rehearing of an appeal against any deduction (including a case where no deduction is granted) granted on the basis of the determination.

Revenue precedents

Issue: Is the cost of providing accommodation for a foreign potential customer an allowable deduction?

Decision: No. The provision of accommodation for a foreign potential customer would appear to come within the definition of business entertainment and therefore would not be an allowable deduction.

Definitions

Appeal Commissioners: s 2(1); Circuit Court: IA 1937 Sch; company: ss 4(1), 5(1); inspector: ss 2(1), 5(1), 852; person: IA 1937 s 11(*c*); profession: ss 2(1), 5(1); trade: s 3(1); year of assessment: ss 2(1), 5(1).

Former enactments

FA 1982 s 20(1)–(6) and (8).

Corresponding UK tax provision

Income and Corporation Taxes Act 1988 s 577.

841 Voluntary Health Insurance Board: restriction of certain losses and deemed disposal of certain assets

(1) In this section—

"the Board" means the Voluntary Health Insurance Board;

"market value" shall be construed in accordance with section 548.

(2) Section 396 shall not apply to a loss incurred by the Board in an accounting period ending before the 1st day of March, 1997.

(3) Notwithstanding any other provision of the Tax Acts, bonds and shares held by the Board on the 28th day of February, 1997, in the course of the business of carrying out schemes of voluntary health insurance shall be deemed to have been disposed of and immediately reacquired by the Board on that date at the assets' market value on that date.

Former enactments

FA 1997 s 61(1), (3) and (5).

842 Replacement of harbour authorities by port companies

(1) In this section, **"relevant port company"** has the same meaning as in paragraph 1 of Schedule 26.

(2) Schedule 26 shall apply where assets are vested in, or transferred to, a relevant port company pursuant to the Harbours Act, 1996.

(3) This section and Schedule 26 shall apply from the 1st day of March, 1997.

Former enactments

FA 1997 s 48.

843 Capital allowances for buildings used for third level educational purposes

(1) In this section—

[**"approved institution"** means—

(*a*) an institution of higher education within the meaning of section 1 of the Higher Education Authority Act, 1971, or

(*b*) an institution in the State in receipt of public funding which provides courses to which a scheme approved by the Minister for Education and Science under the Local Authorities (Higher Education Grants) Acts, 1968 to 1992, [applies, or][1]][2]

[(*c*) any body engaged in the provision of third level health and social services education or training which is approved by the Minister for Health and

Children for the purposes of this section and is in receipt of public funding in respect of the provision of such education or training;][3]

"qualifying expenditure" means capital expenditure incurred on—

(*a*) the construction of a qualifying premises, or

(*b*) the provision of machinery or plant,

[which—

(i) in the case of an institution referred to in paragraph (*a*) or (*b*) of the definition of "approved institution", is, following the receipt of the advice of An tÚdarás, approved for that purpose by the Minister for Education and Science with the consent of the Minister for Finance, and

(ii) in the case of a body referred to in paragraph (*c*) of the definition of "approved institution", is approved for that purpose by the Minister for Health and Children with the consent of the Minister for Finance;][4]

[**"qualifying period"** means the period commencing on 1 July 1997 and ending on 31 July 2006;][5]

"qualifying premises" means a building or structure which—

(*a*) apart from this section is not an industrial building or structure within the meaning of section 268, and

(*b*) (i) is in use for the purposes of third level education [or associated sporting or leisure activities][6] provided by an approved institution,

[(ii) is let to an approved institution,][7]

but does not include any part of a building or structure in use as or as part of a dwelling-house;

"An tÚdarás" means the Body established by section 2 of the Higher Education Authority Act, 1971.

(2) [Subject to subsections (2A) to (7)][8], the provisions of the Tax Acts (other than section 317(2)) relating to the making of allowances or charges in respect of capital expenditure incurred on the construction of an industrial building or structure shall, notwithstanding anything to the contrary in those provisions, apply in relation to qualifying expenditure on a qualifying premises—

(*a*) as if the qualifying premises were, at all times at which it is a qualifying premises, a building or structure in respect of which an allowance is to be made for the purposes of income tax or corporation tax, as the case may be, under Part 9 by reason of its use for a purpose specified in section 268(1)(*a*), and

(*b*) where any activity carried on in the qualifying premises is not a trade, as if it were a trade.

[(2A) An allowance shall be given by virtue of subsection (2) in relation to any qualifying expenditure on a qualifying premises only in so far as that expenditure is incurred in the qualifying period.][9]

(3) In relation to qualifying expenditure [incurred in the qualifying period][10] on a qualifying premises section 272 shall apply as if—

(*a*) in subsection (3)(*a*)(ii) of that section the reference to 4 per cent were a reference to 15 per cent, and

(*b*) in subsection (4)(*a*)(ii) of that section the reference to 25 years were a reference to 7 years.

(4) No allowance shall be made under subsection (2) unless, before the commencement of construction of a qualifying premises, [or, in the case of the construction of a qualifying premises which consists of a building or structure which is to be used for the purposes of sporting or leisure activities associated with third level education provided by an approved institution where in relation to that premises an application for certification under this subsection was made, and the construction of that premises commenced, prior to 15 February 2001, before 1 July 2001,][11] the Minister for Finance certifies that—

(*a*) an approved institution has procured or otherwise secured a sum of money, none of which has been met directly or indirectly by the State, which sum is not less than 50 per cent of the qualifying expenditure to be incurred on the qualifying premises, and

(*b*) such sum is to be used solely by the approved institution for the following purposes—

(i) paying interest on money borrowed for the purpose of funding the construction of the qualifying premises,

(ii) paying any rent on the qualifying premises during such times as the qualifying premises is the subject of a letting on such terms as are referred to in paragraph (*b*)(ii) of the definition of **"qualifying premises"**, and

(iii) purchasing the qualifying premises following the termination of the letting referred to in subparagraph (ii).

(5) Notwithstanding section 274(1), no balancing charge shall be made in relation to a qualifying premises by reason of any of the events specified in that section which occurs more than 7 years after the qualifying premises was first used.

(6) This section shall come into operation on the 1st day of July, 1997.

[(7) The Minister for Finance may not give a certificate under subsection (4) unless an application for certification was made before 1 January 2005.][12]

[(8) Notwithstanding the powers conferred and duties imposed—

(*a*) on the Minister for Education and Science and the Minister for Finance to approve or give consent to the approval of, respectively, certain capital expenditure by virtue of [paragraph (i) of the definition of "qualifying expenditure"][13] in subsection (1), and

(*b*) [in so far as that expenditure is concerned,][14] on the Minister for Finance—

(i) to certify compliance with the requirements of subsection (4), or

(ii) not to give a certificate under that subsection at any time later than a particular day by virtue of subsection (7), the Minister for Education and Science and the Minister for Finance may, [either generally in the case of institutions referred to in paragraphs (*a*) and (*b*) of the definition of "approved institution" or in respect of capital expenditure to be incurred on any particular type of qualifying premises to be used by any such institution],[15] and subject to such conditions, if any, which they may see fit to impose, agree to delegate and may so delegate, in writing, to An tUdarás the authority to exercise the powers and carry out the duties referred to in paragraphs (*a*) and (*b*) and where these Ministers of the Government so delegate that authority [, then, as respects the matters so delegated][16]—

[(I) the definition of "qualifying expenditure" in subsection (1) shall apply as if the reference in paragraph (i) of that definition to "is, following the receipt of the advice of An tÚdarás, approved for that purpose by the Minister for Education and Science with the consent of the Minister for Finance" were a reference to "is approved for that purpose by An tÚdarás", and][17]

(II) subsections (4) and (7) shall apply as if the references in those subsections to "the Minister for Finance" were references to "An tUdarás".][18]

[(9) For the purposes only of determining, in relation to a claim for an allowance by virtue of subsection (2), whether and to what extent capital expenditure incurred on the construction of a qualifying premises is incurred or not incurred in the qualifying period, only such an amount of that capital expenditure as is properly attributable to work on the construction of the premises actually carried out during the qualifying period shall (notwithstanding any other provision of the Tax Acts as to the time when any capital expenditure is or is to be treated as incurred) be treated as having been incurred in that period.][19]

Amendments

1 Substituted by FA 2001 s 76(1)(*a*)(i)(I) with effect from 6 April 2001; previously "applies;".

2 Definition of "approved institution" substituted by FA 1998 s 44(*a*) with effect from 6 April 1998.

3 Definition of "approved institution" para (*c*) inserted by FA 2001 s 76(1)(*a*)(i)(II) with effect from 6 April 2001.

4 Substituted by FA 2001 s 76(1)(*a*)(ii) with effect from 6 April 2001.

5 Subs (1)(definition of "qualifying period") inserted by FA 2004 s 27(*a*) with effect from 1 January 2004.

6 Inserted by FA 2001 s 76(1)(*a*)(iii) as respects capital expenditure incurred on or after 1 October 1999.

7 Definition of "qualifying premises" para (*b*)(ii) substituted by FA 1998 s 44(*b*) with effect from 6 April 1998.

8 Substituted by FA 2004 s 27(*b*) with effect from 1 January 2004; previously "Subject to subsections (3) to (7)".

9 Subs (2A) inserted by FA 2004 s 27(*c*) with effect from 1 January 2004.

10 Inserted by FA 2004 s 27(*c*) with effect from 1 January 2004.

11 Inserted by FA 2001 s 76(1)(*b*) with effect from 6 April 2001.

12 Subs (7) substituted by FA 2005 s 33 with effect from 1 January 2005.

13 Substituted by FA 2001 s 76(1)(*c*)(i) with effect from 6 April 2001; previously "the definition of 'qualifying expenditure'".

14 Inserted by FA 2001 s 76(1)(*c*)(ii) with effect from 6 April 2001.

15 Substituted by FA 2001 s 76(1)(*c*)(iii) with effect from 6 April 2001; previously "either generally or in respect of capital expenditure to be incurred on any particular type of qualifying premises".

16 Inserted by FA 2001 s 76(1)(*c*)(iv) with effect from 6 April 2001.

17 Subs (8)(I) substituted by FA 2001 s 76(1)(*c*)(v) with effect from 6 April 2001.

18 Subs (8) inserted by FA 1999 s 51(*b*) with effect from 6 April 1999.

19 Subs (9) inserted by FA 2004 s 27(*e*) with effect from 1 January 2004.

Cross-references

Restriction on use of capital allowances on certain industrial buildings and other premises: s 409A(1) (specified building).

Ring-fence on use of certain capital allowances on certain industrial buildings and other premises: s 409E(1)(specified building).

Revenue precedents

Issue: An approved institution within the meaning of section 843 [capital allowances for certain third level educational institutions] uses a subsidiary company to manage all its properties. If a premises is let to the subsidiary will it be regarded as a qualifying premises within the meaning of the section?

Decision: A qualifying premises for the purpose of section 843 Taxes Consolidation Act 1997 means, inter alia, one which is let to an approved institution. A wholly owned subsidiary of an approved institution may be regarded as such an institution. Accordingly, if a company is a wholly owned subsidiary of the approved institution the premises may be let to the company and as long as it is used by the approved institution for the purposes of third level education it will be a qualifying premises.

Tax Briefing

TB44 June 2001 p 41 — Expenditure on plant and machinery that comes within TCA 1997 s 843 is treated as expenditure that qualifies for industrial buildings allowance. A balancing charge will not apply to the plant of machinery by reason of any of the effects specified in TCA 1997 s 274(1) which occurs more than 7 years after the plant and machinery is first used. The ring-fencing provisions of TCA 1997 s 404 do not apply to plant and machinery that qualifies as expenditure for the purposes of TCA 1997 s 843.

Definitions

person: IA 1937 s 11(*c*); Tax Acts: s 1(2); trade: ss 3(1), 4(1); writing: IA 1937 Sch.

Former enactments

FA 1997 s 25.

843A Capital allowances for buildings used for certain childcare purposes

[(1) In this section—

"pre-school child" and **"pre-school service"** have the meanings respectively assigned to them by section 49 of the Child Care Act, 1991;

[**"property developer"** means a person carrying on a trade which consists wholly or mainly of the construction or refurbishment of buildings or structures with a view to their sale;][1]

[**"qualifying expenditure"** means capital expenditure incurred on the construction, conversion or refurbishment of a qualifying premises;][2]

"qualifying premises" means a building or structure which—

(*a*) apart from this section is not an industrial building or structure within the meaning of section 268, and

(*b*) is in use for the purposes of providing—

(i) a pre-school service, or

(ii) a pre-school service and a day-care or other service to cater for children other than pre-school children,

and in respect of which it can be shown (to the extent that it is being used for the purposes of providing a pre-school service) that the requirements of Article 9, 10(1) or 11, as appropriate, of the Child Care (Pre-School Services) Regulations, 1996 (SI No 398 of 1996), have been complied with, but does not include any part of a building or structure in use as or as part of a dwelling-house.

(2) Subject to subsections (3) to (5), the provisions of the Tax Acts relating to the making of allowances or charges in respect of capital expenditure incurred on the construction or refurbishment of an industrial building or structure shall, notwithstanding anything to the contrary in those provisions, apply in relation to qualifying expenditure on a qualifying premises—

(*a*) as if a qualifying premises were, at all times at which it is a qualifying premises, a building or structure in respect of which an allowance is to be made for the purposes of income tax or corporation tax, as the case may be, under Part 9 by reason of its use for a purpose specified in section 268(1)(*a*), and

(*b*) where any activity carried on in the qualifying premises is not a trade, as if it were a trade.

(3) In relation to qualifying expenditure [incurred on or after 2 December 1998][3] on a qualifying premises section 272 shall apply as if—

(*a*) in subsection (3)(*a*)(ii) of that section the reference to 4 per cent were a reference to 15 per cent, and

(*b*) in subsection (4)(*a*)(ii) of that section the reference to 25 years were a reference to 7 years.

[(3A) For the purposes of the application, by subsection (2), of sections 271 and 273 in relation to qualifying expenditure incurred on or after 1 December 1999 on a qualifying premises—

(*a*) section 271 shall apply—

(i) as if in subsection (1) of that section the definition of "industrial development agency" were deleted,

(ii) as if in subsection (2)(*a*)(i) of that section "to which subsection (3) applies" were deleted,

(iii) as if subsection (3) of that section were deleted,

(iv) as if the following subsection were substituted for subsection (4) of that section:

"(4) An industrial building allowance shall be an amount equal to 100 per cent of the capital expenditure mentioned in subsection (2)."

and

(v) as if subsection (5) of that section were deleted,

and

(*b*) section 273 shall apply—

(i) as if in subsection (1) of that section the definition of "industrial development agency" were deleted, and

(ii) as if subsections (2)(*b*) and (3) to (7) of that section were deleted.][4]

(4) Notwithstanding section 274(1), no balancing allowance or balancing charge shall be made in relation to a qualifying premises by reason of any event referred to in that section which occurs—

(*a*) more than 10 years after the qualifying premises was first used, or

(*b*) in a case where section 276 applies, more than 10 years after the qualifying expenditure on refurbishment of the qualifying premises was incurred.

[(5) Subsections (3) and (3A) shall not apply in respect of qualifying expenditure incurred on a qualifying premises on or after 1 December 1999—

(*a*) where a property developer is entitled to the relevant interest, within the meaning of section 269, in that qualifying premises, and

(*b*) either the person referred to in paragraph (*a*) or a person connected (within the meaning of section 10) with that person incurred the qualifying expenditure on that qualifying premises.][5]][6]

Amendments

1 Definition of "property developer" inserted by FA 2000 s 63(1)(*a*)(i) with effect from such date as the Minister for Finance may by order appoint, viz 21 June 2000, by virtue of Finance Act 2000 (Section 63) (Commencement) Order 2000, SI No 183 of 2000 refers.

2 Definition of "qualifying expenditure" substituted by FA 2000 s 63(1)(*a*)(ii) with effect from such date as the Minister for Finance may by order appoint, viz 21 June 2000, by virtue of Finance Act 2000 (Section 63) (Commencement) Order 2000, SI No 183 of 2000 refers; previously **"'qualifying expenditure'** means capital expenditure incurred on or after the 2nd day of December, 1998, on the construction, conversion or refurbishment of a qualifying premises;".

3 Inserted by FA 2000 s 63(*b*) with effect from such date as the Minister for Finance may by order appoint, viz 21 June 2000, by virtue of Finance Act 2000 (Section 63) (Commencement) Order 2000, SI No 183 of 2000 refers.

4 Subs (3A) inserted by FA 2000 s 63(*c*) with effect from such date as the Minister for Finance may by order appoint, viz 21 June 2000, by virtue of Finance Act 2000 (Section 63) (Commencement) Order 2000, SI No 183 of 2000 refers.

5 Subs (5) inserted by FA 2000 s 63(*d*) with effect from such date as the Minister for Finance may by order appoint, viz 21 June 2000, by virtue of Finance Act 2000 (Section 63) (Commencement) Order 2000, SI No 183 of 2000 refers.

6 Section 843A inserted by FA 1999 s 49(*b*) with effect from 6 April 1999.

Cross-references

Restriction of relief in respect of loans applied in acquiring interest in companies: s 250A(1)("specified building").

Restriction on use of capital allowances on certain industrial buildings and other premises: s 409A(1) (specified building).

Ring-fence on use of certain capital allowances on certain industrial buildings and other premises: s 409E(1)(specified building).

Tax Briefing

TB37 Oct 1999 p 11 — Childcare Services — capital allowances for buildings used for certain childcare services.

TB41 Sept 2000 pp 16–18 — Industrial and Commercial Buildings Capital Allowances — Finance Act 2000 Restrictions.

Definitions

person: IA 1937 s 11(*c*); Tax Acts: s 1(2); trade: ss 3(1), 4(1).

844 Companies carrying on mutual business or not carrying on a business

(1) Subject to subsection (2), where a company carries on any business of mutual trading or mutual insurance or other mutual business, the provisions of the Corporation Tax Acts and of Schedule F relating to distributions shall apply to distributions made by the company, notwithstanding that they are made to persons participating in the mutual activities of that business and derive from those activities, but shall so apply only to the

extent to which the distributions are made out of profits of the company which are brought into charge to corporation tax or out of franked investment income.

(2) In the case of a company carrying on any mutual life assurance business, the provisions of the Corporation Tax Acts and of Schedule F relating to distributions shall not apply to distributions made to persons participating in the mutual activities of that business and derived from those activities; but, if the business includes annuity business, the annuities payable in the course of that business shall not be treated as charges on the income of the company to any greater extent than if that business were not mutual but were being carried on by the company with a view to the realisation of profits for the company.

(3) Subject to subsections (1) and (2), the fact that a distribution made by a company carrying on any such business is derived from the mutual activities of that business and the recipient is a person participating in those activities shall not affect the character which the payment or other receipt has for the purposes of corporation tax or income tax in the hands of the recipient.

(4) Where a company does not carry on and never has carried on a trade or a business of holding investments, and is not established for purposes which include the carrying on of a trade or of such a business, the provisions of the Corporation Tax Acts and of Schedule F relating to distributions shall apply to distributions made by the company only to the extent to which the distributions are made out of profits of the company which are brought into charge to corporation tax or out of franked investment income.

Definitions

company: ss 4(1), 5(1); distribution: ss 4(1), 436, 437; franked investment income: ss 4(1), 156; person: IA 1937 s 11(*c*); profits: s 4(1); trade: ss 3(1), 4(1), 5(1).

Former enactments

CTA 1976 s 29.

Corresponding UK tax provision

Income and Corporation Taxes Act 1988 s 490.

845 Corporation tax: treatment of tax-free income of non-resident banks, insurance businesses, etc

(1) In this section, **"insurance business"** includes assurance business within the meaning of section 3 of the Insurance Act, 1936.

(2) In this section and in section 846, **"tax-free securities"** means securities to which section 43, 49 or 50 applies and which were issued with a condition regulating the treatment of the interest on the securities for tax purposes such that the interest on the securities is excluded in computing income or profits.

(3) (*a*) In this subsection, **"securities"** includes stocks and shares.

(*b*) Where a banking business, an insurance business or a business consisting wholly or partly in dealing in securities is carried on in the State by a person not resident in the State, then—

(i) in computing for the purposes of the Tax Acts the profits arising from, or loss sustained in, the business, and

(ii) in the case of an insurance business, also in computing the profits or loss from pension business and general annuity business under section 715,

section 76 shall not prevent the inclusion of interest, dividends and other payments to which section 35 or 63 extends notwithstanding the exemption from tax conferred by those sections respectively.

(4) Where—

(*a*) any business referred to in subsection (3)(*b*) is carried on in the State by a person not ordinarily resident in the State, and

(*b*) in making any computation referred to in that subsection with respect to that business, interest on tax-free securities is excluded by virtue of a condition of the issue of such securities,

any expenses attributable to the acquisition or holding of, or to any transaction in, the securities (but not including in those expenses any interest on borrowed money), and any profits or losses so attributable, shall also be excluded in making that computation.

(5) In the case of an overseas life assurance company (within the meaning of section 706), in computing for the purposes of section 726 the income from the investments of the life assurance fund of the company, any interest, dividends and other payments to which section 35 or 63 extends shall be included notwithstanding the exemption from tax conferred by those sections respectively.

Cross-references

Tax free securities, exclusion of interest on borrowed money, subs (4): s 846(1).

Definitions

company: ss 4(1), 5(1); interest: s 4(1); person: IA 1937 s 11(*c*); profits: s 4(1); shares: s 5(1).

Former enactments

CTA 1976 s 51(1)–(3)(*a*), (4)–(6).

Corresponding UK tax provision

Income and Corporation Taxes Act 1988 s 474 [repealed].

845A Non-application of section 130 in the case of certain interest paid by banks

[(1) In this section, **"bank"** means—

(*a*) a person who is a holder of a licence granted under section 9 of the Central Bank Act, 1971, or

(*b*) a person who holds a licence or other similar authorisation under the law of any other Member State of the European Communities which corresponds to a licence granted under the said section 9.

(2) This subsection shall apply to so much of any interest as—

(*a*) is a distribution by virtue only of section 130(2)(*d*)(iv),

(*b*) is payable by a bank carrying on a bona fide banking business in the State and would but for section 130(2)(*d*)(iv) be deductible as a trading expense in computing the amount of the bank's income from its banking business, and

(*c*) represents no more than a reasonable commercial return for the use of the principal in respect of which the interest is paid by the bank.

(3) Where a bank proves that subsection (2) applies to any interest payable by it for an accounting period and elects to have that interest treated as not being a distribution for the purposes of section 130(2)(*d*)(iv), then, section 130(2)(*d*)(iv) shall not apply to that interest.

(4) An election under subsection (3) in relation to interest payable by a bank for an accounting period shall be made in writing to the inspector together with the bank's return of its profits for the period.][1]

Amendments

1 Section 845A inserted by FA 2001 s 88 with effect from 6 April 2001.

Cross-references

Allowance of charges on income, meaning of "bank" applied: s 243(1A).
Matters to be treated as distributions: s 130(2B).

Definitions

inspector: ss 2(1); 852; interest: s 4(1); person: IA 1937 s 11(*c*); profits: s 4(1); writing: IA 1937 Sch.

845B Set-off of surplus advance corporation tax

[(1) In this section—

"surplus advance corporation tax", in relation to an accounting period of a company, means an amount of advance corporation tax—

(*a*) to which the company was liable under section 159 in respect of a distribution made before 6 April 1999,

(*b*) which was paid by the company and not repaid to it, and

(*c*) which was not set against the company's liability to corporation tax for any preceding accounting period.

(2) Where in the case of an accounting period of a company there is an amount of surplus advance corporation tax, that amount shall be set against the company's liability to corporation tax on any income charged to corporation tax for that accounting period and shall accordingly discharge a corresponding amount of that liability.

(3) For the purposes of this section—

(*a*) the income of a company charged to corporation tax for any accounting period shall be taken to be the amount of its profits for that period on which corporation tax falls finally to be borne exclusive of the part of the profits attributable to chargeable gains, and

(*b*) the part of the profits so attributable shall be taken to be the amount brought into the company's profits for that period for the purposes of corporation tax in respect of chargeable gains before any deduction for charges on income, expenses of management or other amounts which can be deducted from or set against or treated as reducing profits of more than one description.

(4) For the purposes of this section, a notice under section 884 may require the inclusion in the return to be delivered by a company under that section of particulars of any surplus advance corporation tax carried forward in relation to that company under subsection (2).

(5) Where an inspector discovers that any set-off of surplus advance corporation tax under this section ought not to have been made, or is or has become excessive, the

inspector may make any such assessments as may in his or her judgment be required for recovering any tax that ought to have been paid and generally for securing that the resulting liabilities to tax (including interest on unpaid tax) of the person concerned are what they would have been if only such set-offs had been made as ought to have been made.][1]

Amendments

1 Section 845B inserted by FA 2003 s 41(1)(*n*) as respects accounting periods ending on or after 6 February 2003.

Definitions

chargeable gain: s 5(1); company: s 4(1); distribution: s 4(1); inspector: s 2(1); profits: s 4(1).

846 Tax-free securities: exclusion of interest on borrowed money

(1) This section shall apply where section 845(4) applies to a business for any accounting period.

(2) Up to the amount determined under this section (in this section referred to as **"the amount ineligible for relief"**), interest becoming due for payment on money borrowed for the purposes of the business—

(*a*) shall be excluded in any computation under the Tax Acts of the profits or loss arising from the business, and

(*b*) shall be excluded from the definition of **"charges on income"** in section 243.

(3) In determining the amount ineligible for relief, account shall be taken of all money borrowed for the purposes of the business outstanding in the accounting period up to the total cost of the tax-free securities held for the purposes of the business in that period; but account shall not be taken of any borrowed money carrying interest which apart from subsection (2) would not be included in the computation under paragraph (*a*) of that subsection and would not be treated as a charge on income for the purposes of the Corporation Tax Acts.

(4) The amount ineligible for relief shall be equal to a year's interest on the amount of money borrowed which is to be taken into account under subsection (3) at a rate equal to the average rate of interest in the accounting period on money borrowed for the purposes of the business, except that in the case of an accounting period of less than 12 months interest shall be taken for that shorter period instead of for a year.

(5) For the purposes of this section, the cost of a holding of tax-free securities which has fluctuated in the accounting period shall be the average cost of acquisition of the initial holding, and of any subsequent acquisitions in the accounting period, applied to the average amount of the holding in the accounting period, and this subsection shall be applied separately to securities of different classes.

Cross-references

Corporation tax: treatment of tax free income of non resident banks, insurance businesses etc: s 845(1).

Definitions

charges on income: ss 4(1), 243(1); company: ss 4(1), 5(1); interest: s 4(1); month: IA 1937 Sch; profits: s 4(1).

Former enactments

CTA 1976 s 52(1)–(4) and (6).

Corresponding UK tax provision

Income and Corporation Taxes Act 1988 s 475.

847 Tax relief for certain branch profits

(1) (*a*) In this section—

"investment plan" means a plan of a company resident in the State—

(i) which involves the investment by the company or by a company associated with it of substantial permanent capital in the State for the purposes of the creation before a date specified in the plan of substantial new employment in the State in trading operations carried on or to be carried on in the State by the company or the company associated with it, and

(ii) which has been submitted before the commencement of its implementation to the Minister by the company for the purpose of enabling it to obtain relief under this section;

"the Minister" means the Minister for Finance;

"qualified company" means a company to which the Minister, following consultation with the Minister for Enterprise and Employment, [has before 15 February 2001 given a certificate],[1] which certificate has not been revoked, under subsection (2);

"qualified foreign trading activities" means trading activities carried on by a qualified company through a branch or agency outside the State in a territory specified in the certificate given under subsection (2) to the company by the Minister following consultation with the Minister for Enterprise, Trade and Employment.

(*b*) For the purposes of this section—

(i) a company shall be associated with another company where one of the companies is a 75 per cent subsidiary of the other company or both companies are 75 per cent subsidiaries of a third company; but, in determining whether one company is a 75 per cent subsidiary of another company, the other company shall be treated as not being the owner of—

(I) any share capital which it owns directly in a company if a profit on the sale of the shares would be treated as a trading receipt of its trade, or

(II) any share capital which it owns indirectly and which is owned directly by a company for which a profit on the sale of the shares would be a trading receipt,

(ii) sections 412 to 418 shall apply for the purposes of this paragraph as they would apply for the purposes of Chapter 5 of Part 12 if section 411(1)(*c*) were deleted,

(iii) where a trade carried on by a qualified company consists partly of qualified foreign trading activities and partly of other trading activities, the company shall be treated as if it were carrying on distinct trades consisting of such qualified foreign trading activities and of such other trading activities,

(iv) there shall be attributed to each trade carried on, or treated under subparagraph (iii) as carried on, such profits or gains or losses as might have been expected to be made if each trade had been carried on under the same or similar conditions by a person independent of, and dealing at arm's length with, the person carrying on the other trade, and

(v) there shall be made all necessary apportionments as are just and reasonable for the purposes of computing—

(I) profits or gains or losses arising from, and

(II) the amount of any charges on income, expenses of management or other amount which can be deducted from or set off against or treated as reducing profits of more than one description as is incurred for the purposes of,

a trade carried on, or treated under subparagraph (iii) as carried on, by a qualified company.

(2) Where a plan has been duly submitted by a company resident in the State and the Minister, following consultation with the Minister for Enterprise, Trade and Employment, is satisfied that—

(*a*) the plan is an investment plan,

(*b*) the company, or a company associated with it, will, before a date specified in the plan and approved by the Minister, make the substantial permanent capital investment in the State under the investment plan for the purposes of the creation of the substantial new employment in the State,

(*c*) the creation of substantial new employment in the State under the investment plan will be achieved, and

(*d*) the maintenance of the employment so created in trading operations in the State will be dependent on the carrying on by the company of qualified foreign trading activities,

then, the Minister may give a certificate certifying that the company is a qualified company with effect from a date specified in the certificate.

(3) (*a*) The Minister shall draw up guidelines for determining whether for the purposes of subsection (2) a company and companies associated with it will create substantial new employment and will make a substantial permanent capital investment in the State.

(*b*) Without prejudice to the generality of paragraph (*a*), guidelines under that paragraph may—

(i) include a requirement for specified levels of—

(I) employment in the State, and

(II) permanent capital investment in the State,

and

(ii) specify such criteria for the purposes of this subsection as the Minister considers appropriate.

(4) A certificate issued under subsection (2) may be given subject to such conditions as the Minister, following consultation with the Minister for Enterprise and Employment, considers proper and specifies in the certificate.

(5) Where in the case of a company in relation to which a certificate under subsection (2) has been given the Minister, following consultation with the Minister for Enterprise and Employment, forms the opinion that such certificate ought to be revoked because any condition subject to which the certificate was given has not been complied with, the

Minister may by notice in writing served by registered post on the company revoke the certificate with effect from such date as may be specified in the notice.

(6) Notwithstanding any other provision of the Corporation Tax Acts—

(*a*) profits or gains or losses arising from the carrying on of qualified foreign trading activities shall be disregarded for the purposes of those Acts, and

(*b*) no amount of any charges on income, expenses of management or other amount which apart from this paragraph may be deducted from or set off against or treated as reducing profits of more than one description, shall be so deducted, set off or treated, as is incurred for the purposes of a trade carried on, or treated under subsection (1)(*b*)(iii) as carried on, by a qualified company which consists of qualified foreign trading activities.

(7) A gain shall not be a chargeable gain for the purposes of the Capital Gains Tax Acts if it accrues to a qualified company on the disposal of an asset, other than an asset specified in paragraphs (*a*) to (*d*) of section 980(2), used wholly and exclusively for the purposes of a trade carried on, or treated under subsection (1)(*b*)(iii) as carried on, by a qualified company which consists of qualified foreign trading activities.

(8) An inspector may by notice in writing require a qualified company to furnish him or her with such information or particulars as may be necessary for the purposes of giving relief under this section.

[(9) (*a*) The provisions of this section shall not apply to an accounting period ending after 31 December 2010.

(*b*) Where an accounting period begins before 31 December 2010 and ends after that date, it shall be divided into 2 parts, one beginning on the date on which the accounting period begins and ending on 31 December 2010 and the other beginning on 1 January 2011 and ending on the date on which the accounting period ends, and both parts shall be treated as if they were separate accounting periods of the company.][2]

Amendments

1 Substituted by FA 2001 s 89 with effect from 6 April 2001; previously "has given a certificate".

2 Subs (9) inserted by FA 2004 s 89 and Sch 3 para 1(*z*) with effect from 25 March 2004.

Definitions

branch or agency: ss 4(1), 5(1); inspector: ss 2(1), 852; person: IA 1937 s 11(*c*); trade: s 3(1); resident: s 5(1); writing: IA 1937 Sch.

Former enactments

FA 1995 s 29.

847A Donations to certain sports bodies

[(1) In this section—

"Acts" means—

(*a*) the Tax Acts,

(*b*) the Capital Gains Tax Acts, and

(*c*) the Value-Added Tax Act, 1972 and the enactments amending or extending that Act,

and any instruments made thereunder;

"appropriate certificate", in relation to a relevant donation by a donor who is an individual (other than an individual referred to in subsection (9)), means a certificate which is in such form as the Revenue Commissioners may prescribe and which contains—

(*a*) statements to the effect that—

(i) the donation satisfies the requirements of subsection (5), and

(ii) the donor has paid or will pay to the Revenue Commissioners income tax of an amount equal to income tax at the standard rate or the higher rate or partly at the standard rate and partly at the higher rate, as the case may be, for the relevant year of assessment on the grossed up amount of the donation, but not being—

(I) income tax which the donor is entitled to charge against any other person or to deduct, retain or satisfy out of any payment which the donor is liable to make to any other person, or

(II) appropriate tax within the meaning of Chapter 4 of Part 8,

(*b*) a statement specifying how much of the grossed up amount referred to in paragraph (*a*)(ii) has been or will be liable to income tax at the standard rate and the higher rate for the relevant year of assessment, and

(*c*) the identifying number, known as the Personal Public Service Number (PPSN) of the donor;

"approved project" means a project in respect of which the Minister has given a certificate under subsection (4), which certificate has not been revoked under that subsection;

"approved sports body" means a body which is in possession of—

(*a*) a certificate from the Revenue Commissioners stating that in their opinion the body is a body of persons to which section 235 applies, and

(*b*) a valid tax clearance certificate,

but does not include a body to whom the Revenue Commissioners have given a notice under section 235(1);

"Minister" means the Minister for Tourism, Sport and Recreation;

"project", in relation to an approved sports body, means one or more of the following:

(*a*) the purchase, construction or refurbishment of a building or structure, or part of a building or structure, to be used for sporting or recreation activities provided by the approved sports body,

(*b*) the purchase of land to be used by the approved sports body in the provision of sporting or recreation facilities,

(*c*) the purchase of permanently based equipment (excluding personal equipment) for use by the approved sports body in the provision of sporting or recreation facilities,

(*d*) the improvement of the playing pitches, surfaces or facilities of the approved sports body, and (*e*) the repayment of, or the payment of interest on, money borrowed by the approved sports body on or after 1 May 2002 for any of the purposes mentioned in paragraphs *(a)* to (*d*);

"relevant accounting period", in relation to a relevant donation made by a company, means the accounting period in which that donation is made by the company;

"relevant donation" means a donation which satisfies the requirements of subsection (5) and takes the form of the payment by a person (in this section referred to as the "donor") of a sum or sums of money amounting to at least €250 to an approved sports body which is made—

(*a*) where the donor is an individual, in a year of assessment, and

(*b*) where the donor is a company, in an accounting period,

but where an accounting period of a company is less than 12 months in length the amount of €250 shall be proportionately reduced;

"relevant year of assessment", in relation to a relevant donation made by an individual, means the year of assessment in which that donation is made by the individual;

"tax clearance certificate" shall be construed in accordance with subsection (3).

(2) For the purposes of this section and in relation to a donation by a donor who is an individual (other than an individual referred to in subsection (9)), references to the grossed up amount are to the amount which after deducting income tax at the standard rate or the higher rate or partly at the standard rate and partly at the higher rate, as the case may be, for the relevant year of assessment leaves the amount of the donation.

(3) (*a*) Where a body which is in compliance with the obligations imposed on it by the Acts in relation to—

(i) the payment or remittance of any taxes, interest or penalties required to be paid or remitted under the Acts to the Revenue Commissioners, and

(ii) the delivery of any returns required to be made under the Acts,

applies to the Collector-General in that behalf, the Collector-General shall issue to the body a certificate (in this section referred to as a "tax clearance certificate") for the purposes of this section stating that the body is in compliance with those obligations.

(*b*) Subsections (5) to (9) of section 1094 shall apply to an application for a tax clearance certificate under this subsection as they apply to an application for a tax clearance certificate under that section.

(4) (*a*) The Minister, on the making of an application by an approved sports body in advance of the undertaking by that body of a project, may give a certificate to that body stating that the project to be undertaken by that body may be treated as an approved project for the purposes of this section.

(*b*) An application under this subsection shall be in such form and contain such information as the Minister may direct.

(*c*) The Minister may, by notice in writing given to the body, revoke the certificate given in respect of a project under paragraph *(a)*, and the project shall cease to be an approved project as respects any donations made to the body after the date of the Minister's notice.

(*d*) The Minister shall not give a certificate to any body in respect of a project under paragraph (*a*) if the aggregate cost of the project is, or is estimated to be, in excess of €40,000,000.

(5) A donation shall satisfy the requirements of this subsection if—

(*a*) it is made to the approved sports body for the sole purpose of funding an approved project,

(*b*) it is or will be applied by the approved sports body for that purpose,

(*c*) apart from this section, it is neither deductible in computing for the purposes of tax the profits or gains of a trade or profession nor an expense of management deductible in computing the total profits of a company,

(*d*) it is not a relevant donation to which section 848A applies,

(*e*) it is not subject to a condition as to repayment,

(*f*) neither the donor nor any person connected with the donor receives, either directly or indirectly, a benefit in consequence of making the donation, including, in particular, a right to membership of the approved sports body or a right to use the facilities of that body,

(*g*) it is not conditional on or associated with, or part of an arrangement involving, the acquisition of property by the approved sports body, otherwise than by way of gift, from the donor or a person connected with the donor, and

(*h*) in the case of a donation made by an individual, the individual—

(i) is resident in the State for the relevant year of assessment,

(ii) has (except in the case of an individual referred to in subsection (9)) given an appropriate certificate in relation to the donation to the approved sports body, and

(iii) has (except in the case of an individual referred to in subsection (9)) paid the tax referred to in such appropriate certificate and is not entitled to claim a repayment of that tax or any part of that tax.

(6) Where it is proved to the satisfaction of the Revenue Commissioners that a person has made a relevant donation, subsection (7), (9) or (11), as the case may be, shall apply.

(7) Where a company makes a relevant donation, other than a relevant donation to which subsection (18) applies, then, for the purposes of corporation tax, the amount of that donation shall be treated as—

(*a*) a deductible trading expense of a trade carried on by the company in, or

(*b*) an expense of management deductible in computing the total profits of the company for,

the relevant accounting period.

(8) A claim by a company under this section shall be made with the return required to be delivered by it under section 951 for the relevant accounting period.

(9) (*a*) Where a relevant donation, other than a relevant donation to which subsection (18) applies, is made by an individual who is a chargeable person (within the meaning of Part 41) for the relevant year of assessment, then—

(i) the amount of the donation shall be deducted from or set off against any income of the individual chargeable to income tax for that year of assessment and tax shall, where necessary, be discharged or repaid accordingly, and

(ii) the total income of the individual or, where the individual's spouse is assessed to income tax in accordance with section 1017, the total income of the spouse shall be calculated accordingly.

(*b*) For the purposes of paragraph *(a)*, any such deduction or set-off shall not be taken into account in determining the net relevant earnings (within the meaning of section 787) of the individual or, as the case may be, the individual's spouse for the relevant year of assessment.

(10) Where a relevant donation is made by an individual who is an individual referred to in subsection (9), a claim under this section shall be made with the return required to be delivered by that individual under section 951 for the relevant year of assessment.

(11) Where a relevant donation, other than a relevant donation to which subsection (18) applies, is made by an individual who is not an individual referred to in subsection (9), the Tax Acts shall apply in relation to the approved sports body to which that donation is made as if—

(*a*) the grossed up amount of the donation were an annual payment which was the income of that body received by it under deduction of tax, in the amounts and at the rates specified in the statement referred to in paragraph (*b*) of the definition of "appropriate certificate", for the relevant year of assessment, and

(*b*) the provisions of the Tax Acts which apply in relation to a claim to repayment of tax applied in relation to any claim to repayment of such tax by that body;

but, if the total amount of the tax referred to in paragraph (*b*) of the definition of "appropriate certificate" is not paid, the amount of any repayment which would otherwise be made to that body in accordance with this section shall not exceed the amount of tax actually paid by that individual.

(12) The details contained in an appropriate certificate shall be given by the approved sports body to the Revenue Commissioners in an electronic format approved by the Revenue Commissioners in connection with the making of a claim to repayment of tax to which subsection (11)(*b*) refers and, where those details are so given, those details shall be accompanied by a declaration made by the approved sports body, on a form prescribed or authorised for that purpose by the Revenue Commissioners, to the effect that those details are correct and complete.

(13) Where the Revenue Commissioners are satisfied that an approved sports body does not have the facilities to give the details contained in an appropriate certificate in the electronic format referred to in subsection (12), such details shall be given in writing in a form prescribed or authorised by the Revenue Commissioners and shall be accompanied by a declaration made by the approved sports body to the effect that the claim is correct and complete.

(14) Every approved sports body, when required to do so by notice in writing from the Minister, shall within the time limited by the notice prepare and deliver to the Minister a return containing particulars of the aggregate amount of relevant donations received by the body in respect of each approved project.

(15) Where any question arises as to whether for the purposes of this section a project is an approved project, or a donation is a relevant donation, the Revenue Commissioners may consult with the Minister.

(16) For the purposes of a claim to relief under this section, but subject to subsection (17), an approved sports body shall, on acceptance of a relevant donation, give to the person making the relevant donation a receipt which shall—

(*a*) contain a statement that—

(i) it is a receipt for the purposes of this section,

(ii) the body is an approved sports body for the purposes of this section,

(iii) the donation in respect of which the receipt is given is a relevant donation for the purposes of this section, and

(iv) the project in respect of which the relevant donation has been made is an approved project,

(*b*) show—

(i) the name and address of the person making the relevant donation,

(ii) the amount of the relevant donation in both figures and words,

(iii) the date the relevant donation was made,

(iv) the full name of the approved sports body,

(v) the date on which the receipt was issued, and

(vi) particulars of the approved project in respect of which the relevant donation has been made,

and

(*c*) be signed by a duly authorised official of the approved sports body.

(17) An approved sports body shall not be required to give a receipt under subsection (16) to a donor—

(*a*) who is an individual but who is not an individual to which subsection (9) applies, or

(*b*) in respect of a relevant donation to which subsection (18) applies.

(18) Relief under this section shall not be given in respect of a relevant donation which is made at any time to an approved sports body in respect of an approved project if, at that time, the aggregate of the amounts of that relevant donation and all other relevant donations made to the approved sports body in respect of the approved project at or before that time exceeds €40,000,000.

(19) Where relief under this section has been granted in respect of a relevant donation and—

(*a*) that donation has not been used by the sports body concerned for the purpose of undertaking the approved project concerned, or

(*b*) which relief is otherwise found not to have been due,

section 235(2) shall not apply to the amount of that relevant donation.

(20) The Revenue Commissioners may nominate any of their officers to perform any acts and discharge any functions authorised by this section to be performed or discharged by them.][1]

Amendments

[1] Section 847A inserted by FA 2002 s 41 with effect from 1 May 2002.

Cross-references

Tax clearance certificates, general scheme: s 1095(2)(*b*)(i).

Tax Briefing

TB47 Apr 2002 p 13 — Donations to certain Sports Bodies.

Definitions

Capital Gains Tax Acts: s 1(2); Collector-General: s 2(1); company: s 4(1); connected: s 10; higher rate: s 3(1); land: IA 1937 Sch; person: IA 1937 s 11(*c*); profession: s 2(1); profits: s 4(1); profits or gains: s 3(4); resident: s 2(1); total income: s 3(1); trade: ss 3(1), 4(1); writing: IA 1937 Sch; year of assessment: s 2(1).

848 Designated charities: repayment of tax in respect of donations

Amendments

Section 848 repealed by TCA 1997 s 848A(13) (inserted by FA 2001 s 45) with effect from 6 April 2001.

848A Donations to approved bodies

[(1) (*a*) In this section—

"appropriate certificate", in relation to a relevant donation by a donor who is an individual, other than an individual referred to in subsection (7), to an approved body, means a certificate which is in such form as the Revenue Commissioners may prescribe and which contains—

(i) statements to the effect that—

(I) the donation satisfies the requirements of subsection (3), and

(II) the donor has paid or will pay to the Revenue Commissioners income tax of an amount equal to income tax at the standard rate or the higher rate or partly at the standard rate and partly at the higher rate, as the case may be, for the relevant year of assessment on the grossed up amount of the donation, but not being—

(A) income tax which the donor is entitled to charge against any other person or to deduct, retain or satisfy out of any payment which the donor is liable to make to any other person, or

(B) appropriate tax within the meaning of Chapter 4 of Part 8,

(ii) a statement specifying how much of the grossed up amount referred to in subparagraph (i)(II) has been or will be liable to income tax at the standard rate and the higher rate for the relevant year of assessment, and

(iii) the identifying number, known as the Personal Public Service Number (PPSN), of the donor;

"approved body" means a body specified in Part 1 of Schedule 26A;

"relevant accounting period" in relation to a relevant donation means the accounting period in which the relevant donation is made;

"relevant donation" means [, subject to subsection (3A),][1] a donation which satisfies the requirements of subsection (3) and takes the form of the payment by a person (in this section referred to as the **"donor"**) of a sum or sums of money amounting to at least [€250][2] to an approved body which is made—

(i) where the donor is a company, in an accounting period, and

(ii) where the donor is an individual, in a year of assessment;

"relevant year of assessment", in relation to a relevant donation, means the year of assessment in which the relevant donation is made.

(*b*) For the purposes of this section and in relation to a donation by a donor who is an individual (other than an individual referred to in subsection (7)), references to the grossed up amount are to the amount which after deducting income tax at the standard rate or the higher rate or partly at the standard rate and partly at the higher rate, as the case may be, for the relevant year of assessment leaves the amount of the donation.

(*c*) This section shall be construed together with Schedule 26A.

(2) Where it is proved to the satisfaction of the Revenue Commissioners that a person has made a relevant donation the provisions of subsection (4), subsection (7) or subsection (9) as the case may be, shall apply.

(3) A donation will satisfy the requirements of this section if—

(*a*) it is not subject to a condition as to repayment,

(*b*) neither the donor nor any person connected with the donor receives a benefit in consequence of making the donation, either directly or indirectly,

(*c*) it is not conditional on or associated with, or part of an arrangement involving, the acquisition of property by the approved body, otherwise than by way of gift, from the donor or a person connected with the donor,

(*d*) subject to subsection (4)—

(i) it would not be deductible in computing for the purposes of corporation tax the profits or gains of a trade or profession, and

(ii) it would not be an expense of management deductible in computing the total profits of a company,

(*e*) in respect of a donation made by an individual, the individual—

(i) is resident in the State for the relevant year of assessment,

(ii) has, except in the case of an individual referred to in subsection (7), given an appropriate certificate in relation to the donation to the approved body, and

(iii) has, except in the case of an individual referred to in subsection (7), paid the tax referred to in such appropriate certificate and is not entitled to claim a repayment of that tax or any part of that tax.

[(3A)(*a*) Notwithstanding any other provision of this section, where the aggregate of the amounts of all donations made by an individual in any year of assessment to an approved body or approved bodies with which the individual is associated is in excess of 10 per cent of the total income of the individual for that year of assessment, the amount of the excess shall not be treated as a relevant donation for the purposes of this section.

(*b*) For the purposes of this subsection—

(i) an individual is associated with an approved body if, at the time the donation is made, the individual is an employee or member of, the approved body or another approved body which is associated with that approved body, and

(ii) an approved body is associated with another approved body if, at the time the donation is made, it could reasonably be considered that—

(I) any person or any group of persons or groups of persons having a reasonable commonality of identity has or have, or had the means or power, either directly or indirectly, to determine the activities carried on or to be carried on by both approved bodies, or

(II) any person or any group of persons or groups of persons having a reasonable commonality of identity exercises or exercise, or is or are able to exercise, control over the affairs of both approved bodies.][3]

(4) Where a company makes a relevant donation in any accounting period and claims relief from tax by reference thereto, the amount thereof shall, for the purposes of corporation tax, be treated as—

(*a*) a deductible trading expense of a trade carried on by the company in, or

(*b*) an expense of management deductible in computing the total profits of the company for,

that accounting period.

(5) A claim by a company under this section shall be made with the return required to be delivered under section 951 for the accounting period in which the relevant donation is made.

(6) Where a relevant donation is made by a donor in an accounting period of a company or in a year of assessment which is less than 12 months, the amounts specified in the definition of "relevant donation" shall be proportionately reduced.

(7) Where a relevant donation is made to an approved body in a year of assessment by an individual who is a chargeable person (within the meaning of Part 41) for the year of assessment, the amount of the donation shall be deducted from or set off against any income of the individual chargeable to income tax for that year of assessment and tax shall where necessary be discharged or repaid accordingly, and the total income of the individual or, where the individual's spouse is assessed to income tax in accordance with section 1017, the total income of the spouse shall be calculated accordingly; but any such deduction or set-off shall not be taken into account in determining the net relevant earnings (within the meaning of section 787) of the individual or, as the case may be, the individual's spouse for the year of assessment.

(8) Where a relevant donation is made to an approved body by an individual who is a chargeable person (within the meaning of Part 41) a claim under this section shall be made with the return required to be made by that individual under section 951 for the year of assessment in which the donation is made.

(9) Where a donation is a relevant donation made by a donor who is an individual (other than an individual referred to in subsection (7)) to an approved body, the Tax Acts shall apply in relation to the approved body as if—

(*a*) the grossed up amount of the donation were an annual payment which was the income of the approved body received by it under deduction of tax, in the amounts and at the rates specified in the statement referred to in paragraph (ii) of the definition of "appropriate certificate" for the relevant year of assessment, and

(*b*) the provisions of those Acts which apply in relation to a claim to repayment of tax applied in relation to any claim to repayment of such tax by an approved body;

but, if the total amount of the tax referred to in paragraph (ii) of the definition of "appropriate certificate" is not paid, the amount of any repayment which would otherwise be made to an approved body in accordance with this section shall not exceed the amount of tax actually paid by the donor.

(10) The details contained in an appropriate certificate shall be given by the approved body to the Revenue Commissioners in an electronic format approved by the Revenue Commissioners in connection with the making of a claim to repayment of tax to which subsection (9)(*b*) refers and where it is so given it shall be accompanied by a declaration made by the approved body, on a form prescribed or authorised for that purpose by the Revenue Commissioners, to the effect that the details are correct and complete.

(11) Where the Revenue Commissioners are satisfied that an approved body does not have the facilities to give the details contained in an appropriate certificate in the electronic format referred to in subsection (10), such details shall be given in writing in a form prescribed or authorised by the Revenue Commissioners and shall be accompanied by a declaration made by the approved body to the effect that the claim is correct and complete.

(12) Section 764 shall apply as if subsection (1)(*b*) were deleted and subsection (2) shall be construed accordingly.

(13) Sections 88, 484, 485, 485A, 485B, 486, 486A and 767, subparagraphs (ii) and (iii) of subsection (1)(*b*), and subsection (3), of section 792 and section 848 are repealed.

(14) Where any body to which Part 2 or Part 3 of Schedule 26A relates has been approved or is the holder of an authorisation, as the case may be, under any enactment and, that approval or authorisation has not been withdrawn on the day prior to the coming into operation of this section, such body shall be deemed to be an approved body for the purposes of this section.][4]

Amendments

1 Inserted by FA 2003 s 21(1)(*a*) as respects donations made on or after 6 February 2003.

2 Substituted by FA 2001 s 45(3) in respect of donations made on or after 1 January 2002; previously "£200".

3 Subs (3A) inserted by FA 2003 s 21(1)(*b*) as respects donations made on or after 6 February 2003.

4 Section 848A inserted by FA 2001 s 45(1) with effect from 6 April 2001.

Cross-references

Deductions allowed in ascertaining taxable income and provisions relating to reductions in tax: s 458(1), (2); s 459(1), (2).

Donations to certain sports bodies: s 847A(5)(*d*).

Method of apportioning reliefs and charging tax in cases of separate assessments, subs (7): s 1024(2)(*a*)(*xa*).

Revenue information

Information leaflet CHY2 — Scheme of tax relief for donations to eligible charities and approved bodies under the terms of section 45 of the Finance Act 2001.

A list of eligible charities for the purposes of the scheme of tax relief on donations is available on Revenue's website — www.revenue.ie — under Publications/Lists.

Tax Briefings

TB44 June 2001 pp 16–19 — Donations to Approved Bodies — Tax Relief.

TB52 May 2003 pp 10–11 — Donations to Approved Bodies (Finance Act 2003 changes).

Definitions

company: s 4(1); higher rate: ss 3(1), 15; person: IA 1937 s 11(*c*); profession: s 2(1); resident: s 819; standard rate: ss 3(1), 15; Tax Acts: s 1(2).

[PART 36A
SPECIAL SAVINGS INCENTIVE ACCOUNTS][1]

Amendments

[1] Part 36A inserted by FA 2001 s 33(1) with effect from 6 April 2001.

Cross-references

Power of inspection, qualifying savings managers: s 904H(2).

Special Savings Incentive Account Regulations, SI No 176 of 2001, regs 4(1)(*a*) (indemnity) and 10(1), (2), (3), (6) and (7) (cessation).

Tax Briefing

TB43 April 2001 pp 25–26 — Special Savings Incentive Accounts.

Revenue information

Guidance Notes for Qualifying Savings Managers in relation to the management of Special Savings Incentive Accounts — Revised April 2002.

Information Leaflet CG12 — Special Savings Incentive Account.

A Revenue Press Release on SSIA maturity arrangements, and an information note on the maturity of SSIAs, are available on Revenue's website — www. revenue.ie — under Whats New/Archive March 2005.

848B Interpretation

[(1) In this Part—

"deposit account" means an account beneficially owned by an individual, which is—

(*a*) an account into which a deposit (within the meaning of section 256(1)) is made, or

(*b*) an account with a relevant European institution into which repayable funds are lodged;

"investment undertaking" has the meaning assigned to it in section 739B and "units in an investment undertaking" shall be construed accordingly;

"PPS Number", in relation to an individual, means that individual's Personal Public Service Number within the meaning of section 223 of the Social Welfare (Consolidation) Act, 1993;

"qualifying assets", subject to section 848G, means—

(*a*) deposit accounts,

(*b*) shares within the meaning of section 2(1) of the Credit Union Act, 1997,

(*c*) units in an investment undertaking,

(*d*) units in, or shares of, a relevant UCITS,

(*e*) relevant life assurance policies,

(*f*) shares issued by a company, wherever incorporated, officially listed on a recognised stock exchange, and

(*g*) securities issued by or on behalf of a government;

"qualifying individual" means an individual who at the time of opening a special savings incentive account—

(*a*) is 18 years of age, or older, and

(*b*) is resident in the State;

"qualifying savings manager" means—

(*a*) a person who is a holder of a licence granted under section 9 of the Central Bank Act, 1971, or a person who holds a licence or other similar authorisation under the law of any other Member State of the European Communities which corresponds to a licence granted under that section,

(*b*) a building society within the meaning of section 256,

(*c*) a trustee savings bank within the meaning of the Trustee Savings Banks Act, 1989,

(*d*) ACC Bank plc,

(*e*) the Post Office Savings Bank,

(*f*) a credit union within the meaning of the Credit Union Act, 1997,

(*g*) an investment undertaking,

(*h*) the holder of—

(i) an authorisation issued by the Minister for Enterprise, Trade and Employment under the European Communities (Life Assurance) Regulations of 1984 (SI No 57 of 1984), as amended, or,

(ii) an authorisation granted by the authority charged by law with the duty of supervising the activities of insurance undertakings in a Member State of the European Communities, other than the State, in accordance with Article 6 of Directive No. 79/267/EEC (OJ No L63 of 13 March, 1979, p 1), who is carrying on the business of life assurance in the State, or

(iii) an official authorisation to undertake insurance in Iceland, Liechtenstein and Norway pursuant to the EEA Agreement within the meaning of the European Communities (Amendment) Act, 1993, and who is carrying on the business of life assurance in the State,

(*i*) a person which is an authorised member firm of the Irish Stock Exchange, within the meaning of the Stock Exchange Act, 1995, or a member firm (which carries on a trade in the State through a branch or agency) of a stock exchange of any other Member State of the European Communities,

(*j*) a firm approved under section 10 of the Investment Intermediaries Act, 1995, which is authorised to hold client money, other than a firm authorised as a Restricted Activity Investment Product Intermediary, where the firm's authorisation permits it to engage in the proposed activities, or a business firm which has been authorised to provide similar investment business services under the laws of a Member State of the European Communities which correspond to that Act, or

(*k*) the Minister for Finance, acting through the Agency (within the meaning of section (1) of the National Treasury Management Agency Act, 1990);

"relevant European institution" means an institution which is a credit institution (within the meaning of the European Communities (Licensing and Supervision of Credit Institutions) Regulations, 1992 (SI No. 395 of 1992)) which has been authorised by the Central Bank of Ireland to carry on business of a credit institution in accordance with the provisions of the supervisory enactments (within the meaning of those Regulations);

"relevant UCITS" means a UCITS situated in a Member State of the European Communities, other than the State, which has been authorised by the competent authorities of the Member State in which it is situated;

"relevant life assurance policy", means a policy of assurance which satisfies the conditions specified in subsection (3);

"special savings incentive account" has the meaning assigned to it in section 848C;

"tax credit" in relation to a subscription, has the meaning assigned to it in section 848D(1);

"UCITS" means undertakings for collective investment in transferable securities within the meaning of Article 1 of Council Directive 85/611 (OJ No L375 of 31 December, 1985, p 3) and references to—

(*a*) "the Member State in which UCITS is situated", and

(*b*) a UCITS which has been "authorised by the competent authorities of the Member State in which it is situated",

shall have the same meanings as in Articles 3 and 4 respectively of that Directive;

"units in, or shares of, a relevant UCITS" means the rights or interests (however described) of the holder of units or shares in that relevant UCITS.

(2) Nothing in this Part shall be construed as authorising or permitting a person who is a qualifying savings manager to provide any services which that person would not otherwise be authorised or permitted to provide in the State.

(3) The conditions referred to in the definition of **"relevant life assurance policy"** in subsection (1) are that the policy of assurance is on the life of a person who beneficially owns the policy, and that the terms and conditions of the policy provide—

(*a*) for an express prohibition of any transfer of the policy, or the rights conferred by the policy or any share or interest in the policy or rights respectively, other than the cash proceeds from the termination of the policy or a partial surrender of the rights conferred by the policy, to that person,

(*b*) the policy, the rights conferred by the policy and any share or interest in the policy or rights respectively, shall not be capable of assignment, other than that the proceeds on the termination of the policy (other than on the death of the policyholder) may be transferred from a qualifying savings manager to another qualifying savings manager in accordance with the provisions of this Part, and

(*c*) the policy is not issued in the course of annuity business or pension business, within the meaning of section 706.][1]

Amendments

[1] Section 848B inserted by FA 2001 s 33(1) with effect from 6 April 2001.

Cross-references

Acquisition of qualifying assets, definition of "qualifying assets" para (*f*): s 848G(2).

Dividend withholding tax, interpretation, meaning of "qualifying savings manager" applied: s 172A(1)(*a*).

Investment undertakings, meaning of "qualifying savings manager" and "special savings incentive account" applied: s 739B(1).

Life assurance companies, taxation of policyholders — new basis, gains arising on a chargeable event, meaning of "special savings incentive account" applied: s 730D(2)(*c*); declarations, meaning of "qualifying savings manager" applied: s 730E(3A)(*a*).
Power of inspection, qualifying savings managers, meaning of "qualifying savings manager" and "special savings incentive account" applied: s 904H(1).
Special Savings Incentive Account Regulations, SI No 176 of 2001, regs 2 (interpretation).

Definitions

person: IA 1937 s 11(*c*); resident: s 819.

848C Special savings incentive account

[A special savings incentive account is a scheme of investment commenced on or after 1 May 2001 and on or before 30 April 2002 by a qualifying individual with a qualifying savings manager (who is registered in accordance with section 848R) under terms which include the following—

(*a*) apart from tax credits, in relation to subscriptions, subscribed by the qualifying savings manager under section 848E(I)(*b*)(ii) only the qualifying individual, or the spouse of that individual, may subscribe to the account,

(*b*) such subscriptions are funded by the qualifying individual, or the spouse of that individual, from funds available to either or both of them out of their own resources without recourse to borrowing, or the deferral of repayment (whether in respect of capital or interest) of sums already borrowed,

(*c*) subject to paragraph (*d*), such subscriptions, ignoring any amounts withdrawn from the account by the qualifying individual—

(i) in the month the account is commenced and in each of the 11 months immediately after that month, are of an amount agreed between the qualifying individual and the qualifying savings manager when the account is commenced, which amount shall not be less than [€12.50],[1] and

(ii) in any one month, do not exceed [€254],[2]

(*d*) such subscriptions, made in the month which is the month in which the fifth anniversary of the day of commencing the account falls, or thereafter, shall not be subscriptions for the purposes of section 848D,

(*e*) such subscriptions and tax credits, in relation to such subscriptions, are to be used, and used only, by the qualifying savings manager to acquire qualifying assets which—

(i) are held in the account and managed by the qualifying savings manager, and

(ii) are beneficially owned by the qualifying individual,

(*f*) all or any of the qualifying assets can not be assigned or otherwise pledged, as security for a loan,

(*g*) on commencing the account, the qualifying individual makes a declaration of a kind referred to in section 848F,

[(*h*) for the account to be treated as maturing (otherwise than in respect of the death of the qualifying individual) in accordance with section 848H(1), the qualifying individual shall make a declaration of a kind referred to in section 848I at any time within the period of 3 months ending on the fifth anniversary of the end of the month in which a subscription was first made to the account,][3] (*i*) that at the request of the qualifying individual, and within such time as shall be agreed, the account, with all rights and obligations of the parties thereto may be transferred to another qualifying savings manager in accordance with the provisions of this Part,

(*j*) that the qualifying savings manager will notify the qualifying individual if he or she ceases to be a qualifying savings manager, or ceases to be registered in accordance with section 848R, and

(*k*) that the qualifying savings manager will take reasonable measures—

(i) to establish that the PPS Number, contained in the declaration referred to in paragraph (*g*), made by a qualifying individual, is the PPS Number in relation to that individual, and

(ii) to ensure that the terms, provided for in this section, under which the account is commenced are and continue to be complied with, and

(*l*) that the qualifying savings manager will retain a copy of all material used to establish the correctness of each PPS Number contained in a declaration in accordance with paragraph (*k*)(i), for so long as the declaration is required to be retained under section 848R(11) and on being so required by an inspector, will make such material available for inspection.][4]

Amendments

1 Substituted by FA 2001 s 33(2)(*a*)(i) with effect from 1 January 2002; previously "£10".

2 Substituted by FA 2001 s 33(2)(*a*)(ii) with effect from 1 January 2002; previously "£200".

3 Para (*h*) substituted by FA 2002 s 49(*a*) with effect from 1 January 2002.

4 Section 848C inserted by FA 2001 s 33(1) with effect from 6 April 2001.

Cross-references

Annual returns by qualifying savings managers: s 848Q(*b*)(i).
Declaration on commencement of special savings incentive account, para (*g*): s 848F.
Declaration on maturity of special savings incentive account, para (*h*): s 848I.
Disclosure of information by qualifying savings managers: s 848U.
Interpretation, meaning of special savings incentive account applied for purposes of this Part: s 848B(1).
Power of inspection in relation to qualifying savings managers: s 904H(2)(*c*)(ii).
Regulations by Revenue Commissioners: s 848S(1)(*f*).
Special Savings Incentive Account Regulations, SI No 176 of 2001, reg 10(4) (cessation).
Termination of special savings incentive accounts: s 848H(2)(*a*).
Transfer of special savings incentive accounts: s 848N(6).

Definitions

inspector: ss 2(1), 852; month: IA 1937 Sch; PPS number, qualifying asset, qualifying individual, qualifying savings manager, tax credits: s 848B(1).

848D Tax credits

[Where a qualifying individual, or the spouse of that individual, subscribes to a special savings incentive account—

(*a*) the qualifying individual shall be treated, for the purposes of the Tax Acts, as having paid a grossed up amount, which amount, after deducting income tax at the standard rate for the year of assessment 2001, leaves the amount of the subscription, and

(*b*) the qualifying individual shall be entitled to be credited with the amount of income tax (in this Part referred to as the "tax credit", in relation to the subscription) treated as having been so deducted, in accordance with the provisions of this Part and not under any other provision of the Tax Acts.][1]

Amendments

1 Section 848D inserted by FA 2001 s 33(1) with effect from 6 April 2001.

Cross-references

Interpretation, meaning of "tax credit" in this section applies for purposes of this Part: s 848B(1).

Special savings incentive account: s 848C(*d*).

Definitions

qualifying individual: s 848B(1); special savings incentive account: s 848B(1); standard rate: ss 3(1), 15; Tax Acts: s 1(2); year of assessment 2001: s 2(1).

848E Payment of tax credit

[(1) Where a qualifying individual subscribes to a special savings incentive account, and the qualifying savings manager of that account complies with the provisions of section 848P in relation to that subscription—

(*a*) the Revenue Commissioners shall, subject to that section, pay to the qualifying savings manager the tax credit in relation to that subscription, and

(*b*) that tax credit shall—

(i) be beneficially owned by the qualifying individual, and

(ii) on receipt, be immediately subscribed by the qualifying savings manager to the special savings incentive account.

(2) Subject to this Part, exemption from income tax and capital gains tax shall be allowed in respect of the income and chargeable gains arising in respect of qualifying assets held in a special savings incentive account.

(3) A deposit (within the meaning of section 256(1)) made to a deposit account which is a qualifying asset, shall not be a relevant deposit (within the meaning of that section) for the purposes of Chapter 4 of Part 8.

[(3A) The provisions of section 267B(2) shall not apply to shares held in a special share account (within the meaning of section 267A) where the shares are a qualifying asset.][1]

(4) Notwithstanding subsection (2), where in a year of assessment an individual commences a special savings incentive account, the individual is obliged to include in a return, required to be delivered by the individual under section 951, or as the case may be, section 879, in respect of that year of assessment, a statement to the effect that the individual has commenced such an account.][2]

Amendments

1 Subs (3A) inserted by FA 2002 s 49(*b*) with effect from 1 January 2002.

2 Section 848E inserted by FA 2001 s 33(1) with effect from 6 April 2001.

Cross-references

Gain on maturity of special savings incentive account, subs (1)(*b*)(ii): s 848J(2), (3).

Investment undertakings, gain arising on a chargeable event: s 739D(6)(*h*).

Regulations: s 848S(1)(*d*).

Special savings incentive accounts, subs (1)(*b*)(ii): s 848C(1)(*a*).

Termination of special savings incentive account: s 848H(3)(*a*).

Definitions

chargeable gain: ss 5(1), 545, deposit account, qualifying assets, qualifying individual, qualifying savings manager, special savings incentive account, tax credit: s 848B(1); year of assessment: s 2(1).

848F Declaration on commencement

[The declaration referred to in section 848C(*g*) is a declaration in writing made by the qualifying individual to the qualifying savings manager which—

(*a*) is made and signed by the qualifying individual,

(*b*) is made in such form—

(i) as may be prescribed or authorised by the Revenue Commissioners, and

(ii) which contains a reference to the offence of making a false declaration under section 848T,

(*c*) contains the qualifying individual's—

(i) name,

(ii) address of his or her permanent residence,

(iii) PPS Number, and

(iv) date of birth,

(*d*) declares at the time the declaration is made, that the qualifying individual—

(i) is resident in the State,

(ii) has not commenced another special savings incentive account,

(iii) is the person who will beneficially own the qualifying assets to be held in the account,

(iv) will subscribe to the account from funds available to him or her, or his or her spouse, from their own resources, without recourse to borrowing, or the deferral of repayment (whether in respect of capital or interest) of sums already borrowed, and

(v) will not assign or otherwise pledge qualifying assets to be held in the account as security for a loan,

and

(*e*) contains an undertaking that if at any time the declaration ceases to be materially correct, the qualifying individual will advise the qualifying savings manager accordingly.][1]

Amendments

1 Section 848F inserted by FA 2001 s 33(1) with effect from 6 April 2001.

Cross-references

Offences in relation to false declarations: s 848T(1).

Power of inspection in relation to qualifying savings managers: s 904H(2)(*c*)(iii).

Registration as qualifying savings manager: s 848R(11)(*a*), (*b*).

Special savings incentive account: s 848C(*g*).

Special Savings Incentive Account Regulations, SI No 176 of 2001, reg 5(1) (declaration on commencement).

Definitions

PPS Number, qualifying assets, qualifying individual, qualifying savings manager: s 848B(1); resident: s 819; special savings incentive account: s 848B(1); writing: IA 1937 Sch.

848G Acquisition of qualifying assets

[(1) Qualifying assets held in a special savings incentive account, managed by a qualifying savings manager and beneficially owned by a qualifying individual may not at any time—

(*a*) be purchased (or otherwise acquired) by the qualifying savings manager, otherwise than—

(i) out of money which the qualifying savings manager holds in the account, and

(ii) by way of a bargain made at arm's length,

(*b*) be purchased from the qualifying individual or any person connected with that individual (within the meaning of section 10), or

(*c*) be connected with any other asset or liability of the qualifying individual or any other person connected with that individual (within the meaning of section 10) and for this purpose a qualifying asset is connected with another asset or a liability if the terms under which either asset or the liability is acquired and held would be different if the qualifying asset, the other asset or the liability, had not been acquired and held.

(2) Shares fulfil the condition as to official listing in paragraph (*f*) of the definition of "qualifying assets" in section 848B(1) if in pursuance of a public offer, a qualifying savings manager applies for the allotment or allocation to him or her of shares in a company which are due to be admitted to such listing within 30 days of the allocation or allotment, and which, when admitted to such a listing, would be qualifying assets.][1]

Amendments

[1] Section 848G inserted by FA 2001 s 33(1) with effect from 6 April 2001.

Cross-references

Interpretation: s 848B(1)(qualifying assets).

Definitions

company: ss 4(1), 5(1); person: IA 1937 s 11(*c*); qualifying assets, qualifying individual, qualifying savings manager, special savings incentive account: s 848B(1).

848H Termination of special savings incentive account

[(1) A special savings incentive account is treated as maturing—

[(*a*) on the fifth anniversary of the end of the month in which a subscription was first made to the account where the qualifying individual has made a declaration of a kind referred to in section 848I and the qualifying savings manager is in possession of that declaration at that time, or,][1]

(*b*) on the day of the death of the qualifying individual,

whichever event first occurs.

(2) A special savings incentive account is treated as ceasing, where at any time before the account is treated as maturing—

(*a*) any of the terms referred to in section 848C are not complied with, or

(*b*) the qualifying individual is neither resident nor ordinarily resident in the State.

(3) Where a special savings incentive account is treated as maturing or ceasing—

(*a*) the account thereafter shall not be a special savings incentive account for the purposes of section 848E, and

(*b*) the assets remaining in the account after having regard to all liabilities to tax on gains treated as accruing to the account under this Part shall—

(i) where the assets are shares, securities, or units in, or shares of, a relevant UCITS, be treated for the purposes of the Capital Gains Tax Acts, as having been acquired by the qualifying individual at their then market value at that time,

(ii) where the asset is a relevant life assurance policy, be treated as if it were a policy commenced at that time and in respect of which premiums in an amount equal to the market value of the policy at that time had been paid at that time, for the purposes of Chapter 5 of Part 26, and

(iii) where the asset is units in an investment undertaking, be treated as if the units had been acquired at that time, for their market value at that time, for the purposes of Chapter IA of Part 27.

[(4) Where at any time a special savings incentive account is treated as maturing or, as the case may be, ceasing, the amount of any income which accrues in respect of qualifying assets held in the account, in so far as it was not, but for this subsection, taken into account in determining a gain under section 848J, 848K or 848L, shall, when received, be treated as an amount of cash withdrawn from the account before the account is treated as maturing, or as the case may be, ceasing, and the qualifying savings manager shall be liable to tax in accordance with section 848M on the gain thereby arising under section 848L.][2]][3]

Amendments

1 Subs (1)(*a*) substituted by FA 2002 s 49(*c*)(i) with effect from 1 January 2002.

2 Subs (4) inserted by FA 2002 s 49(*c*)(ii) with effect from 1 January 2002.

3 Section 848H inserted by FA 2001 s 33(1) with effect from 6 April 2001.

Cross-references

Special savings incentive accounts: s 848C(*h*).

Definitions

Capital Gains Tax Acts: s 1(2); month: IA 1937 Sch; ordinarily resident: s 820; qualifying individual: s 848B(1); qualifying savings manager: s 848B(1); relevant life assurance policy: s 848B(1); resident: s 819; special savings incentive account: s 848B(1); units in an investment undertaking: s 848B(1); units in, or shares of, a relevant UCITS: s 848B(1).

848I Declaration on maturity

[The declaration referred to in section 848C(*h*) is a declaration in writing made by the qualifying individual to the qualifying savings manager which—

(*a*) is made and signed by the qualifying individual,

(*b*) is made in such form—

(i) as may be prescribed or authorised by the Revenue Commissioners, and

(ii) which contains a reference to the offence of making a false declaration under section 848T, (*c*) contains the qualifying individual's—

(i) name,

(ii) address of his or her permanent residence,

(iii) PPS Number, and

(iv) date of birth,

(*d*) declares that at all times in the period from which the account was commenced until the date the declaration is made, the qualifying individual—

(i) was the beneficial owner of the qualifying assets held in the account,

(ii) had only one special savings incentive account,

(iii) was resident or ordinarily resident in the State,

(iv) subscribed to the account from funds available to the qualifying individual or his or her spouse without recourse to borrowing, or the deferral of repayment (whether of capital or interest) of sums borrowed when the account was commenced, and

(v) did not assign or otherwise pledge qualifying assets held in the account as security for a loan.][1]

Amendments

1 Section 848I inserted by FA 2001 s 33(1) with effect from 6 April 2001.

Cross-references

Offences in relation to false declarations: s 848T(1).

Power of inspection in relation to qualifying savings managers: s 904H(2)(*c*)(iii).

Registration as qualifying savings manager: s 848R(11)(*a*).

Special savings incentive accounts: s 848C(*h*).

Termination of special savings incentive account: s 848H(1).

Definitions

ordinarily resident: s 820; PPS Number, qualifying assets, qualifying individual, qualifying savings manager, special savings incentive account: s 848B(1); resident: s 810; writing: IA 1937 Sch.

848J Gain on maturity

[(1) On the day on which a special savings incentive account is treated as maturing, a gain shall be treated as accruing on the account in an amount determined under subsection (2).

(2) The amount of the gain referred to in subsection (1) is an amount equal to the aggregate market value of all assets (including cash) held in the account on the day the account is treated as maturing, less the sum of all subscriptions (including subscriptions made by the qualifying savings manager under section 848E(1)(*b*)(ii)), made to the account on or before that day to the extent that they have not previously been treated, in accordance with subsection (3), as having been withdrawn from the account.

(3) For the purposes of subsection (2) where there is a withdrawal from an account, the amount withdrawn (before being reduced by any tax liability arising under this Part in respect of any gain treated as accruing to the account as a result of the withdrawal) shall be treated as a withdrawal of subscriptions to the extent that the amount withdrawn does not exceed the total amount of subscriptions (including subscriptions made by the qualifying savings manager in accordance with section 848E(1)(*b*)(ii)) made to the

account since commencement, reduced by the amount of such subscriptions previously treated as subscriptions withdrawn from the account under this subsection.

(4) For the purposes of subsection (3) where there is a withdrawal of assets (other than cash) from an account the amount withdrawn shall be the amount which is the market value of those assets at the time of their withdrawal.][1]

Amendments

[1] Section 848J inserted by FA 2001 s 33(1) with effect from 6 April 2001.

Cross-references

Annual returns by qualifying savings managers: s 848Q(*a*)(vii)(II).
Termination of special savings incentive account: s 848H(4).

Definitions

qualifying savings manager, special savings incentive account: s 848B(1).

848K Gain on cessation

[(1) On the day on which a special savings incentive account is treated as ceasing, a gain shall be treated as accruing on the account in an amount determined under subsection (2).

(2) The amount of the gain referred to in subsection (1) is an amount equal to the aggregate market value of all assets (including cash) held in the account on the day the account is treated as ceasing.][1]

Amendments

[1] Section 848K inserted by FA 2001 s 33(1) with effect from 6 April 2001.

Cross-references

Annual returns by qualifying savings manager: s 848Q(*a*)(vii)(II).
Termination of special savings incentive account: s 848H(4).

Definitions

special savings incentive account: s 848B(1).

848L Gain on withdrawal

[(1) Where before a special savings incentive account is treated as maturing or ceasing (as the case may be) a qualifying individual withdraws cash or other assets from the account, a gain shall be treated as accruing on the account in an amount determined under subsection (2).

(2) The amount of the gain referred to in subsection (1) is—

(*a*) where the withdrawal is in cash, the amount of that cash, and

(*b*) where the withdrawal is of assets (other than cash) an amount equal to the market value of such assets on the day of withdrawal.][1]

Amendments

[1] Section 848L inserted by FA 2001 s 33(1) with effect from 6 April 2001.

Cross-references

Annual returns by qualifying savings managers: s 848Q(*a*)(vii)(II).
Termination of special savings incentive account: s 848H(4).

Definitions

qualifying individual, special savings incentive account: s 848B(1).

848M Taxation of gains

[[(1) A qualifying savings manager shall be liable to tax (in this Part referred to as "relevant tax") representing income tax on a gain treated under this Part as accruing to a special savings incentive account in an amount equal to 23 per cent of the amount of that gain.][1]

(2) A qualifying savings manager who becomes liable under subsection (1) to an amount of relevant tax shall be entitled to withdraw sufficient funds from the account to which the gain is treated as accruing to satisfy that liability and the qualifying individual shall allow such withdrawal; but where there are no funds or insufficient funds available in the account out of which the qualifying savings manager may satisfy, or fully satisfy, such liability, the amount of relevant tax for which there are insufficient funds so available shall be a debt due to the qualifying savings manager from the qualifying individual.

(3) Subject to section 848P, the relevant tax in respect of a gain which in accordance with that section, is required to be included in a return, shall be due at the time by which the return is to be made and shall be paid by the qualifying fund manager without the making of an assessment; but relevant tax which has become so due may be assessed on the qualifying savings manager (whether or not it has been paid when the assessment is made) if that tax or any part of it is not paid on or before the due date.

(4) Where it appears to the inspector that there is any amount of relevant tax which ought to have been, but has not been, included in a return, or where the inspector is dissatisfied with any return, the inspector may make an assessment on the qualifying savings manager [to the best of the inspector's judgement][2], and any amount of relevant tax due under an assessment made by virtue of this subsection shall be treated for the purposes of interest on unpaid tax as having been payable at the time when it would have been payable if a correct return had been made.

(5) (*a*) Any relevant tax assessed on a qualifying savings manager under this Chapter shall be due within one month after the issue of the notice of assessment (unless that tax is due earlier under subsection (3)) subject to any appeal against the assessment, but no such appeal shall affect the date when any amount is due under subsection (3).

(*b*) On the determination of an appeal against an assessment under this section any relevant tax overpaid shall be repaid.

(6) (*a*) The provisions of the Income Tax Acts relating to—

(i) assessments to income tax,

(ii) appeals against such assessments (including the rehearing of appeals and the statement of a case for the opinion of the High Court), and

(iii) the collection and recovery of income tax,

shall, in so far as they are applicable, apply to the assessment, collection and recovery of relevant tax.

(*b*) Any amount of relevant tax payable in accordance with this Part without the making of an assessment shall carry interest at the rate of [0.0322 per cent for each day or part of a day][4] from the date when the amount becomes due and payable.

(*c*) [Subsections (3) to (5) of section 1080][5] shall apply in relation to interest payable under paragraph (*b*) as they apply in relation to interest payable under section 1080.

(*d*) In its application to any relevant tax charged by any assessment made in accordance with this section, section 1080 shall apply as if [subsection (2)(*b*)][6] of that section were deleted.][7]

Amendments

1 Subs (1) substituted by FA 2002 s 49(*d*)(i) with effect from 1 January 2002.

2 Substituted by FA 2002 s 49(*d*)(ii) with effect from 1 January 2002; previously "to the best of his or their judgement".

3 Substituted by FA 2002 s 129(1)(*a*) with effect from 1 September 2002 in respect of an amount due to be paid or remitted, whether before, on, or after that date; previously "1 per cent for each month or part of a month".

4 Substituted by FA 2002 s 129(1)(*a*) with effect from 1 September 2002 as regards interest chargeable in respect of an amount due to be paid or remitted, whether before, on, or after that date; previously "1 per cent for each month or part of a month".

5 Substituted by FA 2005 s 145(7)(*a*) and Sch 5 Pt 1 in relation to any unpaid income tax, corporation tax or capital gains tax, as the case may be, that has not been paid before 1 April 2005 regardless of when that tax became due and payable and notwithstanding anything to the contrary in any other enactment other than TCA 1997 s 1082; previously "Subsections (2) to (4) of section 1080".

6 Substituted by FA 2005 s 145(7)(*a*) and Sch 5 Pt 1 in relation to any unpaid income tax, corporation tax or capital gains tax, as the case may be, that has not been paid before 1 April 2005 regardless of when that tax became due and payable and notwithstanding anything to the contrary in any other enactment other than TCA 1997 s 1082; previously "subsection (1)(*b*)".

7 Section 848M inserted by FA 2001 s 33(1) with effect from 6 April 2001.

Cross-references

Dividend withholding tax, interpretation, meaning of "special savings incentive account" applied: s 172A(1)(*a*).

Termination of special savings incentive account: s 848H(4).

Definitions

High Court: IA 1937 Sch; inspector: ss 2(1); 852; month: IA 1937 Sch; qualifying individual, qualifying savings manager: s 848B(1); special savings incentive account: s 848B(1).

848N Transfer of special savings incentive account

[(1) Where arrangements are made by a qualifying individual to transfer his or her special savings incentive account from one qualifying savings manager (in this section referred to as the **"transferor"**) to another qualifying savings manager (in this section referred to as the **"transferee"**) or the account is transferred in consequence of the transferor ceasing to act or to be a qualifying savings manager, the following provisions of this section shall apply.

(2) Where a transfer takes place under subsection (1)—

(*a*) all subscriptions to the special savings incentive account in so far as they have not been applied to acquire qualifying assets, and all qualifying assets in the account, must be made to a single transferee,

(*b*) the qualifying individual shall make a declaration of a kind referred to in section 848O to the transferee, and

(*c*) the transferee shall thereafter for the purposes of this Part be the qualifying savings manager of the special savings incentive account transferred.

(3) The transferor shall within 30 days after the date of transfer—

(*a*) give to the transferee a notice containing the information specified in subsection (4) and the declaration specified in subsection (5), and

(*b*) pay to the transferee the aggregate of the amounts referred to in subsection (4)(*b*)(vi).

(4) The information referred to in subsection (3) is—

(*a*) as regards the qualifying individual his or her—

(i) name,

(ii) address of permanent residence,

(iii) date of birth,

(iv) PPS Number, and

(*b*) as respects the special savings incentive account transferred pursuant to this section—

(i) the date of transfer,

(ii) the date the account was commenced,

(iii) the identification of the assets held in the account,

(iv) the total of all subscriptions made to the account by the qualifying individual, or the spouse of that individual,

(v) the total of all tax credits, in relation to subscriptions, subscribed to the account,

(vi) the amount of any dividends, and other amounts payable in respect of qualifying assets held in the account and amounts of tax credits, which have not been received by the transferor at the date of transfer, and

(vii) the amount of each withdrawal from the account and the date of each such withdrawal.

(5) The declaration referred to in subsection (3) is a declaration in writing made and signed by the transferor to the effect that—

(*a*) the transferor has fulfilled all obligations under this Part,

(*b*) the transferor has transferred to the transferee all money and qualifying assets held in the account and that where registration of any such transfer is required, the transferor has taken the necessary steps to ensure that those qualifying assets can be registered in the name of the transferee, and

(*c*) that, to the best of the qualifying savings manager's knowledge and belief, the information contained in the notice referred to in subsection (3) is correct.

(6) Notwithstanding section 848C, where a special savings incentive account is being transferred in accordance with this section it shall not be treated as ceasing should, during the period of the transfer, the qualifying assets held in the account, temporarily cease to be managed by a qualifying savings manager, or a qualifying savings manager who is registered in accordance with section 848R.][1]

Amendments

1 Section 848N inserted by FA 2001 s 33(1) with effect from 6 April 2001.

Cross-references

Declaration on transfer of special savings incentive account, subs (2)(*b*): s 848O.

Offences in relation to false declarations, subs (5): s 848T.

Power of inspection in relation to qualifying savings managers, subs (3): s 904H(2)(*d*).

Registration as a qualifying savings manager: s 848R(8).
Special Savings Account Regulations 2001, SI No 176 of 2001, reg 12(*a*) (procedure on transfer).

Definitions

PPS Number, tax credits, qualifying assets, qualifying individual, qualifying savings manager, special savings incentive account: s 848B(1).

848O Declaration on transfer

[The declaration referred to in section 848N(2)(*b*) is a declaration in writing made by the qualifying individual to the qualifying savings manager who is the transferee referred to in that section, which—

(*a*) is made and signed by the qualifying individual,

(*b*) is made in such form—

(i) as may be prescribed or authorised by the Revenue Commissioners, and

(ii) which contains a reference to the offence of making a false declaration under section 848T,

(*c*) contains the qualifying individual's—

(i) name,

(ii) address of his or her permanent residence,

(iii) PPS Number, and

(iv) date of birth,

and

(*d*) declares—

(i) at the time the declaration is made, that the qualifying individual—

(I) has not commenced another special savings incentive account, and

(II) is the person who beneficially owns the qualifying assets held in the account being transferred,

(ii) at the time the special savings incentive account was commenced, the qualifying individual was resident in the State,

(iii) that subscriptions to the account have been and will continue to be made from funds available to him or her, or his or her spouse, out of their own resources without recourse to borrowing, or the deferral of repayment (whether in respect of capital or interest) of sums borrowed when the account was commenced, and

(iv) has not and will not assign or otherwise pledge qualifying assets held in the account as security for a loan.][1]

Amendments

1 Section 848O inserted by FA 2001 s 33(1) with effect from 6 April 2001.

Cross-references

Offences in relation to false declarations: s 848T(1).
Power of inspection in relation to qualifying savings manager: s 904H(2)(*c*)(iii).
Registration as qualifying savings manager: s 848R(11)(*a*), (*b*).
Transfer of special savings incentive account: s 848N(2)(*b*).
Special Savings Account Regulations 2001, SI No 176 of 2001, reg 12(*b*) (procedure on transfer).

Definitions

PPS Number, qualifying individual, qualifying savings manager: s 848B(1); resident: s 819; special savings incentive account: s 848B(1); writing: IA 1937 Sch.

848P Monthly returns

[A qualifying savings manager who is or was registered in accordance with section 848R, shall, within 15 days of the end of every month, make a return (including, where it is the case, a nil return) to the Revenue Commissioners, which—

(*a*) specifies in respect of all special savings incentive accounts managed by the qualifying savings manager in that month—

(i) the aggregate amount of tax credits, in relation to the aggregate of subscriptions made to those accounts in that month,

(ii) the aggregate amount of relevant tax to which the qualifying savings manager is liable in respect of gains treated as accruing on those accounts in that month, and

(iii) the net amount (being the difference between the amounts specified in paragraphs (*a*) and (*b*)) due from or, as the case may be, to, the Revenue Commissioners, and

(*b*) contains a declaration in a form prescribed or authorised by the Revenue Commissioners that, to the best of the qualifying savings manager's knowledge and belief, the information referred to in paragraph (*a*) is correct.][1]

Amendments

1 Section 848P inserted by FA 2001 s 33(1) with effect from 6 April 2001.

Cross-references

Payment of tax credit in relation to subscriptions to special savings incentive accounts: s 848E(1).

Power of inspection in relation to qualifying savings managers: s 904H(2)(*a*).

Registration as qualifying savings manager: s 848R(9), (10).

Regulations: s 848S(1)(*a*); para (*a*)(iii): s 848S(1)(*d*).

Special Savings Account Regulations 2001, SI No 176 of 2001, regs 2 (interpretation), 7(*b*) (payment of net amount), 8 (additional information).

Taxation of gains accruing to special savings incentive accounts: s 848M(3).

Definitions

month: IA 1937 Sch; qualifying savings manager: s 848B(1); relevant tax: s 848M(1); special savings incentive account, tax credit: s 848B(1).

848Q Annual returns

[A qualifying savings manager who is or was registered in accordance with section 848R shall in respect of each year of assessment, on or before 28 February in the year following the year of assessment, make a return (including, where it is the case, a nil return), to the Revenue Commissioners which in respect of the year of assessment—

(*a*) specifies in respect of each special incentive savings account managed by the qualifying savings manager—

(i) the name of the qualifying individual,

(ii) the address of that individual's permanent residence,

(iii) the PPS Number of the individual,

(iv) the date the account was commenced,

(v) the total amount of subscriptions made by the qualifying individual, or the spouse of that individual, to the account,

(vi) the total amount of tax credits, in respect of subscriptions, subscribed to the account, and

(vii) in respect of each gain accruing on the account—

(I) the amount of relevant tax to which the qualifying savings manager has thereby become liable, and

(II) whether the gain accrued under section 848J, 848K or 848L,

and

(*b*) containing a declaration, in a form prescribed or authorised by the Revenue Commissioners, that to the best of the qualifying savings manager's knowledge and belief—

(i) in respect of each special savings incentive account referred to in the return, the terms referred to in section 848C have been and are being complied with, and

(ii) the information referred to in paragraph (*a*) and the declaration referred to in subparagraph (i) is correct.][1]

Amendments

1 Section 848Q inserted by FA 2001 s 33(1) with effect from 6 April 2001.

Cross-references

Power of inspection in relation to qualifying savings managers: s 904H(2)(*a*).

Registration as qualifying savings manager s 848R(10), (11).

Regulations: s 848S(1)(*c*).

Special Savings Account Regulations 2001, SI No 176 of 2001, regs 2 (interpretation), 13 (additional information).

Definitions

PPS Number, qualifying savings manager: s 848B(1); relevant tax: s 848M(1); special savings incentive account, tax credits: s 848B(1); year of assessment: s 2(1).

848R Registration etc

[(1) A person can not be a qualifying savings manager unless the person is included in a register maintained by the Revenue Commissioners of persons registered in accordance with subsection (5).

(2) Where at any time a qualifying savings manager does not have a branch or business establishment in the State, or has such a branch or business establishment but does not intend to carry out all the functions as a qualifying savings manager at that branch or business establishment, the qualifying savings manager shall not be registered in accordance with subsection (5) unless the qualifying savings manager appoints for the time being a person, who—

(*a*) where an individual, is resident in the State, and

(*b*) where not an individual, has a business establishment in the State,

to be responsible for securing the discharge of the obligations which fall to be discharged by the qualifying savings manager under this Part, and advises the Revenue Commissioners of the identity of that person and the fact of that person's appointment.

(3) Where a person has been appointed in accordance with subsection (2), and subject to subsection (4) that person shall—

(*a*) be entitled to act on the qualifying savings manager's behalf for any of the purposes of the provisions of this Part,

(*b*) shall secure (where appropriate by acting on the qualifying savings manager's behalf) the qualifying savings manager's compliance with and discharge of the obligations under this Part, and

(*c*) shall be personally liable in respect of any failure of the qualifying savings manager to comply with or discharge any such obligations as if the obligations imposed on the qualifying savings manager were imposed jointly and severally on the qualifying savings manager and the person concerned.

(4) The appointment of a person in accordance with subsection (2) shall be treated as terminated in circumstances where—

(*a*) the Revenue Commissioners have reason to believe that the person concerned—

(i) has failed to secure the discharge of any of the obligations imposed on a qualifying savings manager under this Part, or

(ii) does not have adequate resources to discharge those obligations, and

(*b*) the Revenue Commissioners have notified the qualifying savings manager and that person that they propose to treat the appointment of that person as having terminated with effect from the date of the notice.

(5) If the Revenue Commissioners are satisfied that an applicant for registration is entitled to be registered, they shall register the applicant with effect from such date as may be specified by them.

(6) If it appears to the Revenue Commissioners at any time that a qualifying savings manager who is registered under this section—

(*a*) would not be entitled to be registered if it applied for registration at that time, or

(*b*) has not complied with the provisions of this Part,

the Revenue Commissioners may, by written notice given to the qualifying savings manager, cancel its registration with effect from such date as may be specified in the notice.

(7) Any qualifying savings manager who is aggrieved by the failure of the Revenue Commissioners to register it or by the cancellation of its registration, may, by notice given to the Revenue Commissioners before the end of the period of 30 days beginning with the date on which the qualifying savings manager was notified of the Revenue Commissioners decision, require the matter to be determined by the Appeal Commissioners and the Appeal Commissioners shall hear and determine the matter in like manner as an appeal.

(8) A qualifying savings manager shall give notice to the Revenue Commissioners and the qualifying individuals whose special savings incentive accounts he or she manages of his or her intention to cease to act as the qualifying savings manager not less than 30

days before he or she so ceases so that his or her obligations to the Revenue Commissioners can be conveniently discharged at or about the time he or she ceases to so act, and the notice to the qualifying individuals shall inform them of their right to transfer their special savings incentive accounts under section 848N.

(9) Subject to subsection (10), every return to be made by a qualifying savings manager under section 848P and 848Q shall be made in electronic format approved by the Revenue Commissioners and shall be accompanied by a declaration made by the qualifying savings manager, in a form prescribed or authorised for that purpose by the Revenue Commissioners, to the effect that the return is correct.

(10) Where the Revenue Commissioners are satisfied that a qualifying savings manager does not have the facilities to make a return under sections 848P or 848Q in the format referred to in subsection (9), such returns shall be made in writing in a form prescribed or authorised by the Revenue Commissioners, and shall be accompanied by a declaration made by the qualifying savings manager, on a form prescribed or authorised for that purpose by the Revenue Commissioners, to the effect that the return is correct.

(11) A qualifying savings manager shall retain—

(*a*) in respect of each special savings incentive account which is treated as maturing, the declarations of a kind referred to in sections 848F, 848I, and 848O for a period of 3 years after the date on which the account was treated as maturing, and

(*b*) in respect of each special savings incentive account which is treated as ceasing, the declarations of a kind referred to in sections 848F and 848O for a period of 3 years after the date on which the account was treated as ceasing,

and on being so required by notice given to him or her in writing by an inspector, make available for inspection all or any such declarations.][1]

Amendments

1 Section 848R inserted by FA 2001 s 33(1) with effect from 6 April 2001.

Cross-references

Annual returns by qualifying savings managers: s 848Q.
Monthly returns by qualifying savings managers: s 848P.
Power of inspection in relation to qualifying savings managers: s 904H(2).
Regulations: s 848S(1)(*a*).
Special savings incentive accounts: s 848C; s 848C(*j*); subs (11): s 848C(*l*).
Special Savings Account Regulations 2001, SI No 176 of 2001, regs 2 (indemnity), 3(1) (registration).
Transfer of special savings incentive account: s 848N(6).

Definitions

inspector: s 2(1), 852; person: IA 1937 s 11(*c*); qualifying individual, qualifying savings manager, special savings incentive account: s 848B(1); writing: IA 1937 Sch.

848S Regulations

[(1) The Revenue Commissioners shall make regulations providing generally as to the administration of this Part and those regulations may, in particular and without prejudice to the generality of the foregoing include provisions—

(*a*) as to the manner in which a qualifying savings manager is to register under section 848R, (*b*) as to the manner in which a return is to be made under section 848P,

(*c*) as to the manner in which a return is to be made under section 848Q,

(*d*) as to the manner in which tax credits are to be paid under section 848E(1), or the net amount referred to in section 848P(*a*)(iii),

(*e*) as to the circumstances in which the Revenue Commissioners may require a qualifying savings manager to give a bond or guarantee to the Revenue Commissioners which is sufficient to indemnify the Commissioners against any loss arising by virtue of the fraud or negligence of the qualifying savings manager in relation to the operation of the provisions of this Part, and

(*f*) as to the manner in which a qualifying savings manager ensures compliance with the terms of special savings incentive accounts provided for in section 848C.

(2) Every regulation made under this section shall be laid before Dáil Éireann as soon as may be after it is made and, if a resolution annulling the regulation is passed by Dáil Éireann within the next 21 days on which Dáil Éireann has sat after the regulation is laid before it, the regulation shall be annulled accordingly but without prejudice to the validity of anything previously done thereunder.][1]

Amendments

1 Section 848S inserted by FA 2001 s 33(1) with effect from 6 April 2001.

Regulations

Special Savings Incentive Accounts Regulations, 2001 (SI No 176 of 2001).

Definitions

Dáil Éireann: IA 1937 Sch; qualifying savings manager, special savings incentive account, tax credit: s 848B(1).

848T Offences

[(1) A person who makes a declaration under section 848F, section 8481, section 848O or section 848N(5) which is false, shall be guilty of an offence and shall be liable on summary conviction to a fine of [€1,900],[1] or, at the discretion of the court, to imprisonment for a term not exceeding 6 months or to both the fine and the imprisonment.][2]

Amendments

1 Substituted by FA 2001 s 33(2)(iii) with effect from 1 January 2002; previously "£1,500".

2 Section 848T inserted by FA 2001 s 33(1) with effect from 6 April 2001.

Cross-references

Declaration on commencement of special savings incentive account: s 848F(*b*)(ii).

Declaration on maturity of special savings incentive account: s 848I(*b*)(ii).

Declaration on transfer of special savings incentive account: s 848O(*b*)(ii).

848U Disclosure of information

[Notwithstanding any obligation as to secrecy or other restriction upon disclosure of information imposed by or under statute or otherwise, where a qualifying savings manager has reasonable grounds to suspect that the terms, provided for under section 848C, under which a special savings incentive account was commenced, are not being complied with, the qualifying savings manager shall inform the Revenue Commissioners accordingly.][1]

Amendments

1 Section 848U inserted by FA 2001 s 33(1) with effect from 6 April 2001.

Definitions

qualifying savings manager, special savings incentive account: s 848B(1).

MANAGEMENT PROVISIONS

PART 37
ADMINISTRATION

849 Taxes under care and management of Revenue Commissioners

(1) In this section, **"tax"** means income tax, corporation tax and capital gains tax.

(2) All duties of tax shall be under the care and management of the Revenue Commissioners.

(3) The Revenue Commissioners may do all such acts as may be deemed necessary and expedient for raising, collecting, receiving and accounting for tax in the like and in as full and ample a manner as they are authorised to do in relation to any other duties under their care and management and, unless the Minister for Finance otherwise directs, shall appoint such officers and other persons for collecting, receiving, managing and accounting for any duties of tax as are not required to be appointed by some other authority.

(4) All such appointments shall continue in force, notwithstanding the death, or the ceasing to hold office, of any Revenue Commissioner, and the holders shall have power to execute the duties of their respective offices and to enforce in the execution of those offices all laws and regulations relating to tax in every part of the State.

(5) The Revenue Commissioners may suspend, reduce, discharge or restore, as they see fit, any such officer or person.

(6) Any act or thing required or permitted by this or any other statute to be done by the Revenue Commissioners in relation to tax may be done by any one Revenue Commissioner.

Definitions

inspector: ss 2(1), 5(1), 852; person: IA 1937 s 11(*c*); statute: IA 1937 s 3; s 1(1).

Former enactments

ITA 1967 s 155; CGTA 1975 s 51(1) and Sch 4 paras 1(1) and 2; CTA 1976 s 6(5); FA 1996 s 132(1) and Sch 5 Pt I para 10(1).

Corresponding UK tax provision

Taxes Management Act 1970 s 1.

850 Appeal Commissioners

(1) The Minister for Finance shall appoint persons to be Appeal Commissioners for the purposes of the Income Tax Acts (in the Tax Acts and the Capital Gains Tax Acts referred to as **"Appeal Commissioners"**) and the persons so appointed shall, by virtue

of their appointment and without other qualification, have authority to execute such powers and to perform such duties as are assigned to them by the Income Tax Acts.

(2) Appeal Commissioners shall be allowed such sums in respect of salary and incidental expenses as the Minister for Finance directs.

(3) The Minister for Finance shall cause an account of all appointments of Appeal Commissioners and their salaries to be laid before each House of the Oireachtas within 20 days of their appointment or, in the case of a House not then sitting, within 20 days after the next sitting of that House.

(4) Anything required to be done under the Income Tax Acts by the Appeal Commissioners or any other Commissioners may, except where otherwise expressly provided by those Acts, be done by any 2 or more Commissioners.

Cross-references

Capital acquisitions tax, appeals, meaning of "Appeal Commissioners" applied: CATCA 2003 s 67(1).

Income Tax (Relevant Contracts) Regulations 2000, SI No 71 of 2000, meaning of "Collector-General" applied: ITRCR 2000 reg 2.

Public Service Management (Recruitment and Appointments) Act 2004, s 7 (excluded positions generally) — reference to "Appeal Commissioner" appointed under TCA 1997 s 850.

Definitions

Income Tax Acts: s 1(2); the Oireachtas: IA 1937 Sch; person: IA 1937 s 11(*c*).

Former enactments

ITA 1967 s 156; F(MP)A 1968 s 1(1), s3(2) and Sch Pt II.

Corresponding UK tax provision

Taxes Management Act 1970 s 2.

851 Collector-General

(1) There shall be a Collector-General, who shall be appointed by the Revenue Commissioners from among their officers and who shall hold such office at their will and pleasure.

(2) The Collector-General shall collect and levy the tax from time to time charged in all assessments to income tax, corporation tax and capital gains tax of which particulars have been transmitted to him or her under section 928.

(3) (*a*) The Revenue Commissioners may nominate persons to exercise on behalf of the Collector-General any or all of the powers and functions conferred on the Collector-General by the Tax Acts and the Capital Gains Tax Acts.

(*b*) Those powers and functions, as well as being exercisable by the Collector-General, shall also be exercisable on his or her behalf by persons nominated under this subsection.

(*c*) A person shall not be nominated under this subsection unless he or she is an officer or employee of the Revenue Commissioners.

(4) If and so long as the office of Collector-General is vacant or the holder of that office is unable through illness, absence or other cause to fulfil his or her duties, a person nominated in that behalf by the Revenue Commissioners from among their officers shall act as the Collector-General, and any reference in this or any other Act to the Collector-

General shall be construed as including, where appropriate, a reference to a person nominated under this subsection.

(5) The Revenue Commissioners may revoke a nomination under this section.

Cross-references

Capital acquisitions tax, general interpretation: CATCA 2003 s 2(1)("Collector").

Collection of capital gains tax: s 976(1).

Income Tax (Employments) (Consolidated) Regulations 2001, SI No 559 of 2001, meaning of "Collector-General" applied: reg 2(1).

Income Tax (Relevant Contracts) Regulations 2000, SI No 71 of 2000, meaning of "Collector-General" applied: ITRCR 2000 reg 2.

Private Security Services Act 2004, s 24 (tax clearance), meaning of "Collector-General" applied.

Standards in Public Office Act 2001 s 1(1), meaning of "Collector-General" applied.

Taxes (Offset of Repayments) Regulations 2002, SI No 471 of 2002, meaning of "Collector-General" applied: reg 2(1) (interpretation).

Case law

Subs (2): Collector-General not entitled to take into consideration when dealing with an application for a tax clearance certificate by a company the circumstances of a liquidated company having tax arrears engaged in a similar business and which had common directors and other employees: *Melbarien Enterprises v Revenue Commissioners* (High Court, 19 April 1985).

Subs (3): An arrangement for allocation of payments between the Collector-General and a company was not affected by the fact that a new managing director was unaware of the arrangement: *Metal Products Ltd, (In receivership) v Hearne* (High Court, January 1988).

Definitions

person: IA 1937 s 11(*c*).

Former enactments

ITA 1967 s 162; FA 1974 s 86 Sch 2 Pt I; CGTA 1975 s 51(1) and Sch 4 para 1(3); CTA 1976 s 145(1); FA 1987 s 52; FA 1997 s 157.

Corresponding UK tax provision

Taxes Management Act 1970 s 1.

852 Inspectors of taxes

(1) The Revenue Commissioners may appoint inspectors of taxes, and all such inspectors and all other officers or persons employed in the execution of the Income Tax Acts shall observe and follow the orders, instructions and directions of the Revenue Commissioners.

(2) The Revenue Commissioners may revoke an appointment made under this section.

(3) Inspectors of taxes appointed by the Minister for Finance before the 27th day of May, 1986, shall be deemed to have been appointed by the Revenue Commissioners.

Cross-references

Company acquiring its own shares: s 173(1).

Special investment policies, meaning of "inspector" applied: s 723(1).

Definitions

person: IA 1937 s 11(*c*).

Former enactments

ITA 1967 s 161; FA 1986 s 116.

Corresponding UK tax provision

Taxes Management Act 1970 s 1.

853 Governor and directors of Bank of Ireland

For the purpose of assessing and charging income tax in the cases mentioned in this section, the Governor and directors of the Bank of Ireland—

(*a*) shall be Commissioners,

(*b*) shall have all the necessary powers for that purpose, and

(*c*) shall make assessments under and subject to the Income Tax Acts in respect of—

(i) interest, annuities, dividends and shares of annuities and the profits attached to the same, payable to the Bank of Ireland out of the public revenue of the State,

(ii) interest, annuities, dividends and shares of annuities entrusted to the Bank of Ireland for payment,

(iii) all other interest, annuities and dividends, and

(iv) all other profits chargeable with tax arising within any office or department under the management or control of the Bank of Ireland.

Cross-references

Making of assessments under Schedules C, D, E and F: s 918(1)(*b*).

Definitions

Bank of Ireland: IA 1937 Sch.

Former enactments

ITA 1967 s 157; FA 1969 s 12; FA 1976 s 81(1) and Sch 5 Pt I.

854 Appointment of persons for purposes of assessment of certain public offices

Where the Minister for Finance determines that, by reason of special circumstances existing in any particular public office, it is not expedient that the powers and duties of assessing and charging income tax in relation to that office or any one or more of such powers and duties should be exercised and performed in relation to that office by the inspector or other officer appointed in that behalf, the Revenue Commissioners shall appoint such officers or persons as may be approved of by the Minister for Finance to exercise such powers and duties in relation to that office.

Cross-references

Making of assessments under Schedules C, D, E and F: s 918(1)(*c*).
Functions of assessors: s 923(1)(*a*).

Definitions

inspector: ss 2(1), 5(1), 852; person: IA 1937 s 11(*c*).

Former enactments

ITA 1967 s 158.

855 Declaration to be made by Commissioners

The respective Commissioners for executing the Income Tax Acts in relation to offices and employments of profit and pensions and stipends shall, as soon as practicable after their appointment, meet and make and subscribe the declaration contained in Part 2 of Schedule 27 and may respectively elect a clerk and assessors and, if the tax cannot be deducted at the department or office of the Commissioners or at the office for which they act, they may, from among the officers in their respective departments, appoint separate assessors and collectors for each such department.

Cross-references

Forms of declaration to be made by persons appointed under this section: Sch 27 Pt 1.
Functions of assessors: s 923(1)(*a*).

Former enactments

ITA 1967 s 159.

Corresponding UK tax provision

Taxes Management Act 1970 s 6.

856 Disqualification of Commissioners in cases of personal interest

(1) Every Commissioner acting in the execution of the Income Tax Acts shall be chargeable with tax in the same manner as any other person, but shall take no part in the proceedings, and shall not be present, when any assessment, statement or schedule is under consideration, or any controversy or appeal is being determined, with reference to any case in which he or she is interested, either in his or her own right or in the right of any other person as his or her agent, except during the hearing of an appeal for the purpose of being examined orally by the Commissioners, and he or she shall withdraw during the consideration and determination of the controversy or appeal.

(2) A Commissioner who, in any case referred to in subsection (1), takes any part in the determination of any such controversy or appeal, or fails to withdraw, shall incur a penalty of [€60][1].

(3) For the purposes of corporation tax, where an Appeal Commissioner is interested in his or her own right or in the right of any other person in any matter under appeal, he or she shall not take part in, or be present at, the hearing or determination of the appeal.

Amendments

1 Substituted by FA 2001 s 240(1) and (2)(*k*) and Sch 5 Pt 1 as respects any act or omission which takes place or begins on or after 1 January 2002; previously "£50".

Definitions

Corporation Tax Acts: s 1(2); Income Tax Acts: s 1(2); person: IA 1937 s 11(*c*); year of assessment: ss 2(1), 5(1).

Former enactments

ITA 1967 s 160; CTA 1976 s 146(2).

Corresponding UK tax provision

Taxes Management Act 1970 s 5.

857 Declarations on taking office

(1) Every person appointed to one of the offices named in Part 1 of Schedule 27 shall, before he or she commences to act in the execution of the Income Tax Acts in so far as those Acts relate to tax under Schedule D, make and subscribe the declaration contained in that Part in respect of his or her office.

(2) The declaration may be made before a Peace Commissioner.

(3) A person who acts in the execution of his or her office in relation to tax under Schedule D (otherwise than in respect of any such declaration made before him or her) before he or she has made the prescribed declaration shall forfeit the sum of [€125][1].

(4) All Commissioners and other persons employed for any purpose in connection with the assessment or collection of corporation tax shall be subject to the same obligations as to secrecy with respect to corporation tax as those persons are subject to with respect to income tax, and any declaration made by any such person as to secrecy with respect to income tax shall be deemed to extend also to secrecy with respect to corporation tax.

Amendments

1 Substituted by FA 2001 s 240(1) and (2)(*k*) and Sch 5 Pt 1 as respects any act or omission which takes place or begins on or after 1 January 2002; previously "£100".

Cross-references

Forms of declarations: Sch 27 Pt 1.

Definitions

person: IA 1937 s 11(*c*).

Former enactments

ITA 1967 s 163; F(MP)A 1968 s 3(4) and Sch Pt III; CTA 1976 s 147(5).

Corresponding UK tax provision

Taxes Management Act 1970 s 6.

858 Evidence of authorisation

(1) In this section, except where the context otherwise requires—

"the Acts" means—

(*a*) (i) the Customs Acts,

(ii) the statutes relating to the duties of excise and to the management of those duties,

(iii) the Tax Acts,

(iv) the Capital Gains Tax Acts,

(v) the Value-Added Tax Act, 1972, and the enactments amending or extending that Act,

(vi) the [Capital Acquisitions Tax Consolidation Act 2003],[1] and the enactments amending or extending that Act,

(vii) the statutes relating to stamp duty and to the management of that duty,

and any instruments made thereunder or under any other enactment and relating to tax, and

(*b*) the European Communities (Intrastat) Regulations, 1993 (SI No 136 of 1993);

"authorised officer" means an officer of the Revenue Commissioners who is authorised, nominated or appointed under any provision of the Acts to exercise or perform any functions under any of the specified provisions, and **"authorised"** and **"authorisation"** shall be construed accordingly;

"functions" includes powers and duties;

"identity card", in relation to an authorised officer, means a card which is issued to the officer by the Revenue Commissioners and which contains—

(*a*) a statement to the effect that the officer—

(i) is an officer of the Revenue Commissioners, and

(ii) is an authorised officer for the purposes of the specified provisions,

(*b*) a photograph and signature of the officer,

(*c*) a hologram showing the logo of the Office of the Revenue Commissioners, (*d*) the facsimile signature of a Revenue Commissioner, and

(*e*) particulars of the specified provisions under which the officer is authorised;

"specified provisions", in relation to an authorised officer, means either or both the provisions of the Acts under which the authorised officer—

(*a*) is authorised and which are specified on his or her identity card, and

(*b*) exercises or performs functions under the Customs Acts or any statutes relating to the duties of excise and to the management of those duties;

"tax" means any tax, duty, levy or charge under the care and management of the Revenue Commissioners.

(2) Where, in the exercise or performance of any functions under any of the specified provisions in relation to him or her, an authorised officer is requested to produce or show his or her authorisation for the purposes of that provision, the production by the authorised officer of his or her identity card—

(*a*) shall be taken as evidence of authorisation under that provision, and

(*b*) shall satisfy any obligation under that provision which requires the authorised officer to produce such authorisation on request.

(3) This section shall come into operation on such day as the Minister for Finance may appoint by order.

Amendments

1 Substituted by CATCA 2003 s 119 and Sch 3 with effect from 21 February 2003; previously "Capital Acquisitions Tax Act 1976".

Operative Date

The section came into operation from 1 July 1998 — Taxes Consolidation Act, 1997 (Section 858) (Commencement) Order, SI No 212 of 1998, refers.

Cross-references

This section to be construed together with the Customs Acts, in so far as relating to customs: s 1104(2).

This section to be construed together with the Value Added Tax Acts 1972–1997, in so far as relating to value added tax: s 1104(3).

This section to be construed together with the Stamp Act 1891 and the enactments amending or extending that Act, in so far as relating to stamp duties: s 1104(4).

This section to be construed together with the Capital Acquisitions Tax Act 1976, and the enactments amending or extending that Act, in so far as relating to capital acquisitions tax: s 1104(5).

Former enactments

FA 1997 s 159.

859 Anonymity of authorised officers in relation to certain matters

(1) In this section—

"authorised officer" means an officer of the Revenue Commissioners nominated by them to be a member of the staff of the body;

"the body" has the meaning assigned to it by section 58;

"proceedings" includes any hearing before the Appeal Commissioners (within the meaning of the Revenue Acts);

"the Revenue Acts" means—

(*a*) the Customs Acts,

(*b*) the statutes relating to the duties of excise and to the management of those duties,

(*c*) the Tax Acts,

(*d*) the Capital Gains Tax Acts,

(*e*) the Value-Added Tax Act, 1972, and the enactments amending or extending that Act,

(*f*) the [Capital Acquisitions Tax Consolidation Act 2003],[1] and the enactments amending or extending that Act,

(*g*) the statutes relating to stamp duty and the management of that duty,

(*h*) Chapter IV of Part II of the Finance Act, 1992, and

(*i*) Part VI of the Finance Act, 1983,

and any instruments made thereunder or under any other enactment and relating to tax;

"tax" means any tax, duty, levy or charge under the care and management of the Revenue Commissioners.

(2) Notwithstanding any requirement made by or under any enactment or any other requirement in administrative and operational procedures, including internal procedures, all reasonable care shall be taken to ensure that the identity of an authorised officer shall not be revealed.

(3) In particular and without prejudice to the generality of subsection (2):

(*a*) where, for the purposes of exercising or performing his or her powers or duties under the Revenue Acts in pursuance of the functions of the body, an authorised officer may apart from this section be required to produce or show any written authority or warrant of appointment under those Acts or otherwise to identify himself or herself, the authorised officer shall—

(i) not be required to produce or show any such authority or warrant of appointment or to so identify himself or herself, for the purposes of exercising or performing his or her powers or duties under those Acts, and

(ii) be accompanied by a member of the Garda Síochána who shall, on request by a person affected, identify himself or herself as a member of the Garda Síochána and shall state that he or she is accompanied by an authorised officer;

(*b*) where, in pursuance of the functions of the body, an authorised officer exercises or performs in writing any of his or her powers or duties under the Revenue Acts or any provision of any other enactment, whenever passed, which relates to Revenue, such exercise or performance of his or her powers or duties shall be done in the name of the body and not in the name of the individual authorised officer involved, notwithstanding any provision to the contrary in any of those enactments;

(*c*) in any proceedings arising out of the exercise or performance, in pursuance of the functions of the body, of powers or duties by an authorised officer, any documents relating to such proceedings shall not reveal the identity of any authorised officer, notwithstanding any requirements to the contrary in any provision, and in any proceedings the identity of such officer other than as an authorised officer shall not be revealed other than to the judge or the Appeal Commissioner, as the case may be, hearing the case;

(*d*) where, in pursuance of the functions of the body, an authorised officer is required, in any proceedings, to give evidence and the judge or the Appeal Commissioner, as the case may be, is satisfied that there are reasonable grounds in the public interest to direct that evidence to be given by such authorised officer should be given in the hearing and not in the sight of any person, he or she may so direct.

Amendments

1 Substituted by CATCA 2003 s 119 and Sch 3 with effect from 21 February 2003; previously "Capital Acquisitions Tax Act 1976".

Cross-references

This section to be construed together with the Customs Acts, in so far as relating to customs: s 1104(2).

This section to be construed together with the Value Added Tax Acts 1972–1997, in so far as relating to value added tax: s 1104(3).

This section to be construed together with the Stamp Act 1891 and the enactments amending or extending that Act, in so far as relating to stamp duties: s 1104(4).

This section to be construed together with the Capital Acquisitions Tax Act 1976, and the enactments amending or extending that Act, in so far as relating to capital acquisitions tax: s 1104(5).

This section to be construed together with FA 1983 Pt VI and the enactments amending or extending that Part, in so far as relating to residential property tax: s 1104(6).

Former enactments

FA 1993 s 19A; DCITPA 1996 s 12; CABA 1996 s 23.

860 Administration of oaths

(1) A Peace Commissioner may administer an oath to be taken before a Commissioner by any officer or person in any matter relating to the execution of the Tax Acts.

(2) An Appeal Commissioner may administer an oath to be taken before the Appeal Commissioners under the Tax Acts by any officer or person in any matter relating to the execution of the Tax Acts.

Former enactments

ITA 1967 s 164; F(MP)A 1968 s 3(1) and (3) and Sch Pt I; CTA 1976 s 147(1)–(2).

861 Documents to be in accordance with form prescribed by Revenue Commissioners

(1) Every assessment, charge, bond, warrant, notice of assessment or of demand, or other document required to be used in assessing, charging, collecting and levying income tax, corporation tax or capital gains tax shall be in accordance with the forms prescribed from time to time in that behalf by the Revenue Commissioners, and a document in the form prescribed and supplied or approved by them shall be valid and effectual.

(2) (*a*) In this subsection, **"return"** includes any statement, declaration or list.

(*b*) Any return under the Corporation Tax Acts shall be in such form as the Revenue Commissioners prescribe.

Former enactments

ITA 1967 s 165; CGTA 1975 s 51(1) and Sch 4 para 2; CTA 1976 s 143(12)(*b*) and (*c*) and s147(1)–(2).

Corresponding UK tax provision

Taxes Management Act 1970 s 113.

862 Exercise of powers, etc of Minister for Finance under Tax Acts

Anything required under the Tax Acts to be done by the Minister for Finance may be signified under the hand of the Secretary General, a Deputy Secretary or an Assistant Secretary of the Department of Finance.

Former enactments

ITA 1967 s 166(2); CTA 1976 s 147(1)–(2).

863 Loss, destruction or damage of assessments and other documents

(1) Subject to subsection (2), where any assessment to income tax or capital gains tax for any year, or any assessment to corporation tax for any accounting period or any return or other document relating to income tax, corporation tax or capital gains tax has been lost or destroyed, or has been so defaced or damaged as to be illegible or otherwise useless, the Revenue Commissioners, the Collector-General, inspectors and other officers respectively having powers in relation to income tax, corporation tax or capital gains tax may, notwithstanding anything to the contrary in any enactment, do all such acts and things as they might have done, and all acts and things done under or in accordance with this section shall be as valid and effectual for all purposes as they would have been if the assessment had not been made, or the return or other document had not been made or furnished, or required to be made or furnished.

(2) Where any person who is charged with income tax, corporation tax or capital gains tax in consequence or by virtue of any act or thing done under or in accordance with this section proves to the satisfaction of the Revenue Commissioners that that person has already paid any income tax or capital gains tax for the same year, or corporation tax for the same accounting period, in respect of the subject matter and on the account in respect of and on which that person is so charged, relief shall be given to the extent to which the liability of that person has been discharged by the payments so made either by abatement from the charge or by repayment, as the case may require.

Definitions

Collector-General: s 2(1); inspector: ss 2(1), 5(1), 852; person: IA 1937 s 11(*c*).

Former enactments

ITA 1967 s 188(1); CGTA 1975 s 51(1) and Sch 4 para 2; CTA 1976 s 147(1)–(2).

Corresponding UK tax provision

Taxes Management Act 1970 s 112.

864 Making of claims, etc

(1) Notwithstanding any other provision of the Tax Acts or the Capital Gains Tax Acts—

(*a*) all claims of exemption or for any allowance or deduction under those Acts,

(*b*) all claims for repayment of income tax, corporation tax or capital gains tax under those Acts, and (*c*) (i) all claims to relief under those Acts where the relief is measured in the provision under which it is given, and

(ii) all matters and questions relating to any relief so measured,

in relation to which a right of appeal from a decision is, otherwise than by section 949, not specifically provided,

shall be stated in such manner and form as the Revenue Commissioners may prescribe, and shall be made to and determined by the Revenue Commissioners or such officer of the Revenue Commissioners (including an inspector) as they may authorise in that behalf.

(2) Effect shall be given—

(*a*) to section 21(2) and to that section as modified by sections 24(2) and 25(3), and

(*b*) in so far as the exemptions from income tax conferred by the Corporation Tax Acts call for repayment of tax, to those exemptions,

by means of a claim.

Cross-references

Appeals against determinations of certain claims etc: s 949(1).

Relief for investment in films: s 481(14)(*b*).

Repayment of tax: s 865(7).

Former enactments

ITA 1967 s 432(1) (part of); CGTA 1975 s 51(1) and Sch 4 para 2; CTA 1976 s 4 and s 146(1); FA 1984 s 6(*a*).

Corresponding UK tax provision

Taxes Management Act 1970 Sch 1A(2).

864A Electronic claims

[(1) (*a*) In this section—

"approved electronic communications" means such form of electronic communications as the Revenue Commissioners approve of for the purposes of this section;

"electronic communications" means communication by electrical, digital, magnetic, optical, electromagnetic, biometric or photonic technology, and related technology, by means of which data is transmitted, including telephone apparatus, and **"electronic means"** shall be construed accordingly;

"telephone apparatus" means telegraphy apparatus designed or adapted for the purposes of transmitting and receiving, by way of a public telecommunications service, spoken messages or information or both of them.

(*b*) In paragraph (*a*)—

"information" has the meaning assigned to it by the Electronic Commerce Act 2000;

"public telecommunications service" has the meaning assigned to it by the European Communities (Telecommunications Infrastructure) Regulations 1997 (SI No 338 of 1997).

(*c*) Except where the Revenue Commissioners otherwise direct, this section applies to a claim for an allowance, deduction or relief which falls to be taken into account—

(i) in the making of deductions or repayments of tax under Chapter 4 of Part 42 and the regulations made under that Chapter, or

(ii) except in the case of a chargeable person (within the meaning of section 950), in relation to a repayment of tax deducted under that Chapter and those regulations.

(*d*) References in this section to **"a claim for an allowance, deduction or relief"** include references to—

(i) the making of an election,

(ii) the giving of a notification or notice,

(iii) the amendment of a claim, election, notification or notice, and

(iv) the withdrawal of any claim, election, notification or notice,

in relation to an allowance, deduction or relief, and also include references to an election, notice or application for the purposes of Chapter 1 of Part 44 or a claim under Regulation 26(5) of the Income Tax (Employments) (Consolidated) Regulations 2001 (SI No 559 of 2001).

(*e*) Notwithstanding any other enactment, references in this section to a claim in writing do not include a reference to a claim made by representing or reproducing words in visible form using electronic means.

(2) Notwithstanding any other provision of the Income Tax Acts or instruments made thereunder requiring claims to which this section applies to be made in writing or by notice or in such form as may be prescribed by the Revenue Commissioners, such claims as may be specified by the Revenue Commissioners may be made by an individual by means of approved electronic communications, but subject to such terms and conditions as the Revenue Commissioners may from time to time consider appropriate and specify for the purposes of this section.

(3) The Revenue Commissioners shall make known, in such manner as they think fit, any terms and conditions for the time being specified by them for the purposes of this section.

(4) Where terms and conditions specified by the Revenue Commissioners under this section are for the time being in force with respect to the making of claims to which this section applies, such claims that are made by electronic communications are required to be made in accordance with those terms and conditions.

(5) (*a*) Terms and conditions specified by the Revenue Commissioners for the purposes of this section shall not be capable of modifying any requirement by or under any enactment as to the period within which any claim is to be made, or as to the contents of any claim.

(*b*) Such terms and conditions may include provision as to how any requirement as to the contents of a claim is to be fulfilled when the claim is not produced in writing.

(6) Where a claim is made by a person in accordance with this section, the claim shall—

(*a*) unless and until the contrary is proved, be deemed to have been made by the person purporting to have made the claim, and (*b*) be treated as having been made when it is acknowledged, howsoever, by the Revenue Commissioners as having been received by them.

(7) The making of a claim by a person in accordance with this section shall not prevent an officer of the Revenue Commissioners from enquiring into the claim in accordance with section 886A (inserted by the Finance Act 2005).

(8) Where a claim made in accordance with this section results in the issue to the claimant of a notice, or an amended notice, of determination of tax credits and standard rate cut-off point, the inspector shall, as may be appropriate, be deemed to have determined the amount of the tax credits and standard rate cut-off point appropriate to the claimant in accordance with Regulation 10, or amended the amount in accordance with Regulation 13, of the Income Tax (Employments)(Consolidated) Regulations 2001.

(9) Section 917M (as amended by the Finance Act 2001) shall apply in respect of proceedings in relation to this section, in the same manner as it applies in respect of proceedings in relation to Chapter 6 of Part 38, subject to any necessary modifications including substituting in section 917M a reference to section 864A for a reference to section 917F(1) in each place where it occurs.

(10) Any act to be performed or function to be discharged by the Revenue Commissioners which is authorised by this section may be performed or discharged by any of their officers acting under their authority.][1]

Amendments

1 Section 864A inserted by FA 2005 s 23 with effect from 25 March 2005.

Definitions

Income Tax Acts: s 1(2); inspector: ss 2(1), 852; person: IA 1937 s 11(*c*).

865 Repayment of tax

[(1) (*a*) In this section and section 865A—

the **"Acts"** means the Tax Acts and the Capital Gains Tax Acts and instruments made thereunder;

"chargeable period" has the meaning assigned to it by section 321;

"correlative adjustment" means an adjustment of profits under the terms of arrangements entered into by virtue of [section 826(1)(*a*)][1];

"tax" means any tax, including interest thereon, paid by a person under or in accordance with any provision of the Acts;

"valid claim" shall be construed in accordance with paragraph (*b*).

(*b*) For the purposes of subsection (3)—

[(i) where a person furnishes a statement or return which is required to be delivered by the person in accordance with any provision of the Acts for a chargeable period, such a statement or return shall be treated as a valid claim in relation to a repayment of tax where—

(I) all the information which the Revenue Commissioners may reasonably require to enable them determine if and to what extent a repayment of tax is due to the person for that chargeable period is contained in the statement or return, and

(II) the repayment treated as claimed, if due—

(A) would arise out of the assessment to tax, made by the inspector within the meaning of section 950 (in this clause referred to as the "inspector") at the time the statement or return was furnished, on foot of the statement or return, or

(B) would have arisen out of the assessment to tax, that would have been made by the inspector at the time the statement or return was furnished, on foot of the statement or return if an assessment to tax had been made by the inspector at that time,][2]

(ii) where all information which the Revenue Commissioners may reasonably require, to enable them determine if and to what extent a repayment of tax is due to a person for a chargeable period, is not contained in such a statement or return as is referred to in subparagraph (i), a claim to repayment of tax by that person for that chargeable period shall be treated as a valid claim when that information has been furnished by the person, and

(iii) to the extent that a claim to repayment of tax for a chargeable period arises from a correlative adjustment, the claim shall not be regarded as a valid claim until the quantum of the correlative adjustment is agreed in writing by the competent authorities of the two Contracting States.

(2) Subject to the provisions of this section, where a person has, in respect of a chargeable period, paid, whether directly or by deduction, an amount of tax which is not due from that person or which, but for an error or mistake in a return or statement made by the person for the purposes of an assessment to tax, would not have been due from the person, the person shall be entitled to repayment of the tax so paid.

(3) The Revenue Commissioners shall not make a repayment of the tax referred to in subsection (2) unless a valid claim has been made to them for that purpose.

[(3A)(*a*) Subject to paragraph (*b*), subsection (3) shall not prevent the Revenue Commissioners from making, to a person other than a chargeable person (within the meaning of section 950), a repayment in respect of tax deducted, in accordance with Chapter 4 of Part 42 and the regulations made thereunder, from that person's emoluments for a year of assessment where, on the basis of the information available to them, they are satisfied that the tax so deducted, and in respect of which the person is entitled to a credit, exceeds the person's liability for that year.

(*b*) A repayment referred to in paragraph (*a*) shall not be made at a time at which a claim to the repayment would not be allowed under subsection (4).][3]

(4) Subject to subsection (5), a claim for repayment of tax under the Acts for any chargeable period shall not be allowed unless it is made—

(*a*) in the case of claims made on or before 31 December 2004, under any provision of the Acts other than subsection (2), in relation to any chargeable period ending on or before 31 December 2002, within 10 years,

(*b*) in the case of claims made on or after 1 January 2005 in relation to any chargeable period referred to in paragraph (*a*), within 4 years, and (*c*) in the case of claims made—

(i) under subsection (2) and not under any other provision of the Acts, or

(ii) in relation to any chargeable period beginning on or after 1 January 2003,

within 4 years,

after the end of the chargeable period to which the claim relates.

(5) Where a person would, on due claim, be entitled to a repayment of tax for any chargeable period under any provision of the Acts other than this section, and—

(*a*) that provision provides for a shorter period, within which the claim for repayment is to be made, which ends before the relevant period referred to in subsection (4), then this section shall apply as if that shorter period were the period referred to in subsection (4), and

(*b*) that provision provides for a longer period, within which the claim for repayment is to be made, which ends after the relevant period referred to in subsection (4), then that provision shall apply as if the longer period were the period referred to in subsection (4).

(6) Except as provided for by this section, section 865A or by any other provision of the Acts, the Revenue Commissioners shall not—

(*a*) repay an amount of tax paid to them, or

(*b*) pay interest in respect of an amount of tax paid to them.

(7) Where any person is aggrieved by a decision of the Revenue Commissioners on a claim to repayment by that person, in so far as that decision is made by reference to any provision of this section, the provisions of section 949 shall apply to such decision as if it were a determination made on a matter referred to in section 864.][4]

Amendments

1 Substituted by FA 2004 s 89 and Sch 3 para 1(*aa*) with effect from 25 March 2004; previously "section 826".

2 Subs (1)(*b*)(i) substituted by FA 2005 s 24(1)(*c*)(i) as respects statements or returns made on or after 3 February 2005.

3 Subs (3A) inserted by FA 2005 s 24(1)(*c*)(ii) with effect from 25 March 2005.

4 Section 865 substituted by FA 2003 s 17(*a*) with effect from: (*a*) such day or days as the Minister for Finance may by order or orders appoint either generally or with reference to any particular purpose or provision and different days may be so appointed for different purposes or different provisions and (*b*) notwithstanding the generality of (*a*), any order made by the Minister for Finance in accordance with the provisions of that paragraph may contain, and be subject to, such conditions as the Minister considers appropriate and which are specified in the order; previously "**865 Limit of time for repayment claims**". Except where otherwise expressly provided by any provision of the Tax Acts or the Capital Gains Tax Act, no claim for repayment of income tax, corporation tax or capital gains tax under those Acts shall be allowed unless it is made within 10 years after the end of the year of assessment or, as the case may be, accounting period to which it relates.". By virtue of Finance Act 2003 (Commencement of Section 17) Order 2003, SI No 508 of 2003, this subsection came into operation on 31 October 2003.

Tax Briefing

TB52 May 2003 p 10 — Repayment, Interest and Time Limits (Finance Act 2003 changes).

TB56 July 2004 pp 6–11 — Repayments, Interest and Time Limits — Section 17 FA 2003 changes.

TB57 Oct 2004 pp 7–9 — New Time Limits - Section 17 FA 2003 changes.

TB57 Oct 2004 p 15 — Repayments, Interest and Time Limits — correction to TB56 p 8.

Definitions

Capital Gains Tax Acts: s 1(2); person: IA 1937 s 11(*c*); Tax Acts: s 1(2); writing: IA 1937 Sch; year of assessment: s 2(1).

Former enactments

ITA 1967 s 498; F(MP)A 1968 s 4(5)(*a*); CGTA 1975 s 51(1) and Sch 4 para 2; CTA 1976 s 147(1)–(2).

865A Interest on repayments

[(1) Where a person is entitled to a repayment of tax for a chargeable period and that repayment, or part of the repayment, arises because of a mistaken assumption made by the Revenue Commissioners in the application of any provision of the Acts, that repayment or that part of the repayment shall, subject to section 1006A(2A), carry interest for each day or part of a day for the period commencing with the day after the end of the chargeable period or, as the case may be, the end of each of the chargeable periods for which the repayment is due or the date on which the tax was paid (whichever is the later) and ending on the day on which the repayment is made.

(2) Where, for any reason other than that mentioned in subsection (1), a repayment of tax or a part of a repayment is due to a person for a chargeable period, that repayment or the part of the repayment shall, subject to section 1006A(2A), carry interest for the period beginning on the day which is 6 months after the day on which the claim to repayment becomes a valid claim and ending on the day the repayment is made.

(3) (*a*) Interest payable in accordance with this section shall be simple interest payable at the rate of 0.011 per cent per day or part of a day.

(*b*) The Minister for Finance may, from time to time, make an order prescribing a rate for the purpose of paragraph (*a*).

(*c*) Every order made by the Minister for Finance under paragraph (*b*) shall be laid before Dáil Éireann as soon as may be after it is made and, if a resolution annulling the order is passed by Dáil Éireann within the next 21 days on which Dáil Éireann has sat after the order is laid before it, the order shall be annulled accordingly, but without prejudice to the validity of anything previously done under it.

(4) (*a*) Interest shall not be payable under this section if it amounts to less than €10.

(*b*) Income tax shall not be deductible on payment of interest under this section and such interest shall not be reckoned in computing income, profit or gains for the purposes of the Tax Acts.

(5) This section shall not apply in relation to any repayment or part of a repayment in respect of which interest is payable under any other provision of the Acts.][1]

Amendments

1 Section 865A inserted by FA 2003 s 17(*a*) with effect from: (*a*) such day or days as the Minister for Finance may by order or orders appoint either generally or with reference to any particular purpose or provision and different days may be so appointed for different purposes or different provisions and (*b*) notwithstanding the generality of (*a*), any order made by the Minister for Finance in accordance with the provisions of that paragraph may contain, and be subject to, such conditions as the Minister considers appropriate and which are specified in the order. By virtue of Finance Act 2003 (Commencement of Section 17) Order 2003, SI No 508 of 2003, this subsection came into operation in relation to repayments of tax made on or after 1 November 2003.

Cross-references

Appeals to Circuit Court, subss (3) and (4): s 942(6)(*b*).
Repayment of tax: s 865(6).
Statement of case for High Court: s 941(9).

Tax Briefing

TB52 May 2003 p 10 — Repayment, Interest and Time Limits (Finance Act 2003 changes).
TB56 July 2004 pp 6–11 — Repayments, Interest and Time Limits — Section 17 FA 2003 changes.
TB57 Oct 2004 pp 7–9 — New Time Limits - Section 17 FA 2003 changes.
TB57 Oct 2004 p 15 — Repayments, Interest and Time Limits - correction to TB56 p 8.

Definitions

Acts: s 865(1); chargeable period: s 865(1); Dáil Éireann: IA 1937 Sch; person: IA 1937 s 11(*c*); Tax Acts: s 1(2).

866 Rules as to delivery of statements

Any person who, on that person's own behalf or on behalf of another person or body of persons, delivers a statement of the amount of the profits on which any income tax is chargeable shall observe the rules and directions contained in Schedule 28 in so far as those rules and directions are respectively applicable.

Cross-references

Statements, lists, declarations: Sch 28.

Definitions

body of persons: s 2(1); person: IA 1937 s 11(*c*).

Former enactments

ITA 1967 s 533; FA 1969 s 65(1) and Sch 5 Pt I.

867 Amendment of statutory forms

It shall be lawful for the Revenue Commissioners from time to time to make such amendments of the forms of declarations, lists and statements contained in Schedules 27 and 28 as appear to them to be necessary to give effect to the Income Tax Acts.

Cross-references

Forms of declarations: Sch 27 Pt 1.
Statements, lists, declarations: Sch 28.

Former enactments

ITA 1967 s 189.

868 Execution of warrants

(1) Warrants issued under the authority of the Tax Acts shall be executed by the respective persons to whom they are directed.

(2) Members of the Garda Síochána shall aid in the execution of the Tax Acts.

Definitions

person: IA 1937 s 11(*c*).

Former enactments

ITA 1967 s 536; F(MP)A 1968 s 3(4) and Sch Pt III, s 3(5) and Sch Pt IV; CTA 1976 s 147(1)–(2).

869 Delivery, service and evidence of notices and forms

(1) (*a*) In this subsection, except where in paragraph (*d*) the context otherwise requires, **"company"** means any body corporate.

(*b*) Any notice, form or other document which under the Tax Acts or the Capital Gains Tax Acts is to be given, served, sent or delivered to or on a person by the Revenue Commissioners or by an inspector or other officer of the Revenue Commissioners may be either delivered to the person or left—

(i) in a case where the person is a company, at the company's registered office or place of business, or

(ii) in any other case, at the person's usual or last known place of abode or place of business or, if the person is an individual, at his or her place of employment.

(*c*) Any notice, form or other document referred to in paragraph (*b*) may be served by post addressed—

(i) in a case where the person is a company, to the company at either of the places specified in paragraph (*b*)(i), or

(ii) in any other case, to the person at any of the places specified in paragraph (*b*)(ii).

(*d*) Without prejudice to paragraphs (*b*) and (*c*), section 379 of the Companies Act, 1963, shall apply in relation to the service on a company of any notice, form or other document referred to in this subsection as it applies in relation to the service of documents under that section on a company within the meaning of that Act.

(2) Any notice which under the Tax Acts or the Capital Gains Tax Acts is authorised or required to be given by the Revenue Commissioners may be signed and given by any officer of the Revenue Commissioners authorised by them for the purpose of giving notices of the class to which the notice belongs and, where so signed and given, shall be as valid and effectual as if signed under the hands of the Revenue Commissioners and given by them.

[(3) Prima facie evidence of any notice given or served under the Tax Acts or the Capital Gains Tax Acts by the Revenue Commissioners or an inspector or other officer of the Revenue Commissioners may be given in any proceedings by the production of a document purporting—

(*a*) to be a copy of the notice, or

(*b*) if the details specified in the notice are contained in an electronic, photographic or other record maintained by the Revenue Commissioners, to reproduce those details in so far as they relate to the said notice,

and it shall not be necessary to prove the official positions or position of the persons or person by whom the notice purports to be given or served or, where it is signed, the signatures or signature or that the persons or person signing and giving or serving it were or was authorised to do so.][1]

(4) Notices to be given or delivered to, or served on, the Appeal Commissioners shall be valid and effectual if given or delivered to or served on their Clerk.

(5) This section shall apply notwithstanding any other provision of the Tax Acts or the Capital Gains Tax Acts.

Amendments

[1] Subs (3) substituted by FA 1999 s 22 with effect from 6 April 1999.

Case law

Subs (1)(*a*): Held service to the last known place of business is not effective service: *Ex parte the debtor v IRC* [1992] STC 751.

Definitions

Appeal Commissioners: s 2(1); Capital Gains Tax Acts: s 1(2); inspector: ss 2(1), 5(1), 852; person: IA 1937 s 11(*c*); Tax Acts: s 1(2).

Former enactments

ITA 1967 s 542(2) and (4)–(7); F(MP)A 1968 s 3(2) and Sch Pt I; CGTA 1975 s 51(1) and Sch 4 para 2; FA 1975 s 25; CTA 1976 s 147(1)–(2).

Corresponding UK tax provision

Taxes Management Act 1970 s 115.

870 Effect of want of form, error, etc on assessments, charges, warrants and other proceedings

(1) An assessment, charge, warrant or other proceeding which purports to be made in accordance with the Income Tax Acts, the Corporation Tax Acts or the Capital Gains Tax Acts shall not be quashed, or deemed to be void or voidable, for want of form, or be affected by reason of a mistake, defect, or omission therein, if the same is in substance and effect in conformity with or according to the intent and meaning of those Acts, and if the person or property charged or intended to be charged or affected thereby is designated therein according to common intent and understanding.

(2) For the purposes of the Tax Acts and the Capital Gains Tax Acts but subject to subsection (3), an assessment or a charge made on an assessment shall not be impeached or affected—

(*a*) by reason of a mistake in the assessment or the charge made on the assessment as to—

(i) the name or surname of a person liable,

(ii) the description of any profits or property, or

(iii) the amount of the tax charged;

(*b*) by reason of any variance between the notice and the certificate of charge or assessment.

(3) In cases of charge, the notice of charge shall be duly served on the person intended to be charged, and the notice and certificate shall respectively contain, in substance and effect, the particulars on which the charge is made, and every such charge shall be heard and determined on its merits by the Appeal Commissioners.

Case law

Estimated assessments showing an incorrect trading description and signed by a subordinate inspector held to be valid: *Deighan v Hearne* ITR Vol III p 533.

Interpretation, misclassification of goods under customs tariff, negligence of Revenue Commissioners, legitimate expectation: *Carbery Milk Products Ltd v Minister for Agriculture* ITR Vol IV p 492.

Definitions

Appeal Commissioners: s 2(1); person: IA 1937 s 11(*c*).

Former enactments

ITA 1967 s 537; F(MP)A 1968 s 3(2) and Sch Pt I; CGTA 1975 s 51(1) and Sch 4 para 2; CTA 1976 s 147(1)-(2).

Corresponding UK tax provision

Taxes Management Act 1970 s 114.

871 Power to combine certain returns and assessments

Any return, assessment or other document relating to chargeable gains or capital gains tax may be combined with one relating to income or income tax.

Definitions

chargeable gain: ss 5(1), 545.

Former enactments

CGTA 1975 s 51(1) and Sch 4 para 16.

Corresponding UK tax provision

Taxes Management Act 1970 s 113.

872 Use of information relating to other taxes and duties

(1) Any information acquired, whether before or after the passing of this Act, in connection with any tax or duty under the care and management of the Revenue Commissioners may be used by them for any purpose connected with any other tax or duty under their care and management.

(2) The Revenue Commissioners or any of their officers may, for any purpose in connection with the assessment and collection of income tax, corporation tax or capital gains tax, make use of or produce in evidence any returns, correspondence, schedules, accounts, statements or other documents or information to which the Revenue Commissioners or any of their officers have or has had or may have lawful access for the purposes of the Acts relating to any tax, duty, levy or charge under the care and management of the Revenue Commissioners.

Cross-references

Subs (1) to be construed together with the Customs Acts, in so far as relating to customs: s 1104(2).

Subs (1) to be construed together with the Value Added Tax Acts 1972–1997, in so far as relating to value added tax: s 1104(3).

Subs (1) to be construed together with the Stamp Act 1891 and the enactments amending or extending that Act, in so far as relating to stamp duties: s 1104(4).

Subs (1) to be construed together with the Capital Acquisitions Tax Act 1976, and the enactments amending or extending that Act, in so far as relating to capital acquisitions tax: s 1104(5).

Subs (1) to be construed together with FA 1983 Pt VI and the enactments amending or extending that Part, in so far as relating to residential property tax: s 1104(6).

Tax relief at source, provision of certain information, transitional; this section does not apply in relation to such information: FA 2001 s 24(4).

Former enactments

FA 1928 s34(2); FA 1996 s 130.

873 Proof that person is a Commissioner or officer

In any proceedings under or arising out of the Tax Acts before any court or person empowered to take evidence, prima facie proof of the fact that any person was a Commissioner or officer may be given by proving that, at the time when any matter in controversy in any such proceedings arose, that person was reputed to be or had acted as a Commissioner or officer.

Definitions

person: IA 1937 s 11(*c*).

Former enactments

ITA 1967 s 541; CTA 1976 s 147(1) and(2).

874 Limitation of penalties on officers employed in execution of Tax Acts and Capital Gains Tax Acts

(1) A Commissioner, sheriff, county registrar, clerk, inspector, assessor or Collector-General who acts, or is employed, in the execution of the Tax Acts or the Capital Gains Tax Acts shall not be liable to any penalty in respect of such execution other than as provided by those Acts.

(2) Where any civil or criminal proceeding against any officer or person employed in relation to any duty of income tax, corporation tax or capital gains tax on account of the seizure or detention of any goods is brought to trial, and a verdict or judgment is given against the defendant, then, if the court or judge certifies that there was probable cause for the seizure, the plaintiff shall not be entitled to any damages besides the goods seized, or the value of those goods, or to any costs, and the defendant shall not be liable to any punishment.

Definitions

Collector-General: s 2(1); inspector: ss 2(1), 5(1), 852; person: IA 1937 s 11(*c*).

Former enactments

ITA 1967 s 519; CTA 1976 s 147(1)–(2); CGTA 1975 s 51(1) and Sch 4 para 3(2).

875 Exemption of appraisements and valuations from stamp duty

Amendments

Repealed by FA 1999 s 197 and Sch 6 with effect from 25 March 1999.

PART 38
RETURNS OF INCOME AND GAINS, OTHER OBLIGATIONS AND RETURNS, AND REVENUE POWERS

CHAPTER 1

Income Tax: Returns of Income

876 Notice of liability to income tax

Every person who is chargeable to income tax for any year of assessment and who in relation to that year has not been given a notice under section 877 or 879 and has not made a return of such person's total income shall, not later than one year after the end of the year of assessment, give notice to the inspector of taxes that such person is so chargeable.

Cross-references

Capital gains tax, applied by: s 913(2).

Penalty: Sch 29 column 3.

Self assessment: s 959(4).

Revenue precedent

Issue: Non-resident individual did not have an Irish source of income.

Decision: As he exercised an employment in the State, he is regarded as liable to make a Return of Income.

Former enactments

F(MP)A 1968 s 5(1).

Corresponding UK tax provision

Taxes Management Act 1970 s 7.

877 Returns by persons chargeable

(1) Every person chargeable under the Income Tax Acts, when required to do so by a notice given to such person by an inspector, shall, within the time limited by such notice, prepare and deliver to the inspector a statement in writing as required by the Income Tax Acts, signed by such person, containing the amount of the profits or gains arising to such person, from each and every source chargeable according to the respective schedules, estimated for the period specified in the notice and according to the Income Tax Acts.

...[1]

(3) There shall be added to the statement referred to in subsection (1) a declaration that the amounts contained in that statement are estimated in respect of all the sources of income mentioned in the Income Tax Acts, describing those sources, after deducting only such sums as are allowed.

(4) Every such statement shall be made exclusive of any interest of money or other annual payment arising out of the property of any other person charged in respect of that interest of money or other annual payment.

(5) (*a*) Every person to whom a notice has been given by an inspector requiring such person to deliver a statement of any profits, gains or income in respect of which such person is chargeable under Schedule D or E shall deliver a statement in the form required by the notice, whether or not such person is so chargeable.

(*b*) The penalty imposed on any person proceeded against for not complying with this subsection who proves that such person was not chargeable to income tax shall not exceed [€5][2] for any one offence.

Amendments

1 Subs (2) repealed by FA 2000 s 69(2) and Sch 2 Part 2 with effect from 6 April 1999 in the case of income tax and as respects accounting periods commencing on or after that date in the case of corporation tax.

2 Substituted by FA 2001 s 240(1) and (2)(*k*) and Sch 5 Pt 1 as respects any act or omission which takes place or begins on or after 1 January 2002; previously "£5".

Cross-references

Capital gains tax, applied by: s 913(2).
Increased penalties in case of body of persons, subs (5)(*b*): s 1054(4).
Penalties for failure to make certain returns, subs (5)(*b*): s 1052(3).
Penalty: Sch 29 column 1.
Returns by married persons: s 881(1).
Self assessment, meaning of "specified provisions": s 950(1).
Self assessment, obligation to make a return: s 951(1)(*a*)(i), (3)(*a*).
Surcharge for late returns, meaning of "specified provisions": s 1084(1)(*a*).

Case law

Whether returns showing figures equivalent to income exemption limits (with no supporting records) valid: *Bairead v McDonald* ITR Vol IV p 475.

Statement of practice

Documents to be enclosed with returns of income, September 1988.
Finance Act 1992 and directors: SP IT/1/93, January 1993.
Preparation of accounts for Revenue purposes: SP IT/2/92, October 1992.

Definitions

inspector: ss 2(1), 5(1), 852; writing: IA 1937 Sch; person: IA 1937 s 11(*c*).

Former enactments

ITA 1967 s 169; F(MP)A 1968 s 6(2)–(3); FA 1969 s 65(1) and Sch 5 Pt I; CTA 1976 s 140(1) and Sch 2 Pt I para 4; FA 1976 s 11(5).

Corresponding UK tax provision

Taxes Management Act 1970 s 8.

878 Persons acting for incapacitated persons and non-residents

(1) Every person (in this subsection referred to as **"the first-mentioned person"**) acting in any character on behalf of any incapacitated person or person not resident in the State who, by reason of such incapacity or non-residence in the State, may not be personally charged under the Income Tax Acts shall, whenever required to do so by a notice given to the first-mentioned person by an inspector, within the time permitted by such notice and in any district in which the first-mentioned person may be chargeable on the first-mentioned person's own account, deliver a statement described in section 877 of the profits or gains in respect of which income tax is to be charged on the first-mentioned person on account of that other person, together with the prescribed declaration.

(2) Where 2 or more such persons are liable to be charged for the same person—

(*a*) one statement only shall be required to be delivered which may be made by them jointly or by any one or more of them, and

(*b*) notice in writing may be given by any such persons to the inspector for each district in which they are called on for a statement stating in which district or districts they are respectively chargeable on their own account, and in which of those districts they desire to be charged on behalf of the person for whom they act, and they shall, if any one such person is liable to be charged on such person's own account in that district, be charged in that district accordingly by one assessment.

Cross-references

Capital gains tax, applied by: s 913(2), (3).
Self assessment, meaning of "specified provisions": s 950(1).
Surcharge for late returns, meaning of "specified provisions": s 1084(1)(*a*).
Penalty: Sch 29 column 1.

Definitions

incapacitated person: s 3(1) inspector: ss 2(1), 5(1), 852; writing: IA 1937 Sch.
person: IA 1937 s 11(*c*).

Former enactments

ITA 1967 s 170; F(MP)A 1968 s 6(4).

Corresponding UK tax provision

Taxes Management Act 1970 s 72.

879 Returns of income

(1) In this section, **"prescribed"** means prescribed by the Revenue Commissioners and, in prescribing forms for the purposes of this section, the Revenue Commissioners shall have regard to the desirability of securing in so far as may be possible that no individual shall be required to make more than one return annually of the sources of the individual's income and the amounts derived from those sources.

(2) Every individual, when required to do so by a notice given to him or her in relation to any year of assessment by an inspector, shall within the time limited by the notice prepare and deliver to the inspector a return in the prescribed form of—

- (*a*) all the sources of his or her income for the year of assessment in relation to which the notice is given;
- (*b*) the amount of income from each source for the year of assessment computed in accordance with subsection (3);
- (*c*) such further particulars for the purposes of income tax for the year of assessment as may be required by the notice or indicated by the prescribed form.

[(3) The amount of income from any source to be included in a return under this section shall be computed in accordance with the Income Tax Acts; but where under Chapter 3 of Part 4 the profits or gains (or, as respects the year of assessment 2001, 74 per cent of the profits or gains) of a particular 12 month period are to be taken to be the profits or gains of a year of assessment, the computation shall be made by reference to that period.][1]

(4) Where a person delivers to any inspector a return in a prescribed form, the person shall be deemed to have been required by a notice under this section to prepare and deliver that return.

Amendments

1 Subs (3) substituted by FA 2001 s 77(2) and Sch 2 para 47 with effect from 6 April 2001.

Cross-references

Capital gains tax, applied by: s 913(2), (8).

Penalties for failure to make certain returns: s 1052(4)(*a*).

Penalty, subs (2): Sch 29 column 1.

Self assessment, meaning of "specified provisions": s 950(1).

Self assessment, obligation to make a return: s 951(1)(*a*)(ii), (3)(*a*).

Special savings incentive accounts, payment of tax credit: s 848E(4).

Subcontractors' withholding tax: s 531(16).

Surcharge for late returns, meaning of "specified provisions": s 1084(1).

Case law

Requirement to deliver a return held not satisfied where the taxpayer submitted a formula by which his tax liability might be computed: *Horner v Madden* [1995] STC 802.

Definitions

Income Tax Acts: s 1(2); inspector: ss 2(1), 5(1), 852; year of assessment: s 3(1); person: IA 1937 s 11(*c*).

Former enactments

ITA 1967 s 172(1)–(2), (4) and (6); FA 1974 s 86 and Sch 2 Pt I; FA 1990 s 23(2).

Corresponding UK tax provision

Taxes Management Act 1970 s 8.

---

880 Partnership returns

(1) In this section—

"precedent partner" has the same meaning as in Part 43;

"prescribed" means prescribed by the Revenue Commissioners.

(2) The precedent partner of any partnership, when required to do so by a notice given to that partner in relation to any year of assessment by an inspector, shall within the time limited by the notice prepare and deliver to the inspector a return in the prescribed form of—

- (*a*) all the sources of income of the partnership for the year of assessment in relation to which the notice is given;
- (*b*) the amount of income from each source for the year of assessment computed in accordance with subsection (3);
- (*c*) such further particulars for the purposes of income tax for the year of assessment as may be required by the notice or indicated by the prescribed form.

(3) The amount of income from any source to be included in a return under this section shall be computed in accordance with the Income Tax Acts; but where, in the case of a trade or profession, an account has been made up to a date within the year of assessment or more accounts than one have been made up to dates within that year, the computation shall be made by reference to the period, or to all the periods where there is more than one period, for which accounts have been so made up.

[(3A) For the purposes of subsection (3), an account made up for a period of one year to a date falling in the period from 1 January 2002 to 5 April 2002 shall, in addition to being an account made up to a date in the year of assessment 2002, be deemed to be an account made up to a date within the year of assessment 2001.][1]

(4) Where a person delivers to any inspector a return in a prescribed form, the person shall be deemed to have been required by a notice under this section to prepare and deliver that return.

(5) The precedent partner of any partnership, when required to do so by a notice given to that partner by an inspector, shall within the time limited by such notice prepare and deliver to the inspector a statement in writing signed by that partner stating the amount of the profits or gains arising to the partnership from each and every source chargeable according to the respective schedules, estimated for the period specified in the notice and according to the Income Tax Acts.

(6) There shall be added to the statement referred to in subsection (5) a declaration that the amounts contained in that statement are estimated in respect of all the sources of income mentioned in the Income Tax Acts, describing those sources, after deducting only such sums as are allowed.

Amendments

1 Subs (3A) inserted by FA 2001 s 77(2) and Sch 2 para 48 with effect from 6 April 2001.

Cross-references

Capital allowances and balancing charges in partnership cases: s 1010(9)(*a*).

Capital gains tax, applied by: s 913(2).

Penalties for failure to make certain returns: s 1052(4)(*a*).
Penalty: Sch 29 column 1.
Self assessment, meaning of "specified provisions": s 950(1).
Self assessment, obligation to make a return: s 951(2), (3)(*a*).
Subcontractors' withholding tax: s 531(16).
Surcharge for late returns, meaning of "specified provisions": s 1084(1).

Definitions

Income Tax Acts: s 1(2); inspector: ss 2(1), 5(1), 852; person: IA 1937 s 11(*c*); profession: s 2(1); trade: s 3(1); writing: IA 1937 Sch; year of assessment: s 3(1).

Former enactments

ITA 1967 ss 69(3), 70(1)–(3A) and (5); FA 1974 s 86 and Sch 2 Pt I; FA 1979 s 30; FA 1990 s 23(1).

Corresponding UK tax provision

Taxes Management Act 1970 s 12AA.

881 Returns by married persons

(1) Where an individual is required by a notice given under section 877 to deliver a statement in writing of the total income in respect of which the individual is chargeable to income tax and that income is or includes income of his or her spouse, the individual may, within 21 days from the date of the receipt of the notice, notify the inspector by whom the notice was given that the income in respect of which the individual is chargeable to income tax is or includes income of his or her spouse.

(2) Where an inspector receives a notification under subsection (1) or is of the opinion that the spouse of the individual concerned is in receipt of income, the inspector may by notice given to the individual's spouse require him or her to prepare and deliver to the inspector, within the time limited by the notice and in the form required by the notice, a statement in writing signed by him or her, setting out the amount of income arising to him or her from each and every source chargeable according to the respective schedules, estimated for the period specified in the notice and according to the Income Tax Acts, whether or not the individual's spouse or the individual concerned is the person chargeable to income tax in respect of that income.

(3) The delivery of a statement under subsection (2) shall not affect Chapter 1 of Part 44.

Cross-references

Self assessment, meaning of "specified provisions": s 950(1).
Surcharge for late returns, meaning of "specified provisions": s 1084(1).
Penalty: Sch 29 column 2.

Definitions

Income Tax Acts: s 1(2); inspector: ss 2(1), 5(1), 852; person: IA 1937 s 11(*c*); total income: s 3(1).

Former enactments

ITA 1967 s 195B(3) and (6); FA 1976 s 11(1)–(3); FA 1980 s 19 and Sch 1 Pt III para 6; FA 1993 s 10(1).

CHAPTER 2
Corporation Tax: Returns of Profits

882 Particulars to be supplied by new companies

[(1) (*a*) In this section—

"secretary" includes persons mentioned in section 1044(2) and, in the case of a company not resident in the State, the agent, manager, factor or other representative of the company;

"settlor" and **"settlement"** have the same meanings as in section 10;

"tax", in relation to a territory other than the State, means any tax imposed in that territory which corresponds to income tax or corporation tax;

"ultimate beneficial owners", in relation to a company, means—

(i) the individual or individuals who have control of the company, or

(ii) where a person, whether alone or together with other persons, who controls the company controls it in the capacity as the trustee of a settlement, any person who in relation to the settlement—

(I) is a settlor, or

(II) is, or can under any scheme or arrangement reasonably expect to become, a beneficiary under the settlement, or

(III) where such settlor or beneficiary, as the case may be, is a company, the ultimate beneficial owners of that company.

(*b*) For the purposes of this section, control shall be construed in accordance with section 432.

(2) Every company which is incorporated in the State or which commences to carry on a trade, profession or business in the State shall, in every case within 30 days of—

(*a*) the date on which it commences to carry on a trade, profession or business, wherever carried on,

(*b*) the date at which there is a material change in information previously delivered by the company under this section, and

(*c*) the giving of a notice to the company by an inspector requiring a statement under this section,

deliver to the Revenue Commissioners a statement in writing containing particulars of—

(i) in the case of every company—

(I) the name of the company,

(II) the address of the company's registered office,

(III) the address of its principal place of business,

(IV) the name and address of the secretary of the company,

(V) the date of commencement of the trade, profession or business,

(VI) the nature of the trade, profession or business,

(VII) the date up to which accounts relating to such trade, profession or business will be made up, and

(VIII) such other information as the Revenue Commissioners consider necessary for the purposes of the Tax Acts;

(ii) in the case of a company which is incorporated, but not resident, in the State—

(I) the name of the territory in which the company is, by virtue of the law of that territory, resident for tax purposes,

(II) where subsection (2) of section 23A does not apply by virtue of subsection (3) of that section, the name and address of the company referred to in that latter subsection which carries on a trade in the State, and

(III) where the company is treated as not resident in the State by virtue only of subsection (4) of section 23A—

(A) if the company is controlled by another company the principal class of the shares of which is substantially and regularly traded on one or more than one recognised stock exchange in a relevant territory (within the meaning of section 23A) or territories, the name of the other company and the address of its registered office, and

(B) in any other case, the name and address of the individuals who are the ultimate beneficial owners of the company,

and

(iii) in the case of a company which is neither incorporated in the State nor resident in the State but which carries on a trade, profession or business in the State—

(I) the address of the company's principal place of business in the State,

(II) the name and address of the agent, manager, factor or other representative of the company, and

(III) the date of commencement of the company's trade, profession or business in the State.

[(3) Where a company fails to deliver a statement which it is required to deliver under this section, then, notwithstanding any obligations as to secrecy or other restriction upon disclosure of information imposed by or under any statute or otherwise—

(*a*) the Revenue Commissioners, or

(*b*) such officer of the Revenue Commissioners as is nominated by the Commissioners for the purposes of this section,

may give a notice in writing, or in such other form as the Revenue Commissioners may decide, to the registrar of companies (within the meaning of the Companies Act, 1963) stating that the company has so failed to deliver a statement under this section.][1]][2]

Amendments

1 Subs (3) substituted by FA 2000 s 78 with effect from 6 April 2000.

2 Section 882 substituted by FA 1999 s 83 with effect from 11 February 1999 for companies incorporated on or after from 11 February 1999, and from 1 October 1999 for companies which were incorporated before 11 February 1999.

Cross-references

Penalties for failure to furnish particulars required to be furnished by new companies: s 1073(1), (2).

Revenue information

Information leaflet IT48 — Starting in Business — A Revenue Guide.

Tax Briefing

TB37 Oct 1999 pp 5–6 Irish Registered Non-Resident Companies Update.

Definitions

company: s 4(1); person: IA 1937 s 11(*c*); Tax Acts: s 1(2); trade: ss 3(1), 4(1), 5(1); writing: IA 1937 Sch.

Former enactments

CTA 1976 s 141(1), (1A), (1B) and (3) and s 154; FA 1995 s 58.

883 Notice of liability to corporation tax

Every company which is chargeable to corporation tax for any accounting period and which has not made a return of its profits for that accounting period shall, not later than one year after the end of that accounting period, give notice to the inspector that it is so chargeable.

Cross-references

Penalties for failure to give notice of liability to corporation tax: s 1074.

Definitions

company: ss 4(1), 5(1); inspector: ss 2(1), 5(1), 852; profits: s 4(1).

Former enactments

CTA 1976 s 142(1).

Corresponding UK tax provision

Taxes Management Act 1970 s 10 [repealed].

884 Returns of profits

(1) In this section, **"return"** includes any statement, declaration or list.

(2) A company may be required by a notice served on it by an inspector or other officer of the Revenue Commissioners to deliver to the officer within the time limited by the notice a return of—

(*a*) the profits of the company computed in accordance with the Corporation Tax Acts—

(i) specifying the income taken into account in computing those profits, with the amount from each source,

(ii) giving particulars of all disposals giving rise to chargeable gains or allowable losses under the Capital Gains Tax Acts and the Corporation Tax Acts and particulars of those chargeable gains or allowable losses, and

(iii) giving particulars of all charges on income to be deducted against those profits for the purpose of the assessment to corporation tax, other than those included in paragraph (*d*),

[(*aa*) such further particulars for the purposes of corporation tax as may be required by the notice or specified in the prescribed form in respect of the return,][1]

(*b*) the distributions received by the company from companies resident in the State ...,[2]

...[3]

(*d*) payments made from which income tax is deductible and to which subsections (3) to (5) of section 238 apply, and

(*e*) all amounts which under section 438 are deemed to be annual payments.

(3) An event which, apart from section 584(3) as applied by section 586 or 587, would constitute the disposal of an asset giving rise to a chargeable gain or an allowable loss under the Capital Gains Tax Acts and the Corporation Tax Acts shall for the purposes of this section constitute such a disposal.

(4) A notice under this section may require a return of profits arising in any period during which the company was within the charge to corporation tax, together with

particulars of distributions received in that period from companies resident in the State ...[4].

(5) Every return under this section shall include a declaration to the effect that the return is correct and complete.

(6) A return under this section which includes profits which are payments on which the company has borne income tax by deduction shall specify the amount of income tax so borne.

(7) A notice under this section may require the inclusion in the return of particulars of management expenses, capital allowances and balancing charges which have been taken into account in determining the profits included in the return.

(8) Subsections (3), (4) and (5)(*b*) of section 913 shall apply in relation to a notice under this section as they apply in relation to a notice under any provision of the Income Tax Acts applied in relation to capital gains tax by section 913.

(9) (*a*) In this subsection, **"authorised officer"** means an inspector or other officer of the Revenue Commissioners authorised by them in writing to exercise the powers conferred by this subsection.

(*b*) Where a company which has been duly required to deliver a return under this section fails to deliver the return, or where the inspector is not satisfied with the return delivered by any such company, an authorised officer may serve on that company a notice or notices in writing requiring the company to do any of the following—

(i) to deliver to the inspector or to the authorised officer copies of such accounts (including balance sheets) of the company as may be specified or described in the notice, within such period as may be specified in the notice, including, where the accounts have been audited, a copy of the auditor's certificate;

(ii) to make available for inspection by an inspector or by an authorised officer within such time as may be specified in the notice all such books, accounts and documents in the possession or power of the company as may be specified or described in the notice, being books, accounts and documents which contain information as to profits, assets or liabilities of the company.

(*c*) The inspector or authorised officer may take copies of or extracts from any books, accounts or documents made available for his or her inspection under this subsection.

Amendments

1 Subs (2)(*aa*) inserted by FA 1999 s 210 with effect from 25 March 1999.

2 Repealed by FA 2000 s 69(2) and Sch 2 Part 2 with effect from 6 April 1999 in the case of income tax and as respects accounting periods commencing on or after that date in the case of corporation tax; previously "and the tax credits to which the company is entitled in respect of those distributions".

3 Subs (2)(*c*) deleted FA 2003 s 41(1)(*o*) as respects accounting periods ending on or after 6 February 2003.

4 Repealed by FA 2000 s 69(2) and Sch 2 Part 2 with effect from 6 April 1999 in the case of income tax and as respects accounting periods commencing on or after that date in the case of corporation tax; previously "and of tax credits to which the company is entitled in respect of those distributions".

Cross-references

Appeals against assessments: s 933(6)(*c*)(ii)(I), (7)(*d*)(i).
Company buying its own shares, returns: s 182(4).
Penalties for failure to make certain returns: s 1071(1), (2A); subs (9): s 1071(3).
Penalties for fraudulently or negligently making incorrect returns, etc: s 1072(1)(*a*).
Self assessment, meaning of "specified provisions": s 950(1).
Self assessment, obligation to make a return: s 951(1)(*b*), (3)(*a*).
Set-off of surplus advance corporation tax: s 845B(4).
Surcharge for late returns, meaning of "specified provisions": s 1084(1).

Statement of practice

Company's self-assessment, return of director's details, completion of form CT1: SP CT/2/90.
Preparation of accounts for Revenue purposes: SP IT/2/92, October 1992.

Case law

Subs (7): Tax on deposit interest arising during a voluntary liquidation preferential: *Noyek and Sons Ltd v Hearne* ITR Vol III p 523. However, the tax on such interest arising on official liquidations is not preferential: *In re Hibernian Transport Companies Ltd* [1984] ILRM 583.

Definitions

allowable loss: ss 4(1), 5(1), 546; Appeal Commissioners: ss 2(1), 850; capital allowance: s 2(1); chargeable gain: ss 5(1), 545; charges on income: ss 4(1), 243(1); company: ss 4(1), 5(1); distribution: ss 4(1), 436, 437; Income Tax Acts: s 1(2); inspector: ss 2(1), 5(1), 852; profits: s 4(1); within the charge to (tax): s 2(1); writing: IA 1937 Sch.

Former enactments

CTA 1976 s 143(1)–(6), (7)(*a*), (*b*) and (*d*) and (12)(*c*); FA 1981 s 16; FA 1983 s 36; FA 1990 s 54; FA 1992 s 247.

Corresponding UK tax provision

Taxes Management Act 1970 s 11 [repealed].

CHAPTER 3

Other Obligations and Returns

885 Obligation to show tax reference number on receipts

(1) In this section—

"business" means—

(*a*) a profession, or

(*b*) a trade consisting solely of the supply (within the meaning of the Value-Added Tax Acts, 1972 to 1997) of a service and includes, in the case of a trade part of which consists of the supply of a service, that part, and also includes, in the case of a trade the whole or part of which consists of the supply of a service which incorporates the supply of goods in the course of the supply of that service, that trade or that part, as the case may be;

"specified person", in relation to a business, means—

(*a*) where the business is carried on by an individual, that individual, and

(*b*) where the business is carried on by a partnership, the precedent partner;

"tax reference number", in relation to a specified person, means each of the following—

[(*a*) the Personal Public Service Number (PPSN) stated on any certificate of tax credits and standard rate cut-off point issued to that person by an inspector, not being a certificate issued to an employer in respect of an employee,][1]

(*b*) the reference number stated on any return of income form or notice of assessment issued to that person by an inspector, and

(*c*) the registration number of that person for the purposes of value-added tax.

(2) For the purposes of the Tax Acts and the Capital Gains Tax Acts, the specified person in relation to a business shall ensure that the specified person's tax reference number or, if the specified person has more than one tax reference number, one of those tax reference numbers or, if the specified person has no tax reference number, the specified person's full names and address is or are stated on any document (being an invoice, credit note, debit note, receipt, account, statement of account, voucher or estimate relating to an amount of [€7][2] or more) issued in the course of that business.

Amendments

1 Definition of "tax reference number" para (*a*) substituted by FA 2001 s 2(3) and Sch 1 para 1(*q*) for short tax "year" 2001 and later tax years.

2 Substituted by FA 2001 s 240(1) and (2)(*a*) and Sch 5 Pt 1 for 2002 and later tax years; previously "£5".

Cross-references

Approved retirement fund, meaning of "tax reference number" applied: s 784A(1)(*a*).

Capital gains tax, deduction from consideration on disposal of certain assets, meaning of "tax reference number" applied: s 980(8)(*c*).

Deposit interest retention tax, deposits of companies and pension schemes, meaning of "tax reference number" applied: s 265; interpretation, meaning of "tax reference number" applied: s 256(1) ("relevant deposit", para (*f*)(ii).

Dividend withholding tax (interpretation), meaning of "tax reference number" applied: s 172A(1)(*a*).

Implementation of Council Directive 2003/48/EC of 3 June 2003 on Taxation of Savings Income in the Form of Interest Payments, returns of interest payments made to or secured for beneficial owners, meaning of "tax reference number" applied: s 898H(2)(*c*).

Interest in respect of wholesale debt instuments, meaning of "tax reference number" applied: s 246A(1).

Intesest payments by companies and to non-residents, meaning of "tax reference number" applied: s 246(5)(*a*)(iii)(II)(B).

Investment undertakings, declarations, meaning of "tax reference number" applied: Sch 2B para 1; gain arising on a chargable event, meaning of "tax reference number" applied: s 739D(6)(*k*)(I)(B).

Penalty: Sch 29 column 3.

Returns in relation to certain offshore products, meaning of "tax reference number" applied: s 896(1).

Returns in relation to foreign accounts, meaning of "tax reference number" applied: s 895(1).

Returns of fees, commissions, etc, paid by certain persons, meaning of "tax reference number" applied: s 889(1).

Definitions

inspector: ss 2(1), 5(1), 852; profession: s 2(1); trade: s 3(1).

Former enactments

FA 1983 s 22(1)–(2).

---

886 Obligation to keep certain records

(1) In this section—

"linking documents" means documents drawn up in the making up of accounts and showing details of the calculations linking the records to the accounts;

"records" includes accounts, books of account, documents and any other data maintained manually or by any electronic, photographic or other process, relating to—

(*a*) all sums of money received and expended in the course of the carrying on or exercising of a trade, profession or other activity and the matters in respect of which the receipt and expenditure take place,

(*b*) all sales and purchases of goods and services where the carrying on or exercising of a trade, profession or other activity involves the purchase or sale of goods or services,

(*c*) the assets and liabilities of the trade, profession or other activity referred to in paragraph (*a*) or (*b*), and

(*d*) all transactions which constitute an acquisition or disposal of an asset for capital gains tax purposes.

(2) (*a*) Every person who—

(i) on that person's own behalf or on behalf of any other person, carries on or exercises any trade, profession or other activity the profits or gains of which are chargeable under Schedule D,

(ii) is chargeable to tax under Schedule D or F in respect of any other source of income, or

(iii) is chargeable to capital gains tax in respect of chargeable gains,

shall keep, or cause to be kept on that person's behalf, such records as will enable true returns to be made for the purposes of income tax, corporation tax and capital gains tax of such profits or gains or chargeable gains.

(*b*) The records shall be kept on a continuous and consistent basis, that is, the entries in the records shall be made in a timely manner and be consistent from one year to the next.

(*c*) Where accounts are made up to show the profits or gains from any such trade, profession or activity, or in relation to a source of income, of any person, that person shall retain, or cause to be retained on that person's behalf, linking documents.

(*d*) Where any such trade, profession or other activity is carried on in partnership, the precedent partner (within the meaning of section 1007) shall for the purposes of this section be deemed to be the person carrying on that trade, profession or other activity.

(3) Records required to be kept or retained by virtue of this section shall be kept—

(*a*) in written form in an official language of the State, or

(*b*) subject to section 887(2), by means of any electronic, photographic or other process.

(4) (*a*) Subject to paragraph (*b*), linking documents and records kept in accordance with subsections (2) and (3) shall be retained by the person required to keep the records—

(i) for a period of 6 years after the completion of the transactions, acts or operations to which they relate, or

(ii) in the case of a person who fails to comply with section 951(1) requiring the preparation and delivery of a return on or before the specified return date for a year of assessment or an accounting period, as the case may be, until the expiry of a period of 6 years from the end of the year of assessment or accounting period, as the case may be, in which a return has been delivered showing the profits or gains or chargeable gains derived from those transactions, acts or operations.

(*b*) Paragraph (*a*) shall not—

(i) require the retention of linking documents and records in respect of which the inspector notifies in writing the person who is required to retain them that retention is not required, or

(ii) apply to the books and papers of a company which have been disposed of in accordance with section 305(1) of the Companies Act, 1963.

(5) Any person who fails to comply with subsection (2), (3) or (4) in respect of any records or linking documents in relation to a return for any year of assessment or accounting period shall be liable to a penalty of [€1,520][1]; but a penalty shall not be imposed under this subsection if it is proved that no person is chargeable to tax in respect of the profits or gains for that year of assessment or accounting period, as the case may be.

Amendments

1 Substituted by FA 2001 s 240(1) and (2)(*k*) and Sch 5 Pt 1 as respects any act or omission which takes place or begins on or after 1 January 2002; previously "£1,200".

Cross-references

Power of inspection, tax deduction from payments to certain subcontractors, meaning of "records" applied: s 904(1).

Power to obtain information from certain persons particulars of transactions with and documents concerning tax liability of taxpayer, meaning of "documents" applied: s 902(1)(*a*).

Profits from occupation of certain woodlands, meaning of "records" applied: s 232(3)(*d*).

Profits or gains from stallion fees, meaning of "records" applied: s 231(2)(*d*).

Recovery of penalties: s 1061(1).

Relief for investment in films: s 481(2C)(*c*).

Stud greyhound services, meaning of "records" applied: s 233(3)(*d*).

Subcontractors' withholding tax, subs (2): s 531(11)(*a*)(iii).

Case law

Linking documents are taxpayer's property: *Quigley v Burke* ITR Vol IV p 332.

Revenue precedents

Issue: Are personal bank statements "records" within the meaning of s 886?

Decision: Not if they relate solely to personal transactions and are not such as would be used so as to enable true returns to be made of the profits or gains or chargeable gains of the trade, profession or other activity carried on by the person.

Statement of practice

Revenue powers: SP GEN/1/94, May 1994.

Tax Briefing

TB52 May 2003 p 19 — Retention of Records.

Definitions

person: IA 1937 s 11(*c*); profession: s 2(1); trade: s 3(1); year of assessment: ss 2(1), 5(1).

Former enactments

FA 1968 s 6(1)–(5); CTA 1976 s 147(1)–(2); FA 1992 s 231.

Corresponding UK tax provision

Taxes Management Act 1970 s 12B.

886A Retention and inspection of records in relation to claims by individuals

[(1) An individual who, in relation to a year of assessment, may wish to make a claim for an allowance, deduction or relief in relation to income tax shall keep and preserve all such records as may be requisite for the purpose of enabling the individual to make a correct and complete claim.

(2) The records which an individual is required to keep and preserve in accordance with subsection (1) shall be retained by the individual for the longer of the following periods—

(*a*) where enquiries into the claim or any amendment of the claim are made by an officer of the Revenue Commissioners, the period ending on the day on which those enquiries are treated as completed by the officer, and

(*b*) a period of 6 years beginning at the end of the year of assessment to which the claim relates.

(3) Subject to subsection (4), an individual who fails to comply with subsection (1) in relation to any claim which is made for a year of assessment, shall be liable to a penalty of €1,520 and, for the purposes of recovery of a penalty under this subsection, section 1061 shall apply in the same manner as it applies for the purposes of the recovery of a penalty under any of the sections referred to in that section.

(4) Subsection (3) shall not apply where an officer of the Revenue Commissioners is satisfied that any facts which the officer reasonably requires to be proved, and which would have been proved by the records, are proved by other documentary evidence furnished to the officer.

(5) Subject to the provisions of section 956, an officer of the Revenue Commissioners may enquire into—

(*a*) a claim made by an individual, or

(*b*) any amendment made by an individual of a claim made by the individual,

if, within 4 years from the end of the year of assessment in which the claim, or (as the case may be) any amendment of the claim, is made, the officer gives notice of his or her intention to do so to that individual.

(6) Where an officer of the Revenue Commissioners gives notice under subsection (5) to any individual (in this subsection referred to as the "claimant") of his or her intention to enquire into—

(*a*) a claim made by the claimant, or

(*b*) any amendment made by the claimant of such a claim,

then the officer may at the same or any subsequent time by notice in writing require the claimant, within such time (which shall not be less than 30 days) as may be specified in the notice—

(i) to produce to the officer such documents as are in the claimant's possession or power and as the officer may reasonably require for the purpose of determining whether and, if so, the extent to which the claim or amendment is correct, and

(ii) to furnish the officer with such accounts or particulars as the officer may reasonably require for that purpose.

(7) In complying with a notice under subsection (6) an individual may furnish to the officer copies of documents instead of originals, but—

(*a*) the copies must be photographic or other facsimiles, and

(*b*) the officer may by notice require the original to be produced for inspection.

(8) The officer may take copies of, or make extracts from, any document produced to him or her under this section.][1].

Amendments

1 Section 886A inserted by FA 2005 s 25 with effect from 25 March 2005.

Cross-references

Electronic claims, PAYE: s 864A(7).

Definitions

writing: IA 1937 Sch; year of assessment: s 2(1).

887 Use of electronic data processing

[(1) In this section—

"the Acts" means—

(*a*) the Tax Acts,

(*b*) the Capital Gains Tax Acts,

(*c*) the Value-Added Tax Act, 1972, and the enactments amending or extending that Act,

(*d*) the [Capital Acquisitions Tax Consolidation Act 2003],[1] and the enactments amending or extending that Act, and

(*e*) Part VI of the Finance Act, 1983,

and any instrument made under any of these enactments;

"record" means any document which a person is obliged by the Acts to keep, to issue or to produce for inspection, and any other written or printed material.

(2) For the purposes of the Acts, but subject to section 17 of the Value-Added Tax Act, 1972, a record may be stored, maintained, transmitted, reproduced or communicated, as the case may be, by any electronic, photographic or other process that—

(*a*) provides a reliable assurance as to the integrity of the record from the time when it was first generated in its final form by such electronic, photographic or other process,

(*b*) permits the record to be displayed in intelligible form and produced in an intelligible printed format,

(*c*) permits the record to be readily accessible for subsequent reference in accordance with paragraph (*b*), and

(*d*) conforms to the information technology and procedural requirements drawn up and published by the Revenue Commissioners in accordance with subsection (3).

(3) The Revenue Commissioners shall from time to time draw up and publish in Iris Oifigiúil the information technology and procedural requirements to which any

electronic, photographic or other process used by a person for the storage, maintenance, transmission, reproduction and communication of any record shall conform.

(4) The authority conferred on the Revenue Commissioners by this section to draw up and publish requirements shall be construed as including the authority exercisable in a like manner to revoke and replace or to amend any such requirements.

(5) (*a*) Every person who preserves records by any electronic, photographic or other process, when required to do so by a notice in writing from the Revenue Commissioners, shall, within such period as is specified in the notice, not being less than 21 days from the date of service of the notice, supply to the Revenue Commissioners full particulars relating to the process used by that person, including full particulars relating to software (within the meaning of section 912).

(*b*) A person who fails or refuses to comply with a notice served on the person under paragraph (*a*) shall be liable to a penalty of [€1,265].[2]

(6) (*a*) Subject to paragraph (*b*), where records are kept by a person (being a person who is obliged by the Acts to keep such records) by any electronic, photographic or other process which does not conform with the requirements referred to in paragraphs (*a*) to (*d*) of subsection (2), then the person shall be deemed to have failed to comply with that obligation and that person shall be liable to the same penalties as the person would be liable to if the person had failed to comply with any obligation under the Acts in relation to the keeping of records.

(*b*) Paragraph (*a*) shall not apply where the person referred to in that paragraph complies with any obligation under the Acts in relation to the keeping of records other than in accordance with the provisions of subsection (2).

(7) Where records are preserved by any electronic, photographic or other process, information contained in a document produced by any such process shall, subject to the rules of court, be admissible in evidence in any proceedings, whether civil or criminal, to the same extent as the records themselves.

(8) The Revenue Commissioners may nominate any of their officers to discharge any function authorised by this section to be discharged by the Revenue Commissioners.][3]

Amendments

1 Substituted by CATCA 2003 s 119 and Sch 3 with effect from 21 February 2003; previously "Capital Acquisitions Tax Act 1976".

2 Substituted by FA 2001 s 232(3)(*a*)(i) with effect from 1 January 2002; previously "£1,000".

3 Substituted by FA 2001 s 232(1)(*a*) with effect from 15 February 2001 (as a result of FA 2002 s 138 and Sch 6 paras 5(*f*) and 6(*e*)(i)).

Cross-references

Capital acquisitions tax, obligation to retain certain records, subs (2): CATCA 2003 s 45A(3)(*b*).

Obligation to keep records, subs (2): s 886(3)(*b*).

Power of inspection, PAYE: s 903(1)("records").

This section to be construed together with the Value Added Tax Acts 1972–1997, in so far as relating to value added tax: s 1104(3).

This section to be construed together with the Capital Acquisitions Tax Act 1976, and the enactments amending or extending that Act, in so far as relating to capital acquisitions tax: s 1104(5).

This section to be construed together with FA 1983 Pt VI and the enactments amending or extending that Part, in so far as relating to residential property tax: s 1104(6).

Tax Briefing

TB46 Dec 2001 pp 24–25 — Electronic Storage — Retention of Tax Records in Electronic Format.

Definitions

Capital Gains Tax Acts: s 1(2); person: IA 1937 s 11(*c*); rules of court: IA 1937 Sch; Tax Acts: s 1(2); writing: IA 1937 Sch.

Former enactments

FA 1986 s 113(1)–(3); FA 1993 s 99.

Corresponding UK tax provision

Taxes Management Act 1970 s 115A.

888 Returns, etc by lessors, lessees and agents

(1) In this section, **"lease"**, **"lessee"**, **"lessor"**, **"premises"** and **"rent"** have the same meanings respectively as in Chapter 8 of Part 4.

(2) For the purpose of obtaining particulars of profits or gains chargeable to tax under Case IV or V of Schedule D by virtue of Chapter 8 of Part 4, the inspector may by notice in writing require—

(*a*) any lessor or former lessor of premises to give, within the time limited by the notice, such information as may be specified in the notice as to the provisions of the lease, the terms subject to which the lease was granted and the payments made to or by that lessor or former lessor, as the case may be, in relation to the premises;

(*b*) any lessee, occupier or former lessee or occupier of premises (including any person having or having had the use of premises) to give such information as may be specified in the notice as to the terms applying to the lease, occupation or use of the premises and, where any of those terms are established by any written instrument, to produce the instrument to the inspector for inspection;

(*c*) any lessee or former lessee of premises to give such information as may be specified in the notice as to any consideration given for the grant to that lessee or former lessee, as the case may be, of the lease;

(*d*) any person who as an agent manages premises or is in receipt of rent or other payments arising from premises to prepare and deliver to the inspector a return containing—

(i) the full address of all such premises,

(ii) the name and address of every person to whom such premises belong,

(iii) a statement of all rents and other such payments arising from such premises, and

(iv) such other particulars relating to all such premises as may be specified in the notice;

(*e*) any Minister of the Government [who, or the Health Service Executive or any local authority][1] (within the meaning of section 2(2) of the Local Government Act, 1941) or other board or authority, or other similar body, established by or under statute which, makes any payment either in the nature of or for the purpose of rent or rent subsidy in relation to any premises to prepare and deliver to the inspector a return containing—

(i) the full address of all such premises,

(ii) the name and address of every person to whom such premises belong,
(iii) a statement of all such payments arising in respect of such premises, and
(iv) such other particulars relating to all such premises as may be specified in the notice.

Amendments

1 Substituted by FA 2005 s 147 and Sch 6 para 1(*n*) with effect from 25 March 2005; previously "who, or any health board, local authority".

Cross-references

Capital gains tax, applied by: s 913(2), (6).
Inspector's right to make enquiries, subs (2)(*d*), (*e*): s 899(1).
Returns of certain information by third parties, subs (2)(*d*), (*e*): s 894(1).
Self assessment, meaning of "specified provisions", subs (2)(*a*), (*d*): s 950(1).
Surcharge for late returns, meaning of "specified provisions", subs (2)(*a*), (*d*): s 1084(1).

Statement of practice

Revenue powers: SP GEN/1/94, May 1994.

Definitions

rent: s 5(1); person: IA 1937 s 11(*c*); writing: IA 1937 Sch.

Former enactments

ITA 1967 ss 80(1) and 94; FA 1969 s 33(1) and Sch 4 Pt I; FA 1992 s 227(*a*); FA 1995 s 14(1).

Corresponding UK tax provision

Taxes Management Act 1970 s 19.

889 Returns of fees, commissions, etc paid by certain persons

(1) In this section—

"tax reference number", in relation to a person, has the meaning assigned to it by section 885 in relation to a specified person within the meaning of that section;

references to payments for services include references to payments in the nature of commission of any kind and references to payments in respect of expenses incurred in connection with rendering of services;

references to payments made include references to the giving of any valuable consideration, and the requirement imposed by subsection (5) to state the amount of a payment shall, in relation to any consideration given otherwise than in the form of money, be construed as a requirement to give particulars of the consideration.

(2) Every person carrying on a trade or business shall, if required to do so by notice from an inspector, make and deliver to the inspector a return of all payments of any kind specified in the notice made during the period so specified, being—

(*a*) payments made in the course of the trade or business, or of such part of the trade or business as may be specified in the notice, for services rendered in connection with the trade or business by persons ordinarily resident in the State and not employed in the trade or business,

(*b*) payments for services rendered in connection with the formation, acquisition, development or disposal of the trade or business, or any part of it, by persons ordinarily resident in the State and not employed in the trade or business, or

(*c*) periodical or lump sum payments made to persons ordinarily resident in the State in respect of any copyright.

(3) Every body of persons (which for the purposes of this section shall be deemed to include a Minister of the Government and any body established by or under statute) carrying on any activity which does not constitute a trade or business shall, if required to do so by a notice from an inspector, make and deliver to the inspector a return of all payments of a kind specified in the notice made during the period specified in the notice, being—

(*a*) payments made in the course of carrying on the activity, or such part of the activity as may be specified in the notice, for services rendered in connection with the activity by persons ordinarily resident in the State and not employed by that body of persons, or

(*b*) periodical or lump sum payments made to persons ordinarily resident in the State in respect of any copyright.

(4) A return required under subsection (2) or (3) shall, if the trade or business or other activity is carried on by an unincorporated body of persons, be made and delivered by the person who is, or performs the duties of, secretary of the body, and the notice shall be framed accordingly.

(5) A return under this section shall give the name and tax reference number of the person to whom each payment was made, the amount of the payment and such other particulars as may be specified in the notice, including particulars as to—

(*a*) the services or rights in respect of which the payment was made,

(*b*) the period over which any services were rendered, and

(*c*) any business name and any business or home address of the person to whom payment was made.

(6) A return under this section shall include payments made by the person or body of persons in the course of the trade, business or activity on behalf of any other person.

(7) No person shall be required under this section to include in a return—

(*a*) particulars of any payment from which income tax is deductible,

(*b*) particulars of payments made to any one person where the total of the payments to that person which would otherwise have to be included in the return does not exceed [€635][1], or

(*c*) particulars of any payment made in a year of assessment ending more than 3 years before the service of the notice requiring the person to make the return.

(8) A person who fails to deliver, within the period limited in any notice served on the person under this section, a true and correct return which the person is required by the notice to deliver shall be liable to a penalty of [€1,520][2].

(9) Penalties under this section may, without prejudice to any other method of recovery, be proceeded for and recovered summarily in the like manner as in summary proceedings for the recovery of any fine or penalty under any Act relating to the excise.

(10) In proceedings for the recovery of a penalty under this section, a certificate by an officer of the Revenue Commissioners which certifies that he or she has inspected the relevant records of the Revenue Commissioners and that it appears from them that during a stated period a stated return was not received from the defendant shall be evidence until the contrary is proved that the defendant did not during that period deliver that return, and any such certificate, purporting to be signed by an officer of the

Revenue Commissioners, may be tendered in evidence without proof and shall be deemed until thc contrary is proved to have been signed by an officer of the Revenue Commissioners.

Amendments

1 Substituted by FA 2001 s 240(1) and (2)(*a*) and (*c*) and Sch 5 Pt 1 for 2002 and later tax years in the case of income tax and for accounting periods ending on or after 1 January 2002 in the case of corporation tax; previously "£500".

2 Substituted by FA 2001 s 240(1) and (2)(*k*) and Sch 5 Pt 1 as respects any act or omission which takes place or begins on or after 1 January 2002; previously "£1,200".

Cross-references

Inspector's right to make enquiries: s 899(1).
Returns of certain information by third parties: s 894(1).
Time limit for summary proceedings: s 1064.

Revenue precedents

Issue: Details to be included on form 46G by solicitors.
Decision: Agreed that payments out of clients accounts need not be included on form 46G (completed in accordance with s 889).

Statement of practice

Revenue powers: SP GEN/1/94, May 1994.

Definitions

body of persons: s 2(1); inspector: ss 2(1), 5(1), 852; person: IA 1937 s 11(*c*), trade: s 3(1); year of assessment: s 3(1).

Former enactments

ITA 1967 s 173(1)–(7) and (9)–(10); FA 1982 s 60; FA 1992 s 227(*b*) and s 248.

Corresponding UK tax provision

Taxes Management Act 1970 s 16.

---

890 Returns by persons in receipt of income belonging to others

(1) Every person (in this section referred to as **"the first-mentioned person"**) who, in whatever capacity, is in receipt of any money or value, or of profits or gains arising from any of the sources mentioned in the Income Tax Acts, of or belonging to any other person who is chargeable in respect of such money, value, profits or gains, or who would be so chargeable if that other person were resident in the State and not an incapacitated person, shall, whenever required to do so by a notice given to the first- mentioned person by an inspector, prepare and deliver, within the period mentioned in such notice, a return in the prescribed form, signed by the first-mentioned person, containing—

- (*a*) a statement of all such money, value, profits or gains;
- (*b*) the name and address of every person to whom all such money, value, profits or gains belong;
- (*c*) a declaration whether every such person is of full age, a married woman, resident in the State or an incapacitated person.

(2) Where the first-mentioned person is acting jointly with any other person, the first-mentioned person shall, in the like manner, deliver a list of the names and addresses of all persons joined with the first-mentioned person at the time of delivery of the return mentioned in subsection (1).

(3) No person shall be required under this section to include in a return particulars of receipts (to which subsection (1) applies) of or belonging to any one person where the

total of the receipts relating to that person which would otherwise have to be included in the return does not exceed [€635][1].

Amendments

1 Substituted by FA 2001 s 240(1) and (2)(*a*) and Sch 5 Pt 1 for 2002 and later tax years; previously "£500".

Cross-references

Inspector's right to make enquiries: s 899(1).
Penalty: Sch 29 column 2.
Protection for trustees, agents and receivers: s 1050.
Returns of certain information by third parties: s 894(1).

Case law

Held an auctioneer of livestock was not obliged to deliver a return as the proceeds of sale held by him did not constitute 'profits or gains' but were merely an element to be taken into account in ascertaining profits or gains: *Fawcett v Special Commissioners & Lancaster Farmer's Auction Mart Co Ltd* [1995] STC 61.

Statement of practice

Revenue powers: SP GEN/1/94, May 1994.

Definitions

incapacitated person: s 3(1); inspector: ss 2(1), 5(1), 852; person: IA 1937 s 11(*c*).

Former enactments

ITA 1967 s 176; F(MP)A 1968 s 6(5); FA 1992 s 227(*c*).

Corresponding UK tax provision

Taxes Management Act 1970 s 13.

891 Returns of interest paid or credited without deduction of tax

(1) Subject to subsection (2), every person carrying on a trade or business who, in the ordinary course of the operations of the trade or business, receives or retains money in such circumstances that interest becomes payable on that money which is paid or credited without deduction of income tax, and in particular every person carrying on the trade or business of banking, shall, if required to do so by notice from an inspector, make and deliver to the inspector, within the time specified in the notice, a return of all interest so paid or credited by that person during a year specified in the notice in the course of that person's trade or business or any such part of that person's trade or business as may be so specified, giving the names and addresses of the persons to whom the interest was paid or credited and stating in each case the amount of the interest.

[(1A)(*a*) In this subsection, **"credit union"** means a society registered under the Credit Union Act, 1997, including a society deemed to be so registered under section 5(3) of that Act.

(*b*) This section shall not apply in relation to any interest paid or credited by a credit union in respect of money received or retained by it.][1]

(2) (*a*) No interest paid or credited to any person shall be required to be included in any return under subsection (1) where the total amount of the interest paid or credited to that person which would otherwise have had to be included in the return does not exceed [€65][2].

(*b*) The year specified in a notice under subsection (1) shall not be a year ending more than 3 years before the date of the service of the notice.

(3) Without prejudice to the generality of so much of subsection (1) as enables different notices to be served under that subsection in relation to different parts of a trade or

business, separate notices may be served under that subsection as respects the transactions carried on at any branch or branches respectively specified in the notices, and any such separate notice shall, if served on the manager or other person in charge of the branch or branches in question, be deemed to have been duly served on the person carrying on the trade or business and, where such a separate notice is so served as respects the transactions carried on at any branch or branches, any notice subsequently served under subsection (1) on the person carrying on the trade or business shall not be deemed to extend to any transaction to which that separate notice extends.

(4) (*a*) This section shall, with any necessary modifications, apply in relation to the Post Office Savings Bank as if it were a trade or business carried on by An Post.

(*b*) This subsection shall apply notwithstanding section 4 of the Post Office Savings Bank Act, 1861; but, subject to paragraph (*a*), that section shall remain in full force and effect.

(5) Subsections (1) to (4) shall apply only to money received or retained in the State.

(6) (*a*) Subject to paragraphs (*b*) and (*c*), where a person to whom any interest is paid or credited in respect of any money received or retained in the State by notice in writing served on the person paying or crediting the interest—

(i) declares that the person who was beneficially entitled to that interest when it was paid or credited was not then resident in the State, and

(ii) requests that the interest shall not be included in any return under this section,

the person paying or crediting the interest shall not be required to include the interest in any such return.

(*b*) Where the person on whom a notice under paragraph (*a*) is served is not satisfied that the person who served the notice was resident outside the State when the interest was paid or credited—

(i) there shall be given to the person on whom the notice is served an affidavit, made by the person who served the notice, stating that person's name and address and the country in which that person was resident when the interest was paid or credited, and

(ii) if the person who served the notice was not beneficially entitled to that interest when it was paid or credited, the affidavit shall state, in addition to the particulars specified in subparagraph (i), the name and address of the person who was so entitled and the country in which that person was resident when the interest was paid or credited.

(*c*) Where the person on whom a notice under paragraph (*a*) is served is satisfied that the person who served the notice (in this paragraph referred to as **"the server"**) was not resident in the State when the interest was paid or credited and, if the server declares in the notice, or in a subsequent notice served on the person on whom the first-mentioned notice was served, that the server was not beneficially entitled to the interest when it was paid or credited, the server shall, if the person so entitled (in this paragraph referred to as **"the beneficial owner"**) is resident in the State, state in one of those notices or in a subsequent notice served on the person on whom the first-mentioned notice was served the name and address of the beneficial owner.

(7) A person to whom subsection (1) applies—

(*a*) shall keep and retain any notice served on that person in accordance with subsection (6), and any affidavit that accompanied the notice, for a period of 6 years from the date of the service of the notice,

(*b*) shall, if requested in writing by the Revenue Commissioners to do so, inform the Revenue Commissioners within the time specified in the request whether a notice has been served on that person in accordance with subsection (6) by such person as is named, and whose address is stated, in the request, and

(*c*) shall, if requested in writing by the Revenue Commissioners to do so, furnish to the Revenue Commissioners within the time specified in the request such notice served on that person in accordance with subsection (6) as is specified in the request and the affidavit that accompanied that notice.

Amendments

1 Subs (1A) inserted by FA 1998 s 131(*b*) as respects chargeable periods (within the meaning of TCA 1998 s 321(2)) beginning on or after 1 October 1997.

2 Substituted by FA 2001 s 240(1) and (2)(*a*) and (*c*) and Sch 5 Pt 1 for 2002 and later tax years in the case of income tax and for accounting periods ending on or after 1 January 2002 in the case of corporation tax; previously "£50".

Cross-references

Deposit interest retention tax, company, pension scheme or charity receiving interest free of tax, requirement to state tax reference number or charity number: s 265, s 266.

Implementation of Council Directive 2003/48/EC of 3 June 2003 on Taxation of Savings Income in the Form of Interest Payments, returns of interest payments made to or secured for beneficial owners: s 898H(5).

Inspector's right to make enquiries: s 899(1).

Interest in respect of wholesale debt instruments: s 246A(4)(*a*)(i), (iii), (*b*).

Penalty: Sch 29 column 2.

Returns of certain information by third parties: s 894(1).

Returns of interest paid to non-residents: s 891A(2)(*b*).

Definitions

affidavit: IA 1937 Sch; inspector: ss 2(1), 5(1), 852; person: IA 1937 s 11(*c*); trade: s 3(1); writing: IA 1937 Sch.

Former enactments

ITA 1967 s 175; FA 1983 s 17(2); FA 1995 s 168; Postal and Telecommunications Services Act, 1983 s 8(1) and Sch 4 Pt I.

Corresponding UK tax provision

Taxes Management Act 1970 s 17.

891A Returns of interest paid to non-residents

[(1) In this section—

"appropriate inspector" has the same meaning as in section 950(1);

"chargeable period" has the same meaning as in section 321(2);

"relevant interest" means interest to which subsection (2) of section 246 does not apply by virtue only of paragraph (*h*) (inserted by the Finance Act, 1999) of subsection (3) of that section;

"relevant person" has the same meaning as in section 246;

"specified return date for the chargeable period" has the same meaning as in section 894(1).

(2) (*a*) Subject to paragraph (*c*), every relevant person who pays relevant interest in a chargeable period shall prepare and deliver to the appropriate inspector on or before the specified return date for the chargeable period a return of all relevant interest so paid by the relevant person in the chargeable period stating in the case of each person to whom that relevant interest was paid—

(i) the name and address of the person,

(ii) the amount of relevant interest paid to the person in the chargeable period, and

(iii) the territory in which the person is resident for tax purposes.

(*b*) Section 891 shall not apply, in respect of the payment of relevant interest, to any relevant person to whom paragraph (*a*) applies.

(*c*) Sections 1052 and 1054 shall apply to a failure by a relevant person to deliver a return required by paragraph (*a*) and to each and every such failure, as they apply to a failure to deliver a return referred to in section 1052.][1]

Amendments

1 Section 891A inserted by FA 1999 s 40 with effect from 6 April 1999.

Cross-references

Implementation of Council Directive 2003/48/EC of 3 June 2003 on Taxation of Savings Income in the Form of Interest Payments, returns of interest payments made to or secured for beneficial owners: s 898H(5).

Inspector's right to make enquiries: s 899(1).

Definitions

person: IA 1937 s 11(*c*).

892 Returns by nominee holders of securities

(1) In this section, **"securities"** includes—

(*a*) shares, stocks, bonds, debentures and debenture stock of a company (within the meaning of section 4(1)) and also any promissory note or other instrument evidencing indebtedness issued to a loan creditor (within the meaning of section 433(6)) of a company,

(*b*) securities created and issued by the Minister for Finance under the Central Fund (Permanent Provisions) Act, 1965, or under any other statutory powers conferred on that Minister and any stock, debenture, debenture stock, certificate of charge or other security which is issued with the approval of the Minister for Finance given under any Act of the Oireachtas and in respect of which the payment of interest and the repayment of capital is guaranteed by the Minister for Finance under that Act, and

(*c*) securities of the government of any country or territory outside the State.

(2) Where for any purpose of the Tax Acts any person (in this subsection referred to as **"the holder"**) in whose name any securities are registered is so required by notice in writing given by an inspector, the holder shall, within the time specified in the notice, state whether or not the holder is the beneficial owner of the securities and, if not the

beneficial owner of the securities or any of them, shall furnish in respect of each person on whose behalf the securities are registered in the holder's name—

(*a*) the name and address of such person,

(*b*) the nominal value of the securities so registered on behalf of such person and, in so far as the securities consist of shares in a company, the number and class of such shares, and

(*c*) the date on which each security was so registered in the holder's name on behalf of such person.

Cross-references

Inspector's right to make enquiries: s 899(1).

Penalty: Sch 29 column 2.

Returns of certain information by third parties: s 894(1), (2)(*c*).

Statement of practice

Revenue powers: SP GEN/1/94, May 1994.

Definitions

class (of shares): s 5(1); company: ss 4(1), 5(1); inspector: ss 2(1), 5(1), 852; the Oireachtas: IA 1937 Sch; Tax Acts: s 1(2); writing: IA 1937 Sch.

Former enactments

FA 1983 s 21(1)–(2).

Corresponding UK tax provision

Taxes Management Act 1970 s 26.

893 Returns by certain intermediaries in relation to UCITS

Amendments

1 Section 893 deleted by FA 2001 s 232(1)(*b*) as respects any chargeable period (within the meaning of s 321(2)) commencing on or after 15 February 2001.

Cross-references

Inspector's right to make enquiries: s 899(1).

Returns of certain information by third parties: s 894(1).

Former enactments

FA 1989 s 19(1)–(3); FA 1992 s 229.

894 Returns of certain information by third parties

(1) In this section—

"appropriate inspector", in relation to a person to whom this section applies, means—

(*a*) the inspector who has last given notice in writing to that person that he or she is the inspector to whom that person is required to deliver the return specified in subsection (3),

(*b*) where there is no such inspector as is referred to in paragraph (*a*), the inspector to whom it is customary for that person to deliver [any return, statement, list or declaration],[1] or

(*c*) where there is no such inspector as is referred to in paragraphs (*a*) and (*b*), the inspector of returns specified in section 950;

"chargeable period" has the same meaning as in section 321(2);

"relevant person" has the meaning assigned to it by subsection (2);

"specified provisions" means paragraphs (*d*) and (*e*) of section 888(2) and sections 889 to 893,

"specified return date for the chargeable period", in relation to a chargeable period, means—

[(*a*) (i) where the chargeable period is the year of assessment 2000–2001, 31 January 2002, and

(ii) where the chargeable period is the year of assessment 2001 or any subsequent year of assessment, 31 October in the year of assessment following that year,

and][2]

(*b*) where the chargeable period is an accounting period of a company, the last day of the period of 9 months commencing on the day immediately following the end of the accounting period.

(2) (*a*) Subject to paragraphs (*b*) to (*e*), **"relevant person"** means any person who—

(i) has information of a kind,

(ii) makes a payment of a kind,

(iii) pays or credits interest of a kind, or

(iv) is in receipt of money or value or of profits or gains of a kind,

referred to in a specified provision.

(*b*) Subject to paragraph (*e*), any person who would be excluded from making a return under a specified provision for a chargeable period shall not be a relevant person.

(*c*) A person with information of the kind referred to in section 892 shall, subject to paragraph (*e*), be a relevant person only where the person is not the beneficial owner of the securities referred to in that section.

...[3]

(*e*) A person who is not a relevant person by virtue of any of the provisions of paragraphs (*b*) to (*d*) shall not be excluded from being a relevant person by virtue of any other provision of this subsection.

(3) Every relevant person shall as respects a chargeable period prepare and deliver to the appropriate inspector on or before the specified return date for the chargeable period a return of all such matters and particulars as would be required to be contained in a return delivered pursuant to a notice given to the relevant person by the appropriate inspector under any of the specified provisions for the chargeable period.

(4) An inspector may exclude any person from the application of this section by giving that person a notice in writing that that person is excluded from the application of this section, and the notice shall have effect for such chargeable period or periods, or until such chargeable period or the happening of such event, as shall be specified in the notice.

(5) Where it appears appropriate to an inspector, the inspector may notify any relevant person that a return to be made under this section may be confined to a particular type or

category of information, payment or receipt and, where the relevant person has been so notified, a return made on that basis shall satisfy this section.

(6) This section shall not affect the giving of a notice under any of the specified provisions and shall not remove from any person any obligation or requirement imposed on a person by such a notice, and the giving of a notice under any of the specified provisions to a person shall not remove from that person any obligation to prepare and deliver a return under this section.

(7) Sections 1052 and 1054 shall apply to a failure by a relevant person to deliver a return required by subsection (3), and to each and every such failure, as they apply to a failure to deliver a return referred to in section 1052.

Amendments

1 Substituted by FA 2001 s 78(2)(*d*) for the short tax "year" 2001 and later tax years (income tax and capital gains tax) and as respects accounting periods of companies ending on or after 1 April 2001; previously "a return or statement of income or profits".

2 Definition of "specified return date for the chargeable period" para (*a*) substituted by FA 2003 s 34(1)(*b*) with effect from 6 April 2001.

3 Subs (2)(*d*) deleted by FA 2001 s 232(1)(*c*) as respects any chargeable period (within the meaning of s 321(2)) commencing on or after 15 February 2001.

Cross-references

Inspector's right to make enquiries: s 899(1).

Interest in respect of wholesale debt instruments: s 246A(4)(*a*)(ii).

Penalty, subs (3): Sch 29 column 2.

Returns of interest paid to non-residents, meaning of "specified return date for the chargeable period" applied: s 891A(1).

Revenue information

Information leaflet IT16 — Third Party Returns.

Tax Briefing

TB12 Oct 1993 para 2.1 — Third Party Returns and Solicitors.

Statements of practice

Revenue powers: SP GEN/1/94, May 1994.

Third party returns, return of certain information: SP IT/1/92, October 1992.

Definitions

inspector: ss 2(1), 850; profits: s 4(1); year of assessment: ss 2(1), 5(1).

Former enactments

FA 1992 s 226; FA 1995 s 14(2)(i).

895 Returns in relation to foreign accounts

(1) In this section—

"appropriate inspector", in relation to an intermediary or, as may be appropriate, a resident, means—

(*a*) the inspector who has last given notice in writing to the intermediary or, as the case may be, the resident that he or she is the inspector to whom the intermediary or, as the case may be, the resident is required [to deliver a return, statement, declaration or list by reason of a notice given to the person by the inspector],[1] (*b*) where there is no such inspector as is referred to in paragraph (*a*), the inspector to whom it is customary for the intermediary or, as the case may be, the resident to deliver [such return, statement, declaration or list],[2] or

(*c*) where there is no such inspector as is referred to in paragraphs (*a*) and (*b*), the inspector of returns specified in section 950;

"chargeable period" has the same meaning as in section 321(2);

"deposit" means a sum of money paid to a person on terms under which it will be repaid with or without interest and either on demand or at a time or in circumstances agreed by or on behalf of the person making the payment and the person to whom it is made;

"foreign account" means an account in which a deposit is held at a location outside the State;

"intermediary" means any person carrying on in the State a trade or business in the ordinary course of the operations of which that person provides a relevant service;

"relevant person" means a person who in the normal course of that person's trade or business receives or holds deposits;

"relevant service" means the acting in the State as an intermediary in or in connection with the opening of foreign accounts with relevant persons by or on behalf of residents;

"resident" means a person resident in the State;

"specified return date for the chargeable period", in relation to a chargeable period, means—

[(*a*) (i) where the chargeable period is the year of assessment 2000–2001, 31 January 2002, and

(ii) where the chargeable period is the year of assessment 2001 or any subsequent year of assessment, 31 October in the year of assessment following that year,

and][3]

(*b*) where the chargeable period is an accounting period of a company, the last day of the period of 9 months commencing on the day immediately following the end of the accounting period;

"tax reference number", in relation to a resident, has the meaning assigned to it by section 885 in relation to a specified person within the meaning of that section.

(2) Every intermediary shall as respects a chargeable period prepare and deliver to the appropriate inspector on or before the specified return date for the chargeable period a return specifying in respect of every resident in respect of whom that intermediary has acted in the chargeable period as an intermediary in the opening of a foreign account—

(*a*) the full name and permanent address of the resident,

(*b*) the resident's tax reference number,

(*c*) the full name and address of the relevant person with whom the foreign account was opened,

(*d*) the date on which the foreign account was opened, and

(*e*) the amount of the deposit made in opening the foreign account.

(3) Where a resident requests an intermediary to provide the resident with a relevant service, the resident shall furnish to the intermediary the details which the intermediary is required to include in the return to the appropriate inspector in accordance with subsection (2) and the intermediary shall take all reasonable care (including, where necessary, the requesting of documentary evidence) to confirm that the details furnished are true and correct.

(4) (*a*) Where an intermediary fails—

(i) for any chargeable period to make a return required to be made by the intermediary in accordance with subsection (2),

(ii) to include in such a return for a chargeable period details of any resident to whom the intermediary provided a relevant service in the chargeable period, or

(iii) to take reasonable care to confirm the details of the kind referred to in subsection (2) furnished to the intermediary by a resident to whom the intermediary has provided a relevant service in a chargeable period,

the intermediary shall in respect of each such failure be liable to a penalty of [€2,535][4].

(*b*) Where a resident fails—

(i) to furnish details of the kind referred to in subsection (2) to an intermediary who has provided the resident with a relevant service, or

(ii) knowingly or wilfully furnishes that intermediary with incorrect details of that kind,

the resident shall be liable to a penalty of [€2,535][4].

(5) Penalties under subsection (4) may, without prejudice to any other method of recovery, be proceeded for and recovered summarily in the like manner as in summary proceedings for the recovery of any fine or penalty under any Act relating to the excise.

(6) Where in any chargeable period a resident opens, either directly or indirectly, a foreign account, or causes to be opened a foreign account in relation to which the resident is the beneficial owner of the deposit held in that account, the resident shall, notwithstanding anything to the contrary in section 950 or 1084, be deemed for that chargeable period to be a chargeable person for the purposes of sections 951 and 1084, and the return of income (within the meaning of section 1084) to be delivered by the resident for that chargeable period shall include the following particulars in relation to the account—

(*a*) the name and address of the relevant person with whom the account was opened,

(*b*) the date on which the account was opened,

(*c*) the amount of the deposit made in opening the account, and

(*d*) the name and address of the intermediary, if any, who provided a relevant service in relation to the opening of the account.

Amendments

1 Substituted by FA 2001 s 78(2)(*e*) for the short tax "year" 2001 and later tax years (income tax and capital gains tax) and as respects accounting periods of companies ending on or after 1 April 2001; previously "to deliver a return or statement of income or profits".

2 Substituted by FA 2001 s 78(2)(*f*) for the short tax "year" 2001 and later tax years (income tax and capital gains tax) and as respects accounting periods of companies ending on or after 1 April 2001; previously "such return or statement".

3 Definition of "specified return date for the chargeable period" para (*a*) substituted by FA 2003 s 34(1)(*c*) with effect from 6 April 2001.

4 Substituted by FA 2001 s 240(1) and (2)(*k*) and Sch 5 Pt 1 as respects any act or omission which takes place or begins on or after 1 January 2002; previously "£2,000".

Cross-references

Inspector's right to make enquiries: s 899(1).

Returns in relation to certain offshore products, meaning of "specified return date for the chargeable period" applied: s 896(1).

Seed capital investments, meaning of sum of money on deposit applied: s 494(5).

Self assessment, meaning of "chargeable person": s 950(1).

Statement of practice

Revenue powers: SP GEN/1/94, May 1994.

Tax Briefing

TB23 Sept 1996 p 14 — Returns to be made by Intermediaries in the Financial Services Area.

TB49 Aug 2002 pp 18–20 — Returns to be made by Intermediaries in relation to certain offshore products.

Definitions

inspector: ss 2(1), 5(1), 852; person: IA 1937 s 11(*c*); year of assessment: ss 2(1), 5(1).

Former enactments

FA 1992 s 230(1)–(6).

896 Returns in relation to certain offshore products

[(1) In this section—

"appropriate inspector", in relation to an intermediary, means—

(*a*) the inspector who has last given notice in writing to the intermediary, that he or she is the inspector to whom the intermediary is required to deliver the return specified in subsection (2),

(*b*) where there is no such inspector as is referred to in paragraph (*a*), the inspector to whom it is customary for the intermediary to deliver a return or statement of income or profits, or

(*c*) where there is no such inspector as is referred to in paragraphs (*a*) or (*b*), the inspector of returns specified in section 950;

"chargeable period" has the same meaning as in section 321(2);

"foreign life policy" means a policy of assurance on the life of a person commenced—

(*a*) by a branch or agency (carrying on business in a State other than the State) of an assurance company, or

(*b*) by an assurance company (carrying on business in a State other than the State) other than by its branch or agency carrying on business in the State;

"intermediary" means any person carrying on in the State a trade or business in the course of operations of which that person provides relevant facilities;

"material interest" shall be construed in accordance with section 743(2);

"offshore fund" has the meaning assigned to it by section 743(1);

"offshore product" means—

(*a*) a material interest in an offshore fund, or

(*b*) a foreign life policy;

"relevant facilities" means—

(*a*) the marketing in the State of offshore products,

(*b*) the acting in the State as an intermediary in relation to the acquisition or disposal, in whole or in part, of offshore products by or on behalf of persons who are resident or ordinarily resident in the State, or

(*c*) the provision in the State of facilities for the making of payments from an offshore product to persons who are entitled to the offshore product, whether on the disposal, in whole or in part of the offshore product, or otherwise;

"specified return date for the chargeable period", in relation to a chargeable period, has the meaning assigned to it by section 895(1);

"tax reference number" in relation to a person has the meaning assigned to it by section 885 in relation to a specified person within the meaning of that section.

(2) Every intermediary shall as respects a chargeable period prepare and deliver to the appropriate inspector on or before the specified return date for the chargeable period a return specifying in respect of every person in respect of whom that intermediary has acted in the chargeable period as an intermediary—

(*a*) the full name and permanent address of the person,

(*b*) the person's tax reference number,

(*c*) a description of the relevant facilities provided, including a description of the offshore product concerned and the name and address of the person who provided the offshore product, and

(*d*) details of all payments made (directly or indirectly) by or to the person in respect of the offshore product.

(3) Where an intermediary fails—

(*a*) for any chargeable period to make a return required to be made by the intermediary in accordance with subsection (2),

(*b*) to include in such a return for a chargeable period details of any person to whom the intermediary provided relevant facilities in the chargeable period, or

(*c*) to take reasonable care to confirm the details of the kind referred to in subsection (2) furnished to the intermediary by a person to whom the intermediary has provided relevant facilities in the chargeable period,

the intermediary shall in respect of each such failure be liable to a penalty of [€1,900].[1]

(4) Where a person fails—

(*a*) to furnish details of the kind referred to in subsection (2) to an intermediary who has provided the person with relevant facilities, or

(*b*) knowingly or wilfully furnishes that intermediary with incorrect details of that kind,

the person shall be liable to a penalty of [€1,900].[1]

(5) Where in any chargeable period a person acquires an offshore product to which section 730I or 747C (inserted by the Finance Act, 2001) does not relate, the person shall, notwithstanding anything to the contrary in section 950 or 1084, be deemed for that chargeable period to be a chargeable person for the purposes of sections 951 and 1084, and the return of income to be delivered by the person for that chargeable period shall include the following particulars—

(*a*) the name and address of the offshore fund or, as the case may be, the person who commenced the life policy,

(*b*) a description, including the cost to the person, of the material interest acquired or, as the case may be, a description of the terms of the life policy including premiums payable, and

(*c*) the name and address of the person through whom the offshore product was acquired.][2]

Amendments

1 Substituted by FA 2001 s 232(3)(*a*)(ii) with effect from 1 January 2002; previously "£1,500".

2 Section 896 substituted by FA 2001 s 232(1)(*d*) as respects any chargeable period (within the meaning of section 321(2)) commencing on or after 15 February 2001.

Cross-references

Inspector's right to make enquiries: s 899(1).

Penalties: Sch 29, cols 2 and 3.

Statement of Practice

Third Party Returns Return of Certain Information — SP/IT/2/92 October 1992

Revenue Powers SP-GEN/1/94 May 1994

Tax Briefing

TB20 No 4 of 1995 par1.3 — Offshore Funds — extension of automatic reporting.

TB23 Sept 1996 p 14 — Returns to be made by Intermediaries in the Financial Services Area.

Definitions

branch or agency: s 4(1); inspector: ss 2(1), 852; ordinarily resident: ss 2(1); 820; person: IA 1937 s 11(*c*); resident: ss 2(1), 819; trade: ss 3(1), 4(1), 5(1); writing: IA 1937 Sch.

Former enactments

FA 1992 s 230A; FA 1995 s 41.

---

897 Returns of employees' emoluments, etc

(1) (*a*) In this section, the references to payments made to persons in respect of their employment and to the remuneration of persons in their employment shall be deemed to include references to—

(i) any payments made to employed persons in respect of expenses,

(ii) any payments made on behalf of employed persons and not repaid, and

(iii) any payments made to the employees in a trade or business for services rendered in connection with the trade or business, whether the services were rendered in the course of their employment or not.

(*b*) The reference in paragraph (*a*)(i) to payments made to employed persons in respect of expenses includes a reference to sums put at the disposal of an employed person and paid away by the employed person.

(2) Every employer, when required to do so by notice from an inspector, shall within the time limited by the notice prepare and deliver to the inspector a return containing—

(*a*) the names and places of residence of all persons employed by that employer,

(*b*) particulars of any car (within the meaning of section 121) made available to those persons by reason of that employment,

(*c*) particulars of any preferential loan (within the meaning of section 122) made, released or written off by that employer in whole or in part and particulars of any interest released, written off or refunded by that employer in whole or in part and which was payable or paid on such loan,

(*d*) particulars of any relevant scholarships (within the meaning of section 193) in relation to those persons, not being a payment made before the 6th day of April, 1998, in respect of a scholarship (within the meaning of that section) awarded before the 26th day of March, 1997, and

(*e*) particulars of the payments made to those persons in respect of that employment, except persons who are not employed in any other employment and whose remuneration in the employment for the year does not exceed [€1,905][1].

(3) Where the employer is a body of persons, the secretary of the body or other officer (by whatever name called) performing the duties of secretary shall be deemed to be the employer for the purposes of this section, and any director (within the meaning of section 116) of a body corporate (including a company), or person engaged in the management of that body corporate, shall be deemed to be a person employed.

(4) Where an employer is a body corporate (including a company), that body corporate, as well as the secretary or other officer performing the duties of secretary of the body corporate, shall be liable to a penalty for failure to deliver a return under this section.

(5) An employer shall not be liable to any penalty for omitting from any return under subsection (2) the name or place of residence of any person employed by the employer and not employed in any other employment, where it appears to the Revenue Commissioners that such person is entitled to total exemption from tax.

(6) Where for the purposes of a return under this section an employer apportions expenses incurred partly in or in connection with a particular matter and partly in or in connection with other matters—

(*a*) the return shall contain a statement that the sum included in the return is the result of such an apportionment,

(*b*) the employer, if required to do so by notice from the inspector, shall prepare and deliver to the inspector within the time limited by the notice a return containing full particulars as to the amount apportioned and the manner in which and the grounds on which the apportionment has been made, and

(*c*) where the inspector is dissatisfied with any such apportionment of expenses, the inspector may for the purposes of assessment apportion the expenses, but the employer may, on giving notice in writing to the inspector within 21 days after being notified of any such apportionment made by the inspector, appeal against that apportionment to the Appeal Commissioners.

(7) The Appeal Commissioners shall hear and determine an appeal to them under subsection (6) as if it were an appeal to them against an assessment to income tax, and the provisions of the Income Tax Acts relating to the rehearing of an appeal and to the statement of a case for the opinion of the High Court on a point of law shall, with the necessary modifications, apply accordingly.

Amendments

1 Substituted by FA 2001 s 240(1) and (2)(*a*) and Sch 5 Pt 1 for 2002 and later tax years; previously "£1,500" (short tax "year" 2001: £1,110 (FA 2001 s 77(2) and Sch 2 paras 51 and 61(*a*))).

Cross-references

Benefit in kind charge: s 118(1).
Duty of employer as to tax payable by employees, subss (3)–(4): s 972(4).
Increased penalties in case of body of persons, subs (5): s 1054(4).
Penalties for failure to make certain returns, subs (5): s 1052(3).
Penalty: Sch 29 column 2.

Tax Briefing

TB39 Mar 2000 p 19 — Fringe Benefits — What are the Employer's Reporting Obligations?

Definitions

Appeal Commissioners: s 2(1); body of persons: s 2(1); High Court: IA 1937 Sch; inspector: ss 2(1), 5(1), 852; person: IA 1937 s 11(*c*); trade: s 3(1); writing: IA 1937 Sch.

Former enactments

ITA 1967 s 120(1)–(2), 123 and s178; F(MP)A 1968 s 3(2) and Sch Pt I; FA 1982 s 4(7) and s 8(6); FA 1997 s 11(4).

Corresponding UK tax provision

Taxes Management Act 1970 s 15.

897A Returns by employers in relation to pension products

[(1) In this section—

"Consolidated Regulations" means the Income Tax (Employments) (Consolidated) Regulations 2001 (SI No 559 of 2001);

"emoluments" means emoluments to which Chapter 4 of Part 42 applies;

"employee"—

(*a*) in relation to an employee pension contribution, has the same meaning as it has for the purposes of Chapter 1 of Part 30, and

(*b*) in relation to a PRSA contribution, has the same meaning as in subsection (1) of section 787A;

"employee pension contribution", in relation to a year of assessment and a scheme referred to in either section 774 or 776, means an allowable contribution within the meaning of paragraph (*b*) of Regulation 41 (inserted by the Income Tax (Employments) Regulations 2002 (SI No 511 of 2002)) of the Consolidated Regulations;

"employer"—

(*a*) in relation to an employee pension contribution and an employer pension contribution, shall be construed for the purposes of this section in the same way as it is construed for the purposes of Chapter 1 of Part 30, and (*b*) in relation to a PRSA employee contribution and a PRSA employer contribution, has the same meaning as in section 787A(1);

"employer pension contribution", in relation to a year of assessment and an exempt approved scheme (within the meaning of section 774), means any sum paid by an employer in the year of assessment by means of a contribution under the scheme in respect of employees in a trade or undertaking in respect of the profits of which the employer is assessable to tax;

"PRSA" shall be construed in accordance with section 787A(1);

"PRSA contribution" has the meaning assigned to it by section 787A(1);

"PRSA employee contribution", in relation to a year of assessment, means any PRSA contribution made by an employee in the year of assessment which is an allowable contribution within the meaning of paragraph (*c*) of Regulation 41 (inserted by the Income Tax (Employments) Regulations 2002) of the Consolidated Regulations;

"PRSA employer contribution", in relation to a year of assessment, means any PRSA contribution referred to in section 787E(2) made by an employer to a PRSA in the year of assessment;

"RAC premium", in relation to a year of assessment, means any qualifying premium (within the meaning of section 784) paid by an individual in the year of assessment which is an allowable contribution within the meaning of paragraph (*d*) (inserted by the Income Tax (Employments) Regulations 2003 (SI No 613 of 2003)) of Regulation 41 of the Consolidated Regulations.

(2) Any person who, in relation to a year of assessment, is required by Regulation 31 of the Consolidated Regulations to send prescribed or approved forms to the Collector-General shall include, in one of those forms, details of the following matters in the manner specified in that form—

(*a*) the respective numbers of employees in respect of whom that person deducted—

(i) an employee pension contribution,

(ii) a PRSA contribution,

(iii) a RAC premium,

from emoluments due to the employee in the year of assessment in relation to which the return is being made,

(*b*) the respective numbers of employees in respect of whom that person made—

(i) an employer pension contribution,

(ii) a PRSA employer contribution,

in that year,

(*c*) the respective total amounts of—

(i) employee pension contributions,

(ii) PRSA contributions,

(iii) RAC premiums,

deducted by the person from emoluments due to the employees of that person in that year,

(*d*) the respective total amounts of—

(i) employer pension contributions,

(ii) PRSA employer contributions,

made by that person in respect of the employees of that person in that year.

(3) Sections 1052 and 1054 shall apply to a failure by a person to make the return required by subsection (2) as they apply to a failure to deliver a return referred to in section 1052.][1]

Amendments

1 Section 897A inserted by FA 2004 s 86(1) as respects the year of assessment 2005 and subsequent years of assessment.

Tax Briefing

TB55 April 2004 pp 10–11 — Information in respect of certain tax expenditure.

TB58 Dec 2004 p 15 — P35 2005 — Employer obligations relating to pension contributions.

Definitions

Collector-General: s 2(1); person: IA 1937 s 11(*c*); profits: s 4(1); trade: ss 3(1), 4(1); year of assessment: s 2(1).

898 Returns of copies of rates and production of certain valuations

(1) In this section, **"rating authority"** means—

(*a*) the corporation of a county or other borough,

(*b*) the council of a county, or

(*c*) the council of an urban district.

(2) For the purpose of assessing tax chargeable under Schedule D, the secretary, clerk, or person acting as such, to a rating authority shall, when required by notice from an inspector, transmit to the inspector within such time as may be specified in the notice true copies of the last county rate or municipal rate made by the authority for its rating area or any part of that area.

(3) The Revenue Commissioners shall pay to any such person the expenses of making all such copies, not exceeding the rate of [€2][1] for every 100 ratings.

(4) Every person shall, at the request of any inspector or other officer acting in the execution of the Tax Acts, produce as soon as may be to such inspector or officer, as appropriate, any survey, valuation or record on which the rates for any rating area or part of any such area are assessed, made or collected, or any rate or assessment made under any Act relating to the county rate or municipal rate, which is in that person's custody or possession, and shall permit the inspector or other officer to inspect the same and to take copies of or extracts from any such survey, valuation or record, without any payment.

Amendments

1 Substituted by FA 2001 s 240(1) and (2)(*a*) and Sch 5 Pt 1 for 2002 and later tax years; previously "£1".

Cross-references

Disclosure of information to rating authorities, meaning of "rating authority" applied: s 1092(3).

Penalty: Sch 29 column 2.

Definitions

Income Tax Acts: s 1(2); inspector: ss 2(1), 5(1), 852; person: IA 1937 s 11(*c*).

Former enactments

FA 1974 s 73(1)–(4); CTA 1976 s 147(1)–(2).

898A Format of returns etc

[Where a person is required under this Chapter—

(*a*) to deliver a return, or

(*b*) to give or furnish information,

then such return or such information shall, be made, given, or as the case may be, furnished in such form as the Revenue Commissioners may require.][1]

Amendments

1 Section 898A inserted by FA 2002 s 134 with effect from 25 March 2002.

Definitions

person: IA 1937 s 11(*c*).

[CHAPTER 3A

Implementation of Council Directive 2003/48/EC of 3 June 2003 on Taxation of Savings Income in the Form of Interest Payments and Related Matters

Amendments

1 Chapter 3A (ss 898B–898R) substituted by FA 2004 s 90(1) and Sch 4 with effect from 25 March 2004.

Revenue Information

Guidance Notes for Paying Agents on the Irish legislation implementing the Savings Directive (Council Directive 2003/48/EC) can be downloaded from Revenue's website — **www.revenue.ie** — under Publications/ Technical Guidelines.

898B Interpretation (Chapter 3A)

[(1) In this Chapter and in any regulations made under this Chapter, except where the context otherwise requires—

"arrangements" has the meaning assigned to it by section 898P;

"beneficial owner" has the meaning assigned to it by section 898C(1);

"building society" and **"credit union"** have the same meanings, respectively, as in section 256;

"certificate of residence for tax purposes", in relation to a third country, means a certificate given by the competent authority of that country certifying that an individual is by virtue of the law of that country resident for the purposes of tax in that country, and references to a tax residence certificate shall be construed accordingly;

"competent authority" means—

(*a*) in relation to a Member State, the authority notified to the European Commission by the Member State for the purposes of the Directive, and

(*b*) in relation to a third country, the competent authority for the purposes of bilateral or multilateral tax conventions or, in the absence of any such authority, the authority competent in that country to issue certificates of residence for tax purposes;

"deemed interest payment" has the meaning assigned to it by section 898E(7)(*a*);

"deemed UCITS" has the meaning assigned to it by section 898D(3)(*a*);

[**"the Directive"** means Council Directive 2003/48/EC of 3 June 2003 (OJ No L157, 26.6.2003, p 38) as amended;][1]

"electronic means" includes electrical, digital, magnetic, optical, electromagnetic, biometric and photonic means of transmission of data and other forms of related technology by means of which data is transmitted;

"interest payment" has the meaning assigned to it by section 898E;

"Member State" means a Member State of the European Communities;

"money" includes money expressed in a currency other than euro;

"money debt" means a debt arising from a transaction for the lending of money and which may be settled by—

(*a*) the payment of money, or

(*b*) the transfer of a right to settlement under a debt which may be settled by the payment of money,

whether or not the debt creates or evidences a charge on assets and whether or not the debt carries a right to participate in the profits of the debtor;

"official identity card" has the meaning assigned to it by section 898G(1);

"paying agent" has the meaning assigned to it by section 898D(1);

"PPS number", in relation to an individual resident in the State, means that individual's Personal Public Service Number within the meaning of section 223 of the Social Welfare (Consolidation) Act 1993;

"residual entity" has the meaning assigned to it by section 898D(1);

"relevant territory" means—

(*a*) a Member State other than the State, or

(*b*) a territory with which arrangements have been made;

"Revenue officer" means an officer of the Revenue Commissioners;

"securities" includes—

(*a*) assets which are not chargeable assets for the purposes of capital gains tax by virtue of section 607,

(*b*) stocks, bonds and obligations of any government, municipal corporation, company or other body corporate, whether or not creating or evidencing a charge on assets, and

(*c*) any other money debts whether or not evidenced in writing, but does not include shares (within the meaning of the Companies Act 1963) of a company (within the meaning of that Act) or similar body;

"strip of a security" shall be construed in accordance with section 55;

"UCITS" has the meaning assigned to it by section 898D(2)(*c*);

"UCITS Directive" means Council Directive 85/611/EEC of 20 December 1985 (OJ No L 375, 31.12.1985, p. 3);

"tax year" means a year of assessment for income tax or capital gains tax, as appropriate;

"third country" means a territory other than a Member State;

"TIN", in relation to a relevant territory, means a unique identification number allocated by the relevant territory to an individual for the purposes of taxation and, in relation to the State, means an individual's PPS number.

(2) (*a*) Subject to paragraph (*b*), for the purposes of this Chapter an individual's residence is to be treated as situated in the country in which the individual has his or her permanent address, and any reference in this Chapter to an individual being resident in a country shall be construed accordingly.

(*b*) Paragraph (*a*) shall not apply for the purposes of—

(i) the definition of **"certificate of residence for tax purposes"** in subsection (1) and any use of that definition or of the term tax residence certificate in this Chapter, and

(ii) subsection (3) and any reference in this Chapter to a person being a resident of a territory for tax purposes.

(3) For the purposes of this Chapter, a person is to be regarded as being a resident of a territory for tax purposes if the person is by virtue of the law of that territory resident for the purposes of tax in that territory.

(4) A word or expression that is used in this Chapter and is also used in the Directive has, unless the contrary intention appears, the meaning in this Chapter that it has in the Directive.][2]

Amendments

1 Definition of "the Directive" substituted by FA 2005 s 144(1)(*a*) with effect from 25 March 2005.

2 Section 898B substituted by FA 2004 s 90(1) and Sch 4 with effect from 25 March 2004, but by virtue of section 898R (Commencement) is deemed to have applied as on and from 1 January 2004.

Definitions

company: ss 4(1), 5(1); profits: s 4(1); writing: IA 1937 Sch; year of assessment: ss 2(1), 5(1).

898C Beneficial owner

[(1) In this Chapter **"beneficial owner"**, in relation to an interest payment, means an individual who receives the interest payment or an individual for whom the interest payment is secured, but does not include an individual to whom subsection (2) applies.

(2) This subsection applies to an individual (in this section referred to as the **"intermediary"**) who provides evidence to the person making an interest payment to, or

securing an interest payment for, the intermediary that, in relation to the interest payment, the intermediary—

(*a*) is a paying agent,

(*b*) acts on behalf of a person (not being an individual) or an undertaking referred to in section 898D(2),

(*c*) acts on behalf of a residual entity, where both of the conditions set out in subsection (3) are met, or

(*d*) acts on behalf of another individual (in this section referred to as the **"other individual"**) who receives the interest payment or for whom the interest payment is secured, where the condition set out in subsection (4) is met in relation to the other individual.

(3) The conditions of this subsection are that—

(*a*) the intermediary provides the name and address of the residual entity to the person making or securing the interest payment, and

(*b*) the person making the interest payment makes a return to the Revenue Commissioners within 3 months of the end of the tax year in which the information referred to in paragraph (*a*) is provided to the person of each name and address so provided in that tax year.

(4) The condition of this subsection is that the intermediary provides the person from whom he or she receives an interest payment with the identity of the other individual established in accordance with section 898F or 898G, as appropriate.

(5) If a paying agent has information to the effect, or information indicating, that an individual is not the beneficial owner of an interest payment and paragraph (*a*), (*b*) or (*c*) of subsection (2) does not apply to that individual, the paying agent shall take reasonable steps to identify the beneficial owner in accordance with the provisions of section 898F or 898G, as appropriate.

(6) A paying agent shall treat an individual as the beneficial owner in relation to an interest payment received by, or secured for, the individual if the paying agent is otherwise unable to identify a beneficial owner.][1]

Amendments

1 Section 898C substitued by FA 2004 s 90(1) and Sch 4 with effect from 25 March 2004, but by virtue of section 898R (Commencement) is deemed to have applied as on and from 1 January 2004.

Cross-references

Interpretation: s 898B(1)("beneficial owner").

Definitions

interest payment: ss 898B(1); 898E; month: IA 1937 Sch; paying agent: ss 898B(1); 898D(1); person: IA 1937 s 11(c); residual entity: ss 898B(1); 898D(1); tax year: s 898B(1).

898D Paying agent and residual entity

[(1) In this Chapter—

"paying agent", in relation to any interest payment, means a person who in the course of the person's business or profession carried on in the State makes the interest payment to, or secures the interest payment for, the immediate benefit of a beneficial owner and includes, in particular, a residual entity but only as respects a deemed interest payment, a Minister of the Government and any agency or body established by statute;

"residual entity", in relation to any interest payment, means a person or undertaking established in the State or in a relevant territory to which the interest payment is made for the benefit of a beneficial owner or for which the interest payment is secured for the benefit of a beneficial owner, unless the person making the payment is satisfied on the basis of evidence produced by the person or the undertaking that subsection (2) applies to that person or that undertaking.

(2) This subsection applies to a person or undertaking which—

(*a*) is a legal person (not being an individual) other than the legal persons referred to in Article 4.5 of the Directive,

(*b*) is a person within the charge to corporation tax or within the charge to a tax in a relevant territory which corresponds to corporation tax in the State, or

(*c*) is an undertaking for collective investment in transferable securities (in this Chapter referred to as a **"UCITS"**) recognised as such under the UCITS Directive or an equivalent undertaking for collective investment established in a relevant territory other than a Member State.

(3) (*a*) A residual entity shall be entitled to elect for the purposes of this Chapter to be treated in the same manner as a UCITS recognised as such under the UCITS Directive is treated (in this Chapter referred to as a **"deemed UCITS"**).

(*b*) Where this election is exercised a reference in this Chapter to a UCITS recognised as such under the UCITS Directive includes a reference to a residual entity which has elected to be treated in the same manner as such a UCITS.

(*c*) An election under this subsection shall not be valid unless the person or undertaking concerned presents a certificate issued to it by the competent authority of the relevant territory in which it is resident for tax purposes to the person making an interest payment to it, or securing an interest payment for it, certifying that the election provided for by this subsection has been made by the person or undertaking named on the certificate.

(*d*) As respects a person or undertaking to which this subsection applies who is resident in the State for tax purposes, the Revenue Commissioners shall make regulations —

(i) prescribing the form in which the election provided for by this subsection is to be made,

(ii) providing for the issue of a certificate to a person or undertaking exercising the election provided for by this subsection,

(iii) prescribing the details to be included on any such certificate,

(iv) requiring a residual entity making such an election to provide them with such information as respects its constitution, legal status, ownership, investments, income and customers as may be set out in such regulations, and

(v) providing for such incidental matters as may be necessary for the purposes of the preceding provisions of this paragraph.][1]

Amendments

1 Section 898D substituted by FA 2004 s 90(1) and Sch 4 with effect from 25 March 2004, but by virtue of section 898R (Commencement) is deemed to have applied as on and from 1 January 2004.

Cross-references

Beneficial owner, subs (2): s 898C(2)(*b*).
Interest payment, subs (3): s 898E(7)(*a*).
Interpretation: s 898B(1)("deemed UCITS", "paying agent", "residual entity", "UCITS").

Definitions

beneficial owner: ss 898B(1), 898C(1); competent authority: s 898B(1); interest payment: ss 898B(1); 898E; person: IA 1937 s 11(*c*); relevant territory: s 898B(1); UCITS Directive: s 898B(1).

898E Interest payment

[(1) Subject to section 898K, in this Chapter **"interest payment"** means—

(*a*) any payment of interest of money, whether yearly or otherwise, including any bonus or interest payable under an instalment savings scheme (within the meaning of section 53 of the Finance Act 1970) and any accumulated interest payable in respect of any savings certificate referred to in section 42;

(*b*) any dividend or other distribution made in respect of shares in a building society;

(*c*) any dividend or other distribution made in respect of shares in a credit union;

(*d*) the excess of any amount received in respect of the redemption of a security, a unit of a security or a strip of a security over the amount paid for the security, unit or strip on issue;

(*e*) any prize attaching to a security, including a prize in respect of a prize bond issued under section 22 of the Finance (Miscellaneous Provisions) Act 1956;

(*f*) any amount realised on the sale, refund or redemption of a security, unit of a security, or a strip of a security, which is referable to accrued or capitalised interest, whether or not any such accrued or capitalised interest is separately identified;

(*g*) subject to subsections (2), (5) and (6), income distributed by—

(i) a UCITS authorised in accordance with the UCITS Directive or an equivalent undertaking for collective investment established in a relevant territory other than a Member State,

(ii) a deemed UCITS, or

(iii) an undertaking for collective investment established in a territory other than a relevant territory,

which income derives from an interest payment within the meaning of any of the preceding paragraphs of this subsection and which income is received by any of these undertakings either directly or indirectly from a residual entity;

(*h*) subject to subsections (2) to (6), income realised on the sale, refund or redemption of shares or units in—

(i) a UCITS authorised in accordance with the UCITS Directive or an equivalent undertaking for collective investment established in a relevant territory other than a Member State,

(ii) a deemed UCITS, or

(iii) an undertaking for collective investment established in a territory other than a relevant territory.

(2) Where a paying agent has no information with which to establish the proportion of any income referred to in paragraphs (*g*) and (*h*) of subsection (1) which is income derived from an interest payment that paragraphs (*a*) to (*f*) of that subsection relates, then the paying agent is to treat the full amount of any such income as an **"interest payment"** within the meaning of this section.

(3) (*a*) Income referred to in paragraph (*h*) of subsection (1) is only to be regarded as an interest payment where the UCITS or equivalent undertaking for collective investment established in a relevant territory other than a Member State, deemed UCITS or undertaking concerned has invested directly, or by way of the acquisition of shares or units in another such UCITS or equivalent undertaking, deemed UCITS or undertaking, more than 40 per cent of its assets in investments which produce or have the potential to produce interest or other income such as is referred to in paragraphs (*a*) to (*f*) of subsection (1); but where a paying agent has no information with which to establish the percentage of such assets so invested, then for the purposes of this Chapter more than 40 per cent of such assets are to be treated as so invested.

(*b*) As on and from 1 January 2011, paragraph (*a*) shall apply with the substitution of "25 per cent" for "40 per cent" in both places in which it occurs.

(4) Where a paying agent is unable to determine the amount of income realised by a beneficial owner from the sale, refund or redemption of any shares or units referred to in paragraph (*h*) of subsection (1), then the full proceeds from the sale, refund or redemption of the shares or units shall be treated as the amount of income realised by the beneficial owner for the purposes of that paragraph.

(5) Income referred to in paragraphs (*g*) and (*h*) of subsection (1) shall not be regarded as an interest payment in the case of such income from a UCITS (being an undertaking for collective investment in transferable securities within the meaning of the European Communities (Undertakings for Collective Investment in Transferable Securities) Regulations 1989 (S. I. No 78 of 1989)) or a deemed UCITS (being a person resident in the State) where the UCITS or deemed UCITS investment in assets referred to in paragraphs (*a*) to (*e*) of subsection (1) do not exceed 15 per cent of its total assets.

(6) (*a*) Income referred to in paragraphs (*g*) and (*h*) of subsection (1) shall not be regarded as an interest payment in the case of income from a UCITS authorised in accordance with the UCITS Directive or a deemed UCITS established in a Member State other than the State where the Member State concerned has exercised the option in paragraph 6 of Article 6 of the Directive to derogate from subparagraphs (*c*) and (*d*) of paragraph 1 of that Article.

(*b*) Income referred to in paragraphs (*g*) and (*h*) of subsection (1) shall not be regarded as an interest payment in the case of income from an undertaking for collective investment which is equivalent to a UCITS or from a deemed UCITS established in a relevant territory not being a Member State where the relevant territory concerned has exercised, under arrangements, an option equivalent to the option in paragraph 6 of Article 6 of the Directive to derogate from a provision equivalent to subparagraphs (*c*) and (*d*) of paragraph 1 of that Article.

(7) (*a*) An interest payment to a residual entity which has not elected to be treated as a UCITS in accordance with section 898D(3) shall, at the time the interest payment is received by the residual entity, be treated for the purposes of this Chapter as an interest payment (in this Chapter referred to as a **"deemed interest payment"**) made by the residual entity at that time.

(*b*) This subsection shall not apply to—

(i) a residual entity resident in the State where the residual entity's investment in assets referred to in subsection (1) does not exceed 15 per cent of the total investments of the residual entity, and

(ii) (I) a residual entity established in a Member State other than the State where the Member State concerned has exercised the option in paragraph 6 of Article 6 of the Directive to derogate from paragraph 4 of that Article, or

(II) a residual entity established in a relevant territory not being a Member State where the relevant territory concerned has exercised, under arrangements, an option equivalent to the option in paragraph 6 of Article 6 of the Directive to derogate from a provision equivalent to paragraph 4 of that Article.

(8) For the purposes of this Chapter—

(*a*) the percentages referred to in subsections (3), (5) and (7)(*b*)(i) shall be determined by reference to the most recent investment policy of the person or undertaking concerned as laid down in the instrument of incorporation of the person or the rules of the undertaking,

(*b*) in the absence of the information referred to in paragraph (*a*) or where a paying agent is in possession of information to suggest that the investment policy is not being implemented, the percentages shall be determined by the actual composition of the assets of the undertaking or the person.

(9) For the purposes of this Chapter any amount credited as interest shall be treated as a payment of interest, and references in this Chapter to interest being paid shall be construed accordingly.

(10) For the purposes of this Chapter any reference in this Chapter to the amount of an interest payment in a case where the interest payment is subject to deduction of tax shall be construed as a reference to the amount which would be the amount of that payment if no tax were to be deducted from that payment.

(11) For the purposes of this Chapter penalty charges for the late payment of any interest or other payment referred to in paragraphs (*a*) to (*f*) of subsection (1) shall not be regarded as an **"interest payment"** within the meaning of that subsection.][1]

Amendments

1 Section 898E substituted by FA 2004 s 90(1) and Sch 4 with effect from 25 March 2004, but by virtue of section 898R (Commencement) is deemed to have applied as on and from 1 January 2004.

Cross-references

Interpretation: s 898B(1)("deemed interest payment", "interest payment").
Return of interest payments made to or secured for beneficial owners, subs (1): s 898H(4)(*b*).
Special arrangements for certain securities: s 898K(1).

Definitions

arrangements: ss 898B(1), 898P; beneficial owner: ss 898B(1), 898C(1); building society: s 898B(1); credit union: s 898B(1); deemed UCITS: ss 898B(1), 898D(3)(a); money: s 898B(1); paying agent: ss 898B(1), 898D(1); person: IA 1937 s 11(*c*); residual entity: ss 898B(1); 898D(1); relevant territory: s 898B(1); security: s 898B(1); strip of a security: s 898B(1); UCITS: s 898B(1).

898F Obligations of paying agents where contractual relations entered into before 1 January 2004

[(1) This section applies for the purposes of enabling a paying agent to establish the identity and residence of an individual to whom the agent may make an interest payment or for whom the agent may secure an interest payment where the agent entered into contractual relations with the individual before 1 January 2004.

(2) A paying agent shall as respects contractual relations entered into before 1 January 2004 between the paying agent and an individual establish—

(*a*) the identity of each such individual consisting of his or her name and address in accordance with the procedure set out in subsection (3), and

(*b*) the residence of each such individual in accordance with the procedure set out in subsection (4).

(3) A paying agent shall establish the name and address of an individual using all relevant information at its disposal, in particular information it acquires by virtue of section 32 of the Criminal Justice Act 1994.

(4) A paying agent shall establish the residence of an individual using all relevant information at its disposal, in particular information it acquires by virtue of section 32 of the Criminal Justice Act 1994.

(5) A paying agent who establishes the identity and residence of an individual in accordance with this section shall retain or, in a case where the relevant documentation is held by another person, have access to—

(*a*) a copy of all materials used to identify the individual,

(*b*) a copy of all materials used to establish the residence of the individual, and

(*c*) the original documents or copies admissible in legal proceedings relating to the making of any interest payment to or the securing of any interest payment for the individual where the payment is made or secured on or after [1 July 2005][1],

for a period of at least 5 years after the relationship between the paying agent and the individual has ended.

(6) (*a*) Where a paying agent has established the identity and residence of an individual in accordance with the procedures set out in this section, the paying agent shall continue to treat that individual as so identified and so resident until such time as the paying agent is in possession, or aware, of information which can reasonably be taken to indicate that the individual has been incorrectly identified or is not so resident or has changed his or her residence.

(*b*) Where in accordance with paragraph (*a*) a paying agent becomes aware or has reason to believe that the individual's circumstances have changed or have been incorrectly established, the paying agent shall make all reasonable efforts to establish the individual's correct identity and residence in accordance with the procedures set out in subsection (4) or (5) of section 898G, as appropriate.

(7) Where an individual informs a paying agent that his or her circumstances as established in accordance with the procedure set out in this section have changed, the paying agent shall establish his or her new circumstances in accordance with the procedure set out in subsection (4) or (5) of section 898G, as appropriate.][2]

Amendments

1 Substituted by FA 2005 s 144(1)(*b*) with effect from 25 March 2005; previously "1 January 2005".

2 Section 898F substituted by FA 2004 s 90(1) and Sch 4 with effect from 25 March 2004, but by virtue of section 898R (Commencement) is deemed to have applied as on and from 1 January 2004.

Cross-references

Audit: s 898N(1)("books, records or other documents"), (5).
Beneficial owner: 898C(4), (5).
Penalty for failure to make returns, etc: s 898O(1).
Returns of interest payments made to or secured for beneficial owners: s 898H(3).

Definitions

interest payment: ss 898B(1), 898E; paying agent: ss 898B(1), 898D(1); person: IA 1937 s 11(*c*); year: IA 1937 Sch.

898G Obligations of paying agents in other contractual relations entered into

[(1) In this section **"official identity card"**, in relation to an individual resident in the State, means an official document issued by the Revenue Commissioners or the Minister for Social and Family Affairs which document contains the individual's name, address and PPS number and includes any other official document which may be specified in regulations made by the Revenue Commissioners.

(2) This section applies for the purposes of enabling a paying agent to establish the identity and residence of an individual to whom the agent may make an interest payment or for whom the agent may secure an interest payment where—

(*a*) the agent enters into contractual relations with the individual on or after 1 January 2004, or

(*b*) in the absence of contractual relations, the agent carries out a transaction on behalf of the individual on or after 1 January 2004,

but where, on the basis of documentary proof of identity and residence presented by the individual which is acceptable for the purposes of section 32 of the Criminal Justice Act 1994, the paying agent is satisfied that the individual is resident in the State this section shall not apply to that individual as respects contractual relations entered into or transactions carried out before 1 June 2004, but where the paying agent comes into possession of, or becomes aware of, information which can reasonably be taken to indicate that the individual is not, or may not be, so resident the paying agent shall make all reasonable efforts to determine the individual's correct identity and residence in accordance with the procedures set out in subsections (4) and (5).

(3) A paying agent shall as respects contractual relations entered into, or as respects a transaction carried out in the absence of contractual relations, on or after 1 January 2004 between the paying agent and an individual establish—

(*a*) the identity of each such individual consisting of his or her—

(i) name,

(ii) address, and

(iii) in a case where the [territory][1] in which the individual is resident for tax purposes allocates a TIN, the individual's TIN,

in accordance with the procedure set out in subsection (4), and

(*b*) the residence of each such individual in accordance with the procedure set out in subsection (5).

(4) (*a*) A paying agent shall establish the name, address and, where relevant, the TIN of an individual by reference to the details of the person's name, address and TIN as set out in the person's passport or official identity card as presented by the individual.

(*b*) If an individual's address does not appear on his or her passport or official identity card the paying agent shall establish the individual's address on the basis of any other documentary proof of identity presented by the individual which is acceptable for the purposes of section 32 of the Criminal Justice Act 1994.

(*c*) If there is no TIN or if an individual's TIN does not appear on his or her passport, official identity card or any other documentary proof of identity referred to in paragraph (*b*) as presented by the individual, such as the individual's certificate of residence for tax purposes, the individual's identity as established in accordance with either or both paragraphs (*a*) and (*b*) shall be supplemented by the paying agent establishing the individual's date of birth and place of birth by reference to his or her passport or official identity card.

(5) A paying agent shall establish the residence of an individual—

(*a*) in the case of an individual who presents a passport or official identity card issued by a relevant territory and who at the time of such presentation claims to be resident in a third country, by reference to a tax residence certificate issued by the competent authority of the third country in which the individual claims to be so resident, and in the absence of such a certificate the individual is to be regarded as resident in the relevant territory which issued the passport or other official identity card presented,

(*b*) in any other case, by reference to the address of the individual as set out—

(i) in his or her passport,

(ii) in his or her official identity card, or

(iii) if the paying agent has reason to believe that the person's residence is other than that shown on his or her passport or official identity card, in any other documentary proof of identity presented by the individual which is acceptable for the purposes of section 32 of the Criminal Justice Act 1994.

(6) A paying agent who establishes the identity and residence of an individual in accordance with this section shall retain or, in a case where the documentation is held by another person, have access to—

(*a*) a copy of all materials used to identify the individual,

(*b*) a copy of all materials used to establish the residence of the individual, and

(*c*) the original documents or copies admissible in legal proceedings relating to the making of any interest payment to or the securing of any interest payment for the individual made on or after [1 July 2005][2],

for a period of at least 5 years after the relationship between the paying agent and the individual has ended or, in the case of a transaction carried out in the absence of contractual relations, for a period of at least 5 years after the interest payment was made or secured.

(7) The Revenue Commissioners may make regulations governing the application of this section in a case where contractual relations are entered into, or any other transaction to which this section applies takes place, by postal, telephonic or electronic means. Any such regulations may provide for the use of notarised or certified copies of the documents referred to in this section.

(8) (*a*) Where a paying agent has established the identity and residence of an individual in accordance with the procedure set out in this section, the paying agent shall continue to treat that individual as so identified and so resident until such time as the paying agent is in possession, or aware, of information which can reasonably be taken to indicate that the individual has been incorrectly identified or is not so resident or has changed his or her residence.

(*b*) Where in accordance with paragraph (*a*) a paying agent becomes aware or has reason to believe that the individual's circumstances have changed or have been incorrectly established, the paying agent shall make all reasonable efforts to determine the individual's correct identity and residence in accordance with the procedures set out in this section.

(9) Where an individual informs a paying agent that his or her circumstances as established in accordance with the procedures set out in this section have changed, the paying agent shall establish his or her new circumstances in accordance with the procedure set out in subsection (4) or (5), as appropriate.][3]

Amendments

1 Substituted by FA 2005 s 144(1)(*c*) with effect from 25 March 2005; previously "relevant territory".

2 Substituted by FA 2005 s 144(1)(*b*) with effect from 25 March 2005; previously "1 January 2005".

3 Section 898G substituted by FA 2004 s 90(1) and Sch 4 with effect from 25 March 2004, but by virtue of section 898R (Commencement) is deemed to have applied as on and from 1 January 2004.

Cross-references

Audit: 898N(1)("books, records or other documents").

Beneficial owner: s 898C(4), (5).

Interpretation: s 898B(1)("official identity card"), (5).

Obligations of paying agents where contractual relations entered into before 1 January 2004, subs (4) and (5): s 898F(6), (7).

Returns of interest payments made to or secured for beneficial owners: s 898H(3)(b).

Penalty for failure to make returns, etc: s 898O(1).

Definitions

certificate of residence for tax purposes: s 898B(1); competent authority: s 898B(1); electronic means: s 898B(1); interest payment: ss 898B(1), 898E; paying agent: ss 898B(1), 898D(1); person: IA 1937 s 11(*c*); PPS number: s 898B(1); relevant territory: s 898B(1); third country: s 898B(1); TIN: s 898B(1); year: IA 1937 Sch.

898H Return of interest payments made to or secured for beneficial owners

[(1) [Every paying agent shall, as respects an interest payment made for the immediate benefit of a beneficial owner on or after 1 July 2005 who is resident in a relevant territory, make and deliver to the Revenue Commissioners within 3 months of the end of a tax year (being the tax year 2005 and subsequent years) a return of all interest payments, as respects the tax year 2005, so made during the period 1 July 2005 to 31 December 2005 by that paying agent and, as respects any other tax year, so made by that paying agent during that year consisting of—][1]

(*a*) the details relating to the paying agent set out in subsection (2),

(*b*) the details relating to each beneficial owner to which an interest payment is so made as set out in subsection (3), and

(*c*) the details relating to the total amount of interest payments so made as set out in subsection (4).

(2) The details relating to the paying agent are—

(*a*) name,

(*b*) address (in the case of a company, the address of the company's registered office, if different), and

(*c*) tax reference number and for this purpose **"tax reference number"** has the meaning assigned to it by section 885 in relation to a specified person within the meaning of that section.

(3) The details relating to a beneficial owner are—

(*a*) in a case where contractual relations were entered into before 1 January 2004—

(i) name,

(ii) address, and

(iii) residence (being the individual's country of residence),

as established in accordance with the procedure set out in section 898F, and

(*b*) in a case where contractual relations were entered into on or after 1 January 2004 or, as respects a transaction carried out on or after 1 January 2004, where there are no contractual relations—

(i) name,

(ii) address,

(iii) residence (being the individual's country of residence), and

(iv) (I) TIN, or

(II) if there is no TIN or the TIN has not been made available to the paying agent, date and place of birth,

as established in accordance with the procedure set out in section 898G.

(4) The details relating to an interest payment are—

(*a*) (i) the account number associated with the interest payment, or

(ii) in a case where there is no account number associated with the interest payment, information capable of identifying the asset giving rise to the interest payment,

[(*b*) (i) (I) the total amount of interest payments which are within the meaning of paragraphs (*a*), (*b*), (*c*), (*d*), (*e*) and (*g*) of subsection (1) of section 898E, and

(II) the total amount of interest payments which are within the meaning of paragraphs (*f*) and (*h*) of that subsection, or

(ii) in a case where the paying agent is a residual entity—

(I) the total amount of deemed interest payments which are within the meaning of paragraphs (*a*), (*b*), (*c*), (*d*), (*e*) and (*g*) of subsection (1) of section 898E, and

(II) the total amount of deemed interest payments which are within the meaning of paragraphs (*f*) and (*h*) of that subsection.][2]

(5) Sections 891 and 891A shall not apply to an interest payment which has been included in a return made under this section.][3]

Amendments

1 Substituted by FA 2005 s 144(1)(*d*)(i) with effect from 25 March 2005.

2 Subs (4)(*b*) substituted by FA 2005 s 144(1)(*d*)(ii) with effect from 25 March 2005.

3 Section 898H substituted by FA 2004 s 90(1) and Sch 4 with effect from 25 March 2004, but by virtue of section 898R (Commencement) comes into operation on such day, not being earlier than 1 July 2005, as the Minister for Finance may specify by order.

Cross-references

Commencement: s 898R(1), (3).

Exchange of information between Member States: s 898J(1).

Definitions

beneficial owner: ss 898B(1), 898C(1); company: ss 4(1), 5(1); deemed interest payment: ss 898B(1), 898E(7)(*a*); interest payment: ss 898B(1); 898E; month: IA 1937 Sch; paying agent: ss 898B(1), 898D(1); relevant territory: s 898B(1); residual entity: ss 898B(1); 898D(1); tax year: s 898B(1); TIN: s 898B(1).

898I Return of interest payments to residual entities

[Every person who in the course of the person's business or profession carried on in the State makes an interest payment to, or secures an interest payment for, a residual entity in a tax year which residual entity is established in a relevant territory, shall make and deliver to the Revenue Commissioners within 3 months of the end of the tax year (being the tax year 2005 and subsequent tax years) a return consisting of—

(*a*) the name of the residual entity,

(*b*) the address of the residual entity, and

[(*c*) the total amount of the interest payments so made or so secured by it in the tax year (and for this purpose the tax year 2005 shall be deemed to begin on 1 July 2005 and end on 31 December 2005).][1]][2]

Amendments

1 Para (*c*) substituted by FA 2005 s 144(1)(*e*) with effect from 25 March 2005.

2 Section 898I substituted by FA 2004 s 90(1) and Sch 4 with effect from 25 March 2004, but by virtue of section 898R (Commencement) comes into operation on such day, not being earlier than 1 July 2005, as the Minister for Finance may specify by order.

Cross-references

Commencement: s 898R(1), (3).
Exchange of information: s 898J(2).

Definitions

interest payment: ss 898B(1); 898E; month: IA 1937 Sch; person: IA 1937 s 11(*c*); relevant territory: s 898B(1); residual entity: ss 898B(1); 898D(1); tax year: s 898B(1).

898J Exchange of information between Member States

[(1) The Revenue Commissioners are authorised to communicate information contained in a return made under section 898H in relation to a beneficial owner of any interest payment to the competent authority of the relevant territory of residence of the beneficial owner.

(2) The Revenue Commissioners are authorised to communicate information contained in a return made under section 898I in relation to a residual entity to the competent authority of the relevant territory in which the residual entity is resident.

(3) The Revenue Commissioners are to communicate the information referred to in subsections (1) and (2) to the relevant competent authority within 6 months of the end of the tax year in which an interest payment is made.][1]

Amendments

1 Section 898J substituted by FA 2004 s 90(1) and Sch 4 with effect from 25 March 2004, but by virtue of section 898R (Commencement) comes into operation on such day, not being earlier than 1 July 2005, as the Minister for Finance may specify by order.

Cross-references

Commencement: s 898R(1), (3).

Definitions

beneficial owner: ss 898B(1), 898C(1); competent authority: s 898B(1); interest payment: ss 898B(1); 898E; month: IA 1937 Sch; relevant territory: s 898B(1); residual entity: ss 898B(1); 898D(1); tax year: s 898B(1).

898K Special arrangements for certain securities

[(1) Subject to subsection (2), section 898E shall not apply to a security (being a security issued under a programme)—

(*a*) which issued before 1 March 2001, or

(*b*) where the issuing prospectus was approved before that date by the competent authorities of a Member State (within the meaning of Council Directive 80/390/EEC (OJ No L 100, 17.4.1980, p 1)) or by the responsible authorities of a third country.

(2) Subsection (1) shall cease to apply—

(*a*) in the case of a security issued under a programme promoted by any Government or an entity referred to in the Annex to the Directive, to all securities issued under that programme if on or after 1 March 2002 any further security is issued under that programme, and

(*b*) in any other case, to any security issued under that programme on or after 1 March 2002.

(3) Subject to subsection (4), this section shall cease to apply as on and from the earlier of—

(*a*) the end of the transitional period referred to in Article 10 of the Directive, and

(*b*) 31 December 2010.

(4) If the transitional period referred to in Article 10 of the Directive continues after 31 December 2010, this section shall continue to apply to interest paid in respect of a security referred to in subsection (1) which contains gross-up or early redemption clauses or both.][1]

Amendments

1 Section 898K substituted by FA 2004 s 90(1) and Sch 4 with effect from 25 March 2004, but by virtue of section 898R (Commencement) is deemed to have applied as on and from 1 January 2004.

Cross-references

Interest payment: s 898E(1).

Definitions

the Directive: s 898B(1); security: s 898B(1); third country: s 898B(1).

898L Certificate for the purposes of Article 13.2 of the Directive

[(1) Where an individual resident in the State for tax purposes makes an application to the Revenue Commissioners containing such information in relation to—

(*a*) the individual,

(*b*) the individual's contractual relations with a paying agent, and

(*c*) the identification of the asset which may give rise to an interest payment to be paid or secured by the paying agent,

as the Revenue Commissioners may require, the Revenue Commissioners shall, within 2 months of the receipt of the application, issue a certificate to the applicant containing details of—

(i) the name, address and PPS number of the applicant,

(ii) the name and address of the paying agent identified by the applicant, and

(iii) the account number or other information supplied by the applicant to identify the asset which may give rise to an interest payment to be paid or secured by the paying agent.

(2) A certificate issued in accordance with subsection (1) shall be valid—

(*a*) for a period of 3 years from its date of issue, or

(*b*) until such time as any of the information contained in the certificate becomes inaccurate.][1]

Amendments

1 Section 898L substituted by FA 2004 s 90(1) and Sch 4 with effect from 25 March 2004, but by virtue of section 898R (Commencement) comes into operation on such day, not being earlier than 1 July 2005, as the Minister for Finance may specify by order.

Cross-references

Commencement: s 898R(1), (3).

Arrangements with third countries and dependent and associated territories of Member States, this section applied for purposes of Article 9 (voluntary disclosure) of the agreement to the Council Decision on signing of agreement with Andorra in the same way as it applies for purposes of the Directive: s 898P(2)(*e*).

Definitions

interest payment: ss 898B(1); 898E; month: IA 1937 Sch; paying agent: ss 898B(1); 898D(1); PPS number: 898B(1); year: IA 1937 Sch.

898M Credit for withholding tax

[[(1) Subject to subsections (3) and (4), where tax has been deducted from an interest payment in a relevant territory under provisions applicable in such territory in accordance with the Directive or the arrangements and—

(*a*) the interest payment is, or but for an exemption or relief from tax would be, taken into account in computing the total income of an individual for the tax year in which the tax was deducted for the purposes of income tax, and

(*b*) the individual is resident in the State for that tax year,

then—

(i) the individual may claim a credit for the tax deducted from the payment against any income tax chargeable on that individual for that year and, in determining the amount of tax payable on the individual's total income for that year, credit shall be given for the tax deducted from the interest payment and the amount of the credit shall be the amount of tax deducted from the interest payment, and

(ii) where—

(I) the tax deducted from the interest payment exceeds any such income tax chargeable, the excess shall be repaid, or

(II) no such income tax is chargeable, an amount equal to the tax deducted from the interest payment shall be repaid to the individual.

(2) Subject to subsections (3) and (4), where tax has been deducted from an interest payment in a relevant territory under provisions applicable in such territory in accordance with the Directive or the arrangements and—

(*a*) the interest payment is, or but for an exemption or relief from tax would be, taken into account in computing the chargeable gains of an individual for the tax year in which the tax was deducted for the purposes of the Capital Gains Tax Acts, and

(*b*) the individual is resident in the State for that tax year,

then—

(i) the individual may claim a credit for the tax deducted from the payment against the capital gains tax chargeable on that individual for that year and, in determining the amount of tax payable on the chargeable gains of that individual for that year, credit shall be given for the tax deducted from the interest payment and the amount of the credit shall be the amount of tax deducted from the interest payment, and

(ii) where—

(I) the tax deducted exceeds any such capital gains tax, the excess shall be repaid to the individual, or

(II) no such capital gains tax is chargeable, an amount equal to the tax deducted shall be repaid to the individual.

(3) (*a*) The credit referred to in subsection (1) or (2), as the case may be, shall apply only after the application of any other credit to which the individual may be entitled under any arrangement made under section 826 in respect of any tax deducted from the payment under provisions other than those referred to in subsection (1) or (2).

(*b*) Subsection (1) or (2) shall not apply where—

(i) the individual referred to in the subsection concerned has obtained relief under the law of a territory outside the State in respect of tax that has been deducted from an interest payment in a relevant territory under provisions applicable in such territory in accordance with the Directive or the arrangements, and

(ii) the individual was resident in that territory or was treated as being resident in that territory under arrangements made under section 826 for the year of assessment in which the tax was deducted.][1]

(4) The credit or repayment referred to in subsection (1) or (2), as the case may be, shall not be given—

(*a*) unless the individual claiming the credit or repayment—

(i) makes a claim in that behalf to the Revenue Commissioners,

(ii) makes a return in the prescribed form of the individual's total income or chargeable gains, as the case may be, for the tax year in which the interest payment is, or but for an exemption from tax would be, taken into account for the purposes of income tax or capital gains tax, as the case may be, and

(iii) provides to the Revenue Commissioners the statement referred to in subsection (5), and

(*b*) the Revenue Commissioners are satisfied that tax has been deducted from the interest payment concerned under provisions applicable in the territory concerned in accordance with the Directive or the arrangements.

(5) The statement referred to in subsection (4) is a statement in writing given to the individual by the person who deducted the tax certifying—

(*a*) the name and address of the person deducting the tax,

(*b*) the name and address of the beneficial owner of the interest payment,

(*c*) the date of the interest payment,

(*d*) the amount of the interest payment, and

(*e*) the amount of tax deducted from the interest payment.][2]

Amendments

1 Subss (1)–(3) substituted by FA 2005 s 144(1)(*f*) with effect from 25 March 2005.

2 Section 898M substituted by FA 2004 s 90(1) and Sch 4 with effect from 25 March 2004, but by virtue of section 898R (Commencement) comes into operation on such day, not being earlier than 1 July 2005, as the Minister for Finance may specify by order.

Cross-references

Arrangements with third countries and dependent and associated territories of Member States, this section applies: s 898P(2)(*c*).

Commencement: s 898R(1), (3).

Penalty for failure to make returns: s 898O(2).

Definitions

arrangements: ss 898B(1), 898P; beneficial owner: ss 898B(1), 898C(1); Capital Gains Tax Acts: s 1(2); chargeable gain: ss 5(1); 545; the Directive: s 898B(1); interest payment: ss 898B(1), 898E; person: IA 1937 s 11(*c*); relevant territory: s 898B(1); tax year: s 898B(1); total income: s 3(1); writing: IA 1937 Sch; year of assessment: s 2(1).

898N Audit

[(1) In this section—

"associated company", in relation to a paying agent, means a company which is itself a paying agent and which is the paying agent's associated company within the meaning of section 432;

"authorised officer" means an officer of the Revenue Commissioners authorised by them in writing to exercise the powers conferred by this section;

"books, records or other documents" includes—

(*a*) any records used in the business of a paying agent or used in the transfer department of a paying agent acting as a registrar of securities, whether—

(i) comprised in bound volumes, loose-leaf binders or other loose-leaf filing system, loose leaf ledger sheets, pages, folios or cards, or

(ii) kept on microfilm, magnetic tape or in any non-legible form (by the use of electronics or otherwise) which is capable of being reproduced in a legible form,

(*b*) every electronic or other automated means, if any, by which any such thing in non-legible form is so capable of being reproduced,

(*c*) documents in manuscript, documents which are typed, printed, stencilled or created by any other mechanical or partly mechanical process in use from time to time and documents which are produced by any photographic or photostatic process,

(*d*) correspondence and records of other communications (including e-mails) between a paying agent and a beneficial owner or between a paying agent and a residual entity, and

(*e*) the materials and documents referred to in sections 898F(5) and 898G(6).

(2) A Revenue officer may by notice in writing require a paying agent, or a person who appears to that officer to be a paying agent, to furnish him or her within such time, not being less than 14 days, as may be provided by the notice, with such information (including copies of any relevant books, records or other documents) as he or she may reasonably require for the purposes of determining whether information contained in a report under this Chapter by that paying agent was correct and complete.

(3) Any person who has been required by a notice under subsection (2) to furnish information (including copies of any relevant books, records or other documents) and that person fails to comply with the notice shall be liable to a penalty of €1,265.

(4) An authorised officer may at all reasonable times enter any premises or place of business of a paying agent or a person who appears to that officer to be a paying agent for the purposes of determining whether information—

(*a*) included in a report under this Chapter by that paying agent was correct and complete, or

(*b*) not included in a report under this Chapter was correctly not so included.

(5) Without prejudice to the generality of subsection (4), an authorised officer may—

(*a*) examine the procedures put in place by the paying agent for the purpose of ensuring compliance by the paying agent with the paying agent's obligations under sections 898F and 898G,

(*b*) check a sample of accounts or transactions in respect of which interest has been paid to a beneficial owner to determine whether—

(i) the procedures referred to in paragraph (*a*) have been observed in practice and whether they are adequate, and

(ii) the paying agent is, in respect of each account or transaction in the sample, in possession of the materials and documents referred to in section 898F(5) or 898G(6), as appropriate.

(6) An authorised officer may require a paying agent or an employee of the paying agent to produce books, records or other documents and to furnish information, explanations and particulars and to give all assistance, which the authorised officer reasonably requires for the purposes of the determination and examination referred to in subsections (4) and (5).

(7) An authorised officer may require an associated company in relation to a paying agent or an employee of such an associated company to produce books, records or other documents and to furnish information, explanations and particulars and to give all assistance, which the authorised officer reasonably requires for the purposes of the determination and examination referred to in subsections (4) and (5).

(8) An authorised officer may make extracts from or copies of all or any part of the books, records or other documents or other materials made available to him or her or require that copies of books, records or other documents be made available to him or her, in exercising or performing his or her powers under this section.

(9) An employee of a paying agent or of an associated company in relation to a paying agent who fails to comply with the requirements of an authorised officer in the exercise or performance of the authorised officer's powers or duties under this section shall be liable to a penalty of €1,265.

(10) A paying agent or an associated company in relation to a paying agent which fails to comply with the requirements of the authorised officer in the exercise or performance of the authorised officer's powers or duties under this section shall be liable to a penalty of €19,045 and if that failure continues a further penalty of €2,535 for each day on which the failure continues.

Amendments

1 Section 898N substituted by FA 2004 s 90(1) and Sch 4 with effect from 25 March 2004, but by virtue of section 898R (Commencement) is deemed to have applied as on and from 1 January 2004.

Definitions

beneficial owner: ss 898B(1), 898C(1); company: ss 4(1), 5(1); electronic means: s 898B(1); paying agent: ss 898B(1), 898D(1); person: IA 1937 s 11(*c*); residual entity: ss 898B(1); 898D(1); Revenue officer: s 898B(1); securities: 898B(1); writing: IA 1937 Sch.

898O Penalty for failure to make returns, etc

[[(1) Where any person required to make a return under this Chapter—

(*a*) fails, without reasonable excuse, to comply with any of the requirements of section 898F or 898G,

(*b*) makes an incorrect or incomplete return under this Chapter, or

(*c*) fails, without reasonable excuse, to make such a return,

that person shall be liable to a penalty of €19,045 and, in the case of paragraphs (*a*) and (*c*), if the failure continues that person shall be liable to a further penalty of €2,535 for each day on which the failure continues.][1]

(2) For the purposes of the recovery of a penalty under this section or section 898N, section 1061 applies in the same manner as it applies for the purposes of the recovery of a penalty under any of the sections referred to in that section.

(3) (*a*) A certificate signed by a Revenue officer which certifies that he or she has examined the relevant records and that it appears from those records that during a stated period a stated return was not received from the defendant shall be evidence until the contrary is proved that the defendant did not during that period deliver that return.

(*b*) A certificate certifying as provided for in paragraph (*a*) and purporting to be signed by a Revenue officer may be tendered in evidence without proof and shall be deemed until the contrary is proved to have been signed by such officer.][2]

Amendments

1 Subs (1) substituted by FA 2005 s 144(1)(*g*) with effect from 25 March 2005.

2 Section 898O substituted by FA 2004 s 90(1) and Sch 4 with effect from 25 March 2004, but by virtue of section 898R (Commencement) applies as respects an act or omission which takes place or begins on or after 25 March 2005.

Cross-references

Commencement: s 898R(1), (2).

Definitions

person: IA 1937 s 11(*c*); Revenue officer: s 898B(1).

898P Arrangements with third countries and dependent and associated territories of Member States

[(1) This Chapter shall apply for the purposes of implementing any arrangements made with a territory being a dependent or associated territory of a Member State (in this Chapter referred to as the "arrangements") in relation to the automatic exchange of information and the application of a withholding tax referred to in paragraph 2(ii) of Article 17 of the Directive.

(2) (*a*) In this subsection—

"Council Decision on signing of agreement with Andorra" means Council Decision (2004/828/EC) of 2 November 2004 concerning the signature of the Agreement between the European Community and the Principality of Andorra providing for measures equivalent to those laid down in Council Directive 2003/48/EC on taxation of savings income in the form of interest payments and the approval and signature of the accompanying Memorandum of Understanding (OJ No L359, 4.12.2004, p 32);

"Council Decision on signing of agreement with Liechtenstein" means Council Decision (2004/897/EC) of 29 November 2004 on the signing of the Agreement between the European Community and the Principality of Liechtenstein providing for measures equivalent to those laid down in Council Directive 2003/48/EC on taxation of savings income in the form of interest payments and the approval and signing of the accompanying Memorandum of Understanding (OJ No 379, 24.12.2004, p 83);

"Council Decision on signing of agreement with Monaco" means Council Decision (2005/35/EC) of 7 December 2004 on the signing of the Agreement between the European Community and the Principality of Monaco providing for measures equivalent to those laid down in Council Directive 2003/48/EC on taxation of savings income in the form of interest payments and the approval and signing of the accompanying Memorandum of Understanding (OJ No L19, 21.1.2005, p 53);

"Council Decision on signing of agreement with San Marino" means Council Decision (2004/903/EC) of 29 November 2004 on the signing of the Agreement between the European Community and Republic of San Marino providing for measures equivalent to those laid down in Council Directive 2003/48/EC on taxation of savings income in the form of interest payments and the approval and signing of the accompanying Memorandum of Understanding (OJ No L381, 28.12.2004, p 32);

"Council Decision on signing and conclusion of agreement with the Swiss Confederation" means Council Decision (2004/911/EC) of 2 June 2004 on the signing and conclusion of the Agreement between the European Community and the Swiss Confederation providing for measures equivalent to those laid down in Council Directive 2003/48/EC on taxation of savings income in the form of interest payments and the accompanying Memorandum of Understanding (OJ No L385, 29.12.2004, p 28).

(*b*) (i) Article 12 (Exchange of information on request) of the agreement attached to the Council Decision on signing of agreement with Andorra,

(ii) Article 10 (Exchange of information) of the agreement attached to the Council Decision on signing of agreement with Liechtenstein,

(iii) Article 12 (Transmission of information on request) of the agreement attached to the Council Decision on signing of agreement with Monaco,

(iv) Article 13 (Exchange of information on request) of the agreement attached to the Council Decision on signing of agreement with San Marino, and

(v) Article 10 (Exchange of information) of the agreement attached to the Council Decision on signing and conclusion of agreement with the Swiss Confederation,

shall, notwithstanding any other enactment, have the force of law.

(*c*) Section 898M shall apply for the purposes of implementing—

(i) Article 10 (Elimination of double taxation) of the agreement attached to the Council Decision on signing of agreement with Andorra,

(ii) Article 9 (Elimination of double taxation) of the agreement attached to the Council Decision on signing of agreement with Liechtenstein,

(iii) Article 10 (Elimination of double taxation and/or repayment of withholding tax) of the agreement attached to the Council Decision on signing of agreement with Monaco,

(iv) Article 10 (Elimination of double taxation) of the agreement attached to the Council Decision on signing of agreement with San Marino, and

(v) Article 9 (Elimination of double taxation) of the agreement attached to the Council Decision on signing and conclusion of agreement with the Swiss Confederation,

in the same way as it applies for the purposes of the Directive or the arrangements, and references in that section to tax deducted from an interest payment in a relevant territory under provisions applicable in such territory in accordance with the Directive or the arrangements shall be construed as references to—

(I) in the case of Liechtenstein or the Swiss Confederation, as the case may be, a retention from an interest payment under provisions applicable in that country in accordance with the agreement, and

(II) in the case of Andorra, Monaco or San Marino, as the case may be, tax withheld from an interest payment under provisions applicable in that country in accordance with the agreement,

and references to tax deducted and cognate expressions shall be construed accordingly.

(*d*) (i) The Revenue Commissioners may make regulations generally for the purposes of implementing the provisions of any arrangements the Government may make with the Government of any of the countries referred to in article 17(2)(i) of the Directive for the purposes of supplementing paragraph (*b*).

(ii) For the purposes of subparagraph (i), arrangements made with the head of a State shall be regarded as made with the Government of that State.

(*e*) Section 898L shall apply for the purposes of Article 9 (Voluntary disclosure) of the agreement attached to the Council Decision on signing of agreement with Andorra in the same way as it applies for the purposes of the Directive.][1]

Amendments

1 Section 898P substituted by FA 2005 s 144(1)(*h*) with effect from 25 March 2005.

Cross-references

Commencement: s 898R(3).

Information for tax authorities in other territories, subs (2): s 912A(1) ("foreign tax").

Interpretation: s 898B(1)("arrangements").

Definitions

the Directive: s 898B(1); Member State: s 898B(1).

898Q Miscellaneous and supplemental

[(1) Where a person is required under this Chapter or under regulations made under this Chapter to—

(*a*) deliver a return,

(*b*) give or furnish a certificate,

(*c*) make a declaration or election,

(*d*) make an application,

the return, certificate, declaration, election or application is to be made, given or furnished in such form as the Revenue Commissioners may require.

(2) The Revenue Commissioners may nominate any Revenue officer to perform any acts and discharge any functions authorised by this Chapter or by regulations made under this Chapter to be performed or discharged by the Revenue Commissioners apart from the making of regulations under this Chapter.

(3) Every regulation made under this Chapter shall be laid before Dáil Éireann as soon as may be after it is made and, if a resolution annulling the regulation is passed by Dáil Éireann within the next 21 days on which Dáil Éireann has sat after the regulation is laid before it, the regulation shall be annulled accordingly but without prejudice to the validity of anything previously done under the regulation.

(4) Regulations made by the Revenue Commissioners under this Chapter may contain such supplemental and incidental matters as appear to the Revenue Commissioners to be necessary—

(*a*) to enable persons to fulfil their obligations under this Chapter, or

(*b*) for the general administration of this Chapter.][1]

Amendments

1 Section 898Q substituted by FA 2004 s 90(1) and Sch 4 with effect from 25 March 2004, but by virtue of section 898R (Commencement) is deemed to have applied as on and from 1 January 2004.

Definitions

Dáil Éireann: IA 1937 Sch; person: IA 1937 s 11(*c*); Revenue officer: s 898B(1).

898R Commencement (Chapter 3A)

[(1) This Chapter, other than sections 898H, 898I, 898J, 898L, 898M and [898O][1], is deemed to have applied as on and from 1 January 2004.

[(2) Section 898O shall apply as respects an act or omission which takes place or begins on or after the date of the passing of the Finance Act 2005.][2]

(3) The provisions of sections 898H, 898I, 898J, 898L and 898M shall come into operation on such day, being a day not earlier than [1 July 2005][3], as the Minister for Finance may specify by order.][4]

Amendments

1 Substituted by FA 2005 s 144(1)(*i*)(i) with effect from 25 March 2005; previously "898P".

2 Subs (2) substituted by FA 2005 s 144(1)(*i*)(ii) with effect from 25 March 2005.

3 Substituted by FA 2005 s 144(1)(*i*)(iii) with effect from 25 March 2005; previously "1 January 2005".

4 Section 898R substituted by FA 2004 s 90(1) and Sch 4 with effect from 25 March 2004.

[CHAPTER 4
Revenue Powers

Cross-references

Failure to act within required time: s 1068.

Recovery of penalties: s 1061(1).

899 Inspector's right to make enquiries

(1) In this section, **"specified provisions"** means paragraphs (*d*) and (*e*) of section 888(2) [and sections 889 to 896][1].

(2) An inspector may make such enquiries or take such action within his or her powers as he or she considers necessary to satisfy himself or herself as to the accuracy or otherwise of any return, list, statement or particulars prepared and delivered under a specified provision.

...[2]

Amendments

1 Substituted by FA 2003 s 158(*a*) with effect from 28 March 2003; previously ", sections 889 to 890, and sections 892 to 894".

2 Subs (3) deleted by FA 2003 s 158(*b*) with effect from 28 March 2003.

Revenue information

Code of Practice for Revenue Auditors — August 2002 (may be downloaded from Revenue's website at www.revenue.ie).

Statement of practice

Revenue powers: SP GEN/1/94, May 1994.

Revenue Internal Review Procedures — Audit and Use of Powers: SP GEN/2/99, May 1999.

Tax Briefing

TB49 Aug 2002 pp 6–13 — Code of Practice Revenue Audits.

Definitions

inspector: ss 2(1), 5(1), 852.

Former enactments

FA 1992 s 228; FA 1995 s 14(2)(ii).

900 Power to call for production of books, information, etc

[(1) In this section and in section 901—

"authorised officer" means an officer of the Revenue Commissioners authorised by them in writing to exercise the powers conferred by this section, or as the case may be, section 901;

"books, records or other documents" includes—

(*a*) accounts (including balance sheets) relating to a trade or profession and where the accounts have been audited, a copy of the auditor's certificate,

(*b*) books, accounts, rolls, registers, papers and other documents, whether—

(i) comprised in bound volume, loose-leaf binders or other loose-leaf filing system, loose-leaf ledger sheets, pages, folios or cards, or

(ii) kept on microfilm, magnetic tape or in any non-legible form (by the use of electronics or otherwise) which is capable of being reproduced in a legible form,

(*c*) every electronic or other automatic means, if any, by which any such thing in non-legible form is so capable of being reproduced, and

(*d*) documents in manuscript, documents which are typed, printed, stencilled or created by any other mechanical or partly mechanical process in use from time to time and documents which are produced by any photographic or photostatic process;

"judge" means a judge of the High Court;

"liability" in relation to a person, means any liability in relation to tax to which the person is or may be, or may have been, subject, or the amount of such liability;

"tax" means any tax, duty, levy or charge under the care and management of the Revenue Commissioners.

(2) Subject to this section, an authorised officer may serve on a person a notice in writing, requiring the person, within such period as may be specified in the notice, not being less than 21 days from the date of the service of the notice, to do either or both of the following, namely—

(*a*) to deliver to, or to make available for inspection by, the authorised officer such books, records or other documents as are in the person's possession, power or procurement and as contain, or may (in the authorised officer's opinion formed on reasonable grounds) contain, information relevant to a liability in relation to the person,

(*b*) to furnish to the authorised officer, in writing or otherwise, such information, explanations and particulars as the authorised officer may reasonably require, being information, explanations and particulars that are relevant to any such liability,

and which are specified in the notice.

(3) A notice shall not be served on a person under subsection (2) unless the person has first been given a reasonable opportunity to deliver, or as the case may be, to make

available to the authorised officer concerned the books, records or other documents in question, or to furnish the information, explanations and particulars in question.

(4) Nothing in this section shall be construed as requiring a person who is carrying on a profession, and on whom a notice under subsection (2) has been served, to furnish any information, explanations and particulars relating to a client to an authorised officer, or to deliver to, or make available for inspection by, an authorised officer any books, records or other documents relating to a client, other than such—

(*a*) as pertain to the payment of fees to the person carrying on the profession or to other financial transactions of the person carrying on the profession, or

(*b*) as are otherwise material to the liability in relation to the person carrying on the profession,

and in particular that person shall not be required to disclose any information or professional advice of a confidential nature given to a client.

(5) Where, in compliance with the requirements of a notice served on a person under subsection (2), the person makes available for inspection by an authorised officer, books, records or other documents, the person shall afford the authorised officer reasonable assistance, including information, explanations and particulars, in relation to the use of all the electronic or other automatic means, if any, by which the books, records or other documents, in so far as they are in a non-legible form, are capable of being reproduced in a legible form, and any data equipment or any associated apparatus or material.

(6) Where, under subsection (2), a person makes books, records or other documents available for inspection by the authorised officer, the authorised officer may make extracts from or copies of all or any part of the books, records or other documents.

(7) A person who refuses or fails to comply with a notice served on the person under subsection (2) or fails to afford the assistance referred to in subsection (5) shall be liable to a penalty of [€1,900][1].][2]

Amendments

1 Substituted by FA 2001 s 240(1) and (2)(*k*) and Sch 5 Pt 1 as respects any act or omission which takes place or begins on or after 1 January 2002; previously "£1,500".

2 Section 900 substituted by FA 1999 s 207(*a*) with effect from 25 March 1999.

Cross-references

Capital gains tax, applied by: s 913(2).

Information for tax authorities in other territories, this section is to have effect as if references to tax included references to foreign tax (within meaning of TCA 1997 s 912A(1)) and as if references to liability, in relation to a person, included liability to foreign tax (within meaning of TCA 1997 s 912A(1)) in relation to a person: s 912A(2).

Information to be furnished by third party: request of an authorised officer, meaning of "books, records or other documents" and "liability" applied: s 902(1).

Penalty: Sch 29 column 2.

Revenue offences: s 1078(2)(*hh*).

Surcharge for late returns: s 1084(1)(*b*)(iii).

Tonnage tax, transactions between associated persons and between tonnage tax trade and other activities of same company, meaning of "books, records or documents" applied: s 697LA(7); this section applied: s 697LA(7).

Case law

Nominal ledger not part of accountant's working papers and should have been produced to inspector on request: *Quigley v Burke* ITR Vol IV p 332.

Revenue information

Finance Act 1999 — Revenue Powers: Guidance Notes and Instructions, May 1999.

Code of Practice for Revenue Auditors — August 2002 (may be downloaded from Revenue's website at www.revenue.ie).

Statement of practice

Revenue powers: SP GEN/1/94, May 1994.

Revenue Powers (Finance Act 1999): SP GEN/1/99, May 1999.

Revenue Internal Review Procedures — Audit and Use of Powers: SP GEN/2/99, May 1999.

Tax Briefing

TB49 Aug 2002 pp 6–13 — Code of Practice Revenue Audits.

Definitions

person: IA 1937 s 11(*c*); profession: s 2(1); trade: ss 3(1), 4(1); writing: IA 1937 Sch.

Former enactments

ITA 1967 s 70(3B) and s174; FA 1976 s 3; FA 1979 s 30.

Corresponding UK tax provision

Taxes Management Act 1970 s 20.

901 Application to High Court: production of books, information, etc

[(1) An authorised officer may make an application to a judge for an order requiring a person, to do either or both of the following, namely—

(*a*) to deliver to the authorised officer, or to make available for inspection by the authorised officer, such books, records or other documents as are in the person's power, possession or procurement and as contain, or may (in the authorised officer's opinion formed on reasonable grounds) contain, information relevant to a liability in relation to the person,

(*b*) to furnish to the authorised officer such information, explanations and particulars as the authorised officer may reasonably require, being information, explanations and particulars that are relevant to any such liability,

and which are specified in the application.

(2) Where the judge, to whom an application is made under subsection (1), is satisfied that there are reasonable grounds for the application being made, that judge may, subject to such conditions as he or she may consider proper and specify in the order, make an order requiring the person to whom the application relates—

(*a*) to deliver to the authorised officer, or to make available for inspection by the authorised officer, such books, records or other documents, and

(*b*) to furnish to the authorised officer such information, explanations and particulars,

as may be specified in the order.

(3) Nothing in this section shall oblige a person who is carrying on a profession to furnish any information, explanations or particulars relating to a client to an authorised officer, or to deliver to, or make available for inspection by, an authorised officer any

books, records or other documents relating to the client, without the consent of the client, other than such—

(*a*) as pertain to the payment of fees to the person carrying on the profession or to other financial transactions of the person carrying on the profession, or

(*b*) as are otherwise material to the liability in relation to the person carrying on the profession,

and in particular that person shall not be required to disclose any information or professional advice of a confidential nature given to the client.

[(4) Where in compliance with an order made under subsection (2), a person makes available for inspection by an authorised officer, books, records or other documents, the person shall afford the authorised officer reasonable assistance, including information, explanations and particulars, in relation to the use of all the electronic or other automatic means, if any, by which the books, records or other documents, in so far as they are in a non-legible form, are capable of being reproduced in a legible form, and any data equipment or any associated apparatus or material.

(5) Where in compliance with an order made under subsection (2), a person makes books, records or other documents available for inspection by the authorised officer, the authorised officer may make extracts from or copies of all or any part of the books, records or other documents.][1]][2]

Amendments

1 Subss (4)–(5) inserted by FA 2002 s 132(*a*) with effect from 25 March 2002.

2 Section 901 substituted by FA 1999 s 207(*b*) with effect from 25 March 1999.

Cross-references

Information for tax authorities in other territories, this section is to have effect as if references to tax included references to foreign tax (within meaning of TCA 1997 s 912A(1)) and as if references to liability, in relation to a person, included liability to foreign tax (within meaning of TCA 1997 s 912A(1)) in relation to a person: s 912A(2).

Power to call for production of books, information, etc: s 900(1) (authorised officer).

Revenue offences: s 1078(2)(*hh*)(ii).

Tonnage tax, transactions between associated persons and between tonnage tax trade and other activities of same company, this section applied: s 697LA(7).

Revenue information

Finance Act 1999 — Revenue Powers: Guidance Notes and Instructions, May 1999.

Code of Practice for Revenue Auditors — August 2002 (may be downloaded from Revenue's website at www.revenue.ie).

Statement of practice

Revenue Powers (Finance Act 1999): SP GEN/1/99, May 1999.

Revenue Internal Review Procedures — Audit and Use of Powers: SP GEN/2/99, May 1999.

Tax Briefing

TB49 Aug 2002 pp 6–13 — Code of Practice Revenue Audits.

Definitions

authorised officer, books, records or other documents, judge, liability: s 900(1); person: IA 1937 s 11(*c*); profession: s 2(1).

Former enactments

ITA 1967 s 539; FA 1974 s 86 and Sch 2 Pt I; CTA 1976 s 147(1)–(2).

Corresponding UK tax provision

Taxes Management Act 1970 s 20.

902 Information to be furnished by third party: request of an authorised officer

[(1) In this section and in section 902A—

"authorised officer" means an officer of the Revenue Commissioners authorised by them in writing to exercise the powers conferred by this section, or as the case may be, section 902A;

"books, records or other documents" and **"liability"**, in relation to a person, have, respectively, the meaning assigned to them by section 900(1).

(2) Notwithstanding any obligation as to secrecy or other restriction upon disclosure of information imposed by or under statute or otherwise, and subject to this section, an authorised officer may for the purpose of enquiring into a liability in relation to a person (in this section referred to as **"the taxpayer"**) serve on any other person (not being a financial institution within the meaning of section 906A) a notice in writing requiring that other person, within such period as may be specified in the notice, not being less than 30 days from the date of the service of the notice, to do either or both of the following, namely—

(*a*) to deliver to, or make available for inspection by, the authorised officer, such books, records or other documents as are in the other person's power, possession or procurement and as contain, or may (in the authorised officer's opinion formed on reasonable grounds) contain, information relevant to a liability in relation to the taxpayer,

(*b*) to furnish to the authorised officer, in writing or otherwise, such information, explanations and particulars as the authorised officer may reasonably require, being information, explanations and particulars that are relevant to any such liability,

and which are specified in the notice.

(3) A notice shall not be served on a person under subsection (2) unless the authorised officer concerned has reasonable grounds to believe that the person is likely to have information relevant to the establishment of a liability in relation to the taxpayer.

(4) The persons who may be treated as a taxpayer for the purposes of this section include a company which has been dissolved and an individual who has died.

(5) A notice under subsection (2) shall name the taxpayer in relation to whose liability the authorised officer is enquiring.

(6) Where an authorised officer serves a notice under subsection (2), a copy of such notice shall be given by the authorised officer to the taxpayer concerned.

(7) Where, under subsection (2), a person has delivered any books, records or other documents and those books, records or other documents are retained by the authorised officer, the person shall, at all reasonable times and subject to such reasonable conditions as may be determined by the authorised officer, be entitled to inspect those books, records or other documents and to obtain copies of them.

(8) Where, under subsection (2), a person makes books, records or other documents available for inspection by the authorised officer, the authorised officer may make extracts from or copies of all or any part of the books, records or other documents.

(9) Nothing in this section shall be construed as requiring any person carrying on a profession, and on whom a notice is served under subsection (2), to furnish any information, explanations and particulars relating to a client to an authorised officer or to deliver to, or make available for inspection by, an authorised officer any books, records or other documents relating to a client, other than such—

(*a*) as pertain to the payment of fees or other financial transactions, or

(*b*) as are otherwise material to a liability in relation to the client,

and in particular such person shall not be required to disclose any information or professional advice of a confidential nature.

(10) Where, in compliance with the requirements of a notice under subsection (2), a person makes available for inspection by an authorised officer, books, records or other documents, the person shall afford the authorised officer reasonable assistance, including information, explanations and particulars, in relation to the use of all the electronic or other automatic means, if any, by which the books, records or other documents, in so far as they are in non-legible form, are capable of being reproduced in a legible form and any data equipment or any associated apparatus or material.

(11) A person who fails or refuses to comply with a notice served on the person under subsection (2) or to afford the assistance referred to in subsection (10) shall be liable to a penalty of [€1,900][1], but nothing in section 1078 shall be construed as applying to such failure or refusal.][2]

Amendments

1 Substituted by FA 2001 s 240(1) and (2)(*k*) and Sch 5 Pt 1 as respects any act or omission which takes place or begins on or after 1 January 2002; previously "£1,500".

2 Section 902 substituted by FA 1999 s 207(*c*) with effect from 25 March 1999.

Cross-references

Information for tax authorities in other territories, this section is to have effect as if references to tax included references to foreign tax (within meaning of TCA 1997 s 912A(1)) and as if references to liability, in relation to a person, included liability to foreign tax (within meaning of TCA 1997 s 912A(1)) in relation to a person: s 912A(2).

Revenue offences: s 1078(2)(*hh*)(ii).

Revenue information

Finance Act 1999 — Revenue Powers: Guidance Notes and Instructions, May 1999.

Code of Practice for Revenue Auditors — August 2002 (may be downloaded from Revenue's website at www.revenue.ie).

Statement of practice

Revenue Powers (Finance Act 1999): SP GEN/1/99, May 1999.

Revenue Internal Review Procedures — Audit and Use of Powers: SP GEN/2/99, May 1999.

Tax Briefing

TB49 Aug 2002 pp 6–13 — Code of Practice Revenue Audits.

Definitions

company: ss 4(1), 5(1); person: IA 1937 s 11(*c*); profession: ss 2(1), 5(1); writing: IA 1937 Sch.

Former enactments

FA 1979 s 31; FA 1992 s 238.

902A Application to High Court: information from third party

[(1) In this section—

"the Acts" has the meaning assigned to it by section 1078(1);

"judge" means a judge of the High Court;

"a taxpayer" means any person including a person whose identity is not known to the authorised officer, and a group or class of persons whose individual identities are not so known.

(2) An authorised officer may make an application to a judge for an order requiring a person (other than a financial institution within the meaning of section 906A) to do either or both of the following, namely—

(*a*) to deliver to the authorised officer, or to make available for inspection by the authorised officer, such books, records or other documents as are in the person's power, possession or procurement and as contain, or may (in the authorised officer's opinion formed on reasonable grounds) contain, information relevant to a liability in relation to a taxpayer,

(*b*) to furnish to the authorised officer such information, explanations and particulars as the authorised officer may reasonably require, being information, explanations and particulars that are relevant to any such liability,

and which are specified in the application.

(3) An authorised officer shall not make an application under subsection (2) without the consent in writing of a Revenue Commissioner, and without being satisfied—

(*a*) that there are reasonable grounds for suspecting that the taxpayer, or, where the taxpayer is a group or class of persons, all or any one of those persons, may have failed or may fail to comply with any provision of the Acts,

(*b*) that any such failure is likely to have led or to lead to serious prejudice to the proper assessment or collection of tax (having regard to the amount of a liability in relation to the taxpayer, or where the taxpayer is a group or class of persons, the amount of a liability in relation to all or any one of those persons, that arises or might arise from such failure), and

(*c*) that the information—

(i) which is likely to be contained in the books, records or other documents to which the application relates, or

(ii) which is likely to arise from the information, explanations and particulars to which the application relates,

is relevant to the proper assessment or collection of tax.

(4) Where the judge, to whom an application is made under subsection (2), is satisfied that there are reasonable grounds for the application being made, that judge may, subject to such conditions as he or she may consider proper and specify in the order, make an order requiring the person to whom the application relates—

(*a*) to deliver to the authorised officer, or to make available for inspection by the authorised officer, such books, records or other documents, and (*b*) to furnish to the authorised officer such information, explanations and particulars,

as may be specified in the order.

(5) The persons who may be treated as a taxpayer for the purposes of this section include a company which has been dissolved and an individual who has died.

(6) Nothing in this section shall oblige any person carrying on a profession to furnish any information, explanation or particulars relating to a client to an authorised officer, or to deliver to, or make available for inspection by, an authorised officer any books, records or other documents relating to a client, without the client's consent, other than such—

(*a*) as pertain to the payment of fees or other financial transactions, or

(*b*) as are otherwise material to a liability in relation to the client,

and in particular such person shall not be required to disclose any information or professional advice of a confidential nature.

[(6A) Where in compliance with an order made under subsection (4), a person makes available for inspection by an authorised officer, books, records or other documents, the person shall afford the authorised officer reasonable assistance, including information, explanations and particulars, in relation to the use of all the electronic or other automatic means, if any, by which the books, records or other documents, in so far as they are in a non-legible form, are capable of being reproduced in a legible form, and any data equipment or any associated apparatus or material.

(6B) Where in compliance with an order made under subsection (4), a person makes books, records or other documents available for inspection by the authorised officer, the authorised officer may make extracts from or copies of all or any part of the books, records or other documents.][1]

(7) Every hearing of an application for an order under this section and of any appeal in connection with that application shall be held in camera.][2]

Amendments

1 Subss (6A)–(6B) inserted by FA 2002 s 132(*b*) with effect from 25 March 2002.

2 Section 902A inserted by FA 1999 s 207(*d*) with effect from 25 March 1999.

Cross-references

Information for tax authorities in other territories, this section to have effect as if references to tax included references to foreign tax (within meaning of TCA 1997 s 912A(1)) and as if reference to liability, in relation to a person, included liability to foreign tax (within meaning of TCA 1997 s 912A(1)) in relation to a person; but where this section has effect by virtue only of TCA 1997 s 912A, this section is to have effect as if "a 'taxpayer' means a person;" were substituted for the definition of "a taxpayer" in subs (1) and as if references in this section to tax were references to foreign tax and references to any provision of the Acts were references to any provision of the law of a territory in accordance with which foreign tax is charged or collected: s 912(2),(3).

Information to be furnished by third party: request of an authorised officer: s 902(1) (authorised officer).

Powers of inspection, life policies, meaning of "authorised officer" applied: s 902B(7).

Revenue offences: s 1078(2)(*hh*)(ii).

Revenue information

Finance Act 1999 — Revenue Powers: Guidance Notes and Instructions, May 1999.

Code of Practice for Revenue Auditors — August 2002 (may be downloaded from Revenue's website at www.revenue.ie).

Statement of practice

Revenue Powers (Finance Act 1999): SP GEN/1/99, May 1999.

Revenue Internal Review Procedures — Audit and Use of Powers: SP GEN/2/99, May 1999.

Tax Briefing

TB49 Aug 2002 pp 6–13 — Code of Practice Revenue Audits.

Definitions

books, records or other documents: s 902(1); company: ss 4(1), 5(1); liability: s 902(1); person: IA 1937 s 11(*c*); profession: s 2(1); writing: IA 1937 Sch.

902B Powers of inspection: life policies

[(1) In this section—

"assurance company" has the same meaning as in section 3 of the Insurance Act 1936;

"authorised officer" means an officer of the Revenue Commissioners who is authorised by them in writing to exercise the powers conferred by this section;

"policy" and "premium" have the same meanings, respectively, as in section 3 of the Insurance Act 1936;

"relevant records", in relation to a policy, means any document or any other written or printed material in any form, and includes any information stored, maintained or preserved by means of any mechanical, photographic or electronic device whether or not stored, maintained or preserved in a legible form, but does not include so much of any record that is of a medical nature.

(2) A Revenue Commissioner may, subject to subsection (3) and for the purposes of subsection (7), direct an authorised officer to investigate a class or classes of policies issued by an assurance company and the policyholders to whom they were issued.

(3) Directions may be given by a Revenue Commissioner under subsection (2) where he or she forms the opinion that there are circumstances suggesting that a class of policy or classes of policies issued by an assurance company may have been issued to policyholders, some of whom have paid one or more than one premium in respect of any policy concerned out of income or gains which were required to be, but were not, included in a return made by those policyholders under the Tax Acts or the Capital Gains Tax Acts; and for the purposes of this subsection the Revenue Commissioner may take into consideration information in relation to policies issued by other assurance companies and the policyholders of such policies.

(4) An authorised officer, when investigating a class or classes of policies and the policyholders to whom they were issued, may at all reasonable times, enter any premises or place of business of an assurance company to inspect the relevant records held by the assurance company in respect of a sample of policies of that class or those classes and the policyholders of those policies.

(5) Where an authorised officer has entered any premises or place of business of an assurance company for the purposes of this section, he or she may require the assurance company, or any employee of the assurance company, to produce the relevant records in a form which is legible and to furnish such information and explanations as the authorised officer requires in relation to the relevant records.

(6) Where in accordance with this section an authorised officer inspects relevant records he or she may copy or make extracts from those records.

(7) Information obtained by an authorised officer from inspecting relevant records may only be used for the purposes of enabling an authorised officer, within the meaning of section 902A, to make an application under that section to a judge of the High Court.][1]

Amendments

1 Section 902B inserted by FA 2005 s 140 with effect from 25 March 2005.

Definitions

Capital Gains Tax Acts: s 1(2); High Court: IA 1937 Sch; Tax Acts: s 1(2); writing: IA 1937 Sch.

903 Power of inspection: PAYE

(1) In this section—

"authorised officer" means an officer of the Revenue Commissioners authorised by them in writing to exercise the powers conferred by this section;

"emoluments", **"employer"** and **"tax deduction card"** have the same meanings respectively as in Chapter 4 of Part 42;

"records" means any personnel records relating to the payment of emoluments or the provision of benefits in kind or perquisites, payroll files, wages sheets, [certificates of tax credits and standard rate cut-off point],[1] tax deduction cards, certificates issued in accordance with [Regulation 20 of the Income Tax (Employments) (Consolidated) Regulations 2001 (SI No 559 of 2001)][2], including any data (within the meaning of section 912) [stored in accordance with section 887][3] or by any other means or any other information or documents which the authorised officer may reasonably require.

(2) An authorised officer may at all reasonable times enter any premises or place where the authorised officer has reason to believe that—

(*a*) an employer is or has been carrying on any activity as an employer,

(*b*) any person is or was either paying emoluments or providing benefits in kind or perquisites,

(*c*) any person is or was in receipt of emoluments, benefits in kind or perquisites, or

(*d*) records are or may be kept,

and the authorised officer—

(i) may require any employer or any other person who is on those premises or in that place, other than a person who is there to purchase goods or to receive a service, to produce any records which the authorised officer requires for the purposes of his or her enquiry,

(ii) may, if the authorised officer has reason to believe that any of the records he or she has required to be produced to him or her under paragraph (i) have not been so produced, search on those premises or in that place for those records, and

(iii) may examine, make copies of, take extracts from, remove and retain any records for further examination or for the purposes of any legal proceedings instituted by an officer of the Revenue Commissioners or for the purposes of any criminal proceedings.

[(2A)(*a*) An authorised officer shall not, without the consent of the occupier, enter any premises, or that portion of any premises, which is occupied wholly and exclusively as a private residence, except on production by such officer of a warrant issued by a Judge of the District Court expressly authorising the authorised officer to so enter.

(*b*) A Judge of the District Court may issue a warrant under paragraph (*a*) if satisfied by information on oath that it is proper to do so for the purposes of this section.][4]

(3) An authorised officer may require any person, other than a person purchasing goods or receiving a service from an employer, to give the authorised officer all reasonable assistance, including providing information and explanations and furnishing documents required by the authorised officer.

(4) An authorised officer when exercising or performing his or her powers or duties under this section shall on request produce his or her authorisation for the purposes of this section.

(5) A person who does not comply with the requirements of an authorised officer in the exercise or performance of the authorised officer's powers or duties under this section shall be liable to a penalty of [€1,265][5].

(6) The records referred to in this section shall be retained by the employer for a period of 6 years after the end of the year to which they refer or for such shorter period as the Revenue Commissioners may authorise in writing to the employer.

Amendments

1 Substituted by FA 2001 s 2(3) and Sch 1 para 1(*r*) for short tax "year" 2001 and later tax years; previously "certificates of tax-free allowances".

2 Substituted by FA 2002 s 138 and Sch 6 paras 3(*n*) and 6(*c*)(i) with effect from 1 January 2002; previously "regulation 22 of the Income Tax (Employment) Regulations, 1960 (SI No 28 of 1960)".

3 Substituted by FA 2001 s 232(1)(*e*) with effect from 15 February 2001 (as a result of FA 2002 s 138 and Sch 6 paras 5(*f*) and 6(*e*)(i)); previously "stored by any means approved under section 887".

4 Subs (2A) inserted by FA 2005 s 138 with effect from 25 March 2005.

5 Substituted by FA 2001 s 240(1) and (2)(*k*) and Sch 5 Pt 1 as respects any act or omission which takes place or begins on or after 1 January 2002; previously "£1,000".

Cross-references

Authorised officers and Garda Síochána: s 906.

Revenue information

Information leaflet IT32 — Revenue Audit — Guide for Small Businesses.

Code of Practice for Revenue Auditors — August 2002 (may be downloaded from Revenue's website at www.revenue.ie).

Statement of practice

Revenue powers: SP GEN/1/94, May 1994.

Revenue Internal Review Procedures — Audit and Use of Powers: SP GEN/2/99, May 1999.

Tax Briefing

TB49 Aug 2002 pp 6–13 — Code of Practice Revenue Audits.

Definitions

District Court: IA 1937 Sch; person: IA 1937 s 11(*c*).

Former enactments

ITA 1967 s 127A; FA 1992 s 233.

---

904 Power of inspection: tax deduction from payments to certain subcontractors

(1) In this section—

"authorised officer" means an officer of the Revenue Commissioners authorised by them in writing to exercise the powers conferred by this section;

"principal", **"relevant contract"**, **"relevant operations"** and **"subcontractor"** have the same meanings respectively as in Chapter 2 of Part 18;

"records" means those records required to be kept—

(*a*) under section 531 and regulations made under that section, and

(*b*) under section 886.

(2) An authorised officer may at all reasonable times enter any premises or place where the authorised officer has reason to believe that—

(*a*) any relevant operations are or have been carried on,

(*b*) any person is making or has made payments to a subcontractor in connection with the performance by the subcontractor of a relevant contract in relation to which that person is the principal,

(*c*) any person is or has been in receipt of such payments, or

(*d*) records are or may be kept,

and the authorised officer may—

(i) require any principal or subcontractor, or any employee of, or any other person providing bookkeeping, clerical or other administrative services to, any principal or subcontractor, who is on that premises or in that place to produce any records which the authorised officer requires for the purpose of his or her enquiry,

(ii) if the authorised officer has reason to believe that any of the records he or she has required to be produced to him or her under this subsection have not been so produced, search on those premises or in that place for those records, and

(iii) examine, make copies of, take extracts from, remove and retain any records for a reasonable period for their further examination or for the purpose of any legal proceedings instituted by an officer of the Revenue Commissioners or for the purposes of any criminal proceedings.

[(2A)(*a*) An authorised officer shall not, without the consent of the occupier, enter any premises, or that portion of any premises, which is occupied wholly and exclusively as a private residence, except on production by such officer of a warrant issued by a Judge of the District Court expressly authorising the authorised officer to so enter.

(*b*) A Judge of the District Court may issue a warrant under paragraph (*a*) if satisfied by information on oath that it is proper to do so for the purposes of this section.][1]

(3) An authorised officer may require any principal or subcontractor, or any employee of, or any other person providing bookkeeping, clerical or other administrative services

to, any principal or subcontractor, to give the authorised officer all reasonable assistance, including providing information and explanations and furnishing documents required by the authorised officer.

(4) An authorised officer when exercising or performing his or her powers or duties under this section shall on request produce his or her authorisation for the purposes of this section.

(5) A person who does not comply with the requirements of an authorised officer in the exercise or performance of the authorised officer's powers or duties under this section shall be liable to a penalty of [€1,265][2].

(6) The records referred to in this section shall be retained for a period of 6 years after the end of the year to which they refer or for such shorter period as the Revenue Commissioners may authorise in writing.

Amendments

1 Subs (2A) inserted by FA 2005 s 139 with effect from 25 March 2005.

2 Substituted by FA 2001 s 240(1) and (2)(*k*) and Sch 5 Pt 1 as respects any act or omission which takes place or begins on or after 1 January 2002; previously "£1,000".

Cross-references

Authorised officers and Garda Síochána: s 906.

Penalty: Sch 29 column 3.

Definitions

District Court: IA 1937 Sch; person: IA 1937 s 11(*c*); writing: IA 1937 Sch.

Revenue information

Information leaflet IT32 — Revenue Audit — Guide for Small Businesses.

Code of Practice for Revenue Auditors — August 2002 (may be downloaded from Revenue's website at www.revenue.ie).

Statement of practice

Revenue powers: SP GEN/1/94, May 1994.

Revenue Internal Review Procedures — Audit and Use of Powers: SP GEN/2/99, May 1999.

Tax Briefing

TB49 Aug 2002 pp 6–13 — Code of Practice Revenue Audits.

Former enactments

FA 1970 s 17A; FA 1992 s 235.

904A Power of inspection: returns and collection of appropriate tax

[(1) In this section—

"amount on account of appropriate tax", **"appropriate tax"**, **"deposit"**, **"interest"**, **"relevant deposit taker"**, **"relevant interest"** and **"return"** have, respectively, the meaning assigned to them by section 256(1);

[**"auditor"** means a person who is qualified, for the purposes of Part X of the Companies Act, 1990, for appointment as auditor of a company, or any other person whom the Revenue Commissioners consider suitable, having regard to his or her qualifications or experience, for appointment as an authorised officer;

"authorised officer" means—

(*a*) an officer of the Revenue Commissioners who is authorised by them in writing to exercise the powers conferred by this section, and

(*b*) an auditor who is authorised by the Revenue Commissioners in writing to exercise the powers conferred by this section in relation to an audit of the return of a named relevant deposit taker for a specified year or years of assessment;

"associated company", in relation to a relevant deposit taker, means a company which is itself a relevant deposit taker and which is the relevant deposit taker's associated company within the meaning of section 432;][1]

"books, records or other documents" includes—

(*a*) any records used in the business of a financial institution, or used in the transfer department of a financial institution acting as registrar of securities, whether—

(i) comprised in bound volume, loose-leaf binders or other loose-leaf filing system, loose-leaf ledger sheets, pages, folios or cards, or

(ii) kept on microfilm, magnetic tape or in any non-legible form (by the use of electronics or otherwise) which is capable of being reproduced in a legible form, and

(*b*) every electronic or other automatic means, if any, by which any such thing in non-legible form is so capable of being reproduced, and

(*c*) documents in manuscript, documents which are typed, printed, stencilled or created by any other mechanical or partly mechanical process in use from time to time and documents which are produced by any photographic or photostatic process, and

(*d*) correspondence and records of other communications between a relevant deposit taker and a person to whom it pays interest;

"liability" in relation to a person means any liability in relation to tax to which the person is or may be, or may have been, subject, or the amount of such liability;

"tax" means any tax, duty, levy or charge under the care and management of the Revenue Commissioners.

(2) An authorised officer, having regard to Chapter 4 of Part 8, may at all reasonable times enter any premises or place of business of a relevant deposit taker for the purposes of auditing for a year of assessment—

(*a*) the return made by the relevant deposit taker of—

(i) the relevant interest paid by it in that year,

(ii) the appropriate tax in relation to the payment of that interest,

(iii) the amount of interest in respect of which an amount on account of appropriate tax is due and payable for that year, and

(iv) the amount on account of appropriate tax so due and payable, and

(*b*) whether payments of interest were properly made by the relevant deposit taker without deducting appropriate tax in relation to the payments.

(3) Without prejudice to the generality of subsection (2), the authorised officer may—

(*a*) examine the procedures put in place by the relevant deposit taker for the purpose of ensuring compliance by the relevant deposit taker with its obligations under section 257(2), and

(*b*) check a sample of accounts into which deposits, which have not been treated by the relevant deposit taker as relevant deposits, have been paid, to determine whether—

(i) the procedures referred to in paragraph (*a*) have been observed in practice and whether they are adequate,

[(ii) the relevant deposit taker is, in respect of each deposit in the sample of deposits, in possession of—

(I) a declaration mentioned in section 246A(3)(*b*)(ii)(III) or 263,

(II) the number referred to in paragraph (*f*)(ii) or (*h*)(ii) of the definition of "relevant deposit" in section 256, or

(III) as respects a case within paragraph (*b*)(ii)(I) or (*b*)(ii)(II) of subsection (3) of section 246A, the tax reference number referred to in subsection (4) of that section,

as the case may be, and][7]

(iii) there is information in the relevant deposit taker's possession which can reasonably be taken to indicate that one or more of such deposits is or may be a relevant deposit.

(4) Where an authorised officer in exercising or performing his or her powers and duties under this section has reason to believe that in respect of one or more deposits, the relevant deposit taker has incorrectly treated them as not being relevant deposits, the authorised officer may make such further enquiries as are necessary to establish whether there is a liability in relation to any person.

(5) An authorised officer may require a relevant deposit taker or an employee of the relevant deposit taker to produce books, records or other documents and to furnish information, explanations and particulars and to give all assistance, which the authorised officer reasonably requires for the purposes of his or her audit and examination under subsections (2) and (3), and, as the case may be, enquiries under subsection (4).

[(6) An authorised officer may require an associated company in relation to a relevant deposit taker or an employee of such an associated company to produce books, records or other documents and to furnish information, explanations and particulars and to give all assistance, which the authorised officer reasonably requires for the purposes of his or her audit and examination under subsections (2) and (3) and, as the case may be, enquiries under subsection (4).

(7) An authorised officer may make extracts from or copies of all or any part of the books, records or other documents or other material made available to him or her or require that copies of books, records, or other documents be made available to him or her, in exercising or performing his or her powers or duties under this section.

(8) An employee of a relevant deposit taker or of an associated company in relation to a relevant deposit taker, who fails to comply with the requirements of the authorised

officer in the exercise or performance of the authorised officer's powers or duties under this section shall be liable to a penalty of [€1,265][3].

(9) A relevant deposit taker or an associated company in relation to a relevant deposit taker which fails to comply with the requirements of the authorised officer in the exercise or performance of the authorised officer's powers or duties under this section shall be liable to a penalty of [€19,045][4] and if that failure continues a further penalty of [€2,535][5] for each day on which the failure continues.][6]][7]

Amendments

1 Definitions of "auditor", "authorised officer" and "associated company" substituted for definition of "authorised officer" by FA 2000 s 68(*a*)(i) with effect from 6 April 20000.

2 Subs (3)(*b*)(ii) inserted by FA 2003 s 49(4) with effect from 1 January 2003.

3 Substituted by FA 2001s 240(1) and (2)(*k*) and Sch 5 Pt 1 as respects any act or omission which takes place or begins on or after 1 January 2002; previously "£1,000".

4 Substituted by FA 2001 s 240(1) and (2)(*k*) and Sch 5 Pt 1 as respects any act or omission which takes place or begins on or after 1 January 2002; previously "£15,000".

5 Substituted by FA 2001 s 240(1) and (2)(*k*) and Sch 5 Pt 1 as respects any act or omission which takes place or begins on or after 1 January 2002; previously "£2,000".

6 Subs (6)–(9) substituted for subs (6)–(7) by FA 2000 s 68(*a*)(ii) with effect from 6 April 2000.

7 Section 904A inserted by FA 1999 s 207(*e*) with effect from 25 March 1999.

Cross-references

Dividend payments by credit unions, supplementary provisions, this section applies to a credit union treated under Pt 8 Ch 5 as paying relevant interest: s 267F(1).

Report to Committee of Public Accounts: publication, etc, meaning of "authorised officer" applied: s 904B(1); s 904B(2).

Revenue information

Finance Act 1999 — Revenue Powers: Guidance Notes and Instructions, May 1999.

Code of Practice for Revenue Auditors — August 2002 (may be downloaded from Revenue's website at www.revenue.ie).

Statement of practice

Revenue Powers (Finance Act 1999): SP GEN/1/99, May 1999.

Revenue Internal Review Procedures — Audit and Use of Powers: SP GEN/2/99, May 1999.

Tax Briefing

TB49 Aug 2002 pp 6–13 — Code of Practice Revenue Audits.

Definitions

company: ss 4(1), 5(1); person: IA 1937 s 11(*c*); writing: IA 1937 Sch; year of assessment: s 2(1).

904B Report to Committee of Public Accounts: publication etc

[(1) In this section—

"appropriate tax" and **"relevant deposit taker"** have, respectively, the meanings assigned to them by section 256(1);

"authorised officer" has the meaning assigned to it by section 904A.

(2) Notwithstanding any obligation as to secrecy or other restriction upon disclosure of information imposed by or under statute or otherwise, the Revenue Commissioners—

(*a*) shall, before 1 November 2000, make a report in writing to the Committee of Public Accounts of Dáil Éireann, and

(*b*) may, at any time, cause to be made public a report, in such manner as they consider fit, of the results (including interim results) of any audit carried out by an authorised officer under section 904A during the period from 25 March 1999 to the date the report is made.

(3) The report under subsection (2) shall be in respect of audits of relevant deposit takers for the years of assessment 1986–1987 to 1998–1999, and may specify, in respect of each such audit—

(*a*) the name of the relevant deposit taker concerned,

(*b*) the amount of additional appropriate tax payable by the relevant deposit taker as a result of the audit,

(*c*) the amount of interest payable in respect of any such amount,

(*d*) the amount of any fine or penalty imposed by a court on the relevant deposit taker under the Tax Acts, or accepted by the Revenue Commissioners in place of initiating proceedings for recovery of such fine or penalty,

(*e*) whether an assessment has been made in respect of appropriate tax and, if so, whether the assessment has been appealed,

(*f*) whether the audit has been completed as at the date of the report,

(*g*) the amount of any payment on account of appropriate tax paid by the relevant deposit taker in anticipation of an audit being carried out or during the course of an audit, and

(*h*) such further particulars as the Revenue Commissioners consider fit.][1]

Amendments

1 Section 904B inserted by FA 2000 s 68(1)(*b*) with effect from 6 April 2000.

Definitions

Dáil Éireann: IA 1937 Sch; Tax Acts: s 1(2); writing: IA 1937 Sch; year of assessment: s 2(1).

904C Power of inspection (returns and collection of appropriate tax): assurance companies

[(1) In this section—

"assurance company" and **"life business"** have, respectively, the meanings assigned to them in section 706;

"appropriate tax" has the meaning assigned to it in section 730F;

"authorised officer" means an officer of the Revenue Commissioners authorised by them in writing to exercise the powers conferred by this section;

"books, records or other documents" includes—

(*a*) any records used in the business of an assurance company whether—

(i) comprised in bound volume, loose-leaf binders or other loose-leaf filing system, loose-leaf ledger sheets, pages, folios or cards, or

(ii) kept on microfilm, magnetic tape or in any non-legible form (by use of electronics or otherwise) which is capable of being reproduced in a legible form, and

(*b*) every electronic or other automatic means, if any, by which any such thing in non-legible form is so capable of being reproduced, and (*c*) documents in manuscript, documents which are typed, printed, stencilled or created by any other mechanical means or partly mechanical process in use from time to time and documents which are produced by any photographic or photostatic process, and

(*d*) correspondence and records of other communications by, or on behalf of, policyholders with the assurance company carrying on life business;

"chargeable event", in relation to a life policy, has the meaning assigned to it by section 730C;

"declaration" means a declaration referred to in section 730E;

"liability", in relation to a person, means any liability in relation to tax to which the person is or may be, or may have been, subject, or the amount of such liability;

"life policy" has the meaning assigned to it in section 730B;

"policyholder" has the meaning assigned to it in section 730E;

[**"return"** means a return under section 730FA or section 730G;][1]

"tax" means any tax, duty, levy or charge under the care and management of the Revenue Commissioners.

(2) An authorised officer may at all reasonable times enter any premises or place of business of an assurance company carrying on life business for the purposes of auditing for a financial year the returns made by the company of appropriate tax.

(3) Without prejudice to the generality of subsection (2) the authorised officer may—

(*a*) examine the procedures put in place by the assurance company for the purpose of ensuring compliance by the assurance company with its obligations under Chapter 5 of Part 26,

(*b*) examine all or a sample of the declarations made to the assurance company,

(*c*) examine a sample of life policies to determine whether—

(i) the procedures referred to in paragraph (*a*) have been observed in practice and whether they are adequate,

(ii) the assurance company has on the happening of chargeable events in relation to each life policy, paid the correct amount of appropriate tax in connection with the chargeable events, and

(iii) there is information in the assurance company's possession which can reasonably be taken to indicate that the assurance company incorrectly failed to pay appropriate tax in connection with a chargeable event.

(4) Where an authorised officer in exercising or performing his or her powers and duties under this section has reason to believe that in respect of one or more life policies, the assurance company has incorrectly failed to pay appropriate tax in connection with a chargeable event, the authorised officer may make such further enquiries as are necessary to establish whether there is a liability in relation to any person.

(5) An authorised officer may require an assurance company or an employee of the assurance company to produce books, records or other documents and to furnish information, explanations and particulars and to give all assistance, which the authorised

officer reasonably requires for the purposes of his or her audit and examination under subsections (2) and (3), and, as the case may be, enquiries under subsection (4).

(6) An authorised officer may make extracts from or copies of all or any part of the books, records or other documents or other material made available to him or her or require that copies of books, records or other documents be made available to him or her, in exercising or performing his or her powers or duties under this section.

(7) An employee of an assurance company who fails to comply with the requirements of the authorised officer in the exercise or performance of the authorised officer's powers or duties under this section shall be liable to a penalty of [€1,265][2].

(8) An assurance company which fails to comply with the requirements of the authorised officer in the exercise or performance of the authorised officer's powers or duties under this section shall be liable to a penalty of [€19,045][3] and if that failure continues a further penalty of [€2,535][4] for each day on which the failure continues.][5]

Amendments

1 Definition of "return" substituted by FA 2002 s 40(3) with effect from 5 December 2001.

2 Substituted by FA 2001 s 240(1) and (2)(*k*) and Sch 5 Pt 1 as respects any act or omission which takes place or begins on or after 1 January 2002; previously "£1,000".

3 Substituted by FA 2001 s 240(1) and (2)(*k*) and Sch 5 Pt 1 as respects any act or omission which takes place or begins on or after 1 January 2002; previously "£15,000".

4 Substituted by FA 2001 s 240(1) and (2)(*k*) and Sch 5 Pt 1 as respects any act or omission which takes place or begins on or after 1 January 2002; previously "£2,000".

5 Section 904C inserted by FA 2000 s 68(1)(*b*) with effect from 6 April 2000.

Cross-references

Taxation of policyholders: s 730B(4)(*e*).

Definitions

company: ss 4(1), 5(1); person: IA 1937 s 11(*c*); writing: IA 1937 Sch.

Revenue information

Finance Act 1999 — Revenue Powers: Guidance Notes and Instructions, May 1999.
Code of Practice for Revenue Auditors — August 2002 (may be downloaded from Revenue's website at www.revenue.ie).

Statement of practice

Revenue Powers (Finance Act 1999): SP GEN/1/99, May 1999.
Revenue Internal Review Procedures — Audit and Use of Powers: SP GEN/2/99, May 1999.

Tax Briefing

TB49 Aug 2002 pp 6–13 — Code of Practice Revenue Audits.

904D Power of inspection (returns and collection of appropriate tax; investment undertakings

[(1) In this section—

"appropriate tax" has the meaning assigned to it in section 739E.

"authorised officer" means an officer of the Revenue Commissioners authorised by them in writing to exercise the powers conferred by this section;

"books, records or other documents" includes—

(*a*) any records used in the business of an investment undertaking whether—

(i) comprised in bound volume, loose-leaf binders or other loose-leaf filing system, loose-leaf ledger sheets, pages, folios or cards, or

(ii) kept on microfilm, magnetic tape or in any non-legible form (by use of electronics or otherwise) which is capable of being reproduced in a legible form, and

(*b*) every electronic or other automatic means, if any, by which any such thing in non-legible form is so capable of being reproduced, and

(*c*) documents in manuscript, documents which are typed, printed, stencilled or created by any other mechanical means or partly mechanical process in use from time to time and documents which are produced by any photographic or photostatic process, and

(*d*) correspondence and records of other communications by, or on behalf of, unit holders with the investment undertaking;

"declaration" means a declaration referred to in Schedule 2B;

"investment undertaking" and **"unit holder"** have, respectively, the meanings assigned to them by section 739B;

"liability", in relation to a person, means any liability in relation to tax to which the person is or may be, or may have been, subject, or the amount of such liability;

"return" means a return under section 739F.

"tax" means any tax, duty, levy or charge under the care and management of the Revenue Commissioners.

(2) An authorised officer may at all reasonable times enter any premises or place of business of an investment undertaking for the purposes of auditing for a financial year the returns made by the investment undertaking of appropriate tax.

(3) Without prejudice to the generality of subsection (2) the authorised officer may—

(*a*) examine the procedures put in place by the investment undertaking for the purpose of ensuring compliance by the investment undertaking with its obligations under Chapter 1A of Part 27,

(*b*) examine all or a sample of the declarations made to the investment undertaking,

(*c*) examine transactions in relation to a sample of unit holders to determine whether—

(i) the procedures referred to in paragraph (*a*) have been observed in practice and whether they are adequate,

(ii) the investment undertaking has, on the happening of a chargeable event in relation to a unit holder, paid the correct amount of appropriate tax in connection with the chargeable event, and

(iii) there is information in the investment undertaking's possession which can reasonably be taken to indicate that the investment undertaking incorrectly failed to pay appropriate tax in connection with a chargeable event.

(4) Where an authorised officer in exercising or performing his or her powers and duties under this section has reason to believe that in respect of one or more unit holders, the

investment undertaking has incorrectly failed to pay appropriate tax in connection with a chargeable event, the authorised officer may make such further enquiries as are necessary to establish whether there is a liability in relation to any person.

(5) An authorised officer may require an investment undertaking or an employee of the investment undertaking to produce books, records or other documents and to furnish information, explanations and particulars and to give all assistance, which the authorised officer reasonably requires for the purposes of his or her audit and examination under subsections (2) and (3), and, as the case may be, enquiries under subsection (4).

(6) An authorised officer may make extracts from or copies of all or any part of the books, records or other documents or other material made available to him or her or require that copies of books, records or other documents be made available to him or her, in exercising or performing his or her powers or duties under this section.

(7) An employee of an investment undertaking who fails to comply with the requirements of the authorised officer in the exercise or performance of the authorised officer's powers or duties under this section shall be liable to a penalty of [€1,265][1].

(8) An investment undertaking which fails to comply with the requirements of the authorised officer in the exercise or performance of the authorised officer's powers or duties under this section shall be liable to a penalty of [€19,045][2] and if that failure continues a further penalty of [€2,535][3] for each day on which the failure continues.][4]

Amendments

1 Substituted by FA 2001 s 240(1) and (2)(*k*) and Sch 5 Pt 1 as respects any act or omission which takes place or begins on or after 1 January 2002; previously "£1,000".

2 Substituted by FA 2001 s 240(1) and (2)(*k*) and Sch 5 Pt 1 as respects any act or omission which takes place or begins on or after 1 January 2002; previously "£15,000".

3 Substituted by FA 2001 s 240(1) and (2)(*k*) and Sch 5 Pt 1 as respects any act or omission which takes place or begins on or after 1 January 2002; previously "£2,000".

4 Section 904D inserted by FA 2000 s 68(1)(*b*) with effect from 6 April 2000.

Cross-references

Investment undertakings (interpretation and application), construction of references to an investment undertaking in this section: s 739B(2), (2A)(*a*).

Revenue information

Finance Act 1999 — Revenue Powers: Guidance Notes and Instructions, May 1999.

Code of Practice for Revenue Auditors — August 2002 (may be downloaded from Revenue's website at www.revenue.ie).

Statement of practice

Revenue Powers (Finance Act 1999): SP GEN/1/99, May 1999.

Revenue Internal Review Procedures — Audit and Use of Powers: SP GEN/2/99, May 1999.

Tax Briefing

TB49 Aug 2002 pp 6–13 — Code of Practice Revenue Audits.

Definitions

person: IA 1937 s 11(*c*); writing: IA 1937 Sch.

904E Power of inspection: claims by authorised insurers

[(1) In this section—

"authorised insurer" has the same meaning as in section 470;

"authorised officer" means an officer of the Revenue Commissioners authorised by them in writing to exercise the powers conferred by this section.

(2) An authorised officer may at all reasonable times enter any premises or place of business of an authorised insurer for the purpose of auditing for a year of assessment claims made by the authorised insurer under section 470(3)(*b*)(ii).

(3) Without prejudice to the generality of subsection (2), the authorised officer may—

(*a*) examine the procedures put in place by the authorised insurer in relation to the vouching of claims referred to in that subsection, and

(*b*) check a sample of the cases in respect of which such a claim has been made to determine whether the procedures referred to in paragraph (*a*) have been observed in practice and whether they are adequate.

(4) An authorised officer may require an authorised insurer or an employee of the authorised insurer to furnish information, explanations and particulars and to give all assistance which the authorised officer reasonably requires for the purposes of his or her audit and examination under subsections (2) and (3).

(5) An authorised officer when exercising or performing his or her powers or duties under this section shall, on request, produce his or her authorisation for the purposes of this section.

(6) An employee of an authorised insurer who fails to comply with the requirements of the authorised officer in the exercise or performance of the authorised officer's powers or duties under this section shall be liable to a penalty of [€1,265][1].

(7) An authorised insurer which fails to comply with the requirements of the authorised officer in the exercise or performance of the authorised officer's powers or duties under this section shall be liable to a penalty of [€19,045][2] and, if that failure continues, a further penalty of [€2,535][3] for each day on which the failure continues.][4]

Amendments

1 Substituted by FA 2001 s 22(2)(*a*) for 2002 and later tax years; previously "£1,000".

2 Substituted by FA 2001 s 22(2)(*b*)(i) for 2002 and later tax years; previously "£15,000".

3 Substituted by FA 2001 s 22(2)(*b*)(ii) for 2002 and later tax years; previously "£2,000".

4 Section 904E inserted by FA 2001 s 22(1) for short tax "year" 2001 and later tax years.

Definitions

writing: IA 1937 Sch; year of assessment: s 2(1).

904F Power of inspection: claims by qualifying lenders

[(1) In this section—

"authorised officer" means an officer of the Revenue Commissioners authorised by them in writing to exercise the powers conferred by this section;

"books, records or other documents" includes—

(*a*) any records used in the business of a qualifying lender whether—

(i) comprised in bound volume, loose-leaf binders or other loose-leaf filing system, loose-leaf ledger sheets, pages, folios or cards, or

(ii) kept on microfilm, magnetic tape or in any non-legible form (by the use of electronics or otherwise) which is capable of being reproduced in a legible form, and

(*b*) every electronic or other automatic means, if any, by which any such thing in non-legible form is so capable of being reproduced, and

(*c*) documents in manuscript, documents which are typed, printed, stencilled or created by any other mechanical or partly mechanical process in use from time to time and documents which are produced by any photographic or photostatic process, and

(*d*) correspondence and records of other communications between a qualifying lender and an individual having a qualifying mortgage loan from that qualifying lender;

"qualifying lender" and **"qualifying mortgage loan"** have the same meanings respectively as in section 244A.

(2) An authorised officer may at all reasonable times enter any premises or place of business of a qualifying lender for the purpose of auditing for a year of assessment claims made by the qualifying lender under section 244A(2)(*b*)(ii).

(3) Without prejudice to the generality of subsection (2), the authorised officer may

(*a*) examine the procedures put in place by the qualifying lender in relation to the vouching of claims referred to in that subsection, and

(*b*) check a sample of the cases in respect of which such a claim has been made to determine whether the procedures referred to in paragraph (*a*) have been observed in practice and whether they are adequate.

(4) An authorised officer may require a qualifying lender or an employee of the qualifying lender to produce books, records or other documents and to furnish information, explanations and particulars and to give all assistance, which the authorised officer reasonably requires for the purposes of his or her audit and examination under subsections (2) and (3).

(5) An authorised officer may make extracts from or copies of all or any part of the books, records or other documents or other material made available to him or her or require that copies of books, records, or other documents be made available to him or her, in exercising or performing his or her powers or duties under this section.

(6) An authorised officer when exercising or performing his or her powers or duties under this section shall, on request, produce his or her authorisation for the purposes of this section.

(7) An employee of a qualifying lender who fails to comply with the requirements of the authorised officer in the exercise or performance of the authorised officer's powers or duties under this section shall be liable to a penalty of €1,265.

(8) A qualifying lender which fails to comply with the requirements of the authorised officer in the exercise or performance of the authorised officer's powers or duties under this section shall be liable to a penalty of €19,045 and if that failure continues a further penalty of €2,535 for each day on which the failure continues.][1]

Amendments

1 Section 904F inserted by FA 2001 s 22(3) for 2002 and later tax years.

Cross-references

Mortgage Interest (Relief at Source) Regulations 2001, SI No 558 of 2001, reg 2(1) (interpretation).

Revenue information

Finance Act 1999 — Revenue Powers: Guidance Notes and Instructions, May 1999.

Code of Practice for Revenue Auditors — August 2002 (may be downloaded from Revenue's website at www.revenue.ie).

Statement of practice

Revenue Powers (Finance Act 1999): SP GEN/1/99, May 1999.

Revenue Internal Review Procedures — Audit and Use of Powers: SP GEN/2/99, May 1999.

Tax Briefing

TB49 Aug 2002 pp 6–13 — Code of Practice Revenue Audits.

Definitions

writing: IA 1937 Sch; year of assessment: s 2(1).

904G Power of inspection: claims by qualifying insurers

[(1) In this section—

"authorised officer" means an officer of the Revenue Commissioners authorised by them in writing to exercise the powers conferred by this section;

"qualifying insurer" and **"qualifying long-term care policies"** have the same meanings respectively as in section 470A.

(2) An authorised officer may at all reasonable times enter any premises or place of business of a qualifying insurer for the purpose of auditing for a year of assessment claims made by the qualifying insurer under section 470A(8)(*b*)(ii).

(3) Without prejudice to the generality of subsection (2), the authorised officer may—

(*a*) examine the procedures put in place by the qualifying insurer in relation to the vouching of claims referred to in that subsection, and

(*b*) check a sample of the cases in respect of which such a claim has been made to determine whether the procedures referred to in paragraph (*a*) have been observed in practice and whether they are adequate.

(4) An authorised officer may require a qualifying insurer or an employee of the qualifying insurer to furnish information, explanations and particulars and to give all assistance which the authorised officer reasonably requires for the purposes of his or her audit and examination under subsections (2) and (3).

(5) An authorised officer when exercising or performing his or her powers or duties under this section shall, on request, produce his or her authorisation for the purposes of this section.

(6) An employee of a qualifying insurer who fails to comply with the requirements of the authorised officer in the exercise or performance of the authorised officer's powers or duties under this section shall be liable to a penalty of [€1,265][1].

(7) A qualifying insurer which fails to comply with the requirements of the authorised officer in the exercise or performance of the authorised officer's powers or duties under

this section shall be liable to a penalty of [€19,045][2] and, if that failure continues, a further penalty of [€2,535][3] for each day on which the failure continues.][4]

Amendments

1 Substituted by FA 2001 s 22(5)(*a*)(i) for 2002 and later tax years; previously "£1,000".
2 Substituted by FA 2001 s 22(5)(*a*)(ii)(I) for 2002 and later tax years; previously "£15,000".
3 Substituted by FA 2001 s 22(5)(*a*)(ii)(II) for 2002 and later tax years; previously "£2,000".
4 Section 904G inserted by FA 2001 s 22(4) for short tax "year" 2001 and later tax years.

Revenue information

Finance Act 1999 — Revenue Powers: Guidance Notes and Instructions, May 1999.
Code of Practice for Revenue Auditors — August 2002 (may be downloaded from Revenue's website at www.revenue.ie).

Statement of practice

Revenue Powers (Finance Act 1999): SP GEN/1/99, May 1999.
Revenue Internal Review Procedures — Audit and Use of Powers: SP GEN/2/99, May 1999.

Tax Briefing

TB49 Aug 2002 pp 6–13 — Code of Practice Revenue Audits.

Definitions

writing: IA 1937 Sch; year of assessment: s 2(1).

904H Power of inspection: qualifying savings managers

[(1) In this section—

"authorised officer" means an officer of the Revenue Commissioners authorised by them in writing to exercise the powers conferred by this section;

"qualifying savings manager" has the same meaning as in section 848B (inserted by the Finance Act, 2001);

"special savings incentive account" has the same meaning as in section 848B (inserted by the Finance Act, 2001).

(2) An authorised officer may at all reasonable times enter any premises or place of business of a qualifying savings manager, or a person (in this section referred to as an "appointed person") appointed by a qualifying savings manager in accordance with section 848R (inserted by the Finance Act, 2001), for the purposes of auditing compliance with the provisions of Part 36A (inserted by the Finance Act, 2001) and without prejudice to the generality of the foregoing the authorised officer may—

(*a*) audit the returns made in accordance with sections 848P and 848Q (inserted by the Finance Act, 2001),

(*b*) examine the procedures put in place by the qualifying savings manager, or as the case may be, the appointed person, so as to ensure compliance with the obligations imposed by Part 36A (inserted by the Finance Act, 2001),

(*c*) examine all, or a sample of, special savings incentive accounts to determine—

(i) whether those procedures have been observed in practice,

(ii) whether the terms under which each such account was commenced and continues, are in accordance with the terms referred to in section 848C (inserted by the Finance Act, 2001), and

(iii) whether the qualifying savings manager, in respect of each such account, is, where appropriate, in possession of a declaration referred to in sections 848F, 848I, and 848O (inserted by the Finance Act, 2001), and is not in possession of any information which would reasonably suggest that any such declaration is incorrect,

and

(*d*) examine any notice and declaration referred to in section 848N(3) (inserted by the Finance Act, 2001).

(3) An authorised officer may require a qualifying savings manager, or (as the case may be) the appointed person, or an employee of either such person, to produce all or any of the records relating to the management by him or her of special savings incentive accounts and furnish information, explanations and particulars and to give all assistance, which the authorised officer reasonably requires for the purposes of his or her audit and examination under subsection (2).

(4) An employee of a qualifying savings manager or of an appointed person who fails to comply with the requirements of the authorised officer in the exercise or performance of the authorised officer's powers or duties under this section shall be liable to a penalty of [€1,265][1].

(5) A qualifying savings manager or an appointed person who fails to comply with the requirements of the authorised officer in the exercise or performance of the authorised officer's powers or duties under this section shall be liable to a penalty of [€19,045][2] and, if that failure continues, a further penalty of [€2,535][3] for each day on which the failure continues.][4]

Amendments

1 Substituted by FA 2001 s 22(5)(*b*)(i) for 2002 and later tax years; previously "£1,000".

2 Substituted by FA 2001 s 22(5)(*b*)(ii)(I) for 2002 and later tax years; previously "£15,000".

3 Substituted by FA 2001 s 22(5)(*b*)(ii)(II) for 2002 and later tax years; previously "£2,000".

4 Section 904H inserted by FA 2001 s 22(4) for short tax "year" 2001 and later tax years.

Revenue information

Finance Act 1999 — Revenue Powers: Guidance Notes and Instructions, May 1999.

Code of Practice for Revenue Auditors — August 2002 (may be downloaded from Revenue's website at www.revenue.ie).

Statement of practice

Revenue Powers (Finance Act 1999): SP GEN/1/99, May 1999.

Revenue Internal Review Procedures — Audit and Use of Powers: SP GEN/2/99, May 1999.

Tax Briefing

TB49 Aug 2002 pp 6–13 — Code of Practice Revenue Audits.

Definitions

writing: IA 1937 Sch; year of assessment: s 2(1).

904I Power of inspection: returns and collection of dividend withholding tax

[(1) In this section—

"accountable person" means—

(*a*) a company resident in the State which makes, and

(*b*) an authorised withholding agent who is treated under section 172H as making,

a relevant distribution;

"authorised withholding agent", **"dividend withholding tax"**, and **"relevant distribution"** have, respectively, the meanings assigned to them by section 172A;

"authorised officer" means an officer of the Revenue Commissioners, authorised by them in writing to exercise the powers conferred by this section;

"records" means all records which relate to compliance by an accountable person with obligations under Chapter 8A of Part 6 including all declarations (and accompanying certificates) and notifications which are made, or, as the case may be, given to an accountable person in accordance with that Chapter of that Part and Schedule 2A.

(2) An authorised officer, having regard to Chapter 8A of Part 6, may at all reasonable times enter any premises or place of business of an accountable person for the purposes of auditing a return made by the accountable person under section 172K.

(3) Without prejudice to the generality of subsection (2), the authorised officer may—

(*a*) examine the procedures put in place by the accountable person for the purpose of ensuring compliance by the accountable person with its obligations under Chapter 8A of Part 6, and

(*b*) check all, or a sample of or a class of, the records in the power, possession or procurement of the accountable person to determine whether—

(i) the procedures referred to in paragraph *(a)* have been observed in practice and whether they are adequate, and

(ii) there is information in the accountable person's possession which can reasonably be taken to indicate that the information contained in one or more of the records is or may be incorrect.

(4) An authorised officer may require an accountable person or an employee of the accountable person to produce records and to furnish information, explanations and particulars and to give all assistance which the authorised officer reasonably requires for the purposes of his or her audit and examination under subsections (2) and (3).

(5) An authorised officer may make extracts from or copies of all or any part of the records made available to him or her or require that copies of such records be made available to him or her, in exercising or performing his or her powers or duties under this section.

(6) An employee of an accountable person who fails to comply with the requirements of the authorised officer in the exercise or performance of the authorised officer's powers or duties under this section shall be liable to a penalty of €1,265.

(7) An accountable person who fails to comply with the requirements of the authorised officer in the exercise or performance of the authorised officer's powers or duties under this section shall be liable to a penalty of €19,045 and if that failure continues a further penalty of €2,535 for each day on which the failure continues.][1]

Amendments

1 Section 904I inserted by FA 2002 s 132(*c*) with effect from 25 March 2002.

Revenue information

Finance Act 1999 — Revenue Powers: Guidance Notes and Instructions, May 1999.

Code of Practice for Revenue Auditors — August 2002 (may be downloaded from Revenue's website at www.revenue.ie).

Statement of practice

Revenue Powers (Finance Act 1999): SP GEN/1/99, May 1999.

Revenue Internal Review Procedures — Audit and Use of Powers: SP GEN/2/99, May 1999.

Tax Briefing

TB49 Aug 2002 pp 6–13 — Code of Practice Revenue Audits.

Definitions

company: s 4(1); writing: IA 1937 Sch.

904J Power of inspection: tax deduction from payments in respect of professional services by certain persons

[(1) In this section—

"accountable person" has the same meaning as in section 521;

"authorised officer" means an officer of the Revenue Commissioners authorised by them in writing to exercise the powers conferred by this section;

"books, records or other documents" includes—

(*a*) any records used in the business of an accountable person whether—

(i) comprised in bound volume, loose-leaf binders or other loose-leaf filing system, loose-leaf ledger sheets, pages, folios or cards, or

(ii) kept on microfilm, magnetic tape or in any non-legible form (by the use of electronics or otherwise) which is capable of being reproduced in a legible form,

and

(*b*) every electronic or other automatic means, if any, by which any such thing in non-legible form is so capable of being reproduced, and

(*c*) documents in manuscript, documents which are typed, printed, stencilled or created by any other mechanical or partly mechanical process in use from time to time and documents which are produced by any photographic or photostatic process, and

(*d*) correspondence and records of other communications between an accountable person and a specified person;

"specified person" has the same meaning as in section 520.

(2) An authorised officer may at all reasonable times enter any premises or place of business of an accountable person for the purpose of auditing for a year of assessment returns made by the accountable person under section 525.

(3) Without prejudice to the generality of subsection (2), the authorised officer may—

(*a*) examine the procedures put in place by the accountable person for the purpose of ensuring compliance by the accountable person with that person's obligations under Chapter 1 of Part 18, and

(*b*) examine all or a sample of the returns made by the accountable person to determine whether the procedures referred to in paragraph (*a*) have been observed in practice and whether they are adequate.

(4) An authorised officer may require an accountable person or an employee of the accountable person to produce books, records or other documents and to furnish

information, explanations and particulars and to give all assistance, which the authorised officer reasonably requires for the purposes of his or her audit and examination under subsections (2) and (3).

(5) An authorised officer may make extracts from or copies of all or any part of the books, records or other documents or other material made available to him or her or require that copies of books, records, or other documents be made available to him or her, in exercising or performing his or her powers or duties under this section.

(6) An authorised officer when exercising or performing his or her powers or duties under this section shall, on request, produce his or her authorisation for the purposes of this section.

(7) An employee of an accountable person who fails to comply with the requirements of the authorised officer in the exercise or performance of the authorised officer's powers or duties under this section is liable to a penalty of €1,265.

(8) An accountable person who fails to comply with the requirements of the authorised officer in the exercise or performance of the authorised officer's powers or duties under this section is liable to a penalty of €19,045 and if that failure continues a further penalty of €2,535 for each day on which the failure continues.][1]

Amendments

1 Section 904J inserted by FA 2003 s 159 with effect from 28 March 2003.

Definitions

person: IA 1937 s 11(*c*); writing: IA 1937 Sch; year of assessment: s 2(1).

905 Inspection of documents and records

(1) In this section—

"authorised officer" means an officer of the Revenue Commissioners authorised by them in writing to exercise the powers conferred by this section;

"property" means any asset relating to a tax liability;

[**"records"** means any document or any other written or printed material in any form, and includes any information stored, maintained or preserved by means of any mechanical or electronic device, whether or not stored, maintained or preserved in a legible form—

(i) which relates to a business carried on by a person, or

(ii) which a person is obliged by any provision relating to tax to keep, retain, issue or produce for inspection or which may be inspected under any provision relating to tax;][1]

"tax" means any tax, duty, levy or charge under the care and management of the Revenue Commissioners;

"tax liability" means any existing liability to tax or further liability to tax which may be established by an authorised officer following the exercise or performance of his or her powers or duties under this section.

(2) (*a*) An authorised officer may at all reasonable times enter any premises or place where the authorised officer has reason to believe that—

(i) any trade, profession or other activity, the profits or gains of which are chargeable to tax, is or has been carried on,

(ii) anything is or has been done in connection with any trade, profession or other activity the profits or gains of which are chargeable to tax,

(iii) any records relating to—

(I) any trade, profession, other source of profits or gains or chargeable gains,

(II) any tax liability, or

(III) any repayments of tax in regard to any person,

are or may be kept, or

(iv) any property is or has been located,

and the authorised officer may—

(A) require any person who is on those premises or in that place, other than a person who is there to purchase goods or to receive a service, to produce any records or property,

(B) if the authorised officer has reason to believe that any of the records or property which he or she has required to be produced to him or her under this subsection have not been produced, search on those premises or in that place for those records or property,

(C) examine any records or property and take copies of or extracts from any records,

(D) remove any records and retain them for a reasonable time for the purposes of their further examination or for the purposes of any legal proceedings instituted by an officer of the Revenue Commissioners or for the purposes of any criminal proceedings, and

(E) examine property listed in any records.

(*b*) An authorised officer may in the exercise or performance of his or her powers or duties under this section require any person whom he or she has reason to believe—

(i) is or was carrying on any trade, profession or other activity the profits or gains of which are chargeable to tax,

(ii) is or was liable to any tax, or

(iii) has information relating to any tax liability,

to give the authorised officer all reasonable assistance, including providing information and explanations or furnishing documents and making available for inspection property as required by the authorised officer in relation to any tax liability or any repayment of tax in regard to any person.

(*c*) Nothing in this subsection shall be construed as requiring any person carrying on a profession, or any person employed by any person carrying on a profession, to produce to an authorised officer any documents relating to a client, other than such documents—

(i) as pertain to the payment of fees to the person carrying on the profession or to other financial transactions of the person carrying on the profession,

(ii) as are otherwise material to the tax liability of the person carrying on the profession, or

(iii) as are already required to be provided following a request issued under [section 128 of the Stamp Duties Consolidation Act, 1999],[2]

and in particular that person shall not be required to disclose any information or professional advice of a confidential nature given to a client.

...[3]

(*e*) An authorised officer shall not, without the consent of the occupier, enter any premises, or that portion of any premises, which is occupied wholly and exclusively as a private residence, except on production by such officer of a warrant issued by a Judge of the District Court expressly authorising the authorised officer to so enter.

(*f*) A Judge of the District Court may issue a warrant under paragraph (*e*) if satisfied by information on oath that it is proper to do so for the purposes of this section.

[(2A)(*a*) In this subsection **"the Acts"** has the meaning assigned to it by section 1078(1).

(*b*) Without prejudice to any power conferred by subsection (2), if a Judge of the District Court is satisfied by information on oath that there are reasonable grounds for suspecting—

(i) that a person may have failed or may fail to comply with any provision of the Acts,

(ii) that any such failure is likely to have led or to lead to serious prejudice to the proper assessment or collection of tax (having regard to the amount of any tax liability that arises or might arise from such failure), and

(iii) that records, which are material to the proper assessment or collection of tax are likely to be kept or concealed at any premises or place,

the Judge may issue a search warrant.

(*c*) A search warrant issued under this subsection shall be expressed and shall operate to authorise an authorised officer accompanied by such other named officers of the Revenue Commissioners and such other named persons as the authorised officer considers necessary, at any time or times within one month of the date of issue of the warrant, to enter (if need be by force) the premises or other place named or specified in the warrant, to search such premises or other place, to examine anything found there, to inspect any records found there and, if there are reasonable grounds for suspecting that any records found there are material to the proper assessment or collection of tax, or that the records may be required for the purpose of any legal proceedings instituted by an officer of the Revenue Commissioners or for the purpose of any criminal proceedings, remove such records and retain them for so long as they are reasonably required for the purpose aforesaid.][4]

(3) A person who does not comply with any requirement of an authorised officer in the exercise or performance of the authorised officer's powers or duties under this section shall be liable to a penalty of [€1,265][5].

(4) An authorised officer when exercising or performing his or her powers or duties under this section shall on request show his or her authorisation for the purposes of this section.

Amendments

1 Defintion of "records" substituted by FA 2002 s 132(*d*) with effect from 25 March 2002.

2 Substituted by SDCA 1999 s 162 and Sch 4 with effect from 15 December 1999; previously "section 16 of the Stamp Act, 1891".

3 Subs (2)(*d*) deleted by FA 1999 s 207(*f*)(i) with effect from 25 March 1999.

4 Subs (2A) inserted by FA 1999 s 207(*f*)(ii) with effect from 25 March 1999.

5 Substituted by FA 2001 s 240(1) and (2)(*k*) and Sch 5 Pt 1 as respects any act or omission which takes place or begins on or after 1 January 2002; previously "£1,000".

Cross-references

Authorised officers and Garda Síochána: s 906.
This section to be construed together with the Customs Acts, in so far as relating to customs: s 1104(2).
This section to be construed together with the Value Added Tax Acts 1972–1997, in so far as relating to value added tax: s 1104(3).
This section to be construed together with the Stamp Act 1891 and the enactments amending or extending that Act, in so far as relating to stamp duties: s 1104(4).
This section to be construed together with the Capital Acquisitions Tax Act 1976, and the enactments amending or extending that Act, in so far as relating to capital acquisitions tax: s 1104(5).
This section to be construed together with FA 1983 Pt VI and the enactments amending or extending that Part, in so far as relating to residential property tax: s 1104(6).

Revenue information

Information leaflet IT32 — Revenue Audit — Guide for Small Businesses.
Finance Act 1999 — Revenue Powers: Guidance Notes and Instructions, May 1999.
Code of Practice for Revenue Auditors — August 2002 (may be downloaded from Revenue's website at www.revenue.ie).

Statement of practice

Revenue powers: SP GEN/1/94, May 1994.
Revenue Powers (Finance Act 1999): SP GEN/1/99, May 1999.
Revenue Internal Review Procedures — Audit and Use of Powers: SP GEN/2/99, May 1999.

Tax Briefing

TB49 Aug 2002 pp 6–13 — Code of Practice Revenue Audits.

Case law

Held was a clear implication that the time and place for such inspection set by the taxpayer had to be reasonable: *Johnson v IRC* [1996] STI 270.

Definitions

oath: IA 1937 Sch; person: IA 1937 s 11(*c*); profession: ss 2(1), 5(1); trade: ss 3(1), 4(1), 5(1).

Former enactments

FA 1976 s 34; FA 1992 s 232.

---

906 Authorised officers and Garda Síochána

Where an authorised officer (within the meaning of section 903, 904 or 905, as the case may be) in accordance with section 903, 904 or 905 enters any premises or place, the authorised officer may be accompanied by a member or members of the Garda Síochána, and any such member may arrest without warrant any person who obstructs or interferes with the authorised officer in the exercise or performance of his or her powers or duties under any of those sections.

Cross-references

This section to be construed together with the Customs Acts, in so far as relating to customs: s 1104(2).

This section to be construed together with the Value Added Tax Acts 1972–1997, in so far as relating to value added tax: s 1104(3).

This section to be construed together with the Stamp Act 1891 and the enactments amending or extending that Act, in so far as relating to stamp duties: s 1104(4).

This section to be construed together with the Capital Acquisitions Tax Act 1976, and the enactments amending or extending that Act, in so far as relating to capital acquisitions tax: s 1104(5).

This section to be construed together with FA 1983 Pt VI and the enactments amending or extending that Part, in so far as relating to residential property tax: s 1104(6).

Revenue information

Code of Practice for Revenue Auditors — August 2002 (may be downloaded from Revenue's website at www.revenue.ie).

Statement of practice

Revenue Powers: SP GEN/1/94, May 1994.

Tax Briefing

TB49 Aug 2002 pp 6–13 — Code of Practice Revenue Audits.

Former enactments

FA 1992 s 236.

906A Information to be furnished by financial institutions

[(1) In this section and in sections 907 and 908—

"the Acts" has the meaning assigned to it by section 1078(1);

"authorised officer" means an officer of the Revenue Commissioners authorised by them in writing to exercise the powers conferred by this section, or, as the case may be, section 907 or 908;

"books, records or other documents" includes—

(*a*) any records used in the business of a financial institution, or used in the transfer department of a financial institution acting as registrar of securities, whether—

(i) comprised in bound volume, loose-leaf binders or other loose-leaf filing system, loose-leaf ledger sheets, pages, folios or cards, or

(ii) kept on microfilm, magnetic tape or in any non-legible form (by the use of electronics or otherwise) which is capable of being reproduced in a legible form,

(*b*) every electronic or other automatic means, if any, by which any such thing in non-legible form is so capable of being reproduced,

(*c*) documents in manuscript, documents which are typed, printed, stencilled or created by any other mechanical or partly mechanical process in use from time to time and documents which are produced by any photographic or photostatic process, and

(*d*) correspondence and records of other communications between a financial institution and its customers;

"connected person" has the same meaning as in section 10; but an individual (other than in the capacity as a trustee of a settlement) shall be connected with another individual only if that other individual is the spouse of or a minor child of the first-mentioned individual;

"deposit" and **"interest"** have, respectively, the meaning assigned to them by section 256(1);

[**"financial institution"** means—

(*a*) a person who holds or has held a licence under section 9 of the Central Bank Act, 1971,

(*b*) a person referred to in section 7(4) of the Central Bank Act, 1971, or

(*c*) a credit institution (within the meaning of the European Communities (Licensing and Supervision of Credit Institutions) Regulations, 1992 (SI No 395 of 1992)) which has been authorised by the Central Bank of Ireland to carry on business of a credit institution in accordance with the provisions of the supervisory enactments (within the meaning of those Regulations);][1]

"liability" in relation to a person means any liability in relation to tax to which the person is or may be, or may have been, subject, or the amount of such liability;

"tax" means any tax, duty, levy or charge under the care and management of the Revenue Commissioners.

(2) Notwithstanding any obligation as to secrecy or other restriction upon disclosure of information imposed by or under statute or otherwise, and subject to this section, an authorised officer may, for the purpose of enquiring into a liability in relation to a person (in this section referred to as the **"taxpayer"**), serve on a financial institution a notice in writing requiring the financial institution, within such period as may be specified in the notice, not being less than 30 days from the date of the service of the notice, to do either or both of the following, namely—

(*a*) to make available for inspection by the authorised officer such books, records or other documents as are in the financial institution's power, possession or procurement and as contain, or may (in the authorised officer's opinion formed on reasonable grounds) contain, information relevant to a liability in relation to the taxpayer,

(*b*) to furnish to the authorised officer, in writing or otherwise, such information, explanations and particulars as the authorised officer may reasonably require, being information, explanations and particulars that are relevant to any such liability,

and which are specified in the notice.

(3) Where, in compliance with the requirements of a notice under subsection (2), a financial institution makes available for inspection by an authorised officer, books, records or other documents, it shall afford the authorised officer reasonable assistance, including information, explanations and particulars, in relation to the use of all the electronic or other automatic means, if any, by which the books, records or other documents, in so far as they are in a non-legible form, are capable of being reproduced in a legible form and any data equipment or any associated apparatus or material.

(4) An authorised officer shall not serve a notice on a financial institution under subsection (2) without the consent in writing of a Revenue Commissioner and without having reasonable grounds to believe that the financial institution is likely to have information relevant to a liability in relation to the taxpayer.

(5) Without prejudice to the generality of subsection (2), the books, records or other documents which a financial institution may be required by notice under that subsection to deliver or to make available and the information, explanations and particulars which it may likewise be required to furnish, may include books, records or other documents and information, explanations and particulars relating to a person who is connected with the taxpayer.

(6) The persons who may be treated as a taxpayer for the purposes of this section include a company which has been dissolved and an individual who has died.

(7) A notice served under subsection (2) shall name the taxpayer in relation to whose liability the authorised officer is enquiring.

(8) Where an authorised officer serves a notice under subsection (2), a copy of such notice shall be given by the authorised officer to the taxpayer concerned.

(9) Where, in compliance with a notice served under subsection (2), a financial institution makes books, records or other documents available for inspection by an authorised officer, the authorised officer may make extracts from or copies of all or any part of the books, records or other documents.

(10) A financial institution which fails or refuses to comply with a notice issued under subsection (2) or which fails or refuses to afford reasonable assistance to an authorised officer as required under subsection (3), shall be liable to a penalty of [€19,045][2] and, if the failure or refusal to comply with such notice continues after the expiry of the period specified in the notice served under subsection (2), a further penalty of [€2,535][3] for each day on which the failure or refusal continues.][4]

Amendments

1 Definition of "financial institution" substituted by FA 2000 s 68(*c*) with effect from 6 April 2000.

2 Substituted by FA 2001 s 240(1) and (2)(*k*) and Sch 5 Pt 1 as respects any act or omission which takes place or begins on or after 1 January 2002; previously "£15,000".

3 Substituted by FA 2001 s 240(1) and (2)(*k*) and Sch 5 Pt 1 as respects any act or omission which takes place or begins on or after 1 January 2002; previously "£2,000".

4 Section 906A inserted by FA 1999 s 207(*g*) with effect from 25 March 1999.

Cross-references

Application to High Court: information from third party, meaning of "financial institution" applied: s 902A(2).

Information for tax authorities in other territories, this section is to have effect as if references to tax included references to foreign tax (within meaning of TCA 1997 s 912A(1)) and as if references to liability, in relation to a person, included liability to foreign tax (within meaning of TCA 1997 s 912A(1)) in relation to a person: s 912A(2).

Information to be furnished by third party: request of an authorised officer, meaning of "financial institution" applied: s 902(2).

Interest in respect of wholesale debt instruments, meaning of "financial institution" applied: s 246A(1).

Relief for lessors in respect of expenditure incurred on the provision of certain residential premises, qualifying premises and special qualifying premises, meaning of "financial institution" applied: s 372AM(9A)(*b*)(i).

Revenue information

Finance Act 1999 — Revenue Powers: Guidance Notes and Instructions, May 1999.
Code of Practice for Revenue Auditors — August 2002 (may be downloaded from Revenue's website at www.revenue.ie).

Statement of practice

Revenue Powers (Finance Act 1999): SP GEN/1/99, May 1999.
Revenue Internal Review Procedures — Audit and Use of Powers: SP GEN/2/99, May 1999.

Tax Briefing

TB49 Aug 2002 pp 6–13 — Code of Practice Revenue Audits.

Definitions

company: ss 4(1), 5(1); person: IA 1937 s 11(*c*); writing: IA 1937 Sch.

907 Application to Appeal Commissioners: information from financial institutions

[(1) In this section **"a taxpayer"** means any person including—

(*a*) a person whose identity is not known to the authorised officer, and a group or class of persons whose individual identities are not so known, and

(*b*) a person by or in respect of whom a declaration has been made under section 263(1) declaring that the person is beneficially entitled to all or part of the interest in relation to a deposit.

(2) An authorised officer may, subject to this section, make an application to the Appeal Commissioners for their consent, under subsection (5), to the service by him or her of a notice on a financial institution requiring the financial institution to do either or both of the following, namely—

(*a*) to make available for inspection by the authorised officer, such books, records or other documents as are in the financial institution's power, possession or procurement as contain, or may (in the authorised officer's opinion formed on reasonable grounds) contain, information relevant to a liability in relation to a taxpayer,

(*b*) to furnish to the authorised officer such information, explanations and particulars as the authorised officer may reasonably require, being information, explanations and particulars that are relevant to any such liability,

and which are specified in the application.

(3) An authorised officer shall not make an application under subsection (2) without the consent in writing of a Revenue Commissioner, and without being satisfied—

(*a*) that there are reasonable grounds for suspecting that the taxpayer, or where the taxpayer is a group or class of persons, all or any one of those persons, may have failed or may fail to comply with any provision of the Acts,

(*b*) that any such failure is likely to have led or to lead to serious prejudice to the proper assessment or collection of tax (having regard to the amount of a liability in relation to the taxpayer, or where the taxpayer is a group or class of persons, the amount of a liability in relation to all or any one of those persons, that arises or might arise from such failure), and

(*c*) that the information—

(i) which is likely to be contained in the books, records or other documents to which the application relates, or

(ii) which is likely to arise from the information, explanations and particulars to which the application relates,

is relevant to the proper assessment or collection of tax.

(4) Without prejudice to the generality of subsection (2), the authorised officer may make an application under that subsection to the Appeal Commissioners for their consent, under subsection (5), to the service by him or her of a notice on a financial institution in respect of the matters referred to in paragraphs (*a*) and (*b*) of subsection (2) in so far as they relate to a person who is connected with the taxpayer.

(5) Where the Appeal Commissioners determine that in all the circumstances there are reasonable grounds for the application being made, they may give their consent to the service by the authorised officer concerned of a notice on the financial institution, requiring the financial institution—

(*a*) to make available for inspection by the authorised officer, such books, records or other documents, and

(*b*) to furnish to the authorised officer such information, explanations and particulars,

of the kind referred to in subsection (2) as may, with the Appeal Commissioners' consent, be specified in the notice.

(6) The persons who may be treated as a taxpayer for the purposes of this section include a company which has been dissolved and an individual who has died.

(7) Where the Appeal Commissioners have given their consent in accordance with this section, the authorised officer shall, as soon as practicable, but not later than 14 days from the time that such consent was given, serve a notice on the financial institution concerned and stating that—

(*a*) such consent has been given, and

(*b*) the financial institution should, within a period of 30 days from the date of the service of the notice, comply with the requirements specified in the notice.

[(7A) Where in compliance with the requirements of a notice served under subsection (7), a financial institution makes available for inspection by an authorised officer, books, records or other documents, the financial institution shall afford the authorised officer reasonable assistance, including information, explanations and particulars, in relation to the use of all the electronic or other automatic means, if any, by which the books, records or other documents, in so far as they are in a non-legible form, are capable of being reproduced in a legible form, and any data equipment or any associated apparatus or material.

(7B) Where in compliance with the requirements of a notice served under subsection (7), a financial institution makes books, records or other documents available for inspection by the authorised officer, the authorised officer may make extracts from or copies of all or any part of the books, records or other documents.][1]

(8) (*a*) Subject to paragraph (*b*), an application by an authorised officer under subsection (2) shall, with any necessary modifications, be heard by the Appeal Commissioners as if it were an appeal against an assessment to income tax.

(*b*) Notwithstanding section 933(4), a determination by the Appeal Commissioners under this section shall be final and conclusive.

(9) A financial institution which fails to comply with a notice served on the financial institution by an authorised officer in accordance with this section shall be liable to a penalty of [€19,045][2] and, if the failure continues after the expiry of the period specified in subsection (7)(*b*), a further penalty of [€2,535][3] for each day on which the failure so continues.][4]

Amendments

1 Subss (7A)–(7B) inserted by FA 2002 s 130(1)(*e*) with effect from 25 March 2002.

2 Substituted by FA 2001 s 240(1) and (2)(*k*) and Sch 5 Pt 1 as respects any act or omission which takes place or begins on or after 1 January 2002; previously "£15,000".

3 Substituted by FA 2001 s 240(1) and (2)(*k*) and Sch 5 Pt 1 as respects any act or omission which takes place or begins on or after 1 January 2002; previously "£2,000".

4 Subs 907 substituted by FA 1999 s 207(*h*) with effect from 25 March 1999.

Cross-references

Information for tax authorities in other territories, this section to have effect as if references to tax included references to foreign tax (within meaning of TCA 1997 s 912A(1)) and as if reference to liability, in relation to a person, included liability to foreign tax (within meaning of TCA 1997 s 912A(1)) in relation to a person; but where this section has effect by virtue only of TCA 1997 s 912A, this section is to have effect as if "a 'taxpayer' means a person;" were substituted for the definition of "a taxpayer" in subs (1) and as if references in this section to tax were references to foreign tax and references to any provision of the Acts were references to any provision of the law of a territory in accordance with which foreign tax is charged or collected: s 912(2),(3).
Information to be furnished by financial institution: s 906A(1) (authorised officer).
Revenue offences: s 1078(2)(*hh*)(ii).

Revenue information

Finance Act 1999 — Revenue Powers: Guidance Notes and Instructions, May 1999.
Code of Practice for Revenue Auditors — August 2002 (may be downloaded from Revenue's website at www.revenue.ie).

Statement of practice

Revenue Powers (Finance Act 1999): SP GEN/1/99, May 1999.
Revenue Internal Review Procedures — Audit and Use of Powers: SP GEN/2/99, May 1999.

Definitions

the Acts: s 906A(1); Appeal Commissioners: s 2(1); authorised officer: s 906A(1); books, records or other documents: s 906A(1); company: ss 4(1), 5(1); connected person: s 906A(1); deposit: s 906A(1); interest: s 906A(1); financial institution: s 906A(1); liability: s 906A(1); profession: s 2(1); person: IA 1937 s 11(*c*); tax: s 906A(1); writing: IA 1937 Sch.

Tax Briefing

TB49 Aug 2002 pp 6–13 — Code of Practice Revenue Audits.

Former enactments

WCTIPA 1993 s 13.

908 Application to High Court seeking order requiring information: financial institutions

[(1) In this section—

"judge" means a judge of the High Court;

"a taxpayer" means any person including—

(*a*) a person whose identity is not known to the authorised officer, and a group or class of persons whose individual identities are not so known, and (*b*) a person by or in respect of whom a declaration has been made under section 263(1) declaring that the person is beneficially entitled to all or part of the interest in relation to a deposit.

(2) An authorised officer may, subject to this section, make an application to a judge for an order requiring a financial institution, to do either or both of the following, namely—

(*a*) to make available for inspection by the authorised officer, such books, records or other documents as are in the financial institution's power, possession or procurement as contain, or may (in the authorised officer's opinion formed on reasonable grounds) contain information relevant to a liability in relation to a taxpayer,

(*b*) to furnish to the authorised officer such information, explanations and particulars as the authorised officer may reasonably require, being information, explanations and particulars that are relevant to any such liability,

and which are specified in the application.

(3) An authorised officer shall not make application under subsection (2) without the consent in writing of a Revenue Commissioner, and without being satisfied—

(*a*) that there are reasonable grounds for suspecting that the taxpayer, or, where the taxpayer is a group or class of persons, all or any one of those persons, may have failed or may fail to comply with any provision of the Acts,

(*b*) that any such failure is likely to have led or to lead to serious prejudice to the proper assessment or collection of tax (having regard to the amount of a liability in relation to the taxpayer, or where the taxpayer is a group or class of persons, the amount of a liability in relation to all or any one of them, that arises or might arise from such failure), and

(*c*) that the information—

(i) which is likely to be contained in the books, records or other documents to which the application relates, or

(ii) which is likely to arise from the information, explanations and particulars to which the application relates,

is relevant to the proper assessment or collection of tax.

(4) Without prejudice to the generality of subsection (2), the authorised officer may make an application under that subsection to the judge for an order in respect of the matters referred to in paragraphs (*a*) and (*b*) of that subsection in so far as they relate to a person who is connected with the taxpayer.

(5) Where the judge, to whom an application is made under subsection (2), is satisfied that there are reasonable grounds for the application being made, the judge may, subject to such conditions as he or she may consider proper and specify in the order, make an order requiring the financial institution—

(*a*) to make available for inspection by the authorised officer, such books, records or other documents, and

(*b*) to furnish to the authorised officer such information, explanations and particulars,

as may be specified in the order.

(6) The persons who may be treated as a taxpayer for the purposes of this section include a company which has been dissolved and an individual who has died.

[(6A) Where in compliance with an order made under subsection (5), a financial institution makes available for inspection by an authorised officer, books, records or other documents, the financial institution shall afford the authorised officer reasonable assistance, including information, explanations and particulars, in relation to the use of all the electronic or other automatic means, if any, by which the books, records or other documents, in so far as they are in a non-legible form, are capable of being reproduced in a legible form, and any data equipment or any associated apparatus or material.

(6B) Where in compliance with an order made under subsection (5), a financial institution makes books, records or other documents available for inspection by the authorised officer, the authorised officer may make extracts from or copies of all or any part of the books, records or other documents.][1]

(7) Every hearing of an application for an order under this section and of any appeal in connection with that application shall be held in camera.

(8) Where a judge makes an order under this section, he or she may also, on the application of the authorised officer concerned, make a further order prohibiting, for such period as the judge may consider proper and specify in the order, any transfer of, or any dealing with, without the consent of the judge, any assets or moneys of the person to whom the order relates that are in the custody of the financial institution at the time the order is made.

(9) (*a*) Where—

(i) a copy of any affidavit and exhibits grounding an application under subsection (2) or (8) and any order made under subsection (5) or (8) are to be made available to the taxpayer, or the taxpayer's solicitor or to the financial institution or the financial institution's solicitor, as the case may be, and

(ii) the judge is satisfied on the hearing of the application that there are reasonable grounds in the public interest that such copy of an affidavit, exhibits or order, as the case may be, should not include the name or address of the authorised officer,

such copy, or copies or order shall not include the name or address of the authorised officer.

(*b*) Where, on any application to the judge to vary or discharge an order made under this section, it is desired to cross-examine the deponent of any affidavit filed by or on behalf of the authorised officer and the judge is satisfied that there are reasonable grounds in the public interest to so order, the judge shall order either or both of the following—

(i) that the name and address of the authorised officer shall not be disclosed in court, and

(ii) that such cross-examination shall only take place in the sight and hearing of the judge and in the hearing only of all other persons present at such cross-examination.][2]

Amendments

1 Subss (6A)–(6B) inserted by FA 2002 s 132(1)(*f*) with effect from 25 March 2002.

2 Section 908 substituted by FA 1999 s 207(*i*) with effect from 25 March 1999.

Case law

A prior demand for a return of income must have been made before any official application for an order is allowable: *JB O'C v PCD and another* ITR Vol III p 153. See also *In the matter of G O'C and A O'C* (Supreme Court, Keane J, 22 May 1996).

Cross-references

Information for tax authorities in other territories, this section to have effect as if references to tax included references to foreign tax (within meaning of TCA 1997 s 912A(1)) and as if reference to liability, in relation to a person, included liability to foreign tax (within meaning of TCA 1997 s 912A(1)) in relation to a person; but where this section has effect by virtue only of TCA 1997 s 912A, this section is to have effect as if "a 'taxpayer' means a person;" were substituted for the definition of "a taxpayer" in subs (1) and as if references in this section to tax were references to foreign tax and references to any provision of the Acts were references to any provision of the law of a territory in accordance with which foreign tax is charged or collected: s 912(2),(3).
Information to be furnished by financial institutions: s 906A(1) (authorised officer).

Revenue information

Finance Act 1999 — Revenue Powers: Guidance Notes and Instructions, May 1999.
Code of Practice for Revenue Auditors — August 2002 (may be downloaded from Revenue's website at www.revenue.ie).

Statement of practice

Revenue Powers (Finance Act 1999): SP GEN/1/99, May 1999.
Revenue Internal Review Procedures — Audit and Use of Powers: SP GEN/2/99, May 1999.

Tax Briefing

TB49 Aug 2002 pp 6–13 — Code of Practice Revenue Audits.

Definitions

the Acts: s 906A(1); affidavit: IA 1937 Sch; authorised officer: s 906A(1); books, records or other documents: s 906A(1); company: ss 4(1), 5(1); connected person: s 906A(1); financial institution: s 906A(1), liability: s 906A(1), tax: s 906A(1); writing: IA 1937 Sch.

Former enactments

FA 1983 s 18; DCITPA1996 s 10.

908A Revenue offence: power to obtain information from financial institutions

[(1) In this section—

"authorised officer" means an officer of the Revenue Commissioners authorised by them in writing to exercise the powers conferred by this section;

[**"the Acts"** means the Waiver of Certain Tax, Interest and Penalties Act, 1993, together with the meaning assigned to it by section 1078(1) and;][1]

"books, records or other documents" includes—

(*a*) any records used in the business of a financial institution, or used in the transfer department of a financial institution acting as registrar of securities, whether—

(i) comprised in bound volume, loose-leaf binders or other loose-leaf filing system, loose-leaf ledger sheets, pages, folios or cards, or

(ii) kept on microfilm, magnetic tape or in any non-legible form (by the use of electronics or otherwise) which is capable of being reproduced in a legible form, and (*c*) documents in manuscript, documents which are typed, printed, stencilled or created by any other mechanical or partly mechanical process in use from time to time and documents which are produced by any photographic or photostatic process;

"judge" means a judge of the Circuit Court or of the District Court;

[**"financial institution"** means—

(*a*) a person who holds or has held a licence under section 9 of the Central Bank Act, 1971,

(*b*) a person referred to in section 7(4) of the Central Bank Act, 1971, or

(*c*) a credit institution (within the meaning of the European Communities (Licensing and Supervision of Credit Institutions) Regulations, 1992 (SI No 395 of 1992)) which has been authorised by the Central Bank of Ireland to carry on business of a credit institution in accordance with the provisions of the supervisory enactments (within the meaning of those Regulations);][2]

"liability" in relation to a person means any liability in relation to tax to which the person is or may be, or may have been, subject, or the amount of such liability;

[**"offence"** means an offence falling within any provision of the Acts;][3]

"tax" means any tax, duty, levy or charge under the care and management of the Revenue Commissioners.

[(2) (*a*) In this subsection **"documentation"** includes information kept on microfilm, magnetic tape or in any non-legible form (by use of electronics or otherwise) which is capable of being reproduced in a permanent legible form.

(*b*) If, on application made by an authorised officer, with the consent in writing of a Revenue Commissioner, a judge is satisfied, on information given on oath by the authorised officer, that there are reasonable grounds for suspecting—

(i) that an offence, which would result (or but for its detection would have resulted) in serious prejudice to the proper assessment or collection of tax, is being, has been, or is about to be committed (having regard to the amount of a liability in relation to any person which might be, or might have been, evaded but for the detection of the relevant facts), and

(ii) that there is material in the possession of a financial institution specified in the application which is likely to be of substantial value (whether by itself or together with other material) to the investigation of the relevant facts,

the judge may make an order authorising the authorised officer to inspect and take copies of any entries in the books, records or other documents of the financial institution, and any documentation associated with or relating to an entry in such books, records or other documents, for the purposes of investigation of the relevant facts.][4]

(3) An offence the commission of which, if considered alone, would not be regarded as resulting in serious prejudice to the proper assessment or collection of tax for the purposes of this section may nevertheless be so regarded if there are reasonable grounds for suspecting that the commission of the offence forms part of a course of conduct which is, or but for its detection would be, likely to result in serious prejudice to the proper assessment or collection of tax.

(4) Subject to subsection (5), a copy of any entry in books, records or other documents of a financial institution shall in all legal proceedings be received as prima facie evidence of such an entry, and of the matters, transactions, and accounts therein recorded.

(5) A copy of an entry in the books, records or other documents of a financial institution shall not be received in evidence in legal proceedings unless it is further proved that—

(*a*) in the case where the copy sought to be received in evidence has been reproduced in a legible form directly by either mechanical or electronic means, or both such means, from a financial institution's books, records or other documents maintained in a non-legible form, it has been so reproduced;

(*b*) in the case where the copy sought to be received in evidence has been made (either directly or indirectly) from a copy to which paragraph (*a*) would apply—

(i) the copy sought to be so received has been examined with a copy so reproduced and is a correct copy, and

(ii) the copy so reproduced is a copy to which paragraph (*a*) would apply if it were sought to have it received in evidence,

and

(*c*) in any other case, the copy has been examined with the original entry and is correct.

(6) Proof of the matters to which subsection (5) relates shall be given—

(*a*) in respect of paragraph (*a*) or (*b*)(ii) of that subsection, by some person who has been in charge of the reproduction concerned, and

(*b*) in respect of paragraph (*b*)(i) of that subsection, by some person who has examined the copy with the reproduction concerned, and

(*c*) in respect of paragraph (*c*) of that subsection, by some person who has examined the copy with the original entry concerned, and

and may be given either orally or by an affidavit sworn before any commissioner or person authorised to take affidavits.][5]

Amendments

1 Definition of "the Acts" inserted by FA 2002 s 132(1)(*g*)(i)(I) with effect from 25 March 2002.

2 Definition of "financial institution" substituted by FA 2000 s 68(*c*) with effect from 6 April 2000.

3 Definition of "offence" substituted by FA 2002 s 132(1)(*g*)(i)(II) with effect from 25 March 2002.

4 Subs (2) substituted by FA 2004 s 88 with effect from 25 March 2004.

5 Section 908A inserted by FA 1999 s 207(*j*) with effect from 25 March 1999.

Revenue information

Finance Act 1999 — Revenue Powers: Guidance Notes and Instructions, May 1999.

Code of Practice for Revenue Auditors — August 2002 (may be downloaded from Revenue's website at www.revenue.ie).

Statement of practice

Revenue Powers (Finance Act 1999): SP GEN/1/99, May 1999.

Revenue Internal Review Procedures — Audit and Use of Powers: SP GEN/2/99, May 1999.

Tax Briefing

TB49 Aug 2002 pp 6–13 — Code of Practice Revenue Audits.

Definitions

Circuit Court: IA 1937 Sch; District Court: IA 1937 Sch; person: IA 1937 s 11(*c*); writing: IA 1937 Sch.

908B Application to High Court seeking order requiring information: associated institutions

[(1) In this section—

"the Acts" has the meaning assigned to it by section 1078(1);

"associated institution", in relation to a financial institution, means a person that—

(*a*) is controlled by the financial institution (within the meaning of section 432), and

(*b*) is not resident in the State;

"authorised officer" means an officer of the Revenue Commissioners authorised by them in writing to exercise the powers conferred by this section;

"books, records or other documents" includes—

(*a*) any records used in the business of an associated institution, or used in the transfer department of an associated institution acting as registrar of securities, whether—

(i) comprised in bound volume, loose-leaf binders or other loose-leaf filing system, loose-leaf ledger sheets, pages, folios or cards, or

(ii) kept on microfilm, magnetic tape or in any non-legible form (by the use of electronics or otherwise) which is capable of being reproduced in a legible form,

(*b*) every electronic or other automatic means, if any, by which any such thing in non-legible form is so capable of being reproduced,

(*c*) documents in manuscript, documents which are typed, printed, stencilled or created by any other mechanical or partly mechanical process in use from time to time and documents which are produced by any photographic or photostatic process, and

(*d*) correspondence and records of other communications between an associated institution and its customers;

"financial institution" means—

(*a*) a person who holds or has held a licence under section 9 of the Central Bank Act 1971,

(*b*) a person referred to in section 7(4) of the Central Bank Act 1971, or

(*c*) a credit institution (within the meaning of the European Communities (Licensing and Supervision of Credit Institutions) Regulations 1992 (SI No 395 of 1992)) which has been authorised by the Central Bank and Financial Services Authority of Ireland to carry on business of a credit institution in accordance with the provisions of the supervisory enactments (within the meaning of those Regulations);

"judge" means a judge of the High Court;

"liability" in relation to a person means any liability in relation to tax which the person is or may be, or may have been, subject, or the amount of such liability;

"tax" means any tax, duty, levy or charge under the care and management of the Revenue Commissioners;

"a taxpayer" means any person including a person whose identity is not known to the authorised officer, and a group or class of persons whose individual identities are not so known.

(2) An authorised officer may, subject to this section, make an application to a judge for an order requiring a financial institution to do either or both of the following, namely—

(*a*) to make available for inspection by the authorised officer, such books, records or other documents as are in the power, possession or procurement of an associated institution, in relation to the financial institution, as contain, or may (in the authorised officer's opinion formed on reasonable grounds) contain information relevant to a liability in relation to a taxpayer, or

(*b*) to furnish to the authorised officer such information, explanations and particulars held by, or available from, the financial institution or an associated institution, in relation to the financial institution, as the authorised officer may reasonably require, being information, explanations or particulars that are relevant to any such liability,

and which are specified in the application.

(3) An authorised officer shall not make an application under subsection (2) without the consent in writing of a Revenue Commissioner, and without being satisfied—

(*a*) that there are reasonable grounds for suspecting that the taxpayer, or where the taxpayer is a group or class of persons, all or any one of those persons, may have failed or may fail to comply with any provision of the Acts,

(*b*) that any such failure is likely to have led or to lead to serious prejudice to the proper assessment or collection of tax (having regard to the amount of a liability in relation to the taxpayer, or where the taxpayer is a group or class of persons, the amount of a liability, in relation to all or any one of them, that arises or might arise from such failure), and

(*c*) that the information—

(i) which is likely to be contained in the books, records or other documents to which the application relates, or

(ii) which is likely to arise from the information, explanations and particulars to which the application relates,

is relevant to the proper assessment or collection of tax.

(4) Where the judge, to whom an application is made under subsection (2), is satisfied that there are reasonable grounds for the application being made, then the judge may, subject to such conditions as he or she may consider proper and specify in the order, make an order requiring the financial institution—

(*a*) to make available for inspection by the authorised officer, such books, records or other documents, and

(*b*) to furnish to the authorised officer such information, explanations and particulars,

as may be specified in the order.

(5) The persons who may be treated as a taxpayer for the purposes of this section include a company which has been dissolved and an individual who has died.

(6) Where in compliance with an order made under subsection (4) a financial institution makes available for inspection by an authorised officer, books, records or other documents, then the financial institution shall afford the authorised officer reasonable assistance, including information, explanations and particulars, in relation to the use of all the electronic or other automatic means, if any, by which the books, records or other documents, in so far as they are in a non-legible form, are capable of being reproduced in a legible form, and any data equipment or any associated apparatus or material.

(7) Where in compliance with an order made under subsection (4) a financial institution makes books, records or other documents available for inspection by the authorised officer, then the authorised officer may make extracts from or copies of all or any part of the books, records or other documents.

(8) Every hearing of an application for an order under this section and of any appeal in connection with that application shall be held in camera.][1]

Amendments

[1] Section 908B inserted by FA 2004 s 87 with effect from 25 March 2004.

Definitions

company: ss 4(1), 5(1); High Court: IA 1937 Sch; person: IA 1937 s 11(*c*); writing: IA 1937 Sch.

909 Power to require return of property

(1) (*a*) In this section—

"asset" includes any interest in an asset;

"limited interest" means—

(i) an interest (other than a leasehold interest) for the duration of a life or lives or for a period certain, or

(ii) any other interest which is not an absolute interest;

"prescribed" means prescribed by the Revenue Commissioners;

"property" includes interests and rights of any description and, without prejudice to the generality of the foregoing, includes—

(i) in the case of a limited interest, the property in which the limited interest subsists or on which it is charged or secured or on which there exists a right to have it charged or secured,

(ii) an interest in expectancy,

(iii) an interest or share in a partnership, joint tenancy or estate of a deceased person,

(iv) stock or shares in a company which is in the course of liquidation,

(v) an annuity, and

(vi) property comprised in a settlement which the person concerned is empowered to revoke;

"settlement" has the same meaning as in section 794;

"specified date", in relation to a notice under subsection (2), means the date specified in the notice;

"tax" means income tax and capital gains tax.

(*b*) For the purposes of this section, the cost of acquisition to a person of an asset shall include—

(i) the amount or value of the consideration, in money or money's worth, given by the person or on the person's behalf for the acquisition of the asset, together with the incidental costs to the person of the acquisition or, if the asset was not acquired by the person, any expenditure incurred by the person in providing the asset, and

(ii) the amount of any expenditure incurred on the asset by the person or on the person's behalf for the purpose of enhancing the value of the asset, being expenditure reflected in the state or nature of the asset at the specified date, and any expenditure incurred by the person in establishing, preserving or defending the person's title to, or to a right over, the asset.

(2) Where for the purposes of tax a person is required under any provision of the Tax Acts or the Capital Gains Tax Acts [to deliver a tax return, an inspector of taxes or the inspector of returns (within the meaning of section 951(11)), as the case may be,][1] may require—

(*a*) that person, by notice in writing given to that person, and

(*b*) where that person and his or her spouse are, for the year of assessment to which the tax return relates, treated as living together for the purpose of section 1015, that person's spouse, by notice in writing given to the spouse,

to deliver to the inspector within the time specified in the notice or within such further period as the inspector may allow a statement of affairs in the prescribed form as at the date specified in the notice, and that person or that person's spouse shall, if required by further notice or notices in writing by the inspector, deliver to the inspector within such time, not being less than 30 days, as may be specified in such further notice or notices, a statement verifying such statement of affairs together with such evidence, statement or documents required by the inspector in respect of any asset or liability shown on the statement of affairs, or in respect of any asset or liability which the inspector has reason to believe has been omitted from the statement of affairs.

(3) (*a*) In this section, **"statement of affairs"**, in relation to a notice under subsection (2), means—

(i) where the person to whom notice is given is an individual who is a chargeable person and the tax return concerned relates to income or capital gains in respect of which that individual is chargeable to tax otherwise than in a representative capacity or as a trustee, a statement of all the assets wherever situated to which that individual is beneficially entitled on the specified date and all the liabilities for which that individual is liable on the specified date,

(ii) where the person to whom notice is given is the spouse of an individual referred to in subparagraph (i), a statement of all the assets wherever situated to which that spouse is beneficially entitled on the specified date and all the liabilities for which that spouse is liable on the specified date,

(iii) where the person to whom notice is given is a chargeable person in a representative capacity and the tax return concerned relates to income or capital gains of a person (in this paragraph referred to as **"the second-mentioned person"**) in respect of which that chargeable person is so chargeable, a statement of all the assets wherever situated to which the second-mentioned person is beneficially entitled and which give rise to income or capital gains in respect of which that chargeable person is chargeable to tax in a representative capacity and all the liabilities for which the second-mentioned person is liable, or which are assets or liabilities in relation to which that chargeable person performs functions or duties in such a capacity on the specified date, or

(iv) where the person to whom notice is given is a chargeable person as a trustee of a trust and the tax return concerned relates to income or capital gains of a trust, a statement of all the assets and liabilities comprised in the trust on the specified date.

(*b*) Any assets to which a minor child of an individual referred to in subparagraph (i) or (ii) of paragraph (*a*) is beneficially entitled shall be included in that individual's statement of affairs under this section where—

(i) such assets at any time before their acquisition by the minor child were disposed of by that individual whether to the minor child or not, or

(ii) the consideration for the acquisition of such assets by the minor child was provided directly or indirectly by that individual.

(4) (*a*) A statement of affairs delivered under this section shall contain in relation to each asset included in the statement—

(i) a full description,

(ii) its location on the specified date,

(iii) the cost of acquisition to the person beneficially entitled to that asset,

(iv) [the date of acquisition,][2]

(v) if it was acquired otherwise than by means of a bargain at arm's length, the name and address of the person from whom it was acquired and the consideration, if any, [given to that person in respect of its acquisition, and][3]

[(vi) details of all policies of insurance (if any) whereby the risk of any kind of damage or injury, or the loss or depreciation of the asset is insured.][4]

(*b*) A statement of affairs delivered under this section shall, in the case of an asset which is an interest other than an absolute interest, contain particulars of the title under which the beneficial entitlement arises.

(*c*) A statement of affairs delivered under this section shall be signed by the person by whom it is delivered and shall include a declaration by that person that it is to the best of that person's knowledge, information and belief correct and complete.

(*d*) The Revenue Commissioners may require the declaration mentioned in paragraph (*c*) to be made on oath.

Amendments

1 Substituted by FA 2001 s 78(2)(*g*) for the short tax "year" 2001 and later tax years (income tax and capital gains tax) and as respects accounting periods of companies ending on or after 1 April 2001; previously "to deliver a tax return to an inspector of taxes or to the inspector of returns (within the meaning of section 951(11)), as the case may be, the inspector".

2 Substituted by FA 1999 s 207(*k*)(i); previously "the date of acquisition, and" with effect from 25 March 1999.

3 Substituted by FA 1999 s 207(*k*)(ii); previously "given to that person in respect of its acquisition." with effect from 25 March 1999.

4 Subs (4)(*a*)(vi) inserted by FA 1999 s 207(*k*)(iii) with effect from 25 March 1999.

Cross-references

Penalty: Sch 29 column 2.

Revenue information

Finance Act 1999 — Revenue Powers: Guidance Notes and Instructions, May 1999.

Code of Practice for Revenue Auditors — August 2002 (may be downloaded from Revenue's website at www.revenue.ie).

Statement of practice

Revenue Powers (Finance Act 1999): SP GEN/1/99, May 1999.

Revenue Internal Review Procedures — Audit and Use of Powers: SP GEN/2/99, May 1999.

Tax Briefing

TB49 Aug 2002 pp 6–13 — Code of Practice Revenue Audits.

Definitions

company: ss 4(1), 5(1); inspector: ss 2(1), 5(1), 852; oath: IA 1937 Sch; settlement: s 5(1); writing: IA 1937 Sch; year of assessment: ss 2(1), 5(1).

Former enactments

FA 1983 s 20; FA 1992 s 239.

910 Power to obtain information from Minister of the Government

[(1) For the purposes of the assessment, charge, collection and recovery of any tax or duty placed under their care and management, the Revenue Commissioners may, by notice in writing, request any Minister of the Government or any body established by or under statute to provide them with such information in the possession of that Minister or body in relation to payments for any purposes made by that Minister or by that body, whether on that Minister's or that body's own behalf or on behalf of any other person, to such persons or classes of persons as the Revenue Commissioners may specify in the notice and a Minister of the Government or body of whom or of which such a request is made shall provide such information as may be so specified.][1]

(2) The Revenue Commissioners may nominate any of their officers to perform any acts and discharge any functions authorised by this section to be performed or discharged by the Revenue Commissioners.

Amendments

1 Subs (1) substituted by FA 1999 s 208 with effect from 25 March 1999.

Cross-references

This section to be construed together with the Customs Acts, in so far as relating to customs: s 1104(2).

This section to be construed together with the Value Added Tax Acts 1972–1997, in so far as relating to value added tax: s 1104(3).

This section to be construed together with the Stamp Act 1891 and the enactments amending or extending that Act, in so far as relating to stamp duties: s 1104(4).

This section to be construed together with the Capital Acquisitions Tax Act 1976, and the enactments amending or extending that Act, in so far as relating to capital acquisitions tax: s 1104(5).
This section to be construed together with FA 1983 Pt VI and the enactments amending or extending that Part, in so far as relating to residential property tax: s 1104(6).

Definitions

person: IA 1937 s 11(*c*); tax: s 3(1); writing: IA 1937 Sch.

Former enactments

FA 1995 s 175.

911 Valuation of assets: power to inspect

(1) For the purposes of the Capital Gains Tax Acts, an inspector or other officer mentioned in section 931(1) shall be authorised to inspect any property for the purpose of ascertaining its market value and the person having the custody or possession of that property shall permit the inspector or other officer so authorised, on producing if so required evidence of his or her authority, to inspect it at such reasonable times as the Revenue Commissioners may consider necessary.

(2) Section 1057 shall apply to an inspector or other officer referred to in subsection (1) and to a person acting in the aid of such an inspector or officer as it applies in relation to the persons referred to in paragraphs (*a*) and (*b*) of subsection (1) of that section.

Definitions

inspector: ss 2(1), 5(1), 852; person: IA 1937 s 11(*c*).

Former enactments

CGTA 1975 s 51(1) and Sch 4 para 14.

Corresponding UK tax provision

Taxes Management Act 1970 s 111.

912 Computer documents and records

(1) In this section—

"the Acts" means—

(*a*) the Customs Acts,
(*b*) the statutes relating to the duties of excise and to the management of those duties,
(*c*) the Tax Acts,
(*d*) the Capital Gains Tax Acts,
(*e*) the Value-Added Tax Act, 1972, and the enactments amending or extending that Act,
(*f*) the [Capital Acquisitions Tax Consolidation Act 2003],[1] and the enactments amending or extending that Act, and
(*g*) Part VI of the Finance Act, 1983,

and any instruments made thereunder;

"data" means information in a form in which it can be processed;

"data equipment" means any electronic, photographic, magnetic, optical or other equipment for processing data;

"processing" means performing automatically logical or arithmetical operations on data, or the storing, maintenance, transmission, reproduction or communication of data;

"records" means documents which a person is obliged by any provision of the Acts to keep, issue or produce for inspection, and any other written or printed material;

"software" means any sequence of instructions used in conjunction with data equipment for the purpose of processing data or controlling the operation of the data equipment.

(2) Any provision under the Acts which—

(*a*) requires a person to keep, retain, issue or produce any records or cause any records to be kept, retained, issued or produced, or

(*b*) permits an officer of the Revenue Commissioners—

(i) to inspect any records,

(ii) to enter premises and search for any records, or

(iii) to take extracts from or copies of or remove any records,

shall, where the records are processed by data equipment, apply to the data equipment together with any associated software, data, apparatus or material as it applies to the records.

(3) An officer of the Revenue Commissioners may in the exercise or performance of his or her powers or duties require—

(*a*) the person by or on whose behalf the data equipment is or has been used, or

(*b*) any person having charge of, or otherwise concerned with the operation of, the data equipment or any associated apparatus or material,

to afford him or her all reasonable assistance in relation to the exercise or performance of those powers or duties.

Amendments

1 Substituted by CATCA 2003 s 119 and Sch 3 wtih effect from 21 February 2003; previously "Capital Acquisitions Tax Act 1976".

Cross-references

This section to be construed together with the Customs Acts, in so far as relating to customs: s 1104(2).

This section to be construed together with the Value Added Tax Acts 1972–1997, in so far as relating to value added tax: s 1104(3).

This section to be construed together with the Capital Acquisitions Tax Act 1976, and the enactments amending or extending that Act, in so far as relating to capital acquisitions tax: s 1104(5).

This section to be construed together with FA 1983 Pt VI and the enactments amending or extending that Part, in so far as relating to residential property tax: s 1104(6).

Use of electronic data processing, meaning of "software" applied: s 887(5)(*a*).

Revenue information

Code of Practice for Revenue Auditors — August 2002 (may be downloaded from Revenue's website at www.revenue.ie).

Statement of practice

Revenue powers: SP GEN/1/94, May 1994.

Revenue Internal Review Procedures — Audit and Use of Powers: SP GEN/2/99, May 1999.

Tax Briefing

TB49 Aug 2002 pp 6–13 — Code of Practice Revenue Audits.

Definitions

Tax Acts: s 1(2); person: IA 1937 s 11(*c*).

Former enactments

FA 1992 s 237.

912A Information for tax authorities in other territories

[(1) In this section—

[**"foreign tax"** means a tax chargeable under the laws of a territory in relation to which arrangements (in this section referred to as "the arrangements") having the force of law by virtue of section 826, 898P(2) or section 106 of the Capital Acquisitions Tax Consolidation Act 2003 apply;][1]

"liability to foreign tax", in relation to a person, means any liability in relation to foreign tax to which the person is or may be, or may have been, subject, or the amount of any such liability.

(2) For the purposes of complying with provisions with respect to the exchange of information contained in the arrangements, sections 900, 901, 902, 902A, 906A, 907 and 908 shall, subject to subsection (3), have effect—

(*a*) as if references in those sections to tax included references to foreign tax, and

(*b*) as if references in those sections to liability, in relation to a person, included references to liability to foreign tax, in relation to a person.

(3) Where sections 902A, 907 and 908 have effect by virtue only of this section, they shall have effect as if—

(*a*) there were substituted "'**a taxpayer**' means a person;" for the definition of "a taxpayer" in subsection (1) of each of those sections, and

(*b*) the references in those sections to—

(i) tax, were references to foreign tax, and

(ii) any provision of the Acts, were references to any provision of the law of a territory in accordance with which foreign tax is charged or collected.][2]

Amendments

1 Definition of "foreign tax" substituted by FA 2005 s 144(2) with effect from 25 March 2005.

2 Section 912A inserted by FA 2003 s 38(*b*) with effect from 1 January 2003.

Definitions

person: IA 1937 s 11(*c*).

CHAPTER 5

Capital Gains Tax: Returns, Information, etc

913 Application of income tax provisions relating to returns, etc

(1) The provisions of the Income Tax Acts relating to the making or delivery of any return, statement, declaration, list or other document, the furnishing of any particulars, the production of any document, the making of anything available for inspection, the delivery of any account or the making of any representation, shall, subject to any

necessary modifications, apply in relation to capital gains tax as they apply in relation to income tax.

(2) In particular and without prejudice to subsection (1), sections 876 to 880, sections 888 and 900 and paragraph 1 of Schedule 1 shall, subject to any necessary modifications, apply in relation to capital gains tax.

(3) A notice under any provision of the Income Tax Acts as applied by this section may require particulars of any assets acquired by the person on whom the notice was served (or, if the notice relates to income or chargeable gains of some other person for whom the person who receives the notice is required to make a return under section 878, as so applied by this section, of any assets acquired by that other person) in the period specified in the notice, being a period beginning not earlier than the 6th day of April, 1974, but excluding—

- (*a*) any assets exempted by section 607 or 613, or
- (*b*) any assets acquired as trading stock.

(4) The particulars required under this section may include particulars of the person from whom the asset was acquired and of the consideration for the acquisition.

(5) (*a*) An event which, apart from section 584(3) as applied by section 586 or 587, would constitute the disposal of an asset shall for the purposes of this section constitute such a disposal.

(*b*) An event which, apart from section 584(3) as applied by section 586 or 587, would constitute the acquisition of an asset shall for the purposes of this section constitute such an acquisition.

(6) Section 888 as applied by this section shall apply to property or leases of property other than premises as it applies to premises or leases of premises.

(7) A return of income of a partnership under section 880 shall include—

- (*a*) with respect to any disposal of partnership assets during a period to which any part of the return relates, the like particulars as if the partnership were liable to tax on any chargeable gain accruing on the disposal, and
- (*b*) with respect to any acquisition of partnership assets, the particulars required by subsection (3).

(8) A return under section 879 as applied by this section in relation to chargeable gains accruing to a married woman in a year of assessment, or part of a year of assessment, during which she is a married woman and living with her husband may be required either from her or, if her husband is liable under section 1028(1), from him.

Cross-references

Penalties for failure to make returns etc, and for fraudulently or negligently making incorrect returns: s 1077(1); subs (1): s 1077(2).

Returns of profits, subss (3), (4), (5)(*b*): s 884(8).

Self assessment: s 959(6).

Surcharge for late returns: s 1084(1)(*b*)(iv).

Tax treatment of profits, losses and capital gains of a European Economic Interest Grouping, subs (7): s 1014(3).

Case law

Held, taxpayer had not complied with the obligation to provide details of capital gains where he had submitted a complicated formula with clues from which the gain could be calculated: *Horner v Madden* [1995] STC 802.

Definitions

chargeable gain: ss 5(1), 545; incapacitated person: s 3(1); Income Tax Acts: s 1(2); lease: s 5(1); person: IA 1937 s 11(*c*); trading stock: ss 5(1), 89.

Former enactments

CGTA 1975 s 51(1) and Sch 4 para 3(1), (2) (part of) and (3)–(5), para 10(1) and para 19; FA 1992 s 246.

Corresponding UK tax provision

Taxes Management Act 1970 s 8.

914 Returns by issuing houses, stockbrokers, auctioneers, etc

(1) For the purpose of obtaining particulars of chargeable gains, an inspector may by notice in writing require a return under any provision of this section.

(2) (*a*) In this subsection, **"shares"** includes units in a unit trust.

(*b*) An issuing house or other person carrying on a business of effecting public issues of shares or securities in any company, or placings of shares or securities in any company, either on behalf of the company or on behalf of holders of blocks of shares or securities which have not previously been the subject of a public issue or placing, may be required to make a return of all such public issues or placings effected by that person in the course of the business in the period specified in the notice requiring the return, giving particulars of the persons to or with whom the shares or securities are issued, allotted or placed, and the number or amount of the shares or securities so obtained by them respectively.

(3) A person not carrying on such a business may be required to make a return as regards any such issue or placing effected by that person and specified in the notice, giving particulars of the persons to or with whom the shares or securities are issued, allotted or placed and the number or amount of the shares or securities so obtained by them respectively.

(4) A member of a stock exchange in the State may be required to make a return giving particulars of any transactions effected by that member in the course of that member's business in the period specified in the notice requiring the return and giving particulars of—

(*a*) the parties to the transactions,

(*b*) the number or amount of the shares or securities dealt with in the respective transactions, and

(*c*) the amount or value of the consideration.

(5) A person (other than a member of a stock exchange in the State) who acts as an agent in the State in transactions in shares or securities may be required to make a return giving particulars of—

(*a*) any such transactions effected by that person in the period specified in the notice,

(*b*) the parties to the transactions,

(*c*) the number or amount of the shares or securities dealt with in the respective transactions, and

(*d*) the amount or value of the consideration.

(6) An auctioneer and any person carrying on a trade of dealing in any description of tangible movable property, or of acting as an agent or intermediary in dealings in any description of tangible movable property, may be required to make a return giving particulars of any transactions effected by or through that auctioneer or that person, as the case may be, in which any asset which is tangible movable property is disposed of for a consideration the amount or value of which, in the hands of the recipient, exceeds—

(*a*) as respects transactions effected on or after the 6th day of April, 1994, but before the 6th day of April, 1995, [€6,350][1], and

(*b*) as respects transactions effected on or after the 6th day of April, 1995, [€19,050][2].

(7) No person shall be required under this section to include in a return particulars of any transaction effected more than 3 years before the service of the notice requiring that person to make the return.

Amendments

1 Substituted by FA 2001 s 240(1) and (2)(*b*) and Sch 5 Pt 1 for 2002 and later tax years; previously "£5,000".

2 Substituted by FA 2001 s 240(1) and (2)(*b*) and Sch 5 Pt 1 for 2002 and later tax years; previously "£15,000".

Cross-references

Capital gains tax, penalties for failure to make returns etc, and for fraudulently or negligently making incorrect returns, applied by: s 1077(1)(*a*), (2).

Definitions

chargeable gain: ss 5(1), 545; company: s 5(1); person: IA 1937 s 11(*c*); shares: s 5(1); trade: s 5(1); unit trust: s 5(1); units: s 5(1); writing: IA 1937 Sch; year: IA 1937 Sch.

Former enactments

CGTA 1975 s 51(1) and Sch 4 para 4; FA 1994 s 63; FA 1995 s 70.

Corresponding UK tax provision

Taxes Management Act 1970 s 25.

915 Returns by nominee shareholders

(1) In this section, references to shares include references to securities and loan capital.

(2) Where, for the purpose of obtaining particulars of chargeable gains, any person in whose name any shares of a company are registered is so required by notice in writing by the Revenue Commissioners or by an inspector, that person shall state whether or not that person is the beneficial owner of those shares and, if that person is not the beneficial owner of those shares or any of them, shall furnish the name and address of the person or persons on whose behalf the shares are registered in that person's name.

Cross-references

Capital gains tax, penalties for failure to make returns etc, and for fraudulently or negligently making incorrect returns, applied by: s 1077(1)(*a*), (2).

Definitions

chargeable gain: ss 5(1), 545; company: s 5(1); inspector: ss 2(1), 5(1), 852; person: IA 1937 s 11(*c*); shares: s 5(1); writing: IA 1937 Sch.

Former enactments

CGTA 1975 s 51(1) and Sch 4 para 5.

Corresponding UK tax provision

Taxes Management Act 1970 s 26.

916 Returns by party to a settlement

The Revenue Commissioners may by notice in writing require any person, being a party to a settlement, to furnish them within such time as they may direct (not being less than 28 days) with such particulars relating to the settlement as they think necessary for the purposes of the Capital Gains Tax Acts.

Cross-references

Capital gains tax, penalties for failure to make returns etc, and for fraudulently or negligently making incorrect returns, applied by: s 1077(1)(*a*), (2).

Definitions

person: IA 1937 s 11(*c*); settlement: ss 5(1), 10; writing: IA 1937 Sch.

Former enactments

CGTA 1975 s 51(1) and Sch 4 para 6.

Corresponding UK tax provision

Taxes Management Act 1970 s 27.

917 Returns relating to non-resident companies and trusts

A person who—

(*a*) holds shares or securities in a company not resident or ordinarily resident in the State, or

(*b*) is beneficially interested or acts as agent for or on behalf of a person who is beneficially interested in settled property under a settlement the trustees of which are not resident or ordinarily resident in the State,

may be required by a notice by the Revenue Commissioners to give such particulars as the Revenue Commissioners may consider are required to determine whether the company or trust is [within sections 579 to 579F and section 590],[1] and whether any chargeable gains have accrued to that company, or to the trustees of that settlement, in respect of which the person to whom the notice is given is liable to capital gains tax [under sections 579 to 579F or section 590].[2]

Amendments

1 Substituted by FA 1999 s 92(1)(*a*)(i) with effect from 11 February 1999; previously "within section 579 or 590".

2 Inserted by FA 1999 s 92(1)(*a*)(ii) with effect from 11 February 1999; previously "under section 579 or 590".

Cross-references

Capital gains tax, penalties for failure to make returns etc, and for fraudulently or negligently making incorrect returns, applied by: s 1077(1)(*a*), (2).

Offshore income gains accruing to persons resident or domiciled abroad, for "chargeable gains" read "offshore income gains" and for "capital gains tax under section 579 to 579F" read "income tax or corporation tax under section sections 579 to 579F or section 590, as applied by section 746": s 746(4).

Definitions

chargeable gain: ss 5(1), 545; company: s 5(1); person: IA 1937 s 11(*c*); resident: s 5(1); settled property: s 5(1); settlement: ss 5(1), 10; shares: s 5(1).

Former enactments

CGTA 1975 s 51(1) and Sch 4 para 7.

917A Return of property transfers to non-resident trustees

[(1) In this section and in sections 917B and 917C **"appropriate inspector"** shall be construed in accordance with section 950.

(2) This section applies where—

(*a*) on or after the 11th day of February, 1999, a person (in this section referred to as the **"transferor"**) transfers property to the trustees of a settlement otherwise than under a transaction entered into at arm's length,

(*b*) the trustees of the settlement are neither resident nor ordinarily resident in the State at the time the property is transferred, and

(*c*) the transferor knows or has reason to believe, that the trustees are not so resident and ordinarily resident.

(3) Where this section applies, the transferor shall, before the expiry of 3 months beginning with the day on which the transfer is made, deliver to the appropriate inspector a statement which—

(*a*) identifies the settlement, and

(*b*) specifies the property transferred, the day on which the transfer was made, and the consideration (if any) for the transfer.

(4) Where a transferor fails—

(*a*) to make a statement required to be made by the transferor in accordance with subsection (3), or

(*b*) to include in such a statement the details referred to in subsection (3),

the transferor shall in respect of each such failure be liable to a penalty of [€2,535][1].

(5) Penalties under subsection (4) may, without prejudice to any other method of recovery, be proceeded for and recovered summarily in like manner as in summary proceedings for the recovery of any fine or penalty under any act relating to the excise.][2]

Amendments

1 Substituted by FA 2001 s 240(1) and (2)(*k*) and Sch 5 Pt 1 as respects any act or omission which takes place or begins on or after 1 January 2002; previously "£2,000".

2 Section 917A inserted by FA 1999 s 92(1)(*b*) with effect from 11 February 1999.

Definitions

month: IA 1937 Sch; ordinarily resident: s 5(1); person: IA 1937 s 11(*c*); resident: s 5(1); settlement: s 5(1).

917B Return by settlor in relation to non-resident trustees

[(1) In this section and in section 917C **"arrangements"** means arrangements having the force of law by virtue of [section 826(1)(*a*)][1] (as extended to capital gains tax by section 828);

(2) This section applies where a settlement is created on or after the 11th day of February, 1999, and at the time it is created—

(*a*) the trustees are neither resident nor ordinarily resident in the State, or

(*b*) the trustees are resident and ordinarily resident in the State but fall to be regarded for the purposes of any arrangements as resident in a territory outside the State.

(3) Where this section applies, any person who—

(*a*) is a settlor in relation to the settlement at the time it is created, and

(*b*) at that time fulfils the condition mentioned in subsection (4),

shall, before the expiry of the period of 3 months beginning with the day on which the settlement is created, deliver to the appropriate inspector a statement specifying—

(i) the day on which the settlement was created;

(ii) the name and address of the person making the statement; and

(iii) the names and addresses of the persons who are the trustees immediately before the delivery of the statement.

(4) The condition is that the person concerned is domiciled in the State and is either resident or ordinarily resident in the State.

(5) Where a person fails—

(*a*) to make a statement required to be made by the person in accordance with subsection (2), or

(*b*) to include in such a statement the details referred to in subsection (2), the person shall in respect of each such failure be liable to a penalty of [€2,535][2].

(6) Penalties under subsection (5) may, without prejudice to any other method of recovery, be proceeded for and recovered summarily in like manner as in summary proceedings for the recovery of any fine or penalty under any act relating to the excise.][3]

Amendments

1 Substituted by FA 2004 s 89 and Sch 3 para 1(*ab*) with effect from 25 March 2004; previously "section 826".

2 Substituted by FA 2001 s 240(1) and (2)(*k*) and Sch 5 Pt 1 as respects any act or omission which takes place or begins on or after 1 January 2002; previously "£2,000".

3 Section 917B inserted by FA 1999 s 92(1)(*b*) with effect from 11 February 1999.

Cross-references

Return of property transfers to non-resident trustees: s 917A(1).

Definitions

appropriate inspector: s 917A(1); month: IA 1937 Sch; ordinarily resident: s 5(1); person: IA 1937 s 11(*c*); resident: s 5(1); settlement: s 5(1); settlor: s 5(1).

917C Return by certain trustees

[(1) This section applies where—

(*a*) the trustees of a settlement become at any time (in this section referred to as **"the relevant time"**) on or after the 11th day of February, 1999, neither resident nor ordinarily resident in the State, or

(*b*) the trustees of a settlement, while continuing to be resident and ordinarily resident in the State, become at any time (in this section also referred to as **"the relevant time"**) on or after the 11th day of February, 1999, trustees who fall to be regarded for the purposes of any arrangements as resident in a territory outside the State.

(2) Where this section applies, any person who was a trustee of the settlement immediately before the relevant time shall, before the expiry of the period of 3 months beginning with the day when the relevant time falls, deliver to the appropriate inspector a statement specifying—

(*a*) the day on which the settlement was created,

(*b*) the name and address of each person who is a settlor in relation to the settlement immediately before the delivery of the statement, and

(*c*) the names and addresses of the persons who are the trustees immediately before the delivery of the statement.

(3) Where a person fails—

(*a*) to make a statement required to be made by the person in accordance with subsection (2), or

(*b*) to include in such a statement the details referred to in subsection (2), the person shall in respect of each such failure be liable to a penalty of [€2,535][1].

(4) Penalties under subsection (3) may, without prejudice to any other method of recovery, be proceeded for and recovered summarily in like manner as in summary proceedings for the recovery of any fine or penalty under any act relating to the excise.][2]

Amendments

1 Substituted by s 240(1) and (2)(*k*) and Sch 5 Pt 1 as respects any act or omission which takes place or begins on or after 1 January 2002; previously "£2,000".

2 Section 917C inserted by FA 1999 s 92(1)(*b*) with effect from 11 February 1999.

Cross-references

Returns by settlor in relation to non-resident trustees: s 917B(1).

Returns of property transfers to non-resident trustees: s 917A(1).

Definitions

appropriate inspector: s 917A(1); arrangements: s 917B(1); month: IA 1937 Sch; ordinarily resident: s 5(1); person: IA 1937 s 11(*c*); resident: s 5(1); settlement: s 5(1); settlor: s 5(1).

[CHAPTER 6
Electronic Transmission of Returns of Income, Profits, etc., and of Other Revenue Returns][1]

Amendments

1 Ch 6 (ss 917D–917N) inserted by FA 1999 s 209.

Cross-references

Electronic claims, PAYE: s 864A(9).

Tax Briefing

TB40 June 2000 pp 14–16 — Revenue On-Line Service (ROS) — How to register.

TB42 Dec 2000 pp 36–38 ROS Update.

TB43 Apr 2001 pp 11–12 — ROS — New Developments.

TB44 June 2001 pp 13–15 ROS — Latest News.

TB45 Oct 2001 pp 4–6 ROS — eFiling Income Tax and Corporation Tax.

TB46 Dec 2001 pp 1–13 ROS — Questions and Answers, and Sample Accounts Menus.

TB49 Aug 2002 pp 16–17 — ROS — Payments.

TB52 May 2003 p 32 — ROS Update — Enhancements April 2003.

TB53 Aug 2003 pp 27–28 ROS Update — Enhancements June 2003.

TB54 Dec 2003 pp 14–15 ROS Update.

TB56 July 2004 pp 19–20 — ROS Update.
TB57 Oct 2004 pp 4–6 ROS — Performance Enhancements and Pay and File Tips.
TB58 Dec 2004 p 7 — ROS Release December 2004; What is the ROS Offline Application?
eBriefing
eBrief 05–2005 — ROS Payments and auditor independence (US SEC Regulations).

917D Interpretation (Chapter 6)

[(1) In this Chapter—

"the Acts" means—

(*a*) the statutes relating to the duties of excise and to the management of those duties,
(*b*) the Tax Acts,
(*c*) the Capital Gains Tax Acts,
(*d*) the Value-Added Tax Act, 1972, and the enactments amending or extending that Act,
(*e*) the [Capital Acquisitions Tax Consolidation Act 2003][1], and the enactments amending or extending that Act, and
(*f*) the Stamp Act, 1891, and the enactments amending or extending that Act,

and any instruments made under any of the statutes and enactments referred to in paragraphs (*a*) to (*f*);

"approved person" shall be construed in accordance with section 917G;

"approved transmission" shall be construed in accordance with section 917H;

"authorised person" has the meaning assigned to it by section 917G(3)(*b*);

[**"digital signature"**, in relation to a person, means an advanced electronic signature (within the meaning of the Electronic Commerce Act, 2000) provided to the person by the Revenue Commissioners solely for the purpose of making an electronic transmission of information which is required to be included in a return to which this Chapter applies and for no other purpose and a qualified certificate (within the meaning of that Act) provided to the person by the Revenue Commissioners or a person appointed in that behalf by the Revenue Commissioners;][2]

[**"electronic identifier"**, in relation to a person, means—

(*a*) the person's digital signature, or
(*b*) such other means of electronic identification as may be specified or authorised by the Revenue Commissioners for the purposes of this Chapter;][3]

"hard copy", in relation to information held electronically, means a printed out version of that information;

[**"return"** means any return, claim, application, notification, election, declaration, nomination, statement, list, registration, particulars or other information which a person is or may be required by the Acts to give to the Revenue Commissioners or any Revenue officer;][4]

"revenue officer" means the Collector-General, an inspector or other officer of the Revenue Commissioners (including an inspector or other officer who is authorised under any provision of the Acts (however expressed) to receive a return or to require a return to be prepared and delivered);

"tax" means any income tax, corporation tax, capital gains tax, value-added tax, gift tax, inheritance tax, excise duty or stamp duty.

...[5]

(3) Any references in this Chapter to the making of a return include references in any provision of the Acts to—

(*a*) the preparing and delivering of a return;
(*b*) the sending of a return;
(*c*) the furnishing of a return or of particulars;
(*d*) the delivering of a return;
(*e*) the presentation of a return;
(*f*) the rendering of a return;
(*g*) the giving of particulars or of any information specified in any provision; and
(*h*) any other means whereby a return is forwarded, however expressed.][6]

Amendments

1 Substituted by CATCA 2003 s 119 and Sch 3 with effect from 21 February 2003; previously "Capital Acquisitions Tax Act 1976".

2 Definition of "digital signature" substituted by FA 2001 s 235(*a*)(i)(I) with effect from 15 February 2001.

3 Definition of "electronic identifier" inserted by FA 2005 s 22(*a*) with effect from 25 March 2005.

4 Definition of "return" substituted by FA 2001 s 235(*a*)(i)(II) with effect from 15 February 2001.

5 Subs (2) deleted by FA 2001 s 235(*a*)(ii) with effect from 15 February 2001.

6 Section 917D inserted by FA 1999 s 209 with effect from 25 March 1999.

Cross-references

Mandatory electronic filing and payment of tax: s 917EA(2).

Definitions

Collector-General: ss 2(1), 851; person: IA 1937 s 11(*c*).

917E Application

[This Chapter shall apply to a return if—

(*a*) the provision of the Acts under which the return is made is specified for the purpose of this Chapter by order made by the Revenue Commissioners, and

(*b*) the return is required to be made after the day appointed by such order in relation to returns to be made under the provision so specified.][1]

Amendments

1 Section 917E inserted by FA 1999 s 209 with effect from 25 March 1999.

Notes

The Taxes (Electronic Transmission of Certain Revenue Returns) (Specified Provisions and Appointed Day) Order 2000 (SI No 289 of 2000) specified the following provisions for the purposes of this Chapter:

Value Added Tax Act 1972 s 19(3)(*a*) [VAT3]
Value Added Tax Act 1972 s 19(3)(*aa*) [VAT3]
Income Tax (Employments) Regulations 1960 (SI No 28 of 1960) r 22(1) [P45]
Income Tax (Employments) Regulations 1960 (SI No 28 of 1960) r 25(6) [P45]
Income Tax (Employments) Regulations 1960 (SI No 28 of 1960) r 31 [P30]
Income Tax (Employments) Regulations 1960 (SI No 28 of 1960) r 31A [P30]

and appointed 28 September 2000 as the appointed day in relation to returns to be made under each of those provisions.

The Taxes (Electronic Transmission of Certain Revenue Returns) (Specified Provision and Appointed Day) Order 2001 (SI No 112 of 2001) specified Income Tax (Employments) Regulations 1960 (SI No 28 of 1960) r 35 [P35 and P35L] for the purposes of this Chapter and appointed 5 April 2001 as the appointed day in relation to returns to be made under that provision.

The Taxes (Electronic Transmission of Income Tax and Capital Gains Tax Returns under Self Assessment) (Specified Provision and Appointed Day) Order 2001 (SI No 441 of 2001) specified TCA 1997 s 951(1) other than paragraph (*b*) thereof, for the purposes of this Chapter, and appointed 30 September 2001 as the appointed day in relation to the return (income tax and capital gains tax returns under self assessment) to be made under that section.

The Taxes (Electronic Transmission of Corporation Tax Returns under Self Assessment) (Specified Provision and Appointed Day) Order 2001 (SI No 522 of 2001) specified TCA 1997 s 951(1), for the purposes of this Chapter (in so far as that section had not already been so specified, and appointed 23 November 2001 as the appointed day in relation to the returns (corporation tax returns under self assessment) to be made under that section.

The Taxes (Electronic Transmission of Certain Revenue Returns) (Specified Provisions and Appointed Day) Order 2002 (SI No 194 of 2002) specified TCA 1997 ss 172K(1) (dividend withholding tax), 258(2) (deposit interest retention tax), 525(2) (professional services withholding tax), 730G(2) (life assurance exit tax), 739F(2) (investment undertaking exit tax), 848P (special savings incentive accounts relevant tax — monthly returns) and 848Q (special savings incentive accounts relevant tax — annual returns) for the purposes of this Chapter, and appointed 10 May 2002 as the appointed day in relation to the returns to be made under those sections.

The Taxes (Electronic Transmission of Vehicle Registration Returns) (Specified Provisions and Appointed Day) Order 2002 (SI No 464 of 2002) specified section 131(2)(*a*) of the Finance Act 1992, section 133(2)(*a*) of the Finance Act 1992, Regulation 13(2) of the Vehicle Registration and Taxation Regulations 1992 (SI No 318 of 1992) and Regulation 15 of the Vehicle Registration and Taxation Regulations for the purposes of this Chapter, and appointed 4 October 2002 as the appointed day in relation to returns to be made under those sections and regulations.

The Taxes (Electronic Transmission of Relevant Contracts Returns) (Specified Provisions and Appointed Day) Order 2003 (SI No 127 of 2003) specified TCA 1997 s 531(3A)(*a*) [RCT 30] for the purposes of this Chapter, and appointed 12 April 2003 as the appointed day in relation to returns to be made under that section.

The Taxes (Electronic Transmission of Capital Acquisitions Tax Returns) (Specified Provisions and Appointed Day) Order 2003 (SI No 443 of 2003) specified section section 46 of the Capital Acquisitions Tax Consolidation Act 2003, apart from subsections (3), (7), (13) and (15) thereof, for the purposes of this Chapter, and appointed 28 September 2003 as the appointed day in relation to returns to be made under that section.

The Taxes (Electronic Transmission of Betting Duty Returns) (Specified Provisions and Appointed Day) Order 2004 (SI No 803 of 2004) specified section 70 of the Finance Act 2002 and Paragraphs (1) and (3) of Regulation 5 of the Betting Duty Regulations 2004 for the purposes of this Chapter, and appointed 31 December 2004 as the appointed day in relation to returns to be made under those provisions.

Cross-references

mandatory electronic filing and payment of tax: s 917EA(3)(*a*).

Definitions

the Acts: s 917D; return: s 917D.

917EA Mandatory electronic filing and payment of tax

[(1) In this section—

"electronic means" includes electrical, digital, magnetic, optical, electromagnetic, biometric, photonic means of transmission of data and other forms of related technology by means of which data is transmitted;

"repayment of tax" includes any amount relating to tax which is to be paid or repaid by the Revenue Commissioners;

"specified person" means any person, group of persons or class of persons specified in regulations made under this section for the purposes of either or both paragraphs (*a*) and (*b*) of subsection (3);

"specified return" means a return specified in regulations made under this section;

"specified tax liabilities" means liabilities to tax including interest on unpaid tax specified in regulations made under this section.

(2) Section 917D shall apply for the purposes of regulations made under this section in the same way as it applies for the purposes of this Chapter.

(3) The Revenue Commissioners may make regulations—

(*a*) requiring the delivery by specified persons of a specified return by electronic means where an order under section 917E has been made in respect of that return,

(*b*) requiring the payment by electronic means of specified tax liabilities by specified persons, and

(*c*) for the repayment of any tax specified in the regulations to be made by electronic means.

(4) Regulations made under this section shall include provision for the exclusion of a person from the requirements of regulations made under this section where the Revenue Commissioners are satisfied that the person could not reasonably be expected to have the capacity to make a specified return or to pay the specified tax liabilities by electronic means, and allowing a person, aggrieved by a failure to exclude such person, to appeal that failure to the Appeal Commissioners.

(5) Regulations made under this section may, in particular and without prejudice to the generality of subsection (3), include provision for—

(*a*) the electronic means to be used to pay or repay tax,

(*b*) the conditions to be complied with in relation to the electronic payment or repayment of tax,

(*c*) determining the time when tax paid or repaid using electronic means is to be taken as having been paid or repaid,

(*d*) the manner of proving, for any purpose, the time of payment or repayment of any tax paid or repaid using electronic means, including provision for the application of any conclusive or other presumptions,

(*e*) notifying persons that they are specified persons, including the manner by which such notification may be made, and

(*f*) such supplemental and incidental matters as appear to the Revenue Commissioners to be necessary.

(6) The Revenue Commissioners may nominate any of their officers to perform any acts and discharge any functions authorised by regulation made under this section to be performed or discharged by the Revenue Commissioners.

(7) Where a specified person—

(*a*) makes a return which is a specified return for the purposes of regulations made under this section, or (*b*) makes a payment of tax which is specified tax liabilities for the purposes of regulations made under this section,

in a form other than that required by any such regulation, the specified person shall be liable to a penalty of €1,520 and, for the purposes of the recovery of a penalty under this subsection, section 1061 applies in the same manner as it applies for the purposes of the recovery of a penalty under any of the sections referred to in that section.

(8) Every regulation made under this section shall be laid before Dáil Éireann as soon as may be after it is made and, if a resolution annulling the regulation is passed by Dáil Éireann within the next 21 days on which Dáil Éireann has sat after the regulation is laid before it, the regulation shall be annulled accordingly but without prejudice to the validity of anything previously done under the regulation.][1]

Amendments

1 Section 917EA inserted by FA 2003 s 164(1)(*a*) with effect from such day as the Minister for Finance may appoint by order.

Cross-references

Surcharge for late returns: s 1084(1)(*b*)(i*a*).

Definitions

Appeal Commissioners: s 2(1); person: IA 1937 s 11(*c*); return: s 917D; tax: s 917D.

917F Electronic transmission of returns

[(1) Notwithstanding any other provision of the Acts, the obligation of any person to make a return to which this Chapter applies shall be treated as fulfilled by that person if information is transmitted electronically in compliance with that obligation, but only if—

(*a*) the transmission is made by an approved person or an authorised person,

(*b*) the transmission is an approved transmission,

[(*c*) the transmission bears the electronic identifier of that person, and][1]

(*d*) the receipt of the transmission is acknowledged in accordance with section 917J.

(2) In subsection (1), the reference to the information which is required to be included in the return includes any requirement on a person to—

(*a*) make any statement,

(*b*) include any particulars, or

(*c*) make or attach any claim.

(3) Where the obligation of any person to make a return to which this Chapter applies is treated as fulfilled in accordance with subsection (1) then, any provision of the Acts which—

(*a*) requires that the return include or be accompanied by any description of declaration whatever by the person making the return, apart from a declaration of an amount,

(*b*) requires that the return be signed or accompanied by a certificate,

(*c*) requires that the return be in writing,

(*d*) authorises the return to be signed by a person acting under the authority of the person obliged to make the return, (*e*) authorises the Revenue Commissioners to prescribe the form of a return or which requires a return to be in or on any prescribed form, or

(*f*) for the purposes of any claim for exemption or for any allowance, deduction or repayment of tax under the Acts which is required to be made with the return, authorises the Revenue Commissioners to prescribe the form of a claim,

shall not apply.

(4) Where the obligation of any person to make a return to which this Chapter applies is treated as fulfilled in accordance with subsection (1) then, the time at which any requirement under the Acts to make a return is fulfilled shall be the day on which the receipt of the information referred to in that subsection is acknowledged in accordance with section 917J.

[(5) Where an approved transmission is made by—

(*a*) an approved person on behalf of another person, or

(*b*) an authorised person on behalf of another person (not being the person who authorised that person),

a hard copy of the information shall be made and authenticated in accordance with section 917K.][2]

(6) (*a*) Where the obligation of any person to make a return to which this Chapter applies is treated as fulfilled in accordance with subsection (1) then, any requirement that—

(i) the return or any claim which is to be made with or attached to the return should be accompanied by any document (in this subsection referred to as a "supporting document") other than the return or the claim, and

(ii) the supporting document be delivered with the return or the claim,

shall be treated as fulfilled by the person subject to the requirement if the person or the approved person referred to in subsection (1)(*a*) retains the document for inspection on request by a revenue officer.

(*b*) Any person subject to the requirement referred to in paragraph (*a*) shall produce any supporting documents requested by a revenue officer within 30 days of that request.

(*c*) The references in this subsection to a document include references to any accounts, certificate, evidence, receipts, reports or statements.][3]

Amendments

1 Subs (1)(*c*) substituted by FA 2005 s 22(*b*) with effect from 25 March 2005.

2 Subs (5) substituted by FA 2001 s 235(*b*)(ii) with effect from 15 February 2001.

3 Section 917F inserted by FA 1999 s 209 with effect from 25 March 1999.

Cross-references

Electronic claims, PAYE, subs (1): s 864A(9).
Exercise of powers, subs (1): s 917L(1), (3).
Hard copies, subs (1): s 917K(1)(*a*); subs (3): s 917K(2).
Proceedings, subs (1): s 917M(1), (3), (4).

Definitions

the Acts: s 917D(1); approved transmission: s 917D(1); approved person: s 917D(1); authorised person: s 917D(1); digital signature: s 917D(1); hard copy: s 917D(1); person: IA 1937 s 11(*c*); return: s 917D(1); writing: IA 1937 Sch.

917G Approved persons

[(1) A person shall be an approved person for the purposes of this Chapter if the person is approved by the Revenue Commissioners for the purposes of transmitting electronically information which is required to be included in a return to which this Chapter applies (in this section referred to as **"the transmission"**) and [complies with the condition specified in subsection (3)(*a*) in relation to authorised persons and the condition specified in subsection (3)(*b*) in relation to the making of transmissions and the use of [electronic identifiers][1].[2]

(2) A person seeking to be approved under this section shall make application in that behalf to the Revenue Commissioners [by such means as the Revenue Commissioners may determine][3] for the purposes of this section.

[(3) The conditions referred to in subsection (1) are that—

(*a*) the person notifies the Revenue Commissioners in a manner to be determined by the Revenue Commissioners of the persons (each of whom is referred to in this section as an **"authorised person"**), in addition to the person, who are authorised to make the transmission, and

(*b*) the person and each person who is an authorised person in relation to that person in making the transmission complies with the requirements referred to in subsections (2) and (3) of section 917H.][4]

(4) A person seeking to be approved under this section shall be given notice by the Revenue Commissioners of the grant or refusal by them of the approval and, in the case of a refusal, of the reason for the refusal.

(5) An approval under this section may be withdrawn by the Revenue Commissioners by notice in writing or by such other means as the Revenue Commissioners may decide with effect from such date as may be specified in the notice.

(6) (*a*) A notice withdrawing an approval under the section shall state the grounds for the withdrawal.

(*b*) No approval under this section may be withdrawn unless an approved person or an authorised person has failed to comply with one or more of the requirements referred to in section 917H(2).

(7) A person who is refused approval under this section or whose approval under this section is withdrawn may appeal to the Appeal Commissioners against the refusal or withdrawal.

(8) The appeal under subsection (7) shall be made by notice to the Revenue Commissioners before the end of the period of 30 days beginning with the day on which notice of the refusal or withdrawal was given to the person.

(9) The Appeal Commissioners shall hear and determine an appeal made to them under subsection (7) as if it were an appeal against an assessment to income tax, and the provisions of the Tax Acts relating to appeals shall apply accordingly.][5]

Amendments

1 Substituted by FA 2005 s 22(*c*) with effect from 25 March 2005; previously "digital signatures".

2 Substituted by FA 2001 s 235(*c*)(i) with effect from 15 February 2001; previously "complies with the provisions of this section and, in particular, with the conditions specified in subsection (3)".

3 Subs (3) substituted by FA 2001 s 235(*c*)(ii) with effect from 15 February 2001; previously "in writing or by such other means as may be approved by the Revenue Commissioners".

4 Subs (3) substituted by FA 2001 s 235(*c*)(iii) with effect from 15 February 2001.

5 Section 917G inserted by FA 1999 s 209.

Cross-references

Interpretation, meaning of "approved person" and "authorised person" applied for Chapter: s 917D(1).

Definitions

Appeal Commissioners: ss 2(1), 850; approved person: s 917D(1); authorised person: s 917D(1); person: IA 1937 s 11(*c*); Tax Acts: s 1(2); writing: IA 1937 Sch.

917H Approved transmissions

[(1) Where an approved person transmits electronically information which is required to be included in a return to which this Chapter applies the transmission shall not be an approved transmission unless it complies with the requirements of this section.

[(2) The Revenue Commissioners shall publish and make known to each approved person and each authorised person any requirement for the time being determined by them as being applicable to—

(*a*) the manner in which information which is required to be included in a return to which this Chapter applies is to be transmitted electronically, and

(*b*) the use of a person's [electronic identifier][1].

(3) The requirements referred to in subsection (2) include—

(*a*) requirements as to the software or type of software to be used to make a transmission,

(*b*) the terms and conditions under which a person may make a transmission, and

(*c*) the terms and conditions under which a person may use that person's [electronic identifier][1].][2][3]

[(4) For the purposes of subsection (3), the Revenue Commissioners may determine different terms and conditions in relation to different returns or categories of a return, different categories of persons and different returns or categories of a return made by different categories of persons.][4]

Amendments

1 Substituted by FA 2005 s 22(*d*)(i) with effect from 25 March 2005; previously "digital signature".

2 Subss (2)–(3) substituted by FA 2001 s 235(*d*) with effect from 15 February 2001.

3 Section 917H inserted by FA 1999 s 209 with effect from 25 March 1999.

4 Subs (4) inserted by FA 2005 s 22(*d*)(ii) with effect from 25 March 2005.

Cross-references

Approved person, subs (2): s 917G(3)(*b*), (6)(*b*); subs (3): s 917G(3)(*b*).

Interpretation, meaning of "approved transmission" applied for Chapter: s 917A(1).

Definitions

approved person: s 917D(1); authorised person: s 917D(1); digital signature: s 917D(1); return: s 917D(1).

917I Digital signatures

Amendments

Section 917I deleted by FA 2001 s 235(*e*) with effect from 15 February 2001.

917J Acknowledgement of electronic transmissions

[For the purposes of this Chapter, where an electronic transmission of information which is required to be included in a return to which this Chapter applies is received by the Revenue Commissioners, the Revenue Commissioners shall send an electronic acknowledgement of receipt of that transmission to the person from whom it was received.][1]

Amendments

1 Section 917J inserted by FA 1999 s 209 with effect from 25 March 1999.

Cross-references

Electronic transmission of returns: s 917F(1)(*d*), (4).

Definitions

person: IA 1937 s 11(*c*); return: s 917D(1).

917K Hard copies

[(1) A hard copy shall be made in accordance with this subsection only if—

(*a*) the hard copy is made under processes and procedures which are designed to ensure that the information contained in the hard copy shall only be the information [transmitted or to be transmitted][1] in accordance with section 917F(1),

(*b*) the hard copy is in a form approved by the Revenue Commissioners which is appropriate to the information so transmitted, and

(*c*) the hard copy is authenticated in accordance with subsection (2).

(2) For the purposes of this Chapter, a hard copy made in accordance with subsection (1) shall be authenticated only if the hard copy is signed by the person who would have been required to make the declaration, sign the return or furnish the certificate, as the case may be, but for paragraph (*a*), (*b*) or (*d*) of section 917F(3).][2]

Amendments

1 Substituted by FA 2001 s 235(*f*) with effect from 15 February 2001; previously "to be transmitted".

2 Section 917K inserted by FA 1999 s 209 with effect from 25 March 1999.

Cross-references

Electronic transmission of returns: s 917F(5).

Definitions

person: IA 1937 s 11(*c*); return: s 917D(1).

917L Exercise of powers

[(1) This section shall apply where the obligation of any person to make a return to which this Chapter applies is treated as fulfilled in accordance with section 917F(1).

(2) Where this section applies the Revenue Commissioners and a revenue officer shall have all the powers and duties in relation to the information contained in the transmission as they or that officer would have had if the information had been contained in a return made by post.

(3) Where this section applies the person whose obligation to make a return to which this Chapter applies is treated as fulfilled in accordance with section 917F(1) shall have all the rights and duties in relation to the information contained in the transmission as

the person would have had if that information had been contained in a return made by post.][1]

Amendments

1 Section 917L inserted by FA 1999 s 209 with effect from 25 March 1999.

Definitions

person: IA 1937 s 11(3); return: s 917D(1); Revenue officer: s 917D(1).

917M Proceedings

[(1) This section shall apply where the obligation of any person to make a return to which this Chapter applies is treated as fulfilled in accordance with section 917F(1).

(2) In this section, **"proceedings"** means civil and criminal proceedings, and includes proceedings before the Appeal Commissioners or any other tribunal having jurisdiction by virtue of any provision of the Acts.

(3) Where this section applies a hard copy certified by a revenue officer to be a true copy of the information transmitted electronically in accordance with section 917F(1) shall be treated [for the purposes of the Acts][1] as if the hard copy

(*a*) were a return or, as the case may be, a claim made by post, and

(*b*) contained any declaration, certificate or signature required by the Acts on such a return or, as the case may be, such a claim.

(4) For the purposes of any proceedings under the Acts, unless a Judge or any other person before whom proceedings are taken determines at the time of the proceedings that it is unjust in the circumstances to apply this provision, any rule of law restricting the admissibility or use of hearsay evidence shall not apply to a representation contained in a document recording information which has been transmitted in accordance with section 917F(1) in so far as the representation is a representation as to—

(*a*) the information so transmitted,

(*b*) the date on which, or the time at which, the information was so transmitted, or

(*c*) the identity of the person by whom or on whose behalf the information was so transmitted.][2]

Amendments

1 Substituted by FA 2001 s 235(*g*) with effect from 15 February 2001; previously "for the purposes of any proceedings in relation to which the certificate is given".

2 Section 917M inserted by FA 1999 s 209 with effect from 25 March 1999.

Cross-references

Electronic claims, PAYE, application of this section in respect of proceedings in relation to s 864A in the same manner as this section applies in respect of proceedings in relation to Chapter 6 of Part 38, subject to any necessary modifications including substituting in this section a reference to s 864A for a reference to s 917F(1) in each place where it occurs: s 864A(9).

Definitions

the Acts: s 917D(1); Appeal Commissioners: ss 2(1), 850; hard copy: s 917D(1); person: IA 1937 s 11(*c*); return: s 917D(1); Revenue officer: s 917D(1).

917N Miscellaneous

[The Revenue Commissioners may nominate any of their officers to perform any acts and discharge any functions authorised by this Chapter to be performed or discharged by the Revenue Commissioners.][1]

Amendments

1 Section 917N inserted by FA 1999 s 209 with effect from 25 March 1999.

PART 39
ASSESSMENTS

Cross-references

Rectification of excessive set off etc, of tax credit: s 927(1).

CHAPTER 1
Income Tax and Corporation Tax

918 Making of assessments under Schedules C, D, E and F

(1) Assessments under Schedules D, E and F, except—

(*a*) such assessments as the Revenue Commissioners are empowered to make under Chapter 2 of Part 4,

(*b*) assessments to which section 853 applies, and

(*c*) such assessments as officers or persons appointed by the Revenue Commissioners are empowered to make under section 854,

shall be made by the inspectors or such other officers as the Revenue Commissioners shall appoint in that behalf.

(2) The inspector shall give due notice to each person assessed of every such assessment made by him or her, the amount of the assessment and the time allowed for giving notice of appeal against the assessment.

(3) Anything required to be done by the Revenue Commissioners in relation to the making of assessments under Schedule C or D may be done by such officer of the Revenue Commissioners as they may authorise in that behalf.

(4) Where for any year of assessment profits or gains chargeable to tax under Case IV of Schedule D by virtue of section 98, 99 or 100 arise to any person from 2 or more sources, the several amounts of profits or gains so chargeable may be assessed in one assessment.

Cross-references

Capital gains tax, subss (2)–(3) applied by: s 931(3).

Definitions

inspector: ss 2(1), 5(1), 852; person: IA 1937 s 11(*c*); year of assessment: s 3(1).

Former enactments

ITA 1967 s 88(1) and s181; F(MP)A 1968 s 2, s 3(3) and Sch Pt II; CTA 1976 s 140(1) and Sch 2 Pt I para 5.

Corresponding UK tax provision

Taxes Management Act 1970 s 29.

919 Assessments to corporation tax

(1) Assessments to corporation tax shall be made by an inspector.

(2) (*a*) Where a company on whose profits the tax is to be assessed is resident in the State, the tax shall be assessed on the company.

(*b*) Where a company on whose profits the tax is to be assessed is not resident in the State, the tax shall be assessed on the company in the name of any agent, manager, factor or other representative of the company.

(3) The inspector shall give notice to the company assessed or, in the case of a company not resident in the State, to the agent, manager, factor or other representative of the company assessed of every assessment made by the inspector.

(4) (*a*) In this section, **"information"** includes information received from a member of the Garda Síochána.

(*b*) Where—

(i) a company makes default in the delivery of a statement in respect of corporation tax, or

(ii) the inspector is not satisfied with a statement which has been delivered, or has received information as to its insufficiency,

the inspector shall make an assessment on the company concerned in such sum as according to the best of the inspector's judgment ought to be charged on that company.

(5) (*a*) In this subsection, **"neglect"** means negligence or a failure to give any notice, to make any return, statement or declaration, or to produce or furnish any list, document or other information required by or under the enactments relating to corporation tax; but a company shall be deemed not to have failed to do anything required to be done within a limited time if the company did it within such further time, if any, as the Revenue Commissioners or officer concerned may have allowed and, where a company had a reasonable excuse for not doing anything required to be done, the company shall be deemed not to have failed to do it if the company did it without unreasonable delay after the excuse had ceased.

(*b*) Where an inspector discovers that—

(i) any profits which ought to have been assessed to corporation tax have not been assessed,

(ii) an assessment to corporation tax is or has become insufficient, or

(iii) any relief which has been given is or has become excessive,

the inspector shall make an assessment in the amount or the further amount which ought in the inspector's opinion to be charged.

(*c*) Subject to paragraph (*d*) and any other provision allowing a longer period in any class of case, no assessment to corporation tax shall be made more than [4 years][1] after the end of the accounting period to which it relates.

(*d*) In a case in which any form of fraud or neglect has been committed by or on behalf of any company in connection with or in relation to corporation tax, an assessment may be made on that company at any time for any accounting period for which by reason of the fraud or neglect corporation tax would otherwise be lost to the Exchequer.

(*e*) An objection to the making of any assessment on the ground that the time limited for the making of the assessment has expired shall be made only on appeal against the assessment.

(6) An assessment on a company's profits for an accounting period which falls after the commencement of the winding up of the company shall not be invalid because made before the end of the accounting period.

Amendments

1 Substituted by FA 2003 s 17(*f*) with effect from: (*a*) such day or days as the Minister for Finance may by order or orders appoint either generally or with reference to any particular purpose or provision and different days may be so appointed for different purposes or different provisions and (*b*) notwithstanding the generality of (*a*), any order made by the Minister for Finance in accordance with the provisions of that paragraph may contain, and be subject to, such conditions as the Minister considers appropriate and which are specified in the order; previously "10 years". By virtue of Finance Act 2003 (Commencement of Section 17) Order 2003, SI No 508 of 2003, this amendment comes into operation in relation to the making, on or after 1 January 2005, of an assessment referred to in section 919.

Cross-references

Group relief, claims and adjustments, subs (5)(*b*)(iii): s 429(4).

Interest on overdue income tax and corporation tax in cases of fraud or neglect, subs (5)(*a*): s 1082(1).

Self assessment, amendment of and time limit for assessments: s 955(5)(*b*).

Self assessment, appeals, subs (4): s 957(2)(*a*).

Self assessment, making of assessments, subs (4): s 954(3).

Tax Briefing

TB56 July 2004 pp 6–11 — Repayments, Interest and Time Limits — Section 17 FA 2003 changes.

TB57 Oct 2004 pp 7–9 — New Time Limits - Section 17 FA 2003 changes.

TB57 Oct 2004 p 15 — Repayments, Interest and Time Limits - correction to TB56 p 8.

Definitions

company: ss 4(1), 5(1); inspector: ss 2(1), 5(1), 852; profits: s 4(1).

Former enactments

CTA 1976 s 7 and s 144; DCITPA 1996 s 6; CABA 1996 s 24(2).

Corresponding UK tax provision

Taxes Management Act 1970 ss 28D–28F [repealed].

920 Granting of allowances and reliefs

(1) Notwithstanding anything in the Income Tax Acts, the inspector or such other officer as the Revenue Commissioners shall appoint in that behalf may at any time grant, in relation to any assessment in respect of income tax chargeable for any year of assessment, any allowance, deduction or relief authorised by the Income Tax Acts.

(2) Whenever such inspector or other officer so grants any such allowance, deduction or relief in relation to an assessment, such assessment shall be deemed to be amended accordingly.

Cross-references

Capital gains tax, applied by: s 931(3).

Definitions

inspector: ss 2(1), 5(1), 852; year of assessment: s 3(1).

Former enactments

ITA 1967 s 182.

921 Aggregation of assessments

(1) In this section, **"personal reliefs"** means relief under any of the provisions specified in the Table to section 458.

(2) Where 2 or more assessments to income tax are to be made on a person under Schedule D, E or F or under 2 or more of those Schedules, the tax in the assessments may be stated in one sum, and the notice of assessment may be stated correspondingly.

(3) A notice of appeal in a case in which subsection (2) applies shall, to be valid, indicate each assessment appealed against.

(4) Pending the determination of an appeal against any one or more assessments referred to in subsection (2), an amount of tax (being a portion of the one sum referred to in that subsection) shall be payable on the due date or dates and shall be the amount which results when the appropriate personal reliefs are deducted from the assessments not under appeal or allowed from the tax charged in those assessments, as may be appropriate.

(5) The tax stated in one sum under subsection (2) or the amount payable under subsection (4) shall for the purposes of sections 1080 and 1081 be deemed to be tax charged by an assessment to income tax.

(6) Where for any of the purposes of the Income Tax Acts other than subsection (4) it becomes necessary to determine what amount of the tax charged is applicable to any one of 2 or more assessments referred to in subsection (2), a certificate from the inspector indicating the manner in which the deductions, allowances or reliefs were allocated and stating the separate amounts of tax, if any, and the instalments of tax applicable to any one or more assessments or to each assessment shall be sufficient evidence of the charge to tax in and by each such assessment.

Definitions

inspector: ss 2(1), 5(1), 852; person: IA 1937 s 11(*c*).

Former enactments

ITA 1967 s 183(1)–(5)(*a*) and (7); FA 1969 s 65(1) and Sch 5 Pt I; CTA 1976 s 140(1) and Sch 2 Pt I para 6; FA 1980 s 19 and Sch 1 Pt III para 1; FA 1997 s 146(1) and Sch 9 Pt I para 1(11).

922 Assessment in absence of return

(1) In this section, **"information"** includes information received from a member of the Garda Síochána.

(2) Where the inspector does not receive a statement from a person liable to be charged to income tax, the inspector shall to the best of his or her information and judgment, but subject to section 997, make an assessment on that person of the amount at which that person ought to be charged under Schedule E.

(3) Where—

(*a*) a person makes default in the delivery of a statement in respect of any income tax under Schedule D or F, or

(*b*) the inspector is not satisfied with a statement which has been delivered, or has received any information as to its insufficiency, the inspector shall make an assessment on the person concerned in such sum as according to the best of the inspector's judgment ought to be charged on that person.

Cross-references

Capital gains tax, applied by: s 931(3).
Self assessment, appeals, subs (4): s 957(2)(*a*).
Self assessment, making of assessments: s 954(3).

Definitions

inspector: ss 2(1), 5(1), 852; person: IA 1937 s 11(*c*).

Former enactments

ITA 1967 s 184; FA 1969 s 33(1) and Sch 4 Pt I; CTA 1976 s 140(1) and Sch 2 Pt I para 7; DCITPA 1996 s5; CABA 1996 s24(1).

Corresponding UK tax provision

Taxes Management Act 1970 s 28C.

923 Function of certain assessors

(1) (*a*) A person appointed under section 855 to be an assessor and a person (in this section also referred to as an **"assessor"**) appointed under section 854 shall on request be furnished free of charge by any officer in the relevant department or office or by any agent by whom the same are payable with true accounts of any salaries, fees, wages, perquisites, profits, pensions or stipends chargeable under Schedule E.

(*b*) Every such assessor shall have access to all documents in his or her department or office which concern any such payments.

(*c*) Every such assessor may, if he or she is dissatisfied with any account referred to in paragraph (*a*) or in any case in which it may be necessary, require from any person to be charged an account of any salary, fees, wages, perquisites, profits, pensions or stipend, within the like period as is limited for the delivery of statements of profits or gains under the Income Tax Acts, and under the like penalty as is provided in the case of failure to deliver such statements.

(2) The assessors shall assess the persons who hold offices, or are entitled to pensions or stipends, in accordance with the annual amount thereof from the documents, accounts and papers in their respective departments.

(3) Every assessment shall set out—

(*a*) the full and just annual emoluments of every office and employment of profit, and the full annual amount of every pension or stipend,

(*b*) the names of the persons entitled to those emoluments, pensions or stipends, and

(*c*) the tax payable in each case.

(4) An assessor who fails to comply with this section shall be liable to a penalty not exceeding [€125][1] and not less than [€25][2].

Amendments

1 Substituted by FA 2001 s 240(1) and (2)(*k*) and Sch 5 Pt 1 as respects any act or omission which takes place or begins on or after 1 January 2002; previously "£100".

2 Substituted by FA 2001 s 240(1) and (2)(*k*) and Sch 5 Pt 1 as respects any act or omission which takes place or begins on or after 1 January 2002; previously "£20".

Definitions

person: IA 1937 s 11(*c*).

Former enactments

ITA 1967 s 185.

924 Additional assessments

(1) (*a*) Where the inspector discovers that—

(i) any properties or profits chargeable to income tax have been omitted from the first assessments,

(ii) a person chargeable—

(I) has not delivered any statement,

(II) has not delivered a full and proper statement,

(III) has not been assessed to income tax, or

(IV) has been undercharged in the first assessments, or

(iii) a person chargeable has been allowed, or has obtained from and in the first assessments, any allowance, deduction, exemption, abatement or relief not authorised by the Income Tax Acts,

then, where the tax is chargeable under Schedule D, E or F, the inspector shall make an additional first assessment.

(*b*) Any additional first assessment made by the inspector in accordance with paragraph (*a*) shall be subject to appeal and other proceedings as in the case of a first assessment.

(2) (*a*) In this subsection, **"neglect"** means negligence or a failure to give any notice, to make any return, statement or declaration, or to produce or furnish any list, document or other information required by or under the Income Tax Acts; but a person shall be deemed not to have failed to do anything required to be done within a limited time if such person did it within such further time, if any, as the Revenue Commissioners or officer concerned may have allowed and, where a person had a reasonable excuse for not doing anything required to be done, such person shall be deemed not to have failed to do it if such person did it without unreasonable delay after the excuse had ceased.

(*b*) Subject to paragraph (*c*) and any other provision allowing a longer period in any class of case, an assessment or an additional first assessment may be made at any time not later than [4 years][1] after the end of the year to which the assessment relates.

(*c*) In a case in which any form of fraud or neglect has been committed by or on behalf of any person in connection with or in relation to income tax, an assessment or an additional first assessment may be made at any time for any year for which by reason of the fraud or neglect income tax would otherwise be lost to the Exchequer.

(*d*) (i) In a case in which emoluments to which this subparagraph applies are received in a year of assessment subsequent to that for which they are assessable, paragraph (*b*) shall apply in the case of assessments or additional first assessments in respect of the emoluments subject to the substitution of a reference to the end of the year of assessment in which the emoluments were received for the reference to the end of the year to which the assessment relates.

(ii) The emoluments to which subparagraph (i) applies are emoluments within the meaning of section 112(2), including any payments chargeable to tax by virtue of section 123 and any sums which by virtue of Chapter 3 of Part 5 are to be treated as perquisites of a person's office or employment, being emoluments, payments or sums other than those taken into account in an assessment to income tax for the year of assessment in which they are received, and for the purposes of this paragraph—

(I) any such payment shall, notwithstanding anything in section 123(4), be treated as having been received at the time it was actually received, and

(II) any such sums which are not actually paid to that person shall be treated as having been received at the time when the relevant expenses were incurred or are treated for the purposes of Chapter 3 of Part 5 as having been incurred.

(*e*) An objection to the making of any assessment or additional first assessment on the ground that the time limited for the making of that assessment has expired shall only be made on appeal against the assessment.

(3) Any assessments not made at the time when the first assessments are made shall as soon as they are made be added to the first assessments by means of separate forms of assessment.

Amendments

1 Substituted by FA 2003 s 17(*f*) with effect from: (*a*) such day or days as the Minister for Finance may by order or orders appoint either generally or with reference to any particular purpose or provision and different days may be so appointed for different purposes or different provisions and (*b*) notwithstanding the generality of (*a*), any order made by the Minister for Finance in accordance with the provisions of that paragraph may contain, and be subject to, such conditions as the Minister considers appropriate and which are specified in the order; previously "10 years". By virtue of Finance Act 2003 (Commencement of Section 17) Order 2003, SI No 508 of 2003, this amendment comes into operation in relation to the making of an assessment referred to in section 924, on or after 1 January 2005.

Cross-references

Capital gains tax, applied by: s 931(3).

Interest on overdue income tax and corporation tax in cases of fraud or neglect, subs (2)(*a*): s 1082(1).

Self assessment, amendment of and time limit for assessments, subs (5)(*b*): ss 955(5)(*b*).

Withdrawal of BES relief, subs (2)(*c*): s 504(6).

Case law

Irish

Additional assessment made on the "discovery" of inadmissible deductions for earlier accounting periods upheld: *W Ltd v Wilson* ITR Vol II p 627.

Figures agreed between a company and inspector following an appeal were open to a further charge on a later discovery being made by the inspector: *Hammond Lane Metal Co Ltd v O'Culacháin* ITR Vol IV p 187.

The Commissioners of Inland Revenue were prevented, on a later discovery of errors, from amending as a basis of charge for later years a figure which had been agreed by the courts for an earlier period: *Boland's Ltd v Commissioners of Inland Revenue* ITR Vol I p 34.

UK

Subs (2): Held loss to the Exchequer would not simply be potential loss: *Billingham v Myers* [1996] STI Issue 14 p 36.

Tax Briefing

TB56 July 2004 pp 6–11 — Repayments, Interest and Time Limits — Section 17 FA 2003 changes.
TB57 Oct 2004 pp 7–9 — New Time Limits - Section 17 FA 2003 changes.
TB57 Oct 2004 p 15 — Repayments, Interest and Time Limits — correction to TB56 p 8.

Definitions

Income Tax Acts: s 1(2); inspector: ss 2(1), 5(1), 852; person: IA 1937 s 11(*c*); year of assessment: s 3(1).

Former enactments

ITA 1967 s 186; F(MP)A 1968 s 4(1); FA 1969 s 65(1) and Sch 5 Pt I; CTA 1976 s 140(1) and Sch 2 Pt I para 8; FA 1996 s 132(2) and Sch 5 Pt II.

925 Special rules relating to assessments under Schedule E

(1) Where at any time, either during the year of assessment or in respect of that year, a person becomes entitled to any additional salary, fees or emoluments over and above the amount for which an assessment to income tax has been made on that person, or for which at the commencement of that year that person was liable to be charged to income tax, an additional assessment shall, as often as the case may require, be made on that person in respect of any such additional salary, fees or emoluments, so that he or she may be charged in respect of the full amount of his or her salary, fees or emoluments for that year.

(2) Where any person proves to the satisfaction of the inspector that the amount for which an assessment to income tax has been made in respect of that person's salary, fees or emoluments for any year of assessment exceeds the amount of the salary, fees or emoluments for that year, the assessment shall be adjusted and any amount overpaid by means of tax shall be repaid.

Cross-references

Schedule E: s 19(1).

Former enactments

ITA 1967 Sch 2 para 1(1)–(2).

926 Estimation of certain amounts

(1) Where—

(*a*) the total income of any individual from all sources, whether chargeable with income tax by deduction or otherwise, includes income from any source or sources which is to be computed on the basis of the actual amounts receivable in the year of assessment or where any deductions allowable on account of any annual sums paid out of the property or profits of an individual are to be allowed as deductions in respect of the year in which they are payable, and

(*b*) an assessment to income tax is being made before the end of the year of assessment to which such assessment to tax relates,

the inspector in making the assessment shall, in computing the total amount of income assessable to income tax, estimate the amount of income from each such source or the amount of any such allowable deductions and, in making any such estimate, the inspector shall have due regard to any corresponding amount of income or allowable deductions in the year preceding the year of assessment and shall, in computing the income tax payable, estimate the amount of tax to be credited under sections 59 and 997.

[(1A)(*a*) A certificate to be issued by the Collector-General under this section may—

(i) be issued in an electronic or other format, and

(ii) where the certificate is issued in a non-paper format, be reproduced in a paper format by the county registrar or sheriff or by persons authorised by the county registrar or sheriff to do so.

(*b*) A certificate issued in a non-paper format in accordance with paragraph (*a*) shall—

(i) constitute a valid certificate for all the purposes of this section,

(ii) be deemed to have been made by the Collector-General, and

(iii) be deemed to have been issued on the date that the Collector-General caused the certificate to issue.

(*c*) (i) Where a certificate issued by the Collector-General in a non-paper format is reproduced in a paper format in accordance with paragraph (*a*)(ii) and—

(I) the reproduction contains, or there is appended to it, a note to the effect that it is a copy of a certificate so issued, and

(II) the note contains the signature of the county registrar or sheriff or of the person authorised under paragraph (*a*)(ii) and the date of such signing,

then the copy of the certificate with the note so signed and dated shall, for all purposes, have effect as if it was the certificate itself.

(ii) A signature and date in a note, on a copy of, or appended to, a certificate issued in a non-paper format by the Collector-General, and reproduced in a paper format in accordance with paragraph (*a*)(ii) that—

(I) in respect of such signature, purports to be that of the county registrar or sheriff or of a person authorised to make a copy, shall be taken until the contrary is shown to be the signature of the county registrar or sheriff or of a person who at the material time was so authorised, and

(II) in respect of such date, shall be taken until the contrary is shown to have been duly dated.

(*d*) For the purposes of this subsection—

"electronic" has the meaning assigned to it by the Electronic Commerce Act 2000 and an **"electronic certificate"** shall be construed accordingly;

"issued in a non-paper format" includes issued by facsimile.][1]

(2) Where—

(*a*) an estimate has been made under subsection (1),

(*b*) notice of an appeal against the assessment to income tax has not been given, and

(*c*) the person assessed gives to the inspector within a period of one year from the end of the year of assessment particulars of the correct amount of the income or deductions in respect of which the estimate was made, the inspector shall adjust the assessment by reference to the difference between the correct amount of income assessable to income tax and the amount of the assessment, and any amount of income tax overpaid shall be repaid.

Amendments

1 Subs (1A) inserted by FA 2004 s 84 with effect from 1 January 2004.

Cross-references

Self assessment: s 959(7).

Definitions

inspector: ss 2(1), 5(1), 852; person: IA 1937 s 11(*c*); total income: s 3(1); year of assessment: s 3(1).

Former enactments

ITA 1967 s 528; FA 1974 s 11 and Sch 1 Pt II.

927 Rectification of excessive set-off, etc of tax credit

(1) Where an inspector discovers that any set-off or payment of tax credit ought not to have been made or is or has become excessive, the inspector may make any such assessments as may in his or her judgment be required for recovering any tax that ought to have been paid or any payment of tax credit that ought not to have been made and generally for securing that the resulting liabilities to tax of the persons concerned are what they would have been if only such set-offs or payments had been made as ought to have been made.

(2) This Part, Part 40 and Part 42 shall apply to any assessment under this section for recovering a payment of tax credit as if it were an assessment to income tax for the year of assessment, or, in the case of a company, corporation tax for the accounting period, in respect of which the payment was claimed and as if that payment represented a loss of tax to the Exchequer, and any sum charged by any such assessment shall, subject to any appeal against the assessment, be due within 14 days after the issue of the notice of assessment.

Definitions

company: ss 4(1), 5(1); inspector: ss 2(1), 5(1), 852; tax credit: ss 2(1), 136; year of assessment: ss 2(1), 5(1).

Former enactments

CTA 1976 s 161.

928 Transmission to Collector-General of particulars of sums to be collected

(1) After assessments to income tax and corporation tax have been made, the inspectors shall transmit particulars of the sums to be collected to the Collector-General for collection.

(2) The entering by an inspector or other authorised officer of details of an assessment to income tax or corporation tax and of the tax charged in such an assessment in an electronic, photographic or other record from which the Collector-General may extract such details by electronic, photographic or other process shall constitute transmission of such details by the inspector or other authorised officer to the Collector-General.

(3) Subsection (2) shall apply for the purposes of value-added tax as it applies for the purposes of income tax or corporation tax with the substitution of "value-added tax" for "income tax or corporation tax".

Cross-references

Capital acquisitions tax, application of certain income tax provisions in relation to collection and recovery of, subs (1): CATCA 2003 s 64(3).

Capital gains tax, applied by: s 931(3).

Collection of capital gains tax: s 976(1).

Collector-General: s 851(2).

Corporation tax, subs (1): s 973.

Evidence of electronic transmission of particulars of income tax to be collected in proceedings for recovery of tax, subs (2): s 967.

Generation of estimates by electronic, photographic or other process: s 990A(*b*).

Income Tax (Relevant Contracts) Regulations 2000, SI No 71 of 2000: ITRCR 2000 Reg 15(2).

Subss (2)–(3) to be construed together with the Value Added Tax Acts 1972–1997, in so far as relating to value added tax: s 1104(3).

Definitions

inspector: ss 2(1), 5(1), 852.

Former enactments

ITA 1967 s 187(1); FA 1974 s 86 and Sch 2 Pt I; CTA 1976 s 147(1)–(2); FA 1986 s 113(5); FA 1996 s 132(2) and Sch 5 Pt II.

CHAPTER 2
Provision Against Double Assessment and Relief for Error or Mistake

929 Double assessment

(1) A person who, either on the person's own account or on behalf of another person, has been assessed to income tax or corporation tax, and is by any error or mistake again assessed for the same year of assessment or the same accounting period, as the case may be, for the same cause and on the same account, may apply for relief to the Appeal Commissioners who, on proof to their satisfaction of the double assessment, shall cause the assessment, or so much of the assessment as constitutes a double assessment, to be vacated.

(2) Where it appears to the satisfaction of the Revenue Commissioners that a person has been assessed more than once for the same cause and for the same year of assessment or the same accounting period, as the case may be, they shall direct the whole, or such part, of any assessment as appears to be an overcharge to be vacated, and thereupon the whole, or such part, of the assessment shall be vacated accordingly.

(3) Where it is proved to the satisfaction of the Revenue Commissioners that any such double assessment has been made and that payment has been made on both assessments, they shall order the amount of the overpayment to be repaid to the applicant.

Cross-references

Capital gains tax, applied by: s 931(3).

Definitions

Appeal Commissioners: s 2(1); person: IA 1937 s 11(*c*).

Former enactments

ITA 1967 s 190; F(MP)A 1968 s 3(2) and Sch Pt I; CTA 1976 s 147(1)–(2).

Corresponding UK tax provision

Taxes Management Act 1970 s 32.

930 Error or mistake

Amendments

Section 930 deleted by FA 2003 s 17(*d*) with effect from: (*a*) such day or days as the Minister for Finance may by order or orders appoint either generally or with reference to any particular purpose or provision and different days may be so appointed for different purposes or different provisions and (*b*) notwithstanding the generality of (*a*), any order made by the Minister for Finance in accordance with the provisions of that paragraph may contain, and be subject to, such conditions as the Minister considers appropriate and which are specified in the order; previously "(1) Where any person who has paid tax charged under an assessment to—

(*a*) income tax made for any year of assessment, or

(*b*) corporation tax made for any accounting period,

alleges that the assessment was excessive by reason of some error or mistake in the return or statement made by that person for the purposes of the assessment, that person may, at any time not later than 6 years after the end of the year of assessment or the accounting period, as the case may be, within which the assessment was made, make an application in writing to the Revenue Commissioners for relief.

(2) On receiving any such application, the Revenue Commissioners shall inquire into the matter and shall, subject to this section, give by means of repayment such relief in respect of the error or mistake as is just and reasonable; but no relief shall be given under this section in respect of an error or mistake as to the basis on which the liability of the applicant ought to have been computed where the return or statement was in fact made on the basis of, or in accordance with, the practice generally prevailing at the time when the return or statement was made.

(3) In determining any application under this section, the Revenue Commissioners shall have regard to all the relevant circumstances of the case and in particular shall consider whether the granting of relief would result in the exclusion from the charge to income tax or corporation tax, as the case may be, of any part of the profits or income of the applicant, and for this purpose the Revenue Commissioners may take into consideration the liability of the applicant and assessments made on the applicant in respect of other years of assessment or accounting periods, as the case may be.

(4) Any person aggrieved by the determination of the Revenue Commissioners on an application made by that person under this section may, on giving notice in writing to the Revenue Commissioners within 21 days after the notification to that person of their determination, appeal to the Appeal Commissioners.

(5) The Appeal Commissioners shall thereupon hear and determine the appeal in accordance with the principles to be followed by the Revenue Commissioners in determining applications under this section and, subject to those principles, in the like manner as in the case of an appeal to them against an assessment to income tax, and the provisions of the Income Tax Acts relating to such an appeal (including the provisions relating to the rehearing of an appeal and to the statement of a case for the opinion of the High Court on a point of law) shall apply accordingly with any necessary modifications; but neither the appellant nor the Revenue Commissioners shall be entitled to require a case to be stated for the opinion of the High Court otherwise than on a point of law arising in connection with the computation of profits or income.".

By virtue of Finance Act 2003 (Commencement of Section 17) Order 2003, SI No 508 of 2003, this deletion comes into operation on 1 January 2005, but without prejudice to any application for relief made under section 930 before that day.

Cross-references

Capital gains tax, applied by: s 931(3).

Revenue precedents

Issue: Whether a repayment under s 930 could attract interest as a repayment of Preliminary Tax.

Decision: The repayment made under s 930 is not a repayment of Preliminary Tax. It is a repayment which takes its character from s 930. There is no provision in that section for the payment of interest - the section speaks only of giving relief by way of repayment - there is no mention of payment of interest.

Tax Briefing

TB56 July 2004 pp 6–11 — Repayments, Interest and Time Limits — Section 17 FA 2003 changes.

TB57 Oct 2004 pp 7–9 — New Time Limits — Section 17 FA 2003 changes.

TB57 Oct 2004 p 15 — Repayments, Interest and Time Limits — correction to TB56 p 8.

Definitions

Appeal Commissioners: s 2(1); High Court: IA 1937 Sch; person: IA 1937 s 11(*c*); writing: IA 1937 Sch; year of assessment: s 3(1).

Former enactments

ITA 1967 s 191(1)–(5); F(MP)A 1968 s 3(2) and Sch Pt I; FA 1974 s 86 and Sch 2 Pt I; CTA 1976 s 143(12)(*a*); FA 1995 s 15(*a*) and (*b*).

Corresponding UK tax provision

Taxes Management Act 1970 s 33.

CHAPTER 3
Capital Gains Tax

931 Making of assessments and application of income tax assessment provisions

(1) Assessments under the Capital Gains Tax Acts shall be made by inspectors or such other officers as the Revenue Commissioners shall appoint in that behalf.

(2) The provisions of the Income Tax Acts relating to the assessment of income tax shall, subject to any necessary modifications, apply in relation to capital gains tax as they apply in relation to income tax chargeable under Schedule D.

(3) In particular and without prejudice to the generality of subsection (2), subsections (2) and (3) of section 918 and [sections 920, 922, 924, 928 and 929][1] shall, subject to any necessary modifications, apply to capital gains tax.

Amendments

1 Substituted by FA 2003 s 17(*e*) with effect from: (*a*) such day or days as the Minister for Finance may by order or orders appoint either generally or with reference to any particular purpose or provision and different days may be so appointed for different purposes or different provisions and (*b*) notwithstanding the generality of (*a*), any order made by the Minister for Finance in accordance with the provisions of that paragraph may contain, and be subject to, such conditions as the Minister considers appropriate and which are specified in the order; previously "sections 920, 922, 924 and 928 to 930". By virtue of Finance Act 2003 (Commencement of Section 17) Order 2003, SI No 508 of 2003, this amendment comes into operation on 1 January 2005, but without prejudice to any application for relief made under section 930 before that day.

Cross-references

Appeals against capital gains tax assessments, subs (1): s 945(1), (2)(*c*).

Charging and assessment of persons not resident or ordinarily resident, subs (2): s 1043.

Interest on overdue capital gains tax in cases of fraud or neglect, subs (2): s 1083.

Self assessment: s 959(6).

Valuation of assets, power to inspect, subs (1): s 911(1).

Former enactments

CGTA 1975 s 51(1) and Sch 4 paras 1(2) and 2.

Corresponding UK tax provision

Taxes Management Act 1970 s 29.

PART 40
APPEALS

Cross-references

Rectification of excessive set off etc, of tax credit: s 927(2).

Income Tax (Employments) (Consolidation) Regulations 2001, SI No 559 of 2001: reg 38 (objections and appeals against assessment).

CHAPTER 1
Appeals Against Income Tax and Corporation Tax Assessments

932 Prohibition on alteration of assessment except on appeal

Except where expressly authorised by the Tax Acts, an assessment to income tax or corporation tax shall not be altered before the time for hearing and determining appeals and then only in cases of assessments appealed against and in accordance with such determination, and if any person makes, causes, or allows to be made in any assessment any unauthorised alteration, that person shall incur a penalty of [€60][1].

Amendments

1 Substituted by FA 2001 s 240(1) and (2)(*k*) and Sch 5 Pt 1 as respects any act or omission which takes place or begins on or after 1 January 2002; previously "£50".

Definitions

person: IA 1937 s 11(*c*).

Former enactments

ITA 1967 s 415; CTA 1976 s 146(1); FA 1983 s 37.

933 Appeals against assessment

(1) (*a*) A person aggrieved by any assessment to income tax or corporation tax made on that person by the inspector or such other officer as the Revenue Commissioners shall appoint in that behalf (in this section referred to as **"other officer"**) shall be entitled to appeal to the Appeal Commissioners on giving, within 30 days after the date of the notice of assessment, notice in writing to the inspector or other officer.

(*b*) Where on an application under paragraph (*a*) the inspector or other officer is of the opinion that the person who has given the notice of appeal is not entitled to make such an appeal, the inspector or other officer shall refuse the application and notify the person in writing accordingly, specifying the grounds for such refusal.

(*c*) A person who has had an application under paragraph (*a*) refused by the inspector or other officer shall be entitled to appeal against such refusal by notice in writing to the Appeal Commissioners within 15 days of the date of issue by the inspector or other officer of the notice of refusal.

(*d*) On receipt of an application under paragraph (*c*), the Appeal Commissioners shall request the inspector or other officer to furnish them with a copy of the notice issued to the person under paragraph (*b*) and, on receipt of the copy of the notice, they shall as soon as possible—

(i) refuse the application for an appeal by giving notice in writing to the applicant specifying the grounds for their refusal,

(ii) allow the application for an appeal and give notice in writing accordingly to both the applicant and the inspector or other officer, or

(iii) notify in writing both the applicant and the inspector or other officer that they have decided to arrange a hearing at such time and place specified in the notice to enable them determine whether or not to allow the application for an appeal.

(2) (*a*) The Appeal Commissioners shall from time to time appoint times and places for the hearing of appeals against assessments and the Clerk to the Appeal Commissioners shall give notice of such times and places to the inspector or other officer.

(*b*) The inspector or other officer shall give notice in writing to each person who has given notice of appeal of the time and place appointed for the hearing of that person's appeal; but—

(i) notice under this paragraph shall not be given in a case in which subsection (3)(*b*) applies either consequent on an agreement referred to in that subsection or consequent on a notice referred to in subsection (3)(*d*), and

(ii) in a case where it appears to the inspector or other officer that an appeal may be settled by agreement under subsection (3), he or she may refrain from giving notice under this paragraph or may by notice in writing and with the agreement of the appellant withdraw a notice already given.

(*c*) Where, on application in writing in that behalf to the Appeal Commissioners, a person who has given notice of appeal to the inspector or other officer in accordance with subsection (1)(*a*) satisfies the Appeal Commissioners that the information furnished to the inspector or other officer is such that the appeal is likely to be determined on the first occasion on which it comes before them for hearing, the Appeal Commissioners may direct the inspector or other officer to give the notice in writing first mentioned in paragraph (*b*) and the inspector or other officer shall comply forthwith with such direction, and accordingly subparagraph (ii) of that paragraph shall not apply to that notice of appeal.

(3) (*a*) This subsection shall apply to any assessment in respect of which notice of appeal has been given, not being an assessment the appeal against which has been determined by the Appeal Commissioners or which has become final and conclusive under subsection (6).

(*b*) Where, in relation to an assessment to which this subsection applies, the inspector or other officer and the appellant come to an agreement, whether in writing or otherwise, that the assessment is to stand, is to be amended in a particular manner or is to be discharged or cancelled, the inspector or other officer shall give effect to the agreement and thereupon, if the agreement is that the assessment is to stand or is to be amended, the assessment or the amended assessment, as the case may be, shall have the same force and effect as if it were an assessment in respect of which no notice of appeal had been given.

(*c*) An agreement which is not in writing shall be deemed not to be an agreement for the purposes of paragraph (*b*) unless—

(i) the fact that an agreement was come to, and the terms agreed on, are confirmed by notice in writing given by the inspector or other officer to the appellant or by the appellant to the inspector or other officer, and

(ii) 21 days have elapsed since the giving of that notice without the person to whom it was given giving notice in writing to the person by whom it was given that the first-mentioned person desires to repudiate or withdraw from the agreement.

(*d*) Where an appellant desires not to proceed with the appeal against an assessment to which this subsection applies and gives notice in writing to that effect to the inspector or other officer, paragraph (*b*) shall apply as if the appellant and the inspector or other officer had, on the appellant's notice being received, come to an agreement in writing that the assessment should stand.

(*e*) References in this subsection to an agreement being come to with an appellant and the giving of notice to or by an appellant include references to an agreement being come to with, and the giving of notice to or by, a person acting on behalf of the appellant in relation to the appeal.

(4) All appeals against assessments to income tax or corporation tax shall be heard and determined by the Appeal Commissioners, and their determination on any such appeal shall be final and conclusive, unless the person assessed requires that that person's appeal shall be reheard under section 942 or unless under the Tax Acts a case is required to be stated for the opinion of the High Court.

(5) An appeal against an assessment may be heard and determined by one Appeal Commissioner, and the powers conferred on the Appeal Commissioners by this Part may be exercised by one Appeal Commissioner.

(6) (*a*) In default of notice of appeal by a person to whom notice of assessment has been given, the assessment made on that person shall be final and conclusive.

(*b*) Where a person who has given notice of appeal against an assessment does not attend before the Appeal Commissioners at the time and place appointed for the hearing of that person's appeal, the assessment made on that person shall, subject to subsection (8), have the same force and effect as if it were an assessment in respect of which no notice of appeal had been given.

(*c*) Where on the hearing of an appeal against an assessment—

(i) no application is or has been made to the Appeal Commissioners before or during the hearing of the appeal by or on behalf of the appellant for an adjournment of the proceedings on the appeal or such an application is or has been made and is or was refused, and

(ii) (I) a return of the appellant's income for the relevant year of assessment or, as the case may be, a return under section 884 has not been made by the appellant, or

(II) such a return has been made but—

(A) all the statements of profits and gains, schedules and other evidence relating to such return have not been furnished by or on behalf of the appellant,

(B) information requested from the appellant by the Appeal Commissioners in the hearing of the appeal has not been supplied by the appellant,

(C) the terms of a precept issued by the Appeal Commissioners under section 935 have not been complied with by the appellant, or

(D) any questions as to an assessment or assessments put by the Appeal Commissioners under section 938 have not been answered to their satisfaction, the Appeal Commissioners shall make an order dismissing the appeal against the assessment and thereupon the assessment shall have the same force and effect as if it were an assessment in respect of which no notice of appeal had been given.

(*d*) An application for an adjournment of the proceedings on an appeal against an assessment, being an application made before or during the hearing of the appeal, shall not be refused before the expiration of 9 months from the earlier of—

(i) the end of the year of assessment or, as the case may be, accounting period to which the assessment appealed against relates, and

(ii) the date on which the notice of assessment was given to the appellant.

(*e*) Paragraph (*c*) shall not apply if on the hearing of the appeal the Appeal Commissioners are satisfied that sufficient information has been furnished by or on behalf of the appellant to enable them to determine the appeal at that hearing.

(7) (*a*) A notice of appeal not given within the time limited by subsection (1) shall be regarded as having been so given where, on an application in writing having been made to the inspector or other officer in that behalf within 12 months after the date of the notice of assessment, the inspector or other officer, being satisfied that owing to absence, sickness or other reasonable cause the applicant was prevented from giving notice of appeal within the time limited and that the application was made thereafter without unreasonable delay, notifies the applicant in writing that the application under this paragraph has been allowed.

(*b*) Where on an application under paragraph (*a*) the inspector or other officer is not so satisfied, he or she shall by notice in writing inform the applicant that the application under this paragraph has been refused.

(*c*) Within 15 days after the date of a notice under paragraph (*b*) the applicant may by notice in writing require the inspector or other officer to refer the application to the Appeal Commissioners and, in relation to any application so referred, paragraphs (*a*) and (*b*) shall apply as if for every reference in those paragraphs to the inspector or other officer there were substituted a reference to the Appeal Commissioners.

(*d*) Notwithstanding paragraph (*a*), an application made after the expiration of the time specified in that paragraph which but for that expiration would have been allowed under paragraph (*a*) may be allowed under that paragraph if at the time of the application—

(i) there has been made to the inspector or other officer a return of income or, as the case may be, a return under section 884, statements of profits and gains and such other information as in the opinion of the inspector or other officer would enable the appeal to be settled by agreement under subsection (3), and

(ii) the income tax or corporation tax charged by the assessment in respect of which the application is made has been paid together with any interest on that tax chargeable under section 1080.

(*e*) Where on an application referred to in paragraph (*d*) the inspector or other officer is not satisfied that the information furnished would be sufficient to enable the appeal to be settled by agreement under subsection (3) or if the tax and interest mentioned in paragraph (*d*)(ii) have not been paid, the inspector or other officer shall by notice in writing inform the applicant that the application has been refused.

(*f*) Within 15 days after the date of a notice under paragraph (*e*) the applicant may by notice in writing require the inspector or other officer to refer the application to the Appeal Commissioners and, in relation to an application so referred, if—

(i) the application is one which but for the expiration of the period specified in paragraph (*a*) would have been allowed under paragraph (*c*) if the application had been referred to the Appeal Commissioners under that paragraph,

(ii) at the time the application is referred to the Appeal Commissioners the income tax or corporation tax charged by the assessment in respect of which the application is made, together with any interest on that tax chargeable under section 1080, has been paid, and

(iii) the information furnished to the inspector or other officer is such that in the opinion of the Appeal Commissioners the appeal is likely to be determined on the first occasion on which it comes before them for hearing,

the Appeal Commissioners may allow the application.

(8) In a case in which a person who has given notice of appeal does not attend before the Appeal Commissioners at the time and place appointed for the hearing of that person's appeal, subsection (6)(*b*) shall not apply if—

(*a*) at that time and place another person attends on behalf of the appellant and the Appeal Commissioners consent to hear that other person,

(*b*) on an application in that behalf having been made to them in writing or otherwise at or before that time, the Appeal Commissioners postpone the hearing, or

(*c*) on an application in writing having been made to them after that time the Appeal Commissioners, being satisfied that, owing to absence, sickness or other reasonable cause, the appellant was prevented from appearing before them at that time and place and that the application was made without unreasonable delay, direct that the appeal be treated as one the time for the hearing of which has not yet been appointed.

(9) (*a*) Where action for the recovery of income tax or corporation tax charged by an assessment has been taken, being action by means of the institution of proceedings in any court or the issue of a certificate under section 962, neither subsection (7) nor subsection (8) shall apply in relation to that assessment until that action has been completed.

(*b*) Where, in a case within paragraph (*a*), an application under subsection (7)(*a*) is allowed or, on an application under subsection (8)(*c*), the Appeal Commissioners direct as provided in that subsection, the applicant shall in no case be entitled to repayment of any sum paid or borne by the applicant in respect of costs of any such court proceedings or, as the case may be, of any fees or expenses charged by the county registrar or sheriff executing a certificate under section 962.

Cross-references

Appeal to Circuit Court, subs (3)(*b*), (*c*), (*e*): s 942(8).

Appeals against determination made under ss 98–100, subs (7): s 947(2).

Appeals against determinations of certain claims etc: s 949(2); subss (5) and (7)–(9): s 949(4).

Application to Appeal Commissioners: information from financial institutions: s 907(8)(*b*).

Farming, averaging of farming profits: s 657(4)(*a*)(i).

Income Tax (Purchased Life Annuities) Regulations 1959, SI No 152 of 1959 reg 7.

Schemes to avoid liability to tax under Sch F, meaning of "appeal": s 817(1)(*a*).

Self assessment, meaning of "appeal" applied: s 950(1).

Self assessment, meaning of "determination of the appeal", subss (3), (4), (6): s 950(1).

Case law

Irish

The prerequistes to a valid appeal are not optional and can only be circumscribed in limited circumstances – *Keogh v Criminal Assets Bureau, Revenue Commissioners* 2003 ITR 59.

Subs (1): Appeal procedures to be used in priority to direct court proceedings by a taxpayer; time limits and Revenue powers under this section not unconstitutional: *Deighan v Hearne* ITR Vol III p 533.

Proceedings for fraud instituted by the Revenue did not prohibit further official action for the same liabilities by way of assessments and the use of the appeal procedures: *Revenue Commissioners v Calcul International Ltd* (High Court, 18 December 1986).

The "giving of notice of appeal within 30 days", emphasise the deed of "giving" rather than the receipt of notice. Also the computation of the 15 day period for bringing an appeal against a refusal should include the date of issue of the refusal letter: *Criminal Asset Bureau v P McS.*

Subs (4): Function of Appeal Commissioners to make a final determination of an assessment, which allows for revisions of earlier interim decisions on other connected matters: *The State v Smidic* ITR Vol I p 576.

Mandamus proceedings to amend a final determination of the Appeal Commissioners not competent: *The King (E Spain) v Special Commissioners*, 1 ITC 227 [1934] IR 27.

The High Court refused to overrule a factual decision by the Appeal Commissioners on the nature of an "ex gratia" payment made to a President of the University College Dublin on his retirement: *Mulvey v Coffey*, 2 ITC 239; [1942] IR 277. See also *O'Dwyer v Irish Exporters and Importers Ltd (In liquidation)* ITR Vol I p 629.

Primary facts as determined by the Appeal Commissioners are only to be set aside where there is no evidence to support them: *Mara v Hummingbird Ltd* ITR Vol II p 667. See also *McMahon v Murphy* ITR Vol IV p 125, a capital gains tax case; *Revenue Commissioners v O'Loinsigh* (High Court, 21 December 1994).

Time limits and Revenue powers under this section not unconstitutional: *Deighan v Hearne* ITR Vol III p 573.

Subs (7): The phrase "other reasonable cause" must be read eiusden generis with the words absense and sickness: *Criminal Assets Bureau v D(K)*.

In enacting elaborate procedures for the determination of a taxpayer's liability by assessment and appeal, the Oireachtas provided exclusive machinery for the ascertainment of a taxpayer's liability. The High Court does not retain an inherent jurisdiction to determine a person's liability to tax – *Criminal Assets Bureau v Sean and Rosaleen Hunt (nee) Maher* 2003 ITR 93.

UK

Subs (3): Where agreement based on erroneous view of the law, the parties could enter into a corrective agreement which was operative under the section: *Tod v South Essex Motors* [1988] STC 392.

Error in amended assessment followed by taxpayer's silence held not an agreement: *Schutdenfrei v Hilton* [1998] STC 404.

Held assessment based on error in an agreement could be amended by the Court: *Richart v Bass Holdings Ltd*; *R v HMIT (ex parte Bass Holdings Ltd)* [1993] STC 122.

Held accountant who had been suspended from practice for criminal convictions had no right of audience: *Cassell v Crutchfield* [1995] STC 663.

Is only in exceptional circumstances that judicial review of an assessment would be entertained when appeal procedure was in place: *R v IRC, Ex Parte Caglar* [1995] STC 741; *Development Inc v CIR* [1996] STC 440.

Held was no breach of Commissioners' duty of confidentiality to hear more than one appeal together: *Johnson v Walden* [1996] STI 592.

Definitions

Appeal Commissioners: s 2(1); Circuit Court: IA 1937 Sch; High Court: IA 1937 Sch; inspector: ss 2(1), 5(1), 852; month: IA 1937 Sch; person: IA 1937 s 11(*c*); writing: IA 1937 Sch; year of assessment: s 3(1).

Former enactments

ITA 1967 s 416(1)–(7)(*f*), (8) and (9); F(MP)A 1968 s 3(1), s 3(2) and Sch Pt I; CTA 1976 s 146(1); FA 1980 s 54(1); FA 1983 s 9(*a*)(i) and s37; FA 1995 s 173(1)(*a*).

Corresponding UK tax provision

Taxes Management Act 1970 ss 31–31D.

934 Procedure on appeals

(1) The inspector or such other officer as the Revenue Commissioners shall authorise in that behalf (in this section referred to as **"other officer"**) may attend every hearing of an appeal, and shall be entitled—

(*a*) to be present during all the hearing and at the determination of the appeal,

(*b*) to produce any lawful evidence in support of the assessment, and

(*c*) to give reasons in support of the assessment.

(2) (*a*) On any appeal, the Appeal Commissioners shall permit any barrister or solicitor to plead before them on behalf of the appellant or the inspector or other officer either orally or in writing and shall hear—

(i) any accountant, being any person who has been admitted a member of an incorporated society of accountants, or

(ii) any person who has been admitted a member of the body incorporated under the Companies Act, 1963, on the 31st day of December, 1975, as **"The Institute of Taxation in Ireland"**.

(*b*) Notwithstanding paragraph (*a*), the Appeal Commissioners may permit any other person representing the appellant to plead before them where they are satisfied that such permission should be given.

(3) Where on an appeal it appears to the Appeal Commissioners by whom the appeal is heard, or to a majority of such Appeal Commissioners, by examination of the appellant on oath or affirmation or by other lawful evidence that the appellant is overcharged by any assessment, the Appeal Commissioners shall abate or reduce the assessment accordingly, but otherwise the Appeal Commissioners shall determine the appeal by ordering that the assessment shall stand.

(4) Where on any appeal it appears to the Appeal Commissioners that the person assessed ought to be charged in an amount exceeding the amount contained in the assessment, they shall charge that person with the excess.

(5) Unless the circumstances of the case otherwise require, where on an appeal against an assessment which assesses an amount which is chargeable to income tax or corporation tax it appears to the Appeal Commissioners—

(*a*) that the appellant is overcharged by the assessment, they may in determining the appeal reduce only the amount which is chargeable to income tax or corporation tax,

(*b*) that the appellant is correctly charged by the assessment, they may in determining the appeal order that the amount which is chargeable to income tax or corporation tax shall stand, and (*c*) that the appellant ought to be charged in an amount exceeding the amount contained in the assessment, they may charge the excess by increasing only the amount which is chargeable to income tax or corporation tax.

(6) Where an appeal is determined by the Appeal Commissioners, the inspector or other officer shall give effect to the Appeal Commissioners' determination and thereupon, if the determination is that the assessment is to stand or is to be amended, the assessment or the amended assessment, as the case may be, shall have the same force and effect as if it were an assessment in respect of which no notice of appeal had been given.

(7) Every determination of an appeal by the Appeal Commissioners shall be recorded by them in the prescribed form at the time the determination is made and the Appeal Commissioners shall within 10 days after the determination transmit that form to the inspector or other officer.

Cross-references

Appeal to Circuit Court, subs (2): s 942(4).

Value added tax, this section applied by: VATA 1972 s 25(2)(*c*).

Definitions

Appeal Commissioners: s 2(1); inspector: ss 2(1), 5(1), 852; oath: IA 1937 Sch; person: IA 1937 s 11(*c*); writing: IA 1937 Sch.

Former enactments

ITA 1967 s 421; FA 1968 s 16; CTA 1976 s 146(1); FA 1980 s 54(2); FA 1983 s 9(*a*)(ii) and s 37; FA 1990 s 28; FA 1995 s 173(1)(*b*).

---

935 Power to issue precepts

(1) Where notice of appeal has been given against an assessment, the Appeal Commissioners may, whenever it appears to them to be necessary for the purposes of the Tax Acts, issue a precept to the appellant ordering the appellant to deliver to them, within the time limited by the precept, a schedule containing such particulars for their information as they may demand under the authority of the Tax Acts in relation to—

(*a*) the property of the appellant,

(*b*) the trade, profession or employment carried on or exercised by the appellant,

(*c*) the amount of the appellant's profits or gains, distinguishing the particular amounts derived from each separate source, or

(*d*) any deductions made in determining the appellant's profits or gains.

(2) The Appeal Commissioners may issue further precepts whenever they consider it necessary for the purposes of the Tax Acts, until complete particulars have been furnished to their satisfaction.

(3) A precept may be issued by one Appeal Commissioner.

(4) A person to whom a precept is issued shall deliver the schedule required within the time limited by the precept.

(5) Any inspector or such other officer as the Revenue Commissioners shall authorise in that behalf may at all reasonable times inspect and take copies of or extracts from any such schedule.

Cross-references

Appeals against assessments: s 933(6)(*c*)(ii)(II)(C).
Objection by inspector or other officer to schedules: s 936(1).
Penalty: Sch 29 column 2.

Definitions

Appeal Commissioners: s 2(1); inspector: ss 2(1), 5(1), 852; person: IA 1937 s 11(*c*); profession: s 2(1); trade: s 3(1).

Former enactments

ITA 1967 s 422; F(MP)A 1968 s 3(1), s 3(2) and Sch Pt I; CTA 1976 s 146(1); FA 1983 s 37; FA 1995 s 173(1)(*b*).

936 Objection by inspector or other officer to schedules

(1) The inspector or such other officer as the Revenue Commissioners shall authorise in that behalf (in this section referred to as **"other officer"**) may, within a reasonable time to be allowed by the Appeal Commissioners after examination by the inspector or other officer of any schedule referred to in section 935, object to that schedule or any part of that schedule, and in that case shall state in writing the cause of his or her objection according to the best of his or her knowledge or information.

(2) In every such case the inspector or other officer shall give notice in writing of his or her objection to the person chargeable in order that that person may, if that person thinks fit, appeal against the objection.

(3) A notice under subsection (2) shall be under cover and sealed, and addressed to the person chargeable.

(4) No assessment shall be confirmed or altered until any appeal against the objection has been heard and determined.

Definitions

Appeal Commissioners: s 2(1); inspector: ss 2(1), 5(1), 852; person: IA 1937 s 11(*c*); writing: IA 1937 Sch.

Former enactments

ITA 1967 s 423; F(MP)A 1968 s 3(2) and Sch Pt I; CTA 1976 s 146(1); FA 1995 s 173(1)(*b*).

937 Confirmation and amendment of assessments

Where—

(*a*) the Appeal Commissioners see cause to disallow an objection to a schedule by the inspector or such other officer as the Revenue Commissioners shall authorise in that behalf, or

(*b*) on the hearing of an appeal, the Appeal Commissioners are satisfied with the assessment, or if, after the delivery of a schedule, they are satisfied with the schedule and have received no information as to its insufficiency,

they shall confirm or alter the assessment in accordance with the schedule, as the case may require.

Definitions

Appeal Commissioners: s 2(1); inspector: ss 2(1), 5(1), 852.

Former enactments

ITA 1967 s 424; F(MP)A 1968 s 3(2) and Sch Pt I; CTA 1976 s 146(1); FA 1995 s 173(1)(*b*).

938 Questions as to assessments or schedules

(1) Whenever the Appeal Commissioners are dissatisfied with a schedule or require further information relating to a schedule, they may at any time and from time to time by precept put any questions in writing concerning the schedule, or any matter which is contained or ought to be contained in the schedule, or concerning any deductions made in arriving at the profits or gains, and the particulars thereof, and may require true and particular answers in writing signed by the person chargeable to be given within 7 days after the service of the precept.

(2) The person chargeable shall within the time limited either answer any such questions in writing signed by that person, or shall present himself or herself to be examined orally before the Appeal Commissioners, and may object to and refuse to answer any question; but the substance of any answer given by that person orally shall be taken down in writing in that person's presence and be read over to that person and, after that person has had liberty to amend any such answer, he or she may be required to verify the answer on oath to be administered to him or her by any one of the Appeal Commissioners, and the oath shall be subscribed by the person by whom it is made.

(3) Where any clerk, agent or servant of the person chargeable presents himself or herself on behalf of that person to be examined orally before the Appeal Commissioners, the same provisions shall apply to his or her examination as in the case of the person chargeable who presents himself or herself to be examined orally.

Cross-references

Appeals against assessments: s 933(6)(*c*)(ii)(II)(D).

Definitions

Appeal Commissioners: s 2(1); oath: IA 1937 Sch; person: IA 1937 s 11(*c*); writing: IA 1937 Sch.

Former enactments

ITA 1967 s 425; F(MP)A 1968 s 3(2) and Sch Pt I; CTA 1976 s 146(1).

939 Summoning and examination of witnesses

(1) (*a*) The Appeal Commissioners may summon any person whom they think able to give evidence as respects an assessment made on another person to appear before them to be examined, and may examine such person on oath.

(*b*) The clerk, agent, servant or other person confidentially employed in the affairs of a person chargeable shall be examined in the same manner, and subject to the same restrictions, as in the case of a person chargeable who presents himself or herself to be examined orally.

(2) The oath shall be that the evidence to be given, touching the matter in question, by the person sworn shall be the truth, the whole truth and nothing but the truth, and the oath shall be subscribed by the person by whom it is made.

(3) A person who after being duly summoned—

(*a*) neglects or refuses to appear before the Appeal Commissioners at the time and place appointed for that purpose,

(*b*) appears but refuses to be sworn or to subscribe the oath, or (*c*) refuses to answer any lawful question touching the matters under consideration,

shall be liable to a penalty of [€950][1]; but the penalty imposed in respect of any offence under paragraph (*b*) or (*c*) shall not apply to any clerk, agent, servant or other person referred to in subsection (1)(*b*).

Amendments

1 Substituted by FA 2001 s 240(1) and (2)(*k*) and Sch 5 Pt 1 as respects any act or omission which takes place or begins on or after 1 January 2002; previously "£750".

Definitions

Appeal Commissioners: s 2(1); oath: IA 1937 Sch; person: IA 1937 s 11(*c*).

Former enactments

ITA 1967 s 426; F(MP)A 1968 s 3(2) and Sch Pt I; CTA 1976 s 146(1); FA 1982 s 60(2)(*c*); FA 1992 s 248.

940 Determination of liability in cases of default

Where—

(*a*) a person has neglected or refused to deliver a schedule in accordance with a precept of the Appeal Commissioners,

(*b*) any clerk, agent or servant of, or any person confidentially employed by, a person chargeable, having been summoned, has neglected or refused to appear before the Appeal Commissioners to be examined,

(*c*) the person chargeable or that person's clerk, agent or servant or any person confidentially employed by the person chargeable has declined to answer any question put to him or her by the Appeal Commissioners,

(*d*) an objection has been made to a schedule and the objection has not been appealed against, or

(*e*) the Appeal Commissioners decide to allow any objection made by the inspector or such other officer as the Revenue Commissioners shall authorise in that behalf,

the Appeal Commissioners shall ascertain and settle according to the best of their judgment the sum in which the person chargeable ought to be charged.

Definitions

inspector: ss 2(1), 5(1), 852; person: IA 1937 s 11(*c*).

Former enactments

ITA 1967 s 427; F(MP)A 1968 s 3(2) and Sch Pt I; CTA 1976 s 146(1); FA 1995 s 173(1)(*b*).

941 Statement of case for High Court

(1) Immediately after the determination of an appeal by the Appeal Commissioners, the appellant or the inspector or such other officer as the Revenue Commissioners shall authorise in that behalf (in this section referred to as **"other officer"**), if dissatisfied with the determination as being erroneous in point of law, may declare his or her dissatisfaction to the Appeal Commissioners who heard the appeal.

(2) The appellant or inspector or other officer, as the case may be, having declared his or her dissatisfaction, may within 21 days after the determination by notice in writing

addressed to the Clerk to the Appeal Commissioners require the Appeal Commissioners to state and sign a case for the opinion of the High Court on the determination.

(3) The party requiring the case shall pay to the Clerk to the Appeal Commissioners a fee of [€25][1] for and in respect of the case before that party is entitled to have the case stated.

(4) The case shall set forth the facts and the determination of the Appeal Commissioners, and the party requiring it shall transmit the case when stated and signed to the High Court within 7 days after receiving it.

(5) At or before the time when the party requiring the case transmits it to the High Court, that party shall send notice in writing of the fact that the case has been stated on that party's application, together with a copy of the case, to the other party.

(6) The High Court shall hear and determine any question or questions of law arising on the case, and shall reverse, affirm or amend the determination in respect of which the case has been stated, or shall remit the matter to the Appeal Commissioners with the opinion of the Court on the matter, or may make such other order in relation to the matter, and may make such order as to costs as to the Court may seem fit.

(7) The High Court may cause the case to be sent back for amendment and thereupon the case shall be amended accordingly, and judgment shall be delivered after it has been amended.

(8) An appeal shall lie from the decision of the High Court to the Supreme Court.

(9) Notwithstanding that a case has been required to be stated or is pending, income tax or, as the case may be, corporation tax shall be paid in accordance with the determination of the Appeal Commissioners; but if the amount of the assessment is altered by the order or judgment of the Supreme Court or the High Court, then—

[(*a*) if too much tax has been paid, the amount overpaid shall be refunded with interest in accordance with the provisions of section 865A, or][2]

(*b*) if too little tax has been paid, the amount unpaid shall be deemed to be arrears of tax (except in so far as any penalty is incurred on account of arrears) and shall be paid and recovered accordingly.

Amendments

1 Substituted by FA 2001 s 240(1) and (2)(*a*) and Sch 5 Pt 1 for 2002 and later tax years; previously "£20".

2 Subs (9)(*a*) substituted by FA 2003 s 17(*b*) with effect from: (*a*) such day or days as the Minister for Finance may by order or orders appoint either generally or with reference to any particular purpose or provision and different days may be so appointed for different purposes or different provisions and (*b*) notwithstanding the generality of (*a*), any order made by the Minister for Finance in accordance with the provisions of that paragraph may contain, and be subject to, such conditions as the Minister considers appropriate and which are specified in the order; previously "(*a*) if too much tax has been paid, the amount overpaid shall be refunded with such interest, if any, as the Court may allow, or". By virtue of Finance Act 2003 (Commencement of Section 17) Order 2003, SI No 508 of 2003, this substitution came into operation in relation to any repayment of tax arising under this section by virtue of any order or judgment of the Supreme Court or the High Court made on or after 1 November 2003.

Cross-references

Application to Appeal Commissioners seeking determination that authorised officer justified in requiring information to be furnished by financial institution: s 907(4).

Extension of this section: s 943(1); subs (2): s 943(2); subs (3): s 943(3).

Income Tax (Purchased Life Annuities) Regulations 1959, SI No 152 of 1959, reg 9.
Value added tax, this section applied by: VATA 1972 s 25(2)(i).

Case law

Irish

Subs (1): Failure to express dissatisfaction, Revenue were entitled to proceed with collection: *Bairead v Carr* (High Court, 21 May 1993).

Subs (2): Where appeals heard by more than one Appeal Commissioner the signature of all the Commissioners concerned are required on a case stated under this section. A retired Appeal Commissioner may sign a case stated: *O'Dwyer v Irish Exporters and Importers Ltd (In liquidation)* ITR Vol I p 629.

The requirement that an expression of dissatisfaction is to be given immediately after the determination of an appeal is not to be construed to require it to be declared at the conclusion of the proceedings: *Multiprint Label Systems Ltd v Neylon* [1984] ILRM 545.

A refusal by the Special Commissioners to state a case as there was no point of law involved was upheld by the Courts: *The King (H Stein) v Special Commissioners*, 1 ITC 71.

Subs (5): A case stated lodged with the High Court struck out as appellants did not advise the inspector of the position until after that action had taken place: *A & B v Davis* ITR Vol II p 60.

Subs (6): Held a judge who determines a point of law decided by the Appeal Commissioners is incorrect, has a discretion which must be exercised at that point as to whether or not the case should be remitted. A final order should only be amended in special and unusual circumstances: *Belville Holdings v Revenue Commissioners* ITR Vol III p 340.

Subs (9): interest on tax overpaid may be decided by the court; the court is not obliged to apply the rate used in s 1080: *Texaco (Ireland) Ltd v Murphy* ITR Vol IV p 91.

UK

Held was open to Revenue to raise a new question of law and they were not confined to the points of law in the case stated: *Muir v CIR* [1966] 1 WLR 1269; 43 TC 367.

A complaint that the taxpayer was not fairly treated in proceedings before the general commissioners was not a proper subject for a case stated but was more appropriate to judicial review proceedings: *Read v Rolliston* [1982] STC 370; *Brittain v Gibb* [1986] STC 418; *Mellor v Gurney* [1994] STC 1025.

Held a strict compliance with the time limit for an appeal to the High was an essential prerequisite for the Court to hear the appeal: *Petch v Gurney* [1994] STC 689; *IRC v McGuckian* [1994] STC 888.

Held the High Court has no jurisdiction to hear fresh evidence: *Kudehinbu v Cutts* [1994] STC 560.

Where assessment made under the wrong section, the High Court could uphold the assessment as if it had been made under the appropriate section: *IRC v McGuckian* [1994] STC 888.

Held where the appellant is a partnership, a dissenting partner can declare dissatisfaction: *Re Sutherland & Partners' v Barnes* [1993] STC 399. On appeal by way of case stated the court could not rely on a matter in the transcript of evidence but not found as a fact: *Bradley v London Electric plc* [1996] STC 231 [1996] STC 1054.

Held Court could not remit the matter to the Special Commissioners where the taxpayer wished to present argument not made at the original hearing: *DeneKamp v Pearce* [1998] STC 1120.

Revenue precedents

Issue: Whether tax is to be repaid pending where a Case Stated has been requested. Whether assessment should be amended in accordance with the Appeal Commissioners determination where a case stated has been requested.

Decision: The reference in s 941(9) to "tax shall be paid in accordance with the determination of the Appeal Commissioners" does not entitle the taxpayer demanding a case stated to repayment. Repayment arises only in accordance with subs (9) itself. Section 30(3) FA 1976 (now repealed and s 942(6)(*b*) do not apply where a case stated has been demanded. There is no obligation under s 934 TCA 1997 on the Inspector to amend the assessment where there is an appeal from the Appeal Commissioners decision, since to amend the assessment in accordance with this section would give it the same force and effect as if it were "an assessment in respect of which no appeal had been given". If it were such an assessment, ss 942(6) and 941(9) would be redundant.

Tax Briefing

TB56 July 2004 pp 6–11 — Repayments, Interest and Time Limits — Section 17 FA 2003 changes.
TB57 Oct 2004 pp 7–9 — New Time Limits — Section 17 FA 2003 changes.
TB57 Oct 2004 p 15 — Repayments, Interest and Time Limits — correction to TB56 p 8.

Definitions

Appeal Commissioners: s 2(1); High Court: IA 1937 Sch; inspector: ss 2(1), 5(1), 852; the Supreme Court: IA 1937 Sch; writing: IA 1937 Sch.

Former enactments

ITA 1967 s 428; F(MP)A 1968 s 3(2) and Sch Pt I; FA 1971 s 19(2); CTA 1976 s 146(1); FA 1983 s 9(*a*)(iii) and s 37; FA 1995 s 173(1)(*c*).

Corresponding UK tax provision

Taxes Management Act 1970 s 56.

942 Appeals to Circuit Court

(1) Any person aggrieved by the determination of the Appeal Commissioners in any appeal against an assessment made on that person may, on giving notice in writing to the inspector or such other officer as the Revenue Commissioners shall authorise in that behalf (in this section referred to as **"other officer"**) within 10 days after such determination, require that the appeal shall be reheard by the judge of the Circuit Court (in this section referred to as **"the judge"**) in whose circuit is situate, in the case of—

(*a*) a person who is not resident in the State,

(*b*) the estate of a deceased person,

(*c*) an incapacitated person, or

(*d*) a trust,

the place where the assessment was made and, in any other case, the place to which the notice of assessment was addressed, and the Appeal Commissioners shall transmit to the judge any statement or schedule in their possession which was delivered to them for the purposes of the appeal.

(2) At or before the time of the rehearing of the appeal by the judge, the inspector or other officer shall transmit to the judge the prescribed form in which the Appeal Commissioners' determination of the appeal is recorded.

(3) The judge shall with all convenient speed rehear and determine the appeal, and shall have and exercise the same powers and authorities in relation to the assessment appealed against, the determination, and all consequent matters, as the Appeal Commissioners might have and exercise, and the judge's determination shall, subject to section 943, be final and conclusive.

(4) Section 934(2) shall, with any necessary modifications, apply in relation to a rehearing of an appeal by a judge of the Circuit Court as it applies in relation to the hearing of an appeal by the Appeal Commissioners.

(5) The judge shall make a declaration in the form of the declaration required to be made by an Appeal Commissioner as set out in Part 1 of Schedule 27.

(6) (*a*) Notwithstanding that a person has under subsection (1) required an appeal to the Appeal Commissioners against the assessment to be reheard by a judge of the Circuit Court, income tax or, as the case may be, corporation tax shall be paid in accordance with the determination of the Appeal Commissioners.

[(*b*) Notwithstanding paragraph (*a*), where the amount of tax is altered by the determination of the judge or by giving effect to an agreement under subsection (8), then, if too much tax has been paid, the amount or amounts overpaid shall be repaid and in so far as the amount to be repaid represents tax paid in accordance with this subsection it shall, subject to the provisions of subsection (4) of section 865A, be repaid with interest at the rate specified in subsection (3) of section 865A from the date or dates of payment of the amount or amounts giving rise to the overpayment to the date on which the repayment is made.][1]

...[2]

(8) Where following an application for the rehearing of an appeal by a judge of the Circuit Court in accordance with subsection (1) there is an agreement within the meaning of paragraphs (*b*), (*c*) and (*e*) of section 933(3) between the inspector or other officer and the appellant in relation to the assessment, the inspector shall give effect to the agreement and, if the agreement is that the assessment is to stand or is to be amended, the assessment or the amended assessment, as the case may be, shall have the same force and effect as if it were an assessment in respect of which no notice of appeal had been given.

(9) Every rehearing of an appeal by the Circuit Court under this section shall be held in camera.

...[3]

Amendments

1 Subs (6)(*b*) substituted by FA 2003 s 17(*c*) with effect from: (*a*) such day or days as the Minister for Finance may by order or orders appoint either generally or with reference to any particular purpose or provision and different days may be so appointed for different purposes or different provisions and (*b*) notwithstanding the generality of (*a*), any order made by the Minister for Finance in accordance with the provisions of that paragraph may contain, and be subject to, such conditions as the Minister considers appropriate and which are specified in the order; previously "(*b*) Notwithstanding paragraph (*a*), where the amount of tax is altered by the determination of the judge or by giving effect to an agreement under subsection (8), then, if too much tax has been paid, the amount or amounts overpaid shall be repaid and (except where the interest amounts to less than [€10][1]) in so far as the amount to be repaid represents tax paid in accordance with this subsection it shall be repaid with interest at the rate of [0.0161 per cent, or such other rate (if any) prescribed by the Minister for Finance by regulations, for each day or part of a day][2] from the date or dates of payment of the amount or amounts giving rise to the overpayment to the date on which the repayment is made.

  1 Substituted by FA 2001 s 240(1) and (2)(*a*) and Sch 5 Pt 1 for 2002 and later tax years; previously '£10'.

  2 Substituted by FA 2002 s 129(1)(*c*) with effect from 1 September 2002 as regards interest payable in respect of an amount due to be repaid or retained, whether before, on, or after that date; previously '0.6 per cent, or such other rate (if any) prescribed by the Minister for Finance by regulations, for each month or part of a month'.".

  By virtue of Finance Act 2003 (Commencement of Section 17) Order 2003, SI No 508 of 2003, this substitution came into operation in relation to any repayment of tax arising from a determination made by a judge of the Circuit Court under section 942, or an agreement referred to in subsection (8) of that section entered into, on or after 1 November 2003.

2 Subs (7) deleted by FA 2005 s 147 and Sch 6 para 1(*o*) with effect from 25 March 2005.

3 Subs (10) deleted by FA 2005 s 147 and Sch 6 para 1(*o*) with effect from 25 March 2005.

Cross-references

Appeals against assessments: s 933(4).
Case stated: s 943(1).
Evidence of electronic transmission of particulars of income tax to be collected in proceedings for recovery of tax, subs (6): s 967(*a*)(ii).
Forms of declaration: Sch 27 Pt 1.
High Court proceedings, subs (6): s 966(5)(*a*)(ii).
Income Tax (Purchased Life Annuities) Regulations 1959, SI No 152 of 1959, reg 9.
Value added tax, this section applied by: VATA 1972 s 25(2)(*h*).

Case law

Circuit Court judge has discretionary power to award costs on an appeal from the Appeal Commissioners: *Inspector of Taxes v Arida Ltd* [1996] ILRM 74.

Subs (3): The function of a Circuit Court Judge limited to deciding the quantum of the charge under an assessment before him: *Bourke v Lyster*, 3 ITC 247. Closed cases are not to be re-opened: *In re McGahon* (High Court,8 February 1982).

Where a Circuit Court Judge overruled the determination of the Appeal Commissioner the High Court refused to disturb the decision of the lower court which was considered to be a factual one: *O'Srianáin v Lakeview Ltd* (High Court, 8 October 1984), TL 125. See also *McMahon v Murphy* (High Court, 25 November 1988); *Cassell v Crutchfield* [1997] STC 423; *Rigby v Samson* [1997] STC 524; *Eurofire Ltd v Davison* [1997] STC 538.

Tax Briefing

TB56 July 2004 pp 6–11 — Repayments, Interest and Time Limits — Section 17 FA 2003 changes.

TB57 Oct 2004 pp 7–9 — New Time Limits — Section 17 FA 2003 changes.

TB57 Oct 2004 p 15 — Repayments, Interest and Time Limits — correction to TB56 p 8.

Definitions

Appeal Commissioners: s 2(1); Circuit Court: IA 1937 Sch; Dáil Éireann: IA 1937 Sch; incapacitated person: s 3(1); inspector: ss 2(1), 5(1), 852; Income Tax Acts: s 1(2); month: IA 1937 Sch; person: IA 1937 s 11(*c*); tax: s 3(1); writing: IA 1937 Sch.

Former enactments

ITA 1967 s 416(10) and s 429; F(MP)A 1968 s 3(1), s 3(2) and Sch Pt I; FA 1971 s 19(1); FA 1974 s 69; CTA 1976 s 146(1); FA 1983 s 9(*a*)(iv) and (*b*)(i) and s 37; FA 1995 s 173(1)(*d*); FA 1997 s 146(1) and Sch 9 Pt I para 1(27).

Corresponding UK tax provision

Taxes Management Act 1970 s 56A.

943 Extension of section 941

(1) Section 941 shall, subject to this section, apply to a determination given by a judge pursuant to section 942 in the like manner as it applies to a determination by the Appeal Commissioners, and any case stated by a judge pursuant to section 941 shall set out the facts, the determination of the Appeal Commissioners and the determination of the judge.

(2) The notice in writing required under section 941(2) to be addressed to the Clerk to the Appeal Commissioners shall, in every case in which a judge is under the authority of this section required by any person to state and sign a case for the opinion of the High Court on the determination, be addressed by such person to the county registrar.

(3) The fee required under section 941(3) to be paid to the Clerk to the Appeal Commissioners shall in any case referred to in subsection (2) be paid to the county registrar.

Cross-references

Appeals to Circuit Court: s 942(3).

Case law

Failure to express dissatisfaction, Revenue were entitled to proceed with collection; Circuit Court judge can allow application for case stated to High Court but is not bound to do so having regard to lapse of time: *Bairead v Carr* (High Court, 21 May 1993).

Definitions

Appeal Commissioners: s 2(1); High Court: IA 1937 Sch; person: IA 1937 s 11(*c*); writing: IA 1937 Sch.

Former enactments

ITA 1967 s 430; F(MP)A 1968 s 3(2) and Sch Pt I; CTA 1976 s 146(1); FA 1983 s 9(*a*)(v) and s 37.

944 Communication of decision of Appeal Commissioners

(1) Where the Appeal Commissioners have entertained an appeal against an assessment for any year of assessment or any accounting period and, after hearing argument on the appeal, have postponed giving their determination either for the purpose of considering the argument or for the purpose of affording to the appellant an opportunity of submitting in writing further evidence or argument, the Appeal Commissioners may, unless they consider a further hearing to be necessary, cause their determination to be sent by post to the parties to the appeal.

(2) Where the determination of an appeal by the Appeal Commissioners is sent to the parties by post under this section, a declaration of dissatisfaction under section 941(1) or a notice requiring a rehearing under section 942(1) may be made or given in writing within 12 days after the day on which the determination is so sent to the person making the declaration or giving the notice.

Definitions

Appeal Commissioners: s 2(1); person: IA 1937 s 11(*c*); writing: IA 1937 Sch; year of assessment: s 3(1).

Former enactments

ITA 1967 s 431; F(MP)A 1968 s 3(2) and Sch Pt I; CTA 1976 s 146(1); FA 1983 s 37.

944A Publication of determinations of Appeal Commissioners

[The Appeal Commissioners may make arrangements for the publication of reports of such of their determinations as they consider appropriate, but they shall ensure that any such report is in a form which, in so far as possible, prevents the identification of any person whose affairs are dealt with in the determination.][1]

Amendments

1 Section 944A inserted by FA 1998 s 134(1)(*a*) as respects appeals determined by the Appeal Commissioners after 27 March 1998.

Definitions

Appeal Commissioners: s 2(1); person: IA 1937 s 11(*c*).

CHAPTER 2
Appeals Against Capital Gains Tax Assessments

945 Appeals against assessments

(1) A person aggrieved by any assessment under the Capital Gains Tax Acts made on the person by the inspector or other officer mentioned in section 931(1) shall be entitled to appeal to the Appeal Commissioners on giving, within 30 days after the date of the notice of assessment, notice in writing to the inspector or other officer, and in default of notice of appeal by a person to whom notice of assessment has been given the assessment made on such person shall be final and conclusive.

(2) The provisions of the Income Tax Acts relating to—

(*a*) the appointment of times and places for the hearing of appeals,

(*b*) the giving of notice to each person who has given notice of appeal of the time and place appointed for the hearing of that person's appeal, (*c*) the determination of an appeal by agreement between the appellant or the appellant's agent and an inspector of taxes or other officer mentioned in section 931(1),

(*d*) the determination of an appeal by the appellant giving notice of the appellant's intention not to proceed with the appeal,

(*e*) the hearing, determination or dismissal of an appeal by the Appeal Commissioners, including the hearing, determination or dismissal of an appeal by one Appeal Commissioner,

[(*ee*) the publication of reports of determinations of the Appeal Commissioners,][1]

(*f*) the assessment having the same force and effect as if it were an assessment in respect of which no notice of appeal had been given where the person who has given notice of appeal does not attend before the Appeal Commissioners at the time and place appointed,

(*g*) the extension of the time for giving notice of appeal and the readmission of appeals by the Appeal Commissioners and the provisions which apply where action by means of court proceedings has been taken,

(*h*) the rehearing of an appeal by a judge of the Circuit Court and the statement of a case for the opinion of the High Court on a point of law,

(*i*) the payment of tax in accordance with the determination of the Appeal Commissioners notwithstanding that an appeal is required to be reheard by a judge of the Circuit Court or that a case for the opinion of the High Court on a point of law has been required to be stated or is pending, and

(*j*) the procedures for appeal,

shall, with any necessary modifications, apply to an appeal under any provision of the Capital Gains Tax Acts providing for an appeal to the Appeal Commissioners as if the appeal were an appeal against an assessment to income tax.

Amendments

1 Subs (2)(*ee*) inserted by FA 1998 s 134(1)(*b*) as respects appeals determined by the Appeal Commissioners after 27 March 1998.

Cross-references

Capital gains tax, penalties for failure to make returns etc, and for fraudulently or negligently making incorrect returns, applied by: s 1077(1)(*b*), (2).

Self assessment, meaning of "appeal" applied: s 950(1).

Definitions

Appeal Commissioners: s 2(1); Circuit Court: IA 1937 Sch; High Court: IA 1937 Sch; Income Tax Acts: s 1(2); inspector: ss 2(1), 5(1), 852; person: IA 1937 s 11(*c*); writing: IA 1937 Sch.

Former enactments

CGTA 1975 s 51(1) and Sch 4 para 8; CGT(A)A 1978 s 17 and Sch 2; FA 1983 s 55.

946 Regulations with respect to appeals

(1) The Revenue Commissioners may make regulations—

(*a*) for the conduct of appeals against assessments and decisions on claims under the Capital Gains Tax Acts;

(*b*) entitling persons, in addition to those who would be so entitled apart from the regulations, to appear on such appeals;

(*c*) regulating the time within which such appeals or claims may be brought or made;

(*d*) where the market value of an asset on a particular date or an apportionment or any other matter may affect the liability to capital gains tax of 2 or more persons, enabling any such person to have the matter determined by the tribunal having jurisdiction to determine that matter if arising on an appeal against an assessment, and prescribing a procedure by which the matter is not determined differently on different occasions;

(*e*) authorising an inspector or other officer of the Revenue Commissioners, notwithstanding the obligation as to secrecy imposed by the Income Tax Acts or any other Act, to disclose—

(i) to a person entitled to appear on such an appeal, the market value of an asset as determined by an assessment or decision on a claim, or

(ii) to a person whose liability to tax may be affected by the determination of the market value of an asset on a particular date or an apportionment or any other matter, any decision on the matter made by an inspector or other officer of the Revenue Commissioners.

(2) Regulations under this section may contain such supplemental and incidental provisions as appear to the Revenue Commissioners to be necessary.

(3) Every regulation made under this section shall be laid before Dáil Éireann as soon as may be after it is made and, if a resolution annulling the regulation is passed by Dáil Éireann within the next 21 days on which Dáil Éireann has sat after the regulation is laid before it, the regulation shall be annulled accordingly, but without prejudice to the validity of anything previously done thereunder.

Definitions

Dáil Éireann: IA 1937 Sch; Income Tax Acts: s 1(2); inspector: ss 2(1), 5(1), 852; person: IA 1937 s 11(*c*).

Former enactments

CGTA 1975 s 51(1) and Sch 4 para 9.

CHAPTER 3
Miscellaneous

947 Appeals against determination under sections 98 to 100

(1) Where it appears to the inspector that the determination of any amount on which a person may be chargeable to income tax or corporation tax by virtue of section 98, 99 or 100 may affect the liability to income tax or corporation tax of other persons, the inspector shall give notice in writing to those persons as well as to the first-mentioned person of the determination the inspector proposes to make and of the rights conferred on them by this section.

(2) Any person to whom such a notice is given may within 21 days after the date on which it is given object to the proposed determination by notice in writing given to the inspector, and section 933(7) shall apply, with any necessary modifications, in relation to any such notice as it applies in relation to a notice of appeal under section 933.

(3) (*a*) Subject to paragraph (*b*), where notices have been given under subsection (1) and no notice of objection is duly given under subsection (2), the inspector shall make the determination as proposed in his or her notices and the determination shall not be called in question in any proceedings.

(*b*) This subsection shall not operate to prevent any person to whom notice has not been given under subsection (1) from appealing against any such determination of the inspector which may affect that person's liability to income tax or corporation tax, as the case may be.

(4) Where a notice of objection is duly given, the amount mentioned in subsection (1) shall be determined in the like manner as an appeal and shall be so determined by the Appeal Commissioners.

(5) All persons to whom notices have been given under subsection (1) may take part in any proceedings under subsection (4) and in any appeal arising out of those proceedings and shall be bound by the determination made in the proceedings or on appeal, whether or not they have taken part in the proceedings, and their successors in title shall also be so bound.

(6) A notice under subsection (1) may, notwithstanding any obligation as to secrecy or other restriction on the disclosure of information, include a statement of the grounds on which the inspector proposes to make the determination.

(7) An inspector may by notice in writing require any person to give, within 21 days after the date of the notice or within such longer period as the inspector may allow, such information as appears to the inspector to be required for deciding whether to give a notice under subsection (1) to any person.

Cross-references

Penalty: Sch 29 column 2.

Definitions

Appeal Commissioners: s 2(1); inspector: ss 2(1), 5(1), 852; person: IA 1937 s 11(*c*); writing: IA 1937 Sch.

Former enactments

FA 1975 s 21(1)–(7); CTA 1976 s 147(1)–(2).

948 Appeals against amount of income tax deducted under Schedule E

(1) Any person charged to income tax under Schedule E may appeal to the Appeal Commissioners against the amount of tax deducted from that person's emoluments for any year.

(2) The Appeal Commissioners shall hear and determine an appeal to them under subsection (1) as if it were an appeal to them against an assessment to income tax, and the provisions of the Income Tax Acts relating to the rehearing of an appeal and to the statement of a case for the opinion of the High Court on a point of law shall, with the necessary modifications, apply accordingly.

Definitions

Appeal Commissioners: s 2(1); High Court: IA 1937 Sch; person: IA 1937 s 11(*c*).

Former enactments

ITA 1967 s 113; F(MP)A 1968 s 3(2) and Sch Pt I.

949 Appeals against determinations of certain claims, etc

(1) Any person aggrieved by any determination by the Revenue Commissioners, or such officer of the Revenue Commissioners (including an inspector) as they may have authorised in that behalf, on any claim, matter or question referred to in section 864 may, subject to section 957 and on giving notice in writing to the Revenue Commissioners or the officer within 30 days after notification to the person aggrieved of the determination, appeal to the Appeal Commissioners.

(2) The Appeal Commissioners shall hear and determine an appeal to them under subsection (1) as if it were an appeal against an assessment to income tax and the provisions of section 933 with respect to such appeals, together with the provisions of the Tax Acts relating to the rehearing of an appeal and to the statement of a case for the opinion of the High Court on a point of law, shall apply accordingly with any necessary modifications.

(3) Where—

(*a*) a right of appeal to the Appeal Commissioners is given by any provision of the Tax Acts or the Capital Gains Tax Acts other than section 1037, and

(*b*) such provision, while applying the provisions of the Tax Acts relating to appeals against assessments, does not apply the provisions of those Acts relating to the rehearing of appeals,

such provision shall be deemed to apply those provisions relating to the rehearing of appeals.

(4) In a case in which—

(*a*) a notice of appeal is not given within the time limited by subsection (1), or

(*b*) a person who has given notice of appeal does not attend before the Appeal Commissioners at the time and place appointed for the hearing of the person's appeal,

subsections (5) and (7) to (9) of section 933 shall apply with any necessary modifications.

Cross-references

Making of claims etc: s 864(1)(*c*).
Relief for investment in films: s 481(14)(*b*).
Repayment of tax: s 865(7).

Definitions

Appeal Commissioners: s 2(1); High Court: IA 1937 Sch; inspector: ss 2(1), 5(1), 852; person: IA 1937 s 11(*c*); writing: IA 1937 Sch.

Former enactments

ITA 1967 s 432(1) (part only) and (2)–(4); F(MP)A 1968 s 3(2) and Sch Pt I; CGTA 1975 s 51(1) and Sch 4 para 2; CTA 1976 s 146(1) and s 164 and Sch 3 Pt I; FA 1983 s 37.

PART 41
SELF ASSESSMENT

Cross-references

Capital gains tax, temporary non-residents: s 29A(5).
Donations to approved bodies, meaning of "chargeable person" applied: s 848A(7), (8).
Donations to certain sports bodies, meaning of "chargeable person" applied: s 847A(9)(*a*).

Double tax relief, meanings of "appropriate inspector", "chargeable period" and "specified return date for the chargeable period" applied: s 450(1)(*a*).
Due date for payment of income tax other than under self assessment: s 960.
Exchange of Irish Government bonds: s 751B(5), (6)(*a*).
Income Tax (Relevant Contracts) Regulations 2000, SI No 71 of 2000: ITRCR 2000 Reg 14(3).
Nature and amount of relief for qualifying premiums, meaning of "specified return date for the chargeable period" applied: s 787(7).
Occupational pension schemes, approved schemes, exemptions and reliefs, meaning of "specified return date for the chargeable period" applied: s 774(8); statutory schemes, exemptions and reliefs, meaning of "specified return date for the chargeable period" applied: s 776(3).
Personal Retirement Savings Accounts (PRSAs), method of granting relief for PRSA contributions, meaning of "specified return date for the chargeable period" applied: s 787C(3).
Profits from occupation of woodlands: s 232(3)(*b*).
Profits or gains from stallion fees: s 231(2)(*b*).
Shipping tonnage tax, company termporarily ceasing to operate qualifying ships, meaning of "specified return date for the chargeable period" applied: Sch 18B para 7(4).
Stud greyhound service fees: s 233(3)(*a*).
Surcharge for late returns: s 1084(5); meaning of "chargeable person" applied: s 1084(1)(*a*).
Tax treatment of directors of companies and employees granted rights to acquire shares or other assets: s 128(2A).
Wear and tear allowances in respect of machinery or plant, meaning of "chargeable person" applied: s 284(2)(*ac*)(i).

Revenue information

Information leaflet IT10 — Guide to the Self-Assessment System for the Self-Employed.
Information leaflet IT23 — Main features of Income Tax Self Assessment.
Information leaflet CGT2 — Capital Gains Tax — Self Assessment.
Information leaflet CG2 — Due Dates — Payments and Returns.
Information leaflet CG3 — Payments to the Collector-General.
Information leaflet CG4 — Change of Address.
Information leaflet CG9 — Direct Debit — Preliminary Income Tax.

eBrief

eBrief no 7 — 2005 — For taxpayers who submit their payment **and** file their return through the Revenue Online Service (ROS) for preliminary tax for 2005, income tax balance due for 2004 and capital gains tax on gains arising in initial period 2005 (1 Jan–30 Sept), the filing date is extended to Thursday 17 November 2005.

Tax Briefing

TB44 June 2001 pp 4–6 — Changes to Return Filing and Payment Dates under Self Assessment (Finance Act 2001) — Pay and File system.
TB47 April 2002 pp 1–7 — Pay and File.
TB48 June 2002 pp 5–10 — Pay and File Questions and Answers.
TB49 Aug 2002 pp 15–16 — Pay and File — The 2001 Income Tax Return.
TB50 Oct 2002 pp 8–12 — Pay and File Payment Options.
TB51 Jan 2003 p 8 — Preliminary Income Tax — "Top up payments" for 2002 preliminary tax.
TB51 Jan 2003 p 10 — Self Assessment Return for Individuals for 2002.
TB52 May 2003 p 6 — Form 11 and CTI — No attachments with these forms.
TB52 May 2003 p 7 — Pay and File 2003 IT and CT.
TB53 Aug 2003 p 19 — Form 11 and CT1 attachments — Clarification.
TB53 Aug 2003 pp 1–3 — Capital Gains Tax Payments — Finance Act 2003 changes.
TB53 Aug 2003 pp 4–13 — Extracts from Accounts ("Accounts Menus") Forms 11/CT1, Frequently Asked Questions.
TB53 Aug 2003 pp 25–26 Pay and File 2003 IT and CT.
TB54 Dec 2003 pp 17–19 Extracts from Accounts — Queries.
TB56 July 2004 pp 1–5 — First Active Shares.
TB56 July 2004 pp 17–18 — Form CT1 2004.
TB56 July 2004 pp 22–23 — Pay and File 2004 — IT and CT.
TB57 Oct 2004 pp 1–3 — Pay and File 2004.
TB57 Oct 2004 pp 5–6 — ROS Pay and File Tips.
TB57 Oct 2004 p 6 –CGT First Active Shares — Personal Exemption.
TB58 Dec 2004 pp 10–12 — IT Returns — Property Based Incentives.

950 Interpretation (Part 41)

(1) In this Part, except where the context otherwise requires—

"appeal" means an appeal under section 933 or, as respects capital gains tax, an appeal under section 945;

"appropriate inspector", in relation to a chargeable person, means—

(*a*) the inspector who has last given notice in writing to the chargeable person that he or she is the inspector to whom the chargeable person is required to deliver a return or statement of income or profits or chargeable gains,

(*b*) in the absence of an inspector referred to in paragraph (*a*), the inspector to whom it is customary for the chargeable person to deliver such return or statement, or

(*c*) in the absence of an inspector referred to in paragraphs (*a*) and (*b*), the inspector of returns;

"assessment" means an assessment to tax made under the Income Tax Acts, the Corporation Tax Acts or the Capital Gains Tax Acts, as the case may be;

"chargeable gain" has the same meaning as in section 545(3);

"chargeable period" has the same meaning as in section 321(2);

"chargeable person" means, as respects a chargeable period, a person who is chargeable to tax for that period, whether on that person's own account or on account of some other person but, as respects income tax, does not include a person—

[(*a*) whose only source or sources of income for the chargeable period is or are sources the income from which consists of emoluments to which Chapter 4 of Part 42 applies, but for this purpose a person who, in addition to such source or sources of income, has another source or other sources of income shall be deemed for the chargeable period to be a person whose only source or sources of income for the chargeable period is or are sources the income from which consists of emoluments to which Chapter 4 of Part 42 applies if the income from that other source or those other sources is taken into account in determining the amount of his or her tax credits and standard rate cut-off point for the chargeable period applicable to those emoluments, and, for the purposes of deciding whether such income should be so taken into account, the Revenue Commissioners may have regard to the amount for that, or any previous, chargeable period of the income of the person from that other source or those other sources before deductions, losses, allowances and other reliefs,][1]

(*b*) who for the chargeable period has been exempted by an inspector from the requirements of section 951 by reason of a notice given under subsection (6) of that section, or

(*c*) who is chargeable to tax for the chargeable period by reason only of section 237, 238 or 239,

but paragraph (*a*) shall not apply to a person who is a director or, in the case of a person to whom section 1017 applies, whose spouse is a director (within the meaning of section

116) of a body corporate other than a body corporate which during a period of 3 years ending on the 5th day of April in the chargeable period—

(i) was not entitled to any assets other than cash on hands, or a sum of money on deposit within the meaning of section 895, not exceeding [€130][2],

(ii) did not carry on a trade, business or other activity including the making of investments, and

(iii) did not pay charges on income within the meaning of section 243;

"determination of the appeal" means a determination by the Appeal Commissioners under section 933(4), and includes an agreement referred to in section 933(3) and an assessment becoming final and conclusive by virtue of section 933(6);

"due date for the payment of an amount of preliminary tax" has the meaning assigned to it by section 958(2);

"inspector", in relation to any matter, includes such other officer as the Revenue Commissioners shall appoint in that behalf;

"inspector of returns" means the inspector nominated by the Revenue Commissioners under section 951(11) to be the inspector of returns;

"precedent partner" has the same meaning as in Part 43;

"prescribed form" means a form prescribed by the Revenue Commissioners or a form used under the authority of the Revenue Commissioners, and includes a form which involves the delivery of a return by any electronic, photographic or other process approved of by the Revenue Commissioners;

"preliminary tax" means the amount of tax which a chargeable person is required to pay in accordance with section 952;

"specified provisions" means sections 877 to 881 and 884, paragraphs (*a*) and (*d*) of [section 888(2)],[3] and section 1023;

"specified return date for the chargeable period", in relation to a chargeable period, means—

[(*a*) (i) where the chargeable period is a year of assessment for income tax or capital gains tax purposes, being the year of assessment 2000–2001, 31 January 2002, and

(ii) where the chargeable period is a year of assessment for income tax or capital gains tax purposes, being the year of assessment 2001 or any subsequent year of assessment, 31 October in the year of assessment following that year,][4]

[(*b*) where the chargeable period is an accounting period of a company and subject to paragraph (c), the last day of the period of 9 months commencing on the day immediately following the end of the accounting period, but in any event not later than day 21 of the month in which that period of 9 months ends, and

(*c*) where the chargeable period is an accounting period of a company which ends on or before the date of commencement of the winding up of the company and the specified return date in respect of that accounting period would apart for this paragraph fall on a day after the date of commencement of the winding up but not within a period of 3 months after that date, the day which falls 3 months after the date of commencement of the winding up but in any event not later than day 21 of the month in which that period of 3 months ends.][5]

"tax" means income tax, corporation tax or capital gains tax, as the case may be.

(2) Except in so far as otherwise expressly provided, this Part shall apply notwithstanding any other provision of the Tax Acts or the Capital Gains Tax Acts.

(3) (*a*) Where any obligation or requirement is imposed on a person in any capacity under this Part and a corresponding obligation or requirement is imposed on that person in another capacity, the discharge of any one of those obligations or requirements shall not release the person from the other obligation or requirement.

(*b*) A person shall not in any capacity have an obligation or requirement imposed on that person under this Part by reason only that such obligation or requirement is imposed on that person in any other capacity.

(*c*) Where but for any of the subsequent provisions of this Part any such obligation or requirement would have been imposed on a person in more than one capacity, a release from such obligation or requirement under any of those provisions by reason of any fact or circumstance applying in relation to that person's liability to tax in any one capacity shall not release that person from such obligation or requirement as is imposed on that person in a capacity other than that in which that fact or circumstance applies.

Amendments

1 Definition of "chargeable person" para (*a*) substituted by FA 2005 s 14 for 2005 and subsequent years of assessment.

2 Substituted by FA 2001 s 240(1), (2)(*a*) and Sch 5 Pt 1 for 2002 and later tax years; previously "£100".

3 Substituted by FA 1998 s 136 and Sch 9 para 7 with effect from 6 April 1997; previously "section 888(1)".

4 Definition of "specified return date for the chargeable period" para (*a*) substituted by FA 2003 s 34(1)(*d*) with effect from 6 April 2001.

5 Definition of "specified return date for the chargeable period" paras (*b*)–(*c*) substituted by FA 2003 s 42(1)(*a*) as respects accounting periods ending on or after 1 January 2003.

Cross-references

Bank levy credit, meaning of "appropriate inspector" applied: s 487(3).

Corporation tax — late returns, restriction of relief, meaning of "specified return date for the chargeable period" applied: s 1085(1)(*a*).

Dealers in securities, meaning of "specified return date for the chargeable period" applied: s 749(2A)(*b*).

Deductions allowed in ascertaining taxable income and provisions relating to reductions in tax, meaning of "chargeable person" applied: s 458(1B)(*b*).

Designated areas or streets, double rent allowance: meaning of "appropriate inspector" applied: s 345(5)(*a*).

Dividend payments by credit unions, return of special term share accounts by credit unions: s 267E(1).

Dublin Docklands area, double rent allowance, meaning of "appropriate inspector" applied: s 370(5)(*a*).

Electronic claims, PAYE, meaning of "chargeable person" applied: s 864A(1)(*c*)(ii).

EU Council Directive 90/434/EEC, meaning of "appropriate inspector" applied: s 636(1).

Farming, capital allowances for construction of farm buildings for control of pollution, meaning of "specified return date for the chargeable period" applied: s 659(3C)(*a*).

Farming stock relief, meaning of "specified return date for the chargeable period" applied: s 665.

Farming, trading stock of discontinued trade, meaning of "specified return date for the chargeable period" applied: s 656(1).

Foreign life policies, taxation and returns, interpretation and application, meaning of "specified return date for the chargeable period" applied: s 730H(1); returns on acquisition of policy: s 730I.

General provisions relating to allowances, deductions and reliefs, meaning of "chargeable person" applied: s 459(5)(*b*).

Holiday cottages, disclaimer of capital allowances, meaning of "appropriate inspector": s 355(2)(*a*).

Interest on overdue income tax, corporation tax and capital gains tax, meaning of "chargeable person" applied: s 1080(1).

Offshore funds, taxation and returns of certain funds, interpretation and application, meaning of "specified return date" applied: s 747B(1); return on acquisition of material interest: s 747C.

Past trustees: liability to tax; meaning of "specified return date for the year of assessment" applied: s 579D(1).

Profits from occupation of woodlands meaning of "chargeable person" applied: s 232(3), (3)(*b*).

Profits or gains from stallion fees, meaning of "chargeable person" applied: s 231(2), (2)(*b*).

Qualifying areas, double rent allowance: meaning of "appropriate inspector" applied: s 372E(5)(*a*).

Relief from income tax in respect of income from dealing in residential development land, meaning of "specified return date for the chargeable period" applied: s 644A(5).

Repayment of tax, meaning of "inspector" applied: s 865(1)(*b*)(i)(II)(A); meaning of "chargeable person" applied: s 865(3A)(*a*).

Research and development expenditure, meaning of "appropriate inspector" applied: s 766(1)(*a*).

Returns, and payments of tax, by qualifying fund managers, meaning of "chargeable period" and "appropriate inspector" applied: s 784E(8)(*a*).

Returns of interest paid to non-residents, meaning of "appropriate inspector" applied: s 891A(1).

Returns in relation to certain offshore products: s 896(1)("appropriate inspector"), (5).

Returns in relation to foreign accounts: s 950(6); meaning of "appropriate inspector" applied: s 895(1).

Returns of certain information by third parties, meaning of "appropriate inspector" applied: s 894(1).

Return of property transfers to non-resident trustees, meaning of "appropriate inspector" applied: s 917A(1).

Returns of special term accounts by relevant deposit takers: s 264B(1)("appropriate inspector").

Securitisation, meaning of "specified return date for the accounting period" applied: s 110(6)(*b*).

Self assessment, obligation to make a return, meaning of "appropriate inspector" applied, subs (1): s 951(11)(*b*).

Short-lived businesses, meaning of "return date" applied: s 68(2).

Special trusts for permanently incapacitated individuals, meaning of "specified return date for the chargeable period" applied: s 189A(1).

Stud greyhound service fees, meaning of "chargeable person" applied: s 233(3), (3)(*b*).

Surcharge for late returns, meaning of "specified return date for the chargeable period" applied: s 1084(1)(*a*).

Tax on non-resident company recoverable from another group member or controlling director, meaning of "specified return date for the chargeable period" applied: s 629(1).

Tax rate applicable to certain interest (arising in a Member State of the European Community other than the State) received by individuals, meaning of "specified return date for the chargeable period" applied: s 267M(2)(*b*).

Revenue precedents

Issue: Are non-proprietary directors whose benefits in kind exceed their allowances or who do not provide reasonable estimates of their benefits etc to the Inspector regarded as chargeable persons?

Decision: Yes - see paragraphs 4.1 and 4.2 of Statement of Practice SP- IT/1/93.

Issue: Whether non-resident with no income in the State is a chargeable person.

Decision: Not a chargeable person.

Issue: Chargeable person - does Revenue have to prove that a taxpayer is a chargeable person?

Decision: Where the taxpayer is potentially chargeable (eg is not the non-assessable spouse) and where Revenue assess the taxpayer, s/he thereupon becomes a chargeable person, pending the discharge of the assessment.

Definitions

Appeal Commissioners: s 2(1); chargeable gain: ss 4(1), 5(1), 534; company: ss 4(1), 5(1); Corporation Tax Acts: s 1(2); Income Tax Acts: s 1(2); inspector: ss 2(1), 5(1), 852; month: IA 1937 Sch; person: IA 1937 s 11(*c*); profits: s 4(1); month: IA 1937 Sch; Tax Acts: s 1(2); total income: s 3(1); writing: IA 1937 Sch; year of assessment: ss 2(1), 5(1).

Former enactments

FA 1988 s 9(1)–(3); FA 1990 s 23(3)(*a*); FA 1991 s 45(*a*)(i)–(v) and (vii)–(viii); FA 1992 s 244.

Corresponding UK tax provision

Taxes Management Act 1970 s 9.

951 Obligation to make a return

[Every chargeable person shall as respects a chargeable period prepare and deliver to the Collector-General on or before the specified return date for the chargeable period a return in the prescribed form of—][1]

(*a*) in the case of a chargeable person who is chargeable to income tax or capital gains tax for a chargeable period which is a year of assessment—

(i) all such matters and particulars as would be required to be contained in a statement delivered pursuant to a notice given to the chargeable person by the appropriate inspector under section 877, if the period specified in such notice were the year of assessment which is the chargeable period, and

(ii) where the chargeable person is an individual who is chargeable to income tax or capital gains tax for a chargeable period, in addition to those matters and particulars referred to in subparagraph (i), all such matters and particulars as would be required to be contained in a return for the period delivered to the appropriate inspector pursuant to a notice given to the chargeable person by the appropriate inspector under section 879, or

(*b*) in the case of a chargeable person who is chargeable to corporation tax for a chargeable period which is an accounting period, all such matters and particulars in relation to the chargeable period as would be required to be contained in a return delivered pursuant to a notice given to the chargeable person by the appropriate inspector under section 884,

and such further particulars [(including particulars relating to the preceding year of assessment where the profits or gains of that preceding year are determined in accordance with section 65(3))][2] as may be required by the prescribed form.

(2) The precedent partner of any partnership shall be deemed to be a chargeable person for the purposes of this section and shall as respects any chargeable period deliver to the [Collector-General][3] on or before the specified return date for that chargeable period the return which that partner would be required to deliver for that period under section 880, if [the appropriate inspector][4] had given notice under that section before that specified date.

(3) (*a*) Where under subsection (1) or (2) a person delivers a return to [the Collector-General],[5] the person shall be deemed to have been required by a notice under section 877 to deliver a statement containing the matters and particulars contained in the return or to have been required by a notice under section 879, 880 or 884 to deliver the return, as the case may be.

(*b*) Any provision of the Tax Acts relating to the taking of any action on the failure of a person to deliver a statement or return pursuant to a notice given under any of the sections referred to in paragraph (*a*) shall apply to a chargeable person in a case where such a notice has not been given as if the chargeable person had been given a notice on the specified return date for the chargeable period under such one or more of those sections as is appropriate to the provision in question.

(4) A chargeable person shall prepare and deliver to the [the Collector-General][6],][7] a return for a chargeable period as required by this section notwithstanding that the

chargeable person has not received a notice from an inspector to prepare and deliver a statement or return for that period under any of the sections referred to in subsection (3)(*a*).

(5) (*a*) A return required by this section may be prepared and delivered by the chargeable person or by another person acting under the chargeable person's authority in that regard.

(*b*) Where a return is prepared and delivered by such other person, the Tax Acts shall apply as if it had been prepared and delivered by the chargeable person.

(*c*) A return purporting to be prepared and delivered by or on behalf of any chargeable person shall for the purposes of the Tax Acts be deemed to have been prepared and delivered by that person or by that person's authority, as the case may be, unless the contrary is proved.

(6) An inspector may exclude a person from the application of this section by giving the person a notice in writing stating that the person is excluded from the application of this section, and the notice shall have effect for such chargeable period or periods or until such chargeable period or until the happening of such event as shall be specified in the notice; but—

(*a*) where, before the 25th day of May, 1988, a person has been given notice by the inspector that the person need not prepare and deliver a return for or until a specified chargeable period or until the happening of any event, the person shall be deemed to have been given notice to that effect under this subsection;

(*b*) where a person who has been given a notice under this subsection is chargeable to capital gains tax for any chargeable period, this subsection shall not operate so as to remove the person's obligation under subsection (1) to make a return of the person's chargeable gains for that chargeable period.

(7) (*a*) This section shall not affect the giving of a notice by an inspector under any of the specified provisions and shall not remove from any person any obligation or requirement imposed on the person by such a notice.

(*b*) The giving of a notice under any of the specified provisions to a person shall not remove from that person any obligation to prepare and deliver a return under this section.

(8) In a case to which section 1023(5) applies, a return containing for both the husband and the wife the matters and particulars required by subsection (1) shall, if delivered by one spouse, satisfy the obligation of the other spouse under this section.

(9) Nothing in the specified provisions or in a notice given under any of those provisions shall operate so as to require a chargeable person to deliver a return for a chargeable period on a date earlier than the specified return date for the chargeable period.

(10) A certificate signed by [an officer of the Revenue Commissioners][8] which certifies that he or she has examined the relevant records and that it appears from those records—

(*a*) that as respects a chargeable period a named person is a chargeable person, and

(*b*) that on or before the specified return date for the chargeable period a return in the prescribed form was not received from that chargeable person,

shall be evidence until the contrary is proved that the person so named is a chargeable person as respects that chargeable period and that that person did not on or before the specified return date deliver that return, and a certificate certifying as provided by this subsection and purporting to be signed by [an officer of the Revenue Commissioners][8] may be tendered in evidence without proof and shall be deemed until the contrary is proved to have been signed by [such officer].[9]

(11)(*a*) The Revenue Commissioners may nominate an inspector to be the inspector of returns for the purposes of this Part.

(*b*) The inspector of returns shall take delivery of returns under this section which he or she has directed to be delivered to him or her and of returns from persons in relation to whom he or she is the appropriate inspector in the circumstances specified in paragraph (*c*) of the definition of **"appropriate inspector"** in section 950(1).

(*c*) The name of an inspector nominated under paragraph (*a*) and the address to which returns being delivered to him or her shall be directed shall be published annually in Iris Oifigiúil.

[[(*d*) The Collector-General may designate an address for the delivery of returns which in accordance with this section are required to be delivered to the Collector-General by chargeable persons.][10]

(*e*) Where the Collector-General designates an address under paragraph (*d*), that address shall be published in Iris Oifigiúil as soon as is practicable after such designation.][11]

(12) Sections 1052 and 1054 shall apply to a failure by a chargeable person to deliver a return in accordance with subsections (1) and (2) as they apply to a failure to deliver a return referred to in section 1052.

Amendments

1 Substituted by FA 2003 s 42(1)(*b*)(i) with effect from 1 January 2003 in relation to income tax and capital gains tax and as respects accounting periods ending on or after that date in relation to corporation tax.

2 Inserted by FA 2001 s 78(1)(*b*)(i)(II) for short tax "year" 2001 and later tax years (income tax and capital gains tax) and as respects accounting periods of companies ending on or after 1 April 2001.

3 Substituted by FA 2001 s 78(1)(*b*)(ii) for short tax "year" 2001 and later tax years (income tax and capital gains tax) and as respects accounting periods of companies ending on or after 1 April 2001; previously "appropriate inspector".

4 Substituted by FA 2001 s 78(1)(*b*)(ii) for short tax "year" 2001 and later tax years (income tax and capital gains tax) and as respects accounting periods of companies ending on or after 1 April 2001; previously "the inspector".

5 Substituted by FA 2003 s 42(1)(*b*)(ii) with effect from 1 January 2003 in relation to income tax and capital gains tax and as respects accounting periods ending on or after that date in relation to corporation tax; previously "the Collector-General or an inspector, as the case may be".

6 Substituted by FA 2003 s 42(1)(*b*)(iii) with effect from 1 January 2003 in relation to income tax and capital gains tax and as respects accounting periods ending on or after that date in relation to corporation tax; previously "the Collector-General or the appropriate inspector, as the case may be".

7 Substituted by FA 2001 s 78(1)(*b*)(iv) for short tax "year" 2001 and later tax years (income tax and capital gains tax) and as respects accounting periods of companies ending on or after 1 April 2001; previously "appropriate inspector".

8 Substituted by FA 2001 s 78(1)(*b*)(v)(I) for short tax "year" 2001 and later tax years (income tax and capital gains tax) and as respects accounting periods of companies ending on or after 1 April 2001; previously "an inspector".

9 Substituted by FA 2001 s 78(1)(*b*)(v)(II) for short tax "year" 2001 and later tax years (income tax and capital gains tax) and as respects accounting periods of companies ending on or after 1 April 2001; previously "that inspector".

[10] Subs (11)(*d*) substituted by FA 2003 s 42(1)(*b*)(iv) with effect from 1 January 2003 in relation to income tax and capital gains tax and as respects accounting periods ending on or after that date in relation to corporation tax.

[11] Subs (11)(*d*) and (*e*) inserted by FA 2002 s 52 with effect from 1 January 2002.

Cross-references

Basis at commencement of trade or profession: s 66(3).
Capital gains tax share reinvestment, withdrawal of relief: s 591(10).
Corporation tax — late returns, restriction of relief, meaning of "return of income" applied: s 1085(1)(*a*).
Dealers in securities: s 749(2B)(*a*).
Designated areas, double rent allowance election: s 345(5)(*b*), (*d*).
Donations to approved bodies: s 848A(5), (8).
Donations to certain sports bodies: s 847A(8), (10).
Dublin Docklands Area, double rent allowance election: s 370(5)(*b*), (*d*).
EU Council Directive 90/434/EEC, mergers, divisions: s 631(5)(*b*).
Farming, averaging of farming profits: s 657(7).
Foreign life policies, returns on acquisition of: s 730I.
Holiday cottages, double rent allowance election: s 355(2)(*b*).
Interest payments by companies and to non-residents: s 246(5)(*a*)(iii)(I).
Leased plant and machinery, restriction on use of allowances: s 404(4)(*b*).
Mine rehabilitation expenditure: s 681(6)(*d*).
Offshore funds, taxation and returns of certain offshore funds, returns on acquisition of material interest: s 747C.
Payment of tax under section 128 (tax treatment of share options): s 128B(13).
Past trustees: liability to tax: s 579D(1).
Penalty, subss (1), (2): Sch 29 column 1.
Power to require return of property, subs (11): s 909(2).
Profits from occupation of woodlands: s 232(3); subs (6): s 232(3)(*c*).
Profits or gains from stallion fees: s 231(2); subs (6): s 231(2)(*c*).
Qualifying areas, double rent allowance election: s 372E(5)(*b*), (*d*).
Returns in relation to certain offshore products: s 896(5).
Returns in relation to foreign accounts: s 895(6).
Securitisation of assets: s 110(3)(*b*)(ii).
Self assessment, meaning of "inspector of returns", subs (11): s 950(1).
Self assessment, obligation to make return: s 959(4).
Shipping tonnage tax, plant and machinery, provisions relating to balancing charges: Sch 18B para 15(3).
Special savings incentive accounts, payment of tax credit: s 848E(4).
Stud greyhound service fees: s 233(3); subs (6): s 233(3)(*c*).
Surcharge for late returns, meaning of "return of income" applied: s 1084(1)(*a*).
Tax credit for research and development expenditure: s 766(5).
Tax credit on expenditure on buildings or structures used for research and development: s 766A(5).
Taxation of certain short-term leases of plant and machinery: s 80A(3).
Tax on non-resident company recoverable from another group member or from controlling director, return due date: s 629(1).
Tax treatment of directors of companies and employees granted rights to acquire shares or other assets, subs (6): s 128(2A)(*b*).
Valuation of trading stock on discontinuance of a trade: s 89(3)(*c*).
Wear and tear allowances in respect of machinery or plant: s 284(2)(*ac*)(i).

Revenue information

Information leaflet CG9 — Direct Debit Preliminary Tax.
Pay and File and the 2001 Income Tax Return.
A guide to completing 2002 tax returns may be downloaded from Revenue's website (www.revenue.ie) under What's New/New Publications.

Statements of practice

Documents to be enclosed with returns of income, September 1988.
Self-Assessment-Income Tax-Payment of Preliminary Tax and Filing of Returns for Commencing Sources Under Current Year Basis of Assessment: SP IT/2/91 September 1991.
Directors: SP IT/1/93, January 1993.
Preparation of accounts for Revenue purposes: SP IT/2/92, October 1992.

eBrief

eBrief no 7 — 2005 — For taxpayers who submit their payment **and** file their return through the Revenue Online Service (ROS) for preliminary tax for 2005, income tax balance due for 2004 and capital gains tax on gains arising in initial period 2005 (1 Jan–30 Sept), the filing date is extended to Thursday 17 November 2005.

Tax Briefing

TB14 May 1994 par3.1 — Tax Returns by Liquidators.

TB29 Dec 1997 p 9 — Completion of Form CT1 where reduced rate of corporation tax applies and also where manufacturing relief applies in conjunction with reduced rate.

TB29 Dec 1997 p 13 — Completion of income tax returns.

TB35 Mar 1999 p 30 — Direct Debit Payment of Income Tax Preliminary Tax.

TB36 June 1999 pp 8–9 Directors and Self Assessment.

TB44 June 2001 pp 4–6 — Changes to Return Filing and Payment Dates under Self Assessment (Finance Act 2001) — Pay and File system.

TB47 Apr 2002 pp 1–7 — Pay and File.

TB48 June 2002 pp 5–10 — Pay and File Questions and Answers.

TB49 Aug 2002 pp 15–16 — Pay and File — The 2001 Income Tax Return.

TB51 Jan 2003 p 19 — Self Assessment Tax Return for Individuals for 2002.

TB52 May 2003 p 6 — Form 11 and CTI — No attachments with these forms.

TB52 May 2003 p 7 — Pay and File 2003 IT and CT.

TB53 Aug 2003 p 19 — Form 11 and CT1 attachments — Clarification.

TB53 Aug 2003 pp 1–3 — Capital Gains Tax Payments — Finance Act 2003 changes.

TB53 Aug 2003 pp 4–13 — Extracts from Accounts ("Accounts Menus") Forms 11/CT1, Frequently Asked Questions.

TB53 Aug 2003 pp 25–26 Pay and File 2003 IT and CT.

TB54 Dec 2003 pp 17–19 Extracts from Accounts — Queries.

TB56 July 2004 pp 17–18 — Form CT1 2004.

TB56 July 2004 pp 22–23 — Pay and File 2004 IT and CT.

TB57 Oct 2004 pp 1–3 — Pay and File 2004.

TB57 Oct 2004 pp 5–6 — ROS Pay and File Tips.

TB57 Oct 2004 p 6 — CGT First Active Shares — Personal Exemption on disposal of free shares.

TB58 Dec 2004 pp 10–12 — IT Returns — Property Based Incentives.

Definitions

chargeable gain: ss 4(1), 5(1), 534; Collector-General: ss 2(1), 851; inspector: ss 2(1), 5(1), 852; person: IA 1937 s 11(*c*); Tax Acts: s 1(2); writing: IA 1937 Sch; year of assessment: ss 2(1), 5(1).

Former enactments

FA 1988 s 10; FA 1990 s 23(3)(*b*); FA 1991 s 46.

Corresponding UK tax provision

Taxes Management Act 1970 s 9.

952 Obligation to pay preliminary tax

(1) Every person who is a chargeable person as respects any chargeable period shall be liable to pay to the Collector-General in accordance with this section and section 958 the amount of that person's preliminary tax appropriate to that chargeable period.

(2) The amount of a chargeable person's preliminary tax appropriate to a chargeable period shall be the amount of tax which in the opinion of the chargeable person is likely to become payable by that person for the chargeable period by reason of an assessment or assessments for the chargeable period made or to be made by the inspector or which would be made by the inspector if the inspector did not elect under section 954(4) not to make an assessment.

...[1]

(4) Where on or before the due date for the payment of an amount of preliminary tax appropriate to a chargeable period the chargeable person by whom the tax is payable has

received notice of an assessment for the period, the chargeable person shall not be liable to pay preliminary tax for that chargeable period.

(5) Any amount of preliminary tax appropriate to a chargeable period which is paid by and not repaid to a chargeable person in any capacity shall, to the extent of the amount of that payment or the extent of the amount of that payment less any amount that has been repaid, be treated as a payment on foot of the tax payable by the chargeable person for the chargeable period, being tax which is specified in an assessment or assessments made or to be made for that period on the chargeable person in that capacity.

[(6) This section shall not apply to capital gains tax.][2]

Amendments

1 Subs (3) deleted by FA 2001 s 78(1)(*c*)(i) for short tax "year" 2001 and later tax years (income tax and capital gains tax) and as respects accounting periods of companies ending on or after 1 April 2001.

1 Subs (6) inserted by FA 2001 s 78(1)(*c*)(ii) for short tax "year" and later tax years (income tax and capital gains tax) and as respects accounting periods of companies ending on or after 1 April 2001.

Cross-references

Payment of tax under section 128 (tax treatment of share options): s 128B(11); subs (2): s 128B(12)(*a*).
Self assessment, making of assessments: s 954(7).
Self assessment, meaning of "preliminary tax": s 950(1).
Surcharge for late returns: s 1084(5).

Statement of practice

Payment by direct debit: SP CG 1/96.

Definitions

Collector-General: ss 2(1), 851; inspector: ss 2(1), 5(1), 852; person: IA 1937 s 11(*c*).

Former enactments

FA 1988 s 11.

953 Notices of preliminary tax

Amendments

1 Section 953 deleted by FA 2003 s 17(*d*) with effect from: (*a*) such day or days as the Minister for Finance may by order or orders appoint either generally or with reference to any particular purpose or provision and different days may be so appointed for different purposes or different provisions and (*b*) notwithstanding the generality of (*a*), any order made by the Minister for Finance in accordance with the provisions of that paragraph may contain, and be subject to, such conditions as the Minister considers appropriate and which are specified in the order; previously "...[1]

(7) Where the amount of preliminary tax paid by a chargeable person for any chargeable period exceeds that person's tax liability for that period, the excess shall be repaid and the amount repaid shall carry interest at the rate of [0.0161 per cent, or such other rate (if any) prescribed by the Minister for Finance by regulations, for each day or part of a day][2] for the period from the date or dates of the payment of the amount or amounts giving rise to the overpayment, as the case may require, to the date on which the repayment is made; but—

(*a*) interest shall not be payable under this subsection—

(i) if it amounts to less than [€10][3], or

(ii) to the extent that the excess arises from relief provided for by section 438(4),

and

(*b*) income tax shall not be deductible on payment of interest under this subsection and such interest shall not be reckoned in computing income for the purposes of the Tax Acts.

...[4]

(12) Every regulation made under this section shall be laid before Dáil Éireann as soon as may be after it is made and, if a resolution annulling the regulation is passed by Dáil Éireann within the next 21 days on

which Dáil Éireann has sat after the regulation is laid before it, the regulation shall be annulled accordingly, but without prejudice to the validity of anything previously done thereunder.

[1] Subs (1)–(6) deleted by FA 2001 s 78(1)(*d*) for short tax "year" 2001 and later tax years (income tax and capital gains tax) and as respects accounting periods of companies ending on or after 1 April 2001.

[2] Substituted by FA 2002 s 129(1)(*d*) with effect from 1 September 2002 as regards interest payable in respect of an amount due to be repaid or retained, whether before, on, or after that date; previously "0.5 per cent, or such other rate (if any) prescribed by the Minister for Finance by regulations, for each month or part of a month".

[3] Substituted by FA 2001 s 240(1) and (2)(*a*), (*c*) and Sch 5 Pt 1 for 2002 and later tax years (income tax) and accounting periods ending on or after 1 January 2002 (corporation tax); previously "£10".

[4] Subs (8)–(11) deleted by FA 2001 s 78(1)(*d*) for short tax "year" 2001 and later tax years (income tax and capital gains tax) and as respects accounting periods of companies ending on or after 1 April 2001.".

By virtue of Finance Act 2003 (Commencement of Section 17) Order 2003, SI No 508 of 2003, this deletion comes into operation (I) as respects payments of preliminiary tax made on or after 1 November 2003, and (II) 1 November 2004, as respects payments of preliminary tax made before 1 November 2003 unless the return, for the chargeable period in respect of which the preliminary tax was paid, required by section 951 is lodged with the Collector-General on or before 31 October 2004.

Cross-references

Wear and tear allowances for licences for public (taxis) vehicles; subs (7): s 286A(6).

Revenue precedents

Issue: Whether a repayment of Preliminary Tax which was generated by a BES claim made while case not under appeal carries interest.
Decision: An overpayment of Preliminary Tax (where PT exceeds the liability) carries interest. This includes where the repayment is generated by a BES claim.
Issue: Repayment of preliminary tax carries interest. Whether repayment of excess PSWT carries interest.
Decision: Repayment of excess PSWT does not carry interest.

Tax Briefing

TB56 July 2004 pp 6–11 — Repayments, Interest and Time Limits — Section 17 FA 2003 changes.
TB57 Oct 2004 pp 7–9 — New Time Limits — Section 17 FA 2003 changes.
TB57 Oct 2004 p 15 — Repayments, Interest and Time Limits — correction to TB56 p 8.

Definitions

Dáil Éireann: IA 1937 Sch; person: IA 1937 s 11(*c*); Tax Acts: s 1(2).

Former enactments

FA 1988 s 12; FA 1991 s 47; FA 1997 s 146(1) and Sch 9 Pt I para 15.

954 Making of assessments

(1) An assessment shall not be made on a chargeable person for a chargeable period at any time before the specified return date for the chargeable period unless at that time the chargeable person has delivered a return for the chargeable period, and an assessment shall not be made at a time when the making of the assessment is precluded under section 955(2).

(2) Subject to subsection (3), an assessment made on a chargeable person for a chargeable period shall be made by the inspector by reference to the particulars contained in the chargeable person's return.

(3) Where—

(*a*) a chargeable person makes default in the delivery of a return for a chargeable period, or (*b*) the inspector is not satisfied with the return which has been delivered, or has received any information as to its insufficiency,

nothing in this section shall prevent the inspector from making an assessment in accordance with section 919(4) or 922, as appropriate.

(4) (*a*) Where as respects a chargeable period the inspector is satisfied that a chargeable person has paid all amounts of tax which, if the inspector were to make an assessment on the chargeable person for the chargeable period, would be payable by the chargeable person for the chargeable period, the inspector may elect not to make an assessment on the chargeable person for the chargeable period and, where the inspector so elects, he or she shall give notice of the election to the chargeable person, and the amounts paid by the chargeable person shall be deemed to have been payable in all respects as if the inspector had made the assessment.

(*b*) Subject to section 955(2), nothing in this subsection shall prevent an inspector from making an assessment on the chargeable person for the chargeable period at any time after the giving of the notice of election under this section.

(5) Where an inspector makes an assessment—

(*a*) under either of the provisions referred to in subsection (3) in default of the delivery of a return, or

(*b*) in circumstances where the chargeable person has calculated the amount of tax which will be payable by that person on foot of an assessment and the inspector does not at the time of the making of the assessment disagree with the tax as so calculated,

it shall not be necessary to set out in the notice of assessment any particulars other than particulars as to the amount of tax to be paid by the chargeable person.

(6) Notwithstanding subsections (1) to (5) but subject to section 955(2), where a chargeable person has delivered a return for a chargeable period, the chargeable person may by notice in writing given to the inspector require the inspector to make an assessment for the chargeable period and the inspector shall make the assessment forthwith.

(7) Nothing in this section shall prevent an inspector from making an assessment in accordance with—

(*a*) section 977(3) or subsection (2) or (3) of section 978, as appropriate, and, notwithstanding sections 952 and 958, tax specified in such an assessment shall be due and payable in accordance with section 979,

(*b*) subsection (5) or (6), as appropriate, of section 980 and, notwithstanding sections 952 and 958, tax specified in such an assessment shall be due and payable in accordance with section 980(10), or

(*c*) section 1042 and, notwithstanding sections 952 and 958, tax specified in such an assessment shall be due and payable in accordance with section 1042.

Cross-references

Self assessment, obligation to pay preliminary tax, subs (4): ss 952(2).

Definitions

inspector: ss 2(1), 5(1), 852; person: IA 1937 s 11(*c*); writing: IA 1937 Sch.

Former enactments

FA 1988 s 13; FA 1991 s 48.

955 Amendment of and time limit for assessments

(1) Subject to subsection (2) and to section 1048, an inspector may at any time amend an assessment made on a chargeable person for a chargeable period by making such alterations in or additions to the assessment as he or she considers necessary, notwithstanding that tax may have been paid or repaid in respect of the assessment and notwithstanding that he or she may have amended the assessment on a previous occasion or on previous occasions, and the inspector shall give notice to the chargeable person of the assessment as so amended.

(2) [(*a*) Where a chargeable person has delivered a return for a chargeable period and has made in the return a full and true disclosure of all material facts necessary for the making of an assessment for the chargeable period, an assessment for that period or an amendment of such an assessment shall not be made on the chargeable person after the end of 4 years commencing at the end of the chargeable period in which the return is delivered and—

(i) no additional tax shall be payable by the chargeable person after the end of that period of 4 years, and

(ii) no tax shall be repaid after the end of a period of 4 years commencing at the end of the chargeable period for which the return is delivered,

by reason of any matter contained in the return.][1]

(*b*) Nothing in this subsection shall prevent the amendment of an assessment—

(i) where a relevant return does not contain a full and true disclosure of the facts referred to in paragraph (*a*),

(ii) to give effect to a determination on any appeal against an assessment,

(iii) to take account of any fact or matter arising by reason of an event occurring after the return is delivered,

(iv) to correct an error in calculation, or

(v) to correct a mistake of fact whereby any matter in the assessment does not properly reflect the facts disclosed by the chargeable person,

and tax shall be paid or repaid where appropriate in accordance with any such amendment, and nothing in this section shall affect the operation of section 804(3).

(3) A chargeable person who is aggrieved by an assessment or the amendment of an assessment on the grounds that the chargeable person considers that the inspector was precluded from making the assessment or the amendment, as the case may be, by reason of subsection (2) may appeal against the assessment or amended assessment on those grounds and, if on the hearing of the appeal the Appeal Commissioners determine—

(*a*) that the inspector was so precluded, the Tax Acts shall apply as if the assessment or the amendment, as the case may be, had not been made, and the assessment or the amendment of the assessment as appropriate shall be void, or (*b*) that the inspector was not so precluded, the assessment or the assessment as amended shall stand, except to the extent that any amount or matter in that assessment is the subject of a valid appeal on any other grounds.

(4) (*a*) Where a chargeable person is in doubt as to the application of law to or the treatment for tax purposes of any matter to be contained in a return to be delivered by the chargeable person, that person may deliver the return to the best of that person's belief as to the application of law to or the treatment for tax purposes of that matter but that person shall draw the inspector's attention to the matter in question in the return by specifying the doubt and, if that person does so, that person shall be treated as making a full and true disclosure with regard to that matter.

(*b*) This subsection shall not apply where the inspector is, or on appeal the Appeal Commissioners are, not satisfied that the doubt was genuine and is or are of the opinion that the chargeable person was acting with a view to the evasion or avoidance of tax, and in such a case the chargeable person shall be deemed not to have made a full and true disclosure with regard to the matter in question.

(5) (*a*) In this subsection, **"relevant chargeable period"** means—

(i) where the chargeable period is a year of assessment for income tax, the year 1988–89 and any subsequent year of assessment,

(ii) where the chargeable period is a year of assessment for capital gains tax, the year 1990–91 and any subsequent year of assessment, and

(iii) where the chargeable period is an accounting period of a company, an accounting period ending on or after the 1st day of October, 1989.

(*b*) Sections 919(5)(*b*) and 924 shall not apply in the case of a chargeable person for any relevant chargeable period, and all matters which would have been included in an additional first assessment under those sections shall be included in an amendment of the first assessment or first assessments made in accordance with this section.

(*c*) For the purposes of paragraph (*b*), where any amount of income, profits or gains or, as respects capital gains tax, chargeable gains was omitted from the first assessment or first assessments or the tax stated in the first assessment or first assessments was less than the tax payable by the chargeable person for the relevant chargeable period concerned, there shall be made such adjustments or additions (including the addition of a further first assessment) to the first assessment or first assessments as are necessary to rectify the omission or to ensure that the tax so stated is equal to the tax so payable by the chargeable person.

Amendments

[1] Subs (2)(*a*) substituted by FA 2003 s 17(*g*) with effect from: (*a*) such day or days as the Minister for Finance may by order or orders appoint either generally or with reference to any particular purpose or provision and different days may be so appointed for different purposes or different provisions and (*b*) notwithstanding the generality of (*a*), any order made by the Minister for Finance in accordance with the provisions of that paragraph may contain, and be subject to, such conditions as the Minister considers appropriate and which are specified in the order; previously "(*a*) Where a chargeable person has delivered a return for a chargeable period and has made in the return a full and true disclosure of all material facts necessary for the making of an assessment for the chargeable period, an assessment for that period or an amendment of such an assessment shall not be made on the chargeable person after the end of the period of 6 years commencing

at the end of the chargeable period in which the return is delivered and no additional tax shall be payable by the chargeable person and no tax shall be repaid to the chargeable person after the end of the period of 6 years by reason of any matter contained in the return.". By virtue of Finance Act 2003 (Commencement of Section 17) Order 2003, SI No 508 of 2003, this amendment comes into operation on 1 January 2005 in relation to the making or amending of assessments, additional tax being payable or the repayment of tax by reason of a matter contained in a return for a chargeable period.

Cross-references

Evidence of income: s 1069(1)(*b*).
Inspector's right to make enquiries and amend assessments, subs (2): s 956(1)(*b*)(ii).
Self assessment, appeals: s 957(3).
Self assessment, making of assessments: s 954(2); subs (2): s 954(1), (4)(*b*), (6).

Case law

The protection provided by s 955(2)(*a*) in respect of any claim dating back 6 years from the date of the claim is subject to TCA 1997 s 924. Section 924 provides for the raising of additional assessments where income tax has been omitted from the first assessment: *Criminal Assets Bureau v Hutch.*

Revenue precedents

Issue: Whether repayment should be made pending examination of an expression of doubt under s 955(4).
Decision: While Revenue would have good reason to withhold repayment where the taxpayer has not given sufficient information to quantify the effect of an expression of doubt, in general, Revenue should either amend the assessment to reflect Revenue's view on the disputed item or make the repayment in accordance with the assessment made in line with the return.

Tax Briefing

TB56 July 2004 pp 6–11 — Repayments, Interest and Time Limits — Section 17 FA 2003 changes.
TB57 Oct 2004 pp 7–9 — New Time Limits - Section 17 FA 2003 changes.
TB57 Oct 2004 p 15 — Repayments, Interest and Time Limits — correction to TB56 p 8.

Definitions

Appeal Commissioners: s 2(1); chargeable gain: ss 4(1), 5(1), 534; inspector: ss 2(1), 5(1), 852; person: IA 1937 s 11(*c*); profits: s 4(1); Tax Acts: s 1(2).

Former enactments

FA 1988 s 9(1) (part of) and s 14; FA 1991 s 45(*a*)(vi) and s 49.

956 Inspector's right to make enquiries and amend assessments

(1) (*a*) For the purpose of making an assessment on a chargeable person for a chargeable period or for the purpose of amending such an assessment, the inspector—

(i) may accept either in whole or in part any statement or other particular contained in a return delivered by the chargeable person for that chargeable period, and

(ii) may assess any amount of income, profits or gains or, as respects capital gains tax, chargeable gains, or allow any deduction, allowance or relief by reference to such statement or particular.

(*b*) The making of an assessment or the amendment of an assessment by reference to any statement or particular referred to in paragraph (*a*)(i) shall not preclude the inspector—

(i) from making such enquiries or taking such actions within his or her powers as he or she considers necessary to satisfy himself or herself as to the accuracy or otherwise of that statement or particular, and

(ii) subject to section 955(2), from amending or further amending an assessment in such manner as he or she considers appropriate.

(*c*) Any enquiries and actions referred to in paragraph (*b*) shall not be made in the case of any chargeable person for any chargeable period at any time after the expiry of the period of [4 years][1] commencing at the end of the chargeable period in which the chargeable person has delivered a return for the chargeable period unless at that time the inspector has reasonable grounds for believing that the return is insufficient due to its having been completed in a fraudulent or negligent manner.

(2) (*a*) A chargeable person who is aggrieved by any enquiry made or action taken by an inspector for a chargeable period, after the expiry of the period referred to in subsection (1)(*c*) in respect of that chargeable period, on the grounds that the chargeable person considers that the inspector is precluded from making that enquiry or taking that action by reason of subsection (1)(*c*) may, by notice in writing given to the inspector within 30 days of the inspector making that enquiry or taking that action, appeal to the Appeal Commissioners, and the Appeal Commissioners shall hear the appeal in all respects as if it were an appeal against an assessment.

(*b*) Any action required to be taken by the chargeable person and any further action proposed to be taken by the inspector pursuant to the inspector's enquiry or action shall be suspended pending the determination of the appeal.

(*c*) Where on the hearing of the appeal the Appeal Commissioners—

(i) determine that the inspector was precluded from making the enquiry or taking the action by reason of subsection (1)(*c*), the chargeable person shall not be required to take any action pursuant to the inspector's enquiry or action and the inspector shall be prohibited from pursuing his enquiry or action, or

(ii) decide that the inspector was not so precluded, it shall be lawful for the inspector to continue with his or her enquiry or action.

Amendments

1 Substituted by FA 2003 s 17(*h*) with effect from: (*a*) such day or days as the Minister for Finance may by order or orders appoint either generally or with reference to any particular purpose or provision and different days may be so appointed for different purposes or different provisions and (*b*) notwithstanding the generality of (*a*), any order made by the Minister for Finance in accordance with the provisions of that paragraph may contain, and be subject to, such conditions as the Minister considers appropriate and which are specified in the order; previously "6 years". By virtue of Finance Act 2003 (Commencement of Section 17) Order 2003, SI No 508 of 2003, this amendment comes into operation in relation to enquiries and actions referred to in section 956(1)(*b*) made on or after 1 January 2005.

Cross-references

Retention and inspection of records in relation to claims by individuals: s 886A(5).

Tax Briefing

TB56 July 2004 pp 6–11 — Repayments, Interest and Time Limits — Section 17 FA 2003 changes.

TB57 Oct 2004 pp 7–9 — New Time Limits - Section 17 FA 2003 changes.

TB57 Oct 2004 p 15 — Repayments, Interest and Time Limits — correction to TB56 p 8.

Definitions

Appeal Commissioners: s 2(1); chargeable gain: ss 4(1), 5(1), 534; inspector: ss 2(1), 5(1), 852; person: IA 1937 s 11(*c*); profits: s 4(1); writing: IA 1937 Sch.

Former enactments

FA 1988 s 15; FA 1991 s 50.

957 Appeals

(1) No appeal may be made against—

...[1]

(*b*) the amount of any income, profits or gains or, as respects capital gains tax, chargeable gains, or the amount of any allowance, deduction or relief specified in an assessment or an amended assessment made on a chargeable person for a chargeable period, where the inspector has determined that amount by accepting without the alteration of and without departing from the statement or statements or the particular or particulars with regard to income, profits or gains or, as respects capital gains tax, chargeable gains, or allowances, deductions or reliefs specified in the return delivered by the chargeable person for the chargeable period, or

(*c*) the amount of any income, profits or gains or, as respects capital gains tax, chargeable gains, or the amount of any allowance, deduction or relief specified in an assessment or an amended assessment made on a chargeable person for a chargeable period, where that amount had been agreed between the inspector and the chargeable person, or any person authorised by the chargeable person in that behalf, before the making of the assessment or the amendment of the assessment, as the case may be.

(2) (*a*) Where—

(i) a chargeable person makes default in the delivery of a return, or

(ii) the inspector is not satisfied with the return which has been delivered by a chargeable person, or has received any information as to its insufficiency,

and the inspector makes an assessment in accordance with section 919(4) or 922, no appeal shall lie against that assessment until such time as—

(I) in a case to which subparagraph (i) applies, the chargeable person delivers the return, and

(II) in a case to which either subparagraph (i) or (ii) applies, the chargeable person pays or has paid an amount of tax on foot of the assessment which is not less than the tax which would be payable on foot of the assessment if the assessment were made in all respects by reference to the statements and particulars contained in the return delivered by the chargeable person,

and the time for bringing an appeal against the assessment shall be treated as commencing at the earliest date on which both the return has been delivered and that amount of tax has been paid, and references in this subsection to an assessment shall be construed as including references to any amendment of the assessment which is made before that earliest date.

(*b*) References in this subsection to an amount of tax shall be construed as including any amount of interest which would be due and payable under section 1080 on that tax at the date of payment of the tax, together with any costs incurred or other amounts which may be charged or levied in pursuing the collection of the tax contained in the assessment or the assessment as amended, as the case may be.

(3) Subject to subsections (1) and (2), where an assessment is amended under section 955 (not being an amendment made by reason of the determination of an appeal), the chargeable person may appeal against the assessment as so amended in all respects as if it were an assessment made on the date of the amendment and the notice of the assessment as so amended were a notice of the assessment, except that the chargeable person shall have no further right of appeal, in relation to matters other than additions to, deletions from, or alterations in the assessment, made by reason of the amendment, than the chargeable person would have had if the assessment had not been amended.

(4) Where an appeal is brought against an assessment or an amended assessment made on a chargeable person for any chargeable period, the chargeable person shall specify in the notice of appeal—

(*a*) each amount or matter in the assessment or amended assessment with which the chargeable person is aggrieved, and

(*b*) the grounds in detail of the chargeable person's appeal as respects each such amount or matter.

(5) Where, as respects an amount or matter to which a notice of appeal relates, the notice does not comply with subsection (4), the notice shall, in so far as it relates to that amount or matter, be invalid and the appeal concerned shall, in so far as it relates to that amount or matter, be deemed not to have been brought.

(6) The chargeable person shall not be entitled to rely on any ground of appeal that is not specified in the notice of appeal unless the Appeal Commissioners, or the judge of the Circuit Court, as the case may be, are or is satisfied that the ground could not reasonably have been stated in the notice.

Amendments

[1] Subs (1)(*a*) deleted by FA 2001 s 78(1)(*e*) for short tax "year" 2001 and later tax years (income tax and capital gains tax) and as respects accounting periods of companies ending on or after 1 April 2001.

Cross-references

Appeals against determinations of certain claims etc: s 949(1).
Self assessment, date for payment of tax, subs (2)(*a*)(II): s 958(9)(*a*).

Definitions

Appeal Commissioners: s 2(1); chargeable gain: ss 4(1), 5(1), 534; Circuit Court: IA 1937 Sch; inspector: ss 2(1), 5(1), 852; person: IA 1937 s 11(*c*); profits: s 4(1).

Former enactments

FA 1988 s 17; FA 1991 s 51.

958 Date for payment of tax

[(1) (*a*) In this section—

"corresponding corporation tax for the preceding chargeable period", in relation to a chargeable period which is an accounting period of a company, means an amount determined by the formula—

$$T \times \frac{C}{P}$$

where—

T is the corporation tax payable by the chargeable person for the preceding chargeable period,

C is the [number of days][1] in the chargeable period, and

P is the [number of days][1] in the preceding chargeable period;

[**"tax payable for the initial period"**, in relation to a chargeable period which is a year of assessment for capital gains tax (being the year of assessment 2003 or any subsequent year of assessment), means the tax which would be payable by the chargeable person if the year of assessment ended on 30 September in that year instead of 31 December in that year;

"tax payable for the later period", in relation to a chargeable period which is a year of assessment for capital gains tax (being the year of assessment 2003 or any subsequent year of assessment), means the tax payable for the year of assessment less the tax payable for the initial period in relation to that year of assessment;][2]

"pre-preceding chargeable period", in relation to a chargeable period, means the chargeable period next before the preceding chargeable period;

"relevant limit", in relation to a chargeable period which is an accounting period of a company, means €50,000; but where the length of a chargeable period is less than 12 months the relevant limit in relation to the chargeable period shall be proportionately reduced.

(*b*) For the purposes of this section, a chargeable person being a company shall be a small company in relation to a chargeable period if the corresponding corporation tax for the preceding chargeable period payable by the chargeable person does not exceed the relevant limit in relation to the accounting period.][3]

[[(2) Subject to subsection (10), preliminary tax appropriate to a chargeable period which is a year of assessment for income tax shall be due and payable on or before 31 October in the year of assessment and, accordingly, references in this Part to the due date for the payment of an amount of preliminary tax shall, in the case where that tax is due for a chargeable period which is a year of assessment, be construed as a reference to 31 October in the year of assessment.

(2A)(*a*) Preliminary tax appropriate to a chargeable period which is an accounting period of a company ending in the period from 1 January 2002 to 31 December 2005 shall be due and payable in 2 instalments.

[(*b*) The first of the 2 instalments referred to in paragraph (*a*) (in this section referred to as the **"first instalment"**) shall be due and payable not later than the day which is 31 days before the day on which the accounting period ends, but where that day is later than day 21 of the month in which the first-mentioned day occurs, the first instalment shall be due and payable not later than day 21 of that month.

(*c*) Notwithstanding paragraph (*b*), in a case where an accounting period of a company is less than one month and one day in length, the first instalment shall be due and payable not later than the last day of the accounting period, but where that day is later than day 21 of the month in which that day occurs, the first instalment shall be due and payable not later than day 21 of that month.

(*d*) The second of the 2 instalments referred to in paragraph (*a*) (in this section referred to as the **"second instalment"**) shall be due and payable within the period of 6 months from the end of the accounting period, but in any event the second instalment shall be due and payable not later than day 21 of the month in which that period of 6 months ends.][4]

[(2B)(*a*) Preliminary tax appropriate to a chargeable period which is an accounting period of a company ending on or after 1 January 2006 shall be due and payable not later than the day which is 31 days before the day on which the accounting period ends, but where that day is later than day 21 of the month in which the first-mentioned day occurs, that tax shall be due and payable not later than day 21 of that month.

(*b*) Notwithstanding paragraph (*a*), in a case where an accounting period of a company ending on or after 1 January 2006 is less than one month and one day in length, preliminary tax shall be due and payable not later than the last day of the accounting period, but where that day is later than day 21 of the month in which that day occurs, that tax shall be due and payable not later than day 21 of that month.][5]

(2C)(*a*) References in this Part to the due date for the payment of the first instalment, or the second instalment, of preliminary tax shall be construed in accordance with subsection (2A).

(*b*) References in this Part to the due date for the payment of an amount of preliminary tax shall, in the case where that tax is due for a chargeable period which is an accounting period of a company ending on or after 1 January 2006, be construed in accordance with subsection (2B).][6]

[(3) (*a*) Subject to subsections (3A), (4), (4B), (4C), (4D) and (4E), tax payable by a chargeable person for a chargeable period shall be due and payable—

(i) subject to subparagraphs (ii) and (iii), where an assessment is made on the chargeable person for the chargeable period before the due date for the payment of an amount of preliminary tax for the chargeable period, on or before that date,

(ii) where an assessment is made on the chargeable person for the chargeable period (being a year of assessment for income tax) before the specified return date for the chargeable period, on or before that date,

(iii) where an assessment has not been made on the chargeable person for the chargeable period (being a year of assessment for income tax) on or before the specified return date for the chargeable period,

(iv) where an assessment has not been made on the chargeable person for the chargeable period (being the year of assessment 2002 for capital gains tax), on or before the specified return date for the chargeable period,

(v) where the chargeable period is a year of assessment for capital gains tax (being the year of assessment 2003 for capital gains tax or any subsequent year of assessment for capital gains tax) and an assessment has not been made on the chargeable person for the year of assessment—

(I) as respects tax payable for the initial period, on or before 31 October in the year of assessment, and

(II) as respects tax payable for the later period, on or before 31 January in the next following year of assessment, or

(vi) where the chargeable period is an accounting period of a company, on or before the specified return date for the chargeable period.

(*b*) Where in relation to a chargeable period (being a year of assessment for income tax) the tax payable by a chargeable person for a year of assessment is due and payable in accordance with paragraph (*a*)(iii), then, the tax specified in any subsequent assessment made on the chargeable person for that year shall be deemed to have been due and payable on or before the specified return date for the chargeable period.

(*c*) (i) Where in relation to a chargeable period (being the year of assessment 2002 for capital gains tax) the tax payable by a chargeable person for the year of assessment is due and payable in accordance with paragraph (*a*)(iv), then, the tax specified in any subsequent assessment made on the chargeable person for that year shall be deemed to have been due and payable on or before the specified return date for the chargeable period.

(ii) Where in relation to a chargeable period (being the year of assessment for capital gains tax 2003 or any subsequent year of assessment for capital gains tax) the tax payable by a chargeable person for a year of assessment is due and payable in accordance with paragraph (*a*)(v), then, the tax specified in any subsequent assessment made on the chargeable person for that year shall be deemed to have been due and payable—

(I) on or before 31 October in the year of assessment as respects tax payable for the initial period, and

(II) on or before 31 January in the next following year of assessment as respects tax payable for the later period.

(*d*) Where in relation to a chargeable period (being an accounting period of a company) the tax payable by a chargeable person for an accounting period is due and payable in accordance with paragraph (*a*)(vi), then, the tax specified in any subsequent assessment made on the chargeable person for that accounting period shall be deemed to have been due and payable on or before the specified return date for the chargeable period.][7]

[(3A)(*a*) In this paragraph the **"specified amount"**, in relation to a year of assessment for income tax and the year of assessment 2002 for capital gains tax, means the greater of—

(i) 5 per cent of the tax payable by that person for that year or €3,175, whichever is the lesser, and

(ii) €635.

(*b*) Subject to subsection (3), where—

(i) an assessment to tax has not been made on a chargeable person on or before the specified return date for the chargeable period (being a year of assessment for income tax and the year of assessment 2002 for capital gains tax), and

(ii) the chargeable person has—

(I) delivered a return for the year of assessment by the specified return date for the chargeable period,

(II) made in the return a full and true disclosure of all material facts necessary for the making of a correct assessment for the year of assessment, and

(III) paid an amount of tax for the year of assessment on or before the specified return date, being an amount which is less than the tax payable by the chargeable person for that year of assessment by not more than the specified amount,

then, subject to subsection (8), any additional tax payable by that person for that year shall be due and payable on or before 31 December in the next following year of assessment.][8]

(4) Where but for this subsection tax payable by a chargeable person for a chargeable period [which is a year of assessment][9] would be due and payable in accordance with subsection (3), other than paragraph (*a*)(i) of that subsection, and—

(*a*) the chargeable person has defaulted in the payment of preliminary tax for the chargeable period,

(*b*) the preliminary tax paid by the chargeable person for the chargeable period is less than, or less than the least of, as the case may be—

(i) 90 per cent of the tax payable by the chargeable person for the chargeable period,

(ii) (I) where the chargeable period is a year of assessment other than the year of assessment 2001 or 2002, the income tax payable by the chargeable person for the preceding chargeable period,

(II) where the chargeable period is the year of assessment 2002, 135 per cent of the income tax payable by the chargeable person for the preceding chargeable period,

(III) where the chargeable period is the year of assessment 2001, 74 per cent of the income tax payable by the chargeable person for the preceding chargeable period,

(iii) in the case of a chargeable person to whom subsection (10) applies (other than a chargeable person in relation to whom the amount of income tax payable, or taken in accordance with subsection (5)(*a*) to be payable, for the pre-preceding chargeable period was nil)—

(I) where the chargeable period is a year of assessment other than the year of assessment 2001 or 2003, 105 per cent of the income tax payable by the chargeable person for the pre-preceding chargeable period,

(II) where the chargeable period is the year of assessment 2003, 142 per cent of the income tax payable by the chargeable person for the pre-preceding chargeable period,

(III) where the chargeable period is the year of assessment 2001, 78 per cent of the income tax payable by the chargeable person for the pre-preceding chargeable period,

or

(*c*) the preliminary tax payable by the chargeable person for the chargeable period was not paid by the date on which it was due and payable,

the tax payable by the chargeable person shall be deemed to have been due and payable on the due date for the payment of an amount of preliminary tax for the chargeable period.

(4A) Where—

(*a*) after the due date for the payment of an amount of preliminary tax for a chargeable period (being a year of assessment for income tax), an amount of additional income tax to which subsection (3A) applies is paid for the preceding chargeable period, and

(*b*) an additional amount of preliminary tax (which is not more than the additional amount of income tax so paid) is paid on or before 31 December in the year of assessment such that the total amount of preliminary tax paid by the chargeable person for the chargeable period is not less than the amount specified in subsection (4)(*b*)(ii),

then, the additional amount of preliminary tax so paid shall be deemed for the purposes of subsection (4)(*b*)(ii) to have been paid on the due date for the payment of an amount of preliminary tax for the chargeable period.][10]

[(4B)(*a*) Subject to subsection (4D), where but for this subsection tax payable by a chargeable person for a chargeable period which is an accounting period of a company ending in the period from 1 January 2002 to 31 December 2005 would be due and payable in accordance with subsection (3), and—

(i) the chargeable person has defaulted in the payment of the first instalment or the second instalment of preliminary tax for the chargeable period,

(ii) where the chargeable person is a small company in relation to the accounting period, the first instalment of the preliminary tax paid by the chargeable person for the chargeable period is less than, or less than the lower of—

(I) where the chargeable period is an accounting period of the company ending in the year 2002, 18 per cent of the tax payable by the chargeable person for the chargeable period or 20 per cent of the corresponding corporation tax for the preceding chargeable period,

(II) where the chargeable period is an accounting period of the company ending in the year 2003, 36 per cent of the tax payable by the chargeable person for the chargeable period or 40 per cent of the corresponding corporation tax for the preceding chargeable period,

(III) where the chargeable period is an accounting period of the company ending in the year 2004, 54 per cent of the tax payable by the chargeable person for the chargeable period or 60 per cent of the corresponding corporation tax for the preceding chargeable period, or

(IV) where the chargeable period is an accounting period of the company ending in the year 2005, 72 per cent of the tax payable by the chargeable person for the chargeable period or 80 per cent of the corresponding corporation tax for the preceding chargeable period,

(iii) where the chargeable person is not a small company in relation to the accounting period, the first instalment of the preliminary tax paid by the chargeable person for the chargeable period is less than—

(I) where the chargeable period is an accounting period of the company ending in the year 2002, 18 per cent,

(II) where the chargeable period is an accounting period of the company ending in the year 2003, 36 per cent,

(III) where the chargeable period is an accounting period of the company ending in the year 2004, 54 per cent, or

(IV) where the chargeable period is an accounting period of the company ending in the year 2005, 72 per cent,

of the tax payable by the chargeable person for the chargeable period,

(iv) the aggregate of the first instalment and the second instalment of the preliminary tax paid by the chargeable person for the chargeable period is less than 90 per cent of the tax payable by the chargeable person for the chargeable period, or

(v) the first instalment or the second instalment of the preliminary tax payable by the chargeable person for the chargeable period was not paid by the date on which it was due and payable,

then the tax payable by the chargeable person for the chargeable period shall be deemed to have been due and payable in accordance with paragraph (*b*).

(*b*) (i) Tax due and payable in accordance with this paragraph by a chargeable person for a chargeable period which is an accounting period of a company shall be due and payable in 2 instalments.

(ii) The first of the 2 instalments referred to in subparagraph (i) (in this paragraph and in paragraphs (*c*) and (*d*) referred to as the "first relevant instalment") shall be due and payable not later than the day on which the first instalment of preliminary tax is due and payable in accordance with subsection (2A).

(iii) The second of the 2 instalments referred to in subparagraph (i) (in this paragraph and in paragraphs (*c*) and (*d*) referred to as the "second relevant instalment") shall be due and payable not later than the day on which the second instalment of preliminary tax is due and payable in accordance with subsection (2A).

(*c*) The amount of the first relevant instalment shall be—

(i) where the chargeable period is an accounting period of the company ending in the year 2002, 20 per cent,

(ii) where the chargeable period is an accounting period of the company ending in the year 2003, 40 per cent,

(iii) where the chargeable period is an accounting period of the company ending in the year 2004, 60 per cent, and

(iv) where the chargeable period is an accounting period of the company ending in the year 2005, 80 per cent, of the tax payable by the chargeable person for the chargeable period.

(*d*) The amount of the second relevant instalment shall be an amount equal to the excess of the tax payable by the chargeable person for the chargeable period over the amount of the first relevant instalment.

(4C) Subject to subsection (4E), where but for this subsection tax payable by a chargeable person for a chargeable period which is an accounting period of a company ending on or after 1 January 2006 would be due and payable in accordance with subsection (3), and—

(*a*) the chargeable person has defaulted in the payment of preliminary tax for the chargeable period,

(*b*) the preliminary tax paid by the chargeable person for the chargeable period is—

(i) where the chargeable person is a small company in relation to the accounting period, less than, or less than the lower of—

(I) 90 per cent of the tax payable by the chargeable person for the chargeable period, or

(II) the corresponding corporation tax for the preceding chargeable period,

and

(ii) where the chargeable person is not a small company in relation to the accounting period, less than 90 per cent of the tax payable by the chargeable person for the chargeable period,

or

(*c*) the preliminary tax payable by the chargeable person for the chargeable period was not paid by the date on which it was due and payable,

then the tax payable by the chargeable person for the chargeable period shall be deemed to have been due and payable on the due date for the payment of an amount of preliminary tax for the chargeable period.

(4D) Where as respects a chargeable period which is an accounting period of a company ending in the period 1 January 2002 to 31 December 2005—

(*a*) the first instalment of preliminary tax paid by the chargeable person for the chargeable period in accordance with subsection (2A) is less than—

(i) where the chargeable period is an accounting period ending in 2002, 18 per cent,

(ii) where the chargeable period is an accounting period ending in 2003, 36 per cent,

(iii) where the chargeable period is an accounting period ending in 2004, 54 per cent, or

(iv) where the chargeable period is an accounting period ending in 2005, 72 per cent,

of the tax payable by the chargeable person for the chargeable period, (*b*) the preliminary tax so paid by the chargeable person for the chargeable period is not less than—

(i) where the chargeable period is an accounting period ending in 2002, 18 per cent,

(ii) where the chargeable period is an accounting period ending in 2003, 36 per cent,

(iii) where the chargeable period is an accounting period ending in 2004, 54 per cent, or

(iv) where the chargeable period is an accounting period ending in 2005, 72 per cent,

of the amount which would be payable by the chargeable person for the chargeable period if no amount were included in the chargeable person's profits for the chargeable period in respect of chargeable gains on the disposal by the person of assets in the part of the chargeable period which is after the date by which the first instalment for the chargeable period is payable in accordance with subsection (2A),

(*c*) the chargeable person makes a further payment of preliminary tax for the chargeable period within one month after the end of the chargeable period and the aggregate of that payment and the first instalment paid by the chargeable person for the chargeable period in accordance with subsection (2A) is not less than the percentage specified in paragraph (*a*) in relation to the chargeable period of the tax payable by the chargeable person for the chargeable period, and

(*d*) the aggregate of those payments and the second instalment paid by the chargeable person for the chargeable period in accordance with [subsection (2A)][11] is not less than 90 per cent of the tax payable by the chargeable person for the chargeable period,

then the preliminary tax paid by the chargeable person for the chargeable period shall be treated for the purposes of subsection (4B) as having been paid by the date by which it is due and payable.

(4E) Where as respects a chargeable period which is an accounting period of a company ending on or after 1 January 2006—

(*a*) the preliminary tax paid by the chargeable person for the chargeable period in accordance with subsection (2B) is less than 90 per cent of the tax payable by the chargeable person for the chargeable period,

(*b*) the preliminary tax so paid by the chargeable person for the chargeable period is not less than 90 per cent of the amount which would be payable by the chargeable person for the chargeable period if no amount were included in the chargeable person's profits for the chargeable period in respect of chargeable gains on the disposal by the person of assets in the part of the chargeable period which is after the date by which preliminary tax for the chargeable period is payable in accordance with subsection (2B), and

(*c*) the chargeable person makes a further payment of preliminary tax for the chargeable period within one month after the end of the chargeable period and the aggregate of that payment and the preliminary tax paid by the chargeable person for the chargeable period in accordance with subsection (2B) is not less than 90 per cent of the tax payable by the chargeable person for the chargeable period,

then the preliminary tax paid by the chargeable person for the chargeable period shall be treated for the purposes of subsection (4C) as having been paid by the date by which it is due and payable.][12]

(5) For the purposes of subparagraphs (ii) and (iii) of subsection (4)(*b*)—

(*a*) subject to subsection (7), where the chargeable person was not a chargeable person for the preceding chargeable period or for the pre-preceding chargeable period, the income tax payable for the preceding chargeable period or the pre-preceding chargeable period, as the case may be, shall be taken to be nil, and

(*b*) where, after the due date for the payment of an amount of preliminary tax for a chargeable period which is a year of assessment, an amount of additional income tax for the preceding chargeable period or, in the case of a chargeable person to whom subsection (10) applies, the pre-preceding chargeable period becomes payable, that additional income tax shall not be taken into account only if it became due and payable one month following the amendment to the assessment or the determination of the appeal, as the case may be, by virtue of subsection (8)(*b*) or (9)(*b*).

(6) For the purpose of subparagraphs (ii) and (iii) of subsection (4)(*b*), where the chargeable person is chargeable to income tax for a chargeable period—

(*a*) the tax payable for the preceding chargeable period or, in the case of a chargeable person to whom subsection (10) applies, the pre-preceding chargeable period shall be determined without regard to any relief to which the chargeable person is or may become entitled for the preceding chargeable period or the pre-preceding chargeable period, as the case may be, under Part 16, and

(*b*) the tax payable for the preceding chargeable period or, in the case of a chargeable person to whom subsection (10) applies, the pre-preceding chargeable period shall be determined without regard to any relief to which the chargeable person is or may become entitled for the preceding chargeable period or the pre-preceding chargeable period, as the case may be, under section 481.

(7) Where for a chargeable period, being a year of assessment for income tax, a chargeable person is assessed to tax in accordance with section 1017, and that person was not so assessed for the preceding chargeable period or for the pre-preceding chargeable period or for both of those periods either—

(*a*) because the person's spouse was so assessed for either or both of those periods, or

(*b*) because the person and the person's spouse were assessed to tax in accordance with section 1016 or 1023 for either or both of those periods,

subparagraphs (ii) and (iii) of subsection (4)(*b*) and subsection (5)(*a*) shall apply as if the person and the person's spouse had elected in accordance with section 1018 or 1019, as the case may be, for the person to be assessed to tax in accordance with section 1017 for any of those periods for which the person or the person's spouse were entitled to so elect or would have been so entitled if section 1019 had applied.

(8) (*a*) Subject to paragraph (*b*) and subsection (9), any additional tax due by reason of the amendment of an assessment for a chargeable period shall be deemed to be due and payable on the same day as the tax charged by the assessment before its amendment was due and payable.

(*b*) Where—

(i) the assessment was made after the chargeable person had delivered a return containing a full and true disclosure of all material facts necessary for the making of the assessment, or

(ii) the assessment had previously been amended following the delivery of the return containing such disclosure,

any additional tax due by reason of the amendment of the assessment shall be deemed to have been due and payable not later than one month from the date of the amendment.

[(8A)(*a*) Where, in relation to a chargeable period being a year of assessment for income tax, the profits or gains of a corresponding period relating to the preceding year of assessment are taken to be the profits or gains of that preceding year of assessment in accordance with section 65(3), then, notwithstanding that the assessment for that preceding year of assessment has not been amended, any tax payable for that preceding year of assessment which exceeds the tax due and payable for that year without regard to the operation of section 65(3) shall be due and payable on or before the specified return date for the chargeable period.

(*b*) An amount of income tax to which paragraph (*a*) applies shall not be taken into account for the purposes of subsection (4).

(*c*) Notwithstanding subsection (8), where, in relation to a chargeable period being a year of assessment for income tax, any additional tax for the preceding year of assessment is due and payable by virtue of an amendment of the assessment for that year made in accordance with section 65(3), then, such additional tax as specified in the amendment to the assessment for that year shall be deemed to have been due and payable on or before the specified return date for the chargeable period.][13]

(9) (*a*) The amount by which the tax, found to be payable for a chargeable period on the determination of an appeal against an assessment made on a chargeable person for the chargeable period, is in excess of the amount of the tax for the chargeable period referred to in section 957(2)(*a*)(II) which the chargeable person had paid before the making of the appeal shall be deemed to be due and payable on the same date as the tax charged by the assessment is due and payable.

(*b*) Notwithstanding paragraph (*a*), where—

(i) the tax which the chargeable person had paid before the making of the appeal is not less than 90 per cent of the tax found to be payable on the determination of the appeal, and

(ii) the tax charged by the assessment was due and payable in accordance with subsection (3),

the excess referred to in that paragraph shall be deemed to be due and payable not later than one month from the date of the determination of the appeal.

[(10)(*a*) This subsection shall apply to a chargeable person who authorises the Collector-General to collect preliminary tax by the debiting of the bank account of that person in accordance with paragraph (*b*) and complies with such conditions as the Collector-General may reasonably impose to ensure that an amount of preliminary tax payable by a chargeable person for a chargeable period will be paid by the chargeable person in accordance with this subsection.

(*b*) Preliminary tax appropriate to a chargeable period where the chargeable period is a year of assessment for income tax shall be due and payable in the case of a chargeable person to whom this subsection applies—

(i) as respects the first year of assessment for which the Collector-General is authorised in accordance with paragraph (*a*) to debit that person's bank account, by way of a minimum of 3 equal monthly instalments in that year, and

(ii) as respects any subsequent year of assessment in which the Collector-General is so authorised, by way of a minimum of 8 equal monthly instalments in that year,

and the Collector-General shall debit the bank account of that person with such instalments on day 9 of each month for which the Collector-General is so authorised.

(*c*) The Collector-General may, in any particular case, in order to facilitate the payment of preliminary tax in accordance with this subsection, agree at the Collector-General's discretion to vary the number of equal monthly instalments to be collected in a year or agree at the Collector-General's discretion to an increase or decrease in the amount to be collected in any subsequent instalment to be made in that year.

(*d*) A chargeable person shall not be treated as having paid an amount of preliminary tax in accordance with this subsection unless that person pays in the year of assessment the monthly instalments due in accordance with paragraph (*b*) or (*c*), as appropriate.

(*e*) For the purposes of this section, a chargeable person who pays an amount of preliminary tax appropriate to a chargeable period in accordance with this subsection shall be deemed to have paid that amount of preliminary tax on the due date for the payment of an amount of preliminary tax for the chargeable period.][14]

Amendments

1 Substituted by FA 2003 s 42(1)(*c*)(i)(I) as respects accounting periods ending on or after 1 January 2003; previously "number of months".

2 Definitions of "tax payable for the initial period" and "tax payable for the later period" inserted by FA 2003 s 42(1)(*c*)(i)(II) with effect from 1 January 2003.

3 Subs (1) substituted by FA 2002 s 58(*a*) with effect from 1 January 2002.

4 Subs (2A)(*b*) to (*e*) substituted by FA 2003 s 42(1)(*c*)(ii) as respects, in the case of the amendment made to TCA 1997 s 958(2A)(*b*) and (*c*), accounting periods ending on or after 2 July 2003 and in any other case, as respects accounting periods ending on or after 1 January 2003; previously:

"(*b*) The first of the 2 instalments referred to in paragraph *(a)* (in this section referred to as the "first instalment") shall be due and payable not later than the day which is 31 days before the day on which the accounting period ends; but where that day is later than day 28 of the month in which the first-mentioned day occurs, the first instalment shall be due and payable not later than day 28 of that month or such earlier day in that month as may be specified by order made by the Minister for Finance.

(*c*) Notwithstanding paragraph (*b*), in the case where an accounting period of a company is less than one month and one day in length, the first instalment shall be due and payable not later than the last day of the accounting period; but where that day is later than day 28 of the month in which that day occurs, the first instalment shall be due and payable not later than day 28 of that month or such earlier day in that month as may be specified by order made by the Minister for Finance.

(*d*) Notwithstanding paragraphs (*b*) and (*c*), in the case of an accounting period of a company ending in the year 2002, the first instalment shall not be due and payable earlier than 28 June 2002.

(*e*) The second of the 2 instalments referred to in paragraph *(a)* (in this section referred to as the "second instalment") shall be due and payable within the period of 6 months from the end of the accounting period, but in any event not later than day 28 of the month in which that period of 6 months ends, or such earlier day in that month as may be specified by order made by the Minister for Finance.".

5 Subs (2B) substituted by FA 2003 s 42(1)(*c*)(iii) as respects accounting periods ending on or after 1 January 2003.

6 Subs (2) substituted and subs (2A)–(2C) inserted by FA 2002 s 58(*b*) with effect from 1 January 2002.

7 Subs (3) substituted by FA 2003 s 42(1)(*c*)(iv) with effect from 1 January 2003 in relation to income tax and capital gains tax and as respects accounting periods ending on or after 1 January 2003 in relation to corporation tax.

8 Subs (3A) substituted by FA 2003 s 42(1)(*c*)(v) with effect from 1 January 2003 in relation to income tax and capital gains tax.

9 Inserted by FA 2002 s 58(*d*) with effect from 1 January 2002.

10 Subs (2)–(4) substituted and subs (4A) inserted by FA 2001 s 78(1)(*f*)(ii) for short tax "year" 2001 and later tax years (income tax and capital gains tax) and as respects accounting periods of companies ending on or after 1 April 2001.

11 Substituted by FA 2004 s 89 and Sch 3 para 1(*ac*) with effect from 1 January 2002; previously "subsection (2)".

12 Subss (4B)–(4E) inserted by FA 2002 s 58(*e*) with effect from 1 January 2002.

13 Subs (8A) inserted by FA 2001 s 78(1)(*f*)(iii) for short tax "year" 2001 and later tax years (income tax and capital gains tax) and as respects accounting periods of companies ending on or after 1 April 2001.

14 Subs (10) substituted by FA 2001 s 78(1)(*f*)(iv) for short tax "year" 2001 and later tax years (income tax and capital gains tax) and as respects accounting periods of companies ending on or after 1 April 2001.

Cross-references

Accounting standards, transitional measures (gains and losses in financial instruments), this section to apply with certain modifications to subss (4D)(*b*) and (4E)(*b*): Sch 17A para 4(6)(*a*) and (*b*).

Payment of tax due under section 128 (tax treatment of share options): s 128B(11); subs (3A): s 128B(12)(*b*); subs (4): s 128B(12)(*c*).

Self assessment, making of assessments: s 954(7).

Self assessment, meaning of "due date for the payment of an amount of preliminary tax", subs (2): s 950(1).

Self assessment, obligation to pay preliminary tax: s 952(1).

Revenue precedents

Issue: Due date for balance of tax where taxpayer submits incomplete return.

Decision: The due date is the same as that for the tax charged in the original assessment. However, if the taxpayer is relying on the 90% rule, the amendment may mean that the Preliminary Tax payment is made inadequate by the amendment in which case the due date reverts to the Preliminary Tax due date.

Issue: Whether the capital allowances figure in a return of income is a material fact for the purposes of determining whether a full and true disclosure of all the material facts was made.

Decision: The capital allowances figure is a material fact for the purposes of determining whether a full and true disclosure of all the material facts was made.
Issue: Should surcharge under s 1084 be taken into account in considering if Preliminary Tax payment adequate.
Decision: No; in applying the 90% or 100% rule, surcharge is ignored.

Revenue information

Information leaflet CG9 Direct Debit Preliminary Tax.

Pay and File and the 2001 Income Tax Return.

Statements of Practice

Direct Debit Payment of Income Tax Preliminary Tax CG/1/99.

eBrief

eBrief no 7 — 2005 — For taxpayers who submit their payment **and** file their return through the Revenue Online Service (ROS) for preliminary tax for 2005, income tax balance due for 2004 and capital gains tax on gains arising in initial period 2005 (1 Jan–30 Sept), the filing date is extended to Thursday 17 November 2005.

Tax Briefing

TB35 Mar 1999 p 30 — Direct Debit Payment of Income Tax Preliminary Tax.
TB37 Oct 1999 pp 3–4 Preliminary Tax Calculation.
TB44 June 2001 pp 5–6 — Pay and File System (Finance Act 2001) — Preliminary Tax.
TB47 April 2002 pp 1–7 — Pay and File.
TB47 April 2002 p 14 — Preliminary Corporation Tax payment dates.
TB48 June 2002 pp 1–4 — Revised arrangements for payment of preliminary corporation tax.
TB48 June 2002 pp 5–10 — Pay and File Questions and Answers.
TB49 pp 15–16 — Pay and File — The 2001 Income Tax Return.
TB50 Oct 2002 pp 8–12 — Pay and File Payment Options.
TB51 Jan 2003 p 8 — Preliminary Income Tax — "Top up payments" for 2002 preliminary tax.
TB52 May 2003 p 7 — Pay and File 2003 IT and CT.
TB53 Aug 2003 pp 1–3 — Capital Gains Tax Payments (Finance Act 2003 Changes).
TB55 April 2004 p 14 — Relevenat Tax on Share Options and interaction with Preliminary Tax obligations.
TB56 July 2004 pp 1–5 — First Active Shares.
TB56 July 2004 pp 22–23 — Pay and File 2004 IT and CT.
TB57 Oct 2004 pp 1–3 — Pay and File 2004.
TB57 Oct 2004 pp 5–6 — ROS Pay and File Tips.
TB57 Oct 2004 p 6 — CGT First Active Shares — Personal Exemption on disposal of free shares.

Definitions

chargeable gain: s 5(1); Collector-General: ss 2(1), 851; company: ss 4(1), 5(1); month: IA 1937 Sch; person: IA 1937 s 11(*c*); tax: s 3(1); year of assessment: ss 2(1), 5(1).

Former enactments

FA 1988 s 18; FA 1990 s 24(*d*)(iii), (iv) and (v); FA 1991 s 52(*a*); FA 1992 s 32; FA 1993 s 40; FA 1994 s 13; FA 1995 s 31.

---

959 Miscellaneous (Part 41)

(1) Section 1048 shall apply to an amendment of an assessment under section 955 as it applies to an additional first assessment under section 924.

(2) Where the inspector or any other officer of the Revenue Commissioners acting with the knowledge of the inspector causes to issue, manually or by any electronic, photographic or other process, ...[1] a notice of an amendment of an assessment bearing the name of the inspector, ...[1] [that assessment or amended assessment][2] to which the notice of assessment or notice of amended assessment relates, as the case may be, shall for those purposes be deemed to have been made by the inspector to the best of his or her judgment.

(3) An assessment which is otherwise final and conclusive shall not for any purpose of the Tax Acts and the Capital Gains Tax Acts be regarded as not final and conclusive or as ceasing to be final and conclusive by reason only of the fact that the inspector has amended or may amend the assessment pursuant to section 955 and, where in the case of a chargeable person the inspector elects under section 954(4) not to make an assessment for any chargeable period, the Tax Acts and the Capital Gains Tax Acts shall apply as if an assessment for that chargeable period made on the chargeable person had become final and conclusive on the date on which the notice of election is given.

(4) The giving by a chargeable person of a notice pursuant to section 876 shall not remove from the person an obligation to deliver a return under section 951.

(5) The provisions of this Part as respects due dates for payment of tax shall apply subject to sections 579(4)(*b*) and 981.

(6) References in this Part to any provision of the Income Tax Acts shall, where appropriate for capital gains tax and unless the contrary intention appears, be construed as a reference to those provisions as applied in relation to capital gains tax by sections 913, 931, 976, 1051, 1077 or 1083, as appropriate.

(7) Section 926 shall not apply to a chargeable person as respects any chargeable period.

Amendments

1 Deleted by FA 2001 s 78(1)(*g*) for short tax "year" 2001 and later tax years (income tax and capital gains tax) and as respects accounting periods of companies ending on or after 1 April 2001; previously "a notice of preliminary tax bearing the name of the inspector or" and "that notice of preliminary tax shall for the purposes of the Tax Acts and the Capital Gains Tax Acts be deemed to have been given by the inspector to the best of his or her opinion,".

2 Substituted by FA 2002 s 138 and Sch 6 paras 3(*o*) and 6(*c*)(iv) as respects the year of assessment 2002 and subsequent years of assessment and as respects accounting periods of companies ending on or after 1 January 2001; previously "and that assessment or amended assessment".

Definitions

chargeable gain: ss 4(1), 5(1), 534; Income Tax Acts: s 1(2); inspector: ss 2(1), 5(1), 852; person: IA 1937 s 11(*c*); Tax Acts: s 1(2); year of assessment: ss 2(1), 5(1).

Former enactments

FA 1988 ss 20(5), 21(1), (3)–(5) and (7)–(8); FA 1991 s 53; FA 1992 s 33(1).

PART 42
COLLECTION AND RECOVERY

Cross-references

Rectification of excessive set off etc, of tax credit: s 927(2).

CHAPTER 1
Income Tax

960 Date for payment of income tax other than under self assessment

Income tax contained in an assessment (other than an assessment made under Part 41) for any year of assessment shall be payable on or before [31 October][1] in that year, except that income tax included in any such assessment for any year of assessment which is made on or after [31 October][1] in that year shall be deemed to be due and payable not later than one month from the date on which the assessment is made.

Amendments

[1] Substituted by FA 2001 s 77(2) and Sch 2 paras 52 and 61(*c*) for short tax "year" 2001 and later tax years; previously "the 1st day of November".

Cross-references

Interest on overdue income tax and corporation tax: s 1080(2)(*b*).

Definitions

month: IA 1937 Sch; year of assessment: s 3(1).

Former enactments

ITA 1967 s 477(1); FA 1990 s 24(*a*).

961 Issue of demand notes and receipts

(1) When income tax becomes due and payable, the Collector-General shall make demand of the respective sums given to him or her in charge to collect from the persons charged with those sums, or at the places of their last abode, or on the premises in respect of which the tax is charged, as the case may require.

[(2) On payment of income tax, the Collector-General shall furnish the person concerned with a receipt in respect of that payment; such a receipt shall consist of whichever of the following the Collector-General considers appropriate, namely—

(*a*) a separate receipt on the prescribed form in respect of each such payment, or

(*b*) a receipt on the prescribed form in respect of all such payments that have been made within a period specified in the receipt.][1]

Amendments

[1] Subs (2) substituted by FA 1999 s 23 with effect from 6 April 1999.

Cross-references

Collection of capital gains tax: s 976(3).

Definitions

Collector-General: s 2(1); person: IA 1937 s 11(*c*).

Former enactments

ITA 1967 s 478; FA 1996 s 132(2) and Sch 5 Pt II.

Corresponding UK tax provision

Taxes Management Act 1970 s 60.

962 Recovery by sheriff or county registrar

(1) Whenever any person makes default in paying any sum which may be levied on that person in respect of income tax, the Collector-General may issue a certificate to the county registrar or sheriff of the county in which the defaulter resides or has a place of business certifying the amount of the sum so in default and the person on whom the sum is leviable.

[(1A)(*a*) A certificate to be issued by the Collector-General under this section may—

(i) be issued in an electronic or other format, and

(ii) where the certificate is issued in a non-paper format, be reproduced in a paper format by the county registrar or sheriff or by persons authorised by the county registrar or sheriff to do so.

(*b*) A certificate issued in a non-paper format in accordance with paragraph (*a*) shall—

(i) constitute a valid certificate for all the purposes of this section,

(ii) be deemed to have been made by the Collector-General, and

(iii) be deemed to have been issued on the date that the Collector-General caused the certificate to issue.

(*c*) (i) Where a certificate issued by the Collector-General in a non-paper format is reproduced in a paper format in accordance with paragraph (*a*)(ii) and—

(I) the reproduction contains, or there is appended to it, a note to the effect that it is a copy of a certificate so issued, and

(II) the note contains the signature of the county registrar or sheriff or of the person authorised under paragraph (*a*)(ii) and the date of such signing,

then the copy of the certificate with the note so signed and dated shall, for all purposes, have effect as if it was the certificate itself.

(ii) A signature and date in a note, on a copy of, or appended to, a certificate issued in a non-paper format by the Collector-General, and reproduced in a paper format in accordance with paragraph (*a*)(ii) that—

(I) in respect of such signature, purports to be that of the county registrar or sheriff or of a person authorised to make a copy, shall be taken until the contrary is shown to be the signature of the county registrar or sheriff or of a person who at the material time was so authorised, and

(II) in respect of such date, shall be taken until the contrary is shown to have been duly dated.

(*d*) For the purposes of this subsection—

"electronic" has the meaning assigned to it by the Electronic Commerce Act 2000 and an **"electronic certificate"** shall be construed accordingly;

"issued in a non-paper format" includes issued by facsimile.][1]

(2) Immediately on receipt of the certificate the county registrar or sheriff shall proceed to levy the sum certified in the certificate to be in default by seizing all or any of the goods, animals and other chattels within his or her bailiwick belonging to the defaulter, and for such purposes the county registrar or sheriff shall (in addition to the rights, powers and duties conferred on him or her by this section) have all such rights, powers and duties as are for the time being vested in him or her by law in relation to the execution of a writ of fieri facias in so far as those rights, powers and duties are not inconsistent with the additional rights, powers and duties conferred on him or her by this section.

(3) A county registrar or sheriff executing a certificate under this section shall be entitled—

(*a*) if the sum certified in the certificate to be in default exceeds [€19,050][2], to charge and (where appropriate) to add to that sum and (in any case) to levy under the certificate such fees and expenses, calculated according to the scales appointed by the Minister for Justice, Equality and Law Reform under section 14(1)(*a*) of the Enforcement of Court Orders Act, 1926, and for the time being in force, as the county registrar or sheriff would be entitled so to charge or add and to levy if the certificate were an execution order within the meaning of the Enforcement of Court Orders Act, 1926, (in this section referred to as an **"execution order"**) of the High Court,

(*b*) if the sum certified in the certificate to be in default exceeds [€3,175][3] but does not exceed [€19,050][2], to charge and (where appropriate) to add to that sum and (in any case) to levy under the certificate such fees and expenses, calculated according to the scales referred to in paragraph (*a*), as the county registrar or sheriff would be entitled so to charge or add and to levy if the certificate were an execution order of the Circuit Court, and

(*c*) if the sum certified in the certificate to be in default does not exceed [€3,175][3], to charge and (where appropriate) to add to that sum and (in any case) to levy under the certificate such fees and expenses, calculated according to the scales referred to in paragraph (*a*), as the county registrar or sheriff would be entitled so to charge or add and to levy if the certificate were an execution order of the District Court.

Amendments

1 Subs (1A) inserted by FA 2004 s 84 with effect from 25 March 2004.

2 Substituted by FA 2001 s 240(1) and (2)(*a*) and Sch 5 Pt 1 for 2002 and later tax years; previously "£15,000".

3 Substituted by FA 2001 s 240(1) and (2)(*a*) and Sch 5 Pt 1 for 2002 and later tax years; previously "£2,500".

Cross-references

Appeals against assessments: s 933(9)(*b*).

Collection of capital gains tax: s 976(3).

Criminal Justice (Terrorist Offences) Act 2005, subs (4)(*b*) of section 14 (interim order freezing certain funds) and subs (6)(*b*) of section 15 (interlocutory order) — references to certificates issued under TCA 1997 s 962.

Estimation of tax due for year: s 990(1A)(*c*).

Income Tax (Relevant Contracts) Regulations 2000, SI No 71 of 2000, this section applied: ITRCR 2000 regs 12(1)(*b*), 13(2)(*d*).

PAYE system, estimation of tax due for income tax months: s 989(3)(*d*).

PAYE system, recovery of tax: s 993(1)(*b*).

Poundage and fees due to sheriffs and county registrars: s 1006(1).

Proceeds of Crime Act 1996, subs (3A) (inserted by Proceeds of Crime (Amendment) Act 2005 s 4(*b*)) of section 2 (interim order) and subs (3A) (inserted by Proceeds of Crime (Amendment) Act 2005 s 5(*c*)) of section 3 (interlocutory order) — references to certificates issued under TCA 1997 s 962.

Self-assessment, notices of preliminary tax: s 953(5)(*b*).

Taxes (Offset of Repayments) Regulations 2002, SI No 471 of 2002, reg 2(1) (interpretation — "liability at enforcement" para (*a*)).

Value added tax, this section applied by: VATA 1972 s 24(1)(*b*) and VATR 1979 reg 15(2) but in subs (1) construe the words "any sum which may be levied on that person in respect of income tax" as referring to value added tax payable by the person concerned.

Case law

No infringement of constitutional rights arises from the operation of this section: *Kennedy v Hearne and others* [1988] IR 481.

Tax Briefing

TB33 Sept 1998 p 1 — Revenue Debt and Sheriff Action — new arrangements from 1 Nov, 1998.

Definitions

Circuit Court: IA 1937 Sch; Collector-General: s 2(1); "District Court": IA 1937 Sch; High Court: IA 1937 Sch; land: IA 1937 Sch; person: IA 1937 s 11(*c*).

Former enactments

ITA 1967 s 485(1), (2) and (5); FA 1969 s 65(1) and Sch 5 Pt I; FA 1982 s 10.

Corresponding UK tax provision

Taxes Management Act 1970 s 61.

963 Power of Collector-General and authorised officer to sue in Circuit Court or District Court

(1) Where the amount due in respect of income tax does not exceed the amount which is the monetary limitation on the jurisdiction of the Circuit Court provided for in an action founded on quasi-contract at reference number 1 of the Third Schedule to the Courts (Supplemental Provisions) Act, 1961, the Collector-General or other officer of the Revenue Commissioners duly authorised to collect the tax may sue in that officer's own name in the Circuit Court for the amount so due as a debt due to the Minister for Finance.

(2) Where the amount so due does not exceed the amount which is the monetary limitation on the jurisdiction of the District Court provided for in an action founded on contract by clause (i) of paragraph A of section 77 of the Courts of Justice Act, 1924 (as amended by the Courts Act, 1991), the Collector-General or other officer of the Revenue Commissioners duly authorised to collect the tax may sue in that officer's own name in the District Court for the amount so due as a debt due to the Minister for Finance.

(3) The cost of any such proceedings brought by the Collector-General or other officer under this section shall be subject to the law and practice applicable to the costs of a like proceeding for the recovery of an ordinary civil debt of like amount in the same Court.

Cross-references

Collection of capital gains tax: s 976(3).

Continuance of pending proceedings: s 964(1)(*a*).

Income Tax (Relevant Contracts) Regulations 2000, SI No 71 of 2000, this section applied: ITRCR 2000 Reg 12(1)(*b*).

PAYE system, recovery of tax: s 993(1)(*b*).

Value added tax, this section applied by: VATA 1972 s 24(1)(*b*) and VATR 1979 r 15(3) but:

In subs (1), construe the words "income tax" as referring to value added tax.

In subss (1)–(2) construe the expressions "the Collector-General or other officer of the Revenue Commissioners, duly authorised to collect the tax" and "the Collector-General or other officer under this section" as referring to the Collector General.

Definitions

Circuit Court: IA 1937 Sch; Collector-General: s 2(1); District Court: IA 1937 Sch; tax: s 3(1).

Former enactments

ITA 1967 s 486(1), (2) and (4); FA 1994 s 162(1).

Corresponding UK tax provision

Taxes Management Act 1970 ss 65–68.

964 Continuance of pending proceedings

[(1) (*a*) Notwithstanding subsection (2) of section 966, where the Collector-General duly appointed to collect any income tax has instituted proceedings under section 963 or 966, or continues under this section any proceedings brought under those sections, for the recovery of such tax and, while such proceedings are pending, such Collector-General ceases for any reason to be the Collector-General so appointed to collect such tax, the proceedings may be continued in the name of that Collector-General by any person (in this subsection referred to as the **"successor"**) duly appointed to collect such tax in succession to that Collector-General or any subsequent Collector-General.

(*b*) In any case where paragraph (*a*) applies, the successor shall inform by notice the person or persons against whom the proceedings concerned are pending that those proceedings are being so continued and on service of such notice, notwithstanding any rule of court, it shall not be necessary for the successor to obtain an order of court substituting him or her for the Collector-General who has instituted or continued the proceedings.

(*c*) Any affidavit or oath to be made by a Collector-General for the purposes of the Judgment Mortgage (Ireland) Act 1850 or the Judgment Mortgage (Ireland) Act 1858 may be made by a successor.][1]

(2) Where the Collector-General duly appointed to collect any income tax in succession to another Collector-General institutes or continues proceedings under section 963 for the recovery of the tax or any balance of the tax, the other Collector-General shall for the purposes of the proceedings be deemed until the contrary is proved to have ceased to be the Collector-General appointed to collect the tax.

Amendments

1 Subs (1) substituted by FA 2005 s 146 with effect from 25 March 2005.

Cross-references

Capital acquisitions tax, application of certain income tax provisions in relation to collection and recovery of, subs (2): CATCA 2003 s 64(3).
Collection of capital gains tax: s 976(3).
Income Tax (Relevant Contracts) Regulations 2000, SI No 71 of 2000, this section applied: ITRCR 2000 Reg 12(1)(*b*).
Priority for corporation tax: s 975(1).
Value added tax, this section applied by: VATA 1972 s 24(1)(*b*) and by VATR 1979 r 15(4) but construe references to income tax as references to value added tax.

Definitions

Collector-General: s 2(1); person: IA 1937 s 11(*c*).

Former enactments

ITA 1967 s 187(3) and s 487.

---

965 Evidence in proceedings in Circuit Court or District Court for recovery of income tax

(1) In any proceedings in the Circuit Court or the District Court for or in relation to the recovery of income tax an affidavit duly made by an officer of the Revenue Commissioners deposing to any of the following matters—

(*a*) that the assessment of tax was duly made,

(*b*) that the assessment has become final and conclusive,

(*c*) that the tax or any specified part of the tax is due and outstanding,

(*d*) that demand for the payment of the tax has been duly made,

shall be evidence until the contrary is proved of the matters so deposed to.

(2) Where the averments in the affidavit are not disputed by the defendant or respondent, it shall not be necessary for the officer by whom the affidavit was made to attend or give oral evidence at the hearing of the proceedings nor shall it be necessary to produce or put in evidence at the hearing any register, file, book of assessment or other record relating to the tax.

(3) Where any averment contained in the affidavit is disputed by the defendant or respondent, the judge shall, on such terms as to costs as he or she thinks just, give a reasonable opportunity by adjournment of the hearing or otherwise for the officer by whom the affidavit was made to attend and give oral evidence in the proceedings and for any register, file, book of assessment or other record relating to the tax to be produced and put in evidence in the proceedings.

Cross-references

Collection of capital gains tax: s 976(3).

Definitions

affidavit: IA 1937 Sch; Circuit Court: IA 1937 Sch; District Court: IA 1937 Sch.

Former enactments

ITA 1967 s 489; FA 1974 ss 70, 86 and Sch 2 Pt I.

Corresponding UK tax provision

Taxes Management Act 1970 s 70.

966 High Court proceedings

(1) Without prejudice to any other means by which payment of sums due in respect of income tax may be enforced, an officer of the Revenue Commissioners authorised by them for the purposes of this subsection may sue in his or her own name in the High Court for the recovery of any sum due in respect of that tax, as a debt due to the Minister for Finance for the benefit of the Central Fund, from the person charged with that tax or from that person's executors or administrators or from any person from whom the sum in question is collectable, whether the person so charged was so charged before or after the passing of this Act, and the proceedings may be commenced by summary summons.

(2) Where an officer who has commenced proceedings pursuant to this section, or who has continued the proceedings by virtue of this subsection, dies or otherwise ceases for any reason to be an officer authorised for the purposes of subsection (1)—

(*a*) the right of such officer to continue the proceedings shall cease and the right to continue the proceedings shall vest in such other officer so authorised as may be nominated by the Revenue Commissioners,

(*b*) where such other officer is nominated, he or she shall be entitled accordingly to be substituted as a party to the proceedings in the place of the first-mentioned officer, and

(*c*) where an officer is so substituted, he or she shall give notice in writing of the substitution to the defendant.

(3) In proceedings pursuant to this section, a certificate signed by a Revenue Commissioner certifying the following facts, that a person is an officer of the Revenue Commissioners and that he or she has been authorised by them for the purpose of subsection (1), shall be evidence until the contrary is proved of those facts.

(4) In proceedings pursuant to this section, a certificate signed by a Revenue Commissioner certifying the following facts—

(*a*) that the plaintiff has ceased to be an officer of the Revenue Commissioners authorised by them for the purposes of subsection (1),

(*b*) that another person is an officer of the Revenue Commissioners,

(*c*) that such other person has been authorised by them for the purposes of subsection (1), and

(*d*) that such other person has been nominated by them, in relation to the proceedings, for the purposes of subsection (2),

shall be evidence until the contrary is proved of those facts.

[(5) In proceedings pursuant to this section a certificate signed by an officer of the Revenue Commissioners certifying the following facts:

(*a*) that before the institution of the proceedings a stated sum for income tax became due and payable by the defendant—

(i) under an assessment which had become final and conclusive, or

(ii) under section 942(6),

and

(*b*) (i) that before the institution of the proceedings payment of that stated sum was duly demanded from the defendant, and

(ii) that that stated sum or a stated part of that sum remains due and payable by the defendant,

shall be evidence until the contrary is proved of those facts.][1]

(6) In proceedings pursuant to this section, a certificate certifying the fact or facts referred to in subsection (3) or (4) or paragraph (*a*) or (*b*) of subsection (5) and purporting to be signed as specified in that subsection or paragraph may be tendered in evidence without proof and shall be deemed until the contrary is proved to have been signed by a person holding at the time of the signature the office or position indicated in the certificate as the office or position of the person signing.

(7) All or any of the sums due from any one person in respect of income tax may be included in the same summons.

(8) Subject to this section, the rules of the High Court for the time being applicable to civil proceedings commenced by summary summons shall apply to proceedings pursuant to this section.

Amendments

1 Subs (5) substituted by FA 2001 s 236(*a*)(i) with effect from 30 March 2001.

Case law

Proceedings pursuant to s 966 may be brought by way of summary but the institution of proceedings by plenary summons is not excluded – *Criminal Assets Bureau v Sean and Rosaleen Hunt (nee) Maher* 2003 ITR 93.

Cross-references

Collection of capital gains tax: s 976(3).

Continuance of pending proceedings: s 964(1)(*a*).

Income Tax (Relevant Contracts) Regulations 2000, SI No 71 of 2000, this section applied: ITRCR 2000 Reg 12(1)(*b*).

PAYE system, recovery of tax: s 993(1)(*b*).

Definitions

High Court: IA 1937 Sch; person: IA 1937 s 11(*c*); writing: IA 1937 Sch.

Former enactments

ITA 1967 s 488; FA 1974 s 11 and Sch 1 Pt II; FA 1979 s 12; FA 1980 s 57(1).

Corresponding UK tax provision

Taxes Management Act 1970 s 68.

967 Evidence of electronic transmission of particulars of income tax to be collected in proceedings for recovery of tax

[In any proceedings in the District Court, the Circuit Court or the High Court for or in relation to the recovery of any income tax, a certificate signed by an officer of the Revenue Commissioners certifying that before the institution of proceedings a stated sum of income tax transmitted in accordance with section 928(2) became due and payable by the defendant—

(*a*) (i) under an assessment which had become final and conclusive, or

(ii) under section 942(6),

and

(*b*) demand for the payment of the tax has been duly made,

shall be prima facie evidence until the contrary is proved of those facts, and a certificate so certifying and purporting to be signed as specified in this section may be tendered in evidence without proof and shall be deemed until the contrary is proved to have been signed by an officer of the Revenue Commissioners.][1]

Amendments

[1] Section 967 substituted by FA 2001 s 236(*a*)(ii) with effect from 30 March 2001.

Cross-references

Collection of capital gains tax: s 976(3).

Income Tax (Relevant Contracts) Regulations 2000, SI No 71 of 2000, this section applied: ITRCR 2000 Reg 12(1)(*b*).

Definitions

District Court, Circuit Court, High Court: IA 1937 Sch.

Former enactments

FA 1986 s 113(6).

968 Judgments for recovery of income tax

(1) In this section, **"judgment"** includes any order or decree.

(2) Where in any proceedings for the recovery of income tax judgment is given against the person against whom the proceedings are brought and the judgment provides for the arrest and imprisonment of that person, and a sum is accepted on account or in part payment of the amount for which the judgment was given—

(*a*) such acceptance shall not prevent or prejudice the recovery under the judgment of the balance remaining unpaid of that amount,

(*b*) the judgment shall be capable of being executed and enforced in respect of the balance as fully in all respects and by the like means as if the balance were the amount for which the judgment was given,

(*c*) the law relating to the execution and enforcement of the judgment shall apply in respect of the balance accordingly, and

(*d*) a certificate by a Secretary or an Assistant Secretary of the Revenue Commissioners stating the amount of the balance shall, for the purposes of the enforcement and execution of the judgment, be evidence until the contrary is proved of the amount of the balance.

Cross-references

Collection of capital gains tax: s 976(3).

Income Tax (Relevant Contracts) Regulations 2000, SI No 71 of 2000, this section applied: ITRCR 2000 Reg 12(1)(*b*).

Definitions

person: IA 1937 s 11(*c*).

Former enactments

ITA 1967 s 492; FA 1974 s 86 and Sch 2 Pt I; FA 1997 s 146(1) and Sch 9 Pt I para 1(34).

969 Duration of imprisonment for non-payment of income tax

Amendments

Repealed by FA 1999 s 197 and Sch 6 with effect from 25 March 1999 but with continued application to persons committed to prison before that date.

970 Recovery of income tax charged on profits not distrainable

Where income tax is charged on the profits of royalties, markets or fairs, or on tolls, fisheries or any other annual or casual profits not distrainable, the owner or occupier or receiver of those profits shall be answerable for the income tax so charged, and may retain and deduct that tax out of any such profits.

Cross-references

Collection of capital gains tax: s 976(3).

Definitions

Collector-General: s 2(1); person: IA 1937 s 11(*c*).

Former enactments

ITA 1967 s 494(1).

971 Priority of income tax debts over other debts

(1) No goods or chattels whatever, belonging to any person at the time any income tax becomes in arrear, shall be liable to be taken by virtue of any execution or other process, warrant or authority whatever, or by virtue of any assignment, on any account or pretence whatever, except at the suit of the landlord for rent, unless the person at whose suit the execution or seizure is made or to whom the assignment was made pays or causes to be paid to the Collector-General before the sale or removal of the goods or

chattels all arrears of income tax due at the time of seizure, or payable for the year in which the seizure is made.

(2) Where income tax is claimed for more than one year, the person at whose instance the seizure has been made may, on paying to the Collector-General the income tax which is due for one whole year, proceed in that person's seizure in the like manner as if no income tax had been claimed.

Cross-references

Collection of capital gains tax: s 976(3).

Definitions

Collector-General: s 2(1); person: IA 1937 s 11(*c*).

Former enactments

ITA 1967 s 482(1)–(2).

972 Duty of employer as to income tax payable by employees

(1) Where any employed person has omitted to make payment of any income tax under Schedule D, E or F due and payable by that person for any year, the Revenue Commissioners may give notice to that person's employer at any time after a period of 3 months has elapsed since such income tax became due and payable requiring the employer to deduct the amount of income tax so in arrear from any remuneration payable by the employer to the employed person.

(2) On receipt of the notice, the employer shall deduct such sums, not exceeding in the aggregate the total amount of income tax so in arrear, at such times and in such manner as the Revenue Commissioners may direct and shall forthwith pay over the amounts so deducted to the Collector-General.

(3) Where any employer refuses or neglects to pay over to the Collector-General any sums within the time specified in the notice, the employer shall be liable to pay any such sum as if it had been duly assessed on the employer, and proceedings for the recovery of that sum may be taken in any manner prescribed by the Income Tax Acts, and failure on the part of the employer to deduct any such sum from the employed person shall not be any bar to the recovery of the sum by proceedings.

(4) Where the employer is a body of persons, subsections (3) and (4) of section 897 and subsections (2) and (3) of section 1044 shall apply in relation to anything required to be done under this section.

(5) An employer who pays over to the Collector-General any such sum of income tax as is required by the notice shall be acquitted and discharged of so much money as is represented by the payment as if that sum of money had actually been paid as remuneration to the employed person.

(6) The Revenue Commissioners may nominate any of their officers to perform any acts and discharge any functions authorised by this section to be performed or discharged by the Revenue Commissioners.

Cross-references

Penalty: Sch 29 column 3.

Definitions

body of persons: s 2(1); Collector-General: s 2(1); month: IA 1937 Sch; person: IA 1937 s 11(*c*).

Former enactments

ITA 1967 s 484(1)–(4) and (6)–(7); F(MP)A 1968 s 3(3) and Sch Pt II; FA 1996 s 132(2) and Sch 5 Pt II; FA 1997 s 146(1) and Sch 9 Pt I para 1(33).

CHAPTER 2
Corporation Tax

973 Collection of corporation tax

(1) The Collector-General shall collect and levy the tax from time to time charged on all assessments to corporation tax of which particulars have been transmitted to him or her under section 928(1).

(2) All such powers as are exercisable with respect to the collecting and levying of sums of income tax under Schedule D of which particulars are transmitted under section 928(1) shall extend with respect to sums of corporation tax of which particulars are transmitted under that section.

Definitions

inspector: ss 2(1), 5(1), 852; month: IA 1937 Sch; person: IA 1937 s 11(*c*).

Former enactments

CTA 1976 s 145(1)–(2).

974 Priority for corporation tax

The priority attaching to assessed taxes under sections 98 and 285 of the Companies Act, 1963, shall apply to corporation tax.

Former enactments

CTA 1976 s 145(5).

975 Application of sections 964(2), 980(8) and 981 for purposes of corporation tax

(1) Subsection (2) of section 964 shall apply in relation to corporation tax as it applies in relation to income tax, and accordingly the reference in that subsection to income tax shall apply as if it was or included a reference to corporation tax.

(2) Section 980(8) shall apply for corporation tax as for capital gains tax, and references to capital gains tax in that section shall apply accordingly as if they were or included references to corporation tax.

(3) Section 981 shall apply for the purposes of corporation tax as it applies for the purposes of capital gains tax.

Former enactments

CTA 1976 ss 140(2), 147(1)–(2) and Sch 2 Pt II para 6 and para 12.

CHAPTER 3
Capital Gains Tax

976 Collection of capital gains tax

(1) The Collector-General for the time being appointed under section 851 shall collect and levy capital gains tax from time to time charged in all assessments made under the Capital Gains Tax Acts of which particulars have been transmitted to him or her under section 928(1) as applied to capital gains tax by section 931, and the provisions of section 851 relating to the nomination by the Revenue Commissioners of persons to act as the Collector-General or to exercise the powers of the Collector-General shall apply to capital gains tax as they apply to income tax.

(2) The provisions of the Income Tax Acts relating to the collection and recovery of income tax shall, subject to any necessary modifications, apply in relation to capital gains tax as they apply in relation to income tax chargeable under Schedule D.

(3) In particular and without prejudice to the generality of subsection (2), Chapter 1 of this Part (other than sections 960 and 972) shall, subject to any necessary modifications, apply to capital gains tax.

Cross-references

Interest on overdue capital gains tax in cases of fraud or neglect, subs (2): s 1083.
Self assessment: s 959(6).

Former enactments

CGTA 1975 s 51(1) and Sch 4 paras 1(3), 2(1) and 2(2) and table insofar as it relates to collection.

977 Recovery of capital gains tax from shareholder

(1) In this section, **"capital distribution"** has the same meaning as in section 583.

(2) This section shall apply where a person (in this section referred to as **"the beneficiary"**) connected with a company resident in the State receives or becomes entitled to receive in respect of shares in the company any capital distribution from the company, other than a capital distribution representing a reduction of capital, and—

(*a*) the capital so distributed derives from the disposal of assets in respect of which a chargeable gain accrues to the company, or

(*b*) the distribution constitutes such a disposal of assets.

(3) Where—

(*a*) the capital gains tax assessed on the company for the year of assessment in which the chargeable gain referred to in subsection (2) accrues includes any amount in respect of that chargeable gain, and

(*b*) any of the capital gains tax assessed on the company for that year is not paid within 6 months from the date when it becomes payable by the company,

the beneficiary may by an assessment made within 2 years from that date be assessed and charged (in the name of the company) to an amount of that capital gains tax—

(i) not exceeding the amount or value of the capital distribution which the beneficiary has received or became entitled to receive, and

(ii) not exceeding a proportion equal to the beneficiary's share of the capital distribution made by the company of capital gains tax on the amount of that gain at the rate in force when the gain accrued.

(4) A beneficiary paying any amount of tax under this section shall be entitled to recover a sum equal to that amount from the company.

(5) This section is without prejudice to any liability of the beneficiary receiving or becoming entitled to receive the capital distribution in respect of a chargeable gain accruing to that beneficiary by reference to the capital distribution as constituting a disposal of an interest in shares in the company.

Cross-references

Self assessment, making of assessments, subs (3): s 954(7)(*a*).
Time for payment of capital gains tax, subs (3): s 979.

Definitions

chargeable gain: ss 5(1), 545; company: s 5(1); month: IA 1937 Sch; person: IA 1937 s 11(*c*); resident: s 5(1); shares: s 5(1); year: IA 1937 Sch; year of assessment: ss 2(1), 5(1).

Former enactments

CGTA 1975 s 51(1) and Sch 4 para 17.

978 Gifts: recovery of capital gains tax from donee

(1) In this section—

"old asset" and **"new asset"** have the same meanings respectively as in section 597;

references to a donor include, in the case of an individual who has died, references to his or her personal representatives;

references to a gift include references to any transaction otherwise than by means of a bargain made at arm's length in so far as money or money's worth passes under the transaction without full consideration in money or money's worth, and **"donor"** and **"donee"** shall be construed accordingly.

(2) Where—

(*a*) a chargeable gain accrues in any year of assessment to any person on the disposal of an asset by means of a gift, and

(*b*) any amount of capital gains tax assessed on that person for that year of assessment is not paid within 12 months from the date when the tax becomes payable,

the donee may by an assessment made not later than 2 years from the date when the tax became payable be assessed and charged (in the name of the donor) to capital gains tax on an amount—

(i) not exceeding the amount of the chargeable gain so accruing, and

(ii) not exceeding such an amount of chargeable gains as would, if charged at the rate provided in section 28(3), result in liability to an amount of capital gains tax equal to that amount of capital gains tax which was not paid by the donor.

(3) Where the gift consists of a new asset, the donee may, in addition to being assessed and charged under subsection (2) in respect of the new asset, be assessed and charged as

if the chargeable gain on the disposal of the old asset were a chargeable gain on the disposal of the new asset the capital gains tax in respect of which was not paid within 12 months from the date when the tax had become payable.

(4) (*a*) Where a person on whom capital gains tax is assessed and charged in respect of the disposal of an asset transfers directly or indirectly by means of a gift to a donee—

(i) the whole of the proceeds of the disposal, or

(ii) in a case where the asset is a new asset acquired by the use of the proceeds of the disposal of an old asset, the whole of the proceeds of the disposal of the new asset,

subsections (2) and (3) shall apply to the amount of capital gains tax so assessed and charged.

(*b*) Where a person on whom capital gains tax is assessed and charged in respect of the disposal of an asset transfers directly or indirectly by means of a gift to a donee—

(i) part of the proceeds of the disposal, or

(ii) in a case where the asset is a new asset acquired by the use of the proceeds of the disposal of an old asset, part of the proceeds of the disposal of the new asset,

subsections (2) and (3) shall apply to such part of the amount of capital gains tax so assessed and charged as bears to the whole of such tax the same proportion that that part of the proceeds bears to the whole of those proceeds.

(5) The donee of a gift paying any amount of tax in pursuance of this section shall, subject to any terms or conditions of the gift, be entitled to recover a sum of that amount from the donor of the gift as a simple contract debt in any court of competent jurisdiction.

(6) This section shall apply in relation to a gift made to 2 or more donees with any necessary modifications and subject to the condition that each such donee shall be liable to be assessed and charged in respect only of such part of the amount of capital gains tax payable by the donees by virtue of this section as bears to the whole of such tax the same proportion as the part of the gift made to that donee bears to the whole of the gift.

Cross-references

Capital gains tax, deduction from consideration on disposal of certain assets: s 980(9)(*a*)(i).

Self assessment, making of assessments, subss (2)–(3): s 954(7)(*a*).

Time for payment of capital gains tax, subss (2)–(3): s 979.

Definitions

chargeable gain: ss 5(1), 545; month: IA 1937 Sch; person: IA 1937 s 11(*c*); personal representatives: ss 5(1), 799; year: IA 1937 Sch; year of assessment: ss 2(1), 5(1).

Former enactments

CGTA 1975 s 51(1) and Sch 4 para 18.

979 Time for payment of capital gains tax assessed under sections 977(3) or 978(2) and (3)

Capital gains tax assessed on any person under section 977(3) or subsections (2) and (3) of section 978 in respect of gains accruing in any year shall be payable by that person at or before the expiration of 3 months following that year, or at the expiration of a period of 2 months beginning with the date of the making of the assessment, whichever is the later.

Cross-references

Capital gains tax, deduction from consideration on disposal of certain assets: s 980(10).

Charging and assessment of persons not resident or ordinarily resident, modification of general rules: s 1042(1).

Self assessment, making of assessments: s 954(7)(*a*).

Former enactments

CGTA 1975 s 5(2); FA 1988 s 13(7)(*c*); FA 1991 s 48.

980 Deduction from consideration on disposal of certain assets

(1) In this section—

"designated area" means an area designated by order under section 2 of the Continental Shelf Act, 1968;

"exploration or exploitation rights" has the same meaning as in section 13;

"shares" includes stock and any security.

(2) This section shall apply to assets that are—

(*a*) land in the State,

(*b*) minerals in the State or any rights, interests or other assets in relation to mining or minerals or the searching for minerals,

(*c*) exploration or exploitation rights in a designated area,

(*d*) shares in a company deriving their value or the greater part of their value directly or indirectly from assets specified in paragraph (*a*), (*b*) or (*c*), other than shares quoted on a stock exchange,

(*e*) shares, other than shares quoted on a stock exchange, to which section 584 applies, whether by virtue of that section or any other section, so that, as respects a person disposing of those shares, they are treated as the same shares as shares specified in paragraph (*d*), acquired as the shares so specified were acquired, and

(*f*) goodwill of a trade carried on in the State.

(3) This section shall not apply where the amount or value of the consideration in money or money's worth on a disposal does not exceed the sum of [€500,000][1]; but if an asset owned at one time by one person, being an asset to which this section would but for this subsection apply, is disposed of by that person in parts—

(*a*) to the same person, or

(*b*) to persons who are acting in concert or who are connected persons,

whether on the same or different occasions, the several disposals shall for the purposes of this subsection, but not for any other purpose, be treated as a single disposal.

[(3A) This section shall not apply to a disposal by a body specified in Schedule 15.][2]

(4) (*a*) Subject to paragraph (*b*), on payment of the consideration for acquiring an asset to which this section applies—

(i) the person by or through whom any such payment is made shall deduct from that payment a sum representing an amount of capital gains tax equal to 15 per cent of that payment,

(ii) the person to whom the payment is made shall allow such deduction on receipt of the residue of the payment, and

(iii) the person making the deduction shall, on proof of payment to the Revenue Commissioners of the amount so deducted, be acquitted and discharged of so much money as is represented by the deduction as if that sum had been actually paid to the person making the disposal.

[(*b*) Where the person disposing of the asset produces to the person acquiring the asset—

(i) a certificate issued under subsection (8) in relation to the disposal, or

(ii) if the asset concerned is land on which a new house has been built or land on which a new house is in the course of being built, a certificate issued under subsection (8) in relation to the disposal or one of the certificates specified in subsection (8A) which, in either case, has been issued to the person disposing of the asset,

no deduction referred to in paragraph (*a*) shall be made.

(*c*) In paragraph (*b*)(ii)—

"house" has the same meaning as it has in [section 372AK][3];

"new house" means a house which has been developed or is being developed by or on behalf of the person disposing of it and which has not been used at any time before its disposal.][4]

(5) Where any payment referred to in subsection (4)(*a*) is made by or on behalf of any person, that person shall forthwith deliver to the Revenue Commissioners an account of the payment and of the amount deducted from the payment, and the inspector shall, notwithstanding any other provision of the Capital Gains Tax Acts, assess and charge that person to capital gains tax for the year of assessment in which the payment was made on the amount of the payment at the rate of 15 per cent.

(6) Where, in relation to any payment referred to in subsection (4)(*a*), any person has made default in delivering an account required by this section, or where the inspector is not satisfied with the account, the inspector may estimate the amount of the payment to the best of his or her judgment and, notwithstanding section 31, may assess and charge that person to capital gains tax for the year of assessment in which the payment was made on the amount so estimated at the rate of 15 per cent.

(7) Where the amount of capital gains tax assessed and charged under subsection (5) or (6) is paid, appropriate relief shall, on a claim being made in that behalf, be given to the person chargeable in respect of the gain on the disposal, whether by discharge or repayment or otherwise.

[(8) (*a*) A person chargeable to capital gains tax on the disposal of an asset to which this section applies, or another person (in this section referred to as an **"agent"**) acting under the authority of such person, may apply to the inspector for a certificate that tax should not be deducted from the consideration for the disposal of the asset and that the person acquiring the asset should not be required to give notice to the Revenue Commissioners in accordance with subsection (9)(*a*).

(*b*) If the inspector is satisfied that the person making the application is either the person making the disposal, or an agent, and that—

(i) the person making the disposal is resident in the State,

(ii) no amount of capital gains tax is payable in respect of the disposal, or

(iii) the capital gains tax chargeable for the year of assessment for which the person making the disposal is chargeable in respect of the disposal of the asset and the tax chargeable on any gain accruing in any earlier year of assessment (not being a year ending earlier than the 6th day of April, 1974) on a previous disposal of the asset has been paid,

the inspector shall issue the certificate to the person making the disposal or, as the case may be, the agent, and shall issue a copy of the certificate to the person acquiring the asset.

(*c*) Where an application is made under this subsection by an agent, it must include the name and address of the person making the disposal and where such person is resident in the State, that person's tax reference number (within the meaning of section 885).][5]

[(8A)(*a*) The certificates referred to in subsection (4)(*b*) are—

(i) a certificate of authorisation (within the meaning of section 531) issued for the purposes of that section, the period of validity of which, as provided for by regulations under subsection (6) of that section, has not expired,

(ii) a tax clearance certificate (within the meaning of section 1094) issued for the purposes of that section, the period of validity of which has not expired,

(iii) a tax clearance certificate (within the meaning of section 1095) issued for the purposes of that section, the period of validity of which has not expired, or

(iv) where a person has not been issued with such a certificate of authorisation or such a tax clearance certificate, a certificate such as is referred to in paragraph (*b*).

(*b*) Where a person has not been issued with a certificate of authorisation or a tax clearance certificate such as is referred to in subparagraph (i), (ii) or (iii) of paragraph (*a*), the person disposing of an asset referred to in subsection (4)(*b*)(ii) may apply in that behalf, for the purposes of this paragraph, to the Collector-General for the issue of a certificate and such an application shall be deemed to be an application made under section 1095 for the issuing of a tax clearance certificate thereunder and that section shall, accordingly, apply with the following and any other necessary modifications, that is to say, for the reference in subsection (2) of section 1095 to the scheme there shall be substituted a reference to subsection (4)(*b*) of this section.][6]

(9) (*a*) Where—

(i) after the 2nd day of June, 1995, a person acquires an asset to which this section applies and section 978 does not apply,

(ii) the consideration for acquiring the asset is of such a kind that the deduction mentioned in subsection (4) cannot be made out of the consideration, and

[(iii) the person disposing of the asset does not, at or before the time at which the acquisition is made, produce to the person acquiring the asset a certificate under subsection (8) in relation to the disposal or one of the certificates specified in subsection (8A), being a certificate which, in either case, has been issued to the person disposing of the asset.][7]

the person acquiring the asset shall within 7 days of the time at which the acquisition is made—

(I) notify the Revenue Commissioners of the acquisition in a notice in writing containing particulars of—

(A) the asset acquired,

(B) the consideration for acquiring the asset,

(C) the market value of that consideration estimated to the best of that person's knowledge and belief, and

(D) the name and address of the person making the disposal,

and

(II) pay to the Collector-General an amount of capital gains tax equal to 15 per cent of the market value of the consideration so estimated.

(*b*) Capital gains tax which by virtue of paragraph (*a*)(II) is payable by a person acquiring an asset shall—

(i) be payable by that person in addition to any capital gains tax which by virtue of any other provision of the Capital Gains Tax Acts is payable by that person,

(ii) be due within 7 days of the time at which that person acquires the asset, and

(iii) be payable by that person without the making of an assessment;

but tax which has become so due may be assessed on the person acquiring the asset (whether or not it has been paid when the assessment is made) if that tax or any part of that tax is not paid on or before the due date.

(*c*) Where any person acquiring an asset has in pursuance of paragraph (*a*)(II) paid any amount of capital gains tax by reference to the market value of the consideration for acquiring the asset, that person shall be entitled to recover a sum of that amount from the person disposing of the asset as a simple contract debt in any court of competent jurisdiction; but where a copy of a certificate under subsection (8) is issued to the person acquiring the asset, being a copy of a certificate in relation to the disposal by which the person acquired the asset, that person—

(i) shall not be entitled thereafter to so recover that sum, and

(ii) shall be repaid that amount of tax.

(*d*) This section shall apply in relation to the acquisition of an asset by 2 or more persons with any necessary modifications and subject to the condition that each such person shall be liable to be assessed and charged in respect only of such part of the amount of capital gains tax payable by those persons by virtue of paragraph (*b*) as bears to the whole of such tax the same proportion as the part of the asset acquired by that person bears to the whole of the asset.

[(*e*) Where a person acquiring an asset has paid to the Collector-General an amount of capital gains tax in accordance with paragraph (*a*)(II) and recovered a sum of that amount from the person disposing of the asset, then, on proof being given in that regard, appropriate relief shall be given to the person disposing of the asset, whether by discharge, repayment or otherwise.][8]

(10) Notwithstanding sections 979 and 1042, where an amount of capital gains tax is assessed and charged pursuant to this section, such amount shall be due and payable on the day after the day on which the assessment is made.

(11)(*a*) Subject to paragraph (*b*), where there is a disposal of assets by virtue of a capital sum being derived from those assets, the person paying the capital sum shall, notwithstanding that no asset is acquired by that person, be treated for the purposes of this section as acquiring the assets disposed of for a consideration equal to the capital sum, whether that sum is paid in money or money's worth, and this section shall, subject to any necessary modifications, apply accordingly.

(*b*) Paragraph (*a*) shall not apply where there is a disposal of an asset by virtue of a capital sum being derived from the asset under a policy of insurance of the risk of any kind of damage to the asset.

Amendments

1 Substituted by FA 2002 s 63 with effect from 1 January 2002; previously "€381,000"; previously "£300,000".

2 Subs (3A) inserted by FA 2005 s 56(1)(*a*) with effect from 25 March 2005.

3 Substituted by FA 2005 s 56(1)(*b*) with effect from 25 March 2002; previously "section 329".

4 Subs (4)(*b*) substituted by FA 2000 s 87(1)(*b*) with effect from 23 March 2000.

5 Subs (8) substituted by FA 2003 s 71(1) as respects applications made on or after 28 March 2003.

6 Subs (8A) inserted by FA 2000 s 87(1)(*c*) with effect from 23 March 2000.

7 Subs (9)(*a*)(iii) substituted by FA 2000 s 87(1)(*d*) with effect from 23 March 2000.

8 Subs (9)(*e*) inserted by FA 2005 s 56(1)(*c*) with effect from 25 March 2005.

Cross-references

Capital gains tax, penalties for failure to make returns etc, and for fraudulently or negligently making incorrect returns, applied by: s 1077(1)(*c*), (2).

Corporation tax, subs (8) applied by: s 975(2).

Self assessment, making of assessments, subss (4)–(5), (10): s 954(7)(*b*).

Case law

Subss (2) and (7): No basis for withholding 15% tax as the taxpayer was ordinarily resident in the State: *Pine Valley Developments Ltd and others v Minister for the Environment and others* ITR Vol IV p 543.

Subss (3) and (5): See note under corresponding heading for s 537(2).

Subs (7): Issue of a clearance certificate mandatory where the conditions are satisfied: *E O'Ceallaigh v Financial Indemnity Co Ltd* (High Court, 9 November 1983).

Tax Briefing

TB21 Mar 1996 p 12 — Disposal of certain assets in excess of £100,000.

TB35 Mar 1999 p 22–24 — Procedure for obtaining CGT Clearance Certificates (CG 50A's).

TB51 Jan 2003 p 5 — Where the signing and closing of a contract are scheduled to occur on or about the same time, and a draft Form CG50 and draft contract are submitted by fax not later than 5 days prior to the closing date, Revenue will examine and process the application, and prepare a Form CG50A for issue. On production

of the original CG50 and a copy of the final contract, providing both are unaltered from the faxed versions, Revenue will, where appropriate, issue the Form CG50A.
TB56 July 2004 p 5 — Deduction from consideration on disposal of certain assets: relief for tax deducted (Form CG 50B.

Definitions

chargeable gain: ss 5(1), 545; Collector-General: ss 2(1), 851; company: s 5(1); inspector: ss 5(1), 852; land: IA 1937 Sch; minerals: s 5(1); mining: s 5(1); month: IA 1937 Sch; person: IA 1937 s 11(*c*); resident: s 5(1); shares: s 5(1); trade: s 5(1); writing: IA 1937 Sch; year: IA 1937 Sch; year of assessment: ss 2(1), 5(1).

Former enactments

CGTA 1975 s 51(1) and Sch 4 para 11(1)–(10A); FA 1989 s 29; FA 1995 s 76; FA 1996 s 59.

Corresponding UK tax provision

Taxation of Chargeable Gains Act 1992 s 7[repealed].

981 Payment by instalments where consideration due after time of disposal

Where the consideration or part of the consideration taken into account in the computation of a chargeable gain is payable by instalments over a period beginning not earlier than the time when the disposal is made, being a period exceeding 18 months, then, if the person making the disposal satisfies the Revenue Commissioners that such person would otherwise suffer undue hardship, the capital gains tax on such a chargeable gain accruing on a disposal may, at such person's option, be paid by such instalments as the Revenue Commissioners may allow over a period not exceeding 5 years and ending not later than the time at which the last of the first-mentioned instalments is payable.

Cross-references

Corporation tax, applied by: s 975(3).
Self assessment, due dates for payment: s 959(5).

Definitions

chargeable gain: ss 5(1), 534; inspector: ss2(1), 5(1), 835; month: IA 1937 Sch: person: IA 1937 s 11(c).

Former enactments

CGTA 1975 s 44(1).

Corresponding UK tax provision

Taxation of Chargeable Gains Act 1992 s 48.

982 Preferential payment

The priority attaching to assessed taxes under section 81 of the Bankruptcy Act, 1988, and sections 98 and 285 of the Companies Act, 1963, shall apply to capital gains tax.

Former enactments

CGTA 1975 s 51(1) and Sch 4 para 15.

CHAPTER 4

Collection and Recovery of Income Tax on Certain Emoluments (PAYE System)

Cross-references

Approved retirement fund: s 784A(3)(*a*), (4)(*c*)(II).
Charge to income tax of pensions under Schedule E: s 779(1).
Deductions allowed in ascertaining taxable income and provisions relating to reductions in tax: s 458(1B)(*a*).
Duties of auditors and advisors, in relation to Revenue offences: s 1079(2).
Electronic claims: s 864A(1)(*c*)(i).

Employee (PAYE) allowance, meaning of "emoluments" applied: s 472(1), (3)(*b*).
General provisions relating to allowances, deductions and reliefs: s 459(5)(*a*).
Health Contributions Act 1979, s 1, definitions, meaning of "emoluments" in this Chapter applied in a modified manner.
Income Tax (Employments) (Consolidated) Regulations 2001, SI No 559 of 2001, meaning of "emoluments" applied: reg 2(1) (interpretation); reg 28(3), (4) (payment of tax by employer); reg 42 (deduction or repayment by reference to superannuation contribution).
Income Tax (Relevant Contracts) Regulations 2000, SI No 71 of 2000: ITRCR 2000 reg 17(2).
Liability to tax of holder of fixed charge on book debts of company: s 1001(1)(*a*).
National Training Fund Act 2000, s 5(1), collection of levy, meaning of "emoluments" applied.
Payment of tax by donation of heritage items: s 1003(1)(*a*).
Permanent health benefit scheme benefits, emoluments: s 125(3)(*a*)(ii).
Personal Retirement Saving Accounts (PRSAs), taxation of payments from a PRSA: s 787G(1).
Power of inspection, PAYE, meanings of "emoluments", "employer" and "tax deduction card" applied: s 903(1).
Professional services withholding tax, relevant payment: s 520(1); interim refunds: s 527(3)(*b*).
Rate of charge: s 15(5).
Repayment of tax: s 865(3A)(*a*).
Retirement annuities: relief for premiums: s 784(2B)(*a*), (7).
Returns by employers in relation to pension products, meaning of "emoluments" applied: s 897A(1).
Revenue offences: s 1078(2)(i).
Self assessment, meaning of "chargeable person": s 950(1).
Social welfare benefits, emoluments: s 126(2)(*b*).
Social Welfare (Consolidation) Act 1993, s 2(1), definitions, meaning of "emoluments" applied.
Subcontractors' withholding tax: s 531(5)(*c*)(ii)(III), (6).
Surcharge for late returns: s 1084(3).
Taxes (Offset of Repayments) Regulations 2002, SI No 471 of 2002, regs 2(1) (interpretation — "taxhead" para (*b*)), 3(*a*)(iii), (vi) (order of priority of offset against liabilities) and 4(*a*)(iii), (vi) (special arrangements regarding corporation tax, income tax and capital gains tax).

Revenue information

Employers Guide to PAYE
An Employer's Guide to operating PAYE and PRSI on certain benefits is available on Revenue's website (www.revenue.ie) under PAYE/Benefit in kind.
Information leaflet IT4 — Understanding PAYE Tax Tables.
Information leaflet IT11 — Employees Guide to PAYE.
Information leaflet IT50 — PAYE/PRSI for Small Employers — A Revenue Guide.
Information leaflet IT67 — First Job — A Guide for First Time Entrants to the PAYE Tax System.
Information leaflet IT69 — eWorking and Tax.
Information leaflet CG2 — Due Dates — Payments and Returns.
Information leaflet CG3 — Payments to the Collector-General.
Information leaflet CG4 — Change of Address.
Information leaflet CG6 — P35 — End of Year Returns.
Information leaflet CG7 — Direct Debit — PAYE/PRSI and VAT.

Tax Briefing

TB58 Dec 2004 pp 8–9 P35 End of Year Return 2004.
TB58 Dec 2004 p 15 — P35 2005 — Employer obligations relating to pension contributions.

983 Interpretation (Chapter 4)

In this Chapter, except where the context otherwise requires—

"emoluments" means anything assessable to income tax under Schedule E, and references to payments of emoluments include references to payments on account of emoluments;

"employee" means any person in receipt of emoluments;

"employer" means any person paying emoluments;

[**"income tax month"** means—

(*a*) in relation to a period prior to 6 December 2001, a month beginning on the 6th day of a month and ending on the 5th day of the next month,

(*b*) the period beginning on 6 December 2001 and ending on 31 December 2001, and

(*c*) thereafter, a calendar month;][1]

[**"reliefs from income tax"** means allowances, deductions and tax credits;][2]

[**"tax credits"** means personal tax credits and general tax credits;][2]

"tax deduction card" means a tax deduction card in the form prescribed by the Revenue Commissioners or such other document corresponding to a tax deduction card as may be authorised by the Revenue Commissioners in any particular case.

Amendments

1 Definition of "income tax month" substituted by FA 2001 s 77(2) and Sch 2 para 53 with effect from 6 April 2001.

2 Definitions of reliefs from income tax" and "tax credits" inserted by FA 2001 s 2(3) and Sch 1 para 1(*s*) for short tax "year" 2001 and later tax years.

Cross-references

Taxation of certain perquisites, meaning of "employer" applied: s 112A(3).

Definitions

general tax credit, personal tax credit: s 3(1); year of assessment: s 2(1).

Former enactments

ITA 1967 s 124.

984 Application

(1) This Chapter shall apply to all emoluments except emoluments which are emoluments in respect of which the employer has been notified by the inspector that they are emoluments which arise from an office or employment and from which, in the opinion of the inspector, having regard to the circumstances of the office or employment or to the amount of the emoluments, the deduction of tax by reference to this Chapter is impracticable.

(2) The inspector may, if a change in the circumstances of the office or employment or in the amount of the emoluments so warrants, cancel a notification given under subsection (1) by notice in writing given to the employer, and this Chapter shall then apply to payments of emoluments arising from the office or employment made after the date of such notice.

(3) Any notice issued by or on behalf of the Revenue Commissioners under section 125 of the Income Tax Act, 1967, before the 6th day of April, 1986, shall not have effect in relation to emoluments arising in the year 1997–98 or any subsequent year of assessment.

Cross-references

Oireachtas severance payments deemed to be emoluments within Part 42 Chapter 4 as applied by this section: s 124(2)(*b*).

Restrictive covenants, sum paid deemed to be emoluments within Part 42 Chapter 4 as applied by this section: s 127(2).

Social welfare benefits deemed to be emoluments within Part 42 Chapter 4 as applied by this section: s 126(3)(*b*)(ii).

Definitions

emoluments, employer: s 983; inspector: ss 2(1), 5(1), 852; writing: IA 1937 Sch.

Former enactments

ITA 1967 s 125; FA 1985 s 6(1)–(2).

985 Method of collection

On the making of any payment of any emoluments to which this Chapter applies, income tax shall, subject to this Chapter and in accordance with regulations under this Chapter, be deducted or repaid by the person making the payment notwithstanding that—

(*a*) when the payment is made no assessment has been made in respect of the emoluments, or

(*b*) the emoluments are in whole or in part emoluments for some year of assessment other than that during which the payment is made.

Case law

Irish

The deduction of PAYE, the charging of interest on overdue payments and the enforcement of liabilities not unconstitutional: *Kennedy v Hearne and others* ITR Vol III p 590.

UK

An employer must deduct tax from tips under the PAYE system where there is no tronc: *Figael Ltd v Fox* [1992] STC 83.

On recovering lost wages by way of damages, injured employee, in receipt of sick pay net of PAYE from his employer, held obliged to repay only net amount: *British Railways Board v Franklin* [1993] STC 487.

Definitions

emoluments, employee, employer, income tax month, tax deduction card: s 983; year of assessment: s 3(1).

Former enactments

ITA 1967 s 126; FA 1972 s 46(1) and Sch 4 Pt I.

985A Application of section 985 to certain perquisites, etc

[(1) [Subject to subsection (1A), this section applies][1] to emoluments in the form of—

(*a*) perquisites and profits whatever which are chargeable to tax under section 112 ...[2] including—

(i) an expense incurred by a body corporate in the provision of a benefit, other than a contribution to a PRSA (within the meaning of Chapter 2A of Part 30), for an employee which is treated as a perquisite for the purposes of section 112 by virtue of section 118,

(ii) the benefit arising from a preferential loan which is treated as a perquisite for the purposes of section 112 by virtue of section 122, and

(iii) a perquisite to which section 112A applies,

(*b*) the benefit of the private use of a car which is chargeable to tax by virtue of section 121, and

(*c*) the benefit of the private use of a van which is chargeable to tax by virtue of section 121A.

[(1A) Subsection (1) shall not apply to emoluments in the form of perquisites or profits whatever received by an employee in the form of shares (including stock) being shares or stock in—

(*a*) the company in which the employee holds his or her office or employment, or

(*b*) a company which has control (within the meaning of section 432) of that company.][3]

(2) Where an employee is in receipt of any emolument to which this section applies, the employer shall be treated for the purposes of this Chapter and regulations under this Chapter as making a payment (in this section referred to as a **"notional payment"**) of an amount equal to the amount referred to in subsection (3).

(3) The amount referred to in this subsection, is the amount which, on the basis of the best estimate that can reasonably be made, is the amount of income likely to be chargeable to tax under Schedule E in respect of the emolument.

(4) Where, by reason of an insufficiency of payments actually made to or on behalf of an employee, the employer is unable to deduct the amount (or full amount) of the income tax required to be deducted by virtue of this Chapter and regulations made under this Chapter, the employer shall be liable to remit to the Revenue Commissioners at such time as may be prescribed by regulation an amount of income tax equal to the amount of income tax that the employer would be required, but is unable, to deduct.

[(4A) Any amount of tax which an employer remits in accordance with subsection (4) and any regulations made under that subsection in respect of a notional payment shall be treated as an amount of tax which, at the time the notional payment is made, is deducted in respect of the employee's liability to income tax.][4]

(5) In any case where—

(*a*) an employee is in receipt of an emolument to which this section applies,

(*b*) the employer is required by virtue of this section and regulations made thereunder to remit an amount of income tax (in this subsection referred to as the **"due amount"**) in respect of that emolument, and

(*c*) the employee does not, before the end of the year of assessment, make good the due amount to the employer,

the employee shall be chargeable to tax under Schedule E in respect of the due amount for the next following year of assessment and the due amount shall be treated for that year as an emolument to which this section applies.

(6) The Revenue Commissioners may make regulations to make provision—

(*a*) with respect to the deduction, collection and recovery of amounts to be accounted for in respect of notional payments;

(*b*) applying (with or without modifications) any specified provisions of regulations for the time being in force in relation to deductions from actual payments to amounts to be accounted for in respect of any notional payments.

[(7) Every regulation made under this section shall be laid before Dáil Éireann as soon as may be after it is made and, if a resolution annulling the regulation is passed by Dáil Éireann within the next 21 days on which Dáil Éireann has sat after the regulation is laid before it, the regulation shall be annulled accordingly, but without prejudice to the validity of anything previously done thereunder.][5][6]

Amendments

1 Substituted by FA 2004 s 9(1)(*a*)(i)(I) with effect from 25 March 2004; previously "This section applies".

2 Deleted by FA 2004 s 9(1)(*a*)(i)(II) with effect from 25 March 2004; previously "excluding perquisites or profits whatever in the form of shares (including stock) in a company, but".

3 Subs (1A) inserted by FA 2004 s 9(1)(*a*)(ii) with effect from 25 March 2004.

4 Subs (4A) inserted by FA 2004 s 9(1)(*a*)(iii) for 2004 and subsequent years of assessment.

5 Subs (7) inserted by FA 2004 s 9(1)(*a*)(iv) with effect from 25 March 2005

6 Section 985A inserted by FA 2003 s 6(1)(*d*) with effect from 1 January 2004.

Cross-references

Income Tax (Employments) (Consolidated) Regulations 2001, interpretation, subs (2): ITECR reg 1(1)("notional payment"); subs (4): ITECR reg 1(1)("temporary tax deduction form", "total net tax deducted"), reg 1(1A); deduction of tax in respect of notional payments, subs (4): ITECR 2001 reg 16A; tax borne by the employer in respect of notional payments, subs (4), (5): ITECR 2001 reg 16B; deduction of tax in respect of certain notional payments, subs (4): ITECR 2001 reg 17A(2)(*b*); payment of tax by employer, subs (4): ITECR 2001 reg 28(1)(*b*); payment of tax for periods greater than one month but not exceeding one year; subs (4): ITECR 2001 reg 29(1)(*b*); inspection of employer's records, subs (4): ITECR 2001 reg 32(1).

Priority in bankruptcy of certain amounts: s 994(1)(*b*).

Priority in winding up of certain amounts: s 955.

Health Contribution Act 1979, s 6(3), health contribution by individuals with emoluments other than reckonable earnings, meaning of "notional payment" in this section applied.

National Training Fund Act 2003, s 4(13), rate of levy and supplemental provisions, meaning of "notional payment" in this section applied.

Social Welfare (Consolidation) Act 1993, s 10(1)(*e*), employment contribution, meaning of "notional payment" in this section applied.

State employees, foreign service allowances: s 196A(2) ("emoluments").

Tax Briefing

TB52 May 2003 p 8 — Benefits-in-kind — application of PAYE and PRSI.

Definitions

emoluments, employee, employer: s 983; company: s 4(1); Dáil Éireann: IA 1937 Sch; tax: s 3(1); year of assessment: s 2(1).

985B PAYE settlement agreements

[(1) In this section **"qualifying emoluments"** means emoluments, other than emoluments in the form of a payment of money, which are—

(*a*) minor, as regards the amount or type of emolument involved, and

(*b*) irregular, as to the frequency in which or the times at which, the emoluments are provided.

(2) Subject to this section, the Revenue Commissioners may, on application in that behalf from an employer, enter into an agreement with the employer under which the employer shall account to them in accordance with the provisions of this section in respect of income tax in respect of qualifying emoluments for a year of assessment of one or more employees of the employer which the employer would otherwise have to account for in accordance with the other provisions of this Chapter and any regulations made under those provisions.

(3) Where an employer accounts for income tax under an agreement made in accordance with this section—

(*a*) the employer shall not be liable to account for that tax under the other provisions of this Chapter and any regulations made under those provisions,

(*b*) qualifying emoluments covered by the agreement shall not be reckoned in computing, for the purposes of the Income Tax Acts, the total income of the employee concerned,

(*c*) the amount accounted for shall not be treated as having been deducted in accordance with the other provisions of this Chapter and any regulations under those provisions,

(*d*) an employee shall not be treated as having paid any part of the income tax accounted for by his or her employer and, accordingly, the employee shall not be entitled to a credit in respect of, or to claim or receive repayment of, any part of that tax, and

(*e*) emoluments covered by the agreement shall not be included in a return by the employer under Regulation 31 of the Income Tax (Employments) (Consolidated) Regulations 2001 (SI No 559 of 2001).

(4) The amount in respect of income tax to be accounted for by an employer under an agreement entered into under this section shall be specified in the agreement and shall be—

(*a*) determined in accordance with the factors specified in subsection (5)(*a*), and

(*b*) comprised of the amounts specified in subsection (5)(*b*).

(5) (*a*) The factors specified for the purposes of subsection (4)(*a*) are—

(i) the aggregate amount of the qualifying emoluments covered by the agreement on which income tax is chargeable,

(ii) the total number of employees in receipt of qualifying emoluments covered by the agreement,

(iii) the number of those employees respectively chargeable to income tax—

(I) only at the standard rate for the year of assessment to which the agreement relates, and

(II) at both the standard rate and the higher rate for that year,

and

(iv) such other matters as are agreed by the Revenue Commissioners and the employer to be relevant in relation to the qualifying emoluments covered by the agreement.

(*b*) The amounts specified for the purposes of subsection (4)(*b*) are—

(i) an amount equal to income tax on the aggregate of the amounts computed in accordance with paragraph (*a*)(i), calculated so as to take account of the factor specified in paragraph (*a*)(iii), and

(ii) a further amount reflecting the income tax on the benefit to the employees of receiving the qualifying emoluments included in the agreement without liability to tax.

(6) Where an employer wishes to avail of this section for a year of assessment, the employer shall make application in writing in that behalf to the Revenue Commissioners which is received by them on or before 31 December in that year.

(7) If the amount of income tax which an employer is to account for in relation to a year of assessment in accordance with an agreement entered into under this section is not paid to the Collector-General within 46 days of the end of that year, the agreement shall be null and void and, accordingly, this Chapter and any regulations made thereunder shall apply as if this section had not been enacted.

(8) Any act to be performed or function to be discharged by the Revenue Commissioners which is authorised by this section may be performed or discharged by any of their officers acting under their authority.][1]

Amendments

1 Section 985B inserted by FA 2004 s 9(1)(*b*) with effect from 25 March 2004.

Definitions

Collector-General: s 2(1); emoluments, employee, employer: s 983; higher rate: s 3(1); Income Tax Acts: s 1(2); standard rate) s 3(1); total income: s 3(1); writing: IA 1937 Sch: year of assessment: s 2(1).

986 Regulations

(1) The Revenue Commissioners shall make regulations with respect to the assessment, charge, collection and recovery of income tax in respect of emoluments to which this Chapter applies or of income tax for any previous year of assessment remaining unpaid, and those regulations may, in particular and without prejudice to the generality of the foregoing, include provision—

(*a*) for requiring any employer making any payment of emoluments to which this Chapter applies, when that employer makes the payment, to make a deduction or repayment of tax calculated by reference to such rate or rates of tax for the year as may be specified and any [reliefs from income tax][1] appropriate in the case of the employee as indicated by the particulars on the tax deduction card supplied in respect of the employee by the Revenue Commissioners;

(*b*) for rendering persons who are required to make any such deduction or repayment, in the case of a deduction (whether or not made), accountable for the amount of the tax and liable to pay that amount to the Revenue Commissioners and, in the case of a repayment, entitled (if a repayment has been made) to be paid it, or given credit for it, by the Revenue Commissioners;

(*c*) for the production to and inspection by persons authorised by the Revenue Commissioners of wages sheets and other documents and records for the purpose of satisfying themselves that tax in respect of emoluments to which this Chapter applies has been and is being duly deducted, repaid and accounted for;

(*d*) for the collection and recovery, whether by deduction from emoluments paid in any year or otherwise, of tax in respect of emoluments to which this Chapter applies which has not been deducted or otherwise recovered during the year;

(*e*) for appeals with respect to matters arising under the regulations which would not otherwise be the subject of an appeal;

(*f*) for the deduction of tax at the standard rate and at the higher rate in such cases or classes of cases as may be provided for by the regulations;

[(*g*) for requiring any employer making any payment of emoluments to which this Chapter applies, when making a deduction or repayment of tax in accordance with this Chapter and regulations under this Chapter, to make such deduction or repayment as would require to be made if the amount of emoluments were the emoluments reduced by the amount of any contributions payable by the employee and deductible by the employer from the emoluments being paid and which—

(i) by virtue of section 471 are allowed as a deduction in ascertaining the amount of income on which the employee is to be charged to income tax, or

(ii) by virtue of [Chapter 1, Chapter 2 or Chapter 2A of Part 30][2] are for the purposes of assessment under Schedule E allowed as a deduction from the emoluments;][3]

(*h*) for requiring every employer who pays emoluments to which this Chapter applies exceeding the limit specified in subsection (5) to notify the Revenue Commissioners within the period specified in the regulations that that employer is such an employer;

(*i*) for requiring every employer who pays emoluments to which this Chapter applies exceeding the limits specified in subsection (5) to keep and maintain a register of that employer's employees in such manner as may be specified in the regulations and, on being required to do so by the Revenue Commissioners, to deliver the register to the Revenue Commissioners within the period specified in the notice;

(*j*) for treating persons who are not employers as employers in such cases or classes of cases as may be provided for by the regulations.

(2) Regulations under this section shall apply notwithstanding anything in the Income Tax Acts, but shall not affect any right of appeal which a person would have apart from the regulations.

(3) (*a*) Tax deduction cards shall be prepared with a view to securing that in so far as may be practicable the total tax payable for the year of assessment in respect of any emoluments is deducted from the emoluments paid during that year.

(*b*) In paragraph (*a*), any reference to the total tax payable for a year shall be construed as a reference to the total tax estimated to be payable for the year in respect of the emoluments, subject to [provisional reliefs from income tax][4] and subject also, if necessary, to making an addition to that estimated amount (including a nil amount) for amounts remaining unpaid on account of income tax for any previous year of assessment and to making a deduction from that estimated amount for amounts overpaid on account of any such income tax.

(4) Notwithstanding any other provision of this section, when stating on a tax deduction card an amount in respect of [reliefs from income tax][5] the amount may be rounded up to a convenient greater amount and stated accordingly, and, as respects the amount of tax which is not deducted in the year of assessment as a result of such statement, the adjustment appropriate for its recovery shall be made in a subsequent year of assessment.

(5) (*a*) The limits referred to in paragraphs (*h*) and (i) of subsection (1) shall be emoluments at a rate equivalent to a rate of [€8][6] per week, or in the case of an employee with other employment, [€2][7] per week.

(*b*) In the case of employees paid monthly or at longer intervals, the references in paragraph (*a*) to a rate of [€8][6] per week and a rate of [€2][7] per week shall be treated as references to a rate of [€36][8] per month and a rate of [€9][9] per month respectively.

(6) (*a*) In this subsection—

"domestic employee" means an employee who is employed solely on domestic duties (including the minding of children) in the employer's private dwelling house;

"domestic employment" means employment by reference to which an employee is a domestic employee.

(*b*) Notwithstanding subsection (5), as on and from the 6th day of June, 1997, regulations made in accordance with paragraphs (*h*) and (i) of subsection (1) shall not apply to an employer (being an individual) who pays emoluments to an employee engaged by that employer in a domestic employment where—

(i) the emoluments from that employment are less than [€40][10] per week, and

(ii) the employer has only one such employee.

(7) Every regulation made under this section shall be laid before Dáil Éireann as soon as may be after it is made and, if a resolution annulling the regulation is passed by Dáil Éireann within the next 21 days on which Dáil Éireann has sat after the regulation is laid before it, the regulation shall be annulled accordingly, but without prejudice to the validity of anything previously done thereunder.

Amendments

1 Substituted by FA 2001 s 2(3) and Sch 1 para 1(*t*)(i)(I) for short tax "year" 2001 and later tax years; previously "allowances, deductions and reliefs".

2 Substituted by FA 2003 s 14(1)(*f*) with effect from 28 March 2003; previously "Chapter 1 or Chapter 2A of Part 30".

3 Subs (1)(*g*) substituted by FA 2001 s 2(3) and Sch 1 para 1(*t*)(i)(II) for short tax "year" 2001 and later tax years.

4 Substituted by FA 2001 s 2(3) and Sch 1 para 1(*t*)(ii) for short tax "year" 2001 and later tax years; previously "a provisional deduction for allowances and reliefs".

5 Substituted by FA 2001 s 2(3) and Sch 1 para 1(*t*)(iii) for short tax "year" 2001 and later tax years; previously "allowances, deductions and reliefs".

6 Substituted by FA 2001 s 240(1) and (2)(*a*) and Sch 5 Pt 1 for 2002 and later tax years; previously "£6".

7 Substituted by FA 2001 s 240(1) and (2)(*a*) and Sch 5 Pt 1 for 2002 and later tax years; previously "£1".

8 Substituted by FA 2001 s 240(1) and (2)(*a*) and Sch 5 Pt 1 for 2002 and later tax years; previously "£26".

9 Substituted by FA 2001 s 240(1) and (2)(*a*) and Sch 5 Pt 1 for 2002 and later tax years; previously "£4.50".

10 Substituted by FA 2001 s 240(1) and (2)(*a*) and Sch 5 Pt 1 for 2002 and later tax years; previously "£30".

Cross-references

BES investments: s 503(7); withdrawal of BES relief: s 504(7)(*d*)(i).

Film investments: s 481(17).

PAYE system, recovery of tax: s 993(1)(*c*).

Subcontractors' withholding tax: s 531(6).

Tax treatment of directors of companies and employees granted rights to acquire shares (share options): s 128(2A)(*a*).

Case law

Enforcement proceedings under the operation of the PAYE regulations valid, as they are not criminal proceedings: *Director of Public Prosecutions v Downes* ITR Vol III p 641.

Regulations

Income Tax (Employments) (Consolidated) Regulations 2001 (SI 559/2001).

Revenue information

Information leaflet IT53 — Domestic Employee Scheme

Definitions

Dáil Éireann: IA 1937 Sch; higher rate: ss 3(1), 15; month: IA 1937 Sch; standard rate: s 3(1); week: IA 1937 Sch; year of assessment: s 3(1).

Former enactments

ITA 1967 s 127(1), (2), (3)(*a*)(i) and (*b*) (part of), (4), (5) and (7); FA 1972 s 2(1); FA 1974 s 11 and Sch 1 Pt II; FA 1993 Sch 1 Pt I para 2; FA 1997 s 6.

Corresponding UK tax provision

Income and Corporation Taxes Act 1988 s 203.

987 Penalties for breach of regulations

[(1) Where any person does not comply with any provision of regulations under this Chapter requiring that person to send any return, statement, notification or certificate, other than the end of year return required under [Regulation 31 of the Income Tax (Employments) (Consolidated) Regulations 2001 (SI No 559 of 2001)][1], or to remit income tax to the Collector-General or fails to make any deduction or repayment in accordance with any regulation made pursuant to section 986(1)(*g*), that person shall be liable to a penalty of [€1,520][2].][3]

[(1A) Where any person fails to send an end of year return to the Collector-General in accordance with [Regulation 31 of the Income Tax (Employments) (Consolidated) Regulations 2001 (SI No 559 of 2001)][1], that person shall be liable to a penalty of [€630][4] for each month or part of a month during which the said return remains outstanding, subject to a maximum penalty of [€2,535][5].][6]

(2) Where the person mentioned in [subsection (1) or (1A)][7] is a body of persons, the secretary of the body shall be liable to a separate penalty of [€950][8].

(3) All penalties for failure to comply with any provision of regulations under this Chapter may, without prejudice to any other method of the recovery, be proceeded for and recovered summarily in the like manner as in summary proceedings for the recovery of any fine or penalty under any Act relating to the excise.

(4) In proceedings for recovery of a penalty under this section—

(*a*) a certificate signed by an officer of the Revenue Commissioners which certifies that he or she has inspected the relevant records of the Revenue Commissioners and that it appears from them that during a stated period—

(i) a stated return, statement, notification or certificate was not received from the defendant,

(ii) stated wages sheets or other records or documents were not produced by the defendant,

(iii) the defendant did not remit stated tax to the Collector-General, or

(iv) the defendant did not make a stated deduction or repayment of tax, shall be evidence until the contrary is proved that the defendant did not during that period send that return, statement, notification or certificate or did not produce those wages sheets or other records or documents or did not remit that tax to the Collector-General or did not make that deduction or repayment of tax;

(*b*) a certificate signed by an officer of the Revenue Commissioners which certifies that he or she has inspected the relevant records of the Revenue Commissioners and that it appears from them that a stated return or other document was duly sent to the defendant on a stated day shall be evidence until the contrary is proved that that person received that return or other document in the ordinary course;

(*c*) a certificate signed by an officer of the Revenue Commissioners which certifies that he or she has inspected the relevant records of the Revenue Commissioners and that it appears from them that during a stated period the defendant was an employer or a person whose name and address were registered in the register kept and maintained under [Regulation 7(4) of the Income Tax (Employments) (Consolidated) Regulations 2001 (SI No 559 of 2001)][9], shall be evidence until the contrary is proved that the defendant was during that period an employer or, as the case may be, a person whose name and address were so registered;

(*d*) a certificate certifying as provided for in paragraph (*a*), (*b*) or (*c*) and purporting to be signed by an officer of the Revenue Commissioners may be tendered in evidence without proof and shall be deemed until the contrary is proved to have been signed by an officer of the Revenue Commissioners.

Amendments

1 Substituted by FA 2002 s 138 and Sch 6 paras 3(*p*)(i) and 6(*c*)(i) with effect from 1 January 2002; previously "Regulation 35 of the Income Tax (Employments) Regulations, 1960 (SI No 28 of 1960)".

2 Substituted by FA 2001 s 240(1) and (2)(*k*) and Sch 5 Pt 1 as respects any act or omission which takes place or begins on or after 1 January 2002; previously "£1,200".

3 Subs (1) substituted by FA 1999 s 25(*a*) with effect from 6 April 1999.

4 Substituted by FA 2001s 240(1) and (2)(*k*) and Sch 5 Pt 1 as respects any act or omission which takes place or begins on or after 1 January 2002; previously "£500".

5 Substituted by FA 2001 s 240(1) and (2)(*k*) and Sch 5 Pt 1 as respects any act or omission which takes place or begins on or after 1 January 2002; previously "£2,000".

6 Subs (1A) inserted by FA 1999 s 25(*b*) with effect from 6 April 1999.

7 Substituted by FA 1999 s 25(*c*) with effect from 6 April 1999; previously "subsection (1)".

8 Substituted by FA 2001 s 240(1) and (2)(*k*) and Sch 5 Pt 1 as respects any act or omission which takes place or begins on or after 1 January 2002; previously "£750".

9 Substituted by FA 2002 s 138 and Sch 6 paras 3(*p*)(ii) and 6(*c*)(i) with effect from 1 January 2002; previously "regulation 8(4) of the Income Tax (Employments) Regulations, 1960 (SI No 28 of 1960)".

Cross-references

Capital acquisitions tax, penalties, subs (4) applies, with any necessary modifications, to a penalty under CATCA 2003 as if the penalty were a penalty under the Income Tax Acts: CATCA 2003 s 58(9).

PAYE system, registration of employers: s 988(4).

Revenue offences, subs (4): s 1078(9).

Subcontractors' withholding tax, subs (4): s 531(16).

Time limit for summary proceedings: s 1064.

Definitions

body of persons: s 2(1); Collector-General: s 2(1); person: IA 1937 s 11(*c*).

Former enactments

ITA 1967 s 128(1), (1A), (2) and (4); FA 1972 s 2(2); FA 1973 s 43; FA 1976 s 1; FA 1981 s 4; FA 1982 s 60; FA 1992 s 234 and s 248.

988 Registration of certain persons as employers and requirement to send certain notifications

(1) Where the Revenue Commissioners have reason to believe that a person is liable to send them a notification under [Regulation 7 of the Income Tax (Employments) (Consolidated) Regulations 2001 (SI No 559 of 2001)][1], and has not done so, they may register that person's name and address in the register kept and maintained under paragraph (4) of that regulation (in this section referred to as **"the register"**) and serve a notice on that person stating that that person has been so registered.

(2) Where a notice is served under subsection (1) on a person, the following provisions shall apply:

(*a*) if the person claims to be not liable to send the notification referred to in subsection (1), the person may, by giving notice in writing to the Revenue Commissioners within the period of 14 days from the service of the notice under subsection (1), require the claim to be referred to the Appeal Commissioners and their decision on the claim shall be final and conclusive;

(*b*) if no such claim is, within the time specified in paragraph (*a*), required to be referred, or if such claim is required to be referred and there is a determination by the Appeal Commissioners against the appellant, the appellant shall be regarded for the purposes of the Regulations referred to in subsection (1) as an employer who had sent a notification under paragraph (1) of regulation 8 of those Regulations;

(*c*) if a claim is required to be referred and there is a determination by the Appeal Commissioners in favour of the appellant, the Revenue Commissioners shall on that determination delete the appellant's name and address from the register.

(3) (*a*) Where a person whose name and address is registered in the register is not liable, under [Regulation 28][2] of the Regulations referred to in subsection (1), to remit to the Collector-General any amount of tax for an income tax month, such person shall, within the period of 9 days from the end of that month, make a declaration to that effect in a form prescribed by the Revenue Commissioners and shall send that form to the Collector-General.

(*b*) Where a person whose name and address is registered in the register ceases to pay emoluments to which this Chapter applies, such person shall, within the period of 14 days from the date on which such person ceased to pay such emoluments, notify the Revenue Commissioners to that effect.

(4) Section 987 shall apply to a non-compliance with subsection (3) as it applies to a non-compliance with regulations under this Chapter.

Amendments

1 Substituted by FA 2002 s 138 and Sch 6 paras 3(*q*)(i) and 6(*c*)(i) with effect from 1 January 2002; previously "regulation 8 of the Income Tax (Employments) Regulations, 1960 (SI No 28 of 1960)".

2 Substituted by FA 2002 s 138 and Sch 6 paras 3(*q*)(ii) and 6(*c*)(i) with effect from 1 January 2002; previously "regulation 31".

Definitions

Appeal Commissioners: s 2(1); Collector-General: s 2(1); month: IA 1937 Sch; person: IA 1937 s 11(*c*); writing: IA 1937 Sch.

Former enactments

FA 1974 s 72.

989 Estimation of tax due for income tax months

(1) In this section and in sections 990 and 991, **"the regulations"** means any regulations under section 986.

(2) Where the Revenue Commissioners have reason to believe that a person was liable under the regulations to remit income tax in relation to any income tax month, and the person has not remitted any income tax in relation to that income tax month, they may—

(*a*) estimate the amount of tax which should have been remitted by the person within the period specified in the regulations for the payment of such tax, and

(*b*) serve notice on the person of the amount so estimated.

(3) Where a notice is served under subsection (2) on a person, the following provisions shall apply:

(*a*) the person, if claiming to be not liable to remit any tax for the income tax month to which the notice relates, may by giving notice in writing to the Revenue Commissioners within the period of 14 days from the service of the notice require the claim to be referred for decision to the Appeal Commissioners and their decision shall be final and conclusive;

(*b*) on the expiration of that period, if no such claim is required to be so referred or, if such claim is required to be referred, on final determination by the Appeal Commissioners against the claim, the estimated tax specified in the notice shall be recoverable in the like manner and by the like proceedings as if—

(i) the person were an employer, and

(ii) the amount specified in the notice were the amount of tax which the person was liable under the regulations to deduct from emoluments paid by the person during the income tax month specified in the notice reduced by any amounts which the person was liable under the regulations to repay during the income tax month;

(*c*) if at any time after the service of the notice the person furnishes a declaration of the amount which the person is liable under the regulations to remit in respect of the income tax month specified in the notice and pays the tax in accordance with the declaration together with any interest and costs which may have been incurred in connection with the default, the notice shall, subject to paragraph (*d*), stand discharged and any excess of tax which may have been paid shall be repaid;

(*d*) where action for the recovery of tax specified in a notice under subsection (2) has been taken, being action by means of the institution of proceedings in any court or the issue of a certificate under section 962, paragraph (*c*) shall not, unless the Revenue Commissioners otherwise direct, apply in relation to that notice until that action [has been completed;][1]

[(*e*) where—

(i) the amount of tax estimated in the notice is remitted and a declaration referred to in paragraph (*c*) is not furnished, or

(ii) the Revenue Commissioners have reason to believe that the amount estimated in the notice is less than the amount which the person was liable to remit,

the Revenue Commissioners may amend the amount so estimated by increasing it and serve notice on the person concerned of the revised amount estimated and such notice shall supersede any previous notice issued under subsection (2).][2]

(4) A notice given by the Revenue Commissioners under subsection (2) [or subsection (3)(*e*)][3] may extend to 2 or more consecutive income tax months.

(5) The Revenue Commissioners may nominate any of their officers to perform any acts and discharge any functions authorised by this section to be performed or discharged by the Revenue Commissioners.

Amendments

1 Substituted by FA 2003 s 157(*a*)(i) with effect from 28 March 2003; previously "has been completed.".

2 Subs (3)(*e*) inserted by FA 2003 s 157(*a*)(ii) with effect from 28 March 2003.

3 Inserted by FA 2003 s 157(*a*)(iii) with effect from 28 March 2003.

Cross-references

Appeals, subs (3): s 992.
Generation of estimates by electronic, photographic or other process: s 990A(*a*).
Interest: s 991(2)(*a*).
PAYE system, recovery of tax: s 993(5)(*a*).
Priority in winding up: s 1000(*b*).
Taxes (Offset of Repayments) Regulations 2002, SI No 471 of 2002 reg 2(1) (interpretation — "estimate" para (*a*)).

Definitions

Appeal Commissioners: s 2(1); commencement: IA 1937 Sch; employer: s 983; person: IA 1937 s 11(*c*); writing: IA 1937 Sch; year of assessment: ss 2(1), 5(1).

Statutory instrument

Income Tax (Employments) (Consolidated) Regulations 2001 (SI 559/2001).

Former enactments

FA 1968 s 7(1), (2), (4), (5) and (8); FA 1985 s 9(*a*).

990 Estimation of tax due for year

(1) Where the inspector or such other officer as the Revenue Commissioners may nominate to exercise the powers conferred by this section (in this section referred to as **"other officer"**) has reason to believe that the total amount of tax which an employer was liable under the regulations to remit in respect of the respective income tax months comprised in any year of assessment was greater than the amount of tax (if any) paid by

the employer in respect of those months, then, without prejudice to any other action which may be taken, the inspector or other officer—

(*a*) may make an estimate in one sum of the total amount of tax which in his or her opinion should have been paid in respect of the income tax months comprised in that year, and

(*b*) may serve notice on the employer specifying—

(i) the total amount of tax so estimated,

(ii) the total amount of tax (if any) remitted by the employer in relation to the income tax months comprised in that year, and

(iii) the balance of tax remaining unpaid.

[(1A)(*a*) Where—

(i) a notice is served on an employer under subsection (1) in relation to a year of assessment (being the year of assessment 2000–2001 or a subsequent year of assessment), and

(ii) prior to the service of the notice, the employer had failed to submit to the Collector-General, in relation to that year of assessment, the return required by [Regulation 31 of the Income Tax (Employments) (Consolidated) Regulations 2001 (SI No 559 of 2001)][1],

then, if, within 14 days after the service of the notice, the employer—

(I) sends that return to the Collector-General, and

(II) pays any balance of tax remaining unpaid for the year of assessment in accordance with the return, together with any interest and costs which may have been incurred in connection with the default,

the notice shall, subject to paragraph (*c*), stand discharged and any excess of tax which may have been paid shall be repaid.

(*b*) If, on expiration of the period referred to in paragraph (*a*), the employer has not complied with subparagraphs (I) and (II) of paragraph (*a*), the balance of tax remaining unpaid as specified in the notice shall become due and recoverable in the like manner as if the balance of tax had been charged on the employer under Schedule E.

(*c*) Where action for the recovery of tax specified in a notice under subsection (1) has been taken, being action by means of the institution of proceedings in any court or the issue of a certificate under section 962, so much of paragraph (*a*) as relates to the discharge of the notice shall not, unless the Collector-General otherwise directs, apply in relation to that notice until that action has been completed.][2]

[(*d*) Where—

(i) the amount of tax estimated in a notice under subsection (1) is remitted and the return required by Regulation 31 of the Income Tax (Employments) (Consolidated) Regulations 2001 (SI No 559 of 2001) is not submitted, or

(ii) the inspector or other officer has reason to believe that the amount estimated in the notice is less than the amount which the employer was liable to remit, the inspector or other officer may amend the amount so estimated by increasing it and serve notice on the employer concerned of the revised amount estimated and such notice shall supersede any previous notice issued under subsection (1).][3]

(2) Where a notice is served on an employer under subsection (1) [and prior to such service the employer had sent to the Collector-General the return required by [Regulation 31 of the Income Tax (Employments) (Consolidated) Regulations 2001 (SI No 559 of 2001)][4]][5]—

(*a*) the employer may, if claiming that the total amount of tax or the balance of tax remaining unpaid is excessive, on giving notice in writing to the inspector or other officer within the period of 30 days from the service of the notice, appeal to the Appeal Commissioners;

(*b*) on the expiration of that period, if no notice of appeal is received or, if notice of appeal is received, on determination of the appeal by agreement or otherwise, the balance of tax remaining unpaid as specified in the notice or the amended tax as determined in relation to the appeal shall become due and be recoverable in the like manner and by the like proceedings as if the balance of tax or the amended tax had been charged on the employer under Schedule E.

(3) A notice given by the inspector or other officer under subsection (1) may extend to 2 or more years of assessment.

Amendments

1 Substituted by FA 2002 s 138 and Sch 6 paras 3(*r*)(i) and 6(*c*)(i) with effect from 1 January 2002; previously "Regulation 35 of the Income Tax (Employments) Regulations, 1960 (SI No 28 of 1960)".

2 Subs (1A) inserted by FA 2001 s 237(*a*)(i) with effect from 6 April 2001.

3 Subs (1A)(*d*) inserted by FA 2003 s 157(*b*) with effect from 28 March 2003.

4 Substituted by FA 2002 s 138 and Sch 6 paras 3(*r*)(ii) and 6(*c*)(i) with effect from 1 January 2002; previously "Regulation 35 of the Income Tax (Employment) Regulations, 1960 (SI No 28 of 1960)".

5 Inserted by FA 2001 s 237(*a*)(ii) with effect from 6 April 2001.

Cross-references

Appeals, subs (2): s 992.

Estimation of tax due for income tax months, meaning of "regulations" applied: s 989(1).

Generation of estimates by electronic, photographic or other process: s 990A.

Interest: s 991(2)(*b*).

PAYE system, recovery of tax: s 993(5)(*b*).

Priority in winding up: s 1000(*c*).

Definitions

Appeal Commissioners: s 2(1); Collector-General: ss 2(1), 851; employer: s 983; inspector: ss 2(1), 5(1), 852; writing: IA 1937 Sch; year of assessment: ss 2(1), 5(1).

Former enactments

FA 1968 s 8(1), (2) and (4); FA 1985 s 9(*b*).

990A Generation of estimates by electronic, photographic or other process

[For the purposes of this Chapter—

(*a*) where the inspector, any officer of the Revenue Commissioners nominated by them for the purposes of section 989 or 990 (in this section referred to as "the nominated officer") or any other officer of the Revenue Commissioners acting with the knowledge of the inspector or the nominated officer causes, for the purposes of section 989 or 990, to be issued, manually or by any electronic, photographic or other process, and to be served, a notice bearing the name of the inspector or the nominated officer, the estimate to which that notice relates shall be deemed—

(i) if that notice was issued for the purposes of section 989, to have been made by the nominated officer, and

(ii) if that notice was issued for the purposes of section 990, to have been made by the inspector or the nominated officer, as the case may be, to the best of his or her opinion,

and

(*b*) the provisions of section 928 shall, subject to any necessary modifications, apply in relation to estimates made in accordance with the provisions of section 990 as they apply in relation to assessments to income tax.][1]

Amendments

1 Section 990A inserted by FA 1999 s 24 with effect from 6 April 1999.

Definitions

inspector: ss 2(1), 5(1), 852.

991 Interest

[(1) Where any amount of tax which an employer is liable under this Chapter and any regulations under this Chapter to pay to the Revenue Commissioners is not so paid, simple interest on the amount shall be paid by the employer to the Revenue Commissioners, and such interest shall be calculated from the expiration of the period specified in the regulations for the payment of the amount and at the rate of 0.0322 per cent for each day or part of a day on which the amount remains unpaid.][1]

[(1A) Notwithstanding anything in subsection (1) but subject to subsection (1B), where an amount of tax (in this subsection referred to as **"the relevant amount"**) in respect of a year of assessment (being the year of assessment 2000–2001 or a subsequent year of assessment) is paid later than 14 days after the end of that year of assessment, interest in accordance with subsection (1) shall be payable and calculated—

(*a*) where the relevant amount does not exceed 10 per cent of the total amount of tax which the employer was liable under this Chapter and any regulations made under this Chapter to pay to the Revenue Commissioners for that year of assessment, as if the due date for payment of the relevant amount was the 14th day immediately following the end of the year of assessment, and

(*b*) where the relevant amount exceeds 10 per cent of the amount so payable, as if the due date for payment of the relevant amount was—

(i) as respects the year of assessment 2000–2001, 31 October, 2000,

(ii) as respects the year of assessment 2001, 30 September, 2001, and

(iii) as respects the year of assessment 2002 and subsequent years of assessment, 31 July in the year.

(1B) Where, within 1 month of interest being demanded by the Collector-General in accordance with subsection (1A), the employer declares in writing to the Collector-General the amounts of tax which he or she was liable to remit, but had not remitted, for each of the income tax months comprised in the year of assessment, interest shall be calculated and payable in respect of those amounts in accordance with subsection (1), without regard to subsection (1A).][2]

(2) This section shall apply—

(*a*) to tax recoverable by virtue of a notice under section 989 as if the tax were tax which the person was liable under the regulations to pay for the respective income tax month or months referred to in the notice, and

(*b*) to tax recoverable by virtue of a notice under section 990 as if the tax were tax which the person was liable under the regulations to remit for the last income tax month of the year of assessment to which the notice relates.

Amendments

1 Subs (1) substituted by FA 2002 s 129(1)(*e*) with effect from 1 September 2002 as regards interest chargeable in respect of an amount due to be paid or remitted, whether before, on, or after that date.

2 Subss (1A)–(1B) inserted by FA 2001 s 237(*b*) with effect from 6 April 2001.

Cross-references

Estimation of tax due for income tax months, meaning of "regulations" applied: s 989(1).
Priority in bankruptcy: s 994(1).
Priority in winding up: s 995(*a*)(iii).

Definitions

Collector-General: ss 2(1), 851; employer: s 983; income tax month: s 983; month: IA 1937 Sch; person: IA 1937 s 11(*c*); writing: IA 1937 Sch; year of assessment: s 2(1).

Former enactments

ITA 1967 s 129; FA 1968 s 9; FA 1973 s 1(1); FA 1974 s 71; FA 1975 s 26; FA 1978 s 46.

991A Payment of tax by direct debit

[Where, for a year of assessment (being the year of assessment 2000–2001 or a subsequent year of assessment)—

(*a*) an employer has been authorised by the Collector-General in accordance with [Regulation 29 of the Income Tax (Employments) (Consolidated) Regulations 2001 (SI No 559 of 2001)][1], to remit income tax for a period longer than an income tax month, and

(*b*) such authorisation is subject to the condition that the employer is required each month to pay an amount to the Collector-General by direct debit from the employer's bank account,

then, the provisions of section 991 shall apply to any tax in respect of that year of assessment which is paid by the employer after the end of that year.][2]

Amendments

1 Substituted by FA 2002 s 138 and Sch 6 paras 3(*s*) and 6(*c*)(i) with effect from 1 January 2002; previously "Regulation 31A (inserted by the Income Tax (Employments) Regulations, 1989 (SI No 58 of 1989)) of the Income Tax (Employments) Regulations, 1960 (SI No 28 of 1960)".

2 Section 991A substituted by FA 2001 s 237(*c*) with effect from 6 April 2001.

Definitions

Collector-General: ss 2(1), 851; employer: s 983; income tax month: s 983; month: IA 1937 Sch; year of assessment: s 2(1).

992 Appeals against estimates under section 989 or 990

The provisions of the Income Tax Acts relating to appeals shall apply with any necessary modifications to claims and appeals under sections 989(3) and 990(2) as if those claims or appeals were appeals against assessments to income tax but, in relation to claims under section 989(3), only in so far as those provisions apply to appeals to the Appeal Commissioners.

Definitions

Appeal Commissioners: s 2(1); Income Tax Acts: s 1(2).

Former enactments

FA 1968 s 10.

993 Recovery of tax

(1) (*a*) The provisions of any enactment relating to the recovery of income tax charged under Schedule E shall apply to the recovery of any amount of tax which an employer is liable under this Chapter and any regulations under this Chapter to pay to the Revenue Commissioners by reference to any income tax month as if that amount had been charged on the employer under Schedule E.

(*b*) In particular and without prejudice to the generality of paragraph (*a*), this subsection applies sections 962, 963, 966 and 998.

(*c*) Provisions as applied by this subsection shall so apply subject to any modifications specified by regulations under section 986.

(2) Proceedings may be brought for the recovery of the total amount which the employer is liable under this Chapter and any regulations under this Chapter to pay to the Revenue Commissioners by reference to any income tax month without distinguishing the amounts which the employer is liable to pay by reference to each employee and without specifying the employees in question, and for the purposes of the proceedings that total amount shall be one single cause of action or one matter of complaint; but nothing in this subsection shall prevent the bringing of separate proceedings for the recovery of each of the several amounts which the employer is so liable to pay by reference to any income tax month and to the employer's several employees.

(3) In proceedings instituted by virtue of this section for the recovery of any amount of tax—

(*a*) a certificate signed by an officer of the Revenue Commissioners which certifies that a stated amount of tax is due and payable by the defendant shall be evidence until the contrary is proved that that amount is so due and payable, and

(*b*) a certificate so certifying and purporting to be signed by an officer of the Revenue Commissioners may be tendered in evidence without proof and shall be deemed until the contrary is proved to have been signed by an officer of the Revenue Commissioners.

(4) Any reference in this section to an amount of tax shall include a reference to interest payable in the case in question under section 991.

(5) This section shall apply to the recovery of—

(*a*) any amount of tax estimated under section 989, and

(*b*) any amount of tax estimated under section 990 or any balance of tax so estimated but remaining unpaid,

as if the amount so estimated or the balance of tax so estimated but remaining unpaid were an amount of tax which any person paying emoluments was liable under this Chapter and any regulations under this Chapter to pay to the Revenue Commissioners.

Former enactments

ITA 1967 s 131; FA 1973 s 22.

994 Priority in bankruptcy, etc of certain amounts

[(1) In this section **"employer's liability for the period of 12 months"** means the aggregate of—

(*a*) all sums which an employer was liable under this Chapter and any regulations under this Chapter to deduct from emoluments to which this Chapter applies paid by the employer, and

(*b*) all sums that were not so deducted but which an employer was liable, in accordance with section 985A and any regulations under that section, to remit to the Collector-General in respect of notional payments made by the employer,

during the period of 12 months referred to in subsection (2), reduced by any amounts which the employer was liable under this Chapter and any regulations under this Chapter to repay during the same period, and subject to the addition of interest payable under section 991.][1]

(2) There shall be included among the debts which under section 81 of the Bankruptcy Act, 1988, are to be paid in priority to all other debts in the distribution of the property of a bankrupt, arranging debtor or person dying insolvent so much as is unpaid of the employer's liability for the period of 12 months before the date on which the order of adjudication of the bankrupt was made, the petition of arrangement of the debtor was filed or, as the case may be, the person died insolvent.

Amendments

1 Subs (1) substituted by FA 2004 s 9(1)(*c*) with effect from 25 March 2004.

Cross-references

Priority in winding up, subs (1): s 1000.

Definitions

Collector-General: s 2(1); emoluments, employee, employer: s 983.

Former enactments

ITA 1967 s 132.

995 Priority in winding up of certain amounts

For the purposes of subsection (2)(*a*)(iii) of section 285 of the Companies Act, 1963—

(*a*) the amount referred to in that subsection shall be deemed to include any amount—

[(i) which, apart from Regulation 29 of the Income Tax (Employments) (Consolidated) Regulations 2001 (SI No 559 of 2001), would otherwise have been an amount due at the relevant date in respect of—

(I) sums which an employer is liable under this Chapter and any regulations under this Chapter (other than Regulation 29 of those Regulations) to deduct from emoluments, to which this Chapter applies, paid by the employer, and

(II) sums that were not so deducted but which the employer was liable, in accordance with section 985A and any regulations under that section, to remit to the Collector-General in respect of notional payments made by the employer,

during the period of 12 months next before the relevant date,][1]

(ii) reduced by any amount which the employer was liable under this Chapter and any regulation under this Chapter to repay during that period, and

(iii) with the addition of any interest payable under section 991,

and

(*b*) the relevant date shall, notwithstanding subsection (1) of section 285 of the Companies Act, 1963, be deemed to be the date which is the ninth day after the end of the income tax month in which the relevant date (within the meaning of that subsection) occurred.

Amendments

1 Para (*a*)(i) substituted by FA 2004 s 9(1)(*d*) with effect from 25 March 2004.

Definitions

Collector-General: s 2(1); emoluments, employer, income tax month: s 983.

Former enactments

FA 1989 s 10.

996 Treatment for tax purposes of certain unpaid remuneration

(1) In this section—

"accounting period", in relation to a trade or profession, means a period of 12 months ending on the date up to which the accounts of the trade or profession are usually made up and, where accounts of the trade or profession have not been made up, such period not exceeding 12 months as the Revenue Commissioners may determine;

"date of cessation", in relation to an office or employment, means the date on which a person ceases to hold the office or employment;

"date of commencement", in relation to an office or employment, means the date on which a person commences to hold the office or employment;

"period of account", in relation to a trade or profession, means any period, other than an accounting period, for which the accounts of the trade or profession have been made up;

"period of accrual", in relation to remuneration in respect of an office or employment in a trade or profession, means the period beginning on the later of—

(*a*) the first day of an accounting period, or period of account, of the trade or profession, or

(*b*) the date of commencement of the office or employment,

and ending on the earlier of—

(i) the last day of an accounting period, or period of account, or

(ii) the date of cessation of the office or employment;

"relevant date" means—

(*a*) in relation to an accounting period, the last day of the period, and

(*b*) in relation to a period of account—

(i) where the period of account is less than 12 months, the last day of the period, and

(ii) where the period of account is more than 12 months, each [31st day of December][1] within the period and the last day of the period;

"remuneration" includes all salaries, fees, wages, perquisites or profits whatever from an office or employment.

(2) Where remuneration (in this section referred to as **"unpaid remuneration"**) which is deductible as an expense in computing the profits or income of a trade or profession for an accounting period or period of account for the purposes of Schedule D is unpaid at a relevant date—

(*a*) the unpaid remuneration shall be deemed to be emoluments to which this Chapter applies and shall be deemed to have been paid in accordance with subsection (3), and

(*b*) this Chapter and the regulations made under this Chapter shall, with any necessary modifications, apply to the unpaid remuneration as if it had been so paid.

(3) Unpaid remuneration shall be deemed to have accrued from day to day throughout the period of accrual and there shall be deemed to have been paid on each relevant date so much of that remuneration as accrued up to that date or, if it is earlier, the date of cessation of the office or employment in respect of which the unpaid remuneration is payable—

(*a*) where there was no preceding relevant date, from the beginning of the period of accrual or, if it is later, the date of commencement of the office or employment in respect of which the unpaid remuneration is payable, and

(*b*) where there was a preceding relevant date, from the day following that date or, if it is later, the date of commencement of the office or employment in respect of which the unpaid remuneration is payable.

(4) This section shall not apply to unpaid remuneration paid before—

(*a*) the date of expiry of 6 months after the date (in this subsection referred to as **"the deemed date"**) on which that remuneration is by virtue of subsection (3) deemed to have been paid, or (*b*) in the case where the period of account is one of more than 12 months, the date of expiry of 18 months from the first day of that period of account if the date of expiry is later than the deemed date.

Amendments

1 Substituted by FA 2001 s 77(2) and Sch 2 para 54 with effect from 6 April 2001; previously "the 5th day of April".

Definitions

person: IA 1937 s 11(*c*); profession: ss 2(1), 5(1); trade: ss 3(1), 4(1), 5(1).

Former enactments

FA 1976 s 17(1)–(3)(*a*) and (4)(*b*).

997 Supplementary provisions (Chapter 4)

(1) No assessment under Schedule E for any year of assessment need be made in respect of emoluments to which this Chapter applies except where—

(*a*) the person assessable, by notice in writing given to the inspector ...[1], requires an assessment to be made,

(*b*) the emoluments paid in the year of assessment are not the same in amount as the emoluments which are to be treated as the emoluments for that year, or

(*c*) there is reason to suppose that the emoluments would, if assessed, be taken into account in computing the total income of a person who is liable to tax at the higher rate or would be so liable if an assessment were made in respect of the emoluments;

but where any such assessment is made credit shall be given for the amount of any tax deducted ...[2] from the emoluments.

[(1A) Notwithstanding subsection (1), an assessment under Schedule E in respect of emoluments to which this Chapter applies shall not be made for any year of assessment—

(*a*) where paragraph (*a*) of that subsection applies, unless the person assessable has requested the assessment—

(i) in the case of any year of assessment prior to the year of assessment 2003, within 5 years, and

(ii) in the case of the year of assessment 2003 or any subsequent year of assessment, within 4 years,

from the end of the year of assessment concerned, and

(*b*) where paragraph (*b*) or (*c*) of that subsection applies, at any time later than 4 years from the end of the year of assessment concerned.][3]

(2) Where an employer pays to the Revenue Commissioners any amount of tax which, pursuant to this Chapter and any regulations under this Chapter, the employer has deducted from emoluments, the employer shall be acquitted and discharged of the sum represented by the payment as if the employer had actually paid that sum to the employee.

[(3) Where the inspector, in accordance with the provisions of Regulation 37 of the Income Tax (Employments) (Consolidated) Regulations 2001 (S. I. No 559 of 2001) sends a statement of liability to an employee, that statement shall, if the inspector so directs and gives notice accordingly in or with the statement sent to the employee, be treated in all respects as if it were an assessment raised on the employee, and all the provisions of the Income Tax Acts relating to appeals against assessments and the collection and recovery of tax charged in an assessment shall accordingly apply to the statement.][4]

Amendments

1 Deleted by FA 2003 s 17(1)(*i*)(*a*)(i)(I) with effect from: (*a*) such day or days as the Minister for Finance may by order or orders appoint either generally or with reference to any particular purpose or provision and different days may be so appointed for different purposes or different provisions and (*b*) notwithstanding the generality of (*a*), any order made by the Minister for Finance in accordance with the provisions of that paragraph may contain, and be subject to, such conditions as the Minister considers appropriate and which are specified in the order; previously "within 5 years from the end of the year of assessment". By virtue of Finance Act 2003 (Commencement of Section 17) Order 2003, SI No 508 of 2003, this amendment comes into operation on 1 January 2005 in relation to the making of assessments referred to in section 997.

2 Deleted by FA 2003 s 17(1)(*i*)(*a*)(i)(II) with effect from: (*a*) such day or days as the Minister for Finance may by order or orders appoint either generally or with reference to any particular purpose or provision and different days may be so appointed for different purposes or different provisions and (*b*) notwithstanding the generality of (*a*), any order made by the Minister for Finance in accordance with the provisions of that paragraph may contain, and be subject to, such conditions as the Minister considers appropriate and which are specified in the order; previously "or estimated to be deductible". By virtue of Finance Act 2003 (Commencement of Section 17) Order 2003, SI No 508 of 2003, this amendment comes into operation on 31 October 2003 in relation to the making of assessments referred to in section 997.

3 Subs (1A) inserted by FA 2003 s 17(1)(*i*)(*b*) with effect from: (*a*) such day or days as the Minister for Finance may by order or orders appoint either generally or with reference to any particular purpose or provision and different days may be so appointed for different purposes or different provisions and (*b*) notwithstanding the generality of (*a*), any order made by the Minister for Finance in accordance with the provisions of that paragraph may contain, and be subject to, such conditions as the Minister considers appropriate and which are specified in the order. By virtue of Finance Act 2003 (Commencement of Section 17) Order 2003, SI No 508 of 2003, this amendment comes into operation in relation to the making, on or after 1 January 2005, of assessments referred to in section 997.

4 Subs (3) inserted by FA 2005 s 26 with effect from 25 March 2005.

Case law

Subs (1): A director of a private company was not taxed on certain remuneration payments made to him before the end of an accounting period. While PAYE was accounted for on the full sum in the following year an assessment for the statutory undercharge arising for the earlier year was upheld: *Bedford v Hannon* (High Court, 30 May 1968) TL 105.

Definitions

higher rate: ss 3(1), 15; Income Tax Acts: s 1(2); inspector: ss 2(1), 5(1), 852; total income: s 3(1); writing: IA 1937 Sch; year of assessment: s 3(1).

Former enactments

ITA 1967 s 133; FA 1974 s 11 and Sch 1 Pt II; FA 1993 Sch 1 Pt I para 2.

997A Credit in respect of tax deducted from emoluments of certain directors

[(1) (*a*) In this section—

"control" has the same meaning as in section 432;

"ordinary share capital", in relation to a company, means all the issued share capital (by whatever name called) of the company.

(*b*) For the purposes of this section—

(i) a person shall have a material interest in a company if the person, either on the person's own or with any one or more connected persons, or if any person connected with the person with or without any such other connected persons, is the beneficial owner of, or is able, directly or through the medium of other companies or by any other indirect means, to control, more than 15 per cent of the ordinary share capital of the company, and

(ii) the question of whether a person is connected with another person shall be determined in accordance with section 10.

(2) This section applies to a person to who, in relation to a company (hereafter in this section referred to as "the company"), has a material interest in the company.

(3) Notwithstanding any other provision of the Income Tax Acts or the regulations made under this Chapter, no credit for tax deducted from the emoluments paid by the company to a person to whom this section applies shall be given in any assessment raised on the person or in any statement of liability sent to the person under Regulation 37 of the Income Tax (Employments) (Consolidated) Regulations 2001 (SI No 559 of 2001) unless there is documentary evidence to show that the tax deducted has been remitted by the company to the Collector-General in accordance with the provisions of those regulations.

(4) Where the company remits tax to the Collector-General which has been deducted from emoluments paid by the company, the tax remitted shall be treated as having been deducted from emoluments paid to persons other than persons to whom this section applies in priority to tax deducted from persons to whom this section applies.

(5) Where, in accordance with subsection (4), tax remitted to the Collector-General by the company is to be treated as having been deducted from emoluments paid by the company to persons to whom this section applies, the tax to be so treated shall, if there is more than one such person, be treated as having been deducted from the emoluments paid to each such person in the same proportion as the emoluments paid to the person bears to the aggregate amount of emoluments paid by the company to all such persons.][1]

Amendments

1 Section 997A inserted by FA 2005 s 13 for 2005 and subsequent years of assessment.

Definitions

Collector-General: ss 2(1), 851; company: s 4(1); Income Tax Acts: s 1(2); person: IA 1937 s 11(*c*).

CHAPTER 5

Miscellaneous Provisions

Cross-references

Health Contributions Act 1979, s 10(3)(*a*)(i), power to make regulations and to recover health contributions.
National Training Fund Act 2000, s 5(6), collection of levy.
Social Welfare (Consolidation) Act 1993 s 14(4) (inserted by Social Welfare (Miscellaneous Provisions) Act 2002 s 14(*a*)) — payment of contributions and keeping of record — and s 20(3) (inserted by Social Welfare (Miscellaneous Provisions) Act 2002 s 14(*b*)) — regulations for collection of self-employment contributions.

998 Recovery of moneys due

(1) Every sum due in respect of income tax, corporation tax and capital gains tax and every fine, penalty or forfeiture incurred in connection with any of those taxes shall be deemed to be a debt due to the Minister for Finance for the benefit of the Central Fund, and shall be payable to the Revenue Commissioners and may (without prejudice to any

other mode of recovery of such sum, fine, penalty or forfeiture) be sued for and recovered by action, or other appropriate proceedings, at the suit of the Attorney General in any court of competent jurisdiction.

(2) Moneys so due or payable to or for the benefit of the Central Fund shall have attached to them all such rights, privileges and priorities as have heretofore attached to such moneys, but this subsection shall not operate to make such moneys payable in priority to other debts.

Cross-references

PAYE system, recovery of tax: s 993(1)(*b*).

Value added tax, this section applied by: VATA 1972 s 24(1)(*b*) and VATR 1979 r 15(6) but construe the words "income tax" as referring to value added tax.

Former enactments

ITA 1967 s 491; FA 1974 s 86 and Sch 2 Pt I; CTA 1976 s 147(1)–(2); CGTA 1975 s 51(1) and Sch 4 para 2.

999 Taking by Collector-General of proceedings in bankruptcy

(1) The Collector-General may sue out a debtor's summons and present a petition in bankruptcy in his or her own name in respect of taxes or duties due to the Minister for Finance for the benefit of the Central Fund, being taxes or duties which the Collector-General is empowered to collect and levy.

(2) Subject to this section, the rules of court for the time being applicable and the enactments relating to bankruptcy shall apply to proceedings taken by the Collector-General by virtue of this section.

Former enactments

F(MP)A 1968 s 27; CGTA 1975 s 51(1) and Sch 4 para 2.

1000 Priority in bankruptcy, winding up, etc for sums recovered or deducted under section 531, 989 or 990

For the purposes of section 285 of the Companies Act, 1963, and of section 994, the sums referred to in section 285(2)(*a*)(iii) of the Companies Act, 1963, and in section 994(1) shall be deemed to include—

(*a*) amounts of tax deducted under section 531(1) and amounts of tax recoverable under regulation 12 of the Income Tax (Construction Contracts) Regulations, 1971 (SI No 1 of 1971),

(*b*) amounts of tax recoverable under section 989, and

(*c*) amounts of tax recoverable under section 990,

which relate to a period or periods falling in whole or in part within the period of 12 months referred to in section 285(2)(*a*)(iii) of the Companies Act, 1963, or in section 994(1), as may be appropriate, and in the case of any such amount for a period falling partly within and partly outside whichever of those periods of 12 months is appropriate, it shall be lawful to apportion the total sum or amount according to the respective lengths of the periods falling within the period of 12 months and outside the period of 12 months in order to determine the amount of tax which relates to the period of 12 months.

Definitions

month: IA 1937 Sch.

Former enactments

FA 1968 s 11; FA 1976 s 14.

1001 Liability to tax, etc of holder of fixed charge on book debts of company

(1) In this section, **"relevant amount"** means any amount which the company is liable to remit under—

(*a*) Chapter 4 of this Part, and

(*b*) the Value-Added Tax Act, 1972.

(2) Subject to this section, where a person holds a fixed charge (being a fixed charge created on or after the 27th day of May, 1986) on the book debts of a company (within the meaning of the Companies Act, 1963), such person shall, if the company fails to pay any relevant amount for which it is liable, become liable to pay such relevant amount on due demand, and on neglect or refusal of payment may be proceeded against in the like manner as any other defaulter.

(3) This section shall not apply—

(*a*) unless the holder of the fixed charge has been notified in writing by the Revenue Commissioners that a company has failed to pay a relevant amount for which it is liable and that by virtue of this section the holder of the fixed charge—

(i) may become liable for payment of any relevant amount which the company subsequently fails to pay, and

(ii) where paragraph (*c*) does not apply, has become liable for the payment of the relevant amount which the company has failed to pay,

(*b*) to any amounts received by the holder of the fixed charge from the company before the date on which the holder is notified in writing by the Revenue Commissioners in accordance with paragraph (*a*), and

(*c*) where, within the period from the 2nd day of June, 1995, to the 22nd day of June, 1995, or within 21 days of the creation of the fixed charge, whichever is the later, the holder of the fixed charge furnishes to the Revenue Commissioners a copy of the prescribed particulars of the charge delivered or to be delivered to the registrar of companies in accordance with section 99 of the Companies Act, 1963, to any relevant amount which the company was liable to pay before the date on which the holder is notified in writing by the Revenue Commissioners in accordance with paragraph (*a*).

(4) The amount or aggregate amount which a person shall be liable to pay in relation to a company in accordance with this section shall not exceed the amount or aggregate amount which the person has, while the fixed charge on book debts in relation to the company is in existence, received directly or indirectly from that company in payment or in part payment of any debts due by the company to the person.

(5) The Revenue Commissioners may, at any time and by notice in writing given to the holder of the fixed charge, withdraw with effect from a date specified in the notice a

notification issued by them in accordance with subsection (3); but such withdrawal shall not—

(*a*) affect in any way any liability of the holder of the fixed charge under this section which arose before such withdrawal, or

(*b*) preclude the issue under subsection (3) of a subsequent notice to the holder of the fixed charge.

(6) The Revenue Commissioners may nominate any of their officers to perform any acts and discharge any functions authorised by this section to be performed or discharged by the Revenue Commissioners.

Cross-references

This section to be construed together with the Value Added Tax Acts 1972–1997, in so far as relating to value added tax: s 1104(3).

Definitions

company: ss 4(1), 5(1); person: IA 1937 s 11(*c*); writing: IA 1937 Sch.

Former enactments

FA 1986 s 115; FA 1995 s 174.

1002 Deduction from payments due to defaulters of amounts due in relation to tax

(1) (*a*) In this section, except where the context otherwise requires—

"the Acts" means—

(i) the Customs Acts,

(ii) the statutes relating to the duties of excise and to the management of those duties,

(iii) the Tax Acts,

(iv) the Capital Gains Tax Acts,

(v) the Value-Added Tax Act, 1972, and the enactments amending or extending that Act,

(vi) the [Capital Acquisitions Tax Consolidation Act 2003],[1] and the enactments amending or extending that Act, and

(vii) the [Stamp Duties Consolidation Act, 1999],[2] and the enactments amending or extending that Act,

and any instruments made thereunder;

"additional debt", in relation to a relevant person who has received a notice of attachment in respect of a taxpayer, means any amount which, at any time after the time of the receipt by the relevant person of the notice of attachment but before the end of the relevant period in relation to the notice, would be a debt due by the relevant person to the taxpayer if a notice of attachment were received by the relevant person at that time;

"debt", in relation to a notice of attachment given to a relevant person in respect of a taxpayer and in relation to that relevant person and taxpayer, means, subject to paragraphs (*b*) to (*e*), the amount or aggregate amount of any money which, at the time the notice of attachment is received by the relevant person, is due by the relevant person (whether on that person's own account or as an agent or trustee) to the taxpayer, irrespective of whether the taxpayer has applied for the payment (to the taxpayer or any other person) or for the withdrawal of all or part of the money;

"deposit" means a sum of money paid to a financial institution on terms under which it will be repaid with or without interest and either on demand or at a time or in circumstances agreed by or on behalf of the person making the payment and the financial institution to which it is made;

"emoluments" means anything assessable to income tax under Schedule E;

"financial institution" means a holder of a licence issued under section 9 of the Central Bank Act, 1971, or a person referred to in section 7(4) of that Act, and includes a branch of a financial institution which records deposits in its books as liabilities of the branch;

"further return" means a return made by a relevant person under subsection (4);

"interest on unpaid tax", in relation to a specified amount specified in a notice of attachment, means interest that has accrued to the date on which the notice of attachment is given under any provision of the Acts providing for the charging of interest in respect of the unpaid tax, including interest on an undercharge of tax which is attributable to fraud or neglect, specified in the notice of attachment;

"notice of attachment" means a notice under subsection (2);

"notice of revocation" means a notice under subsection (10);

"penalty" means a monetary penalty imposed on a taxpayer under a provision of the Acts;

"relevant period", in relation to a notice of attachment, means, as respects the relevant person to whom the notice of attachment is given, the period commencing at the time at which the notice is received by the relevant person and ending on the earliest of—

(i) the date on which the relevant person completes the payment to the Revenue Commissioners out of the debt, or the aggregate of the debt and any additional debt, due by the relevant person to the taxpayer named in the notice, of an amount equal to the specified amount in relation to the taxpayer,

(ii) the date on which the relevant person receives a notice of revocation of the notice of attachment, and

(iii) where the relevant person or the taxpayer named in the notice—

(I) is declared bankrupt, the date the relevant person or the taxpayer is so declared, or

(II) is a company which commences to be wound up, the relevant date within the meaning of section 285 of the Companies Act, 1963, in relation to the winding up;

"relevant person", in relation to a taxpayer, means a person whom the Revenue Commissioners have reason to believe may have, at the time a notice of attachment is received by such person in respect of a taxpayer, a debt due to the taxpayer;

"return" means a return made by a relevant person under subsection (2)(*a*)(iii);

"specified amount" has the meaning assigned to it by subsection (2)(*a*)(ii);

"tax" means any tax, duty, levy or charge which in accordance with any provision of the Acts is placed under the care and management of the Revenue Commissioners;

"taxpayer" means a person who is liable to pay, remit or account for tax to the Revenue Commissioners under the Acts.

(*b*) Where a relevant person is a financial institution, any amount or aggregate amount of money, including interest on that money, which at the time the notice of attachment is received by the relevant person is a deposit held by the relevant person—

(i) to the credit of the taxpayer for the taxpayer's sole benefit, or

(ii) to the credit of the taxpayer and any other person or persons for their joint benefit,

shall be regarded as a debt due by the relevant person to the taxpayer at that time.

(*c*) Any amount of money due by the relevant person to the taxpayer as emoluments under a contract of service shall not be regarded as a debt due to the taxpayer.

(*d*) Where there is a dispute as to an amount of money which is due by the relevant person to the taxpayer, the amount in dispute shall be disregarded for the purposes of determining the amount of the debt.

(*e*) In the case referred to in paragraph (*b*), a deposit held by a relevant person which is a financial institution to the credit of the taxpayer and any other person or persons (in this paragraph referred to as **"the other party or parties"**) for their joint benefit shall be deemed (unless evidence to the contrary is produced to the satisfaction of the relevant person within 10 days of the giving of the notices specified in subsection (2)(*e*)) to be held to the benefit of the taxpayer and the other party or parties to the deposit equally, and accordingly only the portion of the deposit so deemed shall be regarded as a debt due by the relevant person to the taxpayer at the time the notice of attachment is received by the relevant person and, where such evidence is produced within the specified time, only so much of the deposit as is shown to be held to the benefit of the taxpayer shall be regarded as a debt due by the relevant person to the taxpayer at that time.

(2) (*a*) Subject to subsection (3), where a taxpayer has made default whether before or after the passing of this Act in paying, remitting or accounting for any tax, interest on unpaid tax, or penalty to the Revenue Commissioners, the Revenue Commissioners may, if the taxpayer has not made good the default, give to a relevant person in relation to the taxpayer a notice in writing (in this section referred to as **"the notice of attachment"**) in which is entered—

(i) the taxpayer's name and address,

(ii) (I) the amount or aggregate amount, or

(II) in a case where more than one notice of attachment is given to a relevant person or relevant persons in respect of a taxpayer, a portion of the amount or aggregate amount,

of the taxes, interest on unpaid taxes and penalties in respect of which the taxpayer is in default at the time of the giving of the notice or notices of attachment (the amount, aggregate amount, or portion of the amount or aggregate amount, as the case may be, being referred to in this section as **"the specified amount"**), and

(iii) a direction to the relevant person—

(I) subject to paragraphs (*b*) and (*c*), to deliver to the Revenue Commissioners, within the period of 10 days from the time at which the notice of attachment is received by the relevant person, a return in writing specifying whether or not any debt is due by the relevant person to the taxpayer at the time the notice is received by the relevant person and, if any debt is so due, specifying the amount of the debt, and

(II) if the amount of any debt is so specified, to pay to the Revenue Commissioners within the period referred to in clause (I) a sum equal to the amount of the debt so specified.

(*b*) Where the amount of the debt due by the relevant person to the taxpayer is equal to or greater than the specified amount in relation to the taxpayer, the amount of the debt specified in the return shall be an amount equal to the specified amount.

(*c*) Where the relevant person is a financial institution and the debt due by the relevant person to the taxpayer is part of a deposit held to the credit of the taxpayer and any other person or persons to their joint benefit, the return shall be made within a period of 10 days from—

(i) the expiry of the period specified in the notices to be given under paragraph (*e*), or

(ii) the production of the evidence referred to in paragraph (*e*)(II).

(*d*) A relevant person to whom a notice of attachment has been given shall comply with the direction in the notice.

(*e*) Where a relevant person which is a financial institution is given a notice of attachment and the debt due by the relevant person to the taxpayer is part of a deposit held by the relevant person to the credit of the taxpayer and any other person or persons (in this paragraph referred to as **"the other party or parties"**) for their joint benefit, the relevant person shall on receipt of the notice of attachment give to the taxpayer and the other party or parties to the deposit a notice in writing in which is entered—

(i) the taxpayer's name and address,

(ii) the name and address of the person to whom a notice under this paragraph is given,

(iii) the name and address of the relevant person, and

(iv) the specified amount,

and which states that—

(I) a notice of attachment under this section has been received in respect of the taxpayer,

(II) under this section a deposit is deemed (unless evidence to the contrary is produced to the satisfaction of the relevant person within 10 days of the giving of the notice under this paragraph) to be held to the benefit of the taxpayer and the other party or parties to the deposit equally, and

(III) unless such evidence is produced within the period specified in the notice given under this paragraph—

(A) a sum equal to the amount of the deposit so deemed to be held to the benefit of the taxpayer (and accordingly regarded as a debt due to the taxpayer by the relevant person) shall be paid to the Revenue Commissioners, where that amount is equal to or less than the specified amount, and

(B) where the amount of the deposit so deemed to be held to the benefit of the taxpayer (and accordingly regarded as a debt due to the taxpayer by the relevant person) is greater than the specified amount, a sum equal to the specified amount shall be paid to the Revenue Commissioners.

(3) An amount in respect of tax, interest on unpaid tax or a penalty, as respects which a taxpayer is in default as specified in subsection (2), shall not be entered in a notice of attachment unless—

(*a*) a period of [14 days][3] has expired from the date on which such default commenced, and

(*b*) the Revenue Commissioners have given the taxpayer a notice in writing (whether or not the document containing the notice also contains other information being communicated by the Revenue Commissioners to the taxpayer), not later than 7 days before the date of the receipt by the relevant person or relevant persons concerned of a notice of attachment, stating that if the amount is not paid it may be specified in a notice or notices of attachment and recovered under this section from a relevant person or relevant persons in relation to the taxpayer.

(4) If, when a relevant person receives a notice of attachment, the amount of the debt due by the relevant person to the taxpayer named in the notice is less than the specified amount in relation to the taxpayer or no debt is so due and, at any time after the receipt of the notice and before the end of the relevant period in relation to the notice, an additional debt becomes due by the relevant person to the taxpayer, the relevant person shall within 10 days of that time—

(*a*) if the aggregate of the amount of any debt so due and the additional debt so due is equal to or less than the specified amount in relation to the taxpayer—

(i) deliver a further return to the Revenue Commissioners specifying the additional debt, and

(ii) pay to the Revenue Commissioners the amount of the additional debt, and so on for each subsequent occasion during the relevant period in relation to the notice of attachment on which an additional debt becomes due by the relevant person to the taxpayer until—

(I) the aggregate amount of the debt and the additional debt or debts so due equals the specified amount in relation to the taxpayer, or

(II) paragraph (*b*) applies in relation to an additional debt, and

(*b*) if the aggregate amount of any debt and the additional debt or debts so due to the taxpayer is greater than the specified amount in relation to the taxpayer—

(i) deliver a further return to the Revenue Commissioners specifying such portion of the latest additional debt as when added to the aggregate of the debt and any earlier additional debts is equal to the specified amount in relation to the taxpayer, and

(ii) pay to the Revenue Commissioners that portion of the additional debt.

(5) Where a relevant person delivers, either fraudulently or negligently, an incorrect return or further return that purports to be a return or further return made in accordance with this section, the relevant person shall be deemed to be guilty of an offence under section 1078.

(6) (*a*) Where a notice of attachment has been given to a relevant person in respect of a taxpayer, the relevant person shall not, during the relevant period in relation to the notice, make any disbursements out of the debt, or out of any additional debt, due by the relevant person to the taxpayer except to the extent that any such disbursement—

(i) will not reduce the debt or the aggregate of the debt and any additional debts so due to an amount that is less than the specified amount in relation to the taxpayer, or

(ii) is made pursuant to an order of a court.

(*b*) For the purposes of this section, a disbursement made by a relevant person contrary to paragraph (*a*) shall be deemed not to reduce the amount of the debt or any additional debts due by the relevant person to the taxpayer.

(7) (*a*) Sections 1052 and 1054 shall apply to a failure by a relevant person to deliver a return required by a notice of attachment within the time specified in the notice or to deliver a further return within the time specified in subsection (4) as they apply to a failure to deliver a return referred to in section 1052.

(*b*) A certificate signed by an officer of the Revenue Commissioners which certifies that he or she has examined the relevant records and that it appears from those records that during a specified period a specified return was not received from a relevant person shall be evidence until the contrary is proved that the relevant person did not deliver the return during that period.

(*c*) A certificate certifying as provided by paragraph (*b*) and purporting to be signed by an officer of the Revenue Commissioners may be tendered in evidence without proof and shall be deemed until the contrary is proved to have been so signed.

(8) Where a relevant person to whom a notice of attachment in respect of a taxpayer has been given—

(*a*) delivers the return required to be delivered by that notice but fails to pay to the Revenue Commissioners within the time specified in the notice the amount specified in the return or any part of that amount, or

(*b*) delivers a further return under subsection (4) but fails to pay to the Revenue Commissioners within the time specified in that subsection the amount specified in the further return or any part of that amount,

the amount specified in the return or further return or the part of that amount, as the case may be, which the relevant person has failed to pay to the Revenue Commissioners may, if the notice of attachment has not been revoked by a notice of revocation, be sued for and recovered by action or other appropriate proceedings at the suit of an officer of the Revenue Commissioners in any court of competent jurisdiction.

(9) Nothing in this section shall be construed as rendering any failure by a relevant person to make a return or further return required by this section, or to pay to the Revenue Commissioners the amount or amounts required by this section to be paid by the relevant person, liable to be treated as a failure to which section 1078 applies.

(10)(*a*) A notice of attachment given to a relevant person in respect of a taxpayer may be revoked by the Revenue Commissioners at any time by notice in writing given to the relevant person and shall be revoked forthwith if the taxpayer has paid the specified amount to the Revenue Commissioners.

(*b*) Where in pursuance of this section a relevant person pays any amount to the Revenue Commissioners out of a debt or an additional debt due by the relevant person to the taxpayer and, at the time of the receipt by the Revenue Commissioners of that amount, the taxpayer has paid to the Revenue Commissioners the amount or aggregate amount of the taxes, interest on unpaid taxes and penalties in respect of which the taxpayer is in default at the time of the giving of the notice or notices of attachment, the first-mentioned amount shall be refunded by the Revenue Commissioners forthwith to the taxpayer.

(11) Where a notice of attachment or a notice of revocation is given to a relevant person in relation to a taxpayer, a copy of such notice shall be given by the Revenue Commissioners to the taxpayer forthwith.

(12)(*a*) Where in pursuance of this section any amount is paid to the Revenue Commissioners by a relevant person, the relevant person shall forthwith give the taxpayer concerned a notice in writing specifying the payment, its amount and the reason for which it was made.

(*b*) On the receipt by the Revenue Commissioners of an amount paid in pursuance of this section, the Revenue Commissioners shall forthwith notify the taxpayer and the relevant person in writing of such receipt.

(13) Where in pursuance of this section a relevant person pays to the Revenue Commissioners the whole or part of the amount of a debt or an additional debt due by the relevant person to a taxpayer, or any portion of such an amount, the taxpayer shall

allow such payment and the relevant person shall be acquitted and discharged of the amount of the payment as if it had been paid to the taxpayer.

(14) Where in pursuance of this section a relevant person is prohibited from making any disbursement out of a debt or an additional debt due to a taxpayer, no action shall lie against the relevant person in any court by reason of a failure to make any such disbursement.

(15) Any obligation on the Revenue Commissioners to maintain secrecy or any other restriction on the disclosure of information by the Revenue Commissioners shall not apply in relation to information contained in a notice of attachment.

(16) A notice of attachment in respect of a taxpayer shall not be given to a relevant person at a time when the relevant person or the taxpayer is an undischarged bankrupt or a company being wound up.

(17) The Revenue Commissioners may nominate any of their officers to perform any acts and discharge any functions authorised by this section to be performed or discharged by the Revenue Commissioners.

Amendments

1 Substituted by CATCA 2003 s 119 and Sch 3 with effect from 21 February 2003; previously "Capital Acquisitions Tax Act 1976".

2 Substituted by SDCA 1999 s 162 and Sch 4 with effect from 15 December 1999; previously "Stamp Act, 1891".

3 Substituted by FA 2001 s 238 with effect from 6 April 2001; previously "one month".

Cross-references

Taxes (Offset of Repayments) Regulations 2002, SI No 471 of 2002, reg 2(1) (interpretation — "liability at enforcement" para (*c*)).

This section to be construed together with the Customs Acts, in so far as relating to customs: s 1104(2).

This section to be construed together with the Value Added Tax Acts 1972–1997, in so far as relating to value added tax: s 1104(3).

This section to be construed together with the Stamp Act 1891 and the enactments amending or extending that Act, in so far as relating to stamp duties: s 1104(4).

This section to be construed together with the Capital Acquisitions Tax Act 1976, and the enactments amending or extending that Act, in so far as relating to capital acquisitions tax: s 1104(5).

Penalty, subss (2)(*a*)(iii)(I), (*c*), (4)(*a*)(i), (*b*)(i): Sch 29 column 1.

Definitions

company: ss 4(1), 5(1); person: IA 1937 s 11(*c*); Tax Acts: s 1(2); writing: IA 1937 Sch.

Former enactments

FA 1988 s 73(1)(*b*)–(16) and (18); FA 1992 s 241(*a*)–(*d*).

1003 Payment of tax by means of donation of heritage items

(1) (*a*) In this section—

"the Acts" means—

(i) the Tax Acts (other than Chapter 8 of Part 6, Chapter 2 of Part 18 and Chapter 4 of this Part),

(ii) the Capital Gains Tax Acts, and

(iii) the [Capital Acquisitions Tax Consolidation Act 2003],[1] and the enactments amending or extending that Act,

and any instruments made thereunder;

"approved body" means—

(i) the National Archives,

(ii) the National Gallery of Ireland,

(iii) the National Library of Ireland,

(iv) the National Museum of Ireland,

(v) the Irish Museum of Modern Art, or

(vi) in relation to the offer of a gift of a particular item or collection of items, any other such body (being a body owned, or funded wholly or mainly, by the State or by any public or local authority) as may be approved, with the consent of the Minister for Finance, by the Minister for Arts, Heritage, Gaeltacht and the Islands for the purposes of this section;

"arrears of tax" means tax due and payable in accordance with any provision of the Acts (including any interest and penalties payable under any provision of the Acts in relation to such tax)—

(i) in the case of income tax, corporation tax or capital gains tax, in respect of the relevant period, or

(ii) in the case of gift tax or inheritance tax, before the commencement of the calendar year in which the relevant gift is made,

which has not been paid at the time a relevant gift is made;

"current liability" means—

(i) in the case of income tax or capital gains tax, any liability to such tax arising in the year of assessment in which the relevant gift is made,

(ii) in the case of corporation tax, any liability to such tax arising in the accounting period in which the relevant gift is made,

(iii) in the case of gift tax or inheritance tax, any liability to such tax which becomes due and payable in the calendar year in which the relevant gift is made;

"designated officer" means—

(i) the member of the selection committee who represents the appropriate approved body on that committee where the approved body is so represented, or

(ii) in any other case, a person nominated in that behalf by the Minister for Arts, Heritage, Gaeltacht and the Islands;

"heritage item" has the meaning assigned to it by subsection (2)(*a*);

"market value" has the meaning assigned to it by subsection (3);

"relevant gift" means a gift of a heritage item to an approved body in respect of which no consideration whatever (other than relief under this section) is received by the person making the gift, either directly or indirectly, from the approved body or otherwise;

"relevant period" means—

(i) in the case of income tax and capital gains tax, any year of assessment preceding the year in which the relevant gift is made, and

(ii) in the case of corporation tax, any accounting period preceding the accounting period in which the relevant gift is made;

"selection committee" means a committee consisting of—

[(i) an officer of the Minister for Arts, Sports and Tourism, who shall act as Chairperson of the committee,

(ii) the Chief Executive of the Heritage Council,

(iii) the Director of the Arts Council,

(iv) the Director of the National Archives,

(v) the Director of the National Gallery of Ireland,

(vi) the Director of the National Library of Ireland,

(vii) the Director of the National Museum of Ireland, and

(viii) the Director and Chief Executive of the Irish Museum of Modern Art,][2]

and includes any person duly acting in the capacity of any of those persons as a result of the person concerned being unable to fulfil his or her duties for any of the reasons set out in paragraph (*b*)(ii);

"tax" means income tax, corporation tax, capital gains tax, gift tax or inheritance tax, as the case may be, payable in accordance with any provision of the Acts;

"valuation date" means the date on which an application is made to the selection committee for a determination under subsection (2)(*a*).

(*b*) (i) The selection committee may act notwithstanding one or more vacancies among its members and may regulate its own procedure.

(ii) If and so long as a member of the selection committee is unable through illness, absence or other cause to fulfil his or her duties, a person nominated in that behalf by the member shall act as the member of the committee in the place of the member.

[(iii) For the purposes of making a decision in relation to an application made to it for a determination under subsection (2)(*a*), the selection committee shall not include the member of that committee who represents the approved body to which it is intended that the gift of the heritage item is to be made where that approved body is so represented but that member may participate in any discussion of the application by that committee prior to the making of the decision.][3]

(2) (*a*) In this section, **"heritage item"** means any kind of cultural item, including—

(i) any archaeological item, archive, book, estate record, manuscript and painting, and

(ii) any collection of cultural items and any collection of such items in their setting,

which, on application to the selection committee in writing in that behalf by a person who owns the item or collection of items, as the case may be, [is, subject to the provisions of paragraphs (*aa*) and (*ab*), determined by the selection committee][4] to be an item or collection of items which is—

(I) an outstanding example of the type of item involved, pre-eminent in its class, whose export from the State would constitute a diminution of the accumulated cultural heritage of Ireland [or whose import into the State would constitute a significant enhancement of the accumulated cultural heritage of Ireland][5], and

(II) suitable for acquisition by an approved body.

[(*aa*) In considering an application under paragraph (*a*), the selection committee shall—

(i) consider such evidence as the person making the application submits to it, and

(ii) seek and consider the opinion in writing in relation to the application of—

(I) the approved body to which it is intended the gift is to be made, and

(II) the Heritage Council, the Arts Council or such other person or body of persons as the committee considers to be appropriate in the circumstances.

(*ab*) Where an application under paragraph (*a*) is in respect of a collection of items, the selection committee shall not make a determination under that paragraph in relation to the collection unless, in addition to the making of a determination in relation to the collection as a whole, the selection committee is satisfied that, on the basis of its consideration of the application in accordance with paragraph (*aa*), it could make a determination in respect of at least one item comprised in the collection, if such were required.][6]

(*b*) On receipt of an application for a determination under paragraph (*a*), the selection committee shall request the Revenue Commissioners in writing to value the item or collection of items, as the case may be, in accordance with subsection (3).

(*c*) The selection committee shall not make a determination under paragraph (*a*) where the market value of the item or collection of items, as the case may be, as determined by the Revenue Commissioners in accordance with subsection (3), at the valuation date—

[(i) is less than,

(I) subject to clause (II), €150,000, and

(II) in the case of at least one item comprised in a collection of items, €50,000, or][7]

(ii) exceeds an amount (which shall not be less than [€150,000][8]) determined by the formula—

[€6,000,000][9] – M

where M is an amount (which may be nil) equal to the market value at the valuation date of the heritage item (if any) or the aggregate of the market values at the respective valuation dates of all the heritage items (if any), as the case may be, in respect of which a determination or determinations, as the case may be, under this subsection has been made by the selection committee in any one calendar year and not revoked in that year.

(*d*) (i) An item or collection of items shall cease to be a heritage item for the purposes of this section if—

(I) the item or collection of items is sold or otherwise disposed of to a person other than an approved body,

(II) the owner of the item or collection of items notifies the selection committee in writing that it is not intended to make a gift of the item or collection of items to an approved body, or

(III) the gift of the item or collection of items is not made to an approved body within the calendar year following the year in which the determination is made under paragraph (*a*).

(ii) Where the selection committee becomes aware, at any time within the calendar year in which a determination under paragraph (*a*) is made in respect of an item or collection of items, that clause (I) or (II) of subparagraph (i) applies to the item or collection of items, the selection committee may revoke its determination with effect from that time.

(3) (*a*) For the purposes of this section, the market value of any item or collection of items (in this subsection referred to as **"the property"**) [shall, subject to paragraph (*d*), be estimated][10] to be the price which in the opinion of the Revenue Commissioners the property would fetch if sold in the open market on the valuation date in such manner and subject to such conditions as might reasonably be calculated to obtain for the vendor the best price for the property.

(*b*) The market value of the property shall be ascertained by the Revenue Commissioners in such manner and by such means as they think fit, and they may authorise a person to inspect the property and report to them the value of the property for the purposes of this section, and the person having custody or possession of the property shall permit the person so authorised to inspect the property at such reasonable times as the Revenue Commissioners consider necessary.

(*c*) Where the Revenue Commissioners require a valuation to be made by a person authorised by them, the cost of such valuation shall be defrayed by the Revenue Commissioners.

[(*d*) Where the property is acquired at auction by the person making the gift, the market value of the property shall, for the purposes of this section, be deemed to include the auctioneer's fees in connection with the auction together with—

(i) any amount chargeable under the Value-Added Tax Act, 1972, by the auctioneer to the purchaser of the property in respect of those fees and in respect of which the purchaser is not entitled to any deduction or refund under that Act or any other enactment relating to value-added tax, or

(ii) in the case of an auction in a country other than the State, the amount chargeable to the purchaser of the property in respect of a tax chargeable under the law of that country which corresponds to value-added tax in the State and in relation to which the purchaser is not entitled to any deduction or refund.][11]

(4) Where a relevant gift is made to an approved body—

(*a*) the designated officer of that body shall give a certificate to the person who made the relevant gift, in such form as the Revenue Commissioners may prescribe, certifying the receipt of that gift and the transfer of the ownership of the heritage item the subject of that gift to the approved body, and

(*b*) the designated officer shall transmit a duplicate of the certificate to the Revenue Commissioners.

(5) Subject to this section, where a person has made a relevant gift the person shall, on submission to the Revenue Commissioners of the certificate given to the person in accordance with subsection (4), be treated as having made on the date of such submission a payment on account of tax of an amount equal to the market value of the relevant gift on the valuation date.

(6) A payment on account of tax which is treated as having been made in accordance with subsection (5) shall be set in so far as possible against any liability to tax of the person who is treated as having made such a payment in the following order—

(*a*) firstly, against any arrears of tax due for payment by that person and against an arrear of tax for an earlier period in priority to a later period, and for this purpose the date on which an arrear of tax became due for payment shall determine whether it is for an earlier or later period, and

(*b*) only then, against any current liability of the person which the person nominates for that purpose,

and such set-off shall accordingly discharge a corresponding amount of that liability.

(7) To the extent that a payment on account of tax has not been set off in accordance with subsection (6), the balance remaining shall be set off against any future liability to tax of the person who is treated as having made the payment which that person nominates for that purpose.

(8) Where a person has power to sell any heritage item in order to raise money for the payment of gift tax or inheritance tax, such person shall have power to make a relevant gift of that heritage item in or towards satisfaction of that tax and, except as regards the nature of the consideration and its receipt and application, any such relevant gift shall be subject to the same provisions and shall be treated for all purposes as a sale made in exercise of that power, and any conveyances or transfers made or purporting to be made to give effect to such a relevant gift shall apply accordingly.

(9) A person shall not be entitled to any refund of tax in respect of any payment on account of tax made in accordance with this section.

(10) Interest shall not be payable in respect of any overpayment of tax for any period which arises directly or indirectly by reason of the set-off against any liability for that period of a payment on account of tax made in accordance with this section.

(11) Where a person makes a relevant gift and in respect of that gift is treated as having made a payment on account of tax, the person concerned shall not be allowed relief under any other provision of the Acts in respect of that gift.

(12)(*a*) The Revenue Commissioners shall as respects each year compile a list of the titles (if any), descriptions and values of the heritage items (if any) in respect of which relief under this section has been given.

(*b*) Notwithstanding any obligation as to secrecy imposed on them by the Acts or the Official Secrets Act, 1963, the Revenue Commissioners shall include in their annual report to the Minister for Finance the list (if any) referred to in paragraph (*a*) for the year in respect of which the report is made.

Amendments

1 Substituted by CATCA 2003 s 119 and Sch 3 with effect from 21 February 2003; previously "Capital Acquisitions Tax Act 1976".

2 Definition of "selection committee" paras (i)–(vii) substituted by FA 2004 s 85(*a*)(i) as respects determinations made under TCA 1997 s 1003(2)(*a*) on or after 25 March 2004.

3 Subs (1)(*b*)(iii) inserted by FA 2004 s 85(*a*)(ii) as respects determinations made under TCA 1997 s 1003(2)(*a*) on or after 25 March 2004.

4 Substituted by FA 2004 s 85(*b*)(i) as respects determinations made under TCA 1997 s 1003(2)(*a*) on or after 25 March 2004; previously "is determined by the selection committee, after consideration of any evidence in relation to the matter which the person submits to the committee and after such consultation (if any) as may seem appropriate to the committee to be necessary with such person or body of persons as in the opinion of the committee may be of assistance to them,".

5 Inserted by FA 2002 s 124(*a*) with effect from 25 March 2002.

6 Subs (2)(*aa*)–(*ab*) inserted by FA 2004 s 85(*b*)(ii) as respects determinations made under TCA 1997 s 1003(2)(*a*) on or after 25 March 2004.

7 Subs (2)(*c*)(i) substituted by FA 2004 s 85(*b*)(iii)(I) as respects determinations made under TCA 1997 s 1003(2)(*a*) on or after 25 March 2004.

8 Substituted by FA 2004 s 85(*b*)(iii)(II) as respects determinations made under TCA 1997 s 1003(2)(*a*) on or after 25 March 2004; previously "€100,000".

9 Substituted by FA 2002 s 124(*b*)(ii) with effect from 25 March 2002; previously "€3,810,000".

10 Substituted by FA 2002 s 124(*c*) with effect from 25 March 2002; previously "shall be estimated".

11 Subs (3)(*d*) inserted by FA 2002 s 124(*d*) with effect from 25 March 2002.

Revenue information

Information leaflet HET1 — Relief for Donation of Heritage Items.

Tax Briefing

TB20 No 4 of 1995 para 1.6 — Relief for Donation of Heritage Items.

Definitions

person: IA 1937 s 11(*c*); tax: s 3(1); Tax Acts: s 1(2); year of assessment: ss 2(1), 5(1).

Former enactments

FA 1995 s 176; FA 1996 s 139.

1004 Unremittable income

(1) In this section, **"particular income"** means income arising outside the State, the amount of which is or is included in the amount (in this section referred to as **"the relevant amount"**) on which in accordance with the Tax Acts income tax or corporation tax is computed.

(2) Subject to subsections (3) to (5), this section shall apply where income tax or corporation tax is charged by an assessment for any period and the tax has not been paid.

(3) In any case in which, on or after the date on which the income tax or corporation tax has become payable, such proof is given to the Revenue Commissioners as satisfies them that particular income cannot, by reason of legislation in the country in which it

arises or of executive action of the government of that country, be remitted to the State, the Revenue Commissioners may for the purposes of collection treat the assessment as if the relevant amount did not include the particular income, but such treatment shall terminate on the Revenue Commissioners ceasing to be so satisfied.

(4) The Revenue Commissioners may for the purposes of this section call for such information as they consider necessary.

(5) Any person who is dissatisfied with a decision of the Revenue Commissioners under subsection (3) may, by giving notice in writing to the Revenue Commissioners within 21 days after the notification of the decision to that person, apply to have the matter referred to the Appeal Commissioners as if it were an appeal against an assessment, and the provisions of the Tax Acts relating to the rehearing of an appeal and to the statement of a case for the opinion of the High Court on a point of law shall apply accordingly with any necessary modifications.

Definitions

Appeal Commissioners: s 2(1); High Court: IA 1937 Sch; person: IA 1937 s 11(*c*); writing: IA 1937 Sch.

Former enactments

ITA 1967 s 549; F(MP)A 1968 s 3(2) and Sch Pt I; FA 1974 s 86 and Sch 2 Pt I; CTA 1976 s 147(1)–(2).

Corresponding UK tax provision

Income and Corporation Taxes Act 1988 s 584.

1005 Unremittable gains

(1) In this section, **"particular gains"** means chargeable gains accruing from the disposal of assets situated outside the State, the amount of which is or is included in the amount (in this section referred to as **"the relevant amount"**) on which in accordance with the Capital Gains Tax Acts the tax is computed.

(2) Subject to subsections (3) to (5), this section shall apply where capital gains tax has been charged by an assessment for the year in which the particular gains accrued and the tax has not been paid.

(3) In any case in which, on or after the date on which the capital gains tax has become payable, such proof is given to the Revenue Commissioners as satisfies them that particular gains cannot, by reason of legislation in the country in which they have accrued or of executive action of the government of that country, be remitted to the State, the Revenue Commissioners may for the purposes of collection treat the assessment as if the relevant amount did not include the particular gains, but such treatment shall terminate on the Revenue Commissioners ceasing to be so satisfied.

(4) The Revenue Commissioners may for the purposes of this section call for such information as they consider necessary.

(5) Any person who is dissatisfied with a decision of the Revenue Commissioners under subsection (3) may, by giving notice in writing to the Revenue Commissioners within 21 days after the notification of the decision to that person, apply to have the matter referred to the Appeal Commissioners as if it were an appeal against an assessment, and the provisions of the Income Tax Acts relating to the rehearing of an appeal and to the

statement of a case for the opinion of the High Court on a point of law shall apply accordingly with any necessary modifications.

Case law

Held relief did not apply where a UK resident assessed to tax on portion of gain accruing to a Rhodesian company, the company not having distributed the gain, even though payment of dividends to UK shareholders prohibited in Rhodesia: *Van-Arkadie v Plunket* [1983] STC 54.

Definitions

Appeal Commissioners: ss 2(1), 5(1); chargeable gain: ss 5(1), 545; High Court: IA 1937 Sch; person: IA 1937 s 11(*c*); writing: IA 1937 Sch.

Former enactments

CGTA 1975 s 43.

1006 Poundage and certain other fees due to sheriffs or county registrars

(1) In this section—

"the Acts" means—

(*a*) the Tax Acts,

(*b*) the Capital Gains Tax Acts,

(*c*) the Value-Added Tax Act, 1972, and the enactments amending or extending that Act,

(*d*) the [Capital Acquisitions Tax Consolidation Act 2003],[1] and the enactments amending or extending that Act, and

(*e*) Part VI of the Finance Act, 1983, and the enactments amending or extending that Part,

and any instruments made thereunder;

"certificate" means a certificate issued under section 962;

"county registrar" means a person appointed to be a county registrar under section 35 of the Court Officers Act, 1926;

"defaulter" means a person specified or certified in an execution order or certificate on whom a relevant amount specified or certified in the order or certificate is leviable;

"execution order" has the same meaning as in the Enforcement of Court Orders Act, 1926;

"fees" means the fees known as poundage fees payable under section 14(1) of the Enforcement of Court Orders Act, 1926, and orders made under that section for services in or about the execution of an execution order directing or authorising the execution of an order of a court by the seizure and sale of a person's property or, as may be appropriate, the fees corresponding to those fees payable under section 962 for the execution of a certificate;

"interest on unpaid tax" means interest which has accrued under any provision of the Acts providing for the charging of interest in respect of unpaid tax, including interest on an undercharge of tax which is attributable to fraud or neglect;

"relevant amount" means an amount of tax or interest on unpaid tax;

"tax" means any tax, duty, levy or charge which, in accordance with any provision of the Acts, is placed under the care and management of the Revenue Commissioners;

references, as respects an execution order, to a relevant amount include references to any amount of costs specified in the order.

(2) Where—

(*a*) an execution order or certificate specifying or certifying a defaulter and relating to a relevant amount is lodged with the appropriate sheriff or county registrar for execution,

(*b*) the sheriff or, as the case may be, the county registrar gives notice to the defaulter of the lodgment or of his or her intention to execute the execution order or certificate by seizure of the property of the defaulter to which it relates, or demands payment by the defaulter of the relevant amount, and

(*c*) the whole or part of the relevant amount is paid to the sheriff or, as the case may be, the county registrar or to the Collector-General, after the giving of that notice or the making of that demand,

then, for the purpose of the liability of the defaulter for the payment of fees and of the exercise of any rights or powers in relation to the collection of fees for the time being vested by law in sheriffs and county registrars—

(i) the sheriff or, as the case may be, the county registrar shall be deemed to have entered, in the execution of the execution order or certificate, into possession of the property referred to in paragraph (*b*), and

(ii) the payment mentioned in paragraph (*c*) shall be deemed to have been levied, in the execution of the execution order or certificate, by the sheriff or, as the case may be, the county registrar,

and fees shall be payable by the defaulter to such sheriff or, as the case may be, country registrar accordingly in respect of the payment mentioned in paragraph (*c*).

Amendments

1 Substituted by CATCA 2003 s 119 and Sch 3 with effect from 21 February 2003; previously "Capital Acquisitions Tax Act 1976".

Cross-references

This section to be construed together with the Value Added Tax Acts 1972–1997, in so far as relating to value added tax: s 1104(3).

This section to be construed together with the Capital Acquisitions Tax Act 1976, and the enactments amending or extending that Act, in so far as relating to capital acquisitions tax: s 1104(5).

This section to be construed together with FA 1983 Pt VI and the enactments amending or extending that Part, in so far as relating to residential property tax: s 1104(6).

Definitions

person: IA 1937 s 11(*c*); Tax Acts: s 1(2).

Former enactments

FA 1988 s 71(1)–(2)(*a*).

1006A Offset between taxes

[(1) In this section—

"Acts" means—

(*a*) the Tax Acts,

(*b*) the Capital Gains Tax Acts,

(*c*) the Value-Added Tax Act, 1972, and the enactments amending or extending that Act,

(*d*) the statutes relating to the duties of excise and to the management of those duties,

(*e*) the [Capital Acquisitions Tax Consolidation Act 2003],[1] and the enactments amending or extending that Act,

(*f*) the Stamp Duties Consolidation Act, 1999,

(*g*) Part VI of the Finance Act, 1983, and the enactments amending or extending that Part,

(*h*) Chapter IV of Part II of the Finance Act, 1992,

and any instrument made thereunder;

[**"claim"** means a claim that gives rise to either or both a repayment of tax and a payment of interest payable in respect of such a repayment under any of the Acts and includes part of such a claim;][2]

[**"liability"** means any tax due or estimated to be due under the Acts for any period or in respect of any event, as may be appropriate in the circumstances, and includes any interest due under the Acts in respect of that tax;][3]

"overpayment" means a payment or remittance under the Acts (including part of such a payment or remittance) which is in excess of the amount of the liability against which it is [credited;][4]

[**"tax"** means any tax, duty, levy or other charge under any of the Acts.][5]

[(2) Notwithstanding any other provision of the Acts, where the Revenue Commissioners are satisfied that a person has not complied with the obligations imposed on the person by the Acts, in relation to either or both—

(*a*) the payment of a liability required to be paid, and

(*b*) the delivery of returns required to be made,

they may, in a case where a repayment is due to the person in respect of a claim or overpayment—

(i) where paragraph (*a*) applies, or where paragraphs (*a*) and (*b*) apply, instead of making the repayment set the amount of the claim or overpayment against any liability due under the Acts, and

(ii) where paragraph (*b*) only applies, withhold making the repayment until such time as the returns required to be delivered have been delivered.

(2A) Where the Revenue Commissioners have set or withheld a repayment by virtue of subsection (2), they shall give notice in writing to that effect to the person concerned and, where subsection (2)(ii) applies, interest shall not be payable under any provision of the Acts from the date of such notice in respect of any repayment so withheld.][6]

(3) The Revenue Commissioners shall make regulations for the purpose of giving effect to this section and, without prejudice to the generality of the foregoing, such regulations shall provide for the order of priority of liabilities due under the Acts against which any claim or overpayment is to be set in accordance with subsection (2).

(4) Every regulation made under this section shall be laid before Dáil Éireann as soon as may be after it is made and, if a resolution annulling the regulation is passed by Dáil Éireann within the next 21 days on which Dáil Éireann has sat after the regulation is laid before it, the regulation shall be annulled accordingly, but without prejudice to the validity of anything previously done thereunder.

[(5) Any act to be performed or function to be discharged (other than the making of regulations) by the Revenue Commissioners which is authorised by this section may be performed or discharged by any of their officers acting under their authority.][7]][8]

Amendments

1 Substituted by CATCA 2003 s 119 and Sch 3 with effect from 21 February 2003; previously "Capital Acquisitions Tax Act 1976".
2 Definition of "claim" substituted by FA 2002 s 125(*a*)(i)(I) with effect from 25 March 2002.
3 Definition of "liability" substituted by FA 2002 s 125(*a*)(i)(II) with effect from 25 March 2002.
4 Substituted by FA 2002 s 125(*a*)(i)(III) with effect from 25 March 2002; previously "credited.".
5 Definition of "tax" substituted by FA 2002 s 125(*a*)(i)(IV) with effect from 25 March 2002.
6 Subs (2) substituted and subs (2A) inserted by FA 2001 s 239(*b*) with effect from 6 April 2001.
7 Subs (5) inserted by FA 2002 s 125(*a*)(ii) with effect from 25 March 2002.
8 Section 1006A inserted by FA 2000 s 164 with effect from 23 March 2000.

Cross-references

Capital acquisitions tax, overpayments, subs (2A): CATCA 2003 s 57(6).
Excise duty, interest on repayments, subs (2A): FA 2001 s 105D(2), (3) (inserted by FA 2003 s 98).
Interest on repayments, subs (2A): s 865A(1), (2).
Relief on retirement for certain income of certain sportsperson: s 480A(2).
Stamp duty, interest on repayments, subs (2A): SDCA 1999 s 159B(1).
Value-added tax, interest on refunds, subs (2A): VATA 1972 s 21A(2), (3).

Regulations

Taxes (Offset of Repayments) Regulations 2002, SI No 471 of 2002.

Tax Briefing

TB45 Oct 2001 pp 10–11 — Offset of Repayment Regulations.

Definitions

Dáil Éireann: IA 1937 Sch; person: IA 1937 s 11(*c*); writing: IA 1937 Sch.

1006B Appropriation of payments

[(1) In this section—

"Acts" means—

(*a*) the Tax Acts,
(*b*) the Capital Gains Tax Acts,
(*c*) the Value-Added Tax Act, 1972, and the enactments amending or extending that Act,

and any instruments made thereunder;

"payment" means a payment or a remittance of a liability under the Acts and includes part of such a payment or remittance;

"liability" means any tax or charge due under the Acts for a taxable period, income tax month, income tax year or chargeable period, as appropriate.

(2) Notwithstanding any other provision of the Acts, where a payment is received by the Revenue Commissioners from a person and it cannot reasonably be determined by the Revenue Commissioners from the instructions, if any, which accompanied the payment which liabilities the person wishes the payment to be set against, the Revenue Commissioners may set the payment against any liability due by the person under the Acts.

(3) The Revenue Commissioners shall make regulations for the purpose of giving effect to this section and, without prejudice to the generality of the foregoing, such regulations shall provide for the order of priority of liabilities due under the Acts against which a payment is to be set in accordance with subsection (2).

(4) Every regulation made under this section shall be laid before Dáil Éireann as soon as may be after it is made and, if a resolution annulling the regulation is passed by Dáil Éireann within the next 21 days on which Dáil Éireann has sat after the regulation is laid before it, the regulation shall be annulled accordingly, but without prejudice to the validity of anything previously done thereunder.

[(5) Any act to be performed or function to be discharged (other than the making of regulations) by the Revenue Commissioners which is authorised by this section may be performed or discharged by any of their officers acting under their authority.][1][2]

Amendments

1 Subs (5) inserted by FA 2002 s 125(*b*) with effect from 25 March 2002.

2 Section 1006B inserted by FA 2000 s FA 2000 s 164 with effect from 23 March 2000.

Definitions

Dáil Éireann: IA 1937 Sch; person: IA 1937 s 11(*c*).

PART 43
PARTNERSHIPS AND EUROPEAN ECONOMIC INTEREST GROUPINGS (EEIG)

Cross-references

European Economic Interest Groupings, this Part applied: s 1014(3).

Farming and market gardening, Schedule D Case I: s 655(2).

Income Tax (Relevant Contracts) Regulations 2000, SI No 71 of 2000: ITRCR 2000 Reg 20(3)(*b*).

Patents, capital sums: effect of death, winding up and partnership changes: s 760(4)(*b*); meaning of "the relevant period" applied: s 760(4)(*a*).

Restriction on use of capital allowances on certain buildings, meaning of "partnership trade" and "several trade" applied: ss 409A(1), 409B(1).

Self assessment, meaning of "precedent partner": s 950(1).

Tax treatment of profits, losses and capital gains of a European Economic Interest Grouping, this Part other than ss 1009, 1010(8) and 1013 applied by: s 1014(3).

Revenue Information

Information Leaflet on Taxation Issues for Milk Production Partnership.

1007 Interpretation (Part 43)

(1) In this Part—

"annual payment" means any payment from which, apart from any insufficiency of profits or gains of the persons making it, income tax is deductible under section 237;

"balancing charge" means a balancing charge under Part 9 or Chapter 1 of Part 29, as the case may be;

"basis period", in relation to a year of assessment, means the period on the profits or gains of which income tax for that year is to be finally computed under Case I of Schedule D in respect of the trade in question or, where by virtue of the Income Tax Acts the profits or gains of any other period are to be taken to be the profits or gains of that period, that other period;

"partnership trade" means a trade carried on by 2 or more persons in partnership;

"precedent partner", in relation to a partnership, means the partner who, being resident in the State—

(*a*) is first named in the partnership agreement,

(*b*) if there is no agreement, is named singly or with precedence over the other partners in the usual name of the firm, or

(*c*) is the precedent acting partner, if the person named with precedence is not an acting partner,

and any reference to precedent partner shall, in a case yin which no partner is resident in the State, be construed as a reference to the agent, manager or factor of the firm resident in the State;

"relevant period", in relation to a partnership trade, means a continuous period the whole or part of which is after the 5th day of April, 1965—

(*a*) beginning at a time when either—

(i) the trade was not carried on immediately before that time by 2 or more persons in partnership, or

(ii) none of the persons then carrying on the trade in partnership was one of the persons who immediately before that time carried on the trade in partnership, and

(*b*) continuing only so long as there has not occurred a time when either—

(i) the trade is not carried on immediately after that time by 2 or more persons in partnership, or

(ii) none of the persons then carrying on the trade in partnership is one of the persons who immediately after that time carry on the trade in partnership,

subject to the condition that, in the case of any such period which apart from this condition would have begun before the 6th day of April, 1965, **"the relevant period"** shall be taken as having begun at the time, or at the last of 2 or more times, at which, a change having occurred in the partnership of persons then engaged in carrying on the trade, the persons so engaged immediately after the time were to be treated for the purposes of income tax as having set up or commenced the trade at that time.

(2) In relation to a case in which a partnership trade is from time to time during a relevant period carried on by 2 or more different partnerships of persons, any reference in this Part to the partnership shall, unless the context otherwise requires, be construed as including a reference to any partnership of persons by whom the trade has been carried on since the beginning of the relevant period and any reference to a partner shall be construed correspondingly.

(3) This Part shall, with any necessary modifications, apply in relation to professions as it applies in relation to trades.

Cross-references

Charging and assessing of non-residents, assessment, meaning of "precedent partner" applied: s 1034.
European Economic Interest Groupings, this Part applied: s 1014(3).

Case law

A taxpayer cannot backdate the commencement of a partnership prior to the date when it actually took legal effect: *Macken v Revenue Commissioners* [1962] IR 302.

A partnership agreement not acted on by the parties to the agreement held not to create partnership: *Hawker v Compton* (1922) 8 TC 306; *Dickenson v Gross* (1927) 11 TC 614; *Alexander Bulloch & Co v IRC* [1976] STC 514.

Partnership agreement held not to be retrospective: *Ayrshire Pullman Motor Services and Ritchie v IRC* (1929) 14 TC 754; *Saywell v Pope* [1979] STC 824.

Vendor continuing to assist the purchaser held not a partner: *Pratt v Strick* (1932) 17 TC 459.

Whether or not a partnership exists is a question of fact: *R v City of London Commissioners (ex parte Gibbs)* (1942) 24 TC 221.

Definitions

person: IA 1937 s 11(*c*); profession: s 2(1); trade: s 3(1); year of assessment: s 3(1).

Former enactments

ITA 1967 s 69; FA 1975 s 33(2) and Sch 1 Pt II.

Corresponding UK tax provision

Income and Corporation Taxes Act 1988 s 111.

1008 Separate assessment of partners

(1) In the case of a partnership trade, the Income Tax Acts shall, subject to this Part, apply in relation to any partner in the partnership as if for any relevant period—

(*a*) any profits or gains arising to that partner from the trade and any loss sustained by that partner in the trade were respectively profits or gains of, and loss sustained in, a trade (in this Part referred to as a **"several trade"**) carried on solely by that partner, being a trade—

(i) set up or commenced at the beginning of the relevant period, or if that partner commenced to be engaged in carrying on the partnership trade at some time in the relevant period other than the beginning of that period, at the time when that partner so commenced, and

(ii) when that partner ceases to be engaged in carrying on the partnership trade either during the relevant period or at the end of that period, permanently discontinued at the time when that partner so ceases, and

(*b*) that partner had paid the part that partner was liable to bear of any annual payment paid by the partnership.

(2) (*a*) For any year or period within the relevant period the amount of the profits or gains arising to any partner from that partner's several trade, or the amount of

loss sustained by that partner in that trade, shall for the purposes of subsection (1) be taken to be so much of the full amount of the profits or gains of the partnership trade or, as the case may be, of the full amount of the loss sustained in the partnership trade as would fall to that partner's share on an apportionment of those profits or gains or, as the case may be, of that loss made in accordance with the terms of the partnership agreement as to the sharing of profits and losses.

(*b*) Where the year or period (in this paragraph referred to as **"the period of computation"**) for which the profits or gains of, or the loss sustained in, the several trade of a partner is to be computed under this subsection is or is part of a year or period for which an account of the partnership trade has been made up, sections 65 and 107 shall apply in relation to the partner as if an account of that partner's several trade had been made up for the period of computation.

(3) (*a*) For the purposes of subsection (2) and subject to paragraph (*b*), the full amount of the profits or gains of the partnership trade for any year or period, or the full amount of the loss sustained in such trade in any year or period, shall, subject to section 1012, be determined by the inspector, and any such determination shall be made as it would have been made if the trade—

(i) had been set up or commenced at the beginning of the relevant period,

(ii) where the relevant period has come to an end, had been permanently discontinued at the end of that period, and

(iii) had at all times within the relevant period been carried on by one and the same person and everything done in the carrying on of the trade to or by the persons by whom it was in fact carried on had been done to or by that person.

(*b*) In a case in which the relevant period began at some time before the 6th day of April, 1965, and the trade was not treated for the purposes of income tax as having been set up or commenced at that time—

(i) the relevant period shall for the purposes of this subsection be deemed to have begun at the time at which the trade was treated for the purposes of income tax as having been set up or commenced, and

(ii) any profits or gains arising to any person from the trade, or any loss sustained by that person in the trade, for any year or period within the relevant period during which that person was engaged in the trade on that person's own account shall be deemed to be profits or gains arising to that person from, or, as the case may be, a loss sustained by that person in, a partnership trade in which that person was entitled during the year or period in question to the full amount of the profits or gains arising or was liable to bear the full amount of the loss.

(4) Where the shares to which the partners are entitled in the basis period for a year of assessment do not exhaust the profits of the trade carried on by the partnership for that period, an assessment shall be made under Case IV of Schedule D on the precedent partner in respect of the unexhausted portion of the profits and the precedent partner shall, if and when such balance is to be paid to a person entitled to such balance, be entitled to deduct from such balance any amounts of tax which have been assessed on

and paid by him or her and he or she shall be acquitted and discharged of any such amounts.

(5) This section shall not cause any income which apart from this section is not earned income to become earned income.

Cross-references

Balancing allowances and charges: s 293(2)(*a*); subs (3): s 293(4).
European Economic Interest Groupings, this Part applied: s 1014(3).
Partnerships, modification of provisions as to appeals, subs (3): s 1012(1); subs (2): s 1012(3).
Schedule D Case V losses, subs (1)(*a*)(ii), permanently discontinued, meaning: s 388.

Case law

A partner who assigned part of his partnership share to a trust, the principal beneficiaries being his wife and children, held to be properly assessed on the whole of his income: *Hadlee v New Zealand Commissioners of Inland Revenue* [1993] STC 294.

Revenue precedents

Issue: Whether a partnership determination necessary in the case of farmers trading in partnership.
Decision: No; in view of TCA 1997 s 655(2), partnership determination not required.
Issue: Whether s 1008(4) applies where the partners in a partnership decide not to allocate the full profits for a basis period to the partners.
Decision: Section 1008(4) applies only where the profits to which the partners are entitled do not exhaust the profits for the period. In a case in which the partners are entitled to all of the profits but do not allocate them to any partner in particular, the subsection does not apply.
Issue: In joint assessment cases, where income was previously returned as income of one spouse, whether a claim that both spouses are and have been in partnership can be sustained and tax treatment allowed accordingly.
Decision: Whether a husband and wife are and have been in partnership is always a question of fact. Onus is on the claimants to show, as a point of fact, that they are and were in partnership.

Definitions

inspector: ss 2(1), 5(1), 852; precedent partner: s 880(1); person: IA 1937 s 11(*c*); relevant period: s 880(1); trade: s 3(1); year of assessment: s 3(1).

Former enactments

ITA 1967 s 71.

Corresponding UK tax provision

Income and Corporation Taxes Act 1988 s 111.

1009 Partnerships involving companies

(1) In this section, profits shall not be taken as including chargeable gains.

(2) Subject to this section, subsections (1), (2)(*a*) and (3) of section 1008 shall apply for the purposes of corporation tax as they apply for the purposes of income tax.

(3) Where the whole or part of an accounting period of a company is or is part of a period for which an account of a partnership trade has been made up, any necessary apportionment shall be made in computing the profits from or loss sustained in the company's several trade for the accounting period of the company.

(4) (*a*) In this subsection, **"the relevant amount"** means—

(i) where the year of assessment and the accounting period coincide, the whole amount of the appropriate share of the joint allowance or, as the case may be, the whole amount of the appropriate share of the joint charge, and

(ii) where part only of the year of assessment is within the accounting period, such portion of the appropriate share of the joint allowance or, as the case may be, such portion of the appropriate share of the joint charge as is apportioned to that part of the year of assessment which falls within the accounting period.

(*b*) Where a capital allowance equal to an appropriate share of a joint allowance would be made, if section 21(2) had not been enacted, in charging to income tax the profits of a company's several trade for any year of assessment, the relevant amount shall for corporation tax purposes be treated as a trading expense of the company's several trade for any accounting period of the company any part of which falls within that year of assessment.

(*c*) Where a balancing charge equal to an appropriate share of a joint charge would be made, if section 21(2) had not been enacted, in charging to income tax the profits of a company's several trade for any year of assessment, the relevant amount shall for corporation tax purposes be treated as a trading receipt of the company's several trade for any accounting period of the company any part of which falls within that year of assessment.

(*d*) Notwithstanding section 1010(8), any reference in this subsection to a joint allowance for a year of assessment shall not include a reference to any capital allowance which is or could be brought forward from a previous year of assessment.

(5) Where under this section an amount is to be apportioned to—

(*a*) a part of an accounting period of a company,

(*b*) a part of a period for which an account of a partnership trade has been made up, or

(*c*) a part of a year of assessment,

the apportionment shall be made by reference to the number of months or fractions of months contained in that part and in the remainder of that accounting period, period or year, as the case may be.

Definitions

capital allowance: s 2(1); chargeable gain: ss 5(1), 545; company: s 4(1); month: IA 1937 Sch; profits: s 4(1); trade: ss 3(1), 4(1), 5(1); year of assessment: ss 2(1), 5(1).

Former enactments

CTA 1976 s 32 (apart from (3)(*c*)(proviso)).

Corresponding UK tax provision

Income and Corporation Taxes Act 1988 ss 114–116.

1010 Capital allowances and balancing charges in partnership cases

(1) The provisions of the Income Tax Acts relating to the making of capital allowances and balancing charges in charging the profits or gains of a trade shall, in relation to the several trade of a partner in a partnership, apply subject to this section.

(2) Where for any year of assessment a claim has been made as provided by subsection (9) by the precedent partner for the time being of any partnership, there shall be made to any partner in the partnership in charging the profits or gains of that partner's several trade a capital allowance in respect of any expenditure or property equal to that partner's appropriate share of any capital allowance for that year, excluding any amount carried forward from an earlier year, (in this section referred to as a **"joint allowance"**) which,

apart from any insufficiency of profits or gains, might have been made in respect of that expenditure or property in charging the profits or gains of the partnership trade if the Income Tax Acts had provided that those profits should be charged by joint assessment on the persons carrying on the trade in the year of assessment as if—

(*a*) those persons had at all times been carrying on the trade and everything done to or by their predecessors in, or in relation to, the carrying on of the trade had been done to or by them, and

(*b*) the trade had been set up or commenced at the beginning of the relevant period and, where the relevant period has come to an end, had been permanently discontinued at the end of that period.

(3) There shall be made for any year of assessment on any partner in a partnership in charging the profits or gains of that partner's several trade a balancing charge equal to that partner's appropriate share of any balancing charge (in this section referred to as a **"joint charge"**) which would have been made for that year in charging the profits or gains of the partnership trade if the Income Tax Acts had provided that those profits should be charged as specified in subsection (2).

(4) Where at the end of the relevant period a person or a partnership of persons succeeds to a partnership trade and any property which immediately before the succession takes place was in use for the purposes of the partnership trade and, without being sold, is immediately after the succession takes place in use for the purposes of the trade carried on by the successor or successors, section 313(1) shall apply as it applies where by virtue of section 69 a trade is to be treated as discontinued.

(5) Where for a partnership trade the relevant period began at some time before the 6th day of April, 1965, and the trade was not treated for the purposes of income tax as having been set up or commenced at that time, the relevant period shall for the purposes of subsections (2) and (3) be deemed to have begun at the time at which the trade was treated for the purposes of income tax as having been set up or commenced.

(6) (*a*) In relation to any partnership trade, the total amount of all joint allowances for any year of assessment and the total amount of all joint charges for that year shall, subject to section 1012, be determined by the inspector.

(*b*) Where after a determination has been made under paragraph (*a*) the inspector becomes aware of any facts or events by reference to which the determination is in his or her opinion incorrect, the inspector may from time to time and as often as appears to him or her to be necessary make a revised determination, and any such revised determination shall supersede any earlier determination and any such additional assessments or repayments of tax shall be made as may be necessary.

(7) (*a*) In this subsection, **"trading period"** means, where the relevant period begins or ends during the year of assessment for which the joint allowance or joint charge is computed, the part of that year of assessment which falls within the relevant period or, in any other case, that year of assessment.

(*b*) Subject to paragraph (*c*), for any year of assessment the partners' appropriate shares of a joint allowance or of a joint charge shall be determined by apportioning the full amount of that allowance or charge between the partners on the same basis as a like amount of profits arising in the trading period from the partnership trade, and accruing from day to day over that period, would be apportioned in accordance with the terms of the partnership if any salary, interest on capital or other sum to which any partner was entitled without regard to the amount of the profits arising from the partnership trade had already been provided for.

(*c*) Where for any year of assessment all the partners (any deceased partner being represented by his or her legal representatives) allege, by notice in writing signed by them and sent to the inspector within 24 months after the end of the year of assessment, that hardship is caused to one or more partners by the apportionment of a joint allowance or joint charge on the basis set out in paragraph (*b*), the Revenue Commissioners may, on being satisfied that hardship has been caused, give such relief as in their opinion is just by making a new apportionment of the joint allowance or joint charge, and any such new apportionment shall for the purposes of the Income Tax Acts apply as if it were an apportionment made under paragraph (*b*), and such additional assessments or repayments of tax shall be made as may be necessary.

(8) (*a*) In this subsection, **"capital allowance brought forward"** means—

(i) any capital allowance or part of a capital allowance due to be made to the partnership for the year 1964–65 or any earlier year of assessment which might, if Part VIII of the Finance Act, 1965, had not been enacted, have been carried forward and made as a deduction in charging the profits or gains of the partnership trade for the year 1965–66, and

(ii) any capital allowance or part of a capital allowance due to be made to a partner for the year 1965–66 or a later year of assessment which but for this subsection might have been carried forward and made as a deduction in charging the profits or gains of the several trade of the partner for a year of assessment subsequent to that for which the capital allowance was computed.

(*b*) For any year of assessment the aggregate amount of all capital allowances brought forward shall for the purposes of making the assessments on the partners be deemed to be a joint allowance for that year, and subsection (7) shall apply accordingly.

(9) In relation to a partnership trade—

(*a*) any claim for a joint allowance for any year of assessment shall be made by the precedent partner as if it were a claim for a capital allowance to be made to that partner and shall be included in the return delivered by that partner under section 880 in relation to that year of assessment, and

(*b*) any claim for a joint allowance shall be deemed to be a claim by every partner for a capital allowance to be made to such partner, being a capital allowance equal to such partner's appropriate share of that joint allowance.

Cross-references

Balancing allowances and charges: s 293(1)(*a*)(i).

European Economic Interest Groupings, this Part applied: s 1014(3).

Partnerships involving companies, subs (8): s 1009(4)(*d*).

Partnerships, charges on capital sums received for sale of patent rights, subs (2): s 1011(1); subs (7): s 1011(2).

Partnerships, modification of provisions as to appeals, subs (6): s 1012(1), (2); subs (7): s 1012(3).

Definitions

Balancing charge, basis period: s 880; month: IA 1937 Sch; person: IA 1937 s 11(*c*); precedent partner, relevant period: s 880; trade: s 3(1); writing: IA 1937 Sch; year of assessment: s 3(1).

Former enactments

ITA 1967 s 72; FA 1980 s 17(2).

1011 Provision as to charges under section 757

(1) Where for any year of assessment a charge under section 757 (in this section referred to as a **"joint charge"**) would have been made in charging the profits or gains of a partnership trade if the Income Tax Acts had provided that those profits or gains should be charged as specified in section 1010(2), there shall be made on any partner in the partnership in charging the profits or gains of that partner's several trade a charge under section 757 equal to that partner's appropriate share of the joint charge.

(2) A partner's appropriate share of a joint charge for the purposes of subsection (1) shall be determined in the same way as the partner's appropriate share of a joint charge within the meaning of section 1010 is to be determined by virtue of subsection (7) of that section.

Cross-references

European Economic Interest Groupings, this Part applied: s 1014(3).

Definitions

trade: s 3(1); year of assessment: s 3(1).

Former enactments

ITA 1967 s 74.

1012 Modification of provisions as to appeals

(1) The inspector may give notice to the partnership concerned of any determination made by him or her under section 1008(3) or 1010(6) by delivering a statement in writing of that determination to the precedent partner for the time being of the partnership, and the provisions of the Income Tax Acts relating to appeals against assessments to income tax shall, with any necessary modifications, apply in relation to any determination and any notice of a determination as if they were respectively such an assessment and notice of such an assessment.

(2) Where a determination has become final and conclusive or, in the case of a determination under subsection (6) of section 1010 has become final and conclusive subject to paragraph (*b*) of that subsection, no question as to its correctness shall be raised on the hearing or on the rehearing of an appeal by any partner either against an assessment in respect of the profits or gains of that partner's several trade or against a determination by the inspector on a claim under section 381.

(3) Where on any appeal mentioned in subsection (2) any question arises as to an apportionment to be made under section 1008(2) or 1010(7) and it appears that the question is material as respects the liability to income tax (for whatever year of assessment) of 2 or more persons, all those persons shall be notified of the time and place of the hearing and shall be entitled to appear and be heard by the Appeal Commissioners or to make representations to them in writing.

Cross-references

Capital allowances and balancing charges in partnership cases: s 1010(6)(*a*).

European Economic Interest Groupings, this Part applied: s 1014(3).

Separate assessment of partners: s 1008(3)(*a*).

Definitions

Appeal Commissioners: s 2(1); person: IA 1937 s 11(*c*); trade: s 3(1); writing: IA 1937 Sch; year of assessment: s 3(1).

Former enactments

ITA 1967 s 73; F(MP)A 1968 s 3(2) and Sch Pt I.

1013 Limited partnerships

(1) In this section—

[**"active partner"**, in relation to a partnership trade, means a partner who works for the greater part of his or her time on the day-to-day management or conduct of the partnership trade;][1]

"the aggregate amount", in relation to a trade, means—

(*a*) in the case of an individual, the aggregate of amounts given or allowed to the individual at any time under any of the specified provisions—

(i) in respect of a loss sustained by him or her in the trade, or of interest paid by him or her by reason of his or her participation in the trade, in any relevant year of assessment, or

(ii) as an allowance to be made to him or her for any relevant year of assessment either in taxing the trade or by means of discharge or repayment of tax to which he or she is entitled by reason of his or her participation in the trade,

and

(*b*) in the case of a company, the aggregate of amounts given or allowed to the company (in this section referred to as **"the partner company"**) or to another company at any time under any of the specified provisions—

(i) in respect of a loss incurred by the partner company in the trade, or of charges paid by it or another company by reason of its participation in the trade, in any relevant accounting period, or

(ii) as an allowance to be made to the partner company for any relevant accounting period either in taxing the trade or by means of discharge or repayment of tax to which it is entitled by reason of its participation in the trade;

"limited partner", in relation to a trade, means—

(*a*) a person carrying on the trade as a limited partner in a limited partnership registered under the Limited Partnerships Act, 1907,

(*b*) a person carrying on the trade as a general partner in a partnership who is not entitled to take part in the management of the trade but is entitled to have the person's liabilities, or those liabilities beyond a certain limit, for debts or obligations incurred for the purposes of the trade, discharged or [reimbursed by some other person,][2] (*c*) a person who carries on the trade jointly with others and, under the law of any territory outside the State, is not entitled to take part in the management of the trade and is not liable beyond a certain limit for debts or obligations [incurred for the purposes of the [trade,][3]];[4]

[(*d*) a person who carries on the trade as a general partner in a partnership otherwise than as an active [partner,][5]][6]

[(*e*) a person who carries on the trade as a partner in a partnership registered under the law of any territory outside the State, otherwise than as an active partner, or

(*f*) a person who carries on the trade jointly with others under any agreement, arrangement, scheme or understanding which is governed by the law of any territory outside the State, otherwise than as a person who works for the greater part of his or her time on the day-to-day management or conduct of that trade;][7]

"relevant accounting period" means an accounting period of the partner company which ends on or after the specified date and at any time during which it carried on the trade as a limited partner;

"the relevant time" means—

(*a*) in the case of an individual, the end of the relevant year of assessment in which the loss is sustained or the interest is paid, or for which the allowance is to be made (except that where the individual ceased to carry on the trade during that year of assessment it is the time when he or she so ceased), and

(*b*) in the case of a partner company, the end of the relevant accounting period in which the loss is incurred or the charges are paid, or for which the allowance is to be made (except that where the partner company ceases to carry on the trade during that accounting period it is the time when the partner company so ceased);

"relevant year of assessment" means a year of assessment which ends after the specified date and at any time during which the individual carried on the trade as a limited partner;

"the specified date" means the 22nd day of May, 1985;

"the specified provisions" means—

(*a*) in the case of an individual, sections 245 to 255, 305 and 381, and

(*b*) in the case of a company, sections 243, 308(4) and 396(2) and subsections (1), (2) and (6) of section 420.

(2) (*a*) Where, in the case of an individual who is a limited partner in relation to a trade, an amount may apart from this section be given or allowed under any of the specified provisions—

(i) in respect of a loss sustained by the individual in the trade, or of interest paid by him or her by reason of his or her participation in the trade, in a relevant year of assessment, or

(ii) as an allowance to be made to the individual for a relevant year of assessment either in taxing the trade or by means of discharge or repayment of tax to which he or she is entitled by reason of his or her participation in the trade, such an amount may be given or allowed—

(I) as respects a contribution by a limited partner to the trade of the limited partnership made before the 24th day of April, 1992, otherwise than against income consisting of profits or [gains arising from the trade,][8]

(II) as respects such a contribution made on or after the 24th day of April, 1992, only against income consisting of [profits or gains arising from the [trade,][9]][10]

[(III) where the individual is a limited partner in relation to a trade by virtue of paragraph (*d*) of the definition of "limited partner" and the relevant year of assessment is—

(A) in the case of such a partner where the activities of the trade include the activity of producing, distributing, or the holding of or of an interest in, films or video tapes or the activity of exploring for, or exploiting, oil or gas resources, the year of assessment 1997–1998 or any subsequent year of assessment, subject to subsection (2A), or

(B) in any other case, the year of assessment 1999–2000 or any subsequent year of assessment, subject to subsection (2B),

only against income consisting of profits or gains arising from the [trade, or][11]][12]

[(IV) where the individual is a limited partner in relation to a trade by virtue of paragraph (*e*) or (*f*) of the definition of "limited partner" and the relevant year of assessment is the year of assessment 2005 or any subsequent year of assessment, only against income consisting of profits or gains arising from the trade,][13]

and only to the extent that the amount given or allowed or, as the case may be, the aggregate amount in relation to that trade does not exceed the amount of his or her contribution to the trade at the relevant time.

(*b*) Where, in the case of a partner company which is a limited partner in relation to a trade, an amount may apart from this section be given or allowed under any of the specified provisions—

(i) in respect of a loss sustained by the partner company in the trade, or of charges paid by the partner company or another company by reason of its participation in the trade, in a relevant accounting period, or

(ii) as an allowance to be made to the partner company for a relevant accounting period either in taxing the trade or by means of discharge or repayment of tax to which it is entitled by reason of its participation in the trade,

such an amount may be given or allowed to the partner company—

(I) as respects a contribution by a limited partner to the trade of the limited partnership made before the 24th day of April, 1992, otherwise than against profits or gains arising from the trade, or to another company, or

(II) as respects such a contribution made on or after the 24th day of April, 1992, only against profits or gains arising from the trade, and only to the extent that the amount given or allowed or, as the case may be, the aggregate amount in relation to that trade does not exceed the partner company's contribution to the trade at the relevant time.

[(2A) [Subparagraph (III)(A)][14] of subsection (2)(*a*) shall not apply to—

(*a*) interest paid on or before the 27th day of February, 1998,

(*b*) an allowance to be made in respect of expenditure incurred on or before the 27th day of February, 1998, or

(*c*) a loss sustained in the year of assessment 1997–98 which would have been the loss sustained in that year if—

(i) that year of assessment had ended on the 27th day of February, 1998, and

(ii) the loss were determined only by reference to accounts made up in relation to the trade for the period commencing on the 6th day of April, 1997, or if later, the date the trade was set up and commenced, and ending on the 27th day of February, 1998, and not by reference to accounts made up for any other period.][15]

[(2B) Subparagraph (III) (B) of subsection (2)(*a*) shall not apply to—

(*a*) interest paid on or before 29 February 2000,

(*b*) an allowance to be made in respect of expenditure incurred on or before 29 February 2000, or

(*c*) a loss sustained in the year of assessment 1999- 2000 which would have been the loss sustained in that year if—

(i) that year of assessment had ended on 29 February 2000, and

(ii) the loss were determined only by reference to accounts made up in relation to the trade for the period commencing on 6 April 1999 or, if later, the date the trade commenced and ending on 29 February 2000 and not by reference to accounts made up for any other period.

(2C)(*a*) In this subsection—

"excepted expenditure" means expenditure to which the provisions of section 409A apply and expenditure to which the provisions of that section or section 409B would apply but for the provisions of—

(i) section 409A(5), or

(ii) paragraph (*a*) of the definition of "specified building" in subsection (1) or (4) of section 409B,

as the case may be;

"specified deduction" means the deduction referred to in section 324(2), 333(2), 345(3), 354(3), 370(3), 372E(3) or 372O(3) as the "second-mentioned deduction" or in paragraph 13 of Schedule 32 as the "further deduction";

"specified individual", in relation to a partnership trade, means an individual who is a limited partner in relation to the trade by virtue only of paragraph (*d*) of the definition of "limited partner", and a reference to a specified individual shall be construed accordingly.

(*b*) (i) Subsection (2)(*a*) shall not apply to a specified individual to which paragraph (*c*), (*d*) or (*e*), as the case may be, applies to the extent that—

(I) the interest referred to in subparagraph (i) of paragraph (*a*) of that subsection is interest paid by the individual by reason of his or her participation in a trade referred to in paragraph (*c*), (*d*) or (*e*), as the case may be, in a relevant year of assessment,

(II) the loss referred to in subparagraph (i) of paragraph (*a*) of that subsection is a loss sustained by the individual in a trade referred to in paragraph (*c*), (*d*) or (*e*), as the case may be, in a relevant year of assessment,

(III) the allowance referred to in subparagraph (ii) of paragraph (*a*) of that subsection is an allowance to be made to the individual for a relevant year of assessment either in taxing a trade or by means of discharge or repayment of tax to which he or she is entitled by reason of his or her participation in a trade referred to in paragraph (*c*), (*d*) or (*e*), as the case may be.

(ii) Subsection (2)(*a*) shall not apply to a specified individual to the extent that—

(I) the interest referred to in subparagraph (i) of paragraph (*a*) of that subsection is interest paid by the individual on a loan where the proceeds of the loan were used by the partnership to incur excepted expenditure in a relevant year of assessment,

(II) the loss referred to in subparagraph (i) of paragraph (*a*) of that subsection arises from the taking into account for the purposes of section 392(1) of an allowance to be made in respect of excepted expenditure, or

(III) the allowance referred to in subparagraph (ii) of paragraph (*a*) of that subsection is an allowance to be made to the individual for a relevant year of assessment in respect of excepted expenditure.

(*c*) This paragraph applies to a specified individual where—

(i) the partnership trade consists wholly of the leasing of machinery or plant to a qualifying company within the meaning of section 486B, and

(ii) the expenditure incurred on the provision of the machinery or plant was incurred under an obligation entered into by the lessor (within the meaning of section 403) and the lessee (within the meaning of section 403) before 1 March 2001.

(*d*) This paragraph applies to a specified individual where in charging the profits or gains of the individual's several trade an allowance in respect of capital expenditure on machinery or plant to which the provisions of section 284(3A) apply has been or is to be made to that individual; but this paragraph shall not apply to such an individual as respects—

(i) interest paid by that individual on a loan taken out on or after 4 September 2000,

(ii) an allowance to be made to that individual for capital expenditure incurred on or after 4 September 2000, or

(iii) a loss sustained in the trade in [the year of assessment 2002][16] or any subsequent year of assessment to the extent that the loss does not arise from the taking into account for the purposes of section 392(1) of an allowance to be made in accordance with the provisions of section 284(3A).

(*e*) This paragraph applies to a specified individual where in computing the amount of the profits or gains, if any, of the partnership trade a specified deduction has been or is to be allowed in respect of a premises occupied by the partnership for the purposes of the partnership trade, and—

(i) the individual became a partner in the partnership before 29 February 2000,

(ii) the individual made a contribution to the partnership trade before that date, and

(iii) the qualifying lease in respect of which a specified deduction has been or is to be allowed was granted to or acquired by the partnership before that date;

but—

(I) subject to clause (II), this paragraph shall not apply to such an individual as respects—

(A) interest paid by that individual in,

(B) an allowance to be made to that individual for, or

(C) any loss sustained in the trade for,

any year of assessment for which a specified deduction in respect of the premises is not allowed in arriving at the amount of the profits or gains of the individual's several trade to be charged to tax or, as the case may be, the loss sustained therein or any subsequent year of assessment, and

(II) where in computing the amount of the profits or gains, if any, of the partnership trade a second-mentioned deduction (within the meaning of section 354(3)) may be made by virtue of section 354(3), this paragraph shall not apply to such an individual as respects—

(A) interest paid by that individual on or after [1 January 2005][17],

(B) an allowance to be made to that individual for [the year of assessment 2005][18] or any subsequent year of assessment, or

(C) any loss sustained in that trade in [the year of assessment 2005][18] or any subsequent year of assessment.][19]

(3) (*a*) A person's contribution to a trade at any time shall be the aggregate of—

(i) the amount which the person has contributed to the trade as capital and has not subsequently, either directly or indirectly, drawn out or received back from the partnership or from a person connected with the partnership (other than anything, in relation to expenditure which the person has incurred on behalf of the partnership trade or in providing facilities for the partnership trade, which the person is or may be entitled so to draw out or receive back at any time when the person carries on the trade as a limited partner or which the person is or may be entitled to require another person to reimburse the person), and

(ii) the amount of any profits or gains of the trade to which the person is entitled but which the person has not received in money or money's worth.

(*b*) A person shall for the purposes of paragraph (*a*) be treated as having received back an amount contributed by the person to the partnership if—

(i) the person received consideration of that amount or value for the sale of the person's interest, or any part of the person's interest, in the partnership,

(ii) the partnership or any person connected with the partnership repays that amount of a loan or an advance from the person, or

(iii) the person receives that amount or value for assigning any debt due to the person from the partnership or from any person connected with the partnership.

(4) (*a*) This subsection shall apply, in relation to an amount given or allowed under any of the specified provisions, as respects a contribution by a partner to the trade of the partnership made on or after the 11th day of April, 1994.

(*b*) For the purposes of this section, where in connection with the making of a contribution to a partnership trade by a general partner in the partnership—

(i) there exists any agreement, arrangement, scheme or understanding under which the partner is required to cease to be a partner in the partnership at any time before the partner is entitled to receive back from the partnership the full amount of the partner's contribution to the trade, or

(ii) by virtue of any agreement, arrangement, scheme or understanding—

(I) any asset owned by the partner is exempt from execution on goods or from a process or mode of enforcement of a debt of the partner or the partnership, or

(II) any other limit or restriction is placed on the creditor's entitlement to recover any such debt from the partner,

the partner shall be treated as a person who is not entitled to take part in the management of the trade but is entitled to have the person's liabilities, or the person's liabilities beyond a certain limit, for debts or obligations incurred for the purposes of the trade, discharged or reimbursed by some other person.

(*c*) In determining whether an amount is given or allowed under any of the specified provisions as respects a contribution to a trade on or after the 11th day of April, 1994, any amount which would not otherwise have been given or allowed by virtue of this section but for a contribution to a trade on or after that date and on the basis that paragraph (*a*) had not been enacted shall be treated as given or allowed as respects such a contribution.

(5) (*a*) In determining whether an amount is given or allowed under any of the specified provisions as respects a contribution to a trade on or after the 24th day of April, 1992, any amount which would not otherwise have been given or allowed by virtue of this section but for a contribution to a trade on or after that date and on the basis that paragraphs (*a*)(II) and (*b*)(II) of subsection (2) had not been enacted shall be treated as given or allowed as respects such a contribution.

(*b*) Notwithstanding paragraph (*a*) and paragraphs (*a*)(II) and (*b*)(II) of subsection (2), this section shall apply in so far as the trade of a limited partnership consists of the management and letting of holiday cottages within the meaning of section 268, where—

(i) a written contract for the construction of the holiday cottages was signed and construction work had commenced before the 24th day of April, 1992, and

(ii) the construction work is completed before the 6th day of April, 1993,

as if references to on or after the 24th day of April, 1992, were references to on or after the 1st day of September, 1992.

Amendments

1 Definition of "active partner" inserted by FA 1998 s 50(1)(*a*)(i) with effect from 28 February 1998.

2 Substituted by FA 1998 s 50(1)(*a*)(ii)(I) with effect from 28 February 1998; previously "reimbursed by some other person, or".

3 Substituted by FA 2005 s 37(*a*)(i) with effect from 1 January 2005; previously "trade, or".

4 Substituted by FA 1998 s 50(1)(*a*)(ii)(II) with effect from 28 February 1998; previously "incurred for the purposes of the trade;".

5 Substituted by FA 2005 s 37(*a*)(ii) with effect from 1 January 2005; previously "partner;".

6 Definition of "limited partner" para (*d*) substituted by FA 2000 s 70(1)(*a*) with effect from 29 February 2000.

7 Subs (1) definition of "limited partner" paras (*e*) and (*f*) inserted by FA 2005 s 37(*a*)(iii) with effect from 1 January 2005.

8 Substituted by FA 1998 s 50(1)(*b*)(i) with effect from 28 February 1998; previously "gains arising from the trade, or".

9 Substituted by FA 2005 s 37(*b*)(i) with effect from 1 January 2005; previously "trade, or".

10 Substituted by FA 1998 s 50(1)(*b*)(ii) with effect from 28 February 1998; previously "profits or gains arising from the trade,".

11 Substituted by FA 2005 s 37(*b*)(ii) with effect from 1 January 2005; previously "trade,".

12 Subs (2)(*a*)(III) substituted by FA 2000 s 70(1)(*b*) with effect from 29 February 2000.

13 Subs (2)(*a*)(IV) inserted by FA 2005 s 37 (*b*)(iii) with effect from 1 January 2005.

14 Substituted by FA 2000 s 70(1)(*c*) with effect from 29 February 2000; previously "Subparagraph (III)".

15 Subs (2A) inserted by FA 1998 s 50(1)(*c*) with effect from 28 February 1998.

16 Substituted by FA 2001 s 77(2) and Sch 2 para 55(*a*) with effect from 6 April 2001; previously "the year of assessment 2001–2002".

17 Substituted by FA 2001 s 77(2) and Sch 2 para 55(*b*)(i) with effect from 6 April 2001; previously "6 April 2004".

18 Substituted by FA 2001 s 77(2) and Sch 2 para 55(*b*)(ii) with effect from 6 April 2001; previously "the year of assessment 2004–2005".

19 Subs (2B)–(2C) inserted by FA 2000 s 70(1)(*d*) with effect from 29 February 2000.

Case law

This section was enacted to counter the effect of transactions involving losses within s 381 allowable against other income which exceeded the amount of investments in limited partnerships: *MacCarthaigh v Daly* ITR Vol III p 253.

Definitions

company: ss 4(1), 5(1); person: IA 1937 s 11(*c*); profits or gains: s 3(4); Tax Acts: s 1(2); trade: s 3(1); year of assessment: ss 2(1), 5(1).

Former enactments

FA 1986 s 46(1)–(4) and (6), FA 1992 s 23; FA 1994 s 29.

Corresponding UK tax provision

Income and Corporation Taxes Act 1988 ss 117 and 118.

1014 Tax treatment of profits, losses and capital gains arising from activities of a European Economic Interest Grouping (EEIG)

(1) In this section, **"grouping"** means a European Economic Interest Grouping formed on the terms, in the manner and with the effects laid down in—

(*a*) Council Regulation (EEC) No 2137/85 of 25 July 1985 (OJ L 119, 31.07.1985 p 1) on the European Economic Interest Grouping (EEIG), and (*b*) the European Communities (European Economic Interest Groupings) Regulations, 1989 (SI No 191 of 1989),

and references to members of a grouping shall be construed accordingly.

(2) Notwithstanding anything in the Tax Acts or in the Capital Gains Tax Acts, a grouping shall be neither—

(*a*) charged to income tax, corporation tax or capital gains tax, as the case may be, in respect of profits or gains or chargeable gains arising to it, nor

(*b*) entitled to relief for a loss sustained by it,

and any assessment required to be made on such profits or gains or chargeable gains, and any relief for a loss, shall as appropriate be made on and allowed to the members of a grouping in accordance with this section.

(3) This Part (other than sections 1009, 1010(8) and 1013) and sections 30 and 913(7) shall apply with any necessary modifications to the activities of a grouping in the same manner as they apply to a trade or profession carried on by 2 or more persons in partnership.

(4) In particular but without prejudice to the generality of subsection (3), the provisions mentioned in that subsection shall in their application for the purposes of this section apply as if—

(*a*) references to a partnership agreement were references to the contract forming or providing for the formation of a grouping,

(*b*) references to a partner were references to a member of a grouping, and

(*c*) anything done or required to be done by the precedent acting partner was done or required to be done by the grouping.

Cross-references

For corporation tax purposes, "company" includes a grouping: s 4(1).

Capital gains tax purposes: s 5(1).

Definitions

chargeable gain: ss 4(1), 5(1), 534; person: IA 1937 s 11(*c*); profits: s 4(1); profession: ss 2(1), 5(1); trade: s 3(1).

Former enactments

FA 1990 s 29(1), (2), (5)–(6).

Corresponding UK tax provision

Income and Corporation Taxes Act 1988 s 510A.

PART 44
MARRIED, SEPARATED AND DIVORCED PERSONS

CHAPTER 1
Income Tax

Cross-references

Electronic claims, PAYE: s 864A(1)(*d*).

Returns by married persons: s 881(3).

Revenue information

Information leaflet IT2 — Taxation of Married Persons
Information leaflet IT3 — What to do about tax when you separate?

1015 Interpretation (Chapter 1)

(1) In this Chapter, **"the inspector"**, in relation to a notice, means any inspector who might reasonably be considered by the person giving notice to be likely to be concerned with the subject matter of the notice or who declares himself or herself ready to accept the notice.

(2) A wife shall be treated for income tax purposes as living with her husband unless either—

(*a*) they are separated under an order of a court of competent jurisdiction or by deed of separation, or

(*b*) they are in fact separated in such circumstances that the separation is likely to be permanent.

(3) (*a*) In this Chapter, references to the income of a wife include references to any sum which apart from this Chapter would be included in computing her total income, and this Chapter shall apply in relation to any such sum notwithstanding that some enactment (including, except in so far as the contrary is expressly provided, an enactment passed after the passing of this Act) requires that that sum should not be treated as income of any person other than her.

(*b*) In the Income Tax Acts, a reference to a person who has duly elected to be assessed to tax in accordance with a particular section includes a reference to a person who is deemed to have elected to be assessed to tax in accordance with that section, and any reference to a person who is assessed to tax in accordance with section 1017 for a year of assessment includes a reference to a case where the person and his or her spouse are assessed to tax for that year in accordance with section 1023.

(4) Any notice required to be served under any section in this Chapter may be served by post.

Cross-references

BES relief, disposal of shares: s 498(2).

Capital gains tax, married woman living with her husband, subs (2): s 5(2).

Deferral of payment of tax under section 128 (tax treatment of share options), subs (2)(*a*), (*b*): s 128A(4A)(i)(II).

Maintenance in the case of separated spouses, meaning of "maintenance arrangement" applied, subs (2): s 1025(1).

Taxation of income deemed to arise from certain sales of securities: s 815(3)(*d*).

Case law

Irish

The legislation underlying ss 1015–1018 and 1022–1024 was originally introduced by FA 1980 ss 192–198 following the Supreme Court's decision that the earlier measures were unconstitutional as they discriminated against married couples: *Murphy v Attorney General* ITR Vol III, pp 127, 188. The Revenue sought to limit the effect of that decision by providing in FA 1980 s 21 that assessments made after the 1980 Supreme Court decision but relating to earlier periods should be excluded from benefiting but failed in the courts to have this position sustained: *Muckley v Ireland* ITR Vol III p 188

UK

A "wife" means wife by a legal marriage and does not include a common-law wife: *Rignell v Andrews* [1990] STC 410.

Although living under the same roof, a couple can maintain two separate households: *Holmes v Mitchell* [1991] STC 25.

Definitions

Income Tax Acts: s 1(2); inspector: ss 2(1), 5(1), 852; person: IA 1937 s 11(*c*).

Former enactments

ITA 1967 s 192; FA 1980 s 18.

Corresponding UK tax provision

Income and Corporation Taxes Act 1988 s 282.

1016 Assessment as single persons

(1) Subject to subsection (2), in any case in which a wife is treated as living with her husband, income tax shall be assessed, charged and recovered, except as is otherwise provided by the Income Tax Acts, on the income of the husband and on the income of the wife as if they were not married.

(2) Where an election under section 1018 has effect in relation to a husband and wife for a year of assessment, this section shall not apply in relation to that husband and wife for that year of assessment.

Cross-references

Election for joint assessment: s 1018(4)(*a*).

Employee (PAYE) allowance, meaning of "the specified amount": s 472(1)(*a*).

Home loan interest: s 244(1)(*b*).

Rent paid: s 473(3).

Self assessment, date for payment of tax: s 958(7)(*b*).

Service charges: s 477(3).

Surcharge for late returns: s 1084(4)(*b*).

Case law

A husband and wife who agreed by a pre-nuptial arrangement to live apart after marriage and in fact did so were to be treated as single persons for income tax purposes: *Donovan v Crofts* ITR Vol I p 115.

Definitions

Income Tax Acts: s 1(2); person: IA 1937 s 11(*c*); year of assessment: s 3(1).

Former enactments

ITA 1967 s 193; FA 1980 s 18.

1017 Assessment of husband in respect of income of both spouses

(1) Where in the case of a husband and wife an election under section 1018 to be assessed to tax in accordance with this section has effect for a year of assessment—

(*a*) the husband shall be assessed and charged to income tax, not only in respect of his total income (if any) for that year, but also in respect of his wife's total income (if any) for any part of that year of assessment during which she is living with him, and for this purpose and for the purposes of the Income Tax Acts that last-mentioned income shall be deemed to be his income, (*b*) the question whether there is any income of the wife chargeable to tax for any year of assessment and, if so, what is to be taken to be the amount of that income for tax purposes shall not be affected by this section, and

(*c*) any tax to be assessed in respect of any income which under this section is deemed to be income of a woman's husband shall, instead of being assessed on her, or on her trustees, guardian or committee, or on her executors or administrators, be assessable on him or, in the appropriate cases, on his executors or administrators.

(2) Any relief from income tax authorised by any provision of the Income Tax Acts to be granted to a husband by reference to the income or profits or gains or losses of his wife or by reference to any payment made by her shall be granted to a husband for a year of assessment only if he is assessed to tax for that year in accordance with this section.

Cross-references

Age tax credit: s 464.
Application for separate assessment: s 1023(2).
Assessment of wife in respect of income of both spouses: s 1019(1), (2)(*a*)(ii), (*b*)(ii), (3).
Basic personal tax credit: s 461(*a*)(i).
BES investments: s 490(1)(*b*); withdrawal of BES relief: s 504(2).
Blind person's tax credit: s 468(2)(*b*).
Deferral of payment of tax under section 128 (tax treatment of share options), subs (2)(*a*), (*b*): s 128A(4A)(i)(II).
Donations to approved bodies: s 848A(7).
Donations to certain sports bodies: s 847A(9)(*a*)(ii).
Election for assessment under this section: s 1018(1), (4)(*a*).
Employed person taking care of incapacitated individual: s 467(2)(*b*).
Employee (PAYE) tax credit: s 472(1)(*a*) (the specified amount): s 472(4).
Employer preferential loan: s 122(2) and (3)(*b*).
Film investments: s 481(6).
Health Contributions Act 1979, s 1 ("emoluments").
Home carer tax credit: s 466A(1)("qualifying claimant").
Home loan interest: s 244(1)(*a*)("relievable interest"), (*b*), (3)(*a*).
Income tax: manner of granting, and effect of, allowances made by means of discharge or repayment of tax: s 305(1)(*b*)(i)(I)(B).
Interpretation of Income Tax Acts: s 3(1)("chargeable tax").
Leased farm land exemption: s 664(3).
Rate of charge: s 15(2), (3).
Relief for health expenses: s 469(3)(*a*).
Relief for insurance against expenses of illness: s 470(2)(*b*).
Relief for fees paid for third level education: s 473A(3).
Reliefs for lessors and owner-occupiers in respect of expenditure incurred on the provision of certain residential accommodation, relief for owner-occupiers: s 372AR(3).
Relief for trade union subscriptions: s 472C(2).
Rent paid: s 473(1)("specified limit"), (3).
Repayment of tax in case of certain husbands and wives: s 1021(1).
Restriction on use of capital allowances on certain industrial buildings and other premises: s 409A(2).
Self assessment, date for payment of tax: s 958(7).
Self assessment, meaning of "chargeable person": s 950(1).
Service charges: s 477(3).
Special provisions relating to tax on wife's income: s 1022(6).
Special provisions relating to year of marriage: s 1020(3)(*a*).
Surcharge for late returns: s 1084(3)(*b*).
Training courses fees: s 476(3).

Case law

Subs (1)(*a*): The separation of spouses arising from the operation of official regulations did not preclude the spouses from being regarded as living together for income tax purposes: *Ua Clothasaigh v McCartan* ITR Vol II p 75.

Subs (1)(*b*): Where husband and wife assessed jointly the basis of charge on the separate sources of the spouses to be determined separately: *Mulvey v Kieran* ITR Vol I p 563.

In the case of a jointly assessed couple, the husband is the chargeable person: *Gilligan v Criminal Assets Bureau* (High Court, 26 February 1997).

Definitions

Income Tax Acts: s 1(2); total income: s 3(1); year of assessment: s 3(1).

Former enactments

ITA 1967 s 194; FA 1980 s 18.

Corresponding UK tax provision

Income and Corporation Taxes Act 1988 s 279 [repealed].

1018 Election for assessment under section 1017

(1) A husband and his wife, where the wife is living with the husband, may at any time during a year of assessment, by notice in writing given to the inspector, jointly elect to be assessed to income tax for that year of assessment in accordance with section 1017 and, where such election is made, the income of the husband and the income of the wife shall be assessed to tax for that year in accordance with that section.

(2) Where an election is made under subsection (1) in respect of a year of assessment, the election shall have effect for that year and for each subsequent year of assessment.

(3) Notwithstanding subsections (1) and (2), either the husband or the wife may, in relation to a year of assessment, by notice in writing given to the inspector before the end of the year, withdraw the election in respect of that year and, on the giving of that notice, the election shall not have effect for that year or for any subsequent year of assessment.

(4) (*a*) A husband and his wife, where the wife is living with the husband and where an election under subsection (1) has not been made by them for a year of assessment (or for any prior year of assessment) shall be deemed to have duly elected to be assessed to tax in accordance with section 1017 for that year unless before the end of that year either of them gives notice in writing to the inspector that he or she wishes to be assessed to tax for that year as a single person in accordance with section 1016.

(*b*) Where a husband or his wife has duly given notice under paragraph (*a*), that paragraph shall not apply in relation to that husband and wife for the year of assessment for which the notice was given or for any subsequent year of assessment until the year of assessment in which the notice is withdrawn, by the person who gave it, by further notice in writing to the inspector.

Cross-references

Assessment as single persons: s 1016(2).

Assessment of husband in respect of income of both spouses: s 1017(1).

Assessment of wife in respect of income of both spouses: s 1019; subs (1): s 1019(4); subs (4): s 1019(2)(*b*)(ii), (4).

Self assessment, date for payment of tax: s 958(7).

Separated and divorced persons, adaptation of special provisions as to married persons, in subs (1) delete "where the life is living with the husband" and delete subs (4): s 1026(1); subs (1): s 1026(2)(*a*).

Special provisions relating to year of marriage: s 1020(2).

Case law

Irish

Married man held not entitled to married person's allowance and double rate bands where his wife was resident and taxable in the UK: *Fennessy v McConnellogue* [1995] IR 500

Revenue precedents

Issue: Individual is resident in the state. Spouse is non-resident. Can they elect for joint assessment.

Decision: An election for joint assessment cannot have effect as the resident spouse cannot be assessed on the income of the non-resident spouse. The resident spouse is therefore incapable of electing for joint assessment.

Issue: Can Common Law Spouses choose to be assessed as married couples?

Decision: Common Law Spouses may not elect to be assessed as married couples.

Issue: Diplomats - allowances applicable to spouses. Is the spouse (eg a UK national) of a Diplomat attached to the UK Embassy, Dublin, entitled to the married allowances if he/she takes up employment in her own right with a private company in Ireland?

Decision: Assuming that both spouses are resident in Ireland for tax purposes, the married personal allowance, reliefs and double rate bands would be applied in full to his/her income, provided they elected to be assessed to tax on the basis of joint assessment.

Definitions

inspector: ss 2(1), 5(1), 852; the inspector: s 1015; person: IA 1937 s 11(*c*); writing: IA 1937 Sch; year of assessment: s 3(1).

Former enactments

ITA 1967 s 195; FA 1980 s 18.

Corresponding UK tax provision

Income and Corporation Taxes Act 1988 s 279.

1019 Assessment of wife in respect of income of both spouses

(1) In this section—

"the basis year", in relation to a husband and wife, means the year of marriage or, if earlier, the latest year of assessment preceding that year of marriage for which details of the total incomes of both the husband and the wife are available to the inspector at the time they first elect, or are first deemed to have duly elected, to be assessed to tax in accordance with section 1017;

"year of marriage", in relation to a husband and wife, means the year of assessment in which their marriage took place.

(2) Subsection (3) shall apply for a year of assessment where, in the case of a husband and wife who are living together—

(*a*) (i) an election (including an election deemed to have been duly made) by the husband and wife to be assessed to income tax in accordance with section 1017 has effect in relation to the year of assessment, and

(ii) the husband and the wife by notice in writing jointly given to the inspector before [1 April][1] in the year of assessment elect that the wife should be assessed to income tax in accordance with section 1017,

or

(*b*) (i) the year of marriage is the year 1993–94 or a subsequent year of assessment,

(ii) not having made an election under section 1018(1) to be assessed to income tax in accordance with section 1017, the husband and wife have been deemed for that year of assessment, in accordance with section 1018(4), to have duly made such an election, but have not made an election in accordance with paragraph (*a*)(ii) for that year, and

(iii) the inspector, to the best of his or her knowledge and belief, considers that the total income of the wife for the basis year exceeded the total income of her husband for that basis year.

(3) Where this subsection applies for a year of assessment, the wife shall be assessed to income tax in accordance with section 1017 for that year, and accordingly references in section 1017 or in any other provision of the Income Tax Acts, however expressed—

(*a*) to a husband being assessed, assessed and charged or chargeable to income tax for a year of assessment in respect of his own total income (if any) and his wife's total income (if any), and

(*b*) to income of a wife being deemed for income tax purposes to be that of her husband,

shall, subject to this section and the modifications set out in subsection (6) and any other necessary modifications, be construed respectively for that year of assessment as references—

(i) to a wife being assessed, assessed and charged or chargeable to income tax in respect of her own total income (if any) and her husband's total income (if any), and

(ii) to the income of a husband being deemed for income tax purposes to be that of his wife.

(4) (*a*) Where in accordance with subsection (3) a wife is by virtue of subsection (2)(*b*) to be assessed and charged to income tax in respect of her total income (if any) and her husband's total income (if any) for a year of assessment—

(i) in the absence of a notice given in accordance with subsection (1) or (4)(*a*) of section 1018 or an application made under section 1023, the wife shall be so assessed and charged for each subsequent year of assessment, and

(ii) any such charge shall apply and continue to apply notwithstanding that her husband's total income for the basis year may have exceeded her total income for that year.

(*b*) Where a notice under section 1018(4)(*a*) or an application under section 1023 is withdrawn and, but for the giving of such a notice or the making of such an application in the first instance, a wife would have been assessed to income tax in respect of her own total income (if any) and the total income (if any) of her husband for the year of assessment in which the notice was given or the application was made, as may be appropriate, then, in the absence of an election made in accordance with section 1018(1) (not being such an election deemed to have been duly made in accordance with section 1018(4)), the wife shall be so assessed to income tax for the year of assessment in which that notice or application is withdrawn and for each subsequent year of assessment.

(5) Where an election is made in accordance with subsection (2)(*a*)(ii) for a year of assessment, the election shall have effect for that year and each subsequent year of assessment unless it is withdrawn by further notice in writing given jointly by the husband and the wife to the inspector before [1 April][1] in a year of assessment and the

election shall not then have effect for the year for which the further notice is given or for any subsequent year of assessment.

(6) For the purposes of the other provisions of this section and as the circumstances may require—

(*a*) a reference in the Income Tax Acts, however expressed, to an individual or a claimant, being a man, a married man or a husband shall be construed respectively as a reference to a woman, a married woman or a wife, and a reference in those Acts, however expressed, to a woman, a married woman or a wife shall be construed respectively as a reference to a man, a married man or a husband, and

(*b*) any provision of the Income Tax Acts shall, in so far as it may relate to the treatment of any husband and wife for the purposes of those Acts, be construed so as to give effect to this section.

Amendments

[1] Substituted by FA 2001 s 77(2) and Sch 2 paras 56 and 61(*e*) for 2002 and later tax years; previously "the 6th day of July".

Cross-references

Self assessment, date for payment of tax: s 958(7).
Special provisions relating to tax on wife's income: s 1022(6).

Definitions

Income Tax Acts: s 1(2); inspector: ss 2(1), 5(1), 852; the inspector: s 1015; total income: s 3(1); writing: IA 1937 Sch; year of assessment: s 3(1).

Former enactments

ITA 1967 s 195B; FA 1993 s 10(1).

Corresponding UK tax provision

Income and Corporation Taxes Act 1988 s 279.

1020 Special provisions relating to year of marriage

(1) In this section—

[**"income tax month"** means—

(*a*) in relation to a period prior to 6 December 2001, a month beginning on the 6th day of a month and ending on the 5th day of the next month,

(*b*) the period beginning on 6 December 2001 and ending on 31 December 2001, and

(*c*) thereafter, a calendar month;][1]

"year of marriage", in relation to a husband and wife, means the year of assessment in which their marriage took place.

(2) Section 1018 shall not apply in relation to a husband and his wife for the year of marriage.

(3) Where, on making a claim in that behalf, a husband and his wife prove that the amount equal to the aggregate of the income tax paid and payable by the husband on his total income for the year of marriage and the income tax paid and payable by his wife on her total income for the year of marriage is in excess of the income tax which would

have been payable by the husband on his total income and the total income of his wife for the year of marriage if—

(*a*) he had been charged to income tax for the year of marriage in accordance with section 1017, and

(*b*) he and his wife had been married to each other throughout the year of marriage,

they shall be entitled, subject to subsection (4), to repayment of income tax of an amount determined by the formula—

$$A \times \frac{B}{[12]^2}$$

where—

A is the amount of the aforementioned excess, and

B is the number of income tax months in the period between the date on which the marriage took place and the end of the year of marriage, part of an income tax month being treated for this purpose as an income tax month in a case where the period consists of part of an income tax month or of one or more income tax months and part of an income tax month.

(4) Any repayment of income tax under subsection (3) shall be allocated to the husband and to the wife concerned in proportion to the amounts of income tax paid and payable by them, having regard to subsection (2), on their respective total incomes for the year of marriage.

(5) Any claim for a repayment of income tax under subsection (3) shall be made in writing to the inspector after the end of the year of marriage and shall be made by the husband and wife concerned jointly.

(6) (*a*) Subsections (1) and (2) of section 459 and section 460 shall apply to a repayment of income tax under this section as they apply to any allowance, deduction, relief or reduction under the provisions specified in the Table to section 458.

(*b*) Subsections (3) and (4) of section 459 and paragraph 8 of Schedule 28 shall, with any necessary modifications, apply in relation to a repayment of tax under this section.

Amendments

1 Definition of "income tax month" substituted by FA 2001 s 77(2) and Sch 2 para 57(*a*) with effect from 6 April 2001.

2 Previously "9" for short tax "year" 2001 only (FA 2001 s 77(2) and Sch 2 paras 57(*b*) and 61(*a*)) and reverted to "12" for 2002 and later tax years.

Cross-references

Withdrawal of BES relief: s 504(2).

Definitions

Income Tax Acts: s 1(2); inspector: ss 2(1), 5(1), 852; the inspector: s 1015; total income: s 3(1); writing: IA 1937 Sch; year of assessment: s 3(1).

Former enactments

ITA 1967 s 195A(1)–(6); FA 1983 s 6; FA 1996 s 132(1) and Sch 5 Pt I para 1(8).

Corresponding UK tax provision

Income and Corporation Taxes Act 1988 s 261 [repealed].

1021 Repayment of tax in case of certain husbands and wives

(1) This section shall apply for a year of assessment in the case of a husband and wife one of whom is assessed to income tax for the year of assessment in accordance with section 1017 and to whom section 1023 does not apply for that year.

(2) Where for a year of assessment this section applies in the case of a husband and wife, any repayment of income tax to be made in respect of the aggregate of the net tax deducted or paid under any provision of the Tax Acts ...[1] in respect of the total income (if any) of the husband and of the total income (if any) of the wife shall be allocated to the husband and the wife concerned in proportion to the net amounts of tax so deducted or paid in respect of their respective total incomes; but this subsection shall not apply where a repayment, which but for this subsection would not be made to a spouse, is less than [€25][2].

(3) Notwithstanding subsection (2), where the inspector, having regard to all the circumstances of a case, is satisfied that a repayment or a greater part of a repayment of income tax arises by reason of some allowance or relief which, if sections 1023 and 1024 had applied for the year of assessment, would have been allowed to one spouse only, the inspector may make the repayment to the husband and the wife in such proportions as the inspector considers just and reasonable.

Amendments

1 Repealed by FA 2000 s 69(2) and Sch 2 Part 2 with effect from 6 April 1999 in the case of income tax and as respects accounting periods commencing on or after that date in the case of corporation tax; previously "(including a tax credit in respect of a distribution from a company resident in the State)".

2 Substituted by FA 2001 s 240(1) and (2)(*a*) and Sch 5 Pt 1 for 2002 and later tax years; previously "£20".

Definitions

distribution: ss 4(1), 436, 437; inspector: ss 2(1), 5(1), 852; the inspector: s 1015; Tax Acts: s 1(2); total income: s 3(1); year of assessment: s 3(1).

Former enactments

ITA 1967 s 195C; FA 1993 s 10(1).

1022 Special provisions relating to tax on wife's income

[(1) Where—

(*a*) an assessment to income tax (in this section referred to as the "original assessment") has been made for any year of assessment on an individual, or on an individual's trustee, guardian or committee (in this section referred to as the "representative"), or on an individual's executors or administrators,

(*b*) the Revenue Commissioners are of the opinion that, if an application for separate assessment under section 1023 had been in force with respect to that year of assessment, an assessment in respect of or of part of the same income would have been made on, or on the representative of, or on the executors or administrators of, an individual who is the spouse of the individual referred to in paragraph (*a*) or who was the spouse of the individual referred to in paragraph (*a*) (in this subsection and in subsection (2) referred to as the "spouse") in that year of assessment, and (*c*) the whole or part of the amount payable under the original assessment has remained unpaid at the expiration of 28 days from the time when it became due,

the Revenue Commissioners may give to the spouse, or, if the spouse is dead, to the spouse's executors or administrators, or, if an assessment referred to in paragraph (*b*) could in the circumstances referred to in that paragraph have been made on the spouse's representative, to the spouse, or to the spouse's representative, a notice stating—

(i) particulars of the original assessment and of the amount remaining unpaid under that assessment, and

(ii) to the best of their judgement, particulars of the assessment (in this subsection referred to as the "last-mentioned assessment") which would have been so made,

and requiring the person to whom the notice is given to pay the lesser of—

(A) the amount which would have been payable under the last-mentioned assessment if it conformed with those particulars, and

(B) the amount remaining unpaid under the original assessment.][1]

(2) The same consequences as respects—

(*a*) the imposition of a liability to pay, and the recovery of, the tax with or without interest,

(*b*) priority for the tax in bankruptcy or in the administration of the estate of a deceased person,

(*c*) appeals to the Appeal Commissioners, the rehearing of such appeals and the stating of cases for the opinion of the High Court, and

(*d*) the ultimate incidence of the liability imposed,

shall follow on the giving of a notice under subsection (1) [to the spouse or to the spouse's representative, or to the spouse's executors or administrators, as would have followed on the making on the spouse, or on the spouse's representative, or on the spouse's executors or administrators],[2] as the case may be, of an assessment referred to in subsection (1)(*b*), being an assessment which—

(i) was made on the day of the giving of the notice,

(ii) charged the same amount of tax as is required to be paid by the notice,

(iii) fell to be made and was made by the authority who made the original assessment, and

(iv) was made by that authority to the best of that authority's judgment,

and the provisions of the Income Tax Acts relating to the matters specified in paragraphs (*a*) to (*d*) shall, with the necessary modifications, apply accordingly.

(3) Where a notice is given under subsection (1), tax up to the amount required to be paid by the notice shall cease to be recoverable under the original assessment and, where the tax charged by the original assessment carried interest under section 1080, such adjustment shall be made of the amount payable under that section in relation to that assessment and such repayment shall be made of any amounts previously paid under that section in relation to that assessment as are necessary to secure that the total sum, if any,

paid or payable under that section in relation to that assessment is the same as it would have been if the amount which ceases to be recoverable had never been charged.

(4) Where the amount payable under a notice under subsection (1) is reduced as the result of an appeal or of a case stated for the opinion of the High Court—

(*a*) the Revenue Commissioners shall, if having regard to that result they are satisfied that the original assessment was excessive, cause such relief to be given by means of repayment or otherwise as appears to them to be just; but

(*b*) subject to any relief so given, a sum equal to the reduction in the amount payable under the notice shall again become recoverable under the original assessment.

(5) The Revenue Commissioners and the inspector or other proper officer shall have the like powers of obtaining information with a view to the giving of, and otherwise in connection with, a notice under subsection (1) as they would have had with a view to the making of, and otherwise in connection with, an assessment referred to in subsection (1)(*b*) if the necessary conditions had been fulfilled for the making of such an assessment.

[(6) Where a husband or a wife dies (in this subsection and subsections (7) and (8) referred to as the "deceased spouse") and at any time before the death the husband and wife were living together, then the other spouse or, if the other spouse is dead, the executors or administrators of the other spouse may, not later than 2 months from the date of the grant of probate or letters of administration in respect of the deceased spouse's estate or, with the consent of the deceased spouse's executors or administrators, at any later date, give to the deceased spouse's executors or administrators and to the inspector a notice in writing declaring that, to the extent permitted by this section, the other spouse or the executors or administrators of the other spouse disclaim responsibility for unpaid income tax in respect of all income of the deceased spouse for any year of assessment or part of a year of assessment, being a year of assessment or a part of a year of assessment for which any income of the deceased spouse was deemed to be the income of the other spouse and in respect of which the other spouse was assessed to tax under section 1017 or under that section as modified by section 1019.][3]

(7) A notice given to the inspector pursuant to subsection (6) shall be deemed not to be a valid notice unless it specifies the names and addresses of [the deceased spouse's executors or administrators].[4]

(8) Where a notice under subsection (6) has been given to [a deceased spouse's executors or administrators][5] and to the inspector—

(*a*) it shall be the duty of the Revenue Commissioners and the Appeal Commissioners to exercise such powers as they may then or thereafter be entitled to exercise under subsections (1) to (5) in connection with any assessment made on or before the date when the giving of that notice is completed, being an assessment in respect of any of the income to which that notice relates, and (*b*) the assessments (if any) to tax which may be made after that date shall, in all respects and in particular as respects the persons assessable and the tax payable, be the assessments which would have been made if—

(i) an application for separate assessment under section 1023 had been in force in respect of the year of assessment in question, and

(ii) all assessments previously made had been made accordingly.

[(9) The Revenue Commissioners may nominate in writing any of their officers to perform any acts and discharge any functions authorised by this section to be [performed or discharged][6] by the Revenue Commissioners.][7]

Amendments

1 Subs (1) substituted by FA 2000 s 29(1)(*a*) as respects assessments made on or after 10 February 2000.

2 Substituted by FA 2000 s 29(1)(*b*) as respects assessments made on or after 10 February 2000; previously "to a woman, or to her trustee, guardian or committee, or to her executors or administrators, as would have followed on the making on her, or on her trustee, guardian or committee, or on her executors or administrators".

3 Subs (6) substituted by FA 2000 s 29(1)(*c*) as respects assessments made on or after 10 February 2000.

4 Substituted by FA 2000 s 29(1)(*d*) as respects assessments made on or after 10 February 2000; previously "the woman's executors or administrators".

5 Substituted by FA 2000 s 29(1)(*e*) as respects assessments made on or after 10 February 2000; previously "a woman's executors or administrators".

6 Substituted by FA 2002 s 138 and Sch 6 paraa 3(*u*) and 6(*c*)(v) with effect from 25 March 2002; previously "performed or authorised".

7 Subs (9) inserted by FA 2000 s 29(1)(*f*) as respects assessments made before, on or after 10 February 2000.

Cross-references

Capital gains, married persons: s 1029.

Definitions

Appeal Commissioners: s 2(1); High Court: IA 1937 Sch; inspector: ss 2(1), 5(1), 852; the inspector: s 1015; month: IA 1937 Sch; person: IA 1937 s 11(*c*); writing: IA 1937 Sch; year of assessment: s 3(1).

Former enactments

ITA 1967 s 196; FA 1980 s 18.

Corresponding UK tax provision

Income and Corporation Taxes Act 1988 s 285 [repealed].

1023 Application for separate assessments

(1) In this section and in section 1024, **"personal reliefs"** means relief under any of the provisions specified in the Table to section 458, apart from relief under sections [461A,][1] 462 and 463.

(2) Where an election by a husband and wife to be assessed to income tax in accordance with section 1017 has effect in relation to a year of assessment and, in relation to that year of assessment, an application is made for the purpose under this section in such manner and form as may be prescribed by the Revenue Commissioners, either by the husband or by the wife, income tax for that year shall be assessed, charged and recovered on the income of the husband and on the income of the wife as if they were not married and the provisions of the Income Tax Acts with respect to the assessment,

charge and recovery of tax shall, except where otherwise provided by those Acts, apply as if they were not married except that—

(*a*) the total deductions from total income [and reliefs][2] allowed to the husband and wife by means of personal reliefs shall be the same as if the application had not had effect with respect to that year,

(*b*) the total tax payable by the husband and wife for that year shall be the same as the total tax which would have been payable by them if the application had not had effect with respect to that year, and

(*c*) section 1024 shall apply.

(3) An application under this section in respect of a year of assessment may be made—

(*a*) in the case of persons marrying during the course of that year, before [1 April][3] in the following year, and

(*b*) in any other case, within 6 months before [1 April][3] in that year.

(4) Where an application is made under subsection (2), that subsection shall apply not only for the year of assessment for which the application was made, but also for each subsequent year of assessment; but, in relation to a subsequent year of assessment, the person who made the application may, by notice in writing given to the inspector before [1 April][3] in that year, withdraw that election and, on the giving of that notice, subsection (2) shall not apply for the year of assessment in relation to which the notice was given or any subsequent year of assessment.

(5) A return of the total incomes of the husband and of the wife may be made for the purposes of this section either by the husband or by the wife but, if the Revenue Commissioners are not satisfied with any such return, they may require a return to be made by the wife or by the husband, as the case may be.

(6) The Revenue Commissioners may by notice require returns for the purposes of this section to be made at any time.

Amendments

1 Inserted by FA 2000 s 14 and Sch 1 para 6(*a*) with effect from 6 April 2000.

2 Inserted by FA 2000 s 14 and Sch 1 para 6(*b*) with effect from 6 April 2000.

3 Substituted by FA 2001 s 77(2) and Sch 2 paras 58 and 61(*e*) for 2002 and later tax years; previously "the 6th day of July".

Cross-references

Assessment of wife in respect of income of both spouses, subss (1), (4): s 1019(1)(*b*)(ii), (4).
Home loan interest: s 244(3)(*b*)(i).
Income Tax (Purchased Life Annuities) Regulations 1959, SI No 152 of 1959, reg 9.
Leased farm land exemption: s 664(3).
Method of apportioning reliefs and charging tax in cases of separate assessment: s 1024(1).
Relief for fees paid for third level education: s 473A(3).
Relief for lessors and owner-occupiers in respect of expenditure incurred on the provision of certain residential accommodation, relief for owner-occupiers: s 372AR(3).
Repayment of tax in case of certain husbands and wives: s 1021(1), (3).
Self assessment, date for payment of tax: s 958(7)(*b*).
Self assessment, meaning of "specified provisions": s 950(1).
Self assessment, obligation to make a return, subs (5): s 951(8).
Separated and divorced persons, adaptation of special provisions as to married persons: s 1026(2)(*c*).
Special provisions relating to tax on wife's income: s 1022(1)(*b*), (8)(*b*)(i).
Surcharge for late returns, meaning of "specified provisions": s 1084(1)(*a*).
Training courses fees: s 476(3).

Definitions

inspector: ss 2(1), 5(1), 852; the inspector: s 1015; month: IA 1937 Sch; person: IA 1937 s 11(*c*); total income: s 3(1); writing: IA 1937 Sch; year of assessment: s 3(1).

Former enactments

ITA 1967 s 197; FA 1980 s 18; FA 1997 s 146(1) and Sch 9 Pt I para 1(12).

Corresponding UK tax provision

Income and Corporation Taxes Act 1988 s 283.

1024 Method of apportioning reliefs and charging tax in cases of separate assessments

(1) This section shall apply where pursuant to an application under section 1023 a husband and wife are assessed to tax for a year of assessment in accordance with that section.

(2) (*a*) Subject to subsection (3), the benefit flowing from the personal reliefs for a year of assessment may be given either by means of reduction of the amount of the tax to be paid or by repayment of any excess of tax which has been paid, or by both of those means, as the case requires, and shall be allocated to the husband and the wife, in so far as it flows from—

[(i) relief under sections 244 and 372AR, in the proportions in which they incurred the expenditure giving rise to the relief;][1]

(ii) relief under sections 461, 464, 465 (other than [subsection (3)][2]) and 468, in the proportions of one-half and one-half;

(iii) relief in respect of a child under [section 465(3)][3] and relief in respect of a dependent relative under section 466, to the husband or to the wife according as he or she maintains the child or dependent relative;

(iv) relief under section 467, in the proportions in which they bear the cost of employing the person in respect of whom the relief is given;

(v) relief under section 469, in the proportions in which they bore the expenditure giving rise to the relief;

[(vi) relief under sections 470, 470A and 473, to the husband or to the wife according as he or she made the payment giving rise to the relief;][4]

(vii) relief under section 471, in the proportions in which they incurred the expenditure giving rise to the relief;

[(viii) relief under sections 472, 472A and 472B, to the husband or to the wife according as the emoluments from which relief under those sections is granted are emoluments of the husband or of the wife;][5]

[(viii*a*) relief under section 472C, to the husband or the wife according as he or she is entitled to the relief under the said section;][6]

(ix) relief under sections [[473A][7], 476],[8] 477, 478 and 479, in the proportions in which they incurred the expenditure giving rise to the relief;

(x) relief under section 481, in the proportions in which they made the relevant investment giving rise to the relief;

[(x*a*) relief under section 848A(7), to the husband and wife according as he or she made the relevant donation giving rise to the relief;][9]

(xi) relief under Part 16, in the proportions in which they subscribed for the eligible shares giving rise to the relief;

(xii) relief under paragraphs 12 and 20 of Schedule 32, in the proportions in which they incurred the expenditure giving rise to the relief.

(*b*) Any reduction of income tax to be made under section 187(4)(*b*) or 188(5) for a year of assessment shall be allocated to the husband and to the wife in proportion to the amounts of income tax which but for section 187(4)(*b*) or 188(5) would have been payable by the husband and by the wife for that year.

[(*c*) Subject to subsection (4), Part 1 of the Table to section 15 shall apply to each of the spouses concerned.][10]

(3) Where the amount of relief allocated to the husband under subsection (2)(*a*) exceeds the income tax chargeable on his income for the year of assessment, the balance shall be applied to reduce the income tax chargeable on the income of the wife for that year, and where the amount of relief allocated to the wife under that paragraph exceeds the income tax chargeable on her income for the year of assessment, the balance shall be applied to reduce the income tax chargeable on the income of the husband for that year.

[(4) Where the part of the taxable income of a spouse chargeable to tax in accordance with subsection (2)(*c*) at the standard rate is less than that of the other spouse and is less than the part of taxable income specified in column (1) of Part 1 of the Table to section 15 (in this subsection referred to as the "appropriate part") in respect of which the first-mentioned spouse is so chargeable to tax at that rate, the part of taxable income of the other spouse which by virtue of subsection (2)(*c*) is to be charged to tax at the standard rate shall be increased, to an amount not exceeding the part of taxable income specified in column (1) of Part 3 of the Table to section 15 in respect of which an individual to whom that Part applies is so chargeable at that rate, by the amount by which the taxable income of the first-mentioned spouse chargeable to tax at the standard rate is less than the appropriate part.][11]

Amendments

1 Subs (2)(*a*)(i) substituted by FA 24(1) and Sch 2 Pt 1 para (*j*) with effect from 1 January 2002.

2 Substituted by FA 2002 s 138 and Sch 6 paras 3(*v*)(i) and 6(*c*)(ii) with effect from 6 April 2001; previously "subsection (4)".

3 Substituted by FA 2002 s 138 and Sch 6 paras 3(*v*)(ii) and 6(*c*)(ii) with effect from 6 April 2001; previously "section 465(4)".

4 Subs (2)(*a*)(vi) substituted by FA 2001 s 20(*b*) with effect from 6 April 2001.

5 Subs (2)(*a*)(viii) substituted by FA 2000 s 14 and Sch 1 para 7(c) with effect from 6 April 2000.

6 Subs (2)(*a*)(viii*a*) inserted by FA 2001 s 11(1)(*c*) for short tax "year" 2001 and later tax years.

7 Substituted by FA 2002 s 138 and Sch 6 paras 3(*v*)(iii) and 6(*c*)(ii) with effect from 6 April 2001; previously "474, 474A, 475, 475A".

8 Substituted by FA 2000 s 21(2) for 2000–2001 and later tax years; previously "475, 476".

9 Para (*xa*) substituted inserted by FA 2002 s 138 and Sch 6 paras 3(*v*)(iv) and 6(*c*)(ii) with effect from 6 April 2001.

10 Subs (2)(*c*) substituted by FA 2000 s 3(*b*)(i) for 2000–2001 and later tax years.

11 Subs (4) substituted by FA 2000 s 3(*b*)(ii) for 2000–2001 and later tax years.

Cross-references

Application for separate assessment, meaning of "personal relief": s 1023(1), (2)(*c*).

Repayment of tax in case of certain husbands and wives: s 1021(3).

Withdrawal of BES relief: s 504(2).

Definitions

relative: s 3(1); person: IA 1937 s 11(*c*); taxable income: ss 3(1), 458; year of assessment: s 3(1).

Former enactments

ITA 1967 s 198; FA 1980 s 18; FA 1981 s 5; FA 1992 s 2(2)(*a*); FA 1997 s 146(1) and Sch 9 Pt I para 1(13).

Corresponding UK tax provision

Income and Corporation Taxes Act 1988 s 284 [repealed].

1025 Maintenance in case of separated spouses

(1) In this section—

"maintenance arrangement" means an order of a court, rule of court, deed of separation, trust, covenant, agreement, arrangement or any other act giving rise to a legally enforceable obligation and made or done in consideration or in consequence of—

(*a*) the dissolution or annulment of a marriage, or

(*b*) such separation of the parties to a marriage as is referred to in section 1015(2),

and a maintenance arrangement relates to the marriage in consideration or in consequence of the dissolution or annulment of which, or of the separation of the parties to which, the maintenance arrangement was made or arises;

"payment" means a payment or part of a payment, as the case may be;

a reference to a child of a person includes a child in respect of whom the person was at any time before the making of the maintenance arrangement concerned entitled to [relief under section 465].[1]

(2) (*a*) This section shall apply to payments made directly or indirectly by a party to a marriage under or pursuant to a maintenance arrangement relating to the marriage for the benefit of his or her child, or for the benefit of the other party to the marriage, being payments—

(i) which are made at a time when the wife is not living with the husband,

(ii) the making of which is legally enforceable, and

(iii) which are annual or periodical;

but this section shall not apply to such payments made under a maintenance arrangement made before the 8th day of June, 1983, unless and until such time as one of the following events occurs, or the earlier of such events occurs where both occur—

(I) the maintenance arrangement is replaced by another maintenance arrangement or is varied, and

(II) both parties to the marriage to which the maintenance arrangement relates, by notice in writing to the inspector, jointly elect that this section shall apply,

and where such an event occurs in either of those circumstances, this section shall apply to all such payments made after the date on which the event occurs.

(*b*) For the purposes of this section and of section 1026 but subject to paragraph (*c*), a payment, whether conditional or not, which is made directly or indirectly by a party to a marriage under or pursuant to a maintenance arrangement relating to the marriage (other than a payment of which the amount, or the method of calculating the amount, is specified in the maintenance arrangement and from which, or from the consideration for which, neither a child of the party to the marriage making the payment nor the other party to the marriage derives any benefit) shall be deemed to be made for the benefit of the other party to the marriage.

(*c*) Where the payment, in accordance with the maintenance arrangement, is made or directed to be made for the use and benefit of a child of the party to the marriage making the payment, or for the maintenance, support, education or other benefit of such a child, or in trust for such a child, and the amount or the method of calculating the amount of such payment so made or directed to be made is specified in the maintenance arrangement, that payment shall be deemed to be made for the benefit of such child, and not for the benefit of any other person.

(3) Notwithstanding anything in the Income Tax Acts but subject to section 1026, as respects any payment to which this section applies made directly or indirectly by one party to the marriage to which the maintenance arrangement concerned relates for the benefit of the other party to the marriage—

(*a*) the person making the payment shall not be entitled on making the payment to deduct and retain out of the payment any sum representing any amount of income tax on the payment,

(*b*) the payment shall be deemed for the purposes of the Income Tax Acts to be profits or gains arising to the other party to the marriage, and income tax shall be charged on that other party under Case IV of Schedule D in respect of those profits or gains, and

(*c*) the party to the marriage by whom the payment is made, having made a claim in that behalf in the manner prescribed by the Income Tax Acts, shall be entitled for the purposes of the Income Tax Acts to deduct the payment in computing his or her total income for the year of assessment in which the payment is made.

(4) Notwithstanding anything in the Income Tax Acts, as respects any payment to which this section applies made directly or indirectly by a party to the marriage to which the maintenance arrangement concerned relates for the benefit of his or her child—

(*a*) the person making the payment shall not be entitled on making the payment to deduct and retain out of the payment any sum representing any amount of income tax on the payment,

(*b*) the payment shall be deemed for the purposes of the Income Tax Acts not to be income of the child,

(*c*) the total income for any year of assessment of the party to the marriage who makes the payment shall be computed for the purposes of the Income Tax Acts as if the payment had not been made, and

(*d*) for the purposes of [section 465(5)][2], the payment shall be deemed to be an amount expended on the maintenance of the child by the party to the marriage who makes the payment and, notwithstanding that the payment is made to the other party to the marriage to be applied for or towards the maintenance of the child and is so applied, it shall be deemed for the purposes of that section not to be an amount expended by that other party on the maintenance of the child.

(5) (*a*) Subsections (1) and (2) of section 459 and section 460 shall apply to a deduction under subsection (3)(*c*) as they apply to any allowance, deduction, relief or reduction under the provisions specified in the Table to section 458.

(*b*) Subsections (3) and (4) of section 459 and paragraph 8 of Schedule 28 shall, with any necessary modifications, apply in relation to a deduction under subsection (3)(*c*).

Amendments

1 Substituted by FA 2000 s 14 and Sch 1 para 8 with effect from 6 April 2000; previously "a deduction under section 465".

2 Substituted by FA 2002 s 138 and Sch 6 paras 3(*w*) and 6(*c*)(ii) with effect from 6 April 2001; previously "section 465(7)".

Cross-references

Separated and divorced persons, adaptation of special provisions as to married persons: s 1026(1), (2)(*b*).

Case law

Foreign divorce recognised where granted in the country in which either spouse was domiciled: *W v W* (Supreme Court,16 December 1992).

Revenue precedents

Issue: Provision in deed of separation for part of retirement gratuity to be paid to separated spouse.
Decision: It is not an annual or periodic payment. Therefore the spouse receiving the payment will not be assessable on it, and the spouse making the payment will not be entitled to a deduction.

Revenue information

Information leaflet IT3 — What to do about tax when you separate?

Tax Briefing

TB22 June 1996 p 8 — Maintenance payments and Levies.

Definitions

Income Tax Acts: s 1(2); inspector: ss 2(1), 5(1), 852; total income: s 3(1); writing: IA 1937 Sch; year of assessment: ss 2(1), 5(1).

Former enactments

FA 1983 s 3; FA 1996 s 132(1) and Sch 5 Pt I para 13(1).

Corresponding UK tax provision

Income and Corporation Taxes Act 1988 s 257F [repealed].

1026 Separated and divorced persons: adaptation of provisions relating to married persons

(1) Where a payment to which section 1025 applies is made in a year of assessment by a party to a marriage (being a marriage which has not been dissolved or annulled) and both parties to the marriage are resident in the State for that year, section 1018 shall apply in relation to the parties to the marriage for that year of assessment as if—

(*a*) in subsection (1) of that section ", where the wife is living with the husband," were deleted, and

(*b*) subsection (4) of that section were deleted.

(2) Where by virtue of subsection (1) the parties to a marriage elect as provided for in section 1018(1), then, as respects any year of assessment for which the election has effect—

(*a*) subject to subsection (1) and paragraphs (*b*) and (*c*), the Income Tax Acts shall apply in the case of the parties to the marriage as they apply in the case of a husband and wife who have elected under section 1018(1) and whose election has effect for that year of assessment,

(*b*) the total income or incomes of the parties to the marriage shall be computed for the purposes of the Income Tax Acts as if any payments to which section 1025 applies made in that year of assessment by one party to the marriage for the benefit of the other party to the marriage had not been made, and

(*c*) income tax shall be assessed, charged and recovered on the total income or incomes of the parties to the marriage as if an application under section 1023 had been made by one of the parties and that application had effect for that year of assessment.

(3) Notwithstanding subsection (1), where a payment to which section 1025 applies is made in a year of assessment by a spouse who is a party to a marriage, that has been dissolved, for the benefit of the other spouse, and—

(*a*) the dissolution was under either—

(i) section 5 of the Family Law (Divorce) Act, 1996, or

(ii) the law of a country or jurisdiction other than the State, being a divorce that is entitled to be recognised as valid in the State,

(*b*) both spouses are resident in the State for tax purposes for that year of assessment, and

(*c*) neither spouse has entered into another marriage,

then, subsections (1) and (2) shall, with any necessary modifications, apply in relation to the spouses for that year of assessment as if their marriage had not been dissolved.

Cross-references

Maintenance in the case of separated spouses: s 1025(2)(*b*), (3).

Revenue information

Information leaflet IT3 — What to do about tax when you separate?

Definitions

Income Tax Acts: s 1(2); total income: s 3(1); year of assessment: ss 2(1), 5(1).

Former enactments

FA 1983 s 4; FA 1997 s 5(*a*).

1027 Payments pursuant to certain orders under Judicial Separation and Family Law Reform Act, 1989, Family Law Act, 1995, and Family Law (Divorce) Act, 1996, to be made without deduction of income tax

Payment of money pursuant to—

(*a*) an order under Part II of the Judicial Separation and Family Law Reform Act, 1989,

(*b*) an order under the Family Law Act, 1995 (other than section 12 of that Act), and (*c*) an order under the Family Law (Divorce) Act, 1996 (other than section 17 of that Act),

shall be made without deduction of income tax.

Former enactments

Judicial Separation and Family Law Reform Act 1989 s 26; Family Law Act 1995 s 37; Family Law (Divorce) Act 1996 s 31.

CHAPTER 2
Capital Gains Tax

1028 Married persons

(1) Subject to this section, the amount of capital gains tax on chargeable gains accruing to a married woman in a year of assessment or part of a year of assessment during which she is a married woman living with her husband shall be assessed and charged on the husband and not otherwise; but this subsection shall not affect the amount of capital gains tax chargeable on the husband apart from this subsection or result in the additional amount of capital gains tax charged on the husband by virtue of this subsection being different from the amount which would otherwise have remained chargeable on the married woman.

(2) (*a*) Subject to paragraph (*b*), subsection (1) shall not apply in relation to a husband and wife in any year of assessment where, before [1 April][1] in the year following that year of assessment, an application is made by either the husband or wife that subsection (1) shall not apply, and such an application duly made shall have effect not only as respects the year of assessment for which it is made but also for any subsequent year of assessment.

(*b*) Where the applicant gives, for any subsequent year of assessment, a notice withdrawing an application under paragraph (*a*), that application shall not have effect with respect to the year for which the notice is given or any subsequent year; but such notice of withdrawal shall not be valid unless it is given before [1 April][1] in the year following the year of assessment for which the notice is given.

(3) In the case of a woman who during a year of assessment or part of a year of assessment is a married woman living with her husband, any allowable loss which under section 31 would be deductible from the chargeable gains accruing in that year of assessment to the one spouse but for an insufficiency of chargeable gains shall for the purposes of that section be deductible from chargeable gains accruing in that year of assessment to the other spouse; but this subsection shall not apply in relation to losses accruing in a year of assessment to either spouse where an application that this subsection shall not apply is made by the husband or the wife before [1 April][1] in the year following that year of assessment.

(4) ...[2]

(5) Where in any year of assessment in which or in part of which the married woman is a married woman living with her husband, the husband disposes of an asset to the wife, or the wife disposes of an asset to the husband, both shall be treated as if the asset was

acquired from the spouse making the disposal for a consideration of such amount as would secure that on the disposal neither a gain nor a loss would accrue to the spouse making the disposal; but this subsection shall not apply if until the disposal the asset formed part of trading stock of a trade carried on by the spouse making the disposal, or if the asset is acquired as trading stock for the purposes of a trade carried on by the spouse acquiring the asset.

(6) Subsection (5) shall apply notwithstanding section 596 or any other provision of the Capital Gains Tax Acts fixing the amount of the consideration deemed to be given on a disposal or acquisition.

(7) Where subsection (5) is applied in relation to a disposal of an asset by a husband to his wife, or by his wife to him, then, in relation to a subsequent disposal of the asset (not within that subsection), the spouse making the disposal shall be treated for the purposes of the Capital Gains Tax Acts as if the other spouse's acquisition or provision of the asset had been his or her acquisition or provision of the asset.

(8) An application or notice of withdrawal under this section shall be in such form and made in such manner as may be prescribed.

Amendments

1 Substituted by FA 2001 s 77(2) and Sch 2 paras 59 and 61(*e*) for 2002 and later tax years; previously "the 6th day of July".

2 Subs (4) deleted by FA 1998 s 75 as respects 1998–99 and later tax years.

Cross-references

Apportionment of expenditure, subs (5): s 544(6)(*a*).

BES investments, subs (5): s 506(1).

Capital gains tax, returns and information, subs (1): s 913(8).

Disposal of business or farm on "retirement", subs (5): s 598(6)(*c*).

Disposals where assets lost or destroyed or become of negligible value: s 538(2A)(*c*)(ii).

Film investments, subs (5): s 481(20)(*d*).

Foreign life assurance and deferred annuities, subs (5): s 594(2)(*e*).

Special portfolio investment accounts, subs (4): s 838(4)(*c*).

Revenue precedents

Issue: Whether disposal of shares by one spouse to the designated broker for a SPIA held in the name of the other spouse would be exempt in accordance with TCA 1997 s 1028(5).

Decision: The disposal of shares by an individual to a designated broker acting as trustee for a SPIA which is beneficially owned by that individual's spouse would not be regarded as a disposal to that individual's spouse. The disposal would be an occasion of charge to CGT by reference to the market value of the assets in question.

Revenue information

Information leaflet IT3 — What to do about tax when you separate?

Definitions

allowable loss: ss 4(1), 5(1), 546; chargeable gain: ss 5(1), 545; person: IA 1937 s 11(*c*); prescribed: s 5(1); trade: s 5(1), ITA 1967 s 1(1); trading stock: ss 5(1), 89; year of assessment: ss 2(1), 5(1).

Former enactments

CGTA 1975 s 13; FA 1980 s 61(*b*); FA 1992 s 59.

1029 Application of section 1022 for purposes of capital gains tax

Section 1022 shall apply with any necessary modifications in relation to capital gains tax as it applies in relation to income tax.

Former enactments

CGTA 1975 s 51(1) and Sch 4 para 10(2).

1030 Separated spouses: transfers of assets

(1) In this section, **"spouse"** shall be construed in accordance with section 2(2)(*c*) of the Family Law Act, 1995.

(2) Notwithstanding any other provision of the Capital Gains Tax Acts, where by virtue or in consequence of—

(*a*) an order made under Part II of the Family Law Act, 1995, on or following the granting of a decree of judicial separation within the meaning of that Act,

(*b*) an order made under Part II of the Judicial Separation and Family Law Reform Act, 1989, on or following the granting of a decree of judicial separation where such order is treated, by virtue of section 3 of the Family Law Act, 1995, as if made under the corresponding provision of the Family Law Act, 1995,

(*c*) a deed of separation, ...[1]

[(*d*) a relief order (within the meaning of the Family Law Act, 1995) made following the dissolution of a marriage or following the legal separation of spouses, or

(*e*) an order or other determination to like effect, which is analogous to an order referred to in paragraph (*d*), of a court under the law of a territory other than the State made under or in consequence of the dissolution of a marriage or the legal separation of spouses, being a dissolution or legal separation that is entitled to be recognised as valid in the State,][2]

either of the spouses concerned disposes of an asset to the other spouse, then, subject to subsection (3), both spouses shall be treated for the purposes of the Capital Gains Tax Acts as if the asset was acquired from the spouse making the disposal for a consideration of such amount as would secure that on the disposal neither a gain nor a loss would accrue to the spouse making the disposal.

(3) Subsection (2) shall not apply if until the disposal the asset formed part of the trading stock of a trade carried on by the spouse making the disposal or if the asset is acquired as trading stock for the purposes of a trade carried on by the spouse acquiring the asset.

(4) Where subsection (2) applies in relation to a disposal of an asset by a spouse to the other spouse, then, in relation to a subsequent disposal of the asset (not being a disposal to which subsection (2) applies), the spouse making the disposal shall be treated for the purposes of the Capital Gains Tax Acts as if the other spouse's acquisition or provision of the asset had been his or her acquisition or provision of the asset.

Amendments

1 Deleted by FA 2000 s 88(1)(*a*) as respects disposals made on or after 10 February 2000; previously "or".

2 Subs (2)(*d*)–(*e*) substituted for subs (2)(*d*) by FA 2000 s 88(1)(*b*) as respects disposals made on or after 10 February 2000.

Revenue information

Information leaflet IT3 — What to do about tax when you separate?

Former enactments

FA 1997 s 72(1)–(3).

1031 Divorced persons: transfers of assets

(1) In this section, **"spouse"** shall be construed in accordance with section 2(2)(*c*) of the Family Law (Divorce) Act, 1996.

(2) Notwithstanding any other provision of the Capital Gains Tax Acts, where by virtue or in consequence of an order made under Part III of the Family Law (Divorce) Act, 1996, on or following the granting of a decree of divorce, either of the spouses concerned disposes of an asset to the other spouse, then, subject to subsection (3), both spouses shall be treated for the purpose of the Capital Gains Tax Acts as if the asset was acquired from the spouse making the disposal for a consideration of such amount as would secure that on the disposal neither a gain nor a loss would accrue to the spouse making the disposal.

(3) Subsection (2) shall not apply if until the disposal the asset formed part of the trading stock of a trade carried on by the spouse making the disposal or if the asset is acquired as trading stock for the purposes of a trade carried on by the spouse acquiring the asset.

(4) Where subsection (2) applies in relation to a disposal of an asset by a spouse to the other spouse, then, in relation to a subsequent disposal of the asset (not being a disposal to which subsection (2) applies), the spouse making the disposal shall be treated for the purposes of the Capital Gains Tax Acts as if the other spouse's acquisition or provision of the asset had been his or her acquisition or provision of the asset.

Revenue information

Information leaflet IT3 — What to do about tax when you separate?

Former enactments

Family Law Divorce Act 1996 s 35; FA 1997 s 71(1)–(3) and (5).

PART 45
CHARGING AND ASSESSING OF NON-RESIDENTS

CHAPTER 1
Income Tax and Corporation Tax

1032 Restrictions on certain reliefs

(1) Except where otherwise provided by this section, an individual not resident in the State shall not be entitled to any of the allowances, deductions, reliefs or reductions under the provisions specified in the Table to section 458.

(2) Where an individual not resident in the State proves to the satisfaction of the Revenue Commissioners that he or she—

(*a*) is a citizen of Ireland,

(*b*) is resident outside the State for the sake or on account of his or her health or the health of a member of his or her family resident with him or her or because of some physical infirmity or disease in himself or herself or any such member of his or her family, and that previous to such residence outside the State he or she was resident in the State,

(*c*) is a citizen, subject or national of another Member State of the European Communities or of a country of which the citizens, subjects or nationals are for the time being exempted by an order under section 10 of the Aliens Act, 1935, from any provision of, or of an aliens order under, that Act, or

(*d*) is a person to whom one of the paragraphs (*a*) to (*e*) of the proviso to section 24 of the Finance Act, 1920, applied in respect of the year ending on the 5th day of April, 1935, or any previous year of assessment,

then, subsection (1) shall not apply to that individual, but the amount of any allowance, deduction or other benefit mentioned in that subsection shall, in the case of that, individual, be reduced to an amount which bears the same proportion to the total amount of that allowance, deduction or other benefit as the portion of his or her income subject to Irish income tax bears to his or her total income from all sources (including income not subject to Irish income tax).

(3) Notwithstanding subsection (2), where an individual not resident in the State proves to the satisfaction of the Revenue Commissioners that the individual is a resident of another Member State of the European Communities and that the proportion which the portion of the individual's income subject to Irish income tax bears to the individual's total income from all sources (including income not subject to Irish income tax) is 75 per cent or greater, subsection (1) or, as the case may be, subsection (2) shall not apply to that individual and he or she shall be entitled to the allowance, deduction or other benefit mentioned in subsection (1).

Cross-references

Charging and assessing of non-residents, entitlement to tax credit in respect of distributions, subss (2)–(3): s 1033.

Case law

The requirements of Article 48 of EC Treaty guaranteeing freedom of movement of EC workers in relation to taxation of non-residents was considered by The Court of Justice (although primarily concerned with German legislation which is dissimilar) in: *Finanzamt Köln-Alstadt v Schumaker* [1995] STI 310.

Definitions

person: IA 1937 s 11(*c*); total income: s 3(1); year of assessment: s 3(1).

Former enactments

ITA 1967 s 153; FA 1974 s 6(2) and Sch 1 Pt I para 1(vii)(*d*); FA 1994 s 155; FA 1996 s 132(1) and Sch 5 Pt I para 1(7).

Corresponding UK tax provision

Income and Corporation Taxes Act 1988 s 278.

1033 Entitlement to tax credit in respect of distributions

Amendments

[1] Section 1033 repealed by FA 1999 s 28(3) in respect of distributions made on or after 6 April 1999.

1034 Assessment

A person not resident in the State, whether a citizen of Ireland or not, shall be assessable and chargeable to income tax in the name of any trustee, guardian, or committee of such person, or of any factor, agent, receiver, branch or manager, whether such factor, agent, receiver, branch or manager has the receipt of the profits or gains or not, in the like manner and to the like amount as such non-resident person would be assessed and charged if such person were resident in the State and in the actual receipt of such profits or gains; but, in the case of a partnership, the precedent partner (within the meaning of section 1007) or, if there is no precedent partner, the factor, agent, receiver, branch or manager shall be deemed to be the agent of a non-resident partner.

Cross-references

Capital gains tax, this section applied by: s 1043.

Rents payable to non-residents, this section does not apply: s 1041(1).

Taxation of collective investment undertakings: s 734(10).

Case law

Irish

A trading enterprise in Australia vested in trustees resident both in Ireland and the United Kingdom, but managed locally, was regarded as being outside the Case I charge: *Executors and Trustees of A C Ferguson (deceased) v Donovan* ITR Vol I p 183.

Revenue precedents

Issue: Charge on non-resident partners.

Decision: The partners are chargeable in the name of the precedent acting partner at the progressive rates ie the lower rate and at the higher rate.

Definitions

person: IA 1937 s 11(*c*).

Former enactments

ITA 1967 s 200.

1035 Profits from agencies, etc

[Subject to section 1035A, a non-resident person][1] shall be assessable and chargeable to income tax in respect of any profits or gains arising, whether directly or indirectly, through or from any factorship, agency, receivership, branch or management, and shall be so assessable and chargeable in the name of the factor, agent, receiver, branch or manager.

Amendments

1 Substituted by FA 2003 s 51(1)(*a*) as respects chargeable periods commending on or after 1 January 2002.

Cross-references

Capital gains tax, this section applied by: s 1043.

Definitions

person: IA 1937 s 11(*c*).

Former enactments

ITA 1967 s 201.

1035A Relieving provision to section 1035

[(1) In this section—

"authorised agent" means—

(*a*) a person acting as an investment business firm, or an authorised member firm—

(i) under an authorisation given by the Central Bank of Ireland under section 10(1) of the Investment Intermediaries Act 1995 or, as the case may be, section 18 of the Stock Exchange Act 1995, and not subsequently revoked, or

(ii) under an authorisation, which corresponds to either of the authorisations referred to in subparagraph (i), given by a competent authority in another

Member State for the purpose of Council Directive 93/22/EEC of 10 May 1993 (OJ No L141, of 11 June 1993, p 27) as amended or extended from time to time, and not subsequently revoked, or

(*b*) a credit institution duly authorised by virtue of Directive No 2000/12/EC of 20 March 2000 (OJ.No L126, of 26 May 2000, p 1) which provides investment business services and in so doing does not exceed the terms of its authorisation and that authorisation has not been revoked,

and **"authorisation"** shall be construed accordingly;

"authorised member firm" has the meaning assigned to it by section 3 of the Stock Exchange Act 1995;

"competent authority" has the meaning assigned to it by section 2 of the Investment Intermediaries Act 1995;

"financial trade" means a trade exercised in the State by a non-resident person through an authorised agent under and within the terms of the authorised agent's authorisation;

"investment business firm" has the meaning assigned to it by section 2 of the Investment Intermediaries Act 1995;

"investment business services" has the meaning assigned to it by section 2 of the Investment Intermediaries Act 1995.

(2) For the purposes of this section—

(*a*) an authorised agent, through whom a non-resident person exercises a financial trade in the State, is independent in relation to the non-resident person for a chargeable period if throughout the chargeable period—

(i) the authorised agent does not otherwise act on behalf of the non-resident person,

(ii) the authorised agent, when acting on behalf of the non-resident person, does so in an independent capacity,

(iii) the authorised agent, when acting on behalf of the non-resident person, does so in the ordinary course of the authorised agent's business, and

(iv) the requirements referred to in subsection (4), in relation to the financial trade, are satisfied,

(*b*) an authorised agent shall not be regarded as acting in an independent capacity when acting on behalf of a non-resident person unless, having regard to its legal, financial and commercial characteristics, the relationship between them is a relationship between persons carrying on independent businesses that deal with each other at arm's length, and

(*c*) references to an amount of profits or gains of a trade, exercised in the State by a non-resident person, to which another person has a beneficial entitlement are references to the amount of profits or gains of the trade to which the other person has, or may acquire, a beneficial entitlement by virtue of—

(i) any interest of the other person (whether or not an interest giving a right to an immediate payment of a share of the profits or gains of the trade) in property in which the whole or any part of the profits or gains of the trade are represented, or

(ii) any interest of the other person in, or other rights in relation to, the non-resident person.

(3) Notwithstanding section 18, a non-resident person shall not be assessable and chargeable to income tax in respect of any profits or gains arising or accruing for a chargeable period to the non-resident person from a financial trade exercised in the State solely through an authorised agent who throughout the chargeable period is independent in relation to the non-resident person.

(4) The requirements of this subsection are satisfied, at any time, in relation to a financial trade exercised in the State by a non-resident person through an authorised agent where at that time—

(*a*) the aggregate of the amount of the profits or gains of the trade, to which the authorised agent and persons, who are both resident in the State and connected with the authorised agent, have a beneficial entitlement, does not exceed 20 per cent of the amount of the profits or gains of the trade, or

(*b*) the Revenue Commissioners are satisfied that it is the intention of the authorised agent, that the aggregate of the amount of the profits or gains of the trade, to which the authorised agent and persons who are resident in the State and connected with the authorised agent have beneficial entitlement, does not exceed 20 per cent of the amount of the profits or gains of the trade and that the reasons for the failure to fulfill that intention, at that time, are of a temporary nature.

(5) The Revenue Commissioners may nominate any of their officers to perform any acts and discharge any functions authorised by this section to be performed or discharged by them.][1]

Amendments

1 Section 1035A inserted by FA 2003 s 51(1)(*b*) as respects chargeable periods commending on or after 1 January 2002.

Revenue information

Guidance notes (Jan 2004) on Investment Management Services and the application of this section are available on Revenue's website (www.revenue.ie) under Publications/Technical Guidelines.

Definitions

connected: s 10; person: IA 1937 s 11(*c*); resident: s 2(1); trade: s 3(1).

1036 Control over residents

Where a non-resident person, not being a citizen of Ireland or an Irish firm or company, or a branch of a non-resident person, carries on business with a resident person, and it appears to the inspector that, owing to the close connection between the resident person and the non-resident person and to the substantial control exercised by the non-resident person over the resident person, the course of business between those persons can be so arranged and is so arranged that the business done by the resident person in pursuance of that person's connection with the non-resident person produces to the resident person either no profits or less than the ordinary profits which might be expected to arise from that business, then, the non-resident person shall be assessable and chargeable to income tax in the name of the resident person as if the resident person were an agent of the non-resident person.

Definitions

inspector: ss 2(1), 5(1), 852; person: IA 1937 s 11(*c*).

Former enactments

ITA 1967 s 202.

1037 Charge on percentage of turnover

(1) Where it appears to the inspector or on appeal to the Appeal Commissioners that the true amount of the profits or gains of any non-resident person chargeable with income tax in the name of a resident person cannot in any case be readily ascertained, the non-resident person may, if it is thought fit by the inspector or the Appeal Commissioners, be assessed and charged on a percentage of the turnover of the business done by the non-resident person through or with the resident person in whose name the non-resident person is so chargeable, and in such a case the provisions of the Income Tax Acts relating to the delivery of statements by persons acting on behalf of others shall extend so as to require returns to be given by the resident person of the business so done by the non-resident person through or with the resident person in the same manner as statements of profits or gains to be charged are to be delivered by persons acting for incapacitated or non-resident persons.

(2) The amount of the percentage under subsection (1) shall in each case be determined, having regard to the nature of the business, by the inspector by whom the assessment on the percentage basis is made, subject to appeal to the Appeal Commissioners.

(3) Where either the resident person or the non-resident person is dissatisfied with the percentage determined either in the first instance or by the Appeal Commissioners on appeal, that person may within 4 months of that determination require the inspector or the Appeal Commissioners, as the case may be, to refer the question of the percentage to a referee or board of referees to be appointed for the purpose by the Minister for Finance, and the decision of the referee or board of referees shall be final and conclusive.

Definitions

Appeal Commissioners: s 2(1); inspector: ss 2(1), 5(1), 852; month: IA 1937 Sch; person: IA 1937 s 11(*c*).

Former enactments

ITA 1967 s 203; F(MP)A 1968 s 3(2) and Sch Pt I.

1038 Merchanting profit

Where a non-resident person is chargeable to income tax in the name of any branch, manager, agent, factor or receiver in respect of any profits or gains arising from the sale of goods or produce manufactured or produced outside the State by the non-resident person, the person in whose name the non-resident person is so chargeable may, if that person thinks fit, apply to—

(*a*) the inspector, or

(*b*) in case of an appeal, to the Appeal Commissioners,

to have the assessment to income tax in respect of those profits or gains made or amended on the basis of the profits which might reasonably be expected to have been earned by—

(i) a merchant, or

(ii) where the goods are retailed by or on behalf of the manufacturer or producer, by a retailer of the goods sold,

who had bought from the manufacturer or producer direct and, on proof to the satisfaction of the inspector or, as the case may be, the Appeal Commissioners of the amount of the profits on that basis, the assessment shall be made or amended accordingly.

Definitions

Appeal Commissioners: s 2(1); inspector: ss 2(1), 5(1), 852; person: IA 1937 s 11(*c*).

Former enactments

ITA 1967 s 204; F(MP)A 68 s3(2) and Sch Pt I.

1039 Restrictions on chargeability

(1) Nothing in this Chapter shall render a non-resident person chargeable in the name of—

(*a*) a broker or general commission agent, or

(*b*) an agent, not being—

(i) an authorised person carrying on the regular agency of the non-resident person, or

(ii) a person chargeable as if that person were an agent in pursuance of this Chapter,

in respect of profits or gains arising from sales or transactions carried out through such a broker or agent.

(2) The fact that a non-resident person executes sales or carries out transactions with other non-residents in circumstances which would make that person chargeable in pursuance of this Chapter in the name of a resident person shall not of itself make that person chargeable in respect of profits arising from those sales or transactions.

Case law

"Regular agency" means an agency that is not a casual or occasional agency and a person can be an agent although engaged in only one transaction: *Wilson v Hooker* [1995] STC 1142.

Definitions

person: IA 1937 s 11(*c*).

Former enactments

ITA 1967 s 205.

1040 Application of sections 1034 to 1039 for purposes of corporation tax

Without prejudice to the general application of income tax procedure to corporation tax, the provisions of this Chapter relating to the assessment and charge of income tax on persons not resident in the State, in so far as they are applicable to tax chargeable on a company, shall apply with any necessary modifications in relation to corporation tax chargeable on companies not resident in the State.

Former enactments

CTA 1976 s 8(4).

1041 Rents payable to non-residents

(1) Section 1034 shall not apply to—

(*a*) tax on profits or gains chargeable to tax under Case V of Schedule D, or

(*b*) tax on any of the profits or gains chargeable under Case IV of Schedule D which arise under the terms of a lease, but to a person other than the lessor, or which otherwise arise out of any disposition or contract such that if they arose to the person making it they would be chargeable under Case V of Schedule D,

where payment is made (whether in the State or elsewhere) directly to a person whose usual place of abode is outside the State; but section 238 shall apply in relation to the payment as it applies to other payments, being annual payments charged with tax under Schedule D and not payable out of profits or gains brought into charge to tax.

(2) Where by virtue of subsection (1) the tax chargeable for any year of assessment on a person's profits or gains chargeable to tax under either or both of the Cases referred to in that subsection would but for this subsection be greater than the tax which would be chargeable on such profits or gains but for subsection (1), then, on a claim in that behalf being made, relief shall be given from the excess, whether by repayment or otherwise.

Cross-references

Annual payments not payable out of taxed income, subs (1): s 238(7).

Amount of s 238 assessment to be allowed as a loss, subs (1): s 390(3).

Tax Briefing

TB42 Dec 2000 p 35 — Non-resident landlords — Taxation of Rental Income.

Definitions

person: IA 1937 s 11(*c*); year of assessment: ss 2(1), 5(1).

Former enactments

FA 1969 s 25.

CHAPTER 2
Capital Gains Tax

1042 Charging and assessment of persons not resident or ordinarily resident: modification of general rules

(1) Notwithstanding section 28(2), 31 or 979, any capital gains tax payable in respect of a chargeable gain which on a disposal accrues to a person not resident or ordinarily resident in the State at the time at which the disposal is made may be assessed and charged before the end of the year of assessment in which the chargeable gain accrues, and the tax so assessed and charged shall be payable at or before the expiration of a period of 3 months beginning with the time at which the disposal is made, or at the expiration of a period of 2 months beginning with the date of making the assessment, whichever is the later.

(2) In computing the amount of capital gains tax payable under subsection (1), section 31 shall apply with any necessary modifications as regards the deduction of any allowable losses which accrued to the person mentioned in subsection (1) before the date of making of the assessment mentioned in that subsection.

Cross-references

Self assessment, making of assessments: s 954(7)(*c*).

Capital gains tax, deduction from consideration on disposal of certain assets: s 980(10).

Former enactments

CGTA 1975 s 5(3); FA 1982 s 33.

1043 Application of sections 1034 and 1035 for purposes of capital gains tax

Without prejudice to the generality of section 931(2), sections 1034 and 1035 shall apply, subject to any necessary modifications, to capital gains tax.

Former enactments

CGTA 1975 s 51(1) and Sch 4 para 2(2).

PART 46
PERSONS CHARGEABLE IN A REPRESENTATIVE CAPACITY

CHAPTER 1
Income Tax and Corporation Tax

Cross-references

Capital gains tax, Chapter 1 (other than section 1050) applied by: s 1051.

1044 Bodies of persons

(1) Subject to section 21, every body of persons shall be chargeable to income tax in the like manner as any person is chargeable under the Income Tax Acts.

(2) The treasurer (or other officer acting as such), auditor or receiver for the time being of any body of persons chargeable to income tax shall be answerable for doing all such acts as are required to be done under the Income Tax Acts for the purpose of the assessment of such body and for payment of the tax, and for the purpose of the assessment of the officers and persons in the employment of such body; but, in the case of a company, the person so answerable shall be the secretary of the company or other officer (by whatever name called) performing the duties of secretary.

(3) Every such officer may from time to time retain out of any money coming into his or her hands on behalf of the body so much of that money as is sufficient to pay the tax charged on the body, and shall be indemnified for all such payments made in pursuance of the Income Tax Acts.

Cross-references

Duty of employer as to tax payable by employees, subss (3)–(4): s 972(4).

Capital gains tax, this section applied by: s 1051.

Increased penalties in case of body of persons, meaning of "secretary", subs (2): s 1054(1).

Corporation tax penalties, meaning of "secretary", subs (2): s 1076(1).

Particulars to be supplied by new companies, meaning of "secretary", subs (2): s 882(1).

Definitions

body of persons: s 2(1); person: IA 1937 s 11(*c*).

Former enactments

ITA 1967 s 207.

Corresponding UK tax provision

Taxes Management Act 1970 s 71.

1045 Trustees, guardians and committees

The trustee, guardian or committee of any incapacitated person having the direction, control or management of the property or concern of any such person, whether such person resides in the State or not, shall be assessable and chargeable to income tax in the like manner and to the like amount as that person would be assessed and charged if he or she were not an incapacitated person.

Cross-references

Capital gains tax, this section applied by: s 1051.

Definitions

incapacitated person: s 3(1); person: IA 1937 s 11(*c*).

Former enactments

ITA 1967 s 208.

1046 Liability of trustees, etc

(1) The person chargeable in respect of an incapacitated person or in whose name a non-resident person is chargeable shall be answerable for all matters required to be done under the Income Tax Acts for the purpose of assessment and payment of income tax.

(2) Any person charged under the Income Tax Acts in respect of any incapacitated or non-resident person may from time to time retain out of money coming into the first-mentioned person's hands on behalf of that incapacitated or non-resident person so much of that money as is sufficient to pay the tax charged, and shall be indemnified for all such payments made in pursuance of the Income Tax Acts.

(3) Without prejudice to the general application of income tax procedure to corporation tax, subsections (1) and (2), in so far as they are applicable to tax chargeable on a company, shall apply with any necessary modifications in relation to corporation tax chargeable on companies not resident in the State.

Cross-references

Capital gains tax, this section applied by: s 1051.

Revenue precedents

Issue: Extent of charge where beneficiaries are not resident in the State.

Decision: Where the whole of the trust income is payable to a beneficiary who is not resident or divisible between two or more beneficiaries, none of whom is resident here, the liability is confined to that on income arising here, subject to any exemption on the basis that the beneficiary is resident in a treaty country.

Definitions

incapacitated person: s 3(1); person: IA 1937 s 11(*c*).

Former enactments

ITA 1967 s 209; CTA 1976 s 8(4).

Corresponding UK tax provision

Taxes Management Act 1970 s 72.

1047 Liability of parents, guardians, executors and administrators

(1) Where a person chargeable to income tax is an infant or dies—

(*a*) the parent or guardian of the infant shall be liable for the tax in default of payment by the infant, and

(*b*) the executor or administrator of the deceased person shall be liable for the tax charged on such deceased person,

and on neglect or refusal of payment any such person so liable may be proceeded against in the like manner as any other defaulter.

(2) A parent or guardian who makes such payment shall be allowed all sums so paid in his or her accounts, and an executor or administrator may deduct all such payments out of the assets and effects of the person deceased.

Cross-references

Capital gains tax, this section applied by: s 1051.

Definitions

person: IA 1937 s 11(*c*).

Former enactments

ITA 1967 s 210(1)–(2).

Corresponding UK tax provision

Taxes Management Act 1970 s 73.

1048 Assessment of executors and administrators

(1) Where a person dies, an assessment or an additional first assessment, as the case may be, may be made for any year of assessment for which an assessment or an additional first assessment could have been made on the person immediately before his or her death, or could be made on the person if he or she were living, in respect of the profits or gains which arose or accrued to such person before his or her death, and the amount of the income tax on such profits or gains shall be a debt due from and payable out of the estate of such person, and the executor or administrator of such person shall be assessable and chargeable in respect of such tax.

(2) No assessment under this section shall be made later than 3 years after the expiration of the year of assessment in which the deceased person died in a case in which the grant of probate or letters of administration was made in that year, and no such assessment shall be made later than 2 years after the expiration of the year of assessment in which such grant was made in any other case; but this subsection shall apply subject to the condition that where the executor or administrator—

(*a*) after the year of assessment in which the deceased person died, delivers an additional affidavit under [section 48 of the Capital Acquisitions Tax Consolidation Act 2003][1], or

(*b*) is liable to deliver an additional affidavit under that section, has been so notified by the Revenue Commissioners and did not deliver the additional affidavit in the year of assessment in which the deceased person died,

such assessment may be made at any time before the expiration of 2 years after the end of the year of assessment in which the additional affidavit was or is delivered.

(3) The executor or administrator of any such deceased person shall, when required to do so by a notice given to the executor or administrator by an inspector, prepare and deliver to the inspector a statement in writing signed by such executor or administrator and containing particulars, to the best of such executor's or administrator's judgment and belief, of the profits or gains which arose or accrued to such deceased person before his or her death and in respect of which such executor or administrator is assessable under this section, and the provisions of the Income Tax Acts relating to statements to be delivered by any person shall apply with any necessary modifications to statements to be delivered under this section.

Amendments

1 Substituted by FA 2004 s 89 and Sch 3 para 1(*ad*) with effect from 21 February 2003; previously "section 38 of the Capital Acquisitions Tax Act, 1976".

Cross-references

Capital gains tax, this section applied by: s 1051.

Proceedings against executor or administrator, subs (2): s 1060(2).

Self assessment, amendment of and time limit for assessments: ss 955(1).

Definitions

affidavit: IA 1937 Sch; inspector: ss 2(1), 5(1), 852; person: IA 1937 s 11(*c*); writing: IA 1937 Sch; year of assessment: s 3(1).

Former enactments

ITA 1967 s 211(1)–(3); F(MP)A 1968 s 4(3)(*a*) and s 6(7); FA 1978 s 11(1).

Corresponding UK tax provision

Taxes Management Act 1970 s 74.

1049 Receivers appointed by court

(1) A receiver appointed by any court in the State which has the direction and control of any property in respect of which income tax or, as the case may be, corporation tax is charged in accordance with the Tax Acts shall be assessable and chargeable with income tax or, as the case may be, corporation tax in the like manner and to the like amount as would be assessed and charged if the property were not under the direction and control of the court.

(2) Every such receiver shall be answerable for doing all matters and things required to be done under the Tax Acts for the purpose of assessment and payment of income tax or, as the case may be, corporation tax.

Cross-references

Capital gains tax, this section applied by: s 1051.

Former enactments

ITA 1967 s 212; CTA 1976 s 147(1) and(2).

Corresponding UK tax provision

Taxes Management Act 1970 s 75.

1050 Protection for trustees, agents and receivers

(1) A trustee who has authorised the receipt of profits arising from trust property by or by the agent of the person entitled to such profits shall not, if—

(*a*) that person or agent actually received the profits under that authority, and (*b*) the trustee makes a return as required by section 890 of the name, address and profits of that person,

be required to do any other act for the purpose of the assessment of that person, unless the Revenue Commissioners require the testimony of the trustee pursuant to the Income Tax Acts.

(2) An agent or receiver of any person resident in the State, other than an incapacitated person, shall not, if that agent or receiver makes a return as required by section 890 of the name, address and profits of that person, be required to do any other act for the purpose of the assessment of that person, unless the Revenue Commissioners require the testimony of the agent or receiver pursuant to the Income Tax Acts.

Definitions

incapacitated person: s 3(1); person: IA 1937 s 11(*c*).

Former enactments

ITA 1967 s 213.

Corresponding UK tax provision

Taxes Management Act 1970 s 76.

CHAPTER 2
Capital Gains Tax

1051 Application of Chapter 1 for purposes of capital gains tax

Chapter 1 other than section 1050 shall, subject to any necessary modifications, apply to capital gains tax.

Cross-references

Self assessment: s 959(6).

Former enactments

CGTA 1975 s 51(1) and Sch 4 para 2(2).

PART 47
PENALTIES, REVENUE OFFENCES, INTEREST ON OVERDUE TAX AND OTHER SANCTIONS

CHAPTER 1
Income Tax and Corporation Tax Penalties

Cross-references

Capital gains tax, penalties for failure to make returns etc, and for fraudulently or negligently making incorrect returns, this Chapter applied by: s 1077(1).

1052 Penalties for failure to make certain returns, etc

(1) Where any person—

(*a*) has been required, by notice or precept given under or for the purposes of any of the provisions specified in column 1 or 2 of Schedule 29, to deliver any return, statement, declaration, list or other document, to furnish any particulars, to produce any document, or to make anything available for inspection, and that person fails to comply with the notice or [precept,][1]

[(*aa*) has delivered a return in the prescribed form for the purposes of any of the provisions specified in column 1 or 2 of Schedule 29 and has failed to include on the prescribed form the details required by that form in relation to any exemption, allowance, deduction, credit or other relief the person is claiming (in this paragraph referred to as the **"specified details"**) where the specified details are stated on the form to be details to which this paragraph refers; but this paragraph shall not apply unless, after the return has been delivered, it had come to the person's notice or had been brought to the person's attention that specified details had not been included on the form and the person failed to remedy matters without unreasonable delay, or][2]

(*b*) fails to do any act, to furnish any particulars or to deliver any account in accordance with any of the provisions specified in column 3 of that Schedule,

that person shall, subject to subsection (2) and to section 1054, be liable to a penalty of [€950][3].

(2) Where the notice referred to in subsection (1) was given under or for the purposes of any of the provisions specified in column 1 of Schedule 29 and the failure continues after the end of the year of assessment following that during which the notice was given, the penalty mentioned in subsection (1) shall be [€1,520][4].

(3) Subsections (1) and (2) shall apply subject to sections 877(5)(*b*) and 897(5).

(4) In proceedings for the recovery of a penalty incurred under this section or under section 1053—

(*a*) a certificate signed by an officer of the Revenue Commissioners, or, in the case of such proceedings in relation to a return referred to in section 879 or 880, by an inspector, which certifies that he or she has examined his or her relevant records and that it appears from those records that a stated notice or precept was duly given to the defendant on a stated day shall be evidence until the contrary is proved that the defendant received that notice or precept in the ordinary course;

(*b*) a certificate signed by an officer of the Revenue Commissioners which certifies that he or she has examined his or her relevant records and that it appears from those records that during a stated period a stated notice or precept has not been complied with by the defendant shall be evidence until the contrary is proved that the defendant did not during that period comply with that notice or precept;

(*c*) in the case of such proceedings in relation to a return referred to in section 879 or 880, a certificate signed by an inspector which certifies that he or she has examined his or her relevant records and that it appears from those records that during a stated period a stated return was not received from the defendant shall be evidence until the contrary is proved that the defendant did not during that period deliver that return;

(*d*) a certificate signed by an officer of the Revenue Commissioners which certifies that he or she has examined his or her relevant records and that it appears from those records that during a stated period the defendant has failed to do a stated act, furnish stated particulars or deliver a stated account in accordance with any of the provisions specified in column 3 of Schedule 29 shall be evidence until the contrary is proved that the defendant did so fail;

(*e*) a certificate certifying as provided for in paragraph (*a*), (*b*), (*c*) or (*d*) and purporting to be signed by an officer of the Revenue Commissioners or, as the case may be, by an inspector may be tendered in evidence without proof and shall be deemed until the contrary is proved to have been signed by such officer or, as the case may be, such inspector.

Amendments

1 Substituted by FA 2004 s 86(2)(*a*) as respects any chargeable period (within the meaning of TCA 1997 s 321(2)) commencing on or after 1 January 2004; previously "precept, or".

2 Subs (1)(*aa*) inserted by FA 2004 s 86(2)(*b*) as respects any chargeable period (within the meaning of TCA 1997 s 321(2)) commencing on or after 1 January 2004.

3 Substituted by FA 2001 s 240(1) and (2)(*k*) and Sch 5 Pt 1 as respects any act or omission which takes place or begins on or after 1 January 2002; previously "£750".

4 Substituted by FA 2001 s 240(1) and (2)(*k*) and Sch 5 Pt 1 as respects any act or omission which takes place or begins on or after 1 January 2002; previously "£1,200".

Cross-references

Approved share option schemes, transitional: Sch 32 para 7(3)(*b*).
Capital gains tax, penalties for failure to make returns etc, and for fraudulently or negligently making incorrect returns, this section applied by: s 1077(1).
Deduction of from payments due to defaulters: s 1002(7)(*a*).
Income Tax (Relevant Contracts) Regulations 2000, SI No 71 of 2000: ITRCR 2000 Reg 7(3).
Increased penalties in case of body of persons: s 1054(2).
Returns by employers in relation to certain pension products, this section applied: s 897A(3).
Returns of interest paid to non-residents, failure to deliver a return, this section applied by: s 891A(2)(*c*).
Returns of special term accounts by relevant deposit takers, this section applied by: s 264B(3).
Returns of special term share accounts by credit unions, this section applied by: s 267E(3).
Revenue offences, subs (4): s 1078(9).
Self assessment, obligation to make a return: s 951(12).
Tonnage tax, transactions between associated persons and between tonnage tax trade and other activities of same company, this section applied by: s 697LA(6).

Case law

Irish

Penalties under this section held to be non criminal in nature, pursuable by civil proceedings: *McLoughlin v Tuite* [1986] IR 235; these penalties not unconstitutional: (Supreme Court, 13 June 1989). See also *Director of Public Prosecutions v Downes* ITR Vol III p 641.

UK

Held penalty properly imposed, where time and place specified by taxpayer for inspection of documents was unreasonable: *Johnson v Blackpool General Commissioners* [1996] STC 277.

Definitions

person: IA 1937 s 11(*c*); year of assessment: s 3(1).

Former enactments

ITA 1967 s 70(4), s 172(5) and s 500; FA 1980 s 57(2); FA 1982 s 60; FA 1992 s 248.

Corresponding UK tax provision

Taxes Management Act 1970 ss 93–94.

1053 Penalty for fraudulently or negligently making incorrect returns, etc

(1) Where any person fraudulently or negligently—

(*a*) delivers any incorrect return or statement of a kind mentioned in any of the provisions specified in column 1 of Schedule 29, (*b*) makes any incorrect return, statement or declaration in connection with any claim for any allowance, deduction or relief, or

(*c*) submits to the Revenue Commissioners, the Appeal Commissioners or an inspector any incorrect accounts in connection with the ascertainment of that person's liability to income tax,

that person shall, subject to section 1054, be liable to a penalty of—

(i) [€125][1], and

(ii) ...[2] the amount of the difference specified in subsection (5).

[(1A) Where any person fails to comply with a requirement to deliver a return or statement of a kind mentioned in any of the provisions specified in column 1 of Schedule 29, by reason of fraud or neglect by that person, that person shall, subject to section 1054, be liable to a penalty of—

(*a*) €125, and

(*b*) ...[3] the amount of the difference specified in subsection (5A).][4]

(2) Where any person fraudulently or negligently furnishes, gives, produces or makes any incorrect return, information, certificate, document, record, statement, particulars, account or declaration of a kind mentioned in any of the provisions specified in column 2 or 3 of Schedule 29, that person shall, subject to section 1054, be liable to a penalty of [€125][1] or, in the case of fraud, [€315][5].

(3) Where any return, statement, declaration or accounts mentioned in subsection (1) was or were made or submitted by a person, neither fraudulently nor negligently, and it comes to that person's notice (or, if the person has died, to the notice of his or her personal representatives) that it was or they were incorrect, then, unless the error is remedied without unreasonable delay, the return, statement, declaration or accounts shall be treated for the purposes of this section as having been negligently made or submitted by that person.

(4) Subject to section 1060(2), proceedings for the recovery of any penalty under subsection (1) or (2) shall not be out of time because they are commenced after the time allowed by section 1063.

(5) The difference referred to in subsection (1)(ii) shall be the difference between—

(*a*) the amount of income tax payable for the relevant years of assessment by the person concerned (including any amount deducted at source and not repayable), and

(*b*) the amount which would have been the amount so payable if the return, statement, declaration or accounts as made or submitted by that person had been correct.

[(5A) The difference referred to in subsection (1A)(*b*) is the difference between—

(*a*) the amount of income tax paid by that person for the relevant years of assessment, and

(*b*) the amount of income tax which would have been payable for the relevant years of assessment if the return or statement had been delivered by that person and the return or statement had been correct.][6]

(6) The relevant years of assessment for the purposes of [subsections (5) and (5A)][7] shall be, in relation to anything delivered, made or submitted in any year of assessment, that year, the next year and any preceding year of assessment, and the references in that subsection to the amount of income tax payable shall not, in relation to anything done in connection with a partnership, include any tax not chargeable in the partnership name.

(7) For the purposes of this section, any accounts submitted on behalf of a person shall be deemed to have been submitted by the person unless that person proves that they were submitted without that person's consent or knowledge.

Amendments

1 Substituted by FA 2001 s 240(1) and (2)(*k*) and Sch 5 Pt 1 as respects any act or omission which takes place or begins on or after 1 January 2002; previously "£100".

2 Deleted by FA 2005 s 141(*a*)(i) in relation to returns, statements, declarations, or accounts delivered, made or, as the case may be, submitted on or after 25 March 2005; previously "the amount or, in the case of fraud, twice".

3 Deleted by FA 2005 s 141(*a*)(ii) in relation to returns, statements, declarations, or accounts delivered, made or, as the case may be, submitted on or after 25 March 2005; previously "the amount or, in the case of fraud, twice".

4 Subs (1A) inserted by FA 2002 s 130(1)(*a*)(i) with effect from 25 March 2002.

5 Substituted by FA 2001 s 240(1) and (2)(*k*) and Sch 5 Pt 1 as respects any act or omission which takes place or begins on or after 1 January 2002; previously "£250".

6 Subs (5A) inserted by FA 2002 s 130(1)(*a*)(ii) with effect from 25 March 2002.

7 Substituted by FA 2002 s 130(1)(*a*)(iii) with effect from 25 March 2002; previously "subsection (5)".

Cross-references

Approved share option schemes, transitional: Sch 32 para 7(3)(*b*).
Capital gains tax, penalties for failure to make returns etc, and for fraudulently or negligently making incorrect returns, this section applied by: s 1077(1).
Increased penalties in case of body of persons, subss (1), (5): s 1054(3)(*a*); subs (2): s 1054(3)(*b*).
Income Tax (Relevant Contracts) Regulations 2000, SI No 71 of 2000: ITRCR 2000 Reg 7(3).
Penalties for failure to furnish certain information and for incorrect information, subs (3): s 1075(5).
Penalties for failure to make certain returns: s 1052(4).
Penalties for fraudulently or negligently making incorrect returns, subs (3): s 1072(3).
Returns by employers in relation to certain pension products, this section applied: s 897A(3).
Returns of interest paid to non-residents, failure to deliver a return, this section applied by: s 891A(2)(*c*).
Revenue offences, subss (3), (7): s 1078(9).
Subcontractors' withholding tax, subss (3), (7): s 531(16).

Case law

Irish

Proceedings for fraud instituted by the Revenue did not prohibit further action for the recovery of the same liabilities by way of assessment and the use of the appeal procedures: *Revenue Commissioners and others v Calcul International Ltd* (High Court, 8 November 1986).

UK

Held the Revenue were entitled to adopt a selective prosecution policy in relation to an accountant's clients and the particular clients who were prosecuted were not unfairly treated: *R v CIR (ex parte Mead & Cook)* [1992] STC 482.

Definitions

inspector: ss 2(1), 5(1), 852; person: IA 1937 s 11(*c*); year of assessment: s 3(1).

Former enactments

ITA 1967 s 501 and s 502; F(MP)A 1968 s 3(2) and Sch Pt I; FA 1974 s 86 and Sch 2 Pt I.

Corresponding UK tax provision

Taxes Management Act 1970 ss 95–97.

1054 Increased penalties in case of body of persons

(1) In this section, **"secretary"** includes persons mentioned in section 1044(2).

(2) Where the person mentioned in section 1052 is a body of persons—

(*a*) the body of persons shall be liable to—

(i) in a case where the notice was given under or for the purposes of any of the provisions specified in column 1 of Schedule 29 and the failure continues after the end of the year of assessment following that during which the notice was given, a penalty of [€1,520][1], and

(ii) in any other case, a penalty of [€950][2] and, if the failure continues after judgment has been given by the court before which proceedings for the penalty have been commenced, a further penalty of [€60][3] for each day on which the failure so continues, and

(*b*) the secretary shall be liable to—

(i) in a case where the notice was given under or for the purposes of any of the provisions specified in column 1 of Schedule 29 and the failure continues after the end of the year of assessment following that during which the notice was given, a separate penalty of [€250][4], and

(ii) in any other case, a separate penalty of [€125][5].

(3) Where the person mentioned in section 1053 is a body of persons—

(*a*) in the case of such fraud or negligence as is mentioned in section 1053(1)—

(i) the body of persons shall be liable to a penalty of—

(I) [€630][6] or, in the case of fraud, [€1,265][7], and

(II) ...[8] the amount of the difference specified in section 1053(5), and

(ii) the secretary shall be liable to a separate penalty of [€125][5] or, in the case of fraud, [€250][4], and

(*b*) in the case of any such fraud or negligence as is mentioned in section 1053(2)—

(i) the body of persons shall be liable to a penalty of [€630][6] or, in the case of fraud, [€1,265][7], and

(ii) the secretary shall be liable to a separate penalty of [€125][5] or, in the case of fraud, [€250][4].

(4) This section shall apply subject to sections 877(5)(*b*) and 897(5), but otherwise shall apply notwithstanding anything in the Income Tax Acts.

Amendments

1 Substituted by FA 2002 s 130(1)(*b*)(i) with effect from 25 March 2002; previously "€1,265".

2 Substituted by FA 2002 s 130(1)(*b*)(ii) with effect from 25 March 2002; previously "€630".

3 Substituted by FA 2001 s 240(1) and (2)(*k*) and Sch 5 Pt 1 as respects any act or omission which takes place or begins on or after 1 January 2002; previously "£50".

4 Substituted by FA 2001 s 240(1) and (2)(*k*) and Sch 5 Pt 1 as respects any act or omission which takes place or begins on or after 1 January 2002; previously "£200".

5 Substituted by FA 2001 s 240(1) and (2)(*k*) and Sch 5 Pt 1 as respects any act or omission which takes place or begins on or after 1 January 2002; previously "£100".

6 Substituted by FA 2001 s 240(1) and (2)(*k*) and Sch 5 Pt 1 as respects any act or omission which takes place or begins on or after 1 January 2002; previously "£500".

7 Substituted by FA 2001 s 240(1) and (2)(*k*) and Sch 5 Pt 1 as respects any act or omission which takes place or begins on or after 1 January 2002; previously "£1,000".

8 Deleted by FA 2005 s 141(*b*) in relation to returns, statements, declarations, or accounts delivered, made or, as the case may be, submitted on or after 25 March 2005; previously "the amount or, in the case of fraud, twice".

Cross-references

Approved share option schemes, transitional: Sch 32 para 7(3)(*b*).
Capital gains tax, penalties for failure to make returns etc, and for fraudulently or negligently making incorrect returns, applied by: s 1077(1).
Deduction of from payments due to defaulters: s 1002(7)(*a*).
Income Tax (Relevant Contracts) Regulations 2000, SI No 71 of 2000: ITRCR 2000 Reg 7(3).
Penalties for failure to make certain returns etc: s 1052(1).
Penalty for fraudulently or negligently making incorrect returns etc: s 1053(1), (1A), (2).
Returns of interest paid to non-residents, failure to deliver a return, this section applied: s 891A(2)(*c*).
Returns of special term accounts by relevant deposit takers, this section applied by s 264B(3).
Returns of special term share accounts by credit unions, this section applied by: s 267E(3).
Self assessment, obligation to make a return: s 951(12).

Definitions

body of persons: s 2(1); person: IA 1937 s 11(*c*); year of assessment: s 3(1).

Former enactments

ITA 1967 s 503 and definition of "secretary" in ITA 1967 s 509; FA 1973 s 46.

1055 Penalty for assisting in making incorrect returns, etc

Any person who assists in or induces the making or delivery for any purposes of income tax or corporation tax of any return, account, statement or declaration which that person knows to be incorrect shall be liable to a penalty of [€630][1].

Amendments

1 Substituted by FA 2001 s 240(1) and (2)(*k*) and Sch 5 Pt 1 as respects any act or omission which takes place or begins on or after 1 January 2002; previously "£500".

Cross-references

Capital gains tax, penalties for failure to make returns etc, and for fraudulently or negligently making incorrect returns, this section applied by: s 1077(1).

Definitions

person: IA 1937 s 11(*c*).

Former enactments

ITA 1967 s 505; FA 1974 s 86 and Sch 2 Pt I; CTA 1976 s 147(1)–(2).

Corresponding UK tax provision

Taxes Management Act 1970 s 99.

1056 Penalty for false statement made to obtain allowance

(1) In this section, **"the specified difference"**, in relation to a person, means the difference between—

(*a*) the amount of income tax or, as the case may be, corporation tax payable in relation to the person's or, as may be appropriate, another person's liability to income tax for a year of assessment or to corporation tax for an accounting period, as the case may be, and

(*b*) the amount which would have been the amount so payable if—

(i) any statement or representation referred to in subsection (2)(*a*) had not been false,

(ii) any account, return, list, declaration or statement referred to in subsection (2)(*b*)(i) had not been false or fraudulent, or

(iii) the full amount of income referred to in subsection (2)(*b*)(ii) had been disclosed.

(2) A person shall, without prejudice to any other penalty to which the person may be liable, be guilty of an offence under this section if—

(*a*) in relation to the person's liability to income tax for a year of assessment or to corporation tax for an accounting period, as the case may be, the person knowingly makes any false statement or false representation—

(i) in any return, statement or declaration made with reference to tax, or

(ii) for the purpose of obtaining any allowance, reduction, rebate or repayment of tax, or

(*b*) in relation to liability to income tax of any other person for a year of assessment or to liability to corporation tax of any other person for an accounting period, as the case may be, the person knowingly and wilfully aids, abets, assists, incites or induces that other person—

(i) to make or deliver a false or fraudulent account, return, list, declaration or statement with reference to property, profits or gains or to tax, or

(ii) unlawfully to avoid liability to tax by failing to disclose the full amount of that other person's income from all sources.

(3) A person guilty of an offence under this section shall be liable—

(*a*) on summary conviction where the amount of the specified difference is—

(i) less than [€1,520][1], to a fine not exceeding 25 per cent of the amount of the specified difference or, at the discretion of the court, to a term of imprisonment not exceeding 12 months or to both;

(ii) equal to or greater than [€1,520][1], to a fine not exceeding [€1,520][1] or, at the discretion of the court, to a term of imprisonment not exceeding 12 months or to both;

or

(*b*) on conviction on indictment where the amount of the specified difference is—

(i) less than [€6,345][2], to a fine not exceeding 25 per cent of the amount of the specified difference or, at the discretion of the court, to a term of imprisonment not exceeding 2 years or to both;

(ii) equal to or greater than [€6,345][2] but less than [€12,695][3], to a fine not exceeding 50 per cent of the amount of the specified difference or, at the discretion of the court, to a term of imprisonment not exceeding 3 years or to both;

(iii) equal to or greater than [€12,695][3] but less than [€31,740][4], to a fine not exceeding the amount of the specified difference or, at the discretion of the court, to a term of imprisonment not exceeding 4 years or to both;

(iv) equal to or greater than [€31,740][4] but less than [€126,970][5], to a fine not exceeding twice the amount of the specified difference or, at the discretion of the court, to a term of imprisonment not exceeding 8 years or to both;

(v) equal to or greater than [€126,970][5], to a fine not exceeding twice the amount of the specified difference and to a term of imprisonment not exceeding 8 years.

(4) Subsections (4) and (6) to (8) of section 1078 shall, with any necessary modifications, apply for the purposes of this section as they apply for the purposes of that section.

(5) This section shall not apply to a declaration given under section 2 or 3 of the Waiver of Certain Tax, Interest and Penalties Act, 1993, by reason only of any false statement or false representation made in relation to subsection (3)(*a*)(iii) of section 2 of that Act or subsection (6)(*b*)(III) of section 3 of that Act, as the case may be.

Amendments

1 Substituted by FA 2001 s 240(1) and (2)(*a*) and (*c*) and Sch 5 Pt 1 for 2002 and later tax years in the case of income tax and accounting periods ending on or after 1 January 2002 in the case of corporation tax; previously "£1,200".

2 Substituted by FA 2001 s 240(1) and (2)(*a*) and (*c*) and Sch 5 Pt 1 for 2002 and later tax years in the case of income tax and accounting periods ending on or after 1 January 2002 in the case of corporation tax; previously "£5,000".

3 Substituted by FA 2001 s 240(1) and (2)(*a*) and (*c*) and Sch 5 Pt 1 for 2002 and later tax years in the case of income tax and accounting periods ending on or after 1 January 2002 in the case of corporation tax; previously "£10,000".

4 Substituted by FA 2001 s 240(1) and (2)(*a*) and (*c*) and Sch 5 Pt 1 for 2002 and later tax years in the case of income tax and accounting periods ending on or after 1 January 2002 in the case of corporation tax; previously "£25,000".

5 Substituted by FA 2001 s 240(1) and (2)(*a*) and (*c*) and Sch 5 Pt 1 for 2002 and later tax years in the case of income tax and accounting periods ending on or after 1 January 2002 in the case of corporation tax; previously "£100,000".

Cross-references

Capital gains tax, penalties for failure to make returns etc, and for fraudulently or negligently making incorrect returns, this section applied by: s 1077(1).

Definitions

month: IA 1937 Sch; person: IA 1937 s 11(*c*); profits: s 4(1); year of assessment: ss 2(1), 5(1).

Former enactments

ITA 1967 s 516; CTA 1976 s 147(1)–(2); WCTIPA 1993 s11.

Corresponding UK tax provision

Taxes Management Act 1970 s 107.

1057 Fine for obstruction of officers in execution of duties

(1) Where any person (in this subsection referred to as **"the first-mentioned person"**) or any person in the first-mentioned person's employ, obstructs, molests or hinders—

(*a*) an officer or any person employed in relation to any duty of income tax or corporation tax in the execution of his or her duty, or of any of the powers or authorities by law given to the officer or person, or

(*b*) any person acting in the aid of an officer or any person so employed,

the first-mentioned person shall for every such offence incur a fine of [€125][1].

(2) Without prejudice to any other mode of recovery, the fine imposed under this section may be proceeded for and recovered in the like manner and, in the case of summary

proceedings, with the like power of appeal as any fine or penalty under any Act relating to the excise.

Amendments

1 Substituted by FA 2001 s 240(1) and (2)(*k*) and Sch 5 Pt 1 as respects any act or omission which takes place or begins on or after 1 January 2002; previously "£100".

Cross-references

Capital gains tax, valuation of assets, power to inspect, subs (1); s 911(2).
Capital gains tax, penalties for failure to make returns etc, and for fraudulently or negligently making incorrect returns, this section applied by: s 1077(1).

Definitions

person: IA 1937 s 11(*c*).

Former enactments

ITA 1967 s 515; CTA 1976 s 147(1)–(2).

Corresponding UK tax provision

Taxes Management Act 1970 s 106.

1058 Refusal to allow deduction of tax

(1) A person who refuses to allow a deduction of income tax or corporation tax authorised by the Tax Acts to be made out of any payment shall forfeit the sum of [€60][1].

(2) Every agreement for payment of interest, rent or other annual payment in full without allowing any such deduction shall be void.

Amendments

1 Substituted by FA 2001 s 240(1) and (2)(*k*) and Sch 5 Pt 1 as respects any act or omission which takes place or begins on or after 1 January 2002; previously "£50".

Cross-references

Capital gains tax, penalties for failure to make returns etc, and for fraudulently or negligently making incorrect returns, this section applied by: s 1077(1).

Definitions

Person: IA 1937 s 11(*c*).

Former enactments

ITA 1967 s 520; CTA 1976 s 147(1)–(2); FA 1996 s 132(1) and Sch 5 Pt I para 10(5).

Corresponding UK tax provision

Taxes Management Act 1970 s 106.

1059 Power to add penalties to assessments

Where an increased rate of income tax or corporation tax is imposed as a penalty, or as part of or in addition to a penalty, the penalty and increased rate of tax may be added to the assessment and collected and levied in the like manner as any tax included in such assessment may be collected and levied.

Cross-references

Capital gains tax, penalties for failure to make returns etc, and for fraudulently or negligently making incorrect returns, this section applied by: s 1077(1).

Former enactments

ITA 1967 s 513; CTA 1976 s 147(3)–(4).

1060 Proceedings against executor or administrator

(1) Where the person who has incurred any penalty has died, any proceedings under the Tax Acts which have been or could have been commenced against that person may be continued or commenced against his or her executor or administrator, as the case may be, and any penalty awarded in proceedings so continued or commenced shall be a debt due from and payable out of his or her estate.

(2) Proceedings may not be commenced by virtue of subsection (1) against the executor or administrator of a person at a time when by virtue of subsection (2) of section 1048 that executor or administrator is not assessable and chargeable under that section in respect of income tax on profits or gains which arose or accrued to the person before his or her death.

Cross-references

Capital gains tax, penalties for failure to make returns etc, and for fraudulently or negligently making incorrect returns, this section applied by: s 1077(1).

Penalty for fraudulently or negligently making incorrect returns etc, subs (2): s 1053(4).

Time limit for recover of fines and penalties: s 1063.

Definitions

person: IA 1937 s 11(*c*).

Former enactments

ITA 1967 s 504; CTA 1976 s 147(3)–(4); FA 1978 s 11(2).

1061 Recovery of penalties

(1) Without prejudice to any other mode of recovery of a penalty under the [preceding provisions of this Part, Chapter 4 of Part 38][1] or under section 305, 783, 789 or 886, an officer of the Revenue Commissioners authorised by them for the purposes of this subsection may sue in his or her own name by civil proceedings [for the recovery of the penalty in any court of competent jurisdiction as a liquidated sum, and, where appropriate, section 94 of the Courts of Justice Act 1924 shall apply accordingly.][2]

(2) Where an officer who has commenced proceedings pursuant to this section, or who has continued the proceedings by virtue of this subsection, dies or otherwise ceases for any reason to be an officer authorised for the purposes of subsection (1)—

(*a*) the right of such officer to continue the proceedings shall cease and the right to continue them shall vest in such other officer so authorised as may be nominated by the Revenue Commissioners,

(*b*) where such other officer is nominated under paragraph (*a*), he or she shall be entitled accordingly to be substituted as a party to the proceedings in the place of the first-mentioned officer, and

(*c*) where an officer is so substituted, he or she shall give notice in writing of the substitution to the defendant.

(3) In proceedings pursuant to this section, a certificate signed by a Revenue Commissioner certifying that—

(*a*) a person is an officer of the Revenue Commissioners, and

(*b*) he or she has been authorised by them for the purposes of subsection (1),

shall be evidence of those facts until the contrary is proved.

(4) In proceedings pursuant to this section, a certificate signed by a Revenue Commissioner certifying that—

(*a*) the plaintiff has ceased to be an officer of the Revenue Commissioners authorised by them for the purposes of subsection (1),

(*b*) another person is an officer of the Revenue Commissioners,

(*c*) such other person has been authorised by them for the purposes of subsection (1), and

(*d*) he or she has been nominated by them in relation to the proceedings for the purposes of subsection (2),

shall be evidence of those facts until the contrary is proved.

(5) In proceedings pursuant to this section, a certificate certifying the facts referred to in subsection (3) or (4) and purporting to be signed by a Revenue Commissioner may be tendered in evidence without proof and shall be deemed until the contrary is proved to have been so signed.

(6) Subject to this section, [the rules of court][3] for the time being applicable to civil proceedings shall apply to proceedings pursuant to this section.

Amendments

1 Substituted by FA 2002 s 130(1)(*c*) with effect from 25 March 2002; previously "preceding provisions of this Part".

2 Substituted by FA 2003 s 162(1)(*a*) as respects civil proceedings commenced on or after 28 March 2003; previously "for the recovery of the penalty in the High Court as a liquidated sum, and section 94 of the Courts of Justice Act 1924, shall apply accordingly.".

3 Substituted by FA 2003 s 162(1)(*b*) as respects civil proceedings commenced on or after 28 March 2003; previously "the rules of the High Court.".

Cross-references

Capital acquisitions tax, penalties; this section applies, with any necessary modifications, to a penalty under CATCA 2003 as if the penalty were a penalty under the Income Tax Acts: CATCA 2003 s 58(9).

Capital gains tax, penalties for failure to make returns etc, and for fraudulently or negligently making incorrect returns, this section applied by: s 1077(1).

Implementation of Council Directive 2003/48/EC of 3 June 2003 on Taxation of Savings Income in the Form of Interest Payments, penalties for failure to make returns: s 898O(2).

Mandatory electronic filing and payment of tax, this section applied by: s 917EA(7).

Retention and inspection of records in relation to claims by individuals, this section applied: s 886A(3).

Stamp duty, instruments executed on or after 1 November 1991, this section applied by: FA 1991 s 109.

Former enactments

ITA 1967 s 508; FA 1968 s 6(6); CTA 1976 s 147(3)–(4).

1062 Proceedings where penalty recoverable cannot be definitely ascertained

Notwithstanding that the amount of a penalty recoverable under the Tax Acts cannot be definitely ascertained by reason of the fact that the amount of income tax or, as the case may be, corporation tax by reference to which such penalty is to be calculated has not been finally ascertained, proceedings may be instituted for the recovery of such penalty and, if at the hearing of such proceedings the amount of such tax has not then been finally ascertained, the Court may, if it is of the opinion that such penalty is recoverable, adjourn such proceedings and shall not give any judgment or make any order for the payment of such penalty until the amount of such tax has been finally ascertained.

Cross-references

Capital acquisitions tax, penalties; this section applies, with any necessary modifications, to a penalty under CATCA 2003 as if the penalty were a penalty under the Income Tax Acts: CATCA 2003 s 58(9).

Capital gains tax, penalties for failure to make returns etc, and for fraudulently or negligently making incorrect returns, this section applied by: s 1077(1).

Stamp duty, instruments executed on or after 1 November 1991, this section applied by: FA 1991 s 109.

Former enactments

ITA 1967 s 510; CTA 1976 s 147(3)–(4).

1063 Time limit for recovery of fines and penalties

Proceedings for the recovery of any fine or penalty incurred under the Tax Acts in relation to or in connection with income tax or corporation tax may, subject to section 1060, be begun at any time within 6 years after the date on which such fine or penalty was incurred.

Cross-references

Capital acquisitions tax, penalties; this section applies, with any necessary modifications, to a penalty under CATCA 2003 as if the penalty were a penalty under the Income Tax Acts: CATCA 2003 s 58(9).

Capital gains tax, penalties for failure to make returns etc, and for fraudulently or negligently making incorrect returns, this section applied by: s 1077(1).

Former enactments

ITA 1967 s 511; FA 1974 s 86 and Sch 2 Pt I; CTA 1976 s 147(3)–(4).

Corresponding UK tax provision

Taxes Management Act 1970 s 103.

1064 Time for certain summary proceedings

Notwithstanding section 10(4) of the Petty Sessions (Ireland) Act, 1851, summary proceedings under section 889, 987 or 1056 may be instituted within 10 years from the date of the committing of the offence or incurring of the penalty, as the case may be.

Cross-references

Capital acquisitions tax, penalties; this section applies, with any necessary modifications, to a penalty under CATCA 2003 as if the penalty were a penalty under the Income Tax Acts: CATCA 2003 s 58(9).

Capital gains tax, penalties for failure to make returns etc, and for fraudulently or negligently making incorrect returns, this section applied by: s 1077(1).

Stamp duty, instruments executed on or after 1 November 1991, this section applied by: FA 1991 s 109.

Former enactments

ITA 1967 s 517; FA 1979 s 29; CTA 1976 s 148.

1065 Mitigation and application of fines and penalties

(1) (*a*) The Revenue Commissioners may in their discretion mitigate any fine or penalty, or stay or compound any proceedings for the recovery of any fine or penalty, and may also, after judgment, further mitigate the fine or penalty, and may order any person imprisoned for any offence to be discharged before the term of his or her imprisonment has expired.

(*b*) The Minister for Finance may mitigate any such fine or penalty either before or after judgment.

(2) Notwithstanding subsection (1)—

(*a*) where a fine or penalty is mitigated or further mitigated, as the case may be, after judgment, the amount or amounts so mitigated shall, subject to paragraph (*b*), not be greater than 50 per cent of the amount of the fine or penalty, and

(*b*) in relation to an individual, being an individual referred to in section 2(2) of the Waiver of Certain Tax, Interest and Penalties Act, 1993, or a person referred to in section 3(2) of that Act, who—

(i) fails to give a declaration required by section 2(3)(*a*) of that Act, or

(ii) gives a declaration referred to in subparagraph (i) or a declaration under section 3(6)(*b*) of that Act which is false or fails to comply with the requirements of subparagraph (iii) or (iv) of section 2(3)(*a*) of that Act or subparagraph (III) of section 3(6)(*b*) of that Act to the extent that any of those subparagraphs apply to that person,

no mitigation shall be allowed.

(3) Moneys arising from fines, penalties and forfeitures, and all costs, charges and expenses payable in respect of or in relation to such fines, penalties and forfeitures, shall be accounted for and paid to the Revenue Commissioners or as they direct.

Cross-references

Capital acquisitions tax, penalties; this section applies, with any necessary modifications, to a penalty under CATCA 2003 as if the penalty were a penalty under the Income Tax Acts: CATCA 2003 s 58(9).

Capital gains tax, penalties for failure to make returns etc, and for fraudulently or negligently making incorrect returns, this section applied by: s 1077(1).

Stamp duty, instruments executed on or after 1 November 1991, this section applied by: FA 1991 s 109.

Tax Briefing

TB36 June 1999 pp 6–7 Code of Practice for Revenue Auditors Update — Mitigation of Penalties.

Definitions

person: IA 1937 s 11(*c*).

Former enactments

ITA 1967 s 512; CTA 1976 s 147(3)–(4); WCTIPA 1993 s10.

1066 False evidence: punishment as for perjury

If any person on any examination on oath, or in any affidavit or deposition authorised by the Tax Acts, wilfully and corruptly gives false evidence, or wilfully and corruptly swears any matter or thing which is false or untrue, that person shall on conviction be subject and liable to such punishment as persons convicted of perjury are subject and liable to.

Cross-references

Capital acquisitions tax, penalties; this section applies, with any necessary modifications, to a penalty under CATCA 2003 as if the penalty were a penalty under the Income Tax Acts: CATCA 2003 s 58(9).

Capital gains tax, penalties for failure to make returns etc, and for fraudulently or negligently making incorrect returns, this section this section applied by: s 1077(1).

Stamp duty, instruments executed on or after 1 November 1991, this section applied by: FA 1991 s 109.

Definitions

affidavit: IA 1937 Sch; oath: IA 1937 Sch; person: IA 1937 s 11(*c*); swear: IA 1937 Sch.

Former enactments

ITA 1967 s 518; CTA 1976 s 147(1)–(2).

1067 Admissibility of statements and documents in criminal and tax proceedings

(1) Statements made or documents produced by or on behalf of a person shall not be inadmissible in any proceedings mentioned in subsection (2) by reason only that it has been drawn to the person's attention that—

(*a*) in relation to income tax or, as the case may be, corporation tax, the Revenue Commissioners may accept pecuniary settlements instead of instituting proceedings, and

(*b*) although no undertaking can be given as to whether or not the Revenue Commissioners will accept such a settlement in the case of any particular person, it is the practice of the Revenue Commissioners to be influenced by the fact that a person has made a full confession of any fraud or default to which the person has been a party and has given full facilities for investigation,

and that the person was or may have been induced thereby to make the statements or produce the documents.

(2) The proceedings referred to in subsection (1) are—

(*a*) any criminal proceedings against the person in question for any form of fraud or wilful default in connection with or in relation to income tax or corporation tax, and

(*b*) any proceedings against the person in question for the recovery of any sum due from that person, whether by means of tax, fine, forfeiture or penalty, in connection with or in relation to income tax or corporation tax.

Cross-references

Capital gains tax, penalties for failure to make returns etc, and for fraudulently or negligently making incorrect returns, this section applied by: s 1077(1).

Definitions

person: IA 1937 s 11(*c*).

Former enactments

ITA 1967 s 521; FA 1974 s 86 and Sch 2 Pt I; CTA 1976 s 147(1)–(2).

1068 Failure to act within required time

[For the purposes of this Chapter, and Chapter 4 of Part 38][1], a person shall be deemed not to have failed to do anything required to be done within a limited time if the person did it within such further time, if any, as the Commissioners or officer concerned may have allowed and, where a person had a reasonable excuse for not doing anything required to be done, the person shall be deemed not to have failed to do it if the person did it without unreasonable delay after the excuse had ceased.

Amendments

1 Substituted by FA 2002 s 130(1)(*d*) with effect from 25 March 2002; previously "For the purposes of this Chapter".

Cross-references

Capital acquisitions tax, penalties; this section applies, with any necessary modifications, to a penalty under CATCA 2003 as if the penalty were a penalty under the Income Tax Acts: CATCA 2003 s 58(9).

Capital gains tax, penalties for failure to make returns etc, and for fraudulently or negligently making incorrect returns, this section applied by: s 1077(1).

Stamp duty, instruments executed on or after 1 November 1991, this section applied by: FA 1991 s 109.

Subcontractors' withholding tax: s 531(16).

Definitions

person: IA 1937 s 11(*c*).

Former enactments

ITA 1967 s 507; CTA 1976 s 147(1)–(2).

1069 Evidence of income

(1) In this section, **"assessment"** includes—

(*a*) an additional assessment, and

(*b*) an assessment as amended under section 955.

(2) For the purposes of this Chapter, any assessment which can no longer be varied by the Appeal Commissioners on appeal or by the order of any court shall be sufficient evidence that the income in respect of which income tax or, as the case may be, corporation tax is charged in the assessment arose or was received as stated in the assessment.

Cross-references

Capital gains tax, penalties for failure to make returns etc, and for fraudulently or negligently making incorrect returns, this section applied by: s 1077(1).

Revenue offences: s 531(16).

Subcontractors' withholding tax: s 531(16).

Definitions

Appeal Commissioners: s 2(1); High Court: IA 1937 Sch; person: IA 1937 s 11(*c*); writing: IA 1937 Sch.

Former enactments

ITA 1967 s 506 and definition of "assessment" in ITA 1967 s 509; F(MP)A 1968 s 3(2) and Sch Pt I; CTA 1976 s 147(1)–(2); FA 1988 s 21(2).

1070 Saving for criminal proceedings

The Tax Acts shall not affect any criminal proceedings for a felony or misdemeanour.

Cross-references

Capital gains tax, penalties for failure to make returns etc, and for fraudulently or negligently making incorrect returns, this section applied by: s 1077(1).

Former enactments

ITA 1967 s 514; CTA 1976 s 147(1)–(2).

CHAPTER 2
Other Corporation Tax Penalties

1071 Penalties for failure to make certain returns

(1) Where any company has been required by notice served under section 884 to deliver a return and the company fails to comply with the notice—

(*a*) the company shall be liable to a penalty of [€630][1] except in the case mentioned in subsection (2) and, if the failure continues after judgment has been given by the court before which proceedings for the penalty have been commenced, to a further penalty of [€60][2] for each day on which the failure so continues, and

(*b*) the secretary of the company shall be liable to a separate penalty of [€125][3] except in the case mentioned in subsection (2).

(2) Where any failure mentioned in subsection (1) continues after the expiration of one year beginning with the date on which the notice was served, the first of the penalties mentioned in that subsection for which the company is liable shall be [€1,265][4], and the secretary of the company shall be liable to a separate penalty of [€250][5].

[(2A)(*a*) Where at any time not earlier than 3 months after the time at which a return is required to be delivered by a company in accordance with section 884, the company has failed to pay any penalty to which it is liable under subsection (1)(*a*) or (2) for failing to deliver the return, the secretary of the company shall, in addition to any penalty to which the secretary is liable under this section, be liable to pay such amount of any penalty to which the company is so liable as is not paid by the company.

(*b*) Where in accordance with paragraph (*a*) the secretary of a company pays any amount of a penalty to which the company is liable, the secretary shall be entitled to recover a sum equal to that amount from the company.][6]

(3) The reference in subsection (1) to the delivery of a return shall be deemed to include a reference to the doing of any of the things specified in subparagraphs (i) and (ii) of paragraph (*b*) of section 884(9).

Amendments

1 Substituted by FA 2001 s 240(1) and (2)(*k*) and Sch 5 Pt 1 as respects any act or omission which takes place or begins on or after 1 January 2002; previously "£500".

2 Substituted by FA 2001 s 240(1) and (2)(*k*) and Sch 5 Pt 1 as respects any act or omission which takes place or begins on or after 1 January 2002; previously "£50".

3 Substituted by FA 2001 s 240(1) and (2)(*k*) and Sch 5 Pt 1 as respects any act or omission which takes place or begins on or after 1 January 2002; previously "£100".

4 Substituted by FA 2001 s 240(1) and (2)(*k*) and Sch 5 Pt 1 as respects any act or omission which takes place or begins on or after 1 January 2002; previously "£1,000".

5 Substituted by FA 2001 s 240(1) and (2)(*k*) and Sch 5 Pt 1 as respects any act or omission which takes place or begins on or after 1 January 2002; previously "£200".

6 Subs (2A) inserted by FA 1999 s 84(1)(*a*) with effect from 1 March 1999.

Cross-references

Company buying its own shares, returns: s 182(4).

Definitions

company: s 4(1); month: IA 1937 Sch.

Former enactments

CTA 1976 s 143(7)(*c*) and (8).

Corresponding UK tax provision

Taxes Management Act 1970 ss 93 and 94.

1072 Penalties for fraudulently or negligently making incorrect returns, etc

(1) Where a company fraudulently or negligently—

(*a*) delivers an incorrect return under section 884,

(*b*) makes any incorrect return, statement or declaration in connection with any claim for any allowance, deduction or relief in respect of corporation tax, or

(*c*) submits to an inspector, the Revenue Commissioners or the Appeal Commissioners any incorrect accounts in connection with the ascertainment of the company's liability to corporation tax,

the company shall be liable to a penalty of—

(i) [€630][1] or, in the case of fraud, [€1,265][2], and

(ii) the amount or, in the case of fraud, twice the amount of the difference specified in subsection (2), and

the secretary of the company shall be liable to a separate penalty of [€125][3] or, in the case of fraud, [€250][4].

(2) The difference referred to in subsection (1) shall be the difference between—

(*a*) the amount of corporation tax payable by the company for the accounting period or accounting periods comprising the period to which the return, statement, declaration or accounts relate, and

(*b*) the amount which would have been the amount so payable if the return, statement, declaration or accounts had been correct.

[(2A) Where any company fails to comply with a requirement to deliver a return of a kind referred to in section 884, by reason of fraud or neglect by that company, that company shall be liable to a penalty of—

(*a*) €630 in the case of neglect or €1,265 in the case of fraud, and

(*b*) (i) the amount in the case of neglect, or

(ii) twice the amount in the case of fraud,

of the difference specified in subsection (2B).

(2B) The difference referred to in subsection (2A)(*b*) is the difference between—

(*a*) the amount of corporation tax paid by the company for the accounting period or accounting periods comprising the period to which the return relates, and

(*b*) the amount of corporation tax which would have been payable for those periods if the return had been delivered by the company and the return had been correct.][5]

(3) Subsection (3) of section 1053 shall apply for the purposes of this section as it applies for the purposes of section 1053.

Amendments

1 Substituted by FA 2001 s 240(1) and (2)(*k*) and Sch 5 Pt 1 as respects any act or omission which takes place or begins on or after 1 January 2002; previously "£500".

2 Substituted by FA 2001 s 240(1) and (2)(*k*) and Sch 5 Pt 1 as respects any act or omission which takes place or begins on or after 1 January 2002; previously "£1,000".

3 Substituted by FA 2001 s 240(1) and (2)(*k*) and Sch 5 Pt 1 as respects any act or omission which takes place or begins on or after 1 January 2002; previously "£100".

4 Substituted by FA 2001 s 240(1) and (2)(*k*) and Sch 5 Pt 1 as respects any act or omission which takes place or begins on or after 1 January 2002; previously "£200".

5 Subss (2A)–(2B) inserted by FA 2002 s 131 with effect from 25 March 2002.

Definitions

Appeal Commissioners: s 2(1); company: s 4(1).

Former enactments

CTA 1976 s 143(9), (10) and (11).

Corresponding UK tax provision

Taxes Management Act 1970 s 96 [repealed].

1073 Penalties for failure to furnish particulars required to be supplied by new companies

[(1) Where a company fails to deliver a statement which it is required to deliver under section 882—

(*a*) the company shall be liable to a penalty of [€630][1] and, if the failure continues after judgement has been given by the court before which proceedings for the penalty have been commenced, to a further penalty of [€60][2] for each day on which the failure so continues, and

(*b*) the secretary of the company shall be liable to a separate penalty of [€125][3].

(2) (*a*) Where at any time not earlier than 3 months after the time at which a statement is required to be delivered by a company in accordance with section 882, the company has failed to pay any penalty to which it is liable under subsection (1)(*a*) for failing to deliver the statement, the secretary of the company shall, in addition to any penalty to which the secretary is liable under subsection (1)(*b*), be liable to pay such amount of any penalty to which the company is so liable as is not paid by the company.

(*b*) Where in accordance with paragraph (*a*) the secretary of a company pays any amount of a penalty to which the company is liable, the secretary shall be entitled to recover a sum equal to that amount from the company.][4]

Amendments

1 Substituted by FA 2001 s 240(1) and (2)(*k*) and Sch 5 Pt 1 as respects any act or omission which takes place or begins on or after 1 January 2002; previously "£500".

2 Substituted by FA 2001 s 240(1) and (2)(*k*) and Sch 5 Pt 1 as respects any act or omission which takes place or begins on or after 1 January 2002; previously "£50".

3 Substituted by FA 2001 s 240(1) and (2)(*k*) and Sch 5 Pt 1 as respects any act or omission which takes place or begins on or after 1 January 2002; previously "£100".

4 Section 1073 substituted by FA 1999 s 84(1)(*b*) with effect from 1 March 1999.

Definitions

company: s 4(1); month: IA 1937 Sch.

Former enactments

CTA 1976 s 141(2).

1074 Penalties for failure to give notice of liability to corporation tax

Where a company fails to give a notice which it is required to give under section 883—

(*a*) the company shall be liable to a penalty of [€630][1] and, if the failure continues after judgment has been given by the court before which proceedings for the penalty have been commenced, to a further penalty of [€60][2] for each day on which the failure so continues, and

(*b*) the secretary of the company shall be liable to a separate penalty of [€125][3].

Amendments

1 Substituted by FA 2001s 240(1) and (2)(*k*) and Sch 5 Pt 1 as respects any act or omission which takes place or begins on or after 1 January 2002; previously "£500".

2 Substituted by FA 2001 s 240(1) and (2)(*k*) and Sch 5 Pt 1 as respects any act or omission which takes place or begins on or after 1 January 2002; previously "£50".

3 Substituted by FA 2001 s 240(1) and (2)(*k*) and Sch 5 Pt 1 as respects any act or omission which takes place or begins on or after 1 January 2002; previously "£100".

Former enactments

CTA 1976 s 142(2).

Corresponding UK tax provision

Taxes Management Act 1970 s 97AA.

1075 Penalties for failure to furnish certain information and for incorrect information

(1) Where any person has been required by notice given under or for the purposes of section 401 or 427 or Part 13 to furnish any information or particulars and that person fails to comply with the notice, that person shall be liable, subject to subsection (3), to a penalty of [€125][1] and, if the failure continues after judgment has been given by the court before which proceedings for the penalty have been commenced, to a further penalty of [€10][2] for each day on which the failure so continues.

(2) Where the person fraudulently or negligently furnishes any incorrect information or particulars of a kind mentioned in section 239, 401 or 427 or Part 13, the person shall be liable, subject to subsection (4), to a penalty of [€125][1] or, in the case of fraud, [€315][3].

(3) Where the person mentioned in subsection (1) is a company—

(*a*) the company shall be liable to a penalty of [€630][4] and, if the failure continues after judgment has been given by the court before which proceedings for the penalty have been commenced, to a further penalty of [€60][5] for each day on which the failure so continues, and

(*b*) the secretary of the company shall be liable to a separate penalty of [€125][1].

(4) Where the person mentioned in subsection (2) is a company—

(*a*) the company shall be liable to a penalty of [€630][4] or, in the case of fraud, [€1,265][6], and

(*b*) the secretary of the company shall be liable to a separate penalty of [€125][1] or, in the case of fraud, [€250][7].

(5) Subsection (3) of section 1053 shall apply for the purposes of this section as it applies for the purposes of section 1053.

Amendments

1 Substituted by FA 2001 s 240(1) and (2)(*k*) and Sch 5 Pt 1 as respects any act or omission which takes place or begins on or after 1 January 2002; previously "£100".

2 Substituted by FA 2001 s 240(1) and (2)(*k*) and Sch 5 Pt 1 as respects any act or omission which takes place or begins on or after 1 January 2002; previously "£10".

3 Substituted by FA 2001 s 240(1) and (2)(*k*) and Sch 5 Pt 1 as respects any act or omission which takes place or begins on or after 1 January 2002; previously "£250".

4 Substituted by FA 2001 s 240(1) and (2)(*k*) and Sch 5 Pt 1 as respects any act or omission which takes place or begins on or after 1 January 2002; previously "£500".

5 Substituted by FA 2001 s 240(1) and (2)(*k*) and Sch 5 Pt 1 as respects any act or omission which takes place or begins on or after 1 January 2002; previously "£50".

6 Substituted by FA 2001 s 240(1) and (2)(*k*) and Sch 5 Pt 1 as respects any act or omission which takes place or begins on or after 1 January 2002; previously "£1,000".

7 Substituted by FA 2001 s 240(1) and (2)(*k*) and Sch 5 Pt 1 as respects any act or omission which takes place or begins on or after 1 January 2002; previously "£200".

Cross-references

Advance corporation tax, application of this section: s 167(8).

Definitions

company: ss 4(1), 5(1); person: IA 1937 s 11(*c*).

Former enactments

CTA 1976 s 149.

Corresponding UK tax provision

Taxes Management Act 1970 s 108.

1076 Supplementary provisions (Chapter 2)

[(1) In this Chapter, **"secretary"** includes—

(*a*) persons mentioned in section 1044(2) and, in the case of a company which is not resident in the State, the agent, manager, factor or other representative of the company, and

(*b*) in the case of a company the secretary (within the meaning of section 175 of the Companies Act, 1963) of which is not an individual resident in the State, an individual resident in the State who is a director of the company.][1]

(2) In proceedings for the recovery of a penalty incurred under the provisions of the Corporation Tax Acts—

(*a*) a certificate signed by an inspector which certifies that he or she has examined his or her relevant records and that it appears from those records that a stated notice was duly given to the defendant on a stated day shall be evidence until the contrary is proved that the defendant received that notice in the ordinary course;

(*b*) a certificate signed by an inspector which certifies that he or she has examined his or her relevant records and that it appears from those records that during a stated period a stated return was not received from the defendant shall be evidence until the contrary is proved that the defendant did not during that period deliver that return;

(*c*) a certificate certifying as provided for in paragraph (*a*) or (*b*) and purporting to be signed by an inspector may be tendered in evidence without proof and shall be deemed until the contrary is proved to have been signed by such inspector.

Amendments

1 Subs (1) substituted by FA 1999 s 84(1)(*c*) with effect from 1 March 1999.

Definitions

company: s 4(1).

Former enactments

CTA 1976 s 154 and s 147(3) and (4) in so far as it refers to ITA 1967 s 172(5).

CHAPTER 3
Capital Gains Tax Penalties

1077 Penalties for failure to make returns, etc and for fraudulently or negligently making incorrect returns, etc

(1) Without prejudice to the generality of section 913(1), Chapter 1 of this Part shall, subject to any necessary modifications, apply in relation to capital gains tax, and sections 1052, 1053 and 1054, as applied by this section, shall for the purposes of the Capital Gains Tax Acts be construed as if in Schedule 29 there were included—

(*a*) in column 1, references to sections 914 to 917,
(*b*) in column 2, a reference to section 945, and
(*c*) in column 3, a reference to section 980.

(2) Where any person has been required by notice or precept given under the provisions of the Income Tax Acts as applied by section 913, or under section 914, 915, 916, 917 or 980, to do any act of a kind mentioned in any of the those provisions or sections, and the person fails to comply with the notice or precept, or where any person fraudulently or negligently makes, delivers, furnishes or produces any incorrect return, statement, declaration, list, account, particulars or other document (or knowingly makes any false statement or false representation) under any of those provisions or sections, Chapter 1 of this Part shall apply to the person for the purposes of capital gains tax as it applies in the case of a like failure or act for the purposes of income tax.

Cross-references

Self assessment: s 959(6).

Former enactments

CGTA 1975 s 51(1) and Sch 4 para 3(2) and (6).

Corresponding UK tax provision

Taxes Management Act 1970 ss 93 and 95.

CHAPTER 4
Revenue Offences

1078 Revenue offences

(1) In this Part—

"the Acts" means—

(*a*) the Customs Acts,
(*b*) the statutes relating to the duties of excise and to the management of those duties,
(*c*) the Tax Acts,
(*d*) the Capital Gains Tax Acts,
(*e*) the Value-Added Tax Act, 1972, and the enactments amending or extending that Act,
(*f*) the [Capital Acquisitions Tax Consolidation Act 2003][1], and the enactments amending or extending that Act,
(*g*) the statutes relating to stamp duty and to the management of that duty, and
(*h*) Part VI of the Finance Act, 1983,

and any instruments made thereunder and any instruments made under any other enactment and relating to tax;

"authorised officer" means an officer of the Revenue Commissioners authorised by them in writing to exercise any of the powers conferred by the Acts;

"tax" means any tax, duty, levy or charge under the care and management of the Revenue Commissioners.

[(1A)(*a*) In this subsection—

"facilitating" means aiding, abetting, assisting, inciting or inducing;

"fraudulent evasion of tax by a person" means the person—

(*a*) evading or attempting to evade any payment or deduction of tax required under the Acts to be paid by the person or, as the case may be, required under the Acts to be deducted from amounts due to the person, or

(*b*) claiming or obtaining, or attempting to claim or obtain, relief or exemption from, or payment or repayment of, any tax, being relief, exemption, payment or repayment, to which the person is not entitled under the Acts,

where, for those purposes, the person deceives, omits, conceals or uses any other dishonest means including—

(i) providing false, incomplete or misleading information, or

(ii) failing to furnish information,

to the Revenue Commissioners or to any other person.

(*b*) For the purposes of this subsection and subsection (5) a person (in this paragraph referred to as the **"first-mentioned person"**) is reckless as to whether or not he or she is concerned in facilitating—

(i) the fraudulent evasion of tax by a person, being another person, or

(ii) the commission of an offence under subsection (2) by a person, being another person,

if the first-mentioned person disregards a substantial risk that he or she is so concerned, and for those purposes **"substantial risk"** means a risk of such a nature and degree that, having regard to all the circumstances and the extent of the information available to the first-mentioned person, its disregard by that person involves culpability of a high degree.

(*c*) A person shall, without prejudice to any other penalty to which the person may be liable, be guilty of an offence under this section if the person—

(i) is knowingly concerned in the fraudulent evasion of tax by the person or any other person,

(ii) is knowingly concerned in, or is reckless as to whether or not the person is concerned in, facilitating—

(I) the fraudulent evasion of tax, or

(II) the commission of an offence under subsection (2) (other than an offence under paragraph (*b*) of that subsection),

by any other person, or

(iii) is knowingly concerned in the fraudulent evasion or attempted fraudulent evasion of any prohibition or restriction on importation for the time being in force, or the removal of any goods from the State, in contravention of any provision of the Acts.][2]

(2) A person shall, without prejudice to any other penalty to which the person may be liable, be guilty of an offence under this section if the person—

(*a*) knowingly or wilfully delivers any incorrect return, statement or accounts or knowingly or wilfully furnishes any incorrect information in connection with any tax,

(*b*) knowingly aids, abets, assists, incites or induces another person to make or deliver knowingly or wilfully any incorrect return, statement or accounts in connection with any tax,

(*c*) claims or obtains relief or exemption from, or repayment of, any tax, being a relief, exemption or repayment to which, to the person's knowledge, the person is not entitled,

(*d*) knowingly or wilfully issues or produces any incorrect invoice, receipt, instrument or other document in connection with any tax,

[(*dd*) (i) fails to make any deduction of dividend withholding tax (within the meaning of Chapter 8A of Part 6) required to be made by the person under section 172B(1),

(ii) fails, having made that deduction, to pay the sum deducted to the Collector-General within the time specified in that behalf in section 172K(2),

(iii) fails to make any reduction required to be made by the person under section 172B(2),

(iv) fails, having made that reduction, to pay to the Collector-General the amount referred to in section 172B(2)(*d*), which amount is treated under that section as if it were a deduction of dividend withholding tax (within the meaning of Chapter 8A of Part 6), within the time specified in that behalf in section 172K(2), or

(v) fails to pay to the Collector-General, within the time specified in that behalf in section 172K(2), an amount referred to in section 172B(3)(*a*) which is required to be paid by the person to the Collector-General and which is treated under that section as if it were a deduction of dividend withholding tax (within the meaning of Chapter 8A of Part 6),][3]

(*e*) (i) fails to make any deduction required to be made by the person under section 257(1),

(ii) fails, having made the deduction, to pay the sum deducted to the Collector-General within the time specified in that behalf in section 258(3), or

(iii) fails to pay to the Collector-General an amount on account of appropriate tax (within the meaning of Chapter 4 of Part 8) within the time specified in that behalf in section 258(4),

[(*f*) fails to pay to the Collector-General appropriate tax (within the meaning of section 739E) within the time specified in that behalf in section 739F,][4]

(*g*) [fails without reasonable excuse][5] to comply with any provision of the Acts requiring—

(i) the furnishing of a return of income, profits or gains, or of sources of income, profits or gains, for the purposes of any tax,

(ii) the furnishing of any other return, certificate, notification, particulars, or any statement or evidence, for the purposes of any tax,

(iii) the keeping or retention of books, records, accounts or other documents for the purposes of any tax, or

(iv) the production of books, records, accounts or other documents, when so requested, for the purposes of any tax,

(*h*) knowingly or wilfully, and within the time limits specified for their retention, destroys, defaces or conceals from an authorised officer—

(i) any documents, or

(ii) any other written or printed material in any form, including any information stored, maintained or preserved by means of any mechanical or electronic device, whether or not stored, maintained or preserved in a legible form, which a person is obliged by any provision of the Acts to keep, to issue or to produce for inspection,

[(*hh*) knowingly or wilfully falsifies, conceals, destroys or otherwise disposes of, or causes or permits the falsification, concealment, destruction or disposal of, any books, records or other document—

(i) which the person has been given the opportunity to deliver, or as the case may be, to make available in accordance with section 900(3), or

(ii) which the person has been required to deliver or, as the case may be, to make available in accordance with a notice served under section 900, 902, 906A or 907, or an order made under section 901, 902A or 908.][6]

(*i*) fails to remit any income tax payable pursuant to Chapter 4 of Part 42, and the regulations under that Chapter, or value-added tax within the time specified in that behalf in relation to income tax or value-added tax, as the case may be, [by the Acts,][7]

[(*ii*) (i) fails to deduct tax required to be deducted by the person under section 531(1), or

(ii) fails, having made that deduction, to pay the sum deducted to the Collector-General within the time specified in that behalf in section 531(3A),

or][8]

(*j*) obstructs or interferes with any officer of the Revenue Commissioners, or any other person, in the exercise or performance of powers or duties under the Acts for the purposes of any tax.

(3) A person convicted of an offence under this section shall be liable—

(*a*) on summary conviction to a fine of [€3,000][9] which may be mitigated to not less than one fourth part of such fine or, at the discretion of the court, to imprisonment for a term not exceeding 12 months or to both the fine and the imprisonment, or

(*b*) on conviction on indictment, to a fine not exceeding [€126,970][10] or, at the discretion of the court, to imprisonment for a term not exceeding 5 years or to both the fine and the imprisonment.

[(3A) Where a person has been convicted of an offence referred to in subparagraph (i), (ii) or (iv) of subsection (2)(*g*), then, if an application is made, or caused to be made to the court in that regard, the court may make an order requiring the person concerned to comply with any provision of the Acts relating to the requirements specified in the said subparagraph (i), (ii) or (iv), as the case may be.][11]

[(3B) A person shall, without prejudice to any other penalty to which the person may be liable, be guilty of an offence under this section if the person fails or refuses to comply with an order referred to in subsection (3A).][12]

(4) Section 13 of the Criminal Procedure Act, 1967, shall apply in relation to an offence under this section as if, in place of the penalties specified in subsection (3) of that section, there were specified in that subsection the penalties provided for by subsection (3)(*a*), and the reference in subsection (2)(*a*) of section 13 of the Criminal Procedure Act, 1967, to the penalties provided for in subsection (3) of that section shall be construed and apply accordingly.

(5) Where an offence under this section is committed by a body corporate and the offence is shown [to have been committed with the consent or connivance of or to be attributable to any recklessness (as provided for by subsection (1A)(*b*)) on the part of][13] any person who, when the offence was committed, was a director, manager, secretary or other officer of the body corporate, or a member of the committee of management or other controlling authority of the body corporate, that person shall also be deemed to be guilty of the offence and may be proceeded against and punished accordingly.

(6) In any proceedings under this section, a return or statement delivered to an inspector or other officer of the Revenue Commissioners under any provision of the Acts and purporting to be signed by any person shall be deemed until the contrary is proved to have been so delivered and to have been signed by that person.

(7) Notwithstanding any other enactment, proceedings in respect of an offence under this section may be instituted within 10 years from the date of the commission of the offence or incurring of the penalty, as the case may be.

(8) Section 1 of the Probation of Offenders Act, 1907, shall not apply in relation to offences under this section.

(9) Sections 987(4) and 1052(4), subsections (3) and (7) of section 1053, and sections 1068 and 1069 and sections 26(6) and 27(7) of the Value-Added Tax Act, 1972, shall, with any necessary modifications, apply for the purposes of this section as they apply for the purposes of those sections, including, in the case of such of those sections as are applied by the Capital Gains Tax Acts, the Corporation Tax Acts, or Part VI of the Finance Act, 1983, the purposes of those sections as so applied.

Amendments

1 Substituted by CATCA 2003 s 119 and Sch 3 with effect from 21 February 2003; previously "Capital Acquisitions Tax Act 1976".

2 Subs (1A) inserted by FA 2005 s 142(*a*) with effect from 25 March 2005.

3 Subs (2)(*dd*) inserted by FA 1999 s 27(*b*) with effect from 6 April 1999.

4 Subs (2)(*f*) inserted by FA 2005 s 142(*b*)(i) with effect from 25 March 2005.

5 Substituted by FA 2002 s 133(*a*) with effect from 25 March 2002; previously "knowingly or wilfully fails".

6 Subs (2)(*hh*) inserted by FA 1999 s 211(*a*) with effect from 25 March 1999.

7 Substituted by FA 2005 s 142(*b*)(ii) with effect from 25 March 2005; previously "by the Acts, or".

8 Subs (2)(*ii*) inserted by FA 2005 s 142(*b*)(iii) with effect from 25 March 2005.

[9] Substituted by FA 2003 s 160(1) as respects an offence committed on or after 28 March 2003; previously "€1,900".

[10] Substituted by FA 2001 s 240(1) and (2)(*k*) and Sch 5 Pt 1 as respects any act or omission which takes place or begins on or after 1 January 2002; previously "£100,000".

[11] Subs (3A) inserted by FA 1999 s 211(*c*) with effect from 25 March 1999.

[12] Subs (3B) inserted by FA 2002 s 133(*b*) with effect from 25 March 2002.

[13] Substituted by FA 2005 s 142(*c*) with effect from 25 March 2005; previously "to have been committed with the consent or connivance of".

Cross-references

Application to High Court: information from third party, meaning of "the Acts" applied: s 902A(1).

Application to High Court seeking order requiring information: associated institutions, meaning of "the Acts" applied: s 908B(1).

Company law, subs (1): Companies Act 1990 s 21(1)(*a*)(i)(V).

Deduction from payments due to defaulters: s 1002(5), (9).

Information to be furnished by financial institutions, meaning of "the Acts" applied: s 906A(1).

Information to be furnished by third party: request of an authorised officer: s 902(11).

Inspection of documents and records, meaning of "the Acts" applied: s 905(2A)(*a*).

Penalty for false statement made to obtain allowance, subss (4), (6)–(8): s 1056(4).

Revenue offence: power to obtain information from financial institutions, meaning of "offence" applied: s 908A(1); subs (1): s 908A(1) ("the Acts").

Stamp duty, new dwelling houses and apartments with, and with no, floor area compliance certificate: Stamp Duties Consolidation Act 1999 s 91A(8); s 92(3).

This section to be construed together with the Customs Acts, in so far as relating to customs: s 1104(2).

This section to be construed together with the Value Added Tax Acts 1972–1997, in so far as relating to value added tax: s 1104(3).

This section to be construed together with the Stamp Act 1891 and the enactments amending or extending that Act, in so far as relating to stamp duties: s 1104(4).

This section to be construed together with the Capital Acquisitions Tax Act 1976, and the enactments amending or extending that Act, in so far as relating to capital acquisitions tax: s 1104(5).

This section to be construed together with FA 1983 Pt VI and the enactments amending or extending that Part, in so far as relating to residential property tax: s 1104(6).

Case law

Meaning of "criminal matter": *Director of Public Prosecutions v Seamus Boyle* ITR Vol IV p 395.

Subs (2)(*e*): District Justice not entitled to conclude, on basis of Revenue certificate, that taxpayer had "knowingly and wilfully" failed to submit return of income; taxpayer not present at District Court hearing and was entitled to defend himself: *O'Callaghan v Clifford and others* ITR Vol IV p 478.

Tax Briefing

TB36 June 1999 pp 3–4 — Revenue's Prosecution Policy.

TB38 Dec 1999 pp 10–11 — Criminal Proceedings.

Definitions

Collector-General: ss 2(1), 851; inspector: ss 2(1), 5(1), 852; month: IA 1937 Sch; person: IA 1937 s 11(*c*); profits: s 4(1); statute: s 2(1), IA 1937 s 3; Tax Acts: s 1(2).

Former enactments

FA 1983 s 94; FA 1986 s 40(2); FA 1989 s 18 and Sch 1 para 3(2); FA 1992 s 243; FA 1996 s 132(1)–(2) and Sch 5 Pt I para 13(2) and Pt II.

1078A Concealing facts disclosed by documents

[(1) Any person who—

(*a*) knows or suspects that an investigation by an officer of the Revenue Commissioners into an offence under the Acts or the Waiver of Certain Tax, Interest and Penalties Act 1993 is being, or is likely to be, carried out, and (*b*) falsifies, conceals, destroys or otherwise disposes of material which the person knows or suspects is or would be relevant to the investigation or causes or permits its falsification, concealment, destruction or disposal,

is guilty of an offence.

(2) Where a person—

(*a*) falsifies, conceals, destroys or otherwise disposes of material, or

(*b*) causes or permits its falsification, concealment, destruction or disposal,

in such circumstances that it is reasonable to conclude that the person knew or suspected—

(i) that an investigation by an officer of the Revenue Commissioners into an offence under the Acts or the Waiver of Certain Tax, Interest and Penalties Act 1993 was being, or was likely to be, carried out, and

(ii) that the material was or would be relevant to the investigation,

the person shall be taken, for the purposes of this section, to have so known or suspected, unless the court or the jury, as the case may be, is satisfied having regard to all the evidence that there is a reasonable doubt as to whether the person so knew or suspected.

(3) A person guilty of an offence under this section is liable—

(*a*) on summary conviction to a fine not exceeding €3,000, or at the discretion of the court, to imprisonment for a term not exceeding 6 months or to both the fine and the imprisonment, or

(*b*) on conviction on indictment, to a fine not exceeding €127,000 or, at the discretion of the court, to imprisonment for a term not exceeding 5 years or to both the fine and the imprisonment.][1]

Amendments

[1] Section 1078A inserted by FA 2003 s 161 with effect from 28 March 2003.

Definitions

person: IA 1937 s 11(*c*).

1078B Presumptions

[(1) In this section—

"return, statement or declaration" means any return, statement or declaration which a person is required to make under the Acts or the Waiver of Certain Tax, Interest and Penalties Act 1993.

(2) The presumptions specified in this section apply in any proceedings, whether civil or criminal, under any provision of the Acts or the Waiver of Certain Tax, Interest and Penalties Act 1993.

(3) Where a document purports to have been created by a person it shall be presumed, unless the contrary is shown, that the document was created by that person and that any statement contained therein, unless the document expressly attributes its making to some other person, was made by that person.

(4) Where a document purports to have been created by a person and addressed and sent to a second person, it shall be presumed, unless the contrary is shown, that the document was created and sent by the first person and received by the second person and that any statement contained therein—

(*a*) unless the document expressly attributes its making to some other person, was made by the first person, and

(*b*) came to the notice of the second person.

(5) Where a document is retrieved from an electronic storage and retrieval system, it shall be presumed unless the contrary is shown, that the author of the document is the person who ordinarily uses that electronic storage and retrieval system in the course of his or her business.

(6) Where an authorised officer in the exercise of his or her powers under subsection (2A) of section 905 has removed records (within the meaning of that section) from any place, gives evidence in proceedings that to the best of the authorised officer's knowledge and belief, the records are the property of any person, the records shall be presumed unless the contrary is proved, to be the property of that person.

(7) Where in accordance with subsection (6) records are presumed in proceedings to be the property of a person and the authorised officer gives evidence that, to the best of the authorised officer's knowledge and belief, the records are records which relate to any trade, profession, or, as the case may be, other activity, carried on by that person, the records shall be presumed unless the contrary is proved, to be records which relate to that trade, profession, or, as the case may be, other activity, carried on by that person.

(8) In proceedings, a certificate signed by an inspector or other officer of the Revenue Commissioners certifying that a return, statement or declaration to which the certificate refers is in the possession of the Revenue Commissioners in such circumstances as to lead the officer to conclude that, to the best of his or her knowledge and belief it was delivered to an inspector or other officer of the Revenue Commissioners, it shall be presumed unless the contrary is proved, to be evidence that the said return, statement, or declaration was so delivered.

(9) In proceedings, a certificate, certifying the fact or facts referred to in subsection (8) and purporting to be signed as specified in that subsection, may be tendered in evidence without proof and shall be deemed until the contrary is proved to have been signed by a person holding, at the time of the signature, the office or position indicated in the certificate as the office or position of the person signing.

(10) References in this section to a document are references to a document in written, mechanical or electronic format and, for this purpose "written" includes any form of notation or code whether by hand or otherwise and regardless of the method by which, or the medium in or on which, the document concerned is recorded.][1]

Amendments

1 Section 1078B inserted by FA 2003 s 161 with effect from 28 March 2003.

Definitions

inspector: s 2(1); person: IA 1937 s 11(*c*); profession: s 2(1); trade: ss 3(1), 4(1).

1078C Provision of information to juries

[(1) In a trial on indictment of an offence under the Acts or the Waiver of Certain Tax, Interest and Penalties Act 1993, the trial judge may order that copies of any or all of the following documents shall be given to the jury in any form that the judge considers appropriate:

(*a*) any document admitted in evidence at the trial,

(*b*) the transcript of the opening speeches of counsel,

(*c*) any charts, diagrams, graphics, schedules or agreed summaries of evidence produced at the trial,

(*d*) the transcript of the whole or any part of the evidence given at the trial,

(*e*) the transcript of the closing speeches of counsel,

(*f*) the transcript of the trial judge's charge to the jury,

(*g*) any other document that in the opinion of the trial judge would be of assistance to the jury in its deliberations including, where appropriate, an affidavit by an accountant or other suitably qualified person, summarising, in a form which is likely to be comprehended by the jury, any transactions by the accused or other persons which are relevant to the offence.

(2) If the prosecutor proposes to apply to the trial judge for an order that a document mentioned in subsection (1)(*g*) shall be given to the jury, the prosecutor shall give a copy of the document to the accused in advance of the trial and, on the hearing of the application, the trial judge shall take into account any representations made by or on behalf of the accused in relation to it.

(3) Where the trial judge has made an order that an affidavit by an accountant or other person mentioned in subsection (1)(*g*) shall be given to the jury, the accountant, or as the case may be, the other person so mentioned—

(*a*) shall be summoned by the prosecution to attend at the trial as an expert witness, and

(*b*) may be required by the trial judge, in an appropriate case, to give evidence in regard to any relevant procedures or principles within his or her area of expertise.][1]

Amendments

[1] Section 1078C inserted by FA 2003 s 161 with effect from 28 March 2003.

Definitions

affidavit: IA 1937 Sch; person: IA 1937 s 11(*c*).

1079 Duties of relevant person in relation to certain revenue offences

(1) In this section—

"the Acts" means—

(*a*) the Customs Acts,

(*b*) the statutes relating to the duties of excise and to the management of those duties,

(*c*) the Tax Acts,

(*d*) the Capital Gains Tax Acts,

(*e*) the Value-Added Tax Act, 1972, and the enactments amending or extending that Act,

(*f*) the [Capital Acquisitions Tax Consolidation Act 2003],[1] and the enactments amending or extending that Act,

(*g*) the statutes relating to stamp duty and to the management of that duty,

and any instruments made thereunder and any instruments made under any other enactment and relating to tax;

"appropriate officer" means any officer nominated by the Revenue Commissioners to be an appropriate officer for the purposes of this section;

"company" means any body corporate;

"relevant person", in relation to a company and subject to subsection (2), means a person who—

(*a*) (i) is an auditor to the company appointed in accordance with section 160 of the Companies Act, 1963 (as amended by the Companies Act, 1990), or

(ii) in the case of an industrial and provident society or a friendly society, is a public auditor to the society for the purposes of the Industrial and Provident Societies Acts, 1893 to 1978, and the Friendly Societies Acts, 1896 to 1977,

or

(*b*) with a view to reward, assists or advises the company in the preparation or delivery of any information, declaration, return, records, accounts or other document which he or she knows will be or is likely to be used for any purpose of tax;

"relevant offence" means an offence committed by a company which consists of the company—

(*a*) knowingly or wilfully delivering any incorrect return, statement or accounts or knowingly or wilfully furnishing or causing to be furnished any incorrect information in connection with any tax,

(*b*) knowingly or wilfully claiming or obtaining relief or exemption from, or repayment of, any tax, being a relief, exemption or repayment to which there is no entitlement,

(*c*) knowingly or wilfully issuing or producing any incorrect invoice, receipt, instrument or other document in connection with any tax, or

(*d*) knowingly or wilfully failing to comply with any provision of the Acts requiring the furnishing of a return of income, profits or gains, or of sources of income, profits or gains, for the purposes of any tax, but an offence under this paragraph committed by a company shall not be a relevant offence if the company has made a return of income, profits or gains to the Revenue Commissioners in respect of an accounting period falling wholly or partly in the period of 3 years preceding the accounting period in respect of which the offence was committed;

"tax" means any tax, duty, levy or charge under the care and management of the Revenue Commissioners.

(2) For the purposes of paragraph (*b*) of the definition of **"relevant person"**, a person who but for this subsection would be treated as a relevant person in relation to a company shall not be so treated if the person assists or advises the company solely in the person's capacity as an employee of the company, and a person shall be treated as assisting or advising the company in that capacity where the person's income from assisting or advising the company consists solely of emoluments to which Chapter 4 of Part 42 applies.

(3) If, having regard solely to information obtained in the course of examining the accounts of a company, or in the course of assisting or advising a company in the preparation or delivery of any information, declaration, return, records, accounts or other document for the purposes of tax, as the case may be, a person who is a relevant person in relation to the company becomes aware that the company has committed, or is in the course of committing, one or more relevant offences, the person shall, if the offence or offences are material—

(*a*) communicate particulars of the offence or offences in writing to the company without undue delay and request the company to—

(i) take such action as is necessary for the purposes of rectifying the matter, or

(ii) notify an appropriate officer of the offence or offences,

not later than 6 months after the time of communication, and

(*b*) (i) unless it is established to the person's satisfaction that the necessary action has been taken or notification made, as the case may be, under paragraph (*a*), cease to act as the auditor to the company or to assist or advise the company in such preparation or delivery as is specified in paragraph (*b*) of the definition of **"relevant person"**, and

(ii) shall not so act, assist or advise before a time which is the earlier of—

(I) 3 years after the time at which the particulars were communicated under paragraph (*a*), and

(II) the time at which it is established to the person's satisfaction that the necessary action has been taken or notification made, as the case may be, under paragraph (*a*).

(4) Nothing in paragraph (*b*) of subsection (3) shall prevent a person from assisting or advising a company in preparing for, or conducting, legal proceedings, either civil or criminal, which are extant or pending at a time which is 6 months after the time of communication under paragraph (*a*) of that subsection.

(5) Where a person, being in relation to a company a relevant person within the meaning of paragraph (*a*) of the definition of **"relevant person"**, ceases under this section to act as auditor to the company, then, the person shall deliver—

(*a*) a notice in writing to the company stating that he or she is so resigning, and

(*b*) a copy of the notice to an appropriate officer not later than 14 days after he or she has delivered the notice to the company.

(6) A person shall be guilty of an offence under this section if the person—

(*a*) fails to comply with subsection (3) or (5), or

(*b*) knowingly or wilfully makes a communication under subsection (3) which is incorrect.

(7) Where a relevant person is convicted of an offence under this section, the person shall be liable—

(*a*) on summary conviction, to a fine of [€1,265][2] which may be mitigated to not less than one-fourth part of such fine, or

(*b*) on conviction on indictment, to a fine not exceeding [€6,345][3] or, at the discretion of the court, to imprisonment for a term not exceeding 2 years or to both the fine and the imprisonment.

(8) Section 13 of the Criminal Procedure Act, 1967, shall apply in relation to this section as if, in place of the penalties specified in subsection (3) of that section, there were specified in that subsection the penalties provided for by subsection (7)(*a*), and the reference in subsection (2)(*a*) of section 13 of the Criminal Procedure Act, 1967, to the penalties provided for in subsection (3) of that section shall be construed and apply accordingly.

(9) Notwithstanding any other enactment, proceedings in respect of this section may be instituted within 6 years from the time at which a person is required under subsection (3) to communicate particulars of an offence or offences in writing to a company.

(10) It shall be a good defence in a prosecution for an offence under subsection (6)(*a*) in relation to a failure to comply with subsection (3) for an accused (being a person who is a relevant person in relation to a company) to show that he or she was in the ordinary scope of professional engagement assisting or advising the company in preparing for legal proceedings and would not have become aware that one or more relevant offences had been committed by the company if he or she had not been so assisting or advising.

(11) Where a person who is a relevant person takes any action required by subsection (3) or (5), no duty to which the person may be subject shall be regarded as having been contravened and no liability or action shall lie against the person in any court for having taken such action.

(12) The Revenue Commissioners may nominate an officer to be an appropriate officer for the purposes of this section, and the name of an officer so nominated and the address to which copies of notices under subsection (3) or (5) shall be delivered shall be published in Iris Oifigiúil.

(13) This section shall apply as respects a relevant offence committed by a company in respect of tax which is—

(*a*) assessable by reference to accounting periods, for any accounting period beginning after the 30th day of June, 1995,

(*b*) assessable by reference to years of assessment, for the year 1995–96 and subsequent years of assessment,

(*c*) payable by reference to a taxable period, for a taxable period beginning after the 30th day of June, 1995,

(*d*) chargeable on gifts or inheritances taken on or after the 30th day of June, 1995,

(*e*) chargeable on instruments executed on or after the 30th day of June, 1995, or

(*f*) payable in any other case, on or after the 30th day of June, 1995.

Amendments

1 Substituted by CATCA 2003 s 119 and Sch 3 with effect from 21 February 2003; previously "Capital Acquisitions Tax Act 1976".

2 Substituted by FA 2001 s 240(1) and (2)(*k*) and Sch 5 Pt 1 as respects any act or omission which takes place or begins on or after 1 January 2002; previously "£1,000".

3 Substituted by FA 2001 s 240(1) and (2)(*k*) and Sch 5 Pt 1 as respects any act or omission which takes place or begins on or after 1 January 2002; previously "£5,000".

Cross-references

This section to be construed together with the Customs Acts, in so far as relating to customs: s 1104(2).
This section to be construed together with the Value Added Tax Acts 1972–1997, in so far as relating to value added tax: s 1104(3).
This section to be construed together with the Stamp Act 1891 and the enactments amending or extending that Act, in so far as relating to stamp duties: s 1104(4).
This section to be construed together with the Capital Acquisitions Tax Act 1976, and the enactments amending or extending that Act, in so far as relating to capital acquisitions tax: s 1104(5).

Definitions

month: IA 1937 Sch; person: IA 1937 s 11(*c*); writing: IA 1937 Sch; year: IA 1937 Sch; year of assessment: ss 2(1), 5(1).

Former enactments

FA 1995 s 172.

CHAPTER 5
Interest on Overdue Tax

1080 Interest on overdue income tax, corporation tax and capital gains tax

[(1) In this section—

"chargeable period" has the same meaning as in section 321(2);

"chargeable person" has the same meaning as in section 950(1);

"period of delay", in relation to any tax due and payable, means the period during which that tax remains unpaid;

"Table" means the Table to subsection (2);

"tax" means income tax, corporation tax or capital gains tax, as appropriate;

"relevant period", in relation to a period of delay which falls into more than one of the periods specified in column (1) of the Table, means any part of the period of delay which falls into, or is the same as, a period specified in that column.

(2) (*a*) Subject to this section and section 1081—

(i) as respects tax due and payable for a chargeable period beginning before 1 January 2005, any tax charged by any assessment to tax shall carry interest from the date when the tax becomes due and payable until payment, and

(ii) as respects tax due and payable for a chargeable period beginning on or after 1 January 2005, any tax due and payable by a chargeable person for a chargeable period shall carry interest from the date when the tax becomes due and payable until payment,

and the amount of that interest shall be determined in accordance with paragraph (*c*).

(*b*) Subject to this section and section 1081, any tax charged by any assessment to income tax shall, notwithstanding any appeal against such assessment, carry interest from the date when, if there were no appeal against the assessment, the tax would become due and payable under section 960 until payment, and the amount of that interest shall be determined in accordance with paragraph (*c*).

(*c*) The interest to be carried by the tax referred to in paragraph (*a*) or (*b*), as the case may be, shall be—

(i) where one of the periods specified in column (1) of the Table includes or is the same as the period of delay, the amount determined by the formula—

$$T \times D \times P$$

where—

T is the tax due and payable which remains unpaid,

D is the number of days (including part of a day) forming the period of delay, and

P is the appropriate percentage in column (2) of the Table opposite the period specified in column (1) of the Table within which the period of delay falls or which is the same as the period of delay,

and

(ii) where a continuous period formed by 2 or more of the periods specified in column (1) of the Table, but not (as in subparagraph (i)) only one such period, includes or is the same as the period of delay, the aggregate of the amounts due in respect of each relevant period which forms part of the period of delay, and the amount due in respect of each such relevant period shall be determined by the formula—

$$T \times D \times P$$

where—

T is the tax due and payable which remains unpaid,

D is the number of days (including part of a day) forming the relevant period, and

P is the appropriate percentage in column (2) of the Table opposite the period specified in column (1) of the Table into which the relevant period falls or which is the same as the relevant period.

TABLE

(Period) (1)	(Percentage) (2)
From 6 April 1963 to 31 July 1971	0.0164%
From 1 August 1971 to 30 April 1975	0.0246%
From 1 May 1975 to 31 July 1978	0.0492%
From 1 August 1978 to 31 March 1998	0.041%
From 1 April 1998 to 31 March 2005	0.0322%
From 1 April 2005 to the date of payment	0.0273%

(3) The interest payable under this section—

(*a*) shall be payable without deduction of income tax and shall not be allowed as a deduction in computing any income, profits or losses for any of the purposes of the Tax Acts, and

(*b*) shall be deemed to be a debt due to the Minister for Finance for the benefit of the Central Fund and shall be payable to the Revenue Commissioners.

(4) Subject to subsection (5)—

(*a*) every enactment relating to the recovery of tax,

(*b*) every rule of court so relating,

(*c*) section 81 of the Bankruptcy Act 1988, and

(*d*) sections 98 and 285 of the Companies Act 1963,

shall apply to the recovery of any amount of interest payable on that tax as if that amount of interest were a part of that tax.

(5) In proceedings instituted by virtue of subsection (4)—

(*a*) a certificate signed by an officer of the Revenue Commissioners certifying that a stated amount of interest is due and payable by the person against whom the proceedings were instituted shall be evidence until the contrary is proven that that amount is so due and payable, and

(*b*) a certificate so certifying and purporting to be signed as specified in this subsection may be tendered in evidence without proof and shall be deemed until the contrary is proved to have been signed by an officer of the Revenue Commissioners.][1]

Amendments

1 Section 1080 substituted by FA 2005 s 145(1) and (8)(*a*) as respects any unpaid income tax, corporation tax or capital gains tax, as the case may be, that has not been paid before 1 April 2005 regardless of when that tax became due and payable and notwithstanding anything to the contrary in any other enactment other than TCA 1997 s 1082 , but shall not apply to the part, if any, before 1 January 1963 of any period of delay (within the meaning of TCA 1997 s 1080 of that Act as substituted by this section).

Cross-references

Aggregation of assessments: s 921(5).

Appeals against assessments: s 933(7)(*d*)(ii), (*f*)(ii).

Appropriate tax due from investment undertakings under an assessment, subs (2)(*b*) treated as deleted: s 739F(7)(*d*).

Appropriate tax due from investment undertakings without making of an assessment, subss (3) to (5) applied: s 739F(7)(*c*).

Appropriate tax due from life assurance companies under an assessment, subs (2)(*b*) treated as deleted: s 730G(7)(*d*).

Appropriate tax due from life assurance companies without making of an assessment, subss (3) to (5) applied: s 730G(7)(*c*).

Appropriate tax due from qualifying fund managers under an assessment, subs (2)(*b*) treated as deleted: s 784E(6)(*d*).

Appropriate tax due from qualifying fund managers without the making of an assessment, subss (3) to (5) applied: s 784E(6)(*c*).

BES investments: s 503(8); withdrawal of BES relief: s 504(7).

Collective investment undertakings, collection of retention tax, subs (2)(*b*) treated as deleted: Sch 18 para 1(7)(*d*); subss (3)–(5) applied by: Sch 18 para 1(7)(*c*).

Deferral of payment of tax under s 128 (tax treatment of share options): s 128A(7).

Deposit interest retention tax due from banks etc, subs (2)(*b*) treated as deleted: s 258(9)(*d*); subss (3)–(5) applied by: s 258(9)(*c*).

Dividend withholding tax due under an assessment, subs (2)(*b*) treated as deleted: s 172K(6)(*d*).

Dividend withholding tax due without the making of an assessment, subss (3) to (5) applied: s 172K(6)(*c*).
Effect on interest of reliefs given by way of discharge or repayment, subs (2): s 1081(1)(*a*).
Extension of charge to tax to profits and income from activities carried on and employments excercised on the Continental Shelf: Sch 1 para 2(1).
Income tax on payments by companies, subs (2)(*b*) treated as deleted: s 240(4); subss (3)–(5) applied by: s 240(3).
Interest on overdue capital gains tax in cases of fraud or neglect: s 1083.
Interest on overdue income tax and corporation tax in cases of fraud or neglect, subs (2): s 1082(3), (5); subss (3)–(5): s 1082(4).
Payment of tax under section 128 (tax treatment of share options), subs (2)(*b*) treated as deleted: s 128B(9)(*d*); subs (3)–(5) applied: s 128B(9)(*c*).
Relevant tax due from qualifying savings managers under an assessment, subs (2)(*b*) treated as deleted: s 848M(6)(*d*).
Relevant tax due from qualifying savings managers without the making of an assessment, subs (3) to (5) applied: s 848M(6)(*c*).
Self assessment, appeals: s 957(2)(*b*).
Special provisions relating to tax on wife's income: s 1022(3).

Definitions

person: IA 1937 s 11(*c*); Tax Acts: s 1(2).

Former enactments

ITA 1967 s 550(1), (3), (4)–(5); FA 1971 s 17(2); FA 1974 s 86 and Sch 2 Pt I; CTA 1976 s 145(4); FA 1978 s 46; FA 1985 s 12; FA 1997 s 146(1) and Sch 9 Pt I para 10(7).

Corresponding UK tax provision

Taxes Management Act 1970 ss 86 and 87.

1081 Effect on interest of reliefs given by discharge or repayment

[(1) Subject to subsection (2)—

(*a*) where for any year of assessment or accounting period, as the case may be, relief from any tax referred to in section 1080(2) is given to any person by a discharge of any of that tax, such adjustment shall be made of the amount of interest payable under that section in relation to that tax, and such repayment shall be made of any amounts of interest previously paid under that section in relation to that tax, as are necessary to secure that the total sum, if any, paid or payable under that section in relation to that tax is the same as it would have been if the tax discharged had never been due and payable, and

(*b*) where relief from tax paid for any year of assessment or accounting period, as the case may be, is given to any person by repayment, that person shall be entitled to require that the amount repaid shall be treated for the purposes of this subsection to the extent possible as if it were a discharge of the tax charged on that person (whether alone or together with other persons) by any assessment for the same year or period; but the relief shall not be applied to any assessment made after the relief was given and shall not be applied to more than one assessment so as to reduce without extinguishing the amount of tax charged thereby.

(2) No relief, whether by discharge or repayment, shall be treated as affecting any tax charged by an assessment to—

(*a*) income tax or any income tax due and payable unless it is a relief from income tax,

(*b*) corporation tax or any corporation tax due and payable unless it is a relief from corporation tax, or (*c*) capital gains tax or capital gains tax due and payable unless it is a relief from capital gains tax.][1]

Amendments

1 Section 1081 substituted by FA 2005 s 145(1) and (8)(*a*) as respects any unpaid income tax, corporation tax or capital gains tax, as the case may be, that has not been paid before 1 April 2005 regardless of when that tax became due and payable and notwithstanding anything to the contrary in any other enactment other than TCA 1997 s 1082 , but shall not apply to the part, if any, before 1 January 1963 of any period of delay (within the meaning of TCA 1997 s 1080 of that Act as substituted by this section).

Cross-references

Aggregation of assessments: s 921(5).
BES investments: s 503(8).
Income tax on payments by companies, subs (1) does not apply: s 240(5).
Interest on overdue capital gains tax in cases of fraud or neglect: s 1083.
Interest on overdue income tax in cases of fraud or neglect: s 1082(4).
Interest on overdue income tax, corporation tax and capital gains tax: s 1080(2)(*a*), (*b*).

Definitions

accounting period: s 27; person: IA 1937 s 11(*c*); year of assessment: s 3(1).

Former enactments

ITA 1967 s 551(1)–(2)(*a*); CTA 1976 s 147(1)–(2).

1082 Interest on overdue income tax and corporation tax in cases of fraud or neglect

(1) In this section, **"neglect"**, in the case of corporation tax, has the same meaning as in section 919(5)(*a*) and, in the case of income tax, has the same meaning as in section 924(2)(*a*).

(2) Where for any year of assessment or accounting period an assessment is made for the purpose of recovering an undercharge to income tax or corporation tax, as the case may be, attributable to the fraud or neglect of any person, the amount of the tax undercharged shall carry interest at the rate of 2 per cent for each month or part of a month from the date or dates on which the tax undercharged for that year or accounting period, as the case may be, would have been payable if it had been included in an assessment made—

(*a*) in the case of income tax, before the 1st day of October in that year, and

(*b*) in the case of corporation tax, on the expiration of 6 months from the end of that accounting period,

to the date of payment of the tax undercharged.

(3) Subject to subsection (5), [section 1080(2)][1] shall not apply to tax carrying interest under this section.

(4) [Subsections (3) to (5) of section 1080][2] and, in the case of income tax, section 1081 shall apply to interest chargeable under this section as they apply to interest chargeable under section 1080.

(5) Where an assessment of the kind referred to in subsection (2) is made—

(*a*) the inspector concerned shall give notice to the person assessed that the tax charged by the assessment will carry interest under this section,

(*b*) the person assessed may appeal against the assessment on the ground that interest should not be charged under this section, and the provisions of the Tax

Acts relating to appeals against assessments shall apply with any necessary modifications in relation to the appeal as they apply in relation to those appeals, and

(*c*) if on the appeal it is determined that the tax charged by the assessment should not carry interest under this section, [section 1080(2)][3] shall apply to that tax.

[(6) This section shall not apply as respects any tax due and payable for a year of assessment or an accounting period beginning on or after 1 January 2005.][4]

Amendments

1 Substituted by FA 2005 s 145(7)(*a*) and Sch 5 Pt 1 in relation to any unpaid income tax, corporation tax or capital gains tax, as the case may be, that has not been paid before 1 April 2005 regardless of when that tax became due and payable and notwithstanding anything to the contrary in any other enactment other than TCA 1997 s 1082; previously "section 1080(1)".

2 Substituted by FA 2005 s 145(7)(*a*) and Sch 5 Pt 1 in relation to any unpaid income tax, corporation tax or capital gains tax, as the case may be, that has not been paid before 1 April 2005 regardless of when that tax became due and payable and notwithstanding anything to the contrary in any other enactment other than TCA 1997 s 1082; previously "Subsections (2) to (4) of section 1080".

3 Substituted by FA 2005 s 145(7)(*a*) and Sch 5 Pt 1 in relation to any unpaid income tax, corporation tax or capital gains tax, as the case may be, that has not been paid before 1 April 2005 regardless of when that tax became due and payable and notwithstanding anything to the contrary in any other enactment other than TCA 1997 s 1082; previously "section 1080(1)".

4 Subs (6) inserted by FA 2005 s 145(2) and (8)(*b*) with effect from 1 January 2005.

Cross-references

Interest on overdue capital gains tax in cases of fraud or neglect: s 1083.

Case law

Held failure by company to notify Revenue in relation to loans to participators constituted neglect and interest on tax which ought to have been paid was properly chargeable: *Joint v Bracken Developments Ltd* [1994] STC 300.

Definitions

inspector: ss 2(1), 5(1), 852; month: IA 1937 Sch; person: IA 1937 s 11(*c*); year of assessment: ss 2(1), 5(1).

Former enactments

FA 1971 s 20(1)–(4) and (6); FA 1974 s 86 and Sch 2 Pt I; CTA 1976 s 145(4); FA 1980 s 14(2); FA 1982 s 59.

1083 Application of sections 1080 to 1082 for capital gains tax purposes

Without prejudice to sections 931(2) and 976(2), sections 1080 to 1082 shall, subject to any necessary modifications, apply to capital gains tax.

Note

By virtue of FA 2005 s 145(6)(*a*) and (*b*)(vii) this section is repealed with effect from 1 April 2005 to the extent that it applies to interest chargeable or payable on capital gains tax, except in so far as it applies TCA 1997 s 1082 to capital gains tax.

Cross-references

Self assessment: s 959(6).

Former enactments

CGTA 1975 s 51(1) and Sch 4 para 2(2).

CHAPTER 6
Other Sanctions

1084 Surcharge for late returns

(1) (*a*) In this section—

"chargeable person", in relation to a year of assessment or an accounting period, means a person who is a chargeable person for the purposes of Part 41;

"return of income" means a return, statement, declaration or list which a person is required to deliver to the inspector by reason of a notice given by the inspector under any one or more of the specified provisions, and includes a return which a chargeable person is required to deliver under section 951;

"specified return date for the chargeable period" has the same meaning as in section 950;

"specified provisions" means sections 877 to 881 and 884, paragraphs (*a*) and (*d*) of section 888(2), and section 1023;

"tax" means income tax, corporation tax or capital gains tax, as may be appropriate.

(*b*) For the purposes of this section—

(i) where a person fraudulently or negligently delivers an incorrect return of income on or before the specified return date for the chargeable period, the person shall be deemed to have failed to deliver the return of income on or before that date unless the error in the return of income is remedied on or before that date,

[(i*a*) where a person who is a specified person in relation to the delivery of a specified return for the purposes of any regulations made under section 917EA delivers a return of income on or before the specified return date for the chargeable period but does so in a form other than that required by any such regulations the person shall be deemed to have delivered an incorrect return on or before the specified return date for the chargeable period and subparagraph (ii) shall apply accordingly,][1]

[(i*b*) where a person delivers a return of income for a chargeable period (within the meaning of section 321(2)) and fails to include on the prescribed form the details required by the form in relation to any exemption, allowance, deduction, credit or other relief the person is claiming (in this subparagraph referred to as the **"specified details"**) and the specified details are stated on the form to be details to which this subparagraph refers, then, without prejudice to any other basis on which a person may be liable to the surcharge referred to in subsection (2), the person shall be deemed to have failed to deliver the return of income on or before the specified return date for the chargeable period and to have delivered the return of income before the expiry of 2 months from that specified return date; but this subparagraph shall not apply unless, after the return has been delivered, it had come to the person's notice or had been brought to the person's attention that specified details had not been included on the form and the person failed to remedy matters without unreasonable delay,][2]

(ii) where a person delivers an incorrect return of income on or before the specified return date for the chargeable period but does so neither fraudulently nor negligently and it comes to the person's notice (or, if he or she has died, to the notice of his or her personal representatives) that it is incorrect, the person shall be deemed to have failed to deliver the return of income on or before the specified return date for the chargeable period unless the error in the return of income is remedied without unreasonable delay,

(iii) where a person delivers a return of income on or before the specified return date for the chargeable period but the inspector, by reason of being dissatisfied with any statement of profits or gains arising to the person from any trade or profession which is contained in the return of income, requires the person, by notice in writing served on the person under section 900, to do any thing, the person shall be deemed not to have delivered the return of income on or before the specified return date for the chargeable period unless the person does that thing within the time specified in the notice, and

(iv) references to such of the specified provisions as are applied, subject to any necessary modifications, in relation to capital gains tax by section 913 shall be construed as including references to those provisions as so applied.

(2) (*a*) Subject to paragraph (*b*), where in relation to a year of assessment or accounting period a chargeable person fails to deliver a return of income on or before the specified return date for the chargeable period, any amount of tax for that year of assessment or accounting period which apart from this section is or would be contained in an assessment to tax made or to be made on the chargeable person shall be increased by an amount (in this subsection referred to as **"the surcharge"**) equal to—

(i) 5 per cent of that amount of tax, subject to a maximum increased amount of [€12,695][3], where the return of income is delivered before the expiry of 2 months from the specified return date for the chargeable period, and

(ii) 10 per cent of that amount of tax, subject to a maximum increased amount of [€63,485][4], where the return of income is not delivered before the expiry of 2 months from the specified return date for the chargeable period,

[and, except where the surcharge arises by virtue of subparagraph (*ib*) of subsection (1)(*b*), if the tax contained in the assessment is not the amount of tax as so increased,][5] then, the provisions of the Tax Acts and the Capital Gains Tax Acts (apart from this section), including in particular those provisions relating to the collection and recovery of tax and the payment of interest on unpaid tax, shall apply as if the tax contained in the assessment to tax were the amount of tax as so increased.

(*b*) In determining the amount of the surcharge, the tax contained in the assessment to tax shall be deemed to be reduced by the aggregate of—

(i) any tax deducted by virtue of any of the provisions of the Tax Acts or the Capital Gains Tax Acts from any income, profits or chargeable gains charged in the assessment to tax in so far as that tax has not been repaid or is not repayable to the chargeable person and in so far as the tax so deducted may be set off against the tax contained in the assessment to tax, [and][6]

...[7]

(iii) any other amounts which are set off in the assessment to tax against the tax contained in that assessment.

(3) In the case of a person—

(*a*) who is a director within the meaning of section 116, or (*b*) to whom section 1017 applies and whose spouse is a director within the meaning of section 116,

subsection (2)(*b*)(i) shall not apply in respect of any tax deducted under Chapter 4 of Part 42 in determining the amount of a surcharge under this section.

(4) (*a*) Notwithstanding subsections (1) to (3), the specified return date for the chargeable period, being a year of assessment (in paragraph (*b*) referred to as **"the first-mentioned year of assessment"**) to which section 66(1) applies, shall be the date which is the specified return date for the year of assessment following that year.

(*b*) Paragraph (*a*) shall only apply if throughout the first-mentioned year of assessment the chargeable person or that person's spouse, not being a spouse in relation to whom section 1016 applies for that year of assessment, was not carrying on a trade or profession set up and commenced in a previous year of assessment.

[(5) This section shall apply in relation to an amount of preliminary tax (within the meaning of Part 41) paid under section 952 as it applies to an amount of tax specified in an assessment.][8]

Amendments

1 Subs (1)(*b*)(*ia*) inserted by FA 2003 s 164(1)(*b*) with effect from such day as the Minister for Finance may appoint by order.

2 Subs (1)(*b*)(*ib*) inserted by FA 2004 s 86(3)(*a*) as respects any chargeable period (within the meaning of TCA 1997 s 321(2)) commencing on or after 1 January 2004.

3 Substituted by FA 2001 s 240(1) and (2)(*k*) and Sch 5 Pt 1 as respects any act or omission which takes place or begins on or after 1 January 2002; previously "£10,000".

4 Substituted by FA 2001 s 240(1) and (2)(*k*) and Sch 5 Pt 1 as respects any act or omission which takes place or begins on or after 1 January 2002; previously "£50,000".

5 Substituted by FA 2004 s 86(3)(*b*) as respects any chargeable period (within the meaning of TCA 1997 s 321(2)) commencing on or after 1 January 2004; previously "and, if the tax contained in the assessment is not the amount of tax as so increased,".

6 Inserted by FA 2000 s 69(1) and Sch 2 Part 1 para (*p*) with effect from 6 April 1999 in the case of income tax and as respects accounting periods commencing on or after that date in the case of corporation tax.

7 Subs (2)(*b*)(ii) repealed by FA 2000 s 69(2) and Sch 2 Part 2 with effect from 6 April 1999 in the case of income tax and as respects accounting periods commencing on or after that date in the case of corporation tax.

8 Subs (5) substituted by FA 2001 s 78(2)(*h*) for the short tax "year" 2001 and later tax years (income tax and capital gains tax) and as respects accounting periods of companies ending on or after 1 April 2001.

Cross-references

Corporation tax — late returns, restriction of relief, subs (1)(*b*)(i)–(iii) applied: s 1085(1)(*b*).

Foreign life policies, interpretation and application, meaning of "return of income" applied: s 730H(1); returns on acquisition of: s 730I.

Offshore funds, taxation and returns of certain funds, interpretation and application, meaning of "return of income" applied: s 747B(1); return on acquisition of material interest: s 747C.

Returns in relation to certain offshore products: s 896(5).

Returns in relation to foreign accounts: s 895(6).

Statements of practice

Company's self-assessment, error or omission in returning director's details (completion of form CT1) will not give rise to surcharge: SP CT/2/90.

Surcharge and other penalties or restriction for late submission of tax returns: SP GEN/1/93, January 1993.

Finance Act, 1992 and Directors: SP IT/1/93, January 1993

Tax Briefing

TB6 Apr 1992 para 1.6 — Surcharge: subcontractors tax — credit for tax deducted.

Definitions

chargeable gain: ss 4(1), 5(1), 534; inspector: ss 2(1), 5(1), 852; month: IA 1937 Sch; person: IA 1937 s 11(*c*); personal representatives: ss 5(1), 799; profession: ss 2(1), 5(1); Tax Acts: s 1(2); trade: s 3(1); writing: IA 1937 Sch; year of assessment: ss 2(1), 5(1).

Former enactments

FA 1986 s 48; FA 1988 s 16; FA 1990 s 25(1); FA 1992 s 245; FA 1995 s 30(1).

1085 Corporation tax — late returns: restriction of certain claims for relief

(1) (*a*) In this section—

"chargeable period" means an accounting period of a company;

"group relief" has the meaning assigned to it by section 411;

"return of income" means a return which a company is required to deliver under section 951;

"specified return date for the chargeable period" has the same meaning as in section 950.

(*b*) Subparagraphs (i), [(*ia*), (*ib*),][1] (ii) and (iii) of paragraph (*b*) of subsection (1) of section 1084 shall apply for the purposes of this section as they apply for the purposes of that section.

(2) Notwithstanding any other provision of the Tax Acts, where in relation to a chargeable period a company fails to deliver a return of income for the chargeable period on or before the specified return date for the chargeable period, then, subject to subsections (3) and (4), the following provisions shall apply:

(*a*) any claim in respect of the chargeable period under section 308(4), 396(2) [, 396A(3)][2] or 399(2) shall be so restricted that the amount by which the company's profits of that or any other chargeable period are to be reduced by virtue of the claim shall be 50 per cent of the amount it would have been if this section had not been enacted,

(*b*) the total amount of group relief which the company may claim in respect of the chargeable period shall not exceed 50 per cent of the company's profits of the chargeable period as reduced by any other relief from tax other than group relief,

[(*ba*) the total amount of the relevant trading loss referred to in subsection (2) of section 396B for the chargeable period shall be treated for the purposes of that section as reduced by 50 per cent,][3]

(*c*) the total amount of the loss referred to in subsection (1) of section 420 for the chargeable period and the total amount of the excess referred to in subsection (2), (3) or (6) of that section for that period shall each be treated for the purposes of Chapter 5 of Part 12 as reduced by 50 per cent,

[(*ca*) the total amount of the loss or excess referred to in subsection (3) of section 420A for the chargeable period shall be treated for the purposes of Chapter 5 of Part 12 as reduced by 50 per cent, (*cb*) the total amount of the relevant trading loss referred to in subsection (2) of section 420B for the chargeable period shall be treated for the purposes of Chapter 5 of Part 12 as reduced by 50 per cent,][4]

...[5]

[(3) Subject to subsection (4), any restriction or reduction imposed by paragraph (*a*), (*b*), (*ba*), (*c*), (*ca*) or (*cb*) of subsection (2) in respect of a chargeable period in the case of a company which fails to deliver a return of income on or before the specified return date for the chargeable period shall apply subject to a maximum restriction or reduction, as the case may be, of €158,715 in each case for the chargeable period.

(4) Where in relation to a chargeable period a company, having failed to deliver a return of income on or before the specified return date for the chargeable period, delivers that return before the expiry of 2 months from the specified return date for the chargeable period, paragraphs (*a*) to (*cb*) of subsection (2) shall apply as if the references in those paragraphs to "50 per cent" were references to "75 per cent" in the case of paragraphs (*a*) and (*b*) and "25 per cent" in the case of paragraphs (*ba*), (*c*), (*ca*) and (*cb*) subject to a maximum restriction or reduction, as the case may be, of €31,740.][6]

Amendments

1 Substituted by FA 2004 s 86(4) as respects any chargeable period (within the meaning of TCA 1997 s 321(2)) commencing on or after 1 January 2004; previously "'(*ia*),".

2 Inserted by FA 2003 s 59(1)(*e*)(i) as respects accounting periods ending on or after 6 February 2003.

3 Subs (2)(*ba*) inserted by FA 2003 s 59(1)(*e*)(ii) as respects accounting periods ending on or after 6 February 2003.

4 Subs (2)(*ca*) and (*cb*) inserted by FA 2003 s 59(1)(*e*)(iii) as respects accounting periods ending on or after 6 February 2003.

5 Subs (2)(*d*) and (*e*) deleted by FA 2003 s 41(1)(*p*)(i) as respects accounting periods ending on or after 6 February 2003.

6 Subs (3) and (4) substituted by FA 2003 s 41(1)(*p*)(ii) as respects accounting periods ending on or after 6 February 2003.

Definitions

company: ss 4(1), 5(1); group relief: ss 4(1), 411; month: IA 1937 Sch; profits: s 4(1).

Former enactments

FA 1992 s 55(1)–(2); FA 1995 s 66(1)–(2).

1086 Publication of names of tax defaulters

(1) In this section—

"the Acts" means—

(*a*) the Tax Acts,

(*b*) the Capital Gains Tax Acts,

(*c*) the Value-Added Tax Act, 1972, and the enactments amending or extending that Act,

(*d*) the [Capital Acquisitions Tax Consolidation Act 2003],[1] and the enactments amending or extending that Act,

[(*e*) the Stamp Duties Consolidation Act, 1999, and the enactments amending or extending that Act][2]

(*f*) Part VI of the Finance Act, 1983,

[(*g*) the Customs Acts,

(*h*) the statutes relating to the duties of excise and to the management of those duties,][3]

and any instruments made thereunder;

[**"tax"** means any tax, duty, levy or charge under the care and management of the Revenue Commissioners.][4]

(2) The Revenue Commissioners shall, as respects each relevant period (being the period beginning on the 1st day of January, 1997, and ending on the 30th day of June, 1997, and each subsequent period of 3 months beginning with the period ending on the 30th day of September, 1997), compile a list of the names and addresses and the occupations or descriptions of every person—

(*a*) on whom a fine or other penalty was imposed by a court under any of the Acts during that relevant period,

(*b*) on whom a fine or other penalty was otherwise imposed by a court during that relevant period in respect of an act or omission by the person in relation to [tax,][5]

(*c*) in whose case the Revenue Commissioners, pursuant to an agreement made with the person in that relevant period, refrained from initiating proceedings for the recovery of any fine or penalty of the kind mentioned in paragraphs (*a*) and (*b*) and, in place of initiating such proceedings, accepted or undertook to accept a specified sum of money in settlement of any claim by the Revenue Commissioners in respect of any specified liability of the person under any of the Acts for—

(i) payment of any tax,

[(ii) except in the case of tax due by virtue of paragraphs (g) and (*h*) of the definition of "the Acts", payment of interest on that tax, and

(iii) a fine or other monetary penalty in respect of that tax including penalties in respect of the failure to deliver any return, statement, declaration, list or other document in connection with the tax, or][6]

[(*d*) in whose case the Revenue Commissioners, having initiated proceedings for the recovery of any fine or penalty of the kind mentioned in paragraphs (*a*) and (*b*), and whether or not a fine or penalty of the kind mentioned in those paragraphs has been imposed by a court, accepted or undertook to accept, in that relevant period, a specified sum of money in settlement of any claim by the Revenue Commissioners in respect of any specified liability of the person under any of the Acts for—

(i) payment of any tax,

[(ii) except in the case of tax due by virtue of paragraphs (g) and (*h*) of the definition of "the Acts", payment of interest on that tax, and

(iii) a fine or other monetary penalty in respect of that tax including penalties in respect of the failure to deliver any return, statement, declaration, list or other document in connection with the tax.][7]][8]

[(2A) For the purposes of subsection (2), the reference to a specified sum in paragraphs (*c*) and (*d*) of that subsection includes a reference to a sum which is the full amount of the claim by the Revenue Commissioners in respect of the specified liability referred to in those paragraphs.][9]

(3) Notwithstanding any obligation as to secrecy imposed on them by the Acts or the Official Secrets Act, 1963—

(*a*) the Revenue Commissioners shall, before the expiration of 3 months from the end of each relevant period, cause each such list referred to in subsection (2) in relation to that period to be published in Iris Oifigiúil, and

[(*b*) the Revenue Commissioners may, at any time after each such list referred to in subsection (2) has been published as provided for in paragraph *(a)*, cause any such list to be publicised or reproduced, or both, in whole or in part, in such manner, form or format as they consider appropriate.][10]

(4) [Paragraph (*c*) and (*d*)][11] of subsection (2) shall not apply in relation to a person in whose case—

(*a*) the Revenue Commissioners are satisfied that, before any investigation or inquiry had been commenced by them or by any of their officers into any matter occasioning a liability referred to in [those paragraphs][12] of the person, the person had voluntarily furnished to them complete information in relation to and full particulars of that matter,

(*b*) section 72 of the Finance Act, 1988, or section 3 of the Waiver of Certain Tax, Interest and Penalties Act, 1993, [applied,][13]

(*c*) the specified sum referred to in [paragraph (*c*) or (*d*), as the case may be,][14] of subsection (2) does not exceed [[€30,000][15], or][16]

[(*d*) the amount of fine or other penalty included in the specified sum referred to in paragraph (*c*) or (*d*), as the case may be, of subsection (2) does not exceed 15 per cent of the amount of tax included in that specified sum.][17]

[(4A)(*a*) In this subsection—

"the consumer price index number" means the All Items Consumer Price Index Number compiled by the Central Statistics Office;

"the consumer price index number relevant to a year" means the consumer price index number at the mid-December before the commencement of that year expressed on the basis that the consumer price index at mid-December 2001 was 100;

"the Minister" means the Minister for Finance.

(*b*) The Minister shall, in the year 2010 and in every fifth year thereafter, by order provide, in accordance with paragraph (*c*), an amount in lieu of the amount referred to in subsection (4)(*c*), or where such an order has been made previously, in lieu of the amount specified in the last order so made.

(*c*) For the purposes of paragraph (*b*) the amount referred to in subsection (4)(*c*) or in the last previous order made under the said paragraph (*b*), as the case may be, shall be adjusted by—

(i) multiplying that amount by the consumer price index number relevant to the year in which the adjustment is made and dividing the product by the consumer price index number relevant to the year in which the amount was previously provided for, and

(ii) rounding the resulting amount up to the next €1,000.

(*d*) An order made under this subsection shall specify that the amount provided for by the order—

(i) takes effect from a specified date, being 1 January in the year in which the order is made, and

(ii) does not apply to any case in which the specified liability referred to in paragraphs (*c*) and (*d*) of subsection (2) includes tax, the liability in respect of which arose before, or which relates to periods which commenced before, that specified date.][18]

(5) Any list referred to in subsection (2) shall specify in respect of each person named in the list such particulars as the Revenue Commissioners think fit—

(*a*) of the matter occasioning the fine or penalty of the kind referred to in subsection (2) imposed on the person or, as the case may be, the liability of that kind to which the person was subject, and

(*b*) of any interest, fine or other monetary penalty, and of any other penalty or sanction, to which that person was liable, or which was imposed on that person by a court, and which was occasioned by the matter referred to in paragraph (*a*).

[(5A) Without prejudice to the generality of paragraph (*a*) of subsection (5), such particulars as are referred to in that paragraph may include—

(*a*) in a case to which paragraph (*a*) or (*b*) of subsection (2) applies, a description, in such summary form as the Revenue Commissioners may think fit, of the act, omission or offence (which may also include the circumstances in which the act or omission arose or the offence was committed) in respect of which the fine or penalty referred to in those paragraphs was imposed, and

(*b*) in a case to which paragraph (*c*) or (*d*) of subsection (2) applies, a description, in such summary form as the Revenue Commissioners may think fit, of the matter occasioning the specified liability (which may also include the circumstances in which that liability arose) in respect of which the Revenue Commissioners accepted, or undertook to accept, a settlement, in accordance with those paragraphs.][19]

Amendments

1 Substituted by CATCA 2003 s 119 and Sch 3 with effect from 21 February 2003; previously "Capital Acquisitions Tax Act 1976".

2 Definition of "the Acts" para (*e*) substituted by FA 2002 s 126(1)(*a*)(i)(I) as respects fines or other penalties, as are referred to in s 1086(2)*(a)* and (*b*), which are imposed by a court, and as respects specified sums, as are referred to in s 1086(2)(*c*) and (*d*), which the Revenue Commissioners accepted, or undertook to accept, in settlement of a specified liability, on or after 25 March 2002.

3 Definition of "the Acts" paras (*g*) and (*h*) inserted by FA 2002 s 126(1)(*a*)(i)(II) as respects fines or other penalties, as are referred to in s 1086(2)*(a)* and (*b*), which are imposed by a court, and as respects specified sums, as are referred to in s 1086(2)(*c*) and (*d*), which the Revenue Commissioners accepted, or undertook to accept, in settlement of a specified liability, on or after 25 March 2002.

4 Definition of "tax" substituted by FA 2002 s 126(1)(*a*)(ii) as respects fines or other penalties, as are referred to in s 1086(2)*(a)* and (*b*), which are imposed by a court, and as respects specified sums, as are

referred to in s 1086(2)(*c*) and (*d*), which the Revenue Commissioners accepted, or undertook to accept, in settlement of a specified liability, on or after 25 March 2002.

5 Substituted by FA 2000 s 162(1)(*a*)(i) as respects fines or other penalties, as are referred to in s 1086(2)(*a*)-(*b*), which are imposed by a court, and as respects specified sums, as are referred to in s 1086(2)(*c*)–(*d*), which the Revenue Commissioners accepted, or undertook to accept, in settlement of a specified liability, on or after 23 March 2000; previously "tax, or".

6 Subs (2)(*c*)(ii)–(iii) substituted by FA 2002 s 126(1)(*b*)(i) as respects fines or other penalties, as are referred to in s 1086(2)*(a)* and (*b*), which are imposed by a court, and as respects specified sums, as are referred to in s 1086(2)(*c*) and (*d*), which the Revenue Commissioners accepted, or undertook to accept, in settlement of a specified liability, on or after 25 March 2002.

7 Subs (2)(*d*)(ii)–(iii) substituted by FA 2002 s 126(1)(*b*)(ii) as respects fines or other penalties, as are referred to in s 1086(2)*(a)* and (*b*), which are imposed by a court, and as respects specified sums, as are referred to in s 1086(2)(*c*) and (*d*), which the Revenue Commissioners accepted, or undertook to accept, in settlement of a specified liability, on or after 25 March 2002.

8 Subs (2)(*d*) inserted by FA 2000 s 162(1)(*a*)(ii) as respects fines or other penalties, as are referred to in s 1086(2)(*a*)–(*b*), which are imposed by a court, and as respects specified sums, as are referred to in s 1086(2)(*c*)–(*d*), which the Revenue Commissioners accepted, or undertook to accept, in settlement of a specified liability, on or after 23 March 2000.

9 Subs (2A) inserted by FA 2000 s 162(1)(*b*) as respects fines or other penalties, as are referred to in s 1086(2)(*a*)–(*b*), which are imposed by a court, and as respects specified sums, as are referred to in s 1086(2)(*c*)–(*d*), which the Revenue Commissioners accepted, or undertook to accept, in settlement of a specified liability, on or after 23 March 2000.

10 Subs (3)(*b*) substituted by FA 2002 s 126(1)(*c*) as respects fines or other penalties, as are referred to in s 1086(2)*(a)* and (*b*), which are imposed by a court, and as respects specified sums, as are referred to in s 1086(2)(*c*) and (*d*), which the Revenue Commissioners accepted, or undertook to accept, in settlement of a specified liability, on or after 25 March 2002.

11 Substituted by FA 2000 s 162(1)(*c*)(i) as respects fines or other penalties, as are referred to in s 1086(2)(*a*)-(*b*), which are imposed by a court, and as respects specified sums, as are referred to in s 1086(2)(*c*)–(*d*), which the Revenue Commissioners accepted, or undertook to accept, in settlement of a specified liability, on or after 23 March 2000; previously "Paragraph (c)".

12 Substituted by FA 2002 s 126(1)(*d*)(i) as respects fines or other penalties, as are referred to in s 1086(2)*(a)* and (*b*), which are imposed by a court, and as respects specified sums, as are referred to in s 1086(2)(*c*) and (*d*), which the Revenue Commissioners accepted, or undertook to accept, in settlement of a specified liability, on or after 25 March 2002; previously "that paragraph".

13 Substituted by FA 2002 s 126(1)(*d*)(ii) as respects fines or other penalties, as are referred to in s 1086(2)*(a)* and (*b*), which are imposed by a court, and as respects specified sums, as are referred to in s 1086(2)(*c*) and (*d*), which the Revenue Commissioners accepted, or undertook to accept, in settlement of a specified liability, on or after 25 March 2002; previously "applied, or".

14 Substituted by FA 2000 s 162(1)(*c*)(ii) as respects fines or other penalties, as are referred to in s 1086(2)(*a*)–(*b*), which are imposed by a court, and as respects specified sums, as are referred to in s 1086(2)(*c*)–(*d*), which the Revenue Commissioners accepted, or undertook to accept, in settlement of a specified liability, on or after 23 March 2000; previously "paragraph (*c*)".

15 Substituted by FA 2005 s 143(1)(*a*) with effect from 25 March 2005, but does not apply where the specified liability referred to in TCA 1997 s 1086(2)(*c*)–(*d*) includes tax, the liability in respect of which arose before, or which relates to periods which commenced before, 1 January 2005; previously "€12,700".

16 Substituted by FA 2002 s 126(1)(*d*)(iii) as respects fines or other penalties, as are referred to in s 1086(2)*(a)* and (*b*), which are imposed by a court, and as respects specified sums, as are referred to in s 1086(2)(*c*) and (*d*), which the Revenue Commissioners accepted, or undertook to accept, in settlement of a specified liability, on or after 25 March 2002; previously "€12,700, or".

17 Subs (4)(*d*) inserted by FA 2002 s 126(1)(*d*)(iv) as respects fines or other penalties, as are referred to in s 1086(2)*(a)* and (*b*), which are imposed by a court, and as respects specified sums, as are referred to in s 1086(2)(*c*) and (*d*), which the Revenue Commissioners accepted, or undertook to accept, in settlement of a specified liability, on or after 25 March 2002.

18 Subs (4A) inserted by FA 2005 s 143(1)(*b*) with effect from 25 March 2005.

19 Subs (5A) inserted by FA 2000 s 162(1)(*d*) as respects fines or other penalties, as are referred to in s 1086(2)(*a*)–(*b*), which are imposed by a court, and as respects specified sums, as are referred to in

s 1086(2)(*c*)–(*d*), which the Revenue Commissioners accepted, or undertook to accept, in settlement of a specified liability, on or after 23 March 2000.

Cross-references

This section to be construed together with the Value Added Tax Acts 1972–1997, in so far as relating to value added tax: s 1104(3).
This section to be construed together with the Stamp Act 1891 and the enactments amending or extending that Act, in so far as relating to stamp duties: s 1104(4).
This section to be construed together with the Capital Acquisitions Tax Act 1976, and the enactments amending or extending that Act, in so far as relating to capital acquisitions tax: s 1104(5).
This section to be construed together with FA 1983 Pt VI and the enactments amending or extending that Part, in so far as relating to residential property tax: s 1104(6).
Health Contributions Act 1979, s 10(3)(*a*)(i), power to make regulatons and to recover health contributions.
National Training Fund Act 2000, s 5(6), collection of levy.

Definitions

statute: s 2(1), IA 1937 s 3; Tax Acts: s 1(2); year: IA 1937 Sch.

Former enactments

FA 1983 s 23; FA 1992 s 240; WCTIPA 1993 s 3(7); FA 1997 s 158.

PART 48
MISCELLANEOUS AND SUPPLEMENTAL

1087 Charge and deduction of income tax not charged or deducted before passing of annual Act

(1) Where in any year of assessment any payments have been made, before the passing of an Act increasing the rate of income tax for that year, on account of any interest, dividends or other annual profits or gains from which under the Tax Acts income tax is required to be deducted and tax has not been charged on or deducted from those payments, or has not been charged on or deducted from those payments at the increased rate of tax for that year—

(*a*) the amount not so charged or deducted shall be charged under Case IV of Schedule D in respect of those payments as profits or gains not charged by virtue of any other Schedule, and

(*b*) the agents entrusted with the payment of the interest, dividends or annual profits or gains shall furnish to the Revenue Commissioners a list containing—

(i) the names and addresses of the persons to whom payments have been made, and

(ii) the amount of those payments,

on a requisition made by the Revenue Commissioners in that behalf.

(2) Any person liable to pay any rent, interest or annuity, or to make any other annual payment, including a payment to which section 104 applies (not being a payment of rent, interest or annuity)—

(*a*) shall be authorised—

(i) to make any deduction on account of income tax for any year of assessment which that person has failed to make before the passing of an Act increasing the rate of tax for that year, or

(ii) to make up any deficiency in any such deduction which has been so made, on the occasion of the next payment of the rent, interest or annuity, or the making of the other annual payment, including a payment to which section 104 applies (not being a payment of rent, interest or annuity), after the passing of the Act so increasing the rate of tax, in addition to any other deduction which that person may be by law authorised to make, and

(*b*) shall also be entitled, if there is no future payment from which the deduction may be made, to recover the sum which might have been deducted as if it were a debt due from the person as against whom the deduction could originally have been made if the Act increasing the rate of tax for the year had been in force.

(3) This section shall not apply to a payment which is a distribution within the meaning of Chapter 2 of Part 6.

Cross-references

A person by or through whom "any annuity or other annual payment (apart from yearly interest)" is paid is obliged to retain tax at the standard rate in force at the time of payment: s 238(2).

A person paying "any annuity or other annual payment" wholly out of taxed income is entitled to retain tax at the rate in force during the period in which the payment was accruing: s 237(1).

Former enactments

ITA 1967 s 8 and s 93(3); FA 1969 s 29; FA 1972 s 12 and Sch 3; CTA 1976 s 140(1) and Sch 2 Pt I para 2.

1088 Restriction on deductions in computing profits

(1) In determining the amount of profits or gains for the purpose of income tax—

(*a*) no deductions shall be made other than those expressly provided for by the Income Tax Acts, and

(*b*) no deduction shall be made on account of any annuity or other annual payment (other than interest) to be paid out of such profits or gains in regard that a proportionate part of the income tax is allowed to be deducted on making any such payment.

(2) In determining the amount of profits or gains from any property described in the Income Tax Acts or from any office or employment of profit, no deduction shall be made on account of diminution of capital employed, or of loss sustained, in any trade or in any profession or employment.

Definitions

profession: s 2(1); trade: s 3(1).

Former enactments

ITA 1967 s 535; FA 1974 s 51.

1089 Status of interest on certain unpaid taxes and duties

(1) Interest payable under—

(*a*) [section 14 and subsections (3) and (4) of section 117 of the Stamp Duties Consolidation Act, 1999],[1]

(*b*) section 21 of the Value-Added Tax Act, 1972, or

(*c*) section 531(9) or 991,

shall be payable without any deduction of income tax and shall not be allowed in computing any income, profits or losses for any of the purposes of the Income Tax Acts.

(2) Interest payable under section 18 of the Wealth Tax Act, 1975, or section 51 of the [Capital Acquisitions Tax Consolidation Act 2003][2] shall not be allowed in computing any income, profits or losses for any of the purposes of the Tax Acts.

Amendments

1 Substituted by SDCA 1999 s 162 and Sch 4 with effect from 15 December 1999; previously "section 15 of the Stamp Act, 1891 and subsections (2) and (3) of section 69 of the Finance Act, 1973".

2 Substituted by CATCA 2003 s 119 and Sch 3 with effect from 21 February 2003; previously "section 41 of the Capital section 51 of the Capital Acquisitions Tax Act 1976".

Definitions

company: ss 4(1), 5(1); Income Tax Acts: s 1(2); Tax Acts: s 1(2).

Former enactments

FA 1973 s 35; FA 1975 s 27; FA 1976 s 29.

1090 Income tax assessment to be conclusive of total income

Where an assessment has become final and conclusive for the purposes of income tax for any year of assessment, that assessment shall also be final and conclusive in estimating total income from all sources for the purposes of the Income Tax Acts, and no allowance or adjustment of liability, on the ground of diminution of income or loss, shall be taken into account in estimating such total income from all sources for such purposes unless that allowance or adjustment has been previously made on an application under the special provisions of the Income Tax Acts relating to that allowance or adjustment.

Definitions

total income: s 3(1); year of assessment: s 3(1).

Former enactments

ITA 1967 s 534.

1091 Annexation of statements to interest warrants, etc

(1) In this section, **"company"** means a company within the meaning of the Companies Act, 1963, and a company created by letters patent or by or in pursuance of any statute.

(2) Every warrant, cheque or other order sent or delivered for the purpose of paying any interest which is not a distribution within the meaning of the Corporation Tax Acts by a company which is entitled to deduct income tax from such interest shall have annexed to it, or be accompanied by, a statement in writing showing—

(*a*) the gross amount which, after deduction of the income tax appropriate to such interest, corresponds to the net amount actually paid,

(*b*) the rate and amount of income tax appropriate to such gross amount, and

(*c*) the net amount actually paid.

(3) A company which fails to comply with subsection (2) shall incur a penalty of [€10][1] in respect of each offence but the aggregate amount of the penalties imposed under this section on any company in respect of offences connected with any one payment or distribution of interest shall not exceed [€125][2].

Amendments

1 Substituted by FA 2001 s 240(1) and (2)(*k*) and Sch 5 Pt 1 as respects any act or omission which takes place or begins on or after 1 January 2002; previously "£10".

2 Substituted by FA 2001 s 240(1) and (2)(*k*) and Sch 5 Pt 1 as respects any act or omission which takes place or begins on or after 1 January 2002; previously "£100".

Definitions

statute: IA 1937 s 3; s 1(1); writing: IA 1937 Sch.

Former enactments

ITA 1967 s 458; CTA 1976 s 140(1) and Sch 2 Pt I para 25.

1092 Disclosure of certain information to rating authorities, etc

(1) This section shall apply to any charge imposed on public moneys, being a charge for the purposes of relief (in this section referred to as **"the relief"**) under the Rates on Agricultural Land (Relief) Acts, 1939 to 1980, and any subsequent enactment together with which those Acts may be cited.

(2) Where a charge to which this section applies is to be made, the Revenue Commissioners or any officer authorised by them for that purpose may, in connection with the establishment of title to the relief of a person (in this subsection referred to as **"the claimant"**), notwithstanding any obligation as to secrecy imposed on them under the Income Tax Acts or under any other enactment, disclose to any person specified in column (1) of the Table to this section information of the kind specified in column (2) of that Table, being information in respect of the claimant which is required by that person when considering the claimant's title to the relief.

(3) In the Table to this section, **"occupation"** has the same meaning as in section 654, and **"rating authority"** has the same meaning as in section 898.

TABLE

(1)	(2)
Persons to whom information to be given	Information to be given
The secretary or clerk, or a person acting as such, to a rating authority or any officer of the Minister for the Environment and Local Government authorised by that Minister for the purpose of this section.	Information relating to the occupation of land by the claimant and the rateable valuation of such land.

Definitions

Income Tax Acts: s 1(2); land: s 5(1), IA 1937 Sch; person: IA 1937 s 11(*c*); rateable valuation: IA 1937 Sch.

Former enactments

FA 1978 s 47; FA 1980 s 89.

1093 Disclosure of information to Ombudsman

Any obligation to maintain secrecy or other restriction on the disclosure or production of information (including documents) obtained by or furnished to the Revenue Commissioners, or any person on their behalf, for taxation purposes, shall not apply to the disclosure or production of information (including documents) to the Ombudsman for the purposes of an examination or investigation by the Ombudsman under the Ombudsman Act, 1980, of any action (within the meaning of that Act) taken by or on behalf of the Revenue Commissioners, being such an action taken in the performance of administrative functions in respect of any tax or duty under the care and management of the Revenue Commissioners.

Cross-references

This section to be construed together with the Customs Acts, in so far as relating to customs: s 1104(2).

This section to be construed together with the Value Added Tax Acts 1972–1997, in so far as relating to value added tax: s 1104(3).

This section to be construed together with the Stamp Act 1891 and the enactments amending or extending that Act, in so far as relating to stamp duties: s 1104(4).

This section to be construed together with the Capital Acquisitions Tax Act 1976, and the enactments amending or extending that Act, in so far as relating to capital acquisitions tax: s 1104(5).

This section to be construed together with FA 1983 Pt VI and the enactments amending or extending that Part, in so far as relating to residential property tax: s 1104(6).

Definitions

person: IA 1937 s 11(*c*).

Former enactments

FA 1992 s 242; FA 1993 s 140; FA 1997 s 160(1).

1094 Tax clearance certificates in relation to certain licences

(1) In this section—

"the Acts" means—

(*a*) the Tax Acts,

(*b*) the Capital Gains Tax Acts, and

(*c*) the Value-Added Tax Act, 1972, and the enactments amending or extending that Act,

and any instruments made thereunder;

"beneficial holder of a licence" means the person who conducts the activities under the licence and, in relation to a licence issued under the Auctioneers and House Agents Act, 1947, includes the authorised individual referred to in section 8(4), or the nominated individual referred to in section 9(1), of that Act;

"licence" [means a licence, permit or authorisation][1], as the case may be, of the kind referred to in—

(*a*) the proviso (inserted by section 156 of the Finance Act, 1992) to section 49(1) of the Finance (1909–1910) Act, 1910,

(*b*) the further proviso (inserted by section 79(1) of the Finance Act, 1993) to section 49(1) of the Finance (1909–1910) Act, 1910,

(*c*) the proviso (inserted by section 79(2) of the Finance Act, 1993) to section 7(3) of the Betting Act, 1931,

(*d*) the proviso (inserted by section 79(3) of the Finance Act, 1993) to section 19 of the Gaming and Lotteries Act, 1956,

(*e*) the proviso (inserted by section 79(4)(*a*) of the Finance Act, 1993) to subsection (1) of section 8 of the Auctioneers and House Agents Act, 1947, (*f*) the proviso (inserted by section 79(4)(*b*) of the Finance Act, 1993) to subsection (1) of section 9 of the Auctioneers and House Agents Act, 1947 (an auction permit under that section being deemed for the purposes of this section to be a licence),

(*g*) the proviso (inserted by section 79(4)(*c*) of the Finance Act, 1993) to subsection (1) of section 10 of the Auctioneers and House Agents Act, 1947,

[(*h*) section 101 of the Finance Act, 1999[,][2]][3]

(*j*) section 93, 116 or 144 of the Consumer Credit Act, 1995[,][2]

[(*k*) subsection (2A) (inserted by section 106 of the Finance Act, 2000) of section 62 of the National Cultural Institutions Act, 1997[,][2]][4]

[(*l*) subsection (1A) (inserted by section 172 of the Finance Act, 2001) of section 2 of the Intoxicating Liquor (National Concert Hall) Act, 1983[,][2]][5]

[(*m*) subsection (3) (inserted by the Finance Act, 2002) of section 122 of the Finance Act, [1992,][6]

(*n*) subsection (1A) (inserted by the Finance Act, 2002) of the Finance (1909–10) Act, [1910, and][7]][8]

[(*o*) section 21 of the Intoxicating Liquor Act 2003;][9]

[**"market value"**, in relation to any property, means the price which such property might reasonably be expected to fetch on a sale in the open market on the date on which the property is to be valued;][10]

"specified date" means the date of commencement of a licence sought to be granted under any of the provisions referred to in [paragraphs (*a*) to [(*o*)][11]][12] of the definition of **"licence"** as specified for the purposes of a tax clearance certificate under subsection (2);

"tax clearance certificate" shall be construed in accordance with subsection (2).

(2) Subject to subsection (3), the Collector-General shall, on an application to him or her by the person who will be the beneficial holder of a licence due to commence on a specified date, issue a certificate (in this section referred to as a **"tax clearance certificate"**) for the purposes of the grant of a licence if—

(*a*) that person and, in respect of the period of that person's membership, any partnership of which that person is or was a partner,

(*b*) in a case where that person is a partnership, each partner,

(*c*) in a case where that person is a company, each person who is either the beneficial owner of, or able directly or indirectly to control, more than 50 per cent of the ordinary share capital of the company,

has or have complied with all the obligations imposed on that person or on them by the Acts in relation to—

(i) the payment or remittance of the taxes, interest and penalties required to be paid or remitted under the Acts, and

(ii) the delivery of returns.

(3) Subject to subsection (4), where a person (in this section referred to as **"the first-mentioned person"**) will be the beneficial holder of a licence due to commence on a specified date and another person (in this section referred to as **"the second-mentioned**

person") was the beneficial holder of the licence at any time during the year ending on that date, and—

(*a*) the second-mentioned person is a company connected (within the meaning of section 10 as it applies for the purposes of the Tax Acts) with the first-mentioned person or would have been such a company but for the fact that the company has been wound up or dissolved without being wound up,

(*b*) the second-mentioned person is a company and the first-mentioned person is a partnership in which—

(i) a partner is or was able, or

(ii) where more than one partner is a shareholder, those partners together are or were able,

directly or indirectly, whether with or without a connected person or connected persons (within the meaning of section 10 as it applies for the purposes of the Tax Acts), to control more than 50 per cent of the ordinary share capital of the company, or

(*c*) the second-mentioned person is a partnership and the first-mentioned person is a company in which—

(i) a partner is or was able, or

(ii) where more than one partner is a shareholder, those partners together are or were able,

directly or indirectly, whether with or without a connected person or connected persons (within the meaning of section 10 as it applies for the purposes of the Tax Acts), to control more than 50 per cent of the ordinary share capital of the company,

then, a tax clearance certificate shall not be issued by the Collector-General under subsection (2) unless, in relation to the activities conducted under the licence, the second-mentioned person has complied with the second-mentioned person's obligations under the Acts as specified in subsection (2).

[(3A) Where—

(*a*) the first-mentioned person will be the beneficial holder of a licence due to commence on a specified date on foot of a certificate granted or to be granted under section 2(1) (as amended by section 23 of the Intoxicating Liquor Act, 1960) of the Licensing (Ireland) Act, 1902,

(*b*) the second-mentioned person was the beneficial holder of the last licence issued prior to the specified date in respect of the premises for which the certificate referred to in paragraph (*a*) was granted, and

(*c*) the acquisition of the premises by the said first-mentioned person was for a consideration of less than market value at the date of such acquisition,

then, subsection (3) shall apply as if—

(i) the reference to the year ending on that date were a reference to 5 years ending on that date, and

(ii) the reference to the activities conducted under the licence was a reference to the activities conducted by the second-mentioned person under the last licence held by the said person prior to the specified date.][13]

(4) Subsection (3) shall not apply to a transfer of a licence effected before the 24th day of April, 1992, or to such transfer effected after that date where a contract for the sale or lease of the premises to which the licence relates was signed before that date.

[(5) An application for a tax clearance certificate under this section shall be made to the Collector-General in a form prescribed by the Revenue Commissioners or in such other manner as the Revenue Commissioners may allow.][14]

(6) Where an application for a tax clearance certificate under this section is refused by the Collector-General, he or she shall as soon as is practicable communicate in writing such refusal and the grounds for such refusal to the person concerned.

(7) (*a*) Where an application under this section to the Collector-General for a tax clearance certificate is refused, the person aggrieved by the refusal may, by notice in writing given to the Collector-General within 30 days of the refusal, apply to have such person's application heard and determined by the Appeal Commissioners; but no right of appeal shall exist by virtue of this section in relation to any amount of tax or interest due under the Acts.

(*b*) A notice under paragraph (*a*) shall be valid only if—

(i) that notice specifies—

(I) the matter or matters with which the person is aggrieved, and

(II) the grounds in detail of the person's appeal as respects each such matter,

and

(ii) any amount under the Acts which is due to be remitted or paid, and which is not in dispute, is duly remitted or paid.

(*c*) The Appeal Commissioners shall hear and determine an appeal made to them under this subsection as if it were an appeal against an assessment to income tax and, subject to paragraph (*d*), the provisions of the Income Tax Acts relating to such an appeal (including the provisions relating to the rehearing of an appeal and to the statement of a case for the opinion of the High Court on a point of law) shall apply accordingly with any necessary modifications.

(*d*) On the hearing of an appeal made under this subsection, the Appeal Commissioners shall have regard to all matters to which the Collector-General is required to have regard under this section.

[(8) A tax clearance certificate to be issued by the Collector-General under this section may—

(*a*) be issued in electronic format, and

(*b*) with the agreement in writing of the applicant, be published in a secure electronic medium and be accessed by persons authorised by the applicant to do so.

(9) A tax clearance certificate shall be valid for the period specified in the certificate.][15]

Amendments

1 Substituted by FA 2002 s 127(*a*)(i)(I)(A) with effect from 25 March 2002; previously "means a licence or authorisation".

2 Substituted by FA 2002 s 127(*a*)(i)(I)(B) with effect from 25 March 2002; previously ";".

3 Definition of "licence" paras (*h*)–(*i*) substituted by FA 1999 s 212(*a*)(i) with effect from 25 March 1999.

4 Definition of "licence" para (*k*) inserted by FA 2000 s 163 with effect from 23 March 2000.

5 Definition of "licence" para (*l*) inserted by FA 2001 s 234 with effect from 6 April 2001.

6 Substituted by Intoxicating Liquor Act 2003, s 21(7)(*a*)(i) with effect from 18 August 2003; previously "1992, and".

7 Substituted by Intoxicating Liquor Act 2003, s 21(7)(*a*)(i), with effect from 18 August 2003; previously "1910;".

8 Definition of "licence" paras (1)(*m*)–(*n*) inserted by FA 2002 s 127(*a*)(i)(I)(C) with effect from 25 March 2002.

9 Definition of "licence" para (*o*) inserted by Intoxicating Liquor Act 2003, s 21(7)(*a*)(ii) with effect from 18 August 2003.

10 Definition of "market value" inserted by FA 1999 s 212(*a*)(ii) with effect from 25 March 1999.

11 Substituted by Intoxicating Liquor Act 2003, s 21(7)(*b*) with effect from 18 August 2003; previously "(*n*)".

12 Substituted by FA 2002 s 127(*a*)(i)(II) with effect from 25 March 2002; previously "paragraphs (*a*) to (*j*)".

13 Subs (3A) inserted by FA 1999 s 212(*b*) with effect from 25 March 1999.

14 Subs (5) substituted by FA 2002 s 127(*a*)(ii) with effect from 25 March 2002.

15 Subss (8)–(9) inserted by FA 2002 s 127(*a*)(iii) with effect from 25 March 2002.

Cross-references

This section to be construed together with the Value Added Tax Acts 1972–1997, in so far as relating to value added tax: s 1104(3).

Deduction from consideration on disposal of certain assets, meaning of "tax clearance certificate" applied: s 980(8A)(*a*)(ii).

Donations to certain sports bodies, tax clearance certificates in respect of, subs (5) to (9) applied: s 847A(3)(*b*).

Intoxicating Liquor Act 2003, s 21(6) and (7), licences to national sporting arenas.

Private Security Services Act 2004, s 24(3), (5), (7) (tax clearance) — references to subs (7) of this section.

Tax clearance certificates for purposes of the Standards in Public Offices Act 2001, subs (6) and (7) applied: Standards in Public Offices Act 2001 s 25(3), (4)(*b*).

Tax clearance certificates, general scheme, meaning of "licence" applied: s 1095(1), subss (5) to (9) applied: s 1095(6).

Case law

Collector of Customs and Excise did not have power to renew a liquor license that had expired six years earlier, although trading had continued for that period: *Connolly v Collector of Customs and Excise* ITR Vol IV p 419.

Revenue information

Information leaflet CG1 — Tax Clearance Scheme.

Tax Briefing

TB47 April 2002 pp 23–24 — Tax Clearance — Finance Act 2002.

eBrief

eBrief no 7–2004 — From 8 March 2004, applications for most categories of Tax Clearance Certificates should be sent directly to the taxpayer's local Revenue District. Non-residents' applications, and applications under the Standards in Public Offices Act 2001 (which sets out the tax clearance requirements for members of the Dáil and Seanad, senior public officials and candidates for appointment to the judiciary), should continue to apply to the Collector-General's Division, Sarsfield House, Limerick.

eBrief 30–2005 — Customers, who require a tax clearance certificate and have outstanding tax issues, are advised to make arrangements to bring their tax affairs up to date in good time to allow for issue of the certificate.

Customers are reminded that for security reasons tax clearance certificates are now being printed and issued from a secure central facility. Therefore, it is not possible to collect a tax clearance certificate at a local Revenue office.

Definitions

Appeal Commissioners: s 2(1); Collector-General: s 2(1); company: ss 4(1), 5(1); ordinary share capital: s 2(1); person: IA 1937 s 11(*c*); Tax Acts: s 1(2); year: IA 1937 Sch.

Former enactments

FA 1992 s 242; FA 1993 s 140; FA 1997 s 160(1).

1095 Tax clearance certificates: general scheme

[(1) In this section—

"the Acts" means—

(*a*) the Tax Acts,

(*b*) the Capital Gains Tax Acts, and

(*c*) the Value-Added Tax Act, 1972, and the enactments amending or extending that Act,

and any instruments made thereunder;

"licence" has the same meaning as in section 1094;

"tax clearance certificate" shall be construed in accordance with subsection (3).

(2) The provisions of this section shall apply in relation to every application by a person to the Collector-General for a tax clearance certificate other than an application for such a certificate made—

(*a*) in relation to a licence, or

(*b*) pursuant to the requirements of—

(i) section 847A (inserted by the Finance Act, 2002),

(ii) the Standards in Public Office Act, 2001, or

(iii) Regulation 6 of the Criminal Justice (Legal Aid) (Tax Clearance Certificate) Regulations 1999 (SI No 135 of 1999).

(3) Subject to this section, where a person who is in compliance with the obligations imposed on the person by the Acts in relation to—

(*a*) the payment or remittance of any taxes, interest or penalties required to be paid or remitted under the Acts, and

(*b*) the delivery of any returns to be made under the Acts,

applies to the Collector-General in that behalf the Collector-General shall issue to the person a certificate (in this section referred to as a "tax clearance certificate") stating that the person is in compliance with those obligations.

(4) A tax clearance certificate shall not be issued to a person unless—

(*a*) that person and, in respect of the period of that person's membership, any partnership of which that person is or was a partner,

(*b*) in a case where that person is a partnership, each partner, and

(*c*) in a case where that person is a company, each person who is either the beneficial owner of, or able directly or indirectly to control, more than 50 per cent of the ordinary share capital of the company, is in compliance with the obligations imposed on the person and each other person (including any partnership) by the Acts in relation to the matters specified in paragraphs *(a)* and *(b)* of subsection (3).

(5) Where a person who applies for a tax clearance certificate in accordance with subsection (3) (in this section referred to as "the first-mentioned person") carries on a business activity which was previously carried on by, or was previously carried on as part of a business activity by, another person (in this section referred to as "the second-mentioned person") and—

(a) the second-mentioned person is a company connected (within the meaning of section 10 as it applies for the purposes of the Tax Acts) with the first-mentioned person or would have been such a company but for the fact that the company has been wound up or dissolved without being wound up,

(b) the second-mentioned person is a company and the first-mentioned person is a partnership in which—

(i) a partner is or was able, or

(ii) where more than one partner is a shareholder, those partners together are or were able,

directly or indirectly, whether with or without a connected person or connected persons (within the meaning of section 10 as it applies for the purposes of the Tax Acts), to control more than 50 per cent of the ordinary share capital of the company, or

(c) the second-mentioned person is a partnership and the first-mentioned person is a company in which—

(i) a partner is or was able, or

(ii) where more than one partner is a shareholder, those partners together are or were able,

directly or indirectly, whether with or without a connected person or connected persons (within the meaning of section 10 as it applies for the purposes of the Tax Acts), to control more than 50 per cent of the ordinary share capital of the company,

then, a tax clearance certificate shall not be issued by the Collector-General under subsection (3) to the first-mentioned person unless, in relation to that business activity, the second-mentioned person is in compliance with the obligations imposed on that person by the Acts in relation to the matters specified in paragraphs *(a)* and *(b)* of subsection (3).

(6) Subsections (5) to (9) of section 1094 shall apply to an application for a tax clearance certificate under this section as they apply to an application for a tax clearance certificate under that section.][1]

Amendments

1 Section 1095 substituted by FA 2002 s 127(*b*) with effect from 25 March 2002.

Cross-references

This section to be construed together with the Value Added Tax Acts 1972–1997, in so far as relating to value added tax: s 1104(3).

Deduction from consideration on disposal of certain assets, meaning of "tax clearance certificate" applied: s 980(8A)(*a*)(ii); s 980(8A)(*b*).

Taxi Regulation Act 2003, s 37(1), tax clearance certification requirements for licence applicants.

Private Security Services Act 2004, s 24 (tax clearance), meaning of "tax clearance certificate" applied; reference to subs (6) of TCA 1997 s 1095.

Public Service Management (Recruitment and Appointment) Act 2004, s 26.

Revenue precedents

Issue: Whether Local Authority obliged to operate Tax Clearance when completing a compulsory purchase of land.

Decision: Not obliged to operate tax clearance, since the Local Authority is not entering into a contract with the landowner. It is exercising its powers under a statutory scheme for land acquisition. This applies whether the price paid for the land has been agreed between the Local Authority and the land owner or has been fixed by arbitration. Where the Local authority enters into a contract with a landowner for purchase of land it would be obliged to operate Tax Clearance, even though it could compulsorily acquire the land.

Issue: Do individuals and companies need to produce a Tax Clearance Certificate in circumstances where rent in excess of £5,000 per annum is payable out of public funds.

Decision: Yes.

Issue: Do the Tax Clearance requirements of Department of Finance Circular F49/13/87 apply to payments made by the Department of Agriculture under the Forest Premium Scheme?

Decision: Yes.

Revenue information

Information leaflet CG1 — Tax Clearance Scheme.

eBrief

eBrief no 7–2004 — From 8 March 2004, applications for most categories of Tax Clearance Certificates should be sent directly to the taxpayer's local Revenue District. Non-residents' applications, and applications under the Standards in Public Offices Act 2001 (which sets out the tax clearance requirements for members of the Dáil and Seanad, senior public officials and candidates for appointment to the judiciary), should continue to apply to the Collector-General's Division, Sarsfield House, Limerick.

eBrief 30–2005 — Customers, who require a tax clearance certificate and have outstanding tax issues, are advised to make arrangements to bring their tax affairs up to date in good time to allow for issue of the certificate.

Customers are reminded that for security reasons tax clearance certificates are now being printed and issued from a secure central facility. Therefore, it is not possible to collect a tax clearance certificate at a local Revenue office.

Tax Briefing

TB47 April 2002 pp 23–24 — Tax Clearance — Finance Act 2002.

Definitions

Capital Gains Tax Acts: s 1(2); Collector-General: s 2(1); company: ss 4(1), 5(1); ordinary share capital: s 2(1); person: IA 1937 s 11(*c*); Tax Acts: s 1(2).

Former enactments

FA 1995 s 177(1)–(6); FA 1996 s 132(1) and Sch 5 Pt I para 19.

1096 Assessment of Electricity Supply Board

For the purpose of determining liability for assessment to and payment of income tax, the Electricity Supply Board is not and never was the State or a branch or department of the Government of the State.

Definitions

the Government: IA 1937 Sch.

Former enactments

ITA 1967 s 545(1).

1096A Construction of reference to oaths, etc

[(1) Without prejudice to any cxpress provision made elsewhere in those Acts in that behalf, references in the Tax Acts and the Capital Gains Tax Acts to an oath shall, in the case of persons for the time being allowed by law to affirm instead of swearing, be construed as including references to an affirmation, and references in those Acts to the administration, taking or swearing of an oath shall be construed accordingly.

(2) In subsection (1) "law" includes the Oaths Act, 1888, and, without prejudice to their application by virtue of any other provision of the Tax Acts or the Capital Gains Tax Acts, the Oaths Act, 1888, and every other enactment for the time being in force authorising an oath to be taken or an affirmation to be made in any particular manner, shall apply to an oath required to be taken or an affirmation required to be made by the Tax Acts or the Capital Gains Tax Acts.][1]

Amendments

1 Section 1096A inserted by FA 1999 s 30 with effect from 6 April 1999.

Definitions

Capital Gains Tax Acts: s 1(2); Tax Acts: s 1(2).

1096B Evidence of computer stored records in court proceedings etc

[(1) In this section—

"copy record" means any copy of an original record or a copy of that copy made in accordance with either of the methods referred to in subsection (2) and accompanied by the certificate referred to in subsection (4), which original record or copy of an original record is in the possession of the Revenue Commissioners;

"original record" means any document, record or record of an entry in a document or record or information stored by means of any storage equipment, whether or not in a legible form, made or stored by the Revenue Commissioners for the purposes of or in connection with tax, and which is in the possession of the Revenue Commissioners;

"provable record" means an original record or a copy record and, in the case of an original record or a copy record stored in any storage equipment, whether or not in a legible form, includes the production or reproduction of the record in a legible form;

"storage equipment" means any electronic, magnetic, mechanical, photographic, optical or other device used for storing information;

"tax" means any tax, duty, levy or charge under the care and management of the Revenue Commissioners.

(2) Where by reason of—

(*a*) the deterioration of,

(*b*) the inconvenience in storing, or

(*c*) the technical obsolescence in the manner of retaining or storing, any original record or any copy record, the Revenue Commissioners may—

(i) make a legible copy of that record, or

(ii) store information concerning that record otherwise than in a legible form so that the information is capable of being used to make a legible copy of that record,

and, they may, thereupon destroy that original record or that copy record.

(3) The legible copy of—

(*a*) a record made, or

(*b*) the information concerning such record stored,

in accordance with subsection (2) shall be deemed to be an original record for the purposes of this section.

(4) In any proceedings a certificate signed by an officer of the Revenue Commissioners stating that a copy record has been made in accordance with the provisions of subsection (2) shall be evidence of the fact of the making of such a copy record and that it is a true copy, unless the contrary is shown.

(5) In any proceedings a document purporting to be a certificate signed by an officer of the Revenue Commissioners, referred to in subsection (4), shall for the purposes of this section be deemed to be such a certificate and to be so signed unless the contrary is shown.

(6) A provable record shall be admissible in evidence in any proceedings and shall be evidence of any fact stated in it or event recorded by it unless the contrary is shown, or unless the court is not satisfied as to the reliability of the system used to make or compile—

(*a*) in the case of an original record, that record, and

(*b*) in the case of a copy record, the original on which it was based.

(7) In any proceedings a certificate signed by an officer of the Revenue Commissioners, stating that a full and detailed search has been made for a record of any event in every place where such records are kept and that no such record has been found, shall be evidence that the event did not happen unless the contrary is shown or unless the court is not satisfied—

(*a*) as to the reliability of the system used to compile or make or keep such records,

(*b*) that, if the event had happened, a record would have been made of it, and

(*c*) that the system is such that the only reasonable explanation for the absence of such record is that the event did not happen.

(8) For the purposes of this section, and subject to the direction and control of the Revenue Commissioners, any power, function or duty conferred or imposed on them may be exercised or performed on their behalf by an officer of the Revenue Commissioners.][1]

Amendments

1 Section 1096B inserted by FA 2002 s 135 with effect from 25 March 2002.

PART 49
COMMENCEMENT, REPEALS, TRANSITIONAL PROVISIONS, ETC

1097 Commencement

(1) Except where otherwise provided by or under this Act, this Act shall be deemed to have come into force—

(*a*) in relation to income tax, for the year 1997–98 and subsequent years of assessment,

(*b*) in relation to corporation tax, for accounting periods ending on or after the 6th day of April, 1997, and

(*c*) in relation to capital gains tax, for the year 1997–98 and subsequent years of assessment.

(2) So much of any provision of this Act as—

(*a*) authorises the making, variation or revocation of any order or regulation or other instrument,

(*b*) relates to the making of a return, the furnishing of a certificate or statement or the giving of any information, including any such provision which imposes a duty or obligation on—

(i) the Revenue Commissioners or on an inspector or other officer of the Revenue Commissioners, or

(ii) any other person,

(*c*) imposes a fine, forfeiture or penalty,

(*d*) (i) except where the tax concerned is all income tax for years of assessment before the year 1997–98, confers any power or imposes any duty or obligation the exercise or performance of which operates or may operate in relation to income tax for more than one year of assessment,

(ii) except where the tax concerned is all corporation tax for accounting periods ending before the 6th day of April, 1997, confers any power or imposes any duty or obligation the exercise or performance of which operates or may operate in relation to corporation tax for more than one accounting period, and

(iii) except where the tax concerned is all capital gains tax for years of assessment before the year 1997–98, confers any power or imposes any duty or obligation the exercise or performance of which operates or may operate in relation to capital gains tax for more than one year of assessment, and

(*e*) relates to any tax or duty, other than income tax, corporation tax or capital gains tax,

shall be deemed to have come into force on the 6th day of April, 1997, in substitution for the corresponding provisions of the repealed enactments.

(3) For the purposes of subsection (2), anything done under or in connection with the provisions of the repealed enactments which correspond to the provisions of this Act referred to in that subsection shall be deemed to have been done under or in connection with the provisions of this Act to which those provisions of the repealed enactments correspond; but nothing in this subsection shall affect the operation of subsections (3) and (4) of section 1102.

(4) Notwithstanding subsection (2), any provision of the repealed enactments which imposes a fine, forfeiture, penalty or punishment for any act or omission shall, in relation to any act or omission which took place or began before the 6th day of April, 1997, continue to apply in substitution for the provision of this Act to which it corresponds.

(5) If, and in so far as, by virtue of subsection (2), a provision of this Act operates from the 6th day of April, 1997, in substitution for a provision of the repealed enactments, any order or regulation made or having effect as if made, and any thing done or having effect as if done, under the excluded provision before that date shall be treated as from that date as if it were an order or regulation made or a thing done under that provision of this Act.

1098 Repeals

(1) The enactments mentioned in column (2) of Schedule 30 (which in this Act are referred to as **"the repealed enactments"**) are hereby repealed as on and from the 6th day of April, 1997, to the extent specified in column (3) of that Schedule.

(2) Subsection (1) shall come into force in accordance with section 1097, and accordingly, except where otherwise provided by that section, this Act shall not apply—

(*a*) to income tax for the year 1996–97 or any previous year of assessment,

(*b*) to corporation tax for accounting periods ending before the 6th day of April, 1997, and

(*c*) to capital gains tax for the year 1996–97 or any previous year of assessment,

and the repealed enactments shall continue to apply—

(i) to income tax for any year mentioned in paragraph (*a*),

(ii) to corporation tax for any period mentioned in paragraph (*b*), and

(iii) to capital gains tax for any year mentioned in paragraph (*c*),

to the same extent that they would have applied if this Act had not been enacted.

1099 Saving for enactments not repealed

This Act (other than subsections (2) to (4) of section 1102) shall apply subject to so much of any Act as contains provisions relating to or affecting income tax, corporation tax or capital gains tax as—

(*a*) is not repealed by this Act, and

(*b*) would have operated in relation to those taxes respectively if this Act had not been substituted for the repealed enactments.

1100 Consequential amendments to other enactments

Schedule 31, which provides for amendments to other enactments consequential on the passing of this Act, shall apply for the purposes of this Act.

1101 Transitional provisions

Schedule 32, which contains transitional provisions, shall apply for the purposes of this Act.

1102 Continuity and construction of certain references to old and new law

(1) The Revenue Commissioners shall have all the jurisdictions, powers and duties in relation to tax under this Act which they had before the passing of this Act.

(2) The continuity of the operation of the law relating to income tax, corporation tax and capital gains tax shall not be affected by the substitution of this Act for the repealed enactments.

(3) Any reference, whether express or implied, in any enactment or document (including this Act and any Act amended by this Act)—

(*a*) to any provision of this Act, or

(*b*) to things done or to be done under or for the purposes of any provision of this Act,

shall, if and in so far as the nature of the reference permits, be construed as including, in relation to the times, years or periods, circumstances or purposes in relation to which the corresponding provision in the repealed enactments applied or had applied, a reference to, or, as the case may be, to things done or to be done under or for the purposes of that corresponding provision.

(4) Any reference, whether express or implied, in any enactment or document (including the repealed enactments and enactments passed and documents made after the passing of this Act)—

(*a*) to any provision of the repealed enactments, or

(*b*) to things done or to be done under or for the purposes of any provision of the repealed enactments,

shall, if and in so far as the nature of the reference permits, be construed as including, in relation to the times, years or periods, circumstances or purposes in relation to which the corresponding provision of this Act applies, a reference to, or as the case may be, to things done or deemed to be done or to be done under or for the purposes of that corresponding provision.

(5) Notwithstanding any other provision of this Act, no act, whether of commission or omission, which was committed or occurred before the 6th day of April, 1997, and was not an offence at the time of commission or omission, shall be an offence in the period from the 6th day of April, 1997, to the date of the passing of this Act.

Cross-references

Commencement, subss (3), (4): s 1097(3).

Savings for enactments not repealed: subss (2)–(4): s 1099.

1103 Continuance of officers, instruments and documents

(1) All officers appointed under the repealed enactments and holding office immediately before the commencement of this Act shall continue in office as if appointed under this Act.

(2) All officers who immediately before the commencement of this Act stood authorised or nominated for the purposes of any provision of the repealed enactments shall be deemed to be authorised or nominated, as the case may be, for the purposes of the corresponding provision of this Act.

(3) All instruments, documents, authorisations and letters or notices of appointment made or issued under the repealed enactments and in force immediately before the commencement of this Act shall continue in force as if made or issued under this Act.

1104 Short title and construction

(1) This Act may be cited as the Taxes Consolidation Act, 1997.

(2) Sections 7, 858, 859, 872(1), 905, 906, 910, 912, 1002, 1078, 1079 and 1093 (in so far as relating to Customs) shall be construed together with the Customs Acts and (in so far as relating to duties of excise) shall be construed together with the statutes which relate to the duties of excise and to the management of those duties.

(3) Sections 7, 811, 858, 859, 872(1), 887, 905, 906, 910 and 912, subsections (2) and (3) of section 928, and sections 1001, 1002, 1006, 1078, 1079, 1086, 1093, 1094 and 1095 (in so far as relating to value-added tax) shall be construed together with the Value-Added Tax Acts, 1972 to 1997.

(4) Sections 7, 8, 811, 858, 859, 872(1), 875, 905, 906, 910, 1002, 1078, 1079, 1086 and 1093 (in so far as relating to stamp duties) shall be construed together with the Stamp Act, 1891, and the enactments amending or extending that Act.

(5) Sections 7, 8, 811, 858, 859, 872(1), 887, 905, 906, 910, 912, 1002, 1003, 1006, 1078, 1079, 1086 and 1093 (in so far as relating to capital acquisitions tax) and Part 34 (in so far as relating to capital acquisitions tax) shall be construed together with the [Capital Acquisitions Tax Consolidation Act 2003],[1] and the enactments amending or extending that Act.

(6) Sections 7, 811, 859, 872(1), 887, 905, 906, 910, 912, 1006, 1078, 1086 and 1093 (in so far as they relate to Part VI of the Finance Act, 1983) shall be construed together with that Part and enactments amending or extending that Part.

Amendments

1 Substituted by CATCA 2003 s 119 and Sch 3 with effect from 21 February 2003; previously "Capital Acquisitions Tax Act 1976".

SCHEDULE 1
Supplementary Provisions Concerning the Extension of Charge to Tax to Profits and Income Derived from Activities Carried on and Employments Exercised on the Continental Shelf

[Sections 13 and 567(4)]

Information

1. The holder of a licence granted under the Petroleum and Other Minerals Development Act, 1960, shall, if required to do so by a notice served on such holder by an inspector, give to the inspector within the time limited by the notice (which shall not be less than 30 days) such particulars as may be required by the notice of—

(*a*) transactions in connection with activities authorised by the licence as a result of which any person is or might be liable to income tax by virtue of section 13 or to corporation tax by virtue of that section as applied by section 23, and

(*b*) emoluments paid or payable in respect of duties performed in an area in which those activities may be carried on under the licence and the persons to whom they were paid or are payable,

and shall take reasonable steps to obtain the information necessary to enable such holder to comply with the notice.

Collection

2. (1) Subject to the following provisions of this Schedule, where any income tax is assessed by virtue of section 13, or any corporation tax is assessed by virtue of that section as applied by section 23, on a person not resident in the State in respect of—

(*a*) profits or gains from activities authorised, or carried on in connection with activities authorised, by a licence granted under the Petroleum and Other Minerals Development Act, 1960, or

(*b*) profits or gains arising from exploration or exploitation rights connected with activities so authorised or carried on,

and any of the tax remains unpaid later than 30 days after it has become due and payable, the Revenue Commissioners may serve a notice on the holder of the licence (in this paragraph referred to as **"the holder"**) specifying particulars of the assessment, the amount of tax remaining unpaid and the date when it became payable, and requiring the holder to pay that amount, together with any interest due on that amount under section 1080, within 30 days of the service of the notice.

(2) Any amount of tax which the holder is required to pay by a notice under this paragraph may be recovered from the holder as if it were tax due and duly demanded from the holder, and the holder may recover any such amount paid by the holder from the person on whom the assessment was made as a simple contract debt in any court of competent jurisdiction.

3. Paragraph 2 shall not apply to any assessment to income tax on emoluments from an office or employment referred to in section 13(5).

4. Paragraph 2 shall not apply if the profits or gains in respect of which the relevant assessment was made arose to the person on whom it was made in consequence of a contract made by the holder of the licence before the 16th day of May, 1973, unless that person is a person connected with the holder of the licence or the contract was varied on or after that date.

5. Where, on an application made by a person who will or might become liable to tax which if remaining unpaid could be recovered under paragraph 2 from the holder of a licence, the Revenue Commissioners are satisfied that the applicant will comply with any obligations imposed on the applicant by the Tax Acts, they may issue a certificate to the holder of the licence exempting that holder from the application of that paragraph with respect to any tax payable by the applicant and, where such a certificate is issued, that paragraph shall not apply to any such tax which becomes due while the certificate is in force.

6. The Revenue Commissioners may, by notice in writing given to the holder of a certificate issued under paragraph 5, cancel the certificate from such date, not earlier than 30 days after the service of the notice, as may be specified in the notice.

7. [In this Schedule a reference to a licence granted under the Petroleum and Other Minerals Development Act, 1960, includes a reference to a lease granted under that Act.][1]

Amendments

1 Para 7 inserted by FA 2001 s 44(*c*) with effect from 6 April 2001.

Cross-references

Capital gains tax, nominees, trustees and agents: s 567(4).

Capital gains tax, para 1 applied by: s 913(2).

Penalty, para 1: Sch 29 column 2.

Definitions

Income Tax Acts: s 1(2); inspector: ss 2(1), 5(1), 852; person: IA 1937 s 11(*c*); writing: IA 1937 Sch.

Former enactments

FA 1973 Sch 3 paras 1, 3, 4, 5, 7 and 8; CTA 1976 Sch 2 Pt I para 36(1) and (3) and Sch 3 Pt II.

SCHEDULE 2
Machinery for Assessment, Charge and Payment of Tax Under Schedule C and, in Certain Cases, Schedule D

[Sections 33, 61 and 62]

PART 1

Interpretation of Parts 2 to 4

1. Section 32 shall apply for the interpretation of Parts 2 to 4 of this Schedule as it applies for the interpretation of Chapter 1 of Part 3 of this Act, except that in Part 4 of this Schedule **"dividends"** shall include all such interest, annuities or payments as are, within the meaning of section 60, dividends to which Chapter 2 of Part 4 of this Act applies.

PART 2

Public Revenue Dividends, etc, Payable to the Bank of Ireland, or Entrusted for Payment to the Bank of Ireland

2. The Bank of Ireland as respects the dividends and the profits attached to the dividends payable to the Bank out of the public revenue of the State, or payable out of any public revenue and entrusted to the Bank for payment and distribution, shall, when any payment becomes due, deliver to the Commissioners appointed to assess and charge the income tax on such dividends and the profits attached to such dividends in books provided for the purpose true accounts of—

- (*a*) the amounts of the dividends, and profits attached to the dividends, payable to the Bank,
- (*b*) all dividends entrusted to the Bank for payment to the persons entitled to such dividends, and
- (*c*) the amount of income tax chargeable on such dividends and the profits attached to such dividends at the standard rate in force at the time of payment without any other deduction than is allowed by the Income Tax Acts.

3. The accounts referred to in paragraph 2 shall distinguish the separate account of each person.

4. The Commissioners shall assess the income tax chargeable on the accounts delivered to the best of their judgment and belief, and shall deliver the assessment books signed by them to the Revenue Commissioners.

5. The Revenue Commissioners shall cause to be made out a certificate showing the total amount of income tax, the total amounts of the dividends and profits attached to the dividends charged with income tax, and the description of the persons or bodies of persons to whom such dividends and profits are payable or who have the distribution or are entrusted with the payment of such dividends.

6. The certificate shall be transmitted to the Commissioners whose duty it is to make the assessment.

7. (1) In the case of dividends and profits attached to dividends payable to the Bank of Ireland out of the public revenue of the State, the Bank of Ireland shall set apart the income tax in respect of the amount payable to the Bank.

(2) In the case of dividends and profits attached to dividends entrusted to the Bank of Ireland for payment and distribution—

- (*a*) the Bank of Ireland shall before making any payment retain the amount of the income tax for the purposes of the Income Tax Acts,
- (*b*) the retaining of the amount shall be deemed to be a payment of the income tax by the persons entitled to the dividends and shall be allowed by those persons on the receipt of the residue of the dividends, and
- (*c*) the Bank of Ireland shall be acquitted and discharged of a sum equal to the amount retained as though that sum had been actually paid.

8. Money set apart or retained under paragraph 7 shall be paid into the general account of the Revenue Commissioners at the Bank of Ireland, and every such payment shall be

accompanied by a certificate, under the hands of 2 or more of the Commissioners who made the assessment, of the amount of the assessment under which the payment is made.

9. Where the Bank of Ireland does all such things as are necessary to enable the income tax to be assessed and paid in respect of British Government Stocks and India Stocks inscribed in its books in Dublin, the Bank shall receive as remuneration an allowance, to be calculated by reference to the amount of dividends paid in respect of such Stocks from which income tax is deducted, and to be fixed by the Minister for Finance.

10. Except where otherwise provided in any other enactments in force at the commencement of this Act, no assessment, charge or deduction of income tax under this Part of this Schedule shall be made where any half-yearly payment in respect of any dividends does not exceed [€3.50][1], but such dividends shall be assessed and charged under Case III of Schedule D.

PART 3

Public Revenue Dividends Payable by Public Offices and Departments

11. Public revenue dividends payable by any public office or Department of State shall be charged under Schedule C by the Revenue Commissioners.

12. The Revenue Commissioners shall exercise the like powers and duties as are possessed by Commissioners empowered to charge dividends payable out of the public revenue in other cases.

13. When any payments of dividends referred to in paragraph 11 are made, the income tax on those payments shall be computed and certified to the proper officer for payment, who shall retain the tax and pay the tax into the general account of the Revenue Commissioners at the Bank of Ireland.

PART 4

Other Public Revenue Dividends, Dividends to Which Chapter 2 of Part 4 Applies, Proceeds of Coupons and Price Paid on Purchase of Coupons

14. (1) Every person, being—

(*a*) a person (other than the Bank of Ireland) who is entrusted with the payment of any dividends which are payable to any persons in the State out of any public revenue other than that of the State,

(*b*) a person in the State who is entrusted with the payment of any dividends to which Chapter 2 of Part 4 applies,

(*c*) a banker or other person in the State who obtains payment of any dividends in such circumstances that the dividends are chargeable to income tax under Schedule C or, in the case of dividends to which Chapter 2 of Part 4 applies, under Schedule D,

(*d*) a banker in the State who sells or otherwise realises coupons in such manner that the proceeds of the sale or realisation are chargeable to income tax under Schedule C or, in the case of dividends to which Chapter 2 of Part 4 applies, under Schedule D, and (*e*) a dealer in coupons in the State who purchases coupons in such manner that the price paid on the purchase is chargeable to income tax under Schedule C or, in the case of dividends to which Chapter 2 of Part 4 applies, under Schedule D,

shall, within one month after being so required by notice published in Iris Oifigiúil, deliver to the Revenue Commissioners an account in writing giving such person's name and residence and a description of those dividends or proceeds or that price paid on purchase, and shall also, on demand by the inspector authorised for that purpose by the Revenue Commissioners, deliver to that inspector true and perfect accounts of the amount of all such dividends, proceeds or price paid on purchase.

(2) The accounts referred to in subparagraph (1) shall distinguish the separate accounts of each of the persons entitled to receive such dividends, proceeds or price paid on purchase, and state the name and address of each such person, and give particulars of the amounts payable and, in the case of amounts payable out of any public revenue other than that of the State, of the public revenue out of which each separate amount is payable.

15. Any person mentioned in clauses (*a*) to (*e*) of paragraph 14(1) is referred to in this Part as a **"chargeable person"**.

16. The Revenue Commissioners shall—

(*a*) have all necessary powers in relation to the examining, auditing, checking and clearing the books and accounts of dividends, proceeds or price paid on purchase delivered under paragraph 14,

(*b*) assess and charge the dividends, proceeds or price paid on purchase at the rate of income tax in force at the time of payment, but reduced by the amount of the exemptions (if any) allowed by the Revenue Commissioners, and

(*c*) give notice of the amount so assessed and charged to the chargeable person.

17. The chargeable person shall out of the moneys in that person's hands pay the income tax on the dividends, proceeds or price paid on purchase on behalf of the persons entitled to the dividends, proceeds or price paid on purchase, and shall be acquitted in respect of all such payments, and the Income Tax Acts shall apply as in the case of dividends payable out of the public revenue of the State and entrusted to the Bank of Ireland for payment and distribution.

18. The chargeable person shall pay the income tax into the general account of the Revenue Commissioners at the Bank of Ireland, and in default of payment the income tax shall be recovered from the chargeable person in the like manner as other income tax assessed and charged on that person may be recovered.

19. A chargeable person who does all such things as are necessary to enable the income tax to be assessed and paid shall receive as remuneration an allowance, to be calculated by reference to the amount of the dividends, proceeds or price paid on purchase paid from which tax has been deducted, and to be fixed by the Minister for Finance at a rate not being less than [€0.675][2] for every [€1,000][3] of that amount.

20. Notwithstanding anything to the contrary in the Income Tax Acts, where the Bank of Ireland (in this paragraph referred to as **"the Bank"**) is entrusted with the payment of any dividends which are payable to any persons in the State out of any public revenue

other than that of the State, this Part shall apply to the Bank and, where the Bank does all things required by this Part to be done by a person entrusted with the payment of such dividends, remuneration shall be payable to the Bank in accordance with paragraph 19.

21. Nothing in this Part shall impose on any banker the obligation to disclose any particulars relating to the affairs of any person on whose behalf that banker may be acting.

22. Where income tax in respect of the proceeds of the sale or realisation of any coupon or in respect of the price paid on the purchase of any coupon has been accounted for under this Part by any banker or any dealer in coupons and the Revenue Commissioners are satisfied that the dividends payable on the coupons in relation to which such proceeds or such price arises have been subsequently paid in such manner that income tax has been deducted from such dividends under any of the provisions of this Schedule, the income tax so deducted shall be repaid.

PART 5

Relief from Obligation to Pay Tax on Certain Interest, Dividends and Other Annual Payments in the Case of Persons Entrusted with Payment

23. When any interest, dividends or other annual payments payable out of any public revenue other than that of the State, or in respect of the stocks, funds, shares or securities of any body of persons not resident in the State, are entrusted to any person in the State for payment to any person in the State, the Revenue Commissioners shall have power to relieve the person so entrusted with payment from the obligation to pay the income tax on such interest, dividends or other annual payments imposed on such person by section 17 and Chapter 1 of Part 3, or Chapter 2 of Part 4 and this Schedule.

24. When granting the relief referred to in paragraph 23 the Revenue Commissioners shall have power to prescribe any conditions which may appear to them to be necessary to ensure the assessment and payment of any income tax assessable and payable in respect of such interest, dividends or other annual payments under the Income Tax Acts.

25. A letter signed by a Secretary or an Assistant Secretary of the Revenue Commissioners stating that the Revenue Commissioners have exercised all or any of the powers conferred by this Part on them or the publication of a notice to that effect in Iris Oifigiúil shall be sufficient evidence that they have done so.

26. When, under the powers conferred on the Revenue Commissioners by this Part, the person entrusted with the payment of the interest, dividends or other annual payments is relieved from payment of the income tax on such interest, dividends or other annual payments, that tax shall be assessable and chargeable under the appropriate case of Schedule D on the person entitled to receive such interest, dividends or other annual payments and shall be payable by that person.

27. Where the person entrusted with the payment of the interest, dividends or other annual payments complies with the conditions prescribed by the Revenue Commissioners under paragraph 24, such person shall be entitled to receive as remuneration an allowance, to be calculated by reference to the amount of the dividends, interest or other annual payments in respect of which such conditions have been

complied with, and to be fixed by the Minister for Finance at a rate or rates not being in any case less than [€0.675][2] for every [€1,000][3] of that amount.

Amendments

1 Substituted by FA 2001 s 240(1) and (2)(*a*) and Sch 5 Pt 1 for 2002 and later tax years; previously "£2.50".

2 Substituted by FA 2001 s 240(1) and (2)(*a*) and Sch 5 Pt 1 for 2002 and later tax years; previously "£0.675".

3 Substituted by FA 2001 s 240(1) and (2)(*a*) and Sch 5 Pt 1 for 2002 and later tax years; previously "£1,000".

Cross-references

Dividends entrusted for payment in the State, Parts 1, 4 and 5 apply: s 61.

Dividends paid outside the State, proceeds of sale of dividend coupons Parts 1, 4 and 5 apply: s 62.

Penalty, para 14: Sch 29 column 3.

Definitions

Bank of Ireland: IA 1937 Sch; body of persons: s 2(1); banker, coupons, dividends: s 32; inspector: ss 2(1), 5(1), 852; month: IA 1937 Sch; person: IA 1937 s 11(*c*); public revenue, public revenue dividends: s 32; writing: IA 1937 Sch.

Former enactments

ITA 1967 Sch 1 Pts I and III to VI; F(MP)A 1968 s 3(3) and Sch Pt II, s 3(4) and Sch Pt III and s 3(5) and Sch Pt IV; FA 1974 s 11 and Sch 1 Pt II.

[SCHEDULE 2A
Dividend Withholding Tax

[Section 172A]

Interpretation

1. In this Schedule—

"appropriate person", in relation to a pension scheme, means—

(*a*) in the case of an exempt approved scheme (within the meaning of section 774), the administrator (within the meaning of section 770) of the scheme,

(*b*) in the case of a retirement annuity contract to which section 784 or 785 applies, the person lawfully carrying on in the State the business of granting annuities on human life with whom the contract is made, and

(*c*) in the case of a trust scheme to which section 784 or 785 applies, the trustees of the trust scheme;

"beneficiary", in relation to a trust, means any person (in this definition referred to as "the first-mentioned person") who, directly or indirectly, is beneficially entitled under the trust, or may, through the exercise of any power or powers conferred on any person or persons, reasonably expect to become so beneficially entitled, to income or capital or to have any income or capital applied for the first-mentioned person's benefit or to receive any other benefit;

"settlor", in relation to a trust, includes any person who has provided or undertaken to provide assets or income directly or indirectly for the purposes of the trust;

"trust" means any trust, disposition, settlement, covenant, agreement or arrangement established, made or entered into by one or more than one settlor, whereby—

(*a*) assets, which may or may not change from time to time in the course of the management of the trust, or (*b*) income, the sources and nature of which may or may not also so change from time to time,

beneficially owned by the settlor or settlors are or is vested in a person or persons (in this Schedule referred to as the **"trustee"** or **"trustees"**) to be—

(i) either or both held and managed for,
(ii) paid over to, or
(iii) applied for,

the benefit of any beneficiary or beneficiaries, but does not include a pension fund, charity or undertaking for collective investment in transferable securities which is established or regulated under the law of any relevant territory.

Currency of certain certificates

2. A certificate referred to in [paragraph 8(*f*) or 9(*f*)][1] shall be treated as a current certificate for the period from the date of the issue of the certificate to the 31st day of December in the fifth year following the year in which the certificate was issued.

Amendments

[1] Substituted by FA 2000 s 30(2)(*a*) with effect from 6 April 2000; previously "paragraph 8(*f*) or subparagraph (*f*) or (*g*) of paragraph 9".

Declaration to be made by company resident in the State

3. The declaration referred to in section 172C(2)(*a*) shall be a declaration in writing to the relevant person in relation to the relevant distributions which—

(*a*) is made by the person (in this paragraph referred to as "the declarer") beneficially entitled to the relevant distributions in respect of which the declaration is made,
(*b*) is signed by the declarer,
(*c*) is made in such form as may be prescribed or authorised by the Revenue Commissioners,
(*d*) declares that, at the time when the declaration is made, the person beneficially entitled to the relevant distributions is a company resident in the State,
(*e*) contains the name and tax reference number of the company,
(*f*) contains an undertaking by the declarer that, if the person mentioned in subparagraph (*d*) ceases to be an excluded person, the declarer will, by notice in writing, advise the relevant person in relation to the relevant distributions accordingly, and
(*g*) contains such other information as the Revenue Commissioners may reasonably require for the purposes of Chapter 8A of Part 6.

Declaration to be made by pension scheme

4. The declaration referred to in section 172C(2)(*b*) shall be a declaration in writing to the relevant person in relation to the relevant distributions which—

(*a*) is made by the person (in this paragraph referred to as "the declarer") beneficially entitled to the relevant distributions in respect of which the declaration is made, (*b*) is signed by the declarer,

(*c*) is made in such form as may be prescribed or authorised by the Revenue Commissioners,

(*d*) declares that, at the time when the declaration is made, the person beneficially entitled to the relevant distributions is a pension scheme,

(*e*) contains the name and tax reference number of the pension scheme,

(*f*) contains a certificate by the appropriate person in relation to the pension scheme that, to the best of that person's knowledge and belief, the declaration made in accordance with subparagraph (*d*) and the information furnished in accordance with subparagraph (*e*) are true and correct,

(*g*) contains an undertaking by the declarer that, if the person mentioned in subparagraph (*d*) ceases to be an excluded person, the declarer will, by notice in writing, advise the relevant person in relation to the relevant distributions accordingly, and

(*h*) contains such other information as the Revenue Commissioners may reasonably require for the purposes of Chapter 8A of Part 6.

[Declaration to be made by qualifying fund manager or qualifying savings manager][1]

4A. [The declaration referred to in section 172C(2)(*ba*)(ii) shall be a declaration in writing to the relevant person which—

(*a*) is made by the person (in this paragraph referred to as the "declarer") beneficially entitled to the relevant distribution in respect of which the declaration is made,

(*b*) is signed by the declarer,

(*c*) is made in such form as may be prescribed or authorised by the Revenue Commissioners,

(*d*) declares that, at the time the declaration is made, the person beneficially entitled to the relevant distribution is a person referred to in section 172C(2)(*ba*)(i),

(*e*) contains the name and tax reference number of the person,

(*f*) contains a statement that, at the time when the declaration is made, the relevant distribution in respect of which the declaration is made will be applied as income of an approved retirement fund, an approved minimum retirement fund or, as the case may be, a special savings incentive account,

(*g*) contains an undertaking that, if the person mentioned in paragraph (*d*) ceases to be an excluded person, the declarer will, by notice in writing, advise the relevant person in relation to the relevant distribution accordingly, and

(*h*) contains such other information as the Revenue Commissioners may reasonably require for the purposes of Chapter 8A of Part 6.][1]

Amendments

1 Para 4A inserted by FA 2001 s 43(2)(*a*) with effect from 6 April 2001.

Declaration to be made by qualifying employee share ownership trust

5. The declaration referred to in section 172C(2)(*c*) shall be a declaration in writing to the relevant person in relation to the relevant distributions which—

(*a*) is made by the person (in this paragraph referred to as "the declarer") beneficially entitled to the relevant distributions in respect of which the declaration is made,

(*b*) is signed by the declarer,

(*c*) is made in such form as may be prescribed or authorised by the Revenue Commissioners,

(*d*) declares that, at the time when the declaration is made, the person beneficially entitled to the relevant distributions is a qualifying employee share ownership trust,

(*e*) contains the name and address of that person,

(*f*) contains a statement that at the time when the declaration is made the relevant distributions in respect of which the declaration is made will form part of the income of the qualifying employee share ownership trust and will be applied in accordance with the provisions of paragraph 13 of Schedule 12,

(*g*) contains an undertaking by the declarer that, if the person mentioned in subparagraph (*d*) ceases to be an excluded person, the declarer will, by notice in writing, advise the relevant person in relation to the relevant distributions accordingly, and

(*h*) contains such other information as the Revenue Commissioners may reasonably require for the purposes of Chapter 8A of Part 6.

Declaration to be made by collective investment undertaking

6. The declaration referred to in section 172C(2)(*d*) shall be a declaration in writing to the relevant person in relation to the relevant distributions which—

(*a*) is made by the person (in this paragraph referred to as "the declarer") beneficially entitled to the relevant distributions in respect of which the declaration is made,

(*b*) is signed by the declarer,

(*c*) is made in such form as may be prescribed or authorised by the Revenue Commissioners,

(*d*) declares that, at the time when the declaration is made, the person beneficially entitled to the relevant distributions is a collective investment undertaking,

(*e*) contains the name and tax reference number of the collective investment undertaking,

(*f*) contains an undertaking by the declarer that, if the person mentioned in subparagraph (*d*) ceases to be an excluded person, the declarer will, by notice in writing, advise the relevant person in relation to the relevant distributions accordingly, and

(*g*) contains such other information as the Revenue Commissioners may reasonably require for the purposes of Chapter 8A of Part 6.

[Declaration to be made by persons entitled to exemption from income tax under Schedule F][1]

6A. [The declaration referred to in section 172C(2)(*da*)(ii) shall be a declaration in writing to the relevant person which—

(*a*) is made by the person (in this paragraph referred to as "the declarer") beneficially entitled to the relevant distributions in respect of which the declaration is made,

(*b*) is signed by the declarer,

(*c*) is made in such form as may be prescribed or authorised by the Revenue Commissioners,

(*d*) declares that, at the time when the declaration is made, the person beneficially entitled to the relevant distribution is a person referred to in section 172C(2)(*da*)(i),

(*e*) contains the name and tax reference number of the person,

(*f*) contains an undertaking by the declarer that, if the person mentioned in subparagraph (*d*) ceases to be an excluded person, the declarer will, by notice in writing, advise the relevant person in relation to the relevant distributions accordingly, and

(*g*) contains such other information as the Revenue Commissioners may reasonably require for the purposes of Chapter 8A of Part 6.][1]

Amendments

1 Para 6A inserted by FA 2001 s 43(2)(*b*) with effect from 6 April 2001.

Declaration to be made by charity

7. The declaration referred to in section 172C(2)(*e*)(ii) shall be a declaration in writing to the relevant person in relation to the relevant distributions which—

(*a*) is made by the person (in this paragraph referred to as "the declarer") beneficially entitled to the relevant distributions in respect of which the declaration is made,

(*b*) is signed by the declarer,

(*c*) is made in such form as may be prescribed or authorised by the Revenue Commissioners,

(*d*) declares that, at the time when the declaration is made, the person beneficially entitled to the relevant distributions is a person referred to in section 172C(2)(*e*)(i),

(*e*) contains the name and address of that person,

(*f*) contains a statement that at the time when the declaration is made the relevant distributions in respect of which the declaration is made will be applied to charitable purposes only and—

(i) form part of the income of a body of persons or trust treated by the Revenue Commissioners as a body or trust established for charitable purposes only, or

(ii) are, according to the rules or regulations established by statute, charter, decree, deed of trust or will, applicable to charitable purposes only and are so treated by the Revenue Commissioners, (*g*) contains an undertaking by the declarer that, if the person mentioned in subparagraph (*d*) ceases to be an excluded person, the declarer will, by notice in writing, advise the relevant person in relation to the relevant distributions accordingly, and

(*h*) contains such other information as the Revenue Commissioners may reasonably require for the purposes of Chapter 8A of Part 6.

Declaration to be made by approved athletic or amateur sports body

7A. [The declaration referred to in section 172C(2)(*f*)(ii) shall be a declaration in writing to the relevant person which—

(*a*) is made by the person (in this paragraph referred to as "the declarer") beneficially entitled to the relevant distributions in respect of which the declaration is made,

(*b*) is signed by the declarer,

(*c*) is made in such form as may be prescribed or authorised by the Revenue Commissioners,

(*d*) declares that, at the time when the declaration is made, the person beneficially entitled to the relevant distribution is a person referred to in section 172C(2)(*f*)(i),

(*e*) contains the name and address of the person,

(*f*) contains a statement that, at the time when the declaration is made, the relevant distributions in respect of which the declaration is made will be applied for the sole purpose of promoting athletic or amateur games or sports and are so treated by the Revenue Commissioners,

(*g*) contains an undertaking by the declarer that, if the person mentioned in subparagraph (*d*) ceases to be an excluded person, the declarer will, by notice in writing, advise the relevant person in relation to the relevant distributions accordingly, and

(*h*) contains such other information as the Revenue Commissioners may reasonably require for the purposes of Chapter 8A of Part 6.][1]

Amendments

[1] Para 7A inserted by FA 2000 s 30(2)(*b*) with effect from 6 April 2000.

Declaration to be made by designated stockbroker operating special portfolio investment account

7B. [The declaration referred to in section 172C(2)(*g*)(ii) shall be a declaration in writing to the relevant person which—

(*a*) is made by the person (in this paragraph referred to as "the declarer") beneficially entitled to the relevant distributions in respect of which the declaration is made,

(*b*) is signed by the declarer,

(*c*) is made in such form as may be prescribed or authorised by the Revenue Commissioners,

(*d*) declares that, at the time when the declaration is made, the person beneficially entitled to the relevant distribution is a person referred to in section 172C(2)(*g*)(i), (*e*) contains the name and tax reference number of the person,

(*f*) contains a statement that, at the time when the declaration is made, the relevant distributions in respect of which the declaration is made will be applied as all or part of the relevant income or gains (within the meaning of section 838) of a special portfolio investment account and are so treated by the Revenue Commissioners,

(*g*) contains an undertaking by the declarer that, if the person mentioned in subparagraph (*a*) ceases to be an excluded person, the declarer will, by notice in writing, advise the relevant person in relation to the relevant distributions accordingly, and

(*h*) contains such other information as the Revenue Commissioners may reasonably require for the purposes of Chapter 8A of Part 6.][1]

Amendments

1 Para 7B inserted by FA 2000 s 30(2)(*b*) with effect from 6 April 2000.

Declaration to be made by qualifying non-resident person, not being a company

8. The declaration referred to in section 172D(3)(*a*)(iii) shall be a declaration in writing to the relevant person in relation to the relevant distributions which—

(*a*) is made by the person (in this paragraph referred to as "the declarer") beneficially entitled to the relevant distributions in respect of which the declaration is made,

(*b*) is signed by the declarer,

(*c*) is made in such form as may be prescribed or authorised by the Revenue Commissioners,

(*d*) declares that, at the time when the declaration is made, the person beneficially entitled to the relevant distributions is a qualifying non-resident person,

(*e*) contains the name and address of that person,

(*f*) is accompanied by a certificate given by the tax authority of the relevant territory in which the person is, by virtue of the law of that territory, resident for the purposes of tax certifying that the person is so resident in that territory,

(*g*) in the case where the relevant distributions (or amounts or other assets representing such distributions) are to be received by a trust, is accompanied by—

(i) a certificate signed by the trustee or trustees of the trust which shall show the name and address of—

(I) the settlor or settlors in relation to the trust, and

(II) the beneficiary or beneficiaries in relation to the trust,

and

[(ii) a notice in writing from the Revenue Commissioners stating that the Commissioners have noted the contents of the certificate referred to in clause (i),][1]

(*h*) contains an undertaking by the declarer that, if the person mentioned in subparagraph (*d*) ceases to be a qualifying non-resident person, the declarer will, by notice in writing, advise the relevant person in relation to the relevant distributions accordingly, and

(i) contains such other information as the Revenue Commissioners may reasonably require for the purposes of Chapter 8A of Part 6.

Amendments

[1] Para 8(*g*)(ii) substituted by FA 2000 s 30(2)(*c*) with effect from 6 April 2000.

Declaration to be made by qualifying non-resident person, being a company

9. The declaration referred to in section 172D(3)(*b*) shall be a declaration in writing to the relevant person in relation to the relevant distributions which—

(*a*) is made by the person (in this paragraph referred to as "the declarer") beneficially entitled to the relevant distributions in respect of which the declaration is made,

(*b*) is signed by the declarer,

(*c*) is made in such form as may be prescribed or authorised by the Revenue Commissioners,

(*d*) declares that, at the time when the declaration is made, the person beneficially entitled to the relevant distributions is a company which is a qualifying non-resident person,

(*e*) contains—

(i) the name and address of that company, and

(ii) the name of the territory in which the company is resident for the purposes of tax,

[(*f*) is accompanied by—

(i) a certificate given by the tax authority of the relevant territory in which the company is, by virtue of the law of that territory, resident for the purposes of tax certifying that the company is so resident in that territory, and a certificate signed by the auditor of the company certifying that in his or her opinion the company is not under the control (within the meaning of section 172D(3A)), whether directly or indirectly, of a person or persons who is or are resident in the State,

(ii) a certificate signed by the auditor of the company certifying that in his or her opinion the company is a company which is not resident in the State and is under the control (within the meaning of section 172D(4)(*a*)), whether directly or indirectly, of a person or persons who, by virtue of the law of a relevant territory, is or are resident for the purposes of tax in such a relevant territory and who is or are, as the case may be, not under the control (within the meaning of section 172D(4)(*b*)), whether directly or indirectly, of a person who is, or persons who are, not so resident, or

(iii) a certificate signed by the auditor of the company certifying that in his or her opinion the principal class of the shares of the company or—

(I) where the company is a 75 per cent subsidiary (within the meaning of section 172D(5)) of another company, of that other company, or

(II) where the company is wholly owned (within the meaning of section 172D(6)) by 2 or more companies, of each of those companies, is substantially and regularly traded on one or more than one recognised stock exchange in a relevant territory or territories or on such other stock exchange as may be approved of by the Minister for Finance for the purposes of Chapter 8A of Part 6,][1]

...[2]

(*h*) contains an undertaking by the declarer that, if the person mentioned in subparagraph (*d*) ceases to be a qualifying non-resident person, the declarer will, by notice in writing, advise the relevant person in relation to the relevant distributions accordingly, and

(i) contains such other information as the Revenue Commissioners may reasonably require for the purposes of Chapter 8A of Part 6.][3]

Amendments

1 Para 9(*f*) substituted by FA 2000 s 30(*d*)(i) with effect from 6 April 2000.
2 Para 9(*g*) deleted by FA 2000 s 30(d)(ii) with effect from 6 April 2000.
3 Schedule 2A inserted by FA 1999 s 27(*c*) with effect from 6 April 1999.

Cross-reference

Authorised withholding agent: s 172G(3)(*a*).
Exemption for certain persons; para 3: s 172C(2)(*a*); para 4: s 172C(2)(*b*); para 4A: s 172C(*ba*); para 5: s 172C(2)(*c*); para 6: s 172C(2)(*d*); para 6A: s 172C(2)(*da*); para 7: s 172C(2)(*e*); para 7A: s 172C(2)(*f*); para 7B: s 172C(2)(*g*).
Exemption for certain non-resident persons, para 8: s 172D(3)(*a*)(iii); para 9 s 172D, (3)(*b*).
Interpretation: s 172A(1)(*b*), (3).
Obligations of qualifying intermediary, para 8: s 172F(3)(*a*)(ii)(I); para 9: s 172F(3)(*a*)(ii)(II).
Power of inspection, returns and collection of dividend withholding tax: s 904I(1)("records).
Qualifying intermediary: s 172E(3)(*b*).

[Declaration to be made by a PRSA administrator

10. The declaration referred to in section 172C(2)(*bb*) shall be a declaration in writing to the relevant person which—

(*a*) is made by the person (in this paragraph referred to as the "declarer") beneficially entitled to the relevant distribution in respect of which the declaration is made,

(*b*) is signed by the declarer,

(*c*) is made in such form as may be prescribed or authorised by the Revenue Commissioners,

(*d*) declares that, at the time when the declaration is made, the person beneficially entitled to the relevant distribution is a person referred to in section 172C(2)(*bb*),

(*e*) contains the name and tax reference number of the person,

(*f*) contains a statement that, at the time when the declaration is made, the relevant distribution in respect of which the declaration is made will be applied as income of a PRSA,

(*g*) contains an undertaking by the declarer that, if the person mentioned in subparagraph (*d*) ceases to be an excluded person, the declarer will, by notice in writing, advise the relevant person in relation to the relevant distribution accordingly, and

(*h*) contains such other information as the Revenue Commissioners may reasonably require for the purposes of Chapter 8A of Part 6.

Declaration to be made by exempt unit trust

11. The declaration referred to in section 172C(2)(*db*) shall be a declaration in writing to the relevant person which—

(*a*) is made by the person (in this paragraph referred to as the "declarer") beneficially entitled to the relevant distributions in respect of which the declaration is made,

(*b*) is signed by the declarer,

(*c*) is made in such form as may be prescribed or authorised by the Revenue Commissioners,

(*d*) declares that, at the time when the declaration is made, the person beneficially entitled to the relevant distribution is a person referred to in section 172C(2)(*db*),

(*e*) contains the name and tax reference number of the person,

(*f*) contains a statement that, at the time when the declaration is made, the relevant distribution in respect of which the declaration is made will be applied as income of an exempt unit trust to which section 731(5)(*a*) applies,

(*g*) contains an undertaking by the declarer that, if the person mentioned in subparagraph (*d*) ceases to be an excluded person, the declarer will, by notice in writing, advise the relevant person in relation to the relevant distribution accordingly, and

(*h*) contains such other information as the Revenue Commissioners may reasonably require for the purposes of Chapter 8A of Part 6.][1]

Amendments

1 Paras 10 and 11 inserted by FA 2005 s 47(2) with effect from 3 February 2005.

[SCHEDULE 2B
Investment Undertakings Declarations

[Section 739B]

Interpretation

1. In this Schedule—

"appropriate person", in relation to a pension scheme, means—

(*a*) in the case of an exempt approved scheme (within the meaning of section 774), the administrator (within the meaning of section 770) of the scheme,

(*b*) in the case of a retirement annuity contract to which section 784 or 785 applies, the person lawfully carrying on in the State the business of granting annuities on human life with whom the contract is made, and

(*c*) in the case of a trust scheme to which section 784 or 785 applies, the trustees of the trust scheme;

"tax reference number", in relation to a person, has the meaning assigned to it by section 885 in relation to a specified person within the meaning of that section.

Declarations of pension schemes

2. The declaration referred to in section 739D(6)(*a*) is a declaration in writing to the investment undertaking which—

(*a*) is made by the person (in this paragraph referred to as the "declarer") entitled to the units in respect of which the declaration is made,

(*b*) is signed by the declarer,

(*c*) is made in such form as may be prescribed or authorised by the Revenue Commissioners,

(*d*) declares that, at the time when the declaration is made, the person entitled to the units is a pension scheme,

(*e*) contains the name and tax reference number of the pension scheme,

(*f*) contains a certificate by the appropriate person in relation to the pension scheme that, to the best of that person's knowledge and belief, the declaration made in accordance with subparagraph (*d*) and the information furnished in accordance with subparagraph (*e*) are true and correct, and

(*g*) contains such other information as the Revenue Commissioners may reasonably require for the purposes of Chapter 1A of Part 27.

Declaration of company carrying on life business

3. The declaration referred to in section 739D(6)(*b*) is a declaration in writing to the investment undertaking which—

(*a*) is made by the person (in this paragraph referred to as the "declarer") entitled to the units in respect of which the declaration is made,

(*b*) is signed by the declarer,

(*c*) is made in such form as may be prescribed or authorised by the Revenue Commissioners,

(*d*) declares that, at the time when the declaration is made, the person entitled to the units is a company carrying on life business within the meaning of section 706,

(*e*) contains the name and tax reference number of the company, and

(*f*) contains such other information as the Revenue Commissioners may reasonably require for the purposes of Chapter 1A of Part 27.

Declarations of investment undertakings

4. The declaration referred to in section 739D(6)(*c*) is a declaration in writing to the investment undertaking which—

(*a*) is made by the person (in this paragraph referred to as the "declarer") entitled to the units in respect of which the declaration is made,

(*b*) is signed by the declarer,

(*c*) is made in such form as may be prescribed or authorised by the Revenue Commissioners,

(*d*) declares that, at the time the declaration is made, the person entitled to the units is an investment undertaking, (*e*) contains the name and tax reference number of the investment undertaking, and

(*f*) contains such other information as the Revenue Commissioners may reasonably require for the purposes of Chapter 1A of Part 27.

Declarations of special investment scheme

5. The declaration referred to in section 739D(6)(*d*) is a declaration in writing to the investment undertaking which—

(*a*) is made by the person (in this paragraph referred to as the "declarer") entitled to the units in respect of which the declaration is made,

(*b*) is signed by the declarer,

(*c*) is made in such form as may be prescribed or authorised by the Revenue Commissioners,

(*d*) declares that, at the time the declaration is made, the person entitled to the units is a special investment scheme,

(*e*) contains the name and tax reference number of the special investment scheme, and

(*f*) contains such other information as the Revenue Commissioners may reasonably require for the purposes of Chapter 1A of Part 27.

Declarations of unit trust

6. The declaration referred to in section 739D(6)(*e*) is a declaration in writing to the investment undertaking which—

(*a*) is made by the person (in this paragraph referred to as the "declarer") entitled to the units in respect of which the declaration is made,

(*b*) is signed by the declarer,

(*c*) is made in such form as may be prescribed or authorised by the Revenue Commissioners,

(*d*) declares that, at the time the declaration is made, the person entitled to the units is a unit trust to which section 731(5)(*a*) applies,

(*e*) contains the name and tax reference number of the unit trust, and

(*f*) contains such other information as the Revenue Commissioners may reasonably require for the purposes of Chapter 1A of Part 27.

Declaration of charity

7. The declaration referred to in section 739D(6)(*f*) is a declaration in writing to the investment undertaking which—

(*a*) is made by the person (in this paragraph referred to as the "declarer") entitled to the units in respect of which the undertaking is made,

(*b*) is signed by the declarer,

(*c*) is made in such form as may be prescribed or authorised by the Revenue Commissioners,

(*d*) declares that, at the time when the declaration is made, the person entitled to the units is a person referred to in section 739D(6)(*f*)(i),

(*e*) contains the name and address of that person,

(*f*) contains a statement that at the time when the declaration is made the units in respect of which the declaration is made are held for charitable purposes only and—

(i) form part of the assets of a body of persons or trust treated by the Revenue Commissioners as a body or trust established for charitable purposes only, or

(ii) are, according to the rules or regulations established by statute, charter, decree, deed of trust or will, held for charitable purposes only and are so treated by the Revenue Commissioners,

(*g*) contains an undertaking by the declarer that if the person mentioned in subparagraph (*d*) ceases to be a person referred to in section 739D(6)(*f*)(i), the declarer will notify the investment undertaking accordingly, and

(*h*) contains such other information as the Revenue Commissioners may reasonably require for the purposes of Chapter 1A of Part 27.

Declaration of qualifying management company and specified company

8. The declaration referred to in section 739D(6)(*g*) is a declaration in writing to the investment undertaking which—

(*a*) is made by a person (in this paragraph referred to as the 'declarer') who is entitled to the units in respect of which the declaration is made,

(*b*) is signed by the declarer,

(*c*) is made in such form as may be prescribed or authorised by the Revenue Commissioners,

(*d*) declares that, at the time the declaration is made, the person entitled to the units is a qualifying management company or, as the case may be, a specified company,

(*e*) contains the name and tax reference number of the declarer, and

(*f*) contains such other information as the Revenue Commissioners may reasonably require for the purposes of Chapter 1A of Part 27.

[Declaration of qualifying fund manager or qualifying savings manager

9. The declaration referred to in section 739D(6)(*h*) is a declaration in writing to the investment undertaking which—

(*a*) is made by a qualifying fund manager or, as the case may be, a qualifying savings manager (in this paragraph referred to as the "declarer') in respect of the units which are assets in an approved retirement fund, an approved minimum retirement fund, or a special savings incentive account,

(*b*) is signed by the declarer,

(*c*) is made in such form as may be prescribed or authorised by the Revenue Commissioners,

(*d*) declares that, at the time the declaration is made, the units in respect of which the declaration is made—

(i) are assets of an approved retirement fund, an approved minimum retirement fund or, as the case may be, a special savings incentive account, and

(ii) are managed by the declarer for the individual who is beneficially entitled to the units, (*e*) contains the name, address and tax reference number of the individual referred to in paragraph (*d*),

(*f*) contains an undertaking by the declarer that if the units cease to be assets of the approved retirement fund, the approved minimum retirement fund or held in the special savings incentive account, including a case where the units are transferred to another such fund or account, the declarer will notify the investment undertaking accordingly, and

(*g*) contains such other information as the Revenue Commissioners may reasonably require for the purposes of Chapter 1A of Part 27.][1]

[Declaration of Credit Union

9B. The declaration referred to in section 739D(6)(*j*) is a declaration in writing to the investment undertaking which—

(*a*) is made by the person (in this paragraph referred to as the "declarer") entitled to the units in respect of which the declaration is made,

(*b*) is signed by the declarer,

(*c*) is made in such form as may be prescribed or authorised by the Revenue Commissioners,

(*d*) contains the name and address of the declarer,

(*e*) declares that, at the time when the declaration is made the person entitled to the units is a credit union,

(*f*) contains such other information as the Revenue Commissioners may reasonably require for the purposes of Chapter 1A of Part 27.][1]

Amendments

1 Sch 2B para 9 substituted by FA 2001 s 75 with effect from 6 April 2001.

[Declaration of PRSA Administrator

9A. The declaration referred to in section 739D(6)(i) is a declaration in writing to the investment undertaking which—

(*a*) is made by a PRSA administrator (in this paragraph referred to as the 'declarer') in respect of units which are assets in a PRSA,

(*b*) is signed by the declarer,

(*c*) is made in such form as may be prescribed or authorised by the Revenue Commissioners,

(*d*) declares that, at the time when the declaration is made, the units in respect of which the declaration is made—

(i) are assets of a PRSA, and

(ii) are managed by the declarer for the individual who is beneficially entitled to the units,

(*e*) contains the name, address and tax reference number of the individual referred to in subparagraph (*d*),

(*f*) contains an undertaking by the declarer that if the units cease to be assets of the PRSA, including a case where the units are transferred to another PRSA, the declarer will notify the investment undertaking accordingly, and

(*g*) contains such other information as the Revenue Commissioners may reasonably require for the purposes of Chapter 1A of Part 27.][1]

Amendments

1 Para 9A inserted by Pensions (Amendment) Act 2002 s 4(1)(*f*) with effect from such date as the Minister for Social, Community and Family Affairs may appoint by order. By virtue of Pensions (Amendment) Act, 2002 (Commencement) Order 2002, SI No 502 of 2002, this amendment comes into operation on 7 November 2002.

[Declaration of Credit Union

9B. The declaration referred to in section 739D(6)(*j*) is a declaration in writing to the investment undertaking which—

(*a*) is made by the person (in this paragraph referred to as the "declarer") entitled to the units in respect of which the declaration is made,

(*b*) is signed by the declarer,

(*c*) is made in such form as may be prescribed or authorised by the Revenue Commissioners,

(*d*) contains the name and address of the declarer,

(*e*) declares that, at the time when the declaration is made the person entitled to the units is a credit union,

(*f*) contains such other information as the Revenue Commissioners may reasonably require for the purposes of Chapter 1A of Part 27.][1]

Amendments

1 Para 9B inserted by FA 2003 s 56(*a*) with effect from 1 January 2003.

Declarations of non-resident on acquisition of units

10. The declaration referred to in section 739(D)(7)(*a*)(i) is a declaration in writing to the investment undertaking which—

(*a*) is made by a person (in this paragraph referred to as the "declarer") who is entitled to the units in respect of which the declaration is made,

(*b*) is made on or about the time when the units are applied for or acquired by the declarer,

(*c*) is signed by the declarer,

(*d*) is made in such form as may be prescribed or authorised by the Revenue Commissioners,

(*e*) declares that, at the time the declaration is made, the declarer is not resident in the State,

(*f*) contains the name and address of the declarer,

(*g*) contains an undertaking by the declarer that if the declarer becomes resident in the State, the declarer will notify the investment undertaking accordingly, and

(*h*) contains such other information as the Revenue Commissioners may reasonably require for the purposes of Chapter 1A of Part 27.

Declaration of non-corporate person

11. The declaration referred to in section 739D(7)(*a*)(ii) is a declaration in writing to the investment undertaking which—

(*a*) is made by the person (in this paragraph referred to as the "declarer") who is entitled to the units in respect of which the declaration is made,

(*b*) is signed by the declarer,

(*c*) is made in such form as may be prescribed or authorised by the Revenue Commissioners,

(*d*) declares that the declarer, at the time the declaration is made, is neither resident nor ordinarily resident in the State,

(*e*) contains the name and address of the declarer,

(*f*) contains an undertaking by the declarer that if the declarer becomes resident in the State, the declarer will notify the investment undertaking accordingly, and

(*g*) contains such other information as the Revenue Commissioners may reasonably require for the purposes of Chapter 1A of Part 27.

Declaration to Collector-General

12. The declaration referred to in section 739D(8)(*a*) is a declaration in writing to the Collector-General which—

(*a*) is made and signed by the investment undertaking,

(*b*) is made in such form as may be prescribed or authorised by the Revenue Commissioners,

(*c*) contains the name, address and tax reference number of the investment undertaking,

(*d*) declares that, to the best of the investment undertaking's knowledge and belief, no units in the investment undertaking were held on 1 April 2000 by a person who was resident in the State at that time, other than such persons whose names and addresses are set out on the schedule to the declaration, and

(*e*) contains a schedule which sets out the name and address of each person who on 1 April 2000 was a unit holder in the investment undertaking and who was on that date, resident in the State.

Declaration of intermediary

13. The declaration referred to in section 739D(9)(*a*) is a declaration in writing to the investment undertaking which—

(*a*) is made and signed by the intermediary,

(*b*) is made in such form as may be prescribed or authorised by the Revenue Commissioners,

(*c*) contains the name and address of the intermediary,

[(*d*) declares that—

(i) at the time of making the declaration, to the best of the intermediary's knowledge and belief, the person who has beneficial entitlement to each of the units in respect of which the declaration is made—

(I) is not resident in the State, where that person is a company, and

(II) where that person is not a company, the person is neither resident nor ordinarily resident in the State, and

(ii) unless the investment undertaking is notified in writing to the contrary, every subsequent application by the intermediary to acquire units in the investment undertaking or an investment undertaking associated with the first-mentioned investment undertaking, shall be on behalf of such a person, (*e*) contains an undertaking that where the intermediary becomes aware at any time that the declaration made in accordance with subparagraph (*d*) is no longer correct, the intermediary will notify the investment undertaking in writing accordingly, and][1]

(*f*) contains such other information as the Revenue Commissioners may reasonably require for the purposes of Chapter 1A of Part 27.][2]

Amendments

1 Para 13(*d*) and (*e*) substituted by FA 2002 s 45(1)(*a*) with effect from 1 January 2002.

2 Schedule 2B inserted by FA 2000 s 58(1)(*b*) with effect from 6 April 2000.

[Certain resident entities: declaration of intermediary

14. The declaration referred to in section 739D(9A)*(a)* is a declaration in writing to the investment undertaking which—

(*a*) is made and signed by the intermediary,

(*b*) is made in such form as may be prescribed or authorised by the Revenue Commissioners,

(*c*) contains the name and address of the intermediary,

(*d*) declares that—

(i) at the time of making the declaration, to the best of the intermediary's knowledge and belief, the person who has beneficial entitlement to each of the units in respect of which the declaration is made is a person referred to in [paragraphs (*a*) to (*k*)][1] of section 739D(6), and

(ii) unless the investment undertaking is notified in writing to the contrary, every subsequent application by the intermediary to acquire units in the investment undertaking or an investment undertaking associated with the first-mentioned investment undertaking, shall be on behalf of such a person,

(*e*) contains an undertaking that where the intermediary becomes aware at any time that the declaration made under subparagraph (*d*) is no longer correct, the intermediary will notify the investment undertaking in writing accordingly, and

(*f*) contains such other information as the Revenue Commissioners may reasonably require for the purposes of Chapter 1A of Part 27.][2]

Amendments

1 Substituted by FA 2003 s 56(*b*) with effect from 1 January 2003; previously "paragraphs (*a*) to (*h*)".

2 Para 14 inserted by FA 2002 s 45(1)(*b*) with effect from 1 January 2002.

Cross-references

Gain arising on a chargeable event: s 739D(10); para 2: s 739D(6)(*a*); para 3: s 739D(6)(*b*); para 4: s 739D(6)(*c*); para 5: s 739D(6)(*d*); para 9B: s 739D(6)(*j*); para 6: s 739D(6)(*e*); para 7: s 739D(6)(*f*)(ii); para 8: s 739D(6)(*g*); para 9: s 739D(6)(*h*); para 9A: s 739D(6)(*i*); para 9B: s 739D(6)(*j*); para 10: s 739D(7)(*a*)(i), (*b*)(ii); para 11: s 739D(7)(*a*)(ii), (*b*)(ii); para 12: s 739D(8)(*a*)(ii); para 13: s 739D(9)(*a*); para 14: s 739D(9A).
Interpretation and application: s 739B(1), (2), (5), (6).

Definitions

approved retirement fund, approved minimum retirement fund: s 739B(1); body of persons: s 2(1); Collector-General: ss 2(1), 851; company: ss 4(1), 5(1); intermediary, investment undertaking, pension scheme: s 739B(1); ordinarily resident: s 2(1); person: IA 1937 s 11(*c*); qualifying management company, special investment scheme, unit: s 739B(1); resident: s 2(1); writing: IA 1937 Sch.

SCHEDULE 3

Reliefs in Respect of Income Tax Charged on Payments on Retirement, etc

[Section 201]

Revenue information

Information leaflet IT21 — Lump Sum Payments on Redundancy/Retirement.

Tax Briefing

TB11 July 1993 par 1.3 — Termination Payments.

TB22 June 1996 p 14 — Redundancy payments and re-engagement of employees.

TB28 Oct 1997 p 7 — Taxation treatment of redundancy/termination payments.

TB47 April 2002 p 10 — Ex gratia redundancy payments — Finance Act 2002 amendments.

PART 1

Interpretation and Preliminary

1. (1) In this Schedule—

"the relevant capital sum in relation to an office or employment" means, subject to subparagraph (2), the aggregate of—

(*a*) the amount of any lump sum (not chargeable to income tax) received,

(*b*) the amount equal to the value at the relevant date of any lump sum (not chargeable to income tax) receivable, and

(*c*) the amount equal to the value at the relevant date of any lump sum (not chargeable to income tax) which, on the exercise of an option or a right to commute, in whole or in part, a pension in favour of a lump sum, may be received in the future,

by the holder in respect of the office or employment in pursuance of any scheme or fund described in section 778(1);

"the standard capital superannuation benefit", in relation to an office or employment, means a sum determined as follows:

(*a*) the average for one year of the holder's emoluments of the office or employment for the last 3 years of his or her service before the relevant date (or for the whole period of his or her service if less than 3 years) shall be ascertained,

(*b*) one-fifteenth of the amount ascertained in accordance with clause (*a*) shall be multiplied by the whole number of complete years of the service of the holder in the office or employment, and

(*c*) an amount equal to the relevant capital sum in relation to the office or employment shall be deducted from the product determined in accordance with clause (*b*).

(2) (*a*) The relevant capital sum in relation to an office or employment shall include the amount mentioned in clause (*c*) of the definition of **"the relevant capital sum in relation to an office or employment"** whether or not the option or right referred to in that clause is exercised.

(*b*) Where, under the conditions or terms of any scheme or fund described in section 778(1), the holder of the office or employment is entitled to surrender irrevocably the option or right referred to in clause (*c*) of the definition of **"the relevant capital sum in relation to an office or employment"** and has done so at the relevant date, the relevant capital sum in relation to an office or employment shall not include the amount mentioned in that clause.

2. Any reference in this Schedule to a payment in respect of which income tax is chargeable under section 123 is a reference to so much of that payment as is chargeable to tax after deduction of the relief applicable to that payment under section 201(5).

3. Any reference in this Schedule to the amount of income tax to which a person is or would be chargeable is a reference to the amount of income tax to which the person is or would be chargeable either by assessment or by deduction.

4. Relief shall be allowed in accordance with this Schedule in respect of income tax chargeable by virtue of section 123 where a claim is duly made in accordance with section 201.

5. A claimant shall not be entitled to relief under this Schedule in respect of any income the tax on which he or she is entitled to charge against any other person, or to deduct, retain or satisfy out of any payment which he or she is liable to make to any other person.

PART 2

Relief by Reduction of Sums Chargeable

6. In computing the charge to tax in respect of a payment chargeable to income tax under section 123, a sum equal to the amount (if any) by which the standard capital superannuation benefit for the office or employment in respect of which the payment is made exceeds the basic exemption shall be deducted from the payment.

7. Where income tax is chargeable under section 123 in respect of 2 or more payments to which paragraph 6 applies, being payments made to or in respect of the same person in respect of the same office or employment or in respect of different offices or employments held under the same employer or under associated employers, then—

(*a*) paragraph 6 shall apply as if those payments were a single payment of an amount equal to their aggregate amount and, where they are made in respect of different offices or employments, as if the standard capital superannuation benefit were an amount equal to the sum of the standard capital superannuation benefits for those offices or employments, and

(*b*) where the payments are treated as income of different years of assessment, the relief to be granted under paragraph 6 in respect of a payment chargeable for any year of assessment shall be the amount by which the relief computed in accordance with subparagraph (*a*) in respect of that payment and any payments chargeable for previous years of assessment exceeds the relief in respect of those payments chargeable for previous years of assessment,

and, where the standard capital superannuation benefit for an office or employment in respect of which 2 or more of the payments are made is not the same in relation to each of those payments, it shall be treated for the purposes of this paragraph as equal to the higher or highest of those benefits.

8. In computing the charge to tax in respect of a payment chargeable to income tax under section 123 in the case of a claimant, if the claimant has not [in the previous 10 years of assessment][1] made a claim under section 201 and the relevant capital sum (if any) in relation to the office or employment in respect of which the payment is made does not exceed [€10,000][2], subsection (5) of section 201 and paragraph 6 shall apply to that payment as if each reference in that subsection and in that paragraph to the basic exemption were a reference to the basic exemption increased by the amount by which [€10,000][2] exceeds that relevant capital sum.

Amendments

1 Substituted by FA 2002 s 15(*a*) for 2002 and later tax years; previously "previously".

2 Substituted by FA 2002 s 15(*b*) for 2002 and later tax years; previously "€5,080" (£4,000).

9. In computing the charge to tax in respect of a payment chargeable to income tax under section 123, being a payment made in respect of an office or employment in which the service of the holder includes foreign service, a sum which bears to the amount which would be chargeable to income tax apart from this paragraph the same proportion as the length of the foreign service bears to the length of the service before the relevant date shall be deducted from the payment (in addition to any deduction allowed under paragraphs 6 to 8 of this Schedule).

PART 3

Relief by Reduction of Tax

10. In the case of any payment in respect of which income tax is chargeable under section 123, relief shall be allowed by means of deduction from the tax chargeable by virtue of that section of an amount equal to the amount determined by the formula—

$$A - (P \times \frac{T}{I})$$

where—

A is the amount of income tax which apart from this paragraph would be chargeable in respect of the total income of the holder or past holder of the office or employment for the year of assessment of which the payment is treated as income after deducting from that amount of tax the amount of tax which would be so chargeable if the payment had not been made,

P is the amount of that payment after deducting any relief applicable to that payment under the preceding provisions of this Schedule,

T is the aggregate of the amounts of [income tax payable][1] in respect of the total income of the holder or past holder of the office or employment for the [3 years][2] of assessment preceding the year of assessment of which the payment is treated as income before taking account of any relief provided by section 826, and

I is the aggregate of the taxable incomes of the holder or past holder of the office or employment for the [3 years][2] of assessment preceding the year of assessment of which the payment is treated as income.

11. Where income tax is chargeable under section 123 in respect of 2 or more payments to or in respect of the same person in respect of the same office or employment and is so chargeable for the same year of assessment, those payments shall be treated for the purposes of paragraph 10 as a single payment of an amount equal to their aggregate amount.

12. Where income tax is chargeable under section 123 in respect of 2 or more payments to or in respect of the same person in respect of different offices or employments and is so chargeable for the same year of assessment, paragraphs 10 and 11 shall apply as if those payments were made in respect of the same office or employment.

Amendments

1 Substituted by FA 2001 s 2(3) and Sch 1 para 1(*u*) for short tax "year" 2001 and later tax years; previously "income tax chargeable".

2 Substituted by FA 2005 s 19(1)(*b*) as respects 2005 and subsequent years of assessment; previously "5 years".

Cross-references

Agreed pay restructuring relief to be reduced: s 202(7); no double deduction: s 202(8).

Revenue precedents

Issue: Calculation of SCSB where the employee has less than 3 years paid service in the immediate period, prior to the "relevant date". Employee may have been on career break, etc.
Decision: To obtain the average under SCSB rules, one has to look at the emoluments of the employment for the "last 3 years of his service". The service in question is the service in the employment in respect of which the termination payment is being made. Where gaps in the service exist, it will be necessary to go back further than 36 months to determine the emoluments for the last 3 years of service.

Definitions

person: IA 1937 s 11(*c*); taxable income: ss 3(1), 458; total income: s 3(1); year of assessment: s 3(1).

Former enactments

ITA 1967 Sch 3; FA 1980 s 10(2); FA 1990 s 12; FA 1993 s 8(*b*).

SCHEDULE 4
Exemption of Specified Non-Commercial State Sponsored Bodies from Certain Tax Provisions

[Section 227]

1. Agency for Personal Service Overseas.
2. Beaumont Hospital Board.
3. Blood Transfusion Service Board.
4. Board for Employment of the Blind.
5. An Bord Altranais.
6. An Bord Bia — The Irish Food Board.
7. Bord Fáilte Éireann.
8. An Bord Glas.
9. An Bord Iascaigh Mhara.
10. Bord na Gaeilge.
11. Bord na Leabhar Gaeilge.
12. Bord na Radharcmhastóirí.
13. An Bord Pleanála.

14. Bord Scoláireachtaí Comalairte.
15. An Bord Tráchtála – The Irish Trade Board.
16. An Bord Uchtála.
17. Building Regulations Advisory Body.
18. The Central Fisheries Board.
19. CERT Limited.
20. The Chester Beatty Library.
21. An Chomhairle Ealaíon.
22. An Chomhairle Leabharlanna.

[22A. An Chomhairle Oidhreachta — The Heritage Council.][1]

23. Coiste An Asgard.
24. Combat Poverty Agency.
25. Comhairle na Nimheanna.
26. Comhairle na n-Ospidéal.
27. Cork Hospitals Board.

[27A. A County Enterprise Board.][2]

28. Criminal Injuries Compensation Tribunal.
29. Dental Council.
30. Drug Treatment Centre Board.
31. Dublin Dental Hospital Board.
32. Dublin Institute for Advanced Studies.
33. Eastern Regional Fisheries Board.
34. Economic and Social Research Institute.
35. Employment Equality Agency.
36. Environmental Protection Agency— An Ghníomhaireacht um Chaomhnú Comhshaoil.
37. Eolas— The Irish Science and Technology Agency.
38. Federated Dublin Voluntary Hospitals.
39. Fire Services Council.
40. An Foras Áiseanna Saothair.
41. Forbairt.
42. Forfás.
43. The Foyle Fisheries Commission.
44. Garda Síochána Appeal Board.
45. Garda Síochána Complaints Board.
46. General Medical Services (Payments) Board.
47. Health Research Board— An Bord Taighde Sláinte.
48. Higher Education Authority.
49. Hospital Bodies Administrative Bureau.
50. Hospitals Trust Board.
51. The Independent Radio and Television Commission – An Coimisiún um Raidio agus Teilifís Neamhspleách.

52. The Industrial Development Agency (Ireland).
53. The Industrial Development Authority.
54. Institiúid Teangeolaíochta Éireann.
55. Institute of Public Administration.
56. The Irish Film Board.
57. The Irish Medicines Board.
[57A. The Irish Sports Council.][3]
58. The Labour Relations Commission.
59. Law Reform Commission.
60. The Legal Aid Board.
61. Leopardstown Park Hospital Board.
62. Local Government Computer Services Board – An Bord Seirbhísí Ríomhaire Rialtais Aitiúil.
63. Local Government Staff Negotiations Board – An Bord Comhchaibidlí Foirne Rialtais Aitiúil.
64. The Marine Institute.
65. Medical Bureau of Road Safety – An Lia-Bhiúró um Shábháiltacht ar Bhóithre.
66. The Medical Council.
67. The National Authority for Occupational Safety and Health – An tÚdarás Náisiúnta um Shábháilteachta agus Sláinte Ceirde.
68. National Cancer Registry.
69. The National Concert Hall Company Limited – An Ceoláras Náisiúnta.
[69A. National Consultative Committee on Racism and Interculturalism.][4]
70. National Council for Educational Awards.
71. National Council for the Elderly.
72. The National Economic and Social Council.
73. The National Economic and Social Forum.
74. National Health Council.
[74A. The National Milk Agency.][5]
[74AB. National Qualifications Authority of Ireland.][6]
...[7]
76. National Rehabilitation Board.
77. The National Roads Authority— An tÚdarás um Bóithre Náisiúnta.
78. National Safety Council— Comhairle Sábháiltacht Náisiúnta.
79. National Social Services Board.
80. The Northern Regional Fisheries Board.
81. The North Western Regional Fisheries Board.
[81A Occupational Safety and Health Institute of Ireland.][8]
82. Office of the Data Protection Commissioner.
83. The Pensions Board.
[83A. The Personal Injuries Assessment Board.][9]

84. Postgraduate Medical and Dental Board.
85. The Radiological Protection Institute of Ireland.
86. The Refugee Agency.
87. Rent Tribunal.
88. Royal Hospital Kilmainham Company.
89. Saint James's Hospital Board.
90. Saint Luke's and St Anne's Hospital Board.
91. Salmon Research Agency of Ireland Incorporated.
92. Shannon Free Airport Development Company Limited.
93. The Shannon Regional Fisheries Board.
94. The Southern Regional Fisheries Board.
95. The South Western Regional Fisheries Board
96. Tallaght Hospital Board.
97. Teagasc.
98. Temple Bar Renewal Limited.
[98A. Tourism Ireland Limited.][10]
99. Údarás na Gaeltachta.

Amendments

1 Inserted by Taxes Consolidation Act 1997 (Amendment of Schedule 4) Order 2001 (SI No 43 of 2001) with effect from 10 July 1995.
2 Inserted by Taxes Consolidation Act 1997 (Amendment of Schedule 4) Order 2001 (SI No 43 of 2001) with effect from 27 November 1995.
3 Inserted by FA 2003 s 64(*a*) with effect from 1 January 2003.
4 Inserted by FA 2003 s 64(*b*) with effect from 1 January 2003.
5 Inserted by Taxes Consolidation Act 1997 (Amendment of Schedule 4) Order 2001 (SI No 43 of 2001) with effect from 30 December 1994.
6 Inserted by FA 2003 s 64(*c*) with effect from 1 January 2003.
7 Deleted by Taxes Consolidation Act 1997 (Amendment of Schedule 4) Order 2001 (SI No 43 of 2001) with effect from 13 February 2001; previously "75. National Heritage Council — Comhairle na Oidhreacha Náisiúnta.".
8 Inserted by FA 2003 s 64(*d*) with effect from 1 January 2003.
9 Inserted by FA 2004 s 40 with effect from 1 January 2004.
10 Inserted by FA 2003 s 64(*e*) with effect from 1 January 2003.

Cross-references

Meaning of non-commercial State-sponsored body: s 227(1).
Minister for Finance may extend this list: s 227(2).

Former enactments

FA 1994 Sch 2; SI 148/1997.

SCHEDULE 5
Description of Custom House Docks Area

[Section 322]

Interpretation

1. In this Schedule—

"thoroughfare" includes any road, street, lane, place, quay, terrace, row, square, hill, parade, diamond, court, bridge, channel and river;

a reference to a line drawn along any thoroughfare is a reference to a line drawn along the centre of that thoroughfare;

a reference to a projection of any thoroughfare is a reference to a projection of a line drawn along the centre of that thoroughfare;

a reference to the point where any thoroughfare or projection of any thoroughfare intersects or joins any other thoroughfare or projection of a thoroughfare is a reference to the point where a line drawn along the centre of one thoroughfare or, in the case of a projection of a thoroughfare, along the projection, would be intersected or joined by a line drawn along the centre of the other thoroughfare or, in the case of another projection of a thoroughfare, along the other projection;

a reference to a point where any thoroughfare or projection of a thoroughfare intersects or joins a boundary is a reference to the point where a line drawn along the centre of such thoroughfare or, in the case of a projection of a thoroughfare, along the projection would intersect or join such boundary.

Description of Custom House Docks Area

2. That part of the county borough of Dublin bounded by a line commencing at the point (in this description referred to as "the first-mentioned point") where a line drawn along the westerly projection of the northern boundary of Custom House Quay would be intersected by a line drawn along Memorial Road, then continuing in a northerly direction along Memorial Road and Amiens Street to the point where it joins Sheriff Street Lower, then continuing, initially in an easterly direction, along Sheriff Street Lower and Commons Street to the point where it intersects the easterly projection of the northern boundary of Custom House Quay, and then continuing in a westerly direction along that projection and that boundary and the westerly projection of that boundary to the first-mentioned point.

Former enactments

FA 1986 Sch 4 Pts I and II.

SCHEDULE 6
Description of Temple Bar Area

[Section 330]

Interpretation

1. In this Schedule—

"thoroughfare" includes any bridge, green, hill, river and street;

a reference to a line drawn along any thoroughfare is a reference to a line drawn along the centre of that thoroughfare;

a reference to a projection of any thoroughfare is a reference to a projection of a line drawn along the centre of that thoroughfare;

a reference to the point where any thoroughfare or projection of any thoroughfare intersects or joins any other thoroughfare is a reference to the point where a line drawn along the centre of one thoroughfare or, in the case of a projection of a thoroughfare, along the projection, would be intersected or joined by a line drawn along the centre of the other thoroughfare.

Description of Temple Bar Area

2. That part of the county borough of Dublin bounded by a line commencing at the point (in this description referred to as **"the first-mentioned point"**) where the River Liffey is intersected by O'Connell Bridge, then continuing, initially in a southerly direction along O'Connell Bridge, Westmoreland Street, College Green, Dame Street, Cork Hill and Lord Edward Street to the point where it joins Fishamble Street, then continuing in a northerly direction along Fishamble Street and the northerly projection of that street to the point where it intersects the River Liffey, then continuing in an easterly direction along the River Liffey to the first-mentioned point.

Former enactments

FA 1991 Sch 2.

SCHEDULE 7
Description of Certain Enterprise Areas

[Section 339]

PART 1

Interpretation

In this Schedule—

"thoroughfare" includes any canal, lane, motorway, railway line and road;

a reference to a line drawn along any thoroughfare is a reference to a line drawn along the centre of that thoroughfare;

a reference to the point where any thoroughfare intersects, joins or traverses any other thoroughfare is a reference to the point where a line drawn along the centre of one thoroughfare would be intersected, joined or traversed by a line drawn along the centre of the other thoroughfare;

a reference to a point where any thoroughfare is intersected by the projection of a boundary is a reference to the point where a line drawn along the centre of such thoroughfare would be intersected by the projection of such boundary.

PART 2

Description of Cherry Orchard/Gallanstown Enterprise Area

That part of the county borough of Dublin and the administrative county of South Dublin bounded by a line commencing at the point (in this description referred to as **"the first-mentioned point"**) where the Grand Canal is traversed by the M50 motorway, then continuing in an easterly direction along the Grand Canal to the point where it is traversed by the unnamed road to the east of the Dublin Corporation Waterworks installation, then continuing in a north-westerly direction along that unnamed road for a distance of 250 metres, then continuing in a straight undefined line in a north-easterly direction to a point on the South Western Railway Line which is 950 metres east of the point where that railway line is traversed by the M50 motorway, then continuing in a westerly direction along that railway line to the point where it is traversed by the M50 motorway, then continuing in a south-easterly direction along that motorway to the first-mentioned point.

PART 3

Description of Finglas Enterprise Area

That part of the county borough of Dublin and the administrative county of Fingal bounded by a line commencing at the point (in this description referred to as **"the first-mentioned point"**) where Jamestown Road is intersected by the western projection of the northern boundary of Poppintree Industrial Estate, then continuing in a northerly direction along Jamestown Road to the point where it joins St. Margaret's Road, then continuing in an easterly direction along St. Margaret's Road for a distance of 110 metres, then continuing in a straight undefined line due north to the point where it intersects the M50 motorway, then continuing in an easterly direction along the M50 motorway to the point where it is traversed by the unnamed road immediately to the west of the playing fields on the northern side of St. Margaret's Road, then continuing in a southerly direction along that unnamed road to the point where it joins St. Margaret's Road, then continuing in an easterly direction along St. Margaret's Road for a distance of 115 metres, then continuing in a straight undefined line in a southerly direction to the point where Balbutcher Lane is intersected by the eastern projection of the northern boundary of Poppintree Industrial Estate, then continuing in a westerly direction along the last-mentioned projection and boundary and the western projection of the last-mentioned boundary to the first-mentioned point.

PART 4

Description of Rosslare Harbour Enterprise Area

Ballygerry Area

That part of the administrative county of Wexford bounded by a line commencing at the point (in this description referred to as **"the first-mentioned point"**) where the N25 road intersects the Ballygerry Road at Kilrane, then continuing initially in a northerly direction along Ballygerry Road to the point where it next joins the N25 road, then continuing initially in a southerly direction along the N25 road to the first-mentioned point.

Harbour Area

That part of the town of Rosslare Harbour in the administrative county of Wexford bounded by a line commencing at the point (in this description referred to as **"the first-mentioned point"**) where the high-water mark joins the south-eastern end of the pier wall to the north-west of the premises known locally as the Old Customs Shed, then continuing in a north-westerly direction along that pier to the point where it intersects the eastern end of the new revetment, then continuing in a south-westerly direction along that revetment to the point which is a distance of 150 metres from the western end of that revetment, then continuing in a straight undefined line due south to the point where it intersects the railway track, then continuing in a north-easterly direction along the railway track to the point where it is intersected by the southern projection of the western boundary of the Old Customs Shed property, then continuing in a northerly direction along the last-mentioned projection and boundary to the point where it joins the north-western boundary of the Old Customs Shed property, then continuing in a north-easterly direction in a straight undefined line to the first-mentioned point.

Former enactments

FA 1997 Sch 10.

SCHEDULE 8
Description of Qualifying Resort Areas

[Section 351]

PART 1

Description of Qualifying Resort Areas of Clare

Kilkee

1. That part of the District Electoral Division of Kilkee comprised in the Townlands of Kilkee Upper, Kilkee Lower and Dough.

2. That part of the District Electoral Division of Kilfearagh comprised in that part of the Townland of Ballyonan or Doonaghboy bounded by a line commencing at the point (in this description referred to as **"the first-mentioned point"**) where the boundaries of the Townlands of Ballyonan or Doonaghboy, Kilkee Lower and Dough converge, then continuing in a south-westerly direction along the boundary of the Townlands of Kilkee Lower and Ballyonan or Doonaghboy for a distance of 568 yards to a point where it intersects a field measuring 1.829 acres, then continuing along the north-eastern boundary of that field to a point where it intersects Local Road (County Road 395), then continuing along the centre of that road in a south-westerly direction for a distance of 20 yards to a point where it intersects the northern projection of the north-eastern boundary of a field measuring 3.517 acres, then continuing along the north-eastern boundary of that field and of the adjoining field in a south-easterly direction, then continuing in that direction to the centre of the Kilkee/Loop Head Regional Road (R487), then continuing along the centre of that road in a southerly direction for 160 yards to a point where it intersects the westerly projection of the southern boundary of a field measuring 1.282 acres, then continuing in an easterly direction along the southern boundary of that field and adjoining fields to a point where it intersects with the eastern boundary of the Townland of Ballyonan or Doonaghboy, and then continuing, initially in a northerly direction, along that boundary to the first-mentioned point.

3. That part of the District Electoral Division of Kilfearagh comprised in that part of the Townland of Corbally bounded by a line commencing at the point (in this description referred to as **"the first-mentioned point"**) being the most westerly point of the boundary between the Townlands of Corbally and Dough, then continuing along that boundary in an easterly direction for approximately 510 yards to a point where it intersects the south-eastern corner of a field measuring 2.020 acres, then continuing in a northerly direction along the eastern boundary of that field and of adjoining fields for a distance of 394 yards, then continuing in a generally westerly direction along the

northern boundary of a field measuring 3.305 acres, then continuing in that direction to the cliff face of George's Head, and then continuing, initially in a southerly direction, along the high water mark to the first-mentioned point.

Lahinch

1. That part of the District Electoral Division of Ennistimon comprised in the Townlands of Lehinch and Dough.

2. That part of the District Electoral Division of Liscannor comprised in the Townland of Ballyellery.

3. That part of the District Electoral Division of Moy comprised in the Townland of Crag.

PART 2

Description of Qualifying Resort Areas of Cork

Clonakilty

1. The administrative area of the urban district of Clonakilty.

2. That part of the District Electoral Division of Ardfield comprised in the Townlands of Dunmore, Muckross, Lonagh, Drombeg and Pallas.

3. That part of the District Electoral Division of Clonakilty Rural comprised in the Townlands of Clogheen, Inchydoney Island, Gallanes, Tawnies Lower (Rural), Tawnies Upper (Rural), Desert (Rural), Youghalls (Rural) and Miles (Rural).

Youghal

1. The administrative area of the urban district of Youghal.

2. That part of the District Electoral Division of Youghal Rural comprised in the Townlands of Summerfield, Ballyvergan East, Ballyclamasy, Knocknacally, Pipersbog, Glanaradotia, Park Mountain, Muckridge Demense, Foxhole and Youghal Mudlands.

3. That part of the District Electoral Division of Clonpriest comprised in the Townlands of Clonard East and Redbarn.

PART 3

Description of Qualifying Resort Areas of Donegal

Bundoran

1. The administrative area of the urban district of Bundoran.

2. That part of the District Electoral Division of Bundoran Rural comprised in that part of the Townland of Magheracar which is situated west of the most westerly boundary of the administrative area of the urban district of Bundoran.

3. That part of the District Electoral Division of Bundoran Rural comprised in that part of the Townland of Finner bounded by a line commencing at the point (in this description referred to as **"the first-mentioned point"**) where the eastern boundary of the administrative area of the urban district of Bundoran, on the southern side of the

National Primary Road (N15), intersects with the centre of that National Primary Road, then continuing in an easterly direction along the centre of that road for a distance of 500 feet, then continuing in a north-westerly direction along the rear boundary to the east of Finner Avenue Housing Estate until the south-eastern corner of Tullan Strand is reached, then continuing in a westerly direction to the point where it joins the most north-easterly point of the boundary of the administrative area of the urban district of Bundoran, then continuing in a southerly direction along the eastern boundary of the urban district to the point where it intersects the centre of the National Primary Road (N15), and then continuing in an easterly direction along the centre of that road to the first-mentioned point.

PART 4

Description of Qualifying Resort Areas of Galway

Salthill

1. That part of the County Borough of Galway bounded by a line commencing at the point (in this description referred to as **"the first-mentioned point"**) where Threadneedle Road meets Salthill Road Upper, then continuing in a northerly direction along the centre of Threadneedle Road to its junction with the road from Seapoint Housing Estate, then continuing in an easterly direction along the southern edge of that estate road and in an easterly projection therefrom to its intersection with a road named Rockbarton West, then continuing in an easterly direction along the centre of Revagh Road to its junction with Rockbarton Road, then continuing in a southerly direction along the centre of Rockbarton Road to its junction with Salthill Road Upper and then continuing in a westerly direction along Salthill Road Upper to the first-mentioned point.

2. That part of the County Borough of Galway bounded by a line commencing at the point (in this description referred to as **"the first-mentioned point"**) where the Seapoint Promenade Road meets Salthill Road Upper, then continuing in a north-easterly direction along the centre of Salthill Road Upper to its junction with Salthill Road Lower, then continuing in an easterly direction along the centre of Grattan Road to its junction with Seapoint Promenade Road and then continuing in a south-westerly direction along the centre of Seapoint Promenade Road to the first-mentioned point.

3. That part of the County Borough of Galway bounded by a line commencing at the point (in this description referred to as **"the first-mentioned point"**) where Dalysfort Road meets Salthill Road Upper, then continuing in an easterly direction along the centre of Salthill Road Upper to a point where it meets Monksfield, then continuing in a north-westerly direction along the centre of Monksfield to the rear of Number 212 Salthill Road Upper, then continuing in a westerly direction along the Commercial Zoning Boundary as set out in the Galway County Borough Development Plan, 1991, to a point at the rear of Western House where it adjoins Dalysfort Road and then continuing in a southerly direction to the first-mentioned point.

4. That part of the County Borough of Galway bounded by a line commencing at the point (in this description referred to as **"the first-mentioned point"**) where Monksfield meets Salthill Road Upper, then continuing in a north-easterly direction along the centre

of Salthill Road Upper to its junction with Salthill Road Lower, then continuing in a northerly direction along the centre of Salthill Road Lower to its junction with Devon Park Road, then continuing in a north-westerly direction along the centre of Devon Park Road to the rear of property known as Number 108 Lower Salthill Road, then continuing in a southerly direction along Devon Park along the rear boundaries of Numbers 108, 110, 112, 114, 116, 118, 120, 122, 124, 126, 128, 130, 132, 134, 136, 138, 140, 142, 144, 146 and 148 Lower Salthill Road to where it meets Lenaboy Park, then continuing along the Commercial Zoning Boundary, as set out in the Galway County Borough Development Plan, 1991, to the rear of Number 160 Upper Salthill Road, then continuing along the rear boundaries of Numbers 160, 162, 164, 166, 168 and 170 Upper Salthill Road, then continuing in a southerly direction to the side boundary of Number 178 Upper Salthill Road, then continuing in a westerly direction along the boundary of Number 178 Upper Salthill Road to its boundary with Lenaboy Gardens, then continuing in a southerly direction along the centre of Lenaboy Gardens to the north-western corner of the Sacre Coeur Hotel, then continuing in a southerly direction along the Commercial Zoning Boundary, as set out in the Galway Borough Development Plan, 1991, to its junction with Monksfield and then continuing in a south-easterly direction to the first-mentioned point.

5. That part of the County Borough of Galway bounded by a line commencing at the point (in this description referred to as **"the first-mentioned point"**) where Lower Salthill Road meets Grattan Road, then continuing in an easterly direction along the centre of Grattan Road to its junction with Salthill Promenade Road, then continuing in a northerly direction along the boundary of the existing private car-park to the rear boundary of that car-park, then continuing in a westerly direction along the rear boundary of properties fronting onto Grattan Road as far as Salthill Road Lower and then continuing in a southerly direction along the centre of Salthill Road Lower to the first-mentioned point.

PART 5

Description of Qualifying Resort Areas of Kerry

Ballybunion

1. That part of the District Electoral Division of Killehenny comprised in the Townlands of Ballyeagh, Killehenny, Ballybunion, Dromin and Doon West.

2. That part of the District Electoral Division of Killehenny comprised in that part of the Townland of Gortnaskeha bounded by a line commencing at the point (in this description referred to as **"the first-mentioned point"**) where the boundaries of the Townlands of Ballyeagh, Gortnaskeha and Ahimma converge, then continuing in an easterly direction along the boundary between the Townlands of Gortnaskeha and Ahimma to a point where it intersects with the centre of the Tralee/Ballybunion Regional Road (R551), then continuing in a north-westerly direction along the centre of that road for 1,192 metres to a point where the road would intersect with a line drawn along the westerly projection of the northern boundary of the existing ESB transformer site, then continuing in a north-easterly direction along the existing field boundary to the centre of the Listowel/Ballybunion Regional Road (R553), then continuing in a northerly direction to the centre of the Local Road (County Road 28), then continuing in

a westerly direction along that road for 230 metres, then continuing in a northerly direction to a point where it intersects with the boundary between the Townlands of Dromin and Gortnaskeha, and then continuing in a southerly direction along the western boundary of the Townland of Gortnaskeha to the first-mentioned point.

3. That part of the District Electoral Division of Killehenny comprised in that part of the Townland of Doon East bounded by a line commencing at the point (in this description referred to as **"the first-mentioned point"**) where the Ballybunion/Beale Local Road (County Road 4) intersects the Ballybunion/Asdee Regional Road (R551), then continuing in a north-easterly direction along the centre of that Regional road for 250 metres, then continuing in a southerly direction along the rear boundary of the existing housing development to the boundary of the Townlands of Doon East and Doon West, then continuing in a westerly direction along that boundary to the centre of the Regional Road (R551), and then continuing in a northerly direction along the centre of that road to the first-mentioned point.

PART 6

Description of Qualifying Resort Areas of Louth

Clogherhead

That part of the District Electoral Division of Clogher comprised in the Townland of Clogher and that part of the Townland of Callystown bounded on the west by the Termonfeckin/Annagassan Local Road (County Road 281) and on the north by the Dunleer/Clogherhead Regional Road (R166).

PART 7

Description of Qualifying Resort Areas of Mayo

Achill

1. The District Electoral Divisions of Slievemore, Dooega, Achill and Corraun Achill.

2. That part of the District Electoral Division of Newport West comprised in the Townland of Mallanranny.

Westport

1. That part of the District Electoral Division of Westport Urban comprised in the Townlands of Ardmore, Cloonmonad, Cahernamart, Carrownalurgan, Knockranny, Westport Demesne (Urban District), Deerpark East, Carrowbeg and those parts of the Townlands of Carrowbaun and Killaghoor contained within the administrative area of the urban district of Westport.

2. That part of the District Electoral Division of Westport Rural comprised in Roman Island and the Townland of Rossbeg.

3. That part of the District Electoral Division of Kilmeena comprised in that part of the Townland of Westport Demesne (Rural District) bounded by a line commencing at the point (in this description referred to as **"the first-mentioned point"**) forming the most north-westerly point of the Townland of Westport Demesne (Urban District), then continuing in a westerly direction for 100 yards, then continuing in a northerly direction

for 320 yards, then continuing in a south-easterly direction for 630 yards following the field boundary south of Kennedy's Wood as far as the administrative boundary of the urban district of Westport and then continuing along that boundary initially in a south-westerly direction to the first-mentioned point.

PART 8

Description of Qualifying Resort Areas of Meath

Bettystown, Laytown and Mosney

1. That part of the District Electoral Division of Julianstown comprised in that part of the Townland of Mornington bounded on the north by a line commencing at the high water mark and continuing in a westerly direction along the northern boundary of Laytown/Bettystown Golf Links to a point where it intersects with the boundary of the Townland of Donacarney Great; and those parts of the Townlands of Betaghstown, Sevitsland, Ministown and Ninch which are situated to the east of the Dublin/Belfast railway line.

2. That part of the District Electoral Division of Julianstown comprised in the Townland of Mosney and that part of the Townland of Briarleas situated to the east of Local Road (County Road 438).

PART 9

Description of Qualifying Resort Areas of Sligo

Enniscrone

1. That part of the District Electoral Division of Kilglass comprised in the Townlands of Carrowhubbock North, Carrowhubbock South, Frankford, Kinard and Trotts.

2. That part of the District Electoral Division of Castleconnor West comprised in the Townlands of Bartragh, Carrowcardin, Muckduff and Scurmore.

PART 10

Description of Qualifying Resort Areas of Waterford

Tramore

1. That part of the District Electoral Division of Islandikane comprised in the Townlands of Westtown, Newtown and Coolnagoppoge.

2. That part of the District Electoral Division of Tramore comprised in the Townlands of Ballycarnane, Monloum, Tramore East, Tramore West, Crobally Upper, Crobally Lower, Tramore Intake and including the land bounded on the west by the Townlands of Tramore West, Crobally Upper and Tramore Intake (part b), on the north by the Townlands of Ballinattin and Tramore Intake (part a), on the east by a line running in a south-easterly direction from Tramore Intake (part a) along the centre of the embankment to the Townland of Tramore Burrow and continuing in that direction as far as the high water mark, and on the south by the high water mark.

PART 11

Description of Qualifying Resort Areas of Wexford

Courtown

1. That part of the District Electoral Division of Courtown comprised in the Townlands of Courtown and Ballinatray Lower.

2. That part of the District Electoral Division of Ardamine comprised in the Townlands of Ballinatray Upper, Seamount, Middletown, Parknacross and Glen (Richards).

PART 12

Description of Qualifying Resort Areas of Wicklow

Arklow

1. The administrative area of the urban district of Arklow.

2. That part of the District Electoral Division of Arklow Rural comprised in the Townlands of Clogga and Askintinny.

3. That part of the District Electoral Division of Kilbride comprised in the Townlands of Seabank and Johnstown South.

Former enactments

FA 1995 Sch 3.

[SCHEDULE 8A
Description of Qualifying Rural Areas

[Section 372L]

Cross-references

Reliefs for lessors and owner-occupiers in respect of expenditure incurred on provision of certain residential accommodation, interpretation: s 372AI(1)("qualifying rural area").

PART 1

Description of Qualifying Rural Areas of Cavan

The District Electoral Divisions of Arvagh, Springfield, Killashandra, Milltown, Carrafin, Grilly, Kilconny, Belturbet Urban, Ardue, Carn, Bilberry, Diamond, Doogary, Lissanover, Ballymagauran, Ballyconnell, Bawnboy, Templeport, Benbrack, Pedara Vohers, Tircahan, Swanlinbar, Kinawley, Derrynananta, Dunmakeever, Dowra, Derrylahan, Tuam, Killinagh, Eskey, Teebane, Scrabby, Loughdawan, Bruce Hall, Drumcarban, Corr, Crossdoney and Killykeen.

PART 2

Description of Qualifying Rural Areas of Leitrim

The administrative county of Leitrim.

PART 3

Description of Qualifying Rural Areas of Longford

The administrative county of Longford.

PART 4

Description of Qualifying Rural Areas of Roscommon

The District Electoral Divisions of Ballintober, Castleteheen, Carrowduff, Kilbride North, Lissonuffy, Killavackan, Termonbarry, Roosky, Kilglass North, Kilglass South, Bumlin, Cloonfinlough, Killukin (in Roscommon Rural District), Strokestown, Annaghmore, Tulsk, Coolougher, Ballinlough, Kiltullagh, Cloonfower, Artagh South, Artagh North, Ballaghaderreen, Edmondstown, Loughglinn, Buckill, Fairymount, Castlereagh, Frenchpark, Bellangare, Castleplunket, Baslick, Breedoge, Altagowlan, Lough Allen, Ballyfarnan, Keadue, Aghafin, Ballyformoyle, Crossna, Kilbryan, Boyle Rural, Boyle Urban, Tivannagh, Rushfield, Tumna North, Tumna South, Killukin (in Boyle No 1 Rural District), Oakport, Rockingham, Danesfort, Cloonteem, Kilmore, Elia, Ballygarden, Aughrim East, Aughrim West, Creeve (in Boyle No 1 Rural District), Creeve (in Roscommon Rural District), Elphin, Rossmore, Cloonyquinn, Ogulla, Mantua, Lisgarve, Kilmacumsy, Kilcolagh, Estersnow, Croghan, Killummod, Cregga, Cloonygormican, Kilbride South, Kilgefin, Cloontuskert, Drumdaff and Kilteevan.

PART 5

Description of Qualifying Rural Areas of Sligo

The District Electoral Divisions of Ballintogher East, Ballynakill, Lisconny, Drumfin, Ballymote, Cloonoghill, Leitrim, Tobercurry, Kilturra, Cuilmore, Kilfree, Coolavin, Killaraght, Templevanny, Aghanagh, Kilmactranny, Ballynashee, Shancough, Drumcolumb, Riverstown, Lakeview, Bricklieve, Drumrat, Toomour, Kilshalvy, Killadoon, Streamstown, Cartron, Coolaney, Owenmore, Temple, Annagh, Carrickbannagher, Collooney and Ballintogher West.][1]

Amendments

[1] Schedule 8A inserted by FA 1998 s 77(*b*) with effect from 6 April 1998.

SCHEDULE 9
Change in Ownership of Company: Disallowance of Trading Losses

[Sections 401 and 679(4)]

Change in Ownership of Company

1. For the purposes of sections 401 and 679(4), there shall be a change in the ownership of a company if—

(*a*) a single person acquires more than 50 per cent of the ordinary share capital of a company,

(*b*) 2 or more persons each acquire a holding of 5 per cent or more of the ordinary share capital of the company and those holdings together amount to more than 50 per cent of the ordinary share capital of the company, or (*c*) 2 or more persons each acquire a holding of the ordinary share capital of the company, and the holdings together amount to more than 50 per cent of the ordinary share capital of the company, but disregarding a holding of less than 5 per cent unless it is an addition to an existing holding and the 2 holdings together amount to 5 per cent or more of the ordinary share capital of the company.

2. In applying paragraph 1—

(*a*) the circumstances at any 2 points in time with not more than 3 years between them may be compared, and a holder at the later time may be regarded as having acquired whatever such holder did not hold at the earlier time, irrespective of what such holder has acquired or disposed of between such 2 points in time;

(*b*) so as to allow for any issue of shares or other reorganisation of capital, the comparison referred to in subparagraph (*a*) may be made in terms of percentage holdings of the total ordinary share capital at the respective times, so that a person whose percentage holding is greater at the later time may be regarded as having acquired a percentage holding equal to the increase;

(*c*) in deciding for the purposes of subparagraphs (*b*) and (*c*) of paragraph 1 whether any person has acquired a holding of at least 5 per cent or a holding which makes at least 5 per cent when added to an existing holding, acquisitions by, and holdings of, persons who are connected with each other shall be aggregated as if they were acquisitions by, and holdings of, one and the same person;

(*d*) any acquisition of shares under the will or on the intestacy of a deceased person and any gift of shares, if it is shown that the gift is unsolicited and made without regard to section 401 or 679(4), shall be disregarded.

3. Where persons, whether members of the company or not, possess extraordinary rights or powers under the articles of association or under any other document regulating the company and as a consequence ownership of ordinary share capital may not be an appropriate test of whether there has been a major change in the persons for whose benefit the losses or capital allowances may ultimately enure, then, in considering whether there has been a change in ownership of the company for the purposes of section 401 or 679(4), holdings of all kinds of share capital, including preference shares, or of any particular category of share capital, or voting power or any other special kind of power, may be taken into account instead of ordinary share capital.

4. Where section 401 or 679(4) has operated to restrict relief by reference to a change in ownership taking place at any time, no transaction or circumstance before that time shall be taken into account in determining whether there is any subsequent change in ownership.

Groups of Companies

5. (1) For the purposes of sections 401 and 679(4), a change in the ownership of a company shall be disregarded if—

(*a*) immediately before the change the company is a 75 per cent subsidiary of another company, and (*b*) that other company continues after the change, despite a change in the direct ownership of the first-mentioned company, to own that first-mentioned company as a 75 per cent subsidiary.

(2) If there is a change in the ownership of a company which has a 75 per cent subsidiary, whether owned directly or indirectly, section 401 or 679(4), as the case may be, shall apply as if there had also been a change in the ownership of that subsidiary unless the change in ownership of the first-mentioned company is to be disregarded under subparagraph (1).

Provisions as to Ownership

6. For the purposes of sections 401 and 679(4) and this Schedule—

(*a*) references to ownership shall be construed as references to beneficial ownership, and references to acquisition shall be construed accordingly,

(*b*) a company shall be deemed to be a 75 per cent subsidiary of another company if and so long as not less than 75 per cent of its ordinary share capital is owned by that other company, whether directly or through another company or other companies, or partly directly and partly through another company or other companies,

(*c*) the amount of ordinary share capital of one company owned by a second company through another company or other companies, or partly directly and partly through another company or other companies, shall be determined in accordance with subsections (5) to (10) of section 9, and

(*d*) **"share"** includes **"stock"**.

Time of Change in Ownership

7. (1) Where any acquisition of ordinary share capital or other property or rights taken into account in determining that there has been a change in ownership of a company—

(*a*) was made in pursuance of a contract of sale or option or other contract, or

(*b*) was made by a person holding such a contract,

the time when the change in ownership took place shall be determined as if the acquisition had been made when the contract was made with the holder or when the benefit of the contract was assigned to the holder so that, in the case of a person exercising an option to purchase shares, such person shall be regarded as having purchased the shares when such person acquired the option.

(2) Subparagraph (1) shall not apply where the contract was made before the 16th day of May, 1973.

Information

8. Any person in whose name any shares or securities of a company are registered shall, if required by notice in writing by an inspector given for the purposes of section 401 or 679(4), state whether or not that person is the beneficial owner of those shares or securities or any of them and, if that person is not the beneficial owner of those shares or securities or any of them, that person shall furnish the name and address of the person or persons on whose behalf those shares or securities are registered in that person's name.

Cross-references

Advance corporation tax (paras 3, 7): s 167(7); para 8: s 167(8).
Expenditure on abortive exploration: s 674(2).
Exploration expenditure: s 679(4)(*d*).
Penalty, para 8: Sch 29 column 2.
Petroleum trade, exploration expenditure incurred by certain companies, para 6: s 694(5).

Definitions

inspector: ss 2(1), 5(1), 852; person: IA 1937 s 11(*c*); writing: IA 1937 Sch; year of assessment: ss 2(1), 5(1).

Former enactments

FA 1973 Sch 5 Pts I (paras 1–7 and 9) and II; FA 1997 s 146(1) and Sch 9 Pt I para 5(3).

SCHEDULE 10
Relief for Investment in Corporate Trades: Subsidiaries

[Section 507]

Finance for Trade of Subsidiary

1. The shares issued by the qualifying company may, instead of or as well as being issued for the purpose mentioned in section 489(1)(*b*), be issued for the purpose of raising money for a qualifying trade being carried on by a subsidiary or which such a subsidiary intends to carry on and, where shares are so issued, paragraph (*b*) of the definition of **"relevant period"** in section 488(1) and subsections (1)(*c*), (7), (8) and (11) of section 489 shall apply as if references to the company were or, as the case may be, included references to the subsidiary.

Individuals Qualifying for Relief

2. (1) In subsections (2), (4) and (6) of section 493, references to a company (except in each subsection the first such reference) include references to a company which is during the relevant period a subsidiary of that company, whether it becomes a subsidiary before, during or after the year of assessment in respect of which the individual concerned claims relief and whether or not it is such a subsidiary while he or she is a partner, director or employee mentioned in subsection (2) of section 493 or while he or she has or is entitled to acquire such capital or voting power or rights as are mentioned in subsections (4) and (6) of that section.

(2) Without prejudice to section 493 as it applies in accordance with subparagraph (1), an individual shall be treated as connected with a company if—

- (*a*) he or she has at any time in the relevant period had control (within the meaning of section 11) of another company which has since that time and before the end of the relevant period become a subsidiary of the company, or
- (*b*) he or she directly or indirectly possesses or is entitled to acquire any loan capital of a subsidiary of that company.

(3) Subsections (5) and (9) of section 493 shall apply for the purposes of this paragraph.

Value Received

3. (1) In sections 499(9) and 501(5), references to the receipt of value from the company shall include references to the receipt of value from any company which during the relevant period is a subsidiary of the company, whether it becomes a subsidiary before

or after the individual concerned receives any value from it, and references to the company in the other provisions of section 499 and in section 501(8) shall be construed accordingly.

(2) In section 501(1), references to the company (except the first such reference) shall include references to a company which during the relevant period is a subsidiary of the company, whether it becomes a subsidiary before or after the repayment, redemption, repurchase or payment referred to in that subsection.

Information

4. Subsections (4) and (5) of section 505 shall apply in relation to any arrangements mentioned in section 507(2)(*c*) as they apply in relation to any arrangement mentioned in section 502.

Cross-references

Individuals qualifying for BES relief, para 2: s 493(1)(*b*); para 2(2)(*b*): 493(11).
Subsidiaries: s 507(4).

Definitions

company: ss 4(1), 5(1); shares: s 5(1); year of assessment: ss 2(1), 5(1).

Former enactments

FA 1984 Sch 2; FA 1987 s 12(2); FA 1991 s 15(2).

SCHEDULE 11
Profit Sharing Schemes

[Section 510]

PART 1

Interpretation

1. In this Schedule, **"control"** shall be construed in accordance with section 432.

2. For the purposes of this Schedule, a company shall be a member of a consortium owning another company if it is one of not more than 5 companies which between them beneficially own not less than 75 per cent of the other company's ordinary share capital and each of which beneficially owns not less than 5 per cent of that capital.

PART 2

Approval of Schemes

3. (1) On the application of a body corporate (in this Schedule referred to as **"the company concerned"**) which has established a profit sharing scheme which complies with subparagraphs (3) and (4), the Revenue Commissioners shall, subject to section 511, approve of the scheme—

(*a*) if they are satisfied in accordance with paragraph 4, and

(*b*) unless it appears to them that there are features of the scheme which are neither essential nor reasonably incidental to the purpose of providing for employees and directors benefits in the nature of interests in shares.

(2) Where the company concerned has control of another company or companies, the scheme may be expressed to extend to all or any of the companies of which it has control, and in this Schedule a scheme which is expressed so to extend is referred to as a **"group scheme"** and, in relation to a group scheme, **"participating company"** means the company concerned or a company of which for the time being the company concerned has control and to which for the time being the scheme is expressed to extend.

(3) The scheme shall provide for the establishment of a body of persons resident in the State (in this Schedule referred to as **"the trustees"**)—

(*a*) who, out of moneys paid to them by the company concerned or, in the case of a group scheme, by a participating company, are required by the scheme to acquire shares in respect of which the conditions in Part 3 of this Schedule are fulfilled,

(*b*) who are under a duty to appropriate shares acquired by them to individuals who participate in the scheme, not being individuals ineligible by virtue of Part 4 of this Schedule, and

(*c*) whose functions with respect to shares held by them are regulated by a trust which is constituted under the law of the State and the terms of which are embodied in an instrument which complies with Part 5 of this Schedule.

[(4) The scheme shall provide that the total of the initial market values of the shares appropriated to any one participant in a year of assessment will not exceed [€12,700][1], or where paragraph (*b*) of subsection (1) of section 515 applies, [€38,100][2].][3]

(5) An application under subparagraph (1) shall be made in writing and shall contain such particulars and be supported by such evidence as the Revenue Commissioners may require.

Amendments

1 Substituted by FA 2001 s 240(1) and (2)(*a*) and Sch 5 Pt 1 for 2002 and later tax years; previously "£10,000" (short tax "year" 2001: £7,400: FA 2001 s 77(2) and Sch 2 paras 60 and 61(*a*))).

2 Substituted by FA 2001 s 240(1) and (2)(*a*) and Sch 5 Pt 1 for 2002 and later tax years; previously "£30,000".

3 Para 3(4) substituted by FA 1999 s 69(1)(*c*)(i) with effect from 6 April 1999.

4. (1) The Revenue Commissioners shall be satisfied that at any time every person who—

(*a*) (i) as respects a profit sharing scheme approved before the 10th day of May, 1997, is then a full-time employee or director of the company concerned or, in the case of a group scheme, of a participating company, or

(ii) as respects a profit sharing scheme approved on or after the 10th day of May, 1997, is then an employee or full-time director of the company concerned or, in the case of a group scheme, of a participating company,

(*b*) has been such an employee or director at all times during a qualifying period, not exceeding [3 years],[1] ending at that time, and

(*c*) is chargeable to income tax in respect of his or her office or employment under Schedule E, will then be eligible, subject to Part 4 of this Schedule, to participate in the scheme on similar terms.

[(1A)(*a*) As respects a profit sharing scheme approved on or after the date of the passing of the Finance Act, 1998, the Revenue Commissioners must be satisfied —

(i) that there are no features of the scheme (other than any which are included to satisfy the requirements of Chapter 1 of Part 17 and this Schedule) which have or would have the effect of discouraging any description of employees or former employees who fulfil the conditions in subparagraph (1) [, having regard to subparagraph (1B),][2] from participating in the scheme, and

(ii) where the company concerned is a member of a group of companies, that the scheme does not and would not have the effect of conferring benefits wholly or mainly on directors of companies in the group or on those employees of companies in the group who are in receipt of higher or the highest levels of remuneration.

[(*b*) For the purposes of this subparagraph—

(i) **"a group of companies"** means a company and any other companies of which it has control or with which it is associated, and

(ii) a company shall be associated with another company where it could reasonably be considered that—

(I) both companies act in pursuit of a common purpose,

(II) any person or any group of persons or groups of persons having a reasonable commonality of identity have or had the means or power, either directly or indirectly, to determine the trading operations carried on or to be carried on by both companies, or

(III) both companies are under the control of any person or group of persons or groups of persons having a reasonable commonality of identity.][3]][4]

[(1B) As respects a scheme which has been established by a relevant company (within the meaning of paragraph 1 of Schedule 12)—

(*a*) any reference in subparagraph (1)(*a*)(ii) to an employee or a full-time director shall be deemed to be a reference to an individual who was such an employee or a full-time director, as the case may be, of that relevant company or of a company within the relevant company's group (within the meaning of paragraph 1(3A) of Schedule 12) on the day the scheme was established, and

(*b*) for the purposes of satisfying the qualifying period requirement referred to in subparagraph (1)(*b*), such periods in which an individual was or is an employee or a director of a company referred to in subparagraphs (3)(*b*) and (13) of paragraph 11A of Schedule 12 shall also be taken into account.][5]

(2) For the purposes of subparagraph (1), the fact that the number of shares to be appropriated to the participants in a scheme varies by reference to the levels of their remuneration, the length of their service or similar factors shall not be regarded as meaning that the participants are not eligible to participate in the scheme on similar terms.

Amendments

1 Substituted by FA 1999 s 69(1)(*c*)(ii) in respect of profit sharing schemes approved of under TCA 1997 Sch 11 Pt 2 on or after 25 March 1999; previously "5 years".

2 Inserted by FA 2001 s 17(1)(*b*)(i)(I) in respect of a profit sharing scheme or an employee share ownership trust approved on or after 12 December 2000.

3 Para 4(1A)(*b*) substituted by FA 2001 s 16(*a*) in respect of profit sharing schemes approved on or after 30 March 2001.

4 Para 4(1A) inserted by FA 1998 s 36(1)(*c*) with effect from 6 April 1998.

5 Para 4(1B) inserted by FA 2001 s 17(1)(*b*)(i)(II) in respect of a profit sharing scheme or an employee share ownership trust approved on or after 12 December 2000.

5. (1) Where at any time after the Revenue Commissioners have approved of a scheme—

(*a*) a participant is in breach of any of his or her obligations under paragraphs (*a*), (*c*) and (*d*) of section 511(4),

(*b*) there is, with respect to the operation of the scheme, any contravention of any provision of Chapter 1 of Part 17, the scheme itself or the terms of the trust referred to in paragraph 3(3)(*c*),

(*c*) any shares of a class of which shares have been appropriated to participants receive different treatment in any respect from the other shares of that class, being in particular different treatment in respect of—

(i) the dividend payable,

(ii) repayment,

(iii) the restrictions attaching to the shares, or

(iv) any offer of substituted or additional shares, securities or rights of any description in respect of the shares,

or

(*d*) the Revenue Commissioners cease to be satisfied in accordance with paragraph 4,

then, the Revenue Commissioners may, subject to subparagraph (3), withdraw the approval with effect from that time or from such later time as they may specify.

(2) Where at any time after the Revenue Commissioners have approved of a scheme an alteration is made in the scheme or the terms of the trust referred to in paragraph 3(3)(*c*), the approval shall not have effect after the date of the alteration unless the Revenue Commissioners have approved of the alteration.

(3) It shall not be a ground for withdrawal of approval of a scheme that shares which have been newly issued receive, in respect of dividends payable with respect to a period beginning before the date on which the shares were issued, treatment less favourable than that accorded to shares issued before that date.

6. (1) Where the company concerned is aggrieved by—

(*a*) the failure of the Revenue Commissioners to approve of a scheme,

(*b*) the failure of the Revenue Commissioners to approve of an alteration as mentioned in paragraph 5(2), or

(*c*) the withdrawal of approval,

the company may, by notice in writing given to the Revenue Commissioners within 30 days from the date on which it is notified of their decision, make an application to have its claim for relief heard and determined by the Appeal Commissioners.

(2) Where an application is made under subparagraph (1), the Appeal Commissioners shall hear and determine the claim in the like manner as an appeal made to them against an assessment, and the provisions of the Income Tax Acts relating to such an appeal (including the provisions relating to the rehearing of an appeal and to the statement of a case for the opinion of the High Court on a point of law) shall apply accordingly with any necessary modifications.

7. ...[1]

Amendments

1 Sch 11 para 7 deleted by FA 2002 s 13(1)(*d*)(i) with effect from 16 April 2001.

PART 3

Conditions as to the Shares

8. [Subject to paragraph 8A, the shares shall form part of the ordinary share capital of—][1]

(*a*) the company concerned,

(*b*) a company which has control of the company [concerned,][2]

(*c*) a company which either is or has control of a company which—

(i) is a member of a consortium owning either the company concerned or a company having control of that company, and

(ii) beneficially owns not less than 15 per cent of the ordinary share capital of the company [so owned, or][3]

[(*d*) a company which issued the shares to the trustees of an employee share ownership trust to which section 519 applies, in an exchange to which section 586 applies, which shares were transferred to the trustees of an approved scheme by the trustees of the employee share ownership trust.][4]

Amendments

1 Substituted by FA 2002 s 13(1)(*d*)(ii) with effect from 16 April 2001; previously "The shares shall form part of the ordinary share capital of—".

2 Substituted by FA 2002 s 13(1)(*d*)(iii) with effect from 16 April 2001; previously "concerned, or".

3 Substituted by FA 2002 s 13(1)(*d*)(iv) with effect from 16 April 2001; previously "so owned.".

4 Para 8(*d*) inserted by FA 2002 s 13(1)(*d*)(v) with effect from 16 April 2001.

8A. [Any reference in subparagraph (*d*) of paragraph 8 to shares shall be construed as including a reference to shares which were issued to the trustees of the employee share ownership trust referred to in that subparagraph as a result of a reorganisation or reduction of share capital (in accordance with section 584) which occurred subsequent to the exchange referred to in that subparagraph and which shares represent—

(*a*) the shares issued in the exchange referred to in that subparagraph, or

(*b*) the specified securities issued in the exchange referred to in paragraph (*b*) of the definition of "specified securities" in section 509(1).][1]

Amendments

1 Para 8A inserted by FA 2002 s 13(1)(*d*)(vi) with effect from 16 April 2001.

9. The shares shall be—

(*a*) shares of a class quoted on a recognised stock exchange,

(*b*) shares in a company not under the control of another company, or

(*c*) shares in a company under the control of a company (other than a company which is, or if resident in the State would be, a close company within the meaning of section 430) whose shares are quoted on a recognised stock exchange.

10. (1) The shares shall be—

(*a*) fully paid up,

(*b*) not redeemable, and

(*c*) not subject to any restrictions other than restrictions which attach to all shares of the same class or, as respects a profits sharing scheme approved on or after the 10th day of May, 1997, a restriction authorised by subparagraph (2).

(2) Subject to subparagraphs (3) and (4), the shares may be subject to a restriction imposed by the company's articles of association—

(*a*) requiring all shares held by directors or employees of the company or of any other company of which it has control to be disposed of on ceasing to be so held, and

(*b*) requiring all shares acquired, in pursuance of rights or interests obtained by such directors or employees, by persons who are not, or have ceased to be, such directors or employees to be disposed of when they are acquired.

(3) A restriction is not authorised by subparagraph (2) unless—

(*a*) any disposal required by the restriction will be by means of sale for a consideration in money on terms specified in the articles of association, and

(*b*) the articles also contain general provisions by virtue of which any person disposing of shares of the same class (whether or not held or acquired as mentioned in subparagraph (2)) may be required to sell them on terms which are the same as those mentioned in [clause (*a*)][1].

(4) Nothing in subparagraph (2) authorises a restriction which would require a person, before the release date, to dispose of his or her beneficial interest in shares the ownership of which has not been transferred to him or her.

Amendments

1 Substituted by FA 2002 s 13(1)(*d*)(vii) with effect from 16 April 2001; previously "paragraph (*a*)".

11. Except where the shares are in a company whose ordinary share capital, at the time of the acquisition of the shares by the trustees, consists of shares of one class only, the majority of the issued shares of the same class shall be held by persons other than—

(*a*) persons who acquired their shares—

(i) in pursuance of a right conferred on them or an opportunity afforded to them as a director or employee of the company concerned or any other company, and

(ii) not in pursuance of an offer to the public,

(*b*) trustees holding shares on behalf of persons who acquired their beneficial interests in the shares in pursuance of a right or opportunity mentioned in subparagraph (*a*), and

(*c*) in a case where the shares are within paragraph 9(*c*) and are not within paragraph 9(*a*), companies which have control of the company whose shares are in question or of which that company is an associated company within the meaning of section 432.

11A. [(1) Notwithstanding any other provision of this Schedule, in the case of specified securities, this Schedule shall, with any necessary modification, apply as if this paragraph were substituted for paragraphs 8 to 11.

(2) The specified securities shall be issued by—

(*a*) a company not under the control of another company, or

(*b*) a company under the control of a company (other than a company which is, or if resident in the State would be, a close company within the meaning of section 430) whose ordinary shares are quoted on a recognised stock exchange.

(3) The specified securities shall not be subject to any restrictions other than restrictions which attach to all specified securities of the same class, or a restriction authorised by subparagraph (4).

(4) Subject to subparagraphs (5) and (6), the specified securities may be subject to a restriction imposed by the company's articles of association—

(*a*) requiring all specified securities held by directors or employees of the company or of any other company of which it has control to be disposed of on ceasing to be so held, and

(*b*) requiring all specified securities acquired, in pursuance of rights or interests obtained by such directors or employees, by persons who are not, or have ceased to be, such directors or employees to be disposed of when they are acquired.

(5) A restriction is not authorised by subparagraph (4) unless—

(*a*) any disposal required by the restriction is to be by means of a sale for a consideration in money on terms specified in the articles of association, and

(*b*) the articles also contain general provisions by virtue of which any person disposing of specified securities of the same class (whether or not held or acquired as mentioned in subparagraph (4)) may be required to sell them on terms which are the same as those mentioned in clause (*a*).][1]

Amendments

1 Para 11A inserted by FA 2002 s 13(1)(*d*)(viii) with effect from 16 April 2001.

PART 4

Individuals Ineligible to Participate

12. An individual shall not be eligible to have shares appropriated to him or her under the scheme at any time unless he or she is at that time or was within the preceding 18

months a director or employee of the company concerned or, if the scheme is a group scheme, of a participating company.

12A. [Notwithstanding paragraph 12, an individual shall be eligible to have shares appropriated to him or her under the scheme at any time if—

(*a*) the shares were transferred to the trustees of the scheme by the trustees of an employee share ownership trust to which section 519 applies, and

(*b*) the individual is at that time, or was within the preceding 30 days, a beneficiary (within the meaning of paragraph 11 [or paragraph 11A, as the case may be,][1] of Schedule 12) of that employee share ownership trust.][2]

Amendments

1 Inserted by FA 2001 s 17(1)(*b*)(ii) in respect of a profit sharing scheme or an employee share ownership trust approved on or after 12 December 2000.

2 Para 12A inserted by FA 1999 s 69(1)(*c*)(iii) in respect of an appropriation of shares made by the trustees of an approved scheme on or after 25 March 1999.

13. An individual shall not be eligible to have shares appropriated to him or her under the scheme at any time in a year of assessment if in that year of assessment shares have been appropriated to him or her under another approved scheme established by the company concerned or by—

(*a*) a company which controls or is controlled by the company concerned or which is controlled by a company which also controls the company concerned, or

(*b*) a company which is a member of a consortium owning the company concerned or which is owned in part by the company concerned as a member of a consortium.

13A. [(1) Notwithstanding paragraph 13, an individual who has had shares appropriated to him or her in a year of assessment under an approved scheme established by a company ("the first-mentioned company") shall, subject to subparagraph (2), be entitled to have shares appropriated to him or her in that year of assessment under an approved scheme established by another company ("the second-mentioned company") if, in that year of assessment, the second-mentioned company acquires control, or is part of a consortium that acquires ownership, of the first-mentioned company under a scheme of reconstruction or amalgamation (within the meaning of section 587).

(2) Section 515 and paragraph 3(4) shall, subject to any necessary modification, apply as if the first-mentioned company and the second-mentioned company were the same company.

(3) This paragraph shall apply to an appropriation of shares made, on or after the date of the passing of the Finance Act, 2000, by the trustees of an approved scheme (within the meaning of section 510(1)).][1]

Amendments

1 Para 13A inserted by FA 2000 s 25 with effect from 6 April 2000.

13B. [(1) Nothing in paragraph 13 shall prevent shares being appropriated to an individual under an approved scheme established by a relevant company (within the meaning of paragraph 1 of Schedule 12) and where, in a year of assessment, shares have been appropriated to an individual under such an approved scheme, paragraph 13 shall apply as if those shares had not been appropriated to that individual in that year of assessment.

(2) Section 515 and paragraph 3(4) shall, subject to any necessary modification, apply in respect of all shares appropriated to that individual in that year of assessment.][1]

Amendments

[1] Para 13B inserted by FA 2001 s 17(1)(*b*)(iii) in respect of a profit sharing scheme or an employee share ownership trust approved on or after 12 December 2000.

14. (1) An individual shall not be eligible to have shares appropriated to him or her under the scheme at any time if at that time he or she has, or at any time within the preceding 12 months had, a material interest in a close company which is—

(*a*) the company whose shares are to be appropriated, or

(*b*) a company which has control of that company or is a member of a consortium which owns that company.

(2) Subparagraph (1) shall apply in relation to a company which would be a close company but for section 430(1)(*a*) or 431.

(3) (*a*) In this paragraph, **"close company"** has the meaning assigned to it by section 430.

(*b*) For the purpose of this paragraph—

(i) subsection (3) of section 433 shall apply—

(I) in a case where the scheme in question is a group scheme, with the substitution of a reference to all participating companies for the first reference to the company in paragraph (*c*)(ii) of that subsection, and

(II) with the substitution of a reference to 15 per cent for the reference in that paragraph to 5 per cent, and

(ii) section 437(2) shall apply, with the substitution of a reference to 15 per cent for the reference in that section to 5 per cent, for the purpose of determining whether a person has or had a material interest in a company.

PART 5

Provisions as to the Trust Instrument

15. The trust instrument shall provide that, as soon as practicable after any shares have been appropriated to a participant, the trustees will give him or her notice in writing of the appropriation—

(*a*) specifying the number and description of those shares, and

(*b*) stating their initial market value.

16. (1) The trust instrument shall contain a provision prohibiting the trustees from disposing of any shares, except as mentioned in paragraphs (*a*), (*b*) or (*c*) of section 511(6), during the period of retention (whether by transfer to the participant or otherwise).

(2) The trust instrument shall contain a provision prohibiting the trustees from disposing of any shares after the end of the period of retention and before the release date except—

(*a*) pursuant to a direction given by or on behalf of the participant or any person in whom the beneficial interest in the participant's shares is for the time being vested, and

(*b*) by a transaction which would not involve a breach of the participant's obligation under paragraph (*c*) or (*d*) of section 511(4).

17. The trust instrument shall contain a provision requiring the trustees—

(*a*) subject to any direction referred to in section 513(3), to pay over to the participant any money or money's worth received by them in respect of, or by reference to, any of the participant's shares, other than money consisting of a sum referred to in section 511(4)(*c*) or money's worth consisting of new shares within the meaning of section 514, and

(*b*) to deal only pursuant to a direction given by or on behalf of the participant (or any person referred to in paragraph 16(2)(*a*)) with any right conferred in respect of any of the participant's shares to be allotted other shares, securities or rights of any description.

18. The trust instrument shall impose an obligation on the trustees—

(*a*) to maintain such records as may be necessary to enable the trustees to carry out their obligations under Chapter 1 of Part 17, and

(*b*) where the participant becomes liable to income tax under Schedule E by reason of the occurrence of any event, to inform the participant of any facts relevant to determining that liability.

Cross-references

"the company concerned", "group scheme", "the trust instrument", "the trustees": s 509(1).
Appropriated shares, Part 2: s 510(3).
Appropriated shares, Part 3: s 510(6).
Company reconstructions, Part 3: s 514(4)(*c*).
Cost of establishing profit sharing schemes: s 518(1).
Distributions, matters treated as: s 130(2)(*f*)(i).
Employee share ownership trusts, Part 2: s 519(8), (9); Sch 12 para 12(2)(*e*), 17.
Excess or unauthorised shares, s 519(10)(*a*): Part 4: s 515(3).
Interpretation: s 509(4).
Shares acquired from an employee share ownership trust, para 12A(*b*): s 511A(1)(*c*).

Definitions

Appeal Commissioners: s 2(1); body of persons: s 2(1); class (of shares): s 5(1); company: ss 4(1), 5(1); close company: ss 4(1), 430, 431; ordinary share capital: s 2(1); person: IA 1937 s 11(*c*); High Court: IA 1937 Sch; Income Tax Acts: s 1(2); year of assessment: ss 2(1), 5(1).

Former enactments

FA 1982 Sch 3; FA 1990 s 136; FA 1995 s 16; FA 1997 s 50(*c*).

SCHEDULE 12
Employee Share Ownership Trusts
[Section 519]

Interpretation

1. (1) For the purposes of this Schedule—

"ordinary share capital" has the same meaning as in section 2;

[**"relevant company"** means—

(*a*) a company into which a trustee savings bank has been reorganised under section 57 of the Trustee Savings Banks Act, 1989, …[1]

(*b*) ICC Bank [plc,][2][3]

[(*c*) ACC Bank plc, or

(*d*) a company which acquired control of the Irish National Petroleum Corporation Limited;][4]

"securities" means shares (including stock) and debentures.

(2) For the purposes of this Schedule, the question whether one company is controlled by another shall be construed in accordance with section 432.

[(3) For the purposes of this Schedule, a company falls within the founding company's group at a particular time if—

(*a*) it is the founding company, or

(*b*) at that time, it is controlled by the founding company and the trust concerned referred to in paragraph 2(1) is expressed to extend to it.][5]

[(3A) For the purposes of this Schedule a company falls within the relevant company's group at a particular time if—

(*a*) it is the relevant company, or

(*b*) at that time, it is controlled by the relevant company and the trust concerned referred to in paragraph 2(1) is expressed to extend to it.][6]

(4) (*a*) In this subparagraph—

[**"associate"** has the meaning assigned to it by subsection (3) of section 433, subject to the reference to the employees in both places where it occurs in subparagraph (ii) of paragraph (*c*) of that subsection being construed as including a reference to former employees;][7]

"control" shall be construed in accordance with section 432.

(*b*) For the purposes of this Schedule, a person shall be treated as having a material interest in a company if the person, either on his or her own or with any one or more of his or her associates, or if any associate of his or her with or without any such other associates, is the beneficial owner of, or able directly or through the medium of other companies or by any other indirect means to control, more than 5 per cent of the ordinary share capital of the company.

(5) For the purposes of this Schedule, a trust shall be established when the deed under which it is established is executed.

Amendments

1 Deleted by FA 2002 s 13(1)(*e*)(i)(I) with effect from 16 April 2001; previously "or".

2 Substituted by FA 2002 s 13(1)(*e*)(i)(II) with effect from 16 April 2001; previously "plc;".

3 Definition of "relevant company" inserted by FA 2001 s 17(1)(*c*)(i)(I) in respect of a profit sharing scheme or an employee share ownership trust approved on or after 12 December 2000.

4 Definition of "relevant company" para (*c*)–(*d*) inserted by FA 2002 s 13(1)(*e*)(i)(III) with effect from 16 April 2001.

5 Subpara (3) substituted by FA 1998 s 36(1)(*d*)(i)(I) as respects employee share ownership trusts approved of under Sch 12 para 2 on or after 27 March 1998.

6 Subpara (3A) inserted by FA 2001 s 17(1)(*c*)(i)(II) in respect of a profit sharing scheme or an employee share ownership trust approved on or after 12 December 2000.

7 Definition of "associate" substituted by FA 1998 s 36(1)(*d*)(i)(II) as respects employee share ownership trusts approved of under TCA 1997 Sch 12 para 2 on or after 27 March 1998.

Approval of Qualifying Trusts

2. [(1) On the application of a body corporate (in this Schedule referred to as "the founding company") which has established an employee share ownership trust, the Revenue Commissioners shall approve of the trust as a qualifying employee share ownership trust if they are satisfied that the conditions in paragraphs 6 to 18 are complied with in relation to the trust.

(2) (*a*) Where the founding company is a member of a group of companies, the Revenue Commissioners shall not approve of a trust under subparagraph (1) unless they are satisfied that the trust does not and would not have the effect of conferring benefits wholly or mainly on directors of companies in the group or on those employees of companies in the group who are in receipt of higher or the highest levels of remuneration.

[(*b*) For the purposes of this subparagraph—

(i) **"a group of companies"** means a company and any other companies of which it has control or with which it is associated, and

(ii) a company shall be associated with another company where it could reasonably be considered that—

(I) both companies act in pursuit of a common purpose,

(II) any person or any group of persons or groups of persons having a reasonable commonality of identity have or had the means or power, either directly or indirectly, to determine the trading operations carried on or to be carried on by both companies, or

(III) both companies are under the control of any person or group of persons or groups of persons having a reasonable commonality of identity.][1]][2]

Amendments

1 Para 2(2)(*b*) substituted by FA 2001 s 16(*b*) as respects employee share ownership trusts approved on or after 30 March 2001.

2 Para 2 substituted by FA 1998 s 36(1)(*d*)(ii) as respects employee share ownership trusts approved of under Sch 12 para 2 on or after 27 March 1998.

3. (1) Where at any time after the Revenue Commissioners have approved of a trust—

(*a*) there is with respect to the operation of the trust any contravention of the conditions in paragraphs 6 to 18, or

(*b*) any shares of a class of which shares have been acquired by the trustees receive different treatment in any respect from the other shares of that class, in particular, different treatment in respect of—

(i) the dividend payable,

(ii) repayment,

(iii) the restrictions attaching to the shares, or

(iv) any offer of substituted or additional shares, securities or rights of any description in respect of the shares,

the Revenue Commissioners may, subject to subparagraph (3), withdraw the approval with effect from that time or from such later time as they may specify.

(2) Where at any time after the Revenue Commissioners have approved of a trust an alteration is made to the terms of the trust, the approval shall not have effect after the date of the alteration unless the Revenue Commissioners have approved of the alteration.

(3) It shall not be a ground for withdrawal of approval of a trust that shares which have been newly issued receive, in respect of dividends payable with respect to a period beginning before the date on which the shares were issued, treatment which is less favourable than that accorded to shares issued before that date.

(4) The Revenue Commissioners may by notice in writing require any person to furnish to them, within such time as they may direct which is not less than 30 days, such information as they think necessary to enable them to either or both—

(*a*) determine whether to approve of an employee share ownership trust or withdraw an approval already given, and

(*b*) determine the liability to tax of any beneficiary under an approved employee share ownership trust.

4. (1) Where the founding company is aggrieved by—

(*a*) the failure of the Revenue Commissioners to approve of an employee share ownership trust,

(*b*) the failure of the Revenue Commissioners to approve of an alteration as mentioned in paragraph 3(2), or

(*c*) the withdrawal of approval,

the company may, by notice in writing given to the Revenue Commissioners within 30 days from the date on which it is notified of their decision, make an application to have its claim for relief heard and determined by the Appeal Commissioners.

(2) Where an application is made under subparagraph (1), the Appeal Commissioners shall hear and determine the claim in the like manner as an appeal made to them against an assessment and the provisions of the Income Tax Acts relating to such an appeal (including the provisions relating to the rehearing of an appeal and to the statement of a

case for the opinion of the High Court on a point of law) shall apply accordingly with any necessary modifications.

5. The Revenue Commissioners may nominate any of their officers, including an inspector, to perform any acts and discharge any functions authorised by this Schedule to be performed or discharged by them.

General

6. (1) The trust shall be established under a deed (in this Schedule and in section 519 referred to as **"the trust deed"**).

(2) The trust shall be established by the founding company which at the time the trust is established is not controlled by another company.

[(3) Nothing in subparagraph (2) shall prohibit a company into which a trustee savings bank has been reorganised under section 57 of the Trustee Savings Banks Act, 1989, from establishing the trust at a time when the company is controlled by another company.][1]

Amendments

1 Para 6(3) inserted by the Trustee Savings Banks (Amendment) Act 2001 with effect from 28 March 2001.

Trustees

7. The trust deed shall provide for the establishment of a body of trustees complying with paragraph 8, 9 or 10.

7A. [Notwithstanding any other provision in this Schedule, in a case to which paragraph 11A applies, any reference in paragraph 8, 9 or 10 to an employee or a director of a company shall be construed as a reference to an individual who—

(*a*) was an employee or a director, as the case may be, of the relevant company or of a company within the relevant company's group on the day the trust was established, and

(*b*) is, at the relevant time (within the meaning, as may be appropriate in the circumstances, of paragraph 8, 9 or 10), an employee or a director, as the case may be, of a company referred to in paragraph 11A(3)(*b*).][1]

Amendments

1 Para 7A inserted by FA 2001 s 17(1)(*c*)(ii) in respect of a profit sharing scheme or an employee share ownership trust approved on or after 12 December 2000.

8. (1) The trust deed shall—

(*a*) appoint the initial trustees;

(*b*) contain rules for the retirement and removal of trustees;

(*c*) contain rules for the appointment of replacement and additional trustees.

(2) The trust deed shall provide that at any time while the trust subsists (in this subparagraph referred to as **"the relevant time"**)—

(*a*) the number of trustees shall not be less than 3;

(*b*) all the trustees shall be resident in the State;

(*c*) the trustees shall include one person who is a trust corporation, a solicitor, or a member of such other professional body as the Revenue Commissioners may from time to time allow for the purposes of this paragraph;

(*d*) the majority of the trustees shall be persons who are not and have never been directors of any company within the founding company's group at the relevant time;

(*e*) the majority of the trustees shall be representatives of the employees of the companies within the founding company's group at the relevant time, and who do not have and have never had a material interest in any such company;

(*f*) the trustees to whom subparagraph (*e*) relates shall, before being appointed as trustees, have been selected by a majority of the employees of the companies within the founding company's group at the time of the selection.

9. (1) The trust deed shall—

(*a*) appoint the initial trustees;

(*b*) contain rules for the retirement and removal of trustees;

(*c*) contain rules for the appointment of replacement and additional trustees.

(2) The trust deed shall be so framed that at any time while the trust subsists the conditions in subparagraph (3) are fulfilled as regards the persons who are then trustees, and in that subparagraph **"the relevant time"** means that time.

(3) The conditions referred to in subparagraph (2) are that—

(*a*) the number of trustees is not less than 3;

(*b*) all the trustees are resident in the State;

(*c*) the trustees include at least one person who is a professional trustee and at least 2 persons who are non-professional trustees;

(*d*) at least half of the non-professional trustees were, before being appointed as trustees, selected in accordance with subparagraph (6) or (7);

(*e*) all the trustees so selected are persons who are employees of companies within the founding company's group at the relevant time, and who do not have and have never had a material interest in any such company.

(4) For the purposes of this paragraph, a trustee shall be a professional trustee at a particular time if—

(*a*) the trustee is then a trust corporation, a solicitor, or a member of such other professional body as the Revenue Commissioners allow for the purposes of this subparagraph,

(*b*) the trustee is not then an employee or director of any company then within the founding company's group, and

(*c*) the trustee meets the requirements of subparagraph (5),

and for the purposes of this paragraph a trustee shall be a non-professional trustee at a particular time if the trustee is not then a professional trustee for those purposes.

(5) A trustee shall meet the requirements of this subparagraph if—

(*a*) he or she was appointed as an initial trustee and, before being appointed as trustee, was selected only by the persons who later became the non-professional initial trustees, or (*b*) he or she was appointed as a replacement or additional trustee and, before being appointed as trustee, was selected only by the persons who were the non-professional trustees at the time of the selection.

(6) Trustees shall be selected in accordance with this subparagraph if the process of selection is one under which—

(*a*) all the persons who are employees of the companies within the founding company's group at the time of the selection, and who do not have and have never had a material interest in any such company, are, in so far as is reasonably practicable, given the opportunity to stand for selection,

(*b*) all the employees of the companies within the founding company's group at the time of the selection are, in so far as is reasonably practicable, given the opportunity to vote, and

(*c*) persons gaining more votes are preferred to those gaining less.

(7) Trustees shall be selected in accordance with this subparagraph if they are selected by persons elected to represent the employees of the companies within the founding company's group at the time of the selection.

10. (1) This paragraph shall apply where the trust deed provides that at any time while the trust subsists there shall be a single trustee.

(2) The trust deed shall—

(*a*) be so framed that at any time while the trust subsists the trustee is a company which at that time is resident in the State and controlled by the founding company;

(*b*) appoint the initial trustee;

(*c*) contain rules for the removal of any trustee and for the appointment of a replacement trustee.

(3) The trust deed shall be so framed that at any time while the trust subsists the company which is then the trustee is a company so constituted that the conditions in subparagraph (4) are then fulfilled as regards the persons who are then directors of the company, and in that subparagraph **"the relevant time"** means that time and **"the trust company"** means that company.

(4) The conditions referred to in subparagraph (3) are that—

(*a*) the number of directors is not less than 3;

(*b*) all the directors are resident in the State;

(*c*) the directors include at least one person who is a professional director and at least 2 persons who are non-professional directors;

(*d*) at least half of the non-professional directors were, before being appointed as directors, selected in accordance with subparagraph (7) or (8);

(*e*) all the directors so selected are persons who are employees of companies within the founding company's group at the relevant time, and who do not have and have never had a material interest in any such company.

(5) For the purposes of this paragraph, a director shall be a professional director at a particular time if —

(*a*) the director is then a solicitor or a member of such other professional body as the Revenue Commissioners may at that time allow for the purposes of this subparagraph,

(*b*) the director is not then an employee of any company then within the founding company's group,

(*c*) the director is not then a director of any such company other than the trust company, and

(*d*) the director meets the requirements of subparagraph (6),

and for the purposes of this paragraph a director shall be a non-professional director at a particular time if the director is not then a professional director for those purposes.

(6) A director shall meet the requirements of this subparagraph if—

(*a*) he or she was appointed as an initial director and, before being appointed as director, was selected only by the persons who later became the non-professional initial directors, or

(*b*) he or she was appointed as a replacement or additional director and, before being appointed as director, was selected only by the persons who were the non-professional directors at the time of the selection.

(7) Directors shall be selected in accordance with this subparagraph if the process of selection is one under which—

(*a*) all the persons who are employees of the companies within the founding company's group at the time of the selection, and who do not have and have never had a material interest in any such company, are, in so far as is reasonably practicable, given the opportunity to stand for selection,

(*b*) all the employees of the companies within the founding company's group at the time of the selection are, in so far as is reasonably practicable, given the opportunity to vote, and

(*c*) persons gaining more votes are preferred to those gaining less.

(8) Directors shall be selected in accordance with this subparagraph if they are selected by persons elected to represent the employees of the companies within the founding company's group at the time of the selection.

Beneficiaries

11. (1) The trust deed shall contain provision as to the beneficiaries under the trust in accordance with this paragraph.

[(2) The trust deed shall provide that a person is a beneficiary at a particular time (in this subparagraph referred to as **"the relevant time"**) if —

(*a*) the person is at the relevant time an employee or director of a company within the founding company's group,

(*b*) at each given time in a qualifying period the person was such an employee or director of a company falling within the founding company's group at that given time, (*c*) in the case of a director, at that given time the person worked as a director of the company concerned at the rate of at least 20 hours a week (disregarding such matters as holidays and sickness), and

(*d*) the person is chargeable to income tax in respect of his or her office or employment under Schedule E.

(2A) The trust deed may provide that a person is a beneficiary at a particular time if, but for subparagraph (2)(*d*), he or she would be a beneficiary within the rule which is included in the deed and conforms with subparagraph (2).][1]

[(2B) Subject to subparagraph (2C), the trust deed may provide that a person is a beneficiary at a particular time (in this subparagraph referred to as **"the relevant time"**) if—

(*a*) the person has at each given time in a qualifying period been an employee or director of a company within the founding company's group at that given time,

(*b*) the person was such an employee or director—

(i) on the date the trust was established or at some time within 9 months prior to that date, or

(ii) at any time in the period of 5 years beginning with such date,

(*c*) the person has ceased to be an employee or director of the company or the company has ceased to be within that group,

[(*d*) at each given time—

(i) in the case of an employee share ownership trust approved under paragraph 2 before the passing of the Finance Act, 2000, in the 5 year period referred to in clause (*b*), and

(ii) in the case of an employee share ownership trust approved under paragraph 2 on or after the passing of the Finance Act, 2000, in the 5 year period, or such lesser period as the Minister for Finance may by order prescribe, commencing on the date referred to in clause (*b*),

50 per cent or such lesser percentage as the Minister for Finance may by order prescribe, of the securities retained by the trustees at that time were pledged by them as security for borrowings, and][2]

(*e*) at the relevant time a period of not more than 15 years has elapsed since the trust was established.

(2C) The trust deed shall not contain a rule that conforms with subparagraph (2B) [or (3)][3] unless the rule is expressed as applying to every person within it.][4]

(3) The trust deed may provide that a person is a beneficiary at a particular time (in this subparagraph referred to as **"the relevant time"**) if—

(*a*) the person has at each given time in a qualifying period been an employee or director of a company within the founding company's group at that given time,

(*b*) the person has ceased to be an employee or director of the company or the company has ceased to be within that group, and

[(*c*) (i) in a case where the founding company is the Electricity Supply Board and as respects securities acquired by the trustees of the trust on or before 31 December 2001, the person was an employee or a director, as the case may be, of a company within the founding company's group on 1 January 1998, and

(ii) in any other case, at the relevant time a period of not more than 18 months has elapsed since the person so ceased or the company so ceased, as the case may be.][5]

(4) The trust deed may provide for a person to be a beneficiary if the person is a charity and the circumstances are such that—

(*a*) there is no person who is a beneficiary within the rule which is included in the deed and conforms with subparagraph (2) or with any rule which is so included and conforms with [subparagraphs (2A), (2B) and (3)],[6] and

(*b*) the trust is in consequence being wound up.

(5) For the purposes of [subparagraphs (2) and (2A)],[7] a qualifying period shall be a period—

(*a*) whose length is not more than [3 years],[8]

(*b*) whose length is specified in the trust deed, and

(*c*) which ends with the relevant time (within the meaning of that subparagraph).

(6) For the purposes of [subparagraphs (2B) and (3)],[9] a qualifying period shall be a period—

(*a*) whose length is equal to that of the period specified in the trust deed for the purposes of a rule which conforms with subparagraph (2), and

(*b*) which ends when the person or company, as the case may be, ceased as mentioned in [subparagraphs; (2B)(*c*) and (3)(*b*)].[10]

(7) The trust deed shall not provide for a person to be a beneficiary unless the person is within the rule which is included in the deed and conforms with subparagraph (2) or any rule which is so included and conforms with [subparagraph (2A), (2B), (3) or (4)].[11]

(8) The trust deed shall provide that, notwithstanding any other rule which is included in it, a person cannot be a beneficiary at a particular time (in this subparagraph referred to as **"the relevant time"**) by virtue of a rule which conforms with [subparagraph (2), (2A), (2B), (3) or (4)][12] if—

(*a*) at the relevant time the person has a material interest in the founding company, or

(*b*) at any time in the period of one year preceding the relevant time the person has had a material interest in that company.

(9) For the purposes of this paragraph, **"charity"** means any body of persons or trust established for charitable purposes only.

[(10) Where an order is proposed to be made under subparagraph (2B)(*d*), a draft of the order shall be laid before Dáil Éireann, and the order shall not be made until a resolution approving of the draft has been passed by Dáil Éireann.][13]

Amendments

1 Para 11(2) substituted by FA 1998 s 36(1)(*d*)(iii)(I) as respects employee share ownership trusts approved of under TCA 1997 Sch 12 para 2 on or after 27 March 1998.

2 Para 11(2B)(*d*) substituted by FA 2000 s 26(a) with effect from 6 April 2000.

3 Inserted by FA 2004 s 15(*a*) with effect from 1 January 2004.

4 Para 11(2B)–(2C) inserted by FA 1999 s 69(1)(*d*)(i)(I) in respect of employee share ownership trusts approved under TCA 1997 Sch 12 para 2 on or after 25 March 1999.

5 Para 11(3)(*c*) substituted by Electricity (Supply) (Amendment) Act 2001 s 8 with effort from 17 April 2001.

6 Substituted by FA 1999 s 69(1)(*d*)(i)(II) in respect of employee share ownership trusts approved under TCA 1997 Sch 12 para 2 on or after 25 March 1999; previously "subparagraphs (2A) and (3)".

7 Substituted by FA 1998 s 36(1)(*d*)(iii)(III) as respects employee share ownership trusts approved of under TCA 1997 Sch 12 para 2 on or after 27 March 1998; previously "subparagraph (2)".

8 Substituted by FA 1999 s 69(1)(*d*)(i)(III) in respect of employee share ownership trusts approved under TCA 1997 Sch 12 para 2 on or after 25 March 1999; previously "5 years".

9 Substituted by FA 1999 s 69(1)(*d*)(i)(IV) in respect of employee share ownership trusts approved under TCA 1997 Sch 12 para 2 on or after 25 March 1999; previously "subparagraph (3)".

10 Substituted by FA 1999 s 69(1)(*d*)(i)(IV) in respect of employee share ownership trusts approved under TCA 1997 Sch 12 para 2 on or after 25 March 1999; previously "subparagraph (3)(*b*)".

11 Substituted by FA 1999 s 69(1)(*d*)(i)(V) in respect of employee share ownership trusts approved under TCA 1997 Sch 12 para 2 on or after 25 March 1999; previously "subparagraph (2A), (3) or (4)".

12 Substituted by FA 1999 s 69(1)(*d*)(i)(VI) in respect of employee share ownership trusts approved under TCA 1997 Sch 12 para 2 on or after 25 March 1999; previously "subparagraph (2), (2A), (3) or (4)".

13 Para 11(10) inserted by FA 2000 s 26(*b*) with effect from 6 April 2000.

11A. [(1) Notwithstanding any other provision of this Schedule, in any case where a trust is established by a company which is a relevant company, this Schedule shall, with any necessary modification, apply as respects the beneficiaries under the trust as if this paragraph were substituted for paragraph 11.

(2) The trust deed shall contain provision as to the beneficiaries under the trust in accordance with this paragraph.

(3) The trust deed shall provide that a person is a beneficiary at a particular time (in this subparagraph referred to as the **"relevant time"**) if—

(*a*) the person was an employee or a director of the relevant company or of a company within the relevant company's group on the day the trust was established by that relevant company,

(*b*) the person is at the relevant time an employee or a director of—

(i) a company (in this subparagraph referred to as the **"first-mentioned company"**) which is, or was at any time since the day the trust was established, within the founding company's group,

(ii) a company within a group of companies (within the meaning of paragraph 2(2)(*b*)) which has acquired control of the first-mentioned company,

(iii) a company to which—

(I) an employee, or

(II) a director,

referred to in clause (*a*) has been transferred under either or both the European Communities (Safeguarding of Employees' Rights on Transfer of Undertaking) Regulations, 1980 and 2000 and the Central Bank Act, 1971, or

(iv) a company within a group of companies (within the meaning of paragraph 2(2)(*b*)), of which the company referred to in subclause (iii) is, or was at any time, a member, (*c*) at each given time in a qualifying period the person was such an employee or a director of a company referred to in clause (*b*),

(*d*) in the case of a director, at that given time the person worked as a director of a company referred to in clause (*b*) or of a company within the relevant company's group at the rate of at least 20 hours a week (disregarding such matters as holidays and sickness), and

(*e*) the person is chargeable to income tax in respect of his or her office or employment under Schedule E.

(4) The trust deed may provide that a person is a beneficiary at a particular time if, but for subparagraph (3)(*e*), he or she would be a beneficiary within the rule which is included in the deed and conforms with subparagraph (3).

(5) Subject to subparagraph (6), the trust deed may provide that a person is a beneficiary at a particular time (in this subparagraph referred to as the **"relevant time"**) if—

(*a*) the person was an employee or a director of the relevant company or of a company within the relevant company's group on the day the trust was established by that relevant company, [or, in the case of a company referred to in clause (*d*) of the definition of "relevant company" in paragraph 1(1), at some time within 9 months prior to that day,][1]

(*b*) the person has at each given time in a qualifying period been an employee or a director of a company referred to in subparagraph (3)(*b*) at that given time,

(*c*) the person has ceased to be an employee or a director of a company referred to in subparagraph (3)(*b*),

(*d*) at each given time in the 5 year period, or such lesser period as the Minister for Finance may by order prescribe, commencing on the date the trust was established, 50 per cent or such lesser percentage as the Minister for Finance may by order prescribe, of the securities retained by the trustees at that time were pledged by them as security for borrowings, and

(*e*) at the relevant time a period of not more than 15 years has elapsed since the trust was established.

(6) The trust deed may provide that a person is a beneficiary at a particular time (in this subparagraph referred to as the **"relevant time"**) if—

(*a*) the person was an employee or a director of the relevant company or of a company within the relevant company's group on the day the trust was established by that relevant company, [or, in the case of a company referred to in clause (*d*) of the definition of "relevant company" in paragraph 1(1), at some time within 9 months prior to that day,][2]

(*b*) the person has at each given time in a qualifying period been an employee or a director of a company referred to in subparagraph (3)(*b*) at that given time,

(*c*) the person has ceased to be an employee or a director of a company referred to in subparagraph (3)(*b*), and

(*d*) at the relevant time a period of not more than 18 months has elapsed since the person so ceased.

(7) The trust deed shall not contain a rule that conforms with subparagraph (5) [or (6)][3] unless the rule is expressed as applying to every person within it.

(8) The trust deed may provide for a person to be a beneficiary if the person is a charity and the circumstances are such that—

(*a*) there is no person who is a beneficiary within the rule which is included in the deed and conforms with subparagraph (3) or with any rule which is so included and conforms with subparagraph (4), (5) or (6), and

(*b*) the trust is in consequence of being wound up.

(9) For the purposes of subparagraph (3), a qualifying period shall be a period—

(*a*) whose length is not more than 3 years,

(*b*) whose length is specified in the trust deed, and

(*c*) which ends with the relevant time (within the meaning of that subparagraph).

(10) For the purposes of subparagraphs (5) and (6), a qualifying period shall be a period—

(*a*) whose length is equal to that of the period specified in the trust deed for the purposes of a rule which conforms with subparagraph (3), and

(*b*) which ends when the person ceased as mentioned in subparagraph (5)(*c*) or (6)(*c*), as the case may be.

(11) The trust deed shall not provide for a person to be a beneficiary unless the person is within the rule which is included in the deed and conforms with subparagraph (3) or any rule which is so included and conforms with subparagraph (4), (5), (6) or (8).

(12) The trust deed shall provide that, notwithstanding any other rule which is included in it, a person cannot be a beneficiary at a particular time (in this subparagraph referred to as the **"relevant time"**) by virtue of a rule which conforms with subparagraph (3), (4), (5), (6) or (8) if—

(*a*) at the relevant time the person has a material interest in a company referred to in subparagraph (3)(*b*), or

(*b*) at any time in the period of one year preceding the relevant time the person has had a material interest in that company,

and for the purposes of this subparagraph any reference to a company shall, in a case to which clause (*a*) of the definition of relevant company applies, also include a reference to a trustee savings bank which has been reorganised into the relevant company concerned.

(13) For the purposes of satisfying the qualifying period requirement referred to in subparagraphs (3)(*c*), (5)(*b*) and (6)(*b*) a person shall also be regarded as such an employee or a director for any period in which that person is an employee or a director of, in a case to which clause (*a*) of the definition of relevant company applies, a trustee savings bank which has been reorganised into that relevant company.

(14) For the purposes of this paragraph **"charity"** means any body of persons or trust established for charitable purposes only.

(15) Where an order is proposed to be made under subparagraph (5)(*d*), a draft of the order shall be laid before Dáil Éireann and the order shall not be made until a resolution approving of the draft has been passed by Dáil Éireann.][4]

Amendments

1 Inserted by FA 2004 s 15(*b*)(i) with effect from 1 January 2004.

2 Inserted by FA 2004 s 15(*b*)(ii) with effect from 1 January 2004.

3 Inserted by FA 2004 s 15(*b*)(iii) with effect from 1 January 2004.

4 Para 11A inserted by FA 2001 s 17(1)(*c*)(iii) in respect of a profit sharing scheme or an employee share ownership trust approved on or after 12 December 2000.

Trustees' Functions

12. (1) The trust deed shall contain provision as to the functions of the trustees.

(2) The functions of the trustees shall be so expressed that it is apparent that their general functions are—

(*a*) to receive sums from the founding company and other sums, by means of loan or otherwise;

(*b*) to acquire securities;

(*c*) to grant rights to acquire shares to persons who are beneficiaries under the terms of the trust deed;

(*d*) to transfer either or both securities and sums to persons who are beneficiaries under the terms of the trust deed;

[(*da*) to pay any sum or to transfer securities to the personal representatives of deceased persons who were beneficiaries under the terms of the trust deed;][1]

(*e*) to transfer securities to the trustees of profit sharing schemes approved under Part 2 of Schedule 11;

(*f*) pending transfer, to retain the securities and to manage them, whether by exercising voting rights or otherwise.

Amendments

1 Para 12(2)(*da*) inserted by FA 2001 s 13(*b*)(i) from 6 April 2001.

Sums

13. (1) The trust deed shall require that any sum received by the trustees—

(*a*) shall be expended within the expenditure period,

(*b*) may be expended only for one or more of the qualifying purposes, and

(*c*) shall, while it is retained by them, be kept as cash, or be kept in an account with a relevant deposit taker (within the meaning of section 256).

(2) For the purposes of subparagraph (1), the expenditure period shall be the period of 9 months beginning on the day determined as follows—

(*a*) in a case where the sum is received from the founding company, or a company which is controlled by that company at the time the sum is received, the day following the end of the accounting period in which the sum is expended by the company from which it is received;

(*b*) in any other case, the day the sum is received.

(3) For the purposes of subparagraph (1), each of the following shall be a qualifying purpose—

(*a*) the acquisition of shares in the founding company [or of securities to which subparagraph (ii) or (iv) of paragraph *(b)* of the definition of "specified securities" in section 509(1) applies][1];

(*b*) the repayment of sums borrowed;

(*c*) the payment of interest on sums borrowed;

(*d*) the payment of any sum to a person who is a beneficiary under the terms of the trust deed;

[(*da*) the payment of any sum to the personal representatives of a deceased person who was a beneficiary under the terms of the trust deed;][2]

(*e*) the meeting of expenses.

(4) The trust deed shall provide that, in ascertaining for the purposes of a relevant rule (being a provision which is included in the trust deed and conforms with subparagraph (1)) whether a particular sum has been expended, sums received earlier by the trustees shall be treated as expended before sums received by them later.

(5) The trust deed shall provide that, where the trustees pay sums to different beneficiaries at the same time, all the sums shall be paid on similar terms.

(6) For the purposes of subparagraph (5), the fact that terms vary according to the levels of remuneration of beneficiaries, the length of their service or similar factors shall not be regarded as meaning that the terms are not similar.

Amendments

1 Inserted by FA 2002 s 13(1)(*e*)(ii) with effect from 16 April 2001.

2 Para 13(3)(*da*) inserted by FA 2001 s 13(*b*)(ii) from 6 April 2001.

Securities

14. (1) Subject to paragraph 15, the trust deed shall provide that securities acquired by the trustees shall be shares in the founding company which—

(*a*) form part of the ordinary share capital of the company,

(*b*) are fully paid up,

(*c*) are not redeemable, and

(*d*) are not subject to any restrictions other than restrictions which attach to all shares of the same class or a restriction authorised by subparagraph (2).

(2) Subject to subparagraph (3), a restriction shall be authorised by this subparagraph if—

(*a*) it is imposed by the founding company's articles of association,

(*b*) it requires all shares held by directors or employees of the founding company, or of any other company which it controls for the time being, to be disposed of on ceasing to be so held, and

(*c*) it requires all shares acquired, in pursuance of rights or interests obtained by such directors or employees, by persons who are not, or have ceased to be, such directors or employees to be disposed of when they are acquired.

(3) A restriction shall not be authorised by subparagraph (2) unless—

(*a*) any disposal required by the restriction will be by means of sale for a consideration in money on terms specified in the articles of association, and

(*b*) the articles also contain general provisions by virtue of which any person disposing of shares of the same class (whether or not held or acquired as mentioned in subparagraph (2)) may be required to sell them on terms which are the same as those mentioned in clause (*a*).

(4) The trust deed shall provide that shares in the founding company may not be acquired by the trustees at a price exceeding the price they might reasonably be expected to fetch on a sale in the open market.

[(5) The trust deed shall provide that shares in the founding company may not be acquired by the trustees at a time when that company is controlled by another company, other than where the founding company is a company into which a trustee savings bank has been reorganised under section 57 of the Trustee Savings Banks Act, 1989.][1]

Amendments

1 Para 14(5) substituted by the Trustee Savings Banks (Amendment) Act 2001 s 3(*b*) with effect from 28 March 2001.

15. The trust deed may provide that the trustees may acquire securities other than shares in the founding company—

(*a*) if they are securities acquired by the trustees as a result of a reorganisation or reduction of share capital ...[1] (construing **"reorganisation or reduction of share capital"** ...[2] in accordance with section 584), or

(*b*) if they are securities issued to the trustees in exchange in circumstances mentioned in section 586.

Amendments

1 Deleted by FA 2002 s 13(1)(*e*)(iii)(I) with effect from 16 April 2001; previously ", and the original shares the securities represent are shares in the founding company".

2 Deleted by FA 2002 s 13(1)(*e*)(iii)(II) with effect from 16 April 2001; previously "and 'original shares'".

16. (1) The trust deed shall provide that—

(*a*) where the trustees transfer securities to a beneficiary, they shall do so on qualifying terms;

(*b*) the trustees shall transfer securities before the expiry of 20 years beginning on the date on which they acquired them.

(2) For the purposes of subparagraph (1), a transfer of securities shall be made on qualifying terms if—

(*a*) all the securities transferred at the same time are transferred on similar terms,

(*b*) securities have been offered to all the persons who are beneficiaries under the terms of the trust deed when the transfer is made, and

(*c*) securities are transferred to all such beneficiaries who have accepted.

(3) For the purposes of subparagraph (2), the fact that terms vary according to the levels of remuneration of beneficiaries, the length of their service or similar factors shall not be regarded as meaning that the terms are not similar.

(4) The trust deed shall provide that, in ascertaining for the purposes of a relevant rule (being a provision which is included in the trust deed and conforms with subparagraph (1)) whether particular securities are transferred, securities acquired earlier by the trustees shall be treated as transferred by them before securities acquired by them later.

Other Features

17. The trust deed shall not contain features which are not essential or reasonably incidental to the purpose of acquiring sums and securities, transferring sums and securities to employees and directors, and transferring securities to the trustees of profit sharing schemes approved under Part 2 of Schedule 11.

18. (1) The trust deed shall provide that for the purposes of the deed the trustees—

(*a*) acquire securities when they become entitled to them;

(*b*) transfer securities to another person when that other person becomes entitled to them;

(*c*) retain securities if they remain entitled to them.

(2) Where the trust deed provides for the matter set out in paragraph 15, the trust deed shall provide for the following exceptions to any rule which is included in it and conforms with subparagraph (1)(*a*), namely—

(*a*) if the trustees become entitled to securities as a result of a reorganisation or reduction of share capital, they shall be treated as having acquired them when they became entitled to the original shares which those securities represent (construing **"reorganisation or reduction of share capital"** and **"original shares"** in accordance with section 584);

(*b*) if securities are issued to the trustees in exchange in circumstances mentioned in section 586, they shall be treated as having acquired them when they became entitled to the securities for which they are exchanged.

(3) The trust deed shall provide that—

(*a*) if the trustees agree to take a transfer of securities, for the purposes of the deed they become entitled to them when the agreement is made [or, if the agreement is subject to one or more specified conditions being satisfied, on that condition or those conditions being satisfied][1] and not on a later transfer made pursuant to the agreement;

(*b*) if the trustees agree to transfer securities to another person, for the purposes of the deed the other person becomes entitled to them when the agreement is made and not on a later transfer made pursuant to the agreement.

Amendments

1 Inserted by FA 1999 s 69(1)(*d*)(ii) in respect of employee share ownership trusts approved under TCA 1997 Sch 12 para 2 on or after 25 March 1999.

Cross-references

Distributions, matters treated as: s 130(2)(*f*)(i); meaning of "securities" applied: s 130(2C); paras 11(2B)(*d*), 11A(5)(*d*) and 13(4): s 130(2C).

Dividend withholding tax, interpretation: s 172A(1)(*a*)(qualifying employee share ownership trust).
Penalties, para 3(4): Sch 29, column 2.
Profit sharing schemes, approval of schemes, paras 1 and 11A: Sch 11 para 4(1B); individuals ineligible to participate, paras 11 and 11A: Sch 11 para 12A(*b*); para 1: Sch 11 para 13B(1).
Profit sharing schemes, shares acquired from employee share ownership trust, paras 11 and 11A: s 511A(1)(*c*).
Profit sharing schemes, interpretation, meaning of "securities" applied: s 509(1)("specified securities").

Definitions

Appeal Commissioners: s 2(1); company: s 4(1); Income Tax Acts: s 1(2); person IA 1937 s 11(*c*); writing: IA 1937 Sch.

Former enactments

FA 1997 Sch 3.

[SCHEDULE 12A
Approved Savings-Related Share Option Schemes

[Section 519A]

Revenue information

A Guide to Savings — Related Share Option Schemes may be downloaded from Revenue's internet site (www.revenue.ie) under Publications/Technical Guidelines.

Interpretation

1. (1) For the purposes of this Schedule—

"approved" in relation to a scheme, means approved under paragraph 2;

"associated company" has the same meaning as in section 432, except that, for the purposes of paragraph 24, subsection (1) of that section shall have effect with the omission of the words "or at any time within one year previously";

"bonus date" has the meaning assigned to it by paragraph 18;

"control" has the same meaning as in section 432;

"full-time director" has the same meaning as in section 250;

"grantor", in relation to a scheme, means the company which has established the scheme;

"group scheme" and, in relation to such a scheme, **"participating company"** have the meanings given by subparagraphs (3) and (4), respectively, of paragraph 2;

"market value" shall be construed in accordance with section 548;

"savings-related share option scheme" means a scheme approved by the Revenue Commissioners in accordance with this Schedule and which approval has not been withdrawn;

"scheme shares" has the meaning assigned to it by paragraph 10;

"shares" includes [stock;][1]

[**"specified age"** means an age that is not less than 60 years and not more than pensionable age (within the meaning of section 2 of the Social Welfare (Consolidation) Act, 1993).][2]

(2) Section 10 shall apply for the purposes of this Schedule.

(3) For the purposes of this Schedule, a company is a member of a consortium that owns another company if it is one of not more than 5 companies which between them beneficially own not less than 75 per cent of the other company's ordinary share capital and each of which beneficially owns not less than 5 per cent of that capital.

(4) For the purposes of this Schedule, the question whether one company is controlled by another shall be determined in accordance with section 432

Amendments

1 Substituted by FA 2000 s 51(*b*)(i)(I) with effect from 6 April 2000; previously "stock.".

2 Definition of "specified age" inserted by FA 2000 s 51(*b*)(i)(II) with effect from 6 April 2000.

Approval of schemes

2. (1) On the application of a body corporate (in this Schedule referred to as "the grantor") which has established a savings-related share option scheme, the Revenue Commissioners shall approve the scheme if they are satisfied that it fulfils the requirements of this Schedule.

(2) An application under subparagraph (1) shall be made in writing and contain such particulars and be supported by such evidence as the Revenue Commissioners may require.

(3) Where the grantor has control of another company or companies, the scheme may be expressed to extend to all or any of the companies of which it has control and in this Schedule a scheme which is expressed so to extend is referred to as a "group scheme".

(4) In relation to a group scheme, "participating company" means the grantor or any other company to which for the time being the scheme is expressed to extend.

[(5) The scheme shall indicate the specified age for the purposes of the scheme.][1]

Amendments

1 Para 2(5) inserted by FA 2000 s 51(*b*)(ii) with effect from 6 April 2000.

3. (1) The Revenue Commissioners shall not approve a scheme under this Schedule if it appears to them that it contains features which are neither essential nor reasonably incidental to the purpose of providing for employees and directors benefits in the nature of rights to acquire shares.

(2) The Revenue Commissioners shall be satisfied—

(*a*) that there are no features of the scheme other than any which are included to satisfy requirements of this Schedule which have or would have the effect of discouraging any description of employees who fulfil the conditions in paragraph 9(1) from actually participating in the scheme, and

(*b*) where the grantor is a member of a group of companies, that the scheme does not and would not have the effect of conferring benefits wholly or mainly on directors of companies in the group or on those employees of companies in the group who are in receipt of the higher or highest levels of remuneration.

[(3) For the purposes of subparagagh (2)—

(*a*) **"a group of companies"** means a company and any other companies of which it has control or with which it is associated, and

(*b*) a company shall be associated with another company where it could reasonably be considered that—

(i) both companies act in pursuit of a common purpose,

(ii) any person or any group of persons or groups of persons having a reasonable commonality of identity have or had the means or power, either directly or indirectly, to determine the trading operations carried on or to be carried on by both companies, or

(iii) both companies are under the control of any person or group of persons or groups of persons having a reasonable commonality of identity.][1]

Amendments

1 Para 3(3) substituted by FA 2001 s 16(*c*) in respect of savings-related share option schemes approved on or after 30 March 2001.

4. (1) If, at any time after the Revenue Commissioners have approved a scheme, any of the requirements of this Schedule cease to be satisfied or the grantor fails to provide information requested by the Revenue Commissioners under paragraph 6, the Revenue Commissioners may withdraw the approval with effect from that time or such later time as the Revenue Commissioners may specify but where rights obtained under a savings-related share option scheme before the withdrawal of approval from the scheme under this paragraph are exercised after the withdrawal, section 519A(3) shall apply in respect of the exercise as if the scheme were still approved.

(2) If an alteration is made in the scheme at any time after the Revenue Commissioners have approved the scheme, the approval shall not have effect after the date of the alteration unless the Revenue Commissioners have approved the alteration.

5. If the grantor is aggrieved by—

(*a*) the failure of the Revenue Commissioners to approve the scheme or to approve an alteration in the scheme,

(*b*) the withdrawal of approval, or

(*c*) the failure of the Revenue Commissioners to decide that a condition subject to which the approval has been given is satisfied,

it may, by notice in writing given to the Revenue Commissioners within 30 days from the date on which it is notified of the Revenue Commissioners' decision, require the matter to be determined by the Appeal Commissioners, and the Appeal Commissioners shall hear and determine the matter in like manner as an appeal made to them against an assessment and all the provisions of the Income Tax Acts relating to such an appeal (including the provisions relating to the rehearing of an appeal and to the statement of a case for the opinion of the High Court on a point of law) shall apply accordingly with any necessary modifications.

Information

6. The Revenue Commissioners may by notice in writing require any person to furnish them, within such time as the Revenue Commissioners may direct (not being less than 30 days), with such information as the Revenue Commissioners think necessary for the performance of their functions under this Schedule, and which the person to whom the notice is addressed has or can reasonably obtain, including in particular information—

(*a*) to enable the Revenue Commissioners to determine—

(i) whether to approve a scheme or withdraw an approval already given, or

(ii) the liability to tax, including capital gains tax, of any person who has participated in a scheme, and

(*b*) in relation to the administration of a scheme and any alteration of the terms of a scheme.

7. The Revenue Commissioners may nominate any of their officers, including an inspector, to perform any acts and discharge any functions authorised by this Schedule to be performed or discharged by them.

Eligibility

8. (1) The scheme shall not provide for any person to be eligible to participate in it, that is to say, to obtain and exercise rights under it at any time if at that time that person has, or has within the preceding 12 months had, a material interest in a close company which is—

(i) a company the shares of which may be acquired pursuant to the exercise of rights obtained under the scheme, or

(ii) a company which has control of such a company or is a member of a consortium which owns such a company.

(2) Subparagraph (1) shall apply in relation to a company which would be a close company but for section 430(1)(*a*) or 431.

(3) (*a*) In this paragraph, "close company" has the meaning assigned to it by section 430.

(*b*) For the purpose of this paragraph—

(i) subsection (3) of section 433 shall apply—

(I) in a case where the scheme in question is a group scheme, with the substitution of a reference to all participating companies for the first reference to the company in paragraph (*c*)(ii) of that subsection, and

(II) with the substitution of a reference to 15 per cent for the reference in that paragraph to 5 per cent, and

(ii) section 437(2) shall apply, with the substitution of a reference to 15 per cent for the reference in that section to 5 per cent, for the purpose of determining whether a person has or had a material interest in a company.

9. (1) Subject to paragraph 8, every person who—

(*a*) is an employee or a full-time director of the grantor or, in the case of a group scheme, a participating company, (*b*) has been such an employee or director at all times during a qualifying period not exceeding three years, and

(*c*) is chargeable to tax in respect of that person's office or employment under Schedule E,

shall be eligible to participate in the scheme, that is to say, to obtain and exercise rights under it, on similar terms.

(2) For the purposes of subparagraph (1), the fact that the rights to be obtained by the persons participating in a scheme vary according to the levels of their remuneration, the length of their service or similar factors shall not be regarded as meaning that they are not eligible to participate in the scheme on similar terms.

(3) Except as provided by paragraph 20 or pursuant to such a provision as is referred to in paragraph 22(1)(*e*) or (*f*), a person shall not be eligible to participate in the scheme at any time unless he or she is at that time a director or employee of the grantor or, in the case of a group scheme, of a participating company.

Conditions as to the shares

10. The scheme shall provide for directors and employees to obtain rights to acquire shares (in this Schedule referred to as **"scheme shares"**) which satisfy the requirements of paragraphs 11 to 15.

11. Scheme shares shall form part of the ordinary share capital of—

(*a*) the grantor,

(*b*) a company which has control of the grantor, or

(*c*) a company which either is, or has control of, a company which—

(i) is a member of a consortium which owns either the grantor or a company having control of the grantor, and

(ii) beneficially owns not less than 15 per cent of the ordinary share capital of the company so owned.

12. Scheme shares shall be—

(*a*) shares of a class quoted on a recognised stock exchange,

(*b*) shares in a company not under the control of another company, or

(*c*) shares in a company which is under the control of a company (other than a company which is, or if resident in the State would be, a close company within the meaning of section 430) whose shares are quoted on a recognised stock exchange.

13. (1) Scheme shares shall be—

(*a*) fully paid up,

(*b*) not redeemable, and

(*c*) not subject to any restrictions other than restrictions which attach to all shares of the same class or a restriction authorised by subparagraph (2).

(2) Subject to subparagraph (3), the shares may be subject to a restriction imposed by the company's articles of association—

(*a*) requiring all shares held by directors or employees of the company or of any other company of which it has control to be disposed of on ceasing to be so held, and

(*b*) requiring all shares acquired, in pursuance of rights or interests obtained by such directors or employees, by persons who are not, or have ceased to be, such directors or employees to be disposed of when they are acquired.

(3) A restriction is not authorised by subparagraph (2) unless—

(*a*) any disposal required by the restriction will be by way of sale for a consideration in money on terms specified in the articles of association, and

(*b*) the articles also contain general provisions by virtue of which any person disposing of shares of the same class (whether or not held or acquired as mentioned in subparagraph (2)) may be required to sell them on terms which are the same as those mentioned in paragraph (*a*).

14. (1) In determining for the purposes of paragraph 13(1)(*c*) whether scheme shares which are or are to be acquired by any person are subject to any restrictions, there shall be regarded as a restriction attaching to the shares any contract, agreement, arrangement or condition by which such person's freedom to dispose of the shares or of any interest in them or of the proceeds of their sale or to exercise any right conferred by them is restricted or by which such a disposal or exercise may result in any disadvantage to that person or to a person connected with that person.

(2) Subparagraph (1) does not apply to so much of any contract, agreement, arrangement or condition as contains provisions similar in purpose and effect to any of the provisions of the Model Code set out in the Listing Rules of the Irish Stock Exchange.

15. Except where scheme shares are in a company whose ordinary share capital consists of shares of one class only, the majority of the issued shares of the same class shall be held by persons other than—

(*a*) persons who acquired their shares—

(i) in pursuance of a right conferred on them or an opportunity afforded to them as a director or employee of the grantor or any other company, and

(ii) not in pursuance of an offer to the public,

(*b*) trustees holding shares on behalf of persons who acquired their beneficial interests in the shares as mentioned in subparagraph (*a*), and

(*c*) in a case where the shares fall within paragraph 12(*c*) and do not fall within paragraph 12(*a*), companies which have control of the company whose shares are in question or of which that company is an associated company within the meaning of section 432.

Exchange provisions

16. (1) The scheme may provide that if any company ("the acquiring company")—

(*a*) obtains control of a company whose shares are scheme shares as a result of making a general offer—

(i) to acquire the whole of the issued ordinary share capital of the company which is made on a condition such that if it is satisfied the person making the offer will have control of the company, or

(ii) to acquire all the shares in the company which are of the same class as the scheme shares,

(*b*) obtains control of a company whose shares are scheme shares in pursuance of a compromise or arrangement sanctioned by the court under section 201 of the Companies Act, 1963, or

(*c*) becomes bound or entitled to acquire shares in a company, under section 204 of the Companies Act, 1963, whose shares are scheme shares,

any participant in the scheme may at any time within the appropriate period, by agreement with the acquiring company, release his or her rights under the scheme (in this paragraph referred to as "the old rights") in consideration of the grant to him or her of rights (in this paragraph referred to as "the new rights") which are equivalent to the old rights but relate to shares in a different company (whether the acquiring company itself or some other company falling within subparagraph (*b*) or (*c*) of paragraph 11).

(2) In subparagraph (1) "the appropriate period" means—

(*a*) in a case falling within clause (*a*) of that subparagraph, the period of six months beginning with the time when the person making the offer has obtained control of the company and any condition subject to which the offer is made is satisfied,

(*b*) in a case falling within clause (*b*) of that subparagraph, the period of six months beginning with the time when the court sanctions the compromise or arrangement, and

(*c*) in a case falling within clause (*c*) of that subparagraph, the period during which the acquiring company remains bound or entitled as mentioned in that clause.

(3) The new rights shall not be regarded for the purposes of this paragraph as equivalent to the old rights unless—

(*a*) the shares to which they relate satisfy the conditions specified, in relation to scheme shares, in paragraphs 11 to 15,

(*b*) the new rights will be exercisable in the same manner as the old rights and subject to the provisions of the scheme as it had effect immediately before the release of the old rights,

(*c*) the total market value, immediately before the release, of the shares which were subject to the participant's old rights is equal to the total market value, immediately after the grant, of the shares in respect of which the new rights are granted to the participant, and

(*d*) the total amount payable by the participant for the acquisition of shares in pursuance of the new rights is equal to the total amount that would have been payable for the acquisition of shares in pursuance of the old rights.

(4) Where any new rights are granted pursuant to a provision included in a scheme by virtue of this paragraph they shall be regarded—

(*a*) for the purposes of section 519A and this Schedule, and

(*b*) for the purposes of the subsequent application (by virtue of a condition complying with subparagraph (3)(*b*)) of the provisions of the scheme,

as having been granted at the time when the corresponding old rights were granted.

Exercise of rights

17. The scheme shall provide for the scheme shares to be paid for with moneys not exceeding the amount of repayments made and any interest paid to them under a certified contractual savings scheme within the meaning of subsection (4) of section 519C.

18. Subject to paragraphs 19 to 22, the rights obtained under the scheme must not be capable of being exercised before the bonus date, that is to say, the date on which repayments under the certified contractual savings scheme are due and for the purposes of this paragraph and paragraph 17—

(*a*) repayments under a certified contractual savings scheme may be taken as including or as not including a bonus,

(*b*) the time when repayments are due shall be, where repayments are taken as including the maximum bonus, the earliest date on which the maximum bonus is payable and, in any other case, the earliest date on which a bonus is payable under the scheme, and

(*c*) the question of what is to be taken as so included must be required to be determined at the time when rights under the scheme are obtained.

19. The scheme shall provide that if a person who has obtained rights under the scheme dies before the bonus date the rights must be exercised, if at all, within 12 months after the date of that person's death and if that person dies within 6 months after the bonus date the rights may be exercised within 12 months after the bonus date.

20. The scheme shall provide that if a person who has obtained rights under it ceases to hold the office or employment by virtue of which that person is eligible to participate in the scheme by reason of—

(*a*) injury or disability or on account of his or her being dismissed by reason of redundancy (within the meaning of the Redundancy Payments Acts, 1967 to 1991), or

(*b*) reaching [the specified age],[1]

then the rights shall be exercised, if at all, within 6 months of that person so ceasing and, if that person so ceases for any other reason within 3 years of obtaining the rights, they may not be exercised at all except pursuant to such a provision of the scheme as is mentioned in paragraph 22(1)(*e*); in relation to the case where that person so ceases, for any other reason, more than 3 years after obtaining the rights, the scheme shall either provide that the rights may not be exercised or that they must be exercised, if at all, within 6 months of that person so ceasing.

Amendments

1 Substituted by FA 2000 s 51(*b*)(iii) with effect from 6 April 2000; previously "pensionable age (within the meaning of section 2 of the Social Welfare (Consolidation) Act, 1993)".

21. The scheme shall provide that where a person who has obtained rights under it continues to hold the office or employment by virtue of which that person is eligible to participate in the scheme after the date on which that person reaches [the specified age],[1] that person may exercise the rights within 6 months of that date.

Amendments

1 Substituted by FA 2000 s 51(*b*)(iv) with effect from 6 April 2000; previously "pensionable age".

22. (1) The scheme may provide that—

(*a*) if any person obtains control of a company whose shares are scheme shares as a result of making a general offer falling within clause (*a*)(i) or (*a*)(ii) of paragraph 16(1), rights obtained under the scheme to acquire shares in the company may be exercised within 6 months of the time when the person making the offer has obtained control of the company and any condition subject to which the offer is made has been satisfied,

(*b*) if under section 201 of the Companies Act, 1963, (compromise between company and its members or creditors) the court sanctions a compromise or arrangement proposed for the purposes of or in connection with a scheme for the reconstruction of a company whose shares are scheme shares or its amalgamation with any other company or companies, rights obtained under the share option scheme to acquire shares in the company may be exercised within 6 months of the court sanctioning the compromise or arrangement,

(*c*) if any person becomes bound or entitled, under section 204 of the Companies Act, 1963, (power to acquire shares of shareholders dissenting from schemes or contract which has been approved by majority), to acquire shares in a company shares in which are scheme shares, rights obtained under the scheme to acquire shares in the company may be exercised at any time when that person remains so bound or entitled,

(*d*) if a company whose shares are scheme shares passes a resolution for voluntary winding up, rights obtained under a scheme to acquire shares in the company may be exercised within 6 months of the passing of the resolution,

(*e*) if a person ceases to hold an office or employment by virtue of which that person is eligible to participate in the scheme by reason only that—

(i) that office or employment is in a company of which the grantor ceases to have control, or

(ii) that office or employment relates to a business or part of a business which is transferred to a person who is neither an associated company of the grantor nor a company of which the grantor has control,

rights under the scheme held by that person may be exercised within 6 months of that person so ceasing, and

(*f*) if, at the bonus date, a person who has obtained rights under the scheme holds an office or employment in a company which is not a participating company but which is—

(i) an associated company of the grantor, or

(ii) a company of which the grantor has control,

those rights may be exercised within 6 months of that date.

(2) For the purposes of this paragraph a person shall be deemed to have obtained control of a company if that person and others acting in concert with that person have together obtained control of it.

23. Except as provided in paragraph 19, rights obtained by a person under the scheme shall not be capable—

(*a*) of being transferred by that person, or

(*b*) of being exercised later than 6 months after the bonus date.

24. No person shall be treated for the purposes of paragraph 20 or 22(1)(*e*) as ceasing to hold an office or employment by virtue of which that person is eligible to participate in the scheme until that person ceases to hold an office or employment in the grantor or in any associated company or company of which the grantor has control.

Acquisition of shares

25. (1) The scheme shall provide for a person's contributions under the certified contractual savings scheme to be of such amount as to secure as nearly as may be repayment of an amount equal to that for which shares may be acquired in pursuance of rights obtained under the scheme, and for this purpose the amount of repayment under the certified contractual savings scheme shall be determined as mentioned in paragraph 18.

(2) The scheme shall not—

(*a*) permit the aggregate amount of a person's contributions under certified contractual savings schemes linked to savings-related share option schemes approved under this Schedule to exceed [€320][1] monthly, nor

(*b*) impose a minimum on the amount of a person's contributions which exceeds [€12][2] monthly.

(3) The Minister for Finance may by order amend subparagraph (2) by substituting for any amount for the time being specified in that subparagraph such amount as may be specified in the order.

Amendments

1 Substituted by FA 2001 s 240(1) and (2)(*a*) and Sch 5 Pt 1 for 2002 and later tax years; previously "£250".

2 Substituted by FA 2001 s 240(1) and (2)(*a*) and Sch 5 Pt 1 for 2002 and later tax years; previously "£10".

Share price

26. The price at which scheme shares may be acquired by the exercise of a right obtained under the scheme—

(*a*) shall be stated at the time the right is obtained, and

(*b*) shall not be manifestly less than 75 per cent of the market value of shares of the same class at that time or, if the Revenue Commissioners and the grantor agree in writing, at such earlier time or times as may be provided in the agreement, but the scheme may provide for such variation of the price as may be necessary to take account of any variation in the share capital of which the scheme shares form part.

Options etc

27. (1) For the purposes of section 437(2), as applied by paragraph 8(3)(*b*)(ii) of this Schedule, a right to acquire shares (however arising) shall be taken to be a right to control them.

(2) Any reference in subparagraph (3) to the shares attributed to an individual is a reference to the shares which, in accordance with section 437(2) as applied by paragraph 8(3)(*b*)(ii) of this Schedule, fall to be brought into account in that individual's case to determine whether their number exceeds a particular percentage of the company's ordinary share capital.

(3) In any case where—

(*a*) the shares attributed to an individual consist of or include shares which that individual or any other person has a right to acquire, and

(*b*) the circumstances are such that, if that right were to be exercised, the shares acquired would be shares which were previously unissued and which the company is contractually bound to issue in the event of the exercise of the right;

then, in determining at any time prior to the exercise of that right whether the number of shares attributed to the individual exceeds a particular percentage of the ordinary share capital of the company, that ordinary share capital shall be taken to be increased by the number of unissued shares referred to in clause (*b*).]1

Amendments

1 Sch 12A inserted by FA 1999 s 68(*b*) with effect from 6 April 1999.

Cross-references

Costs of establishing savings related share option schemes: s 519B(1).

Penalties, para 6: Sch 29, column 2.

Definitions

Appeal Commissioners: s 2(1); class (of shares): s 5(1); company: s 4(1); High Court: IA 1937 Sch; month: IA 1937 Sch; ordinary share capital: s 2(1); person: IA 1937 s 11(*c*); tax: s 3(1); writing: IA 1937 Sch; year: IA 1937 Sch.

[SCHEDULE 12B
Certified Contractual Savings Schemes

[Section 519C]

1. This Schedule shall have effect for the purposes of section 519C.

Specifications by the Minister for Finance

2. (1) The requirements which may be specified under section 519C(4)(*c*) are such requirements as the Minister for Finance thinks fit.

(2) In particular, the requirements may relate to—

(*a*) the descriptions of individuals who may enter into contracts under a scheme;

(*b*) the contributions to be paid by individuals;

(*c*) the sums to be paid or repaid to individuals.

3. (1) Where a specification has been made under section 519C(4)(*c*), the Minister for Finance may withdraw the specification and stipulate the date on which the withdrawal is to become effective and any certification made by the Revenue Commissioners by reference to such specification shall be deemed to have been withdrawn on the same date.

(2) No withdrawal under this paragraph shall affect—

(*a*) the operation of a certified contractual savings scheme before the stipulated date, or

(*b*) any contract under such a scheme entered into before that date.

(3) No withdrawal under this paragraph shall be effective unless the Revenue Commissioners—

(*a*) send a notice by post to each qualifying savings institution informing it of the withdrawal of both the specification and certification, and

(*b*) do so not less than 28 days before the stipulated date.

4. (1) Where a specification has been made under section 519C(4)(*c*), the Minister for Finance may vary the specification and stipulate the date on which the variation is to become effective and any certification made by the Revenue Commissioners by reference to the specification obtaining before the variation shall be deemed to have been withdrawn on the date the variation became effective.

(2) The Revenue Commissioners may at any time certify a scheme as fulfilling the requirements obtaining after the variation.

(3) No variation and withdrawal under this paragraph shall affect—

(*a*) the operation of a certified contractual savings scheme before the stipulated date, or

(*b*) any contract under such a scheme entered into before that date.

(4) No variation and withdrawal under this paragraph shall be effective unless the Revenue Commissioners—

(*a*) send a notice by post to each qualifying savings institution informing it of the variation of the specification and withdrawal of the certification, and

(*b*) do so not less than 28 days before the stipulated date.

Information

5. The Revenue Commissioners may by notice in writing require any person to furnish them, within such time as the Revenue Commissioners may direct (not being less than 30 days), with such information as the Revenue Commissioners think necessary for the performance of their functions under this Schedule, and which the person to whom the notice is addressed has or can reasonably obtain, including in particular information—

(*a*) to enable the Revenue Commissioners to determine—

(i) whether to certify a scheme or withdraw a certification already given, or

(ii) the liability to tax, including capital gains tax, of any person who has participated in a scheme, and

(*b*) in relation to the administration of a scheme and any alteration of the terms of a scheme.

6. The Revenue Commissioners may nominate any of their officers, including an inspector, to perform any acts and discharge any functions authorised by this Schedule to be performed or discharged by them.][1]

Amendments

1 Sch 12B inserted by FA 1999 s 68(*b*) with effect from 6 April 1999.

Cross-references

Penalties, para 5: Sch 29 column 2.

Definitions

person: IA 1937 s 11(*c*); tax: s 3(1); writing: IA 1937 Sch.

[SCHEDULE 12C
Approved Share Option Schemes

[Section 519D]

Revenue information

A guide to approved share option schemes is available on Reveue's website (www.revenue.ie) under Publications/Technical Guidelines.

Interpretation

1. (1) For the purposes of this Schedule—

"approved" in relation to a scheme, means approved under paragraph 2;

"associated company" has the same meaning as in section 432;

"auditor", in relation to a company, means the person or persons appointed as auditor of the company for the purposes of the Companies Acts, 1963 to 1999, or under the law of the territory in which the company is incorporated and which corresponds to those Acts;

"control" has the same meaning as in section 432;

"full-time director", in relation to a company, means a director who is required to devote substantially the whole of his or her time to the service of the company;

"grantor" has the meaning given by paragraph 2(1);

"group scheme" has the meaning given by paragraph 2(3);

"key employee or director", in relation to a company, means an employee or a full-time director of the company whose specialist skills, qualifications and relevant experience are vital to the future success of the company and is so certified to the Revenue Commissioners by the company;

"market value" shall be construed in accordance with section 548;

"participating company", in relation to a group scheme, has the meaning given by paragraph 2(4);

"scheme shares" has the meaning given by paragraph 11;

"shares" includes stock.

(2) Section 10 shall apply for the purposes of this Schedule.

(3) Subsection (3) of section 433 shall have effect in a case where the scheme is a group scheme, with the substitution of a reference to all the participating companies for the first reference to the company in subparagraph (ii) of paragraph (*c*) of that subsection.

(4) For the purposes of this Schedule—

(*a*) a company is a member of a consortium that owns another company if it is one of not more than 5 companies which between them beneficially own not less than 75 per cent of the other company's ordinary share capital and each of which beneficially owns not less than 5 per cent of that capital, and

(*b*) the question of whether one company is controlled by another shall be determined in accordance with section 432.

Approval of schemes

2. (1) On the application of a body corporate (in this Schedule referred to as the **"grantor"**) which has established a share option scheme, the Revenue Commissioners shall approve the scheme if they are satisfied that it fulfils the requirements of this Schedule.

(2) An application under subparagraph (1) shall be made in writing and contain such particulars and be supported by such evidence as the Revenue Commissioners may require.

(3) Where the grantor has control of another company or companies, the scheme may be expressed to extend to all or any of the companies of which it has control and in this Schedule a scheme which is expressed so to extend is referred to as a **"group scheme"**.

(4) In relation to a group scheme, **"participating company"** means the grantor or any other company to which for the time being the scheme is expressed to extend.

3. (1) The Revenue Commissioners shall not approve a scheme under this Schedule if it appears to them that it contains features which are neither essential nor reasonably incidental to the purpose of providing for employees' and full-time directors' benefits in the nature of rights to acquire shares.

(2) The Revenue Commissioners shall be satisfied—

(*a*) that there are no features of the scheme other than any which are included to satisfy requirements of this Schedule which have or would have the effect of discouraging any description of employees who fulfil the conditions in paragraph 8(1) from actually participating in the scheme, and

(*b*) where the grantor is a member of a group of companies, that the scheme does not and would not have the effect of conferring benefits wholly or mainly on directors of companies in the group or on those employees of companies in the group who are in receipt of the higher or highest levels of remuneration.

(3) For the purposes of subparagraph (2), "a group of companies" means a company and any other companies of which it has control or with which it is associated.

(4) For the purposes of subparagraph (3), a company shall be associated with another company where it could reasonably be considered that—

(*a*) both companies act in pursuit of a common purpose,

(*b*) any person or any group of persons or groups of persons having a reasonable commonality of identity have or had the means or power, either directly or indirectly, to determine the trading operations carried on or to be carried on by both companies, or

(*c*) both companies are under the control of any person or group of persons or groups of persons having a reasonable commonality of identity.

4. (1) If, at any time after the Revenue Commissioners have approved a scheme, any of the requirements of this Schedule cease to be satisfied or the grantor fails to provide information requested by the Revenue Commissioners under paragraph 20, the Revenue Commissioners may withdraw the approval with effect from that time or such later time as the Revenue Commissioners may specify.

(2) If an alteration is made in the scheme at any time after the Revenue Commissioners have approved the scheme, the approval shall not have effect after the date of the alteration unless the Revenue Commissioners have approved the alteration.

5. If the grantor is aggrieved by—

(*a*) the failure of the Revenue Commissioners to approve the scheme or to approve an alteration in the scheme,

(*b*) the withdrawal of approval, or

(*c*) the failure of the Revenue Commissioners to decide that a condition subject to which the approval has been given is satisfied,

it may, by notice in writing given to the Revenue Commissioners within 30 days from the date on which it is notified of the Revenue Commissioners' decision, require the matter to be determined by the Appeal Commissioners, and the Appeal Commissioners shall hear and determine the matter in like manner as an appeal made to them against an assessment and all the provisions of the Income Tax Acts relating to such an appeal (including the provisions relating to the rehearing of an appeal and to the statement of a case for the opinion of the High Court on a point of law) shall apply accordingly with any necessary modifications.

6. The Revenue Commissioners may nominate any of their officers, including an inspector, to perform any acts and discharge any functions authorised by this Schedule to be performed or discharged by them.

Eligibility

7. (1) The scheme shall not provide for any person to be eligible to participate in it, that is to say, to obtain and exercise rights under it—

(*a*) unless he or she is an employee or director of the grantor or, in the case of a group scheme, of a participating company, or

(*b*) at any time when he or she has, or has within the preceding 12 months had, a material interest in a close company within the meaning of Chapter 1 of Part 13, which is—

(i) a company the shares of which may be acquired pursuant to the exercise of rights obtained under the scheme, or

(ii) a company which has control of such a company or is a member of a consortium which owns such a company.

(2) Notwithstanding subparagraph 1(*a*), the scheme may provide that a person may exercise rights obtained under it despite having ceased to be an employee or a director.

8. (1) The scheme shall provide that, at any time, every person who—

(*a*) is an employee or a full-time director of the grantor or, in the case of a group scheme, a participating company,

(*b*) has been such an employee or director at all times during a qualifying period not exceeding three years, and

(*c*) is chargeable to tax in respect of that person's office or employment under Schedule E,

shall be eligible to participate in the scheme, that is to say, to obtain and exercise rights under it.

(2) Subject to paragraph 9 every person eligible to participate in the scheme shall do so on similar terms.

(3) For the purposes of subparagraph (2), the fact that—

(*a*) the rights to be obtained by persons participating in a scheme vary or are different—

(i) in the year of assessment in which they commence to hold the office or employment by virtue of which they are entitled to participate in the scheme, or

(ii) according to the levels of their remuneration, the length of their service or similar factors,

or

(*b*) a person is not entitled to receive rights within a stated period of his or her normal retirement date,

shall not be regarded as meaning that they are not eligible to participate in the scheme on similar terms.

9. (1) Subject to the conditions of this paragraph, the scheme may provide for an employee or a director, who is a key employee or director of the grantor or, in the case of a group scheme, a participating company, to obtain and exercise rights under it which do not satisfy the requirement of paragraph 8 regarding participation in the scheme on similar terms.

(2) The conditions of this paragraph are that, in any year of assessment—

(*a*) the total number of shares in respect of which rights have been granted to key employees and directors in accordance with a rule of the scheme which conforms with this paragraph does not exceed 30 per cent of the total number of shares in respect of which rights have been granted to all employees and directors participating in the scheme whether in accordance with this paragraph or paragraph 8, and

(*b*) an individual who obtains rights for a year of assessment by virtue of this paragraph shall not also be entitled to obtain rights for that year in accordance with paragraph 8.

10. In determining for the purposes of paragraph 7—

(*a*) whether a company is a close company, section 430(1)(*a*) and subsections (3) to (7) of section 431 shall be disregarded, and

(*b*) whether a person has or has had a material interest in a company, sections 437(2) and 433(3)(*c*)(ii) shall have effect with the substitution for the references in those provisions to 5 per cent of references to 15 per cent.

Scheme shares

11. The scheme shall provide for directors and employees to obtain rights to acquire shares (in this Schedule referred to as **"scheme shares"**) which satisfy the requirements of paragraphs 12 to 16.

12. Scheme shares shall form part of the ordinary share capital of—

(*a*) the grantor,

(*b*) a company which has control of the grantor, or

(*c*) a company which either is, or has control of, a company which—

(i) is a member of a consortium which owns either the grantor or a company having control of the grantor, and

(ii) beneficially owns not less than 15 per cent of the ordinary share capital of the company so owned.

13. Scheme shares shall be—

(*a*) shares of a class quoted on a recognised stock exchange,

(*b*) shares in a company which is not under the control of another company, or

(*c*) shares in a company which is under the control of a company (other than a company which is, or if resident in the State would be, a close company within the meaning of section 430) whose shares are quoted on a recognised stock exchange.

14. (1) Scheme shares—

(*a*) shall be fully paid up,

(*b*) shall not be redeemable, and

(*c*) shall not be subject to any restrictions other than restrictions which attach to all shares of the same class or a restriction authorised by subparagraph (2).

(2) Subject to subparagraph (3), the shares may be subject to a restriction imposed by the company's articles of association—

(*a*) requiring all shares held by directors or employees of the company or of any other company of which it has control to be disposed of on ceasing to be so held, and

(*b*) requiring all shares acquired, in pursuance of rights or interests obtained by such directors or employees, by persons who are not, or have ceased to be, such directors or employees to be disposed of when they are acquired.

(3) A restriction is not authorised by subparagraph (2) unless—

(*a*) any disposal required by the restriction will be by way of sale for a consideration in money on terms specified in the articles of association, and

(*b*) the articles also contain general provisions by virtue of which any person disposing of shares of the same class (whether or not held or acquired as mentioned in subparagraph (2)) may be required to sell them on terms which are the same as those mentioned in clause (*a*).

15. (1) In determining for the purposes of paragraph 14(1)(*c*) whether scheme shares which are or are to be acquired by any person are subject to any restrictions, there shall be regarded as a restriction attaching to the shares any contract, agreement, arrangement or condition by which such person's freedom to dispose of the shares or of any interest in them or of the proceeds of their sale or to exercise any right conferred by them is restricted or by which such a disposal or exercise may result in any disadvantage to that person or to a person connected with that person.

(2) Subparagraph (1) does not apply to so much of any contract, agreement, arrangement or condition as contains provisions similar in purpose and effect to any of the provisions of the Model Rules set out in the Listing Rules of the Irish Stock Exchange.

16. Except where scheme shares are in a company whose ordinary share capital consists of shares of one class only, the majority of the issued shares of the same class shall be held by persons other than—

(*a*) persons who acquired their shares in pursuance of a right conferred on them or an opportunity afforded to them as a director or employee of the grantor or any other company and not in pursuance of an offer to the public,

(*b*) trustees holding shares on behalf of persons who acquired their beneficial interests in the shares as mentioned in subparagraph (*a*), and

(*c*) in a case where the shares fall within subparagraph (*c*) of paragraph 13 but do not fall within subparagraph (*a*) of that paragraph, companies which have control of the company whose shares are in question or of which that company is an associated company.

Exchange provisions

17. (1) The scheme may provide that if any company (in this paragraph referred to as **"the acquiring company"**)—

(*a*) obtains control of a company whose shares are scheme shares as a result of making a general offer—

(i) to acquire the whole of the issued ordinary share capital of the company which is made on a condition such that if it is satisfied the person making the offer will have control of the company, or

(ii) to acquire all the shares in the company which are of the same class as the scheme shares,

(*b*) obtains control of a company whose shares are scheme shares in pursuance of a compromise or arrangement sanctioned by the court under section 201 of the Companies Act, 1963, or

(*c*) becomes bound or entitled to acquire shares, under section 204 of the Companies Act, 1963, in a company whose shares are scheme shares,

any participant in the scheme may at any time within the appropriate period, by agreement with the acquiring company, release his or her rights under the scheme (in this paragraph referred to as **"the old rights"**) in consideration of the grant to him or her of rights (in this paragraph referred to as **"the new rights"**) which are equivalent to the old rights but relate to shares in a different company (whether the acquiring company itself or some other company falling within subparagraph (*b*) or (*c*) of paragraph 12).

(2) In subparagraph (1) **"the appropriate period"** means—

(*a*) in a case falling within clause (*a*) of that subparagraph, the period of 6 months beginning with the time when the person making the offer has obtained control of the company and any condition subject to which the offer is made is satisfied,

(*b*) in a case falling within clause (*b*) of that subparagraph, the period of 6 months beginning with the time when the court sanctions the compromise or arrangement, and

(*c*) in a case falling within clause (*c*) of that subparagraph, the period during which the acquiring company remains bound or entitled as mentioned in that clause.

(3) The new rights shall not be regarded for the purposes of this paragraph as equivalent to the old rights unless—

(*a*) the shares to which they relate satisfy the conditions specified, in relation to scheme shares, in paragraphs 12 to 16,

(*b*) the new rights will be exercisable in the same manner as the old rights and subject to the provisions of the scheme as it had effect immediately before the release of the old rights,

(*c*) the total market value, immediately before the release, of the shares which were subject to the participant's old rights is equal to the total market value, immediately after the grant, of the shares in respect of which the new rights are granted to the participant, and (*d*) the total amount payable by the participant for the acquisition of shares in pursuance of the new rights is equal to the total amount that would have been payable for the acquisition of shares in pursuance of the old rights.

(4) Where any new rights are granted pursuant to a provision included in a scheme by virtue of this paragraph they shall be regarded—

(*a*) for the purposes of section 519D and this Schedule, and

(*b*) for the purposes of the subsequent application (by virtue of a condition complying with subparagraph (3)(*b*)) of the provisions of the scheme,

as having been granted at the time when the corresponding old rights were granted.

Transfer of rights

18. (1) The scheme shall not permit any person obtaining rights under it to transfer any of them but may provide that if such a person dies before exercising them, they may be exercised after, but not later than one year after, the date of that person's death.

(2) Where the scheme contains the provision permitted by subparagraph (1) and any rights are exercised after the death of the person who obtained them, subsection (3) of section 519D shall apply with the omission of the reference to subsection (4) of that section.

Share price

19. The price at which scheme shares may be acquired by the exercise of a right obtained under the scheme shall be stated at the time the right is obtained and shall not be less than the market value of shares of the same class at that time or, if the Revenue Commissioners and the grantor agree in writing, at such earlier time or times as may be provided in the agreement, but the scheme may provide for such variation of the price so stated as may be necessary to take account of any variation in the share capital of which scheme shares form part.

Information

20. (1) The Revenue Commissioners may by notice in writing require any person to furnish them, within such time as the Revenue Commissioners may direct (not being less than 30 days), with such information as the Revenue Commissioners think necessary for the performance of their functions under this Schedule, and which the person to whom the notice is addressed has or can reasonably obtain, including in particular information—

(*a*) to enable the Revenue Commissioners to determine—

(i) whether to approve a scheme or withdraw an approval already given, or

(ii) the liability to tax, including capital gains tax, of any person who has participated in a scheme,

and

(*b*) in relation to the administration of a scheme and any alteration of the terms of a scheme.

(2) Notwithstanding the generality of subparagraph (1), the Revenue Commissioners may request a certificate from the auditor of a grantor company certifying that, in his or her opinion—

- (*a*) the terms of any rule or rules included in the scheme by virtue of either or both paragraphs 8 and 9 are complied with in relation to a year of assessment, or
- (*b*) as respects rights obtained under the scheme before it was approved under this Schedule, the conditions in subsection (7)(*b*) of section 519D are satisfied.

Options etc

21. (1) For the purposes of section 437(2), as applied by paragraph 10(*b*) of this Schedule, a right to acquire shares (however arising) shall be taken to be a right to control them.

(2) Any reference in subparagraph (3) to the shares attributed to an individual is a reference to the shares which, in accordance with section 437(2) as applied by paragraph 10(*b*) of this Schedule, fall to be brought into account in that individual's case to determine whether their number exceeds a particular percentage of the company's ordinary share capital.

(3) In any case where—

- (*a*) the shares attributed to an individual consist of or include shares which that individual or any other person has a right to acquire, and
- (*b*) the circumstances are such that, if that right were to be exercised, the shares acquired would be shares which were previously unissued and which the company is contractually bound to issue in the event of the exercise of the right,

then, in determining at any time prior to the exercise of that right whether the number of shares attributed to the individual exceeds a particular percentage of the ordinary share capital of the company, that ordinary share capital shall be taken to be increased by the number of unissued shares referred to in clause (*b*).][1]

Amendments

1 Schedule 12C inserted by FA 2001 s 15(*b*) with effect from 30 March 2001.

Cross-references

Penalties, para 20: Sch 29, column 29.

Definitions

Appeal Commissioners: ss 2(1), 850; company: ss 4(1), 5(1); High Court: IA 1937 Sch; Income Tax Acts: s 1(2); month: IA 1937 Sch; ordinary share capital: s 2(1); person: IA 1937 s 11(*c*); tax: ss 2(1), 3(1); writing: IA 1937 Sch; year: IA 1937 Sch; year of assessment: ss 2(1), 5(1).

SCHEDULE 13
Accountable Persons for Purposes of Chapter 1 of Part 18

[Section 521]

1. A Minister of the Government.
2. A local authority within the meaning of section 2(2) of the Local Government Act, 1941.

3. A body established under the Local Government Services (Corporate Bodies) Act, 1971.

4. A health board.

5. The General Medical Services (Payments) Board established under the General Medical Services (Payments) Board (Establishment) Order, 1972 (SI No 184 of 1972).

6. The Attorney General.

7. The Comptroller and Auditor General.

8. The Director of Public Prosecutions.

9. The Commissioner of Valuation.

10. The Chief Boundary Surveyor.

11. The Director of Ordnance Survey.

12. The Revenue Commissioners.

[13. Public Appointments Service.][1]

14. The Commissioners of Public Works in Ireland.

15. The Clerk of Dáil Éireann.

16. The Legal Aid Board.

17. A vocational education committee or a technical college established under the Vocational Education Act, 1930.

18. Teagasc.

19. A harbour authority.

20. An Foras Áiseanna Saothair.

21. Údarás na Gaeltachta.

22. The Industrial Development Agency (Ireland).

...[2]

24. Shannon Free Airport Development Company Limited.

[25. The National Tourism Development Authority.][3]

26. An institution of higher education within the meaning of the Higher Education Authority Act, 1971.

...[4]

28. The Radiological Protection Institute of Ireland.

29. A voluntary public or joint board hospital to which grants are paid by the Minister for Health and Children in the year 1988–89 or any subsequent year of assessment.

30. An authorised insurer within the meaning of section 470.

31. An Bord Glas.

32. An Bord Pleanála.

...[5]

34. Aer Lingus Group plc.

[35. Dublin Airport Authority public limited company.][6]

36. Arramara Teoranta.
37. Blood Transfusion Service Board.
38. An Bord Bia.
39. Bord na gCon.
40. Bord Gáis Éireann.
41. Bord Iascaigh Mhara.

[42. Bord na Móna plc.][7]

...[8]

44. Coillte Teoranta.
45. The Combat Poverty Agency.
46. Coras Iompair Éireann.

...[2]

48. Electricity Supply Board.
49. Housing Finance Agency plc.
50. ...[9]
51. Irish National Petroleum Corporation Limited.
52. Irish National Stud Company Limited.
53. National Building Agency Limited.
54. National Concert Hall Company Limited.
55. The Marine Institute.
56. An Post National Lottery Company.
57. Nítrigin Éireann Teoranta.
58. An Post.
59. Radio Telefís Éireann.

...[10]

61. Royal Hospital Kilmainham Company.
62. The Environmental Protection Agency.

...[2]

64. Forfás.
65. The Irish Aviation Authority.
66. The National Economic and Social Council.
67. The National Economic and Social Forum.
68. The National Roads Authority.
69. Temple Bar Properties Limited.
70. The Irish Film Board.
71. An educational institution established by or under section 3 of the Regional Technical Colleges Act, 1992, as a regional technical college.
72. The Dublin Institute of Technology.
73. Area Development Management Limited.

74. The Commissioner of Irish Lights.
75. Dublin Transportation Office.
76. The Heritage Council.
77. The Higher Education Authority.
78. The Independent Radio and Television Commission.
[79. Horse Racing Ireland.][11]
80. The Labour Relations Commission.
81. National Safety Council.
82. The Pensions Board.
[83. The Commission for Communications Regulation.][12]
84. The Law Reform Commission.
...[8]
86. The Office for Health Management.
...[13]
...[10]
89. National Standards Authority of Ireland.
90. Enterprise Ireland.
91. Dublin Docklands Development Authority.
[92. A Referendum Commission established by order made under section 2(1) of the Referendum Act, 1998.][14]
93. The Office of the Ombudsman.
[94. The Standards in Public Office Commission.][15]
95. The Office of the Information Commissioner.][16]
[96. The Central Fisheries Board.
97. A regional fisheries board established by virtue of an order made under section 10 of the Fisheries Act, 1980.
98. A County Enterprise Board (being a board referred to in the Schedule to the Industrial Development Act, 1995).
99. Western Development Commission.
100. The Equality Authority.
101. Commissioners of Charitable Donations and Bequests for Ireland.
102. Commission for Electricity Regulation.
103. A regional authority established by an order made under section 43(1) of the Local Government Act, 1991.][17]
...[18]][19]
[104. The Eastern Regional Health Authority, the Health Boards Executive or an area health board established under the Health (Eastern Regional Health Authority) Act, 1999.
105. Irish Sports Council.

106. An Bord Uchtála.

107. Council for Children's Hospitals' Care.

108. National Disability Authority.

109. Aquaculture Licences Appeals Board.

110. Office of the President.

111. Director of Equality Investigations.

112. Director of Consumer Affairs.

113. Data Protection Commissioner.

114. Competition Commissioner.

115. Chief State Solicitor.

116. Central Statistics Office.

117. Commission to Inquire into Child Abuse.

118. Campus and Stadium Ireland Development Ltd.

119. Digital Media Development Ltd.

120. Comhairle.][20]

[121. Human Rights Commission.

122. Pensions Ombudsman.

123. Refugee Appeals Tribunal.

124. The Dublin Institute for Advanced Studies.

125. Pre-Hospital Emergency Care Council.

126. Sustainable Energy Ireland — The Sustainable Energy Authority of Ireland.

127. The Health Insurance Authority.

128. Commission for Aviation Regulation.

129. Railway Procurement Agency.

130. The National Council on Ageing and Older People.

131. National Qualifications Authority of Ireland (NQAI).

132. BreastCheck, The National Breast Screening Programme.

133. The National Council for the Professional Development of Nursing and Midwifery.

134. Mater and Children's Hospital Development Ltd.

135. The National Consultative Commission on Racism and Interculturalism.

136. Office of Tobacco Control.

137. The Marine Casualty Investigation Board.

138. National Treasury Management Agency as regards the performance of functions by it conferred on, or delegated to, it by or under Part 2 of the National Treasury Management Agency (Amendment) Act 2000. (State Claims Agency).

139. National Development Finance Agency.][21]

[140. The Personal Injuries Assessment Board.][22]

[141. The National Council for Curriculum and Assessment.

142. The State Examinations Commission.

143. The Special Residential Services Board.][23]

[144. National Treatment Purchase Fund Board.][24]

[145. The Mental Health Commission.][24]

[146. Crisis Pregnancy Agency.][24]

[147. Commission on Electronic Voting.][24]

[148. Irish Medicines Board.][24]

[149. National Educational Welfare Board.][24]

[150. Oifig Choimisinéir na dTeangacha Oifigiúla.][24]

[151. The Health Service Executive.][24]

[152. Commission for Public Service Appointments.][24]

[153. Commission for Taxi Regulation.][24]

Amendments

1 Para 13 substituted by FA 2005 s 15(2)(*a*) with effect from with effect from 19 October 2004; previously "The Civil Service and Local Appointments Commissioners."

2 Deleted by FA 1999 s 17(*a*) with effect from 6 April 1999; previously "23. An Bord Tráchtála — The Irish Trade Board, 47. Custom House Docks Development Authority and 63. Forbairt".

3 Substituted by FA 2004 s 5(1)(*a*) with effect from 28 May 2003; previously "25. Bord Fáilte Éireann.".

4 Deleted by FA 2004 s 5(1)(*b*) with effect from 28 May 2003; previously "27. CERT Limited.".

5 Repealed by ACC Bank Act 2001 s 12(1) and Sch with effect from such date as the Minister for Finance may appoint by order. By virtue of the ACC Bank Act 2001 (Sections 6, 8, 10, 11(2) and (12)) (Commencement) Order 2002, SI No 69 of 2002, this amendment came into operation with effect from 28 February 2002.

6 Para 35 substituted by FA 2005 s 15(2)(*b*) with effect from with effect from 1 October 2004; previously "35. Aer Rianta cuideachta phoiblí theoranta.".

7 Substituted by FA 2001 s 14(*b*) from 6 April 2001; previously "Bord na Móna".

8 Deleted by FA 2000 s 20(*a*) with effect from 6 April 2000; previously "43. Bord Telecom Éireann." and "85. Northern Regional Fisheries Board — Bord Iascaigh Réigiúnach an Tuaisceart.".

9 Repealed by ICC Bank Act 2000 s 7 and the ICC Bank Act 2000 (Sections 5 and 7) (Commencement) Order 2001 (SI No 396 of 2001) with effect from 12 February 2001.

10 Deleted by FA 2001 s 14(*c*) from 6 April 2001; previously "60. National Rehabilitation Board", 88 National Social Services Board.".

11 Substituted by FA 2003 s 10(2)(*a*) with effect from 18 December 2001; previously "79. The Irish Horseracing Authority.".

12 Substituted by FA 2004 s 5(1)(*c*) with effect from 1 December 2002; previously "83. The Office of the Director of Telecommunications Regulation.".

13 Para 87 deleted by FA 2005 s 15(2)(*c*) with effect from with effect from 1 January 2005; previously "87. Hospital Bodies Administration Bureau.".

14 Substituted by FA 2000 s 20(*b*) with effect from 6 April 2000; previously "92. A commission established by the Government or a Minister of the Government for the purpose of providing information to the public in relation to a referendum referred to in section 1 of Article 47 of the Constitution.".

15 Substituted by FA 2004 s 5(1)(*d*) with effect from 10 December 2001; previously "94. The Public Offices Commission.".

16 Paras 83–95 inserted by FA 1999 s 17(*b*) with effect from 6 April 1999.

17 Paras 96–103 inserted by FA 2000 s 20(*c*) with effect from 6 April 2000.

18 Deleted by FA 2003 s 10(2)(*b*) with effect from 1 January 2003; previously "104. The National Pensions Reserve Fund Commission.".

19 Para 104 inserted by National Pensions Reserve Fund Act 2000 s 30(*d*) with effect from 10 December 2000.

20 Paras 104–120 inserted by FA 2001 s 14(*d*) from 6 April 2001.

21 Paras 121–139 inserted by FA 2003 s 10(2)(*c*) with effect from 1 May 2003.

22 Para 140 inserted by Personal Injuries Assessment Board Act 2003, s 85.

23 Paras 140–143 inserted by FA 2004 s 5(1)(*e*) with effect from 1 May 2004.

24 Paras 144–153 inserted by FA 2005 s 15(2)(*d*) with effect from with effect from 1 May 2005.

Cross-references

Professional services withholding tax, meaning of "accountable person": s 521(1).

Former enactments

FA 1992 Sch 2; FA 1994 s 11; FA 1996 s 8.

SCHEDULE 14
Capital Gains Tax: Leases

[Section 566]

Interpretation

1. In this Schedule, **"premium"** includes any like sum, whether payable to the intermediate or a superior lessor and, for the purposes of this Schedule, any sum (other than rent) paid on or in connection with the granting of a tenancy shall be presumed to have been paid by means of a premium except in so far as other sufficient consideration for the payment is shown to have been given.

Leases of Land as Wasting Assets: Restriction of Allowable Expenditure

2. (1) A lease of land shall not be a wasting asset until its duration does not exceed 50 years.

(2) Where at the beginning of the period of ownership of a lease of land it is subject to a sub-lease not at a rent representing the full value of the land together with any buildings on the land, and the value of the lease at the end of the duration of the sub-lease, estimated as at the beginning of the period of ownership, exceeds the expenditure allowable under section 552(1)(*a*) in computing the gain accruing on a disposal of the lease, the lease shall not be a wasting asset until the end of the duration of the sub-lease.

(3) In the case of a wasting asset which is a lease of land, the rate at which expenditure is assumed to be written off shall, instead of being a uniform rate as provided by section 560(3), be a rate fixed in accordance with the Table to this paragraph.

(4) Accordingly, for the purposes of the computation under Chapter 2 of Part 19 of the gain accruing on a disposal of a lease, and where—

(*a*) the percentage derived from the Table to this paragraph for the duration of the lease at the beginning of the period of ownership is P (1),

(*b*) the percentage so derived for the duration of the lease at the time when any item of expenditure attributable to the lease under section 552(1)(*b*) is first reflected in the nature of the lease is P (2), and

(*c*) the percentage so derived for the duration of the lease at the time of the disposal is P (3), then—

(i) there shall be excluded from the expenditure attributable to the lease under section 552(1)(*a*) a fraction equal to—

$$\frac{P(1) - P(2)}{P(1)}$$

and

(ii) there shall be excluded from any item of expenditure attributable to the lease under section 552(1)(*b*) a fraction equal to—

$$\frac{P(2) - P(3)}{P(2)}$$

(5) This paragraph shall apply notwithstanding that the period of ownership of the lease is a period exceeding 50 years, and accordingly no expenditure shall be written off under this paragraph in respect of any period earlier than the time when the lease becomes a wasting asset.

(6) Section 561 shall apply in relation to this paragraph as it applies in relation to subsections (3) to (5) of section 560.

(7) Where the duration of the lease is not an exact number of years, the percentage to be derived from the Table to this paragraph shall be the percentage for the whole number of years plus one-twelfth of the difference between that percentage and the percentage for the next higher number of years for each odd month, counting an odd 14 days or more as one month.

TABLE

Years	*Percentage*	*Years*	*Percentage*
50 (or more)	100.0	25	81.1
49	99.7	24	79.6
48	99.3	23	78.1
47	98.9	22	76.4
46	98.5	21	74.6
45	98.1	20	72.8
44	97.6	19	70.8
43	97.1	18	68.7
42	96.6	17	66.5
41	96.0	16	64.1
40	95.5	15	61.6
39	94.8	14	59.0
38	94.2	13	56.2
37	93.5	12	53.2

36	92.8	11	50.0
35	92.0	10	46.7
34	91.2	9	43.2
33	90.3	8	39.4
32	89.4	7	35.4
31	88.4	6	31.2
30	87.3	5	26.7
29	86.2	4	22.0
28	85.1	3	17.0
27	83.8	2	11.6
26	82.5	1	6.0
		0	0.0

Premiums for Leases

3. (1) Subject to this Schedule, where the payment of a premium is required under a lease of land or otherwise under the terms subject to which a lease of land is granted, there shall be a part disposal of the freehold or other asset out of which the lease is granted.

(2) In applying section 557 to such a part disposal, the property which remains undisposed of shall include a right to any rent or other payments (other than a premium) payable under the lease, and that right shall be valued as at the time of the part disposal.

Payments During Currency of Lease Treated as Premium

4. (1) Where under the terms subject to which a lease of land is granted a sum becomes payable by the lessee in place of the whole or part of the rent for any period or as consideration for the surrender of the lease, the lease shall be deemed for the purposes of this Schedule to have required the payment of a premium to the lessor (in addition to any other premium) of an amount equal to that sum for the period in relation to which the sum is payable.

(2) Where as consideration for the variation or waiver of any of the terms of a lease of land a sum becomes payable by the lessee otherwise than as rent, the lease shall be deemed for the purposes of this Schedule to have required the payment of a premium to the lessor (in addition to any other premium) of an amount equal to that sum for the period from the time when the variation or waiver takes effect to the time when it ceases to have effect.

(3) Where under subparagraph (1) or (2) a premium is deemed to have been received by the lessor otherwise than as consideration for the surrender of the lease, then—

- (*a*) subject to clause (*b*), both the lessor and the lessee shall be treated as if that premium were or were part of the consideration for the grant of the lease due at the time when the lease was granted, but (*b*) if the lessor is a lessee under a lease the duration of which does not exceed 50 years, this Schedule shall apply as if—

(i) that premium had been given as consideration for the grant of the part of the sub-lease covered by the period in respect of which the premium is deemed to have been paid, and

(ii) that consideration were expenditure incurred by the sub-lessee and attributable to that part of the sub-lease under section 552(1)(*b*).

(4) Where subparagraph (3)(*a*) applies, the gain accruing to the lessor on the disposal by means of the grant of the lease shall be recomputed and any necessary adjustments of capital gains tax shall be made accordingly, whether by means of assessment for the year in which the premium is deemed to have been received or by means of discharge or repayment of tax.

(5) Where under subparagraph (1) a premium is deemed to have been received as consideration for the surrender of a lease, that premium shall be regarded as consideration for a separate transaction consisting of the disposal by the lessor of the lessor's interest in the lease.

(6) Subparagraph (2) shall apply in relation to a transaction not at arm's length, and in particular in relation to a transaction entered into gratuitously, as if such sum had become payable by the tenant otherwise than as rent as might have been required of the tenant if the transaction had been at arm's length.

(7) Subparagraph (4) shall apply for the purposes of corporation tax as it applies for the purposes of capital gains tax.

Sub-Leases Out of Short Leases

5. (1) This paragraph shall apply in relation to a lease which is a wasting asset.

(2) In the computation under Chapter 2 of Part 19 of the gain accruing on the part disposal of a lease by means of the grant of a sub-lease for a premium (in this paragraph referred to as **"the actual premium"**), the expenditure attributable to the lease under paragraphs (*a*) and (*b*) of section 552(1) shall be apportioned in accordance with this paragraph, and section 557 shall not apply.

(3) Out of each item of the expenditure attributable to the lease under paragraphs (*a*) and (*b*) of section 552(1) there shall be apportioned to the part disposal—

(*a*) if the amount of the actual premium is not less than the amount which would be obtainable by means of a premium for the sub-lease if the rent payable under the sub-lease were the same as the rent payable under the lease (in this paragraph referred to as **"the full premium"**), the amount (in this paragraph referred to as **"the allowable amount"**) which under paragraph 2(3) is to be written off over the period which is the duration of the sub-lease, and

(*b*) if the amount of the actual premium is less than the full premium, such proportion of the allowable amount as is equal to the proportion which the actual premium bears to the full premium.

(4) Where the sub-lease is a sub-lease of only part of the land comprised in the lease, this paragraph shall apply only in relation to a proportion of the expenditure attributable

to the lease under paragraphs (*a*) and (*b*) of section 552(1) which is the same as the proportion which the value of the land comprised in the sub-lease at the time when the sub-lease is granted bears to the value of that land and the other land comprised in the lease at that time, and the remainder of that expenditure shall be apportioned to the other land.

Exclusion of Premiums Taxed Under Case V of Schedule D

6. (1) Where by reference to any premium income tax has become chargeable under section 98 on any amount, that amount shall be excluded from the consideration taken into account in the computation under Chapter 2 of Part 19 of a gain accruing on a disposal of the interest in respect of which income tax becomes so chargeable, except where in an apportionment under section 557 the value of the consideration is taken into account in the aggregate of that value and the market value of the property which remains undisposed of.

(2) Where by reference to any premium in respect of a sub-lease granted out of a lease, being a lease the duration of which does not at the time of granting the lease exceed 50 years, income tax has become chargeable under section 98 on any amount, that amount shall be deducted from any gain (as computed in accordance with the provisions of the Capital Gains Tax Acts apart from this subparagraph) accruing on the disposal for which the premium is consideration, but not so as to convert the gain into a loss or to increase any loss.

(3) (*a*) Subject to clause (*b*), where income tax has become chargeable under section 100 on any amount (in this subparagraph referred to as **"the relevant amount"**), the relevant amount shall be excluded from the consideration taken into account in the computation under Chapter 2 of Part 19 of a gain accruing on the disposal of the estate or interest in respect of which income tax becomes so chargeable, except where in an apportionment made under section 557 the value of the consideration is taken into account in the aggregate of that value and the market value of the property which remains undisposed of.

(*b*) If the part or interest disposed of is the remainder of a lease or a sub-lease out of a lease the duration of which does not exceed 50 years, clause (*a*) shall not apply, but the relevant amount shall be deducted from any gain (as computed in accordance with the provisions of the Capital Gains Tax Acts apart from this subparagraph) accruing on the disposal, but not so as to convert the gain into a loss or to increase any loss.

(4) References in subparagraphs (1) and (2) to a premium include references to a premium deemed to have been received under subsection (3) or (4) of section 98.

(5) Section 551 shall not be taken as authorising the exclusion of any amount from the consideration for a disposal of assets taken into account in the computation of the gain under Chapter 2 of Part 19 by reference to any amount chargeable to tax under section 75 and Chapter 8 of Part 4.

Disallowance of Premium Treated as Rent Under Superior Lease

7. (1) Where under section 103(2) a person is to be treated as paying additional rent in consequence of having granted a sub-lease, the amount of any loss accruing to such

person on the disposal by means of the grant of the sub-lease shall be reduced by the total amount of the rent which such person is thereby treated as paying over the term of the sub-lease (and without regard to whether relief is thereby effectively given over the term of the sub-lease), but not so as to convert the loss into a gain or to increase any gain.

(2) Nothing in section 551 shall be taken as applying in relation to any amount on which tax is paid under section 99.

(3) Where any adjustment is made under paragraph (*b*) of section 100(2), on a claim under that paragraph, any necessary adjustment shall be made to give effect to the consequences of the claim on the operation of this paragraph or paragraph 6.

Expenditure by Lessee Under Terms of Lease

8. Where under section 98(2) income tax is chargeable on any amount as being a premium the payment of which is deemed to be required by the lease, the person so chargeable shall be treated for the purposes of the computation of any gain accruing to that person on the disposal by means of the grant of the lease, and on any subsequent disposal of the asset out of which the lease was granted, as having incurred at the time the lease was granted expenditure of that amount (in addition to any other expenditure) attributable to the asset under section 552(1)(*b*).

Duration of Leases

9. (1) In ascertaining for the purposes of the Capital Gains Tax Acts the duration of a lease of land, the following provisions of this paragraph shall apply.

(2) Where the terms of the lease include provision for the determination of the lease by notice given by the lessor, the lease shall not be treated as granted for a term longer than one ending at the earliest date on which it could be determined by notice given by the lessor.

(3) Where any of the terms of the lease (whether relating to forfeiture or to any other matter) or any other circumstances render it unlikely that the lease will continue beyond a date falling before the expiration of the term of the lease, the lease shall not be treated as having been granted for a term longer than one ending on that date, and this subparagraph shall apply in particular where the lease provides for the rent to be increased after a given date, or for the lessee's obligations to become in any other respect more onerous after a given date, but includes provision for the determination of the lease on that date by notice given by the lessee, and those provisions render it unlikely that the lease will continue beyond that date.

(4) Where the terms of the lease include provision for the extension of the lease beyond a given date by notice given by the lessee, this paragraph shall apply as if the term of the lease extended for as long as it could be extended by the lessee, but subject to any right of the lessor by notice to determine the lease.

(5) The duration of a lease shall be decided in relation to the grant or any disposal of the lease by reference to the facts which were known or ascertainable at the time when the lease was acquired or created.

Leases of Property Other Than Land

10. (1) Paragraphs 3 to 5 and 9 shall, subject to any necessary modifications, apply in relation to leases of property other than land as they apply to leases of land.

(2) In the case of a lease of a wasting asset which is movable property, the lease shall be assumed to terminate not later than the end of the life of the wasting asset.

Cross-references

Applied by: s 566.

Case law

Payment under lease by lessee of site development costs treated as a premium: *Clarke v United Real (Moorgate) Limited* [1988] STC 273.

Former enactments

CGTA 1975 Sch 3; CTA 1976 s 140(2) and Sch 2 Pt II para 11.

SCHEDULE 15
List of Bodies for Purposes of Section 610

[Section 610]

PART 1

1. An unregistered friendly society whose income is exempt from income tax under section 211(1).
2. A registered friendly society whose income is exempt from income tax under section 211(1).
3. A registered trade union to the extent that its income is exempt from income tax under [section 213 or where the gain is applied solely for the purposes of its registered trade union activities.][1].
4. A local authority within the meaning of section 2(2) of the Local Government Act, 1941.
5. A body established under the Local Government Services (Corporate Bodies) Act, 1971.
6. The Central Bank of Ireland.

[7. The Health Service Executive.][2]

8. A vocational education committee established under the Vocational Education Act, 1930.
9. A committee of agriculture established under the Agriculture Act, 1931.
10. Bord Fáilte Éireann.
11. The Dublin Regional Tourism Organisation Limited.

[12. Dublin Regional Tourism Authority Limited.][3]

[13. The South-East Regional Tourism Authority Limited.][4]

[14. South-West Regional Tourism Authority Limited.][5]

[15. The Western Regional Tourism Authority Limited.][6]

[16. The North-West Regional Tourism Authority Limited.][7]

[17. Midlands-East Regional Tourism Authority Limited.][8]

18. Tramore Fáilte Limited.

19. The National Treasury Management Agency.
20. Eolas— The Irish Science and Technology Agency.
21. Forbairt.
22. Forfás.
23. The Industrial Development Agency (Ireland).
24. The Industrial Development Authority.
25. Shannon Free Airport Development Company Limited.
26. Údarás na Gaeltachta.
27. [Horse Racing Ireland][9]
28. The company incorporated on the 1st day of December, 1994, as Irish Thoroughbred Marketing Limited.
29. The company incorporated on the 1st day of December, 1994, as Tote Ireland Limited.
30. A body designated under section 4(1) of the Securitisation (Proceeds of Certain Mortgages) Act, 1995.
31. The Dublin Docklands Development [Authority and any of its wholly-owned subsidiaries.][10]
32. The Interim Board established under the Milk (Regulation of Supply) (Establishment of Interim Board) Order, 1994 (SI No 408 of 1994).

[33. National Rehabilitation Board.][11]

[34. The National Pensions Reserve Fund Commission.][12]

[35. National Development Finance Agency.][13]

[36. Tourism Ireland Limited.][14]

[37. An approved body (within the meaning of section 235(1)) to the extent that its income is exempt from income tax or, as the case may be, corporation tax.][15]

[38. Any body established by statute for the principal purpose of promoting games or sports and any company wholly owned by such a body, where the gain is applied solely for that purpose.][16]

PART 2

1. The Dublin District Milk Board established under the Dublin District Milk Board Order, 1936 (SR & O, No 254 of 1936).
2. The Cork District Milk Board established under the Cork District Milk Board Order, 1937 (SR & O, No 91 of 1937).
3. The company incorporated on the 19th day of November, 1991, as Dairysan Limited.
4. The company incorporated on the 14th day of February, 1994, as Glenlee (Cork) Limited.

Amendments

1 Substituted by FA 2003 s 72(*a*) with effect from 1 January 2003; previously "section 213.".

2 Substituted by FA 2005 s 57(1)(*a*) with effect from 1 January 2005; previously "7. A health board.".

3 Para 12substituted by FA 2005 s 57(1)(*b*) with effect from 25 March 2005; previously "12. Dublin City and County Regional Tourism Organisation Limited.".

4 Para 13 substituted by FA 2005 s 57(1)(*b*) with effect from 25 March 2005; previously "13. The South-Eastern Regional Tourism Organisation Limited.",.

5 Para 14 substituted by FA 2005 s 57(1)(*b*) with effect from 25 March 2005; previously "14. South-West Regional Tourism Organisation Limited.".

6 Para 15 substituted by FA 2005 s 57(1)(*b*) with effect from 25 March 2005; previously "15. The Western Regional Tourism Organisation Limited.".

7 Para 16 substituted by FA 2005 s 57(1)(*b*) with effect from 25 March 2005; previously "16. The North-West Regional Tourism Organisation Limited.".

8 Para 17 substituted by FA 2005 s 57(1)(*b*) with effect from 25 March 2005; previously "17. Midlands-East Regional Tourism Organisation Limited.".

9 Substituted by Horse and Greyhound Racing Act 2001 s 11 with effect from "the establishment day"; previously "The Irish Horseracing Authority". By virtue of the Horse and Greyhound Racing Act 2001 (Establishment Day) Order 2001, SI No 630 of 2001, 18 December 2001 is "the establishment day".

10 Substituted by FA 2001 s 79(*c*) as respects disposals made on or after 6 April 2001; previously "Authority.".

11 Pt 1 para 33 inserted by FA 1999 s 93 with effect from 6 April 1999.

12 Pt 1 para 34 inserted by National Pensions Reserve Fund Act 2000 s 30(*e*).

13 Para 35 inserted by FA 2003 s 72(*b*) with effect from 1 January 2003.

13 Para 36 inserted by FA 2003 s 72(*b*) with effect from 1 January 2003.

13 Para 37 inserted by FA 2003 s 72(*b*) with effect from 1 January 2003.

13 Para 38 inserted by FA 2003 s 72(*b*) with effect from 1 January 2003.

Cross-references

Deduction from consideration on disposal of certain assets, TCA 1997 s 980 does not apply to a disposal by a body specified in this Schedule: s 980(3A).

Non chargeable bodies: s 610.

Former enactments

CGTA 1975 s 23; FA 1989 s 33; FA 1991 s 20(2) and s 44; FA 1994 s 32(5); FA 1995 s 44(1) and (3); FA 1996 s 39(1) and (6) and s 64.

SCHEDULE 16

Building Societies: Change of Status

[Section 703]

Capital Allowances

1. (1) For the purposes of the allowances and charges provided for by sections 307 and 308, the trade of the society concerned shall not be treated as permanently discontinued and the trade of the successor company shall not be treated as a new trade set up and commenced by the successor company.

(2) There shall be made to or on the successor company in accordance with sections 307 and 308 all such allowances and charges as would have been made to or on the society if the society had continued to carry on the trade, and the amount of any such allowance or charge shall be computed as if the successor company had been carrying on the trade since the society began to do so and as if everything done to or by the society had been done to or by the successor company.

(3) The conversion of the society into the successor company shall not be treated as giving rise to any such allowance or charge.

Financial Assets

2. (1) In this paragraph—

"financial assets" means such assets as are held by the society in accordance with subsections (1) and (3) of section 39 of the Building Societies Act, 1989;

"financial trading stock" means such of the financial assets of the society as would constitute trading stock for the purposes of section 89.

(2) For the purposes of section 89, the financial trading stock of the society concerned shall be valued at an amount equal to its cost to the society.

(3) Where a society converts itself into the successor company, the vesting in the successor company of any financial assets, the profits or gains on the disposal of which would be chargeable to tax under Case I of Schedule D, shall be treated for the purposes of corporation tax as not constituting a disposal of those assets by the society; but, on the disposal of any of those assets by the successor company, the profits or gains accruing to the successor company shall be calculated (for the purposes of corporation tax) as if those assets had been acquired by the successor company at their cost to the society.

Capital Gains: Assets Vested in the Successor Company, etc

3. (1) For the purposes of capital gains tax and corporation tax on chargeable gains, the conversion of a society into the successor company shall not constitute—

(*a*) a disposal by the society of assets owned by it immediately before the conversion, or

(*b*) the acquisition at that time by the successor company of assets which immediately before the conversion were owned by the society.

(2) The Capital Gains Tax Acts, and the Corporation Tax Acts in so far as those Acts relate to chargeable gains, shall apply where a society has converted itself into the successor company as if the successor company had—

(*a*) acquired the assets which vested in the successor company on conversion at the same time and for the same consideration at which they were acquired by the society,

(*b*) been in existence as a company at all times since the society was incorporated,

(*c*) done all things done by the society relating to the acquisition and disposal of the assets which vested in the successor company on conversion, and

(*d*) done all other things done by the society before the conversion.

Capital Gains: Shares, and Rights to Shares, in Successor Company

4. (1) In this paragraph—

"free shares", in relation to a member of the society, means any shares issued by the successor company to that member in connection with the conversion but for no new consideration;

"member", in relation to the society, means a person who is or has been a member of the society, in that capacity, and any reference to a member includes a reference to a member of any particular class or description;

"new consideration" means consideration other than—

(*a*) consideration provided directly or indirectly out of the assets of the society or the successor company, or (*b*) consideration derived from a member's shares or other rights in the society or the successor company.

(2) Where in connection with the conversion there are conferred on members of the society concerned any rights—

(*a*) to acquire shares in the successor company in priority to other persons,
(*b*) to acquire shares in that company for consideration of an amount or value lower than the market value of the shares, or
(*c*) to free shares in that company,

any such rights so conferred on a member shall be regarded for the purposes of capital gains tax as an option (within the meaning of section 540) granted to and acquired by the member for no consideration and having no value at the time of that grant and acquisition.

(3) Where in connection with the conversion shares in the successor company are issued by that company to a member of the society concerned, those shares shall be regarded for the purposes of capital gains tax—

(*a*) as acquired by the member for a consideration of an amount or value equal to the amount or value of any new consideration given by the member for the shares or, if no new consideration is given, as acquired for no consideration, and
(*b*) as having at the time of their acquisition by the member a value equal to the amount or value of the new consideration so given or, if no new consideration is given, as having no value;

but this subparagraph is without prejudice to the application, where appropriate, of subparagraph (2).

(4) Subparagraph (5) shall apply in any case where—

(*a*) in connection with the conversion, shares in the successor company are issued by that company to trustees on terms which provide for the transfer of those shares to members of the society for no new consideration, and
(*b*) the circumstances are such that in the hands of the trustees the shares constitute settled property within the meaning of the Capital Gains Tax Acts.

(5) Where this subparagraph applies, then, for the purposes of capital gains tax—

(*a*) the shares shall be regarded as acquired by the trustees for no consideration,
(*b*) the interest of any member in the settled property constituted by the shares shall be regarded as acquired by that member for no consideration and as having no value at the time of its acquisition, and
(*c*) where on the occasion of a member becoming absolutely entitled as against the trustees to any of the settled property, both the trustees and the member shall be treated as if, on the member becoming so entitled, the shares in question had been disposed of and immediately reacquired by the trustees, in their capacity as trustees within section 567(2), for a consideration of such an amount as would secure that on the disposal neither a gain nor a loss would accrue to the trustees, and accordingly section 576(1) shall not apply in relation to that occasion.

(6) References in this paragraph to the case where a member becomes absolutely entitled to settled property as against the trustees shall be taken to include references to the case where the member would become so entitled but for being a minor or otherwise under a legal disability.

Cross-references

See also: s 703.
Valuation of trading stock on discontinuance of a trade, para 2(2): s 89(3).

Definitions

capital allowance: ss 2(1), 5(1); company: ss 4(1), 5(1); person: IA 1937 s 11(*c*); profits: s 4(1);.settled property: s 5(1); shares: s 5(1); trade: s 3(1).

Former enactments

FA 1990 Sch 3.

SCHEDULE 17
Reorganisation into Companies of Trustee Savings Banks

[Section 705]

Interpretation

1. In this Schedule—

"bank" means either or both a trustee savings bank and a bank within the meaning of section 57(3)(*c*)(i) of the Trustee Savings Banks Act, 1989, as the context requires;

"successor" means the company to which any property, rights, liabilities and obligations are transferred in the course of a transfer;

"transfer" means the transfer by a trustee savings bank of all or part of its property and rights and all of its liabilities or obligations under an order made by the Minister for Finance under section 57 of the Trustee Savings Banks Act, 1989, authorising the reorganisation of one or more trustee savings banks into a company or the reorganisation of a company referred to in subsection (3)(*c*)(i) of that section into a company referred to in subsection (3)(*c*)(ii) of that section.

Capital Allowances

2. (1) This paragraph shall apply for the purposes of—

(*a*) allowances and charges provided for in Part 9, section 670, Chapter 1 of Part 29 and sections 765 and 769, or any other provision of the Tax Acts relating to the making of allowances or charges under or in accordance with that Part or Chapter or those sections, and

(*b*) allowances or charges provided for by sections 307 and 308.

(2) The transfer shall not be treated as giving rise to any such allowance or charge which is provided for under subparagraph (1).

(3) There shall be made to or on the successor in accordance with sections 307 and 308 all such allowances and charges as would, if the bank had continued to carry on the trade, have been made to or on the bank, and the amount of any such allowance or charge shall be computed as if the successor had been carrying on the trade since the

trustee savings bank began to do so and as if everything done to or by the bank had been done to or by the successor; but the successor shall not be entitled to any amount which would have been made to the trustee savings bank by virtue only of section 304(4).

Trading Losses

3. Notwithstanding any other provision of the Tax Acts—

(*a*) a company referred to in subsection (3)(*c*)(i) of section 57 of the Trustee Savings Banks Act, 1989, which becomes a company referred to in subsection (3)(*c*)(ii) of that section shall not be entitled to relief under section 396(1) in respect of any loss incurred by the company in a trade in any accounting period or part of an accounting period in which it was a company referred to in subsection (3)(*c*)(i) of section 57 of the Trustee Savings Banks Act, 1989, and

(*b*) a company referred to in subsection (3)(*c*)(ii) of section 57 of that Act shall not be entitled to relief under section 396(1) in respect of any loss incurred by a company referred to in subsection (3)(*c*)(i) of section 57 of that Act.

Financial Assets

4. (1) In this paragraph, **"financial trading stock"** means such of the assets of the bank as would constitute trading stock for the purposes of section 89.

(2) For the purposes of section 89, the financial trading stock of the bank concerned shall be valued at an amount equal to or treated for the purposes of subparagraph (3) as its cost to that bank.

(3) The acquisition in the course of a transfer by the successor of any assets, the profits or gains on the disposal of which by the bank would be chargeable to tax under Case I of Schedule D, shall be treated for the purposes of income tax and corporation tax as not constituting a disposal of those assets by that bank; but, on the disposal of any of those assets by the successor, the profits or gains accruing to the successor shall be calculated (for the purposes of corporation tax) as if those assets had been acquired by the successor at their cost to the bank.

Capital Gains

5. (1) This paragraph shall apply for the purposes of the Capital Gains Tax Acts, and of the Corporation Tax Acts in so far as those Acts relate to chargeable gains.

(2) The disposal of an asset by a bank to a company in the course of a transfer shall be deemed to be for a consideration of such amount as would secure that on the disposal neither a gain nor a loss would accrue to the bank.

(3) Where subparagraph (2) has applied in relation to the disposal of an asset by the bank, then, in relation to a subsequent disposal of the asset, the successor shall be treated as if the acquisition or provision of the asset by—

(*a*) the trustee savings bank, or

(*b*) if the asset was not acquired or provided by the trustee savings bank, the bank within the meaning of section 57(3)(*c*)(i) of the Trustee Savings Banks Act, 1989,

were the successor's acquisition or provision of the asset.

(4) Any allowable losses accruing at any time to a bank shall, on a transfer and in so far as they have not been allowed as a deduction from chargeable gains, be treated as allowable losses which accrued at that time to the successor.

(5) For the purposes of section 597, the bank and the successor shall be treated as if they were the same person.

(6) Where the liability in respect of any debt owed to a bank is transferred in the course of a transfer to a successor, the successor shall be treated as the original creditor for the purposes of section 541.

Cross-references

Amalgamation of trustee savings banks: s 704(1).
Reorganisation of trustee savings banks into companies: s 705.
Valuation of trading stock at discontinuance of a trade, para 4(2): s 89(3).

Definitions

allowable loss: ss 4(1), 5(1), 546; capital allowance: ss 2(1), 5(1); chargeable gain: ss 4(1), 5(1), 534; company: ss 4(1), 5(1); Income Tax Acts: s 1(2); person: IA 1937 s 11(*c*); Tax Acts: s 1(2); trade: s 3(1); profits: s 4(1).

Former enactments

FA 1990 Sch 4.

[SCHEDULE 17A
Accounting Standards

[Section 76A]

Interpretation

Cross-references

Computation of profits or gains of a company - accounting standards: s 76A(2).
Securisation, this Schedule applies with any necessary modifications, company making election under TCA 1997 s 110(6)(*b*): s 110(6)(*c*).
Treatment of unrealised gains and losses in certain cases, meaning of "relevant accounting standards" applied: s 76B(2); para 4: s 76B(1).

1. In this Schedule **"relevant accounting standards"** means—

(*a*) international accounting standards, or

(*b*) as regards the matters covered by those published standards, Irish generally accepted accounting practice which is based on published standards—

(i) which are stated so as to embody, in whole or in part, international accounting standards, and

(ii) the application of which would produce results which are substantially the same as results produced by the application of international accounting standards.

Transitional Measures (amounts receivable and deductible)

2. (1) In this paragraph—

"deductible amount", in relation to a company, means the aggregate of the amounts of—

(*a*) so much of any amounts receivable by the company which falls to be taken into account as a trading receipt in computing the profits or gains for the purposes of Case I or II of Schedule D of the company for an accounting period computed in accordance with relevant accounting standards as was also taken into account as a trading receipt in computing such profits or gains of the company for any accounting period ending before the first accounting period in respect of which such profits or gains of the company were so computed, and

(*b*) so much of an expense incurred by the company, being an expense which would have been deductible in computing profits or gains for the purposes of Case I or II of Schedule D of the company if the expense had been incurred in an accounting period for which such profits or gains were computed in accordance with relevant accounting standards, as—

(i) was not deducted in computing the profits or gains for the purposes of Case I or II of Schedule D of the company for an accounting period ending before the first accounting period in respect of which such profits or gains of the company are computed in accordance with relevant accounting standards, and

(ii) is not deductible in computing the profits or gains for the purposes of Case I or II of Schedule D of the company for any accounting period for which such profits or gains of the company are so computed;

"taxable amount", in relation to a company, means the aggregate of the amounts of—

(*a*) so much of an amount receivable by the company, being an amount receivable which would have been taken into account as a trading receipt in computing the profits or gains for the purposes of Case I or II of Schedule D of the company if the amount had accrued in an accounting period for which such profits or gains were computed in accordance with relevant accounting standards, as is not so taken into account—

(i) for an accounting period for which such profits or gains of the company are computed in accordance with relevant accounting standards, or

(ii) for an accounting period ending before the first accounting period in respect of which such profits or gains are so computed,

and

(*b*) so much of an expense incurred by the company which is deductible in computing the profits or gains for the purposes of Case I or II of Schedule D of the company for an accounting period for which such profits or gains of the company are computed in accordance with relevant accounting standards as was deducted in computing such profits or gains of the company for any accounting period ending before the first accounting period of the company in respect of which such profits or gains were so computed.

(2) (*a*) An amount equal to the excess of the taxable amount in relation to a company over the deductible amount in relation to the company shall, subject to subparagraph (4), be treated as a trading receipt of the company for the first accounting period of the company in respect of which profits or gains for the purposes of Case I or II of Schedule D of the company are computed in accordance with relevant accounting standards.

(*b*) Notwithstanding clause (*a*), an amount which is treated under clause (*a*) as a trading receipt for an accounting period shall not be taken into account in computing the profits or gains for the purposes of Case I or II of Schedule D of the company for that accounting period but instead, subject to clause (*c*)—

(i) one-fifth of the amount shall be so taken into account for that accounting period, and

(ii) a further one-fifth shall be so taken into account for each succeeding accounting period until the whole amount has been accounted for.

(*c*) Where any accounting period referred to in subclause (i) or (ii) of clause (*b*) is the last accounting period in which a company carried on a trade or profession then such fraction, of the amount referred to in those subclauses, shall be taken into account for that accounting period as is required to ensure that the whole of that amount is accounted for.

(3) (*a*) An amount equal to the excess of the deductible amount in relation to a company over the taxable amount in relation to the company shall, subject to subparagraph (4), be treated as a deductible trading expense of the trade carried on by the company for the first accounting period of the company in respect of which profits or gains for the purposes of Case I or II of Schedule D of the company are computed in accordance with relevant accounting standards.

(*b*) Notwithstanding clause (*a*), an amount which is treated under clause (*a*) as a deductible trading expense for an accounting period shall not be taken into account in computing the profits or gains for the purposes of Case I or II of Schedule D of the company for that accounting period but instead, subject to clause (*c*)—

(i) one-fifth of the amount shall be so taken into account for that accounting period, and

(ii) a further one-fifth shall be so taken into account for each succeeding accounting period until the whole amount has been accounted for.

(*c*) Where any accounting period referred to in subclause (i) or (ii) of clause (*b*) is the last accounting period in which a company carried on a trade or profession then such fraction, of the amount referred to in those subclauses, shall be taken into account for that accounting period as is required to ensure that the whole of that amount is accounted for.

(4) This paragraph does not apply as respects any amount taken into account under paragraph 4.

Transitional Arrangements (bad debts)

3. (1) In this paragraph—

"current bad debts provision", in relation to a period of account of a company, means so much of the aggregate value of debts at the end of the period of account as represents the extent to which they are estimated to be impaired in accordance with relevant accounting standards;

"first relevant period of account", in relation to a company, means the first period of account in respect of which the company prepares its accounts in accordance with relevant accounting standards;

"opening bad debts provision", in relation to a company, means so much of the aggregate value of debts at the beginning of the first relevant period of account of the company as represents the extent to which they are estimated to be impaired in accordance with those standards;

"specific bad debts provision", in relation to a company, means the aggregate of the amounts of doubtful debts which were respectively estimated to be bad at the end of the period of account immediately preceding the first relevant period of account of the company.

(2) This paragraph applies as respects a period of account in respect of which a company prepares its accounts in accordance with relevant accounting standards.

(3) Where, as respects any period of account for which a company prepares its accounts in accordance with relevant accounting standards, the amount of the opening bad debts provision exceeds the higher of—

(*a*) the current bad debts provision, or

(*b*) the specific bad debts provision,

the excess, reduced by any amount treated under this section as a trading expense for any earlier period of account or, if there is more than one such amount, by the aggregate of such amounts, shall be treated as a trading expense of the company's trade for the period of account.

Transitional Measures (gains and losses in financial instruments)

4. (1) In this paragraph—

"changeover day", in relation to a company, means the last day of the accounting period immediately preceding the first accounting period of the company in respect of which profits or gains for the purposes of Case I or II of Schedule D of the company are computed in accordance with relevant accounting standards which are, or include, relevant accounting standards in relation to profits or gains or losses on financial assets and financial liabilities;

"deductible amount", in relation to a company, means the aggregate of—

(*a*) so much of any amount of loss accruing on or before the changeover day on a financial asset or financial liability of the company, being a loss which had not been realised on or before that day and which would have been taken into account in computing profits or gains for the purposes of Case I or II of Schedule D of the company if it had accrued in an accounting period commencing after the changeover day, as, apart from this paragraph, would not be so taken into account for any accounting period of the company, and

(*b*) so much of any amount of profits or gains, accruing and not realised in a period or periods (in this clause referred to as the "first-mentioned period or periods") ending on or before the changeover day on a financial asset or financial liability of the company, which falls to be taken into account in computing the profits or gains for the purposes of Case I or II of Schedule D of the company for an accounting period or periods commencing before the changeover day as would, apart from this paragraph, be taken into account twice in computing profits or gains for the purposes of Case I or II of Schedule D of the company, by virtue of a profit, gain or loss, accruing in a period which includes the first-mentioned period or periods, being taken into account in computing profits or gains for the purposes of Case I or II of Schedule D of the company for an accounting period commencing after the changeover day;

"taxable amount", in relation to a company, means the aggregate of—

(*a*) so much of any amount of profits or gains accruing on or before the changeover day on a financial asset or financial liability of the company, being profits or gains which had not been realised on or before that day and which would have been taken into account in computing the profits or gains for the purposes of Case I or II of Schedule D of the company if they had accrued in an accounting period commencing after the changeover day, as apart from this paragraph, would not be so taken into account for any accounting period of the company, and

(*b*) so much of any amount of loss, accruing and not realised in a period or periods (in this clause referred to as the "first-mentioned period or periods") ending on or before the changeover day on a financial asset or financial liability of the company, which falls to be taken into account in computing the profits or gains for the purposes of Case I or II of Schedule D of the company for an accounting period or periods commencing before the changeover day as would, apart from this paragraph, be taken into account twice in computing profits or gains for the purposes of Case I or II of Schedule D of the company, by virtue of a profit, gain or loss, accruing in a period which includes the first-mentioned period or periods, being taken into account in computing profits or gains for the purposes of Case I or II of Schedule D of the company for an accounting period commencing after the changeover day.

(2) (*a*) An amount equal to the excess of the taxable amount in relation to a company over the deductible amount in relation to the company shall be treated as a trading receipt of the company for the first accounting period of the company commencing after the changeover day.

(*b*) Notwithstanding clause (*a*), an amount which is treated under clause (*a*) as a trading receipt for an accounting period shall not be taken into account in computing the profits or gains for the purposes of Case I or II of Schedule D of the company for that accounting period but instead, subject to clause (*c*)—

(i) one-fifth of the amount shall be so taken into account for that accounting period, and

(ii) a further one-fifth shall be so taken into account for each succeeding accounting period until the whole amount has been accounted for.

(*c*) Where any accounting period referred to in subclause (i) or (ii) of clause (*b*) is the last accounting period in which a company carried on a trade or profession then such fraction, of the amount referred to in those subclauses, shall be taken into account for that accounting period as is required to ensure that the whole of that amount is accounted for.

(3) (*a*) An amount equal to the excess of the deductible amount in relation to a company over the taxable amount in relation to the company shall be treated as a deductible trading expense of the trade carried on by the company for the first accounting period of the company commencing after the changeover day.

(*b*) Notwithstanding clause (*a*), an amount which is treated under clause (*a*) as a deductible trading expense for an accounting period shall not be taken into account in computing the profits or gains for the purposes of Case I or II of

Schedule D of the company for that accounting period but instead, subject to clause (*c*)—

(i) one-fifth of the amount shall be so taken into account for that accounting period, and

(ii) a further one-fifth shall be so taken into account in each succeeding accounting period until the whole amount has been accounted for.

(*c*) Where any accounting period referred to in subclause (i) or (ii) of clause (*b*) is the last accounting period in which a company carried on a trade or profession then such fraction, of the amount referred to in those subclauses, shall be taken into account for that accounting period as is required to ensure that the whole of that amount is accounted for.

(4) (*a*) Subparagraph (5) applies to a loss incurred by a company on the disposal at any relevant time of any financial asset or financial liability where, within a period beginning 4 weeks before and ending 4 weeks after that disposal, the company acquired a financial asset or financial liability of the same class providing substantially the same access to economic benefits and exposure to risk as would have been provided by the reacquisition of the asset or liability disposed of.

(*b*) In this paragraph **"relevant time"** means a time after 1 January 2005 which is in a period of 6 months ending on the changeover day.

(5) A loss to which this subparagraph applies, which would otherwise be taken into account in computing profits or gains or losses of a company for the purposes of Case I or II of Schedule D for an accounting period, shall not be so taken into account but instead—

(*a*) one-fifth of the loss shall be so taken into account for that accounting period,

(*b*) a further one-fifth shall be so taken into account for each succeeding accounting period until the whole amount has been accounted for, and

(*c*) Notwithstanding clauses (*a*) and (*b*), where any accounting period referred to in those clauses is the last accounting period in which a company carried on a trade or profession then such fraction, of the amount referred to in those clauses, shall be taken into account for that accounting period as is required to ensure that the whole of that amount is accounted for.

(6) As respects the first accounting period of a company in respect of which profits or gains for the purposes of Case I or II of Schedule D of the company are computed in accordance with relevant accounting standards, which are, or include, relevant accounting standards in relation to profits or gains or losses on financial assets or liabilities, section 958 shall have effect as if—

(*a*) in subsection (4D)(*b*) the following were substituted for "no amount were included in the chargeable person's profits for the chargeable period in respect of chargeable gains on the disposal by the person of assets in the part of the chargeable period which is after the date by which the first instalment for the chargeable period is payable in accordance with subsection (2A)":

"no amount were included in the chargeable person's profits for the chargeable period in respect of—

(I) chargeable gains on the disposal by the person of assets in the part of the chargeable period which is after the date by which, or

(II) profits or gains or losses accruing, and not realised, in the chargeable period on financial assets or financial liabilities as are attributable to changes in value of those assets or liabilities in the part of the chargeable period which is after the end of the month immediately preceding the month in which,

the first instalment for the chargeable period is payable in accordance with subsection (2A)",

and

(*b*) in subsection (4E)(*b*) the following were substituted for "no amount were included in the chargeable person's profits for the chargeable period in respect of chargeable gains on the disposal by the person of assets in the part of the chargeable period which is after the date by which preliminary tax for the chargeable period is payable in accordance with subsection (2B)":

"no amount were included in the chargeable person's profits for the chargeable period in respect of—

(i) chargeable gains on the disposal by the person of assets in the part of the chargeable period which is after the date by which, or

(ii) profits or gains or losses accruing, and not realised, in the chargeable period on financial assets or financial liabilities as are attributable to changes in value of those assets or liabilities in the part of the chargeable period which is after the end of the month immediately preceding the month in which,

preliminary tax for the chargeable period is payable in accordance with subsection (2B)".][1]

Amendments

1 Sch 17A inserted by FA 2005 s 48(1)(g) as respects any period of account beginning on or after 1 January 2005.

Definitions

accounting period: s 27; chargeable gain: s 4(1); company: s 4(1); international accounting standards: s 4(1); Irish generally accepted accounting practice: s 4(1); month: IA 1937 Sch; period of account: s 4(1); profession: s 2(1); profits: s 4(1); trade: ss 3(1), 4(1).

SCHEDULE 18

Accounting for and Payment of Tax Deducted from Relevant Payments and Undistributed Relevant Income

[Section 734(5)]

Time and Manner of Payment

1. (1) Notwithstanding any other provision of the Acts, this paragraph shall apply for the purpose of regulating the time and manner in which tax deducted in accordance with section 734(5) shall be accounted for and paid.

(2) A collective investment undertaking which is not a specified collective investment undertaking shall, within 15 days from the 5th day of April each year, make a return to the Collector-General of all amounts from which it was required by section 734(5) to

deduct tax in the year ending on that date and of the amount of appropriate tax which it was required to deduct from those amounts.

(3) The appropriate tax required to be included in a return shall be due and payable at the time by which the return is to be made and shall be paid by the collective investment undertaking to the Collector-General, and the appropriate tax so due shall be payable by the collective investment undertaking without the making of an assessment; but the appropriate tax which has become so due may be assessed on the collective investment undertaking (whether or not it has been paid when the assessment is made) if that tax or any part of it is not paid on or before the due date.

(4) Where it appears to the inspector that there is an amount of appropriate tax which ought to have been and has not been included in a return, or the inspector is dissatisfied with any return, he or she may make an assessment on the collective investment undertaking to the best of his or her judgment, and any amount of appropriate tax due under an assessment made by virtue of this subparagraph shall be treated for the purposes of interest on unpaid tax as having been payable at the time when it would have been payable if a correct return had been made.

(5) Where any item has been incorrectly included in a return, the inspector may make such assessments, adjustments or set-offs as may in his or her judgment be required for securing that the resulting liabilities to tax (including interest on unpaid tax) whether of the collective investment undertaking or any other person are, in so far as possible, the same as they would have been if the item had not been so included.

(6) (*a*) Any appropriate tax assessed on a collective investment undertaking under this Schedule shall be due within one month after the issue of the notice of assessment (unless that tax is due earlier under subparagraph (3)) subject to any appeal against the assessment, but no such appeal shall affect the date when any amount is due under subparagraph (3).

(*b*) On the determination of an appeal against an assessment under this Schedule any appropriate tax overpaid shall be repaid.

(7) (*a*) The provisions of the Income Tax Acts relating to—

(i) assessments to income tax,

(ii) appeals against such assessments (including the rehearing of appeals and the statement of a case for the opinion of the High Court), and

(iii) the collection and recovery of income tax,

shall, with any necessary modifications, apply to the assessment, collection and recovery of appropriate tax.

(*b*) Any amount of appropriate tax payable in accordance with this Schedule without the making of an assessment shall carry interest at the rate of 1.25 per cent for each month or part of a month from the date when the amount becomes due and payable until payment.

(*c*) [Subsections (3) to (5) of section 1080][1] shall apply in relation to interest payable under clause (*b*) as they apply in relation to interest payable under section 1080.

(*d*) In its application to any appropriate tax charged by an assessment made in accordance with this Schedule, section 1080 shall apply as if [subsection (2)(*b*)][2] of that section were deleted.

(8) Every return shall be in a form prescribed by the Revenue Commissioners and shall include a declaration to the effect that the return is correct and complete.

Amendments

[1] Substituted by FA 2005 s 145(7)(*a*) and Sch 5 Pt 1 in relation to any unpaid income tax, corporation tax or capital gains tax, as the case may be, that has not been paid before 1 April 2005 regardless of when that tax became due and payable and notwithstanding anything to the contrary in any other enactment other than TCA 1997 s 1082; previously "Subsections (2) to (4) of section 1080".

[1] Substituted by FA 2005 s 145(7)(*a*) and Sch 5 Pt 1 in relation to any unpaid income tax, corporation tax or capital gains tax, as the case may be, that has not been paid before 1 April 2005 regardless of when that tax became due and payable and notwithstanding anything to the contrary in any other enactment other than TCA 1997 s 1082; previously "subsection (1)(*b*)".

Statement to be Given on Making of Relevant Payment

2. Where a collective investment undertaking other than a specified collective investment undertaking makes a relevant payment from which appropriate tax is deductible in accordance with section 734(5), or would be so deductible but for paragraphs (i) and (ii) of the definition of **"appropriate tax"** in section 734(1)(*a*), it shall give to the unit holder to whom the relevant payment is made a statement showing—

(*a*) the amount of the relevant payment,

(*b*) the amount equal to the aggregate of the appropriate tax deducted from the relevant payment and any amount or amounts deducted pursuant to paragraphs (i) and (ii) of the definition of **"appropriate tax"** in section 734(1)(*a*) in determining the appropriate tax or, if by reason of those paragraphs there was no appropriate tax to deduct from the amount of the relevant payment, the aggregate of the amounts referred to in those paragraphs in so far as they refer to the relevant payment,

(*c*) the net amount of the relevant payment,

(*d*) the date of the relevant payment, and

(*e*) such other information in relation to the relevant payment as shall be necessary to enable the correct amount of tax, if any, payable by or repayable to the unit holder in respect of the relevant payment to be determined.

Cross-references

Certain unit trusts not to be collective investment undertakings: s 735(2); option for non-application of s 735: s 736(1).

Penalty, para 1(2): Sch 29 column 2.

Taxation of collective investment undertakings: s 734(1)(*a*).

Definitions

High Court: IA 1937 Sch; Income Tax Acts: s 1(2); inspector: ss 2(1), 5(1), 852; month: IA 1937 Sch; person: IA 1937 s 11(*c*); unit holder: ss 5(1), 734.

Former enactments

FA 1989 Sch 1 paras 1(1)–(7)(*d*) and (8) and para 2; FA 1997 s 146(2) and Sch 9 Pt II.

[SCHEDULE 18A
Restriction on Set-Off of Pre-Entry Losses

[Section 626A]

Application and construction of Schedule

1. (1) This Schedule shall apply in the case of a company which is or has been a member of a group of companies (in this Schedule referred to as **"the relevant group"**) in relation to any pre-entry losses of the company.

(2) In this Schedule **"pre-entry loss"**, in relation to a company, means—

(*a*) an allowable loss that accrued to the company at a time before it became a member of the relevant group in so far as the loss has not been allowed as a deduction from chargeable gains accruing to the company prior to that time, or

(*b*) the pre-entry proportion of an allowable loss accruing to the company on the disposal of a pre-entry asset,

and for the purposes of this Schedule the pre-entry proportion of an allowable loss shall be calculated in accordance with paragraph 2.

(3) In this Schedule **"pre-entry asset"**, in relation to a disposal means, subject to subparagraph (4), an asset which was held [at the time immediately before the relevant event occurred in relation to it by a company which is or was][1] a member of the relevant group.

[(3A)(*a*) In this paragraph references to the relevant event occurring in relation to a company—

(i) in a case in which—

(I) the company was resident in the State at the time when it became a member of the relevant group, or

(II) the asset was a chargeable asset in relation to the company at that time,

are references to the company becoming a member of that group;

(ii) in any other case, are references to whichever is the first of—

(I) the company becoming resident in the State, or

(II) the asset becoming a chargeable asset in relation to the company.

(*b*) For the purposes of paragraph (*a*), an asset is a **"chargeable asset"** in relation to a company at any time if, were the asset to be disposed of by the company at that time, any gain accruing to the company would be a chargeable gain.][2]

(4) An asset is not a pre-entry asset in relation to a disposal where—

(*a*) the company which held the asset at the time [the relevant event occurred in relation to it][3] is not the company which makes the disposal, and

(*b*) since that time the asset has been disposed of otherwise than by a disposal to which section 617 applies,

but, without prejudice to subparagraph (8), where, on a disposal to which section 617 does not apply, an asset would cease to be a pre-entry asset by virtue of this subparagraph and the company making the disposal retains any interest in or over the asset in question, that interest shall be a pre-entry asset for the purposes of this Schedule.

(5) References in this Schedule, in relation to a pre-entry asset, to the relevant time are references to the time when [the relevant event occurred in relation to the company by reference to which that asset is a pre-entry asset][4] and for the purposes of this Schedule—

(*a*) where [a relevant event has occurred in relation to a company][5] on more than one occasion, an asset is a pre-entry asset by reference to the company if the asset would be a pre-entry asset by reference to the company in respect of any one of those occasions, and

(*b*) references in the following provisions of this Schedule to the time when [a relevant event occurred in relation to a company][6], in relation to assets held on more than one such occasion as is mentioned in clause (*a*), are references to the later or latest of those occasions.

(6) Where—

(*a*) the principal company of a group of companies (in this paragraph referred to as "the first group") has at any time become a member of another group (in this paragraph referred to as "the second group") so that the two groups are treated as the same by virtue of subsection (3) of section 616, and

(*b*) the second group, together in pursuance of the said subsection (3) with the first group, is the relevant group,

then, except where subparagraph (7) applies, the members of the first group shall be treated for the purposes of this Schedule as having become members of the relevant group at that time, and not by virtue of the said subsection (3) at the times when they became members of the first group.

(7) This subparagraph applies where—

(*a*) the persons who immediately before the time when the principal company of the first group became a member of the second group owned the shares comprised in the issued share capital of the principal company of the first group are the same as the persons who, immediately after that time, owned the shares comprised in the issued share capital of the principal company of the relevant group, and

(*b*) the company which is the principal company of the relevant group immediately after that time—

(i) was not the principal company of any group immediately before that time, and

(ii) immediately after that time had assets consisting entirely, or almost entirely, of shares comprised in the issued share capital of the principal company of the first group.

(8) For the purposes of this Schedule—

(*a*) an asset (in this subparagraph referred to as "the first asset") acquired or held by a company at any time and an asset (in this subparagraph referred to as "the second asset") held at a later time by the company (or by any company which is or has been a member of the same group of companies as the company) shall be treated as the same asset if the value of the second asset is derived in whole or in part from the first asset, and

(*b*) where—

(i) an asset is treated (whether by virtue of clause (*a*) or otherwise) as the same as an asset held by a company at a later time, and

(ii) the first asset would have been a pre-entry asset in relation to the company,

the second asset shall also be treated as a pre-entry asset in relation to the company,

and clause (*a*) shall apply in particular where the second asset is a freehold and the first asset is a leasehold the lessee of which acquires the reversion.

(9) In determining for the purposes of this Schedule whether an allowable loss accruing to a company on a disposal under section 719 or 738(4)(*a*) is a loss that accrued before the company became a member of the relevant group, the provisions of section 720 or 738(4)(*b*), as the case may be, shall be disregarded.

Amendments

1 Substituted by FA 2001 s 40(1)(*a*) in relation to, where chargeable gains are to be included in a company's total profits, the amount to be included in respect of chargeable gains in the company's total profits for any accounting period ending on or after 15 February 2001, and in any other case, the amount on which a company is chargeable in accordance with s 31 for 2000–2001 and any later tax years. Where the question of whether a company was, at any time before 15 February 2001, a member of a group arises, it is determined by reference to TCA 1997 before its amendment by FA 2001; previously "by a company at the time immediately before the company became".

2 Subs (3A) inserted by FA 2001 s 40(1)(*b*) in relation to, where chargeable gains are to be included in a company's total profits, the amount to be included in respect of chargeable gains in the company's total profits for any accounting period ending on or after 15 February 2001, and in any other case, the amount on which a company is chargeable in accordance with s 31 for 2000–2001 and any later tax years. Where the question of whether a company was, at any time before 15 February 2001, a member of a group arises, it is determined by reference to the TCA 1997 before its amendment by FA 2001.

3 Substituted by FA 2001 s 40(1)(*c*) in relation to, where chargeable gains are to be included in a company's total profits, the amount to be included in respect of chargeable gains in the company's total profits for any accounting period ending on or after 15 February 2001, and in any other case, the amount on which a company is chargeable in accordance with s 31 for 2000–2001 and any later tax years. Where the question of whether a company was, at any time before 15 February 2001, a member of a group arises, it is determined by reference to the TCA 1997 before its amendment by FA 2001; previously "the company became a member of the relevant group".

4 Substituted by FA 2001 s 40(1)(*d*)(i) in relation to, where chargeable gains are to be included in a company's total profits, the amount to be included in respect of chargeable gains in the company's total profits for any accounting period ending on or after 15 February 2001, and in any other case, the amount on which a company is chargeable in accordance with s 31 for 2000–2001 and any later tax years. Where the question of whether a company was, at any time before 15 February 2001, a member of a group arises, it is determined by reference to the TCA 1997 before its amendment by FA 2001; previously "the company by reference to which the asset is a pre-entry asset became a member of the relevant group".

5 Substituted by FA 2001 s 40(1)(*d*)(ii) in relation to, where chargeable gains are to be included in a company's total profits, the amount to be included in respect of chargeable gains in the company's total profits for any accounting period ending on or after 15 February 2001, and in any other case, the amount on which a company is chargeable in accordance with s 31 for 2000–2001 and any later tax years. Where the question of whether a company was, at any time before 15 February 2001, a member of a group arises, it is determined by reference to the TCA 1997 before its amendment by FA 2001; previously "a company has become a member of the relevant group".

[6] Substituted by FA 2001 s 40(1)(*d*)(iii) in relation to, where chargeable gains are to be included in a company's total profits, the amount to be included in respect of chargeable gains in the company's total profits for any accounting period ending on or after 15 February 2001, and in any other case, the amount on which a company is chargeable in accordance with s 31 for 2000–2001 and any later tax years. Where the question of whether a company was, at any time before 15 February 2001, a member of a group arises, it is determined by reference to the TCA 1997 before its amendment by FA 2001; previously "a company became a member of the relevant group".

Calculation of pre-entry loss by reference to market value

2. (1) Where an allowable loss accrues on the disposal by a company of any pre-entry asset, the pre-entry proportion of that loss shall be whichever is the smaller of the amounts mentioned in subparagraph (2).

(2) The amounts referred to in subparagraph (1) are—

(*a*) the amount of the allowable loss which would have accrued if the asset had been disposed of at the relevant time at its market value at that time, and

(*b*) the amount of the allowable loss accruing on the disposal mentioned in subparagraph (1).

Gains from which pre-entry losses are to be deductible

3. (1) Notwithstanding section 78(2) a pre-entry loss that accrued to a company on a disposal before the company became a member of the relevant group shall only be deductible from a chargeable gain accruing to the company where the gain is one accruing—

(*a*) on a disposal made by the company before the date (in this paragraph referred to as "the entry date") on which the company became a member of the relevant group and made in the same accounting period in which the entry date falls,

(*b*) on the disposal of an asset which was held by the company immediately before the entry date, or

(*c*) on the disposal of an asset which—

(i) was acquired by the company on or after the entry date from a person who was not a member of the relevant group at the time of the acquisition, and

(ii) since its acquisition from the person has not been used or held for any purposes other than those of a trade which was being carried on by the company at the time immediately before the entry date and which continued to be carried on by the company until the disposal.

(2) Notwithstanding section 78(2) the pre-entry proportion of an allowable loss accruing to a company on the disposal of a pre-entry asset shall only be deductible from a chargeable gain accruing to the company where—

(*a*) the gain is one accruing on a disposal made by the company before the entry date and made in the same accounting period in which the entry date falls and the company is the one (in this subparagraph referred to as "the initial company") by reference to which the asset on the disposal of which the loss accrues is a pre-entry asset, (*b*) the pre-entry asset and the asset on the disposal of which the gain accrues were each held by the same company at a time immediately before the company became a member of the relevant group, or

(*c*) the gain is one accruing on the disposal of an asset which—

(i) was acquired by the initial company (whether before or after the initial company became a member of the relevant group) from a person who, at the time of the acquisition, was not a member of that group, and

(ii) since its acquisition from the person has not been used or held for any purposes other than those of a trade which was being carried on, immediately before the entry date, by the initial company and which continued to be carried on by the initial company until the disposal.

(3) Where 2 or more companies become members of the relevant group at the same time and those companies were all members of the same group of companies immediately before those companies became members of the relevant group, then—

(*a*) an asset shall be treated for the purposes of subparagraph (1)(*b*) as held, immediately before the company became a member of the relevant group, by the company to which the pre-entry loss in question accrued if the company is one of those companies and the asset was in fact so held by another of those companies,

(*b*) two or more assets shall be treated for the purposes of subparagraph (2)(*b*) as assets held by the same company immediately before the company became a member of the relevant group wherever they would be so treated if all those companies were treated as a single company, and

(*c*) the acquisition of an asset shall be treated for the purposes of subparagraphs (1)(*c*) and (2)(*c*) as an acquisition by the company to which the pre-entry loss in question accrued if the company is one of those companies and the asset was in fact acquired (whether before or after those companies became members of the relevant group) by another of those companies.

Change of a company's nature

4. (1) Where—

(*a*) within any period of 3 years, a company becomes a member of a group of companies and there is (either earlier or later in that period, or at the same time) a major change in the nature or conduct of a trade carried on by the company, or

(*b*) at any time after the scale of the activities in a trade carried on by a company has become small or negligible, and before any considerable revival of the trade, the company becomes a member of a group of companies,

the trade carried on before the change mentioned in clause (*a*), or, as the case may be, the trade mentioned in clause (*b*), shall be disregarded for the purposes of subparagraphs (1)(*c*) and (2)(*c*) of paragraph 3 in relation to any time before the company became a member of the group in question.

(2) In subparagraph (1) the reference to a major change in the nature or conduct of a trade includes a reference to—

(*a*) a major change in the type of property dealt in, or services or facilities provided, in the trade, or

(*b*) a major change in customers, markets or outlets of the trade,

and this paragraph shall apply even if the change is the result of a gradual process which began outside the period of 3 years mentioned in subparagraph (1)(*a*).

(3) Where the operation of this paragraph depends on circumstances or events at a time after the company becomes a member of a group of companies (but not more than 3 years after), an assessment to give effect to this paragraph shall not be out of time if made within 6 years from that time or the latest such time.

Companies changing groups on certain transfers of shares etc.

5. For the purposes of this Schedule, where—

(*a*) a company which is a member of a group of companies becomes at any time a member of another group of companies as the result of a disposal of shares in or other securities of the company or any other company, and

(*b*) that disposal is one on which, by virtue of any provision of the Tax Acts or the Capital Gains Tax Acts, neither a gain nor a loss would accrue,

this Schedule shall apply in relation to the losses that accrued to the company before that time and the assets held by the company at that time as if any time when the company was a member of the first group were included in the period during which the company is treated as having been a member of the second group.][1]

Amendments

[1] Sch 18A inserted by FA 1999 s 57 in respect of a company which becomes a member of a group of companies on or after 1 March 1999.

Definitions

allowable loss: ss 5(1), 546; Capital Gains Tax Acts: s 1(2); chargeable gain: ss 5(1), 545; company: ss 4(1); 5(1); group: s 616(1); person: IA 1937 s 11(*c*); principal company: s 616(1); Tax Acts: s 1(2); trade: ss 3(1), 4(1), 5(1); year: IA 1937 Sch.

[SCHEDULE 18B
Tonnage Tax

PART 1
MATTERS RELATING TO ELECTION FOR TONNAGE TAX

Method of making election

1. (1) A tonnage tax election shall be made by notice to the Revenue Commissioners.

(2) The notice shall contain such particulars and be supported by such evidence as the Revenue Commissioners may require.

When election may be made

2. (1) A tonnage tax election may be made at any time before the end of the period (in this Schedule referred to as the "initial period") of 36 months beginning on the commencement date.

(2) After the end of the initial period a tonnage tax election may only be made in the circumstances specified in subparagraphs (3) and (4) .

(3) (*a*) An election may be made after the end of the initial period in respect of a single company that becomes a qualifying company and has not previously been a qualifying company at any time on or after the commencement date.

(*b*) Any election under this subparagraph shall be made before the end of the period of 36 months beginning with the day on which the company became a qualifying company.

(4) (*a*) An election may be made after the end of the initial period in respect of a group of companies that becomes a qualifying group of companies by virtue of a member of the group becoming a qualifying company, not previously having been a qualifying company, at any time on or after the commencement date.

(*b*) This subparagraph shall not apply if the group of companies—

(i) was previously a qualifying group at any time on or after the commencement date, or

(ii) is substantially the same as a group that was previously a qualifying group of companies at any such time.

(*c*) An election under this subparagraph shall be made before the end of the period of 36 months beginning with the day on which the group of companies became a qualifying group of companies.

(5) This paragraph shall not prevent an election being made under Part 4.

(6) The Minister for Finance may by order provide for further periods within which a tonnage tax election may be made, and any such order may provide for this Part of this Schedule to apply, with any necessary modifications, as appears to the Minister to be appropriate in relation to such further periods as it applies in relation to the initial period.

When election takes effect

3. (1) Subject to this paragraph, a tonnage tax election shall have effect from the beginning of the accounting period in which it is made.

(2) A tonnage tax election shall not have effect in relation to an accounting period beginning before 1 January 2002, but where a tonnage tax election would have effect under subparagraph (1) for an accounting period beginning before 1 January 2002 the election shall have effect from the beginning of the accounting period following that in which it is made.

(3) The Revenue Commissioners may allow a tonnage tax election made before the end of the initial period to have effect from the beginning of an accounting period earlier than that in which it is made (but not one beginning before 1 January 2002).

(4) The Revenue Commissioners may allow a tonnage tax election made before the end of the initial period to have effect from the beginning of the accounting period following that in which it is made or, where the Revenue Commissioners determine that due to exceptional circumstances, unrelated to the avoidance or reduction of tax, it is commercially impracticable for the election to take effect, the beginning of the next following accounting period.

(5) In the case of a group election made in respect of a group of companies where the members have different accounting periods, subparagraph (1) or, if appropriate, subparagraph (3) or (4) shall apply in relation to each qualifying company by reference to that company's accounting periods.

(6) Subject to section 697E(4), a tonnage tax election under paragraph 2(3) or (4) shall have effect from the time at which the company in question became a qualifying company.

Period for which election is in force

4. (1) Subject to subparagraphs (2) and (3) and paragraph 6(3), a tonnage tax election shall remain in force until it expires at the end of the period of 10 years beginning—

(*a*) in the case of a company election, with the first day on which the election has effect in relation to the company, and

(*b*) in the case of a group election, with the first day on which the election has effect in relation to any member of the group.

(2) A tonnage tax election shall cease to be in force—

(*a*) in the case of a company election, if the company ceases to be a qualifying company, and

(*b*) in the case of a group election, if the group of companies ceases to be a qualifying group.

(3) A tonnage tax election may also cease to be in force under Part 4.

Effect of election ceasing to be in force

5. A tonnage tax election that ceases to be in force shall cease to have effect in relation to any company.

Renewal election

6. (1) At any time when a tonnage tax election is in force in respect of a single company or group of companies a further tonnage tax election (in Part 24A and this Schedule referred to as a "renewal election") may be made in respect of that company or group.

(2) Section 697D and paragraphs 1, 4 and 5 shall apply in relation to a renewal election as they apply in relation to an original tonnage tax election.

(3) A renewal election supersedes the existing tonnage tax election.

PART 2
MATTERS RELATING TO QUALIFYING SHIPS

Company temporarily ceasing to operate qualifying ships

7. (1) This paragraph shall apply where a company temporarily ceases to operate any qualifying ships.

(2) This paragraph shall not apply where a company continues to operate a ship that temporarily ceases to be a qualifying ship.

(3) If a company which temporarily ceases to operate any qualifying ships gives notice to the Revenue Commissioners stating—

(*a*) its intention to resume operating qualifying ships, and
(*b*) its wish to remain within tonnage tax,

the company shall be treated for the purposes of Part 24A and this Schedule as if it had continued to operate the qualifying ship or ships it operated immediately before the temporary cessation.

(4) The notice must be given on or before the specified return date for the chargeable period (within the meaning of Part 41) of the company in which the temporary cessation begins.

(5) This paragraph shall cease to apply if and when the company—

(*a*) abandons its intention to resume operating qualifying ships, or
(*b*) again in fact operates a qualifying ship.

Meaning of operating a ship

8. (1) Subject to this paragraph, a company is regarded for the purposes of Part 24A and this Schedule as operating any ship owned by, or chartered to, the company.

(2) (*a*) A company shall not be regarded as the operator of a ship where part only of the ship has been chartered to it.
(*b*) For the purpose of subparagraph *(a)*, a company shall not be taken as having part only of a ship chartered to it by reason only of the ship being chartered to it jointly with one or more other persons.

(3) Except as provided by subparagraphs (4) and (5), a company shall not be regarded as the operator of a ship that has been chartered out by it on bareboat charter terms.

(4) (*a*) A company shall be regarded as operating a ship that has been chartered out by it on bareboat charter terms if the person to whom it is chartered is not a third party.
(*b*) For the purpose of subparagraph *(a)*, a "third party" means—

(i) in the case of a single company, any other person,
(ii) in the case of a member of a group of companies—

(I) any member of the group that is not a tonnage tax company (and does not become a tonnage tax company by virtue of the ship being chartered to it), or
(II) any person who is not a member of the group.

(5) A company shall not be regarded as ceasing to operate a ship that has been chartered out by it on bareboat charter terms if—

(*a*) the ship is chartered out because of short-term over-capacity, and
(*b*) the term of the charter does not exceed 3 years.

(6) A company shall be regarded as operating a qualifying ship for the purposes of the activity described in paragraph (*j*) of the definition of "relevant shipping income" in section 697A if that company has entered contractual arrangements in relation to the

provision of ship management services for the qualifying ship for a stipulated period and the terms of those arrangements give the company—

(*a*) possession and control of the ship,
(*b*) control over the day to day management of the ship, including the right to appoint the master and crew and route planning,
(*c*) control over the technical management of the ship, including decisions on its repair and maintenance,
(*d*) control over the safety management of the ship, including ensuring that all necessary safety and survey certificates are current,
(*e*) control over the training of the officers and crew of the ship, and
(f) the management of the bunkering, victualling and provisioning of the ship,

and those terms are actually implemented for the period in which the company provides ship management services in respect of that ship.

Qualifying ship used as vessel of an excluded kind

9. (1) A qualifying ship that begins to be used as a vessel of an excluded kind ceases to be a qualifying ship when it begins to be so used, but if—

(*a*) a company operates a ship throughout an accounting period of the company, and
(*b*) in that period the ship is used as a vessel of an excluded kind on not more than 30 days, that use shall be disregarded in determining whether the ship is a qualifying ship at any time during that period.

(2) In the case of an accounting period shorter than a year, the figure of 30 days in subparagraph (1) shall be proportionately reduced.

(3) If a company operates a ship during part only of an accounting period of the company, subparagraph (1) shall apply as if for 30 days, or the number of days substituted by subparagraph (2), there were substituted the number of days that bear to the length of that part of the accounting period the same proportion that 30 days bears to a year.

PART 3
CAPITAL ALLOWANCES, BALANCING CHARGES AND RELATED MATTERS

Plant and machinery used wholly for tonnage tax trade

10. (1)(*a*)This subparagraph shall apply where, on a company's entry to tonnage tax, machinery or plant, in respect of which capital expenditure was incurred by the company before its entry into tonnage tax, is to be used wholly and exclusively for the purposes of the company's tonnage tax trade.

(*b*) Where this subparagraph applies—

(i) no balancing charge or balancing allowance shall be made under section 288 as a result of the machinery or plant concerned being used for the purposes of the company's tonnage tax trade,

(ii) any allowance attributable to the machinery or plant referred to in subparagraph *(a)* which, but for this clause, would have been made to the company under Part 9 or under any provision that is construed as one with that Part for any accounting period in which the company is a tonnage tax company shall not be made, and

(iii) section 287 shall not apply as respects any accounting period during which the machinery or plant has been used wholly and exclusively for the purposes of a company's tonnage tax trade.

(2) (*a*) This subparagraph shall apply where the machinery or plant referred to in subparagraph (1)*(a)* begins to be used wholly or partly for purposes other than those of the company's tonnage tax trade.

(*b*) Where this subparagraph applies and the asset begins to be wholly used for purposes other than the company's tonnage tax trade—

(i) no balancing allowance shall be made on the company under section 288(2) for any period in which the company is subject to tonnage tax,

(ii) for the purposes of making a balancing charge under section 288 on the happening of any of the events referred to in subsection (1) of that section—

(I) section 296 shall not apply as respects any accounting period of a company in which the company is subject to tonnage tax,

(II) where the event occurs at a time when the company is subject to tonnage tax, the amount of the capital expenditure of the company still unallowed at the time of the event shall, notwithstanding section 296, be the amount of the capital expenditure of the company on the provision of the machinery or plant which was still unallowed at the time the company's election into tonnage tax had effect, and

(III) where the event occurs at a time when the company is subject to tonnage tax, the references in section 288 to sale, insurance, salvage or compensation moneys and the reference in section 289(3)(*b*) to the open-market price of the machinery or plant shall be taken to be references to the least of—

(A) the actual cost to the company of the machinery or plant for the purpose of the trade carried on by the company,

(B) the price the machinery or plant would have fetched if sold in the open market at the time the company's election into tonnage tax had effect, and

(C) the sale, insurance, salvage or compensation moneys (within the meaning of Part 9) arising from the event or, where paragraph (*b*) of section 289(3) applies, the open-market price of the machinery or plant (within the meaning of that section) at the time of the event.

(*c*) Where this subparagraph applies and the asset begins to be partly used for purposes other than the company's tonnage tax trade—

(i) the machinery or plant shall be treated as 2 separate assets one in use wholly and exclusively for the purposes of the tonnage tax trade and the other in use wholly and exclusively for purposes other than the company's tonnage tax trade,

(ii) subparagraph (2)(*b*) shall apply in relation to the part of the asset treated by virtue of this subparagraph as in use wholly and exclusively for the purposes of the tonnage tax trade as it applies in relation to machinery or plant which begins to be used wholly for purposes other than the company's tonnage tax trade,

(iii) in determining the amount of any capital allowance or balancing charge, if any, to be made under Part 9 or under any other provision to be construed as one with that Part in relation to the part of the asset treated by virtue of this subparagraph as in use wholly and exclusively for purposes other than the company's tonnage tax trade regard shall be had to all relevant circumstances and, in particular, to the extent of the use, if any, of the machinery or plant for the purposes of a trade, and there shall be made to or on the company, in respect of that trade, an allowance of such an amount or a balancing charge of such an amount, as may be just and reasonable.

Plant and machinery used partly for purposes of tonnage tax trade

11. (1) This paragraph shall apply where, on a company's entry into tonnage tax, machinery or plant, in respect of which capital expenditure was incurred by the company before its entry into tonnage tax, is to be used partly for the purposes of the company's tonnage tax trade and partly for purposes other than the company's tonnage tax trade.

(2) Where this paragraph applies—

(*a*) the machinery or plant referred to in subparagraph (1) shall be treated as 2 separate assets one in use wholly and exclusively for the purposes of the tonnage tax trade and the other in use wholly and exclusively for the purposes of the other trade of the company,

(*b*) subject to clause (*c*), in determining the amount of—

(i) any capital allowance or balancing charge to be made in respect of that part of the asset treated as in use wholly and exclusively for purposes other than the company's tonnage tax trade under Part 9 or under any provision which is to be construed as one with that Part, or

(ii) the amount of any balancing charge to be made for the purpose of the tonnage tax trade under Part 9, or under any provision which is to be construed as one with that Part, as applied by this Schedule,

regard shall be had to all relevant circumstances and, in particular, to the extent of the use of the machinery or plant for the purposes of a trade other than the tonnage tax trade, and there shall be made to or on the company, in respect of that trade, an allowance of such an amount, or, in respect of both the tonnage tax trade and the other trade, a balancing charge of such an amount, as may be just and reasonable, and

(*c*) paragraph 10(1)(*b*) and paragraph 10(2)(*b*) shall apply in relation to the part of the asset treated by virtue of this paragraph as in use wholly and exclusively for the purposes of the tonnage tax trade as they apply in relation to the machinery or plant referred to in paragraph 10(1)(*a*).

Plant and machinery: new expenditure partly for tonnage tax purposes

12. (1) This paragraph shall apply where a company subject to tonnage tax incurs capital expenditure on the provision of machinery or plant partly for the purposes of its tonnage tax trade and partly for the purposes of another trade carried on by the company.

(2) Where this paragraph applies the machinery or plant shall be treated as 2 separate assets one in use wholly and exclusively for the purposes of the tonnage tax trade and the other in use wholly and exclusively for the purposes of the other trade of the company and, in determining the amount of any capital allowance, or the amount of any charge to be made, under Part 9 or under any provision which is to be construed as one with that Part in the case of that part of the asset treated as a separate asset for the purposes of the other trade of the company, regard shall be had to all relevant circumstances and, in particular, to the extent of the use of the machinery or plant for the purposes of the other trade, and there shall be made to or on the company, in respect of the other trade, an allowance of such an amount, or a charge of such an amount, as may be just and reasonable.

Plant and machinery: change of use of tonnage tax asset

13. (1) This paragraph shall apply where, at a time when a company is subject to tonnage tax, machinery or plant acquired after the company became so subject and which is used wholly and exclusively for the purposes of the company's tonnage tax trade begins to be used wholly or partly for purposes of another trade.

(2) Where this paragraph applies—

(*a*) if the asset begins to be used wholly for purposes of another trade the provisions of Part 9 shall apply as if capital expenditure had been incurred by the person carrying on the other trade on the provision of the plant or machinery for the purposes of that trade in that person's chargeable period (within the meaning of Part 9) in which the plant or machinery is brought into use for those purposes, and the amount of that expenditure shall be taken as the lesser of—

(i) the amount of the capital expenditure actually incurred by the person, and

(ii) the price which the machinery or plant would have fetched if sold on the open market on the date on which it was so brought into use, and

(*b*) if the asset begins to be used partly for purposes of another trade of the company and partly for the purposes of the tonnage tax trade—

(i) the machinery or plant shall be treated as 2 separate assets one in use wholly and exclusively for the purposes of the tonnage tax trade and the other in use wholly and exclusively for the purposes of the other trade of the company,

(ii) Part 9 shall apply as if the company had incurred capital expenditure on the provision of that part of the asset treated as in use wholly and exclusively for the other trade of the company in the accounting period of the company in which that part of the asset is brought into use for those purposes, and

(iii) in determining the amount of any capital expenditure incurred on the provision of that part of the asset treated as in use as a separate asset for the purposes of the other trade of the company regard shall be had to all relevant circumstances as is just and reasonable.

Plant and machinery: change of use of non-tonnage tax asset

14. (1) This paragraph shall apply where, at a time when a company is subject to tonnage tax, plant or machinery wholly and exclusively used for the purposes of another trade carried on by the company not being a tonnage tax trade begins to be used wholly or partly for the purposes of the company's tonnage tax trade.

(2) Where this paragraph applies and the asset begins to be wholly used for the purposes of the company's tonnage tax trade—

(*a*) no balancing allowance or balancing charge shall be made as a consequence of the change in use, and

(*b*) for the purposes of making a balancing charge under section 288 on the happening subsequent to the change in use of any of the events referred to in subsection (1) of that section—

(i) section 296 shall not apply as respects any accounting period of the company in which the asset is used wholly and exclusively for the purposes of the company's tonnage tax trade,

(ii) where the event occurs at a time when the asset is so used, the amount of the capital expenditure of the company still unallowed at the time of the event shall, notwithstanding section 296, be the amount of the capital expenditure of the company on the provision of the machinery or plant which was still unallowed at the time the asset began to be so used, and

(iii) where the event occurs at a time when the asset is so used, the references in section 288 to sale, insurance, salvage or compensation moneys and the reference in section 289(3)(*b*) to the open-market value of the machinery or plant shall be taken to be references to the least of—

(I) the actual cost to the company of the machinery or plant for the purpose of the trade carried on by the company,

(II) the price the machinery or plant would have fetched if sold in the open market at the time the asset began to be so used, and

(III) the sale, insurance, salvage or compensation moneys (within the meaning of Part 9) arising on the event or, where paragraph (*b*) of section 289(3) applies, the open-market price of the machinery or plant (within the meaning of that section) at the time of the event.

(3) Where this paragraph applies and the asset begins to be partly used for the purposes of the company's tonnage tax trade—

(*a*) the machinery or plant referred to in subparagraph (1) shall be treated as 2 separate assets one in use wholly and exclusively for the purposes of the other trade of the company and the other in use wholly and exclusively for the purposes of the tonnage tax trade of the company,

(*b*) no balancing charge or balancing allowance shall be made in respect of the part treated as in use wholly and exclusively for the purposes of the tonnage tax trade as a consequence of the change in use, (*c*) subparagraph (2)(*b*) shall apply in relation to the part of the asset treated by virtue of this subparagraph as in use wholly and exclusively for the purposes of the tonnage tax trade as it applies in relation to the machinery or plant wholly used for the purposes of the company's tonnage tax trade.

Plant and machinery: provisions relating to balancing charges

15. (1) A balancing charge arising under Part 9 as applied by this Schedule or under this Schedule shall—

(*a*) be treated as arising in connection with a trade carried on by the company other than the company's tonnage tax trade, and

(*b*) be made in taxing that trade.

(2) Subject to paragraph 16 or 17, the charge shall be given effect in the accounting period in which it arises.

(3) On the first occasion of the happening of an event which gives rise to a balancing charge (including such an event arising in respect of more than one asset on the same date) under Part 9 as applied by this Schedule, or under this Schedule, on a tonnage tax company, the tonnage tax company shall by notice in writing to the Revenue Commissioners elect for relief against that charge under either paragraph 16 or, if applicable, paragraph 17 but not for relief under both, and any such election shall be irrevocable and be included in the company's return under section 951 for the accounting period in which the charge arises.

(4) Where a balancing charge arises on a tonnage tax company under Part 9 as applied by this Schedule or under this Schedule subsequent to any charge on the company such as is referred to in subparagraph (3), relief against that charge shall only be available under the paragraph for which the company elected for relief in accordance with that subparagraph.

(5) Relief under paragraph 16 or 17 shall not be available to a company unless the company has made an election under subparagraph (3).

Reduction in balancing charge by reference to time in tonnage tax

16. The amount of any balancing charge under Part 9 as applied by this Schedule or under this Schedule shall be reduced by 20 per cent of the amount of the charge for each whole year in which the company on which the charge is to be made has been subject to tonnage tax calculated by reference to the time of the event giving rise to the charge.

Set-off of accrued losses against balancing charge

17. Where a balancing charge under Part 9 as applied by this Schedule or under this Schedule arises in connection with the disposal of a qualifying ship, then the company may set off against any balancing charge so arising any losses (including any losses referable to capital allowances treated by virtue of section 307 or 308 as trading expenses of the company) which accrued to the company before its entry to tonnage tax and which are attributable to—

(*a*) activities which under tonnage tax became part of the company's tonnage tax trade, or (*b*) a source of income which under tonnage tax becomes relevant shipping income.

Deferment of balancing charge on re-investment

18. (1) Where—

(*a*) a balancing charge under Part 9 as applied by this Schedule arises in connection with the disposal of a qualifying ship, and

(*b*) within the period beginning on the date the company's election for tonnage tax takes effect and ending 5 years after the date of the event giving rise to the balancing charge, the company or another qualifying company which is a member of the same tonnage tax group as the company incurs capital expenditure on the provision of one or more other qualifying ships (in this paragraph referred to as the "new asset"),

then

(i) if the amount on which the charge would have been made, as reduced under paragraph 16 or 17, if applicable, is greater than the capital expenditure on providing the new asset, the balancing charge shall be made only on an amount equal to the difference, and

(ii) if the capital expenditure on providing the new asset is equal to or greater than the amount on which the charge would have been made, as reduced under paragraph 16 or 17, if applicable, the balancing charge shall not be made.

(2) Where an event referred to in section 288(1) occurs in relation to the new asset in the period in which the company which incurs the expenditure on the new asset is subject to tonnage tax then a balancing charge shall be made under this paragraph on that company.

(3) Subject to any reduction under paragraph 16 or 17 and to any further application of this paragraph, the amount of the charge referred to in subparagraph (2) shall be—

(*a*) where subparagraph (1)(i) applies, the difference between the balancing charge which, but for subparagraph (1), would have been made on the disposal referred to in subparagraph (1) and the actual charge made,

(*b*) where subparagraph (1)(ii) applies, the amount of the charge which, but for subparagraph (1), would have been made on the disposal referred to in that subparagraph.

(4) Section 290 shall not apply in relation to balancing charges to which this paragraph applies.

(5) For the purposes of subparagraph (1), where machinery or plant is let to a tonnage tax company on the terms of that company being bound to maintain the machinery or plant and deliver it over in good condition at the end of the lease, and if the burden of the wear and tear on the machinery or plant will in fact fall directly on the company, then the capital expenditure on the provision of the machinery and plant shall be deemed to have been incurred by that company and the machinery and plant shall be deemed to belong to that company.

Exit: plant and machinery

19. (1) Where a company leaves tonnage tax the amount of capital expenditure incurred on the provision of machinery or plant in respect of each asset used by the company for the purposes of its tonnage tax trade which asset was acquired at a time the company was subject to tonnage tax and held by the company at the time it leaves tonnage tax shall be deemed to be the lesser of—

(*a*) the capital expenditure actually incurred by the company on the provision of that machinery or plant for the purposes of the company's tonnage tax trade, and

(*b*) the price the machinery or plant would have fetched if sold in the open market at the date the company leaves tonnage tax.

(2) For the purposes of the making of allowances and charges under Part 9 or any provision construed as one with that Part, the capital expenditure on the provision of the machinery or plant as determined in accordance with subparagraph (1) shall be deemed to have been incurred on the day immediately following the date the company leaves tonnage tax.

(3) (*a*) This subparagraph applies where a company—

(i) leaves tonnage tax having incurred expenditure on the provision of machinery or plant for the purposes of a trade carried on by the company before entry into tonnage tax,

(ii) has used that machinery or plant for the purposes of its tonnage tax trade,

(iii) has been denied allowances in respect of that machinery or plant by virtue of section 697O and the provisions of paragraph 10(1)(*b*)(ii) or paragraph 11(2)(*c*), and

(iv) on leaving tonnage tax starts, recommences or continues to use that machinery or plant for the purposes of a trade carried on by it.

(*b*) Subject to clauses (*c*) and (*d*), where this subparagraph applies any allowance which, but for section 697O and paragraph 10(1)(*b*) or 11(2)(*c*), would have been made under Part 9 or any provision construed as one with that Part to the company for any accounting period in which it was subject to tonnage tax shall, subject to compliance with that Part, be made instead for such accounting periods immediately after the company leaves tonnage tax as will ensure, subject to that Part, that all such allowances are made to the company in those accounting periods as would have been made to the company in respect of that machinery or plant if the company had never been subject to tonnage tax.

(*c*) No wear and tear allowance shall be made by virtue of this subparagraph in respect of any machinery or plant for any accounting period of a company if such allowance when added to the allowances in respect of that machinery or plant made to that company for any previous accounting period will make the aggregate amount of the allowances exceed the actual cost to that company of the machinery or plant, including in that actual cost any expenditure in the nature of capital expenditure on the machinery or plant by means of renewal, improvement or reinstatement.

(*d*) A wear and tear allowance in respect of any machinery or plant made by virtue of this subparagraph for any accounting period shall not exceed the amount appropriate to that machinery or plant as set out in section 284(2).

Industrial buildings

20. (1) Where any identifiable part of a building or structure is used for the purposes of a company's tonnage tax trade, that part is treated for the purposes of Chapter 1 of Part 9 as used otherwise than as an industrial building or structure.

(2) (*a*) This subparagraph applies where, in an accounting period during which a company is subject to tonnage tax, an event giving rise to a balancing charge occurs in relation to an industrial building or structure in respect of which capital expenditure was incurred by the company before its entry into tonnage tax.

(*b*) Where this subparagraph applies—

(i) the sale, insurance, salvage or compensation moneys to be brought into account in respect of any industrial building or structure shall be limited to the market value of the relevant interest when the company entered tonnage tax, and

(ii) the amount of any balancing charge under that Part shall, subject to subparagraphs (3) to (5) of paragraph 15, be reduced in accordance with paragraph 16 or 17, as appropriate.

(3) Where a company subject to tonnage tax disposes of the relevant interest in an industrial building or structure, section 277 shall apply to determine the residue of expenditure in the hands of the person who acquires the relevant interest, as if—

(*a*) the company had not been subject to tonnage tax, and

(*b*) all writing-down allowances, and balancing allowances and charges, had been made as could have been made if the company had not been subject to tonnage tax.

(4) Where a company leaves tonnage tax the amount of capital expenditure qualifying for relief under Chapter 1 of Part 9 shall be determined as if—

(*a*) the company had never been subject to tonnage tax, and

(*b*) all such allowances and charges under that Part had been made as could have been made.

PART 4
GROUPS, MERGERS AND RELATED MATTERS

Company not to be treated as member of more than one group

21. (1) Where a company is a member of both a tonnage tax group and a non-tonnage tax group which if a group election had been made would have been a tonnage tax group (in this paragraph referred to as a qualifying non-tonnage tax group), the company shall be treated as a member of the tonnage tax group and not of the qualifying non-tonnage tax group.

(2) Where a company is a member of 2 tonnage tax groups, the company shall be treated as a member of the group whose tonnage tax election was made first and not of the other

tonnage tax group. In the case of group elections made at the same time, the company shall choose which election it joins in and for the purposes of Part 24A and this Schedule the company shall be treated as a member of the group in respect of which that election is made and not of any other tonnage tax group.

Arrangements for dealing with group matters

22. (1) The Revenue Commissioners may enter into arrangements with the qualifying companies in a group for one of those companies to deal on behalf of the group in relation to matters arising under Part 24A and this Schedule that may conveniently be dealt with on a group basis.

(2) Any such arrangements—

(*a*) may make provision in relation to cases where companies become or cease to be members of a group;

(*b*) may make provision for or in connection with the termination of the arrangements; and

(*c*) may make such supplementary, incidental, consequential or transitional provision as is necessary or expedient for the purposes of the arrangements.

(3) Any such arrangements shall not affect—

(*a*) any requirement under Part 24A and this Schedule that an election be made jointly by all the qualifying companies in the group; or

(*b*) any liability under Part 24A, this Schedule or any other provision of the Tax Acts of a company to which the arrangements relate.

Meaning of "merger" and "demerger"

23. (1) In this Schedule—

"merger" means a transaction by which one or more companies become members of a group, and

"demerger" means a transaction by which one or more companies cease to be members of a group.

(2) References to a merger to which a group is a party include any merger affecting a member of the group.

Merger: between tonnage tax groups or companies

24. (1) This paragraph shall apply where there is a merger—

(*a*) between 2 or more tonnage tax groups,

(*b*) between one or more tonnage tax groups and one or more tonnage tax companies, or

(*c*) between two or more tonnage tax companies.

(2) Where this paragraph applies the group resulting from the merger is a tonnage tax group as if a group election had been made.

(3) The deemed election referred to in subparagraph (2) continues in force, subject to the provisions of this Part, until whichever of the existing tonnage tax elections had the longest period left to run would have expired.

Merger: tonnage tax group/company and qualifying non-tonnage tax group/ company

25. (1) This paragraph shall apply where there is a merger between a tonnage tax group or company and a qualifying non-tonnage tax group or company.

(2) Where this paragraph applies the group resulting from the merger may elect that—

(*a*) it be treated as if a group election had been made which deemed election shall continue in force until the original election made by the tonnage tax group or company would have expired, or

(*b*) the tonnage tax election of the group or company ceases to be in force as from the date of the merger.

(3) Any election under subparagraph (2) shall be made jointly by all the qualifying companies in the group resulting from the merger and by way of notice in writing to the Revenue Commissioners within 12 months of the merger.

Merger: tonnage tax group or company and non-qualifying group or company

26. (1) This paragraph shall apply where there is a merger between a tonnage tax group or company and a non-qualifying group or company.

(2) Where this subsection applies the group resulting from the merger is a tonnage tax group by virtue of the election of the tonnage tax group or company.

Merger: non-qualifying group or company and qualifying non-tonnage tax group or company

27. (1) This paragraph shall apply where there is a merger between a non-qualifying group or company and a qualifying non-tonnage tax group or company.

(2) Where this paragraph applies, the group resulting from the merger may make a tonnage tax election having effect as from the date of the merger.

(3) Any such election shall be made jointly by all the qualifying companies in the group resulting from the merger, by notice in writing to the Revenue Commissioners, within 12 months of the merger.

Demerger: single company

28. (1) This paragraph shall apply where a tonnage tax company ceases to be a member of a tonnage tax group and does not become a member of another group.

(2) Where this paragraph applies—

(*a*) the company in question remains a tonnage tax company as if a single company election had been made, and

(*b*) that deemed election continues in force, subject to the provisions of this Schedule, until the group election would have expired.

(3) If 2 or more members of the previous group remain, and any of them is a qualifying company, the group consisting of those companies shall be a tonnage tax group by virtue of the previous group election.

Demerger: group

29. (1) This paragraph shall apply where a tonnage tax group splits into two or more groups.

(2) Where this paragraph applies each new group that contains a qualifying company that was a tonnage tax company before the demerger shall be a tonnage tax group as if a group election had been made.

(3) That deemed election continues in force, subject to the provisions of this Schedule, until the group election would have expired.

Duty to notify Revenue Commissioners of group changes

30. (1) A tonnage tax company that becomes or ceases to be a member of a group, or of a particular group, shall give notice in writing to the Revenue Commissioners of that fact.

(2) The notice shall be given within the period of 12 months beginning with the date on which the company became or ceased to be a member of the group.

PART 5
MISCELLANEOUS AND SUPPLEMENTAL

Measurement of tonnage of ship

31. (1) References in Part 24A and in this Schedule to the gross or net tonnage of a ship are to that tonnage as determined—

(*a*) in the case of a vessel of 24 metres in length or over, in accordance with the IMO International Convention on Tonnage Measurement of Ships 1969;

(*b*) in the case of a vessel under 24 metres in length, in accordance with tonnage regulations.

(2) A ship shall not be treated as a qualifying ship for the purposes of this Part and this Schedule unless there is in force—

(*a*) a valid International Tonnage Certificate (1969), or

(*b*) a valid certificate recording its tonnage as measured in accordance with tonnage regulations.

(3) In this paragraph "tonnage regulations" means regulations under section 91 of the Mercantile Marine Act, 1955 or the provisions of the law of a country or territory outside the State corresponding to those regulations.

Second or subsequent application of sections 697P and 697Q

32. Where sections 697P and 697Q apply on a second or subsequent occasion on which a company ceases to be a tonnage tax company (whether or not those sections applied on any of the previous occasions)—

(*a*) the references to the company ceasing to be a tonnage tax company shall be read as references to the last occasion on which it did so, and

(*b*) the references to the period during which the company was a tonnage tax company do not include any period before its most recent entry into tonnage tax.

Appeals

33. Where in Part 24A and in this Schedule there is provision for the determination of any matter on a just and reasonable basis and it is not possible for the company concerned and the appropriate inspector (within the meaning of section 950) to agree on what is just and reasonable in the circumstances then there shall be the right of appeal to the Appeal Commissioners in the like manner as an appeal would lie against an assessment to corporation tax and the provisions of the Tax Acts relating to appeals shall apply accordingly.

Delegation of powers and functions

34. The Revenue Commissioners may nominate any of their officers to perform any acts and discharge any functions authorised by Part 24A or this Schedule to be performed or discharged by the Revenue Commissioners.][1].

Amendments

[1] Schedule 18B inserted by FA 2002 s 53(2) with effect from such day as the Minister for Finance may by order appoint.

Cross-references

Application: s 697B.
Capital allowances, general: s 697O; Pt 3: s 697O(3).
Election for tonnage tax: s 697D(1); Pt I: s 697D(4).
Interpretation (Pt 24A): s 697A(3), (4); para 4: s 697A(1)("initial period").
Penalties, para 30: Sch 29, column 2.
Requirement not to enter into tax avoidance arrangements: s 697F(2); para 22: s 697F(3)(*b*).
Requirement that not more than 75 per cent of fleet tonnage is chartered in: s 697E(1); para 22: s 697E(7)(*a*).
Ten year disqualification from re-entry into tonnage tax, Pt 4: s 697Q(3).
Withdrawal of relief on company leaving tonnage tax, paras 16 and 17: s 697P(5).

Definitions

Appeal Commissioners: s 2(1); bareboat charter terms: s 697A(1); company: s 4(1); company election, commencement date, group election, group of companies, qualifying company, qualifying group, qualifying ship: s 697A(1); Tax Acts: s 1(2); tonnage tax, tonnage tax company, tonnage tax election, tonnage tax group, tonnage tax trade: s 697A(1); trade: ss 3(1), 4(1); relevant shipping income, renewal election: s 697A(1); writing: IA 1937 Sch

SCHEDULE 19
Offshore Funds: Distributing Funds

[Section 744]

PART 1
THE DISTRIBUTION TEST

Requirements as to Distributions

1. (1) For the purposes of Chapter 2 of Part 27, an offshore fund pursues a full distribution policy with respect to an account period if—

(*a*) a distribution is made for the account period or for some other period which in whole or in part falls within that account period,

(*b*) subject to Part 2 of this Schedule, the amount of the distribution which is paid to the holders of material and other interests in the fund—

(i) represents at least 85 per cent of the income of the fund for the period, and

(ii) is not less than 85 per cent of the fund's Irish equivalent profits for the period,

(*c*) the distribution is made during the account period or not more than 6 months after the expiry of that period, and

(*d*) the form of the distribution is such that, if any sum forming part of it were received in the State by a person resident in the State and did not form part of the profits of a trade, profession or vocation, that sum would be chargeable to tax under Case III of Schedule D,

and any reference in this subparagraph to a distribution made for an account period includes a reference to any 2 or more distributions so made or, in the case of clause (*b*), the aggregate of those distributions.

(2) Subject to subparagraph (3), with respect to any account period for which—

(*a*) there is no income of the fund, and

(*b*) there are no Irish equivalent profits of the fund,

the fund shall be treated as pursuing a full distribution policy notwithstanding that no distribution is made as mentioned in subparagraph (1).

(3) For the purposes of Chapter 2 of Part 27, an offshore fund shall be regarded as not pursuing a full distribution policy with respect to an account period for which the fund does not make up accounts.

(4) For the purposes of this paragraph—

(*a*) where a period for which an offshore fund makes up accounts includes the whole or part of 2 or more account periods of the fund, then, subject to clause (*c*), income shown in those accounts shall be apportioned between those account periods on a time basis according to the number of days in each account period comprised in the period for which the accounts are made up,

(*b*) where a distribution is made for a period which includes the whole or part of 2 or more account periods of the fund, then, subject to subparagraph (5), the distribution shall be apportioned between those account periods on a time basis according to the number of days in each account period which are comprised in the period for which the distribution is made,

(*c*) where a distribution is made out of specified income but is not made for a specified period, that income shall be attributed to the account period of the fund in which it in fact arose and the distribution shall be treated as made for that account period, and

(*d*) where a distribution is made neither for a specified period nor out of specified income, then, subject to subparagraph (5), the distribution shall be treated as made for the last account period of the fund which ended before the distribution was made.

(5) Where but for this subparagraph the amount of a distribution made, or treated by virtue of subparagraph (4) as made, for an account period would exceed the income of that period, then, for the purposes of this paragraph—

(*a*) if the amount of the distribution was determined by apportionment under subparagraph (4)(*b*), the excess shall be reapportioned, as may be just and reasonable, to any other account period which, in whole or in part, falls within the period for which the distribution was made or, if there is more than one such period, between those periods, and

(*b*) subject to clause (*a*), the excess shall be treated as an additional distribution or series of additional distributions made for preceding account periods in respect of which the distributions or the aggregate distributions, as the case may be, would otherwise be less than the income of the period, applying the excess to later account periods before earlier ones until it is exhausted.

(6) In any case where—

(*a*) for a period which is or includes an account period an offshore fund is subject to any restriction as regards the making of distributions, being a restriction imposed by the law of any territory, and

(*b*) the fund is subject to that restriction by reason of an excess of losses over profits (applying the concept of **"profits"** and **"losses"** in the sense in which, and to the extent to which, they are relevant for the purposes of the law in question),

then, in determining for the purposes of subparagraphs (1) to (5) the amount of the fund's income for that account period, there shall be allowed as a deduction any amount which apart from this subparagraph would form part of the income of the fund for that account period and which may not be distributed by virtue of the restriction.

Funds Operating Equalisation Arrangements

2. (1) In the case of an offshore fund which throughout any account period operates equalisation arrangements, on any occasion in that period when there is a disposal to which this subparagraph applies, the fund shall be treated for the purposes of this Part of this Schedule as making a distribution of an amount equal to so much of the consideration for the disposal as, in accordance with this paragraph, represents income accrued to the date of the disposal.

(2) Subparagraph (1) shall apply to a disposal—

(*a*) which is a disposal of a material interest in the offshore fund concerned,

(*b*) which is a disposal to which Chapter 2 of Part 27 applies (whether by virtue of subsection (3) of section 742 or otherwise) or is one to which that Chapter would apply if subsections (5) and (6) of that section applied generally and not only for the purpose of determining whether, by virtue of subsection (3) of that section, there is a disposal to which that Chapter applies,

(*c*) which is not a disposal with respect to which the conditions in subsection (4) of section 742 are fulfilled, and

(*d*) which is a disposal to the fund itself or to the persons concerned in the management of the fund (in this paragraph referred to as **"the managers of the fund"**) in their capacity as such.

(3) On a disposal to which subparagraph (1) applies, the part of the consideration which represents income accrued to the date of the disposal shall be, subject to subparagraph (4) and paragraph 4(4), the amount which would be credited to the equalisation account of the offshore fund concerned in respect of accrued income if on the date of the

disposal the material interest disposed of were acquired by another person by means of initial purchase.

(4) Where, after the beginning of the period by reference to which the accrued income referred to in subparagraph (3) is calculated, the material interest disposed of by a disposal to which subparagraph (1) applies was acquired by means of initial purchase (whether or not by the person making the disposal), then—

(*a*) the amount which on that acquisition was credited to the equalisation account in respect of accrued income shall be deducted from the amount which in accordance with subparagraph (3) would represent income accrued to the date of the disposal, and

(*b*) if in that period there has been more than one such acquisition of that material interest by means of initial purchase, the deduction to be made under this subparagraph shall be the amount so credited to the equalisation account on the latest such acquisition before the disposal in question.

(5) Where by virtue of this paragraph an offshore fund is treated for the purposes of this Part of this Schedule as making a distribution on the occasion of a disposal, the distribution shall be treated for those purposes as—

(*a*) complying with paragraph 1(1)(*d*),

(*b*) made out of the income of the fund for the account period in which the disposal occurs, and

(*c*) paid immediately before the disposal to the person who was then the holder of the interest disposed of.

(6) In any case where—

(*a*) a distribution in respect of an interest in an offshore fund is made to the managers of the fund,

(*b*) their holding of that interest is in their capacity as such, and

(*c*) at the time of the distribution the fund is operating equalisation arrangements,

then, the distribution shall not be taken into account for the purposes of paragraph 1(1) except to the extent that the distribution is properly referable to that part of the period for which the distribution is made during which that interest has been held by the managers of the fund in their capacity as such.

(7) Subsection (2) of section 742 shall apply for the purposes of this paragraph as it applies for the purposes of that section.

Income Taxable under Case III of Schedule D

3. (1) Subparagraph (2) shall apply if any sums which form part of the income of an offshore fund within paragraph (*b*) or (*c*) of section 743(1) are of such a nature that—

(*a*) the holders of interests in the fund who are either companies resident in the State or individuals domiciled and resident in the State—

(i) are chargeable to tax under Case III of Schedule D in respect of such of those sums as are referable to their interests, or

(ii) if any of that income is derived from assets in the State, would be so chargeable had the assets been outside the State,

and

(*b*) the holders of interests, who are not such companies or individuals, would be chargeable as mentioned in subclause (i) or (ii) of clause (*a*) if they were resident in the State or, in the case of individuals, if they were domiciled and both resident and ordinarily resident in the State.

(2) To the extent that sums within subparagraph (1) do not actually form part of a distribution complying with clauses (*c*) and (*d*) of paragraph 1(1), they shall be treated for the purposes of this Part of this Schedule—

(*a*) as a distribution complying with those clauses and made out of the income of which they form part, and

(*b*) as paid to the holders of the interests to which they are referable.

Commodity Income

4. (1) In this paragraph—

"commodities" means tangible assets (other than currency, securities, debts or other assets of a financial nature) dealt with on a commodity exchange in any part of the world;

"dealing", in relation to dealing in commodities, includes dealing by means of futures contracts and traded options.

(2) To the extent that the income of an offshore fund for any account period includes profits from dealing in commodities, 50 per cent of those profits shall be disregarded in determining for the purposes of paragraphs 1(1)(*b*) and 5—

(*a*) the income of the fund for that period, and

(*b*) the fund's Irish equivalent profits for that period;

but in any account period in which an offshore fund incurs a loss in dealing in commodities the amount of that loss shall not be varied by virtue of this paragraph.

(3) Where the income of an offshore fund for any account period consists of profits from dealing in commodities and other income, then—

(*a*) in determining whether the condition in paragraph 1(1)(*b*) is fulfilled with respect to that account period, the expenditure of the fund shall be apportioned in such manner as is just and reasonable between the profits from dealing in commodities and the other income, and

(*b*) in determining whether and to what extent any expenditure is deductible under section 83 in computing the fund's Irish equivalent profits for that period, so much of the business of the fund as does not consist of dealing in commodities shall be treated as a business carried on by a separate company.

(4) Where there is a disposal to which paragraph 2(1) applies, then, to the extent that any amount which was or would be credited to the equalisation account in respect of accrued income, as mentioned in subparagraph (3) or (4) of paragraph 2, represents profits from dealing in commodities, 50 per cent of that accrued income shall be disregarded in determining under those subparagraphs the part of the consideration for the disposal which represents income accrued to the date of the disposal.

Irish Equivalent Profits

5. (1) In this paragraph, **"profits"** does not include chargeable gains.

(2) A reference in this Schedule to the Irish equivalent profits of an offshore fund for an account period shall be construed as a reference to the amount which, on the assumptions in subparagraph (3), would be the total profits of the fund for that period on which, after allowing for any deductions available against those profits, corporation tax would be chargeable.

(3) The assumptions referred to in subparagraph (2) are that—

(*a*) the offshore fund is a company which in the account period is resident in the State,

(*b*) the account period is an accounting period of that company, and

(*c*) any dividends or distributions which by virtue of section 129 should be disregarded in computing income for corporation tax purposes are nevertheless to be taken into account in that computation in the like manner as if they were dividends or distributions of a company resident outside the State.

(4) Without prejudice to any deductions available apart from this subparagraph, the deductions referred to in subparagraph (2) include—

(*a*) a deduction equal to any amount which by virtue of paragraph 1(6) is allowed as a deduction in determining the income of the fund for the account period in question,

(*b*) a deduction equal to any amount of Irish income tax paid by deduction or otherwise by, and not repaid to, the offshore fund in respect of the income of the account period, and

(*c*) a deduction equal to any amount of tax (paid under the law of a territory outside the State) taken into account as a deduction in determining the income of the fund for the account period in question but which, because it is referable to capital rather than income, is not to be taken into account by virtue of section 71(1) or 77(6);

but section 2(4) shall be disregarded for the purposes of clause (*b*).

(5) For the avoidance of doubt it is hereby declared that, if any sums forming part of the offshore fund's income for any period have been received by the fund without any deduction of or charge to tax by virtue of section 43, 49, 50 or 63, the effect of the assumption in subparagraph (3)(*a*) is that those sums are to be taken into account in determining the total profits referred to in subparagraph (2).

PART 2
MODIFICATIONS OF CONDITIONS FOR CERTIFICATION IN CERTAIN CASES

Exclusion of Investments in Distributing Offshore Funds

6. (1) In this Part of this Schedule, an offshore fund within subparagraph (2)(*c*) is referred to as a **"qualifying fund"**.

(2) In any case where—

(*a*) in an account period of an offshore fund (in this Part of this Schedule referred to as **"the primary fund"**), the assets of the fund consist of or include interests in another offshore fund,

(*b*) those interests (together with other interests which the primary fund may have) are such that, by virtue of paragraph (*a*) of subsection (3) of section 744 or, if the other fund concerned is a company, paragraph (*b*) or (*c*) of that subsection, the primary fund could not apart from this paragraph be certified as a distributing fund in respect of the account period, and

(*c*) without regard to this paragraph, that other fund could be certified as a distributing fund in respect of its account period or, as the case may be, each of its account periods which comprises the whole or any part of the account period of the primary fund,

then, in determining whether in section 744(3) (other than paragraph (*d*)) anything prevents the primary fund being certified as mentioned in clause (*b*), the interests of the primary fund in that other fund shall be disregarded except for the purposes of determining the total value of the assets of the primary fund.

(3) In a case within subparagraph (2)—

(*a*) section 744(3) (other than paragraph (*d*)) shall apply in relation to the primary fund with the modification in paragraph 7 (in addition to that provided for by subparagraph (2)), and

(*b*) Part 1 of this Schedule shall apply in relation to the primary fund with the modification in paragraph 8.

7. The modification referred to in paragraph 6(3)(*a*) is that in any case where—

(*a*) at any time in the account period referred to in paragraph 6(2), the assets of the primary fund include an interest in an offshore fund or in any company (whether an offshore fund or not),

(*b*) that interest is to be taken into account in determining whether in section 744(3) (other than paragraph (*d*)) anything prevents the primary fund being certified as a distributing fund in respect of that account period, and

(*c*) at any time in that account period the assets of the qualifying fund include an interest in the offshore fund or company referred to in clause (*a*),

then, for the purposes of the application in relation to the primary fund of section 744(3) (other than paragraph (*d*)), at any time when the assets of the qualifying fund include the interest referred to in clause (*c*), the primary fund's share of that interest shall be treated as an additional asset of the primary fund.

8. (1) The modification referred to in paragraph 6(3)(*b*) is that, in determining whether the condition in paragraph 1(1)(*b*)(ii) is fulfilled with respect to the account period of the primary fund referred to in paragraph 6(2), the Irish equivalent profits of the primary fund for that account period shall be treated as increased by the primary fund's share of the excess income (if any) of the qualifying fund which is attributable to that account period.

(2) For the purposes of this paragraph, the excess income of the qualifying fund for any account period of that fund shall be the amount (if any) by which its Irish equivalent profits for that account period exceed the amount of the distributions made for that account period, as determined for the purposes of the application of paragraph 1(1) to the qualifying fund.

(3) Where an account period of the qualifying fund coincides with an account period of the primary fund, the excess income (if any) of the qualifying fund for that account period shall be the excess income which is attributable to that account period of the primary fund.

(4) In a case where subparagraph (3) does not apply, the excess income of the qualifying fund attributable to an account period of the primary fund shall be the appropriate fraction of the excess income (if any) of the qualifying fund for any of its account periods which comprises the whole or any part of the account period of the primary fund and, if there is more than one such account period of the qualifying fund, the aggregate of the excess income (if any) of each of them.

(5) For the purposes of subparagraph (4), the appropriate fraction shall be determined by reference to the formula

$$\frac{A}{B}$$

where—

A is the number of days in the account period of the primary fund which are also days in an account period of the qualifying fund, and

B is the number of days in that account period of the qualifying fund or, as the case may be, in each of those account periods of that fund which comprises the whole or any part of the account period of the primary fund.

9. (1) The references in paragraphs 7 and 8(1) to the primary fund's share of—

(*a*) an interest forming part of the assets of the qualifying fund, or

(*b*) the excess income (within the meaning of paragraph 8) of the qualifying fund,

shall be construed as references to the fraction specified in subparagraph (2) of that interest or excess income.

(2) In relation to any account period of the primary fund, the fraction referred to in subparagraph (1) shall be determined by reference to the formula—

where—

$$\frac{C}{D}$$

C is the average value of the primary fund's holding of interests in the qualifying fund during that account period, and

D is the average value of all the interests of the qualifying fund held by any persons during that account period.

Offshore Funds Investing in Trading Companies

10. (1) In this paragraph—

"commodities" has the same meaning as in paragraph 4(1);

"dealing", in relation to commodities, currency, securities, debts or other assets of a financial nature, includes dealing by means of futures contracts and traded options;

"trading company" means a company whose business consists wholly of the carrying on of a trade or trades and does not to any extent consist of—

(*a*) dealing in commodities, currency, securities, debts or other assets of a financial nature, or

(*b*) banking or money-lending.

(2) In any case where the assets of an offshore fund for the time being include an interest in a trading company, section 744(3) shall apply subject to the modifications in subparagraphs (3) and (4).

(3) In the application of section 744(3)(*b*) to so much of the assets of an offshore fund as for the time being consists of interests in a single trading company, **"20 per cent"** shall be substituted for **"10 per cent"**.

(4) In the application of section 744(3)(*c*) to an offshore fund, for **"more than 10 per cent"**, in so far as it would otherwise refer to the share capital of a trading company or to any class of such share capital, **"50 per cent or more"** shall be substituted.

Offshore Funds with Wholly-Owned Subsidiaries

11. (1) In relation to an offshore fund which has a wholly-owned subsidiary which is a company, section 744(3) or Part 1 of this Schedule shall apply subject to the modifications in subparagraph (4).

(2) Subject to subparagraph (3), for the purposes of this paragraph, a company shall be a wholly-owned subsidiary of an offshore fund if and so long as the whole of the issued share capital of the company is—

(*a*) in the case of an offshore fund within section 743(1)(*a*), directly and beneficially owned by the fund,

(*b*) in the case of an offshore fund within section 743(1)(*b*), directly owned by the trustees of the fund for the benefit of the fund, and

(*c*) in the case of an offshore fund within section 743(1)(*c*), owned in a manner which as near as may be corresponds either to clause (*a*) or (*b*).

(3) In the case of a company which has only one class of issued share capital, the reference in subparagraph (2) to the whole of the issued share capital shall be construed as a reference to at least 95 per cent of that share capital.

(4) The modifications referred to in subparagraph (1) are that for the purposes of section 744(3) and Part 1 of this Schedule—

(*a*) the percentage of the receipts, expenditure, assets and liabilities of the subsidiary which is equal to the percentage of the issued share capital of the company concerned which is owned as mentioned in subparagraph (2) shall be regarded as the receipts, expenditure, assets and liabilities of the fund, and

(*b*) there shall be disregarded the interest of the fund in the subsidiary and any distributions or other payments made by the subsidiary to the fund or by the fund to the subsidiary.

Offshore Funds with Interests in Dealing and Management Companies

12. (1) Section 744(3)(*c*) shall not apply to so much of the assets of an offshore fund as consists of issued share capital of a company which is either—

(*a*) a wholly-owned subsidiary of the fund which is within subparagraph (2), or

(*b*) a subsidiary management company of the fund (within the meaning of subparagraph (3)).

(2) A company which is a wholly-owned subsidiary of an offshore fund shall be one to which subparagraph (1)(*a*) applies if—

(*a*) the business of the company consists wholly of dealing in material interests in the offshore fund for the purposes of and in connection with the management and administration of the business of the fund, and

(*b*) the company is not entitled to any distribution in respect of any material interest for the time being held by the company,

and paragraph 11(2) shall apply to determine whether a company is for the purposes of this paragraph a wholly-owned subsidiary of an offshore fund.

(3) A company (being a company in which an offshore fund has an interest) shall be a subsidiary management company of the fund for the purposes of subparagraph (1)(*b*) if—

(*a*) the company carries on no business other than providing services within subparagraph (4) either for the fund alone or for the fund and for any other offshore fund which has an interest in the company, and

(*b*) the company's remuneration for the services it provides to the fund is not greater than it would be if it were determined at arm's length between the fund and a company in which the fund has no interest.

(4) The services referred to in subparagraph (3) are—

(*a*) holding property (being property of any description) occupied or used in connection with the management or administration of the fund, and

(*b*) providing administrative, management and advisory services to the fund.

(5) In determining in accordance with subparagraph (3) whether a company in which an offshore fund has an interest is a subsidiary management company of that fund—

(*a*) every business carried on by a wholly-owned subsidiary of the company shall be treated as carried on by the company,

(*b*) no account shall be taken of so much of the company's business as consists of holding its interests in a wholly-owned subsidiary, and

(*c*) any reference in subparagraph (3)(*b*) to the company shall be taken to include a reference to a wholly-owned subsidiary of the company.

(6) A reference in subparagraph (5) to a wholly-owned subsidiary of a company shall be construed as a reference to another company, the whole of the issued share capital of which is for the time being directly and beneficially owned by the first-mentioned company.

Disregarding of Certain Investments Forming Less Than 5 Per Cent of a Fund

13. (1) In this paragraph, **"excess holding"** means any holding within subparagraph (2).

(2) In any case where—

(*a*) in any account period of an offshore fund the assets of the fund include a holding of issued share capital (or any class of issued share capital) of a company, and

(*b*) that holding is such that by virtue of section 744(3)(*c*) the fund could not (apart from this paragraph) be certified as a distributing fund in respect of that account period,

then, if the condition in subparagraph (3) is fulfilled, that holding shall be disregarded for the purposes of section 744(3)(*c*).

(3) The condition referred to in subparagraph (2) is that at no time in the account period in question does that portion of the fund which consists of—

(*a*) excess holdings, and

(*b*) interests in other offshore funds which are not qualifying funds,

exceed 5 per cent by value of all the assets of the fund.

Power of Revenue Commissioners to Disregard Certain Breaches of Conditions

14. Where in the case of any account period of an offshore fund it appears to the Revenue Commissioners that there has been a failure to comply with any of the conditions in paragraphs (*a*), (*b*) and (*c*) of section 744(3) (as modified, where appropriate, by the preceding provisions of this Part of this Schedule) but they are satisfied that the failure—

(*a*) occurred inadvertently, and

(*b*) was remedied without unreasonable delay,

then, the Revenue Commissioners may disregard the failure for the purposes of determining whether to certify the fund as a distributing fund in respect of that account period.

PART 3
CERTIFICATION PROCEDURE

Application for Certification

15. (1) The Revenue Commissioners shall, in such manner as they consider appropriate, certify an offshore fund as a distributing fund in respect of an account period if—

(*a*) an application in respect of that period is made under this paragraph,

(*b*) the application is accompanied by the accounts of the fund for, or for a period which includes, the account period to which the application relates, (*c*) such information as the Revenue Commissioners may reasonably require for the purpose of determining whether the fund should be so certified is furnished to the Revenue Commissioners, and

(*d*) the Revenue Commissioners are satisfied that nothing in subsection (2) or (3) of section 744 prevents the fund being so certified.

(2) An application under this paragraph shall be made to the Revenue Commissioners by the fund or by a trustee or officer of the fund on behalf of the fund and may be so made before the expiry of the period of 6 months beginning at the end of the account period to which the application relates.

(3) In any case where on an application under this paragraph the Revenue Commissioners determine that the offshore fund concerned should not be certified as a distributing fund in respect of the account period to which the application relates, they shall give notice of that determination to the fund.

(4) Where at any time it appears to the Revenue Commissioners that—

(*a*) the accounts accompanying an application under this paragraph in respect of any account period of an offshore fund are not such, or

(*b*) any information furnished to them in connection with such an application is not such,

as to make full and accurate disclosure of all facts and considerations relevant to the application, the Revenue Commissioners shall give notice to the fund accordingly, specifying the period concerned.

(5) Where a notice is given by the Revenue Commissioners under subparagraph (4), they shall be deemed never to have certified the offshore fund in respect of the account period in question.

Appeals

16. (1) An appeal to the Appeal Commissioners—

(*a*) against a determination referred to in paragraph 15(3), or

(*b*) against a notification under paragraph 15(4),

may be made by the offshore fund or by a trustee or officer of the fund on behalf of the fund, and shall be so made by notice specifying the grounds of appeal and given to the Revenue Commissioners within 30 days of the date of the notice under subparagraph (3) or (4) of paragraph 15 as the case may be.

(2) The Appeal Commissioners shall hear and determine an appeal under subparagraph (1) in accordance with the principles to be followed by the Revenue Commissioners in determining applications under paragraph 15 and, subject to those principles, in the like manner as in the case of an appeal to the Appeal Commissioners against an assessment to income tax, and the provisions of the Income Tax Acts relating to such an appeal (including the provisions relating to the rehearing of an appeal and to the statement of a case for the opinion of the High Court on a point of law) shall apply accordingly with any necessary modifications.

(3) The jurisdiction of the Appeal Commissioners on an appeal under this paragraph shall include jurisdiction to review any decision of the Revenue Commissioners relevant to a ground of the appeal.

PART 4
SUPPLEMENTARY

Assessment: Effect of Non-Certification

17. No appeal may be brought against an assessment to tax on the ground that an offshore fund should have been certified as a distributing fund in respect of an account period of the fund.

18. (1) Without prejudice to paragraph 17, in any case where no application has been made under paragraph 15 in respect of an account period of an offshore fund, any person liable to pay tax which that person would not be liable to pay if the offshore fund were certified as a distributing fund in respect of that period may by notice in writing require the Revenue Commissioners to take action under this paragraph for the purposes of determining whether the fund should be so certified.

(2) Subject to subparagraphs (3) and (5), where the Revenue Commissioners receive a notice under subparagraph (1) they shall by notice, given in such manner as they consider appropriate in the circumstances, invite the offshore fund concerned to make an application under paragraph 15 in respect of the period in question.

(3) Where subparagraph (2) applies, the Revenue Commissioners shall not be required to give notice under that subparagraph before the expiry of the account period to which the notice is to relate nor if an application under paragraph 15 has already been made; but where notice is given under subparagraph (2), an application under paragraph 15 shall not be out of time under paragraph 15(2) if it is made within 90 days of the date of that notice.

(4) Where an offshore fund to which notice is given under subparagraph (2) does not make an application under paragraph 15 in respect of the account period in question within the time allowed by subparagraph (3) or paragraph 15(2), as the case may be, the Revenue Commissioners shall proceed to determine the question of certification in respect of that period as if such an application had been made.

(5) Where the Revenue Commissioners receive more than one notice under subparagraph (1) with respect to the same account period of the same offshore fund, their obligations under subparagraphs (2) and (4) shall be taken to be fulfilled with respect to each of those notices if they are fulfilled with respect to any of them.

(6) Notwithstanding anything in subparagraph (5), for the purpose of a determination under subparagraph (4) with respect to an account period of an offshore fund, the Revenue Commissioners shall have regard to accounts and other information furnished by all persons who have given notice under subparagraph (1) with respect to that account period, and paragraph 15 shall apply as if accounts and information so furnished had been furnished in compliance with subparagraph (1) of that paragraph.

(7) Without prejudice to subparagraph (5), in any case where—

(*a*) at a time after the Revenue Commissioners have made a determination under subparagraph (4) that an offshore fund should not be certified as a distributing fund in respect of an account period, notice is given under subparagraph (1) with respect to that period, and

(*b*) the person giving that notice furnishes the Revenue Commissioners with accounts or information which had not been furnished to them at the time of the earlier determination,

then, the Revenue Commissioners shall reconsider their previous determination in the light of the new accounts or information and, if they consider it appropriate, may determine to certify the fund accordingly.

(8) Where any person has given notice to the Revenue Commissioners under subparagraph (1) with respect to an account period of an offshore fund and no application has been made under paragraph 15 with respect to that period, then —

(*a*) the Revenue Commissioners shall notify that person of their determination with respect to certification under subparagraph (4), and

(*b*) paragraph 16 shall not apply in relation to that determination.

Information as to Decisions on Certification etc

19. Any obligation on the Revenue Commissioners to maintain secrecy or any other restriction upon the disclosure of information by them shall not preclude them from disclosing to any person appearing to them to have an interest in the matter —

(*a*) any determination of the Revenue Commissioners or (on appeal) the Appeal Commissioners as to whether an offshore fund should or should not be certified as a distributing fund in respect of any account period, or

(*b*) the content and effect of any notice given by the Revenue Commissioners under paragraph 15(4).

20. The Revenue Commissioners may nominate any of their officers to perform any acts and discharge any functions authorised by this Schedule to be performed or discharged by the Revenue Commissioners, and references in this Schedule to the Revenue Commissioners shall, with any necessary modifications, be construed as including references to an officer so nominated.

Cross-references

Meanings of "account period", "disposal", "distributing fund", "the equalisation fund", "Irish equivalent profits", "material interest", "non-qualifying fund", "offshore fund" and "offshore income gain": s 740.

Non-qualifying offshore funds: s 744(8)–(10); Part 1: s 744(2); Part 2: s 744(3); Parts 3–4: s 744(11).

Offshore fund operating equalisation arrangements: s 742(1); para 3(1): s 742(4)(*b*).

Revenue precedents

Issue: Would an offshore fund qualify for certification as a distributing fund notwithstanding the fact that no distribution is made and the fund has a nominal level of income?

Decision: Yes, where the level of income does not exceed 1% of the average value of the funds assets held during the accounting period.

Definitions

Appeal Commissioners: ss 2(1), 5(1);. account period: s 744(8)–(10); class (of shares): s 5(1); disposal: s 741(2); distributing fund: s 744(2)–(3); equalisation account: s 742(1); material interest: s 743(2); offshore funds: s 743(1); chargeable gain: ss 4(1), 5(1), 534; company: ss 4(1), 5(1); distribution: ss 4(1), 436, 437; High

Court: IA 1937 Sch; month: IA 1937 Sch; person: IA 1937 s 11(*c*); profession: s 2(1); profits: s 4(1). resident: s 5(1); trade: s 3(1); writing: IA 1937 Sch.

Former enactments

FA 1990 Sch 5.

SCHEDULE 20
Offshore Funds: Computation of Offshore Income Gains

[Section 745]

PART 1
DISPOSAL OF INTERESTS IN NON-QUALIFYING FUNDS

Interpretation

1. In this Part of this Schedule, **"material disposal"** means a disposal to which Chapter 2 of Part 27 applies otherwise than by virtue of section 742.

Calculation of Unindexed Gain

2. (1) Where there is a material disposal, there shall first be determined for the purposes of this Part of this Schedule the amount (if any) which in accordance with this paragraph is the unindexed gain accruing to the person making the disposal.

(2) Subject to subsections (2) to (6) of section 741 and paragraph 3, the unindexed gain accruing on a material disposal shall be the amount which would be the gain on that disposal for the purposes of the Capital Gains Tax Acts if it were computed without regard to—

(*a*) any charge to income tax or corporation tax by virtue of section 745, and

(*b*) any adjustment (in this Part of this Schedule referred to as **"the indexation allowance"**) made under section 556(2) to sums allowable as deductions in the computation of chargeable gains.

3. (1) Where the material disposal forms part of a transfer to which section 600 applies, the unindexed gain accruing on the disposal shall be computed without regard to any deduction to be made under that section in computing a chargeable gain.

(2) Notwithstanding sections 538 and 546, where apart from this subparagraph the effect of any computation under the preceding provisions of this Part of this Schedule would be to produce a loss, the unindexed gain on the material disposal shall be treated as nil, and accordingly for the purposes of this Part of this Schedule no loss shall be treated as accruing on a material disposal.

Gains Since the 6th Day of April, 1990

4. (1) This paragraph shall apply where—

(*a*) the interest in the offshore fund which is disposed of by the person making a material disposal was acquired by that person before the 6th day of April, 1990, or

(*b*) that person is treated by virtue of any provision of subparagraphs (3) and (4) as having acquired the interest before that date.

(2) Where this paragraph applies, the amount which would have been the gain on the material disposal shall be determined for the purposes of this Part of this Schedule—

(*a*) on the assumption that on the 6th day of April, 1990, the interest was disposed of and immediately reacquired for a consideration equal to its market value at that time, and

(*b*) subject to that assumption, on the basis that the gain is computed in the like manner as the unindexed gain on the material disposal is determined under paragraphs 2 and 3,

and that amount is in paragraph 5(2) referred to as **"the gain since the 6th day of April, 1990"**.

(3) Where the person making the material disposal acquired the interest disposed of—

(*a*) on or after the 6th day of April, 1990, and

(*b*) in such circumstances that by virtue of any enactment other than section 556(4) that person and the person (in this subparagraph and subparagraph (4) referred to as **"the previous owner"**) from whom that person acquired the interest disposed of were to be treated for the purposes of the Capital Gains Tax Acts as if that person's acquisition were for a consideration of such an amount as would secure that, on the disposal under which that person acquired the interest disposed of, neither a gain or a loss accrued to the previous owner,

then, the previous owner's acquisition of the interest shall be treated as that person's acquisition of the interest.

(4) Where the previous owner acquired the interest disposed of—

(*a*) on or after the 6th day of April, 1990, and

(*b*) in circumstances similar to those referred to in subparagraph (3),

then, the acquisition of the interest by the predecessor of the previous owner shall be treated for the purposes of this paragraph as the previous owner's acquisition, and so on back through previous acquisitions in similar circumstances until the first such acquisition before the 6th day of April, 1990, or, as the case may be, until an acquisition on a material disposal on or after that date.

The Offshore Income Gain

5. (1) Subject to subparagraph (2), a material disposal shall give rise to an offshore income gain of an amount equal to the unindexed gain on that disposal.

(2) In any case where—

(*a*) paragraph 4 applies, and

(*b*) the gain since the 6th day of April, 1990 (within the meaning of paragraph 4(2)) is less than the unindexed gain on the disposal,

the offshore income gain to which the disposal gives rise shall be an amount equal to the income gain since the 6th day of April, 1990 (within the meaning of that paragraph).

PART 2
Disposals Involving an Equalisation Element

6. (1) Subject to paragraph 7, a disposal to which Chapter 2 of Part 27 applies by virtue of section 742(3) shall give rise to an offshore income gain of an amount equal to the equalisation element relevant to the asset disposed of.

(2) Subject to subparagraphs (4) to (6), the equalisation element relevant to the asset disposed of by a disposal within subparagraph (1) shall be the amount which would be credited to the equalisation account of the offshore fund concerned in respect of accrued income if, on the date of the disposal, the asset disposed of were acquired by another person by means of initial purchase.

(3) In the following provisions of this Part of this Schedule, a disposal within subparagraph (1) is referred to as a **"disposal involving an equalisation element"**.

(4) Where the asset disposed of by a disposal involving an equalisation element was acquired by the person making the disposal after the beginning of the period by reference to which the accrued income referred to in subparagraph (2) is calculated, the amount which apart from this subparagraph would be the equalisation element relevant to that asset shall be reduced by the following amount, that is—

(*a*) if that acquisition took place on or after the 6th day of April, 1990, the amount which on that acquisition was credited to the equalisation account of the offshore fund concerned in respect of accrued income or, as the case may be, would have been so credited if that acquisition had been an acquisition by means of initial purchase, and

(*b*) in any other case, the amount which would have been credited to that account in respect of accrued income if that acquisition had been an acquisition by means of initial purchase taking place on the 6th day of April, 1990.

(5) In any case where—

(*a*) the asset disposed of by a disposal involving an equalisation element was acquired by the person making the disposal at or before the beginning of the period by reference to which the accrued income referred to in subparagraph (2) is calculated, and

(*b*) that period began before the 6th day of April, 1990, and ends after that date,

the amount which apart from this subparagraph would be the equalisation element relevant to that asset shall be reduced by the amount which would have been credited to the equalisation account of the offshore fund concerned in respect of accrued income if the acquisition referred to in clause (*a*) had been an acquisition by means of initial purchase taking place on the 6th day of April, 1990.

(6) Where there is a disposal involving an equalisation element, then, to the extent that any amount which was or would be credited to the equalisation account of the offshore fund in respect of accrued income (as mentioned in subparagraph (2), (3), (4) or (5)) represents profits from dealing in commodities (within the meaning of paragraph 4 of Schedule 19), 50 per cent of that accrued income shall be disregarded in determining

under those subparagraphs the equalisation element relevant to the asset disposed of by that disposal.

7. (1) For the purposes of this Part of this Schedule, the Part 1 gain (if any) on any disposal involving an equalisation element shall be determined in accordance with paragraph 8.

(2) Notwithstanding anything in paragraph 6—

(*a*) where there is no Part 1 gain on a disposal involving an equalisation element, that disposal shall not give rise to an offshore income gain, and

(*b*) where apart from this paragraph the offshore income gain on a disposal involving an equalisation element would exceed the Part 1 gain on that disposal, the offshore income gain to which that disposal gives rise shall be reduced to an amount equal to that Part 1 gain.

8. (1) On a disposal involving an equalisation element, the Part 1 gain shall be the amount (if any) which, by virtue of Part 1 of this Schedule (as modified by subparagraphs (2) and (3)), would be the offshore income gain on that disposal if it were a material disposal within the meaning of that Part.

(2) For the purposes only of the application of Part 1 of this Schedule to determine the Part 1 gain (if any) on a disposal involving an equalisation element, subsections (5) and (6) of section 742 shall apply as if in subsection (5) of that section **"by virtue of subsection (3)"** were deleted.

(3) Where a disposal involving an equalisation element is one which by virtue of any enactment other than section 556(4) is treated for the purposes of the Capital Gains Tax Acts as one on which neither a gain nor a loss accrues to the person making the disposal, then, for the purpose only of determining the Part 1 gain (if any) on the disposal, that enactment shall be deemed not to apply to such a disposal (but without prejudice to the application of that enactment to any earlier disposal).

Cross-references

Offshore income gain, meaning applied, paras 5 and 6(1): s 740.
Offshore fund operating equalisation arrangements: s 742(1).
Charge to income tax of offshore income gain: s 745(1), (5)(*b*).
Deduction of offshore income gain in calculating capital gain, Part 1: s 747(2); Part 2: s 747(7)(*c*).
Meanings of "account period", "disposal", "distributing fund", "the equalisation fund", "Irish equivalent profits", "material interest", "non-qualifying fund", "offshore fund" and "offshore income gain": s 740.

Definitions

chargeable gain: ss 4(1), 5(1), 534; disposal: s 741(2); equalisation account: s 742(1); non-qualifying fund: s 744(1); offshore funds: s 743(1); person: IA 1937 s 11(*c*); profits: s 4(1).

Former enactments

FA 1990 Sch 6.

SCHEDULE 21

Purchase and Sale of Securities: Appropriate Amount in Respect of the Interest

[Sections 749, 750 and 751]

1. For the purposes of section 749, the appropriate amount in respect of the interest shall be the appropriate proportion of the net interest receivable by the first buyer.

2. For the purposes of sections 750 and 751, the appropriate amount in respect of the interest shall be the gross amount corresponding to the appropriate proportion of the net interest receivable by the first buyer.

3. (1) For the purposes of paragraphs 1 and 2, the appropriate proportion shall be the proportion which—

(*a*) the period beginning on the first relevant date and ending on the day before the day on which the first buyer bought the securities,

bears to—

(*b*) the period beginning on the first relevant date and ending on the day before the second relevant date.

(2) In subparagraph (1)—

"the first relevant date" means—

(*a*) in a case where the securities have not been quoted in the official list of the Dublin Stock Exchange at a price excluding the value of the interest payment last payable before the interest receivable by the first buyer or, the securities having been so quoted, the date of the quotation was not the earliest date on which they could have been so quoted if an appropriate dealing in the securities had taken place, that earliest date, and

(*b*) in any other case, the date on which the securities have been first so quoted;

"the second relevant date" means—

(*a*) in a case where the securities have not been quoted in the official list of the Dublin Stock Exchange at a price excluding the value of the interest receivable by the first buyer or, the securities having been so quoted, the date of the quotation was not the earliest date on which they could have been so quoted if an appropriate dealing in the securities had taken place, that earliest date, and

(*b*) in any other case, the date on which the securities have been first so quoted.

(3) Where the interest receivable by the first buyer was the first interest payment payable in respect of the securities, subparagraph (1) shall apply with the substitution for the references to the first relevant date of references to the beginning of the period (in this subparagraph referred to as **"the relevant period"**) for which the interest was payable; but where the capital amount of the securities was not fully paid at the beginning of the relevant period and one or more instalments of capital were paid during the relevant period, then—

(*a*) the interest shall be treated as divided into parts, calculated by reference to the amount of the interest attributable to the capital paid at or before the beginning of the relevant period and the amount of that interest attributable to each such instalment,

(*b*) treating each of those parts as interest payable for the relevant period or, where the part was calculated by reference to any such instalment, as interest payable for the part of the relevant period beginning with the payment of the instalment, the amount constituting the appropriate proportion of each part shall be calculated in accordance with the preceding provisions of this paragraph, and

(*c*) the appropriate proportion of the interest for the purposes of paragraphs 1 and 2 shall be the proportion of the interest constituted by the sum of those amounts.

(4) In relation to securities not the subject of quotations in the official list of the Dublin Stock Exchange, subparagraph (1) shall apply with the substitution for the periods mentioned in that subparagraph of such periods as in the opinion of the Appeal Commissioners correspond with those in the case of the securities in question.

4. Where the securities are of a description such that the bargain price is increased, where interest is receivable by the buyer, by reference to gross interest accruing before the bargain date, paragraphs 1 to 3 shall not apply; but for the purposes of sections 749 to 751 the appropriate amount in respect of the interest shall be the amount of the increase in the bargain price.

Cross-references

Dealers in securities: s 749.

Dividends regarded as paid out of profits accumulated before given date, para (4): Sch 22 para 5(3)(*h*).

Life business, chargeable gains of, in determining "the appropriate amount in respect of the interest", delete "in the opinion of the Appeal Commissioners" from para 3(4): s 711(2)(*a*).

Persons entitled to exemption: s 750.

Purchase and sale of securities: s 748.

Special investment schemes, in determining "the appropriate amount in respect of the interest", delete "in the opinion of the Appeal Commissioners" from para 3(4): s 737(8)(*c*)(i).

Special portfolio investment accounts, in determining "the appropriate amount in respect of the interest", delete "in the opinion of the Appeal Commissioners" from para 3(4): s 838(4)(*d*)(i).

Traders other than dealers in securities: s 751(1)(*a*)(i).

Undertakings for collective investment, in determining "the appropriate amount in respect of the interest", delete "in the opinion of the Appeal Commissioners" from para 3(4): s 738(7)(*a*).

Definitions

Appeal Commissioners: s 2(1).

Former enactments

ITA 1967 Sch 11; F(MP)A 1968 s 3(2) and Sch Pt I.

SCHEDULE 22

Dividends Regarded as Paid out of Profits Accumulated Before Given Date

[Sections 749 and 752]

1. (1) Subject to paragraph 2, a dividend shall be regarded for the purposes of section 752 and of this Schedule as paid wholly out of profits accumulated before a given date (in this Schedule referred to as **"the relevant date"**) if—

(*a*) it is declared for a period falling wholly before the relevant date,

(*b*) there are no profits of the company arising in the period beginning on the relevant date and ending on the date on which the dividend is payable, or

(*c*) having regard to paragraph 3, no part is available for payment of the dividend out of such profits of the company as arose in the period beginning on the relevant date and ending on the date on which the dividend is payable.

(2) Subject to paragraph 2, where out of such profits of the company as arose in the period beginning on the relevant date and ending on the date on which the dividend is payable, some part is, having regard to paragraph 3, available for payment of the dividend but the total amount distributed in payment of the net dividend on all the shares of the class in question exceeds that part of the profits, the dividend shall be regarded for the purposes of section 752 and of this Schedule as paid out of profits accumulated before the relevant date to an extent which is the same as the proportion which the excess bears to that total amount.

(3) For the purposes of this Schedule, a dividend which is declared for a period falling partly before and partly after the relevant date shall be regarded as consisting of 2 dividends respectively declared for the 2 parts of the period and of amounts proportionate to each such part.

2. (1) Notwithstanding paragraph 1, a dividend shall not be regarded as paid to any extent out of profits accumulated before the relevant date if—

(*a*) it became payable within one year from that date, and

(*b*) in the opinion of the Appeal Commissioners the annual rate of dividend on the shares in question in that year—

(i) is not substantially greater than the annual rate of dividend on those shares in the period of 3 years ending on the relevant date, or

(ii) in a case where the shares in question were acquired in the ordinary course of a business of arranging public issues and placings of shares, represents a yield on the cost to the person receiving the dividend not substantially greater than the yield obtainable by investing in comparable shares the prices of which are quoted on stock exchanges in the State.

(2) For the purposes of subparagraph (1)(*b*), the Appeal Commissioners shall have regard to—

(*a*) all dividends paid on the shares in the respective periods,

(*b*) any share issue made in those periods to holders of the shares, and

(*c*) in a case under subparagraph (1)(*b*)(i) where the shares were not in existence 3 years before the relevant date, the dividends paid on, and any share issue made to holders of, any shares surrendered in exchange for the first-mentioned shares or in right of which the first-mentioned shares were acquired,

and shall take such averages and make such adjustments as may appear to them to be required for a fair comparison.

3. (1) The part of the profits of the company arising in the period beginning on the relevant date and ending on the date on which a dividend is payable which is available for payment of the dividend shall be determined in accordance with subparagraphs (2) to (5).

(2) There shall be deducted from those profits such amount, whether fixed or proportionate to the amount of the profits, as in the opinion of the Appeal Commissioners ought justly and reasonably to be treated as set aside for payment of dividends on any other class of shares in the company, having regard to the respective rights attaching to the shares and on the assumption that the total amount available for

distribution by means of net dividend on all the shares in the company over any period will be proportionately greater or less than the profits of the company arising in the period beginning on the relevant date and ending on the date on which the dividend mentioned in subparagraph (1) is payable, according as the first-mentioned period is longer or shorter than the second-mentioned period.

(3) In a case where, in the period beginning on the relevant date and ending on the date on which the dividend is payable, no previous dividend became payable on the shares of the class in question, the whole of the profits of the company arising in the period, less any deduction to be made under subparagraph (2), shall be regarded as available for payment of the dividend.

(4) If any previous dividend became payable on the same shares in the period beginning on the relevant date and ending on the date on which the dividend is payable, there shall be determined in accordance with the preceding paragraphs the extent, if any, to which that previous dividend is to be regarded as paid out of profits accumulated before the relevant date, and the profits of the company arising in that period, less any deduction to be made under subparagraph (2), shall be regarded as primarily available for payment of the net amount of that previous dividend in so far as it is not regarded as paid out of profits accumulated before the relevant date and only such balance, if any, as remains shall be regarded as available for payment of the later dividend.

(5) Where under subparagraph (2) the Appeal Commissioners are to determine what should be set aside for payment of dividends on shares of any class, and dividends on shares of that class have been treated under this Schedule as paid to any extent out of profits accumulated before the relevant date, the Appeal Commissioners may take that fact into account and reduce the amount to be so set aside accordingly.

4. (1) For the purposes of this Schedule, the profits of a company arising in a given period (in this paragraph referred to as **"the specified period"**) shall be determined in accordance with subparagraphs (2) and (3).

(2) Those profits shall be the income of the company for the specified period diminished by—

(*a*) the income tax actually paid by the company for any year of assessment (not being a year of assessment after the year 1975–76) in the specified period, including any sur-tax borne by the company under section 530 of, and Schedule 16 to, the Income Tax Act, 1967,

(*b*) the corporation profits tax payable by the company for any accounting period in the specified period,

(*c*) the corporation tax (including corporation tax charged by virtue of sections 440 and 441) payable by the company for any accounting period in the specified period, and for this purpose the tax credit comprised in any franked investment income shall be treated as corporation tax payable by the company for the accounting period in which the distribution was received, and

(*d*) the capital gains tax payable by the company for any year of assessment (not being a year of assessment after the year 1975–76) in the specified period;

but where relief has been afforded to the company under section 360 of the Income Tax Act, 1967, or under section 826 ...,[1] references in this subparagraph to tax actually borne or to tax payable shall be construed as references to the tax which would have been borne or payable if that relief had not been given.

(3) In ascertaining for the purposes of this paragraph the amount of income tax, corporation profits tax and corporation tax by which the income of the company for the specified period is to be diminished, any tax on the amount to be deducted under clause (*g*) or (*h*) of paragraph 5(3) shall be disregarded.

5. (1) For the purposes of this Schedule, the income of the company for a given period (in this paragraph referred to as **"the specified period"**) shall be determined in accordance with subparagraphs (2) and (3).

(2) There shall be computed the aggregate amount of—

(*a*) any profits or gains arising in the specified period from any trade carried on by the company computed in accordance with the provisions applicable to Case I of Schedule D,

(*b*) any income (including any franked investment income) arising in the specified period (computed in accordance with the Income Tax Acts or, in the case of franked investment income, in accordance with the Corporation Tax Acts), other than profits or gains arising from any trade referred to in clause (*a*), and

(*c*) any capital profits arising in the specified period (whether or not chargeable to capital gains tax or corporation tax).

(3) There shall be deducted from the aggregate amount determined under subparagraph (2) the sum of the following amounts—

(*a*) any loss sustained by the company in the specified period in any trade referred to in subparagraph (2)(*a*) (computed in the same manner as profits or gains under the provisions applicable to Case I of Schedule D),

(*b*) any group relief given to the company in accordance with Chapter 5 of Part 12 for any accounting period in the specified period,

(*c*) any allowances for any year of assessment (not being a year of assessment after the year 1975–76) in the specified period in respect of any such trade under sections 241, 244(3) and 245, Chapter III of Part XIV, and Parts XV and XVI, of the Income Tax Act, 1967,

(*d*) any allowances in respect of any such trade under Chapter III of Part XIV of the Income Tax Act, 1967, which under section 14 of the Corporation Tax Act, 1976, were to be made in taxing the trade for the purposes of corporation tax for any accounting period in the specified period,

(*e*) any allowances in respect of any such trade under Part 9, section 670, Chapter 1 of Part 29 or subsection (1) or (2) of section 765, which under section 307 are to be made in taxing the trade for the purpose of corporation tax for any accounting period in the specified period,

(*f*) (i) any payments made by the company in the specified period to which section 237 or 238 applies, other than payments which are deductible in computing the profits or gains or losses of a trade carried on by the company,

(ii) any amount in respect of which repayment was made under section 496 of the Income Tax Act, 1967, for any year of assessment in the specified period, and

(iii) any charges on income which under section 243(2) are to be allowed as deductions against the total profits for any accounting period in the specified period,

(*g*) if the company is not engaged in carrying on a trade mentioned in section 752(3) and has received in the period—

(i) on or before the 5th day of April, 1976, a dividend which if the company had been engaged in such a trade would have been required by section 371(1) of the Income Tax Act, 1967, to be taken into account to any extent mentioned in that section, such amount as would, after deduction of income tax at the rate authorised by section 456 of that Act, be equal to the amount which would have been so required to be taken into account,

(ii) after the 5th day of April, 1976, a distribution within the meaning of Chapter 2 of Part 6 which if the company had been engaged in such a trade would have been required by section 752(3) to be taken into account to any extent mentioned in that section, an amount equal to so much of the distribution as would be so required to be taken into account increased by so much of the tax credit in respect of that distribution as bears to the amount of such tax credit the same proportion as the part of the distribution which would be so required to be taken into account bears to the distribution, and

(*h*) if the company is not engaged in carrying on a trade mentioned in section 752(3), but were it so engaged any reduction under section 749 would, or would but for section 749(3), be made as respects the price paid by the company for securities (within the meaning of that section) bought by it in the period—

(i) on or before the 5th day of April, 1976, such amount as would, after deduction of income tax at the rate applicable to the payment, be equal to the amount of the reduction, or

(ii) after the 5th day of April, 1976, such amount as would be equal to an amount of gross interest corresponding to an amount of net interest equal to the amount of the reduction,

so however that where the securities are of the description specified in paragraph 4 of Schedule 21, the amount shall be the amount of the reduction,

and the balance shall be the income of the company for the specified period.

6. Any reference in paragraph 4 or 5 to an amount for a year of assessment in the period in question shall be taken as a reference to the full amount for any year of assessment falling wholly within that period and a proportionate part of the amount (on a time basis) for any year of assessment falling partly within that period, and the references in those paragraphs to an amount for an accounting period in that period shall be construed in a corresponding manner.

Amendments

1 Deleted by FA 1998 s 48 and Sch 3 para 11 with effect from 1 January 1998 for corporation tax and 6 April 1998 for income tax and capital gains tax; previously "or 833".

Cross-references

Dealers in securities, para 2: s 749(3).

Purchases of shares by financial concerns and persons exempted from tax: s 752(1), (2), (8).

Definitions

Appeal Commissioners: s 2(1); person: IA 1937 s 11(*c*). trade: s 3(1); year of assessment: s 3(1).

Former enactments

ITA 1967 Sch 12; F(MP)A 1968 s 3(2) and Sch Pt I; CTA 1976 s 140(1) and Sch 2 Pt I par28; FA 1979 s 34.

SCHEDULE 23
Occupational Pension Schemes

[Section 770]

PART 1
GENERAL

Application for Approval of a Scheme

1. An application for the approval for the purposes of Chapter 1 of Part 30 (in this Schedule referred to as **"Chapter 1"**) of any retirement benefits scheme shall be made in writing by the administrator of the scheme to the Revenue Commissioners [in such form and manner as they may specify][1] before the end of the first year of assessment for which approval is required, and shall be supported by—

(*a*) a copy of the instrument or other document constituting the scheme,

(*b*) a copy of the rules of the scheme and, except where the application is being made on the setting up of the scheme, a copy of the accounts of the scheme for the last year for which such accounts have been made up, and

(*c*) such other information and particulars (including copies of any actuarial report or advice given to the administrator or employer in connection with the setting up of the scheme) as the Revenue Commissioners may consider relevant.

Information about Payments under Approved Schemes

2. In the case of every approved scheme, the administrator of the scheme and every employer who pays contributions under the scheme shall, within 30 days from the date of the notice from the inspector requiring them so to do—

(*a*) furnish to the inspector a return containing such particulars of contributions paid under the scheme as the notice may require;

(*b*) prepare and deliver to the inspector a return containing particulars of all payments under the scheme, being—

(i) payments by means of the return of contributions (including interest on contributions, if any),

(ii) payments by means of the commutation of, or in place of, pensions or other lump sum payments, ...[2]

(iii) other payments made to an [employer, and,][3]

[(iv) payments by means of pension, gratuity or other like benefits;][4]

(*c*) furnish to the inspector a copy of the accounts of the scheme to the last date previous to the notice to which such accounts have been made up, together with such other information and particulars (including copies of any actuarial report or advice given to the administrator or employer in connection with the conduct of the scheme in the period to which the accounts relate) as the inspector considers relevant.

[2A. Any such return, copy of accounts, information and particulars required to be provided under paragraph 2 shall be in such form and manner as may be specified in the notice under that paragraph.][5]

Information about Schemes other than Approved Schemes or Statutory Schemes

3. (1) This paragraph shall apply as respects a retirement benefits scheme which is neither an approved scheme nor a statutory scheme.

(2) It shall be the duty of every employer—

(*a*) if there subsists in relation to any of that employer's employees any such scheme, to deliver particulars of that scheme to the inspector within 3 months beginning on the date on which the scheme first comes into operation in relation to any of that employer's employees, and

(*b*) when required to do so by notice given by the inspector to furnish within the time limited by the notice such particulars as the inspector may require with regard to—

(i) any retirement benefits scheme relating to the employer, or

(ii) the employees of that employer to whom any such scheme relates.

(3) It shall be the duty of the administrator of any such scheme, when required to do so by notice given by the inspector, to furnish within the time limited by the notice such particulars as the inspector may require with regard to the scheme.

Responsibility of Administrator of a Scheme

4. (1) Where the administrator of a retirement benefits scheme defaults, cannot be traced or dies, the employer shall be responsible in place of the administrator for the discharge of all duties imposed on the administrator under Chapter 1 and this Schedule and shall be liable for any tax due from the administrator in the capacity as administrator.

(2) No liability incurred under Chapter 1 or this Schedule by the administrator of a scheme, or by an employer, shall be affected by the termination of the scheme or by its ceasing to be an approved scheme or an exempt approved scheme, or by the termination of the appointment of the person mentioned [in section 772(2)(*c*)(ii).][6]

(3) References in this paragraph to the employer include, where the employer is resident outside the State, references to any factor, agent, receiver, branch or manager of the employer in the State.

Regulations

5. (1) The Revenue Commissioners may make regulations generally for the purpose of carrying Chapter 1 and this Schedule into effect.

(2) Every regulation made under this paragraph shall be laid before Dáil Éireann as soon as may be after it is made and, if a resolution annulling the regulation is passed by Dáil Éireann within the next 21 days on which Dáil Éireann has sat after the regulation is laid before it, the regulation shall be annulled accordingly, but without prejudice to the validity of anything previously done thereunder.

Amendments

[1] Inserted by FA 2005 s 21(1)(*f*)(i) with effect from 1 January 2005.
[2] Deleted by FA 2005 s 21(1)(*f*)(ii)(I) with effect from 1 January 2005; previously "and".
[3] Substituted by FA 2005 s 21(1)(*f*)(ii)(II) with effect from 1 January 2005; previously "employer;".
[4] Para 2(*b*)(iv) inserted by FA 2005 s 21(1)(*f*)(ii)(III) with effect from 1 January 2005.
[5] Para 2A inserted by FA 2005 s 21(1)(*f*)(iii) with effect from 1 January 2005.
[6] Substituted by FA 2005 s 21(1)(*f*)(iv) with effect from 1 January 2005; previously "in section 772(2)(*c*).".

PART 2
CHARGE TO TAX IN RESPECT OF UNAUTHORISED AND CERTAIN OTHER PAYMENTS

6. This Part shall apply to any payment to or for the benefit of an employee, otherwise than in course of payment of a pension, being a payment made out of funds which are or have been held for the purposes of a scheme which is or has at any time been approved for the purposes of Chapter 1.

7. Where the payment—

(*a*) is not expressly authorised by the rules of the scheme, or

(*b*) is made at a time when the scheme is not approved for the purposes of Chapter 1 and would not have been expressly authorised by the rules of the scheme when it was last so approved,

the employee (whether or not he or she is the recipient of the payment) shall be chargeable to tax on the amount of the payment under Schedule E for the year of assessment in which the payment is made.

8. Any payment chargeable to tax under this Part shall not be chargeable to tax under section 780 or 781.

9. References in this Part to any payment include references to any transfer of assets or other transfer of money's worth.

Cross-references

General medical services scheme: s 773(2).
Occupational pension schemes, interpretation: s 770(3).
Penalty, paras 2, 3(2)(*b*), (3): Sch 29 column 2.
Penalty, para 3(2)(*a*): Sch 29 column 3.

Definitions

administrator, approved scheme, the Commissioners: s 13(1); Dáil Éireann: IA 1937 Sch; employee, employer, exempt approved scheme: s 770(1); inspector: ss 2(1), 5(1), 852; month: IA 1937 Sch; pension: s 770(1); person: IA 1937 s 11(*c*); statutory scheme: s 770(1); writing: IA 1937 Sch; year of assessment: ss 2(1), 5(1).

Former enactments

FA 1972 Sch 1 Pt I paras 1 to 3(3) and 4 to 5 and Pt VI paras 1 to 4; FA 1996 s 132(1) and Sch 5 Pt I para 6.

[SCHEDULE 23A
Specified Occupations and Professions

[Section 787]

Athlete
Badminton Player
Boxer

Cyclist
Footballer
Golfer
Jockey
Motor Racing Driver
Rugby Player
Squash Player
Swimmer
Tennis Player][1]

Amendments

[1] Schedule 23A inserted by FA 1999 s 19(1)(*c*) for 1999–2000 and later tax years.

Cross-references

Personal Retirement Savings Accounts (PRSAs), interpretation and supplemental: s 787A(1)("specified individual").
Relief on retirement for certain income of certain sportspersons: s 480A(2).

SCHEDULE 24
[Relief from Income Tax and Corporation Tax by Means of Credit in Respect of Foreign Tax

[Sections 826 and 833]

Cross-references

Capital gains tax, temporary non-residents: s 29A(4)(*a*).
Dealers in securities: s 749(2A)(*a*)(ii), (2B)(*a*).

Tax Briefing

TB13 Jan 1994 par2.5 — Double Taxation Relief for Individuals.
TB32 June 1998 p 3 — List of foreign effective rates.
TB55 April 2004 p 6 — Credit for Foreign Tax.

PART 1
Interpretation

1. (1) In this Schedule, except where the context otherwise requires—][1]

"arrangements" means arrangements for the time being in force by virtue of [section 826(1)(*a*)][2] ...;[3]

"the Irish taxes" means income tax and corporation tax;

[**"EEA Agreement"** means the Agreement on the European Economic Area signed at Oporto on 2 May 1992, as adjusted by the Protocol signed at Brussels on 17 March 1993;

"EEA State" means a state which is a contracting party to the EEA Agreement;][4]

[**"foreign tax"** means —

(*a*) in the case of any territory in relation to which arrangements have the force of law, any tax chargeable under the laws of that territory for which credit may be allowed under the arrangements, and (*b*) in any other case, any tax chargeable in respect of which credit may be allowed by virtue of subparagraph (3) of paragraph 9A.][5]

[**"relevant Member State"** means—

(*a*) a Member State of the European Communities, or

(*b*) not being such a Member State, an EEA State which is a territory with the government of which arrangements having the force of law by virtue of [section 826(1)(*a*)][6] have been made;][7]

(2) Any reference in this Schedule to foreign tax shall be construed, in relation to credit to be allowed under any arrangements, as a reference only to tax chargeable under the laws of the territory in relation to which the arrangements are made.

Amendments

1 Substituted by FA 1998 s 60(*a*) as respects accounting periods ending on or after 1 April 1998.

2 Substituted by FA 2004 s 89 and Sch 3 para 1(*ae*)(i)(I) with effect from 25 March 2004; previously "section 826".

3 Deleted by FA 1998 s 48 and Sch 3 para 12 with effect from 1 January 1998 for corporation tax and 6 April 1998 for income tax and capital gains tax; previously "or section 12 of the Finance Act, 1950".

4 Definitions of "EEA" and "EEA State" inserted by FA 2002 s 38(*a*)(i) with effect from 1 January 2002.

5 Definition of "foreign tax" substituted by FA 1998 s 60(*b*) as respects accounting periods ending on or after 1 April 1998.

6 Substituted by FA 2004 s 89 and Sch 3 para 1(*ae*)(i)(II) with effect from 25 March 2004; previously "Section 826".

7 Definition of "relevant Member State" inserted by FA 2002 s 38(*a*)(ii) with effect from 1 January 2002.

General

2. (1) Subject to this Schedule, where under the arrangements credit is to be allowed against any of the Irish taxes chargeable in respect of any income, the amount of the Irish taxes so chargeable shall be reduced by the amount of the credit.

(2) In the case of any income within the charge to corporation tax, the credit shall be applied in reducing the corporation tax chargeable in respect of that income.

(3) Nothing in this paragraph shall authorise the allowance of credit against any Irish tax against which credit is not allowable under the arrangements.

Requirements as to Residence

3. [Subject to paragraphs 9A, 9B and 9C, credit shall not be allowed][1] against income tax for any year of assessment or corporation tax for any accounting period unless the person in respect of whose income the tax is chargeable is resident in the State for that year or accounting period.

Amendments

1 Substituted by FA 2001 s 41(1)(*a*) for accounting periods ending on or after 15 February 2001.

Limit on Total Credit — Corporation Tax

4. (1) The amount of the credit to be allowed against corporation tax for foreign tax in respect of any income shall not exceed the corporation tax attributable to that income.

(2) For the purposes of this paragraph, the corporation tax attributable to any income or gain (in this subparagraph referred to as **"that income"** or **"that gain"**, as the case may be) of a company shall, subject to subparagraphs (3) to (5), be the corporation tax attributable to so much (in this paragraph referred to as **"the relevant income"** or **"the relevant gain"**, as the case may be) of the income or chargeable gains of the company computed in accordance with the Tax Acts and the Capital Gains Tax Acts, as is attributable to that income or that gain, as the case may be.

(3) For the purposes of subparagraph (2), the relevant income of a company attributable to an amount receivable from the sale of goods (within the meaning of section 449) shall be the sum which would for the purposes of that section be taken to be the amount of the income of the company referable to the amount so receivable.

(4) Subject to subparagraph (5), the amount of corporation tax attributable to the relevant income or gain shall be treated as equal to such proportion of the amount of that income or gain as corresponds to the rate of corporation tax payable by the company (before any credit for double taxation relief) on its income or chargeable gains for the accounting period in which the income arises or the gain accrues (in this paragraph referred to as **"the relevant accounting period"**); but, where the corporation tax payable by the company for the relevant accounting period on the relevant income or [gain—

(*a*) is charged at the rate specified in section 21A, the rate of corporation tax payable by the company on its income and chargeable gains for the relevant accounting period shall be the rate so specified,

(*b*) is reduced by virtue of section 448 by any fraction, the rate of tax payable by the company on its income and chargeable gains for the relevant accounting period shall be treated as reduced by that fraction,

(*c*) is to be computed in accordance with section 713(3) or 738(2), the rate of corporation tax payable by the company on its income and chargeable gains for the relevant accounting period shall be treated as the standard rate of income tax,

(*d*) is to be computed in accordance with section 723(6), the rate of corporation tax payable by the company on its income and chargeable gains for the relevant accounting period shall be treated as 20 per cent,

(*e*) is reduced by virtue of section 644B [by any fraction][1], the rate of corporation tax payable by the company on its income and chargeable gains for the relevant accounting period shall be treated as reduced by that fraction,][2]

for the purposes of computing the corporation tax attributable to that relevant income or gain, as the case may be.

(5) Where in the relevant accounting period there is any deduction to be made for charges on income, expenses of management or other amounts which can be deducted from or set off against or treated as reducing profits of more than one description—

(*a*) the company shall for the purposes of [this paragraph, paragraph 9D][3] and sections 449 and 450 allocate every such deduction in such amounts and to such of its profits for that period as it thinks fit, and (*b*) (i) the amount of the relevant income or gain shall be treated for the purposes of subparagraph (4),

(ii) the amount of any income of a company treated for the purposes of section 449 as referable to an amount receivable from the sale of goods (within the meaning of that section) shall be treated for the purposes of that section, ...[4]

(iii) the amount of the income of a company treated for the purposes of section 450 as attributable to relevant payments (within the meaning of that section) shall be treated for the purposes of that section, [and][5]

[(iv) the amount of income of a company treated for the purposes of paragraph 9D as referable to an amount of relevant interest (within the meaning of that paragraph)][6]

as reduced or, as the case may be, extinguished by so much (if any) of the deduction as is allocated to it.

Amendments

1 Inserted by FA 2001 s 41(1)(*b*) for accounting periods ending on or after 15 February 2001.

2 "gain is reduced by virtue of-" and clauses (*a*)–(*c*) substituted by FA 2000 s 71(1)(*a*) as respects accounting periods ending on or after 1 January 2000. For this purpose, where an accounting period of a company begins before 1 January 2000 and ends on or after that day, it is divided into 2 parts, one beginning on the day the accounting period begins and ending on 31 December 1999, and the other beginning on 1 January 2000 and ending on the day the accounting period ends and both parts are treated as separate accounting periods.

3 Substituted by FA 2002 s 57(*a*)(i) with effect from 1 January 2002; previously "this paragraph".

4 Deleted by FA 2002 s 57(*a*)(ii)(I) with effect from 1 January 2002; previously "and".

5 Inserted by FA 2002 s 57(*a*)(ii)(II) with effect from 1 January 2002.

6 Para 4(5)(iv) inserted by FA 2002 s 57(*a*)(ii)(III) with effect from 1 January 2002.

Limit on Total Credit — Income Tax

5. (1) The amount of the credit to be allowed against income tax for foreign tax in respect of any income shall not exceed the sum which would be produced by computing the amount of that income in accordance with the Income Tax Acts, and then charging it to income tax for the year of assessment for which the credit is to be allowed, but at a rate (in this paragraph referred to as **"the specified rate"**) ascertained by dividing the income tax payable by that person for that year by the amount of the total income of that person for that year.

(2) For the purpose of determining the specified rate, the tax payable by any person for any year shall be computed without any reduction of that tax for any credit allowed or to be allowed under any arrangements having effect by virtue of [section 826(1)(*a*)][1] but shall be deemed to be reduced by any tax which the person in question is entitled to charge against any other person, and the total income of any person shall be deemed to be reduced by the amount of any income the income tax on which that person is entitled to charge as against any other person.

(3) Where credit for foreign tax is to be allowed in respect of any income and any relief would but for this subparagraph be allowed in respect of that income under section 830, that relief shall not be allowed.

Amendments

1 Substituted by FA 2004 s 89 and Sch 3 para 1(*ae*)(ii) with effect from 25 March 2004; previously "section 826".

6. Without prejudice to paragraph 5, the total credit to be allowed to a person against income tax for any year of assessment shall not exceed the total income tax payable by the person in question for that year of assessment, less any tax which that person is entitled to charge against any other person.

Effect on Computation of Income of Allowance of Credit

7. (1) Where credit for foreign tax is to be allowed against any of the Irish taxes in respect of any income, this paragraph shall apply in relation to the computation for the purposes of income tax or corporation tax of the amount of that income.

(2) Where the income tax or corporation tax payable depends on the amount received in the State, that amount shall be treated as increased by the amount of the credit allowable against income tax or corporation tax, as the case may be.

(3) Where subparagraph (2) does not apply—

(*a*) no deduction shall be made for foreign tax (whether in respect of the same or any other income), and

(*b*) where the income includes a dividend and under the arrangements foreign tax not chargeable directly or by deduction in respect of the dividend is to be taken into account in considering whether any, and if so what, credit is to be allowed against the Irish taxes in respect of the dividend, the amount of the income shall be treated as increased by the amount of the foreign tax not so chargeable which is to be taken into account in computing the amount of the credit, but

(*c*) notwithstanding anything in clauses (*a*) and (*b*), where any part of the foreign tax in respect of the income (including any foreign tax which under clause (*b*) is to be treated as increasing the amount of the income) cannot be allowed as a credit against any of the Irish taxes, the amount of the income shall be treated as reduced by that part of that foreign tax.

(4) In relation to the computation of the total income of a person for the purpose of determining the rate mentioned in paragraph 5, subparagraphs (1) to (3) shall apply subject to the following modifications:

(*a*) for the reference in subparagraph (2) to the amount of the credit allowable against income tax there shall be substituted a reference to the amount of the foreign tax in respect of the income (in the case of a dividend, foreign tax not chargeable directly or by deduction in respect of the dividend being disregarded), and

(*b*) clauses (*b*) and (*c*) of subparagraph (3) shall not apply,

and, subject to those modifications, shall apply in relation to all income in the case of which credit is to be allowed for foreign tax under any arrangements.

Special Provisions as to Dividends

8. (1) For the purposes of this paragraph, the relevant profits shall be—

(*a*) if the dividend is paid for a specified period, the profits of that period,

(*b*) if the dividend is not paid for a specified period but is paid out of specified profits, those profits, or (*c*) if the dividend is paid neither for a specified period nor out of specified profits, the profits of the last period for which accounts of the body corporate were made up which ended before the dividend became payable;

but if, in a case within clause (*a*) or (*c*), the total dividend exceeds the profits available for distribution of the period mentioned in clause (*a*) or (*c*), as the case may be, the relevant profits shall be the profits of that period together with so much of the profits available for distribution of preceding periods (other than profits previously distributed or previously treated as relevant for the purposes of this paragraph) as is equal to the excess, and for this purpose the profits of the most recent preceding period shall first be taken into account, then the profits of the next most recent preceding period, and so on.

(2) Where, in the case of any dividend, foreign tax not chargeable directly or by deduction in respect of the dividend is under the arrangements to be taken into account in considering whether any, and if so what, credit is to be allowed against the Irish taxes in respect of the dividend, the foreign tax not so chargeable to be taken into account shall be that borne by the body corporate paying the dividend on the relevant profits in so far as it is properly attributable to the proportion of the relevant profits represented by the dividend.

9. Where—

(*a*) the arrangements provide, in relation to dividends of some classes but not in relation to dividends of other classes, that foreign tax not chargeable directly or by deduction in respect of dividends is to be taken into account in considering whether any, and if so what, credit is to be allowed against the Irish taxes in respect of the dividends, and

(*b*) a dividend is paid which is not of a class in relation to which the arrangements so provide,

then, if the dividend is paid to a company which controls, directly or indirectly, not less than 50 per cent of the voting power in the company paying the dividend, credit shall be allowed as if the dividend were a dividend of a class in relation to which the arrangements so provide.

[PART 2

Unilateral Relief][1]

Amendments

1 Part 2 title inserted by FA 1998 s 60(*c*) as respects accounting periods ending on or after 1 April 1998.

9A. [(1) To the extent appearing from the following provisions of this paragraph, relief (in this paragraph referred to as **"unilateral relief"** from corporation tax in respect of profits represented by dividends shall be given in respect of tax payable under the law of any territory other than the State by allowing that tax as a credit against corporation tax, notwithstanding that there are not for the time being in force any arrangements providing for such relief.

(2) Unilateral relief shall be such relief as would fall to be given under this Schedule if arrangements with the government of the territory in question containing the provisions

in subparagraphs (3) to (5) were in force, and a reference in this Schedule to credit under arrangements shall be construed as [including][1] a reference to unilateral relief.

(3) Subject to Part 1 and to subparagraph (5), credit for tax paid under the law of a territory other than the State in relation to a relevant dividend paid by a company resident in the territory to a [company falling within subparagraph (3A)][2] shall be allowed against corporation tax attributable to the profits represented by the dividend.

[(3A)(*a*) A company falls within this subparagraph if—

(i) it is resident in the State, or

(ii) it is, by virtue of the law of a [relevant Member State][3] other than the State, resident for the purposes of tax in such a Member State and the dividend referred to in subparagraph (3) forms part of the profits of a branch or agency of the company in the State.

(*b*) For the purposes of subparagraph (*a*)(ii), **"tax"**, in relation to a [relevant Member State][4] other than the State, means any tax imposed in the Member State which corresponds to corporation tax in the State.][5]

(4) For the purposes of subparagraph (3) —

(*a*) "tax paid under the law of a territory other than the State in relation to a relevant dividend paid by a company" means —

(i) tax which is directly charged on the dividend, whether by charge to tax, deduction of tax at source or otherwise, and the whole of which tax neither the company nor the recipient would have borne if the dividend had not been paid, and

(ii) tax paid in respect of its profits under the law of the territory by the company paying the dividend in so far as that tax is properly attributable to the proportion of the profits represented by the dividend,

(*b*) **"relevant dividend"** means a dividend paid by a company resident in a territory other than the State to a [company falling within subparagraph (3A)][6] which either directly or indirectly owns, or is a subsidiary of a company which directly or indirectly owns, not less than [5 per cent][7] of the ordinary share capital of the company paying the dividend; for the purposes of this subparagraph one company is a subsidiary of another company if the other company owns, directly or indirectly, not less than 50 per cent of the ordinary share capital of the first company.

(5) Credit shall not be allowed by virtue of subparagraph (3) —

(*a*) for tax paid under the law of a territory where there are arrangements with the government of the territory [except ...[8] to the extent that credit may not be given for that tax under those arrangements],[9]

(*b*) for any tax which is relevant foreign tax within the meaning of [section 449 or paragraph 9D][10], or

(*c*) for any tax in respect of which credit may be allowed under section 831.

(6) Where —

(*a*) unilateral relief may be given in respect of a dividend, and (*b*) it appears that the assessment to corporation tax made in respect of the dividends is not made in respect of the full amount thereof, or is incorrect having regard to the credit, if any, which falls to be given by way of unilateral relief,

any such assessment may be made or amended as is necessary to ensure that the total amount of the dividend is assessed, and the proper credit, if any, is given in respect thereof.

(7) In this Schedule in its application to unilateral relief, references to tax payable or paid under the law of a territory outside the State include only references to taxes which are charged on income or capital gains and which correspond to corporation tax and capital gains tax.][11]

Amendments

1 Inserted by FA 1999 s 81(*b*)(i) with effect from 6 April 1999.

2 Substituted by FA 2001 s 41(1)(*c*)(i) for accounting periods ending on or after 15 February 2001; previously "company resident in the State".

3 Substituted by FA 2002 s 38(*b*)(i) with effect from 1 January 2002; previously "Member State of the European Communities".

4 Substituted by FA 2002 s 38(*b*)(ii) with effect from 1 January 2002; previously "Member State of the European Communities".

5 Para 9A(3A) inserted by FA 2001 s 41(1)(*c*)(ii) for accounting periods ending on or after 15 February 2001.

6 Substituted by FA 2001 s 41(1)(*c*)(iii) for accounting periods ending on or after 15 February 2001; previously "company resident in the State".

7 Substituted by FA 2004 s 31(1)(*a*)(i) with effect from such day or days as the Minister for Finance by order appoints, either generally or with reference to any particular purpose or provision, and different days may be so appointed for different purposes or different provisions; previously "25 per cent". By virtue of the Finance Act 2004 (Commencement of Sections 31 and 42) Order 2004, SI No 551 of 2004, this amendment comes into operation with effect from 2 February 2004.

8 Deleted by FA 2004 s 31(1)(*a*)(ii) with effect from such day or days as the Minister for Finance by order appoints, either generally or with reference to any particular purpose or provision, and different days may be so appointed for different purposes or different provisions; previously ", in respect of taxes covered by these arrangements,". By virtue of the Finance Act 2004 (Commencement of Sections 31 and 42) Order 2004, SI No 551 of 2004, this amendment comes into operation with effect from 2 February 2004.

9 Inserted by FA 1999 s 81(*b*)(ii) with effect from 6 April 1999.

10 Substituted by FA 2002 s 57(*b*) with effect from 1 January 2002; previously "section 449".

11 Para 9A inserted by FA 1998 s 60(*c*) as respects accounting periods ending on or after 1 April 1998.

[Dividends Paid Between Related Companies: Relief for Irish and Third Country Taxes

9B. (1) Where a foreign company pays a dividend to [a company falling within subparagraph (1A) (in this paragraph referred to as the **"relevant company"**)][1] and the foreign company is related to [the relevant company][2], then for the purpose of allowing credit under any arrangements against corporation tax in respect of the dividend, there shall, subject to Part 1, be taken into account as if it were tax payable under the law of the territory in which the foreign company is resident —

(*a*) any income tax or corporation tax payable in the State by the foreign company in respect of its profits, and

(*b*) any tax which, under the law of any other territory, is payable by the foreign company in respect of its profits.

[(1A)(*a*) A company falls within this subparagraph if—

(i) it is resident in the State, or

(ii) it is, by virtue of the law of a [relevant Member State][3] other than the State, resident for the purposes of tax in such a Member State and the dividend referred to in subparagraph (1) forms part of the profits of a branch or agency of the company in the State.

(*b*) For the purposes of subparagraph (*a*)(ii), **"tax"**, in relation to a [relevant Member State][4] other than the State, means any tax imposed in the Member State which corresponds to corporation tax in the State.][5]

(2) Where the foreign company has received a dividend from a third company and the third company is related to the foreign company and is connected with [the relevant company][6], then, subject to subparagraph (4), [there shall be treated for the purposes of subparagraph (1) as tax paid by the foreign company in respect of its profits—

(*a*) any underlying tax payable by the third company, and

(*b*) any tax directly charged on the dividend which neither company would have borne had the dividend not been paid,

to the extent to which it would be taken into account][7] under this Schedule if the dividend had been paid by a foreign company to an Irish company and arrangements had provided for [underlying tax to be taken into account: and for this purpose there shall, subject to Part 1, be taken into account as if it were tax payable under the law of the territory in which the third company is resident—

(i) any income tax or corporation tax payable in the State by the foreign company in respect of its profits, and

(ii) any tax which, under the law of any other territory, is payable by the foreign company in respect of its profits.][8]

(3) Where the third company has received a dividend from a fourth company and the fourth company is related to the third company and is connected with [the relevant company],[6] then, subject to subparagraph (4), tax payable by the fourth company [or tax directly charged on the dividend][9] shall similarly be treated for the purposes of subparagraph (2) as tax paid by the third company, and so on for successive companies each of which is related to the one before and is connected with [the relevant company][6].

(4) Subparagraphs (2) and (3) are subject to the following limitations —

(*a*) no tax shall be taken into account in respect of a dividend paid by [a relevant company][10] except corporation tax payable in the State and any tax for which that company is entitled to credit under this Schedule, and

(*b*) no tax shall be taken into account in respect of a dividend paid by a foreign company to another such company unless it could have been taken into account under this Schedule had the other company been [a relevant company][10].

(5) (*a*) In this paragraph —

foreign company" means a company resident outside the State;

...[11]

"underlying tax", in relation to a dividend, means tax borne by the company paying the dividend on the relevant profits (within the meaning of paragraph (8)) in so far as it is properly attributable to the proportion of the relevant profits represented by the dividend.

(*b*) For the purposes of this paragraph —

(i) a company is related to another company if that other company —

(I) [controls][12] directly or indirectly, or

(II) is a subsidiary of a company which [controls][12] directly or indirectly,

not less than [5 per cent][13] of the [voting power][14] of the first-mentioned company,

(ii) one company is a subsidiary of another company if the other company owns, directly or indirectly, not less than 50 per cent of the ordinary share capital of the first-mentioned company,

and

(iii) a company is connected with another company if that other company —

(I) [controls][12] directly or indirectly, or

(II) is a subsidiary of a company which [controls][12] directly or indirectly,

not less than [5 per cent][15] of the [voting power][14] of the first-mentioned company.][16]

Amendments

1 Substituted by FA 2001 s 41(1)(*d*)(i) for accounting periods ending on or after 15 February 2001; previously "an Irish company".

2 Substituted by FA 2001 s 41(1)(*d*)(i) for accounting periods ending on or after 15 February 2001; previously "the Irish company".

3 Substituted by FA 2002 s 38(*c*)(i) with effect from 1 January 2002; previously "Member State of the European Communities".

4 Substituted by FA 2002 s 38(*c*)(ii) with effect from 1 January 2002; previously "Member State of the European Communities".

5 Para 9B(1A) inserted by FA 2001 s 41(1)(*d*)(ii) for accounting periods ending on or after 15 February 2001.

6 Substituted by FA 2001 s 41(1)(*d*)(iii) for accounting periods ending on or after 15 February 2001; previously "the Irish company".

7 Substituted by FA 2000 s 71(1)(*b*)(i) as respects accounting periods ending on or after 1 April 1998; previously "there shall be treated for the purposes of subparagraph (1) as tax paid by the foreign company in respect of its profits any underlying tax payable by the third company, to the extent to which it would be taken into account".

8 Substituted by FA 2004 s 31(1)(*b*)(i) with effect from such day or days as the Minister for Finance by order appoints, either generally or with reference to any particular purpose or provision, and different days may be so appointed for different purposes or different provisions; previously "underlying tax to be taken into account.". By virtue of the Finance Act 2004 (Commencement of Sections 31 and 42) Order 2004, SI No 551 of 2004, this amendment comes into operation with effect from 2 February 2004.

9 Inserted by FA 2000 s 71(1)(*b*)(ii) as respects accounting periods ending on or after 1 April 1998.

10 Substituted by FA 2001 s 41(1)(*d*)(iv) for accounting periods ending on or after 15 February 2001; previously "an Irish company".

11 Definition of "Irish company" deleted by FA 2001 s 41(1)(*d*)(v) for accounting periods ending on or after 15 February 2001.

12 Substituted by FA 1999 s 81(*c*)(i) with effect from 6 April 1999; previously "owns".

13 Substituted by FA 2004 s 31(1)(*b*)(ii)(I) with effect from such day or days as the Minister for Finance by order appoints, either generally or with reference to any particular purpose or provision, and different days may be so appointed for different purposes or different provisions; previously "25 per cent". By virtue of

the Finance Act 2004 (Commencement of Sections 31 and 42) Order 2004, SI No 551 of 2004, this amendment comes into operation with effect from 2 February 2004.

14 Substituted by FA 1999 s 81(*c*)(ii) with effect from 6 April 1999; previously "ordinary share capital".

15 Substituted by FA 2004 s 31(1)(*b*)(ii)(II) with effect from such day or days as the Minister for Finance by order appoints, either generally or with reference to any particular purpose or provision, and different days may be so appointed for different purposes or different provisions; previously "10 per cent". By virtue of the Finance Act 2004 (Commencement of Sections 31 and 42) Order 2004, SI No 551 of 2004, this amendment comes into operation with effect from 2 February 2004.

16 Para 9B inserted by FA 1998 s 60(*c*) as respects accounting periods ending on or after 1 April 1998.

Cross-references

Implementation of Council Directive No 90/435/EEC concerning the common system of taxation applicable in the case of parent companies and subsidiaries of different Member States: s 831(2)(*a*)(iii), 2A(*b*).

9C. [(1) In this paragraph—

"relevant company" means a company which—

(*a*) is not resident in the State,

(*b*) is, by virtue of the law of a [relevant Member State][1] other than the State, resident for the purposes of tax in such a Member State, and

(*c*) carries on a trade in the State through a branch or agency,

and for the purposes of subparagraph (*b*) of this definition **"tax"**, in relation to a [relevant Member State][1] other than the State, means any tax imposed in the Member State which corresponds to corporation tax in the State;

"relevant tax" means foreign tax paid in respect of the income or chargeable gains of a branch or agency in the State of a relevant company, other than such tax paid in a territory in which the company is liable to tax by reason of domicile, residence, place of management or other similar criterion.

(2) A relevant company shall, as respects an accounting period, be entitled to such relief under this Schedule in respect of relevant tax as would, if the branch or agency in the State had been a company resident in the State, have been given under any arrangements to that company resident in the State.][2]

Amendments

1 Substituted by FA 2002 s 38(*d*) with effect from 1 January 2002; previously "Member State of the European Communities".

2 Para 9C inserted by FA 2001 s 41(1)(*e*) for accounting periods ending on or after 15 February 2001.

9D. [(1)(*a*)In this paragraph—

"relevant foreign tax", in relation to interest receivable by a company, means tax—

(i) which under the laws of any foreign territory has been deducted from the amount of the interest,

(ii) which corresponds to income tax or corporation tax,

(iii) which has not been repaid to the company,

(iv) for which credit is not allowable under arrangements, and

(v) which, apart from this paragraph, is not treated under this Schedule as reducing the amount of income;

[**"relevant interest"** means interest receivable by a company—

(*a*) which falls to be taken into account in computing the trading income of a trade carried on by the company, and

(*b*) from which relevant foreign tax is deducted.][1]

(*b*) For the purposes of this paragraph—

(i) the amount of corporation tax which apart from this paragraph would be payable by a company for an accounting period and which is attributable to an amount of relevant interest shall be an amount equal to—

(I) in so far as it is corporation tax charged on profits which under section 26(3) are apportioned to the financial year 2002, 16 per cent, and

(II) in so far as it is corporation tax charged on profits which under section 26(3) are apportioned to the financial year 2003 or any subsequent financial year, 12.5 per cent,

of the amount of the income of the company referable to the amount of the relevant interest [reduced by the relevant foreign tax],[2] and

(ii) the amount of any income of a company referable to an amount of relevant interest in an accounting period shall, subject to paragraph 4(5), be taken to be such sum as bears to the total amount of the trading income of the company for the accounting period [increased by the amount of the relevant foreign tax][3] the same proportion as the amount of relevant interest in the accounting period bears to the total amount receivable by the company in the course of the trade in the accounting period.

(2) Where, as respects an accounting period of a company, the trading income of a trade carried on by the company includes an amount of relevant interest, the amount of corporation tax which, apart from this paragraph, would be payable by the company for the accounting period shall be reduced by so much of—

(*a*) in so far as it is corporation tax charged on profits which under section 26(3) are apportioned to the financial year 2002, 84 per cent, and

(*b*) in so far as it is corporation tax charged on profits which under section 26(3) are apportioned to the financial year 2003 or any subsequent financial year, 87.5 per cent,

of any relevant foreign tax borne by the company in respect of relevant interest in that period as does not exceed the corporation tax which would be so payable and which is attributable to the amount of the relevant interest.

(3) (*a*) This paragraph shall not apply as respects any accounting period of a company which is a relevant accounting period within the meaning of section 442.

(*b*) Subsection (2) of section 442 shall apply for the purposes of this paragraph as it applies for the purposes of Part 14.][4]

Amendments

1 Definition of "relevant interest" substituted by FA 2003 s 60(2)(*a*) as respects accounting periods ending on or after 6 February 2003.

2 Inserted by FA 2003 s 60(2)(*b*)(i) as respects accounting periods ending on or after 6 February 2003.

3 Inserted by FA 2003 s 60(2)(*b*)(ii) as respects accounting periods ending on or after 6 February 2003.

4 Para 9D inserted by FA 2002 s 57(*c*) with effect from 1 January 2002.

[Treatment of unrelieved foreign tax

9E. (1)(*a*)In this paragraph—

"the aggregate amount of corporation tax payable by a company for an accounting period in respect of relevant dividends received by the company in the accounting period from foreign companies" means so much of the corporation tax which, apart from this paragraph, would be payable by the company for that accounting period as would not have been payable had those dividends not been received by the company;

"foreign company" means a company resident outside the State;

"unrelieved foreign tax" has the meaning assigned to it in subparagraph (2).

(*b*) For the purposes of this paragraph, a dividend is a relevant dividend if it is received by a company (in this clause referred to as the **"receiving company"**) from a company which is not resident in the State (in this clause referred to as the **"paying company"**) and the paying company is related to the receiving company (within the meaning of paragraph 9B(5)(*b*)).

(2) Where as respects a relevant dividend received in an accounting period by a company any part of the foreign tax cannot, apart from this paragraph, be allowed as a credit against any of the Irish taxes and, accordingly, the amount of income representing the dividend is treated under paragraph 7(3)(*c*) as reduced by that part of the foreign tax, then an amount determined by the formula—

$$\frac{100 - R}{100} \times D$$

where—

R is the rate per cent specified in section 21A(3), and

D is the amount of the part of the foreign tax by which the income is to be treated under paragraph 7(3)(*c*) as reduced,

shall be treated for the purposes of subparagraph (3) as unrelieved foreign tax of that accounting period.

(3) The aggregate amount of corporation tax payable by a company for an accounting period in respect of relevant dividends received by the company in that accounting period from foreign companies shall be reduced by the unrelieved foreign tax of that accounting period.

(4) Where the unrelieved foreign tax in relation to an accounting period of a company exceeds the aggregate amount of corporation tax payable by the company for the accounting period in respect of relevant dividends received by the company in that accounting period from foreign companies, the excess shall be carried forward and treated as unrelieved foreign tax of the next succeeding accounting period, and so on for succeeding accounting periods.][1]

Amendments

1 Para 9E inserted by FA 2004 s 31(1)(*c*) with effect from such day or days as the Minister for Finance by order appoints, either generally or with reference to any particular purpose or provision, and different days

may be so appointed for different purposes or different provisions. By virtue of the Finance Act 2004 (Commencement of Sections 31 and 42) Order 2004, SI No 551 of 2004, this amendment comes into operation with effect from 2 February 2004.

[PART 3

Miscellaneous

10. Credit shall not be allowed][1] under the arrangements against the Irish taxes chargeable in respect of any income of any person if the person in question elects that credit shall not be allowed in respect of that income.

Amendments

1 Substituted by FA 1998 s 60(*d*) as respects accounting periods ending on or after 1 April 1998.

11. Where under the arrangements relief may be given either in the State or in the territory in relation to which the arrangements are made in respect of any income, and it appears that the assessment to income tax or to corporation tax made in respect of the income is not made in respect of the full amount of that income or is incorrect having regard to the credit, if any, which is to be given under the arrangements, any such additional assessments may be made as are necessary to ensure that the total amount of the income is assessed and the proper credit, if any, is given in respect of that income, and where the income is entrusted to any person in the State for payment, any such additional assessment to income tax may be made on the recipient of the income under Case IV of Schedule D.

12. (1) In this paragraph—

"the relevant year of assessment", in relation to credit for foreign tax in respect of any income, means the year of assessment for which that income is to be charged to income tax or would be so charged if any income tax were chargeable in respect of that income;

"the relevant accounting period", in relation to credit for foreign tax in respect of any income, means the accounting period for which that income is to be charged to corporation tax or would be so charged if any corporation tax were chargeable in respect of that income.

(2) Subject to paragraph 13, any claim for an allowance by means of credit for foreign tax in respect of any income shall be made in writing to the inspector not later than 6 years from the end of the relevant year of assessment or the relevant accounting period, as the case may be, and, if the inspector objects to any such claim, it shall be heard and determined by the Appeal Commissioners as if it were an appeal to the Appeal Commissioners against an assessment to income tax and the provisions of the Income Tax Acts relating to the rehearing of an appeal and to the statement of a case for the opinion of the High Court on a point of law shall, with the necessary modifications, apply accordingly.

13. Where the amount of any credit given under the arrangements is rendered excessive or insufficient by reason of any adjustment of the amount of any tax payable either in the State or in the territory in relation to which the arrangements are made, nothing in the Tax Acts limiting the time for the making of assessments or claims for relief shall apply to any assessment or claim to which the adjustment gives rise, being an assessment or

claim made not later than 6 years from the time when all such assessments, adjustments and other determinations have been made, as are material in determining whether any, and if so what, credit is to be given.

Cross-references

Application in relation to corporation profits tax under old law, para 12: s 827.
Capital gains tax: s 828(1), (2).
Corporation tax, relief to certain companies liable to foreign tax, para 8: s 830(4)(*b*).
Double tax relief, meanings of "arrangements" and "foreign tax" applied, para 1(1): s 450(1); election para 4: s 450(2); para 4(5): s 450(4)(*b*); para 7(3)(*c*): s 450(3)(*b*).
Double taxation agreements etc: s 826(2).
Foreign tax credit: s 449(1)(relevant foreign tax); para 4(5): s 449(2)(*b*).
Foreign tax incentive reliefs: s 829(2).
Implementation of Council Directive 90/435/EEC concerning the common system of taxation applicable in the case of parent companies and subsidiaries of different member States, meaning of "arrangements" applied: s 831(3).
Shipping tonnage tax, exclusion of reliefs, deductions and set-offs, Pt 2: s 697M(3)(*b*).
US agreement: s 833(1).

Definitions

Appeal Commissioners: s 2(1); chargeable gain: ss 4(1), 5(1), 545; charges on income: ss 4(1), 243(1); company: s 4(1); High Court: IA 1937 Sch; inspector: ss 2(1), 5(1), 852; person: IA 1937 s 11(*c*); profits: s 4(1); Tax Acts: s 1(2); total income: s 3(1); trade: ss 3(1), 4(1); writing: IA 1937 Sch; year of assessment: s 3(1)

Case law

"relevant profits" means profits as computed for accounting purposes and not for foreign tax purposes: *Bowater Paper Corporation v Murgatroyd* (1968) 46 TC 52.

Former enactments

ITA 1967 Sch 10; F(MP)A 1968 s 3(2) and Sch Pt I; F(No 2)A 1970 s 1(*c*); FA 1974 s 86 and Sch 2 Pt I; CTA 1976 s 23(2)–(4) and s 166 and Sch 4 Pt I and II; FA 1995 s 60.

SCHEDULE 25

[Section 833]

Convention between the Government of Ireland and the Government of the United States of America for the avoidance of double taxation and the prevention of fiscal evasion with respect to taxes on income.

Amendments

Schedule 25 deleted by FA 1998 s 48 and Sch 3 para 13 with effect from 1 January 1998 for corporation tax and withholding taxes and 6 April 1998 for income tax and capital gains tax.

Revenue precedents

Issue: Transfer pricing - whether to allow a correlative adjustment to compensate for the adjustment imposed by the IRS in the US.
Decision: Agreed to allow a correlative adjustment in the company's liability to Irish tax to compensate for a retrospective adjustment imposed by the U.S. tax authority.
Issue: Whether Article XV(2) of the Ireland/U.S. Double Taxation Convention, 1949 would apply to exempt interest paid to a U.S. partnership and U.S. trusts from Irish tax.
Decision: Confirmed that Article XV(2) of the Ireland/U.S. Double Taxation Convention, 1949 will apply to exempt interest paid to a U.S. partnership and a U.S. trust from Irish tax.
Issue: Ireland/U.S. Double Taxation Convention Article XVIII Professors and Teachers - question of treatment of the exemption from income tax provided for in Article XVIII in cases where the 2 year time limit is exceeded.
Decision: In accordance with the U.S. practice the Revenue Commissioners will not seek to tax the income retroactively where the stay exceeds 2 years.

[SCHEDULE 25A
Exemption from Tax in the Case of Gains on Certain Disposals of Shares

[Section 626B Section 626C]

Effect of earlier no-gain/no-loss transfer

1. (1) For the purposes of this paragraph shares are **"derived"** from other shares only where—

(*a*) one holding of shares is treated by virtue of section 584 as the same asset as another, or

(*b*) there is a sequence of 2 or more of the occurrences mentioned in paragraph (*a*).

(2) The period for which a company has held shares is treated as extended by any earlier period during which the shares concerned, or shares from which they are derived, were held—

(*a*) by a company from which the shares concerned were transferred to the company on a no-gain/no-loss transfer, or

(*b*) by a company from which the shares concerned, or shares from which they are derived, were transferred on a previous no-gain/no-loss transfer—

(i) to a company within clause (*a*), or

(ii) to another company within this clause.

(3) For the purposes of subparagraph (2) a **"no-gain/no-loss transfer"** means a disposal and corresponding acquisition that, by virtue of the Capital Gains Tax Acts, are deemed to be for a consideration such that no gain or loss accrues to the person making the disposal.

(4) Where subparagraph (2) applies to extend the period for which a company (in this paragraph referred to as the **"first-mentioned company"**) is treated as having held any shares, the first-mentioned company shall be treated for the purposes of section 626B(2)(*a*) as having had at any time the same entitlement—

(*a*) to shares, and

(*b*) to any rights enjoyed by virtue of holding shares,

as the company (in this paragraph referred to as the **"other company"**) that at that time held the shares concerned or, as the case may be, the shares from which they are derived.

(5) The shares and rights to be attributed to the first-mentioned company include any holding or entitlement attributed to the other company under section 626B(1)(*b*)(ii).

Effect of deemed disposal and reacquisition

2. (1) In this paragraph—

"deemed disposal and reacquisition" means a disposal and immediate reacquisition treated as taking place under the Capital Gains Tax Acts;

"derived" has the same meaning as in paragraph 1.

(2) A company is not regarded as having held shares throughout a period if, at any time during that period, there is a deemed disposal and reacquisition of—

(*a*) the shares concerned, or

(*b*) shares from which those shares are derived.

Effect of repurchase agreement

3. (1) In this paragraph a **"repurchase agreement"** means an agreement under which—

(*a*) a person (in this paragraph referred to as the **"original owner"**) transfers shares to another person (in this paragraph referred to as the **"interim holder"**) under an agreement to sell them, and

(*b*) the original owner or a person connected with him is required to buy them back either—

(i) in pursuance of an obligation to do so imposed by that agreement or by any related agreement, or

(ii) in consequence of the exercise of an option acquired under that agreement or any related agreement,

and for the purposes of paragraph (*b*) agreements are related if they are entered into in pursuance of the same arrangements (regardless of the date on which either agreement is entered into).

(2) Any reference in this paragraph to the period of a repurchase agreement is a reference to the period beginning with the transfer of the shares by the original owner to the interim holder and ending with the repurchase of the shares in pursuance of the agreement.

(3) This paragraph applies where a company that holds shares in another company transfers the shares under a repurchase agreement.

(4) In determining whether the conditions in paragraph (*a*) of section 626B(2) are satisfied but subject to subparagraph (5)—

(*a*) the original owner shall be treated as continuing to hold the shares transferred and accordingly as retaining entitlement to any rights attached to them, and

(*b*) the interim holder shall be treated as not holding the shares transferred and as not becoming entitled to any such rights,

during the period of the repurchase agreement.

(5) If at any time before the end of the period of the repurchase agreement the original owner, or another member of the same group as the original owner, becomes the holder—

(*a*) of any of the shares transferred, or

(*b*) of any shares directly or indirectly representing any of the shares transferred,

subparagraph (4) does not apply after that time in relation to those shares or, as the case may be, in relation to the shares represented by those shares; and for the purposes of this subparagraph **"group"** means a company which has one or more 51 per cent subsidiaries together with those subsidiaries.

Effect of stock lending arrangements

4. (1) In this paragraph a **"stock lending arrangement"** means arrangements between two persons (in this paragraph referred to as the **"borrower"** and the **"lender"**) under which—

(*a*) the lender transfers shares to the borrower otherwise than by way of sale, and

(*b*) a requirement is imposed on the borrower to transfer those shares back to the lender otherwise than by way of sale.

(2) Any reference in this paragraph to the period of a stock lending arrangement is a reference to the period beginning with the transfer of the shares by the lender to the borrower and ending—

(*a*) with the transfer of the shares back to the lender in pursuance of the arrangement, or

(*b*) when it becomes apparent that the requirement for the borrower to make a transfer back to the lender will not be complied with.

(3) This paragraph applies where a company that holds shares in another company transfers the shares under a stock lending arrangement.

(4) In determining whether the conditions in paragraph (*a*) of section 626B(2) are satisfied but subject to subparagraph (5)—

(*a*) the lender shall be treated as continuing to hold the shares transferred and accordingly as retaining entitlement to any rights attached to them, and

(*b*) the borrower shall be treated for those purposes as not holding the shares transferred and as not becoming entitled to any such rights,

during the period of the stock lending arrangement.

(5) (*a*) If at any time before the end of the period of the stock lending arrangement the lender, or another member of the same group as the lender, becomes the holder—

(i) of any of the shares transferred, or

(ii) of any shares directly or indirectly representing any of the shares transferred,

subparagraph (4) does not apply after that time in relation to those shares or, as the case may be, in relation to the shares represented by those shares.

(*b*) For the purposes of this subparagraph **"group"** means a company which has one or more 51 per cent subsidiaries together with those subsidiaries.

Effect in relation to investee company of earlier company reconstruction etc.

5. (1) In this paragraph **"original shares"** and **"new holding"** shall be construed in accordance with sections 584, 586 and 587.

(2) This paragraph applies where shares in one company (in this paragraph referred to as the **"first company"**)—

(*a*) are exchanged (or deemed to be exchanged) for shares in another company (in this paragraph referred to as the **"second company"**), or (*b*) are deemed to be exchanged by virtue of section 587 for shares in the first company and shares in the second company,

in circumstances such that, under section 584 as that section applies by virtue of section 586 or 587, the original shares and the new holding are treated as the same asset.

(3) Where the second company—

(*a*) is an investee company, and is accordingly the company by reference to which the shareholding requirement under section 626B(2)(*a*) falls to be met, or

(*b*) is a company by reference to which, by virtue of this paragraph, that requirement may be met,

that requirement may instead be met, in relation to times before the exchange, or deemed exchange, by reference to the first company.

(4) If in any case that requirement can be met by virtue of this paragraph, it shall be treated as met.

Negligible value

6. A claim under section 538(2) may not be made in relation to shares held by a company if by virtue of section 626B any loss accruing to the company on a disposal of the shares at the time of the claim, or at any earlier time at or after which the value of the shares becomes negligible, would not be an allowable loss.

Degrouping: time when deemed sale and reacquisition treated as taking place

7. Where—

(*a*) a company, as a result of ceasing at any time (in this paragraph referred to as the **"time of degrouping"**) to be a member of a group, is treated by section 623(4) as having sold and immediately reacquired an asset, and

(*b*) if the company owning the asset at the time of degrouping had disposed of it immediately before that time, any gain accruing on the disposal would by virtue of section 626B not have been a chargeable gain,

then section 623(4) shall have effect as if it provided for the deemed sale and reacquisition to be treated as taking place immediately before the time of degrouping.

Appropriations to trading stock

8. (1) Where—

(*a*) an asset acquired by a company otherwise than as trading stock of a trade carried on by it is appropriated by the company for the purposes of the trade as trading stock (whether on the commencement of the trade or otherwise), and

(*b*) if the company had then sold the asset for its market value, a chargeable gain or allowable loss would have accrued to the company but for the provisions of section 626B,

then the company shall be treated for the purposes of the Capital Gains Tax Acts as if it had thereby disposed of the asset for its market value.

(2) Section 618 applies in relation to this paragraph as it applies in relation to section 596.][1]

Amendments

1 Sch 25A inserted by FA 2004 s 42(1)(b) with effect from such day as the Minister for Finance may appoint by order. By virtue of the Finance Act 2004 (Commencement of Sections 31 and 42) Order 2004, SI No 551 of 2004, this amendment comes into operation with effect from 2 February 2004.

Tax Briefing

TB55 April 2004 pp 8–9 — Note on TCA 1997 ss 626B and 626C and Sch 25A.

Definitions

allowable loss: ss 5(1); 546; Capital Gains Tax Acts: s 1(2); chargeable gain: ss 5(1), 545; company: ss 4(1), 5(1); connected: s 10; market value: ss 5(1), 548; person: IA 1937 s 11(*c*); shares: s 5(1); trade: ss 3(1), 4(1), 5(1); 51 per cent subsidiary: s 9.

SCHEDULE 26
Replacement of Harbour Authorities by Port Companies

[Section 842]

Interpretation

1. In this Schedule—

"relevant port company" means a company formed pursuant to section 7 or 87 of the Harbours Act, 1996;

"relevant transfer" means—

(*a*) the vesting in a relevant port company of assets in accordance with section 96 of the Harbours Act, 1996, and

(*b*) the transfer to a relevant port company of rights and liabilities in accordance with section 97 of that Act.

Capital Allowances

2. (1) This paragraph shall apply for the purposes of—

(*a*) allowances and charges provided for in Part 9, section 670, Chapter 1 of Part 29 and sections 765 and 769, or any other provision of the Tax Acts relating to the making of allowances or charges under or in accordance with that Part or Chapter or those sections, and

(*b*) allowances or charges provided for by sections 307 and 308.

(2) The relevant transfer shall not be treated as giving rise to any such allowance or charge under any of the provisions referred to in subparagraph (1).

(3) There shall be made to or on the relevant port company in accordance with sections 307 and 308 all such allowances and charges in respect of an asset acquired by it in the course of a relevant transfer as would have been made if—

(*a*) allowances in relation to the asset made to the person from whom the asset was acquired had been made to the relevant port company, and

(*b*) everything done to or by that person in relation to the asset had been done to or by the relevant port company.

Capital Gains

3. (1) This paragraph shall apply for the purposes of the Capital Gains Tax Acts, and of the Corporation Tax Acts in so far as those Acts relate to chargeable gains.

(2) The disposal of an asset by a person in the course of a relevant transfer shall be deemed to be for a consideration of such amount as would secure that on the disposal neither a gain nor a loss would accrue to the person.

(3) Where subparagraph (2) has applied in relation to a disposal of an asset, then, in relation to any subsequent disposal of the asset by the relevant port company, the relevant port company shall be treated as if the acquisition or provision of the asset by the person from whom it was acquired by the relevant port company was that company's acquisition or provision of the asset.

(4) For the purposes of section 597, the relevant port company and the person from whom an asset was acquired in the course of a relevant transfer shall be treated as if they were the same person.

Former enactments

FA 1997 Sch 5.

[SCHEDULE 26A
Donations to Approved Bodies, etc

[Section 848A]

PART 1

List of approved bodies for the purposes of section 848A

1. A body approved for education in the arts in accordance with Part 2.

2. A body approved as an eligible charity in accordance with Part 3.

3. An institution of higher education within the meaning of section 1 of the Higher Education Authority Act, 1971, or any body established in the State for the sole purpose of raising funds for such an institution.

4. An institution in the State in receipt of public funding which provides courses to which a scheme approved by the Minister for Education and Science under the Local Authorities (Higher Education Grants) Acts, 1968 to 1992, applies or any body established in the State for the sole purpose of raising funds for such an institution.

5. An institution of higher education in the State which provides courses which are validated by the Higher Education Training and Awards Council under the provisions of the Qualifications (Education and Training) Act, 1999.

6. An institution or other body in the State which provides primary education up to the end of sixth standard, based on a programme prescribed or approved by the Minister for Education and Science.

7. An institution or other body in the State which provides post-primary education up to the level of either or both the Junior Certificate and the Leaving Certificate based on a programme prescribed or approved by the Minister for Education and Science.

8. STEIF which is the Scientific and Technological Education (Investment) Fund established under the Scientific and Technological Education (Investment) Fund Act, 1997 (as amended by the Scientific and Technological Education (Investment) Fund (Amendment) Act, 1998).

9. The company incorporated under the Companies Acts, 1963 to 1990, on 20 September 1990 as First Step Limited.

10. The Malting Research Committee of the Irish Malters Association.

11. The European Research Institute of Ireland.

12. The Equine Foundation.

13. The Dun Research Foundation.

14. The Institute of Ophthalmology.

15. The Mater College for Research and Postgraduate Education.

16. St. Luke's Institute of Cancer Research.

17. A body to which section 209 applies which is a body for the promotion of the observance of the Universal Declaration of Human Rights or the implementation of the European Convention for the protection of Human Rights and Fundamental Freedoms or both the promotion of the observance of that Declaration and the implementation of that Convention.

18. The Foundation for Investing in Communities Limited or any of its 90 per cent subsidiaries as may be approved for the purposes of this Schedule by the Minister for Finance.

[19. The company incorporated under the Companies Acts 1963 to 2001, on 30 January 2003, as US-Ireland Alliance Limited.][1]

Amendments

1 Para 19 inserted by FA 2003 s 22(1) as respects donations made on or after 6 February 2003.

PART 2

Approval of a body for education in the arts

1. In this Part—

"approved body" means any body or institution in the State which may be approved of by the Minister for Finance and which —

(*a*) provides in the State any course one of the conditions of entry to which is related to the results of the Leaving Certificate Examination, a matriculation examination of a recognised university in the State or an equivalent examination held outside the State, or (*b*) (i) is established on a permanent basis solely for the advancement wholly or mainly in the State of one or more approved subjects,

(ii) contributes to the advancement of that subject or those subjects on a national or regional basis, and

(iii) is prohibited by its constitution from distributing to its members any of its assets or profits;

"approved subject" means—

(*a*) the practice of architecture,

(*b*) the practice of art and design,

(*c*) the practice of music and musical composition,

(*d*) the practice of theatre arts,

(*e*) the practice of film arts, or

(f) any other subject approved of for the purpose of this Part by the Minister for Finance.

2. (*a*) The Minister for Finance may, by notice in writing given to the body or institution, as the case may be, withdraw the approval of any body or institution for the purposes of this Part, and on the giving of the notice the body or institution shall cease to be an approved body from the day after the date of the notice referred to in subparagraph (*b*).

(*b*) Where the Minister for Finance withdraws the approval of any body or institution for the purposes of this Part, notice of its withdrawal shall be published as soon as may be in Iris Oifigiúil.

Notes

Where any body to which this Part relates has been approved or is the holder of an authorisation, as the case may be, under any enactment and that approval or authorisation has not been withdrawn on 5 April 2001, that body is deemed to be an "approved body" for the purposes of TCA 1997 s 848A — see TCA 1997 s 848A(14).

A list of approved bodies for Education in the Arts for the purposes of this Part is available on Revenue's website — www.revenue.ie under Publications/Lists.

Tax Briefing

TB Supplement Sept 2002 pp 38–40 — List of approved bodies.

PART 3

Approval of body as eligible charity

1. In this Part—

"authorisation" shall be construed in accordance with paragraph (3);

"eligible charity" means any body in the State that is the holder of an authorisation that is in force.

2. Subject to paragraph (3), the Revenue Commissioners may, on application to them by a body in the State, and on the furnishing of the body to the Revenue Commissioners of such information as they may reasonably require for the purpose of their functions under

this Part, issue to the body a document (in this Part referred to as **"an authorisation"**) stating that the body is an eligible charity for the purposes of this Part.

3. An authorisation shall not be issued to a body unless it shows to the satisfaction of the Revenue Commissioners that—

(*a*) it is a body of persons or a trust established for charitable purposes only,

(*b*) the income of the body is applied for charitable purposes only,

(*c*) before the date of the making of the application concerned under [paragraph 2][1], it has been granted exemption from tax for the purposes of section 207 for a period of not less than [2 years,][2],

(*d*) it provides such other information to the Revenue Commissioners as they may require for the purposes of their functions under this Part, and

(*e*) it complies with such conditions, if any, as the Minister for Social, Community and Family Affairs may, from time to time, specify for the purposes of this Part.

Amendments

1 Substituted by FA 2002 s 138 and Sch 6 paras 3(*x*) and 6(*c*)(iii) with effect from 6 April 2001; previously "subsection (2)".

2 Substituted by FA 2005 s 38 with effect from 1 January 2005; previously "3 years,".

4. An eligible charity shall publish such information in such manner as the Minister for Finance may reasonably require, including audited accounts of the charity comprising—

(*a*) an income and expenditure account or a profit and loss account, as appropriate, for its most recent accounting period, and

(*b*) a balance sheet as at the last day of that period.

5. Notwithstanding any obligations as to secrecy or other restriction upon disclosure of information imposed by or under any statute or otherwise, the Revenue Commissioners may make available to any person the name and address of an eligible charity.

6. Subject to paragraph 7, an authorisation shall have effect for such period, not exceeding 5 years, as the Revenue Commissioners may determine and specify therein.

7. Where the Revenue Commissioners are satisfied that an eligible charity has ceased to comply with paragraph 3 or 4, they shall, by notice in writing served by registered post on the charity, withdraw the authorisation of the charity and the withdrawal shall apply and have effect from such date, subsequent to the date of the notice, as is specified therein.][1]

Amendments

1 Schedule 26A inserted by FA 2001 s 45(4) with effect from 6 April 2001.

Cross-references

Restriction on use of losses on approved buildings, Pt 3 para 1, meaning of "eligible charity" applied: s 409C(1).

Notes

Where any body to which this Part relates has been approved or is the holder of an authorisation, as the case may be, under any enactment and that approval or authorisation has not been withdrawn on 5 April 2001, that body is deemed to be an "approved body" for the purposes of TCA 1997 s 848A — see TCA 1997 s 848A(14).

SCHEDULE 27
Forms of Declarations to be Made by Certain Persons
[Sections 855, 857, 867 and 942]

PART 1

Form of Declaration to be Made by Appeal Commissioners Acting in Respect of Tax under Schedule D

"I, A.B., do solemnly declare, that I will truly, faithfully, impartially and honestly, according to the best of my skill and knowledge, execute the powers and authorities vested in me by the Acts relating to income tax, and that I will exercise the powers entrusted to me by the said Acts in such manner only as shall appear to me necessary for the due execution of the same; and that I will judge and determine upon all matters and things which shall be brought before me under the said Acts without favour, affection, or malice; and that I will not disclose any particular contained in any schedule, statement, return or other document delivered with respect to any tax charged under the provisions relating to Schedule D of the said Acts, or any evidence or answer given by any person who shall be examined, or shall make affidavit or deposition, respecting the same, in pursuance of the said Acts, except to such persons only as shall act in the execution of the said Acts, and where it shall be necessary to disclose the same to them for the purposes of the said Acts, or to the Revenue Commissioners, or in order to, or in the course of, a prosecution for perjury committed in such examination, affidavit or deposition."

Form of Declaration to be Made by Inspectors

"I, A.B., do solemnly declare, that in the execution of the Acts relating to income tax I will examine and revise all statements, returns, schedules and declarations delivered within my district, and, in objecting to the same, I will act according to the best of my information and knowledge; and that I will conduct myself without favour, affection, or malice, and that I will exercise the powers entrusted to me by the said Acts in such manner only as shall appear to me to be necessary for the due execution of the same, or as I shall be directed by the Revenue Commissioners; and that I will not disclose any particular contained in any statement, return, schedule or other document, with respect to any tax charged under the provisions relating to Schedule D of the said Acts, or any evidence or answer given by any person who shall be examined, or shall make affidavit or deposition, respecting the same, in pursuance of the said Acts, except to such persons only as shall act in the execution of the said Acts, and where it shall be necessary to disclose the same to them for the purposes of the said Acts, or to the Revenue Commissioners, or in order to, or in the course of, a prosecution for perjury committed in such examination, affidavit or deposition."

Form of Declaration to be Made by Persons Appointed under Section 854 or Section 855 as Assessors

"I, A.B., do solemnly declare, that in the execution of the Acts relating to income tax, I will in all respects act diligently and honestly, and without favour or affection, to the best of my knowledge and belief, and that I will not disclose any particular contained in any statement, return, schedule or other document delivered to me in the execution of the said Acts with respect to any tax charged under the provisions relating to Schedule D of the said Acts, except to such persons only as shall act in the execution of the said Acts, and where it shall be necessary to disclose the same to them for purposes of the said Acts, or in order to, or in the course of, a prosecution for perjury committed in any matter relating to such statement, return, schedule or other document."

Form of Declaration to be Made by the Collector-General and Officers for Receiving Tax

"I, A.B., do solemnly declare, that in the execution of the Acts relating to income tax, I will not disclose any assessment, or the amount of any sum paid or to be paid by any person, under the said Acts, or the books of assessment which shall be delivered to me in the execution of the said Acts, with respect to any tax charged under the provisions relating to Schedule D of the said Acts, except to such persons only as shall act in the execution of the said Acts, and where it shall be necessary to disclose the same to them for the purposes of the said Acts, or to the Revenue Commissioners, or in order to, or in the course of, a prosecution for perjury committed in relation to the said tax."

Form of Declaration to be Made by the Clerk to the Appeal Commissioners

"I, A.B., do solemnly declare, that I will diligently and faithfully execute the office of a clerk according to the Acts relating to income tax, to the best of my knowledge and judgment; and that I will not disclose any particular contained in any statement, return, declaration, schedule or other document, with respect to the tax charged under the provisions relating to Schedule D of the said Acts, or any evidence or answer given by any person who shall be examined, or shall make affidavit or deposition, respecting the same, except to such persons only as shall act in the execution of the said Acts, and where I shall be directed so to do by the said Acts, or by the commissioners under whom I act, or by the Revenue Commissioners, or in order to, and in the course of, a prosecution for perjury committed in such examination, affidavit or deposition."

PART 2

Form of Declaration to be Made by a Commissioner for Offices

"I, A.B., do solemnly declare, that I will truly, faithfully, impartially and honestly, according to the best of my skill and knowledge, execute the powers and authorities vested in me as a Commissioner for Offices by the Acts relating to income tax, and that I will judge and determine upon all matters and things which shall be brought before me under the said Acts without favour, affection or malice."

Cross-references

Amendment of statutory forms: s 867.

Declaration required to be made by Commissioners, Part 2: s 855.

Declaration on taking office, Part 1: s 857(1).

Definitions

affidavit: IA 1937 Sch; Appeal Commissioners: s 2(1); Clerk to the Appeal Commissioners: s 2(1); Collector-General: s 2(1); inspector: ss 2(1), 5(1), 852; person: IA 1937 s 11(*c*).

Former enactments

ITA 1967 Sch 17; F(MP)A 1968 s 3(4) and Sch Pt III.

SCHEDULE 28
Statements, Lists and Declarations
[Sections 458, 866 and 867]

1.— BY OR FOR EVERY PERSON CARRYING ON ANY TRADE OR EXERCISING ANY PROFESSION TO BE CHARGED UNDER SCHEDULE D.

The amount of the profits or gains thereof arising within the year of assessment.

2.— BY EVERY PERSON ENTITLED TO PROFITS OF AN UNCERTAIN VALUE NOT BEFORE STATED, OR ANY INTEREST, ANNUITY, ANNUAL PAYMENT, DISCOUNT OR DIVIDEND, TO BE CHARGED UNDER SCHEDULE D.

The full amount of the profits or gains arising therefrom within the year of assessment.

3.— BY EVERY PERSON ENTITLED TO OR RECEIVING INCOME FROM SECURITIES OR POSSESSIONS OUT OF THE STATE TO BE CHARGED UNDER SCHEDULE D.

(1) The full amount arising within the year of assessment, and the amount of every deduction or allowance claimed in respect thereof, together with the particulars of such deduction and the grounds for claiming such allowance; or

(2) In the case of any such person who satisfies the Revenue Commissioners that he or she is not domiciled in the State, or that being a citizen of Ireland he or she is not ordinarily resident in the State, or in the case of income arising from such securities and possessions aforesaid which form part of the investments of the foreign life assurance fund of an assurance company the full amount of the actual sums received in the State from remittances payable in the State or from property imported, or from money or value arising from property not imported, or from money or value so received on credit or on account in respect of such remittances, property, money or value brought into the State in the year of assessment without any deduction or abatement.

4.— BY EVERY PERSON ENTITLED TO ANY ANNUAL PROFITS OR GAINS NOT FALLING UNDER ANY OF THE FOREGOING RULES, AND NOT CHARGED BY ANY OF THE OTHER SCHEDULES, TO BE CHARGED UNDER SCHEDULE D.

The full amount thereof received annually, or according to the average directed to be taken by the inspector on a statement of the nature of such profits or gains and the grounds on which the amount has been computed, and the average taken, to the best of the knowledge and belief of such person.

5.— STATEMENT OF PROFITS OF ANY PUBLIC OFFICE, OR EMPLOYMENT OF PROFIT, TO BE CHARGED UNDER SCHEDULE E.

The amount of the salary, fees, wages, perquisites and profits of the year of assessment.

6.— GENERAL DECLARATION BY EACH PERSON RETURNING A STATEMENT OF PROFITS OR GAINS TO BE CHARGED UNDER SCHEDULES D OR E

Declaring the truth thereof, and that the same is fully stated on every description of property, or profits or gains, included in the Act relating to the said tax, and appertaining to such person, estimated to the best of such person's judgment and belief, according to the provisions of the Income Tax Acts.

7.— LISTS AND DECLARATIONS FOR FACILITATING THE EXECUTION OF THE INCOME TAX ACTS IN RELATION TO THE TAX CHARGEABLE ON OTHERS.

First. List containing the name and place of residence of every person in any service or employ, and the payments made to every such person in respect of the service or employment.

Second. List to be delivered by every person chargeable on behalf of another person, and by any person whomsoever who, in whatever capacity, is in receipt of any money or value, or of profits or gains, of or belonging to any other person, describing that other person for whom the person acts, and stating that other person's name and address, and the amount of such money, value, profit or gains, and declaring whether that other person is of full age, or a married woman living with her husband, or a married woman whose husband is not accountable for the payment of tax charged on her, or is resident in the State, or is an incapacitated person. The person delivering such list shall also deliver a list containing the names and addresses of any other person or persons acting jointly with such person.

Third. Declaration on whom the tax is chargeable in respect of any such money, value, profits or gains.

Fourth. List containing the proper description of every body of persons, or trust for which any person is answerable under the Income Tax Acts and where any such person is answerable under the Income Tax Acts for the tax to be charged in respect of the property or profits or gains of other persons, that person shall deliver such lists as aforesaid, together with the required statements of such profits or gains.

8.— LISTS, DECLARATIONS, AND STATEMENTS TO BE DELIVERED IN ORDER TO OBTAIN ANY ALLOWANCE OR DEDUCTION.

First. Declaration of the amount of value of property or profits or gains returned, or for which the claimant has been, or is liable to be, assessed.

Second. Declaration of the amount of rents, interests, annuities, or other annual payments, in respect of which the claimant is liable to allow the tax, with the names of the respective persons by whom such payments are to be made, distinguishing the amount of each payment.

Third. Declaration of the amount of interest, annuities, or other annual payments to be made out of the property or profits or gains assessed on the claimant, distinguishing each source.

Fourth. Statement of the amount of income derived according to the 3 preceding declarations.

Fifth. Statement of any tax which the claimant may be entitled to deduct, retain or charge against any other person.

Cross-references

Age exemption, para 8 applied by s 188(6)(*b*).

Amendment of statutory forms: s 867.

Leased farm land exemption, para 8 applied by s 664(6)(*b*).

Maintenance in the case of separated spouses, para 8 applied by s 1025(5)(*b*).

Patent royalty income exemption, para 8 applied by s 234(8).

Special provisions relating to year of marriage, para 8 applied by s 1020(6)(*b*).

Definitions

person: IA 1937 s 11(*c*); profession: s 2(1); trade: s 3(1); year of assessment: s 3(1).

Former enactments

ITA 1967 Sch 18 paras II to IX; FA 1969 s 33(1) and Sch 4 Pt I; FA 1990 s 20(1); FA 1997 s 146(2) and Sch 9 Pt II.

SCHEDULE 29
Provisions Referred to in Sections 1052, 1053 and 1054

Column 1	Column 2	Column 3
section 121	...[1]	section 123(6)
[section 172K(1)][2]	...[3]	
[section 172L(2)][2]	...[3]	
[section 244A and Regulations under that section][4]		
[section 258(2)][5]		
[section 470 and Regulations under that section][6]		
[section 470A and Regulations under that section][7]		
section 473 or Regulations under that section	section 183	[section 128(11) and (12)][8]
section 477	...[3]	section 238(3)
	[section 264B][9]	
	[section 267E][9]	
section 531 and Regulations under that section		
[section 730FA(2)][10]		
[section 730G(2)		
section 739F(2)][11]		
section 877	section 505(3) and (4)	section 257(1)
		[section 267B][12]
section 878	section 510(7)	section 505(1) and (2)
section 879(2)	section 645	section 531 and Regulations under that section
		section 734(5)
		[section 784A(8)][13]

section 880	section 804(4)	section 876
section 951(1) and (2)	section 808	section 885
[section 986 and Regulations under that section][14]		
paragraphs (*a*)(iii)(I) and (*c*) of subsection (2) and paragraphs (*a*)(i) and (*b*)(i) of subsection (4) of section 1002	section 812(4) section 815 section 881 section 888	[section 896][15] section 904 section 972 Schedule 2, paragraph 14
section 1023	section 890	Schedule 23, paragraph 3(2)(*a*)
Waiver of Certain Tax, Interest and Penalties Act, 1993, sections 2(3)(*a*) and 3(6)(*b*)	section 891 [section 891A][16] section 892 ...[17] section 894(3) [section 896][18] section 897 section 898 section 900 section 909 section 935 section 947 Schedule 1, paragraph 1 Schedule 9, paragraph 8 [Schedule 12, paragraph 3(4)][19] [Schedule 12A, paragraph 6][19] [Schedule 12B, paragraph 5][19] [Schedule 12C, paragraph 20][19] [Schedule 18, paragraph 1(2) [Schedule 18B, paragraph 30][20] Schedule 23, paragraphs 2, 3(2)(*b*) and 3(3)	Waiver of Certain Tax, Interest and Penalties Act, 1993, sections 2(3)(*a*) and 3(6)(*b*)

Amendments

1 Deleted by FA 2000 s 27(*c*)(i) with effect from 6 April 2000; previously "section 128(11)".

2 Inserted by FA 2002 s 128(*a*)(i) with effect from 25 March 2002.

3 Deleted by FA 2002 s 128(*b*) with effect from 25 March 2002; previously "section 172K(1)", "section 172L(2)" and "section 258(2)".

4 Inserted by FA 2001 s 23(2) for 2002 and later tax years.

5 Inserted by FA 2002 s 128(*a*)(ii) with effect from 25 March 2002.

6 Inserted by FA 2001 s 19(3) with effect from 6 April 2001.

7 Inserted by FA 2001 s 20(*c*) with effect from 6 April 2001.

8 Substituted by FA 2003 s 163 and Sch 6 para 1(*h*) with effect from 28 March 2003; previously "section 128(11) and (11A)".

9 Inserted by FA 2001 s 57(1)(*c*)(i) with effect from such date as the Minister for Finance may by order or orders appoint. This amendment came into operation with effect from 1 January 2002 — Finance Act 2001 (Section 57) (Commencement) Order 2001, SI No 596 of 2001, refers.

10 Inserted by FA 2002 s 40(4) with effect from 5 December 2001.
11 Inserted by FA 2000 s 72 with effect from 6 April 2000.
12 Inserted by FA 2001 s 57(1)(*c*)(ii) with effect from such date as the Minister for Finance may by order or orders appoint. This amendment came into operation with effect from 1 January 2002 — Finance Act 2001 (Section 57) (Commencement) Order 2001, SI No 596 of 2001, refers.
13 Inserted by FA 2003 s 14(1)(*g*) with effect from 28 March 2003.
14 Inserted by FA 1999 s 41(*a*) with effect from 6 April 1999.
15 Substituted by FA 2005 s 147 and Sch 6 para 1(*p*)(ii) with effect from 25 March 2005; previously "section 893(3)".
16 Inserted by FA 1999 s 41(*b*) with effect from 6 April 1999.
17 Deleted by FA 2005 s 147 and Sch 6 para 1(*p*)(i)(I) with effect from 25 March 2005; previously "section 893(2)".
18 Inserted by FA 2005 s 147 and Sch 6 para 1(*p*)(i)(II) with effect from 25 March 2005.
19 Inserted by FA 2001 s 15(*c*) with effect from 30 March 2001.
20 Inserted by FA 2002 s 53(4) with effect from such day as the Minister for Finance may by order appoint.

Cross-references

Approved share option schemes, transitional: Sch 32 para 7(3)(*b*).
Increased penalties in case of body of persons, column 1: s 1054(2)(*a*)(i).
Penalties for failure to make certain returns etc, column 1 or 2: s 1052(1)(*a*), (*aa*), (2).
Penalties for failure to make certain returns etc, column 3: s 1052(1)(*b*), (4)(*d*).
Penalty for fraudulently or negligently making incorrect returns etc, column 1: s 1053(1)(*a*).
Penalty for fraudulently or negligently making incorrect returns etc, column 2 or 3: s 1053(2).
Surcharge on certain income of trustees: s 805(2)(*c*).

Former enactments

ITA 1967 Sch 15; F(MP)A 1968 s 5(2); FA 1972 s 13(4) and Sch 1 Pt III para 3; FA 1973 s 33(7) and Sch 3 para 2 and s39 and Sch 5 para 10; FA 1974 s 59(6) and s73(5); FA 1975 s 22(2) and Sch 2 Pt II; FA 1976 s 11(4); FA 1981 s 29(4); FA 1982 s 4(8), s 5(2)(*b*) and s 51(8); FA 1983 s 20(5), s 21(3), and s 22(8); FA 1984 s 24(9) and s 29(6); FA 1985 s 19(4); FA 1986 s 9(11)(*b*) and s40(1); FA 1988 s 10(12) and s 73(7)(*a*); FA 1989 s 18(5)(*b*), s19(4) and Sch 1 par3(1); FA 1991 s 68(4); FA 1992 s 226(7); WCTIPA 1993 s 12; FA 1995 s 7(9)(*b*) and s 236(7); FA 1997 s 13(2).

SCHEDULE 30
Repeals

[Section 1098]

Notes

Repealed:
FA 1928 s 34(2);
ITA 1967;
IT(A)A 1967;
FA 1967 Pt I, s 25, in so far as it relates to income tax, s 27(2) and (6), Sch 3 Pt I, in so far as it relates to income tax;
F(MP)A 1968 Pts I and IV, ss 25 to 27, s 29(2) Sch Pts I to IV;
FA 1968 Pt I ss 37 to 39, s 48(2) and (5);
F(No 2)A 1968 ss 8 and 11(4);
FA 1969 Pts I and II, ss 63, 64, 65(1), s 67(2) and (7), Sch 4 Pt I, Sch 5 Pt I;
FA 1970 Pt I, ss 57 to 59, 62(2) and (7);
F(No 2)A 1970 ss 1, 8(2) and (5);
FA 1971 Pt I, s 55(2) and (6);
FA 1972 Pt I, ss 42, 43, 46, in so far as it relates to income tax, 48(2) and (5), Sch 1, Sch 3 in so far as it relates to income tax, Sch 4 in so far as it relates to income tax;
FA 1973 Pt I s 92, except in so far as it relates to death duties and stamp duty, s 98(2) and (6), Sch 3, Sch 5;
F(TPCM)A 1974;
FA 1974 Pt I, ss 86, 88(2) and (5), Sch 1, Sch 2;
FA 1975 Pt I, s 57(2) and (5), Sch 1, Sch 2;

F(No 2)A 1975 ss 1 and 4(2);
CGTA 1975;
CTA 1976;
FA 1976 Pt 1, ss 81(1) and (3)(*a*), 83(2) and (6), Sch 1, Sch 5 Pt I;
FA 1977 Pt I, ss 53, 54, in so far as it relates to income tax, corporation tax and capital gains tax, 56(2) and (7), Sch 1, Sch 2 in so far as it relates to income tax, corporation tax and capital gains tax;
FA 1978 Pt I s 46, in so far as it relates to income tax, corporation tax and capital gains tax, ss 47, 52(1) and 54(2) and (8), Sch 1, Sch 2, Sch 4 Pt I;
CGT(A)A 1978;
FA 1979 Pt I, s 59(2) and (6), Sch 1, Sch 2;
FA 1980 Pt I, ss 89 and 96(2) and (7), Sch 1;
FA 1981 Pt I, ss 52 and 54(2) and (7), Sch 1;
FA 1982 Pt I, ss 105(2) and (7), Sch 1, Sch 2, Sch 3;
FA 1983 Pt I, Pt V, s 120, in so far as it relates to income tax, corporation tax and capital gains tax, s 122(2) and (6), Sch 4 in so far as it relates to income tax, corporation tax and capital gains tax;
FA 1984 Pt I, s 116(2) and (7), Sch 1, Sch 2;
FA 1985 Pt I, ss 69 and 71(2) and (7), Sch 1;
FA 1986 Pt I, ss 112 to 116, ss 118(2), (7) (in so far as it relates to income tax, corporation tax and capital gains tax) and (8), Sch 1, Sch 2, Sch 3, Sch 4;
IT(A)A 1986;
FA 1987 Pt I, ss 52 and 55(2) and (7);
FA 1988 Pt I, ss 70 to 74, 77(2), (7) (except in so far as it relates to the Local Loans Fund) and (8), Sch 1, Sch 2, Sch 3;
Judicial Separation and Family Law Reform Act 1989 s 26;
FA 1989 Pt I, ss 86 to 89, 95, 98 and 100(2), (7) (except in so far as it relates to capital acquisitions tax) and (8), Sch 1;
FA 1990 Pt I, ss 131, 136, 137, 138 and 140(2) and (8), Schs 1–6;
FA 1991 Pt I, ss 126, 128, 130 and 132(2) and (8), Schs 1–2;
Oireachtas (Allowances to Members) and Ministerial and Parliamentary Offices Act 1992 s 4;
FA 1992 Pt I, Pt VII, except s 248 in so far as it relates to residential property tax, s 254(2), (8) (except in so far as it relates to residential property tax) and (9), Sch 1, Sch 2;
F(No 2)A 1992 Pt I, s 30(2);
FA 1993 Pt I, ss 140 and 143(2) and (8), Sch 1;
Waiver of Certain Tax, Interest and Penalties Act 1993 ss 10–13;
FA 1994 Pt I, Pt VII Ch I, s 161, except in so far as it relates to stamp duty, ss 162, 163(2), 164 and 166(2) and (8), Schs 1–2;
FA 1995 Pt I, Pt VII Ch I, ss 172 to 177, 179(2), (8) and (9), Schs 1–4;
Family Law Act 1995 s 37;
FA 1996 Pt I, Pt VI, ss 139 and 143(2), (7) and (8), Sch 1, Sch 5;
Disclosure of Certain Information for Taxation and Other Purposes Act 1996 ss 5, 6, 10, 11 and 12;
Criminal Assets Bureau Act 1996 ss 23 and 24(1) and (2);
Family Law (Divorce) Act 1996 s 31;
FA 1997 Pts I and VII, ss 157, 158, 159, 160(1), 166(2)(8)(9), Schs 1, 2, 3, 4, 5, 6, 9, 10.

SCHEDULE 31
Consequential Amendments

Section 1100

In the enactments specified in Column (1) of the following Table for the words set out or referred to in Column (2) there shall be substituted the words set out in the corresponding entry in Column (3).

Enactment amended (1)	Words to be replaced (2)	Words to be substituted (3)
The Stamp Act, 1891:		
section 13(1), in the definition of "Appeal Commissioners"	section 156 of the Income Tax Act, 1967	section 850 of the Taxes Consolidation Act, 1997

section 13(4)	Part XXVI (Appeals) of the Income Tax Act, 1967	Chapter 1 of Part 40 (Appeals) of the Taxes Consolidation Act, 1997
The Finance (1909–10) Act, 1910:		
section 49, in the first proviso to subsection (1)	section 242 of the Finance Act, 1992	section 1094 of the Taxes Consolidation Act, 1997
section 49, in the second proviso to subsection (1)	section 242 (as amended by the Finance Act, 1993) of the Finance Act, 1992	section 1094 of the Taxes Consolidation Act, 1997
section 49, in paragraph (a) of subsection (1A)	section 242 of the Finance Act, 1992	section 1094 of the Taxes Consolidation Act, 1997
	subsection (6) of the said section 242	subsection (7) of that section
The Betting Act, 1931, the proviso to section 7(3)	section 242 (as amended by the Finance Act, 1993) of the Finance Act, 1992	section 1094 of the Taxes Consolidation Act, 1997
The Auctioneers and House Agents Act, 1947:		
section 8, in the proviso to subsection (1)	section 242 (as amended by the Finance Act, 1993) of the Finance Act, 1992	section 1094 of the Taxes Consolidation Act, 1997
section 9, in the proviso to subsection (1)	section 242 (as amended by the Finance Act, 1993) of the Finance Act, 1992	section 1094 of the Taxes Consolidation Act, 1997
section 10, in the proviso to subsection (1)	section 242 (as amended by the Finance Act, 1993) of the Finance Act, 1992	section 1094 of the Taxes Consolidation Act, 1997
The Finance Act, 1952, section 19(2)	section 156 of the Corporation Tax Act, 1976	section 9 of the Taxes Consolidation Act, 1997
The Gaming and Lotteries Act, 1956, the proviso to section 19	section 242 (as amended by the Finance Act, 1993) of the Finance Act, 1992	section 1094 of the Taxes Consolidation Act, 1997
The Civil Service Commissioners Act, 1956, section 27(3)	section 156(1) of the Income Tax Act, 1967	section 850(1) of the Taxes Consolidation Act, 1997
The Income Tax (Purchased Life Annuities) Regulations, 1959 (SI No 152 of 1959):		
Regulation 2, in the definition of "the principal section"	section 22 of the Finance Act, 1959	section 788 of the Taxes Consolidation Act, 1997
Regulation 5	subsection (3)	subsection (5)
	subsection (4)	subsection (6)
Regulation 7	Subsection (3) of section 5 of the Finance Act, 1929 (No 32 of 1929), as amended by section 3 of the Finance Act, 1958 (No 25 of 1958)	Subsection (3) of section 933 of the Taxes Consolidation Act, 1997

Regulation 9	Sections 149 and 196 of the Income Tax Act, 1918	Sections 941 and 942 of the Taxes Consolidation Act, 1997
Regulation 17	Rule 17 of the General Rules	Section 1023 of the Taxes Consolidation Act, 1997
Income Tax (Employments) Regulations 1960 (SI No 28 of 1960):		
Regulation 2, in paragraph (1)	"the Act" means the Finance (No 2) Act, 1959 (No 42 of 1959)	"the Act" means the Taxes Consolidation Act, 1997
Regulation 2, paragraph (1), in the definition of "emoluments"	Part II of the Act	Chapter 4 of Part 42 of the Act
Regulation 36, in paragraph (2)	Section 7 of the Finance Act, 1923 (No 21 of 1923), as applied by section 11 of the Act	Section 962 of the Act, as applied by section 993 of the Act
Regulation 36, in paragraph (3)	Section 11 of the Finance Act, 1924 (No 27 of 1924), as applied by section 11 of the Act	Section 963 of the Act, as applied by section 993 of the Act
Regulation 59	section 222 or 223 of the Income Tax Act, 1967 (No 6 of 1967) or by virtue of section 16, 17 or 25 of the Finance Act, 1972 (No 19 of 1972)	section 774 or 776 of the Act
Regulation 60	Chapter IV of Part V of the Income Tax Act, 1967	Chapter 4 of Part 42 of the Act
The Income Tax (Construction Contracts) Regulations, 1971 (SI No 1 of 1971):		
Regulation 2, in the definition of "certified sub-contractor"	subsection (9)(*a*) of the principal section	subsection (13)(*a*) of section 531 of the Act
Regulation 2, in the definition of "principal"	the principal section	section 530 of the Act
	subsection (2) of that section	section 531 of the Act
Regulation 2	"principal section" means section 17 (inserted by the Finance Act, 1976 (No 16 of 1976)) of the Finance Act, 1970 (No 14 of 1970);	"the Act" means the Taxes Consolidation Act, 1997;
Regulation 2, in the definition of "relevant contract"	the principal section	section 530 of the Act
Regulation 2, in the definition of "repayment period"	subsection (4) of the principal section	subsection (5) of section 531 of the Act
Regulation 2, in the definition of "sub-contractor"	subsection (2) of the principal section	subsection (1) of section 531 of the Act
Regulation 2, in the definition of "sub-contractor's certificate"	subsection (7) of the principal section	subsection (11) of section 531 of the Act

Regulation 4	subsection (8)(*a*) of the principal section	subsection (12)(*a*) of section 531 of the Act
Regulation 4A, in paragraph (1)	subsection (8)(*a*) of the principal section	subsection (12)(*a*) of section 531 of the Act
Regulation 4A, in paragraph (2)(c)	section 103(5) of the Corporation Tax Act, 1976	section 433(4) of the Act
	subsection (1) of the principal section	subsection (1) of section 530 of the Act
Regulation 4B, in paragraph (4)	subsection (8)(*a*) of the principal section	subsection (12)(*a*) of section 531 of the Act
Regulation 4C, in paragraph (2)(*a*)(ii)	subsection (7) of the principal section	subsection (11) of section 531 of the Act
Regulation 4C, in paragraph (2)(*b*)	subsection (5)(*a*)(i) of the principal section	subsection (6)(*a*)(i) of section 531 of the Act
Regulation 4C, in paragraph (2)(*c*)	the principal section	section 530 of the Act
Regulation 4C, in paragraph (2)(*d*)	subsection (7) of the principal section	subsection (11) of section 531 of the Act
Regulation 6, in paragraph (3)	subsection (8) of the principal section	subsection (12) of section 531 of the Act
Regulation 8, in paragraph (1)	subsection (2) of the principal section	subsection (1) of section 531 of the Act
Regulation 10, in paragraph (1)	the principal section	section 531 of the Act
Regulation 11, in paragraph (1)	the principal section	section 531 of the Act
	sections 480, 485, 486, 488 and 491 of the Income Tax Act, 1967	sections 962, 963, 966 and 998 of the Act
Regulation 12, in paragraph (1)	the principal section	section 531 of the Act
Regulation 13, in paragraph (1)	subsection (2) of the principal section	subsection (1) of section 531 of the Act
Regulation 13, in paragraph (3)	subsection (4)(*c*)(ii) of the principal section	subsection (5)(*c*)(ii) of section 531 of the Act
Regulation 14	Chapter IV of Part V of the Income Tax Act, 1967	Chapter 4 of Part 42 of the Act
Regulation 19, in paragraph (1)	subsection (8)(*a*) of the principal section	subsection (12)(*a*) of section 531 of the Act
Regulation 20	subsection (9)(*a*) of the principal section	subsection (13)(*a*) of section 531 of the Act
	the said subsection (9)(*a*)	subsection (13)(*a*) of section 531 of the Act
Regulation 21, in paragraph (3)	Chapter III of Part IV of the Income Tax Act, 1967 (No 6 of 1967)	Part 43 of the Act
The Finance Act, 1969, section 49(2B)(*c*)	section 94 of the Finance Act, 1983	section 1078 of the Taxes Consolidation Act, 1997

The Value-Added Tax Act, 1972:		
section 1, in the definition of "Appeal Commissioners"	section 156 of the Income Tax Act, 1967	section 850 of the Taxes Consolidation Act, 1997
section 1, in the definition of "Collector-General"	section 162 of the Income Tax Act, 1967	section 851 of the Taxes Consolidation Act, 1997
section 1, in the definition of "inspector of taxes"	section 161 of the Income Tax Act, 1967	section 852 of the Taxes Consolidation Act, 1997
section 1, in the definition of "secretary"	section 207(2) of the Income Tax Act, 1967	section 1044(2) of the Taxes Consolidation Act, 1997
section 1(2)(*bb*)	section 73 of the Finance Act, 1988	section 1002 of the Taxes Consolidation Act, 1997
section 1(2)(*c*)(i)	Chapter III of Part I of the Finance Act, 1987	Chapter 1 of Part 18 of the Taxes Consolidation Act, 1997
section 1(2)(*c*)(ii)	section 17 of the Finance Act, 1970	Chapter 2 of Part 18 of the Taxes Consolidation Act, 1997
section 18(1)(*a*)(ii*a*)	section 94 (as amended by section 243 of the Finance Act, 1992) of the Finance Act, 1983	section 1078 of the Taxes Consolidation Act, 1997
section 24(1)(*b*)	sections 480, 485, 486, 487, 488 and 491 of the Income Tax Act, 1967	sections 962, 963, 964(1), 966, 967 and 998 of the Taxes Consolidation Act, 1997
section 24(5)	under section 485 of the Income Tax Act, 1967	under section 962 of the Taxes Consolidation Act, 1997
	section 485	section 962
section 27(11)	section 94 (as amended by section 243 of the Finance Act, 1992) of the Finance Act, 1983	section 1078 of the Taxes Consolidation Act, 1997
section 31	section 512 of the Income Tax Act, 1967	section 1065 of the Taxes Consolidation Act, 1997
First Schedule, in paragraph (i)(*g*)	section 18 of the Finance Act, 1989	section 734 of the Taxes Consolidation Act, 1997
The Imposition of Duties (No 221) (Excise Duties) Order, 1975 (SI No 305 of 1975), the proviso to paragraph 12(12)	section 242 (as amended by the Finance Act, 1993) of the Finance Act, 1992	section 1094 of the Taxes Consolidation Act, 1997
The Capital Acquisitions Tax Act, 1976:		
section 16(2), in the definition of "private company"	section 95 of the Corporation Tax Act, 1976	section 431 of the Taxes Consolidation Act, 1997
	subsection (1)	subsection (3)
	subsection (4)	subsection (6)
section 52(1), in the definition of "Appeal Commissioners"	section 156 of the Income Tax Act, 1967	section 850 of the Taxes Consolidation Act, 1997
section 58(2)(*b*)	section 142 of the Income Tax Act, 1967	section 466 of the Taxes Consolidation Act, 1997

section 63(9)	sections 128(4), 507, 508, 510, 511, 512, 517 and 518 of the Income Tax Act, 1967	sections 987(4), 1061, 1062, 1063, 1064, 1065, 1066 and 1068 of the Taxes Consolidation Act, 1997
Second Schedule, Part I, paragraph 9, in the definition of "investment income"	section 2 of the Income Tax Act, 1967	section 3 of the Taxes Consolidation Act, 1997
The Value-Added Tax Regulations, 1979 (SI No 63 of 1979):		
Regulation 15, in paragraph (2)	Section 485 of the Income Tax Act, 1967	Section 962 of the Taxes Consolidation Act, 1997
	the words from "modifications in subsection (1)" to the end of the paragraph	modification in subsection (1), namely, the words "any sum which may be levied on that person in respect of income tax" shall be construed as referring to value-added tax payable by the person concerned
Regulation 15, in paragraph (3)	Section 486 of the Income Tax Act, 1967	Section 963 of the Taxes Consolidation Act, 1997
Regulation 15, in paragraph (3)(*a*)	income tax or sur-tax	income tax
Regulation 15, in paragraph (3)(*b*)	the Collector or other officer of the Revenue Commissioners, duly authorised to collect the said tax	the Collector-General or other officer of the Revenue Commissioners duly authorised to collect the tax
	the Collector or other officer under this section	the Collector-General or other officer under this section
Regulation 15, in paragraph (4)	Section 487 of the Income Tax Act, 1967	Section 964(1) of the Taxes Consolidation Act, 1997
Regulation 15, in paragraph (5)	Section 488 of the Income Tax Act, 1967	Section 966 of the Taxes Consolidation Act, 1997
Regulation 15, in paragraph (5)(*a*)	income tax or sur-tax	income tax
Regulation 15, in paragraph (5)(*b*)	references to an inspector and to the Collector	references to an inspector and to the Collector-General
Regulation 15, in paragraph (6)	Section 491 of the Income Tax Act, 1967	Section 998 of the Taxes Consolidation Act, 1997
	income tax or sur tax	income tax
The Health Contributions Act, 1979:		
section 1, in the definition of "the Collector-General"	section 162 of the Income Tax Act, 1967	section 851 of the Taxes Consolidation Act, 1997
section 1, in the definition of "emoluments"	Chapter IV of Part V of the Income Tax Act, 1967, but without regard to section 192 of that Act	Chapter 4 of Part 42 of the Taxes Consolidation Act, 1997, but without regard to section 1015 of that Act

section 7A	section 3 of the Finance Act, 1983	section 1025 of the Taxes Consolidation Act, 1997
The Health Contribution Regulations, 1979 (SI No 107 of 1979):		
Regulation 3, in the definition of "the Collector"	section 162 of the Income Tax Act, 1967 (No 6 of 1967)	section 851 of the Taxes Consolidation Act, 1997
Regulation 3, in the definition of "excepted farmer"	"an individual to whom section 16 applies" within the meaning of Chapter II of Part I of the Finance Act, 1974 (No 27 of 1974), if paragraphs (*b*) and (*d*) of section 16(1), and section 16(2), of that Act did not apply	"an individual to whom subsection (1) applies" within the meaning of section 657 of the Taxes Consolidation Act, 1997, if paragraphs (*b*) and (*d*) of the definition of "an individual to whom subsection (1) applies" in subsection (1) of that section of that Act and subsection (2) of that section of that Act did not apply
Regulation 3, in the definition of "farm land occupied by the individual"	section 13(1) of the Finance Act, 1974	section 654 of the Taxes Consolidation Act, 1997
Regulation 4	Chapter IV of Part V of the Income Tax Act, 1967, applies but without regard to Chapter I of Part IX of that Act	Chapter 4 of Part 42 of the Taxes Consolidation Act, 1997, applies but without regard to sections 1015 to 1024 of that Act
Regulation 6	Chapter I (inserted by the Finance Act, 1980) (No 14 of 1980) of Part IX of the Income Tax Act, 1967 (No 6 of 1987)	sections 1015 to 1024 of the Taxes Consolidation Act, 1997
	section 33 of the Finance Act, 1975 (No 6 of 1975)	the definition of "capital allowance" in section 2(1) of the Taxes Consolidation Act, 1997
The Youth Employment Agency Act, 1981:		
section 1(1), in the definition of "the Collector-General"	section 162 of the Income Tax Act, 1967	section 851 of the Taxes Consolidation Act, 1997
section 1(1), in the definition of "emoluments"	Chapter IV of Part V of the Income Tax Act, 1967 (but without regard to Chapter I (inserted by the Finance Act, 1980) of Part IX of that Act)	Chapter 4 of Part 42 of the Taxes Consolidation Act, 1997 (but without regard to sections 1015 to 1024 of that Act)
section 18A	section 3 of the Finance Act, 1983	section 1025 of the Taxes Consolidation Act, 1997

The Youth Employment Levy Regulations 1982, (SI No 84 of 1982):		
Regulation 3, in the definition of "the Collector"	section 162 of the Income Tax Act, 1967 (No 6 of 1967)	section 851 of the Taxes Consolidation Act, 1997
Regulation 3, in the definition of "excepted farmer"	an individual to whom section 16 applies within the meaning of Chapter II of Part I of the Finance Act, 1974 (No 27 of 1974), if paragraph (*b*) and (*d*) of subsection (1) and subsection (2) of section 16 of that Act did not apply	an individual to whom subsection (1) applies within the meaning of section 657 of the Taxes Consolidation Act, 1997, if paragraphs (*b*) and (*d*) of the definition of "an individual to whom subsection (1) applies" in subsection (1) of that section of that Act and subsection (2) of that section of that Act did not apply
Regulation 3, in the definition of "farm land occupied by the individual"	section 13(1) of the Finance Act, 1974	section 654 of the Taxes Consolidation Act, 1997
Regulation 6	Chapter I (inserted by the Finance Act, 1980 (No 14 of 1980)) of Part IX of the Income Tax Act, 1967 (No 6 of 1967)	sections 1015 to 1024 of the Taxes Consolidation Act, 1997
	section 33 of the Finance Act, 1975 (No 6 of 1975)	the definition of "capital allowance" in section 2(1) of the Taxes Consolidation Act, 1997
Regulation 16	section 195 of the Income Tax Act, 1967	section 1018 of the Taxes Consolidation Act, 1997
The Income Tax (Rent Relief) Regulations, 1982 (SI No 318 of 1982):		
Regulation 2	Chapter IV of Part IV of the Income Tax Act, 1967 (No 6 of 1967)	Chapter 8 of Part 4 of the Taxes Consolidation Act, 1997
	section 142A (inserted by section 5 of the Finance Act, 1982 (No 14 of 1982)) of the Income Tax Act, 1967	section 473 of the Taxes Consolidation Act, 1997
Regulation 3	subsection (5)(a)(i)	subsection (6)(a)(i)
Regulation 5	section 6 of the Finance Act, 1968 (No 33 of 1968), and section 34 of the Finance Act, 1976 (No 16 of 1976)	sections 886 and 905
The Finance Act, 1984, section 108(1)(*b*)(ii)	subsection (9) of section 235 of the Income Tax Act, 1967	subsection (1) of section 783 of the Taxes Consolidation Act, 1997
	section 235A	section 785

The Finance Act, 1986:		
section 94(1)(*a*), in the definition of "Corporation Tax Acts"	section 155(1) of the Corporation Tax Act, 1976	section 1 of the Taxes Consolidation Act, 1997
section 94(1)(*a*), in the definition of "relevant interest"	section 84(2)(*d*) of the Corporation Tax Act, 1976	section 130(2)(*d*) of the Taxes Consolidation Act, 1997
The Health Contributions (Amendment) Regulations, 1988 (SI No 51 of 1988), Regulation 3, in paragraph (2)	section 195 of the Income Tax Act, 1967	section 1018 of the Taxes Consolidation Act, 1997
The Finance Act, 1989, the proviso to section 45(3)(b)	section 242 (as amended by the Finance Act, 1993) of the Finance Act, 1992	section 1094 of the Taxes Consolidation Act, 1997
The Finance Act, 1990:		
section 112(5)	section 94 of the Finance Act, 1983	section 1078 of the Taxes Consolidation Act, 1997
section 129(1)	subsection (9) of section 235 of the Income Tax Act, 1967	subsection (1) of section 783 of the Taxes Consolidation Act, 1997
The Finance Act, 1991:		
section 108(1)	section 485 of the Income Tax Act, 1967	section 962 of the Taxes Consolidation Act, 1997
section 109(1)	Sections 128(4), 507, 508, 510, 511, 512, 517 and 518 of the Income Tax Act, 1967	Sections 987(4), 1061, 1062, 1063, 1064, 1065, 1066 and 1068 of the Taxes Consolidation Act, 1997
	Income Tax Act, 1967	Taxes Consolidation Act, 1997
section 129(1), in the definition of "the Collector"	section 162 of the Income Tax Act, 1967	section 851 of the Taxes Consolidation Act, 1997
section 129(3)	Section 187 of the Income Tax Act, 1967	Section 928(1) and 964(2) of the Taxes Consolidation Act, 1997
The Finance Act, 1992:		
section 206(*a*), (*aa*) and (*c*)(ii)	section 18 of the Finance Act, 1989	section 734 of the Taxes Consolidation Act, 1997
section 206(*b*)	subsection (5A) (inserted by section 34 of the Finance Act, 1977) of section 31 of the Capital Gains Tax Act, 1975	subsection (6) of section 731 of the Taxes Consolidation Act, 1997
The Finance Act, 1993:		
section 106(2)(*b*)	section 31 of the Finance Act, 1991	section 110 of the Taxes Consolidation Act, 1997
section 109(1), in the definition of "dependent relative"	subsection (9A) (inserted by the Finance Act, 1979) of section 25 of the Capital Gains Tax Act, 1975	subsection (11) of section 604 of the Taxes Consolidation Act, 1997

section 112(*a*)(i)(A)	section 235(9) of the Income Tax Act, 1967	section 783(1) of the Taxes Consolidation Act, 1997
section 112(*a*)(i)(B)	section 235 or section 235A	section 784 or section 785
section 112(*a*)(iii)	section 236 of the Income Tax Act, 1967	section 787 of the Taxes Consolidation Act, 1997
section 112(*d*), proviso (i)	subsection (1A) of section 142 of the Income Tax Act, 1967	subsection (1) of section 466 of the Taxes Consolidation Act, 1997
section 133(1)	section 36 of the Finance Act, 1988	section 451 of the Taxes Consolidation Act, 1997
The Social Welfare (Consolidation) Act, 1993:		
section 2, in the definition of "Collector-General"	section 162 of the Income Tax Act, 1967	section 851 of the Taxes Consolidation Act, 1997
section 2, in the definition of "reckonable emoluments"	Chapter IV of Part V of the Income Tax Act, 1967	Chapter 4 of Part 42 of the Taxes Consolidation Act, 1997
section 2, in the definition of "reckonable income"	section 2 or section 18 of the Finance Act, 1969	section 195, 231 or 232 of the Taxes Consolidation Act, 1997
	Chapter 1 (inserted by the Finance Act, 1980) of Part IX of the Income Tax Act, 1967	Chapter 1 of Part 44 of the Taxes Consolidation Act, 1997
section 2, in the definition of "reckonable income"	section 33 of the Finance Act, 1975	the definition of "capital allowance" in section 2(1) of the Taxes Consolidation Act, 1997
section 18(1)(*b*)	section 48(1) of the Finance Act, 1986	section 1084(1) of the Taxes Consolidation Act, 1997
section 20(5)	section 195 of the Income Tax Act, 1967	section 1018 of the Taxes Consolidation Act, 1997
section 212(5)	section 17 (as amended by section 28 of the Finance Act, 1992) of the Finance Act, 1970	Chapter 2 of Part 18 of the Taxes Consolidation Act, 1997
First Schedule, Part III, paragraph 3(*a*)	section 33 of the Finance Act, 1975	the definition of "capital allowance" in section 2(1) of the Taxes Consolidation Act, 1997
First Schedule, Part III, paragraph 4	Chapter II or III of Part IV of the Income Tax Act, 1967	Chapter 3 of Part 4, or Part 43, of the Taxes Consolidation Act, 1997
First Schedule, Part III, paragraph 6	Chapter II or III of Part IV of the Income Tax Act, 1967	Chapter 3 of Part 4, or Part 43, of the Taxes Consolidation Act, 1997
The Industrial Training (Apprenticeship Levy) Act, 1994, section 1(1)	section 162 of the Income Tax Act, 1967	section 851 of the Taxes Consolidation Act, 1997
The Casual Trading Act, 1995, section 4(2A)	section 161 of the Income Tax Act, 1967	section 852 of the Taxes Consolidation Act, 1997

The Finance Act, 1995:		
section 103	section 156 of the Income Tax Act, 1967	section 850 of the Taxes Consolidation Act, 1997
section 105(3)	Part XXVI (as amended) other than sections 429 and 430 and (in so far as it relates to those sections) section 431, of the Income Tax Act, 1967	Part 40, other than sections 942, 943 and (in so far as it relates to those sections) 944 of the Taxes Consolidation Act, 1997
The Consumer Credit Act, 1995:		
section 93(10)(*d*)	section 242 (as amended by the Finance Act, 1997) of the Finance Act, 1992	section 1094 of the Taxes Consolidation Act, 1997
section 93(10A)(*a*)(i)	section 242 of the Finance Act, 1992	section 1094 of the Taxes Consolidation Act, 1997
section 93(10A)(*a*)(ii)	section 242	section 1094
section 116(9)(*d*)	section 242 (as amended by the Finance Act, 1997) of the Finance Act, 1992	section 1094 of the Taxes Consolidation Act, 1997
section 116(9A)(*a*)(i)	section 242 of the Finance Act, 1992	section 1094 of the Taxes Consolidation Act, 1997
section 116(9A)(*a*)(ii)	section 242	section 1094
section 144(9)(*d*)	section 242 (as amended by the Finance Act, 1997) of the Finance Act, 1992	section 1094 of the Taxes Consolidation Act, 1997
section 144(9A)(*a*)(i)	section 242 of the Finance Act, 1992	section 1094 of the Taxes Consolidation Act, 1997
section 144(9A)(*a*)(ii)	section 242	section 1094
The Finance Act, 1996, section 108(4)	section 94(2)(*d*) of the Finance Act, 1983	section 1078(2)(*d*) of the Taxes Consolidation Act, 1997
The Social Welfare (Consolidated Contributions and Insurability) Regulations, 1996 (SI No 312 of 1996):		
Regulation 3, in the definition of "inspector of taxes"	section 161 of the Act of 1967	section 852 of the Act of 1997
Regulation 3, in the definition of "reckonable earnings"	Chapter IV of Part V of the Act of 1967	Chapter 4 of Part 42 of the Act of 1997
	section 192 of that Act	section 1015 of that Act
	the Act of 1967 (other than Chapter IV of Part V)	the Act of 1997 (other than Chapter 4 of Part 42)
	section 192 of that Act	section 1015 of that Act
Regulation 3, in the definition of "reckonable income"	the Act of 1967	the Act of 1997
	Chapter 11 of Part I of the Finance Act, 1972 (No 19 of 1972)	Chapter 1 of Part 30

Regulation 3, the definition of "the Act of 1967"	"the Act of 1967" means the Income Tax Act, 1967 (No 6 of 1967);	"the Act of 1997" means the Taxes Consolidation Act, 1997;
Regulation 10, in paragraph (1)	section 129 of the Act of 1967	section 991 of the Act of 1997
Regulation 27	section 8(1) of the Finance Act, 1979 (No 11 of 1979)	section 125 of the Act of 1997

SCHEDULE 32
Transitional Provisions

[Section 1101]

Stock of Local Authorities

1. (1) Any stock under section 87 of the Local Government Act, 1946, issued on or after the 13th day of July, 1955, shall be deemed to be securities issued under the authority of the Minister for Finance under section 36, and that section shall apply accordingly.

(2) Section 49 shall apply as if in subsection (1) of that section **"or paragraph 1 of Schedule 32"** were inserted after **"or 41"**.

Former enactments

ITA 1967 s 472(1).

Income Tax: Exemption from Tax of Income from Certain Scholarships

2. Where a payment of income is made before the 6th day of April, 1998, in respect of a scholarship awarded before the 26th day of March, 1997, section 193 shall apply as if—

(*a*) in subsection (1) of that section the definitions of **"relevant body"** and **"relevant scholarship"** and paragraph (*b*) were deleted, and

(*b*) subsections (3) and (4) of that section were deleted.

Former enactments

ITA 1967 s 353; FA 1997 s 11(2).

Corporation Tax: Exemption from Tax of Profits of Custom House Docks Development Authority

3. (1) Notwithstanding any provision of the Corporation Tax Acts, profits arising to the Custom House Docks Development Authority in any accounting period ending on or after the 17th day of November, 1986, shall be exempt from corporation tax.

(2) Subparagraph (1) shall be repealed with effect from the 1st day of May, 1997.

Former enactments

FA 1988 s 42; FA 1997 s 47(4).

Meaning of "Relevant Distributions" for the Purposes of Section 147 in Relation to Distributions Made Before 6th April, 1989

...[1]

Amendments

[1] Para 4 repealed by FA 2000 s 69(2) and Sch 2 Part 2 with effect from 6 April 1999 in the case of income tax and as respects accounting periods commencing on or after that date in the case of corporation tax.

Distributions Out of Certain Income of Manufacturing Companies — Provisions Relating to Relief for Certain Losses and Capital Allowances Carried Forward from 1975–76

...[1]

Amendments

[1] Para 5 deleted by FA 1999 s 71 and Sch 1 para 2(*b*) with effect from 6 April 1999.

Distributions Out of Certain Income of Manufacturing Companies — Provisions Relating to Relief for Certain Corporation Profits Tax Losses

...[1]

Amendments

[1] Para 6 deleted by FA 1999 s 71 and Sch 1 para 2(*d*) with effect from 6 April 1999.

Approved Share Option Schemes

7. (1) This paragraph shall apply where on or after the 6th day of April, 1986, an individual obtains a right to acquire shares in a body corporate—

(*a*) by reason of his or her office or employment as a director or employee of that or any other body corporate, and

(*b*) in accordance with the provisions of a scheme approved under the Second Schedule to the Finance Act, 1986;

but neither this paragraph nor that Schedule shall apply in relation to such a right obtained on or after the 29th day of January, 1992.

(2) Where the individual exercises the right in accordance with the provisions of the scheme referred to in subparagraph (1)(*b*) at a time when it is approved under the Second Schedule to the Finance Act, 1986—

(*a*) income tax shall not be chargeable under section 128 in respect of any gain realised by the exercise of the right, and

(*b*) if but for this clause section 547 would apply, that section shall not apply in calculating the consideration for the acquisition of the shares by the individual or for any corresponding disposal of them to the individual.

(3) (*a*) This paragraph shall apply notwithstanding that the Second Schedule to the Finance Act, 1986, is not re-enacted by this Act, and accordingly this Act shall apply with any modifications necessary to give effect to this paragraph.

(*b*) Without prejudice to the generality of clause (*a*), sections 1052, 1053 and 1054 shall apply for the purposes of that clause as if in Schedule 29 there were included in Column 2 a reference to paragraph 14 of the Second Schedule to the Finance Act, 1986.

Former enactments

FA 1986 s 10(1), (2)(*a*)–(*b*); FA 1992 s 12.

Interest on Certain Loans: Relief from Corporation Tax

8. (1) For the purposes of this paragraph, "permanent loan" means a loan of a permanent character made under an agreement entered into before the 27th day of November, 1975, and which under the agreement is—

(*a*) secured by mortgage or debenture or otherwise on the assets or income of a company, and

(*b*) if subject to repayment, is subject to repayment at not less than 3 months' notice;

but a loan shall not be regarded as a permanent loan for the purposes of this paragraph if under the terms of the loan agreement the rate of interest or other conditions of the loan may be altered during the currency of the loan.

(2) Where for the purposes of corporation tax the income of a company for an accounting period includes interest payable in respect of a permanent loan, the company shall be entitled on a due claim to have its liability to corporation tax for the accounting period reduced as provided by subparagraph (3).

(3) The reduction referred to in subparagraph (2) shall be determined in accordance with subparagraph (4) (apart from clause (*c*)) of paragraph 18 as if the interest were a relevant deficiency within the meaning of subparagraph (1) of that paragraph.

(4) Where in computing the reduction provided for by subparagraph (3) the appropriate amount as determined in accordance with paragraph 18(4)(*a*)(ii) is the company's income for the accounting period, the excess of such interest as is mentioned in subparagraph (2) for the accounting period over that income shall for the purposes of this paragraph be aggregated with the amount of any such interest for the next accounting period and relief shall be allowed for that period in respect of the aggregated amount and, if that aggregated amount exceeds the income for that period, the excess shall be carried forward to the accounting period succeeding that period and so on.

(5) A claim under this paragraph shall be made to the inspector within 2 years from the end of the accounting period.

Former enactments

CTA 1976 s 177.

Allowance for Certain Capital Expenditure on Construction of multi-storey car-parks

9. (1) In this paragraph—

"multi-storey car-park" means a building or structure consisting of 3 or more storeys wholly in use for the purpose of providing, for members of the public generally without preference for any particular class of person, on payment of an appropriate charge, parking space for mechanically propelled vehicles;

"relevant expenditure" means capital expenditure incurred on or after the 29th day of January, 1981, and before the 1st day of April, 1991, on the construction of a multi-storey car-park.

(2) The provisions of the Tax Acts (other than section 273) relating to the making of allowances or charges in respect of capital expenditure on the construction of an industrial building or structure shall apply to relevant expenditure as if it were expenditure incurred on the construction of a building or structure in respect of which an allowance is to be made for the purposes of income tax or corporation tax, as the case may be, under Part 9 by reason of its use for a purpose specified in section 268(1)(*a*).

Revenue precedents

Issue: Whether development of a carpark and shopping area is within meaning of Sch 32 para 9.

Decision: Only where a separate contract is negotiated exclusively for carpark facilities would Revenue consider to be within meaning of Sch 32 para 9.

Definitions

person: IA 1937 s 11(*c*); Tax Acts: s 1(2).

Former enactments

FA 1981 s 25; FA 1986 s 51(2); FA 1988 s 49.

Allowance for Certain Capital Expenditure on Roads, Bridges, etc

10. (1) In this paragraph—

"chargeable period" and **"chargeable period or its basis period"** have the same meanings as in section 321(2);

"qualifying period" means the period commencing on the 29th day of January, 1981, and ending on the 31st day of March, 1989, or, in the case of a relevant agreement entered into on or after the 6th day of April, 1987, ending on the 31st day of March, 1992;

"relevant agreement" means an agreement between a road authority and another person under section 9 of the Local Government (Toll Roads) Act, 1979, by virtue of which that other person incurs relevant expenditure;

"relevant expenditure" means capital expenditure incurred by a person during the qualifying period by virtue of a relevant agreement including, in the case of a relevant agreement entered into on or after the 6th day of April, 1987, interest on money borrowed to meet such capital expenditure, but does not include any expenditure in respect of which any person is entitled to a deduction, relief or allowance under any provision of the Tax Acts other than this paragraph;

"relevant income" means income which arises to a person by virtue of a relevant agreement;

"road authority" has the meaning assigned to it by the Local Government (Toll Roads) Act, 1979.

(2) Where in the case of a relevant agreement entered into before the 6th day of April, 1987, a person, having made a claim in that behalf, proves as respects a chargeable period that relevant income was receivable by such person in that chargeable period or

its basis period and that such person has incurred relevant expenditure, then, such person shall, subject to subparagraph (4), be entitled, for the purpose only of ascertaining the amount (if any) of relevant income on which such person is to be charged to tax for the chargeable period, to an allowance equal to 50 per cent of the relevant expenditure; but the aggregate amount of all allowances made to that person under this subparagraph in relation to any relevant expenditure shall not exceed an amount equal to 50 per cent of that expenditure.

(3) Where a person, having made a claim in that behalf, proves as respects a chargeable period that relevant income was receivable and relevant expenditure was incurred by such person in the chargeable period or its basis period by virtue of the relevant agreement (being a relevant agreement entered into on or after the 6th day of April, 1987) giving rise to the relevant income, such person shall, subject to subparagraph (4), be entitled, for the purpose only of ascertaining the amount (if any) of that relevant income on which such person is to be charged to tax—

- (*a*) to an allowance equal to 50 per cent of the relevant expenditure for that chargeable period, and
- (*b*) to an allowance equal to 10 per cent of the relevant expenditure for each of the next 5 chargeable periods in which that relevant income is receivable by such person;

and, for the purposes of this subparagraph, all relevant expenditure so incurred before the chargeable period in which relevant income is first receivable shall be deemed to have been incurred on the first day of that chargeable period.

(4) Where an allowance to which a person is entitled under this paragraph cannot be given full effect for any chargeable period by reason of a want or deficiency of relevant income, then (so long as the person has relevant income), the amount unallowed shall be carried forward to the succeeding chargeable period and the amount so carried forward shall be treated for the purposes of this paragraph, including any further application of this subparagraph, as the amount of a corresponding allowance for that period.

(5) An appeal to the Appeal Commissioners shall lie on any question arising under this paragraph in the like manner as an appeal would lie against an assessment to income tax or corporation tax, and the provisions of the Tax Acts relating to appeals shall apply accordingly.

Definitions

Appeal Commissioners: s 2(1); person: IA 1937 s 11(*c*); Tax Acts: s 1(2).

Former enactments

FA 1981 s 26; FA 1984 s 39; FA 1989 s 17.

Urban Renewal Scheme, 1986 — Capital Allowances in Relation to Certain Commercial Premises in Designated Areas other than the Custom House Docks Area

11. Where but for the repeal by this Act of the repealed enactments an allowance or charge would be made to or on a person for any chargeable period under Chapter II of Part XV, or Chapter I of Part XVI, of the Income Tax Act, 1967 (including any such allowance as increased under section 25 of the Finance Act, 1978), by virtue of section 42 of the Finance Act, 1986 (in so far as that section applied to areas other than the

Custom House Docks Area within the meaning section 41 of that Act), then, notwithstanding that that section as it so applied is not re-enacted by this Act, that allowance or charge shall be made to or on the person under this Act, and accordingly this Act shall apply with any modifications necessary to give effect to this paragraph.

Former enactments

FA 1986 s 42.

Urban Renewal Scheme, 1986— Allowances to Owner-Occupiers in Relation to Certain Residential Premises in Designated Areas other than the Custom House Docks Area

12. Where but for the repeal by this Act of the repealed enactments a person would, in the computation of his or her total income for any year of assessment, be entitled to a deduction under section 44 of the Finance Act, 1986 (in so far as that section applied to areas other than the Custom House Docks Area within the meaning of section 41 of that Act), then, notwithstanding that that section as it so applied is not re-enacted by this Act, the person shall be entitled to that deduction for that year of assessment under this Act, and accordingly this Act shall apply with any modifications necessary to give effect to this paragraph.

Definitions

Appeal Commissioners: s 2(1); Circuit Court: IA 1937 Sch; Income Tax Acts: s 1(2); inspector: ss 2(1), 852; local authority: ss 2(1), 5(1); person: IA 1937 s 11(*c*); statute: s 2(1), IA 1937 s 3; total income: s 3(1); year of assessment: ss 2(1), 5(1).

Cross-references

Deduction allowed in ascertaining taxable income, ss 458(2); 459(1), (2).

Rate of tax at which repayments are to be made: s 460.

Method of apportioning relief and charging tax in cases of self-assessment: s 1024(2)(*a*)(xii).

Former enactments

FA 1986 s 44.

Urban Renewal Scheme, 1986— Double Rent Allowance in Relation to Certain Premises in Designated Areas other than the Custom House Docks Area

13. Where but for the repeal by this Act of the repealed enactments a further deduction on account of rent in respect of any premises would be made to a person under section 45 of the Finance Act, 1986 (in so far as that section applied to areas other than the Custom House Docks Area within the meaning of section 41 of that Act), in the computation of the amount of the profits or gains of the person's trade or profession, then, notwithstanding that that section as it so applied is not re-enacted by this Act, that further deduction shall be made to the person under this Act, and accordingly this Act shall apply with any modifications necessary to give effect to this paragraph.

Cross-references

Restriction on use by certain partnerships of certain allowances, etc, transitional arrangements: s 1017(2C)(*a*)("specified deduction").

Former enactments

FA 1986 s 45.

Rented Residential Accommodation — Deduction for Expenditure Incurred on Construction, Conversion or Refurbishment in Areas other than the Custom House Docks Area

14. Where, in computing the amount of a surplus or deficiency in respect of rent from any premises in any area other than the Custom House Docks Area (within the meaning of section 41 of the Finance Act, 1986), a person would, but for the repeal by this Act of the repealed enactments—

(*a*) be entitled to a deduction, or

(*b*) be deemed to have received an amount as rent,

under—

(i) section 23 of the Finance Act, 1981,

(ii) section 23 of the Finance Act, 1981, as applied by virtue of section 24 of that Act or section 22 of the Finance Act, 1985, or

(iii) section 23 of the Finance Act, 1981, as applied by section 21 of the Finance Act, 1985,

in so far as those sections applied to areas other than the Custom House Docks Area (within the meaning of section 41 of the Finance Act, 1986), then, notwithstanding that those sections as they so applied are not re-enacted by this Act, the person shall be entitled to that deduction or be deemed to have received that amount as rent, as the case may be, under this Act, and accordingly this Act shall apply with any modifications necessary to give effect to this paragraph.

Definitions

Appeal Commissioners: s 2(1); capital allowance: s 2(1); Circuit Court: IA 1937 Sch; inspector: ss 2(1), 5(1), 852; land: s 5(1), IA 1937 Sch; person: IA 1937 s 11(*c*); trade: s 3(1); writing: IA 1937 Sch.

Former enactments

FA 1981 ss 23–24, FA 1985 ss 21–22, FA 1991 ss 56–58.

Loss Relief, etc

15. The substitution of this Act for the corresponding enactments repealed by this Act shall not alter the effect of any provision enacted before this Act (whether or not there is a corresponding provision in this Act) in so far as it determines whether and to what extent—

(*a*) losses or expenditure incurred in, or an excess of deficiencies over surpluses in, or other amounts referable to, a year of assessment or accounting period earlier than a year of assessment or accounting period to which this Act applies may be taken into account for any tax purposes in a year of assessment or accounting period to which this Act applies, or

(*b*) losses or expenditure incurred in, or an excess of deficiencies over surpluses in, or other amounts referable to, a year of assessment or accounting period to which this Act applies may be taken into account for any tax purposes in a year of assessment or accounting period earlier than a year of assessment or accounting period to which this Act applies.

Relief in Respect of Unrelieved Losses and Capital Allowances Carried Forward from the Year 1975–76

16. (1) In this paragraph—

"relevant amount", in relation to a company, means the aggregate of the following amounts—

(*a*) such part of a loss, including any amount to be treated as a loss under section 316 of the Income Tax Act, 1967, incurred by the company in a trade before the date on which the company comes within the charge to corporation tax in respect of the trade and which, but for the Corporation Tax Act, 1976, could have been carried forward to the year 1976–77 under section 309 of the Income Tax Act, 1967, and

(*b*) such part of any capital allowance to which the company which carries on the trade was entitled in charging the profits or gains of the trade for years before the year 1976–77 and to which effect has not been given by means of relief before that year;

"relevant corporation tax", in relation to an accounting period, means the corporation tax (other than an amount which by virtue of sections 239, 241, 440 and 441 is to be treated as corporation tax of an accounting period) which, apart from this paragraph, paragraph 18 and section 448, would be chargeable for the accounting period exclusive of the corporation tax chargeable on the part of the company's profits attributable to chargeable gains for that period, and that part shall be taken to be the amount brought into the company's profits for that period for the purposes of corporation tax in respect of chargeable gains before any deduction for charges on income, expenses of management or other amounts which can be deducted from or set against or treated as reducing profits of more than one description.

(2) Relief, as provided in subparagraph (3), shall be allowed in respect of a relevant amount against corporation tax payable by the company and such relief shall be given as far as possible from the tax payable for the first accounting period for which the company is within the charge to corporation tax in respect of the trade and, in so far as it cannot be so given, from the tax payable for the next accounting period and so on.

(3) The relief for an accounting period shall be an amount calculated by applying to that part of the relevant amount in respect of which relief from tax has not been allowed a rate equal to—

[(*a*) as respects accounting periods beginning on or after the 1st day of January, 1998, and ending before the 1st day of January, 1999, 17 per cent,

(*b*) as respects accounting periods beginning on or after the 1st day of January, 1999, and ending before the 1st day of January, 2000, 13 per cent,

(*c*) as respects accounting periods beginning on or after the 1st day of January, 2000, and ending before the 1st day of January, 2001, 9 per cent,

(*d*) as respects accounting periods beginning on or after the 1st day of January, 2001, and ending before the 1st day of January, 2002, 5 per cent, and

(*e*) as respects accounting periods beginning on or after the 1st day of January, 2002, and ending before the 1st day of January, 2003, 1 per cent;][1]

but—

(i) the amount to which that rate is applied shall not exceed the amount of income from the trade included in chargeable profits for the accounting period reduced by the amount, if any, included in charges on income paid by the company in the accounting period in respect of payments made wholly and exclusively for the purposes of the trade, and

(ii) where the corporation tax payable by the company for an accounting period is reduced by virtue of a claim under section 448(2), the relief to be given under this paragraph for the accounting period shall be reduced in the same proportion as the corporation tax payable by the company for the accounting period in so far as it is attributable to the income from the trade is so reduced, and the corporation tax attributable to the income from the trade shall be an amount equal to the same proportion of the relevant corporation tax for the accounting period as the income from the trade for the accounting period bears to the total income brought into charge to corporation tax.

(4) Relief under this paragraph shall not be allowed against corporation tax payable by a company which by virtue of agreements between the Government and the Government of the United Kingdom in respect of double income tax was entitled to exemption from income tax for the year 1975–76 in respect of income arising in the State.

[(5) Relief shall not be allowed under this paragraph against corporation tax payable by a company in respect of accounting periods beginning on or after the 1st day of January, 2003.

(6) For the purposes of this paragraph, where an accounting period begins before the 1st day of January of a financial year and ends on or after that day, it shall be divided into two parts, one part beginning on the day on which the accounting period begins and ending on the 31st day of December of the preceding financial year, and another part beginning on the 1st day of January of the financial year and ending on the day on which the accounting period ends, and both parts shall be treated as if they were separate accounting periods.][2]

Amendments

1 Subpara (3)(*a*)–(*c*) substituted by FA 1999 s 71 and Sch 1 para 2(*e*)(i) with effect from 6 April 1999.

2 Subpara (5) substituted by FA 1999 s 71 Sch 1 para 2(*e*)(ii) with effect from 6 April 1999.

Cross-references

Change in ownership of a company, disallowance of trading losses: s 401(2).

Distributions out of profits from trading in Shannon Airport: s 144(8)("S").

Expenditure on abortive exploration: s 674(4).

Exploration expenditure incurred by bodies corporate: s 675(2)(*b*).

Exploration expenditure incurred by person not engaged in trade of mining: s 676(3).

Manufacturing (10%) rate, meaning of "relevant corporation tax": s 448(1)(*d*).

Former enactments

CTA 1976 s 182 (apart from (3)(*c*)(proviso)), (*b*)–(*c*)); FA 1980 s 47(1); FA 1997 s 59 and Sch 6 Pt I para 2(1)–(3).

Relief in Respect of Losses or Deficiencies Within Case IV or V of Schedule D

17. (1) Where—

(*a*) a company was entitled to relief under section 89 or 310 of the Income Tax Act, 1967, or would have been entitled to relief under section 310 of that Act if section 237(5) of that Act had not been enacted, for the year 1975–76 or an earlier year of assessment in respect of a loss within Case IV of Schedule D or a deficiency or an excess of deficiencies within Case V of Schedule D, with the addition of any associated capital allowances in each case, and

(*b*) because of an insufficiency of income of the description concerned, relief could not be fully granted to the company under those sections for any of those years of assessment,

then, the unrelieved amount of loss, deficiency or excess of deficiencies (with the addition of any unrelieved associated capital allowances), as the case may be, shall be treated as if it were a loss in a trade carried on by a company and, if the company so requires, may be relieved under paragraph 16 against income of the same description of the company within the charge to corporation tax as if that income were income of the same trade, and that paragraph shall apply accordingly with any necessary modifications.

(2) Notwithstanding subparagraph (1)—

(*a*) a loss within Case IV of Schedule D, with the addition of any associated capital allowances, shall be relieved under this paragraph only against income of the company chargeable to corporation tax under Case IV of Schedule D,

(*b*) a deficiency or an excess of deficiencies within Case V of Schedule D, with the addition of any associated capital allowances, shall be relieved only against income of the company chargeable to corporation tax under Case V of Schedule D, and

(*c*) so much of any deficiency or so much of any amount treated as a loss as, under section 62 of the Finance Act, 1974, could not have been carried forward or set against profits or gains for income tax purposes if that tax had continued shall be treated as not being a deficiency or loss for the purposes of this paragraph.

Definitions

capital allowance: s 2(1); company: ss 4(1), 5(1); profits: s 4(1); trade: ss 3(1), 4(1), 5(1); within the charge to (tax): s 2(1); year of assessment: ss 2(1), 5(1).

Former enactments

CTA 1976 s 183.

Relief in Respect of Corporation Profits Tax Losses

18. (1) In this paragraph, **"relevant deficiency"**, in relation to a company, means, subject to subparagraph (2), the aggregate of the following amounts—

(*a*) the total of the amounts which under section 25 of the Finance Act, 1964, could (on the assumption that for corporation profits tax purposes an accounting period of the company ended on the 5th day of April, 1976, and a new accounting period commenced on the 6th day of April, 1976, and the enactments in relation to corporation profits tax mentioned in the Third

Schedule to the Corporation Tax Act, 1976, had not been repealed) have been deducted from or set off against profits of the company's business in an accounting period commencing on the 6th day of April, 1976, and

(*b*) the total of the amounts by which under subsections (1) and (3) of section 181 of the Corporation Tax Act, 1976, losses and allowances in respect of capital expenditure were reduced for the purposes of corporation tax;

but any loss or any excess of deficiencies over surpluses which if such loss or excess were a profit or an excess of surpluses over deficiencies would be chargeable to corporation tax on the company for the accounting period shall not be taken into account for the purposes of clause (*a*).

(2) Where for any accounting period an election was made under section 174(3) of the Corporation Tax Act, 1976, all amounts which under section 25 of the Finance Act, 1964, could be deducted from or set off against profits of the company's trade or business for that accounting period, computed without regard to section 174(3) of the Corporation Tax Acts, 1976, shall be deemed to have been so deducted or set off and shall not be included in the computation of any relevant deficiency for the purposes of this paragraph.

(3) (*a*) Subject to clause (*b*), relief as provided in subparagraph (4) shall be allowed in respect of a relevant deficiency against corporation tax payable by the company and such relief shall be given as far as possible from the tax payable for the first accounting period for which the company is within the charge to corporation tax and, in so far as it cannot be so given, from the tax payable for the next accounting period and so on.

(*b*) Relief shall not be allowed against corporation tax payable for any accounting period against the profits of which (if the Corporation Tax Act, 1976, had not been enacted and if the enactments in relation to corporation profits tax referred to in the Third Schedule of that Act had not been repealed) a loss incurred before the 6th day of April, 1976, could not be set off under section 25 of the Finance Act, 1964.

(4) (*a*) For the purposes of this subparagraph—

(i) the income of a company for an accounting period shall be taken to be the amount of its profits for that period on which corporation tax falls finally to be borne exclusive of the part of the profits attributable to chargeable gains, and that part shall be taken to be the amount brought into the company's profits for that period for the purposes of corporation tax in respect of chargeable gains before any deduction for charges on income, expenses of management or other amounts which can be deducted from or set against or treated as reducing profits of more than one description, and

(ii) the appropriate amount shall be the smaller of the amount of the relevant deficiency in respect of which relief has not been allowed and the amount of the company's income for the accounting period.

[(*b*) Subject to clause (*c*), relief for an accounting period shall be an amount determined by the formula —

$$(A - B) - (C - D)$$

where —

A is the amount of corporation tax which, apart from paragraph 16, this paragraph and section 448 is chargeable for the accounting period,

[B is an amount determined by applying a rate equal to—

(*a*) as respects accounting periods beginning on or after the 1st day of January, 1998, and ending before the 1st day of January, 1999, 17 per cent,

(*b*) as respects accounting periods beginning on or after the 1st day of January, 1999, and ending before the 1st day of January, 2000, 13 per cent,

(*c*) as respects accounting periods beginning on or after the 1st day of January, 2000, and ending before the 1st day of January, 2001, 9 per cent,

(*d*) as respects accounting periods beginning on or after the 1st day of January, 2001, and ending before the 1st day of January, 2002, 5 per cent, and

(*e*) as respects accounting periods beginning on or after the 1st day of January, 2002, and ending before the 1st day of January, 2003, 1 per cent,

to the amount of the company's income for the accounting period,][1]

C is the amount of corporation tax which, apart from paragraph 16, this paragraph and section 448, would be chargeable for the accounting period if the amount of the company's income for the accounting period were reduced by the appropriate amount, and

[D is an amount determined by applying a rate equal to—

(*a*) as respects accounting periods beginning on or after the 1st day of January, 1998, and ending before the 1st day of January, 1999, 17 per cent,

(*b*) as respects accounting periods beginning on or after the 1st day of January, 1999, and ending before the 1st day of January, 2000, 13 per cent,

(*c*) as respects accounting periods beginning on or after the 1st day of January, 2000, and ending before the 1st day of January, 2001, 9 per cent,

(*d*) as respects accounting periods beginning on or after the 1st day of January, 2001, and ending before the 1st day of January, 2002, 5 per cent, and

(*e*) as respects accounting periods beginning on or after the 1st day of January, 2002, and ending before the 1st day of January, 2003, 1 per cent,

to the amount of the company's income for the accounting period as reduced by the appropriate amount.][2]][3]

[(*bb*) Subject to clause (*c*), relief for any accounting period beginning on or after the 1st day of January, 2003, shall be an amount determined by the formula—

$$A - B$$

where—

A is the amount of corporation tax which, apart from this paragraph and section 448, is chargeable for the accounting period, and

B is the amount of corporation tax which, apart from this paragraph and section 448, would be chargeable for the accounting period if the amount of the company's income for the accounting period were reduced by the appropriate amount.][4]

(*c*) [Notwithstanding clauses (*b*) and (*bb*)],[5] where the corporation tax payable by a company for an accounting period is reduced by virtue of a claim under section 448(2), the amount of relief to be allowed under the preceding provisions of this paragraph shall be reduced in the same proportion which the amount by which the corporation tax referable to the income from the sale of goods (within the meaning of section 448) for that accounting period is so reduced bears to the relevant corporation tax, and for the purposes of this clause **"relevant corporation tax"** has the same meaning as in paragraph 16.

(5) (*a*) Subparagraphs (3) and (4) shall not apply to a company which by virtue of agreements between the Government and the Government of the United Kingdom in respect of double income tax was entitled to exemption from income tax for the year 1975–76 in respect of income arising in the State; but in such a case the relevant deficiency shall, subject to clause (*b*), be set off against income coming within the charge to corporation tax for the accounting period commencing on the 6th day of April, 1976, and, in so far as the relevant deficiency cannot be so set off, it shall be set off against income coming within the charge to corporation tax for the next accounting period and so on.

(*b*) A relevant deficiency shall not be set off under clause (*a*) against income arising in any accounting period against the profits of which (if the Corporation Tax Act, 1976, had not been enacted and if the enactments in relation to corporation profits tax mentioned in the Third Schedule to that Act had not been repealed) a loss incurred before the 6th day of April, 1976, could not be set off under section 25 of the Finance Act, 1964.

(6) [(*a*) Subparagraph (6) of paragraph 16 shall apply for the purposes of this paragraph as it applies for the purposes of that paragraph.][6]

(*b*) Where under clause (*a*) a part of an accounting period is treated as a separate accounting period, the corporation tax charged for the part which is so treated shall, in so far as it is affected by the rate of corporation tax which is taken to have been charged, be taken for the purposes of this paragraph to be the corporation tax which would have been charged if that part were a separate accounting period.

Amendments

1 Definition of "B" substituted by FA 1999 s 71 and Sch 1 para 2(*f*)(i)(I) with effect from 6 April 1999.

2 Definition of "D" substituted by FA 1999 s 71 and Sch 1 para 2(*f*)(i)(II) with effect from 6 April 1999.

3 Subpara (4)(*b*) substituted by FA 1998 s 55(2) and Sch 6 para 4(*d*)(i) with effect from 6 April 1998.

3 Subpara (4)(*bb*) inserted by FA 1999 s 71 and Sch 1 para 2(*f*)(i)(III) with effect from 6 April 1999.

4 Substituted by FA 1999 s 71 and Sch 1 para 2(*f*)(i)(IV) with effect from 6 April 1999; previously "Notwithstanding clause (*b*)".

5 Subpara (6)(*a*) substituted by FA 1999 s 71 and Sch 1 para 2(*f*)(ii) with effect from 6 April 1999.

Cross-references

Change in ownership of a company, disallowance of trading losses: s 401(2).

Distributions out of profits from trading in Shannon Airport: s 144(8)("S").

Expenditure on abortive exploration: s 674(4).

Exploration expenditure incurred by bodies corporate: s 675(2)(*b*).

Exploration expenditure incurred by person not engaged in trade of mining: s 676(3).

Manufacturing (10%) rate, meaning of "relevant corporation tax": s 448(1).

Definitions

company: ss 4(1), 5(1); the Government: IA 1937 Sch; profits: s 4(1); within the charge to (tax): s 2(1); year of assessment: ss 2(1), 5(1).

Former enactments

CTA 1976 s 174(3)(proviso), 184(proviso)(i)–(iii)); FA 1980 s 48(1); FA 1997 s 59 and Sch 6 Pt I para 2.

Capital Gains Tax Losses Accruing before 6th April, 1976

19. Any losses of a company allowable against chargeable gains for the purposes of capital gains tax in respect of the year of assessment 1974–75 or 1975–76, in so far as they cannot be allowed against chargeable gains for the purposes of that tax, shall be treated for the purposes of corporation tax as if they were allowable losses accruing to the company while within the charge to corporation tax.

Former enactments

CTA 1976 s 175.

Income Tax: Relief for Expenditure on Certain Buildings in Certain Areas

20. (1) Where a person is immediately before the commencement of this Act, entitled to have a deduction made from his or her total income under section 4 of the Finance Act, 1989, he or she shall not cease to be so entitled by reason only of the repeal by this Act of that section, notwithstanding that that section is not re-enacted by this Act, and accordingly this Act shall apply with any modifications necessary to give effect to any such entitlements.

(2) Notwithstanding the repeal by this Act of section 4 of the Finance Act, 1989, relief given under that section, whether before or after the passing of this Act, may be withdrawn in accordance with subsection (4) of that section where the circumstances set out in that subsection apply; and accordingly this Act shall apply with any modifications necessary to give effect to such withdrawal.

Cross-references

Deductions allowed in ascertaining taxable income: ss 458(2), 459(1)–(2).

Method of apportioning reliefs and charging tax in cases of separate assessment: s 1024(2)(*a*)(xii).

Rate of tax at which repayments are to be made: s 460.

Definitions

Appeal Commissioners: s 2(1); Circuit Court: IA 1937 Sch; Income Tax Acts: s 1(2); inspector: ss 2(1), 5(1), 852; local authority: s 2(1); person: IA 1937 s 11(*c*); writing: IA 1937 Sch; year of assessment: ss 2(1), 5(1).

Former enactments

FA 1989 s 4(1)–(6); FA 1993 s 31.

Income Tax: Relief for Income Accumulated Under Trusts

21. (1) Where—

(*a*) in pursuance of any will or settlement any income arising from any fund is accumulated for the benefit of any person contingently on that person attaining a specified age or marrying, and

(*b*) the aggregate amount (in this paragraph referred to as **"the aggregate yearly income"**) in any year of assessment of—

(i) that income,

(ii) the income from any other fund subject to the like trusts for accumulation, and

(iii) the total income of that person from all sources,

is of such an amount only as would entitle an individual either to total exemption from income tax or to relief from income tax,

then, that person shall, on making a claim for the purpose within 6 years after the end of the year of assessment in which the contingency happens, be entitled, on proof of the claim in the manner prescribed by subsections (3) and (4) of section 459 and paragraph 8 of Schedule 28, to have repaid to him or her on account of the income tax which has been paid in respect of the income during the period of accumulation a sum equal to the aggregate amount of relief to which he or she would have been entitled if his or her total income from all sources for each of the several years of that period had been equal to the aggregate yearly income for that year; but in calculating that sum a deduction shall be made in respect of any relief already received.

(2) For the purposes of subparagraph (1), no account shall be taken of any income tax paid in respect of income for a year of assessment beginning after the year 1972–73 or of any relief to which a person would have been entitled for such a year of assessment in the circumstances mentioned in subparagraph (1).

Cross-references

Film investments: s 481(21).

Former enactments

FA 1996 s 31(2)(*a*), (3), (4); FA 1997 s 30(2).

Relief for Investment in Films in Respect of Certain Sums

22. (1) Where an allowable investor company has in the period of 12 months ending on the 22nd day of January, 1997, made a relevant investment, the reference in section 481(4) to [€10,157,904.63][1] shall, in respect of that period, be construed as a reference to [€7,618,428.47][2] or, where the company has in that period paid a sum of money to which subparagraph (2) applies, as a reference to [€7,618,428.47][2] less the amount or, if there are more amounts than one, the aggregate of such amounts of such sums of money.

(2) The amendments effected to section 35 of the Finance Act, 1987, by section 31(1) of the Finance Act, 1996, shall not apply as respects a sum of money paid on or after the 23rd day of January, 1996, and on or before the 31st day of March, 1996, where the sum of money is paid in respect of shares in a qualifying company, and—

(*a*) the Minister for Arts, Culture and the Gaeltacht had received before the 23rd day of January, 1996, an application in writing to give a certificate to the company stating, in relation to a film to be produced by the company, that the film is a qualifying film, and

(*b*) a certificate given by the Minister to the company after the 23rd day of January, 1996, includes a statement that the Minister had received that application before that date.

(3) Where a sum of money is a sum of money—

(*a*) to which the amendments effected to section 35 of the Finance Act, 1987, by section 31(1) of the Finance Act, 1996, do not apply by virtue of subparagraph (2), or

(*b*) which is paid before the 23rd day of January, 1996,

the provisions of section 35 of the Finance Act, 1987, which were in force immediately before the 23rd day of January, 1996, (in this paragraph referred to as "the former provisions") shall, subject to subparagraph (4), continue to apply to that sum of money.

(4) Where the sum of money referred to in subparagraph (3) is a sum of money paid on or after the 6th day of April, 1995, or is a sum of money to which subparagraph (2) applies, and the sum of money is used for the purpose of enabling the qualifying company to produce a qualifying film in respect of which an application (to give a certificate under subsection (1A) of the former provisions) had not been received by the Minister before the 23rd day of January, 1996, the former provisions shall apply as if—

(i) subsection (2) of the former provisions was amended by the substitution for "a deduction of the amount of that investment" of "a deduction of an amount equal to 80 per cent of that investment", and

(ii) subsection (3A) of the former provisions was amended by the substitution for "a deduction of the amount of that investment" of "a deduction of an amount equal to 80 per cent of that investment".

(5) Subparagraphs (2) to (4) shall apply notwithstanding that the former provisions are not re-enacted by this Act and shall be construed together with the former provisions, and accordingly this Act shall apply with any modifications necessary to give effect to those subparagraphs.

(6) As respects a relevant investment made before the 26th day of March, 1997, section 481 shall apply as if in subsection (4)(*b*)(i) of that section the reference to [€3,809,214.24][3] were a reference to [€2,539,476.16][4].

(7) As respects the 12 month period ending on the 22nd day of January, 1996, section 481 shall apply as if in subsection (4)(*b*)(ii) of that section the reference to [€3,809,214.24][3] were a reference to [€2,539,476.16][4].

(8) In relation to a film in respect of which the Minister has received an application before the 26th day of March, 1997, to enable the Minister to consider whether a certificate should be given under subsection (2) of section 481, that subsection shall apply as if paragraph (*c*)(ii)(II) of that subsection were deleted.

Amendments

1 Substituted by FA 2001 s 240(1) and (2) and Sch 5 Pt 1 for 2002 and later tax years; previously "£8,000,000".

2 Substituted by FA 2001 s 240(1) and (2) and Sch 5 Pt 1 for 2002 and later tax years; previously "£6,000,000".

3 Substituted by FA 2001 s 240(1) and (2) and Sch 5 Pt 1 for 2002 and later tax years; previously "£3,000,000".

4 Substituted by FA 2001 s 240(1) and (2) and Sch 5 Pt 1 for 2002 and later tax years; previously "£2,000,000".

Cross-references

Film investments: s 481(21).

Former enactments

FA 1996 s 31(2)(*a*), (3), (4); FA 1997 s 30(2).

Farming: Application of Section 658 in Relation to Expenditure Incurred before 27th January, 1994

23. (1) Section 658 shall apply—

(*a*) as respects capital expenditure incurred before the 27th day of January, 1994, as if the following subsections were substituted for subsection (2) of that section:

"(2) (*a*) Where a person to whom this section applies incurs, for the purpose of a trade of farming land occupied by such person, any capital expenditure on the construction of farm buildings (excluding a building or part of a building used as a dwelling), fences, roadways, holding yards, drains or land reclamation or other works, there shall, subject to paragraph (*b*), be made to such person during a writing-down period of 10 years beginning with the chargeable period related to that expenditure, writing-down allowances (in this section referred to as 'farm buildings allowances') in respect of that expenditure, and such allowances shall be made in taxing the trade.

(*b*) The farm buildings allowance to be granted for any chargeable period shall, subject to paragraphs (*c*) and (*d*), be increased by such amount as is specified in the claim for the allowance by the person to whom the allowance is to be made and, in relation to a case in which this paragraph has applied, any reference in the Tax Acts to a farm buildings allowance made under this section shall be construed as a reference to that allowance as increased under this paragraph.

(*c*) The maximum farm buildings allowance to be made under this section by means of an allowance increased under paragraph (*b*)—

(i) in relation to capital expenditure incurred before the 1st day of April, 1989, shall not for any chargeable period exceed 30 per cent of that capital expenditure,

(ii) in relation to capital expenditure incurred on or after the 1st day of April, 1989, and before the 1st day of April, 1991, whether claimed in one chargeable period or more than one such period, shall not in the aggregate exceed 50 per cent of that capital expenditure, and

(iii) in relation to capital expenditure incurred on or after the 1st day of April, 1991, and before the 1st day of April, 1992, whether claimed in one chargeable period or more than one such period, shall not in the aggregate exceed 25 per cent of that capital expenditure.

(*d*) Notwithstanding paragraph (*c*)(iii), the maximum farm buildings allowances to be made under this section by means of an allowance increased under paragraph (*b*) in relation to capital expenditure incurred—

(i) on or after the 1st day of April, 1991, and before the 1st day of April, 1993,

(ii) for the purposes of the control of farmyard pollution, and

(iii) on works in respect of which grant-aid has been paid under—

(I) the programme, as amended, known as 'the Farm Improvement Programme' implemented by the Minister for Agriculture and Food pursuant to Council Regulation (EEC) No 797/85 of 12 March 1985 (OJ No L 93 of 30.3.1985, p 1), or

(II) the scheme known as 'the Scheme of Investment Aid for the Control of Farmyard Pollution' implemented by the Minister for Agriculture and Food pursuant to an operational programme under Council Regulation (EEC) No 2052/88 of 24 June 1988 (OJ No L 185 of 15.7.1988, p 9),

whether claimed for one chargeable period or more than one such period, shall not in the aggregate exceed 50 per cent of that capital expenditure.

(*e*) The reference in paragraph (*a*) to roadways, holding yards, drains or land reclamation shall apply only as respects expenditure incurred on or after the 1st day of April, 1989.

(2A) (*a*) For the purposes of this subsection, the first relevant year of assessment in relation to expenditure incurred by any person is—

(i) the year of assessment in the basis period for which that person incurs the expenditure, or

(ii) the year of assessment in the basis period for which (if that person's profits or gains from farming for that year of assessment had been chargeable to tax under Case I of Schedule D) that person incurred the expenditure.

(*b*) Where any capital expenditure referred to in subsection (2)(*a*) was incurred by a person on or after the 6th day of April, 1971, and before the 6th day of April, 1974, a farm buildings allowance shall for the purposes of this section be deemed—

(i) to have been made to that person, and

(ii) to have been made in charging the profits or gains of the trade for the first relevant year of assessment and for each subsequent year of assessment before the year 1974–75;

but where that expenditure was incurred in the year 1973–74, a farm buildings allowance shall for the purposes of this section be deemed to have been made in charging the profits or gains of the trade for that year of assessment.

(2B) Notwithstanding any other provision of this section other than subsection (2)(*d*), no farm buildings allowance made in relation to capital expenditure incurred on or after the 1st day of April, 1992, shall be increased under this section.",

and

(*b*) as respects expenditure incurred before the 6th day of May, 1993, as if the following subsection were substituted for subsection (13) of that section:

"(13) Expenditure shall not be regarded for the purposes of this section as having been incurred by a person in so far as it has been met directly or indirectly by the State, by any board established by statute or by any public or local authority."

(2) (*a*) This subparagraph shall apply to expenditure incurred on the construction of fences, roadways, holding yards or drains or on land reclamation.

(*b*) Where on or after the 6th day of April, 1977, and before the 1st day of April, 1989, a person to whom section 658 applies incurs capital expenditure to which this subparagraph applies, being expenditure in respect of which the person is entitled to claim an allowance under that section, the allowance to be granted for the chargeable period related to the expenditure or any subsequent chargeable period shall be increased by such amount as is specified by the person to whom the allowance is to be made in making the person's claim for the allowance, and in relation to a case in which this subsection has applied, any reference in the Tax Acts to a farm buildings allowance made under section 658 shall be construed as a reference to that allowance as increased under this subparagraph.

Former enactments

FA 1974 s 22(2); FA 1977 s 14; FA 1982 s 16; FA 1988 s 52(1)(*a*); FA 1989 s 15; FA 1990 s 77; FA 1991 s 25(*a*).

Transitional Provisions Arising from Amendments Made to the System of Taxation of Life Assurance Companies by Finance Act, 1993

24. Notwithstanding section 713, where chargeable gains and allowable losses accrued on disposals deemed by virtue of section 46A of the Corporation Tax Act, 1976, as applied by section 12(2)(*a*) of the Finance Act, 1993, to have been made by a life assurance company for the accounting period ended on the 31st day of December, 1992, the amount of any fraction of the difference between the aggregate of such chargeable gains and the aggregate of such allowable losses treated by virtue of section 720 (being the re-enactment of section 46B of the Corporation Tax Act, 1976) as a chargeable gain of any accounting period ending on or after the 6th day of April, 1997, shall be deducted

from the amount of the unrelieved profits (within the meaning of section 713) of that accounting period for the purposes of computing the relief due under section 713.

Cross-references

Chargeable gains of life business: s 711(4).

Chargeable gains of life business: s 581(1), (2)–(3) (in so far as a chargeable gain is not thereby disregarded for the purposes of that subsection) apply as if: ss 719, 723(7)(*a*), 711(1)(*a*)(ii) and Sch 32 para 24 had not been enacted: s 711(1)(*b*).

Definitions

allowable loss: ss 4(1), 5(1), 546; chargeable gain: ss 4(1), 5(1), 534; CTA 1976 ss 1(5)(*c*), 155(5); company: ss 4(1), 5(1); profits: s 4(1).

Former enactments

FA 1993 s 12(2)(*b*).

Disposals in the Year 1993–94 of Units in Certain Unit Trusts

25. Where throughout the year of assessment 1993–94 all the assets of a unit trust were assets, whether mentioned in section 19 of the Capital Gains Tax Act, 1975, or in any other provision of that Act, or of any other enactment relating to capital gains tax, to which section 19 of the Capital Gains Tax Act, 1975, applied, the units in the unit trust shall for that year be deemed not to be chargeable assets for the purposes of the Capital Gains Tax Acts.

Cross-references

Undertaking for collective investment, taxation of unit holders: s 739(3)(*a*)(ii)(II).

Former enactments

CGTA 1975 s 31(5); FA 1994 s 64(2).

Application of Section 774(6) in Certain Circumstances

26. In the case of any employer for a chargeable period, being—

(i) where the chargeable period is an accounting period of a company, an accounting period ending on or before the 21st day of April, 1997, and

(ii) where the chargeable period is a year of assessment, any year of assessment the employer's basis period for which ends on a day after that date,

section 774 shall apply as if the following subsection were substituted for subsection (6) of that section:

"(6) (*a*) Any sum paid by an employer by means of contributions under the scheme shall—

(i) in the case of income tax, for the purposes of Case I or II of Schedule D, be allowed to be deducted as an expense incurred in the year in which the sum is paid, and

(ii) in the case of corporation tax, for the purposes of Case I or II of Schedule D and the provisions of sections 83 and 707(4) relating to expenses of management, be allowed to be deducted as an expense or expense of management incurred in the accounting period in which the sum is paid.

(b) The amount of an employer's contributions which may be deducted under paragraph (a) shall not exceed the amount contributed by the employer under the scheme in respect of employees in a trade or undertaking in respect of the profits of which the employer is assessable to income tax or corporation tax, as the case may be.

(c) A sum not paid by means of an ordinary annual contribution shall for the purposes of this subsection be treated, as the Revenue Commissioners may direct, either as an expense incurred in the year or the accounting period, as the case may be, in which the sum is paid, or as an expense to be spread over such period of years as the Revenue Commissioners think proper.".

Former enactments

FA 1972 s 16(4); CTA 1976 s 140(1) and Sch 2 Pt I para 31.

Settlements: Application of Section 792 for the Year of Assessment 1997–98 in Relation to Certain Dispositions to Certain Individuals Residing With, and Sharing Normal Household Expenses With, the Disponer

27. (1) Where—

(a) the conditions set out in subparagraph (3) are satisfied, and

(b) the Revenue Commissioners are satisfied that the application of the amendments to section 439 of the Income Tax Act, 1967, effected by subsections (1) and (2) of section 13 of the Finance Act, 1995, which subsections are re-enacted in subsections (1) and (2) of section 792, would give rise to hardship,

then, those amendments shall not, to the extent that the Revenue Commissioners consider just, apply before the [6th day of April, 2000],[1] in respect of a disposition, to which clause (a) of subparagraph (2) applies, by a person (in this paragraph referred to as **"the disponer"**), in so far as, by virtue or in consequence of such disposition, income is payable in a year of assessment to or for the benefit of an individual to whom clause (b) of subparagraph (2) applies, and accordingly, notwithstanding that section 439 of the Income Tax Act, 1967, as it stood before its amendment by subsections (1) and (2) of section 13 the Finance Act, 1995, is not re-enacted by this Act, this Act shall apply with any modifications necessary to give effect to this paragraph.

(2) (a) This clause shall apply to—

(i) a disposition made before the 6th day of April, 1993, or

(ii) a disposition made on or after the 6th day of April, 1993, to immediately replace a disposition made before that date which has ceased to be effective and only to the extent that the amount payable to or for the benefit of an individual to whom clause (b) applies under such later disposition does not exceed the amount payable to or for the benefit of that individual under the earlier disposition.

(b) This clause shall apply to an individual who is not a child of the disponer and who, for the whole of the year of assessment, is resident with, and shares the normal household expenses with, the disponer.

(3) The conditions referred to in subparagraph (1) are:

(*a*) the making of the disposition referred to in subparagraph (2)(*a*)(i) shall have been notified to the Revenue Commissioners before the 8th day of February, 1995,

(*b*) a child, to whom subparagraph (4) applies, of the disponer or of the individual to whom clause (*b*) of subparagraph (2) applies or of both of them is resident with them for the whole or substantially the whole of the year of assessment, and

(*c*) the child to whom clause (*b*) relates is wholly or mainly maintained by the disponer and the individual jointly at their own expense.

(4) A child to whom this subparagraph applies shall be a child who for a year of assessment—

(i) is under the age of 16 years, or

(ii) if over the age of 16 years at the commencement of the year of assessment, is receiving full-time instruction at any university, college, school or other educational establishment.

Amendments

[1] Substituted by FA 1998 s 7; previously "6th day of April, 1998".

Cross-references

Income under dispositions for short periods: s 792(4).

Income under revocable dispositions: s 791(1).

Tax Briefing

TB18 No. 2 of 1995 par 2.3 p 9 — Covenant relief and the "hardship clause" of subpara (1)(*b*).

Revenue information

Information leaflet IT7 — Covenants to Individuals.

Definitions

disposition: s 791(1); year of assessment: ss 2(1), 5(1).

Former enactments

FA 1995 s 13(3).

Construction of Certain References to Ministers of the Government

28. (1) Subject to subparagraphs (2) and (3), a reference in this Act to a Minister of the Government mentioned in column (1) of the Table to this paragraph shall, in respect of the period from the commencement of this Act to the date mentioned in column (3) of that Table opposite that mention in column (1), be construed as a reference to the Minister of the Government mentioned in column (2) of that Table opposite that mention in column (1).

(2) A reference in Chapter 1 of Part 24 to the Minister for the Marine and Natural Resources shall—

(*a*) in respect of the period from the commencement of this Act to the 11th day of July, 1997, be construed as a reference to the Minister for Transport, Energy and Communications, and

(*b*) in respect of the period from the 12th day of July, 1997, to the 14th day of July, 1997, be construed as a reference to the Minister for Public Enterprise.

(3) A reference in Chapter 2 of Part 24 to the Minister for the Marine and Natural Resources shall—

(*a*) in respect of the period from the commencement of this Act to the 11th day of July, 1997, be construed as a reference to the Minister for Transport, Energy and Communications, and

(*b*) in respect of the period from the 12th day of July, 1997, to the 30th day of September, 1997, be construed as a reference to the Minister for Public Enterprise.

(1)	(2)	(3)
Minister for Justice, Equality and Law Reform	Minister for Justice	8th July, 1997
Minister for Health and Children	Minister for Health	11th July, 1997
Minister for Social, Community and Family Affairs	Minister for Social Welfare	11th July, 1997
Minister for Arts, Heritage, Gaeltacht and the Islands	Minister for Arts, Culture and the Gaeltacht	11th July, 1997
Minister for Enterprise, Trade and Employment	Minister for Tourism and Trade	11th July, 1997
Minister for Tourism, Sport and Recreation	Minister for Tourism and Trade	11th July, 1997
Minister for Agriculture and Food	Minister for Agriculture, Food and Forestry	11th July, 1997
Minister for the Marine and Natural Resources	Minister for the Marine	11th July, 1997
Minister for Public Enterprise	Minister for Transport, Energy and Communications	11th July, 1997
Minister for the Environment and Local Government	Minister for the Environment	21st July, 1997
Minister for Education and Science	Minister for Education	30th September, 1997

Construction of Certain References to Government Departments

29. A reference in this Act to a Government Department mentioned in column (1) of the Table to this paragraph shall, in respect of the period from the commencement of this Act to the date mentioned in column (3) of that Table opposite that mention in column (1), be construed as a reference to the Government Department mentioned in column (2) of that Table opposite that mention in column (1).

(1)	(2)	(3)
Department of Agriculture and Food	Department of Agriculture, Food and Forestry	11th July, 1997
Department of the Environment and Local Government	Department of the Environment	21st July, 1997

Construction of Reference to Secretary General of Department of Finance

30. A reference in this Act to the Secretary General of the Department of Finance shall, in respect of the period from the commencement of this Act to the 31st day of August, 1997, be construed as a reference to the Secretary of the Department of Finance.

31. A reference in this Act to an educational institution mentioned in column (1) of the Table to this paragraph shall, in respect of the period from the commencement of this Act to the date mentioned in column (3) of that Table opposite that mention in column (1), be construed as a reference to the educational institution mentioned in column (2) of that Table opposite that mention in column (1)

Construction of Certain References to Educational Institutions.

(1)	(2)	(3)
National University of Ireland, Dublin	University College, Dublin	15th June, 1997
National University of Ireland, Cork	University College, Cork	15th June, 1997

FINANCE (NO 2) ACT 1998

(No 15 of 1998)

ARRANGEMENT OF SECTIONS

PART 1

INCOME TAX, CORPORATION TAX AND CAPITAL GAINS TAX

An Act to charge and impose certain duties of inland revenue, to amend the law relating to inland revenue and to make further provisions in connection with finance.

[*20th May, 1998*]

BE IT ENACTED BY THE OIREACHTAS AS FOLLOWS:

PART 1

INCOME TAX, CORPORATION TAX AND CAPITAL GAINS TAX

1 Taxation of rents and certain other payments

Notes

Subs (1)(*a*) inserted TCA 1997 s 96(1) definitions of "rented residential premises" and "residential premises" with effect from 23 April 1998.

Subs (1)(*b*) inserted TCA 1997 s 97(2A)–(2E) with effect from 23 April 1998.

Subs (2) inserted TCA 1997 s 71(4A) with effect from 20 May 1998.

2 Restriction of relief in respect of loans applied in acquiring interest in companies and partnerships

Notes

This section inserted TCA 1997 s 248A with effect from 20 May, 1998.

3 Rate of capital gains tax on certain disposals of development land

Notes
This section inserted TCA 1997 s 649A with effect from 20 May 1998.

4 Amendment of section 372L (interpretation (Chapter 8)) of Taxes Consolidation Act, 1997

Notes
This section substituted TCA 1997 s 372L definition of "qualifying period" with effect from 20 May 1998.

PART 3

MISCELLANEOUS

15 Care and management of taxes and duties

All taxes and duties imposed by this Act are hereby placed under the care and management of the Revenue Commissioners.

16 Short title and construction

(1) This Act may be cited as the Finance (No 2) Act, 1998.

(2) Part 1 (so far as relating to income tax) shall be construed together with the Income Tax Acts and (so far as relating to corporation tax) shall be construed together with the Corporation Tax Acts and (so far as relating to capital gains tax) shall be construed together with the Capital Gains Tax Acts.

...

(4) Any reference in this Act to any other enactment shall, except so far as the context otherwise requires, be construed as a reference to that enactment as amended by or under any other enactment including this Act.

(5) In this Act, a reference to a Part, section or Schedule is to a Part or section of, or Schedule to, this Act, unless it is indicated that reference to some other enactment is intended.

(6) In this Act, a reference to a subsection, paragraph or subparagraph is to the subsection, paragraph or subparagraph of the provision (including a Schedule) in which the reference occurs, unless it is indicated that reference to some other provision is intended.

FINANCE ACT 1998

(No 3 of 1998)

ARRANGEMENT OF SECTIONS

PART 1
Income Tax, Corporation Tax And Capital Gains Tax

CHAPTER 1
Interpretation

CHAPTER 2
Income Tax

CHAPTER 3
Income Tax, Corporation Tax and Capital Gains Tax

CHAPTER 4

Corporation Tax

CHAPTER 5

Capital Gains Tax

CHAPTER 6

Income Tax and Corporation Tax: Reliefs for Renewal and Improvement of Certain Urban and Rural Areas

PART 6

Miscellaneous

SCHEDULE 1

Amendments Consequential on Changes in Personal Reliefs

SCHEDULE 2

Provisions Amending Principal Act in consequence of a change in the Currency of Certain States

SCHEDULE 3

Amendment of Principal Act in Consequence of Convention with United States of America relating to Double Taxation, etc

SCHEDULE 4

Amendments Consequential on Changes in Amounts of Tax Credits in Respect of Distributions

SCHEDULE 5
Abolition of Tax Credits

SCHEDULE 6
Change in Rate of Corporation Tax: Further Provisions

SCHEDULE 9
Post-Consolidation Amendments

An Act to charge and impose certain duties of customs and inland revenue (including excise), to amend the law relating to customs and inland revenue (including excise) and to make further provisions in connection with finance.

[*27th March 1998*]

BE IT ENACTED BY THE OIREACHTAS AS FOLLOWS:

PART 1

INCOME TAX, CORPORATION TAX AND CAPITAL GAINS TAX

CHAPTER 1
Interpretation

1 Interpretation

In this Part, "the Principal Act" means the Taxes Consolidation Act, 1997.

CHAPTER 2
Income Tax

2 Amendment of provisions relating to exemption from income tax

Notes

Para (*a*) substituted "£8,200" for "£8,000" and "£4,100" for "£4,000" in TCA 1997 s 187(1) as respects 1998-99 and later tax years.

Para (*b*)(i) substituted ""£10,000" for "£9,200" and "£11,000" for "£10,400" in TCA 1997 s 188(2)(*a*) as respects 1998–99 and later tax years.

Para (*b*)(ii) substituted "£5,000" for "£4,600" and "£5,500" for "£5,200" in TCA 1997 s 188(2)(*b*) as respects 1998–99 and later tax years.

3 Alteration of rates of income tax

Notes

This section substituted TCA 1997 s 15 (Table) as respects 1998–99 and later tax years.

4 Personal reliefs

(1) Where a deduction falls to be made from the total income of an individual for the year of assessment 1998–99 or any subsequent year of assessment in respect of relief to

which the individual is entitled under a provision mentioned in column (1) of the Table to this subsection and the amount of the deduction would, but for this section, be an amount specified in column (2) of the said Table, the amount of the deduction shall, in lieu of being the amount specified in the said column (2), be the amount specified in column (3) of the said Table opposite the mention of the amount in the said column (2).

TABLE

Statutory provision	*Amount to be deducted from total income for the year 1997–98*	*Amount to be deducted from total income for the year 1998–99 and subsequent years*
(1)	(2)	(3)
	£	£
Principal Act:		
section 461		
(married person)	5,800	6,300
(widowed person bereaved in the year of assessment)	5,800	6,300
(widowed person)	3,400	3,650
(single person)	2,900	3,150
section 462		
(additional allowance for widowed persons and others in respect of children)		
(widowed person)	2,400	2,650
(other person)	2,900	3,150
Section 465		
(incapacitated child)	700	800
section 467		
(person employed to take care of an incapacitated person)	7,500	8,500
section 468		
(blind person)	700	1,000
(both spouses blind)	1,600	2,000

(2) Schedule 1 shall apply for the purpose of supplementing subsection (1).

5 Amendment of section 463 (special allowance for widowed parent following death of spouse) of Principal Act

Notes

This section substituted TCA 1997 s 463(2) as respects 1998–99 and later tax years.

6 Amendment of section 126 (tax treatment of certain benefits payable under Social Welfare Acts) of Principal Act

Notes

This section substituted TCA 1997 s 126(8)(*b*) with effect from 6 April 1998.

7 Income under dispositions for short periods

Notes

This section substituted "6th day of April, 2000" for "6th day of April, 1998" in TCA 1997 Sch 32 para 27(1) with effect from 6 April 1998.

8 Amendment of section 66 (special basis at commencement of trade or profession) of Principal Act

Notes

This section substituted TCA 1997 s 66(2) as respects 1998–99 and later tax years.

9 Amendment of section 191 (taxation treatment of Hepatitis C compensation payments) of Principal Act

...

(2) This section shall apply as on and from the 1st day of November, 1997.

Notes

Subs (1) substituted TCA 1997 s 191(1)–(2).

10 Amendment of section 202 (relief for agreed pay restructuring) of Principal Act

Notes

Para (*a*)(i) substituted TCA 1997 s 202(1)(*a*) definition of "relevant agreement" with effect from 6 April 1998.

Para (*a*)(ii) inserted TCA 1997 s 202(1)(*c*) with effect from 6 April 1998.

Para (*b*) substituted TCA 1997 s 202(2)(*b*)(i)–(ii) with effect from 6 April 1998.

11 Amendment of section 479 (relief for new shares purchased on issue by employees) of Principal Act

...

(2) This section shall come into operation on the 12th day of February, 1998.

Notes

Subs (1)(*a*) substituted "the period of 3 years" for "the period of 5 years" in TCA 1997 s 479(1)(*a*) definition of "eligible shares" para (ii).

Subs (1)(*b*)(i) substituted "the period of 3 years" for "the period of 5 years" in TCA 1997 s 479(3).

Subs (1)(*b*)(ii) deleted from "; but" to the end of TCA 1997 s 479(3).

Subs (1)(*c*) substituted TCA 1997 s 479(5).

12 Amendment of Chapter 1 (transfer of assets abroad) of Part 33 of Principal Act

...

(2) This section shall apply irrespective of when the transfer or associated operations took place but shall apply only to income arising on or after the 12th day of February, 1998.

Notes

Subs (1)(*a*)(i) substituted "individuals resident or ordinarily resident in the State" for "individuals ordinarily resident in the State" in TCA 1997 s 806(3).

Subs (1)(*a*)(ii) inserted TCA 1997 s 806(5A).

Subs (1)(*b*) substituted "an individual resident or ordinarily resident in the State" for "an individual ordinarily resident in the State" in TCA 1997 s 808(4)(*a*).

---

13 Reduction in income tax for certain income earned outside the State

---

Notes

This section inserted TCA 1997 s 825A with effect from 6 April 1998.

---

14 Seafarer allowance, etc

...

(2) Paragraph (*b*) of subsection (1) shall come into operation on such day as the Minister for Finance may, by order, appoint.

Notes

Subs (1)(*a*) inserted "Section 472B" after "Section 472A" in TCA 1997 s 458 (Table Part 1) with effect from 6 April 1998.

Subs (1)(*b*) inserted TCA 1997 s 472B from such date as the Minister may appoint by order.

Subs (1)(*c*) inserted TCA 1997 s 823(2A) with effect from 6 April 1998.

Subs (1)(*d*) substituted "sections 472, 472A and 472B" for "section 472" in TCA 1997 s 1024(2)(*a*)(viii) with effect from 6 April 1998.

---

15 Notional loans relating to shares, etc

...

(2) Section 122A, as inserted by this section, shall apply—

(*a*) as regards subsection (2) thereof, as on and from the 4th day of March, 1998, as respects shares acquired (whether before or after that date); but where the shares were acquired before that date, the notional loan referred to in that subsection shall be deemed to have been made on the 4th day of March, 1998, in an amount equal to the amount of that loan outstanding at that date,

(*b*) as regards subsection (6) thereof, in respect of the termination of a loan on or after the 4th day of March, 1998, and

(*c*) as regards subsection (7) thereof, in respect of a disposal made on or after the 4th day of March, 1998.

Notes

Subs (1) inserted TCA 1997 s 122A.

CHAPTER 3

Income Tax, Corporation Tax and Capital Gains Tax

16 Relief for the long-term unemployed

Notes

Para (*a*) inserted TCA 1997 s 88A with effect from 6 April 1998.

Para (*b*)(i) inserted "Section 472A" after "Section 472" in TCA 1997 s 458 (Table Part 1) with effect from 6 April 1998.

Para (*b*)(ii) inserted TCA 1997 s 472A with effect from 6 April 1998.

Para (*c*) substituted "sections 472 and 472A" for "section 472" in TCA 1997 s 1024(2)(*a*)(viii) with effect from 6 April 1998.

17 Relief for gifts made to designated schools

Notes

Para (*a*) inserted "Section 485A(4)" after "Section 478" in TCA 1997 s 458 (Table Part 2) with effect from 6 April 1998.

Para (*b*) inserted TCA 1997 s 485A with effect from 6 April 1998.

Para (*c*) inserted TCA 1997 s 1024(2)(*a*)(*xii*) with effect from 6 April 1998.

18 Amendment of section 200 (certain foreign pensions) of Principal Act

Notes

This section inserted TCA 1997 s 200(2A) with effect from 6 April 1998.

19 Amendment of section 268 (meaning of "industrial building or structure") of Principal Act

Notes

This section substituted "30th day of September, 1998" for "31st day of December, 1997" in TCA 1997 s 268(5)(*a*)(iii) with effect from 6 April 1998.

20 Capital allowances for airport buildings and structures

Notes

Para (*a*)(i) inserted TCA 1997 s 268(1)(*h*) with effect from 6 April 1998.

Para (*a*)(ii) inserted TCA 1997 s 268(9)(*e*) with effect from 6 April 1998.

Para (*a*)(iii) inserted TCA 1997 s 268(10) with effect from 6 April 1998.

Para (*b*)(i) inserted TCA 1997 s 272(3)(*g*) with effect from 6 April 1998.

Para (*b*)(ii) inserted TCA 1997 s 272(3A)–(3B) with effect from 6 April 1998.

Para (*b*)(iii)(I) deleted "and" in TCA 1997 s 272(4)(*d*) with effect from 6 April 1998.

Para (*b*)(iii)(II) substituted TCA 1997 s 272(4)(*e*) with effect from 6 April 1998.

Para (*b*)(iii)(III) inserted TCA 1997 s 272(4)(*g*) with effect from 6 April 1998.

Para (*c*)(i) deleted "and" in TCA 1997 s 274(1)(*b*)(iv) with effect from 6 April 1998.

Para (*c*)(ii) substituted TCA 1997 s 274(1)(*b*)(v) with effect from 6 April 1998.

Para (*c*)(iii) inserted TCA 1997 s 274(1)(*b*)(vi) with effect from 6 April 1998.

Para (*d*) inserted TCA 1997 s 284(8) with effect from 6 April 1998.

21 Amendment of provisions relating to certain capital allowances

Notes

Para (*a*)(i) inserted ", or before the 30th day of June, 1998, if such expenditure would have been incurred before the 31st day of December, 1997, but for the existence of circumstances which resulted in legal proceedings being initiated, being proceedings which were the subject of an order of the High Court made before the 1st day of January, 1998" after "the 31st day of December, 1997", where it first occurs in TCA 1997 ss 271(3)(*c*) and 273(7)(*a*)(i).

Para (*a*)(ii) inserted "where it first occurs," after "as if the reference to the 31st day of December, 1997," in TCA 1997 ss 271(3)(*c*) and 273(7)(*a*)(i).

Para (*b*)(i) inserted ", or before the 30th day of June, 1998, if its provision is solely for use in an industrial building or structure referred to in sections 271(3)(*c*) and 273(7)(*a*)(i) and expenditure in respect of such provision would have been incurred before the 31st day of December, 1997, but for the existence of circumstances which resulted in legal proceedings being initiated, being proceedings which were the subject of an order of the High Court made before the 1st day of January, 1998" after "the 31st day of December, 1997", where it first occurs in TCA 1997 ss 283(5) and 285(7)(*a*)(i).

Para (*b*)(ii) inserted "where it first occurs," after "as if the reference to the 31st day of December, 1997," in TCA 1997 ss 283(5) and 285(7)(*a*)(i).

22 Capital allowances for private nursing homes

Notes

Para (*a*)(i)(I) substituted "section 654," for "section 654, or" in TCA 1997 s 268(1)(*e*) with effect from 6 April 1998.

Para (*a*)(i)(II) inserted TCA 1997 s 268(1)(*g*) with effect from 6 April 1998.

Para (*a*)(ii)(I) deleted "and" in TCA 1997 s 268(9)(*b*) with effect from 6 April 1998.

Para (*a*)(ii)(II) substituted "1992," for "1992." in TCA 1997 s 268(9)(*c*) with effect from 6 April 1998.

Para (*a*)(ii)(III) inserted TCA 1997 s 268(9)(*d*) with effect from 6 April 1998.

Para (*b*)(i)(I) deleted "and" in TCA 1997 s 272(3)(*d*) with effect from 6 April 1998.

Para (*b*)(i)(II) substituted "subsection (2)(*c*)," for "subsection (2)(*c*)." in TCA 1997 s 272(3)(*e*) with effect from 6 April 1998.

Para (*b*)(i)(III) inserted TCA 1997 s 272(3)(*f*) with effect from 6 April 1998.

Para (*b*)(ii) inserted TCA 1997 s 272(4)(*f*) with effect from 6 April 1998.

Para (*b*)(iii) inserted TCA 1997 s 272(7) with effect from 6 April 1998.

Para (*c*) substituted TCA 1997 s 274(1)(*b*)(ii) with effect from 6 April 1998.

23 Capital allowances for certain sea fishing boats

Notes

Para (*a*) inserted TCA 1997 s 284(3A) with effect from such day as the Minister for Finance may appoint by order.

Para (*b*) inserted TCA 1997 s 403(5A) with effect from such day as the Minister for Finance may appoint by order.

24 Amendment of Chapter 3 (designated areas, designated streets, enterprise areas and multi-storey car parks in certain urban areas) of Part 10 of Principal Act

...

(2) Paragraph (*c*)(ii) of subsection (1) shall come into operation on such day as the Minister for Finance may, by order, appoint.

Notes

Subs (1)(*a*)(i) substituted "31st day of December, 1999" for "30th day of June, 2000" in TCA 1997 s 339(1)(*b*) definition of "qualifying period" with effect from 6 April 1998.

Subs (1)(*a*)(ii)(I) substituted "the reference in paragraph (*a*) of the definition of 'qualifying period' in subsection (1) to the period ending on the 31st day of July, 1997, shall be construed as a reference to the period ending on the 31st day of July, 1998." for from "the reference in paragraph (*a*)" to the end of TCA 1997 s 339(2)(*a*) with effect from 6 April 1998.

Subs (1)(*a*)(ii)(II) inserted TCA 1997 s 339(2)(*c*) with effect from 6 April 1998.

Subs (1)(*b*) substituted "31st day of December, 1999" for "30th day of June, 2000" in TCA 1997 s 340(2)(ii) with effect from 6 April 1998.

Subs (1)(*c*)(i) substituted TCA 1997 s 343(1) definition of "qualifying company" para (*a*) with effect from 6 April 1998.

Subs (1)(*c*)(ii) substituted TCA 1997 s 343(1) definition of "qualifying trading operations" paras (*a*)–(*b*) from such date as the Minister for Finance may appoint by order.

Subs (1)(*c*)(iii) substituted TCA 1997 s 343(2)(*a*) with effect from 6 April 1998.

Subs (1)(*d*) substituted TCA 1997 s 345(1) definition of "qualifying lease" with effect from 6 April 1998.

Subs (1)(*e*) inserted TCA 1997 s 350A with effect from 6 April 1998.

25 Amendment of Chapter 1 (Custom House Docks Area) of Part 10 of Principal Act

...

(2) This section shall come into operation on such day as the Minister for Finance may, by order, appoint.

Notes

Subs (1)(*a*)(i) substituted "31st day of December, 1999" for "24th day of January, 1999" in TCA 1997 s 322(1) definition of "the specified period".

Subs (1)(*a*)(ii) substituted "31st day of December, 1999" for "24th day of January, 1999" in TCA 1997 s 322(2)(*b*).

26 Amendment of section 344 (capital allowances in relation to construction or refurbishment of certain multi-storey car parks) of Principal Act

Notes

This section substituted TCA 1997 s 344(1) definition of "qualifying period" with effect from 6 April 1998.

27 Amendment of section 351 (interpretation (Chapter 4)) of Principal Act

Notes

Para (*a*) substituted TCA 1997 s 351 definition of "qualifying period" with effect from 6 April 1998.

Para (*b*) inserted TCA 1997 s 351 definition of "the relevant local authority" with effect from 6 April 1998.

28 Amendment of Chapter 6 (Dublin Docklands Area) of Part 10 of Principal Act

...

(2) This section shall apply as on and from the 6th day of April, 1997.

Notes

Subs (1)(*a*) inserted TCA 1997 s 368(4A).

Subs (1)(*b*) substituted TCA 1997 s 371(2).

29 Capital allowances for, and deduction in respect of, vehicles

Notes

Para (*a*)(i) substituted "mechanically propelled vehicle;" for "mechanically propelled vehicle." in TCA 1997 s 373(2)(*i*) with effect from 6 April 1998.

Para (*a*)(ii) inserted TCA 1997 s 373(2)(*j*) with effect from 6 April 1998.

Para (*b*) substituted TCA 1997 s 376(1) definition of "relevant amount" with effect from 6 April 1998.

30 Treatment of certain losses and capital allowances

Notes

This section inserted TCA 1997 ss 409A and 409B with effect from 6 April 1998.

31 Amendment of section 403 (restriction on use of capital allowances for certain leased assets) of Principal Act

Notes

This section substituted TCA 1997 s 403(9)(*b*) with effect from 6 April 1998.

32 Amendment of section 481 (relief for investment in films) of Principal Act

...

(2) This section shall apply as on and from the 6th day of April, 1997.

Notes

Subs (1)(*a*) substituted "subsection (2), and" for "subsection (2), or" in TCA 1997 s 481(1) definition of "film" para (*a*).

Subs (1)(*b*) substituted "as respects every film" for "as respects any other film" in TCA 1997 s 481(1) definition of "film" para (*b*).

33 Amendment of section 482 (relief for expenditure on significant buildings and gardens) of Principal Act

Notes

This section inserted TCA 1997 s 482(2)(*d*) as respects qualifying expenditure incurred on or after 12 February 1998.

34 Restriction of relief as respects eligible shares issued on or after 3rd December, 1997

Notes

Para (*a*)(i)(I) substituted TCA 1997 s 491(2)–(3), subject to FA 1998 s 35, as respects eligible shares issued on or after 3 December 1997.

Para (*a*)(i)(II) substituted TCA 1997 s 491(5), subject to FA 1998 s 35, as respects eligible shares issued on or after 3 December 1997.

Para (*a*)(ii) deleted TCA 1997 s 492, subject to FA 1998 s 35 as respects eligible shares issued on or after 3 December 1997.

Para (*b*) substituted TCA 1997 s 498(4) with effect from 12 February 1998.

Para (*c*) substituted "500" for "498" in TCA 1997 s 504(7)(*a*) with effect from 6 April 1998.

35 Transitional arrangements in relation to section 34

(1) In this section —

"auditor" means —

(*a*) in relation to a company or its qualifying subsidiary, the person or persons appointed as auditor of the company or its qualifying subsidiary, as appropriate, for all the purposes of the Companies Acts, 1963 to 1990, and

(*b*) in relation to a specified designated fund, the person or persons appointed as auditor of that fund;

"authority" has the meaning assigned to it by section 492 of the Principal Act;

"certifying agency" has the meaning assigned to it by section 488 of the Principal Act;

"certifying Minister" has the meaning assigned to it by section 488 of the Principal Act,

"combined certificate" has the meaning assigned to it by section 492 of the Principal Act;

"County Enterprise Board" means a board referred to in the Schedule to the Industrial Development Act, 1995;

"eligible shares" has the meaning assigned to it by section 488 of the Principal Act;

"industrial development agency" has the meaning assigned to it by section 488 of the Principal Act;

"the principal provisions" mean Chapter 111 of Part 1 of the Finance Act, 1984, or Part 16 of the Principal Act;

"prospectus", in relation to a company, means any prospectus, notice, circular or advertisement, offering to the public for subscription or purchase any eligible shares of the company, and in this definition "the public" includes any section of the public, whether selected as members of the company or as clients of the person issuing the prospectus or in any other manner;

"qualifying subsidiary", in relation to a company, has the same meaning as it has for the purposes of section 495 of the Principal Act;

"qualifying trading operations" has the meaning assigned to it by section 496 of the Principal Act;

"relevant certificate" has the meaning assigned to it by section 492 of the Principal Act;

"specified designated fund" means an investment fund designated under section 27 of the Finance Act, 1984, which closed on or before the 5th day of April, 1997;

"the specified period" means the period beginning on the 1st day of December, 1996, and ending on the 2nd day of December, 1997.

(2) Paragraph (*a*) of section 34 shall not apply as respects eligible shares issued on or after the 3rd day of December, 1997, by a company to which this section applies and in respect of which the conditions in either subsection (5), (6) or (7) are met.

(3) The provisions of Part 16 of the Principal Act which were in force immediately before the 3rd day of December, 1997, shall, as those provisions stand amended by paragraphs (*b*) and (*c*) of section 34, apply as respects eligible shares issued on or after that day by a company to which this section applies and in respect of which the conditions in either subsection (5), (6) or (7) are met.

(4) This section applies to a company which, or whose qualifying subsidiary, either carries on or intends to carry on one or more of the qualifying trading operations.

(5) The conditions of this subsection referred to in subsection (2) are —

(*a*) the eligible shares are issued by the company on or before the 5th day of April, 1998, and

(*b*) the eligible shares are issued following a subscription on behalf of an individual by a person or persons having the management of a specified designated fund, and

(*c*) the company proves to the satisfaction of the Revenue Commissioners that before the 3rd day of December, 1997, it had the intention of raising money, on or before the 5th day of April, 1998, under the principal provisions through the specified designated fund referred to in *paragraph* (*b*) of this subsection,

and in determining whether they are satisfied that the company has complied with the requirements specified in paragraph (*c*) of this subsection the Revenue Commissioners shall have regard to the following —

(i) (I) signed heads of agreement between the company and the fund, or

(II) exchange of correspondence between the company and the fund showing a clear intention that the fund intended, on or before the 5th day of April, 1998, to subscribe for eligible shares in the company,

(ii) a certificate by the auditor of the fund confirming that it is a specified designated fund, and

(iii) any other information the Revenue Commissioners deem necessary for the purpose.

(6) The conditions of this subsection referred to in subsection (2) are —

(*a*) the eligible shares are issued by the company on or before the 30th day of September, 1998, and

(*b*) a relevant certificate or a combined certificate has been issued to the company by an authority before the 3rd day of December, 1997.

(7) The conditions of this subsection referred to in subsection (2) are —

(*a*) the eligible shares are issued by the company on or before the 30th day of September, 1998, and (*b*) the company proves to the satisfaction of the Revenue Commissioners that before the 3rd day of December, 1997, it had an intention to raise money under the principal provisions, and in determining whether they are so satisfied the Revenue Commissioners shall have regard to one or more of the following —

(i) an application in writing made by the company to the Revenue Commissioners in the specified period for the opinion of the Revenue Commissioners as to whether the company would be a qualifying company for the purposes of the principal provisions,

(ii) an application in writing made by the company to an authority in the specified period for a relevant certificate or a combined certificate,

(iii) an application in writing made by the company to an industrial development agency in the specified period for a certificate referred to in section 489(2)(*e*) of the Principal Act,

(iv) an application in writing made to a certifying agency, certifying Minister or County Enterprise Board in the specified period for a certificate under section 497 of the Principal Act, and

(v) the publication in the specified period of a prospectus by, or on behalf of, the company,

and

(*c*) (i) in the case of a company which, or whose qualifying subsidiary, either carries on or intends to carry on a qualifying trading operation as is mentioned in subparagraph (i), (ii), (iii), (v), (viii), (ix), (xi) or (xiii) of paragraph (*a*) of section 496(2) of the Principal Act, that in the specified period the company or its qualifying subsidiary, as the case may be, had entered into a binding contract in writing —

(I) to purchase or lease land or a building,

(II) to purchase or lease plant or machinery, or

(III) for the construction or refurbishment of a building,

to be used in the carrying on of its qualifying trading operation,

(ii) in the case of a company which, or whose qualifying subsidiary, either carries on or intends to carry on a qualifying trading operation as is mentioned in subparagraph (vii) of paragraph (*a*) of section 496(2) of the Principal Act, that in the specified period the company or its qualifying subsidiary, as the case may be, had entered into a binding contract in writing —

(I) to purchase or lease greenhouses,

(II) to purchase or lease plant or machinery, or

(III) for the construction or refurbishment of greenhouses,

to be used in the carrying on of its qualifying trading operation,

(iii) in the case of a company which, or whose qualifying subsidiary, either carries on or intends to carry on a qualifying trading operation as is mentioned in subparagraph (xii) of paragraph (*a*) of section 496(2) of the Principal Act, that in the specified period the company or its qualifying subsidiary, as the case may be, had entered into a binding contract in writing for the production, publication, marketing or promotion of the qualifying recording or qualifying recordings which the company or its qualifying subsidiary, as the case may be, intends to produce,

and the company proves to the satisfaction of the Revenue Commissioners that the contract which it or its qualifying subsidiary, as the case may be, had entered into was integral to, or consistent with, the purpose for which it had intended to raise money under the principal provisions and that the consideration of the contract is equal to 25 per cent or more of the money which it is intended to so raise.

(8) For the purposes of subsection (7) —

(*a*) the date on which a contract was entered into by a company or, as the case may be, its qualifying subsidiary, and

(*b*) the date on which a prospectus was published by, or on behalf of, a company,

shall be confirmed in a certificate by the auditor of the company, or its qualifying subsidiary, as appropriate.

36 Employee share schemes

...

(2) (*a*) Paragraph (*b*) of subsection (1) shall apply as on and from the date of the passing of this Act.

(*b*) Paragraph (*d*) of subsection (1) shall apply as respects employee share ownership trusts approved of under paragraph 2 of Schedule 12 of the Principal Act on or after the date of the passing of this Act.

Notes

Subs (1)(*a*) inserted TCA 1997 s 511A with effect from 6 April 1998.

Subs (1)(*b*) substituted TCA 1997 s 519(7) with effect from 27 March 1998.

Subs (1)(*c*) inserted TCA 1997 Sch 11 para 4(1A) with effect from 6 April 1998.

Subs (1)(*d*)(i)(I) substituted TCA 1997 Sch 12 para 1(3) as respects employee share ownership trusts approved of under TCA 1997 Sch 12 para 2 on or after 27 March 1998.

Subs (1)(*d*)(i)(II) substituted TCA 1997 Sch 12 para 1(4)(*a*) definition of "associate" as respects employee share ownership trusts approved of under TCA 1997 Sch 12 para 2 on or after 27 March 1998.

Subs (1)(*d*)(ii) substituted TCA 1997 Sch 12 para 2 as respects employee share ownership trusts approved of under TCA 1997 Sch 12 para 2 on or after 27 March 1998.

Subs (1)(*d*)(iii)(I) substituted TCA 1997 Sch 12 para 11(2) as respects employee share ownership trusts approved of under TCA 1997 Sch 12 para 2 on or after 27 March 1998.

Subs (1)(*d*)(iii)(II) substituted "subparagraphs (2A) and (3)" for "subparagraph (3)" in TCA 1997 Sch 12 para 11(4)(*a*) as respects employee share ownership trusts approved of under TCA 1997 Sch 12 para 2 on or after 27 March 1998.

Subs (1)(*d*)(iii)(III) substituted "subparagraphs (2) and (2A)" for "subparagraph (2)" in TCA 1997 Sch 12 para 11(5) as respects employee share ownership trusts approved of under TCA 1997 Sch 12 para 2 on or after 27 March 1998.

Subs (1)(*d*)(iii)(IV) substituted of "subparagraph (2A), (3) or (4)" for "subparagraph (3) or (4)" in TCA 1997 Sch 12 para 11(7) as respects employee share ownership trusts approved of under TCA 1997 Sch 12 para 2 on or after 27 March 1998.

Subs (1)(*d*)(iii)(V) substituted "subparagraph (2), (2A), (3) or (4)" for "subparagraph (2), (3) or (4)" in TCA 1997 Sch 12 para 11(8) as respects employee share ownership trusts approved of under TCA 1997 Sch 12 para 2 on or after 27 March 1998.

Definitions

land: IA 1937 Sch; person: IA 1937 s 11(*c*); writing: IA 1937 Sch.

37 Payments to subcontractors in certain industries

...

(2) This section shall apply as on and from the 6th day of October, 1998.

Notes

Subs (1)(*a*) substituted TCA 1997 s 530(1) definition of "meat processing operations".

Subs (1)(*b*) substituted TCA 1997 s 531(1)(*b*)(ii).

38 Amendment of section 659 (farming: allowances for capital expenditure on the construction of farm buildings, etc. for control of pollution) of Principal Act

Notes

This section substituted TCA 1997 s 659(3)(*a*).

39 Amendment of section 667 (special provisions for qualifying farmers) of Principal Act

Notes

Para (*a*) substituted "years of assessment, or" for "years of assessment," in TCA 1997 s 667(2)(*b*)(i) with effect from 6 April 1998.

Para (*b*) substituted TCA 1997 s 667(2)(*b*)(ii)–(iii) with effect from 6 April 1998.

40 Amendment of section 680 (annual allowance for mineral depletion) of Principal Act

Notes

Para (*a*) inserted "at any time" after "qualifying mine" in TCA 1997 s 680(2) with effect from 6 April 1998.

Para (*b*) substituted "time" for "date" in TCA 1997 s 680(2) with effect from 6 April 1998.

41 Amendment of section 681 (allowance for mine rehabilitation expenditure) of Principal Act

Notes

This section inserted "fireclay, coal" after "limestone" in TCA 1997 s 681(1)(*a*) definition of "qualifying mine" with effect from 6 April 1998.

42 Amendment of section 734 (taxation of collective investment undertakings) of Principal Act

Notes

This section substituted TCA 1997 s 734(1)(*a*) definition of "specified company" para (ii) with effect from 6 April 1998.

43 Taxation of shares issued in place of cash dividends

...

(2) This section shall apply as respects shares issued by a company on or after the 3rd day of December, 1997.

Notes

Subs (1)(*a*) substituted TCA 1997 s 816(1)–(3).

Subs (1)(*b*) substituted "sections 436 and 437, and subsection (2)(*b*) of section 816" for "sections 436 and 437" in TCA 1997 s 4(1) definition of "distribution".

Subs (1)(*c*) substituted "sections 436 and 437, and subsections (2)(*b*) of section 816" for "sections 436 and 437" in TCA 1997 s 20(1) Sch F para 1.

Subs (1)(*d*) substituted "sections 436 and 437, and subsections (2)(*b*) of section 816" for "sections 436 and 437" in TCA 1997 s 130(1).

44 Amendment of section 843 (capital allowances for buildings used for third level educational purposes) of Principal Act

Notes

Para (*a*) substituted TCA 1997 s 843(1) definition of "approved institution" with effect from 6 April 1998.

Para (*b*) substituted TCA 1997 s 843(1) definition of "qualifying premises" para (*b*)(ii) with effect from 6 April 1998.

45 Amendment of Part 41 (self assessment) of Principal Act

...

(2) Every order made by the Minister for Finance under this section shall be laid before Dáil Éireann as soon as may be after it is made.

Notes

Subs (1)(*a*) substituted TCA 1997 s 950(1) definition of "specified return date for the chargeable period" para (*a*) with effect from 6 April 1998.

Subs (1)(*b*)(i)(I) substituted TCA 1997 s 958(2)(*a*)–(*b*) with effect from 6 April 1998.

Subs (1)(*b*)(i)(II) substituted "the 1st day of November in the year of assessment, the 30th day of November in the year of assessment, the 1st day of November following the year of assessment, the 30th day of November following the year of assessment" for "the 1st day of November in the year of assessment, the 1st day of November following the year of assessment" in TCA 1997 s 958(2) with effect from 6 April 1998.

Subs (1)(*b*)(ii) substituted TCA 1997 s 958(3)(*b*)(ii) with effect from 6 April 1998.

Subs (1)(*b*)(iii) substituted TCA 1997 s 958(4)(*b*)(i) with effect from 6 April 1998.

Subs (1)(*b*)(iv)(I) substituted:

"on or before —

(i) in the case of the years 1997–98 and 1998–99, the 9th day of December, and

(ii) in the case of the year 1999–2000 and any subsequent year of assessment, the 9th day of March,

in the year of assessment to which the preliminary tax relates by virtue of subsection (2)(*a*)."

for from "on or before the 9th day of December" to the end of TCA 1997 s 958(10)(*a*) with effect from 6 April 1998.

Subs (1)(*b*)(iv)(II) substituted:

"throughout —

(i) in the case of the years 1997–98 and 1998–99, the calendar year or a part of that year in which the due date for the payment of that preliminary tax in accordance with subsection (2)(*a*) falls, and

(ii) in the case of the year 1999–2000 or any subsequent year of assessment, that year,

and the Collector-General shall debit the bank account of that person with such instalments on the 9th day of each month in that calendar year or a part of that calendar year or, as the case may be, in that year."

for from "throughout the calendar year" to the end of TCA 1997 s 958(10)(*b*) with effect from 6 April 1998.

Subs (1)(*b*)(iv)(III) substituted TCA 1997 s 958(10)(*c*) with effect from 6 April 1998.

46 Amendment of section 787 (nature and amount of relief for qualifying premiums) of Principal Act

Notes

This section substituted "on or before the specified return date for the chargeable period (within the meaning of Part 41)" for "on or before the 31st day of January in the year following the year of assessment" in TCA 1997 s 787(7) with effect from 6 April 1998.

47 Amendments of Principal Act in consequence of a change in the currency of certain states

(1) The provisions of the Principal Act referred to in Schedule 2 shall apply subject to the amendments specified in that Schedule (being amendments the purposes of which are, amongst other things, to make provision in consequence of a change in the currency of certain states).

(2) This section shall come into operation on such day or days as the Minister for Finance may appoint by order or orders either generally or with reference to any particular provision of Schedule 2 and different days may be so appointed for different such provisions.

48 Amendment of Principal Act in consequence of convention with United States of America relating to double taxation, etc

(1) Subject to subsection (2), the provisions of the Principal Act referred to in Schedule 3 shall apply subject to the amendments specified in that Schedule.

(2) (*a*) Subject to paragraph (*b*), this section shall apply as on and from the times at which the Convention set out in the Schedule to the Double Taxation Relief (Taxes on Income and Capital Gains) (United States of America) Order, 1997 (SI No 477 of 1997), has effect in accordance with paragraph 2 of Article 29 of that Convention.

(*b*) Where, in relation to a person, paragraph 3 of Article 29 of the said Convention applies in respect of the period specified in that paragraph, the Principal Act shall apply in relation to the person in respect of that period as if subsection (1) had not been enacted.

49 Amendment of Part 26 (life assurance companies) of Principal Act

...

(2) This section shall apply as on and from the 6th day of April, 1997.

Notes

Subs (1) substituted "the rate per cent of corporation tax specified in section 21(1)" for "the rate per cent of corporation tax specified in section 21(1)(*b*)" in TCA 1997 ss 723(6) and 738(2)(*c*).

50 Amendment of section 1013 (limited partnerships) of Principal Act

...

(2) This section shall apply as on and from the 28th day of February, 1998.

Notes

Subs (1)(*a*)(i) inserted TCA 1997 s 1013(1) definition of "active partner".

Subs (1)(*a*)(ii)(I) substiututed "reimbursed by some other person," for "reimbursed by some other person, or" in TCA 1997 s 1013(1) definition of "limited partner" para (*b*).

Subs (1)(*a*)(ii)(II) subsituted "incurred for the purposes of the trade, or" for "incurred for the purposes of the trade;" in TCA 1997 s 1013(1) definition of "limited partner" para (*c*).

Subs (1)(*a*)(ii)(III) inserted TCA 1997 s 1013(1) definition of "limited partner" para (*d*).

Subs (1)(*b*)(i) substituted "gains arising from the trade," for "gains arising from the trade, or" in TCA 1997 s 1013(2)(*a*)(I).

Subs (1)(*b*)(ii) substituted "profits or gains arising from the trade, or" for "profits or gains arising from the trade" in TCA 1997 s 1013(2)(*a*)(II).

Subs (1)(*b*)(iii) inserted TCA 1997 s 1013(2)(*a*)(III).

Subs (1)(*c*) inserted TCA 1997 s 1013(2A).

51 Reduction in tax credits in respect of distributions

...

(2) Schedule 4 shall have effect for the purpose of supplementing subsection (1).

Notes

Subs (1) substituted TCA 1997 s 4(1) definition of "standard credit rate" with effect from 3 December 1997.

52 Abolition of tax credits

The provisions of the Principal Act referred to in Schedule 5 shall apply subject to the amendments specified in that Schedule (being amendments the purposes of which are to provide for the abolition of tax credits as respects distributions made on or after the 6th day of April, 1999).

Definitions

distribution: s 4(1); tax credit: s 2(1).

53 Amendment of definition of specified qualifying shares

Notes

This section substituted "£200,000,000" for "£100,000,000" in the definition of "specified qualifying shares" in TCA 1997 ss 723(1), 737(1) and 838(1).

54 Amendment of section 198 (certain interest not to be chargeable) of Principal Act

Notes

Para (*a*) renumbered the existing provision of TCA 1997 s 198 as subs (1) with effect from 6 April 1998.
Para (*b*) inserted TCA 1997 s 198(2) with effect from 6 April 1998.

CHAPTER 4
Corporation Tax

55 Rate of corporation tax

...

(2) Schedule 6 shall have effect for the purpose of supplementing this section.

Notes

Subs (1)(*a*) substituted "March, 1997," for "March, 1997, and" in TCA 1997 s 21(1)(*a*) with effect from 6 April 1998.
Subs (1)(*b*) substituted TCA 1997 s 21(1)(*b*) with effect from 6 April 1998.

56 Amendment of section 22 (reduced rate of corporation tax for certain income) of Principal Act

Notes

Para (*a*) substituted TCA 1997 s 22(1)(*a*)(I)–(II) with effect from 6 April 1998.
Para (*b*) substituted TCA 1997 s 22(1)(*b*) with effect from 6 April 1998.

57 Amendment of section 713 (investment income reserved for policyholders) of Principal Act

...

(2) This section shall apply as on and from the 6th day of April, 1997.

Notes

Subs (1)(*a*) substituted "specified in section 21(1)" for "specified in section 21(1)(*b*)" in TCA 1997 s 713(3).
Subs (1)(*b*) substituted "in respect of the part specified in subsection (6) of the unrelieved profits" for "in respect of the part specified in subsection (5) of the unrelieved profits" in TCA 1997 s 713(3).

58 Credit unions

Notes

Subs (1) inserted TCA 1997 s 219A with effect from 6 April 1998.
Subs (2) repealed TCA 1997 s 212 with effect from 6 April 1998.

59 Amendment of section 449 (credit for foreign tax not otherwise credited) of Principal Act

Notes

Para (*a*) deleted "and" in TCA 1997 s 449(1) definition of "relevant foreign tax" para (*c*) with effect from 6 April 1998.

Para (*b*) substituted "Schedule 24, and" for "Schedule 24;" in TCA 1997 s 449(1) definition of "relevant foreign tax" para (*d*).
Para (*c*) inserted TCA 1997 s 449(1) definition of "relevant foreign tax" para (*e*).

60 Relief for double taxation

Notes

Para (*a*) substituted:

"Relief from Income Tax and Corporation Tax By Means of Credit in Respect of Foreign Tax

PART 1

Interpretation

1. (1) In this Schedule, except where the context otherwise requires —"

for:

"Relief from Income Tax and Corporation Tax By Means of Credit in Respect of Foreign Tax

Interpretation

1. (1) In this Schedule, except where the context otherwise requires —"

in TCA 1997 Sch 24 as respects accounting period ending on or after 1 April 1998.

Para (*b*) substituted TCA 1997 Sch 24 para 1(1) definition of "foreign tax" as respects accounting period ending on or after 1 April 1998.

Para (*c*) inserted TCA 1997 Sch 24 paras 9A–9B as respects accounting period ending on or after 1 April 1998.

Para (*d*) substituted:

"PART 3

Miscellaneous

10. Credit shall not be allowed"

for:

"Miscellaneous

10. Credit shall not be allowed"

in TCA 1997 Sch 24 para 10 as respects accounting period ending on or after 1 April 1998.

61 Corporate donations to eligible charities

Notes

This section inserted TCA 1997 s 486A with effect from 6 April 1998.

62 Relief for investment in renewable energy generation

...

(2) This section shall come into operation on such day as the Minister for Finance appoints by order.

Notes

Subs (1) inserted TCA 1997 s 486B.

63 Amendment of section 88 (deduction for gifts to Enterprise Trust Ltd.) of Principal Act

Notes

Para (*a*) deleted TCA 1997 s 88(3)(*b*)(ii) with effect from 6 April 1998.
Para (*b*) substituted "£3,000,000" for "£1,500,000" in TCA 1996 s 88(3)(*b*)(iii) with effect from 6 April 1998.

64 Amendment of section 715 (annuity business: separate charge on profits) of Principal Act

...

(2) This section shall apply as respects an accounting period of a company ending on or after the 4th day of March, 1998.

Notes

Subs (1) substituted TCA 1997 s 715(2)(*a*).

CHAPTER 5

Capital Gains Tax

65 Capital gains: rates of charge

...

(2) Subsection (1) shall apply —

(*a*) as respects paragraphs (*a*) and (*c*), in relation to disposals made on or after the 3rd day of December, 1997, and

(*b*) as respects paragraphs (*b*), in relation to disposals made on or after the 12th day of February, 1998.

Notes

Subs (1)(*a*) substituted "20 per cent" for "40 per cent" in TCA 1997 s 28(3).

Subs (1)(*b*) inserted TCA 1997 s 594(2)(*f*).

Subs (1)(*c*) inserted TCA 1997 s 649A.

66 Amendment of Part 27 (unit trusts and offshore funds) of Principal Act

Notes

This section inserted TCA 1997 Pt 27 Ch 3 (s 747A) with effect from 6 April 1998.

67 Amendment of section 538 (disposals where assets lost or destroyed or become of negligible value) of Principal Act

...

(2) This section shall apply as respects a waiver of the right of the State to property on or after the 12th day of February, 1998.

Notes

Subs (1) inserted TCA 1997 s 538(2A).

68 Amendment of section 547 (disposals and acquisitions treated as made at market value) of Principal Act,

...

(2) This section shall apply as respects the acquisition of an asset on or after the 12th day of February, 1998.

Notes

Subs (1) inserted TCA 1997 s 547(1A).

69 Amendment of Chapter 3 (assets held in fiduciary or representative capacity, inheritances and settlements) of Part 19 of Principal Act

...

(2) This section shall apply as respects a disposal deemed to be made on or after the 12th day of February, 1998.

Notes

Subs (1) inserted TCA 1997 s 577A.

70 Repeal of section 592 (reduced rate of capital gains tax on certain disposals of shares by individuals) of Principal Act

...

(2) This section shall apply as respects disposals made on or after the 3rd day of December, 1997.

Notes

Subs (1) repealed TCA 1997 s 592.

71 Amendment of section 597 (replacement of business and other assets) of Principal Act

...

(2) This section shall apply as respects disposals made on or after the passing of this Act.

Notes

Subs (1) substituted TCA 1997 s 597(3)(*c*).

72 Amendment of section 598 (disposals of business or farm on retirement) of Principal Act

...

(2) This section shall apply as respects a disposal of an asset on or after the 6th day of April, 1998.

Notes

Subs (1)(*a*)(i) substituted TCA 1997 s 598(1) definition of "qualifying assets" para (i).
Subs (1)(*a*)(ii) substituted "for a period of not less than 5 years, and" for "for a period of not less than 5 years;" in TCA 1997 s 598(1) definition of "qualifying assets" para (ii).
Subs (1)(*a*)(iii) inserted TCA 1997 598(1) definition of "qualifying assets" para (iii).
Subs (1)(*b*) inserted TCA 1997 598(1) definition of "the Scheme".

73 Amendment of section 652 (non-application of reliefs on replacement of assets in case of relevant disposals) of Principal Act

...

(2) This section shall apply in respect of relevant disposals made on or after the 6th day of April, 1998.

Notes

Subs (1) inserted TCA 1997 s 652(3A)–(3B) in respect of relevant disposals made on or after 6 April 1998.

74 Amendment of section 980 (deduction from consideration on disposal of certain assets) of Principal Act

Notes

This section substituted "£150,000" for "£100,000" in TCA 1997 s 980(3) as respects disposals made on or after 27 March 1998.

75 Amendment of section 1028 (married persons) of Principal Act

Notes

This section deleted TCA 1997 s 1028(4) as respects 1998–99 and later tax years.

CHAPTER 6

Income Tax and Corporation Tax: Reliefs for Renewal and Improvement of Certain Urban and Rural Areas

76 Amendment of Part 10 (income tax and corporation tax: reliefs for renewal and improvement of certain urban areas, certain resort areas and certain islands) of Principal Act

Notes

This section inserted TCA 1997 Pt 10 Ch 7 (ss 372A- 372K) with effect from 6 April 1998.

77 Reliefs for renewal and improvement of certain rural areas

Notes

Para (*a*) inserted TCA 1997 Pt 10 Ch 8 (ss 372L–372T) with effect from 6 April 1998.
Para (*b*) inserted TCA 1997 Sch 8A with effect from 6 April 1998.

PART 6

MISCELLANEOUS

131 Interest payments by certain deposit takers

...

(2) (*a*) Paragraph (*a*) of subsection (1) shall apply as on and from the 6th day of April, 1998.

(*b*) Paragraph (*b*) of subsection (1) shall apply as respects chargeable periods (within the meaning of section 321(2) of the Taxes Consolidation Act, 1997) beginning on or after the 1st day of October, 1997.

Notes

Subs (1)(*a*) substituted TCA 1997 s 256(1) definition of "appropriate tax" para (*a*).
Subs (1)(*b*) inserted TCA 1997 s 891(1A).

133 Interest on unpaid or overpaid taxes

...

(6) This section shall apply as respects interest chargeable or payable under —

(i) sections 240, 531, 953, 991 and 1080 of the Taxes Consolidation Act, 1997,

...

for any month, or any part of a month, commencing on or after the date of the passing of this Act, in respect of an amount due to be paid or retained or an amount due to be repaid or retained, as the case may be, whether before, on or after that date in accordance with those provisions.

Notes

Subs (1)(*a*) substituted "1 per cent" for "1.25 per cent" in each place where it occurs in TCA 1997 ss 240(3)(*a*), 531(9), 991(1) and 1080(1)(*a*)–(*b*).

Subs (1)(*b*) substituted "0.5 per cent" for "0.6 per cent" in TCA 1997 s 953(7).

134 Appeals

...

(4) This section shall apply to appeals determined by the Appeal Commissioners after the date of the passing of this Act.

Notes

Subs (1)(*a*) inserted TCA 1997 s 944A.

Subs (1)(*b*) inserted TCA 1997 s 945(2)(*ee*).

136 Post-consolidation amendments

(1) The provisions of the Taxes Consolidation Act, 1997, referred to in Schedule 9 shall apply subject to the amendments specified in that Schedule.

(2) This section shall be deemed to have come into force on the 6th day of April, 1997.

137 Care and management of taxes and duties

All taxes and duties imposed by this Act are hereby placed under the care and management of the Revenue Commissioners.

138 Short title, construction and commencement

(1) This Act may be cited as the Finance Act, 1998.

(2) Part 1 (so far as relating to income tax) shall be construed together with the Income Tax Acts and (so far as relating to corporation tax) shall be construed together with the Corporation Tax Acts and (so far as relating to capital gains tax) shall be construed together with the Capital Gains Tax Acts.

...

(7) Part 6 (so far as relating to income tax) shall be construed together with the Income Tax Acts and (so far as relating to corporation tax) shall be construed together with the Corporation Tax Acts and (so far as relating to capital gains tax) shall be construed together with the Capital Gains Tax Acts ....

(8) Part 1 shall, save as is otherwise expressly provided therein, apply as on and from the 6th day of April, 1998.

...

(10) Any reference in this Act to any other enactment shall, except so far as the context otherwise requires, be construed as a reference to that enactment as amended by or under any other enactment including this Act.

(11) In this Act, a reference to a Part, section or Schedule is to a Part or section of, or Schedule to, this Act, unless it is indicated that reference to some other enactment is intended.

(12) In this Act, a reference to a subsection, paragraph, subparagraph, clause or subclause is to the subsection, paragraph, subparagraph, clause or subclause of the provision (including a Schedule) in which the reference occurs, unless it is indicated that reference to some other provision is intended.

Definitions

Capital Gains Tax Acts: s 1(2); Corporation Tax Acts: s 1(2); Income Tax Acts: s 1(2).

SCHEDULE 1

AMENDMENTS CONSEQUENTIAL ON CHANGES IN PERSONAL RELIEFS

Notes

Para (*a*)(i) substituted "£6,300" for "£5,800" in TCA 1997 s 461(*a*).

Para (*a*)(ii) substituted "£3,650" for "£3,400" and "£6,300" for "£5,800" in TCA1997 s 461(*b*).

Para (*a*)(iii) substituted "£3,150" for "£2,900" in TCA 1997 s 461(*c*).

Para (*b*) substituted "£2,650" for "£2,400" and "£3,150" for "£2,900" in TCA 199 s 462(2).

Para (*c*) substituted "£800" for "£700" where it occurs in TCA 1997 s 465.

Para (*d*) substituted "£8,500" for "£7,500" where it occurs in TCA 1997 s 467(1).

Para (*e*) substituted "£1,000" for "£700" where it occurs and "£2,000" for "£1,600" in TCA 1997 s 468(2).

SCHEDULE 2

PROVISIONS AMENDING PRINCIPAL ACT IN CONSEQUENCE OF A CHANGE IN THE CURRENCY OF CERTAIN STATES

Notes

Para 1 inserted TCA 1997 s 79(1)(*c*) with effect from such date as the Minister for Finance may appoint by order.

Para 2 substituted TCA 1997 s 80(1) definition of "specified rate" para (*a*) with effect from such date as the Minister for Finance may appoint by order.

Para 3 substituted TCA 1997 s 110(1) definition of "qualifying asset" para (*a*)(i) with effect from such date as the Minister for Finance may appoint by order.

Para 4(*a*) substituted "the rate known as the 3 month European Interbank Offered Rate" for "the rate known as the 3 month Dublin Interbank Offered Rate on Irish pounds (in this subsection referred to as the '3 month Dublin Interbank Offered Rate') a record of which is maintained by the Central Bank of Ireland" in TCA 1997 s 133(13)(*b*) with effect from such date as the Minister for Finance may appoint by order.

Para 4(*b*)(i)–(ii) substituted "the rate known as the 3 month European Interbank Offered Rate" for "the 3 month Dublin Interbank Offered Rate" where it occurs in TCA 1997 s 133(13)(*c*)(i)–(ii) with effect from such date as the Minister for Finance may appoint by order.
Para 5 inserted TCA 1997 s 402(1)(*d*)–(*e*) with effect from such date as the Minister for Finance may appoint by order.
Para 6(*a*) substituted "a rate known as the European Interbank Offered Rate" for "a rate known as the Dublin Interbank Offered Rate and a record of which is kept by the Central Bank of Ireland" in TCA 1997 s 404(1)(*a*) definition of "relevant lease payment" para (ii) with effect from such date as the Minister for Finance may appoint by order.
Para 6(*b*) substituted "the rate known as the 6 month European Interbank Offered Rate" for "the rate known as the 6 month Dublin Interbank Offered Rate and a record of which is maintained by the Central Bank of Ireland" in TCA 1997 s 405(1)(*b*)(ii) with effect from such date as the Minister for Finance may appoint by order.
Para 7 inserted TCA 1997 s 445(2A) with effect from such date as the Minister for Finance may appoint by order.
Para 8(*a*) inserted TCA 1997 s 446(2A) with effect from such date as the Minister for Finance may appoint by order.
Para 8(*b*)(i) substituted TCA 1997 s 446(7)(*c*)(i) with effect from such date as the Minister for Finance may appoint by order.
Para 8(*b*)(ii)(I) substituted TCA 1997 s 446(7)(*c*)(i)(II) with effect from such date as the Minister for Finance may appoint by order.
Para 8(*b*)(ii)(II) substituted TCA 1997 s 446(7)(*c*)(i)(III) with effect from such date as the Minister for Finance may appoint by order.
Para 9 inserted TCA 1997 s 541A with effect from such date as the Minister for Finance may appoint by order.
Para 10 inserted TCA 1997 s 552(1A) with effect from such date as the Minister for Finance may appoint by order.

SCHEDULE 3

AMENDMENT OF PRINCIPAL ACT IN CONSEQUENCE OF CONVENTION WITH UNITED STATES OF AMERICA RELATING TO DOUBLE TAXATION, ETC

Notes

Para 1 deleted "the United States of America or" from TCA 1997 s 44(1) definition of "relevant territory".
Para 2(*a*) deleted "of the United States of America or" from TCA 1997 s 168(1)(*a*)(ii)(II).
Para 2(*b*)(i) deleted the definition of "resident of the United States of America" from TCA 1997 s 168(1)(*b*).
Para 2(*b*)(ii) deleted ", other than the United States of America," from TCA 1997 s 168(1)(*b*).
Para 3(*a*) deleted "of the United States of America or" from TCA 1997 s 222(1)(*b*)(i).
Para 3(*b*)(i) deleted the definition of "resident of the United States of America" from TCA 1997 s 222(1)(*b*)(ii).
Para 3(*b*)(ii) deleted "other than the United States of America" from TCA 1997 s 222(1)(*b*)(ii).
Para 4(*a*)(i) deleted the definition of "resident of the United States of America" from TCA 1997 s 452(1)(*a*).
Para 4(*a*)(ii) deleted ", other than the United States of America," from TCA 1997 s 452(1)(*b*).
Para 4(*b*) deleted "of the United States of America or" from TCA 1997 s 452(2)(*c*).
Para 5 substituted TCA 1997 s 627(2)(*a*) definition of "relevant territory".
Para 6(*a*) deleted "of the United States of America or" from TCA 1997 s 690(2)(*c*).
Para 6(*b*) deleted "'resident of the United States of America' has the meaning assigned to it by the Convention set out in Schedule 25, and" from TCA 1997 s 690(2).
Para 6(*c*) deleted "other than the United States of America," from TCA 1997 s 690(2).
Para 7 substituted TCA 1997 s 730(*b*).
Para 8 deleted "833 to" from TCA 1997 s 826(1).
Para 9 substituted TCA 1997 s 830(2).
Para 10 deleted TCA 1997 ss 833 and 834.
Para 11 deleted "or 833" from TCA 1997 Sch 22 para 4(2).

Para 12 deleted "or section 12 of the Finance Act, 1950" from TCA 1997 Sch 24 para 1(1) definition of "arrangements".

Para 13 deleted TCA 1997 Sch 25.

SCHEDULE 4

AMENDMENTS CONSEQUENTIAL ON CHANGES IN AMOUNTS OF TAX CREDITS IN RESPECT OF DISTRIBUTIONS

Notes

Para 1 substituted TCA 1997 s 145(2)(*b*) as respects a distribution made or treated as having been made by a company on or after 3 December 1997.

Para 2 substituted TCA 1997 s 729(7) with effect from 3 December 1997.

SCHEDULE 5

ABOLITION OF TAX CREDITS

Notes

Para 1 inserted ", before the 6th day of April, 1999," after "Where" in TCA 1997 s 136(1) with effect from 6 April 1998.

Para 2 inserted "and before the 6th day of April, 1999" after "date" in TCA 1997 s 139(1) with effect from 6 April 1998.

Para 3(*a*) inserted "before the 6th day of April, 1999," after "distribution made" in TCA 1997 s 143(2) with effect from 6 April 1998.

Para 3(*b*) inserted ", if any," after "tax credit" in TCA 1997 s 143(5) with effect from 6 April 1998.

Para 3(*c*) inserted ", where the distribution is made before the 6th day of April, 1999," after "50 per cent" in TCA 1997 s 143(7) with effect from 6 April 1998.

Para 4 inserted "made before the 6th day of April, 1999, being a distribution" after "relevant distribution')" in TCA 1997 s 145(1) with effect from 6 April 1998.

Para 5 inserted "made before the 6th day of April, 1999," after "recipient of a relevant distribution" in TCA 1997 s 147(5)(*a*) with effect from 6 April 1998.

Para 6 inserted "before the 6th day of April, 1999," after "distribution made" in TCA 1997 s 150(1) with effect from 6 April 1998.

Para 7 inserted "where the distribution is made before the 6th day of April, 1999," before "(whether" in TCA 1997 s 152(1)(*b*) with effect from 6 April 1998.

Para 8 substituted TCA 1997 s 156 with effect from 6 April 1998.

Para 9 inserted "and the amount of that income is calculated in accordance with subsection (1)(*a*) of section 156" after "receives franked investment income" in TCA 1997 s 157(1) with effect from 6 April 1998.

Para 10 inserted "and the amount of that income is calculated in accordance with subsection (1)(*a*) of section 156" after "receives franked investment income" in TCA 1997 s 158(1) with effect from 6 April 1998.

Para 11 inserted "before the 6th day of April, 1999," after "this Chapter, where" in TCA 1997 s 159 with effect from 6 April 1998.

SCHEDULE 6

CHANGE IN RATE OF CORPORATION TAX: FURTHER PROVISIONS

Notes

Para 1 substituted "31st day of December, 1997" for "31st day of December, 1998" in TCA 1997 s 26(4)(*b*) with effect from 6 April 1998.

Para 2 substituted "31st day of December, 1997" for "31st day of December, 1998" in TCA 1997 s 78(3)(*c*)(ii) with effect from 6 April 1998.

Para 3(*a*) substituted "twenty-two thirty-seconds" for "twenty-six thirty-sixths" in TCA 1997 s 448(2)(*a*) as respects any accounting period beginning on or after 1 January 1998.

Para 3(*b*) substituted TCA 1997 s 448(2)(*b*) with effect from 6 April 1998.

Para 4(*a*)(i)(I) substituted TCA 1997 Sch 32 para 5(2)(i) definition of "S" with effect from 6 April 1998.

Para 4(*a*)(i)(II) substituted TCA 1997 Sch 32 para 5(2)(ii) definition of "S" with effect from 6 April 1998.

Para 4(*a*)(ii) substituted TCA 1997 Sch 32 para 5(3)(*a*) with effect from 6 April 1998.

Para 4(*b*)(i) substituted TCA 1997 Sch 32 para 6(2)(ii) definition of "S" with effect from 6 April 1998.

Para 4(*b*)(ii) substituted TCA 1997 Sch 32 para 6(3)(*a*) with effect from 6 April 1998.

Para 4(*c*)(i) substituted TCA 1997 Sch 32 para 16(3)(*a*)–(*b*) with effect from 6 April 1998.

Para 4(*c*)(ii) substituted TCA 1997 Sch 32 para 16(5) with effect from 6 April 1998.

Para 4(*d*)(i) substituted TCA 1997 Sch 32 para 18(4)(*b*) with effect from 6 April 1998.

Para 4(*d*)(ii) substituted TCA 1997 Sch 32 para 18(6)(*a*) with effect from 6 April 1998.

SCHEDULE 9

POST-CONSOLIDATION AMENDMENTS

Notes

Para 1 substituted "subsection (2)" for "subsection (1)" in TCA 1997 s 82(3) with effect from 6 April 1997.

Para 2 substituted "section 83 or 707" for "section 83 or 709" in TCA 1997 s 109(3) with effect from 6 April 1997.

Para 3 inserted "the right assigned or released but did include the amount or value of" after "did not include the value of" in TCA 1997 s 128(8) with effect from 6 April 1997.

Para 4 substituted "Subsection (3)" for "Subsection (2)" in TCA 1997 s 140(4)(*b*) with effect from 6 April 1997.

Para 5 deleted "'expenditure incurred on the construction of a building or structure' excludes any expenditure within the meaning of section 270(2);" in TCA 1997 s 279(1) with effect from 6 April 1997.

Para 6 substituted "first purchase" for "first sale" in TCA 1997 s 346(7)(*b*)(ii) with effect from 6 April 1997.

Para 7 substituted "section 888(2)" for "section 888(1)" in TCA 1997 s 950(1) with effect from 6 April 1997.

URBAN RENEWAL ACT 1988

Number 27 of 1998

ARRANGEMENT OF SECTIONS

AN ACT TO MAKE NEW PROVISION FOR THE RENEWAL OF CERTAIN URBAN AREAS, FOR THAT PURPOSE TO PROVIDE FOR THE PREPARATION AND SUBMISSION TO THE MINISTER FOR THE ENVIRONMENT AND LOCAL GOVERNMENT BY LOCAL AUTHORITIES OR COMPANIES AUTHORISED BY THEM OF PLANS (TO BE KNOWN AS INTEGRATED AREA PLANS) IN RELATION TO SUCH AREAS, TO DEFINE THE FUNCTIONS OF LOCAL AUTHORITIES OR SUCH COMPANIES IN RELATION TO AND CONSEQUENT UPON THE PREPARATION AND SUBMISSION OF SUCH

PLANS, TO PROVIDE FOR THE REMISSION OF RATES WITHIN AREAS TO WHICH SUCH PLANS RELATE, TO CONFER CERTAIN FUNCTIONS ON THE DUBLIN DOCKLANDS DEVELOPMENT AUTHORITY, TO ENABLE GRANTS TO BE MADE TO LOCAL AUTHORITIES AND CERTAIN OTHER BODIES FOR THE PURPOSES OF, AMONGST OTHER MATTERS, URBAN AND VILLAGE RENEWAL, TO AMEND CERTAIN PROVISIONS OF THE TAXES CONSOLIDATION ACT, 1997 RELATING TO RELIEFS IN RESPECT OF CAPITAL EXPENDITURE, AND TO PROVIDE FOR RELATED MATTERS. [7TH JULY, 1998]

PART I
PRELIMINARY AND GENERAL

1 Short title

This Act may be cited as the Urban Renewal Act, 1998.

2 Commencement

(1) This Act (other than the provisions referred to in subsections (2) to (5)) shall come into operation on such day or days as the Minister may appoint by order or orders either generally or with reference to any particular purpose or provision and different days may be so fixed for different purposes or different provisions.

(2) This Part and sections 7 and 8 shall be deemed to have come into operation on the first day of May, 1997.

(3) Section 13 shall be deemed to have come into operation on the first day of February, 1998.

(4) Sections 18 and 20(2) shall be deemed to have come into operation on the twenty-eighth day of May, 1998.

[(5) Subsection (1) of section 20 shall come into operation on such day or days as the Minister for Finance may appoint by order or orders and different days may be so appointed for different provisions of that subsection or for different purposes and, in particular, different days may be so appointed for the coming into operation of that subsection as respects different provisions of the definition of "specified period" inserted in section 322 of the Taxes Consolidation Act, 1997.][1]

Amendments

1 Subs (5) substituted by FA 1999 s 42 with effect from 6 April 1999.

3 Interpretation

(1) In this Act, except where the context otherwise requires—

"the Act of 1946" means the Local Government Act, 1946;

"the Act of 1997" means the Dublin Docklands Development Authority Act, 1997;

"authorised company" shall be construed in accordance with section 5(2);

"the Authority" means the Dublin Docklands Development Authority established under section 14 of the Act of 1997;

"company" means a company within the meaning of section 2 of the Companies Act, 1963;

"Dublin Docklands Area" has the meaning assigned to it by section 4 of the Act of 1997;

"elective body" means an elective body for the purposes of the County Management Acts, 1940 to 1994;

"functions" includes powers and duties and a reference to the performance of functions includes, with respect to powers and duties, a reference to the exercise of the powers and the carrying out of the duties;

"integrated area plan" has the meaning assigned to it by section 7,

"local authority" means—

(*a*) the corporation of a county borough, or

(*b*) the council of an administrative county,

and the functional area of a local authority for the purposes of this Act is the county borough or, as the case may be, the administrative county of that authority;

"the Minister" means the Minister for the Environment and Local Government;

"rating authority" means a rating authority for the purposes of the Act of 1946;

"reserved function" means—

(a) in the case of the council of a county or an elective body, a reserved function for the purposes of the County Management Acts, 1940 to 1994,

(*b*) in the case of the corporation of a county borough, reserved function for the purposes of the Acts relating to the management of the county borough.

(2) In this Act—

(*a*) a reference to a section is a reference to a section of this Act, unless it is indicated that a reference to some other enactment is intended;

(*b*) a reference to a subsection or paragraph is a reference to a subsection or paragraph of the provision in which the reference occurs, unless it is indicated that a reference to some other provision is intended;

(*c*) a reference to any enactment shall, unless the context otherwise requires, be construed as a reference to that enactment as amended or adapted by or under any subsequent enactment.

Cross-references

Relief for lessors and owner-occupiers in respect of expenditure incurred on the provision of certain residential accommodation, interpretation, meaning of "authorised company" applied: s 372AK ("relevant local authority").

Qualifying urban areas, interpretation and application, meaning of "authorised comapny" applied: s 372A(1)("relevant local authority").

4 Reference to Act in section 372A(2) of Taxes Consolidation Act, 1997

Notwithstanding any discrepancy between the terms in which it is therein so described and the terms of this Act as it is now so enacted, this Act shall be the Act of the Oireachtas referred to in section 372A(2) (inserted by the Finance Act, 1998) of the Taxes Consolidation Act, 1997.

5 Authorised companies

(1) Each local authority may appoint a company (including a company established by a local authority) to be an authorised company for the purposes of this Act.

(2) A reference in this Act to an authorised company shall be construed as a reference to the company appointed under subsection (1) by the particular local authority to which any provision of this Act in which that reference occurs falls to be applied.

(3) A reference in Chapter 7 (inserted by the Finance Act, 1998) of Part 10 of the Taxes Consolidation Act, 1997, to a company established by a local authority shall be construed as including a reference to an authorised company.

(4) A local authority may revoke any appointment made by it under subsection (1).

PART II
INTEGRATED AREA PLANS AND QUALIFYING AREAS

7 Integrated area plans

(1) A local authority or, at the request of that local authority, an authorised company, may prepare and submit to the Minister one or more plans (which or each of which shall be known, and is in this Act referred to, as an "integrated area plan") in respect of an area or areas within the functional area of the local authority and, if the authority or company thinks fit and subject to that subsection, an area referred to in subsection (2).

(2) The area in respect of which an integrated area plan may be prepared may include a part or parts of the functional area or areas of one or more other local authorities if that authority or those authorities consent to that part or those parts being so included.

(3) In preparing an integrated area plan, a local authority or an authorised company, as the case may be, shall have regard to any criteria which the Minister specifies in writing to be criteria to which a local authority or company shall have regard to in preparing such a plan and those criteria may include criteria with respect to the social and economic renewal of the area to which the plan relates.

(4) An integrated area plan shall consist of a written statement and a plan indicating the objectives for—

(*a*) the social and economic renewal, on a sustainable basis, of the area to which the plan relates, and

(*b*) improvements in the physical environment of that area.

(5) Without prejudice to the generality of subsection (4), an integrated area plan shall specify the physical, economic, social and other issues which, in the opinion of the local authority or company, are relevant to the renewal of the area to which it relates.

(6) Without prejudice to the generality of subsection (4), an integrated area plan may, where appropriate, in relation to the area to which it relates—

(*a*) include—

(i) objectives for the renewal, preservation, conservation, restoration, development or redevelopment of the streetscape, layout and building pattern, including the co-ordination and upgrading of shop frontages,

(ii) guidelines with respect to the heights of buildings and to building materials, density of developments and the treatment of spaces between buildings,

(iii) objectives relating to the preservation of the natural, architectural and archaeological heritage,

(iv) objectives for promoting the development or redevelopment of derelict sites or vacant sites,

(v) objectives for employment, training and education, particularly for persons resident in the area,

(vi) objectives for the improvement of existing residential communities and the development of new such communities, including the development of housing for people of different social backgrounds,

(vii) objectives for the development of community facilities,

(viii) objectives for the improvement of the environment, infrastructure and transportation,

and

(*b*) indicate the nature and extent of the investment required to achieve the objectives specified in the plan.

(7) In preparing an integrated area plan the local authority or authorised company concerned may consult with such other persons as appear to it to be concerned with or interested in the matter and shall have regard to any submissions or observations made to it by such persons in the course of that consultation.

8 Recommendations in respect of qualifying areas for the purposes of urban renewal tax reliefs

(1) An integrated area plan submitted to the Minister under section 7 may contain, or be accompanied by, recommendations by the local authority or authorised company concerned that—

(*a*) a part or parts of the area to which the plan relates ought to be a qualifying area for the purposes of one or more sections of [Chapter 7 or 11][1] of Part 10 of the Taxes Consolidation Act, 1997,

[(*b*) the whole of such an area ought to be a qualifying area for the purposes of one or more of the following provisions of the said Chapter 11—

(i) section 372AP, in so far as it relates to conversion expenditure (within the meaning of that Chapter) incurred in relation to a house,

(ii) section 372AP, in so far as it relates to refurbishment expenditure (within the meaning of that Chapter) incurred in relation to a house, and

(iii) section 372AR.][2]

(2) In making any recommendation referred to in subsection (1), the local authority or authorised company concerned shall have regard to the following matters—

(*a*) the consistency between the types of development that are likely to be carried out in the area or areas to which the recommendations relate ("the relevant types of development") and the relevant objectives of the integrated area plan,

(*b*) the significance of the recommendations for the attainment of the objectives of the integrated area plan generally,

(*c*) the market conditions in the area or areas concerned as respects the supply of, and current and anticipated demand for, the relevant types of development, and

(*d*) the nature and extent of any impediments to the carrying out of the relevant types of development.

Amendments

1 Substituted by FA 2002 s 24(2) and Sch 2 Pt 2 para 3(*a*) with effect from 1 January 2002; previously "Chapter 7".

2 Subs (1)(*b*) substituted by FA 2002 s 24(2) and Sch 2 Pt 2 para 3(*b*) with effect from 1 January 2002.

9 Qualifying areas for urban renewal tax reliefs

Having considered an integrated area plan submitted to him or her under section 7 and any recommendations referred to in section 8 which are contained in or have accompanied the plan, the Minister may recommend to the Minister for Finance that he or she make, with respect to the matters concerned, an order under [paragraph *(a)*, (*b*), (*ba*) or (*c*)][1] of section 372B(1) of the Taxes Consolidation Act, 1997.

Amendments

1 Substituted by FA 2002 s 24(2) and Sch 2 Pt 2 para 3(*c*) with effect from 1 January 2002; previously "paragraph *(a)*, (*b*) or (*c*)".

9A Designation of certain areas for rented residential reliefs

[Where, under section 9, the Minister has recommended to the Minister for Finance that he or she make an order under section 372B(1) of the Taxes Consolidation Act, 1997 that a part or parts (in this section referred to as the "specified part or parts"), or the whole, of an area to which an integrated area plan relates ought to be a qualifying area for the purposes of section 372AR of that Act, the Minister may further recommend to the Minister for Finance that he or she make an order under the said section 372B(1) that the specified part or parts or any other part or parts of the area concerned ought to be a qualifying area for the purposes of section 372AP of the Taxes Consolidation Act, 1997 in so far as that section relates to one or more of the following:

(*a*) expenditure on the construction of a house,

(*b*) conversion expenditure in relation to a house, and

(*c*) refurbishment expenditure in relation to a house,

notwithstanding that the integrated area plan does not contain or is not accompanied by a recommendation that the specified part or parts, or the other part or parts, of the area to which the plan relates ought to be a qualifying area for the purposes of the said section 372AP in so far as that section relates to one or more of the matters referred to in paragraphs (*a*), (*b*) and (*c*) of this section.][1]

Amendments

1 Section 9A inserted by FA 2002 s 25(1)(*a*) as respects expenditure incurred on or in relation to a house, where such expenditure is incurred on or after 5 December 2001, or where TCA 1997 372AP(9) or (10) applies, prior to 5 December 2001, but only if a contract for the purchase of the house had not been evidenced in writing by any person prior to that date, but a contract for the purchase of the house is evidenced in writing on or before 1 September 2002.

11 Certain reliefs conditional on buildings etc, being consistent with integrated area plan

(1) No relief from income tax or corporation tax, as the case may be, may be granted under [Chapter 7 or 11][1] of Part 10 of the Taxes Consolidation Act, 1997, in respect of the construction, refurbishment or conversion of a building, structure or house unless the local authority or authorised company which prepared the integrated area plan concerned has certified in writing, in a manner specified by the Minister, that such construction, refurbishment or conversion is consistent with the objectives of that plan, being the particular plan concerned that was taken into consideration by the Minister in the making by him or her to the Minister for Finance of the recommendations referred to in section 9.

[(1A) For the purposes of subsection (1), where the Minister has, under section 9A, recommended to the Minister for Finance that he or she make an order under section 372B(1) of the Taxes Consolidation Act, 1997 that a part of an area to which an integrated area plan relates ought to be a qualifying area for the purposes of section 372AP of that Act, then expenditure referred to in paragraph *(a)*, (*b*) or (*c*), as the case may be, of section 9A which is incurred in relation to a house, the site of which is wholly within that part, may be treated as consistent with the objectives of that plan, notwithstanding that the plan did not contain or was not accompanied by a recommendation that such part ought to be a qualifying area for the purposes of the said section 372AP in so far as that section relates to one or more of the matters referred to in paragraphs *(a)*, (*b*) and (*c*) of section 9A.][2]

(2) In this section **"integrated area plan concerned"** means the integrated area plan, within the boundary of the area to which that plan relates the relevant building, structure or house is situate.

Amendments

1 Substituted by FA 2002 s 24(2) and Sch 2 Pt 2 para 3(*a*) with effect from 1 January 2002; previously "Chapter 7".

2 Subs (1A) inserted by FA 2002 s 25(1)(*b*) as as respects expenditure incurred on or in relation to a house, where such expenditure is incurred on or after 5 December 2001, or where TCA 1997 372AP(9) or (10) applies, prior to 5 December 2001, but only if a contract for the purchase of the house had not been evidenced in writing by any person prior to that date, but a contract for the purchase of the house is evidenced in writing on or before 1 September 2002.

12 Monitoring of inplementation of integrated area plan

(1) Where the Minister for Finance makes an order under section 372B of the Taxes Consolidation Act, 1997, directing that an area or areas shall be a qualifying area for the purposes of one or more sections of [Chapter 7 or 11][1] of Part 10 of that Act, the local authority or authorised company concerned shall make such arrangements as it

considers appropriate in the particular circumstances for monitoring the implementation of the integrated area plan concerned and, in doing so, the authority or company shall have regard to such guidelines as may, from time to time, be issued by the Minister for the purposes of this section.

(2) A local authority or authorised company, as the case may be, shall, in relation to each year in which it causes the monitoring referred to in subsection (1) to be carried out, make, as soon as may be after the end of that year, a report in writing to the Minister of the results of that monitoring.

(3) In this section—

"integrated area plan concerned" means the integrated area plan, within the boundary of the area to which that plan relates the area or areas referred to in subsection (1) are situate;

"local authority or authorised company concerned" means the local authority or authorised company that prepared the integrated area plan concerned.

Amendments

1 Substituted by FA 2002 s 24(2) and Sch 2 Pt 2 para 3(*a*) with effect from 1 January 2002; previously "Chapter 7".

PART III
PROVISIONS RELATING TO DUBLIN DOCKLANDS DEVELOPMENT AUTHORITY

13 Recommendations by Dublin Docklands Development Authority

(1) Having regard to the objectives indicated in the master plan prepared by the Authority under section 24 of the Act of 1997, the Executive Board (within the meaning of section 17 of the Act of 1997) of the Authority may recommend to the Minister for Finance that he or she make, with respect to the matters concerned, an order under paragraph (*a*) or *(b)* of section 367(1) of the Taxes Consolidation Act, 1997.

(2) In making any recommendation under subsection (1), the said Board shall have regard to the criteria set out in subsection (2) of section 367 of the Taxes Consolidation Act, 1997.

14 Certain reliefs conditional on buildings etc, being consistent with master plans

No relief from income tax or corporation tax, as the case may be, may be granted under Chapter 6 of Part 10 of the Taxes Consolidation Act, 1997 in respect of the construction, refurbishment or conversion of a building, structure or house unless the Authority has certified in writing, in a manner specified by the Minister, that such construction, refurbishment or conversion is consistent with the objectives indicated in the master plan prepared by the Authority under section 24 of the Act of 1997.

PART IV
MISCELLANEOUS

18 Amendment of sections 370 and 372E of Taxes Consolidation Act, 1997

Notes

Para (*a*) substituted TCA 1997 s 370(1) definition of "qualifying premises".
Para (*b*) substituted TCA 1997 s 372E definition of "qualifying premises".

19 Amendment of Chapters 7 and 8 of Part 10 of Taxes Consolidation Act, 1997

Notes

Para (*a*) substituted TCA 1997 s 372B(1)(*b*).
Para (*b*)(i) substituted "subsections (3) to (6A)" for "subsections (3) to (6)" in TCA 1997 s 372D .
Para (*b*)(ii) inserted "but subject to section 372B(1)(*b*)" in TCA 1997 s 372D(6)(*a*).
Para (*b*)(iii) inserted TCA 1997 s 372D(6A).
Para (*c*)(i) substituted "subsections (3) to (6B)" for "subsections (3) to (6)" in TCA 1997 s 372N(2)(*a*).
Para (*c*)(ii) inserted TCA 1997 s 372N(6A)–(6B).
Para (*d*)(i) substituted "qualifying trade or profession (being a trade or profession specified by regulations made by the Minister for Finance to be a qualifying trade or profession for the purposes of this section)" for "trade or profession" in TCA 1997 s 372O(3).
Para (*d*)(ii) inserted TCA 1997 372O(6).

20 Amendment of provisions relating to Customs House Docks Area

Notes

Subs (1)(*a*)(i) substituted TCA 1997 s 322(1) definition of "specified period".
Subs (1)(*a*)(ii) substituted TCA 1997 s 322(2)(*b*).
Subs (1)(*b*) deleted TCA 1997 s 323(3)(*b*).
Subs (1)(*c*) substituted in TCA 1997 s 409A(5)(*b*) clauses (I)–(II) for the words "the 1st day of May, 1998," to the end of that subsection. [Note that subs (1)(*c*) was repealed by FA 2000 s 38 with effect from 6 April 2000. The amendment which was to be effected to s 409A(5)(*b*) by subs (1)(*c*) was to come into effect by Ministerial Order — no such order was ever made and subs (1)(*c*), being therefore superfluous, was repealed.]
Subs (2) repealed FA 1998 s 25.

FINANCE ACT 1999

(No 2 of 1999)

ARRANGEMENT OF SECTIONS

PART 1

Income Tax, Corporation Tax and Capital Gains Tax

CHAPTER 1
Interpretation

CHAPTER 5
Savings-Related Share Option Schemes and Employee Share Schemes

CHAPTER 6

Income Tax and Corporation Tax: Tax Reliefs for the Provision of Park and Ride Facilities and for Certain Related Developments

CHAPTER 7

Corporation Tax

CHAPTER 8

Capital Gains Tax

An Act to charge and impose certain duties of customs and inland revenue (including excise), to amend the law relating to customs and inland revenue (including excise) and to make further provisions in connection with finance. [25th March 1999]

BE IT ENACTED BY THE OIREACHTAS AS FOLLOWS:

PART 1

Income Tax, Corporation Tax and Capital Gains Tax

CHAPTER 1

Interpretation

1 Interpretation (Part 1)

In this Part, **"the Principal Act"** means the Taxes Consolidation Act, 1997.

CHAPTER 2

Income Tax

2 Amendment of provisions relating to exemption from income tax

Notes

Para (*a*) substituted TCA 1997 s 187(1)(*a*) for 1999–2000 and later tax years.

Para (*b*) substituted TCA 1997 s 188(2) for 1999–2000 and later tax years.

3 Alteration of rates of income tax

Notes

Section 3 substituted TCA 1997 s 15 (Table) for 1999–2000 and later tax years.

4 Personal reliefs

Notes

Para (*a*) substituted TCA 1997 s 461 and inserted TCA 1997 s 461A for 1999–2000 and later tax years.

Para (*b*)(i) substituted "section 461A" for "section 461" in TCA 1997 s 458 (Table Pt 1) for 1999–2000 and later tax years.

Para (*b*)(ii) inserted "section 461(2)" in TCA 1997 s 458 (Table Pt 2) for 1999–2000 and later tax years.

5 Reliefs for widowed parents and other single parents

Notes

Para (*a*) substituted TCA 1997 s 462 and inserted TCA 1997 s 462A for 1999–2000 and later tax years.

Para (*b*)(i) substituted "section 462A" for "section 462" in TCA 1997 s 458 (Table Pt 1) for 1999–2000 and later tax years.

Para (*b*)(ii) inserted "section 462" in TCA 1997 s 458 (Table Pt 2) for 1999–2000 and later tax years.

6 Amendment of Chapter 1 of Part 15 of the Principal Act

Notes

Para (*a*) substituted "18 years" for "16 years" in TCA 1997 s 465(1)(*a*)(*b*) and TCA 1997 s 465(2)(*a*) with effect from 6 April 1999.

Para (*b*) substituted "18 years" for "16 years" in TCA 1997 s 469(1) definition of "dependant" in each case where it occurs with effect from 6 April 1999.

7 Employee allowance

Notes

Para (*a*)(i) deleted "section 472" from TCA 1997 s 458 (Table Pt 1) for 1999–2000 and later tax years.

Para (*a*)(ii) inserted "section 472" in TCA 1997 s 458 (Table Pt 2) for 1999–2000 and later tax years.

Para (*b*)(i)(I) inserted TCA 1997 s 472(1)(*a*) definition of "appropriate percentage" for 1999–2000 and later tax years.

Para (*b*)(i)(II) inserted TCA 1997 s 472(1)(*a*) definition of "the specified amount" for 1999–2000 and later tax years.

Para (*b*)(ii) substituted TCA 1997 s 472(4) for 1999–2000 and later tax years.

Para (*b*)(iii) substituted TCA 1997 s 472(5) for 1999–2000 and later tax years.

8 Amendment of section 468 (relief for blind persons) of Principal Act

Notes

Section 8 substituted "£1,500" for "£1,000" and "£3,000" for "£2,000" in TCA 1997 s 468(2) for 1999–2000 and later tax years.

9 Employed person taking care of incapacitated individual

Notes

Section 9 substituted TCA 1997 s 467 for 1999–2000 and later tax years.

10 Amendment of section 122 (preferential loan arrangements) of Principal Act

Notes

Para (*a*) substituted "6 per cent" for "7 per cent" in TCA 1997 s 122(1)(*a*) definition of "the specified rate" for 1999–2000 and later tax years.

Para (*b*) substituted "10 per cent" for "11 per cent" in TCA 1997 s 122(1)(*a*) definition of "the specified rate" for 1999–2000 and later tax years.

11 Amendment of section 126 (tax treatment of certain benefits payable under Social Welfare Acts) of Principal Act

Notes

Section 11 substituted TCA 1997 s 126(8)(*b*) with effect from 6 April 1999.

12 Treatment of income arising as a result of certain public subscriptions raised on behalf of incapacitated individuals

Notes

Para (*a*) inserted TCA 1997 s 189A with effect from 6 April 1999.

Para (*b*)(i) inserted "section 189A(2) or" after "by virtue of" in TCA 1997 s 267(2)(*a*) in respect of relevant interest paid on or after 6 April 1999.

Para (*b*)(ii) inserted "or would, but for the provisions of section 189(2), section 189A(3) or section 192(2), have included relevant interest," after "any relevant interest", where those words first occur, in TCA 1997 s 267(3) in respect of relevant interest paid on or after 6 April 1999.

13 Amendment of Chapter 1 (income tax) of Part 7 of Principal Act

Notes

Para (*a*) substituted "(by virtue of section 59 or section 745)" for "(by virtue of section 59)" in TCA 1997 s 189(2) with effect from 6 April 1999.

Para (*b*) substituted of "(by virtue of section 59 or section 745)" for "(by virtue of section 59)" in TCA 1997 s 192(2)(*b*) with effect from 6 April 1999.

14 Amendment of section 201 (exemptions and reliefs in respect of tax under section 123) of Principal Act

...

(2) Subsection (1) shall apply and have effect as respects payments made on or after the 1st day of December 1998.

Notes

Subs (1) substituted "£8,000" for "£6,000" and of "£600" for "£500" in TCA 1997s 201(1)(*a*) definition of "basic exemption".

15 Seafarer allowance, etc

Notes

Section 15 substituted TCA 1997 s 472B(2)(*b*) with effect from 6 April 1999.

16 Amendment of Part 16 (income tax relief for investment in corporate trades — business expansion scheme and seed capital scheme) of Principal Act

Notes

Para (*a*) substituted TCA 1997 s 488(1) definition of "unquoted company" para (*b*) with effect from 6 April 1999.

Para (*b*) substituted "5th day of April, 2001" for "5th day of April, 1999" in TCA 1997 s 489(15) with effect from 6 April 1999.

Para (*c*) substituted "the year 2000–01" for "the year 1998–99" in TCA 1997 s 490(3)(*b*), (4)(*b*) with effect from 6 April 1999.

17 Amendment of Schedule 13 (accountable persons for purposes of Chapter 1 of Part 18) to Principal Act

Notes

Para (*a*) deleted TCA 1997 Sch 13 paras 23, 47 and 63 with effect from 6 April 1999.

Para (*b*) inserted TCA 1997 Sch 13 paras 83–95 with effect from 6 April 1999.

18 Amendment of Chapter 2 (payments to subcontractors in certain industries) of Part 18 of Principal Act

...

(2) (*a*) Paragraphs (*a*) and (*b*), other than subparagraph (v) of paragraph (*b*), of subsection (1) shall apply as respects the year 1999–2000 and subsequent years of assessment.

(*b*) Subparagraph (v) of paragraph (*b*) of subsection (1) shall apply as respects applications for relevant payments cards made on or after the 6th day of October, 1999.

Notes

Subs (1)(*a*)(i) inserted TCA 1997 s 530(1) definition of "income tax month".

Subs (1)(*a*)(ii) substituted TCA 1997 s 530(1) definition of "qualifying period".

Para (1)(*a*)(iii) substituted TCA 1997 s 530(1) definition of "relevant contract" para (*c*).

Para (1)(*b*)(i) inserted TCA 1997 s 531(3A).

Para (1)(*b*)(ii) substituted "assessment (including estimated assessment), estimation, charge, collection and recovery of tax deductible under subsection (1)" for "assessment (including estimated assessment), charge, collection and recovery of tax deductible under subsection (1)" in TCA 1997 s 531(6).

Para (1)(*b*)(iii) substituted TCA 1997 s 531(10).

Para (1)(*b*)(iv)(I) deleted "and" in TCA 1997 s 531(11)(*a*)(iv).

Para (1)(*b*)(iv)(II) substituted "qualifying period, and" for "qualifying period." in TCA 1997 s 531(11)(*a*)(v).

Para (1)(*b*)(iv)(III) inserted TCA 1997 s 531(11)(*a*)(vi).

Para (1)(*b*)(v) substituted TCA 1997 s 531(12).

Para (1)(*b*)(vi) inserted TCA 1997 s 531(17A).

Para (1)(*b*)(vii) inserted "or subsection (17A)" in TCA 1997 s 531(18).

19 Retirement benefits

...

(2) (*a*) Paragraph (*a*) of subsection (1) shall apply as respects any retirements benefit scheme (within the meaning of section 771 of the Principal Act) approved on or after the 6th day of April, 1999.

(*b*) Paragraph (*b*), other than subparagraph (vi), of subsection (1) shall apply as respects any annuity contract for the time being approved by the Revenue Commissioners under section 784 of the Principal Act entered into on or after the 6th day of April, 1999.

(*c*) Subparagraph (vi) of paragraph (*b*), and paragraph (*c*), of subsection (1) shall apply as respects the year of assessment 1999–2000 and subsequent years.

(*d*) Notwithstanding any provision of Part 30 of the Principal Act, a retirement benefits scheme or an annuity contract which was approved by the Revenue Commissioners before the 6th day of April, 1999, shall not cease to be an approved scheme or contract, as the case may be, because the rules of the scheme or the terms of the contract are altered on or after that date to enable an individual to whom the scheme or the contract applies to exercise an option under subsection (3A) of section 772 or subsection (2A) of section 784 of the Principal Act, as may be appropriate, which that individual would be in a position to exercise in accordance with the terms of those subsections as regards a scheme or contract approved on or after the 6th day of April, 1999, and as regards such a scheme or contract, the provisions of this section shall apply as if the scheme or contract were one approved on or after that date.

(*e*) Notwithstanding subsection (3A) of section 772 and subsection (2A) of section 784 of the Principal Act, where a pension or annuity first became payable on or after the 2nd day of December, 1998 and before the 6th day of April, 1999, paragraph (*d*) shall apply as if the references in the said subsections to the exercise of an option on or before the date on which a pension or an annuity would otherwise become payable were a reference to the exercise of an option within six months of the date on which the pension or annuity became payable.

Notes

Subs (1)(*a*)(i)(I) inserted TCA 1997 s 770 definitions of "approved retirement fund" and "approved minimum retirement fund".

Subs (1)(*a*)(i)(II) inserted TCA 1997 s 770 definition of "proprietary director".

Subs (1)(*a*)(ii)(I) substituted of "that, subject to subsection (3A)," for "that" in TCA 1997 s 772(3)(*f*).

Subs (1)(*a*)(ii)(II) inserted TCA 1997 s 772(3A)–(3B).

Subs (1)(*a*)(ii)(III) inserted TCA 1997 s 772(4)(*c*).

Subs (1)(*b*)(i) inserted TCA 1997 s 783(1)(*a*) definitions of "approved retirement fund" and "approved minimum retirement fund".

Subs (1)(*b*)(ii)(I) substituted TCA 1997 s 784(1)(*b*).

Subs (1)(*b*)(ii)(II)(A) substituted "Subject to subsections (2A) and (3) and to section 786," for "Subject to subsection (3)," in TCA 1997 s 784(2)(*a*).

Subs (1)(*b*)(ii)(II)(B) substituted "75 years" for "70 years" in TCA 1997 s 784(2)(*a*)(iii)(II).

Subs (1)(*b*)(ii)(III) substituted TCA 1997 s 784(2)(*b*).

Subs (1)(*b*)(ii)(IV) inserted TCA 1997 s 784(2A)–(2B).

Subs (1)(*b*)(ii)(V) deleted TCA 1997 s 784(3)(*d*).

Subs (1)(*b*)(iii) inserted TCA 1997 ss 784A–784E.

Subs (1)(*b*)(iv) substituted "75 years" for "70 years (or any greater age approved under section 784(3)(*d*))" in TCA 1997 s 785(1)(*b*), (2)(*b*).

Subs (1)(*b*)(v) substituted TCA 1997 s 786(1).

Subs (1)(*b*)(vi)(I) inserted TCA 1997 s 787(2A)–(2B).

Subs (1)(*b*)(vi)(II) substituted TCA 1997 s 787(8) and inserted TCA 1997 s 787(8A)–(8C).

Subs (1)(*c*) inserted TCA 1997 Sch 23A.

20 Purchased life annuities

Notes

Subs (1)(*a*) deleted "or" after "section 787," in TCA 1997 s 788(2)(*d*) with effect from 6 April 1999.

Subs (1)(*b*) substituted "capital), or" for "capital)." in TCA 1997 s 788(2)(*e*) with effect from 6 April 1999.

Subs (1)(*c*) inserted TCA 1997 s 788(2)(*f*) with effect from 6 April 1999.

21 Amendment of section 823 (deduction for income earned outside the State) of Principal Act

...

(2) This section shall apply—

(*a*) as respects the year of assessment 1999–2000 and subsequent years of assessment, and

(*b*) as respects the year of assessment 1998–99 to the extent that the income, profits or gains to be included in computing the specified amount accrues to an individual on or after the 10th day of March, 1999.

Notes

Subs (1)(*a*) substituted TCA 1997 s 823(1) definition of "the specified amount".

Subs (1)(*b*) inserted "in relation to that office or employment or the amount of the income, profits or gains whichever is the lesser." after "the specified amount" in TCA 1997 s 823(3).

22 Amendment of section 869 (delivery, service and evidence of notices and forms) of Principal Act

Notes

Section 22 substituted TCA 1997 s 869(3) with effect from 6 April 1999.

23 Amendment of section 961 (issue of demand notes and receipts) of Principal Act

Notes

Section 23 substituted TCA 1997 s 961(2) with effect from 6 April 1999.

24 Amendment of Chapter 4 (collection and recovery of income tax on certain emoluments (PAYE system)) of Part 42 of Principal Act

Notes

Section 24 inserted TCA 1997 s 990A with effect from 6 April 1999.

25 Amendment of section 987 (penalties for breach of regulations) of Principal Act

Notes

Para (*a*) substituted TCA 1997 s 987(1) with effect from 6 April 1999.

Para (*b*) inserted TCA 1997 s 987(1A) with effect from 6 April 1999.

Para (*c*) substituted "subsection (1) or (1A)" for "subsection (1)" in TCA 1997 s 987(2) with effect from 6 April 1999.

26 Relief for fees paid to publicly funded colleges in the European Union for full-time third level education

Notes

Para (*a*) inserted "Section 474A" in TCA 1997 s 458 (Table Pt 2) with effect from 6 April 1999.

Para (*b*) inserted TCA 1997 s 474A with effect from 6 April 1999.

Para (*c*) inserted "474A," after "474," in TCA 1997 s 1024(2)(*a*)(ix) with effect from 6 April 1999.

CHAPTER 3

Dividend Withholding Tax

27 Dividend withholding tax

Notes

Para (*a*) inserted TCA 1997 Ch 8A (ss 172A–172M) with effect from 6 April 1999.

Para (*b*) inserted TCA 1997 s 1078(2)(*dd*) with effect from 6 April 1999.

Para (*c*) inserted TCA 1997 Sch 2A with effect from 6 April 1999.

Para (*d*) inserted "section 172K(1)" and "section 172L(2)" in TCA 1997 Sch 29 col 2 with effect from 6 April 1999.

28 Distributions to certain non-residents

...

(4) This section shall apply as respects distributions made on or after the 6th day of April, 1999.

Notes

Subs (1) substituted TCA 1997 s 153.

Subs (2) substituted "Section 129 and subsections (4) and (5) of section 153" for "Sections 129 and 153(1)" in TCA 1997 s 712(1).

Subs (3) repealed TCA 1997 s 1033.

29 Amendment of section 831 (implementation of Council Directive No 90/435/EEC concerning the common system of taxation applicable in the case of parent companies and subsidiaries of different Member States) of Principal Act

Notes

Para (*a*) substituted TCA 1997 s 831(1)(*a*) definition of "parent company" with effect from 6 April 1999.

Para (*b*)(i) inserted "which is resident in the State" after "a parent company" in TCA 1997 s 831(2) with effect from 6 April 1999.

Para (*b*)(ii) inserted "which is a company not resident in the State" after "subsidiary" in TCA 1997 s 831(2) with effect from 6 April 1999.

Para (*c*) inserted TCA 1997 s 831(5)–(6) with effect from 6 April 1999.

CHAPTER 4

Income Tax, Corporation Tax and Capital Gains Tax

30 Construction of references to oaths, etc

Notes

Section 30 inserted TCA 1997 s 1096A with effect from 6 April 1999.

31 Amendment of section 97 (computational rules and allowable deductions) of Principal Act

...

(2) This section shall be deemed to have come into force and shall take effect as on and from the 20th day of May, 1998.

Notes

Subs (1) substituted "31st day of March, 1999" for "31st day of December, 1998" in TCA 1997 s 97(2B)(*a*) and TCA 1997 s 97(2C)(*b*).

32 Amendment of section 110 (securitisation of assets) of Principal Act

Notes

Section 32 substituted TCA 1997 s 110 with effect from 6 April 1999.

33 Amendment of section 118 (benefits-in-kind: general charging provision) of Principal Act

Notes

Section 33 inserted TCA 1997 s 118(5A) for 1999–2000 and later tax years.

34 Exemption from benefit-in-kind of certain childcare facilities

Notes

Section 34 inserted TCA 1997 s 120A with effect from 6 April 1999.

35 Amendment of section 472A (relief for the long-term unemployed) of Principal Act

Notes

Para (*a*)(i) inserted TCA 1997 s 472A(1)(*a*) definitions of "the Act of 1993" and "continuous period of unemployment" with effect from 6 April 1999.

Para (*a*)(ii) substituted TCA 1997 s 472A(1)(*a*) definition of "qualifying individual" with effect from 6 April 1999.

Para (*b*)(i) substituted "of such period, and" for "of such period." in TCA 1997 s 472A(1)(*b*) with effect from 6 April 1999.

Para (*b*)(ii) inserted TCA 1997 s 472A(1)(*b*)(iii) with effect from 6 April 1999.

Para (*c*) substituted "subsection (1)(*b*)(i)" for "subsection (2)" in TCA 1997 s 472A(5)(*b*) with effect from 6 April 1999.

36 Amendment of section 485 (relief for gifts to third-level institutions) of Principal Act

...

(2) This section shall apply and have effect as on and from the 6th day of April, 1999.

Notes

Subs (1) substituted TCA 1997 s 485(1) definition of "approved institution".

37 Relief for gifts to the Scientific and Technological Education (Investment) Fund

Notes

Section 37 inserted TCA 1997 s 485B with effect from 6 April 1999.

38 Amendment of section 225 (employment grants) of Principal Act

...

(2) This section shall be deemed to have applied as respects a grant made on or after the 6th day of April, 1996.

Notes

Subs (1) substituted TCA 1997 s 225(1)(*a*)–(*b*).

39 Amendment of section 246 (interest payments by companies and to non-residents) of Principal Act

Notes

Para (*a*)(i) inserted TCA 1997 s 246(1) definitions of "a collective investment undertaking" and "collective investor" with effect from 6 April 1999.

Para (*a*)(ii) inserted TCA 1997 s 246(1) definition of "relevant person" with effect from 6 April 1999.

Para (*a*)(iii)(I) substituted "in the course of carrying on relevant trading operations within the meaning of section 445 or 446" for "on or before the 31st day of December, 2005" in TCA 1997 s 246(1) definition of "relevant security" with effect from 6 April 1999.

Para (*a*)(iii)(II) substituted "issued;" for "issued." in TCA 1997 s 246(1) definition of "relevant security" with effect from 6 April 1999.

Para (*a*)(iv) inserted TCA 1997 s 246(1) definition of "relevant territory" with effect from 6 April 1999.

Para (*b*)(i) substituted "section 700," for "section 700, or" in TCA 1997 s 246(3)(*f*) with effect from 6 April 1999.

Para (*b*)(ii) substituted "distribution, or" for "distribution." in TCA 1997 s 246(3)(*g*) with effect from 6 April 1999.

Para (*b*)(iii) inserted TCA 1997 s 246(3)(*h*) with effect from 6 April 1999.

Para (*c*) substituted TCA 1997 s 246(4)(*a*)–(*b*) with effect from 6 April 1999.

40 Returns of interest paid to non-residents

Notes

Section 40 inserted TCA 1997 s 891A with effect from 6 April 1999.

41 Amendment of Schedule 29 (provisions referred to in sections 1052, 1053 and 1054) to Principal Act

Notes

Para (*a*) inserted "section 986 and Regulations under that section" in TCA 1997 Sch 29 col 1 with effect from 6 April 1999.

Para (*b*) inserted "section 891A" in TCA 1997 Sch 29 col 2 with effect from 6 April 1999.

42 Amendment of section 2 (commencement) of Urban Renewal Act, 1998

Notes

Section 42 substituted Urban Renewal Act 1998 s 2(5) with effect from 6 April 1999.

43 Amendment of section 330 (interpretation (Chapter 2)) of Principal Act

Notes

Section 43 substituted TCA 1997 s 330(1) definition of "qualifying period" with effect from 6 April 1999.

44 Amendment of Chapter 3 (designated areas, designated streets, enterprise areas and multi-storey car parks in certain urban areas) of Part 10 of Principal Act

Notes

Para (*a*) inserted TCA 1997 s 339(2)(*d*) with effect from 6 April 1999.

Para (*b*) inserted ", or, as the case may be, after the day to which the reference to the 31st day of July, 1997, is, by virtue of section 339(2), to be construed" after "the 31st day of July, 1997" in TCA 1997 s 340(1)(*b*) with effect from 6 April 1999.

Para (*c*)(i) substituted TCA 1997 s 343(1) definition of "qualifying company" with effect from 6 April 1999.

Para (*c*)(ii) substituted TCA 1997 s 343(2)(*a*) with effect from 6 April 1999.

Para (*c*)(iii) substituted TCA 1997 s 343(8)(*a*)(iv) with effect from 1 January 1998.

Para (*d*)(i)(I) substituted "of this definition, or" for "of this definition;" in TCA 1997 s 344(1) definition of "qualifying period" para (*b*) with effect from 6 April 1999.

Para (*d*)(i)(II) inserted TCA 1997 s 344(1) definition of "qualifying period" para (*c*) with effect from 6 April 1999.

Para (*d*)(ii) substituted "subsections (3) to (6A)" for "subsections (3) to (6)" in TCA 1997 s 344(2)(*a*) with effect from 6 April 1999.

Para (*d*)(iii) inserted TCA 1997 s 344(6A) with effect from 6 April 1999.

Para (*e*)(i) substituted TCA 1997 s 345(1) definition of "qualifying lease" with effect from 6 April 1999.

Para (*e*)(ii) inserted TCA 1997 s 345(1A) with effect from 6 April 1999.

45 Amendment of section 351 (interpretation (Chapter 4)) of Principal Act

Notes

Section 45 substituted TCA 1997 s 351 definition of "qualifying period" with effect from 6 April 1999.

46 Amendment of section 360 (interpretation (Chapter 5)) of Principal Act

Notes

Para (*a*) substituted TCA 1997 s 360 definition of "qualifying period" with effect from 6 April 1999.

Para (*b*) inserted TCA 1997 s 360 definition of "the relevant local authority" with effect from 6 April 1999.

47 Amendment of Chapter 8 (qualifying rural areas) of Part 10 of Principal Act

Notes

Subs (1)(*a*)(i) substituted TCA 1997 s 372L definition of "qualifying period" para (*b*) with effect from 6 April 1999.

Subs (1)(*a*)(ii) substituted "sections 372R and 372RA" for "section 372R" in TCA 1997 s 372L definition of "refurbishment" with effect from 6 April 1999.

Subs (1)(*b*) substituted "paragraph (*a*) or (*b*) of section 268(1)" for "section 268(1)(*a*)" in TCA 1997 s 372M(1) with effect from 6 April 1999.

Subs (1)(*c*)(i) substituted "3 months" for "12 months" in TCA 1997 s 372P(1) definition of "qualifying lease" with effect from 6 April 1999.

Subs (1)(*c*)(ii) substituted "140 square metres" for "125 square metres" in TCA 1997 s 372P(1) definition of "qualifying premises" with effect from 6 April 1999.

Subs (1)(*d*)(i) substituted "3 months" for "12 months" in TCA 1997 s 372Q(1) definition of "qualifying lease" with effect from 6 April 1999.

Subs (1)(*d*)(ii) substituted "150 square metres" for "125 square metres" in TCA 1997 s 372Q(1) definition of "qualifying premises" with effect from 6 April 1999.

Subs (1)(*e*)(i) substituted "3 months" for "12 months" in TCA 1997 s 372R(1) definition of "qualifying lease" with effect from 6 April 1999.

Subs (1)(*e*)(ii) substituted "150 square metres" for "125 square metres" in TCA 1997 s 372R(1) definition of "qualifying premises" with effect from 6 April 1999.

Subs (1)(*f*) inserted TCA 1997 s 372RA.

Subs (1)(*g*)(i)(I) substituted "In sections 372P to 372RA" for "In sections 372P to 372R" in TCA 1997 s 372S(1) with effect from 6 April 1999.

Subs (1)(*g*)(i)(II) substituted "372Q, 372R or 372RA" for "372Q or 372R" in TCA 1997 s 372S(1) definition of "certificate of reasonable cost" with effect from 6 April 1999.

Subs (1)(*g*)(ii) inserted "or, in so far as it applies to expenditure other than expenditure on refurbishment, section 372RA" after "section 372P" in TCA 1997 s 372S(4)(*a*) with effect from 6 April 1999.

Subs (1)(*g*)(iii) inserted "or, in so far as it applies to expenditure on refurbishment, section 372RA" after "section 372Q or 372R" in TCA 1997 s 372S(4)(*b*) with effect from 6 April 1999.

Subs (1)(*g*)(iv) substituted TCA 1997 s 372S(5) with effect from 6 April 1999.

Subs (1)(*g*)(v)(I) substituted "sections 372P to 372RA" for "sections 372P to 372R" in TCA 1997 s 372S(6) with effect from 6 April 1999.

Subs (1)(*g*)(v)(II) substituted "refurbishment of, or, as the case may be, construction or refurbishment of," for "or refurbishment of," in TCA 1997 s 372S(6) with effect from 6 April 1999.

Subs (1)(*g*)(vi)(I) substituted ", 372R(2) or 372RA(2)" for "or 372R(2)" in TCA 1997 s 372S(7)(*a*) with effect from 6 April 1999.

Subs (1)(*g*)(vi)(II) substituted "refurbishment of, or, as the case may be, construction or refurbishment of," for "or refurbishment of," in TCA 1997 s 372S(7)(*a*) with effect from 6 April 1999.

Subs (1)(*g*)(vii) substituted "refurbishment of, or, as the case may be, construction or refurbishment of," for "or refurbishment of," in TCA 1997 s 372S(7)(*b*) with effect from 6 April 1999.

Subs (1)(*g*)(viii) inserted TCA 1997 s 372S(8)(*c*) with effect from 6 April 1999.

Subs (1)(*g*)(ix) substituted ", 372R or 372RA" for "or 372R" in TCA 1997 s 372S(11) with effect from 6 April 1999.

Subs (2)(*a*) inserted "Section 372I" and "Section 372RA" in TCA 1997 s 458 (Table Pt 1) with effect from 6 April 1999.

Subs (2)(*b*) substituted "364, 371, 372I and 372RA" for "364 and 371" in TCA 1997 s 1024(2)(*a*)(i) with effect from 6 April 1999.

48 Capital allowances for private convalescent homes

Notes

Para (*a*)(i)(I) substituted "section 4 of that Act," for "section 4 of that Act, or" in TCA 1997 s 268(1)(*g*) with effect from 6 April 1999.

Para (*a*)(i)(II) substituted "paragraph (*f*) relates, or" for "paragraph (*f*) relates," in TCA 1997 s 268(1)(*h*) with effect from 6 April 1999.

Para (*a*)(i)(III) inserted TCA 1997 s 268(1)(*i*) with effect from 6 April 1999.

Para (*a*)(ii)(I) deleted "and" in TCA 1997 s 268(9)(*d*) with effect from 6 April 1999.

Para (*a*)(ii)(II) substituted TCA 1997 s 268(9)(*e*)(ii) with effect from 6 April 1999.

Para (*a*)(ii)(III) inserted TCA 1997 s 268(9)(*f*) with effect from 6 April 1999.

Para (*b*)(i) substituted TCA 1997 s 272(3)(*f*) with effect from 6 April 1999.

Para (*b*)(ii) substituted TCA 1997 s 272(4)(*f*) with effect from 6 April 1999.

Para (*c*) substituted TCA 1997 s 274(1)(*b*)(ii) with effect from 6 April 1999.

49 Capital allowances for buildings used for certain childcare purposes

Notes

Para (*a*) inserted "or section 843A" after "section 843" in TCA 1997 s 409A(1) definition of "specified building" para (*b*) with effect from 6 April 1999.

Para (*b*) inserted TCA 1997 s 843A with effect from 6 April 1999.

50 Relief for provision of certain student accommodation

Notes

Section 50 inserted TCA 1997 Pt 11A (ss 380A–380F) with effect from 6 April 1999.

51 Amendment of section 843 (capital allowances for buildings used for third level educational purposes) of Principal Act

Notes

Para (*a*) substituted "31st day of December, 2002" for "1st day of July, 2000" in TCA 1997 s 843(7) with effect from 6 April 1999.

Para (*b*) inserted TCA 1997 s 843(8) with effect from 6 April 1999.

52 Amendment of section 403 (restriction on use of capital allowances for certain leased assets) of Principal Act

...

(2) This section shall apply as on and from the 4th day of March, 1998.

Notes

Subs (1)(*a*) substituted "lessee or lessor" for "lessee" in TCA 1997 s 403(9)(*a*)(i)–(ii).

Subs (1)(*b*) substituted TCA 1997 s 403(9)(*b*)(ii).

53 Capital allowances for, and deduction in respect of, vehicles

Notes

Para (*a*)(i) substituted "mechanically propelled vehicle;" for "mechanically propelled vehicle." in TCA 1997 s 373(2)(*j*) with effect from 6 April 1999.

Para (*a*)(ii) inserted TCA 1997 s 373(2)(*k*) with effect from 6 April 1999.

Para (*b*)(i) substituted "£15,000," for "£15,000, and" in TCA 1997 s 376(1) definition of "relevant amount" with effect from 6 April 1999.

Para (*b*)(ii) substituted TCA 1997 s 376(1) definition of "relevant amount" para (*c*) with effect from 6 April 1999.

54 Amendment of section 666 (deduction for increase in stock values) of Principal Act

Notes

Para (*a*) substituted "2001" for "1999" in TCA 1997 s 666(4)(*a*) with effect from 6 April 1999.

Para (*b*) substituted "2000–01" for "1998–99" in TCA 1997 s 666(4)(*b*) with effect from 6 April 1999.

55 Amendment of section 667 (special provisions for qualifying farmers) of Principal Act

Notes

Section 55 substituted TCA 1997 s 667(2)(*b*)(ii) with effect from 6 April 1999.

56 Amendment of Chapter 1 (general) of Part 20 (companies' chargeable gains) of Principal Act

...

(2) This section shall apply—

(*a*) as respects paragraph (*a*) of subsection (1), in so far as relates to section 616(1)(*a*) of the Principal Act, as respects accounting periods ending on or after the 1st day of July, 1998, and

(*b*) in any other case, as on and from the 11th day of February, 1999.

Notes

Subs (1)(*a*)(i) substituted "of this Chapter" for "of this Part" in TCA 1997 s 616(1).

Subs (1)(*a*)(ii) substituted TCA 1997 s 616(1)(*a*)–(*c*).

Subs (1)(*b*)(i) substituted "an effective 75 per cent subsidiary" for "a 75 percent subsidiary" in TCA 1997 s 616(3).

Subs (1)(*b*)(ii) substituted "effective 75 per cent subsidiary" for "75 per cent subsidiary" in TCA 1997 s 616(4).

Subs (1)(*c*) substituted "effective 75 per cent subsidiary" "75 per cent subsidiary" in TCA 1997 s 621(4).

Subs (1)(*d*) inserted TCA 1997 s 623A.

Subs (1)(*e*) inserted TCA 1997 s 625A.

Subs (1)(*f*) inserted TCA 1997 s 626A.

57 Restriction on set-off of pre-entry losses

...

(2) This section shall apply in respect of a company which becomes a member of a group of companies on or after the 1st day of March, 1999.

Notes

Subs (1) inserted TCA 1997 Sch 18A.

58 Amendment of section 746 (offshore income gains accruing to persons resident or domiciled abroad) of Principal Act

...

(2) This section shall apply as on and from the 11th day of February, 1999.

Notes

Subs (1)(*a*) substituted TCA 1997 s 746(1).

Subs (1)(*b*) inserted TCA 1997 s 746(2A).
Subs (1)(*c*) substituted TCA 1997 s 746(3)(*b*)–(*c*).
Subs (1)(*d*) substituted TCA 1997 s 746(4)(*b*).
Subs (1)(*e*) substituted "sections 806, 807 and 807A" for "sections 806 and 807" in TCA 1997 s 746(5)–(6).

59 Amendment of Chapter 1 (purchase and sale of securities) of Part 28 of Principal Act

...

(2) This section shall apply—

(*a*) as respects section 751A inserted in the Principal Act by subsection (1), as on and from the 11th day of February, 1999,

(*b*) as respects section 751B inserted in the Principal Act by subsection (1), to an exchange of old securities for new securities (within the meaning of the said section 751B) in the period beginning on the 11th day of February, 1999 and ending before the 1st day of January 2000.

Notes

Subs (1) inserted TCA 1997 ss 751A–751B.

60 Amendment of Part 33 (anti-avoidance) of Principal Act

...

(2) (*a*) Subparagraphs (i) and (ii) of paragraph (*a*) and paragraphs (*c*), (*d*) and (*e*), of subsection (1) shall apply as on and from the 11th day of February, 1999.

(*b*) Subparagraph (iii) of paragraph (*a*) of subsection (1) shall apply as respects any sum which a third person referred to in that subparagraph receives or becomes entitled to receive on or after the 11th day of February, 1999.

(*c*) Paragraph (*b*) of subsection (1) shall be deemed to have applied as on and from the 12th day of February, 1998.

Notes

Subs (1)(*a*)(i) substituted "In this section and section 807A—" for "In this section—" TCA 1997 s 806(1).
Subs (1)(*a*)(ii) substituted "For the purposes of this section and section 807A—" for "For the purposes of this section—" in TCA 1997 s 806(2).
Subs (1)(*a*)(iii) inserted TCA 1997 s 806(5)(*c*).
Subs (1)(*b*) inserted TCA 1997 s 807(5).
Subs (1)(*c*) inserted TCA 1997 s 807A.
Subs (1)(*d*) substituted "807, 807A and 809" for "section 807 and 809" in TCA 1997 s 808(2) and TCA 1997 s 808(3)(*b*).
Subs (1)(*e*) substituted "sections 806 and 807A" for "section 806" in TCA 1997 ss 809–810.

61 Amendment of section 481 (relief for investment in films) of Principal Act

Notes

Para (*a*)(i) substituted "5th day of April, 2000" for "22nd day of January, 1999" in TCA 1997 s 481(1) definition of "qualifying period" para (*a*) with effect from 6 April 1999.
Para (*a*)(ii) substituted "5th day of April, 2000" for "22nd day of January, 1999" in TCA 1997 s 481(1) definition of "qualifying period" para (*b*) with effect from 6 April 1999.
Para (*b*)(i) substituted "Subject to paragraph (*b*), where in the period—

(I) being a period of 12 months (in paragraph (*b*) referred to as a "12 month period") ending on an anniversary of the 22nd day of January, 1996, or

(II) commencing on the 23rd day of January, 1999, and ending on the 5th day of April, 2000 (in paragraph (*b*) referred to as the "specified period")

the amount or the aggregate amount of the relevant investments made,"

for "Subject to paragraph (*b*), where in any period of 12 months (in paragraph (*b*) referred to as a '12 month period') ending on an anniversary of the 22nd day of January, 1996, the amount or the aggregate amount of the relevant investments made," in TCA 1997 s 481(4)(*a*) with effect from 6 April 1999.

Para (*b*)(ii) inserted ", or in the specified period," in TCA 1997 s 481(4)(*b*)(ii) with effect from 6 April 1999.

Para (*c*) substituted "1999–2000" for "1998–99" in TCA 1997 s 481(8) with effect from 6 April 1999.

Para (*d*) substituted "1999–2000" for "1998–99" in TCA 1997 s 481(9) with effect from 6 April 1999.

62 Amendment of section 723 (special investment policies) of Principal Act

...

(2) (*a*) Paragraphs (*a*) and (*b*) of subsection (1) shall be deemed to have applied as on and from the 1st day of February, 1993.

(*b*) Paragraph (*c*) of subsection (1) shall apply as respects accounting periods beginning or treated as beginning on or after the 6th day of April, 1999.

(*c*) For the purposes of paragraph (*b*), where an accounting period of a company begins before the 6th day of April, 1999, and ends on or after that day, it shall be divided into 2 parts, one beginning on the day on which the accounting period begins and ending on the 5th day of April, 1999, and the other beginning on the 6th day of April, 1999, and ending on the day on which the accounting period ends, and both parts shall be treated as if they were separate accounting periods of the company.

Notes

Subs (1)(*a*) inserted TCA 1997 s 723(1) definition of "relevant period".

Subs (1)(*b*) substituted "on the date on which each relevant period ends" for "at any time on or after the fifth anniversary of the date on which the first payment was received by it in respect of the policy" in TCA 1997 s 723(3)(*c*).

Subs (1)(*c*) substituted TCA 1997 s 723(6).

63 Amendment of section 737 (special investment schemes) of Principal Act

...

(2) (*a*) Paragraphs (*a*) and (*b*) of subsection (1) shall be deemed to have applied as on and from the 1st day of February, 1993.

(*b*) Paragraph (*c*) of subsection (1) shall apply as on and from the 6th day of April, 1999.

Notes

Subs (1)(*a*) inserted TCA 1997 s 737(1)(*a*) definition of "relevant period".

Subs (1)(*b*) substituted "on the date on which each relevant period ends" for "at any time on or after the fifth anniversary of the date on which the first payment was made by or on behalf of that individual in respect of those units" in TCA 1997 s 737(3)(*a*)(iii).

Subs (1)(*c*) substituted TCA 1997 s 737(6)(*c*).

64 Amendment of section 738 (undertakings for collective investment) of Principal Act

...

(2) This section shall apply in respect of chargeable gains accruing in the year of assessment 1998–99 and subsequent years of assessment.

Notes

Subs (1) substituted TCA 1997 s 738(2)(*d*)(i).

65 Amendment of section 838 (special portfolio investment accounts) of Principal Act

...

(2) This section shall—

(*a*) be deemed to have applied, as respects paragraph (*a*) (ii) and paragraph (*b*) of subsection (1), as on and from the 1st day of February, 1993,

(*b*) be deemed to have applied, as respects paragraphs (*a*)(i), and (*d*) of subsection (1), as on and from the 1st day of December, 1998, and

(*c*) apply, as respects paragraph (*c*) of subsection (1), as on and from the 6th day of April, 1999.

Notes

Subs (1)(*a*)(i)(I) inserted "fully paid-up" after "means an investment in" in TCA 1997 s 838(1)(*a*) definition of "relevant investment".

Subs (1)(*a*)(i)(II) inserted "at market value" after "acquired by a designated broker" in TCA 1997 s 838(1)(*a*) definition of "relevant investment".

Subs (1)(*a*)(ii) inserted TCA 1997 s 838(1)(*a*) definition of "relevant period".

Subs (1)(*b*) substituted "on the date on which each relevant period ends" for "at any time on or after the fifth anniversary of the date on which the first specified deposit was made by an individual in respect of that relevant investment" in TCA 1997 s 838(2)(*c*).

Subs (1)(*c*) substituted ", and in particular the rate of appropriate tax specified in section 256(1) in relation to relevant interest payable in respect of a relevant deposit or relevant deposits held in a special savings account shall apply to special portfolio investment accounts" for "; but that Chapter shall so apply as if, in relation to relevant interest payable in respect of a relevant deposit or relevant deposits held in a special savings account, the rate of appropriate tax were 10 per cent" in TCA 1997 s 838(3).

Subs (1)(*d*) substituted "1028(5)" for "1028(4)" in TCA 1997 s 838(4)(*c*).

66 Amendment of section 839 (limits to special investments) of Principal Act

Notes

Section 66 substituted TCA 1997 s 839(3) with effect from 6 April 1999.

67 Amendment of section 832 (provisions in relation to Convention for reciprocal avoidance of double taxation in the State and the United Kingdom of income and capital gains) of Principal Act

...

(2) This section shall—

(*a*) apply as on and from the 6th day of April, 1999, as respects income tax, and

(*b*) be deemed to apply as on and from the 1st day of January, 1999, as respects corporation tax.

Notes

Subs (1)(*a*)(i) substituted "(S.I. No. 319 of 1976)." for "(S.I. No. 319 of 1976);" in TCA 1997 s 832(1) definition of "the Convention".

Subs (1)(*a*)(ii) deleted TCA 1997 s 832(1) definition of "dividend".

Subs (1)(*b*) deleted TCA 1997 s 832(2).

CHAPTER 5

Savings-Related Share Option Schemes and Employee Share Schemes

68 Savings-related share option schemes

Notes

Para (*a*) inserted TCA 1997 Pt 17 Ch 3 (ss 519A–519C) with effect from 6 April 1999.

Para (*b*) inserted TCA 1997 Schs 12A–12B with effect from 6 April 1999.

69 Employee share schemes

...

(2) (*a*) Paragraphs (*a*)(i), (*a*)(ii) and (*c*)(iii) of subsection (1) shall apply as respects an appropriation of shares made by the trustees of an approved scheme (within the meaning of section 510(1) of the Principal Act) on or after the date of the passing of this Act.

(*b*) Paragraphs (*b*) and (*d*) of subsection (1) shall apply as respects employee share ownership trusts approved under paragraph 2 of Schedule 12 to the Principal Act on or after the date of the passing of this Act.

(*c*) Paragraph (*c*)(ii) of subsection (1) shall apply as respects profit sharing schemes approved of under Part 2 of Schedule 11 to the Principal Act on or after the date of the passing of this Act.

Notes

Subs (1)(*a*)(i) inserted TCA 1997 s 510(5A).

Subs (1)(*a*)(ii) inserted TCA 1997 s 511A(3)–(5).

Subs (1)(*a*)(iii) substituted TCA 1997 s 515(1)–(2).

Subs (1)(*b*)(i) insertion of TCA 1997 s 519(7A).

Subs (1)(*b*)(ii) substituted TCA 1997 s 519(9)(*b*)–(*c*).

Subs (1)(*c*)(i) substituted TCA 1997 Sch 11 para 3(4).

Subs (1)(*c*)(ii) substituted "3 years" for "5 years" in TCA 1997 Sch 11 para 4.

Subs (1)(*c*)(iii) inserted TCA 1997 Sch 11 para 12A.

Subs (1)(*d*)(i)(I) inserted TCA 1997 Sch 12 para 11(2B)–(2C).
Subs (1)(*d*)(i)(II) substituted "subparagraphs (2A), (2B) and (3)" for "subparagraphs (2A) and (3)" in TCA 1997 Sch 12 para 11(4)(*a*).
Subs (1)(*d*)(i)(III) substituted "3 years" for "5 years" in TCA 1997 Sch 12 para 11(5)(*a*).
Subs (1)(*d*)(i)(IV) substituted "subparagraphs (2B) and (3)" for "subparagraph (3)" and by the substitution of "subparagraphs (2B)(*c*) and (3)(*b*)" for "subparagraph (3)(*b*)" in TCA 1997 Sch 12 para 11(6).
Subs (1)(*d*)(i)(V) substituted "subparagraph (2A), (2B), (3) or (4)" for "subparagraph (2A), (3) or (4)" in TCA 1997 Sch 12 para 11(7).
Subs (1)(*d*)(i)(VI) substituted "subparagraph (2), (2A), (2B), (3) or (4)" for "subparagraph (2), (2A), (3) or (4)" in TCA 1997 Sch 12 para 11(8) in respect of employee share ownership trusts approved under TCA 1997 Sch 12 para 2.
Subs (1)(*d*)(ii) inserted "or, if the agreement is subject to one or more specified conditions being satisfied, on that condition or those conditions being satisfied" after "when the agreement is made" in TCA 1997 Sch 12 para 18.

CHAPTER 6

Income Tax and Corporation Tax: Tax Reliefs for the Provision of Park and Ride Facilities and for Certain Related Developments

70 Amendment of Part 10 (income tax and corporation tax: reliefs for renewal and improvement of certain urban areas, certain resort areas and certain islands) of Principal Act

Notes

Subs (1) inserted TCA 1997 Pt 10 Ch 9 (ss 372U–372Z) with effect from 6 April 1999.
Subs (2)(*a*) inserted "Section 372Y" in TCA 1997 s 458 (Table Pt 1) with effect from 6 April 1999.
Subs (2)(*b*) substituted "372I, 372RA and 372Y' for "372I and 372RA" in TCA 1997 s 1024(2)(*a*)(i) with effect from 6 April 1999.

CHAPTER 7

Corporation Tax

71 Rate of corporation tax

....

(2) Schedule 1 shall have effect for the purposes of supplementing this section.

Notes

Subs (1) substituted TCA 1997 s 21(1) with effect from 6 April 1999.

72 Amendment of section 22 (reduced rate of corporation tax for certain income) of Principal Act

Notes

Subs (1)(*a*)(i) substituted TCA 1997 s 22(1)(*a*)(I)–(III) with effect from 6 April 1999.
Subs (1)(*a*)(ii) deleted TCA 1997 s 22(1)(*b*) with effect from 6 April 1999.
Subs (1)(*b*) substituted TCA 1997 s 22(2) with effect from 6 April 1999.
Subs (1)(*c*) inserted TCA 1997 s 22(7A) with effect from 6 April 1999.
Subs (2) repealed TCA 1997 s 22 with effect from 1 January 2000.

73 Higher rate of corporation tax

Notes

Section 73 inserted TCA 1997 s 21A with effect from 6 April 1999.

74 Provisions relating to 10 per cent rate of corporation tax

Notes

Para (*a*)(i)(I) inserted TCA 1997 s 442(1) definitions of "expansion operations" and "industrial development agency" with effect from 6 April 1999.

Para (*a*)(i)(II) substituted TCA 1997 s 442(1) definitions of "relevant accounting period" and "relief under this Part" with effect from 6 April 1999.

Para (*a*)(i)(III) inserted TCA 1997 s 442(1) definition of "specified trade" with effect from 6 April 1999.

Para (*a*)(ii) inserted TCA 1997 s 442(3)–(4) with effect from 6 April 1999.

Para (*b*) substituted "until—

(*a*) in the case of those operations which, on or before the 31st day of May, 1998, were approved by the Minister for carry on in the airport, the 31st day of December, 2005, and

(*b*) in the case of those operations which are so approved after the 31st day of May, 1998, the 31st day of December, 2002"

for "until the 31st day of December, 2005" in TCA 1997 s 445(2) with effect from 6 April 1999.

Para (1)(*c*) substituted "until—

(*a*) in the case of those operations which, on or before the 31st day of July, 1998, were approved by the Minister for carry on in the Area, the 31st day of December, 2005, and

(*b*) in the case of those operations which are so approved after the 31st day of July, 1998, the 31st day of December, 2002"

for "until the 31st day of December, 2005" in TCA 1997 s 446(2) with effect from 6 April 1999.

Para (*d*)(i) substituted TCA 1997 s 454(1)(*b*) with effect from 6 April 1999.

Para (*d*)(ii) substituted "a relevant accounting period" for "an accounting period ending on or before the 31st day of December, 2010," in TCA 1997 s 454(2) with effect from 6 April 1999.

Para (*e*)(i) substituted "a relevant accounting period" for "an accounting period" and "the relevant accounting period" for "the accounting period" in TCA 1997 s 455(2) with effect from 6 April 1999.

Para (*e*)(ii) substituted "a relevant accounting period" for "an accounting period" and "that relevant accounting period" for "that accounting period" in TCA 1997 s 455(3) with effect from 6 April 1999.

Para (*f*) substituted "any relevant accounting period" for "any accounting period ending on or before the 31st day of December, 2010," in TCA 1997 s 456(2)(*a*) with effect from 6 April 1999.

75 Amendment of section 88 (deduction for gifts to Enterprise Trust Ltd.) of Principal Act

Notes

Para (*a*) substituted TCA 1997 s 88(1) with effect from 6 April 1999.

Para (*b*) substituted "31st day of December, 2002" for "31st day of December, 1999" in TCA 1997 s 88(2)(*a*) with effect from 6 April 1999.

Para (*c*) substituted TCA 1997 s 88(3)(*b*)(ii) with effect from 6 April 1999.

Para (*d*) substituted "the amount specified in subparagraph (i)" for "the amounts specified in subparagraphs (i) and (ii)" in TCA 1997 s 88(6) with effect from 6 April 1999.

76 Income of Investor Compensation Company Ltd

...

(2) Paragraph (*b*) of subsection (1) shall be deemed to have come into operation on the 10th day of September, 1998.

Notes

Subs (1)(*a*) inserted TCA 1997 s 219B with effect from 6 April 1999.

Subs (1)(*b*) substituted TCA 1997 s 256(1) definition of "relevant deposit" para (*a*)(iv)–(v).

77 Withdrawal of exemption from corporation tax for Bord Gáis Éireann

Notes

Section 77 deleted TCA 1997 s 220 (Table para 1) for accounting periods beginning on or after 25 March 1999.

78 Amendment of Chapter 5 (group relief) of Part 12 of Principal Act

...

(2) This section shall apply as respects accounting periods ending on or after the 1st day of July, 1998.

Notes

Subs (1)(*a*)(i) inserted TCA 1997 s 410(1)(*a*) definition of "tax".

Subs (1)(*a*)(ii) substituted TCA 1997 s 410(1)(*b*).

Subs (1)(*a*)(iii) substituted "in a Member State of the European Communities" for "in the State" in TCA 1997 s 410(3)(*a*).

Subs (1)(*a*)(iv) substituted "resident in a Member State of the European Communities" for "so resident" in TCA 1997 s 410(4)(*a*)(i).

Subs (1)(*b*)(i) inserted TCA 1997 s 411(1)(*a*) definition of "tax".

Subs (1)(*b*)(ii)(I) substituted "a company which, by virtue of the law of a Member State of the European Communities, is resident for the purposes of tax in such a Member State" for "companies resident in the State" in TCA 1997 s 411(1)(*c*).

Subs (1)(*b*)(ii)(II) substituted "company, not being a company which, by virtue of the law of a Member State of the European Communities, is resident for the purposes of tax in such a Member State" for "company not resident in the State" in TCA 1997 s 411(1)(*c*).

Subs (1)(*c*) inserted "in respect of which the company is within the charge to corporation tax" after "trade" in TCA 1997 s 420(1).

79 Amendment of section 130 (matters to be treated as distributions) of Principal Act

...

(2) This section shall apply as respects accounting periods ending on or after the 1st day of July, 1998.

Notes

Subs (1)(*a*)(i) substituted ", being a company which, by virtue of the law of a Member State of the European Communities, is resident for the purposes of tax in such a Member State" for "also so resident" in TCA 1997 s 130(3)(*b*).

Subs (1)(*a*)(ii) inserted TCA 1997 s 130(3)(*c*).

Subs (1)(*b*) substituted ", not being a company which, by virtue of the law of a Member State of the European Communities, is resident for the purposes of tax in such a Member State" for "not resident in the State" in TCA 1997 s 130(4)(*c*).

80 Amendment of section 486 (corporation tax: relief for gifts to First Step) of Principal Act

Notes

Para (*a*) substituted "on or before the 31st day of December, 2002" for "before the 1st day of January, 2000" in TCA 1997 s 486(2)(*a*) with effect from 6 April 1999.

Subs (*b*)(i) substituted "1999, 2000, 2001 or 2002" for "1996, 1997, 1998 or 1999" in TCA 1997 s 486(4)(*b*)(iii) with effect from 6 April 1999.

Subs (*b*)(ii) substituted "commencing on the 1st day of June, 2002, and ending on the 31st day of December, 2002" for "commencing on the 1st day of June, 1999, and ending on the 31st day of December, 1999" in TCA 1997 s 486(4)(*b*)(iv) with effect from 6 April 1999.

81 Amendment of Schedule 24 (relief from income tax and corporation tax by means of credit in respect of foreign tax) to Principal Act

Notes

Para (*a*) substituted "20 per cent" for "10 per cent" in TCA 1997 Sch 24 para 4(4)(*c*) with effect from 6 April 1999.

Para (*b*)(i) inserted "including" after "shall be construed as" in TCA 1997 Sch 24 para 9A(2) with effect from 6 April 1999.

Para (*b*)(ii) inserted "except, in respect of taxes covered by those arrangements, to the extent that credit may not be given for that tax under those arrangements" after "government of the territory" in TCA 1997 Sch 24 para 9A(5)(*a*) with effect from 6 April 1999.

Para (*c*)(i) substituted "controls" for "owns" in TCA 1997 Sch 24 para 9B(5)(*b*)(i)–(ii) with effect from 6 April 1999.

Para (*c*)(ii) substituted "voting power" for "ordinary share capital" in TCA 1997 Sch 24 para 9B(5)(*b*)(i)–(ii) with effect from 6 April 1999.

82 Company residence

...

(2) This section shall apply—

(*a*) in the case of companies which are incorporated on or after the 11th day of February, 1999, as on and from that day, and

(*b*) in the case of companies which were incorporated before the 11th day of February, 1999, as on and from the 1st day of October, 1999.

Notes

Section 82 inserted TCA 1997 s 23A.

83 Amendment of section 882 (particulars to be supplied by new companies) of Principal Act

...

(2) This section shall apply—

(*a*) in the case of companies which are incorporated on or after the 11th day of February, 1999, as on and from that day, and

(*b*) in the case of companies which were incorporated before the 11th day of February, 1999, as on and from the 1st day of October, 1999.

Notes

Subs (1) substituted TCA 1997 s 882.

84 Amendment of Chapter 2 (other corporation tax penalties) of Part 47 of Principal Act

...

(2) This section shall apply as on and from the 1st day of March, 1999

Notes

Subs (1)(*a*) inserted TCA 1997 s 1071(2A).
Subs (1)(*b*) substituted TCA 1997 s 1073.
Subs (1)(*c*) substituted TCA 1997 s 1076(1).

85 Amendment of sections 198, 710 and 734 of Principal Act

Notes

Para (*a*) substituted TCA 1997 s 198(2)(*a*)–(*b*) with effect from 6 April 1999.
Para (*b*) substituted TCA 1997 s 710(2)(*b*) with effect from 6 April 1999.
Para (*c*) substituted TCA 1997 s 734(1)(*c*)(i)–(ii) with effect from 6 April 1999.

86 Amendment of section 707 (management expenses) of Principal Act

...

(2) This section shall be deemed to have applied as respects income accruing for accounting periods commencing on or after the 1st day of January, 1999.

Notes

Subs (1) substituted TCA 1997 s 707(1)(*b*).

CHAPTER 8

Capital Gains Tax

87 Amendment of section 541A (treatment of debts on a change in currency) of Principal Act

...

(2) This section shall be deemed to have applied as on and from the 31st day of December, 1998.

Notes

Subs (1)(*a*) substituted "Subject to subsection (4) and notwithstanding any other provision of the Capital Gains Tax Acts" for "Notwithstanding any other provision of the Capital Gains Tax Acts" in TCA 1997 s 541A(2).
Subs (1)(*b*) inserted TCA 1997 s 541A(4).

88 Amendment of Chapter 3 (assets held in a fiduciary or representative capacity, inheritances and settlements) of Part 19 of Principal Act

...

(2) This section shall apply as on and from the 11th day of February, 1999.

Notes

Subs (1) inserted TCA 1997 ss 579A–579F.

89 Amendment of Chapter 4 (shares and securities) of Part 19 of Principal Act

...

(2) This section shall apply as respects of chargeable gains accruing to a company on or after the 11th day of February, 1999.

Notes

Subs (1) substituted TCA 1997 s 590.

90 Amendment of Chapter 7 (other reliefs and exemptions) of Part 19 of Principal Act

...

(2) This section shall apply as respects the disposal on or after the 11th day of February, 1999, of an interest created by or arising under a settlement.

Notes

Subs (1)(*a*)(i) substituted "Subject to subsection (5), no chargeable gain" for "No chargeable gain" in TCA 1997 s 613(4)(*a*).

Subs (1)(*a*)(ii) inserted TCA 1997 s 613(5)–(6).

Subs (1)(*b*) inserted TCA 1997 s 613A.

91 Amendment of section 649A (relevant disposals: rate of charge) of Principal Act

...

(2) This section shall apply to a relevant disposal made on or after the 10th day of March, 1999.

Notes

Subs (1)(*a*) substituted TCA 1997 s 649A(2)(*b*)(ii) .

Subs (1)(*b*) inserted TCA 1997 s 649A(2)(*c*).

92 Amendment of Chapter 5 (capital gains tax: returns, information, etc) of Part 38 of Principal Act

...

(2) This section shall apply as on and from the 11th day of February, 1999.

Notes

Subs (1)(*a*)(i) substituted "within sections 579 to 579F and section 590" for "within section 579 or 590" in TCA 1997 s 917.

Subs (1)(*a*)(ii) substituted "under sections 579 to 579F or section 590" for "under section 579 or 590" in TCA 1997 s 917.

Subs (1)(*b*) inserted TCA 1997 ss 917A–917C.

93 Amendment of Schedule 15 (list of bodies for purposes of section 610) to Principal Act

Notes

Section 93 inserted TCA 1997 Sch 15 para 33 with effect from 6 April 1999.

PART 7

MISCELLANEOUS

207 Amendment of Chapter 4 (revenue powers) of Part 18 of Taxes Consolidation Act, 1997

Notes

Para (*a*) substituted TCA 1997 s 900 with effect from 25 March 1999.

Para (*b*) substituted TCA 1997 s 901 with effect from 25 March 1999.

Para (*c*) substituted TCA 1997 s 902 with effect from 25 March 1999.

Para (*d*) inserted TCA 1997 s 902A with effect from 25 March 1999.

Para (*e*) inserted TCA 1997 s 904A with effect from 25 March 1999.

Para (*f*)(i) deleted TCA 1997 s 905(2)(*d*) with effect from 25 March 1999.

Para (*f*)(ii) inserted TCA 1997 s 905(2A) with effect from 25 March 1999.

Para (*g*) inserted TCA 1997 s 906A with effect from 25 March 1999.

Para (*h*) substituted TCA 1997 s 907 with effect from 25 March 1999.

Para (*i*) substituted TCA 1997 s 908 with effect from 25 March 1999.

Para (*j*) inserted TCA 1997 s 908A with effect from 25 March 1999.

Para (*k*)(i) substituted "the date of acquisition," for "the date of acquisition, and" in TCA 1997 s 909(4)(*a*)(iv) with effect from 25 March 1999.

Para (*k*)(ii) substituted "given to that person in respect of its acquisition, and" for "given to that person in respect of its acquisition." in TCA 1997 s 909(4)(*a*)(v) with effect from 25 March 1999.

Para (*k*)(iii) inserted TCA 1997 s 909(4)(*a*)(vi) with effect from 25 March 1999.

208 Power to obtain information from a Minister of the Government or public body

Notes

Section 208 substituted TCA 1997 s 910(1) with effect from 25 March 1999.

209 Electronic filing of tax returns

Notes

Section 209 inserted TCA 1997 Pt 38 Ch 6 (ss 917D–917N) with effect from 25 March 1999, but see TCA s 917E re application of the Chapter to "returns" which requires the Revenue Commissioners to make an order if the Chapter is to apply to a "return".

210 Amendment of section 884 (returns of profits) of Taxes Consolidation Act, 1997

Notes

Section 210 inserted TCA 1997 s 884(2)(*aa*) with effect from 25 March 1999.

211 Amendment of section 1078 (revenue offences) of Taxes Consolidation Act, 1997

Notes

Para (*a*) inserted TCA 1997 s 1078(2)(*hh*) with effect from 25 March 1999.

Para (*b*) substituted "£100,000" for "£10,000" in TCA 1997 s 1078(3)(*b*) with effect from 25 March 1999.

Para (*c*) inserted TCA 1997 s 1078(3A) with effect from 25 March 1999.

212 Amendment of section 1094 (tax clearance in relation to certain licences) of Taxes Consolidation Act, 1997

Notes

Para (*a*)(i) substituted TCA 1997 s 1094(1) definition of "licence" (*h*)–(*i*) with effect from 25 March 1999.

Para (*a*)(ii) inserted TCA 1997 s 1094(1) definition of "market value" with effect from 25 March 1999.

Para (*b*) inserted TCA 1997 s 1094(3A) with effect from 25 March 1999.

216 Care and management of taxes and duties

All taxes and duties imposed by this Act are hereby placed under the care and management of the Revenue Commissioners.

217 Short title, construction and commencement

(1) This Act may be cited as the Finance Act, 1999.

(2) Part 1 (so far as relating to income tax) shall be construed together with the Income Tax Acts and (so far as relating to corporation tax) shall be construed together with the Corporation Tax Acts and (so far as relating to capital gains tax) shall be construed together with the Capital Gains Tax Acts.

...

(8) Part 7 (so far as relating to income tax) shall be construed together with the Income Tax Acts and (so far as relating to corporation tax) shall be construed together with the Corporation Tax Acts and (so far as relating to capital gains tax) shall be construed together with the Capital Gains Tax Acts and (so far as relating to customs) shall be construed together with the Custom Acts and (so far as relating to duties of excise) shall be construed together with the statutes which relate to duties of excise and the management of those duties and (so far as relating to value-added tax) shall be construed together with the Value-Added Tax Acts, 1972 to 1999, and (so far as relating to stamp duty) shall be construed together with the Stamp Act, 1891, and the enactments amending or extending that Act and (so far as relating to residential property tax) shall be construed together with Part VI of the Finance Act, 1983, and the enactments amending or extending that Part and (so far as relating to gift tax or inheritance tax) shall be construed together with the Capital Acquisitions Tax Act, 1976, and the enactments amending or extending that Act.

(9) Part 1 shall, save as is otherwise expressly provided therein, apply as on and from the 6th day of April, 1999.

...

(11) Any reference in this Act to any other enactment shall, except so far as the context otherwise requires, be construed as a reference to that enactment as amended by or under any other enactment including this Act.

(12) In this Act, a reference to a Part, section or Schedule is to a Part or section of, or Schedule to, this Act, unless it is indicated that reference to some other enactment is intended.

(13) In this Act, a reference to a subsection, paragraph, subparagraph, clause or subclause is to the subsection, paragraph, subparagraph, clause or subclause of the provision (including a Schedule) in which the reference occurs, unless it is indicated that reference to some other provision is intended.

SCHEDULE 1

Amendments Consequential on Change in Rate of Corporation Tax

Notes

Para 1(*a*) substituted TCA 1997 s 448(2) with effect from 25 March 1999.
Para 1(*b*) inserted TCA 1997 s 448(5A) with effect from 25 March 1999.
Para 2(*a*)(i)(I) substituted TCA 1997 Sch 32 para 5(2)(i)(I) definition of "S" with effect from 25 March 1999.
Para 2(*a*)(i)(II) substituted TCA 1997 Sch 32 para 5(2)(ii) definition of "S" with effect from 25 March 1999.
Para 2(*a*)(ii) substituted TCA 1997 Sch 32 para 5(3)(*a*) with effect from 25 March 1999.
Para 2(*b*) deleted Sch 32 para 5 with effect from 6 April 1999 with effect from 25 March 1999.
Para 2(*c*)(i) substituted TCA 1997 Sch 32 para 6(2)(ii) definition of "S" with effect from 25 March 1999.
Para 2(*c*)(ii) substituted TCA 1997 Sch 32 para 6(3)(*a*) with effect from 25 March 1999.
Para 2(*d*) deleted TCA 1997 Sch 32 para 6 with effect from 6 April 1999 with effect from 25 March 1999.
Para 2(*e*)(i) substituted TCA 1997 Sch 32 para 16(*a*)–(*c*) with effect from 25 March 1999.
Para 2(*e*)(ii) substituted TCA 1997 Sch 32 para 16(5) with effect from 25 March 1999.
Para 2(*f*)(i)(I) substituted TCA 1997 Sch 32 para 18(4)(*b*) definition of "B" with effect from 25 March 1999.
Para 2(*f*)(i)(II) substituted TCA 1997 Sch 32 para 18(4)(*b*) definition of "D" with effect from 25 March 1999.
Para 2(*f*)(i)(III) inserted TCA 1997 Sch 32 para 18(4)(*bb*) with effect from 25 March 1999.
Para 2(*f*)(i)(IV) substituted "Notwithstanding clauses (*b*) and (*bb*)" for "Notwithstanding clause (*b*)" in TCA 1997 Sch 32 para 18(4)(*c*) with effect from 25 March 1999.
Para 2(*f*)(ii) substituted TCA 1997 Sch 32 para 18(6)(*a*) with effect from 25 March 1999.

FINANCE ACT 2000

(No 3 of 2000)

ARRANGEMENT OF SECTIONS

PART 1

Income Tax, Corporation Tax and Capital Gains Tax

CHAPTER 1
Interpretation

CHAPTER 2
Income Tax

CHAPTER 3
Dividend Withholding Tax

CHAPTER 4
Income Tax, Corporation Tax and Capital Gains Tax

CHAPTER 7

Income Tax and Corporation Tax: Reliefs for Renewal and Improvement of Certain Towns

PART 7

Miscellaneous

SCHEDULE 1

Amendments Consequential on the Introduction of Standard Rated Allowances

SCHEDULE 2

Amendments and Repeals Consequent on Abolition of Tax Credits

An Act to charge and impose certain duties of customs and inland revenue (including excise), to amend the law relating to customs and inland revenue (including excise) and to make further provisions in connection with finance. [23rd March 2000]

PART 1

Income Tax, Corporation Tax and Capital Gains Tax

CHAPTER 1

Interpretation

1 Interpretation (Part 1)

In this Part "Principal Act" means the Taxes Consolidation Act, 1997.

CHAPTER 2

Income Tax

2 Amendment of section 188 (age exemption and associated marginal relief) of Principal Act

Notes

This section substituted TCA 1997 s 188(2) for 2000–2001 and later tax years.

3 Alteration of rates of income tax

Notes

Para (*a*) substituted TCA 1997 s 15(2) and Table for 2000–2001 and later tax years.

Para (*b*)(i) substituted TCA 1997 s 1024(2)(*c*) for 2000–2001 and later tax years.

Para (*b*)(ii) substituted TCA 1997 s 1024(4) for 2000–2001 and later tax years.

4 Amendment of section 461 (standard rated parsonal allowances) of Principal Act

Notes

This section substituted "£9,400" for "£8,400" and "£4,700" for "£4,200" in the definition of "the specified amount" in TCA 1997 s 461(1) for 2000–2001 and later tax years.

5 Additional standard rated allowance for certain widowed persons

Notes

Para (*a*) substituted TCA 1997 s 461A for 2000–2001 and later tax years.

Para (*b*)(i) deleted "Section 461A" from TCA 1997 s 458 (Table Part 1) for 2000–2001 and later tax years.

Para (*b*)(ii) inserted "Section 461A" in TCA 1997 s 458 (Table Part 2) for 2000–2001 and later tax years.

6 Widowed parents and other single parents: standard rated allowance

Notes

Para (*a*) substituted "£4,700" for "£1,050" in TCA 1997 s 462(1) (definition of "the specified amount") for 2000–2001 and later tax years.

Para (*b*) deleted TCA 1997 s 462A for 2000–2001 and later tax years.

Para (*c*) deleted "Section 462A" from TCA 1997 s 458 (Table Part 1) for 2000–2001 and later tax years.

7 Special relief for widowed parent following death of spouse

Notes

Para (*a*) substituted TCA 1997 s 463 for 2000–2001 and later tax years.

Para (*b*)(i) deleted "Section 463" from TCA 1997 s 458 (Table Part 1) for 2000–2001 and later tax years.

Para (*b*)(ii) inserted "Section 463" in TCA 1997 s 458 (Table Part 2) for 2000–2001 and later tax years.

8 Age allowance

Notes

Para (*a*) substituted TCA 1997 s 464 for 2000–2001 and later tax years.

Para (*b*)(i) deleted "Section 464" from TCA 1997 s 458 (Table Part 1) for 2000–2001 and later tax years.

Para (*b*)(ii) inserted "Section 464" in TCA 1997 s 458 (Table Part 2) for 2000–2001 and later tax years.

9 Incapacitated children

Notes

Para (*a*) substituted TCA 1997 s 465 for 2000–2001 and later tax years.

Para (*b*)(i) deleted "Section 465" from TCA 1997 s 458 (Table Part 1) for 2000–2001 and later tax years.

Para (*b*)(ii) inserted "Section 465" in TCA 1997 s 458 (Table Part 2) for 2000–2001 and later tax years.

10 Dependent relative

Notes

Para (*a*) substituted TCA 1997 s 466 for 2000–2001 and later tax years.

Para (*b*)(i) deleted "Section 466" from TCA 1997 s 458 (Table Part 1) for 2000–2001 and later tax years.

Para (*b*)(ii) inserted "Section 466" in TCA 1997 s 458 (Table Part 2) for 2000–2001 and later tax years.

11 Relief for blind persons

Notes

Para (*a*) substituted TCA 1997 s 468 for 2000–2001 and later tax years.

Para (*b*)(i) deleted "Section 468" from TCA 1997 s 458 (Table Part 1) for 2000–2001 and later tax years.

Para (*b*)(ii) inserted "Section 468" in TCA 1997 s 458 (Table Part 2) for 2000–2001 and later tax years.

12 Home carer's allowance

Notes

Para (*a*) inserted TCA 1997 s 466A for 2000–2001 and later tax years.

Para (*b*) inserted "Section 466A" in TCA 1997 s 458 (Table Part 2) for 2000–2001 and later tax years.

13 Amendment of section 473 (allowance for rent paid by certain tenants) of Principal Act

Notes

Para (*a*)(i) inserted TCA 1997 s 473(1)(definition of "appropriate percentage") for 2000–2001 and later tax years.

Para (*a*)(ii) inserted TCA 1997 s 473(1)(definition of "the specified limit" for 2000–2001 and later tax years.

Para (*b*) substituted TCA 1997 s 473(2) for 2000–2001 and later tax years.

Para (*c*) substituted TCA 1997 s 473(3) for 2000–2001 and later tax years.

Para (*d*) substituted TCA 1997 s 473(10) for 2000–2001 and later tax years.

Para (*e*)(i) deleted "Section 473(2) from TCA 1997 s 458 (Table Part 1) for 2000–2001 and later tax years.

Para (*e*)(ii) substituted "Section 473" for "Section 473(3)" in TCA 1997 s 458 (Table Part 2) for 2000–2001 and later tax years.

14 Standard rating of allowances: consequential provisions

The provisions of the Principal Act referred to in Schedule 1 are amended as specified in that Schedule.

15 Amendment of section 122 (preferential loan arrangements) of Principal Act

Notes

This section substituted "4 per cent" for "6 per cent" in TCA 1997 s 122(1)(*a*)(definition of "the specified rate" for 2000–2001 and later tax years.

16 Amendment of section 126 (tax treatment of certain benefits payable under Social Welfare Acts) of Principal Act

Notes

This section substituted TCA 1997 s 126(8)(*b*) with effect from 6 April 2000.

17 Amendment of section 244 (relief for interest paid on certain home loans) of Principal Act

Notes

Para (*a*)(i) substituted TCA 1997 s 244(1) (definition of "dependent relative") for 2000–2001 and later tax years.

Para (*a*)(ii) substituted TCA 1997 s 244(1) (definition of "relievable interest") for 2000–2001 and later tax years.

Para (*a*)(iii) substituted TCA 1997 s 244(1)(*c*) for 2000–2001 and later tax years.

Para (*b*) substituted TCA 1997 s 244(3)(*a*) for 2000–2001 and later tax years.

18 Amendment of section 202 (relief for agreed pay restructuring) of Principal Act

Notes

Subs (1)(*a*) substituted TCA 1997 s 202(1)(*a*) (definition of "specified amount") as respects payments made under a relevant agreement (within the meaning of section 202 of the Principal Act) the relevant date (within that meaning) of which is after 20 July 1999.

Subs (1)(*b*) substituted "6 April 2003" for "the 6th day of April, 2000" in TCA 1997 s 202(2)(*g*) with effect from 6 April 2000.

19 Amendment of Part 16 (income tax relief for investment in corporate trades — business expansion scheme and seed capital scheme) of Principal Act

Notes

Subs (1)(*a*) inserted TCA 1997 s 488(1) (definition of "Exchange Axess") with effect from 1 May 1998.

Subs (1)(*b*) substituted part of TCA 1997 s 491(4) with effect from 1 May 1998.

Subs (1)(*c*)(i) substituted "company," for "company, or" in TCA 1997 s 495(3)(*a*)(ii)(I) with effect from 1 May 1998.

Subs (1)(*c*)(ii) substituted "trades, or" for "trades." in TCA 1997 s 495(3)(*a*)(*ii*)(II) with effect from 1 May 1998.

Subs (1)(*c*)(iii) inserted TCA 1997 s 495(3)(*a*)(ii)(III) with effect from 1 May 1998.

20 Amendment of Schedule 13 (accountable persons for purposes of Chapter 1 of Part 18) to Principal Act

Notes

Para (*a*) deleted TCA 1997 Sch 13 paras 43 and 85 with effect from 6 April 2000.

Para (*b*) substituted TCA 1997 Sch 13 para 92 with effect from 6 April 2000.

Para (*c*) inserted TCA 1997 Sch 13 paras 96–103 with effect from 6 April 2000.

21 Relief for postgraduate and certain third-level fees

Notes

Subs (1)(*a*) inserted TCA 1997 s 475A for 2000–2001 and later tax years.
Subs (1)(*b*) inserted TCA 1997 s 474(2A) for 2000–2001 and later tax years.
Subs (1)(*c*) inserted TCA 1997 s 474A(2A) for 2000–2001 and later tax years.
Subs (1)(*d*)(i) inserted TCA 1997 s 475(1) (definition of "dependent") for 2000–2001 and later tax years.
Subs (1)(*d*)(ii) substituted TCA 1997 s 475(2)–(3) for 2000–2001 and later tax years.
Subs (1)(*e*)(i)(I) inserted TCA 1997 s 476(1) (definition of "appropriate percentage") for 2000–2001 and later tax years.
Subs (1)(*e*)(i)(II) inserted TCA 1997 s 476(1) (definition of "dependant") for 2000–2001 and later tax years.
Subs (1)(*e*)(ii) substituted TCA 1997 s 476(2)–(3) for 2000–2001 and later tax years.
Subs (1)(*f*) inserted "Section 475" in TCA 1997 s 458 (Table Part 2) for 2000–2001 and later tax years.
Subs (2) substituted "475, 475A, 476" for "475, 476" in TCA 1997 s 1024(2)(*a*)(ix) for 2000–2001 and later tax years.

22 Amendment of section 767 (payment to universities and other approved bodies for research in, or teaching of, approved subjects) of Principal Act

Notes

Para (*a*) substituted TCA 1997 s 767(1) (definition of "approved body") with effect from 6 April 2000.
Para (*b*) inserted TCA 1997 s 767(3) with effect from 6 April 2000.

23 Amendment of Part 30 (occupational pension schemes, retirement annuities, purchased life annuities and certain pensions) of Principal Act

(2) ...

(*d*) Notwithstanding the provisions of Part 30 of the Principal Act, a retirement benefits scheme which was approved by the Revenue Commissioners before 6 April 2000 shall not cease to be an approved scheme because the rules of the scheme are altered on or after that date to enable an individual to whom the scheme applies to exercise an option under subsection (3A) (as amended by this Act) of section 772 of the Principal Act, which that individual would be in a position to exercise in accordance with the terms of that subsection as regards a scheme approved on or after 6 April 2000, and, as regards such a scheme, the provisions of this section shall apply as if the scheme were one approved on or after that date.

Notes

Subs (1)(*a*)(i) inserted TCA 1997 s 770(1) (definition of "additional voluntary contributions") with effect from 6 April 2000.
Subs (1)(*a*)(ii) substituted "5 per cent" for "20 per cent" in TCA 1997 s 770(1) (definition of "proprietary director" with effect from 6 April 2000.
Subs (1)(*b*)(i) substituted TCA 1997 s 772(3A)(*a*) with effect from 6 April 2000.
Subs (1)(*b*)(ii) substituted TCA 1997 s 772(3A)(*b*)(i) with effect from 6 April 2000.
Subs (1)(*b*)(iii)(I) deleted TCA 1997 s 772(3B)(*a*)(iii) as regards an approved retirement fund or an approved minimum retirement fund, as the case may be, where the assets in the fund were first accepted into the fund by the qualifying fund manager on or after 6 April 2000.
Subs (1)(*b*)(iii)(II) inserted "in the case of a proprietary director" before "paragraph (*f*)" in TCA 1997 s 772(3B)(*b*) with effect from 6 April 2000.
Subs (1)(*b*)(iv) inserted TCA 1997 s 772(3C) with effect from 6 April 1999.
Subs (1)(*c*) substituted TCA 1997 s 784(2B) with effect from 6 April 2000.
Subs (1)(*d*)(i)(I) substituted TCA 1997 s 784A(1) (definition of "qualifying fund manager") para (*a*) with effect from 6 April 2000.

Subs (1)(*d*)(i)(II) substituted TCA 1997 s 784A(1)(definition of "qualifying fund manager") para (*j*) with effect from 6 April 2000.

Subs (1)(*d*)(i)(III) substituted TCA 1997 s 784A(1)(definition of "qualifying fund manager") para (*l*) with effect from 6 April 2000.

Subs (1)(*d*)(ii) inserted TCA 1997 s 784A(1)(*c*), (*d*) with effect from 6 April 2000.

Subs (1)(*d*)(iii) substituted TCA 1997 s 784A(2)–(7) as regards an approved retirement fund or an approved minimum retirement fund, as the case may be, where the assets in the fund were first accepted into the fund by the qualifying fund manager on or after 6 April 2000.

Subs (1)(*e*)(i) substituted TCA 1997 s 784C(7) as regards an approved retirement fund or an approved minimum retirement fund, as the case may be, where the assets in the fund were first accepted into the fund by the qualifying fund manager on or after 6 April 2000.

Subs (1)(*e*)(ii) deleted TCA 1997 s 784C(8)–(9) as regards an approved retirement fund or an approved minimum retirement fund, as the case may be, where the assets in the fund were first accepted into the fund by the qualifying fund manager on or after 6 April 2000.

Subs (1)(*f*) deleted TCA 1997 s 784E as regards an approved retirement fund or an approved minimum retirement fund, as the case may be, where the assets in the fund were first accepted into the fund by the qualifying fund manager on or after 6 April 2000.

24 Amendment of section 515 (excess or unauthorised shares) of Principal Act

Notes

Para (*a*) substituted "period of 5 years, or such lesser period as the Minister for Finance may by order prescribe," for "5 years" in TCA 1997 s 515(2A)(*b*) with effect from 6 April 2000.

Para (*b*) inserted TCA 1997 s 515(8) with effect from 6 April 2000.

25 Amendment of Schedule 11 (profit sharing schemes) to Principal Act

Notes

This section inserted TCA 1997 Sch 11 para 13A with effect from 6 April 2000.

26 Amendment of Schedule 12 (employee share ownership trusts) to Principal Act

Notes

Para (*a*) substituted TCA 1997 Sch 12 para 11(2B)(*d*) with effect from 6 April 2000.

Para (*b*) inserted TCA 1997 Sch 12 para 11(10) with effect from 6 April 2000.

27 Rights to acquire shares or other assets

Notes

Para (*a*)(i) inserted TCA 1997 s 128(2A) with effect from 6 April 2000.

Para (*a*)(ii) substituted "30 June in the year of assessment following" for "30 days after the end of" in TCA 1997 s 128(11) with effect from 6 April 2000.

Para (*a*)(iii) inserted TCA 1997 s 128(11A) with effect from 6 April 2000.

Para (*b*) inserted TCA 1997 s 128A with effect from 6 April 2000.

Para (*c*)(i) deleted "section 128(11)" in TCA 1997 Sch 29 col 2 with effect from 6 April 2000.

Para (*c*)(ii) inserted "section 128(11) and 128(11A)" in TCA 1997 Sch 29 col 3 with effect from 6 April 2000.

28 Amendment of Chapter 4 (interest payments by certain deposit takers) of Part 8 of Principal Act

Notes

Subs (1) substituted TCA 1997 s 256(1) (definition of "appropriate tax") with effect from 6 April 2000.

Subs (2) substituted TCA 1997 s 261(*c*)(i) with effect from 6 April 2000.

29 Extension of section 1022 (special provisions relating to tax on wife's income) of Principal Act to spouse's income, etc

Notes

Subs (1)(*a*) substituted TCA 1997 s 1022(1) as respects assessments made on or after 10 February 2000.

Subs (1)(*b*) substituted "to the spouse or to the spouse's representative, or to the spouse's executors or administrators, as would have followed on the making on the spouse, or on the spouse's representative, or on the spouse's executors or administrators" for "to a woman, or to her trustee, guardian or committee, or to her executors or administrators, as would have followed on the making on her, or on her trustee, guardian or committee, or on her executors or administrators" in TCA 1997 s 1022(2) as respects assessments made on or after 10 February 2000.

Subs (1)(*c*) substituted TCA 1997 s 1022(6) as respects assessments made on or after 10 February 2000.

Subs (1)(*d*) substituted "the deceased spouse's executors or administrators" for "the woman's executors or administrators" in TCA 1997 s 1022(7) as respects assessments made on or after 10 February 2000.

Subs (1)(*e*) substituted "a deceased spouse's executors or administrators" for "a woman's executors or administrators" in TCA 1997 s 1022(8) as respects assessments made on or after 10 February 2000.

Subs (1)(*f*) inserted TCA 1997 s 1022(9) as respects assessments made before, on or after 10 February 2000.

CHAPTER 3
Dividend Withholding Tax

30 Dividend withholding tax

Notes

Subs (1)(*a*)(i) inserted TCA 1997 s 172A(1)(a) (definition of "approved body of persons") with effect from 6 April 2000.

Subs (1)(*a*)(ii) inserted TCA 1997 s 172A(1)(a) (definition of "designated broker") with effect from 6 April 2000.

Subs (1)(*a*)(iii) inserted TCA 1997 s 172A(1)(a) (definition of "special portfolio investment account" with effect from 6 April 2000.

Subs (1)(*b*)(i) inserted TCA 1997 s 172B(4A) with effect from 6 April 2000.

Subs (1)(*b*)(ii) substituted TCA 1997 s 172B(6) with effect from 6 April 2000.

Subs (1)(*b*)(iii) inserted TCA 1997 s 172B(7) with effect from 6 April 2000.

Subs (1)(*c*)(i)(I) deleted "or" in TCA 1997 s 172C(2)(*d*) and substituted "Schedule 2A," for "Schedule 2A." in TCA 1997 s 172C(2)(*e*)(ii) with effect from 6 April 2000.

Subs (1)(*c*)(i)(II) inserted TCA 1997 s 172C(2)(*f*)–(*g*) with effect from 6 April 2000.

Subs (1)(*c*)(ii) inserted TCA 1997 s 172C(3) with effect from 6 April 2000.

Subs (1)(*d*)(i) substituted TCA 1997 s 172D(3)(*b*) with effect from 6 April 2000.

Subs (1)(*d*)(ii) inserted TCA 1997 s 172D(3A) with effect from 6 April 2000.

Subs (1)(*d*)(iii) substituted "subsection (3)(*b*)(ii)" for "subsection (3)(*b*)(i)" where it occurs in TCA 1997 s 172D(4) with effect from 6 April 2000.

Subs (1)(*d*)(iv)(I) substituted "subsection (3)(*b*)(iii)(I)" for "subsection (3)(*b*)(ii)(II)" in TCA 1997 s 172D(5) with effect from 6 April 2000.

Subs (1)(*d*)(iv)(II) deleted "subparagraph (iii) of" from TCA 1997 s 172D(5) with effect from 6 April 2000.

Subs (1)(*d*)(v) inserted TCA 1997 s 172D(6) with effect from 6 April 2000.

Subs (1)(*e*)(i)(I) substituted TCA 1997 s 172E(3)(*a*)–(*b*) with effect from 6 April 2000.

Subs (1)(*e*)(i)(II) substituted TCA 1997 s 172E(3)(*f*) with effect from 6 April 2000.

Subs (1)(*e*)(ii) inserted TCA 1997 s 172E(3A) with effect from 6 April 2000.

Subs (1)(*e*)(iii) inserted TCA 1997 s 172E(8) with effect from 6 April 2000.

Subs (1)(*f*)(i)(I) substituted "For the purposes of this section, but subject to paragraphs (*g*) and (*h*)" for "For the purposes of paragraph (*d*)" in TCA 1997 s 172F(3)(*e*) with effect from 6 April 2000.

Subs (1)(*f*)(i)(II) substituted "by way of notice in writing or in electronic format" for "by way of notice in writing given in accordance with subsection (1)" and "Liable Fund, and" for "Liable Fund," in TCA 1997 s 172F(3)(*e*)(v) with effect from 6 April 2000.

Subs (1)(*f*)(i)(III) substituted TCA 1997 s 172F(3)(*e*)(vi) and (vii) with effect from 6 April 2000.

Subs (1)(*f*)(i)(IV) inserted TCA 1997 s 172F(3)(*g*) and (*h*) with effect from 6 April 2000.

Subs (1)(*f*)(ii) substituted TCA 1997 s 172F(7) with effect from 6 April 2000.

Subs (1)(*f*)(iii) deleted ", not later than the 21st day of May following the year of assessment to which the return refers," from TCA 1997 s 172F(8) with effect from 6 April 2000.

Subs (1)(*g*)(i)(I) substituted TCA 1997 s 172G(3)(*a*)–(*b*) with effect from 6 April 2000.

Subs (1)(*g*)(i)(II) substituted TCA 1997 s 172G(3)(*g*) with effect from 6 April 2000.

Subs (1)(*g*)(ii) inserted TCA 1997 s 172G(3A) with effect from 6 April 2000.

Subs (1)(*g*)(iii) inserted TCA 1997 s 172G(8) with effect from 6 April 2000.

Subs (1)(*h*)(i) deleted "and" from TCA 1997 s 172K(1)(*f*) and substituted "refers, and" for "refers." in TCA 1997 s 172K(1)(*g*) with effect from 6 April 2000.

Subs (1)(*h*)(ii) inserted TCA 1997 s 172K(1)(*h*) with effect from 6 April 2000.

Subs (1)(*i*) inserted TCA 1997 s 172LA with effect from 10 February 2000.

Subs (2)(*a*) substituted "paragraph 8(*f*) or 9(*f*)" for "paragraph 8(*f*) or subparagraph (*f*) or (*g*) of paragraph 9" in TCA 1997 Sch 2A para 2 with effect from 6 April 2000.

Subs (2)(*b*) inserted TCA 1997 Sch 2A paras 7A–7B with effect from 6 April 2000.

Subs (2)(*c*) substituted TCA 1997 Sch 2A para 8(*g*)(ii) with effect from 6 April 2000.

Subs (2)(*d*)(i) substituted TCA 1997 Sch 2A para 9(*f*) with effect from 6 April 2000.

Subs (2)(*d*)(ii) deleted TCA 1997 Sch 2A para 9(*g*) with effect from 6 April 2000.

31 Amendment of section 153 (distributions to certain nonresidents) of Principal Act

Notes

Para (*a*) substituted TCA 1997 s 153(1) (definition "non-resident person") as respects distributions made on or after 6 April 2000.

Para (*b*) inserted TCA 1997 s 153(1A) as respects distributions made on or after 6 April 2000.

Para (*c*) substituted "paragraph (*b*)(ii)(I) of the definition of 'qualifying non-resident person'" for "paragraph (*b*)(i) of the definition of 'non-resident person'" in TCA 1997 s 153(2) as respects distributions made on or after 6 April 2000.

Para (*d*)(i) substituted "paragraph (*b*)(iii)(I) of the definition of 'qualifying non-resident person'" for "paragraph (*b*)(ii)(II) of the definition of 'non-resident person'" in TCA 1997 s 153(3) as respects distributions made on or after 6 April 2000.

Para (*e*) inserted TCA 1997 s 153(3A) as respects distributions made on or after 6 April 2000.

Para (*f*) substituted "qualifying non-resident person" for "non-resident person" in TCA 1997 s 153(4) as respects distributions made on or after 6 April 2000.

Para (*g*) inserted TCA 1997 s 153(6) as respects distributions made on or after 6 April 2000.

32 Amendment of section 700 (special computational provisions) of Principal Act

Notes

This section inserted TCA 1997 s 700(1A) with effect from 6 April 1999.

33 Amendment of section 831 (implementation of Council Directive No 90/435/ EEC concerning the common system of taxation applicable in the case of parent companies and subsidiaries of different Member States) of Principal Act

Notes

Para (*a*) substituted TCA 1997 s 831(1)(*a*) (definition of "company") as respects distributions made on or after 6 April 2000.

Para (*b*) inserted TCA 1997 s 831(5A) as respects distributions made on or after 6 April 2000.

CHAPTER 4

Income Tax, Corporation Tax and Capital Gains Tax

34 Amendment of section 198 (certain interest not to be chargeable) of Principal Act

Notes

This section substituted TCA 1997 s 198(1) as respects interest paid in the year of assessment 2000–2001 and subsequent years of assessment.

35 Capital allowances for, and deduction in respect of, vehicles

Notes

Para (*a*)(i) substituted "mechanically propelled vehicle;" for "mechanically propelled vehicle." in TCA 1997 s 373(2)(*k*) with effect from 6 April 2000.

Para (*a*)(ii) inserted TCA 1997 s 373(2)(*l*) with effect from 6 April 2000.

Para (*b*)(i) substituted "£ 15,500," for "£15,500, and" in TCA 1997 s 376(1) (definition of "relevant amount") para (*c*) with effect from 6 April 2000.

Para (*b*)(ii) substituted TCA 1997 s 376(1) (definition of "relevant amount") para (*d*) with effect from 6 April 2000.

Para (*b*)(iii) inserted TCA 1997 s 376(1)(*e*) with effect from 6 April 2000.

36 Amendment of section 268 (meaning of "industrial building or structure") of Principal Act

Notes

This section substituted TCA 1997 s 268(1)(*i*) with effect from 6 April 2000.

37 Amendment of section 333 (double rent allowance in respect of rent paid for certain business premises) of Principal Act

Notes

This section substituted TCA 1997 s 333(1)(*a*) (definition of "qualifying lease") with effect from 6 April 2000.

38 Amendment of section 20 (amendment of provisions relating to Custom House Docks Area) of Urban Renewal Act, 1998

Notes

This section repealed Urban Renewal Act 1998 s 20(1)(*c*) with effect from 6 April 2000.

39 Amendment of section 324 (double rent allowance in respect of rent paid for certain business premises) of Principal Act

Notes

Subs (1) inserted TCA 1997 s 324(5) with effect from 3 December 1998.

40 Amendment of Part 9 (principal provisions relating to relief for capital expenditure) of Principal Act

Notes

Para (*a*) deleted "and, where it is so made, section 304(4) shall not apply" from TCA 1997 s 278(2) with effect from 6 April 2000.

Para (*b*)(i) substituted "section 284(6) or 298" for "section 298" in TCA 1997 s 300(1) with effect from 6 April 2000.

Para (*b*)(ii) inserted TCA 1997 s 300(4) with effect from 6 April 2000.

Para (*c*)(i) deleted "as it applies" from TCA 1997 s 304(1) with effect from 6 April 2000.
Para (*c*)(ii)(I) deleted "Subject to section 278(2)," from TCA 1997 s 304(4) with effect from 6 April 2000.
Para (*c*)(ii)(II) inserted ", or in charging profits or gains of any description, as the case may be," in TCA 1997 s 304(4) with effect from 6 April 2000.
Para (*c*)(ii)(III) inserted "or in charging the profits or gains, as the case may be," in TCA 1997 s 304(4) with effect from 6 April 2000.
Para (*c*)(iii) inserted TCA 1997 s 304(6)(*c*) with effect from 6 April 2000.
Para (*d*)(i) inserted "or in charging income under Case V of Schedule D" in TCA 1997 s 305(1)(*a*) with effect from 6 April 2000.
Para (*d*)(ii) substituted TCA 1997 s 305(1)(*b*) with effect from 6 April 2000.
Para (*e*) substituted TCA 1997 s 405(1)(*a*) with effect from 6 April 2000.
Para (*f*) substituted TCA 1997 s 406 with effect from 6 April 2000.

41 Capital allowances for computer software

Notes

Subs (1)(*a*)(i) substituted "that machinery or plant" for "the computer software concerned" in TCA 1997 s 288(1)(*d*) with effect from 29 February 2000.
Subs (1)(*a*)(ii) inserted TCA 1997 s 288(3A) with effect from 29 February 2000.
Subs (1)(*a*)(iii) inserted TCA 1997 s 288(4)(*c*) with effect from 29 February 2000.
Subs (1)(*b*) inserted TCA 1997 s 318(*aa*) with effect from 29 February 2000.

42 Amendment of Chapter 3 (designated areas, designated streets, enterprise areas and multi-storey car parks in certain urban areas) of Part 10 of Principal Act

Notes

Subs (1)(*a*)(i) substituted "paragraph (*a*) or (*e*) of subsection (2)" for "subsection (2)(*a*)" in TCA 1997 s 339(1) (definition of "the relevant local authority") with effect from 1 July 1999.
Subs (1)(*a*)(ii) inserted TCA 1997 s 339(2)(*e*) with effect from 1 July 1999.
Subs (1)(*b*) substituted TCA 1997 s 340(2)(ii) with effect from 1 July 1999.
Subs (1)(*c*)(i) inserted TCA 1997 s 343(1) (definition of "property developer") with effect from 1 July 1999.
Subs (1)(*c*)(ii) substituted "subsections (8), (9) and (11)" for "subsections (8) and (9)" in TCA 1997 s 343(7)(*a*) with effect from 1 July 1999.
Subs (1)(*c*)(iii) inserted TCA 1997 s 343(11) with effect from 1 July 1999.
Subs (1)(*d*)(i)(I) substituted "30 September 1999" for "the 30th day of June, 1999" in TCA 1997 s 344(1) (definition of "qualifying period") with effect from 1 July 1999.
Subs (1)(*d*)(i)(II) substituted TCA 1997 s 344(1)(definition of "qualifying period") para (*c*) with effect from 1 July 1999.
Subs (1)(*d*)(ii) substituted TCA 1997 s 344(1) (definition of "the relevant local authority") para (*b*) with effect from 1 July 1999.
Subs (1)(*e*) substituted "30 September 1998" for "the 30th day of June, 1998" in TCA 1997 s 345(1A)(*b*) with effect from 1 July 1999.

43 Amendment of section 360 (interpretation (Chapter 5)) of Part 10 of Principal Act

Notes

This section substituted "15 per cent" for "50 per cent" in TCA 1997 s 360(1) with effect from 6 April 1999.

44 Amendment of Chapter 7 (qualifying areas) of Part 10 of Principal Act

Notes

Subs (1)(*a*)(i) inserted TCA 1997 s 372A(1) (definition of "property developer") with effect from 1 July 1999.
Subs (1)(*a*)(ii) substituted "31 December 2002;" for "the 31st day of July, 2001;" in TCA 1997 s 372A(1) (definition of "qualifying period") with effect from 1 July 1999.
Subs (1)(*b*)(i) substituted TCA 1997 s 372B(1)(b) with effect from 1 July 1999.

Subs (1)(*b*)(ii) substituted "or end after 31 December 2002." for the words from "or end after" to the end of the paragraph in TCA 1997 s 372B(1)(*c*) with effect from 1 July 1999.
Subs (1)(*c*)(i) substituted TCA 1997 s 372C(1) with effect from 1 July 1999.
Subs (1)(*c*)(ii) substituted "50 per cent" for "25 per cent" in TCA 1997 s 372C(2)(*d*) with effect from 1 July 1999.
Subs (1)(*d*)(i) inserted "or part of a building or structure" in TCA 1997 s 372D(1) with effect from 1 July 1999.
Subs (1)(*d*)(ii) substituted "subsection (3) to (5)" for "subsection (3) to (6A)" in TCA 1997 s 372D(2)(*a*) with effect from 1 July 1999.
Subs (1)(*d*)(iii)(I) deleted "and" from TCA 1997 s 372D(4)(*b*)(i) with effect from 1 July 1999.
Subs (1)(*d*)(iii)(II) substituted TCA 1997 s 372D(2)(*b*)(ii) with effect from 1 July 1999.
Subs (1)(*d*)(iv) deleted TCA 1997 s 372D(6)–(6A) with effect from 1 July 1999.
Subs (1)(*e*) inserted "or part of a building" in TCA 1997 s 372G(1) (definition of "conversion expenditure" paras (*a*) and (*b*)) with effect from 1 July 1999.
Subs (1)(*f*) by the insertion of "or part of a building" in TCA 1997 s 372H(1) (definition of "specified building") with effect from 1 July 1999.
Subs (1)(*g*) inserted TCA 1997 s 372I(2)(*aa*) with effect from 1 July 1999.
Subs (1)(*h*) substituted TCA 1997 s 372K with effect from 1 July 1999.

45 Amendment of Chapter 8 (qualifying rural areas) of Part 10 of Principal Act

Notes

Subs (1)(*a*)(i) inserted TCA 1997 s 372L (definition of "property developer") with effect from 1 July 1999.
Subs (1)(*a*)(ii) substituted "31 December 2002" for "the 31st day of December, 2001" where it occurs in TCA 1997 s 372L with effect from 1 July 1999.
Subs (1)(*b*) substituted "50 per cent" for "25 per cent" in TCA 1997 s 372M(2)(*d*) with effect from 1 July 1999.
Subs (1)(*c*)(i) substituted "subsections (3) to (5)" for "subsections (3) to (6B)" in TCA 1997 s 372N(2)(*a*) with effect from 1 July 1999.
Subs (1)(*c*)(ii)(I) deleted "and" from TCA 1997 s 372N(4)(*b*) with effect from 1 July 1999.
Subs (1)(*c*)(ii)(II) substituted TCA 1997 s 372N(4)(*b*)(ii) with effect from 1 July 1999.
Subs (1)(*c*)(iii) deleted TCA 1997 s 372N(6)–(6B) with effect from 1 July 1999.
Subs (1)(*e*) substituted TCA 1997 s 372T with effect from 1 July 1999.

46 Amendment of Chapter 9 (park and ride facilities and certain related developments) of Part 10 of Principal Act

Notes

Para (*a*) inserted TCA 1997 s 372Y(2)(*aa*) with effect from 6 April 2000.
Para (*b*) substituted "section 372X(6)" for "section 372X(5)" in TCA 1997 s 372Z(10) with effect from 6 April 2000.

47 Amendment of section 823 (deduction for income earned outside the State) of Principal Act

Notes

Subs (1)(*a*) substituted "11 consecutive days" for "14 consecutive days" in TCA 1997 s 823(1) (definition of "qualifying day") para (*a*) with effect from 29 February 2000.
Subs (1)(*b*) substituted "11 consecutive days" for "14 consecutive days" in TCA 1997 s 823(2A)(*b*) with effect from 29 February 2000.
Subs (1)(*c*) substituted "whichever is the lesser; but that amount, or the aggregate of those amounts where there is more than one such office or employment, shall not exceed £25,000." for "whichever is the lesser." in TCA 1997 s 823(3) for 2000–2001 and later tax years; for 1999–2000, as if the reference to "that amount, or the aggregate of those amounts where there is more than one such office or employment" were a reference to "such portion of that amount, or such portion of the aggregate of those amounts where there is more than one such office or employment, which arises by virtue of income, profits or gains accruing or paid on or after 29 February 2000".

48 Amendment of section 481 (relief for investment in films) of Principal Act

Notes

Para (*a*)(i) substituted TCA 1997 s 481(1) (definition of "qualifying company") with effect from such date as the Minister may appoint by order.

Para (*a*)(ii) substituted TCA 1997 s 481(1) (definition of "qualifying period") with effect from such date as the Minister may appoint by order.

Para (*b*) substituted TCA 1997 s 481(2)(c) with effect from such date as the Minister may appoint by order.

49 Amendment of section 482 (relief for expenditure on significant buildings and gardens) of Principal Act

Notes

Para (*a*) substituted "1957;" for "1957." in TCA 1997 s 482(1)(*a*) (definition of "tourist accommodation facility" and inserted TCA 1997 s 482(1)(*a*) (definition of "weekend day") with effect from 23 March 2000.

Para (*b*) substituted TCA 1997 s 482(5)(*b*)(ii) with effect from 23 March 2000.

Para (*c*) substituted TCA 1997 s 482(8) with effect from 23 March 2000.

50 Amendment of section 485 (relief for gifts to third-level institutions) of Principal Act

Notes

Para (*a*)(i) inserted TCA 1997 s 485(1) (definition of "approved development fund") with effect from 6 April 2000.

Para (*a*)(ii) inserted TCA 1997 s 485(1) (definition of "development fund") with effect from 6 April 2000.

Para (*a*)(iii)(I) substituted "relevant guidelines," for "guidelines referred to in subsection (2)(*a*)(i), and" in TCA 1997 s 485(1) (definition of "project") para (c) with effect from 6 April 2000.

Para (*a*)(iii)(II) substituted "skills needs, and" for "skills needs;" in TCA 1997 s 485(1) (definition of "project") para (*d*) with effect from 6 April 2000.

Para (*a*)(iii)(III) inserted TCA 1997 s 485(1)(definition of "project") para (*e*) with effect from 6 April 2000.

Para (*a*)(iv) substituted TCA 1997 s 485(1) (definition of "relevant gift") with effect from 6 April 2000.

Para (*a*)(v) inserted TCA 1997 s 485(1) (definition of "relevant guidelines") with effect from 6 April 2000.

Para (*b*)(i) substituted TCA 1997 s 485(2)(*a*)(i) with effect from 6 April 2000.

Para (*b*)(ii) substituted "relevant guidelines" for "guidelines referred to in subparagraph (i)" in TCA 1997 s 485(2)(*a*)(ii) with effect from 6 April 2000.

Para (*b*)(iii) deleted TCA 1997 s 485(2)(*a*)(iii) with effect from 6 April 2000.

Para (*b*)(iv) substituted TCA 1997 s 485(2)(*c*) with effect from 6 April 2000.

Para (*c*) substituted TCA 1997 s 485(6) and (7) with effect from 6 April 2000.

Para (*d*) substituted "£250" for "£1,000" in TCA 1997 s 485(8) with effect from 6 April 2000.

Para (*e*) inserted "each approved project" in TCA 1997 s 485(9) with effect from 6 April 2000.

Para (*f*) substituted TCA 1997 s 485(10)(*b*) with effect from 6 April 2000.

Para (*g*)(i) substituted TCA 1997 s 485(11)(*a*)(iv) with effect from 6 April 2000.

Para (*g*)(ii) substituted TCA 1997 s 485(11)(*b*)(vi) with effect from 6 April 2000.

Para (*h*) inserted TCA 1997 s 485(12)–(14) with effect from 6 April 2000.

51 Savings-related share option schemes

Notes

Para (*a*)(i) inserted TCA 1997 s 519A(3A) with effect from 6 April 2000.

Para (*a*)(ii)(I) substituted "Subject to subsection (2A) this section shall apply" for "This section shall apply" in TCA 1997 s 519B(1) with effect from 6 April 2000.

Para (*a*)(ii)(II) inserted TCA 1997 s 519B(2A) with effect from 6 April 2000.

Para (*b*)(i)(I) substituted "stock;" for "stock." in TCA 1997 Sch 12A para 1(1) (definition of "shares") with effect from 6 April 2000.

Para (b)(i)(II) inserted TCA 1997 Sch 12A para 1(1) (definition of "specified age") with effect from 6 April 2000.

Para (*b*)(ii) inserted TCA 1997 Sch 12A para 2(5) with effect from 6 April 2000.
Para (*b*)(iii) substituted "the specified age" for "pensionable age (within the meaning of section 2 of the Social Welfare (Consolidation) Act, 1993)" in TCA 1997 Sch 12A para 20(*b*) with effect from 6 April 2000.
Para (*b*)(iv) substituted "the specified age" for "pensionable age" in TCA 1997 Sch 12A para 21 with effect from 6 April 2000.

52 Reduction in tax on certain transactions in land

Notes

Subs (1) inserted TCA 1997 ss 644A–644B as respects income tax, in relation to profits or gains arising on or after 1 December 1999, and as respects corporation tax, in relation to accounting periods ending on or after 1 January 2000. For the purposes of this section where an accounting period of a company begins before 1 January 2000 and ends on or after that day, it shall be divided into two parts, one beginning on the day on which the accounting period begins and ending on 31 December 1999 and the other beginning on 1 January 2000 and ending on the day on which the accounting period ends, and both parts shall be treated for the purpose of this section as if they were separate accounting periods of the company.

53 Amendment of Part 26 (life assurance companies) of Principal Act

Notes

This section inserted TCA 1997 ss 730A–730G (Chs 4–5) with effect from 6 April 2000.

54 Amendment of section 420 (losses, etc which may be surrendered by means of group relief) of Principal Act

Notes

This section substituted TCA 1997 s 420(9) with effect from 6 April 2000.

55 Amendment of section 595 (life assurance policy or deferred annuity contract entered into or acquired by a company) of Principal Act

Notes

This section substituted TCA 1997 s 595(1)(*a*) (definition of "relevant policy") with effect from 6 April 2000.

56 Amendment of section 710 (profits of life business) of Principal Act

Notes

Subs (1)(*a*) substituted "where a company's trading operations on 31 December 2000 consisted solely of foreign life assurance business" for "where a company's trading operations consist solely of a foreign life assurance business" in TCA 1997 s 710(2)(*a*) as respects 2001 and later financial years.
Subs (1)(*b*) deleted TCA 1997 s 710(2)(*a*)(iii) and (iv) as respects 2001 and later financial years.

57 Amendment of Chapter 1 (unit trusts) of Part 27 of Principal Act

Notes

Para (*a*) substituted TCA 1997 s 737(1) (definition of "special investment units") with effect from 6 April 2000.
Para (*b*) substituted TCA 1997 s 738(2)(*b*)(i) with effect from 6 April 2000.
Para (*c*) inserted TCA 1997 s 739A with effect from 6 April 2000.

58 Investment undertakings

Notes

Para (*a*) inserted TCA 1997 ss 739G–739H (Ch 1A) with effect from 6 April 2000.
Para (*b*) inserted TCA 1997 Sch 2B with effect from 6 April 2000.

59 Amendment of section 172A (interpretation) of Principal Act

Notes

This section substituted TCA 1997 s 172A(1)(*a*)(definition of "collective investment undertaking") with effect from 6 April 2000.

60 Amendment of section 659 (farming: allowance for capital expenditure on the construction of farm buildings, etc for control of pollution) of Principal Act

Notes

Para (*a*) substituted "6 April 2003" for "the 6th day of April, 2000," in TCA 1997 s 659(1)(*c*) with effect from 6 April 2000.

Para (*b*)(i) substituted TCA 1997 s 659(2) with effect from 6 April 2000.

Para (*b*)(ii) substituted TCA 1997 s 659(3)(*a*) with effect from 6 April 2000.

Para (*b*)(iii) inserted TCA 1997 s 659(3A)–(3C) with effect from 6 April 2000.

61 Amendment of Part 23 (farming and market gardening) of Principal Act

Notes

Para (*a*) substituted TCA 1997 s 2(1) (definition of "capital allowance") para (*b*) which is to come into operation from such date as the Minister for Finance, with the consent of the Minister for Agriculture, Food and Rural Development, may by order appoint.

Para (*b*) inserted TCA 1997 ss 669A–669F which are to come into operation from such date as the Minister for Finance, with the consent of the Minister for Agriculture, Food and Rural Development, may by order appoint.

62 Amendment of section 723 (special investment policies) of Principal Act

Notes

This section substituted TCA 1997 s 723(1) (definition of "special investment policy") with effect from 6 April 2000.

63 Amendment of section 843A (capital allowances for buildings used for certain childcare purposes) of Principal Act

Notes

Subs (1)(*a*)(i) inserted TCA 1997 s 843A(1) (definition of "property developer") with effect from such date that the Minister for Finance may by order appoint.

Subs (1)(*a*)(ii) substituted TCA 1997 s 843A(1) definition of "qualifying expenditure") with effect from such date that the Minister for Finance may by order appoint.

Subs (1)(*b*) inserted "incurred on or after 2 December 1998" in TCA 1997 s 843A(3) with effect from such date that the Minister for Finance may by order appoint.

Subs (1)(*c*) inserted TCA 1997 s 843A(3A) with effect from such date that the Minister for Finance may by order appoint.

Subs (1)(*d*) inserted TCA 1997 s 843A(5) with effect from such date that the Minister for Finance may by order appoint.

64 Amendment of Part 29 (patents, scientific and certain other research, know-how and certain training) of Principal Act

Notes

This section inserted TCA 1997 ss 769A–769F (Ch 4) with effect from such day as the Minister for Finance may by order appoint.

65 Amendment of section 243 (allowance of charges on income) of Principal Act

Notes

Subs (1) substituted "except where-

(I) the company has been authorised by the Revenue Commissioners to do otherwise, or

(II) the interest is interest referred to in paragraph (*b*) or (*h*) of section 246(3),

the company deducts income tax which it accounts for under sections 238 and 239, or under sections 238 and 241, as the case may be, or"
for "except where the company has been authorised by the Revenue Commissioners to do otherwise, the company deducts income tax which it accounts for under sections 238 and 239, or under sections 238 and 241, as the case may be, or" in TCA 1997 s 243(5) with effect from 10 February 2000.

66 Amendment of section 246 (interest payments by companies and to non-residents) of Principal Act

Notes

Subs (1)(*a*) substituted "made;" for "made." in TCA 1997 s 246(1) (definition of "relevant territory") and inserted TCA 1997 s 246(1) (definition of "tax") with effect from 10 February 2000.

Subs (1)(*b*) substituted "which, by virtue of the law of a relevant territory, is resident for the purposes of tax in the relevant territory," for "resident in a relevant territory" in TCA 1997 s 246(3)(*h*) with effect from 10 February 2000.

67 Amendment of section 247 (relief to companies on loans applied in acquiring interest in other companies) of Principal Act

Notes

Subs (1) substituted TCA 1997 s 247(5) with effect from 6 April 1997.

68 Amendment of Chapter 4 (revenue powers) of Part 38 of Principal Act

Notes

Para (*a*)(i) inserted TCA 1997 s 904A (definitions of "auditor" and "associated company") and substituted TCA 1997 s 904A (definition of "authorised officer") with effect from 6 April 2000.

Para (*a*)(ii) substituted TCA 1997 s 904A(6)–(7) with effect from 6 April 2000.

Para (*b*) inserted TCA 1997 ss 904B–904D with effect from 6 April 2000.

Para (*c*) substituted the definition of "financial institution" in TCA 1997 ss 906A(1) and 908A(1) with effect from 6 April 2000.

Para (*d*) substituted TCA 1997 s 908A(2) with effect from 6 April 2000.

69 Amendments and repeals consequential on abolition of tax credits

(1) The provisions of the Taxes Consolidation Act, 1997, referred to in Part 1 of Schedule 2 shall apply subject to the amendments specified in that Schedule.

(2) Every provision of the Taxes Consolidation Act, 1997, specified in column (1) of Part 2 of Schedule 2 to this Act is repealed to the extent specified in column (2) of that Schedule.

(3) This section shall apply—

(*a*) in the case of income tax, as on and from 6 April 1999, and

(*b*) in the case of corporation tax, as respects accounting periods commencing on or after that date.

70 Restrictions on the use by certain partnerships of losses, etc, and transitional arrangements concerning those restrictions

Notes

Subs (1)(*a*) substituted TCA 1997 s 1013(1) (definition of "limited partner") para (d) with effect from 29 February 2000.

Subs (1)(*b*) substituted TCA 1997 s 1013(2)(III) with effect from 29 February 2000.

Subs (1)(*c*) substituted "Subparagraph (III)(A)" for "Subparagraph (III)" in TCA 1997 s 1013(2A) with effect from 29 February 2000.

Subs (1)(*d*) inserted TCA 1013(2B)–(2C) with effect from 29 February 2000.

71 Amendment of Schedule 24 (relief from income tax and corporation tax by means of credit in respect of foreign tax) to Principal Act

Notes

Subs (1)(*a*) substituted TCA 1997 Sch 24 para 4(4)(*a*)–(*c*) and the words "gain is reduced by virtue of-" which precedes those clauses. The substitution applies as respects accounting periods ending on or after 1 January 2000, and where an accounting period of a company begins before 1 January 2000 and ends on or after that day, it shall be divided into two parts, one beginning on the day on which the accounting period begins and ending on 31 December 1999 and the other beginning on 1 January 2000 and ending on the day on which the accounting period ends, and both parts shall be treated for the purposes of this section as if they were separate accounting periods of the company.

Subs (1)(*b*)(i) substituted "there shall be treated for the purposes of subparagraph (1) as tax paid by the foreign company in respect of its profits—

(*a*) any underlying tax payable by the third company, and

(*b*) any tax directly charged on the dividend which neither company would have borne had the dividend not been paid,

to the extent to which it would be taken into account" for "there shall be treated for the purposes of subparagraph (1) as tax paid by the foreign company in respect of its profits any underlying tax payable by the third company, to the extent to which it would be taken into account" in TCA 1997 Sch 24 para 9B(2) as respects accounting periods ending on or after 1 April 1998.

Subs (1)(*b*)(ii) inserted "or tax directly charged on the dividend" in TCA 1997 Sch 24 para 9B(3) as respects accounting periods ending on or after 1 April 1998.

72 Amendment of Schedule 29 to Principal Act

Notes

This section inserted "section 730G(2)" and "section 739F(2)" in TCA 1997 Sch 29 col 1 with effect from 6 April 2000.

73 Treatment of interest in certain circumstances

Notes

Subs (1) inserted TCA 1997 s 817A as respects interest paid on or after 29 February 2000 and TCA 1997 s 817B as respects interest received on or after 29 February 2000.

74 Amendment of section 213 (trade unions) of Principal Act

Notes

This section substituted TCA 1997 s 213(2)–(3) with effect from 6 April 2000.

CHAPTER 5
Corporation Tax

75 Amendment of section 21A (higher rate of corporation tax) of Principal Act

Notes

Subs (1)(*a*)(i) substituted TCA 1997 s 21A(1) (definition of "excepted operations") para (*a*) for 2000 and later financial years.

Subs (1)(*a*)(ii) inserted TCA 1997 s 21A(1) (definition of "exempt development") for 2000 and later financial years.

Subs (1)(*a*)(iii) inserted TCA 1997 s 21A(1) (definition of "qualifying land") for 2000 and later financial years.

Subs (1)(*b*) substituted TCA 1997 s 21A(3)–(4) for 2000 and later financial years.

76 Reduction of corporation tax liability in respect of certain trading income

Notes

This section inserted TCA 1997 s 22A with effect from 6 April 2000.

77 Amendment of section 23A (company residence) of Principal Act

Notes

Subs (1)(*a*) substituted TCA 1997 s 23A(1)(*b*)(i)(II) with effect from 10 February 2000.

Subs (1)(*b*) deleted "subparagraph (iii) of" in TCA 1997 s 23A(1)(*b*)(i)(III)(B) with effect from 10 February 2000.

78 Amendment of section 882 (particulars to be supplied by new companies) of Principal Act

Notes

This section substituted TCA 1997 882(3) with effect from 6 April 2000.

79 Amendment of section 411 (surrender of relief between members of groups and consortia) of Principal Act

Notes

This section substituted "a company shall be owned by a consortium if 75 per cent or more of the ordinary share capital" for "a company shall be owned by a consortium if all of the ordinary share capital" in TCA 1997 s 411(1)(*a*) with effect from 6 April 2000.

80 Amendment of section 446 (certain trading operations carried on in Custom House Docks Area) of Principal Act

Notes

Para (*a*) inserted TCA 1997 s 446(2B)–(2D) with effect from 6 April 2000.

Para (*b*) substituted TCA 1997 s 446(7)(*c*)(ii)(V) with effect from 6 April 2000.

Para (*c*) inserted TCA 1997 s 446(8A) with effect from 6 April 2000.

81 Amendment of Chapter 1 (general provisions) of Part 26 of Principal Act

Notes

Subs (1)(*a*) substituted TCA 1997 s 711(1) with effect for 1999 and later financial years.

Subs (1)(*b*)(i) deleted TCA 1997 s 713(2) with effect for 2000 and later financial years.

Subs (1)(*b*)(ii) substituted TCA 1997 s 713(3) with effect for 2000 and later financial years.

Subs (1)(*b*)(iii) deleted TCA 1997 s 713(4) with effect for 2000 and later financial years.

82 Amendment of section 110 (securitisation of assets) of Principal Act

Notes

Subs (1)(*a*) inserted ", apart from a transaction where the provisions of paragraph (*a*) of subsection (3) apply to any interest or other distribution payable under the transaction unless the transaction concerned is excluded from the provisions of that paragraph (*a*) by virtue of paragraph (*b*) of that subsection" in TCA 1997 s 110(1) as respects any interest paid on or after 10 February 2000.
Subs (1)(*b*) inserted TCA 1997 s 1997 s 110(3) as respects any interest paid on or after 10 February 2000.

83 Amendment of Part 14 (taxation of companies engaged in manufacturing trades, certain trading operations carried on in Shannon Airport and certain trading operations carried on in the Custom House Docks Area) of Principal Act

Notes

Subs (1)(*a*) substituted TCA 1997 s 445(6) with effect from 1 January 2000.
Subs (1)(*b*)(i) substituted "subsection (4), (5), (5A) or (6)" for "subsection (4), (5) or (6)" in TCA 1997 s 446(2) with effect from 23 March 2000.
Subs (1)(*b*)(ii) inserted TCA 1997 s 446(5A) with effect from 23 March 2000.
Subs (1)(*b*)(iii) substituted TCA 1997 s 446(6) with effect from 1 January 2000.
Subs (1)(*c*) substituted TCA 1997 s 447 with effect from 23 March 2000.
Subs (1)(*d*)(i) substituted "sections 22A, 157, 158, 239, 241, 440, 441, 449, 644B" for "sections 157, 158, 239, 241, 440, 441, 442" in TCA 1997 s 448(1) as respects accounting periods ending on or after 1 January 2000.
Subs (1)(*d*)(ii) deleted TCA 1997 ss 448(7) as respects accounting periods beginning after 1 April 2000.
Subs (1)(*e*) deleted TCA 1997 ss 448(4) and 450(5) as respects accounting periods beginning after 1 April 2000.

84 Amendment of section 220 (profits of certain bodies corporate) of Principal Act

Notes

Subs (1) inserted TCA 1997 s 220 para 8 with effect from 14 July 1999.

CHAPTER 6
Capital Gains Tax

85 Amendment of section 598 (disposals of business or farm on "retirement") of Principal Act

Notes

This section substituted "£375,000" for "£250,000" in TCA 1997 s 598(2)(*a*) as respects disposals made on or after 1 December 1999.

86 Amendment of section 649A (relevant disposals: rate of charge) of Principal Act

Notes

This section substituted TCA 1997 s 649A(1)–(2) with effect from 6 April 2000.

87 Amendment of section 980 (deduction from consideration on disposal of certain assets) of Principal Act

Notes

Subs (1)(*a*) substituted "£300,000" for £150,000" in TCA 1997 s 980(3) as respects disposals made on or after 23 March 2000.

Subs (1)(*b*) substituted TCA 1997 s 980(4)(*b*) as respects disposals made on or after 23 March 2000.
Subs (1)(*c*) inserted TCA 1997 s 980(8A) as respects disposals made on or after 23 March 2000.
Subs (1)(*d*) substituted TCA 1997 s 980(9)(*a*)(iii) as respects disposals made on or after 23 March 2000.

88 Amendment of section 1030 (separated spouses: transfers of assets) of Principal Act

Notes

Subs (1)(*a*) deleted "or" in TCA 1030(2)(*c*) as respects disposals made on or after 10 February 2000.
Subs (1)(*b*) substituted TCA 1030(2)(*d*) as respects disposals made on or after 10 February 2000.

CHAPTER 7

Income Tax and Corporation Tax: Reliefs for Renewal and Improvement of Certain Towns

89 Amendment of Part 10 (income tax and corporation tax: reliefs for renewal and improvement of certain urban areas, certain resort areas and certain islands) of Principal Act

Notes

Para (*a*) inserted TCA 1997 ss 372AA–372AJ with effect from 6 April 2000.
Para (*b*) inserted "Section 372AH" to TCA 1997 s 458 (Table Part 1) with effect from 6 April 2000.
Para (*c*) substituted "372RA, 372Y and 372AH" for "372RA and 372Y" in TCA 1997 s 1024(2)(*a*)(i) with effect from 6 April 2000.

PART 7

Miscellaneous

154 Interpretation (Part 7)

In this Part **"Principal Act"** means the Taxes Consolidation Act, 1997.

160 Amendment of section 824 (appeals) of Principal Act

Notes

This section substituted "Part" for "Chapter" in TCA 1997 s 824(1) with effect from 23 March 2000.

161 Amendment of section 1003 (payment of tax by means of donation of heritage items) of Principal Act

Notes

This section substituted "£3,000,000" for "£750,000" in TCA 1997 s 1003(2)(*c*) as respects the calendar year 2000 and subsequent years.

162 Amendment of section 1086 (publication of names of tax defaulters) of Principal Act

Notes

Subs (1)(*a*)(i) substituted "tax," for "tax, or" in TCA 1997 s 1086(2)(*b*) and "tax, or" for "tax." in TCA 1997 s 1086(2)(*c*)(iii) as respects fines or other penalties, as are referred to in s 1086(2)(*a*)–(*b*), which are imposed by a court, and as respects specified sums, as are referred to in s 1086(2)(*c*)–(*d*), which the Revenue

Commissioners accepted, or undertook to accept, in settlement of a specified liability, on or after 23 March 2000.
Subs (1)(*a*)(ii) inserted TCA 1997 s 1086(2)(*d*) as respects fines or other penalties, as are referred to in s 1086(2)(*a*)–(*b*), which are imposed by a court, and as respects specified sums, as are referred to in s 1086(2)(*c*)–(*d*), which the Revenue Commissioners accepted, or undertook to accept, in settlement of a specified liability, on or after 23 March 2000.
Subs (1)(*b*) inserted TCA 1997 s 1086(2A) as respects fines or other penalties, as are referred to in s 1086(2)(*a*)–(*b*), which are imposed by a court, and as respects specified sums, as are referred to in s 1086(2)(*c*)–(*d*), which the Revenue Commissioners accepted, or undertook to accept, in settlement of a specified liability, on or after 23 March 2000.
Subs (1)(*c*)(i) substituted "Paragraph (*c*) and (*d*)" for "Paragraph (*c*)" in TCA 1997 s 1086(4) as respects fines or other penalties, as are referred to in s 1086(2)(*a*)–(*b*), which are imposed by a court, and as respects specified sums, as are referred to in s 1086(2)(*c*)–(*d*), which the Revenue Commissioners accepted, or undertook to accept, in settlement of a specified liability, on or after 23 March 2000.
Subs (1)(*c*)(ii) substituted "paragraph (*c*) or (*d*), as the case may be," for "paragraph (*c*)" in TCA 1997 s 1086(4)(*c*) as respects fines or other penalties, as are referred to in s 1086(2)(*a*)–(*b*), which are imposed by a court, and as respects specified sums, as are referred to in s 1086(2)(*c*)–(*d*), which the Revenue Commissioners accepted, or undertook to accept, in settlement of a specified liability, on or after 23 March 2000.
Subs (1)(*d*) inserted TCA 1997 s 1086(5A) as respects fines or other penalties, as are referred to in s 1086(2)(*a*)–(*b*), which are imposed by a court, and as respects specified sums, as are referred to in s 1086(2)(*c*)–(*d*), which the Revenue Commissioners accepted, or undertook to accept, in settlement of a specified liability, on or after 23 March 2000.

163 Amendment of section 1094 (tax clearance in relation to certain licences) of Principal Act

Notes

This section inserted para (*k*) in the definition of "licence" in TCA 1997 s 1094(1) with effect from 23 March 2000.

164 Amendment of Chapter 5 (miscellaneous provisions) of Part 42 (collection and recovery) of Principal Act

Notes

This section inserted TCA 1997 ss 1006A–1006B with effect from 23 March 2000.

165 Care and management of taxes and duties

All taxes and duties imposed by this Act are by virtue of this section placed under the care and management of the Revenue Commissioners.

166 Short title, construction and commencement

(1) This Act may be cited as the Finance Act, 2000.

(2) Part 1 (so far as relating to income tax) shall be construed together with the Income Tax Acts and (so far as relating to corporation tax) shall be construed together with the Corporation Tax Acts and (so far as relating to capital gains tax) shall be construed together with the Capital Gains Tax Acts.

...

(8) Part 7 (so far as relating to income tax) shall be construed together with the Income Tax Acts and (so far as relating to corporation tax) shall be construed together with the Corporation Tax Acts and (so far as relating to capital gains tax) shall be construed together with the Capital Gains Tax Acts and (so far as relating to customs) shall be

construed with the Customs Acts and (so far as relating to duties of excise) shall be construed together with the statutes which relate to duties of excise and the management of those duties and (so far as relating to value-added tax) shall be construed together with the Value-Added Tax Acts, 1972 to 2000, and (so far as relating to stamp duty) shall be construed together with the Stamp Duties Consolidation Act, 1999, and (so far as relating to residential property tax) shall be construed together with Part VI of the Finance Act, 1983, and the enactments amending or extending that Part and (so far as relating to gift tax or inheritance tax) shall be construed together with the Capital Acquisitions Tax Act, 1976, and the enactments amending or extending that Act.

(9) Except where otherwise expressly provided in Part 1, that Part shall apply as on and from 6 April 2000.

...

(11) Any reference in this Act to any other enactment shall, except so far as the context otherwise requires, be construed as a reference to that enactment as amended by or under any other enactment including this Act.

(12) In this Act, a reference to a Part, section or Schedule is to a Part or section of, or Schedule to, this Act, unless it is indicated that reference to some other enactment is intended.

(13) In this Act, a reference to a subsection, paragraph, subparagraph, clause or subclause is to the subsection, paragraph, subparagraph, clause or subclause of the provision (including a Schedule) in which the reference occurs, unless it is indicated that reference to some other provision is intended.

SCHEDULE 1

Amendments Consequential on the Introduction of Standard Rated Allowances

(Section 14)

Notes

Para 1 substituted "relief" for "a deduction" in TCA 1997 s 3(1) (definition of "relative") with effect from 6 April 2000.

Para 2 substituted "relief" for "a deduction" in TCA 1997 s 7(2) with effect from 6 April 2000.

Para 3 substituted "relief under section 461(2) as an individual referred to in paragraph (*a*)(i) of the definition of "specified amount" in subsection (1) of that section" for "a deduction specified in section 461(*a*)" in TCA 1997 s 188(3) with effect from 6 April 2000.

Para 4 substituted "entitled to relief" for "entitled to a deduction" in TCA 1997 s 467(4) with effect from 6 April 2000.

Para 5(*a*)(i) substituted "relief under section 461(2) as an individual referred to in paragraph (*a*)(i) of the definition of 'specified amount' in subsection (1) of that section" for "a deduction mentioned in section 461(*a*)" in TCA 1997 s 469(1)(definition of "dependant") with effect from 6 April 2000.

Para 5(*a*)(ii) substituted "relief" for "a deduction" in TCA 1997 s 469(1) (definition of "dependant") with effect from 6 April 2000.

Para 5(*b*) substituted TCA 1997 s 469(4) with effect from 6 April 2000.

Para 6(*a*) inserted "461A," in TCA 1997 s 1023(1) with effect from 6 April 2000.

Para 6(*b*) inserted "and reliefs" in TCA 1997 s 1023(2)(*a*) with effect from 6 April 2000.

Para 7(*a*) substituted "subsection (4)" for "subsection (3)" in TCA 1997 s 1024(2)(*a*)(ii) with effect from 6 April 2000.

Para 7(*b*) substituted "section 465(4)" for "section 465(3)" in TCA 1997 s 1024(2)(*a*)(iii) with effect from 6 April 2000.

Para 7(*c*) substituted TCA 1997 s 1024(2)(*a*)(viii) with effect from 6 April 2000.
Para 8 substituted "relief under section 465" for "a deduction under section 465" in TCA 1997 s 1025(1) with effect from 6 April 2000.

SCHEDULE 2
Amendments and Repeals Consequential on Abolition of Tax Credits
(Section 69)

PART 1
Amendments

PART 2
Repeals

Taxes Consolidation Act, 1997

Notes
Amendments and repeals apply with effect from 6 April 1999 in the case of income tax and as respects accounting periods commencing on or after that date in the case of corporation tax.
Part 1 — Amendments
Para (*a*) inserted TCA 1997 s 2(3A).
Para (*b*) substituted "subsections (2) and (3)" for "subsections (2) to (4)" in TCA 1997 s 137(5).
Para (*c*) substituted TCA 1997 s 140(8).
Para (*d*) substituted "Subsections (8) and (9) of section 140" for "Subsections (6) and (7) of section 145" in TCA 1997 s 141(10).
Para (*e*) substituted "subsections (8) and (9) of section 140" for "subsections (6) and (7) of section 145" in TCA 1997 s 142(6).
Para (*f*)(i) substituted "which consists of a distribution made out of relieved income" for "the tax credit comprised in which has been reduced under this section" in TCA 1997 s 143(1)(*c*).
Para (*f*)(ii) substituted "subsections (8) and (9) of section 140" for "subsections (6) and (7) of section 145" in TCA 1997 s 143(10).
Para (*g*)(i) substituted "where R, S and T have the same meanings respectively as in section 147(1)(*a*)" in TCA 1997 s 144(8).
Para (*g*)(ii) substituted "Subsections (8) and (9) of section 140" for "Subsections (6) and (7) of section 145" in TCA 1997 s 144(9).
Para (*h*) inserted "and" in TCA 1997 s 152(1)(*a*).
Para (*i*)(i)(I) substituted "144 and 145" for "144, 145 and 147(2)" and of "144 and 145" for "144, 145 and 147" in TCA 1997 s 154(1)(*a*).
Para (*i*)(i)(II) deleted ", and subsections (1), (2) and (4) of subsection 147," from TCA 1997 s 154(1)(*b*).
Para (*i*)(ii) substituted TCA 1997 s 154(6).
Para (*k*) inserted "and" in TCA 1997 s 155(3)(*a*).
Para (*l*) substituted "Sections 160 and 162" for "Sections 160, 162 and 171" in TCA 1997 s 167(3).
Para (*m*) inserted "and" in TCA 1997 s 174(2)(i).
Para (*n*) substituted "section 713" for "sections 707 and 713" in TCA 1997 s 714(1).
Para (*o*) substituted TCA 1997 s 834(4)(*f*).
Para (*p*) inserted "and" in TCA 1997 s 1084(2)(*b*)(i).
Part 2 — Repeals
Section 2(1): The definition of "tax credit"; Section 2(4): The, whole subsection; Section 20(1): Paragraph 3 of Schedule F; Section 136: The whole section; Section 137(1): The words from ", and 'relevant tax credit'" to "in respect of the bonus issue"; Section 137(2): The words "or relevant tax credit"; Section 137(4): The whole subsection; Section 137(5): The words "; and nothing in those subsections shall affect the like proportion of the relevant tax credit relating to that bonus issue"; Section 138(3)(*a*): The whole paragraph; Section 139: The whole section; Section 140(3)(*b*): The whole paragraph; Section 140(4): The whole subsection; Section

140(5): The words "(not being a supplementary distribution under this section)"; Section 140(6): The whole subsection; Section 141(3)(*b*): The whole paragraph; Section 141(6): The whole subsection; Section 141(7): The words "(not being a supplementary distribution under this section)"; Section 141(8): The whole subsection; Section 142(2): The words "and, notwithstanding section 136, the recipient of the distribution shall not be entitled to a tax credit in respect of it"; Section 142(5): The whole subsection; Section 142(7): The words "(not being a supplementary distribution under this section)"; Section 143(2): The whole subsection; Section 143(3): The words ", and the tax credit in respect of each such distribution shall be calculated in accordance with subsection (2) and section 136 respectively"; Section 143(5): The whole subsection; Section 143(7): The words from ", and, where" to "so reduced"; Section 143(8): The whole subsection; Section 143(9): The whole subsection; Section 143(11): The words "(not being a supplementary distribution under this section)", and "and the amount of the tax credit which would apply in respect of the distribution if it were not made out of relieved income"; Section 144(3)(*b*): The whole paragraph; Section 144(4): The whole subsection; Section 144(5): The words "(not being a supplementary distribution under this section)"; Section 144(6): The whole subsection; Section 145: The whole section; Section 146: The whole section; Part 6, Chapter 5 (sections 147 to 151): The whole Chapter; Section 152(1)(*b*): The whole paragraph; Section 152(3)(*a*): The words from "and (whether" to "entitled in respect of the distribution"; Section 154(4): The whole subsection; Section 154(5): The whole subsection; Section 155(3)(*b*): The whole paragraph; Section 165: The whole section; Section 168: The whole section; Section 169: The whole section; Section 170: The whole section; Section 171: The whole section; Section 172: The whole section; Section 174(2)(ii): The whole subparagraph; Section 434(1): In the definition of "distributable income" the words "reduced by the tax credit comprised in that income" in paragraph (*a*) and the words "as so reduced" in paragraph (*b*); Section 434(5): In paragraph (*b*) of the definition of "distributable investment income" the words "(as reduced by the tax credit comprised in that income)" in each place it occurs; Section 434(5): In the definition of "distributable estate income" the words "(as reduced by the tax credit comprised in that income)"; Section 440(5): The whole subsection; Section 519(7): The words ", but the trustees shall not be entitled to the set-off or payment of a tax credit under section 136 in respect of those dividends"; Section 707(5)(*a*)(i): The whole subparagraph; Section 707(5)(*a*)(ii): The whole subparagraph; Section 712(1): The words ", and the income represented by the distribution shall be equal to the aggregate of the amount of the distribution and the amount of the tax credit in respect of the distribution"; Section 712(2): The whole subsection; Section 713(1)(*b*): The words "or under section 136, 712(2) or 730"; Section 714(2): The whole subsection; Section 729(5): The whole subsection; Section 729(7): The whole subsection; Section 730: The whole section; Section 737(7)(*a*): The whole paragraph; Section 737(7)(*b*): The whole paragraph; Section 737(9)(*b*): The words "; but, notwithstanding subsection (7) or section 136, the tax credit in respect of a distribution to which this paragraph applies shall be disregarded for the purposes of the Tax Acts and the Capital Gains Tax Acts"; Section 738(3)(*a*)(i): The words ", and the income represented by the distribution shall be equal to the aggregate of the distribution and the amount of the tax credit in respect of the distribution"; Section 738(3)(*a*)(ii): The whole subparagraph; Section 738(3)(*b*): The whole paragraph; Section 838(4)(*g*): The whole paragraph; Section 838(5)(*c*): The words from "; but notwithstanding" to "the Capital Gains Tax Acts"; Section 877(2): The whole subsection; Section 884(2)(*b*): The words "and the tax credits to which the company is entitled in respect of those distributions"; Section 884(4): The words "and of tax credits to which the company is entitled in respect of those distributions"; Section 1021(2): The words "(including a tax credit in respect of a distribution from a company resident in the State)"; Section 1084(2)(*b*)(ii): The whole subparagraph; Schedule 32, paragraph 4: The whole paragraph.

140(5). The words "(not being a supplementary distribution under this section)". Section 140(6). The whole subsection. Section 141(3)(f). The whole paragraph. Section 141(6). The whole subsection. Section 141(7). The words "(not being a supplementary distribution under this section)". Section 141(8). The whole subsection. Section 142(2). The words "and notwithstanding section 136 the recipient of the distributions shall not be entitled to a tax credit in respect of it". Section 142(6). The whole subsection. Section 143. The words "(not being a supplementary distribution under this section)". Section 143(2). The whole subsection. Section 143(3). The words "and the tax credit in respect of each such distribution shall be calculated in accordance with subsection (2) and section 136 respectively". Section 143(4). The whole subsection. Section 143(5). The words "due", and "where" "or so reduced". Section 143(6). The whole subsection. Section 143(9). The whole subsection. Section 143(11). The words "(not being a supplementary distribution under this section)" and "and the amount of the tax credit which would apply in respect of the distribution if it were not made out of exempted income". Section 144(3)(c). The whole paragraph. Section 144(4). The whole subsection. Section 144(6). The words "(not being a supplementary distribution under this section)". Section 144(7). The whole subsection. Section 145. The whole section. Section 146. The whole section. Part 6, Chapter 7 (sections 147 to 150). The whole Chapter. Section 152(1)(a). The whole paragraph. Section 152(3)(a). The words "(or would" "(whether" "has entitled in respect of the distribution". Section 154(4). The whole subsection. Section 154(5). The whole subsection. Section 158(3)(b). The whole paragraph. Section 164. The whole section. Section 168. The whole section. Section 169. The whole section. Section 170. The whole section. Section 171. The whole section. Section 172. The whole section. Section 172A(1)(b). The whole subparagraph. Section 172A(1)(a), in the definition of "distributable income", the words "reduced by the tax credit comprised in that income", in paragraph (a) and the words "as so reduced" in paragraph (b). Section 172B. In paragraph (a) of the definition of "distributable investment income", the words "less reduced by the tax credit comprised in that income" in each place it occurs. Section 184(5). In the definition of "distributable profits" the words "as reduced by the tax credit comprised in that income". Section 440(3). The whole subsection. Section 519(2). The words ", but the trustees shall not be entitled to the set-off or payment of a tax credit under section 136 in respect of those dividends". Section 707(5)(a)(i). The whole subparagraph. Section 707(5)(a)(ii). The whole subparagraph. Section 712(1). The words ", and the income represented by the distribution shall be equal to the aggregate of the amount of the distribution and the amount of the tax credit in respect of the distribution". Section 712(2). The whole subsection. Section 712(3)(a). The words "or under section 136, 137(2) or 730". Section 713(3). The whole subsection. Section 732(2). The whole subsection. Section 732(6). The whole subsection. Section 733. The whole section. Section 737. The whole paragraph. Section 737(6). The whole paragraph. Section 738(3)(b). The words "Notwithstanding subsection (4) of section 136, the tax credit in respect of a distribution to which this paragraph applies shall be disregarded for the purposes of the Tax Acts and the Capital Gains Tax Acts". Section 738(4)(b). The words "and the income represented by the distribution shall be equal to the aggregate of the distribution and the amount of the tax credit in respect of the distribution". Section 738(5)(c)(ii). The whole subparagraph. Section 738(6). The whole paragraph. Section 739(4)(e). The whole paragraph. Section 739(5)(c). The words "notwithstanding section 136 of the Capital Gains Tax Acts". Section 831(7). The whole subsection. Section 831(2)(c). The words "and the tax credits to which the company is entitled in respect of those distributions". Section 831(4). The words "and of tax credits to which the company is entitled in respect of those distributions". Section 1032(2). The words "(including any tax credit in respect of a distribution from a company resident in the State)". Section 1035(4)(b)(i). The whole subparagraph. Schedule 32, paragraph 3. The whole paragraph.

TOWN RENEWAL ACT 2000

(2000 Number 18)

ARRANGEMENT OF SECTIONS

Section

AN ACT TO MAKE NEW PROVISION FOR THE RENEWAL OF CERTAIN TOWNS, OR AN AREA OR AREAS OF CERTAIN TOWNS, FOR THAT PURPOSE TO PROVIDE FOR THE PREPARATION AND SUBMISSION TO THE MINISTER FOR THE ENVIRONMENT AND LOCAL GOVERNMENT BY COUNTY COUNCILS OF PLANS (TO BE KNOWN AS TOWN RENEWAL PLANS) IN RELATION TO SUCH TOWNS OR SUCH AREA OR AREAS, TO DEFINE THE FUNCTIONS OF THE COUNTY COUNCILS IN RELATION TO AND CONSEQUENT UPON THE PREPARATION AND SUBMISSION OF SUCH PLANS, TO MAKE PROVISION IN RELATION TO THE APPLICATION OF CERTAIN PROVISIONS OF THE TAXES CONSOLIDATION ACT, 1997, CONCERNING RELIEFS FROM INCOME TAX AND CORPORATION TAX AND TO PROVIDE FOR RELATED MATTERS [4TH JULY, 2000]

BE IT ENACTED BY THE OIREACHTAS AS FOLLOWS:

1 Interpretation

(1) In this Act, unless the context otherwise requires—

"Act of 1997" means the Taxes Consolidation Act, 1997;

"county council" means the council of an administrative county and the functional area of a county council for the purposes of this Act is the administrative county;

"eligible town" means a town other than a town—

(*a*) in respect of which any part of that town—

(i) is within a qualifying resort area within the meaning of section 351 of the Act of 1997,

(ii) is within an area described as a qualifying area in an order made under section 372B (inserted by the Finance Act, 1998) of the Act of 1997, or

(iii) is within a qualifying rural area within the meaning of section 372L (inserted by the Finance Act, 1998) of the Act of 1997,

or

(*b*) within an administrative county that is specified in the Schedule to this Act;

"environs" means, in relation to a town, environs for the purposes of the census of population concerned;

"functions" includes powers and duties and a reference to the performance of functions includes, with respect to powers and duties, a reference to the exercise of the powers and the carrying out of the duties;

"Minister" means the Minister for the Environment and Local Government;

"qualifying area" has the meaning assigned to it by section 372AA(1) (inserted by the Finance Act, 2000) of the Act of 1997;

"town" means a town, the population of which, including the population of the environs of that town, exceeded 500 persons but did not exceed 6,000 persons in the census of population most recently published before section 3 falls to be applied to that town;

"town renewal plan" has the meaning assigned to it by section 3.

(2) In this Act—

(*a*) a reference to a section is a reference to a section of this Act, unless it is indicated that a reference to some other enactment is intended,

(*b*) a reference to a subsection or paragraph is a reference to the subsection or paragraph of the provision in which the reference occurs, unless it is indicated that a reference to some other provision is intended,

(*c*) a reference to any enactment shall, unless the context otherwise requires, be construed as a reference to that enactment as amended or adapted by or under any subsequent enactment.

2 Reference to Act in section 372AA(2) of Act of 1997

Notwithstanding any discrepancy between the terms in which it is therein so described and the terms of this Act as it is now so enacted, this Act shall be the Act of the Oireachtas referred to in section 372AA(2) (inserted by the Finance Act, 2000) of the Act of 1997.

3 Town renewal plans

(1) A county council may, subject to subsections (3) and (4), prepare and submit to the Minister one or more plans (which or each of which shall be known, and is in this Act referred to, as a **"town renewal plan"**) in respect of an eligible town, or an area or areas

of an eligible town, within the functional area of the county council and, if the county council thinks fit and subject to that subsection, an area referred to in subsection (2).

(2) The area in respect of which a town renewal plan may be prepared may include a part or parts of the functional areas of one or more other county councils if that county council or those county councils consent to that part or parts being included.

(3) A county council, when selecting an eligible town or an area or areas of an eligible town for the purpose of preparing a town renewal plan, shall have regard to any criteria which the Minister specifies in writing to be criteria which a county council shall have regard to in making such a selection and when specifying those criteria the Minister shall have regard, and only have regard to, the need for—

(*a*) the promotion of the physical renewal and revitalisation of towns,

(*b*) the promotion of towns as cultural, commercial, social and residential centres,

(*c*) the promotion of sustainable development patterns, and

(*d*) the enhancement of the amenities, heritage and environment of towns.

(4) A county council, when preparing a town renewal plan, shall have regard to any criteria which the Minister specifies in writing to be criteria to which a county council shall have regard when preparing a town renewal plan and, when so specifying, the Minister shall, having regard to the matters referred to in paragraphs (a) to (d) of subsection (3), include criteria for—

(*a*) the format of, and matters to be included in, a town renewal plan,

(*b*) design considerations,

(*c*) the selection of buildings and areas for the purposes of applying relief from income tax and corporation tax under Chapter 10 (inserted by the Finance Act, 2000) [or Chapter 11 (inserted by the Finance Act, 2002)][1] of Part 10 of the Act of 1997, and

(*d*) the procedure for consultation by a county council in respect of the preparation of a town renewal plan.

(5) The Minister may from time to time make and publish guidelines to which a county council shall have regard in performing its functions under this Act; those guidelines shall include the criteria referred to in subsections (3) and (4).

(6) A town renewal plan shall consist of a written statement and a plan indicating the objectives for—

(*a*) the renewal, on a sustainable basis, of an area comprising the whole or part of the eligible town to which the town renewal plan relates, and

(*b*) improvements in the physical environment of the area comprising the whole or part of the eligible town to which the town renewal plan relates.

(7) Without prejudice to the generality of subsection (6) a town renewal plan may, where appropriate, in relation to the area comprising the whole or part of the eligible town to which it relates, include objectives for—

(*a*) the renewal, preservation, conservation, restoration, development or redevelopment of the townscape, layout and building pattern of that area, including facades of buildings and shop frontages, (*b*) the restoration, refurbishment, consolidation and improvement of the building fabric of the area,

(*c*) the density of development and the treatment of spaces between buildings,

(*d*) the preservation and protection of the natural, architectural and archaeological heritage,

(*e*) the development or redevelopment, for residential or other appropriate use, of—

(i) derelict or vacant sites, or

(ii) buildings or parts of buildings,

(*f*) the promotion of sustainable development patterns, including the protection and improvement of the environment and amenities,

(*g*) the removal of barriers to development, and

(*h*) the enhanced use of infrastructural capacity.

(8) In preparing a town renewal plan the county council may consult with such other persons as appear to it to be concerned with or interested in the matter and shall have regard to any submissions or observations made to it by such persons in the course of that consultation.

Amendments

1 Inserted by FA 2002 s 24(2) and Sch 2 Pt 2 para 4(*a*) with effect from 1 January 2002.

4 Consultation by Minister

(1) The Minister may, for the purposes of this Act, consult with and seek the advice of such persons as appear to the Minister to have relevant expertise in respect of the renewal of towns and may have regard to any advice submitted to him or her by such persons in the course of that consultation.

(2) Without prejudice to the generality of subsection (1) the Minister may consult with the persons referred to in subsection (1) in respect of a town renewal plan submitted to him or her under this Act.

(3) A person referred to in subsections (1) and (2) shall not provide any advice to the Minister of the kind referred to in those subsections if that person has an interest in the matter, the subject of the advice.

5 Recommendations in respect of qualifying areas for purposes of town renewal tax reliefs

(1) A town renewal plan submitted to the Minister under section 3 may contain, or be accompanied by, recommendations by the county council concerned that—

(*a*) a part or parts of the area to which the town renewal plan relates ought to be a qualifying area for the purposes of one or more sections of Chapter 10 (inserted by the Finance Act, 2000) [or Chapter 11 (inserted by the Finance Act, 2002)][1] of Part 10 of the Act of 1997, or

[(*b*) the whole of the area to which the town renewal plan relates ought to be a qualifying area for the purposes of one or more of the following provisions of the said Chapter 11—

(i) section 372AP, in so far as it relates to conversion expenditure (within the meaning of that Chapter) incurred in relation to a house,

(ii) section 372AP, in so far as it relates to refurbishment expenditure (within the meaning of that Chapter) incurred in relation to a house, and

(iii) section 372AR in so far as it relates to expenditure incurred on the refurbishment of a house.][2]

(2) In making a recommendation referred to in subsection (1) the county council concerned shall have regard to—

(*a*) the consistency between the types of development that are likely to be carried out in the area or areas to which the recommendations relate (**"the relevant types of development"**) and the relevant objectives of the town renewal plan,

(*b*) the significance of the recommendations for the overall objectives of the town renewal plan generally,

(*c*) the market conditions in the eligible town or the area or areas of the eligible town concerned as respects the supply of, and current and anticipated demand for, the relevant types of development, and

(*d*) the nature and extent of any impediments to the carrying out of the relevant types of development.

Amendments

1 Inserted by FA 2002 s 24(2) and Sch 2 Pt 2 para 4(*a*) with effect from 1 January 2002.

2 Subs (1)(*b*) substituted by FA 2002 s 24(2) and Sch 2 Pt 2 para 4(*b*) with effect from 1 January 2002.

6 Qualifying areas for town renewal tax reliefs

Having considered a town renewal plan submitted to him or her under section 3, any recommendations referred to in section 5 which are contained in or have accompanied the town renewal plan and advices provided under section 4, the Minister may recommend to the Minister for Finance that he or she make, with respect to the matters concerned, an order under [paragraph (*a*), (*b*), (*b*a) or (*c*)][1] of section 372AB(1) (inserted by the Finance Act, 2000) of the Act of 1997.

Amendments

1 Substituted by FA 2002 s 24(2) and Sch 2 Pt 2 para 4(*c*) with effect from 1 January 2002; previously "paragraph (*a*), (*b*) or (*c*)".

6A Designation of certain areas for rented residential reliefs

[Where, under section 6, the 5 Minister has recommended to the Minister for Finance that he or she make an order under section 372AB(1) of the Act of 1997 that a part or parts of an area to which a town renewal plan relates ought to be a qualifying area for the purposes of section 372AR of that Act, the Minister may further recommend to the Minister for Finance that he or she make an order under the said section 372AB(1) that that part or those parts of the area concerned ought to be a qualifying area for the purposes of section 372AP of the Act of 1997 in so far as that section relates to one or more of the following:

(*a*) expenditure on the construction of a house,
(*b*) conversion expenditure in relation to a house, and
(*c*) refurbishment expenditure in relation to a house,

notwithstanding that the town renewal plan does not contain or is not accompanied by a recommendation or advice that that part or those parts of the area to which the plan relates ought to be a qualifying area for the purposes of the said section 372AP in so far as that section relates to one or more of the matters referred to in paragraphs *(a)*, (*b*) and (*c*) of this section.][1]

Amendments

1 Section 6A inserted by FA 2002 s 25(2)(*a*) as as respects expenditure incurred on or in relation to a house, where such expenditure is incurred on or after 5 December 2001, or where TCA 1997 372AP(9) or (10) applies, prior to 5 December 2001, but only if a contract for the purchase of the house had not been evidenced in writing by any person prior to that date, but a contract for the purchase of the house is evidenced in writing on or before 1 September 2002.

7 Certain reliefs conditional on buildings, etc., being consistent with town renewal plan

(1) No relief from income tax or corporation tax, as the case may be, may be granted under Chapter 10 (inserted by the Finance Act, 2000) [or Chapter 11 (inserted by the Finance Act, 2002)][1] of Part 10 of the Act of 1997, in respect of the construction, refurbishment or conversion of a building, structure or house unless the county council which prepared the town renewal plan concerned has certified in writing, in a manner specified by the Minister, that such construction, refurbishment or conversion is consistent with the objectives of that town renewal plan, being the particular plan concerned that was taken into consideration by the Minister in the making by him or her to the Minister for Finance of the recommendations referred to in section 6.

[(1A) For the purposes of subsection (1), where the Minister has, under section 6A, recommended to the Minister for Finance that he or she make an order under section 372AB(1) (inserted by the Finance Act, 2000) of the Act of 1997 that a part of an area to which a town renewal plan relates ought to be a qualifying area for the purposes of section 372AP of that Act, then expenditure referred to in paragraph *(a)*, (*b*) or (*c*), as the case may be, of section 6A which is incurred in relation to a house, the site of which is wholly within that part, may be treated as consistent with the objectives of that plan, notwithstanding that the plan did not contain or was not accompanied by a recommendation that such part ought to be a qualifying area for the purposes of the said section 372AP in so far as that section relates to one or more of the matters referred to in paragraphs *(a)*, (*b*) and (*c*) of section 6A.][2]

(2) In this section, **"town renewal plan concerned"** means the town renewal plan, within the boundary of the area to which that plan relates, the relevant building, structure or house is situate.

Amendments

1 Inserted by FA 2002 s 24(2) and Sch 2 Pt 2 para 4(*a*) with effect from 1 January 2002.

2 Subs (1A) inserted by FA 2002 s 25(2)(*b*) as as respects expenditure incurred on or in relation to a house, where such expenditure is incurred on or after 5 December 2001, or where TCA 1997 372AP(9) or (10) applies, prior to 5 December 2001, but only if a contract for the purchase of the house had not been

evidenced in writing by any person prior to that date, but a contract for the purchase of the house is evidenced in writing on or before 1 September 2002.

8 Monitoring of implementation of town renewal plans

(1) Where the Minister for Finance makes an order under section 372AB(1) (inserted by the Finance Act, 2000) of the Act of 1997, directing that an area or areas of an eligible town shall be a qualifying area for the purposes of one or more sections of Chapter 10 (inserted by the Finance Act, 2000) [or Chapter 11 (inserted by the Finance Act, 2002)][1] of Part 10 of the Act of 1997, the county council concerned shall make such arrangements as it considers appropriate in the particular circumstances for monitoring the implementation of the town renewal plan concerned and, in doing so, the county council shall have regard to such guidelines as may, from time to time, be issued by the Minister for the purposes of this section.

(2) A county council shall, in relation to each year in which it causes the monitoring referred to in subsection (1) to be carried out, make, as soon as may be after the end of that year, a report in writing to the Minister of the results of that monitoring.

(3) The guidelines referred to in subsection (1) shall specify criteria for monitoring progress having regard to the matters specified in paragraphs (*a*) to (*d*) of section 3(3) and paragraphs (*a*) to (*h*) of section 3(7).

(4) In this section—

"county council concerned" means the county council that prepared the town renewal plan concerned;

"town renewal plan concerned" means the town renewal plan, within the boundary of the area to which that plan relates the area or areas referred to in subsection (1) are situate.

Amendments

1 Inserted by FA 2002 s 24(2) and Sch 2 Pt 2 para 4(*a*) with effect from 1 January 2002.

9 Expenses

The expenses incurred by the Minister in the administration of this Act shall, to such extent as may be sanctioned by the Minister for Finance, be paid out of moneys provided by the Oireachtas.

10 Short title and commencement

(1) This Act may be cited as the Town Renewal Act, 2000.

(2) This Act (other than the provisions referred to in subsection (3)) shall come into operation on such day or days as the Minister may appoint by order or orders either generally or with reference to any particular purpose or provision and different days may be so appointed for different purposes or different provisions.

(3) Sections 3, 4, 5 and 6 shall be deemed to have come into operation on 16 February, 1999.

SCHEDULE

[Section 1(1)]

Administrative county of Fingal

Administrative county of South Dublin

Administrative county of Dún Laoghaire-Rathdown

FINANCE ACT 2001

(2001 Number 7)

ARRANGEMENT OF SECTIONS

PART 1

INCOME TAX, CORPORATION TAX AND CAPITAL GAINS TAX

Chapter 1
Interpretation

Chapter 2
Income Tax

Chapter 4
Corporation Tax

Chapter 5
Capital Gains Tax

PART 8

MISCELLANEOUS

AN ACT TO PROVIDE FOR THE IMPOSITION, REPEAL, REMISSION, ALTERATION AND REGULATION OF TAXATION, OF STAMP DUTIES AND OF DUTIES RELATING TO EXCISE AND OTHERWISE TO MAKE FURTHER PROVISION IN CONNECTION WITH FINANCE INCLUDING THE REGULATION OF CUSTOMS. [30TH MARCH 2001]

PART 1
INCOME TAX, CORPORATION TAX AND CAPITAL GAINS TAX

Chapter 1
Interpretation

1 Interpretation (Part 1)

In this Part **"Principal Act"** means the Taxes Consolidation Act, 1997.

Chapter 2
Income Tax

2 Tax credits

(1) Where an individual is entitled under a provision of the Principal Act mentioned in column (1) of the Table to this subsection to have the income tax to be charged on the individual, other than in accordance with the provisions of section 16(2) of the Principal Act, reduced for the year of assessment 2001 or any subsequent year of assessment and the amount of the reduction would, but for this section, be an amount which is the lesser of—

(*a*) an appropriate percentage of an amount (in this section referred to as the **"standard-rated allowance"**) specified in column (2) of that Table, and

(*b*) the amount which reduces that liability to nil,

the amount of the reduction in accordance with paragraph (*a*) shall, in lieu of being the standard-rated allowance, be the amount of the tax credit specified in column (3) or column (4), as may be appropriate, of the Table opposite the mention of the amount in column (2).

TABLE

Statutory Provision (1)	Standard rated allowance for the year (2)	Tax credit for the year 2001 (3)	Tax credit for the year 2002 and subsequent years (4)
Section 461			
(married person)	£9,400	£1,628	€2,794
(widowed person bereaved in the year of assessment)	£9,400	£1,628	€2,794
(single person)	£4,700	£814	€1,397
Section 461A (additional relief for certain widowed persons)	£1,000	£148	€254
Section 462 (additional relief for single parents)	£4,700	£814	€1,397
Section 463 (additional relief for widowed parent following death of spouse)			
(1st year)	£10,000	£2,000	€2,540
(2nd year)	£8,000	£1,600	€2,032
(3rd year)	£6,000	£1,200	€1,524
(4th year)	£4,000	£800	€1,016
(5th year)	£2,000	£400	€508
Section 464			
(aged person)			
(married person)	£1,600	£238	€408
(single person)	£800	£119	€204
Section 465			
(incapacitated child)	£1,600	£238	€408
Section 466			
(dependent relative)	£220	£33	€56

Section 466A			
(home carer)	£3,000	£444	€762
Section 468			
(blind person)	£3,000	£444	€762
(both spouses blind)	£6,000	£888	€1,524
Section 472			
(employee)	£1,000	£296	€508

(2) Section 7 of the Finance Act, 1999, and sections 4, 5, 6, 7, 8, 9, 10, 11 and 12 of the Finance Act, 2000, shall apply subject to the provisions of this section.

(3) Schedule 1 shall have effect for the purposes of supplementing subsection (1).

3 Alteration of rates of income tax

Notes

Para (*a*) substituted TCA 1997 s 15(4) for short tax "year" 2001 and later tax years.

Para (*b*)(i) substituted "£8,140" for "£6,000" in TCA 1997 s 15(3) for short tax "year" 2001.

Para (*b*)(ii) substituted TCA 1997 s 15 (Table) for short tax "year" 2001.

Para (*c*)(i) substituted "€13,967" for "£6,000" in TCA 1997 s 15(3) for 2002 and later tax years.

Para (*c*)(ii) substituted TCA 1997 s 15 (Table) for 2002 and later tax years.

4 Age Exemption

Notes

Para (*a*)(i) substituted TCA 1997 s 188(1)–(2) for short tax "year" 2001 and later tax years.

Para (*a*)(ii) substituted "a tax credit specified in section 461(*a*)" for "relief under section 461(2) as an individual referred to in paragraph (*a*)(i) of the definition of 'specified amount' in subsection (1) of that section" in TCA 1997 s 188(3) for short tax "year" 2001 and later tax years.

Para (*b*) substituted "€21,586" for "£12,580" and of "€10,793" for "£6,290" in TCA 1997 s 188(2) for 2002 and later tax years.

5 Amendment of section 122 (preferential loan arrangements) of Principal Act

Notes

Para (*a*) substituted "6 per cent" for "4 per cent" in both places where it occurs in TCA 1997 s 122(1)(*a*) (definition of "the specified rate") for short tax "year" 2001 and later tax years.

Para (*b*) substituted "12 per cent" for "10 per cent" in TCA 1997 s 122(1)(*a*) (definition of "the specified rate") for short tax "year" 2001 and later tax years.

6 Amendment of section 126 (tax treatment of certain benefits payable under Social Welfare Acts) of Principal Act

Notes

This section substituted TCA 1997 s 126(8)(*b*) with effect from 6 April 2001.

7 Amendment of section 467 (employed person taking care of incapacitated individual) of Principal Act

Notes

Para (*a*) substituted "£7,400" for "£8,500" in both places where it occurs in TCA 1997 s 467 for short tax "year" 2001.
Para (*b*) substituted "€12,700" for "£8,500" in both places where it occurs in TCA 1997 s 467 for 2002 and later tax years.

8 Amendment of section 469 (relief for health expenses) of Principal Act

Notes

Para (*a*)(i) substituted "under section 465," for "under section 465 or 466, and" in TCA 1997 s 469(1) definition of "dependant" para (*b*) for short tax "year" 2001 and later tax years.
Para (*a*)(ii) substituted "year of assessment, and" for "year of assessment;" in TCA 1997 s 469(1) definition of "dependant" para (*c*)(ii) for short tax "year" 2001 and later tax years.
Para (*a*)(iii) inserted TCA 1997 s 469(1) definition of "dependant" para (*d*) for short tax "year" 2001 and later tax years.
Para (*b*) inserted TCA 1997 s 469(1) definition of "educational psychologist" for short tax "year" 2001 and later tax years.
Para (*c*) deleted "other than routine maternity care" from the definition of "health care" in TCA 1997 s 469(1) for short tax "year" 2001 and later tax years.
Para (*d*) inserted TCA 1997 s 469(1) definition of "health expenses" para (*i*) for short tax "year" 2001 and later tax years.
Para (*e*) deleted TCA 1997 s 469(1) definition of "routine maternity care" for short tax "year" 2001 and later tax years.
Para (*f*) inserted TCA 1997 s 469(1) definition of "speech and language therapist" for short tax "year" 2001 and later tax years.

9 Amendment of section 473 (allowance for rent paid by certain tenants) of Principal Act

Notes

Para (*a*) substituted TCA 1997 s 473(1) definition of "specified limit" for short tax "year" 2001.
Para (*b*) substituted TCA 1997 s 473(1) definition of "specified limit" for 2002 and later tax years.

10 Amendment of section 477 (relief for service charges) of Principal Act

Notes

Para (*a*) substituted "subject to paragraph (*d*)," for "subject to paragraph (*c*)," in TCA 1997 s 477(6)(*a*) for short tax "year" 2001 and later tax years.
Para (*b*) substituted "£150" for "£50" in TCA 1997 s 477(7)(*a*) for short tax "year" 2001.
Para (*c*) substituted "€195" for "£50" in TCA 1997 s 477(7)(*a*) for 2002 and later tax years.

11 Relief for trade union subscriptions

Notes

Subs (1)(*a*) inserted "section 472C" in TCA 1997 s 458(Table Part 2) for short tax "year" 2001 and later tax years.
Subs (1)(*b*) inserted TCA 1997 s 472C for short tax "year" 2001 and later tax years.
Subs (1)(*c*) inserted TCA 1997 s 1024(2)(*a*)(viiia) for short tax "year" 2001 and later tax years.
Subs (2) substituted "€130" for "£74" in TCA 1997 s 472C(1) definition of "specified amount" for 2002 and later tax years.

12 Amendment of Part 16 (income tax relief for investment in corporate trades — business expansion scheme and seed capital scheme) of Principal Act

Notes

Para (*a*) substituted "commencing on 6 April 1984 and ending on 31 December 2001" for "commencing on the 6th day of April, 1984, and ending on the 5th day of April, 2001" in TCA 1997 s 489(15) with effect from 6 April 2001.

Para (*b*) substituted "the year of assessment 2001" for "the year 2000–01" in TCA 1997 s 490(3)(*b*) and (4)(*b*) with effect from 6 April 2001.

Para (*c*)(i) substituted "Shannon Free Airport Development Company Limited," for "Shannon Free Airport Development Company Limited, or" in TCA 1997 s 496(2)(*a*)(ii)(II) with effect from 6 April 2001.

Para (*c*)(ii) substituted "Udarás na Gaeltachta Act, 1979, or" for "Udarás na Gaeltachta Act, 1979," in TCA 1997 s 496(2)(*a*)(ii)(III) with effect from 6 April 2001.

Para (*c*)(iii) inserted TCA 1997 s 496(2)(*a*)(ii)(IV) with effect from 6 April 2001.

13 Employee share ownership trusts — deceased beneficiaries

Notes

Para (*a*)(i)(I) substituted "the trust deed," for "the trust deed, and" in TCA 1997 s 519(5)(*a*)(iv) with effect from 6 April 2001.

Para (*a*)(i)(II) inserted TCA 1997 s 519(5)(*a*)(iv*a*) with effect from 6 April 2001.

Para (*a*)(ii) substituted TCA 1997 s 519(7A) with effect from 6 April 2001.

Para (*a*)(iii) inserted TCA 1997 s 519(8A)–(8B) with effect from 6 April 2001.

Para (*a*)(iv)(I) substituted "subsections (1) to (8B)" for "subsections (1) to (8)" in TCA 1997 s 519(9) with effect from 6 April 2001.

Para (*a*)(iv)(II) substituted "Schedule 11," for "Schedule 11, or" in TCA 1997 s 519(9) with effect from 6 April 2001.

Para (*a*)(iv)(III) inserted TCA 1997 s 519(9)(*ca*) with effect from 6 April 2001.

Para (*a*)(v) inserted TCA 1997 s 519(10) with effect from 6 April 2001.

Para (*b*)(i) inserted TCA 1997 Sch 12 para 12(2)(*da*) with effect from 6 April 2001.

Para (*b*)(ii) inserted TCA 1997 Sch 12 para 13(3)(*da*) with effect from 6 April 2001.

14 Amendment of Schedule 13 (accountable persons for purposes of Chapter 1 of Part 18) to Principal Act

Notes

Para (*a*) substituted "13. The Civil Service and Local Appointments Commissioners." for paragraph 13 in TCA 1997 Sch 13 with effect from 6 April 2001.

Para (*b*) substituted "42. Bord na Móna plc." for paragraph 42 in TCA 1997 Sch 13 with effect from 6 April 2001.

Para (*c*) deleted TCA 1997 Sch 13 paras 60 and 88 with effect from 6 April 2001.

Para (*d*) inserted TCA 1997 Sch 13 paras 104 to 120 with effect from 6 April 2001.

15 Approved share option schemes

Notes

Para (*a*) inserted TCA 1997 Pt 17 Ch 4 s 519D with effect from 30 March 2001.

Para (*b*) inserted TCA 1997 Sch 12C with effect from 30 March 2001.

Para (*c*) inserted "Schedule 12, paragraph 3(4)", "Schedule 12A, paragraph 6", "Schedule 12B, paragraph 5" and "Schedule 12C, paragraph 20" in TCA 1997 Sch 29 Col 2 with effect from 30 March 2001.

16 Amendment of provisions relating to employee share schemes

Notes

Para (*a*) substituted TCA 1997 Sch 11 para 4(1A)(*b*) as respects profit sharing schemes approved on or after 30 March 2001.
Para (*b*) substituted TCA 1997 Sch 12 para 2(2)(*b*) as respects employee share ownership trusts approved on or after 30 March 2001.
Para (*c*) substituted TCA 1997 Sch 12A para 3(3) as respects savings-related share option schemes approved on or after 30 March 2001.

17 Provisions relating to certain approved profit sharing schemes and employee share ownership trusts

Notes

Subs (1)(*a*)(i) inserted "or paragraph 11A, as the case may be," after "paragraph 11" in TCA 1997 s 511A(2)(*c*) as respects a profit sharing scheme or an employee share ownership trust approved on or after 12 December 2000.
Subs (1)(*a*)(ii) inserted "or paragraph 11A, as the case may be," after "paragraph 11" in TCA 1997 s 511A(5) as respects a profit sharing scheme or an employee share ownership trust approved on or after 12 December 2000.
Subs (1)(*b*)(i)(I) inserted ", having regard to subparagraph (1B)," after "subparagraph (1)" in TCA 1997 Sch 11 para 4 as respects a profit sharing scheme or an employee share ownership trust approved on or after 12 December 2000.
Subs (1)(*b*)(i)(II) inserted TCA 1997 Sch 11 para 4(1B) as respects a profit sharing scheme or an employee share ownership trust approved on or after 12 December 2000.
Subs (1)(*b*)(ii) inserted "or paragraph 11A, as the case may be," after "paragraph 11" in TCA 1997 Sch 11 para 12A(*b*) as respects a profit sharing scheme or an employee share ownership trust approved on or after 12 December 2000.
Subs (1)(*b*)(iii) inserted TCA 1997 Sch 11 para 13B as respects a profit sharing scheme or an employee share ownership trust approved on or after 12 December 2000.
Subs (1)(*c*)(i)(I) inserted TCA 1997 Sch 12 para 1(1) definition of "relevant company" as respects a profit sharing scheme or an employee share ownership trust approved on or after 12 December 2000.
Subs (1)(*c*)(i)(II) inserted TCA 1997 Sch 12 para 1(3A) as respects a profit sharing scheme or an employee share ownership trust approved on or after 12 December 2000.
Subs (1)(*c*)(ii) inserted TCA 1997 Sch 12 para 7A as respects a profit sharing scheme or an employee share ownership trust approved on or after 12 December 2000.
Subs (1)(*c*)(iii) inserted TCA 1997 Sch 12 para 11A as respects a profit sharing scheme or an employee share ownership trust approved on or after 12 December 2000.

18 Amendment of Part 30 (occupational pension schemes, retirement annuities, purchased life annuities and certain pensions) of Principal Act

Notes

Para (*a*)(i)(I) inserted TCA 1997 s 770(1) definition of "pension adjustment order" with effect from 6 April 2001.
Para (*a*)(i)(II) inserted TCA 1997 s 770(1) definition of "proprietary director" with effect from 6 April 2001.
Para (*a*)(i)(III) inserted TCA 1997 s 770(1) definition of "relevant date" with effect from 6 April 2001.
Para (*a*)(ii) substituted TCA 1997 s 772(3A)(i) with effect from 6 April 2001.
Para (*b*)(i) inserted TCA 1997 s 784(7) with effect from 6 April 2001.
Para (*b*)(ii) substituted "subsections (2) to (4)" for "subsections (2) and (4)" in TCA 1997 s 784E(6) with effect from 25 March 1999.
Para (*b*)(iii)(I) deleted TCA 1997 s 787(9) with effect from 6 April 2001.
Para (*b*)(iii)(II) substituted TCA 1997 s 787(10) with effect from 6 April 2001.
Para (*b*)(iii)(III) deleted TCA 1997 s 787(12) with effect from 6 April 2001.

19 Amendment of section 470 (relief for insurance against expenses of illness) of Principal Act

...

(2) Notwithstanding any other provision to the contrary, in relation to the year of assessment 2001 an individual shall be entitled to relief under section 470 of the Principal Act in respect of premiums paid to an authorised insurer under a relevant contract both in that year and in the year preceding that year of assessment.

Notes

Subs (1)(*a*)(i) substituted TCA 1997 s 470(1) definition of "relevant contract" for short tax "year" 2001 and later tax years.

Subs (1)(*a*)(ii) inserted TCA 1997 s 470(1) definition of "relievable amount" for short tax "year" 2001 and later tax years.

Subs (1)(*b*) substituted TCA 1997 s 470(2)–(3) and later tax years.

Subs (1)(*c*) inserted TCA 1997 s 470(5)–(6) and later tax years.

Subs (3) inserted "section 470 and Regulations under that section" after "section 121" in TCA 1997 Sch 29 col 1 with effect from 6 April 2001.

20 Relief for premiums under qualifying long-term care policies, etc

Notes

Para (*a*)(i) inserted "Section 470A" after "Section 470" in TCA 1997 s 458 (Table Pt 2) with effect from 6 April 2001.

Para (*a*)(ii) inserted TCA 1997 s 470A with effect from 6 April 2001.

Para (*b*) substituted TCA 1997 s 1024(2)(*a*)(vi) with effect from 6 April 2001.

Para (*c*) inserted "section 470A and Regulations under that section" in TCA 1997 Sch 29 col 1 with effect from 6 April 2001.

21 Taxation of certain perquisites

Notes

This section inserted TCA 1997 s 112A for short tax "year" 2001 and later tax years.

22 Amendment of Chapter 4 (revenue powers) of Part 38 of Principal Act

Notes

Subs (1) inserted TCA 1997 s 904E for short tax "year" 2001 and later tax years.

Subs (2)(*a*) substituted "€1,265" for "£1,000" in TCA 1997 s 904E(6) for 2002 and later tax years.

Subs (2)(*b*)(i) substituted "€19,045" for "£15,000" in TCA 1997 s 904E(7) for 2002 and later tax years.

Subs (2)(*b*)(ii) substituted "€2,535" for "£2,000" in TCA 1997 s 904E(7) for 2002 and later tax years.

Subs (3) inserted TCA 1997 s 904F for 2002 and later tax years.

Subs (4) inserted TCA 1997 ss 904G, 904H for short tax "year" 2001 and later tax years.

Subs (5)(*a*)(i) substituted "€1,265" for "£1,000" in TCA 1997 s 904G(6) for 2002 and later tax years.

Subs (5)(*a*)(ii)(I) substituted "€19,045" for "£15,000" in TCA 1997 s 904G(7) for 2002 and later tax years.

Subs (5)(*a*)(ii)(II) substituted "€2,535" for "£2,000" in TCA 1997 s 904G(7) for 2002 and later tax years.

Subs (5)(*b*)(i) substituted "€1,265" for "£1,000" in TCA 1997 s 904H(4) for 2002 and later tax years.

Subs (5)(*b*)(ii)(I) substituted "€19,045" for "£15,000" in TCA 1997 s 904H(5) for 2002 and later tax years.

Subs (5)(*b*)(ii)(II) substituted "€2,535" for "£2,000" in TCA 1997 s 904H(5) for 2002 and later tax years.

23 Tax relief at source for certain interest

Notes

Subs (1) inserted TCA 1997 s 244A for 2002 and later tax years.

Subs (2) inserted "section 244A and Regulations under that section" after "section 121" in TCA 1997 Sch 29 col 1 for 2002 and later tax years.

24 Provision of certain information: transitional

(1) In this section **"qualifying lender"** has the same meaning as in section 244A (inserted by this Act) of the Principal Act.

(2) (*a*) A qualifying lender shall, on receipt of a request from the Revenue Commissioners, furnish to them the information specified in paragraph (*b*) in relation to every individual having a loan or loans, secured by the mortgage of freehold or leasehold estate or interest in a dwelling, with that qualifying lender in the year of assessment 2001.

(*b*) The information referred to in paragraph (*a*) is as follows—

(i) the name and address of the individual, and

(ii) the account number of the qualifying lender relating to the loan or loans referred to in paragraph (*a*).

(3) The information referred to in subsection (2) shall be used by the Revenue Commissioners for the purpose of facilitating the granting of relief under section 244A of the Principal Act and shall not be used for any other purpose.

(4) The provisions of section 872 of the Principal Act shall not apply or have effect in relation to information acquired by the Revenue Commissioners under the provisions of this section.

25 Amendment of section 120A (exemption from benefit-in-kind of certain childcare facilities) of Principal Act

Notes

Para (*a*) substituted "service" for "service, or" in TCA 1997 s 120A definition of "qualifying premises" para (*b*), and inserted "or" after "service," in TCA 1997 s 120A definition of "qualifying premises" para (*c*), with effect from 6 April 2001.

Para (*b*) inserted TCA 1997 s 120A definition of "qualifying premises" para (*d*) with effect from 6 April 2001.

Para (*c*) inserted TCA 1997 s 120A(3) with effect from 6 April 2001.

26 Amendment of section 669A (interpretation (Chapter 3)) of Principal Act

Notes

This section substituted TCA 1997 s 669A definition of "qualifying quota" para (*b*) with effect from 6 April 2001.

27 Amendment of section 669C (effect of sale of quota) of Principal Act

Notes

This section substituted "chargeable period" for "accounting period" in TCA 1997 s 669C(2) with effect from 6 April 2001.

28 Amendment of section 530 (interpretation (Chapter 2)) of Principal Act

Notes

Para (*a*) inserted TCA 1997 s 530(1) definition of "certified subcontractor" with effect from 6 April 2001.

Para (*b*) inserted TCA 1997 s 530(1) definition of "uncertified subcontractor" with effect from 6 April 2001.

29 Relief for fees paid for third level education, etc

Notes

Subs (1) inserted TCA 1997 s 473A with effect from 6 April 2001.

Subs (2) deleted "section 474", "section 474A", "section 475" and "section 475A" from, and inserted "section 473A" in, TCA 1997 s 458 (Table Pt 2) with effect from 6 April 2001.

Subs (3) repealed TCA 1997 ss 474, 474A, 475 and 475A with effect from 6 April 2001.

30 Seafarer allowance, etc

Notes

Para (*a*)(i) substituted "125 days" and "£3,700" for "169 days" and "£5,000" in TCA 1997 s 472B(4) for short tax "year" 2001.

Para (*a*)(ii) substituted "€6,350" for "£5,000" in TCA 1997 s 472B(4) for 2002 and later tax years.

Para (*b*) inserted TCA 1997 s 472B(4A) with effect from 6 April 2001.

31 Amendment of section 823 (deduction for income earned outside the State) of Principal Act

Notes

Subs (1)(*a*)(i) substituted TCA 1997 s 823(1) definition of "qualifying day" with effect from 26 January 2001.

Subs (1)(*a*)(ii) substituted "270" for "365" in TCA 1997 s 823(1) definition of "the specified amount" formula for short tax "year" 2001.

Subs (1)(*b*)(i) inserted "or, in the case where subparagraph (i) applies and the year of assessment concerned is the year of assessment 2001, 67 days" in TCA 1997 s 823(3) with effect from 6 April 2001.

Subs (1)(*b*)(ii) substituted "£18,500" for "£25,000" in TCA 1997 s 823(3) for short tax "year" 2001.

32 Rent-a-room relief

Notes

Subs (1) inserted TCA 1997 s 216A with effect from 6 April 2001.

Subs (2)(*a*) substituted "€7,620" for "£6,000" in TCA 1997 s 216A(5) for 2002 and later tax years.

Subs (2)(*b*) deleted TCA 1997 s 216A(6) for 2002 and later tax years.

CHAPTER 3

Income Tax, Corporation Tax and Capital Gains Tax

33 Special savings incentive accounts

Notes

Subs (1) inserted TCA 1997 Pt 36A (ss 848B–848U) with effect from 6 April 2001.

Subs (2)(*a*)(i) substituted "€12.50" for "£10" in TCA 1997 s 848C(*c*)(i) for 2002 and later tax years.

Subs (2)(*a*)(ii) substituted "€254" for "£200" in TCA 1997 s 848C(*c*)(ii) for 2002 and later tax years.

Subs (2)(*a*)(iii) substituted "€1,900" for "£1,500" in TCA 1997 s 848T for 2002 and later tax years.

34 Amendment of section 97 (computational rules and allowable deductions) of Principal Act

Notes

Para (*a*)(i) substituted "1997," for "1997, or" in TCA 1997 s 97(2B)(*d*) with effect from 6 April 2001.
Para (*a*)(ii) substituted "during the year, or" for "during the year." in TCA 1997 s 97(2B)(*e*) with effect from 6 April 2001.
Para (*a*)(iii) inserted TCA 1997 s 97(2B)(*f*) with effect from 6 April 2001.
Para (*b*) inserted TCA 1997 s 97(2F) with effect from 6 April 2001.

35 Amendment of section 177 (conditions as to residence and period of ownership) of Principal Act

Notes

This section substituted TCA 1997 s 177(6) as respects a redemption, repayment or purchase of its own shares by a company to which TCA 1997 s 176 applies on or after 15 February 2001.

36 Amendment of section 198 (certain interest not to be chargeable) of Principal Act

Notes

Subs (1)(*a*) substituted "income tax or corporation tax, as is appropriate," for "corporation tax" in TCA 1997 s 198(1)(*a*) definition of "tax" as respects interest paid on or after 30 March 2001.
Subs (1)(*b*) substituted "person" for "company" in TCA 1997 s 198(1)(*b*) as respects interest paid on or after 30 March 2001.
Subs (1)(*c*) deleted "and" from TCA 1997 s 198(1)(*c*)(i) as respects interest paid on or after 30 March 2001.
Subs (1)(*d*) substituted "relevant territory," for "relevant territory." and inserted "and" in TCA 1997 s 198(1)(*c*)(ii)(II) as respects interest paid on or after 30 March 2001.
Subs (1)(*e*) inserted TCA 1997 s 198(1)(*c*)(iii) as respects interest paid on or after 30 March 2001.

37 Treatment of certain interest payments

Notes

Subs (1)(*a*)(i) inserted TCA 1997 s 243(1A) as respects interest paid on or after 30 March 2001.
Subs (1)(*a*)(ii)(I) deleted "or" from TCA 1997 s 243(5)(*a*)(I) as respects interest paid on or after 30 March 2001.
Subs (1)(*a*)(ii)(II) substituted TCA 1997 s 243(5)(*a*)(II) as respects interest paid on or after 30 March 2001.
Subs (1)(*b*)(i) substituted TCA 1997 s 246(1) definitions of "bank" for definitions of "a collective investment undertaking" and "collective investor" as respects interest paid on or after 30 March 2001.
Subs (1)(*b*)(ii) inserted TCA 1997 s 246(1) definition of "investment undertaking" and "relevant person" as respects interest paid on or after 30 March 2001.

38 Amendment of Part 20 (companies' chargeable gains) of Principal Act

Notes

Subs (1)(*a*) substituted TCA 1997 s 615(2) as respects a disposal on or after 15 February 2001.
Subs (1)(*b*)(i)(I) substituted TCA 1997 s 616(1)(*a*) with effect from 15 February 2001.
Subs (1)(*b*)(i)(II) substituted "State;" for "State." in TCA 1997 s 616(1)(*e*) with effect from 15 February 2001.
Subs (1)(*b*)(i)(III) inserted TCA 1997 s 616(1)(*f*) with effect from 15 February 2001.
Subs (1)(*b*)(ii) deleted "(although resident in the State)" from TCA 1997 s 616(2)(*b*)with effect from 15 February 2001.
Subs (1)(*c*) substituted TCA 1997 s 617(1) as respects a disposal on or after 15 February 2001.
Subs (1)(*d*)(i) substituted TCA 1997 s 618(1) as respects an acquisition or disposal on or after 15 February 2001.

Subs (1)(*d*)(ii) inserted "to which this section applies" in TCA 1997 s 618(2) as respects an acquisition or disposal on or after 15 February 2001.
Subs (1)(*d*)(iii) inserted TCA 1997 s 618(3) as respects an acquisition or disposal on or after 15 February 2001.
Subs (1)(*e*) substituted "in the course of a disposal to which section 617 applies" for "at a time when both were members of the group" in TCA 1997 s 619(1)–(2) as respects an acquisition on or after 15 February 2001.
Subs (1)(*f*) substituted TCA 1997 s 620 in relation to cases in which either the disposal or acquisition is on or after 15 February 2001 (any question of whether a company was, at the time of the acquisition or disposal corresponding to such disposal or acquisition a member of a group is determined in accordance with TCA 1997 s 616), or both the disposal and acquisition are on or after that date.
Subs (1)(*g*) inserted TCA 1997 s 620A with effect from 15 February 2001.
Subs (1)(*h*) substituted TCA 1997 s 621 definition of "a group of companies" as respects a case in which the depreciatory transaction (within the meaning of TCA 1997 s 621) is on or after 15 February 2001.
Subs (1)(*i*) substituted TCA 1997 s 623(2) as respects an asset acquired on or after 15 February 2001.
Subs (1)(*j*) substituted "a company which is not resident in a Member State of the European Communities" for "a company resident outside the State" in TCA 1997 s 624(5) with effect from 15 February 2001.
Subs (1)(*k*) substituted "a Member State of the European Communities" for "the State" in TCA 1997 s 629(1) definition of "group" with effect from 15 February 2001.

39 Amendment of section 590 (attribution to participants of chargeable gains accruing to non-resident company) of Principal Act

Notes

Subs (1)(*a*) substituted "section 617 (other than paragraphs (*b*) and (*c*) of subsection (1)), section 618 (with the omission of the words 'to which this section applies' in subsections (1)(*a*) and (2), of 'such' in subsection (1)(*c*) and of subsection (3)), section 619(2) (with the substitution for 'in the course of a disposal to which section 617 applies' of 'at a time when both were members of the group') and section 620(2) (with the omission of the words 'to which this section applies')" for "sections 617 to 620" in TCA 1997 s 590(16)(*b*)(i) for cases in which TCA 1997 s 617, 618, 619(2) or 620(2) as amended by FA 2001 apply.
Subs (1)(*b*) inserted "(apart from paragraphs (c) and (*d*) of subsection (2))" in TCA 1997 s 590(16)(*b*)(ii) for cases in which TCA 1997 s 617, 618, 619(2) or 620(2) as amended by FA 2001 apply.

40 Amendment of Schedule 18A (restriction on set-off of pre-entry losses) to Principal Act

Notes

Subs (1)(*a*) substituted "at the time immediately before the relevant event occurred in relation to it by a company which is or was" for "by a company at the time immediately before the company became" in TCA 1997 Sch 18A para 1(3) in relation to, where chargeable gains are to be included in a company's total profits, the amount to be included in respect of chargeable gains in the company's total profits for any accounting period ending on or after 15 February 2001, and in any other case, the amount on which a company is chargeable in accordance with s 31 for 2000–2001 and any later tax years. Where the question of whether a company was, at any time before 15 February 2001, a member of a group arises, it is determined by reference to TCA 1997 before its amendment by FA 2001.
Subs (1)(*b*) inserted TCA 1997 Sch 18A para 1(3A) in relation to where chargeable gains are to be included in a company's total profits, the amount to be included in respect of chargeable gains in the company's total profits for any accounting period ending on or after 15 February 2001, and in any other case, the amount on which a company is chargeable in accordance with s 31 for 2000–2001 and any later tax years. Where the question of whether a company was, at any time before15 February 2001, a member of a group arises, it is determined by reference to TCA 1997 before its amendment by FA 2001.
Subs (1)(*c*) substituted "the relevant event occurred in relation to it" for "the company became a member of the relevant group" in TCA 1997 Sch 18A para 1(4)(*a*) in relation to where chargeable gains are to be included in a company's total profits, the amount to be included in respect of chargeable gains in the company's total profits for any accounting period ending on or after 15 February 2001, and in any other case, the amount on which a company is chargeable in accordance with s 31 for 2000–2001 and any later tax years. Where the question of whether a company was, at any time before 15 February 2001, a member of a group arises, it is determined by reference to TCA 1997 before its amendment by FA 2001.

Subs (1)(*d*)(i) substituted "the relevant event occurred in relation to the company by reference to which that asset is a pre-entry asset" for "the company by reference to which the asset is a pre-entry asset became a member of the relevant group" in TCA 1997 Sch 18A para 1(5) in relation to where chargeable gains are to be included in a company's total profits, the amount to be included in respect of chargeable gains in the company's total profits for any accounting period ending on or after 15 February 2001, and in any other case, the amount on which a company is chargeable in accordance with s 31 for 2000–2001 and any later tax years. Where the question of whether a company was, at any time before 15 February 2001, a member of a group arises, it is determined by reference to TCA 1997 before its amendment by FA 2001.

Subs (1)(*d*)(ii) substituted "a relevant event has occurred in relation to a company" for "a company has become a member of the relevant group" in TCA 1997 Sch 18A para 1(5)(*a*) in relation to where chargeable gains are to be included in a company's total profits, the amount to be included in respect of chargeable gains in the company's total profits for any accounting period ending on or after 15 February 2001, and in any other case, the amount on which a company is chargeable in accordance with s 31 for 2000–2001 and any later tax years. Where the question of whether a company was, at any time before 15 February 2001, a member of a group arises, it is determined by reference to TCA 1997 before its amendment by FA 2001.

Subs (1)(*d*)(iii) substituted "a relevant event occurred in relation to a company" for "a company became a member of the relevant group" in TCA 1997 Sch 18A para 1(5)(*b*) in relation to where chargeable gains are to be included in a company's total profits, the amount to be included in respect of chargeable gains in the company's total profits for any accounting period ending on or after 15 February 2001, and in any other case, the amount on which a company is chargeable in accordance with s 31 for 2000–2001 and any later tax years. Where the question of whether a company was, at any time before 15 February 2001, a member of a group arises, it is determined by reference to TCA 1997 before its amendment by FA 2001.

41 Amendment of Schedule 24 (relief from income tax and corporation tax by means of credit in respect of foreign tax) to Principal Act

Notes

Subs (1)(*a*) substituted "Subject to paragraphs 9A, 9B and 9C, credit shall not be allowed" for "Credit shall not be allowed" in TCA 1997 Sch 24 para 3 as respects accounting periods ending on or after 15 February 2001.

Subs (1)(*b*) inserted "by any fraction" after "644B" in TCA 1997 Sch 24 para 4(4)(*e*) as respects accounting periods ending on or after 15 February 2001.

Subs (1)(*c*)(i) substituted "company falling within subparagraph (3A)" for "company resident in the State" in TCA 1997 Sch 24 para 9A(3) as respects accounting periods ending on or after 15 February 2001.

Subs (1)(*c*)(ii) inserted TCA 1997 Sch 24 para 9A(3A) as respects accounting periods ending on or after 15 February 2001.

Subs (1)(*c*)(iii) substituted "company falling within subparagraph (3A)" for "company resident in the State" in TCA 1997 Sch 24 para 9A(4)(*b*) as respects accounting periods ending on or after 15 February 2001.

Subs (1)(*d*)(i) substituted "a company falling within subparagraph (1A) (in this paragraph referred to as the 'relevant company')" for "an Irish company" and "the relevant company" for "the Irish company" in TCA 1997 Sch 24 para 9B(1) as respects accounting periods ending on or after 15 February 2001.

Subs (1)(*d*)(ii) inserted TCA 1997 Sch 24 para 9B(1A) as respects accounting periods ending on or after 15 February 2001.

Subs (1)(*d*)(iii) substituted "the relevant company" for "the Irish company" in TCA 1997 Sch 24 para 9B(2)–(3) as respects accounting periods ending on or after 15 February 2001.

Subs (1)(*d*)(iv) substituted "a relevant company" for "an Irish company" in TCA 1997 Sch 24 para 9B(4) as respects accounting periods ending on or after 15 February 2001.

Subs (1)(*d*)(v) deleted TCA 1997 Sch 24 para 9B(5) definition of "Irish company" as respects accounting periods ending on or after 15 February 2001.

Subs (1)(*e*) inserted TCA 1997 Sch 24 para 9C as respects accounting periods ending on or after 15 February 2001.

42 Amendment of section 89 (valuation of trading stock at discontinuance of trade) of Principal Act

Notes

Subs (1)(*a*) substituted TCA 1997 s 89(1)(*b*) with effect from 6 December 2000.

Subs (1)(*b*) substituted "the amount determined in accordance with subsections (3) and (4)" for "the price paid for such trading stock on such sale or the value of the consideration given for such trading stock on such transfer, as the case may be" in TCA 1997 s 89(2)(*a*) with effect from 6 December 2000.

Subs (1)(*c*) inserted TCA 1997 s 89(3)–(6) with effect from 6 December 2000.

43 Dividend withholding tax

Notes

Subs (1)(*a*)(i) inserted TCA 1997 s 172A(1)(*a*) definitions of "approved minimum retirement fund" and "approved retirement fund" with effect from 6 April 2001.

Subs (1)(*a*)(ii) inserted TCA 1997 s 172A(1)(*a*) definition of "qualifying fund manager" with effect from 6 April 2001.

Subs (1)(*a*)(iii) inserted TCA 1997 s 172A(1)(*a*) definition of "qualifying savings manager" with effect from 6 April 2001.

Subs (1)(*a*)(iv) inserted TCA 1997 s 172A(1)(*a*) definition of "special savings incentive account" with effect from 6 April 2001.

Subs (1)(*b*) inserted TCA 1997 s 172B(8) with effect from 6 April 2001.

Subs (1)(*c*)(i)(I) inserted ", but this paragraph is without prejudice to the operation of section 172B(8)" in TCA 1997 s 172C(2)(*a*) with effect from 6 April 2001.

Subs (1)(*c*)(i)(II) inserted TCA 1997 s 172C(2)(*ba*) with effect from 6 April 2001.

Subs (1)(*c*)(i)(III) inserted TCA 1997 s 172C(2)(*da*) with effect from 6 April 2001.

Subs (1)(*c*)(ii)(I) deleted "and" from TCA 1997 s 172C(3)(*a*) with effect from 6 April 2001.

Subs (1)(*c*)(ii)(II) inserted TCA 1997 s 172C(3)(*c*)–(*d*) with effect from 6 April 2001.

Subs (1)(*d*) deleted TCA 1997 s 172D(1) with effect from 6 April 2001.

Subs (1)(*e*) substituted "paragraph 9(*f*)" for "subparagraphs (*f*) and (*g*) of paragraph 9" in TCA 1997 s 172F(3)(*a*)(ii)(II) with effect from 6 April 2001.

Subs (2)(*a*) inserted TCA 1997 Sch 2A para 4A with effect from 6 April 2001.

Subs (2)(*b*) inserted TCA 1997 Sch 2A para 6A with effect from 6 April 2001.

44 Amendment of provisions relating to exploration and exploitation activities

Notes

Para (*a*) substituted TCA 1997 s 13(4) with effect from 6 April 2001.

Para (*b*) substituted TCA 1997 s 567(3) with effect from 6 April 2001.

Para (*c*) inserted TCA 1997 Sch 1 para 7 with effect from 6 April 2001.

45 Donations to approved bodies, etc

Notes

Subs (1) inserted TCA 1997 s 848A with effect from 6 April 2001.

Subs (2) substituted "section 848A(7)" for "section 485A(4)" in TCA 1997 s 458 (Table Pt 2) with effect from 6 April 2001.

Subs (3) substituted "€250" for "£200" in TCA 1997 s 848A(1)(*a*) in respect of a donation made on or after 1 January 2002.

Subs (4) inserted TCA 1997 Sch 26A with effect from 6 April 2001.

46 Amendment of section 665 (interpretation (Chapter 2)) of Principal Act

Notes

This section deleted the definition of "person" from TCA 1997 s 665 with effect from 6 April 2001.

47 Amendment of section 666 (deduction for increase in stock values) of Principal Act

Notes

Subs (1) substituted TCA 1997 s 666(4) from such date as the Minister for Finance may by order appoint.

48 Amendment of section 667 (special provisions for qualifying farmers) of Principal Act

Notes

Subs (1) substituted TCA 1997 s 667(2)(*b*)(ii) from such date as the Minister for Finance may by order appoint.

49 Amendment of section 668 (compulsory disposal of livestock) of Principal Act

Notes

This section substituted TCA 1997 s 668 definition of "stock to which this section applies" with effect from 6 April 2001.

50 Amendment of section 310 (allowances in respect of certain contributions to capital expenditure of local authorities) of Principal Act

Notes

Subs (1)(*a*) inserted TCA 1997 s 310 definition of "local authority" from such date as the Minister for Finance may by order appoint.

Subs (1)(*b*) substituted TCA 1997 s 310(2) from such date as the Minister for Finance may by order appoint.

Subs (1)(*c*) inserted TCA 1997 s 310(2A) from such date as the Minister for Finance may by order appoint.

51 Wear and tear allowances for licences for public hire vehicles

Notes

This section inserted TCA 1997 s 286A with effect from 6 April 1997.

52 Wear and tear allowances for certain sea fishing boats

Notes

Subs (1)(*a*) substituted "6 years" for "3 years" in TCA 1997 s 284(3A)(*a*) from such date as the Mininster for Finance may by order appoint.

Subs (1)(*b*) substituted "paragraph (*ba*) and subsection (4)" for "subsection (4)" in TCA 1997 s 284(3A)(*b*) from such date as the Mininster for Finance may by order appoint.

Subs (1)(*c*) inserted TCA 1997 s 284(3A)(*ba*) from such date as the Mininster for Finance may by order appoint.

Subs (1)(*d*) inserted "or in subparagraph (i) or (ii), as may be appropriate, of paragraph (*ba*)," in TCA 1997 s 284(3A)(*c*) from such date as the Mininster for Finance may by order appoint.

Subs (2) substituted "6 years" for "3 years" in TCA 1997 s 403(5A)(*b*)(ii) from such date as the Mininster for Finance may by order appoint.

53 Wear and tear allowances

Notes

Para (*a*) inserted "paragraph (*aa*) and" in TCA 1997 s 284(2)(*a*) as respects capital expenditure incurred on or after 1 January 2001.
Para (*b*) inserted TCA 1997 s 284(2)(*aa*) as respects capital expenditure incurred on or after 1 January 2001.
Para (*c*) inserted "or the amount specified in paragraph (*aa*)" in TCA 1997 s 284(2)(*b*) as respects capital expenditure incurred on or after 1 January 2001.

54 Amendment of section 274 (balancing allowances and balancing charges) of Principal Act

Notes

This section substituted "or that consideration; but this subsection shall not apply in the case of consideration of the type referred to in subsection (1)(*a*)(iv) which is received on or after 5 March 2001." for "or that consideration." in TCA 1997 s 274(3) with effect from 6 April 2001.

55 Amendment of Chapter 4 (interest payment by certain deposit takers) of Part 8 of Principal Act

Notes

Para (*a*)(i)(I) substituted TCA 1997 s 256(1) definition of "appropriate tax" with effect from 6 April 2000.
Para (*a*)(i)(II) substituted TCA 1997 s 256(1) definition of "appropriate tax" with effect from 6 April 2001.
Para (*a*)(ii) substituted TCA 1997 s 256(1) definition of "deposit" as respects a deposit made on or after 6 April 2001.
Para (*a*)(iii) substituted TCA 1997 s 256(1) definition of "interest" as respects a deposit made on or after 6 April 2001.
Para (*a*)(iv) substituted "on or after 1 January 1993 and before 6 April 2001" for "on or after the 1st day of January, 1993" in TCA 1997 s 256(1) definition of "special savings account" with effect from 6 April 2001.
Para (*b*) substituted ["Subsections (2) to (4)"] [1] for ["Subsections (2) and (4)"][1] in TCA 1997 s 258(9)(*c*) with effect from 6 April 1997.
Para (*c*) substituted "paragraph (*b*) of the definition" for "paragraph (*b*) or the definition" in TCA 1997 s 261(*c*)(i)(II) with effect from 6 April 2001.
Para (*d*) substituted "true and correct; but in the case of a company no such certificate shall be required where the declarer includes a written statement, as part of the declaration to the relevant deposit taker, confirming that the company has availed of the exemption under Part III of the Companies (Amendment) (No 2) Act, 1999" for "true and correct" in TCA 1997 s 265(2)(*e*) with effect from 6 April 2001.

Amendments

1 Substituted by FA 2002 s 138 and Sch 6 paras 5(*a*) and 6(*e*)(i) with effect on and from 30 March 2001; previously "Subsections 2 to 4" and "Subsections 2 and 4".

56 Amendment of section 838 (special portfolio investment accounts) of Principal Act

Notes

Para (*a*)(i) substituted "on or after 1 February 1993 and before 6 April 2001" for "on or after the 1st day of February, 1993" in TCA 1997 s 838(1) definition of "special portfolio investment account" with effect from 6 April 2001.
Para (*a*)(ii) deleted TCA 1997 s 838(1) definition of "relevant period" with effect from 6 April 2001.
Para (*b*)(i) deleted TCA 1997 s 838(2)(*c*) with effect from 6 April 2001.
Para (*b*)(ii) substituted "on or after 1 February 1996 and before 31 December 2000" for "on or after the 1st day of February, 1996" in TCA 1997 s 838(2)(*g*) with effect from 6 April 2001.

57 Taxation of certain savings in credit unions and other financial institutions

Notes

Subs (1)(*a*)(i)(I) substituted TCA 1997 s 256(1) definition of "appropriate tax" para (*a*) with effect from such date as the Minister for Finance may by order or orders appoint.

Subs (1)(*a*)(i)(II) inserted TCA 1997 s 256(1) definition of "credit union" with effect from such date as the Minister for Finance may by order or orders appoint.

Subs (1)(*a*)(i)(III) inserted TCA 1997 s 256(1) definitions of "long term account" and "medium term account" with effect from such date as the Minister for Finance may by order or orders appoint.

Subs (1)(*a*)(i)(IV) inserted TCA 1997 s 256(1) definition of "relevant deposit taker" para (*ca*) with effect from such date as the Minister for Finance may by order or orders appoint.

Subs (1)(*a*)(i)(V) substituted TCA 1997 s 256(1) definition of "relevant interest" with effect from such date as the Minister for Finance may by order or orders appoint.

Subs (1)(*a*)(i)(VI) substituted "deposit taker;" for "deposit taker." in TCA 1997 s 256(1) definition of "special savings account" with effect from such date as the Minister for Finance may by order or orders appoint.

Subs (1)(*a*)(i)(VII) inserted TCA 1997 s 256(1) definition of "special term account" with effect from such date as the Minister for Finance may by order or orders appoint.

Subs (1)(*a*)(ii) inserted TCA 1997 s 261A with effect from such date as the Minister for Finance may by order or orders appoint.

Subs (1)(*a*)(iii)(I) substituted "€480" for "£278" in TCA 1997 s 261A(2) for 2002 and later tax years.

Subs (1)(*a*)(iii)(II) substituted "€635" for "£370" in TCA 1997 s 261A(3) and (5) for 2002 and later tax years.

Subs (1)(*a*)(iv) inserted TCA 1997 ss 264A–264B with effect from such date as the Minister for Finance may by order or orders appoint.

Subs (1)(*a*)(v)(I) substituted "€635" for "£500" in TCA 1997 s 264A(1)(*l*) for 2002 and later tax years.

Subs (1)(*a*)(v)(II) substituted "€7,620" for "£6,000" in TCA 1997 s 264A(1)(*n*) for 2002 and later tax years.

Subs (1)(*a*)(vi) inserted Ch 5 (ss 267A–267F of Pt 8) with effect from such date as the Minister for Finance may by order or orders appoint.

Subs (1)(*a*)(vii)(I) substituted "€480" for "£278" in TCA 1997 s 267C(1) for 2002 and later tax years.

Subs (1)(*a*)(vii)(II) substituted "€635" for "£370" in TCA 1997 s 267C(2) and (4) for 2002 and later tax years.

Subs (1)(*a*)(viii)(I) substituted "€635" for "£500" in TCA 1997 s 267D(1)(*l*) for 2002 and later tax years.

Subs (1)(*a*)(viii)(II) substituted "€7,620" for "£6,000" in TCA 1997 s 267D(1)(*n*) for 2002 and later tax years.

Subs (1)(*b*) inserted "other than Chapter 5 of Part 8," in TCA 1997 s 700(1) with effect from such date as the Minister for Finance may by order or orders appoint.

Subs (1)(*c*)(i) inserted "section 264B" and "section 267E" in TCA 1997 Sch 29 col 2 with effect from such date as the Minister for Finance may by order or orders appoint.

Subs (1)(*c*)(ii) inserted "section 267B" in TCA 1997 Sch 29 col 3 with effect from such date as the Minister for Finance may by order or orders appoint.

58 Amendment of Chapter 9 (park and ride facilities and certain related developments) of Part 10 of Principal Act

Notes

Para (*a*)(i) substituted "subsections (2) to (4A)" for "subsections (2) to (4)" in TCA 1997 s 372V(1)(*a*) with effect from 6 April 2001.

Para (*a*)(ii)(I) inserted "or, where subsection (4A) applies, first used as a qualifying park and ride facility," in TCA 1997 s 372V(4)(*a*) with effect from 6 April 2001.

Para (*a*)(ii)(II) substituted "qualifying park and ride facility" for "park and ride facility" in TCA 1997 s 372V(4)(*b*) with effect from 6 April 2001.

Para (*a*)(iii) inserted TCA 1997 s 372V(4A) with effect from 6 April 2001.

Para (*b*)(i)(I) deleted "and" from TCA 1997 s 372W(1)(*a*) with effect from 6 April 2001.

Para (*b*)(i)(II) substituted TCA 1997 s 372W(1)(*c*) with effect from 6 April 2001.

Para (*b*)(ii) substituted "subsections (3) to (5A)" for "subsections (3) to (5)" in TCA 1997 s 372W(2)(*a*) with effect from 6 April 2001.

Para (*b*)(iii) inserted "or, where subsection (5A) applies, first used as a qualifying premises" in TCA 1997 s 372W(5)(*a*) with effect from 6 April 2001.

Para (v)(iv) inserted TCA 1997 s 372W(5A) with effect from 6 April 2001.

59 Amendment of Part 10 (income tax and corporation tax: reliefs for renewal and improvement of certain urban areas, certain resort areas and certain islands) of Principal Act

Notes

Subs (1)(*a*) substituted "31 December 2001" for "31 December 2000" and "30 September 2001" for "30 September 2000" in TCA 1997 s 344(1) definition of "qualifying period" para (*c*) with effect from 6 April 2000.

Subs (1)(*b*)(i) substituted "paragraph (*b*)" for "paragraph (i)" in TCA 1997 s 372M(3)(*b*) with effect from 6 April 2001.

Subs (1)(*b*)(ii) substituted "175 square metres" for "140 square metres" in TCA 1997 s 372P(1) definition of "qualifying premises" para (*c*) as respects expenditure incurred on or after 6 December 2000, which is expenditure on the construction of a qualifying premises as defined in TCA 1997 s 372P.

Subs (1)(*b*)(iii) substituted "175 square metres" for "150 square metres" in TCA 1997 s 372Q(1) definition of "qualifying premises" para (*b*) as respects expenditure incurred on or after 6 December 2000, which is conversion expenditure within the meaning of TCA 1997 s 372Q.

Subs (1)(*b*)(iv) substituted "175 square metres" for "150 square metres" in TCA 1997 s 372R(1) definition of "qualifying premises" para (*b*) as respects expenditure incurred on or after 6 December 2000, which is relevant expenditure within the meaning of TCA 1997 s 372R.

Subs (1)(*b*)(v) inserted TCA 1997 s 372T(1)(*aa*) with effect from 6 April 2001.

60 Living over the shop scheme

Notes

Para (*a*)(i)(I) inserted TCA 1997 s 372A(1) definition of "existing building" with effect from 6 April 2001.

Para (*a*)(i)(II) inserted TCA 1997 s 372A(1) definition of "necessary construction" with effect from 6 April 2001.

Para (*a*)(i)(III) substituted TCA 1997 s 372A(1) definition of "qualifying period" with effect from 6 April 2001.

Para (*a*)(i)(IV) inserted TCA 1997 s 372A(1) definition of "qualifying street" with effect from 6 April 2001.

Para (*a*)(i)(V) substituted "the building or structure;" for "the building or structure." in TCA 1997 s 372A(1) definition of "refurbishment" with effect from 6 April 2001.

Para (*a*)(i)(VI) inserted TCA 1997 s 372A(1) definitions of "replacement building", "relevant local authority" and "street" with effect from 6 April 2001.

Para (*a*)(ii) inserted "in relation to qualifying areas" in TCA 1997 s 372A(2) with effect from 6 April 2001.

Para (*b*) inserted "in respect of the construction, refurbishment or converstion of a building, structure or house, the site of which is wholly within a qualifying area," in TCA 1997 s 372B(4) with effect from 6 April 2001.

Para (*c*) inserted TCA 1997 s 372BA with effect from 6 April 2001.

Para (*d*)(i) inserted ", or which fronts on to a qualifying street," in TCA 1997 s 372D(1) with effect from 6 April 2001.

Para (*d*)(ii) inserted TCA 1997 s 372D(3A) with effect from 6 April 2001.

Para (*e*)(i) inserted ", or which fronts on to a qualifying street" in TCA 1997 s 372F(1) definition of "qualifying premises" para (*a*) with effect from 6 April 2001.

Para (*e*)(ii) inserted "the site of which is wholly within a qualifying area, or on the necessary construction of a qualifying premises which fronts on to a qualifying street" in TCA 1997 s 372F(2) with effect from 6 April 2001.

Para (*f*) inserted ", or which fronts on to a qualifying street" after "qualifying area" in TCA 1997 s 372G(1) definition of "conversion expenditure" paras (*a*)(i) and (*b*)(i) with effect from 6 April 2001.

Para (*g*) inserted ", or which fronts on to a qualifying street" after "qualifying area" in TCA 1997 s 372H(1) definition of "specified building" para (*a*) with effect from 6 April 2001.

Para (*h*)(i)(I) substituted "local authority; but in the case of a qualifying premises which fronts on to a qualifying street or which is comprised in a building or part of a building which fronts on to a qualifying street, this definition shall apply as if the reference to 'construction' were a reference to 'necessary construction'" for "local authority" in TCA 1997 s 372I(1) definition of "qualifying expenditure" with effect from 6 April 2001.

Para (*h*)(i)(II) inserted ", or which fronts on to a qualifying street or which is comprised in a building or part of a building which fronts on to a qualifying street" after "qualifying area" in TCA 1997 s 372I(1) definition of "qualifying premises" para (*a*) with effect from 6 April 2001.

Para (*h*)(ii) substituted TCA 1997 s 372I(2)(*a*)(i) with effect from 6 April 2001.
Para (*i*) inserted TCA 1997 s 372J(5A) with effect from 6 April 2001.
Para (*j*) inserted TCA 1997 s 372K(1)(*aa*) with effect from 6 April 2001.

61 Amendment of Part 11 (capital allowances and expenses for certain road vehicles) of Principal Act

Notes

Subs (1)(*a*)(i) substituted "mechanically propelled vehicle;" for "mechanically propelled vehicle." in TCA 1997 s 373(2)(*l*) with effect from 6 April 2001.
Subs (1)(*a*)(ii) inserted TCA 1997 s 373(2)(*m*) with effect from 6 April 2001.
Subs (1)(*a*)(iii) substituted "€21,585.55" for "£17,000" in TCA 1997 s 373(2)(*m*) for 2002 and later tax years.
Subs (1)(*b*)(i) inserted TCA 1997 s 376(1) definition of "basis period" with effect from 6 April 2001.
Subs (1)(*b*)(ii)(I) substituted "£16,500," for "£16,500;" in TCA 1997 s 376(1) definition of "relevant amount" with effect from 6 April 2001.
Subs (1)(*b*)(ii)(II) inserted TCA 1997 s 376(1) definition of "relevant amount" para (*f*) with effect from 6 April 2001.
Subs (1)(*b*)(ii)(III) substituted "€21,585.55" for "£17,000" in TCA 1997 s 376(1) definition of "relevant amount" for 2002 and later tax years.
Subs (1)(*c*) substituted TCA 1997 s 376(2) for expenditure incurred in an accounting period ending on or after 1 January 2001, or in a basis period for 2000–2001 or a later tax year, where that basis period ends on or after 1 January 2001.

62 Amendment of provisions relating to treatment of certain losses and certain capital allowances

Notes

Subs (1)(*a*)(i)(I) substituted "Subject to subsections (2) and (3)" for "Subject to subsection (2)" in TCA 1997 s 405(1) with effect from 6 April 2001.
Subs (1)(*a*)(i)(II) substituted TCA 1997 s 405(1)(*a*) with effect from 6 April 2001.
Subs (1)(*a*)(ii) inserted TCA 1997 s 405(3) with effect from 6 April 2001.
Subs (1)(*b*) substituted TCA 1997 s 406 with effect from 6 April 2001.
Subs (1)(*c*)(i)(I) substituted TCA 1997 s 409A(2) as respects an allowance to be made for short tax "year" 2001 and later tax years.
Subs (1)(*c*)(i)(II) substituted "€31,750" for "£18,500" in TCA 1997 s 409A(2) as respects an allowance to be made for short tax "year" 2002 and later tax years.
Subs (1)(*c*)(ii)(I) substituted "£18,500" for "£25,000" in TCA 1997 s 409A(3) as respects an allowance to be made for short tax "year" 2001.
Subs (1)(*c*)(ii)(II) substituted "€31,750" for "£18,500" in TCA 1997 s 409A(3) as respects an allowance to be made for short tax "year" 2002 and later tax years.
Subs (2) repealed FA 2000 s 40(*e*)–(*f*) with effect from 6 April 2001.

63 Relief for certain rented accommodation

Notes

This section inserted Part 11B (ss 380G–380J) with effect from 6 April 2001.

64 Capital allowances for certain hospitals

Notes

Subs (1)(*a*)(i)(I) deleted "or," from TCA 1997 s 268(1)(*h*) from such date as the Minister for Finance may by order appoint.
Subs (1)(*a*)(i)(II) substituted "that Act, or" for "that Act." in TCA 1997 s 268(1)(*i*) from such date as the Minister for Finance may by order appoint.

Subs (1)(*a*)(i)(III) inserted TCA 1997 s 268(1)(*j*) from such date as the Minister for Finance may by order appoint.
Subs (1)(*a*)(ii) inserted TCA 1997 s 268(2A) from such date as the Minister for Finance may by order appoint.
Subs (1)(*a*)(iii)(I) deleted "and" from TCA 1997 s 268(9)(*e*) from such date as the Minister for Finance may by order appoint.
Subs (1)(*a*)(iii)(II) substituted "1998, and" for "1998." in TCA 1997 s 268(9)(*f*) from such date as the Minister for Finance may by order appoint.
Subs (1)(*a*)(iii)(III) inserted TCA 1997 s 268(9)(*g*) from such date as the Minister for Finance may by order appoint.
Subs (1)(*b*)(i)(I) deleted "and" from TCA 1997 s 272(3)(*f*) from such date as the Minister for Finance may by order appoint.
Subs (1)(*b*)(i)(II) substituted "subsection (2)(*c*), and" for "subsection (2)(*c*)." in TCA 1997 s 272(3)(*g*) from such date as the Minister for Finance may by order appoint.
Subs (1)(*b*)(i)(III) inserted TCA 1997 s 272(3)(*h*) from such date as the Minister for Finance may by order appoint.
Subs (1)(*b*)(ii)(I) deleted "and" from TCA 1997 s 272(4)(*f*) from such date as the Minister for Finance may by order appoint.
Subs (1)(*b*)(ii)(II) substituted "1998," for "1998." in TCA 1997 s 272(4)(*g*)(ii)(II) from such date as the Minister for Finance may by order appoint.
Subs (1)(*b*)(ii)(III) inserted TCA 1997 s 272(4)(*h*) from such date as the Minister for Finance may by order appoint.
Subs (1)(*c*)(i) deleted "and" from TCA 1997 s 274(1)(*b*)(v)(II) from such date as the Minister for Finance may by order appoint.
Subs (1)(*c*)(ii) substituted "1998," for "1998." in TCA 1997 s 274(1)(*b*)(vi)(II)(B) from such date as the Minister for Finance may by order appoint.
Subs (1)(*c*)(iii) inserted TCA 1997 s 274(1)(*b*)(vii) from such date as the Minister for Finance may by order appoint.

65 Amendment of section 420 (losses, etc which may be surrendered by means of group relief) of Principal Act

Notes

Subs (1) substituted TCA 1997 s 420(1) as respects accounting periods commencing on or after 1 January 1999.

66 Amendment of section 594 (foreign life assurance and deferred annuities: taxation and returns) of Principal Act

Notes

Subs (1)(*a*)(i) deleted ", on or after the 20th day of May, 1993" from TCA 1997 s 594(1)(*c*)(ii) with effect from 20 March 2001.
Subs (1)(*a*)(ii) inserted TCA 1997 s 594(1)(*c*)(iii)–(v) with effect from 20 March 2001.
Subs (1)(*a*)(iii) inserted TCA 1997 s 594(2)(*g*) with effect from 20 March 2001.
Subs (1)(*b*) deleted TCA 1997 s 594(3) in respect of any chargeable period (within the meaning of s 321(2)) commencing on or after 15 February 2001
Subs (1)(*c*) substituted TCA 1997 s 594(4)(*a*) with effect from 1 January 2001.

67 Amendment of Part 26 (life assurance companies) of Principal Act

Notes

This section inserted Part 26 Ch 6 (ss 730H–730K) with effect from 1 January 2001.

68 Amendment of section 723 (special investment policies) of Principal Act

Notes

Subs (1)(*a*) deleted TCA 1997 s 723(1) definition of "relevant period" with effect from 1 January 2001.
Subs (1)(*b*) substituted TCA 1997 s 723(2)(*g*) with effect from 1 January 2001.

Subs (1)(*c*) deleted TCA 1997 s 723(3)(*c*) with effect from 1 January 2001.

69 Amendment of section 730A (profits of life business: new basis) of Principal Act

Notes

Subs (1)(*a*)(i) substituted TCA 1997 s 730A(1) definition of "new basis business" para (*a*)(i) with effect from 1 January 2001.

Subs (1)(*a*)(ii) substituted "from the time it began to carry on life business;" for "from the time it began to carry on life business." in TCA 1997 s 730A(1) definition of "new basis business" para (*c*) with effect from 1 January 2001.

Subs (1)(*b*) inserted TCA 1997 s 730A(1) definition of "sinking fund or capital redemption business" with effect from 1 January 2001.

Subs (1)(*c*) inserted TCA 1997 s 730A(6)–(8) with effect from 1 January 2001.

70 Amendment of Chapter 5 (policyholders — new basis) of Part 26 of Principal Act

Notes

Subs (1)(*a*) substituted TCA 1997 s 730B(2) with effect from 1 January 2001[1].

Subs (1)(*b*) substituted TCA 1997 s 730C with effect from 15 February 2001[1].

Subs (1)(*c*)(i) substituted TCA 1997 s 730D(2) with effect from 1 January 2001[1].

Subs (1)(*c*)(ii) substituted TCA 1997 s 730D(4)(*a*) with effect from 1 January 2001[1].

Subs (1)(*d*)(i)(I) substituted "section 730D(2)(*a*)" for "section 730D(2)(*a*)(i)" in TCA 1997 s 730E(2) with effect from 1 January 2001[1].

Subs (1)(*d*)(i)(II) substituted TCA 1997 s 730E(2)(*a*) with effect from 1 January 2001[1].

Subs (1)(*d*)(i)(III) substituted TCA 1997 s 730E(2)(*d*) with effect from 1 January 2001[1].

Subs (1)(*d*)(ii) TCA 1997 s 730E(3) and inserted TCA 1997 s 730E(3A) with effect from 1 January 2001[1].

Subs (1)(*e*) substituted "Subsections (2) to (4)" for "Subsections (2) and (4)" in TCA 1997 s 730G(7)(*c*) with effect from 1 January 2001[1].

Subs (1)(*f*) inserted TCA 1997 ss 730GA–730GB with effect from 1 January 2001[1].

Amendments

1 FA 2002 s 138 and Sch 6 paras 5(*b*) and 6(*e*)(i) substituted "Subsection (1) shall" for "This section shall" in FA 2001 s 70(2) with effect from 30 March 2001.

71 Amendment of section 731 (chargeable gains accruing to unit trusts) of Principal Act

Notes

Subs (1)(*a*) substituted "all the issued units in a unit trust which neither is, nor is deemed to be, an authorised unit trust scheme (within the meaning of the Unit Trusts Act, 1990)" for "all the issued units in a unit trust" in TCA 1997 s 731(5)(*a*) with effect from 1 January 2001[1].

Subs (1)(*b*) inserted TCA 1997 s 731(5)(*c*) for 2000–01 and later tax years[1].

Amendments

1 FA 2002 s 138 and Sch 6 paras 5(*c*) and 6(*e*)(i) substituted "Subsection (1) shall" for "This section shall" in FA 2001 s 71(2) with effect from 30 March 2001.

72 Amendment of Part 27 (unit trusts and offshore funds) of Principal Act

Notes

Subs (1) inserted Part 27 Ch 3 (ss 747B–747E) with effect from 1 January 2001.

73 Amendment of section 737 (special investment schemes) of Principal Act

Notes

Subs (1)(*a*) deleted TCA 1997 s 737(1) definition of "relevant period" with effect from 1 January 2001.

Subs (1)(*b*) substituted TCA 1997 s 737(2)(*a*)(v) with effect from 1 January 2001.

Subs (1)(*c*) deleted TCA 1997 s 737(3)(*a*)(iii) with effect from 1 January 2001.

74 Amendment of Chapter 1A (investment undertakings) of Part 27 of Principal Act

Notes

Subs (1)(*a*)(i)(I)(A) deleted "other than a payment made on the death of a unit holder" from TCA 1997 s 739B(1) definition of "chargeable event" para (*b*) with effect from 15 February 2001.

Subs (1)(*a*)(i)(I)(B) deleted "(other than as a result of the death of the unit holder)" from TCA 1997 s 739B(1) definition of "chargeable event" para (*c*) with effect from 15 February 2001.

Subs (1)(*a*)(i)(I)(C) substituted TCA 1997 s 739B(1) definition of "chargeable event" para (A)–(B) with effect from 15 February 2001.

Subs (1)(*a*)(i)(II) inserted TCA 1997 s 739B(1) definition of "qualifying savings manager" with effect from 15 February 2001.

Subs (1)(*a*)(i)(III) inserted TCA 1997 s 739B(1) definition of "special savings incentive account" with effect from 15 February 2001.

Subs (1)(*a*)(ii) substituted TCA 1997 s 739B(3) with effect from 1 April 2000.

Subs (1)(*b*)(i) substituted TCA 1997 s 739D(1)(*a*) with effect from 1 April 2000.

Subs (1)(*b*)(ii) substituted TCA 1997 s 739D(3)–(5) with effect from 1 April 2000.

Subs (1)(*b*)(iii) substituted TCA 1997 s 739D(6)(*h*) with effect from 1 April 2000.

Subs (1)(*b*)(iv) inserted TCA 1997 s 739D(7A) with effect from 1 April 2000.

Subs (1)(*b*)(v) substituted TCA 1997 s 739D(8) and inserted TCA 1997 s 739D(8A)–(8D) with effect from 1 April 2000.

Subs (1)(*b*)(vi) substituted "A gain shall not be treated as arising to an investment undertaking on the happening of a chargeable event in respect of a unit holder" for "A gain shall not be treated as arising to an investment undertaking on the happening of a chargeable event in respect of a unit holder who is an intermediary" in TCA 1997 s 739D(9) with effect from 1 April 2000.

Subs (1)(*b*)(vii) substituted TCA 1997 s 739D(10) with effect from 1 April 2000.

Subs (1)(*c*) substituted TCA 1997 s 739F(5) with effect from 1 April 2000.

Subs (1)(*d*) substituted TCA 1997 s 739F(7)(*c*) with effect from 1 April 2000.

Subs (1)(*e*)(i)(I) substituted TCA 1997 s 739G(2)(*b*) with effect from 1 April 2000.

Subs (1)(*e*)(i)(II) substituted TCA 1997 s 739G(2)(*e*)–(*f*) with effect from 1 April 2000.

Subs (1)(*e*)(i)(III) substituted "chargeable to income tax," for "chargeable to income tax, and" in TCA 1997 s 739G(2)(*h*) with effect from 1 April 2000.

Subs (1)(*e*)(i)(IV) substituted TCA 1997 s 739G(2)(*i*) and inserted TCA 1997 s 739G(2)(*j*) with effect from 1 April 2000.

Subs (1)(*e*)(ii) inserted TCA 1997 s 739G(3)–(5) with effect from 1 April 2000.

Amendments

1 FA 2002 s 138 and Sch 6 paras 5(*d*) and 6(*e*)(i) substituted "Subsection (1) shall" for "This section shall" in FA 2001 s 74(2) with effect from 30 March 2001.

75 Amendment of Schedule 2B (investment undertakings declarations) of Principal Act

Notes

This section substituted TCA 1997 Sch 2B para 9 with effect from 6 April 2001.

76 Amendment of section 843 (capital allowances for buildings used for third level educational purposes) of Principal Act

Notes

Subs (1)(*a*)(i)(I) substituted "applies, or" for "applies;" in TCA 1997 s 843(1) definition of "approved institution" with effect from 6 April 2001.

Subs (1)(*a*)(i)(II) inserted TCA 1997 s 843(1) definition of "approved institution" para (*c*) with effect from 6 April 2001.

Subs (1)(*a*)(ii) substituted from "which, following" to the end of the definition of "qualifying expenditure" in TCA 1997 s 843(1) with effect from 6 April 2001.

Subs (1)(*a*)(iii) inserted "or associated sporting or leisure activities" in TCA 1997 s 843(1) definition of "qualifying premises" para (*b*)(i) as respects capital expenditure incurred on or after 1 October 1999.

Subs (1)(*b*) inserted "or, in the case of the construction of a qualifying premises which consists of a building or structure which is to be used for the purposes of sporting or leisure activities associated with third level education provided by an approved institution where in relation to that premises an application for certification under this subsection was made, and the construction of that premises commenced, prior to 15 February 2001, before 1 July 2001," in TCA 1997 s 843(4) with effect from 6 April 2001.

Subs (1)(*c*)(i) substituted "paragraph (i) of the definition of 'qualifying expenditure'" for "the definition of 'qualifying expenditure'" in TCA 1997 s 843(8)(*a*) with effect from 6 April 2001.

Subs (1)(*c*)(ii) inserted "in so far as that expenditure is concerned," before "on the Minister for Finance" in TCA 1997 s 843(8)(*b*) with effect from 6 April 2001.

Subs (1)(*c*)(iii) substituted "either generally in the case of institutions referred to in paragraphs (*a*) and (*b*) of the definition of 'approved institution' or in respect of capital expenditure to be incurred on any particular type of qualifying premises to be used by any such institution" for "either generally or in respect of capital expenditure to be incurred on any particular type of qualifying premises" in TCA 1997 s 843(8) with effect from 6 April 2001.

Subs (1)(*c*)(iv) inserted ", then, as respects the matters so delegated" in TCA 1997 s 843(8) with effect from 6 April 2001.

Subs (1)(*c*)(v) substituted TCA 1997 s 843(8)(I) with effect from 6 April 2001.

77 Changeover to calendar year of assessment

...

(2) The Principal Act is amended in the manner and to the extent specified in Schedule 2.

Notes

Subs (1)(*a*) substituted TCA 1997 s 2(1) definition of "year of assessment" with effect from 6 April 2001.

Subs (1)(*b*) substituted TCA 1997 s 5(1) definition of "year of assessment" with effect from 6 April 2001.

Subs (1)(*c*) substituted TCA 1997 s 14(2) with effect from 6 April 2001.

78 Provisions relating to making of returns of income and chargeable gains and payment of income tax and capital gains tax

Notes

Subs (1)(*a*)(i) substituted TCA 1997 s 950(1) definition of "chargeable person" para (*a*) for short tax "year" 2001 and later tax years for income tax and capital gains tax and for accounting periods of companies ending on or after 1 April 2001.

Subs (1)(*a*)(ii) substituted TCA 1997 s 950(1) definition of "specified return date for the chargeable period" para (*a*) for short tax "year" 2001 and later tax years for income tax and capital gains tax and for accounting periods of companies ending on or after 1 April 2001.

Subs (1)(*b*)(i)(I) substituted "Every chargeable person shall as respects a chargeable period prepare and deliver to, in the case of a chargeable person who is chargeable to income tax or capital gains tax for a chargeable period which is a year of assessment, the Collector-General and, in any other case, the appropriate inspector" for "Every chargeable person shall as respects a chargeable period prepare and deliver to the appropriate inspector"

in TCA 1997 s 951(1) for short tax "year" 2001 and later tax years for income tax and capital gains tax and for accounting periods of companies ending on or after 1 April 2001.
Subs (1)(*b*)(i)(II) inserted "(including particulars relating to the preceding year of assessment where the profits or gains of that preceding year are determined in accordance with section 65(3))" in TCA 1997 s 951(1) for short tax "year" 2001 and later tax years for income tax and capital gains tax and for accounting periods of companies ending on or after 1 April 2001.
Subs (1)(*b*)(ii) substituted "Collector-General" for "appropriate inspector" and "the appropriate inspector" for "the inspector" in TCA 1997 s 951(2) for short tax "year" 2001 and later tax years for income tax and capital gains tax and for accounting periods of companies ending on or after 1 April 2001.
Subs (1)(*b*)(iii) substituted "the Collector-General or an inspector, as the case may be" for "an inspector" in TCA 1997 s 951(3)(*a*) for short tax "year" 2001 and later tax years for income tax and capital gains tax and for accounting periods of companies ending on or after 1 April 2001.
Subs (1)(*b*)(iv) substituted "the Collector-General or the appropriate inspector, as the case may be," for "appropriate inspector" in TCA 1997 s 951(4) for short tax "year" 2001 and later tax years for income tax and capital gains tax and for accounting periods of companies ending on or after 1 April 2001.
Subs (1)(*b*)(v)(I) substituted "an officer of the Revenue Commissioners" for "an inspector" in TCA 1997 s 951(10) for short tax "year" 2001 and later tax years for income tax and capital gains tax and for accounting periods of companies ending on or after 1 April 2001.
Subs (1)(*b*)(v)(II) substituted "such officer" for "that inspector" in TCA 1997 s 951(10) for short tax "year" 2001 and later tax years for income tax and capital gains tax and for accounting periods of companies ending on or after 1 April 2001.
Subs (1)(*c*)(i) deleted TCA 1997 s 952(3) for short tax "year" 2001 and later tax years for income tax and capital gains tax and for accounting periods of companies ending on or after 1 April 2001.
Subs (1)(*c*)(ii) inserted TCA 1997 s 953(6) for short tax "year" 2001 and later tax years for income tax and capital gains tax and for accounting periods of companies ending on or after 1 April 2001.
Subs (1)(*d*) deleted TCA 1997 s 953(1)–(6) and (8)–(11) for short tax "year" 2001 and later tax years for income tax and capital gains tax and for accounting periods of companies ending on or after 1 April 2001.
Subs (1)(*e*) deleted TCA 1997 s 957(1)(*a*) for short tax "year" 2001 and later tax years for income tax and capital gains tax and for accounting periods of companies ending on or after 1 April 2001.
Subs (1)(*f*)(i) deleted TCA 1997 s 958 definition of "specified due date" for short tax "year" 2001 and later tax years for income tax and capital gains tax and for accounting periods of companies ending on or after 1 April 2001.
Subs (1)(*f*)(ii) substituted TCA 1997 s 958(2)–(4A) for short tax "year" 2001 and later tax years for income tax and capital gains tax and for accounting periods of companies ending on or after 1 April 2001.
Subs (1)(*f*)(iii) inserted TCA 1997 s 958(8A) for short tax "year" 2001 and later tax years for income tax and capital gains tax and for accounting periods of companies ending on or after 1 April 2001.
Subs (1)(*f*)(iv) substituted TCA 1997 s 958(10) for short tax "year" 2001 and later tax years for income tax and capital gains tax and for accounting periods of companies ending on or after 1 April 2001.
Subs (1)(*g*) deleted "a notice of preliminary tax bearing the name of the inspector or" and "that notice of preliminary tax shall for the purposes of the Tax Acts and the Capital Gains Tax Acts be deemed to have been given by the inspector to the best of his or her opinion," from TCA 1997 s 959(2) for short tax "year" 2001 and later tax years for income tax and capital gains tax and for accounting periods of companies ending on or after 1 April 2001.
Subs (2)(*a*) substituted "on including a claim in that behalf with the return required under section 951 for the year of assessment" for "on giving notice in writing to the inspector with the return required under section 951 for the year of assessment" in TCA 1997 s 66(3) for short tax "year" 2001 and later tax years for income tax and capital gains tax and for accounting periods of companies ending on or after 1 April 2001.
Subs (2)(*b*) substituted "when a return under section 951 for the chargeable period is delivered to the Collector-General" for "when a return under section 951 for the chargeable period is delivered to the appropriate inspector (within the meaning of section 950)" in TCA 1997 s 579D(1) and in TCA 1997 s 629(1) definition of "specified period" for short tax "year" 2001 and later tax years for income tax and capital gains tax and for accounting periods of companies ending on or after 1 April 2001.
Subs (2)(*c*) substituted "on including a claim in that behalf with the return required under section 951 for the year of assessment" for "by notice in writing given to the inspector with the return required under section 951 for the year of assessment" in TCA 1997 s 657(7) for short tax "year" 2001 and later tax years for income tax and capital gains tax and for accounting periods of companies ending on or after 1 April 2001.
Subs (2)(*d*) substituted "any return, statement, list or declaration" for "a return or statement of income or profits" in TCA 1997 s 894(1) definition of "appropriate inspector" for short tax "year" 2001 and later tax years for income tax and capital gains tax and for accounting periods of companies ending on or after 1 April 2001.

Subs (2)(*e*) substituted "to deliver a return, statement, declaration or list by reason of a notice given to the person by the inspector" for "to deliver a return or statement of income or profits" in TCA 1997 s 895(1) definition of "appropriate inspector" para (*a*) for short tax "year" 2001 and later tax years for income tax and capital gains tax and for accounting periods of companies ending on or after 1 April 2001.
Subs (2)(*f*) substituted "such return, statement, declaration or list" for "such return or statement" in TCA 1997 s 895(1) definition of "appropriate inspector" para (*b*) for short tax "year" 2001 and later tax years for income tax and capital gains tax and for accounting periods of companies ending on or after 1 April 2001.
Subs (2)(*g*) substituted "to deliver a tax return, an inspector of taxes or the inspector of returns (within the meaning of section 951(11)), as the case may be," for "to deliver a tax return to an inspector of taxes or to the inspector of returns (within the meaning of section 951(11)), as the case may be, the inspector" in TCA 1997 s 909(2) for short tax "year" 2001 and later tax years for income tax and capital gains tax and for accounting periods of companies ending on or after 1 April 2001.
Subs (2)(*h*) substituted TCA 1997 s 1084(5) for short tax "year" 2001 and later tax years for income tax and capital gains tax and for accounting periods of companies ending on or after 1 April 2001.
Subs (3) substituted "€3,175" for "£2,500" and "€635" for "£500" of in TCA 1997 s 958(3A)(*b*)(iii) for 2002 and later tax years.

79 Amendment of provisions relating to Dublin Docklands Development Authority

Notes

Para (*a*)(i) substituted "company," or "company." in TCA 1997 s 9(1)(*c*) with effect from 6 April 2001.
Para (*a*)(ii) inserted TCA 1997 s 9(1)(*d*) with effect from 6 April 2001.
Para (*b*) substituted "Authority and any of its wholly-owned subsidiaries." for "Authority." in TCA 1997 s 220 (Table para 3) as respects accounting periods ending on or after 6 April 2001.
Para (*c*) substituted "Authority and any of its wholly-owned subsidiaries." for "Authority." in TCA 1997 Sch 15 para 31 as respects disposals made on or after 6 April 2001.

80 Amendment of Chapter 10 (designated areas of certain towns) of Part 10 of Principal Act

Notes

Subs (1)(*a*) substituted "31 December 2003" for "31 March 2003" in TCA 1997 s 372AA(1) definition of "qualifying period" with effect from 6 April 2001.
Subs (1)(*b*) substituted "31 December 2003" for "31 March 2003" in TCA 1997 s 372AB(1)(*c*) with effect from 6 April 2001.
Subs (1)(*c*) substituted "150 sq metres" for "125 square metres" in TCA 1997 s 372AF(1) definition of "qualifying premises" para (*b*) for expenditure incurred on or after 6 April 2001 which is conversion expenditure within the meaning of TCA 1997 s 372AF.
Subs (1)(*d*) substituted "150 square metres" for "125 square metres" in TCA 1997 s 372AG(1) definition of "qualifying premises" para (*b*) for expenditure incurred on or after 6 April 2001 which is relevant expenditure within the meaning of TCA 1997 s 372AG.
Subs (1)(*e*) substituted TCA 1997 s 372AH(1) definition of "qualifying premises" para (*d*) for expenditure incurred on or after 6 April 2001 which is qualifying expenditure within the meaning of TCA 1997 s 372AH.
Subs (1)(*f*) inserted TCA 1997 s 372AJ(1)(*aa*)–(*ac*) with effect from 6 April 2001.

81 Capital allowances for hotels

Notes

This section inserted TCA 1997 s 268(11)–(12) with effect from 6 April 2001.

Chapter 4
Corporation Tax

82 Amendment of provisions relating to a shipping trade

Notes

Subs (1)(*a*) inserted TCA 1997 s 21(1A) with effect from 1 January 2001.

Subs (1)(*b*) substituted "1 January 1987 to 31 December 2002" for "the 1st day of January, 1987, to the 31st day of December, 2000" in TCA 1997 s 407(1) definition of "relevant period" with effect from 1 January 2001.

83 Amendment of section 22A (reduction of corporation tax in respect of certain trading income) of Principal Act

Notes

Subs (1)(*a*) substituted TCA 1997 s 22A(2)(*b*)(i)–(iii) for the financial year 2001 and later financial years.

Subs (1)(*b*)(i) substituted "£200,000" for "£50,000" and "£250,000" for "£75,000" in TCA 1997 s 22A(3) for financial year 2001.

Subs (1)(*b*)(ii) substituted "€254,000" for "£50,000" and "€317,500" for "£75,000" in TCA 1997 s 22A(3) for the financial year 2002 and later years.

84 Foundation for investing in Communities

Notes

Subss (1) and (2) inserted TCA 1997 s 87A with effect from 1 August 2000.

Subs (3) repealed TCA 1997 s 87A with effect from 6 April 2001.

85 Amendment of section 130 (matters to be treated as distributions) of Principal Act

Notes

Subs (1) inserted TCA 1997 s 130(2A) for payments made on or after 15 February 2001.

86 Amendment of section 222 (certain dividends from a non-resident subsidiary) of Principal Act

Notes

This section substituted "specified in a certificate given before 15 February 2001 by the Minister" for "specified in a certificate given by the Minister" in TCA 1997 s 222(1)(*a*) definition of "relevant dividends" para (i) with effect from 6 April 2001.

87 Amendment of Chapter 2 of Part 14 of Principal Act

Notes

This section substituted TCA 1997 s 452 with effect from 6 April 2001.

88 Amendment of Part 36 of Principal Act

Notes

This section inserted TCA 1997 s 845A with effect from 6 April 2001.

89 Amendment of section 847 (tax relief for certain branch profits) of Principal Act

Notes

This section substituted "has before 15 February 2001 given a certificate" for "has given a certificate" in TCA 1997 s 847(1) definition of "qualified company" with effect from 6 April 2001.

90 Restriction of certain losses and charges

...

(3) Sections 454, 455 and 456 shall cease to have effect as on and from 1 January 2003.

[(4) *(a)* For the purposes of—

(i) computing the amount of—

(I) relevant trading charges on income within the meaning of section 243A of the Principal Act, and

(II) relevant trading losses within the meaning of section 396A of the Principal Act, and

(ii) this section insofar as it applies to sections 454 and 456 of the Principal Act,

where an accounting period of a company begins before 6 March 2001 and ends on or after that date, it shall be divided into 2 parts, one beginning on the date on which the accounting period begins and ending on 5 March 2001 and the other beginning on 6 March 2001 and ending on the date on which the accounting period ends, and both parts shall be treated as if they were separate accounting periods of the company.

(b) For the purposes of computing the amount of—

(i) charges on income paid for the purposes of the sale of goods within the meaning of section 454 of the Principal Act, and

(ii) a loss from the sale of goods within the meaning of section 455 of the Principal Act,

where an accounting period of a company begins before 1 January 2003 and ends on or after that date, it shall be divided into two parts, one beginning on the date on which the accounting period begins and ending on 31 December 2002 and the other beginning on 1 January 2003 and ending on the date which the accounting period ends, and both parts shall be treated as if they were separate accounting periods of the company.][1]

Amendments

[1] Subs (4) substituted by FA 2002 s 55, and FA 2001 s 90 is to apply, and is deemed always to have applied, as if that substitution were made.

Notes

Subs (1)(*a*) inserted TCA 1997 s 243A as respects an accounting period ending on or after 6 March 2001.
Subs (1)(*b*)(i) inserted TCA 1997 s 396A as respects an accounting period ending on or after 6 March 2001.
Subs (1)(*b*)(ii) inserted TCA 1997 s 420A as respects an accounting period ending on or after 6 March 2001.
Subs (1)(*c*)(i)(I) substituted TCA 1997 s 448(3)–(4) as respects an accounting period ending on or after 6 March 2001.
Subs (1)(*c*)(i)(II) substituted TCA 1997 s 448(5A)(*b*)(i) as respects an accounting period ending on or after 6 March 2001.
Subs (1)(*c*)(ii) substituted TCA 1997 s 454(2)–(3) as respects an accounting period ending on or after 6 March 2001.

Subs (1)(*c*)(iii)(I) substituted "Notwithstanding sections 396(2) and 396A(2) but subject to subsections (6) and (7), for the purposes of those sections" for "Notwithstanding section 396(2) but subject to subsections (6) and (7), for the purposes of that section" in TCA 1997 s 455(2) as respects an accounting period ending on or after 6 March 2001.
Subs (1)(*c*)(iii)(II) deleted TCA 1997 s 455(5) as respects an accounting period ending on or after 6 March 2001.
Subs (1)(*c*)(iv)(I) substituted TCA 1997 s 456(2)–(3) as respects an accounting period ending on or after 6 March 2001.
Subs (1)(*c*)(iv)(II) deleted TCA 1997 s 456(5)(*b*) as respects an accounting period ending on or after 6 March 2001.
Subs (1)(*c*)(v) deleted TCA 1997 s 457 as respects an accounting period ending on or after 6 March 2001.

91 Close company surcharges

Notes

Subs (1)(*a*)(i) substituted TCA 1997 s 434(1) definition of "distributable income" as respects an accounting period ending on or after 14 March 2001.
Subs (1)(*a*)(ii) inserted TCA 1997 s 434(1) definitions of "franked investment income" and "income" as respects an accounting period ending on or after 14 March 2001.
Subs (1)(*a*)(iii) inserted TCA 1997 s 434(1) definition of "relevant charges" as respects an accounting period ending on or after 14 March 2001.
Subs (1)(*b*)(i) substituted "The income" for "For the purposes of subsection (1), the income" in TCA 1997 s 434(4) as respects an accounting period ending on or after 14 March 2001.
Subs (1)(*b*)(ii) substituted TCA 1997 s 434(4)(*g*)–(*h*) as respects an accounting period ending on or after 14 March 2001.
Subs (1)(*c*) substituted TCA 1997 s 434(5) and inserted TCA 1997 s 434(5A) as respects an accounting period ending on or after 14 March 2001.
Subs (2)(*a*) substituted "distributable estate and investment income" for "aggregate of the distributable investment income and distributable estate income" in TCA 1997 s 440(1)(*a*) as respects an accounting period ending on or after 14 March 2001.
Subs (2)(*b*) inserted TCA 1997 s 440(2A) as respects an accounting period ending on or after 14 March 2001.
Subs (3)(*a*)(i) substituted TCA 1997 s 441(4)(*a*)(i)–(ii) as respects an accounting period ending on or after 14 March 2001.
Subs (3)(*a*)(ii) substituted "distributable estate and investment income" for "aggregate of distributable investment income and the distributable estate income" in TCA 1997 s 441(4)(*b*)(iii) as respects an accounting period ending on or after 14 March 2001.
Subs (3)(*b*) substituted "'distributable estate and investment income' and 'distributable trading income'" for "distributable income', 'distributable investment income' and 'distributable estate income'" in TCA 1997 s 441(6)(*b*)(ii) as respects an accounting period ending on or after 14 March 2001.

Chapter 5
Capital Gains Tax

92 Amendment of Chapter 6 (transfers of business assets) of Part 19 of Principal Act

Notes

Subs (1) inserted TCA 1997 s 600A for disposals on or after 5 January 2001.

93 Amendment of Chapter 7 (other reliefs and exemptions) of Part 19 of Principal Act

Notes

Subs (1)(*a*) inserted TCA 1997 s 603A for disposals on or after 6 December, 2000.
Subs (2) substituted "€254,000" for "£200,000" in TCA 1997 s 603A(1) with effect from 1 January 2002.

94 Amendment of section 649A (relevant disposals: rate of charge) of Principal Act

Notes

Para (*a*) substituted TCA 1997 s 649A(1)(*a*)–(*b*) with effect from 6 April 2001.
Para (*b*) deleted TCA 1997 s 649A(1)(*c*) with effect from 6 April 2001.

95 Amendment of section 652 (non-application of reliefs on replacement of assets in case of relevant disposals) of Principal Act

Notes

Subs (1) substituted TCA 1997 s 652(5) for relevant disposals made on or after 6 December 2000.

PART 8
MISCELLANEOUS

231 Interpretation (Part 8)

In this Part **"Principal Act"** means the Taxes Consolidation Act, 1997.

232 Amendment of Chapter 3 (other obligations and returns) of Part 38 of Principal Act

Notes

Subs (1)(*a*) substituted TCA 1997 s 887 [with effect from 15 February 2001][1].
Subs (1)(*b*) deleted TCA 1997 s 893 as respects any chargeable period (within the meaning of s 321(2)) commencing on or after 15 February 2001.
Subs (1)(*c*) deleted TCA 1997 s 894(2)(*d*) as respects any chargeable period (within the meaning of s 321(2)) commencing on or after 15 February 2001.
Subs (1)(*d*) substituted TCA 1997 s 896 as respects any chargeable period (within the meaning of s 321(2)) commencing on or after 15 February 2001.
Subs (1)(*e*) substituted "stored in accordance with section 887" for "stored by any means approved under section 887" in TCA 1997 s 903(1) definition of "records" [with effect from 15 February 2001][1].
Subs (3)(*a*)(i) substituted "€1,265" for "£1,000" in TCA 1997 s 887(5)(*b*) with effect from 1 January 2002.
Subs (3)(*a*)(ii) substituted "€1,900" for "£1,500" in TCA 1997 s 896(3)–(4) with effect from 1 January 2002.

Amendments

1 Substituted by FA 2002 s 138 and Sch 6 paras 5(*f*) and 6(*e*)(i) with effect from 30 March 2001; previously "as respects any chargeable period (within the meaning of s 321(2)) commencing on or after 15 February 2001".

233 Amendment of section 1078 (revenue offences) of Principal Act

Notes

Subs (1) substituted "£1,500" for "£1,000" in TCA 1997 s 1078(3)(*a*) with effect from 6 April 2001.
Subs (2)(*a*) substituted "€1,900" for "£1,500" in TCA 1997 s 1078(3)(*a*) with effect from 1 January 2002.

234 Amendment of section 1094 (tax clearance in relation to certain licences) of Principal Act

Notes

This section inserted TCA 1997 s 1094(1) definition of "licence" para (*l*) with effect from 6 April 2001.

235 Amendment of Chapter 6 (electronic transmission of returns of income, profits, etc, and of other Revenue returns) of Part 38 of Principal Act

Notes

Para (*a*)(i)(I) substituted TCA 1997 s 917D(1) definition of "digital signature" with effect from 15 February 2001.

Para (*a*)(i)(II) substituted TCA 1997 s 917D(1) definition of "return" with effect from 15 February 2001.

Para (*a*)(ii) deleted TCA 1997 s 917D(2) with effect from 15 February 2001.

Para (*b*)(i) substituted "the approved person"s or the authorised person"s digital signature" for "the approved person's digital signature" in TCA 1997 s 917F(1)(*c*) with effect from 15 February 2001.

Para (*b*)(ii) substituted TCA 1997 s 917F(5) with effect from 15 February 2001.

Para (*c*)(i) substituted "complies with the condition specified in subsection (3)(*a*) in relation to authorised persons and the condition specified in subsection (3)(*b*) in relation to the making of transmissions and the use of digital signatures" for "complies with the provisions of this section and, in particular, with the conditions specified in subsection (3)" in TCA 1997 s 917G(1) with effect from 15 February 2001.

Para (*c*)(ii) substituted "by such means as the Revenue Commissioners may determine" for "in writing or by such other means as may be approved by the Revenue Commissioners" in TCA 1997 s 917G(2) with effect from 15 February 2001.

Para (*c*)(iii) substituted TCA 1997 s 917G(3) with effect from 15 February 2001.

Para (*d*) substituted TCA 1997 s 917H(2)–(3) with effect from 15 February 2001.

Para (*e*) deleted TCA 1997 s 917I with effect from 15 February 2001.

Para (*f*) substituted "transmitted or to be transmitted" for "to be transmitted" in TCA 1997 s 917K(1)(*a*) with effect from 15 February 2001.

Para (*g*) substituted "for the purposes of the Acts" for "for the purposes of any proceedings in relation to which the certificate is given" in TCA 1997 s 917M(3) with effect from 15 February 2001.

236 Certificates in court procedings

Notes

Para (*a*)(i) substituted TCA 1997 s 966(5) with effect from 30 March 2001.

Para (*a*)(ii) substituted TCA 1997 s 967 with effect from 30 March 2001.

Para (*b*) substituted TCA 1997 s 1080(4) with effect from 30 March 2001.

237 Amendment of Chapter 4 (collection and recovery of income tax on certain emoluments (PAYE system)) of Part 42 of Principal Act

Notes

Para (*a*)(i) inserted TCA 1997 s 990(1A) with effect from 6 April 2001.

Para (*a*)(ii) inserted "and prior to such service the employer had sent to the Collector-General the return required by Regulation 35 of the Income Tax (Employment) Regulations 1960 (SI No 28 of 1960)" in TCA 1997 s 990(2) with effect from 6 April 2001.

Para (*b*) inserted TCA 1997 s 991(1A)–(1B) with effect from 6 April 2001.

Para (*c*) inserted TCA 1997 s 991A with effect from 6 April 2001.

238 Amendment of section 1002 (deduction from payments due to defaulters of amounts due in relation to tax) of Principal Act

Notes

This section substituted "14 days" for "one month" in TCA 1997 s 1002(3)(*a*).

239 Amendment of section 1006A (offset between taxes) of Principal Act

Notes

Para (*a*) inserted ", and includes any interest due under the Acts in relation to such tax, duty, levy or other charge" in TCA 1997 s 1006A(1) definition of "liability" with effect from 6 April 2001.
Para (*b*) substituted TCA 1997 s 1006A(2) with effect from 6 April 2001.

240 Amendment of enactments consequent on changeover to Euro

(1) (*a*) Subject to subsection (2), in each provision specified in column (1) of Schedule 5 for the words or amount set out in column (2) of that Schedule at that entry there shall be substituted the words or amount set out at the corresponding entry in column (3) of that Schedule.

(*b*) Where words are or an amount is mentioned more than once in a provision specified in column (1) of Schedule 5, then the substitution provided for by paragraph (*a*) shall apply as respects those words or that amount to each mention of those words or that amount in that provision.

(2) Subsection (1) shall apply—

(*a*) to the extent that the amendments relate to income tax and related matters, other than the amendments relating to such matters referred to in subparagraphs (ii), (iii), (iv), (v) and (vi) of paragraph (*l*), as respects the year of assessment 2002 and subsequent years of assessment,

(*b*) to the extent that the amendments relate to capital gains tax and related matters, other than the amendments relating to such matters referred to in paragraph (*l*)(vii), as respects the year of assessment 2002 and subsequent years of assessment,

(*c*) to the extent that the amendments relate to corporation tax and related matters, other than the amendments relating to such matters referred to in subparagraphs (i), (iii) and (iv) of paragraph (*l*), for accounting periods ending on or after 1 January 2002,

...

(*i*) to the extent that section 1086 of the Taxes Consolidation Act, 1997 is amended, as respects specified sums such as are referred to in paragraphs (*c*) and (*d*) of section 1086(2) of that Act which the Revenue Commissioners accept or undertake to accept on or after 1 January 2002,

...

(*k*) to the extent that the enactment amended imposes any fine, forfeiture, penalty or punishment for any act or omission, as respects any act or omission which takes place or begins on or after 1 January 2002,

and

(*l*) to the extent that—

(i) section 110 of the Taxes Consolidation Act, 1997 (in this paragraph referred to as the **"Act of 1997"**) is amended, as respects a company acquiring qualifying assets on or after 1 January 2002,

(ii) sections 201 and 202 of the Act of 1997 and Schedule 3 to that Act are amended, as respects payments made on or after 1 January 2002,

(iii) section 404(6) of the Act of 1997 is amended, as respects a lease entered into on or after 1 January 2002,

(iv) section 481(2)(*c*) of the Act of 1997 is amended, as respects a certificate issued under subsection (2)(*a*)(i) of that section on or after 1 January 2002,

(v) section 491 of the Act of 1997 is amended, as respects eligible shares (within the meaning of section 488 of that Act) issued on or after 1 January 2002,

(vi) [section 494(2)][1] of the Act of 1997 is amended, as respects a relevant investment (within the meaning of section 488 of that Act) being an individual's first such investment made on or after 1 January 2002, and sections 494(5) and 494(6)(*b*) of that Act are amended, as respects a subscription for eligible shares (within the meaning of section 488 of that Act) where the specified date (within the meaning of section 494 of that Act) in relation to that subscription is a date on or after 1 January 2002,

(vii) sections 598 and 602 of the Act of 1997 are amended, as respects disposals made on or after 1 January 2002,

...

Amendments

1 Substituted by FA 2002 s 138 and Sch 6 paras 5(*g*) and 6(*e*)(i) with effect from 30 March 2001; previously "section 494(1)".

241 Deletion of certain references to Bord Telecom Éireann and Irish Telecommunications Investments plc in Principal Act

Notes

Subs (1)(*a*) deleted "Securities issued on or after the 25th day of May, 1988 by Bord Telecom Éireann" and "Securities issued on or after the 25th day of May, 1988, by Irish Telecommunications Investments plc." from TCA 1997 s 37 (Table) as respects any securities issued by Bord Telecom Éireann or Irish Telecommunications Investments plc on or after 15 February 2001.

Subs (1)(*b*) deleted "Bord Telecom Éireann, Irish Telecommunications Investments plc," from TCA 1997 s 607(1)(*d*) as respects any securities issued by Bord Telecom Éireann or Irish Telecommunications Investments plc on or after 15 February 2001.

Subs (1)(*c*) deleted "Bord Telecom Éireann, Irish Telecommunications Investments plc," from TCA 1997 s 838(1)(*a*) definition of "securities" para (ii) as respects any securities issued by Bord Telecom Éireann or Irish Telecommunications Investments plc on or after 15 February 2001.

242 Care and management of taxes and duties

All the taxes and duties imposed by this Act are placed under the care and management of the Revenue Commissioners.

243 Short title, construction and commencement

(1) This Act may be cited as the Finance Act, 2001.

(2) Part 1 (so far as relating to income tax) shall be construed together with the Income Tax Acts and (so far as relating to corporation tax) shall be construed together with the Corporation Tax Acts and (so far as relating to capital gains tax) shall be construed together with the Capital Gains Tax Acts.

...

(8) Part 8 (so far as relating to income tax) shall be construed together with the Income Tax Acts and (so far as relating to corporation tax) shall be construed together with the Corporation Tax Acts and (so far as relating to capital gains tax) shall be construed together with the Capital Gains Tax Acts and (so far as relating to value-added tax) shall be construed together with the Value-Added Tax Acts, 1972 to 2001 and (so far as relating to residential property tax) shall be construed together with Part VI of the Finance Act, 1983, and the enactments amending or extending that Part and (so far as relating to gift tax or inheritance tax) shall be construed together with the Capital Acquisitions Tax Act, 1976, and the enactments amending or extending that Act.

(9) Part 1 shall, save as is otherwise expressly provided therein, apply as on and from 6 April 2001.

...

(11) Any reference in this Act to any other enactment shall, except so far as the context otherwise requires, be construed as a reference to that enactment as amended by or under any other enactment including this Act.

(12) In this Act, a reference to a Part, section or Schedule is to a Part or section of, or Schedule to, this Act, unless it is indicated that reference to some other enactment is intended.

(13) In this Act, a reference to a subsection, paragraph, subparagraph, clause or subclause is to the subsection, paragraph, subparagraph, clause or subclause of the provision (including a Schedule) in which the reference occurs, unless it is indicated that reference to some other provision is intended.

SCHEDULE 1
AMENDMENTS CONSEQUENTIAL ON CHANGES IN PERSONAL RELIEFS

[Section 2]

Notes

Para 1(*a*)(i) inserted TCA 1997 s 3(1) definitions of "chargeable tax" and "general tax credit" for short tax "year" 2001 and later tax years.
Para 1(*a*)(ii) inserted TCA 1997 s 3(1) definitions of "income tax payable" and "personal tax credit" for short tax "year" 2001 and later tax years.
Para 1(*b*) substituted TCA 1997 s 126(7)(*a*)–(*b*) for short tax "year" 2001 and later tax years.
Para 1(*c*) substituted TCA 1997 s 128(2A)(*a*) for short tax "year" 2001 and later tax years.
Para 1(*d*)(i) substituted TCA 1997 s 187(1) for short tax "year" 2001 and later tax years.
Para 1(*d*)(ii) substituted "£333" for "£450" and of "£481" for "£650" in TCA 1997 s 187(2)(*a*) for short tax "year" 2001 and later tax years.
Para 1(*e*)(i) substituted TCA 1997 s 458(1)(*b*) for short tax "year" 2001 and later tax years.
Para 1(*e*)(ii) inserted TCA 1997 s 458(1A) for short tax "year" 2001 and later tax years.
Para 1(*e*)(iii) substituted TCA 1997 s 458(2)(*b*) for short tax "year" 2001 and later tax years.
Para 1(*e*)(iv) substituted "Section 461" for "Section 461(2)" in TCA 1997 s 458 (Table Part 2) for short tax "year" 2001 and later tax years.
Para 1(*f*) substituted TCA 1997 s 461 for short tax "year" 2001 and later tax years.
Para 1(*g*) substituted TCA 1997 s 461A for short tax "year" 2001 and later tax years.
Para 1(*h*) substituted TCA 1997 s 462 for short tax "year" 2001 and later tax years.
Para 1(*i*) substituted TCA 1997 s 463 for short tax "year" 2001 and later tax years.
Para 1(*j*) substituted TCA 1997 s 464 for short tax "year" 2001 and later tax years.
Para 1(*k*) substituted TCA 1997 s 465 for short tax "year" 2001 and later tax years.
Para 1(*l*) substituted TCA 1997 s 466 for short tax "year" 2001 and later tax years.

Para 1(*m*) substituted TCA 1997 s 466A for short tax "year" 2001 and later tax years.
Para 1(*n*) substituted TCA 1997 s 468 for short tax "year" 2001 and later tax years.
Para 1(*o*) substituted TCA 1997 s 472 for short tax "year" 2001 and later tax years.
Para 1(*p*) substituted "certificate of tax credits and standard rate cut-off point" for "certificate of tax-free allowances" in TCA 1997 s 784A(3)[(*b*)][1] for short tax "year" 2001 and later tax years.
Para 1(*q*) substituted TCA 1997 s 885(1) definition of "tax reference number" para (*a*) for short tax "year" 2001 and later tax years.
Para 1(*r*) substituted "certificates of tax credits and standard rate cut-off point" for "certificates of tax-free allowances" in TCA 1997 s 903(1) definition of "records" for short tax "year" 2001 and later tax years.
Para 1(*s*) inserted TCA 1997 s 983 definitions of "reliefs from income tax" and "tax credits" for short tax "year" 2001 and later tax years.
Para 1(*t*)(i)(I) substituted "reliefs from income tax" for "allowances, deductions and reliefs" in TCA 1997 s 986(1)(*a*) for short tax "year" 2001 and later tax years.
Para 1(*t*)(i)(II) substituted TCA 1997 s 986(1)(*g*) for short tax "year" 2001 and later tax years.
Para 1(*t*)(ii) substituted "provisional reliefs from income tax" for "a provisional deduction for allowances and reliefs" in TCA 1997 s 986(3)(*b*) for short tax "year" 2001 and later tax years.
Para 1(*t*)(iii) substituted "reliefs from income tax" for "allowances, deductions and reliefs" in TCA 1997 s 986(4) for short tax "year" 2001 and later tax years.
Para 1(*u*) substituted "income tax payable" for "income tax chargeable" in TCA 1997 Sch 3 para 10 (Formula T) for short tax "year" 2001 and later tax years.
Para 2(*a*)(i) substituted "€10,420" for "£6,068" and "€5,210" for "£3,034" in TCA 1997 s 187(1) for 2002 and later tax years.
Para 2(*a*)(ii) substituted €575" for "£333" and "€830" for "£481" in TCA 1997 s 187(2)(*a*) for 2002 and later tax years.
Para 2(*b*) substituted "€2,794" for "£1,628" and "€1,397" for "£814" in TCA 1997 s 461 for 2002 and later tax years.
Para 2(*c*) substituted "€254" for "£148" in TCA 1997 s 461A for 2002 and later tax years.
Para 2(*d*) substituted "€1,397" for "£814" in TCA 1997 s 462(2) for 2002 and later tax years.
Para 2(*e*) substituted €2,540", "€2,032", "€1,524", "€1,016" and "€508" for "£2,000", "£1,600", "£1,200", "£800" and "£400" in TCA 1997 s 463(2) for 2002 and later tax years.
Para 2(*f*) substituted "€408" and "€204" for "£238" and "£119" in TCA 1997 s 464 for 2002 and later tax years.
Para 2(*g*) substituted "€408" for "£238" in TCA 1997 s 465[(1)][2] for 2002 and later tax years.
Para 2(*h*)(i) substituted "€280" for "£163" in TCA 1997 s 466(1) for 2002 and later tax years.
Para 2(*h*)(ii) substituted "€56" for "£33" in TCA 1997 s 466(2) for 2002 and later tax years.
Para 2(*i*)(i) substituted "€762" for "£444" in TCA 1997 s 466A(2) for 2002 and later tax years.
Para 2(*i*)(ii) substituted "€5,080" for "£2,960" in TCA 1997 s 466A(6)(*a*) for 2002 and later tax years.
Para 2(*j*) substituted "€762" and "€1,524" for "£444" and "£888" in TCA 1997 s 468(2) for 2002 and later tax years.
Para 2(*k*)(i) substituted "€4,572" for "£2,664" in TCA 1997 s 472(2) for 2002 and later tax years.
Para 2(*k*)(ii) substituted "€508" for "£296" in TCA 1997 s 472(4) for 2002 and later tax years.

Amendments

1 Substituted by FA 2002 s 138 and Sch 6 paras 5(*h*)(i) and 6(*e*)(i) with effect from 30 March 2001; previously "(*a*)".

2 Substituted by FA 2002 s 138 and Sch 6 paras 5(*h*)(ii) and 6(*e*)(i) with effect from 30 March 2001; previously "(1)".

SCHEDULE 2
CHANGEOVER TO CALENDAR YEAR OF ASSESSMENT

[Section 77]

AMENDMENT OF TAXES CONSOLIDATION ACT, 1997

Notes

Para 1 substituted "31 December" for "the 5th day of April" in TCA 1997 s 55(1) definition of "relevant day" para (*a*) with effect from 6 April 2001.

Para 2 inserted TCA 1997 s 65(3A)–(3F) with effect from 6 April 2001.
Para 3 inserted TCA 1997 s 66(3A)–(3C) with effect from 6 April 2001.
Para 4(*a*) substituted "the first day of the year of assessment" for "the 6th day of April in that year" in TCA 1997 s 67(1)(*a*) with effect from 6 April 2001.
Para 4(*b*) substituted TCA 1997 s 67(1)(*a*)(ii) with effect from 6 April 2001.
Para 5 substituted "shall be charged for each year of assessment" for "shall be charged annually" in TCA 1997 s 112(1) with effect from 6 April 2001.
Para 6 substituted "the average amount for a year of assessment" for "the average annual amount" in TCA 1997 s 115 with effect from 6 April 2001.
Para 7 substituted "£1,110" for "£1,500" in TCA 1997 s 116(3) for short tax "year" 2001 only.
Para 8(*a*) inserted TCA 1997 s 121(3)(*c*) with effect from 6 April 2001.
Para 8(*b*) inserted TCA 1997 s 121(4A) with effect from 6 April 2001.
Para 8(*c*) inserted TCA 1997 s 121(5)(*aa*) with effect from 6 April 2001.
Para 8(*d*) inserted TCA 1997 s 121(6)(*bb*) with effect from 6 April 2001.
Para 9(*a*) substituted "31 October" for "31 January" in TCA 1997 s 128A(3) for short tax "year" 2001 and later tax years.
Para 9(*b*) substituted "31 October" for "1 November" in TCA 1997 s 128A(4) with effect from 6 April 2001.
Para 10 substituted "1 January 2003" for "the 6th day of April, 2002," in TCA 1997 s 154(3)(*a*) with effect from 6 April 2001.
Para 11 substituted "15 February" for "the 21st day of May" in TCA 1997 s 172LA(7) for short tax "year" 2001 and later tax years.
Para 12 substituted "1 January 2004" for "6 April 2003" in 202(2)(*g*) with effect from 6 April 2001.
Para 13 substituted "£2,960", "£1,480", "£3,700" and "£1,850" for "£4,000", "£2,000", "£5,000" and "£2,500" in TCA 1997 s 244(1)(*a*) definition of "relievable interest" for short tax "year" 2001 only.
Para 14 substituted "£1,776" for "£2,400" in TCA 1997 s 250(3) for short tax "year" 2001 only.
Para 15 substituted "1 January" for "the 6th day of April" in TCA 1997 s 252(1)(*b*) definition of "the specified date" as on and from 1 January 2002.
Para 16(*a*) substituted "1 January" for "the 6th day of April" in TCA 1997 s 258(4)(*b*) for 2002 and later tax years.
Para 16(*b*) inserted TCA 1997 s 258(4A)–(4B) for short tax "year" 2001 and later tax years.
Para 17(*a*) substituted "the period of 270 days" for "the period of 12 months" in TCA 1997 s 259(2) for short tax "year" 2001 only.
Para 17(*b*) substituted "31 December" for "the 5th day of April" in TCA 1997 s 259(2)(*c*) for short tax "year" 2001 and later tax years.
Para 18 substituted "1 January" for "the 6th day of April" in TCA 1997 s 260(4)(*a*)(i) for 2002 and later tax years.
Para 19 inserted TCA 1997 s 284(3B) with effect from 6 April 2001.
Para 20 inserted TCA 1997 ss 328(2A), 337(2A), 349(2A), 371(2A), 372I(2A), 372RA(2A) and 372AH(2A) with effect from 6 April 2001.
Para 21 inserted TCA 1997 ss 364(2A) and 372Y(2A) with effect from 6 April 2001.
Para 22(*a*) substituted "£74" for "£100" in TCA 1997 s 469(2)(*a*) for short tax "year" 2001 only.
Para 22(*b*) substituted "£148" for "£200" in TCA 1997 s 469(2)(*b*) for short tax "year" 2001 only.
Para 23(*a*) substituted "£148" for "£200" in TCA 1997 s 481(6) for short tax "year" 2001 only.
Para 23(*b*) substituted "£18,500" for "£25,000" in TCA 1997 s 481(7) for short tax "year" 2001 only.
Para 24(*a*) inserted "or, where the chargeable period is the year of assessment 2001, £3,700" in TCA 1997 s 482(1)(*a*) definition of "qualifying expenditure" para (ii) for short tax "year" 2001 only.
Para 24(*b*) inserted "or, where the chargeable period is the year of assessment 2001, £3,700" to TCA 1997 s 482(1)(*a*) definition of "relevant expenditure" para (i)(II) for short tax "year" 2001 only.
Para 25(*a*) substituted "£148" for "£200" in TCA 1997 s 490(1) for short tax "year" 2001 only.
Para 25(*b*) substituted "£18,500" for "£25,000" in TCA 1997 s 490(2) for short tax "year" 2001 only.
Para 26 inserted "or, in the case of the year of assessment 2001, £11,100" in TCA 1997 s 494(2)(*a*)(II).
Para 27 substituted "£7,400" for "£10,000" in TCA 1997 s 515(1)–(2) for short tax "year" 2001 only.
Para 28(*a*)(i) substituted TCA 1997 s 520(1) definition of "basis period for a year of assessment" para (*a*)(i) with effect from 6 April 2001.
Para 28(*a*)(ii) substituted TCA 1997 s 520(1) definition of "income tax month" with effect from 6 April 2001.
Para 28(*b*) inserted TCA 1997 s 520(3) with effect from 6 April 2001.
Para 29 substituted "14 days" for "10 days" in TCA 1997 s 525(1) as on and from 1 January 2002.
Para 30 inserted TCA 1997 s 527(3A) with effect from 6 April 2001.
Para 31(*a*) substituted TCA 1997 s 530(1) definition of "income tax month" with effect from 6 April 2001.

Para 31(*b*) substituted "31 December" and "1 January" for "the 5th day of April" and "the 6th day of April" in 530(1) definition of "qualifying period" as on and from 1 January 2002.
Para 32(*a*) substituted "Not later than the 14th day of an income tax month" and "the previous income tax month" for "Within 9 days from the end of an income tax month" and "that income tax month" in TCA 1997 s 531(3A)(*a*) as on and from 1 January 2002.
Para 32(*b*) substituted "commencing on the 1st day of a year of assessment and ending on the last day of the income tax month in which the payment was made" for "commencing on the 6th day of April in a year of assessment and ending on the 5th day of the month following the date of the payment or, if the payment was made on or before the 5th day of a month, ending on the 5th day of that month" in TCA 1997 s 531(5)(*b*) as on and from 1 January 2002.
Para 32(*c*) substituted "year of assessment" for "income tax year" in TCA 1997 s 531(12)(*d*) with effect from 6 April 2001.
Para 33 substituted "mid-November" for "mid-February" in TCA 1997 s 556(1) definition of "the consumer price index number relevant to any year of assessment" with effect on and from 1 January 2002.
Para 34 substituted "£740" for "£1,000" in TCA 1997 s 601(1)–(3) for short tax "year" 2001 only.
Para 35 substituted "£11,100" for "£15,000" in TCA 1997 s 604(12)(*c*) for short tax "year" 2001 only.
Para 36 substituted "£11,100" for "£15,000" in TCA 1997 s 650 for short tax "year" 2001 only.
Para 37(*a*)(i) substituted "31 December" for "the 5th day of April" in TCA 1997 s 657(5)(*a*) with effect from 6 April 2001.
Para 37(*a*)(ii) inserted TCA 1997 s 657(5)(*aa*)–(*ab*) with effect from 6 April 2001.
Para 37(*b*) inserted TCA 1997 s 657(8A)–(8C) with effect from 6 April 2001.
Para 37(*c*) inserted TCA 1997 s 657(11A) with effect from 6 April 2001.
Para 38 substituted "1 January 2004" for "6 April 2003" in TCA 1997 s 659(1)(*c*) with effect from 6 April 2001.
Para 39(*a*) substituted "31 January" for "the 1st day of May" in TCA 1997 s 700(3) in relation to a return due under TCA 1997 s 700(3) in respect of the 2001 or any later tax year.
Para 39(*b*) substituted "£52" for "£70" in TCA 1997 s 700(3)(*a*) for short tax "year" 2001 only.
Para 40 substituted "31 December" for "the 5th day of April" in TCA 1997 s 737(8)(*a*)(i) for short tax "year" 2001 and later tax years.
Para 41 substituted "£148,000" for "£200,000" in TCA 1997 s 787(2A) for short tax "year" 2001 only.
Para 42(*a*)(i) substituted "135 days" for "183 days" in TCA 1997 s 819(1)(*a*) for short tax "year" 2001 only.
Para 42(*a*)(ii) substituted "244 days" for "280 days" in TCA 1997 s 819(1)(*b*) for short tax "year" 2001 and 2002.
Para 42(*b*) substituted "22 days" for "30 days" in TCA 1997 s 819(2) for short tax "year" 2001 only.
Para 43 substituted "£2,220" for "£3,000" in TCA 1997 s 821(1)(*b*) for short tax "year" 2001 only.
Para 44 substituted "135 days" for "182 days" in TCA 1997 s 825(1) definition of "visits" para (*a*) for short tax "year" 2001 only.
Para 45 substituted "10 weeks" for "13 weeks" in TCA 1997 s 825A(1) definition of "qualifying employment" para (*b*) for short tax "year" 2001 only.
Para 46(*a*) substituted "31 December" for "the 5th day of April" in TCA 1997 s 838(4)(*e*) for short tax "year" 2001 and later tax years.
Para 46(*b*)(i) substituted "31 December" for "the 5th day of April" in TCA 1997 s 838(6)(*a*)(i) for short tax "year" 2001 and later tax years.
Para 46(*b*)(ii) substituted "31 October" for "the 1st day of November" in TCA 1997 s 838(6)(*c*) for short tax "year" 2001 and later tax years.
Para 47 substituted TCA 1997 s 879(3) with effect from 6 April 2001.
Para 48 inserted TCA 1997 s 880(3A) with effect from 6 April 2001.
Para 49 substituted "31 October" for "the 31st day of January" in TCA 1997 s 894(1) definition of "specified return date for the chargeable period" para (*a*) for short tax "year" 2001 and later tax years.
Para 50 substituted "31 October" for "the 31st day of January" in TCA 1997 s 895(1) definition of "specified return date for the chargeable period" para (*a*) for short tax "year" 2001 and later tax years.
Para 51 substituted "£1,110" for "£1,500" in TCA 1997 s 897(2)(*e*) for short tax "year" 2001 only.
Para 52 substituted "31 October" for "the 1st day of November" in TCA 1997 s 960 for short tax "year" 2001 and later tax years.
Para 53 substituted TCA 1997 s 983 definition of "income tax month" with effect from 6 April 2001.
Para 54 substituted "31st day of December" for "5th day of April" in TCA 1997 s 996(1) definition of "relevant date" with effect from 6 April 2001.
Para 55(*a*) substituted "the year of assessment 2002" for "the year of assessment 2001–2002" in TCA 1997 s 1013(2C)(*d*)(iii) with effect from 6 April 2001.

Para 55(*b*)(i) substituted "1 January 2005" for "6 April 2004" in TCA 1997 s 1013(2C)(*e*)(II) with effect from 6 April 2001.
Para 55(*b*)(ii) substituted "the year of assessment 2005" for "the year of assessment 2004–2005" in TCA 1997 s 1013(2C)(*e*)(II) with effect from 6 April 2001.
Para 56 substituted "1 April" for "the 6th day of July" in TCA 1997 s 1019 for 2002 and later tax years.
Para 57(*a*) substituted TCA 1997 s 1020(1) definition of "income tax month" with effect from 6 April 2001.
Para 57(*b*) substituted substituted "9" for "12" in TCA 1997 s 1020(3) (Formula) for short tax "year" 2001 only.
Para 58 substituted "1 April" for "the 6th day of July" in TCA 1997 s 1023(3)–(4) for 2002 and later tax years.
Para 59 substituted "1 April" for "the 6th day of July" in TCA 1997 s 1028(2)–(3) for 2002 and later tax years.
Para 60 substituted "£7,400" for "£10,000" in TCA 1997 Sch 11 para 3(4) for short tax "year" 2001 only.

SCHEDULE 5
AMENDMENT OF ENACTMENTS CONSEQUENT ON CHANGEOVER TO EURO

[Section 240]

Notes

Sch 5 and s 240 make the following substitutions.
Taxes Consolidation Act 1997:
s 14(1): "one pound" substituted by "one euro"; s 14(1): "one penny" substituted by "one cent"; para 6 of Schedule C in s 17(1): "one pound" substituted by "one euro"; para 1 of Schedule D in s 18(1): "one pound" substituted by "one euro"; para 2 of Schedule E in s 19(1): "one pound" substituted by "one euro"; s 110(1): "£10,000,000" substituted by "€12,690,000"; s 116(3)(*a*): "£1,500" substituted by "€1,905"; s 126(4)(*b*): "£10" substituted by "€13"; s 133(8)(*c*): "£170,000,000" substituted by "€215,855,473.33"; s 133(11)(*a*): "£250,000,000" substituted by "€317,434,519.61"; s 133(11)(*b*): "£170,000,000" substituted by "€215,855,473.33"; s 152(2): "£10" substituted by "€10"; s 152(2): "£100" substituted by "€125"; s 178(7)(*a*): "£100" substituted by "€100"; s 189A: "£300,000" substituted by "€381,000"; s 201(1)(*a*): "£8,000" substituted by "€10,160"; s 201(1)(*a*): "£600" substituted by "€765"; para (*a*) of the definition of "specified amount" in s 202(1): "£6,000" substituted by "€7,620"; para (*a*) of the definition of "specified amount" in s 202(1): "£200" substituted by "€255"; para (*b*) of the definition of "specified amount" in s 202(1): "£6,000" substituted by " €7,620"; para (*b*) of the definition of "specified amount" in s 202(1) : "£500" substituted by "€635"; para (*c*) of the definition of "specified amount" in s 202(1): "£8,000" substituted by "€10,160"; para (*c*) of the definition of "specified amount" in s 202(1): "£600" substituted by "€765"; s 207(4): "£100" substituted by "€125"; s 211(1): "£160" substituted by "€205"; s 211(1): "£1,000" substituted by "€1,270"; s 211(1): "£52" substituted by "€70"; s 211(6): "£100" substituted by "€125"; s 213(2): "£8,000" substituted by "€10,160"; s 213(2): "£2,000" substituted by "€2,540"; s 213(4): "£100" substituted by "€125"; s 236(4)(*c*): "£500" substituted by "€630"; s 244(1)(*a*): "£4,000" substituted by "€5,080"; s 244(1)(*a*): "£2,000" substituted by "€2,540"; s 244(1)(*a*): "£5,000" substituted by "€6,350"; s 244(1)(*a*): "£2,500" substituted by "€3,175"; s 250(3): "£2,400" substituted by "€3,050"; s 264(1): "£50,000" substituted by "€63,500"; s 305(4): "£500" substituted by "€630"; s 373(2)(*a*): "£2,500" substituted by "€3,174.35"; s 373(2)(*b*): "£3,500" substituted by "€4,444.08"; s 373(2)(*c*): "£4,000" substituted by "€5,078.95"; s 373(2)(*d*): "£6,000" substituted by "€7,618.43"; s 373(2)(*e*): "£7,000" substituted by "€8,888.17"; s 373(2)(*f*): "£10,000" substituted by "€12,697.38"; s 373(2)(*g*): "£13,000" substituted by "€16,506.60"; s 373(2)(*h*): "£14,000" substituted by "€17,776.33"; s 373(2)(i): "£15,000" substituted by "€19,046.07"; s 373(2)(*j*): "£15,500" substituted by "€19,680.94"; s 373(2)(*k*): "£16,000" substituted by "€20,315.81"; s 373(2)(*l*): "£16,500" substituted by "€20,950.68"; para (*a*) of the definition of "relevant amount" in s 376(1): "£14,000" substituted by "€17,776.33"; para (*b*) of the definition of "relevant amount" in s 376(1): "£15,000" substituted by "€19,046.07"; para (*c*) of the definition of "relevant amount" in s 376(1): "£15,500" substituted by "€19,680.94"; para (*d*) of the definition of "relevant amount" in s 376(1): "£16,000" substituted by "€20,315.81"; para (*e*) of the definition of "relevant amount" in s 376(1): "£16,500" substituted by "€20,950.68"; s 404(1)(*b*)(iii): "£2,000" substituted by "€2,540"; s 404(6)(*c*)(ii): "£50,000" substituted by "€63,500"; s 414(1)(*b*): "£100" substituted by "€100"; s 415(1)(*b*): "£100" substituted by "€100"; s 438(3): "£15,000" substituted by "€19,050"; s 440(1)(*b*)(i)(I): "£500" substituted by "€635"; s 440(1)(*b*)(i)(II): "£500" substituted by "€635"; s 441(4)(*b*)(i)(I): "£500" substituted by "€635"; s 441(4)(*b*)(i)(II): "£500" substituted by "€635"; s 469(2)(*a*): "£100" substituted by "€125"; s 469(2)(*b*): "£200" substituted by "€250";

s 472A(2): "£3,000" substituted by "€3,810"; s 472A(2): "£2,000" substituted by "€2,540"; s 472A(2): "£1,000" substituted by "€1,270"; s 472A(3)(*a*): "£1,000" substituted by "€1,270"; s 472A(3)(*a*): "£666" substituted by "€850"; s 472A(3)(*a*): "£334" substituted by "€425"; s 472A(3)(*b*): "£1,000" substituted by "€1,270"; s 472A(3)(*b*): "£666" substituted by "€850"; s 472A(3)(*b*): "£334" substituted by "€425"; s 476(1): "£250" substituted by "€315"; s 476(1): "£1,000" substituted by "€1,270"; s 477(1)(*a*): "£150" substituted by "€195"; s 478(2): "£800" substituted by "€1,015.79"; s 479(2): "£5,000" substituted by "€6,350"; s 481(2)(*c*)(i): "£4,000,000" substituted by "€5,080,000"; s 481(2)(*c*)(ii): "£4,000,000" substituted by " €5,080,000"; s 481(2)(*c*)(ii): "£5,000,000" substituted by "€6,350,000"; the formula in s 481(2)(*c*)(ii): "£100,000" substituted by "€127,000"; s 481(2)(*c*)(iii): "£5,000,000" substituted by "€6,350,000"; s 481(2)(*c*): "£8,250,000" substituted by "€10,480,000"; s 481(4)(*a*): "£8,000,000" substituted by "€10,160,000"; s 481(4)(*b*)(i): "£3,000,000" substituted by "€3,810,000"; s 481(4)(*b*)(ii): "£3,000,000" substituted by "€3,810,000"; s 481(4)(*b*)(ii): "£4,000,000" substituted by "€5,080,000"; s 481(7): "£25,000" substituted by "€31,750"; s 481(16): "£500" substituted by "€630"; s 481(16): "£1,000" substituted by "€1,265"; para (ii) of the definition of "qualifying expenditure" in s 482(1)(*a*): "£5,000" substituted by "€6,350"; para (i)(II) of the definition of "relevant expenditure" in s 482(1)(*a*): "£5,000" substituted by "€6,350"; s 482(7)(*c*): "£500" substituted by "€630"; s 486B(4): "£10,000,000" substituted by "€12,700,000"; s 486B(5): "£7,500,000" substituted by "€9,525,000"; s 486B(11)(i): "£500" substituted by "€630"; s 486B(11)(i): "£1,000" substituted by "€1,265"; s 490(1)(*a*): "£200" substituted by "€250"; s 490(2): "£25,000" substituted by "€31,750"; s 491(2): "£100,000" substituted by "€127,000"; s 491(2): "£500,000" substituted by "€635,000"; s 491(2): "£1,000,000" substituted by "€1,270,000"; s 491(2): "£250,000" substituted by "€317,500"; s 491(2): "£400,000" substituted by "€508,000"; s 491(3): "£100,000" substituted by "€127,000"; s 491(3): "£500,000" substituted by "€635,000"; s 491(3): "£1,000,000" substituted by "€1,270,000"; s 491(3): "£250,000" substituted by "€317,500"; s 491(3): "£400,000" substituted by "€508,000"; s 493(8)(*a*)(i): "£250,000" substituted by "€317,500"; s 494(2)(*a*): "£15,000" substituted by "€19,050"; s 494(5)(*a*): "£100" substituted by "€130"; s 494(6)(*b*)(ii): "£100,000" substituted by "€127,000"; s 496(5)(*c*): "£2,000,000" substituted by "€2,539,476.16"; s 503(6): "£500" substituted by "€630"; s 503(6): "£1,000" substituted by "€1,265"; s 513(6): "£10" substituted by "€13"; s 515(1)(*a*): "£10,000" substituted by "€12,700"; s 515(1)(*b*): "£30,000" substituted by "€38,100"; s 515(2): "£10,000" substituted by "€12,700"; s 515(2): "£30,000" substituted by "€38,100"; s 515(2B): "£30,000" substituted by "€38,100"; s 531(14)(*a*): "£1,000" substituted by "€1,265"; s 531(14)(*b*): "£1,000" substituted by "€1,265"; s 531(14)(*c*): "£1,000" substituted by "€1,265"; s 598(2)(*a*)(i): "£375,000" substituted by "€476,250"; s 598(2)(*a*)(ii): "£375,000" substituted by "€476,250"; s 601(1): "£1,000" substituted by "€1,270"; s 601(2): "£1,000" substituted by "€1,270"; s 601(3): "£1,000" substituted by "€1,270"; s 602(2): "£2,000" substituted by "€2,540"; s 602(3)(*a*): "£2,000" substituted by "€2,540"; s 602(4): "£2,000" substituted by "€2,540"; s 602(6)(*b*): "£2,000" substituted by "€2,540"; s 602(6)(*c*): "£2,000" substituted by "€2,540"; s 604(12)(*c*): "£15,000" substituted by "€19,050"; s 606(1)(*a*): "£25,000" substituted by "€31,740"; s 650: "£15,000" substituted by "€19,050"; s 659(3)(*a*)(i): "£10,000" substituted by "€12,700"; s 659(3)(*a*)(ii): "£15,000" substituted by "€19,050"; s 659(3B)(*a*): "£25,000" substituted by "€31,750"; para (ii)(I) of the definition of "the specified amount" in s 664(1)(*a*): "£2,000" substituted by "€2,539.48"; para (ii)(II) of the definition of "the specified amount" in s 664(1)(*a*): "£2,800" substituted by "€3,555.27"; para (ii)(III) of the definition of "the specified amount" in s 664(1)(*a*): "£2,000" substituted by "€2,539.48"; para (ii)(IV)(A) of the definition of "the specified amount" in s 664(1)(*a*): "£4,000" substituted by "€5,078.95"; para (ii)(IV)(B)of the definition of "the specified amount" in s 664(1)(*a*): "£3,000" substituted by "€3,809.21"; para (ii)(V)(A) of the definition of "the specified amount" in s 664(1)(*a*): "£6,000" substituted by "€7,618.43"; para (ii)(V)(B) of the definition of "the specified amount" in s 664(1)(*a*): "£4,000" substituted by "€5,078.95"; s 664(1)(*b*)(i): "£2,800" substituted by "€3,555.27"; s 664(1)(*b*)(ii)(I): "£4,000" substituted by "€5,078.95"; s 664(1)(*b*)(ii)(II): "£3,000" substituted by "€3,809.21"; s 664(1)(*b*)(iii)(I): "£6,000" substituted by "€7,618.43"; s 664(1)(*b*)(iii)(II): "£4,000" substituted by "€5,078.95"; s 700(3): "£70" substituted by "€90"; s 723(1): "£200,000,000" substituted by "€255,000,000"; s 723(3)(*b*): "£50,000" substituted by "€63,500"; s 723(3)(*c*): "£50,000" substituted by "€63,500"; s 737(1): "£200,000,000" substituted by "€255,000,000"; s 737(3)(*a*)(ii): "£50,000" substituted by "€63,500"; s 737(3)(*a*)(iii): "£50,000" substituted by "€63,500"; the formula in the definition of "qualifying group expenditure on research and development" in s 766(1)(*a*): "£25,000" substituted by "€31,743.45"; para (A) of the definition of "qualifying group expenditure on research and development" in s 766(1)(*a*): "£150,000" substituted by "€190,460.71"; s 766(1)(*b*)(v)(I): "£50,000" substituted by "€63,486.90"; s 783(6): "£500" substituted by "€630"; s 784C(2)(*b*)(ii): "£50,000" substituted by "€63,500"; s 784C(3)(*b*): "£50,000" substituted by "€63,500"; s 784C(4)(*a*): "£10,000" substituted by "€12,700"; s

787(2A): "£200,000" substituted by "€254,000"; s 789(5): "£500" substituted by "€630"; s 821(1)(*b*): "£3,000" substituted by "€3,810"; s 823(3): "£25,000" substituted by "€31,750"; s 838(1)(*a*): "£200,000,000" substituted by "€255,000,000"; s 838(2)(*b*)(i): "£50,000" substituted by "€63,500"; s 838(2)(*b*)(i)(B): "£10,000" substituted by "€12,700"; s 838(2)(*b*)(ii): "£50,000" substituted by "€63,500"; s 838(2)(*c*): "£50,000" substituted by "€63,500"; s 839(2)(*a*)(i): "£25,000" substituted by "€31,750"; s 839(2)(*a*)(i): "£50,000" substituted by "€63,500"; s 839(2)(*a*)(ii): "£25,000" substituted by "€31,750"; s 839(2)(*a*)(ii): "£50,000" substituted by "€63,500"; s 839(2)(*b*)(ii)(I): "£25,000" substituted by "€31,750"; s 839(2)(*b*)(ii)(I): "£50,000" substituted by "€63,500"; s 839(2)(*b*)(ii)(II): "£25,000" substituted by "€31,750"; s 839(2)(*b*)(ii)(II): "£50,000" substituted by "€63,500"; s 839(3): "£50,000" substituted by "€63,500"; s 839(3): "£75,000" substituted by "€95,250"; s 839(4): "£25,000" substituted by "€31,750"; s 839(4): "£50,000" substituted by "€63,500"; s 856(2): "£50" substituted by "€60"; s 857(3): "£100" substituted by "€125"; s 877(5)(*b*): "£5" substituted by "€5"; s 885(2): "£5" substituted by "€7"; s 886(5): "£1,200" substituted by "€1,520"; s 889(7)(*b*): "£500" substituted by "€635"; s 889(8): "£1,200" substituted by "€1,520"; s 890(3): "£500" substituted by "€635"; s 891(2)(*a*): "£50" substituted by "€65"; s 895(4)(*a*): "£2,000" substituted by "€2,535"; s 895(4)(*b*): "£2,000" substituted by "€2,535"; s 897(2)(*e*): "£1,500" substituted by "€1,905"; s 898(3): "£1" substituted by "€2"; s 900(7): "£1,500" substituted by "€1,900"; s 902(11): "£1,500" substituted by "€1,900"; s 903(5): "£1,000" substituted by "€1,265"; s 904(5): "£1,000" substituted by "€1,265"; s 904A(8): "£1,000" substituted by "€1,265"; s 904A(9): "£15,000" substituted by "€19,045"; s 904A(9): "£2,000" substituted by "€2,535"; s 904C(7): "£1,000" substituted by "€1,265"; s 904C(8): "£15,000" substituted by "€19,045"; s 904C(8): "£2,000" substituted by "€2,535"; s 904D(7): "£1,000" substituted by "€1,265"; s 904D(8): "£15,000" substituted by "€19,045"; s 904D(8): "£2,000" substituted by "€2,535"; s 905(3): "£1,000" substituted by "€1,265"; s 906A(10): "£15,000" substituted by "€19,045"; s 906A(10): "£2,000" substituted by "€2,535"; s 907(9): "£15,000" substituted by "€19,045"; s 907(9): "£2,000" substituted by "€2,535"; s 914(6)(*a*): "£5,000" substituted by "€6,350"; s 914(6)(*b*): "£15,000" substituted by "€19,050"; s 917A(4): "£2,000" substituted by "€2,535"; s 917B(5)(*b*): "£2,000" substituted by "€2,535"; s 917C(3)(*b*): "£2,000" substituted by "€2,535"; s 923(4): "£100" substituted by "€125"; s 923(4): "£20" substituted by "€25"; s 932: "£50" substituted by "€60"; s 939(3): "£750" substituted by "€950"; s 941(3): "£20" substituted by "€25"; s 942(6)(*b*): "£10" substituted by "€10"; para (i) of the definition of "chargeable person" in s 950(1): "£100" substituted by "€130"; s 953(7)(*a*)(i): "£10" substituted by "€10"; s 962(3)(*a*): "£15,000" substituted by "€19,050"; s 962(3)(*b*): "£2,500" substituted by "€3,175"; s 962(3)(*b*): "£15,000" substituted by "€19,050"; s 962(3)(*c*): "£2,500" substituted by "€3,175"; s 980(3): "£300,000" substituted by "€381,000"; s 986(5)(*a*): "£6" substituted by "€8"; s 986(5)(*a*): "£1" substituted by "€2"; s 986(5)(*b*): "£6" substituted by "€8"; s 986(5)(*b*): "£1" substituted by "€2"; s 986(5)(*b*): "£26" substituted by "€36"; s 986(5)(*b*): "£4.50" substituted by "€9"; s 986(6)(*b*)(i): "£30" substituted by "€40"; s 987(1): "£1,200" substituted by "€1,520"; s 987(1A): "£500" substituted by "€630"; s 987(1A): "£2,000" substituted by "€2,535"; s 987(2): "£750" substituted by "€950"; s 991(1): "£5" substituted by "€6"; s 1003(2)(*c*)(i): "£75,000" substituted by "€95,250"; s 1003(2)(*c*)(ii): "£75,000" substituted by "€95,250"; s 1003(2)(*c*)(ii): "£3,000,000" substituted by "€3,810,000"; s 1021(2): "£20" substituted by "€25"; s 1052(1): "£750" substituted by "€950"; s 1052(2): "£1,200" substituted by "€1,520"; s 1053(1)(i): "£100" substituted by "€125"; s 1053(2): "£100" substituted by "€125"; s 1053(2): "£250" substituted by "€315"; s 1054(2)(*a*)(i): "£1,000" substituted by "€1,265"; s 1054(2)(*a*)(ii): "£500" substituted by "€630"; s 1054(2)(*a*)(ii): "£50" substituted by "€60"; s 1054(2)(*b*)(i): "£200" substituted by "€250"; s 1054(2)(*b*)(ii): "£100" substituted by "€125"; s 1054(3)(*a*)(i)(I): "£500" substituted by "€630"; s 1054(3)(*a*)(i)(I): "£1,000" substituted by "€1,265"; s 1054(3)(*a*)(ii): "£100" substituted by "€125"; s 1054(3)(*a*)(ii): "£200" substituted by "€250"; s 1054(3)(*b*)(i): "£500" substituted by "€630"; s 1054(3)(*b*)(i): "£1,000" substituted by "€1,265"; s 1054(3)(*b*)(ii): "£100" substituted by "€125"; s 1054(3)(*b*)(ii): "£200" substituted by "€250"; s 1055: "£500" substituted by "€630"; s 1056(3)(*a*)(i): "£1,200" substituted by "€1,520"; s 1056(3)(*a*)(ii): "£1,200" substituted by "€1,520"; s 1056(3)(*b*)(i): "£5,000" substituted by "€6,345"; s 1056(3)(*b*)(ii): "£5,000" substituted by "€6,345"; s 1056(3)(*b*)(ii): "£10,000" substituted by "€12,695"; s 1056(3)(*b*)(iii): "£10,000" substituted by "€12,695"; s 1056(3)(*b*)(iii): "£25,000" substituted by "€31,740"; s 1056(3)(*b*)(iv): "£25,000" substituted by "€31,740"; s 1056(3)(*b*)(iv): "£100,000" substituted by "€126,970"; s 1056(3)(*b*)(v): "£100,000" substituted by "€126,970"; s 1057(1): "£100" substituted by "€125"; s 1058(1): "£50" substituted by "€60"; s 1071(1)(*a*): "£500" substituted by "€630"; s 1071(1)(*a*): "£50" substituted by "€60"; s 1071(1)(*b*): "£100" substituted by "€125"; s 1071(2): "£1,000" substituted by "€1,265"; s 1071(2): "£200" substituted by "€250"; s 1072(1): "£500" substituted by "€630"; s 1072(1): "£1,000" substituted by "€1,265"; s 1072(1): "£100" substituted by "€125"; s 1072(1): "£200" substituted by "€250"; s 1073(1)(*a*): "£500" substituted by "€630"; s 1073(1)(*a*): "£50" substituted by "€60"; s 1073(1)(*b*): "£100" substituted by "€125"; s 1074(*a*): "£500" substituted by "€630"; s 1074(*a*): "£50" substituted by "€60"; s 1074(*b*): "£100" substituted by "€125"; s 1075(1): "£100" substituted by "€125"; s 1075(1): "£10" substituted by "€10"; s 1075(2): "£100" substituted by "€125"; s 1075(2): "£250" substituted by "€315"; s 1075(3)(*a*): "£500" substituted by "€630"; s 1075(3)(*a*): "£50" substituted by "€60"; s 1075(3)(*b*): "£100" substituted by "€125"; s 1075(4)(*a*): "£500" substituted by "€630"; s 1075(4)(*a*): "£1,000" substituted by "€1,265"; s 1075(4)(*b*): "£100" substituted by "€125"; s 1075(4)(*b*): "£200" substituted by "€250"; s 1078(3)(*b*): "£100,000" substituted by "€126,970"; s 1079(7)(*a*): "£1,000" substituted by "€1,265"; s 1079(7)(*b*): "£5,000" substituted by "€6,345"; s 1080(2): "£1" substituted by "€2"; s 1084(2)(*a*)(i): "£10,000" substituted by "€12,695"; s 1084(2)(*a*)(ii): "£50,000" substituted by "€63,485"; s 1085(3)(*a*): "£125,000" substituted by "€158,715"; s 1085(3)(*b*): "£50,000" substituted by "€63,485"; s 1085(4)(*b*)(i): "£25,000" substituted by "€31,740"; s 1085(4)(*b*)(ii): "£10,000" substituted by "€12,695"; s 1086(4)(*c*): "£10,000" substituted by "€12,700"; s 1091(3): "£10" substituted by "€10"; s 1091(3): "£100" substituted by "€125"; Schedule 2, para 10: "£2.50" substituted by "€3.50"; Schedule 2, para 19: "£0.675" substituted by "€0.675"; Schedule 2, para 19: "£1,000" substituted by "€1,000"; Schedule 2, para 27: "£0.675" substituted by "€0.675"; Schedule 2, para 27: "£1,000" substituted by "€1,000"; Schedule 3, para 8: "£4,000" substituted by "€5,080"; Schedule 3, para 8: "£4,000" substituted by "€5,080"; Schedule 11, para 3(4): "£10,000" substituted by "€12,700"; Schedule 11, para 3(4): "£30,000" substituted by "€38,100"; Schedule 12A, para 25 (2)(*a*): "£250" substituted by "€320"; Schedule 12A, para 25 (2)(*b*): "£10" substituted by "€12"; Schedule 32, para 22(1): "£8,000,000" substituted by "€10,157,904.63"; Schedule 32, para 22(1): "£6,000,000" substituted by "€7,618,428.47"; Schedule 32, para 22(1): "£6,000,000" substituted by "€7,618,428.47"; Schedule 32, para 22(6): "£3,000,000" substituted by "€3,809,214.24"; Schedule 32, para 22(6): "£2,000,000" substituted by "€2,539,476.16"; Schedule 32, para 22(7): "£3,000,000" substituted by "€3,809,214.24"; Schedule 32, para 22(7): "£2,000,000" substituted by "€2,539,476.16".

FINANCE ACT 2002

(2002 Number 5)

ARRANGEMENT OF SECTIONS

PART 1
Income Tax, Corporation Tax and Capital Gains Tax

Chapter 1
Interpretation

Chapter 2
Income Tax

Chapter 3
Income Tax, Corporation Tax and Capital Gains Tax

AN ACT TO PROVIDE FOR THE IMPOSITION, REPEAL, REMISSION, ALTERATION AND REGULATION OF TAXATION, OF STAMP DUTIES AND OF DUTIES RELATING TO EXCISE AND OTHERWISE TO MAKE FURTHER PROVISION IN CONNECTION WITH FINANCE INCLUDING THE REGULATION OF CUSTOMS [*25TH MARCH 2002*]

PART 1
INCOME TAX, CORPORATION TAX AND CAPITAL GAINS TAX

Chapter 1
Interpretation

1 Interpretation (Part 1)

In this Part, "Principal Act" means the Taxes Consolidation Act, 1997.

CHAPTER 2
Income Tax

2 Amendment of section 15 (rate of charge) of Principal Act

Notes

Para (*a*) substituted "€19,000" for "€13,967" in TCA 1997 s 15(3) for 2002 and later tax years.

Para (*b*) substituted TCA 1997 s 15(3)(Table) for 2002 and later tax years.

3 Personal tax credits

(1) Where an individual is entitled under a provision of the Principal Act mentioned in column (1) of the Table to this subsection to have the income tax to be charged on the individual, other than in accordance with the provisions of section 16(2) of the Principal Act, reduced for the year of assessment 2002 or any subsequent year of assessment and the amount of the reduction would, but for this section, be an amount which is the lesser of—

(*a*) the amount specified in column (2) of that Table, and
(*b*) the amount which reduces that liability to nil,

the amount of the reduction in accordance with paragraph *(a)* shall be the amount of the tax credit specified in column (3) of the Table.

TABLE

Statutory Provision	Existing tax credit (full year)	Tax credit for the year 2002 and subsequent years
(1)	(2)	(3)
Section 461		
(basic personal tax credit)		
(married person)	€2,794	€3,040
(widowed person bereaved in the year of assessment)	€2,794	€3,040
(single person)	€1,397	€1,520
Section 461A		
(additional tax credit for certain widowed persons)	€254	€300
Section 462		
(one-parent family tax credit)	€1,397	€1,520
Section 463		
(widowed parent tax credit)		
(1st year)	€2,540	€2,600
(2nd year)	€2,032	€2,100
(3rd year)	€1,524	€1,600
(4th year)	€1,016	€1,100
(5th year)	€508	€600
Section 464		
(age tax credit)		
(married person)	€408	€410
(single person)	€204	€205

Section 465 (incapacitated child tax credit)	€408	€500
Section 466 (dependent relative tax credit)	€56	€60
Section 466A (home carer tax credit)	€762	€770
Section 468 (blind person's tax credit)		
(blind person)	€762	€800
(both spouses blind)	€1,524	€1,600
Section 472 (employee tax credit)	€508	€660

(2) Section 2 of the Finance Act, 2001, shall have effect subject to the provisions of this section.

(3) Schedule (1) shall apply for the purpose of supplementing subsection (1).

4 Age exemption

Notes

Section 4 substituted "€26,000" for "€21,586" and "€13,000" for "€10,793". in TCA 1997 s 188(2) for 2002 and later tax years.

5 Amendment of section 467 (employed person taking care of incapacitated individual) of Principal Act

Notes

Section 5 substituted "€30,000" for "€12,700" in both places where it occurs in TCA 1997 s 467 for 2002 and later tax years.

6 Amendment of section 477 (relief for service charges) of Principal Act

Notes

Para (*a*) deleted TCA 1997 s 477(1) definition of "specified limit" with effect from 1 January 2002.
Para (*b*) deleted TCA 1997 s 477(2)(*b*) with effect from 1 January 2002.
Para (*c*) deleted "paragraph (*a*)(i) of" and substituted "paragraph (*c*) of that subsection" for "clause (III) of that paragraph" in TCA 1997 s 477(5)(*a*) with effect from 1 January 2002.
Para (*d*) substituted TCA 1997 s 477(6)(*c*) with effect from 1 January 2002.
Para (*e*) substituted TCA 1997 s 477(7) and inserted TCA 1997 s 477(7A)–(7B) with effect from 1 January 2002.

7 Amendment of section 126 (tax treatment of certain benefits payable under Social Welfare Acts) of Principal Act

Notes

Section 7 substituted TCA 1997 s 126(8)(*b*) with effect from 1 January 2002.

8 Amendment of section 122 (preferential loan arrangements) of Principal Act

Notes

Section 8 substituted "5 per cent" for "6 per cent" in both places where it occurs in TCA 1997 s 122(1)(*a*) definition of "the specified rate" for 2002 and later tax years.

9 Amendment of section 469 (relief for health expenses) of Principal Act

Notes

Para (*a*)(i) substituted TCA 1997 s 469(1) definition of "dependant" for 2002 and later tax years.
Para (*a*)(ii)(I) deleted "or" in TCA 1997 s 469(1) definition of "health expenses" para (*g*) for 2002 and later tax years.
Para (*a*)(ii)(II) substituted "ambulance, or" for "ambulance," in TCA 1997 s 469(1) definition of "health expenses" para (*h*) for 2002 and later tax years.
Para (*a*)(iii) substituted "contact lenses;" for "contact lenses." in TCA 1997 s 469(1) definition of "routine ophthalmic treatment" for 2002 and later tax years.
Para (*a*)(iv) inserted TCA 1997 s 469(1) definition of "relative" for 2002 and later tax years.
Para (*b*) deleted TCA 1997 s 469(4) for 2002 and later tax years.

10 Amendment of Part 30 (occupational pension schemes, retirement annuities, purchased life annuities and certain pensions) of Principal Act

Notes

Subs (1)(*a*)(i)(I) substituted TCA 1997 s 772(3)(*b*) with effect from 25 March 2002.
Subs (1)(*a*)(i)(II) substituted TCA 1997 s 772(3)(*d*) with effect from 25 March 2002.
Subs (1)(*a*)(i)(III) deleted TCA 1997 s 772(3)(*e*) with effect from 25 March 2002.
Subs (1)(*a*)(ii) substituted TCA 1997 s 774(7)(*c*) for 2002 and later tax years.
Subs (1)(*a*)(iii) substituted TCA 1997 s 776(2)(*c*) for 2002 and later tax years.
Subs (1)(*a*)(iv) substituted "the standard rate in force at the time of payment" for "25 per cent" in TCA 1997 s 780(5) as respects any repayment of contributions referred to in TCA 1997 s 780 made on or after 5 December 2001.
Subs (1)(*b*) substituted TCA 1997 s 784(1) for 2002 and later tax years.

11 Amendment of section 128 (tax treatment of directors of companies and employees granted rights to acquire shares or other assets) of Principal Act

Notes

Subs (1)(*a*) inserted TCA 1997 s 128(1)(*a*) definition of "branch or agency" with effect from 25 March 2002.
Subs (1)(*b*) substituted "31 March" for "30 June" in TCA 1997 s 128(11) for 2002 and later tax years.
Subs (1)(*c*) substituted TCA 1997 s 128(12) for TCA 1997 s 128(11A) with effect from 25 March 2002.

12 Relief on retirement for certain income of certain sportspersons

Notes

Section 12 inserted TCA 1997 s 480A with effect from 1 January 2002.

13 Amendment of provisions relating to approved profit sharing schemes and employee share ownership trusts

Notes

Subs (1)(*a*)(i) substituted TCA 1997 s 509(1) definition of "shares" and inserted definition of "specified shares" with effect from 16 April 2001.
Subs (1)(*a*)(ii) inserted TCA 1997 s 509(4) with effect from 16 April 2001.

Subs (1)(*b*) substituted TCA 1997 s 511A with effect from 16 April 2001.
Subs (1)(*c*)(i) substituted TCA 1997 s 519(7A) with effect from 16 April 2001.
Subs (1)(*c*)(ii) substituted TCA 1997 s 519(9)(*d*) with effect from 16 April 2001.
Subs (1)(*c*)(iii) substituted "securities" for "shares" in both places it occurs in TCA 1997 s 519(10) definition of "deceased beneficiary" para (*a*) with effect from 16 April 2001.
Subs (1)(*d*)(i) deleted TCA 1997 Sch 11 para 7 with effect from 16 April 2001.
Subs (1)(*d*)(ii) substituted "Subject to paragraph 8A, the shares shall form part of the ordinary share capital of—" for "The shares shall form part of the ordinary share capital of—" in TCA 1997 Sch 11 para 8 with effect from 16 April 2001.
Subs (1)(*d*)(iii) substituted "concerned," for "concerned, or" in TCA 1997 Sch 11 para 8(*b*) with effect from 16 April 2001.
Subs (1)(*d*)(iv) substituted "so owned, or" for "so owned." in TCA 1997 Sch 11 para 8(*c*)(ii) with effect from 16 April 2001.
Subs (1)(*d*)(v) inserted TCA 1997 Sch 11 para 8(*d*) with effect from 16 April 2001.
Subs (1)(*d*)(vi) inserted TCA 1997 Sch 11 para 8A with effect from 16 April 2001.
Subs (1)(*d*)(vii) substituted "clause (*a*)" for "paragraph (*a*)" in TCA 1997 Sch 11 para 10(3)(*b*) with effect from 16 April 2001.
Subs (1)(*d*)(viii) inserted TCA 1997 Sch 11 para 11A with effect from 16 April 2001.
Subs (1)(*e*)(i)(I) deleted "or" in TCA 1997 Sch 12 para 1(1) definition of "relevant company" clause (*a*) with effect from 16 April 2001.
Subs (1)(*e*)(i)(II) substituted "plc," for "plc;" in TCA 1997 Sch 12 para 1(1) definition of "relevant company" clause (*b*) with effect from 16 April 2001.
Subs (1)(*e*)(i)(III) inserted TCA 1997 Sch 12 para 1(1) definition of "relevant company" clause (*c*)–(*d*) with effect from 16 April 2001.
Subs (1)(*e*)(ii) inserted "or of securities to which subparagraph (ii) or (iv) of paragraph *(b)* of the definition of 'specified securities' in section 509(1) applies" in TCA 1997 Sch 12 para 13(3)(*a*) with effect from 16 April 2001.
Subs (1)(*e*)(iii)(I) deleted ", and the original shares the securities represent are shares in the founding company" in TCA 1997 Sch 12 para 15(*a*) with effect from 16 April 2001.
Subs (1)(*e*)(iii)(II) deleted "and 'original shares'" in TCA 1997 Sch 12 para 15(*a*) with effect from 16 April 2001.

14 Income tax: restriction on use of losses on approved buildings

Notes

Section 14 inserted TCA 1997 409C with effect from 1 January 2002.

15 Amendment of Schedule 3 (reliefs in respect of income tax charged on payments on retirement, etc) to Principal Act

Notes

Para (*a*) substituted "in the previous 10 years of assessment" for "previously" in TCA 1997 Sch 3 para 8 for 2002 and later tax years.
Para (*b*) substituted "€10,000" for "€5,080" in both places where it occurs in TCA 1997 Sch 3 para 8 for 2002 and later tax years.

Chapter 3

Income Tax, Corporation Tax and Capital Gains Tax

16 Amendment of Part 16 (income tax relief for investment in corporate trades — business expansion scheme and seed capital scheme) of Principal Act

Notes

Para (*a*)(i) inserted TCA 1997 s 489(4A) with effect from 1 January 2002.
Para (*a*)(ii) substituted "6 years" for "5 years" in TCA 1997 s 489(5)(*a*)–(*b*) with effect from 1 January 2002.

Para (*a*)(iii) substituted "31 December 2003" for "31 December 2001" in TCA 1997 s 489(15) with effect from 1 January 2002.

Para (*b*)(i) inserted "or (4A)" to TCA 1997 s 490(3)(*a*) with effect from 1 January 2002.

Para (*b*)(ii) substituted "2003" for "2001" in TCA 1997 s 490(3)(*b*) and s 490(4)(*b*) for 2002 with effect from 1 January 2002.

Para (*c*)(i) substituted TCA 1997 s 491(2)(*a*) with effect from 1 January 2002.

Para (*c*)(ii) substituted TCA 1997 s 491(3)(*a*) with effect from 1 January 2002.

17 Rental income: relief for certain interest

Notes

Para (*a*) inserted TCA 1997 s 97(2G) with effect from 1 January 2002.

Para (*b*) inserted TCA 1997 s 248A(3) with effect from 1 January 2002.

18 Amendment of Chapter 8 (taxation of rents and certain other payments) of Part 4 of Principal Act

Notes

Subs (1) inserted TCA 1997 s 98A with effect from 7 June 2001 in respect of a reverse premium received on or after that date.

19 Amendment of section 246 (interest payments by companies and to non-residents) of Principal Act

Notes

Subs (1)(*a*) inserted TCA 1997 s 246(3)(*bb*) as respects interest paid on or after 25 March 2002.

Subs (1)(*b*) inserted TCA 1997 s 246(5) as respects interest paid on or after 25 March 2002.

20 Amendment of Chapter 4 (interest payments by certain deposit takers) of Part 8 of Principal Act

[(2) (*a*) Subject to paragraph (*b*), subsection (1) applies as respects deposits made or after the date of the passing of this Act.

(*b*) Paragraph (*b*) (in so far as it relates to a pension scheme) and paragraph (*c*) of subsection (1) apply to interest paid or credited on or after 1 January 2003 in respect of a deposit made on or after the date of the passing of this Act.][1]

Notes

Subs (1)(*a*)(i) substituted TCA 1997 s 256(1) definition of "relevant deposit" para (*f*)(ii).

Subs (1)(*a*)(ii) substituted TCA 1997 s 256(1) definition of "relevant deposit" para (*h*)(ii).

Subs (1)(*b*) substituted TCA 1997 s 265.

Subs (1)(*c*) substituted TCA 1997 s 266.

Amendments

1 Substituted by FA 2003 s 49(5) with effect from 1 January 2003.

21 Amendment of Part 8 (annual payments, charges and interest) of Principal Act

Notes

Para (*a*)(i) substituted "taker;" for "taker." in TCA 1997 s 256(1) definition of "special term account" para (ii) with effect from 1 January 2002.

Para (*a*)(ii) inserted TCA 1997 s 256(1) definition of "special term share account" with effect from 1 January 2002.

Para (*b*)(i) substituted TCA 1997 s 261A(2)–(3) definition of "special term share account" with effect from 1 January 2002.
Para (*b*)(ii) substituted TCA 1997 s 261A(5) with effect from 1 January 2002.
Para (*c*)(i) substituted TCA 1997 s 264A(1)(*j*) with effect from 1 January 2002.
Para (*c*)(ii) deleted "is payable" in TCA 1997 s 264A(2)(*a*) with effect from 1 January 2002.
Para (*d*)(i) inserted TCA 1997 s 267A(1) definition of "special term account" with effect from 1 January 2002.
Para (*d*)(ii) inserted TCA 1997 s 267A(2) with effect from 1 January 2002.
Para (*e*)(i) substituted TCA 1997 s 267C(1)–(2) with effect from 1 January 2002.
Para (*e*)(ii) substituted TCA 1997 s 267C(4) with effect from 1 January 2002.
Para (*f*)(i) substituted TCA 1997 s 267D(1)(*j*) with effect from 1 January 2002.
Para (*f*)(ii) deleted "is payable" in TCA 1997 s 267D(2)(*a*) with effect from 1 January 2002.

22 Amendment of section 268 (meaning of "industrial building or structure") of Principal Act

Notes

Para (1)(*a*) substituted "grant assistance or any other assistance which is granted by or through the State, any board established by statute, any public or local authority or any other agency of the State" for "grant assistance from the State or from any other person" in TCA 1997 s 268(11) as respects expenditure incurred on or after 1 January 2002.
Para (1)(*b*)(i) deleted "and" in TCA 1997 s 268(12) as respects expenditure incurred on or after 1 January 2002.
Para (1)(*b*)(ii) substituted TCA 1997 s 268(12)(*b*) and inserted TCA 1997 s 268(12)(*c*), (*d*) as respects expenditure incurred on or after 1 January 2002.

23 Amendment of Part 10 (income tax and corporation tax: reliefs for renewal and improvement of certain urban areas, certain resort areas and certain islands) of Principal Act

Notes

Para (1)(*a*)(i) substituted "31 December 2004" for "31 December 2002" in TCA 1997 s 344(1) definition of "qualifying period" para (*c*) with effect from 1 January 2002.
Para (1)(*a*)(ii) substituted "31 December 2003" for "31 December 2001" in TCA 1997 s 344(1) definition of "qualifying period" para (*c*) with effect from 1 January 2002.
Para (1)(*a*)(iii) substituted "30 September 2003" for "30 September 2001" in TCA 1997 s 344(1) definition of "qualifying period" para (*c*) with effect from 1 January 2002.
Para (1)(*b*)(i)(I) substituted TCA 1997 s 372A(1) definition of "qualifying period" para (*a*) with effect from such day or days as the Minister for Finance may by order or orders appoint and different days may be appointed for different provisions.
Para (1)(*b*)(i)(II) substituted TCA 1997 s 372A(1) definition of "relevant local authority" with effect from such day or days as the Minister for Finance may by order or orders appoint and different days may be appointed for different provisions.
Para (1)(*b*)(ii) inserted TCA 1997 s 372A(1A) with effect from such day or days as the Minister for Finance may by order or orders appoint and different days may be appointed for different provisions.
Para (1)(*c*)(i) substituted TCA 1997 s 372B(1)(*c*) with effect from such day or days as the Minister for Finance may by order or orders appoint and different days may be appointed for different provisions.
Para (1)(*c*)(ii) inserted TCA 1997 s 372B(1)(*d*) with effect from 1 January 2002.
Para (1)(*d*) substituted "31 December 2004," for "31 December 2002, and" in TCA 1997 s 372L(1) definition of "qualifying period" para (*a*) with effect from such day or days as the Minister for Finance may by order or orders appoint and different days may be appointed for different provisions.
Para (1)(*e*)(i)(I) inserted TCA 1997 s 372U(1) definition of "property developer" as respects expenditure incurred on or after 7 February 2002.
Para (1)(*e*)(i)(II) substituted TCA 1997 s 372U(1) definition of "qualifying period" as respects expenditure incurred on or after 7 February 2002.
Para (1)(*e*)(ii) inserted TCA 1997 s 372V(2A) as respects expenditure incurred on or after 7 February 2002.
Para (1)(*e*)(iii) inserted TCA 1997 s 372W(3A) as respects expenditure incurred on or after 7 February 2002.

24 Codification of reliefs for lessors and owner-occupiers in respect of certain residential accommodation

(1) The Principal Act is amended in the manner and to the extent specified in Part 1 of Schedule 2.

(2) The Urban Renewal Act, 1998 and the Town Renewal Act, 2000 are amended in the manner and to the extent specified in Part 2 of Schedule 2.

Notes

Subs (3)(*a*) repealed TCA 1997 ss 325 to 329 with effect from 1 January 2002.
Subs (3)(*b*) repealed TCA 1997 ss 334 to 338 with effect from 1 January 2002.
Subs (3)(*c*) repealed TCA 1997 ss 346 to 350 with effect from 1 January 2002.
Subs (3)(*d*) repealed TCA 1997 ss 356 to 359 with effect from 1 January 2002.
Subs (3)(*e*) repealed TCA 1997 Pt 10 Chs 5 and 6 (ss 360–372) with effect from 1 January 2002.
Subs (3)(*f*) repealed TCA 1997 ss 372E to 372J with effect from 1 January 2002.
Subs (3)(*g*) repealed TCA 1997 ss 372O–372R, 372S, 372RA with effect from 1 January 2002.
Subs (3)(*h*) repealed TCA 1997 ss 372X to 372Z with effect from 1 January 2002.
Subs (3)(*i*) repealed TCA 1997 ss 372AE to 372AI with effect from 1 January 2002.
Subs (3)(*j*) repealed TCA 1997 Pt 11A (ss 380A–380F) with effect from 1 January 2002.
Subs (3)(*k*) repealed TCA 1997 Pt 11B (ss 380G–380J) with effect from 1 January 2002.

25 Designation of certain areas for rented residential reliefs

Notes

Subs (1)(*a*) inserted Urban Renewal Act 1998 s 9A as respects expenditure incurred on or in relation to a house, where such expenditure is incurred on or after 5 December 2001, or where TCA 1997 s372AP(9)–(10) applies, prior to 5 December 2001, but only if a contract for the purchase of the house had not been evidenced in writing by any person prior to that date, but a contract for the purchase of the house is evidenced in writing on or before 1 September 2002.

Subs (1)(*b*) inserted Urban Renewal Act 1998 s 11(1A) as respects expenditure incurred on or in relation to a house, where such expenditure is incurred on or after 5 December 2001, or where TCA 1997 s372AP(9)–(10) applies, prior to 5 December 2001, but only if a contract for the purchase of the house had not been evidenced in writing by any person prior to that date, but a contract for the purchase of the house is evidenced in writing on or before 1 September 2002.

Subs (2)(*a*) inserted Town Renewal Act 2000 s 6A as respects expenditure incurred on or in relation to a house, where such expenditure is incurred on or after 5 December 2001, or where TCA 1997 s372AP(9)–(10) applies, prior to 5 December 2001, but only if a contract for the purchase of the house had not been evidenced in writing by any person prior to that date, but a contract for the purchase of the house is evidenced in writing on or before 1 September 2002.

Subs (2)(*b*) inserted Town Renewal Act 2000 s 7(1A) as respects expenditure incurred on or in relation to a house, where such expenditure is incurred on or after 5 December 2001, or where TCA 1997 s372AP(9)–(10) applies, prior to 5 December 2001, but only if a contract for the purchase of the house had not been evidenced in writing by any person prior to that date, but a contract for the purchase of the house is evidenced in writing on or before 1 September 2002.

26 Denial of capital allowances where grant or other assistance received

Notes

Subs (1)(*a*) substituted "grant assistance or any other assistance which is granted by or through the State, any board established by statute, any public or local authority or any other agency of the State" for "grant assistance from the State or from any other person" in TCA 1997 s 372K(1)(*aa*) as respects expenditure incurred on or after 7 February 2002.

Subs (1)(*b*) substituted "grant assistance or any other assistance which is granted by or through the State, any board established by statute, any public or local authority or any other agency of the State" for "grant assistance

from the State or from any other person" in TCA 1997 s 372T(1)(*aa*) as respects expenditure incurred on or after 7 February 2002.
Subs (1)(*c*) substituted substituting "grant assistance or any other assistance which is granted by or through the State, any board established by statute, any public or local authority or any other agency of the State" for "grant assistance from the State or from any other person" in TCA 1997 s 372AJ(1)(*aa*) as respects expenditure incurred on or after 7 February 2002.

27 Amendment of section 372AJ (non-application of relief in certain cases and provision against double relief) of Principal Act

Notes

Section 27 deleted TCA 1997 s 372AJ(1)(*ac*) with effect from 6 April 2001.

28 Amendment of Part 11 (capital allowances and expenses for certain road vehicles) of Principal Act

Notes

Subs (1)(*a*)(i) substituted "January 2001;" for "January 2001." in TCA 1997 s 373(2)(*m*)(ii) with effect from 1 January 2002.
Subs (1)(*a*)(ii) inserted TCA 1997 s 373(2)(*n*) with effect from 1 January 2002.
Subs (1)(*b*) substituted "the purposes of that section" for "the purpose of subsection (3) of that section" in TCA 1997 s 374(1) as respects capital expenditure incurred on or after 1 January 2001.
Subs (1)(*c*) deleted TCA 1997 s 376 as respects expenditure incurred in an accounting period ending on or after 1 January 2002, or in a basis period for a year of assessment, where that basis period ends on or after 1 January 2002.

29 Amendment of section 668 (compulsory disposals of livestock) of Principal Act

Notes

Subs (1)(*a*)(i) substituted "paragraph (*b*) and subsection (3A)" for "paragraph (*b*)" and "the 4 immediately succeeding accounting periods" for "the 2 immediately succeeding accounting periods" in TCA 1997 s 668(3)(*a*) as respects disposals made on or after 21 February 2001.
Subs (1)(*a*)(ii) substituted "Notwithstanding paragraph (*a*) but subject to subsection (3A)" for "Notwithstanding paragraph (*a*)" and "the 3 immediately succeeding accounting periods" for "the immediately succeeding accounting period" in TCA 1997 s 668(3)(*b*) as respects disposals made on or after 21 February 2001.
Subs (1)(*b*) inserted TCA 1997 s 668(3A) as respects disposals made on or after 21 February 2001.
Subs (1)(*c*) substituted TCA 1997 s 668(4) and inserted TCA 1997 s 668(4A) as respects disposals made on or after 21 February 2001.
Subs (1)(*d*) inserted TCA 1997 s 668(6)–(7) with effect from 6 April 2001.

30 Amendment of section 669A (interpretation) of Principal Act

Notes

Subs (1)(*a*) deleted TCA 1997 s 669A definition of "lessee" with effect on and from 6 April 2000.
Subs (1)(*b*) substituted TCA 1997 s 669A definition of "qualifying quota" para (*b*) with effect from 6 April 2000.

31 Capital allowances in respect of machinery or plant

Notes

Subs (1)(*a*)(i) substituted "paragraphs (*aa*) and (*ab*)" for "paragraph (*aa*)" in TCA 1997 s 284(2)(*a*) with effect from 1 January 2002.
Subs (1)(*a*)(ii) inserted TCA 1997 s 284(2)(*ab*)–(*ac*) with effect from 1 January 2002.

Subs (1)(*a*)(iii) substituted ", the amount specified in paragraph (*aa*) or, as the case may be, the amount specified in subparagraph (i) or (ii) of paragraph (*ab*)" for "or the amount specified in paragraph (*aa*), as the case may be," in TCA 1997 s 284(2)(*b*) with effect from 1 January 2002.

Subs (1)(*d*) substituted "For the purposes of paragraphs (*a*)(ii) and (*ab*)(ii) of subsection (2), the value at the commencement of a chargeable period" for "For the purposes of subsection (2)(*a*)(ii), the value at the commencement of the chargeable period" in TCA 1997 s 284(3) with effect from 1 January 2002.

Subs (2) inserted TCA 1997 s 288(3B) with effect from 1 January 2002.

32 Capital allowances for certain hospitals

Notes

Para (*a*) inserted TCA 1997 s 268(1A) with effect from 1 January 2002.

Para (*b*)(i) deleted TCA 1997 s 268(2A) definition of "qualifying hospital" para (*b*) with effect from 1 January 2002.

Para (*b*)(ii) substituted "70 in-patient beds" for "100 in-patient beds" in TCA 1997 s 268(2A) definition of "qualifying hospital" para (*d*) with effect from 1 January 2002.

Para (*b*)(iii) substituted "gives, during the period of 7 years referred to in section 272(4)(*h*), an annual certificate in writing" for "gives a certificate in writing" in TCA 1997 s 268(2A) definition of "qualifying hospital" para (*h*) with effect from 1 January 2002.

Para (*b*)(iv) substituted "and— (I) includes any part of the hospital which consists of rooms used exclusively for the assessment or treatment of patients, but (II) does not include any part of the hospital which consists of consultants' rooms or offices." for "but does not include any part of the hospital which consists of consultants' rooms or offices" in TCA 1997 s 268(2A) definition of "qualifying hospital" (*a*) with effect from 1 January 2002.

33 Registered nursing homes: capital allowances for associated housing units for the aged or infirm

Notes

Para (*a*) inserted "(in this section referred to as a 'registered nursing home')" in TCA 1997 s 268(1)(g) with effect from 1 January 2002.

Para (*b*) inserted TCA 1997 s 268(3A)–(3C) with effect from 1 January 2002.

Para (*c*) inserted inserting "or a qualifying residential unit" in TCA 1997 s 268(7)(*b*) with effect from 1 January 2002.

34 Capital allowances for certain sports injuries clinics

Notes

Para (1)(*a*)(i)(I) deleted "or" in TCA 1997 s 268(1)(*i*) and substituted "qualifying hospital, or" for "qualifying hospital," in TCA 1997 s 268(1)(*j*) from such day as the Minister for Finance may by order appoint.

Para (1)(*a*)(i)(II) inserted TCA 1997 s 268(1)(*k*) from such day as the Minister for Finance may by order appoint.

Para (1)(*a*)(ii) inserted TCA 1997 s 268(1B) from such day as the Minister for Finance may by order appoint.

Para (1)(*a*)(iii) inserted TCA 1997 s 268(2B) from such day as the Minister for Finance may by order appoint.

Para (1)(*a*)(iv)(I) deleted "and" in TCA 1997 s 268(9)(*f*) and substituted "2001, and" for "2001." in TCA 1997 s 268(9)(*g*) from such day as the Minister for Finance may by order appoint.

Para (1)(*a*)(iv)(II) inserted TCA 1997 s 268(9)(*h*) from such day as the Minister for Finance may by order appoint.

Para (1)(*b*) substituted "paragraph (*j*) or (*k*) of section 268(1)" for "section 268(1)(*j*)" in TCA 1997 s 272(3)(*h*) and (4)(*h*) and s 274(1)(*b*)(vii) from such day as the Minister for Finance may by order appoint.

35 Amendment of section 843 (capital allowances for buildings used for third level educational purposes) of Principal Act

Notes

Section 35 substituted "31 December 2004" for "the 31st day of December, 2002" in TCA 1997 s 843(7).

36 Amendment of Part 20 (companies' chargeable gains) of Principal Act

Notes

Para (*a*) substituted "relevant Member State" for "Member State of the European Communities" in TCA 1997 s 615(2)(*b*)(ii) with effect from 1 January 2002.

Para (*b*)(i) substituted "relevant Member State" for "Member State of the European Communities" in TCA 1997 s 616(1)(*a*) with effect from 1 January 2002.

Para (*b*)(ii) inserted TCA 1997 s 616(7) with effect from 1 January 2002.

Para (*c*) substituted "relevant Member State" for "Member State of the European Communities" in TCA 1997 s 621(1) definition of "group of companies" with effect from 1 January 2002.

Para (*d*) substituted "relevant Member State" for "Member State of the European Communities" in TCA 1997 s 624(5) with effect from 1 January 2002.

Para (*e*) substituted "relevant Member State" for "Member State of the European Communities" in TCA 1997 s 629(1) definition of "group" with effect from 1 January 2002.

37 Amendment of Chapter 5 (group relief) of Part 12 of Principal Act

Notes

Para (*a*)(i)(I) inserted TCA 1997 s 410(1)(*a*) definitions of "EEA Agreement", "EEA State" and "relevant Member State" with effect from 1 January 2002.

Para (*a*)(i)(II) substituted "relevant Member State" for "Member State of the European Communities" in TCA 1997 s 410(1)(*a*) definition of "tax" with effect from 1 January 2002.

Para (*a*)(ii)(I) substituted "relevant Member State" for "Member State of the European Communities" in TCA 1997 s 410(1)(*b*) with effect from 1 January 2002.

Para (*a*)(ii)(II) substituted TCA 1997 s 410(1)(*b*)(ii) with effect from 1 January 2002.

Para (*a*)(iii) substituted "relevant Member State" for "Member State of the European Communities" in TCA 1997 s 410(3)(*a*) with effect from 1 January 2002.

Para (*a*)(iv) substituted "relevant Member State" for "Member State of the European Communities" in TCA 1997 s 410(4)(*a*)(i) with effect from 1 January 2002.

Para (*b*)(i)(I) inserted TCA 1997 s 411(1)(*a*) definitions of "EEA Agreement" and "EEA State" with effect from 1 January 2002.

Para (*b*)(i)(II) inserted TCA 1997 s 411(1)(*a*) definition of "relevant Member State" with effect from 1 January 2002.

Para (*b*)(i)(III) substituted "relevant Member State" for "Member State of the European Communities" in TCA 1997 s 411(1)(*a*) definition of "tax" with effect from 1 January 2002.

Para (*b*)(ii) substituted "relevant Member State" for "Member State of the European Communities" in TCA 1997 s 411(1)(*c*) with effect from 1 January 2002.

38 Amendment of Schedule 24 (relief from income tax and corporation tax by means of credit in respect of foreign tax) to Principal Act

Notes

Para (*a*)(i) inserted TCA 1997 Sch 24 para 1(1) definitions of "EEA Agreement" and "EEA State" with effect from 1 January 2002.

Para (*a*)(ii) inserted TCA 1997 Sch 24 para 1(1) definition of "relevant Member State" with effect from 1 January 2002.

Para (*b*)(i) substituted "relevant Member State" for "Member State of the European Communities" in TCA 1997 Sch 24 para 9A(3A)(*a*)(ii) with effect from 1 January 2002.

Para (*b*)(ii) substituted "relevant Member State" for "Member State of the European Communities" in TCA 1997 Sch 24 para 9A(3A)*(b)* with effect from 1 January 2002.
Para (*c*)(i) substituted "relevant Member State" for "Member State of the European Communities" in TCA 1997 Sch 24 para 9B(1A)*(a)*(ii) with effect from 1 January 2002.
Para (*c*)(ii) substituted "relevant Member State" for "Member State of the European Communities" in TCA 1997 Sch 24 para 9B(1A)*(b)* with effect from 1 January 2002.
Para (*d*) substituted "relevant Member State" for "Member State of the European Communities" in TCA 1997 Sch 24 para 9C(1) with effect from 1 January 2002.

39 Application of section 130 (matters to be treated as distributions) of Principal Act

Notes

Para (*a*)(i) substituted "relevant Member State" for "Member State of the European Communities" in TCA 1997 s 130(3)(*b*) with effect from 1 January 2002.
Para (*a*)(ii) substituted "relevant Member State" for "Member State of the European Communities" in TCA 1997 s 130(3)(*c*) with effect from 1 January 2002.
Para (*a*)(iii) inserted TCA 1997 s 130(3)(*d*) with effect from 1 January 2002.
Para (*b*) substituted "relevant Member State" for "Member State of the European Communities" in TCA 1997 s 130(4)(*c*) with effect from 1 January 2002.

40 Life assurance: taxation of personal portfolio life policies

Notes

Subs (1)(*a*) inserted TCA 1997 s 730BA as respects the happening of a chargeable event in relation to a life policy (within the meaning of Chapter 5 of Part 26), or the receipt by a person of a payment in respect of a foreign life policy (within the meaning of Chapter 6 of that Part) or the disposal in whole or in part of a foreign life policy (within that meaning), on or after 26 September 2001.
Subs (1)(*b*)(i) substituted TCA 1997 s 730F(1)(*a*)–(*b*) as respects the happening of a chargeable event in relation to a life policy (within the meaning of Pt 26 Ch 5) on or after 26 September 2001.
Subs (1)(*b*)(ii) inserted TCA 1997 s 730F(4) as respects the happening of a chargeable event in relation to a life policy (within the meaning of Pt 26 Ch 5) on or after 26 September 2001.
Subs (1)(*c*) inserted TCA 1997 s 730FA as respects the happening of a chargeable event in relation to a life policy (within the meaning of Pt 26 Ch 5) on or after 26 September 2001.
Subs (2)(*a*) inserted TCA 1997 s 730J(*a*) as respects the receipt by a person of a payment in respect of a foreign life policy (within the meaning of Pt 26 Ch 6 of Part 26) or the disposal in whole or in part of a foreign life policy (within that meaning) on or after 26 September 2001.
Subs (2)(*b*) substituted TCA 1997 s 730K(1)(formula) as respects the receipt by a person of a payment in respect of a foreign life policy (within the meaning of Pt 26 Ch 6 of Part 26) or the disposal in whole or in part of a foreign life policy (within that meaning) on or after 26 September 2001.
Subs (3) substituted TCA 1997 s 904C(1) definition of "return" with effect from 5 December 2001.
Subs (4) inserted "section 730FA(2)" in TCA 1997 Sch 29 col 1 with effect from 5 December 2001.

41 Donations to certain sports bodies

Notes

Section 41 inserted TCA 1997 s 847A with effect from 1 May 2002.

42 Amendment of section 482 (relief for expenditure on significant buildings and gardens) of Principal Act

Notes

Subs (1)(*a*) substituted TCA 1997 s 482(1)(*a*) definition of "relevant expenditure" subpara (ii) with effect from 30 November 1997.

Subs (1)(*b*) substituted "on or before the 1st day of November" for "on or before the 1st day of January" in TCA 1997 s 482(2)(*b*)(ii) as respects a chargeable period, being the year of assessment 2002 and any subsequent year of assessment or an accounting period of a company beginning on or after 1 January 2002.
Subs (1)(*c*) substituted "on or before 1 November" for "on or before 1 January" in TCA 1997 s 482(8) as respects a chargeable period, being the year of assessment 2002 and any subsequent year of assessment or an accounting period of a company beginning on or after 1 January 2002.
Subs (1)(*d*) inserted TCA 1997 s 482(11) with effect from 6 March 2001.

43 Amendment of section 486B (relief for investment in renewable energy generation) of Principal Act

Notes

Subs (1) substituted TCA 1997 s 486B(1) definition of "qualifying period" with effect from such day as the Minister for Finance appoints by order.

44 Amendment of section 739D (gain arising on a chargeable event) of Principal Act

Notes

Para (*a*) substituted "In this Chapter and Schedule 2B" for "In this Chapter" in TCA 1997 s 739D(1) with effect from 1 January 2002.
Para (*b*) substituted TCA 1997 s 739D(6)(*f*) with effect from 1 January 2002.
Para (*c*) substituted TCA 1997 s 739D(8D)(*a*)–(*b*) with effect from 1 January 2002.
Para (*d*) substituted TCA 1997 s 739D(9) and inserted TCA 1997 s 739D(9A) with effect from 1 January 2002.

45 Amendment of Schedule 2B (investment undertakings declarations) to Principal Act

Notes

Subs (1)(*a*) substituted TCA 1997 Sch 2B para 13(*d*)–(*e*) with effect from 1 January 2002.
Subs (1)(*b*) inserted TCA 1997 Sch 2B para 14 with effect from 1 January 2002.

46 Amendment of Chapter 4 (certain offshore funds — taxation and returns) of Part 27 of Principal Act

Notes

Subs (1)(*a*) substituted TCA 1997 s 747D(*b*) with effect from 1 January 2001.
Subs (1)(*b*) substituted TCA 1997 s 747E(1) with effect from 1 January 2001.

47 Amendment of section 579A (attribution of gains to beneficiaries) of Principal Act

Notes

Subs (1)(*a*) substituted TCA 1997 s 579A(2) with effect from 11 February 1999.
Subs (1)(*b*) deleted TCA 1997 s 579A(10)–(11) with effect from 11 February 1999.

48 Amendment of Chapter 5 (policyholders — new basis) of Part 26 of Principal Act

Notes

Subs (1)(*a*) substituted TCA 1997 s 730D(2)(*b*)(iii) with effect from 1 January 2002.
Subs (1)(*b*) inserted TCA 1997 s 730D(2A) with effect from 1 January 2002.

Subs (1)(*c*) substituted TCA 1997 s 730E(3)(*e*)(iii) with effect from 1 January 2002.

49 Amendment of Part 36A (special savings incentive accounts) of Principal Act

Notes

Para (*a*) substituted TCA 1997 s 848C(*h*) with effect from 1 January 2002.
Para (*b*) inserted TCA 1997 s 848E(3A) with effect from 1 January 2002.
Para (*c*)(i) substituted TCA 1997 s 848H(1)(*a*) with effect from 1 January 2002.
Para (*c*)(ii) inserted TCA 1997 s 848H(4) with effect from 1 January 2002.
Para (*d*)(i) substituted TCA 1997 s 848M(1) with effect from 1 January 2002.
Para (*d*)(ii) substituted "to the best of the inspector's judgement" for "to the best of his or their judgement" in TCA 1997 s 848M(4) with effect from 1 January 2002.

50 Amendment of section 838 (special portfolio investment accounts) of Principal Act

Notes

Section 50 inserted TCA 1997 s 838(4)(*bb*) with effect from 1 January 2002.

51 Amendment of Chapter 2 (payments to subcontractors in certain industries) of Part 18 of Principal Act

Notes

Subs (1)(*a*)(i) inserted "telecommunication apparatus," in TCA 1997 s 530(1) definition of "construction operations" para (*b*) with effect from 1 April 2002.
Subs (1)(*a*)(ii) inserted TCA 1997 s 530(1) definition of "meat processing operations" para (*fa*) with effect from 1 April 2002.
Subs (1)(*b*)(i) substituted "the Income Tax (Relevant Contracts) Regulations 2000 (SI No 71 of 2000)" for "the Income Tax (Construction Contracts) Regulations, 1971 (SI No 1 of 1971)," in TCA 1997 s 531(8) with effect from 6 April 2000.
Subs (1)(*b*)(ii) substituted "the Income Tax (Relevant Contracts) Regulations 2000" for "the Income Tax (Construction Contracts) Regulations, 1971 (SI No 1 of 1971)," in TCA 1997 s 531(10) with effect from 6 April 2000.
Subs (1)(*b*)(iii)(I) substituted "taxes, interest and penalties" for "taxes" in TCA 1997 s 531(11)(*a*)(iv)(A) with effect from 1 April 2002.
Subs (1)(*b*)(iii)(II) substituted "subparagraphs (i) to (iv) and (vi)" for "subparagraphs (i) to (iv)" in TCA 1997 s 531(11)(*b*) with effect from 1 January 2002.

52 Amendment of section 951 (obligation to make a return) of Principal Act

Notes

Section 52 inserted TCA 1997 s 951(11)(*d*)–(*e*) with effect from 1 January 2002.

CHAPTER 4
Corporation Tax

53 Tonnage tax

Notes

Subs (1) inserted TCA 1997 Pt 24A (ss 697A–697Q) with effect from 28 March 2003.
Subs (2) inserted TCA 1997 Sch 18B with effect from 28 March 2003.
Subs (3) inserted TCA 1997 s 21(1A)(c) with effect from 28 March 2003.

Subs (4) inserted "Schedule 18B, paragraph 30" in TCA 1997 Sch 29, column 2, with effect from 28 March 2003.

Subs (5) substituted by FA 2003 s 62(2) with effect from 28 March 2003, and provides that FA 2002 s 53 comes into operation as on and from date of passing of FA 2003, ie 28 March 2003.

54 Relief for certain losses on a value basis

...

(2) For the purposes of computing the amount of—

(*a*) charges on income paid for the purposes of the sale of goods (within the meaning of section 454 of the Principal Act),

(*b*) a loss from the sale of goods (within the meaning of section 455 of the Principal Act),

(*c*) relevant trading charges on income (within the meaning of section 243A of the Principal Act), and

(*d*) relevant trading losses (within the meaning of section 396A of the Principal Act),

in respect of which relief may be claimed by virtue of this section, where an accounting period of a company begins before 6 March 2001 and ends on or after that date, it shall be divided into 2 parts, one beginning on the date on which the accounting period begins and ending on 5 March 2001 and the other beginning on 6 March 2001 and ending on the date on which the accounting period ends, and both parts shall be treated as if they were separate accounting periods of the company.

Notes

Subs (1)(*a*) inserted TCA 1997 s 243B as respects an accounting period ending on or after 6 March 2001.

Subs (1)(*b*)(i)(I) substituted "subsection (2) or section 396A(3), 396B(2) or 455(3)" for "subsection (2) or section 455(3)" in TCA 1997 s 396(1) as respects an accounting period ending on or after 6 March 2001.

Subs (1)(*b*)(i)(II) inserted "net of any part of those charges relieved under section 243B" after "a company" in TCA 1997 s 396(7) as respects an accounting period ending on or after 6 March 2001.

Subs (1)(*b*)(ii) inserted TCA 1997 s 396B as respects an accounting period ending on or after 6 March 2001.

Subs (1)(*b*)(iii) inserted TCA 1997 s 420B as respects an accounting period ending on or after 6 March 2001.

Subs (1)(*c*) inserted "(within the meaning of section 243A)" in TCA 1997 s 454(2) as respects an accounting period ending on or after 6 March 2001.

55 Amendment of section 90 (restriction of certain losses and charges) of Finance Act 2001

Notes

Section 55 substituted FA 2001 s 90(4), and FA 2001 s 90 is to apply, and is deemed always to have applied, as if that substitution were made.

56 Amendment of section 483 (relief for certain gifts) of Principal Act

Notes

Subs (1) inserted TCA 1997 s 483(5) with effect from 6 March 2001.

57 Credit for certain withholding tax

Notes

Para (*a*)(i) substituted "this paragraph, paragraph 9D" for "this paragraph" in TCA 1997 Sch 24 para 4(5)(*a*) with effect from 1 January 2002.

Para (*a*)(ii)(I) deleted "and" in TCA 1997 Sch 24 para 4(5)(*b*)(ii) with effect from 1 January 2002.

Para (*a*)(ii)(II) inserted "and" in TCA 1997 Sch 24 para 4(5)(*b*)(iii) with effect from 1 January 2002.

Para (*a*)(ii)(III) inserted TCA 1997 Sch 24 para 4(5)(*b*)(iv) with effect from 1 January 2002.

Para (*b*) substituted "section 449 or paragraph 9D" for "section 449" in TCA 1997 Sch 24 para 9A(5)(*b*) with effect 1 January 2002.

Para (*c*) inserted TCA 1997 Sch 24 para 9D with effect from 1 January 2002.

58 Amendment of section 958 (date for payment of tax) of Principal Act

Notes

Subs (1)(*a*) substituted TCA 1997 s 958(1) with effect from 1 January 2002.

Subs (1)(*b*) substituted TCA 1997 s 958(2) and inserted TCA 1997 s 958(2A)–(2C) with effect from 1 January 2002.

Subs (1)(*c*) substituted "subsections (3A), (4), (4B), (4C), (4D) and (4E)" for "subsections (3A) and (4)" in TCA 1997 s 958(3) with effect from 1 January 2002.

Subs (1)(*d*) inserted "which is a year of assessment" in TCA 1997 s 958(4) with effect from 1 January 2002.

Subs (1)(*e*) inserted TCA 1997 s 958(4B)–(4E) with effect from 1 January 2002.

CHAPTER 5
Capital Gains Tax

59 Amendment of section 598 (disposal of business or farm on "retirement") of Principal Act

Notes

Section 59 substituted TCA 1997 s 598(1) definition of "qualifying assets" paras (ii)–(iii) and inserted TCA 1997 s 598(1) definition of "qualifying assets" para (iv) with effect from 1 January 2002.

60 Amendment of section 600A (replacement of qualifying premises) of Principal Act

Notes

Para (*a*) substituted TCA 1997 s 600A (1) definition of "qualifying premises" para (*a*) with effect from 1 January 2002.

Para (*b*) substituted TCA 1997 s 600A(1) definition of "replacement premises" para (*b*) with effect from 1 January 2002.

61 Amendment of section 605 (disposals to authority possessing compulsory purchase powers) of Principal Act

Notes

Para (*a*) substituted TCA 1997 s 605(1)(*c*) with effect from 1 January 2002.

Para (*b*) inserted TCA 1997 s 605(4A) with effect from 1 January 2002.

62 Amendment of section 542 (time of disposal and acquisition) of Principal Act

Notes

Section 62 inserted TCA 1997 s 542(1)(*d*) with effect from 1 January 2002.

63 Amendment of section 980 (deduction from consideration on disposal of certain assets) of Principal Act

Notes

Section 63 substituted "€500,000" for "€381,000" in TCA 1997 s 980(3) with effect from 1 January 2002.

PART 6
MISCELLANEOUS

123 Interpretation (Part 6)

In this Part "Principal Act" means the Taxes Consolidation Act, 1997.

124 Amendment of section 1003 (payment of tax by means of donation of heritage items) of Principal Act

Notes

Para (*a*) inserted "or whose import into the State would constitute a significant enhancement of the accumulated cultural heritage of Ireland" in TCA 1997 s 1003(2)(a)(I) with effect from 25 March 2002.
Para (*b*)(i) substituted "€100,000" for "€95,250" in TCA 1997 s 1003(2)(*c*) with effect from 25 March 2002.
Para (*b*)(ii) substituted "€6,000,000" for "€3,810,000" in TCA 1997 s 1003(2)(*c*) with effect from 25 March 2002.
Para (*c*) substituted "shall, subject to paragraph (*d*), be estimated" for "shall be estimated" in TCA 1997 s 1003(3)(*a*) with effect from 25 March 2002.
Para (*c*) inserted TCA 1997 s 1003(3)(*d*) with effect from 25 March 2002.

125 Amendment of Chapter 5 (miscellaneous provisions) of Part 42 of Principal Act

Notes

Para (*a*)(i)(I) substituted TCA 1997 s 1006A(1) definition of "claim" with effect from 25 March 2002.
Para (*a*)(i)(II) substituted TCA 1997 s 1006A(1) definition of "liability" with effect from 25 March 2002.
Para (*a*)(i)(III) substituted "credited;" for "credited." in TCA 1997 s 1006A(1) definition of "overpayment" with effect from 25 March 2002.
Para (*a*)(i)(IV) inserted TCA 1997 s 1006A(1) definition of "tax" with effect from 25 March 2002.
Para (*a*)(ii) inserted TCA 1997 s 1006A(5) with effect from 25 March 2002.
Para (*b*) inserted TCA 1997 s 1006B(5) with effect from 25 March 2002.

126 Amendment of section 1086 (publication of names of tax defaulters) of Principal Act

Notes

Subs (1)(*a*)(i)(I) substituted TCA 1997 s 1086(1) definition of "the Acts" para (*e*) as respects fines or other penalties, as are referred to in TCA 1997 s 1086(2)*(a)*–(*b*), which are imposed by a court, and as respects specified sums, as are referred to in TCA 1997 s 1086(2)(*c*)–(*d*), which the Revenue Commissioners accepted, or undertook to accept, in settlement of a specified liability, on or after 25 March 2002.
Subs (1)(*a*)(i)(II) inserted TCA 1997 s 1086(1) definition of "the Acts" paras (*g*)–(*h*) as respects fines or other penalties, as are referred to in TCA 1997 s 1086(2)*(a)*–(*b*), which are imposed by a court, and as respects

specified sums, as are referred to in TCA 1997 s 1086(2)(*c*)–(*d*), which the Revenue Commissioners accepted, or undertook to accept, in settlement of a specified liability, on or after 25 March 2002.
Subs (1)(*a*)(ii) substituted TCA 1997 s 1086(1) definition of "tax" as respects fines or other penalties, as are referred to in TCA 1997 s 1086(2)*(a)*–(*b*), which are imposed by a court, and as respects specified sums, as are referred to in TCA 1997 s 1086(2)(*c*)–(*d*), which the Revenue Commissioners accepted, or undertook to accept, in settlement of a specified liability, on or after 25 March 2002.
Subs (1)(*b*)(i) substituted TCA 1997 s 1086(2)(*c*)(ii)–(iii) as respects fines or other penalties, as are referred to in TCA 1997 s 1086(2)*(a)*–(*b*), which are imposed by a court, and as respects specified sums, as are referred to in TCA 1997 s 1086(2)(*c*)–(*d*), which the Revenue Commissioners accepted, or undertook to accept, in settlement of a specified liability, on or after 25 March 2002.
Subs (1)(*b*)(ii) substituted TCA 1997 s 1086(2)(*d*)(ii)–(iii) as respects fines or other penalties, as are referred to in TCA 1997 s 1086(2)*(a)*–(*b*), which are imposed by a court, and as respects specified sums, as are referred to in TCA 1997 s 1086(2)(*c*)–(*d*), which the Revenue Commissioners accepted, or undertook to accept, in settlement of a specified liability, on or after 25 March 2002.
Subs (1)(*c*) substituted TCA 1997 s 1086(3)(*b*) as respects fines or other penalties, as are referred to in TCA 1997 s 1086(2)*(a)*–(*b*), which are imposed by a court, and as respects specified sums, as are referred to in TCA 1997 s 1086(2)(*c*)–(*d*), which the Revenue Commissioners accepted, or undertook to accept, in settlement of a specified liability, on or after 25 March 2002.
Subs (1)(*d*)(i) substituted "those paragraphs" for "that paragraph" in TCA 1997 s 1086(4)(*a*) as respects fines or other penalties, as are referred to in TCA 1997 s 1086(2)*(a)*–(*b*), which are imposed by a court, and as respects specified sums, as are referred to in TCA 1997 s 1086(2)(*c*)–(*d*), which the Revenue Commissioners accepted, or undertook to accept, in settlement of a specified liability, on or after 25 March 2002.
Subs (1)(*d*)(ii) substituted "applied," for "applied, or" in TCA 1997 s 1086(4)(*b*) as respects fines or other penalties, as are referred to in TCA 1997 s 1086(2)*(a)*–(*b*), which are imposed by a court, and as respects specified sums, as are referred to in TCA 1997 s 1086(2)(*c*)–(*d*), which the Revenue Commissioners accepted, or undertook to accept, in settlement of a specified liability, on or after 25 March 2002.
Subs (1)(*d*)(iii) substituted "€12,700, or" for "€12,700." in TCA 1997 s 1086(4)(*c*) as respects fines or other penalties, as are referred to in TCA 1997 s 1086(2)*(a)*–(*b*), which are imposed by a court, and as respects specified sums, as are referred to in TCA 1997 s 1086(2)(*c*)–(*d*), which the Revenue Commissioners accepted, or undertook to accept, in settlement of a specified liability, on or after 25 March 2002.
Subs (1)(*d*)(iii) inserted TCA 1997 s 1086(4)(*d*) as respects fines or other penalties, as are referred to in TCA 1997 s 1086(2)*(a)*–(*b*), which are imposed by a court, and as respects specified sums, as are referred to in TCA 1997 s 1086(2)(*c*)–(*d*), which the Revenue Commissioners accepted, or undertook to accept, in settlement of a specified liability, on or after 25 March 2002.

127 Tax clearance

Notes

Para (*a*)(i)(I)(A) substituted "means a licence, permit or authorisation" for "means a licence or authorisation" in TCA 1997 s 1094(1) definition of "licence" with effect from 25 March 2002.
Para (*a*)(i)(I)(B) substituted "," for ";" in TCA 1997 s 1094(1) definition of "licence" paras (*h*), (*j*), (*k*) and (*l*) with effect from 25 March 2002.
Para (*a*)(i)(I)(C) inserted TCA 1997 s 1094(1) definition of "licence" paras (*m*)–(*n*) with effect from 25 March 2002.
Para (*a*)(i)(II) substituted "paragraphs (*a*) to (*n*)" for "paragraphs (*a*) to (*j*)" in TCA 1997 s 1094(1) definition of "specified date" with effect from 25 March 2002.
Para (*a*)(ii) substituted TCA 1997 s 1094(5) with effect from 25 March 2002.
Para (*a*)(iii) inserted TCA 1997 s 1094(8)–(9) with effect from 25 March 2002.
Para (*b*) substituted TCA 1997 s 1095 with effect from 25 March 2002.

128 Amendment of Schedule 29 (provisions referred to in sections 1052, 1053 and 1054) to Principal Act

Notes

Para (*a*)(i) inserted "section 172K(1)", "section 172L(2)" in TCA 1997 Sch 29 Col 1 with effect from 25 March 2002.
Para (*a*)(ii) inserted "section 258(2)" in TCA 1997 Sch 29 Col 1 with effect from 25 March 2002.

Para (*b*) deleted "section 172K(1)", "section 172L(2)" and "section 258(2)" in TCA 1997 Sch 29 Col 2 with effect from 25 March 2002.

129 Interest on unpaid and overpaid tax

Notes

Subs (1)(*a*) substituted "0.0322 per cent for each day or part of a day" for "1 per cent for each month or part of a month" in TCA 1997 ss 172K(6)(*b*), 240(3), 730G(7)(*b*), 739F(7)(*b*), 784E(6)(*b*) and 848M(6)(*b*) with effect from 1 September 2002 as regards interest chargeable or payable in respect of amount due to be paid or remitted or to be repaid or retained, whether before, on, or after that date.

Subs (1)(*b*) substituted "0.0322 per cent for each day or part of a day on" for "1 per cent for each month or part of a month during" in TCA 1997 s 531(9) with effect from 1 September 2002 as regards interest chargeable or payable in respect of amount due to be paid or remitted or to be repaid or retained, whether before, on, or after that date.

Subs (1)(*c*) substituted "0.0161 per cent, or such other rate (if any) prescribed by the Minister for Finance by regulations, for each day or part of a day" for "0.6 per cent, or such other rate (if any) prescribed by the Minister for Finance by regulations, for each month or part of a month" in TCA 1997 s 942(6)(*b*) with effect from 1 September 2002 as regards interest chargeable or payable in respect of amount due to be paid or remitted or to be repaid or retained, whether before, on, or after that date.

Subs (1)(*d*) substituted "0.0161 per cent, or such other rate (if any) prescribed by the Minister for Finance by regulations, for each day or part of a day" for "0.5 per cent, or such other rate (if any) prescribed by the Minister for Finance by regulations, for each month or part of a month" in TCA 1997 s 953(7) with effect from 1 September 2002 as respects interest chargeable or payable in respect of amount due to be paid or remitted or to be repaid or retained, whether before, on, or after that date.

Subs (1)(*e*) substituted TCA 1997 s 991(1) with effect from 1 September 2002 as regards interest chargeable or payable in respect of amount due to be paid or remitted or to be repaid or retained, whether before, on, or after that date.

Subs (1)(*f*)(i) substituted "0.0322 per cent for each day or part of a day" for "1 per cent for each month or part of a month" in TCA 1997 s 1080(1)(*a*)–(*b*) with effect from 1 September 2002 as regards interest chargeable or payable in respect of amount due to be paid or remitted or to be repaid or retained, whether before, on, or after that date.

Subs (1)(*f*)(ii) deleted TCA 1997 s 1080(2) with effect from 1 September 2002 as regards interest chargeable or payable in respect of amount due to be paid or remitted or to be repaid or retained, whether before, on, or after that date.

130 Amendment of Chapter 1 (income tax and corporation tax penalties) of Part 47 of Principal Act

Notes

Subs (1)(*a*)(i) inserted TCA 1997 s 1053(1A) with effect from 25 March 2002.

Subs (1)(*a*)(ii) inserted TCA 1997 s 1053(5A) with effect from 25 March 2002.

Subs (1)(*a*)(iii) substituted "subsections (5) and (5A)" for "subsection (5)" in TCA 1997 s 1053(6) with effect from 25 March 2002.

Subs (1)(*b*)(i) substituted "€1,520" for "€1,265" in TCA 1997 s 1054(2)(*a*)(i) with effect from 25 March 2002.

Subs (1)(*b*)(ii) substituted "€950" for "€630" in TCA 1997 s 1054(2)(*a*)(ii) with effect from 25 March 2002.

Subs (1)(*c*) substituted "preceding provisions of this Part, Chapter 4 of Part 38" for "preceding provisions of this Part" in TCA 1997 s 1061(1) with effect from 25 March 2002.

Subs (1)(*d*) substituted "For the purposes of this Chapter, and Chapter 4 of Part 38" for "For the purposes of this Chapter" in TCA 1997 s 1068 with effect from 25 March 2002.

131 Amendment of section 1072 (penalties for fraudulently or negligently making incorrect returns, etc) of Principal Act

Notes

Section 131 inserted TCA 1997 s 1072(2A)–(2B) with effect from 25 March 2002.

132 Amendment of Chapter 4 (revenue powers) of Part 38 of Principal Act

Notes

Para (*a*) inserted TCA 1997 s 901(4)–(5) with effect from 25 March 2002.
Para (*b*) inserted TCA 1997 s 902A(6A)–(6B) with effect from 25 March 2002.
Para (*c*) inserted TCA 1997 s 904I with effect from 25 March 2002.
Para (*d*) substituted TCA 1997 s 905(1) definition of "records" with effect from 25 March 2002.
Para (*e*) inserted TCA 1997 s 907(7A)–(7B) with effect from 25 March 2002.
Para (*f*) inserted TCA 1997 s 908A(6A)–(6B) with effect from 25 March 2002.
Para (*g*)(i)(I) inserted TCA 1997 s 908A definition "the Acts" with effect from 25 March 2002.
Para (*g*)(i)(II) inserted TCA 1997 s 908A definition "offence" with effect from 25 March 2002.
Para (*g*)(ii) substituted TCA 1997 s 908A(2) with effect from 25 March 2002.

133 Amendment of section 1078 (revenue offences) of Principal Act

Notes

Para (*a*) substituted "fails without reasonable excuse" for "knowingly or wilfully fails" in TCA 1997 s 1078(2)(*g*) with effect from 25 March 2002.
Para (*b*) inserted TCA 1997 s 1078(3B) with effect from 25 March 2002.

134 Amendment of Chapter 3 (returns of income and capital gains, etc) of Part 38 of Principal Act

Notes

Section 134 inserted TCA 1997 s 898A with effect from 25 March 2002.

135 Amendment of Part 48 (miscellaneous and supplemental) of Principal Act

Notes

Section 135 inserted TCA 1997 s 1096B with effect from 25 March 2002.

139 Amendment of Provisional Collection of Taxes Act, 1927

Notes

Para (*a*) substituted Provisional Collection of Taxes 1927 s 1 definition of "new tax" with effect from 25 March 2002.
Para (*b*) substituted "immediately before the date on which the resolution is expressed to take effect or, where no such date is expressed, the passing of the resolution by Dáil Éireann" for "immediately before the end of the previous financial year" in Provisional Collection of Taxes 1927 ss 2–3 with effect from 25 March 2002.

140 Care and management of taxes and duties

All taxes and duties imposed by this Act are placed under the care and management of the Revenue Commissioners.

141 Short title, construction and commencement

(1) This Act may be cited as the Finance Act, 2002.

(2) Part 1 (so far as relating to income tax) shall be construed together with the Income Tax Acts and (so far as relating to corporation tax) shall be construed together with the Corporation Tax Acts and (so far as relating to capital gains tax) shall be construed together with the Capital Gains Tax Acts.

...

(7) Part 6 (so far as relating to income tax) shall be construed together with the Income Tax Acts and (so far as relating to corporation tax) shall be construed together with the Corporation Tax Acts and (so far as relating to capital gains tax) shall be construed together with the Capital Gains Tax Acts and (so far as relating to value-added tax) shall be construed together with the Value-Added Tax Acts, 1972 to 2002 and (so far as relating to residential property tax) shall be construed together with Part VI of the Finance Act, 1983, and the enactments amending or extending that Part and (so far as relating to gift tax or inheritance tax) shall be construed together with the Capital Acquisitions Tax Act, 1976, and the enactments amending or extending that Act.

(8) Except when otherwise expressly provided in Part 1, that Part applies as on and from 1 January 2002.

...

(10) Any reference in this Act to any other enactment shall, except so far as the context otherwise requires, be construed as a reference to that enactment as amended by or under any other enactment including this Act.

(11) In this Act, a reference to a Part, section or Schedule is to a Part or section of, or Schedule to, this Act, unless it is indicated that reference to some other enactment is intended.

(12) In this Act, a reference to a subsection, paragraph, subparagraph, clause or subclause is to the subsection, paragraph, subparagraph, clause or subclause of the provision (including a Schedule) in which the reference occurs, unless it is indicated that reference to some other provision is intended.

SCHEDULE 1
AMENDMENTS CONSEQUENTIAL ON CHANGES IN PERSONAL TAX CREDITS

Notes

Para 1(*a*) substituted "€3,040" for "€2,794" and "€1,520" for "€1,397" in TCA 1997 s 461 for 2002 and later tax years.

Para 1(*b*) substituted "€300" for "€254" in TCA 1997 s 461A for 2002 and later tax years.

Para 1(*c*) substituted "€1,520" for "€1,397" in TCA 1997 s 462(2) for 2002 and later tax years.

Para 1(*d*) substituted "€2,600" for "€2,540", "€2,100" for "€2,032","€1,600" for "€1,524", "€1,100" for "€1,016" and "€600" for "€508" in TCA 1997 s 463(2) for 2002 and later tax years.

Para 1(*e*) substituted "€410" for "€408" and "€205" for "€204" in TCA 1997 s 464 for 2002 and later tax years.

Para 1(*f*) substituted "€500" for "€408" in TCA 1997 s 465(1) for 2002 and later tax years.

Para 1(*g*) substituted "€60" for "€56" in TCA 1997 s 466(2) for 2002 and later tax years.

Para 1(*h*)(i) substituted "€770" for "€762" in TCA 1997 s 466A(2) for 2002 and later tax years.

Para 1(*h*)(ii) substituted "total income" for "an income" in TCA 1997 s 466A(6)(*a*) for 2002 and later tax years.

Para 1(*i*) substituted "€800" for "€762" and "€1,600" for "€1,524" in TCA 1997 s 468(2) for 2002 and later tax years.

Para 1(*j*) substituted "€660" for "€508" in TCA 1997 s 472(4) for 2002 and later tax years.

SCHEDULE 2

CODIFICATION OF RELIEFS FOR LESSORS AND OWNER-OCCUPIERS IN RESPECT OF CERTAIN EXPENDITURE INCURRED ON CERTAIN RESIDENTIAL ACCOMMODATION

PART 1

AMENDMENT OF TAXES CONSOLIDATION ACT 1997

Notes

Para 1 inserted TCA 1997 Pt 10 Ch 11 (ss 327AK–372AV) with effect from 1 January 2002.

Para 2(*a*)(i)(I) substituted "Chapter 11 of this Part" for "section 372F or 372I" in TCA 1997 s 372A(1) definition of "necessary construction" para (*a*) with effect from 1 January 2002.

Para 2(*a*)(i)(II) deleted "and other than for the purposes of sections 372H and 372I" in TCA 1997 s 372A(1) definition of "refurbishment" with effect from 1 January 2002.

Para 2(*a*)(ii) substituted "This Chapter and Chapter 11 of this Part" for "This Chapter" in TCA 1997 s 372A(2) with effect from 1 January 2002.

Para 2(*b*)(i)(I) substituted "this Chapter or Chapter 11 of this Part" for "this Chapter" in TCA 1997 s 372B(1)(*a*) with effect from 1 January 2002.

Para 2(*b*)(i)(II) inserted TCA 1997 s 372B(1)(*ba*) with effect from 1 January 2002.

Para 2(*b*)(ii) substituted "this Chapter or Chapter 11 of this Part" for "this Chapter" in TCA 1997 s 372B(4) with effect from 1 January 2002.

Para 2(*c*)(i)(I) substituted "this Chapter or Chapter 11 of this Part" for "this Chapter" in TCA 1997 s 372BA(1)(*a*) with effect from 1 January 2002.

Para 2(*c*)(i)(II) inserted TCA 1997 s 372BA(1)(*ba*) with effect from 1 January 2002.

Para 2(*c*)(i)(III) inserted "and section 372AL" in TCA 1997 s 372BA(1)(*c*) with effect from 1 January 2002.

Para 2(*c*)(ii) inserted "under this Chapter or Chapter 11 of this Part" in TCA 1997 s 372BA(4) with effect from 1 January 2002.

Para 2(*d*)(i) deleted TCA 1997 s 372L definition of "qualifying period" paras (*b*)–(*c*) with effect from 1 January 2002.

Para 2(*d*)(ii) deleted "and other than for the purposes of sections 372R and 372RA" in TCA 1997 s 372L definition of "refurbishment" with effect from 1 January 2002.

Para 2(*e*)(i) substituted "section 372W or 372AK" for "section 372W, 372X or 372Y" in TCA 1997 s 372U(1) definition of "park and ride facility" para (*b*) with effect from 1 January 2002 with effect from 1 January 2002.

Para 2(*e*)(ii) deleted "or the construction of a qualifying premises within the respective meanings assigned in sections 372X and 372Y" in TCA 1997 s 372U(1) definition of "the relevant local authority" with effect from 1 January 2002.

Para 2(*f*) substituted "section 372AP or 372AR" and "section 372AP(5) or 372AR(5)" for "section 372X or 372Y" and "section 372X(4) or 372Y(2)(*c*)" in TCA 1997 s 372W(2)(*c*)(i) with effect from 1 January 2002.

Para 2(*g*)(i)(I) substituted TCA 1997 s 372AA(1) definition of "qualifying period" with effect from 1 January 2002.

Para 2(*g*)(i)(II) deleted "and other than for the purposes of sections 372AG and 372AH" in TCA 1997 s 372AA(1) definition of "refurbishment" with effect from 1 January 2002.

Para 2(*g*)(ii) substituted "This Chapter and Chapter 11 of this Part" for "This Chapter" in TCA 1997 s 372AA(2) with effect from 1 January 2002.

Para 2(*h*)(i)(I) substituted "This Chapter and Chapter 11 of this Part" for "This Chapter" in TCA 1997 s 372AB(1)(*a*) with effect from 1 January 2002.

Para 2(*h*)(i)(II) substituted "section 372AR" for "section 372AH" in TCA 1997 s 372AB(1)(*b*) with effect from 1 January 2002.

Para 2(*h*)(i)(III) inserted TCA 1997 s 372AB(1)(*ba*) with effect from 1 January 2002.

Para 2(*h*)(i)(IV)(A) inserted "and section 372AL" in TCA 1997 s 372AB(1)(*c*) with effect from 1 January 2002.

Para 2(*h*)(i)(IV)(B) substituted "any provision of Chapter 11 of this Part" for "sections 372AE, 372AF, 372AG, 372AH and 372AI" in TCA 1997 s 372AB(1)(*c*)(ii) with effect from 1 January 2002.

Para 2(*h*)(ii) substituted "this Chapter or Chapter 11 of this Part" for "this Chapter" in TCA 1997 s 372AB(4) with effect from 1 January 2002.

Para 2(*i*) substituted "Section 372AR" for "Section 328", "Section 337", "Section 349", "Section 364", "Section 371", "Section 372I", "Section 372RA", "Section 372Y" and "Section 372AH" in TCA 1997 s 458 (Table) with effect from 1 January 2002.

Para 2(*j*) substituted TCA 1997 s 1024(2)(*a*)(i) with effect from 1 January 2002.

PART 2

CONSEQUENTIAL AMENDMENTS TO OTHER ENACTMENTS

Notes

Para 3(*a*) substituted "Chapter 7 or 11" for "Chapter 7" in Urban Renewal Act 1998 ss 8(1)(*a*), 11(1) and 12(1) with effect from 1 January 2002.

Para 3(*b*) substituted Urban Renewal Act 1998 s 8(1)(*b*) with effect from 1 January 2002.

Para 3(*c*) substituted "paragraph *(a)*, *(b)*, *(ba)* or *(c)*" for "paragraph *(a)*, *(b)* or *(c)*" in Urban Renewal Act 1998 s 9 with effect from 1 January 2002.

Para 4(*a*) inserted "or Chapter 11 (inserted by the Finance Act 2002)" in Town Renewal Act 2000 ss 3(4)(*c*), 5(1)(*a*), 7(1) and 8(1) with effect from 1 January 2002.

Para 4(*b*) substituted Town Renewal Act 2000 s 5(1)(*b*) with effect from 1 January 2002.

Para 4(*c*) substituted "paragraph *(a)*, *(b)*, *(ba)* or *(c)*" for "paragraph *(a)*, *(b)* or *(c)*" in Town Renewal Act 2000 s 6 with effect from 1 January 2002.

SCHEDULE 6
MISCELLANEOUS TECHNICAL AMENDMENTS IN RELATION TO TAX

Notes

Para 3(*a*) substituted "€1,905" for "£1,500" in TCA 1997 s 116(3)(*b*) with effect from 1 January 2002.

Para 3(*b*) substituted "Income Tax (Employments) (Consolidated) Regulations 2001 (SI No 559 of 2001)" for "Income Tax (Employments) Regulations, 1960 (SI No 28 of 1960)" in TCA 1997 s 121(6)(*c*) with effect from 1 January 2002.

Para 3(*c*) substituted "Income Tax (Employments) (Consolidated) Regulations 2001 (SI No 559 of 2001)" for "Income Tax (Employments) Regulations, 1960 (SI No 28 of 1960)" in TCA 1997 s 126(7)(*a*) with effect from 1 January 2002.

Para 3(*d*) substituted "subsections (1)(*b*), (2) and (3) of that section." for "subsections (1)(*b*), (2), (3) and (5) of that section." in TCA 1997 s 187(2)(*b*) with effect from 6 April 2001.

Para 3(*e*) substituted TCA 1997 s 244(1) definition of "dependent relative" with effect from 6 April 2001.

Para 3(*f*) substituted "qualifying street" for "designated street" in TCA 1997 s 372D(3A)(*a*) with effect from 6 April 2001.

Para 3(*g*)(i) substituted TCA 1997 s 434(5)(*a*)(ii) as respects the accounting period ending on or after 14 March 2001.

Para 3(*g*)(ii) substituted TCA 1997 s 434(5)(*b*)(i) as respects accounting period ending on or after 14 March 2001.

Para 3(*h*) substituted "earlier" for "later" in TCA 1997 s 470A(7)(*a*)(i)(II) with effect from 6 April 2001.

Para 3(*i*) substituted "Income Tax (Employments) (Consolidated) Regulations 2001 (SI No 559 of 2001)" for "Income Tax (Employments) Regulations, 1960 (SI No 28 of 1960)" in TCA 1997 s 472(2)(*a*)(ii) with effect from 1 January 2002.

Para 3(*j*) substituted "subsections (4) and (5)" for "subsections (4) and (6)" in TCA 1997 s 472A(1)(*a*) definition of "qualifying child" with effect from 6 April 2001.

Para 3(*k*) substituted "€250" for "£200" in TCA 1997 s 481(6) with effect from 1 January 2002.

Para 3(*l*) substituted "Regulation 22(2)(*b*)(ii) of the Income Tax (Employments) (Consolidated) Regulations 2001 (SI No 559 of 2001)" for "Regulation 25(2)(*b*) of the Income Tax (Employments) Regulations, 1960 (SI No 28 of 1960)" in TCA 1997 s 784A(4)(*c*)(ii)(II) with effect from 1 January 2002.

Para 3(*m*) substituted "this section and section 835, the arrangements shall, notwithstanding any enactment" for "this section and sections 168 and 835, the arrangements shall, notwithstanding any enactment other than section 168" in TCA 1997 s 826(1) with effect from 25 March 2002.

Para 3(*n*) substituted "Regulation 20 of the Income Tax (Employments) (Consolidated) Regulations 2001 (SI No 559 of 2001)" for "regulation 22 of the Income Tax (Employment) Regulations, 1960 (SI No 28 of 1960)" in TCA 1997 s 903(1) definition of "records" with effect from 1 January 2002.

Para 3(*o*) substituted "that assessment or amended assessment" for "and that assessment or amended assessment" in TCA 1997 s 959(2) as respects the year of assessment 2002 and subsequent years of assessment and as respects accounting periods of companies ending on or after 1 January 2001.

Para 3(*p*)(i) substituted "Regulation 31 of the Income Tax (Employments) (Consolidated) Regulations 2001 (SI No 559 of 2001)" for "Regulation 35 of the Income Tax (Employments) Regulations, 1960 (SI No 28 of 1960)" in TCA 1997 s 987(1)–(1A) with effect from 1 January 2002.

Para 3(*p*)(ii) substituted "Regulation 7(4) of the Income Tax (Employments) (Consolidated) Regulations 2001 (SI No 559 of 2001)" for "regulation 8(4) of the Income Tax (Employments) Regulations, 1960 (SI No 28 of 1960)" in TCA 1997 s 987(4)(*c*) with effect from 1 January 2002.
Para 3(*q*)(i) substituted "Regulation 7 of the Income Tax (Employments) (Consolidated) Regulations 2001 (SI No 559 of 2001)" for "regulation 8 of the Income Tax (Employments) Regulations, 1960 (SI No 28 of 1960)" in TCA 1997 s 988(1) with effect from 1 January 2002.
Para 3(*q*)(ii) substituted "Regulation 28" for "regulation 31" in TCA 1997 s 988(3)(*a*) with effect from 1 January 2002.
Para 3(*r*)(i) substituted "Regulation 31 of the Income Tax (Employments) (Consolidated) Regulations 2001 (SI No 559 of 2001)" for "Regulation 35 of the Income Tax (Employments) Regulations, 1960 (SI No 28 of 1960)" in TCA 1997 s 990(1A)*(a)*(ii) with effect from 1 January 2002.
Para 3(*r*)(ii) substituted "Regulation 31 of the Income Tax (Employments) (Consolidated) Regulations 2001 (SI No 559 of 2001)" for "Regulation 35 of the Income Tax (Employment) Regulations, 1960 (SI No 28 of 1960)" in TCA 1997 s 990(2) with effect from 1 January 2002.
Para 3(*s*) substituted "Regulation 29 of the Income Tax (Employments) (Consolidated) Regulations 2001 (SI No 559 of 2001)" for "Regulation 31A (inserted by the Income Tax (Employments) Regulations, 1989 (SI No 58 of 1989)) of the Income Tax (Employments) Regulations, 1960 (SI No 28 of 1960)" in TCA 1997 s 991A*(a)* with effect from 1 January 2002.
Para 3(*t*)(i) substituted "Regulation 29 of the Income Tax (Employments) (Consolidated) Regulations 2001 (SI No 559 of 2001)" for "regulation 31A of the Income Tax (Employments) Regulations, 1960 (SI No 28 of 1960)" in TCA 1997 s 995*(a)*(i) with effect from 1 January 2002.
Para 3(*t*)(ii) substituted "Regulation 29 of those Regulations" for "regulation 31A of those Regulations" in TCA 1997 s 995*(a)*(i) with effect from 1 January 2002.
Para 3(*u*) substituted "performed or discharged" for "performed or authorised" in TCA 1997 s 1022(9) with effect from 25 March 2002.
Para 3(*v*)(i) substituted "subsection (3)" for "subsection (4)" in TCA 1997 s 1024(2)*(a)*(ii) with effect from 6 April 2001.
Para 3(*v*)(ii) substituted "section 465(3)" for "section 465(4)" in TCA 1997 s 1024(2)*(a)*(iii) with effect from 6 April 2001.
Para 3(*v*)(iii) substituted "473A" for "474, 474A, 475, 475A" in TCA 1997 s 1024(2)*(a)*(ix) with effect from 6 April 2001.
Para 3(*v*)(iv) substituted TCA 1997 s 1024(2)*(a)*(x*a*) with effect from 6 April 2001.
Para 3(*w*) substituted "section 465(5)" for "section 465(7)" in TCA 1997 s 1025(4)(*d*) with effect from 6 April 2001.
Para 3(*x*) substituted "paragraph 2" for "subsection (2)" in TCA 1997 Sch 26A para 3(*c*) with effect from 6 April 2001.
Para 5(*a*) substituted "'Subsections (2) and (4)' of 'Subsections (2) to (4)'" for "'Subsections 2 and 4' of 'Subsections 2 to 4'" in FA 2001 s 55(*b*) with effect from 30 March 2001.
Para 5(*b*) substituted "Subsection (1) shall" for "This section shall" in FA 2001 s 70(2) with effect from 30 March 2001.
Para 5(*c*) substituted "Subsection (1) shall" for "This section shall" in FA 2001 s 71(2) with effect from 30 March 2001.
Para 5(*d*) substituted "Subsection (1) shall" for "This section shall" in FA 2001 s 74(2) with effect from 30 March 2001.
Para 5(*f*) substituted FA 2001 s 232(2) with effect from 30 March 2001.
Para 5(*g*) substituted "section 494(2)" for "section 494(1)" in FA 2001 s 240(2)(*l*)(vi) with effect from 30 March 2001.
Para 5(*h*)(i) substituted "paragraph (*b*)" for "paragraph *(a)*" in FA 2001 Sch 1 para 1(*p*) with effect from 30 March 2001.
Para 5(*h*)(ii) substituted "subsection (1)" for "subsection (2)" in FA 2001 Sch 1 para 2(*g*) with effect from 30 March 2001.

PENSIONS (AMENDMENT) ACT 2002

(2002 Number 18)

ARRANGEMENT OF SECTIONS

PART 1
Preliminary and General

Section

PART 2
Personal Retirement Savings Accounts

AN ACT TO AMEND AND EXTEND THE PENSIONS ACT, 1990, AND TO PROVIDE FOR RELATED MATTERS. [*13TH APRIL 2002*]

PART 1
PRELIMINARY AND GENERAL

1 Short title, collective citation, construction and commencement

(1) This Act may be cited as the Pensions (Amendment) Act, 2002.

(2) The Principal Act, the Pensions (Amendment) Act, 1996, and this Act may be cited together as the Pensions Acts, 1990 to 2002, and shall be construed together as one.

(3) This Act shall come into operation on such day or days as the Minister may appoint by order or orders either generally or with reference to any particular purpose or provision and different days may be so appointed for different purposes or different provisions.

(4) Without prejudice to the generality of the foregoing, different days may be so appointed for the coming into operation of section 3 of this Act as respects different provisions of the Part inserted in the Principal Act by that section.

2 Definitions

In this Act—

"Minister" means the Minister for Social, Community and Family Affairs;

"Principal Act" means the Pensions Act, 1990.

4 Amendment of Taxes Consolidation Act, 1997

Notes

Subs (1)(*a*) substituted TCA 1997 s 118(5) with effect from such date as the Minister for Social, Community and Family Affairs may appoint by order.

Subs (1)(*b*)(i) inserted TCA 1997 s 706(3)(*d*) with effect from such date as the Minister for Social, Community and Family Affairs may appoint by order.
Subs (1)(*b*)(ii)(I) deleted "or" from TCA 1997 s 730D(2)(*b*)(ii) with effect from such date as the Minister for Social, Community and Family Affairs may appoint by order.
Subs (1)(*b*)(ii)(II) substituted "207(1)(*b*), or" for "207(1)(*b*)," in TCA 1997 s 730D(2)(*b*)(iii) with effect from such date as the Minister for Social, Community and Family Affairs may appoint by order.
Subs (1)(*b*)(ii)(III) inserted TCA 1997 s 730D(2)(*b*)(iv) with effect from such date as the Minister for Social, Community and Family Affairs may appoint by order.
Subs (1)(*b*)(iii)(I)(A) deleted "or, as the case may be," from TCA 1997 s 730E(3)(*e*)(ii) with effect from such date as the Minister for Social, Community and Family Affairs may appoint by order.
Subs (1)(*b*)(iii)(I)(B) inserted "or, as the case may be," in TCA 1997 s 730E(3)(*e*)(iii) with effect from such date as the Minister for Social, Community and Family Affairs may appoint by order.
Subs (1)(*b*)(iii)(I)(C) inserted TCA 1997 s 730E(3)(*e*)(iv) with effect from such date as the Minister for Social, Community and Family Affairs may appoint by order.
Subs (1)(*b*)(iii)(II) substituted TCA 1997 s 730E(3)(*f*) with effect from such date as the Minister for Social, Community and Family Affairs may appoint by order.
Subs (1)(*c*)(i) substituted "Schedule 2B," for "Schedule 2B, or" in TCA 1997 s 739D(6)(*g*) with effect from such date as the Minister for Social, Community and Family Affairs may appoint by order.
Subs (1)(*c*)(ii) substituted "Schedule 2B, or," for "Schedule 2B," in TCA 1997 s 739D(6)(*h*) with effect from such date as the Minister for Social, Community and Family Affairs may appoint by order.
Subs (1)(*c*)(iii) inserted TCA 1997 s 739D(6)(*i*) with effect from such date as the Minister for Social, Community and Family Affairs may appoint by order.
Subs (1)(*d*)(i) inserted TCA 1997 s 770(1) definition of "Personal Retirement Savings Account" with effect from such date as the Minister for Social, Community and Family Affairs may appoint by order.
Subs (1)(*d*)(ii) inserted TCA 1997 s 772(3D) with effect from such date as the Minister for Social, Community and Family Affairs may appoint by order.
Subs (1)(*d*)(iii) inserted TCA 1997 s 780(2A) with effect from such date as the Minister for Social, Community and Family Affairs may appoint by order.
Subs (1)(*d*)(iv) inserted TCA 1997 s 784(2C) with effect from such date as the Minister for Social, Community and Family Affairs may appoint by order.
Subs (1)(*d*)(v) inserted TCA 1997 Pt 30 Ch 2A (ss 787A–787L) with effect from such date as the Minister for Social, Community and Family Affairs may appoint by order.
Subs (1)(*d*)(vi)(I) substituted "capital)," for "capital), or," in TCA 1997 s 788(2)(*e*) with effect from such date as the Minister for Social, Community and Family Affairs may appoint by order.
Subs (1)(*d*)(vi)(II) substituted "784C, or" for "784C."in TCA 1997 s 788(2)(*f*) with effect from such date as the Minister for Social, Community and Family Affairs may appoint by order.
Subs (1)(*d*)(vi)(III) inserted TCA 1997 s 788(2)(*g*) with effect from such date as the Minister for Social, Community and Family Affairs may appoint by order.
Subs (1)(*e*) substituted "Chapter 1 or Chapter 2A of Part 30" for "Chapter 1 of Part 30" in TCA 1997 s 986(1)(*g*)(ii) with effect from such date as the Minister for Social, Community and Family Affairs may appoint by order.
Subs (1)(*f*) inserted TCA 1997 Sch 2B para 9A with effect from such date as the Minister for Social, Community and Family Affairs may appoint by order.

FINANCE ACT 2003

(2003 No 3)

ARRANGEMENT OF SECTIONS

PART 1
INCOME TAX, CORPORATION TAX AND CAPITAL GAINS TAX

Chapter 1
Interpretation

Chapter 2
Income Tax

Chapter 3
Income Tax, Corporation Tax and Capital Gains Tax

AN ACT TO PROVIDE FOR THE IMPOSITION, REPEAL, REMISSION, ALTERATION AND REGULATION OF TAXATION, OF STAMP DUTIES AND OF DUTIES RELATING TO EXCISE AND OTHERWISE TO MAKE FURTHER PROVISION IN CONNECTION WITH FINANCE INCLUDING THE REGULATION OF CUSTOMS. [*28th March 2003*]

PART 1
INCOME TAX, CORPORATION TAX AND CAPITAL GAINS TAX

Chapter 1
Interpretation

1 Interpretation (Part 1)

In this Part **"Principal Act"** means the Taxes Consolidation Act 1997.

Chapter 2
Income Tax

2 Age exemption

Notes

Section 2 substituted "€30,000" for "€26,000" and "€15,000" for "€13,000" in TCA 1997 s 188(2) as respects the tax year 2003 and later years.

3 Employee tax credit

(2) Section 3 of the Finance Act 2002, shall have effect subject to the provisions of this section.

Notes

Subs (1) substituted "€800" for "€660" in TCA 1997 s 472(4) for 2003 and later tax years.

4 Amendment of section 122 (preferential loan arrangements) of Principal Act

Notes

Para (*a*) substituted "4.5 per cent" for "5 per cent" in both places where it occurs in TCA 1997 s 122(1)(*a*)(definition of "the specified rate) for 2003 and later tax years.

Para (*b*) substituted "11 per cent" for "12 per cent" in TCA 1997 s 122(1)(*a*)(definition of "the specified rate) for 2003 and later tax years.

5 Amendment of section 126 (tax treatment of certain benefits payable under Social Welfare Acts) of Principal Act

Notes

Section 5 substituted TCA 1997 s 126(8)(*b*).

6 Application of PAYE to perquisites, benefits-in-kind, etc

Notes

Subs (1)(*a*) substituted TCA 1997 s 119(4) with effect from 1 January 2004.

Subs (1)(*b*)(i)(I) substituted TCA 1997 s 121(1)(*a*)(definition of "car") with effect from 1 January 2004.

Subs (1)(*b*)(i)(II) inserted TCA 1997 s 121(1)(*a*)(definition of "motor-cycle") with effect from 1 January 2004.

Subs (1)(*b*)(ii) substituted TCA 1997 s 121(2)(*b*)(ii) with effect from 1 January 2004.

Subs (1)(*b*)(iii) substituted TCA 1997 s 121(3)(*a*) with effect from 1 January 2004.

Subs (1)(*b*)(iv)(I) substituted TCA 1997 s 121(4)(*a*) with effect from 1 January 2004.

Subs (1)(*b*)(iv)(II) inserted TCA 1997 s 121(4)(*c*) with effect from 1 January 2004.

Subs (1)(*b*)(iv)(III) inserted TCA 1997 s 121(4)(Table) with effect from 1 January 2004.

Subs (1)(*b*)(v) deleted TCA 1997 s 121(6)(*c*) with effect from 1 January 2004.

Subs (1)(*c*) inserted TCA 1997 s 121A with effect from 1 January 2004.

Subs (1)(*d*) inserted TCA 1997 s 985A with effect from 1 January 2004.

7 Payment of tax in respect of share options in certain circumstances

Notes

Para (*a*) substituted "in the period from 6 April 2000 to the date of the passing of the Finance Act 2003" for "on or after 6 April 2000" in TCA 1997 s 128A(1)(*a*) with effect from 1 January 2003.

Para (*b*) inserted TCA 1997 s 128A(4A) and (4B) with effect from 1 January 2003.

Para (*c*) substituted "subsections (4)(*a*) and (4A)" for "subsection (4)(*a*)" in TCA 1997 s 128A(5) with effect from 1 January 2003.

Para (*d*) substituted "subsections (4) and (4A) but notwithstanding any provisions of subsection (4A) that subsection shall have no effect as respects the payment of any tax in relation to a gain realised by the exercise on or after 6 February 2003 of a right to acquire shares." for "subsection (4)." in TCA 1997 s 128A(7) with effect from 1 January 2003.

8 Payment of tax under section 128 (tax treatment of directors of companies and employees granted rights to acquire shares or other assets) of Principal Act

Notes

Subs (1)(*a*) inserted TCA 1997 s 128B with effect from 30 June 2003.

Subs (1)(b) deleted TCA 1997 s 128(2A) in respect of the exercise, assignment or release of a right (within the meaning of section 128 of the Principal Act) on or after 30 June 2003.

9 Amendment of section 244 (relief for interest paid on certain home loans) of Principal Act

Notes

Subs (1)(*a*) substituted "7 years" for "5 years" in TCA 1997 s 244(1)(*a*)(definition of "relievable interest") with effect from 1 January 2003 but shall not apply to an individual for whom the fifth year of assessment for which he or she had an entitlement to relief under TCA 1997 s 244 in respect of a qualifying loan (within the meaning of that section) was prior to the year of assessment 2002.

Subs (1)(*b*) substituted "€8,000" for "€6,350" in TCA 1997 s 244(1)(*a*)(definition of "relievable interest") with effect from 1 January 2003 but shall not apply to an individual for whom the fifth year of assessment for which he or she had an entitlement to relief under TCA 1997 s 244 in respect of a qualifying loan (within the meaning of that section) was prior to the year of assessment 2002.

Subs (1)(*c*) substituted "€4,000" for "€3,175" in TCA 1997 s 244(1)(*a*)(definition of "relievable interest") with effect from 1 January 2003 but shall not apply to an individual for whom the fifth year of assessment for which he or she had an entitlement to relief under TCA 1997 s 244 in respect of a qualifying loan (within the meaning of that section) was prior to the year of assessment 2002.

10 Amendment of Chapter 1 (payments in respect of professional services by certain persons) of Part 18 of, and Schedule 13 to, Principal Act

Notes

Subs (1)(*a*)(i) substituted "applies," for "applies, and" in TCA 1997 s 520(1)("relevant payment")(i) with effect from 1 January 2003;

Subs (1)(*a*)(ii) substituted "section, and" for "section;" in TCA 1997 s 520(1)("relevant payment")(ii) with effect from 1 January 2003;

Subs (1)(*a*)(iii) inserted TCA 1997 s 520(1)("relevant payment")(iii) with effect from 1 January 2003;

Subs (1)(*b*) substituted TCA 1997 s 525(6) with effect from 1 January 2003;

Subs (2)(*a*) substituted TCA 1997 Sch 13 para 79 with effect from 18 December 2001;

Subs (2)(*b*) deleted TCA 1997 Sch 13 para 104 with effect from 1 January 2003;

Subs (2)(*c*) inserted TCA 1997 Sch 13 paras 121–139 with effect from 1 May 2003;

11 Amendment of section 65 (Cases I and II: basis of assessment) of Principal Act

Notes

This section inserted "notwithstanding anything to the contrary in section 66(2)," after "then," in TCA 1997 s 65(3) with effect from 1 January 2003.

12 Restriction of reliefs where individual is not actively participating in certain trades

Notes

Subs (1) inserted TCA 1997 s 409D as respects an allowance under [TCA 1997][1] Part 9 in respect of machinery or plant to be made for 2002 or later tax year in relation to a trade consisting of or including the generation of electricity, and 2003 or later tax year in relation to any other trade, and as respects any loss sustained in a trade consisting of or including the generation of electricity in 2002 or later tax year, and any other trade in 2003 or later tax year.

1 Amended by FA 2004 s 89 and Sch 3 para 4 with effect on and from 28 March 2003.

13 Income tax: ring-fence on use of certain capital allowances on certain industrial buildings and other premises

Notes

Subs (1) inserted TCA 1997 s 409E with effect from 1 January 2003.

Subs (2) inserted TCA 1997 s 305(1)(*c*) with effect from 1 January 2003.

14 Pension arrangements

Notes

Subs (1)(*a*) substituted TCA 1997 s 608(2) with effect from 28 March 2003;
Subs (1)(*b*)(i)(I) substituted "in the case of a contribution to which paragraph (*ba*) applies, be apportioned" for "be apportioned" in TCA 1997 s 774(7)(*b*)(ii) with effect from 6 February 2003;
Subs (1)(*b*)(i)(II) inserted TCA 1997 s 774(7)(*ba*) with effect from 6 February 2003.
Subs (1)(*b*)(i)(III) inserted TCA 1997 s 774(7)(*d*)–(*e*) with effect from 6 February 2003;
Subs (1)(*b*)(i)(IV) inserted TCA 1997 s 774(8) with effect from 6 February 2003;
Subs (1)(*b*)(ii)(I) substituted "in the case of a contribution to which paragraph (*ba*) applies, be apportioned" for "be apportioned" in TCA 1997 s 776(2)(*b*)(ii) with effect from 6 February 2003;
Subs (1)(*b*)(ii)(II) inserted TCA 1997 s 776(2)(*ba*) with effect from 6 February 2003;
Subs (1)(*b*)(ii)(III) inserted TCA 1997 s 776(2)(*d*)–(*e*) with effect from 6 February 2003;
Subs (1)(*b*)(ii)(IV) inserted TCA 1997 s 776(3) with effect from 6 February 2003;
Subs (1)(*c*)(i)(I)(A) substituted "In this Chapter" for "In this section" in TCA 1997 s 783(1)(*a*) with effect from 6 February 2003;
Subs (1)(*c*)(i)(I)(B) inserted TCA 1997 s 783(1)(*a*)(definitions of "close company" and "connected person") with effect from 6 February 2003;
Subs (1)(*c*)(i)(I)(C) inserted TCA 1997 s 783(1)(*a*)(definition of "participator") with effect from 6 February 2003;
Subs (1)(*c*)(i)(II)(*a*) substituted "benefits of a kind referred to in paragraphs (*b*) and (*c*) of section 772(3) including any similar benefit provided under a statutory scheme established under a public statute" for "a lump sum payable on the termination of the service through death before the age of 70 years or some lower age or disability before the age of 70 or some lower age" in TCA 1997 s 783(2) with effect from 1 January 2003;
Subs (1)(*c*)(i)(II)(*b*) inserted TCA 1997 s 783(2)(*c*) with effect from 1 January 2003;
Subs (1)(*c*)(ii) inserted TCA 1997 s 784A(1A)–(1E) with effect from 6 February 2003;
Subs (1)(*c*)(iii) inserted TCA 1997 s 784A(8) with effect from 28 March 2003.
Subs (1)(*c*)(iv) substituted ", including any distribution or amount treated under this Chapter as a distribution, other than—" for "other than—" in TCA 1997 s 784C(5) with effect from 6 February 2003;
Subs (1)(*d*)(i) substituted TCA 1997 s 787E(1)(*a*)–(*c*) with effect from 1 January 2003;
Subs (1)(*d*)(ii) substituted "Where during a year of assessment an individual is a member of either of an approved scheme or of a statutory scheme (hereafter referred to as a "scheme") in relation to an office or employment, not being a scheme under which the benefits provided in respect of that service are limited to benefits of a kind referred to in paragraphs (*b*) and (*c*) of section 772(3), including any similar benefit provided under a statutory scheme established under a public statute" for "Where during a year of assessment an individual is a member of either of an approved scheme or of a statutory scheme (hereafter referred to as a "scheme") in relation to an office or employment" in TCA 1997 s 787E(3) with effect from 1 January 2003;
Subs (1)(*d*)(iii) inserted TCA 1997 s 787G(4A) with effect from 1 January 2003;
Subs (1)(*e*) inserted TCA 1997 s 790A with effect from 1 January 2002, but shall not apply in respect of any employee's contribution, qualifying premium or PRSA contribution made before 4 December 2002;
Subs (1)(*f*) substituted "Chapter 1, Chapter 2 or Chapter 2A of Part 30" for "Chapter 1 or Chapter 2A of Part 30" in TCA 1997 s 986(1)(*g*)(ii) with effect from 28 March 2003;
Subs (1)(*g*) inserted "section 784A(8)" after "section 734(5)" in TCA 1997 Sch 29 Column 3 with effect from 28 March 2003;

Chapter 3
Income Tax, Corporation Tax and Capital Gains Tax

15 Amendment of Part 16 (income tax relief for investment in corporate trades — business expansion scheme and seed capital scheme) of Principal Act

Notes

Para (*a*) substituted "sections 496(2)(*a*)(iv) and 496(2)(*a*)(xv)" for "section 496(2)(*a*)(iv)" in TCA 1997 s 494(2)(*b*) with effect from 1 January 2003.

Para (*b*) inserted "and, in the case of a company to which this clause applies, its business shall be regarded as having complied with the conditions of this clause throughout the relevant period (where, otherwise, it would not have done so) if it so complied for that part of the relevant period up to and including 31 December 2002" in TCA 1997 s 495(3)(*a*)(ii)(III) with effect from 1 January 2003.
Para (*c*)(i) substituted "1979," for "1979, or" in TCA 1997 s 496(2)(*a*)(ii)(III) with effect from 1 January 2003.
Para (*c*)(ii)(I) inserted "and before the passing of the Finance Act 2003" after "6 April 2001" in TCA 1997 s 496(2)(*a*)(ii)(IV) with effect from 1 January 2003.
Para (*c*)(ii)(II) substituted "concerned, or" for "concerned," in TCA 1997 s 496(2)(*a*)(ii)(IV) with effect from 1 January 2003.
Para (*c*)(iii) inserted TCA 1997 s 496(2)(*a*)(ii)(V) with effect from 1 January 2003.
Para (*c*)(iv) inserted "and in the case of a relevant investment made on or before 31 December 2002, trading operations undertaken on or after 1 January 2003 on an exchange facility established in the Customs House Docks Area will be deemed to be relevant trading operations for the purposes of this section notwithstanding the expiry, in accordance with the provisions of section 446(2)(*b*), of the certificate given by the Minister for Finance under that subsection" in TCA 1997 s 496(2)(*a*)(iv) with effect from 1 January 2003.
Para (*c*)(v) inserted TCA 1997 s 496(2)(*a*)(xv) with effect from 1 January 2003.
Para (*c*)(vi) deleted TCA 1997 s 496(2)(*b*) with effect from 1 January 2003.
Para (*c*)(vii) substituted "subsections (2)(*a*)(iv) and (2)(*a*)(xv)" for "subsection (2)(*a*)(iv)" in TCA 1997 s 496(4)(*b*)(III) with effect from 1 January 2003.
Para (*d*) substituted "sections 496(2)(*a*)(iv) and 496(2)(*a*)(xv)" for "section 496(2)(*a*)(iv)" in TCA 1997 s 497(4)(*a*) with effect from 1 January 2003.

16 Rental income: restriction of relief for certain interest

Notes

Subs (1)(*a*)(i) substituted "in the purchase, other than from the spouse of the person chargeable" for "in the purchase" in TCA 1997 s 97(2G) in relation to interest referred to in s 97(2G) which accrues on or after 6 February 2003 and, for the purposes of this subsection, such interest shall be treated as accruing from day to day.
Subs (1)(*a*)(ii) inserted TCA 1997 s 97(2H) in relation to interest referred to in s 97(2G) which accrues on or after 6 February 2003 and, for the purposes of this subsection, such interest shall be treated as accruing from day to day.
Subs (1)(*b*) inserted TCA 1997 s 248A(4) and (5) in relation to interest referred to in s 248A(2) which accrues on or after 6 February 2003 and, for the purposes of this subsection, such interest shall be treated as accruing from day to day.

17 Claims for repayment, interest on repayments and time limits for assessment

Notes

Subs (1)(*a*) substituted TCA 1997 s 865 and inserted s 865A with effect from: (*a*) such day or days as the Minister for Finance may by order or orders appoint either generally or with reference to any particular purpose or provision and different days may be so appointed for different purposes or different provisions and (*b*) notwithstanding the generality of (*a*), any order made by the Minister for Finance in accordance with the provisions of that paragraph may contain, and be subject to, such conditions as the Minister considers appropriate and which are specified in the order.
Subs (1)(*b*) substituted TCA 1997 s 941(9)(*a*) with effect from: (*a*) such day or days as the Minister for Finance may by order or orders appoint either generally or with reference to any particular purpose or provision and different days may be so appointed for different purposes or different provisions and (*b*) notwithstanding the generality of (*a*), any order made by the Minister for Finance in accordance with the provisions of that paragraph may contain, and be subject to, such conditions as the Minister considers appropriate and which are specified in the order.
Subs (1)(*c*) substituted TCA 1997 s 942(6)(*b*) with effect from: (*a*) such day or days as the Minister for Finance may by order or orders appoint either generally or with reference to any particular purpose or provision and different days may be so appointed for different purposes or different provisions and (*b*) notwithstanding the generality of (*a*), any order made by the Minister for Finance in accordance with the provisions of that paragraph may contain, and be subject to, such conditions as the Minister considers appropriate and which are specified in the order.
Subs (1)(*d*) deleted TCA 1997 ss 930 and 953 with effect from: (*a*) such day or days as the Minister for Finance may by order or orders appoint either generally or with reference to any particular purpose or provision and

different days may be so appointed for different purposes or different provisions and (*b*) notwithstanding the generality of (*a*), any order made by the Minister for Finance in accordance with the provisions of that paragraph may contain, and be subject to, such conditions as the Minister considers appropriate and which are specified in the order.

Subs (1)(*e*) substituted "sections 920, 922, 924, 928 and 929" for "sections 920, 922, 924 and 928 to 930" in TCA 1997 s 931(3) with effect from: (*a*) such day or days as the Minister for Finance may by order or orders appoint either generally or with reference to any particular purpose or provision and different days may be so appointed for different purposes or different provisions and (*b*) notwithstanding the generality of (*a*), any order made by the Minister for Finance in accordance with the provisions of that paragraph may contain, and be subject to, such conditions as the Minister considers appropriate and which are specified in the order.

Subs (1)(*f*) substituted "4 years" for "10 years" in TCA 1997 ss 401(6), 504(3), 599(4)(*b*), 611(1)(*c*), 919(5)(*c*) and 924(2)(*b*) with effect from: (*a*) such day or days as the Minister for Finance may by order or orders appoint either generally or with reference to any particular purpose or provision and different days may be so appointed for different purposes or different provisions and (*b*) notwithstanding the generality of (*a*), any order made by the Minister for Finance in accordance with the provisions of that paragraph may contain, and be subject to, such conditions as the Minister considers appropriate and which are specified in the order.

Subs (1)(*g*) substituted TCA 1997 s 955(2)(*a*) with effect from: (*a*) such day or days as the Minister for Finance may by order or orders appoint either generally or with reference to any particular purpose or provision and different days may be so appointed for different purposes or different provisions and (*b*) notwithstanding the generality of (*a*), any order made by the Minister for Finance in accordance with the provisions of that paragraph may contain, and be subject to, such conditions as the Minister considers appropriate and which are specified in the order.

Subs (1)(*h*) substituted "4 years" for "6 years" in TCA 1997 s 956(1)(*c*) with effect from: (*a*) such day or days as the Minister for Finance may by order or orders appoint either generally or with reference to any particular purpose or provision and different days may be so appointed for different purposes or different provisions and (*b*) notwithstanding the generality of (*a*), any order made by the Minister for Finance in accordance with the provisions of that paragraph may contain, and be subject to, such conditions as the Minister considers appropriate and which are specified in the order.

Subs (1)(*i*)(*a*)(i)(I) deleted "within 5 years from the end of the year of assessment" from TCA 1997 s 997(1)(*a*) with effect from: (*a*) such day or days as the Minister for Finance may by order or orders appoint either generally or with reference to any particular purpose or provision and different days may be so appointed for different purposes or different provisions and (*b*) notwithstanding the generality of (*a*), any order made by the Minister for Finance in accordance with the provisions of that paragraph may contain, and be subject to, such conditions as the Minister considers appropriate and which are specified in the order.

Subs (1)(*i*)(*a*)(i)(II) deleted "or estimated to be deductible" from TCA 1997 s 997(1)(*a*) with effect from: (*a*) such day or days as the Minister for Finance may by order or orders appoint either generally or with reference to any particular purpose or provision and different days may be so appointed for different purposes or different provisions and (*b*) notwithstanding the generality of (*a*), any order made by the Minister for Finance in accordance with the provisions of that paragraph may contain, and be subject to, such conditions as the Minister considers appropriate and which are specified in the order.

Subs (1)(*i*)(*b*) inserted TCA 1997 s 997(1A) with effect from: (*a*) such day or days as the Minister for Finance may by order or orders appoint either generally or with reference to any particular purpose or provision and different days may be so appointed for different purposes or different provisions and (*b*) notwithstanding the generality of (*a*), any order made by the Minister for Finance in accordance with the provisions of that paragraph may contain, and be subject to, such conditions as the Minister considers appropriate and which are specified in the order.

18 Amendment of section 666 (deduction for increase in stock values) of Principal Act

Notes

Subs (1) substituted TCA 1997 s 666(4) with effect from 6 February 2003.

19 Amendment of section 667 (special provisions for qualifying farmers) of Principal Act

Notes

Subs (1) substituted TCA 1997 s 667(2)(*b*)(ii) with effect from such day as the Minister for Finance may by order appoint.

20 Amendment of Chapter 4 (transmission capacity rights) of Part 29 of Principal Act

Notes

Subs (1)(*a*) inserted TCA 1997 s 769A(1) definitions of "control" and "qualifying expenditure" with effect from 28 March 2003.

Para (1)(*b*)(i) substituted "qualifying expenditure" for "capital expenditure" in TCA 1997 s 769B(1),(2)(*b*)("A") where it occurs with effect from 28 March 2003.

Para (1)(*b*)(ii) inserted TCA 1997 s 769B(3) with effect from 28 March 2003.

Para (1)(*c*) substituted "qualifying expenditure" for "capital expenditure" in TCA 1997 s 769C(1)–(5) with effect from 28 March 2003.

Para (1)(*d*) substituted "qualifying expenditure" for "capital expenditure" in TCA 1997 s 769E(2) with effect from 28 March 2003.

Para (1)(*e*) substituted "on the date of the passing of the Finance Act 2003" for "on such day as the Minister for Finance may, by order, appoint" in TCA 1997 s 769E(2) with effect from 28 March 2003.

21 Amendment of section 848A (donations to approved bodies) of Principal Act

Notes

Subs (1)(a) inserted ", subject to subsection (3A)," after "means" in TCA 1997 s 848A(1)(a) definition of "relevant donation" as respects donations made on or after 6 February 2003.

Subs (1)(*b*) inserted TCA 1997 s 848A(3A) as respects donations made on or after 6 February 2003.

22 Amendment of Schedule 26A (donations to approved bodies, etc.) to Principal Act

Notes

Subs (1) inserted TCA 1997 Sch 26A para 19 as respects donations made on or after 6 February 2003.

23 Wear and tear allowances

Notes

Subs (1)(*a*)(i) substituted "paragraphs (*aa*), (*ab*) and (*ad*)" for "paragraphs (*aa*) and (*ab*)" in TCA 1997 s 284(2)(*a*) with effect from 4 December 2002.

Subs (1)(*a*)(ii) inserted TCA 1997 s 284(2)(*ad*) with effect from 4 December 2002.

Subs (1)(*a*)(iii) substituted "the amount specified in any other provision of this subsection" for "the amount specified in subparagraph (i) or (ii) of paragraph (*a*), the amount specified in paragraph (*aa*) or, as the case may be, the amount specified in subparagraph (i) or (ii) of paragraph (*ab*)" in TCA 1997 s 284(2)(*b*) with effect from 4 December 2002.

Subs (1)(*b*) inserted TCA 1997 s 310(2A) with effect from 4 December 2002.

Subs (1)(*c*) substituted "as if the references in paragraphs (*a*)(i), (*aa*) and (*ad*) of that section to 15 per cent, 20 per cent and 12.5 per cent, respectively, were each a reference to 100 per cent" for "as if the reference to paragraph (*a*)(i) of that section to 15 per cent were a reference to 100 per cent" in TCA 1997 s 692(2) with effect from 4 December 2002.

24 Capital allowances for certain day hospitals

Notes

Subs (1) substituted TCA 1997 s 268(2A) definition of "qualifying hospital" para (*d*) as respects capital expenditure incurred on or after 28 March 2003 on the construction (within the meaning of TCA 1997 s 270) of a building or structure.

25 Provisions relating to industrial buildings or structures

Notes

Subs (1)(*a*)(i) substituted "shall, subject to subsection (13), be deemed" for "shall be deemed" in TCA 1997 s 268(3) with effect from 4 December 2002.
Subs (1)(*a*)(ii)(I) substituted "6 April 2001 (being capital expenditure in respect of which but for this subsection a writing-down allowance in excess of 4 per cent would be available under section 272 for a chargeable period)," for "6 April 2001," in TCA 1997 s 268(12) with effect from 4 December 2002.
Subs (1)(*a*)(ii)(II) substituted TCA 1997 s 268(12)(*c*) with effect from 1 January 2003.
Subs (1)(*a*)(iii) inserted TCA 1997 s 268(13) with effect from 4 December 2002.
Subs (1)(*b*)(i)(I) deleted "or" from TCA 1997 s 272(3)(*c*)(i) with effect from 4 December 2002.
Subs (1)(*b*)(i)(II) inserted "or" in TCA 1997 s 272(3)(*c*)(ii) with effect from 4 December 2002.
Subs (1)(*b*)(i)(III) inserted TCA 1997 s 272(3)(*c*)(iii) with effect from 4 December 2002.
Subs (1)(*b*)(ii)(I) deleted "or" from TCA 1997 s 272(4)(*c*)(i) with effect from 4 December 2002.
Subs (1)(*b*)(ii)(II) inserted "or" in TCA 1997 s 272(4)(*c*)(ii) with effect from 4 December 2002.
Subs (1)(*b*)(ii)(III) inserted TCA 1997 s 272(4)(*c*)(iii) with effect from 4 December 2002.
Subs (1)(*b*)(iii) inserted TCA 1997 s 272(8) with effect from 4 December 2002.
Subs (1)(*c*)(i)(I) deleted "or" from TCA 1997 s 274(1)(*b*)(iii)(I) with effect from 4 December 2002.
Subs (1)(*c*)(i)(II) inserted "or" in TCA 1997 s 274(1)(*b*)(iii)(II) with effect from 4 December 2002.
Subs (1)(*c*)(i)(III) inserted TCA 1997 s 274(1)(*b*)(iii)(III) with effect from 4 December 2002.
Subs (1)(*c*)(ii) inserted TCA 1997 s 274(1A) with effect from 4 December 2002.

26 Amendment of Part 10 (income tax and corporation tax: reliefs for renewal and improvement of certain urban areas, certain resort areas and certain islands) of Principal Act

Notes

Para (*a*)(i) substituted TCA 1997 s 372A(1) definition of "relevant local authority" para (*a*) with effect from 1 January 2003.
Para (*a*)(ii) substituted TCA 1997 s 372A(1A)(*a*) with effect from 1 January 2003.
Para (*b*) substituted "31 December 2004" for "30 June 2004" in TCA 1997 s 372U(1) definition of "qualifying period" with effect from 1 January 2003.
Para (*c*) substituted TCA 1997 s 372AA(1) definition of "qualifying period" with effect from 1 January 2003.
Para (*d*) substituted TCA 1997 s 372AK definition of "relevant local authority" with effect from 1 January 2003.
Para (*e*)(i)(I) substituted "31 December 2004" for "30 June 2004" in TCA 1997 s 372AL(1)(*d*) with effect from 1 January 2003.
Para (*e*)(i)(II) substituted "31 December 2004" for "31 December 2003" in TCA 1997 s 372AL(1)(*e*) with effect from 1 January 2003.
Para (*e*)(i)(III) substituted "31 December 2004" for "30 September 2005" in TCA 1997 s 372AL(1)(*f*)(ii) with effect from 1 January 2003.
Para (*e*)(ii) substituted in TCA 1997 s 372AL(2)(*a*) with effect from 1 January 2003.

27 Amendment of Chapter 7 (qualifying areas) of Part 10 of Principal Act

Notes

Subs (1)(*a*) inserted TCA 1997 s 372A(1) definition of "facade" with effect from 1 March 1999.
Subs (1)(*b*)(i) substituted TCA 1997 s 372B(1)(*b*) with effect from 1 March 1999.
Subs (1)(*b*)(ii) substituted TCA 1997 s 372B(2) with effect from 1 March 1999.

Subs (1)(*b*)(iii) inserted TCA 1997 s 372B(2A) with effect from 1 March 1999.
Subs (1)(*c*) inserted TCA 1997 s 372BA(2A) with effect from 6 April 2001.
Subs (1)(*d*)(i) substituted TCA 1997 s 372D(2)(*a*)(ii) with effect from 1 March 1999.
Subs (1)(*d*)(ii)(I) substituted TCA 1997 s 372D(3A)(*a*)(ii) with effect from 1 January 2002.
Subs (1)(*d*)(ii)(II) substituted TCA 1997 s 372D(3A)(*b*) with effect from 1 January 2002.
Subs (1)(*e*)(i) substituted TCA 1997 s 372K(1)(*c*) with effect from 1 January 2003.
Subs (1)(*e*)(ii) substituted "sections 372C and 372D" for "sections 372C, 372D, 372G and 372H" in TCA 1997 s 372K(2) with effect from 1 January 2002.

28 Amendment of section 372T (non-application of relief in certain circumstances and provision against double relief) of Principal Act

Notes

This section inserted TCA 1997 s 372T(1)(*ab*) with effect from 1 January 2003.

29 Amendment of Chapter 10 (designated areas of certain towns) of Part 10 of Principal Act

Notes

Subs (1)(*a*)(i) inserted TCA 1997 s 372AA(1) definition of "facade" with effect from 6 April 2000.
Subs (1)(*a*)(ii) substituted "structure;" for "structure." in TCA 1997 s 372AA(1) definition of "refurbishment" with effect from 6 April 2000.
Subs (1)(*a*)(iii) inserted TCA 1997 s 372AA(1) definition of "street" with effect from 6 April 2000.
Subs (1)(*b*)(i) substituted TCA 1997 s 372AB(1)(*b*) with effect from 6 April 2000.
Subs (1)(*b*)(ii) substituted TCA 1997 s 372AB(1)(*ba*)(ii)–(iii) and inserted TCA 1997 s 372AB(1)(*ba*)(iv) with effect from 6 April 2000.
Subs (1)(*b*)(iii) substituted TCA 1997 s 372AB(2) with effect from 6 April 2000.
Subs (1)(*b*)(iv) inserted TCA 1997 s 372AB(2A) with effect from 6 April 2000.
Subs (1)(*c*) substituted TCA 1997 s 372AD(2)(*a*)(ii) with effect from 6 April 2000.
Subs (1)(*d*)(i) substituted TCA 1997 s 372AJ(1)(*c*) with effect from 1 January 2003.
Subs (1)(*d*)(ii) substituted "sections 372AC and 372AD" for "sections 372AC, 372AD, 372AF and 372AG" in TCA 1997 s 372AJ(2) with effect from 1 January 2002.

30 Amendment of Chapter 11 (reliefs for lessors and owner-occupiers in respect of expenditure incurred on the provision of certain residential accommodation) of Part 10 of Principal Act

Notes

Subs (1)(*a*) inserted "carried out" after "renewal" in TCA 1997 s 372AK definition of "refurbishment" with effect from 1 January 2002.
Subs (1)(*b*) substituted "the conversion or the refurbishment of the house" for "the refurbishment of the house" in TCA 1997 s 372AM(4)(*c*)(ii)(II) with effect from 1 January 2002.
Subs (1)(*c*) inserted TCA 1997 s 372AS(2A) with effect from 1 January 2002.

31 Amendment of section 749 (dealers in securities) of Principal Act

Notes

Subs (1) inserted TCA 1997 s 749(2A) and (2B) as respects securities purchased on or after 1 January 2003.

32 Conditions relating to relief in respect of expenditure incurred on provision of certain student accommodation

Notes

Subs (1) inserted TCA 1997 s 372AM(9A)–(9C) with effect from 18 July 2002.

33 Relevant contracts tax

Notes

Subs (1)(*a*) inserted TCA 1997 s 531(3B) with effect for 2003 and later tax years.

Subs (1)(*b*) substituted TCA 1997 s 531(10)(ii) with effect for 2003 and later tax years.

Subs (1)(*c*)(i) substituted TCA 1997 s 531(12)(*c*) as respects applications made under TCA 1997 s 531(12)(*c*) on or after 28 March 2003.

Subs (1)(*c*)(ii) substituted "the making of an application under paragraph (*a*), (*b*) or (*c*)" for "such application" in TCA 1997 s 531(12)(*d*) as respects applications made under TCA 1997 s 531(12)(*c*) on or after 28 March 2003.

34 Filing date for certain returns and elections

Notes

Subs (1)(*a*) substituted TCA 1997 s 128A(3) with effect from 6 April 2001.

Subs (1)(*b*) substituted TCA 1997 s 894(1) definition of "specified return date for the chargeable period" para (*a*) with effect from 6 April 2001.

Subs (1)(*c*) substituted TCA 1997 s 895(1) definition of "specified return date for the chargeable period" para (*a*) with effect from 6 April 2001.

Subs (1)(*d*) substituted TCA 1997 s 950(1) definition of "specified return date for the chargeable period" para (*a*) with effect from 6 April 2001.

35 Amendment of certain provisions relating to exempt income

Notes

Subs (1)(*a*)(i) renumbered TCA 1997 s 231 as TCA 1997 s 231(1) as respects any chargeable period (within the meaning of TCA 1997 s 321(2)) commencing on or after 1 January 2004.

Subs (1)(*a*)(ii) substituted "shall be exempt from income tax and corporation tax" for "shall not be taken into account for any purpose of the Tax Acts" in TCA 1997 s 231(1) as respects any chargeable period (within the meaning of TCA 1997 s 321(2)) commencing on or after 1 January 2004.

Subs (1)(*a*)(iii) inserted TCA 1997 s 231(2) and (3) as respects any chargeable period (within the meaning of TCA 1997 s 321(2)) commencing on or after 1 January 2004.

Subs (1)(*b*)(i) substituted "shall be exempt from income tax and corporation tax" for "shall not be taken into account for any purpose of the Tax Acts" in TCA 1997 s 232(2) as respects any chargeable period (within the meaning of TCA 1997 s 321(2)) commencing on or after 1 January 2004.

Subs (1)(*b*)(ii) inserted TCA 1997 s 232(3) and (4) as respects any chargeable period (within the meaning of TCA 1997 s 321(2)) commencing on or after 1 January 2004.

Subs (1)(*c*)(i) substituted "shall be exempt from income tax and corporation tax" for "shall not be taken into account for any purpose of the Tax Acts" in TCA 1997 s 233(2) as respects any chargeable period (within the meaning of TCA 1997 s 321(2)) commencing on or after 1 January 2004.

Subs (1)(*c*)(ii) inserted TCA 1997 s 233(3) and (4) as respects any chargeable period (within the meaning of TCA 1997 s 321(2)) commencing on or after 1 January 2004.

36 Transfer of rent

Notes

Subs (1) inserted TCA 1997 s 106A which applies, in the case of subs (2) of that section, as respects any capital sum received on or after 6 February 2003 and, in the case of subs (3) of that section, as respects amounts received on or after that date.

37 Matching of relevant foreign currency assets with foreign currency liabilities

Notes

Subs (1) inserted TCA 1997 s 79A as respects accounting periods ending on or after 6 February 2003.

38 Exchange of information

Notes

Para (*a*) substituted TCA 1997 s 826(1) with effect from 1 January 2003.

Para (*b*) inserted TCA 1997 s 912A with effect from 1 January 2003.

39 Amendment of section 404 (restriction on use of capital allowances for certain machinery or plant) of Principal Act

Notes

This section substituted "it is a lease of machinery or plant provided for leasing by a lessor to a lessee" for "the leasing of the asset is carried on" in TCA 1997 s 404(6)(*b*) with effect from 1 January 2003.

40 Amendment of section 407 (restriction on use of losses and capital allowances for qualifying shipping trade) of Principal Act

Notes

This section substituted "31 December 2006" for "31 December 2002" in TCA 1997 s 407(1) definition of "the relevant period" with effect from 1 January 2003.

41 Amendment and repeals consequential on abolition of tax credits and advance corporation tax

Notes

Subs (1)(*a*)(i) deleted "(other than subsection (5))" from TCA 1997 s 83(3) as respects accounting periods ending on or after 6 February 2003.

Subs (1)(*a*)(ii) deleted TCA 1997 s 83(5) and (6) as respects accounting periods ending on or after 6 February 2003.

Subs (1)(*b*) deleted "and the relevant tax credit" from TCA 1997 s 137(3) as respects accounting periods ending on or after 6 February 2003.

Subs (1)(*c*) substituted TCA 1997 s 144(8) (meaning of T) as respects accounting periods ending on or after 6 February 2003.

Subs (1)(*d*)(i) substituted "and 144" for ", 144 and 145" where it occurs in TCA 1997 s 154(1) as respects accounting periods ending on or after 6 February 2003.

Subs (1)(*d*)(ii) substituted "the day in question" for ", 144(3)(*a*) or 145" in TCA 1997 s 155(3) as respects accounting periods ending on or after 6 February 2003.

Subs (1)(*e*) substituted "or 144(3)(*a*)" for ", 144(3)(*a*) or 145" as respects accounting periods ending on or after 6 February 2003.

Subs (1)(*f*)(i) substituted TCA 1997 s 156 as respects accounting periods ending on or after 6 February 2003.

Subs (1)(*f*)(ii) deleted TCA 1997 ss 157 and 158 as respects accounting periods ending on or after 6 February 2003.

Subs (1)(*g*) deleted TCA 1997 ss 159–164, 166 and 167 as respects accounting periods ending on or after 6 February 2003.

Subs (1)(*h*) deleted "157, 158," from TCA 1997 s 448(1)(*a*) as respects accounting periods ending on or after 6 February 2003.

Subs (1)(*i*) deleted "section 157," from TCA 1997 s 679(3)(*a*) as respects accounting periods ending on or after 6 February 2003.

Subs (1)(*j*) deleted "(including, where a claim is made under section 157 for the purposes mentioned in subsection (2)(*a*) of that section, any franked investment income)" from TCA 1997 s 716(3) as respects accounting periods ending on or after 6 February 2003.

Subs (1)(*k*) deleted "157 or" from TCA 1997 s 751(1)(*b*) as respects accounting periods ending on or after 6 February 2003.

Subs (1)(*l*) deleted "157 or" from TCA 1997 s 753(*b*) as respects accounting periods ending on or after 6 February 2003.

Subs (1)(*m*) deleted TCA 1997 s 817(6) as respects accounting periods ending on or after 6 February 2003.

Subs (1)(*n*) inserted TCA 1997 s 845B as respects accounting periods ending on or after 6 February 2003.

Subs (1)(*o*) inserted TCA 1997 s 884(2)(*c*) as respects accounting periods ending on or after 6 February 2003.

Subs (1)(*p*)(i) deleted TCA 1997 s 1085(2)(*d*) and (*e*) as respects accounting periods ending on or after 6 February 2003.

Subs (1)(*p*)(ii) substituted TCA 1997 s 1085(3) and (4) as respects accounting periods ending on or after 6 February 2003.

Subs (1)(*q*) deleted TCA 1997 s 691 as respects accounting periods ending on or after 6 February 2003.

42 Amendment of Part 41 (self assessment) of Principal Act

Notes

Subs (1)(*a*) substituted definition of "specified return date for the chargeable period" paras (*b*)–(*c*) in relation to corporation tax as respects accounting periods ending on or after 1 January 2003.

Subs (1)(*b*)(i) substituted "Every chargeable person shall as respects a chargeable period prepare and deliver to the Collector-General on or before the specified return date for the chargeable period a return in the prescribed form of—" for all words from "Every chargeable person" down to "a return in the prescribed form of—" in TCA 1997 s 950(1) with effect from 1 January 2003 in relation to income tax and capital gains tax and as respects accounting periods ending on or after that date in relation to corporation tax.

Subs (1)(*b*)(ii) substituted "the Collector-General" for "the Collector-General or an inspector, as the case may be" in TCA 1997 s 950(3) with effect from 1 January 2003 in relation to income tax and capital gains tax and as respects accounting periods ending on or after that date in relation to corporation tax.

Subs (1)(*b*)(iii) substituted "the Collector-General" for "the Collector-General or the appropriate inspector, as the case may be" in TCA 1997 s 950(4) with effect from 1 January 2003 in relation to income tax and capital gains tax and as respects accounting periods ending on or after that date in relation to corporation tax.

Subs (1)(*b*)(iv) substituted TCA 1997 s 950(11)(*d*) with effect from 1 January 2003 in relation to income tax and capital gains tax and as respects accounting periods ending on or after that date in relation to corporation tax.

Subs (1)(*c*)(i)(I) substituted "number of days" for "number of months" where it occurs in TCA 1997 s 958(1)(*a*) definition of "corresponding corporation tax for the preceding chargeable period" as respects accounting periods ending on or after 1 January 2003.

Subs (1)(*c*)(i)(II) inserted TCA 1997 s 958(1)(*a*) definitions of "tax payable for the initial period" and "tax payable for the later period" as respects accounting periods ending on or after 1 January 2003.

Subs (1)(*c*)(ii) substituted TCA 1997 s 958(2A)(*b*) to (*e*), in the case of the amendments to TCA 1997 s 958(2A)(*b*) and (*c*), as respects accounting periods ending on or after 2 July 2003 and, in any other case, as respects accounting periods ending on or after 1 January 2003.

Subs (1)(*c*)(iii) substituted TCA 1997 s 958(2B) as respects accounting periods ending on or after 1 January 2003.

Subs (1)(*c*)(iv) substituted TCA 1997 s 958(3) in relation to income tax and capital gains tax with effect from 1 January 2003 and in relation to corporation tax as respects accounting periods ending on or after 1 January 2003.

Subs (1)(*c*)(v) substituted TCA 1997 s 958(3A) with effect from 1 January 2003.

43 National Development Finance Agency

Notes

Subs (1)(*a*) substituted TCA 1997 s 38(1) with effect from 6 February 2003.

Subs (1)(*b*) inserted TCA 1997 s 230AB with effect from 6 February 2003.

Subs (1)(*c*) inserted TCA 1997 s 256(1) definition of "relevant deposit" para (*a*)(iii*c*) with effect from 6 February 2003.

Subs (1)(*d*) inserted TCA 1997 s 607(1)(*fa*) with effect from 6 February 2003.

44 Restriction on deductibility of certain interest

Notes

This section inserted TCA 1997 s 817C as respects any chargeable period ending on or after 6 February 2003.

45 Amendment of Chapter 2 (additional matters to be treated as distributions, charges to tax in respect of certain loans and surcharges on certain undistributed income) of Part 13 of Principal Act

Notes

Subs (1)(*a*) substituted "to a company not resident in a Member State of the European Communities and, for the purposes of this subsection, a company is a resident of a Member State of the European Communities if the company is by virtue of the law of that Member State resident for the purposes of tax (being, in the case of the State, corporation tax and, in any other case, being any tax imposed in the Member State which corresponds to corporation tax in the State) in such Member State" for the words "to a company not resident in the State" in TCA 1997 s 438(6) as respects the making of a loan, the advance of any money, the incurring of any debt, or the assignment of any debt, on or after 6 February 2003.

Subs (1)(*b*) inserted TCA 1997 s 438A as respects the making of a loan, the advance of any money, the incurring of any debt, or the assignment of any debt, on or after 6 February 2003.

46 Amendment of section 249 (rules relating to recovery of capital and replacement loans) of Principal Act

Notes

Subs (1)(*a*) substituted TCA 1997 s 249(1)(*a*) as respects any recovery of capital or deemed recovery of capital (within the meaning of TCA 1997 s s 249) effected from 6 February 2003.

Subs (1)(*b*) substituted TCA 1997 s 249(2)(*a*) as respects any recovery of capital or deemed recovery of capital (within the meaning of TCA 1997 s s 249) effected from 6 February 2003.

47 Amendment of section 289 (calculation of balancing allowances and balancing charges in certain cases) of Principal Act

Notes

Subs (1)(*a*) substituted "Subject to subsection (6A), where in a case within subsection (5)" for "Where in a case within subsection (5)" in TCA 1997 s 289(6) as respects a gift or sale of machinery or plant on or after 6 February 2003.

Subs (1)(*b*) inserted TCA 1997 s 289(6A) as respects a gift or sale of machinery or plant on or after 6 February 2003.

48 Securitisation and related matters

Notes

Subs (1) substituted TCA 1997 s 110 as respects for any asset acquired or, as a result of an arrangement with another person, held or managed, by a qualifying company (within the meaning of TCA 1997 s 110), or in relation to which a qualifying company (within that meaning) has entered into a legally enforceable arrangement with another person, on or after 6 February 2003.

Subs (2) inserted TCA 1997 s 246(3)(*cc*) and (*ccc*) as respects interest paid on or after 6 February 2003.

Subs (3)(*a*) deleted "and" in TCA 1997 s 198(1) (*c*)(ii)(II) as respects interest paid on or after 6 February 2003.

Subs (3)(*b*)(i) substituted "paid" for "payable" in TCA 1997 s 198(1)(*c*)(iii) as respects interest paid on or after 6 February 2003.

Subs (3)(*b*)(ii) substituted "section 3 of the Asset Covered Securities Act 2001, and" for "section 2 of the Asset Covered Securities Act 2001." in TCA 1997 s 198(1)(*c*)(iii) as respects interest paid on or after 6 February 2003.

Subs (3)(*c*) inserted TCA 1997 s 198(1)(*c*)(iv) as respects interest paid on or after 6 February 2003.

49 Wholesale debt instruments and related matters

(5) Section 20 of the Finance Act 2002 is amended by substituting the following for subsection (2):

"(2)(*a*) Subject to paragraph (*b*), subsection (1) applies as respects deposits made on or after the date of the passing of this Act.

(*b*) Paragraph (*b*) (in so far as it relates to a pension scheme) and paragraph (*c*) of subsection (1) apply to interest paid or credited on or after 1 January 2003 in respect of a deposit made on or after the date of the passing of this Act.".

Notes

Subs (1) inserted TCA 1997 s 246A as respects a wholesale debt instrument (within the meaning of TCA 1997 s 246A) issued on or after such day as the Minister for Finance may appoint by order.

Subs (3)(*a*)(i) deleted TCA 1997 s 64 definition of "recognised clearing system" as respects a "quoted eurobond" (within the meaning of TCA 1997 s 64) issued on or after 28 March 2003.

Subs (3)(*a*)(ii) inserted TCA 1997 s 64(1A) as respects a "quoted eurobond" (within the meaning of TCA 1997 s 64) issued on or after 28 March 2003.

Subs (3)(*a*)(iii) deleted TCA 1997 s 64(6) as respects a "quoted eurobond" (within the meaning of TCA 1997 s 64) issued on or after 28 March 2003.

Subs (3)(*b*) repealed The Interest On Quoted Eurobonds (Designation of Registered Clearing Systems) Order 1995 (SI No 15 of 1995) with effect from 1 January 2003.

Subs (3)(*c*)(i) deleted TCA 1997 s 739B definition of "recognised clearing system" as respects a "quoted eurobond" (within the meaning of TCA 1997 s 64) issued on or after 28 March 2003.

Subs (3)(*c*)(ii) inserted TCA 1997 s 739B(1A) as respects a "quoted eurobond" (within the meaning of TCA 1997 s 64) issued on or after 28 March 2003.

Subs (4) inserted TCA 1997 s 904A(3)(*b*)(ii) with effect from 1 January 2003.

Subs (5) substituted FA 2002 s 20(2).

FA 2002 s 20

Subs (1)(*a*)(i) substituted TCA 1997 s 256(1) definition of "relevant deposit" para (*f*)(ii).

Subs (1)(*a*)(ii) substituted TCA 1997 s 256(1) definition of "relevant deposit" para (*h*)(ii).

Subs (1)(*b*) substituted TCA 1997 s 265.

Subs (1)(*c*) substituted TCA 1997 s 266.

50 Amendment of section 737 (special investment schemes) of Principal Act

Notes

This section inserted TCA 1997 s 737(8)(*bb*) with effect from 1 January 2003.

51 Amendment of Chapter 1 (income tax and corporation tax) of Part 45 of Principal Act

Notes

Subs (1)(*a*) substituted "Subject to section 1035A, a non-resident person" for "A non-resident person" in TCA 1997 s 1035 as respects chargeable periods commending on or after 1 January 2002.

Subs (1)(*b*) inserted TCA 1997 s 1035A as respects chargeable periods commending on or after 1 January 2002.

52 Cessation of special investment business as separate business

Notes

Subs (1)(*a*)(i)(I) substituted TCA 1997 s 707(2)(*a*) as respects accounting periods ending in 2003 and later years.

Subs (1)(*a*)(i)(II) inserted TCA 1997 s 707(2)(*c*) as respects accounting periods ending in 2003 and later years.

Subs (1)(*a*)(ii) deleted TCA 1997 s 707(5)(*a*)(iii) as respects accounting periods ending in 2003 and later years.

Subs (1)(*b*) inserted TCA 1997 s 708(6) as respects accounting periods ending in 2003 and later years.

Subs (1)(*c*)(i) deleted ", otherwise than in respect of the special investment fund," from TCA 1997 s 711(1)(*c*) as respects accounting periods ending in 2003 and later years.

Subs (1)(*c*)(ii) substituted "(excluding pension business and general annuity business)" for "(excluding pension business, general annuity business and special investment business)" in TCA 1997 s 711(4) as respects accounting periods ending in 2003 and later years.

Subs (1)(*d*) deleted ", other than special investment business," from TCA 1997 s 713(3)(*b*) as respects accounting periods ending in 2003 and later years.

Subs (1)(*e*)(i) deleted "other than its special investment business" from TCA 1997 s 719(1) definition of "life business fund" as respects accounting periods ending in 2003 and later years.

Subs (1)(*e*)(ii)(I) deleted "or special investment business" from TCA 1997 s 719(3)(*b*) as respects accounting periods ending in 2003 and later years.

Subs (1)(*e*)(ii)(II) substituted "(excluding pension business and general annuity business)" for "(excluding pension business, general annuity business and special investment business)" in TCA 1997 s 719(3) as respects accounting periods ending in 2003 and later years.

Subs (1)(*e*)(iii)(I) substituted TCA 1997 s 719(4)(*a*)(i)(I) as respects accounting periods ending in 2003 and later years.

Subs (1)(*e*)(iii)(II) deleted "or special investment business" from TCA 1997 s 719(4)(*b*)(i)(I) as respects accounting periods ending in 2003 and later years.

Subs (1)(*e*)(iv) deleted "or special investment business" from TCA 1997 s 719(5)(*a*) as respects accounting periods ending in 2003 and later years.

Subs (1)(*e*)(v) substituted "(excluding pension business or general annuity business)" for "(excluding pension business, general annuity business or special investment business)" in TCA 1997 s 719(6) as respects accounting periods ending in 2003 and later years.

Subs (1)(*e*)(vi) substituted TCA 1997 s 719(7) as respects accounting periods ending in 2003 and later years.

Subs (1)(*f*)(i)(I) substituted TCA 1997 s 723(1) definition of "special investment fund" as respects accounting periods ending in 2003 and later years.

Subs (1)(*f*)(i)(II) substituted TCA 1997 s 723(1) definition of "special investment policy" para (*a*) as respects accounting periods ending in 2003 and later years.

Subs (1)(*f*)(i)(III) deleted TCA 1997 s 723(6) and (7) as respects accounting periods ending in 2003 and later years.

Subs (1)(*g*) substituted "Where, in an accounting period ending on or before 31 December 2002, an assurance company transfers" for "Where an assurance company transfers" in TCA 1997 s 724 as respects accounting periods ending in 2003 and later years.

Subs (1)(*h*)(i) substituted "at any particular time on or before 31 December 2002," for "at any particular time" in TCA 1997 s 725(1) as respects accounting periods ending in 2003 and later years.

Subs (1)(*h*)(ii) substituted "at any time on or before 31 December 2002," for "at any time" in TCA 1997 s 725(2) as respects accounting periods ending in 2003 and later years.

Subs (1)(*i*)(i) deleted TCA 1997 s 839(1)(*b*) as respects accounting periods ending in 2003 and later years.

Subs (1)(*i*)(ii) substituted "paragraph (*c*) or (*d*)" for "paragraph (*b*), (*c*) or (*d*)" in TCA 1997 s 839(2)(*a*) as respects accounting periods ending in 2003 and later years.

Subs (1)(*i*)(iii) substituted "section 737(3)(*a*)(ii) or 838(2)(*b*)" for "section 723(3)(*b*), 737(3)(*a*)(ii) or 838(2)(*b*)" in TCA 1997 s 839(2)(*a*)(ii) as respects accounting periods ending in 2003 and later years.

Subs (1)(*i*)(iv) substituted "paragraph (*c*) or (*d*)" for "paragraph (*b*), (*c*) or (*d*)" in TCA 1997 s 839(2)(*b*)(i) as respects accounting periods ending in 2003 and later years.

Subs (1)(*i*)(v) substituted "paragraph (*c*) or (*d*)" for "paragraph (*b*), (*c*) or (*d*)" in TCA 1997 s 839(2)(*b*)(ii) as respects accounting periods ending in 2003 and later years.

Subs (1)(*i*)(vi) substituted "section 737(3)(*a*)(ii) or 838(2)(*b*)" for "section 723(3)(*b*), 737(3)(*a*)(ii) or 838(2)(*b*)" in TCA 1997 s 839(2)(*b*)(ii)(II) as respects accounting periods ending in 2003 and later years.

Subs (1)(*i*)(vii) deleted "723" from TCA 1997 s 839(3) as respects accounting periods ending in 2003 and later years.

---

53 Amendment of Chapter 1A (investment undertakings) of Part 27 of Principal Act

Notes

Para (*a*)(i)(I) inserted TCA 1997 s 739B definition of "credit union" with effect from 1 January 2003.

Para (*a*)(i)(II) inserted TCA 1997 s 739B definition of "money market fund" with effect from 1 January 2003.

Para (*a*)(i)(III) substituted TCA 1997 s 739B definition of "relevant Regulations" with effect from 1 January 2003.

Para (*a*)(i)(IV) inserted TCA 1997 s 739B definition of "Service" with effect from 1 January 2003.

Para (*a*)(ii) inserted TCA 1997 s 739B(2A) with effect from 1 January 2003.

Para (*b*) substituted TCA 1997 s 739C(1) and inserted TCA 1997 s 739C(1A) with effect from 1 January 2003.

Para (*c*)(i) substituted "Schedule 2B," for "Schedule 2B, or" in TCA 1997 s 739D(6) with effect from 1 January 2003.
Para (*c*)(ii) inserted TCA 1997 s 739D(6)(*j*)–(*k*) with effect from 1 January 2003.
Para (*d*) substituted "paragraphs (*a*) to (*k*)" for "paragraphs (*a*) to (*h*)" in TCA 1997 s 739D(9A)(*b*) with effect from 1 January 2003.
Para (*e*) substituted TCA 1997 s 739G(2)(*b*) with effect from 1 January 2003.

54 Amendment of section 706 (interpretation and general (Part 26)) of Principal Act

Notes

Para (*a*) substituted "an individual who, at the time the contract is made, is" for "an individual who is" in TCA 1997 s 706(3)(*a*) with effect from 1 January 2003.
Para (*b*) substituted TCA 1997 s 706(3)(*d*) with effect from 1 January 2003.

55 Amendment of section 747E (disposal of an interest in offshore funds) of Principal Act

Notes

Subs (1) substituted TCA 1997 s 747E(1)(*a*) with effect from 1 January 2001.

56 Amendment of Schedule 2B (investment undertaking declarations) of Principal Act

Notes

Para (*a*) inserted TCA 1997 Sch 2B para 9B with effect from 1 January 2003.
Para (*b*) substituted "paragraphs (*a*) to (*k*)" for "paragraphs (*a*) to (*h*)" in TCA 1997 Sch 2B para 14(*d*)(i) with effect from 1 January 2003.

57 Amendment of Part 26 (life assurance companies) of Principal Act

Notes

Para (*a*)(i) inserted TCA 1997 s 730A(1) definitions of "credit union" and "financial institution" with effect from 1 January 2003.
Para (*a*)(ii) inserted TCA 1997 s 730A(1) definition of "Service" with effect from 1 January 2003.
Para (*b*) inserted TCA 1997 s 730B(4) with effect from 1 January 2003.
Para (*c*) deleted "(within the meaning of section 906A)" from TCA 1997 s 730C(2)(*a*) with effect from 1 January 2003.
Para (*d*)(i) substituted TCA 1997 s 730D(2)(*b*) with effect from 1 January 2003.
Para (*e*)(i) substituted TCA 1997 s 730E(3)(*e*) and (*f*) with effect from 1 January 2003.
Para (*e*)(ii) inserted TCA 1997 s 730E(5) with effect from 1 January 2003.
Para (*f*) inserted TCA 1997 s 730GB with effect from 1 January 2003.

58 Amendment of section 481 (relief for investment in films) of Principal Act

Notes

Subs (1)(*a*) substituted "31 December 2004" for "5 April 2005" in TCA 1997 s 481(1) definition of "qualifying period" with effect from 28 March 2003.
Subs (1)(*b*) substituted the formula in TCA 1997 s 481(2)(*c*)(ii) with effect from 1 January 2002.
Subs (1)(*c*) substituted "the year of assessment 2004" for "the year 1999–2000" in TCA 1997 s 481(8) with effect from 20 July 2000.
Subs (1)(*d*) substituted "the year of assessment 2004" for "the year 1999–2000" in TCA 1997 s 481(9) with effect from 20 July 2000.
Subs (1)(*e*) substituted TCA 1997 s 481(14) with effect from 28 March 2003.

Chapter 4

Corporation Tax

59 Provisions relating to loss relief

Notes

Subs (1)(*a*) substituted "The" for "Subject to paragraph (*c*), the" in TCA 1997 s 243B(4)(*b*) as respects accounting periods ending on or after 6 February 2003.

Subs (1)(*b*) inserted TCA 1997 s 396A(5) as respects accounting periods ending on or after 6 February 2003.

Subs (1)(*c*)(i) substituted "amounts which could, if a timely claim for such set off had been made by the company, have been set off" for "amounts set off" in TCA 1997 s 396B(2) as respects a claim made under TCA 1997 s 396B on or after 6 February 2003.

Subs (1)(*c*)(ii) substituted TCA 1997 s 396B(6) as respects a claim made under TCA 1997 s 420B on or after 6 February 2003.

Subs (1)(*d*) substituted TCA 1997 s 420B(2) as respects a claim in made under TCA 1997 s 420B on or after 6 February 2003.

Subs (1)(*e*)(i) inserted ", 396A(3)" in TCA 1997 s 1085(2)(*a*) as respects accounting periods ending on or after 6 February 2003.

Subs (1)(*e*)(ii) inserted TCA 1997 s 1085(2)(*ba*) as respects accounting periods ending on or after 6 February 2003.

Subs (1)(*e*)(iii) inserted TCA 1997 s 1085(2)(*ca*) and (*cb*) as respects accounting periods ending on or after 6 February 2003.

60 Unilateral credit relief

Notes

Subs (1)(*a*) inserted "reduced by the relevant foreign tax" after "the amount so receivable" in TCA 1997 s 449(2)(*a*) as respects accounting periods ending on or after 6 February 2003.

Subs (1)(*b*) inserted "increased by the amount of the relevant foreign tax," after "for the relevant accounting period" in TCA 1997 s 449(2)(*b*) as respects accounting periods ending on or after 6 February 2003.

Subs (2)(*a*) substituted TCA 1997 Sch 24 para 9D(1)(*a*) definition of "relevant interest" as respects accounting periods ending on or after 6 February 2003.

Subs (2)(*b*)(i) inserted "reduced by the relevant foreign tax" after "the amount of the relevant interest" in TCA 1997 Sch 24 para 9D(1)(*b*)(i) as respects accounting periods ending on or after 6 February 2003.

Subs (2)(*b*)(ii) inserted "increased by the amount of the relevant foreign tax" after "for the accounting period" in TCA 1997 Sch 24 para 9D(1)(*b*)(ii) as respects accounting periods ending on or after 6 February 2003.

61 Amendment of section 130 (matters to be treated as distributions) of Principal Act

Notes

This section inserted TCA 1997 s 130(2B) as respects any interest paid or other distribution made on or after 6 February 2003.

62 Amendment of Part 24A (tonnage tax) of Principal Act

(2) Section 53 of the Finance Act 2002 is amended by substituting the following for subsection (5):

"(5) This section shall come into operation as on and from the date of passing of the Finance Act 2003."

Notes

Subs (1)(*a*)(i) substituted TCA 1997 s 697A(1) definition of "commencement date" with effect from 28 March 2003.

Subs (1)(*a*)(ii)(I) deleted ", including income in respect of which the conditions set out in section 697I are met" from TCA 1997 s 697A(1) definition of "relevant shipping income" para (a) with effect from 28 March 2003.
Subs (1)(*a*)(ii)(II) deleted ", including income in respect of which the conditions set out in section 697I are met" from TCA 1997 s 697A(1) definition of "relevant shipping income" para (*b*) with effect from 28 March 2003.
Subs (1)(*a*)(ii)(III) substituted TCA 1997 s 697A(1) definition of "relevant shipping income" para (*c*) with effect from 28 March 2003.
Subs (1)(*a*)(ii)(IV) substituted TCA 1997 s 697A(1) definition of "relevant shipping income" para (*e*) with effect from 28 March 2003.
Subs (1)(*a*)(ii)(V) deleted TCA 1997 s 697A(1) definition of "relevant shipping income" paras (*h*) and (*m*) with effect from 28 March 2003.
Subs (1)(*b*) deleted TCA 1997 s 697I with effect from 28 March 2003.
Subs (1)(*c*) inserted TCA 1997 s 697L(3) with effect from 28 March 2003.
Subs (1)(*d*) inserted TCA 1997 ss 697LA and 697LB with effect from 28 March 2003.
Subs (2) substituted FA 2002 s 53(5) with effect from 28 March 2003.

FA 2002 s 53

Subs (1) inserted TCA 1997 Pt 24A (ss 697A–697Q).
Subs (2) inserted TCA 1997 Sch 18B.
Subs (3) inserted TCA 1997 s 21(1A)(c).
Subs (4) inserted "Schedule 18B, paragraph 30" in TCA 1997 Sch 29, column 2.

63 Amendment of section 430 (meaning of "close company") of Principal Act

Notes

Para (*a*)(i) deleted "or" in the second place in which it occur in TCA 1997 s 430(1)(*d*) with effect from 1 January 2003.
Para (*a*)(ii) inserted TCA 1997 s 430(1)(*da*) with effect from 1 January 2003.
Para (*b*) inserted TCA 1997 s 430(2A) with effect from 1 January 2003.

64 Amendment of Schedule 4 (exemption of specified non-commercial State sponsored bodies from certain tax provisions) to Principal Act

Notes

Para (*a*) inserted "57A. The Irish Sports Council." in TCA 1997 Sch 4 with effect from 1 January 2003.
Para (*b*) inserted "69A. National Consultative Committee on Racism and Interculturalism." in TCA 1997 Sch
Para (*c*) inserted "74AB. National Qualification Authority of Ireland." in TCA 1997 Sch 4 with effect from 1 January 2003.
Para (*d*) inserted "81A. Occupational Safety and Health Institute of Ireland." in TCA 1997 Sch 4 with effect from 1 January 2003.
Para (*e*) inserted "98A. Tourism Ireland Limited." in TCA 1997 Sch 4 with effect from 1 January 2003.

Chapter 5
Capital Gains Tax

65 Amendment of section 556 (adjustment of allowable expenditure by reference to consumer price index) of Principal Act

Notes

Para (*a*) substituted "specified in subsection (5), determined under subsection (6) or specified in subsection (6A), as the case may be." for "specified in subsection (5) or determined under subsection (6), as the case may be." in TCA 1997 s 556(2)(*a*) with effect from 1 January 2003.
Para (*b*) substituted "in each subsequent year of assessment up to and including the year of assessment 2003." for "each subsequent year of assessment." in TCA 1997 s 556(6)(*a*) with effect from 1 January 2003.
Para (*c*) substituted "any subsequent year of assessment up to and including the year of assessment 2003," for "any subsequent year of assessment," in TCA 1997 s 556(6)(*b*) with effect from 1 January 2003.
Para (*d*) inserted TCA 1997 s 556(6A) and Table with effect from 1 January 2003.

66 Restriction of relief on issue of debentures etc

Notes

Para (*a*)(i) substituted "Subject to subsections (4) to (9)" for "Subject to subsections (4) to (8)" in TCA 1997 s 584(3) with effect from 1 January 2003.
Para (*a*)(ii) inserted TCA 1997 s 584(9) with effect from 1 January 2003.
Para (*b*) inserted TCA 1997 s 585(1) definition of "conversion of securities" para (*b*) with effect from 1 January 2003.
Para (*c*) inserted TCA 1997 s 586(3)(*c*) with effect from 1 January 2003.
Para (*d*) inserted TCA 1997 s 587(4)(*c*) with effect from 1 January 2003.

67 Restriction of deferral of capital gains tax

Notes

Subs (1)(*a*) substituted "obtains for any material disposal, before 4 December 2002, by" for "obtains for any material disposal by" in TCA 1997 s 591(2)(*a*) with effect from 1 January 2003.
Subs (1)(*b*) substituted "obtains for the disposal, before 4 December 2002, of" for "obtains for the disposal of" in TCA 1997 s 597(4)(*a*)(i) but does not apply to a disposal made by a person, on or after 4 December 2002 and on or before 31 December 2003, of an asset used for the purposes of the person's trade (or any other activity of the person as is referred to in TCA 1997 s 597(2)), where the person claims that, but for the provisions of subs (1)(*b*), the person would have been entitled to claim that the chargeable gain accruing on that disposal could not accrue to the person until assets, which were acquired by the person before 4 December 2002 or acquired under an unconditional contract entered into by the person before that date, ceased to be used for the purposes of that trade of the person, or, as the case may be, that other activity of the person.
Subs (1)(*c*) substituted "for the disposal, before 4 December 2002, of" for "for the disposal of" in TCA 1997 s 600A(2)(*a*) but does not apply to a disposal made by a person, on or after 4 December 2002 and on or before 31 December 2003, of a qualifying premises (within the meaning of TCA 1997 s 600A) where the person claims that, but for the provisions of subs (1)(*c*), the person would have been entitled to claim that the chargeable gain accruing on that disposal could not accrue to the person until a replacement premises (within that meaning) which were acquired by the person before 4 December 2002, or acquired by the person under an unconditional contract entered into before that date was disposed of by the person, or ceased to be a replacement premises.
Subs (1)(*d*) substituted "Where a person makes a disposal, before 4 December 2002, of" for "Where a person makes a disposal of" in TCA 1997 s 605(1) but does not apply to a disposal made by a person, on or after 4 December 2002 and on or before 31 December 2003, of original assets (within the meaning of TCA 1997 s 605), where the person claims and proves to the satisfaction of the Revenue Commissioners that, but for the provisions of subs (1)(*d*), the person would have been entitled to claim that that disposal would not be treated as a disposal for the purposes of the Capital Gains Tax Acts by virtue of the person having, before 4 December 2002, acquired, or entered into an unconditional contract to acquire, new assets (within that meaning).

68 Amendment of section 598 (disposal of business or farm on "retirement") of Principal Act

Notes

Subs (1)(*a*) substituted TCA 1997 s 598(1)(*a*) definition of "the Scheme" as respects a disposal of an asset on or after 27 November 2000.
Subs (1)(*b*) substituted TCA 1997 s 598(1)(*d*)(i) as respects a disposal of an asset on or after 6 February 2003.
Subs (1)(*c*) inserted TCA 1997 s 598(1)(*d*)(ii*a*) as respects a disposal of an asset on or after 6 February 2003.
Subs (1)(*d*) substituted "€500,000" for "€476,250" in TCA 1997 s 598(2)(*a*)(i) and (ii) as respects a disposal of an asset on or after 6 February 2003.

69 Amendment of Chapter 3 (capital gains tax) of Part 2 of Principal Act

Notes

Subs (1) inserted TCA 1997 s 29A as respects an individual who ceases to be resident in the State for the year of assessment 2003, or a subsequent year of assessment but does not apply as respects an individual who before 24 February 2003 ceases to be resident in the State for the year of assessment 2003, but who would not have so ceased, if he could be taxed in the State for that year in respect of gains on a disposal, on each day of that year, of his or her relevant assets, if such a disposal were made by the individual on that day and gains accrued on the disposal (an for these purposes individual is resident in the State for a year of assessment so long as he or she is resident in the State for the year of assessment, and could be taxed in the State for that year in respect of gains on a disposal, on each day of that year, of his or her relevant assets, if such a disposal were made by the individual on that day and gains accrued on the disposal).

70 Amendment of Chapter 1 (assets and acquisition and disposal of assets) of Part 19 of Principal Act

Notes

Subs (1) inserted TCA 1997 s 541B as respects the giving of an undertaking by a person on or after 6 February 2003, the tenor or effect of which is to restrict the person as to the person's conduct or activities.

71 Amendment of section 980 (deduction from consideration on disposal of certain assets) of Principal Act

Notes

Subs (1) substituted TCA 1997 s 980(8) as respects applications made on or after 28 March 2003.

72 Amendment of Schedule 15 (list of bodies for the purposes of section 610) to Principal Act

Notes

Para (*a*) substituted "section 213 or where the gain is applied solely for the purposes of its registered trade union activities." for "section 213." in TCA 1997 Sch 15 para 3 with effect from 1 January 2003.
Para (*b*) inserted TCA 1997 Sch 15 Pt 1 paras 35–38 with effect from 1 January 2003.

PART 7
MISCELLANEOUS

156 Interpretation (Part 6)

In this Part **"Principal Act"** means the Taxes Consolidation Act 1997.

157 Amendment of Chapter 4 (collection and recovery of income tax on certain emoluments (PAYE system)) of Part 42 of Principal Act

Notes

Para (*a*)(i) substituted "has been completed;" for "has been completed." in TCA 1997 s 989(3)(*d*) with effect from 28 March 2003.
Para (*a*)(ii) inserted TCA 1997 s 989(3)(*e*) with effect from 28 March 2003.
Para (*a*)(iii) inserted "or subsection (3)(*e*)" after "subsection (2)" in TCA 1997 s 989(4) with effect from 28 March 2003.
Para (*b*) inserted TCA 1997 s 990(1A)(*d*) with effect from 28 March 2003.

158 Amendment of section 899 (inspector's right to make enquiries) of Principal Act

Notes

Para (*a*) substituted "and sections 889 to 896" for ", sections 889 to 890, and sections 892 to 894" in TCA 1997 s 899(1) with effect from 28 March 2003.
Para (*b*) deleted TCA 1997 s 899(3) with effect from 28 March 2003.

159 Amendment of Chapter 4 (revenue powers) of Part 38 of Principal Act

Notes

This section inserted TCA 1997 s 904J with effect from 28 March 2003.

160 Amendment of section 1078 (revenue offences) of Principal Act

Notes

Subs (1) substituted "€3,000" for "€1,900" in TCA 1997 s 1078(3)(*a*) as respects an offence committed on or after 28 March 2003.

161 Amendment of Chapter 4 (revenue offences) of Part 47 of Principal Act

Notes

This section inserted TCA 1997 ss 1078A–1078C with effect from 28 March 2003.

162 Amendment of section 1061 (recovery of penalties) of Principal Act

Notes

Subs (1)(*a*) substituted "for the recovery of the penalty in any court of competent jurisdiction as a liquidated sum, and, where appropriate, section 94 of the Courts of Justice Act 1924 shall apply accordingly." for "for the recovery of the penalty in the High Court as a liquidated sum, and section 94 of the Courts of Justice Act 1924, shall apply accordingly." in TCA 1997 s 1061(1) as respects civil proceedings commenced on or after 28 March 2003.

Subs (1)(*b*) substituted "the rules of court" for "the rules of the High Court." in TCA 1997 s 1061(6) as respects civil proceedings commenced on or after 28 March 2003.

163 Miscellaneous technical amendments in relation to tax

The enactments specified in Schedule 6 are amended to the extent and in the manner specified in that Schedule.

164 Mandatory electronic filing and payment of tax

Notes

Subs (1)(*a*) inserted TCA 1997 s 917EA with effect from such day as the Minister for Finance may appoint by order.

Subs (1)(*b*) inserted TCA 1997 1084(1)(*b*)(*ia*) with effect from such day as the Minister for Finance may appoint by order.

Subs (1)(*c*) substituted "(*ia*)," after "(i)," in TCA 1997 1085(1)(*b*) with effect from such day as the Minister for Finance may appoint by order.

166 Payments from Central Fund to certain persons

(1) In this section—

"Accounting Officer" means the Accounting Officer of the Office of the Revenue Commissioners;

"CPI number" means the All Items Consumer Price Index Number compiled by the Central Statistics Office;

"relevant period" means the period commencing on the first day of the year of assessment next following the year of assessment in which the tax repaid was paid and concluding on the date of the issue of the repayment of the tax;

"specified judgement" means the decision of the High Court in the case of *O'Coindealbhain (Inspector of Taxes) v Breda O'Carroll* reported in the Irish Tax Reports, Volume IV, at page 221;

"specified payment", in relation to a repayment of tax made for a year of assessment, means a payment made in respect of the loss of purchasing power in respect of that repayment for the relevant period.

(2) In this section the CPI number applicable to the commencement of a relevant period shall be the CPI number relating to the immediately preceding survey date, and the CPI number applicable to the conclusion of the relevant period shall be the CPI number relating to the immediately succeeding survey date.

(3) This section shall apply for the purpose of permitting the Revenue Commissioners to make a specified payment in respect of the repayment of tax in a particular case to which subsection (4) applies where, at the discretion of the Accounting Officer, that Officer considers it appropriate that such payment should be made and approves the making of that payment.

(4) Subject to the approval of the Accounting Officer as mentioned in subsection (3), a specified payment may be made by the Revenue Commissioners in respect of a repayment of income tax made by reference to the specified judgement.

(5) Where a specified payment is made under this section—

(*a*) the amount of the specified payment shall be computed solely by reference to the amount of the repayment concerned and to the movement in the CPI number for the relevant period;

(*b*) it shall be made without deduction of income tax, and

(*c*) it shall not be reckoned in computing total income for the purposes of the Income Tax Acts.

(6) Where a specified payment is made by the Revenue Commissioners in accordance with this section—

(*a*) it shall be paid out of the Central Fund or the growing produce thereof, and

(*b*) the aggregate of all such payments made by virtue of this section shall not exceed €7,000,000.

170 Care and management of taxes and duties

All taxes and duties imposed by this Act are placed under the care and management of the Revenue Commissioners.

171 Short title, construction and commencement

(1) This Act may be cited as the Finance Act 2003.

(2) Part 1 shall be construed together with—

(*a*) in so far as it relates to income tax, the Income Tax Acts,

(*b*) in so far as it relates to corporation tax, the Corporation Tax Acts, and

(*c*) in so far as it relates to capital gains tax, the Capital Gains Tax Acts.

...

(8) Part 7 shall be construed together with—

(*a*) in so far as it relates to income tax, the Income Tax Acts,

(*b*) in so far as it relates to corporation tax, the Corporation Tax Acts,

(*c*) in so far as it relates to capital gains tax, the Capital Gains Tax Acts,

...

(9) Except where otherwise expressly provided in Part 1, that Part applies as on and from 1 January 2003.

...

(11) Any reference in this Act to any other enactment shall, except in so far as the context otherwise requires, be construed as a reference to that enactment as amended by or under any other enactment including this Act.

(12) In this Act, a reference to a Part, section or Schedule is to a Part or section of, or Schedule to, this Act, unless it is indicated that reference to some other enactment is intended.

(13) In this Act, a reference to a subsection, paragraph, subparagraph, clause or subclause is to the subsection, paragraph, subparagraph, clause or subclause of the provision (including a Schedule) in which the reference occurs, unless it is indicated that reference to some other provision is intended.

SCHEDULE 6

Miscellaneous Technical Amendments in Relation to Tax

[Section 148]

Notes

Para 1(*a*) inserted "under a passive investment scheme" after "transferee" in TCA 1997 s 409C(3)(*b*) with effect from 1 January 2002.

Para 1(*b*)(i) deleted TCA 1997 s 434(1) definitions of "distributable income" and "trading income" as respects accounting periods ending on or after 14 March 2001.

Para 1(*b*)(ii) substituted TCA 1997 s 434(5)(*a*)(ii) as respects accounting periods ending on or after 14 March 2001.

Para 1(*c*) deleted TCA 1997 s 440(2A) as respects accounting periods ending on or after 14 March 2001.

Para 1(*d*) substituted TCA 1997 s 469(1) definition of "health expenses" para (*i*) with effect from 28 March 2003.

Para 1(*e*) substituted "€2,540" for "£2,000" in TCA 1997 s 496(2)(*a*)(v) with effect from 1 January 2002.

Para 1(*f*) substituted "A is the amount of the qualifying expenditure incurred on the purchase of the milk quota," for "A is the amount of the capital expenditure incurred on the purchase of the milk quota," in TCA 1997 s 669B(3) with effect from 1 November 2001.

Para 1(*g*) substituted "certificate of tax credits and standard rate cut-off point" for "certificate of tax free allowances" in TCA 1997 s 784(2B)(*b*) with effect from 6 April 2001.

Para 1(*h*) substituted "section 128(11) and (12)" for "section 128(11) and (11A)" in TCA 1997 Sch 29 Col 3 with effect from 28 March 2003.

FINANCE ACT 2004

(2004 Number 8)

ARRANGEMENT OF SECTIONS

PART 1

INCOME TAX, CORPORATION TAX AND CAPITAL GAINS TAX

Chapter 1
Interpretation

Section

Chapter 2
Income Tax

Chapter 3
Income Tax, Corporation Tax and Capital Gains Tax

Chapter 4
Corporation Tax

PART 6
MISCELLANEOUS

SCHEDULE 1
EXEMPTION FROM TAX FOR CERTAIN INTEREST AND ROYALTIES PAYMENTS

SCHEDULE 3
MISCELLANEOUS TECHNICAL AMENDMENTS IN RELATION TO TAX

SCHEDULE 4
TAXATION OF SAVINGS INCOME IN THE FORM OF INTEREST PAYMENTS

AN ACT TO PROVIDE FOR THE IMPOSITION, REPEAL, REMISSION, ALTERATION AND REGULATION OF TAXATION, OF STAMP DUTIES AND OF DUTIES RELATING TO EXCISE AND OTHERWISE TO MAKE FURTHER PROVISION IN CONNECTION WITH FINANCE INCLUDING THE REGULATION OF CUSTOMS [25TH MARCH 2004]

BE IT ENACTED BY THE OIREACHTAS AS FOLLOWS:

PART 1
INCOME TAX, CORPORATION TAX AND CAPITAL GAINS TAX

CHAPTER 1
Interpretation

1 Interpretation (Part 1)

In this Part **"Principal Act"** means the Taxes Consolidation Act 1997.

CHAPTER 2
Income Tax

2 Age exemption

Notes

Section 2 substituted "€31,000" for "€30,000" and "€15,500" for "€15,000" in TCA 1997 s 188(2) for 2004 and subsequent years of assessment.

3 Employee tax credit

(2) Section 3 of the Finance Act 2002, shall have effect subject to the provisions of this section.

Notes

Subs (1) substituted "€1,040" for "€800" in TCA 1997 s 472(4) for 2004 and subsequent years of assessment.

4 Amendment of section 472C (relief for trade union subscriptions) of Principal Act

Notes

Section 4 substituted "€200" for "€130" in TCA 1997 s 472C(1)("specified amount") for 2004 and subsequent years of assessment.

5 Amendment of Schedule 13 (accountable persons for purposes of Chapter 1 of Part 18) to Principal Act

Notes

Subs (1)(*a*) substituted TCA 1997 Sch 13 para 25 with effect from 28 May 2003.
Subs (1)(*b*) deleted TCA 1997 Sch 13 para 27 with effect from 28 May 2003.
Subs (1)(*c*) substituted TCA 1997 Sch 13 para 83 with effect from 1 December 2002.
Subs (1)(*d*) substituted TCA 1997 Sch 13 para 94 with effect from 10 December 2001.
Subs (1)(*e*) inserted TCA 1997 Sch 13 paras 141–143 with effect from 1 May 2004.

6 Amendment of section 189 (payments in respect of personal injuries) of Principal Act

Notes

Section 6 substituted TCA 1997 s 189(1)(*b*) with effect from 1 January 2004.

7 Exemption in respect of certain payments under employment law

Notes

Section 7 inserted TCA 1997 s 192A with effect from 1 January 2004.

8 Exemption in respect of certain benefits-in-kind

Notes

Subs (1)(*a*)(i) inserted TCA 1997 s 116(definition of "business use") with effect from 1 January 2004.
Subs (1)(*a*)(ii) inserted TCA 1997 s 116(definition of "private use") with effect from 1 January 2004.
Subs (1)(*b*) substituted TCA 1997 s 118(5A)–(5F) with effect from 1 January 2004.
Subs (1)(*c*)(i)(I) inserted TCA 1997 s 121A(1)(definition of "gross vehicle weight") with effect from 1 January 2004.

Subs (1)(*c*)(i)(II)(A) deleted "and" from TCA 1997 s 121A(1)(definition of "van", para (*b*)) with effect fom 1 January 2004.
Subs (1)(*c*)(i)(II)(B) substituted "areas, and" for "areas." in TCA 1997 s 121A(1)(definition of "van", para (*c*)) with effect from 1 January 2004.
Subs (1)(*c*)(i)(II)(C) inserted TCA 1997 s 121A(1)(definition of "van", para (*d*)) with effect from 1 January 2004.
Subs (1)(*c*)(ii) inserted TCA 1997 s 121A(2A) with effect from 1 January 2004.

9 Amendment of Chapter 4 (collection and recovery of income tax on certain emoluments (PAYE system)) of Part 42 of Principal Act

Notes

Subs (1)(*a*)(i)(I) substituted "Subject to subsection (1A), this section applies" for "This section applies" in TCA 1997 s 985A(1) with effect from 25 March 2004.
Subs (1)(*a*)(i)(II) deleted "excluding perquisites or profits whatever in the form of shares (including stock) in a company, but" from TCA 1997 s 985A(1)(*a*) with effect from 25 March 2004.
Subs (1)(*a*)(ii) inserted TCA 1997 s 985A(1A) with effect from 25 March 2004.
Subs (1)(*a*)(iii) inserted TCA 1997 s 985A(4A) for 2004 and subsequent years of assessment.
Subs (1)(*a*)(iv) inserted TCA 1997 s 985A(7) with effect for 2004 and subsequent years of assessment.
Subs (1)(*b*) inserted TCA 1997 s 985B with effect from 25 March 2004.
Subs (1)(*c*) substituted TCA 1997 s 994(1) with effect from 25 March 2004.
Subs (1)(*d*) substituted TCA 1997 s 995(*a*)(i) with effect from 25 March 2004.

10 Amendment of section 122 (preferential loan arrangements) of Principal Act

Notes

Subs (1)(*a*) substituted TCA 1997 s 122(1)(definition of "employer")(i) as respects loans made on or after 4 February 2004.
Subs (1)(*b*) substituted "3.5 per cent" for "4.5 per cent" in TCA 1997 s 122(1)(*a*)(definition of "the specified rate") with effect from 1 January 2004.

11 Amendment of section 470 (relief for insurance against expenses of illness) of Principal Act

Notes

Para (*a*) substituted TCA 1997 s 470(1)(definition of "authorised insurer") with effect from 25 March 2004.
Para (*b*) substituted TCA 1997 s 470(1)(definition of "relevant contract") with effect from 25 March 2004.

12 Payments under Scéim na bhFoghlaimeoirí Gaeilge

Notes

Section 12 inserted TCA 1997 s 216B with effect from 1 January 2004.

13 Amendment of Chapter 2 (farming: relief for increase in stock values) of Part 23 of Principal Act

Notes

Subs (1)(*a*)(i) substituted "In this section, but subject to section 667A," for "In this section," in TCA 1997 s 667(1) with effect from 1 January 2004.
Subs (1)(*a*)(ii)(I) inserted "or" after "so set out" in TCA 1997 s 667(1)(definition of "qualifying farmer")(*b*)(iii)(I) with effect from 1 January 2004.
Subs (1)(*a*)(ii)(II) substituted "180 hours." for "180 hours," in, and deleted "or" where it last occurs from, TCA 1997 s 667(1)(definition of "qualifying farmer")(*b*)(iii)(II) with effect from 1 January 2004.

Subs (1)(*a*)(ii)(III) deleted TCA 1997 s 667(1)(definition of "qualifying farmer")(*b*)(iii)(III) with effect from 1 January 2004.
Subs (1)(*b*) inserted TCA 1997 s 667A with effect from 1 January 2004.

14 Amendment of section 664 (relief for certain income from leasing of farm land) of Principal Act

Notes
Subs (1)(*a*)(i) substituted "40 years" for "55 years" in TCA 1997 s 664(1)(*a*)(definition of "qualifying lessor")(i) with effect from 1 January 2004.
Subs (1)(*a*)(ii)(I) substituted "in any other case," for "in any other case, or" in TCA 1997 s 664(1)(*a*)(definition of "the specified amount")(ii)(IV)(B) with effect from 1 January 2004.
Subs (1)(*a*)(ii)(II) substituted TCA 1997 s 664(1)(*a*)(definition of "the specified amount")(ii)(V) with effect from 1 January 2004.
Subs (1)(*b*) substituted TCA 1997 s 664(1)(*b*)(iii) with effect from 1 January 2004.

15 Amendment of Schedule 12 (employee share ownership trusts) to Principal Act

Notes
Para (*a*) inserted "or (3)" in TCA 1997 Sch 12 para 11(2C) with effect from 1 January 2004.
Para (*b*)(i) inserted "or, in the case of a company referred to in clause (*d*) of the definition of 'relevant company' in paragraph 1(1), at some time within 9 months prior to that day," after "established by that relevant company", in TCA 1997 Sch 12 para 11A(5)(*a*) with effect from 1 January 2004.
Para (*b*)(ii) inserted "or, in the case of a company referred to in clause (*d*) of the definition of 'relevant company' in paragraph 1(1), at some time within 9 months prior to that day," in TCA 1997 Sch 12 para 11A(6)(*a*) with effect from 1 January 2004.
Para (*b*)(iii) inserted "or (6)" after "subparagraph (5)" in TCA 1997 Sch 12 para 11A(7) with effect from 1 January 2004.

16 Occupational pension schemes

Notes
Subs (1) inserted TCA 1997 s 772(3E) with effect from 25 March 2004.
Subs (2) substituted TCA 1997 s 774(7)(*b*)(ii) with effect from 6 February 2003.
Subs (3) substituted TCA 1997 s 776(2)(*b*)(ii) with effect from 6 February 2003.

CHAPTER 3
Income Tax, Corporation Tax and Capital Gains Tax

17 Exemption from tax on certain income and gains

Notes
Subs (1)(*a*) substituted TCA 1997 s 189(2) with effect for 2004 and subsequent years of assessment.
Subs (1)(*b*) substituted TCA 1997 s 189A(3) and (4) with effect for 2004 and subsequent years of assessment.
Subs (1)(*c*) substituted "the Income Tax Acts and the Capital Gains Tax Acts" for "the Income Tax Acts" in TCA 1997 s 191(3) with effect for 2004 and subsequent years of assessment.
Subs (1)(*d*) inserted TCA 1997 s 192(3) and (4) with effect for 2004 and subsequent years of assessment.

18 Amendment of Part 16 (income tax relief for investment in corporate trades — business expansion scheme and seed capital scheme) of Principal Act

Notes
Subs (1)(*a*)(i) inserted TCA 1997 s 489(4B) with effect with effect from 1 January 2004.
Subs (1)(*a*)(ii) substituted "4 February 2004"[1] for "31 December 2003" in TCA 1997 s 489(15) with effect from 1 January 2004.

Subs (1)(*b*)(i) substituted "subsection (4), (4A) or (4B) of section 489" for "section 489(4) or (4A)" in TCA 1997 s 490(3)(*a*) with effect with effect from 1 January 2004.
Subs (1)(*b*)(ii) substituted "2006" for "2003" in TCA 1997 s 490(3)(*b*) and (4)(*b*) with effect from 1 January 2004.
Subs (2)(*a*) substituted "31 December 2006" for "4 February 2004" in TCA 1997 s 489(15) with effect from 5 February 2004 on the making of an order to that effect by the Minister for Finance (start date amended from 4 February 2004 to 5 February 2004 by FA 2005 s 27(*b*)(i)).
Subs (2)(*b*)(i) substituted "€1,000,000" for "€750,000" in TCA 1997 s 491(2)(*a*) and (3)(*a*) in relation to eligible shares issued on or after 1 January 2004 (see FA 2005 s 27(*a*)(i) and (*b*)(ii)).
Subs (2)(*b*)(ii) (inserted by FA 2005 s 27(*a*)(i)) inserted TCA 1997 s 491(3A) in relation to eligible shares issued on or after 5 February 2004.
Subs (2)(*c*) substituted TCA 1997 s 494(2)(*a*)(ii)(II) in relation to relevant investments made on or after 5 February 2004, coming into operation on the making of an order to that effect by the Minister for Finance (start date amended from 4 February 2004 to 5 February 2004 by FA 2005 s 27(*b*)(iii)).
Subs (2)(*cc*)(i) (inserted by FA 2005 s 27(*a*)(ii)) substituted TCA 1997 s 495(1)–(2) with effect from 5 February 2004.
Subs (2)(*cc*)(ii) (inserted by FA 2005 s 27(*a*)(ii)) substituted "which is resident in the State, or is resident in an EEA State other than the State and carries on business in the State through a branch or agency," for "which is resident in the State and not resident elsewhere," in TCA 1997 s 496(3)(*a*) with effect from 5 February 2004.
Subs (2)(*cc*)(iii) (inserted by FA 2005 s 27(*a*)(ii)) inserted TCA 1997 s 495(3A) with effect from 5 February 2004.
Subs (2)(*cc*)(iv) (inserted by FA 2005 s 27(*a*)(ii)) inserted TCA 1997 s 495(16) with effect from 5 February 2004.
Subs (2)(*d*)(i)(I)(A) (as amended by FA 2005 s 27(*a*)(iii)) substituted "this Part," for "this Part, and" in TCA 1997 s 496(2)(*a*)(i)(I)(A) as respects subscriptons for eligible shares made on or after 5 February 2004, coming into operation on the making of an order to that effect by the Minister for Finance.
Subs (2)(*d*)(i)(I)(B) (as amended by FA 2005 s 27(*a*)(iii)) substituted "this Part, and" for "this Part," in TCA 1997 s 496(2)(*a*)(i)(II) as respects subscriptons for eligible shares made on or after 5 February 2004, coming into operation on the making of an order to that effect by the Minister for Finance.
Subs (2)(*d*)(i)(I)(C) (as amended by FA 2005 s 27(*a*)(iii)) inserted TCA 1997 s 496(2)(*a*)(i)(III) as respects subscriptons for eligible shares made on or after 5 February 2004, coming into operation on the making of an order to that effect by the Minister for Finance.
Subs (2)(*d*)(i)(II) (as amended by FA 2005 s 27(*a*)(iii)) substituted "on or after 1 January 2003 and on or before 31 December 2004" for "on or after 1 January 2003" in TCA 1997 s 496(2)(*a*)(iv) and (xv) as respects subscriptons for eligible shares made on or after 5 February 2004, coming into operation on the making of an order to that effect by the Minister for Finance.
Subs (2)(*d*)(ii) (as amended by FA 2005 s 27(*a*)(iii)) inserted TCA 1997 s 496(4A) as respects subscriptons for eligible shares made on or after 5 February 2004, coming into operation on the making of an order to that effect by the Minister for Finance.
Subs (2)(*e*) inserted TCA 1997 s 499(3A) with effect from 5 February 2004 on the making of an order to that effect by the Minister for Finance (start date amended from 4 February 2004 to 5 February 2004 by FA 2005 s 27(*b*)(i)).

19 Transitional arrangements in relation to section 18(1)(*a*)(ii)

(1) In this section—

"auditor" means—

(*a*) in relation to a company or its qualifying subsidiary, the person or persons appointed as auditor of the company or its qualifying subsidiary, as appropriate, for all the purposes of the Companies Acts, 1963 to 2003, and

(*b*) in relation to a specified designated fund, the person or persons appointed as auditor of that fund;

"certifying agency" has the meaning assigned to it by section 488 of the Principal Act;

"certifying Minister" has the meaning assigned to it by section 488 of the Principal Act;

"County Enterprise Board" means a board referred to in the Schedule to the Industrial Development Act 1995;

"eligible shares" has the meaning assigned to it by section 488 of the Principal Act;

"industrial development agency" has the meaning assigned to it by section 488 of the Principal Act;

"the principal provisions" means Part 16 of the Principal Act;

"prospectus", in relation to a company, means any prospectus, notice, circular or advertisement, offering to the public for subscription or purchase any eligible shares of the company, and in this definition "the public" includes any section of the public, whether selected as members of the company or as clients of the person issuing the prospectus or in any other manner;

"qualifying subsidiary", in relation to a company, has the same meaning as it has for the purposes of section 495 of the Principal Act;

"qualifying trading operations" has the meaning assigned to it by section 496 of the Principal Act;

"specified designated fund" means an investment fund designated under section 508 of the Principal Act which closed on or before 4 February 2004;

"the specified period" means the period beginning on 5 February 2003 and ending on 4 February 2004.

(2) This section applies to a company which, or whose qualifying subsidiary, either carries on or intends to carry on one or more of the qualifying trading operations.

(3) Subject to subsection (7) where the conditions in either subsection (4) or (5) are met, section 18(1)(*a*)(ii) shall apply as if, in the case of a company to which this section applies, "31 December 2004" were substituted for "4 February 2004".

(4) The conditions of this subsection referred to in subsection (3) are—

(*a*) the eligible shares are issued by the company on or before 31 December 2004, and

(*b*) the eligible shares are issued following a subscription on behalf of an individual by a person or persons having the management of a specified designated fund, and

(*c*) the company proves to the satisfaction of the Revenue Commissioners that on or before 4 February 2004 it had the intention of raising money before that date under the principal provisions through the specified designated fund referred to in paragraph (*b*),

and in determining whether they are satisfied that the company has complied with the requirements specified in paragraph (*c*) the Revenue Commissioners shall have regard to the following—

(i) (I) signed heads of agreement between the company and the fund, or

(II) exchange of correspondence between the company and the fund showing a clear intention that the fund intended to subscribe for eligible shares in the company,

(ii) a certificate by the auditor of the fund confirming that it is a specified designated fund, and

(iii) any other information the Revenue Commissioners deem necessary for the purpose.

(5) The conditions of this subsection referred to in subsection (3) are—

(*a*) the eligible shares are issued by the company on or before 31 December 2004, and

(*b*) the company proves to the satisfaction of the Revenue Commissioners that on or before 4 February 2004 it had an intention to raise money under the principal provisions, and in determining whether they are so satisfied the Revenue Commissioners shall have regard to one or more of the following—

(i) an application in writing made by the company to the Revenue Commissioners in the specified period for the opinion of the Revenue Commissioners as to whether the company would be a qualifying company for the purposes of the principal provisions,

(ii) an application in writing made by the company to an industrial development agency in the specified period for a certificate referred to in section 489(2)(*e*) of the Principal Act,

(iii) an application in writing made to a certifying agency, certifying Minister or County Enterprise Board in the specified period for a certificate under section 497 of the Principal Act, and

(iv) the publication in the specified period of a prospectus by, or on behalf of, the company,

and

(*c*) (i) in the case of a company which, or whose qualifying subsidiary, either carries on or intends to carry on a qualifying trading operation as is mentioned in subparagraph (i), (ii), (iii), (v), (viii), (ix), (xi) or (xiii) of paragraph (*a*) of section 496(2) of the Principal Act, that in the specified period the company or its qualifying subsidiary, as the case may be, had entered into a binding contract in writing—

(I) to purchase or lease land or a building,

(II) to purchase or lease plant or machinery, or

(III) for the construction or refurbishment of a building,

to be used in the carrying on of its qualifying trading operation,

(ii) in the case of a company which, or whose qualifying subsidiary, either carries on or intends to carry on a qualifying trading operation as is mentioned in subparagraph (vii) of paragraph (*a*) of section 496(2) of the Principal Act, that in the specified period the company or its qualifying subsidiary, as the case may be, had entered into a binding contract in writing—

(I) to purchase or lease greenhouses,

(II) to purchase or lease plant or machinery, or

(III) for the construction or refurbishment of greenhouses,

to be used in the carrying on of its qualifying trading operation, and

(iii) in the case of a company which, or whose qualifying subsidiary, either carries on or intends to carry on a qualifying trading operation as is mentioned in subparagraph (xii) of paragraph (*a*) of section 496(2) of the Principal Act, that in the specified period the company or its qualifying subsidiary, as the case may be, had entered into a binding contract in writing for the production, publication, marketing or promotion of the qualifying recording or qualifying recordings which the company or its qualifying subsidiary, as the case may be, intends to produce,

and the company proves to the satisfaction of the Revenue Commissioners that the contract which it or its qualifying subsidiary, as the case may be, had entered into was integral to, or consistent with, the purpose for which it had intended to raise money under the principal provisions and that the consideration of the contract is equal to 25 per cent or more of the money which it is intended to so raise.

(6) For the purposes of subsection (5)—

(*a*) the date on which a contract was entered into by a company or, as the case may be, its qualifying subsidiary, and

(*b*) the date on which a prospectus was published by, or on behalf of, a company,

shall be confirmed in a certificate by the auditor of the company, or its qualifying subsidiary, as appropriate.

(7) If, in accordance with an order made by the Minister for Finance under subsection (3)(*c*) of section 18, subsection (2) of that section comes into operation on a date earlier than 1 January 2005, this section shall cease to apply and have effect as on and from that earlier date.

20 Amendment of section 531 (payments to subcontractors in certain industries) of Principal Act

Notes

Subs (1)(*a*) inserted TCA 1997 s 531(6)(*ba*) with effect from the 25 March 2004.

Subs (1)(*b*) inserted TCA 1997 s 531(11)(*ba*) with effect from 1 January 2004.

Subs (1)(*c*) substituted "subsection (17) or subsection (17A)" for "subsection (17)" in TCA 1997 s 531(20) with effect for the year of assessment 1999–2000 and later years of assessment.

21 Amendment of section 659 (farming: allowances for capital expenditure on the construction of farm buildings, etc. for control of pollution) of Principal Act

Notes

Section 21 substituted "1 January 2007" for "1 January 2004" in TCA 1997 s 659(1)(*c*) with effect from 1 January 2004.

22 Restriction of relief to individuals in respect of loans applied in acquiring interest in companies

Notes

Subs (1) inserted TCA 1997 s 250A which applies in relation to any payment or payments of interest by an individual (*a*) or after 19 March 2003, or (*b*) where this section applies by virtue of definition of "specified amount" para (*c*) in TCA 1997 s 250A, on or after 20 February 2004, and for this purpose interest shall be deemed to accrue from day to day.

23 Qualifying residential units

Notes

Subs (1)(*a*) substituted "comprised in a building of one or more storeys in relation to which building a fire safety certificate under Part III of the Building Control Regulations 1997 (SI No 496 of 1997) (as amended from time to time) is required, and prior to the commencement of the construction works on the building, is granted by the building control authority (within the meaning of section 2 of the Building Control Act 1990, as amended by the Local Government (Dublin) Act 1993 and the Local Government Act 2001) in whose functional area the building is situated" for "comprised in a two storey building" in TCA 1997 s 268(3A)(*b*)(ii) as respects capital expenditure incurred on or after 4 February 2004.
Subs (1)(*b*) substituted "not less than 10 qualifying residential units" for "not less than 20 qualifying residential units" in TCA 1997 s 268(3A)(*c*) as respects capital expenditure incurred on or after 4 February 2004.

24 Qualifying hospitals and qualifying sports injuries clinics

Notes

Subs (1)(*a*) substituted "shall not, as regards a claim for any allowance under this Part by any such person, be regarded as an industrial building or structure" for "shall not be regarded as an industrial building or structure". in TCA 1997 s 268(1A) as respects capital expenditure incurred on the construction or refurbishment of a building or structure on or after 1 May 2004.
Subs (1)(*b*) substituted "shall not, as regards a claim for any allowance under this Part by any such person, be regarded as an industrial building or structure" for "shall not be regarded as an industrial building or structure" in TCA 1997 s 268(1A) as respects capital expenditure incurred on the construction or refurbishment of a building or structure on or after 1 May 2004.

25 Capital allowances for hotels, holiday camps and holiday cottages

Notes

Subs (1)(*a*)(i) substituted "31 July 2006" for "31 December 2004" in TCA 1997 s 268(13)(*b*) with effect from 1 January 2004.
Subs (1)(*a*)(ii) inserted ", in so far as planning permission is required," after "Development Act 2000)" in TCA 1997 s 268(13)(*b*)(i)(I) with effect from 4 December 2002.
Subs (1)(*a*)(iii) substitued "31 December 2004" for "31 May 2003" in TCA 1997 s 268(13)(*b*)(i)(II) with effect from 1 January 2004.
Subs (1)(*a*)(iv) deleted "or" after TCA 1997 s 268(13)(*b*)(i) with effect from 4 December 2002.
Subs (1)(*a*)(v) substituted "a planning application, in so far as planning permission was required," for "a planning application" n TCA 1997 s 268(13)(*b*)(ii)(I) with effect from 1 January 2004.
Subs (1)(*a*)(vi) substituted "regulations," for "regulations." in TCA 1997 s 268(13)(*b*)(ii)(I) with effect from 1 January 2004.
Subs (1)(*a*)(vii) inserted TCA 1997 s 268(13)(*b*)(iii) with effect from 1 January 2004.
Subs (1)(*b*)(i) substituted "31 July 2006" for "31 December 2004" in TCA 1997 s 272(8) with effect from 1 January 2004.
Subs (1)(*b*)(ii) inserted ", in so far as planning permission is required," after "Development Act 2000)" in TCA 1997 s 272(8)(*a*)(i) with effect from 4 December 2002.
Subs (1)(*b*)(iii) substituted "31 December 2004" for "'31 May 2003" in TCA 1997 s 272(8)(*a*)(ii) with effect from 4 December 2002.

Subs (1)(*b*)(iv) substituted "a planning application, in so far as planning permission was required," for "a planning application" in TCA 1997 s 272(8)(*b*)(i) with effect from 1 January 2004.
Subs (1)(*b*)(v) inserted TCA 1997 s 272(8)(*ba*) with effect from 1 January 2004.
Subs (1)(*b*)(vi) substituted "31 December 2004" for "31 May 2003" in TCA 1997 s 272(8)(*c*)(ii) with effect from 1 January 2004.
Subs (1)(*c*)(i) substituted "31 July 2006" for "31 December 2004" in TCA 1997 s 274(1A) with effect from 1 January 2004.
Subs (1)(*c*)(ii) inserted ", in so far as planning permission is required," after "Development Act 2000)" in TCA 1997 s 274(1A)(*a*)(i) with effect from 4 December 2002.
Subs (1)(*c*)(iii) substituted "31 December 2004" for "31 May 2003" in TCA 1997 s 274(1A)(*a*)(ii) with effect from 4 December 2002.
Subs (1)(*c*)(iv) substituted "a planning application, in so far as planning permission was required," for "a planning application" in TCA 1997 s 274(1A)(*b*)(i) with effect from 1 January 2004.
Subs (1)(*c*)(v) inserted TCA 1997 s 274(1A)(*ba*) with effect from 1 January 2004.
Subs (1)(*c*)(vi) substituted "31 December 2004" for 31 May 2003" in TCA 1997 s 274(1A)(*c*)(ii) with effect from 1 January 2004.
Subs (1)(*d*) inserted TCA 1997 s 316(2A) with effect from 1 January 2004.

26 Amendment of Part 10 (income tax and corporation tax: reliefs for renewal and improvement of certain urban areas, certain resort areas and certain islands) of Principal Act

Notes

Subs (1)(*a*) substituted "31 July 2006" for "31 December 2004" in TCA 1997 s 344(1)(definition of "qualifying period")(*c*) with effect from 1 January 2004.
Subs (1)(*b*)(i)(I) substituted "31 July 2006" for "31 December 2004" in TCA 1997 s 372A(1)(definition of "qualifying period")(*a*)(ii) and shall come into operation on the making of an order to that effect by the Minister for Finance.
Subs (1)(*b*)(i)(II) substituted TCA 1997 s 372A(1)(definition of "qualifying period")(*b*) and shall come into operation on the making of an order to that effect by the Minister for Finance.
Subs (1)(*b*)(ii) inserted TCA 1997 s 372A(1B) and shall come into operation on the making of an order to that effect by the Minister for Finance.
Subs (1)(*c*)(i) substituted "31 July 2006" for "31 December 2004" in TCA 1997 s 372B(*c*)(ii) and shall come into operation on the making of an order to that effect by the Minister for Finance.
Subs (1)(*c*)(ii) substituted "31 July 2006" for "31 December 2004" in TCA 1997 s 372B(*d*)(ii) with effect from 1 January 2004.
Subs (1)(*d*)(i) substituted "where such a street is to be a qualifying street for the purposes of section 372AP, that section shall apply in relation to that street" for "where such an area or areas is or are to be a qualifying area for the purposes of section 372AP, that section shall apply in relation to that area or those areas" in TCA 1997 s 372L(1)(*ba*) with effect from 1 January 2002.
Subs (1)(*d*)(ii) inserted TCA 1997 s 372BA(1)(*bb*) and shall come into operation on the making of an order to that effect by the Minister for Finance.
Subs (1)(*d*)(iii) substituted TCA 1997 s 372BA(1)(*c*) with effect from 1 January 2004.
Subs (1)(*e*)(i) renumbered TCA 1997 s 372L(1) and shall come into operation on the making of an order to that effect by the Minister for Finance.
Subs (1)(*e*)(ii) substituted "and ending on— (i) 31 December 2004, or (ii) where subsection (2) applies, 31 July 2006" for "and ending on 31 December 2004" in TCA 1997 s 372L(1)(definition of "qualifying period")(*a*) and shall come into operation on the making of an order to that effect by the Minister for Finance.
Subs (1)(*e*)(iii) inserted TCA 1997 s 372L(2) and shall come into operation on the making of an order to that effect by the Minister for Finance.
Subs (1)(*f*)(i) substituted TCA 1997 s 372U(1)(definition of "qualifying period") with effect from 1 January 2004.
Subs (1)(*f*)(ii) inserted TCA 1997 s 372U(1A) with effect from 1 January 2004.
Subs (1)(*g*) substituted "this Chapter or Chapter 11" for "this Chapter" in TCA 1997 s 372W(2)(*c*)(i) with effect from 1 January 2002.
Subs (1)(*h*)(i) substituted TCA 1997 s 372AA(1)(definition of "qualifying period") with effect from 1 January 2004.
Subs (1)(*h*)(ii) inserted TCA 1997 s 372AA(1A) with effect from 1 January 2004.

Subs (1)(*i*)(i) substituted "6 April 2001" for "the day referred to in paragraph (*a*) of the definition of 'qualifying period' in section 372AA" in TCA 1997 s 372AB(1)(*c*)(i) with effect from 1 January 2002.

Subs (1)(*i*)(ii) substituted "or end after 31 December 2004, or— (I) in the case of sections 372AC and 372AD where section 372AA(1A) applies, end after 31 July 2006, and (II) in the case of any provision of Chapter 11 of this Part where section 372AL(1A) applies, end after 31 July 2006." for "or end after 31 December 2003" in TCA 1997 s 372AB(1)(*c*) with effect from 1 January 2004.

Subs (1)(*j*)(i)(I) substituted "31 July 2006" for "31 December 2004" in TCA 1997 s 372AL(1)(*a*)(ii) with effect from 1 January 2004.

Subs (1)(*j*)(i)(II) substituted "and ending on 31 December 2004 or, where subsection (1A) applies, ending on 31 July 2006" for "and ending on 31 December 2004" in TCA 1997 s 372AL(1)(*b*) with effect from 1 January 2004.

Subs (1)(*j*)(i)(III) substituted "and ending on 31 December 2004 or, where subsection (1A) applies, ending on 31 July 2006" for "and ending on 31 December 2004" in TCA 1997 s 372AL(1)(*c*)(i) and (ii) with effect from 1 January 2004.

Subs (1)(*j*)(i)(IV) substituted "and ending on 31 December 2004 or, where subsection (1A) applies, ending on 31 July 2006" for "and ending on 31 December 2004" in TCA 1997 s 372AL(1)(*d*) with effect from 1 January 2004.

Subs (1)(*j*)(i)(V) substituted "and ending on 31 December 2004 or, where subsection (1A) applies, ending on 31 July 2006" for "and ending on 31 December 2004" in TCA 1997 s 372AL(1)(*e*) with effect from 1 January 2004.

Subs (1)(*j*)(i)(VI) substituted TCA 1997 s 372AL(1)(*f*)(ii) with effect from 1 January 2004.

Subs (1)(*j*)(ii) inserted TCA 1997 s 372AL(1A) with effect from 1 January 2004.

27 Amendment of section 843 (capital allowances for buildings used for third level education purposes) of Principal Act

Notes

Para (*a*) inserted TCA 1997 s 843(1)(definition of "qualifying period") with effect from 1 January 2004.

Para (*b*) substituted "Subject to subsections (2A) to (7)" for "Subject to subsections (3) to (7)" in TCA 1997 s 843(2) with effect from 1 January 2004.

Para (*c*) inserted TCA 1997 s 843(2A) with effect from 1 January 2004.

Para (*d*) inserted "incurred in the qualifying period" after "qualifying expenditure" in TCA 1997 s 843(3) with effect from 1 January 2004.

Para (*e*) inserted TCA 1997 s 843(9) with effect from 1 January 2004.

28 Amendment of section 481 (relief for investment in films) of Principal Act

Notes

Subs (1)(*a*)(i) inserted TCA 1997 s 481(1)(definition of "eligible individual") with effect from such day or days as the Minister for Finance may by order or orders appoint and different days may be appointed for different purposes or different provisions.

Subs (1)(*a*)(ii) substituted TCA 1997 s 481(1)(definition of "film")(*a*) with effect from such day or days as the Minister for Finance may by order or orders appoint and different days may be appointed for different purposes or different provisions.

Subs (1)(*a*)(iii) substituted "Arts, Sport and Tourism" for "Arts, Heritage, Gaeltacht and the Islands" in TCA 1997 s 481(1)(definition of "Minister") with effect from such day or days as the Minister for Finance may by order or orders appoint and different days may be appointed for different purposes or different provisions.

Subs (1)(*a*)(iv) substituted TCA 1997 s 481(1)(definition of "qualifying film") with effect from such day or days as the Minister for Finance may by order or orders appoint and different days may be appointed for different purposes or different provisions.

Subs (1)(*a*)(v) substituted "31 December 2008" for "31 December 2004" in TCA 1997 s 481(1)(definition of "qualifying period") with effect from such day or days as the Minister for Finance may by order or orders appoint and different days may be appointed for different purposes or different provisions.

Subs (1)(*a*)(vi)(I) substituted TCA 1997 s 481(1)(definition of "relevant investment")(*b*) with effect from such day or days as the Minister for Finance may by order or orders appoint and different days may be appointed for different purposes or different provisions.

Subs (1)(*a*)(vi)(II) substituted "other than a provision for its repayment in the event of the Revenue Commissioners not giving a certificate under subsection (2A)" for "other than a provision for its repayment in the event of the Minister not giving a certificate under subsection (2)" in TCA 1997 s 481(1)(definition of "relevant investment") with effect from such day or days as the Minister for Finance may by order or orders appoint and different days may be appointed for different purposes or different provisions.

Subs (1)(*b*)(i) substituted TCA 1997 s 481(2)(*a*) and (*b*) with effect from such day or days as the Minister for Finance may by order or orders appoint and different days may be appointed for different purposes or different provisions.

Subs (1)(*b*)(ii) substituted "€15,000,000" for "€10,480,000" in TCA 1997 s 481(2)(*c*) with effect from such day or days as the Minister for Finance may by order or orders appoint and different days may be appointed for different purposes or different provisions.

Subs (1)(*b*)(iii) deleted TCA 1997 s 481(2)(*d*) and (*e*) with effect from such day or days as the Minister for Finance may by order or orders appoint and different days may be appointed for different purposes or different provisions.

Subs (1)(*c*) inserted TCA 1997 s 481(2A)–(2E) with effect from such day or days as the Minister for Finance may by order or orders appoint and different days may be appointed for different purposes or different provisions.

Subs (1)(*d*) substituted "the year of assessment 2008" for "the year of assessment 2004" in TCA 1997 s 481(8) with effect from such day or days as the Minister for Finance may by order or orders appoint and different days may be appointed for different purposes or different provisions.

Subs (1)(*d*) substituted "the year of assessment 2008" for "the year of assessment 2004" in TCA 1997 s 481(9) with effect from such day or days as the Minister for Finance may by order or orders appoint and different days may be appointed for different purposes or different provisions.

Subs (1)(*f*) substituted "the revocation, under subsection (2D), by the Revenue Commissioners of a certificate issued by them under subsection (2A)" for "the revocation by the Minister of a certificate under subsection (2)" in TCA 1997 s 481(11)(*a*) with effect from such day or days as the Minister for Finance may by order or orders appoint and different days may be appointed for different purposes or different provisions.

Subs (1)(*g*) deleted TCA 1997 s 481(13)(*b*) and (*c*) with effect from such day or days as the Minister for Finance may by order or orders appoint and different days may be appointed for different purposes or different provisions.

Subs (1)(*h*) inserted TCA 1997 s 481(22)–(23) with effect from such day or days as the Minister for Finance may by order or orders appoint and different days may be appointed for different purposes or different provisions.

---

29 Amendment of Chapter 1A (investment undertakings) of Part 27 of Principal Act

Subs (1)(*a*)(i) deleted "and" from TCA 1997 s 739B(1)(*c*) as respects the appropriation or cancellation of a unit (within the meaning of TCA 1997 s 739B) on or after 4 February 2004.

Subs (1)(*a*)(ii) inserted TCA 1997 s 739B(1)(*cc*) as respects the appropriation or cancellation of a unit (within the meaning of TCA 1997 s 739B) on or after 4 February 2004.

Subs (1)(*b*)(i) deleted "and" after "unit holder" from TCA 1997 s 739D(2)(*d*)(ii) as respects the appropriation or cancellation of a unit (within the meaning of TCA 1997 s 739B) on or after 4 February 2004.

Subs (1)(*b*)(ii) inserted TCA 1997 s 739D(2)(*dd*) as respects the appropriation or cancellation of a unit (within the meaning of TCA 1997 s 739B) on or after 4 February 2004.

Subs (1)(*b*)(iii) inserted TCA 1997 s 739D(5A) as respects the appropriation or cancellation of a unit (within the meaning of TCA 1997 s 739B) on or after 4 February 2004.

Subs (1)(*c*)(i) substituted "paragraph (*b*), (*c*), (*d*) or (*dd*)" for "paragraph (*b*), (*c*) or (*d*)" in TCA 1997 s 739E(1)(*b*) as respects the appropriation or cancellation of a unit (within the meaning of TCA 1997 s 739B) on or after 4 February 2004.

Subs (1)(*c*)(ii)(I) deleted "or" from TCA 1997 s 739E(3)(*b*)(i) as respects the appropriation or cancellation of a unit (within the meaning of TCA 1997 s 739B) on or after 4 February 2004.

Subs (1)(*c*)(ii)(II) inserted TCA 1997 s 739E(3)(*b*)(*ia*) as respects the appropriation or cancellation of a unit (within the meaning of TCA 1997 s 739B) on or after 4 February 2004.

---

30 Amendment of Chapter 4 (certain offshore funds — taxation and returns) of Part 27 of Principal Act

Notes

Para (*a*) substituted "section 396, 396B" for "section 396" in TCA 1997 s 747E(4)(*b*) with effect from 1 January 2004.

Para (*b*) inserted TCA 1997 s 747F with effect from 1 January 2004.

31 Amendment of Schedule 24 (relief from income tax and corporation tax by means of credit in respect of foreign tax) to Principal Act

Notes

Para (1)(*a*)(i) substituted "5 per cent" for "25 per cent" in TCA 1997 Sch 24 para 9A(4)(*b*) with effect from such day or days as the Minister for Finance by order appoints, either generally or with reference to any particular purpose or provision, and different days may be so appointed for different purposes or different provisions.

Para (1)(*a*)(ii) deleted ", in respect of taxes covered by these arrangements," in TCA 1997 Sch 24 para 9A(5)(*a*) with effect from such day or days as the Minister for Finance by order appoints, either generally or with reference to any particular purpose or provision, and different days may be so appointed for different purposes or different provisions.

Para (1)(*b*)(i) substituted "underlying tax to be taken into account: and for this purpose there shall, subject to Part 1, be taken into account as if it were tax payable under the law of the territory in which the third company is resident— (i) any income tax or corporation tax payable in the State by the foreign company in respect of its profits, and (ii) any tax which, under the law of any other territory, is payable by the foreign company in respect of its profits." for "underlying tax to be taken into account." in TCA 1997 Sch 24 para 9B(2) with effect from such day or days as the Minister for Finance by order appoints, either generally or with reference to any particular purpose or provision, and different days may be so appointed for different purposes or different provisions.

Para (1)(*b*)(ii)(I) substituted "5 per cent" for "25 per cent" in TCA 1997 Sch 24 para 9B(5)(*b*)(i) with effect from such day or days as the Minister for Finance by order appoints, either generally or with reference to any particular purpose or provision, and different days may be so appointed for different purposes or different provisions.

Para (1)(*b*)(ii)(II) substituted "5 per cent" for "10 per cent" in TCA 1997 Sch 24 para 9B(5)(*b*)(iii) with effect from such day or days as the Minister for Finance by order appoints, either generally or with reference to any particular purpose or provision, and different days may be so appointed for different purposes or different provisions.

Para (1)(*c*) inserted TCA 1997 Sch 24 para 9E with effect from such day or days as the Minister for Finance by order appoints, either generally or with reference to any particular purpose or provision, and different days may be so appointed for different purposes or different provisions.

32 Amendment of section 817C (restriction on deductibility of certain interest) of Principal Act

Notes

Subs (1)(*a*) substituted "Subject to subsection (2A), this section applies where" for "This section applies where" in TCA 1997 s 817C(2) as respects any chargeable period ending on or after 6 February 2003.

Subs (1)(*b*) inserted TCA 1997 s 817C(2A) as respects any chargeable period ending on or after 6 February 2003.

CHAPTER 4
Corporation Tax

33 Tax credit for research and development expenditure, etc

Notes

Subs (1)(*a*) substituted TCA 1997 s 766 with effect from such day as the Minister for Finance may appoint by order and has effect as respects expenditure incurred on or after that day.

Subs (1)(*a*) inserted TCA 1997 s 766A with effect from such day as the Minister for Finance may appoint by order and has effect as respects expenditure incurred on or after that day.

Subs (1)(*b*) substituted TCA 1997 s 141(5)(*a*)(definition of "research and development activities") with effect from such day as the Minister for Finance may appoint by order and has effect as respects expenditure incurred on or after that day.

34 Amendment of section 831 (implementation of Council Directive 90/435/EEC concerning the common system of taxation applicable in the case of parent companies and subsidiaries of different Member States) of Principal Act

Notes

Para (*a*)(i) deleted ", other than in the expression 'unlimited company' in subsection (5A)," from TCA 1997 s 831(1)(definition of "company") with effect from 1 January 2004.

Para (*a*)(ii) inserted ", as amended by Council Directive No 2003/123/EC of 22 December 2003 (OJ No L. 7 of 13.1.2004, p. 41)," in TCA 1997 s 831(1)(definition of "the Directive") with effect from 1 January 2004.

Para (*a*)(iii)(I) substituted TCA 1997 s 831(1)(definition of "parent company")(i) with effect from 1 January 2004.

Para (*a*)(iii)(II) substituted "5 per cent" for "25 per cent" in TCA 1997 s 831(1)(definition of "parent company")(ii), (I) and (II) with effect from 1 January 2004.

Para (*b*)(i) deleted "which is resident in this State" from TCA 1997 s 831(2) with effect from 1 January 2004.

Para (*b*)(ii)(I) substituted TCA 1997 s 831(2)(*a*)(i) with effect from 1 January 2004.

Para (*b*)(ii)(II) substituted "resident, and" for "resident," in TCA 1997 s 831(2)(*a*)(ii) with effect from 1 January 2004.

Para (*b*)(ii)(III) inserted TCA 1997 s 831(2)(*a*)(iii) with effect from 1 January 2004.

Para (*c*) inserted TCA 1997 s 831(2A) with effect from 1 January 2004.

Para (*d*) inserted "or (2A)" in TCA 1997 s 831(3) with effect from 1 January 2004.

Para (*e*) deleted TCA 1997 s 831(5A) with effect from 1 January 2004.

35 Taxation of certain short-term leases of plant and machinery

Notes

Subs (1) inserted TCA 1997 s 80A as respects accounting periods ending on or after 4 February, 2004.

36 Amendment of section 434 (distributions to be taken into account and meaning of "distributable income", "investment income", "estate income", etc) of Principal Act

Notes

Section 36 substituted TCA 1997 s 434(1)(definition of "investment income") with effect from 1 January 2004.

37 Amendment of section 396B (relief for certain trading losses on a value basis) of Principal Act

Notes

Subs (1) substituted TCA 1997 s 396B(1)(definition of "relevant corporation tax") as respects any claim for relief made on or after 4 February 2004.

38 Amendment of section 420B (group relief: relief for certain losses on a value basis) of Principal Act

Notes

Subs (1) substituted TCA 1997 s 420B(1)(definition of "relevant corporation tax") as respects any claim for relief made on or after 4 February 2004.

39 Amendment of section 486B (relief for investment in renewable energy generation) of Principal Act

Notes

Subs (1) substituted "31 December 2006" for "31 December 2004" in TCA 1997 s 486B(1)(definition of "qualifying period") with effect from such day as the Minister for Finance may appoint by order.

40 Amendment of Schedule 4 (exemption of specified non-commercial State sponsored bodies from certain tax provisions) to Principal Act

Notes

Section 40 inserted TCA 1997 Sch 4 para 83A with effect from 1 January 2004.

41 Exemption from tax for certain interest and royalties payments

(1) Part 8 of the Principal Act is amended by substituting the provisions set out in Schedule 1 for Chapter 6 (inserted by the European Communities (Abolition of Withholding Tax on Certain Interest and Royalties) Regulations 2003 (SI No 721 of 2003)).

(2) The European Communities (Abolition of Withholding Tax on Certain Interest and Royalties) Regulations 2003 are revoked.

42 Exemption from tax in the case of gains on certain disposals of shares

Notes

Subs (1)(*a*) inserted TCA 1997 s 626B with effect from such day as the Minister for Finance may appoint by order.

Subs (1)(*a*) inserted TCA 1997 s 626C with effect from such day as the Minister for Finance may appoint by order.

Subs (1)(*b*) inserted TCA 1997 Sch 25A with effect from such day as the Minister for Finance may appoint by order.

PART 6
Miscellaneous

80 Interpretation (Part 6)

In this Part **"Principal Act"** means the Taxes Consolidation Act 1997.

82 Amendment of section 912A (information for tax authorities in other territories) of Principal Act

Notes

Section 82 inserted "or section 106 of the Capital Acquisitions Tax Consolidation Act 2003" in TCA 1997 s 912A(1)(definition of "foreign tax") with effect from 25 March 2004.

83 Amendment of Part 22 (provisions relating to dealing in or developing land and disposals of development land) of Principal Act

Notes

Subs (1)(*a*) substituted "the Local Government (Planning and Development) Acts 1963 to 1999 or the Planning and Development Act 2000," for "section 26 of the Local Government (Planning and Development) Act, 1963," in TCA 1997 s 644A(1)(definition of "residential development land") with effect from 11 March 2002.

Subs (1)(*b*)(i) inserted TCA 1997 s 648(definition of "the Act of 2000") with effect from 21 January 2002.

Subs (1)(*b*)(ii) substituted "(within the meaning of section 3 of the Act of 1963, or, on or after 21 January 2002, within the meaning of section 3 of the Act of 2000)" for "(within the meaning of section 3 of the Act of 1963)" in TCA 1997 s 648(definition of "current use value") with effect from 21 January 2002.

Subs (1)(*b*)(iii) substituted TCA 1997 s 648(definition of "development of a minor nature") with effect from 11 March 2002.

84 Amendment of section 962 (recovery by sheriff or county registrar) of Principal Act

Notes

Section 84 inserted TCA 1997 s 962(1A) with effect from 25 March 2004.

85 Amendment of section 1003 (payment of tax by means of donation of heritage items) of Principal Act

Notes

Subs (1)(*a*)(i) substituted TCA 1997 s 1003(1)(definition of "selection committee")(i)–(vii) as respects determinations made under TCA 1997 s 1003(2)(*a*) on or after 25 March 2004.

Subs (1)(*a*)(ii) inserted TCA 1997 s 1003(1)(*b*)(iii) as respects determinations made under TCA 1997 s 1003(2)(*a*) on or after 25 March 2004.

Subs (1)(*b*)(i) substituted "is, subject to the provisions of paragraphs (*aa*) and (*ab*), determined by the selection committee" for "is determined by the selection committee, after consideration of any evidence in relation to the matter which the person submits to the committee and after such consultation (if any) as may seem appropriate to the committee to be necessary with such person or body of persons as in the opinion of the committee may be of assistance to them," in TCA 1997 s 1003(2)(*a*) as respects determinations made under TCA 1997 s 1003(2)(*a*) on or after 25 March 2004.

Subs (1)(*b*)(ii) inserted TCA 1997 s 1003(2)(*aa*)–(*ab*) as respects determinations made under TCA 1997 s 1003(2)(*a*) on or after 25 March 2004.

Subs (1)(*b*)(iii)(I) substituted TCA 1997 s 1003(2)(*c*)(i) as respects determinations made under TCA 1997 s 1003(2)(*a*) on or after 25 March 2004.

Subs (1)(*b*)(iii)(II) substituted "€150,000" for "€100,000" in TCA 1997 s 1003(2)(*c*)(ii) as respects determinations made under TCA 1997 s 1003(2)(*a*) on or after 25 March 2004.

86 Information in respect of certain tax expenditures

Notes

Subs (1) inserted TCA 1997 s 897A as respects the year of assessment 2005 and subsequent years of assessment.
Subs (2)(*a*) substituted "precept," for "precept, or" in TCA 1997 s 1052(1)(*a*) as respects any chargeable period (within the meaning of TCA 1997 s 321(2)) commencing on or after 1 January 2004.
Subs (2)(*b*) inserted TCA 1997 s 1052(1)(*aa*) as respects any chargeable period (within the meaning of TCA 1997 s 321(2)) commencing on or after 1 January 2004.
Subs (3)(*a*) inserted TCA 1997 s 1084(1)(*b*)(*ib*) as respects any chargeable period (within the meaning of TCA 1997 s 321(2)) commencing on or after 1 January 2004.
Subs (3)(*b*) substituted "and, except where the surcharge arises by virtue of subparagraph (*ib*) of subsection (1)(*b*), if the tax contained in the assessment is not the amount of tax as so increased," for "and, if the tax contained in the assessment is not the amount of tax as so increased," in TCA 1997 s 1084(2)(*a*) as respects any chargeable period (within the meaning of TCA 1997 s 321(2)) commencing on or after 1 January 2004.
Subs (4) substituted "(*ia*), (*ib*)," for "'(*ia*)," in TCA 1997 s 1085(1)(*b*) as respects any chargeable period (within the meaning of TCA 1997 s 321(2)) commencing on or after 1 January 2004.

87 Amendment of Chapter 4 (revenue powers) of Part 38 of Principal Act

Notes

Section 87 inserted TCA 1997 s 908B with effect from 25 March 2004.

88 Amendment of section 908A (revenue offence: power to obtain information from financial institutions) of Principal Act

Notes

Section 88 substituted TCA 1997 s 908A(2) with effect from 25 March 2004.

89 Miscellaneous technical amendments in relation to tax

The enactments specified in Schedule 3 are amended to the extent and in the manner specified in that Schedule.

90 Taxation of savings income in the form of interest payments

Notes

Subs (1) (and Sch 4) substituted TCA 1997 Pt 38 Ch 3A with effect from 25 March 2004.
Subs (2) revoked European Communities (Taxation of Savings Income in the Form of Interest Payments) Regulations 2003 with effect from 25 March 2004.

93 Care and management of taxes and duties

All taxes and duties imposed by this Act are placed under the care and management of the Revenue Commissioners.

94 Short title, construction and commencement

(1) This Act may be cited as the Finance Act 2004.

(2) Part 1 shall be construed together with—

- (*a*) in so far as it relates to income tax, the Income Tax Acts,
- (*b*) in so far as it relates to corporation tax, the Corporation Tax Acts, and
- (*c*) in so far as it relates to capital gains tax, the Capital Gains Tax Acts.

...

(7) Part 6 in so far as it relates to—

(*a*) income tax, shall be construed together with the Income Tax Acts,
(*b*) corporation tax, shall be construed together with the Corporation Tax Acts,
(*c*) capital gains tax, shall be construed together with the Capital Gains Tax Acts,

...

(8) Except where otherwise expressly provided in Part 1, that Part is deemed to have come into force and takes effect as on and from 1 January 2004.

....:

(10) Except where otherwise expressly provided for, where a provision of this Act is to come into operation on the making of an order by the Minister for Finance, that provision shall come into operation on such day or days as the Minister for Finance shall appoint either generally or with reference to any particular purpose or provision and different days may be so appointed for different purposes or different provisions.

(11) Any reference in this Act to any other enactment shall, except in so far as the context otherwise requires, be construed as a reference to that enactment as amended by or under any other enactment including this Act.

(12) In this Act, a reference to a Part, section or Schedule is to a Part or section of, or Schedule to, this Act, unless it is indicated that reference to some other enactment is intended.

(13) In this Act, a reference to a subsection, paragraph, subparagraph, clause or subclause is to the subsection, paragraph, subparagraph, clause or subclause of the provision (including a Schedule) in which the reference occurs, unless it is indicated that reference to some other provision is intended.

SCHEDULE 1
Exemption From Tax For Certain Interest And Royalties Payments

Amendment of Part 8 (Annual Payments, Charges and Interest) of the Taxes Consolidation Act 1997

Notes

Schedule 1 and s 41(1) inserted TCA 1997 Ch 6 (ss 267G–267K).

SCHEDULE 3
Miscellaneous Technical Amendments in Relation to Tax

Notes

Para 1(*a*) and s 89 substituted "826(1)(*a*)" for "section 826" in TCA 1997 s 23A(1)(*a*)(definition of "arrangements") with effect from 25 March 2004.

Para 1(*b*) and s 89 substituted "section 826(1)(*a*)" for "section 826" in TCA 1997 s 29A(4) with effect from 25 March 2004.

Para 1(*c*) and s 89 substituted "section 826(1)(*a*)" for "section 826" in TCA 1997 s 44(1)(definition of "relevant territory" with effect from 25 March 2004.

Para 1(*d*) and s 89 substituted "section 826(1)(*a*)" for "section 826" in TCA 1997 s 130(3)(*d*) with effect from 25 March 2004.

Para 1(*e*) and s 89 substituted "section 826(1)(*a*)" for "section 826" in TCA 1997 s 153(1)(definition of "relevant territory" with effect from 25 March 2004.

Para 1(*f*) and s 89 substituted "section 826(1)(*a*)" for "section 826" in TCA 1997 s 172A(1)(*a*)(definition of "relevant territory" with effect from 25 March 2004.

Para 1(*g*) and s 89 substituted "section 826(1)(*a*)" for "section 826" in TCA 1997 s 198(1)(*a*)(definition of "arrangements" with effect from 25 March 2004.

Para 1(*h*) and s 89 substituted "section 826(1)(*a*)" for "section 826" where it occurs in TCA 1997 s 222(1)(*b*) with effect from 25 March 2004.

Para 1(*i*) and s 89 substituted "section 826(1)(*a*)" for "section 826" in TCA 1997 s 246(1)(*a*)(definition of "relevant territory" with effect from 25 March 2004.

Para 1(*j*) and s 89 substituted "section 826(1)(*a*)" for "section 826" in TCA 1997 s 410(1)(*a*)(definition of "relevant Member State" with effect from 25 March 2004.

Para 1(*k*) and s 89 substituted "section 826(1)(*a*)" for "section 826" in TCA 1997 s 411(1)(*a*)(definition of "relevant Member State" with effect from 25 March 2004.

Para 1(*l*)(i) and s 89 substituted "Section 826(1)(*a*)" for "section 826" in TCA 1997 s 430(1)(*da*) with effect from 25 March 2004.

Para 1(*l*)(ii) and s 89 substituted "section 826(1)(*a*)" for "section 826" in TCA 1997 s 430(2A) with effect from 25 March 2004.

Para 1(*m*) and s 89 substituted "section 826(1)(*a*)" for "section 826" in TCA 1997 s 452(1)(*a*)(definition of "arrangements" with effect from 25 March 2004.

Para 1(*n*) and s 89 substituted "subsection (7A)(iii)" for "subsection (7A)(*c*)" in TCA 1997 s 519(8B) with effect from 25 March 2004.

Para 1(*o*) and s 89 substituted "section 826(1)(*a*)" for "section 826" in TCA 1997 s 579B(1)(definition of "arrangements" with effect from 25 March 2004.

Para 1(*p*) and s 89 substituted "section 826(1)(*a*)" for "section 826" in TCA 1997 s 613(6)(definition of "arrangements" with effect from 25 March 2004.

Para 1(*q*) and s 89 substituted "Section 826(1)(*a*)" for "section 826" in TCA 1997 s 627(2)(*a*)(definition of "relevant territory" with effect from 25 March 2004.

Para 1(*r*) and s 89 substituted "section 826(1)(*a*)" for "section 826" where it occurs in TCA 1997 s 690(2) with effect from 25 March 2004.

Para 1(*s*) and s 89 substituted "section 826(1)(*a*)" for "section 826" in TCA 1997 s 730H(1)(definition of "offshore state") with effect from 25 March 2004.

Para 1(*t*) and s 89 substituted "section 826(1)(*a*)" for "section 826" in TCA 1997 s 747B(1)(definition of "offshore state") with effect from 25 March 2004.

Para 1(*u*) and s 89 substituted "section 826(1)(*a*)" for "section 826" in TCA 1997 s 817C(3) with effect from 25 March 2004.

Para 1(*v*) and s 89 substituted "section 826(1)(*a*)" for "section 826" in TCA 1997 s 825A(1)(definition of "qualifying employment") with effect from 25 March 2004.

Para 1(*w*) and s 89 substituted "section 826(1)(*a*)" for "section 826" in TCA 1997 s 829(2) with effect from 25 March 2004.

Para 1(*x*) and s 89 substituted "section 826(1)(*a*)" for "section 826" in TCA 1997 s 830(2) with effect from 25 March 2004.

Para 1(*y*) and s 89 substituted "section 826(1)(*a*)" for "section 826" in TCA 1997 s 831(1)(*a*) with effect from 25 March 2004.

Para 1(*z*) and s 89 inserted TCA 1997 s 847(9) with effect from 25 March 2004.

Para 1(*aa*) and s 89 substituted "section 826(1)(*a*)" for "section 826" in TCA 1997 s 865(1)(*a*) with effect from 25 March 2004.

Para 1(*ab*) and s 89 substituted "section 826(1)(*a*)" for "section 826" in TCA 1997 s 917B(1) with effect from 25 March 2004.

Para 1(*ac*) and s 89 substituted "subsection (2A)" for "subsection (2)" in TCA 1997 s 958(4D)(*d*) with effect from 1 January 2002.

Para 1(*ad*) and s 89 substituted "section 48 of the Capital Acquisitions Tax Consolidation Act 2003" for "section 38 of the Capital Acquisitions Tax Act, 1976" in TCA 1997 s 1048(2)(*a*) with effect from 21 February 2003.

Para 1(*ae*)(i)(I) and s 89 substituted "section 826(1)(*a*)" for "section 826" in TCA 1997 Sch 24 para 1(1)(definition of "arrangements") with effect from 21 February 2003.

Para 1(*ae*)(i)(II) and s 89 substituted "section 826(1)(*a*)" for "section 826" in TCA 1997 Sch 24 para 1(1)(definition of "relevant Member State") with effect from 21 February 2003.
Para 1(*ae*)(ii) and s 89 substituted "section 826(1)(*a*)" for "section 826" in TCA 1997 Sch 24 para 5(2) with effect from 21 February 2003.
Para 4 and s 89 substituted "Part 9 of the Principal Act" for "Part 9" in FA 2003 1993 s 12(2)(*a*) with effect from 28 March 2003.

SCHEDULE 4
Taxation Of Savings Income In The Form Of Interest Payments

Amendment of Part 38 (Returns of Income and Gains, Other Obligations and Returns, and Revenue Powers) of the Taxes Consolidation Act 1997

Notes

Schedule 4 and s 90(1) inserted TCA 1997 Pt 38 Ch 3A (ss 898B–898R) with effect from 25 March 2004.

FINANCE ACT 2005

No 5 of 2005

ARRANGEMENT OF SECTIONS

PART 1

Income Tax, Corporation Tax and Capital Gains Tax

Chapter 1

Interpretation

Chapter 2

Income Tax

Chapter 3

PAYE: Electronic and Telephone Communications

Chapter 4
Income Tax, Corporation Tax and Capital Gains Tax

Chapter 5
Corporation Tax

Chapter 6
Capital Gains Tax

PART 6
Miscellaneous

SCHEDULE 1
Amendments Consequential on Changes in Personal Tax Credits

SCHEDULE 5
Amendment of Provisions Consequential on Section 145

SCHEDULE 6
Miscellaneous Technical Amendments in Relation to Tax

AN ACT TO PROVIDE FOR THE IMPOSITION, REPEAL, REMISSION, ALTERATION AND REGULATION OF TAXATION, OF STAMP DUTIES AND OF DUTIES RELATING TO EXCISE AND OTHERWISE TO MAKE FURTHER PROVISION IN CONNECTION WITH FINANCE INCLUDING THE REGULATION OF CUSTOMS.

BE IT ENACTED BY THE OIREACHTAS AS FOLLOWS:

PART 1
INCOME TAX, CORPORATION TAX AND CAPITAL GAINS TAX

Chapter 1
Interpretation

1 Interpretation (Part 1)

In this Part "Principal Act" means the Taxes Consolidation Act 1997.

Chapter 2
Income Tax

2 Amendment of section 15 (rate of charge) of Principal Act

Notes

Para (*a*) substituted "€20,400" for "€19,000" in TCA 1997 s 15(3) for 2005 and subsequent years of assessment.

Para (*b*) substituted TCA 1997 s 15 (Table) for 2005 and subsequent years of assessment.

3 Personal tax credits

(1) Where an individual is entitled under a provision of the Principal Act mentioned in column (1) of the Table to this subsection to have the income tax to be charged on the individual, other than in accordance with the provisions of section 16(2) of the Principal Act, reduced for the year of assessment 2005 or any subsequent year of assessment and the amount of the reduction would, but for this section, be an amount which is the lesser of—

(*a*) the amount specified in column (2) of that Table, and

(*b*) the amount which reduces that liability to nil,

the amount of the reduction in accordance with paragraph (*a*) shall be the amount of the tax credit specified in column (3) of the Table.

TABLE

Statutory Provision	Existing tax credit (full year)	Tax credit for the year 2005 and subsequent years
(1)	(2)	(3)
Section 461		
(basic personal tax credit)		
(married person)	€3,040	€3,160
(widowed person bereaved in year of assessment)	€3,040	€3,160
(single person)	€1,520	€1,580
Section 461A		
(additional tax credit for certain widowed persons)	€300	€400
Section 462		

(one-parent family tax credit)	€1,520	€1,580
Section 463		
(widowed parent tax credit)		
(1st year)	€2,600	€2,800
(2nd year)	€2,100	€2,300
(3rd year)	€1,600	€1,800
(4th year)	€1,100	€1,300
(5th year)	€600	€800
Section 465		
(incapacitated child tax credit)	€500	€1,000
Section 468		
(blind person's tax credit)		
(blind person)	€800	€1,000
(both spouses blind)	€1,600	€2,000
Section 472		
(employee tax credit)	€1,040	€1,270

(2) Section 3 (as amended by the Finance Act 2004) of the Finance Act 2002 shall have effect subject to the provisions of this section.

(3) Schedule (1) shall apply for the purposes of supplementing subsection (1).

4 Age exemption

Notes

Section 4 substituted "€33,000" for "€31,000" and "€16,500" for "€15,500" in TCA 1997 s 188(2) for 2005 and subsequent years of assessment.

5 Amendment of section 126 (tax treatment of certain benefits payable under Social Welfare Acts) of Principal Act

Notes

Section 5 substituted TCA 1997 s 126(8)(*b*) with effect from 1 January 2005.

6 Amendment of section 473 (allowance for rent paid by certain tenants) of Principal Act

Notes

Section 6 substituted TCA 1997 s 473(1) definition of "specified limit" for 2005 and subsequent years of assessment.

7 Amendment of section 116 (interpretation (Chapter 3)) of Principal Act

Notes

Section 7 inserted TCA 1997 s 116(1) definition of "premises" with effect from 1 January 2005.

8 Amendment of section 118 (benefits in kind: general charging provision) of Principal Act

Notes

Section 8 substituted TCA 1997 s 118(5A) with effect from 1 January 2005.

9 Preferential loans

Notes

Para (*a*)(i) substituted TCA 1997 s 122(1) definition of "employee" with effect from 1 January 2005.

Para (*a*)(ii) substituted "means, in relation to an individual, a loan, in respect of which no interest is payable or interest is payable at a preferential rate, made directly or indirectly to the individual" for "means a loan, in respect of which no interest is payable or interest is payable at a preferential rate, made directly or indirectly to an individual" in TCA 1997 s 122(1) definition of "preferential loan" with effect from 1 January 2005.

Para (*b*)(i) substituted TCA 1997 s 122(2) with effect from 1 January 2005.

10 Costs and expenses in respect of personal security assets and services

Notes

Section 10 inserted TCA 1997 s 118A with effect from 1 January 2005.

11 Foster care payments etc

Notes

Section 11 inserted TCA 1997 s 192B with effect from 1 January 2005.

12 State employees: foreign service allowances

Notes

Section 12 inserted TCA 1997 s 196A with effect from 1 January 2005.

13 Credit in respect of tax deducted from emoluments of certain directors

Notes

Section 13 inserted TCA 1997 s 997A for 2005 and subsequent years of assessment.

14 Amendment of section 950 (interpretation (Part41)) of Principal Act

Notes

Section 14 substituted TCA 1997 s 950(1) definition of "chargeable person" para (*a*) for 2005 and subsequent years of assessment.

15 Amendment of Chapter 1 (payments in respect of professional services by certain persons) of Part 18 of, and Schedule 13 to, Principal Act

Notes

Subs (1)(*a*) substituted "section," for "section, and" in TCA 1997 s 520(1) definition of "relevant payment" para (ii) with effect from 25 March 2005.

Subs (1)(*b*) substituted "payment, and" for "payment;" in TCA 1997 s 520(1) definition of "relevant payment" para (iii) with effect from 25 March 2005.

Subs (1)(*c*) inserted TCA 1997 s 520(1) definition of "relevant payment" para (iv) with effect from 25 March 2005.

Subs (2)(*a*) substituted TCA 1997 Sch 13 para 13 with effect from 19 October 2004.

Subs (2)(*b*) substituted TCA 1997 Sch 13 para 35 with effect from 1 October 2004.

Subs (2)(*c*) deleted TCA 1997 Sch 13 para 87 with effect from 1 January 2005.

Subs (2)(*d*) inserted TCA 1997 Sch 13 paras 144–153 with effect from 1 May 2005.

16 Amendment of section 128 (tax treatment of directors of companies and employees granted rights to acquire shares or other assets) of Principal Act

(2) (*a*) Subsection (1) applies as respects a right (within the meaning of section 128 of the Principal Act obtained on or after the coming into operation of this section.

(b) This section comes into operation on such day as the Minister for Finance may appoint by order.

Notes

Subs (1) inserted "and shall be so chargeable notwithstanding that he or she was not resident in the State on the date on which the right was obtained" after "in accordance with this section" in TCA 1997 s 128(2) as respects a right (within the meaning of TCA 1997 s 128) obtained on or after such day as the Minister for Finance may appoint by order.

17 Restriction of deductions for employee benefit contributions

Notes

Section 17 inserted TCA 1997 s 81A with effect from 3 February 2005.

18 Amendment of section 130 (matters to be treated as distributions) of Principal Act

Notes

Subs (1)(*a*) substituted "section 131;" for "section 131." in TCA 1997 s 130(2)(*e*) with effect from 3 February 2005.

Subs (1)(*b*) inserted TCA 1997 s 130(2)(*f*) with effect from 3 February 2005.

Subs (1)(*c*) inserted TCA 1997 s 130(2C) with effect from 3 February 2005.

19 Reliefs in respect of income tax charged on payments on retirement

Notes

Subs (1)(*a*)(i) inserted TCA 1997 s 201(2A) as respects payments made on or after 25 March 2005.

Subs (1)(*a*)(ii) substituted "4 years" for "6 years" TCA 1997 s 201(6) as respects payments made on or after 25 March 2005.

Subs (1)(*b*) substituted "3 years" for "5 years" TCA 1997 Sch 3 construction of "T" and "I" for 2005 and subsequent years of assessment.

20 Tax rate applicable to certain deposit interest received by individuals

Notes

Section 20(1) inserted TCA 1997 Part 8, Chapter 7 (s 267M) for 2005 and subsequent years of assessment.

21 Retirement benefits

Notes

Subs (1)(*a*)(i)(I) substituted TCA 1997 s 770(1) definition of "administrator" as respects any retirement benefits scheme approved on or after 1 January 2005.

Subs (1)(*a*)(i)(II) inserted TCA 1997 s 770(1) definition of "overseas pension scheme" as respects any retirement benefits scheme approved on or after 1 January 2005.

Subs (1)(*a*)(i)(III) inserted TCA 1997 s 770(1) definition of "retirement benefits scheme" as respects any retirement benefits scheme approved on or after 1 January 2005.

Subs (1)(*a*)(i)(IV) inserted TCA 1997 s 770(1) definition of "state social security scheme" as respects any retirement benefits scheme approved on or after 1 January 2005.

Subs (1)(*a*)(ii) inserted "contract," after "References in this Chapter to a scheme include references to a" in TCA 1997 s 771(2) as respects any retirement benefits scheme approved on or after 1 January 2005.
Subs (1)(*a*)(iii) substituted TCA 1997 s 772(2)(*c*) as respects any retirement benefits scheme approved on or after 1 January 2005.
Subs (1)(*a*)(iv) substituted TCA 1997 s 774(1) as respects any retirement benefits scheme approved on or after 1 January 2005.
Subs (1)(*a*)(v) substituted TCA 1997 s 779(1) as respects any retirement benefits scheme approved on or after 1 January 2005.
Subs (1)(*b*)(i)(I) substituted TCA 1997 s 784(2)(*a*)(i) as respects any annuity contract approved by the Revenue Commissioners under TCA 1997 s 784 entered into on or after 1 January 2005.
Subs (1)(*b*)(i)(II) substituted "shall, notwithstanding anything in section 18 or 19," for "shall" where it first occurs in TCA 1997 s 784(2B)(*a*) as respects any annuity contract approved by the Revenue Commissioners under TCA 1997 s 784 entered into on or after 1 January 2005.
Subs (1)(*b*)(i)(III) inserted TCA 1997 s 784(4A)–(4B) as respects any annuity contract approved by the Revenue Commissioners under TCA 1997 s 784 entered into on or after 1 January 2005.
Subs (1)(*b*)(ii)(I) substituted "shall, notwithstanding anything in section 18 or 19," for "shall" where it first occurs in TCA 1997 s 784A(3)(*a*) as respects any annuity contract approved by the Revenue Commissioners under TCA 1997 s 784 entered into on or after 1 January 2005.
Subs (1)(*b*)(ii)(II) substituted TCA 1997 s 784A(7)(*a*) as respects any annuity contract approved by the Revenue Commissioners under TCA 1997 s 784 entered into on or after 1 January 2005.
Subs (1)(*b*)(ii)(III) inserted TCA 1997 s 784A(9) as respects any annuity contract approved by the Revenue Commissioners under TCA 1997 s 784 entered into on or after 1 January 2005.
Subs (1)(*b*)(iii) substituted "is in receipt of" for "is entitled to" in TCA 1997 s 784C(4)(*a*) as respects any exercise of an option in accordance with TCA 1997 s 784(2A) on or after 3 February 2005.
Subs (1)(*b*)(iv) inserted TCA 1997 s 785(1A) as respects any annuity contract approved by the Revenue Commissioners under TCA 1997 s 784 entered into on or after 1 January 2005.
Subs (1)(*c*)(i) substituted "in accordance with section 787G(5)(ii)" for "in accordance with section 787G(5)" in TCA 1997 s 787A(1) as respects any PRSA contract entered into on or after 1 January 2005 in respect of a PRSA product approved by the Revenue Commissioners under TCA 1997 s 787K.
Subs (1)(*c*)(ii)(I) substituted "shall, notwithstanding anything in section 18 or 19," for "shall" where it first occurs in TCA 1997 s 787G(1)(*a*) as respects any PRSA contract entered into on or after 1 January 2005 in respect of a PRSA product approved by the Revenue Commissioners under TCA 1997 s 787K.
Subs (1)(*c*)(ii)(II) substituted TCA 1997 s 787G(5) as respects any PRSA contract entered into on or after 1 January 2005 in respect of a PRSA product approved by the Revenue Commissioners under TCA 1997 s 787K.
Subs (1)(*c*)(ii)(III) inserted TCA 1997 s 787G(5A) as respects any PRSA contract entered into on or after 1 January 2005 in respect of a PRSA product approved by the Revenue Commissioners under TCA 1997 s 787K.
Subs (1)(*d*) inserted TCA 1997 Part 30 Chapter 2B (ss 787M–787N) as respects contributions to a qualifying overseas pension plan made on or after 1 January 2005.
Subs (1)(*e*)(i) substituted TCA 1997 s 790A with effect from 1 January 2005.
Subs (1)(*e*)(ii) inserted TCA 1997 s 790B with effect from such day or days as the Minister for Finance may by order appoint and different days may be appointed for different purposes or different provisions.
Subs (1)(*f*)(i) inserted "in such form and manner as they may specify" after "Revenue Commissioners" where it first occurs in TCA 1997 Sch 23 para 1 with effect from 1 January 2005.
Subs (1)(*f*)(ii)(I) deleted "and" from TCA 1997 Sch 23 para 2(*b*)(ii) with effect from 1 January 2005.
Subs (1)(*f*)(ii)(II) substituted "employer, and," for "employer;" in TCA 1997 Sch 23 para 2(*b*)(iii) with effect from 1 January 2005.
Subs (1)(*f*)(ii)(III) inserted TCA 1997 Sch 23 para 2(*b*)(iv) with effect from 1 January 2005.
Subs (1)(*f*)(iii) inserted TCA 1997 Sch 23 para 2A with effect from 1 January 2005.
Subs (1)(*f*)(iv) substituted "in section 772(2)(*c*)(ii)." for "in section 772(2)(*c*)." in TCA 1997 Sch 23 para 4(2) with effect from 1 January 2005.

Chapter 3

PAYE: Electronic and Telephone Communications

22 Amendment of Chapter 6 (electronic transmission of returns of income, profits, etc., and of other Revenue returns) of Part 38 of Principal Act

Notes

Para (*a*) inserted TCA 1997 s 917D definition of "electronic identifier" with effect from 25 March 2005.
Para (*b*) substituted TCA 1997 s 917F(1)(*c*) with effect from 25 March 2005.
Para (*c*) substituted "electronic identifiers" for "digital signatures" in TCA 1997 s 917G(1) with effect from 25 March 2005.
Para (*d*)(i) substituted "electronic identifier" for "digital signature" in TCA 1997 s 917H(2)(*b*) and (3)(*c*) with effect from 25 March 2005.
Para (*d*)(ii) inserted TCA 1997 s 917H(4) with effect from 25 March 2005.

23 Electronic claims

Notes

Section 23 inserted TCA 1997 s 864A with effect from 25 March 2005.

24 Amendment of provisions relating to claims by individuals

Notes

Subs (1)(*a*)(i) inserted ", subject to subsection (1B)," after "a claim in that behalf" in TCA 1997 s 458(1) with effect from 25 March 2005.
Subs (1)(*a*)(ii) inserted TCA 1997 s 458(1B) with effect from 25 March 2005.
Subs (1)(*b*) inserted TCA 1997 s 459(5) with effect from 25 March 2005.
Subs (1)(*c*)(i) substituted TCA 1997 s 865(1)(*b*)(i) as respects statements or returns made on or after 3 February 2005.
Subs (1)(*c*)(ii) inserted TCA 1997 s 865(3A) with effect from 25 March 2005.

25 Retention and inspection of records in relation to claims by individuals

Notes

Section 25 inserted TCA 1997 s 886A with effect from 25 March 2005.

26 Amendment of section 997 (supplementary provisions (Chapter 4)) of Principal Act

Notes

Section 26 inserted TCA 1997 s 997(3) with effect from 25 March 2005.

Chapter 4

Income Tax, Corporation Tax and Capital Gains Tax.

27 Amendment of section 18 (amendment of Part 16 (income tax relief for investment in corporate trades — business expansion scheme and seed capital scheme) of Principal Act) of Finance Act 2004

Notes

Para (*a*)(i) substituted FA 2004 s 18(2)(*b*).
Para (*a*)(ii) inserted FA 2004 s 18(2)(*cc*).
Para (*a*)(iii) substituted FA 2004 s 18(2)(*d*).
Para (*b*)(i) substituted "5 February 2004" for "4 February 2004" in FA 2004 s 18(3)(*b*)(i).
Para (*b*)(ii) substituted FA 2004 s 18(3)(*b*)(ii).

Para (*b*)(iii) substituted "5 February 2004" for "4 February 2004" in FA 2004 s 18(3)(*b*)(iii).

Para (*b*)(iv) inserted FA 2004 s 18(3)(*b*)(iii*a*).

Para (*b*)(v) substituted "5 February 2004" for "4 February 2004" in FA 2004 s 18(3)(*b*)(iv).

28 Amendment of section 482 (relief for expenditure on significant buildings and gardens) of Principal Act

Notes

Para (*a*)(i) substituted "4 hours," for "4 hours, and" in TCA 1997 s 482(5)(*b*)(ii)(II) with effect from 1 January 2005.

Para (*a*)(ii) substituted "access to the building, and" for "access to the building." in TCA 1997 s 482(5)(*b*)(iii) with effect from 1 January 2005.

Para (*a*)(iii) inserted TCA 1997 s 482(5)(*b*)(iv) with effect from 1 January 2005.

Para (*b*) substituted TCA 1997 s 482(7)(*a*) with effect from 1 January 2005.

29 Amendment of Chapter 1 (interpretation and general) of Part 23 (farming and market gardening) of Principal Act

Notes

Section 29 inserted TCA 1997 s 657A with effect from 1 January 2005.

30 Amendment of section 659 (farming: allowances for capital expenditure on the construction of farm buildings, etc., for control of pollution) of Principal Act

Notes

Para (*a*) substituted "1 January 2009" for "1 January 2007" in TCA 1997 s 659(1)(*c*) with effect from 1 January 2005.

Para (*b*)(i) substituted "6 April 2000," for "6 April 2000, or" in TCA 1997 s 659(2)(*b*)(i) with effect from 1 January 2005.

Para (*b*)(ii) substituted "6 April 2000 but before 1 January 2005, or" for "6 April 2000," in TCA 1997 s 659(2)(*b*)(ii) with effect from 1 January 2005.

Para (*b*)(iii) inserted TCA 1997 s 659(2)(*b*)(iii) with effect from 1 January 2005.

Para (*c*) substituted "on or after 6 April 2000 but before 1 January 2005 shall," for "on or after 6 April 2000 shall" in TCA 1997 s 659(3A) with effect from 1 January 2005.

Para (*d*) inserted TCA 1997 s 659(3AA) with effect from 1 January 2005.

Para (*e*)(i) substituted "In this subsection and subsection (3BA)" for "In this subsection" in TCA 1997 s 659(3B)(*a*) with effect from 1 January 2005.

Para (*e*)(ii) substituted "residual amount." for "residual amount;" in TCA 1997 s 659(3B)(*a*) definition of "specified amount" with effect from 1 January 2005.

Para (*e*)(iii) deleted "'specified return date for the chargeable period' has the same meaning as in section 950." from TCA 1997 s 659(3B)(*a*) with effect from 1 January 2005.

Para (*f*) inserted TCA 1997 s 659(3BA) with effect from 1 January 2005.

Para (*g*) substituted TCA 1997 s 659(3C)(*a*) with effect from 1 January 2005.

Para (*h*) substituted "Chapter 1 or Chapter 2" for "Chapter 1" in TCA 1997 s 659(11) with effect from 1 January 2005.

31 Amendment of section 666 (deduction for increase in stock values) of Principal Act

Notes

Subs (1) substituted TCA 1997 s 666(4) with effect from 3 February 2005.

32 Amendment of section 667A (further provisions for qualifying farmers) of Principal Act

Notes

Subs (1) substituted "31 December 2006" for "31 December 2004" in TCA 1997 s 667A(6)(*b*) with effect from such day as the Minister for Finance may by order appoint.

33 Amendment of section 843 (capital allowances for buildings used for third level educational purposes) of Principal Act

Notes

Section 33 substituted TCA 1997 s 843(7) with effect from 1 January 2005.

34 Capital allowances for registered tourist accommodation

Notes

Para (*a*)(i) inserted TCA 1997 s 268(2C) with effect from 1 January 2005.
Para (*a*)(ii) substituted "a holiday camp registered in the register of holiday camps kept under the Tourist Traffic Acts 1939 to 2003" for "a holiday camp" in TCA 1997 s 268(3) with effect from 1 January 2005.
Para (*a*)(iii)(I) substituted TCA 1997 s 268(12)(*a*) with effect from 1 January 2005.
Para (*a*)(iii)(II) substituted "the Regulation or Recommendation" for "the Regulation" in TCA 1997 s 268(12)(*d*)(I) with effect from 1 January 2005.
Para (*a*)(iii)(III) inserted "or, as the case may be, "Community guidelines on State aid for rescuing and restructuring firms in difficulty"(OJ No C244 of 1 October 2004, p 2) prepared by that Commission" after "European Communities" in TCA 1997 s 268(12)(*d*)(ii) with effect from 1 January 2005.
Para (*a*)(iv) inserted TCA 1997 s 268(14)–(15) with effect from 1 January 2005.
Para (*b*)(i)(I) substituted "paragraph (*d*) or (*da*)" for "paragraph (*d*)" in TCA 1997 s 272(3)(*c*) with effect from 1 January 2005.
Para (*b*)(i)(II) inserted TCA 1997 s 272(3)(*da*) with effect from 1 January 2005.
Para (*b*)(ii)(I) substituted "paragraph (*d*) or (*da*)" for "paragraph (*d*)" in TCA 1997 s 272(4)(*c*) with effect from 1 January 2005.
Para (*b*)(ii)(II) inserted TCA 1997 s 272(4)(*da*) with effect from 1 January 2005.
Para (*c*)(i) substituted "subparagraph (iv) or (iv*a*)" for "subparagraph (iv)" in TCA 1997 s 274(1)(*b*)(iii) with effect from 1 January 2005.
Para (*c*)(ii) inserted TCA 1997 s 274(1)(*b*)(iv*a*) with effect from 1 January 2005.

35 Amendment of section 372AJ (non-application of relief in certain cases and provision against double relief) of Principal Act

Notes

Section 35 inserted "or, as the case may be, by a micro, small or medium-sized enterprise within the meaning of the Annex to Commission Recommendation of 6 May 2003 concerning the definition of micro, small and medium-sized enterprises (OJ No L124 of 20 May 2003, p 36)" in TCA 1997 s 372AJ(1)(*ab*) with effect from 1 January 2005.

36 Amendment of section 481 (relief for investment in films) of Principal Act

Notes

Subs (*a*) deleted TCA 1997 s 481(2)(*b*)(I) with effect from 1 January 2005.
Subs (*b*)(i) deleted TCA 1997 s 481(2A)(*g*)(i) with effect from 1 January 2005.
Subs (*b*)(ii) substituted "the amount per cent (in subsection (2)(*c*) referred to as "the specified percentage") specified in the certificate" for "the specified percentage, as referred to in that subsection" in TCA 1997 s 481(2A)(*g*)(iii) with effect from 1 January 2005.
Subs (*b*)(iii) substituted TCA 1997 s 481(2A)(*g*)(iv) with effect from 1 January 2005.
Subs (*b*)(iv) inserted TCA 1997 s 481(2A)(*g*)(v) with effect from 1 January 2005.
Subs (*c*)(i) inserted "subject to paragraph (*ba*)," in TCA 1997 s 481(2C)(*b*) with effect from 1 January 2005.

Subs (*c*)(ii) inserted TCA 1997 s 481(2C)(*ba*) with effect from 1 January 2005.
Subs (*d*)(i) deleted "and" from TCA 1997 s 481(2E)(*k*) with effect from 1 January 2005.
Subs (*d*)(ii) inserted TCA 1997 s 481(2E)(*m*)–(*n*) with effect from 1 January 2005.
Subs (*e*) substituted "1 January 2005" for "the day appointed by order made by the Minister for Finance for the coming into operation of this subsection" and "the day so appointed" respectively in TCA 1997 s 481(22) with effect from 1 January 2005.

37 Amendment of section 1013 (limited partnerships) of Principal Act

Notes

Para (*a*)(i) substituted "trade," for "trade, or" in TCA 1013(1) definition of "limited partner" para (*c*) with effect from 1 January 2005.
Para (*a*)(ii) substituted "partner," for "partner;" in TCA 1013(1) definition of "limited partner" para (*d*) with effect from 1 January 2005.
Para (*a*)(iii) inserted TCA 1013(1) definition of "limited partner" paras (*e*) and (*f*) with effect from 1 January 2005.
Para (*b*)(i) substituted "trade," for "trade, or" in TCA 1013(2)(*a*)(II) with effect from 1 January 2005.
Para (*b*)(ii) substituted "trade, or" for "trade," in TCA 1013(2)(*a*)(III) with effect from 1 January 2005.
Para (*b*)(iii) inserted TCA 1013(2)(*a*)(IV) with effect from 1 January 2005.

38 Amendment of Schedule 26A (donations to approved bodies, etc) to Principal Act

Notes

Section 38 substituted "2 years," for "3 years," in TCA 1997 Sch 26A Pt 3 para 3(*c*) with effect from 1 January 2005.

39 Amendment of section 817 (schemes to avoid liability to tax under Schedule F) of Principal Act

Notes

Subs (1) inserted TCA 1997 s 817(1)(*ca*) as respects any disposal of shares made on or after 1 March 2005.

40 Court funds

Notes

Para (*a*)(i) inserted TCA 1997 s 739B(1) definition of "chargeable event" para (II*a*) with effect from 1 January 2005.
Para (*a*)(ii) inserted TCA 1997 s 739B(1) definition of "court funds manager" with effect from 1 January 2005.
Para (*b*)(i) deleted "and" from TCA 1997 s 739D(1)(*b*) with effect from 1 January 2005.
Para (*b*)(ii) inserted TCA 1997 s 739D(1)(*bb*) with effect from 1 January 2005.

41 Assets of overseas life assurance companies

Notes

Subs (1)(*a*) substituted "agency," for "agency." in TCA 1997 s 29(3) as respects accounting periods ending on or after 1 March 2005.
Subs (1)(*b*) inserted TCA 1997 s 29(3)(*d*) as respects accounting periods ending on or after 1 March 2005.

42 Amendment of Chapter 5 (policyholders — new basis) of Part 26 of Principal Act

Notes

Subs (1)(*a*) inserted TCA 1997 s 730C(1)(*a*)(iv) with effect from such day or days as the Minister for Finance may by order appoint either generally or with reference to any particular provision of this section or class of policy and different days may be so appointed for different provisions of this section or for different classes of policies.

Subs (1)(*b*)(i)(I) deleted "and" from TCA 1997 s 730D(1)(*d*) with effect from such day or days as the Minister for Finance may by order appoint either generally or with reference to any particular provision of this section or class of policy and different days may be so appointed for different provisions of this section or for different classes of policies.

Subs (1)(*b*)(i)(II) inserted TCA 1997 s 730D(1)(*da*) with effect from such day or days as the Minister for Finance may by order appoint either generally or with reference to any particular provision of this section or class of policy and different days may be so appointed for different provisions of this section or for different classes of policies.

Subs (1)(*b*)(ii)(I) deleted "and" from TCA 1997 s 730D(3)(*d*) with effect from such day or days as the Minister for Finance may by order appoint either generally or with reference to any particular provision of this section or class of policy and different days may be so appointed for different provisions of this section or for different classes of policies.

Subs (1)(*b*)(ii)(II) inserted TCA 1997 s 730D(3)(*da*) with effect from such day or days as the Minister for Finance may by order appoint either generally or with reference to any particular provision of this section or class of policy and different days may be so appointed for different provisions of this section or for different classes of policies.

Subs (1)(*b*)(iii) inserted TCA 1997 s 730D(4)(*ba*) with effect from such day or days as the Minister for Finance may by order appoint either generally or with reference to any particular provision of this section or class of policy and different days may be so appointed for different provisions of this section or for different classes of policies.

Subs (1)(*b*)(iv) inserted TCA 1997 s 730D(5) with effect from such day or days as the Minister for Finance may by order appoint either generally or with reference to any particular provision of this section or class of policy and different days may be so appointed for different provisions of this section or for different classes of policies.

Subs (1)(*c*) inserted "at or about the time of the inception of the life policy" after "policyholder" in TCA 1997 s 730E(2)(*a*) with effect from such day or days as the Minister for Finance may by order appoint either generally or with reference to any particular provision of this section or class of policy and different days may be so appointed for different provisions of this section or for different classes of policies.

Subs (1)(*d*) inserted TCA 1997 s 730F(3)(*a*)(ii)(I*a*) with effect from such day or days as the Minister for Finance may by order appoint either generally or with reference to any particular provision of this section or class of policy and different days may be so appointed for different provisions of this section or for different classes of policies.

43 Amendment of section 747E (disposal of an interest in offshore funds) of Principal Act

Notes

Subs (1) substituted "for the purposes of the Tax Acts and the Capital Gains Tax Acts" for "accordingly for the purposes of this Chapter" in TCA 1997 s 747E(3) as respects the disposal of an interest in an offshore fund on or after 3 February 2005.

44 Common contractual funds

Notes

Para (*a*)(i) deleted "or" from TCA 1997 s 172A(1)(*a*) definition of "collective investment undertaking" subpara (ii) with effect from 1 January 2005.

Para (*a*)(ii) inserted "or" in TCA 1997 s 172A(1)(*a*) definition of "collective investment undertaking" subpara (iii) with effect from 1 January 2005.

Para (*a*)(iii) inserted TCA 1997 s 172A(1)(*a*) definition of "collective investment undertaking" subpara (iv) with effect from 1 January 2005.

Para (*b*)(i) deleted "or" from TCA 1997 s 246(1)(*b*) with effect from 1 January 2005.

Para (*b*)(ii) substituted "section 739B, or" for "section 739B;" from TCA 1997 s 246(1)(*c*) with effect from 1 January 2005.

Para (*b*)(iii) inserted TCA 1997 s 246(1)(*d*) with effect from 1 January 2005.

Para (*c*)(i) deleted ", subject to subsection (1A)," from TCA 1997 s 739C(1) with effect from 1 January 2005.

Para (*c*)(ii) deleted TCA 1997 s 739C(1A) with effect from 1 January 2005.

Para (*d*) inserted TCA 1997 s 739I with effect from 1 January 2005.

45 Treatment of leasing

Notes

Subs (1)(*a*) substituted TCA 1997 s 396A(1) definition of "relevant trading loss" as respects any claim made by a company on or after 3 February 2005 for relief for a loss.

Subs (1)(*b*) deleted the words after "section 396A" in TCA 1997 s 396B(1) definition of "relevant trading loss" as respects any claim made by a company on or after 3 February 2005 for relief for a loss.

Subs (1)(*c*) substituted "group relief except to the extent that it could be set off under section 420A against income of a trade of leasing carried on by the claimant company if paragraph (*b*) of the definition of relevant trading loss in section 420A were deleted" for "group relief" in TCA 1997 s 403(4)(*a*)(ii) as respects an accounting period ending on or after 3 February 2005.

Subs (1)(*d*) substituted TCA 19997 s 420A(1) definition of "relevant trading loss" as respects any claim made by a company on or after 3 February 2005 for relief for a loss.

Subs (1)(*e*) deleted the words after "section 396A" in TCA 1997 s 420B definition of "relevant trading loss" with effect from 1 January 2005.

46 Treatment of certain dividends

Notes

Subs (1)(*a*) inserted TCA 1997 s 17(3) as respects any payment on or after 25 March 2005.

Subs (1)(*b*)(i) renumbered existing provision as subs (1) in TCA 1997 s 62 as respects any payment on or after 25 March 2005.

Subs (1)(*b*)(ii) inserted TCA 1997 s 62(2) as respects any payment on or after 25 March 2005.

47 Dividend withholding tax

Notes

Subs (1)(*a*) inserted TCA 1997 s 172A(*a*) definitions of "PRSA administrator" and "PRSA assets" with effect from 3 February 2005.

Subs (1)(*b*)(i)(I) inserted TCA 1997 s 172C(2)(*bb*) with effect from 3 February 2005.

Subs (1)(*b*)(i)(II) inserted TCA 1997 s 172C(2)(*db*) with effect from 3 February 2005.

Subs (1)(*b*)(ii) inserted TCA 1997 s 172C(3)(*ca*)–(*cb*) with effect from 3 February 2005.

Subs (2) inserted TCA 1997 Sch 2A paras 10–11 with effect from 3 February 2005.

Chapter 5
Corporation Tax

48 Generally accepted accounting standards

Notes

Subs (1)(*a*)(i)(I) inserted TCA 1997 s 4(1) definition of "generally accepted accounting practice" as respects any period of account beginning on or after 1 January 2005.

Subs (1)(*a*)(i)(II) inserted TCA 1997 s 4(1) definition of "international accounting standards" and "Irish generally accepted accounting practice" as respects any period of account beginning on or after 1 January 2005.

Subs (1)(*a*)(ii) inserted TCA 1997 s 4(7) as respects any period of account beginning on or after 1 January 2005.

Subs (1)(*b*) inserted TCA 1997 ss 76A–76C as respects any period of account beginning on or after 1 January 2005.

Subs (1)(*c*)(i) substituted "patent;" for "patent." in TCA 1997 s 81(2)(*m*) and inserted TCA 1997 s 81(2)(*n*) as respects any period of account beginning on or after 1 January 2005.

Subs (1)(*c*)(ii) inserted TCA 1997 s 81(3) as respects any period of account beginning on or after 1 January 2005.

Subs (1)(*d*) inserted TCA 1997 s 110(6) as respects any period of account beginning on or after 1 January 2005.

Subs (1)(*e*) inserted TCA 1997 s 321(2A) as respects any period of account beginning on or after 1 January 2005.

Subs (1)(*f*)(i) substituted TCA 1997 s 766(1)(*a*) definition of "expenditure on research and development" subpara (i) as respects any period of account beginning on or after 1 January 2005.
Subs (1)(*f*)(ii) deleted "and" where it lasts occurs in TCA 1997 s 766(1)(*a*) definition of "expenditure on research and development" clause (I) and inserted clause (IA) as respects any period of account beginning on or after 1 January 2005.
Subs (1)(*g*) inserted TCA 1997 Sch 17A as respects any period of account beginning on or after 1 January 2005.

49 Amendment of section 243 (allowance of charges on income) of Principal Act

Notes
Subs (1)(*a*) inserted "has the meaning assigned to it by section 845A and" after " "bank" in TCA 1997 s 243(1A) as respects accounting periods ending on or after 3 February 2005.
Subs (1)(*b*) inserted "in accordance with section 420" after "group relief" in TCA 1997 s 243(2) as respects accounting periods ending on or after 3 February 2005.
Subs (1)(*c*)(i) substituted "interest payable on an advance" for "interest payable in the State on an advance" in TCA 1997 s 243(4)(*b*) as respects accounting periods ending on or after 3 February 2005.
Subs (1)(*c*)(ii) substituted "in a Member State of the European Communities" for "in the State" in each place where it occurs in TCA 1997 s 243(4)(*b*)(i)–(ii) as respects accounting periods ending on or after 3 February 2005.
Subs (1)(*d*)(i) substituted "as the case may be," for "as the case may be, or" in TCA 1997 s 243(5)(*a*) as respects accounting periods ending on or after 3 February 2005.
Subs (1)(*d*)(ii) substituted "the State, or" for "the State." in TCA 1997 s 243(5)(*b*) as respects accounting periods ending on or after 3 February 2005.
Subs (1)(*d*)(iii) inserted TCA 1997 s 243(5)(*c*) as respects accounting periods ending on or after 3 February 2005.

50 Amendment of Chapter 6 (Implementation of Council Directive 2003/49/EC of 3 June 2003 on a common system of taxation applicable to interest and royalty payments made between associated companies of different Member States) of Part 8 of Principal Act

Notes
Subs (1) inserted TCA 1997 s 267L as respects any payment made on or after 1 July 2005.

51 Amendment of Chapter 2 (Miscellaneous) of Part 35 of Principal Act

Notes
Subs (1) inserted TCA 1997 s 831A as respects a distribution made on or after 1 July 2005.

52 Amendment of section 410 (group payments) of Principal Act

Notes
Subs (1)(*a*) substituted "a relevant Member State" for "the State" in TCA 1997 s 410(4) as respects accounting periods ending on or after 1 March 2005.
Subs (1)(*b*) substituted TCA 1997 s 410(5) as respects accounting periods ending on or after 1 March 2005.

53 Amendment of section 448 (relief from corporation tax) of Principal Act

Notes
Subs (1)(*a*) substituted TCA 1997 s 448(1) as respects accounting periods ending on or after 3 February 2005.
Subs (1)(*b*) substituted TCA 1997 s 448(3)(*b*) as respects accounting periods ending on or after 3 February 2005.
Subs (1)(*c*)(i) deleted "or 454" from TCA 1997 s 448(4)(i) as respects accounting periods ending on or after 3 February 2005.
Subs (1)(*c*)(ii) deleted "or 455" from TCA 1997 s 448(4)(ii) as respects accounting periods ending on or after 3 February 2005.

Subs (1)(*c*)(iii) deleted "or 456" from TCA 1997 s 448(4)(iii) as respects accounting periods ending on or after 3 February 2005.

Subs (1)(*d*) deleted TCA 1997 s 448(5A)(*b*)(i) as respects accounting periods ending on or after 3 February 2005.

54 Amendment of section 626B (exemption from tax in the case of gains on certain disposals of shares) of Principal Act

Notes

Subs (1)(*a*) deleted TCA 1997 s 626B(1)(*a*) definition of "relevant time" with effect from 2 February 2004.

Subs (1)(*b*) substituted "5 per cent" for "10 per cent" in TCA 1997 s 626B(1)(*b*)(i)(I)–(III) with effect from 2 February 2004.

Subs (1)(*c*) substituted TCA 1997 s 626B(2)(*a*) with effect from 2 February 2004.

55 Cesser of section 686 (reduction of corporation tax) of Principal Act

Section 686 of the Principal Act shall cease to have effect as respects accounting periods ending on or after 3 February 2005.

Chapter 6
Capital Gains Tax

56 Amendment of section 980 (deduction from consideration on disposal of certain assets) of Principal Act

Notes

Subs (1)(*a*) inserted TCA 1997 s 980(3A) with effect from 25 March 2005.

Subs (1)(*b*) substituted "section 372AK" for "section 329" in TCA 1997 s 980(4)(*c*) definition of "house" with effect from 25 March 2002.

Subs (1)(*c*) inserted TCA 1997 s 980(9)(*e*) with effect from 25 March 2005.

57 Amendment of Schedule 15 (list of bodies for purposes of section 610) to Principal Act

Notes

Subs (1)(*a*) substituted "7. The Health Service Executive." for "7. A health board." in TCA 1997 Sch 15 Pt 1 with effect from 1 January 2005.

Subs (1)(*b*) substituted TCA 1997 Sch 15 Pt 1 paras 12–17 with effect from 25 March 2005.

58 Amendment of section 608 (superannuation funds) of Principal Act

Notes

Section 58 inserted TCA 1997 s 608(2A) with effect from 25 March 2005.

PART 6
MISCELLANEOUS

138 Amendment of section 903 (power of inspection: PAYE) of Taxes Consolidation Act 1997

Notes

Section 138 inserted TCA 1997 s 903(2A) with effect from 25 March 2005.

139 Amendment of section 904 (power of inspection: tax deduction from payments to certain subcontractors) of Taxes Consolidation Act 1997

Notes

Section 139 inserted TCA 1997 s 904(2A) with effect from 25 March 2005.

140 Amendment of Chapter 4 (revenue powers) of Part 38 of Taxes Consolidation Act 1997

Notes

Section 140 inserted TCA 1997 s 902B with effect from 25 March 2005.

141 Amendment of Chapter 1 (income tax and corporation tax penalties) of Part 47 of Taxes Consolidation Act 1997

Notes

Subs (1)(*a*)(i) deleted "the amount or, in the case of fraud, twice" from TCA 1997 s 1053(1)(ii) in relation to returns, statements, declarations, or accounts delivered, made or, as the case may be, submitted on or after 25 March 2005.

Subs (1)(*a*)(ii) deleted "the amount or, in the case of fraud, twice" from TCA 1997 s 1053(1A)(*b*) in relation to returns, statements, declarations, or accounts delivered, made or, as the case may be, submitted on or after 25 March 2005.

Subs (1)(*b*) deleted "the amount or, in the case of fraud, twice" from TCA 1997 s 1054(3)(*a*)(i)(II) in relation to returns, statements, declarations, or accounts delivered, made or, as the case may be, submitted on or after 25 March 2005.

142 Amendment of section 1078 (revenue offences) of Taxes Consolidation Act 1997

Notes

Para (*a*) inserted TCA 1997 s 1078(1A) with effect from 25 March 2005.

Para (*b*)(i) substituted TCA 1997 s 1078(2)(*f*) with effect from 25 March 2005.

Para (*b*)(ii) substituted "by the Acts," for "by the Acts, or" in TCA 1997 s 1078(2)(*i*) with effect from 25 March 2005.

Para (*b*)(iii) inserted TCA 1997 s 1078(2)(*ii*) with effect from 25 March 2005.

Para (*c*) substituted "to have been committed with the consent or connivance of or to be attributable to any neglect on the part of" for "to have been committed with the consent or connivance of" in TCA 1997 s 1078(5) with effect from 25 March 2005.

143 Amendment of section 1086 (publication of names of tax defaulters) of Taxes Consolidation Act 1997

Notes

Subs (1)(*a*) substituted "€30,000" for "€12,700" in TCA 1997 s 1086(4)(*c*) with effect from 25 March 2005, but does not apply where the specified liability referred to in TCA 1997 s 1086(2)(*c*)–(*d*) includes tax, the liability in respect of which arose before, or which relates to periods which commenced before, 1 January 2005.

Subs (1)(*b*) inserted TCA 1997 s 1086(4A) with effect from 25 March 2005.

144 Amendment of Chapter 3A (Implementation of Council Directive 2003/48/EC of 3 June 2003 on Taxation of Savings Income in the Form of Interest Payments and Related Matters) of Part 38 of Taxes Consolidation Act 1997

Notes

Subs (1)(*a*) substituted TCA 1997 s 898B(1) definition of "the Directive" with effect from 25 March 2005.

Subs (1)(*b*) substituted "1 July 2005" for "1 January 2005" in TCA 1997 ss 898F(5)(*c*) and 898G(6)(*c*) with effect from 25 March 2005.
Subs (1)(*c*) substituted "territory" for "relevant territory" in TCA 1997 s 898G(3)(*a*)(iii) with effect from 25 March 2005.
Subs (1)(*d*)(i) substituted the words immediately preceding para (*a*) of TCA 1997 s 898H(1)(*a*) with effect from 25 March 2005.
Subs (1)(*d*)(ii) substituted TCA 1997 s 898H(4)(*b*) with effect from 25 March 2005.
Subs (1)(*e*) substituted TCA 1997 s 898I(*c*) with effect from 25 March 2005.
Subs (1)(*f*) substituted TCA 1997 s 898M(1)–(3) with effect from 25 March 2005.
Subs (1)(*g*) substituted TCA 1997 s 898O(1) with effect from 25 March 2005.
Subs (1)(*h*) substituted TCA 1997 s 898P with effect from 25 March 2005.
Subs (1)(*i*)(i) substituted "898O" for "898P" in TCA 1997 s 898R(1) with effect from 25 March 2005.
Subs (1)(*i*)(ii) substituted TCA 1997 s 898R(2) with effect from 25 March 2005.
Subs (1)(*i*)(iii) substituted "1 July 2005" for "1 January 2005" in TCA 1997 s 898R(3) with effect from 25 March 2005.
Subs (2) substituted TCA 1997 s 912A(1) definition of "foreign tax" with effect from 25 March 2005.

145 Interest on certain overdue tax

...

(6) (*a*) The provisions set out in paragraph (*b*) are, in so far as they are not already repealed, repealed with effect from 1 April 2005 to the extent that they apply to interest chargeable or payable on income tax, corporation tax, capital gains tax, gift tax and inheritance tax that has not been paid before that date regardless of when that tax became due and payable.

(*b*) The provisions referred to in paragraph (*a*) are—

(i) section 14 of the Finance Act 1962;
(ii) sections 550, 551 and 552 of the Income Tax Act 1967;
(iii) section 17 of the Finance Act 1971;
(iv) section 28 of the Finance Act 1975;
(v) section 41 of the Capital Acquisitions Tax Act 1976;
(vi) sections 43 and 46 of the Finance Act 1978;
(vii) the provisions of section 1083 of the Taxes Consolidation Act 1997 except in so far as they apply section 1082 of that Act to capital gains tax;
(viii) section 133 of the Finance Act 1998; and
(ix) section 129 of the Finance Act 2002.

(7) (*a*) In each provision of the Taxes Consolidation Act 1997 set out in column (1) of Part 1 of Schedule 5 for the words in that provision which are set out in column (2) of that Part there shall be substituted the words set out opposite the entry in column (3) of that Part.

...

(8) (*a*) Subsections (1) and (7)(*a*) apply to any unpaid income tax, corporation tax or capital gains tax, as the case may be, that has not been paid before 1 April 2005 regardless of when that tax becomes due and payable and notwithstanding anything to the contrary in any other enactment other than section 1082 of the Taxes Consolidation Act 1997, but subsection (1) shall not apply to the part, if any, before 1 January 1963 of any period of delay (within the meaning of section 1080 of that Act as substituted by this section).

(*b*) Subsection (2) applies and shall be deemed to have always applied from 1 January 2005.

...

Notes

Subs (1) substituted TCA 1997 ss 1080 and 1081 as respects any unpaid income tax, corporation tax or capital gains tax, as the case may be, that has not been paid before 1 April 2005 regardless of when that tax became due and payable and notwithstanding anything to the contrary in any other enactment other than TCA 1997 s 1082 , but shall not apply to the part, if any, before 1 January 1963 of any period of delay (within the meaning of TCA 1997 s 1080 of that Act as substituted by this section).

Subs (2) inserted TCA 1997 s 1082(6) with effect from 1 January 2005.

146 Amendment of section 964 (continuance of pending proceedings) of Taxes Consolidation Act 1997

Notes

Section 146 substituted TCA 1997 s 964(1) with effect from 25 March 2005.

147 Miscellaneous technical amendments in relation to tax

The enactments specified in Schedule 6 are amended to the extent and in the manner specified in that Schedule.

149 Care and management of taxes and duties

All taxes and duties imposed by this Act are placed under the care and management of the Revenue Commissioners.

150 Short title, construction and commencement

(1) This Act may be cited as the Finance Act 2005.

(2) Part 1 shall be construed together with—

(*a*) in so far as it relates to income tax, the Income Tax Acts,

(*b*) in so far as it relates to corporation tax, the Corporation Tax Acts, and

(*c*) in so far as it relates to capital gains tax, the Capital Gains Tax Acts.

...

(7) Part 6 in so far as it relates to—

(*a*) income tax, shall be construed together with the Income Tax Acts,

(*b*) corporation tax, shall be construed together with the Corporation Tax Acts,

(*c*) capital gains tax, shall be construed together with the Capital Gains Tax Acts,

...

(8) Except where otherwise expressly provided in Part 1, that Part is deemed to have come into force and takes effect as on and from 1 January 2005.

(9) Except where otherwise expressly provided for, where a provision of this Act is to come into operation on the making of an order by the Minister for Finance, that provision shall come into operation on such day or days as the Minister for Finance shall appoint either generally or with reference to any particular purpose or provision and different days may be so appointed for different purposes or different provisions.

(10) Any reference in this Act to any other enactment shall, except in so far as the context otherwise requires, be construed as a reference to that enactment as amended by or under any other enactment including this Act.

(11) In this Act, a reference to a Part, section or Schedule is to a Part or section of, or Schedule to, this Act, unless it is indicated that reference to some other enactment is intended.

(12) In this Act, a reference to a subsection, paragraph, subparagraph, clause or subclause is to the subsection, paragraph, subparagraph, clause or subclause of the provision (including a Schedule) in which the reference occurs, unless it is indicated that reference to some other provision is intended.

SCHEDULE 1
Amendments Consequential on Changes in Personal Tax Credits

Section 3

Notes

Para (*a*) and s 3(1) substituted "€3,160" for "€3,040", in both places where it occurs, and "€1,580" for "€1,520", in TCA 1997 s 461 for 2005 and subsequent years of assessment.

Para (*b*) and s 3(1) substituted "€400" for "€300" in TCA 1997 s 461A for 2005 and subsequent years of assessment.

Para (*c*) and s 3(1) substituted "€1,580" for "€1,520" in TCA 1997 s 462(2) for 2005 and subsequent years of assessment.

Para (*d*) and s 3(1) substituted "€2,800", "€2,300", "€1,800", "€1,300" and "€800" for "€2,600", "€2,100", "€1,600", "€1,100" and "€600" in TCA 1997 s 463(2) for 2005 and subsequent years of assessment.

Para (*e*) and s 3(1) substituted "€1,000" for "€500" in TCA 1997 s 465(1) or 2005 and subsequent years of assessment.

Para (*f*) and s 3(1) substituted "€1,000" and "€2,000" for "€800" and "€1,600" in TCA 1997 s 468(2) for 2005 and subsequent years of assessment.

Para (*g*) and s 3(1) substituted "€1,270" for "€1,040", in both places where it occurs, in TCA 1997 s 472(4) for 2005 and subsequent years of assessment.

SCHEDULE 5
Amendment of Provisions Consequential on Section 145

Section 145

Notes

Section 145(7)(*a*) and Sch 5 Pt 1 substituted in relation to any unpaid income tax, corporation tax or capital gains tax, as the case may be, that has not been paid before 1 April 2005 regardless of when that tax became due and payable and notwithstanding anything to the contrary in any other enactment other than TCA 1997 s 1082:

"Subsections (3) to (5) of section 1080" for "Subsections (3) and (4) of section 1080" in TCA 1997 s 128B(9)(*c*);

"subsection (2)(*b*)" for "subsection (1)(*b*)" in TCA 1997 s 128B(9)(*d*);

"Subsections (3) to (5) of section 1080" for "Subsections (2) to (4) of section 1080" in TCA 1997 s 172K(6)(*c*);

"subsection (2)(*b*)" for "subsection (1)(*b*)" in TCA 1997 s 172K(6)(*d*);

"Subsections (3) to (5) of section 1080" for "Subsections (2) to (4) of section 1080" in TCA 1997 s 240(3);

"subsection (2)(*b*)" for "subsection (1)(*b*)" in TCA 1997 s 240(4);

"Subsections (3) to (5) of section 1080" for "Subsections (2) to (4) of section 1080" in TCA 1997 s 258(9)(*c*);

"subsection (2)(*b*)" for "subsection (1)(*b*)" in TCA 1997 s 258(9)(*d*);

"income tax" for "income tax charged by an assessment" in TCA 1997 s 503(8);

"R is 0.083" for "R is the rate per cent specified in section 1080(1)" in TCA 1997 s 591(11)(*c*);

"Subsections (3) to (5) of section 1080" for "Subsections (2) to (4) of section 1080" in TCA 1997 s 730G(7)(*c*);
"subsection (2)(*b*)" for "subsection (1)(*b*)" in TCA 1997 s 730G(7)(*d*);
"Subsections (3) to (5) of section 1080" for "Subsections (2) to (4) of section 1080" in TCA 1997 s 739F(7)(*c*);
"subsection (2)(*b*)" for "subsection (1)(*b*)" in TCA 1997 s 739F(7)(*d*);
"Subsections (3) to (5) of section 1080" for "Subsections (2) to (4) of section 1080" in TCA 1997 s 784E(6)(*c*);
"subsection (2)(*b*)" for "subsection (1)(*b*)" in TCA 1997 s 784E(6)(*d*);
"Subsections (3) to (5) of section 1080" for "Subsections (2) to (4) of section 1080" in TCA 1997 s 848M(6)(*c*);
"subsection (2)(*b*)" for "subsection (1)(*b*)" in TCA 1997 s 848M(6)(*d*);
"section 1080(2)" for "section 1080(1)" in TCA 1997 s 1082(3);
"Subsections (3) to (5) of section 1080" for "Subsections (2) to (4) of section 1080" in TCA 1997 s 1082(4);
"section 1080(2)" for "section 1080(1)" in TCA 1997 s 1082(5);
"Subsections (3) to (5) of section 1080" for "Subsections (2) to (4) of section 1080" in TCA 1997 Sch 18 para 1(7)(*c*);
"subsection (2)(*b*)" for "subsection (1)(*b*)" in TCA 1997 Sch 18 para 1(7)(*d*).

SCHEDULE 6
Miscellaneous Technical Amendments in Relation to Tax

Section 147

Notes

Para 1(*a*) substituting "the Health Service Executive" for "a health board" in TCA 1997 s 4(1) definition of "company" para (*a*) with effect from 25 March 2005.

Para 1(*b*) substituted "Schedule E" for "the Schedule E" in TCA 1997 s 127(2)(i)(I) with effect from 25 March 2005.

Para 1(*c*) substituted "the Health Service Executive" for "a health board" in TCA 1997 s 214(2)(*b*) with effect from 25 March 2005.

Para 1(*d*) substituted TCA 1997 s 267J(2) with effect from 1 January 2004.

Para 1(*e*)(i) substituted "the Health Service Executive" for "the health board in whose functional area the convalescent home is situated," in TCA 1997 s 268(1) definition of "industrial building or structure" para (i) with effect from 25 March 2005.

Para 1(*e*)(ii)(I) deleted TCA 1997 s 268(2A) definition of "health board" with effect from 25 March 2005.

Para 1(*e*)(ii)(II)(A) substituted "the Health Service Executive" for "the health board in whose functional area it is situated" in TCA 1997 s 268(2A) definition of "qualifying hospital" para (*g*) with effect from 25 March 2005.

Para 1(*e*)(ii)(II)(B) substituted "the Health Service Executive" for "the health board" in each place where it occurred in TCA 19997 s 268(2A) definition of "qualifying hospital" para (*g*)(i) with effect from 25 March 2005.

Para 1(*e*)(ii)(II)(C) substituted "the Health Service Executive" for "that health board" in TCA 1997 s 268(2A) definition of "qualifying hospital" para (*h*) with effect from 25 March 2005.

Para 1(*e*)(iii)(I)(A) substituted "the Health Service Executive" for "the health board in whose functional area it is situated" in TCA 1997 s 268(2B)(*e*) with effect from 25 March 2005.

Para 1(*e*)(iii)(I)(B) substituted "the Health Service Executive" for "the health board" in both places where it occurs in TCA 1997 s 268(2B)(*e*)(i) with effect from 25 March 2005.

Para 1(*e*)(iii)(II) substituted "the Health Service Executive" for "that health board" in TCA 1997 s 268(2B)(*f*) with effect from 25 March 2005.

Para 1(*e*)(iv)(I) substituted "the Health Service Executive" for "the health board in whose functional area it is the situated" in TCA 1997 s 268(3A)(*c*)(iv) with effect from 25 March 2005.

Para 1(*e*)(iv)(II) substituted "the Health Service Executive" for "that health board" in both places where it occurs in TCA 1997 s 268(3A)(*c*)(iv) with effect from 25 March 2005.

Para 1(*f*) substituted "section 243 or 243A" for "section 243" in TCA 1997 s 397(3) as respects accounting periods ending on or after 3 February 2005.

Para 1(*g*)(i) substituted "days" for "months" in TCA 1997 s 404(4)(c)(ii) construction of "M" with effect from 3 February 2005.

Para 1(*g*)(ii) substituted "is 0.0273." for "is the rate per cent specified in section 1080(1)." in TCA 1997 s 404(4)(c)(ii) construction of "R" with effect from 3 February 2005.

Para 1(*h*)(i)(I) substituted "the Health Service Executive" for "a health board" in both places where it occurs in TCA 1997 s 469(1) definition of "hospital" with effect from 25 March 2005.

Para 1(*h*)(i)(II) substituted "Health Acts 1947 to 2004" for "Health Acts, 1947 to 1996" in both places where it occurs in TCA 1997 s 469(1) definition of "hospital" with effect from 25 March 2005.
Para 1(*h*)(ii) substituted "practice" for "practise" in TCA 1997 s 469(1) definition of "practitioner" para (*c*) with effect from 25 March 2005.
Para 1(*i*) substituted "in each subsequent year" for "in in each subsequent year" in TCA 1997 s 556(6)(*a*) with effect from 25 March 2005.
Para 1(*j*) substituted "section 826(1)(*a*)" for "section 826" in TCA 1997 s 616(7) definition of "relevant Member State" para (*b*) with effect from 25 March 2005.
Para 1(*k*) substituted "section 104 of the Capital Acquisitions Tax Consolidation Act 2003" for "section 63 of the Finance Act, 1985" in TCA 1997 s 730K(5)(*a*) with effect from 21 February 2003.
Para 1(*l*)(i) substituted "the Health Service Executive" for "health board" in TCA 1997 s 787A(7) definition of "employee" para (*a*) with effect from 25 March 2005.
Para 1(*l*)(ii) substituted "the Executive or the committee" for "board or committee" in TCA 1997 s 787A(7) definition of "employee" para (*a*) with effect from 25 March 2005.
Para 1(*m*) substituted "section 826(1)(*a*)" for "section 826" in TCA 1997 s 825A(3)(*b*) with effect from 25 March 2005.
Para 1(*n*) substituted "who, or the Health Service Executive or any local authority" for "who, or any health board, local authority" in TCA 1997 s 888(2)(*e*) with effect from 25 March 2005.
Para 1(*o*) deleted TCA 1997 s 942(7) and (10) with effect from 25 March 2005.
Para 1(*p*)(i)(I) deleted "section 893(2)" from TCA 1997 Sch 29 col 2 with effect from 25 March 2005.
Para 1(*p*)(i)(II) inserted "section 896" after "section 894(3)" in TCA 1997 Sch 29 col 2 with effect from 25 March 2005.
Para 1(*p*)(ii) substituted "section 896" for "section 893(3)" in TCA 1997 Sch 29 col 3 with effect from 25 March 2005.

INCOME TAX (PURCHASED LIFE ANNUITIES) REGULATIONS 1959

1959 No 152

The Revenue Commissioners, in exercise of the powers conferred on them by section 23 of the Finance Act, 1959 (No 18 of 1959), hereby make the following regulations

1 These Regulations may be cited as the Income Tax (Purchased Life Annuities) Regulations, 1959.

2 In these Regulations —

"the principal section" means [section 788 of the Taxes Consolidation Act, 1997];[1]

"payee" means the person beneficially entitled for the time being to the payments on account of an annuity;

"payer" means any person resident in the State by whom, or any branch or agency in the State of a person not so resident (being a branch or agency through which that person carries on life assurance business) through which, an annuity is paid;

and other expressions have the same meaning as in the Income Tax Acts.

Amendments

[1] Substituted by TCA 1997 s 1100 and Sch 31.

3 A claim for the application of the principal section to an annuity shall be made in writing to the Inspector by the payee and shall give the particulars set out in the Schedule to these Regulations.

4 The Inspector may by notice require the payer of an annuity to furnish him with such particulars relating to the annuity as he may require, including the age of the person during whose life the annuity is payable, the amount or value of the consideration given for the grant of the annuity, and particulars of any other matter appearing to him to be relevant for the purposes of the principal section.

5 On the receipt of a claim under Regulation 3 the Inspector shall determine whether the annuity is a purchased life annuity to which the principal section applies and, if so, what proportion of each payment on account of the annuity constitutes the capital element. The prescribed tables of mortality to be used for this purpose shall be the select tables in the volume of tables published in 1953 at the University Press, Cambridge, for the Institute of Actuaries and the Faculty of Actuaries, entitled **"The a (55) Tables for Annuitants"** and, in using these tables, the age as at the date when the first of the annuity payments begins to accrue, of a person during whose life the annuity is payable, shall be taken to be a number of years of his age at his birthday last preceding that date. If that age is outside the range of the said tables, or in any other case where the tables are insufficient, the actuarial value of the annuity for the purposes of paragraph (*c*) of [subsection (5)][1] of the principal section shall be such amount as may be certified by an actuary nominated by the Minister for Finance. The Inspector shall serve a notice of his determination (hereinafter referred to as the original determination) upon the payee and, unless the payer in not entitled or required to deduct tax from the annuity, upon the payer of the annuity. The determination shall thereupon become effective, and a payer upon whom such notice is served shall be treated as having been notified in the prescribed manner for the purposes of [subsection (6)][2] of the principal section.

6 If the payee is dissatisfied with the original determination he may, within twenty-one days from the date of service upon him of notice thereof, or such further time as the [Appeal Commissioners][3] may allow, give notice to the Inspector of his intention to appeal against the determination and such notice of intention to appeal shall specify the grounds of the appeal.

Amendments

1 Substituted by TCA 1997 s 1100 and Sch 31.
2 Substituted by TCA 1997 s 1100 and Sch 31.
3 Substituted by F(MP)A 1968 s 3(6)(*c*)(ii).

7 [Subsection (3) of section 933 of the Taxes Consolidation Act, 1997],[1] shall, with any necessary modifications, apply to an original determination against which notice of appeal has been given under the last preceding Regulation as if such original determination were an assessment to income tax.

8 If an appeal under Regulation 6 is not withdrawn or settled by agreement, it shall be heard by the [Appeal Commissioners],[2] who shall for this purpose have all such powers as they have in relation to appeals against assessments to income tax under Schedule D.

Amendments

1 Substituted by TCA 1997 s 1100 and Sch 31.
2 Substituted by F(MP)A 1968 s 3(6)(*c*)(ii).

9 [Sections 941 and 942 of the Taxes Consolidation Act, 1997],[1] as amended and extended by subsequent enactments, shall, with any necessary modifications, apply to appeals under these Regulations as they apply to appeals against assessments to income tax.

Amendments

1 Substituted by TCA 1997 s 1100 and Sch 31.

10 If the original determination is amended as the result of an appeal, the inspector shall, unless the payer is not entitled or required to deduct tax from the annuity or any part of it, serve a notice of the determination as so amended upon the payer of the annuity. The amended determination shall become effective as soon as the appeal has been finally determined and any notice as aforesaid has been served, and shall supersede any earlier determination in relation to the first payment made thereafter on account of the annuity, and, subject to the next following Regulation, to all subsequent such payments.

11 If, at any time after a determination has become effective and at least one payment on account of the annuity has been made thereafter, the Inspector or the payee alleges that that determination is erroneous whether by reason of an error or mistake in a claim by the payee or otherwise, the Inspector may make, or the payee may make a claim for, a revised determination. If the Inspector makes a revised determination in accordance with the claim he shall serve notice upon the payee accordingly. If he makes a revised determination without the payee having claimed it, or if he makes a revised determination which is not in accordance with the payee's claim, or if on receipt of the payee's claim he refuses to make a revised determination, he shall serve notice upon the payee accordingly, and Regulations 6, 7, 8 and 9 shall apply, with any necessary modifications, as they apply in relation to the original determination.

12 (1) As soon as the time limit for appealing against a revised determination made under Regulation 11 has expired or, if there is an appeal, as soon as the appeal has been finally determined, the Inspector shall, unless the payer is not entitled or required to deduct tax from the annuity or any part of it, serve notice of the said determination or, as may be appropriate, of that determination as amended on appeal, upon the payer of the annuity. The determination shall thereupon become effective and shall supersede any earlier determination in relation to the first payment made thereafter on account of the annuity, and, subject to Regulation 11, to all subsequent such payments.

(2) If by virtue of Regulation 6 the [Appeal Commissioners][1] extend the time limited for an appeal, the notice of appeal shall be treated as a claim made under Regulation 11 and that Regulation and paragraph (1) of this Regulation shall apply accordingly.

Amendments

1 Substituted by F(MP)A 1968 s 3(6)(*c*)(ii).

13 Where any effective determination is amended on the final determination of an appeal, any amount by which the tax deducted from, or assessed and charged by reference to, payments on account of the annuity on the basis of the said determination exceeds the tax that would have been deducted or assessed and charged if the determination as amended had applied to those payments shall, subject to Regulation 17, be repaid to the payee by the Revenue Commissioners. Any amount by which the tax so deducted or assessed and charged falls short of the tax that would have been deducted or assessed and charged if the determination as amended had applied to those payments shall, subject to Regulation 17 and notwithstanding anything in the Income Tax Acts, be assessed and charged on the payee under Case VI of Schedule D for the relevant years of assessment.

14 (1) Where —

(*a*) income tax has been deducted from or assessed and charged by reference to the whole of any payments on account of any annuity and subsequently an original determination becomes effective, or

(*b*) a revised determination becomes effective,

the difference between —

(i) the tax which the payer was entitled to deduct and did in fact deduct from payments on account of the annuity falling due after the 5th day of April, 1959, but made before the said determination became effective or the tax assessed and charged for the year beginning on the 6th day of April, 1959, or any later year of assessment, by reference to payments made before the said determination became effective,

and

(ii) the tax that would have been deducted from or assessed and charged by reference to the aforesaid payments if it had been deducted or assessed and charged in accordance with the said determination,

shall, except in so far as it has been repaid or assessed and charged under Regulation 13, and subject to Regulation 17, be repaid to the payee by the Revenue Commissioners or, notwithstanding anything in the Income Tax Act, be assessed and charged upon the payee under Case VI of Schedule D for the relevant years of assessment, as the circumstances may require, whether or not, in cases within subparagraph (*b*) hereof, the determination in force before the revised determination became effective had been made or confirmed on appeal.

(2) (*a*) No repayment shall be made under this Regulation in respect of tax for a year of assessment which ended more than six years before the end of the year of assessment in which the claim which gave rise to the said determination was made, or, in a case where the Inspector initiated a revised determination, before the end of the year of assessment in which the Inspector served notice upon the payee under Regulation 11.

(*b*) No assessment shall be made under this Regulation in respect of any year of assessment which ended as aforesaid, except that where any form of fraud or wilful default has been committed by or on behalf of any person in connection with or in relation to the taxation of the annuity, an assessment may be made at any time.

(3) No repayment or assessment shall be made under this Regulation in respect of tax deducted from or assessed and charged by reference to any payment on account of the annuity made before the date of the claim which gave rise to the said determination or, as the case may be, the date of the Inspector's revised determination under Regulation 11 if that deduction or assessment and charge was in fact made on the basis or in accordance with the practice generally prevailing at the time when the said payment was made.

15 In relation to an annuity paid by a person not resident in the State, otherwise than through a branch or agency through which that person carries on life assurance business in the State, to a payee who is resident in the State, the foregoing Regulations, except Regulation 4, shall apply as they apply in relation to an annuity paid by a person who is resident in the State, with the modification that Regulation 11 shall apply as though the reference to at least one payment having been made on account of the annuity were a reference to a payment on account of the annuity having been made on the payee.

17 Where the payee is a married woman living with her husband, any reference in these Regulations to repaying tax to the payee or to charging tax on the payee shall, unless an application for separate assessment under [Section 1023 of the Taxes Consolidation Act, 1997][1] is in force, be read as requiring tax to be repaid to, or charged on, her husband.

Amendments

[1] Substituted by TCA 1997 s 1100 and Sch 31.

18 A determination that becomes effective under these Regulations shall, except to the extent that it may be varied under these Regulations, be final and conclusive for all the purposes of the Income Tax Acts.

19 Where a determination is varied on appeal or by virtue of Regulation 11, and any tax deducted from or assessed and charged by referencc to a payment on account of the annuity is repaid under Regulation 13, 14 or 16, a corresponding adjustment shall be made in estimating for the purposes of the Income Tax Acts the total income of the payee (or if the payee is a married woman living with her husband, of her husband) for the relevant year of assessment, and notwithstanding anything in the Income Tax Acts, such consequential adjustments of his liability to income tax (including sur-tax) as may be necessary shall be made by assessment or by repayment, as the case may require.

20 Any notice or other document authorised or required to be served on any person under these Regulations by the Inspector may be served by post by letter addressed to such person at his usual or last known place of business or abode, or, where such person is a company, by letter addressed to the secretary of the company at its registered office.

21 Anything which is authorised or required by these Regulations to be done by the inspector shall be done by such Inspector of taxes as the Revenue Commissioners may direct.

SCHEDULE

PARTICULARS TO BE GIVEN BY THE PAYEE IN MAKING A CLAIM UNDER REGULATION 3

PART I

1. The name of the payer.
2. The number by which the annuity contract is identified.
3. The amount of each payment on account of the annuity.
4. The frequency with which payments on account of the annuity are made.
5. The name of the person or persons on whose life or lives the annuity are made.
6. The name and address of the annuitant and, if the annuitant is a married woman, the name of her husband.
7. Such particulars of the occupation of the annuitant, or of the husband of an annuitant who is a married woman, as the Revenue Commissioners consider necessary to determine which Inspector should deal with the claim.
8. Such particulars as are necessary to determine whether subsection (8) of the principal section applies to the annuity.

PART II

Additional particulars to be given where the person paying the annuity is not within the definition of payer in Regulation 2.

1. The amount or value of the consideration given for the grant of the annuity.
2. The date of birth of each person on whose life the annuity depends.
3. The date when the first payment on account of the annuity began to accrue.
4. Whether the final payment on account of the annuity will be calculated by reference to the actual date of any person's death.

5. Particulars of any contingencies other than the death of a person on the happening of which the annuity will terminate.

INCOME TAX (RELEVANT CONTRACTS) REGULATIONS 2000

2000 No 71

ARRANGEMENT OF REGULATIONS

PART 1
GENERAL

PART 2
SUB-CONTRACTOR'S CERTIFICATE

PART 3
RECOVERY OF TAX

PART 4
REPAYMENT AND CREDIT TO UNCERTIFIED SUB-CONTRACTORS

PART 5
SPECIAL PROVISIONS IN RELATION TO SUB-CONTRACTOR'S CERTIFICATE, RELEVANT PAYMENTS CARD AND RELEVANT TAX DEDUCTION CARD

THE REVENUE COMMISSIONERS, IN EXERCISE OF THE POWERS CONFERRED ON THEM BY SECTION 531 OF THE TAXES CONSOLIDATION ACT, 1997 (NO 39 OF 1997), HEREBY MAKE THE FOLLOWING REGULATIONS:

PART 1
GENERAL

1 Citation and commencement

(1) These Regulations may be cited as the Income Tax (Relevant Contracts) Regulations, 2000.

(2) These Regulations shall come into operation on the 6th day of April, 2000.

Revenue information

Information leaflet CG 10 — Relevant Contracts Tax (RCT).

eBriefing

eBriefing no 12 — 2004 From 5 April 2004 applications for C2s or payments cards from traders in Counties Dublin, Wicklow, Meath and Kildare should be directed to the local Revenue District (previously dealt with in Tallaght).

Tax Briefing

TB40 June 2000 pp 22–23 — Relevant Contracts Tax — New Regulations.
TB51 Jan 2003 pp 11–12 — Relevant Contracts Tax and Integrated Taxation Processing.
TB52 May 2003 pp 10–11 — Relevant Contracts Tax (Finance Act 2003 changes).
TB54 Dec 2003 p 5 — Only the new 8 digit RCTDC/C45 form should be used from 1 February 2004 when principal contractors are making payments to uncertified subcontractors.

2 Interpretation

In these Regulations, except where the context otherwise requires—

"Act" means the Taxes Consolidation Act, 1997;

"certificate of deduction" has the meaning assigned to it in Regulation 6 of these Regulations;

"certified sub-contractor", in relation to a principal, means a sub-contractor—

(*a*) in respect of whom the principal holds, at the time of making a payment under a relevant contract to the sub-contractor, a relevant payments card for the year in which the payment is made, and

(*b*) in respect of whom the principal has not received a notice under paragraph (*a*) of subsection (13) of section 531 of the Act;

"Collector-General" means the Collector-General appointed under section 851 of the Act;

"director" has the meaning assigned to it by subsection (4) of section 433 of the Act;

"full-time employee" means, in relation to a company or partnership, an employee who is employed on a full-time basis and whose duties are such that he or she is required to devote substantially the whole of his or her time to the service of the company or partnership, as the case may be;

[**"income tax month"** has the meaning (inserted by the Finance Act 2001) assigned to it by subsection (1) of section 530 of the Act;][1]

"inspector" means an inspector of taxes;

"officer of the Revenue Commissioners" includes an inspector;

"payment", in relation to a payment made by a principal to a sub-contractor under a relevant contract, includes a payment on account of an amount due under the relevant contract;

"period of account" means a period for which an account is made up in relation to the business in question;

[**"PPS number"** means a personal public service number within the meaning of section 223 (as amended by section 12(1)(*a*) of the Social Welfare (Miscellaneous Provisions) Act 2002 (No 8 of 2002)) of the Social Welfare (Consolidation) Act 1993;][2]

"prescribed" means prescribed by the Revenue Commissioners under these Regulations;

"principal" means a principal within the meaning of section 530 of the Act of the kind referred to in section 531 of the Act;

"private company" has the meaning assigned to it by section 33 of the Companies Act, 1963;

"proprietary director" has the meaning assigned to it by subsection (1) of section 530 of the Act;

"relevant contract" has the meaning assigned to it in subsection (1) of section 530 of the Act;

"repayment period" has the meaning assigned to it in subsection (5) of section 531 of the Act;

"relevant operations" has the meaning assigned to it in subsection (1) of section 530 of the Act;

"sub-contractor" means a person of the same kind as the person referred to as the sub-contractor in subsection (1) of section 531 of the Act;

"sub-contractor's certificate" means a certificate of authorisation issued to a sub-contractor under subsection (11) of section 531 of the Act;

"uncertified sub-contractor" means a sub-contractor who is not a certified sub-contractor;

"year" means year of assessment;

other words and expressions have the same meaning as in the Income Tax Acts.

Amendments

1 Definition of "income tax month" substituted by Income Tax (Relevant Contracts) Regulations 2001 reg 2(*a*) with effect from 6 April 2001.

2 Definition of "PPS number" inserted by Income Tax (Relevant Contracts) Regulations 2004 reg 2(*a*) with effect from 1 January 2005.

3 Declaration by parties to relevant contract

(1) Prior to entering into a relevant contract, the persons who intend to enter into such a contract shall, in the form which from time to time may be specified for that purpose by the Revenue Commissioners, make a declaration to the effect that, having regard to the guidelines which from time to time may be published by the Revenue Commissioners for the information of such persons as to the distinctions between contracts of employment and relevant contracts, and without prejudice to the question of whether the contract is a contract of employment or a relevant contract, they have satisfied themselves that in their opinion the contract which they propose to enter into is not a contract of employment.

(2) Any declaration made for the purposes of paragraph (1) of this Regulation shall be retained by the principal for the period specified in Regulation 20(4) of these Regulations.

4 Transfer of functions, etc

(1) The Revenue Commissioners may nominate any officer of the Revenue Commissioners to perform any acts and discharge any functions authorised by these Regulations to be performed or discharged by the Revenue Commissioners.

(2) Anything which is authorised or required by these Regulations to be done by an inspector may be done by any inspector.

5 Liability for payment of tax deductible

A person who is required to make any deduction of tax referred to in these Regulations shall, whether the deduction is made or not, be accountable for the amount of the deduction and shall be liable to pay that amount to the Collector-General.

6 Certificate of deduction

When a principal makes a payment to an uncertified sub-contractor from which tax is deductible under subsection (1) of section 531 of the Act, he or she shall, on making such payment, give to the uncertified sub-contractor a certificate in the prescribed form containing such particulars [including the sub-contractor's PPS number or tax reference number as the case may be, and if the sub-contractor is an individual, his or her date of birth][1], as are indicated by the form of the certificate as being required to be entered thereon.

Amendments

1 Substituted by Income Tax (Relevant Contracts) Regulations 2004 reg 2(*b*) with effect from 1 January 2005; previously "including the sub-contractor's date of birth and identifying number, known as the Revenue and Social Insurance (RSI) number,".

7 Service by post, etc

(1) Any notice, notification, certificate, requirement, return, relevant payments card or relevant tax deduction card which is authorised or required to be given, served, made, sent or issued under these Regulations may be sent by post.

(2) If a person delivers to an officer of the Revenue Commissioners any declaration, certificate, statement, return, relevant payments card or relevant tax deduction card in a prescribed form, he or she shall be deemed to have been required by a notice under these Regulations to prepare and deliver that declaration, certificate, statement, return, relevant payments card or relevant tax deduction card.

(3) In proceedings for recovery of a penalty under section 1052, 1053 or 1054 of the Act—

(*a*) a certificate signed by an officer of the Revenue Commissioners which certifies that he or she has examined the relevant records and that it appears from them that a stated notice was duly given to the defendant on a stated day shall be evidence until the contrary is proved that that person received that notice in the ordinary course,

(*b*) a certificate signed by an officer of the Revenue Commissioners which certifies that he or she has examined the relevant records and that it appears from them that, during a stated period, a stated declaration, certificate, statement, return, relevant payments card or relevant tax deduction card was not received from the defendant shall be evidence until the contrary is proved that the defendant did not, during that period, deliver the declaration, certificate, statement, return, relevant payments card or relevant tax deduction card,

(*c*) a certificate certifying as provided for in subparagraph (*a*) or subparagraph (*b*) of this paragraph and purporting to be signed by an officer of the Revenue Commissioners may be tendered in evidence without proof and shall be deemed until the contrary is proved to have been signed by such officer.

[PART 1A
REGISTRATION AS A PRINCIPAl][1]

Amendments

1 Part 1A (Regs 7A–7F) inserted by Income Tax (Relevant Contracts) Regulations 2004 reg 2(*f*) with effect from 1 January 2005.

7A [Operative date

For the purposes of Regulation 7C of these Regulations, "operative date" means 1 January 2005.][1]

Amendments

1 Reg 7A inserted by Income Tax (Relevant Contracts) Regulations 2004 reg 2(*f*) with effect from 1 January 2005.

7B [Keeping and maintaining the register

The Revenue Commissioners shall keep and maintain a register in which shall be included, in respect of each principal, such of the relevant details as they consider necessary for that purpose, in respect of that principal as have been provided, or are taken to have been provided, to them under this Part.][1]

Amendments

1 Reg 7B inserted by Income Tax (Relevant Contracts) Regulations 2004 reg 2(*f*) with effect from 1 January 2005.

7C [Registration and time for registration

(1) (*a*) Subject to paragraph (3) of this Regulation, a person who is a principal on the operative date shall notify the Revenue Commissioners of that fact not later than 21 days after the operative date.

(*b*) A person who is not a principal on the operative date and who enters into a relevant contract, being the first such relevant contract entered into by that person as a principal after the operative date, shall notify the Revenue Commissioners that he or she is a principal not later than 21 days after entering into the relevant contract.

(*c*) The Revenue Commissioners shall give notice to each person to whom subparagraph (*a*) or (*b*) of this paragraph applies that he or she is registered as a principal.

(2) In order to notify the Revenue Commissioners in accordance with subparagraph (*a*) or (*b*) of paragraph (1) of this Regulation, a person to whom either of those subparagraphs applies shall -

(*a*) complete any form furnished by the Revenue Commissioners for that purpose, and

(*b*) provide relevant details required by the Revenue Commissioners as may be indicated on the form.

(3) (*a*) A person who is a principal on the operative date and had indicated this to the Revenue Commissioners before that date is to be taken to have complied with the requirements of paragraphs (1)(*a*) and (2) of this Regulation.

(*b*) The Revenue Commissioners shall give notice to a person to whom subparagraph (*a*) of this paragraph applies that he or she is registered as a principal.

(4) A person who receives a notice pursuant to paragraph (3)(*b*) of this Regulation and who has ceased to be a principal shall notify the Revenue Commissioners in writing of such cessation within 21 days of the receipt of the notice and shall specify the date of such cessation.][1]

Amendments

1 Reg 7C inserted by Income Tax (Relevant Contracts) Regulations 2004 reg 2(*f*) with effect from 1 January 2005.

7D [Notification of change in relevant details

(1) Where a change occurs in any of the relevant details provided, or taken to have been provided, under Regulation 7C of these Regulations, then the following shall notify the Revenue Commissioners in writing of the change —

(*a*) the registered person,

(*b*) if the registered person has died, his or her personal representative, or (*c*) if the registered person is a body of persons which is in liquidation or is otherwise being wound up, the liquidator or any other person who is carrying on business during such liquidation or, as the case may be, winding up.

(2) The notification referred to in paragraph (1) of this Regulation shall be made —

(i) within 21 days of the change, or

(ii) within 21 days of the date of a notice under paragraph (3)(*b*) of Regulation 7C of these Regulations, if the change occurred prior to the issue of the notice.][1]

Amendments

1 Reg 7D inserted by Income Tax (Relevant Contracts) Regulations 2004 reg 2(*f*) with effect from 1 January 2005.

7E [Notification of cessation

A person who is registered as a principal in accordance with Regulation 7C of these Regulations and who ceases to be a principal shall notify the Revenue Commissioners in writing of such cessation by the end of the month following the month in which the cessation takes place and such notification shall specify the date of cessation.][1]

Amendments

1 Reg 7E inserted by Income Tax (Relevant Contracts) Regulations 2004 reg 2(*f*) with effect from 1 January 2005.

7F [Cancellation of registration

Where, in the opinion of the Revenue Commissioners, a person has ceased to be a principal, they may notify that person in writing of their intention to cancel the registration and such cancellation shall be effected as on and from 21 days from the date of the notification unless, within that period the person notifies the Revenue Commissioners in writing that he or she is still a principal and provides such details as may be required by the Revenue Commissioners for the purposes of this Part.][1]

Amendments

1 Reg 7F inserted by Income Tax (Relevant Contracts) Regulations 2004 reg 2(*f*) with effect from 1 January 2005.

PART 2
SUB-CONTRACTOR'S CERTIFICATE

8 Application for sub-contractor's certificate

(1) A person who desires to obtain a sub-contractor's certificate shall make application on the prescribed form for such certificate to the Revenue Commissioners.

(2) Subject to paragraph (3) of this Regulation and Regulation 9 of these Regulations, an application for the certificate referred to in paragraph (1) of this Regulation shall be accompanied by a photograph—

(*a*) where the person applying for the certificate is an individual, of the individual by whom the certificate, if issued, will be produced to a principal in accordance with paragraph (*a*) of subsection (12) (inserted by the Finance Act,

1999) of section 531 of the Act, or would but for paragraphs (*b*) or (*c*) of that subsection be so produced, and

(*b*) where the person applying for the certificate is not an individual, of the individual nominated by the person so applying in accordance with Regulation 9(1) of these Regulations.

(3) The photograph to accompany the application referred to in paragraph (1) of this Regulation shall—

(*a*) be a full face photograph being, in the opinion of the inspector, an adequate facial likeness of the individual referred to in paragraph (2) of this Regulation,

(*b*) be signed on the reverse by that individual, and

(*c*) comply with such conditions as to size, type or other features as the Revenue Commissioners may direct.

9 Nomination of individual who will produce sub-contractor's certificate

(1) Where the person making application for a sub-contractor's certificate in accordance with Regulation 8 of these Regulations is not an individual, or is an individual to whom paragraph (2)(*c*) of this Regulation applies, the person making the application shall nominate, at that time and on the prescribed form, the individual by whom the said certificate, if issued, will be produced to a principal in accordance with paragraph (*a*) of subsection (12) (inserted by the Finance Act, 1999) of section 531 of the Act.

(2) (*a*) The individual nominated in accordance with paragraph (1) of this Regulation shall—

(i) in a case where the applicant for a sub-contractor's certificate is a private company, be a proprietary director of that company, or

(ii) in a case where the applicant for a sub-contractor's certificate is a company other than a private company, be a director of that company, or

(iii) in a case where the applicant for the sub-contractor's certificate is a partnership, be a partner in that partnership.

(*b*) Notwithstanding subparagraph (*a*) of this paragraph, where, in relation to a company or partnership, it would in the opinion of the inspector be impracticable for an individual nominated in accordance with paragraph (1) of this Regulation to be a proprietary director, director or partner, as the case may be, the individual so nominated shall be a full-time employee of the applicant company or partnership, as the case may be, who, in the opinion of the inspector, is a suitable individual to be so nominated.

(*c*) Where the person making the application is an individual and the inspector is satisfied that it is impracticable that the applicant would produce the sub-contractor's certificate in person to each principal contractor, the applicant may nominate an individual by whom the sub-contractor's certificate, if issued, will be so produced and the said individual shall be a full-time employee of the applicant who, in the opinion of the inspector, is a suitable individual to be so nominated.

(3) As soon as the individual nominated in accordance with paragraph (1) of this Regulation ceases to act in the nominated capacity on behalf of the person who nominated him or her, that individual shall immediately surrender the sub-contractor's certificate to the Revenue Commissioners.

10 Ownership and issue of sub-contractor's certificate

(1) A sub-contractor's certificate shall remain the property of the Revenue Commissioners at all times.

(2) A sub-contractor's certificate shall be issued to the individual whose name and photograph appears thereon at such office of the Revenue Commissioners as the inspector may direct.

(3) The individual to whom the sub-contractor's certificate is to be issued in accordance with paragraph (2) of this Regulation may be required to provide such evidence of identity as the inspector may consider necessary and shall, immediately on receipt of the certificate, sign an acknowledgement of such receipt in such form as the inspector may require.

(4) A sub-contractor's certificate shall only be produced to a principal in accordance with paragraph (a) of subsection (12) (inserted by the Finance Act, 1999) of section 531 of the Act by the individual whose photograph appears thereon and to whom the sub-contractor's certificate was issued in accordance with paragraph (2) of this Regulation.

11 Validity of sub-contractor's certificate

(1) A sub-contractor's certificate shall, unless otherwise recalled or cancelled by the Revenue Commissioners, be valid for a period of one year.

[(1A) Notwithstanding paragraph (1) of this Regulation, a sub-contractor's certificate to be issued under that paragraph for a period commencing on 6 April 2001 shall, unless otherwise recalled or cancelled by the Revenue Commissioners, be valid for the period to 31 December 2002.][1]

(2) (*a*) Notwithstanding paragraph (1) of this Regulation, where an applicant for a sub-contractor's certificate has—

(i) average annual sales, arising from relevant operations in the period of three years ending with the end of the last period of account ending prior to the date of the application, exceeding [€6,340,000],[2] and

(ii) satisfied the Revenue Commissioners that he or she has complied with all of the requirements set out in subparagraphs (i) to (iv) and (vi) (inserted by the Finance Act, 1999) of paragraph (*a*) of subsection (11) of section 531 of the Act,

the certificate shall, unless otherwise recalled or cancelled by the Revenue Commissioners, be valid for a period of three years.

(*b*) Where subparagraph (*a*) of this paragraph applies to a sub-contractor, he or she shall be regarded as a class of sub-contractor within the meaning of paragraph (*a*)(i) of subsection (6) of section 531 of the Act.

(c) This paragraph shall not apply in a case where the certificate would not have issued but for the provisions of paragraph (*b*) of subsection (11) of section 531 of the Act being applied.

[(2A) Unless otherwise recalled or cancelled by the Revenue Commissioners, a sub-contractor's certificate to which paragraph (2) applies, which would otherwise be valid for a period commencing before 6 April 2001 and ending after that date shall, notwithstanding anything contained in these Regulations or in any Regulations revoked by these Regulations, be deemed to be valid to 5 April 2001 only.

(2B) Notwithstanding paragraph (2) of this Regulation, a sub-contractor's certificate to which that paragraph applies and which is to be issued for a period commencing on 6 April 2001 shall, unless otherwise recalled or cancelled by the Revenue Commissioners, be valid to 31 December 2004.][3]

Amendments

1 Para (1A) inserted by Income Tax (Relevant Contracts) Regulations 2001 reg 2(*b*)(i) with effect from 6 April 2001.

2 Substituted by Income Tax (Relevant Contracts) Regulations 2001 reg 2(*b*)(iii) with effect from 1 January 2002; previously "£5,000,000".

3 Paras (2A)–(2B) inserted by Income Tax (Relevant Contracts) Regulations 2001 reg 2(*b*)(ii) with effect from 6 April 2001.

PART 3
RECOVERY OF TAX

12 Recovery of tax

(1) (*a*) The provisions of any enactment relating to the recovery of income tax charged under Schedule D shall apply to the recovery of any amount of tax which a principal is liable under section 531 of the Act and these Regulations to pay to the Collector-General as if the said amount had been charged on the principal under Schedule D.

(*b*) In particular and without prejudice to the generality of subparagraph (*a*) of this paragraph, this Regulation applies the provisions of sections 962, 963, 964, 966, 967 and 968 of the Act.

(2) Proceedings may be brought for the recovery of the total amount which a principal is liable to pay as aforesaid without distinguishing the amounts which he or she is liable to pay by reference to each sub-contractor and without specifying the sub-contractors in question, and for the purposes of the proceedings the said total amount shall be one single cause of action or one matter of complaint; but nothing in this paragraph shall prevent the bringing of separate proceedings for the recovery of each of the several amounts which the principal is liable to pay as aforesaid by reference to his or her several sub-contractors.

(3) In proceedings instituted by virtue of this Regulation for the recovery of any amount of tax—

(*a*) a certificate signed by an officer of the Revenue Commissioners which certifies that a stated amount of tax is due and payable by the principal shall be evidence until the contrary is proved that that amount is so due and payable, and

(*b*) a certificate certifying as aforesaid and purporting to be signed by an officer of the Revenue Commissioners may be tendered in evidence without proof and shall be deemed until the contrary is proved to have been signed by an officer of the Revenue Commissioners.

13 Estimation of tax on monthly basis

(1) If within the time specified by subsection (3A) (inserted by the Finance Act, 1999) of section 531 of the Act a person, being a principal or a person who was previously a principal and who has been required to do so in writing by the Revenue Commissioners, fails, in relation to any income tax month, to, either or both—

(*a*) make a return to the Collector-General of the amount of tax, if any, which that person was liable under section 531 to deduct from payments made to uncertified sub-contractors during that income tax month, and

(*b*) remit to the Collector-General the amount of tax, if any, which that person was so liable to deduct,

then, without prejudice to any other action which may be taken, the Revenue Commissioners may—

(i) estimate the amount of tax which, for that income tax month, should have been remitted by the person within the period specified in that subsection (3A) for the payment of such tax, and

(ii) serve notice on the person of the amount so estimated.

(2) Where a notice is served on a person under paragraph (1) of this Regulation, the following provisions shall apply:

(*a*) the person, if claiming to be not liable to remit any tax for the income tax month to which the notice relates, may by giving notice in writing to the Revenue Commissioners within the period of 14 days from the service of the notice require the claim to be referred for decision to the Appeal Commissioners and their decision shall be final and conclusive,

(*b*) on the expiration of that period, if no such claim is required to be so referred or, if such claim is required to be referred, on final determination by the Appeal Commissioners against the claim, the estimated tax specified in the notice shall be recoverable in the like manner and by the like proceedings as if—

(i) the person was a principal, and

(ii) the amount specified in the notice were the amount of tax which the person was liable under section 531 of the Act to deduct from payments made by the person during the income tax month specified in the notice,

(*c*) if, at any time after the service of the notice, the person makes a return as provided for in subsection (3A) (inserted by the Finance Act, 1999) of section 531 of the Act and pays the tax due, if any, together with any interest and costs which may have been incurred in connection with the default, the notice shall, subject to paragraph (*d*), stand discharged and any excess of tax which may have been paid shall be repaid, and

(*d*) where action for the recovery of tax specified in a notice under paragraph (2) has been taken, being action by means of the institution of proceedings in any court or the issue of a certificate under section 962 of the Act, paragraph (c) shall not, unless the Revenue Commissioners otherwise direct, apply in relation to that notice until that action has been completed.

(3) A notice given by the Revenue Commissioners under paragraph (1) may extend to two or more consecutive income tax months.

Cross-references

Taxes (Offset of Repayments) Regulations 2002, SI No 471 of 2002, reg 2(1) (interpretation — "estimate" para (*b*)).

14 Inspector's estimates

(1) Where the inspector, or such other officer as the Revenue Commissioners may nominate to exercise the powers conferred by this Regulation (hereafter in these Regulations referred to as "other officer"), has reason to believe that the total amount of tax which a principal was liable under section 531 of the Act to remit in respect of the respective income tax months comprised in any year was greater than the amount of tax, if any, paid by the principal in respect of the said months then, without prejudice to any other action which may be taken, the inspector or other officer may make an estimate in one sum of the total amount of tax which in his or her opinion should have been paid in respect of the income tax months comprised in that year and may serve notice on the principal specifying—

(*a*) the total amount of tax so estimated,

(*b*) the total amount of tax, if any, remitted by the principal in relation to the income tax months comprised in the said year, and

(*c*) the balance of tax remaining unpaid.

(2) Where notice is served on a principal under paragraph (1) of this Regulation—

(*a*) the principal may, if he or she claims that the total amount of tax or the balance of tax remaining unpaid is excessive, on giving notice in writing to the inspector or other officer within the period of thirty days from the service of the notice, appeal to the Appeal Commissioners,

(*b*) on the expiration of the said period, if no notice of appeal is received or, if notice of appeal is received, on determination of the appeal by agreement or otherwise, the balance of tax remaining unpaid as specified in the notice or the amended tax as determined in relation to the appeal shall become due in the same manner as, and be recoverable by the like proceedings as are provided for, in Regulation 12 of these Regulations.

(3) The provisions of Part 41 of the Act shall, with any necessary modifications, apply to the making and amending of an estimate in accordance with paragraph (1) of this Regulation as if—

(*a*) the said estimate was an assessment made on a chargeable person, and

(*b*) the reference in the said Part 41 to a return was a reference to a return required to be made by the principal in accordance with section 531 of the Act.

(4) The provisions of the Act relating to appeals shall, with any necessary modifications, apply to claims and appeals under this Regulation as if those claims or appeals were appeals against an assessment to income tax.

(5) A notice under paragraph (1) of this Regulation may be issued before the end of the year to which it relates and may extend to two or more years.

15 Notification of estimation

(1) Where the inspector or other officer of the Revenue Commissioners acting with the knowledge of the inspector or other officer causes to issue, manually or by any

electronic, photographic or other process, a notice of estimation of tax, in accordance with Regulation 13 or 14 bearing the name of the inspector or other officer, that estimate to which the notice of estimation of tax relates shall be deemed to have been made by the inspector or other officer to the best of his or her opinion.

(2) The provisions of section 928 of the Act shall, subject to any necessary modifications, apply in relation to estimates made in accordance with the provisions of Regulation 13 or 14 as they apply in relation to assessments to income tax.

PART 4
REPAYMENT AND CREDIT TO UNCERTIFIED SUB-CONTRACTORS

16 Repayment

(1) Any claim for any repayment period by an uncertified sub-contractor for repayment of tax deducted from a payment pursuant to subsection (1) of section 531 of the Act shall be made in the prescribed form.

(2) Where the amount of tax payable by the claimant for the year within which the repayment period falls has not been finally determined on foot of an assessment, or assessments, made on him or her, the Revenue Commissioners shall estimate according to the best of their knowledge and belief and in accordance with the information available to them the amount of tax payable by him or her for that year.

(3) The Revenue Commissioners shall—

(*a*) compute the aggregate of—

(i) the amount of tax which was deducted from payments received by the claimant in the repayment period, and

(ii) the amount of the tax otherwise paid or borne in the repayment period by the claimant for the year within which that period falls,

(*b*) compute the proportion applicable to the repayment period of the amount of tax—

(i) payable by the claimant for the said year on foot of an assessment or assessments made on him or her, or, as the case may be,

(ii) estimated, in accordance with paragraph (2) of this Regulation, to be payable by the claimant for that year,

(*c*) specify—

(i) the amount or amounts of tax for which the claimant is liable for any year or years other than the year referred to in subparagraph (*a*) of this paragraph, and

(ii) any amount or amounts which at the date of making any repayment under subparagraph (*d*) of this paragraph, he or she is liable to remit under any of the enactments referred to in [paragraph (*c*)(ii) of subsection (5)][1] of section 531 of the Act, and

(*d*) repay to the claimant the excess of the aggregate amount computed under subparagraph (*a*) of this paragraph, as reduced by any part of that amount which has been repaid or set off, over the aggregate of—

(i) the proportion computed under subparagraph (*b*) of this paragraph, and

(ii) the amount or total of the amounts specified under subparagraph (*c*) of this paragraph.

(4) If the amount of a repayment calculated by the Revenue Commissioners to be due in respect of any repayment period is not agreed by the claimant, they shall, despite the objection, make the repayment in accordance with their calculation of the amount due to him or her and shall, on determination of any appeal against the amount of the repayment, make such further repayment as may be necessary.

(5) In relation to a case where a sub-contractor is chargeable to corporation tax, unless the context otherwise requires, in this Regulation, references to tax shall include references to corporation tax and references to a year shall include references to an accounting period.

Amendments

1 Substituted by Income Tax (Relevant Contracts) Regulations 2004 reg 2(*c*) with effect from 6 April 2000; previously "paragraph (*c*)(iii) of subsection (5)".

17 Credit against liability to tax of sub-contractor

(1) Subject to paragraph (2), any amount of tax retained on the occasion of any repayment made to an uncertified sub-contractor shall be credited against any tax for which he or she is, or is estimated to be, liable for the year within which the repayment period falls.

(2) Where his or her liability cannot be finally determined until after the end of the year, credit shall not be made during the year against any tax which is deductible in the year from emoluments which fall within Chapter 4 of Part 42 of the Act.

PART 5
SPECIAL PROVISIONS IN RELATION TO SUB-CONTRACTOR'S CERTIFICATE, RELEVANT PAYMENTS CARD AND RELEVANT TAX DEDUCTION CARD

18 Application for relevant payments card

(1) A principal shall, before making an application to the Revenue Commissioners for a relevant payments card in accordance with [paragraph (*a*) of subsection 12][1] (inserted by the Finance Act, 1999) of section 531 of the Act, examine the sub-contractor's certificate produced to him or her and satisfy himself or herself that the individual who produced the sub-contractor's certificate is the individual whose photograph appears thereon.

(2) A sub-contractor, or, as the case may be, the individual nominated in accordance with Regulation 9(1) of these Regulations shall, in the presence of a principal, sign, in the space provided therefor, the form on which the principal makes application to the Revenue Commissioners for a relevant payments card in respect of that sub-contractor in accordance with paragraph (*a*) of subsection (12) (inserted by the Finance Act, 1999) of section 531 of the Act.

(3) Where, in accordance with paragraph (*b*) of subsection 12 (inserted by the Finance Act, 1999) of section 531 of the Act, a principal makes application to the Revenue Commissioners for a relevant payments card in respect of a sub-contractor, the sub-contractor shall provide, on the form on which the principal makes such application, such details as are required by the said form of the nominated bank account (within the

meaning of that paragraph (*b*)) into which all payments to the sub-contractor are to be made and the sub-contractor shall in the space provided sign the said form.

(4) Where, in accordance with paragraph (*c*) of subsection 12 (inserted by the Finance Act, 1999) of section 531 of the Act, a principal makes application to the Revenue Commissioners for a relevant payments card, such an application shall contain such details as are required by the form provided for such applications.

Amendments

1 Substituted by Income Tax (Relevant Contracts) Regulations 2004 reg 2(*d*) with effect from 1 January 2005; previously "paragraphs (*a*), (*b*) and (*c*) of subsection 12".

19 Powers of inspectors

The power—

(*a*) to issue, to refuse to issue or to cancel a sub-contractor's certificate,

(*b*) to receive notice of appeal against refusal to issue a sub-contractor's certificate or against the cancellation of a sub-contractor's certificate, and to act at the hearing or the rehearing of an appeal against such refusal, or cancellation, as the case may be,

(*c*) to give notice, under paragraph (*a*) of subsection (13) of section 531 of the Act, to a principal of the cancellation of a sub-contractor's certificate issued to a sub-contractor, and

(*d*) to advise the person in respect of whom a notice under paragraph (a) of subsection (13) of section 531 of the Act was issued of the issue of such notice and to require that person to return the sub-contractor's certificate issued to him or her,

may be exercised by an inspector of taxes.

20 General provision relating to keeping of records and return by principal at end of year

(1) On making a payment under a relevant contract to a certified sub-contractor, a principal shall enter on the relevant payments card relating to such sub-contractor the particulars, [including the sub-contractor's PPS number or tax reference number as the case may be, and if the sub-contractor is an individual, his or her date of birth,][1] required to be entered on that card regarding such payment.

(2) (*a*) When making the first payment under a relevant contract in any year to an uncertified sub-contractor, a principal shall prepare a relevant tax deduction card, and shall enter thereon at the time of the making of that payment to the uncertified sub-contractor such particulars, [which shall include the sub-contractor's PPS number or tax reference number as the case may be, and if the sub-contractor is an individual, his or her date of birth,][2] as are required to be entered thereon in relation to that payment.

(*b*) When making any subsequent payment to that sub-contractor, the principal shall, at the time of the making of such payment, enter on the said relevant tax deduction card such particulars as are required to be entered thereon in relation to such payment.

(3) (*a*) Within 46 days from the end of each year the principal shall send to the Revenue Commissioners—[1]

(i) a return, in the prescribed form, [which shall include the sub-contractor's PPS number or tax reference number as the case may be, and if the sub-contractor is an individual, his or her date of birth,][2] in respect of each sub-contractor to whom he or she has made a payment or payments in that year, showing the total amount of the payment or payments so made and the total tax, if any, deducted therefrom, and

(ii) a statement and declaration in the prescribed form showing the total of the payments so made and the total tax, if any, deducted therefrom.

(*b*) In a case where the principal is a partnership, the statement and declaration referred to in subparagraph (*a*)(ii) of this Regulation shall be signed by the precedent partner within the meaning of Part 43 of the Act and, in a case where the principal is a body corporate, the statement and declaration shall be signed either by the secretary or by a director of the body corporate.

(4) A principal shall retain relevant payments cards, relevant tax deduction cards and declarations made in accordance with Regulation 3 of these Regulations for a period of six years after the end of the year to which they refer or for such shorter period as the Revenue Commissioners may authorise in writing.

Amendments

1 Substituted by Income Tax (Relevant Contracts) Regulations 2004 reg 2(*e*)(i) with effect from 1 January 2005; previously "including the sub-contractor's date of birth and identifying number, known as the Revenue and Social Insurance (RSI) number,".

2 Substituted by Income Tax (Relevant Contracts) Regulations 2004 reg 2(*e*)(ii) with effect from 1 January 2005; previously "which shall include the sub-contractor's date of birth and identifying number, known as the Revenue and Social Insurance (RSI) number".

21 Records to be kept by certified sub-contractors

Every certified sub-contractor shall keep and maintain throughout the year a record of all payments received by him or her during that year and the record shall state, in relation to each such payments, the date of the payment, the amount of the payment and the name of the person from whom the payment was received.

22 Information to be given to principals by sub-contractors

Every sub-contractor shall furnish to a principal all such information or particulars as are required by the principal to enable the principal to comply with any provision of these Regulations.

PART 6
MISCELLANEOUS

23 Inspection of principal's records, etc

(1) Upon request made to him or her at any premises of a principal by an authorised officer, any person, being the principal or a person employed by the principal at the premises, shall produce to the authorised officer for inspection all such documents and records relating to relevant contracts (including relevant payments cards, relevant tax deduction cards and declarations made in accordance with Regulation 3 of these Regulations) as may be in such person's power, possession or procurement.

(2) Where, in pursuance of this Regulation, an authorised officer requests production of any documents or records, he or she shall, on request, show his or her authorisation for the purposes of this Regulation to the person concerned.

(3) In this Regulation "authorised officer" means an officer of the Revenue Commissioners authorised by them in writing for the purposes of this Regulation or of Regulation 20 of the Income Tax (Relevant Contracts) Regulations, 1971.

24 Death of principal

On the death of a principal anything which the principal would have been liable to do under these Regulations shall be done by the personal representative of the principal.

25 Difference between principal and sub-contractor

(1) If a difference arises between a principal and a sub-contractor as to whether the principal has deducted tax from payments made to the sub-contractor, or as to the amount of tax that has been so deducted, the matter shall be determined by the Appeal Commissioners.

(2) A determination under paragraph (1) of this Regulation may be made by one Appeal Commissioner.

26 Revocations

The Regulations specified in the Schedule to these Regulations are hereby revoked.

SCHEDULE

SI Number (1)	Regulations (2)
SI No 1 of 1971	Income Tax (Construction Contracts) Regulations, 1971
SI No 274 of 1976	Income Tax (Construction Contracts) Regulations, 1976
SI No 239 of 1985	Income Tax (Construction Contracts) Regulations, 1985
SI No 240 of 1991	Income Tax (Construction Contracts) Regulations, 1991
SI No 281 of 1992	Income Tax (Relevant Contracts) Regulations, 1992
SI No 31 of 1993	Income Tax (Relevant Contracts) Regulations, 1993
SI No 163 of 1996	Income Tax (Relevant Contracts) Regulations, 1996

MEDICAL INSURANCE (RELIEF AT SOURCE) REGULATIONS 2001

2001 No 129

ARRANGEMENT OF REGULATIONS

THE REVENUE COMMISSIONERS, IN EXERCISE OF THE POWERS CONFERRED ON THEM BY SECTION 470 OF THE TAXES CONSOLIDATION ACT, 1997 (NO. 39 OF 1997), HEREBY MAKE THE FOLLOWING REGULATIONS:

PART 1
GENERAL

1 Citation and commencement

(1) These Regulations may be cited as the Medical Insurance (Relief at Source) Regulations, 2001.

(2) These Regulations shall come into operation on 6 April 2001.

Revenue Information

Information leaflet CG 11 — Medical Insurance — Tax Relief at Source.

2 Interpretation

(1) In these Regulations, except where the context otherwise requires—

"annual claim" and **"interim claim"** have, respectively, the meanings given by paragraphs (3) and (4) of Regulation 4 of these Regulations;

"authorised insurer" has the meaning assigned to it by subsection (1) of the principal section;

"notice" means notice in writing;

"principal section" means section 470 of the Taxes Consolidation Act, 1997;

"PPS Number", in relation to an individual, means that individual's Personal Public Service Number within the meaning of section 223 of the Social Welfare (Consolidation) Act, 1993 (No. 27 of 1993);

"relevant contract" has the meaning assigned to it by subsection (1) of the principal section;

"year" means year of assessment.

(2) A word or expression that is used in these Regulations and is also used in the Income Tax Acts has, except where the context otherwise requires, the same meaning in these Regulations that it has in those Acts.

3 Refund of payment to individual

Where and for whatever reason an authorised insurer, to which a payment is made in respect of which relief has been given in accordance with subsection (3) of the principal section, makes a refund of that payment to the individual who made it—

(*a*) the amount of that refund shall not exceed the payment actually made to the authorised insurer by that individual, and
(*b*) the authorised insurer shall thereupon repay to the Revenue Commissioners any amount which that insurer had recovered from the Revenue Commissioners on a claim under subsection (3)(*b*)(ii) of the principal section in respect of the amount deducted from that payment.

PART 2

CLAIMS BY AUTHORISED INSURERS

4 Claims by authorised insurers — introductory

(1) A claim made under subsection (3)(*b*)(ii) of the principal section by an authorised insurer to which payments are made for the purpose of recovering amounts from the Revenue Commissioners shall be made in accordance with this Regulation and Regulations 5 and 6.

(2) Before any claim referred to in paragraph (1) of this Regulation can be made, an authorised insurer shall, for the purpose of making such a claim, register with the Revenue Commissioners on a form provided for that purpose and which form shall—

(*a*) provide for the designation of a person or persons authorised to make claims on behalf of the authorised insurer, (*b*) contain the signature or signatures of the person or persons referred to in subparagraph (*a*) of this paragraph, and

(*c*) be completed and signed by—

(i) where the authorised insurer is a company, the secretary of the company, or

(ii) where the authorised insurer is an unincorporated body, the person who is, or performs the duties of, secretary of the body.

(3) Subject to paragraph (4) of this Regulation, a claim shall be made to the Revenue Commissioners for a period of a year and is referred to in these Regulations as an **"annual claim"**.

(4) A claim may also be made in the manner prescribed by Regulation 5 for such period shorter than a year as the Revenue Commissioners may allow and is referred to in these Regulations as an **"interim claim"**.

(5) A claim shall be in such form and contain such particulars as the Revenue Commissioners may prescribe.

5 Interim claims

(1) The Revenue Commissioners shall establish procedures with each authorised insurer in relation to the making of interim claims and, without prejudice to the generality of the foregoing, such procedures shall govern the method by which the claim is to be satisfied, including either or both the debiting by an authorised insurer of a specified bank account set up by the Revenue Commissioners for that purpose and the crediting by the Revenue Commissioners of a bank account within the State nominated by the authorised insurer for that purpose.

(2) If the Revenue Commissioners are satisfied that the amount claimed was deductible in the period for which the claim is made they shall pay the amount to the authorised insurer and, if they are not so satisfied, they shall pay any lesser amount which they are satisfied was deductible.

(3) Where the amount paid by the Revenue Commissioners in accordance with paragraph (2) of this Regulation exceeds the amount actually deducted for the period of the claim, the authorised insurer shall bring the amount of the excess into account in the interim claim next made by that insurer after the actual amount has been ascertained and, if that amount exceeds the amount deducted in respect of the period for which that interim claim is made—

(*a*) the authorised insurer shall repay the amount of the excess to the Revenue Commissioners with the claim, and

(*b*) if the authorised insurer fails to do so, the amount shall be immediately recoverable by the Revenue Commissioners in the same manner as tax charged on the authorised insurer which has become final and conclusive.

6 Annual claims and information returns

(1) Within 2 months after the end of each year, an authorised insurer shall make an annual claim to the Revenue Commissioners for the year in such form and manner as shall be prescribed by them, in respect of all payments in respect of premiums under relevant contracts received by that insurer and in respect of all such premiums refunded

by that insurer in that year and in respect of the amounts deductible from those payments and recoverable from the Revenue Commissioners in accordance with subsection (3) of the principal section.

(2) Within 6 months after the end of a year, an authorised insurer shall make an information return to the Revenue Commissioners in relation to each individual making a payment of premiums in that year to that insurer under a relevant contract and being in such form and manner as shall be prescribed by them, showing in relation to each such individual—

(*a*) his or her name, address and, where available to the authorised insurer, PPS Number,

(*b*) the authorised insurer's membership number relating to that individual,

(*c*) the total amount of premiums paid by the individual for that year, and

(*d*) the amount deducted and retained by that individual under subsection (3)(*a*) of the principal section.

(3) Where the aggregate of the amounts paid by the Revenue Commissioners in respect of interim claims for the year exceeds the amount recoverable from the Revenue Commissioners shown on the annual claim, the authorised insurer shall repay the amount of the excess to the Revenue Commissioners with the claim.

(4) If an authorised insurer fails to make an annual claim and information return within the time limited by this Regulation, the Revenue Commissioners may refuse to make interim payments to that insurer until such time as that claim and return are both received.

(5) Where an annual claim and information return have been made and the authorised insurer which made them subsequently discovers that an error or mistake has been made in either the annual claim or the information return, or both, the insurer shall make either a supplementary annual claim or information return, or both, as the case may require, within 2 months of discovering the error or mistake.

7 Payments to authorised insurers — Revenue Commissioners discretion

An authorised insurer in respect of which the Revenue Commissioners are not satisfied in relation to any one or more of the matters specified in Regulations 4, 5 and 6 shall, nevertheless, for the purposes of the making of payments to that insurer in respect of claims under subsection (3)(*b*)(ii) of the principal section, be treated as an authorised insurer in respect of which they are so satisfied if the Revenue Commissioners are of the opinion that in all the circumstances such insurer's failure to satisfy them in relation to such matter or matters ought to be disregarded for those purposes.

8 Validity of claims

(1) The Revenue Commissioners shall be entitled, in respect of any claim under subsection (3)(*b*)(ii) of the principal section, to make all such enquiries as they consider necessary to establish whether a repayment arising from such a claim is or was properly due.

(2) An authorised insurer shall—

(*a*) keep sufficient records to enable the requirements of this Regulation to be satisfied and shall make these available for inspection within the State, and

(*b*) furnish such information about the claim as may reasonably be required.

PART 3
MISCELLANEOUS

9 Provision of information to the Revenue Commissioners

(1) The Revenue Commissioners may by notice require an authorised insurer to furnish, within such time as may be specified in the notice, such information about any relevant contract provided by that insurer as may reasonably be required by them for the purposes of these Regulations.

(2) An authorised insurer shall keep sufficient records to enable the requirements of this Regulation to be satisfied and shall make those available for inspection within the State.

10 Discharge of functions, etc

The Revenue Commissioners may nominate any officer of the Revenue Commissioners to perform any acts and discharge any functions authorised by these Regulations to be performed or discharged by the Revenue Commissioners.

(2) An authorised insurer shall:

(a) keep sufficient records to enable the requirements of this Regulation to be satisfied and shall make those available for inspection within the State; and

(b) furnish such information about the claim as may reasonably be required.

PART 3
MISCELLANEOUS

9 Provision of information to the Revenue Commissioners

(1) The Revenue Commissioners may by notice require an authorised insurer to furnish, within such time as may be specified in the notice, such information about any relevant contract provided by that insurer as may reasonably be required by them for the purposes of these Regulations.

(2) An authorised insurer shall keep sufficient records to enable the requirements of this Regulation to be satisfied and shall make those available for inspection within the State.

10 Discharge of functions, etc

The Revenue Commissioners may nominate any officer of the Revenue Commissioners to perform any acts and discharge any functions authorised by these Regulations to be performed or discharged by the Revenue Commissioners.

LONG-TERM CARE INSURANCE (RELIEF AT SOURCE) REGULATIONS 2001

2001 No 130

ARRANGEMENT OF REGULATIONS

THE REVENUE COMMISSIONERS, IN EXERCISE OF THE POWERS CONFERRED ON THEM BY SECTION 470A (INSERTED BY THE FINANCE ACT 2001(NO. 7 OF 2001)) OF THE TAXES CONSOLIDATION ACT, 1997 (NO. 39 OF 1997), HEREBY MAKE THE FOLLOWING REGULATIONS:

PART 1
GENERAL

1 Citation and commencement

(1) These Regulations may be cited as the Long-Term Care Insurance (Relief at Source) Regulations, 2001.

(2) These Regulations shall come into operation on 6 April 2001.

2 Interpretation

(1) In these Regulations, except where the context otherwise requires—

"annual claim" and **"interim claim"** have, respectively, the meanings given by paragraphs (2) and (3) of Regulation 5 of these Regulations;

"qualifying insurer" has the meaning assigned to it by subsection (1) of the principal section;

"notice" means notice in writing;

"principal section" means section 470A (inserted by the Finance Act, 2001) of the Taxes Consolidation Act, 1997;

"PPS Number", in relation to an individual, means that individual's Personal Public Service Number within the meaning of section 223 of the Social Welfare (Consolidation) Act, 1993 (No. 27 of 1993);

"qualifying long-term care policy" has the meaning assigned to it by subsection (1) of the principal section;

"year" means year of assessment.

(2) A word or expression that is used in these Regulations and is also used in the Income Tax Acts has, except where the context otherwise requires, the same meaning in these Regulations that it has in those Acts.

3 Registration of qualifying insurers

A person who wants to be entered in the Register maintained by the Revenue Commissioners for the purposes of the principal section and these Regulations shall apply to the Revenue Commissioners on a form provided for that purpose by the Revenue Commissioners, which form shall—

(*a*) provide for—

(i) the full name and address of the person,

(ii) the country in which the person has received an authorisation to carry on the business of life assurance,

(iii) in the case of a person not resident in the State or carrying on business in the State through a fixed place of business, the name and address of the person appointed in accordance with subsection (2)(*b*) of the principal section,

(iv) the designation and signature of each individual authorised to make claims under subsection (8)(*b*)(ii) of the principal section on behalf of the person, and

(v) an undertaking by the person to comply with all the duties and obligations imposed on a qualifying insurer by the principal section and these Regulations,

and

(*b*) be completed and signed by—

(i) where the person is a company, the secretary of the company, or

(ii) where the person is an unincorporated body, the person who is, or who performs the duties of, secretary of the body.

4 Refund of payment to individual

Where and for whatever reason a qualifying insurer, to which a payment is made in respect of which relief has been given in accordance with subsection (8) of the principal section, makes a refund of that payment to the individual who made it—

(*a*) the amount of that refund shall not exceed the payment actually made to the qualifying insurer by that individual, and

(*b*) the qualifying insurer shall thereupon repay to the Revenue Commissioners any amount which that insurer had recovered from the Revenue Commissioners on a claim under subsection (8)(*b*)(ii) of the principal section in respect of the amount deducted from that payment.

PART 2
CLAIMS BY QUALIFYING INSURERS

5 Claims by qualifying insurers — introductory

(1) A claim made under subsection (8)(*b*)(ii) of the principal section by a qualifying insurer to which payments are made for the purpose of recovering amounts from the Revenue Commissioners shall be made in accordance with this Regulation and Regulations 6 and 7.

(2) Subject to paragraph (3) of this Regulation, a claim shall be made to the Revenue Commissioners for a period of a year and is referred to in these Regulations as an **"annual claim"**.

(3) A claim may also be made in the manner prescribed by Regulation 6 for such period shorter than a year as the Revenue Commissioners may allow and is referred to in these Regulations as an **"interim claim"**.

(4) A claim shall be in such form and contain such particulars as the Revenue Commissioners may prescribe.

6 Interim claims

(1) The Revenue Commissioners shall establish procedures with each qualifying insurer in relation to the making of interim claims and, without prejudice to the generality of the foregoing, such procedures shall govern the method by which the claim is to be satisfied, including either or both the debiting by the qualifying insurer of a specified bank account set up by the Revenue Commissioners for that purpose and the crediting by the Revenue Commissioners of a bank account within the State nominated by the qualifying insurer for that purpose.

(2) If the Revenue Commissioners are satisfied that the amount claimed was deductible in the period for which the claim is made they shall pay the amount to the qualifying insurer and, if they are not so satisfied, they shall pay any lesser amount which they are satisfied was deductible.

(3) Where the amount paid by the Revenue Commissioners in accordance with paragraph (2) of this Regulation exceeds the amount actually deducted for the period of the claim, the qualifying insurer shall bring the amount of the excess into account in the interim claim next made by that insurer after the actual amount has been ascertained

and, if that amount exceeds the amount deducted in respect of the period for which that interim claim is made—

(*a*) the qualifying insurer shall repay the amount of the excess to the Revenue Commissioners with the claim, and

(*b*) if the qualifying insurer fails to do so, the amount shall be immediately recoverable by the Revenue Commissioners in the same manner as tax charged on the qualifying insurer which has become final and conclusive.

7 Annual claims and information returns

(1) Within 2 months after the end of each year, a qualifying insurer shall make an annual claim to the Revenue Commissioners for the year in such form and manner as shall be prescribed by them, in respect of all payments in respect of premiums under qualifying long-term care policies received by that insurer and in respect of all such premiums refunded by that insurer in that year and in respect of the amounts deductible from those payments and recoverable from the Revenue Commissioners in accordance with subsection (8) of the principal section.

(2) Within 6 months after the end of a year, a qualifying insurer shall make an information return to the Revenue Commissioners in relation to each individual making a payment of premiums in that year to that insurer under a qualifying long-term care policy and being in such form and manner as shall be prescribed by them, showing in relation to each such individual—

(*a*) his or her name, address and PPS Number,

(*b*) the qualifying insurer's policy number relating to that individual,

(*c*) the total amount of premiums paid by the individual for that year, and

(*d*) the amount deducted and retained by that individual under subsection (8)(*a*) of the principal section.

(3) Where the aggregate of the amounts paid by the Revenue Commissioners in respect of interim claims for the year exceeds the amount recoverable from the Revenue Commissioners shown on the annual claim, the qualifying insurer shall repay the amount of the excess to the Revenue Commissioners with the claim.

(4) If a qualifying insurer fails to make an annual claim and information return within the time limited by this Regulation, the Revenue Commissioners may refuse to make interim payments to that insurer until such time as that claim and return are both received.

(5) Where an annual claim and information return have been made and the qualifying insurer which made them subsequently discovers that an error or mistake has been made in either or both the claim and the information return, the insurer shall make either a supplementary annual claim or information return, or both, as the case may require, within 2 months of discovering the error or mistake.

8 Payments to qualifying insurers — Revenue Commissioners discretion

A qualifying insurer in respect of which the Revenue Commissioners are not satisfied in relation to any one or more of the matters specified in Regulations 5, 6 and 7 shall, nevertheless, for the purposes of the making of payments to that insurer in respect of claims under subsection (8)(*b*)(ii) of the principal section, be treated as a qualifying insurer in respect of which they are so satisfied if the Revenue Commissioners are of the opinion that in all the circumstances such insurer's failure to satisfy them in relation to such matter or matters ought to be disregarded for those purposes.

9 Validity of claims

(1) The Revenue Commissioners shall be entitled, in respect of any claim under subsection (8)*(b)*(ii) of the principal section, to make all such enquiries as they consider necessary to establish whether a repayment arising from such a claim is or was properly due.

(2) A qualifying insurer shall—

(*a*) keep sufficient records to enable the requirements of this Regulation to be satisfied and shall make these available for inspection within the State, and

(*b*) furnish such information about the claim as may reasonably be required.

PART 3
MISCELLANEOUS

10 Provision of information to the Revenue Commissioners

(1) The Revenue Commissioners may by notice require a qualifying insurer to furnish, within such time as may be specified in the notice, such information about any long-term care policy issued by that insurer as may reasonably be required by them for the purposes of these Regulations.

(2) A qualifying insurer shall keep sufficient records to enable the requirements of this Regulation to be satisfied and shall make those available for inspection within the State.

11 Discharge of functions, etc

The Revenue Commissioners may nominate any officer of the Revenue Commissioners to perform any acts and discharge any functions authorised by these Regulations to be performed or discharged by the Revenue Commissioners.

SPECIAL SAVINGS INCENTIVE ACCOUNT REGULATIONS 2001

2001 No 176

ARRANGEMENT OF REGULATIONS

The Revenue Commissioners, in exercise of the powers conferred on them by section 848S (inserted by the Finance Act, 2001 (No. 7 of 2001)) of the Taxes Consolidation Act, 1997 (No. 39 of 1997), hereby make the following Regulations:

General

1 Citation and commencement

(1) These Regulations may be cited as the Special Savings Incentive Accounts Regulations, 2001.

(2) These Regulations shall come into operation on 1 May 2001.

Revenue Information

Information leaflet CG 12 — Special Savings Incentive Accounts.

2 Interpretation

(1) In these Regulations, except where the context otherwise requires—

"annual return" means the return referred to in section 848Q of the Principal Act;

"monthly return" means the return referred to in section 848P of the Principal Act;

"net amount" has the same meaning as it has in section 848P(a)(iii) of the Principal Act;

"PPS Number" has the meaning assigned to it in section 848B(1) of the Principal Act;

"Principal Act " means the Taxes Consolidation Act, 1997;

"qualifying savings manager" has the meaning assigned to it in section 848B(1) of the Principal Act;

"special savings incentive account" has the same meaning as it has in section 848C of the Principal Act;

"tax credit" has the meaning assigned to it in section 848B(1) of the Principal Act.

(2) For the purposes of these Regulations, a special savings incentive account commences on the day the first subscription is made to the special savings incentive account.

(3) A word or expression that is used in these Regulations and is also used in the Tax Acts has, except where the context otherwise requires, the same meaning in these Regulations that it has in those Acts.

(4) In these Regulations–

(*a*) a reference to a Regulation is to a Regulation of these Regulations, and

(*b*) a reference to a paragraph or subparagraph is to the paragraph or subparagraph of the provision in which the reference occurs,

unless it is indicated that reference to some other provision is intended.

Registration of Qualifying Savings Managers, etc

3 Registration

(1) Where a qualifying savings manager applies to the Revenue Commissioners to be registered in accordance with section 848R(5) of the Principal Act, the qualifying

savings manager shall do so in a form prescribed by the Revenue Commissioners for that purpose.

(2) (*a*) Where the Revenue Commissioners are in receipt of an application in accordance with paragraph (1) and they are satisfied that the person making the application is entitled to be registered for the purposes of section 848R(5) of the Principal Act, they shall notify the person in writing that the person has been so registered with effect from the date specified in that notice.

(*b*) In this paragraph **"writing"**, in relation to a notification, includes the use of facsimile or electronic means where a record in a permanent or machine retrievable form of the notification is made or kept at the time of notification.

4 Indemnity

(1) Where at any time, whether before or after a qualifying savings manager has been duly registered, the Revenue Commissioners have reasonable grounds to believe—

(*a*) that the qualifying savings manager does not have, or no longer has, adequate resources to discharge the obligations imposed on qualifying savings managers by Part 36A of the Principal Act, or

(*b*) that the qualifying savings manager may fail, or has failed, to materially comply with those obligations,

then, the Revenue Commissioners may require the qualifying savings manager to give a bond or guarantee to the Revenue Commissioners sufficient to indemnify them against any loss arising by virtue of fraud or negligence of the qualifying savings manager in relation to the operation of that Part of that Act.

(2) Where a qualifying savings manager on being so required by the Revenue Commissioners, fails or refuses to indemnify them in the manner set out in paragraph (1), the Revenue Commissioners may –

(*a*) refuse to register the qualifying savings manager in accordance with section 848R(5) of the Principal Act, or

(*b*) where the qualifying savings manager has already been registered in accordance with that section, the Revenue Commissioners may cancel such registration in accordance with section 848R(6) of the Principal Act.

COMMENCING A SPECIAL SAVINGS INCENTIVE ACCOUNT

5 Declaration on commencement

(1) A qualifying savings manager shall not permit an individual to commence a special savings incentive account unless the qualifying savings manager is in possession of a declaration, of a kind referred to in section 848F of the Principal Act, made by the individual.

(2) Subject to paragraph (3), a declaration of a kind referred to in paragraph (1) may be completed and signed by an individual who intends to commence a special savings incentive account at any time in the month, or in the immediately preceding month, in which the special savings incentive account commences.

(3) A declaration of a kind referred to in paragraph (1) shall not be completed and signed by an individual at any time before 1 May 2001 or after 30 April 2002.

6 Verification of PPS Number

The Revenue Commissioners shall include in the guidance notes provided for by Regulation 17 procedures which set out how a qualifying savings manager is to take reasonable measures to establish that a PPS Number, contained in a declaration referred to in Regulation 5(1), is the PPS Number in relation to the individual who completed the declaration.

MONTHLY RETURNS AND PAYMENT OF NET AMOUNT

7 Payment of net amount

(1) (*a*) The Revenue Commissioners shall establish procedures with each qualifying savings manager who is registered in accordance with section 848R(5) of the Principal Act in relation to the payment of the net amount which is due from or, as the case may be, to the Revenue Commissioners.

(*b*) The net amount referred to in subparagraph (*a*) shall be specified in the monthly return to be made by the qualifying savings manager in accordance with section 848P of the Principal Act.

(*c*) Without prejudice to the generality of paragraph (*a*), such procedures shall govern the method by which the net amount is to be paid, including the debiting or, as the case may be, crediting by the qualifying savings manager of a specified bank account set up by the Revenue Commissioners for that purpose.

(2) If the Revenue Commissioners are satisfied that the net amount specified in a monthly return made by a qualifying savings manager is payable to the qualifying savings manager, they shall pay that amount to the qualifying savings manager and, if they are not so satisfied, they shall pay any lesser amount which they are satisfied is so payable.

8 Additional information

In addition to the matters which a qualifying savings manager is required to include in a monthly return under section 848P of the Principal Act, the qualifying savings manager shall also specify in respect of all special savings incentive accounts managed by the qualifying savings manager in that month the aggregate amount of subscriptions made to those accounts in that month.

9 Correction of errors

(1) Where a qualifying savings manager discovers that the net amount which has been specified in a monthly return is not correct, then, subject to this Regulation, the qualifying savings manager shall take account of that error in the next monthly return required to be made by the qualifying savings manager after that discovery.

(2) (*a*) Subject to subparagraph (*b*), where the holder of a special savings incentive account dies, the qualifying savings manager shall not specify in a monthly

return any subscription made to the special savings incentive account subsequent to the date of death.

(*b*) Where a monthly return includes a subscription which should not have been specified in the return by virtue of subparagraph (a), the qualifying savings manager shall correct that error by accounting for any such subscription and the tax credit in relation to any such subscription in the next monthly return to be made by the qualifying savings manager after the qualifying savings manager is made aware of the death.

(3) (*a*) Subject to subparagraph (*b*), where a special savings incentive account is treated as ceasing on any date, the qualifying savings manager shall not include in a monthly return any subscription made to the special savings incentive account subsequent to that date.

(*b*) Where a monthly return includes a subscription which should not have been specified in the return by virtue of subparagraph (*a*), the qualifying savings manager shall correct that error by accounting for any such subscription and the tax credit in relation to any such subscription in the next monthly return to be made by the qualifying savings manager after the special savings incentive account has been treated as ceasing.

(4) Where a monthly return made by a qualifying savings manager takes account of an error made in a monthly return previously made, and the error has not arisen because of the death of the holder of a special savings incentive account or because a special savings incentive account has been treated as ceasing, the qualifying savings manager shall attach to the monthly return, in a form prescribed by the Revenue Commissioners, details of the adjustment which has been made to the monthly return to account for the error.

CESSATION OF SPECIAL SAVINGS INCENTIVE ACCOUNTS

10 Cessation

(1) Where an individual fails to subscribe an amount to the special savings incentive account in the month the special savings incentive account is commenced and in any of the 11 months immediately succeeding that month, which amount was agreed with the qualifying savings manager when the special savings incentive account was commenced, the qualifying savings manager shall, when such failure first occurs, treat the special savings incentive account as ceasing for the purposes of Part 36A of the Principal Act.

(2) Where an individual who has commenced a special savings incentive account subscribes–

(*a*) in the period from 1 May 2001 to 31 December 2001, an amount greater than £200 in any month, or

(*b*) on or after 1 January 2002, an amount greater than €254 in any month,

the qualifying savings manager shall on the first day of that month treat the special savings incentive account as ceasing for the purposes of Part 36A of the Principal Act.

(3) Where an individual who has commenced a special savings incentive account informs the qualifying savings manager of the account that he or she is neither resident nor ordinarily resident in the State, the qualifying savings manager shall treat the account as ceasing for the purposes of Part 36A of the Principal Act.

(4) Where an individual who has commenced a special savings incentive account fails to complete the declaration referred to in section 848I of the Principal Act within the period provided for in section 848C(*h*) of that Act, the qualifying savings manager shall treat the special savings incentive account as ceasing for the purposes of Part 36A of that Act.

(5) Where a qualifying savings manager has reasonable grounds to suspect that—

(*a*) an individual who has commenced a special savings incentive account was less than 18 years of age at the time the special savings incentive account was commenced,

(*b*) a person, other than the individual who has commenced a special savings incentive account or the spouse of that individual, is subscribing to the special savings incentive account,

(*c*) an individual who has commenced a special savings incentive account is funding subscriptions to it from borrowings or the deferral of repayment (whether in respect of capital or interest) of sums already borrowed,

(*d*) the assets held in a special savings incentive account have been pledged as security for a loan, or

(*e*) the person who completed the declaration referred to in section 848F of the Principal Act on commencing a special savings incentive account, is not the person who beneficially owns all or any of the assets held in that special savings incentive account,

the qualifying savings manager shall inform the Revenue Commissioners accordingly.

(6) Where the Revenue Commissioners have been informed in accordance with paragraph (5), they shall make such enquires as they consider necessary to determine whether the special savings incentive account in respect of which they have been so informed should be treated as ceasing for the purposes of Part 36A of the Principal Act.

(7) Where in accordance with paragraph (6), or otherwise, the Revenue Commissioners determine that a special savings incentive account should be treated as ceasing at any time, they shall so inform the qualifying savings manager of that special savings incentive account by notice in writing accordingly and on receipt of that notice the qualifying savings manager shall treat the account as ceasing for the purposes of part 36A of the Principal Act, at that time.

TRANSFER OF SPECIAL SAVINGS INCENTIVE ACCOUNTS

11 Qualifying savings manager ceasing to act

(1) Where—

(*a*) an individual commences a special savings incentive account managed by a qualifying savings manager, (*b*) the qualifying savings manager acquires qualifying assets to be held in the special savings incentive account, and

(*c*) the individual does not comply with the terms under which the qualifying assets were acquired,

the qualifying savings manager may, subject to paragraph (2), cease to act as the qualifying savings manager of the special savings incentive account.

(2) Where in accordance with paragraph (1) a qualifying savings manager intends to cease to act as the qualifying savings manager of a special savings incentive account, the qualifying savings manager shall –

(*a*) not less than 30 days before the qualifying savings manager intends to cease to act, give notice to the individual concerned of that intention, and

(*b*) inform that individual of their right to transfer the special savings incentive account to another qualifying savings manager.

(3) Where a qualifying savings manager has given notice to an individual in accordance with paragraph (2), and the individual fails or refuses to request the qualifying savings manager to transfer his or her special savings incentive account to another qualifying savings manager, the qualifying savings manager may refuse to accept further subscriptions to the special savings incentive account.

12 Procedure on transfer

Where arrangements are made by an individual to transfer his or her special savings incentive account from one qualifying savings manager (in this Regulation referred to as the **"transferor"**) to another qualifying savings manager (in this Regulation referred to as the **"transferee"**)—

(*a*) the transferor shall give to the transferee, within 30 days after the date of the transfer, the notice referred to in section 848N(3) of the Principal Act, in a form prescribed by the Revenue Commissioners, and

(*b*) the individual shall, on the date of transfer or at any time in the previous 30 days, make a declaration of a kind referred to in section 848O of the Principal Act, to the transferee.

ANNUAL RETURNS

13 Additional information

In addition to the matters which a qualifying savings manager is required to include in an annual return under section 848Q(*a*) of the Principal Act, the qualifying savings manager shall also specify in respect of each special savings incentive account managed by the qualifying savings manager, the date of birth of the individual who commenced the special savings incentive account.

14 Transferred accounts

Where, during a year of assessment, a special savings incentive account has been transferred from a qualifying savings manager (in this Regulation referred to as the

"transferor") to another qualifying savings manager (in this Regulation referred to as the **"transferee"**)—

(*a*) the transferor shall include in the annual return in respect of that year of assessment, the total amount of subscriptions and tax credits in relation to those subscriptions which the transferor included in a monthly return in respect of that year, and

(*b*) the transferee shall include in the annual return in respect of that year of assessment, the total amount of subscriptions and tax credits in relation to those subscriptions which the transferee included in a monthly return in respect of that year.

MISCELLANEOUS

15 Delegation

The Revenue Commissioners may nominate any officer of the Revenue Commissioners to perform any acts and discharge any functions authorised by these Regulations to be performed or discharged by the Revenue Commissioners.

16 Guidance notes

(1) The Revenue Commissioners shall publish guidance notes to assist qualifying savings managers in complying with their statutory obligations in relation to the management of special savings incentive accounts.

(2) The guidance notes referred to in paragraph (1) may be revised by the Revenue Commissioners from time to time.

Notes

The Revenue Commissioners have published (April 2001) guidance notes entitled "Guidance Notes for Qualifying Savings Managers in relation to the management of Special Savings Incentive Accounts.

MORTGAGE INTEREST (RELIEF AT SOURCE) REGULATIONS 2001

2001 No 558

ARRANGEMENT OF REGULATIONS

THE REVENUE COMMISSIONERS, IN EXERCISE OF THE POWERS CONFERRED ON THEM BY SECTION 244A OF THE TAXES CONSOLIDATION ACT, 1997 (NO 39 OF 1997), HEREBY MAKE THE FOLLOWING REGULATIONS:

PART 1
GENERAL

1 Citation and commencement

(1) These Regulations may be cited as the Mortgage Interest (Relief at Source) Regulations, 2001.

(2) These Regulations come into operation on 1 January 2002.

Revenue Information

Information Leaflet CG 13 — Mortgage Interest — Tax Relief at Source.

---

2 Interpretation

(1) In these Regulations, except where the context otherwise requires—

"appropriate percentage", **"qualifying lender"**, **"qualifying mortgage interest"**, **"qualifying mortgage loan"** and **"relievable interest"** have the same meanings, respectively, as they have in the principal section;

"principal section" means section 244A (inserted by section 23(1) of the Finance Act, 2001 (No 7 of 2001)) of the Taxes Consolidation Act, 1997 (No 39 of 1997);

"section 244" means section 244 of the Taxes Consolidation Act, 1997;

"section 904F" means section 904F (inserted by section 22(3) of the Finance Act, 2001) of the Taxes Consolidation Act, 1997;

"year" means year of assessment.

(2) A word or expression that is used in these Regulations and is also used in the Income Tax Acts has, except where the context otherwise requires, the same meaning in these Regulations that it has in those Acts.

PART 2
CLAIMS BY QUALIFYING LENDERS

3 Claims by qualifying lenders — introductory

(1) A claim made under subsection (2)(*b*)(ii) of the principal section by a qualifying lender to which payments of qualifying mortgage interest are made for the purpose of recovering amounts from the Revenue Commissioners shall be made in accordance with this Regulation and Regulation 4 of these Regulations.

(2) Before any claim referred to in paragraph (1) of this Regulation can be made, a qualifying lender shall, on a form provided by the Revenue Commissioners for that purpose—

(*a*) designate a person or persons authorised to make claims on behalf of the qualifying lender,

(*b*) provide the signature or signatures of the person or persons referred to in subparagraph (*a*) of this paragraph, and

(*c*) have the form completed and signed by—

(i) where the qualifying lender is a company, the secretary of the company, or

(ii) where the qualifying lender is an unincorporated body, the person who is, or performs the duties of, secretary of the body.

(3) A claim shall be made to the Revenue Commissioners in the manner prescribed in Regulation 4 of these Regulations and shall be in such form and contain such particulars as the Revenue Commissioners may prescribe.

4 Repayment claims by qualifying lenders

(1) The Revenue Commissioners shall establish procedures with each qualifying lender in relation to the making of claims and, without prejudice to the generality of the foregoing, such procedures shall govern the method by which the claim is to be satisfied,

including either or both the debiting by a qualifying lender of a specified bank account set up by the Revenue Commissioners for that purpose and the crediting by the Revenue Commissioners of a bank account within the State nominated by the qualifying lender for that purpose.

(2) The Revenue Commissioners shall pay the amount claimed to the qualifying lender unless they have specific reason to believe that the amount claimed is not due. Where they so believe, they shall pay any lesser amount which they are satisfied is due.

(3) Where the amount paid by the Revenue Commissioners in accordance with paragraph (2) of this Regulation exceeds the amount actually due for the period of the claim, the qualifying lender shall bring the amount of the excess into account in or before the claim next made by that lender after the actual amount has been ascertained. If the amount of that excess exceeds the amount due in respect of the period for which that claim is made—

(*a*) the qualifying lender shall repay the amount of the excess to the Revenue Commissioners with or in advance of the claim, and

(*b*) if the qualifying lender fails to do so, the amount shall be recoverable by the Revenue Commissioners in the same manner as tax charged on the qualifying lender which has become final and conclusive.

(4) Where the amount paid by the Revenue Commissioners in accordance with paragraph (2) of this Regulation is less than the amount actually due for the period of the claim, the qualifying lender shall bring the amount of the shortfall into account in or before the claim next made by that lender after that actual amount has been ascertained. The Revenue Commissioners shall pay the amount of the shortfall claimed to the qualifying lender unless they have specific reason to believe that the amount claimed is not due.

(5) Where—

(*a*) the amount paid by the Revenue Commissioners in accordance with paragraph (2) of this Regulation is less than the amount claimed by the qualifying lender for the period of the claim, and

(*b*) following the payment, the Revenue Commissioners and the qualifying lender agree on so much of the balance, if any, of the amount of the claim that should be paid,

then the Revenue Commissioners shall repay so much of the amount of the balance as is so agreed to the qualifying lender.

5 Validity of claims

(1) The Revenue Commissioners shall be entitled, in respect of any claim under subsection (2)*(b)*(ii) of the principal section, to make all such enquiries as they consider necessary to establish whether a repayment arising from such a claim is or was properly due.

(2) A qualifying lender shall—

(*a*) keep sufficient records to enable the requirements of this Regulation to be satisfied and shall make these available for inspection within the State, and

(*b*) furnish such information about the claim as may reasonably be required.

PART 3
OPERATION OF RELIEF AT SOURCE

6 Transmission of information by Revenue Commissioners to qualifying lenders

Each month, or such other period as agreed between the Revenue Commissioners and the qualifying lenders, the Revenue Commissioners shall furnish a report to each qualifying lender in the format and containing such information as has been agreed between the Revenue Commissioners and that qualifying lender.

7 Obligations and entitlements of borrowers

(1) The entitlement of an individual to deduct and retain an amount from a payment of qualifying mortgage interest referred to in subsection (2)(*a*) of the principal section shall—

(*a*) apply subject to the fulfilment by the individual of the requirements of this Regulation,

(*b*) apply subject to the provisions of Regulations 8 and 9 of these Regulations, and

(*c*) be given effect to by the granting of relief, in such manner as may be agreed with the Revenue Commissioners, by a qualifying lender in accordance with these Regulations.

(2) In order to obtain relief under subsection (2)(*a*) of the principal section, an individual shall, on drawing down a qualifying mortgage loan from a qualifying lender, make a declaration to the Revenue Commissioners on a prescribed form provided for that purpose—

(*a*) that the loan is in respect of the purchase, repair, development or improvement of the individual's sole or main residence, and

(*b*) that the particulars given on the form are correct.

(3) The individual shall also undertake, on the form referred to in paragraph (2) of this Regulation, to notify the Revenue Commissioners whenever any of the following occur, that is—

(*a*) a change in the personal status of the individual, and

(*b*) a change in the status of the property which would affect the amount of relievable interest in relation to the individual.

(4) The completed form shall be sent by the individual to the Revenue Commissioners.

(5) In the case of any individual in respect of whom information has not been furnished by the Revenue Commissioners to a qualifying lender—

(*a*) in accordance with Regulation 6 of these Regulations, or

(*b*) otherwise to like effect prior to the coming into operation of these Regulations,

then the individual shall not be entitled to deduct and retain, out of a payment of qualifying mortgage interest made to a qualifying lender in respect of which relief is due under section 244, an amount equal to the appropriate percentage of the relievable interest.

8 Obligations and entitlements of qualifying lenders

(1) Each month, or such other period as agreed between the Revenue Commissioners and the qualifying lenders, each qualifying lender shall furnish a report to the Revenue Commissioners, in the format and containing such information as has been agreed between the Revenue Commissioners and that qualifying lender.

(2) A qualifying lender shall—

(*a*) for the purpose of granting, in such manner as may be agreed with the Revenue Commissioners, relief under subsection (2)(*a*) of the principal section to an individual having a qualifying mortgage loan from that qualifying lender, and

(*b*) for the purpose of subsection (2)(*b*) of the principal section,

operate on the basis of the information furnished to it by the Revenue Commissioners—

(i) in accordance with Regulation 6 of these Regulations, or

(ii) otherwise to like effect prior to the coming into operation of these Regulations,

and shall be entitled to rely on that information in so doing.

(3) A qualifying lender shall apply a separate designation to each qualifying mortgage loan in respect of which information has been furnished by the Revenue Commissioners—

(*a*) in accordance with Regulation 6 of these Regulations, or

(*b*) otherwise to like effect prior to the coming into operation of these Regulations,

and shall maintain the accounts relating to such loans in a manner which will facilitate the operation of section 904F.

PART 4
MISCELLANEOUS

9 Exclusion of certain loans

(1) Where the loan repayments in relation to a loan included in the most recent report referred to in Regulation 6 of these Regulations which are due to be made and have not been made in respect of a period agreed with the Revenue Commissioners, a qualifying lender shall notify the Revenue Commissioners, in the report referred to in Regulation 8 of these Regulations, in regard to any such loan and shall furnish the following information in relation to each such loan—

(*a*) the name of the individual having the loan, and

(*b*) account identification details relating to the loan.

(2) In relation to any loan in respect of which paragraph (1) of this Regulation applies, such loan shall, on receipt by the qualifying lender of an instruction from the Revenue Commissioners in a report furnished in accordance with Regulation 6 of these Regulations, cease to be a qualifying mortgage loan for the purposes of the principal section.

(3) A loan which would otherwise be a qualifying mortgage loan shall not be such a loan for the purposes of the principal section unless the loan is administered by a qualifying lender in such manner as is agreed by that lender with the Revenue Commissioners.

10 Disposal of qualifying mortgage loans

(1) A qualifying lender which disposes of all or part of its qualifying mortgage loans or an interest therein, but which continues to administer such loans shall continue to be regarded as a qualifying lender for the purposes of the principal section in relation to those loans.

(2) Notwithstanding paragraph (1) of this Regulation, a qualifying lender which so disposes of qualifying mortgage loans or an interest therein may nominate the person to which the loans are disposed (or an agent of such person) to be regarded as the qualifying lender in relation to such loans and that person (or an agent of such person) shall be regarded as a qualifying lender for the purposes of the principal section.

11 Discharge of functions, etc

The Revenue Commissioners may nominate any officer of the Revenue Commissioners to perform any acts and discharge any functions authorised by these Regulations to be performed or discharged by the Revenue Commissioners.

INCOME TAX (EMPLOYMENTS) (CONSOLIDATED) REGULATIONS 2001

2001 No 559

ARRANGEMENT OF REGULATIONS

PART 1
GENERAL

Regulation

PART 2
REGISTER OF EMPLOYERS AND REGISTERS OF EMPLOYEES

PART 3
TAX CREDITS AND STANDARD RATE CUT-OFF POINT

PART 4
DEDUCTION AND REPAYMENT OF TAX

PART 5
PAYMENT AND RECOVERY OF TAX, ETC

PART 6
ASSESSMENT

PART 7
CONTRIBUTIONS BY EMPLOYEES TO CERTAIN SUPERANNUATION FUNDS AND SCHEMES

PART 8
SPECIAL PROVISIONS WHERE EMPLOYEES ARE IN RECEIPT OF OR ARE ENTITLED TO RECEIVE CERTAIN BENEFITS PAYABLE UNDER THE SOCIAL WELFARE ACTS

PART 9
MISCELLANEOUS

THE REVENUE COMMISSIONERS, IN EXERCISE OF THE POWERS CONFERRED ON THEM BY SECTION 986 OF THE TAXES CONSOLIDATION ACT, 1997 (NO 39 OF 1997), HEREBY MAKE THE FOLLOWING REGULATIONS:

PART 1
GENERAL

1 Citation and commencement

(1) These Regulations may be cited as the Income Tax (Employments) (Consolidated) Regulations, 2001.

(2) These Regulations shall come into operation on 1 January 2002.

Cross-references

Employee tax credit: s 472(2)(*a*)(ii).
Social Welfare (Consolidation) Act 1993, section 14(4) (inserted by Social Welfare (Miscellaneous Provisions) Act 2001), payment of contributions and keeping of record; and section 20(3) (as so inserted), regulations for collection of self-employment contributions.
Tax treatment of certain benefits payable under Social Welfare Acts: s 126(7)(*a*).

Revenue Information

Employers Guide to PAYE.
An Employer's Guide to operating PAYE and PRSI on certain benefits is available on Revenue's website (www.revenue.ie) under PAYE/Benefits in Kind.
Information leaflet IT11 — Employees' Guide to PAYE.
Information leaflet IT50 — PAYE/PRSI for small employers — A Revenue Guide.
Information leaflet IT67 — First job — A Guide for First Time Entrants to the PAYE Tax System.
Information leaflet IT69 — eWorking and Tax.
Information leaflet CG2 — Due Dates — Payments and Returns.
Information leaflet CG3 — Payments to the Collector-General.
Information leaflet CG4 — Change of address.
Information leaflet CG6 — P35 — End of Year Returns.
Information leaflet CG7 — Direct Debit PAYE/PRSI.

Tax Briefing

TB58 Dec 2004 pp 8–9 P35 End of Year Return 2004.
TB58 Dec 2004 p 15 — P35 2005 — Employer obligations relating to pension contributions.

2 Interpretation

(1) In these Regulations, except where the context otherwise requires _

"the Act" means the Taxes Consolidation Act, 1997;

"authorised officer" means an officer of the Revenue Commissioners authorised by them in writing for the purposes of these Regulations;

"authorised person" in relation to Regulations 29 and 30, means an employer who has been authorised in writing by the Collector-General for the purposes of Regulation 29 and, **"authorise"**, **"authorised"** and **"authorisation"** shall be construed accordingly;

"certificate of tax credits and standard rate cut-off point" has the meaning specified in paragraph (2) of Regulation 11;

"Collector-General" means the Collector-General appointed under section 851 of the Act;

"cumulative emoluments" in relation to any date means the sum of all payments of emoluments made by the employer to the employee from the beginning of the year up to and including that date;

"cumulative gross tax" means the sum of cumulative tax due at the standard rate of tax and cumulative tax due at the higher rate of tax;

"cumulative standard rate cut-off point" in relation to any date means the sum of the standard rate cut-off point from the beginning of the year up to and including that date as specified on the employee's tax deduction card;

"cumulative tax" means cumulative gross tax less cumulative tax credits;

"cumulative tax credits" in relation to any date means the sum of the tax credits from the beginning of the year up to and including that date as specified on the employee's tax deduction card;

"cumulative tax due at higher rate of tax" in relation to any date means tax due at the higher rate of tax in respect of the cumulative emoluments to that date to the extent that they exceed the cumulative standard rate cut-off point to that date as specified on the employee's tax deduction card;

"cumulative tax due at standard rate of tax" in relation to any date means tax due by reference to the standard rate of tax for the year in respect of the cumulative emoluments, to that date, up to the amount of the cumulative standard rate cut-off point to that date as specified on the employee's tax deduction card;

"domestic employee" means an employee who is employed solely on domestic duties (including the minding of children) in the employer's private dwelling house;

"domestic employment" means employment by reference to which an employee is a domestic employee;

"emoluments" means emoluments to which Chapter 4 of Part 42 of the Act applies;

"employee" means any person in receipt of emoluments;

"employer" means any person paying emoluments;

"general tax credit" has the same meaning as in section 3 of the Act;

"higher rate of tax" means the rate of income tax known by that description and provided for in section 15 of the Act;

"income tax month" means a calendar month;

"inspector" means an inspector of taxes;

[**"notional payment"** has the meaning assigned to it by subsection (2) of section 985A (inserted by the Finance Act 2003) of the Act;][1]

"personal public service number" has the same meaning as in section 223 of the Social Welfare (Consolidation) Act, 1993;

"personal tax credit" has the same meaning as in section 3 of the Act;

"prescribed" means prescribed by the Revenue Commissioners;

"reliefs from income tax" means allowances, deductions and tax credits;

"standard rate cut-off point" in relation to an employee, means the standard rate cut-off point advised by the inspector on the certificate of tax credits and standard rate cut-off point;

"standard rate of tax" means the rate of income tax known by that description and provided for in section 15 of the Act;

"tax credits" in relation to an employee means the appropriate amount of personal tax credits and general tax credits to which the employee is entitled under the Act;

[**"temporary tax deduction form"** means any form as may be prescribed on which particulars of emoluments paid and the aggregate of —

(i) tax deducted from those emoluments and,

(ii) tax which was not so deducted, but which was remitted by the employer under section 985A(4) of the Principal Act in relation to notional payments,

are to be recorded by the employer pending receipt of a tax deduction card;

"total net tax deducted" means, in relation to the emoluments paid to any employee during any period, the aggregate of —

(i) the total tax deducted from those emoluments, and

(ii) tax which was not so deducted but which was remitted by the employer for that period under section 985A(4) of the Principal Act in relation to notional payments,

less any tax repaid to the employee;][2]

"year" means year of assessment.

[(1A) In these Regulations, except where the context otherwise requires —

(*a*) references to a payment of emoluments shall include references to notional payments in respect of emoluments, and

(*b*) references to tax deducted or to be deducted, or to a requirement to deduct tax, from a payment of emoluments shall include references to —

(i) tax deducted or to be deducted, or to a requirement to deduct tax, from the payment, and

(ii) tax remitted or to be remitted, or a requirement to remit tax, under section 985A(4) of the Principal Act,

in respect of notional payments, as the circumstances may require,

and cognate words shall be construed accordingly .][3]

(2) A word or expression that is used in these Regulations and is also used in the Income Tax Acts has, except where the context otherwise requires, the same meaning in these Regulations that it has in those Acts.

Amendments

1 Definition of "notional payment" inserted by Income Tax (Employments) Regulations 2003 (SI No 613 of 2003) reg 2(*a*)(i)(I) with effect from 1 January 2004.

2 Definitions of "temporary tax deduction form" and "total net tax deducted" substituted by Income Tax (Employments) Regulations 2003 (SI No 613 of 2003) reg 2(*a*)(i)(II) with effect from 1 January 2004.

3 Para (1A) inserted by Income Tax (Employments) Regulations 2003 (SI No 613 of 2003) reg 2(*a*)(ii) with effect from 1 January 2004.

Revenue Information

Penalties for breach of regulations: s 987(4)(*c*).

Registration of certain persons as employers and requirement to sent certain notifications: s 988(1).

3 Intermediate employers

(1) Where an employee works under the general control and management of a person who is not his or her immediate employer, that person (referred to hereafter in this Regulation as the "principal employer") shall be deemed to be the employer for thc purposes of these Regulations, and the immediate employer shall furnish the principal employer with such particulars of the employee's emoluments as may be necessary to enable the principal employer to comply with the provisions of these Regulations.

(2) If the employee's emoluments are actually paid to him or her by the immediate employer—

(*a*) the immediate employer shall be notified by the principal employer of the amount of tax to be deducted or repaid when the emoluments are paid to the employee, and shall deduct or repay accordingly the amount so notified, and

(*b*) the principal employer shall make a corresponding deduction or addition on making to the immediate employer the payment out of which the said emoluments will be paid.

4 Liability for payment of deduction and entitlement to payment of repayment

Persons who are required to make any deduction or repayment referred to in these Regulations shall, in the case of a deduction (whether or not made), be accountable for the amount of the tax, and liable to pay that amount, to the Revenue Commissioners and shall, in the case of a repayment, be entitled, if it has been made, to be paid it, or given credit for it, by the Revenue Commissioners.

5 Powers of inspector

Anything which is authorised or required by these Regulations to be done by the inspector shall be done by such inspector as the Revenue Commissioners may direct.

6 Service by post

Any notice, notification, certificate, requirement or tax deduction card which is authorised or required to be given, served, made, sent or issued under these Regulations may be sent by post.

PART 2
REGISTER OF EMPLOYERS AND REGISTERS OF EMPLOYEES

7 Register of employers

(1) (*a*) Every employer who makes a payment of emoluments to or on behalf of an employee at a rate exceeding a rate equivalent to a rate of €8 a week, or, in the case of an employee with other employment, €2 a week, shall send to the Revenue Commissioners a notification of his or her name and address and of the fact that he or she is paying such emoluments.

(*b*) In the case of an employee paid monthly or at longer intervals, the references in subparagraph (*a*) of this paragraph to a rate of €8 a week and a rate of €2 a week shall be treated as references to a rate of €36 a month and a rate of €9 a month respectively.

(2) Where a change occurs in a name or address which has been notified under this Regulation, the employer shall send to the Revenue Commissioners a notification of the change.

(3) An employer who is liable to send a notification under this Regulation shall do so within the period of 9 days beginning on the day on which the employer becomes so liable.

(4) The Revenue Commissioners shall keep and maintain a register in which names and addresses notified to them under this Regulation shall be registered and, when any name or address has been registered, they shall give notice of the registration to the employer.

Cross-references

Penalties for breach of regulations: s 987(4)(c).

Registration of certain persons as employers and requirement to send certain notification: s 988(1).

8 Registers of employees

(1) Every employer who in any year makes to an employee or employees such payments of emoluments as are referred to in Regulation 7 shall keep and maintain in respect of such employee or employees throughout the year (or throughout the part or parts of a year during which such payments of emoluments are made) a register for that year on the prescribed form.

(2) Where a register is kept and maintained under this Regulation —

(*a*) the employer shall enter in the register, in relation to each employee, the particulars indicated by the form of the register as being required to be entered therein, and

(*b*) the employer, on being required to do so by the Revenue Commissioners by notice, shall deliver the register to the Revenue Commissioners within the period specified in the notice.

9 Domestic employments

Regulations 7 and 8 shall not apply to an employer (being an individual) who pays emoluments to an employee engaged by that employer in a domestic employment where—

(*a*) the emoluments from that employment are less than €40 per week, and
(*b*) the employer has only one such employee.

PART 3
TAX CREDITS AND STANDARD RATE CUT-OFF POINT

10 Determination of appropriate tax credits and standard rate cut-off point by inspector

(1) The amount of the tax credits and standard rate cut-off point appropriate to an employee for any year shall be determined by the inspector who for that purpose may have regard to any of the following matters, namely_

(*a*) the reliefs from income tax to which the employee is entitled for the year in which the amount of the tax credits and standard rate cut-off point is determined, so far as the employee's title to those reliefs has been established at the time of the determination, but, where the amount of the tax credits and standard rate cut-off point is determined before the beginning of the year for which it is to have effect, the inspector shall disregard any such relief from income tax if he or she is not satisfied that the employee will be entitled to it for that year;
(*b*) the emoluments of the employee;
(*c*) where the employee has income (other than emoluments in relation to which the amount of the tax credits and standard rate cut-off point is being determined) the tax credits and standard rate cut-off point appropriate to that employee may be adjusted as necessary to collect the tax due on such income;
(*d*) where the employee is entitled to reliefs from income tax at the higher rate of tax, the tax credits and standard rate cut-off point appropriate to that employee may be adjusted as necessary to give effect to the relief;
(*e*) any tax overpaid for any previous year which has not been repaid;
(*f*) any tax remaining unpaid for any previous year which is not otherwise recovered;
(*g*) such other adjustments as may be necessary to secure that, so far as possible, the tax in respect of the employee's emoluments for the year to which the tax credits and standard rate cut-off point relate shall be deducted from the emoluments paid during the year.

(2) When an employee requests the inspector to disregard any particular relief or income referred to in subparagraph (*a*) or (*c*) of the foregoing paragraph, the inspector shall disregard it for the purposes of that paragraph.

(3) The inspector may disregard part or all of any expenses in respect of which the employee may be entitled to relief from income tax if it is impracticable to take account of all those expenses in determining the appropriate amount of tax credits and standard rate cut-off point, and, where he or she does so, shall direct the employer to disregard an equivalent amount of the employee's emoluments in calculating the tax to be deducted or repaid when any payment of emoluments is made to the employee.

Cross-references
Electronic claims: s 864A(8).

---

11 Notice of determination of tax credits and standard rate cut-off point

(1) After the inspector has determined the amount of the tax credits and standard rate cut-off point for any year in accordance with Regulation 10, he or she shall send notice of his or her determination to the employee.

(2) The inspector shall send to the employer of the employee either a certificate (in these Regulations referred to as a "certificate of tax credits and standard rate cut-off point"), or a tax deduction card incorporating a certificate of tax credits and standard rate cut-off point, certifying the amount of the tax credits and standard rate cut-off point of the employee as determined by the inspector.

(3) If it appears to the inspector that the employee has more than one employment, he or she shall send, in respect of each employment, to the employer a separate certificate of tax credits and standard rate cut-off point or a separate tax deduction card, as appropriate, showing the tax credits and standard rate cut-off point applicable to the particular employment, but the aggregate amount of the tax credits and standard rate cut-off point on the separate certificates of tax credits and standard rate cut-off point or separate tax deduction cards, as the case may be, shall not exceed the total amount of the tax credits and standard rate cut-off point of the employee for the year.

12 Objection and appeal against amount of tax credits and standard rate cut-off point

(1) If the employee is aggrieved by the inspector's determination, he or she may give notice in writing of his or her objection to the inspector, stating the grounds of the objection, within 21 days of the date on which the determination was notified to him or her.

(2) On receipt of the notice of objection, the inspector may amend his or her determination by agreement with the employee, and in default of such agreement the employee, on giving notice in writing to the inspector, may appeal to the Appeal Commissioners.

(3) The Appeal Commissioners on appeal shall determine either or both the amount of tax credits and standard rate cut-off point having regard to the same matters as the inspector may have regard to when the amount of the tax credits and standard rate cut-off point is determined by the inspector, and, subject to the provisions of Regulation 13, their determination shall be final.

(4) Where either or both the amount of the tax credits and standard rate cut-off point is amended, either by the inspector or by the Appeal Commissioners, the inspector shall send to the employee a notice of the new determination.

(5) A certificate of tax credits and standard rate cut-off point or a tax deduction card appropriate to the amount of the tax credits and standard rate cut-off point of an employee as determined by the inspector may be issued to the employer, notwithstanding that the inspector's determination is the subject of an objection or appeal.

(6) An appeal under this Regulation may be heard and determined by one Appeal Commissioner.

13 Amendments of amount of tax credits and standard rate cut-off point

(1) If either or both the amount of tax credits and standard rate cut-off point is found not to be appropriate because the actual circumstances are different from the circumstances by reference to which it was determined by the inspector or the Appeal Commissioners, the inspector may, and if so required by the employee shall, by reference to the actual circumstances, amend, by way of increase or reduction, the previous determination.

(2) After the inspector has amended the determination of the amount of tax credits and standard rate cut-off point, he or she shall give notice of the new determination to the employee not later than the date on which a new certificate of tax credits and standard rate cut-off point or new tax deduction card, as the case may be, is sent to the employer under Regulation 14.

(3) The provisions of Regulation 12 regarding objections and appeals shall apply in relation to the amended determination as they applied in relation to the previous determination.

Cross-references

Electronic claims: s 864A(8).

14 Notice to employer of amended amount of tax credits and standard rate cut-off point

Where a determination of the inspector or of the Appeal Commissioners is amended after a certificate of tax credits and standard rate cut-off point or tax deduction card has been issued, the inspector shall send to the employer, and the employer shall thereafter use, such new certificate of tax credits and standard rate cut-off point or tax deduction card, as may be appropriate.

15 Special provisions for notices and certificates

(1) A determination of the amount of the tax credits and standard rate cut-off point appropriate to an employee for any year under paragraph (1) of Regulation 10 shall, if the inspector deems it proper, have effect for each subsequent year as if a separate determination had been duly made for each such year.

(2) Where the inspector has made a determination of the amount of the tax credits and standard rate cut-off point and the determination is to have effect for each subsequent year under the provisions of paragraph (1) of this Regulation, the notice of determination and the certificate or certificates of tax credits and standard rate cut-off point shall state that the amount of tax credits and standard rate cut-off point indicated thereon shall have effect for that year and for each subsequent year.

(3) The provisions of paragraph (2) of this Regulation shall not preclude an employee from requiring the inspector to determine the amount of the tax credits and standard rate cut-off point for any of the years after the first year included in a notice issued in accordance with the provisions of that paragraph and to send to the employee concerned a notice of such determination, and the provisions of Regulation 12 shall apply to any such determination.

(4) The provisions of Regulation 13 shall apply in relation to each year after the first year included in a notice, certificate or certificates issued under paragraph (2) of this Regulation as they apply in relation to the first year.

(5) The provisions of paragraphs (3) and (4) of this Regulation shall, with the necessary modifications, apply to any new determination of the amount of the tax credits and standard rate cut-off point for any year under Regulation 12 or Regulation 13 as if it were a determination under paragraph (1) of Regulation 10.

PART 4
DEDUCTION AND REPAYMENT OF TAX

16 General provision for deductions and repayments

On payment of emoluments referred to in Regulation 7, deductions or repayments of tax shall be made subject to, and in accordance with, the subsequent provisions of this Part of these Regulations.

16A Deduction of tax in respect of notional payments

[The obligation on an employer to deduct tax in respect of a notional payment shall have effect as an obligation to deduct tax due on that payment from any payment or payments of emoluments actually made by the employer to or on behalf of the employee on—

(*a*) the day the notional payment is made, or

(*b*) if there is no actual payment of emoluments made to the employee on that day, the next pay day following the time when the notional payment is made,

and where, by reason of an insufficiency of payments of emoluments actually made to or on behalf of the employee, the employer is liable to remit under section 985A(4) of the Principal Act an amount of income tax which the employer was unable to deduct from such payments, the employer shall be liable to remit that amount of tax to the Revenue Commissioners as if the amount to be remitted had been deducted in accordance with this Regulation.][1]

Amendments

1 Reg 16A inserted by Income Tax (Employments) Regulations 2003 (SI No 613 of 2003) reg 2(*b*) with effect from 1 January 2004.

16B Tax borne by the employer in respect of notional payments

[Where tax in respect of a notional payment is remitted by the employer in accordance with subsection (4) of section 985A of the Principal Act and subsection (5) of that section applies, the notional payment in respect of the emolument referred to in that subsection (5) shall be treated as if it were made on 31 March in the year of assessment in which the emolument is treated as arising.][1]

Amendments

1 Reg 16B inserted by Income Tax (Employments) Regulations 2003 (SI No 613 of 2003) reg 2(*b*) with effect from 1 January 2004.

17 Calculation and making of deduction or repayment where tax deduction card held

(1) On any payment of emoluments to or on behalf of an employee in respect of whom the employer holds a tax deduction card, the employer, except where these Regulations otherwise provide, shall ascertain—

(*a*) firstly, the cumulative emoluments of that employee at the date of the payment,

(*b*) secondly, by reference to the cumulative standard rate cut-off point specified on the tax deduction card corresponding to the date of payment, the cumulative gross tax in respect of the cumulative emoluments, and

(*c*) finally, by reference to the cumulative tax credits specified on the tax deduction card corresponding to the date of payment, the cumulative tax in respect of the cumulative emoluments.

(2) If the cumulative tax ascertained in accordance with paragraph (1) of this Regulation, exceeds the cumulative tax corresponding to the employee's cumulative emoluments at the date of the last preceding payment of emoluments (hereafter in this Regulation referred to as the "previous cumulative tax"), the employer shall deduct the excess from the emoluments on making the payment in question.

(3) If the cumulative tax as so ascertained is less than the previous cumulative tax, the employer shall repay the difference to the employee on making the payment in question.

(4) If the cumulative tax is equal to the previous cumulative tax, no tax shall be either deducted or repaid when the payment in question is made.

(5) Where the payment in question is the first payment in the year, paragraphs (2), (3) and (4) of this Regulation shall not apply, but the employer shall deduct the cumulative tax as ascertained in accordance with paragraph (1) of this Regulation from the emoluments on making the payment in question.

(6) The employer shall record, either on the tax deduction card or in such other form as may be authorised by the Revenue Commissioners, the following particulars regarding every payment of emoluments which the employer makes to or on behalf of the employee, namely —

(*a*) the date of the payment;

(*b*) the gross amount of the emoluments;

(*c*) in relation to the date of payment—

(i) the cumulative emoluments;

(ii) the cumulative tax due at the standard rate of tax;

(iii) the cumulative tax due at the higher rate of tax; and

(iv) the cumulative gross tax;

(*d*) the corresponding cumulative tax; and

(*e*) the amount of tax, if any, deducted or repaid on making the payment.

17A Deduction of tax in respect of certain notional payments

[(1) This Regulation applies to emoluments being—

(*a*) the benefit of the private use of a car which is chargeable to tax by virtue of section 121 of the Act, (*b*) the benefit of the private use of a van which is chargeable to tax by virtue of section 121A of the Act,

(*c*) the benefit arising from a preferential loan which is treated as a perquisite for the purposes of section 112 by virtue of section 122 of the Act, or

(*d*) a benefit arising from an asset which belongs to the employer and the valuation of which is determined in accordance with subsection (3) of section 119 of the Act.

(2) Where, a notional payment for a year is in respect of an emolument to which this Regulation applies—

(*a*) the amount of the notional payment for the year in relation to the emolument shall be apportioned over the period (referred to in subparagraph (*b*) as the "period of benefit") for which the benefit is available in that year, and

(*b*) the employer shall deduct tax in accordance with this Part of these Regulations or remit tax under section 985A(4) of the Principal Act by reference to the part of the notional payment for the year apportioned to each week, where the employee is paid weekly, or month, where the employee is paid monthly, in the period of benefit.][1]

Amendments

1 Reg 17A inserted by Income Tax (Employments) Regulations 2003 (SI No 613 of 2003) reg 2(*c*) with effect from 1 January 2004.

18 Subsidiary emoluments of employee paid monthly, etc

(1) If the employer makes a payment in respect of overtime or other extra earnings to or on behalf of an employee whose main emoluments are paid monthly, and that payment is made at an earlier date in the income tax month than the date on which the main emoluments are paid, the employer shall repay no tax to the employee on the occasion of that payment, notwithstanding that tax may be repayable under the provisions of Regulation 17, but in such a case, that Regulation shall have effect as if that payment was made on the same date in that income tax month as the date on which the main emoluments are paid.

(2) The provisions of this Regulation shall apply with the necessary modifications to payments in respect of overtime or other extra earnings which are made to or on behalf of an employee whose main emoluments are paid at intervals greater than a month.

19 Deduction in special cases

(1) This Regulation applies to —

(*a*) payments of emoluments made on 31 December in any year or, if that year is a leap year, on 30 or 31 December in that year, to an employee who is paid weekly;

(*b*) payments of emoluments made to or on behalf of an employee after he or she has ceased to be employed by the person making the payments; and

(*c*) any other payments of emoluments made to or on behalf of any employee to which the inspector directs that this Regulation shall apply.

(2) Regulation 17 shall not apply to payments of emoluments to which this Regulation applies, and on making any such payment the employer shall deduct therefrom_

(*a*) by reference to the amount of the employee's tax credits and standard rate cut-off point, the amount of tax which would have been deductible therefrom if the payment had been made on the preceding 1 January or,

(*b*) where the employee has ceased to be employed by the employer and no deduction card is held, tax in accordance with paragraph (2) of Regulation 22.

(3) On making any such payment as mentioned in paragraph (1) of this Regulation, the employer shall record either on the tax deduction card or in such other form as may be authorised by the Revenue Commissioners—

(*a*) the date of the payment,

(*b*) the gross amount of the emoluments,

(*c*) the amount of the appropriate tax credits and standard rate cut-off point, and

(*d*) the amount of tax (if any) deducted on making the payment.

(4) Where the employee has ceased to be employed by the employer and no tax deduction card is held, the particulars referred to in paragraph (3) of this Regulation, except the amounts of the tax credits and standard rate cut-off point, shall be recorded on the emergency card referred to in Regulation 22.

20 Change of employment where certificate of tax credits and standard rate cut-off point or tax deduction card held

(1) If an employer ceases to employ an employee in respect of whom a certificate of tax credits and standard rate cut-off point or tax deduction card has been issued to him or her, he or she shall immediately send to the inspector by whom the certificate of tax credits and standard rate cut-off point or tax deduction card was issued a certificate on the prescribed form containing the following particulars:

(*a*) the name of the employee;

(*b*) the date on which the employment ceased;

(*c*) the week or income tax month in respect of which the last payment of emoluments was recorded on the tax deduction card and the cumulative emoluments at the date of that payment;

and any other particulars as to tax credits and standard rate cut-off point, tax or any other matters which are indicated by such form as being required to be entered thereon.

(2) The employer shall make on the prescribed form 2 copies of the certificate required by paragraph (1) of this Regulation and shall deliver them to the employee on the date the employment ceases.

(3) Immediately on commencing his or her next employment the employee shall deliver to the new employer the 2 copies of the certificate prepared by the former employer and, subject to the provisions of paragraph (4) of this Regulation, the following provisions shall have effect:

(*a*) the new employer shall insert on one copy of the certificate the address of the employee, the date on which the new employment commenced, and the manner in which payment of emoluments is made to the employee, that is to say, weekly, monthly or as the case may be, and shall immediately send that copy to the inspector by whom certificates of tax credits and standard rate cut-off point or tax deduction cards are ordinarily issued to the employer;

(*b*) the inspector shall send to the new employer a certificate of tax credits and standard rate cut-off point or tax deduction card, as appropriate, for the employee;

(*c*) pending the receipt of the certificate of tax credits and standard rate cut-off point or tax deduction card from the inspector, the new employer shall prepare a temporary tax deduction form and, in relation to payments of emoluments by him or her, record on it —

(i) the date of payment,

(ii) the gross amount of emoluments, and

(iii) as respects each week or income tax month (as may be appropriate), the tax credits and standard rate cut-off point for Week 1 or Month 1 as specified on the copies of the certificate prepared by the former employer,

and having regard to the standard rate cut-off point as specified on the copies of the certificate prepared by the former employer, the new employer shall deduct tax on the aggregate amount of the emoluments for the week or income tax month (as may be appropriate) by reference to the tax due at the standard rate of tax and the higher rate of tax (as may be appropriate) on such emoluments reduced by the tax credits for Week 1 or Month 1 as specified on the copies of the certificate prepared by the former employer;

(*d*) when the new employer has received a certificate of tax credits and standard rate cut-off point or tax deduction card from the inspector, he or she shall, having ascertained the aggregate of the amounts of the emoluments and the aggregate of the amounts of the tax by reference to the relevant entries on the copies of the certificate prepared by the former employer and on the temporary tax deduction form (if any), record on the tax deduction card or such other record as may be authorised those aggregates, and those aggregates shall be deemed respectively to be the cumulative emoluments paid and the cumulative tax deducted by him or her.

(4) (*a*) Where the 2 copies of the certificate prepared by the former employer show that the last payment of emoluments was in the year preceding that in which the new employment commences, the new employer shall comply with the provisions of paragraph (3) of this Regulation with the modification that he or she shall not record, or have regard to, the cumulative emoluments and cumulative tax shown on the copies of the certificate.

(*b*) Where the 2 copies of the certificate prepared by the former employer show that the last payment of emoluments was in a year earlier than the year preceding that in which the new employment commences, the new employer shall comply with the provisions of subparagraph (*a*) of paragraph (3) of this Regulation but deduct tax from each payment of emoluments made by him or her to the employee, and keep records on the emergency card referred to in Regulation 22, as if those payments had been payments to which paragraph (2) of that Regulation applied.

(5) If the new employer ceases to employ the employee before he or she receives a certificate of tax credits and standard rate cut-off point or tax deduction card from the inspector, he or she shall comply with the provisions of paragraphs (1) and (2) of this Regulation as if a certificate of tax credits and standard rate cut-off point or tax

deduction card in respect of the employee had been issued to him or her by the inspector, but —

(*a*) for the purposes of subparagraph (*c*) of paragraph (1) of this Regulation, the cumulative emoluments shall be taken to be the aggregate of the cumulative emoluments shown on the copies of the certificate prepared by the former employer and the gross emoluments paid by the new employer; and

(*b*) where, as respects the certificate on the prescribed form referred to in that paragraph (1), entry of particulars of the cumulative tax is required to be made thereon, that tax shall be taken for the purposes of that entry to be the aggregate of the cumulative tax shown on those copies and any tax deducted by the new employer.

(6) If the employee objects to the disclosure to the new employer of his or her cumulative emoluments, he or she may deliver the 2 copies of the certificate prepared by the former employer to the inspector before he or she commences his or her new employment, and the inspector shall send in respect of the employee to the new employer a certificate of tax credits and standard rate cut-off point or tax deduction card not stating the employee's cumulative tax credits and standard rate cut-off point or cumulative emoluments and direct that Regulation 19 shall apply to all payments of emoluments which the new employer makes to or on behalf of the employee.

(7) Retirement on pension shall not be treated as a cessation of employment for the purposes of this Regulation or of Regulation 19 if the emoluments are paid by the same person both before and after the retirement.

Cross-references

Power of inspection, PAYE: s 903(1)("records").

21 Death of employee

(1) On the death of an employee in respect of whom an employer holds a certificate of tax credits and standard rate cut-off point or tax deduction card or in respect of whom a temporary tax deduction form has been prepared by the employer under subparagraph (*c*) of paragraph (3) of Regulation 20 or to whom the provisions of paragraph (2) of Regulation 22 apply, the employer shall immediately send to the inspector by whom certificates of tax credits and standard rate cut-off point or tax deduction cards are ordinarily issued to the employer the certificate (relating to cessation of employment) mentioned in paragraph (1) of Regulation 20 or in paragraph (6) of Regulation 22, as the case may require, and shall insert thereon the name and address of the personal representative of the deceased employee, if they are known to the employer.

(2) If any emoluments are paid by the employer after the date of the employee's death in respect of his or her employment with the employer, the employer shall, on making any such payment, deduct or repay tax as if the deceased employee was still in the employer's employment at the date of the payment, and—

(*a*) if the amount of those emoluments and the date on which they will be paid are known at the time the certificate mentioned in paragraph (1) of this Regulation is completed, the employer shall include thereon the amount of the emoluments, the date on which they will be paid, and the amount of tax which will be deducted or repaid, and

(*b*) in any other case, the employer shall indicate on the certificate that a further payment of emoluments will be made.

22 Emergency basis of deduction

(1) If the employer makes such payments of emoluments as are referred to in Regulation 7 to or on behalf of an employee in respect of whom the employer has not received either a certificate of tax credits and standard rate cut-off point, a tax deduction card or copies of a certificate made by a former employer under paragraph (2) of Regulation 20, the employer on the occasion of the first such payment, shall immediately send to the inspector, by whom certificates of tax credits and standard rate cut-off point or tax deduction cards are ordinarily issued to the employer, a return stating the name and address of the employee, the date on which his or her employment commenced, and such other particulars as may be necessary to secure the issue to the employer of the appropriate certificate of tax credits and standard rate cut-off point or tax deduction card.

[(2) (*a*) Until a certificate of tax credits and standard rate cut-off point or a tax deduction card is received from the inspector, the employer, on making any payment of emoluments to or on behalf of an employee referred to in paragraph (1) of this Regulation, shall deduct tax from such payment in accordance with the following provisions of this paragraph.

(*b*) Subject to subparagraph (*c*) of this paragraph—

(i) during the period of 4 weeks, or in the case of an employee paid monthly, 1 month, from the day on which the employee first holds an employment with the employer in a year, or until the certificate of tax credits and standard rate cut-off point or a tax deduction card is received from the inspector, the employer shall deduct tax at the standard rate of tax and, where appropriate, the higher rate of tax and keep records on an emergency card on the basis that the amount of —

(I) the tax credit is an amount per week equal to one fifty-second of the basic personal tax credit specified in section 461 of the Act, as it applies for that year, or if the employee is paid monthly, an amount equal to one-twelfth of that tax credit, and

(II) the standard rate cut-off point is an amount per week equal to one fifty-second of the amount chargeable to tax at the standard rate specified in Part 1 of the Table to section 15 of the Act, as it applies for that year, or if the employee is paid monthly, one-twelfth of that amount,

and in determining the amount of any tax credits or the standard rate cut-off point under clause (I) or (II) of this subparagraph any part of a euro shall be treated as a whole euro,

(ii) if, within the period of 4 weeks or 1 month referred to in subparagraph (*b*)(i) of this paragraph, the employer has not received the certificate of tax credits and standard rate cut-off point or a tax deduction card, the employer shall, until a certificate of tax credits and standard rate cut-off point or a tax deduction card is received from the inspector, keep records on an emergency card and on the making of any payment of emoluments to or on behalf of the employee deduct tax on the basis that the employee's tax credits are nil and in accordance with the following provisions, that is to say—

(I) in the period of 4 weeks or, in a case where the employee is paid monthly, 1 month, commencing on the day after the end of the period mentioned in subparagraph (*b*)(i) of this paragraph, deduct tax at the standard rate of tax and, where appropriate, the higher rate of tax on the basis that the standard rate cut-off point is the amount referred to in subparagraph (*b*)(i)(II) of this paragraph, and

(II) thereafter deduct tax at the higher rate of tax.

(*c*) In the case of an employee who first holds an employment with an employer on or after 1 January, 2003 and for whom the employer has not been provided with the employee's personal public service number, the provisions of subparagraph (*b*) of this paragraph shall not apply until such time as that number is provided to the employer and the employer shall, until such time, on making any payments of emoluments to or on behalf of the employee, deduct tax at the higher rate of tax and maintain records on an emergency card on the basis that the employee's tax credits are nil.

(2A) Where, for the purposes of this Regulation, an employee furnishes the employer with his or her personal public service number, the employer shall take all reasonable measures to establish that the number furnished is in fact the personal public service number of that employee.][1]

(3) For the purposes of paragraph 2 of this Regulation—

(*a*) all employments which the employee holds with the employer in a year of assessment shall be deemed to be one employment, and

(*b*) that employment, notwithstanding that for a part or parts of the year the employee does not hold an employment with the employer, shall be deemed to be held for a continuous period commencing on the day on which the employee first holds an employment with the employer in that year and ending on the day on which the employee last holds an employment with the employer in that year.

(4) Where the inspector sends a certificate of tax credits and standard rate cut-off point or tax deduction card the employer shall enter on the tax deduction card or such other record as may be authorised the particulars of emoluments and tax deducted as shown on the relevant emergency card.

(5) On making payments of emoluments to or on behalf of the employee after a certificate of tax credits and standard rate cut-off point or tax deduction card relating to the employee sent under paragraph (4) of this Regulation has been received, the following provisions shall have effect for the purposes of Regulation 17 —

(*a*) any cumulative emoluments notified to the employer by the inspector shall be entered by the employer on the tax deduction card and shall be treated as if they represented emoluments paid by the employer, and (*b*) the cumulative tax before the first of the said payments shall be taken to be the sum of any cumulative tax notified to the employer by the inspector and entered by the employer on the tax deduction card and any tax which the employer was liable to deduct from the employee's emoluments under paragraph (2) of this Regulation.

(6) (*a*) Where paragraph (2) of this Regulation applies and the employer ceases to employ the employee before a certificate of tax credits and standard rate cut-off point or tax deduction card in respect of the employee has been received, the employer shall immediately send to the inspector a certificate on the form prescribed for the purposes of paragraph (1) of Regulation 20 and shall make on the prescribed form 2 copies of that certificate which the employer shall deliver to the employee on the date the employment ceases and the said certificate —

(i) shall not contain particulars of the cumulative emoluments or cumulative tax but shall contain particulars of the emoluments paid and tax deducted by the employer, and

(ii) shall indicate that an emergency card was in use when the employment ceased.

(*b*) Immediately on commencing his or her next employment the employee shall deliver to his or her new employer the 2 copies of the certificate referred to above and the new employer —

(i) shall insert on one copy of the certificate the address of the employee, the date on which the new employment commenced, and the manner in which payments of emoluments are made to the employee, that is to say, weekly, monthly or as the case may be, and

(ii) immediately send that copy to the inspector by whom certificates of tax credits and standard rate cut-off point or tax deduction cards are ordinarily issued to him or her,

and paragraphs (2), (3), (4) and (5) of this Regulation shall apply as if the employee had not submitted to the new employer copies of a certificate by a former employer under paragraph (2) of Regulation 20.

(7) This Regulation shall not apply where —

(*a*) the employee performs the duties of his or her employment wholly outside the State, or

(*b*) the employee is outside the State and the emoluments are paid outside the State.

(8) In this Regulation "emergency card" means a card in the form prescribed for the purposes of this Regulation.

Amendments

1 Subs (2) substituted and subs (2A) inserted by Income Tax (Employments) Regulations 2002 (SI 511 of 2002) reg 3(*a*) with effect from 1 January 2003.

Cross-references

Approved retirement fund: s 784A(4)(*c*)(ii)(II).

Tax Briefing

TB50 Oct 2002 p 17 — Emergency Basis of Tax — PAYE.

23 Emoluments not paid weekly or monthly

Where emoluments are paid at regular intervals other than regular intervals of a week or a month, any payment of such emoluments shall be deemed for the purposes of these Regulations to be made on the date on which it would have been made if a payment had been made on the last day of the preceding year, but the employer shall record the actual date of every such payment.

24 Aggregation of emoluments in non-cumulative cases

Where under these Regulations tax is deductible otherwise than by reference to cumulative emoluments and cumulative tax, the amount of tax to be deducted in any week or income tax month shall be calculated by reference to the aggregate of the emoluments paid to or on behalf of the employee in that week or month.

25 Tax-free emoluments

Where the employer makes a payment to or for the benefit of the employee in respect of his or her tax, the amount of the emoluments which the employer pays to or on behalf of the employee shall be deemed for the purposes of deduction and repayment of tax under these Regulations to be such a sum as will include the amount assessable on the employee in respect of the payment made by the employer in respect of the employee's tax.

26 Repayment during sickness and unemployment

(1) If, owing to the absence from work through sickness or other similar cause, the employee is entitled to receive no emoluments on the usual pay day, the employer shall, on application being made in person by the employee or his or her authorised representative, make such repayment of tax to the employee as may be appropriate, having regard to his or her cumulative emoluments at the date of the pay day in question and the corresponding cumulative tax.

(2) If, owing to absence from work otherwise than mentioned in paragraph (1) of this Regulation, the employee is entitled to receive no emoluments on the usual pay day, the employer either—

(*a*) shall make any such repayment of tax to the employee as would be appropriate under paragraph (1) if the absence from work was due to sickness, or

(*b*) not later than the first usual pay day on which no emoluments will be payable to the employee, shall send, to the inspector by whom certificates of tax credits and standard rate cut-off point or tax deduction cards are ordinarily issued to the employer, a notification of the employee's absence from work and of the employer's intention to make no repayment to the employee under subparagraph (*a*) of this paragraph, together with a return containing the same particulars with respect to the employee as the employer would be liable to certify under paragraph (1) of Regulation 20 if the employment had ceased on the day on which emoluments were last paid to or on behalf of the employee.

(3) Where the notification and return referred to in subparagraph (*b*) of paragraph (2) of this Regulation are sent within the time limited by that subparagraph, the employer shall be relieved of the liability to make any repayment under the provisions of subparagraph (*a*) of that paragraph.

(4) On the employee's return to work the employer shall immediately notify the inspector and for the purpose of deducting or repaying tax on the occasion of any subsequent payment of emoluments to or on behalf of the employee during the year shall take into account the amount of any repayment which has been made under paragraph (5) of this Regulation of which he or she is notified by the inspector.

(5) In the case of a person who has ceased to be employed or with respect to whom a notification and return have been sent under the provisions of subparagraph (*b*) of paragraph (2) of this Regulation, any repayment which may be appropriate at any date, having regard to the person's cumulative emoluments at that date and the corresponding cumulative tax, shall be made to him or her by the Revenue Commissioners, and a person who has ceased to be employed shall, on applying for repayment, produce to the inspector the copies of the certificate mentioned in Regulation 20 and such evidence of his or her unemployment as the inspector may require.

Cross-references

Electronic claims: s 864A(1)(*d*).

27 Certificate of tax deducted

(1) Within 46 days from the end of the year the employer shall give to the employee a certificate showing the total amount of the emoluments paid by the employer to or on behalf of the employee during the year, the amount of the employee's tax credits and standard rate cut-off point and the total net tax deducted from the emoluments.

(2) In the case of an employee taken into employment after the beginning of the year, the certificate shall include any emoluments paid to the employee by any previous employer during the year and any tax deducted from those emoluments, being emoluments and tax which the employer giving the certificate was required to take into account for the purposes of deducting or repaying tax in the case of the emoluments paid by him or her.

(3) A certificate shall be given under this Regulation to every employee who is in the employer's employment on the last day of the year and from whose emoluments any tax has been deducted during the year.

PART 5
PAYMENT AND RECOVERY OF TAX, ETC

28 Payment of tax by employer

[(1) Within 14 days from the end of every income tax month the employer shall remit to the Collector-General the total of—

(*a*) all amounts of tax which the employer was liable under these regulations to deduct from emoluments paid by the employer during that income tax month, and (*b*) any amount of tax that was not so deducted but which the employer was liable, in accordance with section 985A(4) of the Act, to remit, in respect of that income tax month, to the Collector-General in respect of notional payments made by the employer,

reduced by any amounts which the employer was liable under these Regulations to repay during that income tax month.][1]

(2) On payment of tax, the Collector-General shall furnish the employer concerned with a receipt in respect of that payment which shall consist of whichever of the following the Collector-General considers appropriate, namely —

(*a*) a separate receipt on the prescribed form in respect of each such payment, or

(*b*) a receipt on the prescribed form in respect of all such payments that have been made within a period specified in the receipt.

[(3) If the amount which the employer is liable to remit to the Collector-General under paragraph (1) of this Regulation exceeds the amount of the total net tax deducted in relation to emoluments paid by the employer during the relevant income tax month, the Revenue Commissioners, on being satisfied that the employer took reasonable care to comply with the provisions of Chapter 4 of Part 42 of the Principal Act and these Regulations and that the under-deduction was due to an error made in good faith, may direct that the amount of the excess shall be recovered from the employee, and where they so direct, the employer shall not be liable to remit the amount of the excess to the Collector-General.

(4) If the amount which the employer is liable to remit to the Collector-General under paragraph (1) of this Regulation exceeds the amount of the total net tax deducted in relation to emoluments paid by the employer during the relevant income tax month and the Revenue Commissioners are of the opinion that an employee has received his or her emoluments knowing that the employer has wilfully failed to either deduct therefrom or to remit in respect thereof in accordance with section 985A(4) of the Principal Act an amount of tax which the employer was liable to deduct or so remit under these Regulations, the Revenue Commissioners may direct that the amount of the excess shall be recovered from the employee, and where they so direct, the employer shall not be liable to remit the amount of the excess to the Collector-General.][2]

(5) If a difference arises between the employer and the employee as to whether the employer has deducted tax, or having regard to Regulation 25 is deemed to have deducted tax, from emoluments paid to or on behalf of the employee, or as to the amount of the tax that has been so deducted or is so deemed to have been deducted, the matter shall, for the purposes of ascertaining the amount of any tax to be recovered from the employee under paragraph (3) or (4) of this Regulation, be determined by the Appeal Commissioners.

(6) If the total of the amounts which the employer was liable to repay during any income tax month exceeds the total of the amounts which the employer was liable to deduct during that income tax month, the employer shall be entitled to deduct the excess from any amount which he or she is subsequently liable to remit to the Collector-General under paragraph (1) of this Regulation or to recover it from the Revenue Commissioners.

(7) A determination under paragraph (5) of this Regulation may be made by one Appeal Commissioner.

Amendments

1 Para (1) substituted by Income Tax (Employments) Regulations 2003 (SI No 613 of 2003) reg 2(*d*)(i) with effect from 1 January 2004.

2 Paras (3) and (4) substituted by Income Tax (Employments) Regulations 2003 (SI No 613 of 2003) reg 2(*d*)(ii) with effect from 1 January 2004.

Cross-references

Registration of certain persons as employers and requirements to send certain notifications: s 988(3)(*a*).

29 Payment of tax for periods greater than one month but not exceeding one year

[(1) Notwithstanding the provisions of Regulation 28, the Collector-General may, from time to time, authorise, in writing, an employer (unless the employer objects) to remit to him or her within 14 days from the end of a period longer than an income tax month but not exceeding a year (which in this Regulation and in Regulation 30 is referred to as the 'accounting period') the total of—

(*a*) all amounts of tax which the employer was liable under these regulations to deduct from emoluments paid by the employer during that accounting period, and

(*b*) any amount of tax that was not so deducted but which the employer was liable, in accordance with section 985A(4) of the Act, to remit, in respect of that accounting period, to the Collector-General in respect of notional payments made by the employer,

reduced by any amounts which the employer was liable under these Regulations to repay during that accounting period.][1]

(2) For the purposes of issuing an authorisation to an employer pursuant to this Regulation, the Collector-General shall, where he or she considers it appropriate, have regard to the following matters:

(*a*) he or she has reasonable grounds to believe that —

(i) the authorisation will not result in a loss of tax, and

(ii) the employer will meet all obligations imposed on the employer under the authorisation,

and

(*b*) the employer —

(i) has been a registered employer within the meaning of Regulation 7 during all of the period consisting of one year immediately preceding the year in which an authorisation for the purposes of this Regulation would, if it were issued, have effect, and

(ii) has made all returns which the employer is required to make in accordance with the provisions of Regulation 31(1).

(3) An authorisation for the purposes of this Regulation may —

(*a*) be issued either without conditions or subject to such conditions as the Collector-General, having regard in particular to the matters set out in paragraph (2) of this Regulation, considers proper and specifies in writing to the employer concerned when issuing the authorisation, and

(*b*) without prejudice to the generality of the foregoing, require an authorised person to agree with the Collector-General a schedule of amounts of money which he or she undertakes to pay on dates specified by the Collector-General by direct debit from his or her account with a financial institution and the total of the amounts specified in that schedule shall be that person's best estimate of his or her total tax liability for his or her accounting period and he or she shall review on an ongoing basis whether the total of the amounts specified in that schedule is likely to be adequate to cover his or her actual liability for his or her accounting period and where this is not the case or is not likely to be the case, he or she shall agree a revised schedule of amounts with the Collector-General and adjust his or her direct debit amounts accordingly.

(4) The Collector-General may terminate an authorisation by notice in writing and, where an employer requests him or her to do so, the Collector-General shall terminate the authorisation.

(5) For the purposes of terminating an authorisation issued pursuant to this Regulation, the Collector-General shall, where he or she considers it appropriate, have regard to thc following matters:

(*a*) he or she has reasonable grounds to believe that the authorisation has resulted or could result in a loss of tax,

(*b*) the employer —

(i) has failed to remit to the Collector-General within 14 days from the end of the preceding accounting period all amounts of tax which the employer was liable under these Regulations to deduct from emoluments paid by the employer during that accounting period, reduced by any amounts which the employer was liable under these regulations to repay during that accounting period, or

(ii) has furnished, or there is furnished on the employer's behalf, any incorrect information for the purposes of the issue to the employer of an authorisation, or

(iii) has failed to make within the required time limit all returns which the employer is required to make in accordance with the provisions of Regulation 31(1), or

(iv) has not complied with the conditions, if any, specified by the Collector-General under paragraph (3) of this Regulation in relation to the issue to the employer of an authorisation.

(6) In relation to each income tax month in respect of which he or she has not remitted an amount of tax in accordance with paragraph (1) of this Regulation or paragraph (1) of Regulation 28, an employer whose authorisation is terminated shall be deemed to have complied with paragraph (1) of Regulation 28 if he or she remits to the Collector-General, within 14 days of issue of a notice of termination, the amount of tax which he or she would have been required to remit in accordance with the provisions of paragraph (1) of Regulation 28 if he or she were an employer to whom an authorisation had not been issued.

(7) (*a*) An authorisation shall be deemed to have been terminated by the Collector-General on the date that an authorised person ceases to be an employer.

(*b*) An employer whose authorisation is deemed to have been terminated shall, in relation to any income tax month (or part of an income tax month) comprised in the accounting period which was in operation in his or her case on the date of such termination, comply with paragraph (1) of Regulation 29 as if he or she were an authorised person whose accounting period ended on the last day of the income tax month during which the termination occurred.

(*c*) The personal representative of a deceased employer shall be deemed to be the employer for the purposes of subparagraph (*b*).

(8) The provisions of paragraphs (2) to (7) of Regulation 28 shall apply to this Regulation as if references therein to "income tax month" were references to "accounting period".

Amendments

1 Para (1) substituted by Income Tax (Employments) Regulations 2003 (SI No 613 of 2003) reg 2(*e*) with effect from 1 January 2004.

Cross-references

Payment of tax by direct debit: s 991A(*a*).
Priority in winding-up of certain amounts: s 995(*a*)(i).

30 Employer failing to pay tax

(1) If within 14 days from the end of any income tax month or accounting period (as provided for in Regulation 29) the employer has remitted no amount of tax to the Collector-General under Regulation 28 or 29 for that income tax month or accounting period, as the case may be, and the Collector-General is unaware of the amount, if any, which the employer is liable so to remit, the Collector-General may give notice to the employer requiring him or her to send to the Collector-General, within the time limited in the notice, a return showing the name of every employee to whom or on behalf of whom he or she made any payment of emoluments or repayment of tax in the period from the preceding 1 January to the day (being the last day of an income tax month or of an accounting period) specified by the notice, together with such particulars with regard to each such employee as the notice may require, being particulars of—

(i) the amount of the tax credits and standard rate cut-off point appropriate to the employee's case;

(ii) the payments of emoluments made to or on behalf of him or her during that period; and

(iii) any other matter affecting the calculation of the tax which the employer was liable under these Regulations to deduct or to repay to the employee during that period,

and the employer shall comply with the requirements of the notice.

(2) In a case referred to in paragraph (1) of this Regulation the Collector-General shall ascertain, in like manner as the employer should, under these Regulations, have ascertained, the amount of tax which the employer should have deducted from the emoluments, and shall notify the amount to the employer.

(3) A notice given by the Collector-General under paragraph (1) of this Regulation may extend to two or more consecutive income tax months or two or more accounting periods, as the case may be.

(4) A notice may be given by the Collector-General under paragraph (1) of this Regulation notwithstanding that an amount of tax has been remitted to the Collector-General by the employer under Regulations 28 or 29 for any income tax month or accounting period, if the Collector-General is not satisfied that the amount so remitted is the full amount which the employer is liable to remit to him for that income tax month or accounting period, as the case may be, and the provisions of this Regulation shall have effect accordingly.

31 Return by employer at end of year

(1) Within 46 days from the end of the year, or from the date on which the employer ceases permanently to be an employer to whom Regulation 7(1) applies, whichever is the earlier, the employer shall send to the Collector-General —

[(*a*) in such form as the Revenue Commissioners may approve or prescribe, a return in respect of each employee showing the total amount of the emoluments, including emoluments in the form of notional payments, paid by the employer to or on behalf of the employee during the year and the total net tax deducted from the emoluments,][1]

(*b*) any temporary tax deduction form, or such other document corresponding to a temporary tax deduction form as may be authorised by the Revenue Commissioners, used by the employer during the year for an employee in respect of whom a tax deduction card was not received,

(*c*) any emergency card, or such other document corresponding to an emergency card as may be authorised by the Revenue Commissioners, used by the employer during the year for an employee in respect of whom a tax deduction card was not received, and

[(*d*) a statement, declaration and certificate in the prescribed form showing—

(i) the total amount of notional payments paid by the employer to or on behalf of every employee during the year, and

(ii) the total net tax deducted or repaid by the employer in respect of every employee during the year.][2]

(2) Where the employer is a body corporate, the declaration and the certificate referred to in subparagraph (*d*) of paragraph (1) of this Regulation shall be signed either by the secretary or by a director of the body corporate.

Amendments

1 Para (1)(*a*) substituted by Income Tax (Employments) Regulations 2003 (SI No 613 of 2003) reg 2(*f*)(i) with effect from 1 January 2004.

2 Para (1)(*d*) substituted by Income Tax (Employments) Regulations 2003 (SI No 613 of 2003) reg 2(*f*)(ii) with effect from 1 January 2004.

Cross-references

Estimation of tax due for year: s 990(1A)(*a*)(ii), (*d*), (2).
PAYE settlement agreements: s 985B(3)(*e*).
Penalties for breach of regulations: s 987(1), (1A).
Returns by employers in relation to certain pension products: s 897A(2).

Tax Briefing

TB58 Dec 2004 pp 8–9 — P35 End of Year Return 2004.

TB58 Dec 2004 p 15 — P35 2005 - Employer obligations relating to pension contributions.

32 Inspection of employer's records

[(1) Upon request made to him or her at any premises of an employer by an authorised officer, any person, being the employer or a person employed by the employer at the premises, shall produce to the authorised officer for inspection all wages sheets, certificates of tax credits and standard rate cut-off point, tax deduction cards, and other documents and records whatsoever relating to the calculation or payment of the emoluments, including notional payments, of employees of the employer or the deduction of tax from, or the remittance of tax under section 985A(4) of the Principal Act in respect of, such emoluments as may be in that person's powers, possession or procurement.][1]

(2) Where in pursuance of this Regulation an authorised officer requests production of any documents or records, he or she shall, on request, show his or her authorisation for the purposes of this Regulation to the person concerned.

(3) The documents and records specified in paragraph (1) of this Regulation, other than certificates of tax credits and standard rate cut-off point and the temporary tax deduction forms, and emergency cards, and the documents corresponding to those forms and cards, referred to in Regulation 31, shall be retained by the employer for a period of six years after the end of the year to which they refer, or for such shorter period as the Revenue Commissioners may authorise by notice in writing to the employer.

Amendments

1 Para (1) substituted by Income Tax (Employments) Regulations 2003 (SI No 613 of 2003) reg 2(*g*) with effect from 1 January 2004.

33 Death of employer

If the employer dies, anything which the employer would have been liable to do under these Regulations shall be done by the employer's personal representative, or, in the case of an employer who paid emoluments on behalf of another person, by the person succeeding the employer or, if there is no such person, the person on whose behalf the employer paid emoluments.

34 Succession to a business, etc

(1) This Regulation applies where there has been a change in the employer from whom an employee receives emoluments in respect of his or her employment in any trade, business, concern or undertaking, or in connection with any property, or from whom an employee receives any annuity or pension.

(2) Where this Regulation applies, the change shall not be treated as a cessation of employment for the purposes of Regulation 20, but, in relation to any matter arising after the change, the employer after the change shall be liable to do anything which the

employer before the change would have been liable to do under these Regulations if the change had not taken place.

(3) The employer after the change shall not be liable for the payment of any tax which was deductible from emoluments paid to the employee before the change took place.

PART 6
ASSESSMENT

35 Assessment of emoluments

(1) Nothing in these Regulations shall prevent an assessment under Schedule E being made on a person in respect of his or her emoluments (income assessed to tax) for any year.

(2) Any assessments on an employee in respect of emoluments may be made in any income tax district and shall be valid notwithstanding that the employee was not in that district, or in the State, during the year in which the assessment was made.

(3) All the emoluments of an employee may be included in one assessment.

36 Return of certain emoluments by employer

The inspector may give notice to the employer requiring the employer to send a return of any emoluments paid by the employer to or on behalf of any employee for any year, being emoluments which are not paid to or on behalf of the employee until after the end of that year, and any such return shall be sent to the inspector within the time limited in the notice.

37 Notification of liability

The inspector shall, in any case where he or she does not propose to make an assessment on an employee with respect to whom tax was deducted during a year, send to the employee, as soon as possible after the end of the year, a statement of his or her liability for the year and showing how it is proposed to deal with any overpayment or underpayment of tax.

Cross-references

Credit in respect of tax deducted from emoluments of certain directors: s 997A(3).

PAYE, supplementary provisions: s 997(3).

38 Objections and appeals against assessment

The provisions of Part 40 of the Act shall, with any necessary modifications, apply in relation to an appeal by an employee against an assessment of emoluments.

39 Recovery of underpayments

(1) If the tax payable under the assessment exceeds the total net tax deducted from the employee's emoluments during the year, the inspector, instead of taking the excess into account in determining the appropriate amount of tax credits and standard rate cut-off point for a subsequent year, may require the employee to remit it to the Collector-General, and, where the inspector so requires, the employee shall remit the excess accordingly on demand made by the Collector-General.

(2) For the purposes of determining the amount of any such excess, any necessary adjustment shall be made to the total net tax in respect of any tax overpaid or remaining unpaid for any year.

40 Recovery of tax from employee

(1) Any tax which is to be remitted to the Collector-General by any employee may be recovered in the manner provided by the Income Tax Acts.

(2) Any tax which is to be remitted to the Collector-General under paragraph (1) of Regulation 39, shall be remitted within 14 days of the date on which the Collector-General first makes application therefor.

PART 7
CONTRIBUTIONS BY EMPLOYEES TO CERTAIN SUPERANNUATION FUNDS AND SCHEMES

41 Interpretation (Part 7)

[In this Part of these Regulations **"allowable contribution"** means a contribution payable by an employee and deductible by an employer from emoluments of the employee and which is —

(*a*) by virtue of section 471 of the Act, allowable as a deduction from such emoluments for the purposes of assessment under Schedule E,

(*b*) an ordinary annual contribution, or any other contribution treated by the Revenue Commissioners, as respects the year in which it is paid, as an ordinary annual contribution paid in that year, allowable by virtue of section 774 or 776 of the Act, as a deduction from such emoluments for the purposes of assessment under Schedule E, ...[1]

(*c*) by virtue of section 787C (inserted by the Pensions (Amendment) Act 2002) of the Act, to be deducted from or set off against the employee's relevant earnings (within the meaning of section 787B (as so inserted) of the Act) for the year of assessment in which it is [paid, or][2]

[(*d*) by virtue of section 787 of the Act, to be deducted from or set off against the employee's relevant earnings (within the meaning of section 783 of the Act) for the year of assessment in which it is paid.][3]][4]

Amendments

1 Deleted by Income Tax (Employments) Regulations 2003 (SI No 613 of 2003) reg 2(*h*)(i) with effect from 1 January 2004; previously "or".

2 Substituted by Income Tax (Employments) Regulations 2003 (SI No 613 of 2003) reg 2(*h*)(ii) with effect from 1 January 2004; previously "paid.".

3 Para (*d*) inserted by Income Tax (Employments) Regulations 2003 (SI No 613 of 2003) reg 2(*h*)(iii) with effect from 1 January 2004.

4 Regulation 41 substituted by Income Tax (Employments) Regulations 2002 (SI 511 of 2002) reg 3(*b*) with effect from such day as the Minister for Social and Family Affairs shall by order, under section 1 of the Pensions (Amendment) Act 2002 (No 18 of 2002), appoint as the day for the coming into operation of section 4 of that Act; previously "In this Part of these Regulations "**'allowable contribution'** means a contribution payable by an employee and deductible by an employer from emoluments of the employee and which is —

(*a*) an ordinary annual contribution, or any other contribution treated by the Revenue Commissioners, as respects the year in which it is paid, as an ordinary annual contribution paid in that year, allowable by virtue of section 774 or 776 of the Act, as a deduction from such emoluments for the purposes of assessment under Schedule E, or

(*b*) by virtue of section 471 of the Act, allowable as a deduction from such emoluments for the purposes of assessment under Schedule E.".

Cross-references

Returns by employers in relation to pension products, meaning of "allowable contribution" (paras (*b*), (*c*) and (*d*)) applied: s 897A(1)("employee pension contribution", "PRSA employee contribution", "RAC premium").

42 Deduction or repayment by reference to superannuation contribution

When making a deduction or repayment of tax in accordance with the provisions of Part 4 of these Regulations from or in respect of emoluments to which Chapter 4 of Part 42 of the Act applies, an employer shall make such deduction or repayment as would require to be made if the amount of the emoluments were those emoluments reduced by the amount of the allowable contribution deductible from those emoluments.

PART 8
SPECIAL PROVISIONS WHERE EMPLOYEES ARE IN RECEIPT OF OR ARE ENTITLED TO RECEIVE CERTAIN BENEFITS PAYABLE UNDER THE SOCIAL WELFARE ACTS

43 Interpretation (Part 8)

In this Part of these Regulations—

"relevant period", in relation to an employee who is absent from work and who in respect of any part of that absence receives, or is entitled to receive, a taxable benefit, means the period commencing with the date on which such taxable benefit first becomes payable to the employee and ending on the earliest of the following dates, that is to say:

(*a*) the date of cessation of employment,

(*b*) the 31 December following the employee's return to work, or

(*c*) such other date as the inspector may specify;

"taxable benefit", in relation to an employee, means any amount payable under the Social Welfare Acts in respect of—

(*a*) disability benefit, and

(*b*) injury benefit which is comprised in occupational injuries benefit,

which is chargeable to income tax by virtue of section 126 of the Act.

44 Tax due in respect of disability or injury benefit

Where, in respect of an absence from work, an employee receives or is entitled to receive a taxable benefit the following provisions shall, notwithstanding any other provision of these Regulations and unless the inspector otherwise directs, apply, that is to say:

(*a*) any payment of emoluments made by the employer to the employee in the relevant period shall be treated as if it were a payment to which Regulation 19 applies, (*b*) (i) where the employee is entitled to receive payment of emoluments during such absence from work, the employer shall, in relation to such payments made by him or her to the employee during the relevant period, reduce the tax credits and standard rate cut-off point for Week 1 or Month 1, as may be appropriate, as specified on the tax deduction card held by the employer in respect of the employee by —

(A) such amount as the Revenue Commissioners, by general notice or otherwise, direct, or

(B) such other amount as the Minister for Social, Community and Family Affairs may notify to the employer in relation to the employee, and

(ii) the reduction of the employee's tax credits and standard rate cut-off point in accordance with the provisions of subparagraph (i) shall be treated as if it were a determination or, as the case may be, an amended determination of tax credits and standard rate cut-off point by the inspector but the inspector need not issue a notice of the determination or the amended determination, as may be appropriate, to the employee or a certificate of tax credits and standard rate cut-off point, an amended certificate of tax credits and standard rate cut-off point, a tax deduction card or an amended tax deduction card, as may be appropriate, to the employer,

and

(*c*) where, on any usual pay day during the period of absence from work which falls within the relevant period, the employee is not entitled to receive payment of emoluments from the employer, the provisions of Regulation 26 shall not apply in respect of such pay day.

PART 9
MISCELLANEOUS

45 Revocations

The Regulations specified in the Schedule to these Regulations are revoked.

SCHEDULE

S.I. Number	Regulations
(1)	(2)
28 of 1960	Income Tax (Employments) Regulations, 1960
166 of 1960	Income Tax (Employments) (No 2) Regulations, 1960
223 of 1970	Income Tax (Employments) Regulations, 1970
182 of 1971	Income Tax (Employments) Regulations, 1971
260 of 1972	Income Tax (Employments) Regulations, 1972
86 of 1974	Income Tax (Employments) Regulations, 1974
292 of 1974	Income Tax (Employments) (No 2) Regulations, 1974

170 of 1975	Income Tax (Employments) Regulations, 1975
368 of 1977	Income Tax (Employments) Regulations, 1977
377 of 1978	Income Tax (Employments) Regulations, 1978
284 of 1980	Income Tax (Employments) Regulations, 1980
67 of 1984	Income Tax (Employments) Regulations, 1984
148 of 1985	Income Tax (Employments) Regulations, 1985
270 of 1987	Income Tax (Employments) Regulations, 1987
58 of 1989	Income Tax (Employments) Regulations, 1989
77 of 1993	Income Tax (Employments) Regulations, 1993
231 of 1997	Income Tax (Employments) Regulations, 1997
66 of 1999	Income Tax (Employments) Regulations, 1999
35 of 2001	Income Tax (Employments) Regulations, 2001

TAXES (OFFSET OF REPAYMENTS) REGULATIONS 2002

(2002 No 471)

ARRANGEMENT OF REGULATIONS

PART 1
GENERAL

PART 2
OFFSETTING

PART 3
MISCELLANEOUS

The Revenue Commissioners, in exercise of the powers conferred on them by section 1006A of the Taxes Consolidation Act 1997 (No. 39 of 1997), make the following regulations:

PART 1
GENERAL

1 Citation

These Regulations may be cited as the Taxes (Offset of Repayments) Regulations 2002.

2 Interpretation

(1) In these Regulations, unless the context otherwise requires—

"Acts", **"claim"**, **"liability"**, **"overpayment"** and **"tax"** have each the same meaning as they have, respectively, in the principal section;

"Collector-General" means the person appointed under section 851 of the Principal Act;

"estimate" means an estimate of tax made in accordance with the provisions of—

(*a*) section 989 of the Principal Act,

(*b*) Regulation 13 of the Income Tax (Relevant Contracts) Regulations 2000 (SI No 71 of 2000), or

(*c*) section 22 of the Value-Added Tax Act 1972 (No 22 of 1972);

"current estimate", in relation to any particular time, means an estimate in respect of either an income tax month or a taxable period, as the case may be, the due date for which is immediately prior to that time or the income tax month or taxable period immediately preceding that month or period;

"due date", in relation to a liability, means the date on which the liability is due and payable under the appropriate provision of the Acts and, in relation to an estimate, the date on which the period for the payment of the tax for the income tax month or taxable period, as the case may be, expires;

"liability at enforcement" means a liability which, at the time at which the repayment is to be made in respect of the claim or overpayment—

(*a*) was certified in a certificate issued, and not withdrawn, under section 962 of the Principal Act,

(*b*) was the subject of proceedings initiated, and not withdrawn, as a debt due to the Minister for Finance, in any court of competent jurisdiction, or

(*c*) was entered as a specified amount in a notice of attachment issued, and not revoked, under section 1002 of the Principal Act;

"Principal Act" means the Taxes Consolidation Act 1997 (No 39 of 1997);

"principal section" means section 1006A of the Principal Act;

"taxhead" means—

(*a*) tax deductible under Chapter 2 of Part 18 of the Principal Act and any regulations made under it,

(*b*) income tax deductible under Chapter 4 of Part 42 of the Principal Act and any regulations made under it,

(*c*) corporation tax,

(*d*) an amount to be collected as income tax by the Collector-General in accordance with the provisions of the European Communities (Mutual Assistance for the Recovery of Claims relating to Certain Levies, Duties, Taxes and Other Measures) Regulations 2002 (SI No 462 of 2002),

(*e*) income tax (other than that referred to in paragraphs (*b*) and (*d*) of this definition),

(*f*) capital gains tax,

(*g*) value-added tax,

(*h*) inheritance tax and gift tax,

(*i*) stamp duties,

(*j*) residential property tax,

(*k*) vehicle registration tax, or

(*l*) excise duties,

as the case may be.

(2) In these Regulations—

(*a*) a reference to a Regulation is to a Regulation of these Regulations, unless it appears that reference to some other provision is intended;

(*b*) a reference to a paragraph is to the paragraph of the provision in which the reference occurs, unless it appears that reference to some other provision is intended.

(3) Subject to paragraph (1), a word or expression that is used in these Regulations and is also used in any provision of the Acts has, except where the context otherwise requires, the same meaning in these Regulations as it has in that provision.

PART 2
OFFSETTING

3 Order of priority of offset against liabilities

Subject to Regulations 4, 5, 6 and 7, the amount of any repayment in respect of a claim or overpayment made by any person, which is, by virtue of subsection (2) of the principal section, to be set against any liability of that person, shall be set against—

(*a*) firstly, any liability, other than a current estimate or a liability at enforcement, in the following sequence:

(i) a liability arising under the same taxhead in respect of which the claim or overpayment is made,

(ii) a liability arising under the Value-Added Tax Act 1972 and the enactments amending or extending that Act,

(iii) a liability arising under Chapter 4 of Part 42 of the Principal Act and the regulations made under it,

(iv) a liability arising under Chapter 2 of Part 18 of the Principal Act and the regulations made under it,

(v) a liability arising under the Corporation Tax Acts,

(vi) a liability arising under any provision (other than Chapter 4 of Part 42 of the Principal Act) of the Income Tax Acts,

(vii) a liability arising under the Capital Gains Tax Acts,

(viii) a liability arising under Part VI of the Finance Act 1983 (No 15 of 1983) and the enactments amending or extending that Part,

(ix) a liability arising under the Capital Acquisitions Tax Act 1976 (No 8 of 1976) and the enactments amending or extending that Act,

(x) a liability arising under the Stamp Duties Consolidation Act 1999 (No 31 of 1999) and the enactments amending or extending that Act,

(xi) a liability arising under Chapter IV of Part II of the Finance Act 1992 (No 9 of 1992),

(xii) a liability arising under the statutes relating to the duties of excise and to the management of those duties,

(*b*) secondly, any liability, being a liability at enforcement, in the sequence set out in paragraph (*a*), and

(*c*) finally, against any amount referred to in paragraph (*d*) of the definition of "taxhead".

4 Special arrangements regarding corporation tax, income tax and capital gains tax

Notwithstanding Regulation 3 but subject to Regulations 5, 6 and 7, in any case where a repayment in respect of a claim or overpayment made by any person, is under a taxhead referred to in paragraph (*c*), (*e*) or (*f*) of the definition of "taxhead", the amount of the repayment, which is, by virtue of subsection (2) of the principal section, to be set against any liability of that person, shall be set against—

(*a*) firstly, any liability, other than a current estimate or a liability at enforcement, in the following sequence:

(i) a liability arising under the same taxhead in respect of which the claim or overpayment is made,

(ii) a liability arising under the Corporation Tax Acts,

(iii) a liability arising under any provision (other than Chapter 4 of Part 42 of the Principal Act) of the Income Tax Acts,

(iv) a liability arising under the Capital Gains Tax Acts,

(v) a liability arising under the Value-Added Tax Act 1972 and the enactments amending or extending that Act,

(vi) a liability arising under Chapter 4 of Part 42 of the Principal Act and the regulations made under it,

(vii) a liability arising under Chapter 2 of Part 18 of the Principal Act and the regulations made under it,

(viii) a liability arising under Part VI of the Finance Act 1983 and the enactments amending or extending that Part,

(ix) a liability arising under the Capital Acquisitions Tax Act 1976 and the enactments amending or extending that Act,

(x) a liability arising under the Stamp Duties Consolidation Act 1999 and the enactments amending or extending that Act,

(xi) a liability arising under Chapter IV of Part II of the Finance Act 1992,

(xii) a liability arising under the statutes relating to the duties of excise and to the management of those duties,

(*b*) secondly, any liability, being a liability at enforcement, in the sequence set out in paragraph (*a*), and

(*c*) finally, against any amount referred to in paragraph (*d*) of the definition of "taxhead".

5 Chronological order of priority of liabilities

For the purposes of Regulation 3 or 4, where, at any time, a repayment is to be set against more than one liability arising under a taxhead, it shall be set against any liability due for an earlier period or event in priority to a later period or event, as the case may be.

6 Nomination of liabilities by taxpayer

Notwithstanding Regulation 3 or 4, a person may, at any time but not later than 30 days after the issue of a notice to him or her under subsection (2A) of the principal section, by notice in writing to the Collector-General request that the repayment concerned be set against liabilities (other than any amount referred to in paragraph (*d*) of the definition of "taxhead") in an order nominated by the person and the Collector-General shall arrange accordingly.

7 Offset of interest

For the purposes of these Regulations, interest due and payable in relation to any liability to tax in respect of any period or event shall be deemed to be due and payable at the same time as the tax in respect of that period or event, as the case may be.

PART 3
MISCELLANEOUS

8 Revocation

The Taxes (Offset of Repayments) Regulations 2001 (SI No 399 of 2001) are revoked.

INCOME TAX (EMPLOYMENTS) REGULATIONS 2002

2002 No 511

The Revenue Commissioners, in exercise of the powers conferred on them by section 986 (as amended by section 4 of the Pensions (Amendment) Act 2002 (No 18 of 2002)) of the Taxes Consolidation Act 1997 (No 39 of 1997), hereby make the following regulations:

1 (1) These Regulations may be cited as the Income Tax (Employments) Regulations 2002.

(2) (*a*) Paragraph (*a*) of Regulation 3 shall come into operation on 1 January 2003.

(*b*) Paragraph (*b*) of Regulation 3 shall come into operation on such day as the Minister for Social and Family Affairs shall by order, under section 1 of the Pensions (Amendment) Act 2002 (No 18 of 2002), appoint as the day for the coming into operation of section 4 of that Act.

2 In these Regulations **"Principal Regulations"** means the Income Tax (Employments) (Consolidated) Regulations 2001 (SI No 559 of 2001).

3

Notes

Para (*a*) substituted Income Tax (Employments) (Consolidated) Regulations 2001 (SI No 559 of 2001) reg 22(2) and inserted reg 22(2A) with effect from 1 January 2003.

Para (*b*) substituted Income Tax (Employments) (Consolidated) Regulations 2001 (SI No 559 of 2001) reg 41 with effect from such day as the Minister for Social and Family Affairs shall by order, under section 1 of the Pensions (Amendment) Act 2002 (No 18 of 2002), appoint as the day for the coming into operation of section 4 of that Act.

EUROPEAN COMMUNITIES (MUTUAL ASSISTANCE FOR THE RECOVERY OF CLAIMS RELATING TO CERTAIN LEVIES, DUTIES, TAXES AND OTHER MEASURES) REGULATIONS 2002

2002 No 462

I, CHARLIE McCREEVY, Minister for Finance, in exercise of the powers conferred on me by section 3 of the European Communities Act 1972 (No 27 of 1972) and for the purpose of giving effect to Council Directive No 76/308/EEC of 15 March 1976 (OJ No L73 of 19 March, 1976, p 18), as amended by Council Directive No 79/1071/EEC of 6 December 1979 (OJ No L331 of 27 December, 1979, p 10), Council Directive No 92/12/EEC of 25 February 1992 (OJ No L076 of 23 march, 1992, p 1), and Council Directive No 2001/44/EC of 15 June 2001 (OJ No L175 of 28 June, 2001, p 17), hereby make the following regulations:

1 Citation

These Regulations may be cited as the European Communities (Mutual Assistance for the Recovery of Claims relating to Certain Levies, Duties, Taxes and Other Measures) Regulations 2002.

2 Interpretation

(1) In these Regulations—

"claim" means any of the claims to which Regulation 3 applies;

"claimant" means the competent authority of a Member State which makes a request for assistance concerning a claim;

[**"Commission Directive"** means Commission Directive No 2002/94/EC of 9 December 2002;][1]

"Council Directive" means Council Directive No 76/308/EEC of 15 March 1976 as amended by Council Directive No 79/1071/EEC of 6 December 1979, Council Directive No 92/12/EEC of 25 February 1992, and Council Directive No 2001/44/EC of 15 June 2001;

"excise duties" means any excise duty in a Member State on—

(*a*) manufactured tobacco,
(*b*) alcohol and alcoholic beverages, or
(*c*) mineral oils;

"export duties" means—

(*a*) customs duties and charges having equivalent effect on exports, and
(*b*) export charges laid down within the framework of—
   (i) the common agricultural policy, or
   (ii) specific arrangements applicable to certain goods resulting from the processing of agricultural products,

which are imposed by, or apply within, a Member State;

"import duties" means—

(*a*) customs duties and charges having equivalent effect on imports, and
(*b*) import charges laid down within the framework of—

(i) the common agricultural policy, or
(ii) specific arrangements applicable to certain goods resulting from the processing of agricultural products,

which are imposed by, or apply within, a Member State;

"Member State" means a Member State of the European Communities other than the State;

"taxes on income and capital" means those taxes set out in Article 1(3) of Council Directive 77/799/EEC of 19 December 1977 (OJ No L336/15 of 27 December 1977, p 15) (as amended by the 1994 Act of Accession (OJ No C241, 29 August 1994, p 21), in so far as it relates to Member States) read in conjunction with article 1(4) of that Directive which are imposed by, or apply within, a Member State;

"taxes on insurance premiums" means those taxes set out in the sixth indent to Article 3 of the Council Directive, read in conjunction with the seventh indent of the Council Directive, which are imposed by, or apply within, a Member State;

"value-added tax", in relation to a Member State, means the tax referred to in Council Directive No 77/388/EEC of 17 May 1977 (OJ No L145 of 13 June 1977, p 1).

(2) A word or expression that is used in these Regulations and is also used in the Council Directive has, unless the contrary intention appears, the meaning in these Regulations that it has in the Council Directive.

(3) A word or expression that is used in these Regulations and is also used in the Tax Acts has, subject to paragraph (2) and unless the contrary intention appears, the meaning in these Regulations that it has in the Tax Acts.

(4) In these Regulations—

(*a*) a reference to a Regulation is to a Regulation of these Regulations, and
(*b*) a reference to a paragraph or subparagraph is to the paragraph or subparagraph of the provision in which the reference occurs,

unless it is indicated that reference to some other provision is intended.

Amendments

1 Substituted by European Communities (Mutual Assistance for the Recovery of Claims relating to Certain Levies, Duties, Taxes and Other Measures) (Amendment) Regulations 2003 reg 2(*a*).

---

3 Claims covered

This Regulation applies to a claim made by a claimant relating to—

(*a*) refunds, interventions and other measures forming part of the system of total or partial financing of the European Agricultural Guidance and Guarantee Fund (EAGGF), including sums to be collected in connection with these actions;
(*b*) levies and other duties provided for under the common organisation of the market for the sugar sector;

(*c*) import duties;

(*d*) export duties;

(*e*) value added tax;

(*f*) excise duties;

(*g*) taxes on income and capital;

(*h*) taxes on insurance premiums;

(*i*) interest, administrative penalties and fines, and costs incidental to a claim referred to in paragraphs (*a*) to (*h*), with the exclusion of any fine or penalty in respect of which the act or commission giving rise to the fine or penalty if committed in the State would have been of a criminal nature.

4 Exchange of information

(1) In this Regulation **"relevant authority"**, in relation to a request for information under this Regulation, means—

(*a*) the Minister for Agriculture and Food, in the case of claims to which Regulation 3 applies which are referred to in paragraph (*a*) or (*b*), or, in so far as relates to any claim referred to in either of those paragraphs, paragraph (*i*), of that Regulation, and

(*b*) the Revenue Commissioners, in the case of any other claim to which Regulation 3 applies.

(2) Subject to paragraph (3), a relevant authority may, at the request of a competent authority of a Member State, disclose to the competent authority any information in relation to a claim which is required to be disclosed by virtue of the Council Directive.

(3) (*a*) A relevant authority shall not disclose any information for the purposes of the Council Directive which would, in the opinion of the relevant authority, be liable to prejudice the security of the State or be contrary to public policy.

(*b*) A relevant authority shall not be obliged to disclose any information for the purposes of the Council Directive—

(i) that the relevant authority concerned would not be able to obtain for the purposes of recovering a similar claim in the State, or

(ii) that would, in the opinion of the relevant authority, be materially detrimental to any commercial, industrial or professional secrets.

(4) In obtaining the information referred to in paragraph (2), it shall be lawful for the relevant authority concerned to make use of the provisions of any enactment or instrument made under statute relating to the recovery of a similar claim in the State.

(5) Nothing in this Regulation shall permit the relevant authority concerned to authorise the use of information disclosed by virtue of the Council Directive to the competent authorities of a Member State other than for the purposes of the recovery of a claim or to facilitate legal proceedings in relation to the recovery of such a claim.

5 Recovery of claims

(1) The Collector-General shall, in accordance with the provisions of these Regulations, collect the amount of a claim specified in any request duly made in accordance with the Council Directive by a claimant.

(2) When the Collector-General duly receives a request from a claimant for the recovery of a claim, the Collector-General shall make demand in writing of the amount stated in the claim made by the claimant from the person against whom the claim is made.

(3) For the purposes of these Regulations, the amount of any claim made by a claimant shall be deemed due and payable not later than 7 days from the date on which the Collector-General makes demand of the amount in accordance with paragraph (2).

(4) The provisions of any enactment relating to the collection or recovery of income tax (other than sections 960, 961, 970, 971, 1000, 1003, 1004 and 1006B, and Chapter 4 of Part 42, of the Taxes Consolidation Act 1997) and the provisions of any rule of court so relating for those purposes shall, with any necessary modifications, apply in relation to the recovery of a claim referred to in paragraph (1) as they apply in relation to income tax, and for this purpose the amount of the claim shall be deemed to be an amount of income tax.

(5) For the purposes of these Regulations, the amount of the claim referred to in paragraph (1) shall be regarded as a debt due to the Minister for Finance, by the person against whom the claim is made by the claimant, in respect of a tax or duty under the care and management of the Revenue Commissioners.

(6) Any reference in this Regulation to the amount of the claim shall include any interest payable in respect of that claim under Regulation 6.

(7) The amount of any claim payable to the Collector-General under these Regulations—

(*a*) shall be payable without any deduction of income tax, and

(*b*) shall not be allowed as a deduction in computing any income, profits or losses for any of the purposes of the Tax Acts (except in so far as any relief is due in respect of the amount of the claim under Part 35 of the Taxes Consolidation Act 1997).

(8) On payment of an amount under these Regulations, the Collector-General shall furnish the person concerned with a receipt in respect of that payment.

6 Interest

(1) The amount of any claim payable in accordance with Regulation 5(1) shall carry interest at the rate of 0.0322 per cent for each day or part of a day from the date when the amount of the claim becomes due and payable in accordance with Regulation 5(3) until payment, and, accordingly, that date is the date on which the instrument permitting enforcement of the recovery of the claim is recognised for the purposes of the second subparagraph of Article 9.2 of the Council Directive.

(2) Subsections (2) to (4) of section 1080 of the Taxes Consolidation Act 1997 shall apply in relation to interest payable in relation to the claim referred to in paragraph (1) as they apply in relation to interest payable under section 1080 of that Act in relation to tax charged by any assessment.

7 Application of rules

The rules laid down in Articles 4 to 12 and 14 to 17 of the Council Directive (to the extent that they are not otherwise given effect to by these Regulations) and [Articles 2 to

28 of the Commission Directive][1] shall apply in relation to claims made by claimants and which are the subject of recovery in accordance with these Regulations.

Amendments

1 Substituted by European Communities (Mutual Assistance for the Recovery of Claims relating to Certain Levies, Duties, Taxes and Other Measures) (Amendment) Regulations 2003 reg 2(*b*); previously "Articles 2 to 21 of the Commission Directive".

8 Stay on proceedings

(1) Subject to paragraph (5), any action taken by the Revenue Commissioners or the Collector-General to recover the amount of any claim, whether by way of legal proceedings or other action, shall be stayed if—

(*a*) in the case of court proceedings, the defendant satisfies the court that court proceedings relevant to that person's liability on the claim to which the proceedings so instituted relate are pending before a court, tribunal or other competent body in a Member State, or

(*b*) in any other case, the person against whom the other action is being taken satisfies the Revenue Commissioners that court proceedings relevant to that person's liability on the claim to which the action relates are pending before a court, tribunal or other competent body in a Member State.

(2) In any legal proceedings instituted under these Regulations it shall be a defence for the defendant to show that a final decision on the claim to which the proceedings relate has been given in the defendant's favour by a court, tribunal or other body of competent jurisdiction in a Member State, and, in relation to any part of a claim to which such legal proceedings relate, it shall be a defence for the defendant to show that such a decision has been given in relation to that part of the claim.

(3) No question shall be raised in any legal proceedings instituted in pursuance of these Regulations as to the liability on the claim to which the proceedings relate of the person against whom the claim is made, [except as provided in paragraph (2)].[1]

(4) For the purposes of this Regulation, legal proceedings shall be regarded as pending so long as an appeal may be brought against any decision in the proceedings; and for these purposes a decision against which no appeal lies, or against which an appeal lies within a period which has expired without an appeal having been brought, shall be regarded as a final decision.

(5) Paragraph (1) shall not apply where a claimant in accordance with the Council Directive so requests, and where the claimant so requests no action shall lie against the State (including the Revenue Commissioners, the Collector-General, any officer of the Revenue Commissioners and any agent of the Revenue Commissioners) in any court by reason of the Revenue Commissioners, the Collector-General or any such officer or agent recovering, or taking any action to recover, the amount of, or part of the amount of, any claim the subject of such a request.

Amendments

1 Substituted by European Communities (Mutual Assistance for the Recovery of Claims relating to Certain Levies, Duties, Taxes and Other Measures) (Amendment) Regulations 2003 reg 2(c); previously "except as provided in paragraph (3)".

9 Remittance of claims

Any amount recovered under these Regulations on foot of a claim made by a claimant under the Council Directive (including any interest under Regulation 6) shall be remitted to that claimant.

10 Application of Council Directive to certain Irish tax, etc. due

(1) In this Regulation—

"tax" means any tax, duty, levy or charge referred to in Article 2 of the Council Directive which is under the care and management of the Revenue Commissioners;

"agricultural levy" means any levy or other measure referred to in Article 2 of the Council Directive for which the Minister for Agriculture and Food is responsible;

"interest on unpaid tax", in relation to an amount of unpaid tax, means the amount of interest that has accrued to the date on which a certificate under this Regulation is signed in respect of the unpaid tax under any provision whatever providing for the charging of interest in respect of that tax, including interest on an undercharge of tax which is attributable to fraud or neglect, as specified in the certificate.

(2) For the purpose of the Council Directive and for the avoidance of doubt, a demand by the Revenue Commissioners or the Minister for Agriculture and Food, as the case may be, for payment of an amount of tax (including, where appropriate, interest on unpaid tax) or agricultural levy where the amount demanded remains unpaid after expiration of the period for payment set out in the demand shall be an instrument permitting enforcement of the debt.

11 Delegation of powers and functions

(1) The Minister for Agriculture and Food may nominate, in writing, any of his or her officers to perform any acts and discharge any functions authorised by these Regulations to be performed or discharged by the Minister.

(2) The Revenue Commissioners may nominate, in writing, any of their officers to perform any acts and discharge any functions authorised by these Regulations to be performed or discharged by them.

(3) The Revenue Commissioners may nominate, in writing, any of their officers to perform any acts and discharge any functions authorised by these Regulations to be performed or discharged by the Collector-General.

12 Repeal and revocations

(1) Section 108 of the Finance Act 2001 is repealed.

(2) The European Communities (Agriculture and Customs) (Mutual Assistance as regards the Recovery of Claims) Regulations 1980 (SI No 73 of 1980) and the European Communities (Value-Added Tax) (Mutual Assistance as regards the Recovery of Claims) Regulations 1980 (SI No 406 of 1980) are revoked.

EUROPEAN COMMUNITIES (MUTUAL ASSISTANCE FOR THE RECOVERY OF CLAIMS RELATING TO CERTAIN LEVIES, DUTIES, TAXES AND OTHER MEASURES) (AMENDMENT) REGULATIONS 2003

2003 No 344

I, CHARLIE McCREEVY, Minister for Finance, in exercise of the powers conferred on me by section 3 of the European Communities Act 1972 (No. 27 of 1972) and for the purposes of giving effect to Commission Directive 2002/94/EC of 9 December 2002 (OJ No L337 of 13 December 2002, p 41), hereby make the following regulations:

1 These Regulations may be cited as the European Communities (Mutual Assistance for the Recovery of Claims relating to Certain Levies, Duties, Taxes and Other Measures)(Amendment) Regulations 2003.

2

Notes

Para (a) substituted definition of "Commission Directive" in European Communities (Mutual Assistance for the Recovery of Claims relating to Certain Levies, Duties, Taxes and Other Measures) Regulations 2002 reg 2(1).

Para (b) substituted "Articles 2 to 28 of the Commission Directive" for "Articles 2 to 21 of the Commission Directive" in European Communities (Mutual Assistance for the Recovery of Claims relating to Certain Levies, Duties, Taxes and Other Measures) Regulations 2002 reg 7.

Para (c) substituted "except as provided in paragraph (2)" for "except as provided in paragraph (3)" in European Communities (Mutual Assistance for the Recovery of Claims relating to Certain Levies, Duties, Taxes and Other Measures) Regulations 2002 reg 8(3).

INCOME TAX (EMPLOYMENTS) REGULATIONS 2003

2003 No 613

THE REVENUE COMMISSIONERS IN EXERCISE OF THE POWERS CONFERRED ON THEM BY SECTIONS 985A (INSERTED BY THE FINANCE ACT 2003 (NO 3 OF 2003)) AND 986 (AS AMENDED BY THAT ACT) OF THE TAXES CONSOLIDATION ACT, 1997 (NO 39 OF 1997) HEREBY MAKE THE FOLLOWING REGULATIONS:

1 (1) These Regulations may be cited as the Income Tax (Employments) Regulations 2003.

(2) These Regulations come into operation on 1 January 2004.

2 In these Regulations, "Principal Regulations" means the Income Tax (Employments) (Consolidated) Regulations 2001 (SI No 559 of 2001).

3

Notes

Para (*a*)(i)(I) inserted Income Tax (Employments) (Consolidated) Regulations 2001 reg 2(1) definition of "notional payment" with effect from 1 January 2004.

Para (*a*)(i)(II) substituted Income Tax (Employments) (Consolidated) Regulations 2001 reg 2(1) definitions of "temporary tax deduction form" and "total net tax deducted" with effect from 1 January 2004.

Para (*a*)(ii) inserted Income Tax (Employments) (Consolidated) Regulations 2001 reg 2(1A) with effect from 1 January 2004.

Para (*b*) inserted Income Tax (Employments) (Consolidated) Regulations 2001 regs 16A and 16B with effect from 1 January 2004.

Para (*c*) inserted Income Tax (Employments) (Consolidated) Regulations 2001 reg 17A with effect from 1 January 2004.

Para (*d*)(i) substituted Income Tax (Employments) (Consolidated) Regulations 2001 reg 28(1) with effect from 1 January 2004.

Para (*d*)(ii) substituted Income Tax (Employments) (Consolidated) Regulations 2001 reg 28(3) and (4) with effect from 1 January 2004.

Para (*e*) substituted Income Tax (Employments) (Consolidated) Regulations 2001 reg 29(1) with effect from 1 January 2004.

Para (*f*)(i) substituted Income Tax (Employments) (Consolidated) Regulations 2001 reg 31(1)(*a*) with effect from 1 January 2004.

Para (*f*)(ii) substituted Income Tax (Employments) (Consolidated) Regulations 2001 reg 31(1)(*d*) with effect from 1 January 2004.

Para (*g*) substituted Income Tax (Employments) (Consolidated) Regulations 2001 reg 32(1) with effect from 1 January 2004.

Para (*h*)(i) deleted "or" after "Schedule E," from Income Tax (Employments) (Consolidated) Regulations 2001 reg 41(*b*) with effect from 1 January 2004.

Para (*h*)(ii) substituted "paid, or" for "paid." in Income Tax (Employments) (Consolidated) Regulations 2001 reg 41(*c*) with effect from 1 January 2004.

Para (*h*)(iii) inserted Income Tax (Employments) (Consolidated) Regulations 2001 reg 41(*d*) with effect from 1 January 2004.

INCOME TAX (EMPLOYMENTS) REGULATIONS 2003

2003 No 613

THE REVENUE COMMISSIONERS IN EXERCISE OF THE POWERS CONFERRED ON THEM BY SECTIONS 985A (INSERTED BY THE FINANCE ACT 2003 (NO 3 OF 2003)) AND 986 (AS AMENDED BY THAT ACT) OF THE TAXES CONSOLIDATION ACT 1997 (NO 39 OF 1997) HEREBY MAKE THE FOLLOWING REGULATIONS:

1. (1) These Regulations may be cited as the Income Tax (Employments) Regulations 2003.

(2) These Regulations come into operation on 1 January 2004.

2. In these Regulations, "Principal Regulations" means the Income Tax (Employments) (Consolidated) Regulations 2001 (SI No 559 of 2001).

3.

Notes

Para (a)(i) inserted Income Tax (Employments) (Consolidated) Regulations 2001 reg 2(1) definition of "notional payment" with effect from 1 January 2004.

Para (a)(ii) substituted Income Tax (Employments) (Consolidated) Regulations 2001 reg 2(1) definitions of "temporary tax deduction form" and "total net tax deducted" with effect from 1 January 2004.

Para (a)(iii) inserted Income Tax (Employments) (Consolidated) Regulations 2001 reg 2(1A) with effect from 1 January 2004.

Para (b) inserted Income Tax (Employments) (Consolidated) Regulations 2001 regs 10A and 10B with effect from 1 January 2004.

Para (c) inserted Income Tax (Employments) (Consolidated) Regulations 2001 reg 17A with effect from 1 January 2004.

Para (d)(i) substituted Income Tax (Employments) (Consolidated) Regulations 2001 reg 28(1) with effect from 1 January 2004.

Para (d)(ii) substituted Income Tax (Employments) (Consolidated) Regulations 2001 reg 28(2) and (4) with effect from 1 January 2004.

Para (e) substituted Income Tax (Employments) (Consolidated) Regulations 2001 reg 29(1) with effect from 1 January 2004.

Para (f)(i) substituted Income Tax (Employments) (Consolidated) Regulations 2001 reg 31(1)(c) with effect from 1 January 2004.

Para (f)(ii) substituted Income Tax (Employments) (Consolidated) Regulations 2001 reg 31(1)(d) with effect from 1 January 2004.

Para (g) substituted Income Tax (Employments) (Consolidated) Regulations 2001 reg 33(1) with effect from 1 January 2004.

Para (h)(i) deleted "or" after "Schedule 5," from Income Tax (Employments) (Consolidated) Regulations 2001 reg 41(c) with effect from 1 January 2004.

Para (h)(ii) substituted "paid, or" for "paid" in Income Tax (Employments) (Consolidated) Regulations 2001 reg 41(c) with effect from 1 January 2004.

Para (h)(iii) inserted Income Tax (Employments) (Consolidated) Regulations 2001 reg 41(d) with effect from 1 January 2004.

EUROPEAN COMMUNITIES (MUTUAL ASSISTANCE IN THE FIELD OF DIRECT TAXATION, CERTAIN EXCISE DUTIES AND TAXATION OF INSURANCE PREMIUMS) REGULATIONS 2003

2003 No 711

I, CHARLIE Mc CREEVY, Minster for Finance, in exercise of the powers conferred on me by section 3 of the European Communities Act 1972 (No 27 of 1972) and for the purpose of giving effect to Council Directive 77/799/EEC of 19 December 1977 (OJ No L336, of 27 December 1977, p 15), as amended by Council Directive No 79/1070/EEC of 6 December 1979 (OJ No L331, of 27 December 1979, p 8), Council Directive No 92/12/EEC of 25 February 1992 (OJ No L76, of 23 March 1992, p 1) and Council Directive 2003/93/EC of 7 October 2003 (OJ No L264, of 15 October 2003, p 23), hereby make the following regulations:

1 (1) These Regulations may be cited as the European Communities (Mutual Assistance in the Field of Direct Taxation, Certain Excise Duties and Taxation of Insurance Premiums) Regulations 2003.

(2) These Regulations come into operation on 31 December 2003.

2 In these Regulations—

"authorised officer" means an officer of the Revenue Commissioners authorised in writing by the Revenue Commissioners for the purpose of these Regulations;

"the Council Directive" means Council Directive 77/799/EEC of 19 December 1977 (OJ No L336, of 27 December 1977, p 15), as amended by Council Directive No 79/1070/EEC of 6 December 1979 (OJ No L331, of 27 December 1979, p 8), Council Directive No 92/12/EEC of 25 February 1992 (OJ No L76, of 23 March 1992, p 1) and Council Directive 2003/93/EC of 7 October 2003 (OJ No L264, of 15 October 2003, p 23).

3 (1) The Revenue Commissioners and authorised officers of those Commissioners may disclose to the competent authorities of another Member State any information required to be to be so disclosed by virtue of the Council Directive.

(2) Neither the Revenue Commissioners nor an authorised officer of those Commissioners shall disclose any information in pursuance of the Council Directive unless satisfied that the competent authorities of the other Member State concerned are bound by, or have undertaken to observe, rules of confidentiality with respect to the information which are not less strict than those applying to it in the State.

(3) Nothing in this Regulation permits the Revenue Commissioners or an authorised officer of those Commissioners to authorise the use of information disclosed by virtue of the Council Directive to the competent authority of another Member State other than for the purposes of taxation or to facilitate legal proceedings for failure to observe the tax laws of that State.

4 (1) Section 107 of the Finance Act 2001 is repealed.

(2) The European Communities (Mutual Assistance in the Field of Direct Taxation) Regulations 1978 (SI No 334 of 1978) and the European Communities (Mutual Assistance in the Field of Value-Added Tax) Regulations 1980 (SI No 407 of 1980) are revoked.

TAXES CONSOLIDATION ACT 1997 (PRESCRIBED RESEARCH AND DEVELOPMENT ACTIVITIES) REGULATIONS 2004

2004 No 434

I, Mary Harney, TD, Tanaiste and Minister for Enterprise, Trade and Employment, in exercise of the powers conferred on me by section 766 of the Taxes Consolidation Act 1997 (No 39 of 1997)(inserted by section 33 of the Finance Act 2004 (No 8 of 2004)), and having consulted with the Minister for Finance, hereby make the following regulations—

1. These Regulations may be cited as the Taxes Consolidation Act 1997 (Prescribed Research and Development Activities) Regulations 2004.

2. These Regulations shall be deemed to have come into operation on 1 January 2004.

3. Without prejudice to Regulation 4 of these Regulations, an activity shall not be a research and development activity for the purposes of section 766 of the Taxes Consolidation Act 1997 (No. 39 of 1997) (inserted by section 33 of the Finance Act 2004 (No.8 of 2004)) unless it is a research and development activity falling within one or more of the following categories:

(1) an activity undertaken in the field of natural sciences, namely—

(*a*) mathematics and computer sciences, including mathematics and other allied fields, computer sciences and other allied subjects and software development,

(*b*) physical sciences, including astronomy and space sciences, physics, and other allied subjects,

(*c*) chemical sciences, including chemistry and other allied subjects,

(*d*) earth and related environmental sciences, including geology, geophysics, mineralogy, physical geography and other geosciences, meteorology and other atmospheric sciences, including climatic research, oceanography, vulcanology, palaeoecology, and other allied sciences, or

(*e*) biological sciences, including biology, botany, bacteriology, microbiology, zoology, entomology, genetics, biochemistry, biophysics and other allied sciences, excluding clinical and veterinary sciences,

(2) an activity undertaken in the field of engineering and technology, namely—

(*a*) civil engineering, including architecture engineering, building science and engineering, construction engineering, municipal and structural engineering and other allied subjects,

(*b*) electrical engineering, electronics, including communication engineering and systems, computer engineering (hardware) and other allied subjects, or

(*c*) other engineering sciences such as chemical, aeronautical and space, mechanical, metallurgical and materials engineering, and their specialised subdivisions, forest products, applied sciences such as geodesy and industrial chemistry, the science and technology of food production, specialised technologies of interdisciplinary fields, for example, systems analysis, metallurgy, mining, textile technology and other allied subjects,

(3) an activity undertaken in the field of medical sciences, namely—

(*a*) basic medicine, including anatomy, cytology, physiology, genetics, pharmacy, pharmacology, toxicology, immunology and immunohaematology, clinical chemistry, clinical microbiology and pathology,

(b) clinical medicine, including anaesthesiology, paediatrics, obstetrics and gynaecology, internal medicine, surgery, dentistry, neurology, psychiatry, radiology, therapeutics, otorhinolaryngology and ophthalmology, or

(c) health sciences, including public health services, social medicine, hygiene, nursing and epidemiology,

(4) an activity undertaken in the field of agricultural sciences, namely—

(*a*) agriculture, forestry, fisheries and allied sciences, including agronomy, animal husbandry, fisheries, forestry, horticulture, and other allied subjects, or

(*b*) veterinary medicine.

4. Without prejudice to the generality of clauses (I) and (II) of the definition of "research and development activities" in section 766 of the Taxes Consolidation Act, an activity falling within any of the following categories shall not be a research and development activity for the purposes of that section—

(*a*) research in the social sciences (including economics, business management and behavioral sciences), arts or humanities,

(*b*) routine testing and analysis for the purposes of quality or quantity control,

(*c*) alterations of a cosmetic or stylistic nature to existing products, services or processes whether or not these alterations represent some improvement,

(*d*) operational research such as management studies or efficiency surveys which are not wholly and exclusively undertaken for the purposes of a specific research and development activity,

(*e*) corrective action in connection with break-downs during commercial production of a product,

(*f*) legal and administrative work in connection with patent applications, records and litigation and the sale or licensing of patents,

(*g*) activity, including design and construction engineering, relating to the construction, relocation, rearrangement or start-up of facilities or equipment other than facilities or equipment which is or are to be used wholly and exclusively for the purposes of carrying on by the company concerned of research and development activities,

(*h*) market research, market testing, market development, sales promotion or consumer surveys,

(*i*) prospecting, exploring or drilling for, or producing, minerals, petroleum or natural gas,

(*j*) the commercial and financial steps necessary for the marketing or the commercial production or distribution of a new or improved material, product, device, process, system or service,

(*k*) administration and general support services (including transportation, storage, cleaning, repair, maintenance and security) which are not wholly and exclusively undertaken in connection with a research and development activity.

EUROPEAN COMMUNITIES (EXEMPTION FROM TAX FOR CERTAIN INTEREST AND ROYALTIES PAYMENTS) REGULATIONS 2004

2004 No 644

I, Charlie McCreevy, Minister for Finance, in exercise of the powers conferred on me by section 3 of the European Communities Act 1972 (No. 27 of 1972) and for the purpose of giving effect to Council Directive 2003/49/EC of 3 June 2003 [OJ No L 157, 26.6.2003, p 49] as amended by Council Directive 2004/66/EC of 26 April 2004 [OJ No L 168, 1.5.2004, p 35] and Council Directive 2004/76/EC of 29 April 2004 [OJ No L 195, 2.6.2004,p.33], hereby make the following regulations:

1. These Regulations may be cited as the European Communities (Exemption from Tax for Certain Interest and Royalties Payments) Regulations 2004.

2. These Regulations apply as respects any payment made on or after 1 May 2004.

Notes

Reg 3 substituted TCA 1997 s 267G(1) definition of "the Directive" with effect for payments made on or after 1 May 2004.
Reg 4 substituted TCA 1997 s 267J(1) with effect for payments made on or after 1 May 2004.

INCOME TAX (RELEVANT CONTRACTS) REGULATIONS 2004

2004 No 761

The Revenue Commissioners, in exercise of the powers conferred on them by section 531 (as amended by section 20 of the Finance Act 2004 (No 8 of 2004)) of the Taxes Consolidation Act 1997 (No 39 of 1997), make the following regulations:

1 (1) These Regulations may be cited as the Income Tax (Relevant Contracts) Regulations 2004.

(2) These Regulations, other than Regulation 2(*c*), come into operation on 1 January 2005.

(3) Regulation 2(c) is to be taken to have come into operation on 6 April 2000.

2

Notes

Para (*a*) inserted Income Tax (Relevant Contracts) Regulations 2000 reg 2 definition of "PPS number" with effect from 1 January 2005.
Para (*b*) substituted "including the sub-contractor's PPS number or tax reference number as the case may be, and if the sub-contractor is an individual, his or her date of birth" for "including the sub-contractor's date of birth and identifying number, known as the Revenue and Social Insurance (RSI) number," in Income Tax (Relevant Contracts) Regulations 2000 reg 6 with effect from 1 January 2005.
Para (*c*) substituted "paragraph (*c*)(ii) of subsection (5)" for "paragraph (*c*)(iii) of subsection (5)" in Income Tax (Relevant Contracts) Regulations 2000 reg 16(3)(*c*)(ii)with effect from 6 April 2000.
Para (*d*) substituted "paragraph (a) of subsection 12" for "paragraphs (*a*), (*b*) and (*c*) of subsection 12" in Income Tax (Relevant Contracts) Regulations 2000 reg 18(1) with effect from 1 January 2005.
Para (*e*)(i) substituted "including the sub-contractor's PPS number or tax reference number as the case may be, and if the sub-contractor is an individual, his or her date of birth," for "including the sub-contractor's date of birth and identifying number, known as the Revenue and Social Insurance (RSI) number," in Income Tax (Relevant Contracts) Regulations 2000 reg 20(1) with effect from 1 January 2005.
Para (*e*)(ii) substituted "which shall include the sub-contractor's PPS number or tax reference number as the case may be, and if the sub-contractor is an individual, his or her date of birth," for "which shall include the sub-contractor's date of birth and identifying number, known as the Revenue and Social Insurance (RSI) number," in Income Tax (Relevant Contracts) Regulations 2000 reg 20(2)(*a*) and (3)(*a*)(i) with effect from 1 January 2005.
Para (*f*) inserted Income Tax (Relevant Contracts) Regulations 2000 Pt 1A (regs 7A–7F) with effect from 1 January 2005.

FILM REGULATIONS 2004

2004 No 869

ARRANGEMENT OF REGULATIONS

PART 1
GENERAL

PART 2
APPLICATION TO THE REVENUE COMMISSIONERS FOR CERTIFICATION AND THE INFORMATION AND DOCUMENTATION TO BE PROVIDED IN OR WITH SUCH APPLICATION

PART 3
CATEGORIES OF FILMS ELIGIBLE FOR CERTIFICATION BY THE REVENUE COMMISSIONERS

PART 4
ISSUE OF AUTHORISATION BY THE MINISTER FOR ARTS, SPORT AND TOURISM

PART 5
RECORDS TO BE MAINTAINED AND PROVIDED BY A QUALIFYING COMPANY

PART 6
NOTIFICATION OF COMPLETION OF PRODUCTION AND PROVISION OF COPIES OF FILM AND COMPLIANCE REPORT

PART 7
THE TYPE OF EXPENDITURE THAT MAY BE ACCEPTED BY THE REVENUE COMMISSIONERS AS EXPENDITURE ON THE PRODUCTION OF A QUALIFYING FILM

The Revenue Commissioners in exercise of the powers conferred on them by section 481 (as amended by the Finance Act 2004 (No 8 of 2004)) of the Taxes Consolidation Act 1997 (No 39 of 1997), with the consent of the Minister for Finance, and with the consent of the Minister for Arts, Sport and Tourism in relation to the matters to be considered regarding the issue of authorisations under subsection (2) of section 481, hereby make the following Regulations:

PART 1
GENERAL

Citation and commencement.

1. (1) These Regulations may be cited as the Film Regulations 2004.

(2) These Regulations come into operation on 1 January 2005 and apply as respects each application made on or after that date by a qualifying company for a certificate under section 481 of the Act in relation to a film.

Interpretation.

2. (1) In these Regulations, except where the context otherwise requires—

"Act" means the Taxes Consolidation Act 1997 (No 39 of 1997);

"auditor" means a person qualified for appointment as auditor of a company in accordance with Part X (as amended) of the Companies Act 1990 (No 33 of 1990);

"eligible goods, services and facilities" means goods, services and facilities which are goods, services and facilities for the purposes of section 481(2A)(g)(iv)(II) of the Act by virtue of Part 8 of these Regulations;

"film" has the same meaning as in section 481 of the Act;

"Minister" means the Minister for Arts, Sport and Tourism;

"qualifying company" has the same meaning as in section 481 of the Act;

"qualifying film" has the same meaning as in section 481 of the Act;

"records", in respect of records to which Part 5 relates, includes records held in a machine readable form;

"relevant investment" has the same meaning as in section 481 of the Act;

"section 481 of the Act" means section 481 (as amended by the Finance Act 2004 (No 8 of 2004)) of the Taxes Consolidation Act 1997 (No 39 of 1997).

(2) Subject to paragraph (1), a word or expression that is used in these Regulations and is also used in the Tax Acts has, except where the context otherwise requires, the same meaning in these Regulations that it has in those Acts.

(3) In these Regulations—

(*a*) a reference to a Regulation is to a Regulation of these Regulations, and

(*b*) a reference to a paragraph or subparagraph is to the paragraph or subparagraph of the Regulation in which the reference occurs,

unless it is indicated that reference to some other provision is intended.

PART 2

APPLICATION TO THE REVENUE COMMISSIONERS FOR CERTIFICATION AND THE INFORMATION AND DOCUMENTATION TO BE PROVIDED IN OR WITH SUCH APPLICATION

Application for certification — general

3. (1) An application made on or after 1 January 2005 for a certificate under section 481 of the Act in relation to a film shall be made by a qualifying company under subsection (2A) of that section and shall be submitted to the Revenue Commissioners at least 7 days prior to the earlier of—

(*a*) the commencement of the raising of relevant investments, and

(*b*) the commencement of the principal photography, the first animation drawings or the first model movement, as the case may be.

(2) An application made in accordance with paragraph (1) shall be made on the form prescribed for that purposes by the Revenue Commissioners.

Application for certification — specific

4. (1) Each application made to the Revenue Commissioners for a certificate under section 481(2A) of the Act shall be accompanied by the supporting documents listed in Schedule 1 to these Regulations and such documents shall be included in the order and manner listed in that Schedule.

(2) The information required at each section of the application form shall be provided in full.

PART 3
CATEGORIES OF FILMS ELIGIBLE FOR CERTIFICATION BY THE REVENUE COMMISSIONERS

Categories of films eligible for certification

5. Subject to Regulation 6, the categories of films listed in Schedule 2 to these Regulations shall be the categories of films eligible for certification by the Revenue Commissioners.

Categories of films not eligible for certification

6. The categories of films listed in Schedule 3 to these Regulations shall not be categories of films eligible for certification by the Revenue Commissioners.

PART 4
ISSUE OF AUTHORISATIONS BY THE MINISTER FOR ARTS, SPORT AND TOURISM

Issue of authorisation

7. An authorisation may not be given by the Minister under section 481(2) of the Act in relation to a film unless—

(*a*) the film is within a category of film eligible for certification by the Revenue Commissioners, and

(*b*) the Minister is satisfied that the film will either or both—

(i) act as an effective stimulus to film making in Ireland, through, among other things, the provision of quality employment and training opportunities, and

(ii) be of importance to the promotion, development and enhancement of the national culture, including, where applicable, the Irish language.

PART 5
RECORDS TO BE MAINTAINED AND PROVIDED BY A QUALIFYING COMPANY

Types of records

8. (1) The records which a qualifying company shall provide to the Revenue Commissioners when requested to do so for the purposes of section 481(2C)(*c*) include—

(*a*) the books of first entry, including a cash receipts book, purchases day book, cheque payments book, creditors ledger and petty cash book,

(*b*) trial balance, all ledgers and journals to which all transactions are posted,

(*c*) the back-up documentation from which the books of first entry were completed, including—

(i) suppliers' invoices, credit notes, statements, and delivery notes,

(ii) cheque stubs and petty cash vouchers, and

(iii) bank statements and correspondence including those items verifying lodgements into bank accounts and transfers out of such accounts,

and

(*d*) auditors' linking documents including documents drawn up in the making up of accounts and showing details of the calculations linking the records to the accounts.

(2) The Revenue Commissioners may request the records to which paragraph (1) relates at any time within a period of up to 6 years after the later of—

(*a*) first delivery and acceptance of the qualifying film, or

(*b*) where the qualifying company fails to submit a complete compliance report on time, within 6 years of the provision of such report.

Records to indicate certain breakdown of expenditure

9. The records which a qualifying company shall provide to the Revenue Commissioners when requested to do so for the purposes of section 481(2C)(*c*) shall include records which provide a breakdown of expenditure to show—

(*a*) the amount of money expended directly on the employment of eligible individuals, and on the provision of eligible goods, services and facilities, and

(*b*) the amount of money expended otherwise than in accordance with paragraph (*a*).

PART 6

NOTIFICATION OF COMPLETION OF PRODUCTION AND PROVISION OF COPIES OF FILM AND COMPLIANCE REPORT

Notification of completion of production.

10. A qualifying company shall, within 4 months of the completion of production of a qualifying film, notify the Revenue Commissioners in writing of the date of such completion of production.

Provision of copies of film

11. (1) A qualifying company shall, within 4 months of the completion of production of a qualifying film, provide 2 copies of the film to the Revenue Commissioners and 2 copies of the film to the Minister.

(2) The copies of the film shall be provided in DVD or VHS PAL format or such other format as may be specified in the certificate issued by the Revenue Commissioners in relation to the film.

(3) The copies of the film shall be forwarded to the Revenue Commissioners and to the Minister by registered post.

Compliance report — certificate issued by the Revenue Commissioners

12. (1) A qualifying company shall, within 4 months of the completion of production of a qualifying film, provide a compliance report in relation to the film to the Revenue Commissioners.

(2) Such report shall be made on the form provided for that purpose by the Revenue Commissioners.

(3) The report shall include the items listed in Schedule 4 to these Regulations.

(4) The report shall be forwarded to the Revenue Commissioners by registered post.

PART 7

THE TYPE OF EXPENDITURE THAT MAY BE ACCEPTED BY THE REVENUE COMMISSIONERS AS EXPENDITURE ON THE PRODUCTION OF A QUALIFYING FILM

Acceptable expenditure

13. Subject to Regulation 14, the type of expenditure which may be accepted by the Revenue Commissioners as expenditure on the production of a qualifying film includes all expenditure necessary to produce the film from the development phase up to and including post-production together with the cost of providing an archive print.

Unacceptable expenditure

14. No sum shall be included in the type of expenditure which may be accepted by the Revenue Commissioners as expenditure on the production of a qualifying film in respect of—

(*a*) costs associated with the distribution or promotion of the film,

(*b*) costs arising after delivery of the materials contracted for with the relevant distributor or broadcaster,

(*c*) legal, accountancy and other costs of raising relevant investments,

(*d*) costs of organising or providing pre-sales monies including those connected with facilitating a return for investors,

(*e*) costs of acquiring rights other than those necessary for the production of the film,

(*f*) expenditure on capital assets used in the production of the film which are not used up in that process,

(*g*) amounts that are paid out of, or are dependent on, or arise from rights in, the receipts, earnings or profits of the film, or

(*h*) fees or other payments deferred unless the payment of such sums is made no later than 4 months after the first occasion on which the completed film is delivered to any financier or distributor thereof.

PART 8

ELIGIBLE GOODS, SERVICES AND FACILITIES AND CONDITIONS TO BE SATISFIED

Interpretation — Part 8

15. In this Part—

"provided within the State" means—

(*a*) (i) in the case of goods which are dispatched or transported, that the dispatch or transportation to the person to whom they are provided begins in the State, and

(ii) in the case of goods which are not dispatched or transported, that the goods are located in the State at the time they are provided;

(*b*) in the case of facilities, that the facilities are located in the State;

(*c*) in the case of transport, that the transportation takes place within the State, or, where transportation takes place across borders, that the journey begins or ends in the State;

(*d*) in the case of a service, that the activities constituting such a service are carried on in the State and that any goods, facilities or transport associated with such service satisfy the conditions of paragraph (*a*), (*b*) or (*c*) of this definition, as the case may be;

"relevant person" means a person carrying on a business in the State from a fixed place of business.

Eligible goods, services and facilities

16. Subject to Regulation 17, goods, services and facilities are goods, services and facilities for the purposes of section 481(2A)(*g*)(iv)(II) of the Act where they are used or consumed in the State in the production of a qualifying film and they are provided within the State by a relevant person directly or indirectly to a qualifying company.

Other person engaged

17. Where a relevant person engages, or arranges for, another person to provide goods, services or facilities such goods, services or facilities shall not be goods, services and facilities for the purposes of section 481(2A)(*g*)(iv)(II) of the Act unless that other person is also a relevant person.

PART 9
MISCELLANEOUS

Currency exchange rate

18. The currency exchange rate to be applied to expenditure on the production of a qualifying film shall be the rate applicable on the date the expenditure is incurred.

SCHEDULE 1
Documentation to accompany an application made for a certificate under section 481(2A) of the Act

1.	Tab A	Covering letter of application.
2.	Tab B	Memorandum and Articles of Association of the Qualifying Company.
3.	Tab C	Certificate of Incorporation of the Qualifying Company.
4.	Tab D	Track record and CVs for Producer; Director; Writer(s).
5.	Tab E	Synopsis of Film.
6.	Tab F	Completed Screenplay, Sample Television Scripts or Storyboard.
7.	Tab G	Production Schedule.
8.	Tab H	Screenplay and Writers' Agreements and Option agreement.
9.	Tab I	Production, Financing and Distribution Agreement.
10.	Tab J	Production Budget.
11.	Tab K	Confirmation that no agreements, arrangements or understandings exist or are proposed that would impact on investor risk.
12.	Tab L	Appendix A — Schedule of Fees.
13.	Tab M	Letters of intent and, if applicable, letters of commitment from sources of funding other than relevant investments.
14.	Tab N	Pre-Sales and Distribution Agreements.
15.	Tab O	Completion Bond Contract, if applicable.
16.	Tab P	Appendix B — Person Hours Schedule.
17.	Tab Q	Full List of Heads of Departments.
18.	Tab R	Other relevant agreements and documentation.
19.	Tab S	A diagram detailing all the parties involved, their respective responsibilities and the flow of funds between them.
20.	Tab T	Details of any issues that might impact on the conditions for relief under section 481 of the Act.
21.	Tab U	Where any agreements, requested above, are unavailable at the time of application, an outline of the proposed agreements, including details of the purpose of each agreement.

22. Tab V Confirmation that no financial arrangements of a type referred to in section 481(2C)(b) of the Act exist or are proposed.

SCHEDULE 2

Categories of films eligible for certification by the Revenue Commissioners

1. Feature film.
2. Television drama.
3. Animation (whether computer generated or otherwise, but excluding computer games).
4. Creative Documentary, where the project—

   (*a*) is based on an original theme, preferably demonstrated by a script or treatment the design and style of which bear the undeniable stamp of creative originality and personal perspective,

   (*b*) contains a certain timeless element so that there is no loss of interest when the event with which it may be linked has passed,

   (*c*) involves production arrangements which give evidence of, in particular, a substantial period of preparation and a significant period devoted to post-production, and

   (*d*) contains significant original filming and does not merely report information.

SCHEDULE 3

Categories of films not eligible for certification by the Revenue Commissioners

Films comprising or substantially based on:

(*a*) public or special performances staged for filming or otherwise,

(*b*) sporting events,

(*c*) games or competitions,

(*d*) current affairs or talk shows,

(*e*) demonstration programmes for tasks, hobbies or projects,

(*f*) review, magazine style or lifestyle programmes,

(*g*) unscripted or reality type programmes, or

(*h*) product produced in-house by a broadcaster or for domestic consumption in one country.

SCHEDULE 4

Documents to accompany a compliance report in relation to a qualifying film

1. Evidence that the film has been shown in a commercial cinema or television or has been commercially distributed in DVD or Video format.
2. A copy of the film in DVD or VHS PAL format or such other format as may be specified in the certificate issued by the Revenue Commissioners in relation to the film.
3. A report by the qualifying company's auditors which includes–

   (*a*) details of the amounts expended in the State on the qualifying film, including the amount of money expended directly on the employment of eligible individuals and on the provision of eligible goods, services and facilities, and

   (*b*) a breakdown of the top sheet production expenditure summaries, covering–

   (i) the amount of money expended directly in the State on the employment of eligible individuals and on the provision of eligible goods, services and facilities, and

   (ii) the entire production expenditure on the qualifying film,

   which must relate line by line to the top sheet production budget summaries furnished with the application for certification.

4. A certificate or report from the auditors in accordance with any guidelines on compliance requirements issued by the Revenue Commissioners.

TABLE OF STATUTORY REFERENCES

All references are to sections in the Taxes Consolidation Act unless otherwise indicated

TABLE OF CASES

All references are to sections in the Taxes Consolidation Act 1997, unless otherwise indicated

D

E

T

U

V

INDEX

Note: Definitions are listed under WORDS AND PHRASES

INDEX

WORDS AND PHRASES